PETERSON'S PRIVATE SECONDARY SCHOOLS

2007

Australia • Canada • Mexico • Singapore • Spain • United Kingdom • United States

About Thomson Peterson's

Thomson Peterson's (www.petersons.com) is a leading provider of education information and advice, with books and online resources focusing on education search, test preparation, and financial aid. Its Web site offers searchable databases and interactive tools for contacting educational institutions, online practice tests and instruction, and planning tools for securing financial aid. Thomson Peterson's serves 110 million education consumers annually.

For more information, contact Thomson Peterson's, 2000 Lenox Drive, Lawrenceville,
NJ 08648; 800-338-3282; or find us on the World Wide Web at www.petersons.com/about.

© 2006 Thomson Peterson's, a part of The Thomson Corporation
Thomson Learning™ is a trademark used herein under license.

Previous editions under the title *Peterson's Guide to Independent Secondary Schools* © 1980, 1981, 1982, 1983, 1984, 1985, 1986, 1987, 1988, 1989, 1990, 1991, 1992 and *Peterson's Private Secondary Schools* 1993, 1994, 1995, 1996, 1997, 1998, 1999, 2000, 2001, 2002, 2003, 2004, 2005

Editor: Fern A. Oram; Production Editor: Susan W. Dilts; Copy Editors: Michael Haines, Sally Ross, Jill C. Schwartz, Mark D. Snider, Pam Sullivan, Valerie Bolus Vaughan; Research Project Manager: Daniel Margolin; Research Associate: Ken Britschge; Programmer: Phyllis Johnson; Manufacturing Manager: Ray Golaszewski; Composition Manager: Linda M. Williams; Client Relations Representative: Karen D. Mount.

ISSN 1066-5366
ISBN-10: 0-7689-2152-X
ISBN-13: 978-0-7689-2152-6

Printed in the United States of America

10 9 8 7 6 5 4 3 2 1   08 07 06

Twenty-seventh Edition

Contents

Contents

INDEX

A Note from the Peterson's Editors

Peterson's Private Secondary Schools 2007 is the authoritative source of information for parents and students who are exploring the alternative of privately provided education. In this edition, you will find information for more than 1,500 schools worldwide. The data published in this guide are obtained directly from the schools themselves to help you make a fully informed decision.

If you've decided to look into private schooling for your son or daughter but aren't sure how to begin, relax. You won't have to go it alone. **What You Should Know About Private Education** can help you plan your search and demystify the admission process. In the articles that follow, you'll find valuable advice from admission experts about applying to private secondary schools and choosing the school that's right for your child. In "Why Choose an Independent School?" Patrick F. Bassett, President of the National Association of Independent Schools (NAIS), describes the reasons why an increasing number of families are considering private schooling. If you want a private education for your child but are hesitant about sending him or her away to a boarding school, read "Another Option: Independent Day Schools" where Lila Lohr, former Head of School at Princeton Day School in Princeton, New Jersey, discusses the benefits of day schools. From The Association of Boarding Schools (TABS) is their "Study Confirms Benefits of Boarding School"—if you are having doubts about boarding schools, you'll want to check out this study! Mark Braun, Head of School at the Outdoor Academy, offers "Semester Schools: Great Opportunities," which explores various options for students to spend an exciting semester in a new "school-away-from-school." To help you compare private schools and make the best choice for your

Schools will be pleased to know that Thomson Peterson's helped you in your private secondary school selection.

child, check out "Finding the Perfect Match" by Helene Reynolds, a former educational planning and placement counselor. "Plan a Successful School Search" gives you an overview of the admission process. If you want more information about the Admission Application Form, read "Understanding the Admission Application Form," by Gregg W. M. Maloberti, Dean of Admission at The Lawrenceville School. For the lowdown on standardized testing, Heather Hoerle describes the two tests most often required by private schools and the role that tests play in admission decisions in "About Standardized Tests." In "Paying for a Private Education," Mark Mitchell, Vice President, School Information Services at NAIS, shares some thoughts on financing options. Then, find out how "Searching for Private Schools Online" can simplify your efforts. Finally, "How to Use This Guide" gives you all the information you need on how to make *Peterson's Private Secondary Schools* work for you!

Next up, the **Quick-Reference Chart**, "Private Secondary Schools At-a-Glance," lists schools by state, U.S. territory, or country and provides essential information about a school's students, range of grade levels, enrollment figures, faculty, and special offerings.

The **School Profiles and Announcements** follow and it's here you can learn more about particular schools. *Peterson's Private Secondary Schools* contains three **School Profiles and Announcements** sections—one for traditional college-preparatory and general academic schools, one for special needs schools that serve students with a variety of special learning

v

A Note from the Peterson's Editors

and social needs, and one for junior boarding schools that serve students in middle school grades.

In-Depth Descriptions follow each **School Profiles and Announcements** section and feature expanded two-page school portraits written exclusively for this guide. There is a reference at the end of a profile directing you to that school's In-Depth Description.

The **Specialized Directories** are generated from responses to our annual school survey. These directories group schools by the categories considered most important when choosing a private school, including type, entrance requirements, curricula, financial aid data, and special programs.

Finally, in the **Index** you'll find the "Alphabetical Listing of Schools" for the page references of schools that have already piqued your interest.

Thomson Peterson's publishes a full line of resources to help guide you and your family through the private secondary school admission process.

Peterson's publications can be found at your local bookstore, library, and high school guidance office, and you can access us online at www.petersons.com.

We welcome any comments or suggestions you may have about this publication and invite you to complete our online survey at **www.petersons.com/ booksurvey.** Or you can fill out the survey at the back of this book, tear it out, and mail it to us at:

Editorial Department
Thomson Peterson's
2000 Lenox Drive
Lawrenceville, NJ 08648

Your feedback will help us to provide personalized solutions for your educational advancement.

Schools will be pleased to know that Thomson Peterson's helped you in your private secondary school selection. Admissions staff members are more than happy to answer questions, address specific problems, and help in any way they can. The editors at Peterson's wish you great success in your search!

What You Should Know About Private Education

Why Choose an Independent School?

Patrick F. Bassett
President of the National Association of Independent Schools (NAIS)

Why do families choose independent schools for their children? Many cite the intimate school size and setting, individualized attention, and high academic standards. The National Educational Longitudinal Study (NELS), conducted by the U.S. Department of Education, confirms what independent school families have known for years: Compared to students in public, parochial, and other private schools, larger percentages of students in independent schools are enrolled in advanced courses. Independent school students:

- Do twice as much homework as their counterparts
- Watch only two-thirds as much television
- Are significantly more likely to participate in varsity or intramural sports
- Are more likely to agree that students and teachers get along well, discipline is fair, and teaching is good

Other longitudinal research confirms the wisdom of choosing an independent school. Roughly speaking, students from independent schools are twice as likely to:

- Take Algebra I and foreign language in the eighth grade
- Enroll in an Advanced Placement course as a sophomore
- Have a teacher who has graduated from a selective college

It is important to note that independent schools, contrary to popular belief and their portrayal in the media, are not "elitist" in any way except in terms of academic expectations.

- Complete precalculus or higher level of mathematics
- Participate in extracurricular sports, arts, academics, and community service

These patterns begin in our elementary schools, which place a strong emphasis on creating a positive learning climate for each child. The patterns are sustained through our middle and upper schools, where children are encouraged and expected to do well academically and urged to participate in extracurricular activities.

Why are these patterns important? Simply stated, they reflect two critical elements that make independent school students well prepared for college and for life: mastery of a serious academic program and being a "player."

What value will I see in an independent school for my child?

Parents often consider independent schools as they would consider any other "investment," expecting a "return" and "value." Research shows that the choice of a child's peer group may be the single most important factor in determining educational success. Parents choose a peer group largely by the school they choose for their child. Data show that virtually all independent school graduates succeed by completing college (as opposed to about 40 percent of the general population). This "persistence factor" is largely attributable to attending a school with high expectations for all students and with a culture that reinforces achievement. The ethos of independent schools contributes to this equation, since "everybody" is expected to work hard and succeed academically and since "everybody" is expected be a "player." Choosing an independent school, and the right independent school for your child, can be one of life's most important and rewarding investments.

Which are the "highest ranking" or "best" independent schools?

Independent schools are as individual as your child. Each has a unique mission, culture, and personality. Among independent schools, there are different shapes and sizes. There are day schools, boarding schools, or combination day-boarding. Some independent schools

have a few dozen students; others have several thousand. Some are coed; others are single-sex. Some independent schools have a religious affiliation; some are nonsectarian. Most serve students of average to exceptional academic ability, but some serve exclusively those with learning differences, and others exclusively serve the gifted. Virtually all independent schools are "college-prep." Because independent schools have different missions and different student populations, NAIS discourages ranking, since no single set of objective criteria could apply.

What are the myths and misconceptions about independent schools?

It is important to note that independent schools, contrary to popular belief and their portrayal in the media, are not "elitist" in any way except in terms of academic expectations. The typical independent school *chooses* to commit to diversity (racial, ethnic, and socioeconomic). Socioeconomic diversity, for example,

is supported by a significant commitment to financial aid: Independent school students come from all family income levels, and approximately 20 percent of them are supported by financial aid. On average nationally, 17 percent of independent school students are students of color.

What kind of relationship does an independent school have with parents?

Independent schools seek a solid partnership with parents. Independent schools seek to speak with a unified voice about a common set of goals and values. It is this coalescing of parental and school voices that points students, like a beacon, toward achievement, decent behaviors, and good citizenship. In the final analysis, children prosper when the key adults in their lives reinforce a common set of values and speak with a common voice. The great achievement of American education is that it offers parents many choices of schooling so that they can find a school with a voice and vision to match their own.

Another Option: Independent Day Schools

Lila Lohr

For those of us who are fortunate enough to be able to send our children to an independent day school, it seems to offer the best of both worlds. Our children are able to reap the enormous benefits of an independent school education and we, as parents, are able to continue to play a vital, daily role in the education of our children. Parents enjoy being seen as partners with day schools in educating their children.

As more and more independent day schools have sprung up in communities across the country, more and more parents are choosing to send their children to them, even when it might involve a lengthy daily commute. Contrary to some old stereotypes, parents of independent school students are not all cut from the same mold, living in the same neighborhood with identical dreams and aspirations for their children. Independent school parents represent a wide range of interests, attitudes, and parenting styles.

They also have several things in common. Most parents send their children to independent day schools because they think their children will get a better education in a safe, value-laden environment. Many parents are willing to pay substantial annual tuition because they believe their children will be held to certain standards, challenged academically, and thoroughly prepared for college.

This willingness to make what is for many substantial financial sacrifices reflects the recognition that much of one's character is formed in school. Concerned parents want their children to go to schools where values are discussed and reinforced. They seek schools that have clear expectations and limits. The nonpublic status allows independent schools to establish specific standards of behavior and performance and to suspend or expel students who don't conform to those expectations.

Understanding the power of adolescent peer pressure, parents are eager to have their children go to school with other teens who are academically ambitious and required to behave. They seek an environment where it is "cool" to be smart, to work hard, and to be involved in the school community. In independent day schools, students spend their evenings doing homework, expect to be called on in class, and participate in sports or clubs.

Successful independent schools, whether elementary or high school, large or small, single-sex or coed, recognize the importance of a school-parent partnership in educating each child. Experienced faculty members and administrators readily acknowledge that, while they are experts on education, parents are the experts on their own children. Gone are the days when parents simply dropped their children off in the morning, picked them up at the end of the day, and assumed the school would do the educating. Clearly, children benefit enormously when their parents and teachers work together, sharing their observations and concerns openly and frequently.

Most independent schools welcome and encourage parental involvement and support.

Independent schools encourage this two-way give-and-take and are committed to taking it well beyond the public school model. Annual back-to-school nights are attended by more than 90 percent of parents. Teacher-parent and student-teacher-parent conferences, extensive written comments as part of the report cards, and adviser systems that encourage close faculty-student relationships are all structures that facilitate this parent-school partnership. Although more and more independent school parents work full-time, they make time for these critical opportunities to sit down and discuss their children's progress.

Most independent schools welcome and encourage parental involvement and support. Although the individual structures vary from school to school, most include opportunities beyond making cookies and chaperoning dances. Many parents enjoy being involved in community service projects, working on school fund raisers, participating in admission activities, sharing their expertise in appropriate academic classes,

and even offering student internships. Most schools have made a concerted effort to structure specific opportunities for working parents to participate in the life of the school.

Twenty years ago, volunteers were plentiful. Today they are a scarce commodity. Independent day schools recognize the benefits of parent volunteers and of extending themselves so that parents feel that they are an important part of the school family. Buddy systems that pair new parents with families who have been at the school for several years help ease the transition for families who are new to the independent school sector.

Independent schools have also responded to increased parental interest in programs focusing on parenting skills. Recognizing the inherent difficulties of raising children, independent day schools have provided forums for discussing and learning about drugs, depression, stress management, peer pressure, and the like. Book groups, panel discussions, and

workshops provide important opportunities for parents to share their concerns and to get to know the parents of their children's classmates. Schools recognize that this parent-to-parent communication and networking strengthens the entire school community.

Many current day school parents would contend that when you choose an independent day school for your child you are really choosing a school for the entire family. The students become so involved in their academic and extracurricular activities and the parents spend so much time at school supporting those activities that it does become the entire family's school.

Lila Lohr is the former Head of School at Princeton Day School in Princeton, New Jersey. She has been a teacher and an administrator in independent day schools for more than thirty years and is the mother of 3 independent day school graduates.

Study Confirms Benefits of Boarding School

Many people have long sung the praises of the boarding school experience. The high-level academics, the friendships, and the life lessons learned are without rival at private day or public schools, they say.

Now, a study released by The Association of Boarding Schools (TABS), a non-profit organization of independent, college-preparatory schools, validates these claims. Not only do boarding school students spend more time studying (and less time watching TV), they are also better prepared for college and progress more quickly in their careers than their counterparts who attended private day or public schools.

The survey, which was conducted by the Baltimore-based research firm the Art & Science Group, involved interviews with 1,000 students and alumni from boarding schools, 1,100 from public schools, and 600 from private day schools (including independent day and parochial schools).

The results not only affirm the benefits enjoyed by boarding school graduates, but those bestowed upon current boarding school students, as well. "The study helps us better understand how the opportunities for interaction and learning beyond the classroom found at boarding schools impact a student's life at school and into adulthood," explains Steve Ruzicka, TABS executive director. Ruzicka says the survey also will provide boarding school alumni with empirical data to help when considering their children's educational options.

Rigorous Academics Prevail

Why do students apply to boarding schools? The TABS study found that the primary motivation for both applicants and their parents is the promise of a better education. And, happily, the vast majority of current and past students surveyed reported that their schools deliver on this promise. Current students indicated significantly higher levels of satisfaction with

their academic experience at boarding schools than their peers at public and private day schools by more than ten percentage points (54 percent of boarding students versus 42 percent of private day students and 40 percent of public school students). Boarders reported in greater relative percentages that they find their schools academically challenging, that their peers are more motivated, and the quality of teaching is very high.

But the boarding environment is valued just as much for the opportunities for interaction and learning beyond the classroom. Interactions in the dining room, the dormitory, and on the playing field both complement and supplement academics, exposing students to a broad geographic and socioeconomic spectrum, challenging their boundaries, and broadening their vision of the world.

The Boarding School Boost

The 24/7 life at boarding schools also gives students a significant leg up when they attend college, the survey documents.

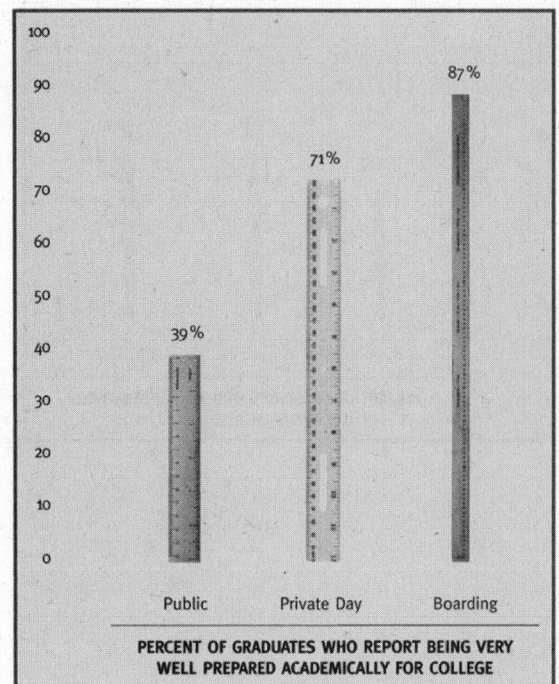

PERCENT OF GRADUATES WHO REPORT BEING VERY WELL PREPARED ACADEMICALLY FOR COLLEGE

Some 87 percent of boarding school graduates said they were very well prepared academically for college, with only 71 percent of private day and just 39 percent of public school alumni saying the same. And 78 percent of boarders reported that their schools also helped better prepare them to face the nonacademic aspects of college life, such as independence, social life, and time management. Only 36 percent of private day

graduates and 23 percent of public school graduates said the same. The TABS survey also documented that a larger percentage of boarding school graduates go on to earn advanced degrees once they finish college: 50 percent, versus 36 percent of private day and 21 percent of public school alumni.

Beyond college, boarding school graduates also reap greater benefits from their on-campus experiences, advancing faster and further in their careers comparatively. The study scrutinized former boarders versus private day and public school graduates in terms of achieving positions in top management and found that by midcareer, 44 percent of boarding school graduates had reached positions in top management versus 33 percent of private day school graduates and 27 percent of public school graduates.

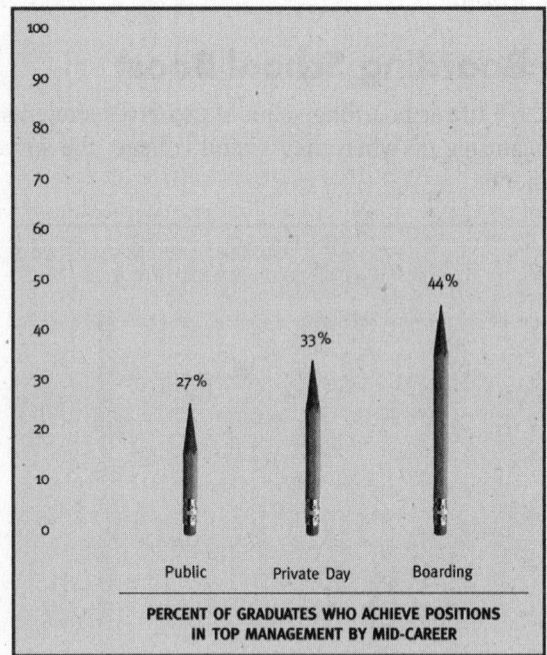

PERCENT OF GRADUATES WHO ACHIEVE POSITIONS IN TOP MANAGEMENT BY MID-CAREER

By late in their careers, more than half of the surveyed boarding school sample, 52 percent, held positions in top management as opposed to 39 percent of private day and 27 percent of public school graduates.

But perhaps the most compelling statistic that the study produced is the extremely high percentage—some 90 percent—of boarding school alumni who say they would, if given the opportunity, repeat their boarding school experience. This alone is a strong argument that validates the enduring value of the boarding school model. It is hoped that the study will help dispel many of the myths and stereotypes that have dogged the image of boarding schools over the last century and spread the good news that boarding schools today are diverse, exciting places for bright, well-adjusted students who are looking for success in their academic lives—and beyond.

For more information on the TABS study please go to www.schools.com.

Used by permission of The Association of Boarding Schools.

Semester Schools: Great Opportunities

Mark Braun
Head of School, The Outdoor Academy

Over the last twenty years, there has been tremendous growth in the range of educational opportunities available to young Americans. The advent of semester schools has played no small part in this trend. Similar in many ways to semester-abroad programs, semester schools provide secondary school students the opportunity to leave their home school for half an academic year to have a very different kind of experience—the experience of living and learning within a small community, among diverse students, and in a new and different place. The curricula of such schools tend to be thematic, interdisciplinary, rigorous, and experiential.

What Are the Benefits?

As a starting point for their programs, semester schools have embraced many of the qualities typical of independent schools. In fact, a number of semester schools were developed as extension programs by existing independent schools, providing unusual opportunities to their own students and those from other schools. Other semester schools have grown from independent educational organizations or foundations that bring their own educational interests and expertise to their semester programs. In both cases, semester schools provide the kind of challenging environment for which independent schools are known.

Across the board, semester school programs provide students with exceptional opportunities for contact with their teachers. Individual instruction and intimate classes are common, as is contact with teachers outside the classroom. At semester schools, students have a full-immersion experience in a tightly knit learning

At semester schools, students have a full-immersion experience in a tightly knit learning community.

community. In such a setting, teachers are able to challenge each student in his or her own area of need, mentoring students to both academic and personal fulfillment.

Semester schools have developed around specialized curricular interests, often involving unique offerings or nontraditional subjects. In almost every case, these specialized curricula are related to the school's location. Indeed, place-based learning is a common thread in semester school education. Whether in New York City or the Appalachian Mountains, semester schools enable students to cultivate a sense of place and develop greater sensitivity to their surroundings. This is often accomplished through a combination of experiential education and traditional instruction. Students develop academic knowledge and practical skills in tandem through active participation in intellectual discourse, creative projects, hands-on exercises, and service learning opportunities. Throughout, emphasis is placed on the importance of combining intellectual exploration with thoughtful self-reflection, often facilitated by journaling exercises or group processing activities.

At semester schools, students inevitably learn their most important lessons through their membership in the school community. Living closely with peers and teachers and working together for the benefit of the group enables students to develop extraordinary communication skills and high levels of interpersonal accountability. Through this experience, students gain invaluable leadership and cooperation skills.

Ultimately, semester education seeks to impart translatable skills to those students who choose to attend. The common goal is for students to return to their schools and families with greater motivation, empathy, self-knowledge, and self-determination. These skills help to prepare students for the college experience and beyond. In addition, semester school participants report that their experiences helped to distinguish them in the college application process. Semester school programs are certainly not for everybody, but they have served an important role for students who are seeking something beyond the ordinary—students who wish to know themselves and the world in a profound way. All of the following semester school programs manifest these same values in their own distinctive way.

CITYterm

Now in its tenth year, CITYterm is an interdisciplinary, experience-based program that takes 30 juniors and seniors from across the country and engages them in a semester-long study of New York City. CITYterm students typically spend three days a week in the classroom, reading, writing, and thinking about New York City, and three days a week in the city working on projects, studying diverse neighborhoods, or meeting with politicians, urban historians, authors, artists, actors, and various city experts. Much of the excitement of CITYterm comes from experiencing firsthand in the city what has been studied in the classroom. Many of the projects are done in collaborative teams where the groups engage not only in formal academic research at the city's libraries but also use the resources of New York City's residents and institutions to gather the information necessary for presentations. Students come to see themselves as the active creators of their own learning both in the classroom and in the world. Learn more about CITYterm by visiting www.themastersschool.com/cityterm.

The Island School

The Island School, founded in 1999 by The Lawrenceville School, is an independent academic program in the Bahamas for high school sophomores or juniors. The fourteen-week academic course of study includes honors classes in science, field research (a laboratory course), history, math, art, English literature, and physical/outdoor education and a weekly community service component. All courses are place-based and explicitly linked, taking advantage of the school's surroundings to both deepen understandings of complex academic and social issues and to make those understandings lasting by connecting course content with experience. Students apply their investigative, interpretive, and problem-solving skills during four- and eight-day kayaking expeditions, SCUBA diving opportunities, teaching environmental issues to local students, and in daily life at the school. In addition to traditional classroom assessments, students conduct research on mangrove communities, coastal management, artificial reefs, permaculture, and marine protected areas. These projects support national research and are conducted under the auspices of the Bahamian government. At the conclusion of the semester, students present their work to a panel of visiting scientists and educators, including local and national government officials from the Bahamas. The opportunity to interact with the local community through research, outreach, and the rigorous physical and academic schedule creates a transformative experience for students. The admissions process is competitive, and selected students demonstrate solid academic performance, leadership potential, and a high degree of self-motivation. Contact The Island School for more information at www.islandschool.org.

The Maine Coast Semester

The Maine Coast Semester (MCS) offers a small group of eleventh-grade students the chance to live and work on a 400-acre saltwater peninsula with the goal of exploring the natural world through courses in natural science, environmental issues, art, history, literature, mathematics, and foreign language. Since 1988, MCS has welcomed more than 1,000 students from more than 200 public and private schools across the country and in Canada. The MCS community is small—38 students and 15 faculty members—and the application process is competitive. In addition to their studies, students work for several hours each afternoon on an organic farm, in a wood lot, or on maintenance and construction projects. Students who attend MCS are highly motivated, capable, and willing to take the risk of leaving friends and family for a portion of their high school career. They enjoy hard work, both intellectual and physical, and they demonstrate a tangible desire to contribute to the world. MCS students return to their schools with self-confidence, an appreciation for the struggles and rewards of community living, and an increased sense of ownership of their education. For information on The Maine Coast Semester, go to www.chewonki.org.

The Mountain School

The Mountain School of Milton Academy, founded in 1984, hosts 45 high school juniors from private and public schools throughout the United States who have chosen to spend four months on a working organic farm in Vermont. Courses provide a demanding and integrated learning experience, taking full advantage of the school's small size and mountain campus. Students and adults develop a social contract of mutual trust that expects individual and communal responsibility, models the values of simplicity and sustainability, and challenges teenagers to engage in meaningful work. Students live with teachers in small houses and help make important decisions concerning how to live together and manage the farm. Courses offered include English, environmental science, U.S history, and all levels of math, physics, chemistry, Spanish, French, Latin, studio art, and humanities. All courses are AP or honors level. To learn more about The Mountain School, please visit www.mountainschool.org.

The Rocky Mountain Semester

The Rocky Mountain Semester (RMS) at the High Mountain Institute is an opportunity for high school juniors to examine the human relationship to the natural world through a combination of rigorous academics and extended wilderness expeditions. During the seventeen-week semester, up to 36 students spend six weeks backpacking, skiing, and studying throughout the wilderness of Colorado, Wyoming, and Utah. The remainder of the semester is spent on campus near Leadville, Colorado, where students pursue a rigorous course of study and learn how to live successfully in a small community environment. While at the RMS, most students take six classes—the only required course is Practices and Principles: Ethics of the Natural World. It is in this class that students are taught the theoretical foundations for all that is done in the field, examine the human relationship to the natural world, and learn the skills necessary to travel safely and comfortably in remote settings. In addition to P&P, students may also take literature of the natural world, natural science, U.S. history or AP U.S. history, Spanish or French, and mathematics. Interested parties can learn more about The Rocky Mountain Semester at www.hminet.org.

The Outdoor Academy of the Southern Appalachians

The Outdoor Academy offers tenth-grade and select eleventh-grade students from across the country a semester away in the mountains of North Carolina. Arising from seventy-eight years of experiential education at Eagle's Nest Foundation, this school-away-from-school provides a college-preparatory curriculum along with special offerings in environmental education, outdoor leadership, the arts, and community service. Each semester, up to 35 students embrace the Southern Appalachians as a unique ecological, historical, and cultural American region. In this setting, students and teachers live as a close-knit community and lessons of cooperation and responsibility abound. Students develop a healthy work ethic as course work and projects are pursued both in and out of the classroom. Courses in English, mathematics, science, history, foreign language, visual arts, and music emphasize hands-on and cooperative learning. Classes often meet outside on the 180-acre wooded campus or in nearby national wilderness areas, where the natural world enhances intellectual pursuits. On weekends and extended trips, the outdoor leadership program teaches hiking, backpacking, caving, canoeing, and rock-climbing skills. The Outdoor Academy is open to students from both public

and private secondary schools, is accredited by the Southern Association of Colleges and Schools, and is a member of the North Carolina Association of Independent Schools. Learn more about The Outdoor Academy at www.enf.org.org.

The Oxbow School

The Oxbow School in Napa, California, is a one-semester visual arts program for high school juniors and seniors from public and private schools nationwide. Oxbow offers students a unique educational experience focused on in-depth study in sculpture, printmaking, drawing and painting, and photography and digital media, including animation. The interdisciplinary, project-based curriculum emphasizes experiential learning, critical thinking, and the development of research skills as a means of focused artistic inquiry. Each semester, 2 Visiting Artists are invited to work collaboratively with students and teachers. By engaging students in the creative process, Oxbow fosters a deep appreciation for creativity in all areas of life beyond the classroom. Since its founding in 1998, students who have spent a semester at The Oxbow School have matriculated to leading universities, colleges, and independent colleges of art and design around the country. Learn more at www.oxbowschool.org.

The Woolman Semester

The Woolman Semester is a community-based, interdisciplinary program for high school juniors and seniors. The mission of the school is to weave together peace, sustainability, and social action into an intensely rigorous academic experience. The school is located on a 230-acre campus complete with forests, fields, gardens, and livestock to use as a living laboratory, as well as for the wood chopping and lettuce harvesting of daily life! Classes generally meet in the morning, while labs, study groups, and farm work take place in the afternoon. Students and faculty also participate in a two-week service project and a one-week hiking trip in the Sierra foothills. Get all the information on The Woolman Semester program at www.woolman.org.

Coastal Studies for Girls

Coastal Studies for Girls (CSG) is an academic, experiential, and inspirational journey. Located in Freeport, Maine, CSG's focus is on marine science and technology for sophomore girls. Although core courses of English, history, foreign language, and mathematics are taught, CSG's "specialties" are Marine Science, Environmental Seminar, and Leadership Adventure. With exciting opportunities already in existence on the

Maine coast, CSG has many educational partners, and students engage in hands-on research projects that are real, meaningful, and ongoing. Leadership Adventure takes students sea kayaking, rock climbing, and on high ropes courses and gives them the opportunity to live aboard a schooner for a week as it makes its way up the Maine coast. In addition, CSG has a guest lecture series, a scholars-in-residence program, and a mentor program designed for students to interact with others from a variety of backgrounds. Each semester, 32 sophomore women arrive from all over the nation. The sophomore year is intentionally chosen so that students may experience a broad spectrum of opportunity that will have an impact on their decisions as

juniors and seniors in college and throughout life. In collaboration with Wolfe Neck Farm, CSG sits on 600 acres of pristine coastline, just minutes from Freeport. Towering white pines, open fields, and lush forests surround the campus, with Casco Bay and the Haraseeket River as backdrops. More information about Coastal Studies for Girls is available at www.coastalstudiesforgirls.org.

The author wishes to acknowledge and thank all the semester school programs for contributing their school profiles and collaborating in order to spread the word about semester school education.

Finding the Perfect Match

Helene Reynolds

One of the real benefits of independent education is that it allows you to deliberately seek out and choose a school community for your child. If you are like most parents, you want your child's school years to reflect an appropriate balance of academic challenge, social development, and exploration into athletics and the arts. You hope that through exposure to new ideas and sound mentoring your child will develop an awareness of individual social responsibility, as well as the study skills and work ethic to make a contribution to his or her world. It is every parent's fondest wish to have the school experience spark those areas of competence that can be pursued toward excellence and distinction.

An increasing number of parents realize that this ideal education is found outside their public school system, that shrinking budgets, divisive school boards, and overcrowded classrooms have resulted in schools where other agendas vie with education for attention and money. In this environment there is less time and energy for teachers to focus on individual needs.

The decision to choose a private school can be made for as many different reasons as there are families making the choice. Perhaps your child would benefit from smaller classes or accelerated instruction. Perhaps your child has needs or abilities that can be more appropriately addressed in a specialized environment. Perhaps you are concerned about the academic quality of your local public school and the impact it may have on your child's academic future. Or perhaps you feel that a private school education is a gift you can give your child to guide him or her toward a more successful future.

Every child is an individual, and this makes school choice a process unique to each family. The fact that your father attended a top-flight Eastern boarding school to prepare for the Ivy League does not necessarily make this educational course suitable for all of his grandchildren. In addition to determining the school's overall quality, you must explore the appropriateness of philosophy, curriculum, level of academic difficulty, and style before making your selection. The right school is the school where your child will thrive, but a famous name and a hallowed reputation are not necessarily the factors that define the right environment. The challenge is in discovering what the factors are that make the match between your child and his or her school the right one.

No matter how good its quality and reputation, a single school is unlikely to be able to meet the needs of all children. The question remains: How do families begin their search with confidence that they will find what they are looking for? How do they make the right connection?

As a parent, there are a number of steps you can follow to establish a reasoned and objective course of information gathering that will lead to a subjective discussion of this information and the way it applies to the student in question. This can only occur if the first step is done thoroughly and in an orderly manner. Ultimately, targeting a small group of schools, any of which could be an excellent choice, is only possible after information gathering and discussion have taken place. With work and a little luck, the result of this process is a school with an academically sound and challenging program based on an educational philosophy that is an extension of the family's views and which will provide an emotionally and socially supportive milieu for the child.

Step 1: Identify student needs

Often the decision to change schools seems to come out of the blue, but, in retrospect, it can be seen as a decision the family has been leading up to for some time. I would urge parents to decide on their own goals for the search first and to make sure, if possible, that they can work in concert toward meeting these goals before introducing the idea to their child. These goals are as different as the parents who hold them. For one parent, finding a school with a state-of-the-art computer program is a high priority. For another, finding a school with a full dance and music

program is important. Others will be most concerned about finding a school that has the best record of college acceptances and highest SAT scores.

Once you have decided your own goals for the search, bring the child into the discussion. I often say to parents that the decision to explore is *not* the decision to change schools but only the decision to gather information and consider options. It is important to be aware that everyone has an individual style of decision making and that the decision to make a change is loaded with concerns, many of which will not be discovered until the process has begun.

If you have already made the decision to change your child's school, it is important to let your child know that this aspect of the decision is open to discussion but not to negotiation. It is equally important that you let your child know that he or she will have responsibility in choosing the specific school. Without that knowledge, your son or daughter may feel that they have no control over the course of their own life.

Some students are responsible enough to take the lead in the exploration; some are too young to do so. But in all cases, children need reassurance about their future and clarity about the reasons for considering other school settings. Sometimes the situation is fraught with disparate opinions that can turn school choice into a family battleground, one in which the child is the ultimate casualty. It is always important to keep in mind that the welfare of the child is the primary goal.

The knowledge that each individual has his or her own agenda and way of making decisions should be warning enough to pursue some preliminary discussion so that you, as parents, can avoid the pitfall of conflicting goals and maintain a united front and a reasonably directed course of action. The family discussion should be energetic, and differences of opinion should be encouraged as healthy and necessary and expressed in a climate of trust and respect.

There are many reasons why you may, at this point, decide to involve a professional educational consultant. Often this choice is made to provide a neutral ground where you and your child can both speak and be heard. Another reason is to make sure that you have established a sound course of

exploration that takes both your own and your child's needs into consideration. Consultants who are up-to-date on school information, who have visited each campus, and who are familiar with the situations of their clients can add immeasurably to the process. They can provide a reality check, reinforcement of personal impressions, and experience-based information support for people who are doing a search of this type for the first time. All the research in the world cannot replace the experience and industry knowledge of a seasoned professional. In addition, if the specific circumstances of the placement are delicate, the educational consultant is in a position to advocate for your child during the placement process. There are also situations in which a family in crisis doesn't have the time or the ability to approach school choice in a deliberate and objective manner.

These are some of the many reasons to engage the services of a consultant, but it is the family guidance aspect that most families overlook at the start of the process and value most highly after they have completed it. A good consultant provides neutral ground and information backup that are invaluable.

If you have already made the decision to change your child's school, it is important to let your child know that this aspect of the decision is open to discussion but not to negotiation.

Step 2: Evaluate your child's academic profile

If your child's academic profile raises questions about his or her ability, learning style, or emotional profile, get a professional evaluation to make sure that your expectations for your child are congruent with the child's actual abilities and needs.

Start gathering information about your child from the current school. Ask guidance counselors and teachers for their observations, and request a formal meeting to review the standardized testing that virtually every school administers. Question their views of your child's behavior, attentiveness, and areas of strength and weakness. Make sure you fully understand the reasons behind their recommendations. Do not feel shy about calling back to ask questions at a later date, after you have had time to think and

consider this important information. Your child's future may depend on the decisions you are making; don't hesitate to keep asking until you have the information you need.

If a picture of concern emerges, ask the guidance counselor, other parents, or your pediatrician for suggestions regarding learning specialists or psychologists in the community who work with children and can provide evaluation of their academic ability, academic achievement, and learning style. The evaluation should be reviewed in-depth with the specialist, who should be asked about specific recommendations for changes in the youngster's schooling.

Remember, as the parent, it is ultimately your responsibility to weigh the ideas of others and to decide if the difficulty lies with your child or the environment, either of which could indicate a need for a change of school.

Step 3: Review the goals of placement

Discuss your differences of opinion about making a change. Identify a list of schools that creates a ballpark of educational possibilities. (An educational consultant can also be helpful at this stage.)

It is important that both you and your child take the time to consider what characteristics, large and small, you would like in the new school and which you would like to avoid. As you each make lists of priorities and discuss them, the process of school choice enters the subjective arena. The impersonal descriptions of school environments transform into very personal visualizations of the ways you and your child view the child in a new setting.

A chance to play ice hockey, a series of courses in Mandarin Chinese, the opportunity to take private flute lessons, or a desire to meet others from all over the world may sound like a bizarre mix of criteria, but the desire to explore and find all of these options in a single environment expresses the expansiveness of the student's mind and the areas he or she wants to perfect, try out, or explore. Don't expect perfectly logical thinking from your child as he or she considers options; don't take everything he or she says literally or too seriously. Open and respectful discussion will allow a child to embrace a new possibility one day and reject it the next—this is part of the process of decision making and affirmation and part of the fun of exploration.

Step 4: Set an itinerary

Set an itinerary for visits and interviews so that you and your child can compare campuses and test your preconceived ideas of the schools you have researched against the reality of the campus community; forward standardized testing scores and transcripts to the schools prior to visits so that the admission office has pertinent information in advance of your meeting.

In order to allow your child the freedom to form opinions about the schools you visit, you may want to keep these pointers in mind:

- Parents should allow their child to be front and center during the visits and interviews—allow your child to answer questions, even if they leave out details you think are important.
- Parents should stay in the background and have confidence that the admission officers know how to engage kids in conversation.
- This may be the first time your child has been treated by a school as an individual and responsible person—enjoy watching him or her adjust to this as an observer, not as a protector or participant.
- Don't let your own anxiety ruin your child's experience.
- Discuss dress in advance so it doesn't become the issue and focus of the trip.

Keep your ideas and impressions to yourself and allow your child first shot at verbalizing opinions. Remember that immediate reactions are not final decisions; often the first response is only an attempt to process the experience.

Step 5: Use the application process for personal guidance

Make sure your child uses the application process not only to satisfy the school's need for information but also to continue the personal guidance process of working through and truly understanding his or her goals and expectations.

Application questions demand your child's personal insight and exploration. Addressing questions about significant experiences, people who have influenced his or her life, or selecting four words that best describe him or her are ways of coming to grips with who your child is and what he or she wants to accomplish both at the new school and in life. Although parents want their children to complete seamless and perfect applications, it is important to remember that the application must be the work of the child and that the parent has an excellent opportunity to discuss the questions and answers to help guide the student in a positive and objective self-review.

It is more important that the application essays accurately reflect the personality and values of the student than that they be technically flawless. Since the

school is basing part of its acceptance decision on the contents of the application, the school needs to meet the real student in the application. The child's own determination of what it is important for the school to know about them is crucial to this process. That being said, parents can play an important role in helping the child understand the difference between unnecessarily brutal honesty and putting his or her best foot forward.

Step 6: Trust your observations

Although the process of school exploration depends on objectivity, it is rare that a family will embrace a school solely because of its computer labs, endowment, library, SAT scores, or football team. These objective criteria frame the search, but it tends to be the intangibles that determine the decision. It is the subjective—instinctive responses to events on campus, people met, quality of interview, unfathomable vibes—that makes the match.

It is important to review what aspects of the school environment made you feel at home. These questions apply equally to parent and child. Did you like the people you met on campus? Was the tour informational but informal, with students stopping to greet you or the tour guide? Was the tone of the campus (austere or homey, modern or traditional) consistent with the kind of educational atmosphere you are looking for? Are the sports facilities beyond your wildest expectation? Does the college-sending record give you confidence that your child will find an intellectually comfortable peer group? How long do the teachers tend to stay with the school, and do they send their own children there? If it is a boarding school, do teachers live on campus? How homey is the dorm setup?

The most fundamental questions are: Do people in the school community like where they are, trust each other, have respect for each other, and feel comfortable there? Is it a family you would care to join? These subjective responses will help you recognize which schools will make your child feel he or she is part of the community, where he or she will fit in and be respected for who he or she is and wants to become.

Helene Reynolds is a former educational consultant from Princeton, New Jersey.

Plan a Successful School Search

Application deadlines, entrance exams, interviews, and acceptance or rejection letters—these are some of the challenges you can expect to encounter when applying to private schools. The school search may seem daunting, but it doesn't have to be. Here are some tips to help get you on your way.

Your first step is to gather information, preferably in the spring before you plan on applying. *Peterson's Private Secondary Schools 2007*, with vital statistics on more than 1,500 leading private schools in the U.S. and abroad, can help you evaluate schools, clarify your choices, and hone your search.

If you're considering boarding schools, you may also want to obtain a free copy of the *Boarding Schools Directory* from The Association of Boarding Schools (TABS) by calling 202-965-8982 or visiting TABS's Web site (http://www.schools.com).

Your next step is to start a list of schools that pique your interest. You'll want to call, fax, e-mail, or write to admissions offices for catalogs and applications. At this stage, don't let cost rule out choices. You'll later learn more about the school—the financing resources it makes available to students and its policies of awarding aid.

With school brochures and catalogs in hand, start planning fall visits and interviews. Review your child's school calendar, noting Saturdays, holidays, and vacations. Try to plan interviews for these days off. Each interview could last about 3 hours, as campus tours and other activities are often included.

Once you have determined which schools you want to see, where they are, and in what order you want to see them, call each school to set the interview date and time.

Keep in mind that there is no "magic number" of schools to see. Some students interview at and apply to only one school, feeling that if they are not accepted, they will stay at their current school.

Some students interview at many, thinking that considering a large number and a variety of schools will help them focus on real needs and desires.

After you've made an appointment to visit the school, reread the school's catalog and its description in this guide so that facts about the school will be fresh in your mind when you visit.

The Application Process

Once you've completed your fact-finding, you'll need to work on applications. Most schools have January or February deadlines, so it pays to begin filling out forms in November.

Applications may ask for all or some of the following: school records, references from teachers, a student statement, a writing sample or essay, an application fee, and medical history form.

Make photocopies of all application pages before you begin to complete them. That way, you'll have at

least one copy for use as a rough draft. You should also make photocopies of each completed application for your records.

References are usually written on specific school forms and are considered confidential. To ensure confidentiality, people providing references mail their comments directly to the school. A school may require four or five references—three academic references, usually from an English teacher, a math teacher, and one other teacher, and one or two references from other evaluators who know the student's personal strengths in areas other than academics. Ask these people in advance if they will write on your child's behalf. Give reference-writers appropriate forms with any special instructions and stamped envelopes addressed to the school; be sure to provide as much lead time before the deadline as possible.

The student application is completed on a special form and consists of factual family information, as well as some long or short essay

Most schools have January or February deadlines, so it pays to begin filling out forms in November.

questions. As tempting as it may be to help, let your child do the writing. The schools need to see the student's style, mechanical skills, and the way he or she looks at life and education. Some schools require a corrected writing sample from an English assignment. In this case, have your child ask his or her English teacher to help choose his or her best work.

Once the applications are mailed, the hard part is done. Ask admission officers when you can expect to hear their decisions. Most schools will let you know in early March. While you wait, you may want to remind your son or daughter that being turned down by a school is not a statement about his or her worth. Schools have many different objectives in putting a class together. And that's a lesson that will come in handy when you face the college application process.

Understanding the Admission Application Form

Gregg W. M. Maloberti
Dean of Admission, The Lawrenceville School in Lawrenceville, New Jersey

Although an attractive option for college applicants for many years, the Admission Application Form (formerly known as the Common Application) for independent boarding and day schools has only recently been made available and has just begun to grow in popularity among candidates. The Admission Application Form has been sanctioned by members of The Association of Boarding Schools (TABS). It represents the collaborative spirit of boarding schools and their commitment to helping students find the right school. Steve Ruzicka, Executive Director of TABS, organized the nationwide effort that led to the publication of the Admission Application Form. "We opened an Internet-driven discussion that led to many suggestions, alterations, and refinements of what is now the Admission Application Form accepted by more than 200 schools. A version of the Admission Application Form is available for day schools as well. My goal is to have every school accept this application." The current version of the Admission Application Form is available in TABS *Boarding Schools Directory* and in electronic form from the TABS Web site: http://www.schools.com/forms/comapp.pdf.

There are a few schools that accept only the recommendation forms from the Admission Application Form. It's best to check with each school to find out which forms are preferred. The list of schools accepting the Admission Application Form is available at this TABS Web site: http://www.schools.com/forms/schools.cfm

Will the Admission Application Form Help or Hinder?

Anxious parents' lingering doubts about the use of the Admission Application Form are hard to ignore: Will the substitution of the Admission Application Form for the individual school's application cause the admission committee to be offended and compromise my child's chances for admission? Parents should rest assured that schools agreeing to accept the Admission Application Form believe that a fair and effective admission decision can be made on the basis of the Admission Application Form and that its use in no way erodes the quality of their selection process.

All applications begin with a biographical sketch of the candidate: name, address, birth date, mailing address, parents' names, and schools attended. Information regarding sibling or legacy relationships, interest in financial aid, citizenship, language spoken, and even racial and ethnic diversity is collected as well. Except for the order in which these questions appear, there is little variation in these question types from one school's application to another. The Admission Application Form certainly relieves candidates of the burden of providing the very same biographical information over and over again.

The second section of an application generally reveals a candidate's accomplishments and ambitions. Often, the applicants are asked to catalog their interests and activities in list or narrative form. Schools want to know what the candidate has done, for how long, with whom, and to what distinction, if any. In a few cases, some schools ask for a series of short answers to a combination of questions or look for the applicant to complete a sentence. There are generally no "right" answers to these questions—but honest answers can help the school begin to characterize the applicant's curiosity, maturity, ambition, and self-esteem. Here again, great similarity exists in the manner and style with which this information is gathered. While the Admission Application Form asks these question types in a more direct manner, it is no less effective than the individual school's application and its use affords a candidate a genuine measure of efficiency without compromising individuality.

Schools that advocate the use of their own applications over that of the Admission Application Form often bitterly defend the third and final portion of their applications since it generally includes essay questions. With few exceptions, these questions, while occasionally posed in a unique or original manner, seek to probe much the same territory covered by the

three choices listed in the essay section of the Admission Application Form:

1. Describe a person who you admire or who has influenced you a great deal.
2. What makes you the interesting person that you are?
3. Explain the impact of an event or activity that has created a change in your life or in your way of thinking.

While the candidate's ability to write well is certainly under review in the essay question, the exercise investigates a candidate's values and explores the individual experiences that have shaped his or her character. These questions give candidates a chance to reveal such qualities as independence, self-reliance, creativity, originality, humility, generosity, curiosity, and genius. Viewed in this light, answering these questions becomes a tall order. The best advice may be to just answer them. In addition, candidates should recognize that although the content of their essays is always of interest, grammar, spelling, punctuation, organization, and the inclusion of evidence or examples are of equal importance.

Candidates who come from disadvantaged backgrounds often find this section of the application the most challenging and occasionally exclusionary. Some schools assume that all applicants have access to such things as summer camps, music instruction, and periodicals and newspapers. Whatever the case, the Admission Application Form is more inclusive of a broader set of experiences. In fact, many outreach agencies who seek to identify and place disadvantaged students in independent schools have either used the Admission Application Form or developed their own applications in lieu of individual school application forms.

If a student fears that using the Admission Application Form will somehow fail to convey a unique aspect of his or her individuality or that the essay question answers will not speak to the unique qualities of why a particular school might be a good match, he or she may want to think about including an extra essay. Just because a candidate uses the Admission Application Form does not mean that he or she must use a common approach to completing it. Imagine how welcome a splash of creativity might

The Admission Application Form makes the process of applying to multiple schools a much more manageable endeavor.

be to an individual reader or committee of admission officers who may read hundreds or even thousands of applications each admission season. An application that parrots the list of school courses, sports, and activities offers little insight into the candidate. A well-written application will be as unique as the individual who wrote it.

Applicants and their parents are not the only winners when the Admission Application Form is used. The teachers who dutifully complete countless recommendation forms enjoy the convenience of having to complete only one form for each of their students applying to independent schools. Practically speaking, if there is ever a time that a student wants to be in good favor with his or her teacher, it is the moment at which a reference is being given. With only one form to complete, most teachers will provide longer and more informative answers that are far more helpful to admission officers. The Admission Application Form is a great remedy for the fatigue and frustration endured by teachers who have been overwhelmed by a barrage of recommendation forms. Currently, there are even more schools accepting the recommendation forms than there are schools accepting the entire Admission Application Form. Before discounting the benefits of the Admission Application Form, be sure to consider at least the use of the recommendation forms.

Counselors and Consultants Speak Out

Lee Cary, from Shore Country Day School in Beverly, Massachusetts, has been advising eighth-graders for many years and finds the workload associated with the application process unreasonable for most of her students. "It is inconceivable to expect a 14-year-old student to write upwards of eight individual essays, all of top quality. From taking time for school visits, making up missed schoolwork, organizing forms, completing paperwork, and polishing writing, the act of applying to secondary school becomes a whole second job for eighth- and ninth-grade students." Considering that the average application includes up to ten documents, some of which must pass between the applicant, the sending school, and back to the applicant or the receiving school, an eighth grader and his or her

parents are now looking at completing more than eighty documents! On top of the testing process and applying for financial aid, this amounts to an enormous administrative challenge.

Karl Koenigsbauer, Secondary School Placement Counselor from Eaglebrook School in Deerfield, Massachusetts, agrees that the Admission Application Form makes the process more efficient, but he worries about how it might erode the process as well. "My goal is to help students find the school that will be the best match for their abilities and interests. The essay questions from some schools really help the candidate to understand more about what qualities of mind and spirit a school values. When a candidate comes to me and says a particular question is too difficult, too simplistic, or just plain confusing, it gives me an opportunity to help him or her see how that question represents the identity of that particular school and why it may or may not be a good match. I worry that the Admission Application Form will homogenize the application process to the point where I lose this opportunity to fine-tune the placement process."

Faith Howland, an independent educational consultant in Boston, Massachusetts, and a member of the Independent Educational Consultants Association (IECA), works with families to find the right school and is also often contacted for help when a student's first round of applications has not been successful. "The application process can be near overwhelming for 13- and 14-year-olds. To write as many as eight different applications, each with different essays, just when you are expected to get great grades, continue your sports commitments, and other extracurriculars—not to mention working to prepare for entrance tests. This is high stress! Use of the Admission Application Form would be supportive to students and would be extremely helpful in streamlining the teacher recommendations. For those kids who need to submit a second round of applications, the Admission Application Form could be invaluable. These youngsters are coping with disappointment while needing to research new possibilities. If schools were willing to share the Admission Application Form, it's conceivable that many more students who might simply give up if not successful on their first applications could be placed."

Many Schools, One Application

Increased acceptance of the Admission Application Form could lead to a marked increase in applications. The Admission Application Form is especially helpful

to the candidate who fails to earn any acceptance letters at the end of the application process. Traditionally, if a candidate wants to apply to a new list of schools, he or she must start from scratch and complete a new set of forms. The Admission Application Form certainly speeds up this process.

More than half of the candidates who apply to independent schools come from public schools and do not enjoy the benefit of placement counselors at their schools nor do they seek the advice of independent counselors. Regardless, most candidates are well served in using the Admission Application Form when applying to multiple schools. One strategy may be to complete a few individual applications and then submit the Admission Application Form to a few other schools—identifying some additional options and increasing the likelihood of having meaningful choices after the decision letters are mailed. Many candidates find it much easier to figure out which school they want once they know which school wants them.

Few schools realize how difficult the application process can be for families who are applying to more than one school. The Admission Application Form makes the process of applying to multiple schools a much more manageable endeavor. The use of the Admission Application Form affords families much more time and energy to devote to other aspects of the application and interview process. By reducing the duplicated paperwork of recommendations and the need to complete so many essays, applicants and their parents are granted a greater opportunity to discuss the real issues surrounding school selection, such as the compatibility of curriculum, style of teaching, and program offerings. Rather than creating folders for each school and chasing down multiple letters of recommendation, applicants and their parents can focus on just a few essays and remove the stress associated with sorting and tracking multiple documents.

Candidates and their families can be assured of the professionalism of admission officers and feel free to use the Admission Application Form. The Admission Application Form represents the efforts of the very best admission officers who have put the interests of the applicant at the fore—shifting the focus away from the school and back to the candidate. Candidates can be confident that the Admission Application Form will more than adequately allow them to make a strong case for their own admission at any school accepting the form.

About Standardized Tests

Heather Hoerle
Vice President, Member Relations, National Association of Independent Schools (NAIS)

Mention the word "testing" to even the most capable student and he or she is likely to freeze in fear. It's no wonder, then, that standardized testing in the independent school admission process causes nail-biting among students and parents alike. While standardized testing is an important part of the application process for most independent schools, it needn't be dreaded. Take the advice of one who has lived through standardized tests for private school, college, and graduate school: Just relax and do the best that you can. Undoubtedly, you will learn something from the experience. I am even more convinced of this admonition, having been an "average" standardized-test-taker all of my life.

You may be wondering why private schools test prospective students in the first place. In most cases, standardized testing is used to evaluate a student's ability to perform outside of the classroom. Often,

> *Often, testing helps schools to understand whether they have an appropriate program for applicants.*

testing helps schools to understand whether they have an appropriate program for applicants. In some cases, private schools find they are best equipped to serve students with test results that fit within a specific range or percentile. Note that standardized testing is also used to place accepted students into appropriate classes in their new school.

Years ago, I took the Secondary School Admission Test (SSAT) as part of the admission process to a boarding school. After my scores came back, my grim-faced mother called the boarding school's admission director to discuss the results. Much to her relief and surprise, I was accepted by the school in spite of mediocre quantitative testing. Indeed, the strength of my application assured school officials that I was ready for their academic challenge, despite the "average" test results. The SSAT, while an important part of my application, did not tell admission officials about my motivation nor did it yield any information about my former academic and creative achievements.

While it is true that some schools assign a great deal of importance to standardized testing, it is just as true that many schools regard testing as only one part of the application process. Many private schools place equal value on the applicant's campus interview, the student's record of achievement, teacher recommendations, and student/parent written statements. In short, test scores cannot tell an individual's full story, and admission officials recognize this limitation, even as they require standardized testing.

The tests that are most frequently used by private secondary schools are the Secondary School Admission Test Board's SSAT and the Educational Records Bureau's Independent School Entrance Exam (ISEE).

Taking the SSAT

The SSAT, which is used to evaluate applicants for admission to grades 5–11, is a multiple-choice test that measures students' ability in math and verbal areas and enables counselors to compare students' scores with those of private school applicants and the national school population. The SSAT takes more than 2 hours to complete. Two levels are administered. The lower level exam is taken by students in grades 5–7. The upper level is administered to students in grades 8–11. Students' scores are compared only to students in the

---

Worried About Taking the SSAT or ISEE?

Here are a few tips to help ban the testing blues.

- Get plenty of rest the day before the test. You will need all of your concentration on the test date, and fatigue can wreak havoc on your ability to focus.
- Eat a meal before you take the test. Your brain needs the energy that food provides!
- Carefully read the materials provided by the sponsoring test group several days before testing is scheduled. Often a "practice test" is included in your registration materials and can be helpful in preparing you for the upcoming test.
- Be well prepared. Advance registration materials offer plenty of guidance on what you will need to bring in order to take the test, such as your registration ticket and No. 2 pencils.
- Allow plenty of time to get to your test site. Be sure that you have directions to the test center, and arrive ahead of the test administration time in order to register on-site, find a bathroom, and get acclimated to the setting.
- As you are taking the test, do not get hung up on hard questions. Skip them and move on. If you have time at the end of each test section, return to unanswered questions and try again.
- Don't forget personal "comfort" items. If you have a cold, be sure to bring tissues and cough drops along. Have extra money on hand, since you may want something to drink during break. Wear layers, just in case you get too hot or too cold while taking the test.
- Finally, relax! While it is important to do your best work on standardized tests, your future does not depend solely on the test results.

---

same grade. The exam contains multiple-choice questions and a writing sample.

The SSAT is given nationally at more than 600 test sites in all fifty states on selected Saturdays during the school year (in November, December, January, February, March, April, and June). It is also given internationally in November, December, January, March, and April at 110 sites in seventy-six countries. In addition, the test is given year-round at some schools and in twelve urban areas where Independent Test Centers (ITCs) are located. There are also five international ITCs in Canada, Hong Kong, Korea, Taiwan, and Thailand. As there is more than one form of the test, students may take the SSAT many times.

Applicants can arrange to have SSAT scores sent to several different schools. Parents can obtain a test registration form and details about specific test sites, dates, and fees by requesting a free copy of the *SSAT Student Guide* at SSAT, CN 5339, Princeton, New Jersey 08543 (609-683-4440) or by visiting www.ssat.org. The Secondary School Admission Test Board also publishes *Preparing and Applying for Independent School Admission and the SSAT*, a sample test booklet that contains an actual test form for student practice.

Taking the ISEE

The ISEE is used to assess the math and verbal abilities and achievement of students entering grades 5 through 12. The test is administered at three levels: a lower level for students applying to grades 5 and 6; a middle level for those students applying to grades 7 and 8; and an upper level for students applying to grades 9 through 12. Students' scores are compared only to students in the same grade.

The test, which takes about 3 hours to complete, has two components—a multiple-choice segment and a 30-minute essay. The essay, although not scored, gives schools a chance to see a student's writing on an informal topic. The turnaround time for score reporting is seven to ten working days.

The ISEE is administered at sites across the U.S. and abroad on dates chosen by the schools. Families can obtain test dates and locations by requesting a free student guide from the Educational Records Bureau, 220 East 42nd Street, New York, New York 10017 (212-672-9800) or by visiting www.erbtest.org. The Educational Records Bureau also publishes *What to Expect on the ISEE*, a sample test booklet that contains half-length practice tests.

How Important Are the Tests?

Parents may want to assure their child that his or her fate does not rely solely on test performance. According to admission counselors, test results are only one part of the admission process. Test scores may not directly relate to the grades a student is capable of achieving in school, and tests cannot measure motivation. Because admission representatives know that a student can contribute to the life of the school community in many different ways, they are careful to keep all of an applicant's talents, abilities, and achievements in mind when evaluating his or her potential for success.

Paying for a Private Education

Mark J. Mitchell
Vice President, School Information Services,
National Association of Independent
Schools (NAIS)

Imagine asking a car dealer to sell you a $15,000 sedan for $5000 because that is all you can afford. When you buy a car, you know that you will be paying more than it cost to design, build, ship, and sell the car. The sales staff will not offer you a price based on your income. At best, you may receive discounts, rebates, or other incentives that allow you to pay the lowest price the dealer is willing to accept. As a buyer, you even accept the notion that the car's value will depreciate as soon as you drive it off the lot. No matter how you look at it, you pay more than the car cost to make and ultimately more than it's worth.

Tuition at many private schools can easily approach the cost of a new car; however, paying for a private school education is not the same as buying a car. One difference is the availability of financial aid at thousands of schools in the United States and abroad to help offset the tuition. Imagine asking a school to accept $5000 for a $15,000 tuition because that is all you can afford to pay. That is exactly what private schools that provide need-based financial aid programs accomplish. Learning about the financing options and procedures available at private schools nationwide can make this imagined scenario a reality for many families.

Need-Based Financial Aid

Many private schools offer assistance to families who demonstrate financial need. They take the tuition of the school and re-evaluate how much of it a family will pay based on financial ability. As a result, the price a family pays varies according to the amount of financial assistance they receive. Through a school's financial aid program, the tuition price listed is not always the tuition price you can expect to pay.

In fact, for academic year 2004–05, 946 NAIS-member schools provided an average of $14,430 for boarding students and $8449 for day students to nearly 18 percent of students in independent schools. The schools themselves fund the vast majority of the $815.7 million in financial aid provided to students. These need-based grants do not require repayment and are used to offset the school's tuition. Schools make this substantial commitment as one way of ensuring a socioeconomically diverse student body and to help ensure that every student qualified for admission has the best chance to enroll, regardless of his or her financial circumstances.

How Financial Need Is Determined

Many schools use a process of determining financial need that requires the completion of applications and the submission of tax forms and other documentation to help them decide how much help each family needs. Currently, more than 2,200 schools nationwide require families to complete a four-page form called the Parents' Financial Statement (PFS), which is available at the school's admission or financial aid office or online at www.nais.org. The PFS gathers information about family size, income and expenses, parents' assets and indebtedness, and the child's assets. From this and other information, schools are provided with an estimate of the amount of discretionary income (after several allowances are made for basic necessities) available for education costs. Schools review each case individually and use this estimate, along with such supporting documentation as most recent income tax forms, to make a final decision on your need for a financial aid grant. You can fill out one form for up to 3 children and send the same form to up to six schools at a time.

The amount of a need-based award varies from person to person and school to school. Just as individuals have different financial resources and obligations that dictate their need for assistance, schools have different resources and policies that dictate their ability to meet your financial need. Tuition costs, endowment incomes, and awarding philosophies are a few of the things that can affect how much a school can offer. If your decision to send your child to a private school depends heavily on getting financial help, you would benefit from applying for aid at more than one school.

Merit-Based Awards

While the majority of aid offered is based on a family's financial situation, not everyone who receives financial assistance must demonstrate financial need. Private schools offer millions of dollars in merit-based scholarships to thousands of students. In the 2004–05

academic year, 317 NAIS-member schools awarded an average annual merit award worth $3225 to students, totaling more than $24.8 million. Even with this level of commitment, such awards are rare (fewer than 5 percent of all enrolled students receive this type of aid) and, therefore, highly competitive. They may serve to reward demonstrated talents or achievements in areas ranging from academics to athletics to the arts.

Some additional resources may be available from organizations and agencies in your community. Civic and religious groups, philanthropies, and even your employer may sponsor scholarships for students at private schools. Unfortunately, these options tend to be few and far between, limited in number and size of award. Be sure to ask a financial aid officer at the school(s) in which you are interested if he or she is aware of such organizations and opportunities.

Whether it is offered by the school or a local organization, be sure to understand the requirements or conditions on which a merit-based scholarship is based. Ask if the award is renewable and, if so, under what conditions. Often, certain criteria must be met (such as minimum GPA, community service, or participation in activities) to ensure renewal of the award in subsequent years. (Some merit awards are available for just one year.)

Tuition Financing Options

Whether or not you qualify for grants or scholarships, another way to get financial help involves finding ways to make tuition payments easier on your family's monthly budget. One common option is the tuition payment plan. These plans allow you to spread tuition payments (less any forms of financial aid you receive) over a period of eight to ten months. In most cases, payments start before the school year begins, but this method can be more feasible than coming up with one or two huge lump sums before the beginning of a semester. Payment plans may be administered by the schools themselves or by a private company approved by the school. They do not normally require credit checks or charge interest; however, they typically

The financial aid officer at the school is the best source of information about your options.

charge an application or service fee, which may include tuition insurance.

Since a high-quality education is one of the best investments they can make in their child's future, many parents finance the cost just as they would any other important investment. Many schools, banks, and other agencies offer tuition loan programs specifically for elementary and secondary school expenses. While such loans are subject to credit checks and must be repaid with interest, they tend to offer rates and terms that are more favorable than those of other consumer loans. These programs are growing in popularity, so it pays to compare the details of more than one type of loan program to find the best one for your needs. Although they should always be regarded as an option of last resort, tuition loan programs can be helpful. Of course, every family must consider both the short- and long-term costs of borrowing and make its decision part of a larger plan for education financing.

A Final Word

Although the primary responsibility to pay for school costs rests with the family, there are options available if you need help. As you can see, financing a private school education can result in a partnership between the family, the school, and sometimes outside agencies or companies, with each making an effort to provide ways to meet the costs. The financial aid officer at the school is the best source of information about your options and is willing to help you in every way he or she can. Always go to the financial aid officer at a school you are interested in whenever you have any questions or concerns about these programs and the application process. Understanding your responsibilities, meeting deadlines, and learning about the full range of options is your best strategy for obtaining assistance. Though there are no guarantees, with proper planning and the right questions, your family just might get that $15,000 education for $5000.

Searching for Private Schools Online

The Internet can be a great tool for parents gathering information about private secondary schools. The majority of private schools maintain their own Web sites, which often devote a large space to admissions information for prospective students and their parents. There are also many worthwhile third-party sites that are ready to help guide you through the various aspects of the selection process, including Petersons.com.

How Petersons.com Can Help

A great place to start your search is at Peterson's High School Planner at www.petersons.com/highschool. The Planner is a comprehensive tool that will help you make sense of the private school admissions process. With a variety of options for finding a day or boarding school, www.petersons.com/highschool is your entry point to a wide range of valuable resources.

Find a Private School

Peterson's High School Planner is organized into various sectors that make it easy for you to find the information you need. You can browse private schools by name or location, for starters, or do a detailed search on the following criteria:

- All-girls schools
- All-boys schools
- Coed schools (boys and girls)
- Boarding schools
- Day schools
- Schools with a postgraduate year
- Junior boarding schools
- Special needs schools

Peterson's High School Planner is organized into various sectors that make it easy for you to find the information you need.

If the schools you are interested in have provided Thomson Peterson's with an **In-Depth Description**, you can do a keyword search on that description. Within the **In-Depth Description**, schools are given the opportunity to communicate unique features of their programs to prospective students.

Once you have found the school of your choice, simply click on it to get information about the institution, including academic programs and facilities, faculty and advisers, student body and conduct, extracurricular opportunities, weekend life, admissions information, athletics, costs and financial aid, and application timetables.

Web Site Visit

For institutions that have provided information about their Web site, simply click the Web Site Visit link to go directly to the institution's Web site. After you arrive at a school's Web site, look around and get a feel for the place. Often, schools offer virtual tours of the campus, complete with photos and commentary. Look at the admissions section to find out what qualities they are looking for in prospective students and what important deadlines must be met. If you have any questions about the admissions process or about the school in general, a visit to their Web site often yields an answer.

E-mail the School

If, after looking at the information provided on both Petersons.com and the school's Web site, you still have questions, you will want to use the "E-mail the School" feature to request more information and/or an application directly from the schools that interest you most. Just click on the "E-mail the School" link and send your message. In most instances, if you keep your questions short and to the point, you will receive an answer in no time at all.

Add to My List

The My List feature is designed to help you with your private school planning. Here you can save the list of schools you're interested in and then revisit at any time, access all the features of the site, and be reminded of important dates.

Prepare for Tests

At Thomson Peterson's, we understand that the private school admissions process can be stressful. With the stakes so high and the competition getting tighter every year, it's easy to feel overwhelmed. Fortunately,

preparing for the SSAT helps to exert some control over the options available. Peterson's SSAT Central's two full-length practice tests can give you some insight into how maximizing test scores can maximize options.

Putting It All Together

Choosing a private school is an involved and complicated process. The tools available to you on the Internet can help you to be more productive in this

process. Put the information you receive from the schools together with the information you've gathered on the Internet, then use what you've learned to narrow your search to a manageable number of choices.

So, what are you waiting for? Fire up the computer; your child's future alma mater may be just a mouse click away.

How to Use This Guide

Quick-Reference Chart

"Private Secondary Schools At-a-Glance" presents data listed in alphabetical order by state and U.S. territories; schools in Canada and other countries follow state listings. If your search is limited to a specific state, turn to the appropriate section and scan the chart for quick information about each school in that state: Are students boarding, day, or both? Is it coeducational? What grade levels are offered? How many students are enrolled? What is the student/faculty ratio? How many Advanced Placement subjects and sports are offered?

School Profiles and Announcements

The **School Profiles and Announcements** contain basic information about the schools and are listed alphabetically in each section. An outline of a profile follows. The items of information found under each section heading are defined and displayed. Any item discussed below that is omitted from a School Profile either does not apply to that particular school or is one for which no information was supplied.

Heading Name and address of school, along with the name of the Head of School.

This icon indicates that the school has purchased an **Announcement** or **In-Depth Description**.

General Information Type (boys', girls', coeducational, boarding/day) and academic emphasis, religious affiliation, grades, founding date, campus setting, nearest major city, housing, campus size, total number of buildings, accreditation and memberships, languages of instruction, endowment, enrollment, upper school average class size, and upper school faculty-student ratio.

Upper School Student Profile Breakdown by grade, gender, boarding/day, geography, and religion.

Faculty Total number; breakdown by gender, number with advanced degrees, and number who reside on campus.

Subjects Offered Academic and general subjects.

Graduation Requirements Subjects and other requirements, including community service.

Special Academic Programs Honors and Advanced Placement courses, accelerated programs, study at local college for college credit, study abroad, independent study, ESL programs, programs for gifted/remedial students and students with learning disabilities.

College Placement Number of recent graduates, representative list of colleges attended. May include mean or median SAT/ACT scores and percentage of students scoring over 600 on each section of the SAT, over 1200 on the combined SAT, or over 26 on the composite ACT.

Student Life Dress code, student council, discipline, and religious service attendance requirements.

Summer Programs Programs offered and focus; location; open to boys, girls, or both and availability to students from other schools; usual enrollment; program dates and application deadlines.

Tuition and Aid Costs, available financial aid.

Admissions New-student figures, admissions requirements, application deadlines, fees.

Athletics Sports, levels, and gender; number of coaching staff.

Computers List of classes that use computers, campus technology.

Contact Person to whom inquiries should be addressed.

Announcements, written by school administrators, present information designed to complement the data already appearing in the School Profile.

In-Depth Descriptions

In-Depth Descriptions, written expressly for Thomson Peterson's by school administrators, provide in-depth information about the schools that have chosen to submit them. These descriptions are all in the same format to provide maximum comparability. **In-Depth Descriptions** follow each School Profile section; there is a page reference at the end of a School Profile directing you to that school's **In-Depth Description**. Schools are listed alphabetically in each section.

Special Needs Schools

One of the great strengths of private schools is their variety. This section is dedicated to the belief that there is an appropriate school setting for every child, one in which he or she will thrive academically, socially, and emotionally. The task for parents, counse-

lors, and educators is to know the child's needs and the schools' resources well enough to make the right match.

Schools in this section serve those students who may have special challenges, including learning differences, dyslexia, language delay, attention deficit disorders, social maladjustment to family and surroundings, or emotional disturbances; these students may need individual attention or are underachieving for some other reason. Parents of children who lag significantly behind their grade level in basic academic skills or who have little or no motivation for schoolwork will also want to consult this section. (For easy reference, schools that offer extra help for students are identified in two directories: "Schools Reporting Programs for Students with Special Needs" and "Schools Reporting That They Accommodate Underachievers.") The schools included here chose to be in this section because they consider special needs education to be their primary focus. It is the mission of these schools, whose curricula and methodologies vary widely, to uncover a student's strengths and, with appropriate academic, social, and psychological counseling, enable him or her to succeed.

Junior Boarding Schools

The boarding schools featured in this section serve students in the middle school grades (6–9); some offer primary programs as well. As parents know, the early adolescent years are ones of tremendous physical and emotional change. Junior boarding schools specialize in this crucial period by taking advantage of children's natural curiosity, zest for learning, and growing self-awareness.

While junior boarding schools enroll students with a wide range of academic abilities and levels of emotional self-assurance, their goal is to meet each youngster's individual needs within a supportive community. They can accomplish this goal through a very low student-teacher ratio—the schools highlighted here have an average of 6 students per teacher. School size is also deliberately kept small; the average enrollment is about 200.

Junior boarding schools have demonstrated a commitment to building a diverse student population. Approximately 1 in 4 students receives financial aid; 11 percent of the student body are students of color; 9 percent are international students.

For more information about junior boarding schools, parents can visit the Junior Boarding Schools Association Web site at www.jbsa.org.

Specialized Directories

These directories are compiled from the information gathered in *Thomson Peterson's Annual Survey of Private Secondary Schools*. The schools that did not return a survey or provided incomplete data are not fully represented in these directories. For ease of reference, the directories are grouped by category: type, curricula, financial data, special programs, and special needs.

Index

The "Alphabetical Listing of Schools" shows page numbers for School Profiles in regular type, page numbers for School Profiles accompanied by Announcements in italic type, and page numbers for In-Depth Descriptions in boldface type.

Data Collection Procedures

The data contained in *Peterson's Private Secondary Schools* **Profiles, Quick-Reference Chart, Specialized Directories,** and **Index** were collected through *Thomson Peterson's Annual Survey of Private Secondary Schools* during fall and winter 2005–06. Questionnaires were posted online for more than 1,500 private secondary schools. With minor exceptions, data for those schools that responded to the questionnaire were submitted by officials at the schools themselves. All usable information received in time for publication has been included. The omission of a particular item from a profile means that it is either not applicable to that school or not available or usable. Because of the extensive system of checks performed on the data collected by Thomson Peterson's, we believe that the information presented in this guide is accurate. Nonetheless, errors and omissions are possible in a data collection and processing endeavor of this scope. Therefore, students and parents should check with a specific school at the time of application to verify all pertinent information.

Criteria for Inclusion in This Book

Most schools in this book have curricula that are primarily college preparatory. If a school is accredited or is a candidate for accreditation by a regional accrediting group, including the European Council of International Schools, and/or is approved by a state Department of Education, and/or is a member of the National Association of Independent Schools or the European Council of International Schools, then such accreditation, approval, or membership is stated. Schools appearing in the **Special Needs Schools** section may not have such accreditation or approval.

Quick-Reference Chart

Private Secondary Schools At-a-Glance

	Boarding Boys	Boarding Girls	Day Boys	Day Girls	Lower	Middle	Upper	Total	Upper	Student/Faculty Ratio	Advanced Placement Subject Areas	Sports
UNITED STATES												
Alabama												
The Altamont School, Birmingham			X	X	5–8		9–12	427	238	5:1	17	17
Bayside Academy, Daphne			X	X	PS–6	7–8	9–12	730	222	8:1	11	25
Indian Springs School, Indian Springs	X	X	X	X			8–PG	274	274	7:1	18	17
Lee-Scott Academy, Auburn			X	X	PK–6		7–12	653	303	12:1	5	10
Madison Academy, Madison			X	X	PS–6		7–12	800	400	15:1		9
Marion Academy, Marion			X	X	K4–3	4–6	7–12	110	43	9:1		7
Mars Hill Bible School, Florence			X	X	K–4	5–8	9–12	605	185	14:1	5	31
McGill-Toolen Catholic High School, Mobile			X	X			9–12	998	998	13:1	9	16
Montgomery Catholic Preparatory School, Montgomery			X	X				910	300	13:1		13
Pickens Academy, Carrollton			X	X	K4–6		7–12	386	187	20:1		10
Randolph School, Huntsville			X	X	K–6	7–8	9–12	804	268	12:1	17	16
Saint James School, Montgomery			X	X	PK–5	6–8	9–12	1,166	366	20:1	13	19
St. Paul's Episcopal School, Mobile			X	X	PK–5	6–8	9–12	1,577	610	16:1	6	15
Sumiton Christian School, Sumiton			X	X	K–5	6–8	9–12	637	231	12:1		20
Three Springs, Huntsville	X	X								10:1		14
Westminster Christian Academy, Huntsville			X	X	K4–6	7–8	9–12	750	230	12:1	5	16
Alaska												
Grace Christian School, Anchorage			X	X	K–6		7–12	675	358	21:1	6	8
Pacific Northern Academy, Anchorage			X	X	K–5	6–8	9–12	115	16	2:1		8
Arizona												
Blueprint Education, Phoenix			X	X								
Brophy College Preparatory, Phoenix			X				9–12	1,233	1,233	14:1	16	44
Green Fields Country Day School, Tucson			X	X	1–5	6–8	9–12	191	87	4:1	9	13
Lourdes Catholic High School, Nogales			X	X	PK–5	6–8	9–12	429	99	12:1		3
Northwest Community Christian School, Phoenix			X	X	PK–6	7–8	9–12	1,350	387	14:1	1	3
Oak Creek Ranch School, West Sedona	X	X				6–8	9–12	83	72	8:1		54
The Orme School, Mayer	X	X	X	X		7–8	9–PG	154	128	6:1	5	41
Phoenix Christian Unified Schools, Phoenix			X	X	PS–6	7–8	9–12	717	373	20:1	5	16
Phoenix Country Day School, Paradise Valley			X	X	PK–4	5–8	9–12	738	255	9:1	15	13
St. Gregory College Preparatory School, Tucson			X	X		6–8	9–PG	351	205	16:1	12	23
Saint Mary's High School, Phoenix			X	X			9–12	818	818	20:1	6	14
St. Paul's Preparatory Academy, Phoenix	X		X				9–12	75	75	10:1		14
Salpointe Catholic High School, Tucson			X	X			9–12	1,245	1,245	22:1	11	22
Southwestern Academy, Rimrock	X	X	X	X		8	9–PG	25	24	4:1	2	31
Spring Ridge Academy, Spring Valley		X					9–12	72	72	9:1		21
Xavier College Preparatory, Phoenix				X			9–12	1,163	1,163	22:1	18	22
Arkansas												
Episcopal Collegiate School, Little Rock			X	X		6–8	9–12	376	206	9:1	16	14
Pulaski Academy, Little Rock			X	X	PK–4	5–8	9–12	1,292	394	13:1	16	21
Subiaco Academy, Subiaco	X		X				9–12	157	157	9:1	10	57
California												
Academy of Our Lady of Peace, San Diego				X			9–12	746	746	15:1	10	10
Anacapa School, Santa Barbara			X	X	7–8		9–12	61	36	12:1	1	12
Archbishop Mitty High School, San Jose			X	X			9–12	1,503	1,503	17:1	20	19
Archbishop Riordan High School, San Francisco			X				9–12	750	750	14:1	7	26
The Archer School for Girls, Los Angeles				X		6–8	9–12	479	282	7:1	12	13
Armona Union Academy, Armona			X	X	K–4	5–8	9–12	118	41	10:1		11
Army and Navy Academy, Carlsbad	X		X			7–8	9–12	325	285	9:1	10	41
Arrowhead Christian Academy, Redlands			X	X		6–8	9–12	585	391	14:1	5	14
The Athenian School, Danville	X	X	X	X		6–8	9–12	450	296	10:1	11	15
Bellarmine College Preparatory, San Jose			X				9–12	1,500	1,500	14:1	7	18
Bentley School, Oakland			X	X	K–5	6–8	9–12	623	263	8:1	15	15
Bishop Conaty-Our Lady of Loretto High School, Los Angeles				X			9–12	448	448	14:1	3	5
Bishop Quinn High School/St. Francis Middle School, Palo Cedro			X	X		7–8	9–12	213	158			24
Brentwood School, Los Angeles			X	X	K–6	7–8	9–12	991	471	8:1	19	40
Bridges Academy, Studio City			X	X		6–8	9–12	83	52	9:1		2
The Buckley School, Sherman Oaks			X	X	K–5	6–8	9–12	750	310	7:1	17	9
Campbell Hall (Episcopal), North Hollywood			X	X	K–6	7–8	9–12	1,073	509	8:1	19	19
Carondelet High School, Concord				X			9–12	830	830	25:1	6	20
Castilleja School, Palo Alto				X		6–8	9–12	415	235	7:1	18	13
Cate School, Carpinteria	X	X	X	X			9–12	265	265	5:1	19	29
Central Catholic High School, Modesto			X	X			9–12	415	415	18:1	8	14
Chadwick School, Palos Verdes Peninsula			X	X	K–6	7–8	9–12	818	339	6:1	16	19
Chaminade College Preparatory, West Hills			X	X			9–12	1,103	1,103	15:1	18	26
Chinese Christian Schools, San Leandro			X	X	K–6	6–8	9–12	939	218	14:1	12	11
Christian Brothers High School, Sacramento			X	X			9–12	1,088	1,088	24:1	12	20
Christian Junior–Senior High School, El Cajon			X	X		7–8	9–12	625	416	14:1	7	12

Private Secondary Schools At-a-Glance

	Students Accepted				Grades			Student/Faculty			School Offerings (number)	
	Boarding		Day									
	Boys	Girls	Boys	Girls	Lower	Middle	Upper	Total	Upper	Student/Faculty Ratio	Advanced Placement Subject Areas	Sports
The College Preparatory School, Oakland			X	X			9–12	329	329	8:1	11	12
Convent of the Sacred Heart High School, San Francisco				X			9–12	210	210	6:1	19	13
Cornelia Connelly School, Anaheim				X			9–12	290	290		12	9
Crespi Carmelite High School, Encino			X				9–12	540	540	23:1	13	13
Crossroads School for Arts & Sciences, Santa Monica			X	X	K–5	6–8	9–12	1,146	500	17:1	13	20
Crystal Springs Uplands School, Hillsborough			X	X		6–8	9–12	355	246	9:1	15	10
De La Salle High School, Concord			X				9–12	1,006	1,006	28:1	9	18
Delphi Academy of Los Angeles, Lake View Terrace			X	X	K–3	4–8	9–12	210	60	18:1		21
Don Bosco High School, Rosemead			X				9–12	900	900	30:1		16
Dunn School, Los Olivos	X	X	X	X		6–8	9–12	250	186	7:1	12	35
Eastside College Preparatory School, East Palo Alto			X	X		6–8	9–12	211	149	8:1		4
Emerson Honors High Schools, Orange	X	X	X	X	K–6		7–12	170	75	15:1	4	10
Francis Parker School, San Diego			X	X	JK–5	6–8	9–12	1,198	459	15:1	15	25
Fresno Christian Schools, Fresno			X	X	K–6	7–8	9–12	720	276	23:1	5	16
The Frostig School, Pasadena			X	X	1–5	6–8	9–12	120	48	6:1		4
Futures High School, Oceanside, Oceanside			X	X		7–8	9–12	36	32	1:1		
Futures High School—San Diego, San Diego			X	X			7–12	42	42	8:1	8	
Garces Memorial High School, Bakersfield			X	X			9–12	668	668	23:1	5	15
Grace Baptist Schools, Redding			X	X	K–6	7–8	9–12	350	150	12:1		9
The Grauer School, Encinitas			X	X		6–8	9–12	84	48	7:1	2	28
Happy Valley School, Ojai	X	X	X	X			9–12	83	83	7:1	3	36
The Harker School, San Jose			X	X	K–5	6–8	9–12	1,685	641	11:1	18	23
Harvard-Westlake School, North Hollywood			X	X		7–9	10–12	1,573	834	8:1	19	21
Head-Royce School, Oakland			X	X	K–5	6–8	9–12	750	319	9:1	19	20
Highland Hall, A Waldorf School, Northridge			X	X	N–6	7–8	9–12	376	107	6:1		7
Hillcrest Christian School, Granada Hills			X	X	K–5	6–8	9–12	757	235	12:1	4	9
Idyllwild Arts Academy, Idyllwild	X	X	X	X		8	9–PG	265	264	12:1	4	22
International High School of FAIS, San Francisco			X	X	PK–5	6–8	9–12	893	313	10:1	14	24
Jesuit High School, Carmichael			X				9–12	1,000	1,000	18:1	12	15
Justin-Siena High School, Napa			X	X			9–12	610	610	19:1	5	20
Kings Christian School, Lemoore			X	X	PK–6	7–8	9–12	327	123	15:1	2	17
La Cheim School, Antioch			X	X	1–5	6–8	9–12	42	24	4:1		7
Laguna Blanca School, Santa Barbara			X	X	K–4	5–8	9–12	411	208	12:1	19	18
La Jolla Country Day School, La Jolla			X	X	N–4	5–8	9–12	1,037	364	12:1	18	28
La Salle High School, Pasadena			X	X			9–12	735	735	12:1	6	18
Le Lycee Francais de Los Angeles, Los Angeles			X	X	K–4	5–8	9–12	808	150	15:1	10	14
Lick-Wilmerding High School, San Francisco			X	X			9–12	418	418	9:1	17	15
Linfield Christian School, Temecula			X	X	K–5	6–8	9–12	924	410	19:1	5	12
Loretto High School, Sacramento				X			9–12	550	550	14:1	6	16
Los Angeles Baptist Junior/Senior High School, North Hills			X	X		7–8	9–12	963	659	22:1	10	11
Los Angeles Lutheran High School, Sylmar			X	X		7–8	9–12	246	174	16:1		11
Louisville High School, Woodland Hills				X			9–12	498	498	25:1	15	13
Loyola High School, Jesuit College Preparatory, Los Angeles			X				9–12	1,210	1,210	15:1	20	14
Lutheran High School, La Verne			X	X			9–12	131	131	12:1	4	15
Lycee International de Los Angeles, Los Angeles			X	X	PK–5	6–8	9–12	461	93	8:1	3	8
Marin Academy, San Rafael			X	X			9–12	413	413	9:1	17	29
Marlborough School, Los Angeles				X		7–9	10–12	530	262	10:1	19	13
Marymount High School, Los Angeles				X			9–12	400	400	8:1	17	20
Mayfield Senior School, Pasadena				X			9–12	305	305	8:1	12	21
Menlo School, Atherton			X	X		6–8	9–12	767	550	11:1	19	16
Mercy High School College Preparatory, San Francisco				X			9–12	530	530	15:1	11	8
Midland School, Los Olivos	X	X					9–12	78	78	5:1	2	18
Mid-Peninsula High School, Menlo Park			X	X			9–12	120	120	8:1		6
Milken Community High School of Stephen Wise Temple, Los Angeles			X	X		7–8	9–12	787	584	7:1	20	23
Montclair College Preparatory School, Van Nuys	X	X	X	X	6–8		9–12	439	319	20:1	14	4
Monte Vista Christian School, Watsonville	X	X	X	X	6–8		9–12	866	676	16:1	7	20
Moreau Catholic High School, Hayward			X	X			9–12	930	930	18:1	13	19
Nawa Academy, French Gulch	X	X				7–8	9–12	48	41	8:1		77
Notre Dame High School, Belmont				X			9–12	733	733	17:1	10	27
Oakwood School, North Hollywood			X	X	K–6		7–12	764	476	10:1	17	39
Ojai Valley School, Ojai	X	X	X	X	PK–5	6–8	9–12	339	118	5:1	10	38
Orangewood Adventist Academy, Garden Grove			X	X	PK–6	7–8		274	90	10:1		7
Orinda Academy, Orinda			X	X		7–8	9–12	129	115	9:1	2	9
Oxford School, Rowland Heights			X	X		7–8	9–12	60	53	14:1	1	2
Pacific Hills School, West Hollywood			X	X		6–8	9–12	289	198	15:1		13
Palma High School, Salinas			X			7–8	9–12	642	454	16:1	11	13
Paraclete High School, Lancaster			X	X			9–12	783	783	18:1	5	12
Polytechnic School, Pasadena			X	X	K–5	6–8	9–12	834	357	17:1		16
Providence High School, Burbank			X	X			9–12	580	580	20:1	11	14
Ramona Convent Secondary School, Alhambra				X		7–8	9–12	497	463	10:1	13	7
Ribet Academy, Los Angeles	X	X	X	X	1–5	6–8	9–12	442	223	8:1	13	31

Quick-Reference Chart
CALIFORNIA

Private Secondary Schools At-a-Glance

| | STUDENTS ACCEPTED | | | | GRADES | | | STUDENT/FACULTY | | | SCHOOL OFFERINGS (number) | |
| | Boarding | | Day | | | | | | | | | |
	Boys	Girls	Boys	Girls	Lower	Middle	Upper	Total	Upper	Student/Faculty Ratio	Advanced Placement Subject Areas	Sports
Rio Lindo Adventist Academy, Healdsburg	X	X	X	X			9–12	145	145	10:1	1	16
Ripon Christian Schools, Ripon			X	X	K–5	6–8	9–12	780	280	18:1	3	13
Rolling Hills Preparatory School, Palos Verdes Estates			X	X		6–8	9–12	256	156	9:1	8	18
Sacramento Country Day School, Sacramento			X	X	PK–5	6–8	9–12	539	142	10:1	12	12
Sacred Heart High School, Los Angeles				X			9–12	370	370	15:1		6
Sacred Heart Preparatory, Atherton			X	X			9–12	485	485	8:1	13	17
Saddleback Valley Christian School, San Juan Capistrano			X	X	PK–6	7–8	9–12	643	176	12:1		11
St. Bernard High School, Playa del Rey			X	X			9–12	644	644	24:1	14	22
St. Catherine's Military Academy, Anaheim	X		X	X	K–6	7–8		160	70	12:1		17
Saint Elizabeth High School, Oakland			X	X			9–12	265	265	15:1	3	8
Saint Lucy's Priory High School, Glendora				X			9–12	871	871	22:1	10	12
St. Margaret's Episcopal School, San Juan Capistrano			X	X	N–5	6–8	9–12	1,221	390	14:1	19	25
Saint Mary's College High School, Berkeley			X	X			9–12	629	629	17:1	7	19
St. Michael's Preparatory School of the Norbertine Fathers, Silverado	X						9–12	64	64	3:1	6	11
Saint Patrick—Saint Vincent High School, Vallejo			X	X			9–12	665	665	30:1	7	13
San Diego Jewish Academy, San Diego			X	X	K–5	6–8	9–12	687	186	20:1	12	20
San Domenico School, San Anselmo		X	X	X	PK–5	6–8	9–12	582	168	9:1	14	15
Santa Catalina School, Monterey		X	X	X	PK–5	6–8	9–12	551	290	7:1	19	39
Southwestern Academy, San Marino	X	X	X	X		6–8	9–PG	111	90	6:1	3	17
Squaw Valley Academy, Olympic Valley	X	X	X	X		6–8	9–12	75	68	7:1	4	47
Stanbridge Academy, San Mateo			X	X	K–6	7–8		83	41	8:1		12
Stevenson School, Pebble Beach	X	X	X	X	PK–5	6–8	9–12	750	549	10:1	18	34
Summerfield Waldorf School, Santa Rosa			X	X	1–6	7–8	9–12	365	96	4:1	3	4
The Thacher School, Ojai	X	X	X	X			9–12	245	245	5:1	17	35
Tri-City Christian Schools, Vista			X	X	PK–6	7–8	9–12	1,132	298	10:1	4	16
The Urban School of San Francisco, San Francisco			X	X			9–12	295	295	9:1	8	34
Ursuline High School, Santa Rosa				X			9–12	336	336	12:1	4	11
Valley Christian School, San Jose			X	X	K–5	6–8	9–12	2,135	1,161	17:1	14	20
Viewpoint School, Calabasas			X	X	K–5	6–8	9–12	1,185	432	10:1	20	24
Village Christian Schools, Sun Valley			X	X	JK–5	6–8	9–12	1,735	610	17:1	9	16
The Waverly School, Pasadena			X	X	PK–6	7–8	9–12	289	80	8:1	10	8
Westridge School, Pasadena				X	4–6	7–8	9–12	510	263	9:1	14	13
Westview School, Los Angeles			X	X		6–8		98	72	8:1		3
Whittier Christian High School, La Habra			X	X			9–12	585	585	10:1	5	13
Windward School, Los Angeles			X	X		7–8	9–12	474	325	7:1	10	6
Woodside International School, San Francisco			X	X		6–8	9–12	85	80	10:1	4	1
Woodside Priory School, Portola Valley	X	X	X	X		6–8	9–12	350	246	10:1	18	17
Colorado												
Alexander Dawson School, Lafayette			X	X	K–4	5–8	9–12	423	188	7:1	15	37
Bridge School, Boulder			X	X		6–8	9–12	105	46	6:1		2
The Colorado Rocky Mountain School, Carbondale	X	X	X	X			9–12	167	167	5:1	8	30
The Colorado Springs School, Colorado Springs			X	X	PS–5	6–8	9–12	462	142	8:1	8	12
Colorado Timberline Academy, Durango	X	X	X	X			9–12	30	30	5:1		27
Denver Academy, Denver			X	X	1–6	7–8	9–12	429	281	6:1		32
Denver Christian High School, Denver			X	X			9–12	296	296	18:1		7
Denver Lutheran High School, Denver			X	X			9–12	211	211	17:1	3	15
Eagle Rock School, Estes Park	X	X	X									32
Forest Heights Lodge, Evergreen	X				K–5	6–8	9–12	24	3	5:1		36
Fountain Valley School of Colorado, Colorado Springs	X	X	X	X			9–12	237	237	5:1	16	39
Kent Denver School, Englewood			X	X		6–8	9–12	656	436	7:1	16	27
The Lowell Whiteman School, Steamboat Springs	X	X	X	X			9–12	95	95	7:1	5	65
St. Mary's Academy, Englewood			X	X	K–5	6–8	9–12	751	277	10:1	11	13
Saint Mary's High School, Colorado Springs			X	X			9–12	380	380	11:1	7	13
Vail Mountain School, Vail			X	X	K–5	6–8	9–12	330	102	10:1	6	41
Connecticut												
Academy of Our Lady of Mercy, Milford				X			9–12	453	453	12:1		12
Avon Old Farms School, Avon	X		X				9–PG	396	396	6:1	19	50
Brunswick School, Greenwich			X		PK–4	5–8	9–12	877	316	6:1	19	16
Canterbury School, New Milford	X	X	X	X			9–PG	361	361	8:1	17	27
Chase Collegiate School, Waterbury			X	X	PK–5	6–8	9–12	475	162	7:1	16	20
Cheshire Academy, Cheshire	X	X	X	X		6–8	9–PG	385	328	7:1	12	25
Choate Rosemary Hall, Wallingford	X	X	X	X			9–12	851	851	6:1	19	49
Christian Heritage School, Trumbull			X	X	K–6	7–8	9–12	522	171	9:1	9	14
Convent of the Sacred Heart, Greenwich				X	PS–4	5–8	9–12	695	243	7:1	14	19
Eagle Hill School, Greenwich	X	X								4:1		40
Eagle Hill-Southport, Southport			X	X				107	20	4:1		6
East Catholic High School, Manchester			X	X			9–12	728	728	14:1	5	19
The Ethel Walker School, Simsbury		X		X		6–8	9–12	243	183	5:1	17	28
The Forman School, Litchfield	X	X	X	X			9–12	170	170	3:1	2	20
The Glenholme School, Washington	X	X	X	X				100	70	12:1		17
Greens Farms Academy, Greens Farms			X	X	K–5	6–8	9–12	589	236	7:1	16	29
Greenwich Academy, Greenwich				X	PK–4	5–8	9–12	784	307	7:1	19	31

Private Secondary Schools At-a-Glance

| | STUDENTS ACCEPTED | | | | GRADES | | | STUDENT/FACULTY | | | SCHOOL OFFERINGS (number) | |
| | Boarding | | Day | | | | | | | | | |
	Boys	Girls	Boys	Girls	Lower	Middle	Upper	Total	Upper	Student/Faculty Ratio	Advanced Placement Subject Areas	Sports
Grove School, Madison	X	X	X	X		7–8	9–13	103	94	4:1		65
The Gunnery, Washington	X	X	X	X			9–PG	290	290	7:1	8	15
Hamden Hall Country Day School, Hamden			X	X	PK–6	7–8	9–12	565	241	8:1		17
Hopkins School, New Haven			X	X		7–8	9–12	655	514	6:1	15	37
The Hotchkiss School, Lakeville	X	X	X	X			9–PG	566	566	5:1	18	43
Hyde School, Woodstock	X	X	X	X			9–12	186	186	12:1	5	17
Indian Mountain School, Lakeville	X	X	X	X	PK–4	5–6	7–9	262	145	4:1		14
Kent School, Kent	X	X	X	X			9–PG	571	571	7:1	19	39
King & Low-Heywood Thomas School, Stamford			X	X	PK–5	6–8	9–12	648	250	7:1	17	22
Kingswood-Oxford School, West Hartford						6–8	9–12	595	393	8:1	16	19
The Loomis Chaffee School, Windsor	X	X	X	X			9–PG	723	723	5:1	13	50
Marianapolis Preparatory School, Thompson	X	X	X	X			9–PG	280	280	10:1	9	35
The Marvelwood School, Kent	X	X	X	X			9–12	150	150	4:1		32
Mercy High School, Middletown				X			9–12	667	667	14:1	11	18
Miss Porter's School, Farmington		X		X			9–12	325	325	8:1	18	40
The Norwich Free Academy, Norwich			X	X						22:1	15	27
The Oxford Academy, Westbrook	X						9–PG	38	38	1:1	8	16
Pomfret School, Pomfret	X	X	X	X			9–PG	353	353	5:1	19	24
The Rectory School, Pomfret	X		X	X		5–9		169	132	3:1		48
Rumsey Hall School, Washington Depot	X	X	X	X	K–5	6–9		307	174	8:1		50
Sacred Heart Academy, Stamford				X			9–12	125	125	10:1	5	6
St. Joseph High School, Trumbull			X	X			9–12	850	850	14:1	7	17
St. Luke's School, New Canaan			X	X		5–8	9–12	485	247	8:1	19	19
Saint Thomas More School, Oakdale	X				8		9–PG	210	194	7:1		38
Salisbury School, Salisbury	X		X				9–PG	285	285	4:1	10	33
South Kent School, South Kent	X		X				9–PG	142	142	4:1	5	25
Suffield Academy, Suffield	X	X	X	X			9–PG	404	404	6:1	11	27
The Taft School, Watertown	X	X	X	X			9–PG	566	566	6:1	19	43
Trinity Catholic High School, Stamford			X	X			9–12	483	483	15:1	8	19
Watkinson School, Hartford			X	X		6–8	9–PG	272	175	5:1		28
Wellspring Foundation, Bethlehem	X	X	X	X				52				
Westminster School, Simsbury	X	X	X	X			9–PG	375	375	5:1	19	22
Westover School, Middlebury		X		X			9–12	205	205	8:1	17	43
The Williams School, New London			X	X		7–8	9–12	321	239	8:1	7	14
The Woodhall School, Bethlehem	X		X				9–PG	44	44	3:1		33
Wooster School, Danbury			X	X	K–5	6–8	9–12	426	144	10:1	12	15
Delaware												
Archmere Academy, Claymont			X	X			9–12	505	505	10:1	18	19
The Cedars Academy, Bridgeville	X	X				5	6–12	40	37	8:1		3
St. Andrew's School, Middletown	X	X					9–12	270	270	5:1	11	30
St. Mark's High School, Wilmington			X	X			9–12	1,585	1,585	15:1	18	18
Salesianum School, Wilmington			X				9–12	1,032	1,032		15	19
Sanford School, Hockessin			X	X	PK–4	5–8	9–12	711	245	7:1	16	11
The Tatnall School, Wilmington			X	X	N–4	5–8	9–12	722	258	8:1	15	18
Tower Hill School, Wilmington			X	X	PK–4	5–8	9–12	755	230	7:1	17	21
Ursuline Academy, Wilmington			X	X	PK–6	7–8	9–12	653	224	7:1	11	15
Wilmington Christian School, Hockessin			X	X	PK–6		7–12	549	290	15:1	3	10
Wilmington Friends School, Wilmington			X	X	PS–5	6–8	9–12	847	254	9:1	4	13
District of Columbia												
The Field School, Washington			X	X		7–8	9–12	308	241	6:1	5	16
Georgetown Day School, Washington			X	X	PK–5	6–8	9–12	1,031	458	7:1	19	16
Georgetown Visitation Preparatory School, Washington				X			9–12	475	475	10:1	10	18
Maret School, Washington			X	X	K–4	5–8	9–12	600	300	6:1	16	19
National Cathedral School, Washington				X	4–6	7–8	9–12	578	306	6:1	17	43
St. Anselm's Abbey School, Washington			X			6–8	9–12	261	141	6:1	17	14
St. John's College High School, Washington			X	X			9–12	1,074	1,074	13:1	12	38
Sidwell Friends School, Washington			X	X	PK–4	5–8	9–12	1,091	466	9:1	11	32
Washington International School, Washington			X	X	PK–5	6–8	9–12	820	246	8:1		11
Florida												
Academy of the Holy Names, Tampa			X	X	PK–4	5–8	9–12	853	346	15:1	12	20
Admiral Farragut Academy, St. Petersburg	X	X	X	X	P4–5	6–8	9–12	425	253	15:1		33
Allison Academy, North Miami Beach			X	X		6–8	9–12	116	85	15:1	4	16
American Academy, Plantation			X	X	1–6	7–8	9–12	498	242	12:1		20
American Heritage School, Plantation			X	X	PK–6		7–12	1,949	1,127	13:1	7	16
Argo Academy, Sarasota	X	X					12	24	24	4:1		10
Belen Jesuit Preparatory School, Miami			X			6–8	9–12	1,315	743	13:1	13	18
The Benjamin School, North Palm Beach			X	X	PK–5	6–8	9–12	1,336	434	16:1	18	21
Berkeley Preparatory School, Tampa			X	X	PK–5	6–8	9–12	1,205	514	8:1	16	26
Bishop Kenny High School, Jacksonville			X	X			9–12	1,440	1,440	15:1		16
Bishop Verot High School, Fort Myers			X	X			9–12	729	729	17:1	9	16
The Bolles School, Jacksonville	X	X	X	X	PK–5	6–8	9–12	1,711	761	9:1	19	20
Bradenton Christian School, Bradenton			X	X	PK–6	7–8	9–12	563	194	14:1		14
Canterbury School, Fort Myers			X	X	PK–5	6–8	9–12	694	211	10:1	14	13

Private Secondary Schools At-a-Glance

	Students Accepted				Grades			Student/Faculty			School Offerings (number)	
	Boarding		Day									
	Boys	Girls	Boys	Girls	Lower	Middle	Upper	Total	Upper	Student/Faculty Ratio	Advanced Placement Subject Areas	Sports
The Canterbury School of Florida, St. Petersburg			X	X	PK–4	5–8	9–12	425	96	8:1	14	24
Cardinal Gibbons High School, Fort Lauderdale			X	X			9–12	1,243	1,243	18:1	12	17
Cardinal Newman High School, West Palm Beach			X	X			9–12	879	879	25:1	5	18
Carrollton School of the Sacred Heart, Miami				X	PK–3	4–6	7–12	710	380	9:1	7	14
Chaminade-Madonna College Preparatory, Hollywood			X	X			9–12	872	872	19:1	10	15
The Community School of Naples, Naples			X	X	PK–5	6–8	9–12	779	259	6:1	19	16
Eckerd Youth Alternatives, Clearwater	X	X			4–5	6–8	9–12	782	319	10:1		5
Episcopal High School of Jacksonville, Jacksonville			X	X		6–8	9–12	891	561	11:1	13	21
Father Lopez High School, Daytona Beach			X	X			9–12	294	294	20:1	5	16
Florida Air Academy, Melbourne	X	X	X	X		6–8	9–12	484	372	16:1	6	52
The Geneva School, Winter Park			X	X	K4–6		7–12	465	129	5:1	5	10
Glades Day School, Belle Glade			X	X	PK–6	7–8	9–12	602	265	10:1	2	14
Gulliver Preparatory School, Miami			X	X	PK–4	5–8	9–12	2,093	908	8:1	20	37
Jesuit High School of Tampa, Tampa			X				9–12	665	665	13:1	6	14
Lake Highland Preparatory School, Orlando			X	X	PK–6	7–8	9–12	1,931	671	12:1	20	23
Miami Country Day School, Miami			X	X	PK–5	6–8	9–12	1,000	351	9:1	17	22
Montverde Academy, Montverde	X	X	X	X	PK–5	6–8	9–PG	431	210	8:1	10	36
The North Broward Preparatory Upper School, Coconut Creek	X	X	X	X	PK–5	6–8	9–12	1,900	815	18:1	14	26
Northside Christian School, St. Petersburg			X	X	PS–5	6–8	9–12	877	221	11:1	5	15
Out-Of-Door-Academy, Sarasota			X	X	PK–6	7–8	9–12	593	176	10:1	13	15
Palmer Trinity School, Miami			X	X		6–8	9–12	600	341	14:1	16	28
Pine Crest School, Fort Lauderdale			X	X	PK–5	6–8	9–12	1,675	770	9:1	19	23
Pope John Paul II High School, Boca Raton			X	X			9–12	871	871	28:1	6	18
Providence School, Jacksonville			X	X	K–5	6–8	9–12	1,170	400	14:1	12	15
Rabbi Alexander S. Gross Hebrew Academy, Miami Beach			X	X	N–5	6–8	9–12	589	143	4:1	8	4
Ransom Everglades School, Miami			X	X		6–8	9–12	991	562	14:1	20	22
Saint Andrew's School, Boca Raton	X	X	X	X	K–5	6–8	9–12	1,135	584	10:1	17	18
Saint Edward's School, Vero Beach			X	X	PK–5	6–8	9–12	932	339	16:1	15	16
St. Johns Country Day School, Orange Park			X	X	PK–5	6–8	9–12	754	232	10:1	17	53
St. Joseph Academy, St. Augustine			X	X			9–12	350	350	13:1	5	13
Saint Stephen's Episcopal School, Bradenton			X	X	PK–6	7–8	9–12	801	300	11:1	14	28
St. Thomas Aquinas High School, Fort Lauderdale			X	X			9–12	2,141	2,141	18:1	18	22
Shorecrest Preparatory School, Saint Petersburg			X	X	PK–4	5–8	9–12	991	237	6:1	19	14
Trinity Preparatory School, Winter Park			X	X		6–8	9–12	822	490	12:1	16	19
Universal Academy of Florida, Tampa			X	X	1–5	6–8	9–12	288	48	16:1		13
University of Miami Online High School, Weston			X	X			8–12	450	450	14:1		9
University School of Nova Southeastern University, Fort Lauderdale			X	X	PK–5	6–8	9–12	1,681	526	11:1	20	18
The Vanguard School, Lake Wales	X	X	X	X		5–8	9–PG	93	81	10:1		19
Westminster Christian School, Miami			X	X	PK–5	6–8	9–12	1,094	418	12:1	13	13

Georgia

	Students Accepted				Grades			Student/Faculty			School Offerings (number)	
	Boys	Girls	Boys	Girls	Lower	Middle	Upper	Total	Upper	Student/Faculty Ratio	Advanced Placement Subject Areas	Sports
Advanced Academy of Georgia, Carrollton	X	X					10–12	67	67	14:1		7
Athens Academy, Athens			X	X	N–4	5–8	9–12	841	312	18:1	8	11
Atlanta International School, Atlanta			X	X	PK–5	6–8	9–12	868	255	8:1		12
Ben Franklin Academy, Atlanta			X	X			9–12	130	130	3:1		4
Brandon Hall School, Atlanta	X		X	X		4–8	9–PG	120	85	3:1	2	9
Brenau Academy, Gainesville		X		X			9–PG	80	80	8:1		12
Brookstone School, Columbus			X	X	PK–4	5–8	9–12	853	283	11:1	13	14
Bulloch Academy, Statesboro			X	X	PK–5	6–8	9–12	517	112	16:1	3	17
Chatham Academy, Savannah			X	X	1–4	5–8	9–12	99	37	10:1		18
The Cottage School, Roswell			X	X		6–8	9–12	165	118	10:1		25
Darlington School, Rome	X	X	X	X	PK–5	6–8	9–PG	928	504	9:1	16	34
First Presbyterian Day School, Macon			X	X	PK–5	6–8	9–12	952	316	12:1	8	16
Frederica Academy, St. Simons Island			X	X	PK–5	6–8	9–12	394	124	9:1	4	11
The Galloway School, Atlanta			X	X	PK–4	5–8	9–12	730	234	10:1	11	12
George Walton Academy, Monroe			X	X	K–6	7–8	9–12	975	334	10:1	10	19
Greater Atlanta Christian Schools, Norcross			X	X	P4–5	6–8	9–12	1,881	620	17:1	19	19
The Heritage School, Newnan			X	X	PK–4	5–8	9–12	384	116	7:1	13	24
Hidden Lake Academy, Dahlonega	X	X					8–PG	141	141	9:1		43
Horizons School, Atlanta	X	X	X	X	K–5	6–7	8–PG	100	60	10:1	2	1
La Grange Academy, La Grange			X	X	K–5	6–8	9–12	229	68	15:1	5	12
The Lovett School, Atlanta			X	X	K–5	6–8	9–12	1,555	612	8:1	16	44
Marist School, Atlanta			X	X			7–12	1,042	1,042	10:1	19	18
North Cobb Christian School, Kennesaw			X	X	PK–6	7–8	9–12	880	242	9:1		19
Oak Mountain Academy, Carrollton			X	X	K–5	6–8	9–12	233	56	4:1	5	10
Pace Academy, Atlanta			X	X	K–5	6–8	9–12	922	380	8:1	16	18
The Paideia School, Atlanta			X	X	N–6	7–8	9–12	915	387	10:1	8	14
Piedmont Academy, Monticello			X	X	K4–5	6–8	9–12	313	88	13:1		13
Rabun Gap-Nacoochee School, Rabun Gap	X	X	X	X		6–8	9–12	314	226	14:1	8	30
Riverside Military Academy, Gainesville	X		X			7–8	9–12	412	353	10:1	6	47
St. Andrew's on the Marsh School, Savannah			X	X	PK–4	5–8	9–12	469	135	9:1	7	14
St. Francis School, Alpharetta			X	X	1–5	6–8	9–12	830	314	14:1		16
St. Pius X Catholic High School, Atlanta			X	X			9–12	1,000	1,000	15:1	19	20

Private Secondary Schools At-a-Glance

	Boarding Boys	Boarding Girls	Day Boys	Day Girls	Lower	Middle	Upper	Total	Upper	Student/Faculty Ratio	Advanced Placement Subject Areas	Sports
Saint Vincent's Academy, Savannah				X			9–12	346	346	12:1	5	12
Savannah Christian Preparatory School, Savannah			X	X	PK–5	6–8	9–12	1,516	455	23:1	4	13
The Savannah Country Day School, Savannah			X	X	PK–5	6–8	9–12	989	309	10:1	16	26
Stratford Academy, Macon			X	X	PK–5	6–8	9–12	931	302	13:1	16	10
Tallulah Falls School, Tallulah Falls	X	X	X	X		7–8	9–12	157	119	8:1	6	57
Three Springs/Prince Mountain Academy, Blue Ridge	X									4:1		25
Trinity Christian School, Dublin			X	X	K4–5	6–8	9–12	389	110	12:1	2	12
The Walker School, Marietta			X	X	PK–5	6–8	9–12	1,075	382	14:1		34
Wesleyan School, Norcross			X	X	K–4	5–8	9–12	1,071	414	7:1	16	18
The Westfield Schools, Perry			X	X	PK–5		6–12	637	337	14:1	5	17
The Westminster Schools, Atlanta			X	X	K–5	6–8	9–12	1,804	782	14:1	17	32
Westminster Schools of Augusta, Augusta			X	X	PK–5	6–8	9–12	511	151	6:1	11	9
Whitefield Academy, Mableton			X	X	PK–5	6–8	9–12	635	236	10:1	8	15
Yeshiva Atlanta, Atlanta			X	X			9–12	80	80	6:1	6	6
Guam												
Saint John's School, Tumon	X	X	X	X	PK–6		7–12	520	225	12:1		17
Hawaii												
Academy of the Pacific, Honolulu			X	X		6–8	9–12	133	108	10:1	3	18
Hale O Ulu School Child and Family Service, Ewa			X	X						12:1		
Hawaiian Mission Academy, Honolulu	X	X	X	X			9–12	128	128	12:1		2
Hawaii Baptist Academy, Honolulu			X	X	K–6		7–12	1,049	652	12:1	9	24
Hawai'i Preparatory Academy, Kamuela	X	X	X	X	K–5	6–8	9–12	613	362	12:1	16	33
Iolani School, Honolulu			X	X	K–6	7–8	9–12	1,833	930	12:1	19	27
La Pietra–Hawaii School for Girls, Honolulu				X		6–8	9–12	240	132	10:1	5	25
Lutheran High School of Hawaii, Honolulu				X			9–12	131	131	10:1	2	18
Maryknoll School, Honolulu			X	X	PK–5	6–8	9–12	1,399	581	11:1	12	32
Mid-Pacific Institute, Honolulu			X	X	K–5	6–8	9–12	1,395	775	19:1	7	31
The Parker School, Kamuela			X	X	K–5	6–8	9–12	269	107	8:1	5	11
Punahou School, Honolulu			X	X	K–5	6–8	9–12	3,768	1,744	12:1	14	23
St. Andrew's Priory School, Honolulu				X	K–4	5–8	9–12	538	139	4:1	8	34
Saint Francis School, Honolulu				X		6–8	9–12	387	322	20:1	8	23
Seabury Hall, Makawao			X	X		6–8	9–12	406	266	12:1	12	14
Idaho												
Bishop Kelly High School, Boise			X	X			9–12	672	672	17:1	9	19
Gem State Adventist Academy, Caldwell	X	X	X	X			9–12	127	127	13:1	1	7
Riverstone Community School, Boise			X	X	K–5	6–8	9–12	252	77	4:1		24
Illinois												
Aquin Central Catholic High School, Freeport			X	X		7–8	9–12	161	112	10:1	4	3
Archbishop Quigley Preparatory High School, Chicago			X				9–12	215	215	7:1	12	18
Aurora Central High School, Aurora			X	X			9–12	431	431	16:1	10	29
Benet Academy, Lisle			X	X			9–12	1,299	1,299	18:1	12	17
Bishop McNamara High School, Kankakee			X	X			9–12	470	470	21:1	8	23
Brehm Preparatory School, Carbondale	X	X	X	X		6–8	9–12	112	84	4:1		10
Broadview Academy, La Fox	X	X	X	X			9–12	82	82	8:1		6
Elgin Academy, Elgin			X	X	PS–4	5–8	9–12	395	125	7:1	7	9
Fox River Country Day School, Elgin	X	X	X	X	PK–5	6–8		180	28	16:1		19
Fox Valley Lutheran Academy, Elgin			X	X			9–12	27	27	4:1		6
Francis W. Parker School, Chicago			X	X	PK–5	6–8	9–12	913	320	6.3:1		30
The Governor French Academy, Belleville	X	X	X	X	1–8		9–12	180	55	6:1	5	24
Guerin College Preparatory High School, River Grove			X	X			9–12	724	724	15:1	12	15
Hales Franciscan High School, Chicago			X				9–12	251	251	18:1		14
Immaculate Conception School, Elmhurst			X	X			9–12	211	211	11:1	4	16
Josephinum High School, Chicago				X		6–8	9–12	156	124	10:1		15
Keith Country Day School, Rockford			X	X	PK–5	6–8	9–12	328	100	9:1	9	6
Lake Forest Academy, Lake Forest	X	X	X	X			9–12	349	349	7:1	19	22
The Latin School of Chicago, Chicago			X	X	JK–5	6–8	9–12	1,079	417	8:1	17	25
Loyola Academy, Wilmette			X	X			9–12	2,000	2,000	17:1	18	55
Marian Central Catholic High School, Woodstock			X	X			9–12	725	725	15:1	3	16
Marist High School, Chicago			X	X			9–12	1,830	1,830	19:1		20
Marmion Academy, Aurora			X				9–12	482	482	11:1	8	20
Mooseheart High School, Mooseheart	X	X	X	X	K–5	6–8	9–12	216	101	6:1		7
Morgan Park Academy, Chicago			X	X	PK–5	6–8	9–12	520	181	5:1	11	18
Mother McAuley High School, Chicago				X			9–12	1,568	1,568	15:1	12	14
Mount Carmel High School, Chicago			X				9–12	805	805	18:1	10	17
Nazareth Academy, LaGrange Park			X	X			9–12	772	772	17:1	11	14
The North Shore Country Day School, Winnetka			X	X	PK–5	6–8	9–12	454	171	7:1	10	14
Notre Dame High School for Girls, Chicago				X			9–12	313	313	14:1	6	7
Quincy Notre Dame High School, Quincy			X	X			9–12	490	490	23:1	3	16
Resurrection High School, Chicago				X			9–12	921	921	14:1	9	13
Rosary High School, Aurora				X			9–12	472	472	14:1	2	10
Routt High School, Jacksonville			X	X			9–12	135	135	8:1	2	13

Private Secondary Schools At-a-Glance

	Students Accepted				Grades			Student/Faculty			School Offerings (number)	
	Boarding		Day									
	Boys	Girls	Boys	Girls	Lower	Middle	Upper	Total	Upper	Student/Faculty Ratio	Advanced Placement Subject Areas	Sports
Roycemore School, Evanston			X	X	PK–4	5–8	9–12	238	73	8:1	12	7
Saint Anthony High School, Effingham			X	X			9–12	209	209	10:1		11
Saint Francis De Sales High School, Chicago			X	X			9–12	360	360	16:1	4	8
Saint Laurence High School, Burbank			X				9–12	650	650	18:1	12	28
Saint Patrick High School, Chicago			X				9–12	1,016	1,016	24:1	8	14
Saint Viator High School, Arlington Heights			X	X						13:1		
Timothy Christian High School, Elmhurst			X	X	K–6	7–8	9–12	1,092	396	13:1	7	12
Trinity High School, River Forest				X			9–12	469	469	12:1		11
University of Chicago Laboratory Schools, Chicago			X	X	N–4	5–8	9–12	1,731	504	10:1	15	15
Wheaton Academy, West Chicago			X	X			9–12	565	565	13:1	5	33
The Willows Academy, Des Plaines				X		6–8	9–12	226	154	10:1	7	6
Woodlands Academy of the Sacred Heart, Lake Forest		X		X			9–12	180	180	9:1	6	8
Indiana												
Bishop Luers High School, Fort Wayne			X	X			9–12	585	585	18:1	4	21
Canterbury High School, Fort Wayne			X	X	K–4	5–8	9–12	754	277	17:1	15	14
Cathedral High School, Indianapolis			X	X			9–12	1,218	1,218	14:1	13	25
The Culver Academies, Culver	X	X	X	X			9–PG	760	760	9:1	19	42
Evansville Day School, Evansville			X	X	PK–4	5–8	9–12	302	63	10:1	10	7
Howe Military School, Howe	X	X	X	X	5–8		9–12	111	74	9:1	3	21
Lakeland Christian Academy, Winona Lake			X	X		7–8	9–12	170	126	15:1		3
La Lumiere School, La Porte	X	X	X	X			9–12	122	119	5:1	2	37
Lutheran High School, Indianapolis			X	X			9–12	291	291	13:1	3	15
Marian High School, Mishawaka			X	X			9–12	816	816	18:1	2	28
Mater Dei High School, Evansville			X	X			9–12	598	598	15:1	3	16
New Horizon Youth Ministries, Marion	X	X				7–8	9–12	24	18	4:1		38
Oldenburg Academy, Oldenburg			X	X			9–12	205	205		9	11
Park Tudor School, Indianapolis			X	X	PK–5	6–8	9–12	984	416	9:1	14	16
Roncalli High School, Indianapolis			X	X			9–12	1,062	1,062	15:1	9	19
Iowa												
Dowling High School, West Des Moines			X	X			9–12	1,158	1,158	14:1		21
Maharishi School of the Age, Fairfield			X	X	PS–6	7–9	10–12	240	93	8:1		6
Rivermont Collegiate, Bettendorf			X	X	PS–5	6–8	9–12	207	42	4:1	8	12
Scattergood Friends School, West Branch	X	X	X	X			9–PG	47	47	2:1		23
Kansas												
Hayden High School, Topeka			X	X			9–12	485	485	15:1	6	19
Kapaun Mount Carmel Catholic High School, Wichita			X	X			9–12	879	879	15:1	7	18
Maur Hill-Mount Academy, Atchison	X	X	X	X			9–12	238	238	8:1		34
St. John's Military School, Salina	X					7–8	9–12	184	157	12:1		20
Saint Thomas Aquinas High School, Overland Park			X	X			9–12	1,275	1,275	16:1		18
Trinity Academy, Wichita			X	X			9–12	242	242	12:1		11
Wichita Collegiate School, Wichita			X	X	PS–4	5–8	9–12	964	268	15:1	17	13
Kentucky												
Assumption High School, Louisville				X			9–12	1,018	1,018	11:1	16	18
Bishop Brossart High School, Alexandria			X	X			9–12	400	400	16:1		10
Calvary Christian Academy, Covington			X	X	K4–6	7–8	9–12	636	197	15:1	7	15
Community Christian Academy, Independence			X	X	PS–6	7–8	9–12	219	58	20:1		3
Kentucky Country Day School, Louisville			X	X	JK–4	5–8	9–12	821	220	7:1	12	19
Lexington Catholic High School, Lexington			X	X			9–12	869	869	15:1	12	20
Oneida Baptist Institute, Oneida	X	X	X	X		6–8	9–12	350	250	11:1	5	14
Saint Patrick's School, Maysville			X	X	1–8		9–12	295	100	13:1		10
Saint Xavier High School, Louisville			X				9–12	1,402	1,402	12:1	18	38
Sayre School, Lexington			X	X	PK–5	6–8	9–12	669	244	10:1	11	12
Trinity High School, Louisville			X				9–12	1,400	1,400	12:1		40
Woodbridge Academy, Lexington			X	X		6–8	9–12	12	6	8:1		
Louisiana												
Academy of the Sacred Heart, Grand Coteau		X		X	PK–4	5–8	9–12	347	115	8:1	5	14
Archbishop Blenk Girls High School, Gretna				X			8–12	606	606	15:1	4	15
The Episcopal School of Acadiana, Cade			X	X	P3–5	6–8	9–12	458	196	6:1	14	15
Isidore Newman School, New Orleans			X	X	PK–5	6–8	9–12	1,130	444	18:1	18	13
Jesuit High School of New Orleans, New Orleans			X			8	9–12	1,401	1,157	13:1	12	20
Notre Dame High School, Crowley			X	X			9–12	530	530	25:1		14
Ridgewood Preparatory School, Metairie			X	X	PK–4	5–8	9–12	281		25:1		6
St. Joseph's Academy, Baton Rouge				X			9–12	872	872	12:1	7	15
St. Mary's Dominican High School, New Orleans				X			8–12	1,068	1,068			18
Teurlings Catholic High School, Lafayette			X	X			9–12	674	674	26:1	2	23
Vandebilt Catholic High School, Houma			X	X			8–12	915	915	25:1		14
Westminster Christian Academy, Opelousas			X	X	PK–6	7–8	9–12	974	253	13:1	4	12
Maine												
Bangor Christian School, Bangor			X	X	K4–5	6–8	9–12	373	123	11:1		9
Berwick Academy, South Berwick			X	X	K–4	5–8	9–12	604	263	12:1	12	10

Private Secondary Schools At-a-Glance

| | STUDENTS ACCEPTED | | | | GRADES | | | STUDENT/FACULTY | | | SCHOOL OFFERINGS (number) | |
| | Boarding | | Day | | | | | | | | | |
	Boys	Girls	Boys	Girls	Lower	Middle	Upper	Total	Upper	Student/Faculty Ratio	Advanced Placement Subject Areas	Sports
Bridgton Academy, North Bridgton	X		X				PG	190	190	10:1		29
Carrabassett Valley Academy, Carrabassett Valley	X	X	X	X		8–9	10–PG	110	80	7:1		38
Cheverus High School, Portland			X	X			9–12	515	515	11:1	9	19
Elan School, Poland	X	X				7–8	9–12	110	108	7:1		47
Fryeburg Academy, Fryeburg	X	X	X	X			9–PG	668	668	10:1	12	61
George Stevens Academy, Blue Hill	X	X	X	X			9–12	314	314	10:1	6	18
Gould Academy, Bethel	X	X	X	X			9–PG	241	241	6:1	5	33
Hebron Academy, Hebron	X	X	X	X		6–8	9–PG	240	208	7:1	9	23
Hyde School, Bath	X	X	X	X			9–12	199	199	6:1		31
Kents Hill School, Kents Hill	X	X	X	X			9–PG	215	215	6:1	11	24
Maine Central Institute, Pittsfield	X	X	X	X			9–PG	522	522	15:1	4	23
North Yarmouth Academy, Yarmouth			X	X		6–8	9–12	313	183	8:1	13	18
Washington Academy, East Machias	X	X	X	X			9–12	359	359	14:1	9	10
Waynflete School, Portland			X	X	PK–5	6–8	9–12	553	250	7:1		27
Maryland												
Academy of the Holy Cross, Kensington				X			9–12	600	600	14:1	12	19
Archbishop Curley High School, Baltimore			X				9–12	622	622	13:1	6	20
The Baltimore Actors' Theatre Conservatory, Baltimore			X	X	1–3	4–8	9–12	26	8	3:1	5	
Baltimore Lutheran Middle and Upper School, Towson			X	X		6–8	9–12	530	350	12:1	3	16
Bishop Walsh Middle High School, Cumberland			X	X	PK–5	6–8	9–12	595	198	15:1		9
The Boys' Latin School of Maryland, Baltimore			X		K–5	6–8	9–12	639	269	8:1	7	17
The Bryn Mawr School for Girls, Baltimore			X	X	K–5	6–8	9–12	798	330	8:1	18	42
The Bullis School, Potomac			X	X	3–5	6–8	9–12	624	356	15:1	17	20
Calvert Hall College High School, Baltimore			X				9–12	1,224	1,224	12:1	19	25
The Calverton School, Huntingtown			X	X	PK–5	6–8	9–12	414	110	11:1		8
The Catholic High School of Baltimore, Baltimore				X			9–12	278	278	12:1	5	8
Charles E. Smith Jewish Day School, Rockville			X	X	K–6		7–12	1,500	715		2	8
Chelsea School, Silver Spring			X	X		5–8	9–12	92	72	3:1		3
Connelly School of the Holy Child, Potomac				X		6–8	9–12	422	293	16:1	9	51
DeMatha Catholic High School, Hyattsville			X				9–12	1,007	1,007	12:1	16	17
Elizabeth Seton High School, Bladensburg				X			9–12	565	565	11:1	10	27
Friends School of Baltimore, Baltimore			X	X	PK–5	6–8	9–12	980	363	11:1	14	16
Garrison Forest School, Owings Mills		X	X		N–5	6–8	9–12	664	232	8:1	11	21
Georgetown Preparatory School, North Bethesda	X		X				9–12	447	447	8:1	20	45
Gilman School, Baltimore			X		P1–5	6–8	9–12	971	427	7:1	19	29
Glenelg Country School, Ellicott City			X	X	PK–5	6–8	9–12	796	260	6:1	19	25
Gunston Day School, Centreville			X	X			9–12	154	154	6:1	7	14
The Holton-Arms School, Bethesda				X	3–6	7–8	9–12	667	328	8:1	10	19
The Key School, Annapolis			X	X	PK–4	5–8	9–12	720	202	8:1	13	29
Landon School, Bethesda			X		3–5	6–8	9–12	675	333	10:1	12	27
Loyola-Blakefield, Baltimore			X			6–8	9–12	1,009	772	12:1	16	25
Maryvale Preparatory School, Brooklandville				X		6–8	9–12	371	266	9:1	6	13
McDonogh School, Owings Mills	X	X	X	X	K–4	5–8	9–12	1,263	566	9:1	16	24
New Dominion School, Oldtown	X							47		6:1		29
The Newport School, Silver Spring			X	X	N–4	5–8	9–12	103	13	4:1	2	3
The Nora School, Silver Spring			X	X			9–12	60	60	5:1		32
Notre Dame Preparatory School, Towson				X		6–8	9–12	742	566	9:1	16	18
Oldfields School, Glencoe		X		X			8–12	174	174	6:1	8	32
The Park School, Brooklandville			X	X	PK–5	6–8	9–12	865	325	8:1	7	11
Queen Anne School, Upper Marlboro			X	X		6–8	9–12	249	141	8:1	7	18
Roland Park Country School, Baltimore				X	K–5	6–8	9–12	709	289	7:1	19	21
St. Andrew's Episcopal School, Potomac			X	X		6–8	9–12	454	316	8:1	8	16
Saint James School, St. James	X	X	X	X	8		9–12	222	196	7:1	13	22
St. John's Literary Institution at Prospect Hall, Frederick			X	X			9–12	300	300	10:1		22
St. Mary's Ryken High School, Leonardtown			X	X			9–12	670	670	13:1	17	15
St. Paul's School, Brooklandville			X	X	P1–4	5–8	9–12	872	312	9:1	12	27
St. Paul's School for Girls, Brooklandville				X		5–8	9–12	477	284	7:1	16	18
Saints Peter and Paul High School, Easton			X	X			9–12	210	210	8:1	8	10
St. Timothy's School, Stevenson		X		X			9–PG	133	133	5:1	12	23
St. Vincent Pallotti High School, Laurel			X	X			9–12	510	510	20:1		17
Sandy Spring Friends School, Sandy Spring	X	X	X	X	PK–5	6–8	9–12	547	232	7:1	10	20
Severn School, Severna Park			X	X		6–8	9–12	592	397	12:1	11	18
Thornton Friends School, Silver Spring			X	X		6–8	9–12	84	51	6:1		11
Washington Waldorf School, Bethesda			X	X	PS–4	5–8	9–12	280	62	8:1	1	6
West Nottingham Academy, Colora	X	X	X	X		6–8	9–PG	190	165	6:1	9	19
Worcester Preparatory School, Berlin			X	X	PK–5	6–8	9–12	563	174	10:1	9	8
Massachusetts												
The Academy at Charlemont, Charlemont	X	X	X	X		7–8	9–PG	114	78	7:1		14
Academy at Swift River, Cummington	X	X					9–12	100	100	8:1		49
Bancroft School, Worcester			X	X	K–5	6–8	9–12	581	242	7:1	14	13
Beacon High School, Brookline			X	X				53	53	2:1		6
Beaver Country Day School, Chestnut Hill			X	X		6–8	9–12	406	291	8:1	10	23

Private Secondary Schools At-a-Glance

	STUDENTS ACCEPTED				GRADES			STUDENT/FACULTY			SCHOOL OFFERINGS (number)	
	Boarding		Day									
	Boys	Girls	Boys	Girls	Lower	Middle	Upper	Total	Upper	Student/Faculty Ratio	Advanced Placement Subject Areas	Sports
Belmont Hill School, Belmont................	X		X			7–9	10–12	419	223	8:1	10	22
The Bement School, Deerfield................	X	X	X	X	K–5		6–9	245	121	7:1		33
Berkshire School, Sheffield................	X	X	X	X			9–PG	372	372	6:1	16	31
Bishop Feehan High School, Attleboro...........			X	X			9–12	966	966	13:1	10	18
Boston University Academy, Boston...........			X	X			9–12	157	157	7:1		28
Brooks School, North Andover................	X	X	X	X			9–12	354	354	5:1	14	18
Buckingham Browne & Nichols School, Cambridge...			X	X	PK–6	7–8	9–12	958	468	7:1	19	26
Buxton School, Williamstown................	X	X	X	X			9–12	90	90	5:1		33
The Cambridge School of Weston, Weston........	X	X	X	X			9–PG	324	324	6:1	10	47
Cape Cod Academy, Osterville................			X	X	K–5	6–8	9–12	402	174	8:1	6	6
Chapel Hill–Chauncy Hall School, Waltham........	X	X	X	X			9–12	146	146	6:1	2	19
Commonwealth School, Boston................			X	X			9–12	154	154	5:1	13	19
Concord Academy, Concord................	X	X	X	X			9–12	364	364	6:1	14	30
Cushing Academy, Ashburnham............	X	X	X	X			9–PG	445	445	8:1	14	35
Dana Hall School, Wellesley................		X		X		6–8	9–12	465	338	8:1	13	34
Deerfield Academy, Deerfield................	X	X	X	X			9–PG	608	608	5:1	19	39
Doctor Franklin Perkins School, Lancaster.......	X	X	X	X								8
Eaglebrook School, Deerfield................	X		X			6–9		273	248	4:1		67
Eagle Hill School, Hardwick................	X	X	X	X		8	9–12	152	143	5:1		35
Falmouth Academy, Falmouth................			X	X		7–8	9–12	213	131	4:1	4	3
Fay School, Southborough................	X	X	X	X	1–5	6–9		382	213	6:1		35
The Fessenden School, West Newton............	X		X		K–4	5–6	7–9	471	186	7:1		24
F. L. Chamberlain School, Middleborough........	X	X	X	X		6–8	9–12	102	92	4:1		14
Fontbonne Academy, Milton................				X			9–12	582	582	13:1	8	21
Governor Dummer Academy, Byfield............	X	X	X	X			9–12	378	378	5:1	14	21
Groton School, Groton................	X	X	X	X		8	9–12	360	339	5:1	13	30
Hillside School, Marlborough................	X		X		5–6	7–9		131	106	4:1		47
Holyoke Catholic High School, Granby.........			X	X			9–12	357	357	12:1	4	16
The John Dewey Academy, Great Barrington.......	X	X					10–PG	30	30	3:1		
The Judge Rotenberg Educational Center, Canton ...	X	X						130	130			
Landmark School, Prides Crossing............	X	X	X	X	1–5	6–7	8–12	447	338	3:1		12
Lawrence Academy, Groton................	X	X	X	X			9–12	391	391	8:1	8	26
Lexington Christian Academy, Lexington..........			X	X		6–8	9–12	343	230	11:1	9	26
Linden Hill School, Northfield................	X							15		3:1		22
The MacDuffie School, Springfield............	X	X	X	X		6–8	9–12	228	167	7:1	10	27
Malden Catholic High School, Malden...........			X				9–12	700	700	14:1	9	18
Matignon High School, Cambridge............			X	X			9–12	345	345	15:1	6	16
Middlesex School, Concord................	X	X	X	X			9–12	355	355	5:1	19	21
Milton Academy, Milton................	X	X	X	X	K–5	6–8	9–12	989	689	5:1	11	28
Miss Hall's School, Pittsfield................		X		X			9–12	172	172	5:1	19	29
Montrose School, Natick................				X		6–8	9–12	131	72	10:1	2	7
The Newman School, Boston................			X	X			9–PG	230	230	14:1	6	17
Newton Country Day School of the Sacred Heart, Newton................				X		5–8	9–12	365	207	7:1	14	27
Noble and Greenough School, Dedham.........	X	X	X	X		7–8	9–12	555	439	7:1	16	18
Northfield Mount Hermon School, Northfield......	X	X	X	X			9–PG	717	717	7:1	15	58
Notre Dame Academy, Worcester................				X			9–12	315	315	11:1	12	21
Phillips Academy (Andover), Andover............	X	X	X	X			9–PG	1,083	1,083	5:1	14	44
The Pingree School, South Hamilton...........			X	X			9–12	311	311	7:1	10	24
The Rivers School, Weston................			X	X		6–8	9–12	418	318	7:1	15	19
Riverview School, East Sandwich................	X	X				6–8	9–12	108	99	4:1		21
The Roxbury Latin School, West Roxbury.........			X				7–12	290	290	8:1	11	11
St. John's Preparatory School, Danvers........			X				9–12	1,217	1,217	13:1	16	42
Saint Mark's School, Southborough............	X	X	X	X			9–12	333	333	5:1	14	24
St. Sebastian's School, Needham................			X			7–8	9–12	354	257	7:1	17	16
Spar Hawk School, Salisbury................			X	X	K–5	6–8	9–12					
Stoneleigh–Burnham School, Greenfield............		X		X		7–8	9–PG	159	140	5:1	9	20
The Sudbury Valley School, Framingham..........			X	X				160	160	16:1		
Tabor Academy, Marion................	X	X	X	X			9–12	486	486	6:1	19	21
Thayer Academy, Braintree................			X	X		6–8	9–12	663	450	7:1	13	31
Trinity Catholic High School, Newton............			X	X			9–12	270	270	15:1	3	16
The Waldorf High School of Massachusetts Bay, Belmont................			X	X			9–12	41	41	4:1		3
Walnut Hill School, Natick................	X	X	X	X			9–12	277	277	6:1	6	4
Waring School, Beverly................			X	X		6–8	9–12	150	99	8:1	5	11
Wilbraham & Monson Academy, Wilbraham.......	X	X	X	X		6–8	9–PG	315	268	7:1	18	43
The Williston Northampton School, Easthampton....	X	X	X	X		7–8	9–PG	568	488	7:1	12	34
Willow Hill School, Sudbury................			X	X		6–8	9–12	61	40	3:1		24
The Winchendon School, Winchendon..........	X	X	X				8–PG	209	209	6:1	5	51
The Winsor School, Boston................				X		5–8	9–12	428	244	5:1	8	13
The Woodward School, Quincy................				X		6–8	9–12	158	104	8:1	4	4
Worcester Academy, Worcester................	X	X	X	X		6–8	9–PG	631	480	7:1	14	20

Michigan

Academy of the Sacred Heart, Bloomfield Hills......			X	X	N–4	5–8	9–12	519	144	14:1	5	9
Brother Rice High School, Bloomfield Hills........			X				9–12	655	655	13:1	18	24

Private Secondary Schools At-a-Glance

	STUDENTS ACCEPTED				GRADES			STUDENT/FACULTY			SCHOOL OFFERINGS (number)	
	Boarding		Day									
	Boys	Girls	Boys	Girls	Lower	Middle	Upper	Total	Upper	Student/Faculty Ratio	Advanced Placement Subject Areas	Sports
Cardinal Mooney Catholic College Preparatory High School, Marine City			X	X			9–12	178	178	11:1	6	11
Cranbrook Schools, Bloomfield Hills	X	X	X	X	PK–5	6–8	9–12	1,620	774	8:1	14	41
Detroit Country Day School, Beverly Hills	X	X	X	X	PK–5	6–8	9–12	1,588	641	8:1	17	28
Greenhills School, Ann Arbor			X	X		6–8	9–12	479	284	14:1	8	13
Hackett Catholic Central High School, Kalamazoo			X	X			9–12	455	455	17:1	6	24
Interlochen Arts Academy, Interlochen	X	X	X	X			9–PG	455	455	6:1	3	44
Kalamazoo Christian High School, Kalamazoo			X		K–5	6–8	9–12	426	426	14:1	5	15
Ladywood High School, Livonia				X			9–12	457	457	14:1		22
The Leelanau School, Glen Arbor	X	X	X	X			9–12	56	56	10:1	3	43
Montcalm School, Albion	X	X				6–8	9–12	44				58
Powers Catholic High School, Flint			X	X			9–12	692	692	18:1	8	21
The Roeper School, Bloomfield Hills			X	X	PK–5	6–8	9–12	609	195	10:1	14	11
St. Mary's Preparatory School, Orchard Lake	X		X				9–12	530	530	10:1	8	34
University Liggett School, Grosse Pointe Woods			X	X	PK–5	6–8	9–12	624	235	9:1	14	15
University of Detroit Jesuit High School and Academy, Detroit			X			7–8	9–12	908	788	15:1	7	16
West Catholic High School, Grand Rapids			X	X			9–12	630	630	16:1	6	25
Minnesota												
Academy of Holy Angels, Richfield			X	X			9–12	865	865	13:1	7	14
Ambassador Preparatory, St. Paul	X	X	X	X		6–9		40	40	5:1		10
Benilde–St. Margaret's School, St. Louis Park			X	X		7–8	9–12	1,153	889	12:1	11	25
The Blake School, Hopkins			X	X	PK–5	6–8	9–12	1,357	517	9:1	14	15
Breck School, Minneapolis			X	X	PK–4	5–8	9–12	1,200	399	7:1	7	19
Concordia Academy, St. Paul			X	X			9–12	476	476	15:1	4	15
Convent of the Visitation School, Mendota Heights			X	X	PK–5	6–8	9–12	605	318	13:1	11	18
Cretin-Derham Hall, Saint Paul			X	X			9–12	1,299	1,299	14:1	7	22
DeLaSalle High School, Minneapolis			X	X			9–12	639	639	13:1	7	19
International School of Minnesota, Eden Prairie			X	X	K–5	6–8	9–12	419	86	17:1	20	30
Lutheran High School, Bloomington			X	X			9–12	86	86	15:1	5	10
Marshall School, Duluth			X	X		5–8	9–12	498	325	9:1	9	18
Mounds Park Academy, St. Paul			X	X	PK–4	5–8	9–12	703	258	9:1	4	16
Nacel International School, Saint Paul	X	X	X	X			9–12	80	80	15:1	3	
St. Agnes High School, St. Paul			X	X	K–6	7–8	9–12	472	227	10:1	3	15
St. Croix Lutheran High School, West St. Paul	X	X	X	X			9–12	396	396	14:1	3	16
Saint John's Preparatory School, Collegeville	X	X	X	X		7–8	9–PG	317	240	11:1	6	32
St. Paul Academy and Summit School, St. Paul			X	X	K–5	6–8	9–12	894	359	7:1		22
Saint Thomas Academy, Mendota Heights			X			7–8	9–12	670	511	10:1	7	23
Shattuck-St. Mary's School, Faribault	X	X	X	X		6–8	9–12	334	275	7:1	14	29
Mississippi												
All Saints' Episcopal School, Vicksburg	X	X	X	X		7–8	9–12	125	94	8:1		85
Chamberlain-Hunt Academy, Port Gibson	X		X	X		7–8	9–12	131	104	4:1	2	42
Copiah Academy, Gallman			X	X	1–3	4–6	7–12	496	250	17:1		12
Jackson Academy, Jackson			X	X	PK–6	7–9	10–12	1,462	310	15:1	10	13
Jackson Preparatory School, Jackson			X	X		7–9	10–12	784	426	11:1	9	15
Madison-Ridgeland Academy, Madison			X	X	K–5	6–8	9–12	921	246	13:1	12	13
New Summit School, Jackson			X	X	K–6	7–8	9–12	74	40	5:1		
Parklane Academy, McComb			X	X	PK–3	4–6	7–12	843	381	27:1	4	10
St. Andrew's Episcopal School, Ridgeland			X	X	PK–4	5–8	9–12	1,153	310	9:1	15	19
St. Stanislaus College, Bay St. Louis	X		X			6–8	9–12	530	352	11:1	3	20
Vicksburg Catholic School, Vicksburg			X	X	PK–6	7–8	9–12	602	167	12:1	1	14
Washington County Day School, Greenville			X	X	PK–5	6–8	9–12	769	256	20:1		11
Missouri												
The Barstow School, Kansas City			X	X	PS–5	6–8	9–12	623	184	9:1	16	10
Chaminade College Preparatory School, St. Louis	X		X			6–8	9–12	905	575	11:1	18	10
Crossroads School, St. Louis			X	X		7–8	9–12	202	144	8:1	6	19
Greenwood Laboratory School, Springfield			X	X	K–6	7–8	9–12	363	112	28:1		7
John Burroughs School, St. Louis			X	X				598	598	8:1	7	26
Lutheran High School North, St. Louis			X	X			9–12	376	376	12:1	3	12
Lutheran High School South, St. Louis			X	X			9–12	605	605	13:1	6	18
Mary Institute and St. Louis Country Day School (MICDS), St. Louis			X	X	JK–4	5–8	9–12	1,223	578	8:1	18	32
Missouri Military Academy, Mexico	X				5–5	6–8	9–PG	226	179	11:1	5	43
Nerinx Hall, Webster Groves				X			9–12	607	607	11:1		13
New Covenant Academy, Springfield			X	X	PK–6	7–8	9–12	377	99			6
Notre Dame High School, St. Louis				X			9–12	425	425	10:1	6	10
The Pembroke Hill School, Kansas City			X	X	PS–5	6–8	9–12	1,193	412	11:1	15	18
Saint Louis Priory School, St. Louis			X			7–8	9–12	392	253	8:1	14	15
St. Mary's Bundschu Memorial High School, Independence			X	X			9–12	207	207	11:1	4	17
Saint Paul Lutheran High School, Concordia	X	X	X	X			9–12	169	169	9:1		17
Saint Teresa's Academy, Kansas City				X			9–12	528	528	12:1		24
Thomas Jefferson School, St. Louis	X	X	X	X		7–8	9–PG	86	62	7:1	12	10

Private Secondary Schools At-a-Glance

| | STUDENTS ACCEPTED | | | | GRADES | | | STUDENT/FACULTY | | | SCHOOL OFFERINGS (number) | |
| | Boarding | | Day | | | | | | | | | |
	Boys	Girls	Boys	Girls	Lower	Middle	Upper	Total	Upper	Student/Faculty Ratio	Advanced Placement Subject Areas	Sports
University of Missouri—Columbia High School, Columbia			X	X							1	
Vianney High School, St. Louis			X				9–12	734	734	22:1	8	22
Visitation Academy of St. Louis County, St. Louis			X	X	PK–6		7–12	692	447	9:1	11	11
Wentworth Military Academy and Junior College, Lexington	X	X	X	X		8	9–12	122	111	8:1		27
Whitfield School, St. Louis			X	X			6–12	470	470	8:1	7	14
Montana												
Lustre Christian High School, Lustre	X	X	X	X			9–12	24	24	4:1		4
Manhattan Christian High School, Manhattan			X	X	PK–5	6–8	9–12	320	122	10:1	3	7
Montana Academy, Marion	X	X						60	60	2:1	4	41
Spring Creek Lodge Academy, Thompson Falls	X	X										6
Summit Preparatory School, Kalispell	X	X						64	64	6:1	1	37
Valley Christian School, Missoula			X	X	K–5	6–8	9–12	434	143	8:1		7
Nebraska												
Brownell-Talbot School, Omaha			X	X	PK–4	5–8	9–12	430	139	9:1	13	19
Central Catholic Mid-High School, Grand Island			X	X		6–8	9–12	304	164			
Duchesne Academy of the Sacred Heart, Omaha				X			9–12	289	289	9:1	5	15
Kearney Catholic High School, Kearny			X	X	6–6	7–8	9–12	288	165	13:1		11
Mercy High School, Omaha				X			9–12	335	335	11:1	5	26
Mount Michael Benedictine High School, Elkhorn	X		X				9–12	170	170	7:1	9	19
Nebraska Christian Schools, Central City	X	X	X	X	K–6	7–8	9–12	182	104	10:1		6
Pius X High School, Lincoln			X	X			9–12	976	976	16:1	5	15
Saint Cecilia High School, Hastings			X	X		6–8	9–12	371	200	11:1		20
Nevada												
Faith Lutheran High School, Las Vegas			X	X		6–8	9–12	1,157	618	17:1	7	17
The Meadows School, Las Vegas			X	X	PK–5	6–8	9–12	898	250	11:1	15	15
Mountain View Christian High School, Las Vegas			X	X	K–6	7–8	9–12	631	127	8:1		17
New Hampshire												
Bishop Brady High School, Concord			X	X			9–12	446	446	15:1	7	26
Bishop Guertin High School, Nashua			X	X			9–12	884	884	23:1	12	34
Brewster Academy, Wolfeboro	X	X	X	X			9–PG	361	361	6:1	8	30
Cardigan Mountain School, Canaan	X		X			6–9		170	158	4:1		39
Coe-Brown Northwood Academy, Northwood			X	X			9–12	681	681	12:1	4	11
The Derryfield School, Manchester			X	X		6–8	9–12	387	239	7:1	10	22
Dublin Christian Academy, Dublin	X	X	X	X	K–6	7–8	9–12	136	81	8:1		11
Dublin School, Dublin	X	X	X	X			9–12	130	130	5:1	4	32
Hampshire Country School, Rindge	X				3–6		7–12	22	16	4:1		26
High Mowing School, Wilton	X	X	X	X			9–12	126	126	4:1		41
Holderness School, Plymouth	X	X	X	X			9–PG	275	275	7:1	11	41
Kimball Union Academy, Meriden	X	X	X	X			9–PG	311	311	6:1	15	34
The Meeting School, Rindge	X	X	X	X			8–12	24	24	2:1		25
New Hampton School, New Hampton	X	X	X	X			9–PG	330	330	5:1	5	45
Phillips Exeter Academy, Exeter	X	X	X	X			9–PG	1,050	1,050	5:1	19	42
Portsmouth Christian Academy, Dover			X	X	PK–5	6–8	9–12	797	244	18:1	4	11
Proctor Academy, Andover	X	X	X	X			9–12	345	345	4:1	11	57
St. Paul's School, Concord	X	X					9–12	533	533	5:1	19	31
St. Thomas Aquinas High School, Dover			X	X			9–12	716	716	15:1	8	19
Tilton School, Tilton	X	X	X	X			9–PG	215	215	5:1	11	27
Trinity High School, Manchester			X	X			9–12	535	535	16:1	4	23
The White Mountain School, Bethlehem	X	X	X	X			9–PG	108	108	4:1		41
New Jersey												
Academy of Saint Aloysius, Jersey City				X				170	167	9:1		13
Academy of Saint Elizabeth, Convent Station				X			9–12	245	245	9:1	8	17
Academy of the Holy Angels, Demarest				X			9–12	577	577	11:1	9	16
Baptist High School, Haddon Heights			X	X	K–6	7–8	9–12	353	184	10:1	4	9
Barnstable Academy, Oakland			X	X		5–8	9–12	145	110	8:1	5	15
Bishop Eustace Preparatory School, Pennsauken			X	X			9–12	765	765	14:1	10	19
Bishop George Ahr High School, Edison			X	X			9–12	900	900		5	16
Blair Academy, Blairstown	X	X	X	X			9–PG	434	434	7:1	17	29
Christian Brothers Academy, Lincroft			X				9–12	919	919	14:1	16	16
Community High School, Teaneck			X	X				170	170			7
The Craig School, Mountain Lakes			X	X	3–5	6–8	9–12	162	60	6:1		4
Delbarton School, Morristown			X			7–8	9–12	540	469	7:1	19	28
Dwight-Englewood School, Englewood			X	X	PK–5	6–8	9–12	942	456	9:1		15
Eastern Christian High School, North Haledon			X	X	PK–4	5–8	9–12	919	378	10:1	6	30
Gill St. Bernard's School, Gladstone			X	X	PK–4	5–8	9–12	600	173	8:1	6	10
The Hudson School, Hoboken			X	X		5–8	9–12	204	91	10:1		15
The Hun School of Princeton, Princeton	X	X	X	X		6–8	9–PG	589	493	8:1	14	37
Immaculata High School, Somerville			X	X			9–12	808	808	15:1	5	12
Immaculate Conception High School, Lodi				X			9–12	187	187	11:1	3	16
Kent Place School, Summit			X	X	N–5	6–8	9–12	633	247	7:1	18	16

Private Secondary Schools At-a-Glance

	Boarding Boys	Boarding Girls	Day Boys	Day Girls	Lower	Middle	Upper	Total	Upper	Student/Faculty Ratio	Advanced Placement Subject Areas	Sports
The King's Christian High School, Cherry Hill			X	X	PK–5	6–8	9–12	428	157	18:1	3	8
Lakewood Prep, Howell			X	X	PK–4	5–8	9–12	167	75	10:1	5	13
The Lawrenceville School, Lawrenceville	X	X	X	X			9–PG	807	807	8:1	11	38
Marist High School, Bayonne			X	X			9–12	485	485	20:1		12
Mary Help of Christians Academy, North Haledon				X			9–12	238	238	10:1	4	9
Marylawn of the Oranges, South Orange				X			9–12	210	210	15:1	5	10
Montclair Kimberley Academy, Montclair			X	X	PK–3	4–8	9–12	1,038	440	7:1	14	21
Moorestown Friends, Moorestown			X	X	PS–4	5–8	9–12	717	278	9:1	12	17
Morristown-Beard School, Morristown			X	X		6–8	9–12	491	368	6:1	10	22
Mt. Saint Dominic Academy, Caldwell				X			9–12	360	360	8:1	4	19
Mount Saint Mary Academy, Watchung				X			9–12	353	353	8:1	9	15
Newark Academy, Livingston			X	X		6–8	9–12	549	412	12:1	19	31
The Newgrange School, Hamilton			X	X				84	29	3:1		6
Notre Dame High School, Lawrenceville			X	X			9–12	1,276	1,276	24:1	10	32
Oak Knoll School of the Holy Child, Summit			X	X	K–6	7–12		549	310	8:1	11	12
Peddie School, Hightstown	X	X	X	X			9–PG	514	514	6:1	10	22
The Pennington School, Pennington	X	X	X	X		6–8	9–12	451	358	8:1	14	20
The Pingry School, Martinsville			X	X	K–6	7–8	9–12	1,017	516	8:1	17	22
Princeton Day School, Princeton			X	X	JK–4	5–8	9–12	895	372	8:1	13	22
Purnell School, Pottersville		X		X			9–12	116	116	8:1		23
Ranney School, Tinton Falls			X	X	N–5	6–8	9–12	785	226		17	16
Rutgers Preparatory School, Somerset			X	X	PK–4	5–8	9–12	726	328	6:1	19	12
Saddle River Day School, Saddle River			X	X	K–5	6–8	9–12	314	150	8:1	13	16
Saint Augustine Preparatory School, Richland			X				9–12	547	547	12:1	14	22
St. Benedict's Preparatory School, Newark			X		7–8		9–12	551	480	11:1		20
Saint Dominic Academy, Jersey City				X			9–12	509	509	12:1	8	11
Saint Joseph's High School, Metuchen			X				9–12	850	850	18:1	8	17
St. Mary's Hall–Doane Academy, Burlington			X	X	PK–6	7–12		197	115	6:1	9	12
St. Peter's Preparatory School, Jersey City			X				9–12	930	930	10:1	10	34
Seton Hall Preparatory School, West Orange			X				9–12	970	970	14:1	16	19
Stuart Country Day School of the Sacred Heart, Princeton				X	PS–5	6–8	9–12	551	165	12:1	15	12
Villa Victoria Academy, Ewing				X	PK–6	7–8	9–12	246	92	6:1	6	7
Villa Walsh Academy, Morristown				X		7–8	9–12	234	202	8:1	11	10
The Wardlaw-Hartridge School, Edison			X	X	PK–5	6–8	9–12	415	155	4:1	19	12
Wildwood Catholic High School, North Wildwood			X	X			9–12	316	316	20:1	5	12
Woodcliff Academy, Wall			X	X	2–6	7–8	9–12	69	30	3:1		10
New Mexico												
Albuquerque Academy, Albuquerque			X	X		6–8	9–12	1,078	640	8:1	18	25
Chamisa Mesa High School, Ranchos de Taos			X	X			9–12	51	51			
Menaul School, Albuquerque			X	X		6–8	9–12	202	120	10:1	5	10
Navajo Preparatory School, Inc., Farmington	X	X	X	X					198	15:1		7
New Mexico Military Institute, Roswell	X	X					9–12	459	459	15:1		35
Rancho Valmora, Valmora	X	X				7–8	9–12	79	73	9:1		28
Santa Fe Preparatory School, Santa Fe			X	X		7–8	9–12	345	239	7:1	4	14
The United World College—USA, Montezuma	X	X					11–12	200	200	8:1		51
New York												
Academy of Mount Saint Ursula, Bronx				X			9–12	433	433	15:1	5	9
The Academy of St. Joseph, Brentwood			X	X	K–5	7–8	9–12	427	221	9:1	5	14
Adelphi Academy, Brooklyn			X	X	PK–4	5–8	9–12	175	85	8:1		26
The Albany Academy, Albany	X		X	X	PK–4	5–8	9–PG	340	187	15:1	17	17
Allendale Columbia School, Rochester			X	X	N–5	6–8	9–12	463	144	6:1	15	12
The Beekman School, New York			X	X			9–PG	78	78	8:1	19	
Berkeley Carroll School, Brooklyn			X	X	N–4	5–8	9–12	785	215	8:1	9	12
The Birch Wathen Lenox School, New York			X	X	K–5	6–8	9–12	450	150	12:1	10	23
The Brearley School, New York				X	K–4	5–8	9–12	675	209	7:1	14	24
Brooklyn Friends School, Brooklyn			X	X	K–4	5–8	9–12	521	154	7:1		6
The Browning School, New York			X		K–4	5–8	9–12	381	111	18:1	14	7
The Calhoun School, New York			X	X	N–4	5–8	9–12	675	180	5:1	6	13
Cascadilla School, Ithaca	X	X	X	X			9–PG	51	51	6:1	10	46
Catholic Central High School, Troy			X	X		7–8	9–12	490	387	13:1	3	14
The Chapin School, New York				X	K–3	4–7	8–12	661	246	4:1	17	63
Charles Finney School, Penfield			X	X	K–5	6–8	9–12	304	192	10:1		9
Christian Brothers Academy, Albany			X			6–8	9–12	504	372	12:1	8	15
Christian Brothers Academy, Syracuse			X	X			7–12	740	740		12	17
Christian Central Academy, Williamsville			X	X	K–6	7–8	9–12	380	84	6:1	3	5
Columbia Grammar and Preparatory School, New York			X	X	PK–6		7–12	1,065	531	7:1	19	24
Convent of the Sacred Heart, New York				X	PK–4	5–7	8–12	655	235	5:1	18	18
The Dalton School, New York			X	X	K–3	4–8	9–12	1,299	452	7:1	11	5
Darrow School, New Lebanon	X	X	X	X			9–PG	124	124	4:1		28
Doane Stuart School, Albany			X	X	N–4	5–8	9–12	275	117	5:1	10	14
The Dwight School, New York			X	X	PK–4	5–8	9–12	435	254	6:1	6	25
Emma Willard School, Troy		X		X			9–PG	318	318	5:1	16	35
The Ethical Culture Fieldston School, Bronx			X	X	PK–6	7–8	9–12	1,608	532	10:1		47

Private Secondary Schools At-a-Glance

| | STUDENTS ACCEPTED | | | | GRADES | | | STUDENT/FACULTY | | | SCHOOL OFFERINGS (number) | |
| | Boarding | | Day | | | | | | | | | |
	Boys	Girls	Boys	Girls	Lower	Middle	Upper	Total	Upper	Student/Faculty Ratio	Advanced Placement Subject Areas	Sports
The Family Foundation School, Hancock	X	X				6–8	9–12	225	222	8:1		14
Fordham Preparatory School, Bronx			X				9–12	922	922	11:1	18	18
French-American School of New York, Larchmont			X	X	N–5	6–8	9–10	652	55	6:1	2	8
Friends Academy, Locust Valley			X	X	N–5	6–8	9–12	749	357	6:1	19	17
Friends Seminary, New York			X	X	K–4	5–8	9–12	653	267	6:1	13	10
Garden School, Jackson Heights			X	X	N–6		7–12	350		11:1	6	7
The Gow School, South Wales	X					7–9	10–PG	142	95	4:1		57
Hackley School, Tarrytown	X	X	X	X	K–4	5–8	9–12	819	381	8:1	19	25
The Harley School, Rochester			X	X	N–4	5–8	9–12	502	154	8:1	15	9
The Harvey School, Katonah	X	X	X	X		6–8	9–12	338	228	7:1	10	22
Hebrew Academy-the Five Towns, Cedarhurst			X	X			9–12	500	500		16	7
The Hewitt School, New York				X	K–3	4–7	8–12	485	155	6:1	8	12
Holy Trinity Diocesan High School, Hicksville			X	X			9–10	1,731	1,731		8	19
Hoosac School, Hoosick	X	X	X	X			8–PG	118	118	5:1	3	23
The Horace Mann School, Riverdale			X	X	N–5	6–8	9–12	1,757	711	9:1	19	38
Houghton Academy, Houghton	X	X	X	X		7–8	9–PG	160	130	17:1		18
Immaculata Academy, Hamburg				X			9–12	207	207	13:1		10
Iona Preparatory School, New Rochelle			X				9–12	754	754	13:1	12	30
The Karafin School, Mount Kisco			X	X			9–12	82	70	6:1		36
Kildonan School, Amenia	X	X	X	X	2–6	7–9	10–PG	134	58	6:1		16
The Knox School, St. James	X	X	X	X		6–8	9–12	115	75	3:1	6	23
Lawrence Woodmere Academy, Woodmere			X	X	PK–4	5–8	9–12	356	174	6:1	14	9
Little Red School House and Elisabeth Irwin High School, New York			X	X	N–4	5–8	9–12	561	162	6:1		16
Long Island Lutheran Middle and High School, Brookville			X	X		6–8	9–12	609	410	11:1	10	19
Loyola School, New York			X	X			9–12	203	203	8:1	9	13
Lycee Français de New York, New York			X	X	PK–5	6–9	10–12	1,263	219	9:1	6	19
Manlius Pebble Hill School, DeWitt			X	X	PK–5	6–8	9–12	584	259	8:1	20	25
Maplebrook School, Amenia	X	X	X	X				78	65	8:1		40
The Mary Louis Academy, Jamaica Estates				X			9–12	1,036	1,036	13:1	7	16
Marymount School, New York			X	X	N–3	4–7	8–12	544	226	16:1	18	22
The Masters School, Dobbs Ferry	X	X	X	X		5–8	9–12	540	402	6:1	17	26
McQuaid Jesuit High School, Rochester			X			7–8	9–12	878	672	16:1	16	44
Millbrook School, Millbrook	X	X	X	X			9–12	262	262	4:1	11	19
National Sports Academy at Lake Placid, Lake Placid	X	X	X	X		8	9–PG	81	78	6:1	4	24
New York Military Academy, Cornwall-on-Hudson	X	X	X	X		7–8	9–12	240	222	14:1	3	33
The Nichols School, Buffalo			X	X		5–8	9–12	589	404	9:1	19	17
North Country School, Lake Placid	X	X	X	X		4–9		75	63	3:1		39
Northwood School, Lake Placid	X	X	X	X			9–12	167	167	8:1	3	49
Oakwood Friends School, Poughkeepsie	X	X	X	X		6–8	9–12	176	145	8:1	8	16
Our Saviour Lutheran School, Bronx			X	X	PK–3	4–6	7–12	340	200	14:1	3	6
The Park School of Buffalo, Snyder			X	X	N–4	5–8	9–12	264	103	9:1	11	8
Polytechnic Preparatory Country Day School, Brooklyn			X	X	N–4	5–8	9–12	976	470	7:1	20	22
Portledge School, Locust Valley			X	X	N–5	6–8	9–12	420	151	8:1	10	10
Poughkeepsie Day School, Poughkeepsie			X	X	PK–4	5–8	9–12	324	110	6:1	6	26
Preston High School, Bronx				X			9–12	600	600	12:1	6	7
Professional Children's School, New York	X	X	X	X		4–8	9–12	201	164	8:1	1	
Regis High School, New York			X				9–12	533	533	12:1		11
Riverdale Country School, Riverdale			X	X	PK–6		7–12	1,060	625	8:1	8	21
Robert Louis Stevenson School, New York			X	X			7–PG	76	76	6:1		27
The Rockland Country Day School, Congers			X	X	PK–5	6–8	9–12	169	60	3:1	14	23
Rye Country Day School, Rye			X	X	PK–4	5–8	9–12	848	368	7:1	15	22
Saint Agnes Boys High School, New York			X				9–12	350	350	16:1	4	8
Saint Raymond High School for Boys, Bronx			X				9–12	806	806	24:1		12
St. Thomas Choir School, New York	X				4–6		7–8	31	15	3:1		24
Saint Vincent Ferrer High School, New York				X			9–12	501	501	16:1		9
Salesian High School, New Rochelle			X				9–12	430	430	11:1	6	21
School for Young Performers, New York			X	X	K–5	6–8	9–12	12	6	1:1	19	
School of the Holy Child, Rye				X		5–8	9–12	324	219	9:1	14	20
Seton Catholic Central High School, Binghamton			X	X			9–12	380	380	23:1	12	16
Smith School, New York			X	X		7–8	9–12	60	45	4:1		6
Soundview Preparatory School, Mount Kisco			X	X		6–8	9–PG	75	58	4:1	5	5
The Spence School, New York				X	K–4	5–8	9–12	644	200	7:1	2	9
Staten Island Academy, Staten Island			X	X	PK–4	5–8	9–12	402	126	5:1	12	11
Stella Maris High School and the Maura Clarke Junior High Program, Rockaway Park			X	X		6–8	9–12	440	401	11:1	2	13
The Stony Brook School, Stony Brook	X	X	X	X		7–8	9–12	336	265	7:1	17	17
Storm King School, Cornwall-on-Hudson	X	X	X	X		7–8	9–12	128	120	6:1	5	52
Trevor Day School, New York			X	X	N–5	6–8	9–12	785	243	6:1	6	12
Trinity-Pawling School, Pawling	X		X			7–8	9–PG	318	290	7:1	17	30
Trinity School, New York			X	X	K–4	5–8	9–12	961	422	7:1	11	15
United Nations International School, New York			X	X	K–4	5–8	9–12	1,460	432	10:1		51
The Waldorf School of Garden City, Garden City			X	X	N–5	6–8	9–12	354	87	7:1	4	13
The Windsor School, Flushing			X	X		6–8	9–13	100	90	14:1	5	11

Private Secondary Schools At-a-Glance

	Boarding Boys	Boarding Girls	Day Boys	Day Girls	Lower	Middle	Upper	Total	Upper	Student/Faculty Ratio	Advanced Placement Subject Areas	Sports
Winston Preparatory School, New York			X	X		6–8	9–12	220	119	3:1		7
York Preparatory School, New York			X	X		6–8	9–12	316	219	6:1	3	30
North Carolina												
Asheville School, Asheville	X	X	X	X			9–12	234	234	4:1	15	58
Auldern Academy, Siler City		X					9–12	50	50	6:1		26
Camelot Academy, Durham			X	X	K–6		7–12	92	47	10:1	6	4
Cannon School, Concord			X	X	PK–4	5–8	9–12	899	294	9:1	14	24
Cape Fear Academy, Wilmington			X	X	PK–5	6–8	9–12	579	183	8:1	13	12
Carolina Day School, Asheville			X	X	PK–5	6–8	9–12	644	181	10:1	18	11
Cary Academy, Cary			X	X		6–8	9–12	698	397	14:1		49
Charlotte Christian School, Charlotte			X	X	JK–5	6–8	9–12	1,017	379	11:1	18	19
Charlotte Country Day School, Charlotte			X	X	PK–4	5–8	9–12	1,626	469	12:1	14	20
Charlotte Latin School, Charlotte			X	X	K–5	6–8	9–12	1,369	477	8:1	14	29
Christ School, Arden	X		X				8–12	185	185	5:1	8	49
Durham Academy, Durham			X	X	PK–4	5–8	9–12	1,129	384	7:1	18	17
Forsyth Country Day School, Lewisville			X	X	PK–4	5–8	9–12	990	392	12:1	8	15
Gaston Day School, Gastonia			X	X	PK–4	5–8	9–12	418	115	9:1	10	13
Greenfield School, Wilson			X	X	PS–4	5–8	9–12	318	67	5:1	3	7
Greensboro Day School, Greensboro			X	X		6–8	9–12	880	330	10:1	17	18
Harrells Christian Academy, Harrells			X	X	K–5	6–8	9–12	471	126	12:1	4	9
The Hill Center, Durham Academy, Durham			X	X	K–5	6–8	9–12	177	78	4:1		
Oak Ridge Military Academy, Oak Ridge	X	X	X	X		6–8	9–12	146	129	7:1	5	25
The Oakwood School, Greenville			X	X	K–5	6–8	9	260	15	4:1		5
The O'Neal School, Southern Pines			X	X	PK–4	5–8	9–12	445	161	10:1	10	11
Ravenscroft School, Raleigh			X	X	PK–5	6–8	9–12	1,119	374	6:1	17	21
Rocky Mount Academy, Rocky Mount			X	X	PK–5	6–8	9–12	446	149	12:1	9	12
St. David's School, Raleigh			X	X	K–4	5–8	9–12	513	201	10:1	15	16
Saint Mary's School, Raleigh		X		X			9–12	268	268	7:1	9	16
Salem Academy, Winston-Salem		X		X			9–12	183	183	9:1	10	21
Stone Mountain School, Black Mountain	X					6–8	9–12	58	39	4:1		42
Wayne Country Day School, Goldsboro			X	X	PK–6		7–12	227	100	15:1	5	10
Westchester Academy, High Point			X	X	K–5	6–8	9–12	410	136	7:1	14	10
North Dakota												
Bismark St. Mary's Central, Bismark			X	X			9–12	365	365	17:1		19
Ohio												
The Andrews School, Willoughby		X		X		7–8	9–12	142	101	5:1	7	22
Beaumont School, Cleveland Heights				X			9–12	449	449	14:1	6	8
Benedictine High School, Cleveland			X				9–12	439	439	11:1	5	20
Bishop Fenwick High School, Franklin			X	X			9–12	521	521	15:1	5	16
Cincinnati Country Day School, Cincinnati			X	X	PK–5	6–8	9–12	850	316	9:1	11	14
The Columbus Academy, Gahanna			X	X	PK–4	5–8	9–12	1,016	334	11:1	17	14
Columbus School for Girls, Columbus				X	PK–5	6–8	9–12	650	219	12:1	15	37
Elyria Catholic High School, Elyria			X	X			9–12	536	536	14:1	5	15
Gilmour Academy, Gates Mills	X	X	X	X	PK–6	7–8	9–12	748	434	10:1	15	39
The Grand River Academy, Austinburg	X						9–12	110	110	7:1	3	51
Hawken School, Gates Mills			X	X	PS–5	6–8	9–12	954	441	9:1	15	16
Lake Ridge Academy, North Ridgeville			X	X	K–5	6–8	9–12	435	164	7:1	13	23
Laurel School, Shaker Heights			X	X	PS–4	5–8	9–12	644	200	8:1	16	12
Lawrence School, Broadview Heights			X	X	1–6	7–8	9–12	220	77	11:1		22
Lehman High School, Sidney			X	X			9–12	284	284	12:1	5	18
Maumee Valley Country Day School, Toledo			X	X	N–6	7–8	9–12	465	171	10:1	9	14
McNicholas High School, Cincinnati			X	X			9–12	810	810	16:1	14	10
Olney Friends School, Barnesville	X	X	X	X			9–12	58	58	4:1	5	26
Padua Franciscan High School, Parma			X	X			9–12	995	995	18:1	6	39
Purcell Marian High School, Cincinnati			X	X			9–12	425	425	11:1	6	19
Regina High School, South Euclid				X			9–12	267	267	14:1	5	10
St. Francis de Sales High School, Toledo			X				9–12	660	660	14:1	18	17
Saint Joseph Central Catholic High School, Fremont			X	X			9–12	276	276	13:1	1	15
Saint Xavier High School, Cincinnati			X				9–12	1,498	1,498	13:1	19	17
The Seven Hills School, Cincinnati			X	X	PK–5	6–8	9–12	1,070	315	9:1	14	13
The Summit Country Day School, Cincinnati			X	X	PK–4	5–8	9–12	1,087	323	9:1	18	18
University School, Hunting Valley			X		K–5	6–8	9–12	869	404	15:1	13	14
The Wellington School, Columbus			X	X	PK–4	5–8	9–12	616	189	12:1	13	13
Western Reserve Academy, Hudson	X	X	X	X			9–12	401	401	6:1	19	47
Oklahoma												
Bishop McGuinness Catholic High School, Oklahoma City			X	X	9–10		11–12	632	299	20:1	9	17
Casady School, Oklahoma City			X	X	PK–4	5–8	9–12	875	338	15:1	17	29
Cascia Hall Preparatory School, Tulsa			X	X		6–8	9–12	576	360	12:1	13	17
Holland Hall, Tulsa			X	X	PK–3	4–8	9–12	994	351	9:1	18	17
Oregon												
The Academy at Sisters, Bend		X				7–8	9–12	30	28	12:1		33

Private Secondary Schools At-a-Glance

| | STUDENTS ACCEPTED | | | | GRADES | | | STUDENT/FACULTY | | | SCHOOL OFFERINGS (number) | |
| | Boarding | | Day | | | | | | | | | |
	Boys	Girls	Boys	Girls	Lower	Middle	Upper	Total	Upper	Student/Faculty Ratio	Advanced Placement Subject Areas	Sports
The Academy for Global Exploration, Ashland	X	X					9–12	5	5	3:1		53
Canyonville Christian Academy, Canyonville	X	X	X	X		6–8	9–12	148	130	13:1	4	8
The Catlin Gabel School, Portland			X	X	PS–5	6–8	9–12	713	273	7:1		51
The Delphian School, Sheridan	X	X	X	X	K–4	5–7	8–12	250				10
Hosanna Christian School, Klamath Falls			X	X	PK–6	7–8	9–12	320	64	8:1		7
Lifegate School, Eugene			X	X	P3–5	6–8	9–12	102	38	8:1	2	4
Mount Bachelor Academy, Prineville	X	X						101		4:1		40
Oregon Episcopal School, Portland	X	X	X	X	PK–5	6–8	9–12	768	235	7:1	8	9
Portland Christian Schools, Portland			X	X	PS–6	7–8	9–12	950	230	10:1	5	9
Portland Lutheran School, Portland	X	X	X	X	PK–5	6–8	9–12	278	112	8:1	1	12
Regis High School, Stayton			X	X			9–12	189	189	15:1	1	15
St. Mary's School, Medford			X	X		6–8	9–12	317	187	10:1	20	25
Salem Academy, Salem			X	X	K–5	6–8	9–12	576	236	17:1	4	10
Santiam Christian School, Corvallis			X	X	PS–6	7–8	9–12	810	297	17:1		11
Thomas A. Edison High School, Portland			X	X						4:1		13
Wellsprings Friends School, Eugene			X	X			9–12	60	60	6:1		7
Western Mennonite School, Salem	X	X	X	X		6–8	9–12	231	132	14:1	1	6

Pennsylvania

| | STUDENTS ACCEPTED | | | | GRADES | | | STUDENT/FACULTY | | | SCHOOL OFFERINGS (number) | |
| | Boarding | | Day | | | | | | | | | |
	Boys	Girls	Boys	Girls	Lower	Middle	Upper	Total	Upper	Student/Faculty Ratio	Advanced Placement Subject Areas	Sports
Academy of Notre Dame de Namur, Villanova				X		6–8	9–12	495	362	8:1		14
The Agnes Irwin School, Rosemont				X	K–4	5–8	9–12	663	249	7:1	14	25
Akiba Hebrew Academy, Merion Station			X	X		6–8	9–12	319	255	7:1	8	9
The Baldwin School, Bryn Mawr				X	PK–5	6–8	9–12	592	190	7:1	11	19
Bishop Carroll High School, Ebensburg			X	X			9–12	257	257	12:1		11
Bishop Hoban High School, Wilkes-Barre			X	X			9–12	650	650	14:1	11	16
Bishop McDevitt High School, Wyncote			X	X			9–12	749	749	20:1	6	20
Blue Mountain Academy, Hamburg	X	X					9–12	249	249	10:1	2	7
Cathedral Preparatory School, Erie			X				9–12	548	548	14:1	19	22
Central Catholic High School, Pittsburgh			X				9–12	850	850	15:1	9	21
CFS, The School at Church Farm, Paoli	X		X			7–8	9–12	181	134	7:1	3	17
Chestnut Hill Academy, Philadelphia			X		PK–5		9–12	568	212	7:1	14	17
Christopher Dock Mennonite High School, Lansdale			X	X			9–12	418	418	13:1	2	10
The Concept School, Westtown			X	X		4–8	9–12	43	30	8:1		16
Country Day School of the Sacred Heart, Bryn Mawr				X	PK–4	5–8	9–12	366	190	10:1	5	9
Delaware County Christian School, Newtown Square			X	X	PK–5		9–12	938	380	12:1	8	13
Delaware Valley Friends School, Paoli			X	X		7–8	9–12	188	138	5:1		13
Devon Preparatory School, Devon			X			6–8	9–12	279	197	10:1	13	13
The Ellis School, Pittsburgh				X	K–4	5–8	9–12	469	173	7:1	12	9
The Episcopal Academy, Merion			X	X	PK–5	6–8	9–12	1,129	445	7:1	14	27
Friends' Central School, Wynnewood			X	X	PK–4	5–8	9–12	993	389	9:1	10	26
George School, Newtown	X	X	X	X			9–12	529	529	7:1	9	34
Germantown Academy, Fort Washington			X	X	PK–5	6–8	9–12	1,122	484	15:1	14	20
Germantown Friends School, Philadelphia			X	X	K–5	6–8	9–12	894	356	9:1		17
Girard College, Philadelphia	X	X			1–5	6–8	9–12	721	209	16:1	2	21
The Grier School, Tyrone		X				7–8	9–PG	200	173	6:1	5	31
The Harrisburg Academy, Wormleysburg			X	X	N–4	5–8	9–12	432	87	8:1	11	7
The Haverford School, Haverford			X		PK–5	6–8	9–12	958	356	8:1	19	24
The Hill School, Pottstown	X	X	X	X			9–PG	495	495	7:1	14	25
The Hill Top Preparatory School, Rosemont			X	X		6–8	9–12	71	46	4:1		37
Holy Name High School, Reading			X	X			9–12	458	458	12:1	5	16
Keystone National High School, Bloomsburg			X	X			9–12	8,700	8,700			
Kimberton Waldorf School, Kimberton			X	X	PK–8		9–12	295	81	7:1		13
The Kiski School, Saltsburg	X		X				9–PG	201	201	5:1	14	31
Lancaster Country Day School, Lancaster			X	X	PS–5	6–8	9–12	495	177	5:1	11	13
Lansdale Catholic High School, Lansdale			X	X			9–12	800	800		6	23
La Salle College High School, Wyndmoor			X				9–12	1,080	1,080	11:1	17	25
Lebanon Catholic Junior / Senior High School, Lebanon			X	X	K4–5	6–8	9–12	458	150	20:1	5	8
Lehigh Valley Christian High School, Allentown			X	X			9–12	184	184	10:1	3	8
Linden Hall School for Girls, Lititz		X		X		6–8	9–PG	121	91	4:1	10	14
Living Word Academy, Lancaster			X	X	K–5	6–8	9–12	339	148	14:1	3	8
Mercersburg Academy, Mercersburg	X	X	X	X			9–PG	442	442	5:1	20	40
Mercyhurst Preparatory School, Erie			X	X			9–12	641	641	15:1		22
Milton Hershey School, Hershey	X	X			PK–5	6–8	9–12	1,301	558	15:1	5	13
MMI Preparatory School, Freeland			X	X		6–8	9–12	190	118	9:1	10	13
Moravian Academy, Bethlehem			X	X	PK–5	6–8	9–12	793	285	7:1	9	9
Mount Alvernia High School, Pittsburgh				X			9–12	87	87	7:1	2	2
Mount Saint Joseph Academy, Flourtown				X			9–12	556	556	10:1	14	15
Notre Dame Junior/Senior High School, East Stroudsburg			X	X			9–12	247	247	15:1	4	17
The Oakland School, Pittsburgh			X	X			8–12	60	60	6:1	3	32
Our Lady of the Sacred Heart, Coraopolis			X	X			9–12	331	331	12:1	1	16
The Pathway School, Norristown	X	X	X	X				158	92	6:1		5
Perkiomen School, Pennsburg	X	X	X	X		5–8	9–PG	249	198	7:1	12	18
The Phelps School, Malvern	X		X			7–8	9–12	138	127	5:1		24
Pine Forge Academy, Pine Forge	X	X	X	X			9–12	186	186	15:1		6

Private Secondary Schools At-a-Glance

	STUDENTS ACCEPTED				GRADES			STUDENT/FACULTY			SCHOOL OFFERINGS (number)	
	Boarding		Day									
	Boys	Girls	Boys	Girls	Lower	Middle	Upper	Total	Upper	Student/Faculty Ratio	Advanced Placement Subject Areas	Sports
Quigley Catholic High School, Baden			X	X			9–12	154	154	12:1	3	17
Saint Basil Academy, Jenkintown				X			9–12	396	396	9:1	9	11
St. Joseph's Preparatory School, Philadelphia			X				9–12	976	976	16:1	14	22
Scranton Preparatory School, Scranton			X	X			9–12	800	800			13
Sewickley Academy, Sewickley			X	X	PK–5	6–8	9–12	795	308	6:1	17	24
Shady Side Academy, Pittsburgh	X	X	X	X	K–5	6–8	9–12	952	499	8:1	6	23
The Shipley School, Bryn Mawr			X	X	PK–5	6–8	9–12	857	334	8:1	17	25
Solebury School, New Hope	X	X	X	X		7–8	9–PG	222	195	6:1	9	25
Springside School, Philadelphia				X	PK–4	5–8	9–12	639	185	7:1	18	26
Valley Forge Military Academy and College, Wayne	X		X			7–8	9–PG	328	293	12:1	6	45
Villa Maria Academy, Erie			X	X			9–12	390	390	11:1	5	13
Villa Maria Academy, Malvern				X			9–12	465	465	9:1	14	16
Westtown School, Westtown	X	X	X	X	PK–5	6–8	9–12	782	394	8:1	10	36
William Penn Charter School, Philadelphia			X	X	K–5	6–8	9–12	896	421	9:1	14	16
Winchester Thurston School, Pittsburgh			X	X	PK–5	6–8	9–12	580	168	7:1	17	23
The Woodlynde School, Strafford			X	X	1–5	6–8	9–12	309	109	6:1	2	10
Wyoming Seminary, Kingston	X	X	X	X	PK–8		9–PG	793	441	8:1	19	30
York Country Day School, York			X	X	PS–5	6–8	9–12	243	61		8	6
Puerto Rico												
Baldwin School of Puerto Rico, Inc., Bayamón			X	X	PK–6	7–8	9–12	820	180	7:1	9	12
Caribbean Preparatory School, San Juan			X	X	PK–6	7–8	9–12	803	195	8:1	6	27
Colegio Puertorriqueno de Ninas, Guaynabo				X	PK–6	7–8		599	169			13
Colegio San Jose, San Juan			X			7–9	10–12	502	234		5	13
Fowlers Academy, Guaynabo			X	X		7–8	9–12	75	55	8:1		4
Guamani Private School, Guayama			X	X						13:1	4	6
St. John's School, San Juan			X	X	PK–5	6–8	9–12	760	276	12:1	10	5
Rhode Island												
La Salle Academy, Providence			X	X		7–8	9–12	1,379	1,295	13:1	10	24
Mount Saint Charles Academy, Woonsocket			X	X			7–12	1,002	1,002	14:1	10	21
Our Lady Of Fatima High School, Warren			X	X		7–8	9–12	162	140	8:1		10
Portsmouth Abbey School, Portsmouth	X	X	X	X			9–12	354	354	7:1	14	19
Providence Country Day School, East Providence			X	X		5–8	9–12	311	211	6:1	11	14
Rocky Hill School, East Greenwich			X	X	PS–5	6–8	9–12	333	151	5:1	8	15
St. Andrew's School, Barrington	X	X	X	X		6–8	9–12	206	168	5:1	1	22
St. George's School, Middletown	X	X	X	X			9–12	347	347	5:1	19	21
The Wheeler School, Providence			X	X	N–5	6–8	9–12	800	325	13:1	11	18
South Carolina												
Ashley Hall, Charleston			X	X	PS–5	6–8	9–12	615	173	13:1	18	29
Beaufort Academy, Beaufort			X	X	PK–4	5–8	9–12	374	101	10:1	5	17
Camden Military Academy, Camden	X					7–8	9–12	305	236	12:1	5	12
Cardinal Newman School, Columbia			X	X		7–8	9–12	430	272	10:1	3	17
Cherokee Creek Boys School, Westminster	X					5–9		20	19	10:1		
Christ Church Episcopal School, Greenville			X	X	K–4	5–8	9–12	1,000	291	9:1	20	16
Hammond School, Columbia			X	X	PK–4	5–8	9–12	980	271	9:1	14	26
Hilton Head Preparatory School, Hilton Head Island			X	X	K–5	6–8	9–12	433	146	12:1	15	15
International Junior Golf Academy, Hilton Head Island	X	X	X	X			7–PG	110	110	10:1	6	1
St. Joseph's Catholic School, Greenville			X	X		6–8	9–12	425	247	11:1	13	17
Shannon Forest Christian School, Greenville			X	X	PK–5		6–12	545	247	17:1	5	11
Spartanburg Day School, Spartanburg			X	X	PK–4	5–8	9–12	472	126	11:1	16	11
Trident Academy, Mt. Pleasant			X	X	K–5	6–8	9–12	131	50	4:1		8
Wilson Hall, Sumter			X	X	PS–5	6–8	9–12	779	209	12:1	14	21
South Dakota												
Freeman Academy, Freeman	X	X	X	X	5–8		9–12	91	53	8:1		6
Lower Brule High School, Lower Brule			X	X	K–6	7–8	9–12	281	75			10
Tennessee												
Battle Ground Academy, Franklin			X	X	K–4	5–8	9–12	919	387	11:1	12	21
Baylor School, Chattanooga	X	X	X	X	6–8		9–12	1,033	704	8:1	17	49
Boyd-Buchanan School, Chattanooga			X	X	K4–5	6–8	9–12	977	351	15:1	7	11
Brentwood Academy, Brentwood			X	X		6–8	9–12	741	435	12:1	8	23
Chattanooga Christian School, Chattanooga			X	X	K–5	6–8	9–12	1,062	410	18:1	10	41
Columbia Academy, Columbia			X	X	K–6		7–12	565	265	13:1		13
Currey Ingram Academy, Brentwood			X	X	K–4	5–8	9–12	261	60			3
David Lipscomb High School, Nashville			X	X	PK–4	5–8	9–12	1,409	526	14:1	4	14
Ezell-Harding Christian School, Antioch			X	X	K–4	5–8	9–12	962	286	12:1	3	15
Father Ryan High School, Nashville			X	X			9–12	935	935	12:1	15	27
Franklin Road Academy, Nashville			X	X	PK–4	5–8	9–12	958	313	9:1	10	24
Girls Preparatory School, Chattanooga				X		6–8	9–12	719	427	8:1	19	45
Harding Academy, Memphis			X	X	PS–6		7–12	1,693	595	13:1	6	15
The Harpeth Hall School, Nashville				X		5–8	9–12	626	378	8:1	13	36
Hutchison School, Memphis				X	PK–4	5–8	9–12	827	218	16:1	16	11
The King's Academy, Seymour	X	X	X	X	K–5	6–8	9–12	369	141	20:1	3	25

Private Secondary Schools At-a-Glance

	Students Accepted				Grades			Student/Faculty			School Offerings (number)	
	Boarding		Day									
	Boys	Girls	Boys	Girls	Lower	Middle	Upper	Total	Upper	Student/Faculty Ratio	Advanced Placement Subject Areas	Sports
Lausanne Collegiate School, Memphis			X	X	PK–4	5–8	9–12	742	217	9:1	14	42
The McCallie School, Chattanooga	X		X			6–8	9–12	890	631	8:1	19	59
Memphis University School, Memphis			X			7–8	9–12	652	438	15:1	19	11
Montgomery Bell Academy, Nashville			X			7–8	9–12	662	445	9:1	16	35
St. Andrew's–Sewanee School, Sewanee	X	X	X	X		6–8	9–12	254	199	7:1	6	31
St. Benedict at Auburndale, Cordova			X	X			9–12	850	850	9:1	5	22
St. Cecilia Academy, Nashville				X			9–12	236	236	9:1	12	18
St. Mary's Episcopal School, Memphis				X	PK–4	5–8	9–12	812	237	19:1	16	13
University School of Nashville, Nashville			X	X	K–4	5–8	9–12	995	347	12:1	19	19
The Webb School, Bell Buckle	X	X	X	X		6–8	9–PG	272	177	7:1	6	63
Webb School of Knoxville, Knoxville			X	X	K–5	6–8	9–12	1,052	471	11:1	20	19
Texas												
Allen Academy, Bryan	X		X	X	PK–5	6–8	9–12	289	69	10:1	14	13
All Saints' Episcopal School of Fort Worth, Fort Worth			X	X	K–6	7–8	9–12	763	233	9:1	9	25
The Awty International School, Houston			X	X	PK–5	6–8	9–12	1,174	345	18:1		15
Bishop Lynch Catholic High School, Dallas			X	X			9–12	1,044	1,044	14:1	13	34
The Brook Hill School, Bullard	X	X	X	X		5–8	9–12	184	109	7:1		16
Cistercian Preparatory School, Irving			X			5–8	9–12	352	176	9:1	19	8
Dallas Academy, Dallas			X		K–6	7–8	9–12	135	93	6:1		11
Dallas Christian School, Mesquite			X		PK–5	6–8	9–12	735	255	15:1		13
Duchesne Academy of the Sacred Heart, Houston				X	PK–4	5–8	9–12	652	249	7:1	11	11
The Emery Weiner School, Houston			X	X		6–8	9–12	371	153	4:1		16
Episcopal High School, Bellaire			X	X			9–12	621	621	9:1	9	20
The Episcopal School of Dallas, Dallas			X	X	PK–4	5–8	9–12	1,138	396	8:1	18	18
Fairhill School, Dallas			X	X	1–5	6–8	9–12	230	89			8
First Baptist Academy, Dallas			X	X	K–4	5–8	9–12	682	273	10:1	4	15
Fort Worth Christian School, Fort Worth			X	X	PK–5	6–8	9–12	763	259	11:1	8	15
Fort Worth Country Day School, Fort Worth			X	X	K–4	5–8	9–12	1,100	378	10:1	18	15
Gateway School, Arlington			X	X		5–8	9–12	30	19	10:1		8
Greenhill School, Addison			X	X	PK–4	5–8	9–12	1,248	442	18:1	13	33
Hillcrest School, Midland			X	X	1–5	6–8	9–12	48	24	10:1		14
The Hockaday School, Dallas		X		X	PK–4	5–8	9–12	1,020	434	8:1	19	55
Houston Learning Academy-Central Campus, Houston			X	X			9–12	54	54	15:1		
Huntington-Surrey School, Austin			X	X			9–12	74	74	4:1	6	
Incarnate Word Academy, Houston				X			9–12	249	249	14:1	10	13
Jesuit College Preparatory School, Dallas			X				9–12	1,021	1,021	11:1	10	22
The John Cooper School, The Woodlands			X	X	K–5	6–8	9–12	898	300	11:1	12	10
The June Shelton School and Evaluation Center, Dallas			X	X	PS–4	5–8	9–12	833	231	8:1		10
Key School, Inc., Fort Worth			X	X	K–4	5–8	9–12	95	36	5:1		
Keystone School, San Antonio			X	X	K–4	5–8	9–12	417	116	10:1	9	9
The Kinkaid School, Houston			X	X	PK–4	5–8	9–12	1,353	532	7:1	20	15
Lakehill Preparatory School, Dallas			X	X	K–4	5–8	9–12	391	110	9:1	12	12
Loretto Academy, El Paso			X	X	PK–5	6–8	9–12	698	429	18:1	6	12
Lutheran High North, Houston			X	X			9–12	313	313	17:1		18
Lydia Patterson Institute, El Paso			X	X		8	9–12	439	279	20:1		6
The Oakridge School, Arlington			X	X	PS–4	5–8	9–12	765	250	9:1	17	14
Prestonwood Christian Academy, Plano			X	X	PK–4	5–8	9–12	1,434	386	10:1	7	13
Providence High School, San Antonio				X		6–8	9–12	348	284	10:1	9	11
St. Agnes Academy, Houston				X			9–12	822	822	15:1	12	17
St. John's School, Houston			X	X	K–5	6–8	9–12	1,217	540	7:1	19	16
St. Mark's School of Texas, Dallas			X		1–4	5–8	9–12	817	350	8:1	17	34
Saint Mary's Hall, San Antonio			X	X	PK–5	6–8	9–PG	918	312	12:1	19	20
St. Michael's Catholic Academy, Austin			X	X			9–12	442	442	11:1	20	13
St. Pius X High School, Houston			X	X			9–12	630	630	13:1	6	15
St. Stephen's Episcopal School, Austin	X	X	X	X		6–8	9–12	656	453	8:1	17	15
St. Thomas High School, Houston			X				9–12	643	643	13:1	10	15
San Marcos Baptist Academy, San Marcos	X	X	X	X		7–8	9–12	219	178	11:1	3	23
Second Baptist School, Houston			X	X	PK–5	6–8	9–12				17	9
Southwest Christian School, Inc., Fort Worth			X	X	PK–6	7–8	9–12	757	253	11:1	7	14
Strake Jesuit College Preparatory, Houston			X				9–12	869	869	12:1	10	10
The Tenney School, Houston			X	X		6–8	9–12	55	43	1:1	2	
Texas NeuroRehab Center, Austin	X	X								10:1		
TMI—The Episcopal School of Texas, San Antonio	X	X	X	X		6–8	9–12	311	227	8:1	14	18
Trinity Christian Academy, Addison			X	X	K–4	5–8	9–12	1,459	468	10:1	14	19
Trinity Valley School, Fort Worth			X	X	K–4	5–8	9–12	946	326	10:1	15	11
Tyler Street Christian Academy, Dallas			X	X	P3–6	7–8	9–12	211	61	10:1	1	5
Vanguard College Preparatory School, Waco			X	X		7–8	9–12	181	122	7:1	6	10
Walden Preparatory School, Dallas			X	X			9–12	50	50	6:1		
Westbury Christian School, Houston			X	X	PK–6	7–8	9–12	500	235	10:1	13	15
The Winston School, Dallas			X	X	1–6	7–8	9–12	239	134	6:1		15
The Winston School San Antonio, San Antonio			X	X	K–6	7–8	9–12	170	60	10:1		17

Private Secondary Schools At-a-Glance

	Boarding Boys	Boarding Girls	Day Boys	Day Girls	Lower	Middle	Upper	Total	Upper	Student/Faculty Ratio	Advanced Placement Subject Areas	Sports
Utah												
Alpine Academy, Salt Lake City		X								4:1		21
Aspen Ranch, Loa	X	X				7–8	9–12	72	66	8:1		24
Cross Creek Programs, LaVerkin	X	X				7–8	9–12	415	390	15:1		37
Island View School, Syracuse	X	X						112	112	15:1		52
Provo Canyon School, Provo	X	X				7–8	9–12	211	187	12:1		23
Rowland Hall-St. Mark's School, Salt Lake City			X	X	PK–5	6–8	9–12	949	275	14:1	15	32
Sorenson's Ranch School, Koosharem	X	X					7–12	95	95	10:1		47
Wasatch Academy, Mt. Pleasant	X	X	X	X			9–12	155	155	6:1	8	70
The Waterford School, Sandy			X	X	PK–5	6–8	9–12	973	293	5:1	14	27
Vermont												
Burke Mountain Academy, East Burke	X	X	X	X			7–PG	61	61	7:1	2	8
Burr and Burton Academy, Manchester	X	X	X	X			9–12	686	686		6	21
The Greenwood School, Putney	X							40		2:1		17
Lyndon Institute, Lyndon Center	X	X	X	X			9–12	658	658	10:1	5	26
Pine Ridge School, Williston	X	X	X	X				98	98	2:1		25
The Putney School, Putney	X	X	X	X			9–12	226	226	5:1	2	55
Rock Point School, Burlington	X	X	X	X			9–12	38	38	5:1		31
St. Johnsbury Academy, St. Johnsbury	X	X	X	X			9–PG	981	981	8:1	18	34
Stratton Mountain School, Stratton Mountain	X	X	X	X		7–8	9–PG	129	108	6:1		12
Vermont Academy, Saxtons River	X	X	X	X			9–PG	267	267	7:1	11	73
Virgin Islands												
Kingshill School, St. Croix			X	X		7–8	9–12	29	21	4:1		19
St. Croix Country Day School, Kingshill			X	X	N–6	7–8	9–12	488	165	12:1	8	11
Virginia												
Bishop Ireton High School, Alexandria			X	X			9–12	810	810	14:1	11	23
The Blue Ridge School, St. George	X						9–12	164	164	6:1		37
Cape Henry Collegiate School, Virginia Beach			X	X	PK–5	6–8	9–12	1,006	344	10:1	12	30
Carlisle School, Axton			X	X	PK–5	6–8	9–12	418	111	12:1	8	17
Chatham Hall, Chatham		X					9–12	131	131	6:1	15	17
Christchurch School, Christchurch	X		X	X			8–PG	220	220	7:1	12	24
The Collegiate School, Richmond			X	X	K–4	5–8	9–12	1,548	490	15:1	11	25
Crawford Day School, Portsmouth			X	X	K–5	6–8	9–12	33	21	2:1		
Eastern Mennonite High School, Harrisonburg			X	X	K–5	6–8	9–12	340	222	10:1	3	10
Episcopal High School, Alexandria	X	X					9–12	444	444	7:1	19	44
Fishburne Military School, Waynesboro	X		X			8	9–12	180	165	8:1	3	29
Flint Hill School, Oakton			X	X	JK–4	5–8	9–12	1,017	432	10:1	18	32
Fork Union Military Academy, Fork Union	X		X			6–8	9–PG	509	446	15:1	5	38
Foxcroft School, Middleburg		X		X			9–12	169	169	7:1	12	25
Fuqua School, Farmville			X	X	PK–5	6–8	9–12	528	151	16:1	5	12
Hampton Roads Academy, Newport News			X	X		6–8	9–12	537	310	10:1	18	18
Hargrave Military Academy, Chatham	X		X	X		7–8	9–PG	410	377	11:1	3	50
Highland School, Warrenton			X	X	PK–5	6–8	9–12	537	214	10:1	16	33
Islamic Saudi Academy, Alexandria			X	X	K–6	7–8	9–12	948	185	15:1	4	16
Little Keswick School, Keswick	X							31	11	4:1		15
Massanutten Military Academy, Woodstock	X	X	X	X		7–8	9–PG	194	169	8:1	1	62
Miller School, Charlottesville	X	X	X	X		7–8	9–12	140	119	6:1	9	43
New Dominion School, Dillwyn	X	X					6–12	110	110	6:1		6
Norfolk Academy, Norfolk			X	X	1–6	7–9	10–12	1,210	340	10:1	17	26
Norfolk Collegiate School, Norfolk			X	X	K–5	6–8	9–12	875	324	10:1	18	15
Oak Hill Academy, Mouth of Wilson	X	X	X	X			8–12	109	109	9:1	2	29
Oakland School, Keswick	X	X	X	X					3	5:1		30
The Potomac School, McLean			X	X	K–3	4–8	9–12	875	309	6:1	15	23
Randolph-Macon Academy, Front Royal	X	X	X	X		6–8	9–PG	397	324	9:1	9	31
St. Anne's–Belfield School, Charlottesville	X	X	X	X	PK–4	5–8	9–12	853	321	12:1	11	15
St. Catherine's School, Richmond				X	PK–5	6–8	9–12	820	292	6:1	17	35
St. Christopher's School, Richmond			X		JK–5	6–8	9–12	941	310	8:1	18	23
Saint Gertrude High School, Richmond				X			9–12	253	253	9:1	7	13
St. Margaret's School, Tappahannock		X		X			8–12	149	149	6:1	5	25
St. Stephen's & St. Agnes School, Alexandria			X	X	JK–5	6–8	9–12	1,155	440	8:1	19	22
Southampton Academy, Courtland			X	X	PK–5	6–8	9–12	432	84	12:1	2	10
Stuart Hall, Staunton		X	X	X		5–8	9–12	156	71	7:1		11
Thornton Friends School/N.V.A., Alexandria			X				9–12	30	30	6:1		12
Timber Ridge School, Cross Junction	X					6–8	9–12	75	57	9:1		10
Trinity Episcopal School, Richmond			X	X			8–12	402	402	10:1	14	28
Virginia Beach Friends School, Virginia Beach			X	X	1–5	6–8	9–12	210	55	5:1	5	8
Virginia Episcopal School, Lynchburg	X	X	X	X			9–12	273	273	8:1	16	27
Wakefield School, The Plains			X	X	PK–5	6–8	9–12	471	133	9:1	19	12
Woodberry Forest School, Woodberry Forest	X						9–12	386	386	8:1	19	59
Washington												
Annie Wright School, Tacoma			X	X	PS–5	6–8	9–12	439	112	7:1	8	8
Bellarmine Preparatory School, Tacoma			X	X			9–12	1,005	1,005	14:1	8	16

Private Secondary Schools At-a-Glance

	STUDENTS ACCEPTED				GRADES			STUDENT/FACULTY			SCHOOL OFFERINGS (number)	
	Boarding		Day									
	Boys	Girls	Boys	Girls	Lower	Middle	Upper	Total	Upper	Student/Faculty Ratio	Advanced Placement Subject Areas	Sports
Bellevue Christian School, Clyde Hill.			X	X	PK–6	7–8	9–12	1,300	360	21:1		19
The Bush School, Seattle.			X	X	K–5	6–8	9–12	557	218	6:1	8	28
Charles Wright Academy, Tacoma			X	X	PK–5	6–8	9–12	688	278	8:1	12	20
Christa McAuliffe Academy, Yakima.			X	X	K–6	7–8	9–12	362	242	23:1	2	
Chrysalis School, Woodinville			X	X	K–6	7–8	9–12	230	160	1:1		
Explorations Academy, Bellingham			X	X				16	10	5:1	2	
Gonzaga Preparatory School, Spokane			X	X			9–12	860	860	19:1	11	19
John F. Kennedy Memorial High School, Burien	X	X	X	X			9–12	866	866	18:1	13	26
King's West School, Bremerton			X	X	K–6		7–12	352	220	11:1	4	7
Lakeside School, Seattle			X	X		5–8	9–12	778	521	10:1		14
The Northwest School, Seattle.	X	X	X	X		6–8	9–12	446	317	9:1		14
Northwest Yeshiva High School, Mercer Island			X	X			9–12	108	108	4:1		6
O'Dea High School, Seattle.			X				9–12	480	480	13:1	2	17
The Overlake School, Redmond			X	X		5–8	9–12	492	282	9:1	14	23
Saint George's School, Spokane			X	X	K–5	6–8	9–12	380	130	5.5:1	12	9
Seattle Academy of Arts and Sciences, Seattle			X	X		6–8	9–12	547	330	7:1		15
Seattle Christian Schools, Seattle.			X	X	K–6	7–8	9–12	695	275	12:1	5	21
Shoreline Christian, Shoreline.			X	X	PS–6	7–8	9–12	287	112	7:1		8
University Prep, Seattle			X	X		6–8	9–12	462	265	9:1	7	10
West Virginia												
The Linsly School, Wheeling.	X	X	X	X	5–8		9–12	425	254	9:1	7	51
Notre Dame High School, Clarksburg			X	X		7–8	9–12	136	95	8:1	7	14
Wisconsin												
Conserve School, Land O' Lakes.	X	X					9–12	135	135	8:1	5	71
Fox Valley Lutheran High School, Appleton			X	X			9–12	616	616	14:1	4	12
Marquette University High School, Milwaukee.			X				9–12	1,067	1,067	15:1	18	19
Newman High School, Wausau			X	X					211	15:1	8	9
The Prairie School, Racine			X	X	PK–4	5–8	9–12	662	245	15:1	11	9
St. John's Northwestern Military Academy, Delafield . .	X					7–8	9–12	300	260	12:1		30
Saint Joseph High School, Kenosha.			X	X		7–8	9–12	495	347	20:1	4	12
University Lake School, Hartland			X	X	JK–5	6–8	9–12	349	96	9:1	9	10
University School of Milwaukee, Milwaukee.			X	X	PK–4	5–8	9–12	1,046	353	9:1	19	22
Wayland Academy, Beaver Dam.	X	X	X	X			9–12	190	190	6:1	12	42
Wisconsin Academy, Columbus	X	X	X	X			9–12	102	102	6:1		7
CANADA												
Academie Sainte Cecile International School, Windsor, ON.	X	X	X	X	1–8		9–12	245	112	10:1		25
The Academy for Gifted Children (PACE), Richmond Hill, ON			X	X	1–3	4–7	8–12	294	126	15:1	2	37
Airdrie Koinonia Christian School, Airdrie, AB			X	X	K–6		7–12	299	126	14:1		15
Albert College, Belleville, ON	X	X	X	X	1–6	7–8	9–PG	294	156	8:1	5	66
Appleby College, Oakville, ON	X	X	X	X		7–8	9–12	683	547	7:1	10	31
Arrowsmith School, Toronto, ON			X	X				60	20	8:1		
Ashbury College, Ottawa, ON	X	X	X	X	4–8		9–12	651	486	16:1		42
Balmoral Hall School, Winnipeg, MB		X	X	X	N–5	6–8	9–12	469	147	7:1	12	65
Bearspaw Christian School, Calgary, AB.			X	X	1–6	7–9	10–12	349	59	20:1		9
The Bethany Hills School, Bethany, ON		X	X	X	JK–6	7–8	9–13	93	45	7:1		47
Bishop's College School, Lennoxville, QC.	X	X	X	X		7–9	10–12	257	160	8:1	13	43
The Bishop Strachan School, Toronto, ON		X		X	PK–6		7–12	893	645	10:1	16	48
Brentwood College School, Mill Bay, BC	X	X	X	X			8–12	425	425	8:1		67
British Columbia Christian Academy, Port Coquitlam, BC			X	X	PK–3	4–7	8–12	266	100	5:1		8
Calgary Academy, Calgary, AB.			X	X	2–6		7–12	570	421	8:1		39
Cambridge International College of Canada, Toronto, ON			X	X			10–13	300	300	13:1		
Centennial Academy, Montreal, QC.			X	X			7–11	340	340	10:1		23
Chedar Chabad, North York, ON	X		X		1–5	6–8	9–12	248	135	25:1		
Columbia International College of Canada, Hamilton, ON	X	X	X	X	9–10	11	12	1,280	760	20:1	5	48
Concordia Continuing Education High School, Edmonton, AB			X	X								
Concordia High School, Edmonton, AB	X	X	X	X				133		10:1		14
The Country Day School, King City, ON.			X	X	JK–6	7–8	9–12	729	320	10:1	2	21
Covenant Canadian Reformed School, Neerlandia, AB			X	X	K–6	7–9	10–12	155	30	10:1		16
Crawford Adventist Academy, Willowdale, ON			X	X	JK–6	7–8	9–12	489	153	16:1		10
Crescent School, Willowdale, ON			X		3–6	7–8	9–12	664	357	12:1	14	21
Crofton House School, Vancouver, BC.		X		X	1–6		7–12	671	443	11:1	6	25
De La Salle College, Toronto, ON.			X	X	5–6	7–8	9–12	584	429	15:1	4	16
Devon Park Christian School, Fredericton, NB			X	X						15:1		3
Edison School, Okotoks, AB			X	X	PK–6		7–12	172	72	12:1	7	7
Equilibrium International Education Institute, Calgary, AB.			X	X			10–12	100	100	15:1		11

Private Secondary Schools At-a-Glance

School	Boarding Boys	Boarding Girls	Day Boys	Day Girls	Lower	Middle	Upper	Total	Upper	Student/Faculty Ratio	Advanced Placement Subject Areas	Sports
Foothills Academy, Calgary, AB			X	X	1–6	7–8	9–12	186	93	12:1		35
Fraser Academy, Vancouver, BC			X	X	1–7		8–12	183	105	5:1		17
Gateway Christian School, Prince George, BC			X	X	K–3	4–6	7–12	118	39			31
Glen Eden School, Vancouver, BC	X	X										
Great Lakes Christian College, Beamsville, ON	X	X	X	X			9–12	104	104	12:1		10
Grenville Christian College, Brockville, ON	X	X	X	X	PK–6	7–8	9–12	203	102	6:1	3	34
Halifax Grammar School, Halifax, NS			X	X	K–4	5–9	10–12	539	196	10:1		15
Hamilton District Christian School, Ancaster, ON			X	X			9–12	576	576	17:1		20
Hamilton Learning Centre, Hamilton, ON			X	X	3–6	7–8	9–12	55	25	5:1		29
Havergal College, Toronto, ON		X		X	JK–6	7–8	9–12	921	485	9:1	4	70
Heritage Christian School, Jordan, ON			X	X	K–8		9–12	558	172	15:1		5
Hillcrest Christian School, Grande Prairie, AB			X	X	K–6	7–9	10–12	48	6	5:1		3
Hillfield Strathallan College, Hamilton, ON			X	X	PK–4	5–8	9–12	1,112	360	9:1	5	25
Hope Christian School, Champion, AB			X	X								
Hudson College, Toronto, ON			X	X	JK–6	7–8	9–12	178	108	10:1		29
Immanuel Christian High School, Lethbridge, AB			X	X		7–9	10–12	300	165	19:1		8
Imperial College of Toronto, Etobicoke, ON	X	X					11–12	201	201	22:1		
King David High School, Vancouver, BC			X	X			8–12	150	150		3	6
King's College School, Caledon, ON			X	X	3–6	7–8	9–12	26	23	6:1		35
Kingsway College, Oshawa, ON	X	X	X	X			9–12	182	182	12:1		13
Lakefield College School, Lakefield, ON	X	X	X	X			7–12	365	365	7:1	5	31
Landmark East School, Wolfville, NS	X	X	X	X	6–9		10–12	60	30	2:1		34
Linden Christian School, Winnipeg, MB			X	X	K–4	5–8	9–12	777	202	13:1		13
Lower Canada College, Montreal, QC			X	X	K–6	7–8	9–12	744	311	22:1	13	58
Luther College High School, Regina, SK	X	X	X	X			9–12	441	441	22:1		15
Malaspina International High School, Nanaimo, BC	X	X	X	X			10–12	130	130	8:1	5	39
Meadowridge Senior School, Maple Ridge, BC			X	X	JK–7		8–12	458	178	9:1		16
Mentor College, Mississauga, ON			X	X	JK–4	5–8	9–12	1,755	640	14:1		31
Metropolitan Preparatory Academy, Toronto, ON			X	X		6–8	9–12	435	335	18:1		15
Miss Edgar's and Miss Cramp's School, Montreal, QC				X	K–5	6–8	9–11	351	118	9:1	2	16
Mississauga Private School, Toronto, ON			X	X	JK–6	7–8	9–12	312	102	13:1		15
Nbisiing Education Centre, North Bay, ON			X	X			9–12	79	79	10:1		7
Niagara Christian Collegiate, Fort Erie, ON	X	X	X	X		7–8	9–12	331	279	17:1	3	16
Notre Dame Regional Secondary, Vancouver, BC			X	X			8–12	630	630	15:1		17
Okanagan Adventist Academy, Kelowna, BC			X	X	K–7		8–12	133	62			6
Pickering College, Newmarket, ON	X	X	X	X	JK–8		9–13	402	230	9:1		28
Pinehurst School, St. Catharines, ON	X	X			7–8	9–10	11–12	25	8	10:1		60
Queen Margaret's School, Duncan, BC		X	X	X	K–7		8–12	260	130	7:1	7	37
Queensway Christian College, Etobicoke, ON			X	X	JK–5	6–8	9–12	183	73	10:1		52
Quinte Christian High School, Belleville, ON			X	X			9–12	135	135	15:1		9
Ridley College, St. Catharines, ON	X	X	X	X		5–8	9–PG	607	503	9:1	10	62
Robert Land Academy, Wellandport, ON	X				6–8	9–10	11–12	148	65	15:1		67
Rocklyn Academy, Meaford, ON		X					9–12	27	27	3:1		25
Rockway Mennonite Collegiate, Kitchener, ON	X	X	X	X		6–8	9–12	422	308	10:1		30
Ron Pettigrew Christian School, Dawson Creek, BC			X	X	K–6	7–8	9–12	78	21	5:1		
Rothesay Netherwood School, Rothesay, NB	X	X	X	X		6–8	9–12	230	174	7:1	11	56
Royal Canadian College, Vancouver, BC			X	X		9–10	11–12	90	70	15:1		5
Sacred Heart School of Halifax, Halifax, NS			X	X	K–6		7–12	429	216	18:1	6	15
St. Andrew's College, Aurora, ON	X		X			6–8	9–12	538	404	10:1	5	60
St. Clement's School, Toronto, ON				X	1–6	7–9	10–13	442	174	9:1	15	34
St. George's School, Vancouver, BC	X		X		1–7		8–12	1,127	748	10:1	13	33
St. George's School of Montreal, Montreal, QC			X	X	PK–6		7–11	538	343	17:1	6	33
St. John's-Kilmarnock School, Breslau, ON			X	X	JK–5	6–8	9–12	454	199	12:1	8	35
St. John's-Ravenscourt School, Winnipeg, MB	X	X	X	X	1–5	6–8	9–12	780	349	9:1	10	20
Saint John's School of Alberta, Stony Plain, AB	X	X				7–9	10–12	106	71	10:1		21
St. Margaret's School, Victoria, BC		X		X	JK–6		7–12	438	288	8:1	5	66
St. Michaels University School, Victoria, BC	X	X	X	X	K–5	6–8	9–12	914	550	10:1	16	54
St. Paul's High School, Winnipeg, MB			X				9–12	589	589	14:1	3	20
Scarborough Christian School, North York, ON			X	X	JK–8		9–12	120	30	12:1		
Sedbergh School, Montebello, QC	X	X	X	X		7–8	9–12	83	63	5:1		56
Selwyn House School, Westmount, QC			X		K–6	7–8	9–11	570	175	9:1		19
SICES International Academy, Edmonton, AB	X	X						102		20:1		3
Smithville District Christian High School, Smithville, ON			X	X			9–12	232	232	11:1		10
Southridge School, Surrey, BC			X	X	K–3	4–7	8–12	674	322	10:1	9	32
Stanstead College, Stanstead, QC	X	X	X	X	7–9		10–12	205	134	8:1	13	39
Strathcona-Tweedsmuir School, Okotoks, AB			X	X	1–6	7–9	10–12	752	291	20:1		15
The Study School, Westmount, QC				X	K–3	4–6	7–11	421	190	8:1		34
Swedish Language School, Calgary, AB			X	X	K–3	4–9	10–12	35	7			
Tapply Binet College, Ancaster, ON			X	X				13	11	3:1		1
Toronto District Christian High School, Woodbridge, ON			X	X			9–12	453	453	13:1		7
Toronto Waldorf School, Thornhill, ON			X	X	1–8		9–12	294	95	5:1		28
Town Centre Montessori School, Markham, ON			X	X	1–6	7–8	9–12	1,400	200	15:1		19
Traditional Learning Academy, Coquitlam, BC			X	X	K–3	4–7	8–12	195	55	15:1		7
Trafalgar Castle School, Whitby, ON		X		X				232	220	9:1	2	30

Private Secondary Schools At-a-Glance

	STUDENTS ACCEPTED				GRADES			STUDENT/FACULTY			SCHOOL OFFERINGS (number)	
	Boarding		Day									
	Boys	Girls	Boys	Girls	Lower	Middle	Upper	Total	Upper	Student/Faculty Ratio	Advanced Placement Subject Areas	Sports
Trinity College School, Port Hope, ON	X	X	X	X		5–8	9–12	602	502	8:1	9	39
United Mennonite Educational Institute, Leamington, ON			X	X			9–12	80	80	15:1		13
University of Toronto Schools, Toronto, ON			X	X		7–8	9–12	619	403	11:1	1	65
Upper Canada College, Toronto, ON	X		X		K–7		8–13	1,116	687	9:1		48
Venta Preparatory School, Ottawa, ON	X	X	X	X	1–7		8–10	85	28	6:1		
Webber Academy, Calgary, AB			X	X	K–6	7–9	10–12	699	98	18:1	5	24
Westgate Mennonite Collegiate, Winnipeg, MB			X	X		7–9	10–12	318	158	15:1	5	31
West Island College, Calgary, AB			X	X		7–9	10–12	437	206	17:1	9	39
Westpark School, Portage la Prairie, MB			X	X	K–4	5–8	9–12	224	51	10:1		9
White Rock Christian Academy, Surrey, BC			X	X	K–5	6–8	9–12	308	93	12:1		10
Windsor Christian Fellowship Academy, Windsor, ON			X	X	K–3	4–7	8–12	66	25	12:1		7
The York School, Toronto, ON			X	X	1–6		7–12	520	300	12:1		26

INTERNATIONAL

Aruba

	Board Boys	Board Girls	Day Boys	Day Girls	Lower	Middle	Upper	Total	Upper	Ratio	AP	Sports
International School of Aruba, Oranjestad			X	X	PK–5	6–8	9–12	130	40	8:1	5	8

Australia

International School of Aruba	Board Boys	Board Girls	Day Boys	Day Girls	Lower	Middle	Upper	Total	Upper	Ratio	AP	Sports
Mercedes College, Springfield			X	X	1–5	6–9	10–12	1,168	440			25

Austria

	Board Boys	Board Girls	Day Boys	Day Girls	Lower	Middle	Upper	Total	Upper	Ratio	AP	Sports
The American International School, Vienna			X	X	PK–5	6–8	9–PG	729	235	7:1	9	18
American International School Salzburg, A-5020 Salzburg	X	X	X	X		7–8	9–PG	71	60	7:1	15	33
Danube International School, Vienna, Vienna			X	X	K–5	6–8	9–12	260	86			

Belgium

	Board Boys	Board Girls	Day Boys	Day Girls	Lower	Middle	Upper	Total	Upper	Ratio	AP	Sports
International School of Brussels, Brussels			X	X	N–6	7–9	10–13	1,400	379	10:1	7	16

Bermuda

	Board Boys	Board Girls	Day Boys	Day Girls	Lower	Middle	Upper	Total	Upper	Ratio	AP	Sports
The Bermuda High School for Girls, Pembroke				X	1–6	7–9	10–13	686	163	7:1		30
Saltus Grammar School, Hamilton HMJX			X	X	K–5	6–8	9–12	994	240	13:1	12	16

Bolivia

	Board Boys	Board Girls	Day Boys	Day Girls	Lower	Middle	Upper	Total	Upper	Ratio	AP	Sports
American Cooperative School, La Paz			X	X	PK–5	6–8	9–12	429	124	10:1	9	15

Brazil

	Board Boys	Board Girls	Day Boys	Day Girls	Lower	Middle	Upper	Total	Upper	Ratio	AP	Sports
Chapel School, Sao Paulo			X	X	PK–6		7–12	700	285	9:1		6
Escola Americana de Campinas, Campinas-SP			X	X	PK–5	6–8	9–12	468	94	7:1	5	27

China

	Board Boys	Board Girls	Day Boys	Day Girls	Lower	Middle	Upper	Total	Upper	Ratio	AP	Sports
Beijing BISS International School, Beijing			X	X	K–6	7–8	9–12			6:1		21

Colombia

	Board Boys	Board Girls	Day Boys	Day Girls	Lower	Middle	Upper	Total	Upper	Ratio	AP	Sports
Colegio Bolivar, Cali			X	X	PK–5	6–8	9–12	1,261	286	10:1	5	14
Colegio Nueva Granada, Bogota			X	X	PK–5	6–8	9–12	1,680	421	20:1	15	11

Cyprus

	Board Boys	Board Girls	Day Boys	Day Girls	Lower	Middle	Upper	Total	Upper	Ratio	AP	Sports
American International School in Cyprus, Nicosia			X	X	K–5	6–8	9–12	258	99	12:1		15

Ecuador

	Board Boys	Board Girls	Day Boys	Day Girls	Lower	Middle	Upper	Total	Upper	Ratio	AP	Sports
Academia Cotopaxi, Quito			X	X	PK–5	6–8	9–12	477	127	7:1		5
Alliance Academy, Quito	X	X	X	X	PK–6	7–8	9–12	400	161	6:1	10	11

Ethiopia

	Board Boys	Board Girls	Day Boys	Day Girls	Lower	Middle	Upper	Total	Upper	Ratio	AP	Sports
International Community School of Addis Ababa, Addis Ababa			X	X	PK–5	6–8	9–12	426	141	13:1		17

France

	Board Boys	Board Girls	Day Boys	Day Girls	Lower	Middle	Upper	Total	Upper	Ratio	AP	Sports
American School of Paris, Saint Cloud			X	X	PK–5	6–8	9–13	747	338	7:1	10	11
The Lycee International, American Section, Saint-Germain-en-Laye Cedex			X	X	PK–5	6–9	10–12	680	179	18:1	1	17

Germany

	Board Boys	Board Girls	Day Boys	Day Girls	Lower	Middle	Upper	Total	Upper	Ratio	AP	Sports
Black Forest Academy, Kandern	X	X	X	X	1–5	6–8	9–12	361	242	8:1	10	26
International School Hamburg, Hamburg			X	X	PK–5	6–8	9–12	670	188	7:1		8
Munich International School, Starnberg			X	X	PK–4	5–8	9–12	1,255	411	9:1		22
Schule Schloss Salem, Salem	X	X	X	X	5–7	8–11	12–13	675	315	5:1		51

Greece

	Board Boys	Board Girls	Day Boys	Day Girls	Lower	Middle	Upper	Total	Upper	Ratio	AP	Sports
American Community Schools of Athens, Athens			X	X	JK–5	6–8	9–12	635	280	17:1		11
Campion School, Athens, Athens			X	X	PK–6	7–9	10–13	485	150	18:1		20
International School of Athens, Kifissia—Athens			X	X	PK–5	6–9	10–12	196	56	9:1		9

Honduras

	Board Boys	Board Girls	Day Boys	Day Girls	Lower	Middle	Upper	Total	Upper	Ratio	AP	Sports
Mazapan School, La Ceiba			X	X	1–6	7–8	9–12	311	111	12:1		10

India

	Board Boys	Board Girls	Day Boys	Day Girls	Lower	Middle	Upper	Total	Upper	Ratio	AP	Sports
Woodstock School, Uttaranchal	X	X	X	X	K–5	6–8	9–12	467	275	15:1	18	18

Indonesia

	Board Boys	Board Girls	Day Boys	Day Girls	Lower	Middle	Upper	Total	Upper	Ratio	AP	Sports
Jakarta International School, Jakarta			X	X	PK–5	6–8	9–12	2,566	938	19:1	14	30
Surabaya International School, Surabaya			X	X	PK–5	6–8	9–12	242	76	8:1	7	12

Private Secondary Schools At-a-Glance

	STUDENTS ACCEPTED				GRADES			STUDENT/FACULTY			SCHOOL OFFERINGS (number)	
	Boarding Boys	Boarding Girls	Day Boys	Day Girls	Lower	Middle	Upper	Total	Upper	Student/Faculty Ratio	Advanced Placement Subject Areas	Sports
Ireland												
St. Andrew's College, Dublin, County Dublin......			X	X			8–12	950	950			32
Italy												
American Overseas School of Rome, Rome.........	X	X	X	X	PK–5	6–8	9–13	605	203	18:1	10	8
American School of Milan, Noverasco di Opera, Milan......			X	X	N–5	6–8	9–12	498	156	8:1		14
CCI The Renaissance School, Lanciano........	X	X	X	X			10–12	120	120	7:1	9	37
Marymount International School, Rome..........			X	X	PK–5	6–8	9–12	753	210	15:1	1	8
St. Stephen's School, Rome, Rome.............	X	X	X	X			9–PG	211	211	6:1	11	8
Japan												
The American School in Japan, Tokyo..........			X	X	N–5	6–8	9–12	1,530	515	10:1	19	15
Canadian Academy, Kobe.................	X	X	X	X	PK–5	6–8	9–13	762	213	11:1	2	9
Columbia International School, Tokorozawa, Saitama.	X	X	X	X	1–6	7–9	10–12	250	144	15:1		19
Hokkaido International School, Sapporo........	X	X	X	X	PK–6	7–9	10–12	182	41	10:1	6	8
St. Mary's International School, Tokyo..........			X		K–6	7–8	9–12	963	267	10:1		20
St. Maur International School, Yokohama..........			X	X	PK–5	6–8	9–12	467	131	4:1	10	7
Seisen International School, Tokyo.............			X	X	K–6	7–8	9–12	693	148	6:1		16
Yokohama International School, Yokohama........			X	X	N–5	6–8	9–12	637	211	10:1		16
Jordan												
Ahliyyah School for Girls, Amman..............				X	1–6		7–12	1,000	500	10:1		42
Kuwait												
The English School, Kuwait, Safat.............			X	X				400	50	19:1		9
Luxembourg												
International School of Luxembourg, L-1430 Luxembourg......			X	X	PS–5	6–8	9–12	683	170	8:1		13
Malaysia												
The International School of Kuala Lumpur, Ampang, Selangor......			X	X	K–5	6–8	9–13	1,242	492	9:1	10	39
Mont'Kiara International School, Kuala Lumpur.....			X	X	1–5	6–8	9–12	711	165	7.1:1		10
Mexico												
The American School Foundation, Mexico City, D.F...			X	X	PK–5	6–8	9–12	2,469	667	10:1	19	14
The American School of Puerto Vallarta, Puerto Vallarta, Jalisco......			X	X	1–6	7–9	10–12	367	69	7:1	3	5
Westhill Institute, Mexico City, DF..............			X	X	PK–6	7–9	10–12	718	107	9:1	6	4
Monaco												
The International School of Monaco, Monte Carlo...			X	X								6
Namibia												
Windhoek International School, Windhoek........			X	X						7:1		10
Netherlands												
The American School of The Hague, 2241 BX Wassenaar......			X	X	K–4	5–8	9–12	1,050	360	7:1	16	12
International School of Amsterdam, Amstelveen.....			X	X	PS–5	6–8	9–12	841	221	11:1		14
Rotterdam International Secondary School, Wolfert van Borselen, Rotterdam......			X	X	6–8	9–10	11–12	162	52	10:1		8
Oman												
The British School, Muscat, Ruwi..............			X	X				765	65	11:1		10
Pakistan												
Karachi American School, Karachi..............			X	X	PS–5	6–8	9–12	332	126	8:1	14	13
Peru												
Colegio Franklin D. Roosevelt, Lima 12...........			X	X	N–5	6–8	9–12	1,265	378	11:1		46
Philippines												
Brent School-Baguio, Baguio City..............	X	X	X	X	PK–5	6–8	9–12	235	71	4:1		14
Poland												
American School of Warsaw, Konstancin-Jeziorna.....			X	X	PK–5	6–8	9–12	837	224	6:1		11
Portugal												
Carlucci American International School of Lisbon, Linho, Sintra......			X	X	N–5	6–8	9–12	494	130	8:1	6	4
St. Dominic's International School, Portugal, Sao Domingos de Rana......			X	X	1–6		7–13	612	345	7:1		15
Qatar												
American School of Doha, Doha...............			X	X	PK–5	6–8	9–12	992	288	20:1	13	14
Republic of Korea												
Seoul Foreign School, Seoul.................			X	X	PK–5	6–8	9–12	1,338	351	10:1	2	10
Seoul International School, Seoul..............			X	X	PK–5	6–8	9–12	1,101	324	13:1	13	8

Private Secondary Schools At-a-Glance

	STUDENTS ACCEPTED				GRADES			STUDENT/FACULTY			SCHOOL OFFERINGS (number)	
	Boarding		Day									
	Boys	Girls	Boys	Girls	Lower	Middle	Upper	Total	Upper	Student/Faculty Ratio	Advanced Placement Subject Areas	Sports
Romania												
American International School of Bucharest, Bucharest			X	X	PK–5	6–8	9–12	550	154	7:1		11
Russian Federation												
Anglo-American School of Moscow, Moscow			X	X	PK–5	6–8	9–12	1,235	327	6:1		34
Saudi Arabia												
American International School-Riyadh, Riyadh			X	X	1–5	6–8	9–12	714	283	15:1		10
The British International School, Jeddah, Jeddah			X	X	6–8	9–10	11–12	623	123	10:1		9
Singapore												
Overseas Family School, Singapore 238515			X	X	PK–5	6–8	9–12	1,950	407	8:1		8
South Africa												
International School of South Africa, Mafikeng	X	X	X	X								
Spain												
The American School of Madrid, Madrid			X	X	PK–5	6–8	9–12	735	215	10:1		6
International College Spain, Madrid			X	X	PK–5	6–8	9–12	616	170	10:1		20
Sweden												
Hvitfeldtska Gymnasiet, International Section, Goteborg			X	X					210	8:1		
Switzerland												
College du Leman International School, Versoix	X	X	X	X	K–5	6–8	9–13	1,754	656	7:1	15	44
Ecole d'Humanite, CH 6085 Hasliberg Goldern	X	X	X	X				146	127	5:1		39
Gstaad International School, Gstaad	X	X	X	X		8–9	10–12	23	10	5:1	5	25
International School Basel, Reinach BL 2			X	X	PK–5	6–10	11–12	913	113	10:1	5	31
International School of Berne, Guemligen 3073			X	X	PK–5		6–12	240	125	5:1		17
The International School of Geneva, Geneva			X	X	PK–6		7–13	3,750	2,100			14
International School of Lausanne, Le Mont-sur-Lausanne			X	X	PK–5	6–8	9–12	551	159	7:1		27
Leysin American School in Switzerland, Leysin	X	X					9–PG	345	345	5:1		67
Neuchatel Junior College, 2002 Neuchâtel	X	X					12	106	106	10:1	11	18
Riverside School, Zug			X	X				112	41	6:1	16	31
St. George's School in Switzerland, 1815 Clarens/ Montreux		X	X	X	K–5	6–8	9–12	313	83	7:1		25
TASIS, The American School in Switzerland, Montagnola-Lugano	X	X	X	X		7–8	9–PG	337	298	5:1	15	34
Zurich International School, Wödenswil			X	X	PS–5	6–8	9–13	931	301	7:1	17	15
Taiwan												
Taipei American School, Taipei			X	X	PK–5	6–8	9–12	2,235	843	9:1	17	12
Thailand												
International School Bangkok, Pakkret	X	X	X	X	PK–5	6–8	9–12	1,873	711	9:1	14	14
Trinidad and Tobago												
International School of Port-of-Spain, Westmorings			X	X	K–5	6–8	9–12	365	115	6:1	6	11
Turkey												
Istanbul International Community School, Istanbul			X	X	1–6		7–10	423	188	9:1		6
United Arab Emirates												
Al-Worood School, Abu Dhabi			X	X	K–6	7–9	10–12	2,239	380	17:1		5
Dubai American Academy, Dubai			X	X	PK–5	6–8	9–12	1,310	390			6
United Kingdom												
ACS Cobham International School, Cobham, Surrey	X	X	X	X	N–4	5–8	9–12	1,296	452	9:1	10	15
ACS Egham International School, Surrey			X	X	N–5	6–8	9–12	466	108	6:1		14
ACS Hillingdon International School, Hillingdon, Middlesex			X	X	PK–4	5–8	9–13	495	198	9:1	12	10
The American School in London, London			X	X	PK–4	5–8	9–12	1,309	462	16:1	19	16
Harrow School, Middlesex	X				9–9	10–11	12–13	805	338	9:1	10	53
Marymount International School, Surrey		X		X		6–8	9–12	217	167	7:1		7
St. Leonards, Fife, Scotland	X	X	X	X	N–7	8–11	12–13	390	97	7:1		51
TASIS The American School in England, Thorpe, Surrey	X	X	X	X	N–5	6–8	9–13	705	300	8:1	19	45
Windermere St. Anne's School, Windermere	X	X	X	X				375	232	6:1		52
Woodside Park International School, London	X	X	X	X	K–6		7–13	404	183	10:1		
Zimbabwe												
Harare International School, Harare			X	X	K–5	6–8	9–12	386	121	10:1		25

Traditional Day and
Boarding Schools

ACADEMIA COTOPAXI

De Las Higuerillas y Alondras
Monteserrin
PO Box 17-01-199
Quito, Ecuador
Head of School: Dr. William Johnston

General Information Coeducational day college-preparatory, International Baccalaureate, and Ecuadorian Diploma school. Grades PK–PG. Founded: 1959. Setting: suburban. 15-acre campus. 3 buildings on campus. Approved or accredited by Ecuadorean Ministry of Education, International Baccalaureate Organization, and Southern Association of Colleges and Schools. Member of Secondary School Admission Test Board. Language of instruction: English. Total enrollment: 477. Upper school average class size: 15. Upper school faculty-student ratio: 1:7.

Upper School Student Profile Grade 9: 41 students (19 boys, 22 girls); Grade 10: 27 students (15 boys, 12 girls); Grade 11: 33 students (16 boys, 17 girls); Grade 12: 26 students (12 boys, 14 girls).

Faculty School total: 67. In upper school: 18 men, 49 women; 35 have advanced degrees.

Subjects Offered Algebra, American history, American literature, art, band, biology, calculus, chemistry, choir, computer literacy, computer programming, computer science, creative writing, drama, English, English literature, ESL, European history, French, geography, geometry, government/civics, history, international relations, journalism, mathematics, music, orchestra, physical education, physical science, physics, psychology, science, social studies, Spanish, swimming, theater, theory of knowledge, world history, world literature, writing, yearbook.

Graduation Requirements Arts and fine arts (art, music, dance, drama), computer science, English, foreign language, mathematics, physical education (includes health), science, social studies (includes history). Community service is required.

Special Academic Programs International Baccalaureate program; honors section; academic accommodation for the gifted, the musically talented, and the artistically talented; remedial reading and/or remedial writing; remedial math; programs in English, mathematics, general development for dyslexic students; special instructional classes for learning disabled students, students with Attention Deficit Disorder and dyslexia; ESL (16 students enrolled).

College Placement 35 students graduated in 2005; all went to college, including Barry University; Clark University; Georgia State University; University of Miami; Virginia Polytechnic Institute and State University. Median SAT verbal: 528, median SAT math: 544, median composite ACT: 24. 16% scored over 600 on SAT verbal, 13% scored over 600 on SAT math, 10% scored over 26 on composite ACT.

Student Life Upper grades have specified standards of dress, student council, honor system. Discipline rests primarily with faculty.

Tuition and Aid Day student tuition: $11,965. Tuition installment plan (monthly payment plans). Tuition reduction for siblings, discounts for longevity and advance payment available. In 2005–06, 10% of upper-school students received aid. Total amount of financial aid awarded in 2005–06: $2500.

Admissions For fall 2005, 32 students applied for upper-level admission, 25 were accepted, 23 enrolled. Any standardized test, MAT 7 Metropolitan Achievement Test, Woodcock-Johnson/Reading Inventory, Woodcock-Munoz in English/Reading Comprehension or writing sample required. Deadline for receipt of application materials: none. Application fee required: $300. Interview required.

Athletics Interscholastic: basketball (boys, girls), soccer (b,g), volleyball (b,g); intramural: weight training (b); coed interscholastic: swimming and diving; coed intramural: swimming and diving. 2 PE instructors, 2 coaches.

Computers Computers are regularly used in business, design, graphic arts classes. Computer network features include campus e-mail, CD-ROMs, Internet access.

Contact Paola Pereira, Director of Admissions. 593-2-467-411 Ext. 210. Fax: 593-2-445-195. E-mail: ppereira@cotopaxi.k12.ec. Web site: www.cotopaxi.k12.ec.

ACADEMIE SAINTE CECILE INTERNATIONAL SCHOOL

925 Cousineau Road
Windsor, Ontario N9G 1V8, Canada
Head of School: Mlle. Thérèse H. Gadoury

General Information Coeducational boarding and day college-preparatory, arts, and bilingual studies school, affiliated with Roman Catholic Church. Boarding grades 7–12, day grades 1–12. Founded: 1993. Setting: urban. Nearest major city is Toronto, Canada. Students are housed in single-sex by floor dormitories. 27-acre campus. 1 building on campus. Approved or accredited by International Baccalaureate Organization, The Association of Boarding Schools, and Ontario Department of Education. Languages of instruction: English and French. Total enrollment: 245. Upper school average class size: 15. Upper school faculty-student ratio: 1:10.

Upper School Student Profile 60% of students are boarding students. 40% are province residents. 60% are international students. International students from Bermuda, Hong Kong, Mexico, Republic of Korea, Taiwan, and Thailand; 7 other countries represented in student body. 70% of students are Roman Catholic.

Faculty School total: 50. In upper school: 13 men, 11 women; 10 have advanced degrees; 4 reside on campus.

Subjects Offered Accounting, advanced chemistry, advanced computer applications, advanced math, algebra, art, art education, art history, audio visual/media, ballet, basketball, biology, business technology, calculus, campus ministry, career education, careers, Catholic belief and practice, chemistry, choir, choral music, civics, classical music, computer information systems, computer keyboarding, computer programming, computer science, concert band, concert bell choir, concert choir, creative dance, creative drama, creative thinking, creative writing, critical thinking, critical writing, dance, dance performance, decision making skills, desktop publishing, desktop publishing, ESL, discrete mathematics, drama performance, drama workshop, dramatic arts, drawing, drawing and design, driver education, earth science, economics, English, English literature, environmental studies, ESL, ethics, expository writing, family living, French, French studies, geography, geometry, German, golf, handbells, health and wellness, health education, history, history of dance, history of music, history of religion, history of the Catholic Church, honors algebra, honors English, honors geometry, honors world history, instrumental music, International Baccalaureate courses, Internet, Internet research, intro to computers, Italian, jazz band, jazz dance, journalism, Latin, leadership skills, library skills, Life of Christ, literature, literature and composition-AP, mathematics, media studies, music, music appreciation, music composition, music history, music performance, music theory, organ, painting, philosophy, photography, physical education, physics, piano, poetry, prayer/spirituality, pre-algebra, pre-calculus, probability and statistics, public speaking, reading, reading/study skills, religion, religions, research skills, research techniques, SAT preparation, science, sculpture, Shakespeare, social studies, softball, Spanish, stage and body movement, stained glass, strings, student government, swimming, tennis, TOEFL preparation, track and field, values and decisions, visual arts, vocal ensemble, voice, volleyball, wind ensemble, wind instruments, world religions, writing, writing fundamentals, writing skills, yearbook.

Graduation Requirements Ontario Ministry of Education requirements.

Special Academic Programs International Baccalaureate program; honors section; accelerated programs; academic accommodation for the gifted, the musically talented, and the artistically talented; remedial reading and/or remedial writing; remedial math; ESL (60 students enrolled).

College Placement 30 students graduated in 2005; all went to college, including McMaster University; The University of British Columbia; The University of Western Ontario; University of Toronto; University of Waterloo; University of Windsor. Median SAT verbal: 370, median SAT math: 620. 60% scored over 600 on SAT math.

Student Life Upper grades have uniform requirement, student council, honor system. Discipline rests primarily with faculty.

Summer Programs Remediation, enrichment, advancement, ESL, art/fine arts programs offered; session focuses on ESL; held on campus; accepts boys and girls; open to students from other schools. 25 students usually enrolled. 2006 schedule: July 3 to September 1.

Tuition and Aid Day student tuition: CAN$10,500; 7-day tuition and room/board: CAN$33,050–CAN$33,900. Tuition installment plan (Insured Tuition Payment Plan). Tuition reduction for siblings, merit scholarship grants, paying campus jobs available. Total upper-school merit-scholarship money awarded for 2005–06: CAN$4500.

Admissions Traditional secondary-level entrance grade is 9. Deadline for receipt of application materials: none. Application fee required: CAN$300. Interview recommended.

Athletics Interscholastic: aquatics (boys, girls), badminton (b,g), basketball (b,g), equestrian sports (b,g), golf (b,g), horseback riding (b,g), ice hockey (g), independent competitive sports (b,g), modern dance (b,g), physical fitness (b,g), soccer (b,g), softball (b,g), swimming and diving (b,g), tennis (b,g), volleyball (b,g); intramural: aquatics (b,g), badminton (b,g), ballet (g), basketball (b,g), bowling (b,g), cross-country running (b,g), dance (b,g), dressage (b,g), equestrian sports (b,g), golf (b,g), horseback riding (b,g), paddle tennis (b,g), soccer (b,g), softball (b,g), swimming and diving (b,g), table tennis (b,g), tennis (b,g), volleyball (b,g); coed interscholastic: aquatics, badminton, basketball, dressage, equestrian sports, fitness, golf, horseback riding, indoor track & field, modern dance, physical fitness, soccer, softball, swimming and diving, tennis, volleyball; coed intramural: aquatics, badminton, basketball, bowling, cross-country running, dance, dressage, equestrian sports, floor hockey, golf, horseback riding, modern dance, soccer, softball, swimming and diving, tennis, volleyball. 2 PE instructors, 8 coaches.

Computers Computers are regularly used in accounting, business, desktop publishing, ESL, information technology, mathematics classes. Computer network features include CD-ROMs, Internet access, file transfer, office computer access.

Contact Ms. Gwen A. Gatt, Admissions Clerk. 519-969-1291. Fax: 519-969-7953. E-mail: info@stececile.ca. Web site: www.stececile.ca.

THE ACADEMY AT CHARLEMONT

1359 Route 2
Charlemont, Massachusetts 01339
Head of School: Mr. Todd A. Sumner

General Information Coeducational boarding and day college-preparatory school. Boarding grades 9–PG, day grades 7–PG. Founded: 1981. Setting: small town. Nearest major city is Springfield. Students are housed in local homes. 12-acre campus. 3 buildings on campus. Approved or accredited by New England Association of Schools and Colleges and Massachusetts Department of Education. Member of National

Association of Independent Schools. Endowment: $250,000. Total enrollment: 114. Upper school average class size: 18. Upper school faculty-student ratio: 1:7.

Upper School Student Profile Grade 9: 20 students (10 boys, 10 girls); Grade 10: 21 students (10 boys, 11 girls); Grade 11: 19 students (9 boys, 10 girls); Grade 12: 18 students (9 boys, 9 girls). 2% of students are boarding students. 88% are state residents. 4 states are represented in upper school student body. 1% are international students. International students from Slovakia.

Faculty School total: 17. In upper school: 8 men, 9 women; 6 have advanced degrees.

Subjects Offered Algebra, American literature, art, art history, biology, calculus, chemistry, computer science, creative writing, drama, earth science, ecology, English, English literature, environmental science, ethics, European history, expository writing, fine arts, French, geography, geometry, government/civics, grammar, health, history, Latin, mathematics, music, philosophy, photography, physical education, physics, religion, Russian, science, social studies, Spanish, speech, theater, trigonometry, world history, world literature, writing.

Graduation Requirements Algebra, American government, American literature, American studies, arts and fine arts (art, music, dance, drama), biology, calculus, chemistry, civics, classical language, computer literacy, English, foreign language, four units of summer reading, geography, geometry, Latin, mathematics, physics, pre-calculus, science, senior project, social studies (includes history).

Special Academic Programs Independent study; study abroad.

College Placement 14 students graduated in 2005; all went to college, including Boston University; Franklin and Marshall College; The College of Wooster; Vassar College; Worcester Polytechnic Institute. Median SAT verbal: 645, median SAT math: 625. 79% scored over 600 on SAT verbal, 57% scored over 600 on SAT math.

Student Life Upper grades have specified standards of dress, student council, honor system. Discipline rests primarily with faculty.

Tuition and Aid Day student tuition: $15,900; 7-day tuition and room/board: $26,900. Tuition installment plan (monthly payment plans, individually arranged payment plans). Need-based scholarship grants, need-based loans available. In 2005–06, 56% of upper-school students received aid. Total amount of financial aid awarded in 2005–06: $450,000.

Admissions Traditional secondary-level entrance grade is 9. For fall 2005, 28 students applied for upper-level admission, 12 were accepted, 9 enrolled. School's own test and writing sample required. Deadline for receipt of application materials: March 1. Application fee required: $30. On-campus interview recommended.

Athletics Interscholastic: alpine skiing (boys, girls), cross-country running (b,g), lacrosse (b,g), soccer (b,g); intramural: winter soccer (b,g); coed interscholastic: basketball; coed intramural: aerobics/dance, alpine skiing, bicycling, canoeing/kayaking, golf, kayaking, tennis, ultimate Frisbee, winter soccer, yoga.

Computers Computers are regularly used in English, foreign language, mathematics, science classes. Computer network features include campus e-mail, on-campus library services, CD-ROMs, Internet access.

Contact Brett A. Carey, Director of Admissions. 413-339-4912. Fax: 413-339-4324. E-mail: bcarey@charlemont.org. Web site: www.charlemont.org.

THE ACADEMY AT SISTERS
Bend, Oregon
See Special Needs Schools section.

ACADEMY AT SWIFT RIVER
Cummington, Massachusetts
See Special Needs Schools section.

THE ACADEMY FOR GIFTED CHILDREN (PACE)
12 Bond Crescent
Richmond Hill, Ontario L4E 3K2, Canada
Head of School: Barbara Rosenberg

General Information Coeducational day college-preparatory and intellectually gifted school. Grades 1–12. Founded: 1993. Setting: suburban. Nearest major city is Toronto, Canada. 2-acre campus. 2 buildings on campus. Approved or accredited by Ontario Department of Education. Language of instruction: English. Total enrollment: 294. Upper school average class size: 17. Upper school faculty-student ratio: 1:15.

Upper School Student Profile Grade 8: 30 students (15 boys, 15 girls); Grade 9: 30 students (14 boys, 16 girls); Grade 10: 13 students (2 boys, 11 girls); Grade 11: 20 students (8 boys, 12 girls); Grade 12: 29 students (14 boys, 15 girls).

Faculty School total: 29. In upper school: 4 men, 8 women; 5 have advanced degrees.

Subjects Offered 20th century world history, Advanced Placement courses, algebra, analytic geometry, biology, calculus, Canadian geography, Canadian history, Canadian law, career education, chemistry, civics, computer information systems, computer programming, computer science, dramatic arts, English, finite math, French, French as a second language, geometry, health education, information technology, language, law, literature, mathematics, modern Western civilization, music, philosophy, physical education, physics, science, sociology, visual arts, world civilizations, writing skills.

Graduation Requirements Advanced chemistry, advanced math, algebra, analytic geometry, biology, calculus, Canadian geography, Canadian history, Canadian literature, career education, chemistry, civics, English literature, French as a second language, healthful living, law, music, philosophy, pre-algebra, pre-calculus, science, senior humanities, social sciences, sociology, theater arts, visual arts, 40 hours of community service, OSSLT.

Special Academic Programs Advanced Placement exam preparation in 2 subject areas; honors section; academic accommodation for the gifted.

College Placement 20 students graduated in 2005; all went to college, including Queen's University at Kingston; The University of Western Ontario; University of Toronto. Median SAT verbal: 780, median SAT math: 800. 100% scored over 600 on SAT verbal, 100% scored over 600 on SAT math.

Student Life Upper grades have specified standards of dress, student council, honor system. Discipline rests primarily with faculty.

Tuition and Aid Day student tuition: CAN$10,000. Tuition installment plan (monthly payment plans).

Admissions Traditional secondary-level entrance grade is 8. For fall 2005, 10 students applied for upper-level admission, 8 were accepted, 8 enrolled. Psychoeducational evaluation, Wechsler Individual Achievement Test and WISC III or other aptitude measures; standardized achievement test required. Deadline for receipt of application materials: none. No application fee required. On-campus interview required.

Athletics Interscholastic: badminton (boys, girls), ball hockey (b), baseball (b,g), basketball (b,g), flag football (b), floor hockey (b), golf (b,g), independent competitive sports (b,g), indoor soccer (b,g), soccer (b,g), softball (b,g), track and field (b,g), volleyball (b,g), winter soccer (b,g); intramural: badminton (b,g), soccer (b,g), softball (b,g); coed interscholastic: badminton, baseball, bowling, cross-country running, flag football, Frisbee, indoor soccer, ultimate Frisbee; coed intramural: alpine skiing, badminton, ball hockey, basketball, cross-country running, curling, floor hockey, handball, ice skating, jogging, jump rope, life saving, martial arts, outdoor activities, outdoor education, outdoor skills, physical fitness, ropes courses, scuba diving, skiing (downhill), snowboarding, snowshoeing, volleyball, wall climbing, yoga. 1 PE instructor, 10 coaches.

Computers Computers are regularly used in information technology, newspaper, photography, programming, science, technology, writing, yearbook classes. Computer network features include CD-ROMs, Internet access, DVD.

Contact Barbara Rosenberg, Director. 905-773-3997. Fax: 905-773-4722. Web site: www.pace.on.ca.

THE ACADEMY FOR GLOBAL EXPLORATION
PO Box 712
Ashland, Oregon 97520
Head of School: Mr. Greg Guevara

General Information Coeducational boarding college-preparatory, outdoor education, and leadership school. Grades 9–12. Founded: 2002. Setting: small town. Nearest major city is Portland. Students are housed in coed dormitories. 50-acre campus. 2 buildings on campus. Approved or accredited by Northwest Association of Accredited Schools and Oregon Department of Education. Total enrollment: 5. Upper school faculty-student ratio: 1:3.

Upper School Student Profile Grade 10: 2 students (2 girls); Grade 11: 2 students (2 boys); Grade 12: 1 student (1 boy). 100% of students are boarding students. 20% are state residents. 5 states are represented in upper school student body.

Faculty School total: 4. In upper school: 1 man, 2 women; 3 have advanced degrees; 3 reside on campus.

Subjects Offered Algebra, biology, chemistry, computer skills, cultural geography, earth science, English, environmental studies, foreign language, geometry, health, mathematics, photography, physical education, science, social studies, space and physical sciences, U.S. history, world history.

Graduation Requirements Cultural geography, electives, English, foreign language, mathematics, outdoor education, physical education (includes health), science, social studies (includes history), cultural studies, outdoor adventure.

Special Academic Programs Honors section; accelerated programs; independent study; study abroad; academic accommodation for the gifted; remedial reading and/or remedial writing; remedial math.

Student Life Upper grades have student council, honor system. Discipline rests primarily with faculty.

Summer Programs Remediation, enrichment, advancement, sports, rigorous outdoor training programs offered; session focuses on outdoor adventure, cultural studies; held both on and off campus; held at various domestic venues and New Zealand, South America, Europe; accepts boys and girls; open to students from other schools. 15 students usually enrolled. 2006 schedule: June 23 to July 15. Application deadline: none.

Tuition and Aid 7-day tuition and room/board: $27,000. Guaranteed tuition plan. Tuition installment plan (monthly payment plans, individually arranged payment plans, semester payment plan). Tuition reduction for siblings, merit scholarship grants, need-based scholarship grants available.

The Academy for Global Exploration

Admissions Traditional secondary-level entrance grade is 10. For fall 2005, 21 students applied for upper-level admission, 17 were accepted, 5 enrolled. Deadline for receipt of application materials: none. Application fee required: $50. Interview required.

Athletics Coed Intramural: alpine skiing, back packing, bicycling, canoeing/kayaking, climbing, combined training, cross-country running, fishing, fitness, fitness walking, fly fishing, Frisbee, hiking/backpacking, independent competitive sports, indoor soccer, jogging, kayaking, life saving, mountain biking, mountaineering, nordic skiing, outdoor activities, outdoor adventure, outdoor education, outdoor recreation, outdoor skills, outdoors, paddling, physical fitness, physical training, project adventure, rafting, rappelling, rock climbing, running, scuba diving, skateboarding, skiing (cross-country), skiing (downhill), skydiving, snowboarding, snowshoeing, soccer, speleology, surfing, telemark skiing, ultimate Frisbee, wall climbing, wilderness, wilderness survival, wildernessways, windsurfing, winter walking. 3 PE instructors.

Computers Computers are regularly used in all classes. Computer resources include Internet access, wireless campus network.

Contact Mr. Greg Guevara, Head of School. 541-913-0660. E-mail: admissions@agexplore.org. Web site: www.AGExplore.org.

See full description on page 636.

ACADEMY OF HOLY ANGELS

6600 Nicollet Avenue South
Richfield, Minnesota 55423-2498
Head of School: Dr. Jill M. Reilly

General Information Coeducational day college-preparatory, arts, business, religious studies, and technology school, affiliated with Roman Catholic Church. Grades 9–12. Founded: 1877. Setting: suburban. Nearest major city is Minneapolis. 26-acre campus. 2 buildings on campus. Approved or accredited by North Central Association of Colleges and Schools. Endowment: $600,000. Total enrollment: 865. Upper school average class size: 20. Upper school faculty-student ratio: 1:13.

Upper School Student Profile 80% of students are Roman Catholic.

Faculty School total: 63. In upper school: 30 men, 30 women; 29 have advanced degrees.

Subjects Offered Algebra, American history, American literature, anatomy, art, art history, astronomy, Bible studies, biology, broadcasting, business, business skills, calculus, ceramics, chemistry, computer math, computer programming, computer science, dance, drafting, drama, economics, electronics, English, English literature, environmental science, ethics, European history, expository writing, fine arts, French, geography, geometry, German, government/civics, grammar, health, history, home economics, industrial arts, journalism, mathematics, mechanical drawing, music, photography, physical education, physics, physiology, psychology, religion, Russian, science, social science, social studies, sociology, Spanish, speech, theater, theology, trigonometry, typing, world history, world literature, writing.

Graduation Requirements Arts and fine arts (art, music, dance, drama), business skills (includes word processing), English, mathematics, physical education (includes health), religion (includes Bible studies and theology), science, social science, social studies (includes history).

Special Academic Programs Advanced Placement exam preparation in 7 subject areas; honors section; independent study; study at local college for college credit; study abroad; academic accommodation for the gifted, the musically talented, and the artistically talented.

College Placement 194 students graduated in 2005; 187 went to college, including Creighton University; Loyola University Chicago; University of Minnesota, Duluth; University of Minnesota, Twin Cities Campus; University of St. Thomas; University of Wisconsin–Madison. Other: 1 went to work, 1 entered military service, 5 had other specific plans. Mean SAT verbal: 577, mean SAT math: 606, mean composite ACT: 25.

Student Life Upper grades have uniform requirement, student council, honor system. Discipline rests equally with students and faculty. Attendance at religious services is required.

Summer Programs Sports, art/fine arts programs offered; session focuses on activities geared toward 9th grade recruiting; held both on and off campus; held at nearby tennis courts; accepts boys and girls; open to students from other schools. 400 students usually enrolled. 2006 schedule: June 12 to July 20. Application deadline: May 26.

Tuition and Aid Day student tuition: $8300. Tuition installment plan (monthly payment plans, individually arranged payment plans, quarterly payment plan). Need-based scholarship grants, minority student scholarships, single-parent family scholarships available. In 2005–06, 26% of upper-school students received aid. Total amount of financial aid awarded in 2005–06: $600,000.

Admissions Traditional secondary-level entrance grade is 9. For fall 2005, 370 students applied for upper-level admission, 350 were accepted, 232 enrolled. ACT-Explore required. Deadline for receipt of application materials: January 13. No application fee required. Interview recommended.

Athletics Interscholastic: baseball (boys), basketball (b,g), cross-country running (b,g), danceline (g), football (b), golf (b,g), ice hockey (b,g), soccer (b,g), softball (g), tennis (b,g), track and field (b,g), volleyball (g); intramural: lacrosse (g); coed interscholastic: bowling; coed intramural: football. 3 PE instructors, 27 coaches, 1 trainer.

Computers Computers are regularly used in English, foreign language, mathematics, science, yearbook classes. Computer network features include campus e-mail, on-campus library services, CD-ROMs, online commercial services, Internet access.

Contact Ms. Emily Dapper, Admissions Associate. 612-798-2613. Fax: 612-798-2610. E-mail: edapper@ahastars.org.

ACADEMY OF MOUNT SAINT URSULA

330 Bedford Park Boulevard
Bronx, New York 10458-2493
Head of School: Sr. Mary Beth Read, OSU

General Information Girls' day college-preparatory, arts, business, religious studies, and technology school, affiliated with Roman Catholic Church. Grades 9–12. Founded: 1855. Setting: urban. Nearest major city is New York. 12-acre campus. 1 building on campus. Approved or accredited by Middle States Association of Colleges and Schools and New York Department of Education. Total enrollment: 433. Upper school average class size: 25. Upper school faculty-student ratio: 1:15.

Upper School Student Profile Grade 9: 121 students (121 girls); Grade 10: 117 students (117 girls); Grade 11: 84 students (84 girls); Grade 12: 111 students (111 girls). 57% of students are Roman Catholic.

Faculty School total: 36. In upper school: 8 men, 28 women; 26 have advanced degrees.

Subjects Offered Accounting, algebra, American history, American literature, anatomy, anthropology, art, Bible studies, biology, biology-AP, business law, calculus-AP, chemistry, community service, composition, computer math, computer programming, computer science, creative writing, driver education, earth science, economics, English, English literature, English-AP, European history, fine arts, French, general science, geometry, government/civics, health, history, history-AP, honors world history, Italian, Latin, mathematics, music, physical education, physics, pre-calculus, religion, science, Shakespeare, social studies, sociology, Spanish, Spanish language-AP, Spanish literature-AP, speech, trigonometry, women's literature, word processing, world history, world literature, writing.

Graduation Requirements Arts and fine arts (art, music, dance, drama), business skills (includes word processing), computer science, English, foreign language, mathematics, physical education (includes health), religion (includes Bible studies and theology), science, social studies (includes history). Community service is required.

Special Academic Programs Advanced Placement exam preparation in 5 subject areas; honors section; study at local college for college credit; academic accommodation for the musically talented and the artistically talented; remedial reading and/or remedial writing; remedial math.

College Placement 117 students graduated in 2005; 115 went to college, including Fordham University; New York University; St. John's University; State University of New York at Binghamton; Villanova University. Other: 2 entered a postgraduate year.

Student Life Upper grades have uniform requirement, student council. Discipline rests primarily with faculty. Attendance at religious services is required.

Summer Programs Remediation programs offered; session focuses on high school prep in math and language arts for new 9th graders; held on campus; not open to students from other schools. 20 students usually enrolled.

Tuition and Aid Day student tuition: $5335. Tuition installment plan (monthly payment plans, semester payment plan, discount for advanced payment for year). Merit scholarship grants, need-based scholarship grants, paying campus jobs, archdiocese program available. In 2005–06, 38% of upper-school students received aid; total upper-school merit-scholarship money awarded: $262,238. Total amount of financial aid awarded in 2005–06: $373,573.

Admissions Traditional secondary-level entrance grade is 9. For fall 2005, 600 students applied for upper-level admission, 385 were accepted, 121 enrolled. New York Archdiocesan Cooperative Entrance Examination required. Deadline for receipt of application materials: September 30. Application fee required: $75. Interview recommended.

Athletics Interscholastic: basketball, cheering, soccer, softball, track and field, volleyball; intramural: basketball, dance, swimming and diving, tennis, track and field, volleyball. 2 PE instructors, 2 coaches.

Computers Computers are regularly used in accounting, English, foreign language, mathematics, science, social studies classes. Computer network features include campus e-mail, on-campus library services, CD-ROMs, Internet access, science labs.

Contact Sr. Barbara Calamari, OSU, Admissions Coordinator. 718-364-5353 Ext. 30. Fax: 718-364-2354. E-mail: bcalamari@amsu.org. Web site: www.amsu.org.

ACADEMY OF NOTRE DAME DE NAMUR

560 Sproul Road
Villanova, Pennsylvania 19085-1220
Head of School: Sr. Mary Anne Broughton, SND

General Information Girls' day college-preparatory school, affiliated with Roman Catholic Church. Grades 6–12. Founded: 1856. Setting: suburban. Nearest major city

is Philadelphia. 38-acre campus. 8 buildings on campus. Approved or accredited by Middle States Association of Colleges and Schools and Pennsylvania Department of Education. Member of National Association of Independent Schools. Endowment: $2 million. Total enrollment: 495. Upper school average class size: 18. Upper school faculty-student ratio: 1:8.

Upper School Student Profile Grade 9: 92 students (92 girls); Grade 10: 89 students (89 girls); Grade 11: 92 students (92 girls); Grade 12: 89 students (89 girls). 90% of students are Roman Catholic.

Faculty School total: 65. In upper school: 6 men, 59 women; 52 have advanced degrees.

Subjects Offered Bible, calculus, calculus-AP, Central and Eastern European history, ceramics, chemistry, chemistry-AP, choral music, Christian and Hebrew scripture, Christian ethics, comparative government and politics-AP, contemporary history, dance, economics, English, English literature, English literature and composition-AP, environmental science, European history, French, French language-AP, geometry, government and politics-AP, health, health education, Hebrew scripture, instrumental music, journalism, Latin, Latin-AP, literature, mathematics, multimedia design, music, music composition, music theory, music theory-AP, physics-AP, pre-algebra, pre-calculus, SAT/ACT preparation, Spanish, Spanish language-AP, U.S. government and politics-AP.

Graduation Requirements 40 hours of social service.

Special Academic Programs Honors section; independent study; study at local college for college credit.

College Placement 87 students graduated in 2005; all went to college, including Saint Joseph's University; The Catholic University of America; The Pennsylvania State University University Park Campus; University of Delaware; University of Notre Dame; University of Pittsburgh.

Student Life Upper grades have uniform requirement, student council, honor system. Discipline rests primarily with faculty. Attendance at religious services is required.

Summer Programs Enrichment, advancement, sports, art/fine arts programs offered; session focuses on academic enrichment; held on campus; accepts boys and girls; open to students from other schools. 100 students usually enrolled.

Tuition and Aid Day student tuition: $12,800–$14,400. Tuition installment plan (Insured Tuition Payment Plan, monthly payment plans). Merit scholarship grants, need-based scholarship grants available. In 2005–06, 11% of upper-school students received aid.

Admissions Traditional secondary-level entrance grade is 9. Admissions testing required. Deadline for receipt of application materials: December 14. Application fee required: $25. Interview recommended.

Athletics Interscholastic: basketball, crew, cross-country running, dance, diving, field hockey, golf, lacrosse, soccer, softball, swimming and diving, tennis, track and field, volleyball. 4 PE instructors, 36 coaches.

Computers Computers are regularly used in all classes. Computer network features include campus e-mail, on-campus library services, CD-ROMs, online commercial services, Internet access, office computer access, DVD.

Contact Mrs. Diane Sander, Director of Admissions. 610-971-0498. Fax: 610-687-1912. E-mail: admissions@ndapa.org. Web site: www.ndapa.org.

ACADEMY OF OUR LADY OF MERCY

200 High Street
Milford, Connecticut 06460
Head of School: Mrs. Barbara C. Griffin

General Information Girls' day college-preparatory school, affiliated with Roman Catholic Church. Grades 9–12. Founded: 1905. Setting: suburban. Nearest major city is New Haven. 30-acre campus. 5 buildings on campus. Approved or accredited by New England Association of Schools and Colleges and Connecticut Department of Education. Total enrollment: 453. Upper school average class size: 18. Upper school faculty-student ratio: 1:12.

Upper School Student Profile Grade 9: 124 students (124 girls); Grade 10: 109 students (109 girls); Grade 11: 97 students (97 girls); Grade 12: 123 students (123 girls). 87% of students are Roman Catholic.

Faculty School total: 48. In upper school: 3 men, 45 women; 39 have advanced degrees.

Subjects Offered Algebra, American history, American literature, anatomy, art, biology, business, calculus, chemistry, computer math, computer programming, English, English literature, environmental science, European history, fine arts, French, geometry, government/civics, health, history, journalism, Latin, mathematics, music, physical education, physics, physiology, religion, science, social studies, Spanish, trigonometry, world history, writing.

Graduation Requirements Arts and fine arts (art, music, dance, drama), English, foreign language, mathematics, physical education (includes health), religion (includes Bible studies and theology), science, social studies (includes history). Community service is required.

Special Academic Programs Honors section.

College Placement 115 students graduated in 2005; all went to college, including Boston College; College of the Holy Cross; Fairfield University; Loyola College in Maryland; Quinnipiac University; University of Connecticut.

Student Life Upper grades have uniform requirement, student council, honor system. Discipline rests primarily with faculty. Attendance at religious services is required.

Tuition and Aid Day student tuition: $10,600. Tuition installment plan (FACTS Tuition Payment Plan, 1- and 2-payment plans). Tuition reduction for siblings, merit scholarship grants, need-based scholarship grants available. In 2005–06, 20% of upper-school students received aid; total upper-school merit-scholarship money awarded: $24,000. Total amount of financial aid awarded in 2005–06: $285,000.

Admissions Traditional secondary-level entrance grade is 9. For fall 2005, 345 students applied for upper-level admission, 212 were accepted, 124 enrolled. High School Placement Test required. Deadline for receipt of application materials: November 15. Application fee required: $50.

Athletics Interscholastic: basketball, cheering, cross-country running, diving, golf, skiing (downhill), soccer, softball, swimming and diving, tennis, track and field, volleyball; intramural: basketball. 1 PE instructor, 27 coaches, 1 trainer.

Computers Computers are regularly used in mathematics classes. Computer network features include campus e-mail, on-campus library services, CD-ROMs, online commercial services, Internet access, wireless campus network.

Contact Mrs. Kathleen O. Shine, Director of Admissions. 203-877-2786 Ext. 125. Fax: 203-876-9760. E-mail: kshine@lauraltonhall.org. Web site: www.lauraltonhall.org.

ACADEMY OF OUR LADY OF PEACE

4860 Oregon Street
San Diego, California 92116-1393
Head of School: Sr. Dolores Anchondo

General Information Girls' day college-preparatory, arts, and religious studies school, affiliated with Roman Catholic Church. Grades 9–12. Founded: 1882. Setting: urban. 20-acre campus. 7 buildings on campus. Approved or accredited by Western Association of Schools and Colleges and California Department of Education. Endowment: $250,000. Total enrollment: 746. Upper school average class size: 28. Upper school faculty-student ratio: 1:15.

Upper School Student Profile Grade 9: 202 students (202 girls); Grade 10: 202 students (202 girls); Grade 11: 163 students (163 girls); Grade 12: 179 students (179 girls). 93% of students are Roman Catholic.

Faculty School total: 52. In upper school: 11 men, 40 women; 36 have advanced degrees.

Subjects Offered Algebra, American literature, art, astronomy, Bible studies, biology, biology-AP, British literature, calculus, ceramics, chemistry, chemistry-AP, creative writing, dance, drama, economics, English, English-AP, ethics, fitness, French, genetics, geometry, government, graphic arts, health, integrated science, marine biology, music appreciation, music theory-AP, oceanography, painting, physical education, physics, pre-calculus, psychology, Spanish, Spanish-AP, speech, statistics-AP, studio art-AP, study skills, trigonometry, U.S. government-AP, U.S. history, U.S. history-AP, Western civilization, yearbook, yoga.

Graduation Requirements Arts and fine arts (art, music, dance, drama), English, foreign language, mathematics, physical education (includes health), religion (includes Bible studies and theology), science, social science, social studies (includes history), speech, 100 hours of community service.

Special Academic Programs Advanced Placement exam preparation in 10 subject areas; honors section.

College Placement 184 students graduated in 2005; 183 went to college, including Loyola Marymount University; San Diego State University; University of Notre Dame; University of San Diego; University of Southern California; Villanova University. Other: 1 went to work. Median SAT verbal: 550, median SAT math: 525. 32% scored over 600 on SAT verbal, 24% scored over 600 on SAT math.

Student Life Upper grades have uniform requirement, student council, honor system. Discipline rests equally with students and faculty. Attendance at religious services is required.

Summer Programs Remediation, advancement, sports, art/fine arts, computer instruction programs offered; session focuses on remedial work and increased course selection coverage during regular school session; held on campus; accepts boys and girls; open to students from other schools. 250 students usually enrolled. 2006 schedule: June 19 to July 28. Application deadline: June 15.

Tuition and Aid Day student tuition: $8500. Tuition installment plan (FACTS Tuition Payment Plan). Need-based scholarship grants available. In 2005–06, 21% of upper-school students received aid. Total amount of financial aid awarded in 2005–06: $566,000.

Admissions For fall 2005, 341 students applied for upper-level admission, 220 were accepted, 212 enrolled. High School Placement Test required. Deadline for receipt of application materials: none. Application fee required: $50. On-campus interview required.

Athletics Interscholastic: basketball, cheering, cross-country running, golf, soccer, softball, swimming and diving, tennis, track and field, volleyball. 6 PE instructors, 30 coaches.

Computers Computer network features include campus e-mail, on-campus library services, CD-ROMs, online commercial services, Internet access, office computer access, DVD.

Contact Mrs. Sue De Winter, Administrative Assistant/Registrar. 619-725-9118. Fax: 619-297-2473. E-mail: sydewinter@yahoo.com. Web site: www.aolp.org.

ACADEMY OF SAINT ALOYSIUS

2495 John F. Kennedy Boulevard
Jersey City, New Jersey 07304-2007
Head of School: Mrs. Tara Brunt

General Information Girls' day college-preparatory and arts school, affiliated with Roman Catholic Church. Grades 9–12. Founded: 1865. Setting: urban. Nearest major city is New York, NY. 1 building on campus. Approved or accredited by Middle States Association of Colleges and Schools, New Jersey Association of Independent Schools, and New Jersey Department of Education. Total enrollment: 170. Upper school average class size: 9. Upper school faculty-student ratio: 1:9.

Upper School Student Profile Grade 9: 55 students (55 girls); Grade 10: 33 students (33 girls); Grade 11: 44 students (44 girls); Grade 12: 35 students (35 girls). 5% of students are Roman Catholic.

Faculty School total: 20. In upper school: 8 men, 12 women; 15 have advanced degrees.

Subjects Offered 20th century American writers, 20th century history, 20th century world history, 3-dimensional art, acting, advanced chemistry, advanced math, algebra, American history, American literature, anatomy and physiology, ancient world history, ancient/medieval philosophy, applied arts, art, art appreciation, art history, basic language skills, Bible as literature, British literature, calculus, campus ministry, career and personal planning, career education, cartooning/animation, Catholic belief and practice, cheerleading, chemistry, choir, Christian and Hebrew scripture, Christian ethics, church history, civil rights, Civil War, civil war history, classical civilization, classical Greek literature, classical language, college admission preparation, college awareness, college counseling, college placement, college planning, college writing, composition, computer education, computer math, constitutional history of U.S., contemporary history, CPR, creative thinking, creative writing, critical writing, drama, dramatic arts, electives, English, English literature, ethics, European civilization, family life, family studies, first aid, fitness, food and nutrition, foreign language, French, gender issues, general science, geometry, great books, health, health and safety, health and wellness, health education, health enhancement, healthful living, Hispanic literature, history, honors algebra, honors English, human anatomy, human biology, human sexuality, independent study, interdisciplinary studies, Internet, Internet research, interpersonal skills, intro to computers, Islamic history, Jewish history, language and composition, language arts, language development, language enhancement and development, Latin American literature, leadership, leadership and service, leadership skills, leadership training, library, library assistant, library research, literary magazine, literature, medieval literature, modern history, modern languages, newspaper, novels, oral communications, oral expression, outdoor education, peace and justice, peer counseling, peer ministry, performing arts, personal and social education, personal development, personal fitness, personal growth, physical education, physical fitness, physics, play production, prayer/spirituality, pre-calculus, pre-college orientation, printmaking, psychology, reading/study skills, research, research skills, research techniques, scripture, senior career experience, Shakespeare, social justice, social skills, society, politics and law, softball, Spanish, Spanish literature, speech, speech and debate, speech and oral interpretations, speech communications, sports, student government, student publications, study skills, tennis, the Web, track and field, trigonometry, U.S. government, U.S. history, United Nations and international issues, values and decisions, visual and performing arts, voice, wellness, Western civilization, Western literature, women in literature, women in society, women in world history, women spirituality and faith, women's health, women's literature, women's studies, work-study, world history, World War I, World War II, writing, writing skills, yearbook.

Special Academic Programs Honors section; independent study; study at local college for college credit; academic accommodation for the musically talented and the artistically talented.

College Placement 55 students graduated in 2005; all went to college.

Student Life Upper grades have uniform requirement, student council, honor system. Discipline rests primarily with faculty. Attendance at religious services is required.

Tuition and Aid Day student tuition: $5200. Tuition installment plan (monthly payment plans). Tuition reduction for siblings, merit scholarship grants, need-based scholarship grants, paying campus jobs available.

Admissions CTB/McGraw-Hill/Macmillan Co-op Test required. Deadline for receipt of application materials: December 2. No application fee required. On-campus interview recommended.

Athletics Interscholastic: basketball, cheering, cross-country running, indoor track & field, soccer, softball, tennis, track and field, volleyball, winter (indoor) track; intramural: aerobics/dance, dance, modern dance. 1 PE instructor.

Computers Computers are regularly used in all academic classes. Computer network features include on-campus library services, CD-ROMs, Internet access, DVD, wireless campus network.

Contact Ms. Prin Dumas, Director of Admissions and Public Relations. 201-433-8877. Fax: 201-433-8839. E-mail: pdumas@academyofstaloysius.org. Web site: www.academyofstaloysius.org.

ACADEMY OF SAINT ELIZABETH

Box 297
Convent Station, New Jersey 07961-0297
Head of School: Sr. Patricia Costello, OP

General Information Girls' day college-preparatory, arts, religious studies, and technology school, affiliated with Roman Catholic Church. Grades 9–12. Founded: 1860. Setting: suburban. Nearest major city is Morristown. 200-acre campus. 2 buildings on campus. Approved or accredited by Middle States Association of Colleges and Schools, National Catholic Education Association, and New Jersey Association of Independent Schools. Total enrollment: 245. Upper school average class size: 15. Upper school faculty-student ratio: 1:9.

Upper School Student Profile Grade 9: 75 students (75 girls); Grade 10: 67 students (67 girls); Grade 11: 49 students (49 girls); Grade 12: 54 students (54 girls). 90% of students are Roman Catholic.

Faculty School total: 30. In upper school: 6 men, 22 women; 12 have advanced degrees.

Subjects Offered 20th century American writers, algebra, American history, American literature, art, Bible studies, biology, calculus, ceramics, chemistry, dance, drama, driver education, ecology, English, English literature, environmental science, European history, expository writing, fine arts, French, geometry, grammar, health, history, journalism, Latin, mathematics, music, photography, physical education, physics, psychology, religion, science, social science, social studies, sociology, Spanish, theater, theology, trigonometry, word processing, world history, world literature.

Graduation Requirements Arts and fine arts (art, music, dance, drama), computer education, English, foreign language, mathematics, physical education (includes health), religion (includes Bible studies and theology), science, social science, social studies (includes history), senior independent study.

Special Academic Programs Advanced Placement exam preparation in 8 subject areas; honors section; independent study; study at local college for college credit.

College Placement 57 students graduated in 2005; all went to college, including American University; Boston College; College of the Holy Cross; Seton Hall University; University of Notre Dame; Villanova University. Mean SAT verbal: 560, mean SAT math: 540.

Student Life Upper grades have uniform requirement, student council, honor system. Discipline rests primarily with faculty. Attendance at religious services is required.

Tuition and Aid Day student tuition: $11,000. Tuition installment plan (monthly payment plans, individually arranged payment plans). Merit scholarship grants, need-based scholarship grants available. In 2005–06, 35% of upper-school students received aid.

Admissions Traditional secondary-level entrance grade is 9. For fall 2005, 150 students applied for upper-level admission, 115 were accepted, 75 enrolled. School's own exam required. Deadline for receipt of application materials: January 15. Application fee required: $100. On-campus interview recommended.

Athletics Interscholastic: aquatics, basketball, cross-country running, field hockey, lacrosse, soccer, softball, swimming and diving, tennis; intramural: aerobics, aerobics/dance, alpine skiing, dance, equestrian sports, horseback riding, independent competitive sports, skiing (downhill). 1 PE instructor, 9 coaches.

Computers Computers are regularly used in English, foreign language, history, mathematics, science, study skills classes. Computer network features include campus e-mail, on-campus library services, CD-ROMs, online commercial services, Internet access.

Contact Sr. Patricia Costello, OP, Principal. 973-290-5200. Fax: 973-290-5232. Web site: academyofsaintelizabeth.org.

THE ACADEMY OF ST. JOSEPH

1725 Brentwood Road
Brentwood, New York 11717-5598
Head of School: Sr. Eileen Kelly, CSJ

General Information Coeducational day college-preparatory school, affiliated with Roman Catholic Church. Boys grades K–8, girls grades K–12. Founded: 1856. Setting: suburban. Nearest major city is New York. 200-acre campus. 2 buildings on campus. Approved or accredited by Commission on Secondary Schools, Middle States Association of Colleges and Schools, and New York Department of Education. Total enrollment: 427. Upper school average class size: 20. Upper school faculty-student ratio: 1:9.

Upper School Student Profile Grade 9: 72 students (72 girls); Grade 10: 69 students (69 girls); Grade 11: 56 students (56 girls); Grade 12: 39 students (39 girls). 71% of students are Roman Catholic.

Faculty School total: 42. In upper school: 3 men, 23 women; 26 have advanced degrees.

Subjects Offered Algebra, American history, American literature, anatomy, art, art history, astronomy, Bible studies, biology, business, calculus, chemistry, computer math, computer programming, computer science, creative writing, culinary arts, drama, earth science, ecology, economics, English, English literature, environmental science, ethics, European history, fine arts, French, geography, geometry, government/civics, grammar, health, history, history of mathematics, humanities, journalism, Latin, mathematics, mechanical drawing, music, oceanography, philosophy, photog-

raphy, physical education, physics, psychology, religion, science, social studies, Spanish, speech, statistics, theology, trigonometry, typing, world history, world literature, writing.

Graduation Requirements Arts and fine arts (art, music, dance, drama), computer science, English, foreign language, humanities, mathematics, physical education (includes health), religion (includes Bible studies and theology), science, social studies (includes history).

Special Academic Programs Advanced Placement exam preparation in 5 subject areas; honors section; study at local college for college credit; study abroad; remedial reading and/or remedial writing; remedial math.

College Placement 51 went to college, including Fordham University; Hofstra University; Saint John's University; Saint Joseph College; Stony Brook University, State University of New York. Other: 1 had other specific plans. 20% scored over 600 on SAT verbal, 8% scored over 600 on SAT math.

Student Life Upper grades have uniform requirement, student council, honor system. Discipline rests equally with students and faculty.

Tuition and Aid Day student tuition: $6200. Tuition installment plan (monthly payment plans, prepayment discount plan, trimester payment plan). Tuition reduction for siblings, merit scholarship grants, need-based scholarship grants available. In 2005–06, 0% of upper-school students received aid; total upper-school merit-scholarship money awarded: $40,000. Total amount of financial aid awarded in 2005–06: $66,530.

Admissions For fall 2005, 225 students applied for upper-level admission, 139 were accepted, 132 enrolled. Admissions testing and Catholic High School Entrance Examination required. Deadline for receipt of application materials: none. Application fee required: $200. On-campus interview required.

Athletics Interscholastic: badminton, basketball, dance, equestrian sports (b), horseback riding (b), modern dance, physical fitness (b), running (b), soccer, softball, swimming and diving, tennis, track and field, volleyball; intramural: track and field. 2 PE instructors, 6 coaches.

Computers Computers are regularly used in foreign language, mathematics, science classes. Computer resources include campus e-mail, on-campus library services, CD-ROMs, online commercial services, Internet access.

Contact Mrs. Kathleen Ventura, Principal. 631-273-2406 Ext. 256. Fax: 631-231-4155 Ext. fax. E-mail: kventura@asjli.org.

ACADEMY OF THE HOLY ANGELS

315 Hillside Avenue
Demarest, New Jersey 07627-2799
Head of School: Sister Virginia Bobrowski

General Information Girls' day college-preparatory, arts, religious studies, bilingual studies, and technology school, affiliated with Roman Catholic Church (Jesuit order). Grades 9–12. Founded: 1879. Setting: suburban. Nearest major city is New York, NY. 25-acre campus. 1 building on campus. Approved or accredited by Middle States Association of Colleges and Schools and National Catholic Education Association. Total enrollment: 577. Upper school average class size: 19. Upper school faculty-student ratio: 1:11.

Upper School Student Profile Grade 9: 168 students (168 girls); Grade 10: 161 students (161 girls); Grade 11: 139 students (139 girls); Grade 12: 109 students (109 girls). 80% of students are Roman Catholic Church (Jesuit order).

Faculty School total: 80. In upper school: 9 men, 47 women; 37 have advanced degrees.

Subjects Offered Accounting, algebra, American history, American literature, anatomy, art, art history, biology, business law, business skills, calculus, ceramics, chemistry, chorus, communications, community service, computer science, creative writing, design, drama, economics, English, English literature, European history, expository writing, film, fine arts, French, geometry, German, government/civics, grammar, graphic arts, health, history, humanities, instrumental music, Italian, journalism, Latin, mathematics, music, musical productions, photography, physical education, physics, physiology, psychology, religion, science, social studies, sociology, Spanish, theater, trigonometry, world history, world literature, writing.

Graduation Requirements Arts and fine arts (art, music, dance, drama), business skills (includes word processing), computer science, English, foreign language, mathematics, physical education (includes health), religion (includes Bible studies and theology), science, social studies (includes history), 20 hours of community service.

Special Academic Programs Advanced Placement exam preparation in 9 subject areas; honors section; independent study; study at local college for college credit; academic accommodation for the gifted, the musically talented, and the artistically talented.

College Placement 126 students graduated in 2005; all went to college, including Boston College; Columbia College; Cornell University; New York University; University of Pennsylvania; University of Southern California. Median SAT verbal: 584, median SAT math: 567.

Student Life Upper grades have uniform requirement, student council, honor system. Discipline rests primarily with faculty. Attendance at religious services is required.

Tuition and Aid Day student tuition: $9100. Tuition installment plan (FACTS Tuition Payment Plan, individually arranged payment plans, single payment plan (with $150 discount)). Merit scholarship grants, need-based scholarship grants, Parents' Scholarship Fund Program (insures continuance of education in event of parental death)

available. In 2005–06, 17% of upper-school students received aid; total upper-school merit-scholarship money awarded: $125,650. Total amount of financial aid awarded in 2005–06: $152,140.

Admissions Traditional secondary-level entrance grade is 9. For fall 2005, 500 students applied for upper-level admission, 200 were accepted, 169 enrolled. CTB/McGraw-Hill/Macmillan Co-op Test required. Deadline for receipt of application materials: none. No application fee required. Interview recommended.

Athletics Interscholastic: basketball, bowling, cross-country running, dance team, fencing, indoor track & field, lacrosse, pom squad, soccer, softball, tennis, track and field, volleyball, winter (indoor) track; intramural: equestrian sports, fencing, martial arts. 3 PE instructors, 15 coaches, 1 trainer.

Computers Computers are regularly used in all classes. Computer network features include on-campus library services, CD-ROMs, online commercial services, Internet access, wireless campus network.

Contact Jennifer Moran, Principal. 201-768-7822 Ext. 202. Fax: 201-768-6933. E-mail: info@holyangels.org. Web site: www.holyangels.org.

ANNOUNCEMENT FROM THE SCHOOL The Academy of the Holy Angels (AHA), founded in 1879 by Sister Mary Nonna Dunphy of the School Sisters of Notre Dame is a private, Catholic, college-preparatory school dedicated to the education of young women. The Academy welcomes students from many different communities, ethnic backgrounds, and religious affiliations. The vision permeating life at the Academy is one of a new global community based on Christian values, especially those of interdependence and a recognition of the role of women in society. The beauty and serenity of the Academy's 25-acre campus in Demarest, New Jersey, is only 15 miles from NYC and Rockland County, offering access to many cultural and educational resources in the area. A National Blue Ribbon School of Excellence and National Service Learning Leader School, AHA features 2 chapels, a Campus Ministry Retreat Center, a Library/Media Center, art studios and dark room, a Business/Computer Lab, the Joseph and Carmen Unanue World Language Lab, a Communications/ Publishing Center, the Spola Science Center, the Luckow Technology Center, a computerized fitness center, 3 fully equipped science labs, a gym, an auditorium, and 19 classrooms. All incoming students are required to purchase a Windows XP Tablet PC to be used in AHA's wireless classrooms. AHA students can choose from 60 diverse clubs and activities as well as participate in a variety of athletics, with 20 teams competing in 12 sports. Summer programs include Humanities Abroad in Austria and Summerfare for girls in grades 5–8. A rotational 8-day schedule allows students to choose classes from a wide variety of academic areas. Students are placed in one of 4 levels: College Preparatory, Honors, High Honors, or Advanced Placement. In 2005, 126 seniors graduated and 99% are enrolled in a 4-year college or university, including Columbia, Cornell, NYU, UCLA, and the University of Pennsylvania. "When you educate a girl to a woman, you transform the world."

ACADEMY OF THE HOLY CROSS

4920 Strathmore Avenue
Kensington, Maryland 20895-1299
Head of School: Sr. Katherine Kase, CSC

General Information Girls' day college-preparatory, arts, and religious studies school, affiliated with Roman Catholic Church. Grades 9–12. Founded: 1868. Setting: suburban. Nearest major city is Rockville. 28-acre campus. 1 building on campus. Approved or accredited by Association of Independent Schools of Greater Washington, Middle States Association of Colleges and Schools, National Catholic Education Association, and Maryland Department of Education. Total enrollment: 600. Upper school average class size: 20. Upper school faculty-student ratio: 1:14.

Upper School Student Profile Grade 9: 157 students (157 girls); Grade 10: 183 students (183 girls); Grade 11: 140 students (140 girls); Grade 12: 120 students (120 girls). 89% of students are Roman Catholic.

Faculty School total: 57. In upper school: 11 men, 46 women; 44 have advanced degrees.

Subjects Offered Acting, algebra, American history, American literature, art, Asian studies, biology, biology-AP, calculus, calculus-AP, ceramics, chemistry, chemistry-AP, Christian scripture, computer programming, computer science, concert choir, creative writing, design, drama, drawing, earth science, economics, English, English language and composition-AP, English literature, English literature and composition-AP, environmental science, ethnic studies, expository writing, fine arts, forensic science, French, geography, geometry, government/civics, grammar, health, Hebrew scripture, history, history of the Catholic Church, honors English, honors geometry, humanities, instrumental music, jazz dance, Latin, Latin American studies, madrigals, mathematics, moral theology, music, music appreciation, musical theater, musical theater dance, painting, peace studies, personal finance, photography, physical education, physical science, physics, physiology, pre-calculus, psychology, public speaking, religion, religious studies, science, Shakespeare, social science, social studies, Spanish, sports medicine, statistics, studio art-AP, tap dance, technology,

television, theater, theater design and production, theology, trigonometry, U.S. government, U.S. government-AP, U.S. history, U.S. history-AP, world history, world studies.

Graduation Requirements Art, electives, English, foreign language, mathematics, performing arts, physical education (includes health), science, senior project, social science, social studies (includes history), theology, Christian service commitment.

Special Academic Programs Advanced Placement exam preparation in 12 subject areas; honors section; independent study; academic accommodation for the gifted and the artistically talented.

College Placement 159 students graduated in 2005; all went to college, including Fordham University; James Madison University; Mount St. Mary's University; The Catholic University of America; University of Maryland, College Park; West Virginia University. Mean SAT verbal: 573, mean SAT math: 550, mean composite ACT: 23.

Student Life Upper grades have uniform requirement, student council, honor system. Discipline rests equally with students and faculty. Attendance at religious services is required.

Summer Programs Enrichment, advancement, sports, art/fine arts, computer instruction programs offered; session focuses on enrichment and athletic skill building; held on campus; accepts girls; open to students from other schools. 200 students usually enrolled. 2006 schedule: June 19 to July 14. Application deadline: May 31.

Tuition and Aid Day student tuition: $12,400. Tuition installment plan (individually arranged payment plans). Tuition reduction for siblings, merit scholarship grants, need-based scholarship grants, alumnae stipends available. In 2005–06, 38% of upper-school students received aid.

Admissions Traditional secondary-level entrance grade is 9. TerraNova required. Deadline for receipt of application materials: December 15. Application fee required: $50. On-campus interview required.

Athletics Interscholastic: archery, basketball, crew, cross-country running, diving, equestrian sports, field hockey, lacrosse, soccer, softball, swimming and diving, tennis, track and field, volleyball; intramural: basketball, cheering, dance, dance team, drill team, golf, lacrosse, soccer. 3 PE instructors, 35 coaches, 1 trainer.

Computers Computers are regularly used in art, foreign language, mathematics, science, social science classes. Computer resources include on-campus library services, CD-ROMs, online commercial services, Internet access, office computer access, DVD.

Contact Mrs. Louise Hendon, Director of Recruitment. 301-929-6442. Fax: 301-929-6440. E-mail: admissions@academyoftheholycross.org. Web site: academyoftheholycross.org.

ANNOUNCEMENT FROM THE SCHOOL The Academy of the Holy Cross, a Catholic college-preparatory school, is dedicated to educating young women in a Christ-centered community that values diversity. The Academy is committed to developing women of courage, compassion, and scholarship who responsibly embrace the social, spiritual, and intellectual challenges of the world.

ACADEMY OF THE HOLY NAMES

3319 Bayshore Boulevard
Tampa, Florida 33629-8899
Head of School: Jacqueline L. Landry

General Information Coeducational day college-preparatory, arts, and religious studies school, affiliated with Roman Catholic Church. Boys grades PK–8, girls grades PK–12. Founded: 1881. Setting: urban. 16-acre campus. 6 buildings on campus. Approved or accredited by National Catholic Education Association, Southern Association of Colleges and Schools, and Florida Department of Education. Languages of instruction: Spanish and French. Endowment: $2.4 million. Total enrollment: 853. Upper school average class size: 20. Upper school faculty-student ratio: 1:15.

Upper School Student Profile 70% of students are Roman Catholic.

Faculty School total: 67. In upper school: 4 men, 29 women; 20 have advanced degrees.

Subjects Offered Advanced Placement courses, algebra, art, communications, computer science, English, French, Latin, mathematics, music, physical education, reading, religion, science, social studies, Spanish, swimming, writing.

Graduation Requirements 75 service hours.

Special Academic Programs Advanced Placement exam preparation in 12 subject areas; honors section.

College Placement 73 students graduated in 2005; all went to college.

Student Life Upper grades have uniform requirement, student council, honor system. Discipline rests primarily with faculty. Attendance at religious services is required.

Tuition and Aid Day student tuition: $11,530. Tuition installment plan (The Tuition Plan, monthly payment plans). Merit scholarship grants, need-based scholarship grants, paying campus jobs available. In 2005–06, 30% of upper-school students received aid; total upper-school merit-scholarship money awarded: $46,560. Total amount of financial aid awarded in 2005–06: $400,000.

Admissions Traditional secondary-level entrance grade is 9. Deadline for receipt of application materials: November 30. Application fee required: $30. On-campus interview required.

Athletics Interscholastic: aerobics/dance (girls), aquatics (g), baseball (b), basketball (b,g), cheering (g), cross-country running (b,g), dance (g), dance squad (g), dance team (g), diving (g), golf (g), lacrosse (b), physical fitness (g), softball (g), swimming and diving (g), tennis (g), track and field (b,g), volleyball (b,g), winter soccer (g); coed interscholastic: aerobics/nautilus. 4 PE instructors.

Computers Computer resources include campus e-mail, on-campus library services, CD-ROMs, Internet access.

Contact Kelly Suske, Admission Assistant. 813-839-5371 Ext. 307. Fax: 813-839-1486. E-mail: ksuske@holynamestpa.org. Web site: www.holynamestpa.org.

ACADEMY OF THE PACIFIC

913 Alewa Drive
Honolulu, Hawaii 96817
Head of School: Mollie Sperry

General Information Coeducational day college-preparatory and arts school. Grades 6–12. Founded: 1961. Setting: suburban. 4-acre campus. 13 buildings on campus. Approved or accredited by Western Association of Schools and Colleges. Member of National Association of Independent Schools. Endowment: $739,807. Total enrollment: 133. Upper school average class size: 10. Upper school faculty-student ratio: 1:10.

Upper School Student Profile Grade 9: 27 students (18 boys, 9 girls); Grade 10: 23 students (17 boys, 6 girls); Grade 11: 34 students (21 boys, 13 girls); Grade 12: 24 students (16 boys, 8 girls).

Faculty School total: 18. In upper school: 8 men, 8 women; 6 have advanced degrees.

Subjects Offered Algebra, American history, American literature, art, biology, ceramics, chemistry, computer math, computer science, creative writing, drama, earth science, economics, English, English literature, environmental science, expository writing, geography, geometry, government/civics, grammar, history, Japanese, journalism, mathematics, music, peer counseling, physical education, physics, pre-calculus, psychology, science, social studies, sociology, Spanish, theater, trigonometry, world culture, world history, world literature, writing.

Graduation Requirements Arts and fine arts (art, music, dance, drama), English, foreign language, mathematics, physical education (includes health), science, social studies (includes history).

Special Academic Programs Advanced Placement exam preparation in 3 subject areas; independent study; academic accommodation for the artistically talented; remedial reading and/or remedial writing; remedial math.

College Placement 45 students graduated in 2005; they went to Chaminade University of Honolulu; University of Hawaii at Manoa. Median SAT verbal: 475, median SAT math: 455, median composite ACT: 19. 11% scored over 600 on SAT verbal.

Student Life Upper grades have specified standards of dress, student council, honor system. Discipline rests primarily with faculty.

Summer Programs Remediation, enrichment programs offered; held on campus; accepts boys and girls; open to students from other schools. 30 students usually enrolled. 2006 schedule: June 12 to July 31. Application deadline: May 30.

Tuition and Aid Day student tuition: $12,900. Tuition installment plan (FACTS Tuition Payment Plan, individually arranged payment plans). Need-based scholarship grants, tuition remission for children of faculty and staff available.

Admissions School's own exam required. Deadline for receipt of application materials: none. No application fee required. On-campus interview required.

Athletics Interscholastic: baseball (boys), basketball (b,g), bowling (b), cross-country running (b,g), football (b), golf (b,g), paddling (b,g), riflery (b), sailing (b), soccer (b,g), swimming and diving (b,g), tennis (b,g), track and field (b,g), volleyball (b,g), water polo (b), weight lifting (b), weight training (b), winter soccer (b); intramural: baseball (b,g), basketball (b,g), cross-country running (b,g), soccer (b,g), volleyball (b,g), weight lifting (b,g).

Computers Computers are regularly used in keyboarding, mathematics, science classes. Computer network features include campus e-mail, CD-ROMs, Internet access, office applications (spreadsheet, word processing), low bandwidth videoconferencing.

Contact Mollie Sperry, Head of School. 808-595-6359. Fax: 808-595-4235. E-mail: msperry@aop.net. Web site: www.aop.net.

ACADEMY OF THE SACRED HEART

1821 Academy Road
Grand Coteau, Louisiana 70541
Head of School: Ms. Mary Burns

General Information Girls' boarding and day college-preparatory, arts, religious studies, bilingual studies, technology, and liberal arts and sciences school, affiliated with Roman Catholic Church. Boarding grades 7–12, day grades PK–12. Founded: 1821. Setting: rural. Nearest major city is Lafayette. Students are housed in single-sex dormitories. 250-acre campus. 9 buildings on campus. Approved or accredited by Independent Schools Association of the Southwest, Network of Sacred Heart Schools, and Louisiana Department of Education. Endowment: $8 million. Total enrollment: 347. Upper school average class size: 18. Upper school faculty-student ratio: 1:8.

Upper School Student Profile Grade 9: 29 students (29 girls); Grade 10: 31 students (31 girls); Grade 11: 28 students (28 girls); Grade 12: 27 students (27 girls). 8% of students are boarding students. 80% are state residents. 7 states are represented in upper school student body. 5% are international students. International students from Mexico; 2 other countries represented in student body. 77% of students are Roman Catholic.

Faculty School total: 50. In upper school: 2 men, 19 women; 6 have advanced degrees; 7 reside on campus.

Subjects Offered Advanced math, Advanced Placement courses, algebra, American literature, art appreciation, biology, biology-AP, British literature, British literature (honors), calculus, calculus-AP, chemistry, chorus, creative dance, creative writing, dance, drama, English, English literature-AP, environmental science, equestrian sports, equine studies, ESL, ethical decision making, fine arts, French, French language-AP, French-AP, geometry, government-AP, government/civics, health, independent study, mathematics, moral reasoning, music theater, photography, physical education, physics, play production, pottery, pre-algebra, religion and culture, scripture, social justice, social science, Spanish, Spanish language-AP, Spanish-AP, studio art, theater, theology, U.S. government, U.S. government-AP, U.S. history, U.S. history-AP, women's studies, world history, world history-AP, yearbook.

Graduation Requirements Arts and fine arts (art, music, dance, drama), English, foreign language, mathematics, physical education (includes health), religion (includes Bible studies and theology), science, social science, social studies (includes history), May project. Community service is required.

Special Academic Programs Advanced Placement exam preparation in 5 subject areas; honors section; independent study; term-away projects; study at local college for college credit; domestic exchange program; study abroad; academic accommodation for the gifted, the musically talented, and the artistically talented; ESL (13 students enrolled).

College Placement 40 students graduated in 2005; all went to college, including Baylor University; Louisiana State University and Agricultural and Mechanical College; Loyola University New Orleans; Tulane University; University of Louisiana at Lafayette; Vanderbilt University. Mean composite ACT: 25.

Student Life Upper grades have uniform requirement, student council, honor system. Discipline rests equally with students and faculty. Attendance at religious services is required.

Tuition and Aid Day student tuition: $8400; 5-day tuition and room/board: $18,650; 7-day tuition and room/board: $19,650. Tuition installment plan (2-payment plan, 3-payment plan, monthly payment plan for day students). Merit scholarship grants, need-based scholarship grants available. In 2005–06, 16% of upper-school students received aid; total upper-school merit-scholarship money awarded: $7500.

Admissions Traditional secondary-level entrance grade is 9. For fall 2005, 20 students applied for upper-level admission, 18 were accepted, 18 enrolled. Metropolitan Achievement Short Form, Stanford Achievement Test and Stanford Achievement Test, Otis-Lennon required. Deadline for receipt of application materials: none. Application fee required: $100. Interview required.

Athletics Interscholastic: basketball, cheering, cross-country running, dance, dance team, dressage, equestrian sports, horseback riding, soccer, softball, swimming and diving, tennis, track and field, volleyball. 2 PE instructors, 3 coaches.

Computers Computers are regularly used in English, history, mathematics, science classes. Computer network features include campus e-mail, on-campus library services, CD-ROMs, Internet access, file transfer, office computer access.

Contact D'Lane Wimberley, Director of Admission. 337-662-5275 Ext. 3036. Fax: 337-662-3011. E-mail: admission@ashcoteau.org. Web site: www.ashcoteau.org.

ANNOUNCEMENT FROM THE SCHOOL The Academy of the Sacred Heart is a Roman Catholic, college-preparatory school for girls in prekindergarten3 through grade 12. Founded in 1821, the Academy is the oldest continuously operating Sacred Heart School in the world and is part of an international group of academic institutions directed by the Society of the Sacred Heart. The Academy is situated on a 250-acre campus in a rural area with lawns, formal gardens, and a lake and ample space for playing fields, cross-country trails, bicycle paths, and equestrian activities. The main building houses the library, elementary school classrooms, 2 computer labs, the chapel, an art studio, and the Shrine of Saint John Berchmans. The Shrine is the location of the only miracle in the United States recognized by the Vatican. A newer building, adjacent to the first, houses administrative offices, high school classrooms, science laboratories, a computer lab, and a large auditorium. Boarding facilities for students in grades 8–12 are located on the top floor. Other features of the Academy include a gymnasium, cafeteria, swimming pool, tennis courts, workout room, and a barn and stables for the equestrian program. Grand Coteau is a small community located about 12 miles north of Lafayette, home to colleges, museums, and other cultural centers. The New Orleans Airport is located approximately 125 miles to the east. The Schools of the Sacred Heart commit themselves to educating to a personal and active faith in God, a deep respect for intellectual values, a social awareness that impels to action, the building of community as a Christian value, and personal growth in an atmosphere of wise freedom.

ACADEMY OF THE SACRED HEART

1250 Kensington Road
Bloomfield Hills, Michigan 48304-3029
Head of School: Bridget Bearss, RSCJ

General Information Coeducational day college-preparatory, arts, religious studies, technology, experiential learning, and community service school, affiliated with Roman Catholic Church. Boys grades N–8, girls grades N–12. Founded: 1851. Setting: suburban. Nearest major city is Detroit. 45-acre campus. 1 building on campus. Approved or accredited by Independent Schools Association of the Central States, Network of Sacred Heart Schools, and Michigan Department of Education. Endowment: $3.4 million. Total enrollment: 519. Upper school average class size: 12. Upper school faculty-student ratio: 1:14.

Upper School Student Profile Grade 9: 43 students (43 girls); Grade 10: 38 students (38 girls); Grade 11: 37 students (37 girls); Grade 12: 26 students (26 girls). 63% of students are Roman Catholic.

Faculty School total: 69. In upper school: 6 men, 15 women; 10 have advanced degrees.

Subjects Offered Advanced Placement courses, American history, American literature, art, band, biology, calculus, calculus-AP, ceramics, chemistry, chorus, community service, computer applications, computer graphics, computer science, drama, earth science, economics, English, environmental science, film, fine arts, forensics, French, genetics, government/civics, Latin, literature, mathematics, minority studies, music, photography, physical education, physics, poetry, pre-calculus, psychology, science, social studies, Spanish, theater, theology, Web site design, women's studies, world history, world literature.

Graduation Requirements Arts and fine arts (art, music, dance, drama), computer science, English, foreign language, government, mathematics, physical education (includes health), science, social studies (includes history), theology, Project Term, arts lab. Community service is required.

Special Academic Programs Advanced Placement exam preparation in 5 subject areas; honors section; independent study; term-away projects; domestic exchange program (with The Network Program Schools); academic accommodation for the artistically talented.

College Placement 28 students graduated in 2005; all went to college, including Albion College; Brandeis University; DePaul University; Miami University; Saint Mary's College; University of Michigan. Median SAT verbal: 555, median SAT math: 556, median composite ACT: 21. 45% scored over 600 on SAT verbal, 17% scored over 600 on SAT math, 24% scored over 26 on composite ACT.

Student Life Upper grades have uniform requirement, student council. Discipline rests primarily with faculty. Attendance at religious services is required.

Summer Programs Enrichment, sports, art/fine arts, computer instruction programs offered; session focuses on enrichment/day camp; held on campus; accepts boys and girls; open to students from other schools. 425 students usually enrolled. 2006 schedule: June 20 to July 29. Application deadline: none.

Tuition and Aid Day student tuition: $16,600. Tuition installment plan (Academic Management Services Plan). Merit scholarship grants, need-based scholarship grants available. In 2005–06, 33% of upper-school students received aid; total upper-school merit-scholarship money awarded: $3000. Total amount of financial aid awarded in 2005–06: $408,610.

Admissions Traditional secondary-level entrance grade is 9. For fall 2005, 43 students applied for upper-level admission, 33 were accepted, 27 enrolled. Scholastic Testing Service High School Placement Test or Stanford Achievement Test required. Deadline for receipt of application materials: none. Application fee required: $50. On-campus interview required.

Athletics Interscholastic: basketball (girls), equestrian sports (g), field hockey (g), figure skating (g), lacrosse (g), skiing (downhill) (g), softball (g), tennis (g), volleyball (g). 1 PE instructor, 14 coaches.

Computers Computer network features include campus e-mail, on-campus library services, CD-ROMs, online commercial services, Internet access, file transfer, office computer access, laptop program with wireless network and print services, classroom multimedia services, computer in each classroom.

Contact Barbara Lopiccolo, Director of Admissions. 248-646-8900 Ext. 129. Fax: 248-646-4143. E-mail: blopiccolo@ashmi.org. Web site: www.ashmi.org.

ANNOUNCEMENT FROM THE SCHOOL The Academy of the Sacred Heart (www.ashmi.org), a member of the Network of Sacred Heart Schools (www.sofie.org), was founded in 1851 and is Michigan's oldest independent school. Located in Bloomfield Hills, it is a Catholic, college-preparatory school for girls (preschool through grade 12) and boys (preschool through grade 8) of many cultures and faiths.

ACCELERATED SCHOOLS

2160 South Cook Street
Denver, Colorado 80210

See full description on page 638.

Student Life Upper grades have specified standards of dress, student council, honor system. Discipline rests primarily with faculty.

Summer Programs Advancement, ESL programs offered; session focuses on EAL support, IB preparation, advancement, revision; held off campus; held at ACS Cobham campus; accepts boys and girls; open to students from other schools. 20 students usually enrolled. 2006 schedule: July to August. Application deadline: none.

Tuition and Aid Day student tuition: £12,100–£15,000. Tuition installment plan (quarterly installment plan). Bursaries available. In 2005–06, 5% of upper-school students received aid. Total amount of financial aid awarded in 2005–06: £65,000.

Admissions Traditional secondary-level entrance grade is 9. English for Non-native Speakers required. Deadline for receipt of application materials: none. Application fee required: £95. Interview recommended.

Athletics Interscholastic: baseball (boys), basketball (b,g), cross-country running (b,g), rugby (b), soccer (b,g), softball (g), swimming and diving (b,g), tennis (b,g), track and field (b,g), volleyball (b,g). 4 PE instructors, 20 coaches.

Computers Computers are regularly used in economics, English, foreign language, geography, graphic arts, information technology, mathematics, music, science classes. Computer network features include campus e-mail, on-campus library services, CD-ROMs, Internet access, file transfer, office computer access, DVD.

Contact Mrs. Deanna Fontanes-Halliday, Dean of Admissions. 44-1895-818402. Fax: 44-1895-818404. E-mail: dhalliday@acs-england.co.uk. Web site: www.acs-england.co.uk.

ADELPHI ACADEMY

8515 Ridge Boulevard
Brooklyn, New York 11209
Head of School: Mrs. Rosemarie B. Ferrara

General Information Coeducational day college-preparatory, arts, business, bilingual studies, technology, and writing school, affiliated with Jewish faith, Christian faith. Grades PK–12. Founded: 1863. Setting: small town. Nearest major city is New York. 1-acre campus. 3 buildings on campus. Approved or accredited by Association of American Schools in South America, Middle States Association of Colleges and Schools, and New York Department of Education. Languages of instruction: Spanish, French, and Italian. Endowment: $2.6 million. Total enrollment: 175. Upper school average class size: 12. Upper school faculty-student ratio: 1:8.

Upper School Student Profile Grade 9: 20 students (10 boys, 10 girls); Grade 10: 21 students (10 boys, 11 girls); Grade 11: 21 students (11 boys, 10 girls); Grade 12: 23 students (12 boys, 11 girls). 80% of students are Jewish, Christian.

Faculty School total: 27. In upper school: 10 men, 11 women; 10 have advanced degrees.

Subjects Offered Acting, adolescent issues, algebra, American history, American literature, art, art history, art history-AP, arts, athletics, biology, biology-AP, bowling, business, business skills, calculus, career and personal planning, chemistry, choir, chorus, classics, college counseling, college placement, communication arts, community service, computer applications, computer education, computer math, computer science, computer skills, computer studies, computers, CPR, creative writing, critical thinking, culinary arts, dance, debate, decision making skills, digital art, digital imaging, digital photography, DNA research, drama, drama performance, drawing, driver education, earth science, English, English composition, English literature, environmental science, European history, expository writing, film, fine arts, first aid, fitness, foreign language, French, French as a second language, French studies, general science, geography, geometry, government, government/civics, grammar, graphic arts, graphic design, great books, Greek culture, guidance, health, health and wellness, health education, health science, history, history of ideas, history of the Americas, independent study, Internet, Internet research, intro to computers, Italian, journalism, junior and senior seminars, keyboarding, lab science, language arts, languages, Latin, leadership, leadership training, learning strategies, library, library research, library skills, life issues, life saving, literacy, literature, martial arts, math analysis, math applications, math methods, mathematics, mathematics-AP, Microsoft, modern history, modern languages, modern politics, music, music appreciation, news writing, newspaper, novel, nutrition, photo shop, photography, photojournalism, physical education, physics, play production, poetry, pre-college orientation, programming, public speaking, publications, publishing, religion, religion and culture, SAT preparation, science, self-defense, senior seminar, senior thesis, set design, Shakespeare, social science, social studies, Spanish, speech, stagecraft, state government, statistics, strategies for success, student teaching, studio art, study skills, technology, telecommunications, tennis, The 20th Century, theater, theater arts, theology, trigonometry, typing, U.S. government, U.S. literature, video, visual arts, voice, volleyball, Web site design, weight fitness, weight training, Western literature, Western philosophy, western religions, word processing, work experience, world civilizations, world culture, world history, world literature, writing, writing, writing skills, writing workshop.

Graduation Requirements Arts and fine arts (art, music, dance, drama), athletics, computer science, English, foreign language, mathematics, physical education (includes health), science, social studies (includes history), 50 hours of community/school service, extracurricular participation.

Special Academic Programs Honors section; independent study; study at local college for college credit; academic accommodation for the gifted, the musically talented, and the artistically talented; remedial reading and/or remedial writing; remedial math; special instructional classes for students with mild learning disabilities and/or Attention Deficit Disorder issues.

College Placement 16 students graduated in 2005; all went to college, including Adelphi University; Cornell University; New York University; Pace University; Polytechnic University, Brooklyn Campus; St. John's University. 50% scored over 600 on SAT verbal, 50% scored over 600 on SAT math.

Student Life Upper grades have uniform requirement, student council, honor system. Discipline rests primarily with faculty.

Summer Programs Remediation, enrichment, advancement, sports, art/fine arts, rigorous outdoor training, computer instruction programs offered; session focuses on enrichment; held on campus; accepts boys and girls; open to students from other schools. 100 students usually enrolled. 2006 schedule: July 10 to August 25. Application deadline: March.

Tuition and Aid Day student tuition: $14,000. Tuition installment plan (Key Tuition Payment Plan, individually arranged payment plans). Tuition reduction for siblings, merit scholarship grants, need-based scholarship grants, need-based loans, middle-income loans, paying campus jobs available. In 2005–06, 35% of upper-school students received aid. Total amount of financial aid awarded in 2005–06: $125,000.

Admissions Traditional secondary-level entrance grade is 9. For fall 2005, 165 students applied for upper-level admission, 65 were accepted, 60 enrolled. School's own exam and Stanford Diagnostic Test required. Deadline for receipt of application materials: none. Application fee required: $75. On-campus interview required.

Athletics Interscholastic: aerobics/dance (girls), baseball (b), basketball (b,g), cheering (g), dance (g), dance squad (g), dance team (g), danceline (g), jogging (b,g), soccer (b), softball (g), volleyball (b,g); coed interscholastic: bowling, cross-country running, fitness, golf, indoor hockey, martial arts, physical fitness, self defense, tennis, weight lifting, weight training; coed intramural: bowling, Cosom hockey, cross-country running, gymnastics, juggling. 3 PE instructors, 9 coaches, 4 trainers.

Computers Computers are regularly used in all classes. Computer network features include campus e-mail, on-campus library services, CD-ROMs, online commercial services, Internet access, file transfer, office computer access.

Contact Mr. Jorge M. Parra, Assist Director of the Academy/Director of Admissions. 718-238-3308 Ext. 202. Fax: 718-238-2894. E-mail: parrag@adelphiacademy.org. Web site: www.adelphiacademy.org.

ANNOUNCEMENT FROM THE SCHOOL As the oldest private, independent, continuing, coeducational, college-preparatory day school in Brooklyn, Adelphi Academy has effectively prepared young people for college, career, and life for more than 140 years. Founded in 1863 and located in the historic Bay Ridge section of Brooklyn, Adelphi enrolls students from prekindergarten through 12th grade. A strong emphasis is placed on small class size within a nurturing and caring environment through Adelphi's founding principles of pride, tradition, spirit, and excellence. The student-teacher ratio is 8 to 1. Adelphi features Project Succeed for College Bound Students with Learning Disabilities. Before- and after-school care, bus service, financial aid, summer school, and summer camp programs are available.

ADMIRAL FARRAGUT ACADEMY
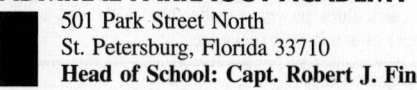
501 Park Street North
St. Petersburg, Florida 33710
Head of School: Capt. Robert J. Fine

General Information Coeducational boarding and day college-preparatory, Naval Junior ROTC, and marine biology school. Boarding grades 6–12, day grades P4–12. Founded: 1933. Setting: suburban. Students are housed in single-sex by floor dormitories. 55-acre campus. 20 buildings on campus. Approved or accredited by Florida Council of Independent Schools, Southern Association of Colleges and Schools, The Association of Boarding Schools, and Florida Department of Education. Member of National Association of Independent Schools and Secondary School Admission Test Board. Endowment: $2 million. Total enrollment: 425. Upper school average class size: 18. Upper school faculty-student ratio: 1:15.

Upper School Student Profile Grade 9: 64 students (44 boys, 20 girls); Grade 10: 77 students (50 boys, 27 girls); Grade 11: 62 students (45 boys, 17 girls); Grade 12: 50 students (37 boys, 13 girls). 35% of students are boarding students. 65% are state residents. 20 states are represented in upper school student body. 5% are international students. International students from Antigua and Barbuda, Belgium, Canada, Costa Rica, Czech Republic, and Kuwait; 8 other countries represented in student body.

Faculty School total: 63. In upper school: 17 men, 8 women; 15 have advanced degrees; 20 reside on campus.

Subjects Offered ACT preparation, advanced math, algebra, American history, American literature, analytic geometry, anatomy and physiology, art, art history, aviation, band, biology, boating, British literature, business communications, calculus, chemistry, chorus, community service, computer programming, computer science, creative writing, drama, driver education, earth science, economics, English, English composition, English literature, environmental science, ESL, ethics and responsibility, fine arts, French, geography, geometry, German, government/civics, grammar, health, history, journalism, keyboarding/computer, library assistant, marching band, marine biology, mathematics, meteorology, military science, music, music history, navigation,

NJROTC, oceanography, physical education, physics, pre-algebra, science, sign language, social studies, sociology, Spanish, speech, statistics, swimming test, trigonometry, world history, world literature, yearbook.

Graduation Requirements Arts and fine arts (art, music, dance, drama), economics, English, ethics, foreign language, government, health education, mathematics, NJROTC, physical education (includes health), science, social studies (includes history), U.S. history, world history, Qualified Boat Handler (QBH) Test, 80 hours of community service.

Special Academic Programs Honors section; study at local college for college credit; academic accommodation for the gifted; remedial reading and/or remedial writing; remedial math; ESL (10 students enrolled).

College Placement 63 students graduated in 2005; all went to college, including Florida State University; Syracuse University; United States Naval Academy; University of Florida; University of South Florida. Mean SAT verbal: 535, mean SAT math: 550, mean composite ACT: 20. 25% scored over 600 on SAT verbal, 24% scored over 600 on SAT math, 20% scored over 26 on composite ACT.

Student Life Upper grades have uniform requirement, student council. Discipline rests equally with students and faculty.

Tuition and Aid Day student tuition: $13,600; 5-day tuition and room/board: $23,950; 7-day tuition and room/board: $29,100. Tuition installment plan (individually arranged payment plans, AFA Payment Plan). Tuition reduction for siblings, need-based scholarship grants, tuition exemption for children of faculty available. In 2005–06, 22% of upper-school students received aid. Total amount of financial aid awarded in 2005–06: $280,000.

Admissions Traditional secondary-level entrance grade is 9. For fall 2005, 195 students applied for upper-level admission, 140 were accepted, 125 enrolled. Any standardized test required. Deadline for receipt of application materials: none. Application fee required: $150. Interview required.

Athletics Interscholastic: baseball (boys), basketball (b,g), cross-country running (b,g), diving (b,g), drill team (b,g), football (b,g), golf (b,g), riflery (b,g), sailing (b,g), softball (g), swimming and diving (b,g), tennis (b,g), track and field (b,g), volleyball (g), wrestling (b); intramural: fishing (b,g), riflery (b,g), wall climbing (b,g), weight training (b,g); coed interscholastic: bowling, cheering, drill team, football, golf, JROTC drill, marksmanship, martial arts, paint ball, riflery, sailing, scuba diving, soccer, volleyball; coed intramural: billiards, fitness, flag football, Frisbee, martial arts, paint ball, physical training, sailing, scuba diving, strength & conditioning, table tennis, volleyball. 4 PE instructors, 3 coaches, 1 trainer.

Computers Computers are regularly used in aviation, computer applications, English, foreign language, history, keyboarding, NJROTC, programming, science, writing, yearbook classes. Computer network features include campus e-mail, on-campus library services, CD-ROMs, online commercial services, Internet access, file transfer, office computer access, DVD, wireless campus network, faculty Web pages, Cisco Networking Academy.

Contact Cmdr. David Graham, Admissions Director. 727-384-5500 Ext. 1. Fax: 727-347-5160. E-mail: admissions@farragut.org. Web site: www.farragut.org.

ANNOUNCEMENT FROM THE SCHOOL Sixty-one graduates of AFA, America's only Honor Naval Academy, earned $5.3-million in scholarships in 2005. With a strong emphasis on values and students from 22 countries, AFA ranks among the best in the nation, with 25% of graduates earning service academy appointments or college ROTC scholarships. Located on a beautiful waterfront campus, AFA's curriculum provides leadership skills and social development in an atmosphere of academic excellence.

See full description on page 642.

ADVANCED ACADEMY OF GEORGIA

Honors House
State University of West Georgia
Carrollton, Georgia 30118
Head of School: Ms. Susan Colgate

General Information Coeducational boarding college-preparatory, arts, business, technology, and mathematics, science, and humanities school. Grades 10–12. Founded: 1995. Setting: small town. Nearest major city is Atlanta. Students are housed in coed dormitories. 394-acre campus. 89 buildings on campus. Approved or accredited by Southern Association of Colleges and Schools and Georgia Department of Education. Total enrollment: 67. Upper school average class size: 14. Upper school faculty-student ratio: 1:14.

Upper School Student Profile 100% of students are boarding students. 86% are state residents. 4 states are represented in upper school student body. 8% are international students. International students from Russian Federation and Spain.

Faculty School total: 270. In upper school: 149 men, 121 women; all have advanced degrees.

Subjects Offered 20th century American writers, 20th century history, 20th century physics, 20th century world history, accounting, acting, advanced chemistry, advanced computer applications, advanced math, advanced studio art-AP, African American history, African American studies, African-American literature, algebra, American biography, American Civil War, American culture, American democracy, American foreign policy, American government, American history, American legal systems, American literature, American sign language, analysis, analysis and differential calculus, analysis of data, analytic geometry, anatomy, ancient world history, ancient/medieval philosophy, animal behavior, anthropology, archaeology, art, art and culture, art appreciation, art education, art history, Asian history, Asian literature, Asian studies, astronomy, astrophysics, athletics, band, banking, Bible as literature, biochemistry, bioethics, DNA and culture, biology, biotechnology, Black history, British history, British literature, British literature (honors), British National Curriculum, business applications, business communications, business education, business law, business mathematics, business skills, business studies, business technology, calculus, cell biology, chemistry, child development, Chinese, Chinese history, Chinese literature, Chinese studies, choir, cinematography, civics/free enterprise, civil rights, Civil War, civil war history, classical civilization, classical Greek literature, classical language, classical music, classical studies, communications, comparative government and politics, comparative politics, computer animation, computer applications, computer art, computer education, computer graphics, computer information systems, computer math, computer multimedia, computer music, computer processing, computer programming, computer science, computer technologies, constitutional history of U.S., constitutional law, consumer economics, critical thinking, critical writing, data analysis, debate, democracy in America, desktop publishing, discrete math, discrete mathematics, DNA, DNA research, DNA science lab, drama, drawing, drawing and design, early childhood, earth and space science, earth science, earth systems analysis, East Asian history, East European studies, Eastern religion and philosophy, Eastern world civilizations, ecology, economics, economics and history, education, English, English composition, English literature, ensembles, entrepreneurship, environmental geography, environmental science, environmental systems, ethics, ethnic literature, ethnic studies, European civilization, European history, film appreciation, film studies, first aid, fitness, forensic science, forensics, French, gender issues, genetics, geography, geology, geometry, German, German literature, global issues, global science, global studies, golf, government/civics, graphic arts, graphic design, graphics, Greek, Greek culture, Holocaust and other genocides, Holocaust legacy, Holocaust seminar, Holocaust studies, honors algebra, honors English, honors geometry, honors U.S. history, honors world history, human anatomy, human sexuality, intro to computers, Japanese, jazz, jazz band, Jewish history, Jewish studies, language arts, Latin, law, law and the legal system, law studies, library, library research, life saving, linear algebra, literature by women, literature seminar, logic, logic, rhetoric, and debate, management information systems, marching band, marine biology, marketing, math analysis, math applications, mathematical modeling, media communications, methods of research, microbiology, microeconomics, Middle East, military history, minority studies, model United Nations, modeling, modern Chinese history, modern civilization, modern European history, modern political theory, modern politics, modern problems, modern Western civilization, modern world history, money management, music, music appreciation, music composition, Native American history, Native American studies, natural history, newspaper, North American literature, oceanography, organic chemistry, painting, parent/child development, performing arts, personal and social education, personal development, personal finance, personal fitness, philosophy, philosophy of government, photography, photojournalism, physical education, physical fitness, physical science, physics, physiology, piano, political economics, political economy, political science, political systems, political thought, post-calculus, pre-calculus, printmaking, probability, probability and statistics, psychology, public policy, public speaking, publications, publishing, radio broadcasting, religion and culture, religious education, religious studies, Roman civilization, Roman culture, ROTC, Russian, Russian history, Russian literature, Russian studies, science and technology, science fiction, Shakespeare, Shakespearean histories, social education, social justice, social psychology, social science, social sciences, social studies, society, society and culture, society challenge and change, society, politics and law, sociology, South African history, Southern literature, Spanish, Spanish literature, speech and debate, speech and oral interpretations, speech communications, sports medicine, sports nutrition, state government, state history, statistics, stock market, student teaching, studio art, technical arts, technical drawing, technical education, technical skills, technical studies, technical theater, technical writing, technology, telecommunications, telecommunications and the Internet, television, The 20th Century, the Presidency, the Sixties, traditional camping, U.S. constitutional history, U.S. government, U.S. government and politics, U.S. history, U.S. literature, U.S. Presidents, United Nations and international issues, Vietnam War, visual and performing arts, visual arts, visual literacy, visual reality, water color painting, weight training, Western civilization, Western literature, Western philosophy, western religions, Western religions, women in literature, women in society, women in the classical world, women in world history, women spirituality and faith, women's health, women's literature, women's studies, world civilizations, world cultures, world geography, world governments, world history, world issues, world literature, world religions, world studies, World War I, World War II, World-Wide-Web publishing, writing.

Graduation Requirements Students must complete Georgia high school requirements which are satisfied through equivalent college courses offered by the university.

Special Academic Programs Honors section; independent study; study at local college for college credit; study abroad; academic accommodation for the gifted, the musically talented, and the artistically talented.

College Placement 32 students graduated in 2005; all went to college, including Agnes Scott College; Brown University; Georgia Institute of Technology; Georgia

State University; Savannah College of Art and Design; University of Georgia. Mean SAT verbal: 648, mean SAT math: 645. 79% scored over 600 on SAT verbal, 75% scored over 600 on SAT math.

Student Life Upper grades have student council, honor system. Discipline rests equally with students and faculty.

Summer Programs Advancement, art/fine arts programs offered; session focuses on arts and humanities; mathematics and science; held on campus; accepts boys and girls; open to students from other schools. 2006 schedule: July 11 to July 24. Application deadline: June 1.

Tuition and Aid 5-day tuition and room/board: $5000; 7-day tuition and room/board: $5000. Merit scholarship grants, need-based scholarship grants, need-based loans, middle-income loans, paying campus jobs available. In 2005–06, 65% of upper-school students received aid; total upper-school merit-scholarship money awarded: $24,000. Total amount of financial aid awarded in 2005–06: $83,700.

Admissions Traditional secondary-level entrance grade is 10. For fall 2005, 80 students applied for upper-level admission, 67 were accepted, 67 enrolled. ACT or SAT required. Deadline for receipt of application materials: August 18. Application fee required: $20. Interview required.

Athletics Coed Intramural: basketball, flag football, Frisbee, paint ball, soccer, softball, ultimate Frisbee.

Computers Computers are regularly used in all classes. Computer network features include campus e-mail, on-campus library services, CD-ROMs, online commercial services, Internet access, file transfer, office computer access, DVD, wireless campus network.

Contact Mrs. Anneliesa Finch, Program Specialist. 678-839-6249. Fax: 678-839-0636. E-mail: afinch@westga.edu. Web site: www.advancedacademy.org.

THE AGNES IRWIN SCHOOL

Ithan Avenue and Conestoga Road
Rosemont, Pennsylvania 19010
Head of School: Ms. Martha C. Cutts

petersons.com

General Information Girls' day college-preparatory school. Grades K–12. Founded: 1869. Setting: suburban. Nearest major city is Philadelphia. 18-acre campus. 5 buildings on campus. Approved or accredited by Middle States Association of Colleges and Schools, Pennsylvania Association of Private Academic Schools, and Pennsylvania Department of Education. Member of National Association of Independent Schools, Secondary School Admission Test Board, and National Coalition of Girls' Schools. Endowment: $17.7 million. Total enrollment: 663. Upper school average class size: 15. Upper school faculty-student ratio: 1:7.

Upper School Student Profile Grade 9: 66 students (66 girls); Grade 10: 65 students (65 girls); Grade 11: 57 students (57 girls); Grade 12: 61 students (61 girls).

Faculty School total: 95. In upper school: 12 men, 27 women; 21 have advanced degrees.

Subjects Offered 20th century world history, advanced studio art-AP, algebra, American history, American history-AP, American literature, American literature-AP, Asian studies, bioethics, biology, biology-AP, calculus, calculus-AP, chemistry, chemistry-AP, computer applications, dance, drama, English, English language-AP, English literature, English literature and composition-AP, environmental science-AP, European history, finite math, French, geometry, Greek, health, history, Japanese history, Latin, media studies, Middle Eastern history, photo shop, photography, physical education, physics, pre-calculus, robotics, Spanish, statistics, studio art, trigonometry.

Graduation Requirements Arts and fine arts (art, music, dance, drama), English, foreign language, history, mathematics, physical education (includes health), science, Senior Assembly. Community service is required.

Special Academic Programs Advanced Placement exam preparation in 14 subject areas; honors section; independent study; academic accommodation for the gifted.

College Placement 54 students graduated in 2005; all went to college, including Boston College; Georgetown University; The Pennsylvania State University University Park Campus; University of Pennsylvania; University of Virginia; Yale University. Mean SAT verbal: 645, mean SAT math: 655. 76% scored over 600 on SAT verbal, 73% scored over 600 on SAT math.

Student Life Upper grades have uniform requirement, student council, honor system. Discipline rests equally with students and faculty.

Summer Programs Remediation, enrichment, advancement, ESL, art/fine arts, computer instruction programs offered; session focuses on arts, academics, athletics; held on campus; accepts boys and girls; open to students from other schools. 1000 students usually enrolled. 2006 schedule: June 12 to July 28. Application deadline: none.

Tuition and Aid Day student tuition: $21,050. Tuition installment plan (monthly payment plans). Need-based scholarship grants, need-based loans, Higher Education Service, Inc available. In 2005–06, 20% of upper-school students received aid. Total amount of financial aid awarded in 2005–06: $1,400,000.

Admissions Traditional secondary-level entrance grade is 9. For fall 2005, 55 students applied for upper-level admission, 24 were accepted, 14 enrolled. ISEE or SSAT required. Deadline for receipt of application materials: February 1. Application fee required: $50. Interview required.

Athletics Interscholastic: basketball, crew, cross-country running, field hockey, golf, lacrosse, soccer, softball, squash, swimming and diving, tennis, volleyball; intramural:

aerobics, aerobics/nautilus, dance, drill team, fencing, fitness, modern dance, nautilus, physical fitness, physical training, strength & conditioning, weight training, yoga. 2 PE instructors, 23 coaches, 1 trainer.

Computers Computers are regularly used in animation, art, English, foreign language, history, mathematics, media arts, photography, science, yearbook classes. Computer network features include on-campus library services, CD-ROMs, online commercial services, Internet access, file transfer, office computer access, DVD, wireless campus network, Blackboard, digital video editing, audio recording studio, online databases.

Contact Ms. Joan M. Brennan, Director of Admissions and Financial Aid. 610-525-8400. Fax: 610-525-8908. E-mail: jbrennan@agnesirwin.org. Web site: www.agnesirwin.org.

See full description on page 644.

AHLIYYAH SCHOOL FOR GIRLS

PO Box 2035
Amman 11181, Jordan
Head of School: Mrs. Haifa Hajjar Najjar

General Information Girls' day college-preparatory, general academic, arts, business, and bilingual studies school, affiliated with Christian faith, Muslim faith; primarily serves underachievers. Grades 1–12. Founded: 1926. Setting: urban. 1-hectare campus. 3 buildings on campus. Approved or accredited by British Accreditation Council and International Baccalaureate Organization. Languages of instruction: English and Arabic. Endowment: 2.5 million Jordanian dinars. Total enrollment: 1,000. Upper school average class size: 25. Upper school faculty-student ratio: 1:10.

Upper School Student Profile Grade 7: 96 students (96 girls); Grade 8: 70 students (70 girls); Grade 9: 86 students (86 girls); Grade 10: 92 students (92 girls); Grade 11: 79 students (79 girls); Grade 12: 77 students (77 girls). 100% of students are Christian, Muslim.

Faculty School total: 121. In upper school: 9 men, 63 women; 28 have advanced degrees.

Subjects Offered Arabic, biology, chemistry, civics, computers, critical thinking, drama, economics, English, geography, geology, history, literature, mathematics, music, physical education, physics, religion, social studies, statistics, theater arts, theory of knowledge, visual arts.

Graduation Requirements Arts and crafts, arts appreciation, athletics, biology, calculus, career education, chemistry, Christianity, computer education, computer programming, computer science, computer skills, creative writing, earth science, economics, English, English literature, history, languages, library, mathematics, painting, physical education (includes health), physics, poetry, religion (includes Bible studies and theology), research, science, Shakespeare, social science, speech and debate, writing skills, Jordanian High School Government Examination, or Cambridge or London Boards, or International Baccalaureate Diploma (non-IB students must complete CAS program).

Special Academic Programs International Baccalaureate program; domestic exchange program; programs in English, mathematics for dyslexic students; special instructional classes for deaf students, students with mild to moderate learning disabilities, Attention Deficit Disorder, and dyslexia; ESL (60 students enrolled).

College Placement 74 students graduated in 2005; they went to American University; McGill University; The American University in Cairo; University of Toronto; York University. Other: 74 entered a postgraduate year.

Student Life Upper grades have uniform requirement, student council. Discipline rests equally with students and faculty.

Tuition and Aid Day student tuition: 1900 Jordanian dinars–3530 Jordanian dinars. Tuition installment plan (monthly payment plans, individually arranged payment plans). Tuition reduction for siblings, bursaries, need-based scholarship grants available. In 2005–06, 9% of upper-school students received aid. Total amount of financial aid awarded in 2005–06: 18,400 Jordanian dinars.

Admissions Traditional secondary-level entrance grade is 7. For fall 2005, 75 students applied for upper-level admission, 30 were accepted, 29 enrolled. Admissions testing and school's own exam required. Deadline for receipt of application materials: February 1. Application fee required: 5 Jordanian dinars. Interview required.

Athletics Interscholastic: artistic gym (girls), ballet (g), basketball (g), climbing (g), combined training (g), cooperative games (g), cross-country running (g), dance (g), dance team (g), fitness (g), fitness walking (g), football (g), gymnastics (g), handball (g), horseback riding (g), indoor soccer (g), indoor track & field (g), jogging (g), jump rope (g), modern dance (g), outdoor activities (g), outdoor adventure (g), outdoor education (g), outdoor recreation (g), outdoor skills (g), paint ball (g), physical fitness (g), physical training (g), rhythmic gymnastics (g), rock climbing (g), running (g), self defense (g), soccer (g), Special Olympics (g), swimming and diving (g), table tennis (g), team handball (g), tennis (g), track and field (g), volleyball (g), walking (g), yoga (g). 4 PE instructors, 9 coaches, 17 trainers.

Computers Computers are regularly used in all classes. Computer network features include campus e-mail, on-campus library services, CD-ROMs, Internet access, file transfer, office computer access, DVD.

Contact Mrs. Badiah Madbak, Academic Deputy. 962-6-4624872 Ext. 109. Fax: 962-6-4621594. E-mail: b.madbak@asg.edu.jo. Web site: www.asg.edu.jo.

AIRDRIE KOINONIA CHRISTIAN SCHOOL

2104 Big Hill Springs Road
Airdrie, Alberta T4B 2A3, Canada
Head of School: Mr. Brian C. Hazeltine

General Information Coeducational day college-preparatory, general academic, and religious studies school, affiliated with Christian faith, Evangelical/Fundamental faith. Grades K–12. Founded: 1987. Setting: rural. Nearest major city is Calgary, Canada. 5-acre campus. 4 buildings on campus. Approved or accredited by Association of Christian Schools International and Alberta Department of Education. Language of instruction: English. Total enrollment: 299. Upper school average class size: 15. Upper school faculty-student ratio: 1:14.

Upper School Student Profile Grade 7: 25 students (8 boys, 17 girls); Grade 8: 28 students (18 boys, 10 girls); Grade 9: 23 students (14 boys, 9 girls); Grade 10: 18 students (6 boys, 12 girls); Grade 11: 15 students (5 boys, 10 girls); Grade 12: 15 students (5 boys, 10 girls). 100% of students are Christian faith, Evangelical/Fundamental faith.

Faculty School total: 17. In upper school: 3 men, 5 women; 2 have advanced degrees.

Subjects Offered Art, biology, career and personal planning, chemistry, Christian doctrine, Christian ethics, Christian scripture, computer information systems, computer keyboarding, computer processing, concert bell choir, drama, English, ethics, family life, French, general math, health education, law studies, mathematics, physics, pre-algebra, science, world religions.

Graduation Requirements 75 hours of community service.

Special Academic Programs Independent study; academic accommodation for the gifted; remedial math; special instructional classes for students with learning disabilities and Attention Deficit Disorder.

College Placement 7 students graduated in 2005; they went to University of Calgary. Other: 6 went to work, 1 entered a postgraduate year.

Student Life Upper grades have specified standards of dress, student council, honor system. Discipline rests primarily with faculty. Attendance at religious services is required.

Tuition and Aid Day student tuition: CAN$1200–CAN$3600. Tuition installment plan (monthly payment plans, individually arranged payment plans). Tuition reduction for siblings, need-based scholarship grants available. In 2005–06, 5% of upper-school students received aid. Total amount of financial aid awarded in 2005–06: CAN$15,000.

Admissions For fall 2005, 13 students applied for upper-level admission, 13 were accepted, 13 enrolled. Deadline for receipt of application materials: none. Application fee required: CAN$25. On-campus interview required.

Athletics Interscholastic: badminton (boys, girls), basketball (b,g), cross-country running (b,g), track and field (b,g), volleyball (b,g); coed interscholastic: badminton, physical fitness; coed intramural: floor hockey, mountain biking, outdoor adventure, outdoor education, rock climbing, skiing (downhill), snowboarding, soccer, softball.

Computers Computer resources include CD-ROMs, Internet access.

Contact Mrs. Mardelle Zieman, Secretary. 403-948-5100. Fax: 403-948-5563. E-mail: secretary@akcs.com. Web site: www.akcs.com.

AKIBA HEBREW ACADEMY

223 North Highland Avenue
Merion Station, Pennsylvania 19066
Head of School: Rabbi Philip D. Field

General Information Coeducational day college-preparatory and religious studies school, affiliated with Jewish faith. Grades 6–12. Founded: 1946. Setting: suburban. Nearest major city is Philadelphia. 7-acre campus. 1 building on campus. Approved or accredited by Middle States Association of Colleges and Schools and Pennsylvania Department of Education. Member of National Association of Independent Schools. Languages of instruction: English and Hebrew. Endowment: $6 million. Total enrollment: 319. Upper school average class size: 16. Upper school faculty-student ratio: 1:7.

Upper School Student Profile Grade 9: 62 students (39 boys, 23 girls); Grade 10: 70 students (41 boys, 29 girls); Grade 11: 65 students (34 boys, 31 girls); Grade 12: 58 students (30 boys, 28 girls). 100% of students are Jewish.

Faculty School total: 62. In upper school: 15 men, 35 women; 41 have advanced degrees.

Subjects Offered Algebra, American history, American literature, art, astronomy, Bible studies, biology, calculus, chemistry, community service, computer math, computer programming, computer science, creative writing, earth science, English, English literature, environmental science, environmental science-AP, ethics, European history, French, geometry, government/civics, grammar, health, Hebrew, history, Jewish studies, Latin, mathematics, music, physical education, physics, public speaking, religion, science, social studies, Spanish, trigonometry, world history, writing.

Graduation Requirements English, foreign language, mathematics, physical education (includes health), religion (includes Bible studies and theology), science, social studies (includes history), senior work project. Community service is required.

Special Academic Programs Advanced Placement exam preparation in 8 subject areas; honors section; term-away projects; study abroad.

College Placement 71 students graduated in 2005; all went to college, including Brandeis University; New York University; University of Maryland, College Park; University of Pennsylvania; University of Pittsburgh. Median SAT verbal: 644, median SAT math: 659.

Student Life Upper grades have specified standards of dress, student council. Discipline rests primarily with faculty.

Tuition and Aid Day student tuition: $18,850. Tuition installment plan (Key Tuition Payment Plan, monthly payment plans, individually arranged payment plans). Need-based scholarship grants available. In 2005–06, 29% of upper-school students received aid. Total amount of financial aid awarded in 2005–06: $610,000.

Admissions Traditional secondary-level entrance grade is 9. For fall 2005, 55 students applied for upper-level admission, 50 were accepted, 43 enrolled. ISEE required. Deadline for receipt of application materials: none. Application fee required: $40. On-campus interview required.

Athletics Interscholastic: baseball (boys), basketball (b,g), soccer (b,g), softball (g), tennis (b,g); intramural: basketball (b,g), field hockey (b,g), soccer (b,g), volleyball (b,g); coed interscholastic: cross-country running, soccer, swimming and diving. 2 PE instructors, 16 coaches.

Computers Computers are regularly used in all academic classes. Computer resources include campus e-mail, on-campus library services, CD-ROMs, online commercial services, Internet access.

Contact Vivian Young, Director of Admissions. 610-667-4070 Ext. 144. Fax: 610-667-1046. E-mail: vyoung@akibaweb.org. Web site: www.akibaweb.org.

THE ALBANY ACADEMY

135 Academy Road
Albany, New York 12208-3196
Head of School: Mrs. Caroline B. Mason

General Information Boys' boarding and coeducational day college-preparatory, arts, and technology school. Boarding boys grades 8–PG, day boys grades PK–PG, day girls grades PK–K. Founded: 1813. Setting: urban. Students are housed in single-sex dormitories. 25-acre campus. 3 buildings on campus. Approved or accredited by New York State Association of Independent Schools. Member of National Association of Independent Schools and Secondary School Admission Test Board. Total enrollment: 340. Upper school average class size: 15. Upper school faculty-student ratio: 1:15.

Upper School Student Profile Grade 9: 34 students (34 boys); Grade 10: 48 students (48 boys); Grade 11: 56 students (56 boys); Grade 12: 41 students (41 boys); Postgraduate: 2 students (2 boys). 8% of students are boarding students. 90% are state residents. 3 states are represented in upper school student body. 2% are international students. International students from Canada, Portugal, Republic of Korea, Serbia and Montenegro, and Sweden.

Faculty School total: 44. In upper school: 22 men, 22 women; 19 have advanced degrees; 1 resides on campus.

Subjects Offered Advanced Placement courses, algebra, American history, American literature, art, band, biology, calculus, chemistry, community service, computer math, computer programming, computer science, drama, economics, English, English literature, European history, fine arts, French, geometry, government/civics, health, history, Latin, mathematics, music, philosophy, physical education, physics, pre-calculus, psychology, science, social studies, Spanish, speech, theater, trigonometry, world history.

Graduation Requirements Arts and fine arts (art, music, dance, drama), English, foreign language, mathematics, physical education (includes health), science, social studies (includes history), participation in the Academy's Leadership Development Program. Community service is required.

Special Academic Programs Advanced Placement exam preparation in 17 subject areas; honors section; accelerated programs; independent study; study at local college for college credit; remedial reading and/or remedial writing.

College Placement 61 students graduated in 2005; 56 went to college, including Middlebury College; New York University; Rensselaer Polytechnic Institute; Siena College; St. Lawrence University; Syracuse University. Other: 1 entered military service. Median composite ACT: 25. Mean SAT verbal: 571, mean SAT math: 601. 46.7% scored over 600 on SAT verbal, 62.2% scored over 600 on SAT math, 53% scored over 26 on composite ACT.

Student Life Upper grades have specified standards of dress, student council, honor system. Discipline rests equally with students and faculty.

Summer Programs Enrichment, sports programs offered; held on campus; accepts boys and girls; open to students from other schools. 2006 schedule: June 27 to August 5. Application deadline: none.

Tuition and Aid Day student tuition: $10,000–$16,500; 7-day tuition and room/board: $23,000–$23,500. Tuition installment plan (Academic Management Services Plan, monthly payment plans, individually arranged payment plans). Need-based scholarship grants, need-based loans available. In 2005–06, 35% of upper-school students received aid. Total amount of financial aid awarded in 2005–06: $454,935.

Admissions Traditional secondary-level entrance grade is 9. For fall 2005, 52 students applied for upper-level admission, 35 were accepted, 23 enrolled. ERB or SSAT required. Deadline for receipt of application materials: none. Application fee required: $50. On-campus interview required.

Athletics Interscholastic: baseball, basketball, cross-country running, diving, drill team, fitness, football, golf, ice hockey, lacrosse, skiing (downhill), soccer, swimming and diving, tennis, track and field, wrestling; intramural: bicycling. 5 PE instructors, 5 coaches, 1 trainer.

Computers Computers are regularly used in all academic, information technology, literary magazine, music, newspaper, yearbook classes. Computer network features include campus e-mail, on-campus library services, CD-ROMs, online commercial services, Internet access, file transfer, office computer access.

Contact Mrs. Barbara McBride, Associate Director of Admission/Director of Financial Aid. 518-429-2416. Fax: 518-427-7016. E-mail: mcbrideb@albany-academy.org. Web site: www.albany-academy.org.

See full description on page 646.

ALBERT COLLEGE

160 Dundas Street West
Belleville, Ontario K8P 1A6, Canada
Head of School: Mr. Keith Stansfield

General Information Coeducational boarding and day college-preparatory, arts, and technology school, affiliated with United Church of Canada. Boarding grades 7–PG, day grades 1–PG. Founded: 1857. Setting: small town. Nearest major city is Toronto, Canada. Students are housed in single-sex dormitories. 25-acre campus. 7 buildings on campus. Approved or accredited by Canadian Educational Standards Institute, The Association of Boarding Schools, and Ontario Department of Education. Affiliate member of National Association of Independent Schools; member of Secondary School Admission Test Board. Language of instruction: English. Endowment: CAN$1.4 million. Total enrollment: 294. Upper school average class size: 15. Upper school faculty-student ratio: 1:8.

Upper School Student Profile Grade 9: 20 students (12 boys, 8 girls); Grade 10: 33 students (19 boys, 14 girls); Grade 11: 46 students (21 boys, 25 girls); Grade 12: 49 students (27 boys, 22 girls); Postgraduate: 8 students (6 boys, 2 girls). 56% of students are boarding students. 65% are province residents. 4 provinces are represented in upper school student body. 34% are international students. International students from Barbados, Bermuda, Hong Kong, Japan, Mexico, and Republic of Korea; 18 other countries represented in student body.

Faculty School total: 34. In upper school: 15 men, 14 women; 4 have advanced degrees; 14 reside on campus.

Subjects Offered Algebra, ancient history, art, art history, art-AP, biology, business, calculus, calculus-AP, Canadian geography, Canadian history, chemistry, computer science, drama, driver education, economics, English, English literature, English-AP, environmental science, ESL, European history, family studies, fine arts, finite math, French, French-AP, geography, history, law, mathematics, music, music-AP, outdoor education, physical education, physics, science, social science, social studies, society challenge and change, world history.

Graduation Requirements Arts and fine arts (art, music, dance, drama), business skills (includes word processing), English, foreign language, mathematics, physical education (includes health), science, social science, social studies (includes history).

Special Academic Programs Advanced Placement exam preparation in 5 subject areas; accelerated programs; independent study; academic accommodation for the gifted, the musically talented, and the artistically talented; ESL (20 students enrolled).

College Placement 50 students graduated in 2005; 46 went to college, including Carleton University; McGill University; Queen's University at Kingston; The University of Western Ontario; University of Ottawa. Other: 3 had other specific plans.

Student Life Upper grades have uniform requirement, student council, honor system. Discipline rests primarily with faculty. Attendance at religious services is required.

Tuition and Aid Day student tuition: CAN$17,200; 5-day tuition and room/board: CAN$28,000; 7-day tuition and room/board: CAN$30,900–CAN$33,600. Tuition installment plan (Insured Tuition Payment Plan, monthly payment plans, individually arranged payment plans, 3-payment plan). Tuition reduction for siblings, bursaries, merit scholarship grants available. In 2005–06, 20% of upper-school students received aid; total upper-school merit-scholarship money awarded: CAN$90,551. Total amount of financial aid awarded in 2005–06: CAN$270,000.

Admissions Traditional secondary-level entrance grade is 9. For fall 2005, 137 students applied for upper-level admission, 108 were accepted, 73 enrolled. Gates MacGinite Reading Tests, Nelson-Denny Reading Test or SSAT required. Deadline for receipt of application materials: none. Application fee required: CAN$100. Interview required.

Athletics Interscholastic: alpine skiing (boys, girls), aquatics (b,g), badminton (b,g), basketball (b,g), cross-country running (b,g), field hockey (g), golf (b), ice hockey (b), lacrosse (g), rugby (b), running (b,g), skiing (cross-country) (b,g), skiing (downhill) (b,g), soccer (b,g), squash (b,g), tennis (b,g), track and field (b,g), volleyball (b,g); intramural: aerobics/nautilus (b,g), ball hockey (b), basketball (b,g), cross-country running (b,g), field hockey (g), floor hockey (b,g), golf (b), hockey (b), ice skating (b), indoor soccer (b,g), kayaking (b,g), lacrosse (g), rowing (b,g), rugby (b), running (b,g), soccer (b,g), tennis (b,g), track and field (b,g), volleyball (b,g), weight training (b); coed interscholastic: nordic skiing, sailing, swimming and diving; coed intramural: aerobics, aerobics/dance, alpine skiing, aquatics, back packing, bicycling, canoeing/kayaking, climbing, dance, fitness, flag football, Frisbee, gymnastics, hiking/backpacking, jogging, modern dance, mountain biking, nordic skiing, outdoor

activities, outdoor recreation, outdoors, paddle tennis, paint ball, physical fitness, physical training, rafting, rappelling, rock climbing, roller blading, ropes courses, sailing, skateboarding, skiing (cross-country), skiing (downhill), snowboarding, squash, swimming and diving, table tennis, triathlon, ultimate Frisbee, wall climbing, wilderness, winter soccer, yoga. 4 PE instructors, 2 coaches.

Computers Computers are regularly used in English, mathematics, science classes. Computer network features include campus e-mail, on-campus library services, CD-ROMs, Internet access.

Contact Heather Kidd, Director of Admission. 800-952-5237 Ext. 2204. Fax: 613-968-9651. E-mail: hkidd@albertc.on.ca. Web site: www.albertc.on.ca.

ALBUQUERQUE ACADEMY

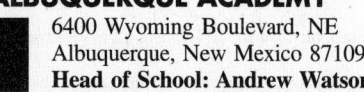

6400 Wyoming Boulevard, NE
Albuquerque, New Mexico 87109
Head of School: Andrew Watson

General Information Coeducational day college-preparatory, arts, and technology school. Grades 6–12. Founded: 1955. Setting: suburban. 312-acre campus. 10 buildings on campus. Approved or accredited by Independent Schools Association of the Southwest and New Mexico Department of Education. Member of National Association of Independent Schools and Secondary School Admission Test Board. Endowment: $205 million. Total enrollment: 1,078. Upper school average class size: 15. Upper school faculty-student ratio: 1:8.

Upper School Student Profile Grade 9: 164 students (81 boys, 83 girls); Grade 10: 164 students (81 boys, 83 girls); Grade 11: 156 students (75 boys, 81 girls); Grade 12: 156 students (80 boys, 76 girls).

Faculty School total: 180. In upper school: 72 men, 52 women; 97 have advanced degrees.

Subjects Offered Advanced Placement courses, algebra, American history, anatomy, Arabic, art, art history, astronomy, band, biochemistry, biology, calculus, chemistry, chemistry-AP, computer science, creative writing, dance, drama, drawing, earth science, economics, electronics, English, English-AP, European history, fine arts, French, French language-AP, genetics, geometry, German, government/civics, history, history-AP, horticulture, jazz, Latin American history, law, library studies, Mandarin, mathematics, media, music, outdoor education, painting, philosophy, photography, physical education, physics, physiology, printmaking, psychology, religion, robotics, science, social studies, Spanish, speech, swimming, theater, trigonometry, weight training, women's studies, world history, writing.

Graduation Requirements English, experiential education, foreign language, mathematics, physical education (includes health), science, social studies (includes history), experiential education (environmental and outdoor activities).

Special Academic Programs Advanced Placement exam preparation in 18 subject areas; independent study; term-away projects; domestic exchange program (with The Catlin Gabel School, Charlotte Latin School, Cincinnati Country Day School, Hamden Hall Country Day School); study abroad.

College Placement 152 students graduated in 2005; 150 went to college, including Brown University; Claremont McKenna College; Occidental College; Stanford University; Trinity University; University of New Mexico. Other: 2 had other specific plans. Mean SAT verbal: 648, mean SAT math: 645, mean composite ACT: 28. 77% scored over 600 on SAT verbal, 80% scored over 600 on SAT math, 80% scored over 26 on composite ACT.

Student Life Upper grades have specified standards of dress, student council, honor system. Discipline rests primarily with faculty.

Summer Programs Remediation, enrichment, advancement, sports, art/fine arts, computer instruction programs offered; session focuses on enrichment; held on campus; open to students from other schools. 2300 students usually enrolled. 2006 schedule: June 5 to July 14. Application deadline: May 31.

Tuition and Aid Day student tuition: $13,954. Tuition installment plan (FACTS Tuition Payment Plan, monthly payment plans, individually arranged payment plans, 1- and 2-payment plans). Need-based scholarship grants available. In 2005–06, 26% of upper-school students received aid. Total amount of financial aid awarded in 2005–06: $1,699,384.

Admissions Traditional secondary-level entrance grade is 9. For fall 2005, 157 students applied for upper-level admission, 56 were accepted, 42 enrolled. ISEE, school's own exam or SSAT required. Deadline for receipt of application materials: February 15. Application fee required: $50. On-campus interview required.

Athletics Interscholastic: baseball (boys), basketball (b,g), cross-country running (b,g), dance (b,g), diving (b,g), football (b), golf (b,g), hiking/backpacking (b,g), life saving (b,g), modern dance (b,g), outdoor education (b,g), outdoor skills (b,g), physical training (b,g), rafting (b,g), rappelling (b,g), rock climbing (b,g), soccer (b,g), softball (g), swimming and diving (b,g), tennis (b,g), track and field (b,g), volleyball (g), wrestling (b,g); coed intramural: basketball, wilderness, wilderness survival. 9 PE instructors, 58 coaches, 3 trainers.

Computers Computers are regularly used in foreign language, history, library science, mathematics classes. Computer network features include campus e-mail, on-campus library services, CD-ROMs, Internet access.

Contact Judy Hudenko, Director of Admission. 505-828-3208. Fax: 505-828-3128. E-mail: hudenko@aa.edu. Web site: www.aa.edu.

ALEXANDER DAWSON SCHOOL

10455 Dawson Drive
Lafayette, Colorado 80026
Head of School: Dr. Anthony Kandel

General Information Coeducational day college-preparatory, arts, and technology school. Grades K–12. Founded: 1970. Setting: rural. Nearest major city is Boulder. 90-acre campus. 11 buildings on campus. Approved or accredited by Association of Colorado Independent Schools, North Central Association of Colleges and Schools, and Colorado Department of Education. Member of National Association of Independent Schools and Secondary School Admission Test Board. Total enrollment: 423. Upper school average class size: 12. Upper school faculty-student ratio: 1:7.

Upper School Student Profile Grade 9: 46 students (20 boys, 26 girls); Grade 10: 43 students (25 boys, 18 girls); Grade 11: 55 students (29 boys, 26 girls); Grade 12: 44 students (23 boys, 21 girls).

Faculty School total: 53. In upper school: 17 men, 12 women; 12 have advanced degrees.

Subjects Offered Algebra, American history, American literature, art, art history, biology, calculus, ceramics, chemistry, computer math, computer multimedia, computer programming, computer science, creative writing, dance, drafting, drama, earth science, economics, English, English literature, European history, expository writing, fine arts, French, geography, geometry, government-AP, government/civics, grammar, health, history, industrial arts, journalism, Latin, mathematics, mechanical drawing, music, photography, physical education, physics, science, social science, social studies, Spanish, speech, theater, trigonometry, world history, world literature, writing.

Graduation Requirements Arts and fine arts (art, music, dance, drama), computer science, English, foreign language, history, mathematics, science.

Special Academic Programs Advanced Placement exam preparation in 15 subject areas; honors section; independent study; term-away projects; study at local college for college credit; study abroad; academic accommodation for the gifted, the musically talented, and the artistically talented; special instructional classes for deaf students.

College Placement 44 students graduated in 2005; all went to college, including Davidson College; Northwestern University; Pomona College; Stanford University; Washington University in St. Louis; Wellesley College. Mean SAT verbal: 640, mean SAT math: 620, mean composite ACT: 27.

Student Life Upper grades have specified standards of dress, student council, honor system. Discipline rests equally with students and faculty.

Summer Programs Enrichment, sports, art/fine arts, computer instruction programs offered; session focuses on athletics, foreign language (grades 4-10); held both on and off campus; held at golf courses, rivers; accepts boys and girls; open to students from other schools. 800 students usually enrolled. 2006 schedule: June 15 to August 5. Application deadline: none.

Tuition and Aid Day student tuition: $15,425. Tuition installment plan (Insured Tuition Payment Plan, monthly payment plans). Need-based scholarship grants, need-based loans available. In 2005–06, 20% of upper-school students received aid. Total amount of financial aid awarded in 2005–06: $570,000.

Admissions Traditional secondary-level entrance grade is 9. For fall 2005, 150 students applied for upper-level admission, 99 were accepted, 77 enrolled. ERB required. Deadline for receipt of application materials: none. Application fee required: $100. Interview required.

Athletics Interscholastic: baseball (boys), basketball (b,g), lacrosse (b), soccer (b,g), softball (g), swimming and diving (b,g), synchronized swimming (g), tennis (b,g), volleyball (g); intramural: lacrosse (b); coed interscholastic: alpine skiing, canoeing/kayaking, cross-country running, equestrian sports, golf, kayaking, martial arts, paddling, skiing (downhill), Special Olympics, track and field; coed intramural: aerobics, back packing, climbing, equestrian sports, fitness, flag football, football, Frisbee, golf, hiking/backpacking, indoor soccer, martial arts, outdoor activities, outdoor adventure, outdoor education, outdoor recreation, outdoor skills, physical fitness, rafting, weight lifting. 3 PE instructors, 22 coaches, 1 trainer.

Computers Computers are regularly used in art, mathematics, science classes. Computer network features include campus e-mail, on-campus library services, CD-ROMs, online commercial services, Internet access, wireless campus network.

Contact Ms. Denise LaRusch, Assistant to the Director of Admissions. 303-665-6679. Fax: 303-381-0415. E-mail: dlarusch@dawsonschool.org. Web site: www.dawsonschool.org.

ALLEN ACADEMY

3201 Boonville Road
Bryan, Texas 77802
Head of School: Mr. Bob Meyer

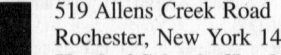

General Information Boys' boarding and coeducational day college-preparatory and ESL school. Boarding boys grades 9–12, day boys grades PK–12, day girls grades PK–12. Founded: 1886. Setting: small town. Nearest major city is Houston. Students are housed in single-sex dormitories. 40-acre campus. 8 buildings on campus. Approved or accredited by Southern Association of Colleges and Schools, Texas Education Agency, The College Board, and Texas Department of Education. Total enrollment: 289. Upper school average class size: 18. Upper school faculty-student ratio: 1:10.

Upper School Student Profile Grade 9: 11 students (6 boys, 5 girls); Grade 10: 13 students (6 boys, 7 girls); Grade 11: 16 students (12 boys, 4 girls); Grade 12: 29 students (22 boys, 7 girls). 4% of students are boarding students. 85% are state residents. 1 state is represented in upper school student body. 15% are international students. International students from Angola, China, Guatemala, Mexico, Republic of Korea, and Taiwan.

Faculty School total: 33. In upper school: 6 men, 10 women; 6 have advanced degrees; 3 reside on campus.

Subjects Offered Algebra, American history, American history-AP, American literature, art, band, biology, biology-AP, British literature, calculus, calculus-AP, chemistry, choir, English language-AP, English literature, English literature and composition-AP, English literature-AP, ESL, European history, European history-AP, French, French-AP, geometry, honors English, journalism, keyboarding/computer, multimedia, outdoor education, physical education, physical fitness, physics-AP, pre-calculus, psychology, Spanish, Spanish-AP, trigonometry, world history, yearbook.

Graduation Requirements Algebra, American history, American literature, arts and fine arts (art, music, dance, drama), biology, British literature (honors), chemistry, English composition, English literature, European history, foreign language, geometry, physics, pre-calculus, world history.

Special Academic Programs Advanced Placement exam preparation in 14 subject areas; honors section; study at local college for college credit; ESL (20 students enrolled).

College Placement 24 students graduated in 2005; 23 went to college, including Abilene Christian University; Sam Houston State University; Texas A&M University; The University of Texas at Austin; The University of Texas at San Antonio; University of Houston. Other: 1 went to work. Median SAT verbal: 562, median SAT math: 560. 35% scored over 600 on SAT verbal, 35% scored over 600 on SAT math.

Student Life Upper grades have uniform requirement, student council, honor system. Discipline rests equally with students and faculty.

Summer Programs Enrichment, ESL programs offered; session focuses on ESL and academics; held on campus; accepts boys and girls; open to students from other schools. 20 students usually enrolled. 2006 schedule: June 1 to June 30. Application deadline: May 1.

Tuition and Aid Day student tuition: $3286–$7292; 7-day tuition and room/board: $26,000. Tuition installment plan (FACTS Tuition Payment Plan, semester payment plan). Need-based scholarship grants available. In 2005–06, 10% of upper-school students received aid. Total amount of financial aid awarded in 2005–06: $50,000.

Admissions Traditional secondary-level entrance grade is 9. For fall 2005, 10 students applied for upper-level admission, 6 were accepted, 4 enrolled. CTP required. Deadline for receipt of application materials: none. Application fee required: $200. Interview recommended.

Athletics Interscholastic: baseball (boys), basketball (b,g), cheering (g), football (b), golf (b,g), softball (g), strength & conditioning (b), tennis (b,g), track and field (b,g), volleyball (g), winter soccer (b); coed intramural: basketball, combined training, weight training. 1 PE instructor, 2 coaches, 1 trainer.

Computers Computers are regularly used in keyboarding, multimedia classes. Computer network features include CD-ROMs, Internet access, office computer access.

Contact Camilla Viator, Director of Admissions. 979-776-0731. Fax: 979-774-7769. E-mail: cviator@allenacademy.org. Web site: www.allenacademy.org.

ANNOUNCEMENT FROM THE SCHOOL Allen provides a rigorous education in the humanities, arts, and sciences in prekindergarten through 12th grade. It compels students to explore a recognized body of scholarship that prepares the individual for life as an informed citizen. The Allen experience develops an awareness of values and viewpoints beyond the self.

ALLENDALE COLUMBIA SCHOOL

519 Allens Creek Road
Rochester, New York 14618-3405
Head of School: Charles Hertrick

General Information Coeducational day college-preparatory school. Grades N–12. Founded: 1890. Setting: suburban. Nearest major city is Buffalo. 30-acre campus. 5 buildings on campus. Approved or accredited by Middle States Association of Colleges and Schools and New York State Association of Independent Schools. Member of National Association of Independent Schools. Endowment: $14 million. Total enrollment: 463. Upper school average class size: 10. Upper school faculty-student ratio: 1:6.

Upper School Student Profile Grade 9: 27 students (15 boys, 12 girls); Grade 10: 50 students (24 boys, 26 girls); Grade 11: 36 students (14 boys, 22 girls); Grade 12: 31 students (12 boys, 19 girls).

Faculty School total: 63. In upper school: 14 men, 13 women; 22 have advanced degrees.

Subjects Offered Algebra, American history, American literature, art, biology, calculus, chemistry, computer science, earth science, English, English literature, European history, expository writing, French, geology, geometry, government/civics,

grammar, health, history, Latin, mathematics, music, physical education, physics, science, social studies, Spanish, trigonometry, world history, writing.

Graduation Requirements Art, computer science, English, foreign language, mathematics, physical education (includes health), science, social studies (includes history), participation in sports.

Special Academic Programs Advanced Placement exam preparation in 15 subject areas; independent study.

College Placement 41 students graduated in 2005; all went to college, including American University; Boston University; Rochester Institute of Technology; Syracuse University; University of Pennsylvania; Williams College. Mean SAT verbal: 628, mean SAT math: 629. 71% scored over 600 on SAT verbal, 68% scored over 600 on SAT math.

Student Life Upper grades have specified standards of dress, student council, honor system. Discipline rests primarily with faculty.

Summer Programs Enrichment, sports, art/fine arts programs offered; session focuses on sports; held on campus; accepts boys and girls; open to students from other schools. 800 students usually enrolled. 2006 schedule: June 12 to August 19. Application deadline: none.

Tuition and Aid Day student tuition: $15,800. Tuition installment plan (monthly payment plans). Need-based scholarship grants available. In 2005–06, 36% of upper-school students received aid. Total amount of financial aid awarded in 2005–06: $528,950.

Admissions Traditional secondary-level entrance grade is 9. For fall 2005, 31 students applied for upper-level admission, 11 were accepted, 9 enrolled. ERB Reading and Math and writing sample required. Deadline for receipt of application materials: none. Application fee required: $25. On-campus interview required.

Athletics Interscholastic: baseball (boys), basketball (b,g), cross-country running (b,g), soccer (b,g), softball (g), tennis (b,g), track and field (b,g), volleyball (g); coed interscholastic: bowling, golf, swimming and diving, winter (indoor) track. 4 PE instructors.

Computers Computers are regularly used in all academic classes. Computer network features include campus e-mail, on-campus library services, Internet access, wireless campus network, county-wide library services.

Contact Alan Carroll, Director of Admissions. 585-381-4560. Fax: 585-249-0230. E-mail: acarroll@allendalecolumbia.org. Web site: www.allendalecolumbia.org.

ALLIANCE ACADEMY

Casilla 17-11-06186
Quito, Ecuador
Head of School: Dr. Rohn Peterson

General Information Coeducational boarding and day college-preparatory, arts, and religious studies school, affiliated with Christian faith. Boarding grades 7–12, day grades PK–12. Founded: 1929. Setting: urban. Students are housed in mission agency dormitories. 8-hectare campus. 6 buildings on campus. Approved or accredited by Association of American Schools in South America, Association of Christian Schools International, and Southern Association of Colleges and Schools. Language of instruction: English. Total enrollment: 400. Upper school average class size: 20. Upper school faculty-student ratio: 1:6.

Upper School Student Profile Grade 9: 37 students (18 boys, 19 girls); Grade 10: 32 students (13 boys, 19 girls); Grade 11: 40 students (16 boys, 24 girls); Grade 12: 52 students (26 boys, 26 girls). 11% of students are boarding students. 71% are international students. International students from Canada, China, Republic of Korea, United Kingdom, and United States; 5 other countries represented in student body. 70% of students are Christian faith.

Faculty School total: 58. In upper school: 16 men, 12 women; 11 have advanced degrees.

Subjects Offered Algebra, American history, American history-AP, American literature, art, auto mechanics, band, Bible, Bible as literature, Bible studies, biology, biology-AP, business, calculus, ceramics, chemistry, choir, Christian doctrine, Christian ethics, Christian studies, church history, computer applications, computer art, computer math, computer programming, computer science, computer science-AP, concert band, creative writing, debate, desktop publishing, drama, earth science, ecology, economics, English, English as a foreign language, English language-AP, English literature, English literature-AP, ESL, family and consumer science, fine arts, French, French as a second language, geography, geometry, government/civics, grammar, health, health education, history, home economics, industrial arts, jazz band, journalism, keyboarding, Life of Christ, marching band, mathematics, music, novel, photography, physical education, physics, piano, pre-algebra, pre-calculus, psychology, public speaking, religion, religion and culture, science, senior seminar, small engine repair, social science, social studies, Spanish, Spanish literature, Spanish literature-AP, speech, speech and debate, theater, trigonometry, U.S. history-AP, video communication, vocal ensemble, woodworking, world geography, world history, world religions, writing, yearbook.

Graduation Requirements Arts and fine arts (art, music, dance, drama), English, foreign language, mathematics, physical education (includes health), religion (includes Bible studies and theology), science, social science, social studies (includes history).

Special Academic Programs Advanced Placement exam preparation in 10 subject areas; independent study; remedial reading and/or remedial writing; programs in

English, mathematics, general development for dyslexic students; special instructional classes for students with developmental and/or learning disabilities; ESL (5 students enrolled).

College Placement 56 students graduated in 2005; all went to college, including Azusa Pacific University; John Brown University; Simpson University. Median SAT verbal: 550, median SAT math: 510. Mean composite ACT: 23. 34% scored over 600 on SAT verbal, 28% scored over 600 on SAT math.

Student Life Upper grades have specified standards of dress, student council. Discipline rests primarily with faculty. Attendance at religious services is required.

Summer Programs ESL programs offered; session focuses on ESL; held on campus; accepts boys and girls; not open to students from other schools. 10 students usually enrolled. 2006 schedule: July 1 to July 31.

Tuition and Aid Day student tuition: $7516. Tuition installment plan (monthly payment plans, individually arranged payment plans). Need-based scholarship grants, tuition reduction for children of missionaries available. In 2005–06, 5% of upper-school students received aid. Total amount of financial aid awarded in 2005–06: $200,000.

Admissions For fall 2005, 33 students applied for upper-level admission, 24 were accepted, 22 enrolled. English entrance exam or WRAT required. Deadline for receipt of application materials: none. Application fee required: $50. On-campus interview required.

Athletics Interscholastic: basketball (boys, girls), soccer (b,g), volleyball (b,g); intramural: badminton (b,g), table tennis (b,g); coed intramural: back packing, basketball, indoor soccer, martial arts, outdoor adventure, soccer, softball, strength & conditioning, table tennis, volleyball. 2 PE instructors.

Computers Computers are regularly used in design, desktop publishing, graphic design, information technology, keyboarding, photography, programming, video film production, yearbook classes. Computer resources include on-campus library services, CD-ROMs, online commercial services, Internet access, DVD.

Contact Mr. Tim Sheppard, Director of Admissions. 593-2-226-6985. Fax: 593-2-226-4350. E-mail: alliance@alliance.k12.ec. Web site: www.alliance.k12.ec.

ALLISON ACADEMY

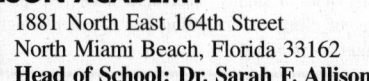 

1881 North East 164th Street
North Miami Beach, Florida 33162
Head of School: Dr. Sarah F. Allison

General Information Coeducational day college-preparatory, general academic, arts, business, and English for Speakers of Other Languages school; primarily serves underachievers. Grades 6–12. Founded: 1983. Setting: urban. Nearest major city is Miami. 1-acre campus. 2 buildings on campus. Approved or accredited by Association of Independent Schools of Florida, CITA (Commission on International and Trans-Regional Accreditation), National Council for Private School Accreditation, Southern Association of Colleges and Schools, and Florida Department of Education. Total enrollment: 116. Upper school average class size: 15. Upper school faculty-student ratio: 1:15.

Upper School Student Profile Grade 9: 21 students (15 boys, 6 girls); Grade 10: 20 students (13 boys, 7 girls); Grade 11: 24 students (14 boys, 10 girls); Grade 12: 20 students (11 boys, 9 girls).

Faculty School total: 17. In upper school: 4 men, 13 women; 7 have advanced degrees.

Subjects Offered Algebra, American government, American history, anatomy, architecture, art history, arts, biology, chemistry, computer science, consumer mathematics, drama, drawing, economics, English, English literature, environmental science, ESL, fine arts, French, general math, geography, geometry, health education, history, humanities, life management skills, life skills, mathematics, painting, peer counseling, photography, physical education, physical science, physics, pre-calculus, psychology, reading, reading/study skills, SAT/ACT preparation, science, social science, social studies, Spanish, speech and debate, sports, trigonometry, world culture, writing, yearbook.

Graduation Requirements Algebra, American government, arts and fine arts (art, music, dance, drama), business skills (includes word processing), chemistry, computer science, creative writing, drama, earth and space science, economics, English, English literature, foreign language, mathematics, physical education (includes health), science, social science, social studies (includes history), U.S. history, 75 hours of community service.

Special Academic Programs Advanced Placement exam preparation in 4 subject areas; honors section; accelerated programs; independent study; term-away projects; study at local college for college credit; academic accommodation for the gifted and the artistically talented; remedial reading and/or remedial writing; remedial math; programs in English, mathematics, general development for dyslexic students; special instructional classes for students with learning disabilities, dyslexia, and Attention Deficit Disorder; ESL (4 students enrolled).

College Placement 19 students graduated in 2005; 18 went to college, including Broward Community College; Florida International University; Miami Dade College; Santa Fe Community College. Other: 1 went to work. Median SAT verbal: 470, median SAT math: 440, median composite ACT: 19. 10% scored over 600 on SAT math.

Student Life Upper grades have uniform requirement, student council. Discipline rests primarily with faculty.

Summer Programs Remediation, enrichment, advancement, ESL, art/fine arts, computer instruction programs offered; session focuses on remediation and enrichment; held on campus; accepts boys and girls; open to students from other schools. 65 students usually enrolled. 2006 schedule: June 12 to August 3. Application deadline: none.

Tuition and Aid Day student tuition: $10,300. Guaranteed tuition plan. Tuition installment plan (SMART Tuition Payment Plan, individually arranged payment plans). Tuition reduction for siblings, merit scholarship grants, need-based scholarship grants available. In 2005–06, 10% of upper-school students received aid; total upper-school merit-scholarship money awarded: $15,000. Total amount of financial aid awarded in 2005–06: $50,000.

Admissions Traditional secondary-level entrance grade is 9. For fall 2005, 52 students applied for upper-level admission, 30 were accepted, 30 enrolled. Admissions testing, CAT, CTBS (or similar from their school) or Woodcock-Johnson Revised Achievement Test required. Deadline for receipt of application materials: none. Application fee required: $350. Interview required.

Athletics Interscholastic: basketball (boys), cheering (g), swimming and diving (b), tennis (b,g), walking (g), weight training (b); intramural: basketball (b,g), cheering (g), golf (b), martial arts (b,g), soccer (b,g), softball (b,g), swimming and diving (b,g), table tennis (b,g), tennis (b,g), walking (g); coed interscholastic: basketball, bowling, flag football, kickball, physical fitness, tennis; coed intramural: martial arts, soccer, softball, swimming and diving, table tennis, tennis, volleyball. 2 PE instructors, 2 coaches.

Computers Computers are regularly used in business applications, history, mathematics, science classes. Computer resources include campus e-mail, on-campus library services, CD-ROMs, online commercial services, Internet access, office computer access, DVD.

Contact Margaret Sheriff, Administrator. 305-940-3922. Fax: 305-940-1820. E-mail: allisonacademy@hotmail.com. Web site: allisonacademy.com.

ANNOUNCEMENT FROM THE SCHOOL Allison Academy continues its commitment to personalized education in which students' needs and strengths are addressed to guide the students in maximizing their academic, social, and physical development. Along with a highly structured academic program, students are offered an array of electives, including piano, art, photography, drama, tennis, basketball, and cheerleading.

ALL SAINTS' EPISCOPAL SCHOOL

2717 Confederate Avenue
Vicksburg, Mississippi 39180-5173
Head of School: Rev. William V. Martin

General Information Coeducational boarding and day college-preparatory, arts, religious studies, and bilingual studies school, affiliated with Episcopal Church. Grades 7–12. Founded: 1908. Setting: suburban. Nearest major city is Jackson. Students are housed in single-sex dormitories. 40-acre campus. 16 buildings on campus. Approved or accredited by National Association of Episcopal Schools, Southern Association of Colleges and Schools, Southern Association of Independent Schools, and The Association of Boarding Schools. Member of National Association of Independent Schools. Endowment: $3.3 million. Total enrollment: 125. Upper school average class size: 8. Upper school faculty-student ratio: 1:8.

Upper School Student Profile Grade 9: 24 students (14 boys, 10 girls); Grade 10: 19 students (4 boys, 15 girls); Grade 11: 29 students (14 boys, 15 girls); Grade 12: 22 students (7 boys, 15 girls). 75% of students are boarding students. 33% are state residents. 10 states are represented in upper school student body. 24% are international students. International students from Belarus, Canada, Jamaica, Republic of Korea, Taiwan, and Viet Nam; 1 other country represented in student body. 50% of students are members of Episcopal Church.

Faculty School total: 25. In upper school: 10 men, 15 women; 15 have advanced degrees; 4 reside on campus.

Subjects Offered Advanced math, algebra, American history, American literature, ancient history, art, biology, botany, calculus, chemistry, computer programming, computer science, creative writing, dance, earth science, English, English literature, environmental science, fine arts, French, geography, geometry, government/civics, grammar, health, history, keyboarding/computer, law studies, mathematics, music, photography, physical education, physical science, physics, poetry, pre-algebra, psychology, religion, science, sculpture, social studies, sociology, Spanish, theology, trigonometry, U.S. history, world history, world literature, writing.

Graduation Requirements Arts and fine arts (art, music, dance, drama), computer science, English, foreign language, mathematics, physical education (includes health), religion (includes Bible studies and theology), science, social studies (includes history).

Special Academic Programs Honors section; independent study; academic accommodation for the gifted, the musically talented, and the artistically talented; special instructional classes for students with learning disabilities, Attention Deficit Disorder, and mild dyslexia; ESL (17 students enrolled).

College Placement 23 students graduated in 2005; all went to college, including Case Western Reserve University; Loyola University New Orleans; Mississippi State University; University of Mississippi; University of Oregon; University of Southern Mississippi.

Student Life Upper grades have specified standards of dress, student council, honor system. Discipline rests primarily with faculty. Attendance at religious services is required.

Tuition and Aid Day student tuition: $6247; 7-day tuition and room/board: $24,072. Tuition installment plan (individually arranged payment plans). Need-based scholarship grants available. In 2005–06, 20% of upper-school students received aid.

Admissions Traditional secondary-level entrance grade is 9. Deadline for receipt of application materials: none. Application fee required: $25. On-campus interview required.

Athletics Interscholastic: basketball (boys), soccer (b), softball (b); intramural: aerobics/nautilus (b,g), archery (b,g), ball hockey (g), ballet (g), basketball (b,g), combined training (b,g), cooperative games (b,g), cricket (b,g), dance (g), fencing (b,g), field hockey (b,g), fitness (b,g), fitness walking (b,g), flag football (b,g), independent competitive sports (b,g), indoor soccer (b,g), modern dance (g), outdoor activities (b,g), outdoor adventure (b,g), outdoor education (b,g), outdoor recreation (b,g), outdoor skills (b,g), outdoors (b,g), physical fitness (b,g), pillo polo (b,g), project adventure (b,g), soccer (b,g), softball (b,g), strength & conditioning (b,g), tennis (b,g), track and field (b,g), ultimate Frisbee (b,g), volleyball (b,g), weight lifting (b,g), weight training (b,g); coed intramural: aerobics, aerobics/dance, aerobics/nautilus, aquatics, archery, back packing, badminton, bicycling, bocce, bowling, canoeing/kayaking, climbing, combined training, cooperative games, cricket, croquet, cross-country running, dance, equestrian sports, fencing, field hockey, fishing, fitness, fitness walking, flag football, floor hockey, Frisbee, golf, gymnastics, hiking/backpacking, horseback riding, horseshoes, independent competitive sports, indoor soccer, jogging, juggling, jump rope, kickball, life saving, marksmanship, martial arts, modern dance, outdoor activities, outdoor adventure, outdoor education, outdoor recreation, outdoor skills, outdoors, paddle tennis, paddling, physical fitness, physical training, pillo polo, pistol, power lifting, project adventure, rappelling, riflery, rock climbing, roller hockey, roller skating, ropes courses, running, self defense, skateboarding, softball, speedball, strength & conditioning, swimming and diving, table tennis, tennis, track and field, ultimate Frisbee, volleyball, walking, wall climbing, wallyball, weight lifting, weight training, whiffle ball, yoga. 5 PE instructors.

Computers Computers are regularly used in data processing, foreign language, keyboarding, media production, science, typing, word processing, writing classes. Computer resources include campus e-mail, on-campus library services, CD-ROMs, Internet access, CollegeView.

Contact Mrs. Carole W. Martin, Admissions Coordinator. 601-636-5266 Ext. 127. Fax: 601-636-8987. E-mail: admissions@allsaintsweb.com. Web site: www.allsaintsweb.com.

ALL SAINTS' EPISCOPAL SCHOOL OF FORT WORTH

9700 Saints Circle
Fort Worth, Texas 76108
Head of School: Thaddeus B. Bird

General Information Coeducational day college-preparatory, arts, and religious studies school, affiliated with Episcopal Church. Grades K–12. Founded: 1951. Setting: suburban. 103-acre campus. 4 buildings on campus. Approved or accredited by Independent Schools Association of the Southwest, National Association of Episcopal Schools, Southwest Association of Episcopal Schools, and Texas Department of Education. Member of National Association of Independent Schools. Endowment: $4.5 million. Total enrollment: 763. Upper school average class size: 12. Upper school faculty-student ratio: 1:9.

Upper School Student Profile Grade 9: 61 students (33 boys, 28 girls); Grade 10: 62 students (35 boys, 27 girls); Grade 11: 60 students (32 boys, 28 girls); Grade 12: 50 students (18 boys, 32 girls). 17% of students are members of Episcopal Church.

Faculty School total: 83. In upper school: 17 men, 11 women; 17 have advanced degrees.

Subjects Offered Algebra, anatomy and physiology, art, ballet, Bible studies, biology, biology-AP, calculus-AP, chemistry, computer science-AP, computers, drama, economics, English, English literature-AP, environmental science, French, geometry, Latin, marketing, physics, physics-AP, pre-calculus, Spanish, Spanish language-AP, speech, studio art-AP, trigonometry, U.S. government-AP, U.S. history, U.S. history-AP, Western civilization.

Graduation Requirements Arts and fine arts (art, music, dance, drama), computer science, English, foreign language, mathematics, religion (includes Bible studies and theology), science, social studies (includes history), speech. Community service is required.

Special Academic Programs Advanced Placement exam preparation in 9 subject areas; honors section.

College Placement 58 students graduated in 2005; all went to college, including Baylor University; Texas A&M University; Texas Christian University; University of Mississippi; University of Oklahoma. Mean SAT verbal: 557, mean SAT math: 569.

Student Life Upper grades have uniform requirement, student council, honor system. Discipline rests equally with students and faculty. Attendance at religious services is required.

Summer Programs Enrichment, sports, art/fine arts, rigorous outdoor training, computer instruction programs offered; session focuses on enrichment; held on campus; accepts boys and girls; open to students from other schools. 55 students usually enrolled. 2006 schedule: June to August.

Tuition and Aid Day student tuition: $10,720. Tuition installment plan (Insured Tuition Payment Plan, monthly payment plans). Merit scholarship grants, need-based scholarship grants available. In 2005–06, 36% of upper-school students received aid; total upper-school merit-scholarship money awarded: $26,000. Total amount of financial aid awarded in 2005–06: $300,000.

Admissions For fall 2005, 32 students applied for upper-level admission, 22 were accepted, 19 enrolled. CTBS/4, ERB or ISEE required. Deadline for receipt of application materials: none. Application fee required: $75. Interview required.

Athletics Interscholastic: ballet (boys, girls), baseball (b), basketball (b,g), cheering (g), combined training (b,g), cross-country running (b,g), dance team (g), field hockey (g), football (b), golf (b,g), rodeo (b,g), soccer (b,g), softball (g), swimming and diving (b,g), tennis (b,g), track and field (b,g), volleyball (g), winter soccer (b,g), wrestling (g); intramural: outdoor adventure (b,g), physical training (b,g), weight lifting (b,g), weight training (b,g); coed intramural: cooperative games, strength & conditioning. 5 PE instructors, 1 trainer.

Computers Computers are regularly used in college planning, data processing, drawing and design, foreign language, library, newspaper, science, yearbook classes. Computer network features include campus e-mail, on-campus library services, CD-ROMs, online commercial services, Internet access, office computer access, wireless campus network.

Contact Robyn Rutkowski, Admissions Assistant. 817-560-5746 Ext. 330. Fax: 817-560-5720. E-mail: robynrutkowski@aseschool.org. Web site: www.asesftw.org.

ALPINE ACADEMY
Salt Lake City, Utah
See Special Needs Schools section.

THE ALTAMONT SCHOOL
4801 Altamont Road
Birmingham, Alabama 35222
Head of School: Mr. Thomas M.S. Wheelock

petersons.com

General Information Coeducational day college-preparatory, arts, and technology school. Grades 5–12. Founded: 1975. Setting: urban. 28-acre campus. 4 buildings on campus. Approved or accredited by National Independent Private Schools Association, Southern Association of Colleges and Schools, Southern Association of Independent Schools, The College Board, and Alabama Department of Education. Member of National Association of Independent Schools. Endowment: $8 million. Total enrollment: 427. Upper school average class size: 16. Upper school faculty-student ratio: 1:5.

Upper School Student Profile Grade 9: 69 students (34 boys, 35 girls); Grade 10: 68 students (40 boys, 28 girls); Grade 11: 51 students (25 boys, 26 girls); Grade 12: 50 students (27 boys, 23 girls).

Faculty School total: 56. In upper school: 19 men, 24 women; 32 have advanced degrees.

Subjects Offered 20th century American writers, acting, advanced chemistry, advanced computer applications, algebra, American history, American literature, anatomy and physiology, art, art history, astronomy, biology, calculus, chemistry, computer keyboarding, computer programming, computer science, concert choir, creative drama, creative writing, earth science, ecology, economics and history, English, English literature, European history, film and new technologies, finite math, French, geography, geometry, government/civics, Greek, health, history, independent study, instruments, Internet research, jazz band, journalism, Latin, mathematics, music, orchestra, photography, physical education, physics, pre-calculus, science, social studies, Spanish, speech, speech and debate, statistics, theater, trigonometry, U.S. history, world literature, writing.

Graduation Requirements American history, computer applications, English, foreign language, history, mathematics, physical education (includes health), science, speech.

Special Academic Programs Advanced Placement exam preparation in 17 subject areas; honors section; independent study; study at local college for college credit; study abroad.

College Placement 50 students graduated in 2005; all went to college, including Vanderbilt University. Mean SAT verbal: 654, mean SAT math: 627, mean composite ACT: 27. 76% scored over 600 on SAT verbal, 65% scored over 600 on SAT math.

Student Life Upper grades have specified standards of dress, student council, honor system. Discipline rests equally with students and faculty.

Summer Programs Remediation, enrichment, advancement, sports, art/fine arts, rigorous outdoor training, computer instruction programs offered; session focuses on

academic credit and fun; held on campus; accepts boys and girls; open to students from other schools. 300 students usually enrolled. 2006 schedule: June 6 to July 17. Application deadline: none.

Tuition and Aid Day student tuition: $13,836. Tuition installment plan (Key Tuition Payment Plan). Merit scholarship grants, need-based scholarship grants, paying campus jobs available. In 2005–06, 25% of upper-school students received aid; total upper-school merit-scholarship money awarded: $75,250. Total amount of financial aid awarded in 2005–06: $521,000.

Admissions Traditional secondary-level entrance grade is 9. For fall 2005, 39 students applied for upper-level admission, 28 were accepted, 20 enrolled. ISEE required. Deadline for receipt of application materials: February 1. Application fee required: $50. On-campus interview required.

Athletics Interscholastic: baseball (boys), basketball (b,g), cross-country running (b,g), indoor track & field (b,g), physical training (b,g), running (b,g), soccer (b,g), softball (g), strength & conditioning (b,g), swimming and diving (b,g), tennis (b,g), track and field (b,g), volleyball (g), weight training (b), winter (indoor) track (b,g); coed interscholastic: golf, running; coed intramural: ultimate Frisbee. 4 PE instructors, 6 coaches, 1 trainer.

Computers Computers are regularly used in all academic, basic skills, multimedia classes. Computer network features include campus e-mail, on-campus library services, CD-ROMs, online commercial services, Internet access, DVD, wireless campus network, virtual library.

Contact Mr. James M. Wiygul, Director of Admissions. 205-879-2006. Fax: 205-871-5666. E-mail: jwiygul@altamontschool.org. Web site: www.altamontschool.org.

ANNOUNCEMENT FROM THE SCHOOL The Altamont School is a coeducational, traditional, college-preparatory school with a history of excellence. Altamont celebrates the spirit of learning, while providing an environment where diligence is expected and freedom is coupled with responsibility. The academic program not only prepares students for a high level of performance in the most rigorous college programs but also provides the intellectual tools required in the most demanding sectors of the adult world. The School also offers many opportunities for children to develop multiple talents by participating in arts, foreign language, community service, clubs, class projects, science competitions, and sports—all at the same time. One of the highlights of Altamont's college search program is the annual College Tour. Altamont is a small family: just over 400 students in grades 5–12 with socioeconomic, ethnic, and religious diversity. The faculty includes 62 teachers who are regionally and nationally recognized as outstanding educators. Sixty-five percent of them hold master's degrees or higher. Athletics are an important part of life at Altamont. Two out of every 3 students compete on one or more of the School's 25 teams. Altamont's main campus sits on Red Mountain, with 40 classrooms, 2 science wings, a Fine Arts Center, a Student Center, an art gallery and sculpture garden, a computer network and science labs, a 20,000-volume library, and special studios for chorus, art, photography, and orchestra. The main campus includes 6 tennis courts, a track, and a soccer field. Two gymnasiums provide 2 basketball courts, 3 volleyball courts, and a weight room. A second campus provides soccer, baseball, and softball fields.

AL-WOROOD SCHOOL
PO Box 46673
Abu Dhabi, United Arab Emirates
Head of School: Dr. Ahmed Osman Mohamed

General Information Coeducational day college-preparatory and general academic school, affiliated with Muslim faith. Grades K–12. Founded: 1982. Setting: urban. 2-hectare campus. 2 buildings on campus. Approved or accredited by CITA (Commission on International and Trans-Regional Accreditation) and Middle States Association of Colleges and Schools. Member of European Council of International Schools. Language of instruction: English. Total enrollment: 2,239. Upper school average class size: 20. Upper school faculty-student ratio: 1:17.

Upper School Student Profile Grade 10: 129 students (71 boys, 58 girls); Grade 11: 111 students (74 boys, 37 girls); Grade 12: 140 students (90 boys, 50 girls). 95% of students are Muslim.

Faculty School total: 131. In upper school: 25 men, 30 women; 10 have advanced degrees.

Graduation Requirements Biology, chemistry, English, language, mathematics, physics.

College Placement 93 students graduated in 2005; 90 went to college, including George Mason University; McMaster University; Michigan State University; Syracuse University; University of Illinois at Chicago; University of Maryland, College Park. Other: 3 had other specific plans. Mean SAT math: 515.

Student Life Upper grades have uniform requirement. Discipline rests primarily with faculty.

Tuition and Aid Day student tuition: 10,200 United Arab Emirates dirhams–22,600 United Arab Emirates dirhams. Tuition installment plan (payment at beginning of each semester plan).

Admissions Traditional secondary-level entrance grade is 10. School's own test required. Deadline for receipt of application materials: September. Application fee required: 250 United Arab Emirates dirhams.

Athletics Intramural: basketball (boys, girls), soccer (b), table tennis (b), tennis (b,g), volleyball (b). 2 PE instructors.

Computers Computers are regularly used in information technology classes. Computer resources include CD-ROMs, Internet access.

Contact Admissions Office. 971-2-444-8855. Fax: 971-2-444-9732. E-mail: alworood@emirates.net.ae. Web site: www.alworood.sch.ae.

AMBASSADOR PREPARATORY

St. Paul, Minnesota

See Junior Boarding Schools section.

AMERICAN ACADEMY

Plantation, Florida

See Special Needs Schools section.

AMERICAN COMMUNITY SCHOOLS OF ATHENS

129 Aghias Paraskevis Street
Halandri
Athens 152 34, Greece
Head of School: Dr. Stefanos Gialamas

General Information Coeducational day college-preparatory, arts, and technology school, affiliated with United Lutheran Church. Grades JK–12. Founded: 1945. Setting: suburban. 3-hectare campus. 4 buildings on campus. Approved or accredited by CITA (Commission on International and Trans-Regional Accreditation) and Middle States Association of Colleges and Schools. Language of instruction: English. Total enrollment: 635. Upper school average class size: 17. Upper school faculty-student ratio: 1:17.

Upper School Student Profile Grade 9: 44 students (22 boys, 22 girls); Grade 10: 85 students (44 boys, 41 girls); Grade 11: 89 students (52 boys, 37 girls); Grade 12: 62 students (31 boys, 31 girls).

Faculty School total: 82. In upper school: 16 men, 44 women; 46 have advanced degrees.

Subjects Offered Algebra, American history, American literature, analysis, Arabic, art, art history, band, biology, business skills, calculus, chemistry, computer programming, computer science, dance, drama, earth science, economics, English, English literature, environmental science, ESL, European history, expository writing, fine arts, French, geometry, German, government/civics, grammar, Greek, history, humanities, information technology, journalism, mathematics, music, peer counseling, photography, physical education, physical science, physics, psychology, science, social science, social studies, sociology, Spanish, speech, statistics, theater, theory of knowledge, trigonometry, writing.

Graduation Requirements Arts and fine arts (art, music, dance, drama), computer science, English, foreign language, mathematics, physical education (includes health), science, social science, social studies (includes history).

Special Academic Programs International Baccalaureate program; honors section; special instructional classes for students with mild special needs; ESL (17 students enrolled).

College Placement 70 students graduated in 2005; all went to college, including Barnard College; Brandeis University; Bryn Mawr College; New York University; University of Toronto; University of Virginia. Mean SAT verbal: 512, mean SAT math: 531. 14% scored over 600 on SAT verbal, 16% scored over 600 on SAT math.

Student Life Upper grades have specified standards of dress, student council. Discipline rests primarily with faculty.

Summer Programs Session focuses on recreational and international leadership; creative thinking through mathematical thinking; held both on and off campus; held at various museums and historical sites (for the leadership program); accepts boys and girls; open to students from other schools. 40 students usually enrolled. 2006 schedule: July 1 to July 30. Application deadline: April 15.

Tuition and Aid Day student tuition: €9900. Tuition installment plan (individually arranged payment plans, semester and quarterly payment plans). Tuition reduction for siblings, need-based scholarship grants available.

Admissions Traditional secondary-level entrance grade is 9. For fall 2005, 89 students applied for upper-level admission, 89 were accepted, 89 enrolled. English for Non-native Speakers or math and English placement tests required. Deadline for receipt of application materials: none. No application fee required. Interview required.

Athletics Interscholastic: basketball (boys, girls), cross-country running (b,g), soccer (b,g), softball (b,g), swimming and diving (b,g), tennis (b,g), track and field (b,g), volleyball (b,g), wrestling (b); coed interscholastic: gymnastics; coed intramural: martial arts. 2 PE instructors.

Computers Computers are regularly used in all academic classes. Computer network features include CD-ROMs, Internet access.

Contact John G. Papadakis, Director of Enrollment Management, Community and Public Affairs. 30-210-639-3200. Fax: 30-210-639-0051. E-mail: papadakisj@acs.gr. Web site: www.acs.gr.

AMERICAN COOPERATIVE SCHOOL

c/o American Embassy
La Paz, Bolivia
Head of School: David P. Cramer

General Information Coeducational day college-preparatory school. Grades PK–12. Founded: 1955. Setting: suburban. 3-hectare campus. 4 buildings on campus. Approved or accredited by Southern Association of Colleges and Schools and US Department of State. Languages of instruction: English and Spanish. Total enrollment: 429. Upper school average class size: 15. Upper school faculty-student ratio: 1:10.

Upper School Student Profile Grade 9: 26 students (15 boys, 11 girls); Grade 10: 41 students (21 boys, 20 girls); Grade 11: 26 students (16 boys, 10 girls); Grade 12: 31 students (17 boys, 14 girls).

Faculty School total: 46. In upper school: 10 men, 17 women; 20 have advanced degrees.

Subjects Offered Advanced Placement courses, algebra, American history, American literature, art, biology, calculus, chemistry-AP, earth science, English, English-AP, environmental science, European literature, French, geography, geometry, government/civics, Latin American history, mathematics, model United Nations, physical education, physical science, science, social studies, Spanish, world history.

Graduation Requirements English, foreign language, mathematics, physical education (includes health), science, social studies (includes history), Spanish.

Special Academic Programs Advanced Placement exam preparation in 9 subject areas; special instructional classes for students with mild learning disabilities; ESL (20 students enrolled).

College Placement 35 students graduated in 2005; 33 went to college, including Brandeis University; Clark University; University of Arkansas; University of Florida; University of Pennsylvania; University of South Carolina. Other: 2 went to work. Mean SAT verbal: 543, mean SAT math: 580.

Student Life Upper grades have student council, honor system. Discipline rests primarily with faculty.

Summer Programs Remediation, enrichment, advancement, ESL, computer instruction programs offered; session focuses on remediation and recreation; held on campus; accepts boys and girls; open to students from other schools. 40 students usually enrolled. 2006 schedule: May 29 to June 23. Application deadline: May 28.

Tuition and Aid Day student tuition: $9900. Tuition installment plan (monthly payment plans).

Admissions Traditional secondary-level entrance grade is 9. For fall 2005, 25 students applied for upper-level admission, 20 were accepted, 20 enrolled. ACT, Iowa Tests of Basic Skills, math and English placement tests, SAT, school's own exam or writing sample required. Deadline for receipt of application materials: none. Application fee required: $100. Interview required.

Athletics Interscholastic: basketball (boys, girls), cheering (g), soccer (b,g), track and field (b,g), volleyball (b,g); intramural: basketball (b,g), climbing (b,g), gymnastics (b,g), mountain biking (b,g), mountaineering (b,g), outdoor adventure (b,g), outdoor education (b,g), rock climbing (b,g), soccer (b,g), swimming and diving (b,g), tennis (b,g), volleyball (b,g), wall climbing (b,g); coed intramural: basketball, climbing, gymnastics, mountain biking, mountaineering, outdoor adventure, outdoor education, rock climbing, soccer, volleyball, wall climbing. 2 PE instructors.

Computers Computers are regularly used in English, journalism, multimedia, music, yearbook classes. Computer network features include campus e-mail, on-campus library services, CD-ROMs, online commercial services, Internet access, office computer access, DVD, wireless campus network.

Contact Dr. David P. Cramer, Superintendent. 591-2-2792302. Fax: 591-2-2797218. E-mail: acs@acslp.org. Web site: www.acslp.org.

AMERICAN HERITAGE SCHOOL

12200 West Broward Boulevard
Plantation, Florida 33325
Head of School: William R. Laurie

General Information Coeducational day college-preparatory, arts, pre-medical, and pre-law school. Grades PK–12. Founded: 1969. Setting: suburban. Nearest major city is Fort Lauderdale. 40-acre campus. 9 buildings on campus. Approved or accredited by Association of Independent Schools of Florida, CITA (Commission on International and Trans-Regional Accreditation), Southern Association of Colleges and Schools, and Florida Department of Education. Total enrollment: 1,949. Upper school average class size: 17. Upper school faculty-student ratio: 1:13.

Upper School Student Profile Grade 7: 147 students (68 boys, 79 girls); Grade 8: 180 students (92 boys, 88 girls); Grade 9: 209 students (114 boys, 95 girls); Grade 10: 221 students (115 boys, 106 girls); Grade 11: 184 students (100 boys, 84 girls); Grade 12: 186 students (94 boys, 92 girls).

Faculty School total: 176. In upper school: 31 men, 61 women; 54 have advanced degrees.

Subjects Offered Algebra, American government, American government-AP, American history, American history-AP, American legal systems, American literature, American literature-AP, anatomy, architectural drawing, art, band, biology, biology-AP, botany, calculus-AP, ceramics, chemistry, chemistry-AP, chorus, community service, computer graphics, computer science, costumes and make-up, creative writing, dance, drama, drawing, economics, economics-AP, English, English language and composition-AP, English literature, English literature and composition-AP, environmental science, environmental science-AP, ESL, fine arts, French, French-AP, geometry, graphic design, guitar, honors algebra, honors English, honors geometry, honors U.S. history, honors world history, journalism, law studies, mathematics, music appreciation, music theory-AP, oceanography, orchestra, painting, photography, physical education, physics, physics-AP, physiology-anatomy, portfolio art, pre-algebra, pre-calculus, probability and statistics, psychology, SAT/ACT preparation, science, sculpture, set design, Spanish, Spanish-AP, sports medicine, stagecraft, studio art, theater, vocal music, Web site design, weight training, word processing, world history, world literature, world religions, writing, yearbook.

Graduation Requirements Arts and fine arts (art, music, dance, drama), computer science, English, foreign language, mathematics, physical education (includes health), science, social studies (includes history). Community service is required.

Special Academic Programs Advanced Placement exam preparation in 7 subject areas; honors section; academic accommodation for the gifted, the musically talented, and the artistically talented; ESL (13 students enrolled).

College Placement 200 students graduated in 2005; all went to college, including Florida Atlantic University; Florida International University; Florida State University; University of Central Florida; University of Florida; University of Miami. Mean SAT verbal: 540, mean SAT math: 540, mean composite ACT: 23. 30% scored over 600 on SAT verbal, 30% scored over 600 on SAT math, 30% scored over 26 on composite ACT.

Student Life Upper grades have uniform requirement, student council. Discipline rests primarily with faculty.

Summer Programs Remediation, enrichment, advancement, ESL, art/fine arts, computer instruction programs offered; session focuses on academics; held on campus; accepts boys and girls; open to students from other schools. 448 students usually enrolled. 2006 schedule: May 30 to July 28. Application deadline: none.

Tuition and Aid Day student tuition: $12,050–$15,166. Tuition installment plan (monthly payment plans, semester payment plan, annual payment plan). Tuition reduction for siblings, merit scholarship grants, need-based scholarship grants, need-based loans available. In 2005–06, 22% of upper-school students received aid; total upper-school merit-scholarship money awarded: $1,334,780. Total amount of financial aid awarded in 2005–06: $2,613,762.

Admissions Traditional secondary-level entrance grade is 9. Slossen Intelligence and Stanford Achievement Test required. Deadline for receipt of application materials: none. Application fee required: $100. On-campus interview required.

Athletics Interscholastic: baseball (boys), basketball (b,g), cross-country running (b,g), diving (b,g), football (b), golf (b,g), soccer (b,g), softball (g), swimming and diving (b,g), tennis (b,g), track and field (b,g), volleyball (b,g), weight training (b,g), winter soccer (b,g), wrestling (b); coed interscholastic: cheering. 7 PE instructors, 4 coaches.

Computers Computers are regularly used in creative writing, graphic arts, journalism, literary magazine, newspaper, Web site design, word processing, yearbook classes. Computer network features include on-campus library services, CD-ROMs, online commercial services, Internet access, Questia.

Contact William R. Laurie, President. 954-472-0022 Ext. 3062. Fax: 954-472-3088. Web site: www.ahschool.com.

See full description on page 648.

THE AMERICAN INTERNATIONAL SCHOOL

Salmannsdorfer Strasse 47
Vienna A-1190, Austria
Head of School: Mr. Kevin Haverty

General Information Coeducational day college-preparatory school. Grades PK–12. Founded: 1959. Setting: suburban. 15-acre campus. 1 building on campus. Approved or accredited by Middle States Association of Colleges and Schools. Affiliate member of National Association of Independent Schools; member of European Council of International Schools. Language of instruction: English. Total enrollment: 729. Upper school average class size: 20. Upper school faculty-student ratio: 1:7.

Upper School Student Profile Grade 9: 63 students (29 boys, 34 girls); Grade 10: 64 students (31 boys, 33 girls); Grade 11: 50 students (28 boys, 22 girls); Grade 12: 58 students (30 boys, 28 girls).

Faculty School total: 107. In upper school: 20 men, 21 women; 28 have advanced degrees.

Subjects Offered Algebra, American history, American literature, art history, band, biology, calculus, ceramics, chemistry, computer science, computers, creative writing, drama, earth science, economics, economics-AP, English, English literature, environmental science, European history, fine arts, French, geography, geometry, German, grammar, health, history, journalism, mathematics, music, physical education,

physical science, physics, pre-calculus, programming, psychology, science, social science, social studies, Spanish, statistics, strings, studio art, theory of knowledge, visual arts, world history, yearbook.

Graduation Requirements Arts and fine arts (art, music, dance, drama), English, foreign language, mathematics, physical education (includes health), science, social studies (includes history).

Special Academic Programs International Baccalaureate program; Advanced Placement exam preparation in 9 subject areas; honors section; ESL (38 students enrolled).

College Placement 66 students graduated in 2005; 40 went to college, including Boston University; Columbus State University; The University of British Columbia; University of Pennsylvania. Other: 3 went to work, 1 entered military service, 2 entered a postgraduate year, 20 had other specific plans. Mean SAT verbal: 583, mean SAT math: 616.

Student Life Upper grades have student council, honor system. Discipline rests equally with students and faculty.

Tuition and Aid Day student tuition: €14,610–€14,900. Tuition installment plan (individually arranged payment plans). Need-based scholarship grants available.

Admissions Deadline for receipt of application materials: none. Application fee required: €150. On-campus interview recommended.

Athletics Interscholastic: baseball (boys), basketball (b,g), cross-country running (b,g), soccer (b,g), softball (g), swimming and diving (b,g), tennis (b,g), track and field (b,g), volleyball (b,g); intramural: ballet (g), weight lifting (b,g); coed interscholastic: aquatics; coed intramural: aerobics/dance, badminton, basketball, dance, golf, gymnastics, martial arts, soccer, softball. 7 PE instructors, 30 coaches.

Computers Computers are regularly used in English, ESL, French, mathematics, science, Spanish, yearbook classes. Computer network features include campus e-mail, on-campus library services, CD-ROMs, Internet access.

Contact Margit Maehrenhorst, Director of Admissions. 43-1-40132 Ext. 218. Fax: 43-1-40132-5. E-mail: m.maehrenhorst@ais.at. Web site: www.ais.at.

AMERICAN INTERNATIONAL SCHOOL IN CYPRUS

11 Kassos Street
Nicosia 1086, Cyprus
Head of School: Ron Joron

General Information Coeducational day college-preparatory, arts, and technology school. Grades K–12. Founded: 1987. 1 building on campus. Approved or accredited by Middle States Association of Colleges and Schools. Member of European Council of International Schools. Language of instruction: English. Total enrollment: 258. Upper school average class size: 15. Upper school faculty-student ratio: 1:12.

Upper School Student Profile Grade 9: 31 students (14 boys, 17 girls); Grade 10: 21 students (11 boys, 10 girls); Grade 11: 27 students (13 boys, 14 girls); Grade 12: 20 students (9 boys, 11 girls).

Faculty School total: 39. In upper school: 7 men, 12 women; 14 have advanced degrees.

Subjects Offered Algebra, American history, art, biology, business mathematics, calculus, chemistry, community service, drama, English, ESL, French, geometry, information technology, International Baccalaureate courses, journalism, mathematics, music, physical education, physical science, physics, pre-calculus, science, social studies, Spanish, Western civilization, yearbook.

Graduation Requirements Arts and fine arts (art, music, dance, drama), computer science, English, foreign language, mathematics, physical education (includes health), science, social studies (includes history). Community service is required.

Special Academic Programs International Baccalaureate program; programs in general development for dyslexic students; ESL (30 students enrolled).

College Placement 22 students graduated in 2005; 20 went to college, including California State University, Long Beach; North Central College; Stony Brook University, State University of New York; University of California, Berkeley. Other: 2 entered military service. 20% scored over 600 on SAT verbal, 40% scored over 600 on SAT math.

Student Life Upper grades have uniform requirement, student council, honor system. Discipline rests primarily with faculty.

Tuition and Aid Day student tuition: 5280 Cyprus pounds.

Admissions Traditional secondary-level entrance grade is 9. For fall 2005, 16 students applied for upper-level admission, 16 were accepted, 16 enrolled. ESL or school's own exam required. Deadline for receipt of application materials: none. Application fee required: 200 Cyprus pounds. Interview required.

Athletics Interscholastic: basketball (boys, girls), field hockey (b,g), gymnastics (b,g), running (b,g), soccer (b,g), swimming and diving (b,g), tennis (b,g), volleyball (b,g); coed intramural: archery, basketball, cross-country running, field hockey, flag football, jogging, softball, table tennis, tennis, weight training. 2 PE instructors, 2 coaches.

Computers Computers are regularly used in English, foreign language, mathematics, science, yearbook classes. Computer network features include campus e-mail, on-campus library services, CD-ROMs, Internet access.

Contact Helen Sphikas, Director's Secretary. 357-22316345. Fax: 357-22316549. E-mail: hsphikas@aisc.ac.cy. Web site: www.aisc.ac.cy/.

AMERICAN INTERNATIONAL SCHOOL OF BUCHAREST

Sos. Pipera-Tunari 196
Commune Voluntari-Pipera
Bucharest, Romania
Head of School: Arnold Bieber

General Information Coeducational day college-preparatory and International Baccalaureate school. Grades PK–12. Founded: 1962. Setting: suburban. 10-hectare campus. 4 buildings on campus. Approved or accredited by European Council of International Schools, International Baccalaureate Organization, and New England Association of Schools and Colleges. Language of instruction: English. Total enrollment: 550. Upper school average class size: 17. Upper school faculty-student ratio: 1:7.

Upper School Student Profile Grade 9: 43 students (20 boys, 23 girls); Grade 10: 42 students (20 boys, 22 girls); Grade 11: 38 students (18 boys, 20 girls); Grade 12: 31 students (13 boys, 18 girls).

Faculty School total: 70. In upper school: 13 men, 21 women; 10 have advanced degrees.

Subjects Offered Art, biology, chemistry, computer programming, computers, design, desktop publishing, drama, economics, English, ESL, filmmaking, French, global issues, history, integrated mathematics, language, literature, mathematics, music, physical education, Spanish, technology, theory of knowledge, world cultures.

Graduation Requirements Art, biology, chemistry, computer literacy, economics and history, English, foreign language, history, International Baccalaureate courses, life skills, math methods, physical education (includes health), 25 hours of community service each year of high school.

Special Academic Programs International Baccalaureate program; ESL (100 students enrolled).

College Placement 24 students graduated in 2005; 19 went to college, including Albright College; Brown University; Drexel University; Meredith College; University of Chicago; University of Notre Dame. Other: 2 entered military service, 3 had other specific plans. Mean SAT verbal: 580, mean SAT math: 600.

Student Life Upper grades have student council. Discipline rests primarily with faculty.

Tuition and Aid Day student tuition: $19,430. Tuition installment plan (individually arranged payment plans, 3-payment installment plan). Need-based scholarship grants available. In 2005–06, 4% of upper-school students received aid. Total amount of financial aid awarded in 2005–06: $200,000.

Admissions Traditional secondary-level entrance grade is 9. For fall 2005, 30 students applied for upper-level admission, 29 were accepted, 29 enrolled. English entrance exam, English proficiency, Macalaitus Test of English, Math Placement Exam, Secondary Level English Proficiency or writing sample required. Deadline for receipt of application materials: none. Application fee required: $1000. On-campus interview recommended.

Athletics Interscholastic: basketball (boys, girls), cross-country running (b,g), soccer (b,g), softball (b,g), swimming and diving (b,g), tennis (b,g), volleyball (b,g); intramural: basketball (b,g); coed intramural: outdoor adventure, outdoor education, physical fitness, sailing, soccer, softball. 2 PE instructors, 4 coaches, 1 trainer.

Computers Computers are regularly used in desktop publishing, graphics, information technology, programming, video film production, yearbook classes. Computer network features include campus e-mail, on-campus library services, CD-ROMs, online commercial services, Internet access, file transfer, office computer access.

Contact Catalina Pieptea, Admission Assistant. 40-1-204-4368. Fax: 40-1-204-4306. E-mail: admiss@aisb.ro. Web site: www.aisb.ro.

AMERICAN INTERNATIONAL SCHOOL-RIYADH

PO Box 990
Riyadh 11421, Saudi Arabia
Head of School: Dr. Til Fullerton

General Information Coeducational day college-preparatory, general academic, and technology school. Grades 1–12. Founded: 1963. Setting: suburban. 29-acre campus. 1 building on campus. Approved or accredited by European Council of International Schools and New England Association of Schools and Colleges. Language of instruction: English. Total enrollment: 714. Upper school average class size: 15. Upper school faculty-student ratio: 1:15.

Upper School Student Profile Grade 9: 69 students (37 boys, 32 girls); Grade 10: 72 students (30 boys, 42 girls); Grade 11: 86 students (46 boys, 40 girls); Grade 12: 56 students (29 boys, 27 girls).

Faculty School total: 69. In upper school: 12 men, 18 women; 20 have advanced degrees.

Subjects Offered Algebra, Arabic, art, biology, calculus, chemistry, college admission preparation, college counseling, computer literacy, concert band, drama, drawing, economics, electives, English, ESL, French, geometry, health, information technology, instrumental music, mathematics, multimedia, music, orchestra, painting, photography, physical education, physics, psychology, SAT preparation, science, social sciences, Spanish, technology, theater arts, theory of knowledge, U.S. history, visual and performing arts, world geography, world history.

Graduation Requirements Arts and fine arts (art, music, dance, drama), electives, English, foreign language, information technology, mathematics, performing arts, physical education (includes health), science, social studies (includes history).

Special Academic Programs International Baccalaureate program; ESL (43 students enrolled).

College Placement 68 students graduated in 2005; 40 went to college, including Boston University; Concordia University; McGill University; University of Illinois at Chicago. Other: 28 had other specific plans. Mean SAT verbal: 517, mean SAT math: 600. 16% scored over 600 on SAT verbal, 44% scored over 600 on SAT math.

Student Life Upper grades have specified standards of dress, student council, honor system. Discipline rests primarily with faculty.

Tuition and Aid Day student tuition: $13,537. Tuition installment plan (individually arranged payment plans).

Admissions Traditional secondary-level entrance grade is 11. Admissions testing required. Deadline for receipt of application materials: none. Application fee required: $1733. On-campus interview required.

Athletics Interscholastic: badminton (boys, girls), basketball (b,g), cricket (b), soccer (b,g), table tennis (b,g), tennis (b), volleyball (b,g); coed interscholastic: cross-country running, softball, track and field. 2 PE instructors.

Computers Computers are regularly used in economics, English, French, geography, history, keyboarding, lab/keyboard, mathematics, psychology, social studies, Spanish, technology, writing classes. Computer network features include campus e-mail, on-campus library services, CD-ROMs, Internet access, file transfer, office computer access, DVD, wireless campus network.

Contact Mrs. Hekam Aghabi, Registration Assistant. 966-1-491 4270 Ext. 270. Fax: 966-1-491 7101. E-mail: haghabi@ais-r.edu.sa. Web site: www.aisr.org.

AMERICAN INTERNATIONAL SCHOOL SALZBURG

Moosstrasse 106
A-5020 Salzburg, Austria
Head of School: Mr. Paul McLean

petersons.com

General Information Coeducational boarding and day college-preparatory school. Grades 7–PG. Founded: 1977. Setting: suburban. Nearest major city is Salzburg. Students are housed in single-sex dormitories. 15-acre campus. 5 buildings on campus. Approved or accredited by Middle States Association of Colleges and Schools, The Association of Boarding Schools, and The College Board. Member of European Council of International Schools. Language of instruction: English. Total enrollment: 71. Upper school average class size: 7. Upper school faculty-student ratio: 1:7.

Upper School Student Profile Grade 9: 13 students (8 boys, 5 girls); Grade 10: 13 students (7 boys, 6 girls); Grade 11: 14 students (7 boys, 7 girls); Grade 12: 20 students (8 boys, 12 girls); Postgraduate: 1 student (1 girl). 90% of students are boarding students. 95% are international students. International students from Bulgaria, Canada, Germany, Japan, and United States; 25 other countries represented in student body.

Faculty School total: 18. In upper school: 7 men, 9 women; 10 have advanced degrees; 5 reside on campus.

Subjects Offered Advanced math, aerobics, algebra, American history, American literature, art, art history, band, biology, calculus-AP, chemistry, chorus, computer applications, computer literacy, computer science, dance, drama, earth science, economics, English, English literature, English literature-AP, ESL, European history, fine arts, French, French language-AP, geometry, German, government and politics-AP, health, history, information technology, journalism, mathematics, model United Nations, modern European history, music, photography, physical education, physical science, physics, pre-algebra, SAT preparation, Spanish, Spanish language-AP, speech, statistics-AP, student government, studio art-AP, swimming, theory of knowledge, U.S. government and politics-AP, U.S. history, U.S. history-AP, visual and performing arts, vocal ensemble, world geography, world history, yearbook.

Graduation Requirements Arts, English, mathematics, music, physical education (includes health), science, social studies (includes history), two foreign languages each year (one of which must be German).

Special Academic Programs Advanced Placement exam preparation in 15 subject areas; honors section; independent study; academic accommodation for the gifted and the musically talented; ESL (8 students enrolled).

College Placement 19 students graduated in 2005; all went to college, including Boston University; Lewis & Clark College; Stanford University; University of California, San Diego; University of Mary Washington. 52% scored over 600 on SAT math.

Student Life Upper grades have specified standards of dress, student council, honor system. Discipline rests primarily with faculty.

Summer Programs Remediation, advancement, ESL programs offered; session focuses on language studies in English and German; held both on and off campus; held at diverse excursion and activity locations; accepts boys and girls; open to students from other schools. 350 students usually enrolled. 2006 schedule: July 2 to August 11. Application deadline: June.

Tuition and Aid Day student tuition: €11,000–€13,000; 5-day tuition and room/board: €18,000–€22,000; 7-day tuition and room/board: €19,000–€24,000. Tuition

reduction for siblings, need-based scholarship grants available. In 2005–06, 5% of upper-school students received aid. Total amount of financial aid awarded in 2005–06: €26,000.

Admissions Traditional secondary-level entrance grade is 9. For fall 2005, 49 students applied for upper-level admission, 35 were accepted, 25 enrolled. English proficiency or TOEFL or SLEP required. Deadline for receipt of application materials: none. Application fee required: €75. Interview recommended.

Athletics Interscholastic: aerobics/dance (girls), baseball (b), basketball (b,g), cross-country running (b,g), dance (b,g), golf (b,g), skiing (downhill) (b,g), soccer (b,g), softball (g), swimming and diving (b,g), tennis (b,g), track and field (b,g), volleyball (b,g); intramural: baseball (b), basketball (b,g), bicycling (b,g), cross-country running (b,g), diving (b,g), fitness walking (b,g), golf (b,g), horseback riding (b,g), independent competitive sports (b,g), indoor soccer (b,g), jogging (b,g), martial arts (b,g), mountaineering (b,g), outdoor recreation (b,g), rock climbing (b,g), sailing (b,g), skiing (cross-country) (b,g), skiing (downhill) (b,g), swimming and diving (b,g), track and field (b,g), volleyball (b,g), walking (b,g); coed interscholastic: track and field; coed intramural: alpine skiing, back packing, bicycling, bowling, climbing, diving, equestrian sports, fitness, golf, horseback riding, independent competitive sports, indoor soccer, jogging, martial arts, mountaineering, outdoor recreation, sailing, skiing (cross-country), skiing (downhill), soccer, swimming and diving, tennis, track and field, walking. 8 PE instructors, 6 coaches.

Computers Computers are regularly used in art, English, ESL, foreign language, information technology, mathematics, science, social science classes. Computer network features include campus e-mail, on-campus library services, CD-ROMs, online commercial services, Internet access, file transfer, DVD, wireless campus network.

Contact Ms. Felicia Gundringer, Office Manager. 43-662-824617 Ext. 12. Fax: 43-662-824555. E-mail: office@ais-salzburg.at. Web site: www.ais-salzburg.at.

See full description on page 650.

AMERICAN OVERSEAS SCHOOL OF ROME

Via Cassia 811
Rome 00189, Italy
Head of School: Dr. Larry W. Dougherty

General Information Coeducational boarding and day college-preparatory and International Baccalaureate school. Boarding grades 9–13, day grades PK–13. Founded: 1946. Setting: suburban. Students are housed in coed dormitories. 6-acre campus. 2 buildings on campus. Approved or accredited by Middle States Association of Colleges and Schools and The Association of Boarding Schools. Member of European Council of International Schools. Language of instruction: English. Total enrollment: 605. Upper school average class size: 18. Upper school faculty-student ratio: 1:18.

Upper School Student Profile Grade 9: 44 students (22 boys, 22 girls); Grade 10: 56 students (28 boys, 28 girls); Grade 11: 48 students (24 boys, 24 girls); Grade 12: 54 students (27 boys, 27 girls); Grade 13: 1 student (1 boy). 8% of students are boarding students. 69% are international students. International students from Canada, China, Israel, Malaysia, United Kingdom, and United States; 44 other countries represented in student body.

Faculty School total: 71. In upper school: 8 men, 15 women; 15 have advanced degrees.

Subjects Offered Advanced computer applications, advanced math, Advanced Placement courses, advanced studio art-AP, algebra, American history, American history-AP, American literature, ancient history, art, art history, art history-AP, band, biology, biology-AP, calculus, calculus-AP, chemistry, chemistry-AP, chorus, computer graphics, computer literacy, computer science, drama, English, English literature, English literature-AP, environmental science, ESL, European history, European history-AP, fine arts, French, French language-AP, French literature-AP, geometry, Italian, Latin, mathematics, model United Nations, music, music history, photojournalism, physical education, physics, physics-AP, psychology, psychology-AP, science, social studies, Spanish, theater, theory of knowledge, trigonometry, world history, writing.

Graduation Requirements Arts and fine arts (art, music, dance, drama), English, foreign language, mathematics, physical education (includes health), science, social studies (includes history).

Special Academic Programs International Baccalaureate program; Advanced Placement exam preparation in 10 subject areas; independent study; academic accommodation for the gifted; remedial reading and/or remedial writing; remedial math; programs in English, mathematics, general development for dyslexic students; ESL (85 students enrolled).

College Placement 51 students graduated in 2005; 47 went to college, including Bryn Mawr College; Duke University; McGill University; Stanford University; United States Military Academy; University of Pennsylvania. Other: 1 went to work, 2 entered military service, 1 had other specific plans. Mean SAT verbal: 550, mean SAT math: 540. 33% scored over 600 on SAT verbal, 20% scored over 600 on SAT math.

Student Life Upper grades have specified standards of dress, student council, honor system. Discipline rests primarily with faculty.

Tuition and Aid Day student tuition: €14,500–€16,700; 7-day tuition and room/board: €18,400. Tuition installment plan (individually arranged payment plans,

semester payment plan, 4-payment plan). Need-based scholarship grants available. In 2005–06, 5% of upper-school students received aid.

Admissions Deadline for receipt of application materials: none. No application fee required. Interview recommended.

Athletics Interscholastic: basketball (boys, girls), cheering (g), cross-country running (b,g), soccer (b,g), tennis (b,g), volleyball (b,g); coed interscholastic: wrestling; coed intramural: lacrosse. 2 PE instructors, 4 coaches.

Computers Computers are regularly used in English, history, mathematics, science classes. Computer network features include campus e-mail, on-campus library services, CD-ROMs, Internet access, DVD.

Contact Mr. Don Levine, Admissions. 39-06-334381. Fax: 39-06-3326-0397. E-mail: admissions@aosr.org. Web site: www.aosr.org.

THE AMERICAN SCHOOL FOUNDATION

Bondojito 215
Colonia Las Americas
Mexico City, D.F. 01120, Mexico
Head of School: Dennis Collins

General Information Coeducational day college-preparatory, arts, bilingual studies, and technology school. Grades PK–12. Founded: 1888. Setting: urban. 17-acre campus. 4 buildings on campus. Approved or accredited by International Baccalaureate Organization and Southern Association of Colleges and Schools. Affiliate member of National Association of Independent Schools. Languages of instruction: English and Spanish. Endowment: 36 million Mexican pesos. Total enrollment: 2,469. Upper school average class size: 17. Upper school faculty-student ratio: 1:10.

Upper School Student Profile Grade 9: 165 students (93 boys, 72 girls); Grade 10: 165 students (92 boys, 73 girls); Grade 11: 162 students (84 boys, 78 girls); Grade 12: 175 students (83 boys, 92 girls).

Faculty School total: 252. In upper school: 27 men, 39 women; 37 have advanced degrees.

Subjects Offered Advanced Placement courses, algebra, American history, American literature, anatomy, anthropology, art, art history, biology, business skills, calculus, ceramics, chemistry, community service, computer programming, computer science, drafting, drama, driver education, earth science, ecology, economics, English, English literature, European history, expository writing, film, fine arts, French, geography, geometry, government/civics, grammar, health, history, humanities, Italian, journalism, mathematics, mechanical drawing, Mexican history, music, personal development, philosophy, photography, physical education, physics, physiology, psychology, religion, science, social science, social studies, Spanish, speech, statistics, theater, trigonometry, typing, world history, world literature, writing, zoology.

Graduation Requirements Arts and fine arts (art, music, dance, drama), business skills (includes word processing), computer science, English, foreign language, foreign policy, mathematics, physical education (includes health), science, social science, social studies (includes history), four years of a non-English language. Community service is required.

Special Academic Programs International Baccalaureate program; Advanced Placement exam preparation in 19 subject areas; honors section; remedial reading and/or remedial writing; remedial math; programs in English, mathematics, general development for dyslexic students; special instructional classes for students with learning disabilities (through the Learning Skills Center), Attention Deficit Disorder, and dyslexia; ESL (20 students enrolled).

College Placement 156 students graduated in 2005; 129 went to college, including Boston University; Loyola University New Orleans; New York University; Suffolk University; The University of Texas at Austin; University of Pennsylvania. Other: 27 had other specific plans. Median SAT verbal: 564, median SAT math: 576, median composite ACT: 24. 27% scored over 600 on SAT verbal, 45% scored over 600 on SAT math, 2% scored over 26 on composite ACT.

Student Life Upper grades have specified standards of dress, student council. Discipline rests primarily with faculty.

Summer Programs Remediation, enrichment, advancement, ESL, art/fine arts, computer instruction programs offered; session focuses on remediation and enrichment; held on campus; accepts boys and girls; open to students from other schools. 781 students usually enrolled. 2006 schedule: June 12 to July 28. Application deadline: none.

Tuition and Aid Day student tuition: 10,000 Mexican pesos. Merit scholarship grants, need-based scholarship grants available. In 2005–06, 16% of upper-school students received aid. Total amount of financial aid awarded in 2005–06: 4,500,000 Mexican pesos.

Admissions Traditional secondary-level entrance grade is 10. For fall 2005, 135 students applied for upper-level admission, 80 were accepted, 79 enrolled. Gates MacGinite Reading Tests required. Deadline for receipt of application materials: none. Application fee required: 700 Mexican pesos. On-campus interview required.

Athletics Interscholastic: baseball (boys), basketball (b,g), cheering (g), football (b), soccer (b,g), softball (g), swimming and diving (b,g), volleyball (b,g); intramural: basketball (b,g), dance (g), football (b), soccer (b), softball (g); coed interscholastic: gymnastics, tennis, track and field; coed intramural: fencing, martial arts, swimming and diving, tennis, track and field, volleyball. 2 PE instructors, 24 coaches.

Computers Computers are regularly used in all academic classes. Computer network features include campus e-mail, on-campus library services, CD-ROMs, online commercial services, Internet access, wireless campus network.

Contact Julie Hellmund, Director of Admission. 52-555-227-4900. Fax: 52-555-272-3589. E-mail: admiss@asf.edu.mx. Web site: www.asf.edu.mx.

THE AMERICAN SCHOOL IN JAPAN

1-1, Nomizu 1-chome
Chofu-shi
Tokyo 182-0031, Japan
Head of School: Timothy S. Carr

General Information Coeducational day college-preparatory school. Grades N–12. Founded: 1902. Setting: suburban. 14-acre campus. 3 buildings on campus. Approved or accredited by Western Association of Schools and Colleges. Affiliate member of National Association of Independent Schools. Language of instruction: English. Endowment: ¥5 million. Total enrollment: 1,530. Upper school average class size: 20. Upper school faculty-student ratio: 1:10.

Upper School Student Profile Grade 9: 139 students (65 boys, 74 girls); Grade 10: 129 students (51 boys, 78 girls); Grade 11: 120 students (56 boys, 64 girls); Grade 12: 127 students (59 boys, 68 girls).

Faculty School total: 150. In upper school: 26 men, 26 women; 37 have advanced degrees.

Subjects Offered Accounting, algebra, American history, American literature, art, arts, Asian studies, biology, calculus, ceramics, chemistry, computer programming, computer science, creative writing, drama, economics, English, English literature, environmental science, European history, expository writing, fine arts, French, geography, geometry, government/civics, health, history, Japanese, jewelry making, journalism, logic, marine biology, mathematics, metalworking, music, photography, physical education, physics, psychology, science, social studies, sociology, Spanish, speech, stained glass, statistics-AP, theater, trigonometry, video film production, world history, world literature, writing.

Graduation Requirements Arts and fine arts (art, music, dance, drama), computer applications, English, foreign language, mathematics, physical education (includes health), science, social studies (includes history), one semester of Japanese studies.

Special Academic Programs Advanced Placement exam preparation in 19 subject areas; honors section; independent study.

College Placement 123 students graduated in 2005; 118 went to college, including Boston University; Brigham Young University; New York University. Other: 5 went to work. Mean SAT verbal: 577, mean SAT math: 630. 45% scored over 600 on SAT verbal, 62% scored over 600 on SAT math.

Student Life Upper grades have specified standards of dress, student council. Discipline rests primarily with faculty.

Summer Programs Enrichment, art/fine arts, computer instruction programs offered; session focuses on enrichment; held on campus; accepts boys and girls; open to students from other schools. 50 students usually enrolled. 2006 schedule: June 12 to June 30. Application deadline: April.

Tuition and Aid Day student tuition: ¥1,922,000. Tuition installment plan (individually arranged payment plans). Need-based scholarship grants available. In 2005–06, 3% of upper-school students received aid.

Admissions Traditional secondary-level entrance grade is 9. Any standardized test required. Deadline for receipt of application materials: none. Application fee required: ¥20,000. On-campus interview recommended.

Athletics Interscholastic: baseball (boys), basketball (b,g), cross-country running (b,g), field hockey (g), football (b), soccer (b,g), swimming and diving (b,g), tennis (b,g), track and field (b,g), volleyball (g), wrestling (b); coed interscholastic: cheering; coed intramural: golf, judo, martial arts. 4 PE instructors, 2 coaches, 1 trainer.

Computers Computers are regularly used in all academic classes. Computer network features include on-campus library services, CD-ROMs, online commercial services, Internet access, Blackboard.

Contact Laura Lyons, Director of Admissions. 81-422-34-5300 Ext. 721. Fax: 81-422-34-5339. E-mail: enroll@asij.ac.jp. Web site: www.asij.ac.jp.

THE AMERICAN SCHOOL IN LONDON

petersons.com

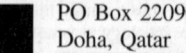

One Waverley Place
London NW8 0NP, United Kingdom
Head of School: William C. Mules

General Information Coeducational day college-preparatory school. Grades PK–12. Founded: 1951. Setting: urban. 3-acre campus. 1 building on campus. Approved or accredited by European Council of International Schools and Middle States Association of Colleges and Schools. Affiliate member of National Association of Independent Schools; member of Secondary School Admission Test Board. Language of instruction: English. Endowment: £500,000. Total enrollment: 1,309. Upper school average class size: 16. Upper school faculty-student ratio: 1:16.

Upper School Student Profile Grade 9: 122 students (54 boys, 68 girls); Grade 10: 116 students (60 boys, 56 girls); Grade 11: 108 students (46 boys, 62 girls); Grade 12: 116 students (59 boys, 57 girls).

Faculty School total: 163. In upper school: 26 men, 29 women; 44 have advanced degrees.

Subjects Offered Acting, African studies, algebra, American literature, anatomy and physiology, art, art history-AP, Asian literature, astronomy, athletics, biology, biology-AP, British literature, calculus, calculus-AP, chemistry, chemistry-AP, Chinese, Chinese studies, comparative cultures, computer animation, computer applications, concert band, concert choir, digital art, digital imaging, digital music, digital photography, drawing, ecology, economics, economics-AP, European history, European literature, film, French, French language-AP, French literature-AP, geometry, German, German-AP, guitar, health, human geography—AP, independent study, Japanese, jazz band, journalism, meteorology, Middle East, modern European history-AP, music theory-AP, mythology, orchestra, painting, photography, physical education, physics-AP, play production, poetry, pre-calculus, printmaking, psychology, Russian literature, Russian studies, Shakespeare, Spanish, Spanish language-AP, Spanish literature-AP, statistics-AP, studio art—AP, trigonometry, U.S. history, U.S. history-AP, video and animation, video film production, Web site design, Western civilization, woodworking, world geography, world literature, writing, yearbook.

Graduation Requirements Arts and fine arts (art, music, dance, drama), computer science, English, foreign language, mathematics, physical education (includes health), science, social studies (includes history).

Special Academic Programs Advanced Placement exam preparation in 19 subject areas; independent study; programs in general development for dyslexic students; ESL.

College Placement 94 students graduated in 2005; 91 went to college, including Dartmouth College; Georgetown University; New York University; Tufts University; University of Pennsylvania. Other: 3 had other specific plans. Mean SAT verbal: 628, mean SAT math: 630.

Student Life Upper grades have student council, honor system. Discipline rests primarily with faculty.

Tuition and Aid Day student tuition: £17,730. Tuition installment plan (monthly payment plans, individually arranged payment plans). Need-based scholarship grants available. In 2005–06, 5% of upper-school students received aid. Total amount of financial aid awarded in 2005–06: £410,000.

Admissions Any standardized test required. Deadline for receipt of application materials: none. Application fee required: £75. On-campus interview recommended.

Athletics Interscholastic: baseball (boys), basketball (b,g), cheering (g), crew (b,g), cross-country running (b,g), field hockey (g), golf (b,g), rugby (b), soccer (b,g), softball (g), swimming and diving (b,g), tennis (b,g), track and field (b,g), volleyball (b,g), wrestling (b); intramural: fencing (b,g).

Computers Computers are regularly used in animation, English, foreign language, journalism, mathematics, media arts, media production, science, social studies, video film production, yearbook classes. Computer network features include campus e-mail, on-campus library services, CD-ROMs, Internet access.

Contact Jodi Coats, Dean of Admissions. 44-20-7449-1221. Fax: 44-20-7449-1350. E-mail: admissions@asl.org. Web site: www.asl.org.

ANNOUNCEMENT FROM THE SCHOOL The American School in London provides an educational program designed to meet the individual needs of an academically motivated student body. The program emphasizes academic excellence, and intellectual growth is linked with social, moral, and physical development. The School takes full advantage of the unique offerings presented by its location in the United Kingdom, its proximity to continental Europe, and its international student body.

See full description on page 652.

AMERICAN SCHOOL OF DOHA

PO Box 22090
Doha, Qatar
Head of School: Mr. Ed Ladd

General Information Coeducational day college-preparatory, arts, and technology school. Grades K–12. Founded: 1988. Setting: suburban. 10-acre campus. 30 buildings on campus. Approved or accredited by New England Association of Schools and Colleges. Language of instruction: English. Total enrollment: 992. Upper school average class size: 20. Upper school faculty-student ratio: 1:20.

Upper School Student Profile Grade 9: 74 students (48 boys, 26 girls); Grade 10: 76 students (36 boys, 40 girls); Grade 11: 76 students (39 boys, 37 girls); Grade 12: 62 students (28 boys, 34 girls).

Faculty School total: 88. In upper school: 21 men, 27 women; 28 have advanced degrees.

Subjects Offered 20th century American writers, 20th century physics, 20th century world history, 3-dimensional art, 3-dimensional design, ACT preparation, acting, advanced chemistry, advanced math, Advanced Placement courses, African American history, algebra, American biography, American Civil War, American culture, American democracy, American government-AP, American history, American history-AP, American literature-AP, Arabic, art, basketball, biology-AP, calculus-AP, career/college preparation, chemistry-AP, choral music, college placement, computer

science, English, English language-AP, English literature-AP, European history-AP, French, history, mathematics, music, physical education, science, senior seminar, Spanish, speech, yearbook.
Graduation Requirements 1½ elective credits, 1968, 20th century American writers, 20th century history, 20th century physics, 20th century world history, 3-dimensional art, 3-dimensional design, accounting, arts and fine arts (art, music, dance, drama), computer science, electives, English, foreign language, mathematics, physical education (includes health), science, senior seminar, social studies (includes history), speech. Community service is required.
Special Academic Programs Advanced Placement exam preparation in 13 subject areas; honors section; independent study; ESL.
College Placement 53 students graduated in 2005; 51 went to college, including American University; Carnegie Mellon University; Franklin Pierce College; Rice University; Texas A&M University; The Johns Hopkins University. Other: 2 had other specific plans. 20% scored over 600 on SAT verbal, 30% scored over 600 on SAT math.
Student Life Upper grades have specified standards of dress, student council, honor system. Discipline rests primarily with faculty.
Tuition and Aid Day student tuition: 45,212 Qatari rials.
Admissions Traditional secondary-level entrance grade is 9. For fall 2005, 108 students applied for upper-level admission, 64 were accepted, 62 enrolled. Admissions testing, Cognitive Abilities Test, math and English placement tests, math, reading, and mental ability tests or writing sample required. Deadline for receipt of application materials: none. Application fee required: 500 Qatari rials. On-campus interview required.
Athletics Interscholastic: basketball (boys, girls), physical fitness (b,g), physical training (b,g), rock climbing (b,g), soccer (b,g), softball (b,g), strength & conditioning (b,g), swimming and diving (b,g), tennis (b,g), volleyball (b,g), wall climbing (b,g); intramural: basketball (b), swimming and diving (b,g); coed interscholastic: climbing, cross-country running, strength & conditioning, swimming and diving, track and field; coed intramural: physical training, swimming and diving. 5 PE instructors, 20 coaches.
Computers Computers are regularly used in all academic, yearbook classes. Computer network features include campus e-mail, on-campus library services, CD-ROMs, Internet access, file transfer, office computer access, DVD, wireless campus network, Entourage, Virtual School, Blackboard, NewsBank, Rubicon Atlas.
Contact Mrs. Sherin Hamza, Registrar. 974-4421377 Ext. 271. Fax: 974-4420885. E-mail: shamza@asd.edu.qa.

THE AMERICAN SCHOOL OF MADRID

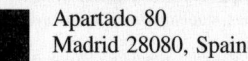
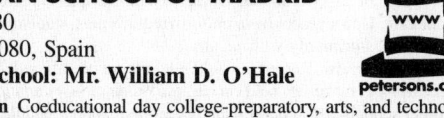

Apartado 80
Madrid 28080, Spain
Head of School: Mr. William D. O'Hale

petersons.com

General Information Coeducational day college-preparatory, arts, and technology school. Grades PK–12. Founded: 1961. Setting: suburban. 4-hectare campus. 5 buildings on campus. Approved or accredited by International Baccalaureate Organization and Middle States Association of Colleges and Schools. Affiliate member of National Association of Independent Schools; member of European Council of International Schools. Language of instruction: English. Total enrollment: 735. Upper school average class size: 20. Upper school faculty-student ratio: 1:10.
Upper School Student Profile Grade 9: 54 students (22 boys, 32 girls); Grade 10: 50 students (28 boys, 22 girls); Grade 11: 62 students (34 boys, 28 girls); Grade 12: 49 students (21 boys, 28 girls).
Faculty School total: 88. In upper school: 19 men, 14 women; 27 have advanced degrees.
Subjects Offered 3-dimensional art, algebra, American history, American literature, art, biology, calculus, chemistry, computer math, computer programming, computer science, earth science, economics, English, English literature, environmental science, European history, expository writing, French, geography, geometry, government/civics, health, history, journalism, mathematics, music, philosophy, physical education, physics, psychology, science, social studies, Spanish, speech, statistics, world history, world literature.
Graduation Requirements English, foreign language, information technology, mathematics, physical education (includes health), science, social studies (includes history).
Special Academic Programs International Baccalaureate program; independent study; ESL (50 students enrolled).
College Placement 56 students graduated in 2005; 55 went to college, including Boston University; Georgetown University; New York University; Purdue University; Saint Louis University; The Pennsylvania State University University Park Campus. Other: 1 entered military service. Mean SAT math: 580.
Student Life Upper grades have specified standards of dress, student council, honor system. Discipline rests equally with students and faculty.
Summer Programs ESL, sports, computer instruction programs offered; session focuses on ESL, soccer; held on campus; accepts boys and girls; open to students from other schools. 275 students usually enrolled. 2006 schedule: July 1 to July 31. Application deadline: June.
Tuition and Aid Day student tuition: €16,044. Tuition installment plan (monthly payment plans, individually arranged payment plans, semester payment plan). Tuition

reduction for siblings, need-based scholarship grants, scholarships for children of employees available. In 2005–06, 11% of upper-school students received aid.
Admissions Traditional secondary-level entrance grade is 11. Achievement/Aptitude/Writing, Comprehensive Test of Basic Skills, ERB, independent norms, Iowa Tests of Basic Skills, PSAT or TAP required. Deadline for receipt of application materials: none. Application fee required: €120. On-campus interview required.
Athletics Interscholastic: basketball (boys, girls), soccer (b), volleyball (g); coed interscholastic: gymnastics, tennis; coed intramural: weight lifting. 4 PE instructors, 3 coaches.
Computers Computers are regularly used in art, English, foreign language, journalism, library, mathematics, photography, science, technology, typing, yearbook classes. Computer network features include campus e-mail, on-campus library services, CD-ROMs, Internet access, DVD, wireless campus network.
Contact Ms. Sholeh Farpour Arab, Admissions Head. 34-91 740 19 00. Fax: 34-9-1-357-2678. E-mail: admissions@asmadrid.org. Web site: www.asmadrid.org.

ANNOUNCEMENT FROM THE SCHOOL Founded in 1961, this college-preparatory coeducational day school enrolls approximately 680 students from more than 50 nations in grade K1 (3 years old) through grade 12. Its primary objective is to provide a traditional US curriculum consistent with that of the best American schools. In addition, students may opt to complete the Spanish *Programa Oficial* and the International Baccalaureate (IB) diploma. Classes are taught in English; Spanish and French are offered as second and third languages. "Experience Spain" allows students from other schools in grades 10–12 to attend ASM for a semester or a year while living with host families. Headmaster: William O'Hale. Accredited by the Middle States Association.

AMERICAN SCHOOL OF MILAN

Villaggio Mirasole
Noverasco di Opera, Milan 20090, Italy
Head of School: Dr. Alan Austen

petersons.com

General Information Coeducational day college-preparatory, bilingual studies, and International Baccalaureate school. Grades N–13. Founded: 1962. Setting: suburban. Nearest major city is Milan. 8-acre campus. 2 buildings on campus. Approved or accredited by International Baccalaureate Organization, Middle States Association of Colleges and Schools, and US Department of State. Affiliate member of National Association of Independent Schools; member of European Council of International Schools. Language of instruction: English. Total enrollment: 498. Upper school average class size: 16. Upper school faculty-student ratio: 1:8.
Upper School Student Profile Grade 9: 41 students (23 boys, 18 girls); Grade 10: 36 students (18 boys, 18 girls); Grade 11: 44 students (21 boys, 23 girls); Grade 12: 35 students (17 boys, 18 girls).
Faculty School total: 59. In upper school: 10 men, 23 women; 28 have advanced degrees.
Subjects Offered Algebra, American history, American literature, art, biology, calculus, chemistry, community service, computer programming, computer science, creative writing, earth science, ecology, English, English literature, environmental science, ESL, European history, expository writing, fine arts, French, geology, geometry, government/civics, grammar, health, history, Italian, mathematics, music, photography, physical education, physics, psychology, science, social science, social studies, theory of knowledge, trigonometry, world history, world literature, writing.
Graduation Requirements Arts and fine arts (art, music, dance, drama), computer science, English, foreign language, mathematics, physical education (includes health), science, social science, social studies (includes history), 100 hours of CAS (Creativity, Action, Service) each year.
Special Academic Programs International Baccalaureate program; independent study; academic accommodation for the gifted, the musically talented, and the artistically talented; remedial reading and/or remedial writing; remedial math; ESL (20 students enrolled).
College Placement 24 went to college. Other: 1 had other specific plans. Median SAT verbal: 620, median SAT math: 650. 24% scored over 600 on SAT verbal, 47% scored over 600 on SAT math.
Student Life Upper grades have specified standards of dress, student council, honor system. Discipline rests equally with students and faculty.
Tuition and Aid Day student tuition: €11,690–€15,100. Tuition installment plan (individually arranged payment plans).
Admissions Traditional secondary-level entrance grade is 9. For fall 2005, 90 students applied for upper-level admission, 60 were accepted, 57 enrolled. English for Non-native Speakers required. Deadline for receipt of application materials: none. Application fee required: €52. On-campus interview recommended.
Athletics Interscholastic: basketball (boys, girls), cross-country running (b,g), soccer (b,g), tennis (b,g), track and field (b,g), volleyball (b,g); intramural: golf (b,g), gymnastics (b,g); coed intramural: aerobics/dance, ballet, basketball, martial arts, soccer, softball, swimming and diving, table tennis, tennis, volleyball. 3 PE instructors, 4 coaches.
Computers Computers are regularly used in college planning, desktop publishing, ESL, English, ESL, history, humanities, journalism, library, library skills, literary magazine, mathematics, media arts, research skills, science, technology, writing,

yearbook classes. Computer network features include campus e-mail, on-campus library services, CD-ROMs, online commercial services, Internet access, file transfer, office computer access, DVD, wireless campus network.
Contact Ms. Vivianne Trobec, Admissions Coordinator. 39-02-53000035. Fax: 39-02-57606274. E-mail: admissions@asmilan.org. Web site: www.asmilan.org.

ANNOUNCEMENT FROM THE SCHOOL The American School of Milan, established in 1962, is a nonprofit, independent college-preparatory school (N–12). One third of the student population is American, one third is Italian, and the remaining third is from 35 different countries. Located in purpose-built facilities on the outskirts of Milan, the School is accredited by the Middle States Association of Colleges and Schools (MSA) and is a member of The National Independent Schools Association (NAIS) and the European Council of International Schools (ECIS). The primary and intermediate schools feature multiage classes. The curriculum of the secondary school is based on the Middle Years Program and the Diploma Program of the International Baccalaureate, enhanced by a wireless laptop computer program for all students from grade 6. To promote learning, the School utilizes the advantages of its location in a modern European city with historical ties.

AMERICAN SCHOOL OF PARIS

41 rue Pasteur
BP 82
Saint Cloud 92210, France
Head of School: Pilar Cabeza de Vaca

General Information Coeducational day college-preparatory school. Grades PK–13. Founded: 1946. Setting: suburban. Nearest major city is Paris. 12-acre campus. 7 buildings on campus. Approved or accredited by European Council of International Schools and Middle States Association of Colleges and Schools. Affiliate member of National Association of Independent Schools; member of Secondary School Admission Test Board. Language of instruction: English. Total enrollment: 747. Upper school average class size: 15. Upper school faculty-student ratio: 1:7.
Upper School Student Profile Grade 9: 87 students (39 boys, 48 girls); Grade 10: 81 students (36 boys, 45 girls); Grade 11: 93 students (47 boys, 46 girls); Grade 12: 74 students (38 boys, 36 girls); Grade 13: 3 students (1 boy, 2 girls).
Faculty School total: 103. In upper school: 30 men, 23 women; 35 have advanced degrees.
Subjects Offered Algebra, American history, American literature, art, band, biology, calculus, ceramics, chemistry, choir, computer graphics, computer programming, computer science, drawing, economics, English, English literature, environmental science, European history, film and new technologies, filmmaking, French, geometry, global issues, global studies, graphic arts, health, humanities, information technology, music, music technology, painting, photography, physical education, physics, pre-calculus, psychology, science, sculpture, social studies, Spanish, theater, theory of knowledge, trigonometry, Web site design, world history, world literature, writing.
Graduation Requirements Arts and fine arts (art, music, dance, drama), computer science, English, foreign language, mathematics, performing arts, physical education (includes health), science, social studies (includes history).
Special Academic Programs International Baccalaureate program; Advanced Placement exam preparation in 10 subject areas; honors section; independent study; academic accommodation for the gifted, the musically talented, and the artistically talented; remedial reading and/or remedial writing; remedial math; programs in English, mathematics, general development for dyslexic students.
College Placement 84 students graduated in 2005; 83 went to college, including Boston University; Columbia College; Duke University; The Johns Hopkins University. Other: 1 had other specific plans. Mean SAT verbal: 591, mean SAT math: 609.
Student Life Upper grades have specified standards of dress, student council. Discipline rests primarily with faculty.
Summer Programs Enrichment, ESL, sports, art/fine arts, computer instruction programs offered; session focuses on teaching English and French as a second language; held on campus; accepts boys and girls; open to students from other schools. 900 students usually enrolled. 2006 schedule: July 4 to July 22. Application deadline: none.
Tuition and Aid Day student tuition: €19,320. Tuition installment plan (monthly payment plans, individually arranged payment plans). Need-based scholarship grants available. In 2005–06, 4% of upper-school students received aid. Total amount of financial aid awarded in 2005–06: €17,000.
Admissions Traditional secondary-level entrance grade is 9. For fall 2005, 180 students applied for upper-level admission, 162 were accepted, 101 enrolled. Deadline for receipt of application materials: none. Application fee required: €690. On-campus interview recommended.
Athletics Interscholastic: baseball (boys), basketball (b,g), cheering (b,g), cross-country running (b,g), soccer (b,g), softball (g), swimming and diving (b,g), tennis (b,g), track and field (b,g), volleyball (b,g); coed intramural: basketball, climbing, soccer, softball, track and field. 4 PE instructors, 5 coaches.

Computers Computers are regularly used in English, foreign language, graphic arts, information technology, mathematics, music, science classes. Computer network features include on-campus library services, CD-ROMs, Internet access.
Contact Mrs. Brenda Heussaff, Admissions Assistant. 331-41.12.82.45. Fax: 331-41.12.82.47. E-mail: admissions@asparis.fr. Web site: www.asparis.org.

THE AMERICAN SCHOOL OF PUERTO VALLARTA

Albatros # 129
PO Box 2-280
Marina Vallarta
Puerto Vallarta, Jalisco 48354, Mexico
Head of School: Mr. Gerald Selitzer

General Information Coeducational day college-preparatory and bilingual studies school. Grades N–12. Founded: 1986. Setting: small town. Nearest major city is Guadalajara. 7-acre campus. 2 buildings on campus. Approved or accredited by European Council of International Schools and Southern Association of Colleges and Schools. Languages of instruction: English and Spanish. Total enrollment: 367. Upper school average class size: 25. Upper school faculty-student ratio: 1:7.
Upper School Student Profile Grade 10: 23 students (11 boys, 12 girls); Grade 11: 25 students (10 boys, 15 girls); Grade 12: 21 students (14 boys, 7 girls). 10% are international students.
Faculty School total: 50. In upper school: 8 men, 10 women; 7 have advanced degrees.
Subjects Offered Advanced Placement courses, algebra, American literature, analytic geometry, biology, British literature, calculus, chemistry, chorus, computers, earth science, English, English literature, English literature and composition-AP, ESL, etymology, geography, geometry, law, life science, literature, literature and composition-AP, Mexican history, Mexican literature, physical science, physics, pre-algebra, pre-calculus, remedial study skills, Spanish, Spanish literature, Spanish literature-AP, trigonometry, U.S. history, U.S. history-AP, world history.
Graduation Requirements Art, biology, British literature, calculus, computer education, conceptual physics, English literature, geometry, health education, Mexican history, Mexican literature, physical education (includes health), Spanish, Spanish literature, U.S. history.
Special Academic Programs Advanced Placement exam preparation in 3 subject areas; independent study; remedial math; ESL (6 students enrolled).
College Placement 24 students graduated in 2005; 23 went to college, including Beloit College; Brown University; Clark University; Hampshire College; The University of British Columbia; University of Guelph. Other: 1 went to work.
Student Life Upper grades have uniform requirement, student council, honor system. Discipline rests primarily with faculty.
Summer Programs Remediation, ESL programs offered; session focuses on remediation and make-up; held on campus; accepts boys and girls; open to students from other schools. 10 students usually enrolled. 2006 schedule: July 8 to August 15. Application deadline: none.
Tuition and Aid Day student tuition: $4331–$7138. Tuition installment plan (monthly payment plans, individually arranged payment plans). Need-based scholarship grants available.
Admissions For fall 2005, 70 students applied for upper-level admission, 30 were accepted, 12 enrolled. Achievement tests, admissions testing, English language and math, reading, and mental ability tests required. Deadline for receipt of application materials: none. No application fee required. On-campus interview required.
Athletics Interscholastic: basketball (boys, girls), golf (b,g), soccer (b,g), tennis (b,g); coed intramural: dance team. 2 PE instructors, 4 coaches, 3 trainers.
Computers Computers are regularly used in keyboarding, lab/keyboard, language development, Spanish, technology, yearbook classes. Computer network features include campus e-mail, on-campus library services, CD-ROMs, Internet access, file transfer, office computer access.
Contact Mrs. Coty Pina, Admissions Coordinator Assistant. 52-322 221 1322. Fax: 52-322 221 2373. E-mail: camerica@aspv.edu.mx. Web site: aspv.edu.mx.

THE AMERICAN SCHOOL OF THE HAGUE

Rijksstraatweg 200
2241 BX Wassenaar, Netherlands
Head of School: Richard Spradling

General Information Coeducational day college-preparatory, arts, and technology school. Grades K–12. Founded: 1953. Setting: suburban. Nearest major city is The Hague. 11-acre campus. 1 building on campus. Approved or accredited by European Council of International Schools, International Baccalaureate Organization, Middle States Association of Colleges and Schools, and The College Board. Language of instruction: English. Total enrollment: 1,050. Upper school average class size: 16. Upper school faculty-student ratio: 1:7.
Upper School Student Profile Grade 9: 74 students (37 boys, 37 girls); Grade 10: 102 students (50 boys, 52 girls); Grade 11: 90 students (48 boys, 42 girls); Grade 12: 94 students (43 boys, 51 girls).

Faculty School total: 130. In upper school: 25 men, 25 women; 50 have advanced degrees.

Subjects Offered 3-dimensional design, advanced chemistry, advertising design, algebra, American literature, art history, art-AP, band, biology, biology-AP, calculus, calculus-AP, ceramics, chemistry, chemistry-AP, choir, comparative government and politics, computer applications, computer multimedia, computer music, computer science, computer-aided design, creative writing, dance, debate, dramatic arts, Dutch, earth science, economics, economics-AP, English, English literature, English-AP, environmental systems, ESL, European history, French, French-AP, geometry, German, German-AP, health and wellness, history of the Americas, honors geometry, information technology, instrumental music, International Baccalaureate courses, jazz band, math analysis, math methods, mathematics-AP, music composition, music theory-AP, music-AP, orchestra, peer counseling, photography, physical education, physics, physics-AP, psychology, public speaking, sociology, Spanish, Spanish-AP, speech and debate, stagecraft, student publications, studio art, theater arts, theater design and production, theory of knowledge, trigonometry, U.S. history, U.S. history-AP, world history, writing, yearbook.

Graduation Requirements Arts and fine arts (art, music, dance, drama), computer information systems, English, health and wellness, mathematics, modern languages, physical education (includes health), science, service learning/internship, social studies (includes history).

Special Academic Programs International Baccalaureate program; Advanced Placement exam preparation in 16 subject areas; honors section; academic accommodation for the gifted, the musically talented, and the artistically talented; ESL (28 students enrolled).

College Placement 90 students graduated in 2005; 84 went to college, including Boston College; Brown University; Cornell University; Duke University; Michigan State University; Northwestern University. Other: 1 entered military service, 1 entered a postgraduate year, 4 had other specific plans. Mean SAT verbal: 556, mean SAT math: 613. 31% scored over 600 on SAT verbal, 55% scored over 600 on SAT math.

Student Life Upper grades have specified standards of dress, student council, honor system. Discipline rests equally with students and faculty.

Tuition and Aid Day student tuition: €16,930. Tuition installment plan (individually arranged payment plans).

Admissions For fall 2005, 105 students applied for upper-level admission, 85 were accepted, 70 enrolled. Deadline for receipt of application materials: none. No application fee required. Interview required.

Athletics Interscholastic: baseball (boys), basketball (b,g), cross-country running (b,g), dance team (g), soccer (b,g), softball (g), track and field (b,g), volleyball (b,g); coed interscholastic: cheering, golf, swimming and diving, tennis. 2 PE instructors, 12 coaches.

Computers Computers are regularly used in all academic classes. Computer network features include campus e-mail, on-campus library services, CD-ROMs, online commercial services, Internet access, file transfer, office computer access, DVD, wireless campus network, Intranet.

Contact Laura Romains, Admissions Director. 31-70-512-1080. Fax: 31-70-512-1076. E-mail: admissions@ash.nl. Web site: www.ash.nl.

ANNOUNCEMENT FROM THE SCHOOL The American School of The Hague (ASH) serves the educational needs of the American and international corporate and diplomatic communities in the Netherlands. Students represent 55 countries; 50% are United States citizens. While ASH reflects the American educational philosophy, the diverse backgrounds of the students foster teaching and learning in the context of international understanding and global citizenship. ASH is a school with a rigorous academic program. The High School curriculum emphasizes preparation for university studies in both the US and around the world. Students may choose to earn a diploma in either the Advanced Placement Program or the International Baccalaureate Program in addition to their high school diploma. ASH students move with confidence to new schools throughout the world, and 94% of each graduating class enters university. The academic program includes a wide range of fine and applied arts courses, and information technology plays a role throughout the disciplines. A full athletic program and extracurricular activities are an important part of student life. The Hague International Model United Nations, a major event for many ASH High School students, is sponsored by the School each January for more than 3,000 international participants. The arts program offers individual and group instruction in vocal and instrumental music, and the ASH Jazz Band is well known throughout Europe. Athletic teams in 9 sports travel throughout Europe to compete with other international schools. The contemporary campus has spacious classrooms, specialized teaching areas, and computer and science labs in separate academic wings for the Elementary School, Middle School, and High School. Three libraries, holding a total of 50,000 volumes, and cafeterias link the academic wings to state-of-the-art facilities for music and theater, 3 gyms, and a double sport hall. The grounds include areas for all age groups, basketball courts, and soccer and baseball fields.

AMERICAN SCHOOL OF WARSAW

Bielawa
u. Warszawska 202
Konstancin-Jeziorna 05-520, Poland
Head of School: Dr. Charles P. Barder

General Information Coeducational day college-preparatory and general academic school. Grades PK–12. Founded: 1953. Setting: suburban. Nearest major city is Warsaw. 10-hectare campus. 1 building on campus. Approved or accredited by European Council of International Schools, New England Association of Schools and Colleges, and US Department of State. Language of instruction: English. Total enrollment: 837. Upper school average class size: 13. Upper school faculty-student ratio: 1:6.

Upper School Student Profile Grade 9: 60 students (30 boys, 30 girls); Grade 10: 55 students (23 boys, 32 girls); Grade 11: 54 students (27 boys, 27 girls); Grade 12: 55 students (24 boys, 31 girls).

Faculty School total: 108. In upper school: 16 men, 18 women.

Subjects Offered 20th century history, 20th century physics, 20th century world history, 3-dimensional art, 3-dimensional design, acting, addiction, adolescent issues, advanced chemistry, advanced computer applications, advanced math, aerobics, algebra, art, art appreciation, band, Basic programming, biochemistry, biology, calculus, ceramics, chemistry, child development, choir, choral music, chorus, clayworking, college admission preparation, college awareness, college counseling, college placement, college planning, comparative civilizations, comparative government and politics, comparative politics, composition, computer applications, computer information systems, computer literacy, computer multimedia, computer programming, computer resources, computer science, computer skills, conceptual physics, concert band, concert choir, contemporary history, contemporary math, CPR, current history, debate, digital photography, discrete math, drama, drama performance, drama workshop, dramatic arts, drawing, drawing and design, Dutch, economics, economics and history, electives, English, English as a foreign language, English composition, English literature, ESL, European history, European literature, foreign language, French, French studies, freshman seminar, geometry, German, German-AP, government, health, history, Holocaust, honors algebra, honors English, honors geometry, honors world history, instrumental music, integrated math, International Baccalaureate courses, lab science, language arts, leadership, linear algebra, model United Nations, modern European history, modern history, modern languages, music appreciation, musical productions, musical theater, non-Western literature, novel, nutrition, oil painting, peer counseling, photography, physical education, physics, play production, Polish, pre-algebra, pre-calculus, pre-college orientation, probability and statistics, psychology, sculpture, senior thesis, service learning/internship, Spanish, speech and debate, sports, strategies for success, student government, student publications, studio art, study skills, substance abuse, Swedish, swimming, tennis, theater, travel, trigonometry, United Nations and international issues, visual and performing arts, visual arts, wellness, wilderness/outdoor program, wind instruments, world history, world literature, world wide web design, writing, yearbook.

Graduation Requirements Arts and fine arts (art, music, dance, drama), electives, English, foreign language, mathematics, physical education (includes health), science, social studies (includes history).

Special Academic Programs International Baccalaureate program; ESL (13 students enrolled).

College Placement 57 students graduated in 2005; 49 went to college. Other: 1 went to work, 7 had other specific plans. Mean SAT verbal: 570, mean SAT math: 580, mean combined SAT: 1750. 38% scored over 600 on SAT verbal, 32% scored over 600 on SAT math.

Student Life Upper grades have student council. Discipline rests primarily with faculty.

Tuition and Aid Day student tuition: $19,802. Tuition installment plan (quarterly payments for self-paying families). Very limited, short-term financial aid for unusual financial situations available. In 2005–06, 1% of upper-school students received aid. Total amount of financial aid awarded in 2005–06: $14,000.

Admissions Traditional secondary-level entrance grade is 11. For fall 2005, 54 students applied for upper-level admission, 40 were accepted, 36 enrolled. Deadline for receipt of application materials: none. Application fee required: $750.

Athletics Interscholastic: basketball (boys, girls), cross-country running (b,g), soccer (b,g), softball (b,g), swimming and diving (b,g), tennis (b,g), volleyball (b,g); intramural: dance team (g), outdoor activities (b,g), outdoor adventure (b,g); coed intramural: hiking/backpacking. 2 PE instructors.

Computers Computers are regularly used in computer applications, science, social studies, Web site design classes. Computer network features include on-campus library services, CD-ROMs, online commercial services, Internet access, DVD, wireless campus network.

Contact Ms. Christiane Majgaard, Registrar. 48-22 702 8542. Fax: 48-22 702 8598. E-mail: admissions@asw.waw.pl. Web site: www.asw.waw.pl/.

ANACAPA SCHOOL

814 Santa Barbara Street
Santa Barbara, California 93101
Head of School: Mr. Gordon Sichi

General Information Coeducational day college-preparatory and arts school. Grades 7–12. Founded: 1981. Setting: urban. Nearest major city is Los Angeles. 2 buildings on campus. Approved or accredited by Western Association of Schools and Colleges and California Department of Education. Total enrollment: 61. Upper school average class size: 12. Upper school faculty-student ratio: 1:12.

Upper School Student Profile Grade 9: 7 students (3 boys, 4 girls); Grade 10: 14 students (8 boys, 6 girls); Grade 11: 9 students (4 boys, 5 girls); Grade 12: 6 students (3 boys, 3 girls).

Faculty School total: 10. In upper school: 5 men, 5 women; 4 have advanced degrees.

Special Academic Programs Advanced Placement exam preparation in 1 subject area.

College Placement 7 students graduated in 2005; all went to college, including Santa Barbara City College; Trinity College; University of California, San Diego; University of California, Santa Cruz.

Student Life Upper grades have specified standards of dress, student council, honor system. Discipline rests primarily with faculty.

Tuition and Aid Day student tuition: $17,400. Tuition installment plan (individually arranged payment plans). Need-based scholarship grants, paying campus jobs available. In 2005–06, 48% of upper-school students received aid.

Admissions Traditional secondary-level entrance grade is 9. Deadline for receipt of application materials: none. Application fee required: $100. On-campus interview required.

Athletics Coed Intramural: aquatics, back packing, basketball, hiking/backpacking, outdoor activities, sailing, soccer, surfing, table tennis, volleyball, walking, yoga.

Computers Computer resources include Internet access.

Contact Ms. Jenny Adams, Admission Associate. 805-965-0228. Fax: 805-899-2758. E-mail: jenny@anacapaschool.org. Web site: www.anacapaschool.org.

THE ANDREWS SCHOOL

38588 Mentor Avenue
Willoughby, Ohio 44094
Head of School: Dr. David N. Rath

petersons.com

General Information Girls' boarding and day college-preparatory and arts school. Grades 7–12. Founded: 1910. Setting: suburban. Nearest major city is Cleveland. Students are housed in single-sex dormitories. 300-acre campus. 16 buildings on campus. Approved or accredited by Independent Schools Association of the Central States, Ohio Association of Independent Schools, The Association of Boarding Schools, and Ohio Department of Education. Member of National Association of Independent Schools and Secondary School Admission Test Board. Endowment: $4 million. Total enrollment: 142. Upper school average class size: 10. Upper school faculty-student ratio: 1:5.

Upper School Student Profile Grade 9: 23 students (23 girls); Grade 10: 25 students (25 girls); Grade 11: 32 students (32 girls); Grade 12: 21 students (21 girls). 42% of students are boarding students. 70% are state residents. 7 states are represented in upper school student body. 19% are international students. International students from China, Japan, Mexico, and Republic of Korea.

Faculty School total: 26. In upper school: 8 men, 15 women; 14 have advanced degrees; 13 reside on campus.

Subjects Offered Algebra, American government, American literature, art, astronomy, biology, biology-AP, calculus, calculus-AP, ceramics, chemistry, chemistry-AP, choir, choral music, community service, computer art, computer programming, computer studies, computer-aided design, CPR, dance, drama, economics, English, English composition, English language-AP, English literature, English literature and composition-AP, environmental science, equine studies, ESL, ethics, film history, fine arts, first aid, French, French language-AP, geometry with art applications, government, grammar, health science, history, honors algebra, honors English, honors geometry, independent study, instrumental music, mathematics, music, painting, physical education, physics, portfolio art, pre-calculus, probability and statistics, science, social studies, Spanish, Spanish language-AP, speech, studio art, studio art-AP, textiles, theater, TOEFL preparation, U.S. history, U.S. history-AP, Web site design, women in literature, world history.

Graduation Requirements Algebra, arts and fine arts (art, music, dance, drama), biology, computer literacy, CPR, English, foreign language, geometry, mathematics, physical education (includes health), science, social studies (includes history), speech, acceptance into at least one U.S. college or university. Community service is required.

Special Academic Programs Advanced Placement exam preparation in 7 subject areas; honors section; independent study; study at local college for college credit; academic accommodation for the gifted and the artistically talented; ESL (16 students enrolled).

College Placement 23 students graduated in 2005; all went to college, including Boston University; Carnegie Mellon University; Emory University, Oxford College; Loyola University Chicago; University of Michigan; Vassar College. Mean SAT verbal: 518, mean SAT math: 533, mean composite ACT: 24.

Student Life Upper grades have uniform requirement, student council, honor system. Discipline rests primarily with faculty.

Summer Programs Sports, art/fine arts programs offered; session focuses on horseback riding, sports, fine and performing arts; held on campus; accepts boys and girls; open to students from other schools.

Tuition and Aid Day student tuition: $16,050; 5-day tuition and room/board: $22,000; 7-day tuition and room/board: $27,000. Tuition installment plan (monthly payment plans, individually arranged payment plans). Merit scholarship grants, need-based scholarship grants available. In 2005–06, 50% of upper-school students received aid; total upper-school merit-scholarship money awarded: $87,190. Total amount of financial aid awarded in 2005–06: $401,000.

Admissions Traditional secondary-level entrance grade is 9. ISEE, SSAT, TOEFL or SLEP or writing sample required. Deadline for receipt of application materials: none. Application fee required: $40. On-campus interview required.

Athletics Interscholastic: basketball, dressage, equestrian sports, horseback riding, lacrosse, soccer, softball, swimming and diving, tennis, volleyball; intramural: alpine skiing, badminton, dressage, equestrian sports, fitness, flag football, hiking/backpacking, horseback riding, modern dance, outdoor activities, outdoor recreation, physical fitness, skiing (downhill), snowboarding, table tennis. 2 PE instructors, 10 coaches, 1 trainer.

Computers Computers are regularly used in art, English, foreign language, graphic design, history, mathematics, music, science classes. Computer network features include campus e-mail, on-campus library services, CD-ROMs, online commercial services, Internet access.

Contact Mrs. Kristina L. Dooley, Director of Admission. 440-942-3600 Ext. 226. Fax: 440-954-5020. E-mail: doolek@andrews-school.org. Web site: www.andrews-school.org.

See full description on page 654.

ANGLO-AMERICAN SCHOOL OF MOSCOW

125367 Moscow, Beregovaya Ulitsa, #1
Moscow 125367, Russian Federation
Head of School: Mr. Drew Noble Alexander

General Information Coeducational day college-preparatory and International Baccalaureate school; primarily serves students with mild learning disabilities. Grades PK–12. Founded: 1949. Setting: urban. 6-hectare campus. 1 building on campus. Approved or accredited by European Council of International Schools, International Baccalaureate Organization, New England Association of Schools and Colleges, and US Department of State. Affiliate member of National Association of Independent Schools. Language of instruction: English. Total enrollment: 1,235. Upper school average class size: 16. Upper school faculty-student ratio: 1:6.

Upper School Student Profile Grade 9: 85 students (40 boys, 45 girls); Grade 10: 91 students (39 boys, 52 girls); Grade 11: 81 students (38 boys, 43 girls); Grade 12: 70 students (33 boys, 37 girls).

Faculty School total: 130. In upper school: 24 men, 22 women; 24 have advanced degrees.

Subjects Offered Art, biology, business, chemistry, choral music, computer keyboarding, computer technologies, concert band, drama, English, environmental systems, ESL, European history, fine arts, French, French as a second language, general science, integrated mathematics, International Baccalaureate courses, literature, mathematics, music, physical education, physical fitness, physics, psychology, Russian, Spanish, theory of knowledge, U.S. history.

Graduation Requirements Arts and fine arts (art, music, dance, drama), English, foreign language, mathematics, physical education (includes health), science, social studies (includes history), theory of knowledge. Community service is required.

Special Academic Programs International Baccalaureate program; ESL (25 students enrolled).

College Placement 55 students graduated in 2005; 54 went to college, including Suffolk University; The College of William and Mary. Other: 1 had other specific plans. Median SAT verbal: 550, median SAT math: 560.

Student Life Upper grades have specified standards of dress, student council. Discipline rests primarily with faculty.

Tuition and Aid Day student tuition: $22,000–$23,200.

Admissions Traditional secondary-level entrance grade is 10. For fall 2005, 136 students applied for upper-level admission, 99 were accepted, 84 enrolled. ESL required. Deadline for receipt of application materials: none. Application fee required: $400.

Athletics Interscholastic: baseball (boys), basketball (b,g), cross-country running (b,g), soccer (b,g), softball (b,g), swimming and diving (b,g), tennis (b,g), volleyball (b,g); intramural: broomball (b,g), ice hockey (b), soccer (b,g); coed intramural: aerobics/dance, badminton, ball hockey, basketball, dance, equestrian sports, fitness, flag football, floor hockey, Frisbee, gymnastics, ice skating, indoor soccer, kickball, martial arts, paddle tennis, physical training, skiing (cross-country), skiing (downhill), snowboarding, softball, strength & conditioning, swimming and diving, table tennis, team handball, ultimate Frisbee, volleyball, weight training. 4 PE instructors, 4 coaches.

Computers Computers are regularly used in art, basic skills, desktop publishing, desktop publishing, ESL, English, foreign language, French, history, humanities,

information technology, introduction to technology, keyboarding, lab/keyboard, language development, library science, library skills, literary magazine, mathematics, multimedia, music, newspaper, SAT preparation, science, social studies, technology, Web site design, word processing, writing, writing, yearbook classes. Computer network features include campus e-mail, on-campus library services, CD-ROMs, online commercial services, Internet access, file transfer, DVD.
Contact Ms. Nicolette Kirk, Admissions Officer. 7-095 231-4486. Fax: 7-095 231-4476. E-mail: admissions@aas.ru. Web site: www.aas.ru.

ANNIE WRIGHT SCHOOL
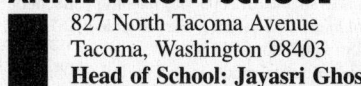 
827 North Tacoma Avenue
Tacoma, Washington 98403
Head of School: Jayasri Ghosh, PhD

General Information Girls' boarding and coeducational day college-preparatory, arts, technology, and mathematics, science and music school, affiliated with Episcopal Church. Boarding girls grades 9–12, day boys grades PS–8, day girls grades PS–12. Founded: 1884. Setting: suburban. Nearest major city is Seattle. Students are housed in single-sex dormitories. 10-acre campus. 2 buildings on campus. Approved or accredited by National Association of Episcopal Schools, National Independent Private Schools Association, Northwest Association of Schools and Colleges, Pacific Northwest Association of Independent Schools, The Association of Boarding Schools, and Washington Department of Education. Member of National Association of Independent Schools and Secondary School Admission Test Board. Endowment: $12 million. Total enrollment: 439. Upper school average class size: 11. Upper school faculty-student ratio: 1:7.
Upper School Student Profile Grade 9: 30 students (30 girls); Grade 10: 38 students (38 girls); Grade 11: 20 students (20 girls); Grade 12: 24 students (24 girls). 44% of students are boarding students. 64% are state residents. 8 states are represented in upper school student body. 31% are international students. International students from China, India, Lithuania, Republic of Korea, Rwanda, and Taiwan; 1 other country represented in student body.
Faculty School total: 65. In upper school: 10 men, 15 women; 15 have advanced degrees; 8 reside on campus.
Subjects Offered Algebra, American history, American literature, anatomy, art, art history, biology, calculus, ceramics, chemistry, computer programming, computer science, creative writing, dance, drama, earth science, economics, English, English literature, ESL, fine arts, French, geometry, government/civics, health, history, Japanese, mathematics, music, music history, physical education, physics, religion, science, social studies, Spanish, theater, world history, world literature.
Graduation Requirements Arts and fine arts (art, music, dance, drama), computer science, English, foreign language, mathematics, physical education (includes health), religion (includes Bible studies and theology), science, social studies (includes history), swim safety test.
Special Academic Programs Advanced Placement exam preparation in 8 subject areas; independent study; term-away projects; study abroad; ESL (27 students enrolled).
College Placement 26 students graduated in 2005; all went to college, including Bryn Mawr College; Columbia College; Haverford College; Seattle University; University of Michigan; University of Washington. Mean SAT verbal: 600, mean SAT math: 645.
Student Life Upper grades have uniform requirement, student council, honor system. Discipline rests equally with students and faculty.
Summer Programs Enrichment, sports, art/fine arts programs offered; session focuses on ; held on campus; accepts boys and girls; open to students from other schools. 2006 schedule: June to August.
Tuition and Aid Day student tuition: $16,438; 7-day tuition and room/board: $32,677. Tuition installment plan (monthly payment plans, individually arranged payment plans). Merit scholarship grants, need-based scholarship grants available. In 2005–06, 30% of upper-school students received aid; total upper-school merit-scholarship money awarded: $40,000. Total amount of financial aid awarded in 2005–06: $300,000.
Admissions Traditional secondary-level entrance grade is 9. SSAT required. Deadline for receipt of application materials: March 16. Application fee required: $30. On-campus interview required.
Athletics Interscholastic: baseball, basketball, crew, cross-country running, golf, soccer, tennis, volleyball. 5 PE instructors, 3 coaches.
Computers Computers are regularly used in all classes. Computer network features include campus e-mail, on-campus library services, CD-ROMs, online commercial services, Internet access, file transfer, office computer access, DVD, wireless campus network, Oracle Academy, Web design.
Contact Mr. Robert Booth, Director of Admission. 253-272-2216. Fax: 253-572-3616. E-mail: admission@aw.org. Web site: www.aw.org.

See full description on page 656.

APPLEBY COLLEGE
540 Lakeshore Road, West
Oakville, Ontario L6K 3P1, Canada
Head of School: Guy S. McLean

General Information Coeducational boarding and day college-preparatory, arts, technology, and service and athletics school, affiliated with Church of England (Anglican). Boarding grades 9–12, day grades 7–11. Founded: 1911. Setting: suburban. Nearest major city is Toronto, Canada. Students are housed in single-sex dormitories. 59-acre campus. 29 buildings on campus. Approved or accredited by Canadian Association of Independent Schools, Canadian Educational Standards Institute, Conference of Independent Schools of Ontario, Ontario Ministry of Education, and The Association of Boarding Schools. Affiliate member of National Association of Independent Schools; member of Secondary School Admission Test Board. Language of instruction: English. Endowment: CAN$5.5 million. Total enrollment: 683. Upper school average class size: 16. Upper school faculty-student ratio: 1:7.
Upper School Student Profile Grade 9: 128 students (66 boys, 62 girls); Grade 10: 133 students (77 boys, 56 girls); Grade 11: 148 students (80 boys, 68 girls); Grade 12: 138 students (70 boys, 68 girls). 44% of students are boarding students. 84% are province residents. 9 provinces are represented in upper school student body. 13% are international students. International students from Australia, Bahamas, Hong Kong, Republic of Korea, Saudi Arabia, and Spain; 21 other countries represented in student body.
Faculty School total: 94. In upper school: 41 men, 53 women; 44 have advanced degrees; 25 reside on campus.
Subjects Offered Algebra, art, biology, business skills, calculus, chemistry, computer programming, computer science, creative writing, drama, ecology, economics, English, English literature, environmental science, European history, fine arts, French, geography, German, history, Latin History, Mandarin, mathematics, modern dance, music, outdoor education, philosophy, physical education, physics, political science, religion, science, social science, social studies, Spanish, theater, world history.
Graduation Requirements Arts and fine arts (art, music, dance, drama), business skills (includes word processing), English, foreign language, mathematics, outdoor education, physical education (includes health), science, social science, social studies (includes history).
Special Academic Programs Advanced Placement exam preparation in 10 subject areas; honors section; term-away projects; domestic exchange program (with The Athenian School); study abroad; academic accommodation for the gifted, the musically talented, and the artistically talented; special instructional classes for blind students.
College Placement 118 students graduated in 2005; 116 went to college, including McGill University; McMaster University; Queen's University at Kingston; The University of Western Ontario; University of Guelph; University of Toronto. Other: 1 entered a postgraduate year, 1 had other specific plans.
Student Life Upper grades have uniform requirement, student council, honor system. Discipline rests equally with students and faculty. Attendance at religious services is required.
Summer Programs Enrichment, ESL, sports, art/fine arts programs offered; session focuses on arts, sports, technology, and outdoor experiences; held on campus; accepts boys and girls; open to students from other schools. 2100 students usually enrolled. 2006 schedule: July 3 to August 25. Application deadline: none.
Tuition and Aid Day student tuition: CAN$20,825–CAN$25,900; 5-day tuition and room/board: CAN$34,525–CAN$35,600; 7-day tuition and room/board: CAN$37,970–CAN$39,900. Tuition installment plan (monthly payment plans, quarterly payments, annual payment plan). Merit scholarship grants available. In 2005–06, 10% of upper-school students received aid; total upper-school merit-scholarship money awarded: CAN$13,500. Total amount of financial aid awarded in 2005–06: CAN$980,000.
Admissions Traditional secondary-level entrance grade is 9. SSAT and TOEFL or SLEP required. Deadline for receipt of application materials: none. Application fee required: CAN$100. Interview required.
Athletics Interscholastic: basketball (boys, girls), field hockey (g), football (b), ice hockey (b,g), rugby (b,g), soccer (b,g), softball (b,g), swimming and diving (b,g), tennis (b,g), volleyball (b,g); intramural: ball hockey (b); coed interscholastic: alpine skiing, aquatics, badminton, cross-country running, freestyle skiing, golf, skiing (downhill), squash, swimming and diving; coed intramural: aerobics, aerobics/nautilus, basketball, climbing, fitness, ice hockey, ice skating, indoor hockey, indoor soccer, martial arts, physical fitness, rock climbing, self defense, squash, swimming and diving, tennis, volleyball, wall climbing. 7 PE instructors, 12 coaches, 1 trainer.
Computers Computers are regularly used in all academic classes. Computer network features include campus e-mail, on-campus library services, CD-ROMs, Internet access, file transfer, office computer access, wireless campus network, media streaming, video conferencing, digital video camera rental, digital still camera rental, HelpDesk, Laptop Repair, Blog Server, Intranet, online course resources.
Contact Bibi Raghubar, Admissions Coordinator. 905-845-4681 Ext. 216. Fax: 905-845-9505. E-mail: braghubar@appleby.on.ca. Web site: www.appleby.on.ca.

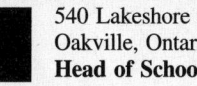

AQUIN CENTRAL CATHOLIC HIGH SCHOOL

1419 South Galena Avenue
Freeport, Illinois 61032-6098
Head of School: Mrs. M. Kathleen Runte

General Information Coeducational day college-preparatory, arts, vocational, religious studies, and technology school, affiliated with Roman Catholic Church. Grades 7–12. Founded: 1923. Setting: small town. Nearest major city is Rockford. 20-acre campus. 1 building on campus. Approved or accredited by North Central Association of Colleges and Schools and Illinois Department of Education. Endowment: $2.7 million. Total enrollment: 161. Upper school average class size: 16. Upper school faculty-student ratio: 1:10.

Upper School Student Profile Grade 9: 27 students (14 boys, 13 girls); Grade 10: 21 students (11 boys, 10 girls); Grade 11: 27 students (15 boys, 12 girls); Grade 12: 37 students (22 boys, 15 girls). 85% of students are Roman Catholic.

Faculty School total: 20. In upper school: 11 men, 7 women; 9 have advanced degrees.

Subjects Offered Algebra, American literature, art, band, biology, British literature, calculus, chemistry, choir, computer applications, computer keyboarding, driver education, economics, English, environmental science, geometry, government, health, humanities, physical education, physical science, physics, pre-calculus, religion, Spanish, speech, U.S. history, world history, yearbook.

Graduation Requirements Arts and fine arts (art, music, dance, drama), English, mathematics, physical education (includes health), religion (includes Bible studies and theology), science, social studies (includes history).

Special Academic Programs Advanced Placement exam preparation in 4 subject areas; study at local college for college credit.

College Placement 23 students graduated in 2005; all went to college, including Highland Community College; Illinois State University; Loras College; Northern Illinois University; University of Illinois at Urbana–Champaign; University of Wisconsin–Madison. Median composite ACT: 21. 9% scored over 26 on composite ACT.

Student Life Upper grades have specified standards of dress, student council. Discipline rests primarily with faculty. Attendance at religious services is required.

Summer Programs Remediation programs offered; session focuses on English, science, and math; held on campus; accepts boys and girls; not open to students from other schools. 5 students usually enrolled. 2006 schedule: June 12 to August 3. Application deadline: May 19.

Tuition and Aid Day student tuition: $3700. Tuition installment plan (monthly payment plans, individually arranged payment plans). Tuition reduction for siblings, need-based scholarship grants available. In 2005–06, 15% of upper-school students received aid. Total amount of financial aid awarded in 2005–06: $18,000.

Admissions Traditional secondary-level entrance grade is 9. For fall 2005, 10 students applied for upper-level admission, 10 were accepted, 10 enrolled. Deadline for receipt of application materials: none. No application fee required. Interview required.

Athletics Interscholastic: baseball (boys), basketball (b,g), football (b). 4 coaches, 1 trainer.

Computers Computers are regularly used in yearbook classes. Computer network features include on-campus library services, CD-ROMs, Internet access, office computer access.

Contact Mrs. M. Kathleen Runte, Superintendent/Principal. 815-235-3154 Ext. 224. Fax: 815-235-3185. E-mail: aquinhs@aeroinc.net.

ARCHBISHOP BLENK GIRLS HIGH SCHOOL

17 Gretna Boulevard
Gretna, Louisiana 70053-4989
Head of School: Mr. David Pooley

General Information Girls' day college-preparatory, arts, business, religious studies, and technology school, affiliated with Roman Catholic Church. Grades 8–12. Founded: 1962. Setting: small town. Nearest major city is New Orleans. 5-acre campus. 5 buildings on campus. Approved or accredited by National Catholic Education Association, Southern Association of Colleges and Schools, and Louisiana Department of Education. Total enrollment: 606. Upper school average class size: 20. Upper school faculty-student ratio: 1:15.

Upper School Student Profile Grade 8: 56 students (56 girls); Grade 9: 144 students (144 girls); Grade 10: 125 students (125 girls); Grade 11: 138 students (138 girls); Grade 12: 143 students (143 girls). 80% of students are Roman Catholic.

Faculty School total: 41. In upper school: 8 men, 33 women; 29 have advanced degrees.

Subjects Offered 20th century history, accounting, advanced math, algebra, American history, American history-AP, art, athletic training, biology, biology-AP, calculus-AP, Catholic belief and practice, chemistry, choir, choral music, civics, computer programming, discrete math, English language and composition-AP, English literature and composition-AP, environmental science, fine arts, French, geometry, honors algebra, honors English, honors geometry, honors U.S. history, honors world history, newspaper, physics, religion, Spanish, yearbook.

Graduation Requirements Algebra, American history, biology, chemistry, civics, computer applications, English, foreign language, geometry, history, physical education (includes health), religion (includes Bible studies and theology), world history.

Special Academic Programs Advanced Placement exam preparation in 4 subject areas; honors section; special instructional classes for deaf students, blind students.

College Placement 126 students graduated in 2005; 121 went to college, including Delgado Community College; Louisiana State University and Agricultural and Mechanical College; University of New Orleans. Other: 5 went to work. Mean composite ACT: 21.

Student Life Upper grades have uniform requirement, student council. Discipline rests primarily with faculty. Attendance at religious services is required.

Tuition and Aid Day student tuition: $4675. Tuition installment plan (monthly payment plans). Merit scholarship grants available. In 2005–06, 1% of upper-school students received aid; total upper-school merit-scholarship money awarded: $67,500. Total amount of financial aid awarded in 2005–06: $67,500.

Admissions Traditional secondary-level entrance grade is 9. For fall 2005, 232 students applied for upper-level admission, 222 were accepted, 206 enrolled. Scholastic Testing Service High School Placement Test required. Deadline for receipt of application materials: none. Application fee required: $20. On-campus interview required.

Athletics Interscholastic: basketball, bowling, cheering, cross-country running, dance team, drill team, golf, gymnastics, soccer, softball, swimming and diving, tennis, track and field, volleyball; intramural: bowling, flag football. 3 PE instructors, 9 coaches, 1 trainer.

Computers Computers are regularly used in accounting, business applications, graphic design, keyboarding, newspaper, science, social studies, Web site design, word processing, yearbook classes. Computer network features include CD-ROMs, Internet access.

Contact Ms. Shannon Manieri, Director of Admissions. 504-367-2626 Ext. 121. Fax: 504-367-7128. E-mail: smanieri@blenkhs.org. Web site: www.blenkhs.org.

ARCHBISHOP CURLEY HIGH SCHOOL

3701 Sinclair Lane
Baltimore, Maryland 21213
Head of School: Michael T. Martin

General Information Boys' day college-preparatory school, affiliated with Roman Catholic Church. Grades 9–12. Founded: 1961. Setting: urban. 33-acre campus. 2 buildings on campus. Approved or accredited by Middle States Association of Colleges and Schools and Maryland Department of Education. Endowment: $3.2 million. Total enrollment: 622. Upper school average class size: 20. Upper school faculty-student ratio: 1:13.

Upper School Student Profile Grade 9: 187 students (187 boys); Grade 10: 169 students (169 boys); Grade 11: 134 students (134 boys); Grade 12: 132 students (132 boys). 80% of students are Roman Catholic.

Faculty School total: 48. In upper school: 39 men, 9 women; 24 have advanced degrees.

Subjects Offered 20th century world history, 3-dimensional design, accounting, advanced chemistry, advanced computer applications, advanced math, algebra, American government, American government-AP, American history, American history-AP, American literature, analytic geometry, art, art appreciation, astronomy, band, Basic programming, biology, biology-AP, British literature, British literature (honors), business law, business mathematics, calculus, calculus-AP, campus ministry, Catholic belief and practice, chemistry, chemistry-AP, choral music, Christian and Hebrew scripture, Christian doctrine, Christian ethics, computer applications, computer keyboarding, computer studies, concert band, consumer law, consumer mathematics, earth science, English, English literature and composition-AP, environmental science, ethical decision making, European history, fine arts, French, freshman seminar, geography, geometry, government, government-AP, health, history of the Catholic Church, HTML design, instrumental music, jazz band, journalism, Life of Christ, music theory, photography, physical science, physics, physics-AP, pre-algebra, pre-calculus, probability and statistics, psychology, psychology-AP, reading/study skills, SAT/ACT preparation, Spanish, Spanish language-AP.

Graduation Requirements Algebra, American government, American history, art appreciation, biology, British literature, chemistry, church history, computer applications, computer keyboarding, English, foreign language, geometry, health, Life of Christ, physical fitness, physics, world history, world religions, 30 hours of community service with a written paper.

Special Academic Programs Advanced Placement exam preparation in 6 subject areas; honors section; independent study; study at local college for college credit; remedial reading and/or remedial writing; remedial math; programs in English, mathematics for dyslexic students.

College Placement 120 students graduated in 2005; they went to Loyola College in Maryland; Towson University; University of Maryland, Baltimore County; University of Maryland, College Park.

Student Life Upper grades have specified standards of dress, student council, honor system. Discipline rests primarily with faculty. Attendance at religious services is required.

Summer Programs Remediation, enrichment, advancement, sports, art/fine arts programs offered; held on campus; accepts boys and girls; open to students from other schools. 200 students usually enrolled. 2006 schedule: June 25 to August 2. Application deadline: June 20.

Tuition and Aid Day student tuition: $8150. Tuition installment plan (Academic Management Services Plan, monthly payment plans, individually arranged payment plans). Tuition reduction for siblings, merit scholarship grants, need-based scholarship grants, paying campus jobs available. In 2005–06, 36% of upper-school students received aid; total upper-school merit-scholarship money awarded: $62,000. Total amount of financial aid awarded in 2005–06: $180,000.

Admissions Traditional secondary-level entrance grade is 9. For fall 2005, 372 students applied for upper-level admission, 193 enrolled. High School Placement Test (closed version) from Scholastic Testing Service required. Deadline for receipt of application materials: January 6. Application fee required: $10. Interview required.

Athletics Interscholastic: baseball, basketball, cross-country running, football, golf, ice hockey, indoor track & field, lacrosse, soccer, swimming and diving, tennis, track and field, wrestling; intramural: basketball, bowling, golf, martial arts, tennis, touch football, volleyball, weight lifting, weight training, whiffle ball, wrestling. 2 PE instructors, 32 coaches, 1 trainer.

Computers Computers are regularly used in English, graphic arts, journalism, library, photography, SAT preparation, science, technology classes. Computer network features include campus e-mail, on-campus library services, CD-ROMs, Internet access, file transfer, office computer access.

Contact Mr. Matthew Sunday, Admissions Director. 410-485-5000 Ext. 289. Fax: 410-485-1090. E-mail: msunday@archbishopcurley.org. Web site: www.archbishopcurley.org.

ARCHBISHOP MITTY HIGH SCHOOL

5000 Mitty Avenue
San Jose, California 95129
Head of School: Mr. Tim Brosnan

General Information Coeducational day college-preparatory, arts, religious studies, and technology school, affiliated with Roman Catholic Church. Grades 9–12. Setting: suburban. 24-acre campus. 11 buildings on campus. Approved or accredited by California Department of Education. Languages of instruction: Spanish and French. Total enrollment: 1,503. Upper school average class size: 27. Upper school faculty-student ratio: 1:17.

Upper School Student Profile Grade 9: 427 students (202 boys, 225 girls); Grade 10: 373 students (173 boys, 200 girls); Grade 11: 350 students (160 boys, 190 girls); Grade 12: 353 students (171 boys, 182 girls). 75% of students are Roman Catholic.

Faculty School total: 86. In upper school: 47 men, 39 women; 47 have advanced degrees.

Subjects Offered 3-dimensional art, acting, American government-AP, American literature-AP, ancient world history, art, biology, biology-AP, British literature, calculus, calculus-AP, Catholic belief and practice, chemistry, chemistry-AP, choral music, chorus, church history, college placement, college writing, community service, computer graphics, computer multimedia, concert band, concert choir, drawing, economics and history, English, English language and composition-AP, English literature, English literature-AP, French, French language-AP, French literature-AP, French studies, French-AP, geometry, history-AP, honors algebra, honors English, honors geometry, honors U.S. history, honors world history, music, music appreciation, music theory-AP, philosophy, physics, physics-AP, political science, religion, social sciences, Spanish, Spanish language-AP, Spanish literature, Spanish literature-AP, student government, theater arts, U.S. government and politics, U.S. government and politics-AP, U.S. history, U.S. history-AP, U.S. literature, visual and performing arts, visual arts, world history.

Graduation Requirements Art, English, foreign language, mathematics, philosophy, physical education (includes health), religious studies, science, social sciences, 100 hours of Christian service.

Special Academic Programs Advanced Placement exam preparation in 20 subject areas; honors section; study at local college for college credit.

College Placement 356 students graduated in 2005; 351 went to college, including Georgetown University; Harvard University; Montserrat College of Art; New York University; Stanford University; University of Notre Dame. Other: 5 entered military service. Mean SAT verbal: 610, mean SAT math: 620.

Student Life Upper grades have specified standards of dress, student council, honor system. Discipline rests primarily with faculty. Attendance at religious services is required.

Summer Programs Remediation, enrichment, advancement, sports programs offered; session focuses on academics and athletics; held on campus; accepts boys and girls; open to students from other schools. 250 students usually enrolled. 2006 schedule: June 17 to July 25. Application deadline: May 31.

Tuition and Aid Day student tuition: $10,405. Tuition installment plan (FACTS Tuition Payment Plan). Need-based scholarship grants, paying campus jobs available. In 2005–06, 10% of upper-school students received aid. Total amount of financial aid awarded in 2005–06: $265,000.

Admissions Traditional secondary-level entrance grade is 9. For fall 2005, 1,300 students applied for upper-level admission, 427 were accepted, 427 enrolled. High

School Placement Test (closed version) from Scholastic Testing Service required. Deadline for receipt of application materials: February 8. Application fee required: $65.

Athletics Interscholastic: badminton (boys, girls), baseball (b), basketball (b,g), cross-country running (b,g), dance team (g), diving (b,g), field hockey (g), football (b), softball (g), swimming and diving (b,g), tennis (b,g), track and field (b,g), volleyball (b,g), water polo (b,g), weight training (b,g), winter soccer (b,g); coed interscholastic: golf, strength & conditioning, wrestling. 4 PE instructors, 90 coaches, 2 trainers.

Computers Computers are regularly used in design classes. Computer network features include campus e-mail, on-campus library services, CD-ROMs, Internet access, file transfer, office computer access.

Contact Ms. Latanya Johnson, Director of Admission. 408-342-4300. Web site: www.mitty.com/.

ARCHBISHOP QUIGLEY PREPARATORY HIGH SCHOOL

103 East Chestnut Street
Chicago, Illinois 60611-2093
Head of School: Rev. Peter Snieg

General Information Boys' day college-preparatory school, affiliated with Roman Catholic Church. Grades 9–12. Founded: 1905. Setting: urban. 1 building on campus. Approved or accredited by North Central Association of Colleges and Schools and Illinois Department of Education. Total enrollment: 215. Upper school average class size: 15. Upper school faculty-student ratio: 1:7.

Upper School Student Profile Grade 9: 59 students (59 boys); Grade 10: 56 students (56 boys); Grade 11: 43 students (43 boys); Grade 12: 62 students (62 boys). 100% of students are Roman Catholic.

Faculty School total: 37. In upper school: 23 men, 9 women; 23 have advanced degrees.

Graduation Requirements Four years of theology/religion.

Special Academic Programs Advanced Placement exam preparation in 12 subject areas; honors section; study at local college for college credit.

College Placement 43 students graduated in 2005; 42 went to college, including DePaul University; Loyola University Chicago; Saint Xavier University; University of Chicago; University of Illinois at Chicago; University of Illinois at Urbana–Champaign. Other: 1 entered military service.

Student Life Upper grades have specified standards of dress, student council, honor system. Discipline rests equally with students and faculty. Attendance at religious services is required.

Tuition and Aid Day student tuition: $6200. Tuition installment plan (SMART Tuition Payment Plan). Tuition reduction for siblings, merit scholarship grants, need-based scholarship grants, paying campus jobs available. In 2005–06, 60% of upper-school students received aid; total upper-school merit-scholarship money awarded: $75,000. Total amount of financial aid awarded in 2005–06: $220,000.

Admissions Traditional secondary-level entrance grade is 9. TerraNova required. Deadline for receipt of application materials: none. Application fee required: $25.

Athletics Interscholastic: baseball, basketball, cross-country running, golf, indoor track & field, soccer, track and field, volleyball, wrestling; intramural: baseball, basketball, fitness, football, indoor soccer, soccer, softball, street hockey, swimming and diving, table tennis, touch football, volleyball, weight training. 1 PE instructor.

Computers Computers are regularly used in all academic classes. Computer network features include on-campus library services, CD-ROMs, online commercial services, Internet access, file transfer, office computer access, DVD.

Contact Mr. Brian Condon, Director of Recruitment/Admissions. 312-787-9343. Fax: 312-787-9343. E-mail: bcondon@quigley.org. Web site: www.quigley.org.

ARCHBISHOP RIORDAN HIGH SCHOOL

175 Phelan Avenue
San Francisco, California 94112
Head of School: Mr. Gabriel A. Crotti

General Information Boys' day college-preparatory school, affiliated with Roman Catholic Church. Grades 9–12. Founded: 1949. Setting: urban. 10-acre campus. 4 buildings on campus. Approved or accredited by National Catholic Education Association, Western Association of Schools and Colleges, and California Department of Education. Endowment: $75,000. Total enrollment: 750. Upper school average class size: 26. Upper school faculty-student ratio: 1:14.

Upper School Student Profile 81% of students are Roman Catholic.

Faculty School total: 59. In upper school: 39 men, 20 women; 35 have advanced degrees.

Subjects Offered 20th century American writers, algebra, American history, American literature, anatomy, art, art appreciation, biology, broadcasting, business, calculus, chemistry, community service, computer science, creative writing, drama, earth science, economics, English, English literature, ethics, European history, expository writing, fine arts, geography, geometry, government/civics, grammar, health, history,

mathematics, music, physical education, physics, physiology, religion, science, social studies, Spanish, statistics, theater, theology, trigonometry, world history, world literature, writing.

Graduation Requirements Arts and fine arts (art, music, dance, drama), computer science, English, foreign language, mathematics, physical education (includes health), religion (includes Bible studies and theology), science, social science, social studies (includes history). Community service is required.

Special Academic Programs Advanced Placement exam preparation in 7 subject areas; honors section; study at local college for college credit; academic accommodation for the gifted; programs in English, mathematics, general development for dyslexic students; special instructional classes for blind students.

College Placement 166 students graduated in 2005; 164 went to college, including City College of San Francisco; San Francisco State University; San Jose State University; Santa Clara University; University of California, Berkeley. Other: 2 had other specific plans.

Student Life Upper grades have specified standards of dress, student council, honor system. Discipline rests primarily with faculty. Attendance at religious services is required.

Tuition and Aid Day student tuition: $10,400. Tuition installment plan (monthly payment plans). Merit scholarship grants, need-based scholarship grants available.

Admissions High School Placement Test required. Deadline for receipt of application materials: December 2. Application fee required: $65. On-campus interview required.

Athletics Interscholastic: baseball, basketball, cross-country running, football, golf, soccer, swimming and diving, tennis, track and field, wrestling; intramural: basketball, bicycling, bowling, field hockey, flag football, floor hockey, hiking/backpacking, indoor hockey, indoor soccer, martial arts, mountain biking, paddle tennis, skiing (downhill), snowboarding, soccer, table tennis, volleyball, weight lifting. 4 coaches, 1 trainer.

Computers Computers are regularly used in English, foreign language, humanities, mathematics, religion, science, social studies, writing fundamentals classes. Computer network features include campus e-mail, on-campus library services, CD-ROMs, online commercial services, Internet access, wireless campus network.

Contact Ms. Sandra Carrillo, Admission Secretary. 415-586-1256. Fax: 415-587-1310. E-mail: scarrillo@riordanhs.org. Web site: www.riordanhs.org.

THE ARCHER SCHOOL FOR GIRLS

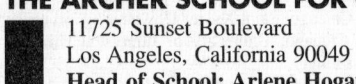

11725 Sunset Boulevard
Los Angeles, California 90049
Head of School: Arlene Hogan

General Information Girls' day college-preparatory school. Grades 6–12. Founded: 1995. Setting: suburban. 6-acre campus. 1 building on campus. Approved or accredited by California Association of Independent Schools, Western Association of Schools and Colleges, and California Department of Education. Total enrollment: 479. Upper school average class size: 16. Upper school faculty-student ratio: 1:7.

Upper School Student Profile Grade 9: 79 students (79 girls); Grade 10: 75 students (75 girls); Grade 11: 88 students (88 girls); Grade 12: 40 students (40 girls).

Faculty School total: 73. In upper school: 18 men, 55 women; 36 have advanced degrees.

Subjects Offered 20th century history, acting, advanced chemistry, advanced math, algebra, American literature, ancient history, archaeology, art, art appreciation, art history, biology, biology-AP, calculus, calculus-AP, career/college preparation, chemistry, chemistry-AP, classical studies, college counseling, computer applications, computer literacy, critical studies in film, digital imaging, drama, earth and space science, English, English composition, English language-AP, English literature, English literature-AP, environmental science-AP, film appreciation, fitness, French, French language-AP, geometry, history, honors U.S. history, human geography—AP, intro to computers, Japanese, Latin, law studies, literary magazine, marine biology, media literacy, modern world history, music, performing arts, photography, physics, pre-calculus, robotics, Roman civilization, self-defense, Spanish, Spanish language-AP, student government, student publications, theater, U.S. history, U.S. history-AP, wilderness experience, yearbook.

Graduation Requirements Arts and fine arts (art, music, dance, drama), English, foreign language, history, mathematics, performing arts, physical education (includes health), science, service learning/internship, annual participation in Arrow Week (experiential education program).

Special Academic Programs Advanced Placement exam preparation in 12 subject areas; honors section.

College Placement 47 students graduated in 2005; all went to college, including University of Southern California. Mean SAT math: 579.

Student Life Upper grades have uniform requirement, student council. Discipline rests primarily with faculty.

Summer Programs Art/fine arts programs offered; session focuses on arts and experiential education; held both on and off campus; held at various locales around the world; accepts girls; open to students from other schools. 100 students usually enrolled. 2006 schedule: June to July. Application deadline: April.

Tuition and Aid Day student tuition: $23,970. Tuition installment plan (FACTS Tuition Payment Plan). Need-based scholarship grants available. In 2005–06, 20% of upper-school students received aid. Total amount of financial aid awarded in 2005–06: $1,000,000.

Admissions Traditional secondary-level entrance grade is 9. For fall 2005, 55 students applied for upper-level admission, 25 were accepted, 12 enrolled. ISEE required. Deadline for receipt of application materials: January 27. Application fee required: $100. On-campus interview required.

Athletics Interscholastic: aerobics/dance, basketball, dance, equestrian sports, soccer, softball, tennis, track and field, volleyball; intramural: cooperative games, fitness, outdoor activities, physical fitness, tennis. 5 PE instructors, 5 coaches.

Computers Computers are regularly used in all academic classes. Computer network features include campus e-mail, on-campus library services, CD-ROMs, online commercial services, Internet access, wireless campus network.

Contact Ashley Burkart, Director of Admissions. 310-873-7037. Fax: 310-873-7052. E-mail: admissions@archer.org. Web site: www.archer.org/.

ARCHMERE ACADEMY

3600 Philadelphia Pike
Box 130
Claymont, Delaware 19703
Head of School: Rev. John C. Zagarella, OPRAEM

petersons.com

General Information Coeducational day college-preparatory, arts, religious studies, and technology school, affiliated with Roman Catholic Church. Grades 9–12. Founded: 1932. Setting: suburban. Nearest major city is Wilmington. 38-acre campus. 6 buildings on campus. Approved or accredited by Middle States Association of Colleges and Schools, National Catholic Education Association, and Delaware Department of Education. Member of National Association of Independent Schools. Endowment: $7.5 million. Total enrollment: 505. Upper school average class size: 15. Upper school faculty-student ratio: 1:10.

Upper School Student Profile Grade 9: 133 students (64 boys, 69 girls); Grade 10: 126 students (62 boys, 64 girls); Grade 11: 120 students (56 boys, 64 girls); Grade 12: 126 students (57 boys, 69 girls). 72% of students are Roman Catholic.

Faculty School total: 62. In upper school: 34 men, 28 women; 44 have advanced degrees.

Subjects Offered Algebra, American history, American literature, architecture, art, art history, Bible studies, biology, calculus, chemistry, computer programming, computer science, creative writing, drama, driver education, ecology, economics, English, English literature, environmental science, ethics, European history, expository writing, French, geometry, German, government/civics, grammar, health, history, mathematics, music, philosophy, physical education, physics, psychology, reading, religion, science, social studies, Spanish, speech, statistics, theater, theology, trigonometry, world history, writing.

Graduation Requirements Computer science, English, foreign language, mathematics, physical education (includes health), religion (includes Bible studies and theology), science, social studies (includes history), speech.

Special Academic Programs Advanced Placement exam preparation in 18 subject areas; honors section; independent study; study abroad; academic accommodation for the gifted, the musically talented, and the artistically talented; programs in English, mathematics for dyslexic students.

College Placement 115 students graduated in 2005; all went to college, including Georgetown University; Saint Joseph's University; The Pennsylvania State University University Park Campus; University of Delaware; University of Pennsylvania; University of Richmond. Median SAT verbal: 620, median SAT math: 615. 55% scored over 600 on SAT verbal, 60% scored over 600 on SAT math.

Student Life Upper grades have uniform requirement, student council, honor system. Discipline rests primarily with faculty. Attendance at religious services is required.

Tuition and Aid Day student tuition: $15,500. Tuition installment plan (10-Month Automatic Debit Plan). Merit scholarship grants, need-based scholarship grants, grants for children of faculty and staff, minority scholarships/grants available. In 2005–06, 46% of upper-school students received aid; total upper-school merit-scholarship money awarded: $117,000. Total amount of financial aid awarded in 2005–06: $991,000.

Admissions Traditional secondary-level entrance grade is 9. For fall 2005, 274 students applied for upper-level admission, 183 were accepted, 133 enrolled. School's own test required. Deadline for receipt of application materials: none. Application fee required: $35. On-campus interview required.

Athletics Interscholastic: baseball (boys), basketball (b,g), cheering (g), cross-country running (b,g), field hockey (g), football (b), golf (b,g), ice hockey (b), indoor track (b,g), lacrosse (b,g), soccer (b,g), softball (g), swimming and diving (b,g), tennis (b,g), track and field (b,g), volleyball (g), wrestling (b); coed interscholastic: winter (indoor) track; coed intramural: basketball, bowling. 1 PE instructor, 15 coaches, 2 trainers.

Computers Computers are regularly used in art, English, foreign language, history, mathematics, multimedia, science classes. Computer network features include campus e-mail, on-campus library services, CD-ROMs, online commercial services, Internet access, file transfer, wireless campus network.

Contact Dr. William J. Doyle, PhD, Academic Dean. 302-798-6632 Ext. 705. E-mail: wdoyle@archmereacademy.com. Web site: www.archmereacademy.com.

ANNOUNCEMENT FROM THE SCHOOL   In an environment that encourages effort and praises accomplishment in and out of the classroom, Archmere students are taught to think rationally, reason intuitively, and communicate clearly. With a philosophy founded on academic excellence but enhanced by a spirit of community and compassion, Archmere maintains a commitment to educating the entire student.

ARGO ACADEMY

PO Box 5477
Sarasota, Florida 34277
Head of School: James Stoll

General Information   Coeducational boarding college-preparatory, vocational, experiential education, marine science, nautical science, and community service school. Grade 12. Founded: 1999. Students are housed in an 88-foot schooner, Ocean Star, or 50-foot yachts. Approved or accredited by Florida Department of Education. Total enrollment: 24. Upper school faculty-student ratio: 1:4.

Upper School Student Profile   100% of students are boarding students. 16 states are represented in upper school student body. 10% are international students. International students from Canada.

Faculty   School total: 8. In upper school: 4 men, 3 women; 3 have advanced degrees; 7 reside on campus.

Subjects Offered   Boating, Caribbean history, communications, community service, CPR, first aid, independent study, leadership training, navigation, oceanography, personal development, scuba diving.

Special Academic Programs   Independent study; study at local college for college credit; study abroad.

College Placement   24 students graduated in 2005; all went to college.

Student Life   Upper grades have specified standards of dress, student council. Discipline rests primarily with faculty.

Tuition and Aid   7-day tuition and room/board: $15,000. Tuition reduction for siblings, Key Education Achiever Loans available.

Admissions   Traditional secondary-level entrance grade is 12. Deadline for receipt of application materials: none. Application fee required: $50. Interview required.

Athletics   Coed Intramural: hiking/backpacking, outdoor activities, outdoor adventure, outdoor education, outdoor recreation, outdoor skills, outdoors, sailing, scuba diving, windsurfing.

Computers   Computer resources include campus e-mail.

Contact   James Stoll, Director. 941-924-6789. Fax: 941-924-6075. E-mail: info@seamester.com. Web site: www.argoacademy.com.

ARLINGTON CHRISTIAN SCHOOL

4500 Ridge Road
Fairburn, Georgia 30213

ANNOUNCEMENT FROM THE SCHOOL   Arlington Christian School is a coeducational, college-preparatory day school. It enrolls 415 students in K5–12. The School is located on 40 acres in south suburban Fulton County. Accreditation: Southern Association of Colleges and Schools, Georgia Accrediting Commission. Membership: GISA. Admission decisions are based on grades, recommendations, standardized testing, and an interview. For more information, visit the School's Web page at http://www.arlingtonchristian.org.

ARMBRAE ACADEMY

1400 Oxford Street
Halifax, Nova Scotia B3H 3Y8, Canada

ANNOUNCEMENT FROM THE SCHOOL   At Armbrae, students and faculty members all know and respect each other. Armbrae Academy aims to provide a first-class university-preparatory programme while maintaining the small classes and personal atmosphere that bring students to the Academy and keep them there. In the past 5 years, 99% of Armbrae graduates have entered university.

ARMONA UNION ACADEMY

14435 Locust Street
PO Box 397
Armona, California 93202
Head of School: Mr. Roderick W. Kerbs

General Information   Coeducational day college-preparatory, general academic, and religious studies school, affiliated with Seventh-day Adventists. Grades K–12. Founded: 1904. Setting: small town. Nearest major city is Fresno. 20-acre campus. 5 buildings on campus. Approved or accredited by Western Association of Schools and Colleges and California Department of Education. Member of Secondary School Admission Test Board. Endowment: $93,000. Total enrollment: 118. Upper school average class size: 11. Upper school faculty-student ratio: 1:10.

Upper School Student Profile   Grade 9: 15 students (8 boys, 7 girls); Grade 10: 12 students (3 boys, 9 girls); Grade 11: 8 students (1 boy, 7 girls); Grade 12: 6 students (1 boy, 5 girls). 90% of students are Seventh-day Adventists.

Faculty   School total: 13. In upper school: 5 men; 2 have advanced degrees.

Subjects Offered   Algebra, American history, American literature, art, Bible studies, biology, business, chemistry, choir, communications, community service, computer science, drama, economics, English, English literature, fine arts, geometry, government, home economics, mathematics, photography, physical education, physical science, physics, religion, science, social science, Spanish, world history, world literature, yearbook.

Graduation Requirements   Arts and fine arts (art, music, dance, drama), business skills (includes word processing), computer science, English, foreign language, mathematics, physical education (includes health), religion (includes Bible studies and theology), science, social science, social studies (includes history). Community service is required.

College Placement   9 students graduated in 2005; 8 went to college, including La Sierra University; Pacific Union College. Other: 1 went to work.

Student Life   Upper grades have specified standards of dress, student council. Discipline rests primarily with faculty.

Tuition and Aid   Day student tuition: $5140. Guaranteed tuition plan. Tuition installment plan (monthly payment plans, individually arranged payment plans). Tuition reduction for siblings, need-based scholarship grants available. In 2005–06, 60% of upper-school students received aid. Total amount of financial aid awarded in 2005–06: $50,000.

Admissions   Traditional secondary-level entrance grade is 9. For fall 2005, 12 students applied for upper-level admission, 10 were accepted, 10 enrolled. Deadline for receipt of application materials: August 20. Application fee required: $75. Interview required.

Athletics   Interscholastic: basketball (boys, girls), flag football (b,g), football (b,g), volleyball (b,g); intramural: basketball (b,g), flag football (b,g); coed interscholastic: baseball, outdoor education, soccer, softball, track and field; coed intramural: baseball, outdoor education, paddle tennis, soccer, softball, table tennis, track and field, volleyball. 1 PE instructor, 1 coach.

Computers   Computers are regularly used in English, history, mathematics, science classes. Computer resources include on-campus library services, CD-ROMs, online commercial services, Internet access.

Contact   Mrs. Aniesha Kleinhammer, School Secretary. 559-582-4468. Fax: 559-582-6609. E-mail: auasecretary@yahoo.com. Web site: www.auaweb.com.

ARMY AND NAVY ACADEMY

2605 Carlsbad Boulevard
PO Box 3000
Carlsbad, California 92018-3000
Head of School: Brig. Gen. Stephen M. Bliss, Retd.

General Information   Boys' boarding and day college-preparatory and Junior ROTC school. Grades 7–12. Founded: 1910. Setting: small town. Nearest major city is San Diego. Students are housed in single-sex dormitories. 16-acre campus. 34 buildings on campus. Approved or accredited by California Association of Independent Schools, The Association of Boarding Schools, and Western Association of Schools and Colleges. Member of National Association of Independent Schools and Secondary School Admission Test Board. Endowment: $276,523. Total enrollment: 325. Upper school average class size: 17. Upper school faculty-student ratio: 1:9.

Upper School Student Profile   Grade 9: 68 students (68 boys); Grade 10: 84 students (84 boys); Grade 11: 92 students (92 boys); Grade 12: 41 students (41 boys). 93% of students are boarding students. 79% are state residents. 14 states are represented in upper school student body. 10% are international students. International students from China, Mexico, Republic of Korea, Russian Federation, and Taiwan; 4 other countries represented in student body.

Faculty   School total: 38. In upper school: 18 men, 14 women; 17 have advanced degrees; 5 reside on campus.

Subjects Offered   Advanced computer applications, algebra, art, art history, biology, biology-AP, calculus-AP, chemistry, chemistry-AP, civics, computers, contemporary issues, drama, economics, English, English-AP, environmental science, ESL, European history-AP, French, French-AP, geography, geometry, honors algebra, honors

English, honors geometry, intro to computers, journalism, marching band, music appreciation, music technology, photography, physical education, physics, physics-AP, pre-calculus, psychology, psychology-AP, SAT preparation, science, Spanish, Spanish-AP, studio art-AP, U.S. history, U.S. history-AP, world history, yearbook.

Graduation Requirements Arts and fine arts (art, music, dance, drama), English, foreign language, leadership education training, mathematics, physical education (includes health), science, social studies (includes history).

Special Academic Programs Advanced Placement exam preparation in 10 subject areas; honors section; remedial reading and/or remedial writing; special instructional classes for students with Attention Deficit Disorder and learning disabilities; ESL (12 students enrolled).

College Placement 54 students graduated in 2005; 50 went to college, including California State University, San Marcos; San Francisco State University; University of California, Irvine; University of California, Los Angeles; University of the Pacific. Other: 2 went to work, 1 entered military service, 1 entered a postgraduate year. Median SAT verbal: 510, median SAT math: 520. 25% scored over 600 on SAT verbal, 26% scored over 600 on SAT math.

Student Life Upper grades have uniform requirement, student council, honor system. Discipline rests primarily with faculty.

Summer Programs Remediation, enrichment, ESL, art/fine arts, computer instruction programs offered; session focuses on enrichment and remediation; held on campus; accepts boys and girls; open to students from other schools. 185 students usually enrolled. 2006 schedule: July 3 to August 5. Application deadline: none.

Tuition and Aid Day student tuition: $16,600; 7-day tuition and room/board: $26,950. Tuition reduction for siblings, merit scholarship grants, need-based scholarship grants available. In 2005–06, 1% of upper-school students received aid; total upper-school merit-scholarship money awarded: $150,000. Total amount of financial aid awarded in 2005–06: $150,000.

Admissions Traditional secondary-level entrance grade is 10. For fall 2005, 329 students applied for upper-level admission, 238 were accepted, 136 enrolled. Any standardized test, Otis-Lennon School Ability Test or TOEFL required. Deadline for receipt of application materials: none. Application fee required: $100. On-campus interview required.

Athletics Interscholastic: aquatics, baseball, basketball, cross-country running, diving, drill team, football, golf, marksmanship, outdoor recreation, power lifting, riflery, running, soccer, strength & conditioning, swimming and diving, tennis, track and field, water polo, wrestling; intramural: aerobics/nautilus, aquatics, basketball, billiards, combined training, fitness, flag football, football, Frisbee, independent competitive sports, jogging, JROTC drill, nautilus, paint ball, physical fitness, physical training, roller hockey, soccer, softball, strength & conditioning, surfing, swimming and diving, touch football, ultimate Frisbee, volleyball, weight lifting, weight training. 11 coaches, 1 trainer.

Computers Computers are regularly used in all academic, occupational education classes. Computer resources include on-campus library services, CD-ROMs, online commercial services, Internet access.

Contact Elizabeth Kalivas, Director of Admissions. 760-729-2385 Ext. 261. Fax: 760-434-5948. E-mail: ekalivas@armyandnavyacademy.org. Web site: www.armyandnavyacademy.org.

See full description on page 658.

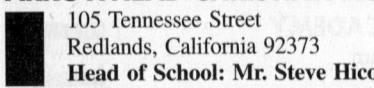

ARROWHEAD CHRISTIAN ACADEMY

105 Tennessee Street
Redlands, California 92373
Head of School: Mr. Steve Hicok

General Information Coeducational day college-preparatory, arts, religious studies, and technology school, affiliated with Christian faith. Grades 6–12. Founded: 1979. Setting: suburban. Nearest major city is San Bernardino. 5-acre campus. 3 buildings on campus. Approved or accredited by Association of Christian Schools International, Western Association of Schools and Colleges, and California Department of Education. Total enrollment: 585. Upper school average class size: 23. Upper school faculty-student ratio: 1:14.

Upper School Student Profile Grade 9: 130 students (69 boys, 61 girls); Grade 10: 96 students (48 boys, 48 girls); Grade 11: 81 students (46 boys, 35 girls); Grade 12: 84 students (38 boys, 46 girls). 100% of students are Christian faith.

Faculty School total: 42. In upper school: 19 men, 17 women; 8 have advanced degrees.

Subjects Offered Advanced math, algebra, American government, American government-AP, American history, American history-AP, American literature, art, ASB Leadership, athletic training, athletics, baseball, basketball, Bible, Bible studies, biology, British literature, British literature (honors), business, calculus, calculus-AP, cheerleading, chemistry, chemistry-AP, choir, choral music, chorus, Christian doctrine, Christian education, Christian ethics, Christian scripture, Christian studies, Christianity, church history, college admission preparation, college awareness, college counseling, college placement, college planning, community service, computer applications, computer graphics, computer keyboarding, computer skills, computer technologies, computers, concert choir, creative writing, desktop publishing, drama, economics, English, English composition, English literature, ESL, food and nutrition, geometry, graphic design, guitar, home economics, honors English, honors geometry,

honors world history, HTML design, instrumental music, international studies, internship, keyboarding/computer, Korean, Korean culture, library, Life of Christ, music theater, musical theater, participation in sports, physical education, physical science, physics, pre-algebra, pre-calculus, psychology, SAT preparation, SAT/ACT preparation, sociology, softball, Spanish, student government, theater arts, track and field, U.S. history-AP, visual and performing arts, volleyball, weight training, world history, world literature, yearbook.

Graduation Requirements Arts and fine arts (art, music, dance, drama), English, foreign language, mathematics, physical education (includes health), religion (includes Bible studies and theology), science, social studies (includes history). Community service is required.

Special Academic Programs Advanced Placement exam preparation in 5 subject areas; honors section; study at local college for college credit; remedial math; programs in general development for dyslexic students; ESL (8 students enrolled).

College Placement 76 students graduated in 2005; 74 went to college, including Azusa Pacific University; Biola University; California State University, San Bernardino; Point Loma Nazarene University; University of California, Los Angeles; University of California, Riverside. Other: 2 went to work. Mean SAT verbal: 520, mean SAT math: 540, mean combined SAT: 1590. 11% scored over 600 on SAT verbal, 30% scored over 600 on SAT math, 14% scored over 1800 on combined SAT.

Student Life Upper grades have specified standards of dress, student council, honor system. Discipline rests primarily with faculty. Attendance at religious services is required.

Summer Programs Remediation, enrichment, advancement, sports, computer instruction programs offered; session focuses on remedial and advancement opportunities; held on campus; accepts boys and girls; not open to students from other schools. 75 students usually enrolled. 2006 schedule: June 20 to July 30. Application deadline: June 10.

Tuition and Aid Day student tuition: $6210. Tuition installment plan (monthly payment plans, 4% discount for full pay up front, 2% discount for two equal payments). Tuition reduction for siblings, need-based scholarship grants, faculty/staff employee discounts available. In 2005–06, 15% of upper-school students received aid. Total amount of financial aid awarded in 2005–06: $130,000.

Admissions Traditional secondary-level entrance grade is 9. For fall 2005, 86 students applied for upper-level admission, 65 were accepted, 65 enrolled. Admissions testing required. Deadline for receipt of application materials: none. Application fee required: $100. On-campus interview required.

Athletics Interscholastic: baseball (boys), basketball (b,g), cheering (g), cross-country running (b,g), football (b), soccer (b,g), softball (g), tennis (b,g), track and field (b,g), volleyball (b,g); intramural: weight lifting (b); coed interscholastic: golf; coed intramural: archery, broomball. 4 PE instructors, 32 coaches, 2 trainers.

Computers Computers are regularly used in all academic, yearbook classes. Computer network features include on-campus library services, CD-ROMs, online commercial services, Internet access, DVD.

Contact Mrs. Patricia Sornoso, Admissions Assistant. 909-793-0601 Ext. 162. Fax: 909-792-5691. E-mail: psornoso@arrowheadchristian.com. Web site: www.arrowheadchristian.org.

ARROWSMITH ACADEMY

2300 Bancroft Way
Berkeley, California 94704

ANNOUNCEMENT FROM THE SCHOOL Arrowsmith Academy is a multicultural, college-preparatory school for grades 9 through 12. The school promotes critical thinking in a structured, innovative, academic, and creative environment. Arrowsmith is coeducational and nonsectarian. The school was founded in 1979 in Lafayette, California. In 1987, Arrowsmith relocated to Berkeley, across the street from the University of California. Approximately 100 students from diverse racial, cultural, and economic backgrounds attend yearly. Arrowsmith Academy is accredited by the Western Association of Schools and Colleges. Courses at Arrowsmith are taught seminar style, with class size averaging 10 to 12 students. The school works with students of varied abilities, including accelerated students and some students with mild learning differences. Students are able to take advantage of resources provided by the on-site learning center, Arrowsmith Center for Educational Success, as well as those provided by the University of California, including libraries, gyms, and museums. More than 90% of Arrowsmith graduates attend a college or university after graduation.

ARROWSMITH SCHOOL

Toronto, Ontario, Canada
See Special Needs Schools section.

ASHBURY COLLEGE

362 Mariposa Avenue
Ottawa, Ontario K1M 0T3, Canada
Head of School: Mr. Tam Matthews

General Information Coeducational boarding and day college-preparatory, bilingual studies, and International Baccalaureate school. Boarding boys grades 9–12, boarding girls grades 9–12, day boys grades 4–12, day girls grades 9–12. Founded: 1891. Setting: urban. Students are housed in single-sex dormitories. 10-acre campus. 2 buildings on campus. Approved or accredited by Canadian Association of Independent Schools, Canadian Educational Standards Institute, European Council of International Schools, International Baccalaureate Organization, The Association of Boarding Schools, and Ontario Department of Education. Affiliate member of National Association of Independent Schools. Language of instruction: English. Endowment: CAN$3 million. Total enrollment: 651. Upper school average class size: 18. Upper school faculty-student ratio: 1:16.

Upper School Student Profile Grade 9: 111 students (62 boys, 49 girls); Grade 10: 121 students (62 boys, 59 girls); Grade 11: 132 students (77 boys, 55 girls); Grade 12: 122 students (64 boys, 58 girls). 20% of students are boarding students. 10% are province residents. 5 provinces are represented in upper school student body. 10% are international students. International students from China, Germany, Ghana, Hong Kong, Mexico, and Saudi Arabia; 25 other countries represented in student body.

Faculty School total: 70. In upper school: 25 men, 30 women; 12 have advanced degrees; 14 reside on campus.

Subjects Offered Accounting, advanced chemistry, advanced math, algebra, American history, art, art history, biology, business, business skills, calculus, Canadian geography, Canadian history, chemistry, computer applications, computer programming, computer science, creative writing, drama, driver education, economics, English, English literature, environmental science, ESL, European history, fine arts, French, geography, geometry, health, history, mathematics, music, physical education, physics, science, social studies, sociology, Spanish, theater, theory of knowledge, world history, world literature.

Graduation Requirements Arts and fine arts (art, music, dance, drama), business skills (includes word processing), computer science, English, French, mathematics, physical education (includes health), science, social studies (includes history), world geography. Community service is required.

Special Academic Programs International Baccalaureate program; ESL (35 students enrolled).

College Placement 122 students graduated in 2005; all went to college, including Carleton University; Dalhousie University; McGill University; Queen's University at Kingston; The University of Western Ontario; University of Ottawa. Median SAT verbal: 600, median SAT math: 610. 53% scored over 600 on SAT verbal, 68.5% scored over 600 on SAT math.

Student Life Upper grades have uniform requirement, student council. Discipline rests primarily with faculty. Attendance at religious services is required.

Summer Programs Advancement programs offered; session focuses on academics; held on campus; accepts boys and girls; open to students from other schools. 85 students usually enrolled. 2006 schedule: July 1 to July 31. Application deadline: June 20.

Tuition and Aid Day student tuition: CAN$16,120; 7-day tuition and room/board: CAN$33,700. Tuition installment plan (monthly payment plans, individually arranged payment plans). Tuition reduction for siblings, bursaries, merit scholarship grants available. In 2005–06, 20% of upper-school students received aid; total upper-school merit-scholarship money awarded: CAN$150,000. Total amount of financial aid awarded in 2005–06: CAN$350,000.

Admissions Traditional secondary-level entrance grade is 9. For fall 2005, 317 students applied for upper-level admission, 221 were accepted, 169 enrolled. Canadian Standardized Test, CAT 2 or TOEFL required. Deadline for receipt of application materials: none. Application fee required: CAN$100. Interview recommended.

Athletics Interscholastic: alpine skiing (boys, girls), baseball (b), basketball (b,g), crew (b,g), cross-country running (b,g), curling (b,g), football (b), golf (b,g), hockey (b), ice hockey (b), independent competitive sports (b,g), rugby (b,g), skiing (downhill) (b,g), soccer (b,g), tennis (b,g), track and field (b,g), volleyball (b,g); intramural: aerobics (g), aerobics/dance (g), badminton (b,g), ball hockey (b,g), dance (g), field hockey (g), ice hockey (b), modern dance (b), outdoor education (b,g), rugby (b,g); coed interscholastic: running; coed intramural: alpine skiing, basketball, bicycling, broomball, cross-country running, curling, hiking/backpacking, martial arts, nautilus, nordic skiing, physical fitness, rowing, skiing (cross-country), skiing (downhill), snowboarding, soccer, softball, squash, swimming and diving, tennis, track and field, ultimate Frisbee, weight training, yoga. 5 PE instructors, 10 coaches.

Computers Computers are regularly used in art, business applications, business education, data processing, economics, geography, graphic arts, humanities, information technology, mathematics, music, science, yearbook classes. Computer network features include campus e-mail, on-campus library services, CD-ROMs, Internet access, DVD, wireless campus network.

Contact Ms. Lisa Lewicki, Director of Admissions. 613-749-5954 Ext. 211. Fax: 613-749-9724. E-mail: admissions@ashbury.on.ca. Web site: www.ashbury.on.ca.

ASHEVILLE SCHOOL

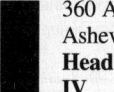 

360 Asheville School Road
Asheville, North Carolina 28806
Head of School: Archibald R. Montgomery, IV

General Information Coeducational boarding and day college-preparatory, arts, and technology school. Grades 9–12. Founded: 1900. Setting: suburban. Nearest major city is Charlotte. Students are housed in single-sex by floor dormitories. 300-acre campus. 19 buildings on campus. Approved or accredited by National Association of Episcopal Schools, North Carolina Association of Independent Schools, Southern Association of Colleges and Schools, Southern Association of Independent Schools, and The Association of Boarding Schools. Member of National Association of Independent Schools and Secondary School Admission Test Board. Endowment: $30 million. Total enrollment: 234. Upper school average class size: 11. Upper school faculty-student ratio: 1:4.

Upper School Student Profile Grade 9: 47 students (22 boys, 25 girls); Grade 10: 71 students (38 boys, 33 girls); Grade 11: 57 students (28 boys, 29 girls); Grade 12: 59 students (31 boys, 28 girls). 75% of students are boarding students. 50% are state residents. 24 states are represented in upper school student body. 14% are international students. International students from Bahamas, Germany, Jamaica, Republic of Korea, and Thailand; 15 other countries represented in student body.

Faculty School total: 63. In upper school: 37 men, 26 women; 23 have advanced degrees; 36 reside on campus.

Subjects Offered Algebra, American history, American literature, ancient history, art, biology, calculus, chemistry, creative writing, driver education, English, English literature, environmental science, European history, finite math, French, general science, geometry, grammar, humanities, Latin, literature, mathematics, medieval/Renaissance history, music, physics, pre-calculus, public speaking, science, social studies, Spanish, studio art, Western civilization, world history, world literature, writing.

Graduation Requirements Arts and fine arts (art, music, dance, drama), English, foreign language, history, mathematics, public speaking, science, Senior Demonstration (series of research papers and oral defense of work), three-day camping trip.

Special Academic Programs Advanced Placement exam preparation in 15 subject areas; honors section; accelerated programs; independent study; study at local college for college credit; study abroad; academic accommodation for the gifted.

College Placement 71 students graduated in 2005; all went to college, including Davidson College; Rhodes College; The University of North Carolina at Chapel Hill; University of the South; University of Virginia.

Student Life Upper grades have specified standards of dress, student council, honor system. Discipline rests equally with students and faculty. Attendance at religious services is required.

Summer Programs Enrichment, ESL, sports, art/fine arts, rigorous outdoor training, computer instruction programs offered; session focuses on leadership, problem solving, mountaineering, and film; held on campus; accepts boys and girls; open to students from other schools. 60 students usually enrolled. 2006 schedule: June 18 to July 29. Application deadline: June 1.

Tuition and Aid Day student tuition: $18,840; 7-day tuition and room/board: $33,210. Tuition installment plan (monthly payment plans, individually arranged payment plans). Need-based scholarship grants, need-based loans, tuition remission for children of faculty available. In 2005–06, 37% of upper-school students received aid. Total amount of financial aid awarded in 2005–06: $1,279,075.

Admissions Traditional secondary-level entrance grade is 9. For fall 2005, 225 students applied for upper-level admission, 141 were accepted, 84 enrolled. ISEE, SSAT and TOEFL required. Deadline for receipt of application materials: February 10. Application fee required: $50. On-campus interview required.

Athletics Interscholastic: baseball (boys), basketball (b,g), cross-country running (b,g), field hockey (g), football (b), soccer (b,g), swimming and diving (b,g), tennis (b,g), track and field (b,g), volleyball (g), wrestling (b); intramural: alpine skiing (b,g), equestrian sports (b,g), skiing (downhill) (b,g); coed interscholastic: bicycling, equestrian sports, golf; coed intramural: aerobics/dance, back packing, ballet, canoeing/kayaking, climbing, dance, fitness, freestyle skiing, Frisbee, hiking/backpacking, horseback riding, jogging, kayaking, lacrosse, life saving, mountain biking, mountaineering, nautilus, outdoor activities, outdoor adventure, outdoor recreation, outdoor skills, paddling, physical fitness, physical training, rafting, rappelling, rock climbing, roller blading, roller skating, ropes courses, running, skateboarding, skiing (cross-country), snowboarding, strength & conditioning, table tennis, wall climbing, weight lifting, weight training, wilderness, yoga. 5 coaches, 1 trainer.

Computers Computers are regularly used in mathematics, science classes. Computer network features include campus e-mail, on-campus library services, Internet access, Microsoft Office, Claris Works.

Contact Bonnie Duffner, Admission Coordinator and Enrollment Assistant. 828-254-6345. Fax: 828-252-8666. E-mail: admission@ashevilleschool.org. Web site: www.ashevilleschool.org.

ANNOUNCEMENT FROM THE SCHOOL Asheville's summer program, Summer Academic Adventures, offers academically talented and high-achieving students entering grades 7–12 the chance to learn through experience. Outdoor

adventure supplements academic enrichment courses such as The Bull and the Bear (stock market), Roller Coaster Physics, Web page design, Film Production (students film and produce a documentary), and many others. Students may attend one or both 3-week sessions.

See full description on page 660.

ASHLEY HALL

172 Rutledge Avenue
Charleston, South Carolina 29403-5877
Head of School: Jill Swisher Muti

General Information Coeducational day (boys' only in lower grades) college-preparatory, arts, technology, and science, mathematics school. Boys grades PS–K, girls grades PS–12. Founded: 1909. Setting: urban. 16-acre campus. 4 buildings on campus. Approved or accredited by South Carolina Independent School Association, Southern Association of Colleges and Schools, and Southern Association of Independent Schools. Member of National Association of Independent Schools. Endowment: $1.3 million. Total enrollment: 615. Upper school average class size: 15. Upper school faculty-student ratio: 1:13.

Upper School Student Profile Grade 9: 45 students (45 girls); Grade 10: 41 students (41 girls); Grade 11: 44 students (44 girls); Grade 12: 43 students (43 girls).

Faculty School total: 68. In upper school: 7 men, 15 women; 18 have advanced degrees.

Subjects Offered 3-dimensional design, algebra, American government-AP, American history, American history-AP, American literature, art, art history, art history-AP, bioethics, biology, biology-AP, calculus, calculus-AP, ceramics, chemistry, chemistry-AP, choir, computer science, creative writing, desktop publishing, drama, economics, economics and history, English, English literature, English-AP, European history, European history-AP, forensics, foundations of civilization, French, French-AP, geography, geometry, government/civics, history, Internet, keyboarding/computer, Latin, Latin-AP, marine biology, mathematics, microeconomics-AP, music, photo shop, photography, physical education, physical science, physics, physics-AP, pre-calculus, programming, psychology, social studies, Spanish, Spanish-AP, speech, statistics, statistics-AP, studio art, studio art-AP, technology, trigonometry, Web site design, world history.

Graduation Requirements Algebra, arts and fine arts (art, music, dance, drama), computer science, English, foreign language, geometry, mathematics, physical education (includes health), science, social studies (includes history).

Special Academic Programs Advanced Placement exam preparation in 18 subject areas; honors section; independent study; term-away projects; study at local college for college credit; academic accommodation for the gifted, the musically talented, and the artistically talented.

College Placement 43 students graduated in 2005; all went to college, including Auburn University; Clemson University; College of Charleston; Davidson College; University of South Carolina; University of Virginia.

Student Life Upper grades have specified standards of dress, student council, honor system. Discipline rests primarily with faculty.

Summer Programs Enrichment, sports, art/fine arts, computer instruction programs offered; session focuses on enrichment, athletics, adventure, and day camps; held on campus; accepts boys and girls; open to students from other schools. 900 students usually enrolled. 2006 schedule: June 1 to July 28. Application deadline: none.

Tuition and Aid Day student tuition: $12,595. Tuition installment plan (monthly payment plans). Merit scholarship grants, need-based scholarship grants, paying campus jobs available. In 2005–06, 15% of upper-school students received aid; total upper-school merit-scholarship money awarded: $74,775. Total amount of financial aid awarded in 2005–06: $120,492.

Admissions Traditional secondary-level entrance grade is 9. For fall 2005, 22 students applied for upper-level admission, 17 were accepted, 9 enrolled. Otis-Lennon School Ability Test required. Deadline for receipt of application materials: January 15. Application fee required: $75. Interview required.

Athletics Interscholastic: basketball, cross-country running, sailing, soccer, softball, strength & conditioning, tennis, track and field, volleyball; intramural: aquatics, back packing, basketball, canoeing/kayaking, climbing, dance squad, dance team, equestrian sports, jump rope, kayaking, kickball, lacrosse, life saving, mountain biking, outdoor adventure, outdoor education, physical fitness, physical training, rock climbing, soccer, softball, swimming and diving, tennis, track and field, volleyball, weight training. 2 PE instructors, 4 coaches, 1 trainer.

Computers Computers are regularly used in animation, art, career exploration, college planning, desktop publishing, graphic design, independent study, introduction to technology, library skills, newspaper, photography, research skills, SAT preparation, video film production, Web site design, yearbook classes. Computer network features include campus e-mail, on-campus library services, CD-ROMs, online commercial services, Internet access, file transfer.

Contact Elizabeth Peters, Director of Admissions. 843-720-2854. Fax: 843-720-2868. E-mail: peterse@ashleyhall.org. Web site: www.ashleyhall.org.

ANNOUNCEMENT FROM THE SCHOOL Ashley Hall was founded in 1909 by Mary Vardrine McBee to establish a curriculum that would prepare young women to enter any college or university in the country. The school's founding mission was remarkably enlightened for its time. Today Ashley Hall upholds those high standards of academic excellence as it strives to prepare its students to meet the challenges of the future. Ashley Hall is an independent, college-preparatory, girls' day school enrolling 615 students in preschool through grade 12. The school's coeducational Ross Early Education Center provides developmentally appropriate curriculum to students ages 2–4. As South Carolina's only all-girls preparatory school, Ashley Hall's single-gender environment provides endless opportunities for girls to become leaders academically, athletically, and socially. The campus is located on 4.5 acres in historic downtown Charleston. The fully networked campus features state-of-the-art technology in classrooms, labs, and the media center. Language, computer skills, University of Chicago's *Everyday Math* program, and athletics begin in kindergarten. A comprehensive sports complex is located off campus and basketball, softball, track, soccer, sailing, tennis, and a championship volleyball program are offered. Advanced Placement and satellite courses enhance the college-preparatory curriculum. Age-appropriate courses in science, social studies, and the arts are offered. College placement is 100 percent, and students regularly receive early acceptance to their first-choice institutions. Year-round coeducational after-school and summer programs are provided to entertain, educate, and challenge all ages. Ashley Hall is committed to a talented and diverse student population and welcomes students of any race, religion, and national or ethnic origin. Ashley Hall has implemented programs to help parents afford an independent school education, including competitive scholarships, tuition grants, flexible payment plans, internships, and financial assistance.

ASPEN RANCH

Loa, Utah
See Special Needs Schools section.

ASSUMPTION HIGH SCHOOL

2170 Tyler Lane
Louisville, Kentucky 40205
Head of School: Mrs. Mary Lee McCoy

General Information Girls' day college-preparatory, arts, business, religious studies, and technology school, affiliated with Roman Catholic Church. Grades 9–12. Founded: 1955. Setting: suburban. 5-acre campus. 3 buildings on campus. Approved or accredited by National Catholic Education Association, Southern Association of Colleges and Schools, and Kentucky Department of Education. Endowment: $500,000. Total enrollment: 1,018. Upper school average class size: 19. Upper school faculty-student ratio: 1:11.

Upper School Student Profile Grade 9: 267 students (267 girls); Grade 10: 254 students (254 girls); Grade 11: 238 students (238 girls); Grade 12: 259 students (259 girls). 86% of students are Roman Catholic.

Faculty School total: 99. In upper school: 15 men, 84 women; 70 have advanced degrees.

Subjects Offered 3-dimensional art, accounting, acting, algebra, American history, American history-AP, American literature, anatomy, art, art history-AP, astronomy, biology, biology-AP, broadcast journalism, business, business law, calculus, calculus-AP, ceramics, chemistry, chemistry-AP, child development, choral music, chorus, community service, computer applications, computer graphics, computer information systems, computer programming, computer science, crafts, creative writing, death and loss, drama, economics, English, English literature, English literature and composition-AP, environmental science, European history, family living, fine arts, finite math, fitness, forensics, French, French language-AP, geography, geometry, government/civics, health, health education, history, home economics, humanities, Internet, journalism, leadership, marine biology, mathematics, music, personal development, physical education, physical science, physics, physiology, pre-calculus, psychology, psychology-AP, public speaking, religion, SAT/ACT preparation, science, social studies, sociology, Spanish, Spanish language-AP, speech, studio art-AP, theater, theology, U.S. government and politics-AP, word processing, world history, world literature.

Graduation Requirements Arts and fine arts (art, music, dance, drama), English, foreign language, humanities, mathematics, personal development, physical education (includes health), public speaking, religion (includes Bible studies and theology), science, social studies (includes history). Community service is required.

Special Academic Programs Advanced Placement exam preparation in 16 subject areas; honors section; study at local college for college credit; academic accommodation for the gifted; special instructional classes for learning disabled students.

College Placement 240 students graduated in 2005; 236 went to college, including Bellarmine University; Eastern Kentucky University; University of Dayton; University of Kentucky; University of Louisville; Western Kentucky University. Other: 3

went to work, I had other specific plans. Median SAT verbal: 550, median SAT math: 550, median composite ACT: 22. 33.3% scored over 600 on SAT verbal, 33.3% scored over 600 on SAT math, 44% scored over 26 on composite ACT.

Student Life Upper grades have uniform requirement, student council, honor system. Discipline rests primarily with faculty. Attendance at religious services is required.

Summer Programs Sports, art/fine arts, computer instruction programs offered; session focuses on academics and sports; held on campus; accepts girls; open to students from other schools. 200 students usually enrolled. 2006 schedule: June 6 to August 2. Application deadline: June 15.

Tuition and Aid Day student tuition: $7825. Tuition installment plan (FACTS Tuition Payment Plan). Merit scholarship grants, need-based scholarship grants available. In 2005–06, 14% of upper-school students received aid; total upper-school merit-scholarship money awarded: $12,450. Total amount of financial aid awarded in 2005–06: $276,475.

Admissions Traditional secondary-level entrance grade is 9. STS required. Deadline for receipt of application materials: none. Application fee required: $100. On-campus interview required.

Athletics Interscholastic: basketball, cheering, cross-country running, dance team, field hockey, golf, ice hockey, lacrosse, rowing, soccer, softball, swimming and diving, tennis, track and field, volleyball; intramural: basketball, bowling, hiking/backpacking, volleyball, walking. 2 PE instructors, 35 coaches.

Computers Computers are regularly used in all academic classes. Computer network features include campus e-mail, on-campus library services, CD-ROMs, online commercial services, Internet access, file transfer, office computer access, DVD, wireless campus network.

Contact Mrs. Mary Ann Steutermann, Principal. 502-458-9551. Fax: 502-454-8411. E-mail: maryann.steutermann@ahsrockets.org. Web site: www.ahsrockets.org.

THE ATHENIAN SCHOOL

2100 Mount Diablo Scenic Boulevard
Danville, California 94506
Head of School: Eleanor Dase

petersons.com

General Information Coeducational boarding and day college-preparatory school. Boarding grades 9–12, day grades 6–12. Founded: 1965. Setting: suburban. Nearest major city is San Francisco. Students are housed in single-sex dormitories. 75-acre campus. 24 buildings on campus. Approved or accredited by California Association of Independent Schools, The Association of Boarding Schools, The College Board, Western Association of Schools and Colleges, and California Department of Education. Member of National Association of Independent Schools and Secondary School Admission Test Board. Endowment: $2.8 million. Total enrollment: 450. Upper school average class size: 15. Upper school faculty-student ratio: 1:10.

Upper School Student Profile Grade 9: 70 students (36 boys, 34 girls); Grade 10: 77 students (39 boys, 38 girls); Grade 11: 76 students (36 boys, 40 girls); Grade 12: 73 students (34 boys, 39 girls). 14% of students are boarding students. 90% are state residents. 2 states are represented in upper school student body. 10% are international students. International students from Hong Kong, Japan, Malaysia, Republic of Korea, Saudi Arabia, and Taiwan; 5 other countries represented in student body.

Faculty School total: 52. In upper school: 19 men, 27 women; 35 have advanced degrees; 25 reside on campus.

Subjects Offered African-American studies, algebra, American history, American literature, American literature-AP, anatomy, art, art history, Asian history, Asian literature, biology, calculus-AP, ceramics, chemistry, classical studies, college writing, community service, comparative cultures, comparative religion, computer programming, computer science, computer skills, contemporary history, creative writing, dance, dance performance, debate, drama, drama performance, drama workshop, drawing, earth science, ecology, economics, economics and history, English, English as a foreign language, English literature, English-AP, environmental studies, ESL, ethics, European history, European history-AP, expository writing, fencing, fine arts, French, French-AP, geography, geology, geometry, government/civics, health, history, humanities, introduction to technology, jazz band, jewelry making, literary magazine, literature seminar, literature-AP, mathematics, modern European history-AP, music, music history, music performance, musical theater, painting, philosophy, photography, physical education, physics, psychology, science, science project, sculpture, sociology, Spanish, Spanish literature-AP, Spanish-AP, stained glass, statistics, statistics-AP, theater, theater design and production, trigonometry, U.S. history-AP, wilderness experience, world cultures, world history, world literature, writing, yearbook, yoga.

Graduation Requirements American history, arts and fine arts (art, music, dance, drama), English, foreign language, history, literature, mathematics, physical education (includes health), science, wilderness experience, world history. Community service is required.

Special Academic Programs Advanced Placement exam preparation in 11 subject areas; honors section; independent study; term-away projects; study at local college for college credit; domestic exchange program; study abroad; ESL (12 students enrolled).

College Placement 71 students graduated in 2005; 70 went to college, including Brown University; Howard University; New York University; University of California, Davis; University of California, Santa Barbara; University of California, Santa Cruz. Other: 1 went to work. Mean SAT verbal: 629, mean SAT math: 648. 70% scored over 600 on SAT verbal, 72% scored over 600 on SAT math.

Student Life Upper grades have specified standards of dress, student council. Discipline rests equally with students and faculty.

Summer Programs Enrichment, advancement, ESL, sports, art/fine arts, computer instruction programs offered; session focuses on academic enrichment, sports, and ESL; held on campus; accepts boys and girls; open to students from other schools. 200 students usually enrolled. 2006 schedule: June 15 to August 15. Application deadline: none.

Tuition and Aid Day student tuition: $23,202; 5-day tuition and room/board: $36,846; 7-day tuition and room/board: $36,846. Tuition installment plan (Insured Tuition Payment Plan, monthly payment plans). Need-based scholarship grants available. In 2005–06, 20% of upper-school students received aid. Total amount of financial aid awarded in 2005–06: $1,230,000.

Admissions Traditional secondary-level entrance grade is 9. For fall 2005, 295 students applied for upper-level admission, 135 were accepted, 50 enrolled. ISEE, SLEP, SSAT or TOEFL required. Deadline for receipt of application materials: January 10. Application fee required: $75. Interview required.

Athletics Interscholastic: baseball (boys), basketball (b,g), cross-country running (b,g), golf (b,g), soccer (b,g), softball (g), swimming and diving (b,g), tennis (b,g); coed interscholastic: volleyball, wrestling; coed intramural: basketball, climbing, cross-country running, dance, fencing, weight training, yoga. 12 coaches.

Computers Computers are regularly used in English, foreign language, history, humanities, information technology, library science, literary magazine, mathematics, publications, science, yearbook classes. Computer network features include campus e-mail, on-campus library services, CD-ROMs, online commercial services, Internet access, file transfer, office computer access, DVD, wireless campus network.

Contact Beverly Gomer, Admission Coordinator. 925-837-5375. Fax: 925-362-7228. E-mail: admission@athenian.org. Web site: www.athenian.org.

ANNOUNCEMENT FROM THE SCHOOL The only nonsectarian San Francisco Bay Area boarding school, Athenian integrates strong academics with the development of students as world citizens. Athenian goes beyond academic excellence to make learning meaningful, interesting, and motivating. Classes average 15-16 students; teachers know each student. The diverse student body comes to this beautiful 75-acre campus from throughout the East Bay and around the world. Distinguishing programs include town meetings, the Athenian Wilderness Experience, international exchanges, robotics, airplane construction, and community service. Virtually 100 percent of the students gain admission to outstanding, carefully matched 4-year colleges; most are accepted to their first-choice school.

See full description on page 662.

ATHENS ACADEMY

1281 Spartan Lane
PO Box 6548
Athens, Georgia 30604
Head of School: J. Robert Chambers Jr.

General Information Coeducational day college-preparatory and technology school. Grades N–12. Founded: 1967. Setting: suburban. Nearest major city is Atlanta. 105-acre campus. 9 buildings on campus. Approved or accredited by Georgia Independent School Association, Southern Association of Colleges and Schools, Southern Association of Independent Schools, and Georgia Department of Education. Member of National Association of Independent Schools. Endowment: $3.5 million. Total enrollment: 841. Upper school average class size: 18. Upper school faculty-student ratio: 1:18.

Upper School Student Profile Grade 9: 70 students (36 boys, 34 girls); Grade 10: 81 students (37 boys, 44 girls); Grade 11: 81 students (44 boys, 37 girls); Grade 12: 80 students (46 boys, 34 girls).

Faculty School total: 106. In upper school: 23 men, 19 women; 32 have advanced degrees.

Subjects Offered Algebra, American history, American literature, anatomy, art, art history, biology, calculus, chemistry, chemistry-AP, computer math, creative writing, drama, ecology, economics, English, English literature, European history, expository writing, fine arts, French, geography, geometry, government/civics, grammar, health, history, Latin, mathematics, music, photography, physical education, physical science, physics, physiology, science, social studies, Spanish, statistics, theater, trigonometry, world history, world literature.

Graduation Requirements Arts and fine arts (art, music, dance, drama), English, foreign language, mathematics, physical education (includes health), science, social studies (includes history).

Special Academic Programs Advanced Placement exam preparation in 8 subject areas; honors section.

College Placement 84 students graduated in 2005; all went to college, including Georgia Institute of Technology; University of Georgia. Median SAT verbal: 652.

Student Life Upper grades have specified standards of dress, student council, honor system. Discipline rests primarily with faculty.

Athens Academy

Summer Programs Remediation, enrichment, computer instruction programs offered; session focuses on enrichment and review; held on campus; accepts boys and girls; open to students from other schools. 80 students usually enrolled. Application deadline: none.

Tuition and Aid Day student tuition: $5440–$11,255. Tuition installment plan (Insured Tuition Payment Plan, monthly payment plans). Tuition reduction for siblings, merit scholarship grants, need-based scholarship grants available. Total upper-school merit-scholarship money awarded for 2005–06: $41,000.

Admissions Traditional secondary-level entrance grade is 9. For fall 2005, 61 students applied for upper-level admission, 39 were accepted, 27 enrolled. CTP III required. Deadline for receipt of application materials: none. Application fee required: $85. On-campus interview required.

Athletics Interscholastic: baseball (boys), basketball (b,g), cheering (g), cross-country running (b,g), football (b), soccer (b,g), swimming and diving (b,g), tennis (b,g), track and field (b,g), volleyball (g); coed interscholastic: cross-country running, golf, swimming and diving, tennis, track and field. 6 PE instructors, 5 coaches.

Computers Computers are regularly used in English, history, mathematics, science classes. Computer network features include campus e-mail, on-campus library services, CD-ROMs, online commercial services, Internet access, wireless campus network.

Contact Stuart A. Todd, Director of Admissions. 706-549-9225. Fax: 706-354-3775. E-mail: stodd@athensacademy.org. Web site: www.athensacademy.org.

ATLANTA INTERNATIONAL SCHOOL

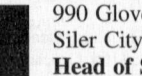

2890 North Fulton Drive
Atlanta, Georgia 30305
Head of School: Dr. Robert Brindley

General Information Coeducational day college-preparatory, bilingual studies, and International Baccalaureate school. Grades PK–12. Founded: 1984. Setting: urban. 10-acre campus. 3 buildings on campus. Approved or accredited by European Council of International Schools, French Ministry of Education, Georgia Independent School Association, International Baccalaureate Organization, Southern Association of Colleges and Schools, and Georgia Department of Education. Member of National Association of Independent Schools. Endowment: $6 million. Total enrollment: 868. Upper school average class size: 15. Upper school faculty-student ratio: 1:8.

Upper School Student Profile Grade 9: 64 students (27 boys, 37 girls); Grade 10: 60 students (33 boys, 27 girls); Grade 11: 62 students (30 boys, 32 girls); Grade 12: 69 students (38 boys, 31 girls).

Faculty School total: 115. In upper school: 20 men, 42 women; 32 have advanced degrees.

Subjects Offered Advanced math, American history, art, athletics, biology, chemistry, choir, chorus, computer science, contemporary issues, English, English literature, environmental studies, ESL, fine arts, French, French as a second language, geography, German, integrated mathematics, International Baccalaureate courses, jazz band, lab/keyboard, Latin, Mandarin, math methods, mathematics, model United Nations, physical education, physics, SAT preparation, science, science and technology, social studies, Spanish, theater, theater arts, theory of knowledge, world history, writing workshop, yearbook.

Graduation Requirements Arts and fine arts (art, music, dance, drama), English, foreign language, mathematics, physical education (includes health), science, social studies (includes history), theory of knowledge, extended essay/research project. Community service is required.

Special Academic Programs International Baccalaureate program; ESL (26 students enrolled).

College Placement 68 students graduated in 2005; 66 went to college, including Barnard College; Carnegie Mellon University; Emory University; Northeastern University; University of Georgia; Yale University. Other: 1 went to work, 1 had other specific plans. Mean SAT verbal: 631, mean SAT math: 611. 60% scored over 600 on SAT verbal, 55% scored over 600 on SAT math.

Student Life Upper grades have specified standards of dress, student council. Discipline rests primarily with faculty.

Summer Programs Remediation, enrichment, advancement, ESL, sports, art/fine arts, computer instruction programs offered; session focuses on language acquisition (French, Spanish, German), middle school math, English review; held on campus; accepts boys and girls; open to students from other schools. 250 students usually enrolled. 2006 schedule: July 3 to July 28. Application deadline: July 17.

Tuition and Aid Day student tuition: $15,625. Tuition installment plan (Insured Tuition Payment Plan). Need-based scholarship grants available. In 2005–06, 16% of upper-school students received aid. Total amount of financial aid awarded in 2005–06: $330,706.

Admissions Traditional secondary-level entrance grade is 9. For fall 2005, 85 students applied for upper-level admission, 33 were accepted, 29 enrolled. SSAT required. Deadline for receipt of application materials: none. Application fee required: $100. Interview recommended.

Athletics Interscholastic: baseball (boys), basketball (b,g), cross-country running (b,g), soccer (b,g), swimming and diving (b,g), track and field (b,g), volleyball (g); intramural: soccer (b,g), strength & conditioning (b,g), track and field (b,g); coed intramural: basketball, fencing, fitness, jogging, running, volleyball. 6 PE instructors, 20 coaches.

Computers Computers are regularly used in English, foreign language, history, lab/keyboard, Latin, library, literary magazine, research skills, science, word processing, writing, yearbook classes. Computer network features include campus e-mail, on-campus library services, CD-ROMs, online commercial services, Internet access, file transfer, server space for file storage, online classroom, multi-user learning software.

Contact Ms. Enid Palmer, Admission Assistant. 404-841-3891. Fax: 404-841-3873. E-mail: epalmer@aischool.org. Web site: www.aischool.org.

AULDERN ACADEMY

990 Glovers Grove Church Road
Siler City, North Carolina 27344
Head of School: Mr. Will Laughlin

petersons.com

General Information Girls' boarding college-preparatory and arts school. Grades 9–12. Founded: 2001. Setting: rural. Nearest major city is Chapel Hill. Students are housed in single-sex dormitories. 86-acre campus. 4 buildings on campus. Approved or accredited by National Independent Private Schools Association, Southern Association of Independent Schools, and North Carolina Department of Education. Candidate for accreditation by Southern Association of Colleges and Schools. Total enrollment: 50. Upper school average class size: 8. Upper school faculty-student ratio: 1:6.

Upper School Student Profile Grade 9: 8 students (8 girls); Grade 10: 13 students (13 girls); Grade 11: 15 students (15 girls); Grade 12: 14 students (14 girls). 100% of students are boarding students.

Faculty School total: 9. In upper school: 4 men, 4 women; 7 have advanced degrees.

Subjects Offered 3-dimensional design, adolescent issues, advanced chemistry, advanced math, algebra, American government-AP, American literature, anatomy and physiology, art, art history, biology, biology-AP, British literature, calculus, calculus-AP, career/college preparation, chemistry, chemistry-AP, computer education, current history, economics, economics-AP, English language and composition-AP, foreign language, geology, geometry, health education, photo shop, physical education, physical fitness, physics, physics-AP, pre-calculus, science, Spanish, Spanish language-AP, study skills, U.S. government, U.S. history, values and decisions, world history.

Graduation Requirements Electives, English, foreign language, mathematics, physical education (includes health), science, social studies (includes history).

Special Academic Programs Advanced Placement exam preparation; independent study; special instructional classes for students with mild learning disabilities, mild Attention Deficit Disorder, and mild behavioral and/or emotional problems (anxiety, depression).

College Placement 9 students graduated in 2005; all went to college, including Austin College; Georgia College & State University; Peace College; University of Denver. Mean SAT verbal: 538, mean SAT math: 510.

Student Life Upper grades have specified standards of dress, student council, honor system. Discipline rests equally with students and faculty.

Summer Programs Remediation, advancement, art/fine arts, computer instruction programs offered; session focuses on academics; held on campus; accepts girls; not open to students from other schools. 35 students usually enrolled. 2006 schedule: June 13 to August 5.

Tuition and Aid 7-day tuition and room/board: $40,000. Guaranteed tuition plan. Tuition installment plan (Key Tuition Payment Plan, monthly payment plans, individually arranged payment plans). Need-based scholarship grants available.

Admissions Comprehensive educational evaluation and psychoeducational evaluation required. Deadline for receipt of application materials: none. No application fee required. Interview required.

Athletics Intramural: aerobics, aerobics/dance, basketball, bicycling, combined training, cooperative games, cross-country running, dance, fitness, fitness walking, horseback riding, indoor soccer, jogging, mountain biking, outdoor activities, physical fitness, running, soccer, strength & conditioning, table tennis, tennis, triathlon, volleyball, walking, weight lifting, weight training. 3 PE instructors.

Computers Computer network features include campus e-mail, on-campus library services, Internet access.

Contact Ms. Brienne McKay, Admissions Counselor. 919-837-2336 Ext. 200. Fax: 919-837-5284. E-mail: brienne.mckay@threesprings.com. Web site: www.auldern. com.

ANNOUNCEMENT FROM THE SCHOOL Auldern Academy is a college-preparatory boarding school with a personal growth curriculum. Auldern offers a traditional boarding school environment with challenging but supportive academics and a personal growth program to prepare young women for college matriculation and independence. Auldern serves academically capable young women, grades 9–12, who would benefit from more structure and support than a typical boarding school provides.

AURORA CENTRAL HIGH SCHOOL

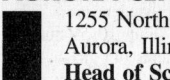

1255 North Edgelawn Drive
Aurora, Illinois 60506-1673
Head of School: Very Rev. F. William Etheredge

General Information Coeducational day college-preparatory school, affiliated with Roman Catholic Church. Grades 9–12. Founded: 1968. Setting: urban. 47-acre campus. 1 building on campus. Approved or accredited by National Catholic Education Association, North Central Association of Colleges and Schools, and Illinois Department of Education. Endowment: $8.1 million. Total enrollment: 431. Upper school average class size: 25. Upper school faculty-student ratio: 1:16.

Upper School Student Profile Grade 9: 104 students (56 boys, 48 girls); Grade 10: 111 students (61 boys, 50 girls); Grade 11: 121 students (56 boys, 65 girls); Grade 12: 95 students (47 boys, 48 girls). 87% of students are Roman Catholic.

Faculty School total: 38. In upper school: 20 men, 18 women; 32 have advanced degrees.

Subjects Offered American government-AP, American history, American literature-AP, ancient history, ancient world history, art, athletics, band, Bible, biology, biology-AP, calculus-AP, campus ministry, chemistry, chemistry-AP, civil war history, comparative religion, computer skills, constitutional history of U.S., consumer economics, contemporary history, CPR, creative writing, earth science, ecology, environmental systems, electives, engineering, English, English composition, English literature, English literature-AP, environmental science, ethics, fine arts, foreign language, French, French-AP, geometry, health, history, home economics, honors algebra, honors English, honors geometry, honors U.S. history, honors world history, instrumental music, Internet, journalism, keyboarding/computer, Latin, math applications, mathematics, medieval history, moral theology, music, newspaper, oral communications, physical education, political science, pre-algebra, pre-calculus, psychology, reading/study skills, science, Shakespeare, social justice, Spanish, Spanish-AP, theology, U.S. government and politics, U.S. government and politics-AP, U.S. history-AP, Western civilization, world history, World War II, yearbook.

Graduation Requirements Algebra, biology, Catholic belief and practice, Christian and Hebrew scripture, constitutional history of U.S., consumer economics, English, English literature, geometry, history, keyboarding/computer, language and composition, moral theology, physical education (includes health), religion (includes Bible studies and theology), science, scripture, U.S. government, U.S. history, retreat programs. Community service is required.

Special Academic Programs Advanced Placement exam preparation in 10 subject areas; honors section; independent study; study abroad; academic accommodation for the gifted; remedial reading and/or remedial writing; remedial math.

College Placement 87 students graduated in 2005; 84 went to college, including Benedictine University; Illinois State University; Loyola University Chicago; Marquette University; Northern Illinois University; University of Illinois at Urbana–Champaign. Other: 1 went to work, 2 entered military service. Median composite ACT: 19.

Student Life Upper grades have uniform requirement, student council, honor system. Discipline rests primarily with faculty. Attendance at religious services is required.

Summer Programs Enrichment, sports, art/fine arts programs offered; session focuses on skill development; held both on and off campus; held at golf course and Park District Facilities; accepts boys and girls; open to students from other schools. 150 students usually enrolled. 2006 schedule: June 7 to August 7. Application deadline: June 7.

Tuition and Aid Day student tuition: $4100. Tuition installment plan (monthly payment plans). Tuition reduction for siblings, merit scholarship grants, need-based scholarship grants, need-based loans available. In 2005–06, 15% of upper-school students received aid; total upper-school merit-scholarship money awarded: $20,000. Total amount of financial aid awarded in 2005–06: $80,000.

Admissions Traditional secondary-level entrance grade is 9. High School Placement Test required. Deadline for receipt of application materials: none. Application fee required: $50. Interview recommended.

Athletics Interscholastic: aerobics/dance (girls), baseball (b,g), basketball (b,g), cheering (g), cross-country running (b,g), dance (g), dance squad (g), dance team (g), football (b), golf (b,g), indoor track (b,g), indoor track & field (b,g), pom squad (g), soccer (b,g), softball (g), tennis (b,g), volleyball (g), wrestling (b); intramural: aerobics/dance (g), baseball (b,g), basketball (b,g), flag football (b), floor hockey (g), football (b), indoor track (b,g), indoor track & field (b,g), jogging (b,g), physical fitness (b,g), physical training (b,g), power lifting (b,g), soccer (b,g), softball (b,g), volleyball (b,g), weight lifting (b,g), weight training (b,g), winter (indoor) track (b,g), wrestling (b); coed intramural: modern dance, physical fitness, physical training, power lifting, soccer, swimming and diving, volleyball, weight lifting, weight training, winter (indoor) track. 2 PE instructors, 50 coaches, 2 trainers.

Computers Computers are regularly used in drafting, engineering, English, French, history, Spanish, technology classes. Computer network features include campus e-mail, on-campus library services, CD-ROMs, online commercial services, Internet access, file transfer, DVD.

Contact Mrs. Peggy Smith, Administrative Assistant. 630-907-0095 Ext. 15. Fax: 630-907-1076. E-mail: psmith@auroracentral.com. Web site: www.auroracentral.com.

AVON OLD FARMS SCHOOL

500 Old Farms Road
Avon, Connecticut 06001
Head of School: Kenneth H. LaRocque

General Information Boys' boarding and day college-preparatory school. Boarding grades 9–PG, day grades 9–12. Founded: 1927. Setting: suburban. Nearest major city is Hartford. Students are housed in single-sex dormitories. 840-acre campus. 39 buildings on campus. Approved or accredited by Connecticut Association of Independent Schools, Department of Education and Employment, United Kingdom, New England Association of Schools and Colleges, The Association of Boarding Schools, and Connecticut Department of Education. Member of National Association of Independent Schools and Secondary School Admission Test Board. Endowment: $35 million. Total enrollment: 396. Upper school average class size: 12. Upper school faculty-student ratio: 1:6.

Upper School Student Profile Grade 9: 75 students (75 boys); Grade 10: 106 students (106 boys); Grade 11: 102 students (102 boys); Grade 12: 94 students (94 boys); Postgraduate: 19 students (19 boys). 76% of students are boarding students. 48% are state residents. 27 states are represented in upper school student body. 7% are international students. International students from Canada, Mexico, Panama, Republic of Korea, Spain, and United Kingdom; 6 other countries represented in student body.

Faculty School total: 56. In upper school: 40 men, 11 women; 34 have advanced degrees; 50 reside on campus.

Subjects Offered Advanced math, advanced studio art-AP, African American studies, algebra, American Civil War, American government-AP, American history-AP, American legal systems, American literature, ancient history, architectural drawing, architecture, art, art-AP, Basic programming, biology, biology-AP, calculus, calculus-AP, ceramics, chamber groups, chemistry, chorus, computer keyboarding, computer programming, computer programming-AP, computer science, concert band, criminal justice, design, digital photography, economics, economics-AP, English, English language and composition-AP, English literature, English literature and composition-AP, English literature-AP, environmental science, environmental science-AP, European history, fine arts, foundations of civilization, French, French language-AP, geology, geometry, government-AP, guitar, honors algebra, honors English, honors geometry, human sexuality, information technology, jazz band, journalism, Latin, macro/microeconomics-AP, modern history, moral reasoning, music theory, photography, physics, physics-AP, pre-calculus, probability and statistics, public speaking, Spanish, Spanish language-AP, statistics-AP, studio art-AP, trigonometry, U.S. government, U.S. government-AP, woodworking, world history, world literature, World War I, World War II.

Graduation Requirements Algebra, American literature, arts and fine arts (art, music, dance, drama), biology, computer applications, computer keyboarding, English, English composition, foreign language, geometry, mathematics, science, social science, U.S. history.

Special Academic Programs Advanced Placement exam preparation in 19 subject areas; honors section; independent study; study abroad; academic accommodation for the gifted, the musically talented, and the artistically talented.

College Placement 112 students graduated in 2005; 111 went to college, including Boston University; Connecticut College; Duke University; Gettysburg College; Hobart and William Smith Colleges; Trinity College. Other: 1 had other specific plans. Median SAT verbal: 544, median SAT math: 591. 24% scored over 600 on SAT verbal, 47% scored over 600 on SAT math.

Student Life Upper grades have specified standards of dress, student council. Discipline rests primarily with faculty.

Tuition and Aid Day student tuition: $24,800; 5-day tuition and room/board: $34,650; 7-day tuition and room/board: $34,650. Tuition installment plan (Insured Tuition Payment Plan, monthly payment plans, individually arranged payment plans). Merit scholarship grants, need-based scholarship grants, need-based loans available. In 2005–06, 32% of upper-school students received aid; total upper-school merit-scholarship money awarded: $53,275. Total amount of financial aid awarded in 2005–06: $2,400,000.

Admissions Traditional secondary-level entrance grade is 9. For fall 2005, 496 students applied for upper-level admission, 277 were accepted, 150 enrolled. PSAT, SAT, SSAT or TOEFL required. Deadline for receipt of application materials: February 1. Application fee required: $50. On-campus interview required.

Athletics Interscholastic: alpine skiing (boys), baseball (b), basketball (b), cross-country running (b), football (b), golf (b), hockey (b), ice hockey (b), indoor hockey (b), lacrosse (b), riflery (b), running (b), skiing (downhill) (b), soccer (b), squash (b), swimming and diving (b), tennis (b), track and field (b), wrestling (b); intramural: alpine skiing (b), ball hockey (b), basketball (b), bicycling (b), combined training (b), cross-country running (b), fishing (b), fitness (b), flag football (b), floor hockey (b), fly fishing (b), freestyle skiing (b), Frisbee (b), golf (b), hockey (b), ice hockey (b), indoor hockey (b), jogging (b), mountain biking (b), nautilus (b), nordic skiing (b), outdoor activities (b), physical training (b), roller blading (b), ropes courses (b), rugby (b), running (b), scuba diving (b), skateboarding (b), skiing (cross-country) (b), skiing (downhill) (b), snowboarding (b), squash (b), street hockey (b), strength & conditioning (b), swimming and diving (b), table tennis (b), tennis (b), touch football (b), ultimate Frisbee (b), water polo (b), weight lifting (b), weight training (b). 1 coach, 1 trainer.

Computers Computers are regularly used in English, foreign language, history, mathematics, science classes. Computer network features include campus e-mail, on-campus library services, CD-ROMs, online commercial services, Internet access, office computer access, DVD, Blackboard, SmartBoards.

Contact Mr. Brendon A. Welker, Director of Admissions. 800-464-2866. Fax: 860-675-6051. E-mail: welkerb@avonoldfarms.com. Web site: www.avonoldfarms.com.

See full description on page 664.

THE AWTY INTERNATIONAL SCHOOL

7455 Awty School Lane
Houston, Texas 77055
Head of School: Dr. David Watson

General Information Coeducational day college-preparatory and bilingual studies school. Grades PK–12. Founded: 1956. Setting: urban. 15-acre campus. 13 buildings on campus. Approved or accredited by European Council of International Schools, French Ministry of Education, Independent Schools Association of the Southwest, International Baccalaureate Organization, and Texas Department of Education. Member of National Association of Independent Schools and Secondary School Admission Test Board. Languages of instruction: English and French. Endowment: $630,000. Total enrollment: 1,174. Upper school average class size: 18. Upper school faculty-student ratio: 1:18.

Upper School Student Profile Grade 9: 110 students (48 boys, 62 girls); Grade 10: 83 students (41 boys, 42 girls); Grade 11: 81 students (28 boys, 53 girls); Grade 12: 71 students (35 boys, 36 girls).

Faculty School total: 145. In upper school: 31 men, 52 women; 39 have advanced degrees.

Subjects Offered Algebra, American history, Arabic, art, biology, calculus, chemistry, community service, computer programming, computer science, computer studies, drama, Dutch, English, ESL, fine arts, French, geography, geometry, German, grammar, history, Italian, mathematics, music, Norwegian, philosophy, physical education, physics, science, social science, social studies, Spanish, theater, theory of knowledge, trigonometry, world history, world literature, writing.

Graduation Requirements Arts and fine arts (art, music, dance, drama), computer science, English, foreign language, mathematics, physical education (includes health), science, social science, social studies (includes history), 4000-word extended essay. Community service is required.

Special Academic Programs International Baccalaureate program; ESL (23 students enrolled).

College Placement 72 students graduated in 2005; all went to college, including Carnegie Mellon University; McGill University; Rice University; The University of Texas at Austin; University of Houston; Vanderbilt University. Median SAT verbal: 600, median SAT math: 620, median composite ACT: 25. 59% scored over 600 on SAT verbal, 74% scored over 600 on SAT math, 45% scored over 26 on composite ACT.

Student Life Upper grades have uniform requirement, student council, honor system. Discipline rests primarily with faculty.

Tuition and Aid Day student tuition: $14,005. Tuition installment plan (monthly payment plans, semi-annual payment plan, Dewar Tuition Refund Plan). Need-based scholarship grants available. In 2005–06, 5% of upper-school students received aid. Total amount of financial aid awarded in 2005–06: $150,000.

Admissions Traditional secondary-level entrance grade is 9. For fall 2005, 100 students applied for upper-level admission, 70 were accepted, 38 enrolled. CTP III, ISEE, OLSAT, ERB, Stanford Achievement Test or writing sample required. Deadline for receipt of application materials: none. Application fee required: $100. On-campus interview required.

Athletics Interscholastic: basketball (boys, girls), cheering (g), cross-country running (b,g), soccer (b,g), tennis (b,g), track and field (b,g), volleyball (g), winter soccer (g); intramural: dance (g), dance squad (g), dance team (g), flag football (b); coed interscholastic: golf, swimming and diving; coed intramural: badminton. 5 PE instructors, 20 coaches.

Computers Computers are regularly used in foreign language, science classes. Computer network features include on-campus library services, CD-ROMs, Internet access.

Contact Beth Anne Browning, Director of Admissions. 713-686-4850 Ext. 305. Fax: 713-686-4956. E-mail: bbrowning@awty.org. Web site: www.awty.org.

THE BALDWIN SCHOOL

701 West Montgomery Avenue
Bryn Mawr, Pennsylvania 19010
Head of School: Blair D. Stambaugh

General Information Girls' day college-preparatory, arts, and technology school. Grades PK–12. Founded: 1888. Setting: suburban. Nearest major city is Philadelphia. 25-acre campus. 3 buildings on campus. Approved or accredited by Middle States Association of Colleges and Schools and Pennsylvania Association of Private Academic Schools. Member of National Association of Independent Schools and

Secondary School Admission Test Board. Endowment: $5.3 million. Total enrollment: 592. Upper school average class size: 16. Upper school faculty-student ratio: 1:7.

Upper School Student Profile Grade 9: 52 students (52 girls); Grade 10: 51 students (51 girls); Grade 11: 42 students (42 girls); Grade 12: 45 students (45 girls).

Faculty School total: 92. In upper school: 6 men, 35 women; 38 have advanced degrees.

Subjects Offered Algebra, American history, American literature, architecture, art, art history, biology, calculus, ceramics, chemistry, computer science, creative writing, drama, earth science, English, English literature, environmental science, ethics, European history, expository writing, fine arts, French, geometry, government/civics, grammar, health, history, human development, Latin, mathematics, music, photography, physical education, physics, science, social science, social studies, Spanish, speech, theater, trigonometry, world history, world literature, writing.

Graduation Requirements Arts and fine arts (art, music, dance, drama), computer science, English, ethics, foreign language, history, life skills, mathematics, physical education (includes health), science, speech, U.S. history.

Special Academic Programs Advanced Placement exam preparation in 11 subject areas; honors section; independent study; study at local college for college credit; academic accommodation for the gifted, the musically talented, and the artistically talented.

College Placement 50 students graduated in 2005; 49 went to college, including Boston University; Brown University; Emory University; University of Pennsylvania; Washington and Lee University; Williams College. Other: 1 had other specific plans. Mean SAT verbal: 660, mean SAT math: 683.

Student Life Upper grades have uniform requirement, student council, honor system. Discipline rests equally with students and faculty.

Tuition and Aid Day student tuition: $19,865. Tuition installment plan (monthly payment plans, individually arranged payment plans). Need-based scholarship grants available. In 2005–06, 22% of upper-school students received aid. Total amount of financial aid awarded in 2005–06: $586,675.

Admissions Traditional secondary-level entrance grade is 9. For fall 2005, 50 students applied for upper-level admission, 33 were accepted, 13 enrolled. ISEE, SSAT, Wechsler Intelligence Scale for Children or writing sample required. Deadline for receipt of application materials: February 1. Application fee required: $50. On-campus interview required.

Athletics Interscholastic: basketball, crew, cross-country running, dance, dance team, diving, field hockey, golf, indoor track, lacrosse, rowing, running, soccer, softball, squash, swimming and diving, tennis, volleyball, winter (indoor) track. 7 PE instructors, 33 coaches, 1 trainer.

Computers Computers are regularly used in all academic classes. Computer network features include campus e-mail, on-campus library services, CD-ROMs, online commercial services, Internet access, file transfer, office computer access.

Contact Sarah J. Goebel, Director of Admissions and Financial Aid. 610-525-2700 Ext. 251. Fax: 610-581-7231. E-mail: sgoebel@baldwinschool.org. Web site: www.baldwinschool.org.

ANNOUNCEMENT FROM THE SCHOOL The Baldwin School provides a rigorous intellectual experience within a respectful and diverse community. Exceptional opportunities exist at Baldwin in competitive athletics and the arts. Baldwin girls are enthusiastic participants in classrooms and on playing fields. Committed faculty members supported by strong school leadership and extensive technology resources make the learning experience an engaging one.

See full description on page 666.

BALDWIN SCHOOL OF PUERTO RICO, INC.

PO Box 1827
Bayamón, Puerto Rico 00960-1827
Head of School: Dr. Günther Brandt

General Information Coeducational day college-preparatory school. Grades PK–12. Founded: 1968. Setting: suburban. Nearest major city is San Juan. 23-acre campus. 6 buildings on campus. Approved or accredited by Middle States Association of Colleges and Schools and Puerto Rico Department of Education. Member of National Association of Independent Schools. Languages of instruction: English and Spanish. Total enrollment: 820. Upper school average class size: 20. Upper school faculty-student ratio: 1:7.

Upper School Student Profile Grade 9: 45 students (26 boys, 19 girls); Grade 10: 39 students (24 boys, 15 girls); Grade 11: 47 students (21 boys, 26 girls); Grade 12: 49 students (28 boys, 21 girls).

Faculty School total: 72. In upper school: 7 men, 27 women; 18 have advanced degrees.

Subjects Offered Algebra, American history, American literature, art, biology, biology-AP, British literature, calculus, calculus-AP, chemistry, computer science, computers, English, English literature, English literature-AP, environmental science, ESL, European history-AP, fine arts, French, geography, geometry, grammar, history, keyboarding, mathematics, music, physical education, physics, pre-calculus, psy-

chology, Puerto Rican history, science, social studies, Spanish, Spanish language-AP, Spanish literature-AP, strings, study skills, visual arts, vocal music, world literature, writing.

Graduation Requirements Algebra, American history, American literature, arts and fine arts (art, music, dance, drama), biology, British literature, chemistry, computer science, English, English literature, geometry, mathematics, physical education (includes health), Puerto Rican history, science, social studies (includes history), Spanish.

Special Academic Programs Advanced Placement exam preparation in 9 subject areas; honors section; ESL (8 students enrolled).

College Placement 43 students graduated in 2005; all went to college, including Boston College; Boston University; The George Washington University; University of Puerto Rico, Mayagüez Campus; University of Puerto Rico, Río Piedras; Villanova University. Median SAT verbal: 601, median SAT math: 590.

Student Life Upper grades have uniform requirement, student council, honor system. Discipline rests equally with students and faculty.

Summer Programs Remediation, enrichment, ESL, computer instruction programs offered; session focuses on remediation; held on campus; accepts boys and girls; open to students from other schools. 175 students usually enrolled. 2006 schedule: June 5 to June 30. Application deadline: May 26.

Tuition and Aid Day student tuition: $8500–$9000. Guaranteed tuition plan. Tuition installment plan (biannual payment plan). Tuition reduction for siblings, need-based scholarship grants, tuition reduction for children of staff, full-scholarship program for eligible students available. In 2005–06, 1% of upper-school students received aid. Total amount of financial aid awarded in 2005–06: $12,000.

Admissions Traditional secondary-level entrance grade is 9. For fall 2005, 22 students applied for upper-level admission, 17 were accepted, 17 enrolled. Brigance Test of Basic Skills and Stanford Achievement Test, Otis-Lennon required. Deadline for receipt of application materials: none. Application fee required: $150. On-campus interview required.

Athletics Interscholastic: basketball (boys, girls), cheering (g), indoor soccer (b,g), soccer (b,g), softball (g), swimming and diving (b,g), tennis (b), volleyball (b,g); intramural: flag football (b,g), touch football (b,g); coed interscholastic: golf, physical fitness. 5 PE instructors, 16 coaches.

Computers Computers are regularly used in art, English, history, mathematics, music, science classes. Computer network features include campus e-mail, on-campus library services, CD-ROMs, Internet access, office computer access, DVD, wireless campus network.

Contact Mrs. Ely Mejías, Director of Admissions. 787-720-2421 Ext. 239. Fax: 787-790-0619. E-mail: emejias@baldwin-school.org. Web site: www.baldwin-school.org.

See full description on page 668.

BALMORAL HALL SCHOOL

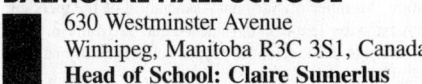

630 Westminster Avenue
Winnipeg, Manitoba R3C 3S1, Canada
Head of School: Claire Sumerlus

petersons.com

General Information Girls' boarding and day (coeducational in lower grades) college-preparatory, arts, and technology school. Boarding girls grades 6–12, day boys grades N–JK, day girls grades N–12. Founded: 1901. Setting: urban. Students are housed in an apartment style residence. 12-acre campus. 2 buildings on campus. Approved or accredited by Canadian Association of Independent Schools, Canadian Educational Standards Institute, The Association of Boarding Schools, and Manitoba Department of Education. Affiliate member of National Association of Independent Schools; member of Secondary School Admission Test Board. Language of instruction: English. Endowment: CAN$365,000. Total enrollment: 469. Upper school average class size: 18. Upper school faculty-student ratio: 1:7.

Upper School Student Profile Grade 9: 32 students (32 girls); Grade 10: 39 students (39 girls); Grade 11: 31 students (31 girls); Grade 12: 36 students (36 girls). 19% of students are boarding students. 79% are province residents. 3 provinces are represented in upper school student body. 17% are international students. International students from China, Hong Kong, Japan, Mexico, Republic of Korea, and Taiwan; 1 other country represented in student body.

Faculty School total: 55. In upper school: 9 men, 13 women; 6 have advanced degrees; 5 reside on campus.

Subjects Offered Architectural drawing, art, band, biology, business, calculus, career/college preparation, chemistry, choir, communications, community service, computer science, consumer mathematics, debate, desktop publishing, drama, driver education, English, English language and composition-AP, English literature, English literature and composition-AP, ESL, European history, French, general science, geography, health, history, home economics, Japanese, journalism, mathematics, modern Western civilization, multimedia, music, musical theater, performing arts, personal development, physical education, physics, pre-calculus, psychology-AP, science, social studies, Spanish, Spanish-AP, technology, world affairs, world history.

Graduation Requirements Minimum of 10 hours per year of Service Learning participation in grades 9 through 12.

Special Academic Programs Advanced Placement exam preparation in 12 subject areas; honors section; accelerated programs; study at local college for college credit; academic accommodation for the gifted; ESL (37 students enrolled).

College Placement 32 students graduated in 2005; all went to college, including McGill University; Queen's University at Kingston; The University of Western Ontario; University of Calgary; University of Manitoba; University of Toronto.

Student Life Upper grades have uniform requirement, student council, honor system. Discipline rests primarily with faculty.

Tuition and Aid Day student tuition: CAN$10,950; 7-day tuition and room/board: CAN$28,900. Tuition installment plan (Insured Tuition Payment Plan, individually arranged payment plans, international students must pay in full prior to official letter of acceptance). Tuition reduction for siblings, bursaries, merit scholarship grants available. In 2005–06, 47% of upper-school students received aid; total upper-school merit-scholarship money awarded: CAN$47,000. Total amount of financial aid awarded in 2005–06: CAN$104,346.

Admissions Traditional secondary-level entrance grade is 9. For fall 2005, 41 students applied for upper-level admission, 34 were accepted, 25 enrolled. School's own exam required. Deadline for receipt of application materials: none. Application fee required: CAN$150. Interview recommended.

Athletics Interscholastic: badminton, basketball, cross-country running, curling, Frisbee, golf, ice hockey, indoor track & field, outdoor skills, running, soccer, track and field, ultimate Frisbee, volleyball; intramural: aerobics, aerobics/dance, aerobics/nautilus, alpine skiing, back packing, badminton, baseball, basketball, bicycling, bowling, broomball, cooperative games, Cosom hockey, cross-country running, curling, dance, fencing, field hockey, figure skating, fitness, fitness walking, flag football, floor hockey, Frisbee, golf, gymnastics, handball, hiking/backpacking, hockey, horseback riding, ice hockey, ice skating, in-line skating, indoor hockey, indoor track & field, jogging, jump rope, modern dance, netball, outdoor activities, outdoor education, outdoor skills, physical fitness, physical training, roller blading, rowing, rugby, running, skiing (cross-country), skiing (downhill), snowboarding, snowshoeing, soccer, softball, strength & conditioning, swimming and diving, table tennis, tennis, track and field, ultimate Frisbee, volleyball, walking, wall climbing, weight training, yoga. 2 PE instructors, 4 coaches.

Computers Computers are regularly used in all classes. Computer network features include campus e-mail, on-campus library services, CD-ROMs, Internet access, office computer access, DVD, wireless campus network.

Contact Pamela K. McGhie, Director of Admissions. 204-784-1621. Fax: 204-774-5534. E-mail: admission@balmoralhall.com. Web site: www.balmoralhall.com.

ANNOUNCEMENT FROM THE SCHOOL Founded in 1901, Balmoral Hall, a university preparatory school, enjoys a reputation as an academic leader, dedicated to educating, encouraging, and empowering young women who excel academically, possess a passion for learning, set high standards for personal achievement, and will be self-confident leaders of tomorrow. A strong faculty delivers a rigorous curriculum in small-class settings that culminates with the challenging Advanced Placement Program in Senior School. Balmoral Hall supports a diverse performing arts and visual arts program. A strong integrated technology program, facilitated by a wireless school community, has resulted in many international-award-winning projects. Numerous opportunities to participate and compete in extracurricular clubs, athletic tournaments, international debating, and public speaking competitions are actively promoted. All programs benefit from a 12-acre campus that includes performing arts and athletic centers, 5 science laboratories, a greenhouse, new-media technology labs, laptop program, library, spacious classrooms, student common room, and dining hall. The International Program welcomes students from around the world, including Mexico, Hong Kong, Korea, Taiwan, Germany, and the United States. The Residence provides a family environment within a fully modernized, apartment-style, 3-story building. The Director of Residence, assistant directors, Coordinator of Student Activities, English as a Second Language (ESL) specialists, school principals, faculty members, and the Head of School comprise the International Team, dedicated to the needs of all Residence Girls. The ESL program excels in developing reading, writing, and communication skills. Fully prepared for postsecondary education, 98% of graduates enter college/university, with more than 60% benefiting from scholarships. A detailed prospectus is accessible from the School's Web site. Early application is advised.

THE BALTIMORE ACTORS' THEATRE CONSERVATORY

The Dumbarton House
300 Dumbarton Road
Baltimore, Maryland 21212-1532
Head of School: Walter E. Anderson

General Information Coeducational day college-preparatory and arts school. Grades K–12. Founded: 1979. Setting: suburban. 35-acre campus. 3 buildings on campus. Approved or accredited by Association of Independent Maryland Schools,

Middle States Association of Colleges and Schools, and Maryland Department of Education. Endowment: $200,000. Total enrollment: 26. Upper school faculty-student ratio: 1:3.

Upper School Student Profile Grade 9: 3 students (1 boy, 2 girls); Grade 10: 2 students (2 boys); Grade 11: 2 students (2 girls); Grade 12: 1 student (1 girl).

Faculty School total: 17. In upper school: 2 men, 11 women; 10 have advanced degrees.

Subjects Offered Acting, algebra, American history-AP, ballet, biology-AP, British literature, chemistry, English language-AP, French, geometry, health science, music history, music theory-AP, novels, physics, pre-calculus, psychology, sociology, theater history, trigonometry, world history.

Graduation Requirements Algebra, American history, ballet, chemistry, English, French, geometry, modern dance, music history, music theory, physical science, psychology, sociology, theater history, world history.

Special Academic Programs Advanced Placement exam preparation in 5 subject areas; honors section; accelerated programs; independent study; study at local college for college credit; academic accommodation for the gifted, the musically talented, and the artistically talented.

College Placement 1 student graduated in 2005 and went to Goucher College; Nazareth College of Rochester. Median SAT verbal: 600, median SAT math: 570, median composite ACT: 26.

Student Life Upper grades have uniform requirement, student council, honor system. Discipline rests primarily with faculty.

Summer Programs Remediation, art/fine arts programs offered; session focuses on music, drama, dance, and art; held off campus; held at our theatre in Oregon Ridge Park, Hunt Valley, Maryland; accepts boys and girls; open to students from other schools. 30 students usually enrolled. 2006 schedule: July 25 to August 9. Application deadline: none.

Tuition and Aid Day student tuition: $8100–$9500. Tuition installment plan (SMART Tuition Payment Plan, FACTS Tuition Payment Plan). Need-based scholarship grants, PLATO Loans, prepGATE Loans available. In 2005–06, 10% of upper-school students received aid. Total amount of financial aid awarded in 2005–06: $12,000.

Admissions Traditional secondary-level entrance grade is 9. For fall 2005, 20 students applied for upper-level admission, 6 were accepted, 4 enrolled. Any standardized test, English, French, and math proficiency and writing sample required. Deadline for receipt of application materials: April 3. Application fee required: $50. On-campus interview required.

Computers Computers are regularly used in all classes. Computer network features include campus e-mail, CD-ROMs, Internet access, DVD, wireless campus network.

Contact Mr. Walter E. Anderson, Headmaster. 410-337-8519. Fax: 410-337-8582. E-mail: batpro@baltimoreactorstheatre.org. Web site: www.baltimoreactorstheatre.org.

BALTIMORE LUTHERAN MIDDLE AND UPPER SCHOOL

1145 Concordia Drive
Towson, Maryland 21286-1796
Head of School: Randal C. Gast

General Information Coeducational day college-preparatory, arts, religious studies, and technology school, affiliated with Lutheran Church. Grades 6–12. Founded: 1965. Setting: suburban. Nearest major city is Baltimore. 25-acre campus. 3 buildings on campus. Approved or accredited by Association of Independent Maryland Schools, Middle States Association of Colleges and Schools, and Maryland Department of Education. Endowment: $1.3 million. Total enrollment: 530. Upper school average class size: 16. Upper school faculty-student ratio: 1:12.

Upper School Student Profile Grade 9: 92 students (39 boys, 53 girls); Grade 10: 90 students (42 boys, 48 girls); Grade 11: 85 students (40 boys, 45 girls); Grade 12: 83 students (35 boys, 48 girls). 40% of students are Lutheran.

Faculty School total: 47. In upper school: 18 men, 16 women; 18 have advanced degrees.

Subjects Offered Advanced Placement courses, algebra, American history, American literature, anatomy, art, Bible studies, biology, biology-AP, calculus, chemistry, Chesapeake Bay studies, computer graphics, computer keyboarding, computer programming, computers, concert band, concert choir, creative writing, dance, drama, drawing and design, earth science, economics, English, English literature, expository writing, French, geometry, German, government/civics, grammar, graphic arts, graphic design, health, honors English, independent study, journalism, Latin, mathematics, music, painting, photography, physical education, physics, pre-algebra, psychology, religion, SAT/ACT preparation, science, social studies, Spanish, speech, street law, studio art, trigonometry, Web site design, word processing, world history, world literature, writing, yearbook.

Graduation Requirements Arts and fine arts (art, music, dance, drama), English, foreign language, mathematics, physical education (includes health), religion (includes Bible studies and theology), science, social studies (includes history).

Special Academic Programs Advanced Placement exam preparation in 3 subject areas; honors section; independent study; study at local college for college credit; academic accommodation for the gifted; programs in general development for dyslexic students.

College Placement 55 students graduated in 2005; 50 went to college, including Concordia College; James Madison University; Loyola College in Maryland; Towson University; University of Maryland; Villa Julie College. Other: 4 went to work, 1 entered military service. Mean SAT verbal: 536, mean SAT math: 508.

Student Life Upper grades have specified standards of dress, student council, honor system. Discipline rests primarily with faculty. Attendance at religious services is required.

Summer Programs Remediation, sports programs offered; session focuses on general activities; held on campus; accepts boys and girls; open to students from other schools. 2006 schedule: June 12 to August 11.

Tuition and Aid Day student tuition: $8200. Tuition installment plan (FACTS Tuition Payment Plan). Tuition reduction for siblings, need-based scholarship grants available. In 2005–06, 22% of upper-school students received aid. Total amount of financial aid awarded in 2005–06: $138,150.

Admissions Traditional secondary-level entrance grade is 9. For fall 2005, 93 students applied for upper-level admission, 73 were accepted, 47 enrolled. School placement exam required. Deadline for receipt of application materials: none. Application fee required: $100. On-campus interview required.

Athletics Interscholastic: baseball (boys), basketball (b,g), cheering (g), cross-country running (b,g), field hockey (g), football (b), golf (b,g), indoor soccer (g), indoor track & field (g), lacrosse (b,g), soccer (b), softball (g), tennis (b,g), volleyball (g), wrestling (b); coed interscholastic: track and field. 5 PE instructors, 3 coaches, 1 trainer.

Computers Computers are regularly used in English, graphic design, history, independent study, journalism, library, mathematics, newspaper, photography, social science, writing, yearbook classes. Computer network features include campus e-mail, on-campus library services, CD-ROMs, Internet access, office computer access, DVD, wireless campus network.

Contact Becky L. Thernes, Director of Admissions. 410-825-2323 Ext. 272. Fax: 410-825-2506. E-mail: admissions@baltimorelutheran.org. Web site: www.baltimorelutheran.org.

BANCROFT SCHOOL

110 Shore Drive
Worcester, Massachusetts 01605
Head of School: Mr. Scott R. Reisinger

General Information Coeducational day college-preparatory school. Grades K–12. Founded: 1900. Setting: suburban. Nearest major city is Boston. 30-acre campus. 7 buildings on campus. Approved or accredited by Association of Independent Schools in New England, New England Association of Schools and Colleges, and Massachusetts Department of Education. Member of National Association of Independent Schools and Secondary School Admission Test Board. Endowment: $20 million. Total enrollment: 581. Upper school average class size: 12. Upper school faculty-student ratio: 1:7.

Upper School Student Profile Grade 9: 61 students (24 boys, 37 girls); Grade 10: 60 students (26 boys, 34 girls); Grade 11: 57 students (24 boys, 33 girls); Grade 12: 64 students (26 boys, 38 girls).

Faculty School total: 75. In upper school: 20 men, 15 women; 28 have advanced degrees.

Subjects Offered Acting, Advanced Placement courses, advanced studio art-AP, algebra, American history, American history-AP, American literature, art, art history, art history-AP, biology, biology-AP, biotechnology, calculus, calculus-AP, ceramics, chamber groups, chemistry, chemistry-AP, chorus, community service, computer graphics, computer science, DNA, drama, dramatic arts, English, English language and composition-AP, English literature, English literature and composition-AP, ethics, European history, European history-AP, French, French-AP, geometry, health, history, jazz band, Latin, Latin-AP, literature by women, marine biology, music, music appreciation, photography, physical education, physics, pre-calculus, psychology, science, senior project, Shakespeare, Spanish, Spanish-AP, theater, theater production, trigonometry, U.S. history-AP, women in world history, world history.

Graduation Requirements Arts and fine arts (art, music, dance, drama), English, foreign language, mathematics, physical education (includes health), science, senior project, social studies (includes history). Community service is required.

Special Academic Programs Advanced Placement exam preparation in 14 subject areas; study at local college for college credit; study abroad; academic accommodation for the gifted.

College Placement 55 students graduated in 2005; all went to college, including Connecticut College; Harvard University; Rensselaer Polytechnic Institute; The George Washington University; Tufts University; University of Pennsylvania. Median SAT verbal: 650, median SAT math: 650.

Student Life Upper grades have specified standards of dress, student council, honor system. Discipline rests primarily with faculty.

Summer Programs Enrichment, advancement, sports, art/fine arts, computer instruction programs offered; session focuses on community outreach; held on campus;

accepts boys and girls; open to students from other schools. 300 students usually enrolled. 2006 schedule: June 19 to August 4. Application deadline: none.

Tuition and Aid Day student tuition: $20,300. Tuition installment plan (Insured Tuition Payment Plan, individually arranged payment plans, 10-month school payment plan). Need-based scholarship grants, scholarship for Worcester residents available. In 2005–06, 22% of upper-school students received aid. Total amount of financial aid awarded in 2005–06: $727,645.

Admissions Traditional secondary-level entrance grade is 9. For fall 2005, 56 students applied for upper-level admission, 25 were accepted, 22 enrolled. SSAT or Wechsler Intelligence Scale for Children required. Deadline for receipt of application materials: February 1. Application fee required: $50. On-campus interview required.

Athletics Interscholastic: baseball (boys), basketball (b,g), cross-country running (b,g), field hockey (g), lacrosse (b,g), soccer (b,g), softball (b,g), tennis (b,g), volleyball (g), wrestling (b); coed interscholastic: golf, skiing (downhill); coed intramural: track and field. 5 PE instructors, 9 coaches, 1 trainer.

Computers Computers are regularly used in all classes. Computer network features include campus e-mail, on-campus library services, CD-ROMs, online commercial services, Internet access, DVD, wireless campus network.

Contact Mrs. Debbie Lamir, Admission Office Assistant. 508-853-2640 Ext. 206. Fax: 508-853-7824. E-mail: dlamir@bancroftschool.org. Web site: www.bancroftschool.org.

ANNOUNCEMENT FROM THE SCHOOL "Bancroft School is a vital, stimulating, and nurturing community of learners. A challenging academic program, a commitment to educating the whole child, and a friendly, supportive environment define the School. From kindergarten through grade 12, Bancroft students are committed, competent, responsible, motivated, and confident young people of high character. Bancroft's faculty is compassionate, professional, and inspiring."—Scott R. Reisinger, Bancroft's Headmaster.

BANGKOK PATANA SCHOOL

2/38 Sukhumvit 105
Bangkok 10260, Thailand

petersons.com

ANNOUNCEMENT FROM THE SCHOOL Bangkok Patana School was founded in 1957 and granted its Charter in 1964 in order to provide a British curriculum education for the children of English-speaking expatriates and others in the Bangkok community. Patana moved to its current site in Bangna in 1990, and the development and expansion of the 17-hectare campus continues to provide purpose-built facilities for the students. The School has 2,120 students representing 50 nationalities; British, US, Australian, and Canadian students are currently 40% of the total. Eighty percent of the teachers are recruited overseas, principally from the UK or from other international schools. The School enrols children from 2½ (Nursery) to 18+ years old (Senior Studies programme). Bangkok Patana is divided into the Elementary Division (including Early Years and Primary) and the Secondary Division. Both follow the English National Curriculum and share a common educational philosophy. Secondary students prepare for GCSE/IGCSE at age 16 and International Baccalaureate Diploma or Certificate at age 18. The excellently resourced campus has full sports, IT, technology, and performing arts facilities. Graduating students have been accepted at major universities worldwide, including Cambridge, Nottingham, London, Yale, University of California, Stanford, Sydney, Chulalongkorn, and Thammasat. All academic results are published annually and can be seen on the Web site at www.patana.ac.th. Students are offered a very comprehensive programme of extracurricular activities, including sports, outdoor education, and the visual and performing arts. Transportation and canteen services are provided. The School is accredited by CIS and NEASC and is a member of the IBO.

BANGOR CHRISTIAN SCHOOL

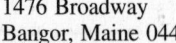
1476 Broadway
Bangor, Maine 04401
Head of School: Mr. Jimmy M. Chasse

General Information Coeducational day college-preparatory and religious studies school, affiliated with Baptist Church. Grades K4–12. Founded: 1970. Setting: suburban. 35-acre campus. 3 buildings on campus. Approved or accredited by New England Association of Schools and Colleges and Maine Department of Education. Total enrollment: 373. Upper school average class size: 20. Upper school faculty-student ratio: 1:11.

Upper School Student Profile Grade 9: 29 students (11 boys, 18 girls); Grade 10: 36 students (18 boys, 18 girls); Grade 11: 22 students (10 boys, 12 girls); Grade 12: 36 students (20 boys, 16 girls). 55% of students are Baptist.

Faculty School total: 25. In upper school: 6 men, 6 women; 2 have advanced degrees.

Special Academic Programs Accelerated programs; independent study; study at local college for college credit.

College Placement 19 students graduated in 2005; 16 went to college. Other: 3 entered military service.

Student Life Upper grades have specified standards of dress, student council, honor system. Discipline rests primarily with faculty.

Summer Programs Sports programs offered; session focuses on sports; held both on and off campus; held at various locations; accepts boys and girls; open to students from other schools. 80 students usually enrolled.

Tuition and Aid Guaranteed tuition plan. Tuition installment plan (monthly payment plans). Tuition reduction for siblings available.

Admissions Traditional secondary-level entrance grade is 9. Deadline for receipt of application materials: none. Application fee required: $100. Interview required.

Athletics Interscholastic: baseball (boys, girls), basketball (b,g), cheering (b,g), cross-country running (b,g), golf (b,g), soccer (b,g), softball (g), track and field (b,g), wrestling (b); intramural: basketball (b,g), cheering (b,g), soccer (b,g); coed interscholastic: cheering. 10 coaches.

Computers Computer network features include campus e-mail, CD-ROMs, Internet access, office computer access, DVD, wireless campus network.

Contact Terri L. Conley, Secretary. 207-947-7356 Ext. 331. Fax: 207-262-9528. E-mail: tconley@bangorchristian.org. Web site: www.bangorchristian.org.

BAPTIST HIGH SCHOOL

Third and Station Avenue
Haddon Heights, New Jersey 08035
Head of School: Mrs. Lynn L. Conahan

General Information Coeducational day college-preparatory, general academic, arts, business, religious studies, and technology school, affiliated with General Association of Regular Baptist Churches. Grades K–12. Founded: 1972. Setting: small town. Nearest major city is Philadelphia, PA. 1 building on campus. Approved or accredited by Association of Christian Schools International, Middle States Association of Colleges and Schools, and New Jersey Department of Education. Total enrollment: 353. Upper school average class size: 25. Upper school faculty-student ratio: 1:10.

Upper School Student Profile Grade 9: 43 students (25 boys, 18 girls); Grade 10: 49 students (20 boys, 29 girls); Grade 11: 38 students (21 boys, 17 girls); Grade 12: 54 students (24 boys, 30 girls). 80% of students are General Association of Regular Baptist Churches.

Faculty School total: 21. In upper school: 8 men, 13 women; 5 have advanced degrees.

Subjects Offered Accounting, advanced chemistry, advanced computer applications, advanced math, algebra, American government, American history-AP, American literature-AP, analytic geometry, anatomy and physiology, applied music, art, art and culture, art appreciation, arts, Basic programming, Bible studies, biology, business mathematics, calculus, calculus-AP, chemistry, choir, church history, civics, communication skills, computer applications, computer programming, creative writing, desktop publishing, dramatic arts, economics, English composition, English literature, English literature and composition-AP, ethics, foreign language, French, general math, general science, geometry, grammar, health, history, jazz band, keyboarding, physics, pre-algebra, pre-calculus, SAT preparation, Spanish, speech, Western civilization, women's health, world history, world history-AP, yearbook.

Graduation Requirements 20th century history, 20th century world history, algebra, American government, American literature, arts appreciation, Bible, biology, British literature, chemistry, computer science, economics, electives, English composition, English literature, ethics, geometry, health, Holocaust studies, lab/keyboard, physical science.

Special Academic Programs Advanced Placement exam preparation in 4 subject areas; honors section; remedial reading and/or remedial writing; remedial math.

College Placement 46 students graduated in 2005; 45 went to college, including Cedarville University; Liberty University; Rutgers, The State University of New Jersey, Rutgers College. Other: 1 entered military service. Mean SAT verbal: 621, mean SAT math: 583. 32% scored over 600 on SAT verbal, 38% scored over 600 on SAT math.

Student Life Upper grades have specified standards of dress, student council, honor system. Discipline rests primarily with faculty. Attendance at religious services is required.

Tuition and Aid Day student tuition: $5400. Tuition installment plan (monthly payment plans). Tuition reduction for siblings, need-based scholarship grants available. In 2005–06, 8% of upper-school students received aid. Total amount of financial aid awarded in 2005–06: $53,000.

Admissions Traditional secondary-level entrance grade is 9. Gates MacGinite Reading Tests and WRAT required. Deadline for receipt of application materials: none. Application fee required: $25. Interview required.

Athletics Interscholastic: baseball (b,g), basketball (b,g), cheering (g), soccer (b,g), softball (g); intramural: floor hockey (b), indoor hockey (b,g); coed interscholastic: cross-country running; coed intramural: volleyball. 2 PE instructors, 11 coaches.

Computers Computers are regularly used in accounting, business applications, mathematics classes. Computer network features include on-campus library services, CD-ROMs, Internet access, office computer access.

Contact Mrs. Phyllis Detwiler, Administrative Assistant. 856-547-2996. Fax: 856-547-6584. E-mail: bhs@baptistregional.org. Web site: www.baptistregional.org.

BARNSTABLE ACADEMY

8 Wright Way
Oakland, New Jersey 07436
Head of School: Mr. David J. Salembier Jr.

General Information Coeducational day college-preparatory, general academic, arts, and technology school. Grades 5–12. Founded: 1978. Setting: suburban. Nearest major city is New York, NY. 4-acre campus. 1 building on campus. Approved or accredited by National Independent Private Schools Association and New Jersey Department of Education. Total enrollment: 145. Upper school average class size: 10. Upper school faculty-student ratio: 1:8.

Upper School Student Profile Grade 9: 24 students (15 boys, 9 girls); Grade 10: 28 students (18 boys, 10 girls); Grade 11: 30 students (19 boys, 11 girls); Grade 12: 28 students (17 boys, 11 girls).

Faculty School total: 17. In upper school: 6 men, 11 women; 12 have advanced degrees.

Subjects Offered Advanced math, algebra, American culture, American government, American legal systems, biology, business mathematics, chemistry, computer applications, contemporary issues, earth and space science, economics, English literature, English-AP, French, geometry, Latin, physical education, physics, psychology, Spanish, U.S. history, world history.

Special Academic Programs Advanced Placement exam preparation in 5 subject areas; honors section; accelerated programs; independent study; study at local college for college credit; academic accommodation for the gifted, the musically talented, and the artistically talented; remedial reading and/or remedial writing; remedial math; programs in English, general development for dyslexic students; special instructional classes for students with learning disabilities and Attention Deficit Disorder, the fragile emotionally disturbed; ESL (8 students enrolled).

College Placement 24 went to college, including Indiana University Bloomington; Pratt Institute; Rutgers, The State University of New Jersey, New Brunswick/Piscataway; University of Vermont. Other: 2 went to work, 1 entered military service, 1 had other specific plans. Median SAT verbal: 520, median SAT math: 530.

Student Life Upper grades have specified standards of dress, student council. Discipline rests primarily with faculty.

Summer Programs Remediation, enrichment, advancement programs offered; held on campus; accepts boys and girls; open to students from other schools. 25 students usually enrolled. 2006 schedule: June 26 to August 4. Application deadline: June 25.

Tuition and Aid Day student tuition: $22,900. Tuition installment plan (monthly payment plans, individually arranged payment plans). Tuition reduction for siblings, merit scholarship grants, need-based scholarship grants available. In 2005–06, 35% of upper-school students received aid; total upper-school merit-scholarship money awarded: $150,000. Total amount of financial aid awarded in 2005–06: $280,000.

Admissions Traditional secondary-level entrance grade is 9. For fall 2005, 175 students applied for upper-level admission, 100 were accepted, 78 enrolled. Deadline for receipt of application materials: none. No application fee required. Interview required.

Athletics Interscholastic: baseball (boys), cheering (g), softball (g); coed interscholastic: aerobics/nautilus, basketball, bowling, dance, nautilus, physical training, soccer, tennis, walking; coed intramural: aerobics, aerobics/dance, aerobics/nautilus, alpine skiing. 2 PE instructors, 3 coaches.

Computers Computer network features include CD-ROMs, Internet access.

Contact Ms. Lizanne M. Coyne, Assistant Headmaster. 201-651-0200. Fax: 201-337-9797. E-mail: lcoyne@barnstableacademy.com. Web site: www.barnstableacademy.com.

THE BARSTOW SCHOOL

11511 State Line Road
Kansas City, Missouri 64114
Head of School: Arthur N. Atkison

petersons.com

General Information Coeducational day college-preparatory school. Grades PS–12. Founded: 1884. Setting: suburban. 41-acre campus. 1 building on campus. Approved or accredited by Independent Schools Association of the Central States and Missouri Independent School Association. Member of National Association of Independent Schools. Language of instruction: English. Endowment: $4 million. Total enrollment: 623. Upper school average class size: 15. Upper school faculty-student ratio: 1:9.

Upper School Student Profile Grade 9: 47 students (27 boys, 20 girls); Grade 10: 42 students (20 boys, 22 girls); Grade 11: 49 students (31 boys, 18 girls); Grade 12: 46 students (22 boys, 24 girls).

Faculty School total: 70. In upper school: 13 men, 14 women; 17 have advanced degrees.

Subjects Offered Acting, advanced chemistry, advanced math, Advanced Placement courses, algebra, American history, American literature, ancient history, art, art history, Asian history, astronomy, biology, biology-AP, calculus, calculus-AP, ceramics, chemistry, chemistry-AP, Chinese, choir, community service, computer programming,

computer science, computer science-AP, creative writing, debate, drawing, English, English language-AP, English literature, English literature-AP, ethics, European history, European history-AP, fine arts, French, French language-AP, French literature-AP, geography, geology, geometry, Japanese, journalism, mathematics, music, photography, physical education, physics, science, social studies, Spanish, Spanish language-AP, speech, statistics, statistics-AP, trigonometry, U.S. government, U.S. history-AP, world history, writing.

Graduation Requirements Arts and fine arts (art, music, dance, drama), computer literacy, English, foreign language, mathematics, physical education (includes health), science, social studies (includes history). Community service is required.

Special Academic Programs Advanced Placement exam preparation in 16 subject areas; honors section; independent study; study at local college for college credit.

College Placement 32 students graduated in 2004; all went to college, including Brown University; Grinnell College; New York University; University of Kansas; University of Pennsylvania; Washington University in St. Louis. Mean composite ACT: 28. 65% scored over 600 on SAT verbal, 50% scored over 600 on SAT math.

Student Life Upper grades have specified standards of dress, student council, honor system. Discipline rests equally with students and faculty.

Tuition and Aid Day student tuition: $13,660. Tuition installment plan (FACTS Tuition Payment Plan). Merit scholarship grants, need-based scholarship grants, need-based loans available. In 2004–05, 13% of upper-school students received aid; total upper-school merit-scholarship money awarded: $40,500. Total amount of financial aid awarded in 2004–05: $349,386.

Admissions Traditional secondary-level entrance grade is 9. For fall 2005, 210 students applied for upper-level admission, 162 were accepted, 119 enrolled. ERB, Otis-Lennon Mental Ability Test and writing sample required. Deadline for receipt of application materials: May. Application fee required: $45. On-campus interview recommended.

Athletics Interscholastic: baseball (boys), basketball (b,g), cheering (g), cross-country running (b,g), dance team (g), soccer (b,g), tennis (b,g), track and field (b,g), volleyball (g); coed interscholastic: golf. 5 PE instructors, 5 coaches.

Computers Computers are regularly used in all academic classes. Computer network features include campus e-mail, on-campus library services, CD-ROMs, online commercial services, Internet access, file transfer.

Contact Mrs. Laura Lyddon Linn, Director of Admission and Financial Aid. 816-942-3255. Fax: 816-942-3227. E-mail: llinn@barstowschool.org. Web site: www.barstowschool.org.

ANNOUNCEMENT FROM THE SCHOOL The Barstow School is a coeducational, independent school of 645 students, preschool through grade 12, who come together with faculty and staff in a mutually supportive, trusting environment that nurtures intellectual, physical, emotional, and moral growth. In academic and extracurricular endeavors, students learn to take risks while pursuing excellence. Mary Louise Barstow and a fellow Wellesley graduate founded the school in 1884. The curriculum at the Barstow School is integrated across academic disciplines and characterized by expansive liberal arts programming. In addition to academic challenge, the Barstow school believes that reason, imagination, and physical activity are necessary aspects of healthy development. This philosophy creates an atmosphere where students learn to take risks; are open-minded, idealistic, and accepting; and develop self-discipline and self-reliance. An honor code helps to ensure Barstow students make ethical choices in their academic and extracurricular endeavors. The Barstow School is structured into three divisions: Lower School (PS–5), Middle School (6–8), and Upper School (9–12). Each division is staffed by administrators and faculty members committed to the academic, emotional, and developmental needs of that specific age group. A new Lower School complex opened in spring 2003. This new facility is designed to meet the learning styles and activities specific to students at that level. The Middle School allows students to continue to foster their love of learning while mastering time-management and study skills necessary to be successful in Upper School. A college-preparatory program, which includes 16 Advanced Placement courses, characterizes the Upper School, which also provides each student opportunities for involvement and leadership and service learning. At every grade level, the approach to learning is dynamic, experiential, active, and engaging. An emphasis on the performing and visual arts ensures students become well-rounded human beings. Students leave Barstow able to write well, think critically, and contribute significantly to their communities.

BATTLE GROUND ACADEMY

PO Box 1889
Franklin, Tennessee 37065-1889
Head of School: Dr. William R Mott

General Information Coeducational day college-preparatory, arts, and technology school. Grades K–12. Founded: 1889. Setting: suburban. Nearest major city is Nashville. 55-acre campus. 10 buildings on campus. Approved or accredited by Southern Association of Colleges and Schools, Southern Association of Independent Schools, Tennessee Association of Independent Schools, and Tennessee Department

of Education. Member of National Association of Independent Schools. Endowment: $7 million. Total enrollment: 919. Upper school average class size: 16. Upper school faculty-student ratio: 1:11.

Upper School Student Profile Grade 9: 110 students (58 boys, 52 girls); Grade 10: 95 students (64 boys, 31 girls); Grade 11: 100 students (51 boys, 49 girls); Grade 12: 82 students (58 boys, 24 girls).

Faculty School total: 72. In upper school: 21 men, 15 women; 25 have advanced degrees.

Subjects Offered Accounting, algebra, American history, American literature, art, art history, biology, calculus, chemistry, chorus, computer programming, computer science, drama, economics, English, English literature, European history, fine arts, French, geography, geometry, government/civics, grammar, health, history, Latin, mathematics, music, music history, physical education, physics, science, social studies, Spanish, speech, theater, trigonometry, world history, world literature, writing, zoology.

Graduation Requirements Arts and fine arts (art, music, dance, drama), computer science, English, foreign language, mathematics, physical education (includes health), science, social studies (includes history).

Special Academic Programs Advanced Placement exam preparation in 12 subject areas; honors section.

College Placement 92 students graduated in 2005; all went to college. Median combined SAT: 1200, median composite ACT: 25.

Student Life Upper grades have uniform requirement, student council, honor system. Discipline rests primarily with faculty.

Summer Programs Remediation, enrichment, sports, art/fine arts, computer instruction programs offered; session focuses on remediation, enrichment, and sports; held both on and off campus; held at local farm; accepts boys and girls; open to students from other schools. 250 students usually enrolled. 2006 schedule: June 5 to August 4. Application deadline: none.

Tuition and Aid Day student tuition: $12,500. Tuition installment plan (The Tuition Plan, monthly payment plans, individually arranged payment plans). Merit scholarship grants, need-based scholarship grants, paying campus jobs available. In 2005–06, 15% of upper-school students received aid; total upper-school merit-scholarship money awarded: $75,000. Total amount of financial aid awarded in 2005–06: $750,000.

Admissions Traditional secondary-level entrance grade is 9. ISEE required. Deadline for receipt of application materials: none. Application fee required: $50. Interview recommended.

Athletics Interscholastic: baseball (boys), basketball (b,g), cheering (b,g), cross-country running (b,g), dance team (g), diving (b,g), fitness (b,g), football (b), golf (b,g), physical fitness (b,g), soccer (b,g), softball (g), strength & conditioning (b,g), swimming and diving (b,g), tennis (b,g), volleyball (g), wrestling (b); intramural: baseball (b,g), basketball (b,g); coed interscholastic: bowling, hockey, ice hockey, outdoor adventure. 4 PE instructors, 1 trainer.

Computers Computers are regularly used in art, college planning, desktop publishing, English, foreign language, geography, history, library, literary magazine, mathematics, newspaper, photography, SAT preparation, science, social studies, Spanish, study skills, technology, theater, writing classes. Computer resources include on-campus library services, CD-ROMs, online commercial services, Internet access, DVD.

Contact Ms. Cathy Irwin, Director of Admissions-Middle and Upper School. 615-567-9014. E-mail: cathyi@battlegroundacademy.org. Web site: www.battlegroundacademy.org.

BAYLOR SCHOOL

PO Box 1337
Chattanooga, Tennessee 37401
Head of School: Dr. Bill Stacy

petersons.com

General Information Coeducational boarding and day college-preparatory school. Boarding grades 9–12, day grades 6–12. Founded: 1893. Setting: suburban. Nearest major city is Atlanta, GA. Students are housed in single-sex dormitories. 670-acre campus. 26 buildings on campus. Approved or accredited by Southern Association of Colleges and Schools, Southern Association of Independent Schools, The Association of Boarding Schools, and Tennessee Department of Education. Member of National Association of Independent Schools and Secondary School Admission Test Board. Language of instruction: English. Endowment: $64 million. Total enrollment: 1,033. Upper school average class size: 13. Upper school faculty-student ratio: 1:8.

Upper School Student Profile Grade 9: 171 students (95 boys, 76 girls); Grade 10: 186 students (101 boys, 85 girls); Grade 11: 169 students (92 boys, 77 girls); Grade 12: 178 students (96 boys, 82 girls). 27% of students are boarding students. 83% are state residents. 22 states are represented in upper school student body. 17% are international students. International students from Bahamas, Bermuda, Mexico, Republic of Korea, Saudi Arabia, and United Kingdom; 2 other countries represented in student body.

Faculty School total: 114. In upper school: 45 men, 33 women; 50 have advanced degrees; 37 reside on campus.

Subjects Offered Algebra, American history, American literature, anthropology, art, art history, biology, calculus, ceramics, chemistry, computer math, computer science, creative writing, dance, drama, driver education, economics, English, English language-AP, English literature, English literature-AP, environmental science, ethics,

European history, European history-AP, film, fine arts, French, French-AP, geography, geometry, German, German-AP, government/civics, history, Latin, Latin-AP, mathematics, music, photography, physical education, physics, physics-AP, religion, science, social studies, Spanish, Spanish-AP, speech, statistics, theater, trigonometry, U.S. history-AP, video, world history, world literature.

Graduation Requirements Arts and fine arts (art, music, dance, drama), English, foreign language, mathematics, physical education (includes health), science, social studies (includes history).

Special Academic Programs Advanced Placement exam preparation in 17 subject areas; honors section; academic accommodation for the gifted, the musically talented, and the artistically talented; special instructional classes for deaf students; ESL (8 students enrolled).

College Placement 169 students graduated in 2004; all went to college, including Auburn University; Boston University; Furman University; The University of Tennessee; University of Georgia; Vanderbilt University. Mean SAT verbal: 575, mean SAT math: 560. 30% scored over 600 on SAT verbal, 45% scored over 600 on SAT math.

Student Life Upper grades have specified standards of dress, student council, honor system. Discipline rests primarily with faculty.

Tuition and Aid Day student tuition: $14,567; 7-day tuition and room/board: $29,920. Tuition installment plan (Key Tuition Payment Plan, monthly payment plans, individually arranged payment plans). Merit scholarship grants, need-based scholarship grants available. In 2004–05, 38% of upper-school students received aid; total upper-school merit-scholarship money awarded: $56,720. Total amount of financial aid awarded in 2004–05: $1,655,953.

Admissions Traditional secondary-level entrance grade is 9. For fall 2005, 212 students applied for upper-level admission, 148 were accepted, 109 enrolled. ISEE, SSAT or TOEFL required. Deadline for receipt of application materials: none. Application fee required: $75. Interview required.

Athletics Interscholastic: aquatics (boys, girls), baseball (b), basketball (b,g), bowling (b,g), cheering (g), crew (b,g), cross-country running (b,g), dance (g), dance team (g), diving (b,g), fencing (b,g), football (b), golf (b,g), modern dance (g), soccer (b,g), softball (g), swimming and diving (b,g), tennis (b,g), track and field (b,g), volleyball (g), wrestling (b); intramural: ballet (g), dance (g), weight lifting (b,g); coed interscholastic: aerobics/dance, rowing, running, strength & conditioning; coed intramural: back packing, bicycling, canoeing/kayaking, climbing, fitness, fly fishing, Frisbee, hiking/backpacking, kayaking, mountain biking, mountaineering, ocean paddling, outdoor activities, outdoor adventure, outdoor education, physical fitness, rafting, rock climbing, scuba diving, ultimate Frisbee, wall climbing, wilderness survival. 5 coaches, 2 trainers.

Computers Computers are regularly used in art, English, history, mathematics, photography, publications, science, Spanish, technology, theater arts, writing, yearbook classes. Computer network features include campus e-mail, on-campus library services, CD-ROMs, online commercial services, Internet access.

Contact Mr. Matt Radtke, Director of Boarding Admission. 423-267-8505 Ext. 260. Fax: 423-757-2525. E-mail: matt_radtke@baylorschool.org. Web site: www.baylorschool.org.

See full description on page 670.

BAYSIDE ACADEMY

303 Dryer Avenue
Daphne, Alabama 36526
Head of School: Mr. Thomas F. Johnson

General Information Coeducational day college-preparatory school. Grades PS–12. Founded: 1970. Setting: small town. Nearest major city is Mobile. 44-acre campus. 10 buildings on campus. Approved or accredited by Southern Association of Colleges and Schools and Alabama Department of Education. Endowment: $1.4 million. Total enrollment: 730. Upper school average class size: 18. Upper school faculty-student ratio: 1:8.

Faculty School total: 112. In upper school: 19 men, 24 women; 25 have advanced degrees.

Subjects Offered Algebra, American history, American literature, art, art history, biology, biology-AP, calculus, chemistry, computer programming, computer science, creative writing, drama, economics, English, English literature, environmental science, ethics, European history, film, fine arts, French, genetics, geography, geometry, government/civics, grammar, histology, history, Latin, marine biology, mathematics, multimedia, music, oceanography, photography, physical education, physics, science, social studies, Spanish, speech, theater, trigonometry, world history, world literature, writing.

Graduation Requirements Arts and fine arts (art, music, dance, drama), computer science, English, foreign language, mathematics, physical education (includes health), science, social studies (includes history).

Special Academic Programs Advanced Placement exam preparation in 11 subject areas; honors section; independent study; programs in English, mathematics, general development for dyslexic students.

College Placement 54 students graduated in 2005; all went to college, including Auburn University; Birmingham-Southern College; College of Charleston; Saint

Louis University; The University of Alabama; Vanderbilt University. 60% scored over 600 on SAT verbal, 50% scored over 600 on SAT math, 50% scored over 26 on composite ACT.

Student Life Upper grades have uniform requirement, student council, honor system. Discipline rests primarily with faculty.

Tuition and Aid Day student tuition: $7000. Tuition installment plan (monthly payment plans, individually arranged payment plans). Tuition reduction for siblings, merit scholarship grants, need-based scholarship grants available. In 2005–06, 15% of upper-school students received aid.

Admissions Traditional secondary-level entrance grade is 9. For fall 2005, 70 students applied for upper-level admission, 46 were accepted, 45 enrolled. Otis-Lennon School Ability Test, Stanford Achievement Test and Stanford Achievement Test, Otis-Lennon School Ability Test required. Deadline for receipt of application materials: none. Application fee required: $100. On-campus interview required.

Athletics Interscholastic: aquatics (boys, girls), baseball (b), basketball (b,g), cheering (g), cross-country running (b,g), dance team (g), football (b), golf (b,g), indoor track (b,g), soccer (b,g), softball (g), swimming and diving (b,g), tennis (b,g), track and field (b,g), volleyball (g); intramural: ballet (g), dance (g), dance team (g), football (b), soccer (b,g); coed intramural: ballet, basketball, bicycling, dance, equestrian sports, physical training, sailing, scuba diving, soccer, strength & conditioning, track and field, weight training, yoga. 5 PE instructors, 16 coaches, 1 trainer.

Computers Computer network features include campus e-mail, on-campus library services, CD-ROMs, online commercial services, Internet access, DVD.

Contact Alan M. Foster, Director of Admissions. 251-626-2840 Ext. 229. Fax: 251-626-2899. E-mail: afoster@baysideacademy.org.

BEACON HIGH SCHOOL

Brookline, Massachusetts
See Special Needs Schools section.

BEARSPAW CHRISTIAN SCHOOL

260055 Range Road 22 NW
Calgary, Alberta T3R 1C5, Canada
Head of School: Mr. Kelly Blake

General Information Coeducational day college-preparatory and religious studies school, affiliated with Christian faith. Grades 1–12. Founded: 1991. Setting: rural. 5-acre campus. 1 building on campus. Approved or accredited by Association of Independent Schools and Colleges of Alberta and Alberta Department of Education. Language of instruction: English. Endowment: CAN$3 million. Total enrollment: 349. Upper school average class size: 20. Upper school faculty-student ratio: 1:20.

Upper School Student Profile Grade 10: 14 students (7 boys, 7 girls); Grade 11: 26 students (12 boys, 14 girls); Grade 12: 19 students (7 boys, 12 girls). 90% of students are Christian faith.

Faculty School total: 26. In upper school: 6 men, 6 women; 1 has an advanced degree.

Subjects Offered 20th century history, 20th century world history, advanced chemistry, advanced math, algebra, applied music, Bible studies, biology, calculus, Canadian history, chemistry, Christian education, computer applications, English composition, general math, keyboarding/computer, physical education, science, social studies, wilderness experience, world history.

Graduation Requirements Bible, English, mathematics, science, social studies (includes history).

Special Academic Programs Special instructional classes for students with learning disabilities, Attention Deficit Disorder, emotional problems, and dyslexia.

College Placement 21 students graduated in 2005; 13 went to college, including University of Calgary. Other: 8 went to work.

Student Life Upper grades have uniform requirement. Discipline rests primarily with faculty. Attendance at religious services is required.

Tuition and Aid Day student tuition: CAN$4200. Tuition installment plan (individually arranged payment plans). Tuition reduction for siblings, need-based scholarship grants, need-based loans available. In 2005–06, 14% of upper-school students received aid. Total amount of financial aid awarded in 2005–06: CAN$27,000.

Admissions Traditional secondary-level entrance grade is 11. For fall 2005, 16 students applied for upper-level admission, 8 were accepted, 8 enrolled. WAIS, WICS required. Deadline for receipt of application materials: September 30. Application fee required: CAN$400. Interview required.

Athletics Interscholastic: badminton (boys, girls), basketball (b,g), cross-country running (b,g), floor hockey (b,g), golf (b), track and field (b,g), volleyball (b,g); intramural: badminton (b,g), basketball (b,g), cross-country running (b,g), flag football (b,g), floor hockey (b,g), track and field (b,g), volleyball (b,g); coed interscholastic: badminton; coed intramural: badminton, basketball, flag football, golf, outdoor education, volleyball. 2 PE instructors.

Computers Computers are regularly used in all academic classes. Computer network features include campus e-mail, Internet access, file transfer.

Contact Mrs. Rene Weiss, School Secretary. 403-295-2566 Ext. 248. Fax: 403-275-8170. E-mail: reneweiss@bearspawschool.ab.ca. Web site: www.bearspawschool.ab.ca.

BEAUFORT ACADEMY

240 Sams Point Road
Beaufort, South Carolina 29907
Head of School: Tim Johnston

General Information Coeducational day college-preparatory and technology school. Grades PK–12. Founded: 1965. Setting: small town. Nearest major city is Savannah, GA. 35-acre campus. 3 buildings on campus. Approved or accredited by South Carolina Independent School Association, Southern Association of Colleges and Schools, Southern Association of Independent Schools, and The College Board. Member of National Association of Independent Schools. Endowment: $650,000. Total enrollment: 374. Upper school average class size: 12. Upper school faculty-student ratio: 1:10.

Upper School Student Profile Grade 9: 33 students (17 boys, 16 girls); Grade 10: 29 students (12 boys, 17 girls); Grade 11: 22 students (10 boys, 12 girls); Grade 12: 17 students (9 boys, 8 girls).

Faculty School total: 48. In upper school: 8 men, 13 women; 16 have advanced degrees.

Subjects Offered Algebra, American history, American literature, anatomy, art, art history, biology, calculus, chemistry, Chinese, composition, computer science, creative writing, debate, drama, earth science, economics, English, English literature, environmental science, European history, fine arts, French, geometry, government/civics, grammar, health, history, journalism, Latin, marine biology, mathematics, modern world history, music, physical education, physics, physiology, pre-calculus, psychology, science, social studies, Spanish, speech, trigonometry, U.S. history, Western civilization, world literature, writing workshop.

Graduation Requirements Arts and fine arts (art, music, dance, drama), computer science, English, ethics and responsibility, foreign language, mathematics, physical education (includes health), science, social studies (includes history), senior seminar (ethics and philosophy).

Special Academic Programs Advanced Placement exam preparation in 5 subject areas; honors section; independent study; study at local college for college credit; study abroad; academic accommodation for the gifted; programs in general development for dyslexic students.

College Placement 19 students graduated in 2005; all went to college, including Clemson University; College of Charleston; University of South Carolina. Median SAT verbal: 579, median SAT math: 586. 33% scored over 600 on SAT verbal, 25% scored over 600 on SAT math.

Student Life Upper grades have specified standards of dress, honor system. Discipline rests primarily with faculty.

Summer Programs Sports programs offered; session focuses on sports/soccer; held on campus; accepts boys and girls; not open to students from other schools. 20 students usually enrolled. 2006 schedule: June 8 to August 1.

Tuition and Aid Day student tuition: $5400–$8495. Tuition installment plan (Insured Tuition Payment Plan, monthly payment plans, individually arranged payment plans). Tuition reduction for siblings, need-based scholarship grants, tuition remission for children of faculty available. In 2005–06, 25% of upper-school students received aid. Total amount of financial aid awarded in 2005–06: $62,000.

Admissions Traditional secondary-level entrance grade is 9. CTP III, ERB CTP III, OLSAT, Stanford Achievement Test or school's own exam or coop required. Deadline for receipt of application materials: none. Application fee required: $60. Interview recommended.

Athletics Interscholastic: baseball (boys), basketball (b,g), football (b), lacrosse (b), soccer (b,g), softball (g), swimming and diving (b,g), tennis (b,g), volleyball (g); coed interscholastic: crew, golf, physical fitness, soccer, swimming and diving, track and field; coed intramural: crew, fitness, floor hockey, rowing, softball, touch football. 2 PE instructors, 2 coaches, 1 trainer.

Computers Computers are regularly used in English, history, journalism, library skills, media, newspaper, publishing, science, yearbook classes. Computer network features include campus e-mail, on-campus library services, CD-ROMs, online commercial services, Internet access, office computer access.

Contact Tim Johnston, Head of School. 843-524-3393. Fax: 843-524-1171. E-mail: tjohnston@beaufortacademy.org. Web site: www.beaufortacademy.org.

BEAUMONT SCHOOL

3301 North Park Boulevard
Cleveland Heights, Ohio 44118
Head of School: Mrs. Margeret Connell

General Information Girls' day college-preparatory, arts, and religious studies school, affiliated with Roman Catholic Church. Grades 9–12. Founded: 1850. Setting: suburban. Nearest major city is Cleveland. 24-acre campus. 2 buildings on campus. Approved or accredited by North Central Association of Colleges and Schools, Ohio Catholic Schools Accreditation Association (OCSAA), and Ohio Department of Education. Endowment: $3.6 million. Total enrollment: 449. Upper school average class size: 20. Upper school faculty-student ratio: 1:14.

Upper School Student Profile Grade 9: 109 students (109 girls); Grade 10: 112 students (112 girls); Grade 11: 124 students (124 girls); Grade 12: 104 students (104 girls). 78% of students are Roman Catholic.

Faculty School total: 47. In upper school: 4 men, 42 women; 28 have advanced degrees.

Subjects Offered Algebra, American history, American literature, art, art history, astronomy, biology, business skills, calculus, ceramics, chemistry, community service, computer programming, computer science, creative writing, culinary arts, economics, English, English literature, ethics, fashion, fine arts, French, geology, geometry, government, health, human relations, journalism, keyboarding, Latin, mathematics, music, photography, physical education, physics, piano, pre-calculus, religion, science, social science, social studies, Spanish, speech, theology, trigonometry, voice, world affairs, world history, world literature, writing.

Graduation Requirements Arts and fine arts (art, music, dance, drama), computer science, English, foreign language, mathematics, physical education (includes health), religion (includes Bible studies and theology), science, social science, social studies (includes history), annual renewal day, Senior Project R.E.A.L, Junior Career Shadowing Day. Community service is required.

Special Academic Programs Advanced Placement exam preparation in 6 subject areas; honors section; independent study; study at local college for college credit; academic accommodation for the gifted.

College Placement 108 students graduated in 2005; all went to college, including John Carroll University; Marquette University; Mercyhurst College; Miami University. Median SAT verbal: 531, median SAT math: 540, median composite ACT: 23. 25% scored over 600 on SAT verbal, 25% scored over 600 on SAT math, 36% scored over 26 on composite ACT.

Student Life Upper grades have uniform requirement, student council, honor system. Discipline rests primarily with faculty. Attendance at religious services is required.

Summer Programs Enrichment, sports, art/fine arts, computer instruction programs offered; session focuses on enrichment and credit courses; held on campus; accepts girls; not open to students from other schools. 175 students usually enrolled.

Tuition and Aid Day student tuition: $7800. Tuition reduction for siblings, merit scholarship grants, need-based scholarship grants, paying campus jobs available. In 2005–06, 41% of upper-school students received aid; total upper-school merit-scholarship money awarded: $55,200. Total amount of financial aid awarded in 2005–06: $100,000.

Admissions Traditional secondary-level entrance grade is 9. For fall 2005, 179 students applied for upper-level admission, 168 were accepted, 109 enrolled. SAS, STS-HSPT required. Deadline for receipt of application materials: May 15. No application fee required. On-campus interview required.

Athletics Interscholastic: basketball, cross-country running, diving, field hockey, softball, swimming and diving, track and field, volleyball. 1 PE instructor, 11 coaches, 1 trainer.

Computers Computers are regularly used in English, foreign language, keyboarding, media, publications, science, social studies, yearbook classes. Computer network features include campus e-mail, on-campus library services, CD-ROMs, Internet access, file transfer, office computer access.

Contact Mrs. Jennifer Lowery, Assistant Director of Admissions. 216-321-2954 Ext. 248. Fax: 216-321-3947. E-mail: jlowery@beaumontschool.org.

BEAVER COUNTRY DAY SCHOOL

791 Hammond Street
Chestnut Hill, Massachusetts 02467
Head of School: Peter R. Hutton

petersons.com

General Information Coeducational day college-preparatory and arts school. Grades 6–12. Founded: 1920. Setting: suburban. Nearest major city is Boston. 17-acre campus. 2 buildings on campus. Approved or accredited by New England Association of Schools and Colleges and Massachusetts Department of Education. Member of National Association of Independent Schools and Secondary School Admission Test Board. Endowment: $5.2 million. Total enrollment: 406. Upper school average class size: 15. Upper school faculty-student ratio: 1:8.

Upper School Student Profile Grade 9: 75 students (40 boys, 35 girls); Grade 10: 75 students (38 boys, 37 girls); Grade 11: 67 students (33 boys, 34 girls); Grade 12: 74 students (41 boys, 33 girls).

Faculty School total: 71. In upper school: 19 men, 25 women; 32 have advanced degrees.

Subjects Offered 20th century history, 3-dimensional art, 3-dimensional design, acting, advanced chemistry, advanced math, Advanced Placement courses, algebra, American history, American literature, anatomy and physiology, art, art history, astronomy, biology, calculus, calculus-AP, ceramics, chamber groups, chemistry, chemistry-AP, child development, China/Japan history, Chinese history, chorus, civil rights, classical music, college counseling, college placement, college writing, community service, comparative civilizations, comparative cultures, comparative government and politics, comparative religion, computer graphics, computer math, computer programming, computer programming-AP, computer skills, contemporary history, costumes and make-up, creative writing, dance, decision making, diversity studies, drafting, drama, driver education, economics, English, English literature, ethical decision making, ethics, European civilization, European history, expository writing, fine arts, French, French as a second language, French language-AP, French literature-AP, French-AP, geography, geometry, government/civics, grammar, health, history, Holocaust studies, honors algebra, honors English, honors geometry, honors U.S. history, human biology, international affairs, jazz, jazz band, journalism, junior

and senior seminars, Latin American history, Latin American studies, mathematics, Middle Eastern history, modern Chinese history, modern European history, music, musical theater, painting, peer counseling, philosophy, photography, physical education, physics, play production, poetry, pre-calculus, programming, psychology, science, Shakespeare, sign language, social justice, social studies, society, politics and law, Spanish, Spanish language-AP, Spanish literature, Spanish literature-AP, Spanish-AP, squash, statistics, studio art, studio art-AP, study skills, theater, trigonometry, typing, U.S. history, world history, writing.

Graduation Requirements Arts, English, foreign language, history, interdisciplinary studies, mathematics, physical education (includes health), science, 40 hours of community service.

Special Academic Programs Advanced Placement exam preparation in 10 subject areas; honors section; independent study; academic accommodation for the artistically talented.

College Placement 64 students graduated in 2005; all went to college, including Boston University; Brandeis University; Connecticut College; New York University; The George Washington University; Tufts University.

Student Life Upper grades have student council, honor system. Discipline rests primarily with students.

Tuition and Aid Day student tuition: $26,560. Tuition installment plan (Academic Management Services Plan, Key Tuition Payment Plan, monthly payment plans, individually arranged payment plans). Need-based scholarship grants available. In 2005–06, 28% of upper-school students received aid. Total amount of financial aid awarded in 2005–06: $2,208,785.

Admissions Traditional secondary-level entrance grade is 9. For fall 2005, 225 students applied for upper-level admission, 113 were accepted, 47 enrolled. ISEE or SSAT required. Deadline for receipt of application materials: February 1. Application fee required: $45. On-campus interview required.

Athletics Interscholastic: baseball (boys), basketball (b,g), cross-country running (b,g), field hockey (g), lacrosse (b,g), soccer (b,g), softball (g), tennis (b,g), volleyball (g), wrestling (b); coed interscholastic: baseball, bicycling, cross-country running, fencing, Frisbee, golf, martial arts, mountain biking, squash, ultimate Frisbee, yoga; coed intramural: aerobics, aerobics/dance, ballet, dance. 3 PE instructors, 15 coaches, 1 trainer.

Computers Computers are regularly used in art, English, foreign language, history, mathematics, science classes. Computer network features include campus e-mail, on-campus library services, CD-ROMs, online commercial services, Internet access, file transfer, office computer access, DVD.

Contact Nedda Bonassera, Admission Office Manager. 617-738-2725. Fax: 617-738-2767. E-mail: admission@bcdschool.org. Web site: www.bcdschool.org.

ANNOUNCEMENT FROM THE SCHOOL Beaver Country Day School, just outside of Boston, offers a balanced college-preparatory curriculum in academics, arts, and athletics for grades 6–12. The diversity of its students (more than 28% are minorities) and faculty members (20% are minorities), together with a mission that emphasizes innovation in learning and teaching, provide a dynamic and challenging curriculum and community. With an average class size of 15, teachers provide attention and encouragement to all students. Included on the 22-acre campus are a professional biotechnology lab, a new Performing and Visual Arts Center, 2 gyms, and an open and spacious library.

THE BEEKMAN SCHOOL

220 East 50th Street
New York, New York 10022
Head of School: George Higgins

petersons.com

General Information Coeducational day college-preparatory, general academic, arts, and technology school. Grades 9–PG. Founded: 1925. Setting: urban. 1 building on campus. Approved or accredited by New York State Board of Regents and New York Department of Education. Total enrollment: 78. Upper school average class size: 8. Upper school faculty-student ratio: 1:8.

Upper School Student Profile Grade 9: 14 students (8 boys, 6 girls); Grade 10: 18 students (11 boys, 7 girls); Grade 11: 21 students (12 boys, 9 girls); Grade 12: 25 students (13 boys, 12 girls); Postgraduate: 2 students (1 boy, 1 girl).

Faculty School total: 16. In upper school: 6 men, 10 women; 13 have advanced degrees.

Subjects Offered Advanced Placement courses, algebra, American history, ancient world history, art, astronomy, bioethics, biology, business mathematics, calculus, calculus-AP, chemistry, computer animation, computer art, computer science, conceptual physics, creative writing, drama, drawing, Eastern religion and philosophy, ecology, economics, electronics, English, environmental science, ESL, European history, film, French, geometry, government, health, journalism, modern politics, modern world history, photography, physical education, physical science, physics, poetry, pre-calculus, psychology, SAT preparation, sculpture, Spanish, TOEFL preparation, trigonometry, U.S. history, Web site design, Western philosophy.

Graduation Requirements Art, computer technologies, electives, English, foreign language, health education, mathematics, physical education (includes health), science, social studies (includes history).

The Beekman School

Special Academic Programs Advanced Placement exam preparation in 19 subject areas; honors section; accelerated programs; independent study; academic accommodation for the gifted, the musically talented, and the artistically talented; remedial reading and/or remedial writing; remedial math; programs in English, mathematics, general development for dyslexic students; ESL (3 students enrolled).

College Placement 28 students graduated in 2005; 27 went to college, including Arizona State University; Boston University; Fordham University; New York University; Sarah Lawrence College; University of Vermont. Other: 1 had other specific plans. Mean SAT verbal: 558, mean SAT math: 509. 33% scored over 600 on SAT verbal, 27% scored over 600 on SAT math.

Student Life Upper grades have honor system. Discipline rests primarily with faculty.

Summer Programs Remediation, enrichment, advancement, ESL programs offered; session focuses on academics; held on campus; accepts boys and girls; open to students from other schools. 35 students usually enrolled. 2006 schedule: July 5 to August 17. Application deadline: July 1.

Tuition and Aid Day student tuition: $23,000. Tuition installment plan (monthly payment plans, individually arranged payment plans).

Admissions Traditional secondary-level entrance grade is 10. For fall 2005, 39 students applied for upper-level admission, 38 were accepted, 33 enrolled. Deadline for receipt of application materials: none. No application fee required. On-campus interview required.

Athletics 1 PE instructor.

Computers Computer resources include campus e-mail, CD-ROMs, online commercial services, Internet access, file transfer, DVD.

Contact George Higgins, Headmaster. 212-755-6666. Fax: 212-888-6085. E-mail: georgeh@beekmanschool.org. Web site: www.BeekmanSchool.org.

ANNOUNCEMENT FROM THE SCHOOL The Beekman School/The Tutoring School offers a traditional academic program taught in a unique and intimate environment. The faculty encourages students to become actively involved in their education and to develop a sense of commitment and responsibility. The Beekman School has a strong tradition of successfully educating virtually all types of students. The School's success is due in part to maintaining small class sizes; flexible, individualized class scheduling; and careful guidance from a devoted staff.

See full description on page 672.

BEIJING BISS INTERNATIONAL SCHOOL

Number 17, Area 4, An Zhen Xi Li, Chaoyang District
Beijing 100029, China
Head of School: Mr. Iain Stirling

General Information Coeducational day college-preparatory, general academic, arts, business, and bilingual studies school. Grades K–12. Founded: 1994. Setting: urban. 2 buildings on campus. Approved or accredited by Western Association of Schools and Colleges. Member of European Council of International Schools. Language of instruction: English. Upper school average class size: 15. Upper school faculty-student ratio: 1:6.

Faculty School total: 54. In upper school: 16 men, 15 women; 28 have advanced degrees.

Special Academic Programs International Baccalaureate program; ESL.

Student Life Upper grades have specified standards of dress, student council, honor system. Discipline rests equally with students and faculty.

Summer Programs Enrichment, advancement, ESL, sports, art/fine arts, rigorous outdoor training, computer instruction programs offered; held on campus; accepts boys and girls; open to students from other schools.

Tuition and Aid Tuition reduction for siblings available.

Admissions Deadline for receipt of application materials: none. Application fee required: $500. On-campus interview required.

Athletics Interscholastic: aquatics (boys, girls), badminton (b,g), basketball (b,g), crew (b), cross-country running (b,g), football (b,g), indoor soccer (b), running (b,g), soccer (b,g), swimming and diving (b,g), track and field (b,g), volleyball (b,g); intramural: aquatics (b,g), badminton (b,g), basketball (b,g), bowling (b,g), climbing (b,g), combined training (b,g), fitness (b,g), floor hockey (b,g), football (b,g), golf (b), indoor soccer (b,g), physical fitness (b,g), rock climbing (b,g), running (b,g), soccer (b,g), track and field (b,g), volleyball (b,g), wall climbing (b,g); coed interscholastic: soccer; coed intramural: floor hockey, football, physical fitness, rock climbing, soccer, volleyball, wall climbing. 2 PE instructors.

Computers Computer network features include on-campus library services, CD-ROMs, Internet access, DVD.

Contact Ms. Rachel SeeToh, Admissions Executive. 86-10-6443 3151 Ext. 253. Fax: 86-10-6443 3156. E-mail: rseetoh@biss.com.cn. Web site: www.biss.com.cn.

BELEN JESUIT PREPARATORY SCHOOL

500 Southwest 127th Avenue
Miami, Florida 33184
Head of School: Fr. Marcelino Garcia, SJ

General Information Boys' day college-preparatory and religious studies school, affiliated with Roman Catholic Church. Grades 6–12. Founded: 1854. Setting: urban. 28-acre campus. 3 buildings on campus. Approved or accredited by CITA (Commission on International and Trans-Regional Accreditation), European Council of International Schools, Jesuit Secondary Education Association, National Catholic Education Association, Southern Association of Colleges and Schools, and Florida Department of Education. Endowment: $4 million. Total enrollment: 1,315. Upper school average class size: 27. Upper school faculty-student ratio: 1:13.

Upper School Student Profile Grade 9: 198 students (198 boys); Grade 10: 233 students (233 boys); Grade 11: 173 students (173 boys); Grade 12: 139 students (139 boys). 98% of students are Roman Catholic.

Faculty School total: 90. In upper school: 35 men, 19 women; 46 have advanced degrees.

Subjects Offered Art, art history, biology, chemistry, composition, computers, English, English literature, French, history, mathematics, music, philosophy, physical education, physics, religion, science, social studies, Spanish.

Graduation Requirements Arts and fine arts (art, music, dance, drama), English, foreign language, mathematics, philosophy, physical education (includes health), religion (includes Bible studies and theology), science, social science, social studies (includes history). Community service is required.

Special Academic Programs Advanced Placement exam preparation in 13 subject areas; honors section; study at local college for college credit.

College Placement 164 students graduated in 2005; all went to college, including Florida International University; Florida State University; Georgetown University; Loyola University New Orleans; University of Florida; University of Miami. Median SAT verbal: 560, median SAT math: 570. Mean composite ACT: 24. 27% scored over 600 on SAT verbal, 26% scored over 600 on SAT math.

Student Life Upper grades have uniform requirement, student council. Discipline rests primarily with faculty.

Tuition and Aid Day student tuition: $9400. Need-based scholarship grants available. In 2005–06, 35% of upper-school students received aid. Total amount of financial aid awarded in 2005–06: $400,000.

Admissions Traditional secondary-level entrance grade is 9. For fall 2005, 122 students applied for upper-level admission, 92 were accepted, 67 enrolled. CTBS, OLSAT required. Deadline for receipt of application materials: none. Application fee required: $30.

Athletics Interscholastic: baseball, basketball, cross-country running, football, golf, rowing, soccer, swimming and diving, tennis, track and field, volleyball, water polo, weight lifting, wrestling; intramural: bowling, fishing, in-line hockey, weight training. 5 PE instructors, 22 coaches, 1 trainer.

Computers Computers are regularly used in art, English, foreign language, history, mathematics, music, science classes. Computer network features include on-campus library services, CD-ROMs, online commercial services, Internet access, DVD.

Contact Mrs. Chris Besil, Admissions Secretary. 786-621-4032. Fax: 305-227-2565. E-mail: admissions@belenjesuit.org. Web site: belenjesuit.org.

BELLARMINE COLLEGE PREPARATORY

960 West Hedding Street
San Jose, California 95126
Head of School: Mr. Mark Pierotti

General Information Boys' day college-preparatory, arts, religious studies, and technology school, affiliated with Roman Catholic Church. Grades 9–12. Founded: 1851. Setting: urban. 21-acre campus. 14 buildings on campus. Approved or accredited by National Catholic Education Association and Western Association of Schools and Colleges. Endowment: $30 million. Total enrollment: 1,500. Upper school average class size: 25. Upper school faculty-student ratio: 1:14.

Upper School Student Profile Grade 9: 390 students (390 boys); Grade 10: 392 students (392 boys); Grade 11: 361 students (361 boys); Grade 12: 357 students (357 boys). 75% of students are Roman Catholic.

Faculty School total: 85. In upper school: 60 men, 25 women; 60 have advanced degrees.

Subjects Offered Algebra, American history, American literature, anatomy, art, arts, biology, calculus, ceramics, chemistry, community service, computer science, drama, English, English literature, ethics, European history, expository writing, fine arts, French, geography, geometry, government/civics, history, international relations, Latin, Mandarin, mathematics, music, physical education, physics, psychology, religion, science, social science, social studies, Spanish, speech, theater, theology, trigonometry, world history, world literature, writing.

Graduation Requirements Arts and fine arts (art, music, dance, drama), English, foreign language, mathematics, physical education (includes health), religion (includes Bible studies and theology), science, social science, social studies (includes history), 100 hours of Christian service.

Special Academic Programs Advanced Placement exam preparation in 7 subject areas; honors section; independent study; special instructional classes for students with learning disabilities and Attention Deficit Disorder.

College Placement 340 students graduated in 2005; all went to college, including California Polytechnic State University, San Luis Obispo; San Jose State University; Santa Clara University; University of California, Berkeley; University of California, Davis; University of Southern California.

Student Life Upper grades have specified standards of dress, student council, honor system. Discipline rests primarily with faculty.

Summer Programs Remediation, enrichment, advancement, sports, art/fine arts, computer instruction programs offered; session focuses on enrichment; held on campus; accepts boys and girls; open to students from other schools. 1320 students usually enrolled. 2006 schedule: June 18 to July 25. Application deadline: June 15.

Tuition and Aid Day student tuition: $10,800. Tuition installment plan (FACTS Tuition Payment Plan, semester payment plan, 10-installment plan). Need-based scholarship grants available. In 2005–06, 16% of upper-school students received aid. Total amount of financial aid awarded in 2005–06: $1,800,000.

Admissions Traditional secondary-level entrance grade is 9. For fall 2005, 950 students applied for upper-level admission, 400 were accepted, 390 enrolled. High School Placement Test required. Deadline for receipt of application materials: February 8. Application fee required: $60.

Athletics Interscholastic: aquatics, baseball, basketball, cross-country running, diving, football, golf, lacrosse, soccer, swimming and diving, tennis, track and field, volleyball, water polo, wrestling; intramural: basketball, flag football, in-line hockey, soccer, softball. 4 PE instructors, 15 coaches, 2 trainers.

Computers Computers are regularly used in art, English, foreign language, mathematics, music, science classes. Computer network features include campus e-mail, on-campus library services, CD-ROMs, online commercial services, Internet access, DVD, wireless campus network.

Contact Terry Council, Admissions Assistant. 408-294-9224. Fax: 408-294-1894. E-mail: admissions@bcp.org. Web site: www.bcp.org.

BELLARMINE PREPARATORY SCHOOL

2300 South Washington Street
Tacoma, Washington 98405
Head of School: John R. Peterson

General Information Coeducational day college-preparatory and religious studies school, affiliated with Roman Catholic Church. Grades 9–12. Founded: 1928. Setting: urban. Nearest major city is Seattle. 42-acre campus. 11 buildings on campus. Approved or accredited by Jesuit Secondary Education Association, National Catholic Education Association, Northwest Association of Schools and Colleges, and Washington Department of Education. Endowment: $15.4 million. Total enrollment: 1,005. Upper school average class size: 20. Upper school faculty-student ratio: 1:14.

Upper School Student Profile Grade 9: 268 students (150 boys, 118 girls); Grade 10: 244 students (118 boys, 126 girls); Grade 11: 254 students (125 boys, 129 girls); Grade 12: 239 students (111 boys, 128 girls). 72% of students are Roman Catholic.

Faculty School total: 85. In upper school: 45 men, 40 women; 47 have advanced degrees.

Subjects Offered 3-dimensional design, accounting, acting, algebra, American government, American history, American literature, anatomy and physiology, art, arts, Asian history, band, bioethics, biology, botany, British literature-AP, business, calculus-AP, Catholic belief and practice, ceramics, chemistry, chemistry-AP, choral music, Christian and Hebrew scripture, church history, community service, composition-AP, computer keyboarding, computer literacy, computer programming, computer science, concert band, concert choir, crafts, creative writing, discrete math, drama, drawing, earth science, electronics, English, English literature, European history, European history-AP, film and literature, fine arts, French, geometry, German, government/civics, grammar, health, health education, history, honors English, honors geometry, honors world history, Japanese, jazz band, journalism, lab science, marine biology, marine studies, mathematics, music, newspaper, photography, physical education, physical fitness, physics, physics-AP, prayer/spirituality, pre-calculus, psychology, psychology-AP, public speaking, religion, science, sculpture, Shakespeare, short story, social studies, Spanish, Spanish-AP, speech, speech communications, statistics, theater, trigonometry, U.S. history-AP, vocal ensemble, vocal music, wind ensemble, world cultures, world history, world religions, writing, yearbook.

Graduation Requirements Arts and fine arts (art, music, dance, drama), English, foreign language, mathematics, physical education (includes health), religion (includes Bible studies and theology), science, social studies (includes history).

Special Academic Programs Advanced Placement exam preparation in 8 subject areas; honors section; independent study; remedial reading and/or remedial writing.

College Placement 230 students graduated in 2005; 228 went to college, including Central Washington University; Gonzaga University; University of Portland; University of Washington; Washington State University; Western Washington University. Other: 2 entered a postgraduate year. Median composite ACT: 25. Mean SAT verbal: 566, mean SAT math: 567. 40% scored over 600 on SAT verbal, 40% scored over 600 on SAT math, 38% scored over 26 on composite ACT.

Student Life Upper grades have specified standards of dress, student council. Discipline rests primarily with faculty. Attendance at religious services is required.

Summer Programs Remediation, enrichment programs offered; session focuses on high school preparedness; held on campus; accepts boys and girls; open to students from other schools. 61 students usually enrolled. 2006 schedule: June 26 to July 28. Application deadline: June 26.

Tuition and Aid Day student tuition: $9247. Tuition installment plan (monthly payment plans, individually arranged payment plans). Need-based scholarship grants, paying campus jobs available. In 2005–06, 32% of upper-school students received aid. Total amount of financial aid awarded in 2005–06: $1,636,971.

Admissions Traditional secondary-level entrance grade is 9. For fall 2005, 354 students applied for upper-level admission, 306 were accepted, 268 enrolled. High School Placement Test (closed version) from Scholastic Testing Service required. Deadline for receipt of application materials: February 9. No application fee required.

Athletics Interscholastic: baseball (boys), basketball (b,g), cheering (g), cross-country running (b,g), football (b), golf (b,g), soccer (b,g), softball (g), tennis (b,g), track and field (b,g), volleyball (g), wrestling (b); coed interscholastic: bowling; coed intramural: basketball, flag football, floor hockey, ultimate Frisbee, volleyball. 4 PE instructors, 3 coaches, 1 trainer.

Computers Computers are regularly used in business education, English, graphic arts, mathematics, newspaper, science, yearbook classes. Computer network features include campus e-mail, on-campus library services, CD-ROMs, Internet access, file transfer.

Contact Elaine Hoelscher, Admissions Secretary. 253-879-9724. Fax: 253-756-3880. E-mail: hoelschere@bellarmineprep.org. Web site: bellarmineprep.org.

BELLEVUE CHRISTIAN SCHOOL

1601 98th Avenue, NE
Clyde Hill, Washington 98004-3400
Head of School: Bill Safstrom

General Information Coeducational day college-preparatory, general academic, arts, business, vocational, religious studies, and technology school, affiliated with Christian faith. Grades PK–12. Founded: 1950. Setting: suburban. Nearest major city is Seattle. 5 buildings on campus. Approved or accredited by Christian Schools International, Northwest Association of Accredited Schools, Northwest Association of Schools and Colleges, and Washington Department of Education. Total enrollment: 1,300. Upper school average class size: 21. Upper school faculty-student ratio: 1:21.

Upper School Student Profile 90% of students are Christian faith.

Faculty School total: 38. In upper school: 18 men, 20 women; 24 have advanced degrees.

Subjects Offered 20th century world history, accounting, advanced chemistry, Advanced Placement courses, algebra, art, art-AP, athletics, band, Bible, biology, calculus-AP, chemistry, chemistry-AP, choral music, church history, community service, drama, economics, English, English-AP, ethics, fine arts, foreign language, geometry, German, German-AP, jazz band, mathematics, physical education, physical science, physics, religion, social science, social studies, Spanish, Spanish language-AP, trigonometry, U.S. history-AP, yearbook.

Graduation Requirements Arts and fine arts (art, music, dance, drama), English, foreign language, mathematics, physical education (includes health), religion (includes Bible studies and theology), science, social science, social studies (includes history). Community service is required.

Special Academic Programs Advanced Placement exam preparation; honors section; academic accommodation for the gifted and the musically talented; ESL (7 students enrolled).

College Placement 78 students graduated in 2005; 74 went to college, including University of Washington. Other: 2 went to work, 2 had other specific plans.

Student Life Upper grades have specified standards of dress, student council. Discipline rests primarily with faculty. Attendance at religious services is required.

Summer Programs Advancement, sports, art/fine arts, computer instruction programs offered; session focuses on providing additional course offerings that might not fit in the schedule during the academic year; held on campus; accepts boys and girls; not open to students from other schools. 100 students usually enrolled. 2006 schedule: July to August.

Tuition and Aid Tuition installment plan (monthly payment plans). Tuition reduction for siblings available. In 2005–06, 15% of upper-school students received aid.

Admissions Traditional secondary-level entrance grade is 9. Deadline for receipt of application materials: none. Application fee required: $75. Interview required.

Athletics Interscholastic: baseball (boys), basketball (b,g), cheering (g), combined training (b,g), cooperative games (b,g), cross-country running (b,g), fitness (b,g), golf (b,g), outdoor activities (b,g), outdoor education (b,g), physical fitness (b,g), physical training (b,g), running (b,g), soccer (b,g), softball (g), track and field (b,g), volleyball (g), weight lifting (b,g), weight training (b,g).

Computers Computer network features include campus e-mail, on-campus library services, Internet access.

Contact Erick Newbill, Admissions Coordinator. 425-454-4402 Ext. 204. Fax: 425-454-4418. E-mail: enewbill@bellevuechristian.org. Web site: www.bellevuechristian.org.

BELMONT HILL SCHOOL

350 Prospect Street
Belmont, Massachusetts 02478-2662
Head of School: Dr. Richard I. Melvoin

petersons.com

General Information Boys' boarding and day college-preparatory, arts, and technology school. Boarding grades 9–12, day grades 7–12. Founded: 1923. Setting: suburban. Nearest major city is Boston. Students are housed in single-sex dormitories. 29-acre campus. 18 buildings on campus. Approved or accredited by New England Association of Schools and Colleges and Massachusetts Department of Education. Member of National Association of Independent Schools and Secondary School Admission Test Board. Language of instruction: English. Endowment: $38 million. Total enrollment: 419. Upper school average class size: 12. Upper school faculty-student ratio: 1:8.

Upper School Student Profile Grade 10: 80 students (80 boys); Grade 11: 72 students (72 boys); Grade 12: 71 students (71 boys). 6% of students are boarding students. 99% are state residents. 2 states are represented in upper school student body. International students from United Kingdom.

Faculty School total: 62. In upper school: 46 men, 14 women; 47 have advanced degrees; 4 reside on campus.

Subjects Offered Algebra, American history, American literature, architecture, art, art history, astronomy, biology, calculus, ceramics, chemistry, Chinese, computer math, computer programming, computer science, creative writing, drafting, drama, earth science, economics, engineering, English, English literature, ethics, European history, expository writing, fine arts, French, geography, geology, geometry, German, government/civics, grammar, health, history, industrial arts, journalism, Latin, mathematics, mechanical drawing, music, philosophy, photography, physical education, physics, psychology, science, social studies, Spanish, speech, statistics, theater, trigonometry, woodworking, world history, writing.

Graduation Requirements Arts and fine arts (art, music, dance, drama), computer science, English, foreign language, mathematics, physical education (includes health), science, social studies (includes history), senior wooden panel carving (a tradition since 1923).

Special Academic Programs Advanced Placement exam preparation in 10 subject areas; honors section; independent study; term-away projects; study at local college for college credit; study abroad.

College Placement Colleges students went to include Boston College; Brown University; Georgetown University; Harvard University; Middlebury College; Tufts University. Mean SAT verbal: 650, mean SAT math: 680.

Student Life Upper grades have specified standards of dress, student council, honor system. Discipline rests equally with students and faculty.

Tuition and Aid Day student tuition: $25,020; 5-day tuition and room/board: $30,070. Tuition installment plan (Key Tuition Payment Plan, FACTS Tuition Payment Plan, monthly payment plans, individually arranged payment plans). Need-based scholarship grants, need-based loans, middle-income loans available. In 2004–05, 25% of upper-school students received aid. Total amount of financial aid awarded in 2004–05: $1,700,000.

Admissions Traditional secondary-level entrance grade is 10. ISEE and SSAT required. Deadline for receipt of application materials: February 1. Application fee required: $40. On-campus interview required.

Athletics Interscholastic: alpine skiing, baseball, basketball, crew, cross-country running, football, golf, ice hockey, lacrosse, rowing, sailing, skiing (cross-country), skiing (downhill), soccer, squash, tennis, track and field, wrestling; intramural: basketball, bicycling, crew, cross-country running, football, ice hockey, skiing (cross-country), squash, strength & conditioning, tennis, touch football, weight lifting. 2 trainers.

Computers Computers are regularly used in foreign language, mathematics, science classes. Computer network features include campus e-mail, on-campus library services, CD-ROMs, online commercial services, Internet access.

Contact Mr. Michael R. Grant, Director of Admission. 617-484-4410 Ext. 257. Fax: 617-484-4829. E-mail: grant@belmont-hill.org. Web site: www.belmont-hill.org.

ANNOUNCEMENT FROM THE SCHOOL Belmont Hill School, founded in 1923 and located in the suburbs of Boston, Massachusetts, is an independent boys' day and boarding school (5 days) that provides a rigorous learning environment for grades 7–12. Small classes and a full schedule from 8 a.m. to 5 p.m. combine classical education with extensive opportunities in athletics, music, theater, visual arts, community service, and other activities. Though diverse in backgrounds and teaching styles, Belmont Hill faculty members share common core values: an insistence upon holding students to high standards; a concern for developing character and values; a recognition that life's lessons can be taught throughout the day, on athletic fields and in rehearsal halls as well as in classrooms; a concern for each student's total development, social and personal as well as academic; and a willingness to provide extra help, whenever and wherever necessary. Belmont Hill is what it is, in large measure, because of the School's single-sex status, which puts the focus on the total development of boys into men. The teachers know the developmental stages of boys and how boys learn best. Boys speak up and stay focused in class, unafraid to take risks and unconcerned about how they are perceived. They feel free to pursue theater, music, or visual arts. They feel free to tutor a child or brighten a senior citizen's day. They feel free, in sum, to develop their talents and to share their humanity, unfettered by juvenile notions of what it means to "be a man" and energized by the spirit of camaraderie that permeates the School. Belmont Hill is a boys' school, but what is more important is that it is a good school. "Goodness" is measured by the character of the students and the citizens they become. Belmont Hill strives to have its students leave with a love of learning and a willingness to work hard, take risks, take a stand, and make a difference.

THE BEMENT SCHOOL

Deerfield, Massachusetts
See Junior Boarding Schools section.

BENEDICTINE HIGH SCHOOL

2900 Martin Luther King, Jr Drive
Cleveland, Ohio 44104
Head of School: Mr. Sal Miroglotta

General Information Boys' day college-preparatory and religious studies school, affiliated with Roman Catholic Church. Grades 9–12. Founded: 1927. Setting: urban. 13-acre campus. 3 buildings on campus. Approved or accredited by North Central Association of Colleges and Schools, Ohio Catholic Schools Accreditation Association (OCSAA), and Ohio Department of Education. Total enrollment: 439. Upper school average class size: 15. Upper school faculty-student ratio: 1:11.

Upper School Student Profile Grade 9: 115 students (115 boys); Grade 10: 112 students (112 boys); Grade 11: 106 students (106 boys); Grade 12: 106 students (106 boys). 85% of students are Roman Catholic.

Faculty School total: 34. In upper school: 31 men, 3 women; 31 have advanced degrees.

Graduation Requirements 1½ elective credits, 20th century American writers, 20th century history, 20th century world history, accounting, algebra, American Civil War, American democracy, American foreign policy, American government, American history, American literature, ancient history, ancient world history, animal science, animation, art, biology, British literature, chemistry, Christian testament, church history, civics, computer applications, English, foreign language, geometry, physical education (includes health), physics, senior project, theology, U.S. history, world history.

Special Academic Programs Advanced Placement exam preparation in 5 subject areas; honors section; study at local college for college credit; remedial reading and/or remedial writing; remedial math.

College Placement 85 students graduated in 2005; 84 went to college, including Ohio University; University of Dayton. Other: 1 went to work. Mean SAT verbal: 509, mean SAT math: 493, mean composite ACT: 19.

Student Life Upper grades have specified standards of dress, student council. Discipline rests primarily with faculty. Attendance at religious services is required.

Tuition and Aid Day student tuition: $6995. Tuition installment plan (monthly payment plans, individually arranged payment plans). Tuition reduction for siblings, merit scholarship grants, need-based scholarship grants, paying campus jobs available. In 2005–06, 65% of upper-school students received aid.

Admissions Traditional secondary-level entrance grade is 9. For fall 2005, 200 students applied for upper-level admission, 150 were accepted, 115 enrolled. High School Placement Test required. No application fee required. Interview recommended.

Athletics Interscholastic: baseball, basketball, bowling, cross-country running, football, golf, hockey, soccer, swimming and diving, track and field, wrestling; intramural: flag football, physical fitness, physical training, skiing (downhill), snowboarding, strength & conditioning, volleyball, weight lifting, weight training. 10 coaches, 2 trainers.

Computers Computers are regularly used in computer applications, information technology, SAT preparation, technical drawing classes. Computer network features include on-campus library services, CD-ROMs, online commercial services, Internet access, file transfer, DVD, wireless campus network.

Contact Mr. Kieran Patton, Director of Admissions. 216-421-2080 Ext. 356. Fax: 216-421-1100. E-mail: kpatton@cbhs.net. Web site: www.cbhs.net.

BENET ACADEMY

2200 Maple Avenue
Lisle, Illinois 60532
Head of School: Mr. Stephen A. Marth

General Information Coeducational day college-preparatory school, affiliated with Roman Catholic Church. Grades 9–12. Founded: 1887. Setting: suburban. Nearest major city is Chicago. 44-acre campus. 8 buildings on campus. Approved or accredited by North Central Association of Colleges and Schools and Illinois Department of Education. Total enrollment: 1,299. Upper school average class size: 27. Upper school faculty-student ratio: 1:18.

Upper School Student Profile Grade 9: 333 students (170 boys, 163 girls); Grade 10: 329 students (175 boys, 154 girls); Grade 11: 314 students (165 boys, 149 girls); Grade 12: 323 students (154 boys, 169 girls). 97% of students are Roman Catholic.
Faculty School total: 69. In upper school: 40 men, 29 women; 56 have advanced degrees.
Subjects Offered Algebra, American history, American literature, art history, biology, business, calculus, chemistry, computer programming, computer science, creative writing, drama, driver education, economics, English, European history, French, geography, geometry, German, government/civics, health, history, Latin, mathematics, music, physical education, physics, religion, science, Spanish, speech, statistics, trigonometry, U.S. history-AP, world history, world literature, writing.
Graduation Requirements Computer science, English, foreign language, mathematics, physical education (includes health), religion (includes Bible studies and theology), science, social studies (includes history).
Special Academic Programs Advanced Placement exam preparation in 12 subject areas; honors section; study at local college for college credit; academic accommodation for the gifted.
College Placement 317 students graduated in 2005; all went to college, including Marquette University; The University of Iowa; University of Illinois; University of Notre Dame. Mean SAT verbal: 643, mean SAT math: 639, mean composite ACT: 28.
Student Life Upper grades have uniform requirement, student council. Discipline rests primarily with faculty. Attendance at religious services is required.
Tuition and Aid Day student tuition: $6675. Tuition installment plan (monthly payment plans). Tuition reduction for siblings, need-based scholarship grants available. In 2005–06, 2% of upper-school students received aid.
Admissions Traditional secondary-level entrance grade is 9. For fall 2005, 650 students applied for upper-level admission, 430 were accepted, 335 enrolled. High School Placement Test required. Deadline for receipt of application materials: January 14. Application fee required: $25. On-campus interview required.
Athletics Interscholastic: baseball (boys), basketball (b,g), cross-country running (b,g), diving (b,g), football (b), golf (b,g), pom squad (g), soccer (b,g), softball (g), strength & conditioning (b), swimming and diving (b,g), tennis (b,g), track and field (b,g), volleyball (b,g); coed intramural: basketball, bowling, flag football, table tennis, volleyball. 3 PE instructors, 30 coaches, 1 trainer.
Computers Computers are regularly used in English, history, mathematics, science, Spanish classes. Computer network features include campus e-mail, on-campus library services, CD-ROMs, online commercial services, Internet access, file transfer, DVD.
Contact Mr. James E. Brown, Assistant Principal. 630-969-6550. Fax: 630-719-0929. E-mail: jbrown@benet.org.

BEN FRANKLIN ACADEMY
1585 Clifton Road
Atlanta, Georgia 30329
Head of School: Dr. Wood Smethurst

General Information Coeducational day college-preparatory school. Grades 9–12. Founded: 1987. Setting: urban. 3-acre campus. 2 buildings on campus. Approved or accredited by Georgia Independent School Association, Southern Association of Colleges and Schools, and Georgia Department of Education. Endowment: $1 million. Total enrollment: 130. Upper school average class size: 1. Upper school faculty-student ratio: 1:3.
Faculty School total: 29. In upper school: 12 men, 17 women; 15 have advanced degrees.
Special Academic Programs Advanced Placement exam preparation; honors section; accelerated programs.
College Placement 62 students graduated in 2005; 57 went to college. Other: 5 went to work.
Student Life Upper grades have specified standards of dress. Discipline rests primarily with faculty.
Tuition and Aid Day student tuition: $20,900. Tuition installment plan (SMART Tuition Payment Plan). Need-based scholarship grants available.
Admissions Traditional secondary-level entrance grade is 10. Deadline for receipt of application materials: none. No application fee required. On-campus interview required.
Athletics Coed Interscholastic: basketball, cross-country running, golf, tennis.
Computers Computer resources include on-campus library services, CD-ROMs, Internet access, file transfer, DVD.
Contact Dr. Martha B. Burdette, Dean of Studies. 404-633-7404. Fax: 404-321-0610. E-mail: bfa@benfranklinacademy.org. Web site: www.benfranklinacademy.org.

ANNOUNCEMENT FROM THE SCHOOL Ben Franklin Academy is a coeducational, college-preparatory, senior high school, accredited by the Southern Association of Colleges and Schools (SACS), for students who are not thriving in traditional classroom settings. The Academy offers individualized instruction to a wide range of students and develops a plan to meet each student's unique needs. For more information, students can visit the Academy's Web site at http://www.benfranklinacademy.org.

BENILDE–ST. MARGARET'S SCHOOL
2501 Highway 100 South
St. Louis Park, Minnesota 55416
Head of School: Robert Tift

General Information Coeducational day college-preparatory, general academic, religious studies, and technology school, affiliated with Roman Catholic Church. Grades 7–12. Founded: 1907. Setting: suburban. Nearest major city is Minneapolis. 33-acre campus. 3 buildings on campus. Approved or accredited by North Central Association of Colleges and Schools and Minnesota Department of Education. Endowment: $3.8 million. Total enrollment: 1,153. Upper school average class size: 21. Upper school faculty-student ratio: 1:12.
Upper School Student Profile Grade 9: 236 students (116 boys, 120 girls); Grade 10: 234 students (117 boys, 117 girls); Grade 11: 222 students (124 boys, 98 girls); Grade 12: 197 students (95 boys, 102 girls). 80% of students are Roman Catholic.
Faculty School total: 96. In upper school: 31 men, 49 women; 49 have advanced degrees.
Subjects Offered Accounting, acting, advanced computer applications, advanced math, Advanced Placement courses, algebra, American government-AP, American history, American history-AP, American literature, ancient history, applied music, art, art appreciation, astronomy, aviation, band, Bible studies, biology, biology-AP, British literature, business, calculus, calculus-AP, career/college preparation, Catholic belief and practice, ceramics, chemistry, choir, church history, civics, comparative government and politics-AP, comparative religion, competitive science projects, computer programming, computer science, creative writing, death and loss, debate, drama, drawing and design, driver education, earth science, ecology, economics, economics and history, English, English literature, English literature-AP, environmental science, European history, European history-AP, film, fine arts, French, French-AP, geography, geometry, government/civics, health, history, journalism, keyboarding, language-AP, Latin, mathematics, music, painting, photography, physical education, physics, psychology, religion, science, social studies, Spanish, Spanish-AP, speech, statistics-AP, stock market, theater, theology, trigonometry, word processing, world history, world literature, world religions, writing.
Graduation Requirements Arts and fine arts (art, music, dance, drama), English, foreign language, mathematics, physical education (includes health), religion (includes Bible studies and theology), science, social studies (includes history).
Special Academic Programs Advanced Placement exam preparation in 11 subject areas; honors section; independent study; study at local college for college credit.
College Placement 229 students graduated in 2005; 222 went to college, including Marquette University; Saint John's University; St. Thomas University; University of Minnesota, Duluth; University of Minnesota, Twin Cities Campus; University of Wisconsin–Madison. Other: 7 had other specific plans. Mean SAT verbal: 580, mean SAT math: 586, mean composite ACT: 25.
Student Life Upper grades have specified standards of dress, student council. Discipline rests primarily with faculty. Attendance at religious services is required.
Summer Programs Sports programs offered; held on campus; accepts boys and girls; open to students from other schools. 550 students usually enrolled. 2006 schedule: June to August. Application deadline: May.
Tuition and Aid Day student tuition: $8850. Tuition installment plan (monthly payment plans, individually arranged payment plans). Merit scholarship grants, need-based scholarship grants, paying campus jobs available. In 2005–06, 15% of upper-school students received aid; total upper-school merit-scholarship money awarded: $33,000. Total amount of financial aid awarded in 2005–06: $581,585.
Admissions Traditional secondary-level entrance grade is 9. For fall 2005, 205 students applied for upper-level admission, 196 were accepted, 142 enrolled. ACT-Explore and any standardized test required. Deadline for receipt of application materials: January 13. No application fee required. On-campus interview recommended.
Athletics Interscholastic: alpine skiing (boys, girls), baseball (b), basketball (b,g), cheering (g), cross-country running (b,g), dance team (g), diving (b,g), football (b), golf (b,g), hockey (b,g), ice hockey (b,g), lacrosse (b,g), nordic skiing (b,g), sailing (b,g), skiing (cross-country) (b,g), skiing (downhill) (b,g), soccer (b,g), softball (g), swimming and diving (b,g), tennis (b,g), track and field (b,g), volleyball (g), weight training (b,g), wrestling (b); intramural: basketball (b,g); coed interscholastic: bowling. 3 PE instructors, 17 coaches, 1 trainer.
Computers Computers are regularly used in all classes. Computer network features include on-campus library services, CD-ROMs, Internet access, file transfer, DVD.
Contact Mary Periolat, Director of Admissions. 952-915-4344. Fax: 952-920-8889. E-mail: mperiolat@bsm-online.org. Web site: bsm-online.org.

ANNOUNCEMENT FROM THE SCHOOL Benilde–St. Margaret's (BSM), a National Service Learning Leader School, is a Catholic community helping students in grades 7–12 develop their own unique place in society. BSM has gained an impressive reputation through a diverse and challenging academic program. An enriching and outstanding extracurricular program appeals to both students and parents. With 2 Presidential Scholars in recent years and 5 students recognized by the National Merit Program this past year, as well as recent state team championships for boys' and girls' hockey, boys' soccer, boys' and girls' alpine skiing, boys' golf, boys' track, girls' swimming, boys' cross country, speech, Math League, Envirothon, and dance, BSM demonstrates a strong

history of high-quality programs. Enhancing the School's legacy of excellence are newly completed facilities, including a chapel, library, theater, and classrooms.

THE BENJAMIN SCHOOL

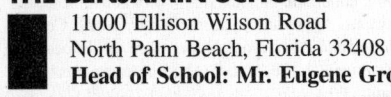

11000 Ellison Wilson Road
North Palm Beach, Florida 33408
Head of School: Mr. Eugene Gross

General Information Coeducational day college-preparatory and arts school. Grades PK–12. Founded: 1960. Setting: suburban. Nearest major city is West Palm Beach. 50-acre campus. 5 buildings on campus. Approved or accredited by Florida Council of Independent Schools, Southern Association of Colleges and Schools, and Florida Department of Education. Member of National Association of Independent Schools and Secondary School Admission Test Board. Total enrollment: 1,336. Upper school average class size: 16. Upper school faculty-student ratio: 1:16.

Upper School Student Profile Grade 9: 108 students (59 boys, 49 girls); Grade 10: 107 students (61 boys, 46 girls); Grade 11: 118 students (58 boys, 60 girls); Grade 12: 101 students (55 boys, 46 girls).

Faculty School total: 167. In upper school: 22 men, 23 women.

Subjects Offered 3-dimensional art, acting, African studies, algebra, American history, American literature, art, art history, Asian studies, band, Basic programming, biology, biology-AP, broadcasting, calculus, calculus-AP, Caribbean history, cartooning/animation, ceramics, chemistry, chemistry-AP, choral music, chorus, communications, community service, comparative government and politics-AP, comparative religion, composition-AP, computer animation, computer math, computer programming, computer science, computer science-AP, creative writing, current events, dance, debate, drama, earth science, ecology, economics, economics-AP, English, English language and composition-AP, English literature, English literature and composition-AP, environmental science, European history, expository writing, film studies, fine arts, French, French language-AP, genetics, geography, geometry, government-AP, government/civics, grammar, history, honors algebra, honors English, honors geometry, journalism, literature and composition-AP, marine biology, mathematics, modern European history-AP, music, mythology, physical education, physical science, physics, physiology-anatomy, piano, political science, pre-calculus, psychology, SAT preparation, science, social science, social studies, Spanish, Spanish language-AP, Spanish literature-AP, speech, statistics, statistics-AP, theater, trigonometry, U.S. government, U.S. government and politics-AP, U.S. government-AP, U.S. history-AP, video film production, world history, writing, writing.

Graduation Requirements Arts and fine arts (art, music, dance, drama), computer science, English, foreign language, mathematics, physical education (includes health), science, social science, social studies (includes history). Community service is required.

Special Academic Programs Advanced Placement exam preparation in 18 subject areas; honors section; accelerated programs; study at local college for college credit; academic accommodation for the gifted, the musically talented, and the artistically talented.

College Placement 72 students graduated in 2005; all went to college, including Duke University; Florida State University; Northwestern University; Southern Methodist University; University of Florida; University of Miami. Mean SAT verbal: 596, mean SAT math: 599, mean composite ACT: 26.

Student Life Upper grades have uniform requirement, student council, honor system. Discipline rests primarily with faculty.

Summer Programs Enrichment, advancement programs offered; session focuses on academic advancement and AP courses; held on campus; accepts boys and girls; open to students from other schools. 40 students usually enrolled. 2006 schedule: June to July. Application deadline: May.

Tuition and Aid Day student tuition: $16,750. Tuition installment plan (Insured Tuition Payment Plan, monthly payment plans). Merit scholarship grants, need-based scholarship grants available. In 2005–06, 12% of upper-school students received aid.

Admissions Traditional secondary-level entrance grade is 9. For fall 2005, 129 students applied for upper-level admission, 68 were accepted, 47 enrolled. ERB required. Deadline for receipt of application materials: February. Application fee required: $100. On-campus interview required.

Athletics Interscholastic: baseball (boys), basketball (b,g), cheering (g), cross-country running (b,g), dance team (g), football (b), golf (b,g), soccer (b,g), softball (g), tennis (b,g), volleyball (g), wrestling (b); intramural: lacrosse (b,g); coed interscholastic: aerobics/dance, bowling, dance, diving, modern dance, swimming and diving, track and field; coed intramural: sailing. 2 PE instructors, 1 trainer.

Computers Computers are regularly used in art, English, foreign language, history, mathematics, science classes. Computer network features include campus e-mail, on-campus library services, Internet access, wireless campus network.

Contact Mrs. Mary Lou Primm, Director of Admission. 561-472-3451. Fax: 561-472-3410. E-mail: mprimm@benjaminschool.com. Web site: www.benjaminschool.com.

BENTLEY SCHOOL

1 Hiller Drive
Oakland, California 94618
Head of School: Richard Fitzgerald

petersons.com

General Information Coeducational day college-preparatory and arts school. Grades K–12. Founded: 1920. Setting: suburban. Nearest major city is Lafayette. 12-acre campus. 4 buildings on campus. Approved or accredited by California Association of Independent Schools and California Department of Education. Candidate for accreditation by Western Association of Schools and Colleges. Member of National Association of Independent Schools. Language of instruction: English. Total enrollment: 623. Upper school average class size: 12. Upper school faculty-student ratio: 1:8.

Upper School Student Profile Grade 9: 88 students (46 boys, 42 girls); Grade 10: 77 students (31 boys, 46 girls); Grade 11: 64 students (30 boys, 34 girls); Grade 12: 34 students (18 boys, 16 girls).

Faculty School total: 76. In upper school: 20 men, 14 women; 20 have advanced degrees.

Subjects Offered 20th century history, algebra, American literature, art history, biology, British literature, European history, geometry, modern European history, physics, public speaking, senior internship, senior thesis, U.S. history, visual and performing arts.

Special Academic Programs Advanced Placement exam preparation in 15 subject areas; honors section; accelerated programs; independent study; term-away projects; study at local college for college credit; study abroad; academic accommodation for the gifted, the musically talented, and the artistically talented.

College Placement 51 students graduated in 2004; all went to college, including New York University; Stanford University; University of California, Berkeley; University of California, Davis; University of California, Santa Cruz; University of Pennsylvania. Median SAT verbal: 720, median SAT math: 710, median composite ACT: 29. 60% scored over 600 on SAT verbal, 70% scored over 600 on SAT math, 75% scored over 26 on composite ACT.

Student Life Upper grades have specified standards of dress, student council, honor system. Discipline rests equally with students and faculty.

Tuition and Aid Day student tuition: $20,085. Tuition installment plan (The Tuition Plan, Key Tuition Payment Plan, SMART Tuition Payment Plan, monthly payment plans, individually arranged payment plans). Merit scholarship grants, need-based scholarship grants available. In 2004–05, 19% of upper-school students received aid; total upper-school merit-scholarship money awarded: $333,400. Total amount of financial aid awarded in 2004–05: $760,000.

Admissions Traditional secondary-level entrance grade is 9. For fall 2005, 230 students applied for upper-level admission, 130 were accepted, 61 enrolled. ISEE or SSAT required. Deadline for receipt of application materials: January 15. Application fee required: $75. Interview recommended.

Athletics Interscholastic: baseball (boys), basketball (b,g), crew (b,g), cross-country running (b,g), soccer (b,g), softball (g), tennis (b,g), volleyball (g); intramural: aerobics (b,g), lacrosse (b,g); coed interscholastic: golf; coed intramural: aerobics, aerobics/dance, aerobics/nautilus, dance, physical fitness. 2 PE instructors, 6 coaches.

Computers Computers are regularly used in science classes. Computer network features include campus e-mail, on-campus library services, CD-ROMs, online commercial services, Internet access, file transfer.

Contact Ms. Yvette Cashmere, Admission Assistant. 510-843-2512 Ext. 2409. Fax: 510-843-5162. E-mail: ycashmere@bentleyschool.net. Web site: www.bentleyschool.net.

ANNOUNCEMENT FROM THE SCHOOL For as long as Bentley has been serving Bay Area students, it has been a school committed to the continued development of a challenging academic environment. Bentley's most profound hope is that the admission process can be a positive one for the whole family. As a community of educators, Bentley has always worked to provide classrooms where enthusiastic and inspiring teachers employ the most effective teaching methods. At the same time, this School is committed to the development of the whole child. Everyone at Bentley loves seeing, every day, how much students love attending Bentley. Indeed, this School is not only a place of profound academic exploration and achievement; it is also a place full of humor, kindness, energy, and excitement. Laughter and thoughtfulness and imagination and creativity round out the Bentley profile.

BERKELEY CARROLL SCHOOL

181 Lincoln Place
Brooklyn, New York 11217
Head of School: Dr. Richard Barter

General Information Coeducational day college-preparatory school. Grades N–12. Founded: 1886. Setting: urban. Nearest major city is New York. 3 buildings on campus. Approved or accredited by New York State Association of Independent Schools and New York Department of Education. Member of National Association of Independent Schools. Endowment: $2.5 million. Total enrollment: 785. Upper school average class size: 15. Upper school faculty-student ratio: 1:8.

Upper School Student Profile Grade 9: 54 students (30 boys, 24 girls); Grade 10: 51 students (27 boys, 24 girls); Grade 11: 50 students (23 boys, 27 girls); Grade 12: 60 students (32 boys, 28 girls).

Faculty School total: 132. In upper school: 28 men, 27 women; 47 have advanced degrees.

Subjects Offered Algebra, American history, American literature, art, art history, astronomy, biology, calculus, ceramics, chemistry, community service, computer applications, computer programming, conceptual physics, creative writing, dance, democracy in America, drama, driver education, economics, engineering, English, English literature, environmental science, European history, expository writing, fine arts, fractals, French, geometry, government/civics, health, history, humanities, Japanese studies, journalism, Latin, marine biology, music, photography, physical education, physics, science, Shakespeare, Spanish, statistics, theater, trigonometry, video and animation, world history, World-Wide-Web publishing, writing.

Graduation Requirements Arts and fine arts (art, music, dance, drama), computer science, English, foreign language, mathematics, physical education (includes health), science, social science, 6-week senior year internship. Community service is required.

Special Academic Programs Advanced Placement exam preparation in 9 subject areas; independent study; study abroad; academic accommodation for the gifted, the musically talented, and the artistically talented.

College Placement 50 students graduated in 2005; all went to college, including Brown University; Columbia College; Tufts University; Vassar College; Wesleyan University.

Student Life Upper grades have specified standards of dress, student council. Discipline rests equally with students and faculty.

Summer Programs Enrichment, sports, art/fine arts programs offered; session focuses on creative arts, athletics; held on campus; accepts boys and girls; open to students from other schools. 250 students usually enrolled. 2006 schedule: July 1 to August 1. Application deadline: none.

Tuition and Aid Day student tuition: $21,250. Tuition installment plan (Insured Tuition Payment Plan, Academic Management Services Plan, Key Tuition Payment Plan, monthly payment plans, individually arranged payment plans). Need-based scholarship grants available. In 2005–06, 30% of upper-school students received aid.

Admissions Traditional secondary-level entrance grade is 9. For fall 2005, 110 students applied for upper-level admission, 40 were accepted, 15 enrolled. ISEE required. Deadline for receipt of application materials: December 15. Application fee required: $50. On-campus interview required.

Athletics Interscholastic: aquatics (boys, girls), baseball (b), basketball (b,g), cheering (g), cross-country running (b,g), indoor track & field (b,g), swimming and diving (b,g), track and field (b,g); intramural: aquatics (b,g), fencing (b,g), swimming and diving (b,g); coed interscholastic: dance, dance squad, judo; coed intramural: swimming and diving. 2 PE instructors, 10 coaches.

Computers Computers are regularly used in art, English, foreign language, history, mathematics, music, science classes. Computer network features include campus e-mail, on-campus library services, CD-ROMs, online commercial services, Internet access, DVD.

Contact Mr. Colm MacMahon, Director of Admissions. 718-789-6060 Ext. 6527. Fax: 718-398-3640. E-mail: cmacmahon@berkeleycarroll.org. Web site: www.berkeleycarroll.org.

BERKELEY PREPARATORY SCHOOL

4811 Kelly Road
Tampa, Florida 33615
Head of School: Joseph A. Merluzzi

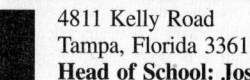

General Information Coeducational day college-preparatory, arts, religious studies, bilingual studies, and technology school, affiliated with Episcopal Church. Grades PK–12. Founded: 1960. Setting: suburban. 64-acre campus. 8 buildings on campus. Approved or accredited by Florida Council of Independent Schools, The College Board, and Florida Department of Education. Member of National Association of Independent Schools and Secondary School Admission Test Board. Total enrollment: 1,205. Upper school average class size: 15. Upper school faculty-student ratio: 1:8.

Upper School Student Profile Grade 9: 133 students (75 boys, 58 girls); Grade 10: 136 students (68 boys, 68 girls); Grade 11: 107 students (59 boys, 48 girls); Grade 12: 138 students (67 boys, 71 girls).

Faculty School total: 145. In upper school: 22 men, 27 women; 37 have advanced degrees.

Subjects Offered African history, algebra, American government, American history, American literature, art, art history, biology, biology-AP, calculus, calculus-AP, ceramics, chemistry, chemistry-AP, China/Japan history, community service, computer math, computer programming, computer science, creative writing, dance, drama, drama performance, drama workshop, early childhood, economics, English, English literature, English-AP, environmental science-AP, etymology, European history, expository writing, fine arts, French, French-AP, freshman seminar, geography, geometry, government/civics, grammar, guitar, health, history, history of China and Japan, honors algebra, honors English, honors geometry, instruments, Latin, Latin American history, Latin-AP, logic, Mandarin, math analysis, mathematics, media arts, microbiology, modern European history, modern European history-AP, music, performing arts, philosophy, physical education, physics, physics-AP, pre-calculus, psychology, religious studies, SAT preparation, science, social studies, Spanish,

Spanish-AP, speech, stage design, statistics, statistics-AP, technical theater, television, theater, theater production, U.S. history, U.S. history-AP, video, video film production, Western civilization, world history, world literature, writing.

Graduation Requirements Arts and fine arts (art, music, dance, drama), computer science, English, foreign language, mathematics, physical education (includes health), religious studies, science, social studies (includes history). Community service is required.

Special Academic Programs Advanced Placement exam preparation in 16 subject areas; honors section; independent study; study abroad.

College Placement 113 students graduated in 2005; all went to college, including Carnegie Mellon University; University of Florida; University of Miami. Mean SAT verbal: 643, mean SAT math: 649, mean composite ACT: 26. 71% scored over 600 on SAT verbal, 79% scored over 600 on SAT math.

Student Life Upper grades have specified standards of dress, student council, honor system. Discipline rests equally with students and faculty.

Summer Programs Remediation, enrichment, advancement, sports, art/fine arts, computer instruction programs offered; session focuses on setting a fun pace for excellence; held on campus; accepts boys and girls; open to students from other schools. 2153 students usually enrolled. 2006 schedule: June 5 to July 28. Application deadline: none.

Tuition and Aid Day student tuition: $15,100. Tuition installment plan (5-installment plan). Merit scholarship grants, need-based scholarship grants available.

Admissions Traditional secondary-level entrance grade is 9. For fall 2005, 106 students applied for upper-level admission, 80 were accepted, 51 enrolled. Otis-Lennon Mental Ability Test and SSAT required. Deadline for receipt of application materials: January 30. Application fee required: $50. On-campus interview required.

Athletics Interscholastic: baseball (boys), basketball (b,g), cheering (g), crew (b,g), cross-country running (b,g), dance squad (g), dance team (g), diving (b,g), football (b), golf (b,g), rowing (b,g), soccer (b,g), softball (g), swimming and diving (b,g), tennis (b,g), track and field (b,g), volleyball (g); coed interscholastic: weight lifting, wrestling; coed intramural: physical fitness, physical training, power lifting, project adventure, strength & conditioning, wall climbing, weight training. 11 PE instructors, 20 coaches, 1 trainer.

Computers Computers are regularly used in art, English, foreign language, history, mathematics, music, science classes. Computer network features include campus e-mail, on-campus library services, CD-ROMs, online commercial services, Internet access, wireless campus network.

Contact Janie McIlvaine, Director of Admissions. 813-885-1673. Fax: 813-886-6933. E-mail: mcilvjan@berkeleyprep.org. Web site: www.berkeleyprep.org.

See full description on page 674.

BERKSHIRE SCHOOL

245 North Undermountain Road
Sheffield, Massachusetts 01257
Head of School: Michael J. Maher

General Information Coeducational boarding and day college-preparatory school. Grades 9–PG. Founded: 1907. Setting: rural. Nearest major city is Hartford, CT. Students are housed in single-sex dormitories. 500-acre campus. 36 buildings on campus. Approved or accredited by Association of Independent Schools in New England, New England Association of Schools and Colleges, and The Association of Boarding Schools. Member of National Association of Independent Schools and Secondary School Admission Test Board. Endowment: $49 million. Total enrollment: 372. Upper school average class size: 12. Upper school faculty-student ratio: 1:6.

Upper School Student Profile Grade 9: 52 students (31 boys, 21 girls); Grade 10: 90 students (53 boys, 37 girls); Grade 11: 110 students (61 boys, 49 girls); Grade 12: 104 students (61 boys, 43 girls); Postgraduate: 16 students (14 boys, 2 girls). 87% of students are boarding students. 21% are state residents. 22 states are represented in upper school student body. 17% are international students. International students from Canada, Germany, Hong Kong, Japan, Republic of Korea, and Taiwan; 16 other countries represented in student body.

Faculty School total: 62. In upper school: 35 men, 27 women; 32 have advanced degrees; 51 reside on campus.

Subjects Offered 3-dimensional design, acting, Advanced Placement courses, algebra, American government, American history, American literature, anatomy, ancient history, animal behavior, art, art history, astronomy, biology, calculus, ceramics, chemistry, Chinese, choral music, chorus, comparative government and politics, comparative religion, composition, computer programming, computer science, constitutional law, creative writing, dance, digital art, drama, drawing and design, economics, English, English literature, environmental science, ESL, ethics, European history, expository writing, French, genetics, geology, geometry, health, history, instrumental music, Latin, mathematics, music, music technology, painting, philosophy, photography, physics, physiology, pre-calculus, psychology, public speaking, science, Spanish, statistics, studio art, theater, trigonometry, writing.

Graduation Requirements Arts and fine arts (art, music, dance, drama), English, foreign language, history, introduction to technology, mathematics, science. Community service is required.

Special Academic Programs Advanced Placement exam preparation in 16 subject areas; honors section; independent study; study abroad; ESL (16 students enrolled).

Berkshire School

College Placement 115 students graduated in 2005; all went to college, including Boston University; Rhode Island School of Design. Mean SAT verbal: 590, mean SAT math: 590. 48% scored over 600 on SAT verbal, 37% scored over 600 on SAT math.

Student Life Upper grades have specified standards of dress, student council, honor system. Discipline rests equally with students and faculty.

Tuition and Aid Day student tuition: $25,850; 7-day tuition and room/board: $35,300. Tuition installment plan (Academic Management Services Plan, Key Tuition Payment Plan, monthly payment plans). Merit scholarship grants, need-based scholarship grants available. In 2005–06, 26% of upper-school students received aid; total upper-school merit-scholarship money awarded: $48,500. Total amount of financial aid awarded in 2005–06: $1,836,591.

Admissions Traditional secondary-level entrance grade is 9. For fall 2005, 714 students applied for upper-level admission, 392 were accepted, 149 enrolled. ACT, PSAT, SAT, SLEP, SSAT or TOEFL required. Deadline for receipt of application materials: February 1. Application fee required: $50. Interview required.

Athletics Interscholastic: baseball (boys), basketball (b,g), crew (b,g), cross-country running (b,g), field hockey (g), football (b), ice hockey (b,g), lacrosse (b,g), soccer (b,g), softball (g), squash (b,g), tennis (b,g), track and field (b,g), volleyball (g); coed interscholastic: alpine skiing, golf, mountain biking; coed intramural: alpine skiing, climbing, dance, hiking/backpacking, modern dance, outdoor adventure, outdoor education, outdoor skills, rappelling, rock climbing, ropes courses, skiing (downhill), snowboarding, wilderness, wilderness survival. 2 trainers.

Computers Computers are regularly used in art, mathematics, music, science, technology classes. Computer network features include campus e-mail, on-campus library services, CD-ROMs, online commercial services, Internet access, file transfer, office computer access, network printing, interactive white boards.

Contact Mr. Andrew L. Bogardus, Director of Admission. 413-229-1003. Fax: 413-229-1016. E-mail: admission@berkshireschool.org. Web site: www.berkshireschool.org.

See full description on page 676.

THE BERMUDA HIGH SCHOOL FOR GIRLS

27 Richmond Road
Pembroke HM 08, Bermuda
Head of School: Robert B. Napier

General Information Girls' day college-preparatory and general academic school. Grades 1–13. Founded: 1894. Setting: small town. Nearest major city is Hamilton. 8-acre campus. 4 buildings on campus. Approved or accredited by state department of education. Affiliate member of National Association of Independent Schools; member of European Council of International Schools. Language of instruction: English. Endowment: 5 million Bermuda dollars. Total enrollment: 686. Upper school average class size: 12. Upper school faculty-student ratio: 1:7.

Upper School Student Profile Grade 10: 52 students (52 girls); Grade 11: 41 students (41 girls); Grade 12: 31 students (3 boys, 28 girls); Grade 13: 39 students (2 boys, 37 girls).

Faculty School total: 85. In upper school: 11 men, 35 women; 20 have advanced degrees.

Subjects Offered Accounting, algebra, art, arts, biology, business, business skills, business studies, calculus, chemistry, computer science, dance, drama, economics, English, English literature, European history, expository writing, fine arts, French, geography, geometry, grammar, health, history, keyboarding, Latin, mathematics, music, physical education, physics, science, social studies, Spanish, theater, trigonometry, world history.

Graduation Requirements Arts and fine arts (art, music, dance, drama), business skills (includes word processing), computer science, English, fitness, foreign language, geography, mathematics, physical education (includes health), science, social studies (includes history).

Special Academic Programs International Baccalaureate program; honors section; remedial reading and/or remedial writing.

College Placement 23 students graduated in 2005; 22 went to college. Other: 1 had other specific plans.

Student Life Upper grades have uniform requirement, student council. Discipline rests primarily with faculty.

Summer Programs Art/fine arts programs offered; held on campus; accepts girls; open to students from other schools.

Tuition and Aid Day student tuition: 12,500 Bermuda dollars–13,560 Bermuda dollars. Tuition installment plan (monthly payment plans, individually arranged payment plans). Bursaries, merit scholarship grants, need-based scholarship grants available. In 2005–06, 34% of upper-school students received aid; total upper-school merit-scholarship money awarded: 125,000 Bermuda dollars. Total amount of financial aid awarded in 2005–06: 300,000 Bermuda dollars.

Admissions Traditional secondary-level entrance grade is 10. For fall 2005, 10 students applied for upper-level admission, 4 were accepted, 2 enrolled. School's own test required. Deadline for receipt of application materials: none. Application fee required: 50 Bermuda dollars. Interview recommended.

Athletics Interscholastic: aquatics (girls), basketball (g), cross-country running (g), field hockey (g), gymnastics (g), netball (g), soccer (g), swimming and diving (g), tennis (g), track and field (g), volleyball (g); intramural: aerobics (g), aerobics/dance (g), aerobics/nautilus (g), back packing (g), badminton (g), ballet (g), basketball (g), cooperative games (g), cross-country running (g), curling (g), dance (g), dressage (g), field hockey (g), fitness (g), fitness walking (g), floor hockey (g), gymnastics (g), nautilus (g), netball (g), outdoor education (g), physical fitness (g), soccer (g), softball (g), squash (g), track and field (g), volleyball (g), wall climbing (g). 4 PE instructors, 2 coaches.

Computers Computers are regularly used in business skills, business studies, English, foreign language, French, geography, history, introduction to technology, mathematics, research skills, Spanish, word processing, yearbook classes. Computer network features include campus e-mail, CD-ROMs, Internet access.

Contact Linda Parker, Head of Secondary Department. 441-295-6153. Fax: 441-295-2754. E-mail: lparker@bhs.bm. Web site: www.bhs.bm.

BERWICK ACADEMY

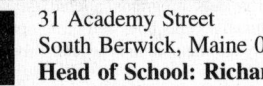

31 Academy Street
South Berwick, Maine 03908
Head of School: Richard W. Ridgway

General Information Coeducational day college-preparatory and arts school. Grades K–PG. Founded: 1791. Setting: small town. Nearest major city is Portsmouth, NH. 72-acre campus. 11 buildings on campus. Approved or accredited by New England Association of Schools and Colleges and Maine Department of Education. Member of National Association of Independent Schools and Secondary School Admission Test Board. Endowment: $15 million. Total enrollment: 604. Upper school average class size: 12. Upper school faculty-student ratio: 1:12.

Upper School Student Profile Grade 9: 64 students (27 boys, 37 girls); Grade 10: 69 students (29 boys, 40 girls); Grade 11: 65 students (24 boys, 41 girls); Grade 12: 63 students (26 boys, 37 girls); Postgraduate: 2 students (2 boys).

Faculty School total: 86. In upper school: 12 men, 16 women; 12 have advanced degrees.

Subjects Offered Algebra, American history, American literature, art, art history, astronomy, biology, calculus, chemistry, computer math, computer programming, computer science, dance, English, ethics, European history, fine arts, French, geology, geometry, government/civics, health, history, journalism, Latin, mathematics, metalworking, music, physical education, physics, science, social studies, Spanish, statistics, theater arts, trigonometry, world history.

Graduation Requirements Algebra, analysis, arts and fine arts (art, music, dance, drama), biology, chemistry, computer science, English, English literature, European civilization, foreign language, languages, mathematics, physical education (includes health), physics, science, social studies (includes history).

Special Academic Programs Advanced Placement exam preparation in 12 subject areas; honors section; independent study; term-away projects; study abroad; academic accommodation for the gifted, the musically talented, and the artistically talented.

College Placement 55 students graduated in 2005; all went to college. 53% scored over 600 on SAT verbal, 62% scored over 600 on SAT math.

Student Life Upper grades have specified standards of dress, student council, honor system. Discipline rests primarily with faculty.

Summer Programs Session focuses on study skills; held on campus; accepts boys and girls; open to students from other schools. 48 students usually enrolled. 2006 schedule: August 1 to August 15. Application deadline: June 30.

Tuition and Aid Day student tuition: $19,200. Tuition installment plan (FACTS Tuition Payment Plan). Need-based scholarship grants, need-based loans available. In 2005–06, 33% of upper-school students received aid. Total amount of financial aid awarded in 2005–06: $960,450.

Admissions Traditional secondary-level entrance grade is 9. For fall 2005, 126 students applied for upper-level admission, 84 were accepted, 45 enrolled. ERB or SSAT or WISC III required. Deadline for receipt of application materials: January 31. Application fee required: $50. Interview required.

Athletics Interscholastic: alpine skiing (boys, girls), baseball (b), basketball (b,g), cross-country running (b,g), dance (b,g), golf (b,g), ice hockey (b,g), lacrosse (b,g); intramural: wilderness (g); coed intramural: bicycling, wilderness. 3 PE instructors, 4 coaches, 2 trainers.

Computers Computers are regularly used in art, dance, English, foreign language, graphic design, history, humanities, independent study, library, mathematics, SAT preparation, science, social studies, theater arts, writing, yearbook classes. Computer network features include campus e-mail, on-campus library services, CD-ROMs, Internet access, office computer access, DVD, wireless campus network.

Contact Diane M. Field, Director of Admission and Financial Aid. 207-384-2164 Ext. 2301. Fax: 207-384-3332. E-mail: dfield@berwickacademy.org. Web site: berwickacademy.org.

Berwick opened its doors in September 2004 with additional classrooms in its Lower School and a new softball field for girls' teams. NEPSAC tournament bids were played in soccer, cross-country running, basketball, lacrosse, and baseball. Upper School students traveled to Guatemala to live with families and renovate a local school.

THE BETHANY HILLS SCHOOL

PO Box 10
727 Bethany Hills Road
Bethany, Ontario L0A 1A0, Canada
Head of School: Mrs. Catherine Benson

General Information Girls' boarding and coeducational day college-preparatory school. Boarding girls grades 7–12, day boys grades JK–6, day girls grades JK–12. Founded: 1981. Setting: rural. Nearest major city is Toronto, Canada. Students are housed in single-sex dormitories. 12-acre campus. 7 buildings on campus. Approved or accredited by Canadian Association of Independent Schools, Canadian Educational Standards Institute, Conference of Independent Schools of Ontario, The Association of Boarding Schools, and Ontario Department of Education. Language of instruction: English. Total enrollment: 93. Upper school average class size: 15. Upper school faculty-student ratio: 1:7.

Upper School Student Profile Grade 9: 13 students (13 girls); Grade 10: 10 students (10 girls); Grade 11: 8 students (8 girls); Grade 12: 2 students (2 girls); Grade 13: 13 students (13 girls). 66% of students are boarding students. 60% are province residents. 3 provinces are represented in upper school student body. 40% are international students. International students from Antigua and Barbuda, Bermuda, British Virgin Islands, China, Hong Kong, and Mexico; 3 other countries represented in student body.

Faculty School total: 18. In upper school: 3 men, 13 women; 5 have advanced degrees; 5 reside on campus.

Subjects Offered Anthropology, arts, biology, business studies, calculus, careers, chemistry, civics, computer science, drama, English, equestrian sports, French, geography, healthful living, history, information technology, mathematics, media studies, music, outdoor education, physical education, physics, psychology, science, sociology, visual arts, world history, world issues, writing skills.

Graduation Requirements Arts, Canadian geography, Canadian history, English, French as a second language, mathematics, physical education (includes health), science. Community service is required.

Special Academic Programs Honors section; ESL (12 students enrolled).

College Placement 14 students graduated in 2005; 13 went to college, including Queen's University at Kingston; The University of British Columbia; Trent University; University of Toronto; York University. Other: 1 had other specific plans.

Student Life Upper grades have uniform requirement, student council, honor system. Discipline rests equally with students and faculty.

Tuition and Aid Day student tuition: CAN$13,000; 7-day tuition and room/board: CAN$31,000.

Admissions Traditional secondary-level entrance grade is 9. SLEP required. Deadline for receipt of application materials: none. Application fee required: CAN$100. Interview recommended.

Athletics Interscholastic: alpine skiing, cricket, field hockey, golf, soccer, track and field; intramural: alpine skiing, field hockey, golf, horseback riding, soccer, track and field; coed interscholastic: aerobics/dance, aerobics/nautilus, alpine skiing, aquatics, archery, back packing, badminton, ball hockey, basketball, bicycling, canoeing/kayaking, climbing, combined training, cooperative games, cross-country running, dressage, equestrian sports, fitness, flag football, hiking/backpacking, horseback riding, ice skating, independent competitive sports, life saving, mountain biking, nordic skiing, outdoor activities, outdoor adventure, outdoor education, outdoor recreation, outdoor skills, outdoors, physical fitness, running, skiing (cross-country), skiing (downhill), snowboarding, snowshoeing, swimming and diving, tennis; coed intramural: aerobics/dance, aerobics/nautilus, alpine skiing, archery, back packing, badminton, ball hockey, baseball, basketball, bicycling, canoeing/kayaking, climbing, combined training, cooperative games, cross-country running, curling, dressage, equestrian sports, fitness, flag football, hiking/backpacking, horseback riding, ice skating, independent competitive sports, life saving, mountain biking, nordic skiing, outdoor activities, outdoor adventure, outdoor education, outdoor recreation, outdoor skills, outdoors, physical fitness, running, skiing (cross-country), skiing (downhill), snowboarding, snowshoeing, tennis. 2 PE instructors, 8 coaches.

Computers Computers are regularly used in all academic classes. Computer network features include campus e-mail, CD-ROMs, Internet access, wireless campus network.

Contact Mrs. Anne E. Scott, Executive Assistant, Admissions. 705-277-2866. Fax: 705-277-1279. E-mail: ascott@bethanyhills.on.ca. Web site: www.bethanyhills.on.ca.

THE BIRCH WATHEN LENOX SCHOOL

210 East 77th Street
New York, New York 10021
Head of School: Frank J. Carnabuci

General Information Coeducational day college-preparatory school. Grades K–12. Founded: 1916. Setting: urban. 1 building on campus. Approved or accredited by New York State Association of Independent Schools and New York Department of Education. Member of National Association of Independent Schools. Endowment: $5.2 million. Total enrollment: 450. Upper school average class size: 12. Upper school faculty-student ratio: 1:12.

Upper School Student Profile Grade 9: 39 students (19 boys, 20 girls); Grade 10: 31 students (16 boys, 15 girls); Grade 11: 39 students (20 boys, 19 girls); Grade 12: 41 students (21 boys, 20 girls).

Faculty School total: 70. In upper school: 15 men, 25 women; 35 have advanced degrees.

Subjects Offered Algebra, American history, American history-AP, American literature, American literature-AP, art, art history, biology, calculus, ceramics, chemistry, community service, computer math, computer science, creative writing, dance, drama, driver education, economics, English, English literature, environmental science, European history, expository writing, fine arts, French, geography, geology, geometry, government/civics, grammar, industrial arts, Japanese, journalism, mathematics, music, philosophy, photography, physical education, physics, science, Shakespeare, social studies, Spanish, speech, swimming, theater, trigonometry, typing, world history, writing.

Graduation Requirements 20th century world history, arts and fine arts (art, music, dance, drama), computer science, English, foreign language, mathematics, physical education (includes health), science, social studies (includes history). Community service is required.

Special Academic Programs Advanced Placement exam preparation in 10 subject areas; honors section; independent study; study abroad; academic accommodation for the gifted.

College Placement 35 students graduated in 2005; all went to college, including Brown University; Columbia University; Harvard University; Lehigh University; The Johns Hopkins University; Trinity College. Mean SAT verbal: 640, mean SAT math: 630.

Student Life Upper grades have specified standards of dress, student council, honor system. Discipline rests equally with students and faculty.

Tuition and Aid Day student tuition: $25,602–$26,199. Tuition installment plan (Key Tuition Payment Plan, monthly payment plans, individually arranged payment plans). Merit scholarship grants, need-based scholarship grants available. In 2005–06, 17% of upper-school students received aid. Total amount of financial aid awarded in 2005–06: $1,200,000.

Admissions Traditional secondary-level entrance grade is 9. For fall 2005, 70 students applied for upper-level admission, 30 were accepted, 20 enrolled. ERB, ISEE, Math Placement Exam or writing sample required. Deadline for receipt of application materials: none. Application fee required: $50. On-campus interview required.

Athletics Interscholastic: baseball (boys), basketball (b,g), cross-country running (b,g), field hockey (g), hockey (b), ice hockey (b), soccer (b,g), softball (g), swimming and diving (b,g), tennis (b,g), track and field (b,g), volleyball (b,g); intramural: aerobics (b,g), baseball (b), basketball (b,g), dance (b), ice hockey (b), indoor soccer (b), running (b,g), skiing (downhill) (b,g), soccer (b,g), softball (g), swimming and diving (b,g), tennis (b,g), track and field (b,g), volleyball (b,g); coed interscholastic: cross-country running, golf, indoor track & field, lacrosse; coed intramural: bicycling, dance, golf, gymnastics, indoor track & field, skiing (cross-country), skiing (downhill). 5 PE instructors, 8 coaches.

Computers Computers are regularly used in all academic classes. Computer network features include campus e-mail, on-campus library services, CD-ROMs, Internet access, file transfer, DVD.

Contact Billie Williams, Admissions Coordinator. 212-861-0404. Fax: 212-879-3388. E-mail: bwilliams@bwl.org. Web site: www.bwl.org.

BISHOP BRADY HIGH SCHOOL

25 Columbus Avenue
Concord, New Hampshire 03301
Head of School: Jean M. Barker

General Information Coeducational day college-preparatory school, affiliated with Roman Catholic Church. Grades 9–12. Founded: 1963. Setting: suburban. 8-acre campus. 1 building on campus. Approved or accredited by New England Association of Schools and Colleges and New Hampshire Department of Education. Total enrollment: 446. Upper school average class size: 17. Upper school faculty-student ratio: 1:15.

Upper School Student Profile Grade 9: 124 students (61 boys, 63 girls); Grade 10: 118 students (57 boys, 61 girls); Grade 11: 98 students (46 boys, 52 girls); Grade 12: 106 students (50 boys, 56 girls). 67% of students are Roman Catholic.

Faculty School total: 31. In upper school: 12 men, 19 women; 25 have advanced degrees.

Subjects Offered Advanced chemistry, advanced math, algebra, anatomy and physiology, art appreciation, arts, biology, biology-AP, calculus-AP, career/college

Bishop Brady High School

preparation, chemistry, chemistry-AP, Christian scripture, college awareness, college counseling, computer education, conceptual physics, drama, English, English literature-AP, English-AP, film studies, French-AP, freshman seminar, geometry, guidance, health education, history, history-AP, honors English, Latin, moral theology, music appreciation, musical theater, physical education, physics-AP, pre-calculus, probability and statistics, psychology, religious studies, research and reference, SAT preparation, social justice, theology, trigonometry, U.S. history-AP, world religions, writing.

Graduation Requirements Algebra, American literature, arts and fine arts (art, music, dance, drama), biology, chemistry, computer education, English, geometry, languages, physical education (includes health), science, social studies (includes history), theology, 70 hours of community service.

Special Academic Programs Advanced Placement exam preparation in 7 subject areas; honors section.

College Placement 90 students graduated in 2005; 85 went to college, including Clarkson University; College of the Holy Cross; Providence College; Saint Anselm College; University of New Hampshire. Other: 4 went to work, 1 entered military service. Mean SAT verbal: 549, mean SAT math: 543, mean composite ACT: 28. 26% scored over 600 on SAT verbal, 25% scored over 600 on SAT math.

Student Life Upper grades have specified standards of dress, student council, honor system. Discipline rests primarily with faculty. Attendance at religious services is required.

Summer Programs Remediation, sports programs offered; session focuses on football and conditioning; mathematics; held on campus; accepts boys and girls; not open to students from other schools. 60 students usually enrolled. 2006 schedule: June to August.

Tuition and Aid Day student tuition: $6400. Tuition installment plan (Insured Tuition Payment Plan, monthly payment plans, individually arranged payment plans). Tuition reduction for siblings, merit scholarship grants, need-based scholarship grants available. In 2005–06, 15% of upper-school students received aid.

Admissions Traditional secondary-level entrance grade is 9. For fall 2005, 135 students applied for upper-level admission, 130 were accepted, 101 enrolled. STS required. Deadline for receipt of application materials: none. Application fee required: $25. Interview required.

Athletics Interscholastic: alpine skiing (boys, girls), baseball (b), basketball (b,g), cheering (g), cross-country running (b,g), field hockey (g), football (b), golf (b,g), ice hockey (b,g), lacrosse (b,g), skiing (downhill) (b,g), soccer (b,g), softball (g), tennis (b,g), track and field (b,g); intramural: basketball (b,g); coed interscholastic: outdoor activities, outdoor adventure; coed intramural: basketball, indoor track, outdoor activities, outdoor adventure, rock climbing, skiing (cross-country), snowboarding, strength & conditioning, table tennis, volleyball, weight lifting, weight training. 1 PE instructor.

Computers Computers are regularly used in business applications, college planning, journalism, literary magazine, newspaper classes. Computer network features include campus e-mail, online commercial services, Internet access.

Contact Mrs. Lonna J. Abbott, Director of Admissions. 603-224-7418 Ext. 300. Fax: 603-228-6664. E-mail: labbott@bishopbrady.edu. Web site: www.bishopbrady.edu.

BISHOP BROSSART HIGH SCHOOL

Grove and Jefferson Streets
Alexandria, Kentucky 41001
Head of School: Mr. Thomas Henry Seither

General Information Coeducational day college-preparatory school, affiliated with Roman Catholic Church. Grades 9–12. Founded: 1950. Setting: small town. Nearest major city is Cincinnati, OH. 2 buildings on campus. Approved or accredited by National Catholic Education Association, Southern Association of Colleges and Schools, and Kentucky Department of Education. Total enrollment: 400. Upper school average class size: 25. Upper school faculty-student ratio: 1:16.

Upper School Student Profile Grade 9: 98 students (49 boys, 49 girls); Grade 10: 93 students (45 boys, 48 girls); Grade 11: 100 students (48 boys, 52 girls); Grade 12: 109 students (45 boys, 64 girls). 98% of students are Roman Catholic.

Faculty School total: 30. In upper school: 17 men, 13 women; 25 have advanced degrees.

Subjects Offered Advanced Placement courses, anatomy, art, arts appreciation, biology, business, business technology, calculus-AP, chemistry, chorus, communication arts, computer programming, computer technologies, earth science, economics, English, English-AP, European history-AP, film, foreign language, French, French-AP, geometry, global issues, government, health, history-AP, introduction to technology, physics, religion, science, social studies, Spanish, Spanish-AP, theater, U.S. history-AP.

College Placement 102 students graduated in 2005; 74 went to college, including Northern Kentucky University; University of Cincinnati; University of Kentucky; University of Louisville. Other: 2 went to work, 19 entered a postgraduate year, 7 had other specific plans.

Student Life Upper grades have uniform requirement, student council, honor system. Discipline rests primarily with faculty. Attendance at religious services is required.

Tuition and Aid Tuition reduction for siblings, need-based scholarship grants available.

Admissions Traditional secondary-level entrance grade is 9. High School Placement Test required. Application fee required: $25.

Athletics Interscholastic: baseball (boys), basketball (b,g), bowling (b,g), cheering (g), dance team (g), golf (b,g), indoor track & field (b,g), soccer (b,g), track and field (b,g), volleyball (g). 5 coaches.

Computers Computer network features include CD-ROMs, Internet access, DVD.

Contact Admissions. 859-635-2108. Fax: 859-635-2135. E-mail: brossart@insightbb.com.

BISHOP CARROLL HIGH SCHOOL

728 Ben Franklin Highway
Ebensburg, Pennsylvania 15931
Head of School: Mrs. Deborah Meckey

General Information Coeducational day college-preparatory, general academic, vocational, and religious studies school, affiliated with Roman Catholic Church. Grades 9–12. Founded: 1960. Setting: small town. Nearest major city is Johnstown. 1 building on campus. Approved or accredited by Middle States Association of Colleges and Schools and Pennsylvania Department of Education. Total enrollment: 257. Upper school average class size: 20. Upper school faculty-student ratio: 1:12.

Upper School Student Profile Grade 9: 60 students (34 boys, 26 girls); Grade 10: 64 students (35 boys, 29 girls); Grade 11: 68 students (32 boys, 36 girls); Grade 12: 65 students (27 boys, 38 girls). 97% of students are Roman Catholic.

Faculty School total: 25. In upper school: 9 men, 16 women; 12 have advanced degrees.

Subjects Offered Accounting, algebra, American government, anatomy and physiology, art, art appreciation, band, biology, calculus, Catholic belief and practice, chemistry, chorus, civics, computer applications, computer keyboarding, earth science, ecology, English, European history, finance, French, government, health, history, home economics, Latin, music appreciation, personal finance, physical education, physics, psychology, public speaking, reading, religion, science, Spanish, trigonometry, U.S. government, U.S. history, Web site design, zoology.

Graduation Requirements Algebra, arts appreciation, biology, Catholic belief and practice, chemistry, civics, computer applications, computer keyboarding, English, geography, government, lab science, language, mathematics, music theory, physical education (includes health), science, social science, U.S. history, world history, 15 hours of community service per year, .25 Accelerated Reader Credit per year.

Special Academic Programs Honors section; independent study; study at local college for college credit; remedial reading and/or remedial writing; special instructional classes for deaf students, blind students.

College Placement 59 students graduated in 2005; 52 went to college, including Indiana University of Pennsylvania; St. Francis College; The Pennsylvania State University University Park Campus; University of Pittsburgh. Other: 1 entered military service, 2 entered a postgraduate year, 4 had other specific plans. Mean SAT verbal: 519, mean SAT math: 503, mean composite ACT: 20.

Student Life Upper grades have uniform requirement. Discipline rests primarily with faculty. Attendance at religious services is required.

Tuition and Aid Day student tuition: $4750. Tuition installment plan (monthly payment plans, individually arranged payment plans). Need-based scholarship grants available. In 2005–06, 88% of upper-school students received aid. Total amount of financial aid awarded in 2005–06: $569,502.

Admissions Traditional secondary-level entrance grade is 9. Diocesan Entrance Exam required. Deadline for receipt of application materials: none. No application fee required. Interview recommended.

Athletics Interscholastic: baseball (boys), basketball (b,g), cheering (g), football (b), golf (b,g), soccer (b,g), softball (g), track and field (b,g), volleyball (g), wrestling (b); coed intramural: bowling. 2 PE instructors, 34 coaches, 1 trainer.

Computers Computers are regularly used in keyboarding classes. Computer network features include on-campus library services, online commercial services, Internet access, office computer access.

Contact Mrs. Deborah Meckey, Principal. 814-472-7500 Ext. 106. Fax: 814-472-8020. Web site: www.bishopcarroll.com.

BISHOP CONATY-OUR LADY OF LORETTO HIGH SCHOOL

2900 West Pico Boulevard
Los Angeles, California 90006
Head of School: Ms. Sharon Morano

General Information Girls' day college-preparatory, general academic, arts, religious studies, and technology school, affiliated with Roman Catholic Church. Grades 9–12. Founded: 1923. Setting: urban. 2-acre campus. 3 buildings on campus. Approved or accredited by National Catholic Education Association, Western Association of Schools and Colleges, Western Catholic Education Association, and California Department of Education. Endowment: $550,000. Total enrollment: 448. Upper school average class size: 27. Upper school faculty-student ratio: 1:14.

Upper School Student Profile Grade 9: 118 students (118 girls); Grade 10: 108 students (108 girls); Grade 11: 115 students (115 girls); Grade 12: 107 students (107 girls). 92% of students are Roman Catholic.

Faculty School total: 28. In upper school: 11 men, 17 women; 18 have advanced degrees.

Subjects Offered Advanced math, algebra, American literature, anatomy and physiology, biology, Catholic belief and practice, chemistry, choir, Christian and Hebrew scripture, computer studies, computers, dance performance, drama, drawing and design, economics, English, French, French-AP, geometry, government, guidance, health, honors algebra, honors English, honors geometry, honors U.S. history, honors world history, integrated science, journalism, mathematics, painting, physical education, physics, pre-calculus, religion, social justice, social studies, Spanish, Spanish language-AP, Spanish literature-AP, U.S. history, visual arts, world history, world literature, world religions.

Graduation Requirements Arts and fine arts (art, music, dance, drama), computer science, English, foreign language, mathematics, physical education (includes health), religion (includes Bible studies and theology), science, social studies (includes history), guidance classes in grades 9 and 10.

Special Academic Programs Advanced Placement exam preparation in 3 subject areas; honors section; remedial reading and/or remedial writing; remedial math.

College Placement 107 students graduated in 2005; 100 went to college, including California State University, Dominguez Hills; California State University, Los Angeles; California State University, Northridge; Mount St. Mary's College; Pasadena City College; Santa Monica College. Other: 3 went to work, 3 entered a postgraduate year, 1 had other specific plans. Mean SAT verbal: 426, mean SAT math: 414, mean composite ACT: 19.

Student Life Upper grades have uniform requirement, student council, honor system. Discipline rests primarily with faculty. Attendance at religious services is required.

Summer Programs Remediation, enrichment, advancement, art/fine arts, computer instruction programs offered; session focuses on make-up courses and strengthening incoming freshmen skills; held on campus; accepts girls; not open to students from other schools. 251 students usually enrolled. 2006 schedule: June 19 to July 21. Application deadline: August 15.

Tuition and Aid Day student tuition: $4450–$4980. Tuition installment plan (monthly payment plans, individually arranged payment plans). Need-based scholarship grants, paying campus jobs available. In 2005–06, 61% of upper-school students received aid. Total amount of financial aid awarded in 2005–06: $300,300.

Admissions Traditional secondary-level entrance grade is 9. For fall 2005, 25 students applied for upper-level admission, 22 were accepted, 18 enrolled. High School Placement Test required. Deadline for receipt of application materials: August 15. Application fee required: $30. On-campus interview required.

Athletics Interscholastic: basketball, dance, soccer, softball, volleyball. 2 PE instructors, 5 coaches.

Computers Computers are regularly used in business applications classes. Computer network features include on-campus library services, CD-ROMs, Internet access.

Contact Director of Admissions. 323-737-0012 Ext. 103. Fax: 323-737-1749. E-mail: hstellern@bishopconatyloretto.org. Web site: bishopconatyloretto.org.

BISHOP EUSTACE PREPARATORY SCHOOL

5552 Route 70
Pennsauken, New Jersey 08109-4798
Head of School: Br. James Beamesderfer, SAC

General Information Coeducational day college-preparatory, arts, and religious studies school, affiliated with Roman Catholic Church. Grades 9–12. Founded: 1954. Setting: suburban. Nearest major city is Philadelphia, PA. 32-acre campus. 7 buildings on campus. Approved or accredited by Middle States Association of Colleges and Schools and New Jersey Department of Education. Endowment: $3.2 million. Total enrollment: 765. Upper school average class size: 21. Upper school faculty-student ratio: 1:14.

Upper School Student Profile Grade 9: 198 students (104 boys, 94 girls); Grade 10: 194 students (94 boys, 100 girls); Grade 11: 190 students (97 boys, 93 girls); Grade 12: 183 students (87 boys, 96 girls). 88% of students are Roman Catholic.

Faculty School total: 60. In upper school: 29 men, 31 women; 34 have advanced degrees.

Subjects Offered Advanced chemistry, Advanced Placement courses, algebra, American history, American history-AP, American literature, anatomy, applied music, art and culture, art history, Bible studies, biology, biology-AP, British literature, British literature (honors), calculus-AP, career exploration, chemistry, chemistry-AP, clinical chemistry, college planning, computer education, creative writing, discrete math, driver education, economics, English, English literature, environmental science, ethics, European history-AP, film, fine arts, French, genetics, geometry, German, government/civics, grammar, health, history, instrumental music, journalism, Latin, law, mathematics, music, music composition, music history, music theory, physical education, physical science, physics, physics-AP, physiology, pre-calculus, science, social studies, sociology, Spanish, statistics-AP, theology, trigonometry, vocal music, women's studies, world affairs, world history.

Graduation Requirements Arts and fine arts (art, music, dance, drama), career exploration, computer science, English, foreign language, mathematics, physical

education (includes health), religion (includes Bible studies and theology), science, sex education, social studies (includes history). Community service is required.

Special Academic Programs Advanced Placement exam preparation in 10 subject areas; honors section; independent study; study at local college for college credit; academic accommodation for the musically talented.

College Placement 183 students graduated in 2005; all went to college, including La Salle University; Loyola College in Maryland; Rutgers, The State University of New Jersey, New Brunswick/Piscataway; Saint Joseph's University; University of Pennsylvania; Villanova University.

Student Life Upper grades have uniform requirement, student council, honor system. Discipline rests primarily with faculty. Attendance at religious services is required.

Summer Programs Enrichment, advancement, sports programs offered; session focuses on student recruitment and enrichment; held on campus; accepts boys and girls; open to students from other schools. 150 students usually enrolled. 2006 schedule: June to July. Application deadline: May.

Tuition and Aid Day student tuition: $10,600. Tuition installment plan (FACTS Tuition Payment Plan). Merit scholarship grants, need-based scholarship grants available. In 2005–06, 35% of upper-school students received aid; total upper-school merit-scholarship money awarded: $155,600. Total amount of financial aid awarded in 2005–06: $520,000.

Admissions Traditional secondary-level entrance grade is 9. For fall 2005, 523 students applied for upper-level admission, 339 were accepted, 200 enrolled. Deadline for receipt of application materials: none. Application fee required: $50.

Athletics Interscholastic: baseball (boys), basketball (b,g), bowling (b,g), cheering (g), crew (b,g), cross-country running (b,g), field hockey (g), football (b), ice hockey (b), indoor track & field (b,g), running (b,g), soccer (b,g), softball (g), swimming and diving (b,g), tennis (b,g), track and field (b,g); coed interscholastic: aquatics, diving, golf. 3 PE instructors, 57 coaches, 1 trainer.

Computers Computers are regularly used in all academic classes. Computer network features include on-campus library services, CD-ROMs, online commercial services, Internet access, wireless campus network.

Contact Mrs. Marylou Williams, Admissions Coordinator. 856-662-2160 Ext. 262. Fax: 856-665-2184. E-mail: mwilliams@eustace.org. Web site: www.eustace.org.

BISHOP FEEHAN HIGH SCHOOL

70 Holcott Drive
Attleboro, Massachusetts 02703
Head of School: Mr. Christopher E. Servant

General Information Coeducational day college-preparatory, arts, and religious studies school, affiliated with Roman Catholic Church. Grades 9–12. Founded: 1961. Setting: suburban. Nearest major city is Providence, RI. 25-acre campus. 3 buildings on campus. Approved or accredited by National Catholic Education Association, New England Association of Schools and Colleges, and Massachusetts Department of Education. Total enrollment: 966. Upper school average class size: 17. Upper school faculty-student ratio: 1:13.

Upper School Student Profile Grade 9: 260 students (129 boys, 131 girls); Grade 10: 233 students (103 boys, 130 girls); Grade 11: 226 students (99 boys, 127 girls); Grade 12: 247 students (113 boys, 134 girls). 90% of students are Roman Catholic.

Faculty School total: 95. In upper school: 35 men, 60 women; 52 have advanced degrees.

Subjects Offered Advanced chemistry, algebra, American literature, analytic geometry, anatomy and physiology, Arabic, art, art history, Bible studies, bioethics, biology, biology-AP, British literature, British literature (honors), business applications, business law, calculus, calculus-AP, campus ministry, Catholic belief and practice, chemistry, chemistry-AP, choir, choral music, chorus, Christian and Hebrew scripture, Christian doctrine, Christian education, Christian ethics, Christian studies, Christian testament, Christianity, college counseling, college planning, composition, computer animation, computer applications, computer graphics, computer keyboarding, computer programming, conceptual physics, concert band, concert choir, dance, drama, drama workshop, drawing, driver education, earth science, ecology, environmental systems, economics, English, English composition, English language and composition-AP, English literature and composition-AP, environmental science, European history, French, genetics, geometry, government and politics-AP, guidance, health and wellness, history of the Catholic Church, honors algebra, honors English, honors geometry, honors U.S. history, honors world history, integrated mathematics, jazz ensemble, lab science, Latin, music theory, mythology, oral communications, physical education, physics, pre-calculus, probability and statistics, psychology, psychology-AP, SAT preparation, Shakespeare, sociology, Spanish, Spanish language-AP, statistics, statistics-AP, studio art-AP, theater arts, theology, U.S. history, U.S. history-AP, Web site design, word processing, world religions.

Graduation Requirements Biology, career education, chemistry, electives, English, foreign language, mathematics, physics, research skills, SAT preparation, study skills, theology, U.S. history, word processing, world history.

Special Academic Programs Advanced Placement exam preparation in 10 subject areas; honors section.

College Placement 281 students graduated in 2005; 245 went to college, including Assumption College; Merrimack College; Providence College; Stonehill College; University of Massachusetts Amherst; University of Rhode Island. Other: 2 went to work. Mean SAT verbal: 560, mean SAT math: 560.

Bishop Feehan High School

Student Life Upper grades have uniform requirement, student council. Discipline rests primarily with faculty. Attendance at religious services is required.

Tuition and Aid Day student tuition: $6600. Tuition installment plan (FACTS Tuition Payment Plan). Merit scholarship grants, need-based scholarship grants available. In 2005–06, 20% of upper-school students received aid; total upper-school merit-scholarship money awarded: $10,000. Total amount of financial aid awarded in 2005–06: $400,000.

Admissions Traditional secondary-level entrance grade is 11. For fall 2005, 535 students applied for upper-level admission, 284 were accepted, 261 enrolled. Scholastic Testing Service High School Placement Test required. Deadline for receipt of application materials: December 15. No application fee required. Interview required.

Athletics Interscholastic: baseball (boys), basketball (b,g), cheering (g), diving (b,g), football (b), indoor track & field (b,g), soccer (b,g), softball (g), swimming and diving (b,g), tennis (b,g), track and field (b,g), volleyball (g); coed interscholastic: cross-country running, dance, dance squad, fencing, golf, ice hockey; coed intramural: fencing. 1 PE instructor, 30 coaches, 1 trainer.

Computers Computers are regularly used in all classes. Computer network features include campus e-mail, on-campus library services, CD-ROMs, Internet access, file transfer, office computer access, DVD, wireless campus network.

Contact Mary O'Brien, Admissions Assistant. 508-226-6223 Ext. 119. Fax: 508-226-7696. E-mail: mobrien@bishopfeehan.com. Web site: www.bishopfeehan.com.

BISHOP FENWICK HIGH SCHOOL

4855 State Route 122
Franklin, Ohio 45005
Head of School: Mrs. Catherine Mulligan

General Information Coeducational day college-preparatory and arts school, affiliated with Roman Catholic Church. Grades 9–12. Founded: 1952. Setting: small town. Nearest major city is Cincinnati. 66-acre campus. 1 building on campus. Approved or accredited by North Central Association of Colleges and Schools, Ohio Catholic Schools Accreditation Association (OCSAA), and Ohio Department of Education. Total enrollment: 521. Upper school average class size: 25. Upper school faculty-student ratio: 1:15.

Upper School Student Profile Grade 9: 160 students (90 boys, 70 girls); Grade 10: 143 students (80 boys, 63 girls); Grade 11: 117 students (64 boys, 53 girls); Grade 12: 101 students (51 boys, 50 girls). 85% of students are Roman Catholic.

Faculty School total: 34. In upper school: 16 men, 16 women; 15 have advanced degrees.

Subjects Offered Accounting, algebra, American democracy, art, art appreciation, art-AP, athletic training, biology, botany, calculus-AP, cell biology, chemistry, chorus, computer graphics, computer processing, computer programming, concert band, creative writing, economics, English, English-AP, ensembles, fine arts, French, functions, general business, geometry, government, health, honors algebra, honors English, honors geometry, integrated math, jazz band, Latin, Latin-AP, leadership skills, marching band, mathematics, multimedia, music appreciation, mythology, Native American studies, physical education, physical science, physics, physiology, portfolio art, pre-algebra, psychology, publications, religion, science, social studies, Spanish, statistics, study skills, technology, theater, theater arts, trigonometry, U.S. history, U.S. history-AP, Web site design, world geography, world history, writing, yearbook, zoology.

Special Academic Programs Advanced Placement exam preparation in 5 subject areas; honors section; study at local college for college credit.

College Placement 85 students graduated in 2005; 83 went to college, including Miami University; Ohio University; The Ohio State University; University of Cincinnati; University of Dayton; Xavier University. Other: 1 went to work, 1 entered military service.

Student Life Upper grades have uniform requirement, student council. Discipline rests primarily with faculty. Attendance at religious services is required.

Tuition and Aid Day student tuition: $5400. Tuition installment plan (SMART Tuition Payment Plan). Tuition reduction for siblings, merit scholarship grants, need-based scholarship grants available. Total upper-school merit-scholarship money awarded for 2005–06: $2000. Total amount of financial aid awarded in 2005–06: $65,000.

Admissions Traditional secondary-level entrance grade is 9. High School Placement Test required. Deadline for receipt of application materials: none. No application fee required.

Athletics Interscholastic: baseball (boys), basketball (b,g), cheering (g), cross-country running (b,g), football (b), golf (b), soccer (b,g), softball (g), swimming and diving (b,g), tennis (b,g), track and field (b,g), volleyball (g), wrestling (b); intramural: basketball (b), in-line hockey (b), weight training (b,g); coed interscholastic: bowling. 1 PE instructor, 17 coaches, 1 trainer.

Computers Computer network features include on-campus library services, CD-ROMs, Internet access, DVD.

Contact Mrs. Jacki George, Coordinator of Institutional Advancement. 513-423-0723 Ext. 206. Fax: 513-420-8690. Web site: www.fenwickfalcons.org.

BISHOP GEORGE AHR HIGH SCHOOL

One Tingley Lane
Edison, New Jersey 08820
Head of School: Sr. Donna Marie Trukowski, CSSF

General Information Coeducational day college-preparatory, arts, and technology school, affiliated with Roman Catholic Church. Grades 9–12. Founded: 1969. Setting: suburban. 24-acre campus. 1 building on campus. Approved or accredited by Accreditation Commission of the Texas Association of Baptist Schools, Middle States Association of Colleges and Schools, and New Jersey Department of Education. Total enrollment: 900. Upper school average class size: 24.

Upper School Student Profile 75% of students are Roman Catholic.

Faculty School total: 55. In upper school: 20 men, 35 women; 30 have advanced degrees.

Special Academic Programs Advanced Placement exam preparation in 5 subject areas; honors section.

College Placement 231 students graduated in 2005.

Student Life Upper grades have uniform requirement, student council. Discipline rests primarily with faculty.

Tuition and Aid Day student tuition: $6900–$7200. Tuition installment plan (The Tuition Plan, SMART Tuition Payment Plan). Merit scholarship grants, need-based scholarship grants available.

Admissions For fall 2005, 600 students applied for upper-level admission, 320 were accepted, 220 enrolled. ACT-Explore required. Deadline for receipt of application materials: none. Application fee required.

Athletics Interscholastic: cheering (girls), dance (g), football (b), golf (b), gymnastics (g), softball (g), volleyball (g), weight training (b), wrestling (b); coed interscholastic: aquatics, baseball, basketball, bowling, cross-country running, physical training, winter (indoor) track. 6 PE instructors, 35 coaches.

Computers Computer resources include on-campus library services, online commercial services, Internet access.

Contact Mrs. Cora Medley, Counseling and Admissions Secretary. 732-549-1108 Ext. 616. Fax: 732-549-9050. E-mail: cmedley@bgahs.org. Web site: www.bgahs.org.

BISHOP GUERTIN HIGH SCHOOL

194 Lund Road
Nashua, New Hampshire 03060-4398
Head of School: Br. Mark Hilton, SC

General Information Coeducational day college-preparatory, arts, religious studies, bilingual studies, and technology school, affiliated with Roman Catholic Church. Grades 9–12. Founded: 1963. Setting: suburban. Nearest major city is Boston, MA. 19-acre campus. 2 buildings on campus. Approved or accredited by New England Association of Schools and Colleges and New Hampshire Department of Education. Total enrollment: 884. Upper school average class size: 25. Upper school faculty-student ratio: 1:23.

Upper School Student Profile Grade 9: 220 students (108 boys, 112 girls); Grade 10: 234 students (122 boys, 112 girls); Grade 11: 220 students (103 boys, 117 girls); Grade 12: 210 students (116 boys, 94 girls). 80% of students are Roman Catholic.

Faculty School total: 67. In upper school: 35 men, 30 women; 55 have advanced degrees.

Subjects Offered 20th century history, acting, advanced chemistry, advanced computer applications, advanced math, algebra, American literature-AP, analysis and differential calculus, anatomy and physiology, art appreciation, art history, band, Bible studies, biology, biology-AP, British history, British literature, British literature (honors), business law, calculus, calculus-AP, campus ministry, career/college preparation, chemistry, chemistry-AP, chorus, Christian and Hebrew scripture, Christian doctrine, Christian education, Christian ethics, Christianity, church history, civics, college admission preparation, college counseling, college writing, community service, comparative government and politics, comparative government and politics-AP, comparative religion, computer applications, computer art, computer education, computer literacy, computer multimedia, computer processing, computer programming, computer programming-AP, computer science, computer technologies, computer-aided design, constitutional history of U.S., consumer economics, contemporary history, CPR, creative writing, death and loss, debate, desktop publishing, digital photography, discrete math, dramatic arts, drawing, driver education, economics, emergency medicine, English, English composition, English literature, English literature and composition-AP, English-AP, environmental science, ethics, European history, fine arts, foreign language, French, geography, geometry, government/civics, grammar, health, health and wellness, health education, history, honors geometry, honors U.S. history, honors world history, human anatomy, human biology, human sexuality, instrumental music, journalism, Latin, Latin-AP, law, literary magazine, marching band, mechanics of writing, moral reasoning, moral theology, music, philosophy, physical education, physics, pre-calculus, psychology, religion, religious studies, science, senior seminar, Shakespeare, social studies, Spanish, statistics, studio art, studio art-AP, The 20th Century, theater, trigonometry, U.S. government and politics, U.S. government and politics-AP, U.S. history, U.S. history-AP, U.S. literature, world history, world literature.

Graduation Requirements Arts and fine arts (art, music, dance, drama), computer science, English, foreign language, mathematics, physical education (includes health), religion (includes Bible studies and theology), science, social studies (includes history). Community service is required.

Special Academic Programs Advanced Placement exam preparation in 12 subject areas; honors section; independent study; study at local college for college credit; study abroad; academic accommodation for the gifted, the musically talented, and the artistically talented.

College Placement 209 students graduated in 2005; 207 went to college, including Boston University; Holy Cross College; Northeastern University; University of Connecticut; University of New Hampshire. Other: 1 entered military service, 1 entered a postgraduate year. Mean SAT verbal: 584, mean SAT math: 570.

Student Life Upper grades have specified standards of dress, student council, honor system. Discipline rests primarily with faculty. Attendance at religious services is required.

Summer Programs Remediation, enrichment, sports, computer instruction programs offered; session focuses on remediation; held on campus; accepts boys and girls; not open to students from other schools. 40 students usually enrolled. 2006 schedule: July 5 to July 29. Application deadline: May 1.

Tuition and Aid Tuition installment plan (FACTS Tuition Payment Plan, individually arranged payment plans). Merit scholarship grants, need-based scholarship grants, paying campus jobs available. In 2005–06, 10% of upper-school students received aid; total upper-school merit-scholarship money awarded: $10,500. Total amount of financial aid awarded in 2005–06: $175,000.

Admissions Traditional secondary-level entrance grade is 9. For fall 2005, 650 students applied for upper-level admission, 230 were accepted. Catholic High School Entrance Examination or STS, Diocese Test required. Deadline for receipt of application materials: January 6. Application fee required: $25.

Athletics Interscholastic: baseball (boys), basketball (b,g), cheering (b,g), cross-country running (b,g), football (b), gymnastics (g), hockey (b,g), ice hockey (b,g), lacrosse (b), skiing (downhill) (b,g), soccer (b,g), softball (g), swimming and diving (b,g), tennis (b,g), track and field (b,g), volleyball (g), wrestling (b); intramural: crew (b,g); coed interscholastic: aquatics, cheering, golf, ice hockey, indoor track, nordic skiing, paint ball, skiing (downhill); coed intramural: aerobics/dance, basketball, bowling, crew, dance, fishing, freestyle skiing, golf, mountain biking, outdoor education, strength & conditioning, swimming and diving, table tennis, tennis, volleyball, weight lifting, weight training. 4 PE instructors, 55 coaches, 2 trainers.

Computers Computers are regularly used in career education, career exploration, career technology, college planning, data processing, desktop publishing, independent study, information technology, introduction to technology, library, library science, library skills, literary magazine, multimedia, music, news writing, newspaper, programming, publications, publishing, research skills, stock market, technology, Web site design, word processing, yearbook classes. Computer network features include campus e-mail, on-campus library services, CD-ROMs, Internet access, file transfer, office computer access, wireless campus network.

Contact Ms. Jamie Gregoire, Director of Admissions. 603-889-4107 Ext. 304. Fax: 603-889-0701. E-mail: admit@bghs.org. Web site: www.bghs.org.

BISHOP HOBAN HIGH SCHOOL

159 South Pennsylvania Boulevard
Wilkes-Barre, Pennsylvania 18701-3394
Head of School: Rev. Walter E. Jenkins

General Information Coeducational day college-preparatory and religious studies school, affiliated with Roman Catholic Church. Grades 9–12. Founded: 1972. Setting: small town. Nearest major city is Harrisburg. 1-acre campus. 1 building on campus. Approved or accredited by Middle States Association of Colleges and Schools and Pennsylvania Department of Education. Total enrollment: 650. Upper school average class size: 26. Upper school faculty-student ratio: 1:14.

Upper School Student Profile Grade 9: 153 students (74 boys, 79 girls); Grade 10: 175 students (80 boys, 95 girls); Grade 11: 168 students (72 boys, 96 girls); Grade 12: 154 students (80 boys, 74 girls). 93% of students are Roman Catholic.

Faculty School total: 47. In upper school: 19 men, 28 women; 31 have advanced degrees.

Subjects Offered 3-dimensional art, accounting, advanced chemistry, advanced computer applications, advanced math, Advanced Placement courses, advanced studio art-AP, algebra, American Civil War, American culture, American foreign policy, American government, American government-AP, American history, American history-AP, American literature, analytic geometry, art, art and culture, art appreciation, art education, art history, arts and crafts, band, bell choir, biology, biology-AP, British literature, British literature (honors), business law, calculus, chemistry, chorus, computer applications, electives, English composition, English literature, English literature-AP, environmental science, first aid, French, geometry, government, government and politics-AP, grammar, guidance, handbells, health education, history of the Catholic Church, history-AP, honors algebra, honors English, honors geometry, honors U.S. history, instruments, journalism, Latin, library, library assistant, Life of Christ, literature, literature-AP, music appreciation, music history, music theory, musical productions, oral communications, physical education, physical science, physics, play production, pottery, prayer/spirituality, pre-calculus, probability and statistics, psychology, psychology-AP, religion, Shakespeare, Spanish, speech com-

munications, studio art-AP, theology, trigonometry, U.S. government, U.S. government and politics-AP, U.S. history-AP, Western civilization, writing.

Graduation Requirements Algebra, American culture, biology, chemistry, communications, computer technologies, English, English literature, geometry, language, music appreciation, physical education (includes health), physical science, research, theology, trigonometry, Western civilization, writing.

Special Academic Programs Advanced Placement exam preparation in 11 subject areas; honors section; study at local college for college credit; remedial reading and/or remedial writing; remedial math; special instructional classes for deaf students, blind students.

College Placement 160 students graduated in 2005; 158 went to college, including Saint Joseph's University; The Pennsylvania State University University Park Campus; The University of Scranton; University of Pittsburgh; Villanova University. Other: 1 went to work, 1 entered military service.

Student Life Upper grades have uniform requirement, student council, honor system. Discipline rests primarily with faculty. Attendance at religious services is required.

Tuition and Aid Day student tuition: $7500. Tuition installment plan (SMART Tuition Payment Plan). Tuition reduction for siblings, merit scholarship grants, need-based scholarship grants available. In 2005–06, 14% of upper-school students received aid; total upper-school merit-scholarship money awarded: $22,450. Total amount of financial aid awarded in 2005–06: $2,832,722.

Admissions Traditional secondary-level entrance grade is 9. For fall 2005, 180 students applied for upper-level admission, 175 were accepted. STS required. Deadline for receipt of application materials: none. Application fee required: $150. On-campus interview required.

Athletics Interscholastic: baseball (boys), basketball (b,g), cheering (g), cross-country running (b,g), diving (b,g), field hockey (g), football (b), soccer (b,g), softball (g), swimming and diving (b,g), track and field (b,g), volleyball (b,g); intramural: ice hockey (b), indoor soccer (b,g), soccer (b,g); coed interscholastic: golf; coed intramural: skiing (downhill). 2 PE instructors.

Computers Computers are regularly used in computer applications, journalism, library, writing, yearbook classes. Computer network features include Internet access.

Contact Mrs. Maria Anna Choman, Guidance Secretary. 570-829-2424 Ext. 37. Fax: 570-829-2241. E-mail: mchoman@bishophoban.com.

BISHOP IRETON HIGH SCHOOL

201 Cambridge Road
Alexandria, Virginia 22314-4899
Head of School: Rev. Matthew Hillyard, OSFS

General Information Coeducational day college-preparatory, arts, religious studies, and technology school, affiliated with Roman Catholic Church. Grades 9–12. Founded: 1964. Setting: suburban. 12-acre campus. 1 building on campus. Approved or accredited by National Catholic Education Association and Southern Association of Colleges and Schools. Endowment: $1 million. Total enrollment: 810. Upper school average class size: 24. Upper school faculty-student ratio: 1:14.

Upper School Student Profile Grade 9: 205 students (93 boys, 112 girls); Grade 10: 209 students (93 boys, 116 girls); Grade 11: 199 students (96 boys, 103 girls); Grade 12: 197 students (92 boys, 105 girls). 93% of students are Roman Catholic.

Faculty School total: 61. In upper school: 28 men, 32 women; 45 have advanced degrees.

Subjects Offered Advanced Placement courses, Catholic belief and practice, computer science, driver education, English, film, fine arts, foreign language, health, mathematics, physical education, religion, science, social studies.

Graduation Requirements Arts and fine arts (art, music, dance, drama), computer science, English, foreign language, mathematics, physical education (includes health), religion (includes Bible studies and theology), science, social studies (includes history), 60 hours of community service.

Special Academic Programs Advanced Placement exam preparation in 11 subject areas; honors section; academic accommodation for the musically talented; special instructional classes for students with Attention Deficit Disorder.

College Placement 196 students graduated in 2005; 193 went to college, including George Mason University; James Madison University; Radford University; The College of William and Mary; Virginia Polytechnic Institute and State University. Other: 3 had other specific plans. Mean SAT verbal: 601, mean SAT math: 591.

Student Life Upper grades have uniform requirement, honor system. Discipline rests primarily with faculty. Attendance at religious services is required.

Summer Programs Remediation, enrichment, computer instruction programs offered; session focuses on remediation; held on campus; accepts boys and girls; open to students from other schools. 25 students usually enrolled. 2006 schedule: June to July.

Tuition and Aid Day student tuition: $8600–$12,700. Tuition installment plan (monthly payment plans). Tuition reduction for siblings, merit scholarship grants, need-based scholarship grants available. In 2005–06, 9% of upper-school students received aid; total upper-school merit-scholarship money awarded: $100,000. Total amount of financial aid awarded in 2005–06: $275,000.

Admissions Traditional secondary-level entrance grade is 9. For fall 2005, 420 students applied for upper-level admission, 346 were accepted, 206 enrolled. High

Bishop Ireton High School

School Placement Test (closed version) from Scholastic Testing Service required. Deadline for receipt of application materials: January 27. Application fee required: $50.

Athletics Interscholastic: baseball (boys), basketball (b,g), football (b), lacrosse (b,g), soccer (b,g), softball (g), swimming and diving (b,g), tennis (b,g), track and field (b,g), volleyball (g), winter (indoor) track (b,g), wrestling (b); intramural: weight training (b,g); coed interscholastic: cheering, crew, cross-country running, diving, golf, ice hockey, indoor track, weight training; coed intramural: dance team, freestyle skiing, skiing (downhill). 4 PE instructors, 3 coaches, 1 trainer.

Computers Computers are regularly used in all academic classes. Computer network features include campus e-mail, on-campus library services, CD-ROMs, online commercial services, Internet access, file transfer, office computer access, DVD.

Contact Mr. Peter J. Hamer, Director of Admissions. 703-212-5190. Fax: 703-212-8173. E-mail: hamerp@bishopireton.org. Web site: www.bishopireton.org.

BISHOP KELLY HIGH SCHOOL

7009 Franklin Road
Boise, Idaho 83709-0922
Head of School: Mr. Robert R. Wehde

General Information Coeducational day college-preparatory and religious studies school, affiliated with Roman Catholic Church. Grades 9–12. Founded: 1964. Setting: suburban. 100-acre campus. 2 buildings on campus. Approved or accredited by National Catholic Education Association, Northwest Association of Accredited Schools, and Idaho Department of Education. Endowment: $3.2 million. Total enrollment: 672. Upper school average class size: 23. Upper school faculty-student ratio: 1:17.

Upper School Student Profile Grade 9: 181 students (99 boys, 82 girls); Grade 10: 164 students (68 boys, 96 girls); Grade 11: 156 students (80 boys, 76 girls); Grade 12: 164 students (92 boys, 72 girls); Grade 13: 7 students (6 boys, 1 girl). 84% of students are Roman Catholic.

Faculty School total: 41. In upper school: 14 men, 27 women; 2 have advanced degrees.

Subjects Offered Algebra, American government, art, art appreciation, biology, calculus, chemistry, choir, Christian and Hebrew scripture, Christianity, comparative religion, computer applications, computer programming, creative writing, earth science, ecology, economics, English, French, geology, geometry, health, horticulture, instrumental music, Japanese, journalism, Latin, physical education, physics, pottery, pre-algebra, pre-calculus, psychology, reading/study skills, Spanish, speech, theater arts, trigonometry, U.S. history, video film production, Western civilization, yearbook.

Graduation Requirements Computer science, English, foreign language, mathematics, physical education (includes health), religion (includes Bible studies and theology), science, social studies (includes history), 30 hours of community service.

Special Academic Programs Advanced Placement exam preparation in 9 subject areas; honors section; independent study; remedial reading and/or remedial writing.

College Placement 153 students graduated in 2005; 146 went to college, including Albertson College of Idaho; Boise State University; Carroll College; Gonzaga University; University of Idaho; University of Portland. Other: 7 went to work. Mean SAT verbal: 573, mean SAT math: 566, mean composite ACT: 25.

Student Life Upper grades have specified standards of dress, student council, honor system. Discipline rests primarily with faculty. Attendance at religious services is required.

Summer Programs Sports programs offered; session focuses on physical education; held on campus; accepts boys; not open to students from other schools. 28 students usually enrolled. 2006 schedule: June 1 to June 30. Application deadline: May.

Tuition and Aid Day student tuition: $5600. Guaranteed tuition plan. Tuition installment plan (The Tuition Plan, monthly payment plans, individually arranged payment plans). Need-based scholarship grants available. In 2005–06, 72% of upper-school students received aid. Total amount of financial aid awarded in 2005–06: $413,000.

Admissions Traditional secondary-level entrance grade is 9. For fall 2005, 672 students applied for upper-level admission, 672 were accepted, 672 enrolled. Deadline for receipt of application materials: none. Application fee required: $205.

Athletics Interscholastic: baseball (boys), basketball (b,g), cheering (g), cross-country running (b,g), dance team (g), football (b), golf (b,g), ice hockey (b), lacrosse (b,g), skiing (downhill) (b,g), snowboarding (b,g), soccer (b,g), softball (g), swimming and diving (b,g), tennis (b,g), track and field (b,g), volleyball (g), weight lifting (b,g), wrestling (b). 2 PE instructors, 34 coaches, 2 trainers.

Computers Computers are regularly used in art, English, foreign language, history, mathematics, science classes. Computer network features include campus e-mail, on-campus library services, CD-ROMs, Internet access.

Contact Kelly Cleary, Admissions. 208-375-6010 Ext. 13. Fax: 208-375-3626. E-mail: kcleary@bk.org. Web site: www.bk.org.

BISHOP KENNY HIGH SCHOOL

1055 Kingman Avenue
Jacksonville, Florida 32207
Head of School: Rev. Michael R. Houle

General Information Coeducational day college-preparatory school, affiliated with Roman Catholic Church. Grades 9–12. Founded: 1952. Setting: urban. 55-acre campus. Approved or accredited by Southern Association of Colleges and Schools and Florida Department of Education. Total enrollment: 1,440. Upper school average class size: 22. Upper school faculty-student ratio: 1:15.

Upper School Student Profile Grade 9: 395 students (194 boys, 201 girls); Grade 10: 338 students (155 boys, 183 girls); Grade 11: 342 students (159 boys, 183 girls); Grade 12: 365 students (172 boys, 193 girls). 82% of students are Roman Catholic.

Faculty School total: 94. In upper school: 35 men, 59 women.

Graduation Requirements 20th century physics, electives, English, foreign language, mathematics, performing arts, personal fitness, practical arts, religion (includes Bible studies and theology), science, social studies (includes history).

Special Academic Programs Advanced Placement exam preparation; honors section.

College Placement 356 students graduated in 2005.

Student Life Upper grades have uniform requirement, student council, honor system. Attendance at religious services is required.

Summer Programs Remediation, advancement, sports programs offered; session focuses on academics ; held on campus; accepts boys and girls; not open to students from other schools. 300 students usually enrolled. 2006 schedule: June to July. Application deadline: April.

Tuition and Aid Tuition installment plan (monthly payment plans, individually arranged payment plans). Tuition reduction for siblings, need-based loans available.

Admissions Traditional secondary-level entrance grade is 9. For fall 2005, 490 students applied for upper-level admission, 485 were accepted, 469 enrolled. Explore required. Deadline for receipt of application materials: none. Application fee required: $300. On-campus interview required.

Athletics Interscholastic: baseball (boys), basketball (b,g), cheering (g), cross-country running (b,g), diving (b,g), drill team (b,g), football (b), golf (b,g), soccer (b,g), softball (g), swimming and diving (b,g), tennis (b,g), track and field (b,g), volleyball (g), weight lifting (b,g), wrestling (b). 5 PE instructors, 5 coaches, 2 trainers.

Computers Computers are regularly used in accounting, computer applications, desktop publishing, journalism, keyboarding, library, newspaper, technology, word processing, yearbook classes. Computer resources include on-campus library services, CD-ROMs, Internet access, DVD.

Contact Mrs. Sheila W. Marovich, Director of Admissions. 904-398-7545. Fax: 904-398-5728. E-mail: development@bishopkenny.org. Web site: Bishopkenny.org.

BISHOP LUERS HIGH SCHOOL

333 East Paulding Road
Fort Wayne, Indiana 46816
Head of School: Mrs. Mary T. Keefer

General Information Coeducational day college-preparatory and religious studies school, affiliated with Roman Catholic Church. Grades 9–12. Founded: 1953. Setting: urban. 5-acre campus. 1 building on campus. Approved or accredited by North Central Association of Colleges and Schools and Indiana Department of Education. Total enrollment: 585. Upper school average class size: 20. Upper school faculty-student ratio: 1:18.

Upper School Student Profile Grade 9: 150 students (80 boys, 70 girls); Grade 10: 159 students (77 boys, 82 girls); Grade 11: 131 students (66 boys, 65 girls); Grade 12: 145 students (75 boys, 70 girls). 84% of students are Roman Catholic.

Faculty School total: 40. In upper school: 14 men, 26 women; 16 have advanced degrees.

Subjects Offered 3-dimensional art, accounting, algebra, Bible, biology, biology-AP, business, business law, calculus-AP, careers, chamber groups, chemistry, chemistry-AP, chorus, church history, computer applications, computer programming, concert band, creative writing, data analysis, discrete mathematics, drawing, economics, English, entrepreneurship, fine arts, French, geometry, government, health education, honors algebra, honors English, honors geometry, honors U.S. history, honors world history, keyboarding, Latin, music appreciation, music theory, painting, physical education, physics, physiology, pre-calculus, psychology, science project, sculpture, sociology, Spanish, speech communications, statistics and probability, strings, student government, student publications, study skills, theater arts, theater production, theology, trigonometry, U.S. history, world civilizations, world geography, world history.

Graduation Requirements Computers, English, mathematics, physical education (includes health), religion (includes Bible studies and theology), science, social studies (includes history).

Special Academic Programs Advanced Placement exam preparation in 4 subject areas; honors section; study at local college for college credit; academic accommodation for the gifted and the musically talented; remedial reading and/or remedial writing; remedial math.

College Placement 138 students graduated in 2005; 120 went to college, including Indiana University–Purdue University Fort Wayne. Other: 6 went to work, 3 entered military service. Mean SAT verbal: 543, mean SAT math: 520.

Student Life Upper grades have specified standards of dress, honor system. Discipline rests equally with students and faculty. Attendance at religious services is required.

Summer Programs Remediation, sports, art/fine arts programs offered; session focuses on camps and enrichment; held on campus; accepts boys and girls; open to students from other schools. 250 students usually enrolled. 2006 schedule: June 15 to August 10. Application deadline: May 30.

Tuition and Aid Day student tuition: $3525. Tuition installment plan (FACTS Tuition Payment Plan). Tuition reduction for siblings, merit scholarship grants, need-based scholarship grants, paying campus jobs available. In 2005–06, 73% of upper-school students received aid.

Admissions Traditional secondary-level entrance grade is 9. For fall 2005, 160 students applied for upper-level admission, 157 were accepted, 150 enrolled. Deadline for receipt of application materials: none. Application fee required: $120.

Athletics Interscholastic: baseball (boys), basketball (b,g), bowling (b,g), cheering (g), cross-country running (b,g), dance (g), dance team (g), diving (b,g), football (b), golf (b,g), lacrosse (b), riflery (b,g), running (b,g), soccer (b,g), softball (g), swimming and diving (b,g), tennis (b,g), track and field (b,g), volleyball (g), wrestling (g); intramural: lacrosse (b,g); coed intramural: lacrosse, riflery, weight training. 2 PE instructors, 25 coaches, 2 trainers.

Computers Computers are regularly used in all academic, business, yearbook classes. Computer network features include campus e-mail, on-campus library services, CD-ROMs, Internet access, office computer access, DVD.

Contact Mrs. Kathy Skelly, Director of Admissions and Public Relations. 260-456-1261 Ext. 3142. Fax: 260-456-1262. E-mail: kskelly@bishopluers.org. Web site: www.bishopluers.org/.

BISHOP LYNCH CATHOLIC HIGH SCHOOL

9750 Ferguson Road
Dallas, Texas 75228
Head of School: Edward E. Leyden

General Information Coeducational day college-preparatory, arts, religious studies, and technology school, affiliated with Roman Catholic Church. Grades 9–12. Founded: 1963. Setting: urban. 22-acre campus. 7 buildings on campus. Approved or accredited by Southern Association of Colleges and Schools, Texas Catholic Conference, and Texas Education Agency. Endowment: $1 million. Total enrollment: 1,044. Upper school average class size: 24. Upper school faculty-student ratio: 1:14.

Upper School Student Profile Grade 9: 264 students (113 boys, 151 girls); Grade 10: 234 students (97 boys, 137 girls); Grade 11: 275 students (111 boys, 164 girls); Grade 12: 271 students (111 boys, 160 girls). 79% of students are Roman Catholic.

Faculty School total: 87. In upper school: 36 men, 51 women; 49 have advanced degrees.

Subjects Offered 3-dimensional design, algebra, American government-AP, American history, American history-AP, American literature, art, Asian history, astronomy, band, Basic programming, biology, biology-AP, business, business law, calculus, calculus-AP, campus ministry, chemistry, chemistry-AP, choir, choreography, Christian and Hebrew scripture, Christian doctrine, Christian ethics, church history, community service, computer math, computer programming, computer science, concert band, creative writing, dance, debate, design, drama, drawing, driver education, economics, English, English literature, English-AP, environmental science, film, fine arts, French, geometry, German, government, government-AP, health, history, Holocaust studies, honors algebra, honors English, honors geometry, honors U.S. history, honors world history, jazz band, keyboarding, Latin, Latin-AP, leadership and service, marching band, mathematics, Mexican history, musical productions, orchestra, painting, peer counseling, personal finance, photography, physical education, physical science, physics, physics-AP, pre-calculus, probability, psychology, psychology-AP, publications, religion, SAT/ACT preparation, science, social studies, sociology, Spanish, speech, statistics, theater, theater arts, theater production, theology, world history, yearbook.

Graduation Requirements Arts and fine arts (art, music, dance, drama), computer science, English, foreign language, mathematics, physical education (includes health), religion (includes Bible studies and theology), science, social studies (includes history), speech, theology, U.S. government, U.S. history, world history. Community service is required.

Special Academic Programs Advanced Placement exam preparation in 13 subject areas; honors section; study at local college for college credit; academic accommodation for the gifted; remedial reading and/or remedial writing; remedial math; programs in English, mathematics for dyslexic students.

College Placement 263 students graduated in 2005; 262 went to college, including Austin College; Southern Methodist University; St. Edward's University; Stephen F. Austin State University; Texas A&M University; University of Oklahoma. Other: 1 entered military service.

Student Life Upper grades have uniform requirement, student council, honor system. Discipline rests primarily with faculty. Attendance at religious services is required.

Summer Programs Remediation, enrichment, art/fine arts, computer instruction programs offered; held on campus; accepts boys and girls; not open to students from other schools. 60 students usually enrolled. 2006 schedule: June 6 to July 8. Application deadline: none.

Tuition and Aid Day student tuition: $9300–$11,500. Tuition installment plan (guaranteed bank loan plan). Tuition reduction for siblings, merit scholarship grants, need-based scholarship grants, paying campus jobs available. In 2005–06, 33% of upper-school students received aid; total upper-school merit-scholarship money awarded: $60,500. Total amount of financial aid awarded in 2005–06: $190,700.

Admissions Traditional secondary-level entrance grade is 9. For fall 2005, 598 students applied for upper-level admission, 400 were accepted, 264 enrolled. ACT-Explore required. Deadline for receipt of application materials: none. Application fee required: $70. On-campus interview required.

Athletics Interscholastic: aquatics (boys, girls), baseball (b), basketball (b,g), cheering (g), cross-country running (b,g), dance team (g), drill team (g), football (b), golf (b,g), lacrosse (b,g), power lifting (b), soccer (b,g), softball (g), strength & conditioning (b,g), swimming and diving (b,g), track and field (b,g), volleyball (g), weight lifting (b), wrestling (b); coed interscholastic: combined training, dance, diving, ice hockey, tennis; coed intramural: bicycling, bowling, climbing, crew, paddle tennis, paint ball, rock climbing, sailing, skateboarding, table tennis. 2 PE instructors, 21 coaches, 2 trainers.

Computers Computers are regularly used in English, foreign language, mathematics, newspaper, publications, science, yearbook classes. Computer network features include campus e-mail, on-campus library services, CD-ROMs, Internet access.

Contact Ann Martin, Director of Admissions. 214-324-3607 Ext. 127. Fax: 214-324-3600. E-mail: ann.martin@bishoplynch.org. Web site: www.bishoplynch.org.

BISHOP MCDEVITT HIGH SCHOOL

125 Royal Avenue
Wyncote, Pennsylvania 19095
Head of School: Salvatore J. DiNenna, EdD

General Information Coeducational day college-preparatory, general academic, arts, business, vocational, religious studies, technology, and science, social studies, mathematics, world languages school, affiliated with Roman Catholic Church. Grades 9–12. Founded: 1958. Setting: suburban. Nearest major city is Philadelphia. 14-acre campus. 1 building on campus. Approved or accredited by Middle States Association of Colleges and Schools, National Catholic Education Association, The College Board, and Pennsylvania Department of Education. Endowment: $100,000. Total enrollment: 749. Upper school average class size: 29. Upper school faculty-student ratio: 1:20.

Upper School Student Profile Grade 9: 191 students (94 boys, 97 girls); Grade 10: 178 students (85 boys, 93 girls); Grade 11: 187 students (83 boys, 104 girls); Grade 12: 193 students (111 boys, 82 girls). 85% of students are Roman Catholic.

Faculty School total: 41. In upper school: 20 men, 21 women; 31 have advanced degrees.

Subjects Offered Accounting, advanced computer applications, advanced math, Advanced Placement courses, algebra, American government, American history, American history-AP, American literature, American literature-AP, analytic geometry, anatomy and physiology, ancient world history, applied arts, applied skills, band, biology, biology-AP, British literature, British literature (honors), business education, business law, business technology, calculus, calculus-AP, chemistry, choral music, Christian doctrine, Christian education, Christian ethics, Christian scripture, Christian studies, Christian testament, church history, competitive science projects, composition, computer keyboarding, computer science, criminal justice, driver education, English, English composition, English literature, English literature-AP, environmental science, European history, fine arts, foreign language, geometry, health, history of the Catholic Church, honors algebra, honors English, honors geometry, honors U.S. history, honors world history, Italian, keyboarding/computer, Latin, life science, physical education, physical science, physics, political economics, psychology, social sciences, Spanish, Spanish-AP, video film production.

Graduation Requirements Algebra, American government, American history, American literature, British literature, chemistry, composition, electives, English, English composition, English literature, environmental science, foreign language, geometry, lab science, physical education (includes health), physical science, religion (includes Bible studies and theology), social science, trigonometry, U.S. history, world history, world literature, service requirement all four years.

Special Academic Programs Advanced Placement exam preparation in 6 subject areas; honors section; study at local college for college credit; remedial reading and/or remedial writing; remedial math.

College Placement 181 students graduated in 2005; 174 went to college, including Drexel University; Gwynedd-Mercy College; La Salle University; Saint Joseph's University; Temple University; Villanova University. Other: 4 went to work, 2 entered military service, 1 had other specific plans. Mean SAT verbal: 547, mean SAT math: 518. 15% scored over 600 on SAT verbal, 15% scored over 600 on SAT math.

Student Life Upper grades have uniform requirement, student council. Discipline rests primarily with faculty. Attendance at religious services is required.

Summer Programs Remediation, enrichment, sports programs offered; session focuses on academic remediation, sport clinics; held on campus; accepts boys and

girls; open to students from other schools. 250 students usually enrolled. 2006 schedule: June 28 to August 1. Application deadline: May 31.

Tuition and Aid Day student tuition: $4140. Tuition installment plan (monthly payment plans, individually arranged payment plans, Archdiocesan Tuition Assistance). Tuition reduction for siblings, merit scholarship grants, need-based scholarship grants, SLM Financial loans available. In 2005–06, 25% of upper-school students received aid; total upper-school merit-scholarship money awarded: $75,000. Total amount of financial aid awarded in 2005–06: $100,000.

Admissions Traditional secondary-level entrance grade is 9. TerraNova required. Deadline for receipt of application materials: none. Application fee required: $170. On-campus interview required.

Athletics Interscholastic: baseball (boys, girls), basketball (b,g), cheering (g), cross-country running (b,g), dance squad (g), drill team (g), field hockey (g), football (b), ice hockey (b), indoor track (b,g), lacrosse (g), soccer (b,g), softball (g), track and field (b,g), volleyball (g), winter (indoor) track (b,g); intramural: flag football (g); coed interscholastic: golf, strength & conditioning, weight training. 1 PE instructor, 15 coaches, 3 trainers.

Computers Computers are regularly used in all academic classes. Computer network features include on-campus library services, CD-ROMs, Internet access, DVD.

Contact Mr. Harry R. Neenhold, Principal. 215-887-5575 Ext. 227. Fax: 215-887-1371. E-mail: hneenhold@mcdevitths.org. Web site: www.mcdevitths.org.

BISHOP MCGUINNESS CATHOLIC HIGH SCHOOL

801 Northwest 50th Street
Oklahoma City, Oklahoma 73118-6001
Head of School: Mr. David L. Morton

General Information Coeducational day college-preparatory, arts, business, religious studies, bilingual studies, and technology school, affiliated with Roman Catholic Church. Grades 9–12. Founded: 1950. Setting: urban. 20-acre campus. 4 buildings on campus. Approved or accredited by North Central Association of Colleges and Schools and Oklahoma Department of Education. Endowment: $1.9 million. Total enrollment: 632. Upper school average class size: 20. Upper school faculty-student ratio: 1:20.

Upper School Student Profile Grade 11: 149 students (93 boys, 56 girls); Grade 12: 150 students (72 boys, 78 girls). 76% of students are Roman Catholic.

Faculty School total: 49. In upper school: 10 men, 12 women; 11 have advanced degrees.

Subjects Offered Accounting, algebra, American literature, American literature-AP, analysis, anatomy and physiology, art, band, biology, biology-AP, business, business law, calculus-AP, Catholic belief and practice, ceramics, chemistry, chorus, church history, computer technologies, creative writing, culinary arts, current events, dance, debate, design, drama, drawing, economics, economics-AP, electives, English, English literature, English literature-AP, ethics, French, geometry, German, government, government-AP, health, history of the Catholic Church, HTML design, international studies, introduction to theater, Latin, leadership and service, newspaper, novels, orchestra, painting, personal finance, photography, physical education, physical science, physics, practical arts, prayer/spirituality, pre-calculus, psychology, scripture, sociology, Spanish, speech, stagecraft, study skills, theater, U.S. history, U.S. history-AP, weight training, world history, world history-AP, world religions, yearbook.

Graduation Requirements Arts and fine arts (art, music, dance, drama), electives, English, foreign language, mathematics, practical arts, science, social studies (includes history), theology, 90 hours of Christian service.

Special Academic Programs Advanced Placement exam preparation in 9 subject areas; honors section; academic accommodation for the gifted and the artistically talented; programs in English, mathematics for dyslexic students; special instructional classes for students with learning differences.

College Placement 171 students graduated in 2005; 163 went to college, including Loyola University New Orleans; Oklahoma City University; Oklahoma State University; Texas Christian University; University of Oklahoma. Other: 5 went to work, 1 entered military service, 2 had other specific plans. Mean SAT verbal: 583, mean SAT math: 564, mean composite ACT: 24. 65% scored over 600 on SAT verbal, 62% scored over 600 on SAT math.

Student Life Upper grades have uniform requirement, student council, honor system. Discipline rests primarily with faculty. Attendance at religious services is required.

Tuition and Aid Day student tuition: $6250. Tuition installment plan (FACTS Tuition Payment Plan). Need-based scholarship grants, paying campus jobs available. In 2005–06, 15% of upper-school students received aid. Total amount of financial aid awarded in 2005–06: $65,600.

Admissions Traditional secondary-level entrance grade is 11. For fall 2005, 8 students applied for upper-level admission, 8 were accepted, 8 enrolled. STS required. Deadline for receipt of application materials: May 31. Application fee required: $350. On-campus interview required.

Athletics Interscholastic: baseball (boys), basketball (b,g), bowling (b,g), cheering (g), cross-country running (b,g), dance team (b,g), football (b), golf (b,g), soccer (b,g), softball (g), swimming and diving (b,g), tennis (b,g), track and field (b,g), volleyball (g), weight training (b,g), winter (indoor) track (b,g), wrestling (b); coed interscholastic: bowling. 1 PE instructor.

Computers Computers are regularly used in all academic classes. Computer resources include campus e-mail, on-campus library services, CD-ROMs, online commercial services, Internet access, office computer access, DVD, wireless campus network, laptop classroom computers.

Contact Ms. Leslie Byers, 9th Grade Counselor/Director of Admissions. 405-842-6638 Ext. 225. Fax: 405-858-9550. E-mail: byersx225@mcguinness.k12.ok.us. Web site: www.bmchs.org.

BISHOP MCNAMARA HIGH SCHOOL

550 West Brookmont Boulevard
Kankakee, Illinois 60901
Head of School: James R. Laurenti

General Information Coeducational day college-preparatory and vocational school, affiliated with Roman Catholic Church. Grades 9–12. Founded: 1926. Setting: suburban. Nearest major city is Joliet. 18-acre campus. 2 buildings on campus. Approved or accredited by National Catholic Education Association and Illinois Department of Education. Endowment: $2.4 million. Total enrollment: 470. Upper school average class size: 21. Upper school faculty-student ratio: 1:21.

Upper School Student Profile Grade 9: 131 students (68 boys, 63 girls); Grade 10: 131 students (75 boys, 56 girls); Grade 11: 102 students (58 boys, 44 girls); Grade 12: 106 students (60 boys, 46 girls). 84% of students are Roman Catholic.

Faculty School total: 33. In upper school: 14 men, 19 women; 19 have advanced degrees.

Subjects Offered Accounting, algebra, American history, American history-AP, American literature, art, auto body, band, biology, business technology, calculus-AP, Catholic belief and practice, chemistry, chemistry-AP, computer technologies, computers, construction, design, drafting, English, English literature, English-AP, French, French-AP, geometry, health, honors geometry, metalworking, physical education, physical science, physics, physics-AP, physiology, pre-algebra, pre-calculus, psychology, psychology-AP, scripture, Spanish, Spanish-AP, studio art, trigonometry, welding, world geography, world history, world religions.

Graduation Requirements Art, electives, English, mathematics, modern languages, physical education (includes health), religion (includes Bible studies and theology), science, social studies (includes history), vocational arts.

Special Academic Programs Advanced Placement exam preparation in 8 subject areas; honors section; independent study; special instructional classes for students with Attention Deficit Disorder.

College Placement 96 students graduated in 2005; 85 went to college, including Eastern Illinois University; Illinois State University; Kankakee Community College; Northern Illinois University; Olivet Nazarene University; University of Illinois at Urbana–Champaign. Other: 6 went to work, 3 entered military service, 2 had other specific plans.

Student Life Upper grades have specified standards of dress, student council. Discipline rests primarily with faculty. Attendance at religious services is required.

Summer Programs Remediation, enrichment, sports programs offered; held on campus; accepts boys and girls; open to students from other schools. 100 students usually enrolled. 2006 schedule: June 10 to August 10. Application deadline: May 1.

Tuition and Aid Day student tuition: $4400. Tuition installment plan (FACTS Tuition Payment Plan). Tuition reduction for siblings, merit scholarship grants, need-based scholarship grants available. In 2005–06, 30% of upper-school students received aid; total upper-school merit-scholarship money awarded: $43,000. Total amount of financial aid awarded in 2005–06: $200,000.

Admissions Traditional secondary-level entrance grade is 9. For fall 2005, 153 students applied for upper-level admission, 146 were accepted, 131 enrolled. High School Placement Test or High School Placement Test (closed version) from Scholastic Testing Service required. Deadline for receipt of application materials: August 23. Application fee required: $30. Interview required.

Athletics Interscholastic: aerobics/dance (girls), baseball (b), basketball (b,g), cheering (g), cross-country running (b,g), dance (g), dance squad (g), dance team (g), flag football (b), football (b), golf (b), gymnastics (g), pom squad (g), soccer (b,g), softball (g), strength & conditioning (b,g), swimming and diving (b,g), tennis (b,g), track and field (b,g), volleyball (g), weight training (b,g), wrestling (b); intramural: basketball (b), bowling (b,g). 2 PE instructors, 7 coaches, 1 trainer.

Computers Computer network features include campus e-mail, on-campus library services, CD-ROMs, Internet access, DVD, wireless campus network.

Contact Jim R. Laurenti, Principal. 815-932-7413 Ext. 225. Fax: 815-932-0926. E-mail: jlaurenti@bishopmac.com. Web site: www.bishopmac.com.

BISHOP QUINN HIGH SCHOOL/ST. FRANCIS MIDDLE SCHOOL

21893 Old 44 Drive
Palo Cedro, California 96073
Head of School: Mr. Karl J. Hanf

General Information Coeducational day college-preparatory and religious studies school, affiliated with Roman Catholic Church. Grades 7–12. Founded: 1994. Setting: small town. Nearest major city is Redding. 40-acre campus. 5 buildings on campus.

Approved or accredited by National Catholic Education Association, Western Association of Schools and Colleges, Western Catholic Education Association, and California Department of Education. Total enrollment: 213. Upper school average class size: 20.

Upper School Student Profile Grade 9: 35 students (18 boys, 17 girls); Grade 10: 22 students (9 boys, 13 girls); Grade 11: 52 students (24 boys, 28 girls); Grade 12: 49 students (27 boys, 22 girls). 60% of students are Roman Catholic.

Faculty School total: 16. In upper school: 6 men, 10 women; 3 have advanced degrees.

Subjects Offered Advanced Placement courses, athletics, band, baseball, cheerleading, choir, choral music, chorus, Christian and Hebrew scripture, Christian doctrine, Christian education, Christian ethics, Christian scripture, Christian studies, Christian testament, Christianity, church history, college admission preparation, college awareness, college counseling, college placement, college planning, community service, comparative religion, computer education, computers, concert band, debate, drama, drama performance, ethics and responsibility, foreign language, French, honors English, physics-AP, portfolio writing, prayer/spirituality, pre-algebra, pre-calculus, reading/study skills, religious education, religious studies, SAT preparation, senior project, social justice, softball, Spanish, Spanish-AP, sports, sports conditioning, statistics, student government, student publications, swimming, theater, theology, trigonometry, U.S. history, U.S. history-AP, vocal music, Web authoring, Web site design, weight fitness, weight training, world religions, yearbook.

Graduation Requirements Senior orals.

Special Academic Programs Advanced Placement exam preparation; honors section; independent study.

College Placement 32 students graduated in 2005; 29 went to college. Other: 2 went to work, 1 entered military service.

Student Life Upper grades have specified standards of dress, student council, honor system. Discipline rests primarily with faculty. Attendance at religious services is required.

Summer Programs Enrichment, sports programs offered; session focuses on enrichment and sports; held on campus; accepts boys and girls; open to students from other schools. 50 students usually enrolled. 2006 schedule: June 12 to July 31. Application deadline: June 9.

Tuition and Aid Day student tuition: $5700. Guaranteed tuition plan. Tuition installment plan (FACTS Tuition Payment Plan). Need-based scholarship grants available. In 2005–06, 60% of upper-school students received aid. Total amount of financial aid awarded in 2005–06: $232,000.

Admissions Traditional secondary-level entrance grade is 9. For fall 2005, 156 students applied for upper-level admission, 156 were accepted, 156 enrolled. Catholic High School Entrance Examination and placement test required. Deadline for receipt of application materials: none. Application fee required: $175. On-campus interview required.

Athletics Interscholastic: baseball (boys), cheering (g), football (b), softball (g), volleyball (g), wrestling (b); coed interscholastic: basketball, bicycling, bowling, cross-country running, fitness, Frisbee, golf, ropes courses, running, skiing (downhill), snowboarding, soccer, strength & conditioning, swimming and diving, tennis, track and field, weight training, winter soccer. 1 PE instructor, 6 coaches.

Computers Computers are regularly used in science, Web site design, yearbook classes. Computer network features include campus e-mail, Internet access, office computer access.

Contact Paula Foster, Administrative Assistant. 530-547-2900. Fax: 530-547-5349. E-mail: pfoster@stfrancis-bquinn.org. Web site: stfrancis-bquinn.org.

BISHOP'S COLLEGE SCHOOL

80 Moulton Hill Road
Lennoxville, Quebec J1M 1Z8, Canada
Head of School: Mr. Lewis Evans

General Information Coeducational boarding and day college-preparatory, arts, and bilingual studies school, affiliated with Church of England (Anglican), United Church of Canada. Grades 7–12. Founded: 1836. Setting: rural. Nearest major city is Montreal, Canada. Students are housed in single-sex dormitories. 350-acre campus. 30 buildings on campus. Approved or accredited by Canadian Association of Independent Schools, Canadian Educational Standards Institute, Quebec Association of Independent Schools, The Association of Boarding Schools, and Quebec Department of Education. Affiliate member of National Association of Independent Schools. Languages of instruction: English and French. Endowment: CAN$9 million. Total enrollment: 257. Upper school average class size: 12. Upper school faculty-student ratio: 1:8.

Upper School Student Profile Grade 10: 59 students (25 boys, 34 girls); Grade 11: 63 students (42 boys, 21 girls); Grade 12: 38 students (23 boys, 15 girls). 73% of students are boarding students. 27% are province residents. 16 provinces are represented in upper school student body. 38% are international students. International students from Bahamas, Bermuda, Germany, Japan, Mexico, and Republic of Korea; 20 other countries represented in student body. 10% of students are members of Church of England (Anglican), United Church of Canada.

Faculty School total: 37. In upper school: 21 men, 16 women; 10 have advanced degrees; 28 reside on campus.

Subjects Offered Algebra, art, biology, calculus, chemistry, computer science, creative writing, drama, ecology, economics, English, environmental science, ESL,

ethics, European history, finite math, French, French as a second language, geography, geometry, history, mathematics, music, philosophy, physical education, physical science, physics, political science, religion, science, sociology, Spanish, study skills, technology, theater, trigonometry, world history.

Special Academic Programs Advanced Placement exam preparation in 13 subject areas; term-away projects; domestic exchange program (with The Athenian School); study abroad; academic accommodation for the gifted, the musically talented, and the artistically talented; remedial math; ESL (40 students enrolled).

College Placement 42 students graduated in 2005; all went to college, including Harvard University; Queen's University at Kingston; The University of Western Ontario; University of Ottawa; University of Toronto; University of Waterloo.

Student Life Upper grades have uniform requirement, student council, honor system. Discipline rests equally with students and faculty. Attendance at religious services is required.

Summer Programs Remediation, enrichment, advancement, ESL, sports, art/fine arts, rigorous outdoor training, computer instruction programs offered; session focuses on English or French as a Second Language; held on campus; accepts boys and girls; open to students from other schools. 150 students usually enrolled. 2006 schedule: July 2 to July 29. Application deadline: none.

Tuition and Aid Tuition installment plan (monthly payment plans, individually arranged payment plans, single payment plan). Tuition reduction for siblings, bursaries, merit scholarship grants, need-based scholarship grants, need-based loans available. In 2005–06, 30% of upper-school students received aid; total upper-school merit-scholarship money awarded: CAN$320,000. Total amount of financial aid awarded in 2005–06: CAN$320,000.

Admissions For fall 2005, 140 students applied for upper-level admission, 100 were accepted, 92 enrolled. Placement test, SLEP or TOEFL required. Deadline for receipt of application materials: none. Application fee required: CAN$100. Interview required.

Athletics Interscholastic: baseball (boys), football (b,g), gymnastics (g), hockey (b), ice hockey (b), softball (g); coed interscholastic: alpine skiing, basketball, bicycling, climbing, cross-country running, equestrian sports, golf, horseback riding, independent competitive sports, nordic skiing, outdoor adventure, skiing (cross-country), skiing (downhill), soccer, swimming and diving, track and field; coed intramural: aerobics, alpine skiing, back packing, badminton, basketball, climbing, Cosom hockey, curling, figure skating, fitness, fitness walking, floor hockey, hiking/ backpacking, hockey, horseback riding, ice hockey, ice skating, indoor hockey, jogging, mountain biking, outdoor education, physical fitness, rock climbing, snowshoeing, squash, strength & conditioning, yoga. 2 PE instructors, 15 coaches, 1 trainer.

Computers Computers are regularly used in English, French as a second language, mathematics, science classes. Computer network features include campus e-mail, on-campus library services, CD-ROMs, Internet access, office computer access, DVD, schoolwide Tablet PC initiative (included in tuition), fiber optic network.

Contact Valerie Scullion, Associate Director of Admissions. 819-566-0227 Ext. 214. Fax: 819-566-8123. E-mail: vscullion@bishopscollegeschool.com. Web site: www. bishopscollegeschool.com.

See full description on page 678.

THE BISHOP STRACHAN SCHOOL

298 Lonsdale Road
Toronto, Ontario M4V 1X2, Canada
Head of School: Mrs. Kim Gordon

General Information Girls' boarding and day college-preparatory, arts, business, religious studies, and technology school, affiliated with Anglican Church of Canada. Boarding grades 7–12, day grades PK–12. Founded: 1867. Setting: urban. Students are housed in single-sex dormitories. 7-acre campus. 1 building on campus. Approved or accredited by Canadian Association of Independent Schools, Canadian Educational Standards Institute, The Association of Boarding Schools, and Ontario Department of Education. Affiliate member of National Association of Independent Schools; member of Secondary School Admission Test Board. Language of instruction: English. Endowment: CAN$11 million. Total enrollment: 893. Upper school average class size: 18. Upper school faculty-student ratio: 1:10.

Upper School Student Profile Grade 7: 92 students (92 girls); Grade 8: 89 students (89 girls); Grade 9: 100 students (100 girls); Grade 10: 128 students (128 girls); Grade 11: 129 students (129 girls); Grade 12: 107 students (107 girls). 16% of students are boarding students. 30% are province residents. 6 provinces are represented in upper school student body. 70% are international students. International students from Antigua and Barbuda, Bahamas, China, Jamaica, Republic of Korea, and United States; 10 other countries represented in student body. 30% of students are members of Anglican Church of Canada.

Faculty School total: 104. In upper school: 7 men, 67 women; 33 have advanced degrees; 5 reside on campus.

Subjects Offered Accounting, algebra, American history, American history-AP, aquatics, art, art history, biology, biology-AP, business, business skills, calculus, calculus-AP, Canadian geography, Canadian history, career and personal planning, career education, chemistry, chemistry-AP, computer programming, computer science, creative writing, drama, earth science, ecology, economics, economics-AP,

The Bishop Strachan School

English, English literature, English literature-AP, English-AP, environmental science, ESL, ethics, European history, expository writing, fine arts, French, geography, geometry, government/civics, graphic arts, health, history, Italian, Latin, Mandarin, mathematics, music, philosophy, physical education, physics, religion, science, social science, social studies, Spanish, theater, trigonometry, U.S. government-AP, world history.

Graduation Requirements Arts, Canadian geography, Canadian history, career education, civics, English, French, mathematics, physical education (includes health), science, 40 hours of community service.

Special Academic Programs Advanced Placement exam preparation in 16 subject areas; honors section; accelerated programs; independent study; term-away projects; study abroad; ESL (8 students enrolled).

College Placement 108 students graduated in 2005; all went to college, including Dalhousie University; McGill University; Queen's University at Kingston; The University of Western Ontario; University of Toronto; University of Waterloo. Mean SAT verbal: 609, mean SAT math: 592.

Student Life Upper grades have uniform requirement, student council, honor system. Discipline rests primarily with faculty. Attendance at religious services is required.

Summer Programs Enrichment, advancement, ESL, art/fine arts, rigorous outdoor training, computer instruction programs offered; session focuses on academics and arts; held both on and off campus; held at Bangalore, India and Algonquin Park; accepts boys and girls; open to students from other schools. 200 students usually enrolled. 2006 schedule: July 4 to July 28. Application deadline: June 15.

Tuition and Aid Day student tuition: CAN$18,900; 7-day tuition and room/board: CAN$38,360. Tuition installment plan (monthly payment plans, 2-installment plan). Bursaries, merit scholarship grants available. In 2005–06, 5% of upper-school students received aid; total upper-school merit-scholarship money awarded: CAN$94,250. Total amount of financial aid awarded in 2005–06: CAN$500,000.

Admissions Traditional secondary-level entrance grade is 7. For fall 2005, 320 students applied for upper-level admission, 159 were accepted, 115 enrolled. SSAT or TOEFL required. Deadline for receipt of application materials: none. Application fee required: CAN$150. Interview required.

Athletics Interscholastic: aerobics (girls), alpine skiing (g), aquatics (g), artistic gym (g), badminton (g), basketball (g), cross-country running (g), curling (g), field hockey (g), golf (g), gymnastics (g), ice hockey (g), nordic skiing (g), rhythmic gymnastics (g), skiing (cross-country) (g), skiing (downhill) (g), soccer (g), softball (g), swimming and diving (g), tennis (g), track and field (g), volleyball (g); intramural: aerobics/dance (g), archery (g), canoeing/kayaking (g), climbing (g), cooperative games (g), crew (g), dance (g), fencing (g), fitness (g), hiking/backpacking (g), kayaking (g), life saving (g), outdoor adventure (g), outdoor education (g), outdoor recreation (g), physical training (g), rappelling (g), rock climbing (g), ropes courses (g), rowing (g), running (g), synchronized swimming (g), wall climbing (g), weight training (g), wilderness survival (g), yoga (g). 11 PE instructors.

Computers Computers are regularly used in art, business studies, career education, career exploration, economics, English, foreign language, geography, history, mathematics, music, science classes. Computer network features include campus e-mail, on-campus library services, CD-ROMs, Internet access, laptop program (grades 9-12).

Contact Ms. Ann Halupka, Admissions Assistant. 416-483-4325 Ext. 1220. Fax: 416-481-5632. E-mail: admissions@bss.on.ca. Web site: www.bss.on.ca.

See full description on page 680.

BISHOP VEROT HIGH SCHOOL

5598 Sunrise Drive
Fort Myers, Florida 33919-1799
Head of School: Fr. J. Christian Beretta, OSFS

General Information Coeducational day college-preparatory, arts, religious studies, technology, Honors, and Advanced Placement school, affiliated with Roman Catholic Church. Grades 9–12. Founded: 1962. Setting: suburban. Nearest major city is Miami. 20-acre campus. 8 buildings on campus. Approved or accredited by Southern Association of Colleges and Schools and Florida Department of Education. Endowment: $500,000. Total enrollment: 729. Upper school average class size: 25. Upper school faculty-student ratio: 1:17.

Upper School Student Profile Grade 9: 191 students (94 boys, 97 girls); Grade 10: 202 students (107 boys, 95 girls); Grade 11: 154 students (72 boys, 82 girls); Grade 12: 182 students (99 boys, 83 girls). 73% of students are Roman Catholic.

Faculty School total: 48. In upper school: 19 men, 29 women; 18 have advanced degrees.

Subjects Offered Acting, Advanced Placement courses, algebra, American government, American government-AP, American history, American history-AP, American literature, American sign language, art, athletic training, band, Bible studies, biology, biology-AP, British literature, British literature (honors), broadcast journalism, business, calculus-AP, ceramics, chemistry, chemistry-AP, choir, church history, computer studies, creative writing, drafting, drama, drawing, driver education, economics, electives, English, English literature and composition-AP, English literature-AP, environmental science, European history-AP, fine arts, foreign language, French, geometry, government, government-AP, health education, history, history of the Catholic Church, history-AP, honors algebra, honors English, honors geometry, honors U.S. history, honors world history, industrial arts, integrated

mathematics, journalism, law studies, marine biology, mathematics, newspaper, painting, personal fitness, photography, physical education, physics, physics-AP, pottery, practical arts, pre-algebra, pre-calculus, probability and statistics, SAT preparation, Spanish, Spanish language-AP, speech, studio art, television, theater, U.S. history, U.S. history-AP, Web site design, weightlifting, world history, world history-AP, writing, yearbook.

Graduation Requirements Algebra, American government, arts and fine arts (art, music, dance, drama), biology, British literature, chemistry, economics, electives, English, English composition, foreign language, geometry, government, health education, mathematics, moral theology, personal fitness, physics, practical arts, psychology, religion (includes Bible studies and theology), science, sociology, U.S. history, world history, world literature.

Special Academic Programs Advanced Placement exam preparation in 9 subject areas; honors section; study at local college for college credit; remedial math; special instructional classes for deaf students.

College Placement 186 students graduated in 2005; 184 went to college, including Florida Gulf Coast University; Florida State University; University of Central Florida; University of Florida; University of Miami; University of Notre Dame. Other: 2 entered military service. Mean SAT verbal: 539, mean SAT math: 531, mean composite ACT: 23.

Student Life Upper grades have specified standards of dress, student council, honor system. Discipline rests primarily with faculty. Attendance at religious services is required.

Summer Programs Enrichment, sports, rigorous outdoor training programs offered; session focuses on elective credit, enrichment; held on campus; accepts boys and girls; not open to students from other schools. 100 students usually enrolled.

Tuition and Aid Day student tuition: $7500. Tuition installment plan (FACTS Tuition Payment Plan, monthly payment plans, individually arranged payment plans, quarterly payment plan). Merit scholarship grants, need-based scholarship grants, tuition reduction for contributing Catholic families available. In 2005–06, 22% of upper-school students received aid; total upper-school merit-scholarship money awarded: $12,500. Total amount of financial aid awarded in 2005–06: $300,000.

Admissions Traditional secondary-level entrance grade is 9. High School Placement Test required. Deadline for receipt of application materials: none. Application fee required: $35.

Athletics Interscholastic: baseball (boys), basketball (b,g), cheering (g), cross-country running (b,g), diving (b,g), football (b), golf (b,g), soccer (b,g), softball (g), swimming and diving (b,g), tennis (b,g), track and field (b,g), volleyball (g), weight lifting (b,g); intramural: weight training (b,g); coed interscholastic: strength & conditioning. 2 PE instructors, 20 coaches, 2 trainers.

Computers Computers are regularly used in career exploration, college planning, drafting, information technology, library, media production, newspaper, photography, publications, SAT preparation, technology, vocational-technical courses, Web site design, yearbook classes. Computer network features include campus e-mail, on-campus library services, CD-ROMs, Internet access, office computer access.

Contact Mrs. Audrey Natarajan, Guidance Assistant. 239-274-6735. Fax: 239-274-6795. E-mail: audrey.natarajan@bvhs.org. Web site: www.bvhs.org.

BISHOP WALSH MIDDLE HIGH SCHOOL

700 Bishop Walsh Road
Cumberland, Maryland 21502
Head of School: Sr. Phyllis McNally, SSND

General Information Coeducational day college-preparatory school, affiliated with Roman Catholic Church. Grades PK–12. Founded: 1966. Setting: small town. 10-acre campus. 1 building on campus. Approved or accredited by Maryland Department of Education. Total enrollment: 595. Upper school average class size: 20. Upper school faculty-student ratio: 1:15.

Upper School Student Profile Grade 9: 46 students (13 boys, 33 girls); Grade 10: 58 students (28 boys, 30 girls); Grade 11: 47 students (25 boys, 22 girls); Grade 12: 47 students (25 boys, 22 girls). 70% of students are Roman Catholic.

Faculty School total: 45. In upper school: 8 men, 12 women; 15 have advanced degrees.

College Placement 54 students graduated in 2005; 52 went to college, including Frostburg State University. Other: 1 went to work, 1 entered military service.

Student Life Upper grades have uniform requirement, student council. Discipline rests primarily with faculty. Attendance at religious services is required.

Tuition and Aid Day student tuition: $4700. Tuition installment plan (FACTS Tuition Payment Plan, monthly payment plans). Need-based scholarship grants available. In 2005–06, 50% of upper-school students received aid. Total amount of financial aid awarded in 2005–06: $30,000.

Admissions Traditional secondary-level entrance grade is 9. Deadline for receipt of application materials: August 31. Application fee required: $30. Interview required.

Athletics Interscholastic: baseball (boys), basketball (b,g), bowling (b,g), cheering (g), football (b), golf (b), soccer (b,g), softball (g), volleyball (g). 1 PE instructor, 8 coaches, 1 trainer.

Computers Computers are regularly used in all classes. Computer network features include Internet access.

Contact Mr. Samuel Torres, Assistant Principal. 301-724-5360 Ext. 104. Fax: 301-722-0555. E-mail: storres@bishopwalsh.org. Web site: bishopwalsh.org.

BISMARK ST. MARY'S CENTRAL

1025 North Second Street
Bismark, North Dakota 58501
Head of School: Mr. John Jankowski

General Information Coeducational day college-preparatory, arts, business, vocational, religious studies, bilingual studies, and technology school, affiliated with Roman Catholic Church. Grades 9–12. Founded: 1908. Setting: suburban. Nearest major city is Bismarck. 4-acre campus. 1 building on campus. Approved or accredited by North Central Association of Colleges and Schools and North Dakota Department of Education. Endowment: $2 million. Total enrollment: 365. Upper school average class size: 22. Upper school faculty-student ratio: 1:17.

Upper School Student Profile 89% of students are Roman Catholic.

Faculty School total: 35. In upper school: 17 men, 18 women; 8 have advanced degrees.

Subjects Offered Accounting, algebra, American history, anatomy, art, auto mechanics, band, biology, business law, business skills, calculus, chorus, computer science, consumer education, current events, desktop publishing, drama, driver education, economics, electronics, English, fashion, fine arts, geography, geometry, government/civics, health, horticulture, industrial arts, international foods, jazz, mathematics, music, music theory, orchestra, physical education, physical science, physics, physiology, pre-calculus, religion, science, social science, social studies, sociology, Spanish, speech, sports nutrition, theater, video film production, weight training, word processing, world history.

Graduation Requirements Arts and fine arts (art, music, dance, drama), business skills (includes word processing), computer science, English, foreign language, mathematics, physical education (includes health), religion (includes Bible studies and theology), science, social science, social studies (includes history). Community service is required.

Special Academic Programs Advanced Placement exam preparation; honors section; independent study; study at local college for college credit; remedial reading and/or remedial writing; remedial math; programs in English, mathematics, general development for dyslexic students.

College Placement 114 students graduated in 2005; 91 went to college, including Bismarck State College; North Dakota State University; Saint John's University; University of Mary; University of Minnesota, Twin Cities Campus; University of North Dakota. Other: 2 entered military service. Median SAT verbal: 530, median SAT math: 550, median composite ACT: 23. 2% scored over 600 on SAT verbal, 3% scored over 600 on SAT math, 49% scored over 26 on composite ACT.

Student Life Upper grades have specified standards of dress, student council, honor system. Discipline rests equally with students and faculty. Attendance at religious services is required.

Summer Programs Enrichment programs offered; session focuses on physical education; held on campus; accepts boys and girls; open to students from other schools.

Tuition and Aid Day student tuition: $2730. Tuition installment plan (SMART Tuition Payment Plan, monthly payment plans, individually arranged payment plans). Merit scholarship grants, need-based scholarship grants, paying campus jobs available. Total upper-school merit-scholarship money awarded for 2005–06: $15,000. Total amount of financial aid awarded in 2005–06: $50,000.

Admissions Traditional secondary-level entrance grade is 9. Deadline for receipt of application materials: none. Application fee required: $25. On-campus interview required.

Athletics Interscholastic: baseball (boys), basketball (b,g), cross-country running (b,g), dance (g), dance squad (g), dance team (g), danceline (g), diving (b,g), football (b), golf (b,g), gymnastics (g), hockey (b,g), ice hockey (b,g), soccer (b,g), swimming and diving (b,g), tennis (b,g), track and field (b,g), volleyball (g), wrestling (b). 2 PE instructors, 1 trainer.

Computers Computers are regularly used in English, foreign language, mathematics, music, science classes. Computer network features include campus e-mail, on-campus library services, CD-ROMs, online commercial services, Internet access, DVD.

Contact Thomas Eberle, Principal. 701-223-4113. Fax: 701-223-8629. Web site: www.smchs.org.

BLACK FOREST ACADEMY

Hammersteiner Strasse 50
Postfach 1109
Kandern 79396, Germany
Head of School: Mr. Mark Wiebe

General Information Coeducational boarding and day college-preparatory, general academic, arts, and religious studies school, affiliated with Christian faith. Boarding grades 7–12, day grades 1–12. Founded: 1956. Setting: small town. Nearest major city is Basel. Students are housed in single-sex dormitories. 2-acre campus. 2 buildings on campus. Approved or accredited by Association of Christian Schools International, European Council of International Schools, and Middle States Association of Colleges and Schools. Language of instruction: English. Total enrollment: 361. Upper school average class size: 20. Upper school faculty-student ratio: 1:8.

Upper School Student Profile Grade 9: 40 students (19 boys, 21 girls); Grade 10: 53 students (29 boys, 24 girls); Grade 11: 75 students (36 boys, 39 girls); Grade 12: 74 students (33 boys, 41 girls). 60% of students are boarding students. 76% are international students. International students from France, Russian Federation, Spain, Switzerland, Turkey, and Uzbekistan; 45 other countries represented in student body. 93% of students are Christian faith.

Faculty School total: 62. In upper school: 21 men, 21 women; 33 have advanced degrees.

Subjects Offered Advanced math, Advanced Placement courses, algebra, American history, art, band, Bible, biology, calculus, calculus-AP, Canadian history, chemistry, chemistry-AP, choir, Christian education, church history, community service, computer keyboarding, computer programming, computer science, drama, English, English literature, English-AP, environmental science, ESL, European history, European history-AP, fine arts, French, French-AP, general math, geography, geometry, German, German-AP, graphic arts, graphic design, health, home economics, industrial technology, journalism, mathematics, music, music appreciation, music theory, physical education, physics, science, social studies, Spanish, statistics, trigonometry, world history.

Graduation Requirements Algebra, American history, arts and fine arts (art, music, dance, drama), Bible, biology, chemistry, computer applications, English, foreign language, physical education (includes health), trigonometry, 30 hours of community service per year.

Special Academic Programs Advanced Placement exam preparation in 10 subject areas; honors section; remedial math; programs in English, mathematics, general development for dyslexic students; special instructional classes for students with learning disabilities; ESL (15 students enrolled).

College Placement 74 students graduated in 2005; 65 went to college, including Bethel College; Grove City College; John Brown University; Seattle Pacific University; Trinity Western University. Other: 2 went to work, 4 entered military service, 3 had other specific plans. Mean SAT verbal: 590, mean SAT math: 570. 47% scored over 600 on SAT verbal, 58% scored over 600 on SAT math, 27% scored over 26 on composite ACT.

Student Life Upper grades have specified standards of dress, student council, honor system. Discipline rests primarily with faculty. Attendance at religious services is required.

Tuition and Aid Day student tuition: €1610–€11,030; 7-day tuition and room/board: €5290–€12,590. Tuition installment plan (monthly payment plans, individually arranged payment plans, quarterly payment plan). Tuition reduction for siblings available.

Admissions Traditional secondary-level entrance grade is 10. Any standardized test or math and English placement tests required. Deadline for receipt of application materials: none. Application fee required: €100. Interview recommended.

Athletics Interscholastic: basketball (boys, girls); skateboarding (b), soccer (b,g), track and field (b,g), volleyball (b,g); intramural: basketball (b,g), cross-country running (b,g), soccer (b,g), volleyball (b,g), weight lifting (b,g); coed interscholastic: aerobics/dance, archery, badminton, baseball, cross-country running, fitness, flag football, floor hockey, Frisbee, gymnastics, ice skating, indoor soccer, jogging, jump rope, outdoor education, physical fitness, roller blading, skiing (downhill), snowboarding, wall climbing, weight lifting. 3 PE instructors, 1 coach.

Computers Computers are regularly used in Bible studies, career exploration, data processing, graphic arts, journalism, media production, music, yearbook classes. Computer network features include campus e-mail, on-campus library services, CD-ROMs, Internet access, DVD, wireless campus network, off-campus e-mail.

Contact Mrs. Judy Thompson, Executive Secretary. 49-7626-91610. Fax: 49-7626-8821. E-mail: jthompson@bfacademy.com. Web site: www.bfacademy.com.

BLAIR ACADEMY

2 Park Street
Blairstown, New Jersey 07825
Head of School: T. Chandler Hardwick III

General Information Coeducational boarding and day college-preparatory and arts school, affiliated with Presbyterian Church. Boarding grades 9–PG, day grades 9–12. Founded: 1848. Setting: rural. Nearest major city is New York, NY. Students are housed in single-sex dormitories. 315-acre campus. 42 buildings on campus. Approved or accredited by Middle States Association of Colleges and Schools, New Jersey Association of Independent Schools, The Association of Boarding Schools, and New Jersey Department of Education. Member of National Association of Independent Schools and Secondary School Admission Test Board. Endowment: $50 million. Total enrollment: 434. Upper school average class size: 12. Upper school faculty-student ratio: 1:7.

Upper School Student Profile Grade 9: 83 students (54 boys, 29 girls); Grade 10: 96 students (52 boys, 44 girls); Grade 11: 128 students (70 boys, 58 girls); Grade 12: 129 students (74 boys, 55 girls); Postgraduate: 14 students (11 boys, 3 girls). 76% of students are boarding students. 55% are state residents. 28 states are represented in upper school student body. 9% are international students. International students from Bermuda, Germany, Hong Kong, Republic of Korea, Taiwan, and United Kingdom; 8 other countries represented in student body.

Faculty School total: 70. In upper school: 45 men, 25 women; 41 have advanced degrees; 60 reside on campus.

Subjects Offered African history, algebra, American history, American literature, anatomy, architecture, art, art history, Asian studies, astronomy, aviation, biology, calculus, ceramics, chemistry, Chinese, Chinese history, computer programming, computer science, creative writing, dance, drafting, drama, drawing, driver education, economics, English, English literature, environmental science, ethics, European history, expository writing, fine arts, French, geometry, government/civics, health, history, Japanese history, jewelry making, Latin, mathematics, mechanical drawing, music, navigation, painting, philosophy, photography, physical education, physics, physiology, pre-calculus, psychology, religion, Russian studies, science, social studies, Spanish, theater, theology, world history, world literature, writing.

Graduation Requirements Arts and fine arts (art, music, dance, drama), English, foreign language, mathematics, physical education (includes health), religion (includes Bible studies and theology), science, social studies (includes history).

Special Academic Programs Advanced Placement exam preparation in 17 subject areas; honors section; independent study; study abroad.

College Placement 130 students graduated in 2005; all went to college, including Columbia College; Cornell University; Dickinson College; Duke University; The George Washington University; University of Pennsylvania. Mean SAT verbal: 610, mean SAT math: 620.

Student Life Upper grades have specified standards of dress, student council, honor system. Discipline rests equally with students and faculty. Attendance at religious services is required.

Tuition and Aid Day student tuition: $26,000; 7-day tuition and room/board: $35,000. Tuition installment plan (Key Tuition Payment Plan, monthly payment plans). Need-based scholarship grants, need-based loans available. In 2005–06, 35% of upper-school students received aid. Total amount of financial aid awarded in 2005–06: $2,264,000.

Admissions Traditional secondary-level entrance grade is 9. For fall 2005, 495 students applied for upper-level admission, 269 were accepted, 149 enrolled. SSAT or TOEFL required. Deadline for receipt of application materials: February 1. Application fee required: $50. On-campus interview required.

Athletics Interscholastic: alpine skiing (boys, girls), baseball (b), basketball (b,g), crew (b,g), cross-country running (b,g), field hockey (g), football (b), golf (b,g), lacrosse (b,g), rowing (b,g), skiing (downhill) (b,g), soccer (b,g), softball (g), squash (b,g), swimming and diving (b,g), tennis (b,g), track and field (b,g), wrestling (b); intramural: crew (b,g), rowing (b,g); coed interscholastic: ice hockey; coed intramural: aerobics, alpine skiing, basketball, dance, equestrian sports, fitness, golf, horseback riding, kayaking, modern dance, outdoor skills, rock climbing, skiing (downhill), soccer, squash, swimming and diving, tennis, weight lifting. 2 trainers.

Computers Computers are regularly used in English, graphic design, history, information technology, mathematics, media production, science, video film production classes. Computer network features include campus e-mail, on-campus library services, CD-ROMs, online commercial services, Internet access, file transfer, DVD.

Contact Barbara Haase, Dean of Admissions. 800-462-5247. Fax: 908-362-7975. E-mail: admissions@blair.edu. Web site: www.blair.edu.

ANNOUNCEMENT FROM THE SCHOOL In its 158th year, Blair offers a strong college-preparatory program with an average class size of 12 and an excellent college placement record. Traditional sports, plus golf, skiing, squash, ice hockey, and crew are offered. Access to the Internet is available from every dorm room. The Academy is located in the foothills of the Pocono Mountains, with easy access to New York City and Philadelphia. Blair's recent capital campaign provided funding for several major improvements to the physical plant, including an arts center, technology center, a new library, a new girls' dormitory, and renovations to existing dorms.

See full description on page 682.

THE BLAKE SCHOOL

110 Blake Road South
Hopkins, Minnesota 55343
Head of School: John C. Gulla

General Information Coeducational day college-preparatory school. Grades PK–12. Founded: 1900. Setting: urban. Nearest major city is Minneapolis. 60-acre campus. 1 building on campus. Approved or accredited by Independent Schools Association of the Central States. Member of National Association of Independent Schools. Endowment: $44 million. Total enrollment: 1,357. Upper school average class size: 15. Upper school faculty-student ratio: 1:9.

Upper School Student Profile Grade 9: 131 students (59 boys, 72 girls); Grade 10: 129 students (61 boys, 68 girls); Grade 11: 131 students (62 boys, 69 girls); Grade 12: 126 students (59 boys, 67 girls).

Faculty School total: 172. In upper school: 37 men, 24 women; 44 have advanced degrees.

Subjects Offered Advanced chemistry, African-American literature, algebra, American history, American literature, art, Asian studies, astronomy, band, biology, biology-AP, calculus, calculus-AP, ceramics, chemistry, chemistry-AP, choir, chorus, communication arts, communications, computer math, creative writing, debate, design, drama, drawing, economics, English, English literature, English-AP, ethics,

European history, European history-AP, fine arts, French, French language-AP, French literature-AP, geology, geometry, German, German-AP, government/civics, history, instrumental music, jazz ensemble, journalism, mathematics, multicultural studies, music, painting, performing arts, photography, physical education, physics, physics-AP, policy and value, political science, printmaking, psychology, religion, science, sculpture, senior project, social psychology, social studies, Spanish, Spanish language-AP, speech, statistics, statistics-AP, studio art, studio art-AP, theater, theater arts, trigonometry, visual and performing arts, vocal ensemble, women's studies, world cultures, world history, world literature, writing.

Graduation Requirements Arts and fine arts (art, music, dance, drama), communications, English, foreign language, mathematics, physical education (includes health), science, social studies (includes history), assembly speech.

Special Academic Programs Advanced Placement exam preparation in 14 subject areas; term-away projects; study at local college for college credit; study abroad.

College Placement 126 students graduated in 2005; all went to college, including Carleton College; Northwestern University; Union College; University of Pennsylvania; University of Wisconsin–Madison. Median SAT verbal: 650, median SAT math: 670, median composite ACT: 28. 61% scored over 600 on SAT verbal, 70% scored over 600 on SAT math, 69% scored over 26 on composite ACT.

Student Life Upper grades have specified standards of dress, student council, honor system. Discipline rests primarily with faculty.

Summer Programs Remediation, enrichment, advancement, sports, art/fine arts programs offered; session focuses on broad-based, academics-arts-sports; held both on and off campus; held at local lakes and beaches, culinary shops, and museums; accepts boys and girls; open to students from other schools. 250 students usually enrolled. 2006 schedule: June 12 to August 6. Application deadline: May 1.

Tuition and Aid Day student tuition: $18,100. Tuition installment plan (local bank-arranged plan). Need-based scholarship grants, need-based loans, academic year low-interest loans, tuition remission for children of faculty available. In 2005–06, 25% of upper-school students received aid. Total amount of financial aid awarded in 2005–06: $1,589,000.

Admissions Traditional secondary-level entrance grade is 9. For fall 2005, 96 students applied for upper-level admission, 56 were accepted, 36 enrolled. ERB or WISC/Woodcock-Johnson required. Deadline for receipt of application materials: January 31. Application fee required: $75. On-campus interview required.

Athletics Interscholastic: alpine skiing (boys, girls), baseball (b), basketball (b,g), cross-country running (b,g), diving (b,g), football (b), golf (b,g), ice hockey (b,g), lacrosse (b,g), skiing (cross-country) (b,g), skiing (downhill) (b,g), soccer (b,g), softball (g), swimming and diving (b,g); coed interscholastic: fencing. 1 PE instructor, 45 coaches, 1 trainer.

Computers Computers are regularly used in English, foreign language, history, mathematics, music, science, social studies, writing classes. Computer network features include campus e-mail, on-campus library services, CD-ROMs, online commercial services, Internet access, DVD, wireless campus network, laptops.

Contact Adaline Shinkle, Director of Admissions. 952-988-3420. Fax: 952-988-3455. E-mail: ashinkle@blakeschool.org. Web site: www.blakeschool.org.

BLUE MOUNTAIN ACADEMY

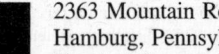

2363 Mountain Road
Hamburg, Pennsylvania 19526
Head of School: Mr. Spencer R. Hannah

General Information Coeducational boarding college-preparatory, religious studies, and leadership school, affiliated with Seventh-day Adventists. Grades 9–12. Founded: 1955. Setting: rural. Students are housed in single-sex dormitories. 735-acre campus. 6 buildings on campus. Approved or accredited by Middle States Association of Colleges and Schools. Total enrollment: 249. Upper school average class size: 24. Upper school faculty-student ratio: 1:10.

Upper School Student Profile Grade 9: 61 students (31 boys, 30 girls); Grade 10: 60 students (34 boys, 26 girls); Grade 11: 65 students (33 boys, 32 girls); Grade 12: 63 students (34 boys, 29 girls). 80% of students are boarding students. 49% are state residents. 19 states are represented in upper school student body. 2% are international students. International students from Republic of Korea and Viet Nam. 88% of students are Seventh-day Adventists.

Faculty School total: 27. In upper school: 15 men, 10 women; 17 have advanced degrees; 20 reside on campus.

Subjects Offered Accounting, Advanced Placement courses, algebra, anatomy and physiology, art, auto body, auto mechanics, band, bell choir, Bible, biology, business mathematics, chemistry, chemistry-AP, choir, computer applications, desktop publishing, digital photography, English, English literature and composition-AP, fiber arts, flight instruction, food and nutrition, French, geometry, golf, gymnastics, health, home economics, honors English, honors world history, leadership, life science, music appreciation, music theory, organ, physical education, physics, piano, pre-algebra, pre-calculus, psychology, sewing, Spanish, U.S. government, U.S. history, U.S. history-AP, weightlifting, Western civilization, world history.

Graduation Requirements Algebra, arts, Bible, biology, computer applications, electives, English, foreign language, mathematics, physical education (includes health), science, social science, U.S. government, U.S. history, work-study, one year of religion for each year enrolled.

Special Academic Programs Advanced Placement exam preparation in 2 subject areas; honors section; accelerated programs; study at local college for college credit; remedial reading and/or remedial writing; remedial math; programs in English, mathematics, general development for dyslexic students.

College Placement 63 students graduated in 2005; 59 went to college, including Andrews University; Columbia Union College; La Sierra University; Southern Adventist University; Walla Walla College. Other: 4 went to work.

Student Life Upper grades have specified standards of dress, student council, honor system. Discipline rests primarily with faculty. Attendance at religious services is required.

Tuition and Aid Day student tuition: $8400; 7-day tuition and room/board: $13,520. Tuition reduction for siblings, need-based scholarship grants, paying campus jobs available. In 2005–06, 28% of upper-school students received aid. Total amount of financial aid awarded in 2005–06: $130,000.

Admissions Traditional secondary-level entrance grade is 9. For fall 2005, 300 students applied for upper-level admission, 265 were accepted. Math Placement Exam required. Deadline for receipt of application materials: none. Application fee required: $15.

Athletics Intramural: basketball (boys, girls), flag football (b,g), floor hockey (b,g), soccer (b,g), softball (b,g), volleyball (b,g); coed intramural: basketball, flag football, floor hockey, gymnastics, soccer, softball, volleyball. 1 PE instructor.

Computers Computers are regularly used in accounting, desktop publishing, history, keyboarding, mathematics, photography, psychology, religion, yearbook classes. Computer network features include on-campus library services, CD-ROMs, Internet access.

Contact Mr. David Morgan, Recruiter. 610-562-2291. Fax: 610-562-8050. E-mail: morg@bma.us. Web site: www.bma.us.

BLUEPRINT EDUCATION

1717 West Northern Avenue
Suite 104
Phoenix, Arizona 85021
Head of School: Barbara Day

General Information Coeducational day college-preparatory, general academic, and distance learning school. Grades 7–12. Founded: 1969. Approved or accredited by CITA (Commission on International and Trans-Regional Accreditation) and North Central Association of Colleges and Schools.

Faculty School total: 40. In upper school: 17 men, 16 women; 33 have advanced degrees.

Subjects Offered Accounting, algebra, American government, American history, art, art history, auto shop, biology, British literature, business, business law, business mathematics, calculus, career and personal planning, career experience, career exploration, character education, chemistry, child development, college planning, computer applications, computer education, computer keyboarding, computer literacy, computer skills, computers, consumer mathematics, decision making skills, drawing, driver education, earth science, economics, English, English composition, environmental education, environmental science, family life, general business, general math, geometry, government, health and wellness, health education, independent study, Internet, interpersonal skills, keyboarding, life management skills, marketing, mathematics, music theory, painting, parenting, personal development, physical education, physical fitness, pre-algebra, psychology, reading, reading/study skills, senior composition, short story, single survival, Spanish, speech, speech communications, statistics, study skills, travel, trigonometry, visual arts, weight training, weightlifting, wellness, wilderness education, work experience, work-study, world geography, world history.

Graduation Requirements Arts and fine arts (art, music, dance, drama), computers, English, foreign language, geography, mathematics, science, social studies (includes history), 12.5 grade level on California Achievement Test.

Special Academic Programs Honors section; accelerated programs; independent study; academic accommodation for the gifted; remedial reading and/or remedial writing; remedial math.

College Placement 30 students graduated in 2005; 15 went to college, including Arizona State University; Northern Arizona University; Pima Community College; The University of Arizona; Utah State University. Other: 10 went to work, 5 entered military service.

Student Life Upper grades have honor system.

Summer Programs Remediation, advancement programs offered; session focuses on remediation and advancement; held both on and off campus; held at various locations for independent study; accepts boys and girls; open to students from other schools. 2006 schedule: June 1 to August 31.

Tuition and Aid Day student tuition: $5000–$5500. Financial aid available to upper-school students. In 2005–06, 2% of upper-school students received aid. Total amount of financial aid awarded in 2005–06: $1000.

Admissions CAT required. Deadline for receipt of application materials: none. Application fee required: $25.

Computers Computers are regularly used in all academic classes. Computer resources include campus e-mail, CD-ROMs, Internet access, office computer access.

Contact Arlene Duston, Curriculum Director. 602-906-4824. Fax: 602-943-9700. E-mail: arlened@blueprinteducation.org. Web site: www.blueprinteducation.org.

THE BLUE RIDGE SCHOOL

Highway 627/Bacon Hollow Road
St. George, Virginia 22935
Head of School: Dr. David A. Bouton

General Information Boys' boarding college-preparatory school, affiliated with Episcopal Church. Grades 9–12. Founded: 1909. Setting: rural. Nearest major city is Charlottesville. Students are housed in single-sex dormitories. 800-acre campus. 11 buildings on campus. Approved or accredited by National Association of Episcopal Schools, Southern Association of Colleges and Schools, The Association of Boarding Schools, Virginia Association of Independent Schools, and Virginia Department of Education. Member of National Association of Independent Schools and Secondary School Admission Test Board. Endowment: $9 million. Total enrollment: 164. Upper school average class size: 8. Upper school faculty-student ratio: 1:6.

Upper School Student Profile Grade 9: 29 students (29 boys); Grade 10: 40 students (40 boys); Grade 11: 54 students (54 boys); Grade 12: 41 students (41 boys). 100% of students are boarding students. 38% are state residents. 23 states are represented in upper school student body. 13% are international students. International students from China, Japan, Lithuania, Republic of Korea, Saudi Arabia, and Taiwan; 4 other countries represented in student body.

Faculty School total: 29. In upper school: 24 men, 5 women; 14 have advanced degrees; 27 reside on campus.

Subjects Offered Algebra, American literature, anatomy, art, astronomy, biology, calculus, chemistry, choir, computer applications, computer programming, computer science, decision making skills, driver education, English, environmental science, ESL, European history, French, geometry, health, honors English, honors geometry, honors U.S. history, integrated science, keyboarding, leadership training, mathematics, music, music history, outdoor education, physics, pre-algebra, pre-calculus, Spanish, trigonometry, U.S. history, world history, world literature, writing, yearbook.

Graduation Requirements Algebra, biology, decision making skills, English, foreign language, geometry, keyboarding, leadership training, mathematics, physical education (includes health), science, social studies (includes history).

Special Academic Programs Honors section; remedial reading and/or remedial writing; ESL (8 students enrolled).

College Placement 40 students graduated in 2005; all went to college, including Hampden-Sydney College; James Madison University; Lynchburg College; Roanoke College; The College of William and Mary.

Student Life Upper grades have specified standards of dress, student council, honor system. Discipline rests primarily with faculty. Attendance at religious services is required.

Tuition and Aid 7-day tuition and room/board: $30,972. Tuition installment plan (Insured Tuition Payment Plan, Academic Management Services Plan). Need-based scholarship grants available. In 2005–06, 23% of upper-school students received aid. Total amount of financial aid awarded in 2005–06: $750,000.

Admissions For fall 2005, 189 students applied for upper-level admission, 111 were accepted, 70 enrolled. Any standardized test required. Deadline for receipt of application materials: February 15. Application fee required: $50. On-campus interview required.

Athletics Interscholastic: baseball, basketball, cross-country running, football, golf, indoor soccer, indoor track, lacrosse, mountain biking, soccer, tennis, track and field, volleyball; intramural: alpine skiing, back packing, bicycling, canoeing/kayaking, climbing, cooperative games, fishing, hiking/backpacking, kayaking, life saving, mountain biking, mountaineering, outdoor activities, outdoor skills, physical training, rafting, rappelling, rock climbing, ropes courses, skiing (downhill), snowboarding, strength & conditioning, weight lifting, weight training, wilderness. 1 trainer.

Computers Computers are regularly used in English, ESL, foreign language, mathematics, science, study skills, word processing, writing, yearbook classes. Computer network features include campus e-mail, on-campus library services, CD-ROMs, online commercial services, Internet access, DVD, wireless campus network.

Contact Mr. David E. Hodgson, Director of Admissions. 434-985-2811. Fax: 434-985-7215. E-mail: admission@blueridgeschool.com. Web site: www. blueridgeschool.com.

ANNOUNCEMENT FROM THE SCHOOL The School has just completed a comprehensive $8-million renovation project that touches nearly every aspect of the campus. The greatest impact has been on the dorms, with all new furniture and an updated interior, and on the academic building, where the entire space has been reallocated and modernized.

See full description on page 684.

THE BOLLES SCHOOL

7400 San Jose Boulevard
Jacksonville, Florida 32217-3499
Head of School: John E. Trainer, Jr.

General Information Coeducational boarding and day college-preparatory and arts school. Boarding grades 7–PG, day grades PK–PG. Founded: 1933. Setting: suburban.

The Bolles School

Students are housed in single-sex dormitories. 52-acre campus. 8 buildings on campus. Approved or accredited by Florida Council of Independent Schools, Southern Association of Colleges and Schools, The Association of Boarding Schools, and Florida Department of Education. Member of National Association of Independent Schools and Secondary School Admission Test Board. Endowment: $9.5 million. Total enrollment: 1,740. Upper school average class size: 18. Upper school faculty-student ratio: 1:9.

Upper School Student Profile Grade 9: 189 students (96 boys, 93 girls); Grade 10: 194 students (92 boys, 102 girls); Grade 11: 205 students (104 boys, 101 girls); Grade 12: 202 students (95 boys, 107 girls PG: 1 boy). 13% of students are boarding students. 93% are state residents. 10 states are represented in upper school student body. 7% are international students. International students from Germany, Indonesia, Mexico, and Republic of Korea; 16 other countries represented in student body.

Faculty School total: 185. In upper school: 51 men, 52 women; 89 have advanced degrees; 12 reside on campus.

Subjects Offered Acting, aerospace science, algebra, American Civil War, American government, American government-AP, American history, American literature, anatomy, art, art history, band, biology, biology-AP, British literature, calculus, calculus-AP, ceramics, chemistry, chemistry-AP, Chinese, chorus, comparative government and politics-AP, composition, computer applications, computer science, computer science-AP, contemporary history, creative writing, dance, data analysis, design, directing, drama, drawing, driver education, earth science, ecology, economics, English, environmental science, ESL, European history, fine arts, fitness, French, geography, geometry, German, government/civics, health, history, history-AP, humanities, Japanese, journalism, Latin, life management skills, life skills, literature, marine science, mathematics, Middle Eastern history, modern European history-AP, music, music history, music theory, mythology, neurobiology, painting, performing arts, philosophy, photography, physical education, physics, physics-AP, physiology, portfolio art, pre-algebra, pre-calculus, programming, psychology, public speaking, publications, science, sculpture, social science, social studies, Spanish, statistics, statistics-AP, studio art, theater, visual arts, Web site design, weight training, Western civilization, world culture, world history.

Graduation Requirements Arts and fine arts (art, music, dance, drama), English, foreign language, mathematics, physical education (includes health), science, social studies (includes history).

Special Academic Programs Advanced Placement exam preparation in 19 subject areas; honors section; independent study; term-away projects; ESL (31 students enrolled).

College Placement 191 students graduated in 2005; all went to college, including College of Charleston; Florida State University; Tulane University; The University of Central Florida; University of Florida; Wake Forest University. Mean SAT verbal: 604, mean SAT math: 604, median composite ACT: 25. 54% scored over 600 on SAT verbal, 53% scored over 600 on SAT math, 43% scored over 26 on composite ACT.

Student Life Upper grades have specified standards of dress, student council, honor system. Discipline rests primarily with faculty.

Tuition and Aid Day student tuition: $14,500; 7-day tuition and room/board: $30,750. Tuition installment plan (major increment payment plan, 10-month plan). Need-based scholarship grants available. In 2005–06, 13.1% of upper-school students received aid. Total amount of financial aid awarded in 2005–06: $1,058,372.

Admissions Traditional secondary-level entrance grade is 9. For fall 2005, 234 students applied for upper-level admission, 109 were accepted, 81 enrolled. ISEE or SSAT required. Deadline for receipt of application materials: none. Application fee required: $45. Interview required.

Athletics Interscholastic: baseball (b), basketball (b,g), cheering (g), crew (b,g), cross-country running (b,g), dance (b,g), football (b), golf (b,g), lacrosse (b), soccer (b,g), softball (g), swimming and diving (b,g), tennis (b,g), track and field (b,g), volleyball (b,g), weight lifting (b), wrestling (b); coed interscholastic: diving, sailing. 2 PE instructors, 5 coaches, 1 trainer.

Computers Computer network features include campus e-mail, on-campus library services, CD-ROMs, online commercial services, Internet access.

Contact Mark I. Frampton, Director of Upper School and Boarding Admission. 904-256-5032. Fax: 904-739-9929. E-mail: framptonm@bolles.org. Web site: www.bolles.org.

See full description on page 686.

BOSTON UNIVERSITY ACADEMY

1 University Road
Boston, Massachusetts 02215
Head of School: Dr. James Tracy

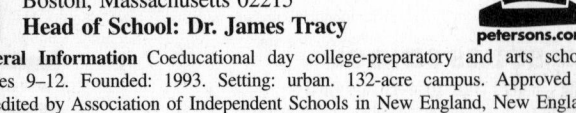

General Information Coeducational day college-preparatory and arts school. Grades 9–12. Founded: 1993. Setting: urban. 132-acre campus. Approved or accredited by Association of Independent Schools in New England, New England Association of Schools and Colleges, and Massachusetts Department of Education. Member of National Association of Independent Schools and Secondary School Admission Test Board. Total enrollment: 157. Upper school average class size: 14. Upper school faculty-student ratio: 1:7.

Upper School Student Profile Grade 9: 38 students (18 boys, 20 girls); Grade 10: 39 students (21 boys, 18 girls); Grade 11: 43 students (23 boys, 20 girls); Grade 12: 37 students (23 boys, 14 girls).

Faculty School total: 23. In upper school: 13 men, 7 women; 15 have advanced degrees.

Subjects Offered Advanced math, algebra, American history, American literature, ancient history, ancient world history, art, art history, biology, calculus, chemistry, Chinese, classical studies, college counseling, community service, computer programming, drama, English, English literature, European history, French, geometry, German, Greek, Hebrew, history, Italian, Japanese, Latin, music, physical education, physics, robotics, Russian, sculpture, senior project, Spanish, statistics, theater, trigonometry, writing.

Graduation Requirements Arts and fine arts (art, music, dance, drama), chemistry, English, history, Latin, mathematics, physical education (includes health), physics, two-semester senior thesis project. Community service is required.

Special Academic Programs Honors section; accelerated programs; independent study; study at local college for college credit; study abroad; academic accommodation for the gifted.

College Placement 25 students graduated in 2005; all went to college, including Boston College; Brown University; Columbia College; Harvard University; Massachusetts Institute of Technology; Yale University. Median SAT verbal: 740, median SAT math: 680. 100% scored over 600 on SAT verbal, 100% scored over 600 on SAT math.

Student Life Upper grades have student council, honor system. Discipline rests equally with students and faculty.

Summer Programs Enrichment, advancement programs offered; session focuses on international education; held off campus; held at London, England; accepts boys and girls; not open to students from other schools. 12 students usually enrolled. 2006 schedule: July to August. Application deadline: January 15.

Tuition and Aid Day student tuition: $22,210. Tuition installment plan (Academic Management Services Plan, monthly payment plans). Tuition reduction for siblings, merit scholarship grants, need-based scholarship grants available. In 2005–06, 38% of upper-school students received aid; total upper-school merit-scholarship money awarded: $132,000. Total amount of financial aid awarded in 2005–06: $545,000.

Admissions Traditional secondary-level entrance grade is 9. For fall 2005, 155 students applied for upper-level admission, 66 were accepted, 32 enrolled. SAT or SSAT required. Deadline for receipt of application materials: January 31. Application fee required: $45. On-campus interview required.

Athletics Interscholastic: basketball (boys, girls), crew (b,g), soccer (b); intramural: aerobics/dance (b,g); coed interscholastic: fencing, Frisbee, golf, sailing, soccer, tennis, ultimate Frisbee, yoga; coed intramural: archery, basketball, blading, canoeing/kayaking, crew, dance, figure skating, floor hockey, Frisbee, ice skating, indoor hockey, kayaking, martial arts, outdoor activities, sailing, skiing (downhill), soccer, softball, swimming and diving, table tennis, team handball, ultimate Frisbee, weight training. 10 PE instructors, 7 coaches.

Computers Computers are regularly used in art, English, foreign language, graphic design, history, mathematics, music, science classes. Computer network features include campus e-mail, on-campus library services, CD-ROMs, online commercial services, Internet access, file transfer, internal electronic bulletin board system.

Contact Ms. Nancy Caruso, Assistant Head of School for External Relations/Director of Admissions and Financial Aid. 617-353-9000. Fax: 617-353-8999. E-mail: nancy_caruso@buacademy.org. Web site: www.buacademy.org.

See full description on page 688.

BOYD-BUCHANAN SCHOOL

4626 Bonnieway Drive
Chattanooga, Tennessee 37411
Head of School: Robert Akins

General Information Coeducational day college-preparatory school, affiliated with Church of Christ. Grades K4–12. Founded: 1952. Setting: urban. 40-acre campus. 5 buildings on campus. Approved or accredited by Southern Association of Colleges and Schools, Tennessee Association of Independent Schools, and Tennessee Department of Education. Endowment: $3 million. Total enrollment: 977. Upper school average class size: 15. Upper school faculty-student ratio: 1:15.

Upper School Student Profile Grade 9: 109 students (52 boys, 57 girls); Grade 10: 82 students (58 boys, 24 girls); Grade 11: 85 students (57 boys, 28 girls); Grade 12: 75 students (39 boys, 36 girls). 40% of students are members of Church of Christ.

Faculty School total: 71. In upper school: 12 men, 26 women; 12 have advanced degrees.

Subjects Offered ACT preparation, Advanced Placement courses, algebra, American government, American history, American studies, art, band, Bible, biology, biology-AP, calculus, calculus-AP, chemistry, chemistry-AP, choir, choral music, chorus, computer applications, computer programming, concert choir, contemporary issues, contemporary problems, data processing, desktop publishing, ecology, economics, English, English composition, English literature, English literature and composition-AP, fitness, French, French-AP, geometry, government, health and wellness, honors algebra, honors English, honors geometry, integrated arts, jazz band, journalism, library assistant, music appreciation, music theory, physical science, physics,

pre-algebra, pre-calculus, psychology, SAT/ACT preparation, sociology, Spanish, Spanish-AP, statistics and probability, theater arts, trigonometry, U.S. history, U.S. history-AP, Web site design, wellness, world geography, world history, yearbook.

Graduation Requirements Arts and fine arts (art, music, dance, drama), Bible, electives, English, foreign language, health and wellness, mathematics, physical education (includes health), science, social sciences.

Special Academic Programs Advanced Placement exam preparation in 7 subject areas; honors section.

College Placement 74 students graduated in 2005; all went to college, including Chattanooga State Technical Community College; Freed-Hardeman University; Lipscomb University; Middle Tennessee State University; The University of Tennessee; The University of Tennessee at Chattanooga.

Student Life Upper grades have uniform requirement, student council, honor system. Discipline rests primarily with faculty. Attendance at religious services is required.

Summer Programs Sports programs offered; held on campus; accepts boys and girls; open to students from other schools. 150 students usually enrolled. 2006 schedule: June 1 to July 31. Application deadline: June 1.

Tuition and Aid Day student tuition: $4875–$6774. Tuition installment plan (FACTS Tuition Payment Plan). Tuition reduction for siblings, need-based scholarship grants available. In 2005–06, 4% of upper-school students received aid. Total amount of financial aid awarded in 2005–06: $80,000.

Admissions Traditional secondary-level entrance grade is 9. For fall 2005, 32 students applied for upper-level admission, 21 were accepted, 17 enrolled. Wide Range Achievement Test or WRAT required. Deadline for receipt of application materials: none. Application fee required: $25. Interview required.

Athletics Interscholastic: baseball (boys), basketball (b,g), cheering (g), cross-country running (b,g), football (b), golf (b,g), soccer (b,g), softball (g), tennis (b,g), volleyball (g), wrestling (b). 3 PE instructors, 18 coaches, 1 trainer.

Computers Computers are regularly used in creative writing, data processing, desktop publishing, journalism, keyboarding, newspaper, programming, study skills, technology, Web site design, word processing, writing, yearbook classes. Computer network features include on-campus library services, Internet access, wireless campus network.

Contact Charlotte H. White, Director of Admissions. 423-629-7610 Ext. 249. Fax: 423-698-5844. E-mail: cwhite@bbschool.org. Web site: www.bbschool.org.

THE BOYS' LATIN SCHOOL OF MARYLAND
822 West Lake Avenue
Baltimore, Maryland 21210
Head of School: Dr. H. Mebane Turner

General Information Boys' day college-preparatory, arts, and technology school. Grades K–12. Founded: 1844. Setting: suburban. 41-acre campus. 4 buildings on campus. Approved or accredited by Association of Independent Maryland Schools, Middle States Association of Colleges and Schools, and Maryland Department of Education. Member of National Association of Independent Schools. Endowment: $14.9 million. Total enrollment: 639. Upper school average class size: 15. Upper school faculty-student ratio: 1:8.

Upper School Student Profile Grade 9: 77 students (77 boys); Grade 10: 66 students (66 boys); Grade 11: 57 students (57 boys); Grade 12: 62 students (62 boys).

Faculty School total: 87. In upper school: 21 men, 12 women; 20 have advanced degrees.

Subjects Offered Advanced computer applications, Advanced Placement courses, African-American history, algebra, American history, American literature, art, art education, biology, calculus, calculus-AP, chemistry, chemistry-AP, community service, computer math, computer programming, computer science, drama, dramatic arts, ecology, economics, English, English literature, English literature-AP, environmental science, European history, European history-AP, expository writing, film, fine arts, French, geometry, government, government/civics, Greek culture, health education, history of mathematics, history-AP, honors algebra, honors English, honors geometry, honors U.S. history, honors world history, journalism, Latin, marine biology, mathematics, media studies, military history, music, music appreciation, physical education, physics, psychology, science, social studies, sociology, Spanish, theater, trigonometry, world history.

Graduation Requirements Arts and fine arts (art, music, dance, drama), computer science, English, foreign language, mathematics, physical education (includes health), science, social studies (includes history), study skills. Community service is required.

Special Academic Programs Advanced Placement exam preparation in 7 subject areas; honors section; independent study; term-away projects; academic accommodation for the gifted, the musically talented, and the artistically talented.

College Placement 61 students graduated in 2005; 58 went to college, including University of Delaware; University of Maryland, College Park. 37% scored over 600 on SAT verbal, 45% scored over 600 on SAT math.

Student Life Upper grades have specified standards of dress, student council, honor system. Discipline rests primarily with faculty.

Summer Programs Remediation, enrichment programs offered; held on campus; accepts boys and girls; open to students from other schools. 2006 schedule: June 16 to August 15. Application deadline: April 1.

Tuition and Aid Day student tuition: $17,300. Tuition installment plan (Academic Management Services Plan). Need-based grants available. In 2005–06, 28% of upper-school students received aid. Total amount of financial aid awarded in 2005–06: $984,900.

Admissions Traditional secondary-level entrance grade is 9. For fall 2005, 94 students applied for upper-level admission, 55 were accepted, 36 enrolled. ERB, ISEE or Otis-Lennon School Ability Test required. Deadline for receipt of application materials: none. Application fee required: $50. On-campus interview required.

Athletics Interscholastic: baseball, basketball, cross-country running, football, golf, ice hockey, lacrosse, outdoor adventure, outdoor education, physical fitness, physical training, soccer, squash, strength & conditioning, tennis, volleyball, wrestling. 5 PE instructors, 18 coaches, 2 trainers.

Computers Computers are regularly used in all academic classes. Computer network features include campus e-mail, on-campus library services, CD-ROMs, online commercial services, Internet access, Intranet combining technology, curricular, and research capabilities.

Contact Mr. James W. Currie Jr., Director of Middle and Upper School Admissions. 410-377-5192 Ext. 1139. Fax: 410-433-2571. E-mail: jcurrie@boyslatinmd.com. Web site: www.boyslatinmd.com.

BRADENTON CHRISTIAN SCHOOL
3304 43rd Street West
Bradenton, Florida 34209
Head of School: Mr. Dan van der Kooy

General Information Coeducational day college-preparatory, arts, business, religious studies, and technology school, affiliated with Christian Reformed Church, Baptist Church. Grades PK–12. Founded: 1960. Setting: suburban. Nearest major city is Tampa. 24-acre campus. 5 buildings on campus. Approved or accredited by Christian Schools of Florida, Florida Council of Independent Schools, Southern Association of Colleges and Schools, and Florida Department of Education. Total enrollment: 563. Upper school average class size: 18. Upper school faculty-student ratio: 1:14.

Upper School Student Profile 45% of students are members of Christian Reformed Church, Baptist.

Faculty School total: 51. In upper school: 13 men, 9 women; 10 have advanced degrees.

Special Academic Programs Honors section; study at local college for college credit.

College Placement 33 students graduated in 2005; all went to college. Mean SAT verbal: 565, mean SAT math: 545, mean composite ACT: 25. 43% scored over 600 on SAT verbal, 25% scored over 600 on SAT math.

Student Life Upper grades have specified standards of dress, student council. Discipline rests primarily with faculty. Attendance at religious services is required.

Tuition and Aid Day student tuition: $8159. Tuition installment plan (monthly payment plans, individually arranged payment plans). Tuition reduction for siblings, need-based scholarship grants available. In 2005–06, 15% of upper-school students received aid. Total amount of financial aid awarded in 2005–06: $42,962.

Admissions Traditional secondary-level entrance grade is 9. Academic Profile Tests or audition required. Deadline for receipt of application materials: none. Application fee required: $100. On-campus interview required.

Athletics Interscholastic: baseball (boys), basketball (b,g), cheering (b,g), cross-country running (b,g), football (b), golf (b), soccer (b,g), softball (g), tennis (b,g), track and field (b,g), volleyball (g); intramural: flag football (b), touch football (b); coed interscholastic: physical fitness. 3 PE instructors, 24 coaches.

Computers Computers are regularly used in accounting, aerospace science, animation, architecture, art, aviation, basic skills, Bible studies, business, business applications, business education, business skills, business studies, cabinet making, career education, career exploration, Christian doctrine, classics, commercial art, construction, creative writing, current events, dance, design, desktop publishing, ESL, drafting, drawing and design, economics, engineering, English, ESL, ethics, foreign language, French as a second language classes. Computer network features include campus e-mail, on-campus library services, Internet access, DVD.

Contact Darlene King, Director of Admissions. 941-792-5454 Ext. 117. Fax: 941-795-7190. E-mail: dking@bcspanthers.org. Web site: www.bcspanthers.org.

BRANDON HALL SCHOOL
Atlanta, Georgia
See Special Needs Schools section.

THE BREARLEY SCHOOL

610 East 83rd Street
New York, New York 10028
Head of School: Dr. Stephanie J. Hull

General Information Girls' day college-preparatory school. Grades K–12. Founded: 1884. Setting: urban. 2 buildings on campus. Approved or accredited by New York State Association of Independent Schools. Member of National Association of Independent Schools. Endowment: $78 million. Total enrollment: 675. Upper school average class size: 11. Upper school faculty-student ratio: 1:7.

Upper School Student Profile Grade 9: 47 students (47 girls); Grade 10: 58 students (58 girls); Grade 11: 49 students (49 girls); Grade 12: 55 students (55 girls).

Faculty School total: 140. In upper school: 22 men, 63 women; 61 have advanced degrees.

Subjects Offered 20th century world history, acting, aerobics, algebra, American history, American literature, Ancient Greek, applied music, art, art history, art history-AP, astronomy, basketball, biology, biology-AP, calculus, calculus-AP, ceramics, chemistry, computer science, contemporary women writers, creative writing, dance, drama, drawing, earth science, English, English literature, environmental science, ethics, expository writing, fine arts, finite math, French, French language-AP, French literature-AP, geometry, government/civics, Greek, gymnastics, health, history, history of China and Japan, independent study, Islamic history, jazz ensemble, junior and senior seminars, Latin, Mandarin, mathematics, multimedia design, music, music history, oil painting, painting, photography, physical education, physics, physics-AP, political thought, research, science, sculpture, senior project, Shakespeare, social studies, softball, Spanish, Spanish language-AP, Spanish literature-AP, squash, statistics, swimming, tennis, theater, track and field, trigonometry, typing, volleyball, water color painting, Web site design, women's literature, world history, writing.

Graduation Requirements Arts and fine arts (art, music, dance, drama), English, foreign language, mathematics, physical education (includes health), science, social studies (includes history).

Special Academic Programs Advanced Placement exam preparation in 14 subject areas; independent study; term-away projects; study abroad.

College Placement 42 students graduated in 2005; all went to college, including Brown University; Cornell University; Harvard University; Macalester College; Princeton University; Yale University. Median SAT verbal: 720, median SAT math: 700. 95% scored over 600 on SAT verbal, 91% scored over 600 on SAT math.

Student Life Upper grades have specified standards of dress, student council. Discipline rests equally with students and faculty.

Tuition and Aid Day student tuition: $28,150. Tuition installment plan (Key Tuition Payment Plan, individually arranged payment plans). Need-based scholarship grants, need-based loans available. In 2005–06, 30% of upper-school students received aid. Total amount of financial aid awarded in 2005–06: $1,340,535.

Admissions For fall 2005, 92 students applied for upper-level admission, 25 were accepted, 13 enrolled. ISEE and school's own exam required. Deadline for receipt of application materials: December 15. Application fee required: $60. On-campus interview required.

Athletics Interscholastic: aquatics, badminton, basketball, cross-country running, field hockey, gymnastics, lacrosse, soccer, softball, squash, swimming and diving, tennis, track and field, volleyball; intramural: aquatics, badminton, baseball, basketball, cooperative games, dance team, field hockey, fitness, gymnastics, jogging, lacrosse, modern dance, physical fitness, running, soccer, softball, squash, strength & conditioning, swimming and diving, tennis, track and field, volleyball, yoga. 12 PE instructors, 3 coaches.

Computers Computers are regularly used in classics, foreign language, history, mathematics, media production, multimedia, science, Web site design classes. Computer network features include campus e-mail, on-campus library services, CD-ROMs, Internet access, file transfer, wireless campus network, Britannica Online, EBSCO, SIRS Researcher, ProQuest, JSTOR.

Contact Ms. Joan Kaplan, Director of Middle and Upper School Admission. 212-744-8582. Fax: 212-472-8020. E-mail: admission@brearley.org. Web site: www.brearley.org.

BRECK SCHOOL

123 Ottawa Avenue, North
Minneapolis, Minnesota 55422
Head of School: Samuel A. Salas

petersons.com

General Information Coeducational day college-preparatory, arts, and religious studies school, affiliated with Episcopal Church. Grades PK–12. Founded: 1886. Setting: suburban. 50-acre campus. 1 building on campus. Approved or accredited by Independent Schools Association of the Central States. Member of National Association of Independent Schools and Secondary School Admission Test Board. Endowment: $40.9 million. Total enrollment: 1,200. Upper school average class size: 18. Upper school faculty-student ratio: 1:7.

Upper School Student Profile 11% of students are members of Episcopal Church.

Faculty School total: 136. In upper school: 25 men, 23 women; 40 have advanced degrees.

Subjects Offered Algebra, American history, American literature, art, astronomy, biology, calculus, ceramics, chemistry, Chinese, chorus, community service, computer math, computer programming, creative writing, dance, drama, ecology, economics, English, English literature, environmental science, ethics, European history, expository writing, fine arts, French, geometry, health, history, mathematics, music, orchestra, physical education, physics, religion, science, social studies, Spanish, statistics, theater, theology, trigonometry, world history, world literature, writing.

Graduation Requirements Arts and fine arts (art, music, dance, drama), English, foreign language, mathematics, physical education (includes health), religion (includes Bible studies and theology), science, social studies (includes history), senior speech, May Program. Community service is required.

Special Academic Programs Advanced Placement exam preparation in 7 subject areas; accelerated programs; independent study; term-away projects; academic accommodation for the gifted, the musically talented, and the artistically talented.

College Placement 88 students graduated in 2005; all went to college, including Boston College; Connecticut College; Gustavus Adolphus College; Middlebury College; Northwestern University; University of Wisconsin–Madison. Median SAT verbal: 626, median SAT math: 619, median composite ACT: 26. 62% scored over 600 on SAT verbal, 59% scored over 600 on SAT math.

Student Life Upper grades have specified standards of dress, student council, honor system. Discipline rests equally with students and faculty. Attendance at religious services is required.

Tuition and Aid Day student tuition: $16,755. Tuition installment plan (Key Tuition Payment Plan). Need-based scholarship grants available. In 2005–06, 18% of upper-school students received aid.

Admissions Traditional secondary-level entrance grade is 9. For fall 2005, 107 students applied for upper-level admission, 41 were accepted, 29 enrolled. CTP III required. Deadline for receipt of application materials: February 1. Application fee required: $75. On-campus interview required.

Athletics Interscholastic: alpine skiing (boys, girls), baseball (b), basketball (b,g), cross-country running (b,g), diving (b,g), football (b), golf (b,g), gymnastics (g), ice hockey (b,g), lacrosse (b,g), nordic skiing (b,g), skiing (cross-country) (b,g), skiing (downhill) (b,g), soccer (b,g), softball (g), swimming and diving (b,g), tennis (b,g), track and field (b,g), volleyball (g). 6 PE instructors, 82 coaches, 1 trainer.

Computers Computers are regularly used in all classes. Computer network features include campus e-mail, on-campus library services, CD-ROMs, online commercial services, Internet access, wireless campus network, multimedia imaging, video presentation, student laptop program.

Contact Michael J. Weiszel, Director of Admissions. 763-381-8200. Fax: 763-381-8288. E-mail: mike.weiszel@breckschool.org. Web site: www.breckschool.org.

ANNOUNCEMENT FROM THE SCHOOL Breck School is a college-preparatory day school that enrolls boys and girls in preschool–grade 12. The School uses the cultural and educational resources of the Twin Cities metropolitan area to offer a vigorous college-preparatory curriculum. All divisions of the School have been honored by the U.S. Department of Education. Named for a pioneer missionary, the Reverend James Lloyd Breck, the School was established in 1886 in Wilder, Minnesota, to provide children with a top-quality education under the auspices of the Episcopal Church. In 1916, Breck moved to St. Paul; in 1956, a new facility was built on the Mississippi River in Minneapolis; and in 1981, the School relocated to the present 50-acre campus just west of downtown Minneapolis. The facilities include a 456-seat production theater, a 5-lane swimming pool, 3 gymnasiums, 3 libraries, 4 art rooms, 8 science laboratories, several playing fields, running tracks, tennis courts, natural wildlife ponds, and a detached ice arena. Campus renovations, completed in fall 2000, include state-of-the-art spaces for performing arts, several new classrooms, and a large fieldhouse. The spiritual and architectural focus of the campus is the Chapel of the Holy Spirit, which seats 1,300. Breck believes that economic, religious, racial, and geographic diversity add vital dimensions to the student educational experience. All educational and administrative policies, financial aid, and athletic and other programs are administered in a manner that applauds such diversity. Students come from 62 communities throughout the Minneapolis–St. Paul metropolitan area. New this year: one-to-one laptop initiative, piloted in grades 4 and 8 and to be expanded to all students in grades 4–12 in 2006–07. Financial aid of nearly $3 million supports approximately 17% of the student body. The enrollment of students of color is 22%. Nearly 70% of Breck's faculty members hold advanced degrees.

BREHM PREPARATORY SCHOOL

Carbondale, Illinois
See Special Needs Schools section.

BRENAU ACADEMY

500 Washington Street SE
Gainesville, Georgia 30501
Head of School: Dr. Frank M. Booth

petersons.com

General Information Girls' boarding and day college-preparatory and arts school. Grades 9–PG. Founded: 1928. Setting: small town. Nearest major city is Atlanta. Students are housed in single-sex dormitories. 56-acre campus. 50 buildings on campus. Approved or accredited by Georgia Independent School Association, Southern Association of Colleges and Schools, Southern Association of Independent Schools, The Association of Boarding Schools, and Georgia Department of Education. Member of National Association of Independent Schools. Endowment: $50 million. Total enrollment: 80. Upper school average class size: 10. Upper school faculty-student ratio: 1:8.

Upper School Student Profile 90% of students are boarding students. 50% are state residents. 10 states are represented in upper school student body. 12% are international students. International students from Australia, Bermuda, China, Republic of Korea, and Taiwan.

Faculty School total: 12. In upper school: 3 men, 9 women; 8 have advanced degrees.

Subjects Offered Algebra, American government, American history, American literature, anatomy, ancient world history, art, biology, calculus, chemistry, chorus, civics, college counseling, composition, computer science, creative writing, dance, drama, driver education, economics, English, English composition, English literature, etymology, fine arts, French, geography, geometry, government, government/civics, grammar, health, history, honors English, human anatomy, journalism, mathematics, music, physical education, physics, poetry, pre-calculus, science, social science, social studies, Spanish, theater, trigonometry, world history.

Graduation Requirements Arts and fine arts (art, music, dance, drama), English, foreign language, mathematics, physical education (includes health), science, social science, social studies (includes history).

Special Academic Programs Honors section; accelerated programs; study at local college for college credit; study abroad; academic accommodation for the gifted, the musically talented, and the artistically talented; programs in English, mathematics, general development for dyslexic students; special instructional classes for students with learning disabilities and Attention Deficit Disorder.

College Placement 13 students graduated in 2005; all went to college, including Auburn University; Boston College; Savannah College of Art and Design; The University of Texas at Austin; University of Georgia.

Student Life Upper grades have specified standards of dress, student council, honor system. Discipline rests primarily with faculty.

Tuition and Aid Day student tuition: $9350; 7-day tuition and room/board: $21,500. Tuition installment plan (Academic Management Services Plan). Tuition reduction for siblings, need-based scholarship grants available. In 2005–06, 10% of upper-school students received aid.

Admissions Traditional secondary-level entrance grade is 9. Deadline for receipt of application materials: none. Application fee required: $25. Interview required.

Athletics Interscholastic: basketball, cheering, cross-country running, tennis, volleyball; intramural: basketball, billiards, bowling, flag football, hiking/backpacking, outdoor activities, soccer, softball, tennis, volleyball. 1 PE instructor, 1 coach.

Computers Computers are regularly used in English, science classes. Computer network features include campus e-mail, on-campus library services, CD-ROMs, online commercial services, Internet access.

Contact Mrs. Leslie N. Miller, Director of Admissions. 770-534-6140. Fax: 770-534-6298. E-mail: enroll@brenau.edu. Web site: www.brenauacademy.org.

ANNOUNCEMENT FROM THE SCHOOL Brenau Academy is the next step on the journey that takes young women into the world as educated, successful professionals. Through exciting classroom environments and challenging curriculum, the Academy offers every student the opportunity to reach her academic goals. Through caring faculty, intramural sports, clubs, community service, field trips, and the arts, students are able to find something that creates a love of learning that extends beyond the classroom. Located on the thriving campus of Brenau Women's College, Academy students are able to take advantage of all the benefits a college offers, while being in the protective environment of a high school. There is a future waiting at Brenau Academy. Come find your place with us.

See full description on page 690.

BRENT SCHOOL-BAGUIO

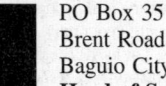

PO Box 35
Brent Road
Baguio City 2600, Philippines
Head of School: Mr. Dick B. Robbins

General Information Coeducational boarding and day college-preparatory school, affiliated with Episcopal Church. Boarding grades 3–12, day grades PK–12. Founded: 1909. Setting: suburban. Nearest major city is Manila. Students are housed in single-sex dormitories. 48-acre campus. 13 buildings on campus. Approved or accredited by Western Association of Schools and Colleges. Member of European Council of International Schools. Language of instruction: English. Total enrollment: 235. Upper school average class size: 17. Upper school faculty-student ratio: 1:4.

Upper School Student Profile Grade 9: 22 students (12 boys, 10 girls); Grade 10: 20 students (10 boys, 10 girls); Grade 11: 17 students (6 boys, 11 girls); Grade 12: 12 students (7 boys, 5 girls). 2% of students are boarding students. 70% are international students. International students from Canada, New Zealand, Republic of Korea, United Kingdom, and United States; 15 other countries represented in student body. 2% of students are members of Episcopal Church.

Faculty School total: 38. In upper school: 11 men, 27 women; 7 have advanced degrees; 18 reside on campus.

Subjects Offered Algebra, American history, art, art history, biology, business, calculus, chemistry, computer applications, computer education, computer information systems, computer literacy, computer multimedia, computer programming, earth science, economics, English, English literature, environmental science, ESL, Filipino, fine arts, French, geography, geometry, health education, history, International Baccalaureate courses, Japanese literature, Korean, Korean literature, mathematics, media studies, music appreciation, outdoor education, Philippine culture, physical education, physics, religion, science, social science, social studies, Spanish, statistics, theory of knowledge, trigonometry, world history, writing, yearbook.

Graduation Requirements Art, art history, Asian history, biology, computer education, computer programming, English, English composition, English literature, ESL, Filipino, foreign language, health education, mathematics, physical education (includes health), religion (includes Bible studies and theology), science, social studies (includes history), theory of knowledge.

Special Academic Programs International Baccalaureate program; ESL (67 students enrolled).

College Placement 15 students graduated in 2005; 12 went to college, including Savannah College of Art and Design; The Ohio State University. Other: 2 went to work, 1 entered military service. Mean SAT verbal: 583, mean SAT math: 666. 67% scored over 600 on SAT verbal, 67% scored over 600 on SAT math.

Student Life Upper grades have uniform requirement, student council, honor system. Discipline rests equally with students and faculty. Attendance at religious services is required.

Tuition and Aid Day student tuition: $1680–$8990. Tuition installment plan (individually arranged payment plans, quarterly, semi-annual, and annual payment plans). Tuition reduction for siblings, merit scholarship grants available. In 2005–06, 9% of upper-school students received aid; total upper-school merit-scholarship money awarded: $34,279. Total amount of financial aid awarded in 2005–06: $78,309.

Admissions Traditional secondary-level entrance grade is 9. For fall 2005, 20 students applied for upper-level admission, 17 were accepted, 16 enrolled. English for Non-native Speakers, Iowa Tests of Basic Skills, Macalaitus Test of English, Metropolitan Achievement Test, SLEP for foreign students, Stanford Achievement Test, Otis-Lennon or writing sample required. Deadline for receipt of application materials: none. Application fee required: $50. On-campus interview required.

Athletics Coed Interscholastic: archery, badminton, baseball, basketball, billiards, bowling, cross-country running, fitness, indoor soccer, outdoor education, soccer, table tennis, track and field, volleyball; coed intramural: basketball. 1 PE instructor, 1 coach.

Computers Computers are regularly used in art, business, career education, career exploration, college planning, computer applications, data processing, English, ESL, foreign language, graphic arts, graphic design, history, information technology, introduction to technology, library, literary magazine, mathematics, music, newspaper, programming, publications, religious studies, science, social science, Spanish, Web site design, word processing, writing, writing, writing fundamentals, yearbook classes. Computer network features include campus e-mail, on-campus library services, CD-ROMs, Internet access, office computer access, wireless campus network.

Contact Mrs. Lourdes C. Balanza, Registrar. 63-74-442-2260 Ext. 105. Fax: 63-74-442-3638. E-mail: registrar@brentschoolbaguio.com. Web site: www. brentschoolbaguio.com.

BRENTWOOD ACADEMY

219 Granny White Pike
Brentwood, Tennessee 37027
Head of School: Curtis G. Masters

General Information Coeducational day college-preparatory, arts, and religious studies school, affiliated with Christian faith. Grades 6–12. Founded: 1969. Setting: suburban. Nearest major city is Nashville. 49-acre campus. 3 buildings on campus. Approved or accredited by Southern Association of Colleges and Schools and Tennessee Association of Independent Schools. Member of National Association of Independent Schools. Endowment: $3 million. Total enrollment: 741. Upper school average class size: 12. Upper school faculty-student ratio: 1:12.

Upper School Student Profile Grade 9: 118 students (63 boys, 55 girls); Grade 10: 98 students (52 boys, 46 girls); Grade 11: 120 students (56 boys, 64 girls); Grade 12: 99 students (49 boys, 50 girls).

Faculty School total: 85. In upper school: 22 men, 28 women; 32 have advanced degrees.

Subjects Offered Advanced math, Advanced Placement courses, algebra, American history, American literature, anatomy and physiology, ancient history, art, Bible

studies, biology, calculus, chemistry, choir, cinematography, composition, computer science, creative writing, dance, drama, earth science, economics, English, English literature, European history, fine arts, forensic science, forensics, French, geography, geometry, government/civics, grammar, history, journalism, Latin, mathematics, modern history, music, physical education, physical science, physics, religion, science, social science, social studies, Spanish, speech, theater, trigonometry, world history, world literature.

Graduation Requirements Arts and fine arts (art, music, dance, drama), business skills (includes word processing), computer science, English, foreign language, mathematics, physical education (includes health), religion (includes Bible studies and theology), science, social science, social studies (includes history).

Special Academic Programs Advanced Placement exam preparation in 8 subject areas; honors section; independent study; academic accommodation for the gifted, the musically talented, and the artistically talented.

College Placement 92 students graduated in 2005; 90 went to college, including The University of Tennessee; University of Mississippi. Other: 2 had other specific plans. 33% scored over 600 on SAT verbal, 33% scored over 600 on SAT math, 30% scored over 26 on composite ACT.

Student Life Upper grades have specified standards of dress, student council, honor system. Discipline rests primarily with faculty.

Summer Programs Remediation, enrichment, sports, art/fine arts, computer instruction programs offered; held on campus; accepts boys and girls; open to students from other schools. 500 students usually enrolled. 2006 schedule: June 1 to August 1. Application deadline: none.

Tuition and Aid Day student tuition: $12,350. Tuition installment plan (monthly payment plans, individually arranged payment plans). Need-based scholarship grants, need-based loans, paying campus jobs available. In 2005–06, 10% of upper-school students received aid. Total amount of financial aid awarded in 2005–06: $362,139.

Admissions Traditional secondary-level entrance grade is 9. For fall 2005, 103 students applied for upper-level admission, 55 were accepted, 32 enrolled. Essay and Otis-Lennon School Ability Test required. Deadline for receipt of application materials: none. Application fee required: $25. On-campus interview required.

Athletics Interscholastic: baseball (boys), basketball (b,g), cheering (g), cross-country running (b,g), dance (g), diving (b,g), football (b), golf (b,g), ice hockey (b), lacrosse (g), physical fitness (b,g), soccer (b,g), softball (g), swimming and diving (b,g), tennis (b,g), track and field (b,g), volleyball (g), wrestling (b); intramural: aerobics/dance (g), physical fitness (b,g), rock climbing (b,g), weight lifting (b,g); coed interscholastic: bowling; coed intramural: strength & conditioning. 29 coaches, 1 trainer.

Computers Computers are regularly used in English, foreign language, mathematics, science classes. Computer network features include on-campus library services, CD-ROMs, Internet access, wireless campus network.

Contact Mrs. Sue Gering, Director of Admission. 615-373-0611. Fax: 615-377-3709. E-mail: admission@brentwoodacademy.com. Web site: www.brentwoodacademy.com.

BRENTWOOD COLLEGE SCHOOL

2735 Mount Baker Road
Mill Bay, British Columbia V0R 2P1, Canada
Head of School: Mrs. Andrea M. Pennells

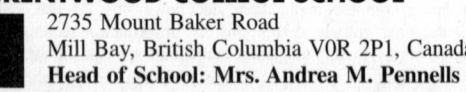

General Information Coeducational boarding and day college-preparatory and arts school. Grades 8–12. Founded: 1923. Setting: rural. Nearest major city is Victoria, Canada. Students are housed in single-sex dormitories. 70-acre campus. 15 buildings on campus. Approved or accredited by Canadian Association of Independent Schools, Headmasters' Conference, The Association of Boarding Schools, and British Columbia Department of Education. Language of instruction: English. Total enrollment: 425. Upper school average class size: 20. Upper school faculty-student ratio: 1:8.

Upper School Student Profile Grade 8: 45 students (26 boys, 19 girls); Grade 9: 66 students (39 boys, 27 girls); Grade 10: 89 students (50 boys, 39 girls); Grade 11: 118 students (53 boys, 65 girls); Grade 12: 106 students (61 boys, 45 girls). 85% of students are boarding students. 60% are province residents. 21 provinces are represented in upper school student body. 22% are international students. International students from Hong Kong, Japan, Mexico, Saudi Arabia, Taiwan, and United States; 4 other countries represented in student body.

Faculty School total: 54. In upper school: 30 men, 11 women; 19 have advanced degrees; 30 reside on campus.

Subjects Offered Algebra, biology, business, calculus, ceramics, chemistry, chorus, computer graphics, computer science, dance, drafting, drama, drawing, economics, English, English literature, fine arts, French, geography, geometry, history, instrumental music, international studies, law, mathematics, painting, photography, physics, psychology, science, sculpture, Spanish.

Graduation Requirements Art, Canadian geography, Canadian history, Canadian law, Canadian literature, career planning, creation science, debate, economics, English literature, French, lab science, mathematics, music, physical education (includes health), social science, speech and debate, vocal music.

Special Academic Programs Advanced Placement exam preparation.

College Placement 109 students graduated in 2005; all went to college, including Harvard University; Princeton University; Stanford University; University of California, Berkeley; University of Washington; Yale University.

Student Life Upper grades have uniform requirement, student council, honor system. Discipline rests primarily with faculty.

Tuition and Aid Day student tuition: CAN$16,300; 7-day tuition and room/board: CAN$30,300–CAN$39,000. Tuition reduction for siblings available.

Admissions Traditional secondary-level entrance grade is 8. For fall 2005, 475 students applied for upper-level admission, 203 were accepted, 147 enrolled. No application fee required. On-campus interview required.

Athletics Interscholastic: aerobics (girls), aerobics/dance (g), ballet (g), field hockey (g), rugby (b); coed interscholastic: badminton, basketball, bicycling, canoeing/kayaking, crew, cross-country running, Frisbee, golf, hiking/backpacking, hockey, ice hockey, kayaking, life saving, martial arts, mountain biking, ocean paddling, outdoor activities, outdoor adventure, outdoor education, outdoor recreation, outdoor skills, outdoors, rowing, running, skiing (downhill), snowboarding, soccer, squash, tennis, track and field, volleyball; coed intramural: aerobics, aerobics/dance, alpine skiing, aquatics, back packing, badminton, ball hockey, ballet, bicycling, canoeing/kayaking, climbing, cooperative games, dance, fishing, fitness, floor hockey, Frisbee, hiking/backpacking, ice skating, indoor soccer, jogging, kayaking, modern dance, mountain biking, ocean paddling, outdoor activities, outdoor adventure, outdoor education, outdoor recreation, outdoor skills, outdoors, paddling, physical fitness, physical training, rock climbing, sailing, skateboarding, strength & conditioning, swimming and diving, table tennis, touch football, triathlon, ultimate Frisbee, wall climbing, weight lifting, weight training, wilderness, winter walking. 6 PE instructors, 36 coaches.

Computers Computer network features include campus e-mail, on-campus library services, CD-ROMs, Internet access, office computer access.

Contact Mr. Andy D. Rodford, Director of Admissions. 250-743-5521. Fax: 250-743-2911. E-mail: andy.rodford@brentwood.bc.ca. Web site: www.brentwood.bc.ca.

ANNOUNCEMENT FROM THE SCHOOL Brentwood is a residential, university-preparatory school with a challenging academic curriculum, including Advanced Placement courses. Beyond the classroom, exceptional athletic and artistic programs build individual confidence and promote teamwork. This oceanfront coeducational campus, set on 65 acres, includes a 62,000-square-foot academic centre, a sports complex, an indoor rowing tank, visual and performing arts studios, 7 residences, and extensive waterfront facilities.

See full description on page 692.

BRENTWOOD SCHOOL

100 South Barrington Place
Los Angeles, California 90049
Head of School: Michael Pratt

General Information Coeducational day college-preparatory and arts school. Grades K–12. Founded: 1972. Setting: suburban. 30-acre campus. 6 buildings on campus. Approved or accredited by California Association of Independent Schools and Western Association of Schools and Colleges. Member of National Association of Independent Schools and Secondary School Admission Test Board. Endowment: $6 million. Total enrollment: 991. Upper school average class size: 17. Upper school faculty-student ratio: 1:8.

Upper School Student Profile Grade 9: 120 students (63 boys, 57 girls); Grade 10: 124 students (67 boys, 57 girls); Grade 11: 110 students (61 boys, 49 girls); Grade 12: 117 students (63 boys, 54 girls).

Faculty School total: 88. In upper school: 43 men, 45 women; 55 have advanced degrees.

Subjects Offered Acting, Advanced Placement courses, advanced studio art-AP, algebra, American government-AP, American history, American literature, Ancient Greek, anthropology, art, art history, art history-AP, art-AP, astronomy, biology, biology-AP, calculus, calculus-AP, ceramics, chemistry, chemistry-AP, choir, choral music, chorus, community service, comparative government and politics-AP, computer programming, computer programming-AP, computer science, computer science-AP, concert choir, creative writing, dance, digital photography, directing, drama, drawing, ecology, economics, economics-AP, English, English literature, environmental science-AP, European history, fine arts, French, French-AP, geometry, global studies, government and politics-AP, government-AP, history, honors algebra, honors English, honors geometry, human development, human geography—AP, Japanese, jazz band, jazz dance, journalism, language-AP, Latin, Latin-AP, literature-AP, math analysis, mathematics, music, music theater, music theory-AP, orchestra, philosophy, photography, physical education, physics, physics-AP, probability and statistics, robotics, science, senior seminar, senior thesis, social science, social studies, Spanish, Spanish-AP, speech, speech and debate, stagecraft, stained glass, statistics-AP, studio art-AP, theater, U.S. government-AP, U.S. history-AP, video, word processing, world history, world literature.

Graduation Requirements Arts and fine arts (art, music, dance, drama), computer science, English, foreign language, mathematics, physical education (includes health), science, senior seminar, senior thesis, social science, social studies (includes history). Community service is required.

Special Academic Programs Advanced Placement exam preparation in 19 subject areas; honors section; independent study; study at local college for college credit; academic accommodation for the gifted and the artistically talented.

College Placement 116 students graduated in 2005; all went to college, including Northwestern University; Stanford University; University of Michigan; University of Pennsylvania; University of Southern California. Mean SAT verbal: 650, mean SAT math: 660, mean combined SAT: 2010. 81% scored over 600 on SAT verbal, 82% scored over 600 on SAT math, 83% scored over 1800 on combined SAT.

Student Life Upper grades have specified standards of dress, student council, honor system. Discipline rests primarily with faculty.

Summer Programs Remediation, enrichment, advancement, sports, art/fine arts, computer instruction programs offered; session focuses on academic enrichment; held on campus; accepts boys and girls; open to students from other schools. 350 students usually enrolled. 2006 schedule: June 26 to August 4. Application deadline: none.

Tuition and Aid Day student tuition: $23,400. Tuition installment plan (Insured Tuition Payment Plan, monthly payment plans, individually arranged payment plans). Need-based scholarship grants available. In 2005–06, 17% of upper-school students received aid. Total amount of financial aid awarded in 2005–06: $2,300,000.

Admissions Traditional secondary-level entrance grade is 9. For fall 2005, 149 students applied for upper-level admission, 24 were accepted, 19 enrolled. ISEE required. Deadline for receipt of application materials: January 27. Application fee required: $125. On-campus interview required.

Athletics Interscholastic: baseball (boys), basketball (b,g), cheering (g), cross-country running (b,g), dance squad (g), dance team (g), flag football (b), football (b), independent competitive sports (b,g), lacrosse (b), soccer (b,g), softball (g), tennis (b,g), track and field (b,g), volleyball (b,g), wrestling (b); intramural: modern dance (g); coed interscholastic: dance, diving, drill team, equestrian sports, fencing, golf, lacrosse, swimming and diving, water polo; coed intramural: bicycling, fitness, Frisbee, jogging, mountain biking, outdoor education, physical fitness, physical training, running, surfing, table tennis, ultimate Frisbee, weight lifting, weight training, yoga. 5 PE instructors, 40 coaches, 2 trainers.

Computers Computers are regularly used in foreign language, mathematics, science classes. Computer network features include campus e-mail, on-campus library services, CD-ROMs, online commercial services, Internet access, file transfer, DVD, wireless library network with laptops.

Contact Judy Wray, Admissions Assistant. 310-889-2657. Fax: 310-476-4087. E-mail: judy_wray@bwscampus.com. Web site: www.bwscampus.com.

BREWSTER ACADEMY

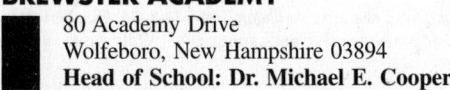

80 Academy Drive
Wolfeboro, New Hampshire 03894
Head of School: Dr. Michael E. Cooper

petersons.com

General Information Coeducational boarding and day college-preparatory, arts, and technology school. Grades 9–PG. Founded: 1820. Setting: small town. Nearest major city is Boston, MA. Students are housed in single-sex dormitories. 80-acre campus. 36 buildings on campus. Approved or accredited by New England Association of Schools and Colleges and The Association of Boarding Schools. Member of National Association of Independent Schools and Secondary School Admission Test Board. Endowment: $12 million. Total enrollment: 361. Upper school average class size: 12. Upper school faculty-student ratio: 1:6.

Upper School Student Profile Grade 9: 54 students (33 boys, 21 girls); Grade 10: 99 students (59 boys, 40 girls); Grade 11: 103 students (63 boys, 40 girls); Grade 12: 89 students (66 boys, 23 girls); Postgraduate: 16 students (15 boys, 1 girl). 80% of students are boarding students. 35% are state residents. 31 states are represented in upper school student body. 16% are international students. International students from Canada, Germany, Japan, Republic of Korea, Taiwan, and Thailand; 6 other countries represented in student body.

Faculty School total: 63. In upper school: 34 men, 27 women; 23 have advanced degrees; 44 reside on campus.

Subjects Offered Algebra, art, art history, biology, biology-AP, calculus, calculus-AP, chemistry, chemistry-AP, chorus, community service, computer graphics, creative writing, dance, dance performance, drama, driver education, English, English language and composition-AP, English literature, English literature-AP, environmental science, ESL, European history, European history-AP, French, geometry, jazz band, journalism, mathematics, music, photography, physics, physics-AP, pottery, science, Spanish, studio art, theater, U.S. history, U.S. history-AP, world history, writing.

Graduation Requirements English, foreign language, mathematics, science, social studies (includes history).

Special Academic Programs Advanced Placement exam preparation in 8 subject areas; honors section; programs in English, mathematics, general development for dyslexic students; ESL (16 students enrolled).

College Placement 105 students graduated in 2005; 103 went to college, including Fordham University; Syracuse University; University of Michigan; University of New Hampshire; University of Vermont. Other: 1 went to work, 1 entered a postgraduate year. Median SAT math: 550. 30% scored over 600 on SAT math, 18% scored over 26 on composite ACT.

Student Life Upper grades have specified standards of dress, student council, honor system. Discipline rests primarily with faculty.

Summer Programs Enrichment, advancement, ESL, sports, art/fine arts, computer instruction programs offered; session focuses on humanities and math, study skills, technology in academics and the arts, outdoor adventure education; held on campus; accepts boys and girls; open to students from other schools. 50 students usually enrolled. 2006 schedule: June 25 to August 4. Application deadline: June 1.

Tuition and Aid Day student tuition: $20,720; 7-day tuition and room/board: $34,980. Tuition installment plan (Insured Tuition Payment Plan, Academic Management Services Plan, Key Tuition Payment Plan). Need-based scholarship grants, Sallie Mae Loans, TERI Loans, PrepGATE Loans available. In 2005–06, 28% of upper-school students received aid. Total amount of financial aid awarded in 2005–06: $1,600,000.

Admissions Traditional secondary-level entrance grade is 9. For fall 2005, 502 students applied for upper-level admission, 275 were accepted, 159 enrolled. SSAT required. Deadline for receipt of application materials: February 1. Application fee required: $35. On-campus interview required.

Athletics Interscholastic: alpine skiing (boys, girls), baseball (b), basketball (b,g), crew (b,g), cross-country running (b,g), field hockey (g), ice hockey (b,g), lacrosse (b,g), nordic skiing (b,g), skiing (cross-country) (b,g), skiing (downhill) (b,g), soccer (b,g), softball (g), tennis (b,g); coed interscholastic: sailing; coed intramural: aerobics, alpine skiing, climbing, dance, equestrian sports, fitness, golf, outdoor skills, rappelling, rock climbing, sailing, skiing (downhill), snowboarding, strength & conditioning, tennis, touch football, wall climbing, weight training, yoga. 1 trainer.

Computers Computers are regularly used in all classes. Computer network features include campus e-mail, on-campus library services, CD-ROMs, online commercial services, Internet access, file transfer, DVD.

Contact Peg Radley, Admission Coordinator. 603-569-7200. Fax: 603-569-7272. E-mail: peg_radley@brewsteracademy.org. Web site: www.brewsteracademy.org.

ANNOUNCEMENT FROM THE SCHOOL Brewster has become known worldwide for innovation and performance in secondary education. The Brewster program is designed to meet students at their current level of performance and accelerate them in their mastery of skills and knowledge, ensuring that Brewster graduates are prepared for the challenges of college and life after college.

See full description on page 694.

BRIDGES ACADEMY

Studio City, California
See Special Needs Schools section.

BRIDGE SCHOOL

6717 South Boulder Road
Boulder, Colorado 80303-4319
Head of School: Ms. Gretchen Lang

General Information Coeducational day college-preparatory, arts, and technology school. Grades 6–12. Founded: 1994. Setting: suburban. 22-acre campus. 1 building on campus. Approved or accredited by North Central Association of Colleges and Schools and Colorado Department of Education. Endowment: $200,000. Total enrollment: 105. Upper school average class size: 10. Upper school faculty-student ratio: 1:6.

Faculty School total: 19. In upper school: 4 men, 8 women; 4 have advanced degrees.

Subjects Offered Advanced math, algebra, American culture, American democracy, American history, American literature, ancient world history, applied arts, applied music, art, art appreciation, art education, Basic programming, British literature, calculus, chemistry, civics, comparative cultures, computer animation, computers, constitutional history of U.S., contemporary history, drama performance, ecology, environmental systems, English, English composition, English literature, European civilization, European history, European literature, foreign language, French, geometry, government/civics, history, Japanese, language arts, mathematics, music, philosophy, physics, pre-algebra, SAT preparation, science and technology, senior project, Shakespeare, Spanish, student government, U.S. government, volleyball, wilderness experience, world governments, world history.

Graduation Requirements Art, arts and fine arts (art, music, dance, drama), computer literacy, English, foreign language, mathematics, social studies (includes history).

Special Academic Programs Accelerated programs; independent study; academic accommodation for the gifted; programs in English, mathematics for dyslexic students.

College Placement 17 students graduated in 2005; 14 went to college, including Colorado State University; University of Colorado at Boulder; University of Oregon. Other: 1 entered military service, 2 had other specific plans.

Student Life Upper grades have student council. Discipline rests equally with students and faculty.

Tuition and Aid Day student tuition: $10,800. Tuition installment plan (individually arranged payment plans). Need-based scholarship grants available. In 2005–06, 10% of upper-school students received aid. Total amount of financial aid awarded in 2005–06: $40,000.

Admissions Achievement tests required. Deadline for receipt of application materials: none. Application fee required: $50. Interview required.

Athletics Interscholastic: basketball (boys, girls), bicycling (b). 2 coaches.

Computers Computers are regularly used in English, history, journalism classes. Computer network features include CD-ROMs, Internet access, file transfer, office computer access.

Contact Ms. Gretchen Lang, Head of schol. 303-494-7551. Fax: 303-494-7558. E-mail: glang4@indra.com. Web site: www.bridgeschool.net.

BRIDGTON ACADEMY

PO Box 292
North Bridgton, Maine 04057
Head of School: Mr. David N. Hursty

petersons.com

General Information Boys' boarding and day college-preparatory and technology school. Grade PG. Founded: 1808. Setting: small town. Nearest major city is Portland. Students are housed in single-sex dormitories. 50-acre campus. 22 buildings on campus. Approved or accredited by Association of Independent Schools in New England, Independent Schools of Northern New England, New England Association of Schools and Colleges, The Association of Boarding Schools, The College Board, and Maine Department of Education. Member of National Association of Independent Schools. Endowment: $3.6 million. Total enrollment: 190. Upper school average class size: 10. Upper school faculty-student ratio: 1:10.

Upper School Student Profile Postgraduate: 190 students (190 boys). 98% of students are boarding students. 15% are state residents. 26 states are represented in upper school student body. 1% are international students. International students from Canada; 1 other country represented in student body.

Faculty School total: 21. In upper school: 18 men, 3 women; 8 have advanced degrees; 17 reside on campus.

Subjects Offered Advanced chemistry, algebra, anatomy and physiology, calculus, chemistry, constitutional history of U.S., contemporary issues, English, English-AP, environmental science-AP, geometry, intro to computers, oceanography, physics, political science, pre-calculus, SAT/ACT preparation, sociology, trigonometry, U.S. constitutional history, U.S. government, Web site design, Western civilization, writing.

Graduation Requirements Computers, English, mathematics, science, social studies (includes history), minimal cumulative GPA of 1.7 (C-) in all classes; students must pass all classes during second semester.

Special Academic Programs Study at local college for college credit; special instructional classes for students with Attention Deficit Disorder.

College Placement 160 students graduated in 2004; 157 went to college, including Bryant University; Plymouth State University; Sacred Heart University; Saint Anselm College; Syracuse University; United States Naval Academy. Other: 3 had other specific plans.

Student Life Upper grades have specified standards of dress, student council. Discipline rests primarily with faculty.

Tuition and Aid Day student tuition: $15,000; 7-day tuition and room/board: $30,400. Tuition installment plan (Academic Management Services Plan, Key Tuition Payment Plan, FACTS Tuition Payment Plan, individually arranged payment plans, 3-payment plan, 8-payment plan). Need-based scholarship grants available. In 2004–05, 50% of upper-school students received aid. Total amount of financial aid awarded in 2004–05: $1,200,000.

Admissions For fall 2005, 352 students applied for upper-level admission, 272 were accepted, 190 enrolled. ACT or SAT required. Deadline for receipt of application materials: none. Application fee required: $45. Interview required.

Athletics Interscholastic: alpine skiing (boys), baseball (b), basketball (b), football (b), golf (b), hockey (b), ice hockey (b), lacrosse (b), skiing (downhill) (b), snowboarding (b), soccer (b), tennis (b); intramural: alpine skiing (b), basketball (b), bicycling (b), canoeing/kayaking (b), hiking/backpacking (b), hockey (b), ice hockey (b), ice skating (b), nautilus (b), nordic skiing (b), outdoor activities (b), paddle tennis (b), paint ball (b), skiing (cross-country) (b), skiing (downhill) (b), snowboarding (b), snowshoeing (b), softball (b), strength & conditioning (b), table tennis (b), volleyball (b), weight lifting (b), weight training (b). 1 trainer.

Computers Computers are regularly used in English, history, mathematics, science classes. Computer network features include on-campus library services, CD-ROMs, online commercial services, Internet access, wireless campus network.

Contact Ms. Lisa M. Antell, Director of Admission and Financial Aid. 207-647-3322 Ext. 208. Fax: 207-647-8513. E-mail: admit@bridgtonacademy.org. Web site: www.bridgtonacademy.org.

See full description on page 696.

BRITISH COLUMBIA CHRISTIAN ACADEMY

3550 Wellington Street
Port Coquitlam, British Columbia V3B 3Y5, Canada
Head of School: Mr. Ian M. Jarvie

General Information Coeducational day college-preparatory, general academic, religious studies, and technology school. Grades PK–12. Founded: 1993. Setting: suburban. Nearest major city is Vancouver, Canada. 12-acre campus. 2 buildings on campus. Approved or accredited by Association of Christian Schools International and British Columbia Department of Education. Language of instruction: English. Total enrollment: 266. Upper school average class size: 20. Upper school faculty-student ratio: 1:5.

Faculty School total: 25. In upper school: 8 men, 4 women; 2 have advanced degrees.

Subjects Offered Acting, applied skills, art, athletic training, athletics, Bible, biology, business education, calculus, career and personal planning, chemistry, choir, computer applications, computer keyboarding, culinary arts, desktop publishing, digital photography, drama, English, fitness, foods, French, geography, golf, guitar, information technology, Japanese, jazz band, leadership, mathematics, multimedia, physics, science, social studies.

Graduation Requirements Applied skills, arts and fine arts (art, music, dance, drama), career and personal planning, English, language, mathematics, science, social studies (includes history).

Special Academic Programs Independent study; ESL (15 students enrolled).

College Placement 17 students graduated in 2005; 15 went to college, including McGill University; Simon Fraser University; The University of British Columbia. Other: 1 went to work, 1 had other specific plans.

Student Life Upper grades have uniform requirement, student council, honor system. Discipline rests primarily with faculty. Attendance at religious services is required.

Summer Programs ESL, sports, computer instruction programs offered; session focuses on ESL and sports; held on campus; accepts boys and girls; open to students from other schools. 100 students usually enrolled. 2006 schedule: July 4 to August 26. Application deadline: June 15.

Tuition and Aid Day student tuition: CAN$3888–CAN$4243. Tuition installment plan (monthly payment plans). Tuition reduction for siblings, bursaries available. In 2005–06, 3% of upper-school students received aid. Total amount of financial aid awarded in 2005–06: CAN$25,000.

Admissions Deadline for receipt of application materials: none. Application fee required: CAN$100. Interview recommended.

Athletics Interscholastic: badminton (boys, girls), baseball (b,g), basketball (b,g), soccer (b), track and field (b,g), volleyball (b,g); intramural: baseball (b,g), basketball (b,g), track and field (b,g), volleyball (b,g); coed intramural: badminton, outdoor recreation, physical fitness, soccer. 2 PE instructors, 4 coaches.

Computers Computers are regularly used in desktop publishing, independent study, information technology, multimedia, publishing, remedial study skills, yearbook classes. Computer network features include campus e-mail, CD-ROMs, Internet access, file transfer, DVD.

Contact Ms. Inez Diikstra, Administrative Assistant. 604-941-8426. Fax: 604-945-6455. E-mail: admissions@bcchristianacademy.ca. Web site: www.bcchristianacademy.ca.

THE BRITISH INTERNATIONAL SCHOOL, JEDDAH

PO Box 6453
Jeddah 21442, Saudi Arabia
Head of School: Mr. Bruce Gamwell

General Information Coeducational day college-preparatory and general academic school. Grades 6–12. Founded: 1977. Setting: suburban. 4-hectare campus. 3 buildings on campus. Approved or accredited by European Council of International Schools and New England Association of Schools and Colleges. Language of instruction: English. Total enrollment: 623. Upper school average class size: 21. Upper school faculty-student ratio: 1:10.

Upper School Student Profile Grade 6: 100 students (55 boys, 45 girls); Grade 7: 100 students (58 boys, 42 girls); Grade 8: 100 students (54 boys, 46 girls); Grade 9: 100 students (57 boys, 43 girls); Grade 10: 100 students (55 boys, 45 girls); Grade 11: 67 students (37 boys, 30 girls); Grade 12: 56 students (31 boys, 25 girls).

Faculty School total: 59. In upper school: 26 men, 33 women; 15 have advanced degrees.

Subjects Offered 20th century world history, 3-dimensional art, advanced chemistry, advanced math, algebra, Arabic, art, arts and crafts, biology, British history, British literature, British National Curriculum, business studies, calculus, career/college preparation, chemistry, community service, computer music, computer studies, concert band, concert choir, desktop publishing, drama, drawing and design, economics, electronic music, English as a foreign language, English composition, English literature, environmental geography, ESL, expository writing, French, French as a second language, general math, general science, geography, geometry, grammar, graphic design, guidance, guitar, information technology, inorganic chemistry, instrumental music, International Baccalaureate courses, Islamic history, jazz band, lab science, language arts, library skills, literature, math methods, mathematics, model United Nations, modern languages, multicultural literature, music appreciation, music composition, music performance, music technology, music theory, natural history, oral

communications, organic chemistry, painting, personal and social education, physical education, physics, piano, poetry, probability and statistics, reading, reading/study skills, SAT preparation, Shakespeare, silk screening, space and physical sciences, Spanish, Spanish literature, swimming competency, wind instruments, world geography, world history, world literature, World War II, writing.

Special Academic Programs International Baccalaureate program; academic accommodation for the gifted, the musically talented, and the artistically talented; remedial reading and/or remedial writing; remedial math; programs in English, general development for dyslexic students; ESL (17 students enrolled).

College Placement 46 students graduated in 2005; all went to college.

Student Life Upper grades have specified standards of dress, student council, honor system. Discipline rests equally with students and faculty.

Tuition and Aid Day student tuition: 33,900 Saudi riyal–50,100 Saudi riyal. Bursaries available. In 2005–06, 1% of upper-school students received aid. Total amount of financial aid awarded in 2005–06: 200,000 Saudi riyal.

Admissions Traditional secondary-level entrance grade is 11. For fall 2005, 12 students applied for upper-level admission, 8 were accepted, 8 enrolled. Admissions testing required. Deadline for receipt of application materials: none. Application fee required: 600 Saudi riyal. Interview required.

Athletics Interscholastic: cricket (boys); intramural: aerobics (g), badminton (b,g), basketball (b,g), canoeing/kayaking (b,g), cricket (b), fitness (b,g); coed interscholastic: basketball; coed intramural: badminton, ball hockey, basketball, bowling, climbing. 2 PE instructors.

Computers Computers are regularly used in English, graphic design, information technology, mathematics, music, science classes. Computer network features include on-campus library services, CD-ROMs, Internet access, office computer access, Intranet.

Contact Mrs. Marina Alibhai, Registrar. 966-26990019 Ext. 219. Fax: 966-26991943. E-mail: conti@conti.sch.sa. Web site: www.continentalschool.com.

THE BRITISH SCHOOL, MUSCAT

PO Box 1907
Ruwi 112, Oman
Head of School: Mr. Steve Howland

General Information Coeducational day college-preparatory and general academic school. Ungraded, ages 3–18. Founded: 1971. Setting: suburban. Nearest major city is Muscat. 7 buildings on campus. Approved or accredited by European Council of International Schools. Language of instruction: English. Total enrollment: 765. Upper school average class size: 18. Upper school faculty-student ratio: 1:11.

Faculty School total: 62. In upper school: 15 men, 15 women.

Subjects Offered Biology, British National Curriculum, business studies, chemistry, community service, drama, English, English literature, French, geography, German, graphics, history, information technology, mathematics, modern languages, music, music technology, personal development, physical education, psychology, reading, science, sports, theater, writing.

Special Academic Programs Special instructional classes for students with Attention Deficit Disorder and dyslexia; ESL (10 students enrolled).

College Placement 15 students graduated in 2005; 14 went to college.

Student Life Upper grades have uniform requirement, student council, honor system. Discipline rests primarily with faculty.

Tuition and Aid Day student tuition: 3210 Omani rials–4470 Omani rials.

Admissions Traditional secondary-level entrance age is 11. ACT, CAT, Cognitive Abilities Test, SAT or school's own test required. Deadline for receipt of application materials: none. No application fee required. Interview required.

Athletics Interscholastic: football (boys); intramural: basketball (b), cricket (b), dance (g), football (b), indoor soccer (b); coed interscholastic: hockey; coed intramural: badminton, equestrian sports, hockey, judo, outdoor education. 5 PE instructors, 1 coach.

Computers Computer network features include CD-ROMs, Internet access, office computer access, wireless campus network.

Contact Mrs. Deirdre Selway, Registrar. 00968 24600842. Fax: 00968 24601062. E-mail: registrar@britishschool.edu.om. Web site: www.britishschool.edu.om.

BROADVIEW ACADEMY

PO Box 307
La Fox, Illinois 60147
Head of School: Dr. Randall J. Siebold

General Information Coeducational boarding and day college-preparatory, general academic, arts, religious studies, bilingual studies, and technology school, affiliated with Seventh-day Adventist Church. Grades 9–12. Founded: 1909. Setting: suburban. Nearest major city is Geneva. Students are housed in single-sex dormitories. 133-acre campus. 5 buildings on campus. Approved or accredited by Board of Regents, General Conference of Seventh-day Adventists, North Central Association of Colleges and Schools, and Illinois Department of Education. Endowment: $550,000. Total enrollment: 82. Upper school average class size: 20. Upper school faculty-student ratio: 1:8.

Upper School Student Profile Grade 9: 21 students (11 boys, 10 girls); Grade 10: 24 students (16 boys, 8 girls); Grade 11: 16 students (8 boys, 8 girls); Grade 12: 21 students (9 boys, 12 girls). 79% of students are boarding students. 85% are state residents. 6 states are represented in upper school student body. 7% are international students. International students from Panama, Republic of Korea, and Thailand. 75% of students are Seventh-day Adventists.

Faculty School total: 14. In upper school: 9 men, 5 women; 5 have advanced degrees; 12 reside on campus.

Subjects Offered ACT preparation, advanced math, algebra, anatomy and physiology, art, auto mechanics, band, Bible, biology, campus ministry, career/college preparation, chemistry, choir, community service, concert band, creative writing, drama, driver education, earth science, English, English composition, ESL, geometry, government, guidance, health, history, music, newspaper, physical education, physics, piano, religion, SAT preparation, Shakespeare, Spanish, U.S. constitutional history, U.S. government, U.S. history, word processing, yearbook.

Graduation Requirements Advanced math, algebra, biology, chemistry, constitutional history of U.S., earth science, English, geometry, government, physical education (includes health), religion (includes Bible studies and theology), Spanish, U.S. government, U.S. history, world history.

Special Academic Programs Accelerated programs; independent study; ESL (6 students enrolled).

College Placement 10 students graduated in 2005; all went to college, including Andrews University; Oakwood College; Southern Adventist University. Median composite ACT: 20.

Student Life Upper grades have specified standards of dress, student council, honor system. Discipline rests primarily with faculty. Attendance at religious services is required.

Tuition and Aid Day student tuition: $7600; 7-day tuition and room/board: $11,900. Guaranteed tuition plan. Tuition installment plan (monthly payment plans). Tuition reduction for siblings, merit scholarship grants, need-based scholarship grants, paying campus jobs available. In 2005–06, 85% of upper-school students received aid; total upper-school merit-scholarship money awarded: $13,935. Total amount of financial aid awarded in 2005–06: $67,000.

Admissions Traditional secondary-level entrance grade is 9. For fall 2005, 51 students applied for upper-level admission, 51 were accepted, 48 enrolled. Deadline for receipt of application materials: none. No application fee required. Interview required.

Athletics Interscholastic: basketball (boys, girls), indoor soccer (b), soccer (b), volleyball (g); coed intramural: flag football, softball. 2 PE instructors, 1 coach.

Computers Computers are regularly used in newspaper, SAT preparation, Spanish, yearbook classes. Computer network features include campus e-mail, on-campus library services, CD-ROMs, Internet access, DVD.

Contact Tamara Keplinger, Registrar. 630-232-7441 Ext. 1221. Fax: 630-232-7443. E-mail: tkeplinger@broadviewacademy.org. Web site: www.broadview.org.

THE BROOK HILL SCHOOL

PO Box 668
Bullard, Texas 75757
Head of School: Rod Fletcher

General Information Coeducational boarding and day college-preparatory, arts, technology, and music school, affiliated with Christian faith. Boarding grades 8–12, day grades 6–12. Founded: 1997. Setting: small town. Nearest major city is Tyler. Students are housed in single-sex houses for 16 students. 120-acre campus. 7 buildings on campus. Approved or accredited by Association of Christian Schools International, Southern Association of Colleges and Schools, The Association of Boarding Schools, and The College Board. Endowment: $30,000. Total enrollment: 184. Upper school average class size: 15. Upper school faculty-student ratio: 1:7.

Upper School Student Profile Grade 9: 36 students (19 boys, 17 girls); Grade 10: 23 students (11 boys, 12 girls); Grade 11: 31 students (20 boys, 11 girls); Grade 12: 19 students (11 boys, 8 girls). 18% of students are boarding students. 88% are state residents. 1 state is represented in upper school student body. 12% are international students. International students from Ghana, Japan, Mexico, Republic of Korea, and Taiwan; 5 other countries represented in student body.

Faculty School total: 35. In upper school: 11 men, 9 women; 16 have advanced degrees; 3 reside on campus.

Subjects Offered 1½ elective credits, ACT preparation, advanced chemistry, advanced math, Advanced Placement courses, algebra, American government, American government-AP, American history-AP, American literature-AP, analysis and differential calculus, anatomy and physiology, ancient history, ancient world history, art, athletics, baseball, basketball, Bible as literature, Bible studies, biology, British literature, British literature-AP, calculus, calculus-AP, career/college preparation, chemistry, chemistry-AP, choir, choral music, Christian ethics, Christian studies, civics/free enterprise, classics, college admission preparation, college awareness, college writing, communication skills, community service, comparative religion, composition, composition-AP, computer applications, computer education, conceptual physics, concert choir, creation science, drama, drama performance, dramatic arts, drawing, economics, economics-AP, English, English composition, English language and composition-AP, English language-AP, English literature, English literature and composition-AP, English literature-AP, English/composition-AP, ensembles, epic

literature, ESL, European history, European history-AP, European literature, fine arts, foreign language, four units of summer reading, French, French as a second language, geometry, government, government and politics-AP, government-AP, great books, health, history-AP, honors algebra, honors English, honors geometry, human biology, lab science, Latin, leadership and service, literary genres, literature and composition-AP, logic, logic, rhetoric, and debate, mathematics-AP, modern European history-AP, modern languages, orchestra, painting, physical education, physics, physiology-anatomy, pre-calculus, public speaking, rhetoric, SAT preparation, SAT/ACT preparation, senior project, Spanish, speech communications, stagecraft, strings, student government, student publications, theater arts, TOEFL preparation, U.S. government and politics, U.S. history, U.S. history-AP, volleyball, yearbook.

Graduation Requirements Arts and fine arts (art, music, dance, drama), Bible, economics, electives, English, foreign language, government, history, lab science, mathematics, physical education (includes health). Community service is required.

Special Academic Programs Honors section; study at local college for college credit; academic accommodation for the musically talented; ESL (10 students enrolled).

College Placement 27 students graduated in 2005; 25 went to college, including Baylor University; Belhaven College; Oklahoma State University; Stephen F. Austin State University; The University of Texas at Austin. Other: 1 went to work, 1 had other specific plans. Mean SAT math: 638, mean composite ACT: 22.

Student Life Upper grades have uniform requirement, student council, honor system. Discipline rests equally with students and faculty. Attendance at religious services is required.

Summer Programs Enrichment, advancement, ESL, sports, art/fine arts programs offered; session focuses on enrichment; held on campus; accepts boys and girls; open to students from other schools. 125 students usually enrolled. 2006 schedule: June 1 to August 1. Application deadline: none.

Tuition and Aid Day student tuition: $7395; 5-day tuition and room/board: $18,155; 7-day tuition and room/board: $23,415. Tuition installment plan (FACTS Tuition Payment Plan, individually arranged payment plans). Need-based scholarship grants available. In 2005–06, 50% of upper-school students received aid. Total amount of financial aid awarded in 2005–06: $280,000.

Admissions Traditional secondary-level entrance grade is 9. For fall 2005, 27 students applied for upper-level admission, 24 were accepted, 24 enrolled. ITBS achievement test, ITBS-TAP, SSAT or TOEFL or SLEP required. Deadline for receipt of application materials: none. Application fee required: $35. Interview recommended.

Athletics Interscholastic: baseball (boys, girls), basketball (b,g), cheering (g), cross-country running (b,g), football (b), golf (b,g), independent competitive sports (b,g), physical fitness (b,g), physical training (b,g), soccer (b), softball (g), tennis (b,g), track and field (b,g), volleyball (g), weight training (b,g); intramural: baseball (b), basketball (b,g), flag football (b,g); coed interscholastic: soccer, tennis; coed intramural: flag football. 3 coaches.

Computers Computers are regularly used in all classes. Computer network features include campus e-mail, CD-ROMs, Internet access, wireless campus network.

Contact Mrs. Terry Ellis, Assistant to Admissions and Marketing. 903-894-5000 Ext. 42. Fax: 903-894-6332. E-mail: admissions@brookhill.org. Web site: www.brookhill.org/.

See full description on page 698.

BROOKLYN FRIENDS SCHOOL

375 Pearl Street
Brooklyn, New York 11201
Head of School: Dr. Michael Nill

General Information Coeducational day college-preparatory, general academic, and arts school, affiliated with Society of Friends. Grades PS–12. Founded: 1867. Setting: urban. Nearest major city is New York. 2 buildings on campus. Approved or accredited by New York State Association of Independent Schools and New York Department of Education. Member of National Association of Independent Schools. Total enrollment: 521. Upper school average class size: 15. Upper school faculty-student ratio: 1:7.

Upper School Student Profile Grade 9: 34 students (15 boys, 19 girls); Grade 10: 42 students (19 boys, 23 girls); Grade 11: 43 students (19 boys, 24 girls); Grade 12: 35 students (13 boys, 22 girls). 3% of students are members of Society of Friends.

Faculty School total: 110. In upper school: 18 men, 20 women; 24 have advanced degrees.

Subjects Offered 20th century world history, 3-dimensional art, acting, advanced chemistry, advanced computer applications, advanced math, Advanced Placement courses, African-American literature, algebra, art, art appreciation, art history, astronomy, biology, biology-AP, calculus-AP, ceramics, chemistry, chorus, civil rights, college counseling, computer animation, computer applications, computer literacy, conflict resolution, contemporary women writers, dance, dance performance, Danish, digital applications, digital photography, directing, drama, drawing, ecology, engineering, environmental science, ethics, European history, fiction, film appreciation, film history, filmmaking, French, French language-AP, freshman foundations, geometry, Harlem Renaissance, health, history of mathematics, Holocaust and other genocides, humanities, Japanese, jazz ensemble, journalism, Latin, Latin American history, Latin-AP, life skills, math analysis, media literacy, media studies, musical

theater, oceanography, orchestra, painting, photography, physical education, physical science, physics, physics-AP, play/screen writing, playwriting, poetry, pre-calculus, programming, psychology, Quakerism and ethics, radio broadcasting, religion, religious studies, research techniques, robotics, science project, science research, Shakespeare, Spanish, Spanish-AP, statistics, student government, study skills, television, theater design and production, theater production, trigonometry, U.S. history, U.S. literature, utopia, video, water color painting, weight training, women's literature, world cultures, writing, yearbook, yoga.

Graduation Requirements Arts, computer literacy, English, foreign language, history, mathematics, physical education (includes health), Quakerism and ethics, religion (includes Bible studies and theology), science, study skills, 100 Hours of community service (20 hours in-school, 80 hours out-of-school), 3-year arts requirement, including 1 visual and 1 performing art.

Special Academic Programs Domestic exchange program; study abroad.

College Placement 40 students graduated in 2005; all went to college, including Amherst College; Fordham University; Oberlin College; Temple University; Wesleyan University.

Student Life Upper grades have specified standards of dress, student council, honor system. Discipline rests equally with students and faculty.

Tuition and Aid Day student tuition: $24,300. Tuition installment plan (Insured Tuition Payment Plan, Key Tuition Payment Plan). Need-based scholarship grants available. In 2005–06, 33% of upper-school students received aid. Total amount of financial aid awarded in 2005–06: $764,200.

Admissions Traditional secondary-level entrance grade is 9. ISEE required. Deadline for receipt of application materials: December 9. Application fee required: $75. On-campus interview required.

Athletics Interscholastic: baseball (boys), basketball (b,g), soccer (b,g), softball (g), volleyball (g); coed interscholastic: cross-country running. 3 PE instructors, 22 coaches.

Computers Computers are regularly used in English, history, library skills, mathematics, media arts, media production, newspaper, science, theology, video film production, yearbook classes. Computer network features include campus e-mail, CD-ROMs, Internet access, DVD, wireless campus network, school-wide Intranet.

Contact Karine Blemur-Chapman, Associate Director of Admissions. 718-852-1029 Ext. 253. Fax: 718-643-4868. E-mail: kbchapman@brooklynfriends.org. Web site: www.brooklynfriends.org.

BROOKS SCHOOL

1160 Great Pond Road
North Andover, Massachusetts 01845-1298
Head of School: Lawrence W. Becker

General Information Coeducational boarding and day college-preparatory school, affiliated with Episcopal Church. Grades 9–12. Founded: 1926. Setting: suburban. Nearest major city is Boston. Students are housed in single-sex dormitories. 251-acre campus. 39 buildings on campus. Approved or accredited by New England Association of Schools and Colleges, The Association of Boarding Schools, and Massachusetts Department of Education. Member of National Association of Independent Schools and Secondary School Admission Test Board. Endowment: $61.4 million. Total enrollment: 354. Upper school average class size: 12. Upper school faculty-student ratio: 1:5.

Upper School Student Profile Grade 9: 86 students (50 boys, 36 girls); Grade 10: 83 students (51 boys, 32 girls); Grade 11: 99 students (47 boys, 52 girls); Grade 12: 86 students (46 boys, 40 girls). 70% of students are boarding students. 28% are state residents. 21 states are represented in upper school student body. 8% are international students. International students from Hong Kong, Nigeria, Republic of Korea, Saudi Arabia, and Thailand; 8 other countries represented in student body.

Faculty School total: 73. In upper school: 38 men, 35 women; 54 have advanced degrees; 39 reside on campus.

Subjects Offered Algebra, American government-AP, American history, American history-AP, American literature, art history, art history-AP, astronomy, Bible studies, biology, biology-AP, calculus, calculus-AP, ceramics, chemistry, chemistry-AP, computer graphics, computer math, computer programming, computer science, creative writing, dance, drama, driver education, earth science, English, English literature, English-AP, environmental science-AP, ethics, etymology, European history, European history-AP, expository writing, film, fine arts, French, French language-AP, French literature-AP, geology, geometry, grammar, Greek, health, history, integrated arts, Irish literature, Italian, journalism, Latin, Latin-AP, mathematics, Middle East, music, oceanography, ornithology, painting, philosophy, photography, physics, physics-AP, poetry, psychology, religion, rhetoric, robotics, Spanish, Spanish language-AP, Spanish literature-AP, statistics, statistics-AP, studio art, theater, theology, trigonometry, world history, world literature, writing.

Graduation Requirements Arts and fine arts (art, music, dance, drama), English, foreign language, history, mathematics, religion (includes Bible studies and theology), science.

Special Academic Programs Advanced Placement exam preparation in 14 subject areas; honors section; independent study; term-away projects; study abroad.

College Placement 86 students graduated in 2005; 84 went to college, including Bates College; Boston College; Georgetown University; Hobart and William Smith

Colleges; Tufts University; University of Vermont. Other: 2 entered a postgraduate year. 43% scored over 600 on SAT verbal, 51% scored over 600 on SAT math.
Student Life Upper grades have specified standards of dress, student council, honor system. Discipline rests primarily with faculty. Attendance at religious services is required.
Summer Programs Enrichment, advancement, sports, computer instruction programs offered; session focuses on English, mathematics, and SAT preparation; held on campus; accepts boys and girls; open to students from other schools. 70 students usually enrolled. 2006 schedule: June 28 to August 20. Application deadline: none.
Tuition and Aid Day student tuition: $25,400; 7-day tuition and room/board: $34,440. Tuition installment plan (Academic Management Services Plan, Key Tuition Payment Plan, individually arranged payment plans). Need-based scholarship grants available. In 2005–06, 21% of upper-school students received aid. Total amount of financial aid awarded in 2005–06: $1,910,000.
Admissions Traditional secondary-level entrance grade is 9. For fall 2005, 824 students applied for upper-level admission, 281 were accepted, 116 enrolled. SSAT, ERB, PSAT, SAT, PLAN or ACT required. Deadline for receipt of application materials: February 1. Application fee required: $75. Interview required.
Athletics Interscholastic: baseball (boys), basketball (b,g), crew (b,g), cross-country running (b,g), field hockey (g), football (b), hockey (b,g), ice hockey (b,g), lacrosse (b,g), soccer (b,g), softball (g), squash (b,g), tennis (b,g), wrestling (b); coed intramural: fitness, golf, sailing, skiing (downhill). 1 trainer.
Computers Computers are regularly used in all academic classes. Computer network features include campus e-mail, on-campus library services, CD-ROMs, online commercial services, Internet access, file transfer, office computer access, DVD, wireless campus network.
Contact Judith S. Beams, Director of Admission. 978-725-6272. Fax: 978-725-6298. E-mail: admission@brooksschool.org. Web site: www.brooksschool.org.

ANNOUNCEMENT FROM THE SCHOOL Brooks School's broad academic curriculum includes 19 Advanced Placement (AP) courses and provides a rigorous college-preparatory program with varied opportunities for challenge. In support of a strong athletic program, the School has just completed a new athletic center.

See full description on page 700.

BROOKSTONE SCHOOL

440 Bradley Park Drive
Columbus, Georgia 31904-2989
Head of School: Scott A. Wilson

petersons.com

General Information Coeducational day college-preparatory school. Grades PK–12. Founded: 1951. Setting: suburban. Nearest major city is Atlanta. 112-acre campus. 11 buildings on campus. Approved or accredited by Georgia Independent School Association, Southern Association of Colleges and Schools, Southern Association of Independent Schools, and Georgia Department of Education. Member of National Association of Independent Schools. Endowment: $18.9 million. Total enrollment: 853. Upper school average class size: 14. Upper school faculty-student ratio: 1:11.
Upper School Student Profile Grade 9: 74 students (42 boys, 32 girls); Grade 10: 67 students (34 boys, 33 girls); Grade 11: 69 students (29 boys, 40 girls); Grade 12: 73 students (31 boys, 42 girls).
Faculty School total: 70. In upper school: 15 men, 16 women; 21 have advanced degrees.
Subjects Offered Algebra, American government, American history, American literature, anatomy, art, band, biology, calculus, calculus-AP, chemistry, chemistry-AP, communications, comparative government and politics-AP, comparative religion, computer applications, computer programming, computer science, computer science-AP, drama, ecology, economics, English, English composition, English literature, European history, European history-AP, fine arts, French, French-AP, geometry, health, history-AP, humanities, Latin, Latin-AP, literature and composition-AP, mathematics, mythology, neuroanatomy, ornithology, physical education, physics, physics-AP, physiology, pre-calculus, psychology, science, social science, social studies, Southern literature, Spanish, Spanish-AP, statistics, statistics-AP, theater, trigonometry, U.S. history-AP, world history, yearbook, zoology.
Graduation Requirements Arts and fine arts (art, music, dance, drama), composition, computer science, English, foreign language, mathematics, physical education (includes health), science, social science, social studies (includes history), speech, senior year speech.
Special Academic Programs Advanced Placement exam preparation in 13 subject areas; honors section; independent study.
College Placement 53 students graduated in 2005; all went to college, including Auburn University; Columbus State University; Furman University; University of Georgia; University of Mississippi; Vanderbilt University. Median SAT verbal: 580, median SAT math: 570. 40% scored over 600 on SAT verbal, 38% scored over 600 on SAT math.
Student Life Upper grades have specified standards of dress, student council, honor system. Discipline rests equally with students and faculty.

Tuition and Aid Day student tuition: $10,270. Tuition installment plan (monthly payment plans, individually arranged payment plans, 3 payments in months July, November, and February (no interest)). Tuition reduction for siblings, merit scholarship grants, need-based scholarship grants, need-based loans, middle-income loans available. In 2005–06, 15% of upper-school students received aid; total upper-school merit-scholarship money awarded: $211,965. Total amount of financial aid awarded in 2005–06: $284,310.
Admissions Traditional secondary-level entrance grade is 9. For fall 2005, 70 students applied for upper-level admission, 51 were accepted, 23 enrolled. Stanford Achievement Test required. Deadline for receipt of application materials: none. Application fee required: $35. On-campus interview required.
Athletics Interscholastic: baseball (boys), basketball (b,g), cheering (g), cross-country running (b,g), football (b), golf (b,g), soccer (b,g), softball (g), tennis (b,g), track and field (b,g), volleyball (g), wrestling (b); intramural: basketball (b,g), ultimate Frisbee (b); coed interscholastic: strength & conditioning. 4 PE instructors.
Computers Computers are regularly used in English, foreign language, French, history, information technology, mathematics, media production, Spanish, yearbook classes. Computer network features include campus e-mail, on-campus library services, CD-ROMs, online commercial services, Internet access, file transfer, DVD.
Contact Mary S. Snyder, Enrollment Director. 706-324-1392. Fax: 706-571-0178. E-mail: msnyder@brookstoneschool.org. Web site: www.brookstoneschool.org.

ANNOUNCEMENT FROM THE SCHOOL Based on the belief that education isn't received but achieved, Brookstone School fosters the high standards and solid values that enable its students to excel both inside and outside the classroom. The goal at Brookstone is to produce not just excellent scholars and athletes but also excellent citizens.

BROPHY COLLEGE PREPARATORY

4701 North Central Avenue
Phoenix, Arizona 85012-1797
Head of School: Mr. Edwin J. Hearn

General Information Boys' day college-preparatory, arts, religious studies, and technology school, affiliated with Roman Catholic Church (Jesuit order). Grades 9–12. Founded: 1928. Setting: urban. 27-acre campus. 9 buildings on campus. Approved or accredited by Jesuit Secondary Education Association, National Catholic Education Association, North Central Association of Colleges and Schools, and Western Catholic Education Association. Endowment: $18 million. Total enrollment: 1,233. Upper school average class size: 25. Upper school faculty-student ratio: 1:14.
Upper School Student Profile Grade 9: 340 students (340 boys); Grade 10: 323 students (323 boys); Grade 11: 292 students (292 boys); Grade 12: 279 students (279 boys). 64% of students are Roman Catholic Church (Jesuit order).
Faculty School total: 91. In upper school: 63 men, 25 women; 63 have advanced degrees.
Subjects Offered Advanced Placement courses, advanced studio art-AP, algebra, American history, American literature, anatomy, art, Bible studies, biology, business, calculus, chemistry, community service, computer math, computer programming, computer science, creative writing, drama, earth science, economics, engineering, English, English literature, ethics, European history, expository writing, fine arts, French, geography, geometry, government/civics, health, history, Latin, mathematics, mechanical drawing, music, physical education, physics, probability and statistics, psychology, religion, science, social science, social studies, sociology, Spanish, speech, theater, theology, trigonometry, video film production, world history, world literature.
Graduation Requirements Arts and fine arts (art, music, dance, drama), computer science, English, foreign language, mathematics, physical education (includes health), religion (includes Bible studies and theology), science, social science, social studies (includes history). Community service is required.
Special Academic Programs Advanced Placement exam preparation in 16 subject areas; honors section; independent study; study at local college for college credit; study abroad.
College Placement 260 students graduated in 2005; all went to college, including Arizona State University; Loyola Marymount University; Santa Clara University; Southern Methodist University; The University of Arizona; University of Southern California. Mean SAT verbal: 606, mean SAT math: 603, mean composite ACT: 26.
Student Life Upper grades have specified standards of dress, student council, honor system. Discipline rests primarily with faculty. Attendance at religious services is required.
Summer Programs Enrichment, advancement, sports, art/fine arts, computer instruction programs offered; session focuses on academic skills and sports; held both on and off campus; held at Manresa Retreat (Sedona, AZ) and Brophy East Campus; accepts boys and girls; open to students from other schools. 1300 students usually enrolled. 2006 schedule: May 30 to June 30. Application deadline: none.
Tuition and Aid Day student tuition: $9600. Tuition installment plan (The Tuition Plan, monthly payment plans, individually arranged payment plans). Paying campus jobs available. In 2005–06, 23% of upper-school students received aid. Total amount of financial aid awarded in 2005–06: $1,570,000.

Admissions Traditional secondary-level entrance grade is 9. For fall 2005, 565 students applied for upper-level admission, 370 were accepted, 340 enrolled. STS required. Deadline for receipt of application materials: January 25. Application fee required: $40. On-campus interview required.

Athletics Interscholastic: aquatics, baseball, basketball, cross-country running, diving, flagball, football, golf, ice hockey, soccer, swimming and diving, tennis, track and field, volleyball, wrestling; intramural: aquatics, badminton, baseball, basketball, bicycling, bowling, cheering, climbing, crew, cricket, fishing, fitness, flag football, Frisbee, golf, handball, hockey, ice hockey, lacrosse, mountain biking, outdoor activities, physical fitness, physical training, rock climbing, skiing (downhill), softball, strength & conditioning, table tennis, touch football, ultimate Frisbee, volleyball, wall climbing, water polo, weight lifting, weight training. 2 PE instructors, 15 coaches, 2 trainers.

Computers Computers are regularly used in all academic classes. Computer network features include campus e-mail, on-campus library services, CD-ROMs, online commercial services, Internet access, Blackboard, computer tablets.

Contact Ms. Amanda Thomson, Assistant Director of Admissions. 602-264-5291 Ext. 6233. Fax: 602-234-1669. E-mail: mthomson@brophyprep.org. Web site: www.brophyprep.org/.

BROTHER RICE HIGH SCHOOL
7101 Lahser Road
Bloomfield Hills, Michigan 48301
Head of School: Mr. John Birney

General Information Boys' day college-preparatory, arts, business, religious studies, and technology school, affiliated with Roman Catholic Church. Grades 9–12. Founded: 1960. Setting: suburban. Nearest major city is Detroit. 20-acre campus. 1 building on campus. Approved or accredited by North Central Association of Colleges and Schools and Michigan Department of Education. Total enrollment: 655. Upper school average class size: 22. Upper school faculty-student ratio: 1:13.

Upper School Student Profile Grade 9: 190 students (190 boys); Grade 10: 170 students (170 boys); Grade 11: 160 students (160 boys); Grade 12: 145 students (145 boys). 75% of students are Roman Catholic.

Faculty School total: 53. In upper school: 35 men, 11 women; 35 have advanced degrees.

Subjects Offered 20th century world history, accounting, algebra, American government, American government-AP, anatomy, anthropology, architectural drawing, art, band, biology, biology-AP, business law, calculus, calculus-AP, chemistry, choir, church history, computer science, computer science-AP, computers, concert band, creative writing, death and loss, debate, drama, earth science, economics, electronics, engineering, English, English composition, English language-AP, ensembles, European history, family living, forensics, French, French-AP, geometry, German, global science, health, jazz band, Latin, library science, literature, mathematics, mechanical drawing, music, music history, music theory, organic chemistry, photography, photojournalism, physical education, physics, physiology, pre-calculus, probability and statistics, psychology, social justice, Spanish, Spanish-AP, speech, studio art—AP, theology, trigonometry, U.S. history, U.S. history-AP, Western civilization, world geography, world religions.

Graduation Requirements Computer science, electives, English, foreign language, mathematics, physical education (includes health), science, social studies (includes history), speech, theology.

Special Academic Programs Advanced Placement exam preparation in 18 subject areas; honors section; remedial reading and/or remedial writing; remedial math.

College Placement 155 students graduated in 2005; all went to college, including Eastern Michigan University; Michigan State University; Oakland University; University of Michigan; Western Michigan University. Median SAT verbal: 630, median SAT math: 670, median composite ACT: 25. 65% scored over 600 on SAT verbal, 65% scored over 600 on SAT math, 55% scored over 26 on composite ACT.

Student Life Upper grades have specified standards of dress, student council, honor system. Discipline rests primarily with faculty. Attendance at religious services is required.

Summer Programs Remediation, enrichment, art/fine arts programs offered; session focuses on camps and enrichment; held on campus; accepts boys and girls; open to students from other schools. 200 students usually enrolled. 2006 schedule: June to August.

Tuition and Aid Day student tuition: $6700. Tuition installment plan (monthly payment plans). Merit scholarship grants, need-based scholarship grants available. In 2005–06, 22% of upper-school students received aid; total upper-school merit-scholarship money awarded: $100,000. Total amount of financial aid awarded in 2005–06: $150,000.

Admissions Traditional secondary-level entrance grade is 9. For fall 2005, 475 students applied for upper-level admission, 250 were accepted, 190 enrolled. SAS, STS-HSPT required. Deadline for receipt of application materials: July 31. No application fee required. Interview recommended.

Athletics Interscholastic: alpine skiing, baseball, basketball, cross-country running, diving, football, golf, hockey, ice hockey, lacrosse, skiing (downhill), soccer, swimming and diving, tennis, track and field, wrestling; intramural: basketball, bowling, fitness, football, paint ball, rugby, skiing (downhill), snowboarding, strength & conditioning, touch football, winter (indoor) track. 50 coaches, 1 trainer.

Computers Computer resources include CD-ROMs, online commercial services, Internet access.

Contact Mr. David D. Sofran, Director of Admissions. 248-647-2531 Ext. 123. Fax: 248-647-2532. E-mail: sofran@brrice.edu.

BROWNELL-TALBOT SCHOOL
400 North Happy Hollow Boulevard
Omaha, Nebraska 68132
Head of School: Dianne Desler

General Information Coeducational day college-preparatory school. Grades PS–12. Founded: 1863. Setting: suburban. 17-acre campus. 4 buildings on campus. Approved or accredited by Independent Schools Association of the Central States, North Central Association of Colleges and Schools, and Nebraska Department of Education. Member of National Association of Independent Schools and Educational Records Bureau. Endowment: $3 million. Total enrollment: 430. Upper school average class size: 15. Upper school faculty-student ratio: 1:9.

Upper School Student Profile Grade 9: 34 students (16 boys, 18 girls); Grade 10: 33 students (14 boys, 19 girls); Grade 11: 37 students (24 boys, 13 girls); Grade 12: 35 students (19 boys, 16 girls).

Faculty School total: 54. In upper school: 16 men, 13 women; 15 have advanced degrees.

Subjects Offered Algebra, American history, American literature, art, biology, business, calculus, chemistry, computer science, creative writing, dance, drama, earth science, economics, English, English literature, environmental science, European history, expository writing, French, geometry, government/civics, history, journalism, Latin, law, mathematics, music, physical education, physics, Spanish, speech, theater, trigonometry, world history, world literature, writing.

Graduation Requirements Arts and fine arts (art, music, dance, drama), computer science, English, foreign language, mathematics, physical education (includes health), religion (includes Bible studies and theology), science, social science, social studies (includes history).

Special Academic Programs Advanced Placement exam preparation in 13 subject areas; study at local college for college credit; academic accommodation for the gifted.

College Placement 29 students graduated in 2005; all went to college, including Boston University; Carnegie Mellon University; Creighton University; University of Pennsylvania; Vanderbilt University; Yale University.

Student Life Upper grades have uniform requirement, student council, honor system. Discipline rests primarily with faculty. Attendance at religious services is required.

Summer Programs Enrichment, sports programs offered; session focuses on chess, foreign language, robotics, sports; held on campus; accepts boys and girls; open to students from other schools. 100 students usually enrolled. 2006 schedule: June 12 to July 14. Application deadline: none.

Tuition and Aid Day student tuition: $11,400–$12,500. Tuition installment plan (FACTS Tuition Payment Plan, monthly payment plans, individually arranged payment plans, 2-payment plan). Need-based scholarship grants available. In 2005–06, 15% of upper-school students received aid. Total amount of financial aid awarded in 2005–06: $280,000.

Admissions Traditional secondary-level entrance grade is 9. For fall 2005, 12 students applied for upper-level admission, 11 were accepted, 8 enrolled. ERB (grade level) and Otis-Lennon School Ability Test required. Deadline for receipt of application materials: none. Application fee required: $25. On-campus interview required.

Athletics Interscholastic: baseball (boys), basketball (b,g), cheering (g), cross-country running (b,g), football (b), golf (b,g), soccer (b,g), swimming and diving (b,g), tennis (b,g), track and field (b,g), volleyball (g); intramural: weight lifting (b,g); coed interscholastic: modern dance, outdoor education; coed intramural: aerobics, aerobics/dance, ballet, dance, yoga. 3 PE instructors, 5 coaches, 1 trainer.

Computers Computers are regularly used in all academic classes. Computer network features include campus e-mail, on-campus library services, CD-ROMs, Internet access, office computer access, DVD, wireless campus network, wireless laptop program (grades 9-12).

Contact Director of Admissions. 402-556-3772. Fax: 402-553-2994. E-mail: admissions@brownell.edu. Web site: www.brownell.edu.

THE BROWNING SCHOOL
52 East 62nd Street
New York, New York 10021
Head of School: Stephen M. Clement III

General Information Boys' day college-preparatory school. Grades K–12. Founded: 1888. Setting: urban. 2 buildings on campus. Approved or accredited by New York State Association of Independent Schools. Member of National Association of Independent Schools and Secondary School Admission Test Board. Endowment: $9 million. Total enrollment: 381. Upper school average class size: 15. Upper school faculty-student ratio: 1:18.

Upper School Student Profile Grade 9: 29 students (29 boys); Grade 10: 32 students (32 boys); Grade 11: 22 students (22 boys); Grade 12: 28 students (28 boys).

Faculty School total: 51. In upper school: 13 men, 10 women; 12 have advanced degrees.

Subjects Offered Algebra, American history, American literature, art, art history, biology, calculus, ceramics, chemistry, computer math, computer programming, computer science, drama, economics, English, English literature, environmental science, ethics, European history, fine arts, French, general science, geography, geometry, government/civics, grammar, health, history, Latin, mathematics, medieval/Renaissance history, music, philosophy, physical education, physics, political science, psychology, public speaking, science, social science, social studies, sociology, Spanish, speech, technology, theater, trigonometry.

Graduation Requirements Arts and fine arts (art, music, dance, drama), computer science, English, foreign language, mathematics, physical education (includes health), public speaking, science, social science, social studies (includes history), senior community service project.

Special Academic Programs Advanced Placement exam preparation in 14 subject areas; honors section; independent study; academic accommodation for the gifted.

College Placement 28 students graduated in 2005; all went to college, including Brown University; Franklin and Marshall College; Georgetown University; The George Washington University; Union College; Vanderbilt University. 48% scored over 600 on SAT verbal, 44% scored over 600 on SAT math.

Student Life Upper grades have specified standards of dress, student council, honor system. Discipline rests equally with students and faculty.

Tuition and Aid Day student tuition: $25,415. Tuition installment plan (Key Tuition Payment Plan). Need-based scholarship grants available. In 2005–06, 20% of upper-school students received aid. Total amount of financial aid awarded in 2005–06: $615,750.

Admissions Traditional secondary-level entrance grade is 9. For fall 2005, 115 students applied for upper-level admission, 31 were accepted, 10 enrolled. ERB and ISEE required. Deadline for receipt of application materials: December. Application fee required: $50. On-campus interview required.

Athletics Interscholastic: baseball, basketball, soccer, tennis; intramural: basketball, cross-country running, soccer, softball; coed intramural: fencing. 4 PE instructors, 6 coaches.

Computers Computers are regularly used in English, foreign language, mathematics, science classes. Computer network features include campus e-mail, on-campus library services, CD-ROMs, online commercial services, Internet access.

Contact Jacqueline A. Casey, Director of Admission. 212-838-6280. Fax: 212-355-5602. E-mail: jcasey@browning.edu. Web site: www.browning.edu.

ANNOUNCEMENT FROM THE SCHOOL The Browning School was founded as a college-preparatory school for boys in 1888 by John A. Browning. A traditional curriculum helps support boys intellectually, physically, and emotionally from preprimary through grade 12. Located in the heart of New York City, the Browning School utilizes the city for all of its vast resources. The 2005–06 school enrollment is 381 boys, with an average grade size of 30. The average class size is about 15 students. Browning is accredited by the New York State Association of Independent Schools (NYSAIS) and the National Association of Independent Schools (NAIS). Browning is a member of Interschool, a consortium of 8 private New York City schools (Browning, Collegiate, Chapin, Brearley, Spence, Nightingale-Bamford, Trinity, and Dalton) that offers opportunities for academic sharing, extracurricular participation in the arts, and social activities for boys and girls. College guidance begins in 9th grade and continues throughout high school. In Form V and Form VI, the boys go on college trips and visit up to 8 colleges each year. The Athletic Program includes intramural offerings, in addition to interscholastic competition in soccer, cross-country, basketball, tennis, track, and baseball. In high school, there are junior varsity and varsity teams. There is an afterschool program (Encore) for students in preprimary through grade 6. Student clubs and activities include the newspaper, yearbook, Student Council, community service, Computer Club, Drama Club, Model UN, Mock Trial, Investment Club, Multicultural Club, and Literary Magazine. Browning operates on a trimester system. Written reports are sent home to parents 6 times a year (at the midpoint and end of each trimester). Letter grades are given to students starting in grade 5. The final grades for each trimester are averaged to determine a final year grade, which becomes part of the student's permanent record. Effort and conduct ratings are also noted in the reports.

BRUNSWICK SCHOOL

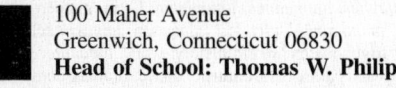

100 Maher Avenue
Greenwich, Connecticut 06830
Head of School: Thomas W. Philip

petersons.com

General Information Boys' day college-preparatory school. Grades PK–12. Founded: 1902. Setting: suburban. Nearest major city is New York, NY. 118-acre campus. 4 buildings on campus. Approved or accredited by Connecticut Association of Independent Schools, New England Association of Schools and Colleges, and Connecticut Department of Education. Member of National Association of Independent Schools. Endowment: $67 million. Total enrollment: 877. Upper school average class size: 14. Upper school faculty-student ratio: 1:6.

Upper School Student Profile Grade 9: 78 students (78 boys); Grade 10: 80 students (80 boys); Grade 11: 82 students (82 boys); Grade 12: 75 students (75 boys).

Faculty School total: 146. In upper school: 41 men, 10 women; 36 have advanced degrees.

Subjects Offered 20th century history, 3-dimensional design, acting, advanced chemistry, African-American literature, algebra, American government-AP, American history, American history-AP, American literature, anthropology, architecture, art, art history, art history-AP, astronomy, biology, biology-AP, calculus, calculus-AP, ceramics, chemistry, chemistry-AP, Chinese, choir, community service, computer graphics, computer programming, computer programming-AP, creative writing, digital art, digital music, drama, earth science, economics, economics-AP, English, environmental science-AP, ethics, European history, European history-AP, film and literature, fine arts, French, French language-AP, French literature-AP, geometry, government-AP, Greek, Greek culture, health, history, honors algebra, honors geometry, human geography—AP, Italian, Japanese history, jazz, jazz band, jazz ensemble, Latin, Latin American literature, Latin-AP, mathematics, media studies, microeconomics, military history, music, oceanography, photography, physical education, physics, physics-AP, poetry, pre-calculus, psychology, psychology-AP, science, senior seminar, Shakespeare, short story, social studies, Spanish, Spanish language-AP, Spanish literature-AP, statistics-AP, studio art, studio art—AP, theater, trigonometry, U.S. government-AP, U.S. history-AP, world cultures, world history-AP, writing.

Graduation Requirements Arts and fine arts (art, music, dance, drama), English, foreign language, mathematics, physical education (includes health), science, social studies (includes history). Community service is required.

Special Academic Programs Advanced Placement exam preparation in 19 subject areas; honors section; independent study; term-away projects; academic accommodation for the gifted, the musically talented, and the artistically talented.

College Placement 76 students graduated in 2005; 75 went to college, including Boston College; Duke University; Middlebury College; Stanford University; University of Colorado at Boulder; University of Southern California. Other: 1 entered a postgraduate year. Mean SAT verbal: 655, mean SAT math: 665. 88% scored over 600 on SAT verbal, 85% scored over 600 on SAT math.

Student Life Upper grades have specified standards of dress, student council, honor system. Discipline rests equally with students and faculty.

Tuition and Aid Day student tuition: $25,000. Tuition installment plan (Key Tuition Payment Plan, monthly payment plans). Need-based scholarship grants available. In 2005–06, 15% of upper-school students received aid. Total amount of financial aid awarded in 2005–06: $828,100.

Admissions Traditional secondary-level entrance grade is 9. For fall 2005, 119 students applied for upper-level admission, 41 were accepted, 28 enrolled. ISEE, PSAT or SSAT required. Deadline for receipt of application materials: December 15. Application fee required: $75. On-campus interview required.

Athletics Interscholastic: baseball, basketball, crew, cross-country running, fencing, football, golf, ice hockey, lacrosse, sailing, soccer, squash, tennis, wrestling; intramural: basketball, softball, squash, touch football. 4 PE instructors, 2 trainers.

Computers Computers are regularly used in all classes. Computer network features include campus e-mail, CD-ROMs, online commercial services, Internet access, wireless campus network.

Contact Jeffry Harris, Director of Admission. 203-625-5842. Fax: 203-625-5889. E-mail: jeffry_harris@brunswickschool.org. Web site: www.brunswickschool.org.

ANNOUNCEMENT FROM THE SCHOOL Brunswick School has coordinate classes and activities at the Upper School level with Greenwich Academy, the neighboring girls' school. The coed environment encompasses 80 percent of the classes and includes art, music, drama, community service, and social activities. The technology program includes laptop computer use starting in the 8th grade. In fall 2004, the Lower School moved to a new building on the 104-acre Edwards Campus where the Middle School has been located since September 2000. In addition, that campus includes 2 athletic buildings with 5 basketball courts, a wrestling room, 8 squash courts, a hockey rink, an artificial turf field, and 4 grass fields.

THE BRYN MAWR SCHOOL FOR GIRLS

109 West Melrose Avenue
Baltimore, Maryland 21210
Head of School: Maureen E. Walsh

General Information Coeducational day (boys' only in lower grades) college-preparatory school. Boys grade PK, girls grades PK–12. Founded: 1885. Setting: suburban. 30-acre campus. 9 buildings on campus. Approved or accredited by Association of Independent Maryland Schools and Maryland Department of Education. Member of National Association of Independent Schools. Endowment: $20.1 million. Total enrollment: 798. Upper school average class size: 13. Upper school faculty-student ratio: 1:8.

Upper School Student Profile Grade 9: 89 students (89 girls); Grade 10: 80 students (80 girls); Grade 11: 83 students (83 girls); Grade 12: 78 students (78 girls).

Faculty School total: 134. In upper school: 10 men, 34 women; 25 have advanced degrees.

The Bryn Mawr School for Girls

Subjects Offered Accounting, algebra, American literature, anatomy, art, art history, astronomy, biology, calculus, ceramics, chemistry, Chinese, computer programming, computer science, creative writing, dance, drama, ecology, economics, emerging technology, English, English literature, ethics, European history, fine arts, French, geography, geometry, German, grammar, Greek, Latin, mathematics, moral theology, music, photography, physical education, physics, public speaking, Russian, science, social studies, Spanish, statistics, technology, theater, trigonometry, urban studies, world history, world literature, writing.

Graduation Requirements Arts and fine arts (art, music, dance, drama), emerging technology, English, foreign language, history, mathematics, physical education (includes health), public speaking, science, 50 hours of community service, convocation speech.

Special Academic Programs Advanced Placement exam preparation in 18 subject areas; honors section; independent study; term-away projects; study abroad; academic accommodation for the gifted, the musically talented, and the artistically talented.

College Placement 75 students graduated in 2005; all went to college, including Brown University; Colby College; Harvard University; Northwestern University; University of Maryland, College Park. Mean SAT verbal: 652, mean SAT math: 638, mean composite ACT: 27.

Student Life Upper grades have uniform requirement, student council, honor system. Discipline rests equally with students and faculty.

Summer Programs Enrichment, sports, art/fine arts programs offered; session focuses on arts, crafts, language, culture, and sports; held on campus; accepts boys and girls; open to students from other schools. 480 students usually enrolled. 2006 schedule: June 13 to August 11. Application deadline: none.

Tuition and Aid Day student tuition: $18,975. Tuition installment plan (Insured Tuition Payment Plan, Academic Management Services Plan, Key Tuition Payment Plan, FACTS Tuition Payment Plan, monthly payment plans). Need-based scholarship grants, need-based loans, middle-income loans available. In 2005–06, 18% of upper-school students received aid. Total amount of financial aid awarded in 2005–06: $745,000.

Admissions Traditional secondary-level entrance grade is 9. For fall 2005, 97 students applied for upper-level admission, 66 were accepted, 23 enrolled. Deadline for receipt of application materials: January 1. Application fee required: $50. On-campus interview required.

Athletics Interscholastic: badminton, ballet, basketball, crew, cross-country running, dance, equestrian sports, field hockey, hockey, indoor soccer, indoor track & field, lacrosse, rowing, running, soccer, softball, squash, tennis, track and field, volleyball, winter (indoor) track, winter soccer; intramural: aerobics, aerobics/dance, aerobics/nautilus, archery, badminton, ball hockey, basketball, bowling, cooperative games, croquet, cross-country running, dance, fitness, flag football, floor hockey, ice hockey, jogging, outdoor activities, physical training, pillo polo, ropes courses, running, strength & conditioning, tennis, touch football, weight training. 7 PE instructors, 50 coaches, 1 trainer.

Computers Computers are regularly used in all academic, animation, art classes. Computer network features include campus e-mail, on-campus library services, CD-ROMs, online commercial services, Internet access, file transfer, off-campus e-mail.

Contact Patricia Nothstein, Director of Admission and Financial Aid. 410-323-8800 Ext. 1237. Fax: 410-435-4678. E-mail: nothsteinp@brynmawrschool.org. Web site: www.brynmawrschool.org.

BUCKINGHAM BROWNE & NICHOLS SCHOOL

80 Gerry's Landing Road
Cambridge, Massachusetts 02138-5512
Head of School: Rebecca T. Upham

General Information Coeducational day college-preparatory and arts school. Grades PK–12. Founded: 1883. Setting: urban. Nearest major city is Boston. 5-acre campus. 6 buildings on campus. Approved or accredited by Association of Independent Schools in New England, New England Association of Schools and Colleges, and Massachusetts Department of Education. Member of National Association of Independent Schools and Secondary School Admission Test Board. Endowment: $35 million. Total enrollment: 958. Upper school average class size: 13. Upper school faculty-student ratio: 1:7.

Upper School Student Profile Grade 9: 124 students (62 boys, 62 girls); Grade 10: 116 students (60 boys, 56 girls); Grade 11: 115 students (56 boys, 59 girls); Grade 12: 113 students (53 boys, 60 girls).

Faculty School total: 132. In upper school: 32 men, 31 women; 56 have advanced degrees.

Subjects Offered Advanced Placement courses, African-American studies, algebra, American history, American literature, ancient history, art, art history, art history-AP, biology, bivouac, calculus, ceramics, chemistry, Chinese, Chinese history, community service, computer science, dance, design, drama, economics, English, English literature, European history, film, fine arts, French, geometry, government/civics, history, Latin, mathematics, medieval history, music, photography, physical education, physics, physiology, psychology, Russian, science, social studies, Spanish, statistics, theater, trigonometry, video, woodworking.

Graduation Requirements Arts and fine arts (art, music, dance, drama), bivouac, English, foreign language, history, mathematics, science, senior spring project. Community service is required.

Special Academic Programs Advanced Placement exam preparation in 19 subject areas; honors section; independent study; term-away projects; study at local college for college credit; study abroad; academic accommodation for the gifted, the musically talented, and the artistically talented.

College Placement 114 students graduated in 2005; 113 went to college, including Harvard University; Middlebury College; New York University; University of Pennsylvania; Wesleyan University; Yale University. Mean SAT verbal: 677, mean SAT math: 672. 85% scored over 600 on SAT verbal, 84% scored over 600 on SAT math.

Student Life Upper grades have specified standards of dress, student council. Discipline rests equally with students and faculty.

Tuition and Aid Day student tuition: $27,850. Tuition installment plan (Insured Tuition Payment Plan, Key Tuition Payment Plan, monthly payment plans). Need-based scholarship grants available. In 2005–06, 23% of upper-school students received aid. Total amount of financial aid awarded in 2005–06: $2,334,090.

Admissions Traditional secondary-level entrance grade is 9. For fall 2005, 417 students applied for upper-level admission, 117 were accepted, 58 enrolled. SSAT required. Deadline for receipt of application materials: February 1. Application fee required: $50. Interview required.

Athletics Interscholastic: baseball (boys), basketball (b,g), crew (b,g), cross-country running (b,g), fencing (b,g), field hockey (g), football (b), hockey (b,g), ice hockey (b,g), lacrosse (b,g), sailing (b,g), skiing (downhill) (b,g), soccer (b,g), softball (g), tennis (b,g), track and field (b,g), volleyball (g), wrestling (b); coed interscholastic: alpine skiing, golf; coed intramural: aerobics, aerobics/dance, aerobics/nautilus, back packing, fitness, physical fitness, sailing, tennis. 2 PE instructors, 20 coaches, 2 trainers.

Computers Computers are regularly used in mathematics, programming, science, video film production classes. Computer network features include campus e-mail, on-campus library services, CD-ROMs, online commercial services, Internet access, file transfer, office computer access.

Contact Natasha Leitch-Huggins, Admission Assistant. 617-800-2136. Fax: 617-547-7696. E-mail: loren_trott@bbns.org. Web site: www.bbns.org.

ANNOUNCEMENT FROM THE SCHOOL BB&N's proximity to the educational and cultural resources of Cambridge and Boston, including Harvard, MIT, and Boston's Museum of Fine Arts, enriches its rigorous, broad curriculum and its vibrant, diverse community of learners. BB&N takes seriously its mission to prepare students for the challenges of an increasingly interdependent world and offers courses in Russian, French, Spanish, Latin, and Mandarin Chinese. Strong programs in the humanities, sciences, mathematics, arts, and athletics prepare students for a wide range of selective colleges. Academic programs with schools in France, Italy, Russia, and Switzerland are available. The new Nicholas Athletic Center includes a rink, fitness center, 3 basketball courts, and an indoor rowing tank.

THE BUCKLEY SCHOOL

3900 Stansbury Avenue
Sherman Oaks, California 91423
Head of School: Elizabeth McGregor

General Information Coeducational day college-preparatory, arts, and technology school. Grades K–12. Founded: 1933. Setting: suburban. Nearest major city is Los Angeles. 19-acre campus. 8 buildings on campus. Approved or accredited by California Association of Independent Schools, Western Association of Schools and Colleges, and California Department of Education. Member of National Association of Independent Schools. Endowment: $2.7 million. Total enrollment: 750. Upper school average class size: 15. Upper school faculty-student ratio: 1:7.

Upper School Student Profile Grade 9: 83 students (40 boys, 43 girls); Grade 10: 93 students (44 boys, 49 girls); Grade 11: 64 students (33 boys, 31 girls); Grade 12: 70 students (35 boys, 35 girls).

Faculty School total: 98. In upper school: 28 men, 27 women; 31 have advanced degrees.

Subjects Offered Algebra, American history, American literature, art history, biology, calculus, ceramics, chemistry, chorus, computer graphics, computer science, creative writing, dance, drama, ecology, English, English literature, fine arts, French, geology, geometry, government/civics, humanities, journalism, Latin, mathematics, music, music theory, orchestra, photography, physical education, physics, science, social science, Spanish, theater, trigonometry, world history, world literature, yoga.

Graduation Requirements Arts and fine arts (art, music, dance, drama), computer science, English, foreign language, humanities, mathematics, performing arts, physical education (includes health), science, social science. Community service is required.

Special Academic Programs Advanced Placement exam preparation in 17 subject areas; honors section; study abroad.

College Placement 57 students graduated in 2005; all went to college, including Columbia College; Loyola Marymount University; Rhode Island School of Design;

University of California, Berkeley; University of Colorado at Boulder; University of Southern California. Median SAT verbal: 640, median SAT math: 650. 63% scored over 600 on SAT verbal, 72% scored over 600 on SAT math, 56% scored over 26 on composite ACT.

Student Life Upper grades have uniform requirement, student council, honor system. Discipline rests equally with students and faculty.

Summer Programs Advancement, art/fine arts, computer instruction programs offered; session focuses on college preparatory courses and enrichment; held on campus; accepts boys and girls; open to students from other schools. 100 students usually enrolled. 2006 schedule: June 13 to July 22. Application deadline: April 1.

Tuition and Aid Day student tuition: $23,250. Tuition installment plan (Academic Management Services Plan, Key Tuition Payment Plan). Need-based scholarship grants available. In 2005–06, 12% of upper-school students received aid. Total amount of financial aid awarded in 2005–06: $487,400.

Admissions Traditional secondary-level entrance grade is 9. For fall 2005, 118 students applied for upper-level admission, 34 were accepted, 11 enrolled. ISEE required. Deadline for receipt of application materials: January 15. Application fee required: $100. On-campus interview required.

Athletics Interscholastic: baseball (boys), basketball (b,g), equestrian sports (b,g), soccer (b,g), softball (g), swimming and diving (b,g), tennis (b,g), volleyball (g); coed interscholastic: cross-country running. 12 PE instructors, 11 coaches, 2 trainers.

Computers Computers are regularly used in art, English, graphic design, music, science, video film production classes. Computer network features include campus e-mail, on-campus library services, online commercial services, Internet access, Web page design, online interaction with UCLA, online syllabi.

Contact Carinne M. Barker, Director of Admission and Financial Aid. 818-783-1610 Ext. 709. Fax: 818-461-6714. E-mail: admissions@buckleyla.org. Web site: www.buckleyla.org.

ANNOUNCEMENT FROM THE SCHOOL Founded in 1933, The Buckley School's educational philosophy encompasses 4 objectives: academic training, creative self-expression through the arts, physical development, and moral education. The School's approach addresses the development of the whole student to become well-rounded, knowledgeable, and independent. The Buckley School, a coeducational day school, enrolls 750 students in kindergarten through grade 12. Contact Carinne M. Barker, Director of Admission and Financial Aid, 3900 Stansbury Avenue, Sherman Oaks, California 91423; telephone: 818-783-1610; fax: 818-461-6714; e-mail: admissions@buckleyla.org; Web site: http://www.buckleyla.org.

THE BULLIS SCHOOL

10601 Falls Road
Potomac, Maryland 20854
Head of School: Mr. Thomas B. Farquhar

General Information Coeducational day college-preparatory school. Grades 3–12. Founded: 1930. Setting: suburban. Nearest major city is Washington, DC. 80-acre campus. 6 buildings on campus. Approved or accredited by Association of Independent Maryland Schools, Middle States Association of Colleges and Schools, and Maryland Department of Education. Member of National Association of Independent Schools and Secondary School Admission Test Board. Language of instruction: English. Endowment: $10.5 million. Total enrollment: 624. Upper school average class size: 15. Upper school faculty-student ratio: 1:15.

Upper School Student Profile Grade 9: 85 students (46 boys, 39 girls); Grade 10: 87 students (43 boys, 44 girls); Grade 11: 84 students (48 boys, 36 girls); Grade 12: 100 students (51 boys, 49 girls).

Faculty School total: 95. In upper school: 28 men, 29 women; 36 have advanced degrees.

Subjects Offered Algebra, American history, American literature, anatomy, art history, art history-AP, basic imaging, biology, calculus, ceramics, chemistry, chemistry-AP, computer keyboarding, computer programming, computer science, concert choir, creative writing, dance, digital art, drama, drawing, earth science, economics, English, English literature, environmental science, European history, European history-AP, expository writing, fine arts, French, geography, geometry, government-AP, government/civics, grammar, graphic design, health, history, humanities, jazz ensemble, journalism, language-AP, Latin, mathematics, media studies, modern European history-AP, music, painting, photography, physical education, physics, physiology, psychology, psychology-AP, science, social studies, Spanish, statistics, statistics-AP, technology, the Sixties, theater, theater history, transition mathematics, trigonometry, U.S. history-AP, Web site design, world history, world literature, world wide web design, writing.

Graduation Requirements Arts and fine arts (art, music, dance, drama), English, foreign language, mathematics, physical education (includes health), science, social studies (includes history), technology.

Special Academic Programs Advanced Placement exam preparation in 17 subject areas; honors section; independent study; academic accommodation for the gifted.

College Placement 79 students graduated in 2004; all went to college, including Boston University; Brigham Young University; Miami University; Syracuse Univer-

sity; The George Washington University; University of Colorado at Boulder. Median SAT verbal: 600, median SAT math: 600.

Student Life Upper grades have uniform requirement, student council, honor system. Discipline rests equally with students and faculty.

Tuition and Aid Day student tuition: $22,690. Tuition installment plan (Academic Management Services Plan, monthly payment plans). Need-based scholarship grants available. In 2004–05, 18% of upper-school students received aid. Total amount of financial aid awarded in 2004–05: $965,600.

Admissions Traditional secondary-level entrance grade is 9. ERB, ISEE, SSAT or Wechsler Intelligence Scale for Children required. Deadline for receipt of application materials: February 1. Application fee required: $60. Interview required.

Athletics Interscholastic: baseball (boys), basketball (b,g), cross-country running (b,g), equestrian sports (b,g), field hockey (g), football (b), golf (b,g), ice hockey (b), lacrosse (b,g), soccer (b,g), softball (g), swimming and diving (b,g), tennis (b,g), track and field (b,g), wrestling (b); intramural: aerobics (b,g), physical training (b,g), strength & conditioning (b,g); coed interscholastic: cheering; coed intramural: outdoor education. 4 PE instructors, 15 coaches, 1 trainer.

Computers Computers are regularly used in art, English, foreign language, history, mathematics, music, science, technology, theater classes. Computer network features include campus e-mail, on-campus library services, CD-ROMs, online commercial services, Internet access, file transfer, office computer access, DVD, wireless campus network, Citrix access from home, faculty web pages.

Contact Ms. Nancy L. Spencer, Director of Admission and Financial Aid. 301-983-5724. Fax: 301-634-3659. E-mail: info@bullis.org. Web site: www.bullis.org.

See full description on page 702.

BULLOCH ACADEMY

873 Westside Road
Statesboro, Georgia 30458
Head of School: Dr. Carolyn Bennett Broucek

General Information Coeducational day college-preparatory school, affiliated with Christian faith. Grades PK–12. Founded: 1971. Setting: rural. Nearest major city is Savannah. 35-acre campus. 3 buildings on campus. Approved or accredited by Association of Independent Maryland Schools, Georgia Accrediting Commission, Georgia Independent School Association, and Southern Association of Colleges and Schools. Total enrollment: 517. Upper school average class size: 16. Upper school faculty-student ratio: 1:16.

Upper School Student Profile Grade 9: 35 students (21 boys, 14 girls); Grade 10: 33 students (15 boys, 18 girls); Grade 11: 15 students (10 boys, 5 girls); Grade 12: 29 students (17 boys, 12 girls). 98% of students are Christian.

Faculty School total: 45. In upper school: 2 men, 9 women; 3 have advanced degrees.

Subjects Offered Advanced Placement courses, American history, art, computer science, economics, English, ethics, foreign language, general science, government/civics, mathematics, music, physical education, psychology, science, social science, social studies, Spanish, world history.

Graduation Requirements Computer science, English, foreign language, mathematics, physical education (includes health), science, social science, social studies (includes history).

Special Academic Programs Advanced Placement exam preparation in 3 subject areas; honors section; independent study; study at local college for college credit; academic accommodation for the gifted, the musically talented, and the artistically talented.

College Placement 27 students graduated in 2005; all went to college, including Georgia Southern University; Mercer University; University of Georgia.

Student Life Upper grades have student council, honor system. Discipline rests primarily with faculty.

Summer Programs Enrichment, sports, art/fine arts, computer instruction programs offered; session focuses on week-long camps; held both on and off campus; held at college campuses; accepts boys and girls; open to students from other schools.

Tuition and Aid Day student tuition: $4628. Tuition installment plan (monthly payment plans, individually arranged payment plans). Tuition reduction for siblings available.

Admissions Traditional secondary-level entrance grade is 9. For fall 2005, 5 students applied for upper-level admission, 5 were accepted, 5 enrolled. Any standardized test and Iowa Tests of Basic Skills required. Deadline for receipt of application materials: none. Application fee required: $300. Interview recommended.

Athletics Interscholastic: baseball (boys), basketball (b,g), cheering (g), cross-country running (b,g), dance team (g), football (b), golf (b,g), physical fitness (b,g), running (b,g), soccer (b,g), softball (g), strength & conditioning (b,g), tennis (b,g), track and field (b,g), weight lifting (b,g), weight training (b,g), wrestling (b); intramural: cross-country running (b,g), physical fitness (b,g); coed interscholastic: physical fitness; coed intramural: basketball, physical fitness. 3 PE instructors, 7 coaches, 1 trainer.

Computers Computers are regularly used in all academic, career education, career exploration, desktop publishing, keyboarding, technology classes. Computer resources include CD-ROMs, Internet access.

Contact Dr. Carolyn Bennett Broucek, Headmaster. 912-764-6297. Fax: 912-764-3165. E-mail: cbroucek@bullochacademy.com. Web site: www.bullochacademy.com.

BURKE MOUNTAIN ACADEMY

PO Box 78
East Burke, Vermont 05832
Head of School: Kirk Dwyer

General Information Coeducational boarding and day college-preparatory school. Grades 7–PG. Founded: 1970. Setting: rural. Nearest major city is St. Johnsbury. Students are housed in coed dormitories. 33-acre campus. 9 buildings on campus. Approved or accredited by New England Association of Schools and Colleges and Vermont Department of Education. Member of National Association of Independent Schools. Total enrollment: 61. Upper school average class size: 17. Upper school faculty-student ratio: 1:7.

Upper School Student Profile Grade 7: 3 students (1 boy, 2 girls); Grade 8: 1 student (1 girl); Grade 9: 8 students (5 boys, 3 girls); Grade 10: 10 students (5 boys, 5 girls); Grade 11: 18 students (7 boys, 11 girls); Grade 12: 17 students (6 boys, 11 girls); Postgraduate: 4 students (2 boys, 2 girls). 90% of students are boarding students. 29% are state residents. 14 states are represented in upper school student body. 3% are international students. International students from Canada and Spain.

Faculty School total: 9. In upper school: 3 men, 6 women; 5 have advanced degrees; 3 reside on campus.

Subjects Offered Algebra, American history, American literature, art, biology, calculus, chemistry, creative writing, current events, English, English literature, European history, fine arts, French, geometry, history, mathematics, physical education, physics, science, social studies, world history, world literature, writing.

Graduation Requirements Arts and fine arts (art, music, dance, drama), English, foreign language, mathematics, physical education (includes health), science, social studies (includes history).

Special Academic Programs Advanced Placement exam preparation in 2 subject areas; independent study; term-away projects; study at local college for college credit; study abroad.

College Placement 14 students graduated in 2005; 5 went to college, including Brown University; Middlebury College; St. Lawrence University; Williams College. Other: 9 entered a postgraduate year.

Student Life Upper grades have honor system. Discipline rests equally with students and faculty.

Tuition and Aid Day student tuition: $23,520; 7-day tuition and room/board: $32,025. Tuition installment plan (monthly payment plans, individually arranged payment plans). Need-based scholarship grants, need-based loans, paying campus jobs available. In 2005–06, 38% of upper-school students received aid. Total amount of financial aid awarded in 2005–06: $384,000.

Admissions SSAT required. Deadline for receipt of application materials: none. Application fee required: $100. Interview recommended.

Athletics Interscholastic: alpine skiing (boys, girls), golf (b,g), lacrosse (g), nordic skiing (b,g), skiing (cross-country) (b,g), skiing (downhill) (b,g), soccer (b,g); intramural: alpine skiing (b,g), nordic skiing (b,g), soccer (b,g); coed interscholastic: cross-country running. 6 coaches.

Computers Computers are regularly used in English, foreign language, mathematics, science classes. Computer resources include campus e-mail, CD-ROMs, Internet access.

Contact Marcia Berry, Office Manager. 802-626-5607. Fax: 802-626-3784. E-mail: mberry@burkemtnacademy.org. Web site: www.burkemtnacademy.org.

BURR AND BURTON ACADEMY

57 Seminary Avenue
Manchester, Vermont 05254
Head of School: Charles Scranton

General Information Coeducational boarding and day college-preparatory, general academic, arts, and technology school. Grades 9–12. Founded: 1829. Setting: small town. Nearest major city is Albany, NY. Students are housed in homes of host families. 29-acre campus. 7 buildings on campus. Approved or accredited by New England Association of Schools and Colleges and Vermont Department of Education. Member of National Association of Independent Schools. Total enrollment: 686. Upper school average class size: 19.

Upper School Student Profile Grade 9: 162 students (88 boys, 74 girls); Grade 10: 176 students (86 boys, 90 girls); Grade 11: 185 students (102 boys, 83 girls); Grade 12: 163 students (82 boys, 81 girls). 1% are international students.

Faculty School total: 43. In upper school: 25 men, 18 women; 25 have advanced degrees.

Subjects Offered Algebra, American history, American literature, anatomy, art, art history, biology, business, calculus, chemistry, computer math, computer programming, computer science, drafting, drama, driver education, earth science, ecology, English, English literature, environmental science, expository writing, French, geometry, German, government/civics, health, history, industrial arts, mathematics,

music, photography, physical education, physics, psychology, science, social studies, Spanish, theater, trigonometry, typing, world history, world literature.

Graduation Requirements Computer literacy, English, mathematics, physical education (includes health), science, social studies (includes history). Community service is required.

Special Academic Programs Advanced Placement exam preparation in 6 subject areas; independent study; term-away projects; study abroad; remedial reading and/or remedial writing; remedial math; programs in English, mathematics, general development for dyslexic students; special instructional classes for deaf students, blind students; ESL.

College Placement 136 students graduated in 2005; 113 went to college, including Middlebury College; Skidmore College; St. Lawrence University; University of Vermont. Other: 12 went to work, 1 entered military service, 10 had other specific plans.

Student Life Upper grades have specified standards of dress, student council. Discipline rests primarily with faculty.

Tuition and Aid 7-day tuition and room/board: $26,300. Tuition installment plan (individually arranged payment plans).

Admissions Traditional secondary-level entrance grade is 9. School's own test and SLEP for foreign students required. Deadline for receipt of application materials: none. No application fee required. Interview recommended.

Athletics Interscholastic: alpine skiing (boys, girls), baseball (b), basketball (b,g), cross-country running (b,g), dance team (g), football (b), golf (b,g), ice hockey (b,g), lacrosse (b,g), nordic skiing (b,g), skiing (cross-country) (b,g), skiing (downhill) (b,g), soccer (b,g), softball (g), tennis (b,g), track and field (b,g); coed intramural: field hockey, floor hockey, outdoor adventure, outdoor education, volleyball. 3 PE instructors, 17 coaches.

Computers Computers are regularly used in English, foreign language, history, mathematics, science classes. Computer network features include campus e-mail, on-campus library services, CD-ROMs, online commercial services, Internet access.

Contact Philip G. Anton, Director of Guidance and Admission. 802-362-1775 Ext. 125. Fax: 802-362-0574. E-mail: panton@burrburton.org. Web site: www.burrburton.org.

THE BUSH SCHOOL

petersons.com

3400 East Harrison Street
Seattle, Washington 98112
Head of School: Mr. Frank E. Magusin

General Information Coeducational day college-preparatory and experiential learning school. Grades K–12. Founded: 1924. Setting: urban. 9-acre campus. 2 buildings on campus. Approved or accredited by Northwest Association of Accredited Schools, Northwest Association of Schools and Colleges, Pacific Northwest Association of Independent Schools, and Washington Department of Education. Member of National Association of Independent Schools. Endowment: $7.5 million. Total enrollment: 557. Upper school average class size: 12. Upper school faculty-student ratio: 1:6.

Upper School Student Profile Grade 9: 60 students (31 boys, 29 girls); Grade 10: 57 students (36 boys, 21 girls); Grade 11: 47 students (26 boys, 21 girls); Grade 12: 54 students (23 boys, 31 girls).

Faculty School total: 80. In upper school: 18 men, 19 women; 28 have advanced degrees.

Subjects Offered Acting, advanced chemistry, advanced math, African American history, African American studies, algebra, American literature, anatomy and physiology, animal behavior, animal science, anthropology, art, art history, astronomy, Bible as literature, biology, biotechnology, calculus, career experience, cartooning/animation, ceramics, chemistry, civics, community service, comparative religion, composition, computer art, computer graphics, computer math, computer multimedia, computer programming, computer science, creative writing, critical writing, dance, digital art, directing, diversity studies, drama, drama workshop, drawing, drawing and design, earth science, ecology, English, English composition, English literature, ensembles, environmental science, environmental studies, ethics, ethics and responsibility, European civilization, European history, experiential education, expository writing, fiber arts, filmmaking, fine arts, fitness, foreign policy, French, genetics, geography, geology, geometry, glassblowing, golf, government/civics, health education, history, history of China and Japan, history of religion, human anatomy, improvisation, Indian studies, instrumental music, internship, Latin American literature, literary magazine, literature, literature by women, logic, marine science, mathematics, metalworking, microbiology, Middle East, music, music composition, music performance, music theater, music theory, musical productions, musical theater, newspaper, nuclear science, oceanography, oil painting, opera, outdoor education, painting, photography, physical education, physics, play production, playwriting and directing, poetry, pre-calculus, printmaking, probability and statistics, programming, psychology, public policy issues and action, religion and culture, Romantic period literature, Russia and contemporary Europe, Russian studies, science, sculpture, senior career experience, senior internship, senior project, service learning/internship, sewing, Shakespeare, short story, social studies, South African history, Spanish, Spanish literature, statistics, student publications, tennis, Thailand and Southeast Asia, theater, theater production, track and field, trigonometry, U.S. history, vocal ensemble, voice ensemble, volleyball, Western civilization, Western philosophy, wilderness camping, wilderness education, wilderness experience, wilderness studies,

wilderness/outdoor program, women's literature, women's studies, woodworking, work experience, world cultures, world history, world literature, world religions, writing, writing workshop, yearbook.

Graduation Requirements Arts and fine arts (art, music, dance, drama), computer science, English, foreign language, mathematics, physical education (includes health), physiology, science, social studies (includes history), experiential learning course every trimester. Community service is required.

Special Academic Programs Advanced Placement exam preparation in 8 subject areas; independent study; term-away projects; domestic exchange program (with The Network Program Schools); study abroad.

College Placement 56 students graduated in 2005; all went to college, including Harvard University; Pitzer College; Santa Clara University; The Colorado College; University of Washington; Washington State University.

Student Life Upper grades have student council, honor system. Discipline rests primarily with faculty.

Summer Programs Enrichment programs offered; session focuses on mathematics; held on campus; accepts boys and girls; open to students from other schools.

Tuition and Aid Day student tuition: $20,175. Tuition installment plan (Insured Tuition Payment Plan, Key Tuition Payment Plan, monthly payment plans, individually arranged payment plans, Dewar Tuition Refund Plan). Need-based scholarship grants available. In 2005–06, 15% of upper-school students received aid. Total amount of financial aid awarded in 2005–06: $456,158.

Admissions Traditional secondary-level entrance grade is 9. ISEE required. Deadline for receipt of application materials: January 19. Application fee required: $60. Interview required.

Athletics Interscholastic: baseball (boys), basketball (b,g), cross-country running (b,g), golf (b,g), running (b,g), skiing (cross-country) (b,g), soccer (b,g), tennis (b,g), track and field (b,g), ultimate Frisbee (b,g), volleyball (g); intramural: lacrosse (g); coed interscholastic: nordic skiing, skiing (cross-country), ultimate Frisbee; coed intramural: back packing, climbing, curling, fencing, Frisbee, hiking/backpacking, outdoor activities, outdoor adventure, outdoor education, outdoor skills, rafting, rock climbing, skiing (downhill), ultimate Frisbee, weight training, wilderness. 3 PE instructors, 3 coaches.

Computers Computers are regularly used in art, English, foreign language, mathematics, multimedia, music, science, yearbook classes. Computer network features include campus e-mail, on-campus library services, CD-ROMs, online commercial services, Internet access, file transfer, DVD, wireless campus network.

Contact Ms. Sheila Hicks, Admissions Assistant. 206-326-7736. Fax: 206-860-3876. E-mail: sheila.hicks@bush.edu. Web site: bush.edu.

ANNOUNCEMENT FROM THE SCHOOL Bush School's progressive educational program balances academic rigor with close student-teacher relationships and wide-ranging experiential education opportunities. Programs emphasize high academic standards and the development of the whole child within a "culture of kindness" that values diversity. Grades K–12, 560 students, 17% of color. Average class size 15.

BUXTON SCHOOL

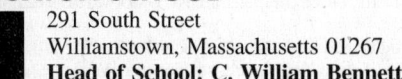

291 South Street
Williamstown, Massachusetts 01267
Head of School: C. William Bennett

petersons.com

General Information Coeducational boarding and day college-preparatory and arts school. Grades 9–12. Founded: 1928. Setting: small town. Nearest major city is Boston. Students are housed in single-sex dormitories. 150-acre campus. 17 buildings on campus. Approved or accredited by Association of Independent Schools in New England, New England Association of Schools and Colleges, The Association of Boarding Schools, and Massachusetts Department of Education. Member of National Association of Independent Schools and Secondary School Admission Test Board. Endowment: $1.2 million. Total enrollment: 90. Upper school average class size: 9. Upper school faculty-student ratio: 1:5.

Upper School Student Profile Grade 9: 11 students (6 boys, 5 girls); Grade 10: 27 students (14 boys, 13 girls); Grade 11: 27 students (12 boys, 15 girls); Grade 12: 25 students (13 boys, 12 girls). 97% of students are boarding students. 10% are state residents. 19 states are represented in upper school student body. 10% are international students. International students from Ecuador, Jamaica, Japan, Republic of Korea, Spain, and Taiwan; 1 other country represented in student body.

Faculty School total: 18. In upper school: 9 men, 9 women; 4 have advanced degrees; 14 reside on campus.

Subjects Offered 20th century history, African studies, algebra, American history, American literature, astronomy, biology, calculus, ceramics, chemistry, comparative religion, contemporary issues, costumes and make-up, creative writing, critical writing, dance performance, drama, drama performance, drawing, economics, English, English literature, ensembles, European history, existentialism, expository writing, fiction, film history, French, geology, geometry, global issues, grammar, instrumental music, lab science, Latin American studies, law studies, marine biology, Middle East, music, music composition, music performance, music theory, oceanography, painting, performing arts, philosophy, photography, physics, poetry, pre-

calculus, printmaking, psychology, set design, social science, society and culture, Spanish, studio art, technical theater, video film production, Vietnam War, voice, writing workshop.

Graduation Requirements American history, English, foreign language, lab science, mathematics, social science.

Special Academic Programs Honors section; academic accommodation for the gifted, the musically talented, and the artistically talented; ESL (4 students enrolled).

College Placement 22 students graduated in 2005; 20 went to college, including Amherst College; Guilford College; Hampshire College; Oberlin College; Sarah Lawrence College; Smith College. Other: 2 had other specific plans.

Student Life Discipline rests primarily with faculty.

Tuition and Aid Day student tuition: $20,700; 7-day tuition and room/board: $33,500. Tuition installment plan (Academic Management Services Plan, Key Tuition Payment Plan, 3-payment plan). Need-based scholarship grants, tuition reduction for priority groups available. In 2005–06, 37% of upper-school students received aid. Total amount of financial aid awarded in 2005–06: $934,000.

Admissions Traditional secondary-level entrance grade is 9. For fall 2005, 55 students applied for upper-level admission, 44 were accepted, 35 enrolled. SSAT required. Deadline for receipt of application materials: February 1. Application fee required: $50. On-campus interview required.

Athletics Interscholastic: soccer (boys, girls); intramural: soccer (b,g), table tennis (b); coed interscholastic: basketball, track and field; coed intramural: basketball, bicycling, bowling, boxing, dance, figure skating, fitness, hiking/backpacking, horseback riding, ice skating, indoor soccer, jogging, kayaking, martial arts, mountain biking, outdoor activities, physical training, rock climbing, roller skating, skateboarding, skiing (cross-country), skiing (downhill), snowboarding, soccer, softball, swimming and diving, ultimate Frisbee, unicycling, weight lifting, winter soccer, yoga.

Computers Computers are regularly used in mathematics, photography, science, video film production classes. Computer resources include CD-ROMs, Internet access, file transfer, DVD, wireless campus network.

Contact Admissions Office. 413-458-3919. Fax: 413-458-9427. E-mail: Admissions@BuxtonSchool.org. Web site: www.BuxtonSchool.org.

ANNOUNCEMENT FROM THE SCHOOL Life at Buxton teaches the importance of a moral and active commitment to a small, diverse community. The sophisticated college-preparatory curriculum also includes art, music, and drama. The student-faculty ratio is 5:1. Individual attention and relationships with adults are emphasized. Work Program and the annual All-School Trip challenge students to meet demands collectively and creatively.

See full description on page 704.

CALGARY ACADEMY

9400-17 Avenue, SW
Calgary, Alberta T3H 4A6, Canada
Head of School: Mr. Peter E. Istvanffy

General Information Coeducational day college-preparatory, arts, and technology school; primarily serves underachievers. Grades 2–12. Founded: 1981. Setting: urban. 17-acre campus. 3 buildings on campus. Approved or accredited by Association of Independent Schools and Colleges of Alberta and Alberta Department of Education. Language of instruction: English. Endowment: CAN$1 million. Total enrollment: 570. Upper school average class size: 16. Upper school faculty-student ratio: 1:8.

Faculty School total: 25. In upper school: 10 men, 15 women; 10 have advanced degrees.

Special Academic Programs Remedial reading and/or remedial writing; remedial math; programs in English, mathematics for dyslexic students.

College Placement 64 students graduated in 2005; 51 went to college. Other: 7 went to work, 6 had other specific plans.

Student Life Upper grades have specified standards of dress, student council, honor system. Discipline rests primarily with faculty.

Tuition and Aid Day student tuition: CAN$7600–CAN$13,750. Tuition installment plan (monthly payment plans, individually arranged payment plans). Bursaries available. In 2005–06, 5% of upper-school students received aid. Total amount of financial aid awarded in 2005–06: CAN$180,000.

Admissions Traditional secondary-level entrance grade is 7. For fall 2005, 150 students applied for upper-level admission, 100 were accepted, 100 enrolled. Wechsler Intelligence Scale for Children III required. Deadline for receipt of application materials: none. Application fee required: CAN$250. Interview required.

Athletics Interscholastic: badminton (boys, girls), basketball (b,g), cross-country running (b,g), golf (b,g), track and field (b,g), volleyball (b,g), wrestling (b,g); intramural: ice hockey (b,g), racquetball (b,g), rock climbing (b,g), self defense (g), squash (b,g), weight training (b,g); coed intramural: aerobics, aerobics/dance, aerobics/nautilus, alpine skiing, aquatics, archery, ball hockey, baseball, bowling, broomball, canoeing/kayaking, climbing, cooperative games, curling, dance, fitness, flag football, football, outdoor education, sailing, scuba diving, skiing (downhill), skydiving, swimming and diving, team handball, walking.

Computers Computers are regularly used in all academic classes. Computer network features include Internet access, wireless campus network.

Contact Ms. Joanne Endacott, Director of Admissions. 403-686-6444 Ext. 236. Fax: 403-686-3427. E-mail: jendacott@calgaryacademy.com. Web site: www.calgaryacademy.com.

THE CALHOUN SCHOOL

433 West End Avenue
New York, New York 10024
Head of School: Steven J. Nelson

petersons.com

General Information Coeducational day college-preparatory and arts school. Grades N–12. Founded: 1896. Setting: urban. 2 buildings on campus. Approved or accredited by New York State Association of Independent Schools and New York Department of Education. Member of National Association of Independent Schools. Endowment: $1.8 million. Total enrollment: 675. Upper school average class size: 15. Upper school faculty-student ratio: 1:5.

Upper School Student Profile Grade 9: 47 students (20 boys, 27 girls); Grade 10: 46 students (23 boys, 23 girls); Grade 11: 48 students (21 boys, 27 girls); Grade 12: 39 students (17 boys, 22 girls).

Faculty School total: 115. In upper school: 16 men, 18 women; 25 have advanced degrees.

Subjects Offered African-American literature, algebra, American history, American literature, anthropology, arts, biology, biology-AP, calculus, chemistry, child development, chorus, community service, computer math, computer programming, computer science, constitutional law, creative writing, English literature, English-AP, ethnic literature, French, geometry, healthful living, human sexuality, independent study, instrumental music, music history, peer counseling, photography, physical education, physics, pre-calculus, psychology, Shakespeare, Spanish, speech, studio art, theater, theater design and production, Web site design, world history, world literature.

Graduation Requirements Arts and fine arts (art, music, dance, drama), computer science, English, foreign language, mathematics, physical education (includes health), science, social studies (includes history), 9th grade Life Skills with peer leaders. Community service is required.

Special Academic Programs Advanced Placement exam preparation in 6 subject areas; honors section; independent study; domestic exchange program (with The Network Program Schools); academic accommodation for the gifted.

College Placement 43 students graduated in 2005; 42 went to college, including Brown University; Columbia College; Goucher College; The George Washington University. Other: 1 went to work. Median SAT verbal: 620, median SAT math: 587. 59% scored over 600 on SAT verbal, 41% scored over 600 on SAT math.

Student Life Upper grades have student council. Discipline rests primarily with faculty.

Tuition and Aid Day student tuition: $27,600. Tuition installment plan (Key Tuition Payment Plan, individually arranged payment plans, 60%/40% payment plan). Need-based scholarship grants available. In 2005–06, 36% of upper-school students received aid. Total amount of financial aid awarded in 2005–06: $1,240,000.

Admissions Traditional secondary-level entrance grade is 9. For fall 2005, 156 students applied for upper-level admission, 30 were accepted, 11 enrolled. ISEE required. Deadline for receipt of application materials: January 15. Application fee required: $50. On-campus interview required.

Athletics Interscholastic: baseball (boys, girls), basketball (b,g), cross-country running (b,g), tennis (b,g), track and field (b,g), volleyball (b,g); coed interscholastic: golf, soccer; coed intramural: aerobics, aerobics/nautilus, basketball, fitness, golf, sailing, soccer, strength & conditioning, tennis. 5 PE instructors, 2 coaches.

Computers Computers are regularly used in basic skills, mathematics, programming, video film production, Web site design classes. Computer network features include Internet access, MS Office, PowerPoint, Basic, Dreameaver, and Flash Software.

Contact Jenny Eugenio, Assistant Director of Admissions. 212-497-6510. Fax: 212-497-6531. E-mail: jenny.eugenio@calhoun.org. Web site: www.calhoun.org.

ANNOUNCEMENT FROM THE SCHOOL Calhoun's progressive program capitalizes on the intellectual curiosity and creative spirit inherent in every child. Classes are small and discussion based, learning experiential and interdisciplinary, the atmosphere lively. In September 2004, Calhoun expanded its facilities with a new center for performing and studio arts, 3 science labs, and a regulation-size gymnasium.

CALVARY CHRISTIAN ACADEMY

5955 Taylor Mill Road
Covington, Kentucky 41015
Head of School: Mr. Don James

General Information Coeducational day college-preparatory, arts, religious studies, and technology school, affiliated with Baptist Church. Grades K4–12. Founded: 1974. Setting: suburban. Nearest major city is Cincinnati, OH. 67-acre campus. 1 building on campus. Approved or accredited by Association of Christian Schools International, CITA (Commission on International and Trans-Regional Accreditation), Southern

Association of Colleges and Schools, and Kentucky Department of Education. Total enrollment: 636. Upper school average class size: 25. Upper school faculty-student ratio: 1:15.

Upper School Student Profile Grade 9: 46 students (22 boys, 24 girls); Grade 10: 53 students (27 boys, 26 girls); Grade 11: 50 students (30 boys, 20 girls); Grade 12: 48 students (16 boys, 32 girls). 65% of students are Baptist.

Faculty School total: 34. In upper school: 10 men, 9 women; 9 have advanced degrees.

Subjects Offered Advanced math, algebra, American literature-AP, ancient history, art, art appreciation, Bible, biology, biology-AP, calculus, chemistry, chemistry-AP, choir, chorus, Christian doctrine, Christian ethics, church history, communication arts, computer applications, computer keyboarding, computer multimedia, computer science, concert band, concert choir, consumer mathematics, creative writing, cultural geography, debate, drama, drama performance, earth science, English, English composition, English language and composition-AP, English language-AP, English literature, English literature and composition-AP, English literature-AP, English-AP, English/composition-AP, ethics, European history-AP, fitness, food and nutrition, general math, general science, geography, geometry, government-AP, grammar, Greek, health education, home economics, honors algebra, independent study, journalism, lab science, language arts, language-AP, library assistant, literature-AP, logic, music theory, newspaper, physical education, physical science, physics-AP, pre-algebra, pre-calculus, rhetoric, Spanish, Spanish-AP, speech and debate, student government, student publications, student teaching, U.S. government, U.S. government-AP, U.S. history, U.S. history-AP, world governments, world history, yearbook.

Graduation Requirements Algebra, art appreciation, Bible, biology, chemistry, Christian doctrine, church history, civics, English, English composition, English literature, European history, foreign language, geometry, health, physical science, U.S. government, U.S. history, world history.

Special Academic Programs Advanced Placement exam preparation in 7 subject areas; honors section; independent study.

College Placement 52 students graduated in 2005; 48 went to college, including Cedarville University; Northern Kentucky University; University of Cincinnati; University of Kentucky; Virginia Polytechnic Institute and State University. Other: 4 went to work. Median composite ACT: 26. 25% scored over 26 on composite ACT.

Student Life Upper grades have uniform requirement, student council. Discipline rests primarily with faculty. Attendance at religious services is required.

Tuition and Aid Day student tuition: $4000. Tuition installment plan (FACTS Tuition Payment Plan, monthly payment plans, individually arranged payment plans). Tuition reduction for siblings, need-based scholarship grants, paying campus jobs available. In 2005–06, 8% of upper-school students received aid. Total amount of financial aid awarded in 2005–06: $25,000.

Admissions Traditional secondary-level entrance grade is 9. For fall 2005, 14 students applied for upper-level admission, 14 were accepted, 14 enrolled. Stanford Achievement Test required. Deadline for receipt of application materials: none. Application fee required: $95. Interview required.

Athletics Interscholastic: baseball (boys), basketball (b,g), boxing (b,g), cheering (g), cross-country running (b,g), golf (b), soccer (b,g), softball (g), volleyball (g); intramural: indoor soccer (b,g), strength & conditioning (b,g); coed intramural: bowling, gymnastics, physical fitness, running. 2 PE instructors, 15 coaches.

Computers Computer network features include on-campus library services, CD-ROMs, Internet access, file transfer, office computer access, DVD, wireless campus network.

Contact Dr. Bill Dickens, Middle and High School Principal. 859-356-9201. Fax: 859-359-8962. E-mail: william.dickens@calvarychristianky.org. Web site: www.calvarychristianky.org.

CALVERT HALL COLLEGE HIGH SCHOOL

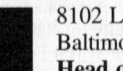

8102 LaSalle Road
Baltimore, Maryland 21286
Head of School: Br. Benedict Oliver, FSC

General Information Boys' day college-preparatory, arts, business, religious studies, and technology school, affiliated with Roman Catholic Church. Grades 9–12. Founded: 1845. Setting: urban. 32-acre campus. 5 buildings on campus. Approved or accredited by Christian Brothers Association, Middle States Association of Colleges and Schools, and Maryland Department of Education. Endowment: $4.3 million. Total enrollment: 1,224. Upper school average class size: 21. Upper school faculty-student ratio: 1:12.

Upper School Student Profile Grade 9: 368 students (368 boys); Grade 10: 282 students (282 boys); Grade 11: 283 students (283 boys); Grade 12: 291 students (291 boys). 77% of students are Roman Catholic.

Faculty School total: 99. In upper school: 73 men, 23 women; 58 have advanced degrees.

Subjects Offered Algebra, American history, American literature, art, art history, band, Bible studies, biology, business, business skills, calculus, chemistry, chorus, computer programming, computer science, creative writing, drama, earth science, economics, English, English literature, ethics, European history, fine arts, French, geography, geometry, German, government/civics, graphic arts, history, journalism, Latin, mathematics, music, painting, physical education, physics, psychology,

religion, science, sculpture, social science, social studies, Spanish, speech, theater, theology, typing, world history, world literature, writing.

Graduation Requirements Arts and fine arts (art, music, dance, drama), business skills (includes word processing), English, foreign language, mathematics, physical education (includes health), religion (includes Bible studies and theology), science, social science, social studies (includes history).

Special Academic Programs Advanced Placement exam preparation in 19 subject areas; honors section; academic accommodation for the gifted, the musically talented, and the artistically talented; remedial reading and/or remedial writing; remedial math; programs in English, mathematics, general development for dyslexic students.

College Placement 260 students graduated in 2005; 256 went to college, including Loyola College in Maryland; Towson University; University of Maryland, Baltimore County; University of Maryland, College Park; Villa Julie College; Virginia Polytechnic Institute and State University. Other: 1 went to work, 1 entered military service, 2 had other specific plans. 31% scored over 600 on SAT verbal, 37% scored over 600 on SAT math.

Student Life Upper grades have specified standards of dress, student council. Discipline rests primarily with faculty. Attendance at religious services is required.

Summer Programs Remediation, enrichment, computer instruction programs offered; session focuses on remediation and make-up courses; held on campus; accepts boys and girls; open to students from other schools. 200 students usually enrolled. 2006 schedule: June to July. Application deadline: June.

Tuition and Aid Day student tuition: $9000. Tuition installment plan (monthly payment plans, individually arranged payment plans). Merit scholarship grants, need-based scholarship grants available. In 2005–06, 40% of upper-school students received aid; total upper-school merit-scholarship money awarded: $280,000. Total amount of financial aid awarded in 2005–06: $1,000,000.

Admissions Traditional secondary-level entrance grade is 9. For fall 2005, 673 students applied for upper-level admission, 525 were accepted, 368 enrolled. STS required. Deadline for receipt of application materials: none. Application fee required: $20.

Athletics Interscholastic: baseball, basketball, cross-country running, diving, football, golf, hockey, ice hockey, indoor track & field, lacrosse, rugby, soccer, swimming and diving, track and field, water polo, winter (indoor) track, wrestling; intramural: archery, basketball, bicycling, billiards, bowling, flag football, mountain biking, rugby, table tennis, weight lifting. 2 PE instructors, 12 coaches, 1 trainer.

Computers Computers are regularly used in business, English, mathematics, science, typing classes. Computer network features include campus e-mail, on-campus library services, CD-ROMs, Internet access, DVD, wireless campus network.

Contact Chris Bengel, Director of Admissions. 410-825-4266 Ext. 126. Fax: 410-825-6826. E-mail: bengelc@calverthall.com. Web site: www.calverthall.com.

THE CALVERTON SCHOOL

300 Calverton School Road
Huntingtown, Maryland 20639
Head of School: Mr. Daniel Hildebrand

General Information Coeducational day college-preparatory, arts, and technology school. Grades PK–12. Founded: 1967. Setting: rural. Nearest major city is Annapolis. 150-acre campus. 3 buildings on campus. Approved or accredited by Association of Independent Maryland Schools, The College Board, and Maryland Department of Education. Member of National Association of Independent Schools. Total enrollment: 414. Upper school average class size: 15. Upper school faculty-student ratio: 1:11.

Upper School Student Profile Grade 9: 31 students (16 boys, 15 girls); Grade 10: 27 students (14 boys, 13 girls); Grade 11: 30 students (17 boys, 13 girls); Grade 12: 22 students (11 boys, 11 girls).

Faculty School total: 49. In upper school: 10 men, 12 women; 15 have advanced degrees.

Subjects Offered Advanced Placement courses, algebra, American history, American literature, art, art history, biochemistry, biology, calculus, chemistry, Chesapeake Bay studies, chorus, computer science, creative writing, drama, economics, engineering, English, English literature, environmental science, European civilization, fine arts, French, French-AP, geometry, government/civics, health, humanities, journalism, literature, mathematics, newspaper, physical education, physics, pre-calculus, public speaking, publications, SAT/ACT preparation, science, social studies, Spanish, Spanish-AP, studio art-AP, theater, trigonometry, U.S. history, U.S. history-AP, visual and performing arts, world civilizations, world history, world literature, yearbook.

Graduation Requirements Algebra, arts and fine arts (art, music, dance, drama), biology, chemistry, English, English composition, English literature, foreign language, geometry, mathematics, physical education (includes health), physics, science, social studies (includes history), trigonometry, U.S. history, world history.

Special Academic Programs Advanced Placement exam preparation; honors section; independent study.

College Placement 35 students graduated in 2004; all went to college.

Student Life Upper grades have specified standards of dress, student council, honor system. Discipline rests equally with students and faculty.

Tuition and Aid Day student tuition: $13,800. Tuition installment plan (Insured Tuition Payment Plan, monthly payment plans, individually arranged payment plans). Need-based scholarship grants, free tuition for fourth child available.

Admissions Traditional secondary-level entrance grade is 9. Admissions testing, Math Placement Exam, Otis-Lennon School Ability Test and writing sample required. Deadline for receipt of application materials: none. Application fee required: $35. On-campus interview required.

Athletics Interscholastic: basketball (boys, girls), cross-country running (b,g), lacrosse (b,g); coed interscholastic: cheering, field hockey, golf, soccer, tennis; coed intramural: basketball. 3 PE instructors, 10 coaches.

Computers Computers are regularly used in all academic classes. Computer network features include on-campus library services, CD-ROMs, online commercial services, Internet access, office computer access, research services and encyclopedia research programs.

Contact Mrs. Erna A. Casalino, Admission Director. 888-678-0216 Ext. 108. Fax: 410-535-6934. E-mail: ecasalino@calvertonschool.org. Web site: www.CalvertonSchool.org.

ANNOUNCEMENT FROM THE SCHOOL The Calverton School, southern Maryland's leader in college-preparatory education, grades PK through 12, offers a challenging student-centered curriculum enhanced by athletics and the arts. A top-notch faculty and 10:1 student-teacher ratio promote a strong sense of community, individual attention, and commitment to the development of well-balanced and well-educated students.

CAMBRIDGE INTERNATIONAL COLLEGE OF CANADA

35 Ourland Avenue
Toronto, Ontario M8Z 4E1, Canada
Head of School: Mr. Irwin Diamond

General Information Coeducational day college-preparatory, arts, business, and science school. Grades 10–13. Founded: 1980. Setting: suburban. 1 building on campus. Approved or accredited by Ontario Department of Education. Language of instruction: English. Total enrollment: 300. Upper school average class size: 16. Upper school faculty-student ratio: 1:13.

Faculty School total: 12. In upper school: 5 men, 5 women; 5 have advanced degrees.

Special Academic Programs ESL (120 students enrolled).

College Placement Colleges students went to include Abilene Christian University.

Student Life Discipline rests equally with students and faculty.

Summer Programs Enrichment, advancement, ESL, art/fine arts programs offered; held on campus; accepts boys and girls; open to students from other schools. 50 students usually enrolled. 2006 schedule: July 10 to August 14. Application deadline: June 25.

Tuition and Aid Day student tuition: $6500. Guaranteed tuition plan.

Admissions Math and English placement tests required. Deadline for receipt of application materials: none. Application fee required: $320.

Computers Computer resources include campus e-mail, CD-ROMs, Internet access, DVD.

Contact Mrs. Atri Dolsingh Hill, Admissions Officer. 416-252-9195. Fax: 416-252-4266. E-mail: cambridge@globalserve.net. Web site: www.CambridgeInternational.com.

THE CAMBRIDGE SCHOOL OF WESTON

45 Georgian Road
Weston, Massachusetts 02493
Head of School: Jane Moulding

General Information Coeducational boarding and day college-preparatory and arts school. Grades 9–PG. Founded: 1886. Setting: suburban. Nearest major city is Boston. Students are housed in single-sex dormitories. 65-acre campus. 25 buildings on campus. Approved or accredited by Association of Independent Schools in New England, New England Association of Schools and Colleges, The Association of Boarding Schools, and The College Board. Member of National Association of Independent Schools and Secondary School Admission Test Board. Endowment: $5 million. Total enrollment: 324. Upper school average class size: 12. Upper school faculty-student ratio: 1:6.

Upper School Student Profile 25% of students are boarding students. 83% are state residents. 8 states are represented in upper school student body. 10% are international students. International students from Canada, China, Japan, Mexico, Republic of Korea, and Taiwan.

Faculty School total: 63. In upper school: 28 men, 35 women; 45 have advanced degrees; 14 reside on campus.

Subjects Offered 3-dimensional art, African American history, African dance, African literature, African studies, African-American literature, African-American studies, algebra, American Civil War, American democracy, American history, American literature, American sign language, anatomy, animal behavior, art, art history, ballet, Bible studies, biology, botany, calculus, calculus-AP, cell biology, ceramics, chemistry, child development, Chinese history, choir, community service, computer math, computer programming, computer science, computer skills, creative

writing, dance, death and loss, digital art, digital photography, discrete math, drama, drama performance, drawing, driver education, earth science, ecology, economics, electronic music, English, English literature, environmental science, environmental systems, ethics, ethnic literature, European history, expository writing, fashion, film history, filmmaking, fine arts, foods, French, geography, geometry, government/civics, grammar, great books, Harlem Renaissance, health, health and wellness, history, history of ideas, history of music, history of science, independent study, interdisciplinary studies, jazz dance, jazz ensemble, journalism, keyboarding, Latin, Latin American literature, marine biology, mathematical modeling, mathematics, Middle East, music, ornithology, painting, philosophy, photography, physical education, physics, physiology, playwriting, poetry, psychology, religion, Roman civilization, science, sculpture, senior project, set design, Shakespeare, short story, social studies, sociology, Spanish, statistics, the Presidency, theater, trigonometry, typing, U.S. constitutional history, wilderness/outdoor program, world history, world literature, World War II, writing, zoology.

Graduation Requirements Art history, arts and fine arts (art, music, dance, drama), computer literacy, computer science, English, foreign language, health education, history, mathematics, physical education (includes health), science, senior project. Community service is required.

Special Academic Programs Advanced Placement exam preparation in 10 subject areas; independent study; term-away projects; study abroad; ESL (25 students enrolled).

College Placement 93 students graduated in 2005; 91 went to college, including Bard College; Massachusetts Institute of Technology; Rhode Island School of Design; Sarah Lawrence College; Stanford University; Wellesley College. Other: 2 had other specific plans. 65% scored over 600 on SAT verbal, 58% scored over 600 on SAT math.

Student Life Upper grades have student council. Discipline rests equally with students and faculty.

Summer Programs Enrichment, advancement, art/fine arts programs offered; session focuses on art and academic enrichment; held on campus; accepts boys and girls; open to students from other schools. 50 students usually enrolled. 2006 schedule: June 29 to July 28. Application deadline: May 1.

Tuition and Aid Day student tuition: $27,000; 7-day tuition and room/board: $36,300. Tuition installment plan (Insured Tuition Payment Plan, Academic Management Services Plan, individually arranged payment plans, Academic Management Services Academic Credit Line). Need-based scholarship grants, paying campus jobs, Achiever Loans (Key Education Resources) available. In 2005–06, 23% of upper-school students received aid. Total amount of financial aid awarded in 2005–06: $1,374,500.

Admissions Traditional secondary-level entrance grade is 9. For fall 2005, 337 students applied for upper-level admission, 211 were accepted, 109 enrolled. ISEE, PSAT, SAT, SSAT or TOEFL required. Deadline for receipt of application materials: February 1. Application fee required: $45. Interview required.

Athletics Interscholastic: baseball (boys), basketball (b,g), field hockey (g), soccer (b,g), softball (g); coed interscholastic: Frisbee, tennis, ultimate Frisbee; coed intramural: aerobics, aerobics/dance, aerobics/nautilus, alpine skiing, back packing, ballet, bicycling, canoeing/kayaking, cheering, climbing, cross-country running, dance, dance team, fencing, fitness, Frisbee, hiking/backpacking, martial arts, modern dance, nordic skiing, outdoor activities, outdoor education, outdoor recreation, outdoor skills, outdoors, physical fitness, physical training, rafting, rock climbing, roller blading, ropes courses, rowing, running, sailing, strength & conditioning, triathlon, ultimate Frisbee, volleyball, weight training, wilderness, yoga. 15 coaches, 1 trainer.

Computers Computers are regularly used in art, college planning, English, ESL, ethics, French, graphic design, history, humanities, independent study, journalism, keyboarding, Latin, library, literary magazine, mathematics, music, newspaper, photography, programming, psychology, publications, science, Spanish, word processing, writing, yearbook classes. Computer network features include campus e-mail, on-campus library services, CD-ROMs, online commercial services, Internet access, file transfer, DVD, wireless campus network.

Contact Trish Saunders, Director of Admissions. 781-642-8650. Fax: 781-398-8344. E-mail: admissions@csw.org. Web site: www.csw.org.

See full description on page 706.

CAMDEN MILITARY ACADEMY

520 Highway 1 North
Camden, South Carolina 29020
Head of School: Col. Eric Boland

petersons.com

General Information Boys' boarding college-preparatory school. Grades 7–PG. Founded: 1892. Setting: small town. Nearest major city is Columbia. Students are housed in single-sex dormitories. 50-acre campus. 15 buildings on campus. Approved or accredited by Southern Association of Colleges and Schools. Member of National Association of Independent Schools. Total enrollment: 305. Upper school average class size: 15. Upper school faculty-student ratio: 1:12.

Upper School Student Profile Grade 9: 54 students (54 boys); Grade 10: 58 students (58 boys); Grade 11: 60 students (60 boys); Grade 12: 64 students (64 boys). 100% of students are boarding students. 39% are state residents. 23 states are represented

in upper school student body. 1% are international students. International students from Bermuda, Cayman Islands, Ghana, Mexico, Republic of Korea, and Trinidad and Tobago.

Faculty School total: 49. In upper school: 35 men, 3 women; 23 have advanced degrees; 9 reside on campus.

Subjects Offered Algebra, American government, anatomy and physiology, band, biology, calculus, chemistry, computer applications, computer literacy, driver education, economics, English, French, geometry, humanities, physical science, physics, pre-calculus, psychology, sociology, Spanish, U.S. history, world geography, world history.

Graduation Requirements Computer literacy, English, foreign language, history, JROTC, mathematics, science.

Special Academic Programs Advanced Placement exam preparation in 5 subject areas; honors section; study at local college for college credit; remedial reading and/or remedial writing.

College Placement 67 students graduated in 2005; they went to University of South Carolina. Other: 1 went to work, 8 entered military service.

Student Life Upper grades have uniform requirement, student council, honor system. Discipline rests primarily with faculty.

Summer Programs Enrichment, advancement programs offered; session focuses on academics; held on campus; accepts boys; open to students from other schools. 2006 schedule: June 19 to July 28. Application deadline: none.

Tuition and Aid 7-day tuition and room/board: $14,995. Tuition reduction for siblings, need-based scholarship grants available. In 2005–06, 15% of upper-school students received aid. Total amount of financial aid awarded in 2005–06: $200,000.

Admissions Traditional secondary-level entrance grade is 9. Deadline for receipt of application materials: none. Application fee required: $100. On-campus interview required.

Athletics Interscholastic: baseball, basketball, cross-country running, football, golf, lacrosse, marksmanship, soccer, tennis, track and field, wrestling; intramural: aerobics. 2 PE instructors, 15 coaches, 1 trainer.

Computers Computers are regularly used in all academic classes. Computer resources include campus e-mail, on-campus library services, CD-ROMs, Internet access, DVD.

Contact Mr. Casey Robinson, Director of Admissions. 803-432-6001. Fax: 803-425-1020. E-mail: admissions@camdenmilitary.com. Web site: www. camdenmilitary.com.

See full description on page 708.

CAMELOT ACADEMY

809 Proctor Street
Durham, North Carolina 27707
Head of School: Thelma DeCarlo Glynn

General Information Coeducational day college-preparatory school. Grades K–12. Founded: 1982. Setting: small town. Nearest major city is Raleigh. 3-acre campus. 1 building on campus. Approved or accredited by National Independent Private Schools Association and North Carolina Department of Education. Total enrollment: 92. Upper school average class size: 10. Upper school faculty-student ratio: 1:10.

Faculty School total: 11. In upper school: 4 men, 3 women.

Graduation Requirements Electives, foreign language, language arts, mathematics, physical education (includes health), science, social studies (includes history).

Special Academic Programs Advanced Placement exam preparation in 6 subject areas; honors section; accelerated programs; independent study; study at local college for college credit; academic accommodation for the gifted; remedial reading and/or remedial writing; remedial math.

College Placement 9 students graduated in 2005; all went to college, including Eckerd College; New York University; San Francisco State University; Savannah College of Art and Design; The University of North Carolina Wilmington. Mean SAT verbal: 558, mean SAT math: 555. 25% scored over 600 on SAT verbal, 38% scored over 600 on SAT math.

Student Life Upper grades have specified standards of dress, honor system. Discipline rests primarily with faculty.

Summer Programs Enrichment, advancement programs offered; session focuses on language arts and mathematics for enrichment and advancement; held on campus; accepts boys and girls; open to students from other schools. 20 students usually enrolled. 2006 schedule: June 12 to July 28.

Tuition and Aid Day student tuition: $8750. Tuition installment plan (monthly payment plan through KeyBank). Tuition reduction for siblings, merit scholarship grants, need-based scholarship grants, need-based loans available. In 2005–06, 60% of upper-school students received aid; total upper-school merit-scholarship money awarded: $38,000.

Admissions Traditional secondary-level entrance grade is 9. California Achievement Test and ERB required. Deadline for receipt of application materials: none. Application fee required: $50. Interview required.

Athletics Interscholastic: soccer (boys); coed interscholastic: basketball; coed intramural: aerobics, fitness. 1 PE instructor.

Contact Ms. Wendy Morris, Office Manager. 919-688-3040. Fax: 919-682-4320. E-mail: wendy@camelotacademy.org. Web site: www.camelotacademy.org/.

CAMPBELL HALL (EPISCOPAL)

4533 Laurel Canyon Boulevard
North Hollywood, California 91607
Head of School: Rev. Julian Bull

petersons.com

General Information Coeducational day college-preparatory, arts, and technology school, affiliated with Episcopal Church. Grades K–12. Founded: 1944. Setting: suburban. Nearest major city is Los Angeles. 15-acre campus. 12 buildings on campus. Approved or accredited by California Association of Independent Schools, The College Board, Western Association of Schools and Colleges, and California Department of Education. Member of National Association of Independent Schools. Languages of instruction: Spanish, French, and Japanese. Endowment: $5 million. Total enrollment: 1,073. Upper school average class size: 15. Upper school faculty-student ratio: 1:8.

Upper School Student Profile Grade 9: 127 students (65 boys, 62 girls); Grade 10: 132 students (68 boys, 64 girls); Grade 11: 124 students (62 boys, 62 girls); Grade 12: 126 students (60 boys, 66 girls). 7% of students are members of Episcopal Church.

Faculty School total: 108. In upper school: 23 men, 32 women; 30 have advanced degrees.

Subjects Offered Algebra, American history, American literature, American studies, ancient history, art, art history, astronomy, band, biology, calculus, ceramics, chemistry, community service, computer programming, computer science, creative writing, dance, drama, drawing, earth science, ecology, economics, English, English literature, environmental science, ethics, European history, fine arts, French, geography, geometry, government/civics, history, human development, humanities, instrumental music, Japanese, law, mathematics, music, orchestra, painting, philosophy, photography, physical education, physics, physiology, pre-calculus, printmaking, psychology, science, sculpture, senior seminar, social studies, sociology, Spanish, speech, statistics, theater, theater arts, trigonometry, voice, yearbook.

Graduation Requirements Arts and fine arts (art, music, dance, drama), computer science, English, foreign language, mathematics, physical education (includes health), science, social studies (includes history). Community service is required.

Special Academic Programs Advanced Placement exam preparation in 19 subject areas; honors section; independent study; study at local college for college credit; study abroad; academic accommodation for the gifted.

College Placement 126 students graduated in 2005; all went to college, including Boston University; New York University; University of California, Berkeley; University of California, Los Angeles; University of Southern California.

Student Life Upper grades have uniform requirement, student council, honor system. Discipline rests primarily with faculty. Attendance at religious services is required.

Summer Programs Enrichment, advancement, sports, art/fine arts, computer instruction programs offered; session focuses on creative arts; held on campus; accepts boys and girls; open to students from other schools. 200 students usually enrolled. 2006 schedule: June 19 to August 4. Application deadline: June 1.

Tuition and Aid Day student tuition: $20,670. Tuition installment plan (Insured Tuition Payment Plan, monthly payment plans, individually arranged payment plans). Tuition reduction for siblings, need-based scholarship grants, paying campus jobs, Episcopal Credit Union tuition loans available. In 2005–06, 21% of upper-school students received aid. Total amount of financial aid awarded in 2005–06: $1,479,425.

Admissions Traditional secondary-level entrance grade is 9. For fall 2005, 596 students applied for upper-level admission, 244 were accepted, 103 enrolled. ISEE required. Deadline for receipt of application materials: February 1. Application fee required: $100. On-campus interview required.

Athletics Interscholastic: aerobics/dance (boys, girls), ballet (g), baseball (b), basketball (b,g), cheering (b,g), cross-country running (b,g), dance (g), dance squad (b,g), equestrian sports (b,g), flag football (b,g), football (b), golf (b,g), modern dance (g), soccer (b,g), softball (g), tennis (b,g), track and field (b,g), volleyball (b,g); intramural: weight lifting (b,g); coed interscholastic: aerobics/dance, cheering, cross-country running, golf, track and field. 5 PE instructors, 13 coaches, 2 trainers.

Computers Computers are regularly used in art, English, foreign language, history, humanities, mathematics, science, theater arts classes. Computer network features include campus e-mail, on-campus library services, CD-ROMs, online commercial services, Internet access.

Contact Ms. Alice Fleming, Director of Admissions. 818-980-7280. Fax: 818-762-3269. E-mail: flemina@campbellhall.org. Web site: www.campbell.pvt.k12.ca.us.

See full description on page 710.

CAMPION SCHOOL, ATHENS

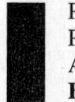

PO Box 67484
Pallini
Athens 15302, Greece
Head of School: Mr. Stephen W. Atherton

petersons.com

General Information Coeducational day college-preparatory, general academic, arts, and music school. Grades PK–13. Founded: 1970. Setting: suburban. 2-hectare campus. 2 buildings on campus. Approved or accredited by European Council of International Schools. Language of instruction: English. Total enrollment: 485. Upper school average class size: 20. Upper school faculty-student ratio: 1:18.

Faculty School total: 65. In upper school: 11 men, 31 women; 16 have advanced degrees.

Subjects Offered Algebra, Arabic, art, biology, calculus, chemistry, design, drama, economics, English, English literature, European history, French, geography, geometry, German, Greek, history, information technology, International Baccalaureate courses, mathematics, music, philosophy, physical education, physics, psychology, SAT preparation, science, Spanish, theater, trigonometry, world history, world literature.

Graduation Requirements Creative arts, English, foreign language, humanities, mathematics, physical education (includes health), science.

Special Academic Programs International Baccalaureate program; academic accommodation for the musically talented and the artistically talented; ESL (11 students enrolled).

College Placement 46 students graduated in 2004; all went to college, including London School of Economics and Political Science; University of Durham. Median SAT verbal: 571, median SAT math: 481. 33% scored over 600 on SAT verbal, 33% scored over 600 on SAT math.

Student Life Upper grades have specified standards of dress, student council. Discipline rests primarily with faculty.

Tuition and Aid Day student tuition: €5240–€9760. Tuition installment plan (individually arranged payment plans). Tuition reduction for siblings, merit scholarship grants, need-based scholarship grants available. In 2004–05, 29% of upper-school students received aid; total upper-school merit-scholarship money awarded: €38,151.

Admissions Traditional secondary-level entrance grade is 12. For fall 2005, 30 students applied for upper-level admission, 20 were accepted, 20 enrolled. School's own test required. Deadline for receipt of application materials: none. No application fee required. On-campus interview required.

Athletics Interscholastic: basketball (boys, girls), cross-country running (b,g), soccer (b,g), tennis (b,g), volleyball (b,g); intramural: basketball (b,g), cricket (b,g), cross-country running (b,g), dance (b,g), field hockey (b,g), gymnastics (b,g), mountain biking (b,g), outdoor activities (b,g), rafting (b,g), rugby (b,g), skiing (downhill) (b,g), snowboarding (b,g), swimming and diving (b,g), table tennis (b,g), tennis (b,g), track and field (b,g), volleyball (b,g), water skiing (b,g), weight lifting (b,g). 3 PE instructors.

Computers Computers are regularly used in English, geography, mathematics, science classes. Computer network features include on-campus library services, CD-ROMs, Internet access.

Contact Ms. Diane Baker, Admissions and Public Relations. 30-2106071700. Fax: 30-2106071750. E-mail: dbaker@hol.gr. Web site: www.campion.edu.gr.

ANNOUNCEMENT FROM THE SCHOOL Campion is an international college-preparatory school that uses a British curriculum modified to reflect the multicultural nature of its student body. The International Baccalaureate Diploma program was selected as the optimum university-preparatory course, allowing students to attain entry to British universities and to American universities with advanced standing.

CANADIAN ACADEMY

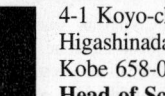

4-1 Koyo-cho Naka
Higashinada-ku
Kobe 658-0032, Japan
Head of School: Mr. Frederic Wesson

General Information Coeducational boarding and day college-preparatory school. Boarding grades 9–13, day grades PK–13. Founded: 1913. Setting: urban. Nearest major city is Osaka. Students are housed in single-sex dormitories. 2-hectare campus. 1 building on campus. Approved or accredited by International Baccalaureate Organization, Ministry of Education, Japan, The College Board, and Western Association of Schools and Colleges. Language of instruction: English. Total enrollment: 762. Upper school average class size: 15. Upper school faculty-student ratio: 1:11.

Upper School Student Profile Grade 9: 51 students (27 boys, 24 girls); Grade 10: 60 students (25 boys, 35 girls); Grade 11: 55 students (22 boys, 33 girls); Grade 12: 46 students (20 boys, 26 girls); Grade 13: 1 student (1 boy). 5% of students are boarding students. International students from Australia, Canada, India, Republic of Korea, and United States; 20 other countries represented in student body.

Faculty School total: 91. In upper school: 17 men, 12 women; 16 have advanced degrees; 20 reside on campus.

Subjects Offered Algebra, American history, art, Asian history, biology, calculus, chemistry, choir, college writing, computer science, concert band, drama, economics, English, ESL, French, geometry, health, Japanese, Japanese history, jazz band, music, orchestra, painting, physical education, physical science, physics, probability and statistics, publications, Spanish, speech, theory of knowledge, trigonometry, U.S. history-AP, world history, world literature.

Graduation Requirements Arts and fine arts (art, music, dance, drama), computer studies, electives, English, mathematics, modern languages, physical education (includes health), science, senior project, social studies (includes history), speech, technology.

Special Academic Programs International Baccalaureate program; Advanced Placement exam preparation in 2 subject areas; honors section; independent study; ESL (2 students enrolled).

College Placement 58 students graduated in 2005; 54 went to college, including Boston University; Bucknell University; Pace University; The Pennsylvania State University at Erie, The Behrend College; Tufts University. Other: 2 went to work, 2 had other specific plans. Median SAT verbal: 520, median SAT math: 600. 31% scored over 600 on SAT verbal, 52% scored over 600 on SAT math.

Student Life Upper grades have specified standards of dress, student council, honor system. Discipline rests primarily with faculty.

Summer Programs Enrichment, sports programs offered; session focuses on SAT preparation and tennis program; held on campus; accepts boys and girls; open to students from other schools. 2006 schedule: June to July. Application deadline: May.

Tuition and Aid Day student tuition: ¥1,616,999; 7-day tuition and room/board: ¥2,956,000. Tuition installment plan (semester payment plan). Need-based scholarship grants available. In 2005–06, 8% of upper-school students received aid. Total amount of financial aid awarded in 2005–06: ¥5,023,550.

Admissions Traditional secondary-level entrance grade is 10. For fall 2005, 30 students applied for upper-level admission, 26 were accepted, 24 enrolled. English for Non-native Speakers, essay, math and English placement tests or SLEP for foreign students required. Deadline for receipt of application materials: none. Application fee required: ¥55,000. On-campus interview required.

Athletics Interscholastic: baseball (boys), basketball (b,g), cheering (g), soccer (b,g), softball (g), tennis (b,g), volleyball (b,g); intramural: baseball (b), basketball (b,g), soccer (b,g), softball (g), table tennis (b,g), volleyball (b,g), weight training (b,g); coed interscholastic: tennis. 4 PE instructors.

Computers Computer network features include campus e-mail, on-campus library services, CD-ROMs, online commercial services, Internet access, file transfer, wireless campus network, campus calendar.

Contact Ms. Sandra Ota, Director of Admissions. 81-78-857-0100. Fax: 81-78-857-4095. E-mail: sandyo@mail.canacad.ac.jp. Web site: www.canacad.ac.jp.

CANNON SCHOOL
5801 Poplar Tent Road
Concord, North Carolina 28027
Head of School: Mr. Richard H. Snyder

General Information Coeducational day college-preparatory school. Grades PK–12. Founded: 1969. Setting: suburban. Nearest major city is Charlotte. 65-acre campus. 3 buildings on campus. Approved or accredited by Southern Association of Colleges and Schools, Southern Association of Independent Schools, and North Carolina Department of Education. Language of instruction: English. Endowment: $977,863. Total enrollment: 899. Upper school average class size: 17. Upper school faculty-student ratio: 1:9.

Upper School Student Profile Grade 9: 94 students (45 boys, 49 girls); Grade 10: 82 students (46 boys, 36 girls); Grade 11: 62 students (35 boys, 27 girls); Grade 12: 56 students (23 boys, 33 girls).

Faculty School total: 85. In upper school: 17 men, 15 women; 21 have advanced degrees.

Subjects Offered Acting, advanced math, algebra, American Civil War, American government-AP, American history, American history-AP, American literature, biology, biology-AP, British literature, calculus-AP, character education, chemistry, chemistry-AP, chorus, college counseling, computer programming-AP, creative writing, debate, directing, discrete mathematics, drawing, English, English-AP, environmental science, environmental science-AP, ethics, film and literature, film history, finance, French, French-AP, functions, geometry, jazz band, Latin, mathematical modeling, modern history, painting, physics, physics-AP, playwriting, poetry, pre-calculus, psychology-AP, publications, sculpture, senior project, Spanish, Spanish language-AP, Spanish literature-AP, speech and oral interpretations, statistics-AP, strings, studio art, theater design and production, trigonometry, visual arts, weight training, wind ensemble, world history, world literature, world religions, yearbook.

Graduation Requirements Arts and fine arts (art, music, dance, drama), biology, chemistry, computer literacy, English, foreign language, history, mathematics, physical education (includes health), science, senior project, trigonometry, U.S. history. Community service is required.

Special Academic Programs Advanced Placement exam preparation in 14 subject areas; honors section; independent study.

College Placement 35 students graduated in 2005; all went to college, including Davidson College; Denison University; East Carolina University; James Madison University; The University of North Carolina at Chapel Hill; The University of North Carolina at Charlotte. Median SAT verbal: 650, median SAT math: 640, median composite ACT: 27. 66% scored over 600 on SAT verbal, 57% scored over 600 on SAT math, 50% scored over 26 on composite ACT.

Student Life Upper grades have specified standards of dress, student council, honor system. Discipline rests primarily with faculty.

Tuition and Aid Day student tuition: $12,940. Tuition installment plan (Insured Tuition Payment Plan, monthly payment plans). Tuition reduction for siblings, merit scholarship grants, need-based scholarship grants, teacher remission available. In

2005–06, 10% of upper-school students received aid; total upper-school merit-scholarship money awarded: $45,000. Total amount of financial aid awarded in 2005–06: $192,020.

Admissions Traditional secondary-level entrance grade is 9. For fall 2005, 49 students applied for upper-level admission, 27 were accepted, 25 enrolled. Admissions testing and ISEE required. Deadline for receipt of application materials: February 25. Application fee required: $90. Interview required.

Athletics Interscholastic: baseball (boys), basketball (b,g), cheering (g), cross-country running (b,g), dance team (g), lacrosse (b), soccer (b,g), swimming and diving (b,g), tennis (b,g), track and field (b,g), volleyball (g); intramural: ballet (g); coed interscholastic: golf, weight training; coed intramural: blading, cheering, croquet, dance, Frisbee, independent competitive sports, jump rope, kickball, Newcombe ball, track and field, weight training, whiffle ball, yoga. 8 coaches, 1 trainer.

Computers Computers are regularly used in all academic, art, music classes. Computer network features include campus e-mail, on-campus library services, CD-ROMs, online commercial services, Internet access, wireless campus network, productivity software.

Contact Dr. Ann Blomquist, Director of Admissions. 704-721-7164. Fax: 704-788-7779. E-mail: ablomquist@cannonschool.org. Web site: www.cannonschool.org.

CANTERBURY HIGH SCHOOL
3210 Smith Road
Fort Wayne, Indiana 46804
Head of School: Jonathan Hancock

General Information Coeducational day college-preparatory, arts, and technology school, affiliated with Christian faith. Grades K–12. Founded: 1977. Setting: suburban. 56-acre campus. 1 building on campus. Approved or accredited by Independent Schools Association of the Central States and Indiana Department of Education. Endowment: $8.1 million. Total enrollment: 754. Upper school average class size: 17. Upper school faculty-student ratio: 1:17.

Upper School Student Profile Grade 9: 68 students (32 boys, 36 girls); Grade 10: 75 students (41 boys, 34 girls); Grade 11: 71 students (44 boys, 27 girls); Grade 12: 63 students (30 boys, 33 girls).

Faculty School total: 88. In upper school: 24 men, 64 women; 51 have advanced degrees.

Subjects Offered Algebra, American history, American literature, analysis and differential calculus, art, band, biology, biology-AP, calculus, chemistry, computer programming, computer science, computer science-AP, concert band, creative writing, diversity studies, drama, dramatic arts, economics, English, English literature, English literature-AP, English-AP, ethics, European history, European history-AP, French, French language-AP, French-AP, geometry, government/civics, health education, history, history-AP, instrumental music, Japanese, Japanese history, jazz band, Latin, Latin-AP, literature, mathematics, music, photography, physical education, physics, physics-AP, pre-calculus, religion, senior seminar, social studies, Spanish, Spanish language-AP, Spanish-AP, speech, theater, trigonometry, vocal music, world history.

Graduation Requirements Arts and fine arts (art, music, dance, drama), college planning, computer science, economics, English, ethics, foreign language, government, mathematics, performing arts, physical education (includes health), religion (includes Bible studies and theology), religion and culture, science, senior internship, social studies (includes history), senior seminars in diversity, ethics, and humanities. Community service is required.

Special Academic Programs Advanced Placement exam preparation in 15 subject areas; independent study; study abroad.

College Placement 62 students graduated in 2005; all went to college, including Butler University; Indiana University Bloomington; Purdue University; University of Notre Dame; Vanderbilt University; Wabash College. Median SAT verbal: 647, median SAT math: 625. Mean composite ACT: 27. 79% scored over 600 on SAT verbal, 58% scored over 600 on SAT math, 67% scored over 26 on composite ACT.

Student Life Upper grades have specified standards of dress, student council, honor system. Discipline rests primarily with faculty. Attendance at religious services is required.

Tuition and Aid Day student tuition: $10,875. Tuition installment plan (pre-approved tuition loans through local bank). Merit scholarship grants, need-based scholarship grants available. In 2005–06, 30% of upper-school students received aid; total upper-school merit-scholarship money awarded: $40,000. Total amount of financial aid awarded in 2005–06: $752,000.

Admissions Traditional secondary-level entrance grade is 9. For fall 2005, 60 students applied for upper-level admission, 30 were accepted, 26 enrolled. ERB required. Deadline for receipt of application materials: none. Application fee required: $35. On-campus interview required.

Athletics Interscholastic: baseball (boys), basketball (b,g), cheering (g), cross-country running (b,g), diving (b,g), golf (b,g), soccer (b,g), softball (g), swimming and diving (b,g), tennis (b,g), track and field (b,g), volleyball (g); intramural: lacrosse (b); coed interscholastic: bowling. 2 PE instructors, 17 coaches, 1 trainer.

Computers Computers are regularly used in art, basic skills, classics, college planning, computer applications, creative writing, desktop publishing, English, ethics, foreign language, French, freshman foundations, health, history, humanities, independent study, information technology, introduction to technology, journalism, keyboarding, lab/keyboard, Latin, library, library skills, literary magazine, mathemat-

ics, music, news writing, newspaper, photography, programming, publications, religion, research skills, SAT preparation, science, senior seminar, social sciences, social studies, Spanish, speech, study skills, technology, theater, Web site design, writing, writing, writing fundamentals, yearbook classes. Computer network features include on-campus library services, CD-ROMs, online commercial services, Internet access, file transfer, wireless campus network, online classroom (assignments, Web sites, grades).

Contact Susan M. Johnson, Director of Admissions. 260-436-7721 Ext. 2011. Fax: 260-407-3551. E-mail: sjohnson@canterburyschool.org. Web site: www.canterburyschool.org.

CANTERBURY SCHOOL

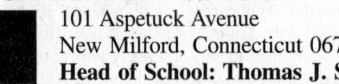

101 Aspetuck Avenue
New Milford, Connecticut 06776
Head of School: Thomas J. Sheehey III

petersons.com

General Information Coeducational boarding and day college-preparatory, arts, business, religious studies, bilingual studies, and technology school, affiliated with Roman Catholic Church. Grades 9–PG. Founded: 1915. Setting: small town. Nearest major city is Hartford. Students are housed in single-sex dormitories. 150-acre campus. 20 buildings on campus. Approved or accredited by New England Association of Schools and Colleges, The Association of Boarding Schools, and Connecticut Department of Education. Member of National Association of Independent Schools and Secondary School Admission Test Board. Endowment: $14 million. Total enrollment: 361. Upper school average class size: 11. Upper school faculty-student ratio: 1:8.

Upper School Student Profile Grade 9: 65 students (36 boys, 29 girls); Grade 10: 82 students (42 boys, 40 girls); Grade 11: 104 students (66 boys, 38 girls); Grade 12: 110 students (73 boys, 37 girls); Postgraduate: 21 students (19 boys, 2 girls). 60% of students are boarding students. 50% are state residents. 18 states are represented in upper school student body. 12% are international students. International students from Australia, Germany, Japan, Republic of Korea, Spain, and Venezuela; 2 other countries represented in student body. 65% of students are Roman Catholic.

Faculty School total: 76. In upper school: 40 men, 36 women; 45 have advanced degrees; 56 reside on campus.

Subjects Offered 1½ elective credits, adolescent issues, algebra, American history, American literature, anthropology, art, art history, astronomy, biochemistry, biology, calculus, ceramics, chemistry, civil rights, computer programming, computer science, creative writing, dance, drama, driver education, earth science, economics, English, English literature, environmental science, ethics, European history, expository writing, fine arts, French, geography, geology, geometry, grammar, history, Irish studies, Latin, marine biology, mathematics, microbiology, music, music theory-AP, oceanography, philosophy, photography, physics, physiology, religion, science, social studies, Spanish, Spanish literature, speech, statistics, theater, theology, trigonometry, women's studies, world history, world literature, writing.

Graduation Requirements Arts and fine arts (art, music, dance, drama), computer science, English, foreign language, mathematics, religion (includes Bible studies and theology), science, social studies (includes history).

Special Academic Programs Advanced Placement exam preparation in 17 subject areas; honors section; independent study; term-away projects; ESL (15 students enrolled).

College Placement 107 students graduated in 2005; 105 went to college, including Boston University; Hobart and William Smith Colleges; Saint Michael's College; United States Military Academy; University of Connecticut. Other: 2 had other specific plans. 25% scored over 600 on SAT verbal, 35% scored over 600 on SAT math.

Student Life Upper grades have specified standards of dress, student council, honor system. Discipline rests primarily with faculty. Attendance at religious services is required.

Summer Programs Sports programs offered; session focuses on basketball and football camps; held on campus; accepts boys and girls; open to students from other schools. 70 students usually enrolled.

Tuition and Aid Day student tuition: $25,650; 5-day tuition and room/board: $34,450; 7-day tuition and room/board: $34,450. Tuition installment plan (Academic Management Services Plan, Key Tuition Payment Plan). Need-based scholarship grants, need-based loans, middle-income loans available. In 2005–06, 46% of upper-school students received aid. Total amount of financial aid awarded in 2005–06: $1,900,000.

Admissions Traditional secondary-level entrance grade is 9. For fall 2005, 510 students applied for upper-level admission, 295 were accepted, 127 enrolled. SLEP, SSAT, TOEFL and writing sample required. Deadline for receipt of application materials: January 20. Application fee required: $50. Interview required.

Athletics Interscholastic: baseball (boys), basketball (b,g), cross-country running (b,g), field hockey (g), football (b), ice hockey (b,g), lacrosse (b,g), soccer (b,g), softball (g), squash (b,g), swimming and diving (b,g), tennis (b,g), track and field (b,g), volleyball (g); intramural: dance (g), equestrian sports (g), hockey (b,g), horseback riding (b,g); coed interscholastic: crew, golf, water polo, wrestling; coed intramural: fitness, softball, Special Olympics, strength & conditioning, weight lifting, weight training. 40 coaches, 2 trainers.

Computers Computers are regularly used in accounting, English, mathematics, multimedia, science classes. Computer network features include campus e-mail, on-campus library services, CD-ROMs, Internet access.

Contact Keith R. Holton, Director of Admission. 860-210-3832. Fax: 860-350-1120. E-mail: admissions@cbury.org. Web site: www.cbury.org.

ANNOUNCEMENT FROM THE SCHOOL Canterbury prides itself on creating a value-based community where every student experiences a broad and challenging program in a small school setting. The School's educational environment fosters academic rigor, athletic development, artistic enrichment, and spiritual growth. The hallmark of a Canterbury education is the School's willingness to accept students as they are, support them when necessary, challenge them when appropriate, and inspire them to become moral leaders in a secular world.

See full description on page 712.

CANTERBURY SCHOOL

8141 College Parkway
Fort Myers, Florida 33919
Head of School: Dr. R. Mason Goss

petersons.com

General Information Coeducational day college-preparatory school. Grades PK–12. Founded: 1964. Setting: suburban. Nearest major city is Tampa. 32-acre campus. 8 buildings on campus. Approved or accredited by Florida Council of Independent Schools, The College Board, and Florida Department of Education. Member of National Association of Independent Schools and Secondary School Admission Test Board. Endowment: $800,000. Total enrollment: 694. Upper school average class size: 17. Upper school faculty-student ratio: 1:10.

Upper School Student Profile Grade 9: 60 students (34 boys, 26 girls); Grade 10: 49 students (19 boys, 30 girls); Grade 11: 48 students (28 boys, 20 girls); Grade 12: 54 students (25 boys, 29 girls).

Faculty School total: 79. In upper school: 15 men, 32 women; 18 have advanced degrees.

Subjects Offered Advanced Placement courses, algebra, American government-AP, American history, American history-AP, American literature, anatomy, art, art history, biology, biology-AP, British literature, calculus, calculus-AP, ceramics, chemistry, chemistry-AP, comparative government and politics-AP, computer programming, constitutional law, creative writing, drama, earth science, ecology, economics, English, English literature, English literature-AP, environmental science-AP, European history, fine arts, French, French language-AP, geography, geometry, government/civics, grammar, health, history, Latin, macroeconomics-AP, marine biology, mathematics, music, nationalism and ethnic conflict, photography, physical education, physics, physics-AP, physiology, psychology, SAT preparation, science, social studies, sociology, Spanish, Spanish language-AP, speech, statistics, theater, U.S. history-AP, United Nations and international issues, world history, world literature, writing, yearbook.

Graduation Requirements Arts and fine arts (art, music, dance, drama), computer science, English, foreign language, mathematics, physical education (includes health), science, social studies (includes history), speech. Community service is required.

Special Academic Programs Advanced Placement exam preparation in 14 subject areas; independent study; study at local college for college credit; study abroad.

College Placement 48 students graduated in 2005; all went to college, including Emory University; Rollins College; University of Florida; University of Miami; University of Pennsylvania; Vanderbilt University. Mean SAT verbal: 600, mean SAT math: 610, mean composite ACT: 26.

Student Life Upper grades have specified standards of dress, student council, honor system. Discipline rests primarily with faculty.

Summer Programs Remediation, enrichment, advancement, sports, art/fine arts programs offered; session focuses on enrichment ; held on campus; accepts boys and girls; open to students from other schools. 100 students usually enrolled. 2006 schedule: June 15 to July 31.

Tuition and Aid Day student tuition: $14,875. Tuition installment plan (monthly payment plans, quarterly payment plan). Merit scholarship grants, need-based scholarship grants available. In 2005–06, 21% of upper-school students received aid; total upper-school merit-scholarship money awarded: $128,792. Total amount of financial aid awarded in 2005–06: $474,658.

Admissions Traditional secondary-level entrance grade is 9. For fall 2005, 65 students applied for upper-level admission, 40 were accepted, 27 enrolled. ERB, SSAT or writing sample required. Deadline for receipt of application materials: none. Application fee required: $75. On-campus interview recommended.

Athletics Interscholastic: baseball (boys), basketball (b,g), cheering (b,g), cross-country running (b,g), lacrosse (b,g), soccer (b,g), softball (g), track and field (b,g), volleyball (b,g), winter soccer (b,g); intramural: basketball (b,g), cross-country running (b,g), soccer (b,g), volleyball (b,g), winter soccer (b,g); coed interscholastic: golf, swimming and diving, tennis; coed intramural: swimming and diving. 6 PE instructors, 27 coaches, 1 trainer.

Computers Computers are regularly used in art, college planning, English, foreign language, French, history, independent study, journalism, Latin, library, mathematics,

science, social sciences, Spanish, speech, theater arts, yearbook classes. Computer network features include campus e-mail, on-campus library services, CD-ROMs, online commercial services, Internet access, file transfer, office computer access, DVD, wireless campus network.

Contact Ms. Julie A. Peters, Director of Admission. 239-415-8945. Fax: 239-481-8339. E-mail: jpeters@canterburyfortmyers.org. Web site: www.canterburyfortmyers.org.

ANNOUNCEMENT FROM THE SCHOOL Canterbury School, founded in 1964, is the only independent prekindergarten through grade 12, nonsectarian, coeducational, college-preparatory day school serving the rapidly growing southwest Florida area. The School's 8-building, 34-acre campus is adjacent to Edison Community College. A member of the National Association of Independent Schools, Canterbury is fully accredited by the Florida Council of Independent Schools and the Florida Kindergarten Council. Canterbury's motto, "Education, Character, Leadership, Service," defines the focus of the School's program and underscores all that is done, in and out of the classroom. At all levels, the academic program emphasizes individual growth, skill development, a high caliber of instruction, collaboration, and high standards. Canterbury provides all students with an opportunity to challenge themselves and take risks in an atmosphere of mutual respect and partnership among students, parents, and teachers. Led by a talented and dedicated faculty, the School seeks to build a close-knit community of learners where the whole child is nurtured and developed and where the model of a liberal arts education thrives. At Canterbury, the life of the mind is complemented by a strong athletics program, a commitment to the arts and creativity, and a fluency in technology. These elements unite in a secure and modern facility to instill in students a love of learning that prepares them for life. An honor code and required community service promote personal integrity and service in the Canterbury community; graduates are expected to be lifelong learners and responsible citizens well-prepared to help shape a changing world. All graduates continue their education. Graduates matriculate at universities and colleges around the country, including Harvard, Northwestern, Notre Dame, Princeton, Davidson, Johns Hopkins, Wake Forest, and the Universities of Florida, Pennsylvania, and Miami.

THE CANTERBURY SCHOOL OF FLORIDA

901 58th Avenue NE
St. Petersburg, Florida 33703
Head of School: Mr. Mac H. Hall

General Information Coeducational day college-preparatory, arts, and marine science school, affiliated with Episcopal Church. Grades PK–12. Founded: 1968. Setting: suburban. Nearest major city is Tampa. 20-acre campus. 3 buildings on campus. Approved or accredited by Florida Council of Independent Schools, National Association of Episcopal Schools, Western Catholic Education Association, and Florida Department of Education. Endowment: $45,000. Total enrollment: 425. Upper school average class size: 14. Upper school faculty-student ratio: 1:8.

Upper School Student Profile Grade 9: 26 students (13 boys, 13 girls); Grade 10: 24 students (15 boys, 9 girls); Grade 11: 24 students (13 boys, 11 girls); Grade 12: 22 students (10 boys, 12 girls). 10% of students are members of Episcopal Church.

Faculty School total: 50. In upper school: 13 men, 18 women; 12 have advanced degrees.

Subjects Offered 20th century world history, Advanced Placement courses, algebra, American government, American literature, anatomy, ancient world history, art, art history, art history-AP, athletics, band, Basic programming, biology, biology-AP, British literature, British literature (honors), calculus, calculus-AP, ceramics, character education, chemistry, chemistry-AP, choral music, chorus, classical language, classical studies, college placement, community service, competitive science projects, computer keyboarding, computer science, computer science-AP, computer skills, contemporary issues, creative writing, earth science, economics, English, English composition, English literature, English literature-AP, environmental studies, ethics, European history, expository writing, film studies, fine arts, foreign language, French, French-AP, freshman seminar, geography, geometry, government/civics, grammar, history, history-AP, interdisciplinary studies, journalism, Latin, leadership and service, library skills, life science, marine biology, marine science, mathematics, mathematics-AP, mentorship program, modern world history, music, musical productions, personal fitness, physical education, physical science, physics, physics-AP, pottery, pre-algebra, pre-calculus, pre-college orientation, psychology-AP, reading/study skills, robotics, SAT preparation, SAT/ACT preparation, science, senior seminar, Shakespeare, social science, social studies, Spanish, Spanish-AP, speech and debate, theater arts, U.S. history, U.S. history-AP, values and decisions, visual and performing arts, weight fitness, world history, world literature, world religions, yearbook.

Graduation Requirements Arts and fine arts (art, music, dance, drama), career/college preparation, electives, English, ethics, foreign language, history, mathematics, physical education (includes health), research, science, senior seminar, writing, Freshman Forum. Community service is required.

Special Academic Programs Advanced Placement exam preparation in 14 subject areas; honors section; independent study; term-away projects; study at local college for college credit; study abroad.

College Placement 21 students graduated in 2005; all went to college, including Auburn University; Florida State University; The College of William and Mary; University of Central Florida; University of Florida; University of South Florida. Mean SAT verbal: 578, mean SAT math: 570. 29% scored over 600 on SAT verbal, 25% scored over 600 on SAT math.

Student Life Upper grades have specified standards of dress, student council, honor system. Discipline rests equally with students and faculty. Attendance at religious services is required.

Summer Programs Enrichment, sports, art/fine arts, computer instruction programs offered; session focuses on multi-discipline skills and abilities; held on campus; accepts boys and girls; open to students from other schools. 50 students usually enrolled. 2006 schedule: June 12 to August 4. Application deadline: March 30.

Tuition and Aid Day student tuition: $11,250. Tuition installment plan (Insured Tuition Payment Plan, monthly payment plans, individually arranged payment plans). Tuition reduction for siblings, need-based scholarship grants available. In 2005–06, 10% of upper-school students received aid. Total amount of financial aid awarded in 2005–06: $213,000.

Admissions Traditional secondary-level entrance grade is 9. For fall 2005, 28 students applied for upper-level admission, 26 were accepted, 21 enrolled. Any standardized test or ERB required. Deadline for receipt of application materials: none. Application fee required: $75. On-campus interview required.

Athletics Interscholastic: baseball (boys), basketball (b,g), cross-country running (b,g), football (b), golf (b), softball (g), swimming and diving (g), tennis (b,g), volleyball (g); intramural: strength & conditioning (b); coed interscholastic: cheering, cross-country running, soccer; coed intramural: canoeing/kayaking, fitness, flag football, floor hockey, hiking/backpacking, kayaking, outdoor activities, outdoor education, physical fitness, ropes courses, ultimate Frisbee, weight training. 4 PE instructors, 21 coaches, 1 trainer.

Computers Computers are regularly used in all academic classes. Computer network features include campus e-mail, on-campus library services, CD-ROMs, online commercial services, Internet access, file transfer, office computer access, DVD, wireless campus network, remote access to second campus.

Contact Ms. Daryl DeBerry, Director of Admissions and Communications. 727-521-6201 Ext. 24. Fax: 727-521-4739. E-mail: ddeberry@canterbury-fl.org. Web site: www.canterbury-fl.org.

CANYONVILLE CHRISTIAN ACADEMY

PO Box 1100
Canyonville, Oregon 97417-1100
Head of School: Cathy Lovato

General Information Coeducational boarding and day college-preparatory, religious studies, and English for Speakers of Other Languages school, affiliated with Christian faith. Boarding grades 9–12, day grades 6–12. Founded: 1924. Setting: rural. Nearest major city is Medford. Students are housed in single-sex dormitories. 10-acre campus. 11 buildings on campus. Approved or accredited by Association of Christian Schools International, Northwest Association of Schools and Colleges, The Association of Boarding Schools, and Oregon Department of Education. Total enrollment: 148. Upper school average class size: 20. Upper school faculty-student ratio: 1:13.

Upper School Student Profile 80% of students are boarding students. 20% are state residents. 10 states are represented in upper school student body. 65% are international students. International students from China, Japan, Mexico, Republic of Korea, Spain, and Taiwan; 7 other countries represented in student body. 80% of students are Christian faith.

Faculty School total: 15. In upper school: 5 men, 9 women; 5 have advanced degrees; 9 reside on campus.

Subjects Offered Advanced Placement courses, algebra, American culture, American history, art, Bible, biology, calculus, calculus-AP, career/college preparation, chemistry, choir, Christian doctrine, computer education, computer keyboarding, computer technologies, computers, consumer economics, culinary arts, desktop publishing, economics, English, English literature, ESL, foreign language, general science, government, grammar, integrative seminar, keyboarding, library assistant, Life of Christ, mathematics, physical education, physical science, physics, pre-calculus, religious education, senior seminar, Spanish, speech and debate, theology, U.S. government, U.S. history, world history.

Graduation Requirements Algebra, Bible, biology, economics, English, foreign language, government, health and wellness, mathematics, physical education (includes health), physical science, speech and debate, U.S. history, world history.

Special Academic Programs Advanced Placement exam preparation in 4 subject areas; honors section; accelerated programs; independent study; remedial math; ESL (35 students enrolled).

College Placement 31 students graduated in 2005; 27 went to college, including George Fox University; Liberty University; Oregon State University; University of Oregon; University of Washington; Vanguard University of Southern California. Other: 4 went to work. Median SAT verbal: 486, median SAT math: 452. 30% scored over 600 on SAT verbal, 30% scored over 600 on SAT math.

Student Life Upper grades have specified standards of dress, student council, honor system. Discipline rests primarily with faculty. Attendance at religious services is required.

Tuition and Aid Day student tuition: $4600; 7-day tuition and room/board: $18,500. Tuition installment plan (monthly payment plans, individually arranged payment plans). Tuition reduction for siblings, merit scholarship grants, need-based scholarship grants, paying campus jobs available. In 2005–06, 20% of upper-school students received aid; total upper-school merit-scholarship money awarded: $3000. Total amount of financial aid awarded in 2005–06: $20,000.

Admissions Traditional secondary-level entrance grade is 9. TOEFL or SLEP required. Deadline for receipt of application materials: none. Application fee required: $100. Interview recommended.

Athletics Interscholastic: basketball (boys, girls), cheering (g), cross-country running (b,g), softball (b), track and field (b,g), volleyball (g); intramural: soccer (b); coed intramural: tennis. 3 PE instructors, 9 coaches.

Computers Computers are regularly used in business applications, keyboarding, technology classes. Computer network features include campus e-mail, CD-ROMs, Internet access, office computer access, wireless campus network.

Contact Noel Schaak, Principal. 541-839-4401. Fax: 541-839-6228. E-mail: cca@canyonville.net. Web site: www.canyonville.net.

CAPE COD ACADEMY

50 Osterville–West Barnstable Road
Osterville, Massachusetts 02655
Head of School: Thomas M. Evans

General Information Coeducational day college-preparatory, arts, and technology school. Grades K–12. Founded: 1976. Setting: small town. Nearest major city is Boston. 46-acre campus. 1 building on campus. Approved or accredited by New England Association of Schools and Colleges. Member of National Association of Independent Schools and Secondary School Admission Test Board. Endowment: $2.2 million. Total enrollment: 402. Upper school average class size: 14. Upper school faculty-student ratio: 1:8.

Upper School Student Profile Grade 9: 46 students (18 boys, 28 girls); Grade 10: 45 students (22 boys, 23 girls); Grade 11: 43 students (25 boys, 18 girls); Grade 12: 40 students (24 boys, 16 girls).

Faculty School total: 54. In upper school: 12 men, 29 women; 39 have advanced degrees.

Subjects Offered Advanced Placement courses, algebra, American history, American literature, art, art-AP, biology, calculus, calculus-AP, chemistry, community service, computer math, computer programming, computer science, drama, earth science, English, English literature, English-AP, environmental science, ethics, European history, expository writing, fine arts, French, French-AP, geography, geometry, health, history, Latin, mathematics, philosophy, photography, physical education, physics, physics-AP, science, social science, social studies, Spanish, Spanish-AP, theater, trigonometry, world history, world literature.

Graduation Requirements Arts and fine arts (art, music, dance, drama), computer science, English, foreign language, independent study, mathematics, physical education (includes health), science, social science, social studies (includes history). Community service is required.

Special Academic Programs Advanced Placement exam preparation in 6 subject areas; honors section; independent study; term-away projects; study abroad.

College Placement 40 students graduated in 2005; all went to college, including Boston College; Brandeis University; Brown University; Connecticut College; Middlebury College. Mean SAT verbal: 595, mean SAT math: 624.

Student Life Upper grades have specified standards of dress, student council, honor system. Discipline rests primarily with faculty.

Tuition and Aid Day student tuition: $14,100–$17,100. Tuition installment plan (Academic Management Services Plan). Need-based scholarship grants available. In 2005–06, 33% of upper-school students received aid. Total amount of financial aid awarded in 2005–06: $275,000.

Admissions Traditional secondary-level entrance grade is 9. ISEE, Otis-Lennon School Ability Test and SSAT required. Deadline for receipt of application materials: February 1. Application fee required: $50. On-campus interview required.

Athletics Interscholastic: basketball (boys, girls), lacrosse (b,g), soccer (b,g); coed interscholastic: cross-country running, golf, tennis. 3 PE instructors, 9 coaches, 1 trainer.

Computers Computers are regularly used in English, mathematics, science classes. Computer network features include campus e-mail, on-campus library services, CD-ROMs, Internet access.

Contact Mr. Warner T. James Jr., Director of Admission. 508-428-5400 Ext. 216. Fax: 508-428-0701. E-mail: admissions@capecodacademy.org. Web site: www.capecodacademy.org.

CAPE FEAR ACADEMY

3900 South College Road
Wilmington, North Carolina 28412
Head of School: Mr. John B. Meehl

General Information Coeducational day college-preparatory and arts school. Grades PK–12. Founded: 1967. Setting: suburban. Nearest major city is Raleigh. 26-acre campus. 3 buildings on campus. Approved or accredited by Southern Association of Colleges and Schools, Southern Association of Independent Schools, and North Carolina Department of Education. Member of National Association of Independent Schools. Endowment: $22,000. Total enrollment: 579. Upper school average class size: 16. Upper school faculty-student ratio: 1:8.

Upper School Student Profile Grade 9: 41 students (21 boys, 20 girls); Grade 10: 53 students (29 boys, 24 girls); Grade 11: 46 students (26 boys, 20 girls); Grade 12: 43 students (16 boys, 27 girls).

Faculty School total: 73. In upper school: 8 men, 14 women; 7 have advanced degrees.

Subjects Offered Algebra, American history, American literature, art, art history, biology, calculus, chemistry, computer science, drama, English, English literature, environmental science, European history, fine arts, geometry, government/civics, grammar, health, history, journalism, literature, mathematics, music, music theory-AP, physical education, physics, science, social studies, Spanish, theater, world history.

Graduation Requirements Arts and fine arts (art, music, dance, drama), computer science, English, foreign language, mathematics, physical education (includes health), science, social studies (includes history). Community service is required.

Special Academic Programs Advanced Placement exam preparation in 13 subject areas; honors section; independent study; study at local college for college credit; study abroad; academic accommodation for the gifted; remedial math; programs in general development for dyslexic students.

College Placement 42 students graduated in 2005; all went to college, including Duke University; North Carolina State University; The University of North Carolina at Chapel Hill; The University of North Carolina at Charlotte; The University of North Carolina Wilmington. Mean SAT verbal: 603, mean SAT math: 602. 54% scored over 600 on SAT verbal, 50% scored over 600 on SAT math.

Student Life Upper grades have specified standards of dress, student council, honor system. Discipline rests primarily with faculty.

Summer Programs Enrichment, sports, art/fine arts programs offered; session focuses on enrichment and sports; held on campus; accepts boys and girls; open to students from other schools. 250 students usually enrolled. 2006 schedule: June 5 to August 18. Application deadline: none.

Tuition and Aid Day student tuition: $11,761. Tuition installment plan (Insured Tuition Payment Plan, FACTS Tuition Payment Plan, monthly payment plans). Merit scholarship grants, need-based scholarship grants available. In 2005–06, 28% of upper-school students received aid; total upper-school merit-scholarship money awarded: $85,285. Total amount of financial aid awarded in 2005–06: $146,961.

Admissions Traditional secondary-level entrance grade is 9. For fall 2005, 38 students applied for upper-level admission, 27 were accepted, 25 enrolled. ERB, ISEE or SSAT required. Deadline for receipt of application materials: none. Application fee required: $75. On-campus interview recommended.

Athletics Interscholastic: basketball (boys, girls), field hockey (g), lacrosse (b,g), soccer (b,g), softball (g), tennis (b,g), volleyball (g); coed interscholastic: cheering, cross-country running, golf, surfing, swimming and diving. 1 PE instructor, 13 coaches, 1 trainer.

Computers Computers are regularly used in all academic classes. Computer network features include campus e-mail, on-campus library services, CD-ROMs, online commercial services, Internet access.

Contact Mrs. Susan Harrell, Director of Admission. 910-791-0287 Ext. 1015. Fax: 910-791-0290. E-mail: sharrell@capefearacademy.org. Web site: www.capefearacademy.org.

CAPE HENRY COLLEGIATE SCHOOL

1320 Mill Dam Road
Virginia Beach, Virginia 23454-2306
Head of School: Dr. John P. Lewis

General Information Coeducational day college-preparatory school. Grades PK–12. Founded: 1924. Setting: suburban. 30-acre campus. 7 buildings on campus. Approved or accredited by Virginia Association of Independent Schools. Member of National Association of Independent Schools. Endowment: $3 million. Total enrollment: 1,006. Upper school average class size: 14. Upper school faculty-student ratio: 1:10.

Upper School Student Profile Grade 9: 86 students (52 boys, 34 girls); Grade 10: 86 students (44 boys, 42 girls); Grade 11: 91 students (52 boys, 39 girls); Grade 12: 81 students (47 boys, 34 girls).

Faculty School total: 134. In upper school: 20 men, 37 women; 34 have advanced degrees.

Subjects Offered Algebra, American history, American literature, art, art history, biology, botany, business skills, calculus, ceramics, chemistry, community service, computer programming, computer science, creative writing, drama, driver education, earth science, ecology, economics, English, English literature, environmental science,

Cape Henry Collegiate School

European history, expository writing, fine arts, French, geography, geology, geometry, government/civics, health, history, journalism, Latin, law, marine biology, mathematics, music, oceanography, photography, physical education, physics, science, social science, social studies, sociology, Spanish, speech, statistics, theater, trigonometry, world history, world literature, writing.

Graduation Requirements Arts and fine arts (art, music, dance, drama), computer science, English, foreign language, mathematics, physical education (includes health), science, social science, social studies (includes history), senior speech. Community service is required.

Special Academic Programs Advanced Placement exam preparation in 12 subject areas; honors section; accelerated programs; independent study; academic accommodation for the gifted, the musically talented, and the artistically talented; remedial reading and/or remedial writing; remedial math; ESL (17 students enrolled).

College Placement 71 students graduated in 2005; 70 went to college, including James Madison University; The College of William and Mary; University of Virginia; Virginia Polytechnic Institute and State University. Other: 1 entered a postgraduate year.

Student Life Upper grades have specified standards of dress, student council, honor system. Discipline rests equally with students and faculty.

Summer Programs Remediation, enrichment, advancement, ESL, sports, art/fine arts, computer instruction programs offered; session focuses on academics and enrichment; held on campus; accepts boys and girls; open to students from other schools. 1200 students usually enrolled. 2006 schedule: June 12 to August 4. Application deadline: none.

Tuition and Aid Day student tuition: $12,815. Tuition installment plan (The Tuition Plan, Insured Tuition Payment Plan, monthly payment plans, individually arranged payment plans, 3-payment plan). Tuition reduction for siblings, need-based scholarship grants available. In 2005–06, 17% of upper-school students received aid. Total amount of financial aid awarded in 2005–06: $300,000.

Admissions Traditional secondary-level entrance grade is 9. For fall 2005, 659 students applied for upper-level admission, 45 were accepted, 40 enrolled. CTBS or ERB or writing sample required. Deadline for receipt of application materials: none. Application fee required: $40. On-campus interview required.

Athletics Interscholastic: baseball (boys), basketball (b,g), cheering (b,g), crew (b,g), cross-country running (b,g), field hockey (g), golf (b,g), lacrosse (b,g), soccer (b,g), softball (g), tennis (b,g), volleyball (b,g), wrestling (b); intramural: cheering (g), wrestling (b); coed interscholastic: crew, cross-country running, golf, swimming and diving, track and field; coed intramural: aerobics/dance, archery, back packing, badminton, ballet, dance, dance squad, golf, handball, lacrosse, modern dance, physical fitness, physical training, soccer, strength & conditioning, swimming and diving, tennis, volleyball, weight lifting, weight training, wilderness. 5 PE instructors, 15 coaches, 1 trainer.

Computers Computers are regularly used in all classes. Computer network features include campus e-mail, on-campus library services, CD-ROMs, online commercial services, Internet access, file transfer, office computer access, DVD, wireless campus network.

Contact Katherine Temme, Director of Admissions. 757-481-2446 Ext. 203. Fax: 757-481-9194. E-mail: kaytemme@capehenry.org. Web site: www.capehenry.org.

ANNOUNCEMENT FROM THE SCHOOL Named for the nearby landing site of the nation's first settlers, Cape Henry Collegiate School prides itself on preparing leaders of the future. Students and faculty have garnered many very impressive accolades; they have conquered both national and international challenges in many areas, including academics, athletics, and the creative and performing arts.

CARDIGAN MOUNTAIN SCHOOL

Canaan, New Hampshire
See Junior Boarding Schools section.

CARDINAL GIBBONS HIGH SCHOOL

2900 Northeast 47th Street
Fort Lauderdale, Florida 33308-5332
Head of School: Paul D. Ott

General Information Coeducational day college-preparatory and religious studies school, affiliated with Roman Catholic Church. Grades 9–12. Founded: 1961. Setting: suburban. 26-acre campus. 8 buildings on campus. Approved or accredited by Florida Council of Independent Schools, National Catholic Education Association, Southern Association of Colleges and Schools, and Florida Department of Education. Total enrollment: 1,243. Upper school average class size: 22. Upper school faculty-student ratio: 1:18.

Upper School Student Profile Grade 9: 335 students (159 boys, 176 girls); Grade 10: 318 students (151 boys, 167 girls); Grade 11: 304 students (145 boys, 159 girls); Grade 12: 286 students (151 boys, 135 girls). 70% of students are Roman Catholic.

Faculty School total: 71. In upper school: 35 men, 31 women; 38 have advanced degrees.

Subjects Offered Art, art history, band, Bible, British literature, British literature-AP, calculus, calculus-AP, chemistry, chemistry-AP, chorus, composition, composition-AP, computer keyboarding, computer programming, computer science, concert band, contemporary history, dance, drama, drawing, economics, ethics, European history-AP, fine arts, French, geography, global studies, government, government-AP, health education, honors algebra, honors English, honors geometry, honors U.S. history, honors world history, integrated math, jazz band, journalism, Latin, library skills, marching band, marine biology, media, music, painting, personal fitness, philosophy, photography, physics, physics-AP, psychology, SAT/ACT preparation, sociology, Spanish, Spanish literature-AP, U.S. history, U.S. history-AP, world history, world religions, yearbook.

Graduation Requirements Algebra, American government, American literature, Bible, biology, chemistry, composition, computer applications, death and loss, economics, electives, ethics, European literature, fitness, foreign language, geometry, global studies, health, senior composition, sociology, trigonometry, U.S. history, world history, world literature, world religions.

Special Academic Programs Advanced Placement exam preparation in 12 subject areas; honors section; independent study; study at local college for college credit; academic accommodation for the gifted, the musically talented, and the artistically talented.

College Placement 295 students graduated in 2005; 293 went to college, including Florida Atlantic University; Florida State University; University of Central Florida; University of Florida; University of Miami; University of North Florida. Other: 2 entered military service. Mean SAT verbal: 560, mean SAT math: 550, mean composite ACT: 23. 24% scored over 600 on SAT verbal, 25% scored over 600 on SAT math, 25% scored over 26 on composite ACT.

Student Life Upper grades have uniform requirement, student council, honor system. Discipline rests equally with students and faculty. Attendance at religious services is required.

Summer Programs Remediation, enrichment, advancement programs offered; session focuses on enrichment/advancement; held on campus; accepts boys and girls; not open to students from other schools. 250 students usually enrolled. 2006 schedule: June 6 to June 24. Application deadline: May 20.

Tuition and Aid Day student tuition: $6700. Tuition installment plan (monthly payment plans). Tuition reduction for siblings, need-based scholarship grants available. In 2005–06, 10% of upper-school students received aid. Total amount of financial aid awarded in 2005–06: $300,000.

Admissions Traditional secondary-level entrance grade is 9. For fall 2005, 575 students applied for upper-level admission, 430 were accepted, 415 enrolled. Scholastic Testing Service High School Placement Test or SSAT, ERB, PSAT, SAT, PLAN or ACT required. Deadline for receipt of application materials: April. Application fee required: $50. Interview recommended.

Athletics Interscholastic: baseball (boys), basketball (b,g), cheering (g), cross-country running (b,g), dance team (g), diving (b,g), drill team (g), football (b), golf (b,g), physical fitness (b,g), soccer (b,g), softball (g), swimming and diving (b,g), tennis (b,g), track and field (b,g), volleyball (b,g), wrestling (b). 2 PE instructors, 50 coaches, 1 trainer.

Computers Computers are regularly used in library, media, technology, typing, writing, yearbook classes. Computer network features include campus e-mail, on-campus library services, CD-ROMs, Internet access, file transfer, office computer access, wireless campus network.

Contact Marie Schramko, Assistant Principal. 954-491-2900 Ext. 105. Fax: 954-772-1025. E-mail: schramko@cghsfl.org. Web site: www.cghsfl.org.

CARDINAL MOONEY CATHOLIC COLLEGE PREPARATORY HIGH SCHOOL

660 South Water Street
Marine City, Michigan 48039
Head of School: Sr. Karen Lietz, OP

General Information Coeducational day college-preparatory school, affiliated with Roman Catholic Church. Grades 9–12. Founded: 1977. Setting: small town. Nearest major city is Mount Clemens. 1-acre campus. 1 building on campus. Approved or accredited by North Central Association of Colleges and Schools and Michigan Department of Education. Total enrollment: 178. Upper school average class size: 17. Upper school faculty-student ratio: 1:11.

Upper School Student Profile Grade 9: 47 students (26 boys, 21 girls); Grade 10: 37 students (15 boys, 22 girls); Grade 11: 42 students (16 boys, 26 girls); Grade 12: 52 students (29 boys, 23 girls). 90% of students are Roman Catholic.

Faculty School total: 20. In upper school: 7 men, 13 women; 9 have advanced degrees.

Special Academic Programs Advanced Placement exam preparation in 6 subject areas; honors section.

College Placement 53 students graduated in 2005; 52 went to college, including Central Michigan University; Grand Valley State University; Michigan State University; Oakland University; University of Detroit Mercy; University of Michigan. Other: 1 had other specific plans.

Student Life Upper grades have uniform requirement, student council, honor system. Discipline rests primarily with faculty. Attendance at religious services is required.

Tuition and Aid Tuition installment plan (monthly payment plans). Tuition reduction for siblings available.

Admissions Traditional secondary-level entrance grade is 9. For fall 2005, 59 students applied for upper-level admission, 59 were accepted, 59 enrolled. High School Placement Test required. Deadline for receipt of application materials: none. Application fee required: $250. Interview required.

Athletics Interscholastic: baseball (boys), basketball (b,g), bowling (b,g), cheering (g), cross-country running (b,g), equestrian sports (g), football (b), golf (b), soccer (g), softball (g), volleyball (g); coed interscholastic: cross-country running. 1 PE instructor, 6 coaches.

Computers Computer resources include on-campus library services, Internet access, DVD.

Contact Sr. Karen Lietz, OP, Principal. 810-765-8825 Ext. 14. Fax: 810-765-7164. E-mail: klietz@cardinalmooneycatholic.com.

CARDINAL NEWMAN HIGH SCHOOL

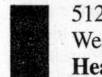

512 Spencer Drive
West Palm Beach, Florida 33409-3699
Head of School: Fr. David W. Carr

General Information Coeducational day college-preparatory school, affiliated with Roman Catholic Church. Grades 9–12. Founded: 1961. Setting: urban. Nearest major city is Miami. 50-acre campus. 5 buildings on campus. Approved or accredited by Southern Association of Colleges and Schools and Florida Department of Education. Total enrollment: 879. Upper school average class size: 25. Upper school faculty-student ratio: 1:25.

Upper School Student Profile Grade 9: 246 students (132 boys, 114 girls); Grade 10: 247 students (123 boys, 124 girls); Grade 11: 190 students (102 boys, 88 girls); Grade 12: 196 students (105 boys, 91 girls). 80% of students are Roman Catholic.

Faculty School total: 68. In upper school: 30 men, 38 women; 25 have advanced degrees.

Subjects Offered Algebra, American government, American history, American literature, anatomy and physiology, art, band, Bible studies, biology, biology-AP, calculus, calculus-AP, chemistry, chorus, church history, college writing, computer applications, computer science, creative writing, desktop publishing, discrete math, drama, economics, English, English literature, English-AP, ethics, European history, family and consumer science, fine arts, French, French-AP, geometry, government/civics, health, history, home economics, honors algebra, honors English, honors geometry, integrated science, International Baccalaureate courses, journalism, Latin, leadership training, marine biology, mathematics, music appreciation, newspaper, physical education, physics, political science, pre-calculus, probability and statistics, religion, social justice, social studies, Spanish, speech, world history, world literature, writing, yearbook.

Graduation Requirements Arts and fine arts (art, music, dance, drama), computer science, English, foreign language, mathematics, physical education (includes health), religion (includes Bible studies and theology), science, social studies (includes history). Community service is required.

Special Academic Programs International Baccalaureate program; Advanced Placement exam preparation in 5 subject areas; honors section; study at local college for college credit; academic accommodation for the gifted; remedial reading and/or remedial writing; remedial math.

College Placement 177 students graduated in 2005; 176 went to college, including Florida Atlantic University; Florida State University; Palm Beach Community College; University of Central Florida; University of Florida; University of North Florida. Other: 1 went to work.

Student Life Upper grades have uniform requirement, student council, honor system. Discipline rests primarily with faculty. Attendance at religious services is required.

Summer Programs Remediation, enrichment programs offered; session focuses on freshmen preparation; held on campus; accepts boys and girls; not open to students from other schools. 50 students usually enrolled.

Tuition and Aid Day student tuition: $6200–$7500. Tuition installment plan (FACTS Tuition Payment Plan). Need-based scholarship grants available.

Admissions Traditional secondary-level entrance grade is 9. STS required. Deadline for receipt of application materials: none. Application fee required: $50. On-campus interview recommended.

Athletics Interscholastic: baseball (boys), basketball (b,g), bowling (b,g), cheering (g), cross-country running (b,g), dance team (g), diving (b,g), football (b), golf (b,g), lacrosse (b,g), physical fitness (b,g), soccer (b,g), softball (g), swimming and diving (b,g), tennis (b,g), track and field (b,g), volleyball (g), wrestling (b). 4 PE instructors.

Computers Computers are regularly used in all academic, Bible studies, yearbook classes. Computer network features include campus e-mail, on-campus library services, CD-ROMs, online commercial services, Internet access.

Contact Mrs. Jan Joy, Admissions Coordinator. 561-242-2268. Fax: 561-683-7307. E-mail: jjoy@cardinalnewman.com. Web site: www.cardinalnewman.com.

ANNOUNCEMENT FROM THE SCHOOL Through academic, religious, service, athletic, and extracurricular programs, Cardinal Newman High School educates the whole person and helps students to develop their God-given talents. The School produces individuals who are academically competitive and

spiritually alive. Cardinal Newman places 98% of its graduating class in national colleges and universities.

CARDINAL NEWMAN SCHOOL

4701 Forest Drive
Columbia, South Carolina 29206-3108
Head of School: Ms. Rose Tindall

General Information Coeducational day college-preparatory and religious studies school, affiliated with Roman Catholic Church. Grades 7–12. Founded: 1858. Setting: urban. 16-acre campus. 4 buildings on campus. Approved or accredited by National Catholic Education Association, South Carolina Independent School Association, Southern Association of Colleges and Schools, and South Carolina Department of Education. Total enrollment: 430. Upper school average class size: 22. Upper school faculty-student ratio: 1:10.

Upper School Student Profile Grade 9: 83 students (40 boys, 43 girls); Grade 10: 71 students (35 boys, 36 girls); Grade 11: 71 students (31 boys, 40 girls); Grade 12: 47 students (20 boys, 27 girls). 73% of students are Roman Catholic.

Faculty School total: 48. In upper school: 24 men, 20 women; 24 have advanced degrees.

Subjects Offered Algebra, American government, art, art history, biology, biology-AP, calculus, calculus-AP, chemistry, computer applications, drama, economics, English composition, English literature, English literature and composition-AP, environmental science, French, geography, government, honors algebra, honors English, honors geometry, honors U.S. history, journalism, keyboarding, Latin, life science, philosophy, physical education, physical science, physics, pre-algebra, pre-calculus, psychology, public speaking, SAT preparation, Spanish, study skills, theology, U.S. history, world civilizations, world geography, yearbook.

Graduation Requirements Algebra, biology, chemistry, computer applications, economics, English, foreign language, geometry, physical education (includes health), physics, theology, U.S. history, world geography, world history, fourth year of either lab science, math or foreign language, 3 years of the same foreign language, government/economics, 40 hours of community service (seniors).

Special Academic Programs Advanced Placement exam preparation in 3 subject areas; honors section; study at local college for college credit.

College Placement 52 students graduated in 2005; all went to college, including Clemson University; College of Charleston; Furman University; The Citadel, The Military College of South Carolina; University of South Carolina; Wofford College.

Student Life Upper grades have uniform requirement, student council, honor system. Discipline rests primarily with faculty. Attendance at religious services is required.

Summer Programs Remediation programs offered; session focuses on remediation and make-up; held on campus; accepts boys and girls; not open to students from other schools. 15 students usually enrolled. 2006 schedule: June 20 to July 26. Application deadline: May 30.

Tuition and Aid Day student tuition: $5986–$6856. Tuition installment plan (FACTS Tuition Payment Plan). Need-based scholarship grants available. In 2005–06, 3% of upper-school students received aid. Total amount of financial aid awarded in 2005–06: $7000.

Admissions Traditional secondary-level entrance grade is 9. For fall 2005, 55 students applied for upper-level admission, 54 were accepted, 54 enrolled. ITBS achievement test and school's own exam required. Deadline for receipt of application materials: March 5. Application fee required: $40. On-campus interview required.

Athletics Interscholastic: aquatics (boys, girls), baseball (b,g), basketball (b,g), cheering (g), cross-country running (b,g), dance team (b,g), football (b), golf (b,g), physical training (b,g), soccer (b,g), softball (g), swimming and diving (b,g), tennis (b,g), triathlon (b), volleyball (g), wrestling (b); coed interscholastic: outdoor adventure. 2 PE instructors, 2 coaches.

Computers Computers are regularly used in all academic classes. Computer network features include campus e-mail, on-campus library services, CD-ROMs, Internet access.

Contact Ms. Theresa Harper, Admissions Coordinator/Registrar. 803-782-2814 Ext. 11. Fax: 803-782-9314. E-mail: tharper@cnhs.org. Web site: www.cnhs.org.

ANNOUNCEMENT FROM THE SCHOOL Cardinal Newman School is a coeducational institution that provides a well-rounded education in a college-preparatory atmosphere for students in grades 7–12. Originally established in 1858 by the Ursuline Sisters, Cardinal Newman was operated on the parish grounds of St. Peter's Catholic Church in Columbia as Ursuline and Catholic High Schools until moving to its current location in 1959. The School is directed by an Advisory Board, representative of the diverse community served by Cardinal Newman, and administered by a principal. Located in beautiful Forest Acres and Columbia, South Carolina, the facilities include the main school building, the chapel, 3 science labs, 2 computer labs, a library, a gymnasium, and a stadium and athletic field. Activities include academic clubs, athletics, yearbook, and drama.

CARIBBEAN PREPARATORY SCHOOL

PO Box 70177
San Juan, Puerto Rico 00936-8177
Head of School: F. Richard Marracino

petersons.com

General Information Coeducational day college-preparatory, arts, and technology school. Grades PK–12. Founded: 1952. Setting: urban. Nearest major city is Hato Rey. 1-acre campus. 3 buildings on campus. Approved or accredited by Middle States Association of Colleges and Schools, The College Board, and Puerto Rico Department of Education. Endowment: $178,650. Total enrollment: 803. Upper school average class size: 13. Upper school faculty-student ratio: 1:8.

Upper School Student Profile Grade 9: 45 students (28 boys, 17 girls); Grade 10: 53 students (27 boys, 26 girls); Grade 11: 58 students (41 boys, 17 girls); Grade 12: 39 students (22 boys, 17 girls).

Faculty School total: 99. In upper school: 13 men, 19 women; 9 have advanced degrees.

Subjects Offered Advanced Placement courses, advanced studio art-AP, African American history, algebra, American history, American literature, anatomy and physiology, art, art history-AP, band, biology, biology-AP, business mathematics, calculus, ceramics, chemistry, chemistry-AP, civics, computer science, computer technologies, creative writing, dance, drama, drawing, earth science, ecology, English, English language and composition-AP, English literature, ethics, European history, forensics, French, geometry, health, jewelry making, journalism, Latin American studies, mathematics, modern world history, music, music appreciation, music history, painting, physical education, physics, play production, pre-calculus, printmaking, psychology, sculpture, sociology, Spanish, Spanish-AP, stained glass, theater, trigonometry, U.S. history-AP, world history.

Graduation Requirements Computer science, English, ethics, foreign language, mathematics, physical education (includes health), Puerto Rican history, science, social studies (includes history), Spanish, Puerto Rican History.

Special Academic Programs Advanced Placement exam preparation in 6 subject areas; honors section; independent study; domestic exchange program (with The Network Program Schools); programs in English, mathematics, general development for dyslexic students; special instructional classes for students with mild learning disabilities and Attention Deficit Disorder.

College Placement 38 students graduated in 2005; all went to college, including Berklee College of Music; Boston University; Florida State University; New York University; University of Massachusetts Amherst; University of Puerto Rico, Río Piedras.

Student Life Upper grades have uniform requirement, student council, honor system. Discipline rests primarily with faculty.

Summer Programs Remediation, enrichment, ESL, sports, computer instruction programs offered; session focuses on improving grades on previously taken courses; held both on and off campus; held at Parkville Campus; accepts boys and girls; open to students from other schools. 50 students usually enrolled. 2006 schedule: June 5 to June 30. Application deadline: June 2.

Tuition and Aid Day student tuition: $8024–$8164. Tuition installment plan (individually arranged payment plans, annual and semester payment plans). Tuition reduction for siblings, merit scholarship grants, need-based scholarship grants available. In 2005–06, 7% of upper-school students received aid; total upper-school merit-scholarship money awarded: $23,000. Total amount of financial aid awarded in 2005–06: $34,000.

Admissions Traditional secondary-level entrance grade is 9. For fall 2005, 31 students applied for upper-level admission, 20 were accepted, 18 enrolled. Stanford Achievement Test required. Deadline for receipt of application materials: none. Application fee required: $85. On-campus interview required.

Athletics Interscholastic: baseball (boys), basketball (b,g), cross-country running (b,g), football (b), indoor soccer (b,g), soccer (b,g), softball (g), track and field (b,g), volleyball (b,g); intramural: soccer (b,g), softball (b,g), volleyball (b,g); coed interscholastic: indoor soccer; coed intramural: aerobics, badminton, basketball, cooperative games, field hockey, fitness, flag football, floor hockey, Frisbee, indoor soccer, jogging, outdoor activities, outdoor education, outdoor recreation, physical fitness, physical training, soccer, softball, strength & conditioning, table tennis, tennis, track and field, volleyball, walking. 3 PE instructors, 8 coaches, 1 trainer.

Computers Computers are regularly used in English, mathematics, science, yearbook classes. Computer resources include on-campus library services, CD-ROMs, Internet access.

Contact Mrs. Jo-Ann Aranguren, Director of Admissions. 787-765-4411 Ext. 32. Fax: 787-764-3809. E-mail: jaranguren@cpspr.org. Web site: www.cpspr.org.

ANNOUNCEMENT FROM THE SCHOOL Unique characteristics include academic rigor, many activities and sports, close relationships between students and teachers, and emphasis on Puerto Rican culture. Parkville and Commonwealth Campuses have been extensively remodeled and expanded. Annual Giving Program initiative has been earmarked to enhance facilities and program areas that include the Permanent Endowment Scholarship Fund.

CARLISLE SCHOOL

300 Carlisle Road
Axton, Virginia 24054
Head of School: Mr. Simon A. Owen-Williams

General Information Coeducational day college-preparatory and arts school. Grades PK–12. Founded: 1968. Setting: rural. Nearest major city is Danville. 50-acre campus. 4 buildings on campus. Approved or accredited by International Baccalaureate Organization, Southern Association of Colleges and Schools, Southern Association of Independent Schools, Virginia Association of Independent Schools, and Virginia Department of Education. Member of National Association of Independent Schools. Endowment: $1.2 million. Total enrollment: 418. Upper school average class size: 14. Upper school faculty-student ratio: 1:12.

Upper School Student Profile Grade 9: 28 students (14 boys, 14 girls); Grade 10: 26 students (19 boys, 7 girls); Grade 11: 26 students (8 boys, 18 girls); Grade 12: 31 students (14 boys, 17 girls).

Faculty School total: 67. In upper school: 6 men, 15 women; 10 have advanced degrees.

Subjects Offered 1½ elective credits, ACT preparation, advanced computer applications, advanced math, Advanced Placement courses, African American history, African American studies, algebra, American government, American government-AP, American history, American history-AP, American literature, art, art history, arts, audio visual/media, band, Basic programming, biology, biology-AP, calculus, calculus-AP, chemistry, chemistry-AP, choir, college counseling, composition-AP, computer information systems, computer programming, computer science, computer science-AP, concert band, creative dance, creative drama, creative writing, dance, drama, earth science, economics, economics-AP, English, English language and composition-AP, English literature, English literature and composition-AP, English literature-AP, environmental science, fine arts, geography, geometry, government, government/civics, grammar, health, health and wellness, history, history of the Americas, honors algebra, honors English, honors geometry, independent study, International Baccalaureate courses, intro to computers, jazz band, jazz ensemble, journalism, lab science, Latin, madrigals, mathematics, mathematics-AP, Microsoft, music, peace education, physical education, physics, physics-AP, play production, pre-algebra, pre-calculus, psychology, psychology-AP, publications, Russian, SAT/ACT preparation, science, senior project, sex education, social studies, Spanish, Spanish literature, Spanish-AP, speech, statistics, statistics-AP, street law, studio art, technical theater, theater, theory of knowledge, U.S. government-AP, U.S. history-AP, wind ensemble, world civilizations, world history, world history-AP, world issues, World War I, World War II, world wide web design, yearbook.

Graduation Requirements Advanced math, algebra, arts and fine arts (art, music, dance, drama), computer science, electives, English, foreign language, mathematics, physical education (includes health), science, social studies (includes history), U.S. and Virginia history, U.S. government.

Special Academic Programs International Baccalaureate program; Advanced Placement exam preparation in 8 subject areas; honors section; independent study; term-away projects; study at local college for college credit.

College Placement 34 students graduated in 2005; all went to college, including Appalachian State University; Hampden-Sydney College; The College of William and Mary; The University of North Carolina at Chapel Hill; University of Virginia; Virginia Polytechnic Institute and State University. Median SAT verbal: 690, median SAT math: 628. 73% scored over 600 on SAT verbal, 73% scored over 600 on SAT math.

Student Life Upper grades have specified standards of dress, student council, honor system. Discipline rests equally with students and faculty.

Summer Programs Remediation, enrichment, advancement, sports, art/fine arts, computer instruction programs offered; session focuses on enrichment, academics, sports, fun; held on campus; accepts boys and girls; open to students from other schools. 60 students usually enrolled. 2006 schedule: June 15 to August 15. Application deadline: June 1.

Tuition and Aid Day student tuition: $8600–$8860. Tuition installment plan (Insured Tuition Payment Plan, FACTS Tuition Payment Plan, monthly payment plans). Need-based scholarship grants available. In 2005–06, 30% of upper-school students received aid. Total amount of financial aid awarded in 2005–06: $112,000.

Admissions Traditional secondary-level entrance grade is 9. For fall 2005, 113 students applied for upper-level admission, 106 were accepted, 85 enrolled. Nelson-Denny Reading Test, Woodcock-Johnson or writing sample required. Deadline for receipt of application materials: none. Application fee required: $35. On-campus interview required.

Athletics Interscholastic: basketball (boys, girls), cheering (g), cross-country running (b,g), field hockey (g), golf (b), soccer (b,g), softball (g), tennis (b,g), volleyball (g); intramural: aerobics/nautilus (b), basketball (b,g), cheering (g), softball (g); coed interscholastic: baseball; coed intramural: aerobics/dance, ballet, basketball, dance, Frisbee, modern dance, weight lifting. 3 PE instructors, 12 coaches.

Computers Computers are regularly used in English, history, humanities, journalism, keyboarding, mathematics, music, science, Spanish, Web site design, word processing, yearbook classes. Computer network features include campus e-mail, on-campus library services, CD-ROMs, online commercial services, Internet access, DVD.

Contact Mrs. Jannelle Sumner, Admissions Assistant. 276-632-7288 Ext. 270. Fax: 276-632-9545. E-mail: jsumner@carlisleschool.org. Web site: www.carlisleschool.org.

CARLUCCI AMERICAN INTERNATIONAL SCHOOL OF LISBON

Rua Antonio dos Reis, 95
Linho, Sintra 2710-301, Portugal
Head of School: Ms. Blannie M. Curtis

General Information Coeducational day college-preparatory and Portuguese Equivalência Program school. Grades N–12. Founded: 1956. Setting: small town. Nearest major city is Lisbon. 4-hectare campus. 4 buildings on campus. Approved or accredited by European Council of International Schools and New England Association of Schools and Colleges. Language of instruction: English. Total enrollment: 494. Upper school average class size: 12. Upper school faculty-student ratio: 1:8.

Upper School Student Profile Grade 9: 31 students (21 boys, 10 girls); Grade 10: 34 students (15 boys, 19 girls); Grade 11: 33 students (16 boys, 17 girls); Grade 12: 32 students (13 boys, 19 girls).

Faculty School total: 56. In upper school: 12 men, 21 women; 21 have advanced degrees.

Subjects Offered Algebra, art, art-AP, biology, biology-AP, business studies, calculus-AP, chemistry, chemistry-AP, choir, computer applications, economics, English, English-AP, French, French-AP, geometry, history and culture of Portugal, International Baccalaureate courses, model United Nations, modern civilization, music, physical education, physics, Portuguese, Portuguese literature, statistics, theory of knowledge, U.S. history, U.S. history-AP, U.S. literature, writing workshop, yearbook.

Graduation Requirements Arts and fine arts (art, music, dance, drama), computer science, English, foreign language, mathematics, physical education (includes health), science, social studies (includes history), community service (for International Baccalaureate diploma candidates).

Special Academic Programs International Baccalaureate program; Advanced Placement exam preparation in 6 subject areas; honors section; academic accommodation for the gifted; remedial reading and/or remedial writing; remedial math; programs in general development for dyslexic students; ESL (20 students enrolled).

College Placement 19 students graduated in 2005; all went to college, including University of Washington; Yale University.

Student Life Upper grades have specified standards of dress, student council, honor system. Discipline rests equally with students and faculty.

Tuition and Aid Day student tuition: €11,632–€15,404. Tuition installment plan (early payment discount, quarterly payment plan). Tuition reduction for siblings, merit scholarship grants, need-based scholarship grants available.

Admissions Traditional secondary-level entrance grade is 9. English for Non-native Speakers, math and English placement tests and Math Placement Exam required. Deadline for receipt of application materials: none. Application fee required: €470. Interview recommended.

Athletics Interscholastic: basketball (boys, girls), cross-country running (b,g); intramural: badminton (b,g), basketball (b,g); coed intramural: golf. 2 PE instructors, 1 coach.

Computers Computers are regularly used in art, economics, English, foreign language, history, mathematics, science classes. Computer network features include on-campus library services, CD-ROMs, Internet access, DVD.

Contact Cynthia Ferrell, Director of Admissions and Marketing. 351-21-923-9800. Fax: 351-21-923-9809. E-mail: info@caislisbon.com. Web site: www.caislisbon.org.

CAROLINA DAY SCHOOL

1345 Hendersonville Road
Asheville, North Carolina 28803
Head of School: Beverly H. Sgro, PhD

General Information Coeducational day college-preparatory and technology school. Grades PK–12. Founded: 1987. Setting: suburban. 28-acre campus. 2 buildings on campus. Approved or accredited by North Carolina Association of Independent Schools, Southern Association of Colleges and Schools, Southern Association of Independent Schools, and North Carolina Department of Education. Member of National Association of Independent Schools. Endowment: $2.6 million. Total enrollment: 644. Upper school average class size: 17. Upper school faculty-student ratio: 1:10.

Upper School Student Profile Grade 9: 39 students (22 boys, 17 girls); Grade 10: 50 students (23 boys, 27 girls); Grade 11: 52 students (25 boys, 27 girls); Grade 12: 40 students (22 boys, 18 girls).

Faculty School total: 102. In upper school: 12 men, 13 women; 18 have advanced degrees.

Subjects Offered Algebra, American history, American literature, ancient history, art, art history, art history-AP, biology, biology-AP, calculus, calculus-AP, chemistry, choral music, chorus, cinematography, computer science, computer science-AP, computer skills, CPR, creative writing, drama, drama performance, ecology, economics, English, English language and composition-AP, English literature, environmental science-AP, environmental systems, European history, European history-AP, evolution, foreign language, French, French-AP, geography, geometry, government, history, literature and composition-AP, martial arts, music theory-AP, physical education, physics, physics-AP, pre-algebra, pre-calculus, psychology-AP, reading/

study skills, SAT preparation, science, senior project, Spanish, Spanish-AP, speech, speech and debate, statistics, statistics-AP, studio art, studio art-AP, U.S. government, U.S. history, U.S. history-AP.

Graduation Requirements Algebra, American history, American literature, arts and fine arts (art, music, dance, drama), biology, chemistry, college counseling, computer literacy, English, geometry, modern languages, physical education (includes health), public speaking, social studies (includes history), CPR/First Aid (non-credit class). Community service is required.

Special Academic Programs Advanced Placement exam preparation in 18 subject areas; honors section; independent study; study at local college for college credit; academic accommodation for the gifted; programs in English, mathematics, general development for dyslexic students; special instructional classes for students with Attention Deficit Disorder and learning disabilities.

College Placement 56 students graduated in 2005; all went to college, including Appalachian State University; Duke University; Elon University; Guilford College; North Carolina State University; The University of North Carolina at Chapel Hill. Mean SAT verbal: 639, mean SAT math: 631. 48% scored over 600 on SAT verbal, 59% scored over 600 on SAT math.

Student Life Upper grades have specified standards of dress, student council, honor system. Discipline rests equally with students and faculty.

Summer Programs Enrichment, sports programs offered; session focuses on recreation and enrichment; held on campus; accepts boys and girls; open to students from other schools. 70 students usually enrolled. 2006 schedule: June 12 to July 28. Application deadline: May 31.

Tuition and Aid Day student tuition: $13,870–$14,990. Tuition installment plan (monthly payment plans, individually arranged payment plans, 1-payment plan or 2-installments plan (August and January)). Need-based scholarship grants available. In 2005–06, 19% of upper-school students received aid. Total amount of financial aid awarded in 2005–06: $161,390.

Admissions Traditional secondary-level entrance grade is 9. For fall 2005, 21 students applied for upper-level admission, 17 were accepted, 12 enrolled. ERB or SSAT required. Deadline for receipt of application materials: none. Application fee required: $100. On-campus interview required.

Athletics Interscholastic: baseball (boys), basketball (b,g), cross-country running (b,g), field hockey (g), martial arts (b,g), soccer (b,g), swimming and diving (b,g), tennis (b,g), track and field (b,g), volleyball (g); coed interscholastic: golf. 1 PE instructor, 2 coaches, 1 trainer.

Computers Computers are regularly used in all academic classes. Computer network features include on-campus library services, CD-ROMs, online commercial services, Internet access, office computer access.

Contact Robin Goertz, Director of Admissions. 828-274-0757 Ext. 310. Fax: 828-274-0756. E-mail: admissions@cdschool.org. Web site: www.cdschool.org.

ANNOUNCEMENT FROM THE SCHOOL Carolina Day School is Asheville's only comprehensive independent school. The School discovers the promise, inspires the journey, and celebrates the achievement of every student. Working in partnership with parents, Carolina Day School challenges young people to pursue their quest for personal excellence by providing them with a rigorous college-preparatory program. The School is situated on 28 wooded acres adjacent to the Blue Ridge Parkway in the mountains of western North Carolina. The School carries on the traditions of academic excellence, social responsibility, and character development, which were strengthened by the 1987 merger of Asheville Country Day School (founded in 1936) and St. Genevieve/Gibbons Hall (founded in 1908). The School serves approximately 640 students in grades PK–12, with class sizes of 12, 16, or 18. Carolina Day students respond to high expectations in a supportive learning environment, as evidenced by consistently high SAT scores and successful college placements. Satisfied parents voice their support for the School with high re-enrollment rates, citing the quality of teaching as the factor most responsible for their children's positive educational experiences. Distinctive features of the curriculum include 18 Advanced Placement courses, a variety of athletic and arts offerings, outdoor and environmental education, leadership training, character education, a college guidance program, and a focus on community service. Successful capital campaigns during the last 10 years have enabled the School to acquire additional acreage, new academic facilities, a gymnasium and fitness center, a center for students with learning differences, and a campuswide telecommunications network.

CARONDELET HIGH SCHOOL

1133 Winton Drive
Concord, California 94518
Head of School: Sr. James Marien Dyer, CSJ

General Information Girls' day college-preparatory, arts, religious studies, and technology school, affiliated with Roman Catholic Church. Grades 9–12. Founded: 1965. Setting: suburban. Nearest major city is Oakland. 9-acre campus. 5 buildings

on campus. Approved or accredited by Western Association of Schools and Colleges. Total enrollment: 830. Upper school average class size: 30. Upper school faculty-student ratio: 1:25.

Upper School Student Profile Grade 9: 215 students (215 girls); Grade 10: 209 students (209 girls); Grade 11: 200 students (200 girls); Grade 12: 204 students (204 girls). 90% of students are Roman Catholic.

Faculty School total: 61. In upper school: 13 men, 48 women; 30 have advanced degrees.

Subjects Offered Algebra, American studies, animation, architectural drawing, art, art history, band, biology, calculus, calculus-AP, cartooning, chemistry, chorus, church history, civics, community service, computer applications, concert band, concert choir, consumer education, creative writing, criminal justice, current events, dance, design, drafting, drawing, economics, English, English-AP, ethics, finite math, fitness, French, geology, geometry, government-AP, health, honors algebra, honors English, honors geometry, Italian, jazz band, journalism, Latin, marching band, marine biology, music history, music theory, musical theater, orchestra, painting, physical education, physics, physics-AP, physiology, pre-algebra, pre-calculus, programming, psychology, psychology-AP, relationships, sculpture, Spanish, Spanish-AP, sports medicine, statistics, strings, studio art-AP, technical drawing, transition mathematics, trigonometry, U.S. history, U.S. history-AP, water color painting, Web site design, women's health, world arts, world civilizations, world religions, writing, yearbook.

Graduation Requirements Computer literacy, English, mathematics, modern languages, physical education (includes health), religious studies, science, social studies (includes history), visual and performing arts, 20 cocurricular credits.

Special Academic Programs Advanced Placement exam preparation in 6 subject areas; honors section; academic accommodation for the gifted.

College Placement 212 students graduated in 2005; 210 went to college, including California Polytechnic State University, San Luis Obispo; Santa Clara University; Stanford University; University of California, Berkeley; University of California, Los Angeles; University of Notre Dame. Other: 2 had other specific plans. Mean SAT verbal: 589, mean SAT math: 574, mean composite ACT: 24.

Student Life Upper grades have uniform requirement, honor system. Discipline rests primarily with faculty. Attendance at religious services is required.

Tuition and Aid Day student tuition: $9250. Tuition installment plan (monthly payment plans, pre-payment plan, semester or quarterly payment plans). Need-based scholarship grants, paying campus jobs available. In 2005–06, 13% of upper-school students received aid.

Admissions Traditional secondary-level entrance grade is 9. For fall 2005, 380 students applied for upper-level admission, 240 were accepted, 220 enrolled. High School Placement Test or High School Placement Test (closed version) from Scholastic Testing Service required. Deadline for receipt of application materials: December 9. Application fee required: $75. On-campus interview required.

Athletics Interscholastic: aquatics, basketball, cheering, combined training, cross-country running, dance, dance squad, diving, drill team, golf, lacrosse, soccer, softball, swimming and diving, tennis, volleyball, water polo; intramural: basketball, flag football, physical fitness, physical training, volleyball. 3 PE instructors, 40 coaches, 1 trainer.

Computers Computer resources include campus e-mail, on-campus library services, CD-ROMs, Internet access.

Contact Ms. Kathy Harris, Director of Admissions. 925-686-5353 Ext. 161. Fax: 925-671-9429. E-mail: kharris@carondeleths.org. Web site: carondelethighschool.com/.

CARRABASSETT VALLEY ACADEMY

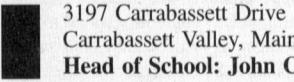

3197 Carrabassett Drive
Carrabassett Valley, Maine 04947
Head of School: John C. Ritzo

petersons.com

General Information Coeducational boarding and day college-preparatory, arts, and technology school. Grades 8–PG. Founded: 1982. Setting: rural. Nearest major city is Waterville. Students are housed in single-sex dormitories. 8-acre campus. 3 buildings on campus. Approved or accredited by New England Association of Schools and Colleges and Maine Department of Education. Endowment: $250,677. Total enrollment: 110. Upper school average class size: 12. Upper school faculty-student ratio: 1:7.

Upper School Student Profile Grade 10: 37 students (27 boys, 10 girls); Grade 11: 20 students (14 boys, 6 girls); Grade 12: 26 students (20 boys, 6 girls); Postgraduate: 2 students (2 boys). 88% of students are boarding students. 63% are state residents. 15 states are represented in upper school student body. 1% are international students. International students from Canada, Ireland, and Japan; 1 other country represented in student body.

Faculty School total: 12. In upper school: 4 men, 8 women; 6 have advanced degrees; 8 reside on campus.

Subjects Offered Algebra, American history, American literature, biology, calculus, chemistry, computer science, earth science, English, ESL, European history, fine arts, French, geography, geometry, government/civics, health, history, mathematics, music, photography, physical education, physics, pre-calculus, publications, science, social studies, Spanish, sports conditioning, studio art, world history.

Graduation Requirements Algebra, American history, applied arts, arts and fine arts (art, music, dance, drama), athletic training, athletics, biology, computer literacy,

English, foreign language, geometry, health education, physical education (includes health), science, senior project, social studies (includes history), participation in snow sports.

Special Academic Programs ESL (2 students enrolled).

College Placement 36 students graduated in 2005; 34 went to college, including Bates College; Colby College; Montana State University; University of Colorado at Boulder; University of Maine. Other: 2 had other specific plans. Median SAT verbal: 525, median SAT math: 520.

Student Life Upper grades have specified standards of dress, student council, honor system. Discipline rests primarily with faculty.

Summer Programs Sports programs offered; session focuses on ski/snowboard training; held both on and off campus; held at Blackcomb, British Columbia, Mt. Hood, Oregon, and New Zealand; accepts boys and girls; open to students from other schools. 60 students usually enrolled. 2006 schedule: June 27 to August 11. Application deadline: May 1.

Tuition and Aid Day student tuition: $24,100; 7-day tuition and room/board: $32,100. Tuition installment plan (monthly payment plans). Need-based scholarship grants available. In 2005–06, 30% of upper-school students received aid.

Admissions Traditional secondary-level entrance grade is 10. Deadline for receipt of application materials: March 31. Application fee required: $40. Interview required.

Athletics Interscholastic: alpine skiing (boys, girls); baseball (b), freestyle skiing (b,g), skiing (downhill) (b,g), snowboarding (b,g), soccer (b,g); intramural: weight lifting (b,g), weight training (b,g); coed interscholastic: baseball, bicycling, mountain biking, skateboarding; coed intramural: aerobics/dance, back packing, bicycling, canoeing/kayaking, climbing, combined training, fitness, golf, hiking/backpacking, in-line skating, kayaking, mountaineering, outdoor activities, outdoor adventure, outdoor education, outdoor skills, outdoors, physical fitness, physical training, rappelling, roller blading, running, Special Olympics, tennis, ultimate Frisbee, volleyball, wall climbing, wilderness. 14 coaches, 1 trainer.

Computers Computers are regularly used in all classes. Computer network features include campus e-mail, on-campus library services, CD-ROMs, online commercial services, Internet access, office computer access, DVD.

Contact Mrs. Dawn Smith, Director of Admissions. 207-237-2250. Fax: 207-237-2213. E-mail: dsmith@gocva.com. Web site: www.gocva.com.

ANNOUNCEMENT FROM THE SCHOOL CVA is an independent, coeducational, boarding and day school for grades 8 through postgraduate. The intent and purpose of the Academy is to foster individual student development by providing the optimum balance of excellence in athletic training with a focus on competitive or big mountain skiing/snowboarding, college-preparatory academics, and responsible living. Located at Sugarloaf/USA.

CARROLLTON SCHOOL OF THE SACRED HEART

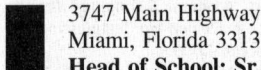

3747 Main Highway
Miami, Florida 33133
Head of School: Sr. Suzanne Cooke

General Information Girls' day college-preparatory, arts, religious studies, bilingual studies, and technology school, affiliated with Roman Catholic Church. Grades PK–12. Founded: 1961. Setting: urban. 10-acre campus. 5 buildings on campus. Approved or accredited by Florida Council of Independent Schools. Endowment: $2 million. Total enrollment: 710. Upper school average class size: 15. Upper school faculty-student ratio: 1:9.

Upper School Student Profile Grade 7: 60 students (60 girls); Grade 8: 60 students (60 girls); Grade 9: 75 students (75 girls); Grade 10: 65 students (65 girls); Grade 11: 60 students (60 girls); Grade 12: 60 students (60 girls). 87% of students are Roman Catholic.

Faculty School total: 74. In upper school: 9 men, 24 women; 20 have advanced degrees.

Subjects Offered Algebra, American history, American literature, anatomy and physiology, art, art history, Bible studies, biology, British literature, calculus, chemistry, computer science, debate, drama, earth systems analysis, economics, English, English literature, environmental science, ethics, expository writing, fine arts, French, general science, geometry, government/civics, grammar, health, history, humanities, journalism, mathematics, music, photography, physical education, physical science, physics, pre-calculus, psychology, religion, science, scripture, social science, social studies, Spanish, speech, theater, trigonometry, vocal ensemble, world history, world literature.

Graduation Requirements Arts and fine arts (art, music, dance, drama), computer science, English, foreign language, mathematics, physical education (includes health), religion (includes Bible studies and theology), science, social studies (includes history). Community service is required.

Special Academic Programs Advanced Placement exam preparation in 7 subject areas; honors section; independent study; study at local college for college credit; domestic exchange program; study abroad.

College Placement 52 students graduated in 2005; all went to college, including Boston College; Florida International University; Northwestern University; University of Miami; Vanderbilt University. Median SAT verbal: 580, median SAT math: 590,

median composite ACT: 24. 51% scored over 600 on SAT verbal, 47% scored over 600 on SAT math, 30% scored over 26 on composite ACT.

Student Life Upper grades have uniform requirement, student council, honor system. Discipline rests primarily with faculty. Attendance at religious services is required.

Tuition and Aid Day student tuition: $17,975. Tuition installment plan (Insured Tuition Payment Plan, monthly payment plans). Merit scholarship grants, need-based scholarship grants available. In 2005–06, 15% of upper-school students received aid; total upper-school merit-scholarship money awarded: $45,000. Total amount of financial aid awarded in 2005–06: $920,000.

Admissions Traditional secondary-level entrance grade is 9. For fall 2005, 132 students applied for upper-level admission, 37 were accepted, 30 enrolled. Admissions testing required. Deadline for receipt of application materials: February 1. Application fee required: $100. On-campus interview required.

Athletics Interscholastic: aquatics, basketball, crew, cross-country running, golf, sailing, soccer, softball, swimming and diving, tennis, track and field, volleyball, water polo, winter soccer. 2 PE instructors, 8 coaches.

Computers Computers are regularly used in all academic classes. Computer network features include campus e-mail, on-campus library services, CD-ROMs, online commercial services, Internet access, laptop program.

Contact Ms. Ana J. Roye, Admissions Director. 305-446-5673 Ext. 1224. Fax: 305-446-4160. E-mail: aluna@carrollton.org. Web site: www.carrollton.org.

CARSON LONG MILITARY INSTITUTE

200 North Carlisle Street
PO Box 98
New Bloomfield, Pennsylvania 17068-0098

petersons.com

ANNOUNCEMENT FROM THE SCHOOL Carson Long is celebrating 170 years of character-building education. A preparatory school for boys of average ability, from parents of average income, Carson Long sends more than 80% to college. The Army Junior ROTC program has earned a rating of Honor School with Distinction. The School emphasizes structure, self-discipline, and family values.

See full description on page 714.

CARY ACADEMY

1500 North Harrison Avenue
Cary, North Carolina 27513
Head of School: Mr. Donald S. Berger

General Information Coeducational day college-preparatory, arts, and technology school. Grades 6–12. Founded: 1996. Setting: suburban. Nearest major city is Raleigh. 52-acre campus. 6 buildings on campus. Approved or accredited by North Carolina Association of Independent Schools, Southern Association of Colleges and Schools, and North Carolina Department of Education. Total enrollment: 698. Upper school average class size: 14. Upper school faculty-student ratio: 1:14.

Upper School Student Profile Grade 9: 106 students (62 boys, 44 girls); Grade 10: 102 students (51 boys, 51 girls); Grade 11: 100 students (47 boys, 53 girls); Grade 12: 89 students (42 boys, 47 girls).

Faculty School total: 73. In upper school: 26 men, 18 women; 33 have advanced degrees.

Subjects Offered Advanced Placement courses, aerobics, algebra, American history, American history-AP, American literature, American literature-AP, anatomy and physiology, astronomy, athletic training, biology, biology-AP, biotechnology, calculus, calculus-AP, ceramics, chamber groups, chemistry, chemistry-AP, Chinese, computer programming, computer programming-AP, concert choir, debate, digital photography, drawing, economics, economics-AP, environmental science, film studies, forensic science, French language-AP, French literature-AP, French-AP, geometry, German, German literature, German-AP, health education, history of mathematics, instruments, international relations, jazz band, journalism, modern European history-AP, multimedia design, music composition, music theory, orchestra, painting, photography, physical education, physics, physics-AP, pre-calculus, programming, psychology, Spanish language-AP, Spanish literature, Spanish literature-AP, Spanish-AP, statistics and probability, statistics-AP, studio art, studio art-AP, technical theater, theater production, trigonometry, video, voice, Web site design, wind ensemble, women in world history, world arts, world history, world literature, yearbook.

Graduation Requirements Algebra, American history, American literature, biology, chemistry, foreign language, physical education (includes health), physics, world history, world literature.

Special Academic Programs Advanced Placement exam preparation; honors section; accelerated programs; independent study; academic accommodation for the gifted, the musically talented, and the artistically talented.

College Placement 94 students graduated in 2005; all went to college, including Davidson College; Georgetown University; North Carolina State University; The George Washington University; The University of North Carolina at Chapel Hill; The

University of North Carolina Wilmington. Median SAT verbal: 680, median SAT math: 670. 82% scored over 600 on SAT verbal, 84.6% scored over 600 on SAT math.

Student Life Upper grades have specified standards of dress, student council, honor system. Discipline rests equally with students and faculty.

Summer Programs Enrichment, sports, art/fine arts, computer instruction programs offered; session focuses on enrichment; held on campus; accepts boys and girls; open to students from other schools. 2006 schedule: June 13 to July 29. Application deadline: none.

Tuition and Aid Day student tuition: $13,775. Tuition installment plan (Academic Management Services Plan). Merit scholarship grants, need-based scholarship grants, need-based loans available. In 2005–06, 15% of upper-school students received aid; total upper-school merit-scholarship money awarded: $10,000. Total amount of financial aid awarded in 2005–06: $568,919.

Admissions Traditional secondary-level entrance grade is 9. For fall 2005, 82 students applied for upper-level admission, 50 were accepted, 37 enrolled. Achievement/Aptitude/Writing, CTP or ERB CTP IV required. Deadline for receipt of application materials: none. Application fee required: $100. Interview required.

Athletics Interscholastic: aquatics (boys, girls), baseball (b), basketball (b,g), cheering (b,g), cross-country running (b,g), field hockey (g), golf (b), lacrosse (b), soccer (b,g), softball (g), swimming and diving (b,g), tennis (b,g), track and field (b,g), volleyball (g), wrestling (g); intramural: baseball (b), basketball (b,g), cooperative games (b,g), dance (b,g), dance squad (g), fitness (b,g), fitness walking (b,g), Fives (b,g), floor hockey (b,g), indoor soccer (b,g), modern dance (g), soccer (b,g), softball (g), strength & conditioning (b,g), tennis (b,g), touch football (b,g), track and field (b,g), ultimate Frisbee (b,g), volleyball (b,g), walking (b,g), weight lifting (b,g), wrestling (b,g); coed intramural: aerobics, aerobics/dance, aerobics/nautilus, badminton, basketball, billiards, bowling, cooperative games, dance, fitness, fitness walking, Fives, floor hockey, Frisbee, golf, gymnastics, handball, indoor soccer, jogging, jump rope, kickball, martial arts, modern dance, Newcombe ball, physical fitness, running, soccer, strength & conditioning, table tennis, tai chi, tennis, touch football, track and field, ultimate Frisbee, volleyball, walking, weight lifting, weight training, winter walking. 2 PE instructors, 40 coaches, 1 trainer.

Computers Computers are regularly used in all academic, animation, desktop publishing, drawing and design, independent study, media arts, media production, music, theater arts, video film production, yearbook classes. Computer network features include campus e-mail, on-campus library services, CD-ROMs, online commercial services, Internet access, file transfer.

Contact Ms. Denise Goodman, Director of Admissions. 919-228-4550. Fax: 919-677-4002. E-mail: denise_goodman@caryacademy.org. Web site: www.caryacademy.org.

CASADY SCHOOL

9500 North Pennsylvania Avenue
PO Box 20390
Oklahoma City, Oklahoma 73120
Head of School: Mr. Charles W. Britton

petersons.com

General Information Coeducational day college-preparatory school, affiliated with Episcopal Church. Grades PK–12. Founded: 1947. Setting: suburban. 80-acre campus. 29 buildings on campus. Approved or accredited by Independent Schools Association of the Southwest, National Independent Private Schools Association, Southwest Association of Episcopal Schools, and The College Board. Member of National Association of Independent Schools and Secondary School Admission Test Board. Endowment: $11.8 million. Total enrollment: 875. Upper school average class size: 15. Upper school faculty-student ratio: 1:15.

Upper School Student Profile Grade 9: 80 students (46 boys, 34 girls); Grade 10: 88 students (45 boys, 43 girls); Grade 11: 87 students (47 boys, 40 girls); Grade 12: 83 students (31 boys, 52 girls). 30% of students are members of Episcopal Church.

Faculty School total: 116. In upper school: 29 men, 20 women; 35 have advanced degrees.

Subjects Offered African-American studies, algebra, American history, American literature, art, art history, Asian history, athletic training, band, Bible studies, biochemistry, biology, biology-AP, British literature, calculus, calculus-AP, ceramics, chemistry, chemistry-AP, choir, choral music, college counseling, college placement, college planning, computer applications, computer programming, computer science, creative writing, data processing, digital imaging, drama, drama performance, drawing, driver education, earth science, economics, English, English language-AP, English literature, English literature-AP, environmental science, European history, expository writing, fine arts, French, French language-AP, French literature-AP, freshman seminar, functions, geology, geometry, German, government/civics, grammar, Greek, health, history, human anatomy, journalism, Latin, Latin-AP, mathematics, Middle Eastern history, modern languages, music, mythology, Native American history, painting, photography, physical education, physics, physiology, religion, Russian history, science, social studies, Spanish, Spanish language-AP, Spanish literature-AP, speech, statistics, theater, theology, trigonometry, U.S. history-AP, water color painting, weight training, word processing, world history, world literature, writing, yearbook.

Graduation Requirements Arts and fine arts (art, music, dance, drama), computer science, English, foreign language, mathematics, physical education (includes health), science, social studies (includes history), service learning.

Special Academic Programs Advanced Placement exam preparation in 17 subject areas; independent study; study abroad; academic accommodation for the gifted, the musically talented, and the artistically talented.

College Placement 79 students graduated in 2005; all went to college, including Oklahoma State University; Stanford University; Trinity University; University of Oklahoma; University of Pennsylvania; Vassar College. Mean SAT verbal: 629, mean SAT math: 622. 55% scored over 600 on SAT verbal, 55% scored over 600 on SAT math.

Student Life Upper grades have specified standards of dress, student council, honor system. Discipline rests equally with students and faculty. Attendance at religious services is required.

Summer Programs Remediation, enrichment, advancement, art/fine arts, computer instruction programs offered; held on campus; accepts boys and girls; open to students from other schools. 500 students usually enrolled. 2006 schedule: June 12 to July 14. Application deadline: June 1.

Tuition and Aid Day student tuition: $5900–$13,790. Tuition installment plan (The Tuition Plan, Insured Tuition Payment Plan, monthly payment plans, individually arranged payment plans, 2-installment plan). Merit scholarship grants, need-based scholarship grants available. In 2005–06, 10% of upper-school students received aid; total upper-school merit-scholarship money awarded: $8000. Total amount of financial aid awarded in 2005–06: $428,828.

Admissions Traditional secondary-level entrance grade is 9. For fall 2005, 70 students applied for upper-level admission, 58 were accepted, 32 enrolled. School's own exam required. Deadline for receipt of application materials: none. Application fee required: $35. On-campus interview required.

Athletics Interscholastic: baseball (boys), basketball (b,g), cheering (g), cross-country running (b,g), field hockey (g), football (b), golf (b,g), soccer (b,g), softball (g), swimming and diving (b,g), tennis (b,g), track and field (b,g), volleyball (b,g), wrestling (b); intramural: aerobics/dance (g), dance (g), martial arts (b,g), modern dance (g), physical fitness (b,g), physical training (b,g); coed intramural: aerobics, bowling, climbing, fencing, fitness walking, racquetball, sailing, weight lifting, yoga. 9 PE instructors, 23 coaches, 2 trainers.

Computers Computers are regularly used in all academic classes. Computer resources include campus e-mail, on-campus library services, CD-ROMs, Internet access, file transfer, office computer access.

Contact Mrs. Kathy Kastens, Admission Office Coordinator. 405-749-3185. Fax: 405-749-3223. E-mail: kastensk@casady.org. Web site: www.casady.org.

ANNOUNCEMENT FROM THE SCHOOL Casady School is Oklahoma City's oldest and finest independent college-preparatory school. It was established in 1947 by the Right Reverend Thomas Casady, and by members of the laity. The focus of the School since its founding has been on the full development of the mind, body, and spirit of each student. Casady offers boys and girls in prekindergarten through grade 12 an outstanding academic foundation that prepares them to lead happy, productive, and fulfilling lives. The School complements its academic program, renowned throughout the state and nation, with an extensive activities program, a comprehensive recreational and interscholastic sports program, and a religious education that provides a firm footing in Christian faith. The uncommonly beautiful 80-acre campus is an exciting place for learning. Children develop at different rates, and they learn best when they are actively involved. Casady's Montessori-based early education program centers on carefully selected activities, including an introduction to computers, which hold great appeal for young children. In the Lower Division, the School nurtures children's love of learning, fosters their creativity, and helps them learn to reason. Casady's Middle Division teachers thoughtfully respond to the natural changes and challenges of adolescence. Teachers serve as advisers and coaches, and they work side-by-side with students on community service projects and school activities. The Upper Division offers a rigorous college preparatory education enhanced by strong arts and sports programs and an extensive activities program. Casady students graduate as creative and analytical thinkers, effective writers and speakers, and ethical decision makers. The average SAT scores for the class of 2005 were 629 verbal and 622 math. In 2005, 79 graduates entered 4-year colleges and universities. These are schools such as Cornell, Oklahoma State, Georgetown, Stanford, Johns Hopkins, Rice, MIT, and Vanderbilt and the Universities of Oklahoma and Texas.

CASCADILLA SCHOOL

116 Summit Street
Ithaca, New York 14850
Head of School: Patricia T. Kendall

www petersons.com

General Information Coeducational boarding and day college-preparatory, arts, and bilingual studies school. Grades 9–PG. Founded: 1870. Setting: urban. Nearest major city is Syracuse. Students are housed in single-sex dormitories. 2-acre campus. 3 buildings on campus. Approved or accredited by Colombian Ministry of Education, Ministry of Education (Thailand), Ministry of Education, Japan, New York State Board of Regents, New York State University, The College Board, US Department of State, and New York Department of Education. Endowment: $1.2 million. Total enrollment: 51. Upper school average class size: 7. Upper school faculty-student ratio: 1:6.

Upper School Student Profile Grade 9: 10 students (5 boys, 5 girls); Grade 10: 10 students (5 boys, 5 girls); Grade 11: 20 students (10 boys, 10 girls); Grade 12: 10 students (4 boys, 6 girls); Postgraduate: 1 student (1 boy). 20% of students are boarding students. 80% are state residents. 6 states are represented in upper school student body. 15% are international students. International students from Ecuador, India, Japan, Mexico, Republic of Korea, and Taiwan; 2 other countries represented in student body.

Faculty School total: 13. In upper school: 5 men, 8 women; 12 have advanced degrees; 4 reside on campus.

Subjects Offered Advanced chemistry, Advanced Placement courses, advanced TOEFL/grammar, African literature, algebra, American history, American literature, anatomy and physiology, art, biochemistry, biology, biology-AP, calculus, calculus-AP, career/college preparation, chemistry, chemistry-AP, college admission preparation, college awareness, college counseling, college placement, college planning, college writing, computer programming, computer science, creative writing, decision making, decision making skills, drama performance, driver education, earth science, economics, English, English as a foreign language, English composition, English literature, English literature and composition-AP, English literature-AP, environmental education, environmental science, ESL, ethics, European history, expository writing, fabric arts, French, French as a second language, geometry, government/civics, health, health and wellness, health education, history, honors algebra, honors English, honors geometry, honors U.S. history, honors world history, lab science, leadership skills, mathematics, philosophy, photography, physical education, physics, psychology, public speaking, reading, reading/study skills, SAT preparation, SAT/ACT preparation, science, Shakespeare, social studies, Spanish, trigonometry, typing, video film production, world history, world history-AP, world literature, writing.

Graduation Requirements Arts and fine arts (art, music, dance, drama), computer science, current events, debate, economics, English, foreign language, international affairs, mathematics, physical education (includes health), political science, public speaking, research, research and reference, science, social studies (includes history), English V course (for college research preparation). Community service is required.

Special Academic Programs Advanced Placement exam preparation in 10 subject areas; honors section; accelerated programs; independent study; study at local college for college credit; academic accommodation for the gifted and the artistically talented; remedial reading and/or remedial writing; remedial math; programs in English, mathematics for dyslexic students; special instructional classes for students with learning disabilities and Attention Deficit Disorder; ESL (15 students enrolled).

College Placement 17 students graduated in 2005; 14 went to college, including Buffalo State College, State University of New York; Georgetown University; New York University; Saint John's University; State University of New York at Binghamton; Tufts University. Other: 1 went to work, 1 had other specific plans. Median SAT verbal: 600, median SAT math: 650. 50% scored over 600 on SAT verbal, 50% scored over 600 on SAT math.

Student Life Upper grades have specified standards of dress, student council, honor system. Discipline rests equally with students and faculty.

Summer Programs Remediation, enrichment, advancement, ESL, art/fine arts programs offered; session focuses on academics; held on campus; accepts boys and girls; open to students from other schools. 40 students usually enrolled. 2006 schedule: July 1 to August 17. Application deadline: June 30.

Tuition and Aid Day student tuition: $10,000; 7-day tuition and room/board: $28,000. Tuition installment plan (monthly payment plans, individually arranged payment plans). Tuition reduction for siblings, merit scholarship grants, need-based scholarship grants, paying campus jobs available. In 2005–06, 40% of upper-school students received aid; total upper-school merit-scholarship money awarded: $50,000. Total amount of financial aid awarded in 2005–06: $60,000.

Admissions Traditional secondary-level entrance grade is 10. For fall 2005, 70 students applied for upper-level admission, 35 were accepted, 34 enrolled. Deadline for receipt of application materials: none. Application fee required: $50. Interview recommended.

Athletics Interscholastic: crew (boys, girls); intramural: crew (b,g), fencing (b), independent competitive sports (b,g), rowing (b,g), sailing (b,g), skiing (cross-country) (b,g), skiing (downhill) (b,g), soccer (b,g); coed interscholastic: aerobics, aerobics/nautilus, alpine skiing, aquatics, back packing, badminton, basketball, billiards, bowling, climbing, combined training, fitness, fitness walking, Frisbee, hiking/backpacking, jogging, kayaking, nordic skiing, physical fitness, physical training, swimming and diving, table tennis, weight lifting, yoga; coed intramural: aerobics, aerobics/dance, badminton, basketball, bowling, horseback riding, independent competitive sports, jogging, nautilus, nordic skiing, outdoor activities, outdoor adventure, physical fitness, physical training, pillo polo, racquetball, rowing, sailboarding, skiing (cross-country), skiing (downhill), snowboarding, strength & conditioning, volleyball, walking, wall climbing, windsurfing. 1 PE instructor.

Computers Computers are regularly used in career exploration, college planning, creative writing, desktop publishing, desktop publishing, ESL, literary magazine, mathematics, media arts, newspaper, photography, publishing, research skills, SAT preparation, senior seminar, Spanish, stock market, theater, theater arts, video film production, Web site design, word processing, writing, writing, yearbook classes. Computer network features include campus e-mail, on-campus library services, CD-ROMs, online commercial services, Internet access, file transfer, office computer access, DVD.

Contact Patricia T. Kendall, Headmistress. 607-272-3110. Fax: 607-272-0747. E-mail: admissions@cascadillaschool.org. Web site: www.cascadillaschool.org.

See full description on page 716.

CASCIA HALL PREPARATORY SCHOOL

2520 South Yorktown Avenue
Tulsa, Oklahoma 74114-2803
Head of School: Rev. Bernard C. Scianna, OSA

General Information Coeducational day college-preparatory and liberal arts school, affiliated with Roman Catholic Church. Grades 6–12. Founded: 1926. Setting: urban. 40-acre campus. 7 buildings on campus. Approved or accredited by National Catholic Education Association, North Central Association of Colleges and Schools, and Oklahoma Department of Education. Endowment: $4 million. Total enrollment: 576. Upper school average class size: 18. Upper school faculty-student ratio: 1:12.

Upper School Student Profile Grade 9: 93 students (52 boys, 41 girls); Grade 10: 97 students (57 boys, 40 girls); Grade 11: 87 students (45 boys, 42 girls); Grade 12: 83 students (39 boys, 44 girls). 50% of students are Roman Catholic.

Faculty School total: 54. In upper school: 20 men, 19 women; 29 have advanced degrees.

Subjects Offered 20th century physics, Advanced Placement courses, algebra, American government-AP, ancient world history, art, art-AP, astronomy, Basic programming, Bible studies, biology, calculus, calculus-AP, career exploration, Catholic belief and practice, Central and Eastern European history, chemistry, chemistry-AP, chorus, Christian ethics, church history, composition, computer science, creative writing, driver education, English language and composition-AP, English literature and composition-AP, ethics, European history-AP, French, gardening, geography, geometry, German, government-AP, grammar, health, Holocaust studies, Latin, literature, philosophy, photography, physics, physics-AP, pre-calculus, psychology, Russian studies, SAT/ACT preparation, senior seminar, senior thesis, Spanish, Spanish language-AP, speech, speech and debate, statistics and probability, theology, trigonometry, U.S. history, world history, yearbook.

Graduation Requirements Arts and fine arts (art, music, dance, drama), career exploration, computer science, English, foreign language, mathematics, religion (includes Bible studies and theology), science, senior seminar, social science, social studies (includes history), 25 hours of community service per year of high school attendance.

Special Academic Programs Advanced Placement exam preparation in 13 subject areas; honors section; independent study; study abroad; academic accommodation for the gifted.

College Placement 92 students graduated in 2005; all went to college, including Oklahoma State University; The University of Texas at Austin; University of Denver; University of Kansas; University of Oklahoma; University of Tulsa. Median SAT verbal: 590, median SAT math: 589, median composite ACT: 25. 45% scored over 600 on SAT verbal, 55% scored over 600 on SAT math, 50% scored over 26 on composite ACT.

Student Life Upper grades have uniform requirement, student council. Discipline rests primarily with faculty. Attendance at religious services is required.

Summer Programs Sports programs offered; session focuses on sports camp and driver's education; held on campus; accepts boys and girls; open to students from other schools. 500 students usually enrolled. 2006 schedule: June to August. Application deadline: May.

Tuition and Aid Day student tuition: $8600. Tuition installment plan (monthly payment plans). Tuition reduction for siblings, need-based scholarship grants available. In 2005–06, 20% of upper-school students received aid. Total amount of financial aid awarded in 2005–06: $350,000.

Admissions Traditional secondary-level entrance grade is 9. For fall 2005, 100 students applied for upper-level admission, 60 were accepted, 40 enrolled. 3-R Achievement Test and ACT-Explore required. Deadline for receipt of application materials: none. Application fee required: $25. On-campus interview required.

Athletics Interscholastic: baseball (boys), basketball (b,g), cheering (g), cross-country running (b,g), football (b), golf (b,g), power lifting (b,g), soccer (b,g), softball (g), strength & conditioning (b,g), swimming and diving (b,g), tennis (b,g), track and field (b,g), volleyball (g), weight training (b,g), wrestling (b), yoga (b,g). 15 coaches, 1 trainer.

Computers Computers are regularly used in all classes. Computer network features include campus e-mail, on-campus library services, CD-ROMs, online commercial services, Internet access, DVD, wireless campus network, InfoTrac Search Bank, Internet access to local and state university library catalogues.

Contact Carol B. Otey, Coordinator of Admissions and Communications. 918-746-2604. Fax: 918-746-2635. E-mail: cotey@casciahall.org. Web site: www.casciahall.org.

CASTILLEJA SCHOOL

1310 Bryant Street
Palo Alto, California 94301
Head of School: Joan Z. Lonergan

General Information Girls' day college-preparatory, arts, and technology school. Grades 6–12. Founded: 1907. Setting: suburban. Nearest major city is San Francisco. 5-acre campus. 7 buildings on campus. Approved or accredited by California Association of Independent Schools and Western Association of Schools and Colleges. Member of National Association of Independent Schools and Secondary School Admission Test Board. Endowment: $30.5 million. Total enrollment: 415. Upper school average class size: 14. Upper school faculty-student ratio: 1:7.

Upper School Student Profile Grade 9: 60 students (60 girls); Grade 10: 60 students (60 girls); Grade 11: 55 students (55 girls); Grade 12: 60 students (60 girls).

Faculty School total: 69. In upper school: 11 men, 27 women; 38 have advanced degrees.

Subjects Offered African studies, algebra, American history, American literature, art, art history, biology, calculus, ceramics, chemistry, computer math, computer science, creative writing, drama, economics, English, English literature, environmental science, European history, expository writing, fine arts, French, geometry, government/civics, grammar, health, history, Japanese, journalism, Latin, marine biology, mathematics, music, philosophy, physical education, physics, psychology, Russian history, science, social studies, Spanish, speech, statistics, theater, trigonometry, world history, writing.

Graduation Requirements Arts and fine arts (art, music, dance, drama), English, foreign language, health and wellness, mathematics, physical education (includes health), science, social studies (includes history).

Special Academic Programs Advanced Placement exam preparation in 18 subject areas; honors section; independent study; academic accommodation for the gifted.

College Placement 48 students graduated in 2005; all went to college, including Harvard University; Stanford University; University of California, Berkeley; University of California, Santa Barbara; University of Southern California. Mean SAT verbal: 718, mean SAT math: 700.

Student Life Upper grades have uniform requirement, student council, honor system. Discipline rests equally with students and faculty.

Tuition and Aid Day student tuition: $24,495. Tuition installment plan (monthly payment plans, individually arranged payment plans). Need-based scholarship grants available. In 2005–06, 15% of upper-school students received aid. Total amount of financial aid awarded in 2005–06: $600,000.

Admissions Traditional secondary-level entrance grade is 9. For fall 2005, 104 students applied for upper-level admission, 19 were accepted, 12 enrolled. ISEE or SSAT required. Deadline for receipt of application materials: January 10. Application fee required: $75. On-campus interview required.

Athletics Interscholastic: basketball, cross-country running, golf, gymnastics, lacrosse, soccer, softball, swimming and diving, tennis, track and field, volleyball, water polo; intramural: triathlon. 4 PE instructors, 15 coaches.

Computers Computers are regularly used in English, foreign language, history, mathematics, science classes. Computer network features include campus e-mail, on-campus library services, CD-ROMs, online commercial services, Internet access, file transfer, wireless campus network.

Contact Jill V. W. Lee, Director of Admission. 650-328-3160. Fax: 650-326-8036. E-mail: jill_lee@castilleja.org. Web site: www.castilleja.org.

ANNOUNCEMENT FROM THE SCHOOL Approximately 41% of the students are students of color, and 14% of the students receive tuition assistance. Innovative internship programs and the career speaker series bring a broader world vision into the daily life of the students. Guest speakers have included former Secretary of State Madeline Albright, the late author and playwright Wendy Wasserstein, primatologist Jane Goodall, Poet Laureate Robert Hass, and economist Muhammad Yunus. Campus renovations totaling $15-million include state-of-the-art language, science, and technology labs; a media center; a new pool; theater; and library.

CATE SCHOOL

1960 Cate Mesa Road
Carpinteria, California 93013
Head of School: Benjamin D. Williams, IV

General Information Coeducational boarding and day college-preparatory school. Grades 9–12. Founded: 1910. Setting: small town. Nearest major city is Santa Barbara. Students are housed in single-sex dormitories. 150-acre campus. 18 buildings on campus. Approved or accredited by California Association of Independent Schools, The Association of Boarding Schools, and Western Association of Schools and Colleges. Member of National Association of Independent Schools and Secondary School Admission Test Board. Endowment: $60 million. Total enrollment: 265. Upper school average class size: 12. Upper school faculty-student ratio: 1:5.

Upper School Student Profile Grade 9: 60 students (29 boys, 31 girls); Grade 10: 66 students (32 boys, 34 girls); Grade 11: 71 students (34 boys, 37 girls); Grade 12: 68 students (33 boys, 35 girls). 83% of students are boarding students. 60% are state

residents. 23 states are represented in upper school student body. 14% are international students. International students from Hong Kong, Jamaica, Republic of Korea, Saudi Arabia, Taiwan, and Thailand; 6 other countries represented in student body.

Faculty School total: 53. In upper school: 31 men, 18 women; 30 have advanced degrees; all reside on campus.

Subjects Offered Advanced studio art-AP, algebra, American government-AP, American history, American literature, art, art history-AP, Asian history, biology, biology-AP, calculus, ceramics, chemistry, chemistry-AP, Chinese, choir, computer programming, computer science, computer science-AP, creative writing, digital art, drama, drama performance, economics-AP, English, English literature, environmental science-AP, ethics, European history, finance, fine arts, French, French-AP, freshman seminar, genetics, geometry, government-AP, human development, international relations, Japanese, marine biology, multimedia, music, photography, physics, physics-AP, physiology-anatomy, pre-calculus, psychology, Spanish, Spanish-AP, statistics, statistics-AP, studio art—AP, the Sixties, theater, trigonometry, U.S. history-AP, world history, writing.

Graduation Requirements Arts and fine arts (art, music, dance, drama), English, foreign language, history, human development, mathematics, science, social science.

Special Academic Programs Advanced Placement exam preparation in 19 subject areas; honors section; independent study; study abroad; academic accommodation for the gifted, the musically talented, and the artistically talented; special instructional classes for deaf students.

College Placement 70 students graduated in 2005; all went to college, including New York University; Northwestern University; Princeton University; University of California, Berkeley; University of Pennsylvania; University of Southern California. Median SAT verbal: 650, median SAT math: 650. 81% scored over 600 on SAT verbal, 81% scored over 600 on SAT math.

Student Life Upper grades have specified standards of dress, student council, honor system. Discipline rests primarily with faculty.

Tuition and Aid Day student tuition: $26,250; 7-day tuition and room/board: $34,750. Tuition installment plan (The Tuition Plan, Key Tuition Payment Plan, monthly payment plans). Need-based scholarship grants available. In 2005–06, 28% of upper-school students received aid. Total amount of financial aid awarded in 2005–06: $1,902,000.

Admissions Traditional secondary-level entrance grade is 9. For fall 2005, 500 students applied for upper-level admission, 125 were accepted, 76 enrolled. ISEE, PSAT and SAT for applicants to grade 11 and 12 or SSAT, ERB, PSAT, SAT, PLAN or ACT required. Deadline for receipt of application materials: January 15. Application fee required: $75. On-campus interview required.

Athletics Interscholastic: baseball (boys), basketball (b,g), cross-country running (b,g), football (b), lacrosse (b,g), soccer (b,g), softball (g), squash (b,g), tennis (b,g), track and field (b,g), volleyball (b,g), water polo (b,g); coed interscholastic: golf, swimming and diving; coed intramural: aerobics, aerobics/nautilus, back packing, bicycling, canoeing/kayaking, climbing, dance, fitness, kayaking, mountain biking, outdoor activities, physical fitness, physical training, ropes courses, surfing. 2 coaches, 1 trainer.

Computers Computers are regularly used in English, history, humanities, literary magazine, mathematics, media arts, media production, multimedia, music, newspaper, photography, science, yearbook classes. Computer network features include campus e-mail, on-campus library services, CD-ROMs, Internet access.

Contact Peter J. Mack, Director of Admission. 805-684-4127 Ext. 216. Fax: 805-684-2279. E-mail: peter_mack@cate.org. Web site: www.cate.org.

See full description on page 718.

CATHEDRAL HIGH SCHOOL

5225 East 56th Street
Indianapolis, Indiana 46226
Head of School: Mr. Stephen J. Helmich

petersons.com

General Information Coeducational day college-preparatory, arts, religious studies, and technology school, affiliated with Roman Catholic Church. Grades 9–12. Founded: 1918. Setting: urban. 39-acre campus. 5 buildings on campus. Approved or accredited by Independent Schools Association of the Central States, National Catholic Education Association, National Independent Private Schools Association, and Indiana Department of Education. Candidate for accreditation by North Central Association of Colleges and Schools. Language of instruction: English. Endowment: $2 million. Total enrollment: 1,218. Upper school average class size: 19. Upper school faculty-student ratio: 1:14.

Upper School Student Profile Grade 9: 331 students (172 boys, 159 girls); Grade 10: 330 students (187 boys, 143 girls); Grade 11: 308 students (171 boys, 137 girls); Grade 12: 249 students (126 boys, 123 girls). 80% of students are Roman Catholic.

Faculty School total: 91. In upper school: 33 men, 57 women; 68 have advanced degrees.

Subjects Offered Algebra, American history, American studies, anatomy, art history, Bible studies, biology, business, calculus, chemistry, computer science, debate, drama, driver education, earth science, economics, English, English literature, environmental science, fine arts, French, geology, geometry, German, history, journalism, Latin, mathematics, music, photography, physical education, physics, physiology, psychol-

ogy, religion, science, social science, social studies, sociology, Spanish, speech, theater, trigonometry, world history, world literature.

Graduation Requirements Arts and fine arts (art, music, dance, drama), biology, composition, economics, English, foreign language, government, mathematics, modern world history, physical education (includes health), religious studies, science, social studies (includes history), speech and debate, technology.

Special Academic Programs Advanced Placement exam preparation in 13 subject areas; honors section; independent study; academic accommodation for the gifted, the musically talented, and the artistically talented; remedial reading and/or remedial writing; remedial math; programs in English, mathematics for dyslexic students; special instructional classes for deaf students, blind students, students with learning disabilities, Attention Deficit Disorder, and dyslexia.

College Placement 249 students graduated in 2004; 246 went to college, including Ball State University; DePauw University; Indiana University Bloomington; Purdue University; University of Dayton; University of Notre Dame. Other: 1 went to work, 2 had other specific plans. Median SAT verbal: 530, median SAT math: 520. Mean composite ACT: 23. 24.3% scored over 600 on SAT verbal, 25.1% scored over 600 on SAT math.

Student Life Upper grades have uniform requirement, student council. Discipline rests primarily with faculty. Attendance at religious services is required.

Tuition and Aid Day student tuition: $8325. Tuition installment plan (Key Tuition Payment Plan, monthly payment plans). Merit scholarship grants, need-based scholarship grants available. In 2004–05, 33% of upper-school students received aid; total upper-school merit-scholarship money awarded: $219,000. Total amount of financial aid awarded in 2004–05: $1,400,000.

Admissions Traditional secondary-level entrance grade is 9. For fall 2005, 607 students applied for upper-level admission, 455 were accepted, 332 enrolled. High School Placement Test and High School Placement Test (closed version) from Scholastic Testing Service required. Deadline for receipt of application materials: January 31. No application fee required. On-campus interview required.

Athletics Interscholastic: baseball (boys), basketball (b,g), bowling (b,g), cheering (g), cross-country running (b,g), diving (b,g), football (b), golf (b,g), soccer (b,g), softball (g), swimming and diving (b,g), tennis (b,g), track and field (b,g), volleyball (g), wrestling (b); intramural: dance squad (g), hockey (b), ice hockey (b), lacrosse (b,g), rugby (b,g), volleyball (b), weight lifting (b,g); coed intramural: crew, fencing, martial arts, skiing (downhill). 3 PE instructors, 1 trainer.

Computers Computers are regularly used in business, foreign language, information technology, mathematics, newspaper, photography, science, yearbook classes. Computer network features include campus e-mail, on-campus library services, CD-ROMs, Internet access, office computer access.

Contact Mr. Duane Emery, Vice President for Enrollment Management. 317-968-7360. Fax: 317-543-5050. E-mail: demery@cathedral-irish.org. Web site: www.cathedral-irish.org.

ANNOUNCEMENT FROM THE SCHOOL Cathedral High School is a private, coeducational, college-preparatory, Catholic school. Founded in 1918, Cathedral was an all-male institution until 1976, when it moved to its current location in northeast Indianapolis. A diverse population of students comes from Marion County and its 7 surrounding counties. This year's students attended more than 110 different schools before entering Cathedral. Cathedral is situated on a 39-acre campus that includes a main academic building (Fr. Patrick J. Kelly Hall), the Robert V. Welch Student Activity Center, and the Joe O'Malia Performing Arts Center. Loretto Hall, recently restored and enhanced, is home to the Language Support Program, which meets the special needs of bright, college-bound students with language-based learning differences. The Cunningham Fine Arts Center houses a variety of fine arts disciplines. A student-centered Student Life Center features classrooms (4 of which are SMART classrooms with advanced technology), a state-of-the-art library/media center, and the student commons, which includes game tables, televisions, music, food, and areas for tutoring and spiritual reflection. Home of the Fighting Irish, Cathedral has a rich tradition of excellence in academics, athletics, and extracurricular activities. A rigorous curriculum that includes 19 Advanced Placement courses prepares students for postgraduate placement. A variety of extracurricular opportunities provides a well-rounded learning experience. Seventy-five percent of the freshman class participates in at least one such activity. Cathedral fields 19 varsity sports teams and 7 club sports teams. Community service is also an integral part of the learning experience at Cathedral. Three full-time college advisers and 3 academic advisers assist students in their holistic development. The college advisers work with students and parents throughout the college search and selection process. Ninety-nine percent of Cathedral's graduates attend college, and the past 4 graduating classes have earned over $38 million in college scholarship offers.

CATHEDRAL PREPARATORY SCHOOL

225 West Ninth Street
Erie, Pennsylvania 16501
Head of School: Rev. Scott William Jabo

General Information Boys' day college-preparatory, arts, religious studies, and technology school, affiliated with Roman Catholic Church. Grades 9–12. Founded: 1921. Setting: urban. 4-acre campus. 1 building on campus. Approved or accredited by Middle States Association of Colleges and Schools and Pennsylvania Department of Education. Endowment: $2.1 million. Total enrollment: 548. Upper school average class size: 22. Upper school faculty-student ratio: 1:14.

Upper School Student Profile Grade 9: 179 students (179 boys); Grade 10: 144 students (144 boys); Grade 11: 121 students (121 boys); Grade 12: 104 students (104 boys). 80% of students are Roman Catholic.

Faculty School total: 46. In upper school: 30 men, 16 women; 15 have advanced degrees.

Subjects Offered Aerospace science, algebra, American history, anatomy and physiology, aviation, Basic programming, biology, calculus, ceramics, chemistry, chemistry-AP, church history, computer literacy, computer programming, creative writing, critical thinking, death and loss, debate, desktop publishing, discrete math, drawing, driver education, English, expository writing, finance, first aid, flight instruction, French, geometry, German, health, history of the Catholic Church, history-AP, human anatomy, integrated science, interpersonal skills, introduction to theater, jazz band, keyboarding, Latin, leadership training, mechanical drawing, men's studies, Microsoft, moral theology, newspaper, physical education, physics, pre-calculus, probability and statistics, public speaking, reading, ROTC, sexuality, social justice, Spanish, studio art, theater, trigonometry, video communication, world geography, world history, writing, yearbook.

Special Academic Programs Advanced Placement exam preparation in 19 subject areas; honors section; accelerated programs; study at local college for college credit.

College Placement 145 students graduated in 2005; 144 went to college, including Edinboro University of Pennsylvania; Gannon University; John Carroll University; The Pennsylvania State University at Erie, The Behrend College; The Pennsylvania State University University Park Campus; University of Pittsburgh. Other: 1 went to work. 21% scored over 600 on SAT verbal, 25% scored over 600 on SAT math.

Student Life Upper grades have uniform requirement, student council, honor system. Discipline rests equally with students and faculty. Attendance at religious services is required.

Summer Programs Remediation, enrichment, advancement, sports programs offered; session focuses on academics; held both on and off campus; held at athletic fields; accepts boys and girls; open to students from other schools. 200 students usually enrolled. 2006 schedule: June 17 to July 26. Application deadline: June 17.

Tuition and Aid Day student tuition: $4550. Tuition installment plan (FACTS Tuition Payment Plan). Tuition reduction for siblings, merit scholarship grants, need-based scholarship grants available. In 2005–06, 65% of upper-school students received aid; total upper-school merit-scholarship money awarded: $2000. Total amount of financial aid awarded in 2005–06: $500,000.

Admissions Traditional secondary-level entrance grade is 9. For fall 2005, 275 students applied for upper-level admission, 189 were accepted, 179 enrolled. Placement test required. Deadline for receipt of application materials: March 1. Application fee required: $10. Interview recommended.

Athletics Interscholastic: baseball, basketball, cross-country running, football, golf, hockey, independent competitive sports, JROTC drill, outdoor recreation, power lifting, skiing (cross-country), skiing (downhill), soccer, swimming and diving, tennis, track and field, water polo, weight lifting, weight training, wrestling; intramural: bowling, table tennis, weight lifting. 2 PE instructors, 1 trainer.

Computers Computers are regularly used in all academic classes. Computer network features include campus e-mail, on-campus library services, CD-ROMs, Internet access, file transfer, office computer access, DVD, wireless campus network.

Contact Mr. Anthony Allegretto, Director of Admissions. 814-453-7737 Ext. 242. Fax: 814-455-5462. E-mail: aallegretto@cathedral-prep.com. Web site: www.cathedral-prep.com.

CATHOLIC CENTRAL HIGH SCHOOL

625 Seventh Avenue
Troy, New York 12182-2595
Head of School: Mr. Michael Piatek

General Information Coeducational day college-preparatory, arts, business, and religious studies school, affiliated with Roman Catholic Church. Grades 7–12. Founded: 1924. Setting: suburban. 4-acre campus. 2 buildings on campus. Approved or accredited by National Catholic Education Association and New York State Board of Regents. Endowment: $500,000. Total enrollment: 490. Upper school average class size: 16. Upper school faculty-student ratio: 1:13.

Upper School Student Profile Grade 9: 95 students (41 boys, 54 girls); Grade 10: 96 students (44 boys, 52 girls); Grade 11: 96 students (38 boys, 58 girls); Grade 12: 100 students (40 boys, 60 girls). 86% of students are Roman Catholic.

Faculty School total: 40. In upper school: 18 men, 22 women; 27 have advanced degrees.

Subjects Offered Accounting, algebra, anatomy and physiology, art, astronomy, band, biology, business communications, business law, calculus, Catholic belief and practice, chemistry, chorus, computer art, drawing and design, driver education, earth science, economics, English, English language-AP, global studies, government, health, history, honors English, honors U.S. history, Internet, keyboarding/computer, library skills, mathematics, physics, pre-calculus, printmaking, religion, social studies, Spanish, U.S. history, yearbook.

Graduation Requirements Art, English, mathematics, physical education (includes health), science, social studies (includes history), theology.

Special Academic Programs Advanced Placement exam preparation in 3 subject areas; remedial reading and/or remedial writing; remedial math; ESL (9 students enrolled).

College Placement Colleges students went to include Rensselaer Polytechnic Institute; Siena College; State University of New York at New Paltz; State University of New York College at Geneseo; University at Albany, State University of New York.

Student Life Upper grades have uniform requirement, student council. Discipline rests primarily with faculty. Attendance at religious services is required.

Tuition and Aid Day student tuition: $4950. Tuition installment plan (FACTS Tuition Payment Plan). Need-based scholarship grants, paying campus jobs available. In 2005–06, 26% of upper-school students received aid. Total amount of financial aid awarded in 2005–06: $45,500.

Admissions Traditional secondary-level entrance grade is 9. For fall 2005, 23 students applied for upper-level admission, 23 were accepted, 23 enrolled. Scholastic Testing Service High School Placement Test required. Deadline for receipt of application materials: none. Application fee required: $100. Interview recommended.

Athletics Interscholastic: baseball (boys), basketball (b,g), bowling (b,g), cross-country running (b,g), football (b), golf (b), indoor track & field (b,g), soccer (b,g), softball (g), tennis (b,g), track and field (b,g), volleyball (g); intramural: figure skating (g); coed interscholastic: cheering. 2 PE instructors, 8 coaches, 1 trainer.

Computers Computers are regularly used in accounting, art, business applications, graphic design classes. Computer network features include on-campus library services, CD-ROMs, Internet access.

Contact Mrs. Mary Virginia Bariteau, Development Director. 518-235-7100 Ext. 211. Fax: 518-237-1796. Web site: www.cchstroy.org.

THE CATHOLIC HIGH SCHOOL OF BALTIMORE

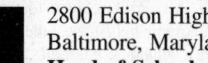

2800 Edison Highway
Baltimore, Maryland 21213
Head of School: Dr. Barbara D. Nazelrod

General Information Girls' day college-preparatory, arts, business, religious studies, and technology school, affiliated with Roman Catholic Church. Grades 9–12. Founded: 1939. Setting: urban. 6-acre campus. 1 building on campus. Approved or accredited by Association of Independent Maryland Schools, Middle States Association of Colleges and Schools, National Catholic Education Association, and Maryland Department of Education. Endowment: $1.9 million. Total enrollment: 278. Upper school average class size: 17. Upper school faculty-student ratio: 1:12.

Upper School Student Profile Grade 9: 80 students (80 girls); Grade 10: 69 students (69 girls); Grade 11: 80 students (80 girls); Grade 12: 49 students (49 girls). 78% of students are Roman Catholic.

Faculty School total: 28. In upper school: 9 men, 16 women; 17 have advanced degrees.

Subjects Offered Algebra, American history, American literature, anatomy, art, band, biology, calculus, chemistry, community service, computer programming, computer science, creative writing, dance, drama, driver education, earth science, economics, English, English literature, expository writing, fine arts, French, geometry, government/civics, grammar, health, history, instrumental music, journalism, keyboarding, literature, mathematics, music, personal development, photography, physical education, physics, physiology, psychology, reading, religion, science, social studies, Spanish, speech, study skills, technology, theater, theology, world history, world literature.

Graduation Requirements Arts and fine arts (art, music, dance, drama), computer science, English, foreign language, mathematics, physical education (includes health), religion (includes Bible studies and theology), science, social studies (includes history). Community service is required.

Special Academic Programs Advanced Placement exam preparation in 5 subject areas; honors section; independent study; study at local college for college credit; remedial reading and/or remedial writing; remedial math; programs in English, mathematics, general development for dyslexic students.

College Placement 84 students graduated in 2005; 78 went to college, including College of Notre Dame of Maryland; Towson University; Villa Julie College. Other: 1 went to work, 5 had other specific plans. Median SAT verbal: 500, median SAT math: 420, median composite ACT: 19. 7% scored over 600 on SAT verbal, 5% scored over 600 on SAT math.

Student Life Upper grades have uniform requirement, student council, honor system. Discipline rests primarily with faculty. Attendance at religious services is required.

Tuition and Aid Day student tuition: $8000. Tuition installment plan (Insured Tuition Payment Plan, FACTS Tuition Payment Plan, biannual payment plan, annual payment plan). Tuition reduction for siblings, merit scholarship grants, need-based scholarship

grants available. In 2005–06, 71% of upper-school students received aid; total upper-school merit-scholarship money awarded: $41,750. Total amount of financial aid awarded in 2005–06: $295,000.

Admissions Traditional secondary-level entrance grade is 9. For fall 2005, 146 students applied for upper-level admission, 128 were accepted, 80 enrolled. High School Placement Test required. Deadline for receipt of application materials: none. Application fee required: $30. On-campus interview required.

Athletics Interscholastic: basketball, cheering, cross-country running, dance team, field hockey; intramural: aerobics, aerobics/dance, cooperative games. 1 PE instructor, 12 coaches.

Computers Computers are regularly used in art, English, foreign language, history, mathematics, music, science, theology classes. Computer network features include on-campus library services, CD-ROMs, online commercial services, Internet access.

Contact Mrs. Barbara Czawlytko, Administrative Assistant. 410-732-6200 Ext. 213. Fax: 410-732-7639. E-mail: bczawlytko@tchs.loyola.edu. Web site: www.tchs.loyola.edu.

THE CATLIN GABEL SCHOOL

8825 Southwest Barnes Road
Portland, Oregon 97225
Head of School: Dr. Lark Palma

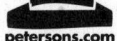

General Information Coeducational day college-preparatory, arts, technology, and sciences school. Grades PK–12. Founded: 1957. Setting: suburban. 54-acre campus. 13 buildings on campus. Approved or accredited by Accreditation Commission of the Texas Association of Baptist Schools, Northwest Association of Schools and Colleges, and Pacific Northwest Association of Independent Schools. Member of National Association of Independent Schools and Secondary School Admission Test Board. Endowment: $19.5 million. Total enrollment: 713. Upper school average class size: 14. Upper school faculty-student ratio: 1:7.

Upper School Student Profile Grade 9: 76 students (30 boys, 46 girls); Grade 10: 68 students (32 boys, 36 girls); Grade 11: 62 students (29 boys, 33 girls); Grade 12: 67 students (31 boys, 36 girls).

Faculty School total: 87. In upper school: 15 men, 19 women; 24 have advanced degrees.

Subjects Offered 3-dimensional art, 3-dimensional design, acting, advanced chemistry, advanced computer applications, advanced math, African-American history, algebra, American democracy, American foreign policy, American history, American literature, applied music, art, art history, arts, astronomy, athletics, baseball, Basic programming, basketball, biology, bookbinding, bookmaking, bowling, calculus, calligraphy, ceramics, chemistry, choir, college admission preparation, college counseling, comedy, communication skills, computer art, computer graphics, computer programming, computer resources, computer science, computer skills, computer studies, concert choir, creative writing, critical studies in film, critical thinking, debate, digital photography, drama, drama performance, dramatic arts, drawing and design, driver education, ecology, economics, English, English literature, ensembles, ethics and responsibility, European history, expository writing, fiber arts, fine arts, foreign language, French, geometry, golf, government/civics, graphic arts, graphic design, health, history, human sexuality, Islamic studies, Japanese, jazz band, mathematics, model United Nations, music, music theory, musical productions, ornithology, outdoor education, peer counseling, performing arts, photo shop, photography, physical education, physical fitness, physics, playwriting and directing, pre-calculus, robotics, science, set design, Shakespeare, social studies, Spanish, Spanish literature, speech and debate, stage design, stagecraft, statistics, statistics and probability, strings, studio art, study skills, technical theater, tennis, textiles, theater, theater arts, theater design and production, track and field, trigonometry, U.S. history, visual and performing arts, vocal ensemble, voice, voice ensemble, volleyball, weight fitness, weight training, wind instruments, woodworking, world affairs, world history, world literature, world wide web design, writing, writing workshop, yearbook.

Graduation Requirements Arts and fine arts (art, music, dance, drama), English, foreign language, mathematics, physical education (includes health), science, social studies (includes history). Community service is required.

Special Academic Programs Honors section; independent study; term-away projects; study at local college for college credit; domestic exchange program; study abroad; academic accommodation for the gifted, the musically talented, and the artistically talented.

College Placement 55 students graduated in 2005; all went to college, including Claremont McKenna College; Columbia College; Cornell University; Dartmouth College; Mount Holyoke College; University of Pennsylvania. Mean SAT verbal: 660, mean SAT math: 668. 76% scored over 600 on SAT verbal, 84% scored over 600 on SAT math.

Student Life Upper grades have student council, honor system. Discipline rests equally with students and faculty.

Tuition and Aid Day student tuition: $18,970. Tuition installment plan (Insured Tuition Payment Plan, monthly payment plans, individually arranged payment plans). Need-based scholarship grants available. In 2005–06, 22% of upper-school students received aid. Total amount of financial aid awarded in 2005–06: $59,000.

Admissions Traditional secondary-level entrance grade is 9. For fall 2005, 95 students applied for upper-level admission, 56 were accepted, 42 enrolled. SSAT

required. Deadline for receipt of application materials: February 15. Application fee required: $75. On-campus interview required.

Athletics Interscholastic: baseball (boys, girls), basketball (b,g), cross-country running (b,g), golf (b,g), racquetball (b,g), soccer (b,g), tennis (b,g), track and field (b,g), volleyball (g); coed interscholastic: racquetball; coed intramural: alpine skiing, back packing, bicycling, bowling, canoeing/kayaking, climbing, fishing, fitness, Frisbee, hiking/backpacking, jogging, kayaking, mountain biking, mountaineering, nordic skiing, ocean paddling, outdoor activities, outdoor adventure, outdoor education, outdoor recreation, outdoor skills, outdoors, paddling, physical fitness, physical training, rafting, rock climbing, ropes courses, running, skiing (cross-country), skiing (downhill), snowshoeing, strength & conditioning, telemark skiing, ultimate Frisbee, walking, wall climbing, weight lifting, weight training, wilderness, wilderness survival, yoga. 6 PE instructors, 20 coaches.

Computers Computers are regularly used in art, engineering, English, foreign language, graphic design, mathematics, science, theater, writing classes. Computer network features include campus e-mail, on-campus library services, CD-ROMs, online commercial services, Internet access, file transfer, wireless campus network, laptop requirement for all upper school students, videoconferencing, SmartBoards.

Contact Ms. Marsha Trump, Assistant Director of Admission. 503-297-1894 Ext. 349. Fax: 503-297-0139. E-mail: trumpm@catlin.edu. Web site: www.catlin.edu.

See full description on page 720.

CCI THE RENAISSANCE SCHOOL

Via Cavour 13
Lanciano 66034, Italy
Head of School: Marisa Di Carlo D'Alessandro

General Information Coeducational boarding and day college-preparatory, arts, and science school. Grades 10–12. Founded: 1995. Setting: small town. Nearest major city is Rome. Students are housed in single-sex residences. 5 buildings on campus. Approved or accredited by Ontario Ministry of Education and state department of education. Member of European Council of International Schools. Language of instruction: English. Total enrollment: 120. Upper school average class size: 16. Upper school faculty-student ratio: 1:7.

Upper School Student Profile 99% of students are boarding students. 99% are international students. International students from Belgium, Brazil, Canada, Germany, Japan, and United States; 4 other countries represented in student body.

Faculty School total: 12. In upper school: 7 men, 5 women; 8 have advanced degrees; 10 reside on campus.

Subjects Offered Algebra, anthropology, art, biology, calculus, Canadian history, career exploration, chemistry, civics, classical civilization, community service, computers, creative writing, data analysis, drama, economics, English, English literature, environmental science, expository writing, finite math, geometry, government/civics, history, information technology, Italian, literature, mathematics, physics, politics, psychology, science, social studies, sociology, trigonometry, world history, world issues, world literature, writing.

Graduation Requirements English, foreign language, mathematics, physical education (includes health), science, social studies (includes history). Community service is required.

Special Academic Programs Advanced Placement exam preparation in 9 subject areas; study abroad.

College Placement 40 students graduated in 2005; 39 went to college, including Acadia University; Dalhousie University; McGill University; Queen's University at Kingston; The University of Western Ontario; University of Toronto. Other: 1 had other specific plans.

Student Life Upper grades have uniform requirement, student council, honor system. Discipline rests equally with students and faculty.

Summer Programs Art/fine arts programs offered; session focuses on credit courses in social sciences, Italian, art; held on campus; accepts boys and girls; open to students from other schools. 120 students usually enrolled. 2006 schedule: July 2 to July 31. Application deadline: April 1.

Tuition and Aid 7-day tuition and room/board: €20,000. Tuition installment plan (monthly payment plans, individually arranged payment plans). Bursaries, merit scholarship grants, need-based scholarship grants, need-based loans available. In 2005–06, 5% of upper-school students received aid. Total amount of financial aid awarded in 2005–06: €30,000.

Admissions Deadline for receipt of application materials: none. Application fee required: $100. Interview recommended.

Athletics Intramural: dance (girls), modern dance (g), rugby (b); coed intramural: aerobics, aerobics/dance, alpine skiing, aquatics, ball hockey, basketball, bicycling, billiards, climbing, cross-country running, equestrian sports, fitness, fitness walking, flag football, hiking/backpacking, horseback riding, jogging, mountain biking, outdoor activities, outdoor recreation, physical fitness, running, sailing, skiing (cross-country), skiing (downhill), snowboarding, soccer, softball, swimming and diving, tennis, touch football, walking, weight training, yoga. 3 coaches.

Computers Computers are regularly used in yearbook classes. Computer resources include campus e-mail, on-campus library services, CD-ROMs, online commercial services, Internet access, DVD.

Contact Jocelyn Manchee, Admissions Officer. 905-508-7108. Fax: 905-508-5480. E-mail: cciren@rogers.com. Web site: www.ccilanciano.com.

See full description on page 722.

THE CEDARS ACADEMY

Bridgeville, Delaware
See Special Needs Schools section.

CENTENNIAL ACADEMY

3641 Prud'homme Avenue
Montreal, Quebec H4A 3H6, Canada
Head of School: Mrs. Angela Burgos

General Information Coeducational day college-preparatory school. Grades 7–11. Founded: 1969. Setting: urban. .5-acre campus. 1 building on campus. Approved or accredited by Canadian Educational Standards Institute and Quebec Department of Education. Language of instruction: English. Total enrollment: 340. Upper school average class size: 17. Upper school faculty-student ratio: 1:10.

Upper School Student Profile Grade 7: 61 students (54 boys, 7 girls); Grade 8: 67 students (49 boys, 18 girls); Grade 9: 67 students (51 boys, 16 girls); Grade 10: 79 students (62 boys, 17 girls); Grade 11: 66 students (47 boys, 19 girls).

Faculty School total: 35. In upper school: 12 men, 23 women; 18 have advanced degrees.

Subjects Offered Advanced chemistry, advanced math, art, art history, athletics, audio visual/media, band, basketball, biology, body human, bowling, Canadian geography, Canadian history, career and personal planning, career/college preparation, chemistry, competitive science projects, computer applications, computer multimedia, computer resources, computer science, creative writing, drama, economics, electives, English, fitness, French as a second language, general science, geography, golf, guidance, jazz band, lab science, language arts, leadership, library, mathematics, media studies, music, physical education, reading, science, sports, student government, swimming, tennis, volleyball, wrestling, yearbook.

Graduation Requirements Canadian history, English, French as a second language, general science, mathematics.

Special Academic Programs Independent study.

College Placement 63 students graduated in 2005; 62 went to college.

Student Life Upper grades have uniform requirement, student council, honor system. Discipline rests primarily with faculty.

Tuition and Aid Day student tuition: CAN$11,500–CAN$14,500. Tuition installment plan (monthly payment plans). Bursaries, merit scholarship grants available. In 2005–06, 9% of upper-school students received aid. Total amount of financial aid awarded in 2005–06: CAN$77,345.

Admissions Traditional secondary-level entrance grade is 7. For fall 2005, 164 students applied for upper-level admission, 141 were accepted, 93 enrolled. Canadian Standardized Test and Otis-Lennon School Ability Test required. Deadline for receipt of application materials: none. Application fee required: CAN$50. Interview required.

Athletics Interscholastic: basketball (boys, girls), soccer (b,g), touch football (g); coed interscholastic: cross-country running, curling, golf, running, swimming and diving, track and field, wrestling; coed intramural: badminton, ball hockey, basketball, bowling, broomball, Cosom hockey, cross-country running, fitness, floor hockey, handball, hockey, ice hockey, Newcombe ball, running, soccer, softball, track and field, volleyball. 2 PE instructors.

Computers Computers are regularly used in all academic classes. Computer network features include on-campus library services, CD-ROMs, Internet access, office computer access, DVD, wireless campus network.

Contact Mrs. Theresa Gilmour, Coordinator of Admissions. 514-486-5533 Ext. 238. Fax: 514-486-1401. E-mail: tgilmour@centennial.qc.ca. Web site: www.centennial.qc.ca.

CENTRAL CATHOLIC HIGH SCHOOL

200 South Carpenter Road
Modesto, California 95351
Head of School: Jim Pecchenino

General Information Coeducational day college-preparatory and religious studies school, affiliated with Roman Catholic Church. Grades 9–12. Founded: 1966. Setting: urban. Nearest major city is Sacramento. 21-acre campus. 12 buildings on campus. Approved or accredited by Western Association of Schools and Colleges and Western Catholic Education Association. Endowment: $946,048. Total enrollment: 415. Upper school average class size: 23. Upper school faculty-student ratio: 1:18.

Upper School Student Profile Grade 9: 96 students (53 boys, 43 girls); Grade 10: 118 students (66 boys, 52 girls); Grade 11: 112 students (62 boys, 50 girls); Grade 12: 89 students (42 boys, 47 girls). 81% of students are Roman Catholic.

Faculty School total: 28. In upper school: 10 men, 13 women; 11 have advanced degrees.

Subjects Offered Algebra, American history, American literature, art, bell choir, Bible studies, biology, broadcast journalism, calculus, chemistry, choir, computer programming, computer science, creative writing, dance, drama, earth science, economics, English, English literature, environmental science, ethics, European history, expository writing, film appreciation, fine arts, geometry, government/civics, grammar, graphics, health, history, mathematics, music, music appreciation, philosophy, physical education, physics, pre-algebra, pre-calculus, psychology, psychology-AP, religion, science, social science, social studies, Spanish, speech, theater, theology, trigonometry, world history, world literature, writing, yearbook.

Graduation Requirements Arts and fine arts (art, music, dance, drama), computer science, English, mathematics, physical education (includes health), religion (includes Bible studies and theology), science, social science, social studies (includes history), speech. Community service is required.

Special Academic Programs Advanced Placement exam preparation in 8 subject areas; honors section; study at local college for college credit; academic accommodation for the gifted; remedial reading and/or remedial writing; remedial math; programs in English, mathematics, general development for dyslexic students.

College Placement 102 students graduated in 2005; all went to college, including California Polytechnic State University, San Luis Obispo; Modesto Junior College; Saint Mary's College of California; University of California, Davis; University of California, Santa Barbara; University of San Diego. Median composite ACT: 22. Mean SAT verbal: 555, mean SAT math: 561.

Student Life Upper grades have specified standards of dress, student council, honor system. Discipline rests primarily with faculty. Attendance at religious services is required.

Summer Programs Remediation programs offered; session focuses on remediation; held on campus; accepts boys and girls; open to students from other schools. 50 students usually enrolled. 2006 schedule: June 5 to July 14. Application deadline: May 5.

Tuition and Aid Day student tuition: $6910–$7205. Guaranteed tuition plan. Tuition installment plan (monthly payment plans, Tuition Management Systems Plan, quarterly and semi-annual payment plans). Tuition reduction for siblings, merit scholarship grants, need-based scholarship grants, paying campus jobs available. In 2005–06, 24% of upper-school students received aid; total upper-school merit-scholarship money awarded: $13,500. Total amount of financial aid awarded in 2005–06: $100,270.

Admissions Traditional secondary-level entrance grade is 9. For fall 2005, 118 students applied for upper-level admission, 95 were accepted, 95 enrolled. Cognitive Abilities Test, Iowa Test of Educational Development or USC/UC Math Diagnostic Test required. Deadline for receipt of application materials: none. Application fee required: $40. On-campus interview required.

Athletics Interscholastic: baseball (boys), basketball (b,g), cheering (g), football (b), golf (b,g), soccer (b,g), softball (g), track and field (b,g), volleyball (g), wrestling (b); coed interscholastic: dance, swimming and diving, tennis; coed intramural: paint ball. 2 PE instructors, 72 coaches.

Computers Computers are regularly used in literacy, science, technology, yearbook classes. Computer network features include campus e-mail, on-campus library services, CD-ROMs, Internet access, file transfer, DVD.

Contact Patricia Crist, Admissions Coordinator/Registrar. 209-524-9611 Ext. 104. Fax: 209-524-4913. E-mail: crist@cchsca.org. Web site: www.cchsca.org.

CENTRAL CATHOLIC HIGH SCHOOL

4720 Fifth Avenue
Pittsburgh, Pennsylvania 15213
Head of School: Br. Richard F. Grzeskiewicz, FSC

General Information Boys' day college-preparatory, arts, business, and religious studies school, affiliated with Roman Catholic Church. Grades 9–12. Founded: 1927. Setting: urban. 2 buildings on campus. Approved or accredited by Middle States Association of Colleges and Schools and Pennsylvania Department of Education. Endowment: $8 million. Total enrollment: 850. Upper school average class size: 21. Upper school faculty-student ratio: 1:15.

Upper School Student Profile Grade 9: 224 students (224 boys); Grade 10: 210 students (210 boys); Grade 11: 200 students (200 boys); Grade 12: 206 students (206 boys). 85% of students are Roman Catholic.

Faculty School total: 65. In upper school: 52 men, 13 women; 44 have advanced degrees.

Subjects Offered Accounting, algebra, American foreign policy, American literature, art, biology, biology-AP, British literature, British literature (honors), business, business mathematics, calculus, calculus-AP, chemistry, chemistry-AP, computer science, computers, consumer education, debate, economics-AP, electives, English, English-AP, environmental science, European history-AP, foreign language, French, geometry, German, health, history, honors algebra, honors English, honors geometry, instrumental music, Italian, Latin, law, marketing, math analysis, mathematics, music, music theory, physical education, physics, physics-AP, pre-calculus, probability and statistics, programming, psychology, religion, science, social studies, sociology, Spanish, Spanish-AP, studio art, theater arts, trigonometry, U.S. history, U.S. history-AP, vocal music, world history, world literature, writing.

Special Academic Programs Advanced Placement exam preparation in 9 subject areas; honors section; study at local college for college credit; academic accommodation for the gifted.

College Placement 202 students graduated in 2005; 197 went to college, including Carnegie Mellon University; Duquesne University; The Pennsylvania State University University Park Campus; University of Dayton; University of Pittsburgh; Villanova University. Other: 2 went to work, 2 entered military service, 1 entered a postgraduate year.

Student Life Upper grades have specified standards of dress, student council. Discipline rests primarily with faculty. Attendance at religious services is required.

Summer Programs Remediation programs offered; session focuses on make-up; held on campus; accepts boys; not open to students from other schools. 60 students usually enrolled. 2006 schedule: June to July.

Tuition and Aid Day student tuition: $6400. Tuition installment plan (SMART Tuition Payment Plan). Need-based scholarship grants available. In 2005–06, 30% of upper-school students received aid. Total amount of financial aid awarded in 2005–06: $550,000.

Admissions Traditional secondary-level entrance grade is 9. For fall 2005, 270 students applied for upper-level admission, 224 enrolled. Scholastic Testing Service High School Placement Test or STS Examination required. Deadline for receipt of application materials: February 1. No application fee required. Interview recommended.

Athletics Interscholastic: baseball, basketball, bowling, crew, cross-country running, fencing, football, golf, hockey, ice hockey, in-line hockey, lacrosse, soccer, swimming and diving, tennis, track and field, volleyball, wrestling; intramural: basketball, flag football, football, Frisbee, touch football. 2 PE instructors, 27 coaches, 2 trainers.

Computers Computers are regularly used in business applications, college planning, data processing, library skills, mathematics, yearbook classes. Computer network features include campus e-mail, on-campus library services, CD-ROMs, online commercial services, Internet access, office computer access, DVD, wireless campus network.

Contact Mr. Brian Miller, Director of Admissions. 412-621-7505. Fax: 412-208-0555. E-mail: admissions@pittcentralcatholic.org. Web site: www.pittcentralcatholic.org.

CENTRAL CATHOLIC MID-HIGH SCHOOL

1200 Ruby Avenue
Grand Island, Nebraska 68803-3799
Head of School: Mr. John Golka

General Information Coeducational day college-preparatory school, affiliated with Roman Catholic Church. Grades 6–12. Founded: 1956. Setting: suburban. 1 building on campus. Approved or accredited by Nebraska Department of Education. Total enrollment: 304. Upper school average class size: 17.

Upper School Student Profile 98% of students are Roman Catholic.

Faculty School total: 38.

Special Academic Programs Honors section.

College Placement 47 students graduated in 2005; 46 went to college, including University of Nebraska at Kearney. Other: 1 entered military service.

Student Life Upper grades have uniform requirement, student council. Attendance at religious services is required.

Admissions No application fee required.

Athletics 3 PE instructors.

Computers Computer network features include Internet access, office computer access.

Contact Admissions. 308-384-2440. Fax: 308-389-3274. Web site: www.gicentralcatholic.org/.

CFS, THE SCHOOL AT CHURCH FARM

PO Box 2000
Paoli, Pennsylvania 19301
Head of School: Charles W. Shreiner III

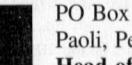

General Information Boys' boarding and day college-preparatory school, affiliated with Episcopal Church. Grades 7–12. Founded: 1918. Setting: suburban. Nearest major city is Philadelphia. Students are housed in single-sex dormitories. 350-acre campus. 19 buildings on campus. Approved or accredited by Middle States Association of Colleges and Schools, National Association of Episcopal Schools, The Association of Boarding Schools, and Pennsylvania Department of Education. Member of National Association of Independent Schools and Secondary School Admission Test Board. Endowment: $114 million. Total enrollment: 181. Upper school average class size: 10. Upper school faculty-student ratio: 1:7.

Upper School Student Profile Grade 9: 40 students (40 boys); Grade 10: 35 students (35 boys); Grade 11: 28 students (28 boys); Grade 12: 31 students (31 boys). 82% of students are boarding students. 48% are state residents. 14 states are represented in upper school student body. 12% are international students. International students from Republic of Korea. 15% are members of Episcopal Church.

Faculty School total: 35. In upper school: 28 men, 7 women; 16 have advanced degrees; 26 reside on campus.

Subjects Offered 20th century history, 3-dimensional design, African-American history, algebra, American history, American history-AP, American literature, art, art history, biology, British literature, calculus-AP, ceramics, chemistry, chemistry-AP, choir, choral music, computer science, creative writing, design, discrete math, drama, driver education, earth science, ecology, economics, English, environmental science, ethics, European history, expository writing, film and literature, fine arts, French, geology, geometry, government/civics, grammar, health, history, history of jazz, industrial arts, instrumental music, journalism, mathematics, music, mythology, photography, physical education, physics, poetry, pre-calculus, psychology, science, Shakespeare, social studies, sociology, Spanish, speech, statistics, technology, theater, trigonometry, Vietnam War, world history, world literature, world religions, writing.

Graduation Requirements Arts and fine arts (art, music, dance, drama), English, foreign language, mathematics, physical education (includes health), religion (includes Bible studies and theology), science, social studies (includes history), technology, Challenge of Required Experience (combination of community service and outdoor educational experience).

Special Academic Programs Advanced Placement exam preparation in 3 subject areas; honors section; independent study; academic accommodation for the musically talented and the artistically talented.

College Placement 35 students graduated in 2005; all went to college, including Johnson & Wales University; Shippensburg University of Pennsylvania; The Pennsylvania State University University Park Campus; University of Delaware; University of Illinois at Urbana–Champaign; University of Michigan. Median SAT verbal: 530, median SAT math: 530. 20% scored over 600 on SAT verbal, 31% scored over 600 on SAT math.

Student Life Upper grades have specified standards of dress, student council. Discipline rests primarily with faculty. Attendance at religious services is required.

Tuition and Aid Day student tuition: $4000–$12,500; 7-day tuition and room/board: $4000–$18,000. Guaranteed tuition plan. Tuition installment plan (monthly payment plans, individually arranged payment plans). Need-based scholarship grants available. In 2005–06, 100% of upper-school students received aid. Total amount of financial aid awarded in 2005–06: $5,464,000.

Admissions Traditional secondary-level entrance grade is 9. For fall 2005, 73 students applied for upper-level admission, 37 were accepted, 25 enrolled. SSAT required. Deadline for receipt of application materials: May 1. Application fee required: $25. Interview required.

Athletics Interscholastic: baseball, basketball, cross-country running, fencing, golf, indoor track, soccer, tennis, track and field, wrestling; intramural: fitness, floor hockey, indoor soccer, physical fitness, strength & conditioning, touch football, weight lifting. 10 coaches.

Computers Computers are regularly used in art, English, foreign language, history, mathematics, music, science classes. Computer network features include campus e-mail, on-campus library services, CD-ROMs, Internet access, DVD.

Contact Rich Lunardi, Admissions Director. 610-363-5346. Fax: 610-280-6746. E-mail: rlunardi@gocfs.net. Web site: www.gocfs.net.

ANNOUNCEMENT FROM THE SCHOOL At CFS, the vision of a connected learning community is now a reality, as all students are issued their own laptop, with network and online access from just about anywhere on campus. In addition, a modern Fine Arts Center is being planned, capable of supporting existing programs in the creative arts, music, and theater.

See full description on page 724.

CHADWICK SCHOOL

26800 South Academy Drive
Palos Verdes Peninsula, California 90274
Head of School: Frederick T. Hill

General Information Coeducational day college-preparatory, arts, and technology school. Grades K–12. Founded: 1935. Setting: suburban. Nearest major city is Los Angeles. 55-acre campus. 5 buildings on campus. Approved or accredited by Association for Experiential Education, California Association of Independent Schools, The College Board, Western Association of Schools and Colleges, and California Department of Education. Member of National Association of Independent Schools. Endowment: $20 million. Total enrollment: 818. Upper school average class size: 16. Upper school faculty-student ratio: 1:6.

Upper School Student Profile Grade 9: 89 students (41 boys, 48 girls); Grade 10: 93 students (49 boys, 44 girls); Grade 11: 79 students (38 boys, 41 girls); Grade 12: 78 students (35 boys, 43 girls).

Faculty School total: 63. In upper school: 27 men, 28 women; 38 have advanced degrees.

Subjects Offered Advanced Placement courses, African history, algebra, American history, American literature, art, art history-AP, art-AP, biology, calculus, calculus-AP, ceramics, chemistry, chemistry-AP, choral music, computer math, computer programming, computer science, creative writing, dance, drama, English, English literature, English literature-AP, European history, expository writing, fine arts, French,

French-AP, geometry, grammar, health, history, history of science, honors algebra, honors geometry, instrumental music, life science, marine biology, mathematics, music, music theory-AP, outdoor education, photography, physical education, physics, pre-calculus, probability, science, social studies, South African history, Spanish, Spanish-AP, speech, statistics, theater, trigonometry, U.S. history-AP, wilderness/outdoor program, world history, world literature, writing, yearbook.

Graduation Requirements Arts and fine arts (art, music, dance, drama), computer programming-AP, English, foreign language, history, mathematics, outdoor education, physical education (includes health), science.

Special Academic Programs Advanced Placement exam preparation in 16 subject areas; honors section; independent study; term-away projects; study abroad; academic accommodation for the gifted, the musically talented, and the artistically talented.

College Placement 76 students graduated in 2005; all went to college, including Georgetown University; Harvard University; Loyola Marymount University; Stanford University; University of California, Berkeley; University of Southern California. Mean SAT verbal: 676, mean SAT math: 686.

Student Life Upper grades have specified standards of dress, student council, honor system. Discipline rests equally with students and faculty.

Summer Programs Enrichment, advancement, sports, art/fine arts, rigorous outdoor training, computer instruction programs offered; session focuses on fine/performing arts, academics, athletics, enrichment; held on campus; accepts boys and girls; open to students from other schools. 600 students usually enrolled. 2006 schedule: June 26 to July 28. Application deadline: none.

Tuition and Aid Day student tuition: $20,375. Tuition installment plan (Academic Management Services Plan, Key Tuition Payment Plan, individually arranged payment plans). Need-based scholarship grants, paying campus jobs, Malone Scholarships (need-/merit-based) available. In 2005–06, 15% of upper-school students received aid. Total amount of financial aid awarded in 2005–06: $1,400,000.

Admissions Traditional secondary-level entrance grade is 9. ISEE required. Deadline for receipt of application materials: February 1. Application fee required: $125. On-campus interview required.

Athletics Interscholastic: baseball (boys), basketball (b,g), cheering (g), cross-country running (b,g), diving (b,g), football (b), golf (b,g), lacrosse (b), soccer (b,g), softball (g), swimming and diving (b,g), tennis (b,g), track and field (b,g), volleyball (b,g), water polo (b,g); intramural: aerobics/dance (g), dance (g), equestrian sports (g), horseback riding (g). 9 coaches, 1 trainer.

Computers Computers are regularly used in art, creative writing, drawing and design, English, foreign language, geography, graphic arts, health, history, humanities, mathematics, music, newspaper, photography, science, social studies, Web site design, yearbook classes. Computer network features include campus e-mail, on-campus library services, CD-ROMs, Internet access, wireless campus network.

Contact Michele Norlin, Assistant Director of Admission. 310-377-1543 Ext. 4029. Fax: 310-377-0380. E-mail: admissions@chadwickschool.org. Web site: www.chadwickschool.org.

ANNOUNCEMENT FROM THE SCHOOL Chadwick School, founded in 1935, is a nonprofit, nondenominational, coeducational day school (grades K–12) that serves a culturally and economically diverse student body. Chadwick's mission encourages personal excellence; the mastery of academic, artistic, and athletic skills; and the development of social and individual responsibility. Chadwick School is located on 55 acres atop the beautiful Palos Verdes Peninsula, with approximately one-third of the faculty living on campus. In the Village School (grades K–6), the class size ranges from 18 to 20 students. Language arts, social studies, mathematics, and science are taught by the classroom teachers in a program coordinated with specialists in art, music, science, technology, foreign languages, and physical education. With an average-class-size of 17 students, the Middle and Upper Schools have a rigorous core curriculum that includes English, history, science, mathematics, foreign language, visual arts, performing arts, technology, and physical education and athletics. In the Upper School, a full range of honors and AP classes is available. Two full-time counselors offer a comprehensive college-counseling program. Numerous extracurricular opportunities are available, including student government, literary magazine, newspaper, yearbook production, and special-interest clubs. Performing arts are housed in the new Laverty Center, with comprehensive drama, dance, and vocal and instrumental programs. Twenty-one athletic teams compete at the varsity level. Technology is integrated into the curriculum and the School has 8 computer labs. The Leavenworth Library, with a total of 25,000 volumes, has a section for grades K–6 and a separate division for grades 7–12. The community service program is part of the afternoon schedule; students have the opportunity to leave campus regularly and volunteer at local agencies and schools. Beginning in the 7th grade, and culminating in a 3-week senior trip just prior to graduation, the outdoor education program presents unique learning opportunities to all Upper and Middle School students. Transportation and need-based financial aid, including the Malone Scholarship, are available.

CHAMBERLAIN-HUNT ACADEMY
124 McComb Avenue
Port Gibson, Mississippi 39150
Head of School: Col. A. Shane Blanton

General Information Boys' boarding and coeducational day college-preparatory, arts, religious studies, bilingual studies, and technology school, affiliated with Presbyterian Church, Reformed Church. Boarding boys grades 7–12, day boys grades 7–12, day girls grades 7–12. Founded: 1879. Setting: small town. Nearest major city is Vicksburg. Students are housed in single-sex dormitories. 120-acre campus. 10 buildings on campus. Approved or accredited by Association of Christian Schools International, Mississippi Private School Association, Southern Association of Colleges and Schools, and Mississippi Department of Education. Endowment: $15 million. Total enrollment: 131. Upper school average class size: 10. Upper school faculty-student ratio: 1:4.

Upper School Student Profile Grade 9: 28 students (27 boys, 1 girl); Grade 10: 24 students (23 boys, 1 girl); Grade 11: 34 students (34 boys); Grade 12: 18 students (16 boys, 2 girls). 92% of students are boarding students. 37% are state residents. 20 states are represented in upper school student body. 1% are international students. International students from Brazil and Russian Federation. 37% of students are Presbyterian, Reformed.

Faculty School total: 32. In upper school: 20 men, 7 women; 18 have advanced degrees; all reside on campus.

Subjects Offered ACT preparation, advanced math, Advanced Placement courses, algebra, American Civil War, American government, American history, American literature-AP, ancient history, art, Bible, biology, British literature, business, calculus, chemistry, choir, Christian doctrine, Christian ethics, church history, classical Greek literature, computer keyboarding, computer programming, computer skills, CPR, earth science, economics, English, English literature, English literature-AP, ethics, French, geometry, government, gymnastics, Latin, logic, men's studies, military history, physics, pre-algebra, rhetoric, Spanish, theology, U.S. government, U.S. history, vocal ensemble, wilderness experience, world history, world wide web design.

Graduation Requirements Oral comprehensive exams, senior speech.

Special Academic Programs International Baccalaureate program; Advanced Placement exam preparation in 2 subject areas; honors section; accelerated programs; academic accommodation for the gifted, the musically talented, and the artistically talented; remedial reading and/or remedial writing; remedial math.

College Placement 8 students graduated in 2005; 5 went to college, including Belhaven College; Thomas Aquinas College; United States Military Academy. Other: 1 went to work, 2 entered military service. Median composite ACT: 21. 17% scored over 26 on composite ACT.

Student Life Upper grades have uniform requirement, student council, honor system. Discipline rests primarily with faculty. Attendance at religious services is required.

Summer Programs Remediation, enrichment, advancement, sports, rigorous outdoor training programs offered; session focuses on remediation and advancement courses along with weekend activities such as rafting, paintball, and ropes course; held both on and off campus; held at rafting trip locale; accepts boys; open to students from other schools. 60 students usually enrolled. 2006 schedule: June 12 to July 14. Application deadline: June 1.

Tuition and Aid Day student tuition: $4000; 7-day tuition and room/board: $12,550. Tuition installment plan (monthly payment plans, individually arranged payment plans). Tuition reduction for siblings, need-based scholarship grants available. In 2005–06, 37% of upper-school students received aid. Total amount of financial aid awarded in 2005–06: $289,700.

Admissions Traditional secondary-level entrance grade is 9. For fall 2005, 159 students applied for upper-level admission, 153 were accepted. Deadline for receipt of application materials: August 1. Application fee required: $50. On-campus interview required.

Athletics Interscholastic: baseball (boys), basketball (b), cross-country running (b), golf (b), soccer (b), tennis (b), track and field (b), winter soccer (b); intramural: back packing (b), baseball (b), basketball (b), canoeing/kayaking (b), climbing (b), cross-country running (b), fishing (b), fitness (b), flag football (b), hiking/backpacking (b), indoor soccer (b), jogging (b), life saving (b), marksmanship (b), outdoor activities (b), outdoor adventure (b), outdoor education (b), outdoor recreation (b), outdoor skills (b), outdoors (b), paint ball (b), physical fitness (b), physical training (b), riflery (b), rock climbing (b), ropes courses (b), running (b), skeet shooting (b), soccer (b), strength & conditioning (b), swimming and diving (b), tennis (b), volleyball (b), wall climbing (b), weight lifting (b), weight training (b), wilderness (b), wilderness survival (b), wildernessways (b). 4 PE instructors, 3 coaches, 3 trainers.

Computers Computers are regularly used in library skills, programming, typing, Web site design classes. Computer resources include on-campus library services, CD-ROMs, online commercial services, Internet access.

Contact Maj. Christopher Michael Blackwell, Director of Admissions. 601-437-8855. Fax: 601-437-3212. E-mail: admissions@chamberlain-hunt.com. Web site: www.chamberlain-hunt.com/.

CHAMINADE COLLEGE PREPARATORY

7500 Chaminade Avenue
West Hills, California 91304
Head of School: Br. Thomas Fahy

General Information Coeducational day college-preparatory, arts, religious studies, and technology school, affiliated with Roman Catholic Church. Grades 9–12. Founded: 1952. Setting: suburban. Nearest major city is Los Angeles. 21-acre campus. 13 buildings on campus. Approved or accredited by Western Association of Schools and Colleges and California Department of Education. Endowment: $3.4 million. Total enrollment: 1,103. Upper school average class size: 26. Upper school faculty-student ratio: 1:15.

Upper School Student Profile Grade 9: 309 students (148 boys, 161 girls); Grade 10: 285 students (150 boys, 135 girls); Grade 11: 259 students (111 boys, 148 girls); Grade 12: 250 students (124 boys, 126 girls). 54% of students are Roman Catholic.

Faculty School total: 77. In upper school: 39 men, 38 women; 49 have advanced degrees.

Subjects Offered Algebra, American history, American literature, anatomy, art, art history, athletic training, band, baseball, basketball, biology, biology-AP, British literature, British literature (honors), calculus, calculus-AP, chemistry, chemistry-AP, Christian and Hebrew scripture, community service, composition, computer programming, computer programming-AP, computer science, creative writing, dance, dance performance, debate, drama, drawing, driver education, economics, English, English language-AP, English literature and composition-AP, environmental science-AP, ethics, European history, expository writing, film studies, finance, fine arts, finite math, French, French language-AP, geography, geometry, government-AP, government/civics, guitar, jazz ensemble, journalism, Latin, literature and composition-AP, macroeconomics-AP, marching band, mathematics, microeconomics-AP, modern European history-AP, music, music appreciation, music performance, physical education, physical science, physics, physics-AP, physiology, physiology-anatomy, play/screen writing, psychology, psychology-AP, religion, science, science fiction, scripture, Shakespeare, social studies, Spanish, Spanish language-AP, speech, speech and debate, sports medicine, statistics and probability, statistics-AP, studio art, theater, trigonometry, U.S. government, U.S. history, U.S. history-AP, United States government-AP, visual and performing arts, visual arts, Western philosophy, Western religions, world history, world history-AP, world literature, writing.

Graduation Requirements Arts and fine arts (art, music, dance, drama), college writing, computer science, English, foreign language, mathematics, physical education (includes health), religious studies, science, social studies (includes history), speech. Community service is required.

Special Academic Programs Advanced Placement exam preparation in 18 subject areas; honors section.

College Placement 249 students graduated in 2005; 242 went to college, including California State University, Northridge; Loyola Marymount University; San Francisco State University; University of California, Davis; University of California, Irvine; University of California, Santa Cruz. Other: 2 entered a postgraduate year, 2 had other specific plans. Median composite ACT: 26. Mean SAT verbal: 586, mean SAT math: 587. 43% scored over 600 on SAT verbal, 53% scored over 600 on SAT math, 41% scored over 26 on composite ACT.

Student Life Upper grades have uniform requirement, student council, honor system. Discipline rests primarily with faculty. Attendance at religious services is required.

Summer Programs Remediation, enrichment, advancement, sports, computer instruction programs offered; session focuses on remediation; held on campus; accepts boys and girls; open to students from other schools. 500 students usually enrolled. 2006 schedule: June 20 to July 30. Application deadline: none.

Tuition and Aid Day student tuition: $8750. Tuition installment plan (monthly payment plans, 2-payment plan, discounted 1-payment plan). Merit scholarship grants, need-based scholarship grants available. In 2005–06, 9% of upper-school students received aid; total upper-school merit-scholarship money awarded: $7500. Total amount of financial aid awarded in 2005–06: $521,070.

Admissions Traditional secondary-level entrance grade is 9. For fall 2005, 318 students applied for upper-level admission, 245 were accepted, 162 enrolled. Non-standardized placement tests required. Deadline for receipt of application materials: January 21. Application fee required: $75. On-campus interview required.

Athletics Interscholastic: aquatics (boys, girls), baseball (b,g), basketball (b,g), cross-country running (b,g), fencing (b,g), football (b), golf (b,g), lacrosse (b,g), soccer (b,g), softball (g), strength & conditioning (b,g), swimming and diving (b,g), tennis (b,g), track and field (b,g), volleyball (b,g), weight training (b,g), wrestling (b); intramural: dance (b,g); coed interscholastic: cheering, physical fitness, strength & conditioning, weight training; coed intramural: back packing, cheering, climbing, dance, dance team, fitness, hiking/backpacking, rock climbing. 3 PE instructors, 76 coaches, 1 trainer.

Computers Computers are regularly used in creative writing, data processing, information technology, introduction to technology, literary magazine, news writing, newspaper, photojournalism, writing, writing, yearbook classes. Computer network features include on-campus library services, CD-ROMs, online commercial services, Internet access, file transfer, wireless campus network.

Contact Mrs. Linda Musgrave, Assistant to Admissions and Registrar. 818-347-8300 Ext. 355. Fax: 818-348-8374. E-mail: lmusgrave@chaminade.org. Web site: www.chaminade.org.

CHAMINADE COLLEGE PREPARATORY SCHOOL

425 South Lindbergh Boulevard
St. Louis, Missouri 63131-2799
Head of School: Rev. Dr. Ralph A. Siefert, SM

General Information Boys' boarding and day college-preparatory and religious studies school, affiliated with Roman Catholic Church. Grades 6–12. Founded: 1910. Setting: suburban. Students are housed in single-sex dormitories. 55-acre campus. 12 buildings on campus. Approved or accredited by Independent Schools Association of the Central States, Midwest Association of Boarding Schools, National Catholic Education Association, North Central Association of Colleges and Schools, The Association of Boarding Schools, and Missouri Department of Education. Member of National Association of Independent Schools and Secondary School Admission Test Board. Endowment: $3 million. Total enrollment: 905. Upper school average class size: 23. Upper school faculty-student ratio: 1:11.

Upper School Student Profile Grade 9: 145 students (145 boys); Grade 10: 145 students (145 boys); Grade 11: 140 students (140 boys); Grade 12: 145 students (145 boys). 5% of students are boarding students. 95% are state residents. 5 states are represented in upper school student body. 3% are international students. International students from Hong Kong, Mexico, Republic of Korea, Rwanda, Taiwan, and Thailand. 84% of students are Roman Catholic.

Faculty School total: 91. In upper school: 60 men, 15 women; 47 have advanced degrees; 5 reside on campus.

Subjects Offered Accounting, algebra, American history, American history-AP, American literature, architecture, art, art history, band, Bible studies, biology, biology-AP, botany, business, business skills, calculus, calculus-AP, chemistry, chemistry-AP, community service, computer programming, computer programming-AP, computer science, creative writing, drama, earth science, ecology, economics, economics-AP, engineering, English, English literature, English literature-AP, English/composition-AP, European history, European history-AP, expository writing, fine arts, French, French-AP, geography, geology, geometry, government/civics, grammar, health, history, industrial arts, Japanese, keyboarding, Latin, Latin-AP, mathematics, physical education, physics, physics-AP, psychology, psychology-AP, religion, science, social studies, sociology, Spanish, Spanish-AP, speech, statistics, statistics-AP, studio art-AP, theater, theology, trigonometry, weight training, world affairs, world history, world literature, writing.

Graduation Requirements Arts and fine arts (art, music, dance, drama), business skills (includes word processing), computer science, English, foreign language, mathematics, physical education (includes health), religion (includes Bible studies and theology), science, social studies (includes history). Community service is required.

Special Academic Programs Advanced Placement exam preparation in 18 subject areas; honors section; study at local college for college credit; academic accommodation for the gifted; ESL (21 students enrolled).

College Placement 148 students graduated in 2005; 147 went to college, including Saint Louis University; Truman State University; University of Dayton; University of Missouri–Columbia; University of Notre Dame; Vanderbilt University. Other: 1 entered military service. Mean SAT verbal: 570, mean SAT math: 587, mean composite ACT: 25. 40% scored over 600 on SAT verbal, 46% scored over 600 on SAT math, 45% scored over 26 on composite ACT.

Student Life Upper grades have specified standards of dress, student council. Discipline rests primarily with faculty. Attendance at religious services is required.

Tuition and Aid Day student tuition: $10,900; 5-day tuition and room/board: $21,650; 7-day tuition and room/board: $22,650.

Admissions Traditional secondary-level entrance grade is 9. For fall 2005, 49 students applied for upper-level admission, 43 were accepted, 33 enrolled. ISEE required. Deadline for receipt of application materials: none. Application fee required: $50. Interview required.

Athletics Interscholastic: baseball, basketball, bowling, cross-country running, diving, football, golf, ice hockey, in-line hockey, lacrosse. 5 PE instructors, 5 coaches, 1 trainer.

Computers Computers are regularly used in all academic classes. Computer network features include campus e-mail, on-campus library services, CD-ROMs, online commercial services, Internet access.

Contact Roger L. Hill, Director of Admissions. 314-993-4400 Ext. 150. Fax: 314-993-4403. E-mail: admissions@chaminade-stl.com. Web site: portal.chaminade-stl.com.

CHAMINADE-MADONNA COLLEGE PREPARATORY

500 Chaminade Drive
Hollywood, Florida 33021-5800
Head of School: Fr. John Thompson, SM

General Information Coeducational day college-preparatory, arts, business, and religious studies school, affiliated with Roman Catholic Church. Grades 9–12. Founded: 1960. Setting: small town. Nearest major city is Fort Lauderdale. 13-acre campus. 10 buildings on campus. Approved or accredited by Southern Association of Colleges and Schools and Florida Department of Education. Total enrollment: 872. Upper school average class size: 26. Upper school faculty-student ratio: 1:19.

Upper School Student Profile Grade 9: 215 students (115 boys, 100 girls); Grade 10: 210 students (110 boys, 100 girls); Grade 11: 230 students (120 boys, 110 girls); Grade 12: 217 students (117 boys, 100 girls). 70% of students are Roman Catholic.
Faculty School total: 67. In upper school: 30 men, 37 women.
Subjects Offered Accounting, advanced chemistry, advanced computer applications, advanced math, advanced studio art-AP, algebra, American history, American literature, anatomy, art, art history, band, biology, business skills, calculus, ceramics, chemistry, choir, community service, computer applications, creative writing, design, directing, drama, economics, English, fine arts, French, geography, geometry, government/civics, health, history, international relations, journalism, keyboarding, law, marine biology, marketing, mathematics, meteorology, music, philosophy, physical education, physics, physiology, play production, practical arts, pre-calculus, psychology, reading, religion, science, Shakespeare, social studies, sociology, Spanish, speech, stagecraft, theater, trigonometry, word processing, world history, writing, yearbook.
Graduation Requirements Arts and fine arts (art, music, dance, drama), business skills (includes word processing), English, foreign language, mathematics, physical education (includes health), practical arts, religion (includes Bible studies and theology), science, social studies (includes history), 80 community service hours.
Special Academic Programs Advanced Placement exam preparation in 10 subject areas; honors section; study at local college for college credit; academic accommodation for the gifted, the musically talented, and the artistically talented; remedial reading and/or remedial writing; remedial math; programs in general development for dyslexic students; special instructional classes for students with learning disabilities, Attention Deficit Disorder, and dyslexia.
College Placement 184 students graduated in 2005; all went to college, including Florida Atlantic University; Florida International University; Florida State University; University of Central Florida; University of Florida; University of Miami. Mean SAT verbal: 512, mean SAT math: 504, mean composite ACT: 20.
Student Life Upper grades have uniform requirement, student council, honor system. Discipline rests primarily with faculty. Attendance at religious services is required.
Tuition and Aid Day student tuition: $7100. Tuition installment plan (monthly payment plans). Need-based scholarship grants available. In 2005–06, 33% of upper-school students received aid. Total amount of financial aid awarded in 2005–06: $400,000.
Admissions Traditional secondary-level entrance grade is 9. For fall 2005, 350 students applied for upper-level admission, 280 were accepted, 260 enrolled. High School Placement Test (closed version) from Scholastic Testing Service required. Deadline for receipt of application materials: January 21. Application fee required: $45. Interview recommended.
Athletics Interscholastic: baseball (boys), basketball (b,g), cheering (g), cross-country running (b,g), flag football (g), football (b), golf (b,g), hockey (b,g), ice hockey (b,g); intramural: aerobics/dance (g), danceline (g), football (b,g); coed intramural: blading, bowling, fishing, in-line hockey. 2 PE instructors, 1 trainer.
Computers Computers are regularly used in English, mathematics, reading classes. Computer resources include campus e-mail, on-campus library services, CD-ROMs, online commercial services, Internet access.
Contact George E. Sayour, Director of Admissions. 954-989-5150 Ext. 112. Fax: 954-983-4663. E-mail: gsayour@cmlions.org. Web site: www.cmlions.org.

CHAMISA MESA HIGH SCHOOL

PO Box 759
Ranchos de Taos, New Mexico 87557
Head of School: Mr. Charles Bush

General Information Coeducational day college-preparatory and arts school. Grades 9–12. Founded: 1990. Setting: small town. Approved or accredited by North Central Association of Colleges and Schools and New Mexico Department of Education. Total enrollment: 51.
Upper School Student Profile Grade 9: 12 students (7 boys, 5 girls); Grade 10: 15 students (9 boys, 6 girls); Grade 11: 15 students (7 boys, 8 girls); Grade 12: 9 students (4 boys, 5 girls).
Faculty School total: 7.
Special Academic Programs Honors section.
College Placement 17 students graduated in 2005; 15 went to college, including University of New Mexico. Other: 2 went to work.
Tuition and Aid Day student tuition: $4600. Tuition installment plan (monthly payment plans).
Admissions Traditional secondary-level entrance grade is 9. No application fee required. Interview required.
Computers Computer network features include Internet access, DVD.
Contact Admissions. 505-751-0943. Fax: 505-751-3715. E-mail: clavalley@chamisamesa.net. Web site: www.chamisamesa.net.

CHAPEL HILL–CHAUNCY HALL SCHOOL

785 Beaver Street
Waltham, Massachusetts 02452
Head of School: Siri Akal Khalsa, EdD

General Information Coeducational boarding and day college-preparatory and arts school. Grades 9–PG. Founded: 1828. Setting: suburban. Nearest major city is Boston. Students are housed in single-sex dormitories. 37-acre campus. 11 buildings on campus. Approved or accredited by Association of Independent Schools in New England, New England Association of Schools and Colleges, The Association of Boarding Schools, and Massachusetts Department of Education. Member of National Association of Independent Schools and Secondary School Admission Test Board. Endowment: $1.6 million. Total enrollment: 146. Upper school average class size: 12. Upper school faculty-student ratio: 1:6.
Upper School Student Profile Grade 9: 23 students (11 boys, 12 girls); Grade 10: 45 students (28 boys, 17 girls); Grade 11: 41 students (26 boys, 15 girls); Grade 12: 37 students (16 boys, 21 girls). 47% of students are boarding students. 76% are state residents. 5 states are represented in upper school student body. 15% are international students. International students from Japan, Republic of Korea, Switzerland, and Taiwan.
Faculty School total: 31. In upper school: 15 men, 16 women; 15 have advanced degrees; 21 reside on campus.
Subjects Offered Acting, adolescent issues, advanced studio art-AP, algebra, American history, American literature, art, biology, calculus, ceramics, chemistry, comparative religion, creative writing, drama, economics, English, English literature, English-AP, ESL, European history, fine arts, geography, geometry, government/civics, grammar, health, history, journalism, mathematics, music, photography, physical education, physics, psychology, science, social studies, Spanish, theater, world history, world literature, writing.
Graduation Requirements Arts and fine arts (art, music, dance, drama), English, foreign language, mathematics, physical education (includes health), science, social studies (includes history), senior presentations. Community service is required.
Special Academic Programs Advanced Placement exam preparation in 2 subject areas; independent study; programs in general development for dyslexic students; special instructional classes for students with mild to moderate learning disabilities; ESL (12 students enrolled).
College Placement 41 students graduated in 2005; 40 went to college, including Boston University; Clark University; Hofstra University; Indiana University of Pennsylvania; Suffolk University; University of Hartford. Other: 1 had other specific plans. Mean SAT verbal: 467, mean SAT math: 518. 6% scored over 600 on SAT verbal, 28% scored over 600 on SAT math.
Student Life Upper grades have student council. Discipline rests equally with students and faculty.
Tuition and Aid Day student tuition: $26,500; 7-day tuition and room/board: $35,800. Tuition installment plan (Key Tuition Payment Plan, monthly payment plans, individually arranged payment plans). Need-based scholarship grants available. In 2005–06, 18% of upper-school students received aid. Total amount of financial aid awarded in 2005–06: $726,000.
Admissions Traditional secondary-level entrance grade is 9. For fall 2005, 190 students applied for upper-level admission, 121 were accepted, 56 enrolled. SSAT or WISC III, TOEFL or SLEP or WISC or WAIS required. Deadline for receipt of application materials: February 1. Application fee required: $50. Interview required.
Athletics Interscholastic: baseball (boys), basketball (b,g), lacrosse (b,g), soccer (b,g), softball (g), volleyball (g), wrestling (b); coed interscholastic: cross-country running, golf, ultimate Frisbee; coed intramural: aerobics/dance, cooperative games, fitness, physical fitness, racquetball, rock climbing, ropes courses, swimming and diving, yoga. 1 PE instructor, 1 trainer.
Computers Computers are regularly used in art, English, history, mathematics, multimedia, newspaper, yearbook classes. Computer network features include campus e-mail, on-campus library services, CD-ROMs, Internet access, office computer access.
Contact Ms. Lisa Zannella, Director of Admissions. 781-894-2644 Ext. 105. Fax: 781-894-5205. E-mail: lisazannella@chch.org. Web site: www.chch.org.

CHAPEL SCHOOL

Escola Maria Imaculada
Rua Vigário João de Pontes, 537
Sao Paulo 04748-000, Brazil
Head of School: John Ciallelo

General Information Coeducational day college-preparatory, religious studies, and bilingual studies school, affiliated with Roman Catholic Church. Grades PK–12. Founded: 1947. Setting: suburban. Nearest major city is São Paulo. 3-hectare campus. 4 buildings on campus. Approved or accredited by Association of American Schools in South America, International Baccalaureate Organization, and Southern Association of Colleges and Schools. Languages of instruction: English and Portuguese. Total enrollment: 700. Upper school average class size: 26. Upper school faculty-student ratio: 1:9.
Upper School Student Profile 90% of students are Roman Catholic.

Faculty School total: 40. In upper school: 15 men, 25 women; 25 have advanced degrees.

Graduation Requirements English, foreign language, mathematics, physical education (includes health), religion (includes Bible studies and theology), science, social studies (includes history).

Special Academic Programs International Baccalaureate program; independent study; ESL (25 students enrolled).

College Placement Colleges students went to include Babson College; Boston College; Boston University; Georgetown University; Savannah College of Art and Design; University of Notre Dame.

Student Life Upper grades have specified standards of dress, student council, honor system. Discipline rests primarily with faculty. Attendance at religious services is required.

Tuition and Aid Day student tuition: 39,600 Brazilian reals.

Admissions Admissions testing required. Deadline for receipt of application materials: none. Application fee required: 200 Brazilian reals. Interview required.

Athletics Interscholastic: basketball (boys, girls), cheering (g), climbing (b,g), soccer (b,g), softball (b,g), volleyball (g). 3 PE instructors, 5 coaches.

Computers Computers are regularly used in all classes. Computer network features include campus e-mail, on-campus library services, CD-ROMs, Internet access, DVD.

Contact Ione Broglia, Admissions Director. 55-11-5687-7455. Fax: 55-11-5521-7763. E-mail: admissions@chapelschool.com. Web site: www.chapelschool.com.

THE CHAPIN SCHOOL

100 East End Avenue
New York, New York 10028
Head of School: Dr. Patricia T. Hayot

General Information Girls' day college-preparatory school. Grades K–12. Founded: 1901. Setting: urban. 1 building on campus. Approved or accredited by New York State Association of Independent Schools and New York Department of Education. Member of National Association of Independent Schools. Endowment: $51 million. Total enrollment: 661. Upper school average class size: 16. Upper school faculty-student ratio: 1:4.

Upper School Student Profile Grade 8: 58 students (58 girls); Grade 9: 43 students (43 girls); Grade 10: 52 students (52 girls); Grade 11: 58 students (58 girls); Grade 12: 35 students (35 girls).

Faculty School total: 118. In upper school: 14 men, 43 women; 39 have advanced degrees.

Subjects Offered Advanced Placement courses, African drumming, African history, African-American history, algebra, American history, American literature, art, art history, Asian history, astronomy, biology, calculus, ceramics, chemistry, Chinese, comparative religion, computer math, computer science, creative writing, dance, design, digital imaging, DNA, drama, drawing, electronics, English, English literature, European history, expository writing, fine arts, French, geography, geometry, government/civics, grammar, Greek, health, history, Latin, Latin American literature, life skills, mathematics, multimedia, music, painting, philosophy, photography, physical education, physics, poetry, psychology, public speaking, religion, Russian literature, science, sculpture, social studies, Spanish, statistics, theater, trigonometry, video, writing.

Graduation Requirements Arts and fine arts (art, music, dance, drama), computer science, English, English literature and composition-AP, foreign language, mathematics, physical education (includes health), science, social studies (includes history).

Special Academic Programs Advanced Placement exam preparation in 17 subject areas; honors section; term-away projects; study abroad.

College Placement 39 students graduated in 2005; all went to college, including Brown University; Bucknell University; Duke University; Stanford University; University of Pennsylvania; Wesleyan University.

Student Life Upper grades have uniform requirement, student council, honor system. Discipline rests primarily with faculty.

Tuition and Aid Day student tuition: $25,600. Need-based scholarship grants, Key Education Resources available. In 2005–06, 23% of upper-school students received aid. Total amount of financial aid awarded in 2005–06: $1,122,020.

Admissions Traditional secondary-level entrance grade is 9. For fall 2005, 58 students applied for upper-level admission, 15 were accepted, 4 enrolled. ISEE and math and English placement tests required. Deadline for receipt of application materials: none. Application fee required: $50. On-campus interview required.

Athletics Interscholastic: badminton, basketball, cross-country running, field hockey, gymnastics, independent competitive sports, lacrosse, soccer, softball, squash, swimming and diving, tennis, track and field, volleyball; intramural: aerobics, aerobics/dance, aerobics/nautilus, aquatics, badminton, ball hockey, ballet, basketball, cooperative games, cross-country running, curling, dance, diving, fencing, field hockey, fitness, fitness walking, flag football, floor hockey, football, Frisbee, gymnastics, handball, indoor hockey, indoor soccer, indoor track & field, jogging, kickball, lacrosse, life saving, martial arts, modern dance, nautilus, outdoor activities, outdoor adventure, outdoor education, outdoor recreation, outdoor skills, physical fitness, physical training, project adventure, ropes courses, self defense, skiing (downhill), snowboarding, soccer, softball, squash, strength & conditioning, swimming and diving, tai chi, team handball, tennis, touch football, track and field, ultimate Frisbee, volleyball, walking, water polo, weight training, whiffle ball, yoga; coed interscholastic: fencing. 14 PE instructors, 17 coaches, 3 trainers.

Computers Computers are regularly used in art, dance, English, foreign language, history, mathematics, music, science classes. Computer network features include campus e-mail, on-campus library services, CD-ROMs, Internet access, DVD, wireless campus network, ProQuest, SIRS Knowledge Source.

Contact Tina I. Herman, Director of Admissions. 212-744-2335. Fax: 212-535-8138. E-mail: admissions@chapin.edu. Web site: www.chapin.edu.

CHARLES E. SMITH JEWISH DAY SCHOOL

11710 Hunters Lane
Rockville, Maryland 20852
Head of School: Mr. Jonathan Cannon

General Information Coeducational day college-preparatory, religious studies, and bilingual studies school, affiliated with Jewish faith. Grades K–12. Founded: 1965. Setting: suburban. Nearest major city is Washington, DC. 9-acre campus. 1 building on campus. Approved or accredited by Middle States Association of Colleges and Schools and Maryland Department of Education. Languages of instruction: English and Hebrew. Total enrollment: 1,500. Upper school average class size: 15.

Upper School Student Profile Grade 7: 132 students (67 boys, 65 girls); Grade 8: 111 students (50 boys, 61 girls); Grade 9: 128 students (64 boys, 64 girls); Grade 10: 116 students (56 boys, 60 girls); Grade 11: 112 students (49 boys, 63 girls); Grade 12: 116 students (58 boys, 58 girls). 100% of students are Jewish.

Faculty School total: 175. In upper school: 23 men, 44 women.

Subjects Offered Algebra, American literature, anatomy, art, art history, Bible studies, biology, business, calculus, chemistry, computer science, creative writing, English, English literature, European history, expository writing, French, geometry, Hebrew, history, human development, Jewish history, journalism, keyboarding, mathematics, microbiology, music, photography, physical education, physics, physiology, psychology, Rabbinic literature, science, social studies, Spanish, sports medicine, technology, trigonometry, yearbook.

Graduation Requirements English, foreign language, mathematics, physical education (includes health), Rabbinic literature, religion (includes Bible studies and theology), science, social studies (includes history).

Special Academic Programs Advanced Placement exam preparation in 2 subject areas; honors section; academic accommodation for the gifted; remedial reading and/or remedial writing; remedial math; programs in English for dyslexic students.

College Placement 108 went to college, including Harvard University; Princeton University; University of Maryland; University of Michigan; University of Pennsylvania; Washington University in St. Louis. Median SAT verbal: 620, median SAT math: 630.

Student Life Upper grades have specified standards of dress, student council. Discipline rests equally with students and faculty. Attendance at religious services is required.

Tuition and Aid Day student tuition: $18,630. Tuition installment plan (monthly payment plans). Need-based scholarship grants available. In 2005–06, 25% of upper-school students received aid.

Admissions Traditional secondary-level entrance grade is 7. For fall 2005, 69 students applied for upper-level admission, 32 were accepted, 30 enrolled. Deadline for receipt of application materials: none. Application fee required: $75. Interview recommended.

Athletics Interscholastic: baseball (boys), basketball (b,g), soccer (b,g), softball (g), tennis (b,g), volleyball (b,g); coed interscholastic: cross-country running, track and field. 4 PE instructors, 11 coaches, 1 trainer.

Computers Computers are regularly used in English, mathematics, science, technology classes. Computer resources include on-campus library services, CD-ROMs, online commercial services, Internet access.

Contact Robin Shapiro, Director of Admissions. 301-881-1400 Ext. 4908.

CHARLES FINNEY SCHOOL

2070 Five Mile Line Road
Penfield, New York 14526
Head of School: Rev. Michael J. Belmont

General Information Coeducational day college-preparatory, arts, business, religious studies, bilingual studies, and technology school, affiliated with Christian faith. Grades K–12. Founded: 1991. Setting: suburban. Nearest major city is Rochester. 8-acre campus. 1 building on campus. Approved or accredited by New York Department of Education. Total enrollment: 304. Upper school average class size: 25. Upper school faculty-student ratio: 1:10.

Upper School Student Profile 100% of students are Christian faith.

Faculty School total: 34. In upper school: 11 men, 12 women; 15 have advanced degrees.

Special Academic Programs Advanced Placement exam preparation; honors section; independent study; academic accommodation for the gifted, the musically talented, and the artistically talented.

College Placement 52 students graduated in 2005; 45 went to college, including Calvin College; Gordon College; Houghton College; Nazareth College of Rochester; Rochester Institute of Technology; University of Rochester. Other: 7 went to work. Median SAT verbal: 580, median SAT math: 570. 71% scored over 600 on SAT verbal, 29% scored over 600 on SAT math.

Student Life Upper grades have specified standards of dress, student council, honor system. Discipline rests primarily with faculty. Attendance at religious services is required.

Tuition and Aid Tuition installment plan (Insured Tuition Payment Plan, monthly payment plans). Tuition reduction for siblings, need-based scholarship grants available.

Admissions Traditional secondary-level entrance grade is 9. Deadline for receipt of application materials: none. Application fee required: $200.

Athletics Interscholastic: baseball (boys), basketball (b,g), cheering (g), football (b), golf (b), soccer (b,g), softball (g), volleyball (g); coed interscholastic: cross-country running. 1 PE instructor, 6 coaches.

Computers Computer resources include on-campus library services, Internet access.

Contact Rev. Dorothy Ross, Director of Admissions and Recruitment. 585-387-3770. Fax: 585-387-3771. E-mail: info@finneyschool.org. Web site: www.finneyschool.org.

CHARLES WRIGHT ACADEMY

7723 Chambers Creek Road
Tacoma, Washington 98467-2099
Head of School: Mr. Robert Camner

petersons.com

General Information Coeducational day college-preparatory and arts school. Grades PK–12. Founded: 1957. Setting: suburban. Nearest major city is Seattle. 90-acre campus. 5 buildings on campus. Approved or accredited by Pacific Northwest Association of Independent Schools and Washington Department of Education. Member of National Association of Independent Schools. Endowment: $10 million. Total enrollment: 688. Upper school average class size: 17. Upper school faculty-student ratio: 1:8.

Upper School Student Profile Grade 9: 82 students (38 boys, 44 girls); Grade 10: 69 students (39 boys, 30 girls); Grade 11: 64 students (33 boys, 31 girls); Grade 12: 63 students (38 boys, 25 girls).

Faculty School total: 87. In upper school: 24 men, 18 women; 30 have advanced degrees.

Subjects Offered Algebra, American history, American literature, art history, biology, calculus, ceramics, chemistry, choir, community service, computer programming, computer science, creative writing, criminology, drama, earth science, economics, English, English literature, environmental science, European history, expository writing, French, geometry, government/civics, history, Japanese, journalism, mathematics, music, outdoor education, performing arts, photography, physical education, physics, Russian history, science, social studies, Spanish, theater, trigonometry, visual arts, world history, world religions.

Graduation Requirements Arts and fine arts (art, music, dance, drama), English, foreign language, mathematics, outdoor education, performing arts, physical education (includes health), science, social studies (includes history), participation in Winterim courses. Community service is required.

Special Academic Programs Advanced Placement exam preparation in 12 subject areas; honors section.

College Placement 69 students graduated in 2005; all went to college.

Student Life Upper grades have specified standards of dress, student council, honor system. Discipline rests equally with students and faculty.

Tuition and Aid Day student tuition: $16,700. Tuition installment plan (Key Tuition Payment Plan, monthly payment plans). Need-based scholarship grants available. In 2005–06, 20% of upper-school students received aid. Total amount of financial aid awarded in 2005–06: $336,815.

Admissions Traditional secondary-level entrance grade is 9. For fall 2005, 71 students applied for upper-level admission, 48 were accepted, 33 enrolled. ISEE, SLEP for foreign students, SSAT or Woodcock-Johnson required. Deadline for receipt of application materials: none. Application fee required: $75. Interview required.

Athletics Interscholastic: baseball (boys), basketball (b,g), cross-country running (b,g), football (b), golf (b,g), soccer (b,g), softball (g), tennis (b,g), track and field (b,g), volleyball (g); intramural: crew (b,g), hiking/backpacking (b,g), outdoor adventure (b,g), outdoor education (b,g), physical fitness (b,g), physical training (b,g), strength & conditioning (b,g), weight training (b,g); coed intramural: climbing, kayaking, outdoor adventure. 6 PE instructors, 7 coaches, 1 trainer.

Computers Computers are regularly used in programming classes. Computer network features include campus e-mail, on-campus library services, CD-ROMs, online commercial services, Internet access, file transfer, DVD.

Contact Mrs. Sue Johnson, Admissions Secretary. 253-620-8373. Fax: 253-620-8357. E-mail: admissions@mail.charleswright.org. Web site: www.charleswright.org.

ANNOUNCEMENT FROM THE SCHOOL Charles Wright Academy is the only PK–12, coed, independent, college-preparatory school in the South Sound. The Academy offers a wide variety of AP classes, visual and performing arts, sports, and community service opportunities. Class sizes are kept small, allowing talented faculty members to connect with every student, in every class, every day.

CHARLOTTE CHRISTIAN SCHOOL

7301 Sardis Road
Charlotte, North Carolina 28270
Head of School: Dr. Leo Orsino

General Information Coeducational day college-preparatory school, affiliated with Christian faith. Grades JK–12. Founded: 1950. Setting: suburban. 55-acre campus. 4 buildings on campus. Approved or accredited by Association of Christian Schools International, North Carolina Association of Independent Schools, Southern Association of Colleges and Schools, Southern Association of Independent Schools, and North Carolina Department of Education. Total enrollment: 1,017. Upper school average class size: 15. Upper school faculty-student ratio: 1:11.

Upper School Student Profile Grade 9: 89 students (48 boys, 41 girls); Grade 10: 94 students (55 boys, 39 girls); Grade 11: 106 students (53 boys, 53 girls); Grade 12: 90 students (53 boys, 37 girls). 100% of students are Christian faith.

Faculty School total: 104. In upper school: 18 men, 18 women; 14 have advanced degrees.

Subjects Offered Accounting, acting, advanced studio art-AP, algebra, American culture, American government, American government-AP, American literature, anatomy and physiology, art, art history-AP, athletic training, band, biology, biology-AP, British literature, business, business law, calculus-AP, chamber groups, chemistry, choreography, Christian education, Christian ethics, church history, civil war history, computer applications, computer science-AP, computer-aided design, economics, English literature, environmental science-AP, European history-AP, French, French-AP, geometry, German, graphic arts, graphic design, health and wellness, language-AP, Latin, leadership, learning strategies, Life of Christ, literature and composition-AP, marketing, math applications, music composition, music theory-AP, newspaper, painting, photography, physical education, physical science, physics, physics-AP, pre-calculus, psychology, public speaking, research skills, SAT preparation, sign language, Spanish, Spanish-AP, speech and debate, sports medicine, stage design, statistics-AP, studio art—AP, theater, theater design and production, trigonometry, U.S. history, U.S. history-AP, video film production, voice, voice and diction, Web site design, weight training, wind ensemble, world civilizations, world literature, World War II, yearbook.

Graduation Requirements Bible studies, English, foreign language, mathematics, physical education (includes health), SAT preparation, science, social studies (includes history), speech, service hours, visual or performing arts.

Special Academic Programs Advanced Placement exam preparation in 18 subject areas; honors section.

College Placement 87 students graduated in 2005; all went to college, including Auburn University; Meredith College; North Carolina State University; The University of North Carolina at Chapel Hill; The University of North Carolina Wilmington; Wake Forest University. Mean SAT verbal: 574, mean SAT math: 582, mean composite ACT: 23.

Student Life Upper grades have specified standards of dress, student council, honor system. Discipline rests primarily with faculty. Attendance at religious services is required.

Summer Programs Enrichment, advancement, sports, art/fine arts, rigorous outdoor training, computer instruction programs offered; session focuses on enrichment; held on campus; accepts boys and girls; open to students from other schools. 300 students usually enrolled. 2006 schedule: June to August. Application deadline: none.

Tuition and Aid Day student tuition: $9000–$12,850. Tuition installment plan (The Tuition Plan, Insured Tuition Payment Plan, monthly payment plans, individually arranged payment plans). Tuition reduction for siblings, need-based scholarship grants available. In 2005–06, 20% of upper-school students received aid. Total amount of financial aid awarded in 2005–06: $389,150.

Admissions Traditional secondary-level entrance grade is 9. For fall 2005, 74 students applied for upper-level admission, 60 were accepted, 37 enrolled. Admissions testing or ISEE required. Deadline for receipt of application materials: none. Application fee required: $75. On-campus interview required.

Athletics Interscholastic: baseball (boys), basketball (b,g), cheering (g), cross-country running (b,g), dance (g), football (b), golf (b), soccer (b,g), softball (g), swimming and diving (b,g), tennis (b,g), track and field (b,g), volleyball (g), wrestling (b); intramural: basketball (b,g), cheering (g); coed interscholastic: physical fitness, physical training, strength & conditioning; coed intramural: basketball, fencing, soccer, tennis, weight training. 2 PE instructors, 25 coaches, 1 trainer.

Computers Computers are regularly used in all classes. Computer network features include on-campus library services, CD-ROMs, Internet access, NewsBank InfoWeb, E-Library, E-Library Classic.

Contact Mrs. Janet Aldridge, Admissions Assistant. 704-366-5657. Fax: 704-366-5678. E-mail: janet.aldridge@charchrist.com. Web site: www.charlottechristian.com.

CHARLOTTE COUNTRY DAY SCHOOL

1440 Carmel Road
Charlotte, North Carolina 28226
Head of School: Margaret E. Gragg

General Information Coeducational day college-preparatory school. Grades JK–12. Founded: 1941. Setting: suburban. 60-acre campus. 11 buildings on campus. Approved or accredited by North Carolina Association of Independent Schools, Southern Association of Colleges and Schools, Southern Association of Independent Schools, and North Carolina Department of Education. Member of National Association of Independent Schools and Secondary School Admission Test Board. Endowment: $15.3 million. Total enrollment: 1,626. Upper school average class size: 15. Upper school faculty-student ratio: 1:12.

Upper School Student Profile Grade 9: 121 students (58 boys, 63 girls); Grade 10: 119 students (59 boys, 60 girls); Grade 11: 118 students (56 boys, 62 girls); Grade 12: 111 students (58 boys, 53 girls).

Faculty School total: 66. In upper school: 30 men, 36 women; 39 have advanced degrees.

Subjects Offered Algebra, American history, American history-AP, anatomy, art, art history-AP, astronomy, biology, biology-AP, biotechnology, calculus-AP, ceramics, chemistry, chemistry-AP, Chinese, computer graphics, computer science, computer science-AP, creative writing, dance, debate, discrete math, drama, ecology, economics, English, English literature, English-AP, environmental science-AP, ESL, European history, European history-AP, French, French-AP, geography, geometry, German, German-AP, Japanese, journalism, Latin, Latin-AP, library studies, music, non-Western societies, novels, photography, physical education, physics, physics-AP, physiology, poetry, political science, pre-calculus, probability and statistics, psychology-AP, sculpture, Shakespeare, short story, Spanish, Spanish-AP, studio art-AP, theater, theory of knowledge, trigonometry, typing, visual arts, yearbook.

Graduation Requirements Arts and fine arts (art, music, dance, drama), computer science, English, foreign language, mathematics, physical education (includes health), science, social sciences, social studies (includes history). Community service is required.

Special Academic Programs International Baccalaureate program; Advanced Placement exam preparation in 14 subject areas; honors section; independent study; term-away projects; study abroad; academic accommodation for the gifted; ESL (8 students enrolled).

College Placement 108 students graduated in 2005; all went to college, including Davidson College; Furman University; The University of North Carolina at Chapel Hill; University of Georgia; University of South Carolina; Wake Forest University. Median SAT verbal: 620, median SAT math: 640, median composite ACT: 26. 65% scored over 600 on SAT verbal, 74% scored over 600 on SAT math, 28% scored over 26 on composite ACT.

Student Life Upper grades have specified standards of dress, student council, honor system. Discipline rests primarily with faculty.

Summer Programs Remediation, enrichment, advancement, ESL, sports, art/fine arts, computer instruction programs offered; session focuses on enrichment classes, academic courses, and sports camps; held on campus; accepts boys and girls; open to students from other schools. 300 students usually enrolled. 2006 schedule: June 12 to July 21. Application deadline: none.

Tuition and Aid Day student tuition: $16,500. Tuition installment plan (The Tuition Plan, Insured Tuition Payment Plan, monthly payment plans). Need-based scholarship grants available. In 2005–06, 8% of upper-school students received aid. Total amount of financial aid awarded in 2005–06: $1,211,136.

Admissions Traditional secondary-level entrance grade is 9. For fall 2005, 89 students applied for upper-level admission, 42 were accepted, 24 enrolled. CTP III, ERB and ISEE required. Deadline for receipt of application materials: January 15. Application fee required: $90. On-campus interview required.

Athletics Interscholastic: baseball (boys), basketball (b,g), cheering (g), crew (g), cross-country running (b,g), dance (g), field hockey (g), fitness (b,g), football (b), golf (b), lacrosse (b), soccer (b,g), softball (g), strength & conditioning (b,g), swimming and diving (b,g), tennis (b,g), track and field (b,g), volleyball (g), weight training (b,g), wrestling (b). 1 PE instructor, 15 coaches, 3 trainers.

Computers Computers are regularly used in English, foreign language, mathematics, science classes. Computer network features include campus e-mail, on-campus library services, CD-ROMs, Internet access, DVD, wireless campus network.

Contact Nancy R. Ehringhaus, Director of Admissions. 704-943-4530 Ext. 4531. Fax: 704-943-4536. E-mail: ehringho@ccds.charlotte.nc.us. Web site: www.charlottecountryday.org.

ANNOUNCEMENT FROM THE SCHOOL Charlotte Country Day School strives to be the benchmark of academic excellence in college-preparatory education through superior teaching of a rigorous curriculum. As one of the largest independent schools in the country, Charlotte Country Day blends the abilities of students, aspirations of parents, and skills of professional educators to create a culture of achievement, honor, and compassion. Students in Junior Kindergarten through grade 12 are offered a premier international studies program, state-of-the-art technology, an innovative lab-based science program, a strong fine arts curriculum, an International Baccalaureate program, more than 50 athletic teams, an award-winning physical education program, and a strong focus on community service.

CHARLOTTE LATIN SCHOOL

9502 Providence Road
Charlotte, North Carolina 28277-8695
Head of School: Mr. Arch N. McIntosh Jr.

General Information Coeducational day college-preparatory, arts, and technology school. Grades K–12. Founded: 1970. Setting: suburban. 122-acre campus. 14 buildings on campus. Approved or accredited by North Carolina Association of Independent Schools, Southern Association of Colleges and Schools, Southern Association of Independent Schools, and North Carolina Department of Education. Member of National Association of Independent Schools and Secondary School Admission Test Board. Endowment: $13.9 million. Total enrollment: 1,369. Upper school average class size: 15. Upper school faculty-student ratio: 1:8.

Upper School Student Profile Grade 9: 118 students (58 boys, 60 girls); Grade 10: 118 students (65 boys, 53 girls); Grade 11: 118 students (69 boys, 49 girls); Grade 12: 123 students (73 boys, 50 girls).

Faculty School total: 162. In upper school: 31 men, 26 women; 33 have advanced degrees.

Subjects Offered 20th century American writers, 20th century history, 20th century physics, 20th century world history, 3-dimensional art, advanced chemistry, Advanced Placement courses, algebra, American culture, American government, American government-AP, American history, American history-AP, American literature, art, aviation, biology, biology-AP, British literature, calculus, calculus-AP, ceramics, chemistry, chemistry-AP, college counseling, computer math, computer programming, computer science, computer science-AP, creative writing, drama, driver education, earth science, ecology, economics, economics and history, engineering, English, English literature, English-AP, environmental science, European history, European history-AP, expository writing, finite math, French, French-AP, geography, geology, geometry, German, German-AP, government/civics, grammar, Greek, health, history, Holocaust and other genocides, international relations, international studies, journalism, Latin, Latin-AP, leadership and service, mathematics, music, music theory-AP, physical education, physics, physics-AP, psychology, science, social studies, Spanish, Spanish language-AP, Spanish-AP, speech, sports medicine, statistics-AP, theater, trigonometry, U.S. government and politics-AP, world history, world literature, writing.

Graduation Requirements English, foreign language, international studies, mathematics, physical education (includes health), science, social studies (includes history).

Special Academic Programs Advanced Placement exam preparation in 14 subject areas; honors section; independent study; study abroad; academic accommodation for the gifted, the musically talented, and the artistically talented.

College Placement 106 students graduated in 2005; all went to college, including Clemson University; Davidson College; Furman University; Hampden-Sydney College; The University of North Carolina at Chapel Hill; University of South Carolina.

Student Life Upper grades have specified standards of dress, student council, honor system. Discipline rests primarily with faculty.

Summer Programs Enrichment, advancement, sports, art/fine arts, computer instruction programs offered; session focuses on enrichment and sports camps; held on campus; accepts boys and girls; open to students from other schools. 850 students usually enrolled. 2006 schedule: June 12 to July 28. Application deadline: none.

Tuition and Aid Day student tuition: $15,170. Tuition installment plan (The Tuition Plan, Insured Tuition Payment Plan, monthly payment plans, individually arranged payment plans). Merit scholarship grants, need-based scholarship grants available. In 2005–06, 16% of upper-school students received aid; total upper-school merit-scholarship money awarded: $91,850. Total amount of financial aid awarded in 2005–06: $809,500.

Admissions Traditional secondary-level entrance grade is 9. For fall 2005, 84 students applied for upper-level admission, 36 were accepted, 29 enrolled. ERB, ISEE, Wechsler Intelligence Scale for Children III or Woodcock-Johnson required. Deadline for receipt of application materials: none. Application fee required: $90. On-campus interview required.

Athletics Interscholastic: aquatics (boys, girls), baseball (b), basketball (b,g), cross-country running (b,g), dance (g), dance squad (g), dance team (g), field hockey (g), football (b), golf (b,g), indoor track (b,g), lacrosse (b), soccer (b,g), softball (g), swimming and diving (b,g), tennis (b,g), track and field (b,g), volleyball (g), wrestling (b); intramural: aerobics (g), badminton (b,g), basketball (b,g), dance (g), fencing (b), fitness (b,g), lacrosse (b,g), outdoor activities (b,g), physical fitness (b,g), physical training (b,g), strength & conditioning (b,g); coed interscholastic: cheering, ultimate Frisbee; coed intramural: badminton, fitness, outdoor activities, physical fitness, physical training, strength & conditioning. 10 PE instructors, 15 coaches, 3 trainers.

Computers Computer network features include campus e-mail, on-campus library services, CD-ROMs, online commercial services, Internet access, file transfer, office computer access.

Contact Kathryn B. Booe, Director of Admissions. 704-846-7207. Fax: 704-847-8776. E-mail: kbooe@charlottelatin.org. Web site: www.charlottelatin.org.

ANNOUNCEMENT FROM THE SCHOOL Charlotte Latin School provides a challenging yet nurturing atmosphere for its students. This balanced environment is fostered by the development of intellectual curiosity, a comprehensive athletic program, a solid commitment to the arts, an emphasis on character education, and an educational approach that is traditional in design but progressive in implementation. The School remains true to its founding parents' vision as a place where a stimulating learning environment is united with a vibrant family life, and where families from diverse backgrounds share the common value of respect for themselves and for others, as well as an enduring dedication to support their children's educational journey. As one of the nation's leading independent day schools, Charlotte Latin's numerous honors, including being the youngest school to receive a Cum Laude chapter, and three times being named a Blue Ribbon School of Excellence by the United States Department of Education, illustrate that from transitional kindergarten through grade 12, its students thrive by all measurable standards. Students benefit from a college-preparatory curriculum. Younger students progress in developmentally appropriate steps, while Upper School students select from among 16 Advanced Placement courses. Guided by an Honor Code, Charlotte Latin's students also are encouraged to participate in community service, special interest clubs, and international studies to better prepare themselves to understand and lead the world they shall inherit as adults. Each year, the students' SAT I scores are at the top of the Charlotte region's scores (1277 average for the class of 2005). Charlotte Latin's seniors, who receive individual guidance from two full-time college counselors, are accepted by the nation's leading colleges and universities, including Ivy League schools. The School's campus, conveniently located in suburban Charlotte, encompasses 14 major buildings and a complete athletics complex amid 122 acres of mature trees dotted with picturesque gardens and one-of-a-kind works of sculpture.

CHASE COLLEGIATE SCHOOL

565 Chase Parkway
Waterbury, Connecticut 06708-3394
Head of School: John D. Fixx

General Information Coeducational day college-preparatory school. Grades PK–12. Founded: 1865. Setting: suburban. 47-acre campus. 6 buildings on campus. Approved or accredited by Connecticut Association of Independent Schools, New England Association of Schools and Colleges, and Connecticut Department of Education. Member of National Association of Independent Schools and Secondary School Admission Test Board. Endowment: $7.4 million. Total enrollment: 475. Upper school average class size: 11. Upper school faculty-student ratio: 1:7.
Upper School Student Profile Grade 9: 58 students (29 boys, 29 girls); Grade 10: 39 students (22 boys, 17 girls); Grade 11: 28 students (8 boys, 20 girls); Grade 12: 37 students (19 boys, 18 girls).
Faculty School total: 67. In upper school: 18 men, 9 women; 15 have advanced degrees.
Subjects Offered Acting, Advanced Placement courses, algebra, archaeology, art, art history-AP, astronomy, band, biology, biology-AP, calculus, calculus-AP, ceramics, chamber groups, chemistry, chemistry-AP, chorus, classical Greek literature, classical language, college writing, computer animation, computer programming, concert band, concert bell choir, current events, digital photography, directing, drama, drawing, ecology, economics, English, English language-AP, English literature and composition-AP, ethics, film studies, filmmaking, fine arts, French, French language-AP, French literature-AP, geometry, Greek, handbells, health and wellness, honors algebra, honors geometry, humanities, independent study, jazz band, jazz ensemble, journalism, Latin, Latin-AP, model United Nations, modern European history, music, music technology, natural history, oceanography, oil painting, photography, physics, physics-AP, playwriting, pre-calculus, public speaking, sculpture, society and culture, socioeconomic problems, sociology, Spanish, Spanish-AP, statistics-AP, technical theater, technology, theater, U.S. history, U.S. history-AP, visual arts, water color painting, Web authoring, Web site design, woodworking, world cultures, world history-AP, yearbook.
Graduation Requirements Adolescent issues, arts and fine arts (art, music, dance, drama), athletics, electives, English, ethics, foreign language, history, mathematics, psychology, public speaking, science, technology, senior speech.
Special Academic Programs Advanced Placement exam preparation in 16 subject areas; honors section; independent study; academic accommodation for the gifted.
College Placement 38 students graduated in 2005; 37 went to college, including Boston College; Gettysburg College; Rochester Institute of Technology; Roger Williams University; Tufts University; Yale University. Other: 1 had other specific plans. Median SAT verbal: 600, median SAT math: 580, median composite ACT: 22. 49% scored over 600 on SAT verbal, 49% scored over 600 on SAT math, 38% scored over 26 on composite ACT.
Student Life Upper grades have specified standards of dress, student council, honor system. Discipline rests equally with students and faculty.
Summer Programs Remediation, enrichment, advancement, art/fine arts, computer instruction programs offered; session focuses on enrichment and advancement; held

on campus; accepts boys and girls; open to students from other schools. 500 students usually enrolled. 2006 schedule: June to July. Application deadline: none.
Tuition and Aid Day student tuition: $22,270. Tuition installment plan (Key Tuition Payment Plan, monthly payment plans). Merit scholarship grants, need-based scholarship grants, Founders' Scholarships available. In 2005–06, 38% of upper-school students received aid; total upper-school merit-scholarship money awarded: $134,815. Total amount of financial aid awarded in 2005–06: $838,084.
Admissions Traditional secondary-level entrance grade is 9. For fall 2005, 55 students applied for upper-level admission, 46 were accepted, 29 enrolled. SSAT required. Deadline for receipt of application materials: none. Application fee required: $60. On-campus interview required.
Athletics Interscholastic: baseball (boys), basketball (b,g), cross-country running (b,g), fitness (b,g), lacrosse (b,g), snowboarding (b,g), soccer (b,g), softball (g), strength & conditioning (b,g), tennis (b,g), volleyball (g), wrestling (b); intramural: skiing (downhill) (b,g); coed interscholastic: cross-country running, golf, snowboarding, strength & conditioning, swimming and diving, ultimate Frisbee, weight training; coed intramural: aerobics/dance, dance, outdoor education, skiing (downhill). 4 PE instructors, 12 coaches, 1 trainer.
Computers Computers are regularly used in art, creative writing, English, foreign language, history, humanities, library, literary magazine, mathematics, music, newspaper, photography, research skills, SAT preparation, science, social science, study skills, technology, yearbook classes. Computer network features include on-campus library services, CD-ROMs, Internet access, DVD, wireless campus network.
Contact Margy Foulk, Director of Admission. 203-236-9560. Fax: 203-236-9503. E-mail: mfoulk@chasemail.org. Web site: www.chasemail.org.

CHATHAM ACADEMY

Savannah, Georgia
See Special Needs Schools section.

CHATHAM HALL

800 Chatham Hall Circle
Chatham, Virginia 24531
Head of School: Dr. Gary J. Fountain

petersons.com

General Information Girls' boarding and day college-preparatory school, affiliated with Episcopal Church. Grades 9–12. Founded: 1894. Setting: small town. Nearest major city is Greensboro, NC. Students are housed in single-sex dormitories. 362-acre campus. 9 buildings on campus. Approved or accredited by National Association of Episcopal Schools, Southern Association of Colleges and Schools, The Association of Boarding Schools, and Virginia Association of Independent Schools. Member of Secondary School Admission Test Board. Endowment: $14.9 million. Total enrollment: 131. Upper school average class size: 8. Upper school faculty-student ratio: 1:6.
Upper School Student Profile Grade 9: 33 students (33 girls); Grade 10: 29 students (29 girls); Grade 11: 29 students (29 girls); Grade 12: 40 students (40 girls). 82% of students are boarding students. 34% are state residents. 20 states are represented in upper school student body. 14% are international students. International students from Bahamas, Bermuda, Costa Rica, Germany, Republic of Korea, and Taiwan; 2 other countries represented in student body.
Faculty School total: 34. In upper school: 11 men, 23 women; 19 have advanced degrees; 25 reside on campus.
Subjects Offered Algebra, American history-AP, American literature, art, art history, biology, biology-AP, calculus, calculus-AP, ceramics, chemistry, chemistry-AP, choir, college counseling, computer art, creative writing, dance, DNA science lab, drama, drama performance, earth science, economics, English, English language-AP, English literature, English-AP, ESL, ethics, European history, European history-AP, fine arts, French, French-AP, general science, geography, geometry, history, instrumental music, journalism, Latin, mathematics, medieval/Renaissance history, model United Nations, modern European history, modern European history-AP, music, music composition, music theory, music theory-AP, photography, physical education, physics, pre-calculus, psychology, religion, robotics, SAT/ACT preparation, science, service learning/internship, social studies, Spanish, Spanish-AP, studio art-AP, swimming, theater design and production, trigonometry, U.S. government and politics, U.S. history, veterinary science, Western civilization, world history, writing workshop, yearbook.
Graduation Requirements Arts and fine arts (art, music, dance, drama), English, ethics, foreign language, mathematics, physical education (includes health), religion (includes Bible studies and theology), science, social studies (includes history).
Special Academic Programs Advanced Placement exam preparation in 15 subject areas; honors section; independent study; study abroad; academic accommodation for the gifted, the musically talented, and the artistically talented; ESL (3 students enrolled).
College Placement 31 students graduated in 2005; all went to college, including Cornell University; Dartmouth College; Duke University; Georgetown University; University of Virginia; Vanderbilt University. Median SAT verbal: 605, median SAT math: 600. 61% scored over 600 on SAT verbal, 55% scored over 600 on SAT math.

Student Life Upper grades have specified standards of dress, student council, honor system. Discipline rests equally with students and faculty. Attendance at religious services is required.

Summer Programs Sports programs offered; session focuses on riding; held on campus; accepts girls; open to students from other schools. 30 students usually enrolled. 2006 schedule: July 2 to July 22. Application deadline: none.

Tuition and Aid Day student tuition: $12,170; 7-day tuition and room/board: $33,800. Tuition installment plan (Key Tuition Payment Plan, increments of 45%, 30%, and 20% due July 1, September 1, and December 1, respectively). Need-based scholarship grants available. In 2005–06, 34% of upper-school students received aid. Total amount of financial aid awarded in 2005–06: $980,680.

Admissions Traditional secondary-level entrance grade is 9. For fall 2005, 114 students applied for upper-level admission, 89 were accepted, 49 enrolled. ISEE, PSAT or SAT, SLEP, SSAT or TOEFL required. Deadline for receipt of application materials: February 10. Application fee required: $45. Interview required.

Athletics Interscholastic: aquatics, basketball, cross-country running, diving, equestrian sports, field hockey, horseback riding, soccer, swimming and diving, tennis, volleyball; intramural: aerobics, aquatics, ballet, basketball, dance, diving, equestrian sports, field hockey, horseback riding, lacrosse, modern dance, soccer, softball, swimming and diving, tennis, volleyball. 2 PE instructors, 3 coaches, 1 trainer.

Computers Computers are regularly used in art, English, foreign language, graphic design, history, independent study, journalism, literary magazine, mathematics, music, newspaper, photography, science, yearbook classes. Computer network features include campus e-mail, on-campus library services, CD-ROMs, online commercial services, Internet access, office computer access, DVD, wireless campus network.

Contact Karen Stewart, Director of College Counseling. 434-432-2941. Fax: 434-432-2405. E-mail: kstewart@chathamhall.org. Web site: www.chathamhall.org.

See full description on page 726.

CHATTANOOGA CHRISTIAN SCHOOL

3354 Charger Drive
Chattanooga, Tennessee 37409
Head of School: Donald J. Holwerda

General Information Coeducational day college-preparatory, arts, religious studies, and technology school, affiliated with Christian faith. Grades K–12. Founded: 1970. Setting: urban. Nearest major city is Atlanta, GA. 40-acre campus. 6 buildings on campus. Approved or accredited by Christian Schools International, Southern Association of Colleges and Schools, and Tennessee Department of Education. Endowment: $9 million. Total enrollment: 1,062. Upper school average class size: 18. Upper school faculty-student ratio: 1:18.

Upper School Student Profile Grade 9: 113 students (51 boys, 62 girls); Grade 10: 101 students (41 boys, 60 girls); Grade 11: 88 students (45 boys, 43 girls); Grade 12: 108 students (55 boys, 53 girls). 100% of students are Christian faith.

Faculty School total: 98. In upper school: 32 men, 32 women; 35 have advanced degrees.

Subjects Offered African-American history, algebra, American government, American history, American literature, art, art appreciation, art history, astronomy, Bible studies, biology, calculus-AP, character education, chemistry, choir, civil rights, community service, computer applications, computer programming, computer science, concert band, creative writing, drama, Eastern world civilizations, economics, English, English literature, environmental science, European history, European history-AP, fine arts, French, geology, geometry, German, grammar, health, industrial arts, Japanese studies, jazz band, journalism, keyboarding, Latin, mathematics, mechanical drawing, music, music appreciation, physical education, physical science, physics, psychology, religion, science, shop, Spanish, speech, theater, trigonometry, U.S. history-AP, Web site design, world literature, writing.

Graduation Requirements Arts and fine arts (art, music, dance, drama), computer science, English, foreign language, mathematics, physical education (includes health), religion (includes Bible studies and theology), science, social science, social studies (includes history). Community service is required.

Special Academic Programs Advanced Placement exam preparation in 10 subject areas; honors section; academic accommodation for the gifted, the musically talented, and the artistically talented; remedial reading and/or remedial writing; remedial math.

College Placement 94 students graduated in 2005; all went to college, including Calvin College; Chattanooga State Technical Community College; Covenant College; The University of Tennessee; The University of Tennessee at Chattanooga; Wheaton College. Median SAT verbal: 580, median SAT math: 550, median composite ACT: 23. 41% scored over 600 on SAT verbal, 36% scored over 600 on SAT math, 40% scored over 26 on composite ACT.

Student Life Upper grades have specified standards of dress, student council, honor system. Discipline rests primarily with faculty. Attendance at religious services is required.

Summer Programs Remediation, sports, art/fine arts, computer instruction programs offered; session focuses on sports camps; held on campus; accepts boys and girls; not open to students from other schools. 100 students usually enrolled. 2006 schedule: June 5 to August 7. Application deadline: May 19.

Tuition and Aid Day student tuition: $7005. Tuition installment plan (monthly payment plans, individually arranged payment plans). Tuition reduction for siblings,

need-based scholarship grants, paying campus jobs available. In 2005–06, 17% of upper-school students received aid. Total amount of financial aid awarded in 2005–06: $250,646.

Admissions Traditional secondary-level entrance grade is 9. For fall 2005, 80 students applied for upper-level admission, 60 were accepted, 50 enrolled. Any standardized test required. Deadline for receipt of application materials: none. Application fee required: $150. Interview required.

Athletics Interscholastic: baseball (boys), basketball (b,g), bowling (b,g), cheering (b,g), cross-country running (b,g), golf (b,g), soccer (b,g), softball (g), tennis (b,g), track and field (b,g), volleyball (g), wrestling (b); intramural: badminton (b,g), basketball (b,g), fencing (b,g), flag football (b,g), indoor soccer (b,g), lacrosse (b,g), paddle tennis (b,g), soccer (b,g), softball (g), speedball (b,g), table tennis (b,g), tennis (b,g), touch football (b), track and field (b,g), volleyball (g), weight lifting (b,g), wrestling (b); coed interscholastic: cheering; coed intramural: aerobics/dance, bowling, cooperative games, dance, fitness, Frisbee, hockey, independent competitive sports, modern dance, outdoor activities, outdoor adventure, outdoor recreation, paddle tennis, physical fitness, physical training, street hockey, strength & conditioning, table tennis, ultimate Frisbee, wall climbing, weight training, whiffle ball. 3 PE instructors, 2 coaches.

Computers Computers are regularly used in drawing and design, English, foreign language, lab/keyboard, library, mathematics, psychology, science, technology classes. Computer network features include campus e-mail, on-campus library services, CD-ROMs, Internet access, DVD.

Contact Ms. Kathy Simmons, Admissions Director. 423-265-6411 Ext. 209. Fax: 423-756-4044. E-mail: ksimmons@ccsk12.com. Web site: ccsk12.com.

CHEDAR CHABAD

900 Alness Street, #202
North York, Ontario M3J 2H6, Canada
Head of School: Mr. Gary Gladstone

General Information Boys' boarding and day college-preparatory and religious studies school, affiliated with Jewish faith. Boarding grades 9–12, day grades 1–8. Founded: 1986. Setting: suburban. Nearest major city is Toronto, Canada. Students are housed in single-sex dormitories. 1 building on campus. Approved or accredited by Ontario Department of Education. Languages of instruction: English and Hebrew. Total enrollment: 248. Upper school faculty-student ratio: 1:25.

Upper School Student Profile Grade 9: 22 students (22 boys); Grade 10: 20 students (20 boys); Grade 11: 28 students (28 boys); Grade 12: 65 students (65 boys). 100% of students are boarding students. 28% are province residents. 18 provinces are represented in upper school student body. 11% are international students. International students from Argentina, Australia, France, Mexico, United Kingdom, and United States; 2 other countries represented in student body. 100% of students are Jewish.

Faculty School total: 8. In upper school: 8 men.

Subjects Offered Hebrew, Hebrew scripture, Jewish history, Jewish studies, Judaic studies, Rabbinic literature, religion, religion and culture, religious education, religious studies, scripture, Talmud, Yiddish.

Student Life Upper grades have specified standards of dress, honor system. Discipline rests primarily with faculty. Attendance at religious services is required.

Summer Programs Advancement programs offered; session focuses on religion; held off campus; held at Collingwood, Ontario; accepts boys; open to students from other schools. 75 students usually enrolled. 2006 schedule: July 10 to August 14.

Tuition and Aid 7-day tuition and room/board: $13,500. Guaranteed tuition plan. Tuition installment plan (monthly payment plans). Need-based scholarship grants available.

Admissions Achievement tests, Achievement/Aptitude/Writing or school's own test required. Deadline for receipt of application materials: none. Application fee required: $125. Interview required.

Contact Gary Gladstone, Admissions. 416-663-1972. Fax: 416-650-9404. E-mail: gary@chederchabad.com. Web site: www.chederchabad.com/.

CHELSEA SCHOOL

Silver Spring, Maryland
See Special Needs Schools section.

CHEROKEE CREEK BOYS SCHOOL

Westminster, South Carolina
See Special Needs Schools section.

CHESHIRE ACADEMY

10 Main Street
Cheshire, Connecticut 06410
Head of School: Mr. Ralph Van Inwagan

petersons.com

General Information Coeducational boarding and day college-preparatory school. Boarding grades 9–PG, day grades 6–PG. Founded: 1794. Setting: small town. Nearest major city is Hartford. Students are housed in single-sex dormitories. 104-acre campus. 22 buildings on campus. Approved or accredited by New England Association of Schools and Colleges and The Association of Boarding Schools. Member of National Association of Independent Schools and Secondary School Admission Test Board. Endowment: $8 million. Total enrollment: 385. Upper school average class size: 12. Upper school faculty-student ratio: 1:7.

Upper School Student Profile Grade 9: 61 students (47 boys, 14 girls); Grade 10: 97 students (61 boys, 36 girls); Grade 11: 79 students (50 boys, 29 girls); Grade 12: 83 students (51 boys, 32 girls); Postgraduate: 18 students (18 boys). 56% of students are boarding students. 63% are state residents. 13 states are represented in upper school student body. 19% are international students. International students from Japan, Republic of Korea, Spain, and Taiwan; 21 other countries represented in student body.

Faculty School total: 48. In upper school: 21 men, 23 women; 36 have advanced degrees; 27 reside on campus.

Subjects Offered African-American history, algebra, American history, American literature, anatomy, art, art history, Asian studies, biology, calculus, ceramics, chemistry, community service, computer programming, computer science, creative writing, drama, earth science, ecology, economics, English, English literature, environmental science, ESL, ethics, European history, expository writing, fine arts, French, geography, geometry, government/civics, grammar, health, history, history of jazz, Latin American studies, logic, mathematics, music, music history, mythology, photography, physical education, physics, physiology, psychology, reading, science, social science, social studies, Spanish, speech, statistics, theater, trigonometry, women's studies, world history, world literature, writing.

Graduation Requirements Arts and fine arts (art, music, dance, drama), computer science, electives, English, foreign language, mathematics, physical education (includes health), science, social science, social studies (includes history), senior speech, 10 hours of community service.

Special Academic Programs Advanced Placement exam preparation in 12 subject areas; honors section; accelerated programs; independent study; study at local college for college credit; academic accommodation for the musically talented and the artistically talented; remedial reading and/or remedial writing; remedial math; programs in English, mathematics, general development for dyslexic students; ESL (30 students enrolled).

College Placement Colleges students went to include Cornell University; Harvey Mudd College; University of Chicago.

Student Life Upper grades have specified standards of dress, student council, honor system. Discipline rests primarily with faculty.

Summer Programs Remediation, enrichment, advancement, ESL, sports, art/fine arts, computer instruction programs offered; session focuses on ESL and study skills; held on campus; accepts boys and girls; open to students from other schools. 125 students usually enrolled. 2006 schedule: June 30 to August 5. Application deadline: May 31.

Tuition and Aid Day student tuition: $24,675; 7-day tuition and room/board: $35,375. Tuition installment plan (Key Tuition Payment Plan). Need-based scholarship grants available. In 2005–06, 32% of upper-school students received aid. Total amount of financial aid awarded in 2005–06: $1,000,000.

Admissions Traditional secondary-level entrance grade is 9. For fall 2005, 343 students applied for upper-level admission, 195 were accepted, 118 enrolled. ACT, ISEE, PSAT, SAT, SSAT or TOEFL or SLEP required. Deadline for receipt of application materials: February 1. Application fee required: $50. Interview required.

Athletics Interscholastic: baseball (boys), basketball (b,g), cross-country running (b,g), diving (b,g), fencing (b,g), field hockey (g), football (b), golf (b), lacrosse (b,g), ropes courses (b,g), soccer (b,g), softball (g), swimming and diving (b,g), tennis (b,g), track and field (b,g), volleyball (g); coed interscholastic: wilderness survival; coed intramural: dance, fitness, martial arts, physical training, ropes courses, skiing (downhill), snowboarding, weight lifting, weight training. 30 coaches, 1 trainer.

Computers Computers are regularly used in foreign language, mathematics, science classes. Computer network features include campus e-mail, on-campus library services, CD-ROMs, Internet access.

Contact Michael McCleery, Dean of Admission. 203-272-5396 Ext. 250. Fax: 203-250-7209. E-mail: michael.mccleery@cheshireacademy.org. Web site: www.cheshireacademy.org.

See full description on page 728.

CHESTNUT HILL ACADEMY

500 West Willow Grove Avenue
Philadelphia, Pennsylvania 19118
Head of School: Mr. Francis P. Steel Jr.

petersons.com

General Information Boys' day college-preparatory, arts, technology, and Advanced Placement school. Grades PK–12. Founded: 1861. Setting: suburban. 25-acre campus. 6 buildings on campus. Approved or accredited by Middle States Association of Colleges and Schools, Pennsylvania Association of Private Academic Schools, and Pennsylvania Department of Education. Member of National Association of Independent Schools and Secondary School Admission Test Board. Endowment: $22.7 million. Total enrollment: 568. Upper school average class size: 16. Upper school faculty-student ratio: 1:7.

Upper School Student Profile Grade 9: 60 students (60 boys); Grade 10: 58 students (58 boys); Grade 11: 51 students (51 boys); Grade 12: 43 students (43 boys).

Faculty School total: 36. In upper school: 27 men, 9 women; 22 have advanced degrees.

Subjects Offered Algebra, American history, American literature, art, art history, biology, calculus, ceramics, chemistry, computer math, computer programming, computer science, creative writing, drama, driver education, earth science, engineering, English, English literature, environmental science, ethics, European history, expository writing, fine arts, French, geology, geometry, government/civics, grammar, health, history, Latin, mathematics, music, photography, physical education, physics, physiology, science, social studies, Spanish, theater, world history.

Graduation Requirements Arts and fine arts (art, music, dance, drama), computer science, English, foreign language, mathematics, physical education (includes health), science, social studies (includes history), speech, senior projects, senior speech. Community service is required.

Special Academic Programs Advanced Placement exam preparation in 14 subject areas; honors section; independent study; term-away projects; study abroad; academic accommodation for the gifted, the musically talented, and the artistically talented.

College Placement 53 students graduated in 2005; all went to college, including Lehigh University; Muhlenberg College; The Citadel, The Military College of South Carolina; University of Miami; University of Pennsylvania; University of Richmond. Mean SAT verbal: 609, mean SAT math: 664, mean composite ACT: 27. 59% scored over 600 on SAT verbal, 86% scored over 600 on SAT math, 50% scored over 26 on composite ACT.

Student Life Upper grades have specified standards of dress, student council. Discipline rests equally with students and faculty.

Tuition and Aid Day student tuition: $19,200. Tuition installment plan (Insured Tuition Payment Plan, Academic Management Services Plan, monthly payment plans, individually arranged payment plans). Merit scholarship grants, need-based scholarship grants, need-based loans available. In 2005–06, 41% of upper-school students received aid; total upper-school merit-scholarship money awarded: $56,540. Total amount of financial aid awarded in 2005–06: $873,500.

Admissions Traditional secondary-level entrance grade is 9. For fall 2005, 78 students applied for upper-level admission, 41 were accepted, 23 enrolled. ISEE or SSAT required. Deadline for receipt of application materials: none. Application fee required: $40. On-campus interview required.

Athletics Interscholastic: baseball, basketball, crew, cross-country running, football, golf, ice hockey, indoor track & field, lacrosse, soccer, squash, tennis, track and field, winter (indoor) track, wrestling; intramural: lacrosse, weight lifting, weight training. 2 PE instructors, 21 coaches, 1 trainer.

Computers Computers are regularly used in all academic classes. Computer network features include campus e-mail, on-campus library services, CD-ROMs, online commercial services, Internet access, file transfer, office computer access, DVD, wireless campus network.

Contact Mr. Andrew T. Weller, Director of Admissions. 215-247-4700 Ext. 1133. Fax: 215-247-1068. E-mail: aweller@chestnuthillacademy.org. Web site: www. chestnuthillacademy.org.

---

is the Coordinate Program, a gradual introduction to learning with the girls of neighboring Springside School. Field trips and sharing grade-level performances are the foundation in the Lower School. In Middle School, activities such as community service, orchestra, drama, and dances are coeducational. Finally, in the Upper School, boys have limited coeducational classes in grades 9 and 10 and fully integrated classes in their last two years. It is truly the best of both worlds.

CHEVERUS HIGH SCHOOL

267 Ocean Avenue
Portland, Maine 04103
Head of School: Mr. John H. R. Mullen

General Information Coeducational day college-preparatory, religious studies, and technology school, affiliated with Roman Catholic Church (Jesuit order). Grades 9–12. Founded: 1917. Setting: suburban. 32-acre campus. 2 buildings on campus. Approved or accredited by New England Association of Schools and Colleges and Maine Department of Education. Endowment: $800,000. Total enrollment: 515. Upper school average class size: 22. Upper school faculty-student ratio: 1:11.

Upper School Student Profile Grade 9: 138 students (91 boys, 47 girls); Grade 10: 139 students (89 boys, 50 girls); Grade 11: 122 students (81 boys, 41 girls); Grade 12: 116 students (77 boys, 39 girls). 65% of students are Roman Catholic Church (Jesuit order).

Faculty School total: 52. In upper school: 29 men, 18 women; 24 have advanced degrees.

Subjects Offered Advanced Placement courses, algebra, American history, art, biology, calculus, chemistry, college counseling, community service, computer programming, computer science, economics, English, European history, fine arts, French, geography, geometry, government/civics, Greek, history, Latin, mathematics, music, physics, religion, science, social studies, Spanish, statistics, trigonometry, world history.

Graduation Requirements 20th century history, arts and fine arts (art, music, dance, drama), computer science, English, foreign language, mathematics, religion (includes Bible studies and theology), science, social studies (includes history). Community service is required.

Special Academic Programs Advanced Placement exam preparation in 9 subject areas; honors section; independent study; study at local college for college credit; programs in general development for dyslexic students.

College Placement 119 students graduated in 2005; 115 went to college, including Boston College; Clemson University; Georgetown University; Holy Cross College; University of Maine; University of Notre Dame. Other: 2 went to work, 2 entered military service. Median SAT verbal: 575, median SAT math: 576.

Student Life Upper grades have specified standards of dress, student council, honor system. Discipline rests primarily with faculty.

Tuition and Aid Day student tuition: $7920. Tuition installment plan (monthly payment plans, individually arranged payment plans). Tuition reduction for siblings, merit scholarship grants, need-based scholarship grants, paying campus jobs available. In 2005–06, 50% of upper-school students received aid. Total amount of financial aid awarded in 2005–06: $800,000.

Admissions Traditional secondary-level entrance grade is 9. For fall 2005, 333 students applied for upper-level admission, 153 were accepted, 142 enrolled. STS required. Deadline for receipt of application materials: none. Application fee required: $25. On-campus interview required.

Athletics Interscholastic: baseball (boys), basketball (b,g), cross-country running (b,g), diving (b,g), football (b), golf (b,g), ice hockey (b), indoor track & field (b,g), lacrosse (b,g), soccer (b,g), swimming and diving (b,g), tennis (b,g), track and field (b,g); intramural: basketball (b,g), football (b); coed interscholastic: alpine skiing; coed intramural: alpine skiing, back packing, bicycling, hiking/backpacking, project adventure, volleyball. 10 coaches, 1 trainer.

Computers Computers are regularly used in desktop publishing, ESL, economics, history, information technology, mathematics, SAT preparation, science, word processing, yearbook classes. Computer network features include campus e-mail, on-campus library services, CD-ROMs, online commercial services, Internet access, file transfer, office computer access.

Contact Mr. Jack Dawson, Director of Admissions. 207-774-6238 Ext. 14. Fax: 207-828-0207. E-mail: dawson@cheverus.org. Web site: www.cheverus.org.

CHINESE CHRISTIAN SCHOOLS

750 Fargo Avenue
San Leandro, California 94579
Head of School: Mr. Robin S. Hom

General Information Coeducational day college-preparatory and religious studies school, affiliated with Bible Fellowship Church, Evangelical/Fundamental faith. Grades K–12. Founded: 1979. Setting: suburban. Nearest major city is Oakland. 10-acre campus. 7 buildings on campus. Approved or accredited by Association of Christian Schools International, Western Association of Schools and Colleges, and

California Department of Education. Total enrollment: 939. Upper school average class size: 20. Upper school faculty-student ratio: 1:14.

Upper School Student Profile Grade 9: 61 students (31 boys, 30 girls); Grade 10: 49 students (28 boys, 21 girls); Grade 11: 56 students (43 boys, 13 girls); Grade 12: 52 students (21 boys, 31 girls). 20% of students are Bible Fellowship Church, Evangelical/Fundamental faith.

Faculty School total: 40. In upper school: 15 men, 20 women; 10 have advanced degrees.

Subjects Offered Advanced computer applications, Advanced Placement courses, aerobics, algebra, American government, American government-AP, American history, American history-AP, American literature, American literature-AP, applied music, art, audio visual/media, Basic programming, basketball, Bible, Bible studies, biology, biology-AP, British literature, calculus, calculus-AP, Cantonese, career/college preparation, chemistry, Chinese, Chinese studies, choir, choral music, Christian doctrine, Christian ethics, Christian studies, civics, civics/free enterprise, college counseling, college placement, college planning, communications, community service, comparative religion, computer applications, computer graphics, computer science, CPR, debate, drama, driver education, economics, economics-AP, electives, English, English language-AP, English literature, English literature-AP, ESL, European history-AP, first aid, foreign language, general science, geometry, government, government and politics-AP, government-AP, graphic arts, honors English, intro to computers, language arts, leadership and service, learning strategies, library assistant, literature and composition-AP, literature-AP, macro/microeconomics-AP, macroeconomics-AP, Mandarin, marching band, marine science, martial arts, mathematics-AP, microeconomics, microeconomics-AP, music, newspaper, participation in sports, physical education, physics, physics-AP, pre-algebra, pre-calculus, probability and statistics, public speaking, religious education, religious studies, ROTC (for boys), SAT preparation, SAT/ACT preparation, science, science research, Spanish, speech, speech and debate, speech communications, sports, state history, statistics, student government, theater, theater arts, trigonometry, U.S. government, U.S. government and politics-AP, U.S. government-AP, U.S. history, U.S. history-AP, visual and performing arts, volleyball, Web authoring, world history, world wide web design, yearbook.

Graduation Requirements Algebra, American government, American history, Bible, Chinese, CPR, driver education, economics, English, first aid, foreign language, geometry, history, lab science, Life of Christ, mathematics, physical education (includes health), physics, pre-algebra, science, visual and performing arts, world history, Mandarin I or Chinese Culture class.

Special Academic Programs Advanced Placement exam preparation in 12 subject areas; honors section; study at local college for college credit; academic accommodation for the gifted; ESL (9 students enrolled).

College Placement 55 students graduated in 2005; all went to college, including California State University, East Bay; San Jose State University; University of California, Davis; University of California, Los Angeles; University of California, San Diego; University of California, Santa Barbara. Mean SAT verbal: 556, mean SAT math: 615, mean composite ACT: 25. 33% scored over 600 on SAT verbal, 54% scored over 600 on SAT math.

Student Life Upper grades have uniform requirement, student council. Discipline rests primarily with faculty. Attendance at religious services is required.

Summer Programs Remediation, enrichment, advancement, ESL, sports programs offered; session focuses on academic enrichment or remediation; held on campus; accepts boys and girls; open to students from other schools. 270 students usually enrolled. 2006 schedule: June 21 to August 4. Application deadline: May 15.

Tuition and Aid Day student tuition: $4950–$6875. Tuition installment plan (monthly payment plans, individually arranged payment plans, eTuition automatic electronic deposit). Tuition reduction for siblings, merit scholarship grants, need-based scholarship grants, paying campus jobs available. In 2005–06, 5% of upper-school students received aid; total upper-school merit-scholarship money awarded: $10,000. Total amount of financial aid awarded in 2005–06: $100,000.

Admissions Traditional secondary-level entrance grade is 9. For fall 2005, 65 students applied for upper-level admission, 63 were accepted, 61 enrolled. Achievement/Aptitude/Writing, admissions testing, California Achievement Test, CTBS (or similar from their school), Math Placement Exam, Stanford Achievement Test or writing sample required. Deadline for receipt of application materials: none. No application fee required. On-campus interview required.

Athletics Interscholastic: basketball (boys, girls), cross-country running (b,g), JROTC drill (b), soccer (b,g), tennis (b,g), track and field (b,g), volleyball (b,g); intramural: drill team (b), outdoor education (b,g), outdoor recreation (b,g); coed interscholastic: cross-country running, swimming and diving; coed intramural: outdoor education, outdoor recreation. 2 PE instructors, 1 coach.

Computers Computers are regularly used in lab/keyboard, library skills, programming, senior seminar, Web site design classes. Computer network features include on-campus library services, CD-ROMs, Internet access, DVD, wireless campus network.

Contact Mrs. Mary Chan, Admissions Director. 510-351-4957. Fax: 510-351-1789. E-mail: mary_chan@ccs-rams.org. Web site: www.ccs-rams.org.

CHOATE ROSEMARY HALL

333 Christian Street
Wallingford, Connecticut 06492-3800
Head of School: Edward J. Shanahan, PhD

General Information Coeducational boarding and day college-preparatory school. Grades 9–PG. Founded: 1890. Setting: small town. Nearest major city is New Haven. Students are housed in single-sex dormitories. 400-acre campus. 116 buildings on campus. Approved or accredited by Connecticut Association of Independent Schools, New England Association of Schools and Colleges, The Association of Boarding Schools, and Connecticut Department of Education. Member of National Association of Independent Schools and Secondary School Admission Test Board. Endowment: $213 million. Total enrollment: 851. Upper school average class size: 12. Upper school faculty-student ratio: 1:6.

Upper School Student Profile Grade 9: 163 students (75 boys, 88 girls); Grade 10: 210 students (101 boys, 109 girls); Grade 11: 245 students (130 boys, 115 girls); Grade 12: 213 students (106 boys, 107 girls); Postgraduate: 20 students (18 boys, 2 girls). 71% of students are boarding students. 49% are state residents. 43 states are represented in upper school student body. 10% are international students. International students from Canada, Hong Kong, Japan, Republic of Korea, Saudi Arabia, and Singapore; 18 other countries represented in student body.

Faculty School total: 151. In upper school: 64 men, 45 women; 65 have advanced degrees; 122 reside on campus.

Subjects Offered Algebra, American history, American literature, anatomy, anthropology, architecture, art, art history, astronomy, Bible studies, biology, calculus, ceramics, chemistry, child development, Chinese, computer math, computer programming, computer science, creative writing, dance, drama, ecology, economics, electronics, English, English literature, ethics, etymology, European history, expository writing, fine arts, French, geography, geometry, German, government/civics, health, history, history of ideas, history of mathematics, interdisciplinary studies, international studies, Italian, Japanese, language, Latin, linear algebra, logic, macroeconomics-AP, marine biology, mathematics, microbiology, microeconomics-AP, music, philosophy, photography, physical education, physics, physiology, political science, psychology, public speaking, religion, Russian, science, social studies, Spanish, speech, statistics, theater, trigonometry, world history, world literature, world wide web design, writing.

Graduation Requirements Art, English, foreign language, history, mathematics, philosophy, physical education (includes health), psychology, religion (includes Bible studies and theology), science, 30 hours of community service.

Special Academic Programs Advanced Placement exam preparation in 19 subject areas; honors section; independent study; term-away projects; study abroad; academic accommodation for the gifted, the musically talented, and the artistically talented.

College Placement 241 students graduated in 2005; 235 went to college, including Brown University; Cornell University; Georgetown University; Harvard University; University of Pennsylvania; Yale University. Other: 6 had other specific plans. 79% scored over 600 on SAT verbal, 86% scored over 600 on SAT math.

Student Life Upper grades have specified standards of dress, student council, honor system. Discipline rests primarily with faculty.

Summer Programs Enrichment, advancement, ESL, art/fine arts programs offered; session focuses on academic growth and enrichment; held on campus; accepts boys and girls; open to students from other schools. 500 students usually enrolled. 2006 schedule: June 26 to July 29. Application deadline: May 1.

Tuition and Aid Day student tuition: $25,680; 7-day tuition and room/board: $35,360. Tuition installment plan (Insured Tuition Payment Plan, Key Tuition Payment Plan, monthly payment plans). Need-based scholarship grants, need-based loans available. In 2005–06, 27% of upper-school students received aid. Total amount of financial aid awarded in 2005–06: $5,700,000.

Admissions Traditional secondary-level entrance grade is 9. For fall 2005, 1,462 students applied for upper-level admission, 465 were accepted, 276 enrolled. ACT, ISEE, PSAT or SAT for applicants to grade 11 and 12, SSAT or TOEFL required. Deadline for receipt of application materials: January 15. Application fee required: $50. Interview required.

Athletics Interscholastic: archery (boys, girls), basketball (b,g), cross-country running (b,g), diving (b,g), field hockey (g), football (b), ice hockey (b,g), lacrosse (b,g), soccer (b,g), squash (b,g), swimming and diving (b,g), volleyball (g), water polo (b), wrestling (b); intramural: crew (b,g), squash (b,g); coed intramural: aerobics, aerobics/dance, aerobics/nautilus, back packing, ballet, basketball, bicycling, cross-country running, dance, equestrian sports, fitness, Frisbee, hiking/backpacking, horseback riding, ice hockey, ice skating, jogging, martial arts, modern dance, mountain biking, mountaineering, nautilus, outdoor activities, physical fitness, physical training, rock climbing, rowing, running, scuba diving, self defense, soccer, strength & conditioning, swimming and diving, tennis, ultimate Frisbee, volleyball, weight lifting, weight training, winter (indoor) track, yoga. 75 coaches, 3 trainers.

Computers Computers are regularly used in all academic, art, college planning, desktop publishing, drawing and design, graphic design, information technology, library skills, literary magazine, media production, music, newspaper, photography, study skills, theater arts, video film production, yearbook classes. Computer network features include campus e-mail, on-campus library services, CD-ROMs, online commercial services, Internet access, file transfer, office computer access, wireless campus network, student-initiated and operated Linux Laboratory.

Contact Raymond M. Diffley III, Director of Admission. 203-697-2239. Fax: 203-697-2629. E-mail: admissions@choate.edu. Web site: www.choate.edu.

ANNOUNCEMENT FROM THE SCHOOL Seniors may create an individualized Capstone Project, which typically includes 2 related courses in the fall and winter terms and an independent project (the "capstone") in the spring. Capstone projects range from mathematical modeling to Chinese studies to international economics to historical trends in American foreign policy to creative writing.

See full description on page 730.

CHRISTA MCAULIFFE ACADEMY

402 East Yakima Avenue
Suite 1100
Yakima, Washington 98901
Head of School: Glen W. Blomgren

General Information Coeducational day college-preparatory, general academic, bilingual studies, technology, and Advanced Placement, distance learning school. Grades K–12. Founded: 1985. Setting: small town. Nearest major city is Seattle. 1 building on campus. Approved or accredited by CITA (Commission on International and Trans-Regional Accreditation), Northwest Association of Schools and Colleges, and Washington Department of Education. Total enrollment: 362. Upper school faculty-student ratio: 1:23.

Faculty School total: 15. In upper school: 3 men, 12 women; 4 have advanced degrees.

Subjects Offered Art, computers, electives, English, health, mathematics, music, occupational education, physical education, science, social studies, standard curriculum.

Graduation Requirements Art, career exploration, computer applications, English, mathematics, music, pre-vocational education, science, social studies (includes history).

Special Academic Programs Advanced Placement exam preparation in 2 subject areas; honors section; accelerated programs; independent study; academic accommodation for the gifted; programs in general development for dyslexic students.

College Placement 31 students graduated in 2005; they went to Florida State University; Texas State University-San Marcos; The Pennsylvania State University University Park Campus; University of Illinois at Chicago; University of Washington; Washington State University.

Student Life Upper grades have student council, honor system. Discipline rests equally with students and faculty.

Summer Programs Remediation, enrichment, advancement, computer instruction programs offered; session focuses on make-up and advancement; held both on and off campus; held at students' homes; accepts boys and girls; open to students from other schools. 40 students usually enrolled. 2006 schedule: June 1 to August 31. Application deadline: none.

Tuition and Aid Day student tuition: $3600. Tuition installment plan (monthly payment plans, individually arranged payment plans). Tuition reduction for siblings, paying campus jobs available.

Admissions Traditional secondary-level entrance grade is 9. Achievement/Aptitude/Writing required. Deadline for receipt of application materials: none. Application fee required: $90. Interview recommended.

Computers Computers are regularly used in all academic classes. Computer network features include campus e-mail, Internet access, file transfer, office computer access.

Contact Debbie Whitecotton, Director of Administrative Services/Registrar. 509-575-4989. Fax: 509-575-4976. E-mail: debbie@cmacademy.org. Web site: www.cmacademy.org.

CHRIST CHURCH EPISCOPAL SCHOOL

245 Cavalier Drive
Greenville, South Carolina 29607
Head of School: Dr. Leland H. Cox Jr.

General Information Coeducational day college-preparatory, arts, religious studies, technology, and International Baccalaureate school, affiliated with Episcopal Church. Grades K–12. Founded: 1959. Setting: suburban. Nearest major city is Charlotte, NC. 68-acre campus. 5 buildings on campus. Approved or accredited by International Baccalaureate Organization, National Association of Episcopal Schools, Southern Association of Colleges and Schools, Southern Association of Independent Schools, and The College Board. Member of National Association of Independent Schools. Endowment: $6.7 million. Total enrollment: 1,000. Upper school average class size: 18. Upper school faculty-student ratio: 1:9.

Upper School Student Profile Grade 9: 86 students (43 boys, 43 girls); Grade 10: 72 students (35 boys, 37 girls); Grade 11: 65 students (29 boys, 36 girls); Grade 12: 68 students (41 boys, 27 girls). 19% of students are members of Episcopal Church.

Faculty School total: 107. In upper school: 10 men, 25 women; 22 have advanced degrees.

Christ Church Episcopal School

Subjects Offered 20th century history, algebra, American history, American literature, American literature-AP, Ancient Greek, art, biology, biology-AP, calculus, calculus-AP, chemistry, chemistry-AP, China/Japan history, Christian education, Christian ethics, Christian scripture, Christian studies, computer art, computer graphics, computer programming, computer programming-AP, computer science, creative writing, drama, earth science, economics, English, English literature, environmental science, ESL, ethics, ethics and responsibility, European history, European history-AP, expository writing, fine arts, French, French-AP, geometry, German, government and politics-AP, government/civics, grammar, history, history-AP, honors English, honors U.S. history, honors world history, humanities, International Baccalaureate courses, journalism, keyboarding, Latin, Latin-AP, marine biology, mathematics, music, music theory-AP, music-AP, physical education, physics, physics-AP, psychology, public speaking, religion, SAT/ACT preparation, science, social studies, Spanish, Spanish-AP, speech, statistics, statistics-AP, theater, theology, theory of knowledge, trigonometry, U.S. history-AP, Web site design, world history, world history-AP, world literature.

Graduation Requirements Arts and fine arts (art, music, dance, drama), electives, English, foreign language, mathematics, physical education (includes health), public speaking, religion (includes Bible studies and theology), science, senior thesis, social studies (includes history), extended essay (for IB diploma candidates).

Special Academic Programs International Baccalaureate program; Advanced Placement exam preparation in 20 subject areas; honors section; independent study; study abroad; ESL (15 students enrolled).

College Placement 71 students graduated in 2005; all went to college, including Clemson University; College of Charleston; Furman University; University of South Carolina; University of the South; Vanderbilt University. Mean SAT verbal: 641, mean SAT math: 644.

Student Life Upper grades have specified standards of dress, student council, honor system. Discipline rests equally with students and faculty. Attendance at religious services is required.

Summer Programs Remediation, enrichment, sports, art/fine arts, computer instruction programs offered; session focuses on enrichment; held on campus; accepts boys and girls; open to students from other schools. 420 students usually enrolled. 2006 schedule: June 7 to July 30. Application deadline: none.

Tuition and Aid Day student tuition: $12,550. Tuition installment plan (Insured Tuition Payment Plan, FACTS Tuition Payment Plan, monthly payment plans). Merit scholarship grants, need-based scholarship grants available. In 2005–06, 11% of upper-school students received aid; total upper-school merit-scholarship money awarded: $89,250. Total amount of financial aid awarded in 2005–06: $137,702.

Admissions Traditional secondary-level entrance grade is 9. For fall 2005, 32 students applied for upper-level admission, 27 were accepted, 26 enrolled. Achievement/Aptitude/Writing and ERB required. Deadline for receipt of application materials: April 15. Application fee required: $150. On-campus interview required.

Athletics Interscholastic: baseball (boys), basketball (b,g), cheering (g), cross-country running (b,g), field hockey (g), football (b), golf (b,g), soccer (b,g), swimming and diving (b,g), tennis (b,g), track and field (b,g), volleyball (g), wrestling (b); intramural: dance team (g), fencing (b), weight training (b,g). 7 PE instructors, 14 coaches, 1 trainer.

Computers Computers are regularly used in all classes. Computer network features include on-campus library services, CD-ROMs, online commercial services, Internet access, classroom computers.

Contact Mrs. Pam Sheftall Matthews, Director of Admissions. 864-299-1522 Ext. 1223. Fax: 864-299-8861. E-mail: matthewp@cces.org. Web site: www.cces.org.

ANNOUNCEMENT FROM THE SCHOOL A coeducational, college-preparatory, Episcopal day school, CCES is one of 3 American independent schools offering International Baccalaureate programs in grades primer–12. Situated on a 68-acre campus, CCES offers small classes, 15 Advanced Placement courses, outstanding fine and performing arts, community service, and chapel. The School's top-rated athletic program fields 35 teams.

CHRISTCHURCH SCHOOL

49 Seahorse Lane
Christchurch, Virginia 23031
Head of School: Mr. John E. Byers

General Information Boys' boarding and coeducational day college-preparatory, arts, religious studies, marine science, and ESL school, affiliated with Episcopal Church. Boarding boys grades 8–PG, day boys grades 8–PG, day girls grades 8–PG. Founded: 1921. Setting: rural. Nearest major city is Richmond. Students are housed in single-sex dormitories. 120-acre campus. 13 buildings on campus. Approved or accredited by National Association of Episcopal Schools, The Association of Boarding Schools, The College Board, Virginia Association of Independent Schools, and Virginia Department of Education. Member of National Association of Independent Schools and Secondary School Admission Test Board. Endowment: $1.9 million. Total enrollment: 220. Upper school average class size: 12. Upper school faculty-student ratio: 1:7.

Upper School Student Profile Grade 8: 11 students (10 boys, 1 girl); Grade 9: 36 students (26 boys, 10 girls); Grade 10: 45 students (43 boys, 2 girls); Grade 11: 63

students (51 boys, 12 girls); Grade 12: 65 students (49 boys, 16 girls). 58% of students are boarding students. 59% are state residents. 16 states are represented in upper school student body. 15% are international students. International students from Germany, Jamaica, Republic of Korea, and Taiwan; 4 other countries represented in student body. 23% of students are members of Episcopal Church.

Faculty School total: 34. In upper school: 25 men, 9 women; 21 have advanced degrees; 24 reside on campus.

Subjects Offered Adolescent issues, advanced math, Advanced Placement courses, advanced studio art-AP, algebra, American Civil War, American history, American history-AP, American literature, art, art history, biology, British literature-AP, calculus, calculus-AP, chemistry, chemistry-AP, comparative government and politics-AP, comparative political systems-AP, composition-AP, computer science, economics, English, English language-AP, English literature, English literature-AP, environmental science-AP, ethics, fine arts, French, French-AP, geography, geometry, government and politics-AP, government/civics, health, marine biology, music, physical education, physics, physics-AP, social studies, Spanish, Spanish-AP, theology, trigonometry, U.S. history-AP, United States government-AP, world history, world history-AP, world wide web design.

Graduation Requirements Arts and fine arts (art, music, dance, drama), English, foreign language, health and wellness, mathematics, physical education (includes health), religion (includes Bible studies and theology), science, social studies (includes history).

Special Academic Programs Advanced Placement exam preparation in 12 subject areas; programs in general development for dyslexic students; special instructional classes for students diagnosed with mild learning disabilities; ESL (18 students enrolled).

College Placement 51 students graduated in 2005; all went to college, including George Mason University; Hampden-Sydney College; James Madison University; Lynchburg College; University of Mary Washington; Virginia Polytechnic Institute and State University. Median SAT verbal: 570, median SAT math: 550. 25% scored over 600 on SAT verbal, 25% scored over 600 on SAT math.

Student Life Upper grades have specified standards of dress, student council, honor system. Discipline rests primarily with faculty. Attendance at religious services is required.

Summer Programs Enrichment, sports programs offered; session focuses on academic enrichment and skills building, marine science, sailing, crew; held on campus; accepts boys and girls; open to students from other schools. 100 students usually enrolled. 2006 schedule: June 18 to July 15. Application deadline: none.

Tuition and Aid Day student tuition: $15,000; 7-day tuition and room/board: $35,500. Guaranteed tuition plan. Tuition installment plan (monthly payment plans, 60% due July 1—40% due January 1). Need-based scholarship grants available. In 2005–06, 30% of upper-school students received aid. Total amount of financial aid awarded in 2005–06: $990,300.

Admissions Traditional secondary-level entrance grade is 9. For fall 2005, 214 students applied for upper-level admission, 129 were accepted, 74 enrolled. SSAT or TOEFL required. Deadline for receipt of application materials: none. Application fee required: $50. Interview required.

Athletics Interscholastic: baseball (boys), basketball (b,g), crew (b,g), cross-country running (b), field hockey (g), football (b), golf (b), lacrosse (b), sailing (b), soccer (b), tennis (b,g), track and field (b,g), volleyball (g), winter (indoor) track (b,g), wrestling (b); intramural: winter soccer (g); coed interscholastic: cross-country running, golf, indoor soccer, indoor track, sailing, soccer, strength & conditioning, weight lifting, winter (indoor) track; coed intramural: fitness, martial arts, outdoor skills, sailing, weight training. 1 trainer.

Computers Computers are regularly used in all academic classes. Computer network features include campus e-mail, on-campus library services, CD-ROMs, online commercial services, Internet access, office computer access, DVD.

Contact Mrs. Nancy M. Nolan, Director of Admission. 804-758-2306. Fax: 804-758-0721. E-mail: admission@christchurchschool.org. Web site: www.christchurchschool.org.

See full description on page 732.

CHRISTIAN BROTHERS ACADEMY

850 Newman Springs Road
Lincroft, New Jersey 07738
Head of School: Br. Stephen Olert, FSC

General Information Boys' day college-preparatory school, affiliated with Roman Catholic Church. Grades 9–12. Founded: 1959. Setting: suburban. Nearest major city is New York, NY. 157-acre campus. 3 buildings on campus. Approved or accredited by Middle States Association of Colleges and Schools. Endowment: $6.2 million. Total enrollment: 919. Upper school average class size: 24. Upper school faculty-student ratio: 1:14.

Upper School Student Profile Grade 9: 249 students (249 boys); Grade 10: 235 students (235 boys); Grade 11: 218 students (218 boys); Grade 12: 217 students (217 boys). 80% of students are Roman Catholic.

Faculty School total: 70. In upper school: 51 men, 19 women; 41 have advanced degrees.

Subjects Offered Algebra, American government, American history, anatomy and physiology, Bible studies, biology, business, business skills, calculus, chemistry, computer science, creative writing, driver education, economics, English, environmental science, European history, French, geometry, health, history, journalism, Latin, mathematics, physical education, physics, psychology, religion, science, social science, social studies, Spanish, theology, trigonometry, world history, world literature, writing.

Graduation Requirements Business skills (includes word processing), computer science, English, foreign language, mathematics, physical education (includes health), religion (includes Bible studies and theology), science, social science, social studies (includes history).

Special Academic Programs Advanced Placement exam preparation in 16 subject areas; honors section; study abroad.

College Placement 212 students graduated in 2005; all went to college, including Drexel University; La Salle University; Loyola College in Maryland; Rutgers, The State University of New Jersey, New Brunswick/Piscataway; Saint Joseph's University; Villanova University. Median SAT verbal: 610, median SAT math: 630.

Student Life Upper grades have specified standards of dress, student council. Discipline rests primarily with faculty. Attendance at religious services is required.

Tuition and Aid Day student tuition: $9650. Tuition installment plan (Academic Management Services Plan, individually arranged payment plans). Merit scholarship grants, need-based scholarship grants available. In 2005–06, 9% of upper-school students received aid; total upper-school merit-scholarship money awarded: $48,000. Total amount of financial aid awarded in 2005–06: $622,800.

Admissions For fall 2005, 458 students applied for upper-level admission, 276 were accepted, 249 enrolled. School's own test required. Deadline for receipt of application materials: none. Application fee required: $75.

Athletics Interscholastic: baseball, basketball, bowling, cross-country running, golf, ice hockey, lacrosse, sailing, soccer, swimming and diving, tennis, track and field, winter (indoor) track, wrestling; intramural: baseball, basketball, bowling, Frisbee, soccer, tennis, volleyball. 3 PE instructors, 21 coaches, 1 trainer.

Computers Computers are regularly used in mathematics, science classes. Computer network features include on-campus library services, CD-ROMs, Internet access.

Contact Br. Ralph Montedoro, FSC, Principal. 732-747-1959 Ext. 101. Fax: 732-747-1643. Web site: www.cbalincroftnj.org.

CHRISTIAN BROTHERS ACADEMY

12 Airline Drive
Albany, New York 12205
Head of School: Mr. David R. McGuire

General Information Boys' day college-preparatory, business, religious studies, and Junior ROTC school, affiliated with Roman Catholic Church. Grades 6–12. Founded: 1859. Setting: suburban. 120-acre campus. 1 building on campus. Approved or accredited by Middle States Association of Colleges and Schools, New York State Board of Regents, and New York Department of Education. Endowment: $2.8 million. Total enrollment: 504. Upper school average class size: 25. Upper school faculty-student ratio: 1:12.

Upper School Student Profile Grade 9: 82 students (82 boys); Grade 10: 110 students (110 boys); Grade 11: 86 students (86 boys); Grade 12: 94 students (94 boys). 74% of students are Roman Catholic.

Faculty School total: 38. In upper school: 23 men, 9 women; 16 have advanced degrees.

Subjects Offered Accounting, algebra, American government, American government-AP, art, astrophysics, band, biology, biology-AP, business law, calculus-AP, chemistry, chemistry-AP, computer technologies, driver education, earth science, economics, English, English-AP, European history-AP, French, geometry, global studies, government-AP, health, keyboarding, Latin, life science, math analysis, mathematics, mechanical drawing, military science, music, physical education, physical science, physics, religion, science, sociology, Spanish, U.S. history, U.S. history-AP, Web site design, world history-AP.

Graduation Requirements Arts and fine arts (art, music, dance, drama), English, foreign language, lab science, mathematics, military science, physical education (includes health), religion (includes Bible studies and theology), social studies (includes history).

Special Academic Programs Advanced Placement exam preparation in 8 subject areas; honors section.

College Placement 898 students graduated in 2005; 97 went to college, including Manhattan College; Northeastern University; Siena College; University at Albany, State University of New York. Other: 1 entered military service. Mean SAT verbal: 530, mean SAT math: 555.

Student Life Upper grades have uniform requirement, student council, honor system. Discipline rests primarily with faculty. Attendance at religious services is required.

Summer Programs Enrichment, sports programs offered; session focuses on basketball for boys; soccer for boys and girls; held on campus; accepts boys and girls; open to students from other schools. 150 students usually enrolled. 2006 schedule: July 10 to July 28.

Tuition and Aid Day student tuition: $8900. Tuition installment plan (monthly payment plans, 3-payment plan). Merit scholarship grants, need-based scholarship

grants available. In 2005–06, 35% of upper-school students received aid; total upper-school merit-scholarship money awarded: $147,098. Total amount of financial aid awarded in 2005–06: $474,000.

Admissions Traditional secondary-level entrance grade is 9. For fall 2005, 38 students applied for upper-level admission, 36 were accepted, 27 enrolled. Iowa Tests of Basic Skills required. Deadline for receipt of application materials: none. No application fee required.

Athletics Interscholastic: baseball, basketball, bowling, cross-country running, football, golf, ice hockey, lacrosse, riflery, skiing (downhill), soccer, tennis, track and field, wrestling; intramural: skiing (downhill), weight lifting. 3 PE instructors, 18 coaches, 1 trainer.

Computers Computers are regularly used in writing classes. Computer network features include campus e-mail, on-campus library services, CD-ROMs, Internet access, wireless campus network.

Contact Mr. Martin McGraw, Director of Admissions. 518-452-9809 Ext. 110. Fax: 518-452-9806. E-mail: mcgrawm@cbaalbany.org. Web site: www.cbaalbany.org.

CHRISTIAN BROTHERS ACADEMY

6245 Randall Road
Syracuse, New York 13214
Head of School: Br. Thomas Zoppo, FSC

General Information Coeducational day college-preparatory and religious studies school, affiliated with Roman Catholic Church. Grades 7–12. Founded: 1900. Setting: suburban. 40-acre campus. 1 building on campus. Approved or accredited by Christian Brothers Association, Middle States Association of Colleges and Schools, and New York Department of Education. Endowment: $800,000. Total enrollment: 740. Upper school average class size: 27.

Upper School Student Profile 85% of students are Roman Catholic.

Faculty School total: 57. In upper school: 29 men, 28 women.

Subjects Offered Advanced Placement courses, American history, American literature, art, art history, biology, business, calculus, chemistry, computer programming, earth science, economics, English, English literature, environmental science, European history, expository writing, fine arts, French, government/civics, grammar, health, history, Latin, mathematics, mechanical drawing, music, physical education, physics, pre-calculus, psychology, public speaking, religion, science, social science, social studies, Spanish, theology, world history, world literature.

Graduation Requirements Arts and fine arts (art, music, dance, drama), computer science, English, foreign language, mathematics, physical education (includes health), religion (includes Bible studies and theology), science, social science, social studies (includes history), community service for seniors.

Special Academic Programs Advanced Placement exam preparation in 12 subject areas; honors section.

College Placement 124 students graduated in 2005; 122 went to college, including Boston College; Le Moyne College; Saint Joseph's University; Syracuse University; University of Notre Dame. Other: 2 had other specific plans. Mean SAT verbal: 580, mean SAT math: 593, mean composite ACT: 26.

Student Life Upper grades have specified standards of dress, student council. Discipline rests primarily with faculty. Attendance at religious services is required.

Tuition and Aid Day student tuition: $7000. Tuition installment plan (SMART Tuition Payment Plan, individually arranged payment plans). Merit scholarship grants, need-based scholarship grants available. In 2005–06, 95% of upper-school students received aid; total upper-school merit-scholarship money awarded: $125,000.

Admissions Traditional secondary-level entrance grade is 9. For fall 2005, 25 students applied for upper-level admission, 20 were accepted, 20 enrolled. Admissions testing required. Deadline for receipt of application materials: February 1. Application fee required: $40. Interview recommended.

Athletics Interscholastic: baseball (boys), basketball (b,g), cheering (g), cross-country running (b,g), diving (b,g), football (b), golf (b,g), gymnastics (b), ice hockey (b), lacrosse (b,g), soccer (b,g), softball (g), swimming and diving (b,g), tennis (b,g), track and field (b,g), volleyball (g); coed interscholastic: bowling. 4 PE instructors, 1 trainer.

Computers Computer network features include on-campus library services, CD-ROMs, Internet access.

Contact Br. Joseph Reed, FSC, Assistant Principal for Student Affairs. 315-446-5960. Fax: 315-446-3393.

CHRISTIAN BROTHERS HIGH SCHOOL

4315 Martin Luther King Jr. Boulevard
Sacramento, California 95820
Head of School: Mr. Raymond Burnell

General Information Coeducational day college-preparatory school, affiliated with Roman Catholic Church. Grades 9–12. Founded: 1876. Setting: urban. 22-acre campus. 10 buildings on campus. Approved or accredited by Christian Brothers Association, National Catholic Education Association, and Western Association of Schools and Colleges. Total enrollment: 1,088. Upper school average class size: 24. Upper school faculty-student ratio: 1:24.

Christian Brothers High School

Upper School Student Profile Grade 9: 274 students (149 boys, 125 girls); Grade 10: 287 students (185 boys, 102 girls); Grade 11: 278 students (150 boys, 128 girls); Grade 12: 249 students (138 boys, 111 girls). 69% of students are Roman Catholic.

Faculty School total: 71. In upper school: 35 men, 36 women; 31 have advanced degrees.

Subjects Offered Algebra, American history, American history-AP, American literature, anatomy, art, audio visual/media, band, biology, biology-AP, calculus-AP, cartooning, chemistry, chemistry-AP, chorus, composition, computer programming, computer programming-AP, computer science-AP, creative writing, drama, driver education, economics, English, English-AP, ensembles, environmental science, fine arts, French, French-AP, general science, geography, geometry, German, German-AP, government/civics, health, jazz, journalism, keyboarding, literature, logic, mathematics, orchestra, painting, philosophy, physical education, physics, physics-AP, physiology, psychology, reading, religion, science, senior seminar, social science, social studies, Spanish, Spanish-AP, statistics, theater, video film production, world history, world history-AP, world literature.

Graduation Requirements Arts and fine arts (art, music, dance, drama), English, foreign language, mathematics, physical education (includes health), religion (includes Bible studies and theology), science, social science, social studies (includes history). Community service is required.

Special Academic Programs Advanced Placement exam preparation in 12 subject areas; honors section; study at local college for college credit.

College Placement 222 students graduated in 2005; 220 went to college, including California Polytechnic State University, San Luis Obispo; California State University, Sacramento; Saint Mary's College of California; University of California, Davis; University of California, San Diego; University of California, Santa Cruz. Other: 2 had other specific plans. Mean SAT verbal: 534, mean SAT math: 527, mean composite ACT: 25.

Student Life Upper grades have specified standards of dress, student council. Discipline rests primarily with faculty. Attendance at religious services is required.

Summer Programs Remediation, enrichment, advancement, sports, art/fine arts, computer instruction programs offered; held on campus; accepts boys and girls; open to students from other schools. 300 students usually enrolled. 2006 schedule: June 13 to July 25. Application deadline: none.

Tuition and Aid Day student tuition: $9800. Tuition installment plan (The Tuition Plan, monthly payment plans). Tuition reduction for siblings, need-based scholarship grants available.

Admissions Traditional secondary-level entrance grade is 9. For fall 2005, 374 students applied for upper-level admission, 300 were accepted, 276 enrolled. High School Placement Test required. Deadline for receipt of application materials: April 1. No application fee required. Interview recommended.

Athletics Interscholastic: baseball (boys), basketball (b,g), cheering (g), football (b), golf (b,g), lacrosse (g), soccer (b,g), softball (g), tennis (b,g), track and field (b,g), volleyball (b,g), water polo (b,g); intramural: drill team (g), strength & conditioning (b), weight training (b), yoga (b,g); coed interscholastic: cross-country running, diving, swimming and diving, wrestling. 3 PE instructors, 40 coaches, 1 trainer.

Computers Computers are regularly used in computer applications, English, journalism, keyboarding, mathematics, science, video film production classes. Computer resources include campus e-mail, on-campus library services, CD-ROMs, Internet access.

Contact Mr. David Jablonsky, Director of Admissions. 916-733-3690. Fax: 916-733-3657. E-mail: djablonsky@cbhs-sacramento.org. Web site: www.cbhs-sacramento.org.

CHRISTIAN CENTRAL ACADEMY

39 Academy Street
Williamsville, New York 14221
Head of School: Nurline Lawrence

General Information Coeducational day college-preparatory, arts, and religious studies school, affiliated with Christian faith. Grades K–12. Founded: 1949. Setting: suburban. Nearest major city is Buffalo. 5-acre campus. 2 buildings on campus. Approved or accredited by Association of Christian Schools International and New York Department of Education. Endowment: $50,000. Total enrollment: 380. Upper school average class size: 20. Upper school faculty-student ratio: 1:6.

Upper School Student Profile Grade 9: 24 students (14 boys, 10 girls); Grade 10: 27 students (17 boys, 10 girls); Grade 11: 18 students (10 boys, 8 girls); Grade 12: 15 students (10 boys, 5 girls). 100% of students are Christian faith.

Faculty School total: 35. In upper school: 6 men, 9 women; 12 have advanced degrees.

Subjects Offered Advanced computer applications, advertising design, algebra, American government, American history, American history-AP, American literature, applied music, art, band, Bible, biology, calculus-AP, career/college preparation, chemistry, choral music, chorus, communications, computer keyboarding, computer studies, design, drawing, driver education, earth science, economics, English, English literature, English-AP, geometry, global studies, health, history, journalism, Latin, music, orchestra, physical education, physics, pre-calculus, Spanish, studio art, trigonometry, world history, world literature, writing.

Graduation Requirements Algebra, American government, American history, American literature, Bible, biology, chemistry, computer keyboarding, earth science,

---

economics, English, geometry, global studies, physical education (includes health), physics, pre-calculus, Spanish, trigonometry, writing, community service hours for all four years.

Special Academic Programs Advanced Placement exam preparation in 3 subject areas; honors section; independent study.

College Placement 15 students graduated in 2005; all went to college, including Gordon College; Grove City College; Houghton College; Niagara University; Philadelphia Biblical University; State University of New York at Buffalo. Median SAT verbal: 580, median SAT math: 550. 33% scored over 600 on SAT verbal, 27% scored over 600 on SAT math.

Student Life Upper grades have specified standards of dress, student council, honor system. Discipline rests primarily with faculty. Attendance at religious services is required.

Tuition and Aid Day student tuition: $5665. Tuition installment plan (monthly payment plans, payment discount plans, Tuition Direct Plan). Tuition reduction for siblings, need-based scholarship grants available. In 2005–06, 18% of upper-school students received aid. Total amount of financial aid awarded in 2005–06: $20,000.

Admissions Traditional secondary-level entrance grade is 9. For fall 2005, 21 students applied for upper-level admission, 18 were accepted, 15 enrolled. Admissions testing and writing sample required. Deadline for receipt of application materials: none. Application fee required: $50. Interview recommended.

Athletics Interscholastic: basketball (boys, girls), soccer (b,g); intramural: soccer (b); coed interscholastic: cross-country running; coed intramural: skiing (downhill), snowboarding. 2 PE instructors, 3 coaches.

Computers Computers are regularly used in college planning, drawing and design, English, journalism, yearbook classes. Computer resources include on-campus library services, CD-ROMs, Internet access.

Contact Deborah White, Director of Admissions. 716-634-4821. Fax: 716-634-5851. E-mail: cca@adelphia.net. Web site: www.christianca.com.

CHRISTIAN HERITAGE SCHOOL

575 White Plains Road
Trumbull, Connecticut 06611-4898
Head of School: Barry Giller

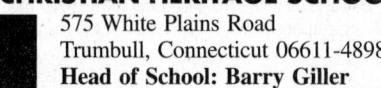

General Information Coeducational day college-preparatory and religious studies school. Grades 7–12. Founded: 1977. Setting: suburban. Nearest major city is Bridgeport. 5-acre campus. 3 buildings on campus. Approved or accredited by Association of Christian Schools International, New England Association of Schools and Colleges, The College Board, and Connecticut Department of Education. Endowment: $300,000. Total enrollment: 522. Upper school average class size: 16. Upper school faculty-student ratio: 1:9.

Upper School Student Profile Grade 9: 49 students (21 boys, 28 girls); Grade 10: 34 students (19 boys, 15 girls); Grade 11: 47 students (29 boys, 18 girls); Grade 12: 41 students (18 boys, 23 girls).

Faculty School total: 57. In upper school: 19 men, 14 women; 16 have advanced degrees.

Subjects Offered 20th century American writers, 20th century history, 20th century physics, 20th century world history, advanced chemistry, advanced math, Advanced Placement courses, algebra, American foreign policy, American government, American history, American history-AP, American literature, architecture, art, band, Bible, Bible studies, biology, biology-AP, British literature, business, calculus, calculus-AP, career and personal planning, career/college preparation, chemistry, choir, choral music, chorus, Christian and Hebrew scripture, Christian doctrine, Christian education, Christian ethics, Christian scripture, Christian studies, Christian testament, classical Greek literature, classics, college awareness, college counseling, college placement, college planning, college writing, communication skills, computer keyboarding, computer processing, computer programming, computer programming-AP, computer science, computer skills, concert band, concert choir, constitutional history of U.S., consumer mathematics, contemporary history, contemporary issues, contemporary issues in science, creative arts, current events, current history, data processing, desktop publishing, drama performance, drawing, earth science, English, English composition, English literature, ensembles, ethics, ethics and responsibility, expository writing, French, functions, general science, geography, geometry, government/civics, grammar, health and wellness, health education, history, history-AP, home economics, honors algebra, honors English, honors geometry, honors U.S. history, human anatomy, human biology, inorganic chemistry, instrumental music, instruments, intro to computers, journalism, keyboarding, keyboarding/computer, language and composition, life issues, Life of Christ, life science, literature, madrigals, marching band, mathematics, mathematics-AP, moral and social development, moral reasoning, moral theology, music, music theory, musical productions, newspaper, novels, oral communications, organic chemistry, painting, philosophy, physical education, physical science, physics, poetry, prayer/spirituality, pre-algebra, pre-calculus, public speaking, publications, reading/study skills, religion, religious education, science, science project, senior seminar, Shakespeare, social studies, Spanish, Spanish-AP, speech, statistics, student government, student publications, U.S. government, U.S. history-AP, vocal ensemble, vocal music, volleyball, work experience, world affairs, world history, writing, yearbook.

Graduation Requirements Electives, English, foreign language, mathematics, physical education (includes health), religion (includes Bible studies and theology), science, social studies (includes history).

Special Academic Programs Advanced Placement exam preparation in 9 subject areas; honors section; independent study.

College Placement 45 students graduated in 2005; 44 went to college, including Evangel University; Messiah College; Southern Connecticut State University. Other: 1 went to work. Median SAT verbal: 550, median SAT math: 530. 40% scored over 600 on SAT verbal, 22% scored over 600 on SAT math.

Student Life Upper grades have specified standards of dress, student council. Discipline rests primarily with faculty. Attendance at religious services is required.

Tuition and Aid Day student tuition: $9160–$10,140. Tuition installment plan (SMART Tuition Payment Plan, monthly payment plans, individually arranged payment plans). Tuition reduction for siblings, need-based scholarship grants available. In 2005–06, 45% of upper-school students received aid. Total amount of financial aid awarded in 2005–06: $564,000.

Admissions Traditional secondary-level entrance grade is 9. For fall 2005, 25 students applied for upper-level admission, 18 were accepted, 12 enrolled. Admissions testing, Otis-Lennon School Ability Test and Stanford Achievement Test required. Deadline for receipt of application materials: none. Application fee required: $40. On-campus interview required.

Athletics Interscholastic: baseball (boys), basketball (b,g), cheering (g), golf (b), soccer (b,g), softball (g), track and field (b,g), volleyball (g); intramural: weight lifting (b), weight training (b); coed interscholastic: cross-country running, tennis, ultimate Frisbee; coed intramural: Frisbee. 1 PE instructor, 9 coaches.

Computers Computers are regularly used in business education, college planning, data processing, desktop publishing, drafting, journalism, keyboarding, mathematics, newspaper, programming, word processing, yearbook classes. Computer network features include campus e-mail, on-campus library services, CD-ROMs, Internet access.

Contact Mrs. Jennifer Thompson, Director of Admissions. 203-261-6230 Ext. 3009. Fax: 203-452-1531. E-mail: jthompson@kingsmen.org. Web site: www.kingsmen.org.

ANNOUNCEMENT FROM THE SCHOOL Christian Heritage School was founded in 1977 to partner with parents by providing a college-preparatory education from an evangelical Christian worldview for children in grades K–12. A rigorous academic program is enriched by a myriad of cocurricular opportunities, including athletics, student government, drama, and a variety of clubs. Students are also encouraged in their faith through weekly chapels, service opportunities, and mission trips. Financial aid is available.

CHRISTIAN JUNIOR–SENIOR HIGH SCHOOL

2100 Greenfield Drive
El Cajon, California 92019
Head of School: Scottt Meadows

General Information Coeducational day college-preparatory, arts, religious studies, and ESL school, affiliated with Protestant Church. Boys grade 7, girls grade 12. Founded: 1965. Setting: suburban. Nearest major city is San Diego. 13-acre campus. 10 buildings on campus. Approved or accredited by Association of Christian Schools International and Western Association of Schools and Colleges. Total enrollment: 625. Upper school average class size: 21. Upper school faculty-student ratio: 1:14.

Upper School Student Profile Grade 9: 118 students (56 boys, 62 girls); Grade 10: 108 students (53 boys, 55 girls); Grade 11: 94 students (37 boys, 57 girls); Grade 12: 96 students (45 boys, 51 girls). 80% of students are Protestant.

Faculty School total: 45. In upper school: 17 men, 25 women; 21 have advanced degrees.

Subjects Offered Advanced chemistry, Advanced Placement courses, algebra, American literature, anatomy and physiology, art, ASB Leadership, Bible studies, biology, British literature-AP, calculus, calculus-AP, ceramics, chemistry, comparative religion, computer applications, computer keyboarding, computer literacy, concert band, concert choir, drafting, drama, drama performance, drama workshop, economics, economics and history, English, English literature and composition-AP, English literature-AP, ensembles, ESL, European history-AP, food and nutrition, geometry, government, health, health education, home economics, honors algebra, honors English, honors geometry, interior design, journalism, leadership and service, library assistant, library science, Life of Christ, marching band, music, music theory, newspaper, physical education, physics, physics-AP, pre-algebra, pre-calculus, relationships, sewing, softball, Spanish, Spanish-AP, speech, speech and debate, sports conditioning, sports medicine, statistics, statistics and probability, swimming, symphonic band, theater arts, TOEFL preparation, U.S. government, U.S. history, U.S. history-AP, visual and performing arts, visual arts, vocal ensemble, vocal music, volleyball, weight training, world history, world literature, yearbook.

Graduation Requirements Arts and fine arts (art, music, dance, drama), English, foreign language, health education, keyboarding/computer, mathematics, physical education (includes health), religion (includes Bible studies and theology), science, social studies (includes history), typing.

Special Academic Programs Advanced Placement exam preparation in 7 subject areas; honors section; ESL (48 students enrolled).

College Placement 97 students graduated in 2005; 96 went to college, including Biola University; Point Loma Nazarene University; San Diego State University; University of California, Riverside; University of California, San Diego; Westmont College. Other: 1 went to work. Mean SAT verbal: 539, mean SAT math: 528, mean composite ACT: 23.

Student Life Upper grades have uniform requirement. Discipline rests primarily with faculty. Attendance at religious services is required.

Summer Programs Remediation, advancement programs offered; session focuses on academics (math, social science, foreign language); held on campus; accepts boys and girls; open to students from other schools. 40 students usually enrolled. 2006 schedule: June 12 to July 25. Application deadline: April 28.

Tuition and Aid Day student tuition: $10,600. Tuition installment plan (monthly payment plans). Tuition reduction for siblings, need-based scholarship grants available. In 2005–06, 5% of upper-school students received aid. Total amount of financial aid awarded in 2005–06: $18,000.

Admissions Traditional secondary-level entrance grade is 9. For fall 2005, 83 students applied for upper-level admission, 64 were accepted, 64 enrolled. Any standardized test, ESL, SCAT or writing sample required. Deadline for receipt of application materials: none. Application fee required: $300. On-campus interview required.

Athletics Interscholastic: baseball (boys), basketball (b,g), cheering (g), football (b), golf (b,g), soccer (b,g), softball (g), tennis (b,g), volleyball (b,g); coed interscholastic: cross-country running, swimming and diving, track and field. 2 PE instructors, 33 coaches, 1 trainer.

Computers Computers are regularly used in drafting, ESL, keyboarding, library science, mathematics, newspaper, reading, science, social sciences, yearbook classes. Computer network features include on-campus library services, CD-ROMs, online commercial services, Internet access, Blackboard.

Contact Karen Andrews, ESL Administrator. 619-440-1531. Fax: 619-590-1717. E-mail: kandrews@christianunified.org. Web site: www.christianunified.com.

CHRISTOPHER DOCK MENNONITE HIGH SCHOOL

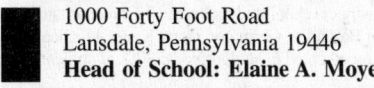

1000 Forty Foot Road
Lansdale, Pennsylvania 19446
Head of School: Elaine A. Moyer

General Information Coeducational day college-preparatory, general academic, and vocational school, affiliated with Mennonite Brethren Church. Grades 9–12. Founded: 1954. Setting: suburban. Nearest major city is Philadelphia. 75-acre campus. 5 buildings on campus. Approved or accredited by Mennonite Schools Council, Middle States Association of Colleges and Schools, and Pennsylvania Department of Education. Endowment: $1 million. Total enrollment: 418. Upper school average class size: 22. Upper school faculty-student ratio: 1:13.

Upper School Student Profile Grade 9: 99 students (53 boys, 46 girls); Grade 10: 115 students (60 boys, 55 girls); Grade 11: 102 students (45 boys, 57 girls); Grade 12: 102 students (53 boys, 49 girls). 62% of students are members of Mennonite Brethren Church.

Faculty School total: 35. In upper school: 16 men, 16 women; 16 have advanced degrees.

Subjects Offered Accounting, algebra, American history, American literature, anatomy, art, art history, astronomy, Bible studies, biology, business, business skills, calculus, ceramics, chemistry, child development, communications, computer programming, computer science, creative writing, drama, driver education, earth science, economics, English, English literature, environmental science, European history, family and consumer sciences, fine arts, geography, geology, geometry, gerontology, government/civics, grammar, health, history, industrial arts, journalism, keyboarding, mathematics, music, photography, physical education, physics, religion, science, social science, social studies, Spanish, speech, statistics, theater, trigonometry, word processing, world history, world literature.

Graduation Requirements Arts and fine arts (art, music, dance, drama), business skills (includes word processing), computer science, English, family and consumer sciences, mathematics, physical education (includes health), religion (includes Bible studies and theology), science, social science, social studies (includes history), five-day urban experience, senior independent study/service experience (one week).

Special Academic Programs Advanced Placement exam preparation in 2 subject areas; honors section; remedial reading and/or remedial writing; remedial math.

College Placement 113 students graduated in 2005; 102 went to college, including Eastern Mennonite University; Eastern University; Goshen College; Messiah College; Montgomery County Community College. Other: 9 went to work, 1 entered a postgraduate year, 1 had other specific plans. 29% scored over 600 on SAT verbal, 24% scored over 600 on SAT math.

Student Life Upper grades have specified standards of dress, student council. Discipline rests primarily with faculty. Attendance at religious services is required.

Tuition and Aid Day student tuition: $10,800. Tuition installment plan (monthly payment plans). Tuition reduction for siblings, need-based scholarship grants available. In 2005–06, 80% of upper-school students received aid. Total amount of financial aid awarded in 2005–06: $400,000.

Christopher Dock Mennonite High School

Admissions Traditional secondary-level entrance grade is 9. For fall 2005, 149 students applied for upper-level admission, 144 were accepted, 120 enrolled. Deadline for receipt of application materials: none. Application fee required: $25. On-campus interview required.

Athletics Interscholastic: baseball (boys), basketball (b,g), cross-country running (b,g), field hockey (g), golf (b), soccer (b,g), softball (g), tennis (b,g), track and field (b,g), volleyball (b,g); coed intramural: basketball, soccer, volleyball. 3 PE instructors, 32 coaches, 1 trainer.

Computers Computers are regularly used in accounting, keyboarding, lab/keyboard, mathematics, music, programming, SAT preparation, science, Web site design, word processing, yearbook classes. Computer network features include campus e-mail, on-campus library services, CD-ROMs, Internet access, office computer access, DVD, K12Planet.

Contact Lois Boaman, Coordinator of Admissions. 215-362-2675 Ext. 111. Fax: 215-362-2943. E-mail: laboaman@christopherdock.org. Web site: www.christopherdock.org.

CHRIST SCHOOL

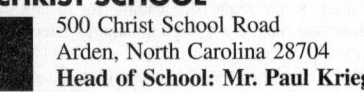

500 Christ School Road
Arden, North Carolina 28704
Head of School: Mr. Paul Krieger

petersons.com

General Information Boys' boarding and day college-preparatory, arts, religious studies, and technology school, affiliated with Episcopal Church. Grades 8–12. Founded: 1900. Setting: rural. Nearest major city is Asheville. Students are housed in single-sex dormitories. 500-acre campus. 15 buildings on campus. Approved or accredited by National Association of Episcopal Schools, North Carolina Association of Independent Schools, Southern Association of Independent Schools, The Association of Boarding Schools, and North Carolina Department of Education. Member of National Association of Independent Schools and Secondary School Admission Test Board. Endowment: $8.5 million. Total enrollment: 185. Upper school average class size: 11. Upper school faculty-student ratio: 1:5.

Upper School Student Profile Grade 8: 13 students (13 boys); Grade 9: 34 students (34 boys); Grade 10: 46 students (46 boys); Grade 11: 42 students (42 boys); Grade 12: 50 students (50 boys). 82% of students are boarding students. 47% are state residents. 15 states are represented in upper school student body. 10% are international students. International students from Barbados, Germany, Hong Kong, Jamaica, and Republic of Korea; 1 other country represented in student body. 30% of students are members of Episcopal Church.

Faculty School total: 39. In upper school: 28 men, 11 women; 27 have advanced degrees; 30 reside on campus.

Subjects Offered Advanced Placement courses, African-American history, algebra, American history, American history-AP, American literature, anatomy and physiology, ancient history, art, art-AP, biology, calculus, calculus-AP, chemistry, computer programming, computer science-AP, drama, economics, English, English literature, English literature-AP, environmental science, ESL, European history, fine arts, French, geography, geometry, government, journalism, Latin, law, mathematics, medieval/Renaissance history, modern European history-AP, music, music theory, photography, physical science, physics, physics-AP, pre-calculus, religion, SAT/ACT preparation, science, social studies, Spanish, statistics, studio art, theater, TOEFL preparation, trigonometry, U.S. government, U.S. history, U.S. history-AP, Vietnam history, world geography, world history.

Graduation Requirements Arts and fine arts (art, music, dance, drama), computer literacy, English, foreign language, mathematics, physical education (includes health), religion (includes Bible studies and theology), science, social studies (includes history).

Special Academic Programs Advanced Placement exam preparation in 8 subject areas; honors section; independent study; academic accommodation for the gifted; ESL (13 students enrolled).

College Placement 43 students graduated in 2005; all went to college, including Furman University; The University of North Carolina Wilmington; University of Mississippi; Virginia Military Institute; Wofford College.

Student Life Upper grades have specified standards of dress, student council, honor system. Discipline rests equally with students and faculty. Attendance at religious services is required.

Tuition and Aid Day student tuition: $15,800; 5-day tuition and room/board: $30,510; 7-day tuition and room/board: $31,500. Tuition installment plan (The Tuition Plan, Key Tuition Payment Plan, monthly payment plans, 2-payment plan, early payment discount plan). Merit scholarship grants, need-based scholarship grants available. In 2005–06, 30% of upper-school students received aid; total upper-school merit-scholarship money awarded: $165,000. Total amount of financial aid awarded in 2005–06: $640,000.

Admissions Traditional secondary-level entrance grade is 9. For fall 2005, 165 students applied for upper-level admission, 111 were accepted, 74 enrolled. ACT, Iowa Subtests, ISEE, PSAT, SAT, SSAT or Wechsler Intelligence Scale for Children III required. Deadline for receipt of application materials: none. Application fee required: $50. On-campus interview required.

Athletics Interscholastic: baseball, basketball, cross-country running, football, golf, lacrosse, soccer, swimming and diving, tennis, track and field, wrestling; intramural: alpine skiing, back packing, bicycling, billiards, bowling, boxing, canoeing/kayaking,

climbing, fishing, flag football, Frisbee, hiking/backpacking, indoor soccer, kayaking, life saving, martial arts, mountain biking, mountaineering, outdoor activities, outdoor adventure, outdoor education, outdoor recreation, outdoor skills, outdoors, paint ball, racquetball, rappelling, rock climbing, running, skeet shooting, skiing (downhill), strength & conditioning, table tennis, ultimate Frisbee, wallyball, weight lifting, weight training, yoga. 3 coaches, 1 trainer.

Computers Computers are regularly used in all classes. Computer network features include campus e-mail, on-campus library services, CD-ROMs, Internet access, wireless campus network.

Contact Mr. Denis Stokes, Director of Admission. 828-684-6232 Ext. 118. Fax: 828-684-4869. E-mail: dstokes@christschool.org. Web site: www.christschool.org.

See full description on page 734.

CHRYSALIS SCHOOL

14241 North East Woodinville-Duvall Road, PMB 243
Woodinville, Washington 98072
Head of School: Karen Fogle

General Information Coeducational day college-preparatory and general academic school. Grades K–12. Founded: 1983. Setting: suburban. Nearest major city is Seattle. 1 building on campus. Approved or accredited by Northwest Association of Schools and Colleges and Washington Department of Education. Total enrollment: 230. Upper school faculty-student ratio: 1:1.

Upper School Student Profile Grade 9: 40 students (20 boys, 20 girls); Grade 10: 40 students (20 boys, 20 girls); Grade 11: 40 students (20 boys, 20 girls); Grade 12: 40 students (20 boys, 20 girls).

Faculty School total: 35. In upper school: 14 men, 21 women; 10 have advanced degrees.

Subjects Offered Career planning, computer technologies, English, filmmaking, French, geography, German, graphics, history, mathematics, physical education, SAT preparation, science, social science, Spanish.

Graduation Requirements Computer literacy, English, foreign language, history, mathematics, physical education (includes health), science.

Special Academic Programs Honors section; accelerated programs; independent study; study at local college for college credit; academic accommodation for the gifted; remedial reading and/or remedial writing; remedial math; programs in English, mathematics, general development for dyslexic students; special instructional classes for students with learning disabilities.

College Placement 60 students graduated in 2005; 50 went to college, including Bellevue Community College; University of Washington; Washington State University; Western Washington University. Other: 4 went to work, 1 entered military service, 5 had other specific plans.

Student Life Discipline rests primarily with faculty.

Summer Programs Remediation, enrichment, advancement, art/fine arts, computer instruction programs offered; session focuses on continuing advancement; held on campus; accepts boys and girls; open to students from other schools. 75 students usually enrolled. 2006 schedule: July 12 to August 24. Application deadline: none.

Tuition and Aid Day student tuition: $10,650–$55,000. Tuition installment plan (monthly payment plans, individually arranged payment plans).

Admissions Traditional secondary-level entrance grade is 9. For fall 2005, 100 students applied for upper-level admission, 90 were accepted, 80 enrolled. Deadline for receipt of application materials: none. Application fee required: $175. On-campus interview required.

Computers Computers are regularly used in English, foreign language, history, mathematics, science classes. Computer resources include campus e-mail, on-campus library services, CD-ROMs, online commercial services, Internet access, DVD.

Contact Wanda Metcalfe, Student and Financial Services Director. 425-481-2228. Fax: 425-486-8107. E-mail: wanda@chrysalis-school.com. Web site: www.chrysalis-school.com.

CINCINNATI COUNTRY DAY SCHOOL

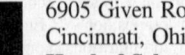

6905 Given Road
Cincinnati, Ohio 45243-2898
Head of School: Dr. Robert Macrae

petersons.com

General Information Coeducational day college-preparatory, arts, and technology school. Grades PK–12. Founded: 1926. Setting: suburban. 62-acre campus. 8 buildings on campus. Approved or accredited by Independent Schools Association of the Central States and Ohio Department of Education. Member of National Association of Independent Schools and Secondary School Admission Test Board. Endowment: $16 million. Total enrollment: 850. Upper school average class size: 13. Upper school faculty-student ratio: 1:9.

Upper School Student Profile Grade 9: 70 students (44 boys, 26 girls); Grade 10: 90 students (52 boys, 38 girls); Grade 11: 82 students (41 boys, 41 girls); Grade 12: 74 students (27 boys, 47 girls).

Faculty School total: 100. In upper school: 25 men, 17 women; 32 have advanced degrees.

Subjects Offered Acting, algebra, American history, American history-AP, American literature, analysis, art, art history, biology, biology-AP, calculus, calculus-AP, ceramics, chemistry, chemistry-AP, choir, computer graphics, computer programming, computer science, CPR, creative writing, dance, drama, earth science, English, English literature, European history, fine arts, French, French language-AP, French literature-AP, genetics, geometry, health, humanities, music, photography, physical education, physics, psychology, public speaking, Spanish, Spanish language-AP, Spanish literature-AP, speech, statistics, theater, trigonometry, world history.

Graduation Requirements Arts and fine arts (art, music, dance, drama), computer science, English, foreign language, health, history, mathematics, science, senior project. Community service is required.

Special Academic Programs Advanced Placement exam preparation in 11 subject areas; honors section; independent study; term-away projects; study abroad.

College Placement 71 students graduated in 2005; all went to college, including DePaul University; Indiana University Bloomington; Miami University; University of Cincinnati; University of Colorado at Boulder; Vanderbilt University. Mean SAT verbal: 600, mean SAT math: 611.

Student Life Upper grades have specified standards of dress, student council, honor system. Discipline rests equally with students and faculty.

Summer Programs Remediation, enrichment, advancement, sports, art/fine arts, computer instruction programs offered; session focuses on camps and academic programs; held on campus; accepts boys and girls; open to students from other schools. 800 students usually enrolled. 2006 schedule: June 1 to August 20. Application deadline: June.

Tuition and Aid Day student tuition: $16,735. Tuition installment plan (Insured Tuition Payment Plan, FACTS Tuition Payment Plan, monthly payment plans). Merit scholarship grants, need-based scholarship grants, Parent Loans available. In 2005–06, 12% of upper-school students received aid; total upper-school merit-scholarship money awarded: $20,000. Total amount of financial aid awarded in 2005–06: $335,120.

Admissions Traditional secondary-level entrance grade is 9. For fall 2005, 64 students applied for upper-level admission, 34 were accepted, 20 enrolled. ISEE, Otis-Lennon Ability or Stanford Achievement Test or SSAT, ERB, PSAT, SAT, PLAN or ACT required. Deadline for receipt of application materials: March 15. Application fee required: $50. Interview recommended.

Athletics Interscholastic: baseball (boys), basketball (b,g), crew (b,g), cross-country running (b,g), football (b), golf (b,g), gymnastics (g), lacrosse (b), softball (g), swimming and diving (b,g), tennis (b,g), track and field (b,g); intramural: dance team (g), lacrosse (g); coed interscholastic: dance squad. 5 PE instructors, 2 trainers.

Computers Computer network features include campus e-mail, on-campus library services, CD-ROMs, online commercial services, Internet access, file transfer, DVD, wireless campus network.

Contact Aaron B. Kellenberger, Director of Admission. 513-979-0220. Fax: 513-527-7614. E-mail: kellenbea@countryday.net. Web site: www.countryday.net.

ANNOUNCEMENT FROM THE SCHOOL From preschool through high school, the Cincinnati Country Day School (CCDS) provides students with opportunities to reach their full potential through a personalized learning experience. CCDS offers coeducational programs for children as young as 18 months of age through grade 12 on a beautiful 62-acre campus in suburban Cincinnati, Ohio. There are numerous activities available for students, including 16 varsity sports, award-winning fine and performing arts, and special interest organizations. Summer programs are also available for students of all ages. The School offers a challenging college-preparatory curriculum that builds a strong foundation in academics, athletics, activities, and the arts. As members of the School community, students are expected to model the virtues of respect, responsibility, integrity, courage, and compassion in their daily lives. The School has become a national leader in integrating technology and education through its commitment to equipping students in grades 5–12 with their own laptop computers. The TabletPC program enhances the classroom learning experience for students and provides a unique atmosphere for learning. With a superior technology program and rich academic curriculum, CCDS provides a *progressive* education in a *traditional* setting. With 100% of the students matriculating to 4-year colleges, each student leaves CCDS with a superior academic preparation, having grown personally in areas of social interaction and self-awareness. Cincinnati Country Day School fulfills its mission by providing superior faculty and staff who build on each student's uniqueness and encourage active participation in a varied curriculum rich in meaning. The School advocates a diverse community as an educational imperative and builds community through opportunities for student leadership, involvement, and personal growth. In superior learning facilities and in a climate conducive to intellectual, social, physical, and artistic development, the School instills a lifelong love of learning.

CISTERCIAN PREPARATORY SCHOOL

3660 Cistercian Road
Irving, Texas 75039
Head of School: Fr. Peter Verhalen

General Information Boys' day college-preparatory, arts, and religious studies school, affiliated with Roman Catholic Church. Grades 5–12. Founded: 1962. Setting: suburban. Nearest major city is Dallas. 62-acre campus. 7 buildings on campus. Approved or accredited by Independent Schools Association of the Southwest and Texas Catholic Conference. Member of National Association of Independent Schools. Endowment: $5.1 million. Total enrollment: 352. Upper school average class size: 22. Upper school faculty-student ratio: 1:9.

Upper School Student Profile Grade 9: 42 students (42 boys); Grade 10: 45 students (45 boys); Grade 11: 43 students (43 boys); Grade 12: 44 students (44 boys). 78% of students are Roman Catholic.

Faculty School total: 42. In upper school: 17 men, 6 women; 20 have advanced degrees.

Subjects Offered Algebra, American history, American literature, anatomy, art, biology, calculus, chemistry, computer science, creative writing, drama, ecology, economics, English, English literature, ethics, European history, expository writing, fine arts, French, geometry, government/civics, health, history, Latin, music, photography, physical education, physics, pre-calculus, religion, science, social studies, Spanish, speech, theology, trigonometry, world history, world literature.

Graduation Requirements Arts and fine arts (art, music, dance, drama), computer science, electives, English, foreign language, mathematics, physical education (includes health), science, senior project, social studies (includes history), theology, completion of an independent senior project during fourth quarter of senior year.

Special Academic Programs Advanced Placement exam preparation in 19 subject areas; independent study; study at local college for college credit.

College Placement 40 students graduated in 2005; all went to college, including Stanford University; Texas A&M University; The University of Texas at Austin; University of Notre Dame; University of San Diego. Median SAT verbal: 710, median SAT math: 710, median composite ACT: 30. 98% scored over 600 on SAT verbal, 95% scored over 600 on SAT math, 95% scored over 26 on composite ACT.

Student Life Upper grades have specified standards of dress, student council. Discipline rests primarily with faculty. Attendance at religious services is required.

Summer Programs Remediation, enrichment, sports, art/fine arts, computer instruction programs offered; session focuses on mathematics and English remediation and enrichment, arts and fine arts, computers, and sports camp; held on campus; accepts boys; open to students from other schools. 125 students usually enrolled. 2006 schedule: June 5 to June 30. Application deadline: none.

Tuition and Aid Day student tuition: $11,500. Tuition installment plan (Tuition Management Systems Plan). Need-based scholarship grants available. In 2005–06, 15% of upper-school students received aid. Total amount of financial aid awarded in 2005–06: $178,650.

Admissions Traditional secondary-level entrance grade is 9. For fall 2005, 20 students applied for upper-level admission, 8 were accepted, 8 enrolled. English language, High School Placement Test, Iowa Tests of Basic Skills, ITBS achievement test, Kuhlmann-Anderson, mathematics proficiency exam or writing sample required. Deadline for receipt of application materials: January 27. Application fee required: $60.

Athletics Interscholastic: baseball, basketball, cross-country running, football, soccer, swimming and diving, tennis, track and field. 6 coaches, 1 trainer.

Computers Computers are regularly used in programming classes. Computer network features include on-campus library services, CD-ROMs, Internet access, online college applications, numerous online databases, reference sources.

Contact Jennifer Kirlin, Registrar. 469-499-5400. Fax: 469-499-5440. E-mail: jkirlin@cistercian.org. Web site: www.cistercian.org.

ANNOUNCEMENT FROM THE SCHOOL At Cistercian, each class, or form, is assigned a Form Master, who accompanies his class from one year to the next. The Form Master is personally responsible for establishing the community within which each student can develop intellectually, emotionally, physically, and spiritually.

COE-BROWN NORTHWOOD ACADEMY

907 First New Hampshire Turnpike
Northwood, New Hampshire 03261
Head of School: Mr. David S. Smith

General Information Coeducational day college-preparatory, general academic, arts, business, vocational, bilingual studies, and technology school. Grades 9–12. Founded: 1867. Setting: rural. Nearest major city is Concord. 5 buildings on campus. Approved or accredited by New England Association of Schools and Colleges and New Hampshire Department of Education. Total enrollment: 681. Upper school average class size: 15. Upper school faculty-student ratio: 1:12.

Upper School Student Profile Grade 9: 191 students (104 boys, 87 girls); Grade 10: 182 students (91 boys, 91 girls); Grade 11: 159 students (77 boys, 82 girls); Grade 12: 149 students (74 boys, 75 girls).

Faculty School total: 65. In upper school: 32 men, 33 women.

Subjects Offered 3-dimensional art, 3-dimensional design, accounting, acting, advanced chemistry, advanced math, Advanced Placement courses, advanced studio art-AP, algebra, American government, American history, American history-AP, American literature, American literature-AP, American studies, analytic geometry, anatomy and physiology, ancient world history, animal science, architecture, art, art appreciation, arts and crafts, auto mechanics, band, Basic programming, biology, British literature, British literature (honors), business law, calculus, calculus-AP, chemistry, child development, chorus, computer applications, computer literacy, computer programming, contemporary problems, drama, drawing and design, earth science, economics, English, English literature-AP, environmental science, family life, film studies, French, freshman seminar, general math, geography, geology, geometry, health, honors algebra, honors English, honors geometry, honors U.S. history, horticulture, intro to computers, music theory, parent/child development, physical education, physics, piano, pre-algebra, psychology, senior project, Spanish, world history, zoology.

Graduation Requirements Algebra, art, biology, civics, economics, English, geometry, intro to computers, physical education (includes health), physical science, U.S. history, world cultures, senior portfolio project.

Special Academic Programs Advanced Placement exam preparation in 4 subject areas; honors section; independent study; remedial reading and/or remedial writing; remedial math; special instructional classes for deaf students, blind students.

College Placement 165 students graduated in 2005; 134 went to college, including Keene State College; Plymouth State University; University of New Hampshire. Other: 28 went to work, 3 entered military service. Mean SAT verbal: 526, mean SAT math: 531.

Student Life Upper grades have specified standards of dress, student council. Discipline rests primarily with faculty.

Summer Programs Remediation programs offered; session focuses on remediation; held on campus; accepts boys and girls; open to students from other schools. 20 students usually enrolled. 2006 schedule: June to August. Application deadline: June.

Tuition and Aid Day student tuition: $9500.

Admissions Traditional secondary-level entrance grade is 9. For fall 2005, 201 students applied for upper-level admission, 187 were accepted, 185 enrolled. Deadline for receipt of application materials: January 27. No application fee required.

Athletics Interscholastic: baseball (boys), basketball (b,g), cheering (g), cross-country running (b,g), soccer (b,g), softball (g), tennis (b,g), track and field (b,g), volleyball (g); coed interscholastic: golf, skiing (downhill). 2 PE instructors, 22 coaches.

Computers Computers are regularly used in accounting, architecture, art, basic skills, business, career exploration, economics, English, foreign language, journalism, keyboarding, library, literary magazine, photography, science, vocational-technical courses, Web site design, yearbook classes. Computer resources include on-campus library services, CD-ROMs, online commercial services, Internet access.

Contact Mrs. Cheri Wolf, Guidance Secretary. 603-942-5531. Fax: 603-942-7537. E-mail: cwolf@coebrownacademy.com.

COLEGIO BOLIVAR

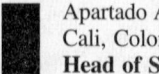

Apartado Aereo 26300
Cali, Colombia
Head of School: Mr. Joseph Nagy

General Information Coeducational day college-preparatory, bilingual studies, and technology school. Grades PK–12. Founded: 1947. Setting: suburban. 13-hectare campus. 7 buildings on campus. Approved or accredited by Association of American Schools in South America, Colombian Ministry of Education, and Southern Association of Colleges and Schools. Languages of instruction: English and Spanish. Total enrollment: 1,261. Upper school average class size: 17. Upper school faculty-student ratio: 1:10.

Upper School Student Profile Grade 9: 79 students (47 boys, 32 girls); Grade 10: 75 students (41 boys, 34 girls); Grade 11: 71 students (34 boys, 37 girls); Grade 12: 61 students (32 boys, 29 girls).

Faculty School total: 154. In upper school: 20 men, 22 women; 13 have advanced degrees.

Subjects Offered Advanced chemistry, Advanced Placement courses, algebra, American history, American literature, art, art history, biology, business, calculus, chemistry, computer science, dance, drama, English, English literature, environmental science, ESL, ethics, French, geology, government/civics, graphic design, history, journalism, mathematics, music, philosophy, photography, physical education, physics, programming, psychology, religion, robotics, social studies, Spanish, theater, trigonometry, world literature.

Graduation Requirements Algebra, American history, American literature, art, biology, calculus, chemistry, computer education, economics, electives, geography, geometry, history of the Americas, music, physical education (includes health), physics, political science, pre-calculus, senior project, Spanish, Spanish literature, trigonometry, world history, world literature, writing, social service hours.

Special Academic Programs Advanced Placement exam preparation in 5 subject areas; independent study; academic accommodation for the gifted; remedial reading and/or remedial writing; ESL.

College Placement 63 students graduated in 2005; 61 went to college, including Brandeis University; College of Charleston; Dalhousie University; Indiana University Bloomington; University of Virginia; Vassar College. Other: 2 had other specific plans. Mean SAT verbal: 509, mean SAT math: 538. 5% scored over 600 on SAT verbal, 7% scored over 600 on SAT math.

Student Life Upper grades have specified standards of dress, student council, honor system. Discipline rests equally with students and faculty.

Tuition and Aid Day student tuition: 13,797,376 Colombian pesos–14,853,123 Colombian pesos. Tuition installment plan (monthly payment plans, annual payment plan). Need-based scholarship grants available. In 2005–06, 7% of upper-school students received aid.

Admissions Traditional secondary-level entrance grade is 9. For fall 2005, 1 student applied for upper-level admission, 1 was accepted, 1 enrolled. School's own exam required. Deadline for receipt of application materials: none. Application fee required: 75,000 Colombian pesos. On-campus interview required.

Athletics Interscholastic: aerobics (girls), aerobics/dance (g), baseball (b), basketball (b,g), dance (g), equestrian sports (b,g), gymnastics (b,g), horseback riding (b,g), running (b,g), soccer (b,g), swimming and diving (b,g), track and field (b,g), volleyball (b,g); intramural: gymnastics (b,g), soccer (b,g), softball (b), swimming and diving (b,g), track and field (b,g), volleyball (b,g). 6 PE instructors, 20 coaches.

Computers Computers are regularly used in graphic design, photography, Web site design, yearbook classes. Computer network features include on-campus library services, CD-ROMs, online commercial services, Internet access, office computer access.

Contact Mrs. Patricia Nasser, Admissions Assistant. 57-2-555-2039 Ext. 274. Fax: 57-2-555-2041. E-mail: pnasser@colegiobolivar.edu.co. Web site: www.colegiobolivar.edu.co.

COLEGIO FRANKLIN D. ROOSEVELT

Av. Las Palmeras 325, Urbanizacion Camacho La Molina
Lima 12, Peru
Head of School: Dr. Carol Kluznik

General Information Coeducational day college-preparatory, general academic, arts, and technology school. Grades N–12. Founded: 1946. Setting: suburban. Nearest major city is Lima. 23-acre campus. 4 buildings on campus. Approved or accredited by Southern Association of Colleges and Schools. Languages of instruction: English and Spanish. Total enrollment: 1,265. Upper school average class size: 20. Upper school faculty-student ratio: 1:11.

Upper School Student Profile Grade 9: 87 students (42 boys, 45 girls); Grade 10: 84 students (56 boys, 28 girls); Grade 11: 104 students (58 boys, 46 girls); Grade 12: 103 students (59 boys, 44 girls).

Faculty School total: 166. In upper school: 20 men, 26 women; 24 have advanced degrees.

Subjects Offered Advanced Placement courses, algebra, American history, American literature, art, biology, calculus, chemistry, computer programming, computer science, debate, digital photography, drama, drama performance, early childhood, earth science, economics, English, English literature, ESL, fine arts, French, French as a second language, geography, geometry, global issues, health, history, journalism, keyboarding, mathematics, model United Nations, music, orchestra, photography, physical education, physical science, physics, psychology, science, social studies, Spanish, theater, theory of knowledge, trigonometry, U.S. history, world history, yearbook.

Graduation Requirements Arts and fine arts (art, music, dance, drama), English, foreign language, information technology, mathematics, physical education (includes health), science, social studies (includes history).

Special Academic Programs International Baccalaureate program; honors section; academic accommodation for the gifted, the musically talented, and the artistically talented; remedial reading and/or remedial writing; special instructional classes for students with mild learning disabilities; ESL (10 students enrolled).

College Placement 82 students graduated in 2005; 74 went to college, including Indiana University Bloomington; Michigan State University; Mount Holyoke College; University of Virginia; Yale University. Other: 8 had other specific plans. Median SAT verbal: 511, median SAT math: 539, median composite ACT: 25. 21% scored over 600 on SAT verbal, 40% scored over 600 on SAT math, 37% scored over 26 on composite ACT.

Student Life Upper grades have uniform requirement, student council, honor system. Discipline rests primarily with faculty.

Tuition and Aid Day student tuition: $7800–$8850. Tuition installment plan (monthly payment plans). Need-based scholarship grants available. In 2005–06, 2% of upper-school students received aid. Total amount of financial aid awarded in 2005–06: $8840.

Admissions Traditional secondary-level entrance grade is 11. For fall 2005, 29 students applied for upper-level admission, 29 were accepted, 29 enrolled. SAT or Stanford Achievement Test, Otis-Lennon School Ability Test required. Deadline for receipt of application materials: none. Application fee required: $200. On-campus interview required.

Athletics Interscholastic: aquatics (boys, girls), baseball (b), basketball (b,g), field hockey (b,g), in-line hockey (b), roller hockey (b), rugby (b), soccer (b,g), softball (b,g), swimming and diving (b,g), tennis (b,g), track and field (b,g), volleyball (b,g);

intramural: basketball (b,g), flag football (b,g), indoor soccer (b,g), rugby (b), soccer (b,g), volleyball (b,g); coed intramural: aerobics, aerobics/nautilus, archery, back packing, badminton, ball hockey, basketball, bowling, cheering, climbing, cooperative games, fitness, flag football, floor hockey, golf, hiking/backpacking, in-line hockey, in-line skating, independent competitive sports, indoor soccer, jogging, jump rope, kickball, lacrosse, martial arts, outdoor activities, outdoor adventure, outdoor education, outdoor recreation, outdoor skills, outdoors, roller blading, roller hockey, surfing, volleyball, wall climbing, yoga. 3 PE instructors, 20 coaches.

Computers Computers are regularly used in art, English, history, mathematics, music, photography, science classes. Computer network features include campus e-mail, on-campus library services, CD-ROMs, online commercial services, Internet access, office computer access, DVD.

Contact Nora Marquez, Director of Admissions. 51-1-435-0890 Ext. 4008. Fax: 51-1-436-0927. E-mail: nmarquez@amersol.edu.pe. Web site: www.amersol.edu.pe.

COLEGIO NUEVA GRANADA

Carrera 2E #70-20
Bogota, Colombia
Head of School: Barry L. McCombs

General Information Coeducational day college-preparatory and Colombian Bachillerato school. Grades PK–12. Founded: 1938. Setting: urban. 17-acre campus. 2 buildings on campus. Approved or accredited by Southern Association of Colleges and Schools. Languages of instruction: English and Spanish. Total enrollment: 1,680. Upper school average class size: 20. Upper school faculty-student ratio: 1:20.

Upper School Student Profile Grade 9: 93 students (45 boys, 48 girls); Grade 10: 95 students (48 boys, 47 girls); Grade 11: 66 students (34 boys, 32 girls); Grade 12: 167 students (88 boys, 79 girls).

Faculty School total: 219. In upper school: 20 men, 27 women; 13 have advanced degrees.

Subjects Offered Algebra, American history, American literature, anatomy, art, art history, biology, botany, calculus, ceramics, chemistry, computer science, creative writing, drama, earth science, ecology, English, English literature, environmental science, ethics, European history, fine arts, French, geography, geometry, government/civics, health, history, journalism, mathematics, music, philosophy, physical education, physics, psychology, religion, science, social science, social studies, sociology, Spanish, speech, theater, trigonometry, world history, writing.

Graduation Requirements Arts and fine arts (art, music, dance, drama), computer science, electives, English, foreign language, mathematics, physical education (includes health), science, social science, social studies (includes history), senior independent project, Colombian High School for those students who choose it.

Special Academic Programs Advanced Placement exam preparation in 15 subject areas; honors section; independent study; academic accommodation for the gifted; programs in English, mathematics, general development for dyslexic students; special instructional classes for students with learning disabilities, students with emotional and behavioral problems, Attention Deficit Disorder; ESL (20 students enrolled).

College Placement 92 students graduated in 2005; 90 went to college, including Boston University; Columbia International University; McGill University; Tufts University; University of Notre Dame; University of Virginia. Other: 2 entered military service. Mean SAT verbal: 517, mean SAT math: 534.

Student Life Upper grades have uniform requirement, student council, honor system. Discipline rests equally with students and faculty.

Tuition and Aid Tuition installment plan (5-installment plan). Need-based scholarship grants available. In 2005–06, 13% of upper-school students received aid. Total amount of financial aid awarded in 2005–06: 74,331,400 Colombian pesos.

Admissions Traditional secondary-level entrance grade is 9. Admissions testing required. Deadline for receipt of application materials: none. No application fee required. On-campus interview required.

Athletics Interscholastic: baseball (boys), basketball (b,g), gymnastics (g), roller hockey (b), soccer (b,g), table tennis (b,g), track and field (b,g), volleyball (b,g); intramural: basketball (b,g), cheering (g), gymnastics (g), mountain biking (b), soccer (b,g), weight lifting (b); coed intramural: track and field, volleyball. 6 PE instructors, 6 coaches.

Computers Computers are regularly used in desktop publishing, introduction to technology, mathematics, science, technology classes. Computer network features include campus e-mail, on-campus library services, CD-ROMs, Internet access, file transfer, office computer access, Blackboard.

Contact Katherine Ancizar, Director of Admissions. 57-1-321-1147. Fax: 57-1-211-3720. E-mail: kancizar@cng.edu. Web site: www.cng.edu.

COLEGIO PUERTORRIQUENO DE NINAS

Turquesa Street, Golden Gate
Guaynabo, Puerto Rico 00968
Head of School: Miss Ivette Nater

General Information Girls' day college-preparatory, arts, bilingual studies, and technology school. Grades PK–12. Founded: 1924. Setting: urban. Nearest major city is San Juan. 1 building on campus. Approved or accredited by Middle States

Association of Colleges and Schools, The College Board, and Puerto Rico Department of Education. Language of instruction: Spanish. Total enrollment: 599. Upper school average class size: 25.

Upper School Student Profile Grade 9: 40 students (40 girls); Grade 10: 44 students (44 girls); Grade 11: 44 students (44 girls); Grade 12: 43 students (43 girls).

Faculty School total: 53. In upper school: 3 men, 20 women; 3 have advanced degrees.

Subjects Offered Algebra, American history, American literature, art, art history, biology, calculus, ceramics, chemistry, computer programming, drama, ecology, English, English literature, French, geometry, grammar, health, history, home economics, mathematics, music, physical education, physics, science, social studies, Spanish, theater, typing, world history.

Graduation Requirements Computers, English, mathematics, science, social studies (includes history).

Special Academic Programs Honors section; ESL.

College Placement 38 students graduated in 2005; all went to college, including American University; Boston College; Georgetown University; Saint Joseph's University; Tufts University.

Student Life Upper grades have uniform requirement, student council, honor system. Discipline rests equally with students and faculty.

Tuition and Aid Day student tuition: $3650. Tuition installment plan (monthly payment plans, individually arranged payment plans). Merit scholarship grants, need-based scholarship grants available. Total upper-school merit-scholarship money awarded for 2005–06: $24,150. Total amount of financial aid awarded in 2005–06: $46,550.

Admissions Traditional secondary-level entrance grade is 9. For fall 2005, 19 students applied for upper-level admission, 10 were accepted, 9 enrolled. Learn Aid Aptitude Test required. Deadline for receipt of application materials: August 7. Application fee required: $30. On-campus interview required.

Athletics Interscholastic: basketball, bowling, cross-country running, paddle tennis, soccer, softball, swimming and diving, table tennis, tennis, track and field, volleyball; intramural: basketball, bowling, cross-country running, jump rope, kickball, paddle tennis, soccer, track and field, volleyball. 2 PE instructors, 4 coaches, 1 trainer.

Computers Computers are regularly used in basic skills, lab/keyboard classes. Computer resources include on-campus library services, CD-ROMs, Internet access, ExPAN, Encarta.

Contact Ritín Santaella, Registrar. 787-782-2618. Fax: 787-782-8370. Web site: www.cpnpr.org/.

COLEGIO SAN JOSE

PO Box 21300
San Juan, Puerto Rico 00928-1300
Head of School: Br. Francisco T. Gonzalez, DMD

General Information Boys' day college-preparatory, arts, business, religious studies, technology, and science, anatomy and marine biology school, affiliated with Roman Catholic Church. Grades 7–12. Founded: 1938. Setting: urban. 6-acre campus. 1 building on campus. Approved or accredited by Middle States Association of Colleges and Schools, National Catholic Education Association, The College Board, and Puerto Rico Department of Education. Language of instruction: Spanish. Endowment: $1.6 million. Total enrollment: 502. Upper school average class size: 25.

Upper School Student Profile Grade 10: 71 students (71 boys); Grade 11: 74 students (74 boys); Grade 12: 89 students (89 boys). 99% of students are Roman Catholic.

Faculty School total: 44. In upper school: 25 men, 19 women; 19 have advanced degrees.

Subjects Offered Accounting, algebra, American history, American literature, anatomy, art, art history, biology, biology-AP, broadcasting, business skills, calculus, chemistry, choir, Christian ethics, computer science, ecology, English, English literature, ethics, European history, French, French as a second language, geography, geometry, government/civics, grammar, health, history, instrumental music, keyboarding, marine biology, mathematics, music, physical education, physics, pre-calculus, psychology, religion, science, social studies, Spanish, world history.

Graduation Requirements Business skills (includes word processing), computer science, English, foreign language, mathematics, physical education (includes health), religion (includes Bible studies and theology), science, social studies (includes history), 40 hours of Christian community service.

Special Academic Programs Advanced Placement exam preparation in 5 subject areas; honors section.

College Placement 76 students graduated in 2005; all went to college, including University of Dayton; University of Puerto Rico, Mayagüez Campus; University of Puerto Rico, Río Piedras.

Student Life Upper grades have uniform requirement, student council, honor system. Discipline rests equally with students and faculty. Attendance at religious services is required.

Summer Programs Remediation, computer instruction programs offered; session focuses on remediation/make-up; held on campus; accepts boys and girls; open to students from other schools. 200 students usually enrolled. 2006 schedule: June 1 to June 30. Application deadline: June 5.

Colegio San Jose

Tuition and Aid Tuition installment plan (The Tuition Plan, individually arranged payment plans). Need-based scholarship grants available. In 2005–06, 13% of upper-school students received aid. Total amount of financial aid awarded in 2005–06: $200,000.

Admissions Traditional secondary-level entrance grade is 10. For fall 2005, 274 students applied for upper-level admission, 142 were accepted, 102 enrolled. Admissions testing, any standardized test and Catholic High School Entrance Examination required. Deadline for receipt of application materials: February 1. Application fee required: $10. On-campus interview required.

Athletics Interscholastic: baseball, basketball, bowling, cross-country running, fitness, golf, indoor soccer, physical fitness, soccer, swimming and diving, tennis, track and field, volleyball; intramural: cross-country running, indoor soccer, soccer, swimming and diving, tennis, track and field, volleyball. 3 PE instructors, 4 coaches, 1 trainer.

Computers Computers are regularly used in accounting, art, data processing, English, foreign language, mathematics, music, psychology, science, Spanish, yearbook classes. Computer resources include campus e-mail, on-campus library services, CD-ROMs, Internet access, DVD, wireless campus network.

Contact Mrs. María E. Guzmán, Guidance—Advisor. 787-751-8177 Ext. 229. Fax: 787-767-1746. E-mail: sanjose.mail@csj-pr.org. Web site: www.csj-pr.org.

COLLEGE DU LEMAN INTERNATIONAL SCHOOL

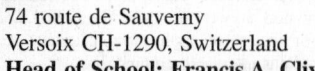

74 route de Sauverny
Versoix CH-1290, Switzerland
Head of School: Francis A. Clivaz

petersons.com

General Information Coeducational boarding and day college-preparatory, arts, business, and bilingual studies school. Boarding grades 5–13, day grades K–13. Founded: 1960. Setting: rural. Nearest major city is Geneva. Students are housed in single-sex dormitories. 18-acre campus. 14 buildings on campus. Approved or accredited by European Council of International Schools and New England Association of Schools and Colleges. Languages of instruction: English and French. Total enrollment: 1,754. Upper school average class size: 18. Upper school faculty-student ratio: 1:7.

Upper School Student Profile 30% of students are boarding students. 80% are international students. International students from China, France, Japan, Russian Federation, United Kingdom, and United States; 99 other countries represented in student body.

Faculty School total: 219. In upper school: 66 men, 40 women; 45 have advanced degrees; 17 reside on campus.

Subjects Offered Accounting, advanced chemistry, advanced computer applications, advanced math, Advanced Placement courses, American history, American history-AP, American literature-AP, analysis and differential calculus, analytic geometry, ancient history, Arabic, art, art education, art-AP, athletics, audio visual/media, baseball, basketball, biology-AP, British literature, business studies, calculus, calculus-AP, career/college preparation, chemistry, chemistry-AP, choir, college counseling, communication arts, computer applications, drama, earth science, economics-AP, English as a foreign language, English composition, English literature-AP, environmental science, ESL, European history, European history-AP, French, French language-AP, French literature-AP, geography, German, German-AP, health, health education, history, human biology, instrumental music, integrated mathematics, International Baccalaureate courses, international relations, languages, macro/microeconomics-AP, mechanics, model United Nations, music, orchestra, philosophy, photography, physical education, physics, physics-AP, piano, pre-calculus, probability and statistics, psychology, religion and culture, SAT preparation, science, sociology, softball, Spanish, Spanish language-AP, Spanish literature, Spanish literature-AP, tennis, volleyball, weight training, world cultures, yearbook.

Graduation Requirements English, foreign language, mathematics, physical education (includes health), science, social studies (includes history).

Special Academic Programs International Baccalaureate program; Advanced Placement exam preparation in 15 subject areas; honors section; academic accommodation for the gifted, the musically talented, and the artistically talented; remedial reading and/or remedial writing; programs in English for dyslexic students; special instructional classes for students with special needs; ESL.

College Placement 117 students graduated in 2005; 87 went to college, including London School of Economics and Political Science; Queen's University at Kingston; Stanford University; Tufts University; University of Cambridge; Yale University. Other: 30 had other specific plans.

Student Life Upper grades have specified standards of dress, student council, honor system. Discipline rests primarily with faculty.

Summer Programs Advancement, ESL, sports, art/fine arts, computer instruction programs offered; session focuses on language study (French and English), sports, excursions; held on campus; accepts boys and girls; open to students from other schools. 250 students usually enrolled. 2006 schedule: June 25 to August 6. Application deadline: none.

Tuition and Aid Day student tuition: 20,600 Swiss francs–21,800 Swiss francs; 7-day tuition and room/board: 50,000 Swiss francs–52,000 Swiss francs. Tuition installment plan (monthly payment plans, individually arranged payment plans). Assistance consideration on an individual basis available.

Admissions Traditional secondary-level entrance grade is 9. For fall 2005, 560 students applied for upper-level admission, 491 were accepted, 491 enrolled. Any standardized test, English entrance exam and mathematics proficiency exam required. Deadline for receipt of application materials: none. Application fee required: 250 Swiss francs. Interview recommended.

Athletics Interscholastic: alpine skiing (boys, girls), badminton (b,g), basketball (b,g), cross-country running (b,g), floor hockey (b,g), golf (b,g), indoor hockey (b,g), indoor soccer (b,g), rugby (b), skiing (downhill) (b,g), snowboarding (b,g), soccer (b,g), swimming and diving (b,g), tennis (b,g), track and field (b,g), volleyball (b,g); intramural: aerobics (g), alpine skiing (b,g), badminton (b,g), baseball (b), basketball (b,g), cricket (b), cross-country running (b,g), dance squad (g), floor hockey (b,g), Frisbee (b,g), gymnastics (g), indoor hockey (b,g), indoor soccer (b,g), physical training (b,g), rugby (b), skiing (downhill) (b,g), snowboarding (b,g), soccer (b,g), softball (b,g), swimming and diving (b,g), table tennis (b,g), team handball (b,g), tennis (b,g), touch football (b), track and field (b,g), ultimate Frisbee (b,g), volleyball (b,g), walking (g), weight training (b); coed interscholastic: archery, baseball, indoor track & field, scooter football; coed intramural: aerobics, aerobics/dance, archery, bicycling, bowling, fitness, Frisbee, golf, horseback riding, jogging, judo, martial arts, physical fitness, physical training, running, softball, ultimate Frisbee, yoga. 8 PE instructors.

Computers Computers are regularly used in English, ESL, foreign language, mathematics, science classes. Computer network features include campus e-mail, on-campus library services, CD-ROMs, online commercial services, Internet access, file transfer, DVD.

Contact Francis A. Clivaz, Director General. 41-22-775-5555. Fax: 41-22-775-5559. E-mail: info@cdl.ch. Web site: www.cdl.ch.

See full description on page 736.

THE COLLEGE PREPARATORY SCHOOL

6100 Broadway
Oakland, California 94618
Head of School: Murray Cohen

General Information Coeducational day college-preparatory school. Grades 9–12. Founded: 1960. Setting: urban. Nearest major city is San Francisco. 6-acre campus. 14 buildings on campus. Approved or accredited by California Association of Independent Schools, Western Association of Schools and Colleges, and California Department of Education. Member of National Association of Independent Schools. Endowment: $8.3 million. Total enrollment: 329. Upper school average class size: 14. Upper school faculty-student ratio: 1:8.

Upper School Student Profile Grade 9: 82 students (38 boys, 44 girls); Grade 10: 83 students (40 boys, 43 girls); Grade 11: 86 students (39 boys, 47 girls); Grade 12: 78 students (39 boys, 39 girls).

Faculty School total: 49. In upper school: 20 men, 29 women; 35 have advanced degrees.

Subjects Offered 3-dimensional art, acting, advanced math, algebra, American government, American history, American literature, animal behavior, art, art-AP, astronomy, biology, biology-AP, British literature, calculus, calculus-AP, chemistry, chemistry-AP, chorus, comparative religion, computer art, computer science, contemporary issues in science, creative writing, dance, dance performance, debate, drama, drawing and design, economics, English, English literature, European history, expository writing, fine arts, French, freshman foundations, genetics, geometry, health and wellness, health education, independent study, Japanese, jazz band, junior and senior seminars, Latin, mathematics, modern Chinese history, music, music theory-AP, orchestra, photography, physical education, physics, poetry, psychology, publications, science, Shakespeare, Spanish, stagecraft, statistics-AP, studio art, studio art-AP, theater design and production, trigonometry, U.S. government, vocal ensemble, vocal jazz, Western civilization, world civilizations, yearbook.

Graduation Requirements Arts and fine arts (art, music, dance, drama), English, foreign language, freshman foundations, history, mathematics, physical education (includes health), science, sophomore health, Intraterm Program.

Special Academic Programs Advanced Placement exam preparation in 11 subject areas; honors section; independent study; study at local college for college credit; academic accommodation for the gifted, the musically talented, and the artistically talented.

College Placement 82 students graduated in 2005; 81 went to college, including Harvard University; Pomona College; Princeton University; Stanford University; Swarthmore College; University of California, Davis. Mean SAT verbal: 724, mean SAT math: 713.

Student Life Upper grades have student council. Discipline rests equally with students and faculty.

Summer Programs Held on campus; accepts boys and girls; not open to students from other schools. 20 students usually enrolled.

Tuition and Aid Day student tuition: $23,275. Tuition installment plan (Insured Tuition Payment Plan, monthly payment plans, individually arranged payment plans).

Need-based scholarship grants, need-based loans available. In 2005–06, 23% of upper-school students received aid. Total amount of financial aid awarded in 2005–06: $1,165,690.

Admissions Traditional secondary-level entrance grade is 9. For fall 2005, 369 students applied for upper-level admission, 128 were accepted, 87 enrolled. Essay and ISEE required. Deadline for receipt of application materials: January 10. Application fee required: $75. On-campus interview required.

Athletics Interscholastic: basketball (boys, girls), cross-country running (b,g), soccer (b,g), softball (g), swimming and diving (b,g), tennis (b,g), track and field (b,g), volleyball (b,g); intramural: basketball (b,g); coed interscholastic: golf; coed intramural: cross-country running, dance, Frisbee, soccer, ultimate Frisbee, volleyball. 4 PE instructors, 11 coaches.

Computers Computers are regularly used in art, drawing and design, freshman foundations, mathematics, music, newspaper, science, theater arts, yearbook classes. Computer network features include campus e-mail, on-campus library services, CD-ROMs, online commercial services, Internet access, file transfer, office computer access, DVD, wireless campus network, remote access to library services, Web publishing, remote file-server access, video recording and editing.

Contact Jonathan Zucker, Assistant Director of Admissions & Financial Aid. 510-652-4364. Fax: 510-652-7467. E-mail: jonathan_zucker@college-prep.org. Web site: www.college-prep.org.

THE COLLEGIATE SCHOOL

North Mooreland Road
Richmond, Virginia 23229
Head of School: Keith A. Evans

General Information Coeducational day college-preparatory, arts, and technology school. Grades K–12. Founded: 1915. Setting: suburban. 115-acre campus. 13 buildings on campus. Approved or accredited by Southern Association of Colleges and Schools, Virginia Association of Independent Schools, and Virginia Department of Education. Member of National Association of Independent Schools and Secondary School Admission Test Board. Endowment: $34.7 million. Total enrollment: 1,548. Upper school average class size: 15. Upper school faculty-student ratio: 1:15.

Upper School Student Profile Grade 9: 119 students (59 boys, 60 girls); Grade 10: 127 students (59 boys, 68 girls); Grade 11: 125 students (61 boys, 64 girls); Grade 12: 119 students (53 boys, 66 girls).

Faculty School total: 184. In upper school: 31 men, 33 women; 56 have advanced degrees.

Subjects Offered Acting, African-American literature, algebra, American history, American history-AP, American literature, art, biology, biology-AP, calculus-AP, ceramics, chemistry, chemistry-AP, community service, computer applications, creative writing, drama, driver education, earth science, economics, economics-AP, English, English literature, ethics, European history, fine arts, French, French-AP, geometry, government/civics, health, journalism, Latin, music, photography, physics, religion, robotics, Spanish, Spanish language-AP, statistics, theater, trigonometry, world history.

Graduation Requirements Arts and fine arts (art, music, dance, drama), English, ethics, foreign language, government, history, mathematics, religion (includes Bible studies and theology), science, sports, senior speech. Community service is required.

Special Academic Programs Advanced Placement exam preparation in 11 subject areas; honors section; independent study; study at local college for college credit; programs in general development for dyslexic students.

College Placement 108 students graduated in 2005; all went to college, including James Madison University; The College of William and Mary; University of Georgia; University of Virginia; Virginia Polytechnic Institute and State University; Wake Forest University. Mean SAT verbal: 632, mean SAT math: 662.

Student Life Upper grades have specified standards of dress, student council, honor system. Discipline rests equally with students and faculty.

Summer Programs Remediation, enrichment, advancement, sports, art/fine arts, computer instruction programs offered; session focuses on advancement, remediation, sports; held on campus; accepts boys and girls; open to students from other schools. 1300 students usually enrolled. 2006 schedule: June 12 to August 4. Application deadline: none.

Tuition and Aid Day student tuition: $15,680. Tuition installment plan (Insured Tuition Payment Plan, monthly payment plans). Need-based scholarship grants available. In 2005–06, 11% of upper-school students received aid. Total amount of financial aid awarded in 2005–06: $571,945.

Admissions Traditional secondary-level entrance grade is 9. For fall 2005, 71 students applied for upper-level admission, 33 were accepted, 22 enrolled. PSAT and SAT for applicants to grade 11 and 12 or SSAT required. Deadline for receipt of application materials: none. Application fee required: $50. Interview required.

Athletics Interscholastic: baseball (boys), basketball (b,g), cross-country running (b,g), diving (b,g), field hockey (g), football (b), indoor track (b,g), indoor track & field (b,g), lacrosse (b,g), soccer (b,g), softball (g), swimming and diving (b,g), tennis (b,g), track and field (b,g), volleyball (g), winter (indoor) track (b,g), wrestling (b); coed interscholastic: golf, indoor soccer; coed intramural: combined training, dance, dance squad, dance team, fitness, modern dance. 3 PE instructors, 31 coaches, 2 trainers.

Computers Computers are regularly used in art, English, foreign language, history, mathematics, science classes. Computer network features include campus e-mail, on-campus library services, CD-ROMs, Internet access, file transfer, office computer access, DVD, wireless campus network.

Contact Amanda L. Surgner, Director of Admission. 804-741-9722. Fax: 804-741-5472. E-mail: asurgner@collegiate-va.org. Web site: www.collegiate-va.org/.

COLORADO ACADEMY

3800 South Pierce Street
Denver, Colorado 80235

ANNOUNCEMENT FROM THE SCHOOL Colorado Academy aspires to fulfill the ideals of the liberal arts tradition in every discipline and with every child. A century of experience has shown that the best way to help students achieve excellence is to provide them with an environment where learning comes alive: in the classroom, on stage, on the playing field, and in service to others.

THE COLORADO ROCKY MOUNTAIN SCHOOL

1493 County Road 106
Carbondale, Colorado 81623
Head of School: Jeff Leahy

General Information Coeducational boarding and day college-preparatory and arts school. Grades 9–12. Founded: 1953. Setting: small town. Nearest major city is Denver. Students are housed in single-sex dormitories. 350-acre campus. 23 buildings on campus. Approved or accredited by Association for Experiential Education, Association of Colorado Independent Schools, The Association of Boarding Schools, and Colorado Department of Education. Member of National Association of Independent Schools and Secondary School Admission Test Board. Endowment: $13.8 million. Total enrollment: 167. Upper school average class size: 10. Upper school faculty-student ratio: 1:5.

Upper School Student Profile Grade 9: 42 students (27 boys, 15 girls); Grade 10: 30 students (15 boys, 15 girls); Grade 11: 41 students (24 boys, 17 girls); Grade 12: 54 students (24 boys, 30 girls). 60% of students are boarding students. 62% are state residents. 19 states are represented in upper school student body. 16% are international students. International students from Australia, Democratic People's Republic of Korea, Germany, India, Japan, and Venezuela; 3 other countries represented in student body.

Faculty School total: 35. In upper school: 21 men, 14 women; 19 have advanced degrees; 33 reside on campus.

Subjects Offered Advanced Placement courses, algebra, American literature, anthropology, art, art history, biology, botany, calculus, ceramics, chemistry, computer programming, computer science, creative writing, drama, earth science, ecology, English, English literature, environmental science, ESL, ethics, European history, expository writing, fine arts, French, gardening, geography, geology, geometry, geopolitics, government/civics, grammar, guitar, history, history of ideas, journalism, mathematics, music, philosophy, photography, physical education, physics, physiology, religion, science, Shakespeare, social studies, Spanish, theater, trigonometry, Western civilization, world history, world literature, writing.

Graduation Requirements Arts and fine arts (art, music, dance, drama), chemistry, English, foreign language, mathematics, science, senior project, social studies (includes history), participation in outdoor program. Community service is required.

Special Academic Programs Advanced Placement exam preparation in 8 subject areas; academic accommodation for the gifted, the musically talented, and the artistically talented; ESL (10 students enrolled).

College Placement 38 students graduated in 2005; all went to college, including Bates College; Dartmouth College; Lewis & Clark College; Middlebury College; The Colorado College; University of Vermont. Mean SAT verbal: 545, mean SAT math: 529, mean composite ACT: 22. 28% scored over 600 on SAT verbal, 23% scored over 600 on SAT math.

Student Life Upper grades have student council, honor system. Discipline rests equally with students and faculty.

Tuition and Aid Day student tuition: $19,200; 7-day tuition and room/board: $31,600. Tuition installment plan (Key Tuition Payment Plan, monthly payment plans, individually arranged payment plans). Merit scholarship grants, need-based scholarship grants, middle-income loans available. In 2005–06, 38% of upper-school students received aid; total upper-school merit-scholarship money awarded: $14,000. Total amount of financial aid awarded in 2005–06: $75,500.

Admissions Traditional secondary-level entrance grade is 9. For fall 2005, 150 students applied for upper-level admission, 117 were accepted, 70 enrolled. SLEP, SLEP for foreign students, SSAT, TOEFL or TOEFL or SLEP required. Deadline for receipt of application materials: February 1. Application fee required: $50. Interview required.

Athletics Intramural: aerobics/dance (girls), basketball (b,g), climbing (b,g), dance (b,g), fly fishing (b,g), freestyle skiing (b,g), kayaking (b,g); coed interscholastic:

alpine skiing, bicycling, canoeing/kayaking, climbing, cross-country running, independent competitive sports, kayaking, nordic skiing; coed intramural: alpine skiing, back packing, basketball, bicycling, canoeing/kayaking, climbing, dance, equestrian sports, fishing, fitness, floor hockey, fly fishing, freestyle skiing, Frisbee, hiking/backpacking, horseshoes, jogging, kayaking, martial arts, mountain biking, mountaineering, nordic skiing, outdoor adventure, outdoor education, outdoor recreation, outdoor skills, outdoors. 4 coaches.

Computers Computers are regularly used in art, college planning, ESL, mathematics, science classes. Computer network features include campus e-mail, on-campus library services, CD-ROMs, online commercial services, Internet access, office computer access, DVD, wireless campus network.

Contact Heather Weymouth, Associate Director of Admission. 970-963-2562. Fax: 970-963-9865. E-mail: hweymouth@crms.org. Web site: www.crms.org.

ANNOUNCEMENT FROM THE SCHOOL Located in Carbondale, Colorado, the Colorado Rocky Mountain School (CRMS) is a boarding and day college-preparatory school for boys and girls in grades 9–12. Founded by John and Anne Holden in 1953, the School has always sustained the Holdens' vision that by nurturing civic courage, critical thought, an international scope of interest, and a responsibility to serve others, a CRMS education would produce citizens who could serve as protectors of democracy and peace. Today, the Colorado Rocky Mountain School continues to aspire to develop the unique potential of each student and believes that the study of Camus and Faulkner, organic chemistry and calculus, and history and photography share equal importance with mending fences, backpacking, kayaking, and other physical activities. CRMS offers a rigorous college-preparatory curriculum that encompasses a full range of academic courses, including selected Advanced Placement classes. The curriculum is designed to prepare students not only to attend college but also to find success there and to nurture a lifelong passion for learning. CRMS believes that the classroom must open onto the world, that learning is not easily contained, and that a scholar's life should encompass action as well as quiet study. In support of this belief, CRMS courses are balanced with a carefully constructed active curriculum, composed of outdoor education, sports, and work crew. The preeminent goal of Colorado Rocky Mountain School is to prepare students in mind, body, and spirit for the challenges they will face in college and beyond. By the time students graduate, they have been trained to think critically and write lucidly. CRMS graduates are well prepared to attend selective colleges and universities across the country. Ultimately, what makes CRMS so special is not its majestic setting at the foot of Mt. Sopris, its new classroom building, or its unparalleled outdoor program. Rather, it is the students and teachers who make up this community and call it home. The only way to feel that is to come and visit and see the School firsthand.

THE COLORADO SPRINGS SCHOOL

21 Broadmoor Avenue
Colorado Springs, Colorado 80906
Head of School: Mr. Mickey Landry

General Information Coeducational day college-preparatory, arts, and experiential learning school. Grades PS–12. Founded: 1961. Setting: suburban. Nearest major city is Denver. 30-acre campus. 10 buildings on campus. Approved or accredited by Association of Colorado Independent Schools and Colorado Department of Education. Member of National Association of Independent Schools, Secondary School Admission Test Board, and National Association for College Admission Counseling. Endowment: $2.9 million. Total enrollment: 462. Upper school average class size: 17. Upper school faculty-student ratio: 1:8.

Upper School Student Profile Grade 9: 42 students (26 boys, 16 girls); Grade 10: 39 students (23 boys, 16 girls); Grade 11: 31 students (18 boys, 13 girls); Grade 12: 30 students (17 boys, 13 girls).

Faculty School total: 55. In upper school: 9 men, 11 women; 16 have advanced degrees.

Subjects Offered 20th century history, acting, African history, African studies, algebra, American literature, anatomy and physiology, art history, band, biology, biology-AP, botany, calculus-AP, chemistry, choir, community service, composition, computer applications, computer programming, directing, drama, drawing, economics, economics-AP, English, English literature-AP, environmental science, European history-AP, European literature, French, French language-AP, French literature-AP, functions, geography, geology, geometry, grammar, history, Latin American history, literature, macro/microeconomics-AP, microeconomics, music, music appreciation, painting, philosophy, photography, physical education, physics, playwriting, pottery, pre-calculus, printmaking, SAT/ACT preparation, sculpture, Spanish, Spanish literature, Spanish literature-AP, speech, statistics, statistics-AP, studio art-AP, textiles, theater, trigonometry, U.S. history, U.S. history-AP, Western civilization, world geography, world history, world literature, writing, writing workshop, yearbook.

Graduation Requirements Arts and fine arts (art, music, dance, drama), athletics, college admission preparation, computer science, English, foreign language, mathematics, science, social studies (includes history), speech and oral interpretations,

---

Experience Centered Seminar each year, college overview course, 24 hours of community service per each year of high school.

Special Academic Programs Advanced Placement exam preparation in 8 subject areas; honors section; independent study; term-away projects; study abroad; academic accommodation for the gifted.

College Placement 36 students graduated in 2005; 35 went to college, including Carnegie Mellon University; Sarah Lawrence College; Spelman College; University of Colorado at Boulder; University of Denver; University of Pennsylvania. Other: 1 went to work. Mean SAT verbal: 544, mean SAT math: 595, mean composite ACT: 25.

Student Life Upper grades have specified standards of dress, student council. Discipline rests equally with students and faculty.

Summer Programs Remediation, sports, art/fine arts programs offered; held both on and off campus; held at various field trip locations; accepts boys and girls; open to students from other schools.

Tuition and Aid Day student tuition: $14,375. Tuition installment plan (monthly payment plans). Merit scholarship grants, need-based scholarship grants available. In 2005–06, 44% of upper-school students received aid; total upper-school merit-scholarship money awarded: $124,100. Total amount of financial aid awarded in 2005–06: $375,950.

Admissions Traditional secondary-level entrance grade is 9. For fall 2005, 33 students applied for upper-level admission, 24 were accepted, 15 enrolled. Deadline for receipt of application materials: none. Application fee required: $50. Interview required.

Athletics Interscholastic: basketball (boys, girls), cross-country running (b,g), golf (b), lacrosse (b), soccer (b,g), tennis (b,g), volleyball (g); coed intramural: mountaineering, outdoor education, rock climbing, skiing (cross-country), skiing (downhill). 2 PE instructors, 8 coaches.

Computers Computers are regularly used in all academic classes. Computer network features include campus e-mail, on-campus library services, CD-ROMs, online commercial services, Internet access, DVD, wireless campus network.

Contact Mrs. Eve Skolnik, Director of Admission and Financial Aid. 719-475-9747 Ext. 112. Fax: 719-475-9864. E-mail: esckolnik@css.org. Web site: www.css.org.

ANNOUNCEMENT FROM THE SCHOOL The Colorado Springs School, preschool through grade 12 college-prep day school, allows students to "learn by doing." Small classes mean teachers know students as individuals and can challenge them in the rigorous academic program. Students have many opportunities for participation and personal growth and receive personalized college counseling.

COLORADO TIMBERLINE ACADEMY

35554 US Highway 550
Durango, Colorado 81301
Head of School: Daniel J. Coey

General Information Coeducational boarding and day college-preparatory, general academic, and arts school; primarily serves underachievers. Grades 9–PG. Founded: 1975. Setting: rural. Nearest major city is Albuquerque, NM. Students are housed in single-sex dormitories and 2-person log cabins. 53-acre campus. 29 buildings on campus. Approved or accredited by Colorado Department of Education. Member of Secondary School Admission Test Board. Total enrollment: 30. Upper school average class size: 5. Upper school faculty-student ratio: 1:5.

Upper School Student Profile 90% of students are boarding students. 10% are state residents. 10 states are represented in upper school student body. 10% are international students. International students from Gambia and Mexico.

Faculty School total: 11. In upper school: 5 men, 4 women; 4 have advanced degrees; 9 reside on campus.

Subjects Offered Algebra, American history, American literature, anatomy, archaeology, art, art history, arts, astronomy, biology, botany, calculus, chemistry, computer science, creative writing, drama, economics, engineering, English, environmental science, fine arts, French, geography, geometry, government/civics, grammar, health, history, industrial arts, mathematics, music, philosophy, photography, physical education, physics, psychology, religion, robotics, SAT/ACT preparation, science, social studies, Spanish, speech, study skills, trigonometry, typing, world history, world literature, writing.

Graduation Requirements Arts and fine arts (art, music, dance, drama), computer science, English, foreign language, mathematics, philosophy, physical education (includes health), religion (includes Bible studies and theology), science, social studies (includes history).

Special Academic Programs Accelerated programs; independent study; term-away projects; study at local college for college credit; study abroad; academic accommodation for the artistically talented; remedial reading and/or remedial writing; remedial math; programs in English for dyslexic students; special instructional classes for students with learning disabilities and Attention Deficit Disorder.

College Placement 12 students graduated in 2005; 10 went to college, including Fort Lewis College. Other: 1 went to work, 1 had other specific plans.

Student Life Upper grades have student council. Discipline rests primarily with faculty.

Tuition and Aid Day student tuition: $12,700; 7-day tuition and room/board: $24,300. Guaranteed tuition plan. Tuition installment plan (individually arranged payment plans). Merit scholarship grants, need-based scholarship grants available. In 2005–06, 12% of upper-school students received aid; total upper-school merit-scholarship money awarded: $4000. Total amount of financial aid awarded in 2005–06: $52,000.

Admissions Traditional secondary-level entrance grade is 9. For fall 2005, 18 students applied for upper-level admission, 15 were accepted, 15 enrolled. Deadline for receipt of application materials: none. Application fee required: $35. Interview required.

Athletics Intramural: aerobics/dance (girls), basketball (b,g); coed intramural: aerobics/nautilus, alpine skiing, aquatics, back packing, bicycling, bowling, canoeing/kayaking, climbing, fishing, fitness, fitness walking, fly fishing, hiking/backpacking, kayaking, mountain biking, outdoor activities, outdoor adventure, outdoor education, outdoor recreation, outdoor skills, rafting, rock climbing, skiing (downhill), snowboarding, soccer.

Computers Computers are regularly used in business education, career exploration, college planning, current events, English, independent study, life skills, mathematics, research skills, SAT preparation, science, technology, typing, video film production, word processing, writing fundamentals, yearbook classes. Computer resources include campus e-mail, CD-ROMs, online commercial services, Internet access.

Contact Alexander Schuhl, Admissions Director. 970-247-5898. Fax: 970-259-8067. E-mail: adm@ctaedu.org. Web site: www.ctaedu.org.

ANNOUNCEMENT FROM THE SCHOOL Colorado Timberline Academy is pleased to announce the addition of an Orton-Gillingham component to the program. As a result of the completion of training of additional staff members, Colorado Timberline Academy has 3 instructors available for this new component as part of the tutoring program.

See full description on page 738.

COLUMBIA ACADEMY

1101 West 7th Street
Columbia, Tennessee 38401
Head of School: Dr. Bill Thrasher

General Information Coeducational day college-preparatory, arts, business, religious studies, and technology school, affiliated with Church of Christ. Grades K–12. Founded: 1978. Setting: small town. Nearest major city is Nashville. 67-acre campus. 6 buildings on campus. Approved or accredited by National Christian School Association, Southern Association of Colleges and Schools, and Tennessee Department of Education. Total enrollment: 565. Upper school average class size: 18. Upper school faculty-student ratio: 1:13.

Upper School Student Profile Grade 7: 49 students (26 boys, 23 girls); Grade 8: 41 students (15 boys, 26 girls); Grade 9: 42 students (22 boys, 20 girls); Grade 10: 38 students (19 boys, 19 girls); Grade 11: 43 students (17 boys, 26 girls); Grade 12: 52 students (20 boys, 32 girls). 60% of students are members of Church of Christ.

Faculty School total: 43. In upper school: 12 men, 11 women; 14 have advanced degrees.

Subjects Offered Accounting, ACT preparation, advanced math, algebra, American history, American literature, anatomy and physiology, art, band, Bible, biology, British literature, calculus, chemistry, chorus, composition, computer keyboarding, computer science, concert band, creative writing, current events, earth science, economics, English, environmental science, fine arts, geography, geometry, government/civics, grammar, health, journalism, music, physical education, physical science, physics, psychology, religion, Spanish, speech, world history.

Graduation Requirements Arts and fine arts (art, music, dance, drama), computer science, economics, electives, English, foreign language, mathematics, physical education (includes health), religion (includes Bible studies and theology), science, social science, social studies (includes history), speech, successfully pass the state Gateway Exams in Algebra I, English II and Biology, successfully pass Bible every year while enrolled.

Special Academic Programs Honors section; independent study; study at local college for college credit.

College Placement 36 students graduated in 2005; 34 went to college, including Columbia State Community College; Freed-Hardeman University; Lipscomb University; Middle Tennessee State University; Tennessee Technological University; The University of Tennessee at Martin. Other: 2 went to work. Median composite ACT: 21. 8% scored over 26 on composite ACT.

Student Life Upper grades have specified standards of dress, student council, honor system. Discipline rests primarily with faculty.

Tuition and Aid Day student tuition: $4850. Tuition installment plan (monthly payment plans, individually arranged payment plans). Tuition reduction for siblings, need-based scholarship grants, paying campus jobs available. In 2005–06, 4% of upper-school students received aid.

Admissions Traditional secondary-level entrance grade is 9. For fall 2005, 270 students applied for upper-level admission, 265 were accepted, 265 enrolled.

Otis-Lennon School Ability Test required. Deadline for receipt of application materials: none. Application fee required: $50. On-campus interview recommended.

Athletics Interscholastic: baseball (boys), basketball (b,g), bowling (b,g), cheering (g), football (b), golf (b,g), soccer (b,g), softball (g), strength & conditioning (b), tennis (b,g), trap and skeet (b,g), volleyball (g); intramural: flag football (g). 1 PE instructor.

Computers Computers are regularly used in accounting, creative writing, journalism, SAT preparation, yearbook classes. Computer network features include campus e-mail, on-campus library services, CD-ROMs, Internet access.

Contact Mrs. Shirley A. Smith, Academic Dean. 931-388-5369. Fax: 931-380-8506. E-mail: sasmith@columbia-academy.net. Web site: www.columbia-academy.net.

COLUMBIA GRAMMAR AND PREPARATORY SCHOOL

5 West 93rd Street
New York, New York 10025
Head of School: Dr. Richard J. Soghoian

General Information Coeducational day college-preparatory and arts school. Grades PK–12. Founded: 1764. Setting: urban. 3 buildings on campus. Approved or accredited by New York State Association of Independent Schools and New York Department of Education. Member of National Association of Independent Schools. Endowment: $12.5 million. Total enrollment: 1,065. Upper school average class size: 14. Upper school faculty-student ratio: 1:7.

Upper School Student Profile Grade 7: 75 students (40 boys, 35 girls); Grade 8: 75 students (39 boys, 36 girls); Grade 9: 104 students (54 boys, 50 girls); Grade 10: 95 students (51 boys, 44 girls); Grade 11: 87 students (50 boys, 37 girls); Grade 12: 95 students (44 boys, 51 girls).

Faculty School total: 171. In upper school: 39 men, 34 women; 48 have advanced degrees.

Subjects Offered 3-dimensional art, acting, advanced computer applications, Advanced Placement courses, American history, American literature, anatomy, anthropology, art, art history, biology, calculus, ceramics, chemistry, community service, comparative religion, computer programming, computer science, creative writing, drama, driver education, economics, English, English literature, environmental science, European history, expository writing, film, fine arts, French, genetics, geography, geology, government/civics, grammar, health, history, Japanese, journalism, Latin, mathematics, music, music history, philosophy, photography, physical education, physics, psychology, religion, science, social studies, sociology, Spanish, theater, world history, world literature, writing.

Graduation Requirements Arts and fine arts (art, music, dance, drama), computer science, English, foreign language, mathematics, physical education (includes health), science, social studies (includes history). Community service is required.

Special Academic Programs Advanced Placement exam preparation in 19 subject areas; honors section; independent study; academic accommodation for the gifted; remedial reading and/or remedial writing; remedial math; programs in English, mathematics, general development for dyslexic students.

College Placement 76 students graduated in 2005; all went to college, including Bard College; Boston University; Emory University; Oberlin College; The George Washington University; Vanderbilt University. Median SAT verbal: 650, median SAT math: 650. 73.4% scored over 600 on SAT verbal, 70.3% scored over 600 on SAT math.

Student Life Upper grades have specified standards of dress, student council. Discipline rests primarily with faculty.

Tuition and Aid Day student tuition: $27,000–$27,200. Tuition installment plan (Insured Tuition Payment Plan, monthly payment plans). Need-based scholarship grants available. In 2005–06, 27% of upper-school students received aid. Total amount of financial aid awarded in 2005–06: $2,007,060.

Admissions Traditional secondary-level entrance grade is 9. For fall 2005, 290 students applied for upper-level admission, 91 were accepted, 45 enrolled. ISEE required. Deadline for receipt of application materials: December 1. Application fee required: $55. On-campus interview required.

Athletics Interscholastic: baseball (boys), basketball (b,g), cross-country running (b,g), golf (b), soccer (b,g), softball (g), swimming and diving (b,g), tennis (b,g), track and field (b,g), volleyball (g); coed interscholastic: ice hockey; coed intramural: aerobics, badminton, basketball, combined training, fitness, floor hockey, jogging, physical fitness, physical training, strength & conditioning, table tennis, touch football, ultimate Frisbee, volleyball, weight training. 4 PE instructors, 11 coaches.

Computers Computers are regularly used in desktop publishing, foreign language, graphics, science, typing, Web site design, writing fundamentals classes. Computer network features include campus e-mail, on-campus library services, CD-ROMs, online commercial services, Internet access, wireless campus network.

Contact Terry Centeno, Admissions Coordinator. 212-749-6200 Ext. 362. Fax: 212-961-3105. Web site: www.cgps.org.

See full description on page 740.

COLUMBIA INTERNATIONAL COLLEGE OF CANADA

1003 Main Street West
Hamilton, Ontario L8S 4P3, Canada
Head of School: Mrs. Anna Shkolnik

General Information Coeducational boarding and day college-preparatory, general academic, and business school. Grades 9–12. Founded: 1979. Setting: urban. Nearest major city is Toronto, Canada. Students are housed in coed dormitories and single-sex dormitories. 8-acre campus. 3 buildings on campus. Approved or accredited by Ontario Ministry of Education, Western Catholic Education Association, and Ontario Department of Education. Language of instruction: English. Total enrollment: 1,280. Upper school average class size: 20. Upper school faculty-student ratio: 1:20.

Upper School Student Profile Grade 9: 80 students (60 boys, 20 girls); Grade 10: 120 students (80 boys, 40 girls); Grade 11: 320 students (170 boys, 150 girls); Grade 12: 760 students (417 boys, 343 girls). 80% of students are boarding students. 6% are province residents. 5 provinces are represented in upper school student body. 94% are international students. International students from China, Indonesia, Jamaica, Mexico, Republic of Korea, and Singapore; 46 other countries represented in student body.

Faculty School total: 70. In upper school: 28 men, 42 women; 18 have advanced degrees.

Subjects Offered 20th century world history, accounting, advanced TOEFL/grammar, algebra, analysis and differential calculus, analytic geometry, art, art and culture, art appreciation, art education, biology, business, Canadian geography, Canadian history, career education, chemistry, civics, college counseling, computer education, computer programming, computer technologies, dramatic arts, economics, English composition, English literature, English literature and composition-AP, ESL, French as a second language, general business, general math, general science, geography, honors algebra, honors English, honors geometry, honors world history, intro to computers, kinesiology, lab science, leadership, leadership education training, leadership training, life management skills, life skills, Mandarin, math applications, math methods, mathematics, mathematics-AP, Mexican history, modern world history, music, outdoor education, physical education, physical fitness, physics, society challenge and change, visual arts.

Graduation Requirements Arts, business, English, mathematics, science, social studies (includes history), community volunteer hours, Ontario Secondary School Literacy Test.

Special Academic Programs Advanced Placement exam preparation in 5 subject areas; accelerated programs; study at local college for college credit; ESL (405 students enrolled).

College Placement 625 students graduated in 2005; all went to college, including McMaster University; The University of Western Ontario; University of Toronto; University of Waterloo; York University.

Student Life Upper grades have uniform requirement, student council. Discipline rests primarily with faculty.

Summer Programs Remediation, advancement, ESL, sports programs offered; session focuses on academics, ESL, and leadership education; held both on and off campus; held at Bark Lake Outdoor Education and Leadership Campus; accepts boys and girls; open to students from other schools. 800 students usually enrolled. 2006 schedule: June 21 to August 21. Application deadline: April 28.

Tuition and Aid Day student tuition: CAN$10,800; 7-day tuition and room/board: CAN$20,000.

Admissions Traditional secondary-level entrance grade is 12. For fall 2005, 600 students applied for upper-level admission, 380 were accepted, 350 enrolled. Math and English placement tests and Math Placement Exam required. Deadline for receipt of application materials: none. Application fee required: CAN$200. Interview recommended.

Athletics Intramural: aerobics (boys, girls), aquatics (b,g), badminton (b,g), ball hockey (b,g), baseball (b,g), basketball (b,g), fitness (b,g), floor hockey (b,g), football (b), indoor soccer (b,g), outdoor activities (b,g), soccer (b), squash (b,g), strength & conditioning (b), swimming and diving (b,g), table tennis (b,g), tennis (b,g), volleyball (b,g), wallyball (b,g), weight training (b); coed intramural: badminton, ball hockey, baseball, basketball, canoeing/kayaking, cooperative games, cross-country running, dance team, fishing, golf, hiking/backpacking, ice skating, in-line skating, jogging, jump rope, martial arts, outdoor activities, outdoor adventure, outdoor education, outdoor recreation, outdoor skills, physical fitness, physical training, roller blading, roller skating, ropes courses, running, self defense, skiing (cross-country), snowshoeing, swimming and diving, table tennis, volleyball, wilderness, wilderness survival, winter walking. 3 PE instructors.

Computers Computers are regularly used in accounting, business, business applications, career education, economics, ESL, geography, science classes. Computer network features include CD-ROMs, Internet access, file transfer, wireless campus network.

Contact Mr. Evan Harris, Admissions Officer. 905-572-7883 Ext. 2835. Fax: 905-572-9332. E-mail: admissions02@cic-totalcare.com. Web site: www.CIC-TotalCare.com.

COLUMBIA INTERNATIONAL SCHOOL

153 Matsugo
Tokorozawa, Saitama 359-0027, Japan
Head of School: Mr. Barrie McCligott

petersons.com

General Information Coeducational boarding and day college-preparatory, bilingual studies, and technology school. Boarding grades 7–12, day grades 1–12. Founded: 1988. Setting: suburban. Nearest major city is Tokyo. Students are housed in single-sex dormitories. 2-acre campus. 2 buildings on campus. Approved or accredited by Ontario Ministry of Education. Candidate for accreditation by Western Association of Schools and Colleges. Language of instruction: English. Endowment: ¥10 million. Total enrollment: 250. Upper school average class size: 15. Upper school faculty-student ratio: 1:15.

Upper School Student Profile Grade 10: 48 students (16 boys, 32 girls); Grade 11: 49 students (18 boys, 31 girls); Grade 12: 47 students (16 boys, 31 girls). 13% of students are boarding students. International students from Canada, China, Philippines, Republic of Korea, United Kingdom, and United States; 7 other countries represented in student body.

Faculty School total: 19. In upper school: 12 men, 4 women; 6 have advanced degrees; 1 resides on campus.

Subjects Offered 20th century world history, algebra, ancient world history, art, Asian history, biology, business, calculus, Canadian geography, Canadian history, chemistry, communications, community service, computer keyboarding, computer science, computers, economics, English, ESL, foreign language, geography, geometry, global issues, history, Internet, keyboarding, literacy, mathematics, media studies, physical education, reading, TOEFL preparation, world issues, yearbook.

Graduation Requirements Ontario Literacy Test, 40 hours of community involvement activities.

Special Academic Programs Study abroad; ESL (45 students enrolled).

College Placement 29 students graduated in 2005; 22 went to college, including Foothill College; Temple University; The University of British Columbia; University of Manitoba; University of Saskatchewan; University of Victoria. Other: 4 went to work, 3 had other specific plans.

Student Life Upper grades have uniform requirement, student council, honor system. Discipline rests equally with students and faculty.

Summer Programs Remediation, ESL, art/fine arts, computer instruction programs offered; session focuses on ESL, computers, science, and art; held both on and off campus; held at Tokyo (Japan), Edmonton (Canada), and Gold Coast (Australia); accepts boys and girls; open to students from other schools. 150 students usually enrolled. 2006 schedule: July 5 to August 6. Application deadline: June 30.

Tuition and Aid Day student tuition: ¥1,575,000; 7-day tuition and room/board: ¥660,000–¥1,230,000. Merit scholarship grants, facility and entrance fees exemption for siblings available. In 2005–06, 5% of upper-school students received aid; total upper-school merit-scholarship money awarded: ¥5,600,000.

Admissions Traditional secondary-level entrance grade is 10. For fall 2005, 69 students applied for upper-level admission, 49 were accepted, 45 enrolled. Any standardized test required. Deadline for receipt of application materials: none. Application fee required: ¥25,000. On-campus interview required.

Athletics Coed Intramural: aerobics, baseball, basketball, bowling, cooperative games, floor hockey, Frisbee, hiking/backpacking, kickball, outdoor activities, rock climbing, snowboarding, soccer, softball, table tennis, tennis, volleyball, weight training, yoga. 2 PE instructors.

Computers Computers are regularly used in all classes. Computer network features include campus e-mail, on-campus library services, CD-ROMs, Internet access, file transfer, office computer access, DVD, wireless campus network.

Contact Mr. Yoshitaka Matsumura, Coordinator. 81-42-946-1911. Fax: 81-42-946-1955. E-mail: admissions@columbia-ca.co.jp. Web site: www.columbia-ca.co.jp.

ANNOUNCEMENT FROM THE SCHOOL CIS encourages personal growth, social awareness, and respect for achievement. The staff helps students develop powers of critical and creative thought, which prepare them for both the demands of postsecondary education and life as international citizens. Varied opportunities for achievement and personal fulfillment are provided through academic studies and extracurricular pursuits.

THE COLUMBUS ACADEMY

PO Box 30745
4300 Cherry Bottom Road
Gahanna, Ohio 43230
Head of School: John M. Mackenzie

petersons.com

General Information Coeducational day college-preparatory school. Grades PK–12. Founded: 1911. Setting: suburban. Nearest major city is Columbus. 230-acre campus. 16 buildings on campus. Approved or accredited by Independent Schools Association of the Central States and Ohio Department of Education. Member of National Association of Independent Schools and Secondary School Admission Test Board. Endowment: $19.5 million. Total enrollment: 1,016. Upper school average class size: 15. Upper school faculty-student ratio: 1:11.

Upper School Student Profile Grade 9: 91 students (52 boys, 39 girls); Grade 10: 91 students (54 boys, 37 girls); Grade 11: 84 students (42 boys, 42 girls); Grade 12: 68 students (38 boys, 30 girls).

Faculty School total: 133. In upper school: 22 men, 22 women; 34 have advanced degrees.

Subjects Offered Advanced chemistry, advanced computer applications, advanced math, Advanced Placement courses, advanced studio art-AP, algebra, American government-AP, American history, American history-AP, American literature, analysis and differential calculus, art history, biology, biology-AP, British literature, calculus, calculus-AP, career/college preparation, ceramics, chemistry, chemistry-AP, China/Japan history, Chinese, choir, choral music, chorus, college counseling, comparative government and politics-AP, comparative political systems-AP, computer applications, computer education, computer programming-AP, computer science, computer science-AP, concert band, concert choir, creative writing, drawing and design, economics, economics-AP, English, European history, European history-AP, fine arts, Finnish, French, French-AP, geology, geometry, government and politics-AP, government-AP, health education, history of China and Japan, instrumental music, integrated science, Latin, Latin-AP, military history, photography, physical education, physics, physics-AP, pre-calculus, Russian history, senior career experience, South African history, Spanish, Spanish language-AP, Spanish literature-AP, speech, strings, theater, trigonometry, U.S. government and politics, U.S. history-AP, weight training, world history, world religions.

Graduation Requirements Arts and fine arts (art, music, dance, drama), English, foreign language, mathematics, science, social studies (includes history), formal speech delivered to the students and faculty of the upper school during junior year.

Special Academic Programs Advanced Placement exam preparation in 17 subject areas; honors section; independent study; study abroad; academic accommodation for the gifted.

College Placement 79 students graduated in 2005; 78 went to college, including Boston University; Case Western Reserve University; Denison University; Miami University; The Ohio State University; University of Pennsylvania. Other: 1 had other specific plans. Median SAT verbal: 640, median SAT math: 670, median composite ACT: 28. 71% scored over 600 on SAT verbal, 75% scored over 600 on SAT math, 64% scored over 26 on composite ACT.

Student Life Upper grades have specified standards of dress, student council. Discipline rests equally with students and faculty.

Summer Programs Remediation, enrichment, advancement, art/fine arts, computer instruction programs offered; session focuses on academic enrichment, fine arts, fun and games; held on campus; accepts boys and girls; open to students from other schools. 400 students usually enrolled. 2006 schedule: June 19 to August 12.

Tuition and Aid Day student tuition: $16,100. Tuition installment plan (The Tuition Plan, Academic Management Services Plan, Tuition Management Systems Plan). Need-based scholarship grants available. In 2005–06, 15% of upper-school students received aid. Total amount of financial aid awarded in 2005–06: $543,300.

Admissions Traditional secondary-level entrance grade is 9. For fall 2005, 47 students applied for upper-level admission, 32 were accepted, 26 enrolled. ISEE or SSAT required. Deadline for receipt of application materials: none. Application fee required: $50. On-campus interview required.

Athletics Interscholastic: ball hockey (boys), baseball (b), basketball (b,g), cross-country running (b,g), diving (b,g), field hockey (g), football (b), lacrosse (g), soccer (b,g), swimming and diving (b,g), track and field (b,g), volleyball (g), wrestling (b); coed intramural: bicycling. 3 PE instructors, 1 trainer.

Computers Computers are regularly used in college planning, current events, economics, English, foreign language, humanities, journalism, Latin, learning cognition, library skills, mathematics, media production, multimedia, music, photography, publications, reading, remedial study skills, research skills, SAT preparation, science, technology, theater, writing classes. Computer network features include campus e-mail, on-campus library services, CD-ROMs, online commercial services, Internet access.

Contact Louis A. Schultz, Director of Admissions. 614-337-4309. Fax: 614-475-0396. Web site: www.ColumbusAcademy.org.

ANNOUNCEMENT FROM THE SCHOOL Committed to its motto, "In Quest of the Best," the Columbus Academy is an academically rigorous school that emphasizes community service, diversity, and moral courage. Serving approximately 1,015 girls and boys in grades preK–12, the Academy offers a comprehensive program in academics, athletics, the arts, and other cocurricular offerings. Learning takes place in impressive facilities on the 230-acre campus located 15 minutes from downtown Columbus.

COLUMBUS SCHOOL FOR GIRLS

56 South Columbia Avenue
Columbus, Ohio 43209
Head of School: Dr. Diane B. Cooper

General Information Girls' day college-preparatory, arts, and technology school. Grades PK–12. Founded: 1898. Setting: urban. 78-acre campus. 1 building on campus. Approved or accredited by Independent Schools Association of the Central States.

Member of National Association of Independent Schools. Endowment: $23.9 million. Total enrollment: 650. Upper school average class size: 15. Upper school faculty-student ratio: 1:12.

Upper School Student Profile Grade 9: 46 students (46 girls); Grade 10: 55 students (55 girls); Grade 11: 61 students (61 girls); Grade 12: 57 students (57 girls).

Faculty School total: 97. In upper school: 11 men, 29 women; 34 have advanced degrees.

Subjects Offered Acting, algebra, American history, American literature, art, art history, art-AP, Asian history, astronomy, biology, biology-AP, calculus, calculus-AP, ceramics, chemistry, chemistry-AP, choir, civics, college admission preparation, comparative government and politics-AP, computer programming, computer science, drawing, earth science, economics, economics and history, English, English literature, English literature-AP, environmental science, European history, European history-AP, French, French language-AP, geography, geometry, German, German-AP, government/civics, health, international relations, Latin, Latin-AP, math applications, music, music history, music theater, musical theater, newspaper, painting, philosophy, photography, physical education, physics, physics-AP, political science, pre-calculus, psychology-AP, public speaking, sculpture, senior seminar, Spanish, Spanish language-AP, Spanish literature-AP, speech, statistics, strings, theater, trigonometry, U.S. government and politics-AP, U.S. history, visual arts, vocal ensemble, vocal music, wind ensemble, world history, world literature, world religions, yearbook.

Graduation Requirements Arts and fine arts (art, music, dance, drama), biology, civics, college planning, electives, English, foreign language, geometry, history, lab science, mathematics, physical education (includes health), physics, public speaking, SAT preparation, science, technology, U.S. history, world history, Senior May Program, service hours.

Special Academic Programs Advanced Placement exam preparation in 15 subject areas; honors section; independent study; study at local college for college credit.

College Placement 71 students graduated in 2005; all went to college, including Duke University; Kenyon College; Miami University; Ohio University; The Ohio State University; University of Michigan. Mean SAT verbal: 621, mean SAT math: 630, mean composite ACT: 26.

Student Life Upper grades have uniform requirement, student council, honor system. Discipline rests primarily with faculty.

Summer Programs Remediation, enrichment, advancement, sports, art/fine arts, rigorous outdoor training, computer instruction programs offered; session focuses on academic areas; held both on and off campus; held at various sites in community and CSG's Kirk Athletic Campus; accepts boys and girls; open to students from other schools. 600 students usually enrolled. 2006 schedule: June 19 to August 11. Application deadline: none.

Tuition and Aid Day student tuition: $14,620–$16,520. Tuition installment plan (Tuition Management Systems Plan). Need-based scholarship grants, tuition reduction for three or more siblings available. In 2005–06, 23% of upper-school students received aid. Total amount of financial aid awarded in 2005–06: $484,153.

Admissions Traditional secondary-level entrance grade is 9. For fall 2005, 55 students applied for upper-level admission, 30 were accepted, 18 enrolled. CTP, ISEE or school's own test required. Deadline for receipt of application materials: February 16. Application fee required: $50. On-campus interview required.

Athletics Interscholastic: basketball, cross-country running, diving, field hockey, golf, lacrosse, soccer, swimming and diving, tennis, track and field, volleyball; intramural: aerobics, aerobics/dance, aerobics/nautilus, aquatics, archery, badminton, basketball, bowling, cooperative games, diving, field hockey, fitness, fitness walking, golf, jump rope, lacrosse, life saving, martial arts, outdoor activities, physical fitness, racquetball, ropes courses, running, self defense, skiing (downhill), soccer, strength & conditioning, swimming and diving, synchronized swimming, table tennis, tennis, track and field, volleyball, walking, weight training, yoga. 6 PE instructors, 21 coaches, 1 trainer.

Computers Computers are regularly used in art, English, foreign language, history, mathematics, music, science, theater classes. Computer network features include campus e-mail, on-campus library services, CD-ROMs, online commercial services, Internet access, DVD, wireless campus network.

Contact Ann Boston Timm, Director of Admission and Financial Aid, Forms VI-XII. 614-252-0781 Ext. 104. Fax: 614-252-0571. E-mail: atimm@columbusschoolforgirls.org. Web site: www.columbusschoolforgirls.org.

COMMONWEALTH SCHOOL

151 Commonwealth Avenue
Boston, Massachusetts 02116
Head of School: William D. Wharton

General Information Coeducational day college-preparatory, arts, and technology school. Grades 9–12. Founded: 1957. Setting: urban. 1 building on campus. Approved or accredited by Association of Independent Schools in New England and Massachusetts Department of Education. Member of National Association of Independent Schools and Secondary School Admission Test Board. Endowment: $9.2 million. Total enrollment: 154. Upper school average class size: 11. Upper school faculty-student ratio: 1:5.

Upper School Student Profile Grade 9: 46 students (27 boys, 19 girls); Grade 10: 36 students (15 boys, 21 girls); Grade 11: 36 students (21 boys, 15 girls); Grade 12: 36 students (17 boys, 19 girls).

Commonwealth School

Faculty School total: 34. In upper school: 14 men, 16 women; 26 have advanced degrees.

Subjects Offered Advanced chemistry, advanced computer applications, advanced math, Advanced Placement courses, African American history, African-American literature, algebra, American history, analysis of data, ancient history, ancient world history, art, art history, biology, biology-AP, calculus, calculus-AP, ceramics, chamber groups, chemistry, choral music, chorus, classics, college counseling, community service, computer programming, computer science, current events, dance, drama, drawing, economics, English, English literature, European history, expository writing, film series, film studies, fine arts, French, geometry, Greek, history of the Americas, honors algebra, honors English, honors geometry, honors U.S. history, Japanese history, jazz, jazz band, jazz ensemble, jazz theory, Latin, Latin American history, mathematics, medieval history, medieval/Renaissance history, modern European history-AP, music, music theory, organic chemistry, philosophy, photography, physical education, physics, printmaking, probability and statistics, science, short story, Spanish, Spanish literature, theater, writing.

Graduation Requirements Algebra, ancient history, art, biology, calculus, chemistry, English, ethics, foreign language, geometry, medieval history, physical education (includes health), physics, U.S. history, City of Boston Course, completion of project each year. Community service is required.

Special Academic Programs Advanced Placement exam preparation in 13 subject areas; honors section; independent study; academic accommodation for the gifted, the musically talented, and the artistically talented.

College Placement 32 students graduated in 2005; 30 went to college, including Brown University; Bryn Mawr College; Columbia College; University of Chicago; Wesleyan University; Yale University. Other: 2 had other specific plans. Median SAT verbal: 720, median SAT math: 690.

Student Life Upper grades have honor system. Discipline rests primarily with faculty.

Tuition and Aid Day student tuition: $26,440. Tuition installment plan (Key Tuition Payment Plan). Need-based scholarship grants, need-based loans available. In 2005–06, 31% of upper-school students received aid. Total amount of financial aid awarded in 2005–06: $782,600.

Admissions Traditional secondary-level entrance grade is 9. For fall 2005, 180 students applied for upper-level admission, 75 were accepted, 47 enrolled. ISEE or SSAT required. Deadline for receipt of application materials: February 1. Application fee required: $45. On-campus interview required.

Athletics Interscholastic: basketball (boys, girls), soccer (b,g); coed interscholastic: fencing, independent competitive sports, squash, ultimate Frisbee; coed intramural: aerobics/nautilus, ballet, cross-country running, dance, fitness, martial arts, physical fitness, running, sailing, squash, tai chi, tennis, weight training, yoga. 12 coaches.

Computers Computers are regularly used in photography, programming classes. Computer network features include campus e-mail, on-campus library services, CD-ROMs, Internet access, wireless campus network.

Contact Susan Young, Admissions Coordinator. 617-266-7525. Fax: 617-266-5769. E-mail: admissions@commschool.org. Web site: www.commschool.org.

See full description on page 742.

COMMUNITY CHRISTIAN ACADEMY

11875 Taylor Mill Road
Independence, Kentucky 41051
Head of School: Tara Montez Bates

General Information Coeducational day college-preparatory and religious studies school, affiliated with Pentecostal Church. Grades PS–12. Founded: 1983. Setting: rural. Nearest major city is Cincinnati, OH. 107-acre campus. 1 building on campus. Approved or accredited by International Christian Accrediting Association and Kentucky Department of Education. Total enrollment: 219. Upper school faculty-student ratio: 1:20.

Upper School Student Profile Grade 9: 16 students (10 boys, 6 girls); Grade 10: 14 students (8 boys, 6 girls); Grade 11: 7 students (3 boys, 4 girls); Grade 12: 21 students (8 boys, 13 girls). 50% of students are Pentecostal.

Faculty School total: 14. In upper school: 1 man, 5 women; 1 has an advanced degree.

Subjects Offered Advanced math, algebra, American history, art appreciation, Bible, biology, business skills, calculus, chemistry, choral music, computer applications, cultural geography, English, geography, health, integrated science, life skills, literature, pre-algebra, pre-calculus, Spanish.

Graduation Requirements Bible, electives, English, foreign language, mathematics, physical education (includes health), science, social studies (includes history), statistics, visual and performing arts.

College Placement 5 students graduated in 2005; 4 went to college, including Cincinnati State Technical and Community College; Northern Kentucky University. Other: 1 went to work. Mean composite ACT: 15.

Student Life Upper grades have specified standards of dress, student council, honor system. Discipline rests primarily with faculty. Attendance at religious services is required.

Tuition and Aid Day student tuition: $2590. Guaranteed tuition plan. Tuition installment plan (The Tuition Plan, monthly payment plans). Financial aid available to upper-school students. In 2005–06, 3% of upper-school students received aid.

Admissions Traditional secondary-level entrance grade is 9. For fall 2005, 12 students applied for upper-level admission, 8 were accepted, 8 enrolled. Admissions testing required. Deadline for receipt of application materials: none. Application fee required: $75. Interview required.

Athletics Interscholastic: basketball (boys, girls), cheering (g), volleyball (g). 1 PE instructor, 2 coaches.

Computers Computers are regularly used in foreign language classes. Computer network features include CD-ROMs, Internet access.

Contact Jackie Foote, Secretary. 859-356-7990 Ext. 112. Fax: 859-356-7991. E-mail: jackie.foote@ccaky.org. Web site: www.ccaky.org.

COMMUNITY HIGH SCHOOL

Teaneck, New Jersey
See Special Needs Schools section.

THE COMMUNITY SCHOOL OF NAPLES

13275 Livingston Road
Naples, Florida 34109
Head of School: John E. Zeller Jr.

petersons.com

General Information Coeducational day college-preparatory, arts, and technology school. Grades PK–12. Founded: 1982. Setting: suburban. Nearest major city is Miami. 135-acre campus. 3 buildings on campus. Approved or accredited by Florida Council of Independent Schools and Florida Department of Education. Member of National Association of Independent Schools and Secondary School Admission Test Board. Endowment: $4.5 million. Total enrollment: 779. Upper school average class size: 12. Upper school faculty-student ratio: 1:6.

Upper School Student Profile Grade 9: 73 students (35 boys, 38 girls); Grade 10: 57 students (27 boys, 30 girls); Grade 11: 64 students (36 boys, 28 girls); Grade 12: 65 students (24 boys, 41 girls).

Faculty School total: 100. In upper school: 22 men, 20 women; 25 have advanced degrees.

Subjects Offered Algebra, American government, American government-AP, American history, American literature, anatomy and physiology, art, art history-AP, band, biology, biology-AP, broadcasting, calculus, calculus-AP, chemistry, chemistry-AP, chorus, clayworking, comparative government and politics-AP, computer programming, computer science, computer science-AP, constitutional law, creative writing, digital photography, drama, dramatic arts, drawing, economics, economics-AP, electives, English, English language and composition-AP, English literature and composition-AP, European history-AP, fine arts, French, French language-AP, French literature-AP, geometry, German, glassblowing, graphic design, health, history, honors algebra, honors English, honors geometry, honors U.S. history, honors world history, Italian, jazz band, journalism, Latin, macro/microeconomics-AP, marine science, mathematics, music, music theory-AP, painting, performing arts, personal fitness, photography, physical education, physics, physics-AP, pre-calculus, psychology, robotics, science, Spanish, Spanish language-AP, Spanish literature-AP, statistics-AP, strings, studio art-AP, theater, U.S. history-AP, vocal music, Web site design, world history, world literature.

Graduation Requirements Arts and fine arts (art, music, dance, drama), computer science, English, foreign language, history, mathematics, physical education (includes health), public speaking, science. Community service is required.

Special Academic Programs Advanced Placement exam preparation in 19 subject areas; honors section; independent study; study at local college for college credit; study abroad.

College Placement 63 students graduated in 2005; all went to college, including Southern Methodist University; University of Colorado at Boulder; University of Florida; University of Miami; Vanderbilt University. Median SAT verbal: 585, median SAT math: 630, median combined SAT: 1805. 44% scored over 600 on SAT verbal, 66% scored over 600 on SAT math, 61% scored over 26 on composite ACT.

Student Life Upper grades have specified standards of dress, student council, honor system. Discipline rests equally with students and faculty.

Summer Programs Enrichment programs offered; session focuses on mathematics, English, foreign language, physics, and SAT preparation; held on campus; accepts boys and girls; not open to students from other schools. 40 students usually enrolled. 2006 schedule: August 2 to August 19.

Tuition and Aid Day student tuition: $18,320. Tuition installment plan (Insured Tuition Payment Plan, monthly payment plans, individually arranged payment plans). Need-based scholarship grants available. In 2005–06, 11% of upper-school students received aid. Total amount of financial aid awarded in 2005–06: $622,152.

Admissions Traditional secondary-level entrance grade is 9. ISEE or school's own exam required. Deadline for receipt of application materials: none. Application fee required: $100. On-campus interview required.

Athletics Interscholastic: baseball (boys), basketball (b,g), cheering (g), cross-country running (b,g), golf (b,g), lacrosse (b), soccer (b,g), softball (g), swimming and diving (b,g), tennis (b,g), volleyball (g); coed interscholastic: sailing, track and field; coed intramural: physical training, strength & conditioning, weight training. 16 coaches.

Computers Computers are regularly used in art, business education, English, foreign language, history, mathematics, music, science classes. Computer network features include campus e-mail, on-campus library services, CD-ROMs, Internet access, DVD. **Contact** Ms. Judy Evans, Director of Admissions. 239-597-7575 Ext. 205. Fax: 239-598-2973. E-mail: jevans@communityschoolnaples.org. Web site: www.communityschoolnaples.org.

ANNOUNCEMENT FROM THE SCHOOL Established in 1982, The Community School of Naples provides an independent, nondenominational, college-preparatory education to more than 770 students in prekindergarten through grade 12. CSN prioritizes academic excellence and character education, while emphasizing fine arts, athletics, and student activities. The School has received national recognition and proudly offers a financial aid program. John Zeller is Head of School.

THE CONCEPT SCHOOL

Route 926 & Westtown Road
Westtown, Pennsylvania 19395
Head of School: Mrs. Lauren Vangieri

petersons.com

General Information Coeducational day college-preparatory, general academic, arts, and technology school. Grades 4–12. Founded: 1972. Setting: suburban. Nearest major city is Philadelphia. 10-acre campus. 1 building on campus. Approved or accredited by Pennsylvania Department of Education. Endowment: $75,000. Total enrollment: 43. Upper school average class size: 8. Upper school faculty-student ratio: 1:8.

Upper School Student Profile Grade 9: 7 students (5 boys, 2 girls); Grade 10: 9 students (6 boys, 3 girls); Grade 11: 8 students (6 boys, 2 girls); Grade 12: 6 students (4 boys, 2 girls).

Faculty School total: 10. In upper school: 1 man, 6 women; 6 have advanced degrees.

Subjects Offered Algebra, American history, anthropology, art, art history, biology, chemistry, comparative religion, computer graphics, consumer mathematics, criminal justice, cultural arts, economics, English, environmental science, film, fine arts, foreign language, general science, geometry, government/civics, health, history, human development, independent study, keyboarding, language arts, Latin, mathematics, physical education, physics, physiology, pre-algebra, pre-calculus, psychology, science, social science, social studies, speech, trigonometry, U.S. government, visual arts.

Graduation Requirements Arts and fine arts (art, music, dance, drama), computer science, English, mathematics, physical education (includes health), science, social science, social studies (includes history).

Special Academic Programs Independent study; study at local college for college credit; academic accommodation for the gifted and the artistically talented; remedial reading and/or remedial writing; remedial math; programs in general development for dyslexic students; special instructional classes for students with learning differences, Attention Deficit Disorder, Asperger's Syndrome, school phobia, dyslexia, Attention Deficit Hyperactivity Disorder, and Non-verbal Learning Disorder.

College Placement 8 students graduated in 2004; 6 went to college, including Pennsylvania State University System; Temple University; University of Delaware; Villanova University; West Chester University of Pennsylvania; Widener University. Other: 2 went to work. Mean SAT verbal: 520, mean SAT math: 490.

Student Life Upper grades have specified standards of dress, student council, honor system. Discipline rests equally with students and faculty.

Tuition and Aid Day student tuition: $14,500. Tuition installment plan (monthly payment plans). Tuition reduction for siblings available.

Admissions Traditional secondary-level entrance grade is 9. For fall 2005, 33 students applied for upper-level admission, 15 were accepted, 12 enrolled. Math and English placement tests and WISC/Woodcock-Johnson required. Deadline for receipt of application materials: none. Application fee required: $50. On-campus interview required.

Athletics Coed Intramural: basketball, bicycling, bowling, canoeing/kayaking, handball, horseback riding, ice skating, in-line skating, physical fitness, physical training, rock climbing, roller skating, ropes courses, skiing (downhill), snowboarding, yoga. 1 PE instructor.

Computers Computers are regularly used in accounting, all academic, English, history, mathematics, science classes. Computer network features include CD-ROMs, Internet access.

Contact Mrs. Carol McAdam, School Secretary. 610-399-1135. Fax: 610-399-0767. E-mail: cmcadam@conceptschool.com. Web site: www.conceptschool.com.

ANNOUNCEMENT FROM THE SCHOOL The Concept School, a unique, small, educational environment, provides personalized learning for students with average or better academic and cognitive abilities. Teachers and the school psychologist work together to identify a student's learning profile, to assess strengths, to accommodate weaknesses, and to address behaviors in a positive way. A structured academic program features experiential learning in the School's nature preserve and during field trips to nearby historic sites and museums. Lessons in drawing, writing, math, and science develop students' appreciation of the variety and complexity in nature and society.

CONCORD ACADEMY

166 Main Street
Concord, Massachusetts 01742
Head of School: Jacob E. Dresden

General Information Coeducational boarding and day college-preparatory, arts, and technology school. Grades 9–12. Founded: 1922. Setting: suburban. Nearest major city is Boston. Students are housed in single-sex dormitories. 26-acre campus. 29 buildings on campus. Approved or accredited by New England Association of Schools and Colleges, The Association of Boarding Schools, and Massachusetts Department of Education. Member of National Association of Independent Schools and Secondary School Admission Test Board. Endowment: $36.5 million. Total enrollment: 364. Upper school average class size: 12. Upper school faculty-student ratio: 1:6.

Upper School Student Profile Grade 9: 77 students (34 boys, 43 girls); Grade 10: 105 students (49 boys, 56 girls); Grade 11: 91 students (45 boys, 46 girls); Grade 12: 93 students (44 boys, 49 girls). 44% of students are boarding students. 75% are state residents. 25 states are represented in upper school student body. 8% are international students. International students from Hong Kong, Japan, Republic of Korea, and Thailand; 5 other countries represented in student body.

Faculty School total: 60. In upper school: 26 men, 34 women; 46 have advanced degrees; 30 reside on campus.

Subjects Offered African-American literature, algebra, American history, American literature, ancient history, architecture, art, art history, astronomy, biology, calculus-AP, ceramics, chamber groups, chemistry, chorus, comparative religion, computer programming, computer science, computer science-AP, creative writing, dance, drama, drawing, earth science, English, English literature, environmental science, European history, expository writing, fiber arts, film history, filmmaking, fine arts, French, French language-AP, French literature-AP, gender issues, geology, geometry, German, German-AP, government/civics, history, history of science, introduction to digital multitrack recording techniques, Irish literature, Islamic history, Japanese history, jazz ensemble, journalism, Latin, Latin American literature, Latin-AP, mathematics, music, music history, music technology, music theory-AP, oceanography, orchestra, painting, photography, physical education, physics, play/screen writing, poetry, pre-calculus, Russian history, science, sculpture, senior project, social studies, Spanish, Spanish language-AP, Spanish literature-AP, statistics and probability, statistics-AP, theater, theater design and production, trigonometry, U.S. history, Web site design, wind ensemble, world history, world literature, writing, writing workshop.

Graduation Requirements Computer science, English, foreign language, history, mathematics, performing arts, physical education (includes health), science, visual arts.

Special Academic Programs Advanced Placement exam preparation in 14 subject areas; independent study; term-away projects; study abroad; academic accommodation for the gifted, the musically talented, and the artistically talented; remedial reading and/or remedial writing.

College Placement 89 students graduated in 2005; all went to college, including Bard College; Bowdoin College; Carnegie Mellon University; Middlebury College; New York University; Skidmore College.

Student Life Upper grades have student council, honor system. Discipline rests equally with students and faculty.

Tuition and Aid Day student tuition: $28,850; 7-day tuition and room/board: $35,680. Tuition installment plan (Key Tuition Payment Plan, monthly payment plans). Need-based scholarship grants, need-based loans, Achiever Loans (Key Education Resources) available. In 2005–06, 19% of upper-school students received aid. Total amount of financial aid awarded in 2005–06: $1,800,000.

Admissions Traditional secondary-level entrance grade is 9. For fall 2005, 830 students applied for upper-level admission, 253 were accepted, 114 enrolled. ISEE, SSAT or TOEFL required. Deadline for receipt of application materials: January 31. Application fee required: $45. Interview required.

Athletics Interscholastic: baseball (boys), basketball (b,g), cross-country running (b,g), field hockey (g), lacrosse (b,g), skiing (downhill) (b,g), soccer (b,g), softball (g), squash (b,g), tennis (b,g), volleyball (g), wrestling (b); coed interscholastic: alpine skiing, golf, sailing, ultimate Frisbee; coed intramural: aerobics, aerobics/dance, ballet, bicycling, cross-country running, dance, fencing, fitness, jogging, martial arts, modern dance, outdoor activities, outdoor adventure, physical fitness, skiing (downhill), strength & conditioning, ultimate Frisbee. 4 coaches, 2 trainers.

Computers Computers are regularly used in English, mathematics, music, science, video film production classes. Computer network features include campus e-mail, on-campus library services, CD-ROMs, online commercial services, Internet access, office computer access, wireless campus network.

Contact Pamela J. Safford, Associate Head for Enrollment and Planning. 978-402-2250. Fax: 978-402-2345. E-mail: admissions@concordacademy.org. Web site: www.concordacademy.org.

CONCORDIA ACADEMY

2400 North Dale Street
St. Paul, Minnesota 55113
Head of School: Mrs. Lynn Henry

General Information Coeducational day college-preparatory, arts, and religious studies school, affiliated with Lutheran Church–Missouri Synod. Grades 9–12. Founded: 1893. Setting: suburban. 14-acre campus. 1 building on campus. Approved or accredited by National Lutheran School Accreditation, North Central Association of Colleges and Schools, and Minnesota Department of Education. Endowment: $300,000. Total enrollment: 476. Upper school average class size: 22. Upper school faculty-student ratio: 1:15.

Upper School Student Profile Grade 9: 98 students (55 boys, 43 girls); Grade 10: 138 students (70 boys, 68 girls); Grade 11: 130 students (63 boys, 67 girls); Grade 12: 110 students (54 boys, 56 girls). 45% of students are Lutheran Church–Missouri Synod.

Faculty School total: 30. In upper school: 14 men, 15 women; 10 have advanced degrees.

Subjects Offered Advanced Placement courses, algebra, American history, American literature, art, art history, Bible studies, biology, British literature, British literature-AP, business, business skills, calculus, calculus-AP, ceramics, chemistry, choir, chorus, communications, computer keyboarding, computer programming, computer science, concert band, concert choir, consumer mathematics, creative writing, drama, earth science, economics, English, English literature, ethics, European history, expository writing, fine arts, French, geography, geometry, German, government/civics, grammar, health, history, honors English, jazz ensemble, journalism, keyboarding/computer, mathematics, modern world history, music, music appreciation, peer ministry, physical education, physics, pre-algebra, pre-calculus, psychology, religion, science, social science, social studies, sociology, Spanish, speech, theater, theology, world history, world literature, writing.

Graduation Requirements Arts and fine arts (art, music, dance, drama), English, keyboarding/computer, mathematics, physical education (includes health), religion (includes Bible studies and theology), science, social studies (includes history).

Special Academic Programs Advanced Placement exam preparation in 4 subject areas; honors section; study at local college for college credit; academic accommodation for the gifted; remedial reading and/or remedial writing; remedial math; programs in general development for dyslexic students.

College Placement 129 students graduated in 2005; 121 went to college, including Concordia College; Concordia University; Gustavus Adolphus College; University of Minnesota, Twin Cities Campus; Valparaiso University. Other: 5 went to work, 3 had other specific plans. Median composite ACT: 23. Mean SAT verbal: 614, mean SAT math: 650. 25% scored over 26 on composite ACT.

Student Life Upper grades have specified standards of dress, student council. Discipline rests primarily with faculty. Attendance at religious services is required.

Tuition and Aid Day student tuition: $5440–$6690. Tuition installment plan (monthly payment plans, quarterly payment plan). Merit scholarship grants, need-based scholarship grants available. In 2005–06, 20% of upper-school students received aid; total upper-school merit-scholarship money awarded: $5200. Total amount of financial aid awarded in 2005–06: $75,000.

Admissions Traditional secondary-level entrance grade is 9. For fall 2005, 540 students applied for upper-level admission, 520 were accepted, 476 enrolled. Math and English placement tests required. Deadline for receipt of application materials: none. Application fee required: $100. On-campus interview required.

Athletics Interscholastic: baseball (boys), basketball (b,g), cheering (g), cross-country running (b,g), dance team (g), football (b), golf (b,g), ice hockey (b,g), soccer (b,g), softball (g), strength & conditioning (b,g), tennis (b), track and field (b,g), volleyball (g); intramural: basketball (b,g), weight training (b,g). 2 PE instructors, 30 coaches, 1 trainer.

Computers Computers are regularly used in English, foreign language, history, keyboarding, mathematics, music, remedial study skills, science, speech, yearbook classes. Computer resources include campus e-mail, on-campus library services, CD-ROMs, online commercial services, Internet access.

Contact Mrs. Becky Berner, Director of Admissions. 651-484-8429 Ext. 136. Fax: 651-484-0594. E-mail: bberner@concordiaacademy.com. Web site: www.concordiaacademy.com.

CONCORDIA CONTINUING EDUCATION HIGH SCHOOL

10537-44 Street
Edmonton, Alberta T6A 1W1, Canada
Head of School: Marilyn Westbury

General Information Coeducational day college-preparatory school, affiliated with Lutheran Church. Grades 11–12. Approved or accredited by Alberta Department of Education. Language of instruction: English.

Upper School Student Profile 20% of students are Lutheran.

Admissions TOEFL or SLEP required. Deadline for receipt of application materials: none. No application fee required.

Contact Gerry Cameron, Coordinator Special Sessions. 780-413-7808. Fax: 780-466-9394. E-mail: gerry.cameron@concordia.ab.ca.

CONCORDIA HIGH SCHOOL

7128 Ada Boulevard
Edmonton, Alberta T5B 4E4, Canada
Head of School: Mr. David Eifert

General Information Coeducational boarding and day college-preparatory, arts, and religious studies school, affiliated with Lutheran Church. Grades 10–12. Founded: 1921. Setting: urban. Students are housed in single-sex dormitories. 12-acre campus. 1 building on campus. Approved or accredited by Association of Independent Schools and Colleges of Alberta, Canadian Association of Independent Schools, and Alberta Department of Education. Language of instruction: English. Total enrollment: 133. Upper school average class size: 16. Upper school faculty-student ratio: 1:10.

Upper School Student Profile 23% of students are boarding students. International students from Brazil, Hong Kong, Mexico, Republic of Korea, Thailand, and United States; 1 other country represented in student body. 20% of students are Lutheran.

Faculty School total: 15. In upper school: 5 men, 10 women; 7 have advanced degrees.

Subjects Offered Art, athletics, biology, career and personal planning, chemistry, choir, Christian education, drama, drama performance, English, French, information processing, mathematics, media arts, physical education, physics, religious studies, service learning/internship, social studies.

Graduation Requirements Advanced chemistry, advanced math, arts and fine arts (art, music, dance, drama), Christian education, French, language, religious studies.

Special Academic Programs Study at local college for college credit.

College Placement 42 students graduated in 2005; 37 went to college. Other: 3 went to work, 1 entered military service, 1 had other specific plans.

Student Life Upper grades have uniform requirement, student council. Discipline rests primarily with faculty. Attendance at religious services is required.

Tuition and Aid Day student tuition: CAN$4160; 5-day tuition and room/board: CAN$6266; 7-day tuition and room/board: CAN$6990. Tuition reduction for siblings, bursaries available.

Admissions TOEFL or SLEP required. Deadline for receipt of application materials: none. Application fee required: CAN$150. Interview required.

Athletics Interscholastic: basketball (boys, girls); intramural: basketball (b,g), soccer (b,g), volleyball (b,g); coed interscholastic: badminton, fitness, lacrosse; coed intramural: alpine skiing, canoeing/kayaking, cheering, cross-country running, curling, golf, outdoor activities, physical fitness.

Computers Computers are regularly used in media arts classes. Computer network features include campus e-mail, on-campus library services, Internet access.

Contact Mr. Keith Kruse, Assistant Principal. 780-479-9390. Fax: 780-479-5050. E-mail: highschool@concordia.ab.ca. Web site: www.concordiahighschool.com.

CONNELLY SCHOOL OF THE HOLY CHILD

9029 Bradley Boulevard
Potomac, Maryland 20854
Head of School: Mrs. Maureen K. Appel

General Information Girls' day college-preparatory, arts, and religious studies school, affiliated with Roman Catholic Church. Grades 6–12. Founded: 1961. Setting: suburban. Nearest major city is Washington, DC. 9-acre campus. 4 buildings on campus. Approved or accredited by Association of Independent Maryland Schools, Association of Independent Schools of Greater Washington, Middle States Association of Colleges and Schools, National Catholic Education Association, and Maryland Department of Education. Member of National Association of Independent Schools and Secondary School Admission Test Board. Total enrollment: 422. Upper school average class size: 16. Upper school faculty-student ratio: 1:16.

Upper School Student Profile Grade 9: 54 students (54 girls); Grade 10: 79 students (79 girls); Grade 11: 70 students (70 girls); Grade 12: 90 students (90 girls). 79% of students are Roman Catholic.

Faculty School total: 54. In upper school: 4 men, 35 women.

Subjects Offered Algebra, American history, American literature, art, biology, biology-AP, calculus, chemistry, community service, creative writing, drama, English, English literature, fine arts, French, French-AP, geometry, government/civics, health, history, humanities, instrumental music, Latin, literature, mathematics, music, photography, physical education, physics, religion, science, social studies, Spanish, Spanish-AP, speech, study skills, theater, trigonometry, world history, world literature, writing.

Graduation Requirements Arts and fine arts (art, music, dance, drama), computer skills, English, foreign language, mathematics, physical education (includes health), religion (includes Bible studies and theology), science, social studies (includes history). Community service is required.

Special Academic Programs Advanced Placement exam preparation in 9 subject areas; honors section; academic accommodation for the gifted, the musically talented, and the artistically talented.

College Placement 72 students graduated in 2005; all went to college, including Elon University; Fairfield University; Saint Joseph's University; The Catholic University of America; University of Maryland.

Student Life Upper grades have uniform requirement, student council, honor system. Discipline rests equally with students and faculty. Attendance at religious services is required.

Tuition and Aid Day student tuition: $17,695. Tuition installment plan (Insured Tuition Payment Plan, Key Tuition Payment Plan, monthly payment plans). Merit scholarship grants, need-based scholarship grants, middle-income loans available.

Admissions Traditional secondary-level entrance grade is 9. High School Placement Test, ISEE or SSAT required. Deadline for receipt of application materials: December 15. Application fee required: $50. Interview required.

Athletics Interscholastic: aerobics/dance, basketball, cross-country running, dance, dance squad, dance team, diving, equestrian sports, field hockey, fitness, horseback riding, indoor track, lacrosse, modern dance, soccer, softball, swimming and diving, tennis, track and field, volleyball, winter (indoor) track; intramural: aerobics, aerobics/dance, archery, badminton, baseball, cooperative games, dance, deck hockey, fencing, field hockey, fitness, fitness walking, flag football, floor hockey, football, Frisbee, golf, independent competitive sports, indoor hockey, indoor soccer, indoor track & field, jogging, jump rope, kickball, lacrosse, physical fitness, running, self defense, soccer, softball, street hockey, strength & conditioning, touch football, track and field, ultimate Frisbee, walking, wall climbing, weight training. 4 PE instructors, 31 coaches, 1 trainer.

Computers Computers are regularly used in English, foreign language, mathematics, religion, science, social studies classes. Computer network features include campus e-mail, on-campus library services, CD-ROMs, online commercial services, Internet access, DVD.

Contact Mrs. Meg Mayo, Director of Admissions. 301-365-0955. Fax: 301-365-0981. E-mail: admissions@holychild.org. Web site: www.holychild.org.

ANNOUNCEMENT FROM THE SCHOOL Connelly School of the Holy Child is a Catholic independent school community committed to the intellectual, spiritual, artistic, social, and physical development of each student; to academic challenge and the joy of learning; and to educating women of faith and action for compassionate service to humanity. The School was founded in 1961 by the Society of the Holy Child Jesus.

CONSERVE SCHOOL

5400 North Black Oak Lake Road
Land O' Lakes, Wisconsin 54540
Head of School: Mr. Stefan Anderson

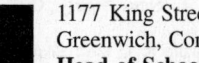

General Information Coeducational boarding college-preparatory, arts, and technology school. Grades 9–12. Founded: 2002. Setting: rural. Nearest major city is Green Bay. Students are housed in single-sex dormitories. 1,200-acre campus. 8 buildings on campus. Approved or accredited by Midwest Association of Boarding Schools. Candidate for accreditation by Independent Schools Association of the Central States. Language of instruction: English. Total enrollment: 135. Upper school average class size: 15. Upper school faculty-student ratio: 1:8.

Upper School Student Profile Grade 9: 30 students (16 boys, 14 girls); Grade 10: 41 students (20 boys, 21 girls); Grade 11: 40 students (19 boys, 21 girls); Grade 12: 24 students (10 boys, 14 girls). 100% of students are boarding students. 52% are state residents. 15 states are represented in upper school student body. 1% are international students. International students from Germany, Iceland, and Republic of Korea; 1 other country represented in student body.

Faculty School total: 23. In upper school: 10 men, 13 women; 19 have advanced degrees; all reside on campus.

Subjects Offered Algebra, American history, anatomy, art history-AP, astronomy, band, biology, biology-AP, calculus, calculus-AP, ceramics, Chinese, choir, computer technologies, creative writing, drama, ecology, English literature, environmental science, environmental science-AP, fine arts, geology, geometry, government, health and wellness, integrated mathematics, journalism, music, orchestra, painting, photography, physics, physics-AP, piano, pre-calculus, printmaking, research, Spanish, statistics, technology, U.S. government, U.S. history-AP, world history, world literature.

Graduation Requirements Arts and fine arts (art, music, dance, drama), English literature, history, mathematics, modern languages, science, technology, wellness, independent research.

Special Academic Programs Advanced Placement exam preparation in 5 subject areas; honors section; ESL (8 students enrolled).

College Placement 13 students graduated in 2004; all went to college, including Brown University; Carleton College; Dartmouth College; The Colorado College; University of Wisconsin–Madison. Mean SAT verbal: 675, mean SAT math: 627.

Student Life Upper grades have specified standards of dress, student council, honor system. Discipline rests equally with students and faculty.

Tuition and Aid 7-day tuition and room/board: $26,500. Tuition installment plan (Key Tuition Payment Plan, monthly payment plans). Merit scholarship grants, need-based scholarship grants available. In 2004–05, 95% of upper-school students

received aid; total upper-school merit-scholarship money awarded: $498,950. Total amount of financial aid awarded in 2004–05: $2,381,500.

Admissions Traditional secondary-level entrance grade is 9. For fall 2005, 83 students applied for upper-level admission, 64 were accepted, 47 enrolled. ISEE or SSAT, ERB, PSAT, SAT, PLAN or ACT required. Deadline for receipt of application materials: February 15. Application fee required: $35. Interview required.

Athletics Interscholastic: baseball (boys), basketball (b,g), cross-country running (b,g), nordic skiing (b,g), skiing (cross-country) (b,g), soccer (b,g), softball (g), track and field (b,g), volleyball (g); coed intramural: aerobics, aerobics/dance, alpine skiing, archery, back packing, badminton, biathlon, bicycling, canoeing/kayaking, climbing, cooperative games, dance, figure skating, fishing, fitness, fitness walking, fly fishing, freestyle skiing, Frisbee, golf, hiking/backpacking, ice skating, jogging, judo, juggling, jump rope, kayaking, life saving, martial arts, modern dance, mountain biking, outdoor activities, outdoor adventure, outdoor education, outdoor recreation, outdoor skills, paddle tennis, paint ball, physical fitness, physical training, racquetball, rock climbing, rowing, running, skateboarding, skiing (downhill), snowboarding, snowshoeing, strength & conditioning, swimming and diving, table tennis, telemark skiing, ultimate Frisbee, walking, wall climbing, wallyball, weight lifting, weight training, wilderness, wilderness survival, windsurfing, winter walking. 2 PE instructors, 5 coaches, 1 trainer.

Computers Computers are regularly used in all academic classes. Computer network features include campus e-mail, on-campus library services, Internet access, file transfer, office computer access, wireless campus network.

Contact Mr. James E. Smith, Head of Admissions. 715-547-1321. Fax: 715-547-1390. E-mail: admissions@conserveschool.org. Web site: www.conserveschool.org.

See full description on page 744.

CONVENT OF THE SACRED HEART

1177 King Street
Greenwich, Connecticut 06831
Head of School: Sr. Joan Magnetti, RSCJ

General Information Girls' day college-preparatory, arts, religious studies, bilingual studies, and technology school, affiliated with Roman Catholic Church. Grades PS–12. Founded: 1848. Setting: suburban. Nearest major city is New York, NY. 110-acre campus. 3 buildings on campus. Approved or accredited by Connecticut Association of Independent Schools, Network of Sacred Heart Schools, New England Association of Schools and Colleges, The College Board, and Connecticut Department of Education. Member of National Association of Independent Schools and Secondary School Admission Test Board. Endowment: $18 million. Total enrollment: 695. Upper school average class size: 13. Upper school faculty-student ratio: 1:7.

Upper School Student Profile Grade 9: 79 students (79 girls); Grade 10: 57 students (57 girls); Grade 11: 55 students (55 girls); Grade 12: 52 students (52 girls). 70% of students are Roman Catholic.

Faculty School total: 111. In upper school: 14 men, 35 women; 34 have advanced degrees.

Subjects Offered Advanced Placement courses, algebra, American history, American literature, American literature-AP, art, art history, astronomy, biology, biology-AP, broadcast journalism, calculus, ceramics, chemistry, choir, choral music, Christian education, Christian ethics, Christian scripture, Christian studies, Christian testament, Christianity, college counseling, college placement, community service, computer programming, computer science, creative writing, dance, dance performance, design, drama, earth science, ecology, English, English language and composition-AP, English literature, environmental science, ethics, European history, expository writing, fine arts, French, French-AP, geography, geometry, government/civics, grammar, health, history, journalism, Latin, logic, madrigals, mathematics, mathematics-AP, media production, moral and social development, music, photography, physical education, physics, pre-calculus, SAT/ACT preparation, science, social studies, Spanish, statistics, student government, student publications, theater, theology, trigonometry, visual and performing arts, world history, world literature, writing, yearbook.

Graduation Requirements Arts and fine arts (art, music, dance, drama), electives, English, foreign language, mathematics, physical education (includes health), religion (includes Bible studies and theology), science, social studies (includes history). Community service is required.

Special Academic Programs Advanced Placement exam preparation in 14 subject areas; honors section; accelerated programs; independent study; term-away projects; domestic exchange program (with Network of Sacred Heart Schools); study abroad; academic accommodation for the gifted and the artistically talented.

College Placement 55 students graduated in 2005; all went to college, including Stanford University; University of Notre Dame. Median SAT verbal: 630, median SAT math: 640.

Student Life Upper grades have uniform requirement, student council, honor system. Discipline rests equally with students and faculty. Attendance at religious services is required.

Tuition and Aid Day student tuition: $24,900. Tuition installment plan (Academic Management Services Plan). Merit scholarship grants, need-based scholarship grants available. In 2005–06, 21% of upper-school students received aid. Total amount of financial aid awarded in 2005–06: $864,150.

Convent of the Sacred Heart

Admissions Traditional secondary-level entrance grade is 9. For fall 2005, 100 students applied for upper-level admission, 45 were accepted, 30 enrolled. ERB Reading and Math or ISEE required. Deadline for receipt of application materials: February 1. Application fee required: $50. On-campus interview required.

Athletics Interscholastic: basketball, crew, cross-country running, diving, field hockey, golf, lacrosse, soccer, softball, squash, swimming and diving, tennis; intramural: aerobics/dance, aerobics/nautilus, aquatics, dance, dance squad, independent competitive sports, yoga. 5 PE instructors, 18 coaches, 1 trainer.

Computers Computers are regularly used in all academic classes. Computer network features include campus e-mail, on-campus library services, CD-ROMs, online commercial services, Internet access, DVD, wireless campus network.

Contact Pamela R. McKenna, Director of Admission. 203-532-3534. Fax: 203-531-3301. E-mail: admission@cshgreenwich.org. Web site: www.cshgreenwich.org.

See full description on page 746.

CONVENT OF THE SACRED HEART

1 East 91st Street
New York, New York 10128-0689
Head of School: Dr. Mary Blake

General Information Girls' day college-preparatory school, affiliated with Roman Catholic Church. Grades N–12. Founded: 1881. Setting: urban. 2 buildings on campus. Approved or accredited by New York State Association of Independent Schools and New York Department of Education. Member of National Association of Independent Schools and Secondary School Admission Test Board. Endowment: $18.2 million. Total enrollment: 655. Upper school average class size: 16. Upper school faculty-student ratio: 1:5.

Upper School Student Profile Grade 8: 47 students (47 girls); Grade 9: 51 students (51 girls); Grade 10: 51 students (51 girls); Grade 11: 39 students (39 girls); Grade 12: 48 students (48 girls). 66% of students are Roman Catholic.

Faculty School total: 109. In upper school: 16 men, 38 women; 43 have advanced degrees.

Subjects Offered Advanced studio art-AP, algebra, American history, American literature, art, audio visual/media, biology, biology-AP, calculus, calculus-AP, campus ministry, ceramics, chemistry, chemistry-AP, chorus, computer applications, computer multimedia, creative writing, dance, desktop publishing, digital photography, drama, earth science, East European studies, English, English literature, English literature-AP, environmental science, ethics, European history, expository writing, film history, fine arts, finite math, forensics, French, French-AP, functions, geography, geometry, government/civics, handbells, health, Hebrew scripture, history, journalism, Latin, madrigals, mathematics, model United Nations, multicultural literature, multimedia design, music, musical theater, performing arts, photography, physical education, physical science, physics, physics-AP, portfolio art, pottery, pre-calculus, religion, science, science research, social studies, Spanish, Spanish-AP, speech, statistics, statistics-AP, theater, theology, trigonometry, U.S. history-AP, visual arts, women's literature, world history, world issues, world literature, world religions, writing.

Graduation Requirements Arts and fine arts (art, music, dance, drama), computer science, English, foreign language, mathematics, physical education (includes health), religion (includes Bible studies and theology), science, social studies (includes history).

Special Academic Programs Advanced Placement exam preparation in 18 subject areas; honors section; independent study; term-away projects; domestic exchange program (with Network of Sacred Heart Schools); study abroad; academic accommodation for the gifted.

College Placement 47 students graduated in 2005; all went to college, including Boston College; Cornell University; Fordham University; New York University; Princeton University; University of Pennsylvania.

Student Life Upper grades have uniform requirement, student council. Discipline rests primarily with faculty. Attendance at religious services is required.

Summer Programs Sports, art/fine arts, computer instruction programs offered; session focuses on visual and performing arts; held on campus; accepts boys and girls; open to students from other schools. 160 students usually enrolled. 2006 schedule: June 30 to July 25. Application deadline: April 15.

Tuition and Aid Day student tuition: $24,410. Tuition installment plan (Key Tuition Payment Plan). Need-based scholarship grants, need-based loans available. In 2005–06, 37% of upper-school students received aid. Total amount of financial aid awarded in 2005–06: $1,392,265.

Admissions Traditional secondary-level entrance grade is 9. For fall 2005, 163 students applied for upper-level admission, 43 were accepted, 19 enrolled. ISEE required. Deadline for receipt of application materials: December 15. Application fee required: $50. On-campus interview required.

Athletics Interscholastic: basketball, cross-country running, indoor track & field, lacrosse, soccer, softball, swimming and diving, tennis, track and field, volleyball, winter (indoor) track; intramural: basketball, fitness, jogging, physical training, roller blading, running, soccer, softball, swimming and diving, tennis, volleyball, weight lifting, weight training. 6 PE instructors, 6 coaches, 1 trainer.

Computers Computers are regularly used in all academic classes. Computer network features include campus e-mail, on-campus library services, CD-ROMs, online commercial services, Internet access, file transfer.

Contact Angela P. Liang, Admissions Office Coordinator. 212-722-4745 Ext. 105. Fax: 212-996-1784. E-mail: aliang@cshnyc.org. Web site: www.cshnyc.org.

ANNOUNCEMENT FROM THE SCHOOL Chartered in 1881, Convent of the Sacred Heart is a member of the international network of Sacred Heart schools and the oldest independent girls' school in New York City. The beautiful facilities are located in two landmark buildings overlooking Central Park. The school is dedicated to the holistic development of young women, and committed to preparing students for the challenges of the modern world. "As we teach children to read, write, listen, think, imagine and create, we need also to educate them to their responsibilities as citizens who will create a more just and compassionate world," states Dr. Mary Blake, headmistress. The Lower School provides a strong learning foundation, and is designed to help students become inquisitive, original thinkers through intensive personal attention and small-group study. By the time students reach the Middle School, comprised of grades 5 through 7, they are ready for more abstract study in the basic subjects. They continue the study of foreign languages, begun in grade 3, while thoroughly preparing for the academic challenges of the Upper School. The Upper School curriculum is rigorous. In addition to demanding college-preparatory courses, a wide variety of electives are offered, many highlighting the unique cultural advantages of New York City. Advanced Placement courses are offered in English, history, modern and classical languages, mathematics, sciences, studio art, and music. In addition, religion courses are required of all Sacred Heart students. Cocurricular activities include student government; Model UN; literary, science, and second-language publications; theatrical productions; mock trial; forensics; women of proud heritage; hand bells; archeology; chorus; math team; and numerous student-run clubs, while numerous athletic teams compete with other independent schools. Students may participate in an exchange program with other Sacred Heart schools in Europe and the United States. Service activities are expected of each student, exemplifying the commitment of Sacred Heart education to social justice and the support of the broader community.

CONVENT OF THE SACRED HEART HIGH SCHOOL

2222 Broadway
San Francisco, California 94115
Head of School: Douglas H. Grant

General Information Girls' day college-preparatory, arts, religious studies, and technology school, affiliated with Roman Catholic Church. Grades 9–12. Founded: 1887. Setting: urban. 2-acre campus. 3 buildings on campus. Approved or accredited by California Association of Independent Schools, Network of Sacred Heart Schools, and Western Association of Schools and Colleges. Member of National Association of Independent Schools and Secondary School Admission Test Board. Endowment: $7 million. Total enrollment: 210. Upper school average class size: 12. Upper school faculty-student ratio: 1:6.

Upper School Student Profile Grade 9: 54 students (54 girls); Grade 10: 60 students (60 girls); Grade 11: 50 students (50 girls); Grade 12: 53 students (53 girls). 51% of students are Roman Catholic.

Faculty School total: 137. In upper school: 10 men, 25 women; 22 have advanced degrees.

Subjects Offered 3-dimensional art, 3-dimensional design, advanced computer applications, algebra, American government-AP, American history, American literature, analysis, applied arts, applied music, art appreciation, art education, art history, art history-AP, Basic programming, biology, biology-AP, British literature, British literature (honors), calculus, calculus-AP, ceramics, chemistry, chemistry-AP, choir, choral music, chorus, college admission preparation, community service, comparative political systems-AP, composition-AP, computer applications, computer education, computer programming, computer programming-AP, computer science, computer science-AP, computer skills, computer studies, creative writing, drama, drawing and design, economics, economics and history, English, English language and composition-AP, English literature, English literature and composition-AP, environmental science, environmental science-AP, ethics, ethics and responsibility, European history, European history-AP, expository writing, film studies, fine arts, French, French language-AP, freshman seminar, geometry, government and politics-AP, government/civics, graphic arts, health, historical foundations for arts, history, honors algebra, honors English, honors U.S. history, honors world history, Japanese, journalism, Latin, Mandarin, marine biology, music, philosophy, photography, photojournalism, physical education, physics, physiology, probability, qualitative analysis, religion, religious studies, social studies, Spanish, statistics and probability, studio art-AP, theology, trigonometry, women's studies, world history, world literature, yearbook.

Graduation Requirements Arts and fine arts (art, music, dance, drama), computer science, English, foreign language, history, mathematics, physical education (includes health), religion (includes Bible studies and theology), science. Community service is required.

Special Academic Programs Advanced Placement exam preparation in 19 subject areas; honors section; accelerated programs; independent study; domestic exchange program (with Network of Sacred Heart Schools).

College Placement 50 students graduated in 2005; all went to college, including University of California, Davis; University of California, Los Angeles; University of Colorado at Boulder; University of Puget Sound; University of San Diego; University of Southern California. Median SAT verbal: 600, median SAT math: 570.

Student Life Upper grades have uniform requirement, student council, honor system. Discipline rests equally with students and faculty. Attendance at religious services is required.

Tuition and Aid Day student tuition: $23,500. Tuition installment plan (Insured Tuition Payment Plan, Key Tuition Payment Plan, 2-payment plan). Need-based scholarship grants available. In 2005–06, 40% of upper-school students received aid. Total amount of financial aid awarded in 2005–06: $700,000.

Admissions Traditional secondary-level entrance grade is 9. For fall 2005, 193 students applied for upper-level admission, 97 were accepted, 61 enrolled. High School Placement Test (closed version) from Scholastic Testing Service or SSAT required. Deadline for receipt of application materials: January 3. Application fee required: $75. On-campus interview required.

Athletics Interscholastic: basketball, crew, cross-country running, golf, soccer, swimming and diving, tennis, volleyball; intramural: badminton, basketball, cross-country running, golf, gymnastics, sailing, soccer, swimming and diving, tennis, volleyball, wall climbing; coed interscholastic: fencing. 1 PE instructor, 3 coaches.

Computers Computers are regularly used in all academic classes. Computer network features include campus e-mail, on-campus library services, CD-ROMs, online commercial services, Internet access, file transfer, wireless campus network, Palm PDA program (beaming station in student center allows students to download homework), announcements and calendars (updated daily).

Contact Ms. Caitlin S. Curran, Admissions Director. 415-292-3125. Fax: 415-929-0553. E-mail: ccurran@sacredsf.org. Web site: www.sacredsf.org.

ANNOUNCEMENT FROM THE SCHOOL Convent of the Sacred Heart High School is an independent, Catholic, college-preparatory high school for 200 girls founded in 1887 by the Religious of the Sacred Heart located in Pacific Heights. CSH was most recently recognized by the U.S. Department of Education as a National Exemplary School.

CONVENT OF THE VISITATION SCHOOL

2455 Visitation Drive
Mendota Heights, Minnesota 55120-1696
Head of School: Dawn Nichols

General Information Coeducational day college-preparatory, arts, religious studies, and technology school, affiliated with Roman Catholic Church. Boys grades PK–6, girls grades PK–12. Founded: 1873. Setting: suburban. Nearest major city is St. Paul. 50-acre campus. 1 building on campus. Approved or accredited by Independent Schools Association of the Central States and Minnesota Department of Education. Member of National Association of Independent Schools and Secondary School Admission Test Board. Endowment: $900,000. Total enrollment: 605. Upper school average class size: 17. Upper school faculty-student ratio: 1:13.

Upper School Student Profile Grade 9: 92 students (92 girls); Grade 10: 77 students (77 girls); Grade 11: 80 students (80 girls); Grade 12: 69 students (69 girls). 84% of students are Roman Catholic.

Faculty School total: 64. In upper school: 9 men, 27 women; 26 have advanced degrees.

Subjects Offered Algebra, American history, American literature, anatomy, art, astronomy, ballet, biology, biology-AP, British literature, calculus, calculus-AP, ceramics, chamber groups, chemistry, child development, choir, Christian scripture, composition, computer science, creative writing, desktop publishing, drawing, economics, English, English literature, English literature-AP, European history, French, French-AP, genetics, geometry, government, graphic design, health, history, history-AP, honors algebra, Latin, literary genres, math analysis, mathematics, music, orchestra, painting, peer ministry, photography, physical education, physical science, physics, physiology, prayer/spirituality, psychology, religion, science, senior seminar, sociology, Spanish, Spanish-AP, speech, theater, U.S. government-AP, U.S. history, Web site design, women spirituality and faith, world culture, world history, world religions.

Graduation Requirements Arts and fine arts (art, music, dance, drama), computer science, English, foreign language, mathematics, physical education (includes health), religion (includes Bible studies and theology), science, social science, social studies (includes history), two-week senior year service project.

Special Academic Programs Advanced Placement exam preparation in 11 subject areas; honors section; independent study; study at local college for college credit.

College Placement 64 students graduated in 2005; all went to college, including College of Saint Benedict; DePaul University; Saint Louis University; St. Olaf College; University of Notre Dame; University of Wisconsin–Madison. Mean SAT verbal: 604, mean SAT math: 584, mean composite ACT: 27.

Student Life Upper grades have uniform requirement, student council, honor system. Discipline rests primarily with faculty. Attendance at religious services is required.

Tuition and Aid Day student tuition: $14,328. Tuition installment plan (monthly payment plans, individually arranged payment plans, semi-annual payment plan). Need-based scholarship grants, funds allocated from the Archdiocese available. In 2005–06, 32% of upper-school students received aid. Total amount of financial aid awarded in 2005–06: $700,000.

Admissions Traditional secondary-level entrance grade is 9. For fall 2005, 102 students applied for upper-level admission, 65 were accepted, 56 enrolled. ERB, Individual IQ and Iowa Tests of Basic Skills required. Deadline for receipt of application materials: January 6. Application fee required: $25. Interview required.

Athletics Interscholastic: alpine skiing, basketball, cross-country running, diving, golf, hockey, ice hockey, lacrosse, nordic skiing, skiing (cross-country), skiing (downhill), soccer, softball, swimming and diving, tennis, track and field, volleyball; intramural: ballet, basketball. 30 coaches, 1 trainer.

Computers Computers are regularly used in all classes. Computer network features include on-campus library services, CD-ROMs, online commercial services, Internet access, file transfer, office computer access, DVD, wireless campus network.

Contact Patty Healy Janssen, Director of Admissions and Marketing. 651-683-1705. Fax: 651-454-7144. E-mail: phealy@vischool.org. Web site: www.visitation.net.

COPIAH ACADEMY

PO Box 125
Gallman, Mississippi 39077
Head of School: Carol Rigby

General Information Coeducational day college-preparatory school. Grades 1–12. Founded: 1967. Setting: rural. Nearest major city is Hazlehurst. 30-acre campus. 3 buildings on campus. Approved or accredited by Mississippi Private School Association and Southern Association of Colleges and Schools. Endowment: $150,000. Total enrollment: 496. Upper school average class size: 19. Upper school faculty-student ratio: 1:17.

Upper School Student Profile Grade 7: 37 students (21 boys, 16 girls); Grade 8: 40 students (22 boys, 18 girls); Grade 9: 36 students (19 boys, 17 girls); Grade 10: 50 students (21 boys, 29 girls); Grade 11: 45 students (21 boys, 24 girls); Grade 12: 43 students (26 boys, 17 girls).

Faculty School total: 36. In upper school: 7 men, 10 women; 9 have advanced degrees.

Subjects Offered Calculus, cheerleading, chemistry, choir, civics, computer technologies, consumer mathematics, current history, driver education, earth science, economics, electives, English, English language-AP, environmental science, foreign language, French, geography, geometry, golf, government, health and wellness, history, history-AP, honors English, honors U.S. history, intro to computers, marching band, music appreciation, oral communications, participation in sports, physics, pre-algebra, softball, space and physical sciences, Spanish, speech, sports, state history, track and field, trigonometry, U.S. government, U.S. history, U.S. history-AP, world history.

Graduation Requirements Algebra, American government, American history, biology, electives, English, science.

Special Academic Programs Honors section; study at local college for college credit.

College Placement Colleges students went to include Mississippi College; Mississippi State University; University of Mississippi. Mean composite ACT: 21. 10% scored over 26 on composite ACT.

Student Life Upper grades have specified standards of dress, student council. Discipline rests primarily with faculty.

Tuition and Aid Day student tuition: $3000. Tuition reduction for siblings, need-based scholarship grants available. In 2005–06, 3% of upper-school students received aid. Total amount of financial aid awarded in 2005–06: $3923.

Admissions Traditional secondary-level entrance grade is 9. For fall 2005, 12 students applied for upper-level admission, 12 were accepted, 12 enrolled. Deadline for receipt of application materials: none. No application fee required.

Athletics Interscholastic: baseball (boys), basketball (b,g), cheering (g), cross-country running (b,g), dance team (g), football (b), soccer (b,g), softball (g), tennis (b,g), track and field (b,g); intramural: basketball (b,g), football (b), strength & conditioning (b,g); coed interscholastic: golf. 1 PE instructor, 7 coaches.

Computers Computers are regularly used in writing classes. Computer resources include on-campus library services, CD-ROMs, online commercial services, Internet access.

Contact Candy Price, Secretary. 601-892-3770. Fax: 601-892-6222. Web site: www.copiahacademy.org.

CORNELIA CONNELLY SCHOOL

2323 West Broadway
Anaheim, California 92804
Head of School: Sr. Francine Gunther, SHCJ

General Information Girls' day college-preparatory, arts, and religious studies school, affiliated with Roman Catholic Church. Grades 9–12. Founded: 1961. Setting: urban. Nearest major city is Los Angeles. 6-acre campus. 7 buildings on campus.

Cornelia Connelly School

Approved or accredited by California Association of Independent Schools, National Catholic Education Association, Western Association of Schools and Colleges, and Western Catholic Education Association. Member of National Association of Independent Schools. Total enrollment: 290. Upper school average class size: 18.

Upper School Student Profile Grade 9: 82 students (82 girls); Grade 10: 88 students (88 girls); Grade 11: 63 students (63 girls); Grade 12: 57 students (57 girls). 80% of students are Roman Catholic.

Faculty School total: 30. In upper school: 8 men, 22 women; 14 have advanced degrees.

Subjects Offered Arts, chemistry, community service, English, fine arts, French, general science, mathematics, physical education, religion, science, social studies, Spanish.

Graduation Requirements Arts and fine arts (art, music, dance, drama), English, foreign language, mathematics, physical education (includes health), religion (includes Bible studies and theology), science, social studies (includes history). Community service is required.

Special Academic Programs Advanced Placement exam preparation in 12 subject areas; honors section; independent study; term-away projects.

College Placement 42 went to college, including California State University, Fullerton; California State University, Long Beach; Chapman University; Santa Clara University; Stanford University; University of San Diego. Other: 1 entered military service.

Student Life Upper grades have uniform requirement, student council, honor system. Discipline rests primarily with faculty. Attendance at religious services is required.

Summer Programs Enrichment, advancement programs offered; held on campus; accepts boys and girls; open to students from other schools. 2006 schedule: June 20 to July 29.

Tuition and Aid Day student tuition: $9400. Tuition installment plan (Key Tuition Payment Plan, FACTS Tuition Payment Plan, 2-payment plan (July and December), 1-payment plan (July)). Merit scholarship grants, need-based scholarship grants available.

Admissions Traditional secondary-level entrance grade is 9. High School Placement Test (closed version) from Scholastic Testing Service required. Deadline for receipt of application materials: none. Application fee required: $50. Interview required.

Athletics Interscholastic: basketball, cheering, cross-country running, golf, soccer, softball, tennis, track and field, volleyball. 2 PE instructors, 7 coaches.

Computers Computers are regularly used in all academic, basic skills, college planning, library, publications, SAT preparation, yearbook classes. Computer network features include CD-ROMs, Internet access, file transfer, DVD, wireless campus network.

Contact Ms. Michele Alcaraz, Director of Admissions and Tuition Assistance. 714-776-1717 Ext. 34. Fax: 714-776-2534. E-mail: malcaraz@connellyhs.org.

ANNOUNCEMENT FROM THE SCHOOL Cornelia Connelly High School is an independent, fully accredited, college-preparatory school for young women. Through small class size, attention to each individual, and a comprehensive educational program, Connelly creates a values-based learning culture that empowers young women to become articulate and self-confident and to use their gifts to contribute to a changing world.

THE COTTAGE SCHOOL

Roswell, Georgia
See Special Needs Schools section.

THE COUNTRY DAY SCHOOL

13415 Dufferin Street
King City, Ontario L7B 1K5, Canada
Head of School: Mr. Paul C. Duckett

General Information Coeducational day college-preparatory, arts, business, and technology school. Grades JK–12. Founded: 1972. Setting: rural. Nearest major city is Toronto, Canada. 100-acre campus. 2 buildings on campus. Approved or accredited by Canadian Association of Independent Schools, Canadian Educational Standards Institute, Conference of Independent Schools of Ontario, and Ontario Department of Education. Language of instruction: English. Total enrollment: 729. Upper school average class size: 15. Upper school faculty-student ratio: 1:10.

Upper School Student Profile Grade 9: 80 students (40 boys, 40 girls); Grade 10: 80 students (40 boys, 40 girls); Grade 11: 80 students (40 boys, 40 girls); Grade 12: 80 students (40 boys, 40 girls).

Faculty School total: 79. In upper school: 28 men, 20 women.

Subjects Offered Advanced chemistry, advanced computer applications, advanced math, algebra, American history, anatomy and physiology, ancient history, ancient/medieval philosophy, art and culture, art history, athletics, band, biology, business studies, Canadian geography, Canadian history, Canadian literature, career education, career/college preparation, choir, comparative politics, computer programming, creative writing, English, environmental geography, European history, French,

government/civics, history, languages, mathematics, modern Western civilization, performing arts, philosophy, physical education, physics, politics, science, society, world history.

Graduation Requirements Ministry Grade 10 Literacy Test (Government of Ontario).

Special Academic Programs Advanced Placement exam preparation in 2 subject areas; accelerated programs.

College Placement 76 students graduated in 2005; all went to college, including McGill University; McMaster University; Queen's University at Kingston; The University of Western Ontario; University of Guelph; University of Toronto.

Student Life Upper grades have uniform requirement, student council, honor system. Discipline rests primarily with faculty.

Summer Programs Enrichment, advancement, art/fine arts programs offered; session focuses on enrichment; held both on and off campus; held at Spain and Temagami, Ontario; accepts boys and girls; open to students from other schools. 15 students usually enrolled. 2006 schedule: July 2 to July 31. Application deadline: March 2.

Tuition and Aid Day student tuition: CAN$17,750.

Admissions Traditional secondary-level entrance grade is 9. For fall 2005, 97 students applied for upper-level admission, 58 were accepted, 37 enrolled. CAT 5, school's own test or writing sample required. Deadline for receipt of application materials: none. Application fee required: CAN$100. On-campus interview required.

Athletics Interscholastic: baseball (girls), basketball (b,g), cross-country running (b,g), golf (b,g), rugby (b,g), running (b,g), soccer (b,g), softball (b,g), track and field (b,g), volleyball (b,g); intramural: alpine skiing (b,g), badminton (b,g), ball hockey (b,g), basketball (b,g), bowling (b,g), cooperative games (b,g), ice hockey (b), ice skating (b,g), skiing (downhill) (b,g), snowboarding (b,g), soccer (b,g), softball (b,g), volleyball (b,g); coed intramural: curling, Frisbee. 5 PE instructors.

Computers Computers are regularly used in accounting, business, career education, English, geography, history, mathematics, media, music, writing, yearbook classes. Computer network features include campus e-mail, on-campus library services, CD-ROMs, Internet access, DVD, wireless campus network, access to online library resources from home.

Contact Mr. Christopher White, Director of Admission and University Placement. 905-833-1220. Fax: 905-833-1350. E-mail: admissions@cds.on.ca. Web site: www.cds.on.ca/.

COUNTRY DAY SCHOOL OF THE SACRED HEART

480 Bryn Mawr Avenue
Bryn Mawr, Pennsylvania 19010
Head of School: Sr. Matthew Anita MacDonald, SSJ

General Information Girls' day college-preparatory, arts, religious studies, and technology school, affiliated with Roman Catholic Church. Grades PK–12. Founded: 1865. Setting: suburban. Nearest major city is Philadelphia. 16-acre campus. 3 buildings on campus. Approved or accredited by Middle States Association of Colleges and Schools, Pennsylvania Association of Private Academic Schools, and Pennsylvania Department of Education. Member of National Association of Independent Schools. Endowment: $5 million. Total enrollment: 366. Upper school average class size: 15. Upper school faculty-student ratio: 1:10.

Upper School Student Profile Grade 9: 53 students (53 girls); Grade 10: 51 students (51 girls); Grade 11: 43 students (43 girls); Grade 12: 43 students (43 girls). 75% of students are Roman Catholic.

Faculty School total: 48. In upper school: 4 men, 23 women; 19 have advanced degrees.

Subjects Offered Algebra, American history, American history-AP, American literature, art, arts, Bible studies, biology, calculus, chemistry, composition, computer science, economics, English, English literature, environmental science, ethics, European history, film, fine arts, French, geometry, government/civics, health, Latin, mathematics, media studies, physical education, physics, pre-calculus, religion, science, social science, social studies, Spanish, trigonometry, word processing, world history, world literature.

Graduation Requirements Arts and fine arts (art, music, dance, drama), English, foreign language, mathematics, physical education (includes health), religion (includes Bible studies and theology), science, social studies (includes history), two weeks of senior independent study with a professional at his or her work, 25 hours of community service per year.

Special Academic Programs Advanced Placement exam preparation in 5 subject areas; honors section; independent study; term-away projects; study at local college for college credit; domestic exchange program (with Network of Sacred Heart Schools); study abroad; academic accommodation for the musically talented.

College Placement 56 students graduated in 2005; all went to college, including The Catholic University of America; The Pennsylvania State University University Park Campus; Villanova University. Mean SAT verbal: 590, mean SAT math: 570.

Student Life Upper grades have uniform requirement, student council. Discipline rests equally with students and faculty. Attendance at religious services is required.

Tuition and Aid Day student tuition: $12,750. Tuition installment plan (SMART Tuition Payment Plan). Tuition reduction for siblings, merit scholarship grants, need-based scholarship grants available. In 2005–06, 31% of upper-school students received aid; total upper-school merit-scholarship money awarded: $250,500. Total amount of financial aid awarded in 2005–06: $300,020.

Admissions Traditional secondary-level entrance grade is 9. For fall 2005, 140 students applied for upper-level admission, 120 were accepted, 35 enrolled. High School Placement Test required. Deadline for receipt of application materials: November 25. Application fee required: $35. Interview required.

Athletics Interscholastic: basketball, crew, field hockey, golf, lacrosse, softball, tennis, track and field, volleyball. 2 PE instructors, 12 coaches.

Computers Computers are regularly used in English, foreign language, history, mathematics, science, technology classes. Computer network features include campus e-mail, on-campus library services, CD-ROMs, online commercial services, Internet access.

Contact Mrs. Laurie Nowlan, Director of Admissions. 610-527-3915 Ext. 214. Fax: 610-527-0942. E-mail: lnowlan@cdssh.org. Web site: www.cdssh.org.

ANNOUNCEMENT FROM THE SCHOOL Sacred Heart, a member of the Network of Sacred Heart Schools, is a Catholic college-preparatory school for girls in preK–grade 12. The 370 students represent all faiths within a family environment. A comprehensive liberal arts education meets the needs of self-motivated, intellectually aware students. Advanced Placement courses, outstanding community service, superior athletics are highlights.

COVENANT CANADIAN REFORMED SCHOOL

PO Box 67
Neerlandia, Alberta T0G 1R0, Canada
Head of School: Harry VanDelden

General Information Coeducational day college-preparatory, general academic, business, religious studies, and technology school, affiliated with Reformed Church. Grades K–12. Founded: 1977. Setting: rural. Nearest major city is Barrhead, Canada. 5-acre campus. 2 buildings on campus. Approved or accredited by Association of Independent Schools and Colleges of Alberta and Alberta Department of Education. Language of instruction: English. Total enrollment: 155. Upper school average class size: 10. Upper school faculty-student ratio: 1:10.

Upper School Student Profile Grade 10: 14 students (7 boys, 7 girls); Grade 11: 8 students (6 boys, 2 girls); Grade 12: 8 students (3 boys, 5 girls). 99% of students are Reformed.

Faculty School total: 12. In upper school: 6 men, 1 woman.

Subjects Offered Accounting, architectural drawing, Bible studies, biology, Canadian geography, Canadian law, career and personal planning, career technology, child development, Christian education, computer information systems, computer keyboarding, computer skills, computer studies, consumer law, desktop publishing, digital photography, drawing and design, early childhood, electronic publishing, English, ESL, French as a second language, geology, health education, HTML design, information processing, intro to computers, introduction to technology, keyboarding/computer, mathematics, physical education, prayer/spirituality, religious studies, science, sewing, social studies, theology and the arts, Web site design, Western religions, work experience, world geography, world religions, yearbook.

Special Academic Programs Independent study; remedial reading and/or remedial writing; remedial math; programs in English, mathematics, general development for dyslexic students; ESL (1 student enrolled).

College Placement 12 students graduated in 2005; 8 went to college, including Grossmont College; University of Alberta. Other: 4 went to work.

Student Life Upper grades have specified standards of dress, student council. Discipline rests primarily with faculty.

Tuition and Aid Day student tuition: CAN$4500. Tuition installment plan (monthly payment plans, individually arranged payment plans).

Admissions Traditional secondary-level entrance grade is 10. For fall 2005, 4 students applied for upper-level admission, 4 were accepted, 4 enrolled. Achievement/Aptitude/Writing or Canadian Standardized Test required. Deadline for receipt of application materials: none. No application fee required. Interview required.

Athletics Coed Intramural: badminton, ball hockey, baseball, basketball, flag football, floor hockey, football, Frisbee, hockey, ice hockey, indoor hockey, indoor soccer, lacrosse, soccer, softball, volleyball.

Computers Computers are regularly used in all classes. Computer resources include on-campus library services, CD-ROMs, Internet access, file transfer, DVD.

Contact Mr. Harry VanDelden, Principal. 780-674-4774. Fax: 780-674-6410. E-mail: hvd@xplornet.com.

THE CRAIG SCHOOL

Mountain Lakes, New Jersey
See Special Needs Schools section.

CRANBROOK SCHOOLS

39221 Woodward Avenue
PO Box 801
Bloomfield Hills, Michigan 48303-0801
Head of School: Arlyce Seibert

General Information Coeducational boarding and day college-preparatory and arts school. Boarding grades 9–12, day grades PK–12. Founded: 1922. Setting: suburban. Nearest major city is Detroit. Students are housed in single-sex dormitories. 315-acre campus. 10 buildings on campus. Approved or accredited by Independent Schools Association of the Central States, Midwest Association of Boarding Schools, The Association of Boarding Schools, The College Board, and Michigan Department of Education. Member of National Association of Independent Schools and Secondary School Admission Test Board. Endowment: $150 million. Total enrollment: 1,620. Upper school average class size: 16. Upper school faculty-student ratio: 1:8.

Upper School Student Profile Grade 9: 174 students (93 boys, 81 girls); Grade 10: 208 students (117 boys, 91 girls); Grade 11: 208 students (103 boys, 105 girls); Grade 12: 184 students (93 boys, 91 girls). 33% of students are boarding students. 51% are state residents. 15 states are represented in upper school student body. 12% are international students. International students from Germany, Hong Kong, Pakistan, Republic of Korea, Saudi Arabia, and Taiwan; 20 other countries represented in student body.

Faculty School total: 191. In upper school: 55 men, 41 women; 76 have advanced degrees; 67 reside on campus.

Subjects Offered Advanced Placement courses, African-American literature, algebra, American history, American literature, anatomy, anthropology, art, art history, astronomy, band, biology, botany, British literature, calculus, ceramics, chemistry, chorus, computer science, creative writing, dance, design, drama, drawing, driver education, earth science, economics, English, English literature, environmental science, ethics, European history, expository writing, fine arts, French, genetics, geology, geometry, German, government/civics, health, history, humanities, interdisciplinary studies, jazz band, jewelry making, Latin, mathematics, metalworking, model United Nations, orchestra, painting, philosophy, photography, physics, precalculus, printmaking, psychology, religion, science, sculpture, social science, social studies, Spanish, speech, statistics, theater, trigonometry, weaving, wilderness/outdoor program, world history, writing.

Graduation Requirements English, foreign language, history, mathematics, religion (includes Bible studies and theology), science.

Special Academic Programs Advanced Placement exam preparation in 14 subject areas; honors section; independent study; term-away projects; study abroad; academic accommodation for the gifted, the musically talented, and the artistically talented; ESL (8 students enrolled).

College Placement 207 students graduated in 2005; 205 went to college, including Duke University; Harvard University; Michigan State University; Northwestern University; University of Illinois at Urbana–Champaign; University of Michigan. Other: 2 had other specific plans. Mean SAT verbal: 639, mean SAT math: 655, mean composite ACT: 28.

Student Life Upper grades have specified standards of dress, student council, honor system. Discipline rests primarily with faculty.

Summer Programs Enrichment programs offered; session focuses on academics; held on campus; accepts boys and girls; open to students from other schools. 250 students usually enrolled. 2006 schedule: June 24 to August 3. Application deadline: none.

Tuition and Aid Day student tuition: $21,730; 7-day tuition and room/board: $30,380. Tuition installment plan (FACTS Tuition Payment Plan). Merit scholarship grants, need-based scholarship grants available. In 2005–06, 30% of upper-school students received aid; total upper-school merit-scholarship money awarded: $182,000. Total amount of financial aid awarded in 2005–06: $6,000,000.

Admissions Traditional secondary-level entrance grade is 9. For fall 2005, 467 students applied for upper-level admission, 225 were accepted, 150 enrolled. SSAT required. Deadline for receipt of application materials: none. Application fee required: $25. Interview required.

Athletics Interscholastic: alpine skiing (boys, girls), baseball (b), basketball (b,g), crew (b,g), cross-country running (b,g), diving (b,g), fencing (b), field hockey (g), football (b), golf (b,g), ice hockey (b,g), lacrosse (b,g), skiing (downhill) (b,g), soccer (b,g), softball (g), swimming and diving (b,g), tennis (b,g), track and field (b,g), volleyball (g); intramural: basketball (b), weight training (b,g); coed intramural: back packing, bicycling, bowling, climbing, dance, fencing, fitness, fitness walking, Frisbee, hiking/backpacking, independent competitive sports, jogging, martial arts, modern dance, mountain biking, outdoor education, running, scuba diving, snowboarding, soccer, softball, strength & conditioning, tai chi, tennis, volleyball, wilderness survival. 18 coaches, 2 trainers.

Computers Computers are regularly used in English, foreign language, history, mathematics, science classes. Computer network features include campus e-mail, on-campus library services, CD-ROMs, online commercial services, Internet access, DVD, SmartBoards.

Contact Drew Miller, Director of Admission. 248-645-3610. Fax: 248-645-3025. E-mail: admission@cranbrook.edu. Web site: schools.cranbrook.edu.

See full description on page 748.

CRAWFORD ADVENTIST ACADEMY

531 Finch Avenue, West
Willowdale, Ontario M2R 3X2, Canada
Head of School: Mr. Norman Brown

General Information Coeducational day college-preparatory, arts, business, religious studies, and technology school, affiliated with Seventh-day Adventist Church. Grades JK–12. Founded: 1954. Setting: urban. Nearest major city is Toronto, Canada. 5-acre campus. 1 building on campus. Approved or accredited by Ontario Ministry of Education. Language of instruction: English. Total enrollment: 489. Upper school average class size: 25. Upper school faculty-student ratio: 1:16.

Upper School Student Profile 90% of students are Seventh-day Adventists.

Faculty School total: 16. In upper school: 10 men, 4 women; 10 have advanced degrees.

Subjects Offered Accounting, advanced computer applications, algebra, American history, band, Bible, biology, business, business mathematics, business technology, calculus, Canadian geography, Canadian history, chemistry, choir, civics, community service, computer applications, computer information systems, discrete mathematics, earth and space science, English, entrepreneurship, French as a second language, guidance, independent study, information technology, marketing, physical education, physics, science, writing skills, yearbook.

College Placement 37 students graduated in 2005; 35 went to college, including Andrews University; Oakwood College; Ryerson University; The University of Western Ontario; University of Toronto; York University. Other: 2 went to work. Median composite ACT: 20. 22% scored over 26 on composite ACT.

Student Life Upper grades have uniform requirement, student council, honor system. Discipline rests primarily with faculty.

Tuition and Aid Day student tuition: CAN$6600. Tuition installment plan (monthly payment plans). Tuition reduction for siblings, need-based scholarship grants, paying campus jobs available. In 2005–06, 10% of upper-school students received aid. Total amount of financial aid awarded in 2005–06: CAN$10,000.

Admissions CAT required. Deadline for receipt of application materials: none. Application fee required: CAN$25. Interview required.

Athletics Interscholastic: basketball (boys, girls), cooperative games (b,g), flag football (b,g), softball (b,g), volleyball (b,g); intramural: basketball (b,g), flag football (b,g), floor hockey (b,g), indoor soccer (b,g), physical fitness (b,g), table tennis (b,g), volleyball (b,g); coed intramural: outdoor education, softball. 1 coach.

Computers Computers are regularly used in introduction to technology classes. Computer network features include CD-ROMs, Internet access, wireless campus network.

Contact Dr. Janice Patricia Maitland, Principal, 7-12. 416-633-0090 Ext. 223. Fax: 416-633-0467. E-mail: janypan@rogers.com.

CRAWFORD DAY SCHOOL

Portsmouth, Virginia
See Special Needs Schools section.

CRESCENT SCHOOL

2365 Bayview Avenue
Willowdale, Ontario M2L 1A2, Canada
Head of School: Geoff Roberts

General Information Boys' day college-preparatory school. Grades 3–12. Founded: 1913. Setting: urban. Nearest major city is Toronto, Canada. 30-acre campus. 2 buildings on campus. Approved or accredited by Canadian Association of Independent Schools, Canadian Educational Standards Institute, Conference of Independent Schools of Ontario, Ontario Ministry of Education, and Ontario Department of Education. Affiliate member of National Association of Independent Schools; member of Secondary School Admission Test Board. Language of instruction: English. Endowment: CAN$3 million. Total enrollment: 664. Upper school average class size: 22. Upper school faculty-student ratio: 1:12.

Upper School Student Profile Grade 9: 89 students (89 boys); Grade 10: 88 students (88 boys); Grade 11: 97 students (97 boys); Grade 12: 83 students (83 boys).

Faculty School total: 66. In upper school: 27 men, 12 women; 4 have advanced degrees.

Subjects Offered Accounting, algebra, American history, art, biology, business skills, calculus, chemistry, computer programming, computer science, creative writing, drama, economics, English, English literature, entrepreneurship, fine arts, finite math, French, geography, health, history, information technology, law, leadership training, mathematics, media arts, music, philosophy, physical education, physics, political science, science, social studies, Spanish, technology/design, theater, world history.

Graduation Requirements Arts and fine arts (art, music, dance, drama), business skills (includes word processing), English, foreign language, mathematics, physical education (includes health), science, social studies (includes history).

Special Academic Programs Advanced Placement exam preparation in 14 subject areas; honors section; accelerated programs.

College Placement 87 students graduated in 2005; all went to college, including Dalhousie University; McGill University; Queen's University at Kingston; The University of Western Ontario; University of Toronto; University of Waterloo. 75% scored over 600 on SAT verbal, 80% scored over 600 on SAT math.

Student Life Upper grades have uniform requirement, student council. Discipline rests primarily with faculty.

Summer Programs Advancement programs offered; session focuses on earning additional credits; held on campus; accepts boys and girls; open to students from other schools. 28 students usually enrolled. 2006 schedule: June 21 to July 28. Application deadline: June 15.

Tuition and Aid Day student tuition: CAN$19,900. Tuition installment plan (monthly payment plans, individually arranged payment plans). Bursaries, merit scholarship grants, need-based scholarship grants available. In 2005–06, 1% of upper-school students received aid; total upper-school merit-scholarship money awarded: CAN$90,000. Total amount of financial aid awarded in 2005–06: CAN$92,000.

Admissions Traditional secondary-level entrance grade is 9. For fall 2005, 136 students applied for upper-level admission, 58 were accepted, 42 enrolled. CAT, ERB CTP III, school's own exam and SSAT required. Deadline for receipt of application materials: December 16. Application fee required: CAN$125. On-campus interview required.

Athletics Interscholastic: alpine skiing, badminton, basketball, cross-country running, golf, ice hockey, rugby, skiing (downhill), soccer, softball, squash, swimming and diving, table tennis, tennis, track and field, volleyball; intramural: ball hockey, basketball, curling, flag football, Frisbee, golf, ice hockey, soccer, softball, squash, table tennis, tennis, track and field, volleyball, weight lifting. 3 PE instructors.

Computers Computers are regularly used in accounting, art, economics, English, foreign language, geography, history, mathematics, music, science, technology classes. Computer network features include campus e-mail, on-campus library services, CD-ROMs, online commercial services, Internet access.

Contact Alanna McIver, Admissions Assistant. 416-449-2556 Ext. 227. Fax: 416-449-7950. E-mail: amciver@crescentschool.org. Web site: www.crescentschool.org.

CRESPI CARMELITE HIGH SCHOOL

5031 Alonzo Avenue
Encino, California 91316-3699
Head of School: Fr. Paul Henson, OCARM

General Information Boys' day college-preparatory, arts, and religious studies school, affiliated with Roman Catholic Church. Grades 9–12. Founded: 1959. Setting: suburban. Nearest major city is Los Angeles. 3-acre campus. 2 buildings on campus. Approved or accredited by Western Association of Schools and Colleges and California Department of Education. Total enrollment: 540. Upper school average class size: 23. Upper school faculty-student ratio: 1:23.

Upper School Student Profile Grade 9: 148 students (148 boys); Grade 10: 155 students (155 boys); Grade 11: 129 students (129 boys); Grade 12: 108 students (108 boys). 72% of students are Roman Catholic.

Faculty School total: 47. In upper school: 33 men, 8 women; 26 have advanced degrees.

Subjects Offered Advanced Placement courses, advanced studio art-AP, algebra, American history-AP, American literature-AP, anatomy and physiology, Ancient Greek, ancient world history, applied music, ASB Leadership, athletic training, audio visual/media, baseball, Basic programming, basketball, biology, biology-AP, British literature, British literature-AP, calculus, calculus-AP, chemistry, Christian scripture, church history, classical Greek literature, computer graphics, constitutional law, drama performance, driver education, earth science, economics and history, economics-AP, English composition, English literature and composition-AP, ethics, European history-AP, film studies, French as a second language, geometry, golf, government, government and politics-AP, Greek, Greek culture, health, history of the Catholic Church, Holocaust, honors English, honors geometry, international studies, journalism, language and composition, Latin-AP, law, media arts, men's studies, model United Nations, moral and social development, music appreciation, music composition, photography, physical science, physics-AP, prayer/spirituality, pre-calculus, probability and statistics, psychology, social justice, Spanish language-AP, sports, sports conditioning, statistics-AP, student government, student publications, U.S. history, U.S. history-AP, video film production, Web site design, Western civilization, western religions, world cultures, world geography, world religions, yearbook.

Graduation Requirements Arts and fine arts (art, music, dance, drama), English, foreign language, mathematics, physical education (includes health), public speaking, religion (includes Bible studies and theology), science, social science, social studies (includes history). Community service is required.

Special Academic Programs Advanced Placement exam preparation in 13 subject areas; honors section.

College Placement 135 students graduated in 2005; all went to college, including California State University, Northridge; Loyola Marymount University; Marymount College, Palos Verdes, California; University of California, Los Angeles; University of California, Santa Cruz; University of Southern California. Median SAT verbal: 540, median SAT math: 530, median composite ACT: 24. 27% scored over 600 on SAT verbal, 24% scored over 600 on SAT math.

Student Life Upper grades have specified standards of dress, student council. Discipline rests primarily with faculty. Attendance at religious services is required.

Summer Programs Remediation, enrichment, advancement, sports, art/fine arts programs offered; session focuses on remediation and/or enrichment in math, science, language, and social studies; held on campus; accepts boys and girls; open to students from other schools. 250 students usually enrolled. 2006 schedule: June 26 to July 28. Application deadline: June 12.

Tuition and Aid Day student tuition: $8025. Tuition installment plan (Tuition Management Systems Plan). Merit scholarship grants, need-based scholarship grants, paying campus jobs available. In 2005–06, 20% of upper-school students received aid; total upper-school merit-scholarship money awarded: $36,750. Total amount of financial aid awarded in 2005–06: $276,525.

Admissions Traditional secondary-level entrance grade is 9. For fall 2005, 334 students applied for upper-level admission, 270 were accepted, 148 enrolled. High School Placement Test and High School Placement Test (closed version) from Scholastic Testing Service required. Deadline for receipt of application materials: none. Application fee required: $55. On-campus interview required.

Athletics Interscholastic: aquatics, baseball, basketball, cross-country running, football, golf, lacrosse, soccer, swimming and diving, tennis, track and field, volleyball, water polo; intramural: basketball. 4 PE instructors, 1 trainer.

Computers Computers are regularly used in English, foreign language, history, mathematics, science classes. Computer network features include campus e-mail, on-campus library services, CD-ROMs, online commercial services, Internet access, DVD.

Contact Mr. Robert Kodama, Director of Admissions. 818-345-1672 Ext. 310. Fax: 818-705-0209. E-mail: rkodama@crespi.org. Web site: www.crespi.org.

CRETIN-DERHAM HALL

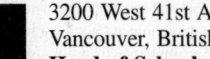

550 South Albert Street
Saint Paul, Minnesota 55116
Head of School: Mr. Richard Engler

General Information Coeducational day college-preparatory, general academic, arts, business, religious studies, technology, and Junior ROTC school, affiliated with Roman Catholic Church. Grades 9–12. Founded: 1987. Setting: urban. 15-acre campus. 5 buildings on campus. Approved or accredited by North Central Association of Colleges and Schools. Total enrollment: 1,299. Upper school average class size: 20. Upper school faculty-student ratio: 1:14.

Upper School Student Profile Grade 9: 331 students (158 boys, 173 girls); Grade 10: 329 students (167 boys, 162 girls); Grade 11: 324 students (157 boys, 167 girls); Grade 12: 315 students (148 boys, 167 girls). 93% of students are Roman Catholic.

Faculty School total: 112. In upper school: 51 men, 61 women; 50 have advanced degrees.

Subjects Offered Aerobics, algebra, American government-AP, American history, American literature, analysis, art history, arts, audio visual/media, biology, business, career exploration, chemistry, computer math, computer programming, computer science, drama, economics, English, environmental science, ethics, fine arts, French, geography, geometry, German, government/civics, history, JROTC, Latin, mathematics, music, physical education, physics, religion, science, social studies, Spanish, speech, theater, theology, trigonometry.

Graduation Requirements Arts and fine arts (art, music, dance, drama), English, foreign language, mathematics, physical education (includes health), religion (includes Bible studies and theology), science, social studies (includes history).

Special Academic Programs Advanced Placement exam preparation in 7 subject areas; honors section; accelerated programs; independent study; study at local college for college credit; academic accommodation for the gifted; remedial reading and/or remedial writing; remedial math.

College Placement 315 students graduated in 2005; 306 went to college, including Saint Mary's University of Minnesota; University of Minnesota, Duluth; University of Minnesota, Twin Cities Campus; University of St. Thomas; University of Wisconsin–Madison. Other: 9 went to work.

Student Life Upper grades have uniform requirement, student council. Discipline rests primarily with faculty. Attendance at religious services is required.

Summer Programs Remediation, enrichment, sports, art/fine arts, computer instruction programs offered; session focuses on enrichment; held on campus; accepts boys and girls; open to students from other schools. 500 students usually enrolled. 2006 schedule: June to July. Application deadline: June 1.

Tuition and Aid Day student tuition: $7950. Tuition installment plan (monthly payment plans, individually arranged payment plans, 2- and 3-payment plans). Need-based scholarship grants, paying campus jobs available. In 2005–06, 44% of upper-school students received aid. Total amount of financial aid awarded in 2005–06: $1,400,000.

Admissions Traditional secondary-level entrance grade is 9. For fall 2005, 563 students applied for upper-level admission, 360 were accepted, 342 enrolled. STS required. Deadline for receipt of application materials: none. No application fee required. Interview recommended.

Athletics Interscholastic: baseball (boys), basketball (b,g), cross-country running (b,g), dance team (g), diving (b,g), football (b), golf (b,g), gymnastics (g), ice hockey (b,g), riflery (b,g), skiing (downhill) (b,g), soccer (b,g), softball (g), swimming and diving (b,g), tennis (b,g), track and field (b,g), volleyball (g); coed interscholastic:

alpine skiing, cheering, JROTC drill, skiing (cross-country), ultimate Frisbee; coed intramural: basketball, volleyball. 4 PE instructors, 1 trainer.

Computers Computers are regularly used in all academic, data processing, publications, yearbook classes. Computer network features include campus e-mail, on-campus library services, CD-ROMs, online commercial services, Internet access, ability to check assignments and contact faculty.

Contact Mary Jo Groeller, Administrator of Admissions. 651-696-3302. Fax: 651-696-3394. E-mail: mjgroeller@cretin-derhamhall.org. Web site: cretin-derhamhall.org.

CROFTON HOUSE SCHOOL

3200 West 41st Avenue
Vancouver, British Columbia V6N 3E1, Canada
Head of School: Dr. Patricia J. Dawson

General Information Girls' day college-preparatory school. Grades 1–12. Founded: 1898. Setting: urban. 10-acre campus. 6 buildings on campus. Approved or accredited by British Columbia Department of Education. Affiliate member of National Association of Independent Schools. Language of instruction: English. Endowment: CAN$2.7 million. Total enrollment: 671. Upper school average class size: 20. Upper school faculty-student ratio: 1:11.

Upper School Student Profile Grade 7: 40 students (40 girls); Grade 8: 92 students (92 girls); Grade 9: 90 students (90 girls); Grade 10: 74 students (74 girls); Grade 11: 69 students (69 girls); Grade 12: 76 students (76 girls).

Faculty School total: 61. In upper school: 5 men, 36 women; 8 have advanced degrees.

Subjects Offered Art, art history, biology, calculus, chemistry, Chinese, comparative religion, computer science, drama, English, English literature, English literature-AP, fine arts, French, geography, history, home economics, Latin, mathematics, music, physical education, physics, science, social studies, Spanish, theater.

Graduation Requirements Arts and fine arts (art, music, dance, drama), English, mathematics, science, social studies (includes history).

Special Academic Programs Advanced Placement exam preparation in 6 subject areas; honors section.

College Placement 76 students graduated in 2005; all went to college, including McGill University; Queen's University at Kingston; The University of British Columbia; The University of Western Ontario; University of Toronto; University of Victoria.

Student Life Upper grades have uniform requirement, student council. Discipline rests primarily with faculty.

Tuition and Aid Day student tuition: CAN$11,660. Tuition installment plan (monthly payment plans, term payment plan (3 terms a year)). Tuition reduction for siblings, bursaries, merit scholarship grants available. In 2005–06, 4% of upper-school students received aid; total upper-school merit-scholarship money awarded: CAN$9500. Total amount of financial aid awarded in 2005–06: CAN$154,438.

Admissions Traditional secondary-level entrance grade is 8. For fall 2005, 140 students applied for upper-level admission, 46 were accepted, 46 enrolled. School's own exam or SSAT required. Deadline for receipt of application materials: December 1. Application fee required: CAN$200. On-campus interview required.

Athletics Interscholastic: badminton, basketball, cross-country running, field hockey, independent competitive sports, netball, rowing, soccer, swimming and diving, tennis, track and field, volleyball; intramural: badminton, baseball, cooperative games, cross-country running, dance, field hockey, fitness, flag football, floor hockey, handball, jogging, netball, soccer, softball, swimming and diving, table tennis, team handball, tennis, touch football, track and field, ultimate Frisbee, volleyball. 5 PE instructors, 25 coaches.

Computers Computers are regularly used in English, foreign language, mathematics, science, social studies, technology, video film production classes. Computer network features include on-campus library services, CD-ROMs, online commercial services, Internet access, file transfer.

Contact Mrs. Louise Kirk, Registrar. 604-266-5423. Fax: 604-263-4941. E-mail: lkirk@croftonhouse.ca. Web site: www.croftonhouse.ca.

CROSS CREEK PROGRAMS

LaVerkin, Utah
See Special Needs Schools section.

CROSSROADS SCHOOL

500 DeBaliviere Avenue
St. Louis, Missouri 63112
Head of School: William B. Handmaker

General Information Coeducational day college-preparatory and arts school. Grades 7–12. Founded: 1974. Setting: urban. 20-acre campus. 1 building on campus. Approved or accredited by Independent Schools Association of the Central States and Missouri Department of Education. Member of National Association of Independent

Schools and Secondary School Admission Test Board. Total enrollment: 202. Upper school average class size: 15. Upper school faculty-student ratio: 1:8.

Upper School Student Profile Grade 9: 40 students (20 boys, 20 girls); Grade 10: 30 students (10 boys, 20 girls); Grade 11: 37 students (16 boys, 21 girls); Grade 12: 37 students (19 boys, 18 girls).

Faculty School total: 27. In upper school: 12 men, 15 women; 12 have advanced degrees.

Subjects Offered 3-dimensional art, African American history, algebra, American literature, anatomy, art, art history, art history-AP, Asian history, biology, biology-AP, botany, calculus, calculus-AP, ceramics, chemistry, chemistry-AP, community service, comparative religion, computer applications, creative writing, drama, ecology, English, English literature, environmental science, environmental science-AP, European history, fine arts, French, geography, geology, geometry, history, Japanese, journalism, keyboarding, Latin, literature and composition-AP, mathematics, music, music theater, photography, physical education, physics, psychology, social science, sociology, Spanish, speech, studio art-AP, theater, trigonometry, women's studies, word processing, world history, world literature.

Graduation Requirements American literature, arts and fine arts (art, music, dance, drama), biology, chemistry, classics, computer science, creative writing, earth science, electives, English composition, English literature, environmental science, foreign language, interdisciplinary studies, mathematics, non-Western literature, physical education (includes health), political science, practical arts, social science, social studies (includes history), U.S. government and politics, world cultures, one course taken at a local university or college during senior year.

Special Academic Programs Advanced Placement exam preparation in 6 subject areas; honors section; study abroad.

College Placement 33 students graduated in 2005; all went to college, including Boston University; Carnegie Mellon University; Knox College; Saint Louis University; Washington University in St. Louis; Wesleyan University. Median SAT verbal: 655, median SAT math: 620, median composite ACT: 27.

Student Life Upper grades have specified standards of dress, student council, honor system. Discipline rests equally with students and faculty.

Tuition and Aid Day student tuition: $13,700. Tuition installment plan (SMART Tuition Payment Plan). Need-based scholarship grants, need-based loans available. In 2005–06, 38% of upper-school students received aid.

Admissions Traditional secondary-level entrance grade is 9. For fall 2005, 68 students applied for upper-level admission, 61 were accepted, 30 enrolled. ISEE required. Deadline for receipt of application materials: February 13. Application fee required: $40. On-campus interview required.

Athletics Interscholastic: baseball (boys), basketball (b,g), indoor soccer (b,g), soccer (b,g), tennis (g), volleyball (g); intramural: soccer (b,g); coed interscholastic: bicycling, fitness; coed intramural: aquatics, basketball, bicycling, cheering, climbing, drill team, fencing, indoor soccer, softball, table tennis, touch football, volleyball, wall climbing, weight training, yoga. 5 PE instructors, 9 coaches.

Computers Computers are regularly used in English, foreign language, history, journalism, mathematics, newspaper, science classes. Computer network features include on-campus library services, CD-ROMs, Internet access.

Contact Kara C. Sheban, Director of Admission. 314-367-8101. Fax: 314-367-9711. E-mail: kara@crossroads-school.org. Web site: www.crossroads-school.org.

CROSSROADS SCHOOL FOR ARTS & SCIENCES

1714— 21st Street
Santa Monica, California 90404-3917
Head of School: Roger H. Weaver

General Information Coeducational day college-preparatory and arts school. Grades K–12. Founded: 1971. Setting: urban. Nearest major city is Los Angeles. 3-acre campus. 16 buildings on campus. Approved or accredited by California Association of Independent Schools, The College Board, Western Association of Schools and Colleges, Western Catholic Education Association, and California Department of Education. Member of National Association of Independent Schools. Endowment: $9 million. Total enrollment: 1,146. Upper school average class size: 14. Upper school faculty-student ratio: 1:17.

Upper School Student Profile Grade 9: 128 students (64 boys, 64 girls); Grade 10: 122 students (55 boys, 67 girls); Grade 11: 126 students (60 boys, 66 girls); Grade 12: 124 students (68 boys, 56 girls).

Faculty School total: 164. In upper school: 36 men, 41 women; 39 have advanced degrees.

Subjects Offered Algebra, American history, American studies, art history, biology, calculus, ceramics, chemistry, community service, computer programming, computer science, creative writing, critical studies in film, cultural arts, dance, earth and space science, English, environmental education, ethics, film studies, French, gender issues, geometry, graphic design, great books, Greek, human development, Japanese, jazz ensemble, jazz theory, journalism, Latin, marine biology, marine ecology, music appreciation, music theory, orchestra, photography, physical education, physics, physiology, pre-calculus, sculpture, Spanish, statistics, studio art, theater, trigonometry, video film production, world civilizations, yoga.

Graduation Requirements Arts and fine arts (art, music, dance, drama), English, foreign language, human development, mathematics, physical education (includes health), science, social studies (includes history). Community service is required.

Special Academic Programs Advanced Placement exam preparation in 13 subject areas; honors section; term-away projects; academic accommodation for the gifted, the musically talented, and the artistically talented.

College Placement 110 students graduated in 2005; 106 went to college, including Bard College; New York University; University of California, Berkeley; University of Pennsylvania; University of Southern California. Other: 1 went to work, 2 entered a postgraduate year, 1 had other specific plans. Mean SAT verbal: 590, mean SAT math: 620.

Student Life Upper grades have student council. Discipline rests primarily with faculty.

Summer Programs Remediation, enrichment, advancement, sports, art/fine arts, computer instruction programs offered; session focuses on enrichment; held on campus; accepts boys and girls; open to students from other schools. 900 students usually enrolled. 2006 schedule: June 26 to August 4.

Tuition and Aid Day student tuition: $23,707. Tuition installment plan (monthly payment plans, individually arranged payment plans). Merit scholarship grants, need-based scholarship grants, need-based loans available. In 2005–06, 18% of upper-school students received aid; total upper-school merit-scholarship money awarded: $57,544. Total amount of financial aid awarded in 2005–06: $1,623,980.

Admissions Traditional secondary-level entrance grade is 9. For fall 2005, 148 students applied for upper-level admission, 32 were accepted, 22 enrolled. ISEE required. Deadline for receipt of application materials: January 4. Application fee required: $125. On-campus interview required.

Athletics Interscholastic: baseball (boys), basketball (b,g), cross-country running (b,g), soccer (b,g), softball (g), tennis (b,g), track and field (b,g), volleyball (b,g); coed interscholastic: golf, swimming and diving; coed intramural: canoeing/kayaking, climbing, hiking/backpacking, kayaking, outdoor activities, outdoor education, rock climbing, ropes courses, snowshoeing, table tennis. 5 PE instructors, 29 coaches, 1 trainer.

Computers Computers are regularly used in foreign language, graphic design, journalism, Latin, mathematics, science classes. Computer network features include campus e-mail, on-campus library services, CD-ROMs, online commercial services, Internet access, file transfer, DVD, wireless campus network.

Contact Gennifer Yoshimaru, Director of Admissions. 310-828-1196 Ext. 704. Fax: 310-392-9011. E-mail: gyoshimaru@xrds.org. Web site: www.xrds.org.

CRYSTAL SPRINGS UPLANDS SCHOOL

400 Uplands Drive
Hillsborough, California 94010
Head of School: Ms. Amy Richards

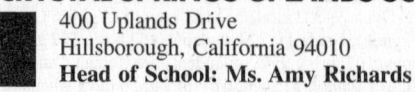

General Information Coeducational day college-preparatory school. Grades 6–12. Founded: 1952. Setting: suburban. Nearest major city is San Francisco. 10-acre campus. 4 buildings on campus. Approved or accredited by California Association of Independent Schools and Western Association of Schools and Colleges. Member of National Association of Independent Schools and Secondary School Admission Test Board. Endowment: $10.8 million. Total enrollment: 355. Upper school average class size: 15. Upper school faculty-student ratio: 1:9.

Upper School Student Profile Grade 9: 60 students (28 boys, 32 girls); Grade 10: 62 students (32 boys, 30 girls); Grade 11: 58 students (26 boys, 32 girls); Grade 12: 66 students (33 boys, 33 girls).

Faculty School total: 45. In upper school: 23 men, 22 women; 28 have advanced degrees.

Subjects Offered Acting, advanced computer applications, algebra, American government-AP, American history, American history-AP, American literature, art, art history-AP, astronomy, biology, biology-AP, calculus, calculus-AP, ceramics, chamber groups, chemistry, chorus, comparative cultures, computer math, computer programming, computer science, concert bell choir, creative writing, dance, dance performance, drama, English, English literature, ensembles, environmental science-AP, European history, European history-AP, fine arts, French, French language-AP, French literature-AP, geometry, government and politics-AP, graphic design, health, history, mathematics, multicultural literature, music, music theory-AP, photography, physical education, physics, physics-AP, poetry, post-calculus, pre-calculus, science, Shakespeare, Spanish, Spanish language-AP, Spanish literature-AP, statistics, theater, video film production, wellness, world history, world literature, writing.

Graduation Requirements Arts and fine arts (art, music, dance, drama), English, foreign language, history, mathematics, physical education (includes health), science, senior project.

Special Academic Programs Advanced Placement exam preparation in 15 subject areas; honors section.

College Placement 56 students graduated in 2005; all went to college, including New York University; Princeton University; Stanford University; University of California, Los Angeles; University of Pennsylvania.

Student Life Upper grades have specified standards of dress, student council, honor system. Discipline rests primarily with faculty.

Tuition and Aid Day student tuition: $24,560. Tuition installment plan (Insured Tuition Payment Plan, monthly payment plans, Tuition Management Systems Plan). Need-based scholarship grants available. In 2005–06, 19% of upper-school students received aid. Total amount of financial aid awarded in 2005–06: $1,000,000.

Admissions Traditional secondary-level entrance grade is 9. For fall 2005, 170 students applied for upper-level admission, 72 were accepted, 31 enrolled. ISEE or SSAT required. Deadline for receipt of application materials: January 10. Application fee required: $75. On-campus interview required.

Athletics Interscholastic: baseball (boys), basketball (b,g), cross-country running (b,g), soccer (b,g), swimming and diving (b,g), tennis (b,g), track and field (b,g), volleyball (b,g); coed interscholastic: badminton, golf. 3 PE instructors, 14 coaches, 1 trainer.

Computers Computers are regularly used in all academic classes. Computer network features include campus e-mail, on-campus library services, CD-ROMs, online commercial services, Internet access, file transfer, DVD, wireless campus network.

Contact Abby H. Wilder, Director of Admission. 650-342-4175 Ext. 1517. Fax: 650-342-7611. E-mail: admission@csus.com. Web site: www.csus.com.

ANNOUNCEMENT FROM THE SCHOOL A CSUS senior recently said, "The friendships I have formed with faculty members have been invaluable. Teachers here are clearly intelligent but, more important, they are excited about their areas of expertise. I have become a better writer, a better thinker, and a better athlete because I have been surrounded by people who give me room to take risks, intellectually and personally. I am now looking for a collegiate CSUS."

THE CULVER ACADEMIES

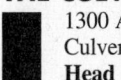

1300 Academy Road
Culver, Indiana 46511
Head of School: Mr. John N. Buxton

petersons.com

General Information Coeducational boarding and day college-preparatory and arts school. Grades 9–PG. Founded: 1894. Setting: small town. Nearest major city is South Bend. Students are housed in single-sex dormitories. 1,800-acre campus. 39 buildings on campus. Approved or accredited by Independent Schools Association of the Central States, North Central Association of Colleges and Schools, and Indiana Department of Education. Member of National Association of Independent Schools and Secondary School Admission Test Board. Endowment: $156 million. Total enrollment: 760. Upper school average class size: 15. Upper school faculty-student ratio: 1:9.

Upper School Student Profile Grade 9: 143 students (83 boys, 60 girls); Grade 10: 220 students (133 boys, 87 girls); Grade 11: 189 students (99 boys, 90 girls); Grade 12: 206 students (112 boys, 94 girls); Postgraduate: 2 students (2 boys). 90% of students are boarding students. 29% are state residents. 38 states are represented in upper school student body. 15% are international students. International students from Canada, China, Mexico, Republic of Korea, Taiwan, and Venezuela; 18 other countries represented in student body.

Faculty School total: 93. In upper school: 59 men, 34 women; 70 have advanced degrees; 4 reside on campus.

Subjects Offered Acting, advanced math, aerospace education, algebra, American government, American government-AP, American history, American history-AP, American literature, anatomy, art, art history, arts, astronomy, aviation, ballet, Basic programming, biology, biology-AP, calculus, calculus-AP, career/college preparation, ceramics, character education, chemistry, chemistry-AP, Chinese, choir, church history, college admission preparation, college placement, college planning, comparative religion, computer math, computer programming, computer science, computer science-AP, dance, drama, dramatic arts, driver education, economics, economics-AP, English, English language-AP, English literature, equestrian sports, equine studies, equitation, ESL, ethics and responsibility, European history, film studies, fine arts, fitness, flight instruction, French, French-AP, freshman seminar, geology, geometry, German, German literature, German-AP, government, government-AP, government/civics, health and wellness, honors English, honors geometry, instrumental music, integrated math, integrated science, jazz band, journalism, Latin, Latin-AP, leadership training, library research, macro/microeconomics-AP, mathematics, mentorship program, music, music theory, music theory-AP, photography, physical education, physics, physics-AP, physiology, piano, play production, pottery, pre-algebra, pre-calculus, science, science research, Shakespeare, social studies, Spanish, Spanish language-AP, Spanish-AP, speech, statistics-AP, strings, theater, trigonometry, U.S. government and politics-AP, U.S. history-AP, world history, world religions, yearbook.

Graduation Requirements Arts and fine arts (art, music, dance, drama), English, foreign language, health education, history, leadership training, mathematics, science, senior community service project.

Special Academic Programs Advanced Placement exam preparation in 19 subject areas; honors section; academic accommodation for the gifted, the musically talented, and the artistically talented; ESL (16 students enrolled).

College Placement 182 students graduated in 2005; 180 went to college, including Florida State University; Indiana University Bloomington; Miami University; Purdue University; Texas A&M University; University of Michigan. Other: 2 had other specific plans. Mean SAT verbal: 560, mean SAT math: 599, mean composite ACT: 24.

Student Life Upper grades have uniform requirement, student council, honor system. Discipline rests equally with students and faculty. Attendance at religious services is required.

Summer Programs Enrichment, advancement, ESL, sports, art/fine arts, computer instruction programs offered; session focuses on leadership training, citizenship, lifetime interests and skills development; held on campus; accepts boys and girls; open to students from other schools. 1300 students usually enrolled. 2006 schedule: June 25 to August 6. Application deadline: May 1.

Tuition and Aid Day student tuition: $21,000; 7-day tuition and room/board: $28,900. Tuition installment plan (Key Tuition Payment Plan). Merit scholarship grants, need-based scholarship grants available. In 2005–06, 51% of upper-school students received aid; total upper-school merit-scholarship money awarded: $782,900. Total amount of financial aid awarded in 2005–06: $1,976,620.

Admissions Traditional secondary-level entrance grade is 9. For fall 2005, 761 students applied for upper-level admission, 431 were accepted, 262 enrolled. SCAT or SSAT required. Deadline for receipt of application materials: July 25. Application fee required: $30. Interview required.

Athletics Interscholastic: baseball (boys), basketball (b,g), cheering (g), crew (b,g), cross-country running (b,g), diving (b,g), equestrian sports (b,g), fencing (b,g), football (b), golf (b,g), horseback riding (b,g), ice hockey (b,g), indoor track & field (b,g), lacrosse (b,g), polo (b,g), rugby (b), soccer (b,g), softball (g), swimming and diving (b,g), tennis (b,g), track and field (b,g), volleyball (g), wrestling (b); intramural: aerobics (b,g), ballet (g), basketball (b,g), dance (b,g), dance team (g), drill team (b,g), fitness (b,g), ice hockey (b,g), marksmanship (b,g), modern dance (g), racquetball (b,g), ropes courses (b,g), soccer (b,g), strength & conditioning (b,g), trap and skeet (b,g), weight training (b,g), yoga (b,g); coed interscholastic: dressage, sailing; coed intramural: outdoor adventure, scuba diving, skiing (downhill). 8 PE instructors, 3 trainers.

Computers Computers are regularly used in all classes. Computer network features include campus e-mail, on-campus library services, CD-ROMs, Internet access, DVD, wireless campus network, school-issued laptops (to all students).

Contact Mr. Michael Turnbull, Director of Admissions. 574-842-7100. Fax: 574-842-8066. E-mail: turnbul@culver.org. Web site: www.culver.org.

ANNOUNCEMENT FROM THE SCHOOL The Batten Scholars Program offers 6 new freshmen and sophomores a renewable, 4-year merit scholarship covering tuition, room and board, books, participation in a service-based work project, and funding for one summer of study abroad. Selection is based upon a superior record of academic achievement, personal character, and demonstrated leadership.

See full description on page 750.

CURREY INGRAM ACADEMY

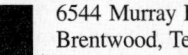

6544 Murray Lane
Brentwood, Tennessee 37027
Head of School: Ms. Kathleen G. Rayburn

General Information Coeducational day college-preparatory, arts, bilingual studies, technology, Spanish, and ethics and character education school. Grades K–12. Founded: 1968. Setting: rural. Nearest major city is Nashville. 83-acre campus. Approved or accredited by Southern Association of Colleges and Schools and Tennessee Department of Education. Total enrollment: 261. Upper school average class size: 11.

Upper School Student Profile Grade 9: 24 students (15 boys, 9 girls); Grade 10: 8 students (6 boys, 2 girls); Grade 11: 14 students (9 boys, 5 girls); Grade 12: 14 students (9 boys, 5 girls).

Faculty In upper school: 7 men, 10 women; 11 have advanced degrees.

Special Academic Programs Independent study; academic accommodation for the gifted, the musically talented, and the artistically talented; remedial reading and/or remedial writing; remedial math; programs in English, mathematics, general development for dyslexic students; special instructional classes for students with LD, ADD, dyslexia, and Nonverbal Learning Disorder.

College Placement 9 students graduated in 2005; all went to college, including Emory University; Lipscomb University; Savannah College of Art and Design; Tennessee Technological University; The University of Alabama; University of the Ozarks.

Student Life Upper grades have uniform requirement, student council, honor system. Discipline rests primarily with faculty.

Summer Programs Remediation, enrichment, sports, art/fine arts, computer instruction programs offered; session focuses on academic skill retention and enhancement of strengths/talents; held on campus; accepts boys and girls; open to students from other schools. 100 students usually enrolled.

Tuition and Aid Day student tuition: $24,080. Tuition installment plan (monthly payment plans). Need-based scholarship grants available. In 2005–06, 28% of upper-school students received aid. Total amount of financial aid awarded in 2005–06: $177,540.

Admissions Traditional secondary-level entrance grade is 9. For fall 2005, 17 students applied for upper-level admission, 11 were accepted, 7 enrolled. Psycho-educational evaluation required. Deadline for receipt of application materials: none. Application fee required: $250. Interview required.

Athletics Interscholastic: basketball (boys), cross-country running (b), softball (b). 2 PE instructors, 2 coaches.

Computers Computer network features include on-campus library services, CD-ROMs, Internet access, file transfer, DVD, wireless campus network, iPods.

Contact Mrs. Kathleen Harrigan Boles, Director of Admission. 615-507-3173 Ext. 250. Fax: 615-507-3170. E-mail: kathy.boles@curreyingram.org. Web site: www.curreyingram.org.

CUSHING ACADEMY

39 School Street
PO Box 8000
Ashburnham, Massachusetts 01430-8000
Head of School: Mr. M. Willard Lampe II

General Information Coeducational boarding and day college-preparatory, arts, and technology school. Grades 9–PG. Founded: 1865. Setting: small town. Nearest major city is Boston. Students are housed in single-sex dormitories. 162-acre campus. 31 buildings on campus. Approved or accredited by Association of Independent Schools in New England, New England Association of Schools and Colleges, The Association of Boarding Schools, and Massachusetts Department of Education. Member of National Association of Independent Schools and Secondary School Admission Test Board. Endowment: $15.5 million. Total enrollment: 445. Upper school average class size: 12. Upper school faculty-student ratio: 1:8.

Upper School Student Profile Grade 9: 65 students (34 boys, 31 girls); Grade 10: 110 students (64 boys, 46 girls); Grade 11: 135 students (75 boys, 60 girls); Grade 12: 113 students (65 boys, 48 girls); Postgraduate: 22 students (16 boys, 6 girls). 86% of students are boarding students. 35% are state residents. 28 states are represented in upper school student body. 26% are international students. International students from Brazil, China, Hong Kong, Mexico, Republic of Korea, and Taiwan; 25 other countries represented in student body.

Faculty School total: 76. In upper school: 39 men, 26 women; 36 have advanced degrees; 52 reside on campus.

Subjects Offered Advanced Placement courses, aerobics, algebra, American government, American government-AP, American history, American literature, American literature-AP, anatomy, architectural drawing, art, biology, biology-AP, calculus, calculus-AP, chemistry, chemistry-AP, chorus, community service, computer programming, computer science, creative writing, dance, developmental language skills, digital photography, drafting, drama, drawing, driver education, ecology, economics, English, English literature, environmental science, ESL, ethics, European history, expository writing, fine arts, French, geometry, government/civics, grammar, health, history, Latin, marine biology, mathematics, mechanical drawing, music, music theory, photography, physics, physiology, pre-calculus, psychology, science, social studies, sociology, Spanish, speech, theater, trigonometry, world history, world literature, World-Wide-Web publishing, writing.

Graduation Requirements Arts and fine arts (art, music, dance, drama), computer science, English, foreign language, health and wellness, mathematics, science, social studies (includes history).

Special Academic Programs Advanced Placement exam preparation in 14 subject areas; honors section; independent study; term-away projects; academic accommodation for the gifted, the musically talented, and the artistically talented; remedial reading and/or remedial writing; remedial math; programs in English, mathematics for dyslexic students; ESL (85 students enrolled).

College Placement 118 students graduated in 2005; 117 went to college, including Bentley College; Boston University; Brown University; Northeastern University; Suffolk University; University of Colorado at Boulder. Other: 1 entered a postgraduate year.

Student Life Upper grades have specified standards of dress, student council. Discipline rests primarily with faculty.

Summer Programs Remediation, enrichment, advancement, ESL, art/fine arts, computer instruction programs offered; session focuses on enrichment; held both on and off campus; held at Chile; accepts boys and girls; open to students from other schools. 325 students usually enrolled. 2006 schedule: July 1 to August 10.

Tuition and Aid Day student tuition: $25,020; 7-day tuition and room/board: $36,135. Tuition installment plan (Academic Management Services Plan, Key Tuition Payment Plan, monthly payment plans). Merit scholarship grants, need-based scholarship grants available. In 2005–06, 23% of upper-school students received aid; total upper-school merit-scholarship money awarded: $50,000. Total amount of financial aid awarded in 2005–06: $2,100,000.

Admissions Traditional secondary-level entrance grade is 9. For fall 2005, 670 students applied for upper-level admission, 415 were accepted, 185 enrolled. ACT, PSAT, SAT, SLEP, SSAT or TOEFL required. Deadline for receipt of application materials: February 1. Application fee required: $50. Interview required.

Athletics Interscholastic: baseball (boys), basketball (b,g), field hockey (g), football (b), ice hockey (b,g), lacrosse (b,g), soccer (b,g), softball (g), tennis (b,g), track and field (b,g), volleyball (g); intramural: flag football (b); coed interscholastic: alpine skiing, cross-country running, golf; coed intramural: aerobics, aerobics/dance, alpine skiing, boxing, dance, equestrian sports, figure skating, fitness, horseback riding, ice hockey, ice skating, independent competitive sports, martial arts, modern dance, outdoor adventure, outdoor education, ropes courses, skiing (downhill), snowboarding, strength & conditioning, wall climbing, weight training. 2 coaches, 2 trainers.

Computers Computers are regularly used in art, English, history, mathematics, science classes. Computer network features include campus e-mail, on-campus library services, CD-ROMs, Internet access, DVD, wireless campus network, CushNet (on campus network).

Contact Mrs. Melanie J. Connors, Director of Admission. 978-827-7300. Fax: 978-827-6253. E-mail: admission@cushing.org. Web site: www.cushing.org.

ANNOUNCEMENT FROM THE SCHOOL Cushing Academy is dedicated to educating the minds and shaping the characters of young men and women. The Academy exists for students and their personal and academic growth. In a community that is academically and culturally diverse, the Academy challenges each individual and supports excellence in every aspect of the learning process. Cushing Academy offers a rigorous college-preparatory curriculum, teaching skills that build confidence and instilling values that endure.

See full description on page 752.

DALLAS ACADEMY

Dallas, Texas
See Special Needs Schools section.

DALLAS CHRISTIAN SCHOOL

1515 Republic Parkway
Mesquite, Texas 75150
Head of School: Allen Norman

General Information Coeducational day college-preparatory and religious studies school, affiliated with Church of Christ. Grades PK–12. Founded: 1957. Setting: suburban. Nearest major city is Dallas. 60-acre campus. 7 buildings on campus. Approved or accredited by National Christian School Association, Southern Association of Colleges and Schools, and Texas Department of Education. Total enrollment: 735. Upper school average class size: 25. Upper school faculty-student ratio: 1:15.

Upper School Student Profile Grade 9: 64 students (33 boys, 31 girls); Grade 10: 70 students (39 boys, 31 girls); Grade 11: 53 students (33 boys, 20 girls); Grade 12: 68 students (32 boys, 36 girls). 36% of students are members of Church of Christ.

Faculty School total: 70. In upper school: 13 men, 14 women; 16 have advanced degrees.

Subjects Offered Algebra, American history, American literature, art, band, Bible studies, biology, calculus, cheerleading, chemistry, chorus, computer math, computer science, creative writing, drama, economics, English, English literature, fine arts, French, geography, geometry, government/civics, health, history, humanities, journalism, mathematics, newspaper, physical education, physics, religion, science, sign language, social studies, Spanish, speech, speech origins of English, theater, world history, world literature, yearbook.

Graduation Requirements Arts and fine arts (art, music, dance, drama), computer science, English, foreign language, mathematics, physical education (includes health), religion (includes Bible studies and theology), science, social studies (includes history), speech origins of English, seniors must take SAT.

Special Academic Programs Study at local college for college credit.

College Placement 91 students graduated in 2005; 88 went to college, including Abilene Christian University; Baylor University; Lubbock Christian University; Texas A&M University; Texas Tech University. Other: 2 went to work, 1 had other specific plans. Median SAT verbal: 560, median SAT math: 560.

Student Life Upper grades have uniform requirement, student council, honor system. Discipline rests primarily with faculty. Attendance at religious services is required.

Tuition and Aid Day student tuition: $9400. Tuition installment plan (FACTS Tuition Payment Plan). Tuition reduction for siblings, need-based scholarship grants available. In 2005–06, 11% of upper-school students received aid. Total amount of financial aid awarded in 2005–06: $121,000.

Admissions Traditional secondary-level entrance grade is 9. For fall 2005, 41 students applied for upper-level admission, 40 were accepted, 31 enrolled. Woodcock-Johnson Revised Achievement Test required. Deadline for receipt of application materials: none. No application fee required. On-campus interview required.

Athletics Interscholastic: baseball (boys), basketball (b,g), cheering (g), cross-country running (b,g), drill team (g), football (b), golf (b,g), soccer (b,g), softball (g), tennis (b,g), track and field (b,g), volleyball (g), wrestling (b). 2 PE instructors.

Computers Computers are regularly used in newspaper, Web site design, yearbook classes. Computer network features include on-campus library services, Internet access.

Contact Ms. Becky Burroughs, High School Principal. 972-270-5495 Ext. 277. Fax: 972-270-7581. E-mail: bburroughs@dallaschristian.com. Web site: www.dallaschristian.com.

THE DALTON SCHOOL

108 East 89th Street
New York, New York 10128-1599
Head of School: Ellen C. Stein

General Information Coeducational day college-preparatory and arts school. Grades K–12. Founded: 1919. Setting: urban. 3 buildings on campus. Approved or accredited by New York State Association of Independent Schools. Member of National Association of Independent Schools and Secondary School Admission Test Board. Endowment: $30 million. Total enrollment: 1,299. Upper school average class size: 15. Upper school faculty-student ratio: 1:7.

Upper School Student Profile Grade 9: 108 students (51 boys, 57 girls); Grade 10: 121 students (59 boys, 62 girls); Grade 11: 112 students (54 boys, 58 girls); Grade 12: 111 students (51 boys, 60 girls).

Faculty School total: 203. In upper school: 60 men, 61 women; 58 have advanced degrees.

Subjects Offered Algebra, American history, American legal systems, American literature, architecture, art, art history, Asian literature, astronomy, biology, calculus, ceramics, chemistry, community service, computer programming, computer science, dance, earth science, ecology, economics, English, English literature, environmental science, ethics, European history, fine arts, French, geometry, government/civics, health, history, Latin, law, mathematics, music, philosophy, photography, physical education, physics, Russian literature, science, social studies, Spanish, theater, trigonometry, world history, world literature.

Graduation Requirements Arts and fine arts (art, music, dance, drama), computer science, English, foreign language, history, mathematics, physical education (includes health), science. Community service is required.

Special Academic Programs Advanced Placement exam preparation in 11 subject areas; honors section; study at local college for college credit.

College Placement 112 students graduated in 2005; all went to college, including Amherst College; Brown University; Columbia College; Cornell University; University of Pennsylvania; Yale University.

Student Life Upper grades have student council. Discipline rests equally with students and faculty.

Tuition and Aid Day student tuition: $27,600. Tuition installment plan (FACTS Tuition Payment Plan, 2-payment plan). Need-based scholarship grants available. In 2005–06, 20% of upper-school students received aid. Total amount of financial aid awarded in 2005–06: $2,014,348.

Admissions Traditional secondary-level entrance grade is 9. ISEE or SSAT required. Deadline for receipt of application materials: December 2. Application fee required: $50. On-campus interview required.

Athletics Interscholastic: baseball (boys), basketball (b,g), football (b), lacrosse (b,g); intramural: baseball (b), basketball (b,g), football (b); coed intramural: gymnastics. 10 PE instructors, 14 coaches, 1 trainer.

Computers Computers are regularly used in English, foreign language, mathematics, science classes. Computer network features include campus e-mail, on-campus library services, CD-ROMs, online commercial services, Internet access, wireless campus network.

Contact Eva Rado, Director, Middle and High School Admissions. 212-423-5200. Fax: 212-423-5259. E-mail: rado@dalton.org. Web site: www.dalton.org.

DANA HALL SCHOOL

45 Dana Road
Wellesley, Massachusetts 02482
Head of School: Blair Jenkins

petersons.com

General Information Girls' boarding and day college-preparatory, arts, technology, and language lab school. Boarding grades 9–12, day grades 6–12. Founded: 1881. Setting: suburban. Nearest major city is Boston. Students are housed in single-sex dormitories. 55-acre campus. 34 buildings on campus. Approved or accredited by Association of Independent Schools in New England, New England Association of Schools and Colleges, The Association of Boarding Schools, and Massachusetts Department of Education. Member of National Association of Independent Schools and Secondary School Admission Test Board. Endowment: $20.1 million. Total enrollment: 465. Upper school average class size: 14. Upper school faculty-student ratio: 1:8.

Upper School Student Profile Grade 9: 85 students (85 girls); Grade 10: 82 students (82 girls); Grade 11: 81 students (81 girls); Grade 12: 90 students (90 girls). 40% of students are boarding students. 82% are state residents. 15 states are represented in upper school student body. 10% are international students. International students from Ecuador, Hong Kong, Mexico, Republic of Korea, Taiwan, and Thailand; 10 other countries represented in student body.

Faculty School total: 60. In upper school: 18 men, 42 women; 29 have advanced degrees; 22 reside on campus.

Subjects Offered African studies, algebra, American history, American literature, architecture, art, art history, astronomy, biology, calculus, ceramics, chemistry, community service, computer math, computer programming, computer science, creative writing, dance, drama, earth science, economics, English, English literature, environmental science, equestrian sports, European history, expository writing, fine arts, French, geography, geology, geometry, government/civics, grammar, health,

history, Latin, logic, marine biology, mathematics, Middle Eastern history, music, philosophy, photography, physical education, physics, Russian studies, science, social studies, Spanish, statistics, theater, trigonometry, women in the classical world, world history, writing.

Graduation Requirements Arts and fine arts (art, music, dance, drama), computer science, English, foreign language, mathematics, physical education (includes health), science, social studies (includes history), 20 hours of community service.

Special Academic Programs Advanced Placement exam preparation in 13 subject areas; honors section; independent study; term-away projects; study at local college for college credit; academic accommodation for the musically talented and the artistically talented.

College Placement 80 students graduated in 2005; all went to college, including Cornell College; Dartmouth College; Georgetown University; Stanford University; University of Pennsylvania. 69% scored over 600 on SAT verbal, 70% scored over 600 on SAT math.

Student Life Upper grades have student council, honor system. Discipline rests equally with students and faculty.

Tuition and Aid Day student tuition: $28,000; 7-day tuition and room/board: $37,000. Tuition installment plan (individually arranged payment plans, 10-month plan). Need-based scholarship grants, need-based loans available. In 2005–06, 19% of upper-school students received aid. Total amount of financial aid awarded in 2005–06: $2,065,785.

Admissions Traditional secondary-level entrance grade is 9. For fall 2005, 434 students applied for upper-level admission, 262 were accepted, 131 enrolled. ISEE, SSAT or TOEFL required. Deadline for receipt of application materials: February 1. Application fee required: $40. Interview required.

Athletics Interscholastic: basketball, cross-country running, dance, equestrian sports, fencing, field hockey, golf, hockey, horseback riding, ice hockey, lacrosse, modern dance, soccer, softball, tennis, volleyball; intramural: aerobics, aerobics/dance, aquatics, ballet, dance, fitness, fitness walking, indoor track, modern dance, nautilus, outdoor education, physical fitness, rock climbing, self defense, swimming and diving, track and field, walking, weight lifting, weight training, yoga. 5 PE instructors, 21 coaches, 1 trainer.

Computers Computers are regularly used in art, English, history, mathematics, science, technology, Web site design classes. Computer network features include campus e-mail, on-campus library services, CD-ROMs, online commercial services, Internet access, file transfer, office computer access, DVD, wireless campus network.

Contact Heather Cameron, Director of Admission and Financial Aid. 781-235-3010. Fax: 781-235-0577. E-mail: admission@danahall.org. Web site: www.danahall.org.

ANNOUNCEMENT FROM THE SCHOOL The Shipley Center for Athletics, Health & Wellness is a 93,000-square-foot facility that is scheduled to open in fall 2005 and will house a swimming pool, squash courts, and a state-of-the-art fencing studio. The 2004–05 Wannamaker Lecture Series welcomes speakers Linda Whitlock, President and Chief Executive Officer of Boys & Girls Clubs of Boston, named one of the Most Powerful Women in Boston in 2003 by *Boston Magazine;* Mark Mathabane, award-winning novelist and author of *Kaffir* Boy, a *New York Times* bestseller; and Pilobolus, a dance theater troupe created by Alison Chase. Their work is an identifiable mix of acrobatics, mime, spectacle, and modern dance.

See full description on page 754.

DANUBE INTERNATIONAL SCHOOL, VIENNA

Josef Gall-gasse 2
Vienna 1020, Austria
Head of School: Mr. Andrew R. Scott

General Information Coeducational day college-preparatory, general academic, business, and bilingual studies school. Grades K–12. Founded: 1992. Setting: urban. 1 building on campus. Member of European Council of International Schools. Language of instruction: English. Total enrollment: 260. Upper school average class size: 20.

Faculty School total: 37. In upper school: 10 men, 10 women.

Special Academic Programs International Baccalaureate program; ESL.

Student Life Upper grades have student council. Discipline rests primarily with faculty.

Tuition and Aid Day student tuition: €13,110–€14,273. Tuition installment plan (monthly payment plans). Merit scholarship grants available.

Admissions Traditional secondary-level entrance grade is 9. Admissions testing required. Deadline for receipt of application materials: none. Application fee required: €185. Interview required.

Athletics 2 PE instructors.

Computers Computer resources include campus e-mail, CD-ROMs, Internet access, DVD, wireless campus network.

Contact Gabi McHale, Registrar. 43-1-7203110 Ext. 10. Fax: 43-1-7203110 Ext. 40. E-mail: registrar@danubeschool.at. Web site: www.danubeschool.at/index.shtml.

DARLINGTON SCHOOL

1014 Cave Spring Road
Rome, Georgia 30161
Head of School: Thomas C. Whitworth III

petersons.com

General Information Coeducational boarding and day college-preparatory, arts, and technology school, affiliated with Christian faith. Boarding grades 9–PG, day grades PK–PG. Founded: 1905. Setting: small town. Nearest major city is Atlanta. Students are housed in single-sex dormitories. 500-acre campus. 15 buildings on campus. Approved or accredited by Georgia Independent School Association, Southern Association of Colleges and Schools, Southern Association of Independent Schools, The Association of Boarding Schools, and Georgia Department of Education. Member of National Association of Independent Schools and Secondary School Admission Test Board. Endowment: $35.6 million. Total enrollment: 928. Upper school average class size: 14. Upper school faculty-student ratio: 1:9.

Upper School Student Profile Grade 9: 110 students (55 boys, 55 girls); Grade 10: 126 students (64 boys, 62 girls); Grade 11: 143 students (71 boys, 72 girls); Grade 12: 125 students (67 boys, 58 girls). 36% of students are boarding students. 73% are state residents. 25 states are represented in upper school student body. 11% are international students. International students from Bermuda, Germany, Jamaica, Republic of Korea, Saudi Arabia, and Thailand; 18 other countries represented in student body. 85% of students are Christian faith.

Faculty School total: 98. In upper school: 34 men, 24 women; 33 have advanced degrees; 55 reside on campus.

Subjects Offered Advanced Placement courses, algebra, American literature, anatomy and physiology, ancient world history, art, art history, band, biology, calculus, chemistry, chorus, computer programming, computer science, creative writing, drama, drawing, economics, English, English literature, environmental science, ESL, European history, expository writing, film, fine arts, French, general science, geometry, government/civics, grammar, graphic arts, graphic design, health, history, humanities, journalism, mathematics, music, natural history, photojournalism, physical education, physics, science, social studies, Spanish, theater, trigonometry, typing, video, world culture, world history, world literature, World-Wide-Web publishing, writing.

Graduation Requirements Arts and fine arts (art, music, dance, drama), English, foreign language, information technology, mathematics, physical education (includes health), science, social studies (includes history), participation in after-school activities.

Special Academic Programs Advanced Placement exam preparation in 16 subject areas; honors section; ESL (8 students enrolled).

College Placement 108 students graduated in 2005; all went to college, including Auburn University; Georgia Institute of Technology; Mercer University; The University of Alabama; University of Georgia; University of the South.

Student Life Upper grades have specified standards of dress, student council, honor system. Discipline rests equally with students and faculty. Attendance at religious services is required.

Summer Programs Enrichment, sports programs offered; session focuses on camps for middle-school aged children (rising 6th-9th grades); held on campus; accepts boys and girls; open to students from other schools. 2000 students usually enrolled. 2006 schedule: June 4 to July 28. Application deadline: none.

Tuition and Aid Day student tuition: $12,800; 7-day tuition and room/board: $30,100. Tuition installment plan (monthly payment plans, individually arranged payment plans). Merit scholarship grants, need-based scholarship grants, need-based loans available. In 2005–06, 18% of upper-school students received aid; total upper-school merit-scholarship money awarded: $339,850. Total amount of financial aid awarded in 2005–06: $1,172,050.

Admissions Traditional secondary-level entrance grade is 9. For fall 2005, 263 students applied for upper-level admission, 180 were accepted, 121 enrolled. SAT for students entering as juniors, SSAT or TOEFL required. Deadline for receipt of application materials: none. Application fee required: $50. Interview required.

Athletics Interscholastic: baseball (boys), basketball (b,g), cheering (g), crew (b,g), cross-country running (b,g), football (b), golf (b,g), lacrosse (b,g), soccer (b,g), softball (g), swimming and diving (b,g), tennis (b,g), track and field (b,g), volleyball (g), wrestling (b); intramural: basketball (b,g), flag football (b,g), indoor soccer (b), tennis (b,g), volleyball (b,g); coed interscholastic: diving; coed intramural: aerobics, back packing, equestrian sports, Frisbee, horseback riding, kayaking, mountain biking, outdoor adventure, paint ball, physical fitness, physical training, soccer, strength & conditioning, table tennis, ultimate Frisbee, water polo, weight lifting. 3 PE instructors, 6 coaches, 1 trainer.

Computers Computers are regularly used in computer applications, English, foreign language, history, mathematics, science, Web site design classes. Computer network features include campus e-mail, on-campus library services, CD-ROMs, Internet access.

Contact Mr. Casey Zimmer, Director of Admission. 706-236-0479. Fax: 706-232-3600. E-mail: czimmer@darlingtonschool.org. Web site: www.darlingtonschool.org.

ANNOUNCEMENT FROM THE SCHOOL Darlington School, Rome, Georgia, is a coeducational, college-preparatory day (prekindergarten through grade 12) and boarding (grade 9 through grade 12) school established in 1905. Located 65 miles northwest of Atlanta, Darlington offers motivated students rigorous academics, numerous fine arts opportunities, and a competitive athletics program in a nurturing environment.

See full description on page 756.

DARROW SCHOOL

110 Darrow Road
New Lebanon, New York 12125
Head of School: Mrs. Nancy Wolf

petersons.com

General Information Coeducational boarding and day college-preparatory and arts school. Grades 9–PG. Founded: 1932. Setting: rural. Nearest major city is Pittsfield, MA. Students are housed in single-sex dormitories. 365-acre campus. 26 buildings on campus. Approved or accredited by Middle States Association of Colleges and Schools, New York State Association of Independent Schools, and The Association of Boarding Schools. Member of National Association of Independent Schools and Secondary School Admission Test Board. Language of instruction: English. Endowment: $745,150. Total enrollment: 124. Upper school average class size: 9. Upper school faculty-student ratio: 1:4.

Upper School Student Profile Grade 9: 25 students (18 boys, 7 girls); Grade 10: 30 students (17 boys, 13 girls); Grade 11: 35 students (13 boys, 22 girls); Grade 12: 33 students (13 boys, 20 girls); Postgraduate: 1 student (1 girl). 92% of students are boarding students. 39% are state residents. 16 states are represented in upper school student body. 13% are international students. International students from Germany, Jamaica, Japan, Republic of Korea, Singapore, and Taiwan.

Faculty School total: 32. In upper school: 15 men, 15 women; 16 have advanced degrees; 30 reside on campus.

Subjects Offered 3-dimensional art, acting, African-American studies, algebra, American history, American literature, art, art history, biology, botany, calculus, ceramics, chemistry, clayworking, computer graphics, computer skills, computer studies, creative writing, drama, drawing, driver education, earth science, ecology, economics, English, English literature, environmental education, environmental science, ethics, European history, expository writing, fine arts, French, French studies, geometry, grammar, health, history, journalism, leadership training, math applications, mathematics, music, oil painting, photo shop, photography, photojournalism, physics, play production, political economics, pottery, pre-calculus, probability and statistics, psychology, reading/study skills, Russian literature, science, science and technology, social science, social studies, Spanish, Spanish literature, theater, trigonometry, woodworking, world history, world literature, writing, yearbook.

Graduation Requirements Arts and fine arts (art, music, dance, drama), computer science, English, foreign language, mathematics, physical education (includes health), science, social science, social studies (includes history).

Special Academic Programs Honors section; independent study; term-away projects; study at local college for college credit; academic accommodation for the musically talented and the artistically talented; special instructional classes for students with Attention Deficit Disorder; ESL (5 students enrolled).

College Placement 34 students graduated in 2004; all went to college, including Cornell University; Goucher College; Ohio Wesleyan University; Pratt Institute; Syracuse University; The Colorado College.

Student Life Upper grades have specified standards of dress, student council. Discipline rests equally with students and faculty.

Tuition and Aid Day student tuition: $18,225; 7-day tuition and room/board: $31,975. Tuition installment plan (Insured Tuition Payment Plan, Academic Management Services Plan, Key Tuition Payment Plan, individually arranged payment plans). Need-based scholarship grants available. In 2004–05, 34% of upper-school students received aid. Total amount of financial aid awarded in 2004–05: $796,000.

Admissions Traditional secondary-level entrance grade is 9. For fall 2005, 134 students applied for upper-level admission, 101 were accepted, 62 enrolled. Deadline for receipt of application materials: none. Application fee required: $50. On-campus interview required.

Athletics Interscholastic: baseball (boys), basketball (b,g), soccer (b,g), softball (g), tennis (b,g); coed interscholastic: fencing, lacrosse; coed intramural: alpine skiing, bicycling, cross-country running, dance, fitness, fitness walking, freestyle skiing, hiking/backpacking, modern dance, mountain biking, outdoor activities, outdoor recreation, physical fitness, power lifting, rock climbing, skiing (cross-country), skiing (downhill), snowboarding, snowshoeing, ultimate Frisbee, weight lifting.

Computers Computer network features include campus e-mail, on-campus library services, CD-ROMs, Internet access, wireless campus network.

Contact J. Kirk Russell III, Director of Admission. 518-794-6008. Fax: 518-794-7065. E-mail: jkr@darrowschool.org. Web site: www.darrowschool.org.

ANNOUNCEMENT FROM THE SCHOOL Living, working, learning in the classroom and beyond. These words have guided Darrow's educational philosophy for more than 70 years. Hands-on learning, innovative teaching methods, and individual attention create an atmosphere that supports the pursuit of individual creativity and the joy of learning for its own sake. The new Joline Arts Center offers exceptional state-of-the-art spaces for all visual arts. Sam, a junior,

De La Salle College

Upper School Student Profile Grade 9: 114 students (55 boys, 59 girls); Grade 10: 110 students (54 boys, 56 girls); Grade 11: 106 students (51 boys, 55 girls); Grade 12: 99 students (46 boys, 53 girls). 90% of students are Roman Catholic.

Faculty School total: 43. In upper school: 30 men, 13 women.

Special Academic Programs Advanced Placement exam preparation in 4 subject areas.

College Placement 100 students graduated in 2005; all went to college, including McGill University; McMaster University; Queen's University at Kingston; The University of Western Ontario; University of Toronto; York University.

Student Life Upper grades have uniform requirement, student council, honor system. Discipline rests primarily with faculty. Attendance at religious services is required.

Summer Programs Enrichment, advancement programs offered; held on campus; accepts boys and girls; open to students from other schools. 150 students usually enrolled.

Tuition and Aid Day student tuition: CAN$9350. Tuition installment plan (monthly payment plans). Tuition reduction for siblings, bursaries, need-based scholarship grants available. In 2005–06, 20% of upper-school students received aid.

Admissions Traditional secondary-level entrance grade is 9. For fall 2005, 151 students applied for upper-level admission, 80 were accepted, 59 enrolled. SSAT required. Deadline for receipt of application materials: December 16. Application fee required: CAN$100. On-campus interview required.

Athletics Interscholastic: baseball (boys), basketball (b,g), field hockey (g), football (b), ice hockey (b,g), soccer (b,g), softball (g), volleyball (b,g); coed interscholastic: alpine skiing, aquatics, badminton, cross-country running, golf, track and field; coed intramural: ball hockey, fencing. 4 PE instructors.

Computers Computer network features include campus e-mail, CD-ROMs, Internet access, office computer access.

Contact Ms. Anna Di Benedetto, Admissions Secretary. 416-969-8771 Ext. 228. Fax: 416-969-9175. E-mail: adib@delasalle.toronto.on.ca.

DE LA SALLE HIGH SCHOOL

1130 Winton Drive
Concord, California 94518
Head of School: Br. Christopher Brady, FSC

General Information Boys' day college-preparatory, arts, and religious studies school, affiliated with Roman Catholic Church. Grades 9–12. Founded: 1965. Setting: suburban. Nearest major city is Oakland. 25-acre campus. 10 buildings on campus. Approved or accredited by Western Association of Schools and Colleges and Western Catholic Education Association. Endowment: $1.5 million. Total enrollment: 1,006. Upper school average class size: 30. Upper school faculty-student ratio: 1:28.

Upper School Student Profile Grade 9: 270 students (270 boys); Grade 10: 260 students (260 boys); Grade 11: 235 students (235 boys); Grade 12: 241 students (241 boys). 80% of students are Roman Catholic.

Faculty School total: 69. In upper school: 45 men, 24 women; 38 have advanced degrees.

Subjects Offered Algebra, American history, anatomy, art, band, Bible studies, biology, calculus, chemistry, chorus, computer science, creative writing, current events, design, drafting, drawing, economics, English, English-AP, ethics, fine arts, first aid, French, geology, geometry, government/civics, health, history, Italian, jazz, Latin, literature, marine biology, mathematics, music history, music theory, orchestra, painting, physical education, physics, physiology, pre-calculus, psychology, religion, science, sculpture, social studies, Spanish, Spanish-AP, sports medicine, statistics, trigonometry, world history, world religions, writing.

Graduation Requirements Arts and fine arts (art, music, dance, drama), English, foreign language, mathematics, physical education (includes health), religion (includes Bible studies and theology), science, social studies (includes history).

Special Academic Programs Advanced Placement exam preparation in 9 subject areas; honors section; independent study; remedial math.

College Placement 246 students graduated in 2005; 243 went to college, including California Polytechnic State University, San Luis Obispo; California State University, Chico; Loyola Marymount University; Saint Mary's College of California; University of California, Berkeley; University of California, Davis. Other: 2 went to work, 1 had other specific plans. Mean SAT verbal: 564, mean SAT math: 576, mean composite ACT: 25. 32% scored over 600 on SAT verbal, 32% scored over 600 on SAT math, 30% scored over 26 on composite ACT.

Student Life Upper grades have specified standards of dress, student council, honor system. Discipline rests primarily with faculty. Attendance at religious services is required.

Summer Programs Remediation, enrichment, advancement, computer instruction programs offered; session focuses on remediation; held on campus; accepts boys; not open to students from other schools. 30 students usually enrolled. 2006 schedule: June 19 to July 14. Application deadline: June 2.

Tuition and Aid Day student tuition: $10,500. Tuition installment plan (10-month, quarterly, semi-annual, and annual payment plans). Need-based grants available. In 2005–06, 17% of upper-school students received aid. Total amount of financial aid awarded in 2005–06: $1,029,000.

Admissions Traditional secondary-level entrance grade is 9. For fall 2005, 413 students applied for upper-level admission, 270 were accepted, 270 enrolled. High

---

School Placement Test required. Deadline for receipt of application materials: none. Application fee required: $75. On-campus interview required.

Athletics Interscholastic: baseball, basketball, cross-country running, diving, football, golf, lacrosse, rugby, soccer, swimming and diving, tennis, track and field, volleyball, water polo, wrestling; intramural: basketball, bowling, flag football, floor hockey. 5 PE instructors, 80 coaches, 1 trainer.

Computers Computers are regularly used in animation, art, business applications, business education, business skills, business studies, career exploration, career technology, college planning, drawing and design, English, French, French as a second language, graphics, history, information technology, introduction to technology, language development, library, mathematics, media production, media services, music, newspaper, science, social studies, Spanish, technology, vocational-technical courses, yearbook classes. Computer network features include on-campus library services, CD-ROMs, Internet access, wireless campus network.

Contact Mr. Joseph Grantham, Director of Admissions. 925-288-8102. Fax: 925-686-3474. E-mail: granthamj@dlshs.org.

DELASALLE HIGH SCHOOL

One DeLaSalle Drive
Minneapolis, Minnesota 55401-1597
Head of School: Br. Michael Collins, FSC

General Information Coeducational day college-preparatory, arts, business, religious studies, and technology school, affiliated with Roman Catholic Church. Grades 9–12. Founded: 1900. Setting: urban. 10-acre campus. 3 buildings on campus. Approved or accredited by National Catholic Education Association, North Central Association of Colleges and Schools, and Minnesota Department of Education. Endowment: $2.8 million. Total enrollment: 639. Upper school average class size: 22. Upper school faculty-student ratio: 1:13.

Upper School Student Profile Grade 9: 174 students (81 boys, 93 girls); Grade 10: 184 students (83 boys, 101 girls); Grade 11: 149 students (77 boys, 72 girls); Grade 12: 132 students (68 boys, 64 girls). 73% of students are Roman Catholic.

Faculty School total: 58. In upper school: 30 men, 28 women; 43 have advanced degrees.

Subjects Offered 20th century American writers, 20th century history, 20th century world history, advanced computer applications, advanced studio art-AP, African-American literature, algebra, American biography, American government, American history, American history-AP, American legal systems, American literature, ancient world history, anthropology, art, art-AP, ballet, band, Bible, biology, biology-AP, business applications, business law, business mathematics, calculus, calculus-AP, campus ministry, Catholic belief and practice, Central and Eastern European history, chamber groups, chemistry, chemistry-AP, child development, choir, choral music, Christian and Hebrew scripture, Christian ethics, Civil War, comparative government and politics, comparative religion, composition, computer applications, computer graphics, computer keyboarding, computer programming, computer programming-AP, computer science, computer science-AP, concert band, concert choir, creative writing, drama performance, drama workshop, economics, English, English language and composition-AP, English language-AP, English literature-AP, ethics, ethnic studies, European history, European history-AP, film, film studies, filmmaking, first aid, fitness, forensic science, French, French-AP, geography, geometry, German, government, graphic arts, graphic design, health and wellness, history of the Catholic Church, history-AP, honors algebra, honors English, honors geometry, honors U.S. history, honors world history, human sexuality, instrumental music, introduction to theater, Japanese, Japanese as Second Language, Japanese history, journalism, mathematics, mathematics-AP, media communications, media literacy, moral and social development, personal finance, philosophy, physical education, physical science, physics, physics-AP, pre-calculus, probability and statistics, psychology, Shakespeare, social justice, Spanish, Spanish language-AP, speech, street law, trigonometry, vocal music, Western civilization, world geography, world religions.

Graduation Requirements Arts and fine arts (art, music, dance, drama), English, foreign language, mathematics, physical education (includes health), religious studies, science, social studies (includes history), 60 hours of documented Christian service.

Special Academic Programs Advanced Placement exam preparation in 7 subject areas; honors section; independent study; study at local college for college credit.

College Placement 129 students graduated in 2005; 123 went to college, including Carleton College; College of Saint Benedict; Saint John's University; Saint Mary's University of Minnesota; University of Minnesota, Twin Cities Campus; University of St. Thomas. Other: 4 went to work, 2 entered military service. Mean composite ACT: 25. 56% scored over 26 on composite ACT.

Student Life Upper grades have uniform requirement, student council, honor system. Discipline rests primarily with faculty. Attendance at religious services is required.

Tuition and Aid Day student tuition: $7625. Tuition installment plan (FACTS Tuition Payment Plan, monthly payment plans). Merit scholarship grants, need-based scholarship grants, off-campus work programs for tuition benefit available. In 2005–06, 53% of upper-school students received aid; total upper-school merit-scholarship money awarded: $150,000. Total amount of financial aid awarded in 2005–06: $1,102,000.

Admissions Traditional secondary-level entrance grade is 9. For fall 2005, 424 students applied for upper-level admission, 305 were accepted, 174 enrolled. High

School Placement Test required. Deadline for receipt of application materials: none. No application fee required. Interview required.

Athletics Interscholastic: baseball (boys), basketball (b,g), cross-country running (b,g), football (b), golf (b,g), soccer (b,g), softball (g), swimming and diving (g), tennis (b,g), track and field (b,g), volleyball (g), wrestling (b); coed interscholastic: cheering, rowing, weight training; coed intramural: aerobics, archery, bowling, strength & conditioning. 3 PE instructors, 44 coaches, 1 trainer.

Computers Computers are regularly used in art, business, English, French, graphic design, independent study, journalism, media, media production, music, science, social studies, Spanish, writing classes. Computer network features include on-campus library services, CD-ROMs, Internet access.

Contact Ms. Sarah Graham, Director of Admission. 612-676-7675. Fax: 612-676-7699. E-mail: sarah.graham@delasalle.com. Web site: www.delasalle.com.

DELAWARE COUNTY CHRISTIAN SCHOOL

462 Malin Road
Newtown Square, Pennsylvania 19073-3499
Head of School: Dr. Stephen P. Dill

General Information Coeducational day college-preparatory and arts school, affiliated with Protestant-Evangelical faith. Grades PK–12. Founded: 1950. Setting: suburban. Nearest major city is Philadelphia. 26-acre campus. 6 buildings on campus. Approved or accredited by Association of Christian Schools International, Middle States Association of Colleges and Schools, and Pennsylvania Department of Education. Endowment: $3 million. Total enrollment: 938. Upper school average class size: 21. Upper school faculty-student ratio: 1:12.

Upper School Student Profile Grade 9: 105 students (47 boys, 58 girls); Grade 10: 90 students (40 boys, 50 girls); Grade 11: 88 students (44 boys, 44 girls); Grade 12: 97 students (45 boys, 52 girls). 100% of students are Protestant-Evangelical faith.

Faculty School total: 108. In upper school: 22 men, 25 women; 27 have advanced degrees.

Subjects Offered Algebra, American history, American literature, art, Bible studies, biology, calculus, chemistry, choir, choral music, concert band, concert bell choir, concert choir, creative writing, digital art, discrete math, drama, earth science, economics, English, English literature, English literature and composition-AP, European history-AP, fine arts, geography, geometry, German, German-AP, government/civics, grammar, graphics, handbells, journalism, literature, mathematics, music, music theory, physical education, physics, physics-AP, religion, science, social studies, Spanish, Spanish-AP, theater, trigonometry, U.S. history-AP, world history, writing workshop, yearbook.

Graduation Requirements Arts and fine arts (art, music, dance, drama), computer science, English, foreign language, mathematics, physical education (includes health), religion (includes Bible studies and theology), science, social studies (includes history).

Special Academic Programs Advanced Placement exam preparation in 8 subject areas; honors section; study abroad; academic accommodation for the gifted, the musically talented, and the artistically talented; ESL (8 students enrolled).

College Placement 102 students graduated in 2005; 100 went to college, including Eastern University; Messiah College; Temple University. Other: 1 went to work. Mean SAT verbal: 558, mean SAT math: 564.

Student Life Upper grades have uniform requirement, student council, honor system. Discipline rests primarily with faculty. Attendance at religious services is required.

Summer Programs Sports, art/fine arts programs offered; held on campus; accepts boys and girls; open to students from other schools. 200 students usually enrolled. 2006 schedule: June 21 to August 6. Application deadline: May 1.

Tuition and Aid Day student tuition: $8745. Tuition installment plan (monthly payment plans). Tuition reduction for siblings, need-based scholarship grants available. In 2005–06, 25% of upper-school students received aid. Total amount of financial aid awarded in 2005–06: $500,000.

Admissions Traditional secondary-level entrance grade is 9. ERB required. Deadline for receipt of application materials: none. Application fee required. On-campus interview required.

Athletics Interscholastic: baseball (boys), basketball (b,g), cheering (g), cross-country running (b,g), field hockey (g), golf (b,g), soccer (b,g), softball (g), tennis (b,g), track and field (b,g), wrestling (b); intramural: ice hockey (b); coed interscholastic: life saving. 3 PE instructors.

Computers Computers are regularly used in art, English, journalism, library, literary magazine, mathematics, newspaper, photography, photojournalism, publications, SAT preparation, writing, yearbook classes. Computer network features include campus e-mail, on-campus library services, CD-ROMs, Internet access, DVD, wireless campus network.

Contact Mrs. Arlene J. Warmhold, Admissions Secretary. 610-353-6522 Ext. 285. Fax: 610-356-9684. E-mail: awarmhold@dccs.org. Web site: www.dccs.org.

ANNOUNCEMENT FROM THE SCHOOL Delaware County Christian School is a parent-owned independent school with an enrollment of 950 students in grades K–12. The School, founded in 1950, provides a strong academic program within an evangelical Christian perspective. The Discovery Center

provides support programs for students with learning disabilities. Students are admitted on the basis of entrance tests, previous school records, and parental spiritual commitment.

DELAWARE VALLEY FRIENDS SCHOOL

Paoli, Pennsylvania
See Special Needs Schools section.

DELBARTON SCHOOL

230 Mendham Road
Morristown, New Jersey 07960
Head of School: Rev. Luke L. Travers, OSB

General Information Boys' day college-preparatory, arts, religious studies, and technology school, affiliated with Roman Catholic Church. Grades 7–12. Founded: 1939. Setting: suburban. Nearest major city is New York, NY. 400-acre campus. 5 buildings on campus. Approved or accredited by Middle States Association of Colleges and Schools, New Jersey Association of Independent Schools, and New Jersey Department of Education. Member of National Association of Independent Schools and Secondary School Admission Test Board. Endowment: $16.6 million. Total enrollment: 540. Upper school average class size: 15. Upper school faculty-student ratio: 1:7.

Upper School Student Profile Grade 9: 125 students (125 boys); Grade 10: 116 students (116 boys); Grade 11: 120 students (120 boys); Grade 12: 108 students (108 boys). 79% of students are Roman Catholic.

Faculty School total: 76. In upper school: 68 men, 8 women; 45 have advanced degrees.

Subjects Offered Accounting, advanced chemistry, algebra, American history, American literature, art, art history, astronomy, biology, calculus, chemistry, computer math, computer programming, computer science, creative writing, driver education, economics, English, English literature, environmental science, ethics, European history, fine arts, French, geography, geometry, German, grammar, health, history, international relations, Latin, mathematics, music, philosophy, physical education, physics, religion, Russian, social studies, Spanish, speech, trigonometry, world history.

Graduation Requirements Arts and fine arts (art, music, dance, drama), computer science, English, foreign language, mathematics, physical education (includes health), religion (includes Bible studies and theology), science, social studies (includes history), speech.

Special Academic Programs Advanced Placement exam preparation in 19 subject areas; independent study.

College Placement 101 students graduated in 2005; all went to college, including Colgate University; Columbia College; Cornell University; Georgetown University; Princeton University; Villanova University. Mean SAT verbal: 680, mean SAT math: 700.

Student Life Upper grades have specified standards of dress, student council, honor system. Discipline rests primarily with faculty. Attendance at religious services is required.

Summer Programs Enrichment, advancement, sports, computer instruction programs offered; session focuses on summer school (co-ed) and summer sports (boys); held on campus; accepts boys and girls; open to students from other schools. 1000 students usually enrolled. 2006 schedule: June 21 to July 28. Application deadline: April 28.

Tuition and Aid Day student tuition: $21,390. Tuition installment plan (Key Tuition Payment Plan, monthly payment plans, individually arranged payment plans). Need-based scholarship grants available. In 2005–06, 11% of upper-school students received aid. Total amount of financial aid awarded in 2005–06: $952,580.

Admissions Traditional secondary-level entrance grade is 9. For fall 2005, 225 students applied for upper-level admission, 107 were accepted, 100 enrolled. Stanford Achievement Test, Otis-Lennon School Ability Test, school's own exam required. Deadline for receipt of application materials: January 6. Application fee required: $70. On-campus interview required.

Athletics Interscholastic: baseball, basketball, bowling, cross-country running, football, golf, ice hockey, indoor track, lacrosse, soccer, squash, swimming and diving, tennis, track and field, winter (indoor) track, wrestling; intramural: bicycling, combined training, fitness, flag football, Frisbee, independent competitive sports, mountain biking, skiing (downhill), strength & conditioning, ultimate Frisbee, weight lifting, weight training. 4 PE instructors.

Computers Computers are regularly used in music, science, word processing classes. Computer network features include campus e-mail, on-campus library services, CD-ROMs, online commercial services, Internet access, wireless campus network.

Contact Mrs. Connie Curnow, Administrative Assistant—Office of Admissions. 973-538-3231 Ext. 3019. Fax: 973-538-8836. E-mail: ccurnow@delbarton.org. Web site: www.delbarton.org.

See full description on page 762.

DELPHI ACADEMY OF LOS ANGELES

11341 Brainard Avenue
Lake View Terrace, California 91342
Head of School: Mrs. Maggie Reinhart

petersons.com

General Information Coeducational day college-preparatory, general academic, arts, business, and technology school. Grades K–12. Founded: 1984. Setting: suburban. Nearest major city is Los Angeles. 10-acre campus. 4 buildings on campus. Approved or accredited by California Department of Education. Total enrollment: 210. Upper school average class size: 18. Upper school faculty-student ratio: 1:18.

Upper School Student Profile Grade 9: 12 students (6 boys, 6 girls); Grade 10: 16 students (8 boys, 8 girls); Grade 11: 16 students (8 boys, 8 girls); Grade 12: 16 students (8 boys, 8 girls).

Faculty School total: 50. In upper school: 1 man, 8 women; 1 has an advanced degree.

Subjects Offered Acting, advanced chemistry, advanced computer applications, advanced math, algebra, American literature, anatomy and physiology, art, art history, ASB Leadership, Basic programming, biology, business skills, calculus, calligraphy, career and personal planning, career education internship, career/college preparation, ceramics, chemistry, choir, college counseling, communication skills, community service, comparative religion, competitive science projects, composition, computer applications, consumer economics, consumer mathematics, current events, decision making skills, drama, drawing, economics, education, electronics, English, English literature, ethical decision making, ethics and responsibility, expository writing, family living, fine arts, first aid, fitness, French, geography, geometry, government, grammar, health, history, honors English, intro to computers, language arts, leadership skills, literature seminar, logic, math applications, mathematics, music, nutrition, personal money management, philosophy, physical education, physical science, physics, pre-algebra, pre-calculus, public speaking, religions, research skills, SAT preparation, science, science project, senior career experience, Shakespeare, social studies, sociology, Spanish, student government, study skills, trigonometry, U.S. constitutional history, U.S. government, Western civilization, world history, yearbook.

Graduation Requirements Advanced chemistry, advanced computer applications, calculus, communication skills, comparative religion, constitutional history of U.S., current events, economics, English literature, foreign language, government/civics, health, physics, public speaking, Shakespeare, student government.

Special Academic Programs Honors section; accelerated programs; independent study; term-away projects; academic accommodation for the gifted; remedial reading and/or remedial writing; remedial math.

College Placement 9 students graduated in 2005; 6 went to college, including California State Polytechnic University, Pomona; California State University, Northridge; Occidental College. Other: 3 went to work. Mean SAT verbal: 660, mean SAT math: 680. 100% scored over 600 on SAT verbal, 100% scored over 600 on SAT math.

Student Life Upper grades have specified standards of dress, student council, honor system. Discipline rests primarily with faculty.

Summer Programs Remediation, enrichment, advancement, ESL, sports, art/fine arts, computer instruction programs offered; session focuses on study skills and outdoor fun; held on campus; accepts boys and girls; open to students from other schools. 200 students usually enrolled. 2006 schedule: June 19 to August 18. Application deadline: none.

Tuition and Aid Day student tuition: $13,500. Tuition installment plan (monthly payment plans, individually arranged payment plans). Tuition reduction for siblings, need-based scholarship grants available. In 2005–06, 5% of upper-school students received aid.

Admissions Traditional secondary-level entrance grade is 9. For fall 2005, 20 students applied for upper-level admission, 10 were accepted, 10 enrolled. Admissions testing and writing sample required. Deadline for receipt of application materials: none. Application fee required: $100. On-campus interview required.

Athletics Interscholastic: baseball (boys); basketball (b,g), softball (b,g), volleyball (b,g); intramural: basketball (b,g), dance team (g), football (b,g), softball (b,g), volleyball (b,g); coed interscholastic: soccer; coed intramural: aerobics, aerobics/dance, cooperative games, field hockey, fitness, flag football, gymnastics, jogging, outdoor activities, outdoor recreation, paddle tennis, physical fitness, running, soccer, tennis. 3 PE instructors, 3 coaches.

Computers Computers are regularly used in all academic, business, business applications, career exploration, college planning, data processing, desktop publishing, engineering, library skills, newspaper, photography, research skills, yearbook classes. Computer network features include campus e-mail, CD-ROMs, Internet access, wireless campus network.

Contact Ms. Sandee Ferman, Head of Admissions. 818-583-1070 Ext. 107. Fax: 818-583-1082. E-mail: pg@delphila.org. Web site: www.delphila.org.

ANNOUNCEMENT FROM THE SCHOOL Delphi Academy of Los Angeles, part of a network of 9 schools across the US, highly acclaimed for its innovative educational approach, employs the breakthrough study methods developed over 40 years ago by American author and educator L. Ron Hubbard. The Los Angeles–area campus, now located in Lake View Terrace, has served the communities of Pasadena, Glendale, Hollywood, Los Angeles, and the San Fernando and San Gabriel Valleys since 1984. The school moved to its brand-new, 9-acre campus, just 10 miles west of its former home in La Canada Flintridge, in January 2003. The school is independent, coeducational, and college- and career-preparatory and offers a full-day program to students from kindergarten through high school. All students are given the tools to attain the highest academic and ethical standards along with the ability to achieve 100% mastery of what they study. A disciplined, fast-paced educational structure allows students to progress independently in individualized programs that address their strengths, weaknesses, and special interests. A wide range of hands-on projects, on- and off-campus apprenticeships, frequent field trips, and community service ensure that each student is able to connect his or her education to the real world. The program also focuses on the 4 points of the Delphi logo: knowledge, ethics, integrity, and leadership. These points are achieved by cultivating students' abilities to take increasing responsibility for their studies, their school, their environment, and their fellow man. Recent Delphi graduates have attended Cornell, Johns Hopkins, UC Berkeley, UCLA, UC Davis, UC Riverside, American University, USC, Harvey Mudd, Randolph-Macon, and NYU. The school also offers a summer program that is an outstanding balance of fun and academics. The session runs for 9 weeks, from the end of June through the end of August each year, with a minimum enrollment of 4 weeks. The program includes week-long camping trips from the Sierras to Santa Barbara to San Diego, with many challenging activities and classes planned throughout the summer. A very popular English-as-a-second-language program is also offered, where students begin building their vocabulary right away and have lots of practice speaking English with their American friends. The school is licensed to use Applied Scholastics® educational services.

THE DELPHIAN SCHOOL

20950 Southwest Rock Creek Road
Sheridan, Oregon 97378
Head of School: Rosemary Didear

petersons.com

General Information Coeducational boarding and day college-preparatory, general academic, arts, business, technology, and computer technology, career orientation school. Boarding grades 3–12, day grades K–12. Founded: 1976. Setting: rural. Nearest major city is Salem. Students are housed in single-sex dormitories. 800-acre campus. 4 buildings on campus. Approved or accredited by Oregon Department of Education. Language of instruction: English. Total enrollment: 250. Upper school average class size: 20.

Upper School Student Profile 80% of students are boarding students. 10% are state residents. 15 states are represented in upper school student body. 15% are international students. International students from Austria, Canada, Japan, Mexico, Republic of Korea, and Taiwan; 8 other countries represented in student body.

Faculty In upper school: 93 reside on campus.

Subjects Offered Advanced chemistry, advanced computer applications, algebra, American history, American literature, anatomy and physiology, art, arts, arts and crafts, Basic programming, biology, biology-AP, business, business applications, business skills, calculus, calculus-AP, career and personal planning, career/college preparation, ceramics, cheerleading, chemistry, choir, communication skills, computer science, computer skills, concert choir, creative writing, drama, drawing, economics, economics-AP, electronics, English, English composition, English language and composition-AP, English literature and composition-AP, ESL, ethical decision making, ethics, ethics and responsibility, fine arts, first aid, French, French studies, general science, geography, geometry, government, grammar, health, history, language arts, leadership, leadership skills, leadership training, literature seminar, logic, math applications, mathematics, music, music history, nutrition, personal money management, photography, physical education, physical fitness, physical science, physics, physiology, physiology-anatomy, public speaking, religion, religions, research skills, SAT preparation, science, science project, senior career experience, Shakespeare, social studies, Spanish, student government, study skills, trigonometry, U.S. constitutional history, U.S. government, volleyball, Western civilization, world history, writing, yearbook.

Graduation Requirements Art, arts and fine arts (art, music, dance, drama), Bible studies, business skills (includes word processing), computer science, dance, drama, English, ethics, foreign language, French, general science, leadership, leadership training, logic, mathematics, music, physical education (includes health), religion (includes Bible studies and theology), religion and culture, science, social studies (includes history), theology, word processing.

Special Academic Programs Accelerated programs; independent study; academic accommodation for the gifted, the musically talented, and the artistically talented; ESL (30 students enrolled).

Student Life Upper grades have specified standards of dress, student council, honor system. Discipline rests equally with students and faculty.

Tuition and Aid Day student tuition: $15,385; 7-day tuition and room/board: $28,210. Tuition installment plan (monthly payment plans). Tuition reduction for siblings, merit scholarship grants, need-based scholarship grants, need-based loans available.

Admissions Traditional secondary-level entrance grade is 8. Deadline for receipt of application materials: none. Application fee required: $50. Interview required.
Athletics Interscholastic: baseball (boys), basketball (b,g), soccer (b), softball (g), tennis (b), volleyball (g); coed intramural: hiking/backpacking, racquetball, skiing (downhill), tennis. 4 PE instructors, 15 coaches.
Computers Computer network features include campus e-mail, on-campus library services, CD-ROMs, Internet access, file transfer.
Contact Donetta Phelps, Director of Admissions. 800-626-6610. Fax: 503-843-4158. E-mail: info@delphian.org. Web site: www.delphian.org.

See full description on page 764.

DEMATHA CATHOLIC HIGH SCHOOL

4313 Madison Street
Hyattsville, Maryland 20781
Head of School: Daniel J. McMahon, PhD

General Information Boys' day college-preparatory, arts, religious studies, and music (instrumental and choral) school, affiliated with Roman Catholic Church. Grades 9–12. Founded: 1946. Setting: suburban. Nearest major city is Washington, DC. 6-acre campus. 5 buildings on campus. Approved or accredited by Association of Independent Schools of Greater Washington, Middle States Association of Colleges and Schools, National Catholic Education Association, and Maryland Department of Education. Endowment: $2 million. Total enrollment: 1,007. Upper school average class size: 22. Upper school faculty-student ratio: 1:12.
Upper School Student Profile Grade 9: 278 students (278 boys); Grade 10: 267 students (267 boys); Grade 11: 223 students (223 boys); Grade 12: 239 students (239 boys). 58% of students are Roman Catholic.
Faculty School total: 76. In upper school: 59 men, 17 women; 39 have advanced degrees.
Subjects Offered Accounting, Advanced Placement courses, African-American literature, algebra, American government, American government-AP, American history, American history-AP, anatomy and physiology, art, art history, art-AP, astronomy, band, biology, biology-AP, biotechnology, British literature, British literature-AP, business, business law, calculus, calculus-AP, campus ministry, Catholic belief and practice, chemistry, chemistry-AP, choral music, chorus, Christian ethics, church history, college admission preparation, community service, computer applications, computer programming, computer science, computer science-AP, computer skills, computer studies, contemporary art, digital photography, English, English composition, English literature, environmental science, ethics, film studies, forensic science, French, French language-AP, geology, geometry, German, German-AP, government, government-AP, health, health education, history, history of religion, history of rock and roll, honors algebra, honors English, honors geometry, honors U.S. history, honors world history, instrumental music, jazz, journalism, Latin, Latin American studies, Latin-AP, literature-AP, mathematics, modern languages, music, music performance, mythology, newspaper, photography, photojournalism, physical education, physical science, physics, physics-AP, pre-calculus, psychology, SAT preparation, science, science research, social studies, Spanish, Spanish-AP, speech, sports medicine, statistics, studio art, studio art—AP, study skills, symphonic band, theology, trigonometry, U.S. government, U.S. history, U.S. literature, vocal music, world history, writing, yearbook.
Graduation Requirements Arts, computer science, English, foreign language, mathematics, physical education (includes health), science, social studies (includes history), theology, 55 hours of Christian service.
Special Academic Programs Advanced Placement exam preparation in 16 subject areas; honors section; independent study; academic accommodation for the gifted, the musically talented, and the artistically talented; remedial reading and/or remedial writing.
College Placement 235 students graduated in 2005; 224 went to college, including Hampton University; Mount St. Mary's University; North Carolina Agricultural and Technical State University; Salisbury University; University of Maryland, Baltimore County; University of Maryland, College Park. Other: 5 went to work, 3 entered a postgraduate year, 3 had other specific plans. Mean SAT verbal: 533, mean SAT math: 543.
Student Life Upper grades have uniform requirement, student council, honor system. Discipline rests primarily with faculty. Attendance at religious services is required.
Summer Programs Remediation, sports, art/fine arts, computer instruction programs offered; held on campus; accepts boys and girls; open to students from other schools. 400 students usually enrolled. 2006 schedule: June 19 to July 18. Application deadline: June 16.
Tuition and Aid Day student tuition: $8375. Tuition installment plan (FACTS Tuition Payment Plan). Tuition reduction for siblings, merit scholarship grants, need-based scholarship grants available. In 2005–06, 43% of upper-school students received aid; total upper-school merit-scholarship money awarded: $173,150. Total amount of financial aid awarded in 2005–06: $760,865.
Admissions Traditional secondary-level entrance grade is 9. For fall 2005, 593 students applied for upper-level admission, 320 were accepted, 275 enrolled. Archdiocese of Washington Entrance Exam required. Deadline for receipt of application materials: December 15. Application fee required: $50.

Athletics Interscholastic: baseball, basketball, crew, cross-country running, diving, football, golf, ice hockey, lacrosse, soccer, swimming and diving, tennis, track and field, winter (indoor) track, wrestling; intramural: basketball, rugby, strength & conditioning. 2 PE instructors, 1 trainer.
Computers Computers are regularly used in computer applications, digital applications, independent study, lab/keyboard, library, newspaper, publishing, science, technology, Web site design, word processing, yearbook classes. Computer network features include on-campus library services, Internet access, wireless campus network.
Contact Mrs. Christine Thomas, Assistant Director of Admissions. 301-864-3666 Ext. 143. Fax: 301-864-2032. E-mail: cthomas@dematha.org. Web site: www.dematha.org.

DENVER ACADEMY

Denver, Colorado
See Special Needs Schools section.

DENVER CHRISTIAN HIGH SCHOOL

2135 South Pearl Street
Denver, Colorado 80210
Head of School: Mr. Dan Vander Ark

General Information Coeducational day college-preparatory, general academic, arts, business, religious studies, bilingual studies, and technology school, affiliated with Christian Reformed Church. Grades 9–12. Founded: 1950. Setting: urban. 4-acre campus. 1 building on campus. Approved or accredited by Association of Christian Schools International, North Central Association of Colleges and Schools, and Colorado Department of Education. Endowment: $1.3 million. Total enrollment: 296. Upper school average class size: 18. Upper school faculty-student ratio: 1:18.
Upper School Student Profile Grade 9: 56 students (27 boys, 29 girls); Grade 10: 64 students (32 boys, 32 girls); Grade 11: 91 students (44 boys, 47 girls); Grade 12: 85 students (43 boys, 42 girls). 20% of students are members of Christian Reformed Church.
Faculty School total: 22. In upper school: 10 men, 12 women; 16 have advanced degrees.
Subjects Offered Acting, advanced chemistry, advanced computer applications, advanced math, algebra, American government, American history, American literature, art, band, Bible, biology, British literature, calculus, chamber groups, chemistry, choir, Christian doctrine, Christian scripture, church history, composition, computer applications, computer keyboarding, concert band, concert choir, consumer economics, drama, driver education, earth science, European history, general math, government, grammar, health, introduction to literature, jazz band, keyboarding/computer, personal fitness, physical education, physical fitness, physics, poetry, pre-algebra, pre-calculus, psychology, research, senior seminar, Shakespeare, Spanish, speech, studio art, symphonic band, the Web, trigonometry, U.S. government, U.S. history, Web site design, weight fitness, Western civilization, world geography, world history, yearbook.
Special Academic Programs Honors section; independent study; special instructional classes for deaf students.
College Placement 88 students graduated in 2005; 85 went to college, including Calvin College; Metropolitan State College of Denver; University of Colorado at Denver and Health Sciences Center—Downtown Denver Campus. Other: 1 went to work, 2 entered military service. Mean SAT verbal: 560, mean SAT math: 545, mean composite ACT: 23.
Student Life Upper grades have specified standards of dress, student council. Discipline rests primarily with faculty. Attendance at religious services is required.
Tuition and Aid Day student tuition: $6760. Tuition installment plan (monthly payment plans). Merit scholarship grants, need-based scholarship grants available. In 2005–06, 15% of upper-school students received aid.
Admissions Traditional secondary-level entrance grade is 9. For fall 2005, 302 students applied for upper-level admission, 296 were accepted, 296 enrolled. WISC/Woodcock-Johnson or Woodcock-Johnson Educational Evaluation, WISC III required. Deadline for receipt of application materials: none. Application fee required: $200. Interview required.
Athletics Interscholastic: baseball (boys), basketball (b,g), cross-country running (b,g), dance team (g), football (b), golf (b,g), soccer (b,g). 3 PE instructors, 25 coaches.
Computers Computer network features include campus e-mail, on-campus library services, CD-ROMs, Internet access, file transfer, wireless campus network.
Contact Sheryl Vriesman, Admissions Secretary. 303-733-2421 Ext. 110. Fax: 303-733-7734. E-mail: sherylv@denver-christian.org.

DENVER LUTHERAN HIGH SCHOOL

3201 West Arizona Avenue
Denver, Colorado 80219
Head of School: Mr. Loren Otte

General Information Coeducational day college-preparatory, general academic, arts, religious studies, and technology school, affiliated with Lutheran Church–Missouri Synod. Grades 9–12. Founded: 1955. Setting: urban. 12-acre campus. 1 building on campus. Approved or accredited by North Central Association of Colleges and Schools and Colorado Department of Education. Total enrollment: 211. Upper school average class size: 18. Upper school faculty-student ratio: 1:17.

Upper School Student Profile Grade 9: 58 students (30 boys, 28 girls); Grade 10: 57 students (39 boys, 18 girls); Grade 11: 44 students (24 boys, 20 girls); Grade 12: 52 students (27 boys, 25 girls). 70% of students are Lutheran Church–Missouri Synod.

Faculty School total: 18. In upper school: 12 men, 6 women; 6 have advanced degrees.

Subjects Offered Algebra, art, band, biology, calculus, chemistry, chorus, computer programming, computer science, consumer mathematics, creative writing, debate, English, fine arts, geography, geometry, international relations, literature, mathematics, physical education, physics, psychology, reading, religion, science, social science, social studies, Spanish, speech, trigonometry.

Graduation Requirements Algebra, American government, arts and fine arts (art, music, dance, drama), biology, chemistry, computer applications, electives, English, English composition, English literature, geography, mathematics, physical education (includes health), science, social science, social studies (includes history), religion class for each year enrolled.

Special Academic Programs Advanced Placement exam preparation in 3 subject areas; honors section; independent study; study at local college for college credit; remedial reading and/or remedial writing; remedial math.

College Placement 60 students graduated in 2005; 49 went to college, including Colorado State University; Concordia University; Concordia University Wisconsin; Metropolitan State College of Denver; University of Colorado at Boulder; University of Northern Colorado. Other: 4 went to work, 3 entered military service, 4 had other specific plans. Mean composite ACT: 23.

Student Life Upper grades have specified standards of dress, student council, honor system. Discipline rests primarily with faculty. Attendance at religious services is required.

Summer Programs Remediation programs offered; session focuses on remediation; held on campus; accepts boys and girls; not open to students from other schools. 12 students usually enrolled. 2006 schedule: June to July. Application deadline: May.

Tuition and Aid Day student tuition: $6600. Tuition reduction for siblings, need-based scholarship grants available. In 2005–06, 30% of upper-school students received aid.

Admissions Traditional secondary-level entrance grade is 9. For fall 2005, 213 students applied for upper-level admission, 213 were accepted, 212 enrolled. High School Placement Test required. Deadline for receipt of application materials: none. Application fee required: $475. On-campus interview required.

Athletics Interscholastic: baseball (boys), basketball (b,g), cheering (g), cross-country running (b,g), floor hockey (b), football (b), golf (b,g), roller hockey (b), soccer (b,g), softball (g), tennis (b,g), track and field (b,g), volleyball (g), wrestling (b); intramural: field hockey (b). 3 PE instructors, 6 coaches, 1 trainer.

Computers Computers are regularly used in art, geography, graphic arts, theater arts, yearbook classes. Computer network features include on-campus library services, CD-ROMs, online commercial services, Internet access.

Contact Mr. Loren Otte, Principal. 303-934-2345 Ext. 3103. Fax: 303-934-0455. Web site: www.denverlhs.org.

THE DERRYFIELD SCHOOL

2108 River Road
Manchester, New Hampshire 03104-1396
Head of School: Mr. Randle B. Richardson

General Information Coeducational day college-preparatory school. Grades 6–12. Founded: 1964. Setting: suburban. Nearest major city is Boston, MA. 84-acre campus. 3 buildings on campus. Approved or accredited by Association of Independent Schools in New England, Independent Schools of Northern New England, New England Association of Schools and Colleges, and New Hampshire Department of Education. Member of National Association of Independent Schools and Secondary School Admission Test Board. Endowment: $3 million. Total enrollment: 387. Upper school average class size: 14. Upper school faculty-student ratio: 1:7.

Upper School Student Profile Grade 9: 64 students (30 boys, 34 girls); Grade 10: 56 students (25 boys, 31 girls); Grade 11: 53 students (24 boys, 29 girls); Grade 12: 66 students (30 boys, 36 girls).

Faculty School total: 52. In upper school: 23 men, 15 women; 26 have advanced degrees.

Subjects Offered 20th century American writers, 3-dimensional art, algebra, American literature, anatomy and physiology, ancient world history, area studies, art, art history, biology, British literature, calculus, calculus-AP, chemistry, China/Japan history, chorus, computer science, contemporary issues, creative writing, drafting, drama, driver education, earth science, economics and history, English, English

composition, English literature, English-AP, European history, expository writing, film, fine arts, French, French language-AP, French literature-AP, geography, geometry, global issues, government/civics, Greek, health, history, Holocaust, independent study, Latin, Latin-AP, mathematics, music, organic chemistry, philosophy, physical education, physics, pre-calculus, psychology, public speaking, science, Shakespeare, social studies, Spanish, Spanish language-AP, Spanish literature-AP, speech, statistics, statistics-AP, studio art, theater, trigonometry, U.S. history-AP, Western civilization, world history, world literature, writing.

Graduation Requirements Arts and fine arts (art, music, dance, drama), athletics, English, foreign language, health and wellness, history, mathematics, science.

Special Academic Programs Advanced Placement exam preparation in 10 subject areas; honors section; independent study; term-away projects; academic accommodation for the gifted.

College Placement 56 students graduated in 2005; 55 went to college, including Boston College; Colby College; Connecticut College; Lehigh University; The George Washington University; University of New Hampshire. Other: 1 entered a postgraduate year.

Student Life Upper grades have specified standards of dress, student council. Discipline rests equally with students and faculty.

Tuition and Aid Day student tuition: $19,750. Tuition installment plan (Key Tuition Payment Plan, FACTS Tuition Payment Plan). Need-based scholarship grants, USS Education Loan Program available. In 2005–06, 16% of upper-school students received aid. Total amount of financial aid awarded in 2005–06: $898,230.

Admissions Traditional secondary-level entrance grade is 9. For fall 2005, 65 students applied for upper-level admission, 60 were accepted, 34 enrolled. SSAT required. Deadline for receipt of application materials: February 10. Application fee required: $50. On-campus interview required.

Athletics Interscholastic: alpine skiing (boys, girls), baseball (b), basketball (b,g), crew (b,g), cross-country running (b,g), field hockey (g), independent competitive sports (b,g), lacrosse (b,g), skiing (cross-country) (b,g), skiing (downhill) (b,g), soccer (b,g), softball (g), tennis (b,g); coed interscholastic: golf, ice hockey; coed intramural: aerobics, ropes courses, snowboarding, swimming and diving, volleyball, weight training, yoga. 7 coaches.

Computers Computers are regularly used in history, mathematics, music, science classes. Computer network features include campus e-mail, on-campus library services, CD-ROMs, online commercial services, Internet access, DVD, online computer linked to New Hampshire State Library.

Contact Mrs. Donna Guerra, Admission Coordinator. 603-669-4524. Fax: 603-641-9521. E-mail: admission@derryfield.org. Web site: www.derryfield.org.

ANNOUNCEMENT FROM THE SCHOOL As a coeducational, college-preparatory day school, Derryfield offers an advanced curriculum, numerous electives, and an emphasis on sound study skills, while enabling students to live at home during their middle and high school years. All students explore talents in required arts and athletics programs.

DETROIT COUNTRY DAY SCHOOL

22305 West Thirteen Mile Road
Beverly Hills, Michigan 48025-4435
Head of School: Gerald T. Hansen

General Information Coeducational boarding and day college-preparatory school. Boarding grades 7–12, day grades PK–12. Founded: 1914. Setting: suburban. Nearest major city is Detroit. Students are housed in on-campus homes. 100-acre campus. 4 buildings on campus. Approved or accredited by Independent Schools Association of the Central States and Michigan Department of Education. Member of National Association of Independent Schools. Endowment: $9 million. Total enrollment: 1,588. Upper school average class size: 15. Upper school faculty-student ratio: 1:8.

Upper School Student Profile Grade 9: 183 students (92 boys, 91 girls); Grade 10: 154 students (90 boys, 64 girls); Grade 11: 149 students (75 boys, 74 girls); Grade 12: 155 students (80 boys, 75 girls). 3% are international students.

Faculty School total: 193. In upper school: 35 men, 37 women; 60 have advanced degrees.

Subjects Offered African-American studies, algebra, American history, American literature, American studies, anatomy, ancient history, art, astronomy, band, biology, botany, calculus, ceramics, chemistry, chorus, college counseling, community service, composition, computer programming, computer science, current events, design, drama, drawing, ecology, economics, economics and history, English, English literature, environmental science, European history, fine arts, finite math, French, genetics, geometry, German, government/civics, grammar, graphic arts, health, history, humanities, Japanese, Latin, literature, mathematics, media, metalworking, microbiology, music, music history, music theory, natural history, orchestra, painting, photography, physical education, physical science, physics, physiology, poetry, pre-calculus, printmaking, science, sculpture, social studies, Spanish, speech, statistics, study skills, theater, theory of knowledge, Western civilization, world literature, zoology.

Graduation Requirements American history, arts and fine arts (art, music, dance, drama), college counseling, computer science, English, foreign language, mathe-

ics, physical education (includes health), science, speech, athletic participation, skill-oriented activities, service-oriented activities.

Special Academic Programs International Baccalaureate program; Advanced Placement exam preparation in 17 subject areas; honors section; academic accommodation for the gifted, the musically talented, and the artistically talented.

College Placement 134 students graduated in 2005; all went to college, including Albion College; Michigan State University; University of Michigan. Mean SAT verbal: 646, mean SAT math: 661, mean composite ACT: 27.

Student Life Upper grades have uniform requirement, student council, honor system. Discipline rests primarily with faculty.

Summer Programs Enrichment, art/fine arts, computer instruction programs offered; session focuses on academic enrichment and sports camps; held on campus; accepts boys and girls; open to students from other schools. 2006 schedule: June 18 to August 3.

Tuition and Aid Day student tuition: $20,690; 7-day tuition and room/board: $28,700. Need-based scholarship grants, need-based loans available. In 2005–06, 21% of upper-school students received aid. Total amount of financial aid awarded in 2005–06: $2,500,000.

Admissions Traditional secondary-level entrance grade is 9. For fall 2005, 904 students applied for upper-level admission, 62 enrolled. ISEE and Otis-Lennon School Ability Test required. Deadline for receipt of application materials: none. Application fee required: $50. On-campus interview required.

Athletics Interscholastic: alpine skiing (boys, girls), ball hockey (g), baseball (b), basketball (b,g), bowling (b,g), cross-country running (b,g), dance squad (g), diving (b,g), field hockey (g), football (b), golf (b,g), hockey (b), ice hockey (b), lacrosse (b,g), skiing (downhill) (b,g), soccer (b,g), softball (g), swimming and diving (b,g), tennis (b,g), track and field (b,g), volleyball (g), wrestling (b); intramural: weight lifting (b,g); coed interscholastic: cheering, outdoor adventure, snowboarding; coed intramural: basketball, project adventure, strength & conditioning. 4 coaches, 2 trainers.

Computers Computers are regularly used in all classes. Computer network features include campus e-mail, on-campus library services, CD-ROMs, online commercial services, Internet access, file transfer, office computer access, DVD.

Contact Jorge Dante Hernandez Prosperi, Director of Admissions. 248-646-7717. Fax: 248-203-2184. E-mail: jprosperi@dcds.edu. Web site: www.dcds.edu.

See full description on page 766.

DEVON PARK CHRISTIAN SCHOOL

PO Box 3510, Station B
Fredericton, New Brunswick E3A 5J8, Canada
Head of School: Mr. Randy Fox

General Information Coeducational day college-preparatory school, affiliated with Baptist Church. Grades 1–12. Founded: 1979. Setting: suburban. 5-acre campus. 1 building on campus. Approved or accredited by New Brunswick Department of Education. Language of instruction: English. Upper school average class size: 15. Upper school faculty-student ratio: 1:15.

Upper School Student Profile 20% of students are Baptist.

Faculty School total: 13. In upper school: 4 men, 4 women; 1 has an advanced degree.

Student Life Upper grades have specified standards of dress, student council, honor system. Discipline rests primarily with faculty. Attendance at religious services is required.

Admissions Application fee required. Interview required.

Athletics Interscholastic: basketball (boys, girls), cross-country running (b,g), soccer (b,g).

Contact Mr. Randy Fox, Principal. 506-458-9379. Fax: 506-458-8702. E-mail: dpcs@devonparkchristianschool.ca. Web site: www.devonparkchristianschool.ca.

DEVON PREPARATORY SCHOOL

363 Valley Forge Road
Devon, Pennsylvania 19333-1299
Head of School: Rev. James J. Shea, Sch.P

General Information Boys' day college-preparatory school, affiliated with Roman Catholic Church. Grades 6–12. Founded: 1956. Setting: suburban. Nearest major city is Philadelphia. 21-acre campus. 7 buildings on campus. Approved or accredited by Middle States Association of Colleges and Schools, Pennsylvania Association of Private Academic Schools, and Pennsylvania Department of Education. Endowment: $500,000. Total enrollment: 279. Upper school average class size: 15. Upper school faculty-student ratio: 1:10.

Upper School Student Profile Grade 9: 67 students (67 boys); Grade 10: 53 students (53 boys); Grade 11: 39 students (39 boys); Grade 12: 38 students (38 boys). 90% of students are Roman Catholic.

Faculty School total: 33. In upper school: 19 men, 8 women; 21 have advanced degrees.

Subjects Offered Advanced Placement courses, algebra, American history, art, biology, calculus, chemistry, community service, computer science, economics, English, European history, French, geography, geometry, German, health, Italian,

Latin, law, mathematics, music, physical education, physics, political science, pre-calculus, religion, science, social studies, Spanish, trigonometry, Vietnam War, world culture.

Graduation Requirements Computer science, English, foreign language, geography, Latin, mathematics, physical education (includes health), political science, religion (includes Bible studies and theology), science, social studies (includes history). Community service is required.

Special Academic Programs Advanced Placement exam preparation in 13 subject areas.

College Placement 53 students graduated in 2005; all went to college, including Fordham University; La Salle University; Saint Joseph's University; University of Pittsburgh; University of Richmond; Villanova University. Median SAT verbal: 639, median SAT math: 643.

Student Life Upper grades have specified standards of dress, student council. Discipline rests primarily with faculty. Attendance at religious services is required.

Tuition and Aid Day student tuition: $13,500. Tuition installment plan (monthly payment plans). Tuition reduction for siblings, merit scholarship grants, need-based scholarship grants available. In 2005–06, 74% of upper-school students received aid; total upper-school merit-scholarship money awarded: $599,125. Total amount of financial aid awarded in 2005–06: $629,175.

Admissions Traditional secondary-level entrance grade is 9. For fall 2005, 142 students applied for upper-level admission, 89 were accepted, 67 enrolled. Math and English placement tests, STS and writing sample required. Deadline for receipt of application materials: none. Application fee required: $25. On-campus interview recommended.

Athletics Interscholastic: baseball, basketball, cross-country running, golf, indoor track & field, outdoors, soccer, tennis, track and field; intramural: bowling, outdoor recreation, paint ball, skiing (downhill). 2 PE instructors, 10 coaches, 1 trainer.

Computers Computers are regularly used in all academic, newspaper, technology, writing, yearbook classes. Computer network features include CD-ROMs, Internet access.

Contact Mr. Peter Crippen, Director of Admissions. 610-688-7337. Fax: 610-688-2409. E-mail: pcrippen@devonprep.com. Web site: www.devonprep.com.

DOANE STUART SCHOOL

799 South Pearl Street
Albany, New York 12202
Head of School: Dr. Richard D. Enemark

General Information Coeducational day college-preparatory, arts, and religious studies school, affiliated with Episcopal Church, Roman Catholic Church. Grades N–12. Founded: 1852. Setting: suburban. 80-acre campus. 3 buildings on campus. Approved or accredited by National Association of Episcopal Schools, Network of Sacred Heart Schools, New York State Association of Independent Schools, and New York Department of Education. Member of National Association of Independent Schools and Secondary School Admission Test Board. Endowment: $1 million. Total enrollment: 275. Upper school average class size: 14. Upper school faculty-student ratio: 1:5.

Upper School Student Profile Grade 9: 27 students (11 boys, 16 girls); Grade 10: 31 students (12 boys, 19 girls); Grade 11: 27 students (11 boys, 16 girls); Grade 12: 32 students (20 boys, 12 girls).

Faculty School total: 41. In upper school: 13 men, 7 women; 12 have advanced degrees.

Subjects Offered Advanced Placement courses, algebra, American history, American literature, art, biology, calculus, chemistry, community service, computer science, creative writing, earth science, economics, English, English literature, environmental science, ethics, fencing, fine arts, French, geometry, government/civics, health, history, mathematics, music, photography, physical education, physics, psychology, religion, science, social studies, Spanish, theater, trigonometry, world history, writing.

Graduation Requirements 4 years of English, 3 to 4 years of math, 3 to 4 years of science, 4 years of history, 3 to 4 years of foreign language, 4 years of comparative religion, 4 years of physical education, 3 to 4 elective courses (may include fine and performing arts), 25 hours of community service per year.

Special Academic Programs Advanced Placement exam preparation in 10 subject areas; independent study; term-away projects; study at local college for college credit; domestic exchange program (with Network of Sacred Heart Schools); study abroad.

College Placement 20 students graduated in 2005; all went to college. Mean SAT verbal: 641, mean SAT math: 631.

Student Life Upper grades have uniform requirement, student council. Discipline rests primarily with faculty. Attendance at religious services is required.

Tuition and Aid Day student tuition: $10,000–$16,800. Tuition installment plan (Academic Management Services Plan, monthly payment plans, individually arranged payment plans, biannual and quarterly payment plans). Need-based scholarship grants available. In 2005–06, 40% of upper-school students received aid. Total amount of financial aid awarded in 2005–06: $625,000.

Admissions Traditional secondary-level entrance grade is 9. School's own test or SSAT required. Deadline for receipt of application materials: none. Application fee required: $75. On-campus interview required.

Doane Stuart School

Athletics Interscholastic: baseball (boys), basketball (b,g), soccer (b,g); coed interscholastic: cross-country running, fencing, martial arts, softball, tai chi, tennis, track and field, yoga; coed intramural: physical fitness, skiing (downhill), weight training. 2 PE instructors, 8 coaches.

Computers Computers are regularly used in all classes. Computer network features include on-campus library services, CD-ROMs, Internet access.

Contact Mr. Eric Stahura, Director of Admission and College Counseling. 518-465-5222 Ext. 241. Fax: 518-465-5230. E-mail: estahura@doanestuart.org. Web site: www.doanestuart.org.

See full description on page 768.

DOCTOR FRANKLIN PERKINS SCHOOL

Lancaster, Massachusetts
See Special Needs Schools section.

DON BOSCO HIGH SCHOOL

1151 San Gabriel Boulevard
Rosemead, California 91770
Head of School: Rev. Carmine Vairo, SDB

General Information Boys' day college-preparatory and technology school, affiliated with Roman Catholic Church. Grades 9–12. Founded: 1955. Setting: suburban. Nearest major city is Los Angeles. 32-acre campus. Approved or accredited by Western Association of Schools and Colleges and California Department of Education. Total enrollment: 900. Upper school faculty-student ratio: 1:30.

Upper School Student Profile Grade 9: 300 students (300 boys); Grade 10: 280 students (280 boys); Grade 11: 200 students (200 boys); Grade 12: 120 students (120 boys). 90% of students are Roman Catholic.

Faculty School total: 90. In upper school: 75 men, 15 women; 10 have advanced degrees.

Subjects Offered Algebra, American history, American literature, architecture, art, art history, Bible studies, biology, calculus, chemistry, computer programming, computer science, construction, creative writing, drafting, drama, economics, electronics, English, English literature, ethics, European history, expository writing, geography, geometry, government/civics, grammar, health, Italian, macroeconomics-AP, mathematics, mechanical drawing, microeconomics-AP, music, photography, physical education, physics, religion, social studies, Spanish, Spanish language-AP, Spanish literature-AP, speech, theater, theology, trigonometry, world history, world literature.

College Placement 172 students graduated in 2005; all went to college, including California State University, Los Angeles.

Student Life Upper grades have specified standards of dress, student council, honor system. Discipline rests primarily with faculty. Attendance at religious services is required.

Summer Programs Remediation, enrichment, advancement, sports, art/fine arts, computer instruction programs offered; session focuses on computers; held on campus; accepts boys and girls; open to students from other schools. 900 students usually enrolled. 2006 schedule: June 21 to August 2. Application deadline: June 21.

Tuition and Aid Day student tuition: $6975. Guaranteed tuition plan. Tuition installment plan (monthly payment plans). Tuition reduction for siblings, merit scholarship grants, need-based scholarship grants available. In 2005–06, 45% of upper-school students received aid; total upper-school merit-scholarship money awarded: $75,000. Total amount of financial aid awarded in 2005–06: $300,000.

Admissions For fall 2005, 480 students applied for upper-level admission, 330 were accepted, 317 enrolled. High School Placement Test and High School Placement Test (closed version) from Scholastic Testing Service required. Deadline for receipt of application materials: January 31. Application fee required: $50. On-campus interview required.

Athletics Interscholastic: baseball, basketball, cross-country running, football, soccer, swimming and diving, tennis, track and field, volleyball; intramural: bicycling, bowling, golf, independent competitive sports, paint ball, power lifting, weight lifting. 4 PE instructors, 20 coaches, 2 trainers.

Computers Computer network features include campus e-mail.

Contact Michael Smith, Director of Admissions. 626-940-2011. Fax: 626-940-2001. E-mail: msmith@boscotech.edu. Web site: www.boscotech.edu.

DOWLING HIGH SCHOOL

1400 Buffalo Road
West Des Moines, Iowa 50265
Head of School: Dr. Jerry M. Deegan

General Information Coeducational day college-preparatory, general academic, arts, business, religious studies, bilingual studies, and technology school, affiliated with Roman Catholic Church. Grades 9–12. Founded: 1918. Setting: suburban. Nearest major city is Des Moines. 60-acre campus. 1 building on campus. Approved or accredited by North Central Association of Colleges and Schools and Iowa Department of Education. Endowment: $9 million. Total enrollment: 1,158. Upper school average class size: 20. Upper school faculty-student ratio: 1:14.

Upper School Student Profile 95% of students are Roman Catholic.

Faculty School total: 80. In upper school: 40 men, 40 women; 36 have advanced degrees.

Subjects Offered 20th century world history, accounting, ACT preparation, acting, advanced chemistry, advanced computer applications, advanced math, Advanced Placement courses, advertising design, algebra, American government, American government-AP, American history, American history-AP, American literature, American literature-AP, applied arts, aquatics, art, art history, athletics, band, baseball, Basic programming, biology, biology-AP, brass choir, British literature, business, business communications, business law, calculus, calculus-AP, career and personal planning, career planning, career/college preparation, ceramics, chamber groups, cheerleading, chemistry, chemistry-AP, choir, choral music, chorus, church history, college counseling, college planning, composition, composition-AP, computer applications, computer information systems, computer keyboarding, computer processing, computer programming, computers, concert band, concert choir, creative writing, digital photography, drama, economics, economics-AP, English, English composition, English language and composition-AP, English literature, environmental science, European history, European history-AP, finance, fine arts, foreign language, French, general business, general science, geography, geometry, German, government, government-AP, health, history, history-AP, honors algebra, honors English, honors geometry, honors U.S. history, honors world history, humanities, information processing, integrated math, jazz band, journalism, keyboarding, Latin, life saving, literature, literature-AP, marching band, metalworking, modern European history, newspaper, painting, personal finance, physical education, physics, physics-AP, play production, poetry, pottery, pre-algebra, pre-calculus, probability and statistics, programming, religion, SAT/ACT preparation, scuba diving, social justice, sociology, Spanish, Spanish language-AP, speech and debate, swimming, tennis, theater production, theology, U.S. government, U.S. government-AP, U.S. history, U.S. history-AP, visual arts, vocal jazz, weight training, world religions, yearbook.

Graduation Requirements Arts and fine arts (art, music, dance, drama), business, English, mathematics, science, social studies (includes history), theology, Reading Across the Curriculum (RAC), 10 service hours per semester/20 per year, 10.5 credits of electives.

Special Academic Programs Advanced Placement exam preparation; honors section; accelerated programs; independent study; study at local college for college credit; academic accommodation for the gifted, the musically talented, and the artistically talented; remedial reading and/or remedial writing; remedial math.

College Placement 252 students graduated in 2005; 225 went to college, including Benedictine College; Creighton University; Iowa State University of Science and Technology; Loras College; The University of Iowa; University of Northern Iowa. Other: 1 entered military service, 1 entered a postgraduate year, 25 had other specific plans. Median composite ACT: 24.

Student Life Upper grades have specified standards of dress, student council, honor system. Discipline rests primarily with faculty. Attendance at religious services is required.

Summer Programs Remediation programs offered; session focuses on advancement for the purpose of freeing up a slot in the schedule to take an elective; held on campus; accepts boys and girls; not open to students from other schools.

Tuition and Aid Day student tuition: $4782. Tuition installment plan (monthly payment plans). Merit scholarship grants, need-based scholarship grants, paying campus jobs available. In 2005–06, 41% of upper-school students received aid; total upper-school merit-scholarship money awarded: $50,000. Total amount of financial aid awarded in 2005–06: $800,000.

Admissions Traditional secondary-level entrance grade is 9. For fall 2005, 335 students applied for upper-level admission, 330 were accepted, 330 enrolled. Placement test required. Deadline for receipt of application materials: none. Application fee required: $85.

Athletics Interscholastic: aerobics/dance (girls), aquatics (b,g), baseball (b), basketball (b,g), bowling (b,g), cheering (g), cross-country running (b,g), dance team (b,g), diving (g), drill team (g), football (b), golf (b,g), hockey (b), soccer (b,g), softball (g), swimming and diving (b,g), tennis (b,g), track and field (b,g), volleyball (g), wrestling (b); coed interscholastic: cheering; coed intramural: ultimate Frisbee.

Computers Computers are regularly used in keyboarding classes. Computer network features include on-campus library services, CD-ROMs, Internet access.

Contact Mrs. Tatia Eischeid, Admissions Assistant. 515-222-1047. Fax: 515-222-1056. E-mail: teischei@dowlingcatholic.org. Web site: www.dowlingcatholic.org.

DUBAI AMERICAN ACADEMY

PO Box 32762
Dubai, United Arab Emirates
Head of School: Mr. Dan Young

General Information Coeducational day college-preparatory school. Grades K–12. Founded: 1997. Setting: urban. 23-acre campus. 2 buildings on campus. Approved or accredited by European Council of International Schools, International Baccalaureate Organization, and New England Association of Schools and Colleges. Language of instruction: English. Total enrollment: 1,310. Upper school average class size: 18.

Faculty In upper school: 15 men, 24 women.

Special Academic Programs International Baccalaureate program.

College Placement 32 students graduated in 2005; all went to college.

Student Life Upper grades have uniform requirement, student council, honor system. Discipline rests primarily with faculty.

Admissions Traditional secondary-level entrance grade is 10. High School Placement Test required. Application fee required: 350 United Arab Emirates dirhams.

Athletics Interscholastic: basketball (boys, girls), soccer (b,g), softball (b,g), swimming and diving (b,g), track and field (b,g), volleyball (b,g).

Computers Computer network features include on-campus library services, CD-ROMs, Internet access, DVD.

Contact Mrs. Camilla Oberg, Rgistrar. 971-43479222. Fax: 971-43476070. E-mail: coberg@daa.sch.ae. Web site: www.dubaiacademy.org.

DUBLIN CHRISTIAN ACADEMY

106 Page Road
Box 521
Dublin, New Hampshire 03444
Head of School: Mr. Kevin E. Moody

General Information Coeducational boarding and day college-preparatory, arts, business, and religious studies school, affiliated with Christian faith. Boarding grades 7–12, day grades K–12. Founded: 1964. Setting: rural. Nearest major city is Boston, MA. Students are housed in single-sex dormitories. 200-acre campus. 5 buildings on campus. Approved or accredited by New Hampshire Department of Education. Total enrollment: 136. Upper school average class size: 15. Upper school faculty-student ratio: 1:8.

Upper School Student Profile 41% of students are boarding students. 59% are state residents. 12 states are represented in upper school student body. 18% are international students. International students from Ethiopia and Republic of Korea; 3 other countries represented in student body.

Faculty In upper school: 9 men, 11 women; 7 have advanced degrees; 17 reside on campus.

Subjects Offered Accounting, algebra, art, Bible studies, biology, business, calculus, ceramics, chemistry, chorus, computer literacy, consumer mathematics, economics, English, French, geometry, history, home economics, instrumental music, law, mathematics, music, physics, piano, religion, science, social studies, Spanish, speech, studio art, study skills, U.S. history, voice, word processing, world history.

Graduation Requirements English, foreign language, mathematics, religion (includes Bible studies and theology), science, social studies (includes history), speech.

Special Academic Programs Academic accommodation for the musically talented; remedial reading and/or remedial writing; remedial math.

College Placement 16 students graduated in 2005; all went to college, including Bob Jones University; Clearwater Christian College. Mean SAT verbal: 620, mean SAT math: 560, mean composite ACT: 23.

Student Life Upper grades have specified standards of dress, student council. Discipline rests primarily with faculty. Attendance at religious services is required.

Tuition and Aid Day student tuition: $5910; 7-day tuition and room/board: $11,140. Need-based scholarship grants available. In 2005–06, 20% of upper-school students received aid.

Admissions Deadline for receipt of application materials: June 30. Application fee required: $35. Interview recommended.

Athletics Interscholastic: basketball (boys, girls), soccer (b), volleyball (g); intramural: baseball (b), bicycling (b,g), cheering (g), flag football (b); coed intramural: alpine skiing, ice skating, snowboarding, softball.

Computers Computers are regularly used in accounting, business, English, foreign language, history, mathematics, music, science classes. Computer resources include campus e-mail, on-campus library services, CD-ROMs, Internet access.

Contact Mrs. Beth Fletcher, Admissions Secretary. 603-563-8505. Fax: 603-563-8008. E-mail: bfletcher@dublinchristian.org. Web site: www.dublinchristian.org.

DUBLIN SCHOOL

Box 522
18 Lehmann Way
Dublin, New Hampshire 03444-0522
Head of School: Christopher R. Horgan

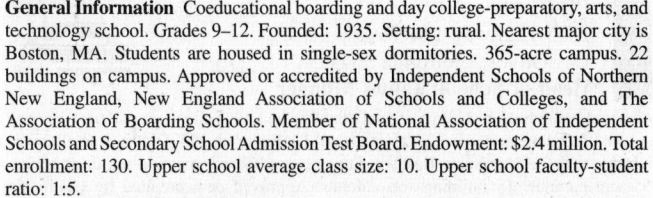
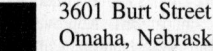
petersons.com

General Information Coeducational boarding and day college-preparatory, arts, and technology school. Grades 9–12. Founded: 1935. Setting: rural. Nearest major city is Boston, MA. Students are housed in single-sex dormitories. 365-acre campus. 22 buildings on campus. Approved or accredited by Independent Schools of Northern New England, New England Association of Schools and Colleges, and The Association of Boarding Schools. Member of National Association of Independent Schools and Secondary School Admission Test Board. Endowment: $2.4 million. Total enrollment: 130. Upper school average class size: 10. Upper school faculty-student ratio: 1:5.

Upper School Student Profile Grade 9: 22 students (10 boys, 12 girls); Grade 10: 27 students (18 boys, 9 girls); Grade 11: 37 students (27 boys, 10 girls); Grade 12: 44 students (22 boys, 22 girls). 72% of students are boarding students. 31% are state

residents. 25 states are represented in upper school student body. 24% are international students. International students from Germany, Jamaica, Republic of Korea, Rwanda, and Taiwan.

Faculty School total: 27. In upper school: 15 men, 12 women; 13 have advanced degrees; 22 reside on campus.

Subjects Offered Acting, advanced math, African-American history, algebra, American foreign policy, American literature, anatomy and physiology, ancient world history, art, arts, biology, biology-AP, British literature, calculus, calculus-AP, carpentry, ceramics, chemistry, choir, chorus, college counseling, college placement, community service, computer education, computer literacy, computer programming, costumes and make-up, creative arts, creative dance, creative drama, cultural arts, dance performance, digital music, drama, drama performance, dramatic arts, drawing and design, electronic music, English, English composition, English literature, ESL, European civilization, European history, film history, fine arts, foreign policy, French, geology, geometry, guitar, honors U.S. history, instrumental music, Latin, library research, library skills, literature, marine biology, mathematics, modern dance, modern European history, music, music composition, music performance, music technology, music theory, musical productions, musical theater, musical theater dance, painting, personal and social education, personal development, philosophy, photography, physics, poetry, pre-algebra, pre-calculus, psychology, research, science, senior project, Shakespeare, social studies, Spanish, Spanish literature, stagecraft, statistics, student government, studio art, study skills, theater, theater arts, U.S. government and politics, U.S. history, U.S. history-AP, video film production, vocal ensemble, voice, weight training, world literature, writing, yearbook.

Graduation Requirements Art, arts, computer skills, English, general science, history, languages, mathematics, independent study in selected disciplines (for seniors), graduation requirements for honors diploma differ.

Special Academic Programs Advanced Placement exam preparation in 4 subject areas; honors section; independent study; term-away projects; domestic exchange program (with The Network Program Schools); academic accommodation for the artistically talented; programs in general development for dyslexic students; ESL (10 students enrolled).

College Placement 30 students graduated in 2005; all went to college, including Boston University; Cornell University; Indiana University Bloomington; New York University; Smith College; University of Vermont. Median SAT verbal: 530, median SAT math: 495. 18% scored over 600 on SAT verbal, 18% scored over 600 on SAT math.

Student Life Upper grades have specified standards of dress, student council. Discipline rests equally with students and faculty.

Tuition and Aid Day student tuition: $22,000; 7-day tuition and room/board: $35,500. Tuition installment plan (monthly payment plans). Need-based financial aid available. In 2005–06, 32% of upper-school students received aid. Total amount of financial aid awarded in 2005–06: $812,000.

Admissions Traditional secondary-level entrance grade is 9. For fall 2005, 151 students applied for upper-level admission, 123 were accepted, 53 enrolled. SSAT required. Deadline for receipt of application materials: January 31. Application fee required: $50. On-campus interview required.

Athletics Interscholastic: basketball (boys, girls), crew (b,g), lacrosse (b,g), snowboarding (b,g), soccer (b,g), tennis (b,g); coed interscholastic: aerobics/dance, alpine skiing, cross-country running, dance, dance squad, dance team, equestrian sports, modern dance, rowing, sailing; coed intramural: basketball, climbing, freestyle skiing, hiking/backpacking, indoor hockey, martial arts, nordic skiing, physical fitness, rock climbing, sailing, skiing (cross-country), skiing (downhill), squash, strength & conditioning, tennis, volleyball, wall climbing, weight lifting, weight training. 23 coaches, 1 trainer.

Computers Computers are regularly used in all academic classes. Computer network features include campus e-mail, on-campus library services, CD-ROMs, Internet access, file transfer, office computer access, DVD, wireless campus network.

Contact Sheila Bogan, Director of Admission and Financial Aid. 603-563-8584 Ext. 233. Fax: 603-563-8671. E-mail: admission@dublinschool.org. Web site: www. dublinschool.org/.

ANNOUNCEMENT FROM THE SCHOOL Dublin School recently added a state-of-the-art recording studio to the campus and renovated Louise Shonk Kelly Recital Hall and a girls' dormitory. The School recently completed a successful capital campaign that raised $3 million. The funds will be focused on upgrading the physical plant and increasing faculty salaries and housing. In order to accommodate a growing interest in the arts, Dublin is improving and expanding current facilities and curriculum.

See full description on page 770.

DUCHESNE ACADEMY OF THE SACRED HEART

3601 Burt Street
Omaha, Nebraska 68131
Head of School: Mrs. Sheila Haggas

General Information Girls' day college-preparatory school, affiliated with Roman Catholic Church. Grades 9–12. Founded: 1881. Setting: urban. 13-acre campus. 3

buildings on campus. Approved or accredited by Network of Sacred Heart Schools, North Central Association of Colleges and Schools, and Nebraska Department of Education. Endowment: $2 million. Total enrollment: 289. Upper school average class size: 15. Upper school faculty-student ratio: 1:9.

Upper School Student Profile Grade 9: 69 students (69 girls); Grade 10: 82 students (82 girls); Grade 11: 70 students (70 girls); Grade 12: 68 students (68 girls). 90% of students are Roman Catholic.

Faculty School total: 37. In upper school: 13 men, 23 women; 26 have advanced degrees.

Subjects Offered 20th century history, 3-dimensional art, ACT preparation, acting, advanced chemistry, advanced math, algebra, American history, American literature, American literature-AP, anatomy and physiology, art, art history, biology, British literature, business, calculus, chemistry, chemistry-AP, child development, choir, choral music, Christian and Hebrew scripture, Christian ethics, Christian testament, Christianity, church history, college counseling, community service, comparative government and politics, constitutional history of U.S., constitutional law, creative writing, dance, driver education, economics, English, environmental science, ethics, forensics, French, geometry, health, healthful living, Hebrew scripture, independent study, instrumental music, introduction to theater, journalism, modern European history, music theory, photography, physical education, physics, physics-AP, precalculus, publications, SAT preparation, senior seminar, sociology, Spanish, speech, technical theater, theater, theater production, U.S. government and politics, world cultures, world literature, world religions, yearbook.

Graduation Requirements Arts and fine arts (art, music, dance, drama), English, foreign language, mathematics, physical education (includes health), religion (includes Bible studies and theology), science, social studies (includes history). Community service is required.

Special Academic Programs Advanced Placement exam preparation in 5 subject areas; honors section; independent study; term-away projects; study at local college for college credit; domestic exchange program (with Network of Sacred Heart Schools); study abroad; academic accommodation for the gifted; special instructional classes for deaf students, blind students.

College Placement 66 students graduated in 2005; all went to college, including Creighton University; Loyola University Chicago; Texas Christian University; University of Nebraska–Lincoln; University of Nebraska at Omaha. Median combined SAT: 1155, median composite ACT: 25.

Student Life Upper grades have uniform requirement, student council, honor system. Discipline rests primarily with faculty. Attendance at religious services is required.

Summer Programs Sports programs offered; session focuses on open gym/fitness training; held on campus; accepts girls; not open to students from other schools. 100 students usually enrolled. 2006 schedule: June to July. Application deadline: May.

Tuition and Aid Day student tuition: $6850. Tuition installment plan (monthly payment plans, quarterly payment plan, semester payment plan). Tuition reduction for siblings, merit scholarship grants, need-based scholarship grants, minority scholarships, reduced tuition for children of Creighton University employees available. In 2005–06, 48% of upper-school students received aid; total upper-school merit-scholarship money awarded: $42,000. Total amount of financial aid awarded in 2005–06: $117,000.

Admissions Traditional secondary-level entrance grade is 9. For fall 2005, 380 students applied for upper-level admission, 335 were accepted, 289 enrolled. Scholastic Testing Service required. Deadline for receipt of application materials: January 7. Application fee required: $25. On-campus interview required.

Athletics Interscholastic: basketball, cross-country running, dance squad, diving, golf, soccer, softball, swimming and diving, tennis, track and field, volleyball; intramural: aerobics, aerobics/dance, cheering, yoga. 2 PE instructors, 12 coaches, 1 trainer.

Computers Computers are regularly used in all classes. Computer network features include campus e-mail, on-campus library services, CD-ROMs, Internet access, file transfer, office computer access, DVD, wireless campus network, computer network with other Sacred Heart schools, mandatory laptop purchase by 10th, 11th and 12th grade students.

Contact Mrs. Meg Jones, Recruitment Director/Exchange Coordinator. 402-558-3800 Ext. 1070. Fax: 402-558-0051. E-mail: mjones@duchesne.creighton.edu. Web site: duchesne.creighton.edu.

Upper School Student Profile Grade 9: 57 students (57 girls); Grade 10: 66 students (66 girls); Grade 11: 70 students (70 girls); Grade 12: 56 students (56 girls). 65% of students are Roman Catholic.

Faculty School total: 34. In upper school: 3 men, 31 women; 25 have advanced degrees.

Subjects Offered Algebra, American government-AP, American literature, art history, arts, band, Bible studies, bioethics, biology, British literature, calculus, calculus-AP, ceramics, chemistry, chemistry-AP, community service, composition, computer graphics, computer programming, creative writing, desktop publishing, drawing, economics, English, English literature, European history, fine arts, French, French-AP, geometry, government/civics, health, human sexuality, Internet, Latin, mathematics, music, photography, physical education, physical fitness, physics, prayer/spirituality, pre-calculus, psychology, religious studies, science, scripture, sexuality, Shakespeare, social justice, social studies, Spanish, Spanish-AP, speech, statistics, statistics-AP, studio art, theater, theater production, theology, U.S. history, U.S. history-AP, Western literature, women's studies, world history, world literature, world religions, writing.

Graduation Requirements Arts and fine arts (art, music, dance, drama), computer science, English, foreign language, history, mathematics, physical education (includes health), religion (includes Bible studies and theology), science, completion of social awareness program. Community service is required.

Special Academic Programs Advanced Placement exam preparation in 11 subject areas; honors section; independent study; domestic exchange program (with Network of Sacred Heart Schools); academic accommodation for the musically talented and the artistically talented.

College Placement 66 students graduated in 2005; all went to college, including Baylor University; Creighton University; Northwestern University; Southern Methodist University; Texas Christian University; Texas Tech University. Median SAT verbal: 640, median SAT math: 620, median composite ACT: 27. 62% scored over 600 on SAT verbal, 59% scored over 600 on SAT math, 62% scored over 26 on composite ACT.

Student Life Upper grades have uniform requirement, student council, honor system. Discipline rests primarily with faculty. Attendance at religious services is required.

Summer Programs Art/fine arts, computer instruction programs offered; session focuses on enrichment, high school credit, and math review; held on campus; accepts girls; open to students from other schools. 200 students usually enrolled. 2006 schedule: June 12 to July 28.

Tuition and Aid Day student tuition: $13,970. Tuition installment plan (monthly payment plans). Merit scholarship grants, need-based scholarship grants available. In 2005–06, 22% of upper-school students received aid; total upper-school merit-scholarship money awarded: $26,300. Total amount of financial aid awarded in 2005–06: $444,205.

Admissions Traditional secondary-level entrance grade is 9. For fall 2005, 90 students applied for upper-level admission, 50 were accepted, 25 enrolled. ISEE or Otis-Lennon School Ability Test required. Deadline for receipt of application materials: January 27. Application fee required: $75. On-campus interview required.

Athletics Interscholastic: basketball, cross-country running, dance, field hockey, golf, softball, swimming and diving, tennis, track and field, volleyball, winter soccer. 2 PE instructors, 12 coaches.

Computers Computers are regularly used in all academic classes. Computer network features include campus e-mail, on-campus library services, CD-ROMs, online commercial services, Internet access, file transfer, office computer access, DVD, wireless campus network.

Contact Mrs. Beth Speck, Director of Admission. 713-468-8211 Ext. 133. Fax: 713-465-9809. E-mail: beth.speck@duchesne.org. Web site: www.duchesne.org.

ANNOUNCEMENT FROM THE SCHOOL Facilities include a chapel; classroom buildings for Upper, Middle, and Lower Schools; a Fine Arts Building; and gymnasium. National Merit Finalists, Commended Scholars, National Achievement Scholarship Program, Advanced Placement Scholars. Active sports program; academic, fine arts, and technology competitions; weekly community service commitment; and technology integrated throughout the curriculum with state-of-the-art equipment, curriculum mapping, and laptops in grades 6–12. Member of the Network of Sacred Heart Schools.

DUCHESNE ACADEMY OF THE SACRED HEART

10202 Memorial Drive
Houston, Texas 77024
Head of School: Sr. Jan Dunn, RSCJ

petersons.com

General Information Girls' day college-preparatory, arts, religious studies, and technology school, affiliated with Roman Catholic Church. Grades PK–12. Founded: 1960. Setting: suburban. 12-acre campus. 4 buildings on campus. Approved or accredited by Independent Schools Association of the Southwest, National Catholic Education Association, Texas Catholic Conference, Texas Education Agency, and Texas Department of Education. Endowment: $7.1 million. Total enrollment: 652. Upper school average class size: 14. Upper school faculty-student ratio: 1:7.

DUNN SCHOOL

PO Box 98
2555 Highway 154 West
Los Olivos, California 93441
Head of School: James Munger

petersons.com

General Information Coeducational boarding and day college-preparatory and arts school. Boarding grades 9–12, day grades 6–12. Founded: 1957. Setting: small town. Nearest major city is Santa Barbara. Students are housed in single-sex dormitories. 55-acre campus. 15 buildings on campus. Approved or accredited by California Association of Independent Schools, The Association of Boarding Schools, Western Association of Schools and Colleges, and California Department of Education. Member of National Association of Independent Schools and Secondary School

Admission Test Board. Languages of instruction: English, Spanish, and French. Endowment: $1 million. Total enrollment: 250. Upper school average class size: 15. Upper school faculty-student ratio: 1:7.

Upper School Student Profile Grade 9: 45 students (17 boys, 28 girls); Grade 10: 44 students (24 boys, 20 girls); Grade 11: 48 students (26 boys, 22 girls); Grade 12: 49 students (32 boys, 17 girls). 60% of students are boarding students. 67% are state residents. 11 states are represented in upper school student body. 16% are international students. International students from Ghana, Hong Kong, Japan, Republic of Korea, and Taiwan; 6 other countries represented in student body.

Faculty School total: 32. In upper school: 17 men, 15 women; 22 have advanced degrees; 30 reside on campus.

Subjects Offered Algebra, American foreign policy, American history, American history-AP, ancient history, art history, biology, biology-AP, calculus, calculus-AP, ceramics, chemistry, chemistry-AP, classical civilization, college counseling, computer programming, computer science, conceptual physics, contemporary history, creative writing, drama, economics, economics and history, English, English language-AP, English literature, English literature-AP, English-AP, environmental science, environmental science-AP, European history, experiential education, fine arts, French, French language-AP, freshman foundations, human development, instrumental music, integrated math, journalism, music, organic gardening, outdoor education, photography, physical education, physics, physics-AP, science, social science, Spanish, Spanish language-AP, statistics and probability, statistics-AP, studio art, studio art-AP, theater, world history, World War II.

Graduation Requirements Arts and fine arts (art, music, dance, drama), computer science, English, foreign language, history, human development, lab science, mathematics, outdoor education, science.

Special Academic Programs Advanced Placement exam preparation in 12 subject areas; honors section; independent study; academic accommodation for the gifted; special instructional classes for students with moderate to mild learning differences.

College Placement 37 students graduated in 2005; 36 went to college, including Boston University; Saint Mary's College of California; San Francisco State University; University of California, Los Angeles; University of California, Santa Barbara; Vassar College. Other: 1 entered military service. Median SAT verbal: 550, median SAT math: 561, median combined SAT: 1111.

Student Life Upper grades have specified standards of dress, student council, honor system. Discipline rests primarily with faculty.

Tuition and Aid Day student tuition: $15,500; 7-day tuition and room/board: $34,500. Tuition installment plan (Key Tuition Payment Plan, monthly payment plans, individually arranged payment plans, 2-payment plan). Need-based scholarship grants available. In 2005–06, 25% of upper-school students received aid. Total amount of financial aid awarded in 2005–06: $500,000.

Admissions Traditional secondary-level entrance grade is 9. For fall 2005, 172 students applied for upper-level admission, 126 were accepted, 75 enrolled. ISEE, SSAT or TOEFL required. Deadline for receipt of application materials: February 15. Application fee required: $50. Interview required.

Athletics Interscholastic: aerobics/dance (girls), baseball (b), basketball (b,g), lacrosse (b,g), soccer (b,g), tennis (b,g), volleyball (b,g), weight training (b); coed interscholastic: canoeing/kayaking, climbing, cross-country running, dance, equestrian sports, fitness, fitness walking, football, golf, hiking/backpacking, horseback riding, kayaking, modern dance, outdoor education, physical fitness, physical training, rafting, rock climbing, ropes courses, strength & conditioning, surfing, swimming and diving, track and field, walking; coed intramural: badminton, horseshoes, table tennis. 3 coaches, 1 trainer.

Computers Computers are regularly used in art, mathematics, multimedia, music, publications, science, Web site design, yearbook classes. Computer network features include on-campus library services, CD-ROMs, Internet access, wireless campus network.

Contact Ann E. Greenough-Coats, Director of Admissions. 800-287-9197. Fax: 805-686-2078. E-mail: admissions@dunnschool.com. Web site: www.dunnschool.com.

ANNOUNCEMENT FROM THE SCHOOL Anthony Dunn, a native of England who was educated at Oxford University, founded Dunn School in 1957. It is located on a 55-acre campus in the beautiful Santa Ynez Valley, 29 miles northeast of Santa Barbara. Dunn School has a rigorous college-preparatory curriculum and offers Advanced Placement in 12 subject areas. The student body is comprised of 112 boarding and 77 day students. The average class size of 15 fosters a deep and meaningful relationship between faculty members and students. In addition, each student is assigned a faculty adviser with whom they meet daily. The adviser is responsible for monitoring each advisee in all academic and nonacademic areas. Dunn School has a Learning Skills Program that accommodates a select number of students with minimal, diagnosed language and learning difficulties. The School believes in the importance of character development through extracurricular activities, including interscholastic sports, outdoor education, and community service. Dunn School is implementing its Personal Education Program, or PEP, in the 2005–06 academic year. The purpose of this plan is to provide a curricular and extracurricular guide for the student, parents, adviser, and the college planner as the student moves toward the goal of successful college placement. The PEP provides a template for planning and an ongoing record of achievements. College counseling at Dunn School is

available to students beginning in the 9th grade and includes individual appointments, group information sessions, meetings with college representatives, preparation for the SAT and TOEFL, and assistance with the application process. All Dunn graduates are prepared for the college of their choice.

DURHAM ACADEMY

3601 Ridge Road
Durham, North Carolina 27705
Head of School: Edward Costello

General Information Coeducational day college-preparatory, arts, and technology school. Grades PK–12. Founded: 1933. Setting: suburban. Nearest major city is Raleigh. 75-acre campus. 11 buildings on campus. Approved or accredited by North Carolina Association of Independent Schools, Southern Association of Colleges and Schools, Southern Association of Independent Schools, and North Carolina Department of Education. Member of National Association of Independent Schools and Secondary School Admission Test Board. Endowment: $7 million. Total enrollment: 1,129. Upper school average class size: 14. Upper school faculty-student ratio: 1:7.

Upper School Student Profile Grade 9: 100 students (54 boys, 46 girls); Grade 10: 99 students (52 boys, 47 girls); Grade 11: 96 students (45 boys, 51 girls); Grade 12: 89 students (45 boys, 44 girls).

Faculty School total: 154. In upper school: 26 men, 21 women; 43 have advanced degrees.

Subjects Offered Accounting, algebra, American history, American literature, art, art history, astronomy, biology, calculus, ceramics, chemistry, community service, computer graphics, computer programming, computer science, creative writing, dance, drama, ecology, economics, English, English literature, environmental science, fine arts, finite math, French, geometry, German, history, Latin, mathematics, music, outdoor education, physical education, physics, psychology, robotics, science, social studies, Spanish, statistics, theater.

Graduation Requirements Arts and fine arts (art, music, dance, drama), computer science, English, foreign language, mathematics, outdoor education, physical education (includes health), science, senior project, social studies (includes history). Community service is required.

Special Academic Programs Advanced Placement exam preparation in 18 subject areas; honors section; independent study; special instructional classes for students with learning disabilities and Attention Deficit Disorder.

College Placement 94 students graduated in 2005; 93 went to college, including Duke University; The University of North Carolina at Chapel Hill; University of Southern California; University of Virginia; Wake Forest University. Other: 1 entered a postgraduate year. Median SAT verbal: 649, median SAT math: 650. 61% scored over 600 on SAT verbal, 70% scored over 600 on SAT math.

Student Life Upper grades have specified standards of dress, student council, honor system. Discipline rests equally with students and faculty.

Summer Programs Enrichment programs offered; session focuses on academic enrichment, non-academic activities; held on campus; accepts boys and girls; open to students from other schools. 550 students usually enrolled. 2006 schedule: June 12 to July 28. Application deadline: none.

Tuition and Aid Day student tuition: $16,025. Tuition installment plan (Key Tuition Payment Plan, monthly payment plans). Need-based scholarship grants available. In 2005–06, 35% of upper-school students received aid. Total amount of financial aid awarded in 2005–06: $368,755.

Admissions Traditional secondary-level entrance grade is 9. For fall 2005, 87 students applied for upper-level admission, 42 were accepted, 32 enrolled. CTP III, ISEE or SSAT required. Deadline for receipt of application materials: January 13. Application fee required: $60. Interview required.

Athletics Interscholastic: baseball (boys), basketball (b,g), cross-country running (b,g), dance (b), field hockey (g), golf (b), lacrosse (b,g), soccer (b,g), softball (g), swimming and diving (b,g), tennis (b,g), track and field (b,g), volleyball (g), weight training (b,g); intramural: dance team (g); coed interscholastic: golf, weight training; coed intramural: indoor soccer, winter soccer. 7 PE instructors, 6 coaches, 1 trainer.

Computers Computers are regularly used in all classes. Computer network features include on-campus library services, CD-ROMs, online commercial services, Internet access, file transfer, DVD, wireless campus network.

Contact Jessica Carothers, Director of Admission and Financial Aid. 919-493-5787. Fax: 919-489-4893. E-mail: admissions@da.org. Web site: www.da.org.

DWIGHT-ENGLEWOOD SCHOOL

315 East Palisade Avenue
Englewood, New Jersey 07631-0489
Head of School: Dr. Ralph E. Sloan

General Information Coeducational day college-preparatory and technology school. Grades PK–12. Founded: 1889. Setting: suburban. Nearest major city is New York, NY. 33-acre campus. 10 buildings on campus. Approved or accredited by Middle States Association of Colleges and Schools. Member of National Association of

Dwight-Englewood School

Independent Schools and Secondary School Admission Test Board. Endowment: $7 million. Total enrollment: 942. Upper school average class size: 15. Upper school faculty-student ratio: 1:9.

Upper School Student Profile Grade 9: 116 students (63 boys, 53 girls); Grade 10: 111 students (56 boys, 55 girls); Grade 11: 108 students (51 boys, 57 girls); Grade 12: 121 students (60 boys, 61 girls).

Faculty School total: 130. In upper school: 32 men, 39 women; 48 have advanced degrees.

Subjects Offered Acting, advanced chemistry, advanced math, Advanced Placement courses, advanced studio art-AP, American government-AP, American history, American history-AP, American literature-AP, analysis, analysis and differential calculus, analysis of data, analytic geometry, ancient history, architecture, art, art history, art history-AP, bell choir, bioethics, bioethics, DNA and culture, biology, biology-AP, calculus-AP, ceramics, chemistry-AP, choir, chorus, community service, computer graphics, computer science-AP, concert bell choir, creative writing, critical thinking, data analysis, digital imaging, digital photography, drama, dramatic arts, drawing, drawing and design, economics and history, engineering, English, English language and composition-AP, English language-AP, English literature, English literature and composition-AP, English literature-AP, English-AP, environmental science, environmental science-AP, ethics, European history, evolution, fine arts, foreign language, fractal geometry, fractals, French, French language-AP, French literature-AP, French-AP, general science, genetics, geometry, government and politics-AP, government-AP, health, health education, history, history of jazz, independent study, Japanese, language-AP, Latin, law, literature and composition-AP, mathematics, orchestra, organic chemistry, painting, photography, physical education, physics-AP, printmaking, psychology, robotics, science, social studies, Spanish, statistics-AP, technology, world history.

Graduation Requirements Arts and fine arts (art, music, dance, drama), English, foreign language, mathematics, physical education (includes health), science, social studies (includes history), technology. Community service is required.

Special Academic Programs Advanced Placement exam preparation; honors section; independent study; study abroad.

College Placement 113 students graduated in 2005; all went to college, including Boston University; Columbia University; New York University; The George Washington University; Tufts University; University of Pennsylvania. Mean SAT verbal: 690, mean SAT math: 641. 44% scored over 600 on SAT verbal, 54% scored over 600 on SAT math.

Student Life Upper grades have student council. Discipline rests primarily with faculty.

Summer Programs Remediation, enrichment, advancement, ESL, sports, art/fine arts, computer instruction programs offered; session focuses on academics and sports; held on campus; accepts boys and girls; open to students from other schools. 1000 students usually enrolled. 2006 schedule: June to August. Application deadline: none.

Tuition and Aid Day student tuition: $22,735. Tuition installment plan (Key Tuition Payment Plan, monthly payment plans). Need-based scholarship grants, need-based loans, middle-income loans available. In 2005–06, 16% of upper-school students received aid. Total amount of financial aid awarded in 2005–06: $1,438,841.

Admissions Traditional secondary-level entrance grade is 9. For fall 2005, 152 students applied for upper-level admission, 84 were accepted, 62 enrolled. ISEE or SSAT required. Deadline for receipt of application materials: none. Application fee required: $65. On-campus interview required.

Athletics Interscholastic: baseball (boys), basketball (b,g), cross-country running (b,g), field hockey (g), football (b), golf (b,g), lacrosse (b,g), soccer (b,g), softball (g), tennis (b,g), track and field (b,g), volleyball (g), wrestling (b); intramural: cheering (g), fencing (g). 10 PE instructors, 15 coaches, 1 trainer.

Computers Computers are regularly used in art, English, history, mathematics, science, technology classes. Computer network features include campus e-mail, on-campus library services, CD-ROMs, online commercial services, Internet access, file transfer, office computer access, DVD, wireless campus network, Tablet PC program.

Contact Ms. Sherronda L. Oliver, Director of Enrollment and External Relations. 201-569-9500 Ext. 3500. Fax: 201-568-9451. E-mail: olives@d-e.org. Web site: www.d-e.org.

ANNOUNCEMENT FROM THE SCHOOL One Community, Infinite Possibilities. Founded in 1889, Dwight-Englewood School is a highly selective, college-preparatory day school, enrolling students from preschool through grade 12. Drawing upon over 80 communities in New Jersey's Bergen and Hudson Counties, New York City, and New York's Rockland County, the School combines a rigorous academic program with a wide range of artistic, athletic, and intellectual activities. D-E is committed to the classical concept of education. In the humanities, as well as in math and science, courses are designed to enhance students' competence and confidence as readers and writers, as well as critical thinkers. The use of computers is also integrated throughout the curriculum. The School offers Tablet PCs, wireless network access, online course content, and "one-click" classrooms. What truly distinguishes a D-E education is the quality and dedication of the faculty. In small classes, teachers create an environment that promotes ethical decision making and the values of integrity and service to others. These men and women serve as role models, instructors, and coaches; they guide students along a path of intellectual and personal development and

prepare them for productive lives in the future. The D-E experience gives students the highest quality preparation to thrive in a world marked by diversity in race, religion, national origin, and point of view. An important thread of D-E's long history is tied to the belief that education involves more than academic and extracurricular development. Character education is an equally important, if less tangible, mission for the School. Everyone at D-E seeks to grow: in respect, honesty, judgment, commitment, courage, and community and everyone is expected to work toward living these shared values. At D-E, the opportunity to grow is a precious gift, one that brings out our best selves.

THE DWIGHT SCHOOL

291 Central Park West
New York, New York 10024
Head of School: Mr. Stephen Spahn

General Information Coeducational day college-preparatory, arts, business, bilingual studies, and technology school. Grades PK–12. Founded: 1880. Setting: urban. 3 buildings on campus. Approved or accredited by European Council of International Schools, International Baccalaureate Organization, Middle States Association of Colleges and Schools, and New York Department of Education. Endowment: $5 million. Total enrollment: 435. Upper school average class size: 15. Upper school faculty-student ratio: 1:6.

Upper School Student Profile Grade 9: 64 students (36 boys, 28 girls); Grade 10: 67 students (39 boys, 28 girls); Grade 11: 61 students (40 boys, 21 girls); Grade 12: 62 students (38 boys, 24 girls).

Faculty School total: 93. In upper school: 24 men, 26 women; 32 have advanced degrees.

Subjects Offered Algebra, American history, American literature, art, art history, biology, calculus, chemistry, community service, computer math, computer science, creative writing, dance, drama, economics, English, English literature, environmental science, ethics, European history, expository writing, film, fine arts, French, geometry, government/civics, grammar, health, history, Italian, Japanese, journalism, Latin, mathematics, music, philosophy, photography, physical education, physics, physiology, psychology, science, social studies, Spanish, technology/design, theater, theory of knowledge, trigonometry, typing, world history, world literature, writing.

Graduation Requirements Arts and fine arts (art, music, dance, drama), computer science, English, foreign language, mathematics, physical education (includes health), science, social studies (includes history). Community service is required.

Special Academic Programs International Baccalaureate program; Advanced Placement exam preparation in 6 subject areas; honors section; independent study; term-away projects; study abroad; remedial reading and/or remedial writing; remedial math; special instructional classes for students with learning disabilities; ESL (15 students enrolled).

College Placement 65 students graduated in 2005; 61 went to college, including Brown University; Dartmouth College; New York University; Northwestern University; The George Washington University; Trinity College. Other: 4 went to work.

Student Life Upper grades have specified standards of dress, student council, honor system. Discipline rests equally with students and faculty.

Summer Programs Remediation, enrichment, advancement, ESL, computer instruction programs offered; session focuses on academics and study abroad; held both on and off campus; held at Costa Rica, Kenya, London; accepts boys and girls; open to students from other schools. 25 students usually enrolled. 2006 schedule: June 15 to June 25. Application deadline: none.

Tuition and Aid Day student tuition: $26,250–$28,000. Tuition installment plan (The Tuition Plan, Insured Tuition Payment Plan, monthly payment plans, individually arranged payment plans). Need-based scholarship grants, prepGATE Loans available. In 2005–06, 20% of upper-school students received aid. Total amount of financial aid awarded in 2005–06: $500,000.

Admissions Traditional secondary-level entrance grade is 9. ERB or ISEE required. Deadline for receipt of application materials: none. Application fee required: $45. On-campus interview required.

Athletics Interscholastic: baseball (boys), basketball (b,g), cross-country running (b,g), dance (g), dance team (g), fencing (b,g), physical training (b,g), soccer (b,g), softball (g), tai chi (b), track and field (b,g), volleyball (g); intramural: basketball (b,g), boxing (b,g), fencing (b,g), physical fitness (b,g), physical training (b,g), soccer (b), weight lifting (b,g), weight training (b,g); coed interscholastic: fencing, physical training, soccer, weight training; coed intramural: boxing, fencing, golf, martial arts, physical fitness, physical training, skiing (downhill), snowboarding, snowshoeing, soccer, strength & conditioning, swimming and diving, tai chi, tennis, weight lifting, weight training, yoga. 6 PE instructors, 16 coaches.

Computers Computers are regularly used in foreign language, mathematics, music, science classes. Computer network features include campus e-mail, on-campus library services, CD-ROMs, online commercial services, Internet access, DVD, wireless campus network.

Contact Marina Bernstein, Director of Admissions. 212-724-2146. Fax: 212-724-2539. E-mail: mbernstein@dwight.edu. Web site: www.dwight.edu.

See full description on page 772.

EAGLEBROOK SCHOOL

Deerfield, Massachusetts

See Junior Boarding Schools section.

EAGLE HILL SCHOOL

Greenwich, Connecticut

See Special Needs Schools section.

EAGLE HILL SCHOOL

Hardwick, Massachusetts

See Special Needs Schools section.

EAGLE HILL-SOUTHPORT

Southport, Connecticut

See Special Needs Schools section.

EAGLE ROCK SCHOOL

Estes Park, Colorado

See Special Needs Schools section.

EAST CATHOLIC HIGH SCHOOL

115 New State Road
Manchester, Connecticut 06040-1898
Head of School: Sr. Bette Gould, SSJ

General Information Coeducational day college-preparatory, arts, and religious studies school, affiliated with Roman Catholic Church. Grades 9–12. Founded: 1961. Setting: suburban. Nearest major city is Hartford. 47-acre campus. 2 buildings on campus. Approved or accredited by Connecticut Association of Independent Schools, New England Association of Schools and Colleges, and Connecticut Department of Education. Endowment: $500,000. Total enrollment: 728. Upper school average class size: 21. Upper school faculty-student ratio: 1:14.

Upper School Student Profile Grade 9: 213 students (116 boys, 97 girls); Grade 10: 174 students (86 boys, 88 girls); Grade 11: 175 students (82 boys, 93 girls); Grade 12: 166 students (81 boys, 85 girls). 90% of students are Roman Catholic.

Faculty School total: 53. In upper school: 23 men, 30 women; 49 have advanced degrees.

Subjects Offered Algebra, American history, American history-AP, American literature, American literature-AP, anatomy, art, Bible studies, biology, biology-AP, business, calculus, calculus-AP, chemistry, chemistry-AP, computer programming, computer science, digital photography, economics, English, English literature, English literature-AP, environmental science, ethics, European history, expository writing, French, geography, geometry, government/civics, grammar, health, history, Latin, mathematics, music, philosophy, physical education, physics, physiology, psychology, religion, science, sculpture, social studies, sociology, Spanish, theology, trigonometry, world history, world literature, writing.

Graduation Requirements English, foreign language, health and wellness, mathematics, physical education (includes health), religion (includes Bible studies and theology), science, social studies (includes history), study skills.

Special Academic Programs Advanced Placement exam preparation in 5 subject areas; honors section.

College Placement 153 students graduated in 2005; 152 went to college, including Central Connecticut State University; Eastern Connecticut State University; Johnson & Wales University; Saint Joseph College; University of Connecticut; University of Hartford. Other: 1 entered military service.

Student Life Upper grades have uniform requirement, student council. Discipline rests primarily with faculty. Attendance at religious services is required.

Tuition and Aid Day student tuition: $8275. Tuition installment plan (SMART Tuition Payment Plan, August pre-payment discount plan). Tuition reduction for siblings, merit scholarship grants, need-based scholarship grants available. In 2005–06, 33% of upper-school students received aid; total upper-school merit-scholarship money awarded: $21,000. Total amount of financial aid awarded in 2005–06: $576,792.

Admissions Traditional secondary-level entrance grade is 9. High School Placement Test (closed version) from Scholastic Testing Service required. Deadline for receipt of application materials: none. Application fee required: $20.

Athletics Interscholastic: baseball (boys), basketball (b,g), cheering (g), cross-country running (b,g), dance team (g), football (b), golf (b,g), ice hockey (b), lacrosse (b,g), soccer (b,g), softball (g), swimming and diving (g), tennis (b,g), track and field

(b,g), volleyball (g), weight lifting (b), winter (indoor) track (b,g), wrestling (b); intramural: volleyball (g); coed interscholastic: indoor track. 2 PE instructors, 40 coaches, 1 trainer.

Computers Computers are regularly used in science, technology classes. Computer resources include on-campus library services, CD-ROMs, online commercial services, Internet access, office computer access.

Contact Ms. Jacqueline Gryphon, Director of Recruitment and Admissions. 860-649-5336 Ext. 238. Fax: 860-649-7191. E-mail: gryphonj@echs.com. Web site: echs.com.

EASTERN CHRISTIAN HIGH SCHOOL

50 Oakwood Avenue
North Haledon, New Jersey 07508
Head of School: Mr. Kurt Kaboth

General Information Coeducational day college-preparatory and general academic school, affiliated with Christian Reformed Church. Grades PK–12. Founded: 1892. Setting: suburban. Nearest major city is New York, NY. 27-acre campus. 1 building on campus. Approved or accredited by Association of Christian Schools International, Middle States Association of Colleges and Schools, and New Jersey Department of Education. Endowment: $5.8 million. Total enrollment: 919. Upper school average class size: 20. Upper school faculty-student ratio: 1:10.

Upper School Student Profile Grade 9: 86 students (42 boys, 44 girls); Grade 10: 90 students (41 boys, 49 girls); Grade 11: 98 students (52 boys, 46 girls); Grade 12: 104 students (47 boys, 57 girls). 50% of students are members of Christian Reformed Church.

Faculty School total: 86. In upper school: 17 men, 22 women; 21 have advanced degrees.

Subjects Offered Accounting, algebra, American history, American literature, art, Bible studies, biology, business, business skills, calculus, chemistry, community service, computer science, computer-aided design, creative writing, driver education, English, English literature, European history, fine arts, French, geometry, government/civics, grammar, health, history, humanities, journalism, Latin, mathematics, music, personal finance, physical education, physical science, physics, psychology, science, social studies, sociology, Spanish, study skills, technical education, trigonometry, world history, writing.

Graduation Requirements Arts and fine arts (art, music, dance, drama), Bible, English, lab science, mathematics, physical education (includes health), science, social studies (includes history), technical skills, word processing, 50 hours of community service.

Special Academic Programs Advanced Placement exam preparation in 6 subject areas; honors section; independent study; academic accommodation for the gifted, the musically talented, and the artistically talented; remedial reading and/or remedial writing; remedial math; programs in English, mathematics for dyslexic students; ESL (7 students enrolled).

College Placement 98 students graduated in 2005; 89 went to college, including Calvin College; Eastern University; Louisiana Tech University; Messiah College; Stevens Institute of Technology; William Paterson University of New Jersey. Other: 4 went to work, 5 had other specific plans. Median SAT verbal: 552, median SAT math: 549. 32% scored over 600 on SAT verbal, 37% scored over 600 on SAT math.

Student Life Upper grades have specified standards of dress, student council. Discipline rests primarily with faculty. Attendance at religious services is required.

Tuition and Aid Day student tuition: $9700. Tuition installment plan (monthly payment plans). Tuition reduction for siblings, need-based scholarship grants available.

Admissions Traditional secondary-level entrance grade is 9. For fall 2005, 59 students applied for upper-level admission, 44 were accepted, 44 enrolled. Deadline for receipt of application materials: none. Application fee required: $75. On-campus interview required.

Athletics Interscholastic: baseball (boys), basketball (b,g), bowling (b,g), cheering (g), cross-country running (b,g), golf (b,g), soccer (b,g), softball (g), tennis (b,g), track and field (b,g), volleyball (g); intramural: aerobics (b,g), badminton (b,g), basketball (b,g), fitness walking (b,g), flag football (b,g), flagball (b,g), football (b,g), Frisbee (b,g), golf (b,g), gymnastics (b,g), indoor soccer (b,g), lacrosse (b,g), paddle tennis (b,g), physical fitness (b,g), roller hockey (b,g), running (b,g), skateboarding (b,g), skiing (downhill) (b,g), soccer (b,g), softball (b,g), street hockey (b,g), table tennis (b,g), volleyball (b,g), weight lifting (b,g); coed intramural: aerobics, badminton, baseball, basketball, fitness walking, flag football, flagball, football, golf, gymnastics, indoor soccer, lacrosse, paddle tennis, physical fitness, roller hockey, running, skateboarding, skiing (downhill), soccer, softball, street hockey, table tennis, volleyball, weight lifting. 2 PE instructors, 18 coaches.

Computers Computers are regularly used in all academic classes. Computer network features include on-campus library services, CD-ROMs, Internet access, file transfer, Microsoft Office, Microsoft Visual Studio, AutoCAD LT 2000, Adobe Photoshop, Adobe GoLive, Adobe Illustrator, Adobe LiveMotion.

Contact Ms. Janyce Bandstra, Admission Director. 973-427-6244 Ext. 207. Fax: 973-427-9775. E-mail: admissions@easternchristian.org. Web site: www.easternchristian.org.

EASTERN MENNONITE HIGH SCHOOL

801 Parkwood Drive
Harrisonburg, Virginia 22802
Head of School: Mr. Paul G. Leaman

General Information Coeducational day college-preparatory, arts, and religious studies school, affiliated with Mennonite Church USA. Grades K–12. Founded: 1917. Setting: small town. Nearest major city is Washington, DC. 24-acre campus. 3 buildings on campus. Approved or accredited by Southern Association of Colleges and Schools, Virginia Association of Independent Schools, and Virginia Department of Education. Endowment: $1.8 million. Total enrollment: 340. Upper school average class size: 20. Upper school faculty-student ratio: 1:10.

Upper School Student Profile Grade 9: 54 students (23 boys, 31 girls); Grade 10: 59 students (34 boys, 25 girls); Grade 11: 61 students (27 boys, 34 girls); Grade 12: 48 students (24 boys, 24 girls). 63% of students are Mennonite Church USA.

Faculty School total: 36. In upper school: 17 men, 16 women; 18 have advanced degrees.

Subjects Offered Acting, advanced math, algebra, American government, American history, American literature, analysis, applied music, art, art history, band, bell choir, Bible studies, biology, British literature, British literature (honors), business, business skills, ceramics, chemistry, choir, choral music, chorus, Christian and Hebrew scripture, Christian doctrine, Christian ethics, Christian studies, Christian testament, Christianity, church history, community service, computer education, computer science, concert choir, consumer mathematics, creative writing, desktop publishing, drama, drawing, driver education, earth science, economics, engineering, English, English composition, English literature, family and consumer sciences, fiction, fine arts, food and nutrition, food science, French, general science, geography, geometry, government, grammar, guitar, handbells, health, health education, history, home economics, honors English, human development, industrial arts, industrial technology, instrumental music, interior design, keyboarding/computer, mathematics, mechanical drawing, music, music composition, music theory, novel, oil painting, orchestra, outdoor education, painting, photography, physical education, physical science, physics, poetry, pottery, pre-algebra, religion, religious education, research skills, science, sculpture, sewing, shop, social science, social studies, sociology, Spanish, speech, speech communications, stained glass, study skills, theater, typing, U.S. government, U.S. history, vocal music, voice, water color painting, woodworking, world cultures, world history, writing.

Graduation Requirements Arts and fine arts (art, music, dance, drama), electives, English, foreign language, home economics, keyboarding/computer, mathematics, physical education (includes health), religion (includes Bible studies and theology), science, social studies (includes history), technical arts.

Special Academic Programs International Baccalaureate program; Advanced Placement exam preparation in 3 subject areas; independent study; study at local college for college credit; academic accommodation for the gifted; remedial reading and/or remedial writing; remedial math; programs in English, mathematics, general development for dyslexic students.

College Placement 49 students graduated in 2005; 38 went to college, including Eastern Mennonite University; Goshen College; Hesston College; James Madison University. Other: 5 went to work, 6 had other specific plans. Median SAT verbal: 569, median SAT math: 554. 35% scored over 600 on SAT verbal, 35% scored over 600 on SAT math.

Student Life Upper grades have specified standards of dress, student council. Discipline rests primarily with faculty. Attendance at religious services is required.

Tuition and Aid Day student tuition: $8513–$10,280. Tuition installment plan (monthly payment plans, individually arranged payment plans). Need-based scholarship grants available. In 2005–06, 28% of upper-school students received aid. Total amount of financial aid awarded in 2005–06: $159,689.

Admissions Traditional secondary-level entrance grade is 9. For fall 2005, 51 students applied for upper-level admission, 45 were accepted, 37 enrolled. Deadline for receipt of application materials: none. Application fee required: $25.

Athletics Interscholastic: basketball (boys, girls), cheering (g), cross-country running (b,g), soccer (b,g), softball (g), tennis (b,g), track and field (b,g), volleyball (g); intramural: baseball (b), basketball (b,g), soccer (g), wrestling (b); coed interscholastic: baseball; coed intramural: volleyball. 3 PE instructors, 9 coaches, 2 trainers.

Computers Computers are regularly used in business skills, graphic design, library, mathematics, music, publications, research skills, science, social science, social studies, yearbook classes. Computer resources include on-campus library services, CD-ROMs, Internet access, DVD.

Contact Jean Smucker Fisher, Director of Admissions. 540-432-4521. Fax: 540-432-4528. E-mail: fisherj@emhs.net. Web site: www.emhs.net.

EASTSIDE COLLEGE PREPARATORY SCHOOL

2101 Pulgas Avenue
East Palo Alto, California 94303
Head of School: Chris Bischof

General Information Coeducational day college-preparatory school. Grades 6–12. Founded: 1996. Setting: suburban. Nearest major city is Oakland. 6-acre campus. 7 buildings on campus. Approved or accredited by Western Association of Schools and Colleges and California Department of Education. Total enrollment: 211. Upper school average class size: 18. Upper school faculty-student ratio: 1:8.

Faculty School total: 25.

Student Life Upper grades have specified standards of dress, student council, honor system.

Summer Programs Remediation, enrichment, advancement, sports programs offered; held on campus; accepts boys and girls; not open to students from other schools.

Admissions Deadline for receipt of application materials: January 13. No application fee required.

Athletics Interscholastic: basketball (boys, girls), soccer (b,g), track and field (b,g), volleyball (b,g).

Contact Helen Kim, Vice Principal. 650-688-0850 Ext. 109. Fax: 650-688-0859. E-mail: helenk@eastside.org. Web site: www.eastside.org.

ECKERD YOUTH ALTERNATIVES

Clearwater, Florida
See Special Needs Schools section.

ECOLE D'HUMANITE

CH 6085 Hasliberg Goldern, Switzerland

Head of School: K. C. Hill

petersons.com

General Information Coeducational boarding and day college-preparatory, general academic, arts, vocational, and bilingual studies school. Ungraded, ages 7–20. Founded: 1934. Setting: rural. Nearest major city is Lucerne. Students are housed in coed dormitories. 5-acre campus. 13 buildings on campus. Approved or accredited by Department of Education of Bern and Swiss Federation of Private Schools. Member of European Council of International Schools. Languages of instruction: English and German. Endowment: 1 million Swiss francs. Total enrollment: 146. Upper school average class size: 5. Upper school faculty-student ratio: 1:5.

Upper School Student Profile 93% of students are boarding students. 49% are international students. International students from Canada, Germany, Japan, Netherlands, Taiwan, and United States; 8 other countries represented in student body.

Faculty School total: 42. In upper school: 15 men, 18 women; 9 have advanced degrees; 40 reside on campus.

Subjects Offered Algebra, American literature, art, art history, Asian history, band, batik, biology, bookmaking, calculus, career and personal planning, carpentry, ceramics, chemistry, choir, choreography, chorus, community service, computer programming, computer skills, costumes and make-up, creative dance, creative writing, culinary arts, cultural geography, current events, dance, dance performance, debate, drama, drama workshop, drawing, ecology, environmental systems, English, English as a foreign language, English composition, English literature, environmental science, ESL, European history, expository writing, fine arts, first aid, folk dance, French, French as a second language, gardening, geography, geometry, German, grammar, guitar, gymnastics, health, history, home economics, independent study, jazz ensemble, jewelry making, Latin, mathematics, modern dance, music, music appreciation, music performance, musical productions, musical theater, musical theater dance, outdoor education, peer counseling, philosophy, photo shop, photography, physical education, physics, piano, poetry, pottery, pre-calculus, psychology, radio broadcasting, religion, research skills, SAT preparation, science, sewing, Shakespeare, single survival, social science, social studies, studio art, swimming, theater, TOEFL preparation, trigonometry, U.S. history, vocal ensemble, voice, weaving, wind ensemble, women's studies, woodworking, world history, world literature, writing, yearbook, yoga.

Graduation Requirements English, foreign language, independent study, mathematics, physical education (includes health), research skills, SAT preparation, science, social science, social studies (includes history), 2x term paper methodology course, balance of courses in arts, sports, handcrafts. Community service is required.

Special Academic Programs Honors section; accelerated programs; independent study; term-away projects; academic accommodation for the gifted, the musically talented, and the artistically talented; remedial reading and/or remedial writing; remedial math; ESL (65 students enrolled).

College Placement 6 students graduated in 2005; 3 went to college, including Bennington College. Other: 1 went to work, 2 had other specific plans. Median SAT verbal: 545, median SAT math: 670. 33% scored over 600 on SAT verbal, 50% scored over 600 on SAT math.

Student Life Upper grades have student council, honor system. Discipline rests equally with students and faculty.

Tuition and Aid Day student tuition: 18,000 Swiss francs; 7-day tuition and room/board: 31,000 Swiss francs–40,000 Swiss francs. Guaranteed tuition plan. Tuition installment plan (monthly payment plans, individually arranged payment plans). Need-based scholarship grants, need-based loans, middle-income loans available. In 2005–06, 21% of upper-school students received aid. Total amount of financial aid awarded in 2005–06: 180,000 Swiss francs.

Admissions Traditional secondary-level entrance age is 14. Deadline for receipt of application materials: none. No application fee required. Interview recommended.

Athletics Intramural: basketball (boys, girls), judo (b,g); coed intramural: aerobics, aerobics/dance, alpine skiing, archery, back packing, badminton, ballet, baseball, basketball, bicycling, canoeing/kayaking, climbing, dance, fitness walking, Frisbee, gymnastics, hiking/backpacking, horseback riding, indoor soccer, judo, juggling, kayaking, martial arts, modern dance, rock climbing, sailing, skiing (downhill), snowboarding, snowshoeing, soccer, softball, strength & conditioning, swimming and diving, table tennis, tennis, ultimate Frisbee, volleyball, walking, yoga. 5 trainers.

Computers Computers are regularly used in career exploration, college planning, creative writing, data processing, English, graphic design, independent study, library, newspaper, photography, typing, yearbook classes. Computer resources include campus e-mail, CD-ROMs, Internet access.

Contact K. C. Hill, Director. 41-33-972-9272. Fax: 41-33-972-9272. E-mail: us.office@ecole.ch. Web site: www.ecole.ch.

ANNOUNCEMENT FROM THE SCHOOL No matter where a child grows up, he or she can benefit from living abroad as a teenager. The Ecole d'Humanité provides not only a global perspective, with its location in the heart of Europe and its international selection of students, but also a safe and happy living environment with its caring staff and community.

See full description on page 774.

EDISON SCHOOL

Box 2, Site 11, RR2
Okotoks, Alberta T1S 1A2, Canada
Head of School: Mrs. Beth Chernoff

General Information Coeducational day college-preparatory and general academic school. Grades PK–12. Founded: 1993. Setting: small town. Nearest major city is Calgary, Canada. 5-acre campus. 2 buildings on campus. Approved or accredited by Association of Independent Schools and Colleges of Alberta and Alberta Department of Education. Languages of instruction: English, Spanish, and French. Total enrollment: 172. Upper school average class size: 12. Upper school faculty-student ratio: 1:12.

Upper School Student Profile Grade 7: 12 students (6 boys, 6 girls); Grade 8: 12 students (6 boys, 6 girls); Grade 9: 12 students (6 boys, 6 girls); Grade 10: 12 students (6 boys, 6 girls); Grade 11: 12 students (6 boys, 6 girls); Grade 12: 12 students (6 boys, 6 girls).

Faculty School total: 18. In upper school: 3 men, 4 women; 4 have advanced degrees.

Subjects Offered Advanced Placement courses, art, biology, chemistry, English, French, gymnastics, mathematics, physical education, physics, science, social studies, Spanish, standard curriculum.

Graduation Requirements Alberta Learning requirements.

Special Academic Programs Advanced Placement exam preparation in 7 subject areas; accelerated programs; independent study; academic accommodation for the gifted.

College Placement 12 students graduated in 2005; 10 went to college, including The University of British Columbia; University of Alberta; University of Calgary; University of Waterloo. Other: 2 went to work.

Student Life Upper grades have uniform requirement, honor system. Discipline rests primarily with faculty.

Tuition and Aid Day student tuition: CAN$6000. Tuition installment plan (monthly payment plans). Tuition reduction for siblings available.

Admissions For fall 2005, 20 students applied for upper-level admission, 4 were accepted, 4 enrolled. Achievement tests or admissions testing required. Deadline for receipt of application materials: none. No application fee required. On-campus interview required.

Athletics Interscholastic: badminton (boys, girls), basketball (b,g), cross-country running (b,g), track and field (b,g), volleyball (b,g); intramural: badminton (b,g), basketball (b,g), cross-country running (b,g), volleyball (b,g); coed interscholastic: badminton, flag football; coed intramural: badminton, flag football, outdoor education. 1 PE instructor.

Computers Computers are regularly used in all classes.

Contact Mrs. Beth Chernoff, Head Mistress. 403-938-7670. Fax: 403-938-7224. E-mail: office@edisonschool.ca. Web site: www.edisonschool.ca.

ELAN SCHOOL

Poland, Maine
See Special Needs Schools section.

ELGIN ACADEMY

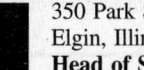

350 Park Street
Elgin, Illinois 60120
Head of School: Dr. John W. Cooper

General Information Coeducational day college-preparatory, arts, and technology school. Grades PS–12. Founded: 1839. Setting: suburban. Nearest major city is Chicago. 20-acre campus. 7 buildings on campus. Approved or accredited by Independent Schools Association of the Central States. Member of National Association of Independent Schools and Secondary School Admission Test Board. Total enrollment: 395. Upper school average class size: 12. Upper school faculty-student ratio: 1:7.

Upper School Student Profile Grade 9: 30 students (19 boys, 11 girls); Grade 10: 34 students (16 boys, 18 girls); Grade 11: 29 students (15 boys, 14 girls); Grade 12: 32 students (16 boys, 16 girls).

Faculty School total: 54. In upper school: 10 men, 13 women; 12 have advanced degrees.

Subjects Offered Algebra, American history, American literature, art, art history, biology, calculus, ceramics, chemistry, computer programming, computer science, creative writing, drama, English, English literature, environmental science, European history, expository writing, fine arts, finite math, French, geometry, government/civics, grammar, history, Latin, Latin-AP, mathematics, music, painting, photography, physical education, psychology, psychology-AP, science, social studies, Spanish, statistics, theater, trigonometry, world history, world literature, writing.

Graduation Requirements Arts and fine arts (art, music, dance, drama), English, foreign language, mathematics, physical education (includes health), science, social studies (includes history).

Special Academic Programs Advanced Placement exam preparation in 7 subject areas; honors section; independent study.

College Placement 32 students graduated in 2005; all went to college, including Lawrence University; Macalester College; New York University; Northwestern University; Washington University in St. Louis; Wellesley College.

Student Life Upper grades have specified standards of dress, student council. Discipline rests primarily with faculty.

Tuition and Aid Day student tuition: $13,550. Tuition installment plan (Key Tuition Payment Plan, monthly payment plans, individually arranged payment plans, 10-month payment plan). Need-based scholarship grants available. In 2005–06, 25% of upper-school students received aid.

Admissions Traditional secondary-level entrance grade is 9. For fall 2005, 27 students applied for upper-level admission, 24 were accepted, 21 enrolled. ERB—verbal abilities, reading comprehension, quantitative abilities (level F, form 1) required. Deadline for receipt of application materials: none. Application fee required: $50. On-campus interview required.

Athletics Interscholastic: baseball (boys), basketball (b,g), cross-country running (b,g), field hockey (g), soccer (b,g), softball (g), tennis (b,g), track and field (b,g); coed interscholastic: golf. 2 PE instructors, 3 coaches.

Computers Computers are regularly used in art, English, foreign language, mathematics, science, social studies classes. Computer network features include campus e-mail, on-campus library services, CD-ROMs, Internet access.

Contact Mr. Erik C. Calhoun, Director of Admission. 847-695-0303. Fax: 847-695-5017. E-mail: ecalhoun@elginacademy.org. Web site: www.elginacademy.org.

ANNOUNCEMENT FROM THE SCHOOL Elgin Academy is celebrating its 166th year, making it the oldest college-preparatory school west of the Alleghenies. From its earliest days, the Academy has been both nonsectarian and coeducational. The campus is located 35 miles northwest of Chicago and serves the suburban communities of the greater Fox River Valley. The 18-acre campus is part of the historic district of Elgin, Illinois, and includes 7 buildings that house the Lower, Middle, and Upper Schools serving preschool through grade 12 students. The total enrollment for the 2005–06 academic year is 386. The educational program is designed to give students a sound academic background in a broad range of the arts and sciences and the knowledge, skills, and attitudes necessary to become intellectually engaged and confident about their place in the world. The personal environment of the Academy encourages students to be active in the arts, cocurricular clubs, athletics, and community service. Team sports include soccer, basketball, tennis, track and cross-country, field hockey, golf, softball, and baseball. Each year, Elgin graduates (all college bound) attend schools in all regions of the country, including Lawrence University, Wellesley, Notre Dame, Columbia, Washington University, Northwestern, Tulane, and William and Mary. The hallmarks of an Elgin Academy education include the following: a nationally recognized academic program, broad exposure to the arts, a close association with faculty as teachers and advisers, opportunities for personal growth and talent development, and complete preparation for successful college placement. The Academy offers selective admission and seeks students from social, economic, and ethnic diversity. Applicants are admitted for the fall semester on a rolling basis beginning January 1 until available spaces in each grade level are filled. Late applicants who are admissible may be given wait-list status. The Academy's financial aid program assists 20% of the students who

---

demonstrate financial need. For further information, please call the Office of Admission at 847-695-0303, visit the Web site at www.elginacademy.org, or e-mail: info@elginacademy.org.

ELIZABETH SETON HIGH SCHOOL

5715 Emerson Street
Bladensburg, Maryland 20710-1844
Head of School: Sr. Virginia Ann Brooks

General Information Girls' day college-preparatory, arts, business, religious studies, bilingual studies, and technology school, affiliated with Roman Catholic Church. Grades 9–12. Founded: 1959. Setting: suburban. Nearest major city is Washington, DC. 24-acre campus. 1 building on campus. Approved or accredited by Middle States Association of Colleges and Schools, National Catholic Education Association, and Maryland Department of Education. Total enrollment: 565. Upper school average class size: 19. Upper school faculty-student ratio: 1:11.

Upper School Student Profile Grade 9: 156 students (156 girls); Grade 10: 149 students (149 girls); Grade 11: 125 students (125 girls); Grade 12: 135 students (135 girls). 65% of students are Roman Catholic.

Faculty School total: 47. In upper school: 7 men, 40 women; 23 have advanced degrees.

Subjects Offered Accounting, advanced chemistry, advanced math, algebra, American government-AP, American history, American history-AP, American literature, analytic geometry, anatomy, art, art-AP, biology, business, calculus, calculus-AP, ceramics, chemistry, choir, chorus, Christian and Hebrew scripture, Christianity, church history, community service, computer keyboarding, computer multimedia, computer science, desktop publishing, earth science, economics, English, English literature, English literature and composition-AP, English literature-AP, environmental science, ethics, European history, fine arts, French, geography, geometry, government-AP, government/civics, grammar, health, history, home economics, honors algebra, honors English, honors geometry, journalism, Latin, mathematics, music, newspaper, philosophy, photography, physical education, physics, physiology, pre-calculus, probability and statistics, psychology, psychology-AP, religion, science, social studies, sociology, Spanish, speech, symphonic band, theology, trigonometry, Web site design, world history, world literature, writing.

Graduation Requirements 1½ elective credits, arts and fine arts (art, music, dance, drama), English, foreign language, health education, mathematics, physical education (includes health), religion (includes Bible studies and theology), science, social studies (includes history), technology. Community service is required.

Special Academic Programs Advanced Placement exam preparation in 10 subject areas; honors section; independent study; academic accommodation for the gifted, the musically talented, and the artistically talented; programs in general development for dyslexic students; special instructional classes for students with mild learning disabilities, organizational deficiencies, Attention Deficit Disorder, and dyslexia.

College Placement 119 students graduated in 2005; all went to college, including Hampton University; Spelman College; The University of North Carolina at Greensboro; Towson University; University of Maryland, Baltimore County; University of Maryland, College Park. Mean SAT verbal: 550, mean SAT math: 505.

Student Life Upper grades have uniform requirement, student council, honor system. Discipline rests equally with students and faculty. Attendance at religious services is required.

Summer Programs Remediation, enrichment, sports, art/fine arts programs offered; held on campus; accepts girls; open to students from other schools. 2006 schedule: June to August.

Tuition and Aid Day student tuition: $7650. Tuition installment plan (monthly payment plans, quarterly payment plan). Tuition reduction for siblings, merit scholarship grants, need-based scholarship grants, paying campus jobs available. In 2005–06, 50% of upper-school students received aid; total upper-school merit-scholarship money awarded: $150,000.

Admissions Traditional secondary-level entrance grade is 9. For fall 2005, 360 students applied for upper-level admission, 214 were accepted, 156 enrolled. High School Placement Test required. Deadline for receipt of application materials: December 15. Application fee required: $35. On-campus interview required.

Athletics Interscholastic: basketball, cheering, crew, cross-country running, dance squad, equestrian sports, field hockey, horseback riding, indoor track, lacrosse, pom squad, rowing, soccer, softball, swimming and diving, tennis, volleyball, winter (indoor) track; intramural: aerobics, aerobics/dance, aerobics/nautilus, combined training, cooperative games, dance, fitness walking, flag football, kickball. 3 PE instructors, 25 coaches, 1 trainer.

Computers Computers are regularly used in desktop publishing, English, keyboarding, lab/keyboard, multimedia, science, typing, Web site design, word processing classes. Computer network features include campus e-mail, on-campus library services, CD-ROMs, online commercial services, Internet access, DVD.

Contact Mrs. Dawn Slone, Director of Admissions. 301-864-4532 Ext. 7115. Fax: 301-864-8946. E-mail: 520@setonhs.org. Web site: www.setonhs.org.

THE ELLIS SCHOOL

6425 Fifth Avenue
Pittsburgh, Pennsylvania 15206
Head of School: Dr. Mary H. Grant

General Information Girls' day college-preparatory school. Grades K–12. Founded: 1916. Setting: urban. 7-acre campus. 9 buildings on campus. Approved or accredited by Middle States Association of Colleges and Schools and Pennsylvania Department of Education. Member of National Association of Independent Schools. Endowment: $23.9 million. Total enrollment: 469. Upper school average class size: 10. Upper school faculty-student ratio: 1:7.

Upper School Student Profile Grade 9: 41 students (41 girls); Grade 10: 41 students (41 girls); Grade 11: 47 students (47 girls); Grade 12: 44 students (44 girls).

Faculty School total: 77. In upper school: 10 men, 27 women; 27 have advanced degrees.

Subjects Offered 20th century history, algebra, American history, American literature, anthropology, archaeology, art, art history, biology, calculus, ceramics, chemistry, computer science, creative writing, dance, drama, economics, English, English literature, European history, expository writing, fine arts, French, geometry, government/civics, health, history, journalism, Latin, linear algebra, mathematics, music, photography, physical education, physics, social studies, Spanish, speech, statistics, theater, trigonometry, world history, world literature, writing.

Graduation Requirements Arts and fine arts (art, music, dance, drama), computer literacy, English, first aid, foreign language, mathematics, physical education (includes health), science, social studies (includes history), completion of three-week mini-course program (grades 9-11), senior projects.

Special Academic Programs Advanced Placement exam preparation in 12 subject areas; honors section; independent study; term-away projects.

College Placement 44 students graduated in 2005; all went to college, including Georgetown University; Lehigh University; The Pennsylvania State University University Park Campus; The University of North Carolina at Chapel Hill; University of Michigan; University of Pittsburgh. Mean SAT verbal: 628, mean SAT math: 615.

Student Life Upper grades have uniform requirement, student council, honor system. Discipline rests primarily with faculty.

Tuition and Aid Day student tuition: $17,950. Tuition installment plan (10-month payment plan; two-payment plan). Need-based scholarship grants available. In 2005–06, 31% of upper-school students received aid. Total amount of financial aid awarded in 2005–06: $616,900.

Admissions Traditional secondary-level entrance grade is 9. For fall 2005, 48 students applied for upper-level admission, 31 were accepted, 20 enrolled. ISEE required. Deadline for receipt of application materials: none. Application fee required: $35. On-campus interview required.

Athletics Interscholastic: basketball, crew, cross-country running, field hockey, gymnastics, lacrosse, softball, swimming and diving, tennis; intramural: crew, field hockey, lacrosse. 3 PE instructors, 6 coaches, 1 trainer.

Computers Computers are regularly used in all classes. Computer network features include campus e-mail, on-campus library services, CD-ROMs, online commercial services, Internet access.

Contact Sara Imbriglia, Director of Admissions. 412-661-4880. Fax: 412-661-7634. E-mail: admissions@theellisschool.org. Web site: www.theellisschool.org.

ELYRIA CATHOLIC HIGH SCHOOL

725 Gulf Road
Elyria, Ohio 44035-3697
Head of School: Mr. Andrew Krakowiak

General Information Coeducational day college-preparatory, general academic, arts, business, and religious studies school, affiliated with Roman Catholic Church. Grades 9–12. Founded: 1948. Setting: suburban. Nearest major city is Cleveland. 16-acre campus. 1 building on campus. Approved or accredited by North Central Association of Colleges and Schools, Ohio Catholic Schools Accreditation Association (OCSAA), and Ohio Department of Education. Total enrollment: 536. Upper school average class size: 24. Upper school faculty-student ratio: 1:14.

Upper School Student Profile Grade 9: 142 students (79 boys, 63 girls); Grade 10: 123 students (60 boys, 63 girls); Grade 11: 136 students (65 boys, 71 girls); Grade 12: 135 students (72 boys, 63 girls). 90% of students are Roman Catholic.

Faculty School total: 40. In upper school: 18 men, 15 women; 19 have advanced degrees.

Subjects Offered Accounting, advanced math, algebra, American government, American history, American history-AP, analysis of data, anatomy and physiology, art, band, biology, business, calculus, calculus-AP, campus ministry, Catholic belief and practice, chamber groups, chemistry, child development, choir, Christian and Hebrew scripture, Christian doctrine, Christian ethics, church history, computer applications, concert band, concert choir, current events, data analysis, drama, drama performance, earth science, English, fine arts, food and nutrition, French, French language-AP, geometry, German, health, history, honors English, industrial arts, introduction to theater, journalism, leadership, life issues, marching band, music appreciation, parent/child development, peer ministry, physical fitness, physics, prayer/spirituality, pre-calculus, psychology, reading/study skills, social justice, Spanish, Spanish language-AP, theater, world religions, yearbook.

Graduation Requirements Arts and fine arts (art, music, dance, drama), computers, English, mathematics, physical education (includes health), religion (includes Bible studies and theology), science, social studies (includes history), school and community service hours, Ohio Proficiency Test.

Special Academic Programs Advanced Placement exam preparation in 5 subject areas; honors section; study at local college for college credit; remedial reading and/or remedial writing; remedial math; special instructional classes for students with learning disabilities and Attention Deficit Disorder.

College Placement 127 students graduated in 2005; 124 went to college, including Bowling Green State University; Kent State University; Ohio University; The Ohio State University; The University of Toledo; University of Dayton. Other: 3 went to work. Mean SAT verbal: 570, mean SAT math: 557.

Student Life Upper grades have specified standards of dress, student council, honor system. Discipline rests primarily with faculty. Attendance at religious services is required.

Tuition and Aid Day student tuition: $5500. Tuition installment plan (monthly payment plans). Tuition reduction for siblings, merit scholarship grants, need-based scholarship grants, paying campus jobs available. In 2005–06, 24% of upper-school students received aid; total upper-school merit-scholarship money awarded: $20,000. Total amount of financial aid awarded in 2005–06: $200,000.

Admissions Traditional secondary-level entrance grade is 9. High School Placement Test (closed version) from Scholastic Testing Service required. Deadline for receipt of application materials: January 13. No application fee required. Interview recommended.

Athletics Interscholastic: baseball (boys), basketball (b,g), cross-country running (b,g), football (b), golf (b), ice hockey (b), soccer (b,g), softball (g), tennis (b,g), volleyball (g), wrestling (b); coed interscholastic: bowling, cheering, swimming and diving, track and field. 2 PE instructors, 47 coaches, 1 trainer.

Computers Computers are regularly used in business studies, journalism, newspaper, typing, word processing, yearbook classes. Computer resources include campus e-mail, on-campus library services, CD-ROMs, Internet access, office computer access.

Contact Mr. Michael Wisnor, Director of Admissions and Public Relations. 440-365-1821 Ext. 16. Fax: 440-365-7536. E-mail: echs_wisnor@leeca.org. Web site: www.elyriacatholic.com.

EMERSON HONORS HIGH SCHOOLS

4100 East Walnut Street
Orange, California 92869
Head of School: Dr. Glory Ludwick

General Information Coeducational boarding and day college-preparatory, general academic, and arts school. Boarding grades 7–12, day grades K–12. Founded: 1958. Setting: suburban. Nearest major city is Los Angeles. Students are housed in homes of host families. 5-acre campus. 8 buildings on campus. Approved or accredited by Western Association of Schools and Colleges and California Department of Education. Total enrollment: 170. Upper school average class size: 15. Upper school faculty-student ratio: 1:15.

Upper School Student Profile Grade 7: 16 students (8 boys, 8 girls); Grade 8: 13 students (8 boys, 5 girls); Grade 9: 11 students (9 boys, 2 girls); Grade 10: 7 students (3 boys, 4 girls); Grade 11: 15 students (5 boys, 10 girls); Grade 12: 12 students (5 boys, 7 girls). 20% of students are boarding students. 80% are state residents. 3 states are represented in upper school student body. 20% are international students. International students from China, Japan, Republic of Korea, and Viet Nam; 4 other countries represented in student body.

Faculty School total: 25. In upper school: 7 men, 6 women; 11 have advanced degrees.

Subjects Offered Acting, advanced chemistry, advanced math, advanced TOEFL/grammar, algebra, American government, American government-AP, American history-AP, analysis and differential calculus, anatomy, ancient world history, applied arts, applied music, Arabic, art, art and culture, art appreciation, art education, art history, Basic programming, biology, biology-AP, calculus, calculus-AP, cell biology, ceramics, chemistry, chemistry-AP, Chinese, civil war history, classical civilization, classical Greek literature, classical music, classics, clayworking, computer keyboarding, computer processing, computer programming, computer skills, concert band, contemporary art, contemporary history, creative drama, creative writing, cultural geography, current events, current history, drama workshop, drawing, earth science, economics and history, Egyptian history, English, English literature, ESL, fine arts, gardening, general math, geography, geometry, grammar, jazz band, library skills, Mandarin, math analysis, physics, physics-AP, pre-algebra, pre-calculus, reading, SAT preparation, science, Shakespeare, Spanish, TOEFL preparation, U.S. history, world history.

Graduation Requirements Art, English, foreign language, mathematics, music, physical education (includes health), science, social studies (includes history). Community service is required.

Special Academic Programs Advanced Placement exam preparation in 4 subject areas; honors section; accelerated programs; independent study; study at local college for college credit; academic accommodation for the gifted, the musically talented, and the artistically talented; ESL (20 students enrolled).

College Placement 14 students graduated in 2005; 12 went to college, including California State University, Fullerton; Chapman University; Fashion Institute of Technology; New York University; University of California, Los Angeles. Other: 1 went to work, 1 entered military service.

Student Life Upper grades have specified standards of dress, honor system. Discipline rests equally with students and faculty.

Summer Programs Remediation, enrichment, advancement, ESL, sports, art/fine arts, computer instruction programs offered; session focuses on continuation of year program with more electives; held on campus; accepts boys and girls; open to students from other schools. 60 students usually enrolled. 2006 schedule: June 19 to July 25. Application deadline: May 15.

Tuition and Aid Day student tuition: $9064; 7-day tuition and room/board: $20,000–$30,000. Tuition installment plan (monthly payment plans, individually arranged payment plans). Tuition reduction for siblings, need-based scholarship grants available. In 2005–06, 10% of upper-school students received aid. Total amount of financial aid awarded in 2005–06: $50,000.

Admissions Traditional secondary-level entrance grade is 10. For fall 2005, 100 students applied for upper-level admission, 80 were accepted, 75 enrolled. Achievement tests or any standardized test required. Deadline for receipt of application materials: none. Application fee required: $200. Interview required.

Athletics Coed Interscholastic: baseball, basketball, cross-country running, fitness, flag football, handball, kickball, physical fitness, soccer, softball. 1 PE instructor, 1 coach.

Computers Computers are regularly used in desktop publishing, yearbook classes. Computer resources include CD-ROMs, Internet access.

Contact Mrs. Cathie Peterson, Administration. 714-633-4774. E-mail: majelix@socal.rr.com. Web site: eldorado-emerson.org.

THE EMERY WEINER SCHOOL

9825 Stella Link
Houston, Texas 77025
Head of School: Mr. Stuart J. Dow

General Information Coeducational day college-preparatory and religious studies school, affiliated with Jewish faith. Grades 6–12. Setting: urban. 12-acre campus. 2 buildings on campus. Approved or accredited by Southern Association of Colleges and Schools and Texas Department of Education. Endowment: $15 million. Total enrollment: 371. Upper school average class size: 12. Upper school faculty-student ratio: 1:4.

Upper School Student Profile Grade 9: 36 students (19 boys, 17 girls); Grade 10: 43 students (21 boys, 22 girls); Grade 11: 34 students (11 boys, 23 girls); Grade 12: 40 students (18 boys, 22 girls).

Faculty School total: 35. In upper school: 23 have advanced degrees.

Subjects Offered Acting, advanced chemistry, advanced math, algebra, American Civil War, art, biology, biology-AP, calculus, calculus-AP, career/college preparation, ceramics, chemistry, chemistry-AP, civil war history, clayworking, college counseling, composition, composition-AP, computer applications, computer graphics, computer-aided design, constitutional history of U.S., crafts, debate, digital art, drama, drama performance, drawing, English, English-AP, foreign language, geometry, Hebrew, Hebrew scripture, history, history of religion, history-AP, honors English, honors U.S. history, Judaic studies, lab science, library, mathematics, mathematics-AP, media, newspaper, painting, physics, play production, play/screen writing, pottery, religion and culture, religious education, religious studies, SAT preparation, Spanish, Spanish-AP, student government, study skills, theater arts, theater design and production, U.S. history, U.S. history-AP, yearbook.

Graduation Requirements Arts, English, foreign language, history, Judaic studies, mathematics, physical education (includes health), science. Community service is required.

Special Academic Programs Advanced Placement exam preparation; honors section.

College Placement 39 students graduated in 2005; all went to college, including Emory University; Northwestern University; The University of Texas at Austin; The University of Texas at San Antonio; Tulane University; Vassar College. Median SAT verbal: 620, median SAT math: 620, median composite ACT: 26. 72% scored over 600 on SAT verbal, 59% scored over 600 on SAT math, 50% scored over 26 on composite ACT.

Student Life Upper grades have uniform requirement, student council, honor system. Discipline rests primarily with faculty. Attendance at religious services is required.

Tuition and Aid Day student tuition: $12,500. Tuition installment plan (monthly payment plans). Need-based scholarship grants available. In 2005–06, 20% of upper-school students received aid. Total amount of financial aid awarded in 2005–06: $204,067.

Admissions Traditional secondary-level entrance grade is 9. ISEE required. Application fee required: $100. Interview required.

Athletics Interscholastic: baseball (boys), basketball (b,g), football (b), golf (b), soccer (b,g), softball (g), tennis (b,g), track and field (b,g), volleyball (g); intramural: dance (g), golf (b,g); coed interscholastic: soccer; coed intramural: fencing, outdoor activities, outdoor adventure, outdoor education, outdoor recreation, outdoor skills. 1 PE instructor, 14 coaches.

Computers Computers are regularly used in Web site design classes. Computer network features include campus e-mail, on-campus library services, CD-ROMs, Internet access, wireless campus network, Adobe PageMaker, Adobe Photoshop, Microsoft Publisher, Word, Excel, PowerPoint.

Contact Mrs. Rosiland Ivie, Registrar. 832-204-5900 Ext. 106. Fax: 832-204-5910. Web site: www.emeryweiner.org.

ANNOUNCEMENT FROM THE SCHOOL Emery High School, a college-preparatory and Jewish community school, offers small class sizes, a strong advisory program, and highly qualified, caring faculty. In addition to the challenging dual-studies curriculum (general and Judaic studies), Emery provides a progressive, pluralistic environment that encourages students to take an active role in defining their community. Students also engage in experiential learning, including a 2-week Interim Term (involving unique course offerings and outdoor-education trips) and a 1-week, culturally oriented spring trip.

EMMA WILLARD SCHOOL

285 Pawling Avenue
Troy, New York 12180
Head of School: Ms. Trudy E. Hall

General Information Girls' boarding and day college-preparatory and arts school. Grades 9–PG. Founded: 1814. Setting: suburban. Nearest major city is Albany. Students are housed in single-sex dormitories. 137-acre campus. 23 buildings on campus. Approved or accredited by New York State Association of Independent Schools, The Association of Boarding Schools, and New York Department of Education. Member of National Association of Independent Schools and Secondary School Admission Test Board. Endowment: $91 million. Total enrollment: 318. Upper school average class size: 11. Upper school faculty-student ratio: 1:5.

Upper School Student Profile Grade 9: 66 students (66 girls); Grade 10: 101 students (101 girls); Grade 11: 79 students (79 girls); Grade 12: 70 students (70 girls); Postgraduate: 2 students (2 girls). 63% of students are boarding students. 53% are state residents. 25 states are represented in upper school student body. 19% are international students. International students from China, Ecuador, Japan, Republic of Korea, Taiwan, and United Kingdom; 13 other countries represented in student body.

Faculty School total: 62. In upper school: 18 men, 41 women; 49 have advanced degrees; 41 reside on campus.

Subjects Offered Advanced Placement courses, advanced studio art-AP, algebra, American history, American literature, ancient world history, art, art history, art history-AP, art-AP, ballet, bioethics, biology, biology-AP, calculus, calculus-AP, ceramics, chemistry, chemistry-AP, chorus, comparative government and politics-AP, computer programming, computer science, computer science-AP, conceptual physics, creative writing, dance, digital imaging, drama, drawing and design, driver education, economics, English, English literature, English literature and composition-AP, ESL, European history, expository writing, fiber arts, fine arts, forensic science, French, French language-AP, geometry, government and politics-AP, government-AP, government/civics, health and wellness, history, internship, Latin, Latin-AP, mathematics, medieval/Renaissance history, music, neuroscience, orchestra, photography, physical education, physics, physics-AP, poetry, practicum, pre-calculus, Russian, SAT preparation, science, social science, Spanish, Spanish language-AP, Spanish-AP, statistics, statistics-AP, studio art—AP, theater, trigonometry, U.S. history-AP, weaving, world history, world literature.

Graduation Requirements Arts and fine arts (art, music, dance, drama), computer science, English, foreign language, mathematics, physical education (includes health), science, social studies (includes history). Community service is required.

Special Academic Programs Advanced Placement exam preparation in 16 subject areas; independent study; term-away projects; study abroad; academic accommodation for the musically talented and the artistically talented (17 students enrolled).

College Placement 84 students graduated in 2005; all went to college, including Columbia College; Goucher College; Massachusetts Institute of Technology; Smith College; Union College; Washington University in St. Louis. Mean SAT verbal: 650, mean SAT math: 620. 72% scored over 600 on SAT verbal, 65% scored over 600 on SAT math.

Student Life Upper grades have specified standards of dress, student council, honor system. Discipline rests primarily with faculty.

Summer Programs Enrichment, computer instruction programs offered; session focuses on academic enrichment for grades 7-12; held on campus; accepts girls; open to students from other schools. 170 students usually enrolled. 2006 schedule: July 6 to August 15. Application deadline: June 1.

Tuition and Aid Day student tuition: $21,200; 7-day tuition and room/board: $33,750. Guaranteed tuition plan. Tuition installment plan (Key Tuition Payment Plan, monthly payment plans). Merit scholarship grants, need-based scholarship grants available. In 2005–06, 41% of upper-school students received aid; total upper-school merit-scholarship money awarded: $51,500. Total amount of financial aid awarded in 2005–06: $2,211,200.

Admissions Traditional secondary-level entrance grade is 9. For fall 2005, 317 students applied for upper-level admission, 175 were accepted, 99 enrolled. ERB, PSAT or SAT, SLEP, SSAT or TOEFL required. Deadline for receipt of application materials: February 15. Application fee required: $45. Interview recommended.

Athletics Interscholastic: aquatics, basketball, crew, cross-country running, diving, field hockey, lacrosse, rowing, soccer, softball, swimming and diving, tennis, track and field, volleyball; intramural: aerobics, aerobics/dance, ballet, basketball, dance, fitness, fitness walking, floor hockey, hiking/backpacking, jogging, martial arts, modern dance, outdoor activities, physical fitness, physical training, running, skiing (downhill), snowboarding, soccer, softball, strength & conditioning, swimming and diving, tennis, ultimate Frisbee, volleyball, water polo, weight training. 3 PE instructors, 2 coaches, 1 trainer.

Computers Computers are regularly used in all academic classes. Computer network features include campus e-mail, on-campus library services, CD-ROMs, online commercial services, Internet access, file transfer, office computer access, DVD, wireless campus network.

Contact Kent H. Jones, Director of Enrollment Management. 518-883-1320. Fax: 518-883-1805. E-mail: admissions@emmawillard.org. Web site: www.emmawillard.org.

See full description on page 776.

THE ENGLISH SCHOOL, KUWAIT

PO Box 379
Safat 13004, Kuwait
Head of School: Mr. John Allcott

General Information Coeducational day college-preparatory and general academic school. Ungraded, ages 3–13. Founded: 1953. Setting: suburban. Nearest major city is Kuwait City. 1 building on campus. Approved or accredited by Independent Schools Joint Council, Jamaica Independent Schools Association, and Kuwait Ministry of Education. Member of European Council of International Schools. Language of instruction: English. Total enrollment: 400. Upper school average class size: 20. Upper school faculty-student ratio: 1:19.

Faculty School total: 40.

Student Life Upper grades have uniform requirement, student council. Discipline rests primarily with faculty.

Tuition and Aid Day student tuition: 2120 Kuwaiti dinars. Tuition installment plan (individually arranged payment plans). Tuition reduction for siblings available.

Admissions Traditional secondary-level entrance age is 11. Any standardized test, English language or English proficiency required. Deadline for receipt of application materials: none. No application fee required. Interview recommended.

Athletics Interscholastic: cricket (boys), netball (g); coed interscholastic: aquatics, ball hockey, basketball, floor hockey, gymnastics, independent competitive sports, roller blading. 1 PE instructor.

Computers Computers are regularly used in all classes. Computer network features include campus e-mail, on-campus library services, CD-ROMs, Internet access, DVD.

Contact Mrs. Liz Brealy, Registrar. 965-5637206. Fax: 965-5637147. E-mail: registrar@tes.edu.kw. Web site: www.tes.edu.kw.

THE EPISCOPAL ACADEMY

376 North Latches Lane
Merion, Pennsylvania 19066-1797
Head of School: Mr. L. Hamilton Clark Jr.

General Information Coeducational day college-preparatory, arts, religious studies, and technology school, affiliated with Episcopal Church. Grades PK–12. Founded: 1785. Setting: suburban. Nearest major city is Philadelphia. 32-acre campus. 10 buildings on campus. Approved or accredited by Middle States Association of Colleges and Schools, Pennsylvania Association of Private Academic Schools, and Pennsylvania Department of Education. Member of National Association of Independent Schools and Secondary School Admission Test Board. Language of instruction: English. Endowment: $15 million. Total enrollment: 1,129. Upper school average class size: 16. Upper school faculty-student ratio: 1:7.

Upper School Student Profile Grade 9: 109 students (62 boys, 47 girls); Grade 10: 107 students (55 boys, 52 girls); Grade 11: 117 students (65 boys, 52 girls); Grade 12: 112 students (55 boys, 57 girls).

Faculty School total: 179. In upper school: 41 men, 38 women; 74 have advanced degrees.

Subjects Offered African history, algebra, American history, American history-AP, American literature, art, art history, Bible studies, biology, calculus, ceramics, chemistry, Chinese history, classical language, college counseling, computer art, computer graphics, computer information systems, computer programming, computer programming-AP, creative writing, drama, drawing, earth science, ecology, economics, English, English-AP, environmental science, ethics, European history, fine arts, French, French language-AP, French literature-AP, French studies, French-AP, geology, geometry, government and politics-AP, Greek, Greek culture, health and safety, history, Latin, Latin-AP, mathematics, mechanical drawing, modern world history, music, painting, photography, physical education, physics, physics-AP, pre-calculus, psychology, religion, religions, Russian history, science, senior project, social studies, Spanish, Spanish language-AP, Spanish literature, Spanish literature-AP, Spanish-AP, statistics-AP, studio art, studio art—AP, The 20th Century, theater history, theater production, theology, U.S. government and politics-AP, U.S. history,

U.S. history-AP, Vietnam history, visual and performing arts, vocal ensemble, vocal music, water polo, weight training, wood lab, woodworking, world cultures, world history, writing.

Graduation Requirements Arts and fine arts (art, music, dance, drama), English, foreign language, mathematics, physical education (includes health), religion (includes Bible studies and theology), science, senior project, social studies (includes history).

Special Academic Programs Advanced Placement exam preparation in 14 subject areas; honors section; independent study; study abroad.

College Placement 101 students graduated in 2004; all went to college, including Cornell University; Denison University; Duke University; Harvard University; The George Washington University; University of Pennsylvania. Mean SAT verbal: 650, mean SAT math: 660.

Student Life Upper grades have specified standards of dress, student council, honor system. Discipline rests primarily with faculty. Attendance at religious services is required.

Tuition and Aid Day student tuition: $19,900. Tuition installment plan (Key Tuition Payment Plan, 60% due August 15—remainder by February 1). Need-based scholarship grants available. In 2004–05, 14% of upper-school students received aid. Total amount of financial aid awarded in 2004–05: $1,700,000.

Admissions Traditional secondary-level entrance grade is 9. For fall 2005, 199 students applied for upper-level admission, 100 were accepted, 57 enrolled. ISEE or SSAT required. Deadline for receipt of application materials: December 31. Application fee required: $50. On-campus interview required.

Athletics Interscholastic: baseball (boys), basketball (b,g), crew (b,g), cross-country running (b,g), diving (b,g), field hockey (g), football (b), golf (b,g), indoor track (b,g), lacrosse (b,g), soccer (b,g), softball (g), squash (b,g), swimming and diving (b,g), tennis (b,g), track and field (b,g), winter (indoor) track (b,g); intramural: aerobics (g), floor hockey (b); coed interscholastic: ice hockey, water polo; coed intramural: basketball, fitness, fitness walking, football, Frisbee, squash, trap and skeet, weight lifting, weight training. 1 PE instructor, 2 trainers.

Computers Computers are regularly used in art, English, foreign language, history, science classes. Computer network features include campus e-mail, on-campus library services, CD-ROMs, Internet access.

Contact Ellen M. Hay, Director of Admission. 610-667-9612 Ext. 3002. Fax: 610-617-2262. E-mail: hay@ea1785.org.

See full description on page 778.

EPISCOPAL COLLEGIATE SCHOOL

1701 Cantrell Road
Little Rock, Arkansas 72201
Head of School: Dr. Mercer Neale

General Information Coeducational day college-preparatory, arts, and technology school, affiliated with Episcopal Church. Grades 6–12. Founded: 2000. Setting: suburban. Nearest major city is Dallas, TX. 10-acre campus. 3 buildings on campus. Approved or accredited by Southwest Association of Episcopal Schools. Endowment: $31 million. Total enrollment: 376. Upper school average class size: 14. Upper school faculty-student ratio: 1:9.

Upper School Student Profile Grade 9: 52 students (27 boys, 25 girls); Grade 10: 56 students (24 boys, 32 girls); Grade 11: 46 students (20 boys, 26 girls); Grade 12: 52 students (29 boys, 23 girls). 20% of students are members of Episcopal Church.

Faculty School total: 28. In upper school: 15 men, 13 women; 25 have advanced degrees.

Special Academic Programs Advanced Placement exam preparation in 16 subject areas; honors section.

College Placement 39 students graduated in 2005; all went to college, including University of Arkansas.

Student Life Upper grades have uniform requirement, student council, honor system. Discipline rests primarily with faculty. Attendance at religious services is required.

Summer Programs Enrichment, sports, art/fine arts, computer instruction programs offered; session focuses on enrichment; held on campus; accepts boys and girls; open to students from other schools. 30 students usually enrolled.

Tuition and Aid Day student tuition: $7820. Tuition installment plan (monthly payment plan, individually arranged payment plans). Need-based scholarship grants available. In 2005–06, 25% of upper-school students received aid. Total amount of financial aid awarded in 2005–06: $525,000.

Admissions Traditional secondary-level entrance grade is 9. Stanford 9 required. Deadline for receipt of application materials: none. Application fee required: $25. Interview required.

Athletics Interscholastic: baseball (boys), basketball (b,g), cheering (g), fitness (b,g), football (b), golf (b,g), physical fitness (b,g), physical training (b,g), soccer (b,g), softball (g), tennis (b,g), track and field (b,g), volleyball (g), weight training (b,g). 2 PE instructors, 8 coaches, 1 trainer.

Computers Computer network features include on-campus library services, CD-ROMs, online commercial services, Internet access, DVD.

Contact Ms. Ashley Honeywell, Director of Admission. 501-372-1194 Ext. 406. Fax: 501-537-0259. E-mail: ahoneywell@episcopalcollegiate.org. Web site: www.episcopalcollegiate.org.

EPISCOPAL HIGH SCHOOL

4650 Bissonnet
Bellaire, Texas 77401
Head of School: Mr. Edward C. Becker

General Information Coeducational day college-preparatory, arts, religious studies, and technology school, affiliated with Episcopal Church. Grades 9–12. Founded: 1984. Setting: urban. Nearest major city is Houston. 35-acre campus. 7 buildings on campus. Approved or accredited by Association for Experiential Education, Independent Schools Association of the Southwest, and Texas Department of Education. Member of National Association of Independent Schools and Secondary School Admission Test Board. Total enrollment: 621. Upper school average class size: 18. Upper school faculty-student ratio: 1:9.

Upper School Student Profile Grade 9: 170 students (82 boys, 88 girls); Grade 10: 139 students (67 boys, 72 girls); Grade 11: 172 students (96 boys, 76 girls); Grade 12: 140 students (66 boys, 74 girls). 28% of students are members of Episcopal Church.

Faculty School total: 93. In upper school: 40 men, 53 women; 50 have advanced degrees.

Subjects Offered Acting, algebra, anatomy, ancient history, art appreciation, art history, band, Bible studies, biology, biology-AP, calculus-AP, ceramics, chemistry, choir, civil rights, dance, debate, design, drawing, English, English-AP, ethics, European history, French, French-AP, geography, geology, geometry, government, government-AP, graphic design, health, history of science, instrumental music, journalism, Latin, Latin American studies, music theory, newspaper, oceanography, orchestra, painting, photography, physical education, physics, physics-AP, physiology, pre-calculus, sculpture, Spanish, Spanish-AP, speech, stagecraft, statistics, theater, theology, U.S. history, U.S. history-AP, video film production, Vietnam War, world religions, World War II, writing, yearbook.

Graduation Requirements Arts and fine arts (art, music, dance, drama), English, foreign language, mathematics, physical education (includes health), religion (includes Bible studies and theology), religious studies, science, social studies (includes history).

Special Academic Programs Advanced Placement exam preparation in 9 subject areas; honors section; independent study; study at local college for college credit.

College Placement 141 students graduated in 2005; all went to college, including Louisiana State University and Agricultural and Mechanical College; Southern Methodist University; Texas Christian University; The University of Texas at Austin. Median SAT verbal: 584, median SAT math: 594.

Student Life Upper grades have uniform requirement, student council, honor system. Discipline rests equally with students and faculty. Attendance at religious services is required.

Summer Programs Remediation, enrichment, art/fine arts programs offered; session focuses on enrichment and remediation; held on campus; accepts boys and girls; open to students from other schools. 275 students usually enrolled. 2006 schedule: June 5 to July 14. Application deadline: May 8.

Tuition and Aid Day student tuition: $16,382. Tuition installment plan (Insured Tuition Payment Plan, SMART Tuition Payment Plan, monthly payment plans). Need-based scholarship grants, middle-income loans available. In 2005–06, 18% of upper-school students received aid. Total amount of financial aid awarded in 2005–06: $1,250,000.

Admissions Traditional secondary-level entrance grade is 9. For fall 2005, 382 students applied for upper-level admission, 296 were accepted, 182 enrolled. ISEE and Otis-Lennon Ability or Stanford Achievement Test required. Deadline for receipt of application materials: January 9. Application fee required: $50. On-campus interview required.

Athletics Interscholastic: ballet (boys, girls), baseball (b), basketball (b,g), cheering (b,g), cross-country running (b,g), dance (b,g), field hockey (b,g), football (b), golf (b,g), lacrosse (b,g), running (b,g), softball (g), strength & conditioning (b,g), swimming and diving (b,g), tennis (b,g), track and field (b,g), volleyball (b,g), weight training (b,g), winter soccer (b,g), wrestling (b). 7 PE instructors, 6 coaches, 1 trainer.

Computers Computers are regularly used in art, English, foreign language, history, mathematics, music, religion, science classes. Computer network features include campus e-mail, on-campus library services, CD-ROMs, online commercial services, Internet access, wireless campus network, CollegeView.

Contact Audrey Koehler, Director of Admission. 713-512-3400. Fax: 713-512-3603. E-mail: kpiper@ehshouston.org. Web site: www.ehshouston.org/.

EPISCOPAL HIGH SCHOOL

1200 North Quaker Lane
Alexandria, Virginia 22302
Head of School: F. Robertson Hershey

General Information Coeducational boarding college-preparatory, arts, religious studies, and technology school, affiliated with Episcopal Church. Grades 9–12. Founded: 1839. Setting: urban. Nearest major city is Washington, DC. Students are housed in single-sex dormitories. 135-acre campus. 26 buildings on campus. Approved or accredited by Southern Association of Colleges and Schools, Virginia Association of Independent Schools, and Virginia Department of Education. Member of National Association of Independent Schools and Secondary School Admission Test

Episcopal High School

Board. Endowment: $123 million. Total enrollment: 444. Upper school average class size: 11. Upper school faculty-student ratio: 1:7.

Upper School Student Profile Grade 9: 95 students (54 boys, 41 girls); Grade 10: 112 students (63 boys, 49 girls); Grade 11: 112 students (59 boys, 53 girls); Grade 12: 125 students (68 boys, 57 girls). 100% of students are boarding students. 29% are state residents. 30 states are represented in upper school student body. 7% are international students. International students from Bermuda, China, Jamaica, Republic of Korea, Saudi Arabia, and Zimbabwe; 12 other countries represented in student body. 25% of students are members of Episcopal Church.

Faculty School total: 63. In upper school: 40 men, 23 women; 46 have advanced degrees; 54 reside on campus.

Subjects Offered Advanced chemistry, advanced math, advanced studio art-AP, algebra, American history, American literature, art, art history, art-AP, astronomy, biology, biology-AP, calculus, calculus-AP, ceramics, chemistry, chemistry-AP, Chinese, choir, composition-AP, computer programming, computer programming-AP, computer science, computer science-AP, creative writing, dance, drama, economics, economics-AP, English, English literature, English literature and composition-AP, English literature-AP, English-AP, English/composition-AP, environmental science, environmental science-AP, ethics, European history, European history-AP, fine arts, French, French language-AP, French literature-AP, geometry, German, German-AP, government-AP, government/civics, Greek, history, honors algebra, honors English, honors geometry, honors U.S. history, honors world history, international relations, international relations-AP, Latin, Latin-AP, mathematics, microeconomics-AP, Middle Eastern history, modern European history-AP, music, music theory-AP, photography, physical education, physics, physics-AP, pre-calculus, psychology-AP, religion, science, senior internship, Shakespeare, social science, social studies, Spanish, Spanish literature-AP, statistics-AP, theater, theology, trigonometry, U.S. history-AP, world history, world history-AP, writing.

Graduation Requirements Arts and fine arts (art, music, dance, drama), computer studies, English, foreign language, mathematics, physical education (includes health), science, social studies (includes history), theology.

Special Academic Programs Advanced Placement exam preparation in 19 subject areas; honors section; independent study; term-away projects; study abroad; academic accommodation for the gifted, the musically talented, and the artistically talented.

College Placement 101 students graduated in 2005; all went to college, including Duke University; The University of North Carolina at Chapel Hill; Trinity College; University of the South; University of Virginia; Washington and Lee University. Mean SAT verbal: 629, mean SAT math: 647. 65% scored over 600 on SAT verbal, 75% scored over 600 on SAT math.

Student Life Upper grades have specified standards of dress, student council, honor system. Discipline rests primarily with faculty. Attendance at religious services is required.

Tuition and Aid 7-day tuition and room/board: $33,300. Tuition installment plan (Insured Tuition Payment Plan, monthly payment plans). Merit scholarship grants, need-based scholarship grants, need-based loans, paying campus jobs available. In 2005–06, 30% of upper-school students received aid; total upper-school merit-scholarship money awarded: $127,000. Total amount of financial aid awarded in 2005–06: $2,700,000.

Admissions Traditional secondary-level entrance grade is 9. For fall 2005, 636 students applied for upper-level admission, 270 were accepted, 157 enrolled. ISEE, PSAT or SAT or SSAT required. Deadline for receipt of application materials: January 31. Application fee required: $50. Interview required.

Athletics Interscholastic: baseball (boys), basketball (b,g), crew (g), cross-country running (b,g), field hockey (g), football (b), golf (b), indoor soccer (g), indoor track & field (b,g), lacrosse (b,g), rowing (g), soccer (b,g), softball (g), squash (b,g), tennis (b,g), track and field (b,g), volleyball (g); intramural: soccer (b), strength & conditioning (b,g); coed interscholastic: aerobics, aerobics/dance, aerobics/nautilus, back packing, ballet, canoeing/kayaking, cheering, climbing, dance, fitness, hiking/backpacking, kayaking, rock climbing; coed intramural: ballet, fitness, modern dance, outdoor activities, outdoor adventure, outdoor education, outdoor recreation, outdoor skills, outdoors, physical fitness, physical training, power lifting, wall climbing, weight lifting, weight training. 4 coaches, 1 trainer.

Computers Computers are regularly used in all academic classes. Computer network features include campus e-mail, on-campus library services, CD-ROMs, online commercial services, Internet access, file transfer, office computer access, DVD.

Contact Douglas C. Price, Director of Admission. 703-933-4062. Fax: 703-933-3016. E-mail: admissions@episcopalhighschool.org. Web site: www.episcopalhighschool.org.

See full description on page 780.

EPISCOPAL HIGH SCHOOL OF JACKSONVILLE

4455 Atlantic Boulevard
Jacksonville, Florida 32207
Head of School: Charles F. Zimmer

petersons.com

General Information Coeducational day college-preparatory, arts, religious studies, and technology school, affiliated with Episcopal Church. Grades 6–12. Founded: 1966. Setting: urban. 58-acre campus. 25 buildings on campus. Approved or accredited by Florida Council of Independent Schools and Southern Association of Colleges and Schools. Member of National Association of Independent Schools. Endowment: $4.6 million. Total enrollment: 891. Upper school average class size: 17. Upper school faculty-student ratio: 1:11.

Upper School Student Profile Grade 9: 150 students (79 boys, 71 girls); Grade 10: 136 students (69 boys, 67 girls); Grade 11: 144 students (82 boys, 62 girls); Grade 12: 131 students (71 boys, 60 girls). 26% of students are members of Episcopal Church.

Faculty School total: 88. In upper school: 36 men, 52 women; 50 have advanced degrees.

Subjects Offered Algebra, American history, American literature, ancient history, art, art history, band, biology, calculus, ceramics, chemistry, computer programming, computer science, dance, drama, earth science, economics, English, English literature, environmental science, European history, fine arts, French, general science, geography, geometry, German, government/civics, health, history, journalism, Latin, marine biology, mathematics, medieval/Renaissance history, music, music history, music theory, photography, physical education, physics, political science, psychology, religion, science, social studies, Spanish, speech, statistics, theater, trigonometry, world history, writing, yearbook.

Graduation Requirements Arts and fine arts (art, music, dance, drama), computer science, English, foreign language, leadership, library skills, mathematics, physical education (includes health), religion (includes Bible studies and theology), science, social studies (includes history). Community service is required.

Special Academic Programs Advanced Placement exam preparation in 13 subject areas; honors section; study abroad.

College Placement 137 students graduated in 2004; 136 went to college, including Boston University; Florida State University; University of Florida; University of North Florida; University of Notre Dame. Other: 1 had other specific plans. Mean SAT verbal: 599, mean SAT math: 604, mean composite ACT: 24. 44% scored over 600 on SAT verbal, 64% scored over 600 on SAT math, 32% scored over 26 on composite ACT.

Student Life Upper grades have specified standards of dress, student council, honor system. Discipline rests equally with students and faculty. Attendance at religious services is required.

Tuition and Aid Day student tuition: $12,900. Tuition installment plan (Insured Tuition Payment Plan, monthly payment plans). Merit scholarship grants, need-based scholarship grants available. In 2004–05, 11% of upper-school students received aid; total upper-school merit-scholarship money awarded: $22,450. Total amount of financial aid awarded in 2004–05: $681,152.

Admissions Traditional secondary-level entrance grade is 9. For fall 2005, 103 students applied for upper-level admission, 65 were accepted, 45 enrolled. ISEE required. Deadline for receipt of application materials: none. Application fee required: $50. On-campus interview required.

Athletics Interscholastic: baseball (boys), basketball (b,g), crew (b,g), cross-country running (b,g), football (b), golf (b,g), lacrosse (b), modern dance (b,g), soccer (b,g), softball (g), swimming and diving (b,g), tennis (b,g), track and field (b,g), volleyball (g), weight lifting (b), weight training (b), wrestling (b); intramural: dance (g); coed interscholastic: cheering, dance, dance squad, dance team. 6 PE instructors, 55 coaches, 2 trainers.

Computers Computers are regularly used in accounting, all classes. Computer network features include campus e-mail, on-campus library services, CD-ROMs, online commercial services, Internet access, file transfer.

Contact Peggy P. Fox, Director of Admissions. 904-396-5751 Ext. 221. Fax: 904-396-0981. E-mail: foxp@episcopalhigh.org. Web site: www.episcopalhigh.org.

THE EPISCOPAL SCHOOL OF ACADIANA

PO Box 380
Cade, Louisiana 70519
Head of School: Mr. Christopher H. Taylor

General Information Coeducational day college-preparatory and arts school, affiliated with Episcopal Church. Grades PK–12. Founded: 1979. Setting: rural.

Nearest major city is Lafayette. 75-acre campus. 15 buildings on campus. Approved or accredited by Independent Schools Association of the Southwest, National Association of Episcopal Schools, and Louisiana Department of Education. Member of National Association of Independent Schools. Endowment: $265,000. Total enrollment: 458. Upper school average class size: 10. Upper school faculty-student ratio: 1:6.

Upper School Student Profile Grade 9: 64 students (28 boys, 36 girls); Grade 10: 51 students (31 boys, 20 girls); Grade 11: 44 students (17 boys, 27 girls); Grade 12: 37 students (18 boys, 19 girls). 22% of students are members of Episcopal Church.

Faculty School total: 58. In upper school: 16 men, 12 women; 14 have advanced degrees.

Subjects Offered Advanced chemistry, algebra, American history, American history-AP, American literature, architectural drawing, art, biology, biology-AP, calculus, calculus-AP, ceramics, chemistry, chemistry-AP, civics, computer programming, computer science, drama, drawing, earth science, English, English literature, environmental science, fine arts, French, French language-AP, French-AP, geography, geometry, government/civics, grammar, honors English, honors geometry, interpersonal skills, mathematics, music, photography, physical education, physics, pre-calculus, public speaking, reading, science, social studies, speech, studio art, U.S. history, Western civilization, Western civilization-AP, world history, writing.

Graduation Requirements Algebra, American history, American literature, arts and fine arts (art, music, dance, drama), biology, British literature, British literature (honors), chemistry, computer science, electives, English, foreign language, geometry, mathematics, physical education (includes health), physics, pre-calculus, Western civilization.

Special Academic Programs Advanced Placement exam preparation in 14 subject areas; honors section; independent study; academic accommodation for the gifted; programs in general development for dyslexic students.

College Placement 40 students graduated in 2005; all went to college, including Emory University; Louisiana State University and Agricultural and Mechanical College; Texas A&M University; Tulane University; University of Louisiana at Lafayette; Vanderbilt University. Median SAT verbal: 625, median SAT math: 640, median composite ACT: 28. 72% scored over 600 on SAT verbal, 72% scored over 600 on SAT math, 75% scored over 26 on composite ACT.

Student Life Upper grades have specified standards of dress, student council, honor system. Discipline rests equally with students and faculty. Attendance at religious services is required.

Summer Programs Remediation, enrichment, advancement, sports programs offered; session focuses on study skills, readiness, enrichment, and academic credit; held on campus; accepts boys and girls; not open to students from other schools. 43 students usually enrolled.

Tuition and Aid Day student tuition: $10,150. Tuition installment plan (monthly payment plans, 2-payment plan, 4-payment plan). Merit scholarship grants, need-based scholarship grants, faculty tuition remission available. In 2005–06, 18% of upper-school students received aid; total upper-school merit-scholarship money awarded: $36,400. Total amount of financial aid awarded in 2005–06: $115,590.

Admissions Traditional secondary-level entrance grade is 9. For fall 2005, 12 students applied for upper-level admission, 10 were accepted, 9 enrolled. ACT, ACT-Explore, ERB, Otis-Lennon Mental Ability Test, PSAT or SAT, SSAT, ERB, PSAT, SAT, PLAN or ACT or writing sample required. Deadline for receipt of application materials: none. Application fee required: $50. On-campus interview required.

Athletics Interscholastic: baseball (boys), basketball (b), cheering (g), cross-country running (b,g), indoor track & field (b,g), rugby (b), soccer (b,g), swimming and diving (b,g), tennis (b,g), track and field (b,g), volleyball (g); coed interscholastic: golf, outdoor adventure; coed intramural: back packing, fly fishing. 5 PE instructors.

Computers Computers are regularly used in all academic, art classes. Computer network features include campus e-mail, on-campus library services, CD-ROMs, online commercial services, Internet access, DVD, wireless campus network, university library link.

Contact Director of Admissions. 337-365-1416. Fax: 337-367-9841. E-mail: adbroussard@esacadiana.com. Web site: www.ESAcadiana.com.

THE EPISCOPAL SCHOOL OF DALLAS

4100 Merrell Road
Dallas, Texas 75229
Head of School: Rev. Stephen B. Swann

petersons.com

General Information Coeducational day college-preparatory, arts, religious studies, and technology school, affiliated with Episcopal Church. Grades PK–12. Founded: 1974. Setting: suburban. 36-acre campus. 5 buildings on campus. Approved or accredited by Independent Schools Association of the Southwest, National Association of Episcopal Schools, National Independent Private Schools Association, Southwest Association of Episcopal Schools, Texas Education Agency, and Texas Department of Education. Member of National Association of Independent Schools and Secondary School Admission Test Board. Languages of instruction: English, Spanish, and French. Endowment: $17.5 million. Total enrollment: 1,138. Upper school average class size: 15. Upper school faculty-student ratio: 1:8.

Upper School Student Profile Grade 9: 96 students (47 boys, 49 girls); Grade 10: 105 students (54 boys, 51 girls); Grade 11: 98 students (40 boys, 58 girls); Grade 12: 97 students (45 boys, 52 girls). 38% of students are members of Episcopal Church.

Faculty School total: 160. In upper school: 33 men, 99 women; 64 have advanced degrees.

Subjects Offered Advanced Placement courses, algebra, American history, anatomy, art, art history, biology, calculus, chemistry, chorus, community service, computer math, computer science, creative writing, drama, earth science, ecology, economics, English, environmental science, ethics, European history, fine arts, French, geometry, government/civics, health, instrumental music, international relations, journalism, Latin, mathematics, Middle Eastern history, music, photography, physical education, physics, political science, pre-calculus, religion, science, social studies, Spanish, speech, theater, trigonometry, world history, world literature, writing.

Graduation Requirements Arts and fine arts (art, music, dance, drama), computer science, economics, English, foreign language, government, mathematics, physical education (includes health), religion (includes Bible studies and theology), science, social studies (includes history), participation in wilderness program. Community service is required.

Special Academic Programs Advanced Placement exam preparation in 18 subject areas; honors section; independent study.

College Placement 92 students graduated in 2005; all went to college, including Baylor University; Emory University; Southern Methodist University; Texas A&M University; The University of Texas at Austin; Vanderbilt University. 67% scored over 600 on SAT verbal, 70% scored over 600 on SAT math, 56% scored over 26 on composite ACT.

Student Life Upper grades have uniform requirement, student council, honor system. Discipline rests equally with students and faculty. Attendance at religious services is required.

Summer Programs Enrichment, advancement, sports, art/fine arts, rigorous outdoor training, computer instruction programs offered; held both on and off campus; held at Wolf Run Outdoor Education Center; accepts boys and girls; open to students from other schools. 200 students usually enrolled. 2006 schedule: June to August. Application deadline: May.

Tuition and Aid Day student tuition: $18,200. Tuition installment plan (Insured Tuition Payment Plan, monthly payment plans). Need-based scholarship grants available. In 2005–06, 10% of upper-school students received aid. Total amount of financial aid awarded in 2005–06: $1,100,000.

Admissions Traditional secondary-level entrance grade is 9. For fall 2005, 117 students applied for upper-level admission, 78 were accepted, 26 enrolled. ISEE, SLEP for foreign students, SSAT or writing sample required. Deadline for receipt of application materials: January 20. Application fee required: $175. On-campus interview required.

Athletics Interscholastic: baseball (boys), basketball (b,g), cheering (g), crew (b,g), cross-country running (b,g), field hockey (g), football (b), golf (b,g), hockey (g), ice hockey (b), lacrosse (b,g), outdoor education (b,g), rowing (b,g), soccer (b,g), softball (g), tennis (b,g), track and field (b,g), volleyball (b,g); coed interscholastic: crew. 2 PE instructors, 32 coaches, 2 trainers.

Computers Computers are regularly used in English, mathematics, science classes. Computer network features include campus e-mail, on-campus library services, CD-ROMs, online commercial services, Internet access, file transfer, office computer access.

Contact Ruth Burke, Director of Admission and Financial Aid. 214-353-5827. Fax: 214-353-5872. E-mail: burker@esdallas.org. Web site: www.esdallas.org.

ANNOUNCEMENT FROM THE SCHOOL The Episcopal School of Dallas (ESD) is a faith-centered, coeducational, college-preparatory school whose mission is to educate young people having a variety of backgrounds and aptitudes. ESD provides a challenging, traditional curriculum along with community service, outdoor education, and a low student to teacher ratio. Activities include athletics, fine arts, publications, and special-interest clubs. The School's Headmaster is the Reverend Stephen B. Swann.

EQUILIBRIUM INTERNATIONAL EDUCATION INSTITUTE

707-14 Street, NW
Calgary, Alberta T2N 2A4, Canada
Head of School: Mrs. Anna Jankowska

General Information Coeducational day college-preparatory, general academic, arts, and business school. Grades 10–12. Founded: 1993. Setting: urban. 1-acre campus. 1 building on campus. Approved or accredited by Alberta Department of Education. Language of instruction: English. Total enrollment: 100. Upper school average class size: 9. Upper school faculty-student ratio: 1:15.

Upper School Student Profile Grade 10: 40 students (20 boys, 20 girls); Grade 11: 30 students (15 boys, 15 girls); Grade 12: 30 students (15 boys, 15 girls).

Faculty School total: 14. In upper school: 4 men, 10 women; 3 have advanced degrees.

Graduation Requirements Arts, computers, English, mathematics, physical education (includes health), science, social studies (includes history).

Equilibrium International Education Institute

Special Academic Programs Accelerated programs; independent study; term-away projects; special instructional classes for deaf students, blind students; ESL.

College Placement 8 students graduated in 2005; 6 went to college, including University of Calgary; University of Toronto. Other: 2 went to work.

Student Life Upper grades have student council, honor system. Discipline rests equally with students and faculty.

Tuition and Aid Day student tuition: CAN$3200. Guaranteed tuition plan. Bursaries available. In 2005–06, 5% of upper-school students received aid.

Admissions Traditional secondary-level entrance grade is 10. For fall 2005, 120 students applied for upper-level admission, 100 were accepted, 100 enrolled. Admissions testing required. Deadline for receipt of application materials: none. Application fee required: CAN$100.

Athletics Coed Interscholastic: baseball, basketball, cooperative games, fitness, outdoors, paint ball, skiing (downhill), snowboarding, soccer, swimming and diving, table tennis. 1 PE instructor.

Computers Computer network features include campus e-mail, CD-ROMs, Internet access.

Contact Mrs. Kasia M. Bluhm, Office Administrator. 403-283-1111. Fax: 403-270-7786. E-mail: school@equilibrium.ab.ca. Web site: www.equilibrium.ab.ca.

ESCOLA AMERICANA DE CAMPINAS

PO Box 978
Campinas-SP 13012-970, Brazil
Head of School: Stephen A. Herrera

General Information Coeducational day college-preparatory, arts, and bilingual studies school. Grades PK–12. Founded: 1956. Setting: urban. Nearest major city is Sao Paulo. 4-acre campus. 4 buildings on campus. Approved or accredited by Association of American Schools in South America and Southern Association of Colleges and Schools. Member of European Council of International Schools. Languages of instruction: English and Portuguese. Endowment: $350,000. Total enrollment: 468. Upper school average class size: 20. Upper school faculty-student ratio: 1:7.

Upper School Student Profile Grade 9: 19 students (10 boys, 9 girls); Grade 10: 22 students (8 boys, 14 girls); Grade 11: 25 students (12 boys, 13 girls); Grade 12: 28 students (11 boys, 17 girls).

Faculty School total: 60. In upper school: 8 men, 14 women; 10 have advanced degrees.

Subjects Offered Algebra, American history, American literature, art, biology, calculus, chemistry, computer science, creative writing, drama, economics, English, English literature, fine arts, geography, geometry, government/civics, grammar, history, journalism, mathematics, music, physical education, physics, Portuguese, psychology, science, social studies, speech, trigonometry, world history, world literature, writing.

Graduation Requirements Arts and fine arts (art, music, dance, drama), computer science, English, foreign language, mathematics, physical education (includes health), science, social studies (includes history). Community service is required.

Special Academic Programs Advanced Placement exam preparation in 5 subject areas; honors section; term-away projects; study at local college for college credit; study abroad; special instructional classes for students with mild learning differences; ESL (22 students enrolled).

College Placement 18 students graduated in 2005; 13 went to college, including Bentley College; Florida Institute of Technology; Vassar College; Webster University; Yale University. Other: 5 had other specific plans. Median SAT verbal: 575, median SAT math: 610. 36% scored over 600 on SAT verbal, 64% scored over 600 on SAT math.

Student Life Upper grades have student council, honor system. Discipline rests equally with students and faculty.

Tuition and Aid Day student tuition: $3100–$5107. Tuition installment plan (monthly payment plans). Need-based scholarship grants available. In 2005–06, 10% of upper-school students received aid. Total amount of financial aid awarded in 2005–06: $113,213.

Admissions Traditional secondary-level entrance grade is 9. For fall 2005, 30 students applied for upper-level admission, 19 were accepted, 17 enrolled. Iowa Tests of Basic Skills, school's own exam and TAP required. Deadline for receipt of application materials: none. No application fee required. On-campus interview recommended.

Athletics Interscholastic: basketball (boys, girls), canoeing/kayaking (g), cheering (g), indoor soccer (b,g), soccer (b,g), volleyball (g); intramural: ballet (g), basketball (b,g), canoeing/kayaking (g), cheering (g), climbing (b,g), indoor soccer (b,g), soccer (b,g); coed intramural: aerobics, baseball, basketball, climbing, cooperative games, fitness, flag football, Frisbee, gymnastics, handball, indoor soccer, jogging, judo, kickball, martial arts, physical fitness, self defense, soccer, softball, strength & conditioning, table tennis, track and field, ultimate Frisbee, volleyball. 3 PE instructors, 9 coaches.

Computers Computers are regularly used in art, English, history, independent study, mathematics, science, yearbook classes. Computer network features include campus e-mail, on-campus library services, CD-ROMs, online commercial services, Internet access, office computer access, DVD.

Contact Davi Sanchez, High School Principal. 55-19-2102-1006. Fax: 55-19-2102-1016. E-mail: davi_sanchez@eac.com.br. Web site: www.eac.com.br.

THE ETHEL WALKER SCHOOL

230 Bushy Hill Road
Simsbury, Connecticut 06070
Head of School: Ms. Susanna A. Jones

General Information Girls' boarding and day college-preparatory and arts school. Boarding grades 9–12, day grades 6–12. Founded: 1911. Setting: suburban. Nearest major city is Hartford. Students are housed in single-sex dormitories. 600-acre campus. 9 buildings on campus. Approved or accredited by Association of Independent Schools in New England, Connecticut Association of Independent Schools, New England Association of Schools and Colleges, The Association of Boarding Schools, and Connecticut Department of Education. Member of National Association of Independent Schools and Secondary School Admission Test Board. Endowment: $10.5 million. Total enrollment: 243. Upper school average class size: 10. Upper school faculty-student ratio: 1:5.

Upper School Student Profile Grade 9: 52 students (52 girls); Grade 10: 38 students (38 girls); Grade 11: 56 students (56 girls); Grade 12: 37 students (37 girls). 52% of students are boarding students. 51% are state residents. 16 states are represented in upper school student body. 13% are international students. International students from Bermuda, El Salvador, Japan, Panama, Republic of Korea, and Spain; 3 other countries represented in student body.

Faculty School total: 50. In upper school: 13 men, 37 women; 40 have advanced degrees; 17 reside on campus.

Subjects Offered African drumming, algebra, American history, American literature, art, art history, Asian history, astronomy, ballet, bell choir, biology, calculus, calculus-AP, ceramics, chemistry, chemistry-AP, choir, choreography, college counseling, community service, computer science, computer science-AP, concert choir, creative writing, dance, dance performance, drama, drawing and design, driver education, earth science, English, English literature, English literature and composition-AP, environmental science, environmental science-AP, equestrian sports, ethics, ethics and responsibility, European history, fine arts, French, French language-AP, geography, geometry, health, history, history-AP, honors algebra, independent study, instrumental music, Latin, Latin American history, Latin-AP, mathematics, modern European history, music, music theory, musical theater, newspaper, peer counseling, personal fitness, photography, physical education, physics, poetry, pre-calculus, psychology-AP, SAT/ACT preparation, science, science project, science research, sculpture, senior project, set design, social science, Spanish, Spanish language-AP, Spanish literature-AP, Spanish-AP, student publications, studio art-AP, tap dance, the Web, trigonometry, U.S. history-AP, visual and performing arts, voice, women's health, world history, world literature, writing, yearbook.

Graduation Requirements Arts and fine arts (art, music, dance, drama), English, ethics, foreign language, history, leadership training, mathematics, physical education (includes health), science, women's health, junior/senior project. Community service is required.

Special Academic Programs Advanced Placement exam preparation in 17 subject areas; honors section; independent study; term-away projects; study at local college for college credit; study abroad; academic accommodation for the gifted, the musically talented, and the artistically talented.

College Placement 37 students graduated in 2005; 36 went to college, including Bates College; Boston University; Skidmore College; Trinity College; Vassar College; Villanova University. Other: 1 entered a postgraduate year. Mean SAT verbal: 570, mean SAT math: 570.

Student Life Upper grades have specified standards of dress, student council, honor system. Discipline rests equally with students and faculty.

Tuition and Aid Day student tuition: $25,900; 7-day tuition and room/board: $36,200. Tuition installment plan (monthly payment plans, individually arranged payment plans, 1-, 2-, and 10-payment plans). Tuition reduction for siblings, need-based scholarship grants available. In 2005–06, 40% of upper-school students received aid. Total amount of financial aid awarded in 2005–06: $2,000,000.

Admissions Traditional secondary-level entrance grade is 9. For fall 2005, 285 students applied for upper-level admission, 158 were accepted, 89 enrolled. SSAT required. Deadline for receipt of application materials: February 1. Application fee required: $60. On-campus interview required.

Athletics Interscholastic: basketball, dressage, equestrian sports, field hockey, horseback riding, lacrosse, soccer, softball, tennis, volleyball; intramural: aerobics, aerobics/dance, aerobics/nautilus, ballet, climbing, dance, dance team, equestrian sports, fitness, hiking/backpacking, judo, modern dance, mountaineering, outdoor activities, outdoor adventure, physical fitness, rock climbing, strength & conditioning, wall climbing. 2 PE instructors, 11 coaches, 1 trainer.

Computers Computers are regularly used in English, foreign language, graphic design, history, mathematics, photography, science classes. Computer network features include campus e-mail, on-campus library services, CD-ROMs, online commercial services, Internet access, DVD, Apple Share, Local Talk/Ethernet.

Contact Ms. Barbara J. Lundberg, Dean of Enrollment Management. 860-408-4200. Fax: 860-408-4201. E-mail: barb_lundberg@ethelwalker.org. Web site: www. ethelwalker.org.

THE ETHICAL CULTURE FIELDSTON SCHOOL

Fieldston Road
Bronx, New York 10471
Head of School: Joseph P. Healey, PhD

General Information Coeducational day college-preparatory and arts school. Grades PK–12. Founded: 1878. Setting: urban. Nearest major city is New York. 19-acre campus. 10 buildings on campus. Approved or accredited by New York State Association of Independent Schools and New York Department of Education. Member of National Association of Independent Schools. Endowment: $47.5 million. Total enrollment: 1,608. Upper school average class size: 18. Upper school faculty-student ratio: 1:10.

Upper School Student Profile Grade 9: 139 students (79 boys, 60 girls); Grade 10: 137 students (60 boys, 77 girls); Grade 11: 127 students (55 boys, 72 girls); Grade 12: 129 students (70 boys, 59 girls).

Faculty School total: 241. In upper school: 55 men, 59 women; 81 have advanced degrees.

Subjects Offered 20th century history, 3-dimensional art, acting, adolescent issues, African studies, African-American history, African-American literature, algebra, American history, American literature, ancient world history, anthropology, architectural drawing, architecture, art, art history, biology, biology-AP, calculus-AP, chamber groups, chemistry, chemistry-AP, Chinese history, chorus, community service, computer graphics, computer programming, computer science-AP, creative writing, dance, directing, drama, dramatic arts, drawing, earth science, electronic music, English, English literature, English literature and composition-AP, English literature-AP, ethics, European civilization, European history, European literature, evolution, French, French language-AP, French literature-AP, genetics, geology, geometry, graphic design, history of science, Japanese history, jazz dance, jazz ensemble, jewelry making, journalism, Latin American history, Latin American literature, leadership, marine biology, meteorology, Middle East, modeling, modern dance, music, music performance, Native American studies, orchestra, painting, philosophy, photography, physical science, physics, physics-AP, poetry, pre-calculus, printmaking, Russian history, Russian literature, science, sculpture, Shakespeare, social issues, social justice, Spanish, Spanish language-AP, Spanish literature-AP, stagecraft, statistics-AP, U.S. history-AP, unified math, visual arts, voice, women's literature, world literature.

Graduation Requirements Arts, biology, English, ethics, history, lab science, languages, mathematics, physical education (includes health), physical science, U.S. history, world history, 60 hours of community service (120 hours during summer).

Special Academic Programs Honors section; independent study.

College Placement 126 students graduated in 2005; 119 went to college, including Carleton College; The George Washington University; Vassar College; Washington University in St. Louis; Wesleyan University; Yale University. Other: 7 had other specific plans. Median SAT verbal: 680, median SAT math: 680.

Student Life Upper grades have student council. Discipline rests equally with students and faculty.

Tuition and Aid Day student tuition: $25,250. Tuition installment plan (Key Tuition Payment Plan). Need-based scholarship grants, need-based loans available. In 2005–06, 24% of upper-school students received aid. Total amount of financial aid awarded in 2005–06: $3,355,538.

Admissions Traditional secondary-level entrance grade is 9. For fall 2005, 451 students applied for upper-level admission, 87 were accepted, 48 enrolled. ISEE required. Deadline for receipt of application materials: November 1. Application fee required: $60. On-campus interview required.

Athletics Interscholastic: baseball (boys), basketball (b,g), cross-country running (b,g), field hockey (g), football (b), lacrosse (g), soccer (b,g), softball (g), swimming and diving (g), tennis (b,g), volleyball (g); intramural: flag football (b,g), lacrosse (b,g), softball (g); coed interscholastic: cross-country running, Frisbee, golf, hockey, ice hockey, indoor track & field, swimming and diving, track and field, ultimate Frisbee; coed intramural: aerobics, aerobics/dance, aerobics/nautilus, dance, deck hockey, fitness, fitness walking, flag football, floor hockey, indoor hockey, indoor soccer, jogging, jump rope, kickball, nautilus, outdoor activities, outdoor education, outdoor recreation, physical fitness, physical training, running, soccer, speedball, street hockey, strength & conditioning, swimming and diving, tai chi, team handball, tennis, walking, weight training, whiffle ball. 7 PE instructors, 16 coaches, 1 trainer.

Computers Computers are regularly used in history, mathematics, science classes. Computer network features include campus e-mail, on-campus library services, CD-ROMs, Internet access.

Contact Ms. Ellen S. Bell, Assistant Head of School for Enrollment Management & Marketing. 718-329-7262. Fax: 718-329-7344. E-mail: ebell@ecfs.org. Web site: www.ecfs.org.

EVANSVILLE DAY SCHOOL

3400 North Green River Road
Evansville, Indiana 47715
Head of School: Mr. Ben Hebebrand

General Information Coeducational day college-preparatory school, affiliated with United Methodist Church. Grades PK–12. Founded: 1946. Setting: suburban. Nearest major city is St. Louis, MO. 55-acre campus. 1 building on campus. Approved or accredited by Independent Schools Association of the Central States and Indiana Department of Education. Member of National Association of Independent Schools. Endowment: $335,000. Total enrollment: 302. Upper school average class size: 15. Upper school faculty-student ratio: 1:10.

Upper School Student Profile Grade 9: 15 students (8 boys, 7 girls); Grade 10: 13 students (5 boys, 8 girls); Grade 11: 14 students (9 boys, 5 girls); Grade 12: 21 students (15 boys, 6 girls).

Faculty School total: 42. In upper school: 9 men, 7 women; 11 have advanced degrees.

Subjects Offered Advanced Placement courses, algebra, American history, American literature, art, biology, calculus, ceramics, chemistry, computer programming, computer science, creative writing, drama, economics, English, English literature, environmental science, expository writing, fine arts, French, geography, geometry, government/civics, grammar, health, history, journalism, mathematics, music, music theory, philosophy, physical education, physics, psychology, science, social science, social studies, sociology, Spanish, speech, theater, trigonometry, world history, world literature, world religions, writing, zoology.

Graduation Requirements Arts and fine arts (art, music, dance, drama), computer science, English, foreign language, mathematics, physical education (includes health), science, social science, social studies (includes history), speech.

Special Academic Programs Advanced Placement exam preparation in 10 subject areas; honors section; study at local college for college credit.

College Placement 22 students graduated in 2005; all went to college, including Ball State University; DePauw University; Indiana University Bloomington; University of Evansville; University of Georgia; University of Kentucky. Mean composite ACT: 25.

Student Life Upper grades have specified standards of dress, student council, honor system. Discipline rests primarily with faculty.

Summer Programs Enrichment, advancement, art/fine arts, computer instruction programs offered; session focuses on enrichment; held both on and off campus; held at University of Evansville; accepts boys and girls; open to students from other schools. 100 students usually enrolled. 2006 schedule: June to July. Application deadline: May.

Tuition and Aid Day student tuition: $10,440. Tuition installment plan (Insured Tuition Payment Plan, monthly payment plans). Tuition reduction for siblings, need-based scholarship grants, Professional Judgment scholarships available. In 2005–06, 25% of upper-school students received aid. Total amount of financial aid awarded in 2005–06: $100,000.

Admissions Traditional secondary-level entrance grade is 9. For fall 2005, 14 students applied for upper-level admission, 13 were accepted, 8 enrolled. English proficiency or ERB required. Deadline for receipt of application materials: none. Application fee required: $30. On-campus interview required.

Athletics Interscholastic: basketball (boys, girls), cheering (g), golf (b), outdoor adventure (b,g), physical fitness (b,g), soccer (b,g), tennis (g); coed interscholastic: cheering. 3 PE instructors.

Computers Computers are regularly used in all academic, yearbook classes. Computer network features include campus e-mail, on-campus library services, CD-ROMs, Internet access.

Contact Gerri A. Rice, Admission Counselor. 812-476-3039 Ext. 205. Fax: 812-476-4061. E-mail: grice@evansvilledayschool.org. Web site: www.evansvilledayschool.org.

EXPLORATIONS ACADEMY

PO Box 3014
Bellingham, Washington 98227
Head of School: Daniel Kirkpatrick

General Information Coeducational day college-preparatory, experiential education, and international field study expeditions school. Ungraded, ages 11–18. Founded: 1995. Setting: urban. Nearest major city is Vancouver, BC, Canada. 1-acre campus. 1 building on campus. Approved or accredited by Northwest Association of Schools and Colleges and Washington Department of Education. Languages of instruction: English and Spanish. Total enrollment: 16. Upper school average class size: 10. Upper school faculty-student ratio: 1:5.

Faculty School total: 7. In upper school: 4 men, 3 women; 4 have advanced degrees.

Subjects Offered Agriculture, American literature, anatomy and physiology, anthropology, archaeology, art, boat building, botany, calculus, carpentry, chemistry, computer graphics, computer programming, conflict resolution, construction, creative writing, desktop publishing, drawing, earth science, ecology, environmental science, first aid, French, gardening, gender issues, geology, government, health, horticulture, human relations, journalism, Latin American studies, leadership training, marine biology, media, meteorology, microbiology, music, music history, painting, philosophy, photography, physical education, physics, poetry, political science, psychology, sculpture, sexuality, short story, Spanish, technology, theater design and production, video film production, world culture, world geography, world history, world literature, writing.

Graduation Requirements Arts and fine arts (art, music, dance, drama), computer science, English, foreign language, human relations, mathematics, occupational education, physical education (includes health), science, social science, social studies (includes history), Washington State and Northwest History, one term of self-designed interdisciplinary studies. Community service is required.

Explorations Academy

Special Academic Programs Advanced Placement exam preparation in 2 subject areas; honors section; accelerated programs; independent study; term-away projects; academic accommodation for the gifted.

College Placement 2 students graduated in 2005; all went to college, including Humboldt State University; The Evergreen State College; Western Washington University.

Student Life Upper grades have honor system. Discipline rests primarily with faculty.

Summer Programs Enrichment, advancement, art/fine arts programs offered; session focuses on experiential learning; held both on and off campus; held at local urban and wilderness areas; accepts boys and girls; open to students from other schools. 12 students usually enrolled. 2006 schedule: June 23 to August 25. Application deadline: none.

Tuition and Aid Day student tuition: $8200. Guaranteed tuition plan. Tuition installment plan (monthly payment plans, individually arranged payment plans, school's own payment plan). Tuition reduction for siblings, need-based scholarship grants, need-based loans, low-interest loans available. In 2005–06, 40% of upper-school students received aid. Total amount of financial aid awarded in 2005–06: $50,000.

Admissions Traditional secondary-level entrance age is 14. For fall 2005, 25 students applied for upper-level admission, 21 were accepted, 18 enrolled. Deadline for receipt of application materials: none. Application fee required: $50. Interview required.

Computers Computers are regularly used in animation, art, English, French, graphics, mathematics, media production, publications, SAT preparation, science, writing, yearbook classes. Computer network features include campus e-mail, CD-ROMs, online commercial services, Internet access, file transfer, office computer access, DVD, wireless campus network.

Contact Betty McMahon, Registrar. 360-671-8085. Fax: 360-671-2521. E-mail: info@explorationsacademy.org. Web site: www.explorationsacademy.org.

EZELL-HARDING CHRISTIAN SCHOOL

574 Bell Road
Antioch, Tennessee 37013
Head of School: Mr. Donald Hutchison

General Information Coeducational day college-preparatory and religious studies school, affiliated with Church of Christ. Grades K–12. Founded: 1973. Setting: suburban. Nearest major city is Nashville. 30-acre campus. 1 building on campus. Approved or accredited by National Christian School Association, Southern Association of Colleges and Schools, and Tennessee Association of Independent Schools. Languages of instruction: English and Spanish. Endowment: $100,000. Total enrollment: 962. Upper school average class size: 19. Upper school faculty-student ratio: 1:12.

Upper School Student Profile Grade 9: 61 students (26 boys, 35 girls); Grade 10: 76 students (24 boys, 52 girls); Grade 11: 77 students (34 boys, 43 girls); Grade 12: 72 students (38 boys, 34 girls). 40% of students are members of Church of Christ.

Faculty School total: 75. In upper school: 12 men, 16 women; 8 have advanced degrees.

Subjects Offered Advanced math, algebra, American history, anatomy and physiology, art, band, Bible, biology, calculus, chemistry, chorus, creative writing, economics, European history, fitness, French, geography, geometry, government, journalism, keyboarding, microcomputer technology applications, physical science, physics, psychology, sociology, Spanish, trigonometry, wellness, world history.

Graduation Requirements American history, Bible, computers, English, mathematics, physical education (includes health), science, wellness, economics or government, world history or European history.

Special Academic Programs Advanced Placement exam preparation in 3 subject areas; honors section.

College Placement 68 students graduated in 2005; 65 went to college, including Freed-Hardeman University; Harding University; Lipscomb University; Middle Tennessee State University; The University of Tennessee; Trevecca Nazarene University. Other: 2 went to work, 1 entered military service. Median composite ACT: 23. 20% scored over 26 on composite ACT.

Student Life Upper grades have specified standards of dress, student council. Discipline rests primarily with faculty.

Tuition and Aid Day student tuition: $5500. Tuition installment plan (The Tuition Plan, monthly payment plans). Need-based scholarship grants available.

Admissions Traditional secondary-level entrance grade is 9. Deadline for receipt of application materials: none. Application fee required: $40. Interview recommended.

Athletics Interscholastic: baseball (boys), basketball (b,g), bowling (b,g), cheering (g), cross-country running (b,g), drill team (g), football (b), golf (b,g), hockey (b), soccer (b,g), softball (g), tennis (b,g), track and field (b,g), volleyball (g), weight training (b,g).

Computers Computer network features include campus e-mail, on-campus library services, Internet access.

Contact Mrs. Carolyn S. Allen, Admissions Officer. 615-367-0532. Fax: 615-399-8747. E-mail: carolyn.allen@ezellharding.com. Web site: ezellharding.com.

FAIRHILL SCHOOL

Dallas, Texas
See Special Needs Schools section.

FAITH LUTHERAN HIGH SCHOOL

2015 South Hualapai Way
Las Vegas, Nevada 89117-6949
Head of School: Mr. Kevin M. Dunning

General Information Coeducational day college-preparatory and religious studies school, affiliated with Lutheran Church–Missouri Synod, Evangelical Lutheran Church in America. Grades 6–12. Founded: 1979. Setting: suburban. 45-acre campus. 3 buildings on campus. Approved or accredited by Lutheran School Accreditation Commission, Northwest Association of Schools and Colleges, and Nevada Department of Education. Endowment: $750,000. Total enrollment: 1,157. Upper school average class size: 24. Upper school faculty-student ratio: 1:17.

Upper School Student Profile Grade 9: 191 students (97 boys, 94 girls); Grade 10: 171 students (80 boys, 91 girls); Grade 11: 144 students (76 boys, 68 girls); Grade 12: 112 students (52 boys, 60 girls). 14% of students are Lutheran Church–Missouri Synod, Evangelical Lutheran Church in America.

Faculty School total: 75. In upper school: 23 men, 33 women; 23 have advanced degrees.

Subjects Offered Algebra, American history, art, biology, chemistry, computer science, earth science, English, fine arts, fitness, geometry, German, health, mathematics, music, physical education, physical science, religion, SAT/ACT preparation, science, social studies, Spanish.

Graduation Requirements Arts and fine arts (art, music, dance, drama), computer science, English, foreign language, mathematics, physical education (includes health), religion (includes Bible studies and theology), science, social studies (includes history).

Special Academic Programs Advanced Placement exam preparation in 7 subject areas; honors section; independent study; study at local college for college credit; academic accommodation for the musically talented; remedial math.

College Placement 113 students graduated in 2005; 108 went to college, including Concordia University; University of Nevada, Las Vegas; University of Nevada, Reno. Other: 3 went to work, 2 entered military service. Mean SAT verbal: 523, mean SAT math: 524, mean composite ACT: 24.

Student Life Upper grades have uniform requirement, student council. Discipline rests primarily with faculty. Attendance at religious services is required.

Tuition and Aid Day student tuition: $6870. Tuition installment plan (monthly payment plans, individually arranged payment plans). Tuition reduction for siblings, need-based scholarship grants available. In 2005–06, 10% of upper-school students received aid. Total amount of financial aid awarded in 2005–06: $175,000.

Admissions Traditional secondary-level entrance grade is 9. For fall 2005, 330 students applied for upper-level admission, 305 were accepted, 289 enrolled. Stanford 9 required. Deadline for receipt of application materials: none. Application fee required: $300. On-campus interview required.

Athletics Interscholastic: aerobics/dance (girls), aquatics (b,g), baseball (b), basketball (b,g), cheering (g), cross-country running (b,g), dance team (g), football (b), golf (b,g), lacrosse (b), soccer (b,g), softball (g), swimming and diving (b,g), track and field (b,g), volleyball (g); intramural: strength & conditioning; coed interscholastic: strength & conditioning; coed intramural: skiing (downhill). 7 PE instructors, 26 coaches.

Computers Computers are regularly used in yearbook classes. Computer network features include on-campus library services, CD-ROMs, Internet access, DVD.

Contact Carol Neal, Registrar. 702-804-4400. Fax: 702-804-4488. Web site: www.faithlutheranlv.org.

FALMOUTH ACADEMY

7 Highfield Drive
Falmouth, Massachusetts 02540
Head of School: Mr. David C. Faus

General Information Coeducational day college-preparatory and arts school. Grades 7–12. Founded: 1976. Setting: small town. Nearest major city is Boston. 34-acre campus. 3 buildings on campus. Approved or accredited by Association of Independent Schools in New England and New England Association of Schools and Colleges. Member of National Association of Independent Schools and Secondary School Admission Test Board. Endowment: $3 million. Total enrollment: 213. Upper school average class size: 12. Upper school faculty-student ratio: 1:4.

Upper School Student Profile Grade 9: 45 students (18 boys, 27 girls); Grade 10: 28 students (12 boys, 16 girls); Grade 11: 28 students (16 boys, 12 girls); Grade 12: 30 students (14 boys, 16 girls).

Faculty School total: 35. In upper school: 10 men, 18 women; 20 have advanced degrees.

Subjects Offered Algebra, American history, American literature, art, biology, calculus, ceramics, chemistry, creative writing, drama, earth science, ecology, English, English literature, environmental science, European history, expository writing, fine

222   *www.petersons.com*   *Peterson's Private Secondary Schools 2007*

arts, French, geography, geology, geometry, German, grammar, health, history, journalism, mathematics, music, photography, physical education, physics, science, sculpture, social studies, statistics, theater, trigonometry, woodworking, world history, world literature, writing.

Graduation Requirements Arts and fine arts (art, music, dance, drama), English, foreign language, history, mathematics, science.

Special Academic Programs Advanced Placement exam preparation in 4 subject areas; independent study; term-away projects; study abroad.

College Placement 33 students graduated in 2005; all went to college, including St. Lawrence University; Wellesley College. Mean SAT verbal: 653, mean SAT math: 624.

Student Life Upper grades have specified standards of dress, student council, honor system. Discipline rests primarily with faculty.

Tuition and Aid Day student tuition: $17,100. Merit scholarship grants, need-based scholarship grants, need-based loans, TERI Loans available. In 2005–06, 35% of upper-school students received aid; total upper-school merit-scholarship money awarded: $3000. Total amount of financial aid awarded in 2005–06: $417,010.

Admissions Traditional secondary-level entrance grade is 9. For fall 2005, 25 students applied for upper-level admission, 9 were accepted, 7 enrolled. SSAT required. Deadline for receipt of application materials: March 1. Application fee required: $50. On-campus interview required.

Athletics Interscholastic: basketball (boys, girls), lacrosse (b,g), soccer (b,g). 1 PE instructor.

Computers Computers are regularly used in design, English, mathematics, science classes. Computer resources include CD-ROMs, Internet access, DVD.

Contact Mr. Michael J. Earley, Director of Admissions. 508-457-9696. Fax: 508-457-4112. E-mail: mearley@falmouthacademy.org. Web site: www.falmouthacademy.org.

ANNOUNCEMENT FROM THE SCHOOL Falmouth Academy is a deliberately small school with a traditional core curriculum that emphasizes reading and writing. Students achieve outstanding results in regional competitions in science, music, art, and athletics. The school offers 7 performing music groups, including a 30-piece string orchestra. Falmouth also conducts exchanges with schools in France and Germany.

THE FAMILY FOUNDATION SCHOOL

Hancock, New York
See Special Needs Schools section.

FATHER LOPEZ HIGH SCHOOL

960 Madison Avenue
Daytona Beach, Florida 32114-1889
Head of School: Mrs. Linda A. Dowdy

General Information Coeducational day college-preparatory, arts, business, and religious studies school, affiliated with Roman Catholic Church. Grades 9–12. Founded: 1959. Setting: urban. 15-acre campus. 8 buildings on campus. Approved or accredited by Southern Association of Colleges and Schools and Florida Department of Education. Total enrollment: 294. Upper school average class size: 25. Upper school faculty-student ratio: 1:20.

Upper School Student Profile Grade 9: 76 students (37 boys, 39 girls); Grade 10: 76 students (34 boys, 42 girls); Grade 11: 51 students (26 boys, 25 girls); Grade 12: 91 students (53 boys, 38 girls). 79% of students are Roman Catholic.

Faculty School total: 27. In upper school: 10 men, 17 women; 14 have advanced degrees.

Subjects Offered Advanced Placement courses, algebra, American government, American government-AP, American history, American history-AP, American literature, anatomy and physiology, art, athletics, audio visual/media, Bible studies, biology, biology-AP, British literature, British literature-AP, calculus-AP, chemistry, computer education, computer graphics, computer keyboarding, computer programming, dance, drama performance, economics, English, English literature, English literature-AP, French, geography, geometry, government, government-AP, graphic design, health education, honors English, honors geometry, integrated math, law studies, leadership skills, marine science, personal fitness, photography, physical education, pre-calculus, psychology, religious education, social justice, Spanish, theology, U.S. history, U.S. history-AP, Web site design, weight training, world geography, world history, world religions, writing.

Graduation Requirements 100 hours of community service.

Special Academic Programs Advanced Placement exam preparation in 5 subject areas; honors section.

College Placement 91 students graduated in 2005; all went to college, including Florida State University; University of Central Florida; University of Florida; University of Miami; University of North Florida. Median combined SAT: 1069, median composite ACT: 23.

Student Life Upper grades have uniform requirement, honor system. Discipline rests primarily with faculty. Attendance at religious services is required.

Tuition and Aid Day student tuition: $6100. Tuition installment plan (FACTS Tuition Payment Plan). Financial aid available to upper-school students. In 2005–06, 21% of upper-school students received aid. Total amount of financial aid awarded in 2005–06: $75,000.

Admissions Traditional secondary-level entrance grade is 9. For fall 2005, 80 students applied for upper-level admission, 80 were accepted, 80 enrolled. Deadline for receipt of application materials: none. No application fee required. Interview recommended.

Athletics Interscholastic: aerobics/dance (girls), baseball (b), basketball (b,g), cheering (g), cross-country running (b,g), dance team (g), diving (b,g), football (b), golf (b,g), soccer (b,g), softball (g), swimming and diving (b,g), tennis (b,g), track and field (b,g), volleyball (g), weight training (b,g). 1 PE instructor, 9 coaches, 1 trainer.

Computers Computer resources include on-campus library services, CD-ROMs, Internet access.

Contact Mrs. Linda A. Dowdy, RSM, Principal. 386-253-5213 Ext. 303. Fax: 386-252-6101. E-mail: ldowdy@fatherlopez.org.

FATHER RYAN HIGH SCHOOL

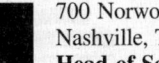

700 Norwood Drive
Nashville, Tennessee 37204
Head of School: Mr. McIntyre Jim

General Information Coeducational day college-preparatory, arts, and religious studies school, affiliated with Roman Catholic Church. Grades 9–12. Founded: 1925. Setting: suburban. 40-acre campus. 5 buildings on campus. Approved or accredited by National Catholic Education Association, Southern Association of Colleges and Schools, Southern Association of Independent Schools, Tennessee Association of Independent Schools, and The College Board. Endowment: $5 million. Total enrollment: 935. Upper school average class size: 23. Upper school faculty-student ratio: 1:12.

Upper School Student Profile Grade 9: 239 students (133 boys, 106 girls); Grade 10: 245 students (130 boys, 115 girls); Grade 11: 215 students (123 boys, 92 girls); Grade 12: 236 students (120 boys, 116 girls); Postgraduate: 935 students (506 boys, 429 girls). 90% of students are Roman Catholic.

Faculty School total: 80. In upper school: 37 men, 40 women; 46 have advanced degrees.

Subjects Offered 3-dimensional design, Advanced Placement courses, aerobics, algebra, American government, American government-AP, American history, American history-AP, American literature, anatomy, art, art history, art-AP, athletic training, Bible studies, biology, British literature, calculus, calculus-AP, Catholic belief and practice, chemistry, chemistry-AP, chorus, church history, college counseling, college planning, college writing, computer programming, computer science, computer studies, dance, dance performance, drama, drama performance, driver education, economics, English, English literature, English-AP, European history, European history-AP, film studies, French, French-AP, geography, geometry, government-AP, government/civics, grammar, health, history, honors geometry, honors U.S. history, journalism, Latin, mathematics, music, physical education, physics, physics-AP, physiology, psychology, religion, SAT preparation, science, Shakespeare, social studies, Spanish, Spanish-AP, speech, statistics-AP, theater, theater production, theology, trigonometry, Web site design, wind ensemble, world history, world literature, world religions, writing.

Graduation Requirements Arts and fine arts (art, music, dance, drama), computer science, English, foreign language, health education, mathematics, physical education (includes health), religion (includes Bible studies and theology), science, social studies (includes history).

Special Academic Programs Advanced Placement exam preparation in 15 subject areas; honors section; academic accommodation for the gifted, the musically talented, and the artistically talented.

College Placement 226 students graduated in 2005; 219 went to college, including Middle Tennessee State University; Saint Louis University; Tennessee Technological University; The University of Tennessee; University of Dayton; Western Kentucky University. Other: 4 went to work, 2 entered military service. Median SAT verbal: 553, median SAT math: 524, median composite ACT: 22. 20% scored over 26 on composite ACT.

Student Life Upper grades have uniform requirement, student council. Discipline rests primarily with faculty. Attendance at religious services is required.

Summer Programs Remediation, enrichment, advancement, sports, art/fine arts, computer instruction programs offered; session focuses on remedial studies; held on campus; accepts boys and girls; open to students from other schools. 150 students usually enrolled. 2006 schedule: June 5 to June 30. Application deadline: none.

Tuition and Aid Day student tuition: $7200. Tuition installment plan (monthly payment plans, individually arranged payment plans). Tuition reduction for siblings, need-based scholarship grants available. In 2005–06, 13% of upper-school students received aid. Total amount of financial aid awarded in 2005–06: $298,000.

Admissions Traditional secondary-level entrance grade is 9. For fall 2005, 301 students applied for upper-level admission, 260 were accepted, 239 enrolled. High School Placement Test required. Deadline for receipt of application materials: none. Application fee required: $25. On-campus interview required.

Athletics Interscholastic: aquatics (boys, girls), baseball (b,g), basketball (b,g), bowling (b,g), cheering (g), cross-country running (b,g), dance (g), dance team (g),

diving (b,g), football (b), golf (b,g), ice hockey (b), lacrosse (b,g), power lifting (b), soccer (b,g), softball (g), Special Olympics (b,g), strength & conditioning (b,g), swimming and diving (b,g), tennis (b,g), track and field (b,g), volleyball (g), weight lifting (b,g), wrestling (b); intramural: fishing (b,g), indoor soccer (b,g), physical fitness (b,g). 6 PE instructors, 4 coaches, 1 trainer.

Computers Computer network features include on-campus library services, CD-ROMs, online commercial services, Internet access, office computer access, DVD.
Contact Ms. Connie Hansom, Director of Admissions. 615-383-4200. Fax: 615-783-0264. E-mail: hansomc@fatherryan.org. Web site: www.fatherryan.org.

FAY SCHOOL

Southborough, Massachusetts
See Junior Boarding Schools section.

THE FENSTER SCHOOL

8500 East Ocotillo Drive
Tucson, Arizona 85750

See full description on page 782.

THE FESSENDEN SCHOOL

West Newton, Massachusetts
See Junior Boarding Schools section.

THE FIELD SCHOOL

2301 Foxhall Road, NW
Washington, District of Columbia 20007
Head of School: Dale T. Johnson

General Information Coeducational day college-preparatory and arts school. Grades 7–12. Founded: 1972. Setting: urban. 10-acre campus. 4 buildings on campus. Approved or accredited by Association of Independent Schools of Greater Washington and Middle States Association of Colleges and Schools. Member of National Association of Independent Schools and Secondary School Admission Test Board. Total enrollment: 308. Upper school average class size: 11. Upper school faculty-student ratio: 1:6.
Upper School Student Profile Grade 9: 62 students (32 boys, 30 girls); Grade 10: 67 students (34 boys, 33 girls); Grade 11: 58 students (31 boys, 27 girls); Grade 12: 54 students (28 boys, 26 girls).
Faculty School total: 49. In upper school: 25 men, 24 women; 19 have advanced degrees.
Subjects Offered Algebra, American history, American literature, ancient history, art, art history, biology, calculus, ceramics, chemistry, computer math, creative writing, drama, earth science, English, English literature, environmental science, European history, expository writing, fine arts, French, geometry, government/civics, grammar, history, journalism, Latin, literature, mathematics, music, photography, physical education, physics, pre-calculus, science, social studies, space and physical sciences, Spanish, theater, trigonometry, typing, world history, world literature, writing.
Graduation Requirements Arts and fine arts (art, music, dance, drama), English, foreign language, mathematics, physical education (includes health), science, social studies (includes history), work internship (2 weeks annually).
Special Academic Programs Advanced Placement exam preparation in 5 subject areas; accelerated programs; independent study; academic accommodation for the gifted and the artistically talented; remedial math.
College Placement 50 students graduated in 2005; all went to college, including College of Charleston; Columbia College; Kenyon College; Oberlin College; University of Virginia; Wesleyan University.
Student Life Upper grades have student council, honor system. Discipline rests primarily with faculty.
Summer Programs Remediation, enrichment programs offered; session focuses on humanities and math; held on campus; accepts boys and girls; not open to students from other schools. 20 students usually enrolled. 2006 schedule: June 15 to July 15.
Tuition and Aid Day student tuition: $24,900. Tuition installment plan (Insured Tuition Payment Plan, Key Tuition Payment Plan, monthly payment plans). Need-based scholarship grants available. In 2005–06, 10% of upper-school students received aid.
Admissions Traditional secondary-level entrance grade is 9. For fall 2005, 196 students applied for upper-level admission, 82 were accepted, 36 enrolled. SSAT required. Deadline for receipt of application materials: January 15. Application fee required: $80. On-campus interview required.
Athletics Interscholastic: baseball (boys), basketball (b,g), cross-country running (b,g), lacrosse (g), soccer (b,g), softball (g), swimming and diving (b,g), tennis (b,g), track and field (b,g), ultimate Frisbee (b,g), volleyball (g); intramural: basketball (b,g),

fitness (b,g); coed interscholastic: Frisbee, swimming and diving; coed intramural: fitness, Frisbee, indoor soccer, physical fitness, ultimate Frisbee, volleyball, yoga.
Computers Computers are regularly used in English, foreign language, history, mathematics, science classes. Computer network features include on-campus library services, CD-ROMs, online commercial services, Internet access, file transfer, office computer access, DVD.
Contact Maureen Miesmer, Associate Director of Admission. 202-295-5840. Fax: 202-295-5850. E-mail: admission@fieldschool.org. Web site: www.fieldschool.org.

FIRST BAPTIST ACADEMY

PO Box 868
Dallas, Texas 75221
Head of School: Mr. Jake Walters

General Information Coeducational day college-preparatory, arts, religious studies, and technology school, affiliated with Baptist Church. Grades K–12. Founded: 1972. Setting: urban. 1 building on campus. Approved or accredited by Accreditation Commission of the Texas Association of Baptist Schools, Southern Association of Colleges and Schools, and Texas Department of Education. Endowment: $100,000. Total enrollment: 682. Upper school average class size: 22. Upper school faculty-student ratio: 1:10.
Upper School Student Profile Grade 9: 75 students (32 boys, 43 girls); Grade 10: 75 students (37 boys, 38 girls); Grade 11: 48 students (20 boys, 28 girls); Grade 12: 75 students (39 boys, 36 girls). 35% of students are Baptist.
Faculty School total: 71. In upper school: 11 men, 15 women; 8 have advanced degrees.
Subjects Offered Algebra, American history, astronomy, biology, calculus, calculus-AP, ceramics, chemistry, economics, English, English literature-AP, English-AP, fine arts, French, geometry, government-AP, history, math analysis, oceanography, photography, physics, pottery, pre-calculus, Spanish, theater arts, world history.
Graduation Requirements Algebra, American history, American literature, arts and fine arts (art, music, dance, drama), Basic programming, Bible, Bible studies, biology, chemistry, computer keyboarding, electives, English, English literature, foreign language, geography, geometry, government, history, keyboarding/computer, mathematics, physical education (includes health), physics, pre-algebra, science, U.S. history, government/economics, human geography. Community service is required.
Special Academic Programs Advanced Placement exam preparation in 4 subject areas; honors section.
College Placement 69 students graduated in 2005; 67 went to college, including Baylor University; Southern Methodist University; Texas A&M University; Texas Tech University. Other: 2 had other specific plans. Mean composite ACT: 24.
Student Life Upper grades have uniform requirement, student council, honor system. Discipline rests primarily with faculty. Attendance at religious services is required.
Tuition and Aid Day student tuition: $9350. Tuition installment plan (FACTS Tuition Payment Plan). Need-based scholarship grants available. In 2005–06, 28% of upper-school students received aid. Total amount of financial aid awarded in 2005–06: $600,000.
Admissions Traditional secondary-level entrance grade is 9. Stanford Achievement Test required. Deadline for receipt of application materials: none. Application fee required: $75. Interview required.
Athletics Interscholastic: aquatics (boys, girls), baseball (b), basketball (b,g), cheering (g), diving (b,g), drill team (g), football (b), golf (b,g), soccer (g), softball (g), swimming and diving (b,g), tennis (b,g), track and field (b,g), volleyball (g), wrestling (b). 4 PE instructors, 2 coaches.
Computers Computers are regularly used in desktop publishing classes. Computer resources include campus e-mail.
Contact Susan Money, Director of Admissions. 214-969-7861. Fax: 214-969-7797. E-mail: smoney@firstdallas.org.

FIRST PRESBYTERIAN DAY SCHOOL

5671 Calvin Drive
Macon, Georgia 31210
Head of School: Mr. Gregg E. Thompson

General Information Coeducational day college-preparatory, arts, and religious studies school, affiliated with Christian faith. Grades PK–12. Founded: 1970. Setting: suburban. Nearest major city is Atlanta. 54-acre campus. 7 buildings on campus. Approved or accredited by Christian Schools International, Georgia Independent School Association, Southern Association of Colleges and Schools, and Georgia Department of Education. Endowment: $2.2 million. Total enrollment: 952. Upper school average class size: 18. Upper school faculty-student ratio: 1:12.
Upper School Student Profile Grade 9: 82 students (43 boys, 39 girls); Grade 10: 82 students (40 boys, 42 girls); Grade 11: 81 students (41 boys, 40 girls); Grade 12: 71 students (36 boys, 35 girls). 96% of students are Christian.
Faculty School total: 73. In upper school: 24 men, 26 women; 34 have advanced degrees.
Subjects Offered Accounting, advanced chemistry, Advanced Placement courses, algebra, American literature, anatomy and physiology, art, art appreciation, band,

Bible, biology, biology-AP, British literature, calculus-AP, chemistry, chorus, comparative religion, computer applications, economics, English, English language and composition-AP, English literature and composition-AP, family life, French, geometry, government, honors algebra, honors English, honors geometry, journalism, Latin, Latin-AP, logic, model United Nations, modern European history, music appreciation, physical science, physics, pre-calculus, psychology, Spanish, statistics, studio art-AP, theater, U.S. history, U.S. history-AP, world history.

Graduation Requirements Arts and fine arts (art, music, dance, drama), Bible, computer skills, electives, English, foreign language, mathematics, physical education (includes health), science, social studies (includes history).

Special Academic Programs Advanced Placement exam preparation in 8 subject areas; honors section.

College Placement 76 students graduated in 2005; all went to college, including Auburn University; Georgia Institute of Technology; Mercer University; Samford University; University of Georgia. 24% scored over 600 on SAT verbal, 28% scored over 600 on SAT math.

Student Life Upper grades have specified standards of dress, student council, honor system. Discipline rests primarily with faculty. Attendance at religious services is required.

Summer Programs Remediation, enrichment, sports, art/fine arts programs offered; session focuses on reading and study skills, mathematics enrichment, sports; held on campus; accepts boys and girls; open to students from other schools. 40 students usually enrolled. 2006 schedule: June 10 to July 30. Application deadline: May 15.

Tuition and Aid Day student tuition: $8730. Tuition installment plan (monthly payment plans). Tuition reduction for siblings, merit scholarship grants, need-based scholarship grants available. In 2005–06, 21% of upper-school students received aid; total upper-school merit-scholarship money awarded: $4000. Total amount of financial aid awarded in 2005–06: $140,000.

Admissions Traditional secondary-level entrance grade is 9. Stanford 9 and writing sample required. Deadline for receipt of application materials: February 1. Application fee required: $50. Interview recommended.

Athletics Interscholastic: baseball (boys), basketball (b,g), cheering (g), cross-country running (b,g), dance team (g), football (b), golf (b,g), soccer (b,g), softball (g), swimming and diving (b,g), tennis (b,g), track and field (b,g), wrestling (b,g); intramural: football (b), indoor soccer (b,g), soccer (b,g), strength & conditioning (b,g), weight training (b,g). 3 PE instructors, 5 coaches, 1 trainer.

Computers Computers are regularly used in all classes. Computer network features include campus e-mail, on-campus library services, CD-ROMs, online commercial services, Internet access, file transfer, office computer access, DVD.

Contact Mr. Terrell Mitchell, Director of Admissions. 478-477-6505 Ext. 107. Fax: 478-477-2804. E-mail: tmitchell@fpdmacon.org. Web site: www.fpdmacon.org.

FISHBURNE MILITARY SCHOOL

225 South Wayne Avenue
Waynesboro, Virginia 22980
Head of School: Col. William W. Alexander Jr.

General Information Boys' boarding and day college-preparatory and Army Junior ROTC school; primarily serves underachievers. Grades 8–12. Founded: 1879. Setting: small town. Nearest major city is Washington, DC. Students are housed in single-sex dormitories. 4 buildings on campus. Approved or accredited by Southern Association of Colleges and Schools, Virginia Association of Independent Schools, Virginia Association of Independent Specialized Education Facilities, and Virginia Department of Education. Endowment: $1.3 million. Total enrollment: 180. Upper school average class size: 9. Upper school faculty-student ratio: 1:8.

Upper School Student Profile Grade 9: 35 students (35 boys); Grade 10: 45 students (45 boys); Grade 11: 50 students (50 boys); Grade 12: 45 students (45 boys). 90% of students are boarding students. 17 states are represented in upper school student body. 5% are international students. International students from Aruba, Italy, Mexico, Saudi Arabia, Singapore, and Thailand; 5 other countries represented in student body.

Faculty School total: 23. In upper school: 20 men, 3 women; 5 have advanced degrees; 5 reside on campus.

Subjects Offered Algebra, American history, American literature, anatomy, art, art history, biology, business, calculus, chemistry, computer programming, computer science, computer technologies, creative writing, driver education, earth science, economics, English, English literature, environmental science, ESL, fine arts, French, geography, geology, geometry, government/civics, grammar, health, history, journalism, JROTC, mathematics, military science, music, physical education, physics, physiology, science, social studies, sociology, Spanish, speech, trigonometry, world history.

Graduation Requirements Arts and fine arts (art, music, dance, drama), computer science, English, foreign language, JROTC, mathematics, physical education (includes health), science, social studies (includes history).

Special Academic Programs Advanced Placement exam preparation in 3 subject areas; honors section; study at local college for college credit; remedial reading and/or remedial writing; remedial math; ESL (5 students enrolled).

College Placement 25 students graduated in 2005; 21 went to college, including Purdue University; The Pennsylvania State University University Park Campus;

United States Military Academy; University of Virginia; Virginia Military Institute; Virginia Polytechnic Institute and State University. Other: 2 went to work, 2 entered military service.

Student Life Upper grades have uniform requirement, student council, honor system. Discipline rests equally with students and faculty.

Summer Programs Remediation, enrichment, advancement, computer instruction programs offered; session focuses on academics; held on campus; accepts boys; open to students from other schools. 100 students usually enrolled. 2006 schedule: July 2 to July 29.

Tuition and Aid Day student tuition: $9300; 7-day tuition and room/board: $20,700. Tuition installment plan (Key Tuition Payment Plan, monthly payment plans, individually arranged payment plans, Tuition Management Systems Plan). Tuition reduction for siblings, merit scholarship grants, need-based scholarship grants, band scholarships, tuition reduction for children of military personnel, PLATO Loans available. In 2005–06, 40% of upper-school students received aid. Total amount of financial aid awarded in 2005–06: $75,000.

Admissions Deadline for receipt of application materials: none. Application fee required: $50. Interview recommended.

Athletics Interscholastic: baseball, basketball, canoeing/kayaking, cooperative games, cross-country running, drill team, football, golf, JROTC drill, lacrosse, marksmanship, outdoor adventure, riflery, soccer, track and field, wrestling; intramural: baseball, basketball, billiards, bowling, martial arts, paint ball, rappelling, ropes courses, self defense, skiing (downhill), snowboarding, strength & conditioning, volleyball, weight lifting, weight training. 1 PE instructor, 15 coaches, 1 trainer.

Computers Computers are regularly used in English, foreign language, history, mathematics, science classes. Computer resources include campus e-mail, on-campus library services, CD-ROMs, Internet access, DVD.

Contact Capt. Carl V. Lambert, Director of Admissions. 800-946-7773. Fax: 540-946-7738. E-mail: lambert@fishburne.org. Web site: www.fishburne.org.

F. L. CHAMBERLAIN SCHOOL

Middleborough, Massachusetts
See Special Needs Schools section.

FLINT HILL SCHOOL

10409 Academic Drive
Oakton, Virginia 22124
Head of School: Mr. John Thomas

petersons.com

General Information Coeducational day college-preparatory, arts, and technology school. Grades JK–12. Founded: 1956. Setting: suburban. Nearest major city is Washington, DC. 50-acre campus. 1 building on campus. Approved or accredited by Association of Independent Schools of Greater Washington, Virginia Association of Independent Schools, and Virginia Department of Education. Member of National Association of Independent Schools and Secondary School Admission Test Board. Endowment: $625,000. Total enrollment: 1,017. Upper school average class size: 12. Upper school faculty-student ratio: 1:10.

Upper School Student Profile Grade 9: 117 students (59 boys, 58 girls); Grade 10: 116 students (67 boys, 49 girls); Grade 11: 106 students (48 boys, 58 girls); Grade 12: 93 students (48 boys, 45 girls).

Faculty School total: 115. In upper school: 19 men, 23 women; 42 have advanced degrees.

Subjects Offered 20th century history, advanced chemistry, algebra, art, biology, British literature, British literature (honors), calculus, calculus-AP, ceramics, chemistry, chemistry-AP, chorus, community service, computer animation, computer graphics, computer programming, computer science-AP, conceptual physics, creative writing, drama, drawing, economics and history, English, English literature, English literature and composition-AP, environmental science, environmental science-AP, European civilization, European history, European history-AP, fine arts, French, French language-AP, French literature-AP, French-AP, geometry, government-AP, history, Latin, Latin-AP, macro/microeconomics-AP, music, music theory-AP, ornithology, photography, physical education, physics, physics-AP, pre-calculus, psychology-AP, religion, science, sculpture, senior project, Spanish, Spanish-AP, statistics-AP, studio art, study skills, theater, trigonometry, U.S. history, U.S. history-AP, world religions.

Graduation Requirements Arts and fine arts (art, music, dance, drama), English, foreign language, mathematics, physical education (includes health), science, social studies (includes history), athletic participation. Community service is required.

Special Academic Programs Advanced Placement exam preparation in 18 subject areas; honors section.

College Placement 74 students graduated in 2005; they went to George Mason University; James Madison University; The College of William and Mary; University of Virginia; Virginia Polytechnic Institute and State University; Wake Forest University. Other: 74 entered a postgraduate year. Median SAT verbal: 620, median SAT math: 630.

Student Life Upper grades have specified standards of dress, student council, honor system. Discipline rests primarily with faculty.

Flint Hill School

Summer Programs Remediation, enrichment, advancement, sports, art/fine arts, rigorous outdoor training, computer instruction programs offered; session focuses on enrichment and athletics; held both on and off campus; held at international venues; accepts boys and girls; open to students from other schools. 347 students usually enrolled. 2006 schedule: June 21 to July 30. Application deadline: none.

Tuition and Aid Day student tuition: $21,480. Tuition installment plan (Insured Tuition Payment Plan, FACTS Tuition Payment Plan, monthly payment plans). Need-based scholarship grants available. In 2005–06, 59% of upper-school students received aid. Total amount of financial aid awarded in 2005–06: $1,012,245.

Admissions Traditional secondary-level entrance grade is 9. For fall 2005, 505 students applied for upper-level admission, 328 were accepted, 214 enrolled. SSAT, SSAT or WISC III, Wechsler Intelligence Scale for Children or WISC-R or WISC-III required. Deadline for receipt of application materials: February 3. Application fee required: $50. On-campus interview required.

Athletics Interscholastic: baseball (boys), basketball (b,g), cross-country running (b,g), dance team (g), diving (b,g), football (b), golf (b), lacrosse (b,g), soccer (b,g), softball (g), swimming and diving (b,g), tennis (b,g), track and field (b,g), volleyball (g); coed interscholastic: canoeing/kayaking, climbing, independent competitive sports, physical fitness, strength & conditioning; coed intramural: aerobics/dance, back packing, canoeing/kayaking, climbing, dance, fitness, martial arts, modern dance, mountaineering, outdoor education, physical fitness, physical training, rock climbing, strength & conditioning, wall climbing, weight training, wilderness. 14 coaches, 2 trainers.

Computers Computers are regularly used in animation, art, basic skills, college planning, English, foreign language, French, history, language development, library, mathematics, newspaper, science, Spanish, writing, yearbook classes. Computer network features include campus e-mail, on-campus library services, CD-ROMs, online commercial services, Internet access.

Contact Ms. Patricia Harden, Director of Admission. 703-584-2300. Fax: 703-242-0718. E-mail: admissions@flinthill.org. Web site: www.flinthill.org.

ANNOUNCEMENT FROM THE SCHOOL Flint Hill School, enrolling 1,017 students in JK–12, encourages both faculty members and students to experience the joy of learning and growing in a diverse society. Academic excellence is engendered within a value-centered community where respect, responsibility, compassion, and honesty are fostered. The School consists of two campuses located on 50 acres, housing well-appointed library facilities, a state-of-the-art media center, learning centers, and spacious science and computer labs. All faculty members work in fully networked classrooms, integrating multimedia and technology into the curriculum. An extensive experiential education program enhances classroom academics. Athletics facilities include 2 full-size gymnasiums, 8 tennis courts, a 400-meter track, and athletics fields. Fine arts facilities include a 300-seat theater and art, dance, and music studios. Headmaster: Mr. John M. Thomas. Director of Admission: Ms. Pat Harden.

FLORIDA AIR ACADEMY

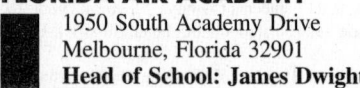

1950 South Academy Drive
Melbourne, Florida 32901
Head of School: James Dwight

General Information Coeducational boarding and day college-preparatory, computer science, and aerospace science school. Grades 6–12. Founded: 1961. Setting: suburban. Nearest major city is Orlando. Students are housed in single-sex dormitories. 30-acre campus. 18 buildings on campus. Approved or accredited by Florida Council of Independent Schools, Southern Association of Colleges and Schools, and Florida Department of Education. Member of Secondary School Admission Test Board. Total enrollment: 484. Upper school average class size: 14. Upper school faculty-student ratio: 1:16.

Upper School Student Profile Grade 9: 76 students (69 boys, 7 girls); Grade 10: 107 students (98 boys, 9 girls); Grade 11: 113 students (103 boys, 10 girls); Grade 12: 76 students (76 boys). 70% of students are boarding students. 80% are state residents. 22 states are represented in upper school student body. 10% are international students. International students from Bahamas, Bermuda, China, Japan, Netherlands Antilles, and Puerto Rico; 15 other countries represented in student body.

Faculty School total: 40. In upper school: 14 men, 20 women; 18 have advanced degrees.

Subjects Offered Aerospace education, aerospace science, algebra, American history, American literature, art, band, biology, calculus, calculus-AP, chemistry, chorus, computer applications, computer art, computer graphics, computer programming, computer science, computer technology certification, driver education, economics, English, English literature and composition-AP, English literature-AP, English-AP, ESL, flight instruction, geometry, government/civics, graphic arts, graphic design, health education, history, history-AP, honors algebra, honors English, honors geometry, honors U.S. history, honors world history, JROTC, mathematics, music, music appreciation, oceanography, physical education, physics, physics-AP,

pre-calculus, psychology, SAT preparation, science, scuba diving, social studies, sociology, Spanish, Spanish language-AP, TOEFL preparation, trigonometry, U.S. government, world history, yearbook.

Graduation Requirements Aerospace education, arts and fine arts (art, music, dance, drama), computer education, English, JROTC, mathematics, physical fitness, science, social sciences, Spanish.

Special Academic Programs Advanced Placement exam preparation in 6 subject areas; honors section; study at local college for college credit; academic accommodation for the gifted; remedial reading and/or remedial writing; remedial math; ESL (35 students enrolled).

College Placement 72 students graduated in 2005; all went to college, including Barry University; Embry-Riddle Aeronautical University; Florida Institute of Technology; Florida International University; University of Central Florida; University of Florida.

Student Life Upper grades have uniform requirement, student council, honor system. Discipline rests equally with students and faculty.

Summer Programs Remediation, enrichment, advancement, ESL, sports, computer instruction programs offered; session focuses on academics and activities; held on campus; accepts boys and girls; open to students from other schools. 120 students usually enrolled. 2006 schedule: June 17 to July 28. Application deadline: April 20.

Tuition and Aid Day student tuition: $8000; 7-day tuition and room/board: $25,000. Tuition installment plan (monthly payment plans, individually arranged payment plans). Tuition reduction for siblings, merit scholarship grants, need-based scholarship grants available. In 2005–06, 40% of upper-school students received aid; total upper-school merit-scholarship money awarded: $350,000.

Admissions Traditional secondary-level entrance grade is 9. For fall 2005, 425 students applied for upper-level admission, 390 were accepted, 372 enrolled. Achievement tests, any standardized test, PSAT and SAT for applicants to grade 11 and 12 or TOEFL required. Deadline for receipt of application materials: none. Application fee required: $100. Interview recommended.

Athletics Interscholastic: baseball (boys), basketball (b,g), cheering (g); cross-country running (b,g), drill team (b,g), football (b), golf (b), power lifting (b), soccer (b,g), softball (b,g), tennis (b,g), volleyball (b,g), weight lifting (b), winter soccer (b,g); intramural: aerobics/nautilus (b), baseball (b), basketball (b,g), cooperative games (b), flag football (b), football (b), Frisbee (b), golf (b), ice skating (b), power lifting (b), soccer (b,g), softball (b,g), touch football (b), volleyball (b,g), weight lifting (b), winter soccer (b,g); coed interscholastic: aerobics/dance, aquatics, bowling, climbing, JROTC drill, martial arts, nautilus, physical fitness, physical training, rock climbing, running, scuba diving, strength & conditioning, swimming and diving, track and field, weight training; coed intramural: bowling, canoeing/kayaking, independent competitive sports, jogging, JROTC drill, life saving, martial arts, nautilus, outdoor activities, outdoor education, outdoor recreation, physical fitness, physical training, rock climbing, roller skating, ropes courses, running, scuba diving, self defense, skateboarding, strength & conditioning, surfing, swimming and diving, table tennis, tai chi, tennis, ultimate Frisbee, weight training, windsurfing. 4 PE instructors, 6 coaches.

Computers Computers are regularly used in aerospace science, aviation, college planning, data processing, desktop publishing, English, foreign language, graphic arts, graphic design, information technology, mathematics, publishing, research skills, SAT preparation, science, social science, writing classes. Computer network features include campus e-mail, on-campus library services, CD-ROMs, Internet access.

Contact Mrs. Louise Orris, Webmaster. 321-723-3211 Ext. 30023. Fax: 321-676-0422. E-mail: lorris@flair.com. Web site: www.flair.com.

See full description on page 784.

FONTBONNE ACADEMY

930 Brook Road
Milton, Massachusetts 02186
Head of School: Dr. Anne Malone

General Information Girls' day college-preparatory school, affiliated with Roman Catholic Church. Grades 9–12. Founded: 1950. Setting: suburban. Nearest major city is Boston. 14-acre campus. 3 buildings on campus. Approved or accredited by National Catholic Education Association, New England Association of Schools and Colleges, and Massachusetts Department of Education. Total enrollment: 582. Upper school average class size: 20. Upper school faculty-student ratio: 1:13.

Upper School Student Profile Grade 9: 144 students (144 girls); Grade 10: 146 students (146 girls); Grade 11: 135 students (135 girls); Grade 12: 157 students (157 girls). 90% of students are Roman Catholic.

Faculty School total: 53. In upper school: 9 men, 40 women; 34 have advanced degrees.

Subjects Offered 20th century American writers, advanced computer applications, algebra, American history, American history-AP, American literature, analytic geometry, applied music, art, art-AP, biology, biology-AP, British literature (honors), calculus-AP, career/college preparation, Catholic belief and practice, chemistry, choral music, chorus, church history, college admission preparation, college counseling, computer music, computer programming, conceptual physics, ecology, environmental systems, electronic music, English, English literature, English-AP, finance, fine arts, French, French-AP, freshman seminar, geometry, guidance, health, instrumental music, integrated mathematics, jazz ensemble, Latin, literature by women, media

communications, physical education, physics, physiology, pre-calculus, research techniques, science, social justice, social studies, sociology, Spanish, Spanish-AP, theater production, theology, trigonometry, vocal jazz, women's literature, world history.

Graduation Requirements Arts and fine arts (art, music, dance, drama), biology, English, foreign language, mathematics, physical education (includes health), physical science, theology, U.S. history, U.S. literature, world history, 100 hours of community service.

Special Academic Programs Advanced Placement exam preparation in 8 subject areas; honors section; independent study.

College Placement 149 students graduated in 2005; all went to college, including Boston College; Boston University; College of the Holy Cross; Providence College; Stonehill College; University of Massachusetts Amherst.

Student Life Upper grades have uniform requirement, student council, honor system. Discipline rests primarily with faculty. Attendance at religious services is required.

Summer Programs Remediation, enrichment, sports programs offered; session focuses on remediation and sports camps; held on campus; accepts girls; not open to students from other schools. 75 students usually enrolled. 2006 schedule: June 26 to July 14.

Tuition and Aid Day student tuition: $8750. Tuition installment plan (FACTS Tuition Payment Plan, 2-payment plan). Merit scholarship grants, need-based scholarship grants, paying campus jobs, tuition reduction for daughters of employees available. In 2005–06, 56% of upper-school students received aid; total upper-school merit-scholarship money awarded: $9200. Total amount of financial aid awarded in 2005–06: $720,650.

Admissions Traditional secondary-level entrance grade is 9. For fall 2005, 570 students applied for upper-level admission, 310 were accepted, 145 enrolled. Archdiocese of Boston or STS required. Deadline for receipt of application materials: December 31. No application fee required.

Athletics Interscholastic: alpine skiing, basketball, cheering, cross-country running, dance team, golf, ice hockey, skiing (downhill), softball, swimming and diving, tennis, track and field, volleyball, winter (indoor) track; intramural: basketball, dance, flag football, floor hockey, lacrosse, physical fitness, physical training, strength & conditioning. 3 PE instructors, 26 coaches, 3 trainers.

Computers Computers are regularly used in all classes. Computer network features include on-campus library services, CD-ROMs, online commercial services, Internet access.

Contact Sr. Josephine Perico, CSJ, Admissions Assistant. 617-696-3241 Ext. 2105. Fax: 617-696-7688. E-mail: jperico@fontbonneacademy.org. Web site: www.fontbonneacademy.org.

FOOTHILLS ACADEMY

Calgary, Alberta, Canada
See Special Needs Schools section.

FORDHAM PREPARATORY SCHOOL

East Fordham Road
Bronx, New York 10458-5175
Head of School: Rev. Kenneth J. Boller, SJ

General Information Boys' day college-preparatory school, affiliated with Roman Catholic Church. Grades 9–12. Founded: 1841. Setting: urban. Nearest major city is New York. 5-acre campus. 2 buildings on campus. Approved or accredited by Jesuit Secondary Education Association, Middle States Association of Colleges and Schools, National Catholic Education Association, New York State Association of Independent Schools, and New York Department of Education. Endowment: $1 million. Total enrollment: 922. Upper school average class size: 24. Upper school faculty-student ratio: 1:11.

Upper School Student Profile Grade 9: 274 students (274 boys); Grade 10: 214 students (214 boys); Grade 11: 237 students (237 boys); Grade 12: 197 students (197 boys). 80% of students are Roman Catholic.

Faculty School total: 84. In upper school: 63 men, 21 women; 68 have advanced degrees.

Subjects Offered Advanced chemistry, algebra, American Civil War, American history, American history-AP, American literature, Ancient Greek, architectural drawing, art history-AP, biochemistry, biology, biology-AP, calculus, calculus-AP, chemistry, chemistry-AP, computer programming, constitutional history of U.S., creative writing, economics, electronics, English, English language and composition-AP, English literature-AP, European history-AP, forensic science, French, geometry, German, global studies, government and politics-AP, graphic design, health, Italian, Latin, Latin-AP, macroeconomics-AP, media communications, modern history, modern world history, music, physical education, physics, physics-AP, poetry, pre-calculus, religious studies, science research, short story, Spanish, Spanish language-AP, Spanish literature-AP, statistics-AP, studio art, studio art-AP, trigonometry, world history-AP.

Graduation Requirements Arts and fine arts (art, music, dance, drama), English, foreign language, mathematics, physical education (includes health), religious studies, science, social studies (includes history), senior service project.

Special Academic Programs Advanced Placement exam preparation in 18 subject areas; honors section; study at local college for college credit.

College Placement 225 students graduated in 2005; 223 went to college, including Fairfield University; Fordham University; Loyola College in Maryland; Manhattan College; New York University; Villanova University. Other: 2 went to work. Mean SAT verbal: 583, mean SAT math: 582.

Student Life Upper grades have specified standards of dress. Discipline rests primarily with faculty. Attendance at religious services is required.

Tuition and Aid Day student tuition: $10,230. Tuition installment plan (monthly payment plans). Merit scholarship grants, need-based scholarship grants available. In 2005–06, 30% of upper-school students received aid; total upper-school merit-scholarship money awarded: $300,000. Total amount of financial aid awarded in 2005–06: $1,000,000.

Admissions Traditional secondary-level entrance grade is 9. For fall 2005, 1,200 students applied for upper-level admission, 600 were accepted, 274 enrolled. Cooperative Entrance Exam (McGraw-Hill), ERB, ISEE, SSAT or STS required. Deadline for receipt of application materials: December 23. No application fee required. On-campus interview recommended.

Athletics Interscholastic: baseball, basketball, bowling, crew, cross-country running, diving, football, golf, ice hockey, indoor track, swimming and diving, tennis, track and field, volleyball, winter (indoor) track, wrestling; intramural: basketball, floor hockey, weight training. 2 PE instructors, 16 coaches, 3 trainers.

Computers Computers are regularly used in English, foreign language, history, mathematics, science classes. Computer network features include campus e-mail, on-campus library services, CD-ROMs, online commercial services, Internet access, file transfer, wireless campus network.

Contact Christopher D. Lauber, Director of Admissions. 718-584-8367. Fax: 718-367-7598. E-mail: lauberc@fordhamprep.org. Web site: fordhamprep.org.

FOREST HEIGHTS LODGE

Evergreen, Colorado
See Special Needs Schools section.

FORK UNION MILITARY ACADEMY

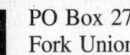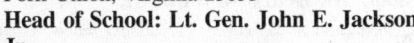

PO Box 278
Fork Union, Virginia 23055
Head of School: Lt. Gen. John E. Jackson Jr.

petersons.com

General Information Boys' boarding and day college-preparatory, arts, religious studies, technology, and Advanced Placement school, affiliated with Baptist Church. Grades 6–PG. Founded: 1898. Setting: rural. Nearest major city is Richmond. Students are housed in single-sex dormitories. 1,000-acre campus. 16 buildings on campus. Approved or accredited by Southern Association of Colleges and Schools, Southern Association of Independent Schools, Virginia Association of Independent Schools, and Virginia Department of Education. Member of National Association of Independent Schools. Endowment: $13 million. Total enrollment: 509. Upper school average class size: 13. Upper school faculty-student ratio: 1:15.

Upper School Student Profile Grade 9: 78 students (78 boys); Grade 10: 89 students (89 boys); Grade 11: 99 students (99 boys); Grade 12: 116 students (116 boys); Postgraduate: 64 students (64 boys). 97% of students are boarding students. 45% are state residents. 32 states are represented in upper school student body. 10% are international students. International students from Egypt, El Salvador, Mexico, Poland, Republic of Korea, and Sudan; 5 other countries represented in student body. 33% of students are Baptist.

Faculty School total: 48. In upper school: 33 men, 3 women; 29 have advanced degrees; 38 reside on campus.

Subjects Offered Algebra, American history, American literature, art, astronomy, Bible studies, biology, calculus, chemistry, creative writing, driver education, earth science, economics, English, English literature, French, geography, geometry, German, government/civics, grammar, health, history, humanities, mathematics, physical education, physics, religion, science, social science, social studies, sociology, Spanish, speech, trigonometry, world history, world literature.

Graduation Requirements English, foreign language, government, mathematics, physical education (includes health), religion (includes Bible studies and theology), science, social science, social studies (includes history).

Special Academic Programs Advanced Placement exam preparation in 5 subject areas; honors section; independent study; study at local college for college credit; remedial reading and/or remedial writing.

College Placement 126 students graduated in 2005; all went to college, including George Mason University; James Madison University; The Citadel, The Military College of South Carolina; University of Virginia; Virginia Military Institute; Virginia Polytechnic Institute and State University. 20% scored over 600 on SAT verbal, 25% scored over 600 on SAT math, 20% scored over 26 on composite ACT.

Student Life Upper grades have uniform requirement, student council, honor system. Discipline rests equally with students and faculty. Attendance at religious services is required.

Fork Union Military Academy

Summer Programs Remediation, enrichment, advancement, ESL, computer instruction programs offered; session focuses on academics; held on campus; accepts boys; open to students from other schools. 200 students usually enrolled. 2006 schedule: June 30 to July 31. Application deadline: none.

Tuition and Aid Day student tuition: $13,655; 7-day tuition and room/board: $19,990. Tuition installment plan (Key Tuition Payment Plan, monthly payment plans). Merit scholarship grants, need-based scholarship grants, need-based loans available. In 2005–06, 35% of upper-school students received aid. Total amount of financial aid awarded in 2005–06: $600,000.

Admissions Traditional secondary-level entrance grade is 9. For fall 2005, 292 students applied for upper-level admission, 250 were accepted, 187 enrolled. Deadline for receipt of application materials: none. Application fee required: $50. On-campus interview recommended.

Athletics Interscholastic: baseball, basketball, cross-country running, diving, drill team, football, golf, indoor soccer, indoor track & field, lacrosse, life saving, marksmanship, paint ball, physical fitness, physical training, power lifting, racquetball, riflery, running, scuba diving, skeet shooting, skydiving, snowboarding, soccer, squash, strength & conditioning, swimming and diving, table tennis, tennis, track and field, trap and skeet, volleyball, weight lifting, weight training, winter (indoor) track, winter soccer, wrestling; intramural: fitness, physical fitness, table tennis. 1 PE instructor, 4 coaches, 2 trainers.

Computers Computer network features include campus e-mail, on-campus library services, CD-ROMs, online commercial services, Internet access.

Contact Lt. Col. Steve Macek, Director of Admissions. 434-842-4205. Fax: 434-842-4300. E-mail: maceks@fuma.org. Web site: www.forkunion.com.

See full description on page 786.

THE FORMAN SCHOOL

Litchfield, Connecticut
See Special Needs Schools section.

FORSYTH COUNTRY DAY SCHOOL

5501 Shallowford Road
PO Box 549
Lewisville, North Carolina 27023-0549
Head of School: Mr. Henry M. Battle Jr.

General Information Coeducational day college-preparatory school. Grades PK–12. Founded: 1970. Setting: suburban. Nearest major city is Winston-Salem. 62-acre campus. 7 buildings on campus. Approved or accredited by North Carolina Association of Independent Schools, Southern Association of Colleges and Schools, Southern Association of Independent Schools, The College Board, and North Carolina Department of Education. Member of National Association of Independent Schools. Endowment: $9 million. Total enrollment: 990. Upper school average class size: 12. Upper school faculty-student ratio: 1:12.

Upper School Student Profile Grade 9: 88 students (47 boys, 41 girls); Grade 10: 106 students (61 boys, 45 girls); Grade 11: 107 students (63 boys, 44 girls); Grade 12: 91 students (55 boys, 36 girls).

Faculty School total: 160. In upper school: 17 men, 32 women; 24 have advanced degrees.

Subjects Offered Advanced Placement courses, advanced studio art-AP, algebra, American history, American history-AP, American literature, art, astronomy, biology, calculus, calculus-AP, ceramics, chemistry, Chinese studies, community service, computer math, computer programming, computer science, creative writing, digital art, drama, English, English literature, European history, fine arts, foreign policy, French, freshman seminar, geometry, grammar, health, history, history of science, humanities, international relations, Japanese studies, journalism, Latin, mathematics, Middle Eastern history, music, photography, physical education, physics, psychology, SAT/ACT preparation, science, social studies, Spanish, statistics-AP, theater, yearbook.

Graduation Requirements Arts and fine arts (art, music, dance, drama), English, foreign language, history, mathematics, physical education (includes health), science. Community service is required.

Special Academic Programs Advanced Placement exam preparation in 8 subject areas; honors section; academic accommodation for the gifted; programs in English, general development for dyslexic students; ESL (2 students enrolled).

College Placement 91 students graduated in 2005; all went to college, including Duke University; Elon University; North Carolina State University; The University of North Carolina at Chapel Hill; The University of North Carolina Wilmington; Wake Forest University. Median SAT verbal: 610, median SAT math: 600. 70% scored over 600 on SAT verbal, 68% scored over 600 on SAT math.

Student Life Upper grades have specified standards of dress, student council, honor system. Discipline rests equally with students and faculty.

Summer Programs Enrichment programs offered; session focuses on leadership training; held both on and off campus; held at various businesses and offices throughout the community; accepts boys and girls; open to students from other schools. 50 students usually enrolled. 2006 schedule: June 15 to July 31.

Tuition and Aid Day student tuition: $13,275. Tuition installment plan (Insured Tuition Payment Plan, monthly payment plans, individually arranged payment plans). Need-based scholarship grants available. In 2005–06, 10% of upper-school students received aid. Total amount of financial aid awarded in 2005–06: $348,502.

Admissions Traditional secondary-level entrance grade is 10. For fall 2005, 73 students applied for upper-level admission, 59 were accepted, 51 enrolled. ERB CTP IV, WRAT and writing sample required. Deadline for receipt of application materials: none. Application fee required: $100. On-campus interview required.

Athletics Interscholastic: baseball (boys), basketball (b,g), cross-country running (b,g), dance team (g), field hockey (g), football (b), lacrosse (b), soccer (b,g), softball (g), tennis (b,g), track and field (b,g), volleyball (g), wrestling (b); coed interscholastic: golf, swimming and diving. 4 PE instructors, 4 coaches, 1 trainer.

Computers Computers are regularly used in art, English, foreign language, history, mathematics, music, science classes. Computer network features include campus e-mail, on-campus library services, CD-ROMs, online commercial services, Internet access, DVD, wireless campus network.

Contact Lu Anne C. Wood, Director of Admission. 336-945-3151 Ext. 340. Fax: 336-945-2907. E-mail: luannewood@fcds.org. Web site: www.fcds.org.

FORT WORTH CHRISTIAN SCHOOL

7517 Bogart Drive
Fort Worth, Texas 76180
Head of School: Mr. Craig Smith

General Information Coeducational day college-preparatory, arts, religious studies, and technology school, affiliated with Church of Christ. Grades PK–12. Founded: 1957. Setting: suburban. Nearest major city is North Richland Hills. 35-acre campus. 6 buildings on campus. Approved or accredited by National Christian School Association, Southern Association of Colleges and Schools, Texas Private School Accreditation Commission, and Texas Department of Education. Endowment: $148,541. Total enrollment: 763. Upper school average class size: 20. Upper school faculty-student ratio: 1:11.

Upper School Student Profile Grade 9: 69 students (40 boys, 29 girls); Grade 10: 68 students (33 boys, 35 girls); Grade 11: 54 students (29 boys, 25 girls); Grade 12: 68 students (45 boys, 23 girls). 46% of students are members of Church of Christ.

Faculty School total: 40. In upper school: 13 men, 13 women; 9 have advanced degrees.

Subjects Offered Advanced Placement courses, algebra, anatomy and physiology, art, band, Bible studies, biology, calculus, chemistry, chorus, computer applications, computer information systems, drama, economics, economics and history, English, English language and composition-AP, English literature and composition-AP, family studies, French, geometry, government, government/civics, health, Latin, photography, physical education, physics, pre-calculus, SAT/ACT preparation, Spanish, U.S. history, video, world geography, world history, yearbook.

Graduation Requirements Arts and fine arts (art, music, dance, drama), business skills (includes word processing), computer science, electives, English, foreign language, mathematics, physical education (includes health), religion (includes Bible studies and theology), science, social science, social studies (includes history), world geography.

Special Academic Programs Advanced Placement exam preparation in 8 subject areas; honors section; independent study; study at local college for college credit.

College Placement 61 students graduated in 2005; 59 went to college, including Abilene Christian University; Baylor University; Texas A&M University; Texas Christian University; The University of Texas at Arlington; University of North Texas. Other: 2 went to work. Mean SAT verbal: 559, mean SAT math: 538, mean composite ACT: 23. 36% scored over 600 on SAT verbal, 19% scored over 600 on SAT math, 28% scored over 26 on composite ACT.

Student Life Upper grades have uniform requirement, student council, honor system. Discipline rests primarily with faculty. Attendance at religious services is required.

Summer Programs Remediation, advancement programs offered; session focuses on advancement; held both on and off campus; held at participants' homes for online courses; accepts boys and girls; not open to students from other schools. 20 students usually enrolled. 2006 schedule: June 7 to July 16. Application deadline: May 29.

Tuition and Aid Day student tuition: $6225–$6950. Tuition installment plan (monthly payment plans, individually arranged payment plans, tuition payment plans arranged through local bank). Tuition reduction for siblings, need-based scholarship grants, tuition reduction for children of faculty and staff available. In 2005–06, 30% of upper-school students received aid. Total amount of financial aid awarded in 2005–06: $138,500.

Admissions Traditional secondary-level entrance grade is 9. For fall 2005, 31 students applied for upper-level admission, 25 were accepted, 25 enrolled. Wechsler Individual Achievement Test required. Deadline for receipt of application materials: none. Application fee required: $475. On-campus interview required.

Athletics Interscholastic: aquatics (boys, girls), baseball (b), basketball (b,g), cheering (b,g), cross-country running (b,g), football (b), golf (b,g), power lifting (b), soccer (b,g), softball (g), swimming and diving (b,g), tennis (b,g), track and field (b,g), volleyball (g), weight lifting (b). 1 coach.

Computers Computers are regularly used in computer applications, desktop publishing, independent study, newspaper, technology, word processing, yearbook classes. Computer network features include on-campus library services, CD-ROMs, Internet access, DVD.

Contact Mrs. Kelly Cantrell, Coordinator of Student Services. 817-520-6511. Fax: 817-281-7063. E-mail: kcantrell@fwc.org. Web site: www.fwc.org.

FORT WORTH COUNTRY DAY SCHOOL

4200 Country Day Lane
Fort Worth, Texas 76109-4299
Head of School: Evan D. Peterson

General Information Coeducational day college-preparatory and arts school. Grades K–12. Founded: 1962. Setting: suburban. 100-acre campus. 13 buildings on campus. Approved or accredited by Independent Schools Association of the Southwest. Member of National Association of Independent Schools. Endowment: $19 million. Total enrollment: 1,100. Upper school average class size: 14. Upper school faculty-student ratio: 1:10.

Upper School Student Profile Grade 9: 96 students (42 boys, 54 girls); Grade 10: 96 students (43 boys, 53 girls); Grade 11: 93 students (42 boys, 51 girls); Grade 12: 93 students (42 boys, 51 girls).

Faculty School total: 125. In upper school: 16 men, 21 women; 29 have advanced degrees.

Subjects Offered Algebra, American history, American literature, art, art history, biology, calculus, ceramics, chemistry, comparative religion, computer math, computer programming, computer science, creative writing, dance, drama, driver education, earth science, ecology, economics, English, English literature, European history, expository writing, fine arts, French, geography, geology, geometry, government/civics, grammar, health, history, journalism, mathematics, modern problems, music, music history, photography, physical education, physics, science, social studies, Spanish, speech, study skills, technology, theater, trigonometry, typing, word processing, world history, writing.

Graduation Requirements Algebra, American government, arts and fine arts (art, music, dance, drama), biology, English, foreign language, lab science, mathematics, physical education (includes health), science, social studies (includes history), participation in athletics. Community service is required.

Special Academic Programs Advanced Placement exam preparation in 18 subject areas; honors section; independent study; term-away projects; study at local college for college credit; study abroad; academic accommodation for the gifted, the musically talented, and the artistically talented.

College Placement 91 students graduated in 2005; 90 went to college, including Texas A&M University; The University of Texas at Austin; Washington University in St. Louis. Other: 1 entered a postgraduate year. Mean SAT verbal: 649, mean SAT math: 656. 76% scored over 600 on SAT verbal, 85% scored over 600 on SAT math.

Student Life Upper grades have uniform requirement, student council, honor system. Discipline rests equally with students and faculty.

Summer Programs Remediation, enrichment, sports, art/fine arts programs offered; session focuses on athletics and enrichment; held both on and off campus; held at local golf course (for enrichment golf and golf team practice); accepts boys and girls; open to students from other schools. 300 students usually enrolled. 2006 schedule: June 1 to July 31. Application deadline: May 30.

Tuition and Aid Day student tuition: $13,335. Tuition installment plan (Key Tuition Payment Plan, monthly payment plans). Merit scholarship grants, need-based scholarship grants, Malone Scholars Program available. In 2005–06, 20% of upper-school students received aid; total upper-school merit-scholarship money awarded: $40,600. Total amount of financial aid awarded in 2005–06: $662,994.

Admissions Traditional secondary-level entrance grade is 9. For fall 2005, 76 students applied for upper-level admission, 38 were accepted, 30 enrolled. ERB or ISEE required. Deadline for receipt of application materials: March 3. Application fee required: $75. Interview required.

Athletics Interscholastic: baseball (boys), basketball (b,g), cheering (g), field hockey (g), football (b), lacrosse (b), swimming and diving (g), track and field (b,g), volleyball (b,g), winter soccer (b,g), wrestling (b); intramural: lacrosse (b); coed interscholastic: cross-country running, golf, independent competitive sports, ropes courses. 12 PE instructors, 45 coaches, 2 trainers.

Computers Computers are regularly used in architecture, college planning, creative writing, desktop publishing, English, foreign language, history, humanities, introduction to technology, library skills, life skills, mathematics, music, newspaper, publications, reading, science, Web site design, writing, yearbook classes. Computer network features include on-campus library services, CD-ROMs, online commercial services, Internet access, file transfer.

Contact Barbara Waldron Jiongo, Director of Admissions and Financial Aid. 817-302-3242. Fax: 817-377-3425. E-mail: bjiongo@fwcds.org. Web site: www.fwcds.org.

FOUNTAIN VALLEY SCHOOL OF COLORADO

6155 Fountain Valley School Road
Colorado Springs, Colorado 80911
Head of School: John E. Creeden, PhD

General Information Coeducational boarding and day college-preparatory, arts, and technology school. Grades 9–12. Founded: 1929. Setting: suburban. Nearest major city is Denver. Students are housed in single-sex dormitories. 1,100-acre campus. 41 buildings on campus. Approved or accredited by Association of Colorado Independent Schools, The Association of Boarding Schools, and Colorado Department of Education. Member of National Association of Independent Schools and Secondary School Admission Test Board. Endowment: $26 million. Total enrollment: 237. Upper school average class size: 12. Upper school faculty-student ratio: 1:5.

Upper School Student Profile Grade 9: 52 students (19 boys, 33 girls); Grade 10: 51 students (25 boys, 26 girls); Grade 11: 63 students (31 boys, 32 girls); Grade 12: 71 students (27 boys, 44 girls). 62% of students are boarding students. 55% are state residents. 20 states are represented in upper school student body. 20% are international students. International students from Germany, Japan, Mexico, Republic of Korea, Saudi Arabia, and Taiwan; 8 other countries represented in student body.

Faculty School total: 48. In upper school: 25 men, 23 women; 32 have advanced degrees; 30 reside on campus.

Subjects Offered 20th century history, 20th century world history, 3-dimensional art, 3-dimensional design, acting, advanced chemistry, advanced computer applications, advanced studio art-AP, algebra, American history, American history-AP, American literature, American politics in film, biology, biology-AP, British literature, calculus, calculus-AP, ceramics, chamber groups, chemistry, chemistry-AP, college counseling, Colorado ecology, composition, computer applications, computer multimedia, computer programming, creative writing, desktop publishing, drama, English, English literature and composition-AP, environmental science-AP, ESL, European history, fiction, film and literature, film history, French, French language-AP, geology, geometry, health, honors algebra, honors English, honors geometry, instrumental music, intro to computers, jewelry making, literature, musical productions, outdoor education, philosophy, photography, physics, physics-AP, pre-calculus, senior project, senior seminar, Shakespeare, short story, South African history, Spanish, Spanish language-AP, statistics and probability, statistics-AP, strings, student government, student publications, studio art, studio art-AP, U.S. government and politics-AP, visual and performing arts, vocal ensemble, Western civilization, wilderness/outdoor program, wind ensemble, world history, world history-AP, world literature, world wide web design, World-Wide-Web publishing, writing.

Graduation Requirements Arts and fine arts (art, music, dance, drama), computer science, English, foreign language, mathematics, physical education (includes health), science, social studies (includes history).

Special Academic Programs Advanced Placement exam preparation in 16 subject areas; honors section; independent study; term-away projects; academic accommodation for the gifted, the musically talented, and the artistically talented; ESL (12 students enrolled).

College Placement 64 students graduated in 2005; all went to college, including Cornell University; Hobart and William Smith Colleges; Kenyon College; The Colorado College; University of Colorado at Boulder. Mean SAT verbal: 585, mean SAT math: 560, mean composite ACT: 24.

Student Life Upper grades have specified standards of dress, student council, honor system. Discipline rests equally with students and faculty.

Summer Programs Rigorous outdoor training programs offered; session focuses on outdoor education, natural sciences, leadership; held both on and off campus; held at FVS' 40-acre Mountain Campus and surrounding Mount Princeton region; accepts boys and girls; open to students from other schools. 20 students usually enrolled. 2006 schedule: June 26 to July 8. Application deadline: none.

Tuition and Aid Day student tuition: $17,500; 7-day tuition and room/board: $31,400. Tuition installment plan (Key Tuition Payment Plan, monthly payment plans, individually arranged payment plans). Merit scholarship grants, need-based scholarship grants available. In 2005–06, 34% of upper-school students received aid; total upper-school merit-scholarship money awarded: $30,000. Total amount of financial aid awarded in 2005–06: $1,300,000.

Admissions Traditional secondary-level entrance grade is 9. For fall 2005, 176 students applied for upper-level admission, 128 were accepted, 81 enrolled. SSAT required. Deadline for receipt of application materials: February 1. Application fee required: $50. Interview required.

Athletics Interscholastic: basketball (boys, girls), cross-country running (b,g), diving (g), field hockey (g), indoor soccer (g), lacrosse (b), soccer (b,g), swimming and diving (g), tennis (b,g), track and field (b,g), volleyball (g); coed interscholastic: back packing, climbing, equestrian sports, fitness, horseback riding, independent competitive sports, outdoor education, outdoor recreation, outdoor skills, Polocrosse, rock climbing, rodeo, skiing (downhill), snowboarding, squash; coed intramural: aerobics/dance, aerobics/nautilus, alpine skiing, back packing, climbing, dance, golf, hiking/backpacking, horseback riding, mountain biking, mountaineering, outdoor education, Polocrosse, rock climbing, skiing (cross-country), skiing (downhill), snowboarding, squash, strength & conditioning, swimming and diving, telemark skiing, tennis, weight training, yoga. 2 coaches, 1 trainer.

Computers Computers are regularly used in all academic, college planning, multimedia, news writing, newspaper, photography, publications, theater, Web site

Fountain Valley School of Colorado

design, yearbook classes. Computer network features include campus e-mail, on-campus library services, CD-ROMs, online commercial services, Internet access, office computer access, DVD, Intranet.

Contact Mr. Randy Roach, Director of Admission. 719-390-7035 Ext. 251. Fax: 719-390-7762. E-mail: admission@fvs.edu. Web site: www.fvs.edu.

See full description on page 788.

FOWLERS ACADEMY

PO Box 921
Guaynabo, Puerto Rico 00970-0921
Head of School: Mrs. Doris N. De Jesús

General Information Coeducational day college-preparatory school, affiliated with Christian faith; primarily serves underachievers. Grades 7–12. Founded: 1986. Setting: suburban. 2-acre campus. 2 buildings on campus. Approved or accredited by Comisión Acreditadora de Instituciones Educativas, Middle States Association of Colleges and Schools, The College Board, and Puerto Rico Department of Education. Language of instruction: Spanish. Total enrollment: 75. Upper school average class size: 10. Upper school faculty-student ratio: 1:8.

Upper School Student Profile Grade 9: 15 students (12 boys, 3 girls); Grade 10: 11 students (8 boys, 3 girls); Grade 11: 17 students (15 boys, 2 girls); Grade 12: 12 students (11 boys, 1 girl).

Faculty School total: 11. In upper school: 6 men, 5 women; 3 have advanced degrees.

Subjects Offered Algebra, American literature, ancient world history, arts and crafts, Bible, career/college preparation, chemistry, Christian education, college counseling, computer literacy, earth science, ecology, English, ESL, film appreciation, geometry, keyboarding/computer, physical education, physics, pre-algebra, pre-college orientation, Puerto Rican history, Spanish, theater, U.S. history, world history.

Graduation Requirements Algebra, ancient world history, chemistry, Christian education, earth science, electives, English, geometry, physical education (includes health), physical science, physics, pre-college orientation, Puerto Rican history, Spanish, U.S. history, world history.

Special Academic Programs Accelerated programs; special instructional classes for students with ADD and LD; ESL (29 students enrolled).

College Placement 16 went to college, including University of Puerto Rico, Río Piedras; University of Puerto Rico at Carolina.

Student Life Upper grades have uniform requirement, student council, honor system. Discipline rests primarily with faculty. Attendance at religious services is required.

Summer Programs Remediation, ESL programs offered; session focuses on academic courses and remediation; held on campus; accepts boys and girls; open to students from other schools. 25 students usually enrolled. 2006 schedule: June 5 to June 30. Application deadline: May 31.

Tuition and Aid Day student tuition: $4200. Guaranteed tuition plan. Tuition installment plan (monthly payment plans). Tuition reduction for siblings, need-based scholarship grants available. In 2005–06, 6% of upper-school students received aid. Total amount of financial aid awarded in 2005–06: $10,500.

Admissions Traditional secondary-level entrance grade is 9. Deadline for receipt of application materials: none. No application fee required. Interview required.

Athletics Intramural: volleyball (boys, girls); coed intramural: basketball, physical fitness, table tennis. 1 PE instructor.

Computers Computers are regularly used in English, ESL, science, Spanish classes. Computer resources include Internet access.

Contact Mr. Carmelo Arbona, Registrar. 787-787-1350. Fax: 787-789-0055. E-mail: fowlers@coqui.net.

FOXCROFT SCHOOL

PO Box 5555
Middleburg, Virginia 20118
Head of School: Mary Louise Leipheimer

General Information Girls' boarding and day college-preparatory school. Grades 9–12. Founded: 1914. Setting: rural. Nearest major city is Washington, DC. Students are housed in single-sex dormitories. 500-acre campus. 52 buildings on campus. Approved or accredited by The Association of Boarding Schools and Virginia Association of Independent Schools. Member of National Association of Independent Schools and Secondary School Admission Test Board. Endowment: $23 million. Total enrollment: 169. Upper school average class size: 10. Upper school faculty-student ratio: 1:7.

Upper School Student Profile Grade 9: 34 students (34 girls); Grade 10: 44 students (44 girls); Grade 11: 55 students (55 girls); Grade 12: 36 students (36 girls). 73% of students are boarding students. 45% are state residents. 22 states are represented in upper school student body. 15% are international students. International students from Bermuda, Costa Rica, Mexico, Republic of Korea, Thailand, and Viet Nam; 4 other countries represented in student body.

Faculty School total: 38. In upper school: 10 men, 20 women; 22 have advanced degrees; 21 reside on campus.

Subjects Offered 3-dimensional art, acting, advanced chemistry, algebra, American literature, analytic geometry, anatomy and physiology, ancient world history, architecture, art, art history, astronomy, ballet, biology, botany, British literature, calculus, calculus-AP, cell biology, ceramics, chemistry, chemistry-AP, choir, chorus, Civil War, college counseling, community service, comparative religion, computer graphics, computer science, conceptual physics, constitutional law, creative dance, creative drama, creative writing, current events, dance, debate, digital photography, discrete math, drama, drawing and design, ecology, economics, economics-AP, English, English composition, English literature, English literature-AP, environmental science, European civilization, European history, European literature, expository writing, fine arts, fitness, forensic science, French, French language-AP, general science, geology, geometry, grammar, health education, history, human anatomy, independent study, leadership training, library, macroeconomics-AP, mathematics, microbiology, music, music theory, music theory-AP, oceanography, painting, performing arts, photography, physical education, physics, piano, poetry, pottery, pre-calculus, printmaking, public speaking, Roman civilization, SAT preparation, sculpture, senior project, social studies, Spanish, Spanish language-AP, Spanish literature, Spanish literature-AP, statistics and probability, studio art, studio art—AP, technology, The 20th Century, trigonometry, U.S. history, U.S. history-AP, vocal ensemble, weight fitness, world cultures, world literature, writing, yearbook, yoga.

Graduation Requirements Arts and fine arts (art, music, dance, drama), English, foreign language, history, mathematics, physical education (includes health), science.

Special Academic Programs Advanced Placement exam preparation in 12 subject areas; honors section; independent study; study abroad; academic accommodation for the gifted, the musically talented, and the artistically talented.

College Placement 42 students graduated in 2005; all went to college, including Goucher College; Radford University; Rhodes College; The George Washington University; University of the South; University of Virginia. Median SAT verbal: 620, median SAT math: 510, median composite ACT: 24. 39% scored over 600 on SAT verbal, 37% scored over 600 on SAT math.

Student Life Upper grades have specified standards of dress, student council. Discipline rests equally with students and faculty.

Tuition and Aid Day student tuition: $25,000; 7-day tuition and room/board: $35,700. Tuition installment plan (The Tuition Plan, Insured Tuition Payment Plan, Key Tuition Payment Plan, monthly payment plans, Tuition Management Systems Plan). Merit scholarship grants, need-based scholarship grants, need-based loans, middle-income loans available. In 2005–06, 22% of upper-school students received aid; total upper-school merit-scholarship money awarded: $98,700. Total amount of financial aid awarded in 2005–06: $890,000.

Admissions Traditional secondary-level entrance grade is 9. For fall 2005, 143 students applied for upper-level admission, 108 were accepted, 52 enrolled. SSAT required. Deadline for receipt of application materials: February 15. Application fee required: $50. Interview required.

Athletics Interscholastic: aerobics/dance, basketball, climbing, cross-country running, dance, dressage, equestrian sports, field hockey, figure skating, horseback riding, lacrosse, rock climbing, soccer, softball, tennis, volleyball; intramural: basketball, climbing, combined training, dance, dance team, dressage, equestrian sports, field hockey, fitness, horseback riding, lacrosse, modern dance, physical fitness, physical training, rock climbing, softball, strength & conditioning, weight training, yoga. 2 PE instructors, 1 trainer.

Computers Computers are regularly used in English, foreign language, history, mathematics, music, science classes. Computer network features include campus e-mail, on-campus library services, CD-ROMs, online commercial services, Internet access, DVD, wireless campus network.

Contact Rebecca B. Gilmore, Director of Admission. 800-858-2364. Fax: 540-687-3627. E-mail: admissions@foxcroft.org. Web site: www.foxcroft.org.

ANNOUNCEMENT FROM THE SCHOOL Foxcroft is dedicated to preparing young women for a future that demands intelligent responses, highly developed skills, and a firmly rooted character. The central components of a Foxcroft education are intellectual, but the School's commitment to the physical, emotional, social, and personal development of students is integrated into the holistic curriculum.

See full description on page 790.

FOX RIVER COUNTRY DAY SCHOOL

Elgin, Illinois
See Junior Boarding Schools section.

FOX VALLEY LUTHERAN ACADEMY

220 Division Street
Elgin, Illinois 60120
Head of School: Janet R. Zimdahl

General Information Coeducational day college-preparatory and religious studies school, affiliated with Lutheran Church. Grades 9–12. Founded: 1974. Setting: suburban. Nearest major city is Chicago. 1 building on campus. Approved or

accredited by North Central Association of Colleges and Schools and Illinois Department of Education. Total enrollment: 27. Upper school average class size: 8. Upper school faculty-student ratio: 1:4.

Upper School Student Profile Grade 9: 9 students (1 boy, 8 girls); Grade 10: 8 students (4 boys, 4 girls); Grade 11: 5 students (4 boys, 1 girl); Grade 12: 5 students (5 boys). 56% of students are Lutheran.

Faculty School total: 9. In upper school: 2 men, 6 women; 5 have advanced degrees.

Subjects Offered Algebra, American history, American literature, Bible studies, biology, business, chemistry, choir, computer science, earth science, economics, English, English literature, environmental science, fine arts, geography, geometry, government/civics, health, mathematics, music, physical education, physics, psychology, religion, science, social science, social studies, sociology, Spanish, speech, theology, trigonometry, typing, world history, world literature, writing.

Graduation Requirements Arts and fine arts (art, music, dance, drama), English, foreign language, mathematics, physical education (includes health), religion (includes Bible studies and theology), science, social science, social studies (includes history).

Special Academic Programs Independent study; study at local college for college credit.

College Placement 16 students graduated in 2005; 15 went to college, including Concordia University Wisconsin; Elgin Community College; Northern Illinois University; Valparaiso University. Other: 1 went to work. 3% scored over 26 on composite ACT.

Student Life Upper grades have specified standards of dress, student council. Discipline rests primarily with faculty. Attendance at religious services is required.

Tuition and Aid Day student tuition: $5600. Tuition installment plan (monthly payment plans, individually arranged payment plans, semi-annual payment plan, annual payment plan). Need-based scholarship grants available. In 2005–06, 25% of upper-school students received aid. Total amount of financial aid awarded in 2005–06: $25,000.

Admissions Traditional secondary-level entrance grade is 9. Deadline for receipt of application materials: none. Application fee required: $150. On-campus interview required.

Athletics Interscholastic: basketball (boys, girls), cheering (g), cross-country running (b,g), soccer (b), track and field (b,g), volleyball (g); coed interscholastic: basketball. 1 PE instructor, 4 coaches.

Computers Computers are regularly used in English, Spanish classes. Computer network features include campus e-mail, CD-ROMs, Internet access, office computer access, DVD.

Contact Jan Burmeister, Assistant Principal. 847-468-8207. Fax: 847-742-2930. E-mail: fvla_jb@yahoo.com. Web site: www.fvla.com.

FOX VALLEY LUTHERAN HIGH SCHOOL

5300 North Meade Street
Appleton, Wisconsin 54913-8383
Head of School: Mr. Paul Hartwig

General Information Coeducational day college-preparatory, general academic, arts, business, vocational, religious studies, and technology school, affiliated with Wisconsin Evangelical Lutheran Synod. Grades 9–12. Founded: 1953. Setting: suburban. Nearest major city is Green Bay. 63-acre campus. 1 building on campus. Approved or accredited by Wisconsin Department of Education. Endowment: $2 million. Total enrollment: 616. Upper school average class size: 25. Upper school faculty-student ratio: 1:14.

Upper School Student Profile Grade 9: 173 students (83 boys, 90 girls); Grade 10: 150 students (74 boys, 76 girls); Grade 11: 139 students (69 boys, 70 girls); Grade 12: 154 students (86 boys, 68 girls). 90% of students are Wisconsin Evangelical Lutheran Synod.

Faculty School total: 43. In upper school: 32 men, 11 women; 15 have advanced degrees.

Subjects Offered Accounting, advanced chemistry, advanced computer applications, advanced math, Advanced Placement courses, algebra, American government, American history, American literature, art, athletics, band, basic language skills, Basic programming, Bible, Bible studies, biology, British literature, British literature (honors), British literature-AP, business, business law, calculus, calculus-AP, choir, Christian doctrine, church history, communication skills, comparative religion, composition, computer applications, computer keyboarding, computer programming, computer skills, computer-aided design, concert band, concert choir, construction, critical writing, digital photography, drama, earth science, economics, economics-AP, English, English composition, foods, general science, geometry, German, government, graphic arts, health and wellness, honors English, keyboarding/computer, language and composition, Latin, Life of Christ, modern Western civilization, modern world history, personal fitness, physical fitness, physics, piano, psychology, reading/study skills, religion, remedial/makeup course work, sewing, Spanish, statistics, symphonic band, woodworking, world geography, world history.

Graduation Requirements 1½ elective credits, arts and fine arts (art, music, dance, drama), English, mathematics, physical education (includes health), religion (includes Bible studies and theology), science.

Special Academic Programs Advanced Placement exam preparation in 4 subject areas; honors section; accelerated programs; study at local college for college credit; academic accommodation for the gifted; remedial reading and/or remedial writing; remedial math.

College Placement 152 students graduated in 2005; 124 went to college, including Martin Luther College; University of Wisconsin–Fox Valley; University of Wisconsin–Green Bay; University of Wisconsin–Milwaukee; University of Wisconsin–Oshkosh; University of Wisconsin–Stevens Point. Other: 13 went to work, 8 entered military service.

Student Life Upper grades have specified standards of dress, student council, honor system. Discipline rests primarily with faculty. Attendance at religious services is required.

Tuition and Aid Day student tuition: $3985–$5600. Tuition installment plan (FACTS Tuition Payment Plan). Tuition reduction for siblings, need-based scholarship grants available. In 2005–06, 25% of upper-school students received aid. Total amount of financial aid awarded in 2005–06: $185,000.

Admissions Traditional secondary-level entrance grade is 9. Explore required. Deadline for receipt of application materials: none. Application fee required: $15. Interview required.

Athletics Interscholastic: baseball (boys), basketball (b,g), cheering (g), cross-country running (b,g), dance team (g), football (b), golf (b,g), ice hockey (b), softball (g), track and field (b,g), volleyball (g), wrestling (b). 2 PE instructors, 1 trainer.

Computers Computers are regularly used in business, current events, economics, English, graphic arts, keyboarding, science classes. Computer network features include campus e-mail, on-campus library services, CD-ROMs, Internet access, file transfer, office computer access.

Contact Mrs. Gloria Knoll, Guidance Assistant. 920-739-4441. E-mail: gknoll@fvlhs.org. Web site: www.fvlhs.org.

FRANCIS PARKER SCHOOL

6501 Linda Vista Road
San Diego, California 92111
Head of School: Mr. Timothy R. McIntire

General Information Coeducational day college-preparatory, arts, bilingual studies, and technology school. Grades JK–12. Founded: 1912. Setting: urban. Approved or accredited by Western Association of Schools and Colleges and California Department of Education. Member of National Association of Independent Schools. Endowment: $5.1 million. Total enrollment: 1,198. Upper school average class size: 15. Upper school faculty-student ratio: 1:15.

Upper School Student Profile Grade 9: 122 students (58 boys, 64 girls); Grade 10: 116 students (53 boys, 63 girls); Grade 11: 109 students (63 boys, 46 girls); Grade 12: 112 students (51 boys, 61 girls).

Faculty School total: 42. In upper school: 30 men, 12 women; 10 have advanced degrees.

Subjects Offered Algebra, American history, American literature, anthropology, art, art history, biology, business, calculus, ceramics, chemistry, community service, computer math, computer programming, computer science, CPR, creative writing, drama, earth science, economics, English, English literature, environmental science, ethics, European history, expository writing, fine arts, fitness, French, geography, geology, geometry, government/civics, grammar, health, history, journalism, Latin, marine biology, mathematics, microbiology, music, philosophy, photography, physical education, physics, physiology, psychology, science, social studies, Spanish, speech, theater, trigonometry, world history, world literature, writing.

Graduation Requirements Arts and fine arts (art, music, dance, drama), computer science, CPR, English, fitness, foreign language, mathematics, physical education (includes health), science, social studies (includes history), speech. Community service is required.

Special Academic Programs Advanced Placement exam preparation in 15 subject areas; honors section; independent study; term-away projects; study at local college for college credit; study abroad.

College Placement 96 students graduated in 2005; all went to college, including Stanford University; University of California, Berkeley; University of California, Los Angeles; University of Southern California. Median SAT verbal: 639, median SAT math: 640, median composite ACT: 26.

Student Life Upper grades have uniform requirement, student council, honor system. Discipline rests primarily with faculty.

Summer Programs Enrichment, advancement, sports, art/fine arts, computer instruction programs offered; held both on and off campus; held at water sports locales; accepts boys and girls; open to students from other schools. 2006 schedule: June 24 to August 2. Application deadline: none.

Tuition and Aid Day student tuition: $17,125. Tuition installment plan (monthly payment plans). Merit scholarship grants, need-based scholarship grants available. In 2005–06, 10% of upper-school students received aid; total upper-school merit-scholarship money awarded: $2000. Total amount of financial aid awarded in 2005–06: $1,900,000.

Admissions Traditional secondary-level entrance grade is 9. For fall 2005, 198 students applied for upper-level admission, 38 were accepted, 35 enrolled. ISEE required. Deadline for receipt of application materials: February 6. Application fee required: $100. Interview required.

Athletics Interscholastic: baseball (boys), basketball (b,g), crew (g), football (b), golf (b,g), hockey (b), independent competitive sports (b,g), lacrosse (b,g), rowing (g), soccer (b,g), softball (g), tennis (b,g), volleyball (b,g), weight training (b,g); coed interscholastic: cheering, cross-country running, dance, sailing, track and field; coed intramural: climbing, fitness, martial arts, physical fitness, physical training, strength & conditioning. 5 PE instructors, 55 coaches, 1 trainer.

Computers Computers are regularly used in English, foreign language, history, mathematics, science classes. Computer network features include campus e-mail, on-campus library services, CD-ROMs, online commercial services, Internet access.

Contact Mrs. Judy Conner, Director of Admissions. 858-569-7900. Fax: 858-569-0621. E-mail: jconner@francisparker.org. Web site: www.francisparker.org.

FRANCIS W. PARKER SCHOOL

330 West Webster Avenue
Chicago, Illinois 60614
Head of School: Dr. Daniel B. Frank

General Information Coeducational day college-preparatory school. Grades PK–12. Founded: 1901. Setting: urban. 5-acre campus. 1 building on campus. Approved or accredited by Independent Schools Association of the Central States, North Central Association of Colleges and Schools, The College Board, and Illinois Department of Education. Member of National Association of Independent Schools. Endowment: $13 million. Total enrollment: 913. Upper school average class size: 16. Upper school faculty-student ratio: 1:6.

Upper School Student Profile Grade 9: 82 students (37 boys, 45 girls); Grade 10: 79 students (40 boys, 39 girls); Grade 11: 80 students (37 boys, 43 girls); Grade 12: 79 students (42 boys, 37 girls).

Faculty School total: 100. In upper school: 24 men, 27 women; 45 have advanced degrees.

Subjects Offered Art, community service, drama, English, French, health, history, Latin, leadership, mathematics, music, physical education, science, social sciences, Spanish, yearbook.

Graduation Requirements Arts and fine arts (art, music, dance, drama), English, foreign language, mathematics, physical education (includes health), science, social studies (includes history). Community service is required.

Special Academic Programs Independent study.

College Placement 76 students graduated in 2005; 75 went to college, including Chapman University; DePaul University; Kenyon College; Middlebury College; University of Michigan; Wesleyan University. Other: 1 went to work.

Student Life Upper grades have specified standards of dress, student council, honor system. Discipline rests equally with students and faculty.

Tuition and Aid Day student tuition: $19,424. Tuition installment plan (Academic Management Services Plan, monthly payment plans, individually arranged payment plans). Need-based scholarship grants available. In 2005–06, 24% of upper-school students received aid. Total amount of financial aid awarded in 2005–06: $1,160,000.

Admissions Traditional secondary-level entrance grade is 9. For fall 2005, 129 students applied for upper-level admission, 53 were accepted, 23 enrolled. ISEE required. Deadline for receipt of application materials: none. Application fee required: $75. On-campus interview required.

Athletics Interscholastic: baseball (boys), basketball (b,g), cross-country running (b,g), field hockey (g), golf (b,g), soccer (b,g), softball (g), tennis (b,g), track and field (b,g); coed interscholastic: aerobics/nautilus, badminton, Cosom hockey, flag football, floor hockey, handball, in-line hockey, in-line skating, indoor hockey, indoor track & field, jogging, nautilus, roller blading, roller hockey, running, table tennis, ultimate Frisbee, volleyball, weight lifting, winter (indoor) track; coed intramural: floor hockey, strength & conditioning, volleyball. 6 PE instructors, 26 coaches, 1 trainer.

Computers Computers are regularly used in all academic, animation, design, engineering, music, video film production classes. Computer network features include campus e-mail, on-campus library services, CD-ROMs, online commercial services, Internet access, office computer access, DVD, wireless campus network, black & white and color printing.

Contact Rolanda Rogers Shepard, Admission Coordinator for Middle and Upper Schools. 773-797-5110. Fax: 773-549-0587. E-mail: rshepard@fwparker.org. Web site: www.fwparker.org.

FRANKLIN ROAD ACADEMY

4700 Franklin Road
Nashville, Tennessee 37220
Head of School: Dr. Margaret Wade

General Information Coeducational day college-preparatory, arts, religious studies, and technology school, affiliated with Christian faith. Grades PK–12. Founded: 1971. Setting: suburban. 55-acre campus. 3 buildings on campus. Approved or accredited by Southern Association of Colleges and Schools, Southern Association of Independent Schools, Tennessee Association of Independent Schools, and Tennessee Department of Education. Member of National Association of Independent Schools. Endowment: $500,000. Total enrollment: 958. Upper school average class size: 17. Upper school faculty-student ratio: 1:9.

Upper School Student Profile Grade 9: 79 students (38 boys, 41 girls); Grade 10: 84 students (39 boys, 45 girls); Grade 11: 82 students (46 boys, 36 girls); Grade 12: 68 students (37 boys, 31 girls). 90% of students are Christian.

Faculty School total: 98. In upper school: 21 men, 14 women; 20 have advanced degrees.

Subjects Offered Advanced chemistry, Advanced Placement courses, algebra, American history, American literature, art, art-AP, band, baseball, basketball, Bible, Bible studies, biology, biology-AP, calculus, calculus-AP, chemistry, chemistry-AP, choral music, Civil War, college counseling, computer education, computer music, computer programming, computer science, current events, dance, drama, dramatic arts, economics, economics and history, electronic music, English, English language-AP, English literature, English literature-AP, environmental science, European history, European history-AP, fine arts, French, French language-AP, French literature-AP, geometry, government/civics, grammar, history, history-AP, honors algebra, honors English, honors geometry, honors U.S. history, human anatomy, jazz band, keyboarding/computer, Latin, Latin-AP, Life of Christ, mathematics, mathematics-AP, model United Nations, music, music theory, personal development, physical education, physics, physics-AP, physiology-anatomy, pottery, pre-calculus, SAT preparation, SAT/ACT preparation, science, social science, social studies, Spanish, Spanish language-AP, Spanish literature-AP, speech, statistics, statistics-AP, student government, student publications, technical theater, theater, theater production, track and field, trigonometry, U.S. government, U.S. history, U.S. history-AP, vocal music, volleyball, weight training, world history, world literature, wrestling, writing.

Graduation Requirements Arts and fine arts (art, music, dance, drama), computer science, English, foreign language, mathematics, physical education (includes health), religion (includes Bible studies and theology), science, social studies (includes history). Community service is required.

Special Academic Programs Advanced Placement exam preparation in 10 subject areas; honors section; independent study; term-away projects; academic accommodation for the gifted, the musically talented, and the artistically talented.

College Placement 81 students graduated in 2005; all went to college, including Auburn University; Belmont University; Middle Tennessee State University; The University of Tennessee; University of Georgia. 40% scored over 600 on SAT verbal, 50% scored over 600 on SAT math, 50% scored over 26 on composite ACT.

Student Life Upper grades have specified standards of dress, student council, honor system. Discipline rests primarily with faculty.

Summer Programs Enrichment, sports, art/fine arts, computer instruction programs offered; session focuses on day camps, the arts, technology, and sports; held both on and off campus; held at swimming pool; accepts boys and girls; open to students from other schools. 400 students usually enrolled. 2006 schedule: June 5 to July 28.

Tuition and Aid Day student tuition: $11,790. Tuition installment plan (Insured Tuition Payment Plan, individually arranged payment plans). Need-based scholarship grants available. In 2005–06, 2% of upper-school students received aid. Total amount of financial aid awarded in 2005–06: $40,000.

Admissions Traditional secondary-level entrance grade is 9. For fall 2005, 104 students applied for upper-level admission, 65 were accepted, 23 enrolled. ISEE required. Deadline for receipt of application materials: none. Application fee required: $35. On-campus interview required.

Athletics Interscholastic: baseball (boys), basketball (b,g), bowling (b,g), cheering (g), cross-country running (b,g), dance (g), diving (b,g), football (b), golf (b,g), hockey (b), ice hockey (b), soccer (b,g), softball (g), swimming and diving (b,g), tennis (b,g), track and field (b,g), volleyball (g), wrestling (b); intramural: aerobics/dance (g), physical fitness (b,g), physical training (b,g), power lifting (b), strength & conditioning (b,g); coed intramural: aerobics/dance, riflery. 2 PE instructors, 2 coaches, 1 trainer.

Computers Computers are regularly used in art, Bible studies, college planning, creative writing, economics, English, foreign language, French, history, journalism, keyboarding, Latin, library skills, literary magazine, mathematics, music, religious studies, science, social sciences, Spanish, technology, theater, theater arts, Web site design, writing, yearbook classes. Computer network features include campus e-mail, on-campus library services, CD-ROMs, online commercial services, Internet access, file transfer, office computer access, DVD, wireless campus network, networked instructional software.

Contact Mrs. Jan Marshall, Associate Director of Admissions. 615-832-8845 Ext. 322. Fax: 615-834-4137. E-mail: marshallj@frapanthers.com. Web site: www.franklinroadacademy.com.

FRASER ACADEMY

Vancouver, British Columbia, Canada
See Special Needs Schools section.

FREDERICA ACADEMY

200 Hamilton Road
St. Simons Island, Georgia 31522
Head of School: Ms. Ellen E. Fleming

General Information Coeducational day college-preparatory, arts, and technology school. Grades PK–12. Founded: 1970. Setting: small town. Nearest major city is Jacksonville, FL. 18-acre campus. 7 buildings on campus. Approved or accredited by

Georgia Independent School Association, Southern Association of Colleges and Schools, and Georgia Department of Education. Member of National Association of Independent Schools. Total enrollment: 394. Upper school average class size: 18. Upper school faculty-student ratio: 1:9.

Upper School Student Profile Grade 9: 37 students (18 boys, 19 girls); Grade 10: 36 students (20 boys, 16 girls); Grade 11: 29 students (15 boys, 14 girls); Grade 12: 22 students (10 boys, 12 girls).

Faculty School total: 35. In upper school: 7 men, 8 women; 10 have advanced degrees.

Subjects Offered Algebra, American history, American literature, anatomy, ancient history, art, biology, biology-AP, calculus-AP, chemistry, choral music, computer applications, drama, economics, English, English literature, environmental science, geometry, government/civics, grammar, keyboarding/computer, literature-AP, photography, physical education, physical science, physics, pre-calculus, psychology, public speaking, science, Spanish, U.S. history-AP, world history, world literature, writing, yearbook.

Graduation Requirements Algebra, American government, American history, arts and fine arts (art, music, dance, drama), biology, chemistry, computer applications, economics, English literature, foreign language, geometry, physical education (includes health), world history.

Special Academic Programs Advanced Placement exam preparation in 4 subject areas; honors section.

College Placement 24 students graduated in 2005; all went to college, including Georgia Institute of Technology; University of Georgia. Mean SAT verbal: 634, mean SAT math: 579. 29% scored over 600 on SAT verbal, 35% scored over 600 on SAT math.

Student Life Upper grades have specified standards of dress, student council, honor system. Discipline rests primarily with faculty.

Summer Programs Enrichment, sports, art/fine arts, computer instruction programs offered; session focuses on enrichment; held both on and off campus; held at the beach (sailing class); accepts boys and girls; open to students from other schools. 200 students usually enrolled. 2006 schedule: June 14 to August 1. Application deadline: May 2.

Tuition and Aid Day student tuition: $11,500. Merit scholarship grants, need-based scholarship grants, local bank financing available. In 2005–06, 36% of upper-school students received aid. Total amount of financial aid awarded in 2005–06: $192,430.

Admissions Traditional secondary-level entrance grade is 9. For fall 2005, 25 students applied for upper-level admission, 20 were accepted, 20 enrolled. Any standardized test, Cognitive Abilities Test, OLSAT/Stanford and writing sample required. Deadline for receipt of application materials: none. Application fee required: $75. Interview required.

Athletics Interscholastic: baseball (boys), basketball (b,g), cheering (g), soccer (b,g), softball (g), tennis (b,g), volleyball (g); coed interscholastic: crew, cross-country running, golf, swimming and diving. 2 PE instructors, 5 coaches, 1 trainer.

Computers Computers are regularly used in all academic, library skills, photography, yearbook classes. Computer network features include on-campus library services, CD-ROMs, online commercial services, Internet access, office computer access.

Contact Ms. Jennifer Daniel, Director of Admission. 912-638-9981 Ext. 106. Fax: 912-638-1442. E-mail: jdaniel@fredericaacademy.org. Web site: www. fredericaacademy.org.

FREEMAN ACADEMY

748 South Main Street
Freeman, South Dakota 57029
Head of School: Mr. Marlan Kaufman

General Information Coeducational boarding and day college-preparatory, arts, and religious studies school, affiliated with Mennonite Church USA. Boarding grades 9–12, day grades 5–12. Founded: 1900. Setting: rural. Nearest major city is Sioux Falls. Students are housed in coed dormitories and host family homes. 80-acre campus. 6 buildings on campus. Approved or accredited by Mennonite Schools Council and South Dakota Department of Education. Endowment: $953,000. Total enrollment: 91. Upper school average class size: 10. Upper school faculty-student ratio: 1:8.

Upper School Student Profile Grade 9: 17 students (8 boys, 9 girls); Grade 10: 15 students (8 boys, 7 girls); Grade 11: 12 students (11 boys, 1 girl); Grade 12: 9 students (4 boys, 5 girls). 13% of students are boarding students. 92% are state residents. 2 states are represented in upper school student body. 5% are international students. International students from Taiwan and Turkey. 70% of students are Mennonite Church USA.

Faculty School total: 13. In upper school: 4 men, 7 women; 1 has an advanced degree; 2 reside on campus.

Subjects Offered Computer science, English, fine arts, mathematics, religion, science, social science, social studies.

Graduation Requirements Arts and fine arts (art, music, dance, drama), computer science, English, foreign language, mathematics, religion (includes Bible studies and theology), science, social studies (includes history).

Special Academic Programs Independent study; academic accommodation for the musically talented and the artistically talented.

College Placement 5 students graduated in 2005; 3 went to college, including Bethel College; Dordt College. Other: 2 went to work. Median composite ACT: 22.

Student Life Upper grades have specified standards of dress, honor system. Discipline rests primarily with faculty. Attendance at religious services is required.

Tuition and Aid Day student tuition: $4075; 5-day tuition and room/board: $8125; 7-day tuition and room/board: $8575. Tuition installment plan (monthly payment plans, semester payment plan). Merit scholarship grants, need-based scholarship grants available. In 2005–06, 13% of upper-school students received aid; total upper-school merit-scholarship money awarded: $500. Total amount of financial aid awarded in 2005–06: $5000.

Admissions Traditional secondary-level entrance grade is 9. For fall 2005, 9 students applied for upper-level admission, 9 were accepted, 9 enrolled. Deadline for receipt of application materials: none. No application fee required. Interview recommended.

Athletics Interscholastic: basketball (boys, girls), cross-country running (b,g), golf (b,g), soccer (b,g), track and field (b,g), volleyball (g). 3 coaches.

Computers Computers are regularly used in English, keyboarding, mathematics, religion, science, social studies, speech, yearbook classes. Computer network features include campus e-mail, on-campus library services, CD-ROMs, Internet access, DVD.

Contact Sara Flohrs, Enrollment Director. 605-925-4237 Ext. 225. Fax: 605-925-4271. E-mail: sflohrs@freemanacademy.pvt.k12.sd.us. Web site: www.freemanacademy.pvt.k12.sd.us.

FRENCH-AMERICAN SCHOOL OF NEW YORK

111 Larchmont Avenue
Larchmont, New York 10538
Head of School: Mr. Robert Leonhardt

General Information Coeducational day college-preparatory and bilingual studies school. Grades N–10. Founded: 1980. Setting: suburban. Nearest major city is White Plains. 1 building on campus. Approved or accredited by Middle States Association of Colleges and Schools, New York State Association of Independent Schools, and New York Department of Education. Languages of instruction: English and French. Total enrollment: 652. Upper school average class size: 19. Upper school faculty-student ratio: 1:6.

Upper School Student Profile Grade 9: 34 students (14 boys, 20 girls); Grade 10: 21 students (6 boys, 15 girls).

Faculty School total: 84. In upper school: 12 men, 22 women; 26 have advanced degrees.

Subjects Offered Algebra, American history, American literature, art, biology, civics, computer applications, computer multimedia, earth science, ecology, economics, English, ESL, European history, expository writing, French, French language-AP, French literature-AP, French studies, geometry, German, government, health, Latin, mathematics, multimedia, music, newspaper, philosophy, physical education, physics, public speaking, science, social studies, Spanish, Spanish language-AP, world history, world literature, writing, yearbook.

Special Academic Programs Advanced Placement exam preparation in 2 subject areas; honors section; ESL (32 students enrolled).

Student Life Upper grades have specified standards of dress, student council. Discipline rests primarily with faculty.

Tuition and Aid Day student tuition: $14,770–$19,750. Tuition installment plan (Academic Management Services Plan, Dewar Tuition Refund Plan). Need-based scholarship grants available. In 2005–06, 20% of upper-school students received aid. Total amount of financial aid awarded in 2005–06: $270,000.

Admissions Traditional secondary-level entrance grade is 9. For fall 2005, 11 students applied for upper-level admission, 8 were accepted, 8 enrolled. Deadline for receipt of application materials: none. Application fee required: $60. Interview recommended.

Athletics Interscholastic: baseball (boys), basketball (b,g), soccer (b,g), tennis (b,g), track and field (b,g); coed interscholastic: cross-country running, in-line hockey; coed intramural: fencing, in-line hockey. 2 PE instructors, 2 coaches.

Computers Computers are regularly used in art, English, foreign language, French, history, mathematics, music, publications, science classes. Computer network features include campus e-mail, on-campus library services, CD-ROMs, Internet access, laptop use (in certain classes).

Contact Mr. Antoine Agopian, Director of Admissions. 914-834-3002 Ext. 233. Fax: 914-834-1284. E-mail: aagopian@fasny.org. Web site: www.fasny.org.

FRESNO CHRISTIAN SCHOOLS

7280 North Cedar Avenue
Fresno, California 93720
Head of School: Gary D. Schultz

General Information Coeducational day college-preparatory, arts, religious studies, and technology school, affiliated with Protestant faith. Grades K–12. Founded: 1977. Setting: suburban. 27-acre campus. 8 buildings on campus. Approved or accredited by Association of Christian Schools International, Western Association of Schools and Colleges, and California Department of Education. Total enrollment: 720. Upper school average class size: 25. Upper school faculty-student ratio: 1:23.

Fresno Christian Schools

Upper School Student Profile Grade 9: 66 students (25 boys, 41 girls); Grade 10: 70 students (32 boys, 38 girls); Grade 11: 72 students (38 boys, 34 girls); Grade 12: 68 students (33 boys, 35 girls). 95% of students are Protestant.

Faculty School total: 53. In upper school: 19 men, 6 women; 14 have advanced degrees.

Subjects Offered Algebra, American government, American history-AP, American literature, art, athletics, band, Bible, Bible studies, biology, biology-AP, British literature, calculus-AP, career and personal planning, career/college preparation, ceramics, chemistry, choir, choral music, Christian education, college planning, computer applications, computer graphics, computer keyboarding, computer literacy, computer programming, concert band, drama, economics, English, English-AP, ensembles, filmmaking, French, geometry, home economics, honors English, humanities, journalism, leadership training, mathematics, physical science, physics, pre-calculus, Spanish, trigonometry, typing, U.S. history, video film production, world geography, world history, yearbook.

Graduation Requirements English, foreign language, mathematics, physical education (includes health), religion (includes Bible studies and theology), science, social science, social studies (includes history). Community service is required.

Special Academic Programs Advanced Placement exam preparation in 5 subject areas; honors section; independent study; study at local college for college credit; remedial reading and/or remedial writing; remedial math; special instructional classes for students with learning disabilities.

College Placement 68 students graduated in 2005; 61 went to college, including Biola University; California State University, Fresno; Fresno City College; Pacific University; Pepperdine University; Point Loma Nazarene University. Other: 3 went to work, 1 entered military service, 3 had other specific plans. Median SAT verbal: 556, median SAT math: 572.

Student Life Upper grades have specified standards of dress, student council, honor system. Discipline rests primarily with faculty. Attendance at religious services is required.

Summer Programs Remediation, advancement, sports programs offered; session focuses on make-up courses; held on campus; accepts boys and girls; not open to students from other schools. 115 students usually enrolled. 2006 schedule: June 1 to August 2. Application deadline: May 5.

Tuition and Aid Day student tuition: $6850. Tuition installment plan (FACTS Tuition Payment Plan, monthly payment plans, individually arranged payment plans). Tuition reduction for siblings, need-based scholarship grants available. In 2005–06, 9% of upper-school students received aid. Total amount of financial aid awarded in 2005–06: $300,000.

Admissions Traditional secondary-level entrance grade is 9. For fall 2005, 45 students applied for upper-level admission, 35 were accepted, 28 enrolled. Any standardized test required. Deadline for receipt of application materials: none. Application fee required: $100. Interview required.

Athletics Interscholastic: baseball (boys), basketball (b,g), cheering (g), drill team (g), football (b), soccer (b,g), softball (g), strength & conditioning (b,g), tennis (b,g), track and field (b,g), volleyball (g); intramural: flag football (b); coed interscholastic: physical training, rock climbing; coed intramural: badminton, climbing, volleyball. 2 PE instructors, 12 coaches, 1 trainer.

Computers Computers are regularly used in keyboarding, media production, publications, yearbook classes. Computer network features include campus e-mail, on-campus library services, CD-ROMs, Internet access, office computer access, wireless campus network.

Contact Jon Endicott, Vice Principal. 209-297-9464 Ext. 126. Fax: 209-299-1051. E-mail: jendicott@fresnochristian.com. Web site: www.fresnochristian.com.

FRIENDS ACADEMY

Duck Pond Road
Locust Valley, New York 11560
Head of School: Mr. William G. Morris Jr.

General Information Coeducational day college-preparatory school, affiliated with Society of Friends. Grades N–12. Founded: 1876. Setting: suburban. Nearest major city is New York. 65-acre campus. 8 buildings on campus. Approved or accredited by New York State Association of Independent Schools and New York Department of Education. Member of National Association of Independent Schools and Secondary School Admission Test Board. Endowment: $22 million. Total enrollment: 749. Upper school average class size: 15. Upper school faculty-student ratio: 1:6.

Upper School Student Profile Grade 9: 92 students (46 boys, 46 girls); Grade 10: 87 students (40 boys, 47 girls); Grade 11: 88 students (41 boys, 47 girls); Grade 12: 90 students (42 boys, 48 girls). 2% of students are members of Society of Friends.

Faculty School total: 109. In upper school: 28 men, 33 women; 43 have advanced degrees.

Subjects Offered Advanced Placement courses, African studies, algebra, American history, American literature, art, art history, Bible studies, biology, calculus, ceramics, chemistry, community service, computer literacy, computer programming, computer science, creative writing, drama, driver education, English, English literature, environmental science, ethics, European history, expository writing, fine arts, French, geography, geometry, grammar, Greek, health, history, Italian, Latin, logic, mathematics, mechanical drawing, music, outdoor education, photography, physical

education, physics, psychology, religion, science, social science, social studies, Spanish, speech, theater, trigonometry, Western civilization, world literature, writing.

Graduation Requirements Arts and fine arts (art, music, dance, drama), computer literacy, English, foreign language, mathematics, outdoor education, physical education (includes health), religion (includes Bible studies and theology), science, social science, social studies (includes history), speech, participation in on-campus work crew program. Community service is required.

Special Academic Programs Advanced Placement exam preparation in 19 subject areas; honors section; independent study.

College Placement 84 students graduated in 2005; all went to college, including Boston College; Boston University; Cornell University; New York University; The George Washington University; Yale University. Mean SAT verbal: 595, mean SAT math: 616.

Student Life Upper grades have specified standards of dress, student council. Discipline rests primarily with faculty. Attendance at religious services is required.

Summer Programs Art/fine arts programs offered; session focuses on using the arts to learn life skills and using life skills to explore the arts (via The Artist's Institute); held on campus; accepts boys and girls; open to students from other schools. 25 students usually enrolled. 2006 schedule: June 19 to July 22.

Tuition and Aid Day student tuition: $22,900. Tuition installment plan (Insured Tuition Payment Plan, monthly payment plans). Need-based scholarship grants, Quaker grants, tuition remission for children of faculty and staff available. In 2005–06, 20% of upper-school students received aid. Total amount of financial aid awarded in 2005–06: $1,000,000.

Admissions Traditional secondary-level entrance grade is 9. For fall 2005, 98 students applied for upper-level admission, 58 were accepted, 44 enrolled. SSAT required. Deadline for receipt of application materials: January 13. Application fee required: $35. On-campus interview required.

Athletics Interscholastic: baseball (boys), basketball (b,g), crew (b,g), cross-country running (b,g), field hockey (g), football (b), golf (b), indoor track & field (b,g), lacrosse (b,g), soccer (b,g), softball (g), tennis (b,g), track and field (b,g), winter (indoor) track (b,g), wrestling (b); coed intramural: dance, volleyball. 7 PE instructors, 1 trainer.

Computers Computers are regularly used in English, mathematics, science, technology classes. Computer network features include campus e-mail, on-campus library services, CD-ROMs, online commercial services, Internet access, file transfer, office computer access, DVD, wireless campus network.

Contact Patty Ziplow, Director of Admissions and Financial Aid. 516-676-0393. Fax: 516-465-1718. E-mail: patty_ziplow@fa.org. Web site: www.fa.org.

ANNOUNCEMENT FROM THE SCHOOL Founded in 1876 by Gideon Frost for "the children of Friends and those similarly sentimented," Friends Academy is a Quaker, coeducational, independent, college-preparatory day school serving students from age 3 through grade 12. The school's philosophy is based on the principles of integrity, simplicity, patience, moderation, peaceful resolution of conflict, and a belief that the silence and simple ministry of the "gathered meeting" brings the presence of God into the midst of busy lives. Friends Academy is committed to developing a diverse community whose members value excellence in learning and growth in knowledge and skills, a genuine commitment to service and ethical action, and a realization that every life is to be explored, celebrated, and enjoyed in the spirit of the Religious Society of Friends. Courses in classical studies, modern and interdisciplinary studies, Quakerism, community service, athletics, and creative and performing arts provide a comprehensive educational experience for all members of the school community. The full program is accredited by the New York State Association of Independent Schools (NYSAIS). All students, faculty, and staff attend a silent Meeting for Worship, in the manner of Friends, each week. Several years ago, the entire school constituency constructed a strategic master plan that provided the framework for the future growth of the school. Success in an ambitious capital campaign has allowed Friends Academy to improve and expand the Middle School; create a new Upper School science center; construct the Helen A. Dolan Center, a state-of-the-art theater, arts center, and commons; build the Kumar Wang Library, the intellectual heart of the school; and renovate and restore Gideon Frost Hall, which houses Upper School classrooms and administrative offices.

FRIENDS' CENTRAL SCHOOL

1101 City Avenue
Wynnewood, Pennsylvania 19096
Head of School: David Felsen

General Information Coeducational day college-preparatory school, affiliated with Society of Friends. Grades PK–12. Founded: 1845. Setting: suburban. Nearest major city is Philadelphia. 23-acre campus. 7 buildings on campus. Approved or accredited by Pennsylvania Association of Private Academic Schools and Pennsylvania Department of Education. Member of National Association of Independent Schools. Endowment: $14 million. Total enrollment: 993. Upper school average class size: 15. Upper school faculty-student ratio: 1:9.

Upper School Student Profile Grade 9: 95 students (51 boys, 44 girls); Grade 10: 96 students (52 boys, 44 girls); Grade 11: 98 students (49 boys, 49 girls); Grade 12: 100 students (53 boys, 47 girls). 4% of students are members of Society of Friends.
Faculty School total: 130. In upper school: 25 men, 23 women; 42 have advanced degrees.
Subjects Offered Advanced math, algebra, American history, American literature, Bible, biology, biology-AP, calculus, calculus-AP, ceramics, chemistry, chemistry-AP, chorus, computer applications, computer programming, conflict resolution, drama, English, French, French-AP, geometry, instrumental music, Latin, Latin-AP, life skills, media studies, modern European history, music history, music theory, philosophy, photography, physical education, physical science, physics, pre-calculus, psychology, sexuality, Spanish, Spanish-AP, statistics-AP, studio art, study skills, Western literature, women in world history, woodworking, world history, writing workshop.
Graduation Requirements Arts and fine arts (art, music, dance, drama), English, foreign language, history, mathematics, science.
Special Academic Programs Advanced Placement exam preparation in 10 subject areas.
College Placement 92 students graduated in 2005; 91 went to college, including Bard College; Brown University; Dickinson College; Syracuse University; University of Pennsylvania. Other: 1 had other specific plans. Mean SAT verbal: 645, mean SAT math: 644. 65% scored over 600 on SAT verbal, 76% scored over 600 on SAT math.
Student Life Upper grades have specified standards of dress, student council. Discipline rests primarily with faculty. Attendance at religious services is required.
Summer Programs Remediation, enrichment programs offered; session focuses on math and English; held on campus; accepts boys and girls; open to students from other schools. 35 students usually enrolled. 2006 schedule: June 26 to August 4. Application deadline: June 1.
Tuition and Aid Day student tuition: $20,185. Tuition installment plan (monthly payment plans, Higher Education Service, Inc). Need-based scholarship grants available. In 2005–06, 25% of upper-school students received aid. Total amount of financial aid awarded in 2005–06: $2,485,625.
Admissions Traditional secondary-level entrance grade is 9. For fall 2005, 140 students applied for upper-level admission, 58 were accepted, 28 enrolled. ISEE, SSAT or Wechsler Intelligence Scale for Children III required. Deadline for receipt of application materials: January 15. Application fee required: $35. On-campus interview required.
Athletics Interscholastic: aquatics (boys, girls), baseball (b), basketball (b,g), cross-country running (b,g), field hockey (g), indoor track & field (b,g), lacrosse (b,g), soccer (b,g), softball (g), swimming and diving (b,g), tennis (b,g), track and field (b,g), winter (indoor) track (b,g); coed interscholastic: cheering, golf, polo, water polo, wrestling; coed intramural: aerobics/dance, aerobics/nautilus, dance, fitness, nautilus, physical fitness, physical training, strength & conditioning. 8 PE instructors, 10 coaches, 1 trainer.
Computers Computers are regularly used in college planning, foreign language, French, health, information technology, introduction to technology, mathematics, publishing, science, Spanish, technology, Web site design, yearbook classes. Computer network features include campus e-mail, on-campus library services, CD-ROMs, online commercial services, Internet access, file transfer, office computer access, DVD, wireless campus network, Intranet collaboration.
Contact Barbara Behar, Director of Admission and Financial Aid. 610-649-7440. Fax: 610-649-5669. E-mail: admission@friendscentral.org. Web site: www.friendscentral.org.

FRIENDS SCHOOL OF BALTIMORE

5114 North Charles Street
Baltimore, Maryland 21210
Head of School: Matthew Micciche

General Information Coeducational day college-preparatory, arts, and technology school, affiliated with Society of Friends. Grades PK–12. Founded: 1784. Setting: urban. 34-acre campus. 8 buildings on campus. Approved or accredited by Association of Independent Maryland Schools, Friends Council on Education, and Middle States Association of Colleges and Schools. Member of National Association of Independent Schools, Secondary School Admission Test Board, and Educational Records Bureau. Endowment: $16.6 million. Total enrollment: 980. Upper school average class size: 17. Upper school faculty-student ratio: 1:11.
Upper School Student Profile Grade 9: 88 students (44 boys, 44 girls); Grade 10: 92 students (46 boys, 46 girls); Grade 11: 94 students (42 boys, 52 girls); Grade 12: 89 students (47 boys, 42 girls). 5% of students are members of Society of Friends.
Faculty School total: 115. In upper school: 17 men, 17 women; 26 have advanced degrees.
Subjects Offered Algebra, American history, American literature, art, art history, biology, calculus, chemistry, computer math, computer science, CPR, creative writing, dance, drama, economics, English, English literature, environmental science, first aid, French, geometry, health, history, history of science, journalism, Latin, mathematics, music, photography, physical education, physics, Russian, science, social studies, Spanish, statistics, theater, trigonometry, world history, world literature.
Graduation Requirements American history, computer science, CPR, English, first aid, mathematics, physical education (includes health), science, social studies (includes history). Community service is required.

Special Academic Programs Advanced Placement exam preparation in 14 subject areas; accelerated programs; term-away projects; study abroad.
College Placement 90 students graduated in 2005; 89 went to college, including Gettysburg College; Skidmore College; State Fair Community College; Tufts University; University of Chicago; University of Maryland, College Park. Other: 1 had other specific plans. Median SAT verbal: 655, median SAT math: 636. 60% scored over 600 on SAT verbal, 56% scored over 600 on SAT math.
Student Life Upper grades have specified standards of dress, student council. Discipline rests equally with students and faculty. Attendance at religious services is required.
Summer Programs Art/fine arts, computer instruction programs offered; session focuses on computers; held on campus; accepts boys and girls; open to students from other schools. 200 students usually enrolled. 2006 schedule: June 17 to July 28. Application deadline: none.
Tuition and Aid Day student tuition: $16,610. Tuition installment plan (Key Tuition Payment Plan, monthly payment plans). Need-based scholarship grants, need-based loans, middle-income loans available. In 2005–06, 30% of upper-school students received aid. Total amount of financial aid awarded in 2005–06: $690,244.
Admissions Traditional secondary-level entrance grade is 9. For fall 2005, 165 students applied for upper-level admission, 55 were accepted, 27 enrolled. ISEE or SSAT required. Deadline for receipt of application materials: none. Application fee required: $45. Interview required.
Athletics Interscholastic: aerobics/dance (girls), badminton (g), baseball (b), basketball (b,g), cross-country running (b,g), field hockey (g), football (b), golf (b,g), indoor soccer (g), lacrosse (b,g), soccer (b,g), softball (g), tennis (b,g); intramural: aerobics/dance (g), fitness (b,g), softball (b); coed interscholastic: cross-country running, dance squad, golf; coed intramural: aerobics/dance, archery, fitness. 7 PE instructors, 5 coaches, 1 trainer.
Computers Computers are regularly used in all academic, English, history, mathematics, science classes. Computer network features include campus e-mail, on-campus library services, CD-ROMs, online commercial services, Internet access, file transfer, office computer access.
Contact Karen E. Dates, Director of Admission and Outreach. 410-649-3207. Fax: 410-649-3302. E-mail: kdates@friendsbalt.org. Web site: www.friendsbalt.org.

FRIENDS SEMINARY

222 East 16th Street
New York, New York 10003
Head of School: Robert N. Lauder

General Information Coeducational day college-preparatory school, affiliated with Society of Friends. Grades K–12. Founded: 1786. Setting: urban. 7 buildings on campus. Approved or accredited by New York State Association of Independent Schools and New York Department of Education. Member of National Association of Independent Schools. Endowment: $6 million. Total enrollment: 653. Upper school average class size: 15. Upper school faculty-student ratio: 1:6.
Upper School Student Profile Grade 9: 74 students (42 boys, 32 girls); Grade 10: 67 students (29 boys, 38 girls); Grade 11: 62 students (34 boys, 28 girls); Grade 12: 64 students (27 boys, 37 girls). 3% of students are members of Society of Friends.
Faculty School total: 103. In upper school: 20 men, 26 women; 31 have advanced degrees.
Subjects Offered Acting, African-American studies, algebra, American history, American literature, anthropology, architecture, art history, biology, calculus, ceramics, chemistry, chorus, community service, computer math, computer programming, computer science, creative writing, drama, driver education, ecology, English, English literature, environmental science, European history, experiential education, fabric arts, fine arts, French, genetics, geology, geometry, government/civics, Greek, health, history, human relations, international relations, Internet, jazz, Latin, law, marine biology, mathematics, media, music, musical productions, philosophy, photography, physical education, physics, playwriting, science, sculpture, social studies, Spanish, statistics, theater, trigonometry, wilderness education, women's studies, world history, world literature, world religions.
Graduation Requirements Arts and fine arts (art, music, dance, drama), computer science, English, experiential education, foreign language, human relations, mathematics, physical education (includes health), science, social studies (includes history), 7 hours in-school and 20 hours out-of-school community service per year.
Special Academic Programs Advanced Placement exam preparation in 13 subject areas; independent study; term-away projects; domestic exchange program; study abroad.
College Placement 61 students graduated in 2005; all went to college, including Cornell University; Harvard University; Haverford College; Northwestern University; Tufts University; Wesleyan University. Median SAT verbal: 660, median SAT math: 640.
Student Life Upper grades have student council, honor system. Discipline rests primarily with faculty.
Summer Programs Session focuses on mathematics and composition; held on campus; accepts boys and girls; open to students from other schools.
Tuition and Aid Day student tuition: $24,950. Tuition installment plan (The Tuition Plan, Insured Tuition Payment Plan, Key Tuition Payment Plan, monthly payment plans, individually arranged payment plans). Need-based scholarship grants, need-

based loans, middle-income loans, PLITT Loans available. In 2005–06, 28% of upper-school students received aid. Total amount of financial aid awarded in 2005–06: $2,548,500.

Admissions Traditional secondary-level entrance grade is 9. ISEE or SSAT required. Deadline for receipt of application materials: January 15. Application fee required: $50. On-campus interview required.

Athletics Interscholastic: baseball (boys), basketball (b,g), soccer (b,g), softball (g), tennis (b,g), volleyball (g); coed interscholastic: golf, squash, swimming and diving, track and field, volleyball. 5 PE instructors, 5 coaches.

Computers Computers are regularly used in all academic classes. Computer network features include campus e-mail, CD-ROMs, online commercial services, Internet access.

Contact Harriet O. Burnett, Director of Admissions. 212-979-5030 Ext. 141. Fax: 212-677-5543. E-mail: hburnett@friendsseminary.org. Web site: www. friendsseminary.org.

THE FROSTIG SCHOOL
Pasadena, California
See Special Needs Schools section.

FRYEBURG ACADEMY
745 Main Street
Fryeburg, Maine 04037-1329
Head of School: Daniel G. Lee Jr.

petersons.com

General Information Coeducational boarding and day college-preparatory, general academic, arts, vocational, bilingual studies, and technology school. Grades 9–PG. Founded: 1792. Setting: small town. Nearest major city is Portland. Students are housed in single-sex dormitories. 34-acre campus. 15 buildings on campus. Approved or accredited by Association of Independent Schools in New England, Independent Schools of Northern New England, New England Association of Schools and Colleges, The Association of Boarding Schools, The College Board, and Maine Department of Education. Member of National Association of Independent Schools and Secondary School Admission Test Board. Endowment: $5.5 million. Total enrollment: 668. Upper school average class size: 15. Upper school faculty-student ratio: 1:10.

Upper School Student Profile 20% of students are boarding students. 5% are state residents. 10 states are represented in upper school student body. 15% are international students. International students from Germany, Republic of Korea, Spain, Taiwan, Thailand, and Viet Nam; 14 other countries represented in student body.

Faculty School total: 63. In upper school: 34 men, 29 women; 22 have advanced degrees; 25 reside on campus.

Subjects Offered Algebra, American literature, anatomy, art, art history, biology, botany, business, calculus, chemistry, computer math, computer programming, computer science, creative writing, drafting, drama, driver education, earth science, ecology, economics, English, English literature, ethics, European history, expository writing, fine arts, French, geography, geometry, government/civics, grammar, health, history, industrial arts, journalism, Latin, linear algebra, marine biology, mathematics, mechanical drawing, music, photography, physical education, physics, physiology, psychology, science, social studies, sociology, Spanish, speech, theater, trigonometry, typing, world history, world literature, writing.

Graduation Requirements Arts and fine arts (art, music, dance, drama), computer science, English, foreign language, mathematics, physical education (includes health), science, social studies (includes history). Community service is required.

Special Academic Programs Advanced Placement exam preparation in 12 subject areas; honors section; independent study; study at local college for college credit; academic accommodation for the musically talented; remedial reading and/or remedial writing; remedial math; programs in English, mathematics, general development for dyslexic students; special instructional classes for students with learning disabilities, Attention Deficit Disorder, and dyslexia; ESL (44 students enrolled).

College Placement 158 students graduated in 2005; 124 went to college, including Bentley College; Boston College; Boston University; Northeastern University; University of Maine; University of New Hampshire. Other: 28 went to work, 6 entered military service. Mean SAT verbal: 493, mean SAT math: 495. 11% scored over 600 on SAT verbal, 17% scored over 600 on SAT math.

Student Life Upper grades have student council. Discipline rests primarily with faculty.

Tuition and Aid Day student tuition: $15,600; 7-day tuition and room/board: $31,200. Tuition installment plan (Academic Management Services Plan, monthly payment plans, individually arranged payment plans). Need-based scholarship grants, paying campus jobs, merit-based aid (some need required) available. In 2005–06, 43% of upper-school students received aid. Total amount of financial aid awarded in 2005–06: $750,000.

Admissions Traditional secondary-level entrance grade is 11. For fall 2005, 170 students applied for upper-level admission, 106 were accepted, 57 enrolled. Writing sample required. Deadline for receipt of application materials: none. Application fee required: $50. Interview required.

Athletics Interscholastic: baseball (boys), basketball (b,g), cross-country running (b,g), field hockey (g), football (b), golf (b), hockey (b,g), ice hockey (b,g), lacrosse (b,g), skiing (cross-country) (b,g), skiing (downhill) (b,g), snowboarding (b,g), soccer (b,g), softball (g), tennis (b,g), track and field (b,g), wrestling (b); intramural: strength & conditioning (b,g), table tennis (b,g); coed interscholastic: alpine skiing, cheering, mountain biking, nordic skiing; coed intramural: alpine skiing, archery, back packing, badminton, ball hockey, basketball, bicycling, billiards, bowling, canoeing/kayaking, climbing, figure skating, fishing, fitness, fitness walking, flag football, floor hockey, fly fishing, freestyle skiing, Frisbee, golf, hiking/backpacking, ice skating, jogging, kayaking, mountain biking, mountaineering, paint ball, physical fitness, physical training, pistol, rock climbing, roller blading, skiing (downhill), snowboarding, snowshoeing, swimming and diving, table tennis, telemark skiing, tennis, volleyball, walking, wall climbing, weight lifting, whiffle ball, winter walking. 1 PE instructor, 3 coaches, 1 trainer.

Computers Computers are regularly used in all classes. Computer network features include campus e-mail, on-campus library services, CD-ROMs, Internet access, file transfer, wireless campus network.

Contact Stephanie S. Morin, Director of Admission. 207-935-2013. Fax: 207-935-4292. E-mail: admissions@fryeburgacademy.org. Web site: www.fryeburgacademy.org.

ANNOUNCEMENT FROM THE SCHOOL Nestled in the foothills of the White Mountains, Fryeburg Academy has been the center of the small village of Fryeburg, Maine, since 1792. The Academy prides itself on its diversity; students from 50 countries and many U.S. states have called Fryeburg Academy home. Such diversity has created an incredibly caring, supportive atmosphere for all Academy students. The Academy's curriculum supports a wide range of classes and programs adapted to meet the needs of such a diverse student body. Recognizing that young people of varying aptitudes, interests, and abilities must be prepared to meet the challenges of a complex world, Fryeburg Academy offers both college-preparatory and business/pre-vocational curricula. Students have the opportunity to study and explore both areas. A minimum of 19 credits is required for graduation; these must include the following courses: English, history, science, mathematics, and computer proficiency. Students must enroll in at least 5 academic subjects each semester, but most elect to carry 6 courses. The curriculum offers English as a second language (ESL) and 11 Advanced Placement courses. Remedial and developmental reading programs are available for students with learning differences. Interscholastic sports include field hockey, soccer, football, cross-country, golf, tennis, lacrosse, wrestling, basketball, baseball, softball, alpine and Nordic skiing, snowboarding, ice hockey, and track and field. A great attraction is the wealth of natural resources, as well as close access to culture and entertainment. The White Mountains present students with the potential for endless outdoor adventures that include skiing, snowboarding, and hiking. Afternoon and weekend activities provide transportation for these and other opportunities, such as shopping in Boston or Portland or seeing a play in nearby Conway, New Hampshire.

FUQUA SCHOOL
605 Fuqua Drive
PO Drawer 328
Farmville, Virginia 23901
Head of School: Ms. Ruth S. Murphy

General Information Coeducational day college-preparatory, arts, business, and technology school. Grades PK–12. Founded: 1993. Setting: small town. Nearest major city is Richmond. 60-acre campus. 19 buildings on campus. Approved or accredited by Southern Association of Colleges and Schools, Virginia Association of Independent Schools, and Virginia Department of Education. Member of Secondary School Admission Test Board. Total enrollment: 528. Upper school average class size: 16. Upper school faculty-student ratio: 1:16.

Upper School Student Profile Grade 9: 36 students (21 boys, 15 girls); Grade 10: 39 students (19 boys, 20 girls); Grade 11: 41 students (17 boys, 24 girls); Grade 12: 35 students (11 boys, 24 girls).

Faculty School total: 58. In upper school: 6 men, 12 women; 6 have advanced degrees.

Subjects Offered Accounting, advanced computer applications, algebra, art, band, biology, biology-AP, business, calculus-AP, chemistry, communications, composition, computer information systems, computer keyboarding, computer-aided design, consumer mathematics, current events, driver education, earth science, English, English-AP, environmental science, ethics, finance, fitness, geometry, government-AP, grammar, health, history-AP, journalism, newspaper, physics, pre-calculus, shop, Spanish, theater, U.S. government, U.S. history, world affairs, world geography, yearbook.

Graduation Requirements Arts and fine arts (art, music, dance, drama), communications, composition, computer information systems, English, fitness, foreign language, grammar, health education, mathematics, physical education (includes health), science, social studies (includes history). Community service is required.

Special Academic Programs Advanced Placement exam preparation in 5 subject areas; honors section; accelerated programs; independent study; study at local college for college credit; academic accommodation for the gifted.

College Placement 40 students graduated in 2005; all went to college, including Christopher Newport University; Hampden-Sydney College; James Madison University; Longwood University; Lynchburg College; United States Air Force Academy. Median SAT verbal: 550, median SAT math: 540, median composite ACT: 22. 20% scored over 600 on SAT verbal, 23% scored over 600 on SAT math, 28% scored over 26 on composite ACT.

Student Life Upper grades have uniform requirement, student council, honor system. Discipline rests primarily with faculty.

Summer Programs Enrichment, sports programs offered; session focuses on sports and sport skills; held on campus; accepts boys and girls; open to students from other schools. 2006 schedule: June to August. Application deadline: May.

Tuition and Aid Day student tuition: $6450. Tuition installment plan (The Tuition Plan, Insured Tuition Payment Plan, monthly payment plans, individually arranged payment plans). Tuition reduction for siblings, merit scholarship grants, need-based scholarship grants available. In 2005–06, 48% of upper-school students received aid; total upper-school merit-scholarship money awarded: $8800. Total amount of financial aid awarded in 2005–06: $44,000.

Admissions Traditional secondary-level entrance grade is 9. For fall 2005, 11 students applied for upper-level admission, 10 were accepted, 9 enrolled. Placement test required. Deadline for receipt of application materials: none. Application fee required: $100. On-campus interview required.

Athletics Interscholastic: baseball (boys), basketball (b,g), cheering (g), football (b), softball (g), tennis (b,g), volleyball (g); intramural: basketball (g); coed interscholastic: cross-country running, golf, soccer, swimming and diving, track and field. 2 PE instructors, 23 coaches.

Computers Computers are regularly used in all classes. Computer network features include campus e-mail, on-campus library services, CD-ROMs, online commercial services, Internet access, file transfer, office computer access, DVD, video editing software, CD-ROM +RW and DVD +RW.

Contact Mrs. Christy M. Murphy, Director of Admissions. 434-392-4131 Ext. 273. Fax: 434-392-5062. E-mail: murphycm@fuquaschool.com. Web site: www.fuquaschool.com.

FUTURES HIGH SCHOOL, OCEANSIDE

2204 El Camino Real
Suite 314
Oceanside, California 92054-8304
Head of School: Mr. Michael Halasz

General Information Coeducational day college-preparatory and general academic school. Grades 7–12. Founded: 1985. Setting: suburban. Nearest major city is San Diego. 1-acre campus. 1 building on campus. Approved or accredited by Western Association of Schools and Colleges and California Department of Education. Total enrollment: 36. Upper school average class size: 3. Upper school faculty-student ratio: 1:1.

Upper School Student Profile Grade 9: 5 students (3 boys, 2 girls); Grade 10: 7 students (3 boys, 4 girls); Grade 11: 10 students (7 boys, 3 girls); Grade 12: 10 students (5 boys, 5 girls).

Faculty School total: 19. In upper school: 4 men, 15 women; 4 have advanced degrees.

Subjects Offered Algebra, American literature, anatomy and physiology, anthropology, art appreciation, astronomy, biology, calculus, chemistry, composition, creative writing, earth and space science, economics, English, English literature, French, geography, geometry, German, integrated mathematics, journalism, Latin, marine biology, math analysis, music appreciation, mythology, oceanography, physics, pre-calculus, printmaking, probability and statistics, psychology, reading, sociology, Spanish, theater, trigonometry, U.S. history, world history, world literature.

Graduation Requirements Arts and fine arts (art, music, dance, drama), English, foreign language, mathematics, personal development, practical arts, science, social science.

Special Academic Programs Accelerated programs; independent study; term-away projects; academic accommodation for the gifted, the musically talented, and the artistically talented; remedial reading and/or remedial writing; remedial math; programs in English, mathematics, general development for dyslexic students; special instructional classes for deaf students.

College Placement 16 students graduated in 2005; 12 went to college, including California State University, San Marcos; MiraCosta College; Palomar College; The American University of Paris; The University of Tennessee; University of California, Los Angeles. Other: 2 went to work, 2 entered military service.

Student Life Upper grades have specified standards of dress, student council. Discipline rests primarily with faculty.

Summer Programs Remediation, enrichment, advancement, art/fine arts, computer instruction programs offered; session focuses on advancement; held on campus; accepts boys and girls; open to students from other schools. 125 students usually enrolled. 2006 schedule: June 19 to August 25. Application deadline: none.

Tuition and Aid Day student tuition: $2900–$7500. Tuition installment plan (monthly payment plans). Tuition reduction for siblings, need-based scholarship grants available. In 2005–06, 1% of upper-school students received aid.

Admissions Traditional secondary-level entrance grade is 10. Achievement/Aptitude/Writing required. Deadline for receipt of application materials: none. Application fee required: $150. On-campus interview required.

Computers Computer network features include campus e-mail, CD-ROMs, Internet access.

Contact Mr. Michael Halasz, Director. 760-721-7577. Fax: 760-721-6069. E-mail: mhalasz@futures.edu. Web site: www.futures.edu.

FUTURES HIGH SCHOOL—SAN DIEGO

5333 Mission Center Road
Suite 350
San Diego, California 92108-4340
Head of School: Carolyn Lindstrom

General Information Coeducational day college-preparatory, general academic, and vocational school; primarily serves underachievers and individuals with Attention Deficit Disorder. Grades 7–12. Founded: 1991. Setting: urban. 1 building on campus. Approved or accredited by Western Association of Schools and Colleges and California Department of Education. Total enrollment: 42. Upper school average class size: 1. Upper school faculty-student ratio: 1:8.

Upper School Student Profile Grade 8: 1 student (1 boy); Grade 9: 3 students (1 boy, 2 girls); Grade 10: 5 students (3 boys, 2 girls); Grade 11: 16 students (7 boys, 9 girls); Grade 12: 14 students (8 boys, 6 girls).

Faculty School total: 20. In upper school: 7 men, 12 women; 10 have advanced degrees.

Subjects Offered Algebra, American literature, anatomy, arts, biology, calculus, chemistry, computer graphics, economics, English, fine arts, French, geometry, mathematics, physical education, physics, physiology-anatomy, pre-calculus, religion, social studies, Spanish, trigonometry, U.S. government, U.S. history, world history.

Graduation Requirements Arts and fine arts (art, music, dance, drama), computer science, English, foreign language, mathematics, personal development, physical education (includes health), science, social studies (includes history), portfolio presentation, proficiency exams, volunteer credit hours. Community service is required.

Special Academic Programs Advanced Placement exam preparation in 8 subject areas; accelerated programs; term-away projects; study at local college for college credit; academic accommodation for the gifted, the musically talented, and the artistically talented; remedial reading and/or remedial writing; remedial math; special instructional classes for students with learning disabilities and Attention Deficit Disorder.

College Placement 21 students graduated in 2005; 17 went to college, including California State University, Chico; Grossmont College; Marymount College, Palos Verdes, California; San Diego State University; University of California, San Diego. Other: 4 went to work. 45% scored over 600 on SAT verbal, 52% scored over 600 on SAT math, 100% scored over 26 on composite ACT.

Student Life Upper grades have student council, honor system. Discipline rests primarily with faculty.

Summer Programs Remediation, enrichment, advancement, art/fine arts, computer instruction programs offered; session focuses on advancement and remedial academic work; held on campus; accepts boys and girls; open to students from other schools. 130 students usually enrolled. 2006 schedule: June 13 to August 20. Application deadline: June 1.

Tuition and Aid Day student tuition: $6800–$8500. Tuition installment plan (monthly payment plans, individually arranged payment plans). Tuition reduction for siblings, need-based scholarship grants available. In 2005–06, 5% of upper-school students received aid.

Admissions Traditional secondary-level entrance grade is 10. Math Placement Exam or PSAT required. Deadline for receipt of application materials: none. Application fee required: $325. On-campus interview required.

Computers Computers are regularly used in business education, English, foreign language, history, mathematics, science classes. Computer network features include campus e-mail, on-campus library services, CD-ROMs, online commercial services, Internet access, file transfer, DVD, wireless campus network.

Contact Hillary Lambrecht, Administrative Assistant. 619-297-5311. Fax: 619-297-5313. E-mail: hlambrecht@futures.edu. Web site: www.futures.edu.

THE GALLOWAY SCHOOL

215 West Wieuca Road, NW
Atlanta, Georgia 30342
Head of School: Linda Martinson, PhD

General Information Coeducational day college-preparatory, arts, and technology school. Grades PK–12. Founded: 1969. Setting: urban. 8-acre campus. 4 buildings on campus. Approved or accredited by Southern Association of Colleges and Schools, Southern Association of Independent Schools, and Georgia Department of Education.

The Galloway School

Member of National Association of Independent Schools and Secondary School Admission Test Board. Endowment: $2.8 million. Total enrollment: 730. Upper school average class size: 12. Upper school faculty-student ratio: 1:10.

Upper School Student Profile Grade 9: 57 students (22 boys, 35 girls); Grade 10: 54 students (32 boys, 22 girls); Grade 11: 63 students (37 boys, 26 girls); Grade 12: 60 students (27 boys, 33 girls).

Faculty School total: 101. In upper school: 14 men, 19 women; 28 have advanced degrees.

Subjects Offered Algebra, American history, American literature, biology, British literature, calculus, chemistry, drama, economics, electives, English, English-AP, fine arts, French, geometry, guidance, history, integrated physics, language arts, Latin, library, mathematics, music, physical education, physical science, political science, pre-calculus, science, senior composition, social studies, Spanish, technology, visual arts, world geography, world history, world literature.

Graduation Requirements Arts and fine arts (art, music, dance, drama), computers, electives, English, foreign language, mathematics, science, social studies (includes history).

Special Academic Programs Advanced Placement exam preparation in 11 subject areas; accelerated programs; independent study; study at local college for college credit; academic accommodation for the gifted, the musically talented, and the artistically talented.

College Placement 64 students graduated in 2005; all went to college, including Emory University; Georgia Institute of Technology; University of Georgia; Vanderbilt University.

Student Life Upper grades have student council. Discipline rests primarily with faculty.

Summer Programs Remediation, enrichment, sports programs offered; held both on and off campus; held at sports camps; accepts boys and girls; open to students from other schools. 55 students usually enrolled. 2006 schedule: June 15 to August 7. Application deadline: May 31.

Tuition and Aid Day student tuition: $14,870. Tuition installment plan (Key Tuition Payment Plan). Need-based scholarship grants available. In 2005–06, 13% of upper-school students received aid. Total amount of financial aid awarded in 2005–06: $271,860.

Admissions Traditional secondary-level entrance grade is 9. For fall 2005, 63 students applied for upper-level admission, 29 were accepted, 14 enrolled. SSAT required. Deadline for receipt of application materials: February 20. Application fee required: $75. Interview required.

Athletics Interscholastic: baseball (boys), basketball (b,g), golf (b,g), soccer (b,g), softball (g), swimming and diving (b,g), tennis (b,g), volleyball (g); coed interscholastic: cross-country running, outdoor adventure, running, track and field. 1 PE instructor, 2 coaches, 1 trainer.

Computers Computers are regularly used in art, desktop publishing, drawing and design, graphic arts, information technology, introduction to technology, journalism, keyboarding, literary magazine, multimedia, music, newspaper, photography, publishing, research skills, Web site design, yearbook classes. Computer network features include campus e-mail, on-campus library services, CD-ROMs, online commercial services, Internet access, file transfer, office computer access, DVD, wireless campus network, print sharing.

Contact Rosetta Gooden, Director of Admission. 404-252-8389. Fax: 404-252-7770. E-mail: r.gooden@gallowayschool.org. Web site: www.gallowayschool.org.

GARCES MEMORIAL HIGH SCHOOL

2800 Loma Linda Drive
Bakersfield, California 93305
Head of School: V. Robert Garcia

General Information Coeducational day college-preparatory school, affiliated with Roman Catholic Church. Grades 9–12. Founded: 1947. Setting: suburban. Nearest major city is Los Angeles. 32-acre campus. 15 buildings on campus. Approved or accredited by Western Association of Schools and Colleges and Western Catholic Education Association. Endowment: $450,000. Total enrollment: 668. Upper school average class size: 23. Upper school faculty-student ratio: 1:23.

Upper School Student Profile Grade 9: 163 students (85 boys, 78 girls); Grade 10: 198 students (105 boys, 93 girls); Grade 11: 140 students (69 boys, 71 girls); Grade 12: 167 students (78 boys, 89 girls). 72% of students are Roman Catholic.

Faculty School total: 41. In upper school: 22 men, 19 women; 22 have advanced degrees.

Subjects Offered Algebra, American history, American literature, anatomy, art, biology, calculus, chemistry, community service, computer science, creative writing, drama, driver education, economics, English, English literature, ethics, fine arts, French, geography, geometry, government/civics, graphic arts, health, history, journalism, mathematics, music, physical education, physics, physiology, psychology, religion, science, social studies, Spanish, theater, world history, world literature.

Graduation Requirements Arts and fine arts (art, music, dance, drama), English, foreign language, mathematics, physical education (includes health), religion (includes Bible studies and theology), science, social studies (includes history), 40 hours of community service.

Special Academic Programs Advanced Placement exam preparation in 5 subject areas; honors section; study at local college for college credit.

College Placement 177 students graduated in 2005; 144 went to college, including Bakersfield College; California Polytechnic State University, San Luis Obispo; California State University, Bakersfield; Loyola Marymount University; San Diego State University; University of Southern California. Other: 1 entered military service. Mean SAT verbal: 528, mean SAT math: 529, mean composite ACT: 23. 15.3% scored over 600 on SAT verbal, 16.9% scored over 600 on SAT math.

Student Life Upper grades have uniform requirement, student council. Discipline rests primarily with faculty. Attendance at religious services is required.

Summer Programs Remediation, enrichment, advancement, sports, art/fine arts, computer instruction programs offered; session focuses on mathematics and English; held on campus; accepts boys and girls; open to students from other schools. 800 students usually enrolled. 2006 schedule: June 7 to July 14. Application deadline: May 12.

Tuition and Aid Day student tuition: $5600–$6275. Tuition installment plan (monthly payment plans, individually arranged payment plans). Merit scholarship grants, need-based scholarship grants available. In 2005–06, 20% of upper-school students received aid; total upper-school merit-scholarship money awarded: $5000. Total amount of financial aid awarded in 2005–06: $257,000.

Admissions Traditional secondary-level entrance grade is 9. For fall 2005, 225 students applied for upper-level admission, 200 were accepted, 185 enrolled. CTBS/4 required. Deadline for receipt of application materials: January 30. Application fee required: $50. Interview required.

Athletics Interscholastic: baseball (boys), basketball (b,g), cheering (g), cross-country running (b,g), dance team (g), diving (b,g), football (b), soccer (b,g), softball (g), swimming and diving (b,g), tennis (b,g), track and field (b,g), volleyball (g), weight training (b); intramural: baseball (b), basketball (b,g), volleyball (b,g); coed interscholastic: golf; coed intramural: basketball, volleyball. 3 PE instructors, 28 coaches, 2 trainers.

Computers Computers are regularly used in graphic arts, journalism, keyboarding classes. Computer resources include CD-ROMs, Internet access.

Contact Mrs. Joan M. Richardson, Registrar. 661-327-2578 Ext. 109. Fax: 661-327-5427. E-mail: jrichardson@garces.org. Web site: www.garces.org.

GARDEN SCHOOL

33-16 79th Street
Jackson Heights, New York 11372
Head of School: Dr. Richard Marotta

General Information Coeducational day college-preparatory school. Grades N–12. Founded: 1923. Setting: urban. Nearest major city is New York. 1 building on campus. Approved or accredited by Middle States Association of Colleges and Schools, New York State Association of Independent Schools, and New York Department of Education. Total enrollment: 350. Upper school average class size: 15. Upper school faculty-student ratio: 1:11.

Faculty School total: 36. In upper school: 10 men, 12 women.

Subjects Offered Algebra, American history, American literature, anthropology, art, biology, calculus, chemistry, computer science, creative writing, economics, English, English literature, European history, expository writing, forensics, French, geometry, grammar, health, history, mathematics, music, physical education, physics, psychology, reading, science, social studies, sociology, Spanish, statistics, trigonometry, world history, world literature, writing.

Graduation Requirements English, foreign language, mathematics, physical education (includes health), science, social studies (includes history).

Special Academic Programs Advanced Placement exam preparation in 6 subject areas; honors section; independent study; ESL (10 students enrolled).

College Placement 30 students graduated in 2004; all went to college, including City College of the City University of New York; Fordham University; New York University; State University of New York at Binghamton.

Student Life Upper grades have specified standards of dress, student council. Discipline rests primarily with faculty.

Tuition and Aid Day student tuition: $9100–$9500. Tuition installment plan (monthly payment plans, 3-part plan (no interest), 10-month plan (with interest)). Tuition reduction for siblings, merit scholarship grants, need-based scholarship grants, need-based loans available. In 2004–05, 15% of upper-school students received aid.

Admissions Traditional secondary-level entrance grade is 9. School's own exam required. Deadline for receipt of application materials: none. Application fee required: $30. On-campus interview required.

Athletics Interscholastic: basketball (boys, girls), softball (b,g), tennis (b,g), volleyball (g); intramural: football (b), tennis (b,g), track and field (b,g); coed interscholastic: soccer. 2 PE instructors, 1 coach.

Computers Computer resources include campus e-mail, on-campus library services, CD-ROMs, Internet access.

Contact Ms. Mary Petruso, Admissions Secretary. 718-335-6363. Fax: 718-565-1169. Web site: www.gardenschool.org.

ANNOUNCEMENT FROM THE SCHOOL Garden School enrolls approximately 400 students, from 2 years old through the senior year of high school. The Garden School Plan rests upon a college-preparatory curriculum that combines traditional academics with an emphasis on the individual student.

Garden School expects its students to pursue rigorous educational and community-directed goals.

GARRISON FOREST SCHOOL

300 Garrison Forest Road
Owings Mills, Maryland 21117
Head of School: Mr. G. Peter O'Neill Jr.

General Information Girls' boarding and day (coeducational in lower grades) college-preparatory and arts school. Boarding girls grades 8–12, day boys grades N–K, day girls grades N–12. Founded: 1910. Setting: suburban. Nearest major city is Baltimore. Students are housed in single-sex dormitories. 115-acre campus. 17 buildings on campus. Approved or accredited by Association of Independent Maryland Schools, Middle States Association of Colleges and Schools, The Association of Boarding Schools, and Maryland Department of Education. Member of National Association of Independent Schools and Secondary School Admission Test Board. Endowment: $31 million. Total enrollment: 664. Upper school average class size: 14. Upper school faculty-student ratio: 1:8.

Upper School Student Profile Grade 9: 61 students (61 girls); Grade 10: 72 students (72 girls); Grade 11: 59 students (59 girls); Grade 12: 40 students (40 girls). 18% of students are boarding students. 9 states are represented in upper school student body. 6% are international students. International students from Armenia, Germany, Mexico, and Republic of Korea.

Faculty School total: 91. In upper school: 6 men, 30 women; 25 have advanced degrees; 25 reside on campus.

Subjects Offered Algebra, American history, American literature, anatomy, animal behavior, art, art history, art history-AP, arts and crafts, biology, calculus, calculus-AP, ceramics, chemistry, chemistry-AP, child development, computer science, computer skills, creative writing, dance, decision making skills, design, drama, drawing, ecology, English, English literature, English-AP, ESL, ethics, fine arts, French, French-AP, geometry, history-AP, Latin, Latin-AP, life skills, mathematics, music, philosophy, photography, physical education, physics, physics-AP, public speaking, science, Spanish, Spanish-AP, statistics, theater, trigonometry, U.S. history-AP, world history.

Graduation Requirements Arts and fine arts (art, music, dance, drama), computer science, decision making skills, English, foreign language, mathematics, physical education (includes health), public speaking, science, social studies (includes history).

Special Academic Programs Advanced Placement exam preparation in 11 subject areas; honors section; independent study; term-away projects; academic accommodation for the gifted, the musically talented, and the artistically talented; ESL (4 students enrolled).

College Placement 49 students graduated in 2005; all went to college, including Boston University; Columbia College; Cornell University; Duke University; University of Maryland, College Park; University of Virginia. 50% scored over 600 on SAT verbal, 50% scored over 600 on SAT math.

Student Life Upper grades have uniform requirement, student council, honor system. Discipline rests equally with students and faculty.

Summer Programs Sports, art/fine arts programs offered; held on campus; accepts boys and girls; open to students from other schools. 200 students usually enrolled. 2006 schedule: June to August. Application deadline: June.

Tuition and Aid Day student tuition: $19,600; 7-day tuition and room/board: $33,400. Tuition installment plan (Tuition Management Systems Plan). Need-based scholarship grants, need-based loans available. In 2005–06, 24% of upper-school students received aid. Total amount of financial aid awarded in 2005–06: $840,650.

Admissions Traditional secondary-level entrance grade is 9. For fall 2005, 150 students applied for upper-level admission, 71 were accepted, 31 enrolled. ISEE and SSAT required. Deadline for receipt of application materials: January 6. Application fee required: $45. Interview required.

Athletics Interscholastic: badminton, basketball, cross-country running, equestrian sports, field hockey, horseback riding, lacrosse, polo, soccer, softball, squash, tennis, winter soccer; intramural: aerobics, aerobics/dance, dance, fitness, golf, modern dance, strength & conditioning, yoga. 5 PE instructors, 27 coaches, 1 trainer.

Computers Computers are regularly used in English, foreign language, history, mathematics, science classes. Computer network features include campus e-mail, on-campus library services, CD-ROMs, Internet access, file transfer, DVD, wireless campus network.

Contact A. Randol Benedict, Director of Admission and Financial Aid. 410-363-1500. Fax: 410-363-8441. E-mail: gfs_info@gfs.org. Web site: www.gfs.org.

See full description on page 792.

GASTON DAY SCHOOL

2001 Gaston Day School Road
Gastonia, North Carolina 28056
Head of School: Dr. Richard E. Rankin

General Information Coeducational day college-preparatory and arts school. Grades PK–12. Founded: 1967. Setting: suburban. Nearest major city is Charlotte.

40-acre campus. 4 buildings on campus. Approved or accredited by Southern Association of Colleges and Schools and North Carolina Department of Education. Member of National Association of Independent Schools. Endowment: $1.7 million. Total enrollment: 418. Upper school average class size: 15. Upper school faculty-student ratio: 1:9.

Upper School Student Profile Grade 9: 36 students (19 boys, 17 girls); Grade 10: 27 students (10 boys, 17 girls); Grade 11: 28 students (16 boys, 12 girls); Grade 12: 24 students (16 boys, 8 girls).

Faculty School total: 49. In upper school: 9 men, 13 women; 16 have advanced degrees.

Subjects Offered Advanced chemistry, advanced computer applications, advanced math, Advanced Placement courses, advanced studio art-AP, algebra, American history-AP, American literature-AP, analytic geometry, ancient world history, art, biology, biology-AP, British literature, British literature (honors), calculus-AP, chemistry, chemistry-AP, choral music, chorus, college counseling, college placement, college writing, composition-AP, creative writing, drama, English, English language and composition-AP, English language-AP, English literature, English literature and composition-AP, English literature-AP, English-AP, English/composition-AP, ensembles, expository writing, fine arts, foreign language, French, French-AP, general science, geometry, government, government-AP, honors algebra, honors English, honors geometry, honors U.S. history, honors world history, internship, language-AP, learning lab, music, physics, physics-AP, pre-algebra, pre-calculus, psychology, psychology-AP, SAT preparation, science, senior internship, Spanish, Spanish-AP, student government, studio art—AP, study skills, U.S. government, U.S. government-AP, U.S. history-AP, U.S. literature, United States government-AP, visual and performing arts, visual arts, weight training, world literature, writing, yearbook.

Graduation Requirements Arts and fine arts (art, music, dance, drama), computer science, electives, English, foreign language, mathematics, physical education (includes health), science, social studies (includes history), 25 hours of community service per year.

Special Academic Programs Advanced Placement exam preparation in 10 subject areas; honors section; independent study; academic accommodation for the gifted.

College Placement 12 students graduated in 2005; all went to college, including Elon University; North Carolina State University; The University of North Carolina at Charlotte. Median SAT verbal: 560, median SAT math: 553.

Student Life Upper grades have specified standards of dress, student council, honor system. Discipline rests primarily with faculty.

Summer Programs Enrichment, sports programs offered; session focuses on academic enrichment; advancement in sports and arts; held on campus; accepts boys and girls; open to students from other schools. 120 students usually enrolled. 2006 schedule: June to August.

Tuition and Aid Day student tuition: $10,920. Tuition installment plan (monthly payment plans, individually arranged payment plans). Merit scholarship grants, need-based scholarship grants available. In 2005–06, 25% of upper-school students received aid; total upper-school merit-scholarship money awarded: $70,000. Total amount of financial aid awarded in 2005–06: $72,000.

Admissions Traditional secondary-level entrance grade is 9. For fall 2005, 40 students applied for upper-level admission, 28 were accepted, 24 enrolled. Battery of testing done through outside agency required. Deadline for receipt of application materials: none. Application fee required: $40. On-campus interview required.

Athletics Interscholastic: baseball (boys), basketball (b,g), cheering (g), cross-country running (b,g), soccer (b,g), softball (g), tennis (b,g), track and field (b,g), volleyball (g), wrestling (b); coed interscholastic: cross-country running, golf, strength & conditioning, swimming and diving, track and field. 3 PE instructors, 23 coaches, 1 trainer.

Computers Computers are regularly used in art, English, foreign language, history, journalism, mathematics, newspaper, science, yearbook classes. Computer network features include campus e-mail, on-campus library services, CD-ROMs, online commercial services, Internet access.

Contact Mrs. Martha Jayne Rhyne, Director of Admission. 704-864-7744 Ext. 228. Fax: 704-865-3813. E-mail: mjrhyne@gastonday.org. Web site: www.gastonday.org.

ANNOUNCEMENT FROM THE SCHOOL Gaston Day School is a traditional, coeducational, independent day school for students in prekindergarten (ages 3 and 4) through grade 12. The School has approximately 425 students and is located within 30 minutes of Charlotte, North Carolina. The Lower School curriculum includes phonics-based reading, hands-on science, and manipulative mathematics. The Middle and Upper School curricula are sequential, with a focused commitment to standard and Advanced Placement courses. The School has a technology center, a state-of-the-art visual and performing arts center, and a student-life complex.

GATEWAY CHRISTIAN SCHOOL

Box 1089
Prince George, British Columbia V2L 4V2, Canada
Head of School: Mrs. Mitra Kostamo

General Information Coeducational day college-preparatory, general academic, arts, vocational, and religious studies school, affiliated with Apostolic Church of

Pentecost; primarily serves underachievers. Grades K–12. Founded: 1981. Setting: suburban. Nearest major city is Vancouver, Canada. 7-acre campus. 1 building on campus. Approved or accredited by Association of Christian Schools International and British Columbia Department of Education. Language of instruction: English. Total enrollment: 118.

Upper School Student Profile Grade 7: 7 students (3 boys, 4 girls); Grade 8: 8 students (5 boys, 3 girls); Grade 9: 10 students (5 boys, 5 girls); Grade 10: 3 students (1 boy, 2 girls); Grade 11: 5 students (3 boys, 2 girls); Grade 12: 6 students (3 boys, 3 girls). 75% of students are Apostolic Church of Pentecost.

Faculty School total: 9. In upper school: 2 men, 3 women.

Subjects Offered Accounting, advanced math, algebra, applied arts, applied music, applied skills, art, athletics, Basic programming, basketball, Bible, Bible studies, biology, biology-AP, business mathematics, Canadian geography, Canadian history, Canadian law, Canadian literature, career and personal planning, career education, cartooning, cell biology, chemistry, Christian education, Christian studies, creation science, creative arts, creative drama, creative writing, critical thinking, critical writing, decision making, drama, drawing, earth science, Eastern world civilizations, economics, English, English composition, food and nutrition, French, general business, general math, general science, geometry, health, history, home economics, human biology, Internet research, intro to computers, Life of Christ, life science, mathematics, musical productions, musical theater, oil painting, physical education, physics, physics-AP, poetry, pre-calculus, religious studies, science, sculpture, social studies, softball, swimming, track and field, volleyball, water polo, wilderness camping, wilderness education, world geography, world history, writing.

Special Academic Programs Independent study.

Student Life Upper grades have uniform requirement, student council, honor system. Discipline rests primarily with faculty. Attendance at religious services is required.

Tuition and Aid Day student tuition: CAN$1000. Tuition installment plan (monthly payment plans). Need-based scholarship grants available.

Admissions Traditional secondary-level entrance grade is 7. Deadline for receipt of application materials: March 15. Application fee required: CAN$250. Interview required.

Athletics Interscholastic: canoeing/kayaking (boys, girls), cross-country running (b,g), hiking/backpacking (b,g), hockey (b), independent competitive sports (b,g), indoor hockey (b,g), indoor soccer (b,g), indoor track (b,g), jogging (b,g), kayaking (b,g), outdoor recreation (g), street hockey (b,g); coed interscholastic: aquatics, baseball, basketball, bicycling, curling, fitness, floor hockey, indoor hockey, indoor track & field, luge, outdoor activities, outdoor education, outdoor recreation, physical fitness, soccer, softball, swimming and diving, track and field, volleyball, water polo, wilderness survival. 1 PE instructor, 1 coach.

Computers Computers are regularly used in creative writing, keyboarding, research skills, science classes. Computer network features include CD-ROMs, Internet access.

Contact Mrs. Carla Paulson, Head Secretary. 250-563-8585. Fax: 250-563-3488. E-mail: gcsadmin@telus.net.

GATEWAY SCHOOL

Arlington, Texas
See Special Needs Schools section.

GEM STATE ADVENTIST ACADEMY

16115 Montana Avenue
Caldwell, Idaho 83607
Head of School: Mike Schwartz

General Information Coeducational boarding and day college-preparatory, religious studies, and technology school, affiliated with Seventh-day Adventist Church. Grades 9–12. Founded: 1918. Setting: rural. Nearest major city is Boise. Students are housed in single-sex dormitories. 4 buildings on campus. Approved or accredited by Accrediting Association of Seventh-day Adventist Schools, Colleges and Universities, Inc., National Council for Private School Accreditation, Northwest Association of Schools and Colleges, and Idaho Department of Education. Total enrollment: 127. Upper school average class size: 20. Upper school faculty-student ratio: 1:13.

Upper School Student Profile Grade 9: 32 students (17 boys, 15 girls); Grade 10: 34 students (19 boys, 15 girls); Grade 11: 40 students (19 boys, 21 girls); Grade 12: 21 students (8 boys, 13 girls). 34% of students are boarding students. 67% are state residents. 7 states are represented in upper school student body. 7% are international students. International students from Hong Kong, Republic of Korea, Spain, and Taiwan. 95% of students are Seventh-day Adventists.

Faculty School total: 13. In upper school: 9 men, 4 women; 4 have advanced degrees; 8 reside on campus.

Subjects Offered Advanced computer applications, algebra, art, bell choir, Bible studies, biology, calculus-AP, chemistry, chorus, computer applications, consumer mathematics, economics, English, general science, geometry, graphic arts, gymnastics, health, Internet, keyboarding, music history, music theory, orchestra, physical education, physics, piano, pre-algebra, pre-calculus, Spanish, speech, U.S. government, U.S. history, voice, work experience, world history, yearbook.

Graduation Requirements Arts and fine arts (art, music, dance, drama), computer education, economics, English, foreign language, humanities, mathematics, physical

education (includes health), religion (includes Bible studies and theology), science, social studies (includes history), speech, U.S. government, U.S. history.

Special Academic Programs Advanced Placement exam preparation in 1 subject area; study at local college for college credit; academic accommodation for the musically talented.

College Placement 37 students graduated in 2005; 32 went to college, including Boise State University; Pacific Union College; Walla Walla College.

Student Life Upper grades have specified standards of dress, student council, honor system. Discipline rests primarily with faculty. Attendance at religious services is required.

Tuition and Aid Day student tuition: $7920; 7-day tuition and room/board: $12,020. Tuition installment plan (monthly payment plans, individually arranged payment plans). Tuition reduction for siblings, need-based scholarship grants, paying campus jobs available.

Admissions Traditional secondary-level entrance grade is 9. Deadline for receipt of application materials: none. No application fee required. Interview required.

Athletics Interscholastic: basketball (boys, girls), flag football (b), volleyball (g); intramural: basketball (b,g), flag football (b,g), floor hockey (b,g), soccer (b,g), softball (b,g); coed intramural: gymnastics, softball. 1 PE instructor, 1 coach.

Computers Computers are regularly used in art, business education, English, graphic arts, health, history, science, typing, writing fundamentals classes. Computer network features include campus e-mail, on-campus library services, CD-ROMs, online commercial services, Internet access, office computer access, DVD.

Contact Karen Davies, Registrar. 208-459-1627. Fax: 208-454-9079. E-mail: registrar@gemstate.org. Web site: www.gemstate.org.

THE GENEVA SCHOOL

2025 State Road 436
Winter Park, Florida 32792
Head of School: Rev. Robert Forrest Ingram

General Information Coeducational day college-preparatory and religious studies school, affiliated with Christian faith. Grades K4–12. Founded: 1993. Setting: suburban. Nearest major city is Orlando. 3-acre campus. 1 building on campus. Approved or accredited by Christian Schools International and Florida Council of Independent Schools. Total enrollment: 465. Upper school average class size: 14. Upper school faculty-student ratio: 1:5.

Upper School Student Profile Grade 7: 28 students (15 boys, 13 girls); Grade 8: 17 students (9 boys, 8 girls); Grade 9: 33 students (17 boys, 16 girls); Grade 10: 18 students (9 boys, 9 girls); Grade 11: 14 students (9 boys, 5 girls); Grade 12: 16 students (7 boys, 9 girls).

Faculty School total: 52. In upper school: 15 men, 9 women; 12 have advanced degrees.

Subjects Offered Advanced Placement courses, aesthetics, algebra, Ancient Greek, art, Bible, biology, British literature (honors), calculus-AP, chemistry, choral music, Christian ethics, classical Greek literature, comparative religion, critical thinking, critical writing, debate, drama, earth science, English-AP, ethics, European history, foreign language, French, French-AP, history, honors algebra, honors English, honors geometry, honors U.S. history, honors world history, independent study, instrumental music, Irish literature, journalism, Latin, life management skills, mathematics, medieval literature, music appreciation, oral communications, personal fitness, philosophy, photography, photojournalism, physical education, physical fitness, physical science, physics, physics-AP, poetry, pre-algebra, pre-calculus, public speaking, reading/study skills, rhetoric, science, senior thesis, Shakespeare, Spanish, speech and debate, studio art—AP, study skills, theater, trigonometry, U.S. history, world history, yearbook.

Graduation Requirements Arts and fine arts (art, music, dance, drama), Bible, electives, English, foreign language, history, mathematics, physical education (includes health), rhetoric, science.

Special Academic Programs Advanced Placement exam preparation in 5 subject areas; honors section; independent study.

College Placement 7 students graduated in 2005; 6 went to college, including Clemson University; Florida Gulf Coast University; Furman University; Rollins College; University of Central Florida; University of Mississippi. Other: 1 had other specific plans. Mean SAT verbal: 591, mean SAT math: 591, mean composite ACT: 24. 71% scored over 600 on SAT verbal, 71% scored over 600 on SAT math, 33% scored over 26 on composite ACT.

Student Life Upper grades have uniform requirement, student council. Discipline rests primarily with faculty. Attendance at religious services is required.

Tuition and Aid Day student tuition: $6900. Tuition installment plan (monthly payment plans). Need-based scholarship grants available. In 2005–06, 30% of upper-school students received aid.

Admissions Traditional secondary-level entrance grade is 8. For fall 2005, 42 students applied for upper-level admission, 36 were accepted, 34 enrolled. Admissions testing, English proficiency, mathematics proficiency exam and writing sample required. Deadline for receipt of application materials: none. Application fee required: $100. Interview required.

Athletics Interscholastic: baseball (boys), basketball (b,g), cheering (g), flag football (b,g), soccer (b,g), softball (g), volleyball (g); coed interscholastic: cross-country running, golf, tennis. 2 PE instructors.

Computers Computers are regularly used in journalism, yearbook classes. Computer network features include Internet access.

Contact Mrs. Caroline Newkirk, Administrative Assistant/Registrar. 407-332-6363 Ext. 206. Fax: 407-332-1664. E-mail: ccnewkirk@genevaschool.org. Web site: www.genevaschool.org.

GEORGE SCHOOL

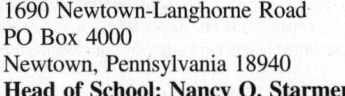

1690 Newtown-Langhorne Road
PO Box 4000
Newtown, Pennsylvania 18940
Head of School: Nancy O. Starmer

petersons.com

General Information Coeducational boarding and day college-preparatory, arts, religious studies, bilingual studies, and technology school, affiliated with Society of Friends. Grades 9–12. Founded: 1893. Setting: suburban. Nearest major city is Philadelphia. Students are housed in single-sex dormitories. 265-acre campus. 18 buildings on campus. Approved or accredited by Friends Council on Education, International Baccalaureate Organization, Middle States Association of Colleges and Schools, The Association of Boarding Schools, The College Board, and Pennsylvania Department of Education. Member of National Association of Independent Schools and Secondary School Admission Test Board. Endowment: $65.8 million. Total enrollment: 529. Upper school average class size: 14. Upper school faculty-student ratio: 1:7.

Upper School Student Profile Grade 9: 118 students (55 boys, 63 girls); Grade 10: 139 students (73 boys, 66 girls); Grade 11: 144 students (71 boys, 73 girls); Grade 12: 128 students (62 boys, 66 girls). 55% of students are boarding students. 22 states are represented in upper school student body. 15% are international students. International students from Germany, Hong Kong, Japan, Republic of Korea, Taiwan, and United Kingdom; 27 other countries represented in student body. 14% of students are members of Society of Friends.

Faculty School total: 86. In upper school: 35 men, 51 women; 55 have advanced degrees; 55 reside on campus.

Subjects Offered African history, African-American history, algebra, American literature, art, Asian history, astronomy, Bible studies, biology, calculus, ceramics, chemistry, community service, composition, computer science, dance, desktop publishing, drama, drawing, driver education, English, English literature, ESL, fine arts, French, geometry, global studies, health, horticulture, hydrology, industrial arts, journalism, Latin, Latin American history, life science, literature, mathematics, meteorology, Middle Eastern history, modern dance, modern European history, music theory, oceanography, orchestra, ornithology, painting, philosophy, photography, physical education, physics, physiology, pre-calculus, probability and statistics, religion, Russian history, science, science and technology, Spanish, stagecraft, theater, theory of knowledge, video film production, visual arts, vocal ensemble, woodworking, world history, world literature.

Graduation Requirements Arts and fine arts (art, music, dance, drama), computer literacy, English, foreign language, mathematics, performing arts, physical education (includes health), religion (includes Bible studies and theology), science, social studies (includes history), swimming competency, word processing, 65 hours of community service.

Special Academic Programs International Baccalaureate program; Advanced Placement exam preparation in 9 subject areas; honors section; independent study; academic accommodation for the gifted; ESL (20 students enrolled).

College Placement 151 students graduated in 2005; all went to college, including Boston University; Connecticut College; Franklin and Marshall College; Guilford College; New York University; University of Pennsylvania.

Student Life Upper grades have specified standards of dress, student council, honor system. Discipline rests equally with students and faculty. Attendance at religious services is required.

Summer Programs Enrichment, advancement, ESL programs offered; session focuses on academic and social preparation; held on campus; accepts boys and girls; not open to students from other schools. 36 students usually enrolled.

Tuition and Aid Day student tuition: $24,700; 7-day tuition and room/board: $33,500. Tuition installment plan (Key Tuition Payment Plan, monthly payment plans, individually arranged payment plans). Merit scholarship grants, need-based scholarship grants, need-based loans available. In 2005–06, 42% of upper-school students received aid; total upper-school merit-scholarship money awarded: $20,823. Total amount of financial aid awarded in 2005–06: $4,800,000.

Admissions Traditional secondary-level entrance grade is 9. For fall 2005, 572 students applied for upper-level admission, 274 were accepted, 166 enrolled. SSAT or TOEFL or SLEP required. Deadline for receipt of application materials: February 15. Application fee required: $50. Interview required.

Athletics Interscholastic: baseball (boys), basketball (b,g), cross-country running (b,g), field hockey (g), football (b), lacrosse (b,g), soccer (b,g), softball (g), swimming and diving (b,g), tennis (b,g), track and field (b,g), volleyball (g), wrestling (b,g); coed interscholastic: cheering, equestrian sports, golf, horseback riding, indoor track, winter (indoor) track; coed intramural: aerobics/dance, aquatics, archery, badminton, basketball, dance, fitness, horseback riding, life saving, martial arts, modern dance, outdoor education, physical fitness, soccer, softball, strength & conditioning, swimming and diving, table tennis, volleyball, weight training, yoga. 4 PE instructors, 4 coaches, 1 trainer.

Computers Computers are regularly used in English, ESL, foreign language, history, mathematics, newspaper, photography, science, yearbook classes. Computer network features include campus e-mail, on-campus library services, CD-ROMs, online commercial services, Internet access, DVD, wireless campus network.

Contact Karen S. Hallowell, Director of Admissions. 215-579-6547. Fax: 215-579-6549. E-mail: admissions@georgeschool.org. Web site: www.georgeschool.org.

See full description on page 794.

GEORGE STEVENS ACADEMY

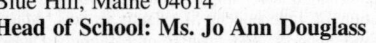

23 Union Street
Blue Hill, Maine 04614
Head of School: Ms. Jo Ann Douglass

petersons.com

General Information Coeducational boarding and day college-preparatory, general academic, arts, and vocational school. Grades 9–12. Founded: 1803. Setting: small town. Nearest major city is Bangor. Students are housed in host family homes. 20-acre campus. 4 buildings on campus. Approved or accredited by Independent Schools of Northern New England, New England Association of Schools and Colleges, The College Board, and Maine Department of Education. Endowment: $1.2 million. Total enrollment: 314. Upper school average class size: 14. Upper school faculty-student ratio: 1:10.

Upper School Student Profile Grade 9: 60 students (26 boys, 34 girls); Grade 10: 104 students (59 boys, 45 girls); Grade 11: 67 students (35 boys, 32 girls); Grade 12: 83 students (36 boys, 47 girls).

Faculty School total: 31. In upper school: 15 men, 16 women; 16 have advanced degrees.

Subjects Offered 20th century history, 3-dimensional design, advanced chemistry, advanced math, Advanced Placement courses, algebra, American literature, American literature-AP, art, art history, art-AP, arts and crafts, band, biology, British literature (honors), business mathematics, calculus-AP, carpentry, chemistry, computer applications, computer literacy, creative writing, critical thinking, desktop publishing, developmental language skills, drafting, drawing, driver education, earth science, electives, English, English-AP, environmental science, environmental science-AP, ESL, European history, fine arts, foreign language, forensics, French, general math, general science, geometry, German, health education, history, history-AP, honors algebra, honors English, honors geometry, honors U.S. history, humanities, independent study, industrial arts, industrial technology, instrumental music, internship, jazz band, jazz ensemble, lab science, languages, Latin, literature, literature-AP, marine science, mathematics, mathematics-AP, mechanics, modern history, modern languages, music, music theory, musical productions, mythology, personal fitness, photo shop, photography, physical education, physics, pre-algebra, pre-calculus, printmaking, psychology, science, senior project, small engine repair, social science, Spanish, sports, statistics-AP, street law, student government, technology/design, TOEFL preparation, transportation technology, U.S. history, U.S. history-AP, Western civilization, woodworking, World-Wide-Web publishing, writing.

Graduation Requirements Arts and fine arts (art, music, dance, drama), electives, English, foreign language, history, honors U.S. history, mathematics, physical education (includes health), science, social sciences, Maine Learning Results Requirements, Senior Debate.

Special Academic Programs Advanced Placement exam preparation in 6 subject areas; honors section; accelerated programs; independent study; academic accommodation for the gifted, the musically talented, and the artistically talented; remedial reading and/or remedial writing; remedial math; ESL (2 students enrolled).

College Placement 82 students graduated in 2005; 54 went to college, including Bates College; Bowdoin College; Lafayette College; Northeastern University; University of Maine; University of Southern Maine. Other: 28 went to work. Median SAT verbal: 540, median SAT math: 490. 31% scored over 600 on SAT verbal, 26% scored over 600 on SAT math.

Student Life Upper grades have student council. Discipline rests primarily with faculty.

Summer Programs Remediation, enrichment, sports, art/fine arts, computer instruction programs offered; held on campus; accepts boys and girls; open to students from other schools. 2006 schedule: July.

Tuition and Aid 7-day tuition and room/board: $25,000. Guaranteed tuition plan. Tuition installment plan (monthly payment plans, individually arranged payment plans).

Admissions Traditional secondary-level entrance grade is 9. PSAT, SSAT or TOEFL or SLEP required. Deadline for receipt of application materials: none. Application fee required: $50. Interview required.

Athletics Interscholastic: baseball (boys), basketball (b,g), cheering (b,g), cross-country running (b,g), golf (b,g), indoor track (b,g), sailing (b,g), soccer (b,g), softball (g), tennis (b,g), track and field (b,g), wrestling (b,g); coed intramural: croquet, flag football, floor hockey, outdoor recreation, ultimate Frisbee, volleyball. 2 PE instructors, 26 coaches.

Computers Computers are regularly used in all academic, computer applications, desktop publishing, Web site design classes. Computer network features include on-campus library services, CD-ROMs, Internet access, office computer access, DVD.

George Stevens Academy

Contact Ms. Sheryl Cole Stearns, International Program Director. 207-374-2808. Fax: 207-374-2982. E-mail: sstearns@georgestevensacademy.org. Web site: www.georgestevensacademy.org.

See full description on page 796.

GEORGETOWN DAY SCHOOL

4200 Davenport Street, NW
Washington, District of Columbia 20016
Head of School: Peter M. Branch

General Information Coeducational day college-preparatory school. Grades PK–12. Founded: 1945. Setting: urban. 6-acre campus. 1 building on campus. Approved or accredited by Association of Independent Maryland Schools, Middle States Association of Colleges and Schools, and District of Columbia Department of Education. Member of National Association of Independent Schools and Secondary School Admission Test Board. Endowment: $7.5 million. Total enrollment: 1,031. Upper school average class size: 15. Upper school faculty-student ratio: 1:7.

Upper School Student Profile Grade 9: 114 students (55 boys, 59 girls); Grade 10: 117 students (63 boys, 54 girls); Grade 11: 114 students (56 boys, 58 girls); Grade 12: 113 students (56 boys, 57 girls).

Faculty School total: 160. In upper school: 30 men, 40 women; 49 have advanced degrees.

Subjects Offered Algebra, American history, American literature, anthropology, art, art history, astronomy, biology, calculus, ceramics, chemistry, community service, computer science, creative writing, dance, drama, driver education, economics, English, environmental science-AP, European history, fine arts, French, geometry, government/civics, history, Latin, law, linear algebra, mathematics, music, photography, physical education, physics, psychology, science, social studies, Spanish, statistics-AP, theater, trigonometry, world history.

Graduation Requirements Arts and fine arts (art, music, dance, drama), English, foreign language, literature, mathematics, physical education (includes health), science, social studies (includes history). Community service is required.

Special Academic Programs Advanced Placement exam preparation in 19 subject areas; honors section; independent study.

College Placement 111 students graduated in 2005; all went to college, including Brown University; Duke University; Harvard University; Oberlin College; Stanford University; Yale University. Median SAT verbal: 680, median SAT math: 668.

Student Life Upper grades have student council, honor system. Discipline rests primarily with faculty.

Tuition and Aid Day student tuition: $21,217–$24,303. Tuition installment plan (Academic Management Services Plan, monthly payment plans). Need-based scholarship grants available. In 2005–06, 18% of upper-school students received aid. Total amount of financial aid awarded in 2005–06: $900,000.

Admissions Traditional secondary-level entrance grade is 9. For fall 2005, 242 students applied for upper-level admission, 84 were accepted, 54 enrolled. ISEE or SSAT required. Deadline for receipt of application materials: January 13. Application fee required: $60. On-campus interview required.

Athletics Interscholastic: baseball (boys), basketball (b,g), crew (b,g), cross-country running (b,g), lacrosse (b,g), soccer (b,g), softball (g), tennis (b,g), track and field (b,g), volleyball (g); intramural: indoor soccer (b,g); coed interscholastic: golf, wrestling; coed intramural: flag football, ropes courses, weight training. 5 PE instructors, 6 coaches, 1 trainer.

Computers Computers are regularly used in art, English, foreign language, history, mathematics, music, science classes. Computer network features include campus e-mail, on-campus library services, CD-ROMs, online commercial services, Internet access, DVD, wireless campus network.

Contact Vincent W. Rowe Jr., Director of Enrollment Management and Financial Aid. 202-274-3210. Fax: 202-274-3211. E-mail: vrowe@gds.org. Web site: www.gds.org.

ANNOUNCEMENT FROM THE SCHOOL Georgetown Day School honors the integrity and worth of each individual within a diverse school community. The School is dedicated to providing a supportive educational atmosphere in which teachers challenge the intellectual, creative, and physical abilities of its students and foster strength of character and concern for others. Georgetown Day encourages its students to wonder, to inquire, and to be self-reliant, laying the foundation for a lifelong love of learning.

GEORGETOWN PREPARATORY SCHOOL

10900 Rockville Pike
North Bethesda, Maryland 20852-3299
Head of School: Rev. William L. George, SJ

General Information Boys' boarding and day college-preparatory, arts, religious studies, and technology school, affiliated with Roman Catholic Church. Grades 9–12. Founded: 1789. Setting: suburban. Nearest major city is Washington, DC. Students are housed in single-sex dormitories. 86-acre campus. 8 buildings on campus.

Approved or accredited by Middle States Association of Colleges and Schools, The Association of Boarding Schools, and Maryland Department of Education. Member of National Association of Independent Schools and Secondary School Admission Test Board. Endowment: $80 million. Total enrollment: 447. Upper school average class size: 16. Upper school faculty-student ratio: 1:8.

Upper School Student Profile Grade 9: 110 students (110 boys); Grade 10: 110 students (110 boys); Grade 11: 110 students (110 boys); Grade 12: 117 students (117 boys). 23% of students are boarding students. 60% are state residents. 25 states are represented in upper school student body. 15% are international students. International students from Canada, Indonesia, Japan, Mexico, Republic of Korea, and United Kingdom; 13 other countries represented in student body. 75% of students are Roman Catholic.

Faculty School total: 53. In upper school: 43 men, 10 women; 45 have advanced degrees; 17 reside on campus.

Subjects Offered Algebra, American history, American literature, art, art history, Bible studies, biology, calculus, chemistry, computer programming, computer science, drama, driver education, economics, English, English literature, ESL, ethics, European history, fine arts, French, geometry, German, government/civics, history, journalism, Latin, mathematics, music, philosophy, physical education, physics, psychology, religion, science, social studies, Spanish, speech, theater, theology, trigonometry, world history, world literature.

Graduation Requirements Arts and fine arts (art, music, dance, drama), computer science, English, foreign language, mathematics, physical education (includes health), religion (includes Bible studies and theology), science, social studies (includes history). Community service is required.

Special Academic Programs Advanced Placement exam preparation in 20 subject areas; honors section; independent study; term-away projects; study abroad; academic accommodation for the gifted; ESL (10 students enrolled).

College Placement 104 students graduated in 2005; all went to college, including Duke University; Georgetown University; Harvard University; Princeton University; University of Virginia; Yale University. 71% scored over 600 on SAT verbal, 67% scored over 600 on SAT math.

Student Life Upper grades have specified standards of dress, student council. Discipline rests primarily with faculty. Attendance at religious services is required.

Summer Programs Advancement, ESL programs offered; session focuses on ESL; held on campus; accepts boys and girls; open to students from other schools. 75 students usually enrolled. 2006 schedule: June 28 to August 6. Application deadline: March 1.

Tuition and Aid Day student tuition: $19,650; 7-day tuition and room/board: $34,650. Tuition installment plan (FACTS Tuition Payment Plan). Need-based scholarship grants, middle-income loans available. In 2005–06, 25% of upper-school students received aid. Total amount of financial aid awarded in 2005–06: $1,570,000.

Admissions Traditional secondary-level entrance grade is 9. For fall 2005, 497 students applied for upper-level admission, 152 were accepted, 125 enrolled. SSAT required. Deadline for receipt of application materials: January 15. Application fee required: $50. Interview required.

Athletics Interscholastic: baseball, basketball, cross-country running, diving, fencing, football, golf, ice hockey, indoor soccer, indoor track & field, lacrosse, rugby, running, soccer, swimming and diving, tennis, track and field, winter (indoor) track, wrestling; intramural: basketball, bicycling, billiards, canoeing/kayaking, climbing, flag football, hiking/backpacking, horseback riding, ice skating, kayaking, life saving, martial arts, mountain biking, nautilus, ocean paddling, paint ball, power lifting, racquetball, rappelling, rock climbing, ropes courses, skiing (downhill), snowboarding, softball, strength & conditioning, table tennis, weight training. 1 PE instructor, 16 coaches, 2 trainers.

Computers Computers are regularly used in art, classics, data processing, English, French, history, Latin, mathematics, music, religious studies, science, Spanish, writing classes. Computer network features include campus e-mail, on-campus library services, CD-ROMs, online commercial services, Internet access, file transfer, DVD, wireless campus network.

Contact Mr. Michael J. Horsey, Dean of Admissions. 301-214-1215. Fax: 301-493-6128. E-mail: admissions@gprep.org. Web site: www.gprep.org.

GEORGETOWN VISITATION PREPARATORY SCHOOL

1524 35th Street, NW
Washington, District of Columbia 20007
Head of School: Daniel M. Kerns

General Information Girls' day college-preparatory and religious studies school, affiliated with Roman Catholic Church. Grades 9–12. Founded: 1799. Setting: urban. 23-acre campus. 7 buildings on campus. Approved or accredited by Association of Independent Schools of Greater Washington, Middle States Association of Colleges and Schools, National Independent Private Schools Association, and District of Columbia Department of Education. Member of National Association of Independent Schools. Total enrollment: 475. Upper school average class size: 17. Upper school faculty-student ratio: 1:10.

Upper School Student Profile Grade 9: 118 students (118 girls); Grade 10: 120 students (120 girls); Grade 11: 113 students (113 girls); Grade 12: 134 students (134 girls). 90% of students are Roman Catholic.
Faculty School total: 52. In upper school: 9 men, 37 women; 32 have advanced degrees.
Subjects Offered Algebra, American history, American literature, anthropology, art, art history, Bible studies, biology, calculus, chemistry, computer programming, computer science, creative writing, dance, English, English literature, ethics, European history, expository writing, fine arts, French, geography, geometry, government/civics, health, history, Latin, mathematics, music, philosophy, physical education, physics, psychology, religion, science, social science, social studies, Spanish, speech, theology, trigonometry, world history.
Graduation Requirements Arts and fine arts (art, music, dance, drama), English, foreign language, mathematics, physical education (includes health), religion (includes Bible studies and theology), science, social science, social studies (includes history).
Special Academic Programs Advanced Placement exam preparation in 10 subject areas; honors section; independent study; study at local college for college credit.
College Placement 106 students graduated in 2005; all went to college, including Boston College; Dartmouth College; Georgetown University; University of Notre Dame; University of Virginia. Mean SAT verbal: 674, mean SAT math: 626.
Student Life Upper grades have uniform requirement, student council, honor system. Discipline rests primarily with faculty. Attendance at religious services is required.
Summer Programs Enrichment, sports, art/fine arts, computer instruction programs offered; held on campus; accepts girls; not open to students from other schools. 100 students usually enrolled. 2006 schedule: June to July. Application deadline: April.
Tuition and Aid Day student tuition: $17,300. Tuition installment plan (FACTS Tuition Payment Plan, individually arranged payment plans). Merit scholarship grants, need-based scholarship grants, paying campus jobs available. In 2005–06, 25% of upper-school students received aid; total upper-school merit-scholarship money awarded: $20,000. Total amount of financial aid awarded in 2005–06: $1,000,000.
Admissions Traditional secondary-level entrance grade is 9. For fall 2005, 400 students applied for upper-level admission, 140 were accepted, 118 enrolled. High School Placement Test required. Deadline for receipt of application materials: December 9. Application fee required: $50. On-campus interview required.
Athletics Interscholastic: basketball, crew, cross-country running, dance, diving, field hockey, fitness, indoor track, lacrosse, soccer, softball, swimming and diving, tennis, track and field, volleyball; intramural: cheering, flag football, strength & conditioning. 4 PE instructors, 23 coaches, 1 trainer.
Computers Computers are regularly used in art, English, French, history, mathematics, religion, science, Spanish classes. Computer network features include campus e-mail, on-campus library services, CD-ROMs, online commercial services, Internet access, office computer access, DVD, wireless campus network.
Contact Meghan K. Burke, Assistant Director of Admissions. 202-337-3350 Ext. 2246. Fax: 202-342-5733. E-mail: mburke@visi.org. Web site: www.visi.org.

ANNOUNCEMENT FROM THE SCHOOL Since 1799, Georgetown Visitation has been educating women of faith, vision, and purpose. A dynamic and well-balanced Catholic education reaches a diverse community intellectually and spiritually. Visitation's core curriculum, AP and honors courses, electives, Georgetown University Bridge Program, Language Consortium, extensive cocurriculars, 11 competitive sports, community service, traditions, and speaker forums make learning creative and challenging.

GEORGE WALTON ACADEMY

1 Bulldog Drive
Monroe, Georgia 30655
Head of School: William M. Nicholson

General Information Coeducational day college-preparatory, arts, and technology school. Grades K4–12. Founded: 1969. Setting: small town. Nearest major city is Atlanta. 42-acre campus. 8 buildings on campus. Approved or accredited by Georgia Accrediting Commission, Georgia Independent School Association, Southern Association of Colleges and Schools, and Georgia Department of Education. Total enrollment: 975. Upper school average class size: 17. Upper school faculty-student ratio: 1:10.
Upper School Student Profile Grade 9: 94 students (47 boys, 47 girls); Grade 10: 84 students (46 boys, 38 girls); Grade 11: 82 students (43 boys, 39 girls); Grade 12: 74 students (38 boys, 36 girls).
Faculty School total: 51. In upper school: 8 men, 18 women; 10 have advanced degrees.
Subjects Offered Algebra, American history, American literature, anatomy, art, art history, Bible studies, biology, calculus, chemistry, computer science, creative writing, drama, economics, English, English literature, environmental science, European history, fine arts, geography, geometry, government/civics, grammar, health, history, journalism, lab/keyboard, Latin, leadership training, mathematics, music, photography, physical education, physics, psychology, science, social science, social studies, sociology, Spanish, theater, trigonometry, typing, world history, world literature, writing.
Graduation Requirements Arts and fine arts (art, music, dance, drama), composition, English, foreign language, mathematics, physical education (includes health), science, social science, social studies (includes history).
Special Academic Programs Advanced Placement exam preparation in 10 subject areas; honors section; academic accommodation for the musically talented and the artistically talented.
College Placement 64 students graduated in 2005; all went to college, including Georgia College & State University; Georgia Institute of Technology; Georgia Southern University; Georgia State University; North Georgia College & State University; University of Georgia.
Student Life Upper grades have specified standards of dress, student council, honor system. Discipline rests primarily with faculty.
Tuition and Aid Day student tuition: $6900. Tuition installment plan (monthly payment plans). Tuition reduction for siblings, need-based scholarship grants available. In 2005–06, 1% of upper-school students received aid.
Admissions Traditional secondary-level entrance grade is 9. CAT 5, CTBS, Stanford Achievement Test, any other standardized test, Otis-Lennon, Stanford Achievement Test, PSAT or SAT required. Deadline for receipt of application materials: none. Application fee required: $150. On-campus interview recommended.
Athletics Interscholastic: aquatics (boys, girls), baseball (b), basketball (b,g), cheering (g), cross-country running (b,g), football (b), golf (b,g), physical fitness (b,g), softball (g), swimming and diving (b,g), tennis (b,g), track and field (b,g), volleyball (g), weight lifting (b), weight training (b,g), wrestling (b); intramural: aerobics (g), aerobics/dance (g), aerobics/nautilus (g). 5 PE instructors, 12 coaches.
Computers Computers are regularly used in all academic classes. Computer network features include campus e-mail, on-campus library services, CD-ROMs, Internet access, file transfer, office computer access, DVD.
Contact Mrs. Chris Stancil, Director of Admissions. 770-207-5172 Ext. 234. Fax: 770-267-4023. E-mail: cstancil@gwalton.com. Web site: gwlton.com.

GERMANTOWN ACADEMY

340 Morris Road
PO Box 287
Fort Washington, Pennsylvania 19034
Head of School: Mr. James W. Connor

General Information Coeducational day college-preparatory, arts, and technology school. Grades PK–12. Founded: 1759. Setting: suburban. Nearest major city is Philadelphia. 110-acre campus. 8 buildings on campus. Approved or accredited by Middle States Association of Colleges and Schools, Pennsylvania Association of Private Academic Schools, and Pennsylvania Department of Education. Member of National Association of Independent Schools. Endowment: $37 million. Total enrollment: 1,122. Upper school average class size: 15. Upper school faculty-student ratio: 1:15.
Upper School Student Profile Grade 9: 120 students (67 boys, 53 girls); Grade 10: 123 students (68 boys, 55 girls); Grade 11: 120 students (64 boys, 56 girls); Grade 12: 121 students (60 boys, 61 girls).
Faculty School total: 138. In upper school: 39 men, 22 women; 47 have advanced degrees.
Subjects Offered Acting, algebra, American history, American literature, art, art history, biology, botany, calculus, ceramics, chemistry, civil rights, computer math, computer science, creative writing, drama, driver education, economics, English, English literature, environmental science, European history, expository writing, film, fine arts, French, geography, geometry, government/civics, grammar, health, health education, history, Latin, marine biology, mathematics, medieval history, music, music history, music theory, philosophy, photography, physical education, physics, Russian, science, sculpture, social studies, society and culture, Spanish, speech, statistics, technology, trigonometry, women in world history, world history, writing.
Graduation Requirements Algebra, arts and fine arts (art, music, dance, drama), biology, chemistry, English, European history, foreign language, geometry, physical education (includes health), physics, U.S. history, ability to swim.
Special Academic Programs Advanced Placement exam preparation in 14 subject areas; honors section; independent study.
College Placement 120 students graduated in 2005; all went to college, including Cornell University; Drexel University; Franklin and Marshall College; The Johns Hopkins University; Trinity College; University of Pennsylvania. Mean SAT verbal: 626, mean SAT math: 633. 64% scored over 600 on SAT verbal, 78% scored over 600 on SAT math.
Student Life Upper grades have specified standards of dress, student council, honor system. Discipline rests equally with students and faculty.
Summer Programs Remediation, enrichment, advancement, art/fine arts, computer instruction programs offered; session focuses on challenging activities, fun and learning; held on campus; accepts boys and girls; open to students from other schools. 1400 students usually enrolled. 2006 schedule: June 20 to July 29. Application deadline: none.
Tuition and Aid Day student tuition: $19,355. Tuition installment plan (Higher Education Service, Inc). Merit scholarship grants, need-based scholarship grants available. In 2005–06, 24% of upper-school students received aid; total upper-school merit-scholarship money awarded: $84,000. Total amount of financial aid awarded in 2005–06: $1,100,000.

Admissions Traditional secondary-level entrance grade is 9. For fall 2005, 168 students applied for upper-level admission, 58 were accepted, 39 enrolled. ISEE or SSAT required. Deadline for receipt of application materials: none. Application fee required: $40. On-campus interview required.

Athletics Interscholastic: baseball (boys), basketball (b,g), cheering (g), cross-country running (b,g), diving (b,g), field hockey (g), football (b), golf (b,g), ice hockey (b), lacrosse (b,g), soccer (b,g), softball (g), swimming and diving (b,g), tennis (b,g), track and field (b,g), volleyball (g), water polo (b,g), wrestling (b); intramural: football (b,g), weight lifting (b,g); coed interscholastic: water polo, winter (indoor) track. 7 PE instructors, 20 coaches, 2 trainers.

Computers Computers are regularly used in English, foreign language, graphic arts, history, mathematics, photography, science classes. Computer network features include campus e-mail, on-campus library services, CD-ROMs, online commercial services, Internet access, file transfer.

Contact Admission Office. 215-643-1331. Fax: 215-646-1216. E-mail: admission@germantownacademy.org. Web site: www.germantownacademy.org.

GERMANTOWN FRIENDS SCHOOL

31 West Coulter Street
Philadelphia, Pennsylvania 19144
Head of School: Richard L. Wade

General Information Coeducational day college-preparatory, arts, and technology school, affiliated with Society of Friends. Grades K–12. Founded: 1845. Setting: urban. 21-acre campus. 20 buildings on campus. Approved or accredited by Friends Council on Education, Middle States Association of Colleges and Schools, and Pennsylvania Association of Private Academic Schools. Member of National Association of Independent Schools and Secondary School Admission Test Board. Endowment: $29.7 million. Total enrollment: 894. Upper school average class size: 18. Upper school faculty-student ratio: 1:9.

Upper School Student Profile Grade 9: 95 students (50 boys, 45 girls); Grade 10: 84 students (42 boys, 42 girls); Grade 11: 91 students (44 boys, 47 girls); Grade 12: 86 students (39 boys, 47 girls). 8.1% of students are members of Society of Friends.

Faculty School total: 136. In upper school: 27 men, 34 women; 40 have advanced degrees.

Subjects Offered 3-dimensional art, advanced chemistry, advanced math, algebra, American history, American literature, ancient history, art, art history, biology, calculus, chemistry, choir, chorus, Civil War, comparative cultures, computer applications, computer programming, creative writing, drama, dramatic arts, drawing, English, environmental science, European history, expository writing, French, geometry, grammar, graphic arts, Greek, health, human sexuality, independent study, instrumental music, jazz ensemble, Latin, Latin History, madrigals, mathematics, music, music theory, opera, orchestra, painting, philosophy, photography, physical education, physics, pre-calculus, science, social studies, Spanish, sports, stagecraft, statistics, studio art, theater, trigonometry, vocal music.

Graduation Requirements Arts and fine arts (art, music, dance, drama), English, foreign language, history, lab science, mathematics, music, physical education (includes health), month-long off-campus independent project.

Special Academic Programs Honors section; independent study; term-away projects; domestic exchange program (with The Network Program Schools, The Catlin Gabel School); study abroad; academic accommodation for the gifted, the musically talented, and the artistically talented.

College Placement 91 students graduated in 2005; 86 went to college, including Haverford College; Oberlin College; Stanford University; The George Washington University; University of Chicago; University of Pennsylvania. Other: 5 had other specific plans. Mean SAT verbal: 669, mean SAT math: 643. 75% scored over 600 on SAT verbal, 70% scored over 600 on SAT math.

Student Life Upper grades have student council. Discipline rests primarily with faculty. Attendance at religious services is required.

Tuition and Aid Day student tuition: $18,645–$18,975. Tuition installment plan (Academic Management Services Plan, Key Tuition Payment Plan, individually arranged payment plans). Need-based scholarship grants, need-based loans available. In 2005–06, 19% of upper-school students received aid. Total amount of financial aid awarded in 2005–06: $624,299.

Admissions Traditional secondary-level entrance grade is 9. For fall 2005, 86 students applied for upper-level admission, 42 were accepted, 25 enrolled. ISEE or SSAT required. Deadline for receipt of application materials: December 10. Application fee required: $40. On-campus interview required.

Athletics Interscholastic: baseball (boys), basketball (b,g), cross-country running (b,g), field hockey (g), indoor soccer (b,g), indoor track & field (b,g), lacrosse (g), soccer (b,g), softball (g), squash (b,g), tennis (b,g), track and field (b,g), wrestling (b); coed intramural: physical training, strength & conditioning, weight lifting, weight training. 5 PE instructors, 24 coaches, 1 trainer.

Computers Computers are regularly used in art, English, foreign language, history, mathematics, music, photography, publications, science classes. Computer network features include campus e-mail, on-campus library services, CD-ROMs, online commercial services, Internet access, file transfer.

Contact Eleanor M. Elkinton, Director, Admissions and Financial Aid. 215-951-2346. Fax: 215-951-2370. E-mail: elliee@gfsnet.org. Web site: www.germantownfriends.org.

GILL ST. BERNARD'S SCHOOL

St. Bernard's Road
Gladstone, New Jersey 07934
Head of School: Mr. S. A. Rowell

General Information Coeducational day college-preparatory, arts, and technology school. Grades PK–12. Founded: 1900. Setting: rural. Nearest major city is New York, NY. 73-acre campus. 22 buildings on campus. Approved or accredited by Middle States Association of Colleges and Schools and New Jersey Association of Independent Schools. Member of National Association of Independent Schools and Secondary School Admission Test Board. Endowment: $1.8 million. Total enrollment: 600. Upper school average class size: 12. Upper school faculty-student ratio: 1:8.

Upper School Student Profile Grade 9: 48 students (20 boys, 28 girls); Grade 10: 46 students (27 boys, 19 girls); Grade 11: 44 students (22 boys, 22 girls); Grade 12: 35 students (17 boys, 18 girls).

Faculty School total: 78. In upper school: 16 men, 14 women; 18 have advanced degrees.

Subjects Offered 20th century world history, 3-dimensional art, advanced chemistry, advanced math, African-American studies, algebra, American democracy, American history, American history-AP, American literature, analysis and differential calculus, analytic geometry, art, astronomy, biology, biology-AP, British literature, British literature (honors), calculus, calculus-AP, chemistry, chemistry-AP, chorus, college counseling, comparative cultures, computer education, computer programming, computer science, contemporary issues, creative writing, drama, earth science, English, English literature, English literature-AP, environmental science, European history, fine arts, French, gender issues, geography, geometry, government/civics, health, history, international relations, Latin, literature, mathematics, music, oceanography, philosophy, photography, physical education, physics, psychology, science, social studies, Spanish, technology, theater, woodworking, world history, world literature.

Graduation Requirements Arts and fine arts (art, music, dance, drama), English, foreign language, history, mathematics, science, unit-intensive 2-week course each year.

Special Academic Programs Advanced Placement exam preparation in 6 subject areas; honors section; independent study; study abroad; academic accommodation for the gifted.

College Placement 38 students graduated in 2004; all went to college, including Bucknell University; Centenary College of Louisiana; Northeastern University; University of Pennsylvania.

Student Life Upper grades have specified standards of dress, student council, honor system. Discipline rests equally with students and faculty.

Tuition and Aid Day student tuition: $20,995. Merit scholarship grants, need-based scholarship grants, Key Education Resources available. In 2004–05, 20% of upper-school students received aid; total upper-school merit-scholarship money awarded: $45,000. Total amount of financial aid awarded in 2004–05: $700,000.

Admissions Traditional secondary-level entrance grade is 9. ERB and SSAT required. Deadline for receipt of application materials: none. Application fee required: $50. On-campus interview required.

Athletics Interscholastic: baseball (boys), basketball (b,g), cross-country running (b,g), fencing (b,g), golf (b,g), roller hockey (b,g), soccer (b,g), softball (g), tennis (b,g), track and field (b,g). 1 PE instructor, 3 trainers.

Computers Computers are regularly used in art, creative writing, English, graphic design, history, humanities, introduction to technology, journalism, library, library skills, literary magazine, mathematics, multimedia, news writing, newspaper, research skills, science, social science, technology classes. Computer network features include campus e-mail, on-campus library services, CD-ROMs, online commercial services, Internet access, file transfer.

Contact Ms. Joyce E. Miller, Director of Admissions. 908-234-1611 Ext. 247. Fax: 908-234-0215. E-mail: jmiller@gsbschool.org. Web site: www.gsbschool.org.

ANNOUNCEMENT FROM THE SCHOOL Gill St. Bernard's School (1900) is a nonsectarian, independent day school, grades PK–12 in Gladstone, New Jersey. The School is the result of a merger between the Gill School for Girls and the St. Bernard's Episcopal School for Boys in 1972. In fall 1996, the two campuses were consolidated on the Gladstone site. The 72-acre campus features several academic buildings, a new athletic center, an art gallery, a theater, 20 acres of playing fields, 6 tennis courts, and a state-of-the-art track. The Lower School curriculum is designed to promote the development of independence, intellectual curiosity, and the academic foundation necessary for students to continue their educational journey. In Middle School, the curriculum emphasizes the development and mastery of skills that prepare each student for high school. The expanding horizons of the middle school student are recognized and encouraged. The Upper School's challenging and diverse curriculum is designed to prepare students for success in college as well as for future life endeavors. AP and honors courses, along with extensive extracurricular options, are offered. The Upper School college guidance program begins in grade 9 with student and parent information sessions. In the junior year, families work with college counselors to identify and investigate various college and university options. Individual guidance and direction with applications, interviews, required testing (AP exams, etc.), and financial assistance applications characterize the senior year. One

hundred percent of GSB students matriculate at colleges or universities. Gill St. Bernard's School is committed to working with exceptional, college-bound students who can think critically and analytically, act with integrity and compassion, and become responsible citizens and leaders in their communities, the nation, and the world. In all aspects of School life, integrity, compassion, and respect for others are ideals that Gill St. Bernard's holds true.

GILMAN SCHOOL

5407 Roland Avenue
Baltimore, Maryland 21210
Head of School: Mr. Jon C. McGill

General Information Boys' day college-preparatory school. Grades P1–12. Founded: 1897. Setting: suburban. 67-acre campus. Approved or accredited by Association of Independent Maryland Schools and Maryland Department of Education. Member of National Association of Independent Schools and Secondary School Admission Test Board. Endowment: $58 million. Total enrollment: 971. Upper school average class size: 16. Upper school faculty-student ratio: 1:7.

Upper School Student Profile Grade 9: 106 students (106 boys); Grade 10: 112 students (112 boys); Grade 11: 103 students (103 boys); Grade 12: 106 students (106 boys).

Faculty School total: 128. In upper school: 44 men, 20 women; 49 have advanced degrees.

Subjects Offered Algebra, American history, American literature, anatomy, Arabic, art, art history, biology, calculus, ceramics, chemistry, Chinese, community service, computer math, computer programming, computer science, creative writing, drafting, drama, driver education, ecology, economics, engineering, English, English literature, environmental science, European history, expository writing, fine arts, French, geometry, German, government/civics, grammar, Greek, history, industrial arts, Latin, mathematics, mechanical drawing, music, photography, physical education, physics, physiology, religion, Russian, science, social studies, Spanish, speech, statistics, theater, trigonometry, writing.

Graduation Requirements Art history, athletics, English, foreign language, history, mathematics, music appreciation, religions, science, senior project.

Special Academic Programs Advanced Placement exam preparation in 19 subject areas; honors section; independent study; academic accommodation for the gifted.

College Placement 109 students graduated in 2005; all went to college, including Georgetown University; Princeton University; The Johns Hopkins University; Tulane University; University of Maryland; Wake Forest University. Mean SAT verbal: 638, mean SAT math: 654. 70% scored over 600 on SAT verbal, 70% scored over 600 on SAT math.

Student Life Upper grades have specified standards of dress, student council, honor system. Discipline rests primarily with faculty.

Summer Programs Remediation, enrichment, advancement programs offered; session focuses on remediation; held on campus; accepts boys and girls; open to students from other schools. 200 students usually enrolled. 2006 schedule: June 19 to July 28. Application deadline: June 19.

Tuition and Aid Day student tuition: $17,835. Tuition installment plan (Key Tuition Payment Plan, Gilman Monthly Payment Plan). Need-based scholarship grants, need-based loans available. In 2005–06, 21% of upper-school students received aid. Total amount of financial aid awarded in 2005–06: $1,100,000.

Admissions Traditional secondary-level entrance grade is 9. For fall 2005, 113 students applied for upper-level admission, 46 were accepted, 26 enrolled. ISEE required. Deadline for receipt of application materials: January 9. Application fee required: $50. On-campus interview required.

Athletics Interscholastic: baseball, basketball, cross-country running, diving, football, golf, ice hockey, indoor track, lacrosse, soccer, squash, swimming and diving, tennis, track and field, volleyball, water polo, winter (indoor) track, wrestling; intramural: basketball, bicycling, crew, cross-country running, fitness, flag football, Frisbee, golf, physical fitness, rugby, table tennis, tennis, touch football, weight lifting, winter soccer. 2 PE instructors, 2 trainers.

Computers Computers are regularly used in mathematics classes. Computer network features include campus e-mail, on-campus library services, CD-ROMs, Internet access, file transfer.

Contact Robert J. Demeule, Director of Admissions. 410-323-3800. Fax: 410-532-6513. E-mail: rdemeule@gilman.edu. Web site: www.gilman.edu.

ANNOUNCEMENT FROM THE SCHOOL Founded in 1897 as the first country day school in the United States, Gilman is a college-preparatory school enrolling 970 boys in pre-first through twelfth grades. The School aims to provide thorough academic instruction, to promote physical vigor, and to develop sound character. The Upper School curriculum, which includes electives, Advanced Placement courses, and a coordinate program with nearby girls' schools, is enriched by many diverse extracurricular activities. A summer session is offered. Tuition for 2005–06 was $16,815–$17,836. Jon C. McGill is Gilman's 12th Headmaster. Gilman is accredited by the Association of Independent Maryland Schools.

GILMOUR ACADEMY

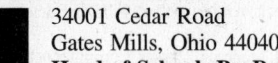

34001 Cedar Road
Gates Mills, Ohio 44040-9356
Head of School: Br. Robert E. Lavelle, CSC

General Information Coeducational boarding and day college-preparatory, arts, religious studies, and technology school, affiliated with Roman Catholic Church. Boarding grades 7–12, day grades PK–12. Founded: 1946. Setting: suburban. Nearest major city is Cleveland. Students are housed in single-sex dormitories and boys' wing and girls' wing dorms. 144-acre campus. 15 buildings on campus. Approved or accredited by Independent Schools Association of the Central States, Midwest Association of Boarding Schools, National Catholic Education Association, North Central Association of Colleges and Schools, Ohio Association of Independent Schools, The Association of Boarding Schools, and Ohio Department of Education. Member of National Association of Independent Schools and Secondary School Admission Test Board. Language of instruction: English. Endowment: $29 million. Total enrollment: 748. Upper school average class size: 15. Upper school faculty-student ratio: 1:10.

Upper School Student Profile Grade 9: 100 students (61 boys, 39 girls); Grade 10: 116 students (64 boys, 52 girls); Grade 11: 102 students (49 boys, 53 girls); Grade 12: 112 students (59 boys, 53 girls); Postgraduate: 4 students (3 boys, 1 girl). 12% of students are boarding students. 87% are state residents. 16 states are represented in upper school student body. 3% are international students. International students from Canada, Mexico, and Republic of Korea; 2 other countries represented in student body. 81% of students are Roman Catholic.

Faculty School total: 106. In upper school: 41 men, 28 women; 50 have advanced degrees; 11 reside on campus.

Subjects Offered Advanced Placement courses, advanced studio art-AP, algebra, American government, American history, American literature, art, band, Bible, biology, biology-AP, British literature, broadcast journalism, calculus, calculus-AP, ceramics, chemistry, chemistry-AP, chorus, community service, computer programming, computer science, computer science-AP, creative writing, drama, drawing, economics, English, English literature, English-AP, ensembles, ESL, ethics, European history, European history-AP, fine arts, French, French language-AP, French-AP, geometry, geometry with art applications, government, government-AP, government/civics, health, history, history of rock and roll, independent study, jazz ensemble, journalism, Latin, Latin-AP, law, leadership, mathematics, mathematics-AP, model United Nations, modern European history-AP, music, musical productions, oil painting, painting, photography, physical education, physical fitness, physics, physics-AP, pre-algebra, pre-calculus, religion, religious studies, SAT/ACT preparation, science, social studies, Spanish, Spanish language-AP, speech, speech and debate, statistics-AP, student government, student publications, studio art, studio art-AP, swimming, theater, trigonometry, U.S. history, U.S. history-AP, weight training, work-study, world history, writing, writing workshop, yearbook.

Graduation Requirements Arts and fine arts (art, music, dance, drama), English, foreign language, mathematics, physical education (includes health), religion (includes Bible studies and theology), science, social studies (includes history), speech, senior project. Community service is required.

Special Academic Programs Advanced Placement exam preparation in 15 subject areas; accelerated programs; independent study; term-away projects; study at local college for college credit; academic accommodation for the gifted, the musically talented, and the artistically talented; ESL (2 students enrolled).

College Placement 110 students graduated in 2004; 108 went to college, including Boston College; Case Western Reserve University; Fordham University; Miami University; Vanderbilt University; Villanova University. Other: 2 entered a post-graduate year. Median SAT verbal: 637, median SAT math: 624. 55% scored over 600 on SAT verbal, 48% scored over 600 on SAT math.

Student Life Upper grades have specified standards of dress, student council, honor system. Discipline rests equally with students and faculty. Attendance at religious services is required.

Tuition and Aid Day student tuition: $6865–$16,460; 5-day tuition and room/board: $26,430–$27,530; 7-day tuition and room/board: $28,030–$29,130. Tuition installment plan (SMART Tuition Payment Plan). Tuition reduction for siblings, merit scholarship grants, need-based scholarship grants, need-based loans, paying campus jobs, endowed scholarships with criteria specified by donors available. In 2004–05, 45% of upper-school students received aid; total upper-school merit-scholarship money awarded: $50,000. Total amount of financial aid awarded in 2004–05: $1,800,000.

Admissions Traditional secondary-level entrance grade is 9. For fall 2005, 412 students applied for upper-level admission, 186 were accepted, 110 enrolled. ACT, ISEE, PSAT, SAT, SSAT or TOEFL required. Deadline for receipt of application materials: none. Application fee required: $25. Interview required.

Athletics Interscholastic: baseball (boys), basketball (b,g), cross-country running (b,g), diving (b,g), football (b), hockey (b,g), ice hockey (b,g), lacrosse (b), running (b,g), soccer (b,g), softball (g), swimming and diving (b,g), tennis (b,g), track and field (b,g), volleyball (g); intramural: cheering (g), indoor soccer (b,g), lacrosse (g); coed interscholastic: figure skating, golf, indoor track, indoor track & field, winter (indoor) track; coed intramural: aerobics, aerobics/nautilus, alpine skiing, aquatics, basketball, bowling, broomball, figure skating, fitness, flag football, floor hockey, golf, ice hockey, ice skating, indoor track, paddle tennis, physical fitness, skiing (downhill),

snowboarding, soccer, strength & conditioning, swimming and diving, tennis, volleyball, weight training, winter (indoor) track, winter soccer. 4 PE instructors, 5 coaches, 2 trainers.

Computers Computers are regularly used in all academic classes. Computer network features include campus e-mail, on-campus library services, CD-ROMs, online commercial services, Internet access, file transfer, office computer access, DVD, wireless campus network, EXPAN (college guidance service).

Contact Mr. Devin K. Schlickmann, Dean of Admissions and Enrollment Management. 440-473-8050. Fax: 440-473-8010. E-mail: admissions@gilmour.org. Web site: www.gilmour.org.

ANNOUNCEMENT FROM THE SCHOOL Gilmour Academy is a premier, Catholic, coeducational, independent boarding and day school, which emphasizes the intellectual, spiritual, moral, social, and physical growth of each student. Through a challenging academic program, including 90-minute classes, Socratic Seminars, and a rigorous core curriculum, students succeed because they learn to think critically and solve problems in a project-oriented world. The college-preparatory program is accented by the collegiate atmosphere of Gilmour's 144-acre campus, 11 academic buildings, exceptional athletics facilities, including 2 NHL-size ice arenas and a new athletic center, and a family-style dormitory for 52 students in grades 7–12.

See full description on page 798.

GIRARD COLLEGE

2101 South College Avenue
Philadelphia, Pennsylvania 19121-4897
Head of School: Hon. Dominic Cermele

General Information Coeducational boarding college-preparatory and general academic school. Grades 1–12. Founded: 1848. Setting: urban. Students are housed in single-sex dormitories. 43-acre campus. 10 buildings on campus. Approved or accredited by Middle States Association of Colleges and Schools, The Association of Boarding Schools, and Pennsylvania Department of Education. Member of National Association of Independent Schools. Endowment: $355 million. Total enrollment: 721. Upper school average class size: 22. Upper school faculty-student ratio: 1:16.

Upper School Student Profile Grade 9: 71 students (28 boys, 43 girls); Grade 10: 48 students (22 boys, 26 girls); Grade 11: 48 students (21 boys, 27 girls); Grade 12: 42 students (19 boys, 23 girls). 100% of students are boarding students. 90% are state residents. 6 states are represented in upper school student body.

Faculty School total: 71. In upper school: 12 men, 9 women; 9 have advanced degrees; 2 reside on campus.

Subjects Offered Algebra, American history, American literature, anatomy, art, biology, calculus, chemistry, choir, college counseling, community service, computer literacy, earth science, English, English literature, European history, French, geometry, government/civics, health, honors algebra, honors English, honors geometry, honors U.S. history, instrumental music, jazz band, life management skills, mathematics, multicultural studies, music appreciation, physical education, physics, poetry, pre-calculus, SAT preparation, senior project, social studies, sociology, Spanish, video film production, world cultures.

Graduation Requirements College counseling, computer literacy, English, foreign language, mathematics, physical education (includes health), science, senior career experience, senior project, social science, social studies (includes history). Community service is required.

Special Academic Programs Advanced Placement exam preparation in 2 subject areas; honors section; study at local college for college credit; remedial reading and/or remedial writing; remedial math.

College Placement 24 students graduated in 2005; 23 went to college, including Albright College; Drexel University; Indiana University of Pennsylvania; Temple University; The Pennsylvania State University University Park Campus; Villanova University. Other: 1 entered military service. Mean SAT verbal: 490, mean SAT math: 477.

Student Life Upper grades have uniform requirement, student council. Discipline rests primarily with faculty.

Tuition and Aid Full scholarships (if admission requirements met) available. In 2005–06, 100% of upper-school students received aid.

Admissions Traditional secondary-level entrance grade is 9. For fall 2005, 124 students applied for upper-level admission, 24 were accepted, 14 enrolled. Admissions testing, math, reading, and mental ability tests and writing sample required. Deadline for receipt of application materials: none. No application fee required. On-campus interview required.

Athletics Interscholastic: baseball (boys), basketball (b,g), cross-country running (b,g), soccer (b,g), softball (g), tennis (g), track and field (b,g), winter (indoor) track (b,g), wrestling (b); intramural: strength & conditioning (b,g); coed interscholastic: cheering; coed intramural: aerobics, dance, flag football, life saving, martial arts, outdoor activities, outdoor adventure, physical fitness, swimming and diving, weight training. 1 PE instructor, 11 coaches.

Computers Computers are regularly used in college planning, English, foreign language, history, library, mathematics, newspaper, reading, research skills, SAT preparation, science, social studies, study skills, word processing, writing, yearbook classes. Computer network features include campus e-mail, on-campus library services, CD-ROMs, online commercial services, Internet access, file transfer.

Contact Admission Receptionist. 215-787-2620. Fax: 215-787-4402. E-mail: admissions@girardcollege.com. Web site: www.girardcollege.com.

ANNOUNCEMENT FROM THE SCHOOL For more than 150 years, Girard College has helped young people find hope, joy, and opportunity in learning and living. In classrooms and residences, on playing fields and in the community, Girard students shine. Girard is a private, coed, boarding school for academically capable students in grades 1–12 who come from families headed by a single parent or guardian with limited financial resources. All Girard students receive full scholarships, enabling them to take part in the School's strong academic program and to live safely on its enclosed 43-acre campus in the Philadelphia Art Museum area of the city. Girard College Elementary School provides solid, comprehensive, academic preparation for children in grades 1–5. Small groupings of no more than 23 students per class create an intimate setting for learning. Highly trained and certified teachers apply the latest educational strategies in thought-provoking and engaging lessons. Specialists provide classes in art, music, physical education, health, science, computer technology, and library. The Middle School is dedicated to the greatest development of its students. A major goal is to enable all students to master the academic skills, concepts, and knowledge necessary to ensure their participation in society as productive citizens. To accomplish this goal, an interdisciplinary team-teaching approach to instruction is provided at all grade levels, with coordinated classroom activities, assemblies, and field trips. With a typical acceptance rate of 100 percent, 95 percent of Girard students choose to attend a 4-year college. Girard's athletic programs reflect the school's emphasis on physical well-being while fostering a sense of teamwork and leadership. Girard's athletic achievements include consecutive District I championships in boys' basketball and District track championships in 1999 and 2001. Girard offers a variety of other sports. For more information, visit www.girardcollege.com.

GIRLS PREPARATORY SCHOOL

205 Island Avenue
Chattanooga, Tennessee 37405
Head of School: Mr. Stanley R. Tucker

General Information Girls' day college-preparatory, arts, and technology school. Grades 6–12. Founded: 1906. Setting: suburban. Nearest major city is Atlanta, GA. 55-acre campus. 8 buildings on campus. Approved or accredited by Southern Association of Colleges and Schools and Southern Association of Independent Schools. Member of National Association of Independent Schools. Endowment: $24.5 million. Total enrollment: 719. Upper school average class size: 13. Upper school faculty-student ratio: 1:8.

Upper School Student Profile Grade 9: 104 students (104 girls); Grade 10: 111 students (111 girls); Grade 11: 110 students (110 girls); Grade 12: 102 students (102 girls).

Faculty School total: 79. In upper school: 16 men, 35 women; 26 have advanced degrees.

Subjects Offered Algebra, American history, American literature, art, art history, Basic programming, Bible studies, biology, calculus, chemistry, computer science, constitutional law, dance, drama, East Asian history, economics, English, English literature, European history, expository writing, fine arts, forensic science, French, geometry, government/civics, graphic design, history, Latin, marine biology, mathematics, music, orchestra, photography, physical education, physics, pottery, pre-calculus, religion, science, Spanish, statistics, trigonometry, world history.

Graduation Requirements Arts and fine arts (art, music, dance, drama), electives, English, foreign language, history, mathematics, physical education (includes health), religion (includes Bible studies and theology), science.

Special Academic Programs Advanced Placement exam preparation in 19 subject areas; honors section; independent study.

College Placement 109 students graduated in 2005; all went to college, including Auburn University; Emory University; The University of Tennessee; University of Georgia; Vanderbilt University; Washington University in St. Louis. Median SAT verbal: 615, median SAT math: 605, median composite ACT: 24. 55% scored over 600 on SAT verbal, 59% scored over 600 on SAT math.

Student Life Upper grades have uniform requirement, student council, honor system. Discipline rests primarily with faculty.

Summer Programs Remediation, enrichment, advancement, sports, art/fine arts, computer instruction programs offered; session focuses on enrichment; held on campus; accepts boys and girls; open to students from other schools. 700 students usually enrolled. 2006 schedule: June 9 to July 25. Application deadline: none.

Tuition and Aid Day student tuition: $15,580. Tuition installment plan (Key Tuition Payment Plan, monthly payment plans, individually arranged payment plans, 60%/40% and 100% payment plans). Merit scholarship grants, need-based scholarship grants, need-based loans available. In 2005–06, 23% of upper-school students received

aid; total upper-school merit-scholarship money awarded: $29,960. Total amount of financial aid awarded in 2005–06: $847,222.

Admissions Traditional secondary-level entrance grade is 9. For fall 2005, 61 students applied for upper-level admission, 39 were accepted, 23 enrolled. ISEE required. Deadline for receipt of application materials: none. Application fee required: $50. On-campus interview required.

Athletics Interscholastic: basketball, cheering, crew, cross-country running, diving, golf, lacrosse, soccer, softball, swimming and diving, tennis, track and field, volleyball; intramural: aerobics, aerobics/dance, back packing, bicycling, canoeing/kayaking, climbing, dance, dance squad, fitness, fitness walking, Frisbee, hiking/backpacking, jogging, kayaking, life saving, modern dance, mountain biking, outdoor activities, outdoor adventure, outdoor education, paddle tennis, physical fitness, rafting, rock climbing, rowing, running, self defense, strength & conditioning, ultimate Frisbee, walking, weight lifting, wilderness. 6 PE instructors, 25 coaches, 2 trainers.

Computers Computers are regularly used in Bible studies, dance, English, foreign language, history, mathematics, photography, science classes. Computer network features include campus e-mail, on-campus library services, CD-ROMs, online commercial services, Internet access, file transfer, office computer access, DVD, wireless campus network, network printing.

Contact Diane Moore, Director of Admissions. 423-634-7647. Fax: 423-634-7643. E-mail: dmoore@gps.edu.

ANNOUNCEMENT FROM THE SCHOOL One of the largest secondary girls' day schools in the United States, GPS enrolls 750 students in grades 6–12. An incubator for educational innovation, GPS began its student-owned, wireless laptop program in 1998. An average of 20% of GPS graduates have been recognized by the National Merit Program. Faculty members who excel at teaching girls and a wide range of honors and AP offerings foster a solid academic preparation. Resources include a superior fine arts department, 13 competitive interscholastic sports, and over 60 student organizations that provide leadership opportunities. Community service and a nationally recognized character education program enrich the students' extracurricular lives.

GLADES DAY SCHOOL

400 Gator Boulevard
Belle Glade, Florida 33430
Head of School: Mr. Armando Perez Jr.

General Information Coeducational day college-preparatory and general academic school. Grades PK–12. Founded: 1965. Setting: small town. Nearest major city is Miami. 20-acre campus. 4 buildings on campus. Approved or accredited by Florida Council of Independent Schools. Total enrollment: 602. Upper school average class size: 20. Upper school faculty-student ratio: 1:10.

Upper School Student Profile Grade 9: 70 students (36 boys, 34 girls); Grade 10: 69 students (38 boys, 31 girls); Grade 11: 65 students (42 boys, 23 girls); Grade 12: 61 students (29 boys, 32 girls).

Faculty School total: 33. In upper school: 14 men, 19 women; 3 have advanced degrees.

Subjects Offered Advanced math, algebra, American government, American history, American literature, anatomy, art, biology, calculus, chemistry, computer applications, computer keyboarding, computer programming, computer skills, computer technologies, concert band, current events, earth science, economics, English, English literature, environmental science, European history, general math, geometry, grammar, health, health education, journalism, keyboarding, law studies, marching band, microeconomics-AP, physical education, physics, play production, pre-calculus, SAT/ACT preparation, Spanish, trigonometry, U.S. history, weightlifting, Western civilization, world history, world history-AP, yearbook.

Graduation Requirements Computer keyboarding, English, foreign language, health education, mathematics, performing arts, physical education (includes health), science, social science, social studies (includes history).

Special Academic Programs Advanced Placement exam preparation in 2 subject areas; honors section; independent study; study at local college for college credit; remedial reading and/or remedial writing; remedial math; programs in general development for dyslexic students.

College Placement 61 students graduated in 2005; 54 went to college, including Florida Atlantic University; Florida Gulf Coast University; Palm Beach Community College; Santa Fe Community College; University of Florida; University of North Florida. Other: 2 went to work, 5 had other specific plans.

Student Life Upper grades have uniform requirement, student council. Discipline rests primarily with faculty.

Summer Programs Remediation programs offered; session focuses on remediation; held on campus; accepts boys and girls; not open to students from other schools. 15 students usually enrolled. 2006 schedule: June 10 to July 10. Application deadline: June 8.

Tuition and Aid Day student tuition: $4800–$5295. Tuition installment plan (FACTS Tuition Payment Plan, monthly payment plans, individually arranged payment plans). Tuition reduction for siblings, need-based scholarship grants, need-based loans available. In 2005–06, 10% of upper-school students received aid.

Admissions Traditional secondary-level entrance grade is 9. For fall 2005, 85 students applied for upper-level admission, 76 were accepted, 72 enrolled. Deadline for receipt of application materials: none. Application fee required: $200. On-campus interview required.

Athletics Interscholastic: baseball (boys), basketball (b,g), cheering (g), cross-country running (b,g), drill team (g), football (b), golf (b), soccer (b,g), softball (g), track and field (b,g), volleyball (g); intramural: strength & conditioning (b,g), tennis (b,g), weight training (b,g). 3 PE instructors, 2 coaches, 2 trainers.

Computers Computers are regularly used in journalism, mathematics, science, Web site design, word processing, yearbook classes. Computer resources include on-campus library services, CD-ROMs, Internet access.

Contact Mrs. Irene Tellechea, High School Secretary. 561-996-6769 Ext. 10. Fax: 561-992-9274. E-mail: admissions@gladesdayschool.com. Web site: gladesdayschool.com.

GLEN EDEN SCHOOL

Vancouver, British Columbia, Canada
See Special Needs Schools section.

GLENELG COUNTRY SCHOOL

12793 Folly Quarter Road
Ellicott City, Maryland 21042
Head of School: Ryland O. Chapman III

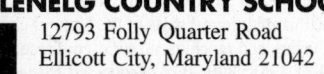 

General Information Coeducational day college-preparatory, arts, and technology school. Grades PK–12. Founded: 1954. Setting: suburban. Nearest major city is Baltimore. 87-acre campus. 1 building on campus. Approved or accredited by Association of Independent Maryland Schools, Middle States Association of Colleges and Schools, and Maryland Department of Education. Member of National Association of Independent Schools. Endowment: $350,000. Total enrollment: 796. Upper school average class size: 16. Upper school faculty-student ratio: 1:6.

Upper School Student Profile Grade 9: 76 students (36 boys, 40 girls); Grade 10: 68 students (37 boys, 31 girls); Grade 11: 56 students (25 boys, 31 girls); Grade 12: 60 students (37 boys, 23 girls).

Faculty School total: 120. In upper school: 18 men, 22 women; 28 have advanced degrees.

Subjects Offered Algebra, American history, American literature, art, art history, biology, biology-AP, calculus, calculus-AP, chemistry, chemistry-AP, Chinese, chorus, community service, computer science, creative writing, drama, English, English literature, English-AP, European history, expository writing, French, French-AP, geometry, history, humanities, integrative seminar, Latin, Latin-AP, mathematics, photography, physical education, physical science, physics, physics-AP, pre-calculus, psychology, publications, science, social studies, Spanish, Spanish-AP, statistics, studio art, theater, trigonometry, world affairs.

Graduation Requirements English, foreign language, integrative seminar, mathematics, physical education (includes health), science, social studies (includes history), participation in Civic Leadership Program, 25 hours of community service per year.

Special Academic Programs Advanced Placement exam preparation in 19 subject areas; honors section; independent study; academic accommodation for the gifted.

College Placement 47 students graduated in 2005; all went to college, including Dickinson College; James Madison University; Randolph-Macon College; University of Maryland, Baltimore County; Vanderbilt University; Virginia Polytechnic Institute and State University. Median SAT verbal: 615, median SAT math: 594. 52% scored over 600 on SAT verbal, 45% scored over 600 on SAT math.

Student Life Upper grades have uniform requirement, student council, honor system. Discipline rests equally with students and faculty.

Summer Programs Remediation, enrichment, sports programs offered; session focuses on academics and athletics; held on campus; accepts boys and girls; open to students from other schools. 220 students usually enrolled. 2006 schedule: June 15 to July 31. Application deadline: March.

Tuition and Aid Day student tuition: $17,260–$17,760. Tuition installment plan (monthly payment plans, individually arranged payment plans, 2-payment plan). Merit scholarship grants, need-based scholarship grants available. In 2005–06, 26% of upper-school students received aid; total upper-school merit-scholarship money awarded: $50,000. Total amount of financial aid awarded in 2005–06: $375,000.

Admissions Traditional secondary-level entrance grade is 9. For fall 2005, 80 students applied for upper-level admission, 45 were accepted, 34 enrolled. ISEE required. Deadline for receipt of application materials: February 1. Application fee required: $75. On-campus interview required.

Athletics Interscholastic: baseball (boys), basketball (b,g), cross-country running (b,g), field hockey (g), golf (b,g), ice hockey (b), indoor soccer (b,g), lacrosse (b,g), soccer (b,g), tennis (b,g), volleyball (g), winter soccer (g); coed interscholastic: equestrian sports, ice hockey; coed intramural: aerobics, aerobics/dance, ball hockey, dance, fitness, flag football, floor hockey, golf, in-line hockey, skiing (downhill), strength & conditioning, ultimate Frisbee, weight training. 5 PE instructors, 9 coaches, 1 trainer.

Computers Computers are regularly used in all academic classes. Computer network features include campus e-mail, on-campus library services, CD-ROMs, Internet access, DVD, wireless campus network.

Contact Mrs. Karen K. Wootton, Director of Admission and Financial Aid. 410-531-7346 Ext. 2203. Fax: 410-531-7363. E-mail: wootton@glenelg.org. Web site: www.glenelg.org.

ANNOUNCEMENT FROM THE SCHOOL Glenelg Country School was founded in 1954 by 5 Howard County families searching for an independent, coeducational, nonsectarian school that would provide small class sizes, excellent teachers, and a strong academic program. The School is located on 87 beautiful acres in the center of Howard County, accessible to both Baltimore and Washington. The Primary, Lower, Middle, and Upper Schools each have separate academic buildings. The Upper School, grades 9–12, opened an academic expansion and new athletic center in spring 2005. There are no boarding options available, and families are responsible for transportation to and from school. Seventy-five percent of the families live in Howard County. The mission of Glenelg Country School is to provide a challenging academic curriculum, enriching opportunities in the arts, and a vigorous athletic program in order to develop intellectual curiosity, personal integrity, compassion for others, and strong citizenship. In addition to strong academic offerings, including 15 Advanced Placement courses, the Upper School offers opportunities in athletics (13 sports), fine and performing arts, special interest clubs, and community service. College preparation and selection are integral parts of the Upper School. A full-time college counselor and advisers and teachers provide guidance. The class of 2005 had a mean SAT total of 1218; 89% took Advanced Placement courses; 85% were accepted by their first-choice college; 97% were accepted by their first or second-choice college. The enrollment for 2005–06, from prekindergarten through grade 12, is 800 students. The Upper School enrolls 260 students (76 in the class of 2009), with enrollment predicted to reach 300 in the next few years. The male:female ratio is 1:1. The School is sensitive to ethnic diversity, with a minority population of 25%. A financial aid program allows for socioeconomic diversity, with 18% of students receiving need-based assistance.

THE GLENHOLME SCHOOL

Washington, Connecticut
See Special Needs Schools section.

GONZAGA PREPARATORY SCHOOL

1224 East Euclid Avenue
Spokane, Washington 99207-2899
Head of School: Mr. Kevin Michael Booth

General Information Coeducational day college-preparatory, general academic, and religious studies school, affiliated with Roman Catholic Church (Jesuit order). Grades 9–12. Founded: 1887. Setting: urban. 20-acre campus. 4 buildings on campus. Approved or accredited by Northwest Association of Schools and Colleges and Washington Department of Education. Endowment: $10 million. Total enrollment: 860. Upper school average class size: 19. Upper school faculty-student ratio: 1:19.
Upper School Student Profile Grade 9: 251 students (115 boys, 136 girls); Grade 10: 204 students (103 boys, 101 girls); Grade 11: 218 students (109 boys, 109 girls); Grade 12: 187 students (78 boys, 109 girls). 73% of students are Roman Catholic Church (Jesuit order).
Faculty School total: 65. In upper school: 36 men, 25 women; 51 have advanced degrees.
Subjects Offered Algebra, American history, American literature, art, art history, Bible studies, biology, business, calculus, ceramics, chemistry, computer programming, computer science, drama, earth science, English, English literature, environmental science, European history, fine arts, French, geography, geometry, government/civics, grammar, Greek, health, history, home economics, journalism, keyboarding, Latin, mathematics, music, occupational education, philosophy, photography, physical education, physics, psychology, religion, science, single survival, social studies, Spanish, theater, theology, trigonometry, world history, world literature, writing, zoology.
Graduation Requirements Arts and fine arts (art, music, dance, drama), English, foreign language, mathematics, occupational education, physical education (includes health), religion (includes Bible studies and theology), science, social studies (includes history). Community service is required.
Special Academic Programs Advanced Placement exam preparation in 11 subject areas; honors section; independent study; study at local college for college credit.
College Placement 214 students graduated in 2005; 209 went to college, including Gonzaga University; Seattle University; University of Portland; University of Washington; Washington State University; Western Washington University. Other: 2 went to work, 1 entered military service, 2 had other specific plans. Median SAT verbal: 557, median SAT math: 557, median combined SAT: 1114, median composite ACT: 23.

Student Life Upper grades have specified standards of dress, student council. Discipline rests primarily with faculty. Attendance at religious services is required.
Summer Programs Remediation, enrichment, art/fine arts, computer instruction programs offered; session focuses on development of basic skills; held on campus; accepts boys and girls; open to students from other schools. 140 students usually enrolled. 2006 schedule: June 20 to July 22. Application deadline: June 20.
Tuition and Aid Day student tuition: $7450. Tuition installment plan (monthly payment plans, individually arranged payment plans). Tuition reduction for siblings, merit scholarship grants, need-based scholarship grants, Fair Share Tuition Program available. In 2005–06, 60% of upper-school students received aid.
Admissions Traditional secondary-level entrance grade is 9. High School Placement Test required. Deadline for receipt of application materials: December 3. No application fee required.
Athletics Interscholastic: baseball (boys), basketball (b,g), cheering (g), cross-country running (b,g), dance team (g), football (b), golf (b,g), soccer (b,g), softball (g), tennis (b,g), track and field (b,g), volleyball (g), wrestling (b); intramural: lacrosse (b); coed interscholastic: strength & conditioning, weight training; coed intramural: bowling, dance team, rock climbing, tennis, yoga. 3 PE instructors, 44 coaches, 1 trainer.
Computers Computers are regularly used in English, foreign language, mathematics, occupational education, science classes. Computer network features include campus e-mail, on-campus library services, CD-ROMs, Internet access, DVD.
Contact Mike Arte, Academic Vice Principal. 509-483-8512. Fax: 509-777-8123. E-mail: marte@gprep.com. Web site: www.gprep.com.

GOULD ACADEMY

PO Box 860
Bethel, Maine 04217
Head of School: Daniel A. Kunkle

General Information Coeducational boarding and day college-preparatory, arts, and technology school. Grades 9–PG. Founded: 1836. Setting: small town. Nearest major city is Portland. Students are housed in single-sex dormitories. 456-acre campus. 30 buildings on campus. Approved or accredited by Association of Independent Schools in New England, Independent Schools of Northern New England, New England Association of Schools and Colleges, The Association of Boarding Schools, and Maine Department of Education. Member of National Association of Independent Schools and Secondary School Admission Test Board. Endowment: $9.5 million. Total enrollment: 241. Upper school average class size: 12. Upper school faculty-student ratio: 1:6.
Upper School Student Profile Grade 9: 44 students (23 boys, 21 girls); Grade 10: 54 students (33 boys, 21 girls); Grade 11: 77 students (47 boys, 30 girls); Grade 12: 63 students (36 boys, 27 girls); Postgraduate: 3 students (2 boys, 1 girl). 74% of students are boarding students. 42% are state residents. 20 states are represented in upper school student body. 17% are international students. International students from China, Czech Republic, Germany, Japan, Republic of Korea, and Taiwan; 16 other countries represented in student body.
Faculty School total: 45. In upper school: 23 men, 19 women; 25 have advanced degrees; 24 reside on campus.
Subjects Offered Acting, Advanced Placement courses, African-American literature, algebra, American foreign policy, American government-AP, American history, American literature, American literature-AP, analytic geometry, art, art history, athletic training, band, bioethics, DNA and culture, biology, biology-AP, British literature, British literature (honors), British literature-AP, calculus, calculus-AP, celestial navigation, ceramics, chemistry, chemistry-AP, chorus, Civil War, clayworking, college placement, computer information systems, computer music, computer programming, computer science, computers, conceptual physics, creative writing, debate, design, digital music, drama, drawing, earth science, Eastern religion and philosophy, ecology, economics, electives, electronic music, English, environmental science, environmental science-AP, ESL, European history, expository writing, foreign policy, French, geography, geometry, government and politics-AP, history, history-AP, honors algebra, honors English, honors world history, introduction to digital multitrack recording techniques, jazz band, jewelry making, Latin, learning strategies, literature by women, mathematics, music, music appreciation, music theory, musicianship, navigation, painting, philosophy, photography, physics, pottery, pre-calculus, printmaking, robotics, science, sculpture, Shakespeare, social studies, software design, Spanish, theater, U.S. government and politics-AP, video film production, women's literature, world history, writing.
Graduation Requirements English, foreign language, mathematics, physical education (includes health), science, social studies (includes history).
Special Academic Programs Advanced Placement exam preparation in 5 subject areas; honors section; independent study; term-away projects; study abroad; academic accommodation for the gifted, the musically talented, and the artistically talented; ESL (10 students enrolled).
College Placement 51 students graduated in 2005; 50 went to college, including Bentley College; Lewis & Clark College; Rochester Institute of Technology; Saint Michael's College; University of Illinois at Urbana–Champaign; University of Vermont. Other: 1 went to work. Mean composite ACT: 24.
Student Life Upper grades have specified standards of dress, student council, honor system. Discipline rests equally with students and faculty.

Tuition and Aid Day student tuition: $20,800; 7-day tuition and room/board: $35,750. Tuition installment plan (individually arranged payment plans, full-payment by August 15, 2/3 payment by August 12, 1/3 by December 1). Merit scholarship grants, need-based scholarship grants, need-based loans available. In 2005–06, 40% of upper-school students received aid; total upper-school merit-scholarship money awarded: $150,000. Total amount of financial aid awarded in 2005–06: $1,242,000.
Admissions Traditional secondary-level entrance grade is 9. For fall 2005, 189 students applied for upper-level admission, 155 were accepted, 92 enrolled. SSAT required. Deadline for receipt of application materials: February 1. Application fee required: $30. Interview required.
Athletics Interscholastic: alpine skiing (boys, girls), baseball (b), basketball (b,g), bicycling (b,g), cross-country running (b,g), field hockey (g), freestyle skiing (b,g), lacrosse (b,g), nordic skiing (b,g), outdoor skills (b,g), skiing (cross-country) (b,g), skiing (downhill) (b,g), snowboarding (b,g), soccer (b,g), softball (g), tennis (b,g); intramural: skiing (cross-country) (b,g), skiing (downhill) (b,g), snowboarding (b,g); coed interscholastic: climbing, dance, dressage, equestrian sports, golf, horseback riding, mountain biking, skateboarding, skiing (cross-country), skiing (downhill), snowboarding; coed intramural: golf, nordic skiing, outdoor activities, outdoor education, outdoor recreation, racquetball, rock climbing, skiing (cross-country), skiing (downhill), snowboarding, squash, strength & conditioning, trap and skeet, weight training. 11 coaches, 1 trainer.
Computers Computers are regularly used in English, foreign language, history, mathematics, music, science, technology classes. Computer network features include campus e-mail, on-campus library services, CD-ROMs, Internet access, file transfer, wireless campus network.
Contact John A. Kerney, Director of Admission. 207-824-7777. Fax: 207-824-2926. E-mail: john.kerney@gouldacademy.org. Web site: www.gouldacademy.org.

See full description on page 800.

GOVERNOR DUMMER ACADEMY

1 Elm Street
Byfield, Massachusetts 01922
Head of School: John Martin Doggett Jr.

petersons.com

General Information Coeducational boarding and day college-preparatory and arts school. Grades 9–12. Founded: 1763. Setting: rural. Nearest major city is Boston. Students are housed in single-sex dormitories. 450-acre campus. 40 buildings on campus. Approved or accredited by Association of Independent Schools in New England and The Association of Boarding Schools. Member of National Association of Independent Schools and Secondary School Admission Test Board. Endowment: $62 million. Total enrollment: 378. Upper school average class size: 12. Upper school faculty-student ratio: 1:5.
Upper School Student Profile Grade 9: 84 students (40 boys, 44 girls); Grade 10: 106 students (47 boys, 59 girls); Grade 11: 99 students (46 boys, 53 girls); Grade 12: 89 students (44 boys, 45 girls). 65% of students are boarding students. 52% are state residents. 21 states are represented in upper school student body. 12% are international students. International students from Germany, Japan, Republic of Korea, and Thailand; 7 other countries represented in student body.
Faculty School total: 76. In upper school: 45 men, 31 women; 43 have advanced degrees; 51 reside on campus.
Subjects Offered Advanced chemistry, algebra, American history, American history-AP, American literature, anatomy, art, band, biology, biology-AP, calculus-AP, ceramics, chemistry, chorus, civics, computer graphics, computer math, computer programming, computer science, constitutional law, creative writing, dance, drama, driver education, ecology, economics, English literature, English literature and composition-AP, environmental science, ESL, European history, expository writing, filmmaking, fine arts, French, French-AP, geometry, German, health, history, Holocaust and other genocides, honors algebra, jazz band, Latin, marine biology, marine science, mathematics, Middle Eastern history, modern European history, modern European history-AP, music, music history, music theory, photography, physics, physics-AP, psychology, psychology-AP, religion, science, social studies, Spanish, Spanish-AP, statistics-AP, studio art—AP, theater, trigonometry, visual and performing arts, women's studies, writing.
Graduation Requirements Arts and fine arts (art, music, dance, drama), English, foreign language, history, mathematics, science, 50 hours of community service.
Special Academic Programs Advanced Placement exam preparation in 14 subject areas; honors section; independent study; study abroad; ESL (4 students enrolled).
College Placement 93 students graduated in 2005; 92 went to college, including Boston University; Colby College; Hobart and William Smith Colleges; Providence College; University of New Hampshire. Other: 1 had other specific plans. Mean SAT verbal: 589, mean SAT math: 616. 45% scored over 600 on SAT verbal, 55% scored over 600 on SAT math, 52% scored over 1800 on combined SAT.
Student Life Upper grades have specified standards of dress, student council, honor system. Discipline rests primarily with faculty.
Tuition and Aid Day student tuition: $27,950; 7-day tuition and room/board: $35,350. Tuition installment plan (The Tuition Plan, Academic Management Services Plan, monthly payment plans). Need-based scholarship grants available. In 2005–06, 27% of upper-school students received aid. Total amount of financial aid awarded in 2005–06: $2,200,000.

Admissions Traditional secondary-level entrance grade is 9. For fall 2005, 733 students applied for upper-level admission, 190 were accepted, 112 enrolled. ISEE, SSAT or TOEFL required. Deadline for receipt of application materials: January 31. Application fee required: $50. Interview required.
Athletics Interscholastic: baseball (boys), basketball (b,g), cross-country running (b,g), field hockey (g), football (b), ice hockey (b,g), lacrosse (b,g), soccer (b,g), softball (g), tennis (b,g), track and field (b,g), volleyball (g), wrestling (b); intramural: dance (g); coed interscholastic: golf; coed intramural: aerobics/dance, alpine skiing, dance, outdoor activities, outdoor recreation, skiing (downhill), yoga. 2 trainers.
Computers Computers are regularly used in art, English, foreign language, history, mathematics, music, science classes. Computer network features include campus e-mail, on-campus library services, CD-ROMs, Internet access, office computer access, DVD, wireless campus network, laptop sign-out in student center and library, Moodle Website for teachers and students to share course data, events, and discussions.
Contact Peter T. Bidstrup, Director of Admission. 978-499-3120. Fax: 978-462-1278. E-mail: admissions@gda.org. Web site: www.gda.org.

See full description on page 802.

THE GOVERNOR FRENCH ACADEMY

219 West Main Street
Belleville, Illinois 62220-1537
Head of School: Phillip E. Paeltz

General Information Coeducational boarding and day college-preparatory school. Boarding grades 9–12, day grades K–12. Founded: 1983. Setting: suburban. Nearest major city is St. Louis, MO. Students are housed in homes of local families. 3 buildings on campus. Approved or accredited by CITA (Commission on International and Trans-Regional Accreditation), North Central Association of Colleges and Schools, and Illinois Department of Education. Languages of instruction: English and Spanish. Endowment: $100,000. Total enrollment: 180. Upper school average class size: 15. Upper school faculty-student ratio: 1:6.
Upper School Student Profile Grade 9: 13 students (5 boys, 8 girls); Grade 10: 14 students (7 boys, 7 girls); Grade 11: 13 students (8 boys, 5 girls); Grade 12: 15 students (9 boys, 6 girls). 6% of students are boarding students. 90% are state residents. International students from Indonesia, Japan, Republic of Korea, Saudi Arabia, Taiwan, and Turkey; 5 other countries represented in student body.
Faculty School total: 22. In upper school: 6 men, 6 women; 8 have advanced degrees.
Subjects Offered Algebra, American history, American literature, anthropology, art, art history, biology, botany, calculus, chemistry, computer science, creative writing, earth science, ecology, economics, English, English literature, environmental science, European history, expository writing, geography, geometry, government/civics, grammar, history, history of ideas, logic, mathematics, music, philosophy, physical education, physics, physiology, psychology, science, social science, social studies, sociology, Spanish, speech, statistics, trigonometry, world history, world literature, zoology.
Graduation Requirements English, foreign language, mathematics, physical education (includes health), science, social science, vote of faculty.
Special Academic Programs Advanced Placement exam preparation in 5 subject areas; accelerated programs; independent study; academic accommodation for the gifted, the musically talented, and the artistically talented; programs in English for dyslexic students; ESL (7 students enrolled).
College Placement 15 students graduated in 2005; 14 went to college, including Saint Louis University; The Ohio State University; University of Illinois at Urbana–Champaign; Washington University in St. Louis. Other: 1 entered military service. Mean SAT verbal: 601, mean SAT math: 638. 50% scored over 600 on SAT verbal, 50% scored over 600 on SAT math.
Student Life Upper grades have uniform requirement, honor system. Discipline rests primarily with faculty.
Summer Programs Remediation, enrichment, advancement, art/fine arts, computer instruction programs offered; session focuses on academics; held both on and off campus; held at local YMCA and sportplex facility; accepts boys and girls; open to students from other schools. 85 students usually enrolled. 2006 schedule: July 10 to August 18. Application deadline: none.
Tuition and Aid Day student tuition: $4900; 7-day tuition and room/board: $12,876. Tuition installment plan (SMART Tuition Payment Plan, monthly payment plans, quarterly payment plan, bi-annual payment plan). Tuition reduction for siblings available. In 2005–06, 5% of upper-school students received aid.
Admissions Traditional secondary-level entrance grade is 9. For fall 2005, 20 students applied for upper-level admission, 17 were accepted, 15 enrolled. Deadline for receipt of application materials: none. No application fee required. Interview required.
Athletics Interscholastic: basketball (boys, girls), volleyball (g); intramural: baseball (b), bowling (g), dance (g); coed interscholastic: bicycling, golf, soccer, tennis; coed intramural: climbing, fencing, fitness, golf, independent competitive sports, marksmanship, martial arts, nautilus, rappelling, riflery, skateboarding, softball, swimming and diving, table tennis, track and field, wall climbing. 2 PE instructors.
Computers Computers are regularly used in science, yearbook classes. Computer network features include campus e-mail, CD-ROMs, Internet access.

The Governor French Academy

Contact Ms. Carol Wilson, Director of Admissions. 618-233-7542. Fax: 618-233-0541. E-mail: admiss@governorfrench.com. Web site: www.governorfrench.com.

THE GOW SCHOOL

South Wales, New York
See Special Needs Schools section.

GRACE BAPTIST SCHOOLS

3782 Churn Creek Road
Redding, California 96002
Head of School: Supt. Stephen L. Roberts

General Information Coeducational day college-preparatory, business, vocational, religious studies, and technology school, affiliated with Baptist Church, Christian faith. Grades K–12. Founded: 1974. Setting: urban. 10-acre campus. 3 buildings on campus. Approved or accredited by Association of Christian Schools International, Western Association of Schools and Colleges, and California Department of Education. Total enrollment: 350. Upper school average class size: 30. Upper school faculty-student ratio: 1:12.

Upper School Student Profile Grade 9: 40 students (18 boys, 22 girls); Grade 10: 30 students (22 boys, 8 girls); Grade 11: 40 students (22 boys, 18 girls); Grade 12: 40 students (15 boys, 25 girls). 80% of students are Baptist, Christian.

Faculty School total: 18. In upper school: 6 men, 8 women; 5 have advanced degrees.

Special Academic Programs Independent study; study at local college for college credit.

College Placement 31 students graduated in 2005; 26 went to college, including The Master's College and Seminary. Other: 3 went to work, 2 entered military service. Median SAT verbal: 450, median SAT math: 450, median composite ACT: 26. 10% scored over 600 on SAT verbal, 20% scored over 600 on SAT math, 30% scored over 26 on composite ACT.

Student Life Upper grades have specified standards of dress, student council, honor system. Discipline rests equally with students and faculty. Attendance at religious services is required.

Tuition and Aid Day student tuition: $3200. Tuition installment plan (individually arranged payment plans, 10-, 11-, or 12-month payment plans). Tuition reduction for siblings available. In 2005–06, 10% of upper-school students received aid.

Admissions Traditional secondary-level entrance grade is 9. For fall 2005, 12 students applied for upper-level admission, 12 were accepted, 12 enrolled. Wide Range Achievement Test required. Deadline for receipt of application materials: none. No application fee required. Interview required.

Athletics Interscholastic: baseball (boys), basketball (b,g), cheering (g), cross-country running (b,g), fitness (b,g), physical fitness (b,g), soccer (b,g), softball (g), volleyball (g); intramural: soccer (b,g). 4 PE instructors, 12 coaches, 3 trainers.

Computers Computer network features include CD-ROMs, Internet access, DVD, wireless campus network.

Contact Hon. Kolene Dutton, Registrar. 530-222-2232. Fax: 530-222-1784. E-mail: gbs.lchs@juno.com. Web site: www.libertygbs.org.

GRACE CHRISTIAN SCHOOL

12407 Pintail Street
Anchorage, Alaska 99516
Head of School: Nathan Davis

General Information Coeducational day college-preparatory and religious studies school, affiliated with Christian faith. Grades K–12. Founded: 1980. Setting: urban. 7-acre campus. 1 building on campus. Approved or accredited by Association of Christian Schools International and Northwest Association of Schools and Colleges. Total enrollment: 675. Upper school average class size: 21. Upper school faculty-student ratio: 1:21.

Upper School Student Profile Grade 7: 56 students (29 boys, 27 girls); Grade 8: 67 students (25 boys, 42 girls); Grade 9: 68 students (39 boys, 29 girls); Grade 10: 56 students (24 boys, 32 girls); Grade 11: 59 students (31 boys, 28 girls); Grade 12: 53 students (31 boys, 22 girls). 99% of students are Christian faith.

Faculty School total: 28. In upper school: 12 men, 16 women; 6 have advanced degrees.

Subjects Offered Algebra, American government, American history, American history-AP, American sign language, anatomy and physiology, art, Bible, biology, biology-AP, calculus-AP, career education, chemistry, chemistry-AP, choir, Christian ethics, computer skills, computer technologies, drama, English, English language and composition-AP, English literature and composition-AP, English literature-AP, English/composition-AP, fine arts, first aid, French, geography, geometry, health, humanities, keyboarding/computer, literature, mathematics, music theory-AP, physical education, physical science, physics, religion, science, social studies, Spanish, speech, trigonometry, U.S. history, world history, yearbook.

Graduation Requirements Arts and fine arts (art, music, dance, drama), English, mathematics, physical education (includes health), religion (includes Bible studies and theology), science, social studies (includes history).

Special Academic Programs Advanced Placement exam preparation in 6 subject areas.

College Placement 53 students graduated in 2005; 51 went to college, including Baylor University; Corban College; Stanford University; University of Alaska Anchorage; Westmont College. Other: 2 went to work. Mean SAT verbal: 549, mean SAT math: 537, mean composite ACT: 25. 30% scored over 600 on SAT verbal, 36% scored over 600 on SAT math, 55% scored over 26 on composite ACT.

Student Life Upper grades have specified standards of dress, student council, honor system. Discipline rests primarily with faculty.

Tuition and Aid Day student tuition: $5300. Tuition installment plan (monthly payment plans, individually arranged payment plans). Tuition reduction for siblings, need-based scholarship grants available. In 2005–06, 7% of upper-school students received aid. Total amount of financial aid awarded in 2005–06: $50,000.

Admissions Traditional secondary-level entrance grade is 7. For fall 2005, 54 students applied for upper-level admission, 44 were accepted, 44 enrolled. Stanford Achievement Test required. Deadline for receipt of application materials: none. Application fee required: $50. Interview required.

Athletics Interscholastic: basketball (boys, girls), cheering (g), cross-country running (b,g), skiing (cross-country) (b,g), soccer (b,g), track and field (b,g), volleyball (g), wrestling (b). 2 PE instructors.

Computers Computers are regularly used in technology, yearbook classes. Computer network features include on-campus library services, online commercial services, Internet access.

Contact Darlene Kuiper, Admissions. 907-345-4814. Fax: 907-644-2260. E-mail: admissions@gcsk12.net. Web site: gcsk12.net.

THE GRAND RIVER ACADEMY

3042 College Street
Austinburg, Ohio 44010
Head of School: Randy Blum

General Information Boys' boarding college-preparatory, arts, and ESL school; primarily serves underachievers. Grades 9–PG. Founded: 1831. Setting: rural. Nearest major city is Cleveland. Students are housed in single-sex dormitories. 200-acre campus. 10 buildings on campus. Approved or accredited by Independent Schools Association of the Central States, Midwest Association of Boarding Schools, North Central Association of Colleges and Schools, The Association of Boarding Schools, and Ohio Department of Education. Member of National Association of Independent Schools. Endowment: $2 million. Total enrollment: 110. Upper school average class size: 7. Upper school faculty-student ratio: 1:7.

Upper School Student Profile Grade 9: 14 students (14 boys); Grade 10: 27 students (27 boys); Grade 11: 33 students (33 boys); Grade 12: 36 students (36 boys). 100% of students are boarding students. 35% are state residents. 16 states are represented in upper school student body. 13% are international students. International students from Canada, Hong Kong, Mexico, Republic of Korea, Russian Federation, and Saudi Arabia; 2 other countries represented in student body.

Faculty School total: 24. In upper school: 17 men, 7 women; 10 have advanced degrees; 23 reside on campus.

Subjects Offered Advanced Placement courses, algebra, American history, American literature, art, biology, British literature (honors), calculus, calculus-AP, chemistry, civics, college writing, community service, computer applications, computer keyboarding, computer science, creative writing, digital photography, driver education, economics, English, English literature, environmental science, ESL, fine arts, French, geography, government, grammar, health, history, integrated science, lab science, mathematics, photography, physical education, physics, physics-AP, pre-calculus, psychology, public speaking, science, social studies, Spanish, speech, TOEFL preparation, Web site design, world history, world literature, writing.

Graduation Requirements Arts and fine arts (art, music, dance, drama), computer science, English, mathematics, physical education (includes health), science, social studies (includes history), acceptance at a college, passage of Ohio state-mandated proficiency tests. Community service is required.

Special Academic Programs Advanced Placement exam preparation in 3 subject areas; honors section; study at local college for college credit; remedial reading and/or remedial writing; special instructional classes for students with Attention Deficit Disorder; ESL (6 students enrolled).

College Placement 33 students graduated in 2005; all went to college, including Baldwin-Wallace College; Case Western Reserve University; Hobart and William Smith Colleges; Indiana University Bloomington; John Carroll University; The University of Texas at Austin.

Student Life Upper grades have specified standards of dress, student council, honor system. Discipline rests primarily with faculty.

Summer Programs Remediation, enrichment, advancement, ESL, sports, art/fine arts, computer instruction programs offered; session focuses on ESL, enrichment, and remediation; held on campus; accepts boys and girls; open to students from other schools. 40 students usually enrolled. 2006 schedule: June 25 to August 4. Application deadline: June 20.

Tuition and Aid 5-day tuition and room/board: $25,100; 7-day tuition and room/board: $26,200. Tuition installment plan (Key Tuition Payment Plan). Merit scholarship grants, need-based scholarship grants, prepGATE Loans, P.L.A.T.O. Junior Loans available. In 2005–06, 10% of upper-school students received aid; total upper-school merit-scholarship money awarded: $11,500. Total amount of financial aid awarded in 2005–06: $100,000.

Admissions Traditional secondary-level entrance grade is 10. For fall 2005, 71 students applied for upper-level admission, 62 were accepted, 43 enrolled. Deadline for receipt of application materials: none. Application fee required: $35. On-campus interview required.

Athletics Interscholastic: baseball, basketball, cross-country running, golf, horseback riding, indoor soccer, soccer, tennis, wrestling; intramural: back packing, baseball, basketball, bicycling, billiards, bocce, bowling, canoeing/kayaking, equestrian sports, fishing, fitness, fitness walking, flag football, fly fishing, football, freestyle skiing, Frisbee, golf, hiking/backpacking, horseback riding, horseshoes, martial arts, nautilus, outdoor activities, outdoor recreation, outdoor skills, paddle tennis, paint ball, power lifting, rafting, roller blading, ropes courses, self defense, skateboarding, skiing (cross-country), skiing (downhill), snowboarding, soccer, softball, strength & conditioning, table tennis, tennis, touch football, ultimate Frisbee, volleyball, walking, weight lifting, whiffle ball, wrestling. 1 PE instructor.

Computers Computers are regularly used in English, ESL, foreign language, history, mathematics, science classes. Computer resources include campus e-mail, on-campus library services, CD-ROMs, online commercial services, Internet access, DVD, wireless campus network, mobile learning lab, classrooms linked to T-1, Smart Board technology.

Contact Sam Corabi, Director of Admission. 440-275-2811 Ext. 25. Fax: 440-275-1825. E-mail: admissions@grandriver.org. Web site: www.grandriver.org.

ANNOUNCEMENT FROM THE SCHOOL In selecting students for admission, the Academy is not concerned primarily with past academic performance; more important is the student's ability to perform successfully in the Grand River program. Through small classes, afternoon activities, supervised evening study halls, and daily help sessions, students learn self-discipline and acquire interests in academics. The curriculum is college preparatory, and all seniors are accepted by a college or university.

See full description on page 804.

THE GRAUER SCHOOL

1500 South El Camino Real
Encinitas, California 92024
Head of School: Dr. Stuart Robert Grauer

General Information Coeducational day college-preparatory, arts, and technology school. Grades 6–12. Founded: 1991. Setting: suburban. Nearest major city is San Diego. 5-acre campus. 6 buildings on campus. Approved or accredited by Western Association of Schools and Colleges and California Department of Education. Endowment: $1.3 million. Total enrollment: 84. Upper school average class size: 12. Upper school faculty-student ratio: 1:7.

Upper School Student Profile Grade 9: 12 students (6 boys, 6 girls); Grade 10: 12 students (6 boys, 6 girls); Grade 11: 12 students (6 boys, 6 girls); Grade 12: 12 students (6 boys, 6 girls).

Faculty School total: 15. In upper school: 8 men, 7 women; 6 have advanced degrees.

Subjects Offered Advanced chemistry, advanced math, algebra, American culture, American literature, ancient history, applied music, art, art appreciation, biology, calculus, character education, chemistry, civics, college planning, community service, computer applications, computer education, computer keyboarding, computer multimedia, drama, earth and space science, economics, English literature, environmental education, ESL, gardening, geography, geometry, global studies, health, Japanese, Latin, marine science, multimedia, music appreciation, outdoor education, personal fitness, physical education, physiology-anatomy, pre-algebra, religion, SAT preparation, Spanish, studio art, study skills, surfing, theater arts, U.S. government, U.S. history, world geography, world history.

Graduation Requirements American literature, art, chemistry, college admission preparation, computer applications, computer skills, economics, English, foreign language, French, geometry, life science, mathematics, non-Western literature, physical education (includes health), physical science, religion (includes Bible studies and theology), religion and culture, science, social studies (includes history), studio art, U.S. government, U.S. literature, Western civilization, Western literature, wilderness/outdoor program, world geography, world literature, portfolio defense. Community service is required.

Special Academic Programs Advanced Placement exam preparation in 2 subject areas; honors section; accelerated programs; independent study; study abroad; academic accommodation for the gifted, the musically talented, and the artistically talented; remedial math; ESL (2 students enrolled).

College Placement 12 students graduated in 2005; all went to college, including California Polytechnic State University, San Luis Obispo; California State Polytechnic University, Pomona; University of California, Berkeley; University of California, Los Angeles; University of California, San Diego; University of San Diego. Median SAT verbal: 650, median SAT math: 500. 60% scored over 600 on SAT verbal, 60% scored over 600 on SAT math.

Student Life Upper grades have specified standards of dress, student council, honor system. Discipline rests equally with students and faculty.

Summer Programs Remediation, enrichment, advancement, ESL, sports, art/fine arts, computer instruction programs offered; session focuses on college preparatory courses and study skills; held on campus; accepts boys and girls; open to students from other schools. 50 students usually enrolled. 2006 schedule: June 27 to August 5. Application deadline: June 22.

Tuition and Aid Day student tuition: $13,000–$15,500. Tuition installment plan (SMART Tuition Payment Plan, individually arranged payment plans). Tuition reduction for siblings, merit scholarship grants, need-based scholarship grants available. In 2005–06, 10% of upper-school students received aid; total upper-school merit-scholarship money awarded: $25,000. Total amount of financial aid awarded in 2005–06: $25,000.

Admissions Traditional secondary-level entrance grade is 9. For fall 2005, 58 students applied for upper-level admission, 23 were accepted, 20 enrolled. ISEE and Stanford 9 required. Deadline for receipt of application materials: none. Application fee required: $95. On-campus interview required.

Athletics Coed Intramural: aerobics, alpine skiing, back packing, ball hockey, basketball, bocce, bowling, canoeing/kayaking, climbing, cross-country running, fitness, fitness walking, flag football, football, golf, hiking/backpacking, independent competitive sports, jogging, outdoor adventure, outdoor education, physical fitness, rock climbing, skiing (downhill), snowboarding, soccer, softball, surfing, tennis. 4 PE instructors, 2 coaches, 1 trainer.

Computers Computers are regularly used in graphic arts, journalism, keyboarding, yearbook classes. Computer network features include campus e-mail, on-campus library services, CD-ROMs, Internet access, file transfer, office computer access, wireless campus network.

Contact Dr. Karen Berger, EdD, Admissions Coordinator. 760-274-2116. Fax: 760-944-6784. E-mail: karen@grauerschool.com. Web site: www.grauerschool.com.

GREATER ATLANTA CHRISTIAN SCHOOLS

1575 Indian Trail Road
Norcross, Georgia 30093
Head of School: Dr. David Fincher

General Information Coeducational day college-preparatory and religious studies school, affiliated with Church of Christ. Grades P4–12. Founded: 1961. Setting: suburban. Nearest major city is Atlanta. 74-acre campus. 17 buildings on campus. Approved or accredited by Georgia Independent School Association, National Christian School Association, Southern Association of Colleges and Schools, Southern Association of Independent Schools, The College Board, and Georgia Department of Education. Total enrollment: 1,881. Upper school average class size: 16. Upper school faculty-student ratio: 1:17.

Upper School Student Profile Grade 9: 173 students (76 boys, 97 girls); Grade 10: 152 students (69 boys, 83 girls); Grade 11: 160 students (72 boys, 88 girls); Grade 12: 135 students (73 boys, 62 girls). 26% of students are members of Church of Christ.

Faculty School total: 181. In upper school: 30 men, 29 women; 32 have advanced degrees.

Subjects Offered 3-dimensional art, accounting, algebra, American history-AP, art history, art-AP, biology-AP, business, calculus-AP, character education, chemistry-AP, computer math, computer science-AP, English language and composition-AP, ethics, European history-AP, expository writing, French, Latin, music theory-AP, philosophy, photography, physics-AP, physiology, psychology-AP, sociology, speech, statistics-AP, theology, world history-AP.

Graduation Requirements Computer science, English, foreign language, mathematics, physical education (includes health), science, social science, social studies (includes history), one year of Bible for each year of attendance.

Special Academic Programs Advanced Placement exam preparation in 19 subject areas; honors section; study abroad; academic accommodation for the gifted, the musically talented, and the artistically talented; ESL (20 students enrolled).

College Placement 134 students graduated in 2005; all went to college, including Auburn University; Georgia Institute of Technology; Harding University; Kennesaw State University; Lipscomb University; University of Georgia. Median SAT verbal: 593, median SAT math: 611, median combined SAT: 1204.

Student Life Upper grades have uniform requirement, student council, honor system. Discipline rests primarily with faculty. Attendance at religious services is required.

Tuition and Aid Day student tuition: $9000–$10,400. Tuition installment plan (monthly payment plans, quarterly tuition plan). Need-based scholarship grants available.

Admissions Traditional secondary-level entrance grade is 9. For fall 2005, 55 students applied for upper-level admission, 26 were accepted, 23 enrolled. CTBS/4 or Stanford Achievement Test required. Deadline for receipt of application materials: none. Application fee required: $150. On-campus interview required.

Athletics Interscholastic: baseball (boys), basketball (b,g), cheering (g), diving (b,g), football (b), golf (b,g), ice hockey (b), lacrosse (b,g), soccer (b,g), softball (g),

swimming and diving (b,g), volleyball (g), weight lifting (b), wrestling (b); intramural: aerobics (g), physical fitness (b,g); coed interscholastic: cross-country running, tennis, track and field. 2 PE instructors.

Computers Computers are regularly used in college planning classes. Computer network features include on-campus library services, CD-ROMs, online commercial services, Internet access.

Contact Mrs. Linda Clovis, Director of Admissions. 770-243-2274. Fax: 770-243-2213. E-mail: lindacl@gacs.pvt.k12.ga.us. Web site: www.greateratlantachristian.org.

GREAT LAKES CHRISTIAN COLLEGE

4875 King Street
Beamsville, Ontario L0R 1B0, Canada
Head of School: Mr. Art Ford

General Information Coeducational boarding and day college-preparatory, general academic, and religious studies school, affiliated with Church of Christ. Grades 9–12. Founded: 1952. Setting: small town. Nearest major city is Hamilton, Canada. Students are housed in single-sex dormitories. 15-acre campus. 6 buildings on campus. Approved or accredited by Ontario Ministry of Education and Ontario Department of Education. Language of instruction: English. Endowment: CAN$500,000. Total enrollment: 104. Upper school average class size: 22. Upper school faculty-student ratio: 1:12.

Upper School Student Profile Grade 9: 19 students (10 boys, 9 girls); Grade 10: 25 students (12 boys, 13 girls); Grade 11: 30 students (13 boys, 17 girls); Grade 12: 30 students (18 boys, 12 girls). 55% of students are boarding students. 73% are province residents. 7 provinces are represented in upper school student body. 27% are international students. International students from Hong Kong, Republic of Korea, Taiwan, and United States; 2 other countries represented in student body. 50% of students are members of Church of Christ.

Faculty School total: 15. In upper school: 9 men, 2 women; 5 have advanced degrees; 2 reside on campus.

Subjects Offered 20th century world history, accounting, algebra, arts appreciation, Bible, biology, calculus, career and personal planning, chemistry, computer science, computer technologies, dramatic arts, economics, English, English composition, English language and composition-AP, English literature, English-AP, ESL, family studies, finite math, French, geography, history, mathematics, mathematics-AP, media, music, music composition, physical education, physics, society, technology, world issues.

Graduation Requirements 20th century history, advanced math, art, Bible, business, Canadian geography, Canadian history, Canadian literature, career planning, civics, computer information systems, conceptual physics, critical thinking, current events, economics, English, English composition, English literature, French as a second language, geography, mathematics, physical education (includes health), science, society challenge and change, world geography, world history.

Special Academic Programs Independent study; study at local college for college credit; ESL (8 students enrolled).

College Placement 35 students graduated in 2005; 26 went to college, including McMaster University; The University of Western Ontario; University of Toronto; University of Waterloo; Wilfrid Laurier University; York University. Other: 8 went to work, 1 had other specific plans.

Student Life Upper grades have uniform requirement, student council. Discipline rests primarily with faculty. Attendance at religious services is required.

Tuition and Aid Day student tuition: CAN$6450; 5-day tuition and room/board: CAN$11,150; 7-day tuition and room/board: CAN$12,600. Tuition installment plan (monthly payment plans, individually arranged payment plans). Tuition reduction for siblings, bursaries, merit scholarship grants, need-based scholarship grants, need-based loans, middle-income loans, paying campus jobs available. In 2005–06, 50% of upper-school students received aid; total upper-school merit-scholarship money awarded: CAN$12,000. Total amount of financial aid awarded in 2005–06: CAN$100,000.

Admissions Traditional secondary-level entrance grade is 9. For fall 2005, 200 students applied for upper-level admission, 150 were accepted, 105 enrolled. SLEP required. Deadline for receipt of application materials: none. Application fee required: CAN$150. Interview recommended.

Athletics Interscholastic: badminton (boys, girls), basketball (b,g), cross-country running (b,g), golf (b), hockey (b,g), ice hockey (b,g), soccer (b,g), track and field (b,g), volleyball (b,g); intramural: badminton (b,g), basketball (b,g), cooperative games (b,g), volleyball (b,g); coed interscholastic: badminton; coed intramural: badminton, cooperative games, volleyball. 1 PE instructor, 1 coach.

Computers Computers are regularly used in accounting, business, music, technology, typing classes. Computer network features include campus e-mail, CD-ROMs, Internet access, office computer access.

Contact Miss Caley D. Cramp, Director of Admissions. 905-563-5374 Ext. 212. Fax: 905-563-0818. E-mail: study@glcc.on.ca. Web site: www.glcc.on.ca.

GREENFIELD SCHOOL

PO Box 3525
Wilson, North Carolina 27895-3525
Head of School: Janet B. Beaman

General Information Coeducational day college-preparatory school. Grades PS–12. Founded: 1969. Setting: small town. Nearest major city is Raleigh. 61-acre campus. 9 buildings on campus. Approved or accredited by North Carolina Association of Independent Schools, Southern Association of Colleges and Schools, and North Carolina Department of Education. Member of National Association of Independent Schools. Total enrollment: 318. Upper school average class size: 17. Upper school faculty-student ratio: 1:5.

Upper School Student Profile Grade 9: 9 students (3 boys, 6 girls); Grade 10: 15 students (9 boys, 6 girls); Grade 11: 18 students (13 boys, 5 girls); Grade 12: 25 students (17 boys, 8 girls).

Faculty School total: 38. In upper school: 5 men, 10 women; 4 have advanced degrees.

Subjects Offered Advanced computer applications, advanced math, Advanced Placement courses, algebra, American history, American literature, ancient world history, art, athletics, biology, British literature, calculus, calculus-AP, chemistry, chorus, college awareness, community service, computer applications, computer education, computer graphics, computer information systems, computer keyboarding, computer math, computer multimedia, computer processing, computer programming, computer programming-AP, computer science, computer skills, computer technologies, desktop publishing, earth science, economics, electives, English, English literature, fine arts, foreign language, geography, geometry, government/civics, grammar, health, history, honors algebra, honors English, honors geometry, honors world history, keyboarding/computer, language arts, mathematics, music, physical education, physical science, physics, pre-algebra, pre-calculus, psychology, SAT preparation, science, social studies, Spanish, sports conditioning, trigonometry, Web site design, world geography, world history, writing, yearbook.

Graduation Requirements Arts and fine arts (art, music, dance, drama), computer science, English, foreign language, mathematics, physical education (includes health), science, social studies (includes history). Community service is required.

Special Academic Programs Advanced Placement exam preparation in 3 subject areas; honors section; independent study; study at local college for college credit; academic accommodation for the gifted; remedial reading and/or remedial writing; remedial math; programs in English, general development for dyslexic students.

College Placement 15 students graduated in 2005; all went to college, including East Carolina University; Meredith College; North Carolina State University; The University of North Carolina at Chapel Hill; The University of North Carolina Wilmington; University of Georgia. Median SAT verbal: 536, median SAT math: 539, median composite ACT: 24. 13% scored over 600 on SAT verbal, 33% scored over 600 on SAT math, 1% scored over 26 on composite ACT.

Student Life Upper grades have specified standards of dress, student council, honor system. Discipline rests primarily with faculty.

Summer Programs Enrichment, sports, art/fine arts, computer instruction programs offered; session focuses on academic enrichment, athletic development, and relaxation; held on campus; accepts boys and girls; open to students from other schools. 300 students usually enrolled. 2006 schedule: May 29 to July 28. Application deadline: none.

Tuition and Aid Day student tuition: $6995. Tuition installment plan (monthly payment plans). Tuition reduction for siblings, merit scholarship grants, need-based scholarship grants available.

Admissions Traditional secondary-level entrance grade is 9. For fall 2005, 6 students applied for upper-level admission, 4 were accepted, 4 enrolled. Comprehensive Test of Basic Skills or CTP III required. Deadline for receipt of application materials: none. Application fee required: $100. On-campus interview required.

Athletics Interscholastic: baseball (boys), basketball (b,g), cheering (g), soccer (b,g), tennis (b,g), volleyball (g); coed interscholastic: golf. 3 PE instructors, 9 coaches.

Computers Computers are regularly used in all academic classes. Computer resources include campus e-mail, on-campus library services, CD-ROMs, Internet access, file transfer.

Contact Diane Oliphant Hamilton, Director of Admissions and Community Relations. 252-237-8046. Fax: 252-237-1825. E-mail: hamiltond@greenfieldschool.org. Web site: www.greenfieldschool.org.

GREEN FIELDS COUNTRY DAY SCHOOL

6000 North Camino de la Tierra
Tucson, Arizona 85741
Head of School: Gerald H. Barkan, EdD

General Information Coeducational day college-preparatory, arts, and technology school. Grades K–12. Founded: 1933. Setting: suburban. 22-acre campus. 15 buildings on campus. Approved or accredited by Arizona Association of Independent Schools, National Independent Private Schools Association, and North Central Association of Colleges and Schools. Member of National Association of Independent Schools. Endowment: $1.2 million. Total enrollment: 191. Upper school average class size: 12. Upper school faculty-student ratio: 1:4.

 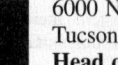

Upper School Student Profile Grade 9: 15 students (8 boys, 7 girls); Grade 10: 24 students (12 boys, 12 girls); Grade 11: 20 students (7 boys, 13 girls); Grade 12: 28 students (19 boys, 9 girls).

Faculty School total: 29. In upper school: 8 men, 12 women; 16 have advanced degrees.

Subjects Offered 3-dimensional art, advanced chemistry, advanced computer applications, advanced math, Advanced Placement courses, advanced studio art-AP, algebra, American government, American government-AP, American history, American history-AP, American literature, art, art-AP, Basic programming, biology, biology-AP, British literature (honors), British literature-AP, calculus, calculus-AP, ceramics, chemistry, chorus, college placement, computer programming, computer science, conceptual physics, discrete math, drama, drama performance, economics, economics-AP, English, European history, European history-AP, expository writing, fine arts, French, French language-AP, French literature-AP, French-AP, geography, geometry, government and politics-AP, government-AP, independent study, journalism, Latin American history, marine biology, music theory, musical theater, newspaper, physical education, physics, political science, pre-calculus, probability and statistics, social studies, Spanish, Spanish-AP, studio art—AP, trigonometry, U.S. government and politics-AP, U.S. history-AP, U.S. literature, Web site design, weight training, world history, writing, yearbook.

Graduation Requirements Advanced math, algebra, American history, American literature, arts and fine arts (art, music, dance, drama), biology, chemistry, computer science, computer skills, discrete mathematics, electives, English, English literature, foreign language, geometry, mathematics, physical education (includes health), science, social studies (includes history), world history, writing.

Special Academic Programs Advanced Placement exam preparation in 9 subject areas; independent study.

College Placement 24 students graduated in 2005; all went to college, including Arizona State University; Gonzaga University; Northern Arizona University; Stanford University; The University of Arizona; Willamette University. Mean SAT verbal: 602, mean SAT math: 583, mean composite ACT: 25. 52% scored over 600 on SAT verbal, 41% scored over 600 on SAT math, 33% scored over 26 on composite ACT.

Student Life Upper grades have specified standards of dress, student council, honor system. Discipline rests primarily with faculty.

Summer Programs Sports programs offered; session focuses on basketball and volleyball; held on campus; accepts boys and girls; open to students from other schools.

Tuition and Aid Day student tuition: $12,900. Tuition installment plan (FACTS Tuition Payment Plan, semester payment plan). Merit scholarship grants, need-based scholarship grants available. In 2005–06, 25% of upper-school students received aid. Total amount of financial aid awarded in 2005–06: $159,193.

Admissions Traditional secondary-level entrance grade is 9. For fall 2005, 15 students applied for upper-level admission, 13 were accepted, 13 enrolled. Achievement tests or Achievement/Aptitude/Writing required. Deadline for receipt of application materials: none. Application fee required: $35. On-campus interview recommended.

Athletics Interscholastic: baseball (boys), basketball (b,g), softball (g), volleyball (g); coed interscholastic: physical fitness, physical training, soccer; coed intramural: climbing, outdoor adventure, outdoor skills, rock climbing, tennis, wall climbing. 2 PE instructors, 8 coaches.

Computers Computers are regularly used in English, mathematics, newspaper, science, yearbook classes. Computer resources include campus e-mail, on-campus library services, CD-ROMs, online commercial services, Internet access.

Contact Carole Knapp, Director of Admission. 520-297-2288 Ext. 105. Fax: 520-297-2072. E-mail: admissions@greenfields.org. Web site: www.greenfields.org.

GREENHILL SCHOOL

4141 Spring Valley Road
Addison, Texas 75001
Head of School: Scott A. Griggs

General Information Coeducational day college-preparatory and arts school. Grades PK–12. Founded: 1950. Setting: suburban. Nearest major city is Dallas. 78-acre campus. 8 buildings on campus. Approved or accredited by Independent Schools Association of the Southwest and Texas Department of Education. Member of National Association of Independent Schools and Secondary School Admission Test Board. Endowment: $18.7 million. Total enrollment: 1,248. Upper school average class size: 18. Upper school faculty-student ratio: 1:18.

Upper School Student Profile Grade 9: 114 students (57 boys, 57 girls); Grade 10: 115 students (60 boys, 55 girls); Grade 11: 109 students (50 boys, 59 girls); Grade 12: 104 students (55 boys, 49 girls).

Faculty School total: 141. In upper school: 28 men, 25 women; 33 have advanced degrees.

Subjects Offered Algebra, American history, American literature, art, art history, biology, calculus, ceramics, chemistry, computer math, computer programming, computer science, creative writing, dance, drama, ecology, economics, English, English literature, European history, expository writing, fine arts, French, geometry, government/civics, grammar, health, history, journalism, Latin, Mandarin, mathemat-

ics, music, oceanography, philosophy, photography, physical education, physics, science, social studies, Spanish, speech, theater, trigonometry, world history, world literature, writing.

Graduation Requirements Arts and fine arts (art, music, dance, drama), classical language, computer studies, English, history, mathematics, modern languages, physical education (includes health), science. Community service is required.

Special Academic Programs Advanced Placement exam preparation in 13 subject areas; honors section; independent study.

College Placement 101 students graduated in 2005; all went to college, including Emory University; Southern Methodist University; The University of Texas at Austin; University of Pennsylvania; University of Southern California; Washington University in St. Louis. Median SAT math: 650, median composite ACT: 27. 76% scored over 600 on SAT math, 73% scored over 26 on composite ACT.

Student Life Upper grades have specified standards of dress, student council, honor system. Discipline rests primarily with faculty.

Summer Programs Enrichment, sports, art/fine arts, computer instruction programs offered; session focuses on enrichment and sports; held on campus; accepts boys and girls; open to students from other schools. 1230 students usually enrolled. 2006 schedule: June 7 to August 5. Application deadline: none.

Tuition and Aid Day student tuition: $18,000. Tuition installment plan (monthly payment plans, individually arranged payment plans). Need-based scholarship grants available. In 2005–06, 16% of upper-school students received aid. Total amount of financial aid awarded in 2005–06: $922,175.

Admissions Traditional secondary-level entrance grade is 9. For fall 2005, 147 students applied for upper-level admission, 48 were accepted, 36 enrolled. ISEE required. Deadline for receipt of application materials: January 6. Application fee required: $175. Interview required.

Athletics Interscholastic: aquatics (boys, girls), baseball (b), basketball (b,g), cheering (g), field hockey (g), football (b), golf (b,g), lacrosse (b,g), rowing (b,g), running (b,g), soccer (b,g), softball (g), swimming and diving (b,g), tennis (b,g), track and field (b,g), volleyball (b,g), winter soccer (b,g); intramural: baseball (b), power lifting (b); coed interscholastic: crew, cross-country running; coed intramural: aquatics, ballet, basketball, dance, fitness, Frisbee, physical fitness, strength & conditioning, table tennis, tai chi, ultimate Frisbee, water volleyball, weight lifting, weight training, yoga. 13 PE instructors, 14 coaches, 2 trainers.

Computers Computers are regularly used in English, mathematics, science classes. Computer network features include campus e-mail, on-campus library services, CD-ROMs, online commercial services, Internet access.

Contact Lynn Switzer Bozalis, Director of Admission. 972-628-5910. Fax: 972-404-8217. E-mail: admission@greenhill.org. Web site: www.greenhill.org.

ANNOUNCEMENT FROM THE SCHOOL Greenhill School combines an exceptionally strong, creative academic program with arts and athletics for students from diverse ethnic, religious, and economic backgrounds. Greenhill encourages the development of individual talent and emphasizes intellectual and moral integrity, sensitivity to others, respect for difference, and a courageous and generous engagement with life.

See full description on page 806.

GREENHILLS SCHOOL

850 Greenhills Drive
Ann Arbor, Michigan 48105
Head of School: Peter B. Fayroian

General Information Coeducational day college-preparatory and arts school. Grades 6–12. Founded: 1968. Setting: suburban. Nearest major city is Detroit. 30-acre campus. 1 building on campus. Approved or accredited by Independent Schools Association of the Central States and Michigan Department of Education. Member of National Association of Independent Schools and Secondary School Admission Test Board. Endowment: $6 million. Total enrollment: 479. Upper school average class size: 15. Upper school faculty-student ratio: 1:14.

Upper School Student Profile Grade 9: 80 students (43 boys, 37 girls); Grade 10: 61 students (35 boys, 26 girls); Grade 11: 76 students (32 boys, 44 girls); Grade 12: 67 students (29 boys, 38 girls).

Faculty School total: 57. In upper school: 14 men, 16 women; 28 have advanced degrees.

Subjects Offered 3-dimensional art, advanced chemistry, Advanced Placement courses, African-American literature, algebra, American history, American literature, ancient history, art, astronomy, biology, calculus, calculus-AP, ceramics, chemistry, chorus, community service, creative writing, discrete math, drama, drawing, economics, economics and history, English, English literature, ethics, European history, expository writing, fine arts, French, geometry, government, health, history, jazz, journalism, Latin, mathematics, music, orchestra, painting, photography, physical education, physical science, physics, science, social studies, Spanish, theater, trigonometry, world history, world literature, writing.

Graduation Requirements Arts and fine arts (art, music, dance, drama), English, foreign language, mathematics, physical education (includes health), science, social studies (includes history). Community service is required.

Greenhills School

Special Academic Programs Advanced Placement exam preparation in 8 subject areas; honors section; independent study; academic accommodation for the gifted.

College Placement 74 students graduated in 2005; all went to college, including Brown University; Northwestern University; University of Michigan; Washington University in St. Louis; Wesleyan University. Median SAT verbal: 649, median SAT math: 657, median composite ACT: 28.

Student Life Upper grades have specified standards of dress, student council, honor system. Discipline rests primarily with faculty.

Summer Programs Enrichment programs offered; session focuses on enrichment, academics, travel; held on campus; accepts boys and girls; open to students from other schools. 30 students usually enrolled. 2006 schedule: July 1 to July 30. Application deadline: none.

Tuition and Aid Day student tuition: $14,965. Tuition installment plan (FACTS Tuition Payment Plan). Need-based scholarship grants available. In 2005–06, 20% of upper-school students received aid. Total amount of financial aid awarded in 2005–06: $441,559.

Admissions Traditional secondary-level entrance grade is 9. For fall 2005, 61 students applied for upper-level admission, 43 were accepted, 40 enrolled. SSAT or TOEFL required. Deadline for receipt of application materials: none. Application fee required: $40. On-campus interview required.

Athletics Interscholastic: baseball (boys), basketball (b,g), cross-country running (b,g), field hockey (g), golf (b,g), soccer (b,g), softball (g), swimming and diving (b), tennis (b,g), track and field (b,g); intramural: basketball (b,g), cross-country running (b,g), field hockey (g), soccer (b,g); coed interscholastic: swimming and diving; coed intramural: hiking/backpacking, outdoor activities, outdoor education. 3 PE instructors, 1 trainer.

Computers Computers are regularly used in all academic classes. Computer resources include campus e-mail, on-campus library services, CD-ROMs, online commercial services, Internet access, file transfer.

Contact Betsy Ellsworth, Director of Admission and Financial Aid. 734-205-4061. Fax: 734-769-5029. E-mail: admission@greenhillsschool.org. Web site: www.greenhillsschool.org.

ANNOUNCEMENT FROM THE SCHOOL Greenhills School is a college-preparatory day school enrolling 228 boys and 248 girls in grades 6–12. Greenhills School offers a challenging, traditional liberal arts program and emphasizes creative expression as well as the development of critical thinking and communication skills. Greenhills encourages a diverse body of motivated, committed, able students to develop their full intellectual, ethical, artistic, and athletic potential and to flourish as curious, creative, and responsible citizens whose lives have meaning, balance, and a capacity for self-renewal. Activities include forensics, publications, athletics, and other groups and clubs. A summer enrichment program is offered each year. Tuition: $14,965. Financial aid: $844,000.

GREENSBORO DAY SCHOOL

PO Box 26805
Greensboro, North Carolina 27429-6805
Head of School: Dr. Dexter Ralph Davison Jr.

petersons.com

General Information Coeducational day college-preparatory, arts, and technology school. Grades K–12. Founded: 1970. Setting: suburban. 55-acre campus. 10 buildings on campus. Approved or accredited by Southern Association of Colleges and Schools. Member of National Association of Independent Schools. Language of instruction: English. Endowment: $4.4 million. Total enrollment: 880. Upper school average class size: 16. Upper school faculty-student ratio: 1:10.

Upper School Student Profile Grade 9: 88 students (52 boys, 36 girls); Grade 10: 84 students (50 boys, 34 girls); Grade 11: 72 students (36 boys, 36 girls); Grade 12: 86 students (43 boys, 43 girls).

Faculty School total: 115. In upper school: 22 men, 22 women; 36 have advanced degrees.

Subjects Offered Algebra, American government, American history, American literature, art, art appreciation, biology, biology-AP, calculus, calculus-AP, chemistry, chorus, college admission preparation, college counseling, college placement, computer programming, computer science-AP, creative writing, drama, economics, English, English language-AP, English literature, ESL, European history, European history-AP, fine arts, French, French language-AP, French literature-AP, geometry, government/civics, health, history, journalism, Latin, Latin-AP, mathematics, music, photography, physical education, physics, physics-AP, psychology, SAT preparation, science, social studies, Spanish, Spanish language-AP, Spanish literature-AP, sports medicine, statistics-AP, theater, trigonometry, U.S. history-AP, world history, writing, yearbook.

Graduation Requirements Arts and fine arts (art, music, dance, drama), English, foreign language, mathematics, physical education (includes health), science, social studies (includes history), senior project (four-week internship).

Special Academic Programs Advanced Placement exam preparation in 17 subject areas; honors section; independent study; term-away projects; study abroad; academic accommodation for the gifted and the artistically talented; special instructional classes for students with learning disabilities and Attention Deficit Disorder; ESL (11 students enrolled).

College Placement 75 students graduated in 2004; all went to college, including The University of North Carolina at Greensboro; Virginia Polytechnic Institute and State University.

Student Life Upper grades have specified standards of dress, student council, honor system. Discipline rests equally with students and faculty.

Tuition and Aid Day student tuition: $12,972. Tuition installment plan (monthly payment plans, individually arranged payment plans). Merit scholarship grants, need-based scholarship grants available. In 2004–05, 12% of upper-school students received aid; total upper-school merit-scholarship money awarded: $12,124. Total amount of financial aid awarded in 2004–05: $308,210.

Admissions Traditional secondary-level entrance grade is 9. For fall 2005, 71 students applied for upper-level admission, 34 enrolled. ERB (CTP-Verbal, Quantitative) required. Deadline for receipt of application materials: none. Application fee required: $50. On-campus interview required.

Athletics Interscholastic: baseball (boys), basketball (b,g), cheering (g), cross-country running (b,g), field hockey (g), golf (b), lacrosse (b,g), soccer (b,g), swimming and diving (b,g), tennis (b,g), track and field (b,g), volleyball (g), wrestling (b); intramural: weight lifting (b,g); coed interscholastic: aquatics; coed intramural: back packing, badminton, basketball, ropes courses. 12 PE instructors, 20 coaches, 1 trainer.

Computers Computers are regularly used in yearbook classes. Computer network features include campus e-mail, on-campus library services, CD-ROMs, online commercial services, Internet access, DVD, wireless campus network.

Contact Danette Morton, Director of Admission. 336-288-8590 Ext. 223. Fax: 336-282-2905. E-mail: dmorton@greensboroday.org. Web site: www.greensboroday.org.

ANNOUNCEMENT FROM THE SCHOOL Greensboro Day School is an independent college-preparatory school offering learning experiences for approximately 870 students in Transitional Kindergarten through grade 12. Outstanding attributes include a strong basic curriculum complemented by parental involvement and programs in athletics, fine and performing arts, computers, and foreign languages. GDS is a laptop school in grades 6–12. Graduates attend universities throughout the nation.

GREENS FARMS ACADEMY

35 Beachside Avenue
PO Box 998
Greens Farms, Connecticut 06838-0998
Head of School: Janet M. Hartwell

General Information Coeducational day college-preparatory, arts, and technology school. Grades K–12. Founded: 1925. Setting: suburban. Nearest major city is New York, NY. 42-acre campus. 2 buildings on campus. Approved or accredited by Connecticut Association of Independent Schools, New England Association of Schools and Colleges, and Connecticut Department of Education. Member of National Association of Independent Schools and Secondary School Admission Test Board. Endowment: $23 million. Total enrollment: 589. Upper school average class size: 12. Upper school faculty-student ratio: 1:7.

Upper School Student Profile Grade 9: 64 students (28 boys, 36 girls); Grade 10: 60 students (33 boys, 27 girls); Grade 11: 47 students (26 boys, 21 girls); Grade 12: 65 students (35 boys, 30 girls).

Faculty School total: 80. In upper school: 23 men, 16 women; 26 have advanced degrees.

Subjects Offered Algebra, American history, American literature, animation, architecture, art, art history, biology, calculus, chemistry, computer graphics, computer math, computer programming, computer science, creative writing, drama, earth science, ecology, economics, English, English literature, environmental science, European history, expository writing, fine arts, French, geography, geology, geometry, government/civics, grammar, health, history, keyboarding, Latin, mathematics, music, philosophy, photography, physical education, physics, science, social studies, Spanish, speech, theater, trigonometry, Web site design, world history, world literature, writing.

Graduation Requirements Algebra, arts and fine arts (art, music, dance, drama), biology, English, foreign language, mathematics, science, social studies (includes history), participation in athletics.

Special Academic Programs Advanced Placement exam preparation in 16 subject areas; honors section; independent study; study abroad.

College Placement 57 students graduated in 2005; all went to college, including Boston College; Cornell University; Dickinson College; Hamilton College; Mount Holyoke College; Tufts University. Median SAT verbal: 644, median SAT math: 647. 77% scored over 600 on SAT verbal, 64% scored over 600 on SAT math.

Student Life Upper grades have specified standards of dress, student council, honor system. Discipline rests equally with students and faculty.

Summer Programs Remediation, enrichment, advancement, sports programs offered; session focuses on academics and athletics; held on campus; accepts boys and girls; open to students from other schools. 50 students usually enrolled. 2006 schedule: June 23 to August 1.

Tuition and Aid Day student tuition: $26,700. Tuition installment plan (Key Tuition Payment Plan). Need-based scholarship grants available. In 2005–06, 15% of upper-school students received aid. Total amount of financial aid awarded in 2005–06: $660,115.

Admissions Traditional secondary-level entrance grade is 9. For fall 2005, 123 students applied for upper-level admission, 47 were accepted, 24 enrolled. ISEE or SSAT required. Deadline for receipt of application materials: January 1. Application fee required: $75. On-campus interview required.

Athletics Interscholastic: baseball (boys), basketball (b,g), cross-country running (b,g), field hockey (g), ice hockey (b), independent competitive sports (b,g), lacrosse (b,g), soccer (b,g), softball (g), squash (b,g), tennis (b,g), volleyball (g), wrestling (b); coed interscholastic: golf; coed intramural: climbing, fencing, figure skating, fitness, Frisbee, ice skating, nautilus, physical fitness, physical training, rock climbing, strength & conditioning, ultimate Frisbee, weight lifting, weight training, yoga. 6 PE instructors, 12 coaches, 1 trainer.

Computers Computers are regularly used in animation, art, English, foreign language, French, graphic arts, graphics, history, library, literary magazine, mathematics, music, newspaper, photography, science, Spanish, video film production, Web site design, yearbook classes. Computer network features include on-campus library services, CD-ROMs, online commercial services, Internet access, file transfer, wireless campus network.

Contact Stephanie Whitney, Director of Admission. 203-256-7514. Fax: 203-256-7591. E-mail: admissions@gfacademy.org. Web site: www.gfacademy.org.

GREENWICH ACADEMY

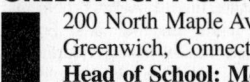

200 North Maple Avenue
Greenwich, Connecticut 06830-4799
Head of School: Molly H. King

petersons.com

General Information Girls' day college-preparatory and arts school. Grades PK–12. Founded: 1827. Setting: suburban. Nearest major city is New York, NY. 39-acre campus. 6 buildings on campus. Approved or accredited by Connecticut Association of Independent Schools, New England Association of Schools and Colleges, and Connecticut Department of Education. Member of National Association of Independent Schools and Secondary School Admission Test Board. Endowment: $78.5 million. Total enrollment: 784. Upper school average class size: 12. Upper school faculty-student ratio: 1:7.

Upper School Student Profile Grade 9: 74 students (74 girls); Grade 10: 80 students (80 girls); Grade 11: 81 students (81 girls); Grade 12: 72 students (72 girls).

Faculty School total: 104. In upper school: 11 men, 30 women; 33 have advanced degrees.

Subjects Offered Algebra, American history, American literature, ancient history, architecture, art, art history, astronomy, biology, calculus, ceramics, chemistry, computer science, creative writing, dance, drama, earth science, ecology, economics, English, English literature, environmental science, European history, expository writing, fine arts, French, geology, geometry, government/civics, health, Latin, mathematics, medieval history, music, oceanography, photography, physical education, physics, pre-calculus, psychology, science, Spanish, speech, statistics, theater, trigonometry, women's studies, world history, world literature, zoology.

Graduation Requirements Arts and fine arts (art, music, dance, drama), English, foreign language, mathematics, physical education (includes health), science, social studies (includes history). Community service is required.

Special Academic Programs Advanced Placement exam preparation in 19 subject areas; honors section; term-away projects; study abroad.

College Placement 66 students graduated in 2005; all went to college, including Colby College; Cornell University; Harvard University; New York University; Princeton University. Median SAT verbal: 675, median SAT math: 662. 88% scored over 600 on SAT verbal, 81% scored over 600 on SAT math.

Student Life Upper grades have uniform requirement, student council, honor system. Discipline rests equally with students and faculty.

Tuition and Aid Day student tuition: $25,000. Tuition installment plan (Key Tuition Payment Plan). Need-based scholarship grants, PLITT Loans, tuition reduction for children of faculty available. In 2005–06, 15% of upper-school students received aid. Total amount of financial aid awarded in 2005–06: $672,100.

Admissions Traditional secondary-level entrance grade is 9. For fall 2005, 110 students applied for upper-level admission, 45 were accepted, 31 enrolled. ERB, ISEE or SSAT required. Deadline for receipt of application materials: December 15. Application fee required: $75. On-campus interview required.

Athletics Interscholastic: basketball, crew, cross-country running, field hockey, golf, ice hockey, independent competitive sports, lacrosse, sailing, soccer, softball, squash, swimming and diving, tennis, volleyball; intramural: aerobics, aerobics/nautilus, basketball, cooperative games, crew, cross-country running, dance, field hockey, fitness, Frisbee, independent competitive sports, modern dance, nautilus, Newcombe ball, physical fitness, physical training, running, self defense, strength & conditioning, tennis, weight lifting, yoga. 6 PE instructors, 43 coaches, 1 trainer.

Computers Computers are regularly used in art, English, foreign language, history, humanities, mathematics, music, science classes. Computer network features include campus e-mail, on-campus library services, CD-ROMs, online commercial services, Internet access, file transfer, office computer access, DVD, wireless campus network, Intranet.

Contact Irene Mann, Admissions Registrar. 203-625-8990. Fax: 203-625-8912. E-mail: imann@greenwichacademy.org. Web site: www.greenwichacademy.org.

ANNOUNCEMENT FROM THE SCHOOL Established in 1827, Greenwich Academy is located on a beautiful 39-acre campus. An independent, college-preparatory school for girls and women, grades PK–12, the Academy seeks to foster excellence. Its mission is to provide a challenging, comprehensive educational experience grounded in a rigorous liberal arts curriculum within an inclusive and diverse community. The school's motto, "Ad Igenium Faciendum: Toward the building of character," reflects a focus on developing independent women of courage, integrity, and compassion. A challenging liberal arts curriculum offers opportunities for even the youngest girls to excel in mathematics, science, writing, technology, and the arts. Within the framework of tradition, Greenwich Academy integrates innovation and technology into all aspects of its program. Computer skills are developed throughout the Lower and Middle Schools. In grades 7–12, each student uses her own laptop in academic classes and for homework assignments. Foreign language instruction begins with conversational Spanish in grades PK–4, followed by Latin and a more formal study of Spanish or French in Middle School. The Lower and Middle Schools continue to foster a love of reading, an understanding of mathematics, a foundation in world history and current events, and the principles of science. The Upper School focuses on liberal arts preparation for college in a wide variety of courses. All students at Greenwich Academy take 4 years of high school math and at least 3 years of high school science, including biology, chemistry, and physics. Twenty-six AP courses are offered. GA's coordinated program with Brunswick School for boys provides coed classes, including Chinese and Italian, as well as many joint music, drama, art, and community service projects. All students participate in intramural and interscholastic sports, dance, art, music, and community service, all of which help to develop team spirit, civic responsibility, and mutual respect. Facilities include a second gymnasium with 2 basketball courts, locker rooms, a fitness center, 5 international squash courts, a performing arts center (with a 400-seat theater), a studio theater for dance and drama productions, acoustically correct choral and music rooms, a visual arts gallery, and a Middle/Upper School library. The PK–K classes are located on a 6.5-acre campus adjacent to soccer/sports fields.

GREENWOOD LABORATORY SCHOOL

901 South National
Springfield, Missouri 65897
Head of School: Dr. Janice Duncan

General Information Coeducational day college-preparatory, arts, and technology school. Grades K–12. Founded: 1908. Setting: urban. 3-acre campus. 1 building on campus. Approved or accredited by North Central Association of Colleges and Schools and Missouri Department of Education. Total enrollment: 363. Upper school average class size: 30. Upper school faculty-student ratio: 1:28.

Upper School Student Profile Grade 9: 29 students (11 boys, 18 girls); Grade 10: 30 students (15 boys, 15 girls); Grade 11: 28 students (14 boys, 14 girls); Grade 12: 25 students (13 boys, 12 girls).

Faculty School total: 28. In upper school: 11 men, 9 women; 17 have advanced degrees.

Subjects Offered Computer science, English, fine arts, foreign language, independent study, instrumental music, mathematics, science, social studies, state government, vocal music, wellness.

Graduation Requirements Students have to pass a Graduation Exhibition and achieve Public Affairs Merits.

Special Academic Programs Independent study.

College Placement 24 students graduated in 2005; 23 went to college, including Missouri State University; University of Arkansas; University of Missouri–Columbia. Other: 1 went to work. Median composite ACT: 25. 42% scored over 26 on composite ACT.

Student Life Upper grades have student council. Discipline rests equally with students and faculty.

Tuition and Aid Day student tuition: $3848. Tuition installment plan (individually arranged payment plans, single payment plan).

Admissions Traditional secondary-level entrance grade is 9. For fall 2005, 8 students applied for upper-level admission, 8 were accepted, 8 enrolled. Deadline for receipt of application materials: none. No application fee required. On-campus interview required.

Athletics Interscholastic: basketball (boys, girls); coed interscholastic: cross-country running, golf, physical fitness, soccer, swimming and diving, tennis. 3 PE instructors, 5 coaches.

Computers Computers are regularly used in English, social studies, word processing, writing, yearbook classes. Computer network features include campus e-mail, on-campus library services, DVD, wireless campus network.

Greenwood Laboratory School

Contact Ms. Ruth Ann Johnson, Counselor. 417-836-7667. Fax: 417-836-8449. E-mail: ruthannjohnson@missouristate.edu. Web site: www.missouristate.edu/contrib/greenwd/.

THE GREENWOOD SCHOOL

Putney, Vermont
See Junior Boarding Schools section.

GRENVILLE CHRISTIAN COLLEGE

Box 610
Brockville, Ontario K6V 5V8, Canada
Head of School: Fr. Gordon Mintz

General Information Coeducational boarding and day college-preparatory, arts, business, technology, and mathematics, social studies, and sciences school, affiliated with Christian faith. Boarding grades 7–12, day grades PK–12. Founded: 1969. Setting: small town. Nearest major city is Ottawa, Canada. Students are housed in single-sex dormitories. 260-acre campus. 11 buildings on campus. Approved or accredited by Canadian Association of Independent Schools, The Association of Boarding Schools, and Ontario Department of Education. Affiliate member of National Association of Independent Schools; member of Secondary School Admission Test Board. Language of instruction: English. Endowment: CAN$193,000. Total enrollment: 203. Upper school average class size: 10. Upper school faculty-student ratio: 1:6.

Upper School Student Profile Grade 9: 16 students (9 boys, 7 girls); Grade 10: 25 students (16 boys, 9 girls); Grade 11: 37 students (26 boys, 11 girls); Grade 12: 24 students (17 boys, 7 girls). 69% of students are boarding students. 62% are province residents. 4 provinces are represented in upper school student body. 37% are international students. International students from Hong Kong, Japan, Republic of Korea, Taiwan, and United States; 3 other countries represented in student body. 25% of students are Christian faith.

Faculty School total: 37. In upper school: 8 men, 14 women; 3 have advanced degrees; 4 reside on campus.

Subjects Offered Algebra, art, art history, biology, business, calculus, career and personal planning, chemistry, civics, computer multimedia, computer programming, computer science, computer studies, drama, economics, English, environmental science, ESL, fine arts, finite math, French, geography, geometry, health education, history, mathematics, music, philosophy, physical education, physics, science, trigonometry, world history, world issues, world religions.

Graduation Requirements Arts and fine arts (art, music, dance, drama), business, Canadian geography, Canadian history, career planning, civics, English, French, mathematics, physical education (includes health), science, social science. Community service is required.

Special Academic Programs Advanced Placement exam preparation in 3 subject areas; independent study; academic accommodation for the gifted; programs in general development for dyslexic students; ESL (20 students enrolled).

College Placement 36 students graduated in 2005; 33 went to college, including Carleton University; McGill University; Queen's University at Kingston; University of Toronto; University of Waterloo; York University. Other: 2 went to work, 1 entered a postgraduate year.

Student Life Upper grades have uniform requirement, student council, honor system. Discipline rests primarily with faculty. Attendance at religious services is required.

Tuition and Aid Day student tuition: CAN$16,900; 5-day tuition and room/board: CAN$28,900; 7-day tuition and room/board: CAN$30,900. Tuition reduction for siblings, bursaries, merit scholarship grants, need-based scholarship grants, need-based loans available. In 2005–06, 22% of upper-school students received aid; total upper-school merit-scholarship money awarded: CAN$29,000. Total amount of financial aid awarded in 2005–06: CAN$327,384.

Admissions Traditional secondary-level entrance grade is 10. For fall 2005, 51 students applied for upper-level admission, 35 were accepted, 28 enrolled. SLEP for foreign students, SSAT or writing sample required. Deadline for receipt of application materials: none. Application fee required: CAN$100. Interview required.

Athletics Interscholastic: badminton (boys, girls), basketball (b,g), cross-country running (b,g), nordic skiing (b,g), skiing (cross-country) (b,g), soccer (b,g), tennis (b,g), track and field (b,g), volleyball (b,g); intramural: dance squad (g), fitness walking (g), floor hockey (b), skiing (downhill) (b,g); coed interscholastic: badminton, cross-country running, nordic skiing, skiing (cross-country), tennis; coed intramural: alpine skiing, badminton, ball hockey, baseball, basketball, bicycling, billiards, cheering, fencing, fitness, flag football, floor hockey, Frisbee, golf, horseback riding, indoor hockey, indoor soccer, lacrosse, paddle tennis, skiing (cross-country), skiing (downhill), snowshoeing, soccer, softball, table tennis, tennis, ultimate Frisbee, volleyball, walking. 1 PE instructor.

Computers Computers are regularly used in business studies, data processing, geography, programming, science, yearbook classes. Computer network features include campus e-mail, CD-ROMs, Internet access, file transfer, office computer access, DVD, wireless campus network.

Contact Mrs. Toni Price, Admission Officer. 613-345-5521 Ext. 3367. Fax: 613-345-3826. E-mail: tprice@grenvillecc.ca. Web site: www.grenvillecc.ca.

THE GRIER SCHOOL

PO Box 308
Tyrone, Pennsylvania 16686-0308
Head of School: Andrea A. Hollnagel

petersons.com

General Information Girls' boarding college-preparatory, general academic, and arts school. Grades 7–PG. Founded: 1853. Setting: rural. Nearest major city is Pittsburgh. Students are housed in single-sex dormitories. 320-acre campus. 12 buildings on campus. Approved or accredited by Middle States Association of Colleges and Schools, Pennsylvania Association of Private Academic Schools, and The Association of Boarding Schools. Member of National Association of Independent Schools and Secondary School Admission Test Board. Endowment: $3 million. Total enrollment: 200. Upper school average class size: 10. Upper school faculty-student ratio: 1:6.

Upper School Student Profile Grade 9: 27 students (27 girls); Grade 10: 41 students (41 girls); Grade 11: 63 students (63 girls); Grade 12: 41 students (41 girls); Postgraduate: 1 student (1 girl). 100% of students are boarding students. 5% are state residents. 22 states are represented in upper school student body. 35% are international students. International students from China, Hong Kong, Mexico, Republic of Korea, Saudi Arabia, and Taiwan; 12 other countries represented in student body.

Faculty School total: 38. In upper school: 14 men, 23 women; 11 have advanced degrees; 17 reside on campus.

Subjects Offered Algebra, American history, American literature, anatomy, art, art history, art history-AP, art-AP, biology, biology-AP, calculus, calculus-AP, ceramics, chemistry, choral music, choreography, community service, computer math, computer programming, computer-aided design, creative writing, dance, desktop publishing, drama, earth science, ecology, English, English literature, English-AP, environmental science, equine studies, ESL, European history, fabric arts, fine arts, French, French-AP, geography, geometry, government/civics, health, history, journalism, linguistics, mathematics, music, photography, physical education, physics, physiology, piano, psychology, science, social studies, Spanish, theater, trigonometry, typing, video film production, voice, world history, writing, yearbook.

Graduation Requirements Arts and fine arts (art, music, dance, drama), computer science, English, foreign language, mathematics, physical education (includes health), science, social science, social studies (includes history).

Special Academic Programs Advanced Placement exam preparation in 5 subject areas; honors section; independent study; study abroad; academic accommodation for the gifted, the musically talented, and the artistically talented; remedial reading and/or remedial writing; remedial math; programs in English, general development for dyslexic students; special instructional classes for students with learning disabilities, Attention Deficit Disorder, and dyslexia; ESL (39 students enrolled).

College Placement 39 students graduated in 2005; all went to college, including Brigham Young University; Duquesne University; Lynn University; Ripon College; University of Michigan; University of Wisconsin–Madison. Median SAT verbal: 520, median SAT math: 550. 25% scored over 600 on SAT verbal, 15% scored over 600 on SAT math.

Student Life Upper grades have specified standards of dress, student council, honor system. Discipline rests primarily with faculty.

Summer Programs ESL, sports, art/fine arts programs offered; session focuses on recreation and ESL; held on campus; accepts girls; open to students from other schools. 25 students usually enrolled. 2006 schedule: June 16 to September 7. Application deadline: none.

Tuition and Aid 7-day tuition and room/board: $33,900. Tuition installment plan (individually arranged payment plans). Tuition reduction for siblings, merit scholarship grants, need-based scholarship grants, need-based loans, paying campus jobs available. In 2005–06, 45% of upper-school students received aid. Total amount of financial aid awarded in 2005–06: $1,150,000.

Admissions For fall 2005, 151 students applied for upper-level admission, 121 were accepted, 99 enrolled. SSAT required. Deadline for receipt of application materials: none. Application fee required: $25. Interview recommended.

Athletics Interscholastic: basketball, dance team, drill team, equestrian sports, martial arts, skiing (downhill), soccer, softball, tennis, track and field; intramural: aerobics, aerobics/dance, alpine skiing, aquatics, ballet, bicycling, bowling, dance, hiking/backpacking, horseback riding, jogging, modern dance, mountain biking, nordic skiing, ropes courses, skiing (cross-country), skiing (downhill), swimming and diving, tennis, volleyball, walking, weight training, yoga. 3 PE instructors, 3 coaches, 3 trainers.

Computers Computers are regularly used in English, foreign language, mathematics, science classes. Computer network features include campus e-mail, on-campus library services, CD-ROMs, online commercial services, Internet access, file transfer.

Contact Andrew M. Wilson, Assistant Head/Director of Admissions. 814-684-3000 Ext. 106. Fax: 814-684-2177. E-mail: admissions@grier.org. Web site: www.grier.org.

ANNOUNCEMENT FROM THE SCHOOL Grier takes pride in offering a highly supportive and nurturing environment for students whose academic backgrounds range from underachievement to high achievement. The Learning Skills Program provides one-on-one tutorial help, while Grier's "Honors Program" and "A" track courses challenge gifted students. Programs in the visual and performing arts are particularly strong.

See full description on page 808.

GROTON SCHOOL

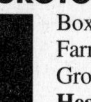

Box 991
Farmers Row
Groton, Massachusetts 01450
Head of School: Richard B. Commons

petersons.com

General Information Coeducational boarding and day college-preparatory school, affiliated with Episcopal Church. Grades 8–12. Founded: 1884. Setting: rural. Nearest major city is Boston. Students are housed in single-sex dormitories. 370-acre campus. 17 buildings on campus. Approved or accredited by Association of Independent Schools in New England, New England Association of Schools and Colleges, and The Association of Boarding Schools. Member of National Association of Independent Schools and Secondary School Admission Test Board. Endowment: $237 million. Total enrollment: 360. Upper school average class size: 13. Upper school faculty-student ratio: 1:5.

Upper School Student Profile Grade 9: 77 students (41 boys, 36 girls); Grade 10: 92 students (42 boys, 50 girls); Grade 11: 83 students (41 boys, 42 girls); Grade 12: 87 students (44 boys, 43 girls). 90% of students are boarding students. 36% are state residents. 34 states are represented in upper school student body. 11% are international students. International students from Canada, China, Jamaica, Japan, Republic of Korea, and United Kingdom; 7 other countries represented in student body.

Faculty School total: 63. In upper school: 36 men, 24 women; 46 have advanced degrees; all reside on campus.

Subjects Offered Advanced chemistry, advanced math, algebra, American literature, American literature-AP, analytic geometry, Ancient Greek, ancient world history, archaeology, art, art history, art history-AP, ballet, Bible studies, biology, biology-AP, botany, Buddhism, calculus, calculus-AP, cell biology, Central and Eastern European history, ceramics, chemistry, chemistry-AP, choir, choral music, civil rights, Civil War, civil war history, classical Greek literature, classical language, classics, composition, composition-AP, computer science-AP, creative writing, dance, discrete math, drawing, earth science, ecology, environmental systems, economics, English, English composition, English-AP, environmental science, environmental science-AP, environmental studies, ethics, European history, European history-AP, expository writing, fine arts, fractal geometry, fractals, French, French language-AP, French literature-AP, geography, geometry, government, grammar, Greek, health, history, Holocaust, honors algebra, honors English, honors geometry, honors U.S. history, honors world history, independent study, lab science, language-AP, Latin, Latin-AP, linear algebra, literature, literature and composition-AP, mathematics, mathematics-AP, modern European history, modern European history-AP, modern history, modern languages, modern world history, music, music history, music theory, organic biochemistry, painting, philosophy, photo shop, photography, physical science, physics, physics-AP, political economics, pre-algebra, pre-calculus, psychology, religion, religions, religious studies, science, Shakespeare, social science, Spanish, Spanish language-AP, Spanish literature, Spanish literature-AP, sports medicine, statistics, studio art, studio art-AP, theology, trigonometry, U.S. constitutional history, U.S. government, U.S. government and politics, U.S. government and politics-AP, U.S. history, U.S. history-AP, Western civilization, wood lab, woodworking, world history, world history-AP, writing.

Graduation Requirements Arts and fine arts (art, music, dance, drama), classical language, English, foreign language, mathematics, religious studies, science, social studies (includes history).

Special Academic Programs Advanced Placement exam preparation in 13 subject areas; honors section; independent study; study abroad; academic accommodation for the gifted, the musically talented, and the artistically talented.

College Placement 78 students graduated in 2005; all went to college, including Bowdoin College; Duke University; Georgetown University; Harvard University; Princeton University; Trinity College. Median SAT verbal: 670, median SAT math: 650. 81% scored over 600 on SAT verbal, 91% scored over 600 on SAT math.

Student Life Upper grades have specified standards of dress, student council, honor system. Discipline rests equally with students and faculty. Attendance at religious services is required.

Tuition and Aid Day student tuition: $28,330; 7-day tuition and room/board: $37,770. Tuition installment plan (Insured Tuition Payment Plan, Key Tuition Payment Plan, monthly payment plans, individually arranged payment plans). Need-based scholarship grants, need-based loans, Key Education Resources available. In 2005–06, 30% of upper-school students received aid. Total amount of financial aid awarded in 2005–06: $2,656,000.

Admissions Traditional secondary-level entrance grade is 9. For fall 2005, 659 students applied for upper-level admission, 170 were accepted, 91 enrolled. SSAT or TOEFL required. Deadline for receipt of application materials: January 15. Application fee required: $40. Interview required.

Athletics Interscholastic: baseball (boys), basketball (b,g), crew (b,g), cross-country running (b,g), field hockey (g), football (b), hockey (g), ice hockey (b,g), lacrosse (b,g), rowing (b,g), soccer (b,g), squash (b,g), tennis (b,g); intramural: Fives (b,g), physical training (b,g), self defense (g), weight training (b,g); coed interscholastic: dance team; coed intramural: aerobics/dance, dance, fitness, Frisbee, golf, ice skating, jogging, modern dance, skiing (cross-country), skiing (downhill), soccer, strength & conditioning, ultimate Frisbee. 2 coaches, 1 trainer.

Computers Computers are regularly used in English, history, mathematics, science classes. Computer network features include campus e-mail, on-campus library services, CD-ROMs, Internet access, office computer access, wireless campus network, wireless environment in classrooms and library.

Contact Mr. John M. Niles, Director of Admission. 978-448-7510. Fax: 978-448-9623. E-mail: jniles@groton.org. Web site: www.groton.org.

ANNOUNCEMENT FROM THE SCHOOL The year 2005 marks the final year of a multiyear facilities enhancement program that saw the renovation or new construction of 17 residence halls, St. John's Chapel, the McCormack Library, the Athletic and Recreation Center, maintenance facilities, the Dillon Center for the Visual Arts, and the Campbell Performing Arts Center.

See full description on page 810.

GROVE SCHOOL

Madison, Connecticut
See Special Needs Schools section.

GSTAAD INTERNATIONAL SCHOOL

Gstaad, Switzerland
See Special Needs Schools section.

GUAMANI PRIVATE SCHOOL

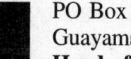

PO Box 3000
Guayama, Puerto Rico 00785
Head of School: Mr. Eduardo Delgado

General Information Coeducational day college-preparatory and bilingual studies school. Grades 1–12. Founded: 1914. Setting: urban. Nearest major city is Caguas, Puerto Rico. 1-acre campus. 1 building on campus. Approved or accredited by Middle States Association of Colleges and Schools, National Catholic Education Association, and Puerto Rico Department of Education. Languages of instruction: English and Spanish. Upper school average class size: 20. Upper school faculty-student ratio: 1:13.

Faculty School total: 32. In upper school: 10 men, 10 women; 3 have advanced degrees.

Subjects Offered Advanced math, Advanced Placement courses, algebra, American government, American history, analysis and differential calculus, chemistry, civics, pre-algebra, pre-calculus, science project, science research, social sciences, social studies, sociology, Spanish, Spanish language-AP, U.S. literature, visual arts, world geography, world history.

Graduation Requirements Mathematics, science, social sciences, Spanish, acceptance into a college or university. Community service is required.

Special Academic Programs Advanced Placement exam preparation in 4 subject areas; honors section; independent study.

College Placement Colleges students went to include Embry-Riddle Aeronautical University; Syracuse University; University of Puerto Rico, Cayey University College; University of Puerto Rico, Mayagüez Campus; University of Puerto Rico, Río Piedras.

Student Life Upper grades have uniform requirement, student council, honor system. Discipline rests primarily with faculty.

Summer Programs Remediation, ESL programs offered; held on campus; accepts boys and girls; open to students from other schools. 30 students usually enrolled. 2006 schedule: June 1 to June 30. Application deadline: May 27.

Admissions School's own test or Test of Achievement and Proficiency required. Deadline for receipt of application materials: none. Application fee required: $30. Interview required.

Athletics Interscholastic: aerobics/dance (girls), basketball (b,g), cheering (g), dance squad (g), volleyball (b,g); coed interscholastic: dance team. 3 PE instructors, 2 coaches.

Computers Computers are regularly used in English, mathematics, science, social sciences, Spanish, word processing classes. Computer resources include on-campus library services, CD-ROMs, Internet access, wireless campus network.

Contact Mrs. Digna Torres, Secretary. 787-864-6880. Fax: 787-866-4947. Web site: www.guamani.com.

GUERIN COLLEGE PREPARATORY HIGH SCHOOL

8001 West Belmont
River Grove, Illinois 60171-1096
Head of School: Mrs. Elizabeth (Bonnie) Brown

General Information Coeducational day college-preparatory, arts, business, religious studies, and technology school, affiliated with Roman Catholic Church. Grades 9–12. Founded: 1962. Setting: suburban. Nearest major city is Chicago. 23-acre campus. 2 buildings on campus. Approved or accredited by National Catholic Education Association, North Central Association of Colleges and Schools, and

Guerin College Preparatory High School

Illinois Department of Education. Endowment: $2 million. Total enrollment: 724. Upper school average class size: 25. Upper school faculty-student ratio: 1:15.

Upper School Student Profile Grade 9: 208 students (106 boys, 102 girls); Grade 10: 157 students (60 boys, 97 girls); Grade 11: 192 students (69 boys, 123 girls); Grade 12: 167 students (66 boys, 101 girls). 90% of students are Roman Catholic.

Faculty School total: 64. In upper school: 19 men, 45 women; 30 have advanced degrees.

Graduation Requirements Arts and fine arts (art, music, dance, drama), computers, electives, English, mathematics, physical education (includes health), science, social science, speech, theology.

Special Academic Programs Advanced Placement exam preparation in 12 subject areas; honors section; study at local college for college credit; ESL (2 students enrolled).

College Placement 215 students graduated in 2005; 205 went to college, including DePaul University; Dominican University; Lewis University; Loyola University Chicago; Northern Illinois University; University of Illinois at Urbana–Champaign. Other: 5 went to work, 5 had other specific plans.

Student Life Upper grades have uniform requirement, student council. Discipline rests primarily with faculty. Attendance at religious services is required.

Summer Programs Remediation, enrichment, sports, art/fine arts programs offered; session focuses on summer camps, freshman experience, and computers; held on campus; accepts boys and girls; open to students from other schools. 250 students usually enrolled. 2006 schedule: June 13 to July 1.

Tuition and Aid Day student tuition: $6700. Tuition installment plan (monthly payment plans, individually arranged payment plans). Tuition reduction for siblings, merit scholarship grants, need-based scholarship grants, paying campus jobs available. In 2005–06, 36% of upper-school students received aid. Total amount of financial aid awarded in 2005–06: $400,000.

Admissions Traditional secondary-level entrance grade is 9. For fall 2005, 750 students applied for upper-level admission, 735 were accepted, 724 enrolled. Explore required. Deadline for receipt of application materials: none. Application fee required: $250. Interview recommended.

Athletics Interscholastic: baseball (boys), basketball (b,g), cheering (g), dance (g), football (b), gymnastics (g), ice hockey (b), soccer (b,g), softball (g), volleyball (g), weight training (b,g); intramural: aerobics (g); coed interscholastic: cross-country running, golf, ice hockey, wrestling. 15 coaches, 1 trainer.

Computers Computers are regularly used in all academic classes. Computer network features include campus e-mail.

Contact Mrs. Valerie Reiss, Director of Admissions. 708-453-6233 Ext. 28. Fax: 708-453-6296. E-mail: vreiss@guerinprep.org. Web site: www.guerinprep.org.

GULLIVER PREPARATORY SCHOOL

6575 North Kendall Drive
Miami, Florida 33156
Head of School: Patrick W. Snay

General Information Coeducational day college-preparatory, arts, technology, International Baccalaureate, and pre-engineering school. Grades PK–12. Founded: 1926. Setting: suburban. 14-acre campus. 3 buildings on campus. Approved or accredited by CITA (Commission on International and Trans-Regional Accreditation), Florida Council of Independent Schools, Southern Association of Colleges and Schools, Southern Association of Independent Schools, and Florida Department of Education. Member of Secondary School Admission Test Board. Total enrollment: 2,093. Upper school average class size: 14. Upper school faculty-student ratio: 1:8.

Upper School Student Profile Grade 9: 231 students (127 boys, 104 girls); Grade 10: 228 students (126 boys, 102 girls); Grade 11: 240 students (132 boys, 108 girls); Grade 12: 209 students (115 boys, 94 girls).

Faculty School total: 116. In upper school: 52 men, 64 women; 65 have advanced degrees.

Subjects Offered Algebra, American history, American literature, anatomy, architectural drawing, architecture, art, art history, biology, calculus, ceramics, chemistry, college admission preparation, college awareness, college counseling, college placement, college planning, college writing, community service, computer animation, computer applications, computer keyboarding, computer processing, computer programming, computer programming-AP, computer science, computer science-AP, computer skills, computer studies, concert band, concert choir, creative writing, critical studies in film, dance, desktop publishing, drafting, drama, economics, engineering, English, English literature, environmental science, European history, fine arts, French, geometry, government/civics, history, Italian, Latin, marine biology, mathematics, mechanical drawing, music, newspaper, philosophy, physical education, physics, psychology, religion, science, social studies, Spanish, speech, statistics, theater, trigonometry, video, world history, world literature, yearbook, zoology.

Graduation Requirements Arts and fine arts (art, music, dance, drama), computer science, English, foreign language, mathematics, physical education (includes health), science, social studies (includes history). Community service is required.

Special Academic Programs International Baccalaureate program; Advanced Placement exam preparation in 20 subject areas; honors section; study at local college for college credit; academic accommodation for the gifted, the musically talented, and the artistically talented.

College Placement 210 students graduated in 2005; all went to college, including Cornell College; Duke University; Florida International University; Florida State University; University of Florida; University of Miami.

Student Life Upper grades have specified standards of dress, student council, honor system. Discipline rests primarily with faculty.

Summer Programs Remediation, enrichment, advancement, art/fine arts, rigorous outdoor training, computer instruction programs offered; session focuses on enrichment and reinforcement; held on campus; accepts boys and girls; open to students from other schools. 175 students usually enrolled. 2006 schedule: June 12 to July 21. Application deadline: June 9.

Tuition and Aid Day student tuition: $18,800–$22,000. Tuition installment plan (monthly payment plans, school's own tuition recovery plan). Tuition reduction for siblings, need-based scholarship grants available. Total amount of financial aid awarded in 2005–06: $2,000,000.

Admissions Traditional secondary-level entrance grade is 9. For fall 2005, 269 students applied for upper-level admission, 106 were accepted, 70 enrolled. School's own exam and SSAT required. Deadline for receipt of application materials: February 20. Application fee required: $100. Interview recommended.

Athletics Interscholastic: baseball (boys), basketball (b,g), cross-country running (b,g), diving (b,g), football (b), golf (b,g), gymnastics (b,g), lacrosse (b), physical training (b,g), power lifting (b), running (b,g), soccer (b,g), softball (g), swimming and diving (b,g), tennis (b,g), track and field (b,g), volleyball (g), water polo (b,g); intramural: weight training (b,g); coed interscholastic: aerobics, aerobics/dance, aquatics, cheering, dance, dance squad, dance team, modern dance; coed intramural: aerobics/dance, aerobics/nautilus, badminton, dance, dance squad, dance team, fitness, flag football, Frisbee, kickball, modern dance, netball, physical fitness, running, strength & conditioning, touch football. 6 PE instructors, 55 coaches, 2 trainers.

Computers Computers are regularly used in architecture, art, college planning, drafting, English, graphic arts, graphic design, keyboarding, newspaper, programming, science, technology, word processing, yearbook classes. Computer network features include campus e-mail, on-campus library services, CD-ROMs, online commercial services, Internet access, file transfer, office computer access, DVD, wireless campus network, modified laptop program.

Contact Carol A. Bowen, Director of Admission. 305-666-7937 Ext. 408. Fax: 305-665-3791. E-mail: bowc@gulliverschools.org. Web site: www.gulliverschools.org.

THE GUNNERY

99 Green Hill Road
Washington, Connecticut 06793
Head of School: Susan G. Graham

General Information Coeducational boarding and day college-preparatory school. Boarding grades 9–PG, day grades 9–12. Founded: 1850. Setting: rural. Nearest major city is Hartford. Students are housed in single-sex dormitories. 220-acre campus. 27 buildings on campus. Approved or accredited by Connecticut Association of Independent Schools, New England Association of Schools and Colleges, The Association of Boarding Schools, and Connecticut Department of Education. Member of National Association of Independent Schools and Secondary School Admission Test Board. Endowment: $19 million. Total enrollment: 290. Upper school average class size: 14. Upper school faculty-student ratio: 1:7.

Upper School Student Profile Grade 9: 52 students (40 boys, 12 girls); Grade 10: 73 students (44 boys, 29 girls); Grade 11: 77 students (49 boys, 28 girls); Grade 12: 70 students (39 boys, 31 girls); Postgraduate: 19 students (19 boys). 70% of students are boarding students. 50% are state residents. 23 states are represented in upper school student body. 14% are international students. International students from China, Germany, Japan, Republic of Korea, Russian Federation, and Taiwan; 13 other countries represented in student body.

Faculty School total: 50. In upper school: 28 men, 22 women; 26 have advanced degrees; 40 reside on campus.

Subjects Offered Advanced chemistry, algebra, American history, American history-AP, American literature, anatomy, art, art history, biology, calculus, ceramics, chemistry, computer graphics, computer math, computer programming, computer science, creative writing, drama, drawing, earth science, economics, English, English language-AP, English literature, English literature-AP, environmental science, environmental studies, ESL, ethics, ethics and responsibility, European history, European history-AP, expository writing, fine arts, French, geometry, government/civics, grammar, health, history, history of rock and roll, honors algebra, honors English, honors geometry, human development, instruments, marine biology, mathematics, modern European history-AP, music, music composition, mythology, painting, photography, physical education, physical science, physics, physics-AP, physiology, physiology-anatomy, political science, pottery, pre-calculus, psychology, public speaking, science, social studies, sociology, Spanish, Spanish language-AP, Spanish literature-AP, speech, studio art, theater, trigonometry, U.S. history-AP, values and decisions, voice, world history, world literature, writing.

Graduation Requirements Arts and fine arts (art, music, dance, drama), English, ethics and responsibility, foreign language, human development, mathematics, physical education (includes health), public speaking, science, social studies (includes history), speech.

Special Academic Programs Advanced Placement exam preparation in 8 subject areas; honors section; independent study; term-away projects; study abroad; academic accommodation for the gifted, the musically talented, and the artistically talented; ESL (11 students enrolled).

College Placement 92 students graduated in 2005; 90 went to college, including Franklin and Marshall College; Northeastern University; Pace University; Purchase College, State University of New York; St. Lawrence University; University of Connecticut. Other: 1 entered a postgraduate year, 1 had other specific plans. Mean SAT verbal: 570, mean SAT math: 570.

Student Life Upper grades have uniform requirement, student council, honor system. Discipline rests equally with students and faculty.

Tuition and Aid Day student tuition: $26,000; 7-day tuition and room/board: $35,200. Tuition installment plan (Insured Tuition Payment Plan, Academic Management Services Plan, Key Tuition Payment Plan). Merit scholarship grants, need-based scholarship grants, need-based loans available. In 2005–06, 40% of upper-school students received aid; total upper-school merit-scholarship money awarded: $50,000. Total amount of financial aid awarded in 2005–06: $1,700,000.

Admissions Traditional secondary-level entrance grade is 9. For fall 2005, 400 students applied for upper-level admission, 200 were accepted, 100 enrolled. PSAT or SAT or SSAT required. Deadline for receipt of application materials: January 31. Application fee required: $50. On-campus interview required.

Athletics Interscholastic: baseball (boys), basketball (b,g), crew (b,g), cross-country running (b,g), field hockey (g), football (b), golf (b,g), ice hockey (b,g), lacrosse (b,g), soccer (b,g), softball (g), strength & conditioning (b,g), tennis (b,g), volleyball (g), wrestling (b). 2 coaches, 1 trainer.

Computers Computers are regularly used in art, English, foreign language, history, mathematics, music, science classes. Computer network features include campus e-mail, on-campus library services, CD-ROMs, Internet access, wireless campus network.

Contact Thomas W. Adams, Director of Admissions. 860-868-7334. Fax: 860-868-1614. E-mail: admissions@gunnery.org. Web site: www.gunnery.org.

See full description on page 812.

GUNSTON DAY SCHOOL

911 Gunston Road
PO Box 200
Centreville, Maryland 21617
Head of School: Jeffrey Woodworth

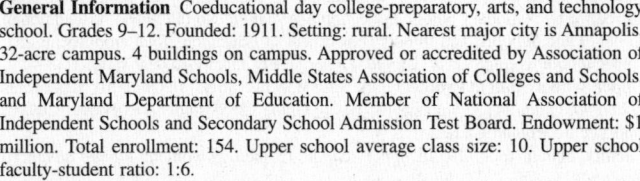
petersons.com

General Information Coeducational day college-preparatory, arts, and technology school. Grades 9–12. Founded: 1911. Setting: rural. Nearest major city is Annapolis. 32-acre campus. 4 buildings on campus. Approved or accredited by Association of Independent Maryland Schools, Middle States Association of Colleges and Schools, and Maryland Department of Education. Member of National Association of Independent Schools and Secondary School Admission Test Board. Endowment: $1 million. Total enrollment: 154. Upper school average class size: 10. Upper school faculty-student ratio: 1:6.

Upper School Student Profile Grade 9: 36 students (19 boys, 17 girls); Grade 10: 42 students (17 boys, 25 girls); Grade 11: 42 students (14 boys, 28 girls); Grade 12: 34 students (18 boys, 16 girls).

Faculty School total: 28. In upper school: 16 men, 12 women; 13 have advanced degrees.

Subjects Offered African history, algebra, American history, American literature, art, biology, biology-AP, calculus, calculus-AP, ceramics, chemistry, chemistry-AP, Chesapeake Bay studies, community service, computer programming, computer science, ecology, English, English literature, environmental science, fine arts, French, French-AP, government/civics, health, history, history-AP, Japanese history, Latin, Latin American history, mathematics, music, performing arts, photography, physics, physics-AP, pre-calculus, pre-college orientation, printmaking, psychology, Russian history, SAT preparation, science, sculpture, senior thesis, silk screening, Spanish, statistics-AP, studio art, trigonometry, world history, world religions.

Graduation Requirements Arts and fine arts (art, music, dance, drama), athletics, computer science, English, foreign language, history, mathematics, science, social science. Community service is required.

Special Academic Programs Advanced Placement exam preparation in 7 subject areas; independent study; study at local college for college credit; academic accommodation for the gifted, the musically talented, and the artistically talented; ESL (3 students enrolled).

College Placement 32 students graduated in 2005; all went to college, including Bowdoin College; Davidson College; Dickinson College; Lehigh University; St. Mary's College of Maryland; Washington College.

Student Life Upper grades have specified standards of dress, student council, honor system. Discipline rests primarily with faculty.

Tuition and Aid Day student tuition: $17,900. Tuition installment plan (Academic Management Services Plan). Merit scholarship grants, need-based scholarship grants available. In 2005–06, 30% of upper-school students received aid. Total amount of financial aid awarded in 2005–06: $405,000.

Admissions Traditional secondary-level entrance grade is 9. ISEE or SSAT required. Deadline for receipt of application materials: February 1. Application fee required: $50. On-campus interview required.

Athletics Interscholastic: basketball (boys, girls), field hockey (g), lacrosse (b,g), swimming and diving (b,g), tennis (b,g); intramural: independent competitive sports (b,g), tennis (b,g); coed interscholastic: golf, sailing, soccer, swimming and diving, tennis; coed intramural: crew, cross-country running, fitness, independent competitive sports, strength & conditioning, tennis, weight training.

Computers Computers are regularly used in English, foreign language, history, mathematics, science classes. Computer network features include campus e-mail, CD-ROMs, online commercial services, Internet access, DVD, wireless campus network.

Contact Michael H. Strannahan, Director of Admission and Financial Aid. 410-758-0620. Fax: 410-758-0628. E-mail: mstrannahan@gunstondayschool.org. Web site: www.gunstondayschool.org/.

ANNOUNCEMENT FROM THE SCHOOL Gunston Day School is an independent, coeducational, college-preparatory school for motivated and capable students. Gunston fosters a supportive and challenging environment where the art of learning is practiced by encouraging critical thinking, creativity, stewardship, and self-discipline. The School community is committed to high standards of academic achievement, ethical behavior, and physical fitness.

HACKETT CATHOLIC CENTRAL HIGH SCHOOL

1000 West Kilgore Road
Kalamazoo, Michigan 49008-3695
Head of School: Mr. Timothy Eastman

General Information Coeducational day college-preparatory, arts, business, vocational, religious studies, bilingual studies, and technology school, affiliated with Roman Catholic Church. Grades 9–12. Founded: 1964. Setting: suburban. Nearest major city is Grand Rapids. 3-acre campus. 1 building on campus. Approved or accredited by Michigan Association of Non-Public Schools, North Central Association of Colleges and Schools, and Michigan Department of Education. Endowment: $2 million. Total enrollment: 455. Upper school average class size: 23. Upper school faculty-student ratio: 1:17.

Upper School Student Profile Grade 9: 107 students (59 boys, 48 girls); Grade 10: 110 students (56 boys, 54 girls); Grade 11: 116 students (67 boys, 49 girls); Grade 12: 122 students (65 boys, 57 girls). 90% of students are Roman Catholic.

Faculty School total: 27. In upper school: 9 men, 18 women; 12 have advanced degrees.

Subjects Offered Acting, algebra, American literature, anatomy and physiology, band, biology, biology-AP, business law, calculus-AP, careers, Catholic belief and practice, chemistry, choir, church history, composition, computer literacy, consumer economics, creative writing, desktop publishing, drawing, earth science, economics, English literature, English-AP, environmental science, fine arts, French, functions, geometry, global issues, health, honors algebra, human development, keyboarding, Latin, Life of Christ, literature, marketing, Microsoft, painting, photography, physical education, pre-calculus, psychology, scripture, sociology, Spanish, speech, statistics, studio art, trigonometry, U.S. government, U.S. history, U.S. history-AP, Web site design, weightlifting, world geography, world history, world history-AP, writing, yearbook.

Graduation Requirements Arts and fine arts (art, music, dance, drama), electives, English, foreign language, mathematics, physical education (includes health), science, social studies (includes history), four years of Catholic classes.

Special Academic Programs Advanced Placement exam preparation in 6 subject areas; honors section; independent study; study at local college for college credit; academic accommodation for the gifted, the musically talented, and the artistically talented; remedial reading and/or remedial writing; remedial math; programs in English, mathematics, general development for dyslexic students; special instructional classes for students with learning disabilities, Attention Deficit Disorder, and dyslexia.

College Placement 117 students graduated in 2005; 110 went to college, including Albion College; Grand Valley State University; Kalamazoo College; Michigan State University; University of Michigan; Western Michigan University. Other: 5 went to work, 2 entered military service. Median composite ACT: 23. Mean SAT verbal: 599, mean SAT math: 540. 34% scored over 600 on SAT verbal, 25% scored over 600 on SAT math, 25% scored over 26 on composite ACT.

Student Life Upper grades have specified standards of dress, student council, honor system. Discipline rests primarily with faculty. Attendance at religious services is required.

Tuition and Aid Day student tuition: $6038. Guaranteed tuition plan. Tuition installment plan (The Tuition Plan, monthly payment plans). Tuition reduction for siblings, need-based scholarship grants available. In 2005–06, 83% of upper-school students received aid. Total amount of financial aid awarded in 2005–06: $400,000.

Admissions Traditional secondary-level entrance grade is 9. Woodcock Reading Mastery Key Math or WRAT required. Deadline for receipt of application materials: none. Application fee required: $200. Interview required.

Athletics Interscholastic: alpine skiing (boys, girls), aquatics (b,g), baseball (b), basketball (b,g), cheering (g), cross-country running (b,g), diving (b,g), football (b),

golf (b,g), ice hockey (b), physical training (b,g), soccer (b,g), softball (g), strength & conditioning (b,g), swimming and diving (b,g), tennis (b,g), volleyball (g), weight lifting (b,g); intramural: polo (b); coed interscholastic: bowling, figure skating, skiing (downhill), track and field; coed intramural: snowboarding. 1 PE instructor, 22 coaches, 1 trainer.

Computers Computers are regularly used in science, typing, yearbook classes. Computer network features include on-campus library services, CD-ROMs, Internet access, office computer access, DVD.

Contact Mr. Jonathon Burhans, Dean of Students. 269-381-2646 Ext. 104. Fax: 269-381-3919. E-mail: jburhans@hackettcc.org. Web site: www.hackettcc.org.

HACKLEY SCHOOL

293 Benedict Avenue
Tarrytown, New York 10591
Head of School: Walter C. Johnson

General Information Coeducational boarding and day college-preparatory and liberal arts school, affiliated with Christian faith. Boarding grades 9–12, day grades K–12. Founded: 1899. Setting: suburban. Nearest major city is New York. Students are housed in single-sex dormitories. 285-acre campus. 15 buildings on campus. Approved or accredited by Middle States Association of Colleges and Schools, New York State Association of Independent Schools, New York State Board of Regents, and The Association of Boarding Schools. Member of National Association of Independent Schools and Secondary School Admission Test Board. Endowment: $22 million. Total enrollment: 819. Upper school average class size: 15. Upper school faculty-student ratio: 1:8.

Upper School Student Profile Grade 9: 99 students (51 boys, 48 girls); Grade 10: 96 students (54 boys, 42 girls); Grade 11: 100 students (48 boys, 52 girls); Grade 12: 86 students (42 boys, 44 girls). 7% of students are boarding students. 96% are state residents. 3 states are represented in upper school student body. 3% are international students. International students from Colombia, Ecuador, Japan, and Peru; 8 other countries represented in student body.

Faculty School total: 115. In upper school: 28 men, 35 women; 42 have advanced degrees; 50 reside on campus.

Subjects Offered 20th century world history, 3-dimensional art, African-American literature, algebra, American government-AP, American history, American history-AP, American literature, ancient history, anthropology, architectural drawing, art, art history, art history-AP, biology, biology-AP, British literature, calculus-AP, ceramics, chemistry, chemistry-AP, chorus, civil rights, comparative government and politics-AP, computer graphics, computer programming, computer science, computer science-AP, concert band, contemporary issues, creative writing, driver education, ecology, economics, electronic publishing, English, English language-AP, English literature-AP, environmental science-AP, environmental systems, European history, film studies, fine arts, finite math, French, French language-AP, French literature-AP, genetics, geometry, German, German-AP, Greek, history, Italian, Latin, Latin American history, Latin-AP, marine biology, marine science, mathematics, modern European history, music, music theory, music theory-AP, natural history, orchestra, organic chemistry, performing arts, photography, physical education, physics, physics-AP, pre-calculus, science, social studies, Spanish, Spanish language-AP, Spanish literature-AP, statistics-AP, studio art-AP, trigonometry, Vietnam War, world history, zoology.

Graduation Requirements Arts and fine arts (art, music, dance, drama), English, foreign language, history, mathematics, physical education (includes health), science.

Special Academic Programs Advanced Placement exam preparation in 19 subject areas; honors section; independent study; ESL (5 students enrolled).

College Placement 89 students graduated in 2005; all went to college, including Boston University; Columbia University; Cornell University; New York University; Princeton University; University of Pennsylvania. Mean SAT verbal: 669, mean SAT math: 658. 80% scored over 600 on SAT verbal, 80% scored over 600 on SAT math.

Student Life Upper grades have specified standards of dress, student council. Discipline rests primarily with faculty.

Tuition and Aid Day student tuition: $25,900; 5-day tuition and room/board: $33,900. Tuition installment plan (Insured Tuition Payment Plan, Academic Management Services Plan, Key Tuition Payment Plan, monthly payment plans). Need-based scholarship grants, need-based loans available. In 2005–06, 15% of upper-school students received aid. Total amount of financial aid awarded in 2005–06: $2,250,000.

Admissions Traditional secondary-level entrance grade is 9. ISEE and SSAT required. Deadline for receipt of application materials: December 16. Application fee required: $55. On-campus interview required.

Athletics Interscholastic: baseball (boys), basketball (b,g), field hockey (g), football (b), golf (b,g), lacrosse (b,g), soccer (b,g), softball (g), squash (b,g), tennis (b,g), wrestling (b); intramural: squash (b,g); coed interscholastic: cheering, cross-country running, fencing, indoor track & field, strength & conditioning, swimming and diving, track and field; coed intramural: aerobics, aerobics/nautilus, fitness, physical fitness, ropes courses, weight training, yoga. 6 PE instructors, 9 coaches, 1 trainer.

Computers Computers are regularly used in newspaper, publishing, Web site design, yearbook classes. Computer network features include on-campus library services, CD-ROMs, Internet access, laptop loaner program.

Contact Fran Demas, Admissions Associate. 914-366-2642. Fax: 914-366-2636. E-mail: fdemas@hackleyschool.org. Web site: www.hackleyschool.org.

ANNOUNCEMENT FROM THE SCHOOL Hackley is beginning construction of a new, state-of-the-art lower school facility with a library. Hackley has just opened a new, state-of-the-art middle/upper school science facility, a new middle school building with a dining hall, a student union, a health center, and a new performance space. The project has added an additional 64,000 square feet of space to Hackley's existing physical plant.

See full description on page 814.

HALE O ULU SCHOOL CHILD AND FAMILY SERVICE

91-1841 Fort Weaver Road
Ewa, Hawaii 96706
Head of School: Ms. Ann Kawahara

General Information Coeducational day college-preparatory school; primarily serves underachievers. Ungraded, ages 12–17. Founded: 1980. Nearest major city is Ewa Beach. 1 building on campus. Approved or accredited by Hawaii Department of Education. Upper school faculty-student ratio: 1:12.

Faculty School total: 8. In upper school: 4 men, 4 women; 3 have advanced degrees.

Special Academic Programs Independent study.

Student Life Upper grades have specified standards of dress, honor system. Discipline rests primarily with faculty.

Admissions TASK Cognitive Abilities Test required. No application fee required. On-campus interview required.

Athletics 1 PE instructor.

Contact Admissions. 808-681-1580. Fax: 808-681-3202. Web site: www.cfs-hawaii.org.

HALES FRANCISCAN HIGH SCHOOL

4930 South Cottage Grove Avenue
Chicago, Illinois 60615
Head of School: Mr. John Young

General Information Boys' day college-preparatory, arts, business, religious studies, and technology school, affiliated with Roman Catholic Church. Grades 9–12. Founded: 1962. Setting: urban. 4-acre campus. 2 buildings on campus. Approved or accredited by National Catholic Education Association, North Central Association of Colleges and Schools, and Illinois Department of Education. Total enrollment: 251. Upper school average class size: 20. Upper school faculty-student ratio: 1:18.

Upper School Student Profile Grade 9: 86 students (86 boys); Grade 10: 72 students (72 boys); Grade 11: 35 students (35 boys); Grade 12: 58 students (58 boys). 20% of students are Roman Catholic.

Faculty School total: 19. In upper school: 13 men, 6 women; 3 have advanced degrees.

Subjects Offered Advanced computer applications, Advanced Placement courses, African-American history, African-American literature, algebra, American government, American literature, art, Bible studies, biology, biology-AP, business skills, calculus-AP, chemistry, community service, computer science, English, fine arts, geography, health, literature, mathematics, physical education, physics, pre-calculus, religion, SAT/ACT preparation, science, social science, social studies, speech, trigonometry, word processing, world history, writing.

Graduation Requirements Arts and fine arts (art, music, dance, drama), business skills (includes word processing), computer science, English, foreign language, mathematics, physical education (includes health), religion (includes Bible studies and theology), science, social science, social studies (includes history). Community service is required.

Special Academic Programs Honors section; independent study; study at local college for college credit; study abroad.

College Placement 41 students graduated in 2005; 38 went to college, including Chicago State University; Eastern Michigan University. Other: 3 went to work. Median SAT verbal: 320, median SAT math: 390, median composite ACT: 17.

Student Life Upper grades have uniform requirement, student council, honor system. Discipline rests equally with students and faculty. Attendance at religious services is required.

Summer Programs Remediation, enrichment, sports, computer instruction programs offered; session focuses on writing, reading, math, and study skills; held on campus; accepts boys; open to students from other schools. 65 students usually enrolled. 2006 schedule: June 21 to July 31. Application deadline: none.

Tuition and Aid Day student tuition: $4500. Tuition installment plan (SMART Tuition Payment Plan, monthly payment plans, individually arranged payment plans). Tuition reduction for siblings, merit scholarship grants, need-based scholarship grants, paying campus jobs available. In 2005–06, 65% of upper-school students received aid; total upper-school merit-scholarship money awarded: $25,000. Total amount of financial aid awarded in 2005–06: $1,500,000.

Admissions Traditional secondary-level entrance grade is 9. For fall 2005, 150 students applied for upper-level admission, 128 were accepted, 88 enrolled. TerraNova required. Deadline for receipt of application materials: none. Application fee required: $25. Interview required.

Athletics Interscholastic: baseball, basketball, bowling, drill team, football, indoor track, strength & conditioning, track and field, weight lifting, weight training, wrestling; intramural: basketball, football, softball, strength & conditioning, touch football, track and field; coed interscholastic: cheering. 1 PE instructor, 16 coaches, 1 trainer.

Computers Computers are regularly used in basic skills, business education, business skills, college planning, introduction to technology, library skills, publications classes. Computer network features include CD-ROMs, Internet access.

Contact Mr. Jasper Strong, Director of Recruitment and Admissions. 773-285-8400 Ext. 225. Fax: 773-285-7025. Web site: www.halesfranciscan.org.

HALIFAX GRAMMAR SCHOOL

5750 Atlantic Street
Halifax, Nova Scotia B3H 1G9, Canada
Head of School: Dr. Paul W. Bennett

General Information Coeducational day college-preparatory and International Baccalaureate school. Grades K–12. Founded: 1958. Setting: urban. 4-acre campus. 2 buildings on campus. Approved or accredited by Canadian Association of Independent Schools, International Baccalaureate Organization, and Nova Scotia Department of Education. Language of instruction: English. Endowment: CAN$100,000. Total enrollment: 539. Upper school average class size: 16. Upper school faculty-student ratio: 1:10.

Upper School Student Profile Grade 10: 79 students (48 boys, 31 girls); Grade 11: 66 students (33 boys, 33 girls); Grade 12: 53 students (30 boys, 23 girls).

Faculty School total: 53. In upper school: 9 men, 13 women; 13 have advanced degrees.

Subjects Offered Algebra, art, art history, biology, business studies, calculus, Canadian history, chemistry, computer science, drama, economics, English, English composition, English literature, European history, French, geography, German, history, Latin, math methods, mathematics, music, music history, music theory, physical education, physics, science, Spanish, theory of knowledge, world history, writing.

Graduation Requirements English, foreign language, mathematics, science, social studies (includes history), theory of knowledge, IB CAS Program.

Special Academic Programs International Baccalaureate program; honors section; academic accommodation for the gifted, the musically talented, and the artistically talented.

College Placement 54 students graduated in 2005; 53 went to college, including McGill University; Mount Allison University; Queen's University at Kingston; University of Toronto. Other: 1 had other specific plans.

Student Life Upper grades have specified standards of dress, student council. Discipline rests primarily with faculty.

Summer Programs Remediation programs offered; session focuses on two-week math and French programs for new students; held on campus; accepts boys and girls; open to students from other schools. 31 students usually enrolled.

Tuition and Aid Day student tuition: CAN$9654. Tuition installment plan (monthly payment plans, term payment plan). Tuition reduction for siblings, bursaries, merit scholarship grants, need-based scholarship grants available. In 2005–06, 15% of upper-school students received aid; total upper-school merit-scholarship money awarded: CAN$45,000. Total amount of financial aid awarded in 2005–06: CAN$184,529.

Admissions Traditional secondary-level entrance grade is 10. For fall 2005, 45 students applied for upper-level admission, 31 were accepted, 31 enrolled. CAT 2, English language and Otis-Lennon School Ability Test required. Deadline for receipt of application materials: none. Application fee required: CAN$100. Interview required.

Athletics Interscholastic: alpine skiing (boys, girls), aquatics (b,g), badminton (b,g), basketball (b,g), cross-country running (b,g), golf (b,g), rugby (b), skiing (downhill) (b,g), soccer (b,g), swimming and diving (b,g), track and field (b,g); coed interscholastic: badminton, Frisbee, ultimate Frisbee; coed intramural: climbing, fencing. 1 PE instructor, 2 coaches.

Computers Computer network features include campus e-mail, on-campus library services, CD-ROMs, online commercial services, Internet access, DVD, wireless campus network.

Contact Ms. Ann Marie Kent, Admissions Officer. 902-431-8550. Fax: 902-423-9315. E-mail: admissions@hgs.ns.ca. Web site: www.hgs.ns.ca.

ANNOUNCEMENT FROM THE SCHOOL The first all-IB-Diploma class graduated with a remarkable success rate. School opened in September with a record enrolment of 540 students and a new Headmaster, Dr. Paul Bennett, at the helm. Halifax is now actively engaged in renewing its Mission Statement and developing a strategic plan for the School's future.

HAMDEN HALL COUNTRY DAY SCHOOL

1108 Whitney Avenue
Hamden, Connecticut 06517
Head of School: Robert J. Izzo

General Information Coeducational day college-preparatory school. Grades PK–12. Founded: 1912. Setting: suburban. Nearest major city is New Haven. 42-acre campus. 8 buildings on campus. Approved or accredited by Connecticut Association of Independent Schools, New England Association of Schools and Colleges, and Connecticut Department of Education. Member of National Association of Independent Schools. Endowment: $3 million. Total enrollment: 565. Upper school average class size: 15. Upper school faculty-student ratio: 1:8.

Upper School Student Profile Grade 9: 67 students (36 boys, 31 girls); Grade 10: 72 students (37 boys, 35 girls); Grade 11: 56 students (28 boys, 28 girls); Grade 12: 46 students (28 boys, 18 girls).

Faculty School total: 78. In upper school: 26 men, 23 women; 36 have advanced degrees.

Subjects Offered Algebra, American literature, anatomy, art history, astronomy, biology, Black history, British literature, calculus, ceramics, chamber groups, chemistry, chorus, computer programming, computer science, creative writing, debate, drama, drawing, economics, electronics, ethics, European history, expository writing, French, geology, geometry, history of architecture, improvisation, jazz, Latin, law, life science, meteorology, multimedia design, music appreciation, music history, music theory, oceanography, painting, peer counseling, philosophy, playwriting, poetry, printmaking, sculpture, sociology, Spanish, speech, statistics, theater, trigonometry, U.S. history, Western civilization, women in literature, world history, world literature, zoology.

Graduation Requirements Arts and fine arts (art, music, dance, drama), computer science, English, foreign language, mathematics, physical education (includes health), science, social studies (includes history), participation in 2 athletic seasons each year.

Special Academic Programs Advanced Placement exam preparation; honors section; independent study.

College Placement 69 students graduated in 2005; all went to college, including American University; Syracuse University; University of Chicago; University of Connecticut; University of Pennsylvania; Vanderbilt University. Median SAT verbal: 600, median SAT math: 600, median combined SAT: 1800, median composite ACT: 26.

Student Life Upper grades have specified standards of dress, student council, honor system. Discipline rests equally with students and faculty.

Summer Programs Remediation, enrichment, advancement, sports, art/fine arts, computer instruction programs offered; held on campus; accepts boys and girls; open to students from other schools. 2006 schedule: June 12 to August 11. Application deadline: none.

Tuition and Aid Day student tuition: $21,800. Tuition installment plan (individually arranged payment plans). Need-based scholarship grants, need-based loans, paying campus jobs, Key Education Resources available. In 2005–06, 30% of upper-school students received aid.

Admissions Traditional secondary-level entrance grade is 9. For fall 2005, 183 students applied for upper-level admission, 125 were accepted, 57 enrolled. ISEE or SSAT required. Deadline for receipt of application materials: February 1. Application fee required: $50. On-campus interview required.

Athletics Interscholastic: baseball (boys), basketball (b,g), field hockey (g), football (b), lacrosse (b,g), soccer (b,g), softball (g), tennis (b,g), volleyball (g), wrestling (b); coed interscholastic: cross-country running, golf; coed intramural: outdoors, physical fitness, running, swimming and diving, weight training. 2 PE instructors, 15 coaches, 1 trainer.

Computers Computer network features include campus e-mail, on-campus library services, CD-ROMs, Internet access, file transfer, office computer access, DVD, wireless campus network.

Contact Janet B. Izzo, Director of Admissions. 203-865-6158 Ext. 238. Fax: 203-776-5852. Web site: www.hamdenhall.org.

ANNOUNCEMENT FROM THE SCHOOL Hamden Hall Country Day School is a coeducational, college-preparatory school enrolling nearly 600 students in PK–12. It is set on 12 acres overlooking Lake Whitney in south-central Connecticut, just north of New Haven and Yale University, with an additional 30 acres of athletics fields. Hamden Hall was founded in 1912 as a day school for boys by Dr. John P. Cushing, its first headmaster. Coeducation was introduced in 1927 and, within 7 years, the School was expanded to encompass grades 9–12. A comprehensive college-preparatory program was implemented in 1935. The mission of Hamden Hall is to provide a challenging education that fosters academic excellence while formulating a student's character, value system, and sense of independence. The faculty members, having earned 88 baccalaureate and 60 advanced degrees, including 3 doctorates, are well qualified in their areas of specialization. They serve as role models and mentors in the classroom, on the playing field, and in other areas of school life. With an 8:1 student-teacher ratio, the School aims to offer a nurturing environment in which young people can reach their full potential intellectually, physically, and socially. The program is specially structured for students making

Hamden Hall Country Day School

the transition from childhood to adolescence. The curriculum builds on the skills acquired in the early grades and combines them with new challenges and techniques designed to maximize learning. Students in the Upper School combine a demanding curriculum of interscholastic sports and a variety of clubs and extracurricular activities, including the Princeton Peer Leadership program. Advanced Placement and honors courses are offered in most major disciplines as is independent study. A full-time college counseling staff works with students and parents. In 2005, all of the 69 graduating students entered such colleges and universities as Brown, Emory, Vanderbilt, Yale, and the University of Pennsylvania.

HAMILTON DISTRICT CHRISTIAN SCHOOL

92 Glancaster Road
Ancaster, Ontario L9G 3K9, Canada
Head of School: Mr. George Van Kampen

General Information Coeducational day college-preparatory, general academic, arts, business, vocational, religious studies, and technology school, affiliated with Christian faith. Grades 9–12. Founded: 1953. Setting: suburban. Nearest major city is Hamilton, Canada. 22-acre campus. 1 building on campus. Approved or accredited by Christian Schools International and Ontario Ministry of Education. Language of instruction: English. Total enrollment: 576. Upper school average class size: 15. Upper school faculty-student ratio: 1:17.

Upper School Student Profile Grade 9: 172 students (86 boys, 86 girls); Grade 10: 133 students (72 boys, 61 girls); Grade 11: 133 students (72 boys, 61 girls); Grade 12: 138 students (63 boys, 75 girls). 100% of students are Christian faith.

Faculty School total: 48. In upper school: 23 men, 25 women; 7 have advanced degrees.

Subjects Offered 20th century history, 3-dimensional art, 3-dimensional design, accounting, acting, adolescent issues, advanced chemistry, advanced computer applications, advanced math, ancient history, ancient world history, applied arts, architectural drawing, art, art history, Bible, biology, business technology, calculus, Canadian geography, Canadian history, Canadian law, career experience, carpentry, chemistry, choir, civics, computer applications, computer keyboarding, computer multimedia, computer programming, computer technologies, computer-aided design, concert band, creative writing, drafting, drama, economics, English literature, environmental science, ESL, family and consumer sciences, finite math, food and nutrition, French, geometry, guidance, history, instrumental music, keyboarding/computer, leadership training, mathematics, media, modern Western civilization, music, peer counseling, personal finance, physical education, physics, religious studies, science, sociology, trigonometry, woodworking.

Graduation Requirements Ancient history, art, Canadian history, civics, computer keyboarding, English, French, history, mathematics, science, 40 hours of community service, senior social science, senior Biblical studies.

Special Academic Programs Remedial reading and/or remedial writing; remedial math; programs in general development for dyslexic students; ESL (12 students enrolled).

College Placement 126 students graduated in 2005; 85 went to college, including Calvin College; Liberty University; McMaster University; Queen's University at Kingston; University of Toronto; Wilfrid Laurier University. Other: 30 went to work, 5 entered a postgraduate year, 3 had other specific plans. Median composite ACT: 24. 30% scored over 26 on composite ACT.

Student Life Upper grades have specified standards of dress, student council. Discipline rests primarily with faculty.

Tuition and Aid Day student tuition: CAN$9200. Tuition installment plan (monthly payment plans, individually arranged payment plans, Christian Economic Assistance Foundation). Tuition reduction for siblings, need-based tuition assistance fund available.

Admissions Traditional secondary-level entrance grade is 9. Deadline for receipt of application materials: none. No application fee required. Interview required.

Athletics Interscholastic: badminton (boys, girls), baseball (g), basketball (b,g), cross-country running (b,g), hockey (b), ice hockey (b), running (b,g), soccer (b,g), softball (g), track and field (b,g), volleyball (b,g); intramural: ball hockey (b,g), basketball (b,g), bicycling (b,g), equestrian sports (b,g), flag football (b,g), floor hockey (b,g), volleyball (b,g), wallyball (b,g), whiffle ball (b,g); coed interscholastic: badminton; coed intramural: bicycling, equestrian sports, floor hockey, horseback riding, mountain biking. 4 PE instructors.

Computers Computers are regularly used in all classes. Computer network features include campus e-mail, on-campus library services, CD-ROMs, online commercial services, Internet access, file transfer, office computer access.

Contact Ms. Emily Prins, Student Services Secretary. 905-648-6655. Fax: 905-648-3139. E-mail: eprins@hdch.org.

HAMILTON LEARNING CENTRE

Hamilton, Ontario, Canada
See Special Needs Schools section.

HAMMOND SCHOOL

854 Galway Lane
Columbia, South Carolina 29209
Head of School: Dr. Herbert B. Barks Jr.

General Information Coeducational day college-preparatory and arts school. Grades PK–12. Founded: 1966. Setting: suburban. 108-acre campus. 10 buildings on campus. Approved or accredited by South Carolina Independent School Association and Southern Association of Colleges and Schools. Member of National Association of Independent Schools and Secondary School Admission Test Board. Endowment: $100,000. Total enrollment: 980. Upper school average class size: 15. Upper school faculty-student ratio: 1:9.

Upper School Student Profile Grade 9: 72 students (38 boys, 34 girls); Grade 10: 80 students (47 boys, 33 girls); Grade 11: 59 students (26 boys, 33 girls); Grade 12: 60 students (26 boys, 34 girls).

Faculty School total: 112. In upper school: 30 men, 30 women; 45 have advanced degrees.

Subjects Offered Advanced Placement courses, African American history, algebra, American government, American history, American literature, art, art history, biology, calculus, chemistry, choir, chorus, computer programming, computer science, creative writing, drama, earth science, economics, electives, English, English literature, European history, film studies, finite math, French, geometry, government/civics, history, journalism, Latin, mathematics, music, physical education, physics, science, social studies, Spanish, speech, trigonometry, world history, world literature.

Graduation Requirements Arts and fine arts (art, music, dance, drama), English, foreign language, mathematics, physical education (includes health), science, social studies (includes history).

Special Academic Programs Advanced Placement exam preparation in 14 subject areas; honors section; independent study; study abroad; academic accommodation for the gifted, the musically talented, and the artistically talented.

College Placement 60 students graduated in 2005; all went to college, including Clemson University; The University of North Carolina at Chapel Hill; University of South Carolina; University of the South; Vanderbilt University; Washington and Lee University. 36% scored over 600 on SAT verbal, 36% scored over 600 on SAT math.

Student Life Upper grades have uniform requirement, student council, honor system. Discipline rests primarily with faculty.

Tuition and Aid Day student tuition: $10,895. Tuition installment plan (Insured Tuition Payment Plan, local bank finance plan). Need-based scholarship grants available. In 2005–06, 12% of upper-school students received aid. Total amount of financial aid awarded in 2005–06: $600,000.

Admissions Traditional secondary-level entrance grade is 9. For fall 2005, 88 students applied for upper-level admission, 41 were accepted, 40 enrolled. ERB, Otis-Lennon School Ability Test or SSAT required. Deadline for receipt of application materials: none. Application fee required: $75. On-campus interview required.

Athletics Interscholastic: back packing (boys, girls), baseball (b), basketball (b,g), canoeing/kayaking (b,g), cheering (b,g), climbing (b,g), combined training (b,g), cross-country running (b,g), fitness (b,g), football (b), golf (b,g), hiking/backpacking (b,g), kayaking (b,g), rafting (b,g), rappelling (b,g), rock climbing (b,g), ropes courses (b,g), soccer (b,g), softball (g), strength & conditioning (b,g), swimming and diving (b,g), tennis (b,g), track and field (b,g), volleyball (g), wilderness (b,g), wrestling (b); coed interscholastic: cross-country running, golf. 3 PE instructors, 1 coach, 1 trainer.

Computers Computer resources include on-campus library services, Internet access.

Contact Mrs. Julia S. Moore, Director of Admission. 803-776-0295. Fax: 803-776-0122. E-mail: admdirector@hammondschool.org. Web site: www.hammondschool.org.

ANNOUNCEMENT FROM THE SCHOOL Hammond School was founded in 1966 by a group of parents who were interested in developing an independent, college-preparatory school in Columbia, South Carolina. The School is located on a 108-acre campus in southeast Columbia. It is a coeducational school with 980 students attending preschool through grade 12. Hammond School has a reputation not only for academic excellence but also for its emphasis on character, honor, and service. An Honor Code dictates the high standards of behavior expected of Hammond students. The primary mission of the School is to provide a challenging academic program that prepares students to attend the finest colleges and universities in the nation. To that end, 112 faculty members teach in a small setting with a curriculum tailored to the individual. The educational plan focuses on skills. From the youngest to the oldest, students are expected to master foundational skills in the core curriculum areas of reading, writing, and computation. Advanced work is available in all disciplines and most students begin college with earned credits from Advanced Placement courses taken at Hammond. One hundred percent of Hammond graduates attend college. The average combined SAT score in 2005–06 was 1222. More Hammond graduates have received National Merit recognition than have graduates of any other area independent school. Hammond graduates attend Vanderbilt, Columbia, Clemson, Boston, Washington and Lee, Virginia, Tufts, UNC at Chapel Hill, Brigham Young, and Furman, among others. College counseling begins in grade 9 and culminates in the application and selection process in grade 12. Eighty-seven percent of the class of 2005 earned academic scholarships to

colleges and universities. Hammond offers a wide variety of extracurricular experiences for students. Beginning grade 7, students may participate in interscholastic athletics in 13 areas. Fine arts at Hammond are a major component of the program. Auditioned music students are traveling to the Vatican to sing in the spring and have previously performed at Dauchau in Austria. Both visual arts and drama are equally recognized for their exhibitions and performances. In addition, an outdoor program offers nature and environmental study, as well as hiking, rock climbing, and white-water rafting. The global facet of the Hammond program includes the full-school study of a specific country each year and opportunities for international travel for upper school students and faculty members.

HAMPSHIRE COUNTRY SCHOOL

Rindge, New Hampshire
See Junior Boarding Schools section.

HAMPTON ROADS ACADEMY

739 Academy Lane
Newport News, Virginia 23602
Head of School: Mr. Thomas D. Harvey

General Information Coeducational day college-preparatory school. Grades 6–12. Founded: 1959. Setting: suburban. Nearest major city is Norfolk. 53-acre campus. 4 buildings on campus. Approved or accredited by Virginia Association of Independent Schools and Virginia Department of Education. Member of National Association of Independent Schools. Total enrollment: 537. Upper school average class size: 16. Upper school faculty-student ratio: 1:10.

Upper School Student Profile Grade 9: 77 students (32 boys, 45 girls); Grade 10: 77 students (42 boys, 35 girls); Grade 11: 84 students (38 boys, 46 girls); Grade 12: 72 students (40 boys, 32 girls).

Faculty School total: 57. In upper school: 16 men, 23 women; 33 have advanced degrees.

Subjects Offered African studies, algebra, American history, American literature, anatomy, art, biology, calculus, ceramics, chemistry, creative writing, drama, driver education, earth science, economics, English, English literature, European history, expository writing, fine arts, French, geography, geometry, German, government/civics, grammar, health, history, Latin, mathematics, music, photography, physical education, physics, physiology, science, social studies, Spanish, speech, statistics, theater, trigonometry, typing, world history, world literature, writing.

Graduation Requirements Arts and fine arts (art, music, dance, drama), English, foreign language, mathematics, physical education (includes health), science, social studies (includes history).

Special Academic Programs Advanced Placement exam preparation in 18 subject areas; honors section; independent study.

College Placement 76 students graduated in 2005; all went to college, including James Madison University; University of South Carolina; University of Virginia; Virginia Commonwealth University; Virginia Polytechnic Institute and State University. Mean SAT verbal: 626, mean SAT math: 619.

Student Life Upper grades have specified standards of dress, student council, honor system. Discipline rests primarily with faculty.

Summer Programs Enrichment, advancement, sports, art/fine arts programs offered; held on campus; accepts boys and girls; open to students from other schools. 75 students usually enrolled. 2006 schedule: June 15 to July 9. Application deadline: none.

Tuition and Aid Day student tuition: $9765–$11,025. Tuition installment plan (Academic Management Services Plan). Need-based scholarship grants available. In 2005–06, 12% of upper-school students received aid.

Admissions Traditional secondary-level entrance grade is 9. CTBS, OLSAT and ERB required. Deadline for receipt of application materials: March 1. Application fee required: $45. On-campus interview required.

Athletics Interscholastic: baseball (boys), basketball (b,g), cheering (g), cross-country running (b,g), field hockey (g), football (b), golf (b,g), lacrosse (b), physical training (b,g), sailing (b,g), soccer (b,g), softball (g), strength & conditioning (b,g), swimming and diving (b,g), tennis (b,g), track and field (b,g), volleyball (g), weight training (b,g). 3 PE instructors, 44 coaches, 1 trainer.

Computers Computers are regularly used in English, mathematics, music, science, yearbook classes. Computer network features include campus e-mail, on-campus library services, CD-ROMs, online commercial services, Internet access, office computer access, DVD, wireless campus network.

Contact Ms. Mary S. Stevens, Director of Admission. 757-884-9148. Fax: 757-884-9147. E-mail: msteve@hra.org. Web site: www.hra.org.

HAPPY VALLEY SCHOOL

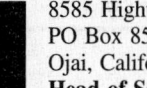

8585 Highway 150
PO Box 850
Ojai, California 93024
Head of School: Mr. Paul Amadio

General Information Coeducational boarding and day college-preparatory and arts school. Grades 9–12. Founded: 1946. Setting: rural. Nearest major city is Los Angeles. Students are housed in single-sex dormitories. 500-acre campus. 11 buildings on campus. Approved or accredited by California Association of Independent Schools, The Association of Boarding Schools, and Western Association of Schools and Colleges. Member of National Association of Independent Schools and Secondary School Admission Test Board. Languages of instruction: English and Spanish. Endowment: $500,000. Total enrollment: 83. Upper school average class size: 12. Upper school faculty-student ratio: 1:7.

Upper School Student Profile Grade 9: 12 students (6 boys, 6 girls); Grade 10: 22 students (13 boys, 9 girls); Grade 11: 25 students (16 boys, 9 girls); Grade 12: 24 students (9 boys, 15 girls). 70% of students are boarding students. 66% are state residents. 13 states are represented in upper school student body. 23% are international students. International students from China, Japan, Mexico, Republic of Korea, Taiwan, and Thailand; 2 other countries represented in student body.

Faculty School total: 16. In upper school: 8 men, 8 women; 10 have advanced degrees; 9 reside on campus.

Subjects Offered Acting, adolescent issues, algebra, American history, art, art history, astronomy, biology, calculus, calculus-AP, ceramics, chemistry, computer science, digital art, drama, driver education, English, English as a foreign language, English language and composition-AP, English literature, English-AP, environmental science, ESL, ethics, expository writing, film, fine arts, geography, geometry, government/civics, history, mathematics, music, music history, music theory, music theory-AP, philosophy, photography, physical education, physics, scene study, science, social science, social studies, Spanish, theater, world history.

Graduation Requirements Arts and fine arts (art, music, dance, drama), English, foreign language, mathematics, physical education (includes health), science, social science, social studies (includes history).

Special Academic Programs Advanced Placement exam preparation in 3 subject areas; honors section; independent study; study at local college for college credit; academic accommodation for the musically talented and the artistically talented; ESL (9 students enrolled).

College Placement 24 students graduated in 2005; 23 went to college, including Pitzer College; Sarah Lawrence College; The Evergreen State College; University of California, Santa Barbara; University of California, Santa Cruz; University of Puget Sound. Other: 1 went to work. Median SAT verbal: 550, median SAT math: 530. 8% scored over 600 on SAT verbal, 15% scored over 600 on SAT math.

Student Life Upper grades have student council, honor system. Discipline rests equally with students and faculty.

Tuition and Aid Day student tuition: $17,900; 7-day tuition and room/board: $33,800. Tuition installment plan (Academic Management Services Plan, Key Tuition Payment Plan, individually arranged payment plans). Tuition reduction for siblings, merit scholarship grants, need-based scholarship grants, paying campus jobs available. In 2005–06, 26% of upper-school students received aid; total upper-school merit-scholarship money awarded: $5000. Total amount of financial aid awarded in 2005–06: $300,000.

Admissions Traditional secondary-level entrance grade is 9. For fall 2005, 148 students applied for upper-level admission, 70 were accepted, 45 enrolled. Deadline for receipt of application materials: none. Application fee required: $50. On-campus interview required.

Athletics Interscholastic: basketball (boys); intramural: baseball (b), basketball (b), soccer (b,g), softball (b), volleyball (g), wrestling (b); coed interscholastic: aerobics, aerobics/dance, back packing, cross-country running, dance, fitness, fitness walking, Frisbee, golf, hiking/backpacking, mountain biking, outdoor activities, outdoor education, outdoor skills, paddle tennis, physical training, ropes courses, skeet shooting, surfing, ultimate Frisbee, walking, yoga; coed intramural: bicycling, billiards, running, skiing (downhill), swimming and diving, table tennis, tennis, track and field. 2 coaches.

Computers Computers are regularly used in desktop publishing, graphic arts, graphic design, mathematics, media arts, publications, video film production classes. Computer network features include campus e-mail, on-campus library services, CD-ROMs, online commercial services, Internet access, office computer access, DVD, wireless campus network.

Contact Ms. Adrian Sweet, Director of Admission. 805-646-4343 Ext. 422. Fax: 805-646-4371. E-mail: asweet@hvalley.org. Web site: www.hvalley.org.

ANNOUNCEMENT FROM THE SCHOOL Happy Valley School is an accredited college-preparatory boarding school with an emphasis on creative expression. The School provides a safe and intimate community where students are able to explore and express their intellectual and creative abilities through challenging academic classes, music, studio art, theater, photography, digital art, and ceramics. Outdoor education, community service, and athletics are important

components of the educational experience. Tuition for boarding students is $33,800; day student tuition is $17,900. Financial aid is available.

See full description on page 816.

HARARE INTERNATIONAL SCHOOL

66 Pendennis Road
Mt. Pleasant
Harare, Zimbabwe
Head of School: Mr. Paul Michael Poore

General Information Coeducational day college-preparatory, arts, and technology school. Grades PK–12. Founded: 1992. Setting: suburban. 22-acre campus. 8 buildings on campus. Approved or accredited by European Council of International Schools and New England Association of Schools and Colleges. Language of instruction: English. Total enrollment: 386. Upper school average class size: 18. Upper school faculty-student ratio: 1:10.
Upper School Student Profile Grade 9: 31 students (15 boys, 16 girls); Grade 10: 30 students (14 boys, 16 girls); Grade 11: 29 students (14 boys, 15 girls); Grade 12: 31 students (17 boys, 14 girls).
Faculty School total: 56. In upper school: 13 men, 16 women; 20 have advanced degrees.
Subjects Offered 20th century world history, acting, advanced computer applications, Advanced Placement courses, advanced studio art-AP, algebra, American literature, applied music, art, band, biology, biology-AP, calculus-AP, ceramics, chemistry, chemistry-AP, college counseling, computer applications, computer programming-AP, computer science-AP, computer studies, concert band, drama, earth science, economics-AP, electives, English, English as a foreign language, English language-AP, English literature-AP, environmental science, environmental studies, ESL, foreign language, French, French language-AP, French literature-AP, geometry, health, health education, honors algebra, independent study, instrumental music, jazz band, language arts, macroeconomics-AP, microeconomics, microeconomics-AP, modern European history, modern European history-AP, modern languages, music, music theory, physical education, physical science, physics, pre-algebra, pre-calculus, programming, psychology, psychology-AP, publications, remedial study skills, science, sociology, Spanish, statistics, studio art-AP, trigonometry, unified math.
Graduation Requirements Arts and fine arts (art, music, dance, drama), computer studies, English, mathematics, modern languages, physical education (includes health), science, social studies (includes history), annual CAS requirement, completion of IT Skills checklist. Community service is required.
Special Academic Programs International Baccalaureate program; honors section; independent study; academic accommodation for the gifted, the musically talented, and the artistically talented; remedial reading and/or remedial writing; remedial math; programs in English, mathematics, general development for dyslexic students; special instructional classes for students with learning disabilities, Attention Deficit Disorder, and dyslexia; ESL (45 students enrolled).
College Placement 26 students graduated in 2005; all went to college.
Student Life Upper grades have specified standards of dress, student council. Discipline rests primarily with faculty.
Tuition and Aid Day student tuition: $10,760–$15,220. Tuition installment plan (monthly payment plans, individually arranged payment plans).
Admissions Traditional secondary-level entrance grade is 9. For fall 2005, 16 students applied for upper-level admission, 15 were accepted, 15 enrolled. Placement test, SLEP or writing sample required. Deadline for receipt of application materials: none. Application fee required: $500. Interview recommended.
Athletics Interscholastic: aquatics (boys, girls), badminton (b,g), basketball (b,g), cricket (b,g), cross-country running (b,g), field hockey (b,g), golf (b,g), gymnastics (g), martial arts (b,g), rugby (b), running (b,g), soccer (b,g), softball (b,g), swimming and diving (b,g), tennis (b,g), track and field (b,g), triathlon (b,g), ultimate Frisbee (b), volleyball (b,g), weight training (b,g); intramural: badminton (b,g), basketball (b,g), bicycling (b,g), cricket (b,g), hiking/backpacking (b,g), judo (b,g), martial arts (b,g), mountain biking (b,g), physical training (b,g), soccer (b,g), softball (b,g), ultimate Frisbee (b,g), volleyball (b,g), weight training (b,g); coed interscholastic: ultimate Frisbee. 2 PE instructors, 15 coaches.
Computers Computers are regularly used in all academic classes. Computer network features include campus e-mail, on-campus library services, CD-ROMs, Internet access, office computer access, wireless campus network.
Contact Mrs. Britta Aryee, Registrar. 263-4-870514. Fax: 263-4-883371. E-mail: baryee@his.ac.zw. Web site: www.his-zim.com.

HARDING ACADEMY

1100 Cherry Road
Memphis, Tennessee 38117
Head of School: Mr. Tom D. Dickson

General Information Coeducational day college-preparatory school, affiliated with Church of Christ. Grades PS–12. Founded: 1952. Setting: suburban. 57-acre campus. 3 buildings on campus. Approved or accredited by National Christian School

Association, Southern Association of Colleges and Schools, and Tennessee Department of Education. Endowment: $2 million. Total enrollment: 1,693. Upper school average class size: 19. Upper school faculty-student ratio: 1:13.
Upper School Student Profile 47% of students are members of Church of Christ.
Faculty School total: 52. In upper school: 26 men, 20 women; 23 have advanced degrees.
Subjects Offered Accounting, algebra, American government, American history, American history-AP, American literature, anatomy and physiology, art, art-AP, band, Bible, biology, biology-AP, British literature, British literature-AP, calculus-AP, chemistry, chorus, computer applications, computer keyboarding, concert band, drama, earth science, English, English language and composition-AP, English literature and composition-AP, etymology, French, geography, geometry, grammar, health, journalism, physical fitness, Spanish, Spanish language-AP, speech, statistics, world history.
Graduation Requirements Algebra, American government, American history, American literature, arts and fine arts (art, music, dance, drama), Bible, biology, British literature, English, fitness, foreign language, geometry, speech, world history.
Special Academic Programs Advanced Placement exam preparation in 6 subject areas; honors section; study abroad.
College Placement 103 students graduated in 2005; all went to college, including Auburn University; Christian Brothers University; Harding University; Mississippi State University; The University of Tennessee. Median SAT verbal: 575, median SAT math: 525, median composite ACT: 24. 34.4% scored over 600 on SAT verbal, 15.1% scored over 600 on SAT math, 31% scored over 26 on composite ACT.
Student Life Upper grades have specified standards of dress, student council, honor system. Discipline rests primarily with faculty. Attendance at religious services is required.
Summer Programs Remediation, enrichment, sports, art/fine arts programs offered; held on campus; accepts boys and girls; open to students from other schools.
Tuition and Aid Day student tuition: $6695–$7495. Tuition installment plan (monthly payment plans, individually arranged payment plans). Tuition reduction for siblings, need-based scholarship grants available. In 2005–06, 10% of upper-school students received aid. Total amount of financial aid awarded in 2005–06: $227,000.
Admissions Traditional secondary-level entrance grade is 9. Metropolitan Achievement Short Form and Otis-Lennon School Ability Test required. Deadline for receipt of application materials: none. No application fee required. Interview recommended.
Athletics Interscholastic: baseball (boys), basketball (b,g), bowling (b,g), cheering (g), cross-country running (b,g), fitness (b,g), football (b), golf (b,g), pom squad (g), soccer (b,g), softball (g), tennis (b,g), track and field (b,g), volleyball (g), wrestling (b). 2 PE instructors, 45 coaches, 1 trainer.
Computers Computers are regularly used in accounting, keyboarding classes. Computer network features include campus e-mail, on-campus library services, CD-ROMs, online commercial services, Internet access.
Contact Mrs. Betty B. Copeland, Director of Admissions. 901-767-4494. Fax: 901-763-4949. E-mail: copeland.betty@hardinglions.org. Web site: www. hardinglions.org.

HARGRAVE MILITARY ACADEMY

200 Military Drive
Chatham, Virginia 24531
Head of School: Col. Wheeler Baker, USMC (Retired), PhD

petersons.com

General Information Boys' boarding and coeducational day college-preparatory, general academic, arts, religious studies, technology, post-graduate academic and standardized testing enhancement, and leadership and ethics school, affiliated with Baptist General Association of Virginia. Boarding boys grades 7–PG, day boys grades 7–PG, day girls grades 9–PG. Founded: 1909. Setting: small town. Nearest major city is Danville. Students are housed in single-sex dormitories. 214-acre campus. 13 buildings on campus. Approved or accredited by Southern Association of Colleges and Schools, The Association of Boarding Schools, and Virginia Association of Independent Schools. Member of National Association of Independent Schools. Endowment: $4 million. Total enrollment: 410. Upper school average class size: 11. Upper school faculty-student ratio: 1:11.
Upper School Student Profile 92% of students are boarding students. 29% are state residents. 34 states are represented in upper school student body. 3% are international students. International students from Canada, China, Haiti, Honduras, Mexico, and Taiwan. 20% of students are Baptist General Association of Virginia.
Faculty School total: 56. In upper school: 24 men, 24 women; 27 have advanced degrees; 23 reside on campus.
Subjects Offered Advanced Placement courses, algebra, American government, American history, American literature, art, astronomy, Bible studies, biology, calculus, chemistry, civics, computer science, creative writing, debate, drama, driver education, earth science, economics, English, English literature, environmental science, ESL, expository writing, French, geography, geometry, government/civics, health, history, journalism, leadership, leadership and service, leadership education training, leadership skills, leadership training, mathematics, meteorology, physical education, physics, psychology, reading, religion, science, social studies, sociology, Spanish, speech, study skills, theater, trigonometry.

Graduation Requirements Bible, computer science, English, foreign language, mathematics, physical education (includes health), religion (includes Bible studies and theology), science, social studies (includes history).

Special Academic Programs Advanced Placement exam preparation in 3 subject areas; honors section; independent study; study at local college for college credit; remedial reading and/or remedial writing; remedial math; programs in general development for dyslexic students; special instructional classes for students with Attention Deficit Disorder; ESL (2 students enrolled).

College Placement 74 students graduated in 2005; 73 went to college, including The Citadel, The Military College of South Carolina; United States Military Academy; United States Naval Academy; Virginia Military Institute; Virginia Polytechnic Institute and State University. Other: 1 entered military service. Median SAT verbal: 519, median SAT math: 531.

Student Life Upper grades have uniform requirement, student council, honor system. Discipline rests equally with students and faculty. Attendance at religious services is required.

Summer Programs Remediation, enrichment, advancement, ESL, sports, rigorous outdoor training, computer instruction programs offered; session focuses on academics/sports camps; held on campus; accepts boys; open to students from other schools. 200 students usually enrolled. 2006 schedule: June 26 to July 22. Application deadline: none.

Tuition and Aid Day student tuition: $12,000; 7-day tuition and room/board: $22,900. Guaranteed tuition plan. Tuition installment plan (individually arranged payment plans). Tuition reduction for siblings, merit scholarship grants, need-based scholarship grants, Achiever Loans (Key Education Resources), prepGATE Loans available. In 2005–06, 25% of upper-school students received aid; total upper-school merit-scholarship money awarded: $37,000. Total amount of financial aid awarded in 2005–06: $280,000.

Admissions Traditional secondary-level entrance grade is 10. For fall 2005, 582 students applied for upper-level admission, 535 were accepted, 304 enrolled. Deadline for receipt of application materials: none. Application fee required: $75. Interview recommended.

Athletics Interscholastic: aquatics (boys, girls), baseball (b), basketball (b), cross-country running (b,g), diving (b,g), football (b), golf (b,g), lacrosse (b), marksmanship (b,g), swimming and diving (b,g), volleyball (g), wrestling (b); intramural: back packing (b), canoeing/kayaking (b), climbing (b), cross-country running (b), hiking/backpacking (b), jogging (b), life saving (b), marksmanship (b), mountaineering (b), outdoor activities (b), outdoor adventure (b), outdoor education (b), outdoor recreation (b), outdoor skills (b), paint ball (b), physical fitness (b), rappelling (b), riflery (b), rock climbing (b), skeet shooting (b), swimming and diving (b), table tennis (b), wall climbing (b), weight lifting (b), weight training (b); coed interscholastic: riflery, soccer, tennis; coed intramural: aquatics, back packing, basketball, billiards, drill team, fitness, jogging, life saving, marksmanship, paddle tennis, physical fitness, physical training, roller blading, ropes courses, running, scuba diving, skateboarding, skiing (downhill), soccer, strength & conditioning, swimming and diving, table tennis, tennis, walking, water polo, weight lifting, weight training. 3 PE instructors, 9 coaches, 2 trainers.

Computers Computers are regularly used in art, English, foreign language, history, mathematics, science classes. Computer network features include campus e-mail, on-campus library services, CD-ROMs, online commercial services, Internet access, various intranets.

Contact Cmdr. Frank Martin, Director of Admissions. 800-432-2480. Fax: 434-432-3129. E-mail: admissions@hargrave.edu. Web site: www.hargrave.edu.

ANNOUNCEMENT FROM THE SCHOOL Hargrave Military Academy is an independent college-preparatory military school that espouses the "whole person" concept through its academic, spiritual, athletic, and military program. *Mens Sana In Corpore Sano* is found on the Hargrave Military Academy's logo, and being of "Sound Mind" and "Sound Body" is extremely important to those who attend Hargrave Military Academy.

See full description on page 818.

THE HARKER SCHOOL

500 Saratoga Avenue
San Jose, California 95129
Head of School: Christopher Nikoloff

General Information Coeducational day college-preparatory, arts, technology, and gifted students school. Grades K–12. Founded: 1893. Setting: urban. 16-acre campus. 6 buildings on campus. Approved or accredited by California Association of Independent Schools, Western Association of Schools and Colleges, and California Department of Education. Member of National Association of Independent Schools. Total enrollment: 1,685. Upper school average class size: 11. Upper school faculty-student ratio: 1:11.

Upper School Student Profile Grade 9: 176 students (89 boys, 87 girls); Grade 10: 152 students (77 boys, 75 girls); Grade 11: 170 students (85 boys, 85 girls); Grade 12: 143 students (73 boys, 70 girls).

Faculty School total: 183. In upper school: 41 men, 37 women; 61 have advanced degrees.

Subjects Offered Acting, advanced math, aerobics, algebra, American literature, architecture, art history-AP, Asian history, Asian literature, astronomy, baseball, basketball, biology, biology-AP, British literature, calculus-AP, ceramics, chemistry, chemistry-AP, choir, college counseling, community service, computer programming, computer science-AP, contemporary women writers, dance, dance performance, debate, drawing, ecology, economics, electronics, engineering, English literature and composition-AP, ethics, European history-AP, evolution, expository writing, fencing, film and literature, fitness, French, French language-AP, French literature-AP, golf, graphic arts, honors algebra, honors geometry, instrumental music, international affairs, Japanese, Latin, Latin-AP, linear algebra, literary magazine, mentorship program, music, music theory-AP, newspaper, orchestra, organic chemistry, painting, physics, physics-AP, physiology-anatomy, play production, political thought, pre-calculus, psychology-AP, public policy, public speaking, radio broadcasting, robotics, scene study, sculpture, self-defense, Shakespeare, softball, Spanish, Spanish language-AP, Spanish literature-AP, statistics, stone carving, student government, study skills, swimming, technical theater, tennis, theater arts, track and field, trigonometry, U.S. government and politics-AP, U.S. history, U.S. history-AP, video and animation, visual arts, vocal ensemble, volleyball, weight training, Western philosophy, world history, wrestling, yearbook, yoga.

Graduation Requirements Algebra, arts and fine arts (art, music, dance, drama), biology, chemistry, computer science, English, ethics, foreign language, geometry, physical education (includes health), physics, public speaking, trigonometry, U.S. history, world history, 30 total hours of community service.

Special Academic Programs Advanced Placement exam preparation in 18 subject areas; honors section; independent study; academic accommodation for the gifted.

College Placement 123 students graduated in 2005; all went to college, including Massachusetts Institute of Technology; Stanford University; University of California, Berkeley; University of California, Davis; University of Pennsylvania; Yale University. Mean SAT verbal: 678, mean SAT math: 698.

Student Life Upper grades have specified standards of dress, student council, honor system. Discipline rests primarily with faculty.

Summer Programs Enrichment, advancement programs offered; session focuses on academics; held both on and off campus; held at venues abroad for upper school students; accepts boys and girls; open to students from other schools. 250 students usually enrolled. 2006 schedule: June 26 to August 4. Application deadline: June 1.

Tuition and Aid Day student tuition: $24,968. Need-based scholarship grants, need-based loans available. In 2005–06, 10% of upper-school students received aid.

Admissions Traditional secondary-level entrance grade is 9. ERB CTP III, essay, ISEE or SSAT required. Deadline for receipt of application materials: January 10. Application fee required: $50. Interview required.

Athletics Interscholastic: baseball (boys), basketball (b,g), cheering (g), cross-country running (b,g), football (b), golf (b,g), lacrosse (g), soccer (b,g), softball (g), swimming and diving (b,g), tennis (b,g), track and field (b,g), volleyball (b,g), water polo (b,g); coed interscholastic: football, wrestling; coed intramural: aerobics/dance, dance, fencing, fitness, martial arts, physical fitness, tennis, weight lifting, yoga. 5 PE instructors, 19 coaches, 1 trainer.

Computers Computers are regularly used in all academic, graphic arts, programming classes. Computer network features include campus e-mail, on-campus library services, CD-ROMs, online commercial services, Internet access, wireless campus network, ProQuest, Gale Group, InfoTrac, Facts On File.

Contact Ruth Tebo, Admissions Secretary. 408-249-2510. Fax: 408-984-2325. E-mail: rutht@harker.org. Web site: www.harker.org.

See full description on page 820.

THE HARLEY SCHOOL

1981 Clover Street
Rochester, New York 14618
Head of School: Mr. Paul Schiffman

General Information Coeducational day college-preparatory and arts school. Grades N–12. Founded: 1917. Setting: suburban. 25-acre campus. 2 buildings on campus. Approved or accredited by National Independent Private Schools Association and New York State Association of Independent Schools. Member of National Association of Independent Schools. Endowment: $8.2 million. Total enrollment: 502. Upper school average class size: 8. Upper school faculty-student ratio: 1:8.

Upper School Student Profile Grade 9: 37 students (20 boys, 17 girls); Grade 10: 46 students (22 boys, 24 girls); Grade 11: 33 students (18 boys, 15 girls); Grade 12: 38 students (19 boys, 19 girls).

Faculty School total: 80. In upper school: 10 men, 13 women; 18 have advanced degrees.

Subjects Offered African history, algebra, American history, anthropology, archaeology, art, art history, biology, calculus, ceramics, chemistry, chorus, community service, computer graphics, computer math, computer programming, computer science, creative writing, desktop publishing, drama, drawing, driver education, economics, English, English literature, environmental science, ethics, European history, expository writing, film, fine arts, French, geometry, graphic arts, Greek, Latin, mathematics, music, music theory, orchestra, philosophy, photography, physical

education, physics, psychology, science, Shakespeare, social studies, Spanish, speech, study skills, theater, Vietnam, voice, world history, writing.

Graduation Requirements Arts and fine arts (art, music, dance, drama), computer science, English, foreign language, mathematics, physical education (includes health), science, social studies (includes history), participation in team sports. Community service is required.

Special Academic Programs Advanced Placement exam preparation in 15 subject areas; honors section; independent study; study abroad.

College Placement 42 students graduated in 2005; all went to college, including Dartmouth College; Harvard University; Oberlin College; St. Bonaventure University; Stanford University; The College of Wooster. Mean SAT verbal: 642, mean SAT math: 608.

Student Life Upper grades have student council, honor system. Discipline rests primarily with faculty.

Summer Programs Remediation, enrichment, sports, art/fine arts, computer instruction programs offered; session focuses on day camp, outdoor skills, swimming, tennis; held on campus; accepts boys and girls; open to students from other schools. 200 students usually enrolled. 2006 schedule: June 12 to August 4. Application deadline: May.

Tuition and Aid Day student tuition: $13,150–$15,150. Tuition installment plan (Insured Tuition Payment Plan, Key Tuition Payment Plan, monthly payment plans, 2-payment plan, prepay discount). Tuition reduction for siblings, need-based scholarship grants available. In 2005–06, 28% of upper-school students received aid.

Admissions Traditional secondary-level entrance grade is 9. For fall 2005, 26 students applied for upper-level admission, 18 were accepted, 14 enrolled. ERB, essay and Otis-Lennon School Ability Test required. Deadline for receipt of application materials: none. Application fee required: $50. On-campus interview required.

Athletics Interscholastic: basketball (boys, girls), golf (b), soccer (b,g), softball (b,g), swimming and diving (b,g), tennis (b,g), volleyball (b,g); coed interscholastic: outdoor education, running. 3 PE instructors, 11 coaches.

Computers Computers are regularly used in all classes. Computer network features include campus e-mail, CD-ROMs, Internet access, office computer access.

Contact Kimberley Moore, Director of Institutional Advancement. 585-442-1770. Fax: 585-442-5758. E-mail: kmoore@harleyschool.org.

THE HARPETH HALL SCHOOL

3801 Hobbs Road
PO Box 150207
Nashville, Tennessee 37215-0207
Head of School: Ann Teaff

www
petersons.com

General Information Girls' day college-preparatory, arts, and technology school. Grades 5–12. Founded: 1951. Setting: suburban. 35-acre campus. 5 buildings on campus. Approved or accredited by Southern Association of Colleges and Schools and Tennessee Association of Independent Schools. Member of National Association of Independent Schools. Endowment: $22 million. Total enrollment: 626. Upper school average class size: 16. Upper school faculty-student ratio: 1:8.

Upper School Student Profile Grade 9: 97 students (97 girls); Grade 10: 96 students (96 girls); Grade 11: 95 students (95 girls); Grade 12: 90 students (90 girls).

Faculty School total: 79. In upper school: 58 have advanced degrees.

Subjects Offered Advanced Placement courses, algebra, American government, American history, American history-AP, American literature, art, art history, art history-AP, biology, biology-AP, botany, calculus, chemistry, chemistry-AP, choral music, comparative politics, computer math, computer programming, computer science, conceptual physics, creative writing, dance, drama, ecology, English, English literature, environmental science, environmental studies, environmental systems, European history, European history-AP, expository writing, fine arts, French, French language-AP, French literature-AP, functions, geometry, government/civics, grammar, health, history, Latin, Latin-AP, mathematics, media arts, music, photography, physical education, physics, physics-AP, psychology, science, social science, social studies, Spanish, Spanish language-AP, Spanish literature-AP, speech, statistics and probability, theater, trigonometry, video, world history, world literature, writing.

Graduation Requirements Arts and fine arts (art, music, dance, drama), communication skills, electives, English, foreign language, mathematics, physical education (includes health), science, social science, participation in Winterim Program each year.

Special Academic Programs Advanced Placement exam preparation in 13 subject areas; honors section; independent study; term-away projects; study abroad; academic accommodation for the gifted, the musically talented, and the artistically talented.

College Placement 86 students graduated in 2005; all went to college, including Auburn University; The University of Tennessee; University of Georgia; University of the South; University of Virginia; Vanderbilt University. Mean SAT verbal: 645, mean SAT math: 615, mean composite ACT: 27.

Student Life Upper grades have uniform requirement, student council, honor system. Discipline rests primarily with faculty.

Summer Programs Enrichment, sports, art/fine arts, computer instruction programs offered; session focuses on enrichment classes and sports; held on campus; accepts boys and girls; open to students from other schools. 300 students usually enrolled. 2006 schedule: June to August. Application deadline: none.

Tuition and Aid Day student tuition: $15,450. Tuition installment plan (The Tuition Plan, individually arranged payment plans, Tuition Management Systems Plan). Merit

scholarship grants, need-based scholarship grants available. In 2005–06, 12% of upper-school students received aid; total upper-school merit-scholarship money awarded: $2500. Total amount of financial aid awarded in 2005–06: $658,450.

Admissions Traditional secondary-level entrance grade is 9. ISEE required. Deadline for receipt of application materials: January 1. Application fee required: $35. On-campus interview required.

Athletics Interscholastic: aquatics, basketball, bowling, cross-country running, diving, golf, lacrosse, soccer, softball, swimming and diving, tennis, track and field, volleyball; intramural: aerobics/dance, back packing, badminton, climbing, dance, fitness, flag football, hiking/backpacking, jogging, modern dance, outdoor activities, outdoor adventure, outdoor education, outdoor recreation, outdoor skills, physical training, rock climbing, self defense, ultimate Frisbee, walking, wall climbing, weight training, yoga. 2 PE instructors, 7 coaches, 2 trainers.

Computers Computers are regularly used in all academic classes. Computer network features include campus e-mail, on-campus library services, CD-ROMs, online commercial services, Internet access, DVD, wireless campus network.

Contact Dianne Wild, Director of Admission and Financial Aid. 615-346-0126. Fax: 615-297-0480. E-mail: wild@harpethhall.org. Web site: www.harpethhall.org.

ANNOUNCEMENT FROM THE SCHOOL The Harpeth Hall School, middle Tennessee's only independent, college-preparatory school for girls (grades 5–12), challenges each student to develop her highest intellectual ability, to discover her creative talents, and to make a meaningful contribution to her community. The School has a rich tradition of education and understands how young women learn and succeed. Harpeth Hall offers an academically challenging, technologically advanced setting in which all students use laptop computers as a significant part of their learning experience. The School's faculty members have been national leaders in integrating technology into the curriculum and are on the forefront of exploring how the laptop can facilitate learning. Small classes and a 9:1 student-teacher ratio ensure that each student actively participates in the learning process. Almost all students take 4 years of math, and Advanced Placement courses are offered in every discipline, including chemistry, biology, and physics. In addition to its academic excellence, Harpeth Hall offers outstanding athletics, arts, service learning, leadership opportunities, and innovative programs. Girls eagerly participate in the 11 varsity sports programs, acquiring self-discipline and teamwork and leadership skills. A rich fine arts program creates many opportunities for growth in the visual and performing arts. The School's service learning program instills leadership and a strong sense of community responsibility. An advisory program allows for personal development and mentoring. Harpeth Hall offers a 3-week Winterim program that allows Upper School students to explore in depth various areas of interest through special course work, work/study internships, academic trips, or independent study. Financial aid is available.

HARRELLS CHRISTIAN ACADEMY

360 Tomahawk Highway
Harrells, North Carolina 28444
Head of School: Dr. Ronald L. Montgomery

General Information Coeducational day college-preparatory, arts, religious studies, and technology school. Grades K–12. Founded: 1969. Setting: rural. Nearest major city is Wilmington. 32-acre campus. 7 buildings on campus. Approved or accredited by North Carolina Association of Independent Schools, Southern Association of Colleges and Schools, Southern Association of Independent Schools, and North Carolina Department of Education. Total enrollment: 471. Upper school average class size: 16. Upper school faculty-student ratio: 1:12.

Upper School Student Profile Grade 9: 26 students (12 boys, 14 girls); Grade 10: 42 students (17 boys, 25 girls); Grade 11: 30 students (15 boys, 15 girls); Grade 12: 28 students (14 boys, 14 girls).

Faculty School total: 38. In upper school: 2 men, 8 women; 4 have advanced degrees.

Subjects Offered Algebra, anatomy, art, biology, business, chemistry, computer science, earth science, English, English literature, government/civics, grammar, history, keyboarding, Latin, mathematics, music, physical education, physical science, physics, religion, SAT/ACT preparation, science, social studies, Spanish.

Graduation Requirements Computer applications, electives, English, foreign language, mathematics, physical education (includes health), religious studies, science, social studies (includes history). Community service is required.

Special Academic Programs Advanced Placement exam preparation in 4 subject areas; honors section; independent study; study at local college for college credit.

College Placement 33 students graduated in 2005; all went to college, including East Carolina University; Meredith College; North Carolina State University; The University of North Carolina Wilmington. Median composite ACT: 18. 17% scored over 26 on composite ACT.

Student Life Upper grades have specified standards of dress, student council, honor system. Discipline rests equally with students and faculty. Attendance at religious services is required.

Tuition and Aid Day student tuition: $6240. Tuition installment plan (monthly payment plans, individually arranged payment plans). Tuition reduction for siblings,

need-based scholarship grants available. In 2005–06, 8% of upper-school students received aid. Total amount of financial aid awarded in 2005–06: $16,650.

Admissions Traditional secondary-level entrance grade is 10. For fall 2005, 24 students applied for upper-level admission, 22 were accepted, 16 enrolled. Admissions testing and Iowa Tests of Basic Skills required. Deadline for receipt of application materials: none. Application fee required: $35. On-campus interview required.

Athletics Interscholastic: baseball (boys), basketball (b,g), cheering (g), football (b), golf (b,g), soccer (g), softball (g), tennis (g), volleyball (g). 2 PE instructors, 6 coaches.

Computers Computers are regularly used in English, journalism, keyboarding, yearbook classes. Computer network features include campus e-mail, on-campus library services, CD-ROMs, Internet access.

Contact Dr. Ronald L. Montgomery, Headmaster. 910-532-4575 Ext. 222. Fax: 910-532-2958. E-mail: hca2@intrstar.net.

THE HARRISBURG ACADEMY

10 Erford Road
Wormleysburg, Pennsylvania 17043
Head of School: Dr. James Newman

General Information Coeducational day college-preparatory school. Grades N–12. Founded: 1784. Setting: suburban. Nearest major city is Harrisburg. 23-acre campus. 1 building on campus. Approved or accredited by Middle States Association of Colleges and Schools and Pennsylvania Association of Private Academic Schools. Member of National Association of Independent Schools. Endowment: $3 million. Total enrollment: 432. Upper school average class size: 9. Upper school faculty-student ratio: 1:8.

Upper School Student Profile Grade 9: 17 students (8 boys, 9 girls); Grade 10: 30 students (15 boys, 15 girls); Grade 11: 10 students (4 boys, 6 girls); Grade 12: 30 students (14 boys, 16 girls).

Faculty School total: 60. In upper school: 3 men, 10 women; 9 have advanced degrees.

Subjects Offered Advanced Placement courses, algebra, American history, American literature, art, biology, business skills, calculus, ceramics, chemistry, computer science, creative writing, drama, economics, English, English literature, environmental science, European history, expository writing, fine arts, French, geography, geometry, grammar, health, history, Latin, mathematics, music, philosophy, physical education, physics, psychology, science, social studies, Spanish, speech, typing, world history, world literature, writing.

Graduation Requirements Arts and fine arts (art, music, dance, drama), business skills (includes word processing), college planning, English, foreign language, mathematics, physical education (includes health), public speaking, science, social studies (includes history). Community service is required.

Special Academic Programs Advanced Placement exam preparation in 11 subject areas; honors section; accelerated programs; independent study; study at local college for college credit.

College Placement 28 students graduated in 2005; 26 went to college, including Bryn Mawr College; Emory University; The George Washington University; Tulane University; University of Pennsylvania; University of Pittsburgh. Mean SAT verbal: 604, mean SAT math: 595, mean composite ACT: 25. 38% scored over 26 on composite ACT.

Student Life Upper grades have specified standards of dress, student council, honor system. Discipline rests primarily with faculty.

Tuition and Aid Day student tuition: $12,196. Tuition installment plan (Insured Tuition Payment Plan, monthly payment plans). Need-based scholarship grants, need-based loans available. In 2005–06, 8% of upper-school students received aid. Total amount of financial aid awarded in 2005–06: $450,811.

Admissions Traditional secondary-level entrance grade is 9. Admissions testing required. Deadline for receipt of application materials: none. Application fee required: $45. On-campus interview required.

Athletics Interscholastic: basketball (boys, girls), field hockey (g), golf (b), lacrosse (b), soccer (b,g); coed interscholastic: swimming and diving; coed intramural: skiing (downhill). 3 PE instructors, 8 coaches, 1 trainer.

Computers Computers are regularly used in art, English, mathematics, music, science classes. Computer network features include campus e-mail, on-campus library services, CD-ROMs, Internet access, wireless campus network.

Contact Mrs. Jessica Warren, Director of Admissions. 717-763-7811 Ext. 313. Fax: 717-975-0894. E-mail: jwarren@harrisburgacademy.org. Web site: www.harrisburgacademy.org.

HARROW SCHOOL

5 High Street
Harrow on the Hill
Middlesex HAI 3HT, United Kingdom
Head of School: Barnaby J. Lenon

General Information Boys' boarding college-preparatory school, affiliated with Church of England (Anglican). Grades 9–13. Founded: 1572. Setting: suburban. Nearest major city is London. Students are housed in individual rooms. 380-acre campus. 50 buildings on campus. Approved or accredited by Headmasters' Conference. Language of instruction: English. Total enrollment: 805. Upper school average class size: 10. Upper school faculty-student ratio: 1:9.

Upper School Student Profile Grade 9: 161 students (161 boys); Grade 10: 150 students (150 boys); Grade 11: 156 students (156 boys); Grade 12: 165 students (165 boys); Grade 13: 173 students (173 boys). 100% of students are boarding students. 15% are international students. International students from Australia, China, Germany, Malaysia, Republic of Korea, and United States; 32 other countries represented in student body. 60% of students are members of Church of England (Anglican).

Faculty School total: 95. In upper school: 85 men, 10 women; 90 have advanced degrees; 90 reside on campus.

Subjects Offered Advanced chemistry, advanced math, algebra, ancient history, Arabic, art, art history, Bible studies, biology, British literature, business studies, calculus, calculus-AP, career education internship, ceramics, character education, chemistry, chemistry-AP, computer science, creative writing, drama, ecology, economics, English, English literature, European history, French, geography, geometry, German, grammar, Greek, history, Italian, Japanese, Latin, mathematics, music, photography, physics, religion, Spanish, statistics, theater, trigonometry, zoology.

Graduation Requirements Completion of at least three advanced level (AP) courses.

Special Academic Programs Advanced Placement exam preparation in 10 subject areas; academic accommodation for the gifted, the musically talented, and the artistically talented; programs in general development for dyslexic students; ESL (15 students enrolled).

College Placement 141 students graduated in 2005; 138 went to college. Other: 2 went to work, 1 entered military service.

Student Life Upper grades have uniform requirement, honor system. Discipline rests primarily with faculty.

Summer Programs Enrichment, ESL, sports, rigorous outdoor training programs offered; session focuses on enrichment; held both on and off campus; held at Oxford, Rugby, Rodean, Stratford; accepts boys and girls; open to students from other schools. 300 students usually enrolled. 2006 schedule: July 20 to August 20. Application deadline: March 18.

Tuition and Aid 7-day tuition and room/board: £24,000. Tuition installment plan (individually arranged payment plans). Tuition reduction for siblings, bursaries, merit scholarship grants available. In 2005–06, 12% of upper-school students received aid.

Admissions Traditional secondary-level entrance grade is 12. For fall 2005, 100 students applied for upper-level admission, 10 were accepted, 10 enrolled. Cognitive Abilities Test and common entrance examinations required. Deadline for receipt of application materials: none. Application fee required: £100. On-campus interview required.

Athletics Interscholastic: alpine skiing, archery, basketball, crew, cricket, cross-country running, equestrian sports, fencing, Fives, golf, judo, marksmanship, martial arts, pistol, polo, racquetball, riflery, rowing, rugby, running, sailing, skiing (downhill), soccer, squash, swimming and diving, tennis, track and field, triathlon, volleyball, water polo; intramural: alpine skiing, archery, back packing, badminton, biathlon, canoeing/kayaking, climbing, cricket, croquet, cross-country running, drill team, fencing, field hockey, fishing, fly fishing, golf, hiking/backpacking, hockey, independent competitive sports, jogging, kayaking, life saving, marksmanship, martial arts, mountaineering, outdoor adventure, physical fitness, rock climbing, rugby, running, soccer, squash, strength & conditioning, swimming and diving, tennis, track and field, wall climbing, water polo, weight training. 2 PE instructors, 8 coaches, 2 trainers.

Computers Computers are regularly used in all academic classes. Computer network features include campus e-mail, on-campus library services, CD-ROMs, online commercial services, Internet access, file transfer, office computer access, DVD, wireless campus network.

Contact Miss Fiona Hogg, Admissions Secretary. 44-208-8728007. Fax: 44-208-8728012. E-mail: admissions@harrowschool.org.uk. Web site: www.harrowschool.org.uk.

HARVARD-WESTLAKE SCHOOL

3700 Coldwater Canyon
North Hollywood, California 91604
Head of School: Thomas C. Hudnut

General Information Coeducational day college-preparatory school, affiliated with Episcopal Church. Grades 7–12. Founded: 1989. Setting: urban. Nearest major city is Los Angeles. 26-acre campus. 12 buildings on campus. Approved or accredited by Western Association of Schools and Colleges. Member of National Association of Independent Schools. Endowment: $39.4 million. Total enrollment: 1,573. Upper school average class size: 16. Upper school faculty-student ratio: 1:8.

Upper School Student Profile Grade 10: 283 students (143 boys, 140 girls); Grade 11: 293 students (152 boys, 141 girls); Grade 12: 258 students (134 boys, 124 girls).

Faculty School total: 125. In upper school: 63 men, 56 women; 85 have advanced degrees.

Subjects Offered 3-dimensional art, advanced studio art-AP, algebra, American government-AP, American history, American literature, American literature-AP, anatomy, architecture, art, art history, art history-AP, Asian studies, astronomy, biology, biology-AP, calculus, calculus-AP, ceramics, chemistry, chemistry-AP,

Chinese, choreography, chorus, classics, community service, computer animation, computer programming, computer science, computer science-AP, creative writing, dance, drama, drawing, economics, economics-AP, electronics, English, English language and composition-AP, English literature, English literature-AP, environmental science, environmental science-AP, European history, expository writing, film, film studies, fine arts, French, French language-AP, French literature-AP, geography, geology, geometry, government and politics-AP, government/civics, grammar, health, human development, Japanese, jazz, journalism, Latin, Latin-AP, logic, macro/microeconomics-AP, Mandarin, mathematics, music, music history, music theory-AP, oceanography, orchestra, painting, photography, physical education, physics, physics-AP, physiology, political science, pre-calculus, psychology, Russian, science, senior project, Shakespeare, social studies, Spanish, Spanish language-AP, Spanish literature-AP, statistics, studio art-AP, technical theater, theater, trigonometry, U.S. history-AP, video, women's studies, world history, world literature, yearbook, zoology.

Graduation Requirements Arts and fine arts (art, music, dance, drama), English, foreign language, history, human development, mathematics, physical education (includes health), science. Community service is required.

Special Academic Programs Advanced Placement exam preparation in 19 subject areas; honors section; independent study; term-away projects; study at local college for college credit; study abroad; academic accommodation for the gifted, the musically talented, and the artistically talented.

College Placement 276 students graduated in 2005; all went to college, including Columbia College; New York University; Stanford University; University of Michigan; University of Pennsylvania; University of Southern California. Mean SAT verbal: 679, mean SAT math: 691. 90% scored over 600 on SAT verbal, 91% scored over 600 on SAT math.

Student Life Upper grades have specified standards of dress, student council, honor system. Discipline rests primarily with faculty.

Summer Programs Enrichment, sports, art/fine arts, rigorous outdoor training, computer instruction programs offered; session focuses on enrichment; held both on and off campus; held at Channel Islands, Catalina, Costa Rica, France, Japan, China, Russia; accepts boys and girls; open to students from other schools. 400 students usually enrolled. 2006 schedule: June 12 to August 18. Application deadline: none.

Tuition and Aid Day student tuition: $22,700. Tuition installment plan (monthly payment plans, semi-annual payment plan, tri-annual payment plan). Need-based scholarship grants, short-term loans (payable by end of year in which loan is made) available. In 2005–06, 14% of upper-school students received aid. Total amount of financial aid awarded in 2005–06: $3,900,000.

Admissions For fall 2005, 61 students applied for upper-level admission, 17 were accepted, 15 enrolled. ISEE required. Deadline for receipt of application materials: February 1. Application fee required: $125. On-campus interview required.

Athletics Interscholastic: baseball (boys), basketball (b,g), cross-country running (b,g), field hockey (g), flag football (b), football (b), golf (b,g), gymnastics (g), lacrosse (b), soccer (b,g), softball (g), swimming and diving (b,g), tennis (b,g), track and field (b,g), volleyball (b,g), water polo (b,g); coed interscholastic: diving, equestrian sports, fencing, martial arts; coed intramural: badminton. 6 PE instructors, 32 coaches, 2 trainers.

Computers Computers are regularly used in art, history, mathematics, music, science classes. Computer resources include on-campus library services, CD-ROMs, Internet access, music composition and editing, foreign language lab.

Contact Elizabeth Gregory, Director of Admission. 310-274-7281. Fax: 310-288-3212. E-mail: egregory@hw.com. Web site: www.harvardwestlake.com.

ANNOUNCEMENT FROM THE SCHOOL Harvard-Westlake, a coeducational school located in Los Angeles, California, is built on the traditions and high academic standards of Harvard School (founded in 1900) and Westlake School (founded in 1904). The curriculum and programs are designed for students who have the motivation and ability to pursue a rigorous college-preparatory course of study.

THE HARVEY SCHOOL

260 Jay Street
Katonah, New York 10536
Head of School: Mr. Barry W. Fenstermacher

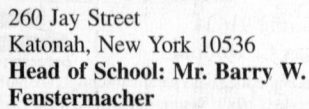
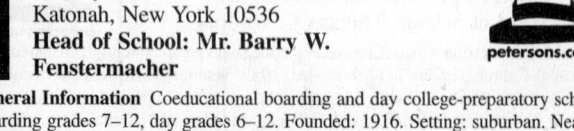

General Information Coeducational boarding and day college-preparatory school. Boarding grades 7–12, day grades 6–12. Founded: 1916. Setting: suburban. Nearest major city is New York. Students are housed in single-sex dormitories. 100-acre campus. 14 buildings on campus. Approved or accredited by New York State Association of Independent Schools and The Association of Boarding Schools. Member of National Association of Independent Schools. Endowment: $1 million. Total enrollment: 338. Upper school average class size: 12. Upper school faculty-student ratio: 1:7.

Upper School Student Profile Grade 9: 57 students (26 boys, 31 girls); Grade 10: 59 students (32 boys, 27 girls); Grade 11: 55 students (30 boys, 25 girls); Grade 12: 57 students (26 boys, 31 girls). 10% of students are boarding students. 85% are state residents. 3 states are represented in upper school student body.

Faculty School total: 62. In upper school: 19 men, 15 women; 23 have advanced degrees; 16 reside on campus.

Subjects Offered Algebra, American history, American literature, art, art history, biology, calculus, ceramics, chemistry, composition-AP, computer programming-AP, creative writing, drama, English, English literature, European history, expository writing, fine arts, French, general science, geology, geometry, government/civics, grammar, Greek, history, Japanese, Latin, logic, mathematics, music, photography, physics, religion, science, social science, social studies, Spanish, speech, theater, trigonometry, women's studies, world history, writing.

Graduation Requirements Arts and fine arts (art, music, dance, drama), English, foreign language, mathematics, science, social science, social studies (includes history).

Special Academic Programs Advanced Placement exam preparation in 10 subject areas; honors section; independent study.

College Placement 48 students graduated in 2005; all went to college, including American University; Bates College; Brown University; Carnegie Mellon University; University of Connecticut; University of Pennsylvania.

Student Life Upper grades have specified standards of dress, student council. Discipline rests primarily with faculty.

Tuition and Aid Day student tuition: $23,500; 5-day tuition and room/board: $30,000. Tuition installment plan (FACTS Tuition Payment Plan, individually arranged payment plans). Merit scholarship grants, need-based scholarship grants available. In 2005–06, 30% of upper-school students received aid; total upper-school merit-scholarship money awarded: $15,000. Total amount of financial aid awarded in 2005–06: $900,000.

Admissions Traditional secondary-level entrance grade is 9. For fall 2005, 250 students applied for upper-level admission, 100 were accepted, 87 enrolled. Deadline for receipt of application materials: none. Application fee required: $50. Interview required.

Athletics Interscholastic: baseball (boys), basketball (b,g), dance team (g), field hockey (g), football (b), ice hockey (b), lacrosse (b,g), rugby (b), soccer (b,g), softball (g); coed interscholastic: baseball, cross-country running, dance, figure skating, fitness, golf, lacrosse, skiing (downhill), soccer, tennis, yoga; coed intramural: aerobics, fitness walking, Frisbee, mountain biking. 1 trainer.

Computers Computers are regularly used in English, foreign language, history, mathematics, science classes. Computer resources include on-campus library services, CD-ROMs, online commercial services, Internet access.

Contact Ronald H. Romanowicz, Director of Enrollment. 914-232-3161 Ext. 138. Fax: 914-232-6034. E-mail: romanowicz@harveyschool.org. Web site: www.harveyschool.org.

See full description on page 822.

HATHAWAY BROWN SCHOOL

19600 North Park Boulevard
Shaker Heights, Ohio 44122

ANNOUNCEMENT FROM THE SCHOOL Hathaway Brown School is Ohio's oldest independent preparatory school for girls in grades K–12. Hathaway Brown School also offers a coeducational early childhood program for boys and girls from 2 to 5 years of age. For more information, contact the Hathaway Brown Office of Admission at 216-320-8767.

THE HAVERFORD SCHOOL

450 Lancaster Avenue
Haverford, Pennsylvania 19041
Head of School: Dr. Joseph T. Cox

General Information Boys' day college-preparatory and arts school. Grades PK–12. Founded: 1884. Setting: suburban. Nearest major city is Philadelphia. 32-acre campus. 7 buildings on campus. Approved or accredited by Middle States Association of Colleges and Schools, Pennsylvania Association of Private Academic Schools, and Pennsylvania Department of Education. Member of National Association of Independent Schools and Secondary School Admission Test Board. Endowment: $32 million. Total enrollment: 958. Upper school average class size: 15. Upper school faculty-student ratio: 1:8.

Upper School Student Profile Grade 9: 96 students (96 boys); Grade 10: 92 students (92 boys); Grade 11: 84 students (84 boys); Grade 12: 84 students (84 boys).

Faculty School total: 130. In upper school: 38 men, 9 women; 33 have advanced degrees.

Subjects Offered Algebra, American history, American literature, animal behavior, art, astronomy, biology, calculus, ceramics, chemistry, Chinese, Chinese studies, drama, ecology, economics, economics and history, English, English literature, European history, fine arts, French, geology, geometry, German, government/civics,

history, Latin, mathematics, music, photography, physical education, physics, physiology, science, social studies, Spanish, statistics, theater, trigonometry, world affairs, world history, world literature.

Graduation Requirements Arts and fine arts (art, music, dance, drama), English, foreign language, mathematics, physical education (includes health), science, social studies (includes history).

Special Academic Programs Advanced Placement exam preparation in 19 subject areas; honors section; independent study; term-away projects; academic accommodation for the gifted; remedial reading and/or remedial writing; remedial math.

College Placement 77 students graduated in 2005; all went to college, including Cornell University; Duke University; Georgetown University; Harvard University; Princeton University; University of Pennsylvania. Median SAT verbal: 650, median SAT math: 660. 65% scored over 600 on SAT verbal, 74% scored over 600 on SAT math.

Student Life Upper grades have specified standards of dress, student council, honor system. Discipline rests equally with students and faculty.

Tuition and Aid Day student tuition: $21,800. Tuition installment plan (Insured Tuition Payment Plan, monthly payment plans, individually arranged payment plans). Need-based scholarship grants available. In 2005–06, 28% of upper-school students received aid. Total amount of financial aid awarded in 2005–06: $1,087,000.

Admissions Traditional secondary-level entrance grade is 9. For fall 2005, 152 students applied for upper-level admission, 73 were accepted, 41 enrolled. ISEE or SSAT or WISC III required. Deadline for receipt of application materials: none. Application fee required: $40. Interview required.

Athletics Interscholastic: aquatics, baseball, basketball, crew, cross-country running, football, golf, hockey, ice hockey, indoor track, lacrosse, soccer, squash, swimming and diving, tennis, track and field, water polo, winter (indoor) track, wrestling; intramural: fitness, physical fitness, physical training, soccer, strength & conditioning, weight training. 6 PE instructors, 2 coaches, 2 trainers.

Computers Computers are regularly used in art, English, history, mathematics, music, science classes. Computer network features include campus e-mail, on-campus library services, CD-ROMs, online commercial services, Internet access.

Contact Mr. Kevin P. Seits, Director of Admissions. 610-642-3020 Ext. 1457. Fax: 610-642-8724. E-mail: kseits@haverford.org. Web site: www.haverford.org.

ANNOUNCEMENT FROM THE SCHOOL The Haverford School aspires to be the premier independent day school for boys, an institution whose graduates are recognized for their character and intellect. The junior kindergarten through grade 12 program provides a superior liberal arts education in a challenging and supportive environment that fosters integrity, leadership, friendship, school spirit, and a commitment to community. The School strives to prepare each student for life by emphasizing the joy of learning, the importance of self-knowledge, and by developing his full intellectual, moral, social, artistic, athletic, and creative potential. The School understands boys' development and provides the support and challenge for 957 boys. The exclusively college-preparatory curriculum features Advanced Placement in English, American and European history, biology, chemistry, physics, math, French, Latin, Spanish, German, music, fine arts, and economics. The state-of-the-art, campus-wide network integrates technology into all aspects of the curriculum. Extracurricular activities include student council, newspaper, yearbook, chorus, community service, and a large variety of clubs. Sixteen varsity sports are offered in upper school, and the School competes in the Inter-Academic League, the oldest such league in the country. From 1999–2005, the colleges matriculating the greatest number of Haverford alumni were Columbia, Cornell, Georgetown, Harvard, Princeton, Trinity, the University of Pennsylvania, and the University of Virginia. SAT averages were 640 verbal and 650 math. In the past 5 years, 35% of the students were recognized as AP Scholars. The School's recently renovated suburban campus, including a state-of-the-art athletic facility, occupies 32 acres. It includes 71 classrooms, a 650-seat auditorium, a 30,000-volume library, 4 computer labs, 10 science labs, and ample art and music studio space. The endowment is more than $32 million. For more information, visit the School's Web site at http://www.haverford.org.

HAVERGAL COLLEGE

1451 Avenue Road
Toronto, Ontario M5N 2H9, Canada
Head of School: Dr. Susan Ditchburn

petersons.com

General Information Girls' boarding and day college-preparatory school, affiliated with Church of England (Anglican). Boarding grades 9–12, day grades JK–12. Founded: 1894. Setting: urban. Students are housed in single-sex dormitories. 22-acre campus. 4 buildings on campus. Approved or accredited by Canadian Association of Independent Schools, Canadian Educational Standards Institute, Conference of Independent Schools of Ontario, The Association of Boarding Schools, and Ontario Department of Education. Affiliate member of National Association of Independent Schools; member of Secondary School Admission Test Board. Language of instruction: English. Endowment: CAN$11 million. Total enrollment: 921. Upper school average class size: 20. Upper school faculty-student ratio: 1:9.

Upper School Student Profile Grade 9: 118 students (118 girls); Grade 10: 119 students (119 girls); Grade 11: 121 students (121 girls); Grade 12: 127 students (127 girls). 12% of students are boarding students. 93% are province residents. 3 provinces are represented in upper school student body. 7% are international students. International students from Cayman Islands, China, Jamaica, Mexico, Republic of Korea, and Saudi Arabia; 6 other countries represented in student body. 20% of students are members of Church of England (Anglican).

Faculty School total: 104. In upper school: 13 men, 62 women; 32 have advanced degrees; 1 resides on campus.

Subjects Offered Algebra, American history, art, art history, biology, biology-AP, calculus, calculus-AP, career planning, chemistry, civics, computer science, creative writing, data processing, drama, economics, English, English literature, environmental geography, European history, French, French literature-AP, general science, geography, geometry, German, health, history, journalism, Latin, law, mathematics, media studies, music, philosophy, physical education, physics, politics, religious studies, social science, social studies, Spanish, Spanish-AP, trigonometry, writing.

Graduation Requirements Arts and fine arts (art, music, dance, drama), business skills (includes word processing), English, foreign language, mathematics, physical education (includes health), science, social science, technology, 40 hours of community service, provincial literacy test.

Special Academic Programs Advanced Placement exam preparation in 4 subject areas; honors section; accelerated programs; independent study; term-away projects; domestic exchange program (with The Brearley School); study abroad.

College Placement 117 students graduated in 2005; all went to college, including Dalhousie University; McGill University; McMaster University; Queen's University at Kingston; The University of Western Ontario; University of Toronto.

Student Life Upper grades have uniform requirement, student council. Discipline rests primarily with faculty. Attendance at religious services is required.

Tuition and Aid Day student tuition: CAN$18,585; 7-day tuition and room/board: CAN$37,170. Tuition installment plan (monthly payment plans, individually arranged payment plans). Bursaries, merit scholarship grants available. In 2005–06, 5% of upper-school students received aid; total upper-school merit-scholarship money awarded: CAN$124,340.

Admissions Traditional secondary-level entrance grade is 9. For fall 2005, 160 students applied for upper-level admission, 86 were accepted, 55 enrolled. SSAT required. Deadline for receipt of application materials: December 16. Application fee required: CAN$150. Interview required.

Athletics Interscholastic: alpine skiing, aquatics, badminton, basketball, crew, cross-country running, field hockey, ice hockey, indoor track & field, rowing, rugby, running, skiing (downhill), soccer, softball, swimming and diving, tennis, track and field, ultimate Frisbee, volleyball; intramural: aerobics, aerobics/dance, aerobics/nautilus, aquatics, badminton, ball hockey, basketball, bicycling, broomball, climbing, cooperative games, cricket, cross-country running, curling, dance, field hockey, fitness, fitness walking, flag football, floor hockey, football, Frisbee, golf, hiking/backpacking, ice skating, in-line skating, independent competitive sports, indoor soccer, indoor track & field, jump rope, lacrosse, life saving, martial arts, modern dance, mountain biking, outdoor activities, outdoor adventure, outdoor education, outdoor recreation, physical fitness, physical training, racquetball, rock climbing, rowing, rugby, running, self defense, skiing (downhill), snowboarding, snowshoeing, soccer, softball, speedball, squash, strength & conditioning, swimming and diving, tennis, touch football, track and field, ultimate Frisbee, volleyball, walking, wall climbing, water polo, weight lifting, whiffle ball, yoga. 6 PE instructors.

Computers Computers are regularly used in English, foreign language, mathematics, science classes. Computer network features include campus e-mail, on-campus library services, CD-ROMs, Internet access, DVD, wireless campus network.

Contact Pamela Newson, Assistant—Upper School Admission. 416-482-4724. Fax: 416-483-9644. E-mail: pam_newson@havergal.on.ca. Web site: www.havergal.on.ca.

ANNOUNCEMENT FROM THE SCHOOL Situated on a beautiful 22-acre campus in Toronto, Havergal College is a leading independent girls' school offering outstanding academic and cocurricular programs from junior kindergarten to senior year. Founded on the values of excellence, leadership, and diversity, Havergal prepares its graduates to take their place as leaders in their chosen pursuits.

HAWAIIAN MISSION ACADEMY

1438 Pensacola Street
Honolulu, Hawaii 96822
Head of School: Mr. Josué Rosado

General Information Coeducational boarding and day college-preparatory, general academic, arts, business, religious studies, bilingual studies, and technology school, affiliated with Seventh-day Adventist Church. Grades 9–12. Founded: 1920. Setting: urban. Students are housed in single-sex by floor dormitories. 4-acre campus. 4 buildings on campus. Approved or accredited by Western Association of Schools and Colleges and Hawaii Department of Education. Total enrollment: 128. Upper school average class size: 25. Upper school faculty-student ratio: 1:12.

Upper School Student Profile Grade 9: 42 students (17 boys, 25 girls); Grade 10: 33 students (15 boys, 18 girls); Grade 11: 26 students (12 boys, 14 girls); Grade 12:

27 students (17 boys, 10 girls). 20% of students are boarding students. 46% are state residents. 2 states are represented in upper school student body. 50% are international students. International students from Hong Kong, Japan, Republic of Korea, and Taiwan. 90% of students are Seventh-day Adventists.

Faculty School total: 13. In upper school: 8 men, 5 women; 8 have advanced degrees; 2 reside on campus.

Subjects Offered Algebra, art, basketball, Bible, biology, business, business education, business skills, calculus, chemistry, choir, Christianity, community service, computer keyboarding, computer literacy, computer science, conceptual physics, concert choir, desktop publishing, digital art, economics, electives, English, English literature, ESL, family and consumer science, family life, general science, geometry, grammar, Hawaiian history, health, independent living, interactive media, Japanese, Japanese as Second Language, journalism, lab science, library, Microsoft, physical education, pre-algebra, pre-calculus, Spanish, student government, student publications, U.S. government, U.S. history, video film production, weight training, woodworking, work experience, work-study, world history, yearbook.

Graduation Requirements Algebra, arts and fine arts (art, music, dance, drama), biology, chemistry, computer keyboarding, computer literacy, English, foreign language, geometry, Hawaiian history, physical education (includes health), physics, practical arts, religion (includes Bible studies and theology), social studies (includes history), U.S. government, work experience, 25 hours of community service per year, 100 hours of work experience throughout the 4 years combined.

Special Academic Programs ESL (11 students enrolled).

College Placement 41 students graduated in 2005; all went to college, including Hawai'i Pacific University; Kapiolani Community College; La Sierra University; Pacific Union College; University of Hawaii at Hilo. Mean SAT verbal: 505, mean SAT math: 535.

Student Life Upper grades have specified standards of dress, student council. Discipline rests primarily with faculty.

Tuition and Aid Day student tuition: $10,000; 7-day tuition and room/board: $18,900. Tuition installment plan (Insured Tuition Payment Plan, monthly payment plans, individually arranged payment plans). Tuition reduction for siblings, need-based scholarship grants, paying campus jobs available. In 2005–06, 23% of upper-school students received aid.

Admissions Traditional secondary-level entrance grade is 9. SSAT required. Deadline for receipt of application materials: none. Application fee required: $25. Interview recommended.

Athletics Interscholastic: basketball (boys, girls), volleyball (b,g). 1 PE instructor, 1 coach.

Computers Computers are regularly used in desktop publishing, economics, graphic arts, journalism, keyboarding, media production, newspaper, publications, video film production, word processing, yearbook classes. Computer network features include on-campus library services, CD-ROMs, Internet access.

Contact Mrs. Nenny Safotu, Registrar. 808-536-2207 Ext. 202. Fax: 808-524-3294. E-mail: registrar@hma4u.org. Web site: www.hma4u.org.

HAWAII BAPTIST ACADEMY

2429 Pali Highway
Honolulu, Hawaii 96817
Head of School: Richard Bento

General Information Coeducational day college-preparatory and Christian education school, affiliated with Baptist Church. Grades K–12. Founded: 1949. Setting: urban. 13-acre campus. 6 buildings on campus. Approved or accredited by Western Association of Schools and Colleges. Member of National Association of Independent Schools and Secondary School Admission Test Board. Endowment: $2 million. Total enrollment: 1,049. Upper school average class size: 20. Upper school faculty-student ratio: 1:12.

Upper School Student Profile Grade 7: 112 students (67 boys, 45 girls); Grade 8: 110 students (54 boys, 56 girls); Grade 9: 113 students (60 boys, 53 girls); Grade 10: 113 students (66 boys, 47 girls); Grade 11: 108 students (55 boys, 53 girls); Grade 12: 96 students (44 boys, 52 girls). 10% of students are Baptist.

Faculty School total: 64. In upper school: 20 men, 33 women; 27 have advanced degrees.

Subjects Offered Advanced Placement courses, algebra, American history, American history-AP, American literature, analytic geometry, anatomy and physiology, art, Asian history, Basic programming, Bible studies, biology, biology-AP, British literature, calculus-AP, ceramics, chemistry, chemistry-AP, Chinese, Christian education, Christian ethics, Christian studies, communication skills, comparative religion, computer applications, conceptual physics, concert band, creation science, creative writing, drama, drama performance, drawing, earth science, East European studies, economics, English, English language and composition-AP, English literature, English literature-AP, European history, European history-AP, fine arts, French, geography, geometry, Hawaiian history, Japanese, journalism, marine biology, mathematics, mechanical drawing, music, music theory-AP, photography, physical education, physics, political science, psychology, religion, science, social studies, sociology, Spanish, speech, statistics, statistics-AP, trigonometry, world history, world literature, writing.

Graduation Requirements Algebra, arts and fine arts (art, music, dance, drama), Asian history, Bible studies, biology, communication skills, computer applications,

conceptual physics, economics, English, foreign language, Hawaiian history, mathematics, physical education (includes health), political science, science, social studies (includes history).

Special Academic Programs Advanced Placement exam preparation in 9 subject areas; independent study.

College Placement 101 students graduated in 2005; all went to college, including Creighton University; University of Hawaii at Manoa; University of Nevada, Las Vegas; University of the Pacific; University of Washington. Mean SAT verbal: 561, mean SAT math: 602, mean composite ACT: 23. 24% scored over 600 on SAT verbal, 59% scored over 600 on SAT math, 25% scored over 26 on composite ACT.

Student Life Upper grades have specified standards of dress, student council. Discipline rests primarily with faculty. Attendance at religious services is required.

Summer Programs Remediation, enrichment, art/fine arts, computer instruction programs offered; session focuses on helping students develop specific skills, enrichment and recreation; held both on and off campus; held at various recreation sites including the beach, bowling alley and park, ice rink, water park, movie theater, golf park, Ultrazone, Windward Sea Yacht Charters; accepts boys and girls; open to students from other schools. 258 students usually enrolled. 2006 schedule: June 19 to July 14. Application deadline: May 12.

Tuition and Aid Day student tuition: $9150. Guaranteed tuition plan. Tuition installment plan (Insured Tuition Payment Plan, monthly payment plans). Need-based scholarship grants available. In 2005–06, 6% of upper-school students received aid. Total amount of financial aid awarded in 2005–06: $30,315.

Admissions Traditional secondary-level entrance grade is 7. For fall 2005, 80 students applied for upper-level admission, 30 were accepted, 13 enrolled. Achievement tests and SSAT required. Deadline for receipt of application materials: February 10. Application fee required: $50. On-campus interview required.

Athletics Interscholastic: aquatics (boys, girls), baseball (b), basketball (b,g), bowling (b,g), canoeing/kayaking (b,g), cheering (g), cross-country running (b,g), diving (b,g), football (b), golf (b,g), gymnastics (g), judo (b,g), kayaking (b,g), riflery (b,g), soccer (b,g), softball (g), swimming and diving (b,g), tennis (b,g), track and field (b,g), volleyball (b,g), water polo (b,g), wrestling (b,g); intramural: basketball (b,g), volleyball (b,g); coed interscholastic: cheering, golf, sailing; coed intramural: volleyball, weight lifting. 3 PE instructors, 30 coaches, 1 trainer.

Computers Computers are regularly used in keyboarding, newspaper, programming, word processing, yearbook classes. Computer resources include CD-ROMs, Internet access.

Contact Katherine Lee, Director of Admissions. 808-595-7585. Fax: 808-595-6354. E-mail: klee@hba.net. Web site: www.hba.net.

HAWAI'I PREPARATORY ACADEMY

65-1692 Kohala Mountain Road
Kamuela, Hawaii 96743-8476
Head of School: Dr. Olaf Jorgenson

General Information Coeducational boarding and day college-preparatory, arts, technology, and marine science school. Boarding grades 6–12, day grades K–12. Founded: 1949. Setting: small town. Nearest major city is Kona. Students are housed in single-sex by floor dormitories and single-sex dormitories. 120-acre campus. 22 buildings on campus. Approved or accredited by The Association of Boarding Schools and Western Association of Schools and Colleges. Member of National Association of Independent Schools and Secondary School Admission Test Board. Endowment: $17 million. Total enrollment: 613. Upper school average class size: 15. Upper school faculty-student ratio: 1:12.

Upper School Student Profile Grade 9: 86 students (39 boys, 47 girls); Grade 10: 88 students (42 boys, 46 girls); Grade 11: 95 students (51 boys, 44 girls); Grade 12: 93 students (44 boys, 49 girls). 49% of students are boarding students. 53% are state residents. 18 states are represented in upper school student body. 21% are international students. International students from Democratic People's Republic of Korea, Germany, Japan, South Africa, Taiwan, and Thailand; 11 other countries represented in student body.

Faculty School total: 65. In upper school: 20 men, 21 women; 27 have advanced degrees; 17 reside on campus.

Subjects Offered Algebra, American literature, American literature-AP, art history-AP, astronomy, biology, biology-AP, calculus, calculus-AP, Cantonese, ceramics, chamber groups, chemistry, chemistry-AP, choir, civics, composition-AP, computer literacy, computer technologies, crafts, creative writing, drawing, economics, economics-AP, English, environmental science-AP, ESL, European history-AP, expository writing, French, French-AP, geology, geometry, Hawaiian history, honors world history, humanities, instrumental music, Japanese, Latin, literary genres, marine biology, mathematics, music appreciation, painting, photography, physical education, physical science, physics, physics-AP, pre-calculus, psychology, psychology-AP, reading, Shakespeare, Spanish, Spanish-AP, sports science, statistics-AP, theater production, trigonometry, U.S. history, U.S. history-AP, video film production, visual arts, vocal ensemble, world history, world literature.

Graduation Requirements Arts and fine arts (art, music, dance, drama), computer science, English, humanities, mathematics, modern languages, physical education (includes health), science, social studies (includes history).

Special Academic Programs Advanced Placement exam preparation in 16 subject areas; honors section; independent study; academic accommodation for the gifted, the

musically talented, and the artistically talented; remedial reading and/or remedial writing; remedial math; ESL (20 students enrolled).

College Placement 78 students graduated in 2005; 76 went to college, including California Polytechnic State University, San Luis Obispo; Santa Clara University; University of Hawaii at Manoa; University of Oregon; University of Puget Sound; University of Washington. Other: 1 entered military service, 1 had other specific plans.

Student Life Upper grades have specified standards of dress, student council, honor system. Discipline rests equally with students and faculty.

Summer Programs Enrichment, ESL, sports, art/fine arts, computer instruction programs offered; session focuses on academic enrichment; held on campus; accepts boys and girls; open to students from other schools. 100 students usually enrolled. 2006 schedule: June 26 to July 20. Application deadline: April 15.

Tuition and Aid Day student tuition: $15,000; 7-day tuition and room/board: $30,000. Guaranteed tuition plan. Tuition installment plan (Key Tuition Payment Plan, monthly payment plans, pre-payment plan, 2-payment plan). Need-based scholarship grants, Hawaii residential boarding grants available. In 2005–06, 22% of upper-school students received aid. Total amount of financial aid awarded in 2005–06: $995,000.

Admissions Traditional secondary-level entrance grade is 9. For fall 2005, 137 students applied for upper-level admission, 97 were accepted, 73 enrolled. Any standardized test, ISEE or SSAT required. Deadline for receipt of application materials: February 3. Application fee required: $75. Interview required.

Athletics Interscholastic: baseball (boys), basketball (b,g), cross-country running (b,g), diving (b,g), golf (b,g), soccer (b,g), swimming and diving (b,g), tennis (b,g), track and field (b,g), volleyball (b,g), water polo (g), wrestling (b); coed interscholastic: dressage, equestrian sports, football, horseback riding; coed intramural: aerobics, aerobics/dance, aquatics, basketball, combined training, cooperative games, dance, dressage, equestrian sports, Frisbee, horseback riding, independent competitive sports, modern dance, paddling, physical fitness, scuba diving, soccer, strength & conditioning, surfing, swimming and diving, tennis, ultimate Frisbee, volleyball, weight lifting, yoga. 1 trainer.

Computers Computers are regularly used in computer applications, economics, graphic arts, science, video film production, yearbook classes. Computer network features include campus e-mail, on-campus library services, CD-ROMs, online commercial services, Internet access, file transfer, office computer access, DVD, wireless campus network.

Contact Mr. Brian K. Chatterley, Esq., Director of Advancement. 808-881-4074. Fax: 808-881-4003. E-mail: bchatterley@hpa.edu. Web site: www.hpa.edu/.

ANNOUNCEMENT FROM THE SCHOOL The Hawai'i Preparatory Academy Middle School boarding program is designed for students seeking a challenging learning environment with equally challenging behavioral expectations. The program is housed in hotel-style facilities where residential faculty members nurture close-knit family relationships. Weekend and after-school activities allow students to take advantage of Hawai'i's beautiful surroundings and rich culture.

See full description on page 824.

HAWKEN SCHOOL

12465 County Line Road
PO Box 8002
Gates Mills, Ohio 44040-8002
Head of School: James S. Berkman

General Information Coeducational day college-preparatory, arts, and business school. Grades PS–12. Founded: 1915. Setting: suburban. Nearest major city is Cleveland. 325-acre campus. 5 buildings on campus. Approved or accredited by Independent Schools Association of the Central States and Ohio Department of Education. Member of National Association of Independent Schools. Endowment: $43.7 million. Total enrollment: 954. Upper school average class size: 15. Upper school faculty-student ratio: 1:9.

Upper School Student Profile Grade 9: 104 students (55 boys, 49 girls); Grade 10: 117 students (57 boys, 60 girls); Grade 11: 105 students (60 boys, 45 girls); Grade 12: 115 students (61 boys, 54 girls).

Faculty School total: 96. In upper school: 41 men, 38 women; 64 have advanced degrees.

Subjects Offered 20th century world history, accounting, acting, advanced chemistry, advanced math, Advanced Placement courses, advanced studio art-AP, African-American literature, algebra, American Civil War, American history, American history-AP, American literature, animal science, art, art appreciation, art history, band, Bible as literature, biology, botany, business, business mathematics, calculus, calculus-AP, ceramics, chemistry, chemistry-AP, choir, choral music, chorus, Civil War, classical Greek literature, community service, computer applications, computer math, computer programming, computer science, computer science-AP, computer skills, concert band, creative dance, creative writing, dance, dance performance, drama, drawing, driver education, ecology, economics, economics and history, electronic music, English, English literature, English-AP, environmental science-AP, ethics, European history, field ecology, film, film studies, fine arts, first aid, French, French studies, French-AP, geography, geometry, government/civics, grammar,

graphic design, health, history, history of jazz, history of rock and roll, Holocaust and other genocides, humanities, improvisation, Latin, Latin-AP, mathematics, mathematics-AP, music, music theory, outdoor education, painting, performing arts, philosophy, photography, physical education, physics, physics-AP, physiology, poetry, probability and statistics, qualitative analysis, science, science research, sculpture, senior project, social science, social studies, Spanish, Spanish literature-AP, speech, statistics-AP, strings, studio art—AP, swimming, theater, theater arts, theater design and production, theater production, trigonometry, U.S. history, U.S. history-AP, world history, world literature, World War I, World War II, writing.

Graduation Requirements Arts and fine arts (art, music, dance, drama), computer science, English, foreign language, history, mathematics, physical education (includes health), science. Community service is required.

Special Academic Programs Advanced Placement exam preparation in 15 subject areas; honors section; accelerated programs; independent study; term-away projects; study abroad; academic accommodation for the gifted and the musically talented.

College Placement 107 students graduated in 2005; all went to college, including Case Western Reserve University; Ohio University; The Ohio State University; University of Rochester. Median SAT verbal: 650, median SAT math: 660, median composite ACT: 27. 74% scored over 600 on SAT verbal, 75% scored over 600 on SAT math, 65% scored over 26 on composite ACT.

Student Life Upper grades have specified standards of dress, student council. Discipline rests primarily with faculty.

Summer Programs Remediation, enrichment, advancement, computer instruction programs offered; session focuses on credit, review, preview and enrichment in English, math, computer studies and health; held on campus; accepts boys and girls; open to students from other schools. 100 students usually enrolled. 2006 schedule: June 19 to July 28. Application deadline: none.

Tuition and Aid Day student tuition: $17,640–$18,955. Tuition installment plan (Key Tuition Payment Plan, individually arranged payment plans, installment payment plan (60 percent by 8/15 and 40 percent by 1/15)). Need-based scholarship grants, need-based loans available. In 2005–06, 23% of upper-school students received aid. Total amount of financial aid awarded in 2005–06: $1,303,700.

Admissions Traditional secondary-level entrance grade is 9. For fall 2005, 256 students applied for upper-level admission, 119 were accepted, 54 enrolled. ISEE required. Deadline for receipt of application materials: March 1. Application fee required: $25. On-campus interview required.

Athletics Interscholastic: baseball (boys), basketball (b,g), cross-country running (b,g), diving (b,g), field hockey (g), football (b), golf (b,g), lacrosse (b,g), soccer (b,g), softball (g), swimming and diving (b,g), tennis (b,g), track and field (b,g); intramural: basketball (b); coed intramural: dance, drill team, outdoor skills. 4 PE instructors, 24 coaches, 2 trainers.

Computers Computers are regularly used in all classes. Computer network features include campus e-mail, on-campus library services, CD-ROMs, Internet access, file transfer, office computer access.

Contact Kelly M. DeShane, Director of Admission and Financial Assistance. 440-423-2955. Fax: 440-423-2973. E-mail: kdesh@hawken.edu. Web site: www.hawken.edu/.

HAYDEN HIGH SCHOOL

401 South West Gage
Topeka, Kansas 66606
Head of School: Mr. Richard L. Strecker

General Information Coeducational day college-preparatory, general academic, arts, business, religious studies, bilingual studies, and technology school, affiliated with Roman Catholic Church. Grades 9–12. Founded: 1911. Setting: suburban. 100-acre campus. 6 buildings on campus. Approved or accredited by North Central Association of Colleges and Schools and Kansas Department of Education. Endowment: $2 million. Total enrollment: 485. Upper school average class size: 18. Upper school faculty-student ratio: 1:15.

Upper School Student Profile Grade 9: 138 students (68 boys, 70 girls); Grade 10: 132 students (72 boys, 60 girls); Grade 11: 105 students (50 boys, 55 girls); Grade 12: 110 students (56 boys, 54 girls). 95% of students are Roman Catholic.

Faculty School total: 42. In upper school: 20 men, 18 women; 26 have advanced degrees.

Subjects Offered 20th century history, 20th century physics, 20th century world history, 3-dimensional art, 3-dimensional design, accounting, ACT preparation, acting, advanced chemistry, advanced computer applications, advanced math, algebra, alternative physical education, American Civil War, American democracy, American government-AP, American history-AP, American legal systems, American literature, analysis, analytic geometry, anatomy and physiology, applied arts, applied music, art, art appreciation, Basic programming, Bible, biology, biology-AP, bookkeeping, British literature, British literature (honors), broadcast journalism, business applications, business law, business mathematics, calculus, calculus-AP, campus ministry, career and personal planning, Catholic belief and practice, chemistry, chemistry-AP, child development, choir, choral music, choreography, Christian and Hebrew scripture, Christian doctrine, Christian ethics, Christianity, civics, classical language, comparative religion, competitive science projects, composition, computer applications, computer education, computer graphics, computer keyboarding, computer programming, computer skills, conceptual physics, concert band, constitutional

history of U.S., creative writing, criminal justice, current events, dance, dance performance, death and loss, desktop publishing, digital photography, drama, drama performance, earth and space science, economics, English, English literature, English literature-AP, English-AP, fine arts, forensics, French, geometry, German, government, government-AP, health education, historiography, history, history of the Catholic Church, honors English, honors geometry, jazz band, keyboarding/computer, Latin, moral reasoning, moral theology, music, music performance, photography, physical education, physics, physics-AP, pre-algebra, pre-calculus, probability and statistics, psychology, reading, religion, science fiction, social justice, sociology, Spanish, speech and debate, studio art, theater, theology, trigonometry, U.S. government, U.S. history, vocal music.

Special Academic Programs Advanced Placement exam preparation in 6 subject areas; honors section; independent study; study at local college for college credit; study abroad; academic accommodation for the gifted and the musically talented; remedial reading and/or remedial writing; remedial math; special instructional classes for students with LD, ADD, dyslexia, emotional and behavioral problems.

College Placement 115 students graduated in 2005; 110 went to college, including Kansas State University; University of Kansas; Washburn University. Other: 4 went to work, 1 entered military service. Median composite ACT: 24. 62% scored over 26 on composite ACT.

Student Life Upper grades have uniform requirement, student council, honor system. Discipline rests primarily with faculty. Attendance at religious services is required.

Summer Programs Remediation, enrichment, advancement, sports, computer instruction programs offered; session focuses on advancement; held on campus; accepts boys and girls; not open to students from other schools. 20 students usually enrolled. 2006 schedule: June to July.

Tuition and Aid Day student tuition: $3850. Tuition installment plan (FACTS Tuition Payment Plan, monthly payment plans). Merit scholarship grants, need-based scholarship grants, paying campus jobs available. In 2005–06, 30% of upper-school students received aid; total upper-school merit-scholarship money awarded: $15,000. Total amount of financial aid awarded in 2005–06: $55,000.

Admissions Traditional secondary-level entrance grade is 9. For fall 2005, 150 students applied for upper-level admission, 148 were accepted, 138 enrolled. ACT, any standardized test or Explore required. Deadline for receipt of application materials: none. No application fee required. Interview recommended.

Athletics Interscholastic: aerobics/dance (girls), baseball (b), basketball (b,g), cheering (b,g), cross-country running (b,g), dance team (g), diving (b,g), drill team (g), football (b), golf (b,g), soccer (b,g), softball (g), strength & conditioning (b,g), swimming and diving (b,g), tennis (b,g), track and field (b,g), volleyball (g), weight training (b,g), wrestling (b); coed interscholastic: cheering. 3 PE instructors, 12 coaches, 2 trainers.

Computers Computers are regularly used in all classes. Computer network features include campus e-mail, on-campus library services, CD-ROMs, online commercial services, Internet access, file transfer, DVD.

Contact Mr. Richard Strecker, President. 785-272-5210 Ext. 19. Fax: 785-272-2975. E-mail: streckerr@haydenhigh.org. Web site: www.haydenhigh.org.

HEAD-ROYCE SCHOOL

4315 Lincoln Avenue
Oakland, California 94602
Head of School: Paul Chapman

petersons.com

General Information Coeducational day college-preparatory, arts, and technology school. Grades K–12. Founded: 1887. Setting: urban. 14-acre campus. 7 buildings on campus. Approved or accredited by California Association of Independent Schools, Western Association of Schools and Colleges, and California Department of Education. Member of National Association of Independent Schools. Endowment: $10 million. Total enrollment: 750. Upper school average class size: 15. Upper school faculty-student ratio: 1:9.

Upper School Student Profile Grade 9: 84 students (37 boys, 47 girls); Grade 10: 88 students (39 boys, 49 girls); Grade 11: 76 students (37 boys, 39 girls); Grade 12: 71 students (38 boys, 33 girls).

Faculty School total: 95. In upper school: 24 men, 19 women; 29 have advanced degrees.

Subjects Offered Algebra, American history, American literature, art, art history, astronomy, biology, calculus, ceramics, chemistry, community service, computer programming, computer science, creative writing, debate, drama, ecology, English, English literature, European history, expository writing, fine arts, French, geometry, graphic arts, health, history, journalism, Latin, marine biology, mathematics, music, neurobiology, photography, physical education, physics, psychology, science, social studies, Spanish, theater, trigonometry, typing, video, world history, world literature, writing.

Graduation Requirements Art history, arts and fine arts (art, music, dance, drama), computer science, English, foreign language, mathematics, physical education (includes health), science, social studies (includes history), 40 hours of community service.

Special Academic Programs Advanced Placement exam preparation in 19 subject areas; honors section; independent study; term-away projects; study at local college for college credit; study abroad; academic accommodation for the gifted, the musically talented, and the artistically talented.

College Placement 77 students graduated in 2005; all went to college, including New York University; University of California, Los Angeles; University of California, Santa Barbara; University of California, Santa Cruz; Wesleyan University; Yale University. Mean SAT verbal: 673, mean SAT math: 678.

Student Life Upper grades have specified standards of dress, student council, honor system. Discipline rests primarily with faculty.

Summer Programs Remediation, enrichment, advancement programs offered; session focuses on sports and enrichment; held on campus; accepts boys and girls; open to students from other schools. 600 students usually enrolled. 2006 schedule: June 19 to July 28. Application deadline: February.

Tuition and Aid Day student tuition: $22,990. Tuition installment plan (Academic Management Services Plan). Need-based scholarship grants, paying campus jobs, tuition remission for children of faculty and staff available. In 2005–06, 21% of upper-school students received aid. Total amount of financial aid awarded in 2005–06: $889,920.

Admissions Traditional secondary-level entrance grade is 9. For fall 2005, 189 students applied for upper-level admission, 82 were accepted, 30 enrolled. ISEE required. Deadline for receipt of application materials: January 10. Application fee required: $75. On-campus interview required.

Athletics Interscholastic: baseball (boys), basketball (b,g), cross-country running (b,g), dance squad (g), golf (b,g), lacrosse (b), modern dance (g), outdoor education (b,g), physical fitness (b,g), soccer (b,g), softball (g), strength & conditioning (b,g), swimming and diving (b,g), tennis (b,g), volleyball (b,g), weight lifting (b,g), weight training (b,g); coed interscholastic: cross-country running, golf, outdoor education, physical fitness, strength & conditioning, swimming and diving; coed intramural: bicycling, dance, ultimate Frisbee. 6 PE instructors, 39 coaches.

Computers Computers are regularly used in English, graphics, mathematics, science, yearbook classes. Computer network features include campus e-mail, on-campus library services, CD-ROMs, online commercial services, Internet access, DVD, wireless campus network.

Contact Catherine Epstein, Director of Admissions. 510-531-1300. Fax: 510-530-8329. E-mail: cepstein@headroyce.org. Web site: www.headroyce.org.

ANNOUNCEMENT FROM THE SCHOOL Head-Royce offers a challenging program in the liberal arts and sciences. Students also participate in fine arts and physical education classes. A variety of student-led clubs and twenty-two athletic teams in ten sports enhance student life. Electives, senior projects, community service, and many Advanced Placement (AP) classes prepare students for outstanding colleges and universities.

HEBREW ACADEMY-THE FIVE TOWNS

635 Central Avenue
Cedarhurst, New York 11516
Head of School: Mr. Stanley Blumenstein

General Information Coeducational day college-preparatory, arts, business, and religious studies school, affiliated with Jewish faith. Grades 9–12. Founded: 1978. Setting: suburban. Nearest major city is New York. 1 building on campus. Approved or accredited by Commission on Secondary Schools, Middle States Association of Colleges and Schools, The College Board, and New York Department of Education. Languages of instruction: English and Hebrew. Total enrollment: 500. Upper school average class size: 20.

Upper School Student Profile 100% of students are Jewish.

Faculty School total: 80.

Subjects Offered Advanced Placement courses, arts, English, fine arts, foreign language, Jewish studies, Judaic studies, mathematics, physical education, religion, science, social science, social studies.

Graduation Requirements Arts and fine arts (art, music, dance, drama), English, foreign language, Judaic studies, mathematics, physical education (includes health), religion (includes Bible studies and theology), science, social science, social studies (includes history).

Special Academic Programs Advanced Placement exam preparation in 16 subject areas; honors section; independent study; study at local college for college credit; study abroad; academic accommodation for the gifted, the musically talented, and the artistically talented; remedial reading and/or remedial writing; remedial math.

College Placement 119 students graduated in 2005; all went to college, including Columbia University; New York University; State University of New York at Binghamton; University of Maryland, College Park; University of Pennsylvania; Yeshiva University. 51% scored over 600 on SAT verbal, 60% scored over 600 on SAT math.

Student Life Upper grades have specified standards of dress, student council, honor system. Discipline rests primarily with faculty. Attendance at religious services is required.

Tuition and Aid Day student tuition: $15,000. Tuition installment plan (monthly payment plans, individually arranged payment plans). Need-based scholarship grants available.

Admissions Traditional secondary-level entrance grade is 9. Board of Jewish Education Entrance Exam required. Deadline for receipt of application materials: November 15. Application fee required. On-campus interview required.

Athletics Interscholastic: baseball (boys, girls); basketball (b,g); field hockey (b), softball (b,g), tennis (b,g); volleyball (g); coed intramural: skiing (downhill). 2 PE instructors, 8 coaches.

Computers Computers are regularly used in computer applications classes. Computer resources include on-campus library services, CD-ROMs, online commercial services, Internet access.

Contact Mr. Stanley Blumenstein, Principal. 516-569-3807. Fax: 516-374-5761.

HEBRON ACADEMY

PO Box 309
Hebron, Maine 04238
Head of School: Mr. John J. King

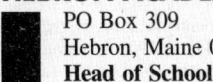

General Information Coeducational boarding and day college-preparatory, arts, religious studies, and technology school. Boarding grades 9–PG, day grades 6–PG. Founded: 1804. Setting: rural. Nearest major city is Portland. Students are housed in single-sex dormitories. 1,500-acre campus. 21 buildings on campus. Approved or accredited by Independent Schools of Northern New England, New England Association of Schools and Colleges, The Association of Boarding Schools, and Maine Department of Education. Member of National Association of Independent Schools and Secondary School Admission Test Board. Endowment: $6 million. Total enrollment: 240. Upper school average class size: 12. Upper school faculty-student ratio: 1:7.

Upper School Student Profile Grade 9: 28 students (13 boys, 15 girls); Grade 10: 53 students (33 boys, 20 girls); Grade 11: 68 students (45 boys, 23 girls); Grade 12: 45 students (29 boys, 16 girls); Postgraduate: 14 students (13 boys, 1 girl). 60% of students are boarding students. 60% are state residents. 19 states are represented in upper school student body. 16% are international students. International students from Brazil, Canada, Germany, Japan, Republic of Korea, and Sweden; 3 other countries represented in student body.

Faculty School total: 44. In upper school: 17 men, 21 women; 12 have advanced degrees; 30 reside on campus.

Subjects Offered Algebra, art, astronomy, Bible as literature, biology, calculus, chemistry, computer studies, current events, drawing and design, English, functions, geology, geometry, history, international relations, jazz, Latin, music theory, painting, photography, physics, physiology-anatomy, portfolio art, pottery, programming, psychology, sculpture, Spanish, studio art, trigonometry, U.S. history, world history, world religions.

Graduation Requirements Algebra, biology, chemistry, English, foreign language, geometry, U.S. history.

Special Academic Programs Advanced Placement exam preparation in 9 subject areas; honors section; academic accommodation for the gifted, the musically talented, and the artistically talented; ESL (9 students enrolled).

College Placement 59 students graduated in 2005; all went to college, including Colby College; Elmira College; Hobart and William Smith Colleges; Purdue University; University of Maine; University of Vermont. Median SAT verbal: 530, median SAT math: 560. 26% scored over 600 on SAT verbal, 29% scored over 600 on SAT math.

Student Life Upper grades have specified standards of dress, student council, honor system. Discipline rests primarily with faculty.

Tuition and Aid Day student tuition: $19,700; 7-day tuition and room/board: $35,500. Tuition installment plan (Insured Tuition Payment Plan, monthly payment plans). Merit scholarship grants, need-based scholarship grants, Achiever Loans (Key Education Resources), prepGATE Loans available. In 2005–06, 45% of upper-school students received aid; total upper-school merit-scholarship money awarded: $15,000. Total amount of financial aid awarded in 2005–06: $1,700,000.

Admissions Traditional secondary-level entrance grade is 9. For fall 2005, 253 students applied for upper-level admission, 184 were accepted, 99 enrolled. PSAT or SAT for applicants to grade 11 and 12, SSAT or TOEFL or SLEP required. Deadline for receipt of application materials: February 1. Application fee required: $40. Interview required.

Athletics Interscholastic: alpine skiing (boys, girls), baseball (b), basketball (b,g), cross-country running (b,g), field hockey (g), football (b), golf (b,g), ice hockey (b,g), lacrosse (b,g), mountain biking (b,g), outdoor education (b,g), outdoor skills (b,g), physical fitness (b,g), skiing (cross-country) (b,g), skiing (downhill) (b,g), snowboarding (b,g), soccer (b,g), softball (g), swimming and diving (b,g), tennis (b,g), track and field (b,g); intramural: weight lifting (b,g); coed intramural: golf, mountain biking, outdoor education, outdoor skills, physical fitness, yoga. 1 PE instructor, 1 coach, 1 trainer.

Computers Computers are regularly used in art, graphic design, introduction to technology classes. Computer network features include campus e-mail, on-campus library services, CD-ROMs, online commercial services, Internet access, file transfer, office computer access, wireless campus network.

Contact Mr. Joseph M. Hemmings, Director of Admissions. 207-966-2100 Ext. 225. Fax: 207-966-1111. E-mail: admissions@hebronacademy.org. Web site: www.hebronacademy.org.

ANNOUNCEMENT FROM THE SCHOOL Applications for fall enrollment are accepted throughout the year; however, as admission is competitive and spaces may fill quickly, students are encouraged to apply early for fall enrollment. Mid-year applications are considered on a space-available basis. All interested students are urged to visit the school early in the admissions process to have their questions and concerns answered and to get a sense of the community.

See full description on page 826.

HERITAGE CHRISTIAN SCHOOL

2850 Fourth Avenue
PO Box 400
Jordan, Ontario L0R 1S0, Canada
Head of School: Mr. A. Ben Harsevoort

General Information Coeducational day college-preparatory, general academic, arts, and religious studies school, affiliated with Reformed Church. Grades K–12. Founded: 1992. Setting: rural. Nearest major city is St. Catharines, Canada. 10-acre campus. 1 building on campus. Approved or accredited by Ontario Department of Education. Language of instruction: English. Total enrollment: 558. Upper school average class size: 25. Upper school faculty-student ratio: 1:15.

Upper School Student Profile Grade 9: 47 students (23 boys, 24 girls); Grade 10: 38 students (19 boys, 19 girls); Grade 11: 45 students (24 boys, 21 girls); Grade 12: 42 students (23 boys, 19 girls). 95% of students are Reformed.

Faculty School total: 30. In upper school: 10 men, 4 women; 4 have advanced degrees.

Subjects Offered 20th century American writers, 20th century physics, 20th century world history, advanced chemistry, advanced math, algebra, analysis and differential calculus, art, Bible, biology, bookkeeping, British literature, business mathematics, business studies, calculus, Canadian geography, Canadian history, Canadian law, Canadian literature, career education, chemistry, choral music, Christian and Hebrew scripture, Christian doctrine, Christian education, Christian ethics, Christian studies, Christian testament, Christianity, church history, civics, classical civilization, computer education, computer keyboarding, computer programming, computer skills, consumer mathematics, creative writing, culinary arts, drafting, English, English composition, English literature, entrepreneurship, environmental education, ethics, European civilization, European history, family studies, finite math, foods, foundations of civilization, French as a second language, general math, geography, geometry, grammar, health, history, honors algebra, honors English, honors geometry, honors world history, humanities, independent living, language and composition, language arts, law and the legal system, life science, literature, marketing, mathematics, media literacy, modern civilization, modern European history, modern Western civilization, music, music appreciation, novels, personal finance, physical education, physics, practicum, public speaking, religion and culture, religious education, religious studies, Shakespeare, society challenge and change, speech communications, technical drawing, vocal music, word processing, world civilizations, world literature, writing.

Graduation Requirements Ontario Secondary School Diploma requirements.

Special Academic Programs Independent study; remedial reading and/or remedial writing; remedial math.

College Placement 29 students graduated in 2005; 20 went to college, including Calvin College; Covenant College. Other: 9 went to work.

Student Life Upper grades have uniform requirement, student council. Discipline rests primarily with faculty. Attendance at religious services is required.

Tuition and Aid Day student tuition: CAN$11,736. Tuition installment plan (monthly payment plans).

Admissions Traditional secondary-level entrance grade is 9. Deadline for receipt of application materials: none. No application fee required. On-campus interview required.

Athletics Interscholastic: badminton (boys, girls), basketball (b,g), ice hockey (b), soccer (b,g), volleyball (b,g). 3 coaches.

Computers Computers are regularly used in accounting, business, economics, information technology, keyboarding, mathematics, newspaper, typing, yearbook classes. Computer network features include CD-ROMs.

Contact Mrs. Mariam Sinke, Administrative Assistant. 905-562-7303. Fax: 905-562-0020. E-mail: heritage@hcsjordan.ca. Web site: hcsjordan.ca.

THE HERITAGE SCHOOL

2093 Highway 29 North
Newnan, Georgia 30263
Head of School: Judith Griffith

General Information Coeducational day college-preparatory school. Grades PK–12. Founded: 1970. Setting: small town. Nearest major city is Atlanta. 63-acre campus. 9 buildings on campus. Approved or accredited by Georgia Independent School Association, Southern Association of Colleges and Schools, Southern Association of Independent Schools, and Georgia Department of Education. Member of National

Association of Independent Schools. Endowment: $934,382. Total enrollment: 384. Upper school average class size: 19. Upper school faculty-student ratio: 1:7.
Upper School Student Profile Grade 9: 40 students (23 boys, 17 girls); Grade 10: 31 students (21 boys, 10 girls); Grade 11: 22 students (9 boys, 13 girls); Grade 12: 23 students (13 boys, 10 girls).
Faculty School total: 49. In upper school: 6 men, 10 women; 4 have advanced degrees.
Subjects Offered Advanced Placement courses, algebra, American history, American literature, art, art history, biology, calculus, chemistry, computer applications, drama, earth science, economics, English, English literature, environmental science, European history, French, geography, geometry, government/civics, grammar, health, history, mathematics, music, physical education, public speaking, science, social science, social studies, Spanish, speech, theater, world history, world literature.
Graduation Requirements Arts and fine arts (art, music, dance, drama), computer science, electives, English, foreign language, mathematics, physical education (includes health), public speaking, science, social studies (includes history), 3 credit units of foreign language.
Special Academic Programs Advanced Placement exam preparation in 13 subject areas; independent study.
College Placement 31 students graduated in 2005; all went to college, including Auburn University; Georgia Institute of Technology; Georgia Southern University; Mercer University; University of Georgia; University of the South.
Student Life Upper grades have specified standards of dress, student council, honor system. Discipline rests primarily with faculty.
Tuition and Aid Day student tuition: $10,590. Tuition installment plan (monthly payment plans). Tuition reduction for siblings, need-based scholarship grants available. In 2005–06, 26% of upper-school students received aid. Total amount of financial aid awarded in 2005–06: $159,385.
Admissions Traditional secondary-level entrance grade is 9. For fall 2005, 20 students applied for upper-level admission, 18 were accepted, 16 enrolled. Otis-Lennon School Ability Test required. Deadline for receipt of application materials: none. Application fee required: $50. On-campus interview required.
Athletics Interscholastic: aerobics/dance (girls), baseball (b), basketball (b,g), cheering (g), cross-country running (b,g), dance team (g), golf (b,g), soccer (b,g), softball (g), swimming and diving (b,g), tennis (b,g); coed interscholastic: physical fitness, weight training; coed intramural: back packing, basketball, canoeing/kayaking, climbing, flag football, hiking/backpacking, kayaking, mountaineering, outdoor adventure, outdoor education, ropes courses, wilderness survival. 3 PE instructors.
Computers Computers are regularly used in college planning, creative writing, English, foreign language, publications, science, yearbook classes. Computer network features include on-campus library services, CD-ROMs, Internet access.
Contact Julie Bowdoin, Director of Admissions. 770-253-9898. Fax: 770-253-4850. E-mail: jbowdoin@heritagehawks.org. Web site: www.heritagehawks.org.

THE HEWITT SCHOOL

45 East 75th Street
New York, New York 10021
Head of School: Ms. Linda MacMurray Gibbs

General Information Girls' day college-preparatory school. Grades K–12. Founded: 1920. Setting: urban. 1 building on campus. Approved or accredited by Middle States Association of Colleges and Schools, National Independent Private Schools Association, and New York State Association of Independent Schools. Member of National Association of Independent Schools and Secondary School Admission Test Board. Endowment: $7.7 million. Total enrollment: 485. Upper school average class size: 15. Upper school faculty-student ratio: 1:6.
Upper School Student Profile Grade 8: 36 students (36 girls); Grade 9: 33 students (33 girls); Grade 10: 34 students (34 girls); Grade 11: 26 students (26 girls); Grade 12: 27 students (27 girls).
Faculty School total: 73. In upper school: 11 men, 15 women; 18 have advanced degrees.
Subjects Offered Algebra, American history, American literature, anatomy and physiology, art, biology, calculus, chemistry, computers, drama, earth science, English, English literature, European history, fine arts, French, genetics, geometry, history, Latin, mathematics, music, photography, physical education, physics, pre-calculus, science, Spanish, world history.
Graduation Requirements Arts and fine arts (art, music, dance, drama), computer science, English, foreign language, mathematics, physical education (includes health), SAT preparation, science, social studies (includes history). Community service is required.
Special Academic Programs Advanced Placement exam preparation in 8 subject areas; honors section; independent study; term-away projects; study abroad; academic accommodation for the musically talented and the artistically talented.
College Placement 26 students graduated in 2005; all went to college, including Brown University; Connecticut College; Duke University; Georgetown University; The George Washington University; University of Michigan. Mean SAT verbal: 600, mean SAT math: 620. 47% scored over 600 on SAT verbal, 52% scored over 600 on SAT math.
Student Life Upper grades have uniform requirement, student council. Discipline rests primarily with faculty.

Summer Programs Enrichment programs offered; session focuses on mathematics, English, and study skills; held on campus; accepts girls; not open to students from other schools. 9 students usually enrolled. 2006 schedule: August 22.
Tuition and Aid Day student tuition: $27,500. Guaranteed tuition plan. Tuition installment plan (Insured Tuition Payment Plan, Key Tuition Payment Plan, monthly payment plans). Need-based scholarship grants available. In 2005–06, 19% of upper-school students received aid. Total amount of financial aid awarded in 2005–06: $1,375,920.
Admissions Traditional secondary-level entrance grade is 9. For fall 2005, 59 students applied for upper-level admission, 21 were accepted, 12 enrolled. ERB or ISEE required. Deadline for receipt of application materials: December 1. Application fee required: $60. On-campus interview required.
Athletics Interscholastic: badminton, basketball, cross-country running, gymnastics, soccer, swimming and diving, tennis, track and field, volleyball; intramural: badminton, basketball, cross-country running, fitness, gymnastics, physical fitness, soccer, swimming and diving, tennis, track and field, volleyball, yoga. 4 PE instructors.
Computers Computers are regularly used in art, English, foreign language, history, humanities, mathematics, music, science classes. Computer network features include campus e-mail, on-campus library services, CD-ROMs, online commercial services, Internet access, file transfer, DVD, wireless campus network.
Contact Ms. Carrie Wessel, Director of Admissions, Lower School. 212-994-2600. Fax: 212-472-7531. E-mail: cwessel@hewittschool.org. Web site: hewittschool.org.

HIDDEN LAKE ACADEMY

Dahlonega, Georgia
See Special Needs Schools section.

HIGHLAND HALL, A WALDORF SCHOOL

17100 Superior Street
Northridge, California 91325
Head of School: Edward J. Eadon

General Information Coeducational day college-preparatory and arts school. Grades N–12. Founded: 1955. Setting: suburban. Nearest major city is Los Angeles. 11-acre campus. 4 buildings on campus. Approved or accredited by Association of Waldorf Schools of North America and Western Association of Schools and Colleges. Total enrollment: 376. Upper school average class size: 27. Upper school faculty-student ratio: 1:6.
Upper School Student Profile Grade 9: 29 students (13 boys, 16 girls); Grade 10: 29 students (15 boys, 14 girls); Grade 11: 27 students (14 boys, 13 girls); Grade 12: 22 students (10 boys, 12 girls).
Faculty School total: 30. In upper school: 15 men, 15 women; 3 have advanced degrees.
Subjects Offered Algebra, American history, American literature, anatomy, ancient history, architecture, art, art history, astronomy, biology, bookbinding, botany, calculus, career/college preparation, cell biology, chemistry, choral music, chorus, clayworking, conflict resolution, CPR, creative writing, drama, drawing, earth science, economics, English, English literature, ethnic studies, European history, eurythmy, expository writing, geography, geology, geometry, German, government/civics, grammar, guidance, guitar, handbells, health, history, honors U.S. history, jazz ensemble, marine biology, mathematics, metalworking, music, music history, Native American history, orchestra, painting, physical education, physics, physiology, pre-algebra, pre-calculus, SAT preparation, sculpture, sewing, social studies, Spanish, speech, stained glass, stone carving, theater, trigonometry, woodworking, world history, world literature, writing, yearbook, zoology.
Graduation Requirements Acting, anatomy, ancient history, art, art history, arts, biology, bookbinding, botany, cell biology, chemistry, clayworking, crafts, design, earth science, economics, English, eurythmy, foreign language, geology, government, history of music, human sexuality, mathematics, music, Native American history, painting, physical education (includes health), physics, science, sculpture, sewing, society and culture, stone carving, U.S. history, world history, zoology. Community service is required.
Special Academic Programs Honors section; independent study; study abroad; academic accommodation for the gifted, the musically talented, and the artistically talented.
College Placement 26 students graduated in 2005; 19 went to college, including Bennington College; Boston University; Gonzaga University; Oberlin College; Occidental College; The Colorado College. Other: 7 went to work. Mean SAT verbal: 645, mean SAT math: 550, mean composite ACT: 27. 50% scored over 600 on SAT verbal, 60% scored over 600 on SAT math, 50% scored over 26 on composite ACT.
Student Life Discipline rests primarily with faculty.
Tuition and Aid Day student tuition: $13,300. Tuition installment plan (Insured Tuition Payment Plan, FACTS Tuition Payment Plan, monthly payment plans). Need-based scholarship grants available. In 2005–06, 15% of upper-school students received aid. Total amount of financial aid awarded in 2005–06: $52,200.
Admissions Traditional secondary-level entrance grade is 9. For fall 2005, 34 students applied for upper-level admission, 23 were accepted, 15 enrolled. Essay, math

and English placement tests and writing sample required. Deadline for receipt of application materials: January 31. Application fee required: $100. On-campus interview required.

Athletics Interscholastic: baseball (boys), basketball (b,g), soccer (b), softball (g), volleyball (b,g); coed interscholastic: cross-country running; coed intramural: golf. 2 PE instructors, 3 coaches.

Computers Computers are regularly used in newspaper, yearbook classes. Computer resources include on-campus library services, Internet access, wireless campus network.

Contact Lynn van Schilfgaarde, Enrollment Director. 818-349-1394 Ext. 211. Fax: 818-349-2390. E-mail: lvs@highlandhall.org. Web site: www.highlandhall.org.

HIGHLAND SCHOOL
597 Broadview Avenue
Warrenton, Virginia 20186
Head of School: Mr. Henry D. Berg

General Information Coeducational day college-preparatory school. Grades PK–12. Founded: 1928. Setting: small town. Nearest major city is Washington, DC. 41-acre campus. 4 buildings on campus. Approved or accredited by Virginia Association of Independent Schools and Virginia Department of Education. Member of National Association of Independent Schools. Endowment: $1.5 million. Total enrollment: 537. Upper school average class size: 12. Upper school faculty-student ratio: 1:10.

Upper School Student Profile Grade 9: 58 students (31 boys, 27 girls); Grade 10: 55 students (22 boys, 33 girls); Grade 11: 57 students (30 boys, 27 girls); Grade 12: 44 students (20 boys, 24 girls).

Faculty School total: 80. In upper school: 11 men, 23 women; 25 have advanced degrees.

Subjects Offered Algebra, American literature, art, art appreciation, biology, biotechnology, calculus-AP, chemistry, chemistry-AP, choir, choral music, chorus, college writing, composition, computer graphics, computer keyboarding, computer literacy, computer programming, computer programming-AP, computer science, computer science-AP, computer skills, computer studies, computer technologies, computer tools, computer-aided design, concert band, concert bell choir, drama, English, English-AP, environmental science, European history-AP, French, French-AP, geometry, Greek, honors English, international relations, intro to computers, journalism, Latin, Latin-AP, law, macroeconomics-AP, marine biology, microeconomics, modern European history, music appreciation, orchestra, physical education, physics, physics-AP, pre-calculus, probability and statistics, SAT preparation, Spanish, Spanish-AP, statistics-AP, study skills, trigonometry, U.S. history-AP, world cultures, world religions.

Graduation Requirements Arts and fine arts (art, music, dance, drama), computer science, English, foreign language, lab science, mathematics, physical education (includes health), social science, 20 hours of community service for each year of attendance.

Special Academic Programs Advanced Placement exam preparation in 16 subject areas; honors section; independent study; term-away projects.

College Placement 48 students graduated in 2005; all went to college, including James Madison University; The College of William and Mary; The University of North Carolina at Chapel Hill; United States Military Academy; University of Virginia; Virginia Polytechnic Institute and State University.

Student Life Upper grades have specified standards of dress, student council, honor system. Discipline rests equally with students and faculty.

Summer Programs Enrichment, sports, art/fine arts, rigorous outdoor training, computer instruction programs offered; session focuses on recreation and academics; held both on and off campus; held at Vint Hill (swimming) and various locations (camping and hiking); accepts boys and girls; open to students from other schools. 200 students usually enrolled. 2006 schedule: June 13 to August 12.

Tuition and Aid Day student tuition: $14,410. Tuition installment plan (Insured Tuition Payment Plan, monthly payment plans, individually arranged payment plans). Merit scholarship grants, need-based scholarship grants, faculty/staff discounts available. In 2005–06, 15% of upper-school students received aid; total upper-school merit-scholarship money awarded: $103,000. Total amount of financial aid awarded in 2005–06: $258,000.

Admissions Traditional secondary-level entrance grade is 9. For fall 2005, 96 students applied for upper-level admission, 66 were accepted, 49 enrolled. SSAT, ERB, PSAT, SAT, PLAN or ACT or TOEFL or SLEP required. Deadline for receipt of application materials: February 4. Application fee required: $75. Interview required.

Athletics Interscholastic: aerobics/dance (girls), ball hockey (g), basketball (b,g), cheering (g), cross-country running (b,g), dance (g), dance squad (g), dance team (g), field hockey (g), lacrosse (b,g), modern dance (g), running (b,g), soccer (b,g), softball (g), tennis (b,g), volleyball (g); intramural: ball hockey (g), basketball (b,g), field hockey (g), lacrosse (b,g), soccer (b,g), volleyball (g); coed interscholastic: aquatics, cross-country running, golf, swimming and diving; coed intramural: aerobics/dance, back packing, climbing, dance, fitness, freestyle skiing, outdoor activities, outdoor adventure, physical fitness, power lifting, ropes courses, running, skiing (downhill), snowboarding, strength & conditioning, volleyball, weight lifting, weight training. 4 PE instructors, 8 coaches.

Computers Computer network features include campus e-mail, on-campus library services, CD-ROMs, Internet access.

Contact Mr. Chris S. Pryor, Director of Admission and Financial Aid. 540-878-2700 Ext. 1201. Fax: 540-341-7164. E-mail: cpryor@highlandschool.org. Web site: www.highlandschool.org.

HIGH MOWING SCHOOL
222 Isaac Frye Highway
Wilton, New Hampshire 03086
Head of School: Cary Hughes

General Information Coeducational boarding and day college-preparatory and arts school. Grades 9–12. Founded: 1942. Setting: rural. Nearest major city is Boston, MA. Students are housed in single-sex dormitories. 125-acre campus. 17 buildings on campus. Approved or accredited by Association of Independent Schools in New England, Association of Waldorf Schools of North America, Independent Schools of Northern New England, New England Association of Schools and Colleges, The Association of Boarding Schools, home study, and New Hampshire Department of Education. Member of National Association of Independent Schools and Secondary School Admission Test Board. Endowment: $1 million. Total enrollment: 126. Upper school average class size: 12. Upper school faculty-student ratio: 1:4.

Upper School Student Profile Grade 9: 28 students (15 boys, 13 girls); Grade 10: 33 students (16 boys, 17 girls); Grade 11: 36 students (14 boys, 22 girls); Grade 12: 29 students (13 boys, 16 girls). 50% of students are boarding students. 45% are state residents. 15 states are represented in upper school student body. 7% are international students. International students from Bermuda, France, Germany, Japan, and Switzerland; 6 other countries represented in student body.

Faculty School total: 30. In upper school: 10 men, 15 women; 16 have advanced degrees; 20 reside on campus.

Subjects Offered Accounting, advanced chemistry, algebra, American history, American literature, anatomy, ancient history, art, astronomy, batik, biology, botany, calculus, ceramics, chemistry, community service, computer math, computer programming, computer science, creative writing, dance, digital art, drama, driver education, earth science, ecology, economics, English, English literature, environmental science, equine studies, ESL, ethics, European history, expository writing, fiber arts, fine arts, French, geography, geology, geometry, German, government/civics, grammar, health, history, history of science, mathematics, meteorology, music, mythology, nature study, philosophy, photography, physical education, physics, physiology, Russian literature, science, social science, social studies, speech, theater, theory of knowledge, trigonometry, wilderness education, world history, world literature, writing, zoology.

Graduation Requirements Algebra, arts and fine arts (art, music, dance, drama), economics, English, foreign language, government, mathematics, performing arts, physical education (includes health), physics, science, social science, social studies (includes history), studio art. Community service is required.

Special Academic Programs Honors section; independent study; term-away projects; study abroad; academic accommodation for the musically talented and the artistically talented; programs in mathematics for dyslexic students; ESL (8 students enrolled).

College Placement 30 students graduated in 2005; 28 went to college, including Bowdoin College; Mount Holyoke College; Sarah Lawrence College; Skidmore College; Smith College; University of Pennsylvania. Other: 2 went to work.

Student Life Upper grades have specified standards of dress, student council. Discipline rests primarily with faculty.

Tuition and Aid Day student tuition: $21,485; 5-day tuition and room/board: $31,299; 7-day tuition and room/board: $34,291. Tuition installment plan (monthly payment plans, individually arranged payment plans). Need-based scholarship grants, middle-income loans available. In 2005–06, 50% of upper-school students received aid. Total amount of financial aid awarded in 2005–06: $370,000.

Admissions Traditional secondary-level entrance grade is 9. For fall 2005, 144 students applied for upper-level admission, 68 were accepted, 57 enrolled. TOEFL or SLEP required. Deadline for receipt of application materials: none. Application fee required: $50. Interview required.

Athletics Interscholastic: basketball (boys, girls), cross-country running (b,g), field hockey (g), running (b,g), soccer (b,g); coed interscholastic: Frisbee, lacrosse; coed intramural: aerobics, aerobics/dance, aerobics/nautilus, alpine skiing, archery, back packing, baseball, bicycling, Circus, climbing, cross-country running, dance, fencing, fitness walking, golf, handball, jogging, juggling, nautilus, outdoor activities, outdoor adventure, outdoor education, outdoor recreation, outdoor skills, outdoors, physical training, running, skiing (cross-country), skiing (downhill), snowboarding, unicycling, walking, wilderness, wilderness survival, wildernessways, yoga. 1 PE instructor, 8 coaches.

Computers Computers are regularly used in graphic arts, graphic design, mathematics, science, technology classes. Computer resources include on-campus library services, CD-ROMs, Internet access.

Contact Sam Rosario, Director of Admissions. 603-654-2391 Ext. 103. Fax: 603-654-6588. E-mail: admissions@highmowing.org. Web site: www.highmowing.org.

ANNOUNCEMENT FROM THE SCHOOL   The Dr. Bruce Bairstow Science and Technology Building opened at High Mowing School in 2003. This beautiful post-and-beam facility is made of steel and wood and houses 2 science labs, an auditorium, a math/science classroom, and a recording studio and digital arts studio, which have state-of-the-art equipment for cinematography, recording, and digital arts. There is also an open studio for rehearsals, performances, filming, and community gatherings.

See full description on page 828.

THE HILL CENTER, DURHAM ACADEMY

Durham, North Carolina
See Special Needs Schools section.

HILLCREST CHRISTIAN SCHOOL

17531 Rinaldi Street
Granada Hills, California 91344
Head of School: Mr. David Kendrick

General Information   Coeducational day college-preparatory, general academic, arts, and religious studies school, affiliated with Christian faith. Grades K–12. Founded: 1976. Setting: suburban. Nearest major city is Los Angeles. 4-acre campus. 3 buildings on campus. Approved or accredited by Association of Christian Schools International, Western Association of Schools and Colleges, and California Department of Education. Total enrollment: 757. Upper school average class size: 25. Upper school faculty-student ratio: 1:12.

Upper School Student Profile   Grade 9: 60 students (28 boys, 32 girls); Grade 10: 60 students (29 boys, 31 girls); Grade 11: 59 students (35 boys, 24 girls); Grade 12: 56 students (27 boys, 29 girls).

Faculty   School total: 40. In upper school: 8 men, 11 women; 7 have advanced degrees.

Subjects Offered   Accounting, algebra, American literature, art, Bible studies, biology, British literature, calculus-AP, chemistry, choir, choral music, computer applications, computer keyboarding, drama, dramatic arts, economics, English, English literature and composition-AP, English literature-AP, foreign language, general math, geometry, journalism, physical education, physics, pre-algebra, pre-calculus, psychology, Spanish, U.S. government, U.S. history, U.S. history-AP, world history.

Graduation Requirements   Advanced math, algebra, Bible, biology, chemistry, economics, English, geometry, performing arts, physical education (includes health), physical science, Spanish, U.S. government, U.S. history, world history, cumulative GPA of 2.0 or higher.

Special Academic Programs   Advanced Placement exam preparation in 4 subject areas; independent study; programs in general development for dyslexic students.

College Placement   39 students graduated in 2005; 37 went to college, including California State University, Northridge; Loyola Marymount University; Pepperdine University; University of California, Berkeley; University of California, Los Angeles; University of Southern California. Other: 1 went to work, 1 entered a postgraduate year. Mean SAT verbal: 520, mean SAT math: 530, mean composite ACT: 25. 8% scored over 600 on SAT verbal, 25% scored over 600 on SAT math.

Student Life   Upper grades have uniform requirement, student council. Discipline rests primarily with faculty. Attendance at religious services is required.

Summer Programs   Remediation, enrichment, sports, art/fine arts, computer instruction programs offered; session focuses on remediation/make-up and summer and sport camps; held on campus; accepts boys and girls; open to students from other schools. 60 students usually enrolled. 2006 schedule: June 12 to August 18. Application deadline: June 2.

Tuition and Aid   Day student tuition: $5269. Tuition installment plan (SMART Tuition Payment Plan). Tuition reduction for siblings, need-based scholarship grants available. In 2005–06, 5% of upper-school students received aid.

Admissions   Traditional secondary-level entrance grade is 9. For fall 2005, 46 students applied for upper-level admission, 35 were accepted, 29 enrolled. 3-R Achievement Test and Math Placement Exam required. Deadline for receipt of application materials: none. No application fee required. On-campus interview required.

Athletics   Interscholastic: baseball (boys), basketball (b,g), cheering (g), football (b), golf (b), softball (g), track and field (b,g), volleyball (b,g); coed interscholastic: soccer.

Computers   Computers are regularly used in accounting, computer applications, English, journalism classes. Computer network features include on-campus library services, CD-ROMs, Internet access, DVD.

Contact   Mrs. Krista Joyner, Registrar. 818-368-7071. Fax: 818-363-4455. E-mail: kjoyner@mail.hillcrestchristianschool.org.

HILLCREST CHRISTIAN SCHOOL

10306-102 Street
Grande Prairie, Alberta T8V 2W3, Canada
Head of School: Mr. Dave Paetkau

General Information   Coeducational day college-preparatory, general academic, arts, and religious studies school; primarily serves underachievers. Grades K–12. Founded: 1981. Setting: urban. 1-acre campus. 1 building on campus. Approved or accredited by Association of Independent Schools and Colleges of Alberta and Alberta Department of Education. Languages of instruction: English and French. Total enrollment: 48. Upper school faculty-student ratio: 1:5.

Faculty   School total: 8. In upper school: 2 men, 2 women; 1 has an advanced degree.

Subjects Offered   Advanced math, art, ballet, Bible studies, biology, career and personal planning, chemistry, Christian education, computer technologies, dance, drama, English, forestry, French as a second language, health, mathematics, music, physical education, science, social studies, work experience.

Graduation Requirements   Alberta Learning requirements.

Special Academic Programs   Accelerated programs; independent study.

Student Life   Upper grades have uniform requirement. Discipline rests primarily with faculty.

Tuition and Aid   Day student tuition: CAN$2800. Tuition installment plan (monthly payment plans, individually arranged payment plans). Tuition reduction for siblings, need-based scholarship grants available. In 2005–06, 11% of upper-school students received aid.

Admissions   Traditional secondary-level entrance grade is 10. Deadline for receipt of application materials: September 6. No application fee required. On-campus interview required.

Athletics   Coed Interscholastic: dance, hiking/backpacking, physical fitness. 1 PE instructor.

Computers   Computers are regularly used in all classes. Computer network features include CD-ROMs, Internet access, office computer access, DVD.

Contact   Mr. Dave Paetkau, Principal. 780-539-9161. Fax: 780-532-6932. E-mail: hcsgp@telus.net. Web site: www.hcsgp.ca.

HILLCREST SCHOOL

Midland, Texas
See Special Needs Schools section.

HILLFIELD STRATHALLAN COLLEGE

299 Fennell Avenue, West
Hamilton, Ontario L9C 1G3, Canada
Head of School: Dr. Tom Matthews

General Information   Coeducational day college-preparatory, general academic, arts, business, and technology school. Grades PK–12. Founded: 1901. Setting: suburban. Nearest major city is Toronto, Canada. 50-acre campus. 8 buildings on campus. Approved or accredited by Canadian Association of Independent Schools, Canadian Council of Montessori Administrators, Canadian Educational Standards Institute, Conference of Independent Schools of Ontario, and Ontario Department of Education. Affiliate member of National Association of Independent Schools. Language of instruction: English. Total enrollment: 1,112. Upper school average class size: 16. Upper school faculty-student ratio: 1:9.

Upper School Student Profile   Grade 9: 95 students (52 boys, 43 girls); Grade 10: 93 students (51 boys, 42 girls); Grade 11: 90 students (44 boys, 46 girls); Grade 12: 82 students (41 boys, 41 girls).

Faculty   School total: 122. In upper school: 18 men, 21 women; 12 have advanced degrees.

Subjects Offered   Accounting, Advanced Placement courses, algebra, American history, art, biology, biology-AP, business, calculus, Canadian geography, Canadian history, chemistry, chemistry-AP, classical studies, communications, computer science, dramatic arts, economics, English, English literature, English literature-AP, ESL, European history, fine arts, French, French as a second language, French language-AP, geography, geometry, German, guidance, health, healthful living, history, information technology, Japanese, law, mathematics, mathematics-AP, music, philosophy, physical education, physics, science, social science, social studies, Spanish, technology, world history, writing.

Graduation Requirements   Arts and fine arts (art, music, dance, drama), English, foreign language, information technology, mathematics, physical education (includes health), science, social science, social studies (includes history), technology.

Special Academic Programs   Advanced Placement exam preparation in 5 subject areas; independent study; academic accommodation for the gifted, the musically talented, and the artistically talented; programs in general development for dyslexic students; ESL (20 students enrolled).

College Placement   85 students graduated in 2005; 81 went to college, including McMaster University; Ryerson University; University of Guelph; University of Ottawa; University of Toronto; Wilfrid Laurier University. Other: 2 went to work, 2 had other specific plans.

Student Life Upper grades have uniform requirement, student council, honor system. Discipline rests primarily with faculty.

Tuition and Aid Day student tuition: CAN$16,840. Tuition installment plan (Insured Tuition Payment Plan, monthly payment plans, individually arranged payment plans). Tuition reduction for siblings, bursaries, merit scholarship grants, paying campus jobs, arts scholarships available. In 2005–06, 10% of upper-school students received aid.

Admissions Traditional secondary-level entrance grade is 9. For fall 2005, 60 students applied for upper-level admission, 50 were accepted, 40 enrolled. School's own test required. Deadline for receipt of application materials: none. Application fee required: CAN$150. On-campus interview required.

Athletics Interscholastic: baseball (boys, girls), basketball (b,g), crew (b,g), cross-country running (b,g), field hockey (g), golf (b,g), rowing (b,g), rugby (b,g), running (b,g), soccer (b,g), softball (b,g), track and field (b,g), volleyball (b,g); intramural: baseball (b,g), basketball (b,g), soccer (b,g), tennis (b,g), volleyball (b,g); coed interscholastic: badminton, tennis; coed intramural: badminton, bicycling, canoeing/kayaking, climbing, fitness, outdoor education, outdoor skills, roller blading, weight lifting, weight training, wilderness survival.

Computers Computers are regularly used in accounting, design, geography, information technology, introduction to technology, language development, library skills, mathematics, music, technology, video film production, Web site design, yearbook classes. Computer network features include campus e-mail, on-campus library services, CD-ROMs, online commercial services, Internet access, file transfer, DVD.

Contact Mr. Raymond Marks, Director of Admissions. 905-389-1367 Ext. 137. Fax: 905-389-6366. E-mail: admissions@hillstrath.on.ca. Web site: www.hillstrath.on.ca.

THE HILL SCHOOL

717 East High Street
Pottstown, Pennsylvania 19464-5791
Head of School: Mr. David R. Dougherty

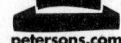
petersons.com

General Information Coeducational boarding and day college-preparatory school. Boarding grades 9–PG, day grades 9–12. Founded: 1851. Setting: small town. Nearest major city is Philadelphia. Students are housed in single-sex dormitories. 200-acre campus. 58 buildings on campus. Approved or accredited by Middle States Association of Colleges and Schools, Pacific Northwest Association of Independent Schools, The Association of Boarding Schools, and Pennsylvania Department of Education. Member of National Association of Independent Schools and Secondary School Admission Test Board. Endowment: $108 million. Total enrollment: 495. Upper school average class size: 12. Upper school faculty-student ratio: 1:7.

Upper School Student Profile Grade 9: 88 students (57 boys, 31 girls); Grade 10: 135 students (76 boys, 59 girls); Grade 11: 141 students (77 boys, 64 girls); Grade 12: 116 students (68 boys, 48 girls); Postgraduate: 15 students (13 boys, 2 girls). 80% of students are boarding students. 48% are state residents. 28 states are represented in upper school student body. 13% are international students. International students from Canada, Hong Kong, Jamaica, Republic of Korea, Spain, and Sweden; 8 other countries represented in student body.

Faculty School total: 86. In upper school: 56 men, 30 women; 61 have advanced degrees; 80 reside on campus.

Subjects Offered Acting, advanced chemistry, advanced computer applications, advanced math, Advanced Placement courses, advanced studio art-AP, algebra, American Civil War, American history, American history-AP, American literature-AP, American studies, Ancient Greek, ancient world history, art, art history, art-AP, arts, astronomy, athletic training, basic language skills, Basic programming, Bible studies, biochemistry, biology, biology-AP, boat building, botany, British literature-AP, calculus, calculus-AP, chamber groups, chemistry, chemistry-AP, Chinese, choral music, Christian ethics, Christian scripture, Christian testament, college admission preparation, college counseling, college placement, college planning, college writing, composition-AP, computer math, computer programming, computer science, computer science-AP, concert choir, creative writing, digital art, earth science, ecology, economics, economics-AP, English, English language and composition-AP, English literature, English literature and composition-AP, environmental science, European history, European history-AP, expository writing, French, French language-AP, French literature-AP, geography, geometry, German, government/civics, grammar, Greek, history, honors algebra, honors English, honors geometry, humanities, independent study, instrumental music, jazz band, journalism, lab science, Latin, Latin-AP, life issues, linear algebra, mathematics, music, oral communications, orchestra, participation in sports, photography, physics, physics-AP, physiology-anatomy, pre-calculus, pre-college orientation, psychology, psychology-AP, radio broadcasting, religion, SAT/ACT preparation, science, sex education, sexuality, social studies, sociology, Spanish, speech, sports medicine, theater, theology, trigonometry, typing, U.S. history-AP, woodworking, world history, world literature, writing, writing.

Graduation Requirements English, foreign language, mathematics, religion (includes Bible studies and theology), science, social studies (includes history).

Special Academic Programs Advanced Placement exam preparation in 14 subject areas; honors section; independent study; study abroad.

College Placement 127 students graduated in 2005; all went to college, including Boston University; Cornell University; Drexel University; Trinity College; United States Naval Academy; University of Pennsylvania. Mean SAT verbal: 625, mean SAT

math: 633, mean composite ACT: 26. 62% scored over 600 on SAT verbal, 66% scored over 600 on SAT math, 53% scored over 26 on composite ACT.

Student Life Upper grades have specified standards of dress, student council, honor system. Discipline rests equally with students and faculty.

Tuition and Aid Day student tuition: $23,300; 7-day tuition and room/board: $34,300. Tuition installment plan (Insured Tuition Payment Plan, monthly payment plans, individually arranged payment plans). Need-based scholarship grants available. In 2005–06, 38% of upper-school students received aid. Total amount of financial aid awarded in 2005–06: $3,500,000.

Admissions Traditional secondary-level entrance grade is 9. For fall 2005, 656 students applied for upper-level admission, 300 were accepted, 174 enrolled. ACT, ISEE, PSAT or SAT for applicants to grade 11 and 12, SSAT or TOEFL required. Deadline for receipt of application materials: February 1. Application fee required: $50. Interview required.

Athletics Interscholastic: baseball (boys), basketball (b,g), cross-country running (b,g), field hockey (g), football (b), ice hockey (b,g), indoor track (b,g), lacrosse (b,g), soccer (b,g), softball (g), squash (b,g), swimming and diving (b,g), tennis (b,g), water polo (b,g), winter (indoor) track (b,g), wrestling (b); coed interscholastic: diving, golf, track and field; coed intramural: aerobics, basketball, golf, martial arts, riflery, soccer, squash, strength & conditioning, tennis, volleyball, weight lifting. 2 coaches, 2 trainers.

Computers Computers are regularly used in all classes. Computer network features include campus e-mail, on-campus library services, CD-ROMs, online commercial services, Internet access, wireless campus network.

Contact Mrs. Sally B. Keidel, Director of Admission and Enrollment Management. 610-326-1000. Fax: 610-705-1753. E-mail: skeidel@thehill.org. Web site: www. thehill.org.

ANNOUNCEMENT FROM THE SCHOOL The Hill School's mission is to prepare young men and women from across the United States and around the world for excellence in school, college, career, and life. To achieve such scholastic excellence and character development, Hill students learn inside and outside the classroom: they learn in the dining hall, in the residence halls, through participation in extracurricular activities, via international exchange programs, and on the playing fields. Athletics are, in fact, part of Hill School's curriculum, teaching sportsmanship and self-discipline. Traditions such as twice-weekly chapel services reinforce students' ethical development and nurture their individual spirituality. The top priority at Hill is to provide an outstanding academic environment. The Hill School's program is based on the liberal arts and sciences and is taught in small classes by faculty members who reside on campus and serve as dorm parents, coaches, and advisers.

See full description on page 830.

HILLSIDE SCHOOL

Marlborough, Massachusetts
See Junior Boarding Schools section.

THE HILL TOP PREPARATORY SCHOOL

Rosemont, Pennsylvania
See Special Needs Schools section.

HILTON HEAD PREPARATORY SCHOOL

8 Fox Grape Road
Hilton Head Island, South Carolina 29928
Head of School: Dr. Susan R. Groesbeck

General Information Coeducational day college-preparatory, arts, and technology school. Grades K–12. Founded: 1965. Setting: small town. Nearest major city is Savannah, GA. 25-acre campus. 5 buildings on campus. Approved or accredited by South Carolina Independent School Association, Southern Association of Colleges and Schools, Southern Association of Independent Schools, The College Board, and South Carolina Department of Education. Member of National Association of Independent Schools and Secondary School Admission Test Board. Total enrollment: 433. Upper school average class size: 12. Upper school faculty-student ratio: 1:12.

Upper School Student Profile Grade 9: 41 students (13 boys, 28 girls); Grade 10: 32 students (18 boys, 14 girls); Grade 11: 38 students (20 boys, 18 girls); Grade 12: 35 students (18 boys, 17 girls).

Faculty School total: 63. In upper school: 12 men, 15 women; 11 have advanced degrees.

Subjects Offered Advanced studio art-AP, algebra, American literature-AP, art, biology-AP, British literature, calculus, calculus-AP, chemistry, chemistry-AP, Chinese, chorus, college counseling, community service, computer science-AP, computer studies, drama, English literature and composition-AP, French language-AP, French-AP, geography, geometry, guidance, guitar, health education, history-AP, journalism,

Latin, leadership and service, library, literature and composition-AP, marine biology, newspaper, peer counseling, performing arts, physical education, physical fitness, physics-AP, piano, pre-calculus, SAT/ACT preparation, senior career experience, senior thesis, Spanish language-AP, Spanish-AP, statistics and probability, statistics-AP, strings, student government, studio art, trigonometry, U.S. history, U.S. history-AP, visual and performing arts, world history, world literature, yearbook.

Graduation Requirements Arts and fine arts (art, music, dance, drama), computer literacy, English, foreign language, internship, mathematics, physical education (includes health), science, social studies (includes history), senior speech, 10 hours of community service per school year.

Special Academic Programs Advanced Placement exam preparation in 15 subject areas; honors section.

College Placement 33 students graduated in 2005; all went to college, including Clemson University; Duke University; Emory University; Furman University; University of Pennsylvania; Wake Forest University. Median SAT verbal: 585, median SAT math: 561.

Student Life Upper grades have specified standards of dress, student council, honor system. Discipline rests primarily with faculty.

Tuition and Aid Day student tuition: $6900–$12,649. Tuition installment plan (monthly payment plans, individually arranged payment plans, bank-arranged plan, self-insured tuition refund plan). Tuition reduction for siblings, need-based scholarship grants, tuition discounts for children of faculty available. In 2005–06, 25% of upper-school students received aid. Total amount of financial aid awarded in 2005–06: $200,000.

Admissions Traditional secondary-level entrance grade is 9. For fall 2005, 25 students applied for upper-level admission, 20 were accepted, 17 enrolled. School's own exam, SSAT or writing sample required. Deadline for receipt of application materials: none. Application fee required: $65. On-campus interview required.

Athletics Interscholastic: aerobics/dance (girls), baseball (b), basketball (b,g), cheering (g), dance team (g), football (b), soccer (b,g), tennis (b,g), volleyball (g); intramural: aerobics/dance (g), basketball (b,g), dance team (g), soccer (b,g); coed interscholastic: aquatics, cross-country running, golf; coed intramural: outdoor activities, physical fitness, strength & conditioning. 2 PE instructors, 5 coaches, 1 trainer.

Computers Computers are regularly used in all academic, art, college planning, journalism, library, music, newspaper, yearbook classes. Computer network features include campus e-mail, on-campus library services, CD-ROMs, Internet access, file transfer, DVD, wireless campus network.

Contact Lauren R. Marlis, Director of Admissions. 843-671-2286. Fax: 843-671-7624. E-mail: lmarlis@hhprep.org. Web site: www.hhprep.org.

THE HOCKADAY SCHOOL

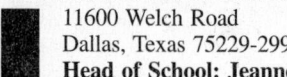

11600 Welch Road
Dallas, Texas 75229-2999
Head of School: Jeanne P. Whitman

petersons.com

General Information Girls' boarding and day college-preparatory school. Boarding grades 8–12, day grades PK–12. Founded: 1913. Setting: suburban. Students are housed in single-sex dormitories. 100-acre campus. 12 buildings on campus. Approved or accredited by Independent Schools Association of the Southwest and The Association of Boarding Schools. Member of National Association of Independent Schools and Secondary School Admission Test Board. Language of instruction: English. Endowment: $100 million. Total enrollment: 1,020. Upper school average class size: 16. Upper school faculty-student ratio: 1:8.

Upper School Student Profile Grade 9: 99 students (99 girls); Grade 10: 120 students (120 girls); Grade 11: 111 students (111 girls); Grade 12: 104 students (104 girls). 13% of students are boarding students. 6 states are represented in upper school student body. 3% are international students. International students from China, Japan, Mexico, Republic of Korea, Taiwan, and United Kingdom; 10 other countries represented in student body.

Faculty School total: 105. In upper school: 17 men, 37 women; 39 have advanced degrees.

Subjects Offered 3-dimensional art, 3-dimensional design, acting, advanced math, advanced studio art-AP, algebra, American biography, American history, American history-AP, American literature, analytic geometry, anatomy, applied arts, applied music, art history, Asian studies, astronomy, athletics, audio visual/media, backpacking, ballet, ballet technique, basketball, biology, biology-AP, body human, British literature, broadcast journalism, broadcasting, Broadway dance, calculus, calculus-AP, cell biology, ceramics, chemistry, chemistry-AP, comparative religion, computer applications, computer science, computer science-AP, concert choir, consumer economics, CPR, creative writing, current events, dance, dance performance, debate, digital art, digital imaging, digital music, digital photography, directing, discrete mathematics, drawing and design, ecology, environmental systems, economics-AP, English, English literature, English literature and composition-AP, environmental science, environmental science-AP, ESL, fencing, finite math, French, French language-AP, French literature-AP, genetics, geometry, guitar, health, health and wellness, honors English, humanities, information technology, interdisciplinary studies, journalism, Latin, Latin-AP, life management skills, madrigals, Mandarin, meteorology, microbiology, modern European history-AP, newspaper, non-Western literature, orchestra, philosophy, photography, physical education, physical fitness,

physics, physics-AP, piano, pre-calculus, printmaking, probability and statistics, psychology, psychology-AP, self-defense, senior internship, set design, short story, Spanish, Spanish language-AP, Spanish literature-AP, stagecraft, studio art, studio art—AP, swimming, tennis, track and field, U.S. government, U.S. history, U.S. history-AP, Vietnam War, voice, volleyball, Web site design, wellness, world history, World War I, yearbook.

Graduation Requirements 1½ elective credits, algebra, American literature, applied arts, British literature, chemistry, computer literacy, English, English literature, foreign language, geometry, information technology, physical education (includes health), physics, trigonometry, U.S. government, U.S. history, world history, History of Art and Music, 60 hours of community of service, Senior project—unpaid week at a workplacein which they have a career interest.

Special Academic Programs Advanced Placement exam preparation in 19 subject areas; honors section; independent study; term-away projects; study abroad; ESL (12 students enrolled).

College Placement 110 students graduated in 2005; all went to college, including Princeton University; Southern Methodist University; The University of Texas at Austin; University of Southern California; Vanderbilt University; Yale University. Mean SAT verbal: 666, mean SAT math: 675. 75% scored over 600 on SAT verbal, 79% scored over 600 on SAT math.

Student Life Upper grades have uniform requirement, student council, honor system. Discipline rests primarily with faculty.

Summer Programs Enrichment, advancement, ESL, sports, art/fine arts, computer instruction programs offered; session focuses on enrichment; held on campus; accepts boys and girls; open to students from other schools. 800 students usually enrolled. 2006 schedule: June 12 to July 21. Application deadline: none.

Tuition and Aid Day student tuition: $15,525–$15,730; 7-day tuition and room/board: $28,120–$28,920. Tuition installment plan (monthly payment plan at J.P. Morgan-Chase Bank). Need-based financial aid available. In 2005–06, 15% of upper-school students received aid. Total amount of financial aid awarded in 2005–06: $786,700.

Admissions Traditional secondary-level entrance grade is 9. Admissions testing required. Deadline for receipt of application materials: none. Application fee required: $150. Interview required.

Athletics Interscholastic: basketball, cheering, crew, cross-country running, diving, fencing, field hockey, golf, lacrosse, rowing, soccer, softball, swimming and diving, tennis, track and field, volleyball, winter soccer; intramural: aerobics, aerobics/dance, aquatics, archery, badminton, bicycling, cooperative games, crew, dance, fitness, fitness walking, Frisbee, golf, hiking/backpacking, in-line hockey, in-line skating, independent competitive sports, jogging, life saving, martial arts, mountain biking, outdoor activities, outdoor adventure, paddle tennis, physical fitness, physical training, project adventure, racquetball, roller blading, ropes courses, running, self defense, strength & conditioning, swimming and diving, table tennis, tennis, ultimate Frisbee, walking, wallyball, weight lifting, weight training, yoga. 10 PE instructors, 10 coaches, 1 trainer.

Computers Computers are regularly used in all academic, animation, art, computer applications, creative writing, dance, engineering, English, French, health, history, humanities, information technology, introduction to technology, journalism, Latin, mathematics, media, media production, media services, multimedia, music, newspaper, photography, photojournalism, psychology, publications, publishing, science, Spanish, technology, Web site design, yearbook classes. Computer network features include campus e-mail, on-campus library services, CD-ROMs, online commercial services, Internet access, file transfer, DVD, wireless campus network.

Contact Jen Liggitt, Director of Admission. 214-363-6311. Fax: 214-363-0942. E-mail: admissions@mail.hockaday.org. Web site: www.hockaday.org.

See full description on page 832.

HOKKAIDO INTERNATIONAL SCHOOL

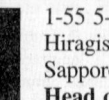

1-55 5-jo 19-chome
Hiragishi, Toyohira-Ku
Sapporo 062-0935, Japan
Head of School: Mr. Wayne D. Rutherford

General Information Coeducational boarding and day college-preparatory school. Boarding grades 7–12, day grades PK–12. Founded: 1958. Setting: urban. Students are housed in coed dormitories. 4-acre campus. 2 buildings on campus. Approved or accredited by CITA (Commission on International and Trans-Regional Accreditation), East Asia Regional Council of Schools, and Western Association of Schools and Colleges. Member of Secondary School Admission Test Board. Language of instruction: English. Endowment: $9 million. Total enrollment: 182. Upper school average class size: 14. Upper school faculty-student ratio: 1:10.

Upper School Student Profile Grade 10: 17 students (10 boys, 7 girls); Grade 11: 14 students (7 boys, 7 girls); Grade 12: 13 students (6 boys, 7 girls). 20% of students are boarding students. 50% are international students. International students from Republic of Korea, Taiwan, United Kingdom, and United States; 12 other countries represented in student body.

Faculty School total: 23. In upper school: 8 men, 3 women; 5 have advanced degrees; 2 reside on campus.

Subjects Offered Algebra, art, arts, biology, calculus, chemistry, English, English literature-AP, fine arts, geography, history, Japanese, language arts, mathematics, music, physical education, physics, physics-AP, pre-calculus, science, social studies, Spanish, U.S. history, world history-AP.

Graduation Requirements Arts and fine arts (art, music, dance, drama), English, foreign language, mathematics, physical education (includes health), science, social science, social studies (includes history), extracurricular involvement requirement (EIR).

Special Academic Programs Advanced Placement exam preparation in 6 subject areas; independent study; ESL (8 students enrolled).

College Placement 13 students graduated in 2005; 9 went to college, including Clark University; Reed College; University of Oregon. Other: 2 went to work, 2 entered a postgraduate year. Mean SAT verbal: 487, mean SAT math: 556. 15% scored over 600 on SAT verbal, 30% scored over 600 on SAT math.

Student Life Upper grades have student council. Discipline rests primarily with faculty.

Tuition and Aid Day student tuition: ¥1,055,000; 7-day tuition and room/board: ¥1,700,000. Tuition reduction for siblings, need-based scholarship grants available. In 2005–06, 20% of upper-school students received aid. Total amount of financial aid awarded in 2005–06: ¥2,000,000.

Admissions Traditional secondary-level entrance grade is 10. For fall 2005, 12 students applied for upper-level admission, 10 were accepted, 10 enrolled. School's own exam required. Deadline for receipt of application materials: none. Application fee required: $142. Interview required.

Athletics Interscholastic: basketball (boys, girls), soccer (b), volleyball (g); coed intramural: back packing, hiking/backpacking, outdoor activities, skiing (downhill), snowboarding. 1 PE instructor.

Computers Computers are regularly used in English, foreign language, history, mathematics, science classes. Computer network features include campus e-mail, CD-ROMs, Internet access, wireless campus network.

Contact Mr. Wayne D. Rutherford, Headmaster. 81-11-816-5000. Fax: 81-11-816-2500. E-mail: his@his.ac.jp. Web site: www.his.ac.jp.

HOLDERNESS SCHOOL

Chapel Lane
PO Box 1879
Plymouth, New Hampshire 03264-1879
Head of School: Mr. R. Phillip Peck

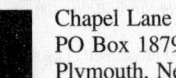

General Information Coeducational boarding and day college-preparatory, arts, religious studies, bilingual studies, and technology school, affiliated with Episcopal Church. Grades 9–PG. Founded: 1879. Setting: small town. Nearest major city is Boston, MA. Students are housed in single-sex dormitories. 620-acre campus. 29 buildings on campus. Approved or accredited by Association of Independent Schools in New England, New England Association of Schools and Colleges, The Association of Boarding Schools, and New Hampshire Department of Education. Member of National Association of Independent Schools and Secondary School Admission Test Board. Endowment: $30.7 million. Total enrollment: 275. Upper school average class size: 12. Upper school faculty-student ratio: 1:7.

Upper School Student Profile Grade 9: 46 students (25 boys, 21 girls); Grade 10: 66 students (44 boys, 22 girls); Grade 11: 83 students (50 boys, 33 girls); Grade 12: 77 students (53 boys, 24 girls); Postgraduate: 3 students (3 boys). 79% of students are boarding students. 40% are state residents. 24 states are represented in upper school student body. 9% are international students. International students from Canada, Ireland, Jamaica, Lithuania, Norway, and Republic of Korea; 2 other countries represented in student body. 20% of students are members of Episcopal Church.

Faculty School total: 50. In upper school: 34 men, 16 women; 27 have advanced degrees; 30 reside on campus.

Subjects Offered Advanced Placement courses, algebra, art, Bible studies, biology, biotechnology, calculus, ceramics, chemistry, chorus, civil rights, community service, drama, driver education, ecology, economics, economics and history, English, environmental science, ethics, ethics and responsibility, European history, fine arts, French, geometry, government/civics, history, human anatomy, human development, humanities, Latin, mathematics, music, music composition, music theory, music theory-AP, photography, physics, politics, religion, science, social studies, Spanish, theater, theology, trigonometry, U.S. history, voice, Web site design, women's studies, world history, world religions, writing.

Graduation Requirements Arts and fine arts (art, music, dance, drama), English, foreign language, history, human development, humanities, mathematics, science, theology. Community service is required.

Special Academic Programs Advanced Placement exam preparation in 11 subject areas; honors section; independent study; term-away projects; study abroad; academic accommodation for the gifted, the musically talented, and the artistically talented.

College Placement 73 students graduated in 2005; all went to college, including Bates College; Brown University; Georgetown University; Middlebury College; University of New Hampshire; University of Vermont. Mean SAT verbal: 569, mean SAT math: 600. 37% scored over 600 on SAT verbal, 39% scored over 600 on SAT math.

Student Life Upper grades have specified standards of dress, student council, honor system. Discipline rests equally with students and faculty. Attendance at religious services is required.

Tuition and Aid Day student tuition: $20,800; 7-day tuition and room/board: $35,100. Tuition installment plan (Insured Tuition Payment Plan, Key Tuition Payment Plan, monthly payment plans). Need-based scholarship grants available. In 2005–06, 21% of upper-school students received aid. Total amount of financial aid awarded in 2005–06: $1,627,100.

Admissions Traditional secondary-level entrance grade is 9. For fall 2005, 346 students applied for upper-level admission, 203 were accepted, 94 enrolled. SSAT or WISC III required. Deadline for receipt of application materials: February 1. Application fee required: $35. Interview required.

Athletics Interscholastic: alpine skiing (boys, girls), baseball (b), basketball (b,g), bicycling (b,g), cross-country running (b,g), field hockey (g), football (b), freestyle skiing (b,g), ice hockey (b,g), lacrosse (b,g), nordic skiing (b,g), skiing (cross-country) (b,g), skiing (downhill) (b,g), snowboarding (b,g), soccer (b,g), softball (g), tennis (b,g); coed interscholastic: golf; coed intramural: back packing, canoeing/kayaking, climbing, fishing, fly fishing, Frisbee, hiking/backpacking, ice hockey, kayaking, mountain biking, mountaineering, outdoor activities, outdoor skills, physical fitness, rock climbing, skiing (cross-country), skiing (downhill), snowboarding, snowshoeing, softball, squash, strength & conditioning, ultimate Frisbee, wall climbing, weight lifting, weight training, wilderness, wilderness survival. 21 coaches, 1 trainer.

Computers Computers are regularly used in Bible studies, creative writing, English, foreign language, graphic arts, history, library, mathematics, music, photography, religious studies, science, technology, theater, video film production, Web site design, yearbook classes. Computer network features include campus e-mail, on-campus library services, CD-ROMs, Internet access, file transfer, office computer access, DVD, 4 computer labs (3 PC, 1 Mac).

Contact Mrs. Nancy Dalley, Assistant to the Director of Admission. 603-536-1747. Fax: 603-536-2125. E-mail: admissions@holderness.org. Web site: www.holderness.org.

See full description on page 834.

HOLLAND HALL

5666 East 81st Street
Tulsa, Oklahoma 74137-2099
Head of School: Dr. Mark D. Desjardins

General Information Coeducational day college-preparatory, arts, religious studies, and technology school, affiliated with Episcopal Church. Grades PK–12. Founded: 1922. Setting: suburban. 162-acre campus. 5 buildings on campus. Approved or accredited by Independent Schools Association of the Southwest and Oklahoma Department of Education. Member of National Association of Independent Schools. Endowment: $75 million. Total enrollment: 994. Upper school average class size: 16. Upper school faculty-student ratio: 1:9.

Upper School Student Profile Grade 9: 91 students (50 boys, 41 girls); Grade 10: 93 students (50 boys, 43 girls); Grade 11: 85 students (55 boys, 30 girls); Grade 12: 82 students (39 boys, 43 girls). 12% of students are members of Episcopal Church.

Faculty School total: 123. In upper school: 30 men, 23 women; 33 have advanced degrees.

Subjects Offered Algebra, American history, American literature, art, art history, biology, biology-AP, calculus, calculus-AP, ceramics, chemistry, chemistry-AP, Chinese, computer programming, computer science, computer science-AP, creative writing, dance, debate, drama, driver education, earth science, ecology, economics, English, English literature, English literature-AP, English-AP, environmental science, ethics, European history, expository writing, fine arts, French, French language-AP, French literature-AP, geology, geometry, government/civics, grammar, history, history-AP, Latin, Latin-AP, mathematics, music, photography, physical education, physics, physics-AP, physiology, religion, science, social studies, Spanish, Spanish language-AP, Spanish-AP, speech, theater, theology, trigonometry, world history, world literature, writing.

Graduation Requirements Arts and fine arts (art, music, dance, drama), English, foreign language, mathematics, physical education (includes health), religion (includes Bible studies and theology), science, social studies (includes history), senior intern program. Community service is required.

Special Academic Programs Advanced Placement exam preparation in 18 subject areas; honors section; independent study; study at local college for college credit.

College Placement 99 students graduated in 2005; all went to college, including New York University; Oklahoma State University; The University of Texas at Austin; University of Colorado at Boulder; University of Oklahoma; University of Tulsa. Median SAT verbal: 630, median SAT math: 620, median composite ACT: 27. 65% scored over 600 on SAT verbal, 62% scored over 600 on SAT math, 65% scored over 26 on composite ACT.

Student Life Upper grades have uniform requirement, student council, honor system. Discipline rests equally with students and faculty. Attendance at religious services is required.

Summer Programs Enrichment, advancement, sports, art/fine arts programs offered; session focuses on academic enrichment; held on campus; accepts boys and girls; open to students from other schools. 855 students usually enrolled. 2006 schedule: June 5 to July 28. Application deadline: none.

Tuition and Aid Day student tuition: $12,950. Tuition installment plan (monthly payment plans, school's own payment plan). Merit scholarship grants, need-based grants available. In 2005–06, 28% of upper-school students received aid; total upper-school merit-scholarship money awarded: $160,640. Total amount of financial aid awarded in 2005–06: $720,910.

Admissions Traditional secondary-level entrance grade is 9. For fall 2005, 90 students applied for upper-level admission, 48 were accepted, 27 enrolled. ERB required. Deadline for receipt of application materials: none. Application fee required: $25. On-campus interview required.

Athletics Interscholastic: baseball (boys), basketball (b,g), cheering (g), cross-country running (b,g), dance (b,g), field hockey (g), football (b), golf (b,g), soccer (b,g), softball (g), tennis (b,g), track and field (b,g), volleyball (g); intramural: aerobics (b,g), modern dance (b,g), soccer (b,g); coed interscholastic: cheering, dance, strength & conditioning, weight lifting; coed intramural: modern dance, soccer, tennis. 1 PE instructor, 6 coaches, 1 trainer.

Computers Computers are regularly used in English, foreign language, history, mathematics, science classes. Computer network features include campus e-mail, on-campus library services, CD-ROMs, online commercial services, Internet access, wireless campus network.

Contact Lori Adams, Director of Admission and Financial Aid. 918-481-1111 Ext. 740. Fax: 918-481-1145. E-mail: ladams@hollandhall.org. Web site: www.hollandhall.org.

ANNOUNCEMENT FROM THE SCHOOL Holland Hall is an independent, coeducational, college-preparatory, Episcopal day school that educates, nurtures, and empowers the individual student for lifelong learning. Holland Hall is recognized for superior college preparation by the Oklahoma State Regents for Higher Education.

THE HOLTON-ARMS SCHOOL

7303 River Road
Bethesda, Maryland 20817
Head of School: Diana Coulton Beebe

General Information Girls' day college-preparatory school. Grades 3–12. Founded: 1901. Setting: suburban. Nearest major city is Washington, DC. 57-acre campus. 8 buildings on campus. Approved or accredited by Association of Independent Maryland Schools, Middle States Association of Colleges and Schools, and Maryland Department of Education. Member of National Association of Independent Schools and Secondary School Admission Test Board. Endowment: $46.1 million. Total enrollment: 667. Upper school average class size: 15. Upper school faculty-student ratio: 1:8.

Upper School Student Profile Grade 9: 90 students (90 girls); Grade 10: 81 students (81 girls); Grade 11: 75 students (75 girls); Grade 12: 82 students (82 girls).

Faculty School total: 57. In upper school: 18 men, 39 women; 45 have advanced degrees.

Subjects Offered African-American studies, algebra, American history, American literature, anatomy and physiology, ancient world history, art, art history-AP, Asian studies, biology, biology-AP, calculus, calculus-AP, ceramics, chemistry, Chinese, community service, computer programming, computer science-AP, contemporary history, creative writing, dance, drama, drawing, ecology, economics, English, English literature, environmental science, European history, expository writing, French, French-AP, geography, government/civics, grammar, health, history, history-AP, Latin, Latin American history, Latin-AP, mathematics, medieval history, Middle Eastern history, music, music technology, painting, philosophy, photography, physical education, physics, physics-AP, psychology, science, science research, social studies, Spanish, Spanish-AP, speech, statistics, theater, trigonometry, women's studies, world history, world literature, writing.

Graduation Requirements Arts, English, foreign language, history, mathematics, physical education (includes health), science. Community service is required.

Special Academic Programs Advanced Placement exam preparation in 10 subject areas; honors section; independent study; academic accommodation for the gifted and the artistically talented.

College Placement 73 students graduated in 2005; all went to college, including Cornell University; Georgetown University; Princeton University; Trinity College; Vassar College; Yale University. Median SAT verbal: 700, median SAT math: 690. 90.4% scored over 600 on SAT verbal, 87.6% scored over 600 on SAT math.

Student Life Upper grades have uniform requirement, student council, honor system. Discipline rests equally with students and faculty.

Tuition and Aid Day student tuition: $23,170–$23,500. Tuition installment plan (Key Tuition Payment Plan, monthly payment plans). Need-based scholarship grants available. In 2005–06, 18% of upper-school students received aid. Total amount of financial aid awarded in 2005–06: $1,674,775.

Admissions Traditional secondary-level entrance grade is 9. ISEE or SSAT required. Deadline for receipt of application materials: February 1. Application fee required: $60. Interview required.

Athletics Interscholastic: basketball, crew, cross-country running, diving, field hockey, ice hockey, lacrosse, soccer, softball, swimming and diving, tennis, track and field, volleyball; intramural: basketball, cross-country running, dance, diving, field hockey, lacrosse, life saving, modern dance, physical fitness, soccer, softball, strength & conditioning, swimming and diving, tennis, track and field, volleyball, weight training. 8 PE instructors, 5 coaches, 1 trainer.

Computers Computers are regularly used in all classes. Computer network features include campus e-mail, on-campus library services, CD-ROMs, online commercial services, Internet access, file transfer, wireless campus network, laptop program (grades 7-12).

Contact Sharron Rodgers, Director of Enrollment and Marketing. 301-365-5300. Fax: 301-365-6071. E-mail: admit@holton-arms.edu. Web site: www.holton-arms.edu.

HOLY NAME HIGH SCHOOL

955 East Wyomissing Boulevard
Reading, Pennsylvania 19611
Head of School: Mr. Keith S. Laser

General Information Coeducational day college-preparatory school, affiliated with Roman Catholic Church. Grades 9–12. Founded: 1964. Setting: urban. 10-acre campus. 1 building on campus. Approved or accredited by Middle States Association of Colleges and Schools and Pennsylvania Department of Education. Total enrollment: 458. Upper school average class size: 25. Upper school faculty-student ratio: 1:12.

Upper School Student Profile Grade 9: 109 students (42 boys, 67 girls); Grade 10: 114 students (51 boys, 63 girls); Grade 11: 96 students (41 boys, 55 girls); Grade 12: 139 students (55 boys, 84 girls). 94% of students are Roman Catholic.

Faculty School total: 35. In upper school: 18 men, 17 women; 11 have advanced degrees.

Graduation Requirements 4 years of theology.

Special Academic Programs Advanced Placement exam preparation in 5 subject areas; honors section; study at local college for college credit.

College Placement 117 students graduated in 2005; 116 went to college. Other: 1 entered military service.

Student Life Upper grades have uniform requirement, student council. Discipline rests primarily with faculty. Attendance at religious services is required.

Summer Programs Sports programs offered; session focuses on basketball and volleyball; held on campus; accepts boys and girls; not open to students from other schools. 300 students usually enrolled. 2006 schedule: June 12 to August 11. Application deadline: none.

Tuition and Aid Day student tuition: $4400. Tuition installment plan (FACTS Tuition Payment Plan). Tuition reduction for siblings, need-based scholarship grants available. In 2005–06, 34% of upper-school students received aid. Total amount of financial aid awarded in 2005–06: $233,222.

Admissions Traditional secondary-level entrance grade is 9. For fall 2005, 125 students applied for upper-level admission, 125 were accepted, 122 enrolled. Math and English placement tests required. Deadline for receipt of application materials: none. Application fee required: $100. On-campus interview recommended.

Athletics Interscholastic: baseball (boys), basketball (b,g), cheering (g), field hockey (g), football (b), soccer (b,g), softball (g), swimming and diving (b,g), tennis (b,g), track and field (b,g), volleyball (b,g); coed interscholastic: cross-country running, golf; coed intramural: bowling, ice hockey, indoor track & field. 1 PE instructor, 52 coaches, 1 trainer.

Computers Computers are regularly used in all academic classes. Computer resources include on-campus library services, CD-ROMs, Internet access.

Contact Mr. Anthony Balistrere, Director of Institutional Advancement. 610-374-8361 Ext. 23. Fax: 610-374-4398. E-mail: tonybalistrere@holynamehighschool.org. Web site: www.holynamehighschool.org.

HOLYOKE CATHOLIC HIGH SCHOOL

66 School Street
Granby, Massachusetts 01033
Head of School: Sr. Cornelia Roy

General Information Coeducational day college-preparatory school, affiliated with Roman Catholic Church. Grades 9–12. Founded: 1963. Setting: rural. Nearest major city is Springfield. 32-acre campus. 2 buildings on campus. Approved or accredited by New England Association of Schools and Colleges and Massachusetts Department of Education. Total enrollment: 357. Upper school average class size: 16. Upper school faculty-student ratio: 1:12.

Upper School Student Profile Grade 9: 83 students (33 boys, 50 girls); Grade 10: 87 students (41 boys, 46 girls); Grade 11: 92 students (43 boys, 49 girls); Grade 12: 95 students (48 boys, 47 girls). 90% of students are Roman Catholic.

Faculty School total: 33. In upper school: 12 men, 21 women; 20 have advanced degrees.

Graduation Requirements Community service hours at each grade level.

Special Academic Programs Advanced Placement exam preparation in 4 subject areas; honors section; independent study.

College Placement 97 students graduated in 2005; 93 went to college. Other: 2 went to work, 2 entered military service.

Student Life Upper grades have uniform requirement, student council. Discipline rests primarily with faculty. Attendance at religious services is required.

Tuition and Aid Day student tuition: $5775. Tuition installment plan (FACTS Tuition Payment Plan, individually arranged payment plans). Need-based scholarship grants available. In 2005–06, 23% of upper-school students received aid. Total amount of financial aid awarded in 2005–06: $287,830.

Admissions Traditional secondary-level entrance grade is 9. For fall 2005, 127 students applied for upper-level admission, 108 were accepted, 81 enrolled. Deadline for receipt of application materials: February 4. Application fee required: $25. Interview recommended.

Athletics Interscholastic: baseball (boys, girls), basketball (b,g), cheering (g), flag football (g), football (b), soccer (b,g), softball (g), tennis (b,g); intramural: volleyball (b,g); coed interscholastic: archery, cross-country running, golf, indoor track, skiing (downhill), swimming and diving; coed intramural: weight training.

Computers Computer network features include on-campus library services, CD-ROMs, Internet access, office computer access, DVD.

Contact Mrs. Theresa Marie Zaborowski, Director of Admissions. 413-467-2477 Ext. 172. Fax: 413-467-3424. E-mail: tzaborowski@gaels.org. Web site: www.gaels.org.

HOLY TRINITY DIOCESAN HIGH SCHOOL

98 Cherry Lane
Hicksville, New York 11801
Head of School: Mr. Gene Fennell

General Information Coeducational day college-preparatory school, affiliated with Roman Catholic Church. Grades 9–12. Founded: 1967. Setting: suburban. Nearest major city is New York. 1 building on campus. Approved or accredited by Middle States Association of Colleges and Schools, New York State Board of Regents, The College Board, and New York Department of Education. Total enrollment: 1,731. Upper school average class size: 28.

Upper School Student Profile Grade 9: 459 students (193 boys, 266 girls); Grade 10: 480 students (220 boys, 260 girls); Grade 11: 419 students (194 boys, 225 girls); Grade 12: 373 students (169 boys, 204 girls). 90% of students are Roman Catholic.

Faculty School total: 110. In upper school: 43 men, 67 women; 91 have advanced degrees.

Subjects Offered Accounting, advanced math, Advanced Placement courses, American government, American government-AP, American history, American history-AP, American literature, American literature-AP, anatomy and physiology, architectural drawing, art, band, biology, biology-AP, British literature, British literature (honors), business law, calculus, calculus-AP, campus ministry, ceramics, chemistry, chemistry-AP, chorus, Christian scripture, Christian studies, Christian testament, comparative religion, composition, computer keyboarding, concert band, criminology, critical studies in film, dance, desktop publishing, earth science, economics, English, English composition, English language and composition-AP, English literature, English literature-AP, environmental science, film, food and nutrition, French, government and politics-AP, health, honors English, honors U.S. history, honors world history, intro to computers, jazz theory, keyboarding/computer, literature and composition-AP, mathematics, music, performing arts, physical education, physics, physics-AP, pre-calculus, public speaking, religion, Spanish, Spanish language-AP, stagecraft, statistics, theater arts, theology, U.S. government and politics, U.S. government and politics-AP, U.S. history, U.S. history-AP, world wide web design.

Graduation Requirements Arts and fine arts (art, music, dance, drama), economics, English, foreign language, mathematics, physical education (includes health), religion (includes Bible studies and theology), science, U.S. government and politics.

Special Academic Programs Advanced Placement exam preparation in 8 subject areas; honors section.

College Placement 369 students graduated in 2005; 362 went to college, including Hofstra University; Nassau Community College; Stony Brook University, State University of New York. Other: 2 went to work, 1 entered military service, 3 had other specific plans. Mean SAT verbal: 526, mean SAT math: 528.

Student Life Upper grades have uniform requirement, student council. Discipline rests primarily with faculty.

Tuition and Aid Day student tuition: $6210. Tuition installment plan (individually arranged payment plans, 10-month tuition plan, 3-payment plan). Need-based scholarship grants available.

Admissions Traditional secondary-level entrance grade is 9. Catholic High School Entrance Examination required. Deadline for receipt of application materials: none. No application fee required.

Athletics Interscholastic: badminton (girls), baseball (b), basketball (b,g), cheering (g), cross-country running (b,g), dance team (g), football (b), golf (b), gymnastics (g), lacrosse (b,g), soccer (b,g), softball (g), swimming and diving (b,g), tennis (b,g), track and field (b,g), volleyball (b,g); intramural: physical training (b), weight training (b); coed interscholastic: bowling. 6 PE instructors, 1 trainer.

Computers Computers are regularly used in English, graphic design, Web site design classes. Computer network features include on-campus library services, Internet access.

Contact Admissions. 516-433-2900. Fax: 516-433-2827. E-mail: hths98@holytrinityhs.echalk.com. Web site: www.holytrinityhs.org.

HOME STUDY INTERNATIONAL

12501 Old Columbia Pike
Silver Spring, Maryland 20904-6600

See full description on page 836.

HOOSAC SCHOOL

PO Box 9
Hoosick, New York 12089
Head of School: Richard J. Lomuscio

General Information Coeducational boarding and day college-preparatory school, affiliated with Episcopal Church. Grades 8–PG. Founded: 1889. Setting: rural. Nearest major city is Albany. Students are housed in single-sex dormitories. 350-acre campus. 16 buildings on campus. Approved or accredited by Middle States Association of Colleges and Schools, National Association of Episcopal Schools, New York State Association of Independent Schools, The Association of Boarding Schools, and New York Department of Education. Member of National Association of Independent Schools and Secondary School Admission Test Board. Endowment: $1 million. Total enrollment: 118. Upper school average class size: 8. Upper school faculty-student ratio: 1:5.

Upper School Student Profile Grade 8: 6 students (4 boys, 2 girls); Grade 9: 18 students (10 boys, 8 girls); Grade 10: 25 students (17 boys, 8 girls); Grade 11: 37 students (30 boys, 7 girls); Grade 12: 38 students (27 boys, 11 girls); Postgraduate: 4 students (4 boys). 88% of students are boarding students. 29% are state residents. 17 states are represented in upper school student body. 27% are international students. International students from Canada, Croatia, Hong Kong, India, Republic of Korea, and Saudi Arabia; 9 other countries represented in student body.

Faculty School total: 23. In upper school: 13 men, 10 women; 8 have advanced degrees; 15 reside on campus.

Subjects Offered Algebra, American history, American literature, art, art history, astronomy, biology, calculus, calculus-AP, ceramics, chemistry, computer science, creative writing, criminology, dance, drama, driver education, earth science, English, English literature, English-AP, ethics, European history, expository writing, fine arts, French, geometry, government/civics, grammar, history, history-AP, marketing, mathematics, music, photography, physical education, physics, science, social studies, theater, world history, world literature, writing.

Graduation Requirements Arts and fine arts (art, music, dance, drama), computer literacy, English, ethics, foreign language, mathematics, physical education (includes health), science, social studies (includes history).

Special Academic Programs Advanced Placement exam preparation in 3 subject areas; accelerated programs; independent study; study at local college for college credit; academic accommodation for the musically talented and the artistically talented; remedial reading and/or remedial writing; remedial math; programs in English, mathematics, general development for dyslexic students; ESL (5 students enrolled).

College Placement 38 students graduated in 2005; all went to college, including Boston College; Boston University; Hamilton College; Hobart and William Smith Colleges; University of Michigan.

Student Life Upper grades have specified standards of dress, student council, honor system. Discipline rests primarily with faculty. Attendance at religious services is required.

Tuition and Aid Day student tuition: $14,000; 7-day tuition and room/board: $26,200. Tuition installment plan (Academic Management Services Plan, monthly payment plans, individually arranged payment plans). Need-based scholarship grants, need-based loans available. In 2005–06, 30% of upper-school students received aid. Total amount of financial aid awarded in 2005–06: $525,000.

Admissions Traditional secondary-level entrance grade is 9. For fall 2005, 192 students applied for upper-level admission, 84 were accepted, 53 enrolled. Deadline for receipt of application materials: none. Application fee required: $30. Interview required.

Athletics Interscholastic: baseball (boys), basketball (b,g), ice hockey (b), lacrosse (b); intramural: bicycling (b,g), flag football (b,g), floor hockey (b,g); coed intramural: alpine skiing, aquatics, billiards, bowling, cross-country running, dance, deck hockey, fishing, golf, indoor hockey, indoor soccer, life saving, outdoor activities, outdoor adventure, outdoor recreation, physical fitness. 1 PE instructor, 15 coaches.

Computers Computers are regularly used in English classes. Computer network features include campus e-mail, CD-ROMs, Internet access, file transfer, wireless campus network.

Contact Dean S. Foster, Assistant Headmaster. 800-822-0159. Fax: 518-686-3370. E-mail: admissions@hoosac.com. Web site: www.hoosac.com.

See full description on page 838.

HOPE CHRISTIAN SCHOOL

PO Box 235
Champion, Alberta T0L 0R0, Canada
Head of School: Mr. Dale Anger

General Information Coeducational day college-preparatory, general academic, arts, vocational, and religious studies school, affiliated with Evangelical Free Church of America. Grades 1–12. Founded: 1980. Setting: small town. Nearest major city is Lethbridge, Canada. 2 buildings on campus. Approved or accredited by Alberta Department of Education. Language of instruction: English. Upper school average class size: 10.

Upper School Student Profile 20% of students are members of Evangelical Free Church of America.

Faculty In upper school: 2 men, 2 women.

Student Life Upper grades have uniform requirement. Discipline rests primarily with faculty. Attendance at religious services is required.

Tuition and Aid Guaranteed tuition plan.

Admissions Deadline for receipt of application materials: none. No application fee required. Interview required.

Contact Mr. Dale Anger, Principal. 403-897-3019. Fax: 403-897-2392. E-mail: principal@hopechristianschool.ca. Web site: hopechristianschool.ca.

HOPKINS SCHOOL

986 Forest Road
New Haven, Connecticut 06515
Head of School: Ms. Barbara Masters Riley

General Information Coeducational day college-preparatory school. Grades 7–12. Founded: 1660. Setting: suburban. Nearest major city is New York, NY. 108-acre campus. 9 buildings on campus. Approved or accredited by Connecticut Association of Independent Schools, New England Association of Schools and Colleges, and Connecticut Department of Education. Member of National Association of Independent Schools. Endowment: $40 million. Total enrollment: 655. Upper school average class size: 14. Upper school faculty-student ratio: 1:6.

Upper School Student Profile Grade 9: 132 students (65 boys, 67 girls); Grade 10: 130 students (68 boys, 62 girls); Grade 11: 124 students (66 boys, 58 girls); Grade 12: 128 students (67 boys, 61 girls).

Faculty School total: 106. In upper school: 52 men, 54 women; 85 have advanced degrees.

Subjects Offered African-American history, algebra, American history, American literature, ancient history, art, art history, art history-AP, art-AP, biology, biology-AP, British history, calculus, calculus-AP, ceramics, chemistry, chemistry-AP, chorus, classical music, computer math, computer programming, computer science, computer science-AP, creative writing, drama, earth science, English, English literature, environmental science-AP, European history, expository writing, film, fine arts, French, French-AP, geometry, government/civics, Greek, history, Holocaust studies, HTML design, human sexuality, Islamic history, Italian, jazz, Latin, Latin American history, Latin-AP, mathematics, military history, music, music theory, photography, physics, physics-AP, politics, psychology, public speaking, Russian history, Spanish, Spanish-AP, studio art, studio art-AP, theater, trigonometry, U.S. history-AP, video, Web site design, woodworking, world history, world literature, writing.

Graduation Requirements Arts and fine arts (art, music, dance, drama), English, foreign language, mathematics, physical education (includes health), science, social studies (includes history), swimming.

Special Academic Programs Advanced Placement exam preparation in 15 subject areas; honors section; independent study; term-away projects; study abroad.

College Placement 134 students graduated in 2005; all went to college, including Boston College; Brown University; Cornell University; Georgetown University; University of Pennsylvania; Yale University. Mean SAT verbal: 695, mean SAT math: 700.

Student Life Upper grades have specified standards of dress, student council, honor system. Discipline rests equally with students and faculty.

Summer Programs Remediation, enrichment, advancement, ESL, sports, art/fine arts, rigorous outdoor training, computer instruction programs offered; session focuses on academics and athletics; held both on and off campus; held at Yale outdoor education center; accepts boys and girls; open to students from other schools. 290 students usually enrolled. 2006 schedule: June 26 to August 4. Application deadline: none.

Tuition and Aid Day student tuition: $24,500. Tuition installment plan (Academic Management Services Plan, Key Tuition Payment Plan). Need-based scholarship grants, paying campus jobs available. In 2005–06, 21% of upper-school students received aid. Total amount of financial aid awarded in 2005–06: $2,245,000.

Admissions Traditional secondary-level entrance grade is 9. For fall 2005, 250 students applied for upper-level admission, 95 were accepted, 60 enrolled. ISEE or SSAT required. Deadline for receipt of application materials: February 1. Application fee required: $50. On-campus interview required.

Athletics Interscholastic: baseball (boys), basketball (b,g), cross-country running (b,g), diving (b,g), fencing (b,g), field hockey (g), football (b), independent competitive sports (b,g), indoor track (b), lacrosse (b,g), soccer (b,g), softball (g), swimming and diving (b,g), tennis (b,g), track and field (b,g), volleyball (g), wrestling (b); intramural: independent competitive sports (b,g); coed interscholastic: aquatics, golf, independent competitive sports, water polo; coed intramural: aerobics, aerobics/dance, aerobics/nautilus, ballet, basketball, climbing, cooperative games, dance, fencing, fitness, floor hockey, independent competitive sports, nautilus, outdoor adventure, project adventure, ropes courses, running, soccer, swimming and diving, tennis, volleyball, weight lifting, weight training, wilderness. 5 coaches, 3 trainers.

Computers Computers are regularly used in art, English, foreign language, history, mathematics, science classes. Computer network features include campus e-mail, on-campus library services, CD-ROMs, Internet access.

Contact Mr. Dana Blanchard, Director of Admissions. 203-397-1001 Ext. 211. Fax: 203-389-2249. E-mail: admissions@hopkins.edu. Web site: www.hopkins.edu.

THE HORACE MANN SCHOOL

231 West 246th Street
Riverdale, New York 10471
Head of School: Dr. Thomas M. Kelly

General Information Coeducational day college-preparatory, arts, and technology school. Grades N–12. Founded: 1887. Setting: suburban. Nearest major city is New York. 18-acre campus. 6 buildings on campus. Approved or accredited by New York State Association of Independent Schools and New York Department of Education. Member of National Association of Independent Schools and Secondary School Admission Test Board. Endowment: $67 million. Total enrollment: 1,757. Upper school average class size: 17. Upper school faculty-student ratio: 1:9.

Upper School Student Profile Grade 9: 179 students (89 boys, 90 girls); Grade 10: 177 students (93 boys, 84 girls); Grade 11: 179 students (91 boys, 88 girls); Grade 12: 176 students (90 boys, 86 girls).

Faculty School total: 245.

Subjects Offered Advanced Placement courses, algebra, American history, anthropology, art, art history, astronomy, biology, business, calculus, ceramics, chemistry, community service, computer math, computer programming, computer science, creative writing, dance, drama, driver education, economics, English, English literature, environmental science, European history, expository writing, fine arts, French, French-AP, geology, geometry, German, government/civics, grammar, health, history, history of science, Italian, Japanese, journalism, Latin, logic, mathematics, music, philosophy, photography, physical education, physics, psychology, religion, Russian, science, social studies, Spanish, statistics, television, theater, trigonometry, typing, video, world history, writing.

Graduation Requirements Algebra, arts and fine arts (art, music, dance, drama), biology, computer science, CPR, English, foreign language, geometry, health and wellness, mathematics, physical education (includes health), science, social studies (includes history), trigonometry, U.S. history, world history. Community service is required.

Special Academic Programs Advanced Placement exam preparation in 19 subject areas; honors section; independent study.

College Placement 176 students graduated in 2005; all went to college, including Brown University; Cornell University; Harvard University; University of Pennsylvania; Washington University in St. Louis; Yale University.

Student Life Upper grades have student council. Discipline rests primarily with faculty.

Summer Programs Remediation, enrichment, advancement, ESL, art/fine arts, computer instruction programs offered; session focuses on academics; held on campus; accepts boys and girls; open to students from other schools. 200 students usually enrolled. 2006 schedule: June 22 to August 4. Application deadline: none.

Tuition and Aid Day student tuition: $27,350. Tuition installment plan (Academic Management Services Plan, 3-payment plan). Need-based scholarship grants available. In 2005–06, 22% of upper-school students received aid. Total amount of financial aid awarded in 2005–06: $2,985,943.

Admissions Traditional secondary-level entrance grade is 9. ERB, ISEE or SSAT required. Deadline for receipt of application materials: December 1. Application fee required: $50. On-campus interview required.

Athletics Interscholastic: baseball (boys), basketball (b,g), cross-country running (b,g), field hockey (g), football (b), gymnastics (g), lacrosse (b,g), soccer (b,g), softball (g), swimming and diving (b,g), tennis (b,g), track and field (b,g), volleyball (g), wrestling (b); intramural: baseball (b), basketball (b,g), field hockey (g), football (b), lacrosse (b,g), soccer (b,g), tennis (b,g); coed interscholastic: fencing, golf, indoor track & field, squash, water polo, winter (indoor) track; coed intramural: bowling, climbing, cross-country running, dance squad, dance team, fitness, Frisbee, golf, modern dance, outdoor education, paddle tennis, physical fitness, physical training, rock climbing, ropes courses, softball, strength & conditioning, swimming and diving, table tennis, track and field, ultimate Frisbee, volleyball, water polo, weight lifting, weight training. 14 PE instructors, 22 coaches, 2 trainers.

Computers Computers are regularly used in English, library skills, mathematics, media production, science classes. Computer network features include campus e-mail, on-campus library services, CD-ROMs, Internet access, file transfer, office computer access, DVD, wireless campus network.

Contact Lisa J. Moreira, Director of Admissions & Financial Aid. 718-432-4100. Fax: 718-432-3610. E-mail: admissions@horacemann.org. Web site: www. horacemann.org/.

HORIZONS SCHOOL

1900 DeKalb Avenue
Atlanta, Georgia 30307
Head of School: Mr. Les Garber

General Information Coeducational boarding and day college-preparatory, arts, and ESL school. Boarding grades 8–PG, day grades K–PG. Founded: 1978. Setting: urban. Students are housed in single-sex-by-hall dormitories. 4-acre campus. 4 buildings on campus. Approved or accredited by Georgia Accrediting Commission and Georgia Department of Education. Endowment: $100,000. Total enrollment: 100. Upper school average class size: 12. Upper school faculty-student ratio: 1:10.
Upper School Student Profile 15% of students are boarding students. 80% are state residents. 3 states are represented in upper school student body. 20% are international students. International students from China, Ethiopia, Germany, Japan, Republic of Korea, and Viet Nam; 5 other countries represented in student body.
Faculty School total: 12. In upper school: 3 men, 5 women; 4 have advanced degrees; 4 reside on campus.
Subjects Offered Algebra, American literature, art, biology, calculus, chemistry, computer literacy, contemporary history, creative writing, drama, economics, English, environmental science, French, geometry, government, photography, physical science, physics, pre-algebra, pre-calculus, psychology, Spanish, U.S. history, world history, world literature, zoology.
Graduation Requirements English, foreign language, independent study, mathematics, physical education (includes health), science, social studies (includes history). Community service is required.
Special Academic Programs Advanced Placement exam preparation in 2 subject areas; independent study; ESL (16 students enrolled).
College Placement 18 students graduated in 2005; 17 went to college, including Emory University; Georgia State University; University of Georgia. Other: 1 went to work.
Student Life Upper grades have specified standards of dress, student council, honor system. Discipline rests equally with students and faculty.
Tuition and Aid Day student tuition: $8800; 5-day tuition and room/board: $17,000; 7-day tuition and room/board: $17,000. Tuition installment plan (monthly payment plans). Paying campus jobs available. In 2005–06, 70% of upper-school students received aid. Total amount of financial aid awarded in 2005–06: $56,000.
Admissions For fall 2005, 25 students applied for upper-level admission, 15 were accepted, 15 enrolled. Deadline for receipt of application materials: none. Application fee required: $200. Interview required.
Athletics Coed Intramural: soccer.
Computers Computers are regularly used in English, ESL, foreign language, history, mathematics, science classes. Computer network features include Internet access.
Contact Mr. Les Garber, Administrator. 404-378-2219. Fax: 404-378-8946. E-mail: horizonsschool@horizonsschool.com. Web site: www.horizonsschool.com.

ANNOUNCEMENT FROM THE SCHOOL Horizons School of Atlanta emphasizes education for families interested in the advantages of a small school community. High school classes (with an average size of 12 students) feature seminar-style approaches that maximize student participation and involvement. Elementary and middle school classes (with an average size of 14 students) provide a forum for optimal personalized and individualized education. Academically, Horizons offers a college-preparatory curriculum, with more than 90% of graduates enrolling in colleges and universities across the country. In addition, Horizons' philosophy and programs incorporate those experiences, skills, and values necessary for success. International students, an integral part of Horizons, graduate and then enroll in an American college or university. Some international students enroll for a transition year between high school and college in order to improve English proficiency and other skills required at a college level. There is no anonymity at Horizons School and no back of the classroom in which to hide. Education is active, not passive, and students learn responsibility by being given responsibility. Leadership skills are gained through experiences, and individual education is the empowerment of each student—the belief that he or she can accomplish anything. Students play an active role in all aspects of the School, from the traditional classroom expectations to the responsibilities each person has to the School community. The campus has 4 buildings, 3 of which (the high school, gymnasium, and theater) were built by students, on 3½ wooded acres. Students are involved in the decision-making process to constantly upgrade the campus. Horizons welcomes new students and families and extends an invitation to call 404-378-2219 for more information or to set up a visit.

HOSANNA CHRISTIAN SCHOOL

5000 Hosanna Way
Kamath Falls, Oregon 97603
Head of School: Mr. Dan Dickey

General Information Coeducational day college-preparatory and general academic school, affiliated with Evangelical faith. Grades PK–12. Founded: 1988. Setting: small town. Nearest major city is Klamath Falls. 26-acre campus. 1 building on campus. Approved or accredited by Association of Christian Schools International, Northwest Association of Schools and Colleges, and Oregon Department of Education. Endowment: $100,000. Total enrollment: 320. Upper school average class size: 25. Upper school faculty-student ratio: 1:8.
Upper School Student Profile Grade 9: 14 students (6 boys, 8 girls); Grade 10: 22 students (8 boys, 14 girls); Grade 11: 13 students (7 boys, 6 girls); Grade 12: 15 students (5 boys, 10 girls).
Faculty School total: 20. In upper school: 4 men, 6 women; 3 have advanced degrees.
Special Academic Programs Study at local college for college credit; remedial reading and/or remedial writing; remedial math.
College Placement 12 students graduated in 2005; they went to Corban College; Oregon Institute of Technology; Whitworth College.
Student Life Upper grades have uniform requirement, student council, honor system. Discipline rests primarily with faculty. Attendance at religious services is required.
Tuition and Aid Day student tuition: $3820. Tuition installment plan (monthly payment plans). Tuition reduction for siblings, need-based scholarship grants available. In 2005–06, 10% of upper-school students received aid. Total amount of financial aid awarded in 2005–06: $9000.
Admissions Traditional secondary-level entrance grade is 9. For fall 2005, 20 students applied for upper-level admission, 15 were accepted, 12 enrolled. Deadline for receipt of application materials: none. No application fee required. On-campus interview required.
Athletics Interscholastic: basketball (boys, girls), cross-country running (b,g), dance team (g), golf (b,g), swimming and diving (b,g), track and field (b,g), volleyball (g). 2 PE instructors, 8 coaches.
Computers Computer network features include on-campus library services, CD-ROMs, online commercial services, Internet access, office computer access.
Contact Mrs. Christi Garrison, Assistant. 541-882-7732. Fax: 541-882-6940. E-mail: admin@hosannachristian.org. Web site: www.hosannachristian.org.

THE HOTCHKISS SCHOOL

11 Interlaken Road
PO Box 800
Lakeville, Connecticut 06039
Head of School: Mr. Robert H. Mattoon Jr.

General Information Coeducational boarding and day college-preparatory school. Grades 9–PG. Founded: 1891. Setting: rural. Nearest major city is Hartford. Students are housed in single-sex dormitories. 550-acre campus. 80 buildings on campus. Approved or accredited by Connecticut Association of Independent Schools, New England Association of Schools and Colleges, The Association of Boarding Schools, and Connecticut Department of Education. Member of National Association of Independent Schools and Secondary School Admission Test Board. Endowment: $356.6 million. Total enrollment: 566. Upper school average class size: 12. Upper school faculty-student ratio: 1:5.
Upper School Student Profile Grade 9: 96 students (49 boys, 47 girls); Grade 10: 151 students (78 boys, 73 girls); Grade 11: 159 students (82 boys, 77 girls); Grade 12: 146 students (73 boys, 73 girls); Postgraduate: 14 students (12 boys, 2 girls). 89% of students are boarding students. 23% are state residents. 33 states are represented in upper school student body. 17% are international students. International students from Canada, China, Hong Kong, Mexico, Republic of Korea, and United Kingdom; 13 other countries represented in student body.
Faculty School total: 128. In upper school: 73 men, 55 women; 79 have advanced degrees; 92 reside on campus.
Subjects Offered 3-dimensional design, acting, advanced math, advanced studio art-AP, algebra, American history, American history-AP, American literature, anatomy and physiology, Ancient Greek, ancient history, architecture, art, art history, art history-AP, astronomy, Bible studies, bioethics, biology, biology-AP, calculus, calculus-AP, ceramics, chemistry, chemistry-AP, Chinese, Chinese history, chorus, classics, comparative government and politics-AP, computer applications, computer math, computer programming, computer programming-AP, computer science, conceptual physics, constitutional history of U.S., creative writing, dance, digital photography, discrete math, drama, dramatic arts, drawing, ecology, economics, economics-AP, English, English literature, English-AP, environmental science, environmental science-AP, environmental studies, ethics, European history, European history-AP, expository writing, film, filmmaking, fine arts, French, French language-AP, French literature-AP, geology, geometry, German, government/civics, Greek, history of jazz, history of music, Holocaust, humanities, independent study, Japanese history, jazz band, jazz dance, jazz ensemble, Latin, Latin American history, Latin-AP, limnology, mathematics, meteorology, modern Chinese history, modern European history-AP, music, music appreciation, music composition, music history, music technology, music theory, music theory-AP, musical productions, musical theater, non-Western literature, orchestra, organic chemistry, philosophy, photography, physics, physics-AP, playwriting, pre-calculus, public speaking, religion, Russian history, science, social science, social studies, Spanish, Spanish literature-AP, statistics-AP, studio art, the Sixties, theater, trigonometry, video, voice, world literature, writing.
Graduation Requirements American history, arts and fine arts (art, music, dance, drama), English, foreign language, mathematics, science.

The Hotchkiss School

Special Academic Programs Advanced Placement exam preparation in 18 subject areas; honors section; independent study; term-away projects; study abroad; academic accommodation for the gifted, the musically talented, and the artistically talented.

College Placement 165 students graduated in 2005; 163 went to college, including Cornell University; Georgetown University; Middlebury College; Trinity College; University of Pennsylvania; Yale University. Other: 2 had other specific plans. Mean SAT verbal: 636, mean SAT math: 653. 75% scored over 600 on SAT verbal, 78% scored over 600 on SAT math.

Student Life Upper grades have specified standards of dress, student council. Discipline rests equally with students and faculty.

Summer Programs Art/fine arts programs offered; session focuses on chamber music, environmental studies; held on campus; accepts boys and girls; open to students from other schools. 30 students usually enrolled. 2006 schedule: June 25 to July 16.

Tuition and Aid Day student tuition: $28,815; 7-day tuition and room/board: $33,810. Tuition installment plan (Key Tuition Payment Plan). Need-based scholarship grants, middle-income loans available. In 2005–06, 34% of upper-school students received aid. Total amount of financial aid awarded in 2005–06: $4,608,000.

Admissions Traditional secondary-level entrance grade is 9. For fall 2005, 1,697 students applied for upper-level admission, 338 were accepted, 185 enrolled. ISEE, PSAT or SAT for applicants to grade 11 and 12, SAT, SSAT or TOEFL required. Deadline for receipt of application materials: January 16. Application fee required: $50. Interview required.

Athletics Interscholastic: baseball (boys), basketball (b,g), cross-country running (b,g), diving (b,g), field hockey (g), football (b), ice hockey (b,g), lacrosse (b,g); coed interscholastic: golf, sailing; coed intramural: aerobics, aerobics/nautilus, ballet, basketball, canoeing/kayaking, climbing, cross-country running, dance, drill team, equestrian sports, fencing, fishing, fitness, fitness walking, fly fishing, freestyle skiing, golf, hiking/backpacking, horseback riding, ice hockey, ice skating, jogging, kayaking, life saving, modern dance, mountain biking, nautilus, outdoor activities, outdoor recreation, paddle tennis, physical fitness, physical training, rafting, rappelling, rock climbing, ropes courses, running. 2 coaches, 2 trainers.

Computers Computers are regularly used in all academic classes. Computer network features include campus e-mail, on-campus library services, CD-ROMs, online commercial services, Internet access, file transfer, DVD.

Contact Mr. William D. Leahy, Dean of Admission. 860-435-3102. Fax: 860-435-0042. E-mail: admission@hotchkiss.org. Web site: www.hotchkiss.org.

See full description on page 840.

HOUGHTON ACADEMY

9790 Thayer Street
Houghton, New York 14744
Head of School: Philip G. Stockin

General Information Coeducational boarding and day college-preparatory, arts, religious studies, and ESL school, affiliated with Wesleyan Church. Boarding grades 9–PG, day grades 7–PG. Founded: 1883. Setting: rural. Nearest major city is Buffalo. Students are housed in single-sex dormitories and staff homes. 25-acre campus. 5 buildings on campus. Approved or accredited by Association of Christian Schools International, Middle States Association of Colleges and Schools, The Association of Boarding Schools, and New York Department of Education. Endowment: $90,000. Total enrollment: 160. Upper school average class size: 17. Upper school faculty-student ratio: 1:17.

Upper School Student Profile Grade 9: 23 students (17 boys, 6 girls); Grade 10: 33 students (22 boys, 11 girls); Grade 11: 30 students (16 boys, 14 girls); Grade 12: 43 students (17 boys, 26 girls); Postgraduate: 1 student (1 boy). 47% of students are boarding students. 70% are state residents. 7 states are represented in upper school student body. 20% are international students. International students from China, Hong Kong, Japan, Mexico, Republic of Korea, and Viet Nam; 3 other countries represented in student body. 25% of students are members of Wesleyan Church.

Faculty School total: 23. In upper school: 7 men, 16 women; 10 have advanced degrees; 3 reside on campus.

Subjects Offered Algebra, American history, American literature, art, band, Bible, Bible studies, biology, business, business skills, calculus, chemistry, chorus, community service, computer science, creative writing, desktop publishing, driver education, earth science, economics, English, English literature, environmental science, ESL, ethics, fine arts, geography, geometry, government/civics, grammar, history, home economics, industrial arts, mathematics, music, photography, physical education, physics, science, social science, social studies, Spanish, speech, trigonometry, word processing, world history, writing.

Graduation Requirements Arts and fine arts (art, music, dance, drama), Bible, electives, English, mathematics, physical education (includes health), science, social studies (includes history).

Special Academic Programs Honors section; independent study; study at local college for college credit; ESL (5 students enrolled).

College Placement 48 students graduated in 2005; 45 went to college, including LeTourneau University; State University of New York College at Geneseo; University at Albany, State University of New York. Other: 2 had other specific plans. Median SAT verbal: 570, median SAT math: 540. 35% scored over 600 on SAT verbal, 42% scored over 600 on SAT math.

Student Life Upper grades have specified standards of dress, student council. Discipline rests primarily with faculty. Attendance at religious services is required.

Tuition and Aid Day student tuition: $5938; 7-day tuition and room/board: $18,427. Tuition installment plan (SMART Tuition Payment Plan, individually arranged payment plans). Need-based scholarship grants available. In 2005–06, 25% of upper-school students received aid. Total amount of financial aid awarded in 2005–06: $95,000.

Admissions For fall 2005, 90 students applied for upper-level admission, 75 were accepted, 65 enrolled. PSAT or SAT for applicants to grade 11 and 12, SLEP, SSAT or TOEFL required. Deadline for receipt of application materials: none. Application fee required: $50. Interview required.

Athletics Interscholastic: baseball (boys), basketball (b,g), cheering (g), soccer (b,g), softball (g), volleyball (g); intramural: badminton (b,g), basketball (b,g), billiards (b,g), floor hockey (b,g), golf (b,g), indoor soccer (b,g), paddle tennis (b,g), racquetball (b,g), skiing (downhill) (b,g), soccer (b,g), table tennis (b,g), tennis (b,g), volleyball (b,g), winter walking (b,g); coed interscholastic: golf; coed intramural: badminton, ball hockey, indoor soccer, paddle tennis, skiing (downhill), softball, table tennis, winter walking. 2 PE instructors, 11 coaches, 1 trainer.

Computers Computers are regularly used in accounting, Bible studies, college planning, English, graphic design, keyboarding, mathematics, multimedia, SAT preparation, science, word processing, yearbook classes. Computer network features include campus e-mail, on-campus library services, CD-ROMs, Internet access, file transfer, office computer access, DVD, electronic access to Houghton College Library holdings.

Contact Ronald J. Bradbury, Director of Admissions. 585-567-8115. Fax: 585-567-8048. E-mail: admissons@houghtonacademy.org. Web site: www.houghtonacademy.org.

HOUSTON LEARNING ACADEMY-CENTRAL CAMPUS

3333 Bering Drive
Houston, Texas 77057
Head of School: Shari Schiffman

General Information Coeducational day college-preparatory, general academic, business, and technology school; primarily serves underachievers. Grades 9–12. Founded: 1983. Setting: urban. 1 building on campus. Approved or accredited by CITA (Commission on International and Trans-Regional Accreditation), Southern Association of Colleges and Schools, and Texas Department of Education. Total enrollment: 54. Upper school average class size: 12. Upper school faculty-student ratio: 1:15.

Upper School Student Profile Grade 9: 7 students (3 boys, 4 girls); Grade 10: 7 students (5 boys, 2 girls); Grade 11: 18 students (8 boys, 10 girls); Grade 12: 22 students (15 boys, 7 girls).

Faculty School total: 4. In upper school: 2 men, 2 women; 3 have advanced degrees.

Graduation Requirements Texas Education Agency requirements.

Special Academic Programs Accelerated programs; independent study; remedial reading and/or remedial writing; remedial math.

College Placement 35 students graduated in 2005; 30 went to college, including Abilene Christian University; Texas A&M University; The University of Texas at Austin; University of Houston. Other: 4 went to work, 1 entered military service.

Student Life Discipline rests primarily with faculty.

Summer Programs Remediation, enrichment, advancement, art/fine arts, computer instruction programs offered; session focuses on earning extra credits required for graduation; held on campus; accepts boys and girls; open to students from other schools. 1300 students usually enrolled. 2006 schedule: June 7 to August 3. Application deadline: May 15.

Tuition and Aid Day student tuition: $5400. Tuition installment plan (monthly payment plans, discounts for paying for the entire semester or year in advance). Tuition reduction for siblings, prepGATE Loans available.

Admissions Traditional secondary-level entrance grade is 10. For fall 2005, 54 students applied for upper-level admission, 54 were accepted, 54 enrolled. Deadline for receipt of application materials: none. No application fee required. On-campus interview required.

Computers Computers are regularly used in business applications classes. Computer resources include CD-ROMs, Internet access.

Contact Linda Stonefield, Administrative Assistant. 713-789-9197. Fax: 713-785-9043. E-mail: nobel1606@nlcinc.com.

HOWE MILITARY SCHOOL

PO Box 240
Howe, Indiana 46746
Head of School: Dr. Duane Van Orden

General Information Coeducational boarding and day college-preparatory, religious studies, bilingual studies, and Junior ROTC school, affiliated with Episcopal Church. Boarding grades 5–12, day grades 5–8. Founded: 1884. Setting: rural. Nearest major city is South Bend. Students are housed in single-sex dormitories. 100-acre campus.

15 buildings on campus. Approved or accredited by Independent Schools Association of the Central States, North Central Association of Colleges and Schools, The Association of Boarding Schools, and Indiana Department of Education. Member of National Association of Independent Schools. Endowment: $26 million. Total enrollment: 111. Upper school average class size: 10. Upper school faculty-student ratio: 1:9.

Upper School Student Profile Grade 9: 16 students (14 boys, 2 girls); Grade 10: 26 students (19 boys, 7 girls); Grade 11: 15 students (7 boys, 8 girls); Grade 12: 17 students (15 boys, 2 girls). 100% of students are boarding students. 25% are state residents. 17 states are represented in upper school student body. 1% are international students. International students from Republic of Korea. 9% of students are members of Episcopal Church.

Faculty School total: 30. In upper school: 12 men, 9 women; 5 have advanced degrees; 6 reside on campus.

Subjects Offered Accounting, algebra, American history, American literature, anatomy, art, band, biology, biology-AP, broadcasting, business skills, cabinet making, calculus, calculus-AP, chemistry, chemistry-AP, chorus, computer graphics, computer literacy, computer programming, computer science, creative writing, drafting, earth science, economics, English, English literature, environmental science, ethics, French, geography, geometry, German, government/civics, grammar, history, industrial arts, journalism, JROTC, leadership training, mathematics, mechanical drawing, military science, music, music theory, painting, philosophy, physical education, physics, pre-algebra, pre-calculus, religion, science, social studies, sociology, Spanish, speech, speech communications, trigonometry, world geography, world history, world literature, yearbook.

Graduation Requirements Computer education, English, foreign language, JROTC, leadership training, mathematics, physical education (includes health), religion (includes Bible studies and theology), science, social studies (includes history).

Special Academic Programs Advanced Placement exam preparation in 3 subject areas.

College Placement 21 students graduated in 2005; 19 went to college, including Adrian College; Lake Superior State University; Michigan State University; Rose-Hulman Institute of Technology; The College of Wooster. Other: 1 entered military service. Median SAT verbal: 470, median SAT math: 482, median composite ACT: 23. 3% scored over 600 on SAT verbal, 6% scored over 600 on SAT math, 9% scored over 26 on composite ACT.

Student Life Upper grades have uniform requirement, student council, honor system. Discipline rests primarily with faculty. Attendance at religious services is required.

Summer Programs Remediation, advancement, sports, rigorous outdoor training programs offered; session focuses on academics with a blend of recreation; held off campus; held at Cedar Lake, IN; accepts boys; open to students from other schools. 150 students usually enrolled. 2006 schedule: June 18 to July 28. Application deadline: June 30.

Tuition and Aid Day student tuition: $6650; 7-day tuition and room/board: $23,000. Tuition installment plan (delayed payment plan). Tuition reduction for siblings, need-based scholarship grants available. In 2005–06, 40% of upper-school students received aid. Total amount of financial aid awarded in 2005–06: $500,000.

Admissions Traditional secondary-level entrance grade is 10. For fall 2005, 44 students applied for upper-level admission, 35 were accepted, 22 enrolled. OLSAT, Stanford Achievement Test required. Deadline for receipt of application materials: none. Application fee required: $100. On-campus interview required.

Athletics Interscholastic: baseball (boys), basketball (b,g), cheering (g), cross-country running (b,g), softball (g), tennis (b,g), volleyball (g), wrestling (b); intramural: baseball (b), football (b), physical training (b); coed interscholastic: basketball, cheering, cross-country running, golf, JROTC drill, riflery, soccer, swimming and diving, track and field, wrestling; coed intramural: basketball, billiards, horseback riding, physical fitness, soccer, softball, swimming and diving, table tennis, volleyball, weight lifting. 1 PE instructor.

Computers Computers are regularly used in English, foreign language, JROTC, mathematics, newspaper, science, yearbook classes. Computer network features include campus e-mail, on-campus library services, CD-ROMs, Internet access, file transfer, office computer access, Lotus 1-2-3, Word Perfect, CAD, Microsoft Office.

Contact Dr. Brent E. Smith, Director of Admissions. 260-562-2131 Ext. 221. Fax: 260-562-3678. E-mail: admissions@howemilitary.com. Web site: www.howemilitary.com.

See full description on page 842.

HUDSON COLLEGE

819 Sheppard Avenue West
Toronto, Ontario M3H 2T3, Canada
Head of School: Mr. Jack Bavington

General Information Coeducational day college-preparatory, arts, business, and technology school. Grades JK–12. Founded: 2003. Setting: suburban. 6-acre campus. 1 building on campus. Approved or accredited by Ontario Ministry of Education and Ontario Department of Education. Language of instruction: English. Total enrollment: 178. Upper school average class size: 12. Upper school faculty-student ratio: 1:10.

Faculty School total: 15. In upper school: 6 men, 9 women; 3 have advanced degrees.

Subjects Offered Accounting, algebra, biology, business, calculus, Canadian history, careers, chemistry, civics, computer information systems, dramatic arts, economics, English, finite math, foreign language, French, geography, geometry, health, history, humanities, instrumental music, law, literature, music, photography, physical education, physics, politics, science, social sciences, Spanish, visual arts, vocal music, world issues, world studies, writing.

Special Academic Programs Accelerated programs; independent study; term-away projects; study at local college for college credit; academic accommodation for the gifted; ESL (26 students enrolled).

College Placement 24 students graduated in 2005; all went to college, including Carleton University; McMaster University; Queen's University at Kingston; The University of Western Ontario; University of Toronto; York University.

Student Life Upper grades have uniform requirement, student council, honor system. Discipline rests primarily with faculty.

Summer Programs Remediation, enrichment, advancement, ESL, sports, art/fine arts, computer instruction programs offered; held on campus; accepts boys and girls; open to students from other schools. 150 students usually enrolled. 2006 schedule: June 29 to September 1. Application deadline: June 1.

Tuition and Aid Day student tuition: CAN$10,800. Tuition installment plan (monthly payment plans, individually arranged payment plans). Tuition reduction for siblings, bursaries, merit scholarship grants, need-based scholarship grants available. In 2005–06, 10% of upper-school students received aid.

Admissions Admissions testing required. Deadline for receipt of application materials: none. Application fee required: CAN$250. Interview required.

Athletics Interscholastic: basketball (boys), soccer (b), softball (b,g), table tennis (b), volleyball (b); intramural: badminton (b,g), ball hockey (b,g), baseball (b,g), basketball (b,g), dance (g), dance team (g), fitness (b,g), flag football (b,g), floor hockey (b,g), golf (b,g), gymnastics (g), indoor hockey (b,g), physical fitness (b,g), soccer (b,g), softball (b,g), swimming and diving (b,g), table tennis (b,g), track and field (b,g), volleyball (b,g), weight lifting (b); coed interscholastic: badminton, cross-country running; coed intramural: alpine skiing, badminton, cross-country running, fitness, golf, indoor hockey, outdoor activities, outdoor adventure, outdoor education, outdoor recreation, skiing (cross-country), snowboarding, swimming and diving, tennis, track and field, volleyball. 2 PE instructors.

Computers Computers are regularly used in all academic classes. Computer network features include campus e-mail, on-campus library services, CD-ROMs, Internet access, DVD.

Contact General Information. 416-631-0082. E-mail: info@hudsoncollege.ca. Web site: www.hudsoncollege.ca.

THE HUDSON SCHOOL

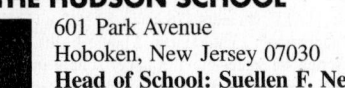

601 Park Avenue
Hoboken, New Jersey 07030
Head of School: Suellen F. Newman

General Information Coeducational day college-preparatory, arts, and music, theater, foreign languages school. Grades 5–12. Founded: 1978. Setting: urban. Nearest major city is New York, NY. 1 building on campus. Approved or accredited by Middle States Association of Colleges and Schools and New Jersey Department of Education. Member of National Association of Independent Schools. Endowment: $900,000. Total enrollment: 204. Upper school average class size: 18. Upper school faculty-student ratio: 1:10.

Upper School Student Profile Grade 9: 20 students (8 boys, 12 girls); Grade 10: 29 students (10 boys, 19 girls); Grade 11: 26 students (8 boys, 18 girls); Grade 12: 16 students (6 boys, 10 girls).

Faculty School total: 50. In upper school: 13 men, 13 women; 25 have advanced degrees.

Subjects Offered Algebra, American literature, art, biology, British literature, calculus, chemistry, computer science, computer science-AP, computers, conceptual physics, contemporary issues, creative writing, English, English literature, English literature-AP, English-AP, environmental science, ethnic literature, film, French, French-AP, German, German-AP, health, Japanese, Latin, Latin-AP, learning strategies, mathematics, media studies, music, music theory, mythology, physical education, physics-AP, psychology, psychology-AP, social science, Spanish, Spanish-AP, U.S. history, U.S. history-AP, world civilizations, world literature.

Graduation Requirements Arts and fine arts (art, music, dance, drama), computer science, English, foreign language, Latin, mathematics, physical education (includes health), science, social studies (includes history). Community service is required.

Special Academic Programs Honors section; accelerated programs; independent study; study at local college for college credit; study abroad; academic accommodation for the gifted, the musically talented, and the artistically talented; remedial reading and/or remedial writing; remedial math; ESL (2 students enrolled).

College Placement 21 students graduated in 2005; all went to college, including Boston College; Brown University; McGill University; Pratt Institute; Swarthmore College. Median SAT verbal: 550, median SAT math: 600. 20% scored over 600 on SAT verbal, 30% scored over 600 on SAT math.

Student Life Upper grades have student council, honor system. Discipline rests primarily with faculty.

Summer Programs Art/fine arts programs offered; session focuses on dramatic arts; held on campus; accepts boys and girls; open to students from other schools.

The Hudson School

Tuition and Aid Day student tuition: $11,200. Tuition installment plan (monthly payment plans, semi-annual and annual payment plans; quarterly by special arrangement). Need-based scholarship grants available. In 2005–06, 35% of upper-school students received aid. Total amount of financial aid awarded in 2005–06: $150,000.

Admissions Traditional secondary-level entrance grade is 9. For fall 2005, 90 students applied for upper-level admission, 60 were accepted, 20 enrolled. ERB, ISEE or SSAT required. Deadline for receipt of application materials: December 15. Application fee required: $50. On-campus interview required.

Athletics Interscholastic: basketball (boys, girls), dance (g), modern dance (g), soccer (b,g), softball (b,g); coed interscholastic: bowling, cheering, swimming and diving, tennis; coed intramural: aerobics/dance, fencing, Frisbee, outdoor education, physical fitness, ultimate Frisbee. 3 PE instructors, 4 coaches.

Computers Computers are regularly used in all academic classes. Computer network features include CD-ROMs, Internet access.

Contact Suellen F. Newman, Director. 201-659-8335 Ext. 107. Fax: 201-222-3669. E-mail: admissions@thehudsonschool.org. Web site: www.thehudsonschool.org.

ANNOUNCEMENT FROM THE SCHOOL The Hudson School provides intellectually inquisitive students in grades 5–12 with a rigorous college-preparatory education that inspires independent thinking, lifelong learning, and a sense of community. Hudson fosters an eclectic and supportive environment that challenges students and teachers to fully develop their talents through a creative and stimulating interdisciplinary curriculum.

THE HUN SCHOOL OF PRINCETON

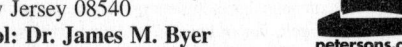

176 Edgerstoune Road
Princeton, New Jersey 08540
Head of School: Dr. James M. Byer

petersons.com

General Information Coeducational boarding and day college-preparatory school. Boarding grades 9–PG, day grades 6–PG. Founded: 1914. Setting: small town. Nearest major city is New York, NY. Students are housed in single-sex dormitories. 45-acre campus. 6 buildings on campus. Approved or accredited by Middle States Association of Colleges and Schools, New Jersey Association of Independent Schools, and The Association of Boarding Schools. Member of National Association of Independent Schools and Secondary School Admission Test Board. Endowment: $10 million. Total enrollment: 589. Upper school average class size: 13. Upper school faculty-student ratio: 1:8.

Upper School Student Profile Grade 9: 106 students (55 boys, 51 girls); Grade 10: 121 students (72 boys, 49 girls); Grade 11: 135 students (76 boys, 59 girls); Grade 12: 118 students (63 boys, 55 girls); Postgraduate: 13 students (12 boys, 1 girl). 33% of students are boarding students. 15 states are represented in upper school student body. 10% are international students. International students from Bahrain, Republic of Korea, Russian Federation, Taiwan, Turkey, and Venezuela; 16 other countries represented in student body.

Faculty School total: 104. In upper school: 58 men, 46 women; 48 have advanced degrees; 30 reside on campus.

Subjects Offered 3-dimensional art, 3-dimensional design, advanced computer applications, Advanced Placement courses, advanced TOEFL/grammar, algebra, American government, American history, American history-AP, American literature, anatomy, architectural drawing, architecture, art, art history, art history-AP, biology, biology-AP, calculus, calculus-AP, ceramics, chemistry, chemistry-AP, chorus, community service, computer programming, computer science, drama, driver education, economics, engineering, English, English-AP, ESL, European history, fine arts, French, French-AP, geometry, government/civics, health, history, interdisciplinary studies, jazz band, Latin, Latin-AP, marine biology, mathematics, mechanical drawing, music, photography, physical education, physics, physics-AP, physiology, public speaking, science, social studies, Spanish, Spanish-AP, statistics-AP, television, theater, trigonometry, U.S. history-AP, video, video film production, world history.

Graduation Requirements Arts and fine arts (art, music, dance, drama), computer science, English, foreign language, health, history, mathematics, science, 10 hours of community service per year, summer reading, extra-curricular activities.

Special Academic Programs Advanced Placement exam preparation in 14 subject areas; honors section; study at local college for college credit; academic accommodation for the gifted; programs in English, mathematics, general development for dyslexic students; special instructional classes for students with mild learning differences; ESL (22 students enrolled).

College Placement 134 students graduated in 2005; 132 went to college, including Boston University; Carnegie Mellon University; Colgate University; Dickinson College; Franklin and Marshall College; Princeton University. Other: 1 entered a postgraduate year, 1 had other specific plans.

Student Life Upper grades have specified standards of dress, student council, honor system. Discipline rests equally with students and faculty.

Summer Programs Remediation, enrichment, advancement, ESL, art/fine arts, computer instruction programs offered; session focuses on make-up courses, enrichment, SAT and TOEFL preparation; held on campus; accepts boys and girls; open to students from other schools. 110 students usually enrolled. 2006 schedule: June 26 to July 28. Application deadline: none.

Tuition and Aid Day student tuition: $24,020; 7-day tuition and room/board: $34,970. Tuition installment plan (Academic Management Services Plan). Merit scholarship grants, need-based scholarship grants, prepGATE Loans available. In 2005–06, 25% of upper-school students received aid; total upper-school merit-scholarship money awarded: $50,000. Total amount of financial aid awarded in 2005–06: $2,150,000.

Admissions Traditional secondary-level entrance grade is 9. PSAT or SAT for applicants to grade 11 and 12, SSAT or TOEFL required. Deadline for receipt of application materials: January 31. Application fee required: $50. On-campus interview required.

Athletics Interscholastic: baseball (boys), basketball (b,g), cheering (g), crew (b,g), cross-country running (b,g), fencing (b,g), field hockey (g), football (b), lacrosse (b,g), soccer (b,g), softball (g), tennis (b,g); intramural: dance squad (g), soccer (b,g), water polo (b,g), weight training (b,g); coed interscholastic: golf, ice hockey, swimming and diving, track and field; coed intramural: aerobics/dance, aerobics/nautilus, ballet, basketball, cross-country running, dance, fitness, flag football, Frisbee, jogging, nautilus, paint ball, physical fitness, running, skiing (downhill), strength & conditioning, touch football, ultimate Frisbee, volleyball, water polo, weight lifting. 3 coaches, 1 trainer.

Computers Computers are regularly used in all academic classes. Computer network features include campus e-mail, on-campus library services, CD-ROMs, online commercial services, Internet access, file transfer, DVD, wireless campus network.

Contact Mr. P. Terence Beach, Director of Admissions. 609-921-7600. Fax: 609-279-9398. E-mail: admiss@hunschool.org. Web site: www.hunschool.org.

ANNOUNCEMENT FROM THE SCHOOL The Hun School of Princeton is located midway between New York City and Philadelphia in the university town of Princeton, New Jersey. Hun provides a traditional college-preparatory program that draws upon the cultural and scientific opportunities in the area. A full range of athletics and activities supplement a strong curriculum designed to stimulate critical thinking and analysis and inspire curiosity. Competent, caring faculty members work closely with students to promote excellence and self-esteem in an environment of high but fair expectations. Extensive weekend activities and a supportive adviser system are outstanding features of residential life. Academic learning skills and instruction in ESL are available.

See full description on page 844.

HUNTINGTON-SURREY SCHOOL

4001 Speedway
Austin, Texas 78751
Head of School: Dr. Light Bailey German

General Information Coeducational day college-preparatory school. Grades 9–12. Founded: 1973. Setting: urban. 1 building on campus. Approved or accredited by Southern Association of Colleges and Schools and Texas Department of Education. Total enrollment: 74. Upper school average class size: 8. Upper school faculty-student ratio: 1:4.

Upper School Student Profile Grade 9: 9 students (6 boys, 3 girls); Grade 10: 22 students (15 boys, 7 girls); Grade 11: 21 students (10 boys, 11 girls); Grade 12: 22 students (9 boys, 13 girls).

Faculty School total: 20. In upper school: 10 men, 10 women; 16 have advanced degrees.

Subjects Offered Algebra, art, biology, calculus, chemistry, college planning, comparative religion, creative drama, discrete math, drama, ecology, environmental systems, English, French, geometry, German, history, Latin, literature, math analysis, math review, mathematics, philosophy, physical science, physics, pre-algebra, pre-calculus, SAT preparation, senior science survey, social studies, Spanish, student publications, study skills, trigonometry, U.S. history, work-study, world history.

Graduation Requirements English, mathematics, science, social studies (includes history), senior research project, school exit examinations: assertion with proof essay exam and mathematical competency exam, senior advisory course.

Special Academic Programs Advanced Placement exam preparation in 6 subject areas; accelerated programs; academic accommodation for the gifted.

College Placement 23 students graduated in 2005; 21 went to college, including Henderson State University; St. Edward's University; Texas State University-San Marcos; The Evergreen State College; The University of Texas at Austin. Other: 1 entered military service, 1 entered a postgraduate year. Mean SAT verbal: 620, mean SAT math: 540, mean combined SAT: 1760. 30% scored over 600 on SAT verbal, 25% scored over 600 on SAT math, 30% scored over 1800 on combined SAT.

Student Life Upper grades have student council, honor system. Discipline rests primarily with faculty.

Tuition and Aid Day student tuition: $7200. Tuition installment plan (monthly payment plans).

Admissions Traditional secondary-level entrance grade is 9. For fall 2005, 28 students applied for upper-level admission, 23 were accepted, 23 enrolled. Deadline for receipt of application materials: none. No application fee required. On-campus interview required.

Computers Computers are regularly used in study skills, writing classes. Computer resources include study hall computers and printers (available for student use).
Contact Ms. Johni Walker-Little, Assistant Director. 512-478-4743. Fax: 512-457-0235. Web site: www.huntingtonsurrey.com.

HUTCHISON SCHOOL

1740 Ridgeway Road
Memphis, Tennessee 38119-5397
Head of School: Dr. Annette C. Smith

petersons.com

General Information Girls' day college-preparatory, arts, and technology school. Grades PK–12. Founded: 1902. Setting: suburban. 52-acre campus. 8 buildings on campus. Approved or accredited by Southern Association of Colleges and Schools, Southern Association of Independent Schools, and Tennessee Association of Independent Schools. Member of National Association of Independent Schools. Endowment: $10 million. Total enrollment: 827. Upper school average class size: 16. Upper school faculty-student ratio: 1:16.
Upper School Student Profile Grade 9: 47 students (47 girls); Grade 10: 48 students (48 girls); Grade 11: 60 students (60 girls); Grade 12: 63 students (63 girls).
Faculty School total: 117. In upper school: 5 men, 27 women; 24 have advanced degrees.
Subjects Offered Acting, advanced studio art-AP, algebra, American government, American history, American history-AP, American literature, American literature-AP, anatomy and physiology, art, art history, biology, biology-AP, British literature, British literature (honors), British literature-AP, calculus, calculus-AP, chemistry, chemistry-AP, choral music, college writing, contemporary issues, creative writing, dance, drama, earth science, economics, English, English language-AP, English literature, English literature-AP, environmental education, environmental science, European history, European history-AP, film and literature, film history, fine arts, foreign language, French, French language-AP, genetics, geography, geometry, global issues, government/civics, health, health and wellness, history, honors algebra, honors English, honors geometry, independent study, Latin, mathematics, music, physical education, physics, pre-calculus, psychology, science, social studies, Spanish, speech, studio art, studio art—AP, theater, women in world history, women's studies, world history, world history-AP.
Graduation Requirements Arts and fine arts (art, music, dance, drama), English, foreign language, mathematics, physical education (includes health), science, social studies (includes history), world history, annual community service.
Special Academic Programs Advanced Placement exam preparation in 16 subject areas; honors section; independent study; academic accommodation for the gifted.
College Placement 63 students graduated in 2005; all went to college, including The University of Alabama; The University of Tennessee; University of Georgia; University of Mississippi; University of Virginia; Vanderbilt University. Mean SAT verbal: 615, mean SAT math: 599, mean composite ACT: 26. 50% scored over 600 on SAT verbal, 45% scored over 600 on SAT math, 32% scored over 26 on composite ACT.
Student Life Upper grades have uniform requirement, student council, honor system. Discipline rests equally with students and faculty.
Summer Programs Remediation, enrichment, advancement, sports, art/fine arts, computer instruction programs offered; session focuses on athletic skill development; held on campus; accepts girls; open to students from other schools. 130 students usually enrolled. 2006 schedule: June 1 to August 10. Application deadline: none.
Tuition and Aid Day student tuition: $13,275. Tuition installment plan (Insured Tuition Payment Plan, monthly payment plans, individually arranged payment plans, 4-payment plan). Need-based scholarship grants available. In 2005–06, 9% of upper-school students received aid. Total amount of financial aid awarded in 2005–06: $126,822.
Admissions Traditional secondary-level entrance grade is 9. For fall 2005, 48 students applied for upper-level admission, 20 were accepted, 11 enrolled. Admissions testing, ISEE or writing sample required. Deadline for receipt of application materials: none. Application fee required: $50. Interview required.
Athletics Interscholastic: basketball (girls), bowling (g), cross-country running (g), dance (g), fitness (g), golf (g), lacrosse (g), swimming and diving (g), tennis (g), volleyball (g); intramural: basketball (g), bowling (g), cross-country running (g), softball (g). 4 PE instructors, 12 coaches, 1 trainer.
Computers Computers are regularly used in all academic, video film production classes. Computer network features include campus e-mail, on-campus library services, CD-ROMs, online commercial services, Internet access, file transfer, office computer access, DVD, wireless campus network.
Contact Candy Covington, Director of Admissions. 901-762-6672. Fax: 901-432-6655. E-mail: ccovington@hutchisonschool.org. Web site: www.hutchisonschool.org.

ANNOUNCEMENT FROM THE SCHOOL Hutchison School, founded in 1902, is located on 50 acres in East Memphis. The School serves more than 800 girls from prekindergarten–grade 12. This college-preparatory day school provides a challenging academic program framed by the balanced development of the mind, body, and spirit. The campus consists of 8 buildings, including 2 gyms, a multimedia library and technology center, and a 630-seat theater. Hutchison offers a variety of athletic competition in 12 sports. The arts play an integral part in the curriculum, and instruction is further enhanced by the Arts Academy, a program that provides additional enrichment of the arts through its afterschool, weekend, and summer offerings. Hutchison is divided into 4 divisions. Early Childhood offers half-day and full-day programs, beginning with 3- and 4-year olds, and full-day programs for senior kindergarten. These programs focus on early literacy, fundamental math skills, Spanish, social studies, and science instruction. Classes of 15–17 girls are taught by a teacher and a teacher assistant. Lower School for grades 1–4 and Middle School for grades 5–8 offer interdisciplinary instruction in English, math, social studies, science, Spanish, the arts, and PE. Latin is taught in grade 8. Upper School for grades 9–12 provides a rigorous college-preparatory program balanced by a variety of extracurricular activities. Hutchison students consistently rank above the national average on SAT/ACT tests, earn college credit through Advanced Placement classes, and are accepted at top colleges and universities across the country. A full-time college counseling staff works with students beginning in 9th grade, and 100% of the School's graduates attend 4-year colleges and universities. With a low student-teacher ratio, the School maintains a focus on instruction that is student engaged and fosters an environment where students are encouraged to think critically, use original expression, and problem solve. The School seeks students who are intellectually inquisitive, strongly motivated, and highly committed to accepting the challenges and opportunities the School offers.

HVITFELDTSKA GYMNASIET, INTERNATIONAL SECTION

Rektorsgatan 2
Goteborg 411 33, Sweden
Head of School: Mrs. Agneta Santesson

General Information Coeducational day college-preparatory, general academic, and bilingual studies school. Grades 10–12. Founded: 1647. Setting: urban. Nearest major city is Gothenburg. 3 buildings on campus. Member of European Council of International Schools. Language of instruction: English. Upper school average class size: 15. Upper school faculty-student ratio: 1:8.
Upper School Student Profile Grade 10: 60 students (35 boys, 25 girls); Grade 11: 80 students (48 boys, 32 girls); Grade 12: 70 students (40 boys, 30 girls).
Faculty School total: 25. In upper school: 10 men, 15 women; all have advanced degrees.
Special Academic Programs International Baccalaureate program; ESL (10 students enrolled).
College Placement 70 students graduated in 2005; 40 went to college. Other: 15 went to work.
Student Life Upper grades have student council, honor system. Discipline rests primarily with faculty.
Admissions Traditional secondary-level entrance grade is 10. For fall 2005, 200 students applied for upper-level admission, 65 were accepted, 60 enrolled. No application fee required.
Computers Computer network features include campus e-mail, on-campus library services, CD-ROMs, Internet access.
Contact Mrs. Maria Nicolai, IB-coordinator. +46-313670694. Fax: +46-313670602. E-mail: maria.nicolai@educ.goteborg.se. Web site: www.hvitfeldt.educ.goteborg.se.

HYDE SCHOOL

PO Box 237
Woodstock, Connecticut 06281
Head of School: Duncan McCrann

petersons.com

General Information Coeducational boarding and day college-preparatory and general academic school. Grades 9–12. Founded: 1966. Setting: rural. Nearest major city is Hartford. Students are housed in single-sex dormitories. 120-acre campus. 6 buildings on campus. Approved or accredited by Association of Independent Schools in New England, New England Association of Schools and Colleges, The Association of Boarding Schools, and Connecticut Department of Education. Endowment: $6.7 million. Total enrollment: 186. Upper school average class size: 15. Upper school faculty-student ratio: 1:12.
Upper School Student Profile Grade 9: 20 students (12 boys, 8 girls); Grade 10: 44 students (26 boys, 18 girls); Grade 11: 84 students (64 boys, 20 girls); Grade 12: 37 students (24 boys, 13 girls); Postgraduate: 1 student (1 boy). 98% of students are boarding students. 15% are state residents. 30 states are represented in upper school student body. 1% are international students.
Faculty School total: 38. In upper school: 22 men, 14 women; 11 have advanced degrees; 21 reside on campus.
Subjects Offered 3-dimensional art, advanced chemistry, advanced math, Advanced Placement courses, algebra, American government, American history, American history-AP, athletics, backpacking, biology, calculus, calculus-AP, character education, chemistry, drama performance, drawing and design, English, English language and composition-AP, English language-AP, English literature, English literature and composition-AP, French as a second language, geometry, honors algebra, honors

geometry, physics, Spanish, sports, studio art, technical theater, U.S. government-AP, U.S. history, visual and performing arts, visual arts, wilderness experience, wilderness/outdoor program.

Graduation Requirements Electives, English, foreign language, mathematics, science, social studies (includes history), Hyde's graduation requirements embody academic achievement and character development. Character growth is determined through an intense 40-hour, evaluation process involving all members of the senior class and faculty. All students make a speech at graduation representing their principles.

Special Academic Programs Advanced Placement exam preparation in 5 subject areas; honors section; independent study; remedial reading and/or remedial writing; remedial math.

College Placement 44 students graduated in 2005; 42 went to college, including Bates College; Boston University; Gettysburg College; University of Vermont; Wheaton College. Other: 2 entered a postgraduate year. Mean SAT verbal: 525, mean SAT math: 513.

Student Life Upper grades have specified standards of dress, honor system. Discipline rests equally with students and faculty.

Summer Programs Enrichment, sports, art/fine arts, rigorous outdoor training programs offered; session focuses on orientation for the fall; held both on and off campus; held at Hyde's Wilderness Campus in Eustis, ME, and on Seguin Island off the coast of Maine; accepts boys and girls; open to students from other schools. 75 students usually enrolled. 2006 schedule: July 5 to August 7. Application deadline: July 1.

Tuition and Aid Day student tuition: $19,500; 7-day tuition and room/board: $34,500. Tuition reduction for siblings, need-based scholarship grants, prepGATE Private School Loan Program, CitiBank CitiAssist K-12 Loans available. In 2005–06, 25% of upper-school students received aid. Total amount of financial aid awarded in 2005–06: $750,000.

Admissions SSAT required. Deadline for receipt of application materials: none. Application fee required: $100. Interview required.

Athletics Interscholastic: basketball (boys, girls), cross-country running (b,g), football (b), ice hockey (b,g), lacrosse (b,g), soccer (b,g), tennis (b,g), track and field (b,g), wrestling (b); coed interscholastic: martial arts, ropes courses, wilderness, wrestling; coed intramural: back packing, canoeing/kayaking, hiking/backpacking, outdoor adventure, outdoor skills, ropes courses, wilderness. 2 trainers.

Computers Computer network features include campus e-mail, on-campus library services, CD-ROMs, online commercial services, Internet access, office computer access.

Contact Holly E. Thompson, Director of Admission. 860-963-4758. Fax: 860-928-0612. E-mail: hthompson@hyde.edu. Web site: www.hyde.edu.

See full description on page 846.

HYDE SCHOOL

616 High Street
Bath, Maine 04530
Head of School: Mrs. Laurie G. Hurd

petersons.com

General Information Coeducational boarding and day college-preparatory and arts school. Grades 9–12. Founded: 1966. Setting: small town. Nearest major city is Portland. Students are housed in single-sex dormitories. 145-acre campus. 32 buildings on campus. Approved or accredited by Association of Independent Schools in New England, New England Association of Schools and Colleges, The Association of Boarding Schools, and Maine Department of Education. Member of National Association of Independent Schools. Endowment: $6.7 million. Total enrollment: 199. Upper school average class size: 12. Upper school faculty-student ratio: 1:6.

Upper School Student Profile Grade 9: 17 students (12 boys, 5 girls); Grade 10: 32 students (22 boys, 10 girls); Grade 11: 77 students (55 boys, 22 girls); Grade 12: 72 students (50 boys, 22 girls); Postgraduate: 1 student (1 boy). 93% of students are boarding students. 19% are state residents. 30 states are represented in upper school student body. 2% are international students.

Faculty School total: 40. In upper school: 26 men, 14 women; 13 have advanced degrees; 30 reside on campus.

Subjects Offered Algebra, American history, American literature, art, art history, biology, calculus, chemistry, computer science, creative writing, earth science, English, English literature, environmental science, European history, French, geography, geology, geometry, government/civics, grammar, history, journalism, mathematics, music, philosophy, photography, physical education, physics, religion, science, social science, Spanish, world history.

Graduation Requirements Electives, English, foreign language, mathematics, science, social studies (includes history), Hyde's graduation requirements embody academic achievement and character development. Character growth is determined through an intense 40-hour, evaluation process involving all members of the senior class and faculty. All students make a speech at graduation representing their principles.

Special Academic Programs Honors section; independent study; study at local college for college credit; remedial reading and/or remedial writing; remedial math.

College Placement 42 students graduated in 2005; 40 went to college, including Bates College; Bucknell University; Clemson University; Syracuse University;

University of Denver. Other: 1 went to work. Median SAT verbal: 540, median SAT math: 519. 15% scored over 600 on SAT verbal, 11% scored over 600 on SAT math.

Student Life Upper grades have specified standards of dress, student council, honor system. Discipline rests equally with students and faculty.

Summer Programs Enrichment, sports, art/fine arts, rigorous outdoor training programs offered; session focuses on orientation for the school year; held both on and off campus; held at wilderness preserve in Eustis, ME and on Seguin Island off the coast of Maine; accepts boys and girls; open to students from other schools. 85 students usually enrolled. 2006 schedule: July 10 to August 13. Application deadline: July 1.

Tuition and Aid Day student tuition: $19,500; 7-day tuition and room/board: $34,500. Tuition reduction for siblings, need-based scholarship grants, prepGATE Private School Loan Program, CitiBank CitiAssist K-12 Loans available. In 2005–06, 35% of upper-school students received aid. Total amount of financial aid awarded in 2005–06: $750,000.

Admissions SSAT required. Deadline for receipt of application materials: none. Application fee required: $100. Interview required.

Athletics Interscholastic: basketball (boys, girls), football (b), lacrosse (b,g), soccer (b,g), track and field (b,g), wrestling (b); coed interscholastic: aquatics, crew, cross-country running, nordic skiing, skiing (cross-country), swimming and diving, tennis; coed intramural: hiking/backpacking, kayaking, life saving, outdoor activities, outdoor education, outdoor skills, outdoors, physical fitness, physical training, project adventure, snowshoeing, strength & conditioning, walking, weight lifting, weight training, wilderness, wilderness survival, wildernessways. 30 coaches, 2 trainers.

Computers Computer network features include campus e-mail, on-campus library services, CD-ROMs, online commercial services, Internet access, file transfer, office computer access, DVD, wireless campus network.

Contact Mrs. Melissa Burroughs, Director of Admissions. 207-443-7101. Fax: 207-442-9346. E-mail: mburroughs@hyde.edu. Web site: www.hyde.edu.

See full description on page 846.

IDYLLWILD ARTS ACADEMY

52500 Temecula Road
PO Box 38
Idyllwild, California 92549
Head of School: William M. Lowman

petersons.com

General Information Coeducational boarding and day college-preparatory and arts school. Grades 9–PG. Founded: 1986. Setting: rural. Nearest major city is Los Angeles. Students are housed in single-sex dormitories. 205-acre campus. 44 buildings on campus. Approved or accredited by California Association of Independent Schools and Western Association of Schools and Colleges. Member of National Association of Independent Schools and Secondary School Admission Test Board. Endowment: $750,000. Total enrollment: 265. Upper school average class size: 13. Upper school faculty-student ratio: 1:12.

Upper School Student Profile Grade 9: 37 students (16 boys, 21 girls); Grade 10: 66 students (25 boys, 41 girls); Grade 11: 69 students (24 boys, 45 girls); Grade 12: 88 students (35 boys, 53 girls); Postgraduate: 4 students (3 boys, 1 girl). 90% of students are boarding students. 40% are state residents. 32 states are represented in upper school student body. 32% are international students. International students from Bulgaria, China, Germany, Mexico, Republic of Korea, and Taiwan; 12 other countries represented in student body.

Faculty School total: 65. In upper school: 24 men, 20 women; 30 have advanced degrees; 21 reside on campus.

Subjects Offered 3-dimensional art, 3-dimensional design, acting, advanced math, algebra, American government, American history, American literature, anatomy, art, art history, audio visual/media, audition methods, ballet, biology, Broadway dance, calculus, career/college preparation, ceramics, chemistry, choir, choral music, choreography, computer graphics, computer science, creative writing, critical studies in film, dance, digital art, directing, drama, drawing and design, driver education, economics, English, English literature, ensembles, environmental science, ESL, fiction, film and literature, film and new technologies, film appreciation, film history, film studies, filmmaking, fine arts, French, geography, geometry, government/civics, grammar, history, illustration, improvisation, jazz dance, jazz ensemble, jazz theory, mathematics, multimedia, music, music theater, music theory, musical productions, musical theater dance, orchestra, performing arts, photography, physical education, physics, play production, play/screen writing, playwriting and directing, poetry, pottery, printmaking, science, social science, social studies, Spanish, tap dance, technical theater, technology/design, theater, video film production, vocal music, voice and diction, voice ensemble, world history, world literature, writing.

Graduation Requirements Art, arts and fine arts (art, music, dance, drama), computer literacy, computer science, English, foreign language, mathematics, performing arts, physical education (includes health), science, social science, social studies (includes history).

Special Academic Programs Advanced Placement exam preparation in 4 subject areas; honors section; accelerated programs; independent study; academic accommodation for the musically talented and the artistically talented; ESL (31 students enrolled).

College Placement 94 students graduated in 2005; 93 went to college, including California Institute of the Arts; New York University; The Johns Hopkins University; The Juilliard School; University of California, Los Angeles; University of Rochester. Other: 1 had other specific plans.

Student Life Upper grades have student council. Discipline rests equally with students and faculty.

Summer Programs ESL, art/fine arts programs offered; session focuses on visual and performing arts; held on campus; accepts boys and girls; open to students from other schools. 600 students usually enrolled. 2006 schedule: July 10 to August 19. Application deadline: none.

Tuition and Aid Day student tuition: $20,775; 7-day tuition and room/board: $37,950. Tuition installment plan (Key Tuition Payment Plan, monthly payment plans, individually arranged payment plans, school's own payment plan). Tuition reduction for siblings, need-based scholarship grants, paying campus jobs available. In 2005–06, 49% of upper-school students received aid. Total amount of financial aid awarded in 2005–06: $290,000.

Admissions Traditional secondary-level entrance grade is 10. For fall 2005, 233 students applied for upper-level admission, 181 were accepted, 140 enrolled. SLEP, SSAT or TOEFL required. Deadline for receipt of application materials: none. Application fee required: $35. Interview required.

Athletics Intramural: aerobics (boys, girls); coed intramural: aerobics, aerobics/dance, aerobics/nautilus, basketball, bicycling, bowling, climbing, cross-country running, fencing, Frisbee, hiking/backpacking, physical fitness, rock climbing, soccer, tennis, ultimate Frisbee, volleyball, walking, wall climbing, water polo, weight lifting, yoga. 1 PE instructor.

Computers Computers are regularly used in art, design, drafting, drawing and design, English, ESL, graphic design, media production, science classes. Computer resources include campus e-mail, on-campus library services, CD-ROMs, Internet access.

Contact Ms. Karen R. Porter, Dean of Admission and Financial Aid. 951-659-2171 Ext. 2343. Fax: 951-659-2058. E-mail: admission@idyllwildarts.org. Web site: www.idyllwildarts.org.

ANNOUNCEMENT FROM THE SCHOOL Idyllwild Arts Academy now offers grades 9–12 and a postgraduate year. Eighth grade is offered only for international students who need English as a second language.

See full description on page 848.

IMMACULATA ACADEMY

5138 South Park Avenue
Hamburg, New York 14075
Head of School: Mr. David T. Christian

General Information Girls' day college-preparatory, arts, business, religious studies, and technology school, affiliated with Roman Catholic Church. Grades 9–12. Founded: 1928. Setting: suburban. Nearest major city is Buffalo. 25-acre campus. 1 building on campus. Approved or accredited by Middle States Association of Colleges and Schools, National Catholic Education Association, New York State Association of Independent Schools, New York State Board of Regents, and New York Department of Education. Endowment: $300,000. Total enrollment: 207. Upper school average class size: 15. Upper school faculty-student ratio: 1:13.

Upper School Student Profile Grade 9: 55 students (55 girls); Grade 10: 60 students (60 girls); Grade 11: 52 students (52 girls); Grade 12: 40 students (40 girls). 94.7% of students are Roman Catholic.

Faculty School total: 25. In upper school: 7 men, 18 women; 18 have advanced degrees.

Subjects Offered Advanced math, Advanced Placement courses, algebra, American government, American history, American history-AP, American literature, art, art appreciation, art-AP, athletics, biology, biology-AP, business, business skills, calculus, chemistry, chemistry-AP, chorus, computer science, earth science, economics, English, English literature, English-AP, fine arts, French, geometry, government/civics, health, instrumental music, Latin, mathematics, music, physical education, physics, psychology, religion, religious education, science, social science, social studies, sociology, Spanish, studio art, studio art—AP, trigonometry, world literature.

Graduation Requirements Advanced studio art-AP, arts and fine arts (art, music, dance, drama), computer science, English, foreign language, mathematics, physical education (includes health), religion (includes Bible studies and theology), science, social studies (includes history), 80 hours of community service (minimum of 20 hours per year), reflection paper about service each year, senior year synthesis paper on service and subsequent interview.

Special Academic Programs Advanced Placement exam preparation; honors section; independent study; study at local college for college credit; academic accommodation for the musically talented and the artistically talented.

College Placement 35 students graduated in 2005; all went to college, including Canisius College; Niagara University; Rochester Institute of Technology; St. Bonaventure University; State University of New York at Buffalo; State University of New York College at Brockport. Mean SAT verbal: 521, mean SAT math: 502, mean composite ACT: 22. 11% scored over 600 on SAT verbal, 11% scored over 600 on SAT math, 23% scored over 26 on composite ACT.

Student Life Upper grades have uniform requirement, student council, honor system. Discipline rests primarily with faculty. Attendance at religious services is required.

Summer Programs Enrichment, sports programs offered; session focuses on enrichment program for 5th through 8th grade girls; held on campus; accepts girls; open to students from other schools. 28 students usually enrolled. 2006 schedule: July 1 to August 31. Application deadline: June 1.

Tuition and Aid Day student tuition: $6035. Tuition installment plan (FACTS Tuition Payment Plan, individually arranged payment plans). Merit scholarship grants, need-based scholarship grants, need-based loans, tuition reduction for daughters of alumnae, tuition reduction for Diocesan employees available. In 2005–06, 49% of upper-school students received aid. Total amount of financial aid awarded in 2005–06: $34,000.

Admissions Traditional secondary-level entrance grade is 9. For fall 2005, 107 students applied for upper-level admission, 100 were accepted, 56 enrolled. Catholic High School Entrance Examination or High School Placement Test required. Deadline for receipt of application materials: June 30. No application fee required. On-campus interview recommended.

Athletics Interscholastic: badminton, basketball, bowling, cross-country running, dance squad, soccer, softball, track and field, volleyball; intramural: badminton, basketball, bowling, cross-country running, dance squad, tennis, track and field, volleyball. 1 PE instructor, 14 coaches.

Computers Computers are regularly used in business applications, desktop publishing, newspaper, typing, word processing classes. Computer network features include on-campus library services, CD-ROMs, Internet access, office computer access, DVD, remote access to homework assignments through Learning Village.

Contact Miss Andrea Agnello, Director of Admissions and Recruitment. 716-649-6161 Ext. 140. Fax: 716-646-1782. E-mail: aagnello@immaculataacademy.com. Web site: www.immaculataacademy.com.

IMMACULATA HIGH SCHOOL

240 Mountain Avenue
Somerville, New Jersey 08876
Head of School: Sr. Mary Birster

General Information Coeducational day college-preparatory and religious studies school, affiliated with Roman Catholic Church. Grades 9–12. Founded: 1962. Setting: suburban. 19-acre campus. 3 buildings on campus. Approved or accredited by Middle States Association of Colleges and Schools, National Catholic Education Association, and New Jersey Department of Education. Total enrollment: 808. Upper school average class size: 25. Upper school faculty-student ratio: 1:15.

Upper School Student Profile Grade 9: 184 students (94 boys, 90 girls); Grade 10: 193 students (92 boys, 101 girls); Grade 11: 234 students (112 boys, 122 girls); Grade 12: 197 students (98 boys, 99 girls). 92% of students are Roman Catholic.

Faculty School total: 75. In upper school: 17 men, 58 women; 43 have advanced degrees.

Subjects Offered Accounting, advanced chemistry, advanced math, Advanced Placement courses, algebra, American history, American literature, anatomy, ancient world history, art, art history-AP, biology, British literature, business, calculus, calculus-AP, chemistry, creative writing, drama, drawing and design, driver education, Eastern world civilizations, ecology, English-AP, environmental science, environmental studies, European history, film history, foreign language, geometry, global issues, global studies, graphic design, health, honors algebra, honors English, honors geometry, marching band, music theory, religious education, science, social studies, speech, trigonometry, U.S. history-AP.

Graduation Requirements Algebra, American literature, biology, British literature, chemistry, driver education, foreign language, geometry, physical education (includes health), physical science, theology, U.S. history, Western civilization.

Special Academic Programs Advanced Placement exam preparation in 5 subject areas; honors section.

College Placement 200 students graduated in 2005; all went to college, including Loyola College in Maryland; Rutgers, The State University of New Jersey, New Brunswick/Piscataway; Saint Joseph's University; Seton Hall University; The Pennsylvania State University University Park Campus; The University of Scranton. Mean SAT verbal: 568, mean SAT math: 570.

Student Life Upper grades have uniform requirement. Discipline rests primarily with faculty. Attendance at religious services is required.

Tuition and Aid Day student tuition: $6700. Tuition installment plan (FACTS Tuition Payment Plan).

Admissions Traditional secondary-level entrance grade is 9. For fall 2005, 300 students applied for upper-level admission, 240 were accepted, 200 enrolled. High School Placement Test required. Deadline for receipt of application materials: December 31. Application fee required: $150. On-campus interview required.

Athletics Interscholastic: baseball (boys), basketball (b,g), cheering (g), cross-country running (b,g), football (b), lacrosse (b,g), soccer (b,g), softball (g), tennis (b,g); coed interscholastic: bowling, golf, swimming and diving. 5 PE instructors, 50 coaches, 1 trainer.

Computers Computers are regularly used in graphic design, word processing classes. Computer network features include on-campus library services, CD-ROMs, online commercial services, Internet access.

Contact Sr. Margaret Peter Carolli, Academic Dean. 908-722-0200 Ext. 118. Fax: 908-218-7765. E-mail: mpeter@immaculatahighschool.org. Web site: www.immaculatahighschool.org.

IMMACULATE CONCEPTION HIGH SCHOOL

258 South Main Street
Lodi, New Jersey 07644-2199
Head of School: Sr. Mary Alicia Adametz, CSSF

General Information Girls' day college-preparatory, arts, and religious studies school, affiliated with Roman Catholic Church. Grades 9–12. Founded: 1915. Setting: suburban. Nearest major city is Paterson. 3-acre campus. 1 building on campus. Approved or accredited by Middle States Association of Colleges and Schools and New Jersey Department of Education. Total enrollment: 187. Upper school average class size: 17. Upper school faculty-student ratio: 1:11.

Upper School Student Profile Grade 9: 49 students (49 girls); Grade 10: 45 students (45 girls); Grade 11: 59 students (59 girls); Grade 12: 34 students (34 girls). 87% of students are Roman Catholic.

Faculty School total: 17. In upper school: 7 men, 10 women.

Subjects Offered Advanced math, algebra, American history, American history-AP, American literature, American literature-AP, anatomy and physiology, art, Bible studies, biology, biology-AP, British literature, calculus, character education, chemistry, chemistry-AP, communications, computer skills, concert choir, driver education, English, English literature-AP, French, geometry, health and safety, honors algebra, honors English, honors geometry, honors U.S. history, journalism, lab science, musical productions, peer ministry, performing arts, physical education, physics, pre-calculus, psychology, religious education, religious studies, social psychology, Spanish, world cultures, writing.

Graduation Requirements Computers, English, foreign language, lab science, mathematics, physical education (includes health), religious studies, social studies (includes history). Community service is required.

Special Academic Programs Advanced Placement exam preparation in 3 subject areas; honors section; study at local college for college credit.

College Placement 41 students graduated in 2005; 40 went to college, including Caldwell College; Felician College; Montclair State University; Rutgers, The State University of New Jersey, New Brunswick/Piscataway; Saint Peter's College; Seton Hall University. Other: 1 had other specific plans. Mean SAT verbal: 490, mean SAT math: 475.

Student Life Upper grades have uniform requirement, student council. Discipline rests primarily with faculty. Attendance at religious services is required.

Summer Programs Advancement programs offered; session focuses on Jump Start Program for incoming freshmen; held on campus; accepts girls; not open to students from other schools. 25 students usually enrolled. 2006 schedule: July 31 to August 17. Application deadline: February.

Tuition and Aid Day student tuition: $6825. Tuition installment plan (FACTS Tuition Payment Plan, annual payment plan). Tuition reduction for siblings, merit scholarship grants, need-based scholarship grants available. In 2005–06, 10% of upper-school students received aid; total upper-school merit-scholarship money awarded: $12,500. Total amount of financial aid awarded in 2005–06: $12,500.

Admissions Traditional secondary-level entrance grade is 9. For fall 2005, 270 students applied for upper-level admission, 228 were accepted, 56 enrolled. Cooperative Entrance Exam (McGraw-Hill) required. Deadline for receipt of application materials: none. Application fee required: $300. Interview recommended.

Athletics Interscholastic: basketball, bowling, cheering, cross-country running, soccer, softball, tennis, volleyball; intramural: aerobics, basketball, fitness, fitness walking, flag football, physical fitness, self defense, tennis, touch football, volleyball, walking. 2 PE instructors, 9 coaches.

Computers Computers are regularly used in graphic arts classes. Computer resources include on-campus library services, Internet access.

Contact Sr. Mary Juanita Arnister, CSSF, Director of Admissions. 973-773-2665. Fax: 973-614-0893. E-mail: jarnister@ichslodi.com. Web site: www.ichslodi.com.

IMMACULATE CONCEPTION SCHOOL

217 Cottage Hill Avenue
Elmhurst, Illinois 60126
Head of School: Pamela M. Levar

General Information Coeducational day college-preparatory, arts, religious studies, and technology school, affiliated with Roman Catholic Church. Grades 9–12. Founded: 1936. Setting: suburban. Nearest major city is Chicago. 2 buildings on campus. Approved or accredited by North Central Association of Colleges and Schools and Illinois Department of Education. Total enrollment: 211. Upper school average class size: 17. Upper school faculty-student ratio: 1:11.

Upper School Student Profile Grade 9: 56 students (31 boys, 25 girls); Grade 10: 63 students (37 boys, 26 girls); Grade 11: 40 students (17 boys, 23 girls); Grade 12: 52 students (25 boys, 27 girls). 95% of students are Roman Catholic.

Faculty School total: 19. In upper school: 7 men, 12 women; 8 have advanced degrees.

Subjects Offered 3-dimensional art, accounting, advanced chemistry, advanced math, algebra, American government, American history, anatomy and physiology, ancient world history, art, biology, biology-AP, British literature, business law, calculus, calculus-AP, campus ministry, career/college preparation, Catholic belief and practice, ceramics, chemistry, college counseling, computer applications, computer keyboarding, computer programming, constitutional history of U.S., consumer education, current events, drawing, ecology, environmental systems, economics, English, English-AP, environmental science, fitness, foreign language, French, geometry, government/civics, health education, honors algebra, honors English, honors geometry, honors U.S. history, humanities, library, musical theater, newspaper, painting, physical education, physics, pre-calculus, SAT/ACT preparation, sociology, Spanish, speech, student government, trigonometry, U.S. history-AP, yearbook.

Graduation Requirements Algebra, American government, American literature, art, biology, British literature, calculus, Catholic belief and practice, chemistry, computer applications, constitutional history of U.S., consumer education, English, environmental science, foreign language, geometry, grammar, health, history, human biology, language and composition, mathematics, physical science, political science, pre-calculus, trigonometry, U.S. history, world history, 40 hours of Christian service, attendance at retreat.

Special Academic Programs Advanced Placement exam preparation in 4 subject areas; honors section; study at local college for college credit.

College Placement 56 students graduated in 2005; all went to college, including DePaul University; Eastern Illinois University; Marquette University; Purdue University; University of Illinois at Urbana–Champaign. Mean composite ACT: 22. 23% scored over 26 on composite ACT.

Student Life Upper grades have uniform requirement, student council. Discipline rests primarily with faculty. Attendance at religious services is required.

Summer Programs Sports programs offered; session focuses on sports; held on campus; accepts boys and girls; not open to students from other schools. 100 students usually enrolled. 2006 schedule: June.

Tuition and Aid Day student tuition: $6600. Tuition installment plan (SMART Tuition Payment Plan). Tuition reduction for siblings, merit scholarship grants, need-based scholarship grants, merit scholarships (for placement test top scorers), externally funded scholarships (alumni, memorials), Catholic School Teacher Grants (1/3 reduction) available. In 2005–06, 20% of upper-school students received aid; total upper-school merit-scholarship money awarded: $19,000. Total amount of financial aid awarded in 2005–06: $50,000.

Admissions Traditional secondary-level entrance grade is 9. For fall 2005, 62 students applied for upper-level admission, 60 were accepted, 56 enrolled. Diocesan Entrance Exam or High School Placement Test (closed version) from Scholastic Testing Service required. Deadline for receipt of application materials: none. No application fee required.

Athletics Interscholastic: baseball (boys), basketball (b,g), bowling (b,g), cross-country running (b,g), dance squad (g), football (b), indoor track (b,g), pom squad (g), soccer (g), softball (g), track and field (b,g), volleyball (g), weight lifting (b), weight training (b,g), winter (indoor) track (b,g); coed interscholastic: golf. 2 PE instructors, 19 coaches, 2 trainers.

Computers Computers are regularly used in business applications, career exploration, college planning, library, news writing, science, stock market, yearbook classes. Computer network features include on-campus library services, CD-ROMs, online commercial services, Internet access.

Contact Mrs. Jean Field, Director of Guidance. 630-530-3460. Fax: 630-530-2290. E-mail: ichighschool@icelmhurst.org. Web site: www.icelmhurst.org/ichs.

IMMANUEL CHRISTIAN HIGH SCHOOL

802 6th Avenue N
Lethbridge, Alberta T1H 0S1, Canada
Head of School: Mr. Ed DeYoung

General Information Coeducational day college-preparatory and general academic school, affiliated with Christian Reformed Church, Reformed Church. Grades 7–12. Founded: 1962. Setting: urban. 4-acre campus. 1 building on campus. Approved or accredited by Christian Schools International and Alberta Department of Education. Language of instruction: English. Total enrollment: 300. Upper school average class size: 22. Upper school faculty-student ratio: 1:19.

Upper School Student Profile 70% of students are members of Christian Reformed Church, Reformed.

Faculty School total: 25. In upper school: 12 men, 13 women.

Graduation Requirements Alberta Learning requirements.

College Placement 53 students graduated in 2005; 27 went to college, including Calvin College; Dordt College; The University of Lethbridge; Trinity Christian College; Trinity Western University; University of Alberta.

Student Life Upper grades have specified standards of dress, student council. Discipline rests primarily with faculty.

Tuition and Aid Day student tuition: CAN$5500–CAN$6100. Tuition installment plan (monthly payment plans, individually arranged payment plans). Tuition reduction for siblings available.

Admissions Deadline for receipt of application materials: none. No application fee required. On-campus interview required.

Athletics Interscholastic: badminton (boys, girls), basketball (b,g), golf (b,g), running (b,g), track and field (b,g), volleyball (b,g); intramural: badminton (b,g), basketball (b,g), track and field (b,g), volleyball (b,g); coed interscholastic: badminton, cross-country running; coed intramural: badminton, scuba diving.

Computers Computers are regularly used in all classes. Computer resources include campus e-mail, on-campus library services, CD-ROMs, Internet access, file transfer.

Contact Mr. Ed DeYoung, Principal. 403-328-4783. Fax: 403-327-6333. E-mail: ed.deyoung@gmail.com. Web site: www.immanuelchristian.org.

IMPERIAL COLLEGE OF TORONTO

20 Queen Elizabeth Boulevard
Etobicoke, Ontario M8Z 1L8, Canada
Head of School: Mr. Jon Austin

General Information Coeducational boarding college-preparatory and general academic school. Grades 11–12. Founded: 1990. Setting: urban. Nearest major city is Toronto, Canada. Students are housed in coed dormitories. 2-acre campus. Approved or accredited by Ontario Department of Education. Language of instruction: English. Total enrollment: 201. Upper school average class size: 22. Upper school faculty-student ratio: 1:22.

Upper School Student Profile Grade 11: 30 students (16 boys, 14 girls); Grade 12: 171 students (87 boys, 84 girls). 25% of students are boarding students. 5% are province residents. 1 province is represented in upper school student body. 95% are international students. International students from China, Hong Kong, Malaysia, Republic of Korea, Taiwan, and Viet Nam; 2 other countries represented in student body.

Faculty School total: 17. In upper school: 10 men, 7 women; 6 have advanced degrees; 2 reside on campus.

Subjects Offered Accounting, advanced TOEFL/grammar, algebra, biology, chemistry, Chinese, college placement, computer applications, economics, finite math, geography, geometry, history, law, physics.

Graduation Requirements Accounting, calculus, computer science, economics, English, mathematics, physics.

Special Academic Programs Accelerated programs; independent study; special instructional classes for students with emotional and behavioral problems; ESL (85 students enrolled).

College Placement 180 students graduated in 2005; 162 went to college, including McGill University; McMaster University; The University of Western Ontario; University of Manitoba; University of Toronto; University of Waterloo. Other: 10 had other specific plans.

Student Life Upper grades have honor system. Discipline rests primarily with faculty.

Summer Programs Advancement, ESL programs offered; session focuses on ESL and pre-university program; held on campus; accepts boys and girls; open to students from other schools. 29 students usually enrolled. 2006 schedule: June 1 to August 26. Application deadline: May 1.

Tuition and Aid Day student tuition: $6000; 7-day tuition and room/board: $12,000. Guaranteed tuition plan.

Admissions For fall 2005, 240 students applied for upper-level admission, 201 were accepted, 201 enrolled. Deadline for receipt of application materials: none. Application fee required: $250.

Computers Computers are regularly used in ESL, Web site design, word processing classes. Computer resources include campus e-mail, CD-ROMs, Internet access, office computer access.

Contact Ms. Pearl Liao, Admission Officer. 416-251-4970. Fax: 416-251-0259. E-mail: info@imperialcollege.org. Web site: www.imperialcollege.org.

INCARNATE WORD ACADEMY

609 Crawford
Houston, Texas 77002-3668
Head of School: Sr. Lauren Beck

General Information Girls' day college-preparatory school, affiliated with Roman Catholic Church. Grades 9–12. Founded: 1873. Setting: urban. 2 buildings on campus. Approved or accredited by National Catholic Education Association, Southern Association of Colleges and Schools, Texas Catholic Conference, Texas Education Agency, Texas Private School Accreditation Commission, and Texas Department of Education. Total enrollment: 249. Upper school average class size: 18. Upper school faculty-student ratio: 1:14.

Upper School Student Profile Grade 9: 78 students (78 girls); Grade 10: 58 students (58 girls); Grade 11: 57 students (57 girls); Grade 12: 56 students (56 girls). 93% of students are Roman Catholic.

Faculty School total: 35. In upper school: 5 men, 30 women; 13 have advanced degrees.

Graduation Requirements 100 hours of community service.

Special Academic Programs Advanced Placement exam preparation in 10 subject areas; honors section; independent study.

College Placement 51 students graduated in 2005; all went to college, including Texas A&M University; The University of Texas at Austin; University of Houston; University of Notre Dame.

Student Life Upper grades have uniform requirement, student council, honor system. Discipline rests primarily with faculty. Attendance at religious services is required.

Summer Programs Sports programs offered; session focuses on sports conditioning camp; held off campus; held at University of St. Thomas; accepts girls; open to students from other schools. 45 students usually enrolled.

Tuition and Aid Day student tuition: $6750. Tuition installment plan (monthly payment plans, individually arranged payment plans). Merit scholarship grants, need-based scholarship grants, paying campus jobs available. In 2005–06, 13% of upper-school students received aid; total upper-school merit-scholarship money awarded: $24,000. Total amount of financial aid awarded in 2005–06: $95,000.

Admissions Traditional secondary-level entrance grade is 9. For fall 2005, 300 students applied for upper-level admission, 280 were accepted, 249 enrolled. High School Placement Test (closed version) from Scholastic Testing Service required. Deadline for receipt of application materials: February 1. Application fee required: $50. Interview recommended.

Athletics Interscholastic: aerobics/dance, basketball, cross-country running, dance team, golf, running, soccer, softball, track and field, volleyball; intramural: cheering, fitness, physical fitness. 2 PE instructors, 6 coaches, 4 trainers.

Computers Computers are regularly used in keyboarding, Web site design, yearbook classes. Computer network features include on-campus library services, CD-ROMs, online commercial services, Internet access, DVD.

Contact Ms. Gabrielle Patout, Director of Admissions. 713-227-3637. Fax: 713-227-1014. E-mail: gpatout@incarnateword.org. Web site: www.incarnateword.org.

INDIAN MOUNTAIN SCHOOL

Lakeville, Connecticut
See Junior Boarding Schools section.

INDIAN SPRINGS SCHOOL

190 Woodward Drive
Indian Springs, Alabama 35124
Head of School: Mr. Melville G. MacKay III

General Information Coeducational boarding and day college-preparatory, arts, and technology school. Boarding grades 9–PG, day grades 8–12. Founded: 1952. Setting: suburban. Nearest major city is Birmingham. Students are housed in single-sex dormitories. 350-acre campus. 38 buildings on campus. Approved or accredited by Southern Association of Colleges and Schools, Southern Association of Independent Schools, and Alabama Department of Education. Member of National Association of Independent Schools and Secondary School Admission Test Board. Endowment: $22 million. Total enrollment: 274. Upper school average class size: 15. Upper school faculty-student ratio: 1:7.

Upper School Student Profile Grade 8: 32 students (10 boys, 22 girls); Grade 9: 63 students (32 boys, 31 girls); Grade 10: 61 students (37 boys, 24 girls); Grade 11: 57 students (30 boys, 27 girls); Grade 12: 61 students (28 boys, 33 girls). 25% of students are boarding students. 83% are state residents. 9 states are represented in upper school student body. 10% are international students. International students from China, Germany, Republic of Korea, Rwanda, and Taiwan.

Faculty School total: 37. In upper school: 21 men, 16 women; 28 have advanced degrees; 21 reside on campus.

Subjects Offered Advanced Placement courses, algebra, American government-AP, American history, American literature, architecture, art, art history, athletics, biology, biology-AP, calculus, calligraphy, ceramics, chemistry, computer applications, computer keyboarding, computer multimedia, computer science, concert choir, constitutional law, contemporary issues, creative writing, drama, economics, English, English literature, English-AP, environmental science-AP, European history, expository writing, film studies, fine arts, French, French-AP, geology, geometry, government-AP, government/civics, history, jazz, Latin, Latin-AP, mathematics, music, painting, philosophy, physical education, physical fitness, physics, play production, precalculus, Russian history, science, Shakespeare, social studies, Spanish, Spanish-AP, statistics-AP, theater, trigonometry, video film production, Western civilization-AP, world history, world literature, world religions, world wide web design, World-Wide-Web publishing, writing, yearbook.

Graduation Requirements Arts and fine arts (art, music, dance, drama), English, foreign language, mathematics, music history, physical education (includes health), science, social studies (includes history).

Special Academic Programs Advanced Placement exam preparation in 18 subject areas; independent study; academic accommodation for the gifted, the musically talented, and the artistically talented.

College Placement 60 students graduated in 2005; all went to college, including Bard College; Birmingham-Southern College; Middlebury College; The University of Alabama; University of Pennsylvania; Wake Forest University. Median SAT verbal: 660, median SAT math: 655. Mean composite ACT: 27. 77% scored over 600 on SAT verbal, 72% scored over 600 on SAT math, 65% scored over 26 on composite ACT.

Indian Springs School

Student Life Upper grades have student council, honor system. Discipline rests equally with students and faculty.

Tuition and Aid Day student tuition: $14,250; 5-day tuition and room/board: $23,815; 7-day tuition and room/board: $25,695. Tuition installment plan (Key Tuition Payment Plan, monthly payment plans, individually arranged payment plans). Need-based scholarship grants, paying campus jobs, Key Education Resources available. In 2005–06, 28% of upper-school students received aid. Total amount of financial aid awarded in 2005–06: $602,377.

Admissions Traditional secondary-level entrance grade is 8. For fall 2005, 171 students applied for upper-level admission, 125 were accepted, 90 enrolled. SSAT or writing sample required. Deadline for receipt of application materials: none. Application fee required: $50. Interview required.

Athletics Interscholastic: baseball (boys), basketball (b,g), soccer (b,g), softball (g), volleyball (g); intramural: basketball (b,g), flag football (b), soccer (b,g); coed interscholastic: cross-country running, golf, tennis, ultimate Frisbee; coed intramural: aerobics, aerobics/nautilus, outdoor activities, paint ball, physical fitness, strength & conditioning, table tennis, ultimate Frisbee. 3 PE instructors, 8 coaches.

Computers Computers are regularly used in English, keyboarding, multimedia, technology, video film production, Web site design classes. Computer network features include on-campus library services, CD-ROMs, Internet access, DVD, wireless campus network.

Contact Shelby S. Hammer, Director of External Affairs. 205-988-3350. Fax: 205-988-3797. E-mail: shammer@indiansprings.org. Web site: www.indiansprings.org.

See full description on page 850.

INTERLOCHEN ARTS ACADEMY

PO Box 199
4000 Highway M-137
Interlochen, Michigan 49643-0199
Head of School: Mr. Jeffrey S. Kimpton

General Information Coeducational boarding and day college-preparatory and arts school. Grades 9–PG. Founded: 1962. Setting: rural. Nearest major city is Traverse City. Students are housed in single-sex dormitories. 1,200-acre campus. 225 buildings on campus. Approved or accredited by Independent Schools Association of the Central States, North Central Association of Colleges and Schools, The Association of Boarding Schools, and Michigan Department of Education. Member of National Association of Independent Schools and Secondary School Admission Test Board. Endowment: $32 million. Total enrollment: 455. Upper school average class size: 12. Upper school faculty-student ratio: 1:6.

Upper School Student Profile Grade 9: 27 students (14 boys, 13 girls); Grade 10: 62 students (18 boys, 44 girls); Grade 11: 160 students (71 boys, 89 girls); Grade 12: 188 students (95 boys, 93 girls); Postgraduate: 18 students (10 boys, 8 girls). 93% of students are boarding students. 22% are state residents. 49 states are represented in upper school student body. 14% are international students. International students from Canada, China, Japan, Republic of Korea, South Africa, and Uzbekistan; 12 other countries represented in student body.

Faculty School total: 77. In upper school: 49 men, 28 women; 60 have advanced degrees; 36 reside on campus.

Subjects Offered Algebra, American history, American literature, art, ballet, ballet technique, biology, British literature, British literature (honors), calculus, ceramics, chamber groups, chemistry, chemistry-AP, choir, choral music, choreography, civil war history, computer math, computer science, contemporary art, creative writing, current events, dance, dance performance, drafting, drama, dramatic arts, earth science, ecology, English, English literature, environmental science, European history, expository writing, fine arts, French, geometry, German, government/civics, health, history, mathematics, music, philosophy, photography, physical education, physics, science, social studies, Spanish, speech, statistics, theater, trigonometry, world history, world literature, writing.

Graduation Requirements Arts and fine arts (art, music, dance, drama), English, mathematics, physical education (includes health), science, social studies (includes history).

Special Academic Programs Advanced Placement exam preparation in 3 subject areas; accelerated programs; independent study; term-away projects; academic accommodation for the gifted, the musically talented, and the artistically talented; ESL (54 students enrolled).

College Placement 225 students graduated in 2005; 214 went to college, including Cleveland Institute of Music; Eastman School of Music; Oberlin College; Peabody Conservatory of Music of The Johns Hopkins University; The Juilliard School; University of Michigan. Other: 5 entered a postgraduate year, 6 had other specific plans. Mean SAT verbal: 609, mean SAT math: 577, mean composite ACT: 25.

Student Life Upper grades have uniform requirement, student council, honor system. Discipline rests primarily with faculty.

Summer Programs Art/fine arts programs offered; session focuses on fine and performing arts; held on campus; accepts boys and girls; open to students from other schools. 2200 students usually enrolled. 2006 schedule: June 25 to August 8. Application deadline: February 15.

Tuition and Aid Day student tuition: $18,600–$19,900; 7-day tuition and room/board: $30,350–$31,650. Tuition installment plan (Key Tuition Payment Plan). Merit scholarship grants, need-based scholarship grants available. In 2005–06, 70% of upper-school students received aid. Total amount of financial aid awarded in 2005–06: $5,000,000.

Admissions Traditional secondary-level entrance grade is 11. For fall 2005, 648 students applied for upper-level admission, 500 were accepted, 455 enrolled. Achievement tests, any standardized test, audition, essay, placement test or SSAT required. Deadline for receipt of application materials: none. Application fee required: $50. Interview recommended.

Athletics Intramural: baseball (boys); coed intramural: aerobics, archery, badminton, basketball, canoeing/kayaking, climbing, cooperative games, cross-country running, fishing, fitness, fitness walking, flag football, floor hockey, fly fishing, Frisbee, hiking/backpacking, indoor soccer, jogging, modern dance, Newcombe ball, outdoor activities, outdoor adventure, outdoor education, outdoor recreation, outdoor skills, physical fitness, pillo polo, project adventure, rappelling, ropes courses, running, skiing (cross-country), skiing (downhill), snowshoeing, soccer, softball, table tennis, touch football, ultimate Frisbee, volleyball, wall climbing, whiffle ball, yoga.

Computers Computers are regularly used in mathematics, music, science classes. Computer network features include campus e-mail, on-campus library services, online commercial services, Internet access, wireless campus network.

Contact Coordinator of Academy Admissions. 231-276-7472. Fax: 231-276-7464. E-mail: admissions@interlochen.org. Web site: www.interlochen.org.

ANNOUNCEMENT FROM THE SCHOOL Interlochen Arts Academy, the nation's first and foremost boarding arts high school, unites students with others who value their highest aspirations in a fast-paced, creative environment that challenges, inspires, and focuses talents. Five hundred of the world's most talented and motivated young artists study music, theater, dance, visual arts, creative writing, and motion picture arts in IAA's college-like setting. Preprofessional arts instruction, college-preparatory education, and life-skills development are vital ingredients in the Interlochen experience. While producing more than 250 artistic presentations in the school year, Academy students also master a rigorous college-preparatory academic curriculum that prepares them to take prominent roles in a whole universe of professional endeavors. Thirty-seven IAA graduates have been chosen as Presidential Scholars in the Arts/Academics, more than from any other high school in the United States. The faculty at IAA is comprised of 81 outstanding artists and educators, 40 of whom hold earned master's degrees and 20 of whom hold earned doctorates. The Academy also offers dozens of guest-artist master classes annually. Interlochen Arts Academy was honored by the National Foundation for Advancement in the Arts as one of its inaugural Distinguished Schools in the Arts; IAA is one of only 5 schools to receive this honor and the only independent school to be recognized. Founded in 1962, IAA is situated on a 1200-acre wooded campus with educational, recreational, and performance facilities, including Corson Auditorium, Harvey Theatre (major additions in 2005), visual arts studios and gallery, the Writing House (dedicated in 2003), Dendrinos Chapel and Recital Hall, the Hildegarde Lewis Dance Building, the Roscoe O. Bonisteel Library (ready in spring 2006), and the Aaron and Helen L. DeRoy Center for Film Studies (ready in 2006). More than half of the students at Interlochen Arts Academy receive some kind of financial aid.

INTERNATIONAL COLLEGE SPAIN

Calle Vereda Norte, #3
La Moraleja
Madrid 28109, Spain
Head of School: Mr. Terry J. Hedger

General Information Coeducational day college-preparatory and bilingual studies school. Grades PK–12. Founded: 1980. Setting: suburban. 3-hectare campus. 3 buildings on campus. Approved or accredited by European Council of International Schools, International Baccalaureate Organization, and New England Association of Schools and Colleges. Language of instruction: English. Total enrollment: 616. Upper school average class size: 10. Upper school faculty-student ratio: 1:10.

Upper School Student Profile Grade 9: 35 students (17 boys, 18 girls); Grade 10: 44 students (21 boys, 23 girls); Grade 11: 51 students (25 boys, 26 girls); Grade 12: 40 students (18 boys, 22 girls).

Faculty School total: 63. In upper school: 15 men, 18 women; 12 have advanced degrees.

Subjects Offered 20th century world history, advanced chemistry, advanced math, art, biology, chemistry, computer programming, computer science, Danish, design, drama, Dutch, economics, English, English literature, European history, expressive arts, French, geography, global studies, history, humanities, information technology, interdisciplinary studies, International Baccalaureate courses, Italian, Japanese, mathematics, model United Nations, music, personal and social education, physical education, physics, science, social education, social studies, Spanish, Spanish literature, Swedish, technology, theory of knowledge, world affairs, world cultures, world history, world literature, world studies.

Graduation Requirements English, foreign language, mathematics, science, social science, social studies (includes history), 90% minimum attendance, minimum average effort grade of satisfactory. Community service is required.

Special Academic Programs International Baccalaureate program; ESL (46 students enrolled).

College Placement 50 students graduated in 2005; 48 went to college, including Boston University; Duke University; University of California, Berkeley; University of Miami; University of Michigan; University of South Florida. Other: 2 entered military service. 75% scored over 600 on SAT verbal, 100% scored over 600 on SAT math.

Student Life Upper grades have specified standards of dress, student council. Discipline rests equally with students and faculty.

Summer Programs ESL, art/fine arts programs offered; session focuses on English and Spanish languages; held on campus; accepts boys and girls; open to students from other schools. 280 students usually enrolled. 2006 schedule: July 1 to July 26. Application deadline: none.

Tuition and Aid Day student tuition: €11,340–€12,360. Tuition installment plan (Insured Tuition Payment Plan). Tuition reduction for siblings, bursaries, merit scholarship grants, need-based scholarship grants available. In 2005–06, 9% of upper-school students received aid; total upper-school merit-scholarship money awarded: €8560. Total amount of financial aid awarded in 2005–06: €38,706.

Admissions Traditional secondary-level entrance grade is 11. For fall 2005, 50 students applied for upper-level admission, 20 were accepted, 20 enrolled. Admissions testing and math and English placement tests required. Deadline for receipt of application materials: none. Application fee required: €500. On-campus interview required.

Athletics Interscholastic: basketball (boys, girls), cross-country running (b,g), soccer (b,g), volleyball (b,g); intramural: aerobics/dance (b,g), badminton (b,g), ballet (b,g), field hockey (b,g), gymnastics (b,g), physical fitness (b,g), soccer (b,g), softball (b,g), swimming and diving (b,g), table tennis (b,g), tennis (b,g), volleyball (b,g); coed interscholastic: track and field; coed intramural: alpine skiing, dance, judo, martial arts, skiing (downhill). 2 PE instructors, 2 coaches.

Computers Computers are regularly used in art, career education, economics, English, ESL, information technology, mathematics, science classes. Computer resources include CD-ROMs, online commercial services, Internet access, DVD, wireless campus network.

Contact Mrs. JoAnn DeCamp, Registrar. 34-9-1-650-2398. Fax: 34-9-1-650-1035. E-mail: registrar@icsmadrid.org. Web site: www.icsmadrid.com.

INTERNATIONAL COMMUNITY SCHOOL OF ADDIS ABABA

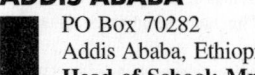

PO Box 70282
Addis Ababa, Ethiopia
Head of School: Mr. Stephen Edward Plisinski

General Information Coeducational day college-preparatory school. Grades PK–12. Founded: 1964. Setting: suburban. 15-acre campus. 2 buildings on campus. Approved or accredited by Academy of Orton-Gillingham Practitioners and Educators and Middle States Association of Colleges and Schools. Member of European Council of International Schools. Language of instruction: English. Total enrollment: 426. Upper school average class size: 16. Upper school faculty-student ratio: 1:13.

Upper School Student Profile Grade 9: 36 students (18 boys, 18 girls); Grade 10: 39 students (21 boys, 18 girls); Grade 11: 32 students (17 boys, 15 girls); Grade 12: 34 students (21 boys, 13 girls).

Faculty School total: 45. In upper school: 13 men, 9 women; 19 have advanced degrees.

Subjects Offered Algebra, American history, American literature, art, biology, ceramics, chemistry, computer programming, computer science, creative writing, current events, earth science, English, English literature, ESL, European history, fine arts, French, geography, geometry, grammar, health, history, mathematics, music, physical education, physics, political science, science, social studies, Spanish, theory of knowledge, world history, world literature, writing.

Graduation Requirements Arts and fine arts (art, music, dance, drama), computer science, electives, English, foreign language, mathematics, physical education (includes health), science, social studies (includes history).

Special Academic Programs International Baccalaureate program; Advanced Placement exam preparation; remedial reading and/or remedial writing; remedial math; ESL (16 students enrolled).

College Placement 21 students graduated in 2005; 20 went to college. Median SAT verbal: 565, median SAT math: 595. 21% scored over 600 on SAT verbal, 21% scored over 600 on SAT math.

Student Life Upper grades have specified standards of dress, student council, honor system. Discipline rests equally with students and faculty.

Tuition and Aid Day student tuition: $4645–$13,015. Tuition installment plan (quarterly payment plan). Tuition reduction for siblings, merit scholarship grants available. Total upper-school merit-scholarship money awarded for 2005–06: $5000.

Admissions Traditional secondary-level entrance grade is 9. For fall 2005, 70 students applied for upper-level admission, 59 were accepted, 59 enrolled. School's

own exam required. Deadline for receipt of application materials: none. No application fee required. On-campus interview required.

Athletics Interscholastic: basketball (boys, girls), cross-country running (b,g), soccer (b,g), tennis (b,g), track and field (b,g); intramural: baseball (b,g), basketball (b,g), cross-country running (b,g), soccer (b,g), softball (b,g), track and field (b,g); coed intramural: ballet, bowling, cheering, dance, golf, martial arts, outdoor activities, outdoor education, outdoor recreation, physical training. 2 PE instructors.

Computers Computers are regularly used in English classes. Computer network features include on-campus library services, CD-ROMs, Internet access, file transfer.

Contact Mr. Michael Archbold, Counselor. 251-11-371-8102. Fax: 251-11-371-0722. E-mail: ics@ethionet.et. Web site: addis.ecis.org/.

INTERNATIONAL HIGH SCHOOL OF FAIS

150 Oak Street
San Francisco, California 94102
Head of School: Ms. Jane Camblin

General Information Coeducational day college-preparatory, arts, bilingual studies, and technology school. Grades PK–12. Founded: 1962. Setting: urban. 3-acre campus. 2 buildings on campus. Approved or accredited by California Association of Independent Schools, European Council of International Schools, French Ministry of Education, International Baccalaureate Organization, Western Association of Schools and Colleges, and California Department of Education. Member of National Association of Independent Schools and Secondary School Admission Test Board. Languages of instruction: English, Spanish, and French. Endowment: $1.3 million. Total enrollment: 893. Upper school average class size: 17. Upper school faculty-student ratio: 1:10.

Upper School Student Profile Grade 9: 73 students (28 boys, 45 girls); Grade 10: 91 students (37 boys, 54 girls); Grade 11: 79 students (33 boys, 46 girls); Grade 12: 70 students (33 boys, 37 girls).

Faculty School total: 139. In upper school: 30 men, 29 women; 35 have advanced degrees.

Subjects Offered Advanced chemistry, advanced computer applications, advanced math, algebra, American history, American literature, art, art history, arts appreciation, biology, calculus, chemistry, community service, computer science, creative writing, current events, drama, earth science, economics, English, English literature, environmental science, ESL, European history, expository writing, fine arts, French, geography, geometry, German, government/civics, history, International Baccalaureate courses, journalism, Mandarin, mathematics, music, philosophy, physical education, physics, science, social studies, Spanish, theater, theory of knowledge, trigonometry, world arts, world history, world literature, writing.

Graduation Requirements Arts and fine arts (art, music, dance, drama), computer science, English, foreign language, International Baccalaureate courses, mathematics, physical education (includes health), science, social studies (includes history), theory of knowledge, extended essay, 150 hours of CAS. Community service is required.

Special Academic Programs International Baccalaureate program; Advanced Placement exam preparation in 14 subject areas; honors section; independent study; term-away projects; study abroad; academic accommodation for the gifted, the musically talented, and the artistically talented; ESL (10 students enrolled).

College Placement 73 students graduated in 2005; 70 went to college, including Brown University; New York University; Northwestern University; Oberlin College; University of California, Berkeley; University of California, Santa Barbara. Other: 3 had other specific plans. Median SAT verbal: 630, median SAT math: 630. 68% scored over 600 on SAT verbal, 79% scored over 600 on SAT math.

Student Life Upper grades have student council. Discipline rests equally with students and faculty.

Summer Programs Enrichment, advancement, art/fine arts programs offered; held on campus; accepts boys and girls; open to students from other schools.

Tuition and Aid Day student tuition: $23,790. Tuition installment plan (Insured Tuition Payment Plan, FACTS Tuition Payment Plan). Need-based scholarship grants, French bourse available. In 2005–06, 25% of upper-school students received aid. Total amount of financial aid awarded in 2005–06: $748,000.

Admissions Traditional secondary-level entrance grade is 9. For fall 2005, 267 students applied for upper-level admission, 170 were accepted, 47 enrolled. ERB required. Deadline for receipt of application materials: none. Application fee required: $75. Interview required.

Athletics Interscholastic: baseball (boys, girls), basketball (b,g), football (b), soccer (b,g), volleyball (b,g); intramural: ballet (b,g), baseball (b), basketball (b,g), floor hockey (b,g), soccer (b,g), softball (g), tennis (b,g), volleyball (b,g); coed interscholastic: cross-country running, golf, swimming and diving, tennis, track and field; coed intramural: badminton, ballet, cross-country running, fencing, flagball, golf, handball, indoor hockey, outdoor activities, outdoor adventure, physical fitness, physical training, swimming and diving, water polo, weight training. 4 PE instructors, 8 coaches, 3 trainers.

Computers Computers are regularly used in graphics, mathematics, multimedia, science classes. Computer network features include on-campus library services, CD-ROMs, online commercial services, Internet access, file transfer, video editing, Web page creation.

Contact Amanda Hamilton, Admission Coordinator. 415-558-2084. Fax: 415-558-2085. E-mail: amandah@fais-ihs.org. Web site: www.ihs-fais.org.

INTERNATIONAL JUNIOR GOLF ACADEMY

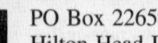

PO Box 22659
Hilton Head Island, South Carolina 29926
Head of School: Beth Johnson

General Information Coeducational boarding and day college-preparatory and arts school; primarily serves individuals with Attention Deficit Disorder and dyslexic students. Grades 6–PG. Founded: 1995. Setting: suburban. Nearest major city is Savannah, GA. Students are housed in single-sex dormitories. 5-acre campus. 2 buildings on campus. Approved or accredited by South Carolina Department of Education. Candidate for accreditation by Southern Association of Colleges and Schools. Languages of instruction: Spanish and French. Total enrollment: 110. Upper school average class size: 12. Upper school faculty-student ratio: 1:10.

Upper School Student Profile 95% of students are boarding students. 24 states are represented in upper school student body. 40% are international students. International students from Canada, Guatemala, Japan, Mexico, Republic of Korea, and United Kingdom; 10 other countries represented in student body.

Faculty School total: 10. In upper school: 3 men, 7 women; all reside on campus.

Special Academic Programs Advanced Placement exam preparation in 6 subject areas; honors section; ESL (20 students enrolled).

College Placement 20 students graduated in 2005; 18 went to college. Other: 2 had other specific plans.

Student Life Upper grades have specified standards of dress, student council, honor system. Discipline rests equally with students and faculty.

Summer Programs ESL, sports programs offered; session focuses on golf; held on campus; accepts boys and girls; open to students from other schools. 350 students usually enrolled. 2006 schedule: June 5 to August 14. Application deadline: June 1.

Tuition and Aid Day student tuition: $21,000; 7-day tuition and room/board: $34,500. Tuition installment plan (individually arranged payment plans). Sallie Mae Loans available. In 2005–06, 5% of upper-school students received aid.

Admissions Deadline for receipt of application materials: none. Application fee required: $35. Interview recommended.

Athletics Interscholastic: golf (boys, girls). 15 coaches, 1 trainer.

Computers Computer resources include Internet access.

Contact Ryley Webb, Director of Admission. 843-686-1500. Fax: 843-785-5116. E-mail: ryley@ijga.com. Web site: www.ijga.com.

INTERNATIONAL SCHOOL BANGKOK

39/7 Soi Nichada Thani, Samakee Road
Pakkret 11120, Thailand
Head of School: Dr. William Gerritz

General Information Coeducational boarding and day college-preparatory school. Grades PK–12. Founded: 1951. Setting: suburban. Nearest major city is Bangkok. 35-acre campus. 2 buildings on campus. Approved or accredited by East Asia Regional Council of Schools and Western Association of Schools and Colleges. Affiliate member of National Association of Independent Schools; member of European Council of International Schools. Language of instruction: English. Total enrollment: 1,873. Upper school average class size: 25. Upper school faculty-student ratio: 1:9.

Upper School Student Profile Grade 9: 185 students (98 boys, 87 girls); Grade 10: 171 students (73 boys, 98 girls); Grade 11: 184 students (82 boys, 102 girls); Grade 12: 171 students (92 boys, 79 girls).

Faculty School total: 181. In upper school: 67 men, 77 women; 124 have advanced degrees.

Subjects Offered Algebra, American history, American literature, art, art history, biology, business, calculus, calculus-AP, ceramics, chemistry, computer math, computer programming, computer science, creative writing, dance, drafting, drama, earth science, ecology, economics, electives, English, English literature, environmental science, ESL, European history, expository writing, fine arts, French, geography, geology, geometry, German, government/civics, grammar, health, history, home economics, humanities, industrial arts, Japanese, journalism, language arts, languages, mathematics, mechanical drawing, music, performing arts, philosophy, photography, physical education, physics, psychology, reading, science, social studies, sociology, Spanish, speech, statistics, Thai, theater, theory of knowledge, trigonometry, typing, world history, world literature, writing.

Graduation Requirements Arts and fine arts (art, music, dance, drama), computers, English, mathematics, physical education (includes health), science, social studies (includes history). Community service is required.

Special Academic Programs International Baccalaureate program; Advanced Placement exam preparation in 14 subject areas; independent study; ESL (300 students enrolled).

College Placement 149 students graduated in 2005; they went to Duke University; The George Washington University; The Johns Hopkins University; University of California, San Diego; University of Colorado at Boulder; University of Virginia. 27% scored over 600 on SAT verbal, 43% scored over 600 on SAT math, 23% scored over 26 on composite ACT.

Student Life Upper grades have specified standards of dress, student council. Discipline rests primarily with faculty.

Summer Programs Remediation, advancement, ESL, art/fine arts programs offered; held on campus; accepts boys and girls; open to students from other schools. 135 students usually enrolled. 2006 schedule: June 5 to July 28. Application deadline: June 2.

Tuition and Aid Day student tuition: 581,600 Thai bahts. Tuition installment plan (semester payment plan).

Admissions Deadline for receipt of application materials: none. Application fee required: 4000 Thai bahts. On-campus interview required.

Athletics Interscholastic: aquatics (boys, girls), badminton (b,g), basketball (b,g), cross-country running (b,g), dance (b,g), physical training (b,g), rugby (b,g), soccer (b,g), softball (b,g), swimming and diving (b,g), tennis (b,g), track and field (b,g), volleyball (b,g); intramural: aquatics (b,g), fencing (b), rugby (b,g). 5 PE instructors.

Computers Computers are regularly used in English, history, science classes. Computer network features include campus e-mail, on-campus library services, CD-ROMs, Internet access, ExPAN.

Contact Mrs. Wendy Chairin, Admissions Director. 662-963-5800 Ext. 125. Fax: 662-583-5432. E-mail: register@isb.ac.th. Web site: www.isb.ac.th.

INTERNATIONAL SCHOOL BASEL

Fleischbachstrasse 2
Reinach BL 2 4153, Switzerland
Head of School: Mrs. Lesley Barron

General Information Coeducational day college-preparatory school. Grades PK–12. Founded: 1979. Setting: suburban. Nearest major city is Basel. 6-acre campus. 1 building on campus. Approved or accredited by European Council of International Schools, International Baccalaureate Organization, and New England Association of Schools and Colleges. Language of instruction: English. Total enrollment: 913. Upper school average class size: 16. Upper school faculty-student ratio: 1:10.

Faculty School total: 140. In upper school: 24 men, 38 women; 27 have advanced degrees.

Subjects Offered Art, biology, business, chemistry, drama, economics, English, English literature, ESL, fine arts, foreign language, French, general science, geography, German, government, health, health education, history, industrial technology, information technology, International Baccalaureate courses, international relations, mathematics, physical education, physical fitness, physics, psychology, SAT preparation, science, social studies, theater.

Graduation Requirements Arts and fine arts (art, music, dance, drama), English, foreign language, mathematics, physical education (includes health), science, social studies (includes history), minimum GPA of 5.0.

Special Academic Programs International Baccalaureate program; Advanced Placement exam preparation in 5 subject areas; honors section; independent study; study at local college for college credit; remedial reading and/or remedial writing; remedial math; ESL.

College Placement 49 students graduated in 2005; 32 went to college, including Columbia College; Harvard University; Stanford University. Other: 14 went to work, 1 entered military service, 2 had other specific plans. 55% scored over 600 on SAT verbal, 36% scored over 600 on SAT math.

Student Life Upper grades have specified standards of dress, student council, honor system. Discipline rests equally with students and faculty.

Tuition and Aid Day student tuition: 16,350 Swiss francs–29,500 Swiss francs. Tuition installment plan (monthly payment plans, individually arranged payment plans, 2-payment plan).

Admissions Deadline for receipt of application materials: none. Application fee required: 4000 Swiss francs. Interview required.

Athletics Interscholastic: basketball (boys, girls); coed interscholastic: alpine skiing, ball hockey, basketball, cross-country running, floor hockey, fly fishing, football, gymnastics, indoor hockey, skiing (downhill), soccer, swimming and diving, track and field, volleyball; coed intramural: alpine skiing, aquatics, back packing, badminton, ball hockey, baseball, basketball, biathlon, blading, climbing, cross-country running, fitness, floor hockey, gymnastics, indoor hockey, indoor soccer, mountain biking, netball, outdoor education, physical training, rock climbing, rowing, skiing (downhill), soccer, softball, swimming and diving, track and field, volleyball, weight training. 7 PE instructors, 5 coaches.

Computers Computers are regularly used in business, economics, English, foreign language, history, humanities, library, mathematics, psychology, science, technology classes. Computer network features include campus e-mail, on-campus library services, CD-ROMs, online commercial services, Internet access, file transfer, DVD, wireless campus network.

Contact Mrs. Jennifer Dunning, Head of Admissions. 41-61-715 33 33. Fax: 41-61-715 33 15. E-mail: info@isbasel.ch. Web site: www.isbasel.ch.

INTERNATIONAL SCHOOL HAMBURG

Holmbrook 20
Hamburg 22605, Germany
Head of School: Peter Gittins

General Information Coeducational day college-preparatory, arts, and technology school. Grades PK–12. Founded: 1957. Setting: suburban. 3-acre campus. 1 building on campus. Approved or accredited by European Council of International Schools and New England Association of Schools and Colleges. Language of instruction: English. Total enrollment: 670. Upper school average class size: 20. Upper school faculty-student ratio: 1:7.

Upper School Student Profile Grade 9: 58 students (32 boys, 26 girls); Grade 10: 42 students (25 boys, 17 girls); Grade 11: 44 students (16 boys, 28 girls); Grade 12: 44 students (26 boys, 18 girls).

Faculty School total: 85. In upper school: 27 men, 18 women; 25 have advanced degrees.

Subjects Offered Art, biology, chemistry, computer math, drama, English, environmental science, ESL, European history, fine arts, French, geography, German, history, mathematics, music, photography, physical education, physics, science, social studies, Spanish, theater, theory of knowledge, world history.

Graduation Requirements Arts and fine arts (art, music, dance, drama), English, foreign language, mathematics, physical education (includes health), science, social studies (includes history).

Special Academic Programs International Baccalaureate program; ESL (80 students enrolled).

College Placement 42 students graduated in 2005; 25 went to college, including University of Edinburgh; Yale University. Other: 4 entered military service, 3 had other specific plans.

Student Life Upper grades have student council. Discipline rests primarily with faculty.

Tuition and Aid Day student tuition: €11,700–€15,300. Tuition installment plan (2-payment plan).

Admissions Traditional secondary-level entrance grade is 9. For fall 2005, 50 students applied for upper-level admission, 45 were accepted, 44 enrolled. ACT, CTBS, Stanford Achievement Test, any other standardized test or PSAT and SAT for applicants to grade 11 and 12 required. Deadline for receipt of application materials: none. Application fee required: €100. On-campus interview required.

Athletics Interscholastic: basketball (boys, girls), soccer (b,g), swimming and diving (b,g), track and field (b,g), volleyball (g); intramural: basketball (b,g), cross-country running (b,g), field hockey (b,g), soccer (b,g), swimming and diving (b,g), tennis (b,g), track and field (b,g), volleyball (b,g). 5 PE instructors, 4 coaches.

Computers Computers are regularly used in English, foreign language, mathematics, music, science classes. Computer network features include campus e-mail, on-campus library services, CD-ROMs, online commercial services, Internet access, file transfer, office computer access, DVD.

Contact Catherine Bissonnet, Director of Admissions. 49-40-883-00-133. Fax: 49-40-881-1405. E-mail: cbissonnet@international-school-hamburg.de. Web site: www.international-school-hamburg.de.

INTERNATIONAL SCHOOL OF AMSTERDAM

Sportlaan 45
Amstelveen 1185 TB, Netherlands
Head of School: Dr. Ed Greene

General Information Coeducational day college-preparatory, arts, and bilingual studies school. Grades PS–12. Founded: 1964. Setting: suburban. Nearest major city is Amsterdam. 1-acre campus. 2 buildings on campus. Approved or accredited by European Council of International Schools and New England Association of Schools and Colleges. Language of instruction: English. Total enrollment: 841. Upper school average class size: 15. Upper school faculty-student ratio: 1:11.

Upper School Student Profile Grade 9: 68 students (33 boys, 35 girls); Grade 10: 70 students (39 boys, 31 girls); Grade 11: 48 students (18 boys, 30 girls); Grade 12: 35 students (17 boys, 18 girls).

Faculty School total: 122. In upper school: 16 men, 23 women; 18 have advanced degrees.

Subjects Offered Addiction, algebra, American literature, art, biology, calculus, chemistry, community service, computer programming, computer science, drama, Dutch, economics, English, English literature, ESL, European history, food science, French, geography, geometry, German, history, Japanese, mathematics, music, photography, physical education, physics, science, social science, social studies, Spanish, technology, theater, theory of knowledge, trigonometry, world history, world literature.

Graduation Requirements Arts, computer science, English, foreign language, mathematics, physical education (includes health), science, social science, social studies (includes history). Community service is required.

Special Academic Programs International Baccalaureate program; independent study; academic accommodation for the gifted, the musically talented, and the artistically talented; remedial reading and/or remedial writing; remedial math; programs in English, mathematics, general development for dyslexic students; ESL (191 students enrolled).

College Placement 46 students graduated in 2005; 42 went to college, including Boston College; Georgetown University; Imperial College; The University of North Carolina at Chapel Hill; University of Bath; University of Edinburgh. Other: 1 went to work, 1 entered military service, 2 had other specific plans.

Student Life Upper grades have student council, honor system. Discipline rests primarily with faculty.

Summer Programs Sports programs offered; session focuses on one-week basketball camp; held on campus; accepts boys and girls; not open to students from other schools.

Tuition and Aid Day student tuition: €18,400–€19,100. Tuition installment plan (monthly payment plans, individually arranged payment plans).

Admissions For fall 2005, 120 students applied for upper-level admission, 84 were accepted, 63 enrolled. Deadline for receipt of application materials: none. No application fee required. On-campus interview required.

Athletics Interscholastic: basketball (boys, girls), soccer (b,g), swimming and diving (b,g), tennis (b,g), track and field (b,g), volleyball (g); intramural: rugby (b); coed interscholastic: soccer, softball, volleyball; coed intramural: badminton, ballet, basketball, gymnastics, judo, modern dance, self defense, soccer, softball, swimming and diving, tennis, volleyball. 7 PE instructors, 14 coaches, 14 trainers.

Computers Computers are regularly used in English, foreign language, information technology, mathematics, science classes. Computer network features include campus e-mail, on-campus library services, CD-ROMs, online commercial services, Internet access.

Contact Julia True, Admissions Officer. 31-20-347-1111. Fax: 31-20-347-1222. E-mail: admissions@isa.nl. Web site: www.isa.nl.

INTERNATIONAL SCHOOL OF ARUBA

Wayaca Residence Z.N.
Oranjestad, Aruba
Head of School: Robert L. Werner

General Information Coeducational day college-preparatory and business school. Grades PK–12. Founded: 1985. Setting: suburban. 5-acre campus. 2 buildings on campus. Approved or accredited by Association of American Schools in South America, European Council of International Schools, Southern Association of Colleges and Schools, and US Department of State. Language of instruction: English. Endowment: $100,000. Total enrollment: 130. Upper school average class size: 12. Upper school faculty-student ratio: 1:8.

Upper School Student Profile Grade 9: 11 students (6 boys, 5 girls); Grade 10: 6 students (4 boys, 2 girls); Grade 11: 11 students (6 boys, 5 girls); Grade 12: 12 students (6 boys, 6 girls).

Faculty School total: 28. In upper school: 8 men, 7 women; 9 have advanced degrees.

Subjects Offered Advanced Placement courses, algebra, American history, art, biology, calculus, chemistry, computer science, Dutch, English, English literature, environmental science, geometry, journalism, mathematics, oceanography, physical education, physics, physics-AP, science, social science, social studies, Spanish, world history.

Graduation Requirements Arts and fine arts (art, music, dance, drama), computer science, English, foreign language, mathematics, physical education (includes health), science, social science, social studies (includes history). Community service is required.

Special Academic Programs Advanced Placement exam preparation in 5 subject areas; independent study; remedial reading and/or remedial writing; ESL (15 students enrolled).

College Placement 10 students graduated in 2005; 8 went to college, including Boston University; Florida International University; Johnson & Wales University; Lynn University; University of Florida; York University. Other: 2 went to work. Median SAT verbal: 500, median SAT math: 625. 25% scored over 600 on SAT verbal, 50% scored over 600 on SAT math.

Student Life Upper grades have uniform requirement, student council, honor system. Discipline rests primarily with faculty.

Summer Programs ESL programs offered; session focuses on reinforcement; held on campus; accepts boys and girls; open to students from other schools. 2006 schedule: July 1 to July 31. Application deadline: May.

Tuition and Aid Day student tuition: $9000–$11,000. Tuition installment plan (individually arranged payment plans, 2-payment plan). Merit scholarship grants available. In 2005–06, 2% of upper-school students received aid. Total amount of financial aid awarded in 2005–06: $20,000.

Admissions Traditional secondary-level entrance grade is 10. For fall 2005, 20 students applied for upper-level admission, 15 were accepted, 15 enrolled. Any standardized test and SLEP required. Deadline for receipt of application materials: none. Application fee required: $1000. On-campus interview required.

Athletics Interscholastic: basketball (boys, girls), golf (b,g), scuba diving (b,g), soccer (b,g), softball (b,g), tennis (b,g), volleyball (b,g); intramural: basketball (b,g), track and field (b,g); coed interscholastic: golf, softball, tennis. 2 PE instructors.

Computers Computers are regularly used in journalism, yearbook classes. Computer resources include campus e-mail, CD-ROMs, Internet access.

Contact Robert Lee Werner, Headmaster. 297-583-5040. Fax: 297-583-6020. E-mail: rwernerwis@yahoo.com.

INTERNATIONAL SCHOOL OF ATHENS

Xenias and Artemidos Streets
PO Box 51051
Kifissia—Athens GR-145 10, Greece
Head of School: Mr. C. N. Dardoufas

General Information Coeducational day college-preparatory and arts school. Grades PK–12. Founded: 1979. Setting: suburban. Nearest major city is Athens. 2-acre campus. 1 building on campus. Approved or accredited by CITA (Commission on International and Trans-Regional Accreditation), Department of Defense Dependents Schools, and Middle States Association of Colleges and Schools. Language of instruction: English. Total enrollment: 196. Upper school average class size: 14. Upper school faculty-student ratio: 1:9.

Upper School Student Profile Grade 10: 16 students (10 boys, 6 girls); Grade 11: 18 students (10 boys, 8 girls); Grade 12: 22 students (16 boys, 6 girls).

Faculty School total: 44. In upper school: 8 men, 25 women; 17 have advanced degrees.

Subjects Offered American literature, Arabic, art, art history, biology, business studies, calculus, chemistry, cultural geography, design, drama, English, English literature, ESL, French, geography, Greek, history, information technology, mathematics, modern world history, music, physical education, physics, science, sociology, Spanish, studio art, theory of knowledge, world history, world literature, writing.

Graduation Requirements Art history, arts and fine arts (art, music, dance, drama), English, foreign language, history, information technology, mathematics, physical education (includes health), science, requirements for students in IB diploma program differ. Community service is required.

Special Academic Programs International Baccalaureate program; independent study; remedial reading and/or remedial writing; remedial math; programs in English, mathematics, general development for dyslexic students; ESL (24 students enrolled).

College Placement 37 students graduated in 2005; 35 went to college, including Brunel University; Kent Institute of Art and Design; Kingston University; Queen Mary (University of London); The American College of Greece; University College London. Other: 1 went to work, 1 had other specific plans.

Student Life Upper grades have uniform requirement, student council. Discipline rests primarily with faculty.

Summer Programs Enrichment, ESL, art/fine arts, computer instruction programs offered; session focuses on ESL, modern Greek, and French (subject to demand); held both on and off campus; held at archaeological sites, beaches for swimming and water sports, and swimming pool; accepts boys and girls; open to students from other schools. 65 students usually enrolled. 2006 schedule: June 27 to July 23. Application deadline: none.

Tuition and Aid Day student tuition: €3800–€8700; 7-day tuition and room/board: €25,400. Tuition installment plan (monthly payment plans, individually arranged payment plans). Tuition reduction for siblings, need-based scholarship grants available. In 2005–06, 15% of upper-school students received aid. Total amount of financial aid awarded in 2005–06: €20,000.

Admissions Traditional secondary-level entrance grade is 10. For fall 2005, 14 students applied for upper-level admission, 13 were accepted, 12 enrolled. Admissions testing, Math Placement Exam, Secondary Level English Proficiency or writing sample required. Deadline for receipt of application materials: none. Application fee required: €800. On-campus interview required.

Athletics Interscholastic: basketball (boys, girls), cross-country running (b,g), soccer (b,g), track and field (b,g), volleyball (b,g); intramural: basketball (b,g), cross-country running (b,g), handball (b,g), soccer (b,g), swimming and diving (b,g), volleyball (b,g); coed intramural: tennis, water volleyball. 3 PE instructors.

Computers Computers are regularly used in English, foreign language, information technology, library, mathematics, science, social studies, yearbook classes. Computer resources include campus e-mail, on-campus library services, CD-ROMs, online commercial services, Internet access, file transfer, office computer access.

Contact Ms. Betty Haniotakis, Director of Admissions. 30-210-623-3888. Fax: 30-210-623-3160. E-mail: bhani@isa.edu.gr. Web site: www.isa.edu.gr/home.htm.

INTERNATIONAL SCHOOL OF BERNE

Mattenstrasse 3
Guemligen 3073, Switzerland
Head of School: Kevin Thomas Page

petersons.com

General Information Coeducational day college-preparatory school. Grades PK–12. Founded: 1961. Setting: suburban. Nearest major city is Berne. 3 buildings on campus. Approved or accredited by European Council of International Schools, International Baccalaureate Organization, New England Association of Schools and Colleges, and Swiss Federation of Private Schools. Language of instruction: English. Total enrollment: 240. Upper school average class size: 15. Upper school faculty-student ratio: 1:5.

Upper School Student Profile Grade 6: 24 students (10 boys, 14 girls); Grade 7: 15 students (9 boys, 6 girls); Grade 8: 19 students (9 boys, 10 girls); Grade 9: 15 students (12 boys, 3 girls); Grade 10: 12 students (8 boys, 4 girls); Grade 11: 18 students (9 boys, 9 girls); Grade 12: 21 students (10 boys, 11 girls).

Faculty School total: 41. In upper school: 14 men, 12 women; 2 have advanced degrees.

Subjects Offered Art, biology, chemistry, drama, economics, English, English literature, ESL, European history, fine arts, French, German, history, mathematics, music, physical education, physics, science, social science, social studies, technology, theater, world history, world literature.

Graduation Requirements Arts and fine arts (art, music, dance, drama), drama, English, foreign language, mathematics, physical education (includes health), science, social science, social studies (includes history), theory of knowledge, extended essay, Creative Acting Service (CAS).

Special Academic Programs International Baccalaureate program; honors section; ESL (25 students enrolled).

College Placement 14 students graduated in 2005; 9 went to college, including Florida Atlantic University; Purdue University; Stanford University. Other: 2 went to work, 3 had other specific plans. Mean SAT verbal: 633, mean SAT math: 560. 50% scored over 600 on SAT verbal, 50% scored over 600 on SAT math.

Student Life Upper grades have student council, honor system. Discipline rests equally with students and faculty.

Tuition and Aid Day student tuition: 22,240 Swiss francs–24,940 Swiss francs. Tuition installment plan (monthly payment plans, individually arranged payment plans). Need-based scholarship grants available.

Admissions For fall 2005, 16 students applied for upper-level admission, 16 were accepted. Admissions testing required. Deadline for receipt of application materials: none. Application fee required: 250 Swiss francs. On-campus interview required.

Athletics Interscholastic: alpine skiing (boys, girls), basketball (b,g), cricket (b), cross-country running (b,g), floor hockey (b,g), football (b,g), indoor soccer (b,g), martial arts (b,g), running (b,g), skiing (downhill) (b,g), snowboarding (b,g), soccer (b,g), swimming and diving (b,g), track and field (b,g), volleyball (b,g); intramural: alpine skiing (b,g), basketball (b,g), cricket (b), cross-country running (b,g), floor hockey (b,g), football (b,g), indoor soccer (b,g), martial arts (b,g), rugby (b), running (b,g), skiing (downhill) (b,g), snowboarding (b,g), soccer (b,g), swimming and diving (b,g), track and field (b,g), volleyball (b,g); coed interscholastic: alpine skiing; coed intramural: alpine skiing, baseball, cricket, martial arts, soccer. 1 PE instructor, 2 coaches.

Computers Computers are regularly used in drawing and design, English, information technology, library skills, mathematics, science, yearbook classes. Computer network features include on-campus library services, CD-ROMs, online commercial services, Internet access.

Contact Kevin Thomas Page, Director. 41-31-951-2358. Fax: 41-31-951-1710. E-mail: office@isberne.ch. Web site: www.isberne.ch.

ANNOUNCEMENT FROM THE SCHOOL The International School of Berne, located in the suburb of Gümligen, 10 minutes from the centre of Berne, capital of Switzerland, offers an education in English for children from ages 3 to 18. A strong educational curriculum follows the widely renowned International Baccalaureate Primary Years, Middle Years, and Diploma Programs with a philosophy of education based on the principles of educating the whole person; of promoting international understanding; of education through a broad, balanced curriculum; and of respect for and tolerance of cultural diversity. The elementary and middle school program includes French and German, music and visual arts, theatre arts, the sciences, humanities, mathematics, and English. The grade 5 students complete their elementary education with an Exhibition, which celebrates their learning over their 6 years in elementary school. The middle school students complete their educational program through a Personal Project in grade 10. This leads into the IB Diploma program in grades 11 and 12. This is a comprehensive and rigorous 2-year curriculum to prepare students for university entrance. Students choose 6 subjects to study, as well as write an extended essay, follow a Theory of Knowledge Course, and complete a Community, Service and Action Program. The school sections, Early Learning Centre, Elementary, and Secondary, are on 3 sites, all within 200 meters of one another. Specialist areas in the school include a gymnasium, 2 computer labs, 3 science labs, 2 art rooms, a theatre arts rehearsal area, and a music room. Extensive use of local facilities for athletics, sports tournaments, and theatre and music productions enable the school to complement its program. The physical education program includes 7 ice skating days for kindergarten and grade 1 and 7 ski/snowboarding days for grades 2–12 during the winter term.

INTERNATIONAL SCHOOL OF BRUSSELS

19 Kattenberg
Brussels 1170, Belgium
Head of School: Mr. Kevin Bartlett

General Information Coeducational day college-preparatory, arts, bilingual studies, and technology school. Grades N–13. Founded: 1951. Setting: suburban. 40-acre campus. 2 buildings on campus. Approved or accredited by European Council of International Schools and Middle States Association of Colleges and Schools. Language of instruction: English. Endowment: €32,500. Total enrollment: 1,400. Upper school average class size: 20. Upper school faculty-student ratio: 1:10.

Upper School Student Profile Grade 10: 127 students (58 boys, 69 girls); Grade 11: 121 students (64 boys, 57 girls); Grade 12: 121 students (58 boys, 63 girls); Grade 13: 10 students (4 boys, 6 girls).

Faculty School total: 171. In upper school: 17 men, 29 women; 38 have advanced degrees.

Subjects Offered Advanced Placement courses, algebra, American history, American literature, anthropology, art, biology, business mathematics, calculus, chemistry, chorus, computer programming, computer science, creative writing, drama, ecology, English, English literature, environmental science, ESL, European history, expository writing, fine arts, French, geometry, grammar, graphic arts, health, history, instrumental music, Japanese, journalism, mathematics, orchestra, philosophy, physical education, physics, science, social science, social studies, Spanish, speech, statistics, theater, theory of knowledge, trigonometry, world history, world literature, writing.

Graduation Requirements Arts and fine arts (art, music, dance, drama), computer science, English, foreign language, mathematics, science, social science, social studies (includes history).

Special Academic Programs International Baccalaureate program; Advanced Placement exam preparation in 7 subject areas; honors section; academic accommodation for the gifted, the musically talented, and the artistically talented; remedial reading and/or remedial writing; remedial math; programs in English, mathematics, general development for dyslexic students; special instructional classes for students with cognitive impairment and those with a range of learning differences, provided their other learning needs can be accommodated; ESL.

College Placement 126 students graduated in 2005; 120 went to college. Other: 2 entered military service. Mean SAT verbal: 526, mean SAT math: 597. 43% scored over 600 on SAT verbal, 48% scored over 600 on SAT math.

Student Life Upper grades have student council, honor system. Discipline rests primarily with faculty.

Summer Programs Remediation, ESL, sports, art/fine arts, computer instruction programs offered; session focuses on mix of fun activities and academics; held on campus; accepts boys and girls; open to students from other schools. 442 students usually enrolled. 2006 schedule: June 26 to July 14.

Tuition and Aid Day student tuition: €23,300. Tuition installment plan (monthly payment plans, individually arranged payment plans). Need-based scholarship grants available. In 2005–06, 18% of upper-school students received aid. Total amount of financial aid awarded in 2005–06: €671,991.

Admissions Traditional secondary-level entrance grade is 10. For fall 2005, 55 students applied for upper-level admission, 50 were accepted, 50 enrolled. English for Non-native Speakers or Math Placement Exam required. Deadline for receipt of application materials: none. Application fee required: €1000. Interview recommended.

Athletics Interscholastic: baseball (boys), basketball (b,g), cross-country running (b,g), field hockey (g), football (b), golf (b,g), rugby (b), soccer (b,g), softball (g), swimming and diving (b,g), tennis (b,g), track and field (b,g), volleyball (b,g); intramural: climbing (b,g), gymnastics (b,g); coed intramural: dance. 3 PE instructors.

Computers Computers are regularly used in all classes. Computer network features include campus e-mail, on-campus library services, CD-ROMs, online commercial services, Internet access, file transfer, office computer access.

Contact Mrs. Annick Buck, Admissions Coordinator. 32-2-6614224. Fax: 32-2-6614213. E-mail: bucka@isb.be. Web site: www.isb.be.

THE INTERNATIONAL SCHOOL OF GENEVA

62 Route de Chene
Geneva 1208, Switzerland
Head of School: Dr. Nicholas Tate

petersons.com

General Information Coeducational day college-preparatory, general academic, and bilingual studies school. Grades PK–13. Founded: 1924. Setting: urban. 15-acre campus. 16 buildings on campus. Approved or accredited by European Council of International Schools, Headmasters' Conference, International Baccalaureate Organization, Middle States Association of Colleges and Schools, Swiss Federation of Private Schools, and The College Board. Member of Secondary School Admission Test Board. Languages of instruction: English and French. Total enrollment: 3,750. Upper school average class size: 20.

Faculty School total: 395.

Subjects Offered Advanced chemistry, advanced math, art, biology, chemistry, computer skills, computer-aided design, drama, economics, English, English literature, ESL, fine arts, French, French as a second language, French literature-AP, general science, geography, German, history, International Baccalaureate courses, Italian, mathematics, music, performing arts, physical education, physics, science, social studies, Spanish, theater, theory of knowledge, world literature.

Graduation Requirements English, foreign language, lab science, mathematics, social studies (includes history).

Special Academic Programs International Baccalaureate program; academic accommodation for the musically talented and the artistically talented; remedial reading and/or remedial writing; remedial math; programs in general development for dyslexic students; ESL.

College Placement 320 students graduated in 2005; 310 went to college. Other: 5 went to work, 5 entered military service.

Student Life Upper grades have student council. Discipline rests primarily with faculty.

Tuition and Aid Day student tuition: 24,190 Swiss francs. Tuition installment plan (individually arranged payment plans, trimester payment plan). Tuition reduction for siblings, bursaries available.

Admissions Deadline for receipt of application materials: none. No application fee required. On-campus interview recommended.

Athletics Interscholastic: alpine skiing (boys, girls), basketball (b,g), cross-country running (b,g), indoor soccer (b,g), skiing (downhill) (b,g), soccer (b,g), swimming and diving (b,g), tennis (b,g), track and field (b,g); intramural: badminton (b,g), basketball (b,g), climbing (b,g), crew (b,g), field hockey (b,g), indoor soccer (b,g), skiing (downhill) (b,g), soccer (b,g), swimming and diving (b,g), table tennis (b,g), tennis (b,g), track and field (b,g).

Computers Computers are regularly used in all academic classes. Computer network features include on-campus library services, CD-ROMs, Internet access, wireless campus network.

Contact Mr. John Douglas, Director of Admissions. 41-22-787 24 00. Fax: 41-22-787 26 32. E-mail: admissions@ecolint.ch. Web site: www.ecolint.ch.

ANNOUNCEMENT FROM THE SCHOOL In 1924, staff of the League of Nations founded The International School of Geneva and committed it to promoting international understanding and values now incorporated into the ideals of the United Nations. The School, with more than 130 nationalities and nearly as many mother tongues, is now one of the largest international schools in the world and Switzerland's largest private school. The School has 3 campuses, all with primary and secondary schools: La Grande Boissière (1,800 students) in Geneva; La Chataigneraie (1,200) in the canton of Vaud; and Campus des Nations (750), in the heart of Geneva's International Quarter. The School is a service school working for the benefit of the international community of Geneva. There are no entrance exams; the School is prepared to accept students throughout the year who can benefit from its programs based on previous academic records and recommendations. It is organized as a nonprofit foundation governed by a board of elected parent members and representatives of local authorities. School fees are the largest contributor to an annual operating budget of SwFr 75 million. Teachers come from more than 30 countries, reinforcing the School's commitment to an appreciation of cultural diversity. The learning languages are English and French; there is also a strong dual-language program. Children are encouraged to maintain contact with their mother languages. The School's educational programs are based on a multicultural view of the world and promote the development of the whole child. The School was the first in the world to offer the International Baccalaureate (IB) to its students. Students can also receive an American high school diploma or prepare for the International GCSE, the French brevet des collèges, and the Swiss maturité. The Council of International Schools and the Middle States Association of Colleges and Schools accredit the School.

THE INTERNATIONAL SCHOOL OF KUALA LUMPUR

Jalan Kolam Air
Ampang, Selangor 68000, Malaysia
Head of School: Mr. William Powell

General Information Coeducational day college-preparatory school. Grades PK–13. Founded: 1965. Setting: suburban. Nearest major city is Kuala Lumpur. 6-acre campus. 1 building on campus. Approved or accredited by Western Association of Schools and Colleges. Affiliate member of National Association of Independent Schools; member of European Council of International Schools. Language of instruction: English. Total enrollment: 1,242. Upper school average class size: 20. Upper school faculty-student ratio: 1:9.

Upper School Student Profile Grade 9: 131 students (67 boys, 64 girls); Grade 10: 122 students (62 boys, 60 girls); Grade 11: 139 students (66 boys, 73 girls); Grade 12: 100 students (53 boys, 47 girls); Grade 13: 1 student (1 boy).

Faculty School total: 142. In upper school: 28 men, 22 women; 40 have advanced degrees.

Subjects Offered Advanced chemistry, advanced math, algebra, anthropology, applied arts, architecture, art, Asian history, biology, biology-AP, calculus, calculus-AP, ceramics, chemistry, chemistry-AP, computer multimedia, computer programming-AP, computer science, drama, economics, English, English literature, English-AP, environmental science, ESL, European history, fine arts, French, French-AP, geometry, health, history, information technology, instrumental music, integrated math, integrated science, International Baccalaureate courses, journalism, keyboarding, Malay, Mandarin, math methods, mathematics, music, photography, physical education, physics, physics-AP, pre-calculus, psychology, science, social

The International School of Kuala Lumpur

studies, sociology, Spanish, Spanish language-AP, statistics, studio art-AP, theater, theater arts, theory of knowledge, trigonometry, U.S. history-AP, world history, world studies.

Graduation Requirements Applied arts, arts and fine arts (art, music, dance, drama), English, foreign language, mathematics, physical education (includes health), science, social studies (includes history), South East Asian studies.

Special Academic Programs International Baccalaureate program; Advanced Placement exam preparation in 10 subject areas; honors section; independent study; special instructional classes for students with mild learning disabilities; ESL (100 students enrolled).

College Placement 111 students graduated in 2005; 99 went to college, including Swarthmore College; The University of British Columbia; The University of Texas at Austin; University of Michigan; University of Victoria. Other: 4 went to work, 4 entered military service, 2 entered a postgraduate year, 2 had other specific plans. Mean SAT verbal: 541, mean SAT math: 694, mean composite ACT: 25. 36% scored over 600 on SAT verbal, 75% scored over 600 on SAT math, 33% scored over 26 on composite ACT.

Student Life Upper grades have uniform requirement, student council, honor system. Discipline rests primarily with faculty.

Summer Programs Enrichment, ESL, art/fine arts, rigorous outdoor training, computer instruction programs offered; session focuses on enrichment and basic skills; held both on and off campus; held at various locations, including science center; accepts boys and girls; open to students from other schools. 36 students usually enrolled. 2006 schedule: June 12 to July 1. Application deadline: May 31.

Tuition and Aid Day student tuition: $10,434. Tuition installment plan (individually arranged payment plans). IB Scholarships to Malaysian students available.

Admissions For fall 2005, 84 students applied for upper-level admission, 82 were accepted, 82 enrolled. English for Non-native Speakers, Gates MacGinitie Reading Tests or Math Placement Exam required. Deadline for receipt of application materials: none. Application fee required: 517 Malaysian ringgits.

Athletics Interscholastic: aerobics/dance (boys, girls), aquatics (b,g), badminton (b,g), basketball (b,g), cross-country running (b,g), dance (b,g), dance team (b,g), rugby (b), running (b,g), soccer (b,g), softball (b,g), swimming and diving (b,g), tennis (b,g), touch football (b,g), track and field (b,g), volleyball (b,g); intramural: aerobics/dance (b,g), aquatics (b,g), basketball (b,g), climbing (b,g), cooperative games (b,g), dance (b,g), fitness (b,g), judo (b,g), martial arts (b,g), outdoor education (b,g), paddle tennis (b,g), physical fitness (b,g), rock climbing (b,g), rugby (b), soccer (b,g), softball (b,g), swimming and diving (b,g), tennis (b,g), touch football (b,g), track and field (b,g), ultimate Frisbee (b,g), volleyball (b,g), water polo (b,g), water volleyball (b,g), weight training (b,g); coed interscholastic: aerobics/dance, aquatics, badminton, dance, dance team, swimming and diving, track and field; coed intramural: aerobics/dance, aquatics, badminton, baseball, basketball, climbing, cooperative games, Cosom hockey, dance, field hockey, fitness, floor hockey, football, golf, kickball, outdoor education, paddle tennis, physical fitness, rock climbing, self defense, soccer, softball, strength & conditioning, swimming and diving, touch football, track and field, ultimate Frisbee, weight training, yoga. 3 PE instructors, 2 coaches.

Computers Computers are regularly used in all academic, multimedia, programming, Web site design classes. Computer network features include campus e-mail, on-campus library services, CD-ROMs, online commercial services, Internet access, Microsoft Office.

Contact Ms. Grace Tan, Secretary. 011-603-4259-5627. Fax: 011-603-4259-5738. E-mail: grace_tan@iskl.edu.my. Web site: www.iskl.edu.my.

INTERNATIONAL SCHOOL OF LAUSANNE

Chemin de la Grangette 2
Le Mont-sur-Lausanne 1052, Switzerland
Head of School: Mr. Simon Taylor

General Information Coeducational day college-preparatory school. Grades PK–12. Founded: 1962. Setting: suburban. Nearest major city is Lausanne. 8-acre campus. 1 building on campus. Approved or accredited by European Council of International Schools and New England Association of Schools and Colleges. Language of instruction: English. Total enrollment: 551. Upper school average class size: 16. Upper school faculty-student ratio: 1:7.

Upper School Student Profile Grade 9: 37 students (25 boys, 12 girls); Grade 10: 38 students (21 boys, 17 girls); Grade 11: 41 students (24 boys, 17 girls); Grade 12: 43 students (27 boys, 16 girls).

Faculty School total: 96. In upper school: 16 men, 28 women; 12 have advanced degrees.

Subjects Offered Art, biology, chemistry, community service, design, drama, economics, English, ESL, French, geography, German, history, information technology, International Baccalaureate courses, library skills, mathematics, music, personal and social education, physics, science, Spanish, sports, Swedish, swimming, theory of knowledge.

Graduation Requirements English, mathematics, modern languages, physical education (includes health), science, social science. Community service is required.

Special Academic Programs International Baccalaureate program; special instructional classes for students with learning disabilities, dyslexia; ESL (6 students enrolled).

College Placement 22 students graduated in 2005; 20 went to college, including Brown University; The Taft School; University of Pennsylvania; University of Virginia. Other: 2 had other specific plans.

Student Life Upper grades have specified standards of dress, student council. Discipline rests equally with students and faculty.

Tuition and Aid Day student tuition: 26,000 Swiss francs. Bursaries available. In 2005–06, 1% of upper-school students received aid. Total amount of financial aid awarded in 2005–06: 26,200 Swiss francs.

Admissions For fall 2005, 49 students applied for upper-level admission, 38 were accepted, 38 enrolled. English for Non-native Speakers required. Deadline for receipt of application materials: none. No application fee required. Interview recommended.

Athletics Interscholastic: basketball (boys), cross-country running (b,g), indoor soccer (b,g), rugby (b), skiing (downhill) (b,g), soccer (b,g), swimming and diving (b,g), tennis (b,g), track and field (b,g), volleyball (g); coed interscholastic: tennis; coed intramural: aerobics/dance, badminton, basketball, climbing, dance, field hockey, fitness, floor hockey, indoor soccer, jogging, kayaking, mountain biking, nordic skiing, outdoor activities, rock climbing, rugby, skiing (downhill), soccer, softball, squash, swimming and diving, track and field, ultimate Frisbee, volleyball, water polo. 2 PE instructors, 3 coaches.

Computers Computers are regularly used in all classes. Computer resources include CD-ROMs, Internet access, wireless campus network.

Contact Admissions Office. 41-21-652 02 02. Fax: 41-21-652 02 03. E-mail: admissions@isl.ch. Web site: www.isl.ch.

INTERNATIONAL SCHOOL OF LUXEMBOURG

36 Boulevard Pierre Dupong
L-1430 Luxembourg, Luxembourg
Head of School: Mr. Clayton W. Lewis

General Information Coeducational day college-preparatory, arts, bilingual studies, technology, and global issues and awareness school. Grades PS–12. Founded: 1963. Setting: suburban. Nearest major city is Luxembourg City. 3-acre campus. 2 buildings on campus. Approved or accredited by European Council of International Schools, International Baccalaureate Organization, and Middle States Association of Colleges and Schools. Affiliate member of National Association of Independent Schools. Language of instruction: English. Endowment: €6 million. Total enrollment: 683. Upper school average class size: 18. Upper school faculty-student ratio: 1:8.

Upper School Student Profile Grade 9: 37 students (21 boys, 16 girls); Grade 10: 43 students (23 boys, 20 girls); Grade 11: 45 students (18 boys, 27 girls); Grade 12: 45 students (19 boys, 26 girls).

Faculty School total: 95. In upper school: 11 men, 40 women; 38 have advanced degrees.

Subjects Offered Advanced math, algebra, art, art history, biology, chemistry, computers, earth science, English, English literature, ESL, European history, French, geography, geometry, German, health, history, International Baccalaureate courses, mathematics, music, physical education, physics, science, social studies, study skills, theory of knowledge, trigonometry, world history, world literature.

Graduation Requirements English, foreign language, mathematics, physical education (includes health), science, social studies (includes history). Community service is required.

Special Academic Programs International Baccalaureate program; ESL (35 students enrolled).

College Placement 41 students graduated in 2005; 38 went to college, including Colgate University. Other: 1 entered military service, 2 had other specific plans. Median SAT verbal: 555, median SAT math: 583, median composite ACT: 24. 27% scored over 600 on SAT verbal, 44% scored over 600 on SAT math.

Student Life Upper grades have student council, honor system. Discipline rests primarily with faculty.

Tuition and Aid Day student tuition: €14,070. Tuition installment plan (monthly payment plans). Merit scholarship grants, need-based scholarship grants available. Total upper-school merit-scholarship money awarded for 2005–06: €29,000. Total amount of financial aid awarded in 2005–06: €1,300,000.

Admissions Traditional secondary-level entrance grade is 10. For fall 2005, 25 students applied for upper-level admission, 22 were accepted, 22 enrolled. Admissions testing and math and English placement tests required. Deadline for receipt of application materials: none. Application fee required: €100. On-campus interview required.

Athletics Interscholastic: basketball (boys, girls), soccer (b,g), track and field (b,g), volleyball (g); intramural: ballet (g), basketball (b,g), soccer (b,g), track and field (b,g), volleyball (g); coed interscholastic: rugby, soccer, swimming and diving; coed intramural: fitness, gymnastics, modern dance, nautilus, physical fitness, strength & conditioning, swimming and diving. 5 PE instructors.

Computers Computers are regularly used in all classes. Computer network features include campus e-mail, on-campus library services, CD-ROMs, Internet access, file transfer, office computer access, DVD.

Contact Mrs. Erica Bastian, Assistant to the Director. 352 260440. E-mail: erica_bastian@islux.lu. Web site: www.islux.lu.

INTERNATIONAL SCHOOL OF MINNESOTA

6385 Beach Road
Eden Prairie, Minnesota 55344
Head of School: Mrs. Susan Berg

petersons.com

General Information Coeducational day college-preparatory, arts, bilingual studies, and Advanced Placement school. Grades PS–12. Founded: 1985. Setting: suburban. Nearest major city is Minneapolis. 55-acre campus. 4 buildings on campus. Approved or accredited by North Central Association of Colleges and Schools and Minnesota Department of Education. Total enrollment: 419. Upper school average class size: 17. Upper school faculty-student ratio: 1:17.

Upper School Student Profile Grade 9: 16 students (8 boys, 8 girls); Grade 10: 31 students (16 boys, 15 girls); Grade 11: 17 students (7 boys, 10 girls); Grade 12: 22 students (11 boys, 11 girls).

Faculty School total: 80. In upper school: 10 men, 18 women; 13 have advanced degrees.

Subjects Offered 20th century physics, advanced computer applications, Advanced Placement courses, advanced studio art-AP, algebra, American government-AP, American history, American literature, art, art history-AP, art-AP, astronomy, baseball, Basic programming, basketball, biology, biology-AP, British literature, calculus, calculus-AP, chemistry, choir, clayworking, college admission preparation, college awareness, college counseling, college placement, college planning, composition-AP, computer applications, computer education, computer information systems, computer keyboarding, computer literacy, computer programming, computer programming-AP, computer science, computer science-AP, computer skills, computer studies, computers, concert choir, current events, earth science, earth systems analysis, English, English language and composition-AP, English language-AP, English literature, English literature and composition-AP, English literature-AP, ESL, European history, European history-AP, French, French language-AP, French literature-AP, French studies, French-AP, geometry, government-AP, health, literature and composition-AP, mathematics, mathematics-AP, modern European history-AP, music, musical productions, performing arts, physical education, physics, physics-AP, pre-algebra, pre-calculus, psychology, reading/study skills, SAT/ACT preparation, science, social studies, softball, Spanish, Spanish language-AP, Spanish literature, Spanish literature-AP, statistics-AP, studio art-AP, swimming, theater, TOEFL preparation, track and field, trigonometry, U.S. history, U.S. history-AP, United States government-AP, vocal ensemble, vocal music, world culture, world history, world history-AP, world issues, world literature, writing, yearbook.

Graduation Requirements Arts and fine arts (art, music, dance, drama), computer literacy, English, foreign language, mathematics, physical education (includes health), science, social studies (includes history), advanced algebra, intermediate geometry, second or third language study.

Special Academic Programs Advanced Placement exam preparation in 20 subject areas; independent study; study at local college for college credit; academic accommodation for the gifted; remedial math; special instructional classes for students with inattentive type Attention Deficit Disorder/Attention Deficit Hyperactivity Disorder; ESL (8 students enrolled).

College Placement 25 students graduated in 2005; all went to college, including Carleton College; Northwestern University; St. Olaf College; University of Minnesota, Twin Cities Campus; University of Pennsylvania. Mean SAT verbal: 656, mean SAT math: 646, mean composite ACT: 26. 77% scored over 600 on SAT verbal, 83% scored over 600 on SAT math, 57% scored over 26 on composite ACT.

Student Life Upper grades have uniform requirement, student council, honor system. Discipline rests equally with students and faculty.

Summer Programs Remediation, enrichment, advancement, ESL programs offered; held on campus; accepts boys and girls; not open to students from other schools. 10 students usually enrolled. 2006 schedule: June 20 to August 12. Application deadline: none.

Tuition and Aid Day student tuition: $12,000. Tuition installment plan (Insured Tuition Payment Plan, FACTS Tuition Payment Plan, monthly payment plans). Tuition reduction for siblings, need-based scholarship grants available. In 2005–06, 3% of upper-school students received aid.

Admissions Traditional secondary-level entrance grade is 9. English Composition Test for ESL students, English entrance exam, English proficiency, ERB (grade level), ERB CTP IV, Math Placement Exam, Otis-Lennon School Ability Test, school's own exam or writing sample required. Deadline for receipt of application materials: none. Application fee required: $75. Interview recommended.

Athletics Interscholastic: baseball (boys), basketball (b,g), soccer (b,g), softball (g), track and field (b,g); intramural: cheering (g), dance (g), flag football (b), physical fitness (b,g), physical training (b,g), weight lifting (b,g), weight training (b,g); coed interscholastic: aquatics, sailing, swimming and diving; coed intramural: alpine skiing, canoeing/kayaking, freestyle skiing, indoor soccer, kayaking, kickball, martial arts, outdoor adventure, outdoor education, outdoor recreation, outdoor skills, physical fitness, physical training, skiing (downhill), snowboarding, snowshoeing, winter soccer. 3 PE instructors, 10 coaches.

Computers Computers are regularly used in computer applications classes. Computer network features include campus e-mail, on-campus library services, CD-ROMs, Internet access, DVD.

Contact Ms. Kay Kendall, Admissions Representative. 952-918-1840. Fax: 952-918-1801. E-mail: kkendall@ism-sabis.net. Web site: www.ism-sabis.net.

ANNOUNCEMENT FROM THE SCHOOL The International School of Minnesota (ISM) is an independent, nondenominational, college-preparatory school for students age 3 through grade 12 in Eden Prairie, Minnesota. ISM, as a member of the worldwide SABIS® School Network, provides a superior education within a state already known for its academic excellence. SABIS® is an educational system that offers a rigorous, internationally oriented, college-preparatory curriculum gleaned from more than 120 years of international "best practices." SABIS® is based on a system of principles requiring sequential and consistent teaching practices that result in the mastery of curriculum and a foundation for lifelong learning—it is established, it is consistent, it is global. A school's success is measured by the value its education adds to each student. ISM gives all its students the advantage of an outstanding college-preparatory education. ISM's core curriculum ensures daily instruction in the areas of mathematics, sciences, English, and world languages. In the Upper School, students have the opportunity to choose from over 20 Advanced Placement courses as well as a wide variety of studio arts, vocal and instrumental music offerings, varsity and junior varsity sports, and clubs and activities—all integral factors in a college-preparatory education. As a result of the SABIS® Educational System, ISM students achieve some of the highest scores in the area on national Advanced Placement exams and the SAT (in addition to a 100% college acceptance rate). From early childhood education to graduation, students enjoy a broad range of learning experiences within a school community that reflects a diversity of cultures, religions, race, economic status, and languages. To accommodate mid-year relocations or school changes, the ISM Admissions Department accepts applications year-round; students are enrolled on a space-available basis. Please contact the Admissions Department at 952-918-1840 or visit the ISM Web site at www.ism-sabis.net for more information about the admissions process or financial aid.

THE INTERNATIONAL SCHOOL OF MONACO

12 Quai Antoine 1er
Monte Carlo 98000, Monaco
Head of School: Mrs. Mary Maccaud

General Information Coeducational day college-preparatory, general academic, bilingual studies, and International Baccalaureate school. Grades K–13. Founded: 1994. Setting: small town. 1 building on campus. Approved or accredited by European Council of International Schools and International Baccalaureate Organization. Languages of instruction: English and French. Upper school average class size: 16.

Faculty School total: 50.

Graduation Requirements International Baccalaureate courses.

Special Academic Programs International Baccalaureate program; ESL.

Student Life Upper grades have specified standards of dress, student council, honor system. Discipline rests primarily with faculty.

Tuition and Aid Day student tuition: €13,920–€15,280. Tuition installment plan (Payments are made in 3 installations but individual payment plans may be made where appropriate). Tuition reduction for siblings, bursaries available.

Admissions School's own exam required. Deadline for receipt of application materials: none. No application fee required. On-campus interview recommended.

Athletics Interscholastic: basketball (boys, girls), independent competitive sports (b,g), outdoor recreation (b,g), soccer (b,g), swimming and diving (b,g), tennis (b,g). 2 PE instructors.

Computers Computers are regularly used in information technology classes. Computer network features include Internet access, wireless campus network.

Contact Mrs. Angela Godfrey, Admissions Department. 377-93256820. Fax: 377-93256830. E-mail: ecoleism@cote-dazur.com. Web site: www.ismonaco.org.

INTERNATIONAL SCHOOL OF PORT-OF-SPAIN

1 International Drive
Westmorings, Trinidad and Tobago
Head of School: Mr. Barney Latham

General Information Coeducational day college-preparatory, general academic, and arts school. Grades K–12. Founded: 1994. Setting: suburban. Nearest major city is Port of Spain. 3-acre campus. 1 building on campus. Approved or accredited by Southern Association of Colleges and Schools and state department of education. Language of instruction: English. Total enrollment: 365. Upper school average class size: 10. Upper school faculty-student ratio: 1:6.

Upper School Student Profile Grade 9: 25 students (16 boys, 9 girls); Grade 10: 32 students (11 boys, 21 girls); Grade 11: 28 students (14 boys, 14 girls); Grade 12: 30 students (17 boys, 13 girls).

Faculty School total: 19. In upper school: 8 men, 11 women; 15 have advanced degrees.

Subjects Offered Advanced math, Advanced Placement courses, algebra, American history, American history-AP, ancient world history, biology, biology-AP, calculus-AP, Caribbean history, chemistry, computer literacy, computers, contemporary studies,

dance, drama, earth science, economics, English, English-AP, environmental science, French, geography, geometry, leadership, model United Nations, modern world history, music, physical education, physics, physics-AP, pre-calculus, psychology-AP, Spanish, Spanish language-AP, statistics-AP, studio art—AP, theater arts, theater production, U.S. history, video film production.

Graduation Requirements Algebra, ancient world history, biology, English, foreign language, geometry, modern world history, physical education (includes health), physical science, technology.

Special Academic Programs Advanced Placement exam preparation in 6 subject areas.

College Placement 21 students graduated in 2005; 13 went to college, including Brock University; Carleton University; The University of Texas at Austin; University of Denver; University of Miami; York University. Other: 7 went to work, 1 entered a postgraduate year. Mean SAT verbal: 522, mean SAT math: 514. 19% scored over 600 on SAT verbal, 31% scored over 600 on SAT math.

Student Life Upper grades have uniform requirement, student council, honor system. Discipline rests primarily with faculty.

Tuition and Aid Day student tuition: $12,000. Tuition installment plan (monthly payment plans). Merit scholarship grants, need-based scholarship grants available. In 2005–06, 10% of upper-school students received aid; total upper-school merit-scholarship money awarded: $42,000. Total amount of financial aid awarded in 2005–06: $42,000.

Admissions Traditional secondary-level entrance grade is 9. For fall 2005, 30 students applied for upper-level admission, 27 were accepted, 25 enrolled. Admissions testing required. Deadline for receipt of application materials: none. Application fee required: $15. Interview required.

Athletics Coed Interscholastic: basketball, rugby, soccer, volleyball; coed intramural: archery, baseball, basketball, cheering, cricket, martial arts, rugby, soccer, softball, ultimate Frisbee, volleyball. 2 PE instructors, 1 coach.

Computers Computers are regularly used in all classes. Computer network features include campus e-mail, on-campus library services, CD-ROMs, online commercial services, Internet access, DVD.

Contact Mrs. Jackie Fung Kee Fung, Director of Admission/Public Relations. 868-632 4591 Ext. 411. Fax: 868-632-4033. E-mail: jfungkeefung@isps.edu.tt. Web site: www.isps.edu.tt.

INTERNATIONAL SCHOOL OF SOUTH AFRICA

Private Bag X 2114
Mafikeng 2745, South Africa
Head of School: Mr. James Haupt

General Information Coeducational boarding and day college-preparatory and general academic school. Boarding grades 3–13, day grades 1–13. Founded: 1990. Setting: small town. Nearest major city is Johannesburg. Students are housed in single-sex dormitories. 54-hectare campus. Member of European Council of International Schools. Language of instruction: English. Upper school average class size: 8.

Faculty In upper school: 2 men, 2 women; 1 has an advanced degree.

Student Life Upper grades have uniform requirement, student council, honor system. Discipline rests primarily with faculty.

Tuition and Aid Day student tuition: 30,000 South African rand; 7-day tuition and room/board: 70,000 South African rand. Tuition installment plan (monthly payment plans, individually arranged payment plans). Tuition reduction for siblings, bursaries, merit scholarship grants available. Total upper-school merit-scholarship money awarded for 2005–06: 500,000 South African rand.

Admissions Admissions testing required. Deadline for receipt of application materials: none. Application fee required: 500 South African rand. On-campus interview recommended.

Athletics 2 PE instructors, 1 coach.

Computers Computer resources include CD-ROMs, Internet access, DVD.

Contact Mrs. Rani Chandramohan, Admissions Officer. 27 18 3811102. Fax: 27 18 3811187. E-mail: admin@issa.co.za. Web site: www.issa.co.za.

IOLANI SCHOOL

563 Kamoku Street
Honolulu, Hawaii 96826
Head of School: Val T. Iwashita

General Information Coeducational day college-preparatory and arts school, affiliated with Episcopal Church. Grades K–12. Founded: 1863. Setting: urban. 25-acre campus. 7 buildings on campus. Approved or accredited by National Association of Episcopal Schools, Western Association of Schools and Colleges, and Hawaii Department of Education. Member of National Association of Independent Schools and Secondary School Admission Test Board. Endowment: $100 million. Total enrollment: 1,833. Upper school average class size: 17. Upper school faculty-student ratio: 1:12.

Upper School Student Profile Grade 9: 238 students (118 boys, 120 girls); Grade 10: 236 students (109 boys, 127 girls); Grade 11: 226 students (104 boys, 122 girls); Grade 12: 230 students (112 boys, 118 girls). 5% of students are members of Episcopal Church.

Faculty School total: 150. In upper school: 63 men, 65 women; 90 have advanced degrees.

Subjects Offered Algebra, American history, American literature, art, Asian studies, band, Bible studies, biology, calculus, ceramics, chemistry, Chinese, chorus, computer programming, computer science, creative writing, dance, drama, economics, English, English literature, European history, expository writing, fine arts, French, geography, geometry, government/civics, Hawaiian history, health, history, Japanese, journalism, Latin, mathematics, money management, music, orchestra, photography, physical education, physics, pre-calculus, psychology, religion, science, social studies, Spanish, speech, statistics, theater, trigonometry, world affairs, world history, world literature, writing.

Graduation Requirements Algebra, arts and fine arts (art, music, dance, drama), Bible, biology, chemistry, computer science, English, European history, geometry, literature, mathematics, physical education (includes health), physics, science, social studies (includes history), 3 years of the same foreign language.

Special Academic Programs Advanced Placement exam preparation in 19 subject areas; honors section; independent study; academic accommodation for the gifted, the musically talented, and the artistically talented; ESL (14 students enrolled).

College Placement 229 students graduated in 2005; all went to college, including Boston University; Santa Clara University; University of California, Los Angeles; University of Hawaii at Manoa; University of Southern California; University of Washington. 57% scored over 600 on SAT verbal, 82% scored over 600 on SAT math, 70% scored over 26 on composite ACT.

Student Life Upper grades have specified standards of dress, student council. Discipline rests primarily with faculty. Attendance at religious services is required.

Summer Programs Enrichment, advancement, ESL, art/fine arts, computer instruction programs offered; session focuses on reinforcement, enrichment, and recreation and sports; held on campus; accepts boys and girls; open to students from other schools. 3000 students usually enrolled. 2006 schedule: June 12 to July 21. Application deadline: February 15.

Tuition and Aid Day student tuition: $12,200. Tuition installment plan (The Tuition Plan, monthly payment plans, semester and annual payment plans). Need-based scholarship grants available. In 2005–06, 12% of upper-school students received aid. Total amount of financial aid awarded in 2005–06: $950,000.

Admissions Traditional secondary-level entrance grade is 9. For fall 2005, 796 students applied for upper-level admission, 85 were accepted, 61 enrolled. SSAT required. Deadline for receipt of application materials: December 1. Application fee required: $85. On-campus interview recommended.

Athletics Interscholastic: aerobics/dance (girls), baseball (b), basketball (b,g), bowling (b,g), canoeing/kayaking (b,g), cheering (g), cross-country running (b,g), dance (b,g), dance team (g), diving (b), football (b), kayaking (b,g), modern dance (g), ocean paddling (b,g), soccer (b,g), softball (g), strength & conditioning (b,g), swimming and diving (b,g), tennis (b,g), track and field (b,g), volleyball (b,g), water polo (b,g), weight training (b,g), wrestling (b,g); coed interscholastic: ballet, golf, judo, tennis. 6 PE instructors, 170 coaches, 3 trainers.

Computers Computers are regularly used in all academic classes. Computer network features include campus e-mail, on-campus library services, CD-ROMs, online commercial services, Internet access, DVD.

Contact Patricia N. Liu, Director of Admission. 808-943-2222. Fax: 808-943-2375. E-mail: admission@iolani.org. Web site: www.iolani.org.

IONA PREPARATORY SCHOOL

255 Wilmot Road
New Rochelle, New York 10804
Head of School: Mr. Richard P. Hazelton

General Information Boys' day college-preparatory, arts, religious studies, and technology school, affiliated with Roman Catholic Church. Grades 9–12. Founded: 1916. Setting: suburban. Nearest major city is New York. 29-acre campus. 3 buildings on campus. Approved or accredited by Christian Brothers Association, Middle States Association of Colleges and Schools, National Catholic Education Association, New York State Association of Independent Schools, and New York State Board of Regents. Endowment: $6 million. Total enrollment: 754. Upper school average class size: 26. Upper school faculty-student ratio: 1:13.

Upper School Student Profile Grade 9: 207 students (207 boys); Grade 10: 213 students (213 boys); Grade 11: 153 students (153 boys); Grade 12: 181 students (181 boys). 90% of students are Roman Catholic.

Faculty School total: 60. In upper school: 44 men, 16 women; 55 have advanced degrees.

Subjects Offered Accounting, algebra, American history, American history-AP, American literature, anatomy, art, biology, biology-AP, British literature, calculus, chemistry, chemistry-AP, communications, community service, computer programming, computer science, economics, English, environmental science, fine arts, French, geometry, government-AP, graphic design, health, history, Italian, Latin, Latin-AP, media, music, painting, physical education, physics, physiology, psychology,

psychology-AP, religion, science, social science, social studies, Spanish, trigonometry, word processing, world literature, world religions.

Graduation Requirements Art, computer science, English, foreign language, mathematics, music, physical education (includes health), religion (includes Bible studies and theology), science, social studies (includes history), 75 hours of community service (senior year).

Special Academic Programs Advanced Placement exam preparation in 12 subject areas; honors section; study at local college for college credit; academic accommodation for the gifted.

College Placement 168 students graduated in 2005; all went to college, including American University; Boston College; Fairfield University; Fordham University; Iona College; New York University. Mean SAT verbal: 542, mean SAT math: 553. 20% scored over 600 on SAT verbal, 21% scored over 600 on SAT math.

Student Life Upper grades have specified standards of dress, student council, honor system. Discipline rests primarily with faculty. Attendance at religious services is required.

Tuition and Aid Day student tuition: $10,650. Tuition installment plan (monthly payment plans, individually arranged payment plans, 6-payment plan, semester payment plan). Tuition reduction for siblings, merit scholarship grants, need-based scholarship grants available. In 2005–06, 24% of upper-school students received aid; total upper-school merit-scholarship money awarded: $190,000. Total amount of financial aid awarded in 2005–06: $203,000.

Admissions Traditional secondary-level entrance grade is 9. For fall 2005, 810 students applied for upper-level admission, 563 were accepted, 207 enrolled. ISEE and New York Archdiocesan Cooperative Entrance Examination required. Deadline for receipt of application materials: none. No application fee required. Interview recommended.

Athletics Interscholastic: baseball, basketball, bowling, cross-country running, diving, football, golf, ice hockey, indoor track, indoor track & field, lacrosse, running, soccer, swimming and diving, tennis, track and field, ultimate Frisbee, volleyball, winter (indoor) track; intramural: baseball, basketball, climbing, fitness, flag football, floor hockey, Frisbee, physical fitness, physical training, rock climbing, soccer, strength & conditioning, tennis, volleyball, wall climbing, weight lifting. 3 PE instructors, 30 coaches, 1 trainer.

Computers Computers are regularly used in all classes. Computer network features include campus e-mail, on-campus library services, CD-ROMs, online commercial services, Internet access, DVD, wireless campus network.

Contact Mrs. Ann V. Slocum, Director of Admissions. 914-632-0714 Ext. 215. Fax: 914-632-9760. E-mail: avs81@ionaprep.org. Web site: www.ionaprep.org.

ISIDORE NEWMAN SCHOOL

1903 Jefferson Avenue
New Orleans, Louisiana 70115
Head of School: Dr. Thomas Price

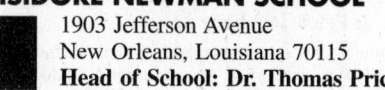

General Information Coeducational day college-preparatory school. Grades PK–12. Founded: 1903. Setting: urban. 9-acre campus. 11 buildings on campus. Approved or accredited by Independent Schools Association of the Southwest, Southern Association of Colleges and Schools, and Louisiana Department of Education. Member of National Association of Independent Schools. Endowment: $27 million. Total enrollment: 1,130. Upper school average class size: 18. Upper school faculty-student ratio: 1:18.

Upper School Student Profile Grade 9: 117 students (55 boys, 62 girls); Grade 10: 115 students (54 boys, 61 girls); Grade 11: 107 students (57 boys, 50 girls); Grade 12: 105 students (61 boys, 44 girls).

Faculty School total: 175. In upper school: 26 men, 45 women; 44 have advanced degrees.

Subjects Offered Advanced computer applications, Advanced Placement courses, algebra, American government-AP, American history, American history-AP, American literature, anatomy, art, art history, art history-AP, biology, biology-AP, calculus, calculus-AP, chemistry, Chinese, choral music, chorus, civics, communications, computer programming, computer science, computer science-AP, drama, English, English literature, environmental science, European history-AP, fine arts, French, French language-AP, French literature-AP, French-AP, genetics, geometry, government/civics, history, human development, humanities, Latin, Latin-AP, mathematics, modern European history, modern European history-AP, music, music theory, photojournalism, physical education, physics, physics-AP, physiology, programming, science, sculpture, social studies, Spanish, Spanish language-AP, Spanish literature-AP, speech, statistics-AP, technical theater, theater, trigonometry, U.S. government-AP, U.S. history, U.S. history-AP, Web site design, world history.

Graduation Requirements Arts and fine arts (art, music, dance, drama), computer science, English, foreign language, humanities, mathematics, physical education (includes health), science, social studies (includes history), speech.

Special Academic Programs Advanced Placement exam preparation in 18 subject areas; honors section; independent study.

College Placement Colleges students went to include Louisiana State University and Agricultural and Mechanical College; Tulane University; University of Chicago; University of Miami; University of Pennsylvania; Vanderbilt University.

Student Life Upper grades have specified standards of dress, student council, honor system. Discipline rests equally with students and faculty.

Summer Programs Remediation, enrichment, art/fine arts, computer instruction programs offered; held both on and off campus; held at Northeast (college tour); accepts boys and girls; open to students from other schools. 2006 schedule: June 1 to July 31. Application deadline: none.

Tuition and Aid Day student tuition: $14,450. Tuition installment plan (Insured Tuition Payment Plan). Need-based scholarship grants, local bank education loans, SLM Financial loans available. In 2005–06, 17% of upper-school students received aid. Total amount of financial aid awarded in 2005–06: $1,537,123.

Admissions Traditional secondary-level entrance grade is 9. For fall 2005, 92 students applied for upper-level admission, 51 were accepted, 38 enrolled. ERB (CTP-Verbal, Quantitative), ERB CTP III, independent norms, Individual IQ, Achievement and behavior rating scale, ISEE, school's own test and writing sample required. Deadline for receipt of application materials: none. Application fee required: $35. Interview required.

Athletics Interscholastic: baseball (boys), basketball (b,g), cross-country running (b,g), football (b), golf (b,g), gymnastics (b,g), soccer (b,g), softball (g), swimming and diving (b,g), tennis (b,g), track and field (b,g), volleyball (g); coed interscholastic: cheering. 11 PE instructors, 2 coaches, 2 trainers.

Computers Computers are regularly used in all academic classes. Computer network features include campus e-mail, on-campus library services, CD-ROMs, online commercial services, Internet access, DVD, wireless campus network.

Contact Mrs. Ladd Sheets, Admission Assistant. 504-896-6323. Fax: 504-896-8597. E-mail: lsheets@newmanschool.org. Web site: www.newmanschool.org.

ANNOUNCEMENT FROM THE SCHOOL For more than 100 years, Isidore Newman School has offered a challenging, sequential curriculum in a supportive learning environment. As they gain knowledge in the humanities, sciences, and fine arts, students demonstrate a mastery of material, meet high academic standards, and develop their capacity for critical thinking and creativity. A variety of extracurricular activities complements the program. For further information, families may access the Isidore Newman School Web site at http://www.newmanschool.org.

ISLAMIC SAUDI ACADEMY

8333 Richmond Highway
Alexandria, Virginia 22309
Head of School: Mr. Abdalla Al-Shabnan

General Information Coeducational day college-preparatory, religious studies, and bilingual studies school, affiliated with Muslim faith. Grades K–12. Founded: 1984. Setting: suburban. 3-acre campus. 1 building on campus. Approved or accredited by CITA (Commission on International and Trans-Regional Accreditation), Southern Association of Colleges and Schools, and Virginia Department of Education. Languages of instruction: English and Arabic. Total enrollment: 948. Upper school average class size: 15. Upper school faculty-student ratio: 1:15.

Upper School Student Profile Grade 9: 55 students (23 boys, 32 girls); Grade 10: 51 students (22 boys, 29 girls); Grade 11: 45 students (15 boys, 30 girls); Grade 12: 34 students (18 boys, 16 girls). 95% of students are Muslim.

Faculty School total: 130. In upper school: 23 men, 14 women; 15 have advanced degrees.

Subjects Offered Advanced Placement courses, algebra, Arabic, Arabic studies, art, biology, biology-AP, calculus-AP, ceramics, chemistry, computer applications, computers, drawing, English, ESL, finite math, geometry, Islamic history, mathematics, painting, photography, physical education, physics, physics-AP, pre-calculus, programming, sculpture, social studies, statistics.

Graduation Requirements Computer education, English, mathematics, science, social studies (includes history), 4 years of Arabic, 4 years of Islamic studies.

Special Academic Programs Advanced Placement exam preparation in 4 subject areas; accelerated programs; independent study; study at local college for college credit; remedial reading and/or remedial writing; remedial math; ESL (133 students enrolled).

College Placement 47 students graduated in 2005; 45 went to college, including American University; George Mason University; The Catholic University of America; The George Washington University; University of Virginia. Other: 1 entered military service, 1 had other specific plans. Median SAT verbal: 469, median SAT math: 498. Mean composite ACT: 18. 38% scored over 600 on SAT verbal, 33% scored over 600 on SAT math.

Student Life Upper grades have uniform requirement, student council, honor system. Discipline rests primarily with faculty.

Summer Programs Remediation, enrichment, advancement, ESL programs offered; session focuses on enrichment and advancement; held on campus; accepts boys and girls; not open to students from other schools. 43 students usually enrolled. 2006 schedule: July 6 to August 20. Application deadline: none.

Tuition and Aid Day student tuition: $2500. Tuition installment plan (individually arranged payment plans, school's own installment plans (2)). Need-based scholarship grants available. In 2005–06, 40% of upper-school students received aid. Total amount of financial aid awarded in 2005–06: $100,000.

Islamic Saudi Academy

Admissions Gates MacGinite Reading Tests, Math Placement Exam and school placement exam required. Deadline for receipt of application materials: March 31. Application fee required: $25. On-campus interview required.

Athletics Interscholastic: basketball (boys, girls), soccer (b,g), wrestling (b); intramural: archery (b), baseball (b), basketball (b,g), flag football (b), football (b), gymnastics (b,g), indoor soccer (b,g), kickball (b,g), physical fitness (b,g), soccer (b,g), strength & conditioning (b), table tennis (b,g), track and field (b,g), weight lifting (b), wilderness (b). 7 PE instructors, 4 coaches, 1 trainer.

Computers Computers are regularly used in data processing, design, desktop publishing, desktop publishing, ESL, drafting, drawing and design, programming, Web site design classes. Computer network features include on-campus library services, CD-ROMs, Internet access, DVD.

Contact Ms. Amal Mustafa, Admissions Officer. 703-780-0606 Ext. 316. Fax: 703-780-8491. E-mail: amalmustafa@hotmail.com. Web site: www.saudiacademy.net.

ISLAND VIEW SCHOOL

2650 West 2700 South
Syracuse, Utah 84075
Head of School: Ms. Judith M. Jacques

General Information Coeducational boarding college-preparatory and general academic school; primarily serves individuals with Attention Deficit Disorder and individuals with emotional and behavioral problems. Ungraded, ages 12–18. Setting: small town. Nearest major city is Salt Lake City. Students are housed in single-sex dormitories. 23-acre campus. 3 buildings on campus. Approved or accredited by Joint Commission on Accreditation of Healthcare Organizations, Northwest Association of Schools and Colleges, and Utah Department of Education. Total enrollment: 112. Upper school average class size: 15. Upper school faculty-student ratio: 1:15.

Faculty School total: 9. In upper school: 4 men, 5 women; 3 have advanced degrees.

Subjects Offered Algebra, American government, American history, American literature, American studies, art, art appreciation, biology, calculus, career education, chemistry, debate, economics, English, English composition, geography, geometry, government, health, history, Holocaust, honors U.S. history, honors world history, integrated science, journalism, literature, mathematics, peer counseling, poetry, pre-calculus, reading, SAT preparation, science, social studies, sociology, Spanish, speech, women's studies, world cultures, world history, world literature, world studies, writing workshop.

Graduation Requirements American history, art, English, mathematics, physical education (includes health), science, world history.

Special Academic Programs Honors section; study at local college for college credit.

College Placement 10 students graduated in 2005; 7 went to college, including Mount St. Mary's College. Other: 3 went to work.

Student Life Upper grades have specified standards of dress, student council, honor system. Discipline rests equally with students and faculty.

Summer Programs Remediation, enrichment, advancement, art/fine arts programs offered; session focuses on remediation and enrichment; held both on and off campus; held at sites within the community; accepts boys and girls; not open to students from other schools. 112 students usually enrolled. 2006 schedule: July 1 to August 30.

Tuition and Aid Tuition installment plan (monthly payment plans).

Admissions Traditional secondary-level entrance age is 15. For fall 2005, 800 students applied for upper-level admission, 125 were accepted, 100 enrolled. Deadline for receipt of application materials: none. No application fee required.

Athletics Interscholastic: aerobics (boys, girls), aerobics/dance (b,g), alpine skiing (b,g), aquatics (b,g), back packing (b,g), badminton (b,g), ball hockey (b,g), baseball (b,g), basketball (b,g), bicycling (b,g), bowling (b,g), canoeing/kayaking (b,g), climbing (b,g), combined training (b,g), cooperative games (b,g), fishing (b,g), fitness (b,g), fitness walking (b,g), flag football (b,g), floor hockey (b,g), Frisbee (b,g), golf (b,g), hiking/backpacking (b,g), jogging (b,g), kickball (b,g), mountain biking (b,g), nordic skiing (b,g), outdoor activities (b,g), outdoor adventure (b,g), outdoor education (b,g), outdoor recreation (b,g), paddle tennis (b,g), physical fitness (b,g), rafting (b,g), rock climbing (b,g), ropes courses (b,g), sailing (b,g), skiing (cross-country) (b,g), skiing (downhill) (b,g), snowboarding (b,g), soccer (b,g), softball (b,g), strength & conditioning (b,g), swimming and diving (b,g), table tennis (b,g), tennis (b,g), touch football (b,g), ultimate Frisbee (b,g), volleyball (b,g), walking (b,g), wall climbing (b,g), weight training (b,g). 4 PE instructors.

Computers Computer resources include CD-ROMs, Internet access.

Contact Laura Burt, Registrar. 801-773-0200. Fax: 801-773-0208. Web site: www.islandview-rtc.com/gen2/home.html.

ISTANBUL INTERNATIONAL COMMUNITY SCHOOL

Karaagac Koyu
Istanbul 34866, Turkey
Head of School: Mr. Jeremy Lewis

General Information Coeducational day college-preparatory, general academic, and International Baccalaureate school. Grades 1–12. Founded: 1911. Setting: rural. 13-hectare campus. 3 buildings on campus. Approved or accredited by European Council of International Schools and New England Association of Schools and Colleges. Language of instruction: English. Endowment: $7 million. Total enrollment: 423. Upper school average class size: 15. Upper school faculty-student ratio: 1:9.

Upper School Student Profile Grade 7: 30 students (15 boys, 15 girls); Grade 8: 33 students (17 boys, 16 girls); Grade 9: 31 students (17 boys, 14 girls); Grade 10: 36 students (16 boys, 20 girls); Grade 11: 28 students (18 boys, 10 girls); Grade 12: 30 students (23 boys, 7 girls).

Faculty School total: 55. In upper school: 13 men, 13 women; 13 have advanced degrees.

Graduation Requirements International Baccalaureate courses.

Special Academic Programs International Baccalaureate program; ESL.

College Placement 23 students graduated in 2005; all went to college, including New York University; Skidmore College; University at Albany, State University of New York. Mean SAT math: 571.

Student Life Upper grades have student council, honor system. Discipline rests equally with students and faculty.

Tuition and Aid Day student tuition: $17,500–$19,500.

Admissions Application fee required: $250. Interview required.

Athletics Interscholastic: basketball (boys, girls), cross-country running (b,g), soccer (b,g), softball (b,g), tennis (b,g), volleyball (b,g). 2 PE instructors, 10 coaches.

Computers Computers are regularly used in information technology classes. Computer resources include on-campus library services, CD-ROMs, Internet access, file transfer, DVD, wireless campus network.

Contact Ms. Berrin Balik, Registrar. 90-212-857-8264 Ext. 105. Fax: 90-212-857-8270. E-mail: registrat@iics.k12.tr. Web site: www.iics.k12.tr.

JACKSON ACADEMY

4908 Ridgewood Road
PO Box 14978
Jackson, Mississippi 39236-4978
Head of School: Mr. J. Peter Jernberg Jr.

General Information Coeducational day college-preparatory and technology school. Grades PK–12. Founded: 1959. Setting: urban. 48-acre campus. 6 buildings on campus. Approved or accredited by Mississippi Private School Association, Southern Association of Colleges and Schools, and Southern Association of Independent Schools. Member of National Association of Independent Schools. Endowment: $1 million. Total enrollment: 1,462. Upper school average class size: 21. Upper school faculty-student ratio: 1:15.

Upper School Student Profile Grade 10: 109 students (56 boys, 53 girls); Grade 11: 103 students (56 boys, 47 girls); Grade 12: 98 students (48 boys, 50 girls).

Faculty School total: 113. In upper school: 14 men, 33 women; 33 have advanced degrees.

Subjects Offered Accounting, algebra, American government, American history, American history-AP, American literature, anatomy and physiology, art, art history, band, Bible, biology, biology-AP, calculus, calculus-AP, chemistry, chemistry-AP, chorus, computer applications, computer programming, creative writing, driver education, economics, English, English language-AP, English literature, English literature-AP, film history, forensics, French, geography, geometry, Latin, physical education, physical science, physics, physics-AP, pre-calculus, sociology, Spanish, speech, state government, studio art, U.S. government and politics-AP, world history, world literature.

Graduation Requirements Electives, English, foreign language, mathematics, science, social studies (includes history).

Special Academic Programs Advanced Placement exam preparation in 10 subject areas; honors section; independent study; study at local college for college credit; programs in general development for dyslexic students.

College Placement 86 students graduated in 2005; all went to college, including Baylor University; Millsaps College; Mississippi College; Mississippi State University; University of Mississippi; University of Southern Mississippi. Median SAT verbal: 650, median SAT math: 620, median composite ACT: 23. 70% scored over 600 on SAT verbal, 58% scored over 600 on SAT math, 50% scored over 26 on composite ACT.

Student Life Upper grades have uniform requirement, student council. Discipline rests primarily with faculty.

Summer Programs Remediation, enrichment, advancement, sports, art/fine arts, computer instruction programs offered; held on campus; accepts boys and girls; open to students from other schools. 125 students usually enrolled. 2006 schedule: June 1 to July 15. Application deadline: none.

Tuition and Aid Day student tuition: $8280. Tuition installment plan (monthly bank draft, bi-annual payment plan). Tuition reduction for siblings, need-based scholarship grants available. In 2005–06, 9% of upper-school students received aid. Total amount of financial aid awarded in 2005–06: $101,680.

Admissions Traditional secondary-level entrance grade is 10. For fall 2005, 23 students applied for upper-level admission, 23 were accepted, 23 enrolled. Otis-Lennon, Stanford Achievement Test required. Deadline for receipt of application materials: none. Application fee required: $50. On-campus interview required.

Athletics Interscholastic: baseball (boys), basketball (b,g), cheering (g), cross-country running (b,g), drill team (g), football (b), golf (b,g), soccer (b,g), softball (g), tennis (b,g), track and field (b,g); intramural: basketball (b,g); coed interscholastic: outdoor activities, swimming and diving. 5 PE instructors, 6 coaches.

Computers Computers are regularly used in English, history, mathematics, publishing, science classes. Computer network features include campus e-mail, on-campus library services, CD-ROMs, Internet access.

Contact Mrs. Patrice Worley, Director of Advancement Services. 601-364-5768. Fax: 601-364-5722. E-mail: psworley@jacksonacademy.org. Web site: www.jacksonacademy.org.

JACKSON PREPARATORY SCHOOL

3100 Lakeland Drive
Jackson, Mississippi 39232
Head of School: Susan Lindsay

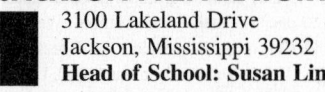

petersons.com

General Information Coeducational day college-preparatory school. Grades 7–12. Founded: 1970. Setting: urban. 74-acre campus. 6 buildings on campus. Approved or accredited by Mississippi Private School Association, Southern Association of Colleges and Schools, Southern Association of Independent Schools, and The College Board. Member of National Association of Independent Schools. Endowment: $993,373. Total enrollment: 784. Upper school average class size: 18. Upper school faculty-student ratio: 1:11.

Upper School Student Profile Grade 10: 156 students (84 boys, 72 girls); Grade 11: 136 students (67 boys, 69 girls); Grade 12: 134 students (62 boys, 72 girls).

Faculty School total: 76. In upper school: 15 men, 36 women; 31 have advanced degrees.

Subjects Offered Accounting, advanced chemistry, Advanced Placement courses, algebra, American government, American history, American history-AP, American literature, art, Asian studies, Bible as literature, biology, biology-AP, British literature, calculus, calculus-AP, chemistry, chemistry-AP, choral music, civics, classical studies, computer science, creative writing, debate, discrete math, drama, driver education, earth science, economics, English, English literature, English literature-AP, European history, film, fine arts, finite math, French, geography, geometry, government-AP, government/civics, grammar, Greek, Greek culture, history, honors algebra, honors English, honors geometry, journalism, Latin, Latin-AP, mathematics, music, physical education, physics, physics-AP, pre-algebra, pre-calculus, science, social studies, Spanish, trigonometry, U.S. government, U.S. government-AP, U.S. history, U.S. history-AP, world history, world literature.

Graduation Requirements Arts and fine arts (art, music, dance, drama), computer applications, English, foreign language, mathematics, science, social studies (includes history).

Special Academic Programs Advanced Placement exam preparation in 9 subject areas; honors section; academic accommodation for the gifted, the musically talented, and the artistically talented; programs in English, mathematics, general development for dyslexic students.

College Placement 113 students graduated in 2005; all went to college, including Mississippi College; Mississippi State University; University of Mississippi; Vanderbilt University. Mean SAT verbal: 612, mean SAT math: 621, mean composite ACT: 26. 58% scored over 600 on SAT verbal, 59% scored over 600 on SAT math, 42% scored over 26 on composite ACT.

Student Life Upper grades have specified standards of dress, student council, honor system. Discipline rests primarily with faculty.

Summer Programs Remediation, enrichment, art/fine arts, computer instruction programs offered; session focuses on enrichment; held on campus; accepts boys and girls; open to students from other schools. 200 students usually enrolled. 2006 schedule: June 5 to July 14. Application deadline: none.

Tuition and Aid Day student tuition: $8100. Tuition installment plan (monthly payment plans). Need-based scholarship grants available. In 2005–06, 11% of upper-school students received aid. Total amount of financial aid awarded in 2005–06: $158,000.

Admissions Traditional secondary-level entrance grade is 10. For fall 2005, 8 students applied for upper-level admission, 6 were accepted, 6 enrolled. OLSAT, Stanford Achievement Test required. Deadline for receipt of application materials: none. Application fee required: $40. Interview recommended.

Athletics Interscholastic: baseball (boys), basketball (b,g), cheering (g), cross-country running (b,g), dance team (g), football (b), Frisbee (b), soccer (b,g), softball (g), swimming and diving (b,g), tennis (b,g), track and field (b,g), ultimate Frisbee (b); intramural: basketball (b,g), Frisbee (b), soccer (b,g), volleyball (b,g); coed interscholastic: cheering, golf. 4 coaches.

Computers Computers are regularly used in all classes. Computer network features include on-campus library services, CD-ROMs, online commercial services, Internet access, Electric Library, EBSCOhost[00ae], GaleNet, Grolier Online, NewsBank, online subscription services.

Contact Lesley W. Morton, Director of Admissions. 601-932-8106 Ext. 1. Fax: 601-936-4068. E-mail: lmorton@jacksonprep.net. Web site: www.jacksonprep.net.

ANNOUNCEMENT FROM THE SCHOOL Specializing in secondary education since 1970, Jackson Preparatory School (Prep) holds the state record with 461 National Merit semifinalists, including 16 from the class of 2006. Statewide, Prep offers the only Classical Heritage Program and is one of four schools to be selected for a cum laude chapter. Students consistently win regional and national awards in language, literature, art, music, and drama. In athletics, Prep teams remain among the leaders of the conference in overall championships.

JAKARTA INTERNATIONAL SCHOOL

PO Box 1078/JKS
Jakarta 12010, Indonesia
Head of School: Dr. Niall Nelson

General Information Coeducational day college-preparatory school. Grades PK–12. Founded: 1951. Setting: suburban. 30-acre campus. 18 buildings on campus. Approved or accredited by European Council of International Schools and Western Association of Schools and Colleges. Affiliate member of National Association of Independent Schools; member of Secondary School Admission Test Board. Language of instruction: English. Total enrollment: 2,566. Upper school average class size: 18. Upper school faculty-student ratio: 1:19.

Upper School Student Profile Grade 9: 208 students (109 boys, 99 girls); Grade 10: 259 students (146 boys, 113 girls); Grade 11: 269 students (134 boys, 135 girls); Grade 12: 197 students (108 boys, 89 girls); Grade 13: 5 students (3 boys, 2 girls).

Faculty School total: 271. In upper school: 48 men, 45 women; 53 have advanced degrees.

Subjects Offered Algebra, American history, American literature, art, art history, Asian studies, band, batik, biology, business studies, calculus, chemistry, community service, computer graphics, computer science, creative writing, dance, drama, drawing, Dutch, economics, English, English literature, ESL, European history, fine arts, French, general science, geography, geometry, German, history, Indonesian, Indonesian studies, information technology, Japanese, journalism, Korean, mathematics, mechanical drawing, music, photography, physical education, physics, political science, psychology, science, science and technology, social studies, Spanish, theater, theory of knowledge, trigonometry, world history, world literature.

Graduation Requirements Arts and fine arts (art, music, dance, drama), computer studies, electives, English, Indonesian studies, mathematics, modern languages, physical education (includes health), science, social studies (includes history), minimum 5 credits in residence, competence in English, student must not turn 21 years of age before July 1 of graduating year.

Special Academic Programs International Baccalaureate program; Advanced Placement exam preparation in 14 subject areas; accelerated programs; independent study; remedial reading and/or remedial writing; remedial math; programs in general development for dyslexic students; ESL (110 students enrolled).

College Placement 210 students graduated in 2005; 200 went to college, including Boston College; Boston University; Kalamazoo College; The University of British Columbia; University of California, Berkeley; University of Illinois at Urbana–Champaign. Other: 4 went to work, 4 entered military service, 2 had other specific plans. Mean SAT verbal: 516, mean SAT math: 609, mean composite ACT: 26. 24% scored over 600 on SAT verbal, 45% scored over 600 on SAT math, 44% scored over 26 on composite ACT.

Student Life Upper grades have specified standards of dress, student council. Discipline rests primarily with faculty.

Summer Programs Enrichment, advancement, ESL, art/fine arts, computer instruction programs offered; session focuses on English for Speakers of Other Languages (ESOL); held on campus; accepts boys and girls; not open to students from other schools. 2006 schedule: June 12 to July 7. Application deadline: May 31.

Tuition and Aid Day student tuition: $15,500. Tuition installment plan (semester payment plan). Need-based scholarship grants available. In 2005–06, 1% of upper-school students received aid. Total amount of financial aid awarded in 2005–06: $49,835.

Admissions Traditional secondary-level entrance grade is 9. For fall 2005, 175 students applied for upper-level admission, 153 were accepted, 153 enrolled. English proficiency, ESOL English Proficiency Test, Math Placement Exam and placement test required. Deadline for receipt of application materials: none. Application fee required: $100. On-campus interview required.

Athletics Interscholastic: badminton (boys, girls), baseball (b), basketball (b,g), rugby (b,g), running (b,g), soccer (b,g), softball (b,g), tennis (b,g), touch football (g), track and field (b,g), volleyball (b,g); intramural: badminton (b,g), baseball (b), basketball (b,g), cricket (b), rugby (b,g), soccer (b,g), volleyball (b,g), yoga (b,g); coed interscholastic: aquatics, cross-country running, dance, dance team, running, swimming and diving; coed intramural: aerobics/dance, aquatics, archery, climbing, cross-country running, dance, dance team, field hockey, flag football, golf, indoor

soccer, martial arts, outdoor adventure, swimming and diving, tennis, touch football, ultimate Frisbee, wall climbing, weight training. 4 PE instructors.

Computers Computers are regularly used in accounting, business studies, creative writing, drawing and design, English, graphic design, information technology, journalism, music, publications, science, technology classes. Computer network features include campus e-mail, on-campus library services, CD-ROMs, online commercial services, Internet access, file transfer.

Contact Mr. Steven Reginald Money, Director of Admissions and Community Activities. 62-21-769-2555 Ext. 80062. Fax: 62-21-750 7650. E-mail: admissions@ jisedu.or.id. Web site: www.jisedu.org.

JESUIT COLLEGE PREPARATORY SCHOOL

12345 Inwood Road
Dallas, Texas 75244
Head of School: Mr. Mike Earsing

General Information Boys' day college-preparatory school, affiliated with Roman Catholic Church (Jesuit order). Grades 9–12. Founded: 1942. Setting: suburban. 27-acre campus. 2 buildings on campus. Approved or accredited by Jesuit Secondary Education Association, National Catholic Education Association, Southern Association of Colleges and Schools, Texas Catholic Conference, and Texas Department of Education. Endowment: $22 million. Total enrollment: 1,021. Upper school average class size: 17. Upper school faculty-student ratio: 1:11.

Upper School Student Profile Grade 9: 274 students (274 boys); Grade 10: 260 students (260 boys); Grade 11: 257 students (257 boys); Grade 12: 230 students (230 boys). 82.5% of students are Roman Catholic Church (Jesuit order).

Faculty School total: 103. In upper school: 74 men, 29 women; 55 have advanced degrees.

Subjects Offered Advanced chemistry, advanced computer applications, advanced math, American literature-AP, American studies, art, art appreciation, art-AP, arts, band, Bible, biology, biology-AP, British literature, British literature-AP, calculus, calculus-AP, Catholic belief and practice, ceramics, chemistry, chemistry-AP, choir, Christian ethics, church history, civics, college counseling, community service, composition, composition-AP, computer applications, computer graphics, computer science, computer science-AP, contemporary issues, discrete mathematics, drama, drama performance, drama workshop, drawing, drawing and design, driver education, earth science, economics, economics-AP, English, English composition, English language and composition-AP, English language-AP, English literature, English literature and composition-AP, English literature-AP, English-AP, English/ composition-AP, ethical decision making, European history, fine arts, French, French-AP, general science, geometry, government, government-AP, grammar, guitar, health, history, history-AP, honors algebra, honors English, honors geometry, honors U.S. history, honors world history, instrumental music, jazz band, journalism, Latin, literature and composition-AP, marching band, mathematics, mathematics-AP, microcomputer technology applications, music, music appreciation, musical productions, orchestra, peace and justice, peer ministry, performing arts, physical education, physics, physics-AP, pottery, prayer/spirituality, pre-calculus, psychology, public speaking, publications, religion, scripture, social studies, Spanish, Spanish language-AP, Spanish literature-AP, Spanish-AP, speech, speech and debate, speech and oral interpretations, statistics, student government, student publications, studio art, studio art-AP, symphonic band, theater, theology, U.S. government, U.S. government-AP, U.S. history, U.S. history-AP, U.S. literature, world history, world history-AP.

Graduation Requirements Arts and fine arts (art, music, dance, drama), computer science, English, foreign language, mathematics, physical education (includes health), science, social studies (includes history), theology. Community service is required.

Special Academic Programs Advanced Placement exam preparation in 10 subject areas; honors section.

College Placement 244 students graduated in 2005; all went to college, including Saint Louis University; Southern Methodist University; Texas Tech University; The University of Texas at Austin. Mean SAT verbal: 600, mean SAT math: 620.

Student Life Upper grades have specified standards of dress, student council, honor system. Discipline rests primarily with faculty. Attendance at religious services is required.

Summer Programs Remediation, enrichment, advancement, sports, art/fine arts, computer instruction programs offered; session focuses on youth recreation; held on campus; accepts boys and girls; open to students from other schools. 800 students usually enrolled. 2006 schedule: June 5 to June 30. Application deadline: May 1.

Tuition and Aid Day student tuition: $10,250. Tuition installment plan (FACTS Tuition Payment Plan, individually arranged payment plans). Merit scholarship grants, need-based scholarship grants, paying campus jobs available. In 2005–06, 26% of upper-school students received aid; total upper-school merit-scholarship money awarded: $58,000. Total amount of financial aid awarded in 2005–06: $1,109,175.

Admissions Traditional secondary-level entrance grade is 9. For fall 2005, 439 students applied for upper-level admission, 290 were accepted, 274 enrolled. ISEE required. Deadline for receipt of application materials: January 6. Application fee required: $75. Interview required.

Athletics Interscholastic: baseball, basketball, crew, cross-country running, diving, fencing, football, golf, ice hockey, lacrosse, power lifting, rugby, soccer, swimming

and diving, tennis, track and field, wrestling; intramural: basketball, flagball, indoor soccer, ultimate Frisbee; coed interscholastic: cheering, drill team. 6 PE instructors, 30 coaches, 1 trainer.

Computers Computers are regularly used in college planning, desktop publishing, English, introduction to technology, literary magazine, newspaper, technology, Web site design, writing, yearbook classes. Computer network features include on-campus library services, CD-ROMs, online commercial services, Internet access, office computer access.

Contact Mrs. Shawn Young, Admissions Assistant. 972-387-8700 Ext. 453. Fax: 972-980-6707. E-mail: syoung@jesuitcp.org. Web site: www.jesuitcp.org.

JESUIT HIGH SCHOOL

1200 Jacob Lane
Carmichael, California 95608
Head of School: Rev. Edward Fassett, SJ

General Information Boys' day college-preparatory and religious studies school, affiliated with Roman Catholic Church. Grades 9–12. Founded: 1963. Setting: suburban. Nearest major city is Sacramento. 45-acre campus. 9 buildings on campus. Approved or accredited by National Catholic Education Association, Western Association of Schools and Colleges, and California Department of Education. Member of Secondary School Admission Test Board. Total enrollment: 1,000. Upper school average class size: 25. Upper school faculty-student ratio: 1:18.

Upper School Student Profile Grade 9: 250 students (250 boys); Grade 10: 250 students (250 boys); Grade 11: 250 students (250 boys); Grade 12: 250 students (250 boys). 80% of students are Roman Catholic.

Faculty School total: 80. In upper school: 58 men, 22 women; 45 have advanced degrees.

Subjects Offered Algebra, American history, American literature, art, art history, arts, biology, business, calculus, chemistry, computer programming, computer science, drama, driver education, earth science, economics, English, English literature, environmental science, ethics, European history, fine arts, French, geography, geometry, German, government/civics, grammar, health, history, journalism, Latin, mathematics, music, physical education, physics, religion, science, social science, social studies, Spanish, speech, theater, theology, trigonometry, typing, world history, world literature, writing.

Graduation Requirements Arts and fine arts (art, music, dance, drama), English, foreign language, mathematics, physical education (includes health), religion (includes Bible studies and theology), science, social studies (includes history), 60 hours of community service.

Special Academic Programs Advanced Placement exam preparation in 12 subject areas; honors section.

College Placement 245 students graduated in 2005; 240 went to college, including California State University, Sacramento; Loyola Marymount University; Santa Clara University; Stanford University; University of California System; University of Southern California. Other: 2 went to work, 3 entered military service. Mean SAT verbal: 570, mean SAT math: 590, mean composite ACT: 24.

Student Life Upper grades have specified standards of dress, student council, honor system. Discipline rests primarily with faculty. Attendance at religious services is required.

Summer Programs Remediation, enrichment, advancement, computer instruction programs offered; held on campus; accepts boys and girls; open to students from other schools. 1200 students usually enrolled. 2006 schedule: June 12 to July 21. Application deadline: June 9.

Tuition and Aid Day student tuition: $9260. Tuition installment plan (monthly payment plans). Need-based scholarship grants, paying campus jobs available. In 2005–06, 15% of upper-school students received aid. Total amount of financial aid awarded in 2005–06: $600,000.

Admissions Traditional secondary-level entrance grade is 9. For fall 2005, 450 students applied for upper-level admission, 290 were accepted, 280 enrolled. High School Placement Test required. Deadline for receipt of application materials: February 14. Application fee required: $20. On-campus interview required.

Athletics Interscholastic: baseball, basketball, cross-country running, diving, football, golf, rugby, soccer, swimming and diving, tennis, track and field, volleyball, water polo, wrestling; intramural: baseball, basketball, bowling, football, soccer, volleyball. 6 PE instructors, 15 coaches, 1 trainer.

Computers Computers are regularly used in English, mathematics, social studies classes. Computer resources include on-campus library services, CD-ROMs, online commercial services, Internet access.

Contact Mr. Gerry Lane, Director of Admissions. 916-482-6060 Ext. 227. Fax: 916-482-2310. E-mail: admissions@jhssac.org. Web site: www.jhssac.org.

JESUIT HIGH SCHOOL OF NEW ORLEANS

4133 Banks Street
New Orleans, Louisiana 70119-6883
Head of School: Fr. Anthony McGinn, SJ

General Information Boys' day college-preparatory school, affiliated with Roman Catholic Church. Grades 8–12. Founded: 1847. Setting: urban. Nearest major city is Baton Rouge. 8-acre campus. 3 buildings on campus. Approved or accredited by Jesuit Secondary Education Association, National Catholic Education Association, Southern Association of Colleges and Schools, and Louisiana Department of Education. Endowment: $17 million. Total enrollment: 1,401. Upper school average class size: 27. Upper school faculty-student ratio: 1:13.

Upper School Student Profile Grade 9: 332 students (332 boys); Grade 10: 314 students (314 boys); Grade 11: 258 students (258 boys); Grade 12: 253 students (253 boys). 88% of students are Roman Catholic.

Faculty School total: 116. In upper school: 80 men, 36 women; 59 have advanced degrees.

Subjects Offered Algebra, American history, American literature, analysis, art history, arts, Bible studies, biology, biology-AP, broadcasting, calculus, calculus-AP, chemistry, chemistry-AP, community service, comparative government and politics-AP, computer applications, computer programming, computer science, creative writing, drama, economics, English, English literature, English literature and composition-AP, European history, fine arts, French, French language-AP, geography, geology, geometry, government/civics, grammar, Greek, health, history, JROTC, Latin, Latin-AP, law, mathematics, military science, music, philosophy, physical education, physical science, physics, physics-AP, politics, psychology, public speaking, radio broadcasting, religion, science, social studies, sociology, Spanish, Spanish language-AP, speech, television, theater, theology, trigonometry, U.S. government and politics-AP, U.S. history-AP, world history, world literature, writing.

Graduation Requirements Arts and fine arts (art, music, dance, drama), computer science, English, foreign language, mathematics, physical education (includes health), religion (includes Bible studies and theology), science, social science, social studies (includes history), speech. Community service is required.

Special Academic Programs Advanced Placement exam preparation in 12 subject areas; honors section.

College Placement 266 students graduated in 2005; 265 went to college, including Louisiana State University and Agricultural and Mechanical College; The University of Alabama; Tulane University; University of New Orleans; University of Southern Mississippi. Other: 1 went to work. Median SAT verbal: 640, median SAT math: 630, median composite ACT: 27. 71% scored over 600 on SAT verbal, 64% scored over 600 on SAT math, 58% scored over 26 on composite ACT.

Student Life Upper grades have uniform requirement, student council. Discipline rests primarily with faculty. Attendance at religious services is required.

Summer Programs Remediation, enrichment programs offered; session focuses on remediation; held on campus; accepts boys; not open to students from other schools. 125 students usually enrolled. 2006 schedule: June 5 to July 14. Application deadline: June 2.

Tuition and Aid Day student tuition: $5400. Need-based scholarship grants, paying campus jobs available. In 2005–06, 9% of upper-school students received aid. Total amount of financial aid awarded in 2005–06: $350,000.

Admissions Traditional secondary-level entrance grade is 9. For fall 2005, 130 students applied for upper-level admission, 86 were accepted, 66 enrolled. High School Placement Test required. Deadline for receipt of application materials: January 7. Application fee required: $20.

Athletics Interscholastic: baseball, basketball, bowling, cross-country running, football, golf, in-line hockey, indoor track & field, JROTC drill, marksmanship, physical fitness, riflery, soccer, swimming and diving, tennis, track and field, wrestling; intramural: baseball, basketball, bicycling, bowling, cheering, flag football, golf, tennis. 5 PE instructors, 26 coaches, 1 trainer.

Computers Computers are regularly used in library skills, mathematics, reading, science, yearbook classes. Computer network features include campus e-mail, on-campus library services, CD-ROMs, Internet access.

Contact Mr. Jack S. Truxillo, Director of Admissions. 504-483-3936. Fax: 504-483-3942. E-mail: truxillo@jesuitnola.org. Web site: www.jesuitnola.org.

JESUIT HIGH SCHOOL OF TAMPA

4701 North Himes Avenue
Tampa, Florida 33614-6694
Head of School: Mr. Joseph Sabin

General Information Boys' day college-preparatory school, affiliated with Roman Catholic Church. Grades 9–12. Founded: 1899. Setting: urban. 30-acre campus. 9 buildings on campus. Approved or accredited by Jesuit Secondary Education Association, National Catholic Education Association, Southern Association of Colleges and Schools, and Florida Department of Education. Total enrollment: 665. Upper school average class size: 21. Upper school faculty-student ratio: 1:13.

Upper School Student Profile Grade 9: 176 students (176 boys); Grade 10: 177 students (177 boys); Grade 11: 147 students (147 boys); Grade 12: 165 students (165 boys). 75% of students are Roman Catholic.

Faculty School total: 50. In upper school: 34 men, 16 women; 37 have advanced degrees.

Subjects Offered Algebra, American history, American literature, anatomy, art, Bible studies, biology, calculus, chemistry, chorus, computer programming, computer science, economics, English, English literature, ethics, European history, French, geometry, government/civics, health, history, Latin, mathematics, music, physical education, physics, physiology, psychology, religion, social studies, Spanish, speech, theology, trigonometry, world history, writing.

Graduation Requirements Arts and fine arts (art, music, dance, drama), English, foreign language, mathematics, physical education (includes health), science, social studies (includes history), theology, 150 hours of community service (additional 20 hours for National Honor Society members).

Special Academic Programs Advanced Placement exam preparation in 6 subject areas; honors section.

College Placement 135 students graduated in 2005; 134 went to college, including Florida State University; University of Central Florida; University of Florida; University of South Florida. Other: 1 entered military service. Median SAT verbal: 590, median SAT math: 600, median composite ACT: 25.

Student Life Upper grades have specified standards of dress, student council. Discipline rests primarily with faculty. Attendance at religious services is required.

Summer Programs Remediation programs offered; session focuses on remediation only; held on campus; accepts boys; not open to students from other schools. 2006 schedule: June 12 to July 10.

Tuition and Aid Day student tuition: $9600. Tuition installment plan (FACTS Tuition Payment Plan). Need-based scholarship grants available.

Admissions Traditional secondary-level entrance grade is 9. For fall 2005, 294 students applied for upper-level admission, 250 were accepted, 176 enrolled. High School Placement Test (closed version) from Scholastic Testing Service or SSAT required. Deadline for receipt of application materials: January 21. Application fee required: $35.

Athletics Interscholastic: baseball, basketball, cross-country running, diving, football, golf, soccer, swimming and diving, tennis, track and field, wrestling; intramural: basketball, football, Frisbee, softball, ultimate Frisbee. 2 PE instructors, 1 trainer.

Computers Computer network features include campus e-mail, on-campus library services, CD-ROMs, online commercial services, Internet access, office computer access.

Contact Ms. Paulette Mack, Registrar. 813-877-5344 Ext. 252. Fax: 813-872-1853. E-mail: pmack@jesuittampa.org. Web site: www.jesuittampa.org.

JOHN BURROUGHS SCHOOL

755 South Price Road
St. Louis, Missouri 63124
Head of School: Keith E. Shahan

General Information Coeducational day college-preparatory school. Grades 7–12. Founded: 1923. Setting: suburban. 47-acre campus. 7 buildings on campus. Approved or accredited by Independent Schools Association of the Central States and North Central Association of Colleges and Schools. Member of National Association of Independent Schools and Secondary School Admission Test Board. Endowment: $38.8 million. Total enrollment: 598. Upper school average class size: 14. Upper school faculty-student ratio: 1:8.

Upper School Student Profile Grade 7: 92 students (46 boys, 46 girls); Grade 8: 101 students (49 boys, 52 girls); Grade 9: 102 students (49 boys, 53 girls); Grade 10: 99 students (51 boys, 48 girls); Grade 11: 98 students (51 boys, 47 girls); Grade 12: 106 students (51 boys, 55 girls).

Faculty School total: 102. In upper school: 44 men, 54 women; 80 have advanced degrees.

Subjects Offered Acting, Advanced Placement courses, African American history, algebra, American history, American literature, Ancient Greek, ancient world history, applied arts, architectural drawing, art, art history, art history-AP, Asian studies, astronomy, bioethics, biology, calculus, calculus-AP, ceramics, chemistry, chemistry-AP, choral music, chorus, classical language, community service, comparative religion, computer math, computer science, computer skills, computer-aided design, concert band, creative writing, dance, debate, drama, earth science, ecology, English, English literature, environmental science, environmental systems, expository writing, fine arts, finite math, foreign language, French, French language-AP, geology, geometry, German, Greek, Greek culture, health, history, home economics, honors English, industrial arts, jazz, jazz band, keyboarding/computer, lab science, Latin, Latin-AP, mathematics, mechanical drawing, meteorology, model United Nations, music, orchestra, organic chemistry, photography, physical education, physics, poetry, pre-algebra, pre-calculus, probability and statistics, psychology, public speaking, reading/study skills, religions, Russian, science, social science, social studies, Spanish, Spanish-AP, speech and debate, statistics, trigonometry, vocal music, word processing, world civilizations, world history, world literature, world religions, writing.

Graduation Requirements Arts and fine arts (art, music, dance, drama), English, foreign language, history, mathematics, performing arts, physical education (includes health), practical arts, science, Senior May Project.

Special Academic Programs Advanced Placement exam preparation in 7 subject areas; honors section; independent study; remedial reading and/or remedial writing; remedial math.

John Burroughs School

College Placement 97 students graduated in 2005; all went to college, including Harvard University; Morehouse College; The University of North Carolina at Chapel Hill; Tufts University; University of Pennsylvania; Washington University in St. Louis. Mean SAT verbal: 691, mean SAT math: 700.

Student Life Upper grades have student council, honor system. Discipline rests equally with students and faculty.

Tuition and Aid Day student tuition: $17,000. Tuition installment plan (monthly payment plans). Need-based scholarship grants, need-based loans available. In 2005–06, 20% of upper-school students received aid. Total amount of financial aid awarded in 2005–06: $1,390,000.

Admissions Traditional secondary-level entrance grade is 7. For fall 2005, 220 students applied for upper-level admission, 123 were accepted, 109 enrolled. ISEE required. Deadline for receipt of application materials: January 16. Application fee required: $40. On-campus interview required.

Athletics Interscholastic: baseball (boys), basketball (b,g), cheering (g), cross-country running (b,g), dance (g), diving (b,g), field hockey (g), fitness (b,g), football (b), golf (b,g), ice hockey (b), modern dance (g), outdoor education (b,g), physical fitness (b,g), physical training (b,g), racquetball (g), soccer (b,g), softball (g), swimming and diving (b,g), tennis (b,g), track and field (b,g), volleyball (g), water polo (b), wrestling (b); intramural: hiking/backpacking (b,g), weight lifting (b,g). 20 PE instructors, 38 coaches, 1 trainer.

Computers Computers are regularly used in all academic classes. Computer network features include on-campus library services, CD-ROMs, online commercial services, Internet access, file transfer, DVD.

Contact Caroline LaVigne, Director of Admissions. 314-993-4040. Fax: 314-567-2896. E-mail: clavigne@jburroughs.org. Web site: www.jburroughs.org.

THE JOHN COOPER SCHOOL

One John Cooper Drive
The Woodlands, Texas 77381
Head of School: Mr. Michael F. Maher

General Information Coeducational day college-preparatory, general academic, arts, technology, and competitive athletics school. Grades K–12. Founded: 1988. Setting: suburban. Nearest major city is Houston. 43-acre campus. 5 buildings on campus. Approved or accredited by Independent Schools Association of the Southwest. Member of National Association of Independent Schools. Endowment: $650,000. Total enrollment: 898. Upper school average class size: 18. Upper school faculty-student ratio: 1:11.

Upper School Student Profile Grade 9: 79 students (38 boys, 41 girls); Grade 10: 84 students (35 boys, 49 girls); Grade 11: 59 students (25 boys, 34 girls); Grade 12: 78 students (38 boys, 40 girls).

Faculty School total: 85. In upper school: 16 men, 24 women; 25 have advanced degrees.

Subjects Offered 3-dimensional art, adolescent issues, advanced chemistry, advanced math, advanced studio art-AP, algebra, American history, American history-AP, American literature, anatomy and physiology, art, art history-AP, athletics, band, baseball, basketball, biology, biology-AP, British literature, calculus, calculus-AP, ceramics, cheerleading, chemistry, chemistry-AP, college planning, computer literacy, computer science, computer science-AP, concert choir, creative writing, drama, drawing, economics, economics and history, English, English literature-AP, European history, European history-AP, French, French-AP, geometry, glassblowing, golf, guitar, health, history, history-AP, jazz band, jewelry making, Latin, linear algebra, literary magazine, literature-AP, mathematical modeling, model United Nations, modern European history-AP, modern political theory, painting, photography, physical education, physics, physics-AP, political thought, pre-calculus, probability and statistics, psychology, social studies, softball, Spanish, Spanish-AP, statistics, statistics-AP, studio art-AP, symphonic band, tennis, theater, trigonometry, U.S. history-AP, volleyball, world history, world literature, world religions, yearbook.

Graduation Requirements Arts and fine arts (art, music, dance, drama), English, foreign language, mathematics, physical education (includes health), science, social studies (includes history).

Special Academic Programs Advanced Placement exam preparation in 12 subject areas; independent study.

College Placement 80 students graduated in 2005; all went to college, including Baylor University; Boston University; Southern Methodist University; Texas A&M University; Trinity University; Vanderbilt University. Median SAT verbal: 632, median SAT math: 642, median composite ACT: 29. 63% scored over 600 on SAT verbal, 74% scored over 600 on SAT math, 80% scored over 26 on composite ACT.

Student Life Upper grades have specified standards of dress, student council, honor system. Discipline rests primarily with faculty.

Summer Programs Enrichment, sports, art/fine arts, rigorous outdoor training, computer instruction programs offered; session focuses on academic enrichment; held both on and off campus; held at zoos, museums, and other field trip locations around town; accepts boys and girls; open to students from other schools. 500 students usually enrolled. 2006 schedule: June 1 to July 1. Application deadline: none.

Tuition and Aid Day student tuition: $13,050. Tuition installment plan (4-part payment plan, 2-part payment plan). Need-based scholarship grants, need-based loans available. In 2005–06, 12% of upper-school students received aid. Total amount of financial aid awarded in 2005–06: $270,408.

Admissions Traditional secondary-level entrance grade is 9. For fall 2005, 61 students applied for upper-level admission, 44 were accepted, 37 enrolled. ISEE or Otis-Lennon School Ability Test required. Deadline for receipt of application materials: none. Application fee required: $125. Interview required.

Athletics Interscholastic: baseball (boys), basketball (b,g), cross-country running (b,g), golf (b,g), softball (g), swimming and diving (b,g), tennis (b,g), track and field (b,g), volleyball (g), winter soccer (b,g). 7 PE instructors, 15 coaches, 1 trainer.

Computers Computers are regularly used in all academic classes. Computer network features include on-campus library services, CD-ROMs, online commercial services, Internet access, DVD.

Contact Mr. Craig Meredith, Director of Admissions. 281-367-0900 Ext. 308. Fax: 281-298-5715. E-mail: cmeredith@johncooper.org. Web site: www.johncooper.org.

THE JOHN DEWEY ACADEMY

Great Barrington, Massachusetts
See Special Needs Schools section.

JOHN F. KENNEDY MEMORIAL HIGH SCHOOL

140 South 140th Street
Burien, Washington 98168-3496
Head of School: Mr. Michael L. Prato

General Information Coeducational boarding and day college-preparatory and religious studies school, affiliated with Roman Catholic Church. Grades 9–12. Founded: 1966. Setting: suburban. Nearest major city is Seattle. Students are housed in 2 separate dorms (international boys and girls). 25-acre campus. 4 buildings on campus. Approved or accredited by CITA (Commission on International and Trans-Regional Accreditation), National Catholic Education Association, Northwest Association of Schools and Colleges, and Washington Department of Education. Endowment: $1.5 million. Total enrollment: 866. Upper school average class size: 23. Upper school faculty-student ratio: 1:18.

Upper School Student Profile Grade 9: 213 students (118 boys, 95 girls); Grade 10: 233 students (121 boys, 112 girls); Grade 11: 232 students (123 boys, 109 girls); Grade 12: 188 students (97 boys, 91 girls). 7% of students are boarding students. 93% are state residents. 1 state is represented in upper school student body. 7% are international students. International students from Hong Kong, Japan, Republic of Korea, Taiwan, Thailand, and Viet Nam; 5 other countries represented in student body. 70% of students are Roman Catholic.

Faculty School total: 67. In upper school: 35 men, 32 women; 34 have advanced degrees.

Subjects Offered Accounting, acting, advanced TOEFL/grammar, algebra, American sign language, art, art appreciation, art history, basic skills, Bible, biology, business mathematics, calculus, carpentry, Catholic belief and practice, chemistry, Christian doctrine, Christian ethics, Christian scripture, community service, comparative religion, composition-AP, computer applications, computer-aided design, concert band, concert choir, construction, contemporary issues, creative writing, current events, drafting, drama, economics, English, English composition, English language and composition-AP, English literature, English literature and composition-AP, English literature-AP, English/composition-AP, ESL, ethical decision making, fiction, fine arts, French, general business, geometry, German, health, Hebrew scripture, honors algebra, honors English, honors geometry, honors U.S. history, ideas, integrated science, interdisciplinary studies, jazz ensemble, journalism, keyboarding, language arts, Latin, law, mathematics, media, physical education, physics, public policy, public service, publications, sign language, social justice, Spanish, speech, statistics-AP, symphonic band, trigonometry, U.S. history, U.S. history-AP, Washington State and Northwest History, woodworking, world history, world religions, yearbook.

Graduation Requirements Arts and fine arts (art, music, dance, drama), English, foreign language, mathematics, physical education (includes health), religion (includes Bible studies and theology), religious education, science, social studies (includes history), culminating project (starting w/ class of 2008), education plan (high school—college) or alternative.

Special Academic Programs Advanced Placement exam preparation in 13 subject areas; honors section; accelerated programs; independent study; study at local college for college credit; study abroad; academic accommodation for the gifted, the musically talented, and the artistically talented; remedial reading and/or remedial writing; remedial math; programs in English, mathematics, general development for dyslexic students; ESL (58 students enrolled).

College Placement 203 students graduated in 2005; 180 went to college, including Central Washington University; Gonzaga University; Seattle University; University of Washington; Washington State University; Western Washington University. Other: 3 went to work, 2 entered military service, 18 had other specific plans.

Student Life Upper grades have specified standards of dress, student council. Discipline rests primarily with faculty. Attendance at religious services is required.

Summer Programs Remediation programs offered; session focuses on remediation, make-up; held on campus; accepts boys and girls; open to students from other schools. 30 students usually enrolled. 2006 schedule: July 3 to July 28. Application deadline: June 28.

Tuition and Aid Day student tuition: $6820–$7425; 7-day tuition and room/board: $15,800. Tuition installment plan (monthly payment plans, individually arranged payment plans). Tuition reduction for siblings, merit scholarship grants, need-based scholarship grants, paying campus jobs available. In 2005–06, 19% of upper-school students received aid; total upper-school merit-scholarship money awarded: $9780. Total amount of financial aid awarded in 2005–06: $390,000.

Admissions Traditional secondary-level entrance grade is 9. Scholastic Testing Service High School Placement Test required. Deadline for receipt of application materials: none. No application fee required. Interview recommended.

Athletics Interscholastic: aquatics (boys, girls), baseball (b), basketball (b,g), cheering (g), cross-country running (b,g), diving (b,g), drill team (g), football (b), golf (b,g), gymnastics (g), soccer (b,g), softball (g), swimming and diving (b,g), tennis (b,g), track and field (b,g), volleyball (b,g), wrestling (b); intramural: basketball (b,g), combined training (b), Frisbee (b,g), physical training (b,g), scuba diving (b,g), strength & conditioning (b,g), table tennis (b,g), ultimate Frisbee (b,g), volleyball (b,g), weight lifting (b,g), weight training (b,g); coed intramural: table tennis, ultimate Frisbee. 3 PE instructors, 53 coaches, 1 trainer.

Computers Computers are regularly used in English, foreign language, history, science classes. Computer network features include campus e-mail, on-campus library services, CD-ROMs, Internet access.

Contact Mr. James Mesick, Director of Admissions, Marketing, and Public Relations. 206-246-0500 Ext. 306. Fax: 206-242-0831. E-mail: mesickj@kennedyhs.org. Web site: www.kennedyhs.org.

JOSEPHINUM HIGH SCHOOL

1501 North Oakley Boulevard
Chicago, Illinois 60622
Head of School: Sr. Martha Roughan

General Information Girls' day college-preparatory, general academic, arts, religious studies, and technology school, affiliated with Roman Catholic Church. Grades 6–12. Founded: 1890. Setting: urban. 2-acre campus. 1 building on campus. Approved or accredited by Network of Sacred Heart Schools, North Central Association of Colleges and Schools, and Illinois Department of Education. Languages of instruction: English and Spanish. Endowment: $3 million. Total enrollment: 156. Upper school average class size: 15. Upper school faculty-student ratio: 1:10.

Upper School Student Profile Grade 9: 29 students (29 girls); Grade 10: 34 students (34 girls); Grade 11: 29 students (29 girls); Grade 12: 32 students (32 girls). 60% of students are Roman Catholic.

Faculty School total: 23. In upper school: 4 men, 17 women; 11 have advanced degrees.

Subjects Offered American literature, applied arts, art, biology, Black history, British literature, chemistry, community service, computer education, constitutional history of U.S., consumer education, dance, drama, early childhood, English, French, health, Latin American history, leadership education training, library research, media production, peer counseling, personal growth, physical education, programming, scripture, sewing, social justice, softball, Spanish, student publications, U.S. history, world geography, yearbook.

Graduation Requirements Arts and fine arts (art, music, dance, drama), biology, computer science, English, foreign language, mathematics, physical education (includes health), religion (includes Bible studies and theology), science, social science, social studies (includes history). Community service is required.

Special Academic Programs Honors section; independent study; remedial math; special instructional classes for deaf students.

College Placement 32 students graduated in 2005; 31 went to college, including DePaul University; University of Illinois at Chicago; University of Illinois at Urbana–Champaign. Other: 1 entered a postgraduate year.

Student Life Upper grades have uniform requirement, student council. Discipline rests primarily with faculty. Attendance at religious services is required.

Tuition and Aid Day student tuition: $5400. Tuition installment plan (monthly payment plans, individually arranged payment plans, Tuition Management Systems Plan). Tuition reduction for siblings, merit scholarship grants, need-based scholarship grants available. In 2005–06, 89% of upper-school students received aid; total upper-school merit-scholarship money awarded: $20,200. Total amount of financial aid awarded in 2005–06: $425,000.

Admissions Traditional secondary-level entrance grade is 9. For fall 2005, 67 students applied for upper-level admission, 61 were accepted, 45 enrolled. ACT, ACT-Explore, Catholic High School Entrance Examination or Scholastic Testing Service High School Placement Test (open version) required. Deadline for receipt of application materials: none. Application fee required: $25. Interview required.

Athletics Interscholastic: badminton, basketball, jump rope, softball, volleyball; intramural: cheering, dance, dance team, kickball, outdoor activities, physical fitness, physical training, soccer, tennis, track and field, volleyball. 1 PE instructor, 3 coaches.

Computers Computers are regularly used in all academic, creative writing, newspaper classes. Computer resources include CD-ROMs, Internet access, DVD.

Contact Courtney Phillips, Admissions Director. 773-276-1261. Fax: 773-292-3963. Web site: josephinum.org.

THE JUDGE ROTENBERG EDUCATIONAL CENTER

Canton, Massachusetts
See Special Needs Schools section.

THE JUNE SHELTON SCHOOL AND EVALUATION CENTER

Dallas, Texas
See Special Needs Schools section.

JUSTIN-SIENA HIGH SCHOOL

4026 Maher Street
Napa, California 94558
Head of School: Gregory J. Schmitz

General Information Coeducational day college-preparatory, arts, business, religious studies, and technology school, affiliated with Roman Catholic Church. Grades 9–12. Founded: 1966. Setting: suburban. Nearest major city is San Francisco. 36-acre campus. 11 buildings on campus. Approved or accredited by Western Association of Schools and Colleges, Western Catholic Education Association, and California Department of Education. Endowment: $1.5 million. Total enrollment: 610. Upper school average class size: 28. Upper school faculty-student ratio: 1:19.

Upper School Student Profile Grade 9: 148 students (75 boys, 73 girls); Grade 10: 151 students (73 boys, 78 girls); Grade 11: 167 students (83 boys, 84 girls); Grade 12: 144 students (72 boys, 72 girls). 68% of students are Roman Catholic.

Faculty School total: 53. In upper school: 30 men, 23 women; 26 have advanced degrees.

Subjects Offered Algebra, American history, American literature, anthropology, art, Bible studies, biology, business, calculus, ceramics, chemistry, chorus, community service, computer math, computer programming, creative writing, dance, drama, driver education, earth science, economics, English, English literature, environmental science, ethics, European history, expository writing, French, geometry, government/civics, grammar, health, history, jazz, journalism, keyboarding, leadership training, mathematics, music, peer counseling, philosophy, photography, physical education, physics, physiology, psychology, religion, science, social science, social studies, Spanish, speech, theater, theology, trigonometry, weight training, word processing, world affairs, world history, world literature, writing, yearbook.

Graduation Requirements English, foreign language, mathematics, physical education (includes health), religion (includes Bible studies and theology), science, social science, social studies (includes history), 100 hours of community service.

Special Academic Programs Advanced Placement exam preparation in 5 subject areas; honors section; study at local college for college credit.

College Placement 150 students graduated in 2005; 148 went to college, including Stanford University; University of California, Berkeley; University of California, Davis; University of California, Los Angeles; University of California, Santa Barbara; University of Southern California. Other: 1 went to work, 1 entered military service. Mean SAT verbal: 542, mean SAT math: 546, mean composite ACT: 23. 32% scored over 600 on SAT verbal, 32% scored over 600 on SAT math, 44% scored over 26 on composite ACT.

Student Life Upper grades have specified standards of dress, student council. Discipline rests equally with students and faculty. Attendance at religious services is required.

Summer Programs Remediation programs offered; session focuses on mathematics and English remediation; held on campus; accepts boys and girls; open to students from other schools. 120 students usually enrolled. 2006 schedule: June 13 to July 25. Application deadline: May 30.

Tuition and Aid Day student tuition: $8950. Tuition installment plan (FACTS Tuition Payment Plan). Tuition reduction for siblings, merit scholarship grants, need-based scholarship grants, paying campus jobs available. In 2005–06, 28% of upper-school students received aid; total upper-school merit-scholarship money awarded: $21,600. Total amount of financial aid awarded in 2005–06: $222,400.

Admissions Traditional secondary-level entrance grade is 9. For fall 2005, 185 students applied for upper-level admission, 181 were accepted, 148 enrolled. Scholastic Testing Service High School Placement Test required. Deadline for receipt of application materials: December 15. No application fee required. Interview recommended.

Athletics Interscholastic: baseball (boys), basketball (b,g), cheering (g), cross-country running (b,g), dance (b,g), dance squad (g), fitness (b,g), football (b), golf (b,g), modern dance (g), physical training (b,g), soccer (b,g), softball (g), tennis (b,g), volleyball (g), water polo (g), weight training (b,g), wrestling (b); coed interscholastic: swimming and diving, track and field. 3 PE instructors, 18 coaches, 1 trainer.

Computers Computers are regularly used in business, business applications, business education, business skills, journalism, keyboarding, library, literary magazine, mathematics, multimedia, newspaper, photography, science, social studies, technology, word processing, yearbook classes. Computer network features include on-campus library services, CD-ROMs, online commercial services, Internet access, DVD, wireless campus network.

Contact Susan Allbritton, Director of Admissions. 707-255-0950 Ext. 603. Fax: 707-255-1334. E-mail: allbrittons@justin-siena.com. Web site: www.justin-siena.com.

KALAMAZOO CHRISTIAN HIGH SCHOOL

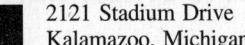

2121 Stadium Drive
Kalamazoo, Michigan 49008-1692
Head of School: Mr. Thomas Kamp

General Information Coeducational day college-preparatory, general academic, arts, business, vocational, religious studies, bilingual studies, and technology school, affiliated with Christian Reformed Church, Reformed Church in America. Grades 9–12. Founded: 1877. Setting: urban. 3-acre campus. 1 building on campus. Approved or accredited by North Central Association of Colleges and Schools and Michigan Department of Education. Endowment: $1 million. Total enrollment: 426. Upper school average class size: 22. Upper school faculty-student ratio: 1:14.

Upper School Student Profile Grade 9: 102 students (57 boys, 45 girls); Grade 10: 113 students (53 boys, 60 girls); Grade 11: 105 students (55 boys, 50 girls); Grade 12: 105 students (45 boys, 60 girls). 75% of students are members of Christian Reformed Church, Reformed Church in America.

Faculty In upper school: 16 men, 15 women; 10 have advanced degrees.

Special Academic Programs Advanced Placement exam preparation in 5 subject areas; honors section; study at local college for college credit.

College Placement 125 students graduated in 2005; 100 went to college, including Hope College. Other: 10 went to work, 4 entered military service. Median composite ACT: 24.

Student Life Upper grades have specified standards of dress, student council, honor system. Discipline rests primarily with faculty. Attendance at religious services is required.

Tuition and Aid Day student tuition: $3500. Tuition installment plan (individually arranged payment plans). Tuition reduction for siblings available. In 2005–06, 5% of upper-school students received aid.

Admissions Deadline for receipt of application materials: none. No application fee required. Interview required.

Athletics Interscholastic: baseball (boys), basketball (b,g), bowling (b,g), cheering (g), cross-country running (b,g), diving (b,g), football (b), golf (b), physical fitness (b,g), soccer (b,g), softball (g), swimming and diving (b,g), tennis (b,g), track and field (b,g), volleyball (g).

Computers Computers are regularly used in accounting, business, business applications, business skills, data processing, graphic arts, graphic design, keyboarding, lab/keyboard classes. Computer network features include on-campus library services, online commercial services, Internet access.

Contact Mr. Thomas Kamp, Principal. 269-381-2250 Ext. 220. Fax: 269-381-0319. E-mail: tkamp@kcsa.org. Web site: www.kcsa.org.

KAPAUN MOUNT CARMEL CATHOLIC HIGH SCHOOL

8506 East Central
Wichita, Kansas 67206
Head of School: Mr. Michael C. Burrus

General Information Coeducational day college-preparatory, arts, business, and religious studies school, affiliated with Roman Catholic Church. Grades 9–12. Setting: suburban. 25-acre campus. 2 buildings on campus. Approved or accredited by North Central Association of Colleges and Schools and Kansas Department of Education. Total enrollment: 879. Upper school average class size: 24. Upper school faculty-student ratio: 1:15.

Upper School Student Profile 99% of students are Roman Catholic.

Faculty School total: 54. In upper school: 22 men, 32 women.

Subjects Offered Business, consumer education, English, fine arts, foreign language, mathematics, physical education, science, social science, theology.

Graduation Requirements Arts and fine arts (art, music, dance, drama), computer science, English, mathematics, physical education (includes health), social science, social sciences, four years of Catholic theology curriculum.

Special Academic Programs Advanced Placement exam preparation in 7 subject areas; honors section; study at local college for college credit; academic accommodation for the gifted; remedial reading and/or remedial writing; remedial math; programs in English, mathematics, general development for dyslexic students; special instructional classes for deaf students.

College Placement 182 students graduated in 2005.

Student Life Upper grades have uniform requirement, student council, honor system. Discipline rests primarily with faculty. Attendance at religious services is required.

Summer Programs Remediation programs offered; held on campus; accepts boys and girls; not open to students from other schools. 30 students usually enrolled.

Admissions School's own test required. Deadline for receipt of application materials: none. Application fee required: $100.

Athletics Interscholastic: baseball (boys), basketball (b,g), bowling (b,g), cheering (g), cross-country running (b,g), dance squad (g), diving (b,g), football (b), golf (b,g),

pom squad (g), soccer (b,g), softball (g), swimming and diving (b,g), tennis (b,g), track and field (b,g), volleyball (g), wrestling (b); intramural: in-line hockey (b). 1 trainer.

Computers Computer network features include Internet access, office computer access, wireless campus network.

Contact Mr. Michael C. Burrus, President. 316-634-0315. Fax: 316-636-2437. E-mail: mburrus@kapaun.org. Web site: kapaun.org/.

KARACHI AMERICAN SCHOOL

Amir Khusro Road, KDA Scheme No. 1
Karachi 75350, Pakistan
Head of School: Peter L. Pelosi, EdD

General Information Coeducational day college-preparatory, arts, bilingual studies, and technology school. Grades PS–12. Founded: 1957. Setting: urban. 10-acre campus. 5 buildings on campus. Approved or accredited by Middle States Association of Colleges and Schools. Language of instruction: English. Total enrollment: 332. Upper school average class size: 25. Upper school faculty-student ratio: 1:8.

Upper School Student Profile Grade 9: 25 students (12 boys, 13 girls); Grade 10: 32 students (19 boys, 13 girls); Grade 11: 43 students (26 boys, 17 girls); Grade 12: 26 students (17 boys, 9 girls).

Faculty School total: 40. In upper school: 8 men, 32 women; 21 have advanced degrees.

Subjects Offered Band, British literature, computer science, concert band, desktop publishing, English, English-AP, French, general science, geometry, health, journalism, mathematics, physical education, psychology, science research, social studies, studio art, Urdu.

Graduation Requirements Arts and fine arts (art, music, dance, drama), computer studies, English, foreign language, mathematics, physical education (includes health), science, social studies (includes history), speech, writing. Community service is required.

Special Academic Programs Advanced Placement exam preparation in 14 subject areas; ESL.

College Placement 26 students graduated in 2005; all went to college, including University of Illinois at Urbana–Champaign. Mean SAT verbal: 563, mean SAT math: 631.

Student Life Upper grades have student council, honor system. Discipline rests equally with students and faculty.

Tuition and Aid Day student tuition: $7220–$11,095. Tuition installment plan (2-payment plan).

Admissions For fall 2005, 45 students applied for upper-level admission, 27 were accepted, 27 enrolled. Admissions testing, any standardized test, English proficiency, ESL, Iowa Test of Educational Development, Iowa Tests of Basic Skills, latest standardized score from previous school, PSAT or SAT, psychoeducational evaluation, SLEP for foreign students or writing sample required. Deadline for receipt of application materials: none. Application fee required: $58. Interview required.

Athletics Interscholastic: cricket (boys); intramural: cricket (b); coed interscholastic: archery, artistic gym, baseball, basketball, cheering, football, gymnastics, physical training, tennis, track and field, volleyball; coed intramural: artistic gym, baseball, basketball, cheering, football, gymnastics, physical training, table tennis, tennis, track and field, volleyball. 2 trainers.

Computers Computer network features include campus e-mail, on-campus library services, CD-ROMs, online commercial services, Internet access, file transfer, office computer access, DVD.

Contact Marilyn Nessel, Director of Admissions. 92-21-453-9096. Fax: 92-21-454-7305. E-mail: guidance@kas.edu.pk. Web site: www.kas.edu.pk.

THE KARAFIN SCHOOL

Mount Kisco, New York
See Special Needs Schools section.

KEARNEY CATHOLIC HIGH SCHOOL

110 East 35th Street
Kearny, Nebraska 68848-1866
Head of School: Terry Torson

General Information Coeducational day college-preparatory, arts, business, and religious studies school, affiliated with Roman Catholic Church. Grades 6–12. Founded: 1960. Setting: small town. Nearest major city is Omaha. 10-acre campus. 1 building on campus. Approved or accredited by National Catholic Education Association, North Central Association of Colleges and Schools, and Nebraska Department of Education. Endowment: $1 million. Total enrollment: 288. Upper school average class size: 15. Upper school faculty-student ratio: 1:13.

Upper School Student Profile Grade 9: 42 students (26 boys, 16 girls); Grade 10: 34 students (18 boys, 16 girls); Grade 11: 34 students (18 boys, 16 girls); Grade 12: 55 students (27 boys, 28 girls). 88% of students are Roman Catholic.

Faculty School total: 24. In upper school: 6 men, 18 women; 10 have advanced degrees.

Subjects Offered Anatomy and physiology, art, art appreciation, art education, art history, band, Basic programming, biology, business, business applications, business communications, business education, business technology, Catholic belief and practice, chemistry, chorus, church history, computer applications, computer programming, CPR, desktop publishing, earth science, economics, English, English literature, geography, government, grammar, graphic arts, history, instrumental music, language arts, modern world history, music appreciation, oil painting, physical science, physics, pre-calculus, reading, religion, social studies, Spanish, speech, theology, U.S. government, vocal music.

Graduation Requirements English, mathematics, physical education (includes health), science, social studies (includes history), speech, theology. Community service is required.

Special Academic Programs Honors section; accelerated programs; study at local college for college credit; academic accommodation for the gifted; special instructional classes for students with learning disabilities and Attention Deficit Disorder.

College Placement 52 students graduated in 2005; 50 went to college, including Creighton University; University of Nebraska–Lincoln; University of Nebraska at Kearney. Other: 2 went to work. Mean composite ACT: 24. 35% scored over 26 on composite ACT.

Student Life Upper grades have uniform requirement, student council. Discipline rests primarily with faculty. Attendance at religious services is required.

Tuition and Aid Day student tuition: $2075–$3000. Tuition installment plan (monthly payment plans, individually arranged payment plans). Tuition reduction for siblings, need-based scholarship grants available. In 2005–06, 5% of upper-school students received aid. Total amount of financial aid awarded in 2005–06: $15,000.

Admissions Traditional secondary-level entrance grade is 9. For fall 2005, 8 students applied for upper-level admission, 7 were accepted, 7 enrolled. Deadline for receipt of application materials: none. Application fee required: $100. Interview required.

Athletics Interscholastic: basketball (boys, girls), cheering (g), cross-country running (b,g), dance team (g), football (b), golf (b,g), soccer (b,g), tennis (b,g), track and field (b,g), volleyball (g), wrestling (b). 1 PE instructor.

Computers Computers are regularly used in accounting, business applications, business education, business skills, business studies, economics, graphic arts, mathematics, science, writing, yearbook classes. Computer network features include CD-ROMs, Internet access, file transfer, office computer access, DVD, wireless campus network, PowerSchool to check classes and grades.

Contact Terry Torson, Principal. 308-234-2610. Fax: 308-234-4986. E-mail: ttorson@esu10.org. Web site: www.kearneycatholic.org.

KEITH COUNTRY DAY SCHOOL

1 Jacoby Place
Rockford, Illinois 61107
Head of School: Mr. Jon S. Esler

General Information Coeducational day college-preparatory, arts, and technology school. Grades PK–12. Founded: 1916. Setting: suburban. Nearest major city is Chicago. 15-acre campus. 1 building on campus. Approved or accredited by Independent Schools Association of the Central States and Illinois Department of Education. Member of National Association of Independent Schools. Endowment: $774,000. Total enrollment: 328. Upper school average class size: 15. Upper school faculty-student ratio: 1:9.

Upper School Student Profile Grade 9: 20 students (11 boys, 9 girls); Grade 10: 20 students (9 boys, 11 girls); Grade 11: 35 students (17 boys, 18 girls); Grade 12: 25 students (12 boys, 13 girls).

Faculty School total: 51. In upper school: 11 men, 17 women; 19 have advanced degrees.

Subjects Offered Advanced math, Advanced Placement courses, algebra, American history, American literature, art, arts, Bible as literature, biology, biology-AP, calculus, ceramics, chemistry, chemistry-AP, college counseling, community service, computer science, design, drama, drawing, economics, English, English literature, English-AP, environmental science, European history, fine arts, French, geography, geometry, government/civics, health, history, Latin, mathematics, music, painting, photography, physical education, physics, pre-calculus, research skills, science, social studies, speech, study skills, theater, trigonometry, world history, world literature.

Graduation Requirements Arts and fine arts (art, music, dance, drama), college counseling, computer science, English, foreign language, mathematics, physical education (includes health), research skills, science, senior project, social studies (includes history), speech. Community service is required.

Special Academic Programs Advanced Placement exam preparation in 9 subject areas; honors section; study at local college for college credit; study abroad; remedial reading and/or remedial writing; programs in general development for dyslexic students.

College Placement 15 students graduated in 2005; all went to college, including Northwestern University; University of Illinois at Urbana–Champaign. Median SAT verbal: 656, median SAT math: 616, median combined SAT: 1272, median composite ACT: 27.

Student Life Upper grades have specified standards of dress, student council, honor system. Discipline rests equally with students and faculty.

Summer Programs Enrichment, sports, art/fine arts programs offered; session focuses on sports skills camps, math camp, music camp; held on campus; accepts boys and girls; open to students from other schools. 80 students usually enrolled. 2006 schedule: June 15 to August 15.

Tuition and Aid Day student tuition: $11,790. Tuition installment plan (monthly payment plans, school's own payment plan). Tuition reduction for siblings, merit scholarship grants, need-based financial aid grants available. In 2005–06, 39% of upper-school students received aid; total upper-school merit-scholarship money awarded: $149,940. Total amount of financial aid awarded in 2005–06: $207,290.

Admissions Traditional secondary-level entrance grade is 9. For fall 2005, 134 students applied for upper-level admission, 92 were accepted, 75 enrolled. ERB and school's own exam required. Deadline for receipt of application materials: none. Application fee required: $50. On-campus interview required.

Athletics Interscholastic: basketball (boys, girls), soccer (b,g), volleyball (g); coed interscholastic: golf, tennis; coed intramural: crew. 3 PE instructors, 6 coaches.

Computers Computers are regularly used in English, mathematics, science, yearbook classes. Computer network features include campus e-mail, on-campus library services, CD-ROMs, Internet access, wireless campus network.

Contact Marcia Aramovich, Director of Admissions. 815-399-8850 Ext. 144. Fax: 815-399-2470. E-mail: admissions@keithschool.com. Web site: www.keithschool.com.

KENT DENVER SCHOOL

4000 East Quincy Avenue
Englewood, Colorado 80113
Head of School: Todd Horn

General Information Coeducational day college-preparatory, arts, and technology school. Grades 6–12. Founded: 1922. Setting: suburban. Nearest major city is Denver. 220-acre campus. 5 buildings on campus. Approved or accredited by Association of Colorado Independent Schools and Colorado Department of Education. Member of National Association of Independent Schools and Secondary School Admission Test Board. Endowment: $21.7 million. Total enrollment: 656. Upper school average class size: 15. Upper school faculty-student ratio: 1:7.

Upper School Student Profile Grade 9: 105 students (53 boys, 52 girls); Grade 10: 112 students (55 boys, 57 girls); Grade 11: 112 students (52 boys, 60 girls); Grade 12: 107 students (52 boys, 55 girls).

Faculty School total: 81. In upper school: 30 men, 29 women; 41 have advanced degrees.

Subjects Offered African-American literature, algebra, American history, American history-AP, American literature, American sign language, ancient history, anthropology, art, art history, art history-AP, Asian studies, biology, calculus, calculus-AP, career education internship, ceramics, chemistry, choir, clayworking, college counseling, community service, computer math, computer programming, computer programming-AP, computer science, creative writing, dance performance, drama, earth science, economics, English, English language and composition-AP, English language-AP, English literature, English literature and composition-AP, environmental science, European history, European history-AP, fine arts, French, French language-AP, French literature-AP, French-AP, general science, genetics, geography, geology, geometry, government/civics, grammar, guitar, health and wellness, history, history-AP, human development, independent study, jazz band, Latin, mathematics, music, music performance, mythology, photography, physical education, physics, pre-calculus, science, social studies, Spanish, Spanish language-AP, Spanish literature-AP, statistics, studio art—AP, theater, Web site design, world history, world literature, writing.

Graduation Requirements Arts and fine arts (art, music, dance, drama), computer science, English, foreign language, history, internship, mathematics, participation in sports, physical education (includes health), science. Community service is required.

Special Academic Programs Advanced Placement exam preparation in 16 subject areas; honors section; independent study; programs in general development for dyslexic students.

College Placement 104 students graduated in 2005; all went to college, including Claremont McKenna College; Middlebury College; Stanford University; The Colorado College; University of San Diego; University of Southern California. Mean SAT verbal: 622, mean SAT math: 631. 67% scored over 600 on SAT verbal, 75% scored over 600 on SAT math.

Student Life Upper grades have specified standards of dress, student council. Discipline rests equally with students and faculty.

Summer Programs Enrichment, sports, art/fine arts, computer instruction programs offered; session focuses on skill building; held on campus; accepts boys and girls; open to students from other schools. 650 students usually enrolled. 2006 schedule: June 12 to June 30. Application deadline: none.

Tuition and Aid Day student tuition: $16,400. Tuition installment plan (Insured Tuition Payment Plan, Key Tuition Payment Plan, monthly payment plans). Need-based scholarship grants, need-based loans available. In 2005–06, 18% of upper-school students received aid. Total amount of financial aid awarded in 2005–06: $1,200,000.

Admissions Traditional secondary-level entrance grade is 9. For fall 2005, 143 students applied for upper-level admission, 55 were accepted, 43 enrolled. ISEE or SSAT required. Deadline for receipt of application materials: January 31. Application fee required: $60. On-campus interview required.

Kent Denver School

Athletics Interscholastic: basketball (boys, girls), cross-country running (b,g), diving (g), field hockey (g), football (b), golf (b,g), hockey (b), ice hockey (b), lacrosse (b,g), soccer (b,g), swimming and diving (g), tennis (b,g), track and field (b,g), volleyball (g), wrestling (b); coed interscholastic: baseball, outdoor education; coed intramural: aerobics/nautilus, bicycling, fitness, mountain biking, outdoor adventure, outdoor education, outdoor skills, physical fitness, physical training, strength & conditioning, weight lifting. 3 PE instructors, 17 coaches, 1 trainer.

Computers Computers are regularly used in art, English, foreign language, history, mathematics, science classes. Computer network features include campus e-mail, on-campus library services, CD-ROMs, online commercial services, Internet access.

Contact Kelly W. Holley, Director of Upper School Admission. 303-770-7660 Ext. 233. Fax: 303-770-1398. E-mail: kholley@kentdenver.org. Web site: www.kentdenver.org.

KENT PLACE SCHOOL

42 Norwood Avenue
Summit, New Jersey 07902-0308
Head of School: Mrs. Susan C. Bosland

petersons.com

General Information Coeducational day (boys' only in lower grades) college-preparatory school. Boys grades N–PK, girls grades N–12. Founded: 1894. Setting: suburban. Nearest major city is New York, NY. 25-acre campus. 6 buildings on campus. Approved or accredited by Middle States Association of Colleges and Schools and New Jersey Association of Independent Schools. Member of National Association of Independent Schools and Secondary School Admission Test Board. Endowment: $14.2 million. Total enrollment: 633. Upper school average class size: 16. Upper school faculty-student ratio: 1:7.

Upper School Student Profile Grade 9: 70 students (70 girls); Grade 10: 62 students (62 girls); Grade 11: 62 students (62 girls); Grade 12: 53 students (53 girls).

Faculty School total: 81. In upper school: 8 men, 26 women; 27 have advanced degrees.

Subjects Offered Advanced Placement courses, algebra, American history, American history-AP, American literature, anatomy and physiology, art, art history-AP, biology, biology-AP, calculus, calculus-AP, ceramics, chemistry, chemistry-AP, computer literacy, computer programming-AP, computer science, creative writing, dance, drama, driver education, economics, English, English language-AP, English literature, English literature-AP, environmental science, environmental science-AP, European history, expository writing, fine arts, French, French language-AP, French literature-AP, geometry, government/civics, grammar, health, history, independent study, Latin, Latin-AP, macroeconomics-AP, mathematics, modern European history-AP, music, music theory-AP, photography, physical education, physics, science, social studies, Spanish, Spanish language-AP, Spanish literature-AP, statistics, statistics-AP, theater, trigonometry, world history.

Graduation Requirements Arts and fine arts (art, music, dance, drama), computer science, English, foreign language, mathematics, physical education (includes health), science, social studies (includes history).

Special Academic Programs Advanced Placement exam preparation in 18 subject areas; independent study.

College Placement 68 students graduated in 2005; all went to college, including Boston College; Brown University; Columbia College; The George Washington University; University of Pennsylvania; Yale University. Median SAT verbal: 660, median SAT math: 670. 78% scored over 600 on SAT verbal, 88% scored over 600 on SAT math.

Student Life Upper grades have specified standards of dress, student council, honor system. Discipline rests equally with students and faculty.

Summer Programs Enrichment programs offered; session focuses on fun and enrichment (via the Summer Explorations Day Camp); held on campus; accepts boys and girls; open to students from other schools. 2006 schedule: June 12 to August 11.

Tuition and Aid Day student tuition: $24,325. Tuition installment plan (Insured Tuition Payment Plan, Key Tuition Payment Plan, monthly payment plans). Need-based scholarship grants available. In 2005–06, 20% of upper-school students received aid. Total amount of financial aid awarded in 2005–06: $1,249,710.

Admissions Traditional secondary-level entrance grade is 9. ISEE or SSAT required. Deadline for receipt of application materials: February 1. Application fee required: $50. On-campus interview required.

Athletics Interscholastic: basketball, cross-country running, field hockey, indoor track, lacrosse, soccer, softball, swimming and diving, tennis, track and field, volleyball; intramural: dance, fencing, modern dance, physical fitness, squash. 4 PE instructors, 19 coaches, 1 trainer.

Computers Computers are regularly used in all classes. Computer network features include campus e-mail, on-campus library services, CD-ROMs, online commercial services, Internet access, file transfer, office computer access, DVD, wireless campus network.

Contact Mrs. Nancy J. Humick, Director of Admission and Financial Aid. 908-273-0900 Ext. 254. Fax: 908-273-9390. E-mail: admission@kentplace.org. Web site: www.kentplace.org.

See full description on page 852.

KENT SCHOOL

PO Box 2006
1 Macedonia Road
Kent, Connecticut 06757
Head of School: Rev. Richardson W. Schell

petersons.com

General Information Coeducational boarding and day college-preparatory, arts, and technology school, affiliated with Episcopal Church. Grades 9–PG. Founded: 1906. Setting: small town. Nearest major city is Hartford. Students are housed in single-sex by floor dormitories and single-sex dormitories. 1,200-acre campus. 15 buildings on campus. Approved or accredited by Association of Independent Schools in New England, Connecticut Association of Independent Schools, National Association of Episcopal Schools, New England Association of Schools and Colleges, The Association of Boarding Schools, and Connecticut Department of Education. Member of National Association of Independent Schools and Secondary School Admission Test Board. Endowment: $64 million. Total enrollment: 571. Upper school average class size: 12. Upper school faculty-student ratio: 1:7.

Upper School Student Profile Grade 9: 90 students (45 boys, 45 girls); Grade 10: 140 students (86 boys, 54 girls); Grade 11: 151 students (79 boys, 72 girls); Grade 12: 160 students (87 boys, 73 girls); Postgraduate: 30 students (23 boys, 7 girls). 91% of students are boarding students. 37 states are state residents. 37 states are represented in upper school student body. 16% are international students. International students from Canada, Germany, Hong Kong, Republic of Korea, Taiwan, and Thailand; 22 other countries represented in student body. 25% of students are members of Episcopal Church.

Faculty School total: 75. In upper school: 45 men, 30 women; 57 have advanced degrees; 30 reside on campus.

Subjects Offered Advanced studio art-AP, African-American history, algebra, American history, American history-AP, American literature, architecture, art, art history-AP, Asian history, astronomy, Bible studies, biology, biology-AP, biotechnology, calculus, calculus-AP, ceramics, chemistry, chemistry-AP, Chinese, classical Greek literature, classical studies, composition-AP, computer math, computer programming, computer science, computer science-AP, constitutional law, digital imaging, drama, ecology, economics, English, English literature, English literature-AP, environmental science-AP, European history, European history-AP, expository writing, fine arts, French, French language-AP, French literature-AP, genetics, geology, geometry, German, German-AP, government and politics-AP, Greek, history, Latin, Latin American history, Latin-AP, law and the legal system, mathematics, meteorology, Middle Eastern history, modern European history-AP, music, music theory-AP, photography, physical education, physics, physics-AP, religion, science, sculpture, social studies, Spanish, Spanish language-AP, Spanish literature-AP, statistics and probability, statistics-AP, theater, theology, trigonometry, world geography, world history, world literature.

Graduation Requirements Arts and fine arts (art, music, dance, drama), English, foreign language, history, mathematics, religion (includes Bible studies and theology), science, theology, U.S. history.

Special Academic Programs Advanced Placement exam preparation in 19 subject areas; honors section; independent study; academic accommodation for the gifted, the musically talented, and the artistically talented; ESL (26 students enrolled).

College Placement 163 students graduated in 2005; all went to college, including Boston University; Hamilton College; Hobart and William Smith Colleges; Syracuse University; United States Naval Academy; University of Pennsylvania.

Student Life Upper grades have specified standards of dress, student council. Discipline rests equally with students and faculty. Attendance at religious services is required.

Summer Programs Enrichment, art/fine arts programs offered; session focuses on creative writing; held on campus; accepts boys and girls; open to students from other schools. 50 students usually enrolled. 2006 schedule: July 9 to July 28. Application deadline: none.

Tuition and Aid Day student tuition: $28,000; 7-day tuition and room/board: $35,500. Guaranteed tuition plan. Tuition installment plan (Key Tuition Payment Plan, monthly payment plans, individually arranged payment plans). Need-based scholarship grants, need-based loans available. In 2005–06, 30% of upper-school students received aid. Total amount of financial aid awarded in 2005–06: $4,300,000.

Admissions Traditional secondary-level entrance grade is 9. For fall 2005, 883 students applied for upper-level admission, 462 were accepted, 221 enrolled. PSAT or SAT for applicants to grade 11 and 12, SSAT or TOEFL required. Deadline for receipt of application materials: January 16. Application fee required: $50. Interview required.

Athletics Interscholastic: baseball (boys), basketball (b,g), crew (b,g), cross-country running (b,g), diving (b,g), field hockey (g), football (b), hockey (b,g), ice hockey (b,g), lacrosse (b,g), rowing (b,g), soccer (b,g), softball (g), squash (b,g), swimming and diving (b,g), tennis (b,g); intramural: basketball (b), crew (b,g), rowing (b,g); coed interscholastic: crew, equestrian sports, golf, horseback riding; coed intramural: aerobics/dance, aerobics/nautilus, alpine skiing, aquatics, ballet, bicycling, dance, equestrian sports, figure skating, fitness, hockey, horseback riding, life saving, modern dance, mountain biking, nautilus, physical fitness, physical training, skiing (downhill), snowboarding, soccer, squash, strength & conditioning, swimming and diving, tennis, weight training, yoga. 1 trainer.

Computers Computers are regularly used in all academic, journalism, newspaper, yearbook classes. Computer network features include campus e-mail, on-campus library services, CD-ROMs, Internet access, wireless campus network.
Contact Ms. Kathryn F. Sullivan, Director of Admissions. 860-927-6111. Fax: 860-927-6109. E-mail: admissions@kent-school.edu. Web site: www.kent-school.edu.

ANNOUNCEMENT FROM THE SCHOOL As part of the Campaign for the Permanent Kent, the School surpassed its original goal of $75-million and reached over $80.5-million with the purpose of endowing student financial aid and improving faculty salaries. Eighty percent of the members of the class of 2005 attend Tier I and Tier II colleges, including one sixth former who received the Morehad Scholar Award and attends the University of North Carolina at Chapel Hill. In the 2004–05 school year, Kent School had 5 New England championships: football, girls' diving, boys' singles tennis, and the first- and second-place girls' crew.

See full description on page 854.

KENTS HILL SCHOOL
PO Box 257
1614 Main Street, Route 17
Kents Hill, Maine 04349-0257
Head of School: Mr. Rist Bonnefond

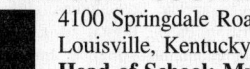

General Information Coeducational boarding and day college-preparatory, arts, and science, environmental studies school, affiliated with Methodist Church. Grades 9–PG. Founded: 1824. Setting: rural. Nearest major city is Portland. Students are housed in single-sex dormitories. 600-acre campus. 24 buildings on campus. Approved or accredited by New England Association of Schools and Colleges, The Association of Boarding Schools, and Maine Department of Education. Member of National Association of Independent Schools and Secondary School Admission Test Board. Endowment: $4.5 million. Total enrollment: 215. Upper school average class size: 11. Upper school faculty-student ratio: 1:6.
Upper School Student Profile Grade 9: 43 students (27 boys, 16 girls); Grade 10: 43 students (28 boys, 15 girls); Grade 11: 48 students (30 boys, 18 girls); Grade 12: 71 students (44 boys, 27 girls); Postgraduate: 10 students (10 boys). 70% of students are boarding students. 47% are state residents. 24 states are represented in upper school student body. 20% are international students. International students from Canada, Germany, Japan, Republic of Korea, Spain, and Taiwan; 12 other countries represented in student body. 3% of students are Methodist.
Faculty School total: 40. In upper school: 21 men, 19 women; 26 have advanced degrees; all reside on campus.
Subjects Offered Acting, Advanced Placement courses, African history, algebra, American history, American literature, art, art history, astronomy, biology, biology-AP, calculus, calculus-AP, ceramics, chemistry, chemistry-AP, concert choir, creative writing, drama, Eastern religion and philosophy, ecology, economics, English, English literature, English literature-AP, environmental science, environmental science-AP, environmental studies, ESL, ethics, European history, European history-AP, fine arts, French, geography, geology, geometry, government/civics, health, history, Holocaust, jazz ensemble, journalism, mathematics, music, photography, physics, physics-AP, psychology, religion, SAT/ACT preparation, science, Shakespeare, social studies, Spanish, statistics-AP, studio art-AP, theater, U.S. history-AP, Western religions, woodworking, world culture, world history, writing, writing.
Graduation Requirements English, environmental studies, foreign language, health, mathematics, science, social studies (includes history), visual and performing arts.
Special Academic Programs Advanced Placement exam preparation in 11 subject areas; honors section; accelerated programs; independent study; term-away projects; study abroad; academic accommodation for the gifted and the artistically talented; programs in general development for dyslexic students; special instructional classes for students with learning differences (through the Learning Skills Center); ESL (15 students enrolled).
College Placement 85 students graduated in 2005; 83 went to college, including Boston University; Cornell University; Harvard University; Rhode Island School of Design; Saint Michael's College; University of Massachusetts Amherst. Other: 1 entered a postgraduate year, 1 had other specific plans. 15% scored over 600 on SAT verbal, 12% scored over 600 on SAT math.
Student Life Upper grades have specified standards of dress, student council, honor system. Discipline rests equally with students and faculty.
Tuition and Aid Day student tuition: $20,820; 7-day tuition and room/board: $35,850. Tuition installment plan (Insured Tuition Payment Plan, Key Tuition Payment Plan, monthly payment plans, individually arranged payment plans, 2-payment plan). Need-based scholarship grants available. In 2005–06, 44% of upper-school students received aid. Total amount of financial aid awarded in 2005–06: $1,600,000.
Admissions Traditional secondary-level entrance grade is 9. SSAT required. Deadline for receipt of application materials: none. Application fee required: $50. Interview required.

Athletics Interscholastic: baseball (boys), basketball (b,g), field hockey (g), football (b), ice hockey (b,g), lacrosse (b,g), mountain biking (b), soccer (b,g), softball (g), tennis (b,g); coed interscholastic: alpine skiing, cross-country running, equestrian sports, golf, horseback riding, nordic skiing, physical training, skiing (cross-country), skiing (downhill), snowboarding; coed intramural: alpine skiing, basketball, fencing, mountain biking, nordic skiing, outdoor skills, skiing (cross-country), skiing (downhill), snowboarding, strength & conditioning, tennis, volleyball. 4 coaches, 1 trainer.
Computers Computers are regularly used in art, college planning, desktop publishing, English, graphic design, history, mathematics, science, Web site design classes. Computer network features include campus e-mail, on-campus library services, CD-ROMs, online commercial services, Internet access.
Contact Ms. Loren B. Mitchell, Director of Admissions. 207-685-4914 Ext. 118. Fax: 207-685-9529. E-mail: lmitchell@kentshill.org. Web site: www.kentshill.org.

See full description on page 856.

KENTUCKY COUNTRY DAY SCHOOL
4100 Springdale Road
Louisville, Kentucky 40241
Head of School: Mr. Bradley E. Lyman

General Information Coeducational day college-preparatory, arts, and technology school. Grades JK–12. Founded: 1972. Setting: suburban. 85-acre campus. 1 building on campus. Approved or accredited by Independent Schools Association of the Central States and Kentucky Department of Education. Member of National Association of Independent Schools. Endowment: $1 million. Total enrollment: 821. Upper school average class size: 18. Upper school faculty-student ratio: 1:7.
Upper School Student Profile Grade 9: 67 students (40 boys, 27 girls); Grade 10: 48 students (20 boys, 28 girls); Grade 11: 54 students (29 boys, 25 girls); Grade 12: 51 students (27 boys, 24 girls).
Faculty School total: 105. In upper school: 20 men, 13 women; 21 have advanced degrees.
Subjects Offered Algebra, American history, American literature, art, biology, calculus, ceramics, chemistry, collage and assemblage, communications, computer math, computer programming, computer science, drama, economics, English, English literature, European history, fine arts, French, geology, geometry, government/civics, history, humanities, instrumental music, Latin, law, mathematics, multimedia, music, physical education, physics, play production, psychology, science, sculpture, social science, social studies, Spanish, speech, statistics, theater, trigonometry.
Graduation Requirements Arts and fine arts (art, music, dance, drama), communications, English, foreign language, mathematics, physical education (includes health), science, social studies (includes history).
Special Academic Programs Advanced Placement exam preparation in 12 subject areas; honors section; independent study; term-away projects; study abroad; academic accommodation for the gifted, the musically talented, and the artistically talented.
College Placement 51 students graduated in 2005; all went to college, including Denison University; Indiana University Bloomington; Miami University; Southern Methodist University; University of Kentucky; Washington and Lee University. Median SAT verbal: 610, median SAT math: 630. 56% scored over 600 on SAT verbal, 62% scored over 600 on SAT math.
Student Life Upper grades have specified standards of dress, student council, honor system. Discipline rests equally with students and faculty.
Summer Programs Remediation, enrichment, advancement, sports, art/fine arts, rigorous outdoor training, computer instruction programs offered; session focuses on enrichment; held on campus; accepts boys and girls; open to students from other schools. 200 students usually enrolled. 2006 schedule: June 7 to August 20. Application deadline: none.
Tuition and Aid Day student tuition: $13,310. Tuition installment plan (FACTS Tuition Payment Plan). Need-based scholarship grants available. In 2005–06, 19% of upper-school students received aid. Total amount of financial aid awarded in 2005–06: $179,245.
Admissions Traditional secondary-level entrance grade is 9. For fall 2005, 45 students applied for upper-level admission, 38 were accepted, 30 enrolled. ERB or Stanford Achievement Test required. Deadline for receipt of application materials: none. Application fee required: $75. On-campus interview required.
Athletics Interscholastic: baseball (boys), basketball (b,g), cross-country running (b,g), diving (b,g), field hockey (g), football (b), golf (b,g), lacrosse (b,g), soccer (b,g), softball (g), swimming and diving (b,g), tennis (b,g), track and field (b,g), volleyball (g), wrestling (b); coed interscholastic: ropes courses; coed intramural: bowling, project adventure, ropes courses, weight lifting. 7 PE instructors, 47 coaches, 1 trainer.
Computers Computers are regularly used in all classes. Computer network features include campus e-mail, on-campus library services, CD-ROMs, online commercial services, Internet access, DVD, wireless campus network.
Contact Ms. Marché Harris, Director of Admission. 502-814-4375. Fax: 502-814-4381. E-mail: admissions@kcd.org. Web site: www.kcd.org.

THE KEY SCHOOL

534 Hillsmere Drive
Annapolis, Maryland 21403
Head of School: Marcella M. Yedid

petersons.com

General Information Coeducational day college-preparatory, arts, and outdoor education school. Grades PK–12. Founded: 1958. Setting: suburban. Nearest major city is Baltimore. 15-acre campus. 10 buildings on campus. Approved or accredited by Association of Independent Maryland Schools and Maryland Department of Education. Member of National Association of Independent Schools. Languages of instruction: Spanish and French. Endowment: $2.3 million. Total enrollment: 720. Upper school average class size: 14. Upper school faculty-student ratio: 1:8.

Upper School Student Profile Grade 9: 48 students (25 boys, 23 girls); Grade 10: 57 students (27 boys, 30 girls); Grade 11: 46 students (21 boys, 25 girls); Grade 12: 51 students (16 boys, 35 girls).

Faculty School total: 109. In upper school: 14 men, 21 women; 25 have advanced degrees.

Subjects Offered Acting, Advanced Placement courses, algebra, American history-AP, American studies, ancient history, art, art history, biology, biology-AP, calculus, calculus-AP, ceramics, chemistry, chemistry-AP, Chesapeake Bay studies, choir, computer science, conceptual physics, creative writing, dance, digital art, digital photography, drama, drama performance, drawing, economics, English, English literature, English literature and composition-AP, European history, fine arts, French, French language-AP, French literature-AP, French-AP, geometry, journalism, Latin, Latin-AP, literature by women, music, photography, physical education, physics-AP, physiology, playwriting, pre-calculus, printmaking, Russian literature, sculpture, Shakespeare, Spanish, Spanish language-AP, Spanish literature-AP, Spanish-AP, statistics, statistics-AP, studio art-AP, theater, theater production, trigonometry.

Graduation Requirements Arts and fine arts (art, music, dance, drama), English, foreign language, history, mathematics, performing arts, physical education (includes health), science.

Special Academic Programs Advanced Placement exam preparation in 13 subject areas; honors section; independent study; academic accommodation for the gifted.

College Placement 48 students graduated in 2005; all went to college, including Barnard College; Boston University; Lehigh University; St. Mary's College of Maryland; University of Maryland, College Park; Wheaton College.

Student Life Upper grades have student council. Discipline rests equally with students and faculty.

Summer Programs Enrichment, rigorous outdoor training programs offered; held both on and off campus; held at Appalachian Trail and Shenandoah Camping; accepts boys and girls; not open to students from other schools. 2006 schedule: June 19 to July 28. Application deadline: June.

Tuition and Aid Day student tuition: $18,985. Tuition installment plan (Academic Management Services Plan, monthly payment plans). Tuition reduction for siblings, need-based scholarship grants available. In 2005–06, 16% of upper-school students received aid. Total amount of financial aid awarded in 2005–06: $320,400.

Admissions Traditional secondary-level entrance grade is 9. For fall 2005, 57 students applied for upper-level admission, 27 were accepted, 16 enrolled. ERB or ISEE required. Deadline for receipt of application materials: none. Application fee required: $45. Interview required.

Athletics Interscholastic: basketball (boys, girls), cross-country running (b), field hockey (g), indoor soccer (g), lacrosse (b,g), soccer (b,g), winter soccer (g); intramural: field hockey (g), lacrosse (b,g); coed interscholastic: golf, sailing, tennis; coed intramural: back packing, basketball, canoeing/kayaking, dance, fitness, fitness walking, golf, hiking/backpacking, modern dance, Newcombe ball, outdoor activities, outdoor adventure, outdoor education, outdoor recreation, outdoor skills, project adventure, roller blading, running, soccer, swimming and diving, tennis, volleyball, walking. 1 PE instructor, 17 coaches, 1 trainer.

Computers Computers are regularly used in all academic classes. Computer network features include campus e-mail, on-campus library services, CD-ROMs, online commercial services, Internet access, file transfer, office computer access, DVD, online supplementary course materials.

Contact Jessie D. Dunleavy, Director of Admission, Communication and Financial Aid. 410-263-9231. Fax: 410-280-5516. E-mail: jdunleavy@keyschool.org. Web site: www.keyschool.org.

ANNOUNCEMENT FROM THE SCHOOL The Key School has a strong academic curriculum that encourages intellectual rigor, independence of thought, curiosity, creativity, and openness to different ideas and perspectives. The tone of the campus is egalitarian, informal, and caring, with an academic focus that is both rigorous and innovative. Key School seeks to develop in its students an interest in learning and a sustaining degree of intellectual curiosity.

KEY SCHOOL, INC.

Fort Worth, Texas
See Special Needs Schools section.

KEYSTONE NATIONAL HIGH SCHOOL

420 West 5th Street
Bloomsburg, Pennsylvania 17815
Head of School: Mark Burke

General Information Coeducational day college-preparatory, general academic, technology, and distance learning school. Grades 9–12. Founded: 1995. Setting: small town. Nearest major city is Harrisburg. Approved or accredited by Distance Education and Training Council, Northwest Association of Accredited Schools, and Pennsylvania Department of Education. Member of Secondary School Admission Test Board. Total enrollment: 8,700.

Faculty School total: 105. In upper school: 45 men, 60 women; 20 have advanced degrees.

Subjects Offered Algebra, alternative physical education, American government, American history, American literature, art and culture, art appreciation, biology, British literature, business law, career and personal planning, chemistry, civics, composition, computer applications, computer technologies, consumer law, contemporary math, creative writing, driver education, earth science, economics, English, English composition, English literature, environmental science, fitness, foreign language, general math, geography, government, grammar, health, health education, history, independent study, intro to computers, lab science, life skills, marketing, math review, mathematics, microcomputer technology applications, music, music appreciation, physical science, physics, pre-algebra, pre-calculus, psychology, science, skills for success, social studies, sociology, trigonometry, wellness, work experience, world arts, writing skills.

Graduation Requirements Algebra, art, electives, English, health, mathematics, science, social sciences, minimum of 5 credits for transfer students.

Special Academic Programs Honors section; accelerated programs; independent study; academic accommodation for the gifted; remedial math.

College Placement Colleges students went to include Kent State University; Temple University; Texas A&M International University; The College of William and Mary; The Pennsylvania State University University Park Campus; University of Michigan. Mean SAT verbal: 534, mean SAT math: 507, mean composite ACT: 24.

Student Life Discipline rests primarily with students.

Summer Programs Remediation, enrichment, advancement, art/fine arts, computer instruction programs offered; session focuses on credit completion ; held off campus; held at students' homes; accepts boys and girls; open to students from other schools.

Tuition and Aid Tuition installment plan (FACTS Tuition Payment Plan). Tuition reduction for siblings, need-based scholarship grants, used book program and re-use book program available.

Admissions Deadline for receipt of application materials: none. No application fee required.

Computers Computers are regularly used in all classes. Computer network features include campus e-mail, on-campus library services, Internet access.

Contact Ms. Deborah Young, Admissions Counselor. 570-784-5220 Ext. 5523. Fax: 570-784-2129. E-mail: dyoung@keystonehighschool.com. Web site: www. keystonehighschool.com.

KEYSTONE SCHOOL

119 East Craig Place
San Antonio, Texas 78212-3497
Head of School: Mr. Hugh McIntosh

petersons.com

General Information Coeducational day college-preparatory and Accelerated Curriculum school. Grades K–12. Founded: 1948. Setting: urban. 3-acre campus. 9 buildings on campus. Approved or accredited by Independent Schools Association of the Southwest. Endowment: $300,000. Total enrollment: 417. Upper school average class size: 14. Upper school faculty-student ratio: 1:10.

Upper School Student Profile Grade 9: 34 students (16 boys, 18 girls); Grade 10: 26 students (13 boys, 13 girls); Grade 11: 30 students (19 boys, 11 girls); Grade 12: 26 students (14 boys, 12 girls).

Faculty School total: 45. In upper school: 8 men, 10 women; 13 have advanced degrees.

Subjects Offered Algebra, American history, ancient history, biology, biology-AP, calculus, chemistry, chemistry-AP, community service, computer science, English, English-AP, French, French-AP, general science, geometry, government/civics, health, history, history-AP, mathematics, mythology, performing arts, physical education, physics, psychology, science, social studies, sociology, Spanish, Spanish-AP, studio art.

Graduation Requirements Arts and fine arts (art, music, dance, drama), English, foreign language, mathematics, physical education (includes health), science, social studies (includes history), 4 Advanced Placement courses. Community service is required.

Special Academic Programs Advanced Placement exam preparation in 9 subject areas; honors section; academic accommodation for the gifted.

College Placement 31 students graduated in 2005; all went to college, including Rice University; Southwestern University; Texas A&M University; Trinity University; Washington University in St. Louis; Yale University. Mean SAT verbal: 684, mean SAT math: 685. 96% scored over 600 on SAT verbal, 96% scored over 600 on SAT math.

Student Life Upper grades have specified standards of dress, student council. Discipline rests primarily with faculty.

Summer Programs Sports programs offered; session focuses on sports camps; held on campus; accepts boys and girls; open to students from other schools. 150 students usually enrolled. 2006 schedule: June 2 to July 30. Application deadline: none.

Tuition and Aid Day student tuition: $10,890–$11,445. Tuition installment plan (monthly payment plans). Need-based scholarship grants available. In 2005–06, 13% of upper-school students received aid. Total amount of financial aid awarded in 2005–06: $139,390.

Admissions Traditional secondary-level entrance grade is 9. For fall 2005, 14 students applied for upper-level admission, 11 were accepted, 10 enrolled. Admissions testing or any standardized test required. Deadline for receipt of application materials: none. Application fee required: $40. On-campus interview required.

Athletics Interscholastic: basketball (boys, girls), golf (b,g), lacrosse (b), soccer (b), softball (g), volleyball (g); coed interscholastic: cross-country running; coed intramural: outdoor education, wall climbing. 3 PE instructors, 4 coaches.

Computers Computer network features include campus e-mail, on-campus library services, CD-ROMs, online commercial services, Internet access, wireless campus network, ProQuest Platinum.

Contact Admissions Coordinator. 210-735-9627. Fax: 210-734-5508. E-mail: admissions@keystoneschool.org. Web site: www.keystoneschool.org.

ANNOUNCEMENT FROM THE SCHOOL Keystone School offers an accelerated curriculum for motivated and talented K–12 students. A diverse student body learns from qualified and experienced teachers in small classes where there is respect for individuality. Campus includes a Performing Arts Center, Gym/Activity Center, Studio Arts Building, computer and science labs, and libraries.

KILDONAN SCHOOL

Amenia, New York
See Special Needs Schools section.

KIMBALL UNION ACADEMY

PO Box 188
Main Street
Meriden, New Hampshire 03770
Head of School: Mr. Michael J. Schafer

General Information Coeducational boarding and day college-preparatory, arts, and environmental science school. Boarding grades 9–PG, day grades 9–12. Founded: 1813. Setting: small town. Nearest major city is Boston, MA. Students are housed in single-sex dormitories. 1,500-acre campus. 35 buildings on campus. Approved or accredited by Independent Schools of Northern New England, New England Association of Schools and Colleges, The Association of Boarding Schools, The College Board, and New Hampshire Department of Education. Member of National Association of Independent Schools and Secondary School Admission Test Board. Endowment: $11.5 million. Total enrollment: 311. Upper school average class size: 12. Upper school faculty-student ratio: 1:6.

Upper School Student Profile Grade 9: 58 students (37 boys, 21 girls); Grade 10: 82 students (51 boys, 31 girls); Grade 11: 77 students (39 boys, 38 girls); Grade 12: 76 students (45 boys, 31 girls); Postgraduate: 18 students (15 boys, 3 girls). 66% of students are boarding students. 30% are state residents. 25 states are represented in upper school student body. 16% are international students. International students from Bahamas, Canada, Colombia, Hong Kong, Japan, and Republic of Korea; 8 other countries represented in student body.

Faculty School total: 46. In upper school: 28 men, 18 women; 30 have advanced degrees; 35 reside on campus.

Subjects Offered Advanced Placement courses, algebra, American history, American literature, anatomy, architecture, art, art history, art history-AP, biology, biology-AP, calculus, calculus-AP, ceramics, chemistry, chemistry-AP, classical civilization, composition-AP, computer applications, computer programming, computer science, creative writing, criminal justice, dance, drama, driver education, English, English language-AP, English literature, English/composition-AP, environmental science, environmental science-AP, environmental studies, European history, expository writing, fine arts, French, French language-AP, French literature-AP, geology, geometry, government/civics, grammar, health, history, history-AP, honors English, honors geometry, independent study, jazz ensemble, Latin, marine biology, marine science, marine studies, mathematics, modern European history-AP, modern world history, music, music history, music theory, peer counseling, philosophy, photo shop, photography, physics, physics-AP, physiology, pottery, probability and statistics, programming, public speaking, science, social studies, Spanish, Spanish-AP, sports psychology, statistics-AP, student publications, studio art, theater, theater arts, trigonometry, U.S. history, U.S. history-AP, world history, world literature, writing.

Graduation Requirements Art, English, foreign language, health, history, mathematics, science.

Special Academic Programs Advanced Placement exam preparation in 15 subject areas; honors section; independent study; study at local college for college credit; academic accommodation for the gifted, the musically talented, and the artistically talented.

College Placement 101 students graduated in 2005; 99 went to college, including Bates College; St. Lawrence University; University of Vermont. Other: 2 had other specific plans. Median SAT verbal: 560, median SAT math: 550. 40% scored over 600 on SAT verbal, 35% scored over 600 on SAT math.

Student Life Upper grades have specified standards of dress, student council, honor system. Discipline rests equally with students and faculty.

Summer Programs Enrichment programs offered; session focuses on environmental leadership (via the EE Just Institute); held both on and off campus; held at Costa Rica; accepts boys and girls; open to students from other schools. 40 students usually enrolled. 2006 schedule: July 1 to July 31. Application deadline: May 1.

Tuition and Aid Day student tuition: $21,500; 7-day tuition and room/board: $33,500. Tuition installment plan (Insured Tuition Payment Plan, Academic Management Services Plan, Key Tuition Payment Plan, monthly payment plans). Need-based scholarship grants, paying campus jobs available. In 2005–06, 37% of upper-school students received aid.

Admissions Traditional secondary-level entrance grade is 9. For fall 2005, 377 students applied for upper-level admission, 254 were accepted, 123 enrolled. PSAT or SAT, SSAT or TOEFL required. Deadline for receipt of application materials: February 1. Application fee required: $35. Interview required.

Athletics Interscholastic: alpine skiing (boys, girls), baseball (b), basketball (b,g), bicycling (b,g), cross-country running (b,g), field hockey (g), fitness walking (b,g), football (b), hockey (b,g), horseback riding (b,g), ice hockey (b,g), lacrosse (b,g), modern dance (b,g), mountain biking (b,g), nordic skiing (b,g), outdoors (b,g), rugby (b), running (b,g), skiing (cross-country) (b,g), skiing (downhill) (b,g), soccer (b,g), softball (g), tennis (b,g); intramural: snowboarding (b,g), snowshoeing (b,g); coed intramural: alpine skiing, dance, fitness, golf, hiking/backpacking, modern dance, outdoor activities, physical fitness, rock climbing, skiing (downhill), snowboarding, strength & conditioning, weight lifting. 1 coach, 2 trainers.

Computers Computers are regularly used in art, English, foreign language, graphic design, history, mathematics, music, newspaper, photography, science, technology, theater arts classes. Computer network features include campus e-mail, on-campus library services, CD-ROMs, Internet access, file transfer, office computer access, DVD, wireless campus network, computer music studio/audio recording.

Contact Mrs. Rachel G. Tilney, Director of Admissions. 603-469-2101. Fax: 603-469-2041. E-mail: rtilney@kua.org. Web site: www.kua.org.

ANNOUNCEMENT FROM THE SCHOOL Founded in 1813, Kimball Union is a coeducational boarding and day school serving 310 students in grades 9–12 and a postgraduate year. Kimball Union's unique location in the Upper Connecticut River Valley and its proximity to Dartmouth College have long made it the preferred choice for students seeking an educational experience that develops the whole person as scholar, athlete, artist, and global citizen.

See full description on page 858.

KIMBERTON WALDORF SCHOOL

Box 350
Kimberton, Pennsylvania 19442
Head of School: Mrs. Paula Moraine

General Information Coeducational day college-preparatory and arts school. Grades PK–12. Founded: 1941. Setting: rural. Nearest major city is Philadelphia. 35-acre campus. 2 buildings on campus. Approved or accredited by Middle States Association of Colleges and Schools and Pennsylvania Department of Education. Member of National Association of Independent Schools. Endowment: $4.5 million. Total enrollment: 295. Upper school average class size: 25. Upper school faculty-student ratio: 1:7.

Upper School Student Profile Grade 9: 21 students (9 boys, 12 girls); Grade 10: 17 students (9 boys, 8 girls); Grade 11: 16 students (6 boys, 10 girls); Grade 12: 27 students (16 boys, 11 girls).

Faculty School total: 45. In upper school: 11 men, 14 women; 3 have advanced degrees.

Subjects Offered Algebra, American history, American literature, anatomy, architecture, art, art history, astronomy, biology, botany, calculus, ceramics, chemistry, community service, computer math, computer programming, computer science, creative writing, drama, earth science, English, English literature, environmental science, European history, expository writing, fine arts, French, gardening, geology, geometry, German, government/civics, grammar, health, history, history of ideas, history of science, mathematics, music, music history, physical education, physics, physiology, science, social studies, Spanish, speech, theater, trigonometry, typing, world history, world literature, writing, zoology.

Graduation Requirements Arts and fine arts (art, music, dance, drama), computer science, English, foreign language, mathematics, physical education (includes health), religion (includes Bible studies and theology), science, social studies (includes history). Community service is required.

Kimberton Waldorf School

Special Academic Programs Honors section; independent study; term-away projects; study abroad.

College Placement 22 students graduated in 2005; 20 went to college, including Bard College; Bates College; Kenyon College; Muhlenberg College; Oberlin College; University of Pennsylvania. Other: 2 had other specific plans. Mean SAT verbal: 612, mean SAT math: 558.

Student Life Upper grades have specified standards of dress, student council. Discipline rests primarily with faculty.

Tuition and Aid Day student tuition: $11,265. Tuition installment plan (monthly payment plans, individually arranged payment plans, biannual payment plan). Tuition reduction for siblings, need-based scholarship grants available. Total amount of financial aid awarded in 2005–06: $246,054.

Admissions Traditional secondary-level entrance grade is 9. For fall 2005, 22 students applied for upper-level admission, 8 were accepted, 8 enrolled. School's own exam required. Deadline for receipt of application materials: none. Application fee required: $35. On-campus interview required.

Athletics Interscholastic: basketball (boys, girls), field hockey (g), hiking/backpacking (b,g), lacrosse (b,g), soccer (b), tennis (b,g), volleyball (b,g); intramural: outdoor activities (b,g), outdoor adventure (b,g), outdoor education (b,g), outdoor skills (b,g), rock climbing (b,g), ropes courses (b,g); coed interscholastic: hiking/backpacking, volleyball; coed intramural: outdoor activities, outdoor adventure, outdoor education, outdoor skills, rock climbing, ropes courses. 3 PE instructors, 8 coaches.

Computers Computer resources include Internet access, office computer access.

Contact Marsha Hill, Director of Admissions. 610-933-3635 Ext. 108. Fax: 610-935-6985. E-mail: marsha@kimberton.org.

ANNOUNCEMENT FROM THE SCHOOL Kimberton Waldorf School is one of 900 Waldorf Schools worldwide. Using the arts to enliven and integrate a rigorous, balanced academic curriculum, the aim is to graduate independent thinkers with a lifelong love of learning. Foreign languages and exchanges, community service, painting, drama, sculpture, music, and gardening are part of each student's school life.

KING & LOW-HEYWOOD THOMAS SCHOOL

1450 Newfield Avenue
Stamford, Connecticut 06905
Head of School: Thomas B. Main

petersons.com

General Information Coeducational day college-preparatory school. Grades PK–12. Founded: 1988. Setting: suburban. Nearest major city is New York, NY. 40-acre campus. 4 buildings on campus. Approved or accredited by Connecticut Association of Independent Schools and New England Association of Schools and Colleges. Member of National Association of Independent Schools. Endowment: $3 million. Total enrollment: 648. Upper school average class size: 11. Upper school faculty-student ratio: 1:7.

Upper School Student Profile Grade 9: 63 students (34 boys, 29 girls); Grade 10: 66 students (35 boys, 31 girls); Grade 11: 60 students (35 boys, 25 girls); Grade 12: 61 students (29 boys, 32 girls).

Faculty School total: 105. In upper school: 18 men, 18 women; 28 have advanced degrees.

Subjects Offered Acting, advanced chemistry, advanced computer applications, advanced math, advanced studio art-AP, algebra, American history, ancient history, ancient world history, art, biology, British literature, calculus, calculus-AP, chemistry, choral music, college counseling, college placement, computer applications, computer graphics, computer multimedia, computer programming, computer programming-AP, computer science, creative writing, discrete math, dramatic arts, economics, economics-AP, English, English literature, English literature-AP, ethics, ethics and responsibility, European history, European history-AP, expository writing, fine arts, French, French language-AP, general science, geometry, health, history, Holocaust, honors algebra, honors English, honors geometry, honors U.S. history, honors world history, independent study, introduction to theater, macroeconomics-AP, mathematics, mathematics-AP, microeconomics-AP, model United Nations, modern European history-AP, modern languages, musical productions, musical theater, performing arts, philosophy, physics, physics-AP, play production, pre-calculus, SAT preparation, science, social studies, Spanish, Spanish literature, Spanish literature-AP, statistics, statistics-AP, student government, student publications, studio art, studio art-AP, theater arts, trigonometry, U.S. history-AP, U.S. literature, world history, writing workshop.

Graduation Requirements Arts and fine arts (art, music, dance, drama), English, ethics, foreign language, history, life skills, mathematics, science, sports.

Special Academic Programs Advanced Placement exam preparation in 17 subject areas; honors section; independent study.

College Placement 65 students graduated in 2005; all went to college, including Boston University; Bucknell University; Cornell University; Franklin and Marshall College; Georgetown University; University of Virginia. Mean SAT verbal: 615, mean SAT math: 624.

Student Life Upper grades have specified standards of dress, student council. Discipline rests equally with students and faculty.

Summer Programs Remediation, enrichment programs offered; session focuses on academics (grades 6-12); enrichment (elementary school); and sports (middle school); held on campus; accepts boys and girls; open to students from other schools. 135 students usually enrolled. 2006 schedule: June 19 to August 4. Application deadline: June 7.

Tuition and Aid Day student tuition: $24,600. Tuition installment plan (Key Tuition Payment Plan). Merit scholarship grants, need-based scholarship grants available. In 2005–06, 15% of upper-school students received aid; total upper-school merit-scholarship money awarded: $36,309. Total amount of financial aid awarded in 2005–06: $496,030.

Admissions Traditional secondary-level entrance grade is 9. For fall 2005, 141 students applied for upper-level admission, 90 were accepted, 34 enrolled. ISEE, school's own test or SSAT required. Deadline for receipt of application materials: February 1. Application fee required: $75. On-campus interview required.

Athletics Interscholastic: baseball (boys), basketball (b,g), cheering (g), cross-country running (b,g), field hockey (g), football (b), golf (b,g), ice hockey (b), independent competitive sports (b,g), lacrosse (b,g), soccer (b,g), softball (g), tennis (b,g), volleyball (g); intramural: dance (g), physical training (b,g); coed interscholastic: cheering, ice hockey, independent competitive sports; coed intramural: aerobics, dance, fitness, physical training, strength & conditioning, weight lifting, weight training, yoga. 13 coaches, 1 trainer.

Computers Computers are regularly used in college planning, creative writing, economics, English, ethics, foreign language, French, history, mathematics, science, technology, writing fundamentals, yearbook classes. Computer network features include campus e-mail, on-campus library services, CD-ROMs, online commercial services, Internet access, file transfer.

Contact Catherine J. Seton, Director of Admission. 203-322-3496 Ext. 347. Fax: 203-461-9988. E-mail: cseton@klht.org. Web site: www.klht.org.

ANNOUNCEMENT FROM THE SCHOOL King & Low-Heywood Thomas School (KLHT) offers a comprehensive college-preparatory program that is responsive to the individual talents and needs of students and their changing environment. The School, which serves students from prekindergarten through grade 12, is noted for high academic standards and individual accountability in scholarship and leadership. KLHT students are consistently recognized for their educational achievements. More than 50% of the Middle School qualifies annually for the Johns Hopkins Talent Search, and many graduating classes have had National Merit Finalists. Honors and Advanced Placement courses are offered in all departments. Academics are balanced with full participation in athletics and a wide variety of clubs and organizations; opportunities for expression in the literary, performing, and visual arts abound. This balance is the framework for the development of the total child. KLHT recognizes and rewards students' efforts to attain their full potential. The School's diverse community focuses on respect for the individual and high standards of conduct and behavior for everyone. College counseling includes full-time professionals, a resource library, and workshops and classes. More than 60 college representatives visit students on campus each year. Prekindergarten and kindergarten are taught by early childhood professionals in a comprehensive learning environment that emphasizes learning readiness within a developmental curriculum. The 5-day program has full- and half-day options. KLHT represents a merger of 3 schools, the oldest of which dates from 1865. Located on 36 acres in North Stamford, KLHT draws from Fairfield and Westchester Counties. Scholarships and financial aid are available. Thomas B. Main (B.A., Bates College; M.A., Wesleyan University) is Head of School. The School is accredited by the New England Association of Schools and Colleges (NEASC).

KING DAVID HIGH SCHOOL

5718 Willow Street
Vancouver, British Columbia V5Z 4S9, Canada
Head of School: Mr. Perry Seidelman

General Information Coeducational day college-preparatory, general academic, arts, business, religious studies, bilingual studies, and technology school, affiliated with Jewish faith. Grades 8–12. Founded: 1986. 2-acre campus. 1 building on campus. Approved or accredited by British Columbia Department of Education. Languages of instruction: English and Hebrew. Total enrollment: 150. Upper school average class size: 18.

Upper School Student Profile Grade 8: 43 students (21 boys, 22 girls); Grade 9: 29 students (11 boys, 18 girls); Grade 10: 32 students (19 boys, 13 girls); Grade 11: 19 students (7 boys, 12 girls); Grade 12: 28 students (13 boys, 15 girls). 100% of students are Jewish.

Faculty School total: 20. In upper school: 8 men, 1 woman.

Special Academic Programs Advanced Placement exam preparation in 3 subject areas; special instructional classes for deaf students.

College Placement 8 students graduated in 2005; 2 went to college, including Austin College. Other: 6 entered a postgraduate year.

Student Life Upper grades have uniform requirement, student council, honor system. Discipline rests primarily with faculty.

Admissions Traditional secondary-level entrance grade is 8. For fall 2005, 36 students applied for upper-level admission, 36 were accepted, 36 enrolled. Deadline for receipt of application materials: none. Application fee required: CAN$1000. On-campus interview recommended.

Athletics Interscholastic: basketball (girls), physical fitness (b,g), soccer (b), track and field (b,g), volleyball (g); coed interscholastic: independent competitive sports. 1 PE instructor.

Computers Computer network features include campus e-mail, on-campus library services, CD-ROMs, Internet access, DVD.

Contact Mr. Perry Seidelman, Principal. 604-263-9700 Ext. 100. Fax: 604-263-4848. E-mail: ghardcastle@kdhs.org. Web site: www.kdhs.org.

THE KING'S ACADEMY

202 Smothers Road
Seymour, Tennessee 37865
Head of School: Walter Grubb

General Information Coeducational boarding and day college-preparatory and religious studies school, affiliated with Baptist Church. Boarding grades 7–12, day grades K–12. Founded: 1880. Setting: suburban. Nearest major city is Knoxville. Students are housed in single-sex dormitories. 67-acre campus. 8 buildings on campus. Approved or accredited by Southern Association of Colleges and Schools and Tennessee Department of Education. Endowment: $1.9 million. Total enrollment: 369. Upper school average class size: 21. Upper school faculty-student ratio: 1:20.

Upper School Student Profile Grade 9: 31 students (16 boys, 15 girls); Grade 10: 44 students (27 boys, 17 girls); Grade 11: 35 students (17 boys, 18 girls); Grade 12: 31 students (16 boys, 15 girls). 34% of students are boarding students. 68% are state residents. 2 states are represented in upper school student body. 32% are international students. International students from Cote d'Ivoire, Ecuador, Hong Kong, Republic of Korea, Taiwan, and United Kingdom; 5 other countries represented in student body. 80% of students are Baptist.

Faculty School total: 35. In upper school: 8 men, 10 women; 7 have advanced degrees; 4 reside on campus.

Subjects Offered Advanced Placement courses, algebra, American history, anatomy, art, Bible studies, biology, calculus, chemistry, choir, computer science, drama, economics, English, English-AP, ESL, fine arts, geometry, government/civics, grammar, health, history, journalism, keyboarding, mathematics, music, orchestra, physical education, physics, physiology, religion, science, social studies, Spanish, world history.

Graduation Requirements Arts and fine arts (art, music, dance, drama), computer science, English, foreign language, mathematics, physical education (includes health), religion (includes Bible studies and theology), science, social studies (includes history).

Special Academic Programs Advanced Placement exam preparation in 3 subject areas; honors section; independent study; ESL (13 students enrolled).

College Placement 28 students graduated in 2005; 25 went to college, including The University of Tennessee. Other: 2 went to work, 1 entered military service. Mean SAT verbal: 550, mean SAT math: 600, mean composite ACT: 22. 1% scored over 600 on SAT verbal, 3% scored over 600 on SAT math, 30% scored over 26 on composite ACT.

Student Life Upper grades have uniform requirement, student council. Discipline rests primarily with faculty. Attendance at religious services is required.

Summer Programs ESL programs offered; session focuses on ESL; held on campus; accepts boys and girls; open to students from other schools. 10 students usually enrolled. 2006 schedule: July to August. Application deadline: none.

Tuition and Aid Day student tuition: $5100; 5-day tuition and room/board: $10,715; 7-day tuition and room/board: $13,990. Tuition installment plan (monthly payment plans, individually arranged payment plans). Need-based scholarship grants, paying campus jobs available. In 2005–06, 6% of upper-school students received aid. Total amount of financial aid awarded in 2005–06: $45,856.

Admissions Traditional secondary-level entrance grade is 10. For fall 2005, 24 students applied for upper-level admission, 24 were accepted, 24 enrolled. Otis-Lennon School Ability Test required. Deadline for receipt of application materials: none. Application fee required: $35. Interview recommended.

Athletics Interscholastic: baseball (boys), basketball (b,g), cheering (g), flagball (b), football (b), golf (b,g), soccer (b,g), softball (g), tennis (b,g), volleyball (g), weight lifting (b), weight training (b), wrestling (b); intramural: basketball (b,g), billiards (b,g), table tennis (b,g), tennis (b,g), volleyball (g), weight lifting (b,g); coed interscholastic: back packing, bowling, canoeing/kayaking, rappelling, rock climbing, strength & conditioning, track and field; coed intramural: cross-country running, outdoor education, physical fitness, volleyball. 4 coaches.

Computers Computers are regularly used in ESL, journalism, keyboarding classes. Computer network features include campus e-mail, CD-ROMs, Internet access.

Contact Janice Mink, Director of Admissions. 865-573-8321. Fax: 865-573-8323. E-mail: jmink@thekingsacademy.net.

THE KING'S CHRISTIAN HIGH SCHOOL

5 Carnegie Plaza
Cherry Hill, New Jersey 08003-1020
Head of School: Rebecca B. Stiegel, EdD

General Information Coeducational day college-preparatory, general academic, and religious studies school, affiliated with Christian faith. Grades PK–12. Founded: 1946. Setting: suburban. Nearest major city is Philadelphia, PA. 10-acre campus. 1 building on campus. Approved or accredited by Association of Christian Schools International. Total enrollment: 428. Upper school average class size: 22. Upper school faculty-student ratio: 1:18.

Upper School Student Profile 100% of students are Christian faith.

Faculty School total: 39. In upper school: 8 men, 30 women; 8 have advanced degrees.

Special Academic Programs Advanced Placement exam preparation in 3 subject areas; honors section; independent study; programs in English, mathematics, general development for dyslexic students; special instructional classes for students with learning disabilities, Attention Deficit Disorder.

College Placement 34 students graduated in 2005; 32 went to college, including Cedarville University. Other: 1 went to work, 1 entered military service. Mean SAT verbal: 536, mean SAT math: 488, mean composite ACT: 25. 16% scored over 600 on SAT verbal, 23% scored over 600 on SAT math, 43% scored over 26 on composite ACT.

Student Life Upper grades have uniform requirement, student council, honor system. Discipline rests primarily with faculty. Attendance at religious services is required.

Tuition and Aid Guaranteed tuition plan. Tuition installment plan (FACTS Tuition Payment Plan). Need-based scholarship grants available. In 2005–06, 23% of upper-school students received aid. Total amount of financial aid awarded in 2005–06: $100,000.

Admissions Traditional secondary-level entrance grade is 9. For fall 2005, 17 students applied for upper-level admission, 17 were accepted, 17 enrolled. Any standardized test required. Deadline for receipt of application materials: none. Application fee required: $75. On-campus interview required.

Athletics Interscholastic: baseball (boys), basketball (b,g), cheering (g), flag football (b), physical fitness (b,g), soccer (b,g), track and field (b,g); intramural: basketball (g), flag football (b), golf (b,g). 2 PE instructors.

Computers Computers are regularly used in all academic classes. Computer resources include on-campus library services, CD-ROMs, Internet access.

Contact Kathleen Trowbridge, Recruitment Director. 856-489-6724. Fax: 856-489-6727. E-mail: ktrowbridge@tkcs.org. Web site: www.tkcs.org.

KINGS CHRISTIAN SCHOOL

900 East D Street
Lemoore, California 93245
Head of School: Mr. Duane E. Daniel

General Information Coeducational day college-preparatory, general academic, arts, religious studies, and technology school. Grades PK–12. Founded: 1979. Setting: small town. Nearest major city is Fresno. 17-acre campus. 10 buildings on campus. Approved or accredited by Association of Christian Schools International and Western Association of Schools and Colleges. Total enrollment: 327. Upper school average class size: 20. Upper school faculty-student ratio: 1:15.

Upper School Student Profile Grade 9: 25 students (12 boys, 13 girls); Grade 10: 35 students (16 boys, 19 girls); Grade 11: 31 students (17 boys, 14 girls); Grade 12: 32 students (13 boys, 19 girls).

Faculty School total: 30. In upper school: 6 men, 7 women; 3 have advanced degrees.

Subjects Offered Accounting, advanced math, algebra, American government, art, Bible studies, biology, business, business law, calculus-AP, career education, chemistry, choir, chorus, community service, computer literacy, computer programming, drama, drama performance, drawing, driver education, economics, English, finance, fine arts, geography, geometry, health, keyboarding, life skills, literature, mathematics, music, music theory, novels, physical education, physical science, physics, pre-algebra, religion, SAT preparation, science, Shakespeare, social science, social studies, Spanish, speech, U.S. history, weight training, word processing, yearbook.

Graduation Requirements Arts and fine arts (art, music, dance, drama), English, foreign language, mathematics, physical education (includes health), science, social science, successfully pass Bible every year of attendance, proof of at least 9th grade proficiency (SAT Test). Community service is required.

Special Academic Programs Advanced Placement exam preparation in 2 subject areas; honors section; accelerated programs; independent study; remedial reading and/or remedial writing; remedial math.

College Placement 32 students graduated in 2005; 26 went to college, including Biola University; California State University, Fresno; The Master's College and Seminary; Vanguard University of Southern California; West Hills Community College. Other: 6 went to work. Median SAT verbal: 490, median SAT math: 465. 14% scored over 600 on SAT verbal, 10% scored over 600 on SAT math.

Student Life Upper grades have specified standards of dress, student council. Discipline rests primarily with faculty.

Kings Christian School

Summer Programs Advancement programs offered; session focuses on advanced math in preparation for calculus; held on campus; accepts boys and girls; not open to students from other schools. 8 students usually enrolled. 2006 schedule: June 12 to June 23. Application deadline: May 19.

Tuition and Aid Day student tuition: $4414. Tuition installment plan (monthly payment plans). Tuition reduction for siblings, need-based scholarship grants, paying campus jobs available. In 2005–06, 18% of upper-school students received aid. Total amount of financial aid awarded in 2005–06: $10,000.

Admissions Traditional secondary-level entrance grade is 9. For fall 2005, 12 students applied for upper-level admission, 7 were accepted, 6 enrolled. PSAT or Stanford Achievement Test required. Deadline for receipt of application materials: none. Application fee required: $50.

Athletics Interscholastic: baseball (boys), basketball (b,g), football (b), golf (b,g), softball (g), track and field (b,g), volleyball (g); intramural: physical fitness (b,g), physical training (b,g), power lifting (b), strength & conditioning (b,g), track and field (b,g), weight training (b,g); coed interscholastic: cheering, cross-country running, track and field; coed intramural: fitness, Frisbee, physical fitness, strength & conditioning, table tennis, track and field. 5 PE instructors, 9 coaches, 2 trainers.

Computers Computers are regularly used in Bible studies, college planning, English, introduction to technology, journalism, library skills, SAT preparation, technical drawing, yearbook classes. Computer network features include campus e-mail, on-campus library services, CD-ROMs, Internet access, file transfer, DVD, wireless campus network.

Contact Leslie Reynolds, Registrar. 559-924-8301 Ext. 107. Fax: 559-924-0607. E-mail: lreynolds@kcsnet.com. Web site: www.kcsnet.com.

KING'S COLLEGE SCHOOL

16379 The Gore Road
Caledon, Ontario L7E 0X4, Canada
Head of School: Mrs. Barbara H. Lord

General Information Coeducational day college-preparatory school. Grades 3–12. Founded: 1994. Setting: rural. Nearest major city is Toronto, Canada. 8-acre campus. 1 building on campus. Approved or accredited by Ontario Department of Education. Language of instruction: English. Total enrollment: 26. Upper school faculty-student ratio: 1:6.

Upper School Student Profile Grade 9: 6 students (6 girls); Grade 10: 6 students (4 boys, 2 girls); Grade 11: 6 students (2 boys, 4 girls); Grade 12: 5 students (1 boy, 4 girls).

Faculty School total: 6. In upper school: 2 men, 2 women; 1 has an advanced degree.

Subjects Offered Algebra, anthropology, band, biology, calculus, Canadian geography, Canadian history, careers, chemistry, civics, discrete math, English, English literature, finite math, French as a second language, geometry, health education, instrumental music, kinesiology, law, mathematics, physical education, physics, psychology, science, sociology, world history.

Graduation Requirements Arts, careers, civics, electives, English, French as a second language, geography, history, mathematics, physical education (includes health), science, social sciences.

Special Academic Programs Accelerated programs; independent study; academic accommodation for the gifted.

College Placement 6 students graduated in 2005; 5 went to college, including Brock University; McGill University; McMaster University; University of Guelph; University of Toronto. Other: 1 had other specific plans.

Student Life Upper grades have uniform requirement, honor system. Discipline rests primarily with faculty.

Tuition and Aid Day student tuition: CAN$13,500. Tuition installment plan (monthly payment plans, individually arranged payment plans).

Admissions Traditional secondary-level entrance grade is 9. For fall 2005, 8 students applied for upper-level admission, 8 were accepted, 8 enrolled. Achievement/ Aptitude/Writing and admissions testing required. Deadline for receipt of application materials: none. Application fee required: CAN$1000. On-campus interview required.

Athletics Coed Interscholastic: alpine skiing, badminton, baseball, basketball, canoeing/kayaking, climbing, equestrian sports, flag football, golf, hiking/ backpacking, horseback riding, outdoor activities, outdoor education, physical fitness, rock climbing, ropes courses, skiing (cross-country), skiing (downhill), snowboarding, snowshoeing, soccer, swimming and diving, volleyball; coed intramural: alpine skiing, back packing, baseball, basketball, canoeing/kayaking, climbing, cooperative games, equestrian sports, flag football, Frisbee, golf, hiking/backpacking, horseback riding, life saving, outdoor education, outdoor skills, outdoors, physical fitness, rafting, rock climbing, ropes courses, skiing (downhill), snowboarding, soccer, softball, swimming and diving, volleyball, walking, wilderness survival, winter soccer, winter walking. 1 PE instructor.

Computers Computers are regularly used in English classes. Computer resources include CD-ROMs.

Contact Mr. John A. Eta, Managing Director. 905-880-7645. Fax: 905-880-9439. Web site: www.kingscollegeschool.ca.

KINGSHILL SCHOOL

St. Croix, Virgin Islands
See Special Needs Schools section.

KINGSWAY COLLEGE

1200 Leland Road
Oshawa, Ontario L1K 2H4, Canada
Head of School: Mr. John Janes

General Information Coeducational boarding and day college-preparatory, general academic, and religious studies school, affiliated with Seventh-day Adventists. Grades 9–12. Founded: 1903. Setting: small town. Nearest major city is Toronto, Canada. Students are housed in single-sex dormitories. 100-acre campus. 9 buildings on campus. Approved or accredited by Ontario Ministry of Education and Ontario Department of Education. Language of instruction: English. Total enrollment: 182. Upper school average class size: 25. Upper school faculty-student ratio: 1:12.

Upper School Student Profile Grade 9: 45 students (31 boys, 14 girls); Grade 10: 44 students (20 boys, 24 girls); Grade 11: 47 students (28 boys, 19 girls); Grade 12: 46 students (26 boys, 20 girls). 48% of students are boarding students. 78% are province residents. 8 provinces are represented in upper school student body. 12% are international students. International students from Hong Kong and United States; 5 other countries represented in student body. 80% of students are Seventh-day Adventists.

Faculty School total: 16. In upper school: 9 men, 7 women; 4 have advanced degrees; 12 reside on campus.

Subjects Offered Accounting, advanced chemistry, advanced computer applications, advanced math, algebra, American history, anthropology, band, biology, business mathematics, business studies, calculus, Canadian geography, Canadian history, Canadian law, career education, ceramics, chemistry, choir, civics, computer applications, computer information systems, computer programming, computer studies, concert band, dramatic arts, English, English literature, ESL, French, healthful living, information processing, intro to computers, music, music performance, physical education, physics, psychology, religious education, science, sociology, U.S. history, visual arts, work-study, world civilizations, world religions.

Special Academic Programs ESL (3 students enrolled).

College Placement 34 students graduated in 2005; 31 went to college, including Andrews University; La Sierra University; Southern Adventist University; University of Toronto; University of Waterloo; Walla Walla College. Other: 3 went to work. 17% scored over 26 on composite ACT.

Student Life Upper grades have specified standards of dress, student council. Discipline rests equally with students and faculty. Attendance at religious services is required.

Tuition and Aid Day student tuition: CAN$8400; 7-day tuition and room/board: CAN$13,700. Tuition installment plan (monthly payment plans, individually arranged payment plans). Tuition reduction for siblings, paying campus jobs available. In 2005–06, 32% of upper-school students received aid.

Admissions Traditional secondary-level entrance grade is 9. For fall 2005, 200 students applied for upper-level admission, 190 were accepted, 175 enrolled. Deadline for receipt of application materials: none. No application fee required. Interview required.

Athletics Intramural: ball hockey (boys, girls), basketball (b,g), flag football (b,g), indoor hockey (b,g), soccer (b,g), softball (b,g); coed intramural: back packing, badminton, canoeing/kayaking, gymnastics, hiking/backpacking, outdoor education, volleyball. 1 PE instructor.

Computers Computers are regularly used in accounting, business, career education, data processing, English, ESL, science, social sciences classes. Computer network features include campus e-mail, CD-ROMs, Internet access, file transfer, DVD.

Contact Mr. Greg Bussey, Director of Enrolment Services. 905-433-1144 Ext. 212. Fax: 905-433-1156. E-mail: busseyg@kingswaycollege.on.ca. Web site: www.kingswaycollege.on.ca.

KING'S WEST SCHOOL

4012 Chico Way NW
Bremerton, Washington 98312-1397
Head of School: Mr. Nick Sweeney

General Information Coeducational day college-preparatory, arts, religious studies, and technology school, affiliated with Christian faith. Grades K–12. Founded: 1991. Setting: small town. Nearest major city is Tacoma. 8-acre campus. 7 buildings on campus. Approved or accredited by Northwest Association of Accredited Schools and Washington Department of Education. Total enrollment: 352. Upper school average class size: 17. Upper school faculty-student ratio: 1:11.

Upper School Student Profile Grade 7: 39 students (21 boys, 18 girls); Grade 8: 30 students (11 boys, 19 girls); Grade 9: 43 students (23 boys, 20 girls); Grade 10: 35 students (19 boys, 16 girls); Grade 11: 28 students (10 boys, 18 girls); Grade 12: 42 students (17 boys, 25 girls). 70% of students are Christian faith.

Faculty School total: 20. In upper school: 9 men, 11 women; 12 have advanced degrees.

Subjects Offered Advanced Placement courses, algebra, American history, American literature, art, band, Bible studies, biology, calculus, chemistry, chorus, creative writing, desktop publishing, drama, earth science, English, English literature, ensembles, European literature, fine arts, geography, geometry, government/civics, health, history, keyboarding, leadership training, life science, mathematics, music, physical education, physical science, physics, practical living, religion, science, Spanish, speech, theater, weight training, world history, yearbook.

Graduation Requirements Arts and fine arts (art, music, dance, drama), Bible, computer science, current events, English, foreign language, history, mathematics, physical education (includes health), practical living, science, speech.

Special Academic Programs Advanced Placement exam preparation in 4 subject areas; academic accommodation for the musically talented and the artistically talented.

College Placement 32 students graduated in 2005; 31 went to college, including Central Washington University; George Fox University; Olympic College; Seattle Pacific University; University of Idaho; University of Washington. Other: 1 had other specific plans. Mean SAT verbal: 584, mean SAT math: 570, mean composite ACT: 25. 48% scored over 600 on SAT verbal, 48% scored over 600 on SAT math, 20% scored over 26 on composite ACT.

Student Life Upper grades have specified standards of dress, student council, honor system. Discipline rests primarily with faculty. Attendance at religious services is required.

Tuition and Aid Day student tuition: $7915. Tuition installment plan (monthly payment plans, prepayment discount plan). Tuition reduction for siblings, need-based scholarship grants available. In 2005–06, 66% of upper-school students received aid.

Admissions Traditional secondary-level entrance grade is 9. For fall 2005, 47 students applied for upper-level admission, 45 were accepted, 42 enrolled. Any standardized test or placement test required. Deadline for receipt of application materials: none. Application fee required: $50. Interview required.

Athletics Interscholastic: basketball (boys, girls), cross-country running (b,g), golf (b), soccer (b,g), softball (g), track and field (b,g), volleyball (g). 2 PE instructors, 20 coaches.

Computers Computers are regularly used in English, foreign language, mathematics, photography, publications, science, technology, Web site design, yearbook classes. Computer network features include CD-ROMs, Internet access.

Contact Mrs. Karin Quinn, Admissions Coordinator. 360-377-7700 Ext. 5011. Fax: 360-377-7795. E-mail: kquinn@crista.net. Web site: www.kingswest.org.

KINGSWOOD-OXFORD SCHOOL

170 Kingswood Road
West Hartford, Connecticut 06119-1496
Head of School: Lee M. Levison

General Information Coeducational day college-preparatory school. Grades 6–12. Founded: 1909. Setting: suburban. Nearest major city is Hartford. 30-acre campus. 10 buildings on campus. Approved or accredited by Connecticut Association of Independent Schools, New England Association of Schools and Colleges, and Connecticut Department of Education. Member of National Association of Independent Schools and Secondary School Admission Test Board. Endowment: $19.4 million. Total enrollment: 595. Upper school average class size: 13. Upper school faculty-student ratio: 1:8.

Upper School Student Profile Grade 9: 102 students (43 boys, 59 girls); Grade 10: 100 students (57 boys, 43 girls); Grade 11: 96 students (55 boys, 41 girls); Grade 12: 95 students (38 boys, 57 girls).

Faculty School total: 93. In upper school: 32 men, 29 women; 43 have advanced degrees.

Subjects Offered Algebra, American history, American literature, anatomy, art, art history, band, biology, calculus, chemistry, chorus, computer programming, computer science, computer science-AP, creative writing, economics, English, English literature, environmental science, fine arts, French, geography, geometry, government/civics, journalism, Latin, marine biology, mathematics, music, orchestra, photography, physics, physiology, political science, public speaking, social studies, Spanish, statistics, theater, trigonometry, world history, world literature, writing.

Graduation Requirements Computer science, English, foreign language, mathematics, performing arts, science, social studies (includes history), visual arts, participation on athletic teams, senior thesis in English. Community service is required.

Special Academic Programs Advanced Placement exam preparation in 16 subject areas; independent study; term-away projects; study at local college for college credit; study abroad.

College Placement 88 students graduated in 2005; 86 went to college, including Boston University; Colgate University; Roger Williams University; Syracuse University; The George Washington University; Wheaton College. Other: 1 entered a postgraduate year, 1 had other specific plans. Median SAT verbal: 620, median SAT math: 600. 61% scored over 600 on SAT verbal, 55% scored over 600 on SAT math.

Student Life Upper grades have specified standards of dress, student council, honor system. Discipline rests equally with students and faculty.

Tuition and Aid Day student tuition: $25,145. Tuition installment plan (Academic Management Services Plan). Need-based scholarship grants available. In 2005–06, 32% of upper-school students received aid. Total amount of financial aid awarded in 2005–06: $1,668,175.

Admissions Traditional secondary-level entrance grade is 9. For fall 2005, 293 students applied for upper-level admission, 135 were accepted, 51 enrolled. SSAT required. Deadline for receipt of application materials: February 1. Application fee required: $50. On-campus interview required.

Athletics Interscholastic: baseball (boys), basketball (b,g), cross-country running (b,g), diving (b,g), field hockey (g), football (b), gymnastics (g), ice hockey (b,g), lacrosse (b,g), soccer (b,g), softball (g), squash (b,g), swimming and diving (b,g), tennis (b,g), track and field (b,g); intramural: basketball (b), soccer (b); coed interscholastic: golf, skiing (downhill); coed intramural: dance, strength & conditioning. 5 coaches, 2 trainers.

Computers Computers are regularly used in English, foreign language, history, mathematics, photography, science classes. Computer resources include campus e-mail, on-campus library services, CD-ROMs, Internet access, wireless campus network.

Contact James J. Skiff, Director of Enrollment and External Affairs. 860-233-9631 Ext. 2272. Fax: 860-236-3651. E-mail: skiff.j@k-o.org. Web site: www.kingswood-oxford.com.

See full description on page 860.

THE KINKAID SCHOOL

201 Kinkaid School Drive
Houston, Texas 77024
Head of School: Donald C. North

General Information Coeducational day college-preparatory and arts school. Grades PK–12. Founded: 1906. Setting: suburban. 40-acre campus. 5 buildings on campus. Approved or accredited by Independent Schools Association of the Southwest, The College Board, and Texas Department of Education. Member of National Association of Independent Schools. Endowment: $63.1 million. Total enrollment: 1,353. Upper school average class size: 14. Upper school faculty-student ratio: 1:7.

Upper School Student Profile Grade 9: 137 students (68 boys, 69 girls); Grade 10: 131 students (66 boys, 65 girls); Grade 11: 123 students (64 boys, 59 girls); Grade 12: 141 students (71 boys, 70 girls).

Faculty School total: 160. In upper school: 35 men, 39 women; 45 have advanced degrees.

Subjects Offered Acting, algebra, American literature, anatomy and physiology, ancient history, anthropology, architecture, art, astronomy, band, biology, biology-AP, calculus, calculus-AP, ceramics, chemistry, chemistry-AP, choir, computer applications, computer programming, computer science-AP, computer studies, creative writing, dance, debate, drama, drawing, economics, English, English-AP, environmental science, ethics, film studies, finance, fine arts, French, French language-AP, French literature-AP, French-AP, geography, geometry, health, history, instrumental music, international relations, journalism, Latin, Latin-AP, mathematics, media, medieval history, Middle East, modern European history-AP, music, music history, music theory-AP, newspaper, orchestra, painting, philosophy, photography, physical education, physics, physics-AP, pre-calculus, printmaking, psychology, science, science research, sculpture, social studies, Spanish, Spanish language-AP, Spanish literature-AP, speech, sports, statistics, statistics-AP, studio art-AP, technical theater, theater, trigonometry, U.S. government, U.S. history, U.S. history-AP, world civilizations, world religions, yearbook.

Graduation Requirements Arts and fine arts (art, music, dance, drama), English, foreign language, mathematics, physical education (includes health), science, social studies (includes history), school service.

Special Academic Programs Advanced Placement exam preparation in 20 subject areas; honors section; independent study; term-away projects; study abroad; academic accommodation for the gifted.

College Placement 115 students graduated in 2005; all went to college, including Princeton University; Rhodes College; Rice University; Southern Methodist University; The University of Texas at Austin; Vanderbilt University. Median SAT verbal: 670, median SAT math: 665. Mean composite ACT: 27. 76% scored over 600 on SAT verbal, 91% scored over 600 on SAT math, 61% scored over 26 on composite ACT.

Student Life Upper grades have specified standards of dress, student council, honor system. Discipline rests primarily with faculty.

Summer Programs Enrichment, advancement, ESL, sports, art/fine arts, computer instruction programs offered; session focuses on arts, academics, and athletics enrichment; held on campus; accepts boys and girls; open to students from other schools. 650 students usually enrolled. 2006 schedule: June 9 to July 11. Application deadline: June 1.

Tuition and Aid Day student tuition: $14,615. Tuition installment plan (monthly payment plans). Merit scholarship grants, need-based scholarship grants available. In 2005–06, 11% of upper-school students received aid; total upper-school merit-scholarship money awarded: $23,850. Total amount of financial aid awarded in 2005–06: $486,815.

Admissions Traditional secondary-level entrance grade is 9. For fall 2005, 214 students applied for upper-level admission, 81 were accepted, 47 enrolled. ISEE and Otis-Lennon School Ability Test required. Deadline for receipt of application materials: December 9. Application fee required: $85. On-campus interview required.

The Kinkaid School

Athletics Interscholastic: baseball (boys), basketball (b,g), cross-country running (b,g), field hockey (g), football (b), golf (b,g), lacrosse (b,g), soccer (b,g), softball (g), swimming and diving (b,g), tennis (b,g), track and field (b,g), volleyball (b,g), wrestling (b); coed interscholastic: cheering. 15 PE instructors, 25 coaches, 2 trainers.

Computers Computers are regularly used in creative writing, English, journalism, literary magazine, mathematics, newspaper, photography, publications, science, Web site design, word processing, writing, writing, yearbook classes. Computer network features include campus e-mail, on-campus library services, CD-ROMs, online commercial services, Internet access, file transfer.

Contact Bettie Hankamer, Director of Admissions. 713-782-1640. Fax: 713-782-3543. E-mail: bettie.hankamer@kinkaid.org. Web site: www.kinkaid.org.

THE KISKI SCHOOL

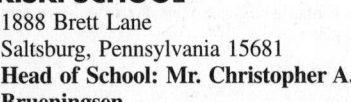 

1888 Brett Lane
Saltsburg, Pennsylvania 15681
Head of School: Mr. Christopher A. Brueningsen

General Information Boys' boarding and day college-preparatory and liberal arts and sciences school. Boarding grades 9–PG, day grades 9–11. Founded: 1888. Setting: rural. Nearest major city is Pittsburgh. Students are housed in single-sex dormitories. 365-acre campus. 42 buildings on campus. Approved or accredited by Middle States Association of Colleges and Schools, Pennsylvania Association of Private Academic Schools, The Association of Boarding Schools, and Pennsylvania Department of Education. Member of National Association of Independent Schools and Secondary School Admission Test Board. Endowment: $10 million. Total enrollment: 201. Upper school average class size: 8. Upper school faculty-student ratio: 1:5.

Upper School Student Profile Grade 9: 25 students (25 boys); Grade 10: 56 students (56 boys); Grade 11: 57 students (57 boys); Grade 12: 57 students (57 boys); Postgraduate: 6 students (6 boys). 95% of students are boarding students. 45% are state residents. 16 states are represented in upper school student body. 35% are international students. International students from Germany, Jamaica, Mexico, Republic of Korea, Spain, and Taiwan; 9 other countries represented in student body.

Faculty School total: 42. In upper school: 34 men, 8 women; 18 have advanced degrees; 38 reside on campus.

Subjects Offered Advanced chemistry, advanced math, algebra, American history-AP, analytic geometry, art, art history, biology, calculus, calculus-AP, ceramics, chemistry, chorus, computer programming, computer science, drama, drama performance, earth science, economics and history, English, English language-AP, English literature, ESL, European history, European history-AP, fine arts, foreign policy, French, French literature-AP, French-AP, geology, geometry, health, history, introduction to theater, music, organic chemistry, physics, physics-AP, political thought, pre-calculus, probability and statistics, psychology, SAT/ACT preparation, senior project, Spanish, speech and debate, The 20th Century, theater arts, theater production, trigonometry, U.S. history, U.S. history-AP, U.S. literature, wellness, world history, writing.

Graduation Requirements Arts and fine arts (art, music, dance, drama), English, ethics, foreign language, lab science, mathematics, personal development, physical education (includes health), social studies (includes history), senior research paper.

Special Academic Programs Advanced Placement exam preparation in 14 subject areas; honors section; academic accommodation for the gifted; ESL (9 students enrolled).

College Placement 53 students graduated in 2005; all went to college, including Carnegie Mellon University; Dartmouth College; Duquesne University; The Johns Hopkins University; The Pennsylvania State University University Park Campus; United States Naval Academy. Mean SAT verbal: 540, mean SAT math: 580.

Student Life Upper grades have specified standards of dress, student council, honor system. Discipline rests primarily with faculty.

Summer Programs ESL, sports programs offered; session focuses on ESL and golf; held on campus; accepts boys and girls; open to students from other schools. 50 students usually enrolled. 2006 schedule: August 2 to September 2. Application deadline: June 15.

Tuition and Aid Day student tuition: $17,500; 7-day tuition and room/board: $29,500. Tuition installment plan (Key Tuition Payment Plan, FACTS Tuition Payment Plan). Merit scholarship grants, need-based scholarship grants, Sallie Mae Loans available. In 2005–06, 38% of upper-school students received aid; total upper-school merit-scholarship money awarded: $50,000. Total amount of financial aid awarded in 2005–06: $1,250,000.

Admissions Traditional secondary-level entrance grade is 9. For fall 2005, 180 students applied for upper-level admission, 140 were accepted, 80 enrolled. ISEE or SSAT required. Deadline for receipt of application materials: none. Application fee required: $50. Interview recommended.

Athletics Interscholastic: baseball, basketball, cross-country running, diving, football, golf, ice hockey, lacrosse, soccer, swimming and diving, tennis, track and field, wrestling; intramural: alpine skiing, basketball, canoeing/kayaking, fishing, flag football, fly fishing, golf, hiking/backpacking, indoor track & field, jogging, martial arts, mountain biking, outdoor activities, paint ball, power lifting, skiing (downhill), snowboarding, strength & conditioning, swimming and diving, weight lifting, weight training. 2 coaches, 1 trainer.

Computers Computers are regularly used in English, mathematics, science classes. Computer network features include campus e-mail, on-campus library services, CD-ROMs, online commercial services, Internet access, file transfer, DVD, wireless campus network.

Contact Mr. Lawrence J. Jensen, Director of Admissions. 877-547-5448. Fax: 724-639-8596. E-mail: admissions@kiski.org. Web site: www.kiski.org.

ANNOUNCEMENT FROM THE SCHOOL Facilities upgrades in 2005 include 2 new dormitories, 5 new tennis courts, and a brand new fitness center. Kiski's campus is completely wireless. Students operate the campus radio station and broadcast athletic events live on the Internet. Kiski students ranked in the top 6% nationally in math competitions in 2005.

See full description on page 862.

THE KNOX SCHOOL

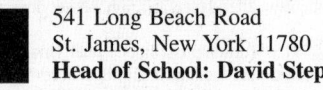 

541 Long Beach Road
St. James, New York 11780
Head of School: David Stephens

General Information Coeducational boarding and day college-preparatory school. Boarding grades 7–12, day grades 6–12. Founded: 1904. Setting: rural. Nearest major city is New York. Students are housed in single-sex dormitories. 50-acre campus. 12 buildings on campus. Approved or accredited by Middle States Association of Colleges and Schools, New York State Association of Independent Schools, New York State Board of Regents, The Association of Boarding Schools, and New York Department of Education. Member of National Association of Independent Schools. Total enrollment: 115. Upper school average class size: 10. Upper school faculty-student ratio: 1:3.

Upper School Student Profile Grade 9: 20 students (6 boys, 14 girls); Grade 10: 22 students (16 boys, 6 girls); Grade 11: 18 students (9 boys, 9 girls); Grade 12: 15 students (5 boys, 10 girls). 57% of students are boarding students. 50% are state residents. 10 states are represented in upper school student body. 20% are international students. International students from China, Japan, Pakistan, Republic of Korea, and Taiwan.

Faculty School total: 31. In upper school: 10 men, 14 women; 12 have advanced degrees; 20 reside on campus.

Subjects Offered 20th century history, algebra, American literature, art history, biology, calculus, calculus-AP, chemistry, chemistry-AP, computer art, computer science, creative writing, current events, earth science, economics, English, environmental science, ESL, European history, French, geometry, government, health and wellness, journalism, music, music history, photo shop, photojournalism, physics, physics-AP, pre-algebra, pre-calculus, Spanish, studio art, U.S. history, vocal music, world history, world literature.

Graduation Requirements Art, electives, English, foreign language, health, history, lab science, mathematics.

Special Academic Programs Advanced Placement exam preparation in 6 subject areas; honors section; independent study; study abroad; remedial reading and/or remedial writing; ESL (17 students enrolled).

College Placement 25 students graduated in 2005; all went to college, including Chapman University; Lynn University; New York University; Sarah Lawrence College; The George Washington University; University of Michigan.

Student Life Upper grades have uniform requirement, student council. Discipline rests primarily with faculty.

Tuition and Aid Day student tuition: $17,030; 5-day tuition and room/board: $30,160; 7-day tuition and room/board: $32,240. Tuition installment plan (individually arranged payment plans, Knight Tuition Plan). Merit scholarship grants, need-based scholarship grants available. In 2005–06, 30% of upper-school students received aid; total upper-school merit-scholarship money awarded: $13,000.

Admissions Traditional secondary-level entrance grade is 9. For fall 2005, 101 students applied for upper-level admission, 64 were accepted, 42 enrolled. SLEP, SSAT or TOEFL required. Deadline for receipt of application materials: February 1. Application fee required: $50. Interview required.

Athletics Interscholastic: baseball (boys), basketball (b,g), dance (b,g), independent competitive sports (b,g), modern dance (b,g), soccer (b), softball (g), tennis (b,g), volleyball (g), weight training (b); intramural: canoeing/kayaking (b,g), tennis (b,g); coed interscholastic: crew, dressage, equestrian sports, golf, horseback riding, soccer; coed intramural: canoeing/kayaking, dance, dressage, equestrian sports, golf, horseback riding, kayaking, modern dance, outdoor adventure, outdoor skills, skiing (cross-country), skiing (downhill), snowboarding, swimming and diving. 3 coaches.

Computers Computer network features include campus e-mail, CD-ROMs, Internet access, wireless campus network.

Contact Meredith M. Stanley, Director of Admissions. 631-686-1600 Ext. 414. Fax: 631-686-1650. E-mail: mstanley@knoxschool.org. Web site: www.theknoxschool.com.

See full description on page 864.

LA CHEIM SCHOOL

Antioch, California
See Special Needs Schools section.

LADYWOOD HIGH SCHOOL

14680 Newburgh Road
Livonia, Michigan 48154
Head of School: Sr. Mary Ann Smith, CSSF

General Information Girls' day college-preparatory, arts, and religious studies school, affiliated with Roman Catholic Church. Grades 9–12. Founded: 1950. Setting: suburban. Nearest major city is Detroit. 1 building on campus. Approved or accredited by North Central Association of Colleges and Schools and Michigan Department of Education. Total enrollment: 457. Upper school average class size: 24. Upper school faculty-student ratio: 1:14.

Upper School Student Profile Grade 9: 100 students (100 girls); Grade 10: 145 students (145 girls); Grade 11: 106 students (106 girls); Grade 12: 106 students (106 girls). 92% of students are Roman Catholic.

Faculty School total: 34. In upper school: 8 men, 26 women; 6 have advanced degrees.

Subjects Offered Advanced chemistry, advanced math, algebra, American government, American history, American history-AP, American literature, anatomy and physiology, art, Asian history, Basic programming, Bible studies, biochemistry, biology, biology-AP, business applications, calculus-AP, career and personal planning, career exploration, Catholic belief and practice, ceramics, character education, chemistry-AP, child development, choir, Christian and Hebrew scripture, college writing, composition, computer education, computer programming, culinary arts, discrete math, drama, drawing and design, economics, English, English composition, English literature and composition-AP, English-AP, environmental science, European civilization, family and consumer sciences, film appreciation, food science, French, French language-AP, French-AP, geometry, global issues, government, graphic arts, health, history of the Catholic Church, independent living, Italian, keyboarding/computer, language and composition, language arts, leadership and service, leadership skills, library assistant, life management skills, literature-AP, novels, oil painting, oral communications, parent/child development, physical education, physics, poetry, prayer/spirituality, pre-calculus, psychology, religion, science, sewing, short story, sociology, Spanish, Spanish-AP, speech, statistics and probability, studio art—AP, theater arts, Vietnam War, visual and performing arts, water color painting, writing, yearbook.

Graduation Requirements Algebra, American government, American history, American literature, arts and fine arts (art, music, dance, drama), Bible studies, biology, business, Catholic belief and practice, chemistry, composition, computer applications, computer keyboarding, computer science, English, English composition, English literature, foreign language, global studies, health education, home economics, literature, mathematics, physical education (includes health), physical fitness, religion (includes Bible studies and theology), science, social science, speech.

Special Academic Programs Honors section; independent study; study at local college for college credit.

College Placement 113 students graduated in 2005; 100 went to college, including Central Michigan University; Michigan State University; University of Michigan; University of Notre Dame; Western Michigan University. Other: 1 entered military service, 1 had other specific plans.

Student Life Upper grades have uniform requirement, student council, honor system. Discipline rests primarily with faculty. Attendance at religious services is required.

Summer Programs Remediation, enrichment programs offered; session focuses on enrichment and remediation; held on campus; accepts girls; not open to students from other schools. 70 students usually enrolled. 2006 schedule: June 21 to July 22. Application deadline: May 19.

Tuition and Aid Day student tuition: $6000. Tuition installment plan (The Tuition Plan, monthly payment plans, individually arranged payment plans). Tuition reduction for siblings, merit scholarship grants, need-based scholarship grants available. In 2005–06, 22% of upper-school students received aid.

Admissions Traditional secondary-level entrance grade is 9. High School Placement Test required. Deadline for receipt of application materials: none. Application fee required. Interview recommended.

Athletics Interscholastic: alpine skiing, basketball, bowling, cheering, cross-country running, diving, equestrian sports, field hockey, figure skating, golf, ice hockey, indoor hockey, lacrosse, skiing (cross-country), skiing (downhill), soccer, softball, swimming and diving, tennis, track and field, volleyball, weight training. 2 PE instructors, 30 coaches, 1 trainer.

Computers Computers are regularly used in accounting, computer applications, data processing, keyboarding, Web site design, word processing, yearbook classes. Computer network features include on-campus library services, Internet access.

Contact Guidance Counselors. 734-591-5492 Ext. 226. Fax: 734-591-4214. Web site: www.ladywood.org.

LA GRANGE ACADEMY

1501 Vernon Road
La Grange, Georgia 30240
Head of School: Dr. Barry Peterson

General Information Coeducational day college-preparatory, arts, and technology school. Grades K–12. Founded: 1970. Setting: small town. Nearest major city is Atlanta. 15-acre campus. 4 buildings on campus. Approved or accredited by Georgia Independent School Association, Southern Association of Colleges and Schools, Southern Association of Independent Schools, and Georgia Department of Education. Member of National Association of Independent Schools. Total enrollment: 229. Upper school average class size: 15. Upper school faculty-student ratio: 1:15.

Upper School Student Profile Grade 9: 20 students (7 boys, 13 girls); Grade 10: 17 students (10 boys, 7 girls); Grade 11: 10 students (5 boys, 5 girls); Grade 12: 21 students (10 boys, 11 girls).

Faculty School total: 26. In upper school: 7 men, 7 women; 5 have advanced degrees.

Subjects Offered Algebra, American history, American literature, anatomy, art, art history, biology, business, calculus, chemistry, chemistry-AP, computer science, creative writing, driver education, earth science, economics, English, English literature, environmental science, expository writing, geography, geometry, government/civics, grammar, health, history, instrumental music, Latin, mathematics, music, physical education, physics, political science, psychology, science, social studies, Spanish, speech, trigonometry, world history, world literature.

Graduation Requirements English, foreign language, mathematics, physical education (includes health), science, social studies (includes history).

Special Academic Programs Advanced Placement exam preparation in 5 subject areas; honors section; independent study; study at local college for college credit; academic accommodation for the gifted, the musically talented, and the artistically talented.

College Placement 20 students graduated in 2005; all went to college, including Auburn University; Converse College; Dartmouth College; LaGrange College; Stetson University; University of Georgia. 33% scored over 600 on SAT verbal, 33% scored over 600 on SAT math.

Student Life Upper grades have specified standards of dress, student council, honor system. Discipline rests primarily with faculty.

Summer Programs Enrichment, art/fine arts, computer instruction programs offered; held on campus; accepts boys and girls; open to students from other schools. 50 students usually enrolled. 2006 schedule: June 3 to August 5. Application deadline: June 1.

Tuition and Aid Day student tuition: $6990. Tuition installment plan (monthly payment plans, quarterly payment plan). Merit scholarship grants, need-based scholarship grants, funded scholarships for specific groups or individuals available. In 2005–06, 20% of upper-school students received aid; total upper-school merit-scholarship money awarded: $25,000. Total amount of financial aid awarded in 2005–06: $59,820.

Admissions School's own exam required. Deadline for receipt of application materials: none. Application fee required: $50. On-campus interview required.

Athletics Interscholastic: baseball (boys), basketball (b,g), cheering (g), soccer (b,g), softball (g), tennis (b,g), weight training (b,g); coed interscholastic: golf, swimming and diving, tennis, weight lifting, yoga; coed intramural: basketball, football, soccer, swimming and diving. 3 PE instructors, 8 coaches.

Computers Computers are regularly used in all classes. Computer network features include campus e-mail, on-campus library services, CD-ROMs, Internet access.

Contact Sharon Hashimoto, Admissions Office. 706-882-8097. Fax: 706-882-8640. Web site: www.lagrangeacademy.org.

LAGUNA BLANCA SCHOOL

4125 Paloma Drive
Santa Barbara, California 93110
Head of School: Douglas W. Jessup

General Information Coeducational day college-preparatory, arts, and technology school. Grades K–12. Founded: 1933. Setting: suburban. 33-acre campus. 10 buildings on campus. Approved or accredited by California Association of Independent Schools, Western Association of Schools and Colleges, and California Department of Education. Member of National Association of Independent Schools. Endowment: $3.3 million. Total enrollment: 411. Upper school average class size: 14. Upper school faculty-student ratio: 1:12.

Upper School Student Profile Grade 9: 55 students (33 boys, 22 girls); Grade 10: 50 students (26 boys, 24 girls); Grade 11: 52 students (27 boys, 25 girls); Grade 12: 51 students (22 boys, 29 girls).

Faculty School total: 61. In upper school: 24 men, 37 women; 36 have advanced degrees.

Subjects Offered Algebra, American history, American history-AP, art, art history, biology, biology-AP, calculus-AP, ceramics, chemistry, chorus, community service, comparative government and politics-AP, computer science, computer science-AP, creative writing, drama, economics, English, English-AP, ethics, fine arts, French, French-AP, geology, geometry, government/civics, history, Latin, marine biology, mathematics, music, music appreciation, photography, physical education, physics,

physics-AP, pre-calculus, science, social studies, Spanish, Spanish-AP, speech, statistics-AP, studio art-AP, theater, U.S. government-AP, Western civilization, world history, yearbook.

Graduation Requirements Arts and fine arts (art, music, dance, drama), computer science, English, foreign language, mathematics, physical education (includes health), science, social studies (includes history), speech, senior internship project. Community service is required.

Special Academic Programs Advanced Placement exam preparation in 19 subject areas; honors section; independent study; special instructional classes for blind students.

College Placement 56 students graduated in 2005; 53 went to college, including Princeton University; Stanford University; University of California, Los Angeles; University of California, Santa Barbara; University of Pennsylvania; University of Southern California. Other: 3 had other specific plans. Mean SAT verbal: 630, mean SAT math: 630, mean combined SAT: 1900. 63% scored over 600 on SAT verbal, 73% scored over 600 on SAT math, 79% scored over 1800 on combined SAT.

Student Life Upper grades have specified standards of dress, student council, honor system. Discipline rests primarily with faculty.

Tuition and Aid Day student tuition: $15,400–$18,500. Tuition installment plan (Insured Tuition Payment Plan, monthly payment plans, individually arranged payment plans). Merit scholarship grants, need-based scholarship grants available. In 2005–06, 6% of upper-school students received aid; total upper-school merit-scholarship money awarded: $28,500. Total amount of financial aid awarded in 2005–06: $174,600.

Admissions Traditional secondary-level entrance grade is 9. For fall 2005, 44 students applied for upper-level admission, 41 were accepted, 31 enrolled. CTP, Otis-Lennon Mental Ability Test or Otis-Lennon School Ability Test required. Deadline for receipt of application materials: February 15. Application fee required: $100. Interview required.

Athletics Interscholastic: baseball (boys), basketball (b,g), cross-country running (b,g), football (b), golf (b), independent competitive sports (b,g), lacrosse (b,g), soccer (b,g), softball (g), tennis (b,g), track and field (b,g), volleyball (b,g); coed intramural: back packing, hiking/backpacking, juggling, skiing (downhill), surfing, yoga. 3 PE instructors, 30 coaches, 1 trainer.

Computers Computers are regularly used in art, college planning, creative writing, French, geography, history, journalism, lab/keyboard, library, literary magazine, mathematics, music, newspaper, publications, science, theater, theater arts, typing, word processing, yearbook classes. Computer network features include campus e-mail, on-campus library services, CD-ROMs, online commercial services, Internet access, office computer access, library access from the home.

Contact Joyce Balak, Director of Admission and Financial Aid. 805-687-2461 Ext. 210. Fax: 805-682-2553. E-mail: jbalak@lagunablanca.org. Web site: www.lagunablanca.org.

LA JOLLA COUNTRY DAY SCHOOL

9490 Genesee Avenue
La Jolla, California 92037
Head of School: Dr. Judith R. Glickman

General Information Coeducational day college-preparatory, arts, and technology school. Grades N–12. Founded: 1926. Setting: suburban. Nearest major city is San Diego. 24-acre campus. 8 buildings on campus. Approved or accredited by California Association of Independent Schools, Western Association of Schools and Colleges, and California Department of Education. Member of National Association of Independent Schools and Secondary School Admission Test Board. Endowment: $1 million. Total enrollment: 1,037. Upper school average class size: 14. Upper school faculty-student ratio: 1:12.

Upper School Student Profile Grade 9: 93 students (47 boys, 46 girls); Grade 10: 93 students (43 boys, 50 girls); Grade 11: 95 students (48 boys, 47 girls); Grade 12: 83 students (37 boys, 46 girls).

Faculty School total: 122. In upper school: 18 men, 24 women; 27 have advanced degrees.

Subjects Offered Advanced studio art-AP, algebra, art, art appreciation, art history, art history-AP, astronomy, biology, biology-AP, calculus-AP, chemistry, chemistry-AP, chorus, comparative religion, computer graphics, computer multimedia, computer programming, computer science, computer science-AP, conceptual physics, creative writing, dance, drama, drama performance, drama workshop, economics, English, English language-AP, English literature, English literature and composition-AP, English literature-AP, environmental science, European history, European history-AP, expository writing, film studies, French, French literature-AP, French-AP, freshman seminar, geometry, geometry with art applications, government, government-AP, history of drama, honors algebra, honors geometry, independent study, instrumental music, linear algebra, madrigals, multimedia, music appreciation, music history, music-AP, painting, performing arts, photography, physical education, physical science, physics, physics-AP, portfolio art, pre-calculus, programming, psychology, Spanish, Spanish literature-AP, Spanish-AP, speech, statistics-AP, strings, studio art, studio art—AP, technical theater, theater, theater arts, theater history, theater production, theory of knowledge, U.S. history-AP, wellness, women's studies, world culture, writing.

Graduation Requirements Arts and fine arts (art, music, dance, drama), English, foreign language, mathematics, performing arts, physical education (includes health), science, senior project, social sciences, speech, 40 hours of community service.

Special Academic Programs Advanced Placement exam preparation in 18 subject areas; honors section.

College Placement 84 students graduated in 2005; all went to college, including San Diego State University; University of California, Berkeley; University of California, Los Angeles; University of California, San Diego; University of California, Santa Barbara; University of Southern California. Mean SAT verbal: 658, mean SAT math: 666. 72% scored over 600 on SAT verbal, 82% scored over 600 on SAT math.

Student Life Upper grades have specified standards of dress, student council. Discipline rests equally with students and faculty.

Summer Programs Remediation, enrichment, advancement, sports, art/fine arts, computer instruction programs offered; session focuses on academics, summer camp, sports camps; held on campus; accepts boys and girls; open to students from other schools. 600 students usually enrolled. 2006 schedule: June 21 to August 2. Application deadline: none.

Tuition and Aid Day student tuition: $18,980. Tuition installment plan (individually arranged payment plans). Need-based scholarship grants available. In 2005–06, 17% of upper-school students received aid. Total amount of financial aid awarded in 2005–06: $1,900,000.

Admissions Traditional secondary-level entrance grade is 9. ISEE required. Deadline for receipt of application materials: February 6. Application fee required: $100. On-campus interview required.

Athletics Interscholastic: aquatics (boys, girls), baseball (b), basketball (b,g), cheering (g), cross-country running (b,g), dance (b,g), fencing (b,g), football (b), golf (b,g), independent competitive sports (b,g), lacrosse (b,g), soccer (b,g), softball (b,g), swimming and diving (b,g), tennis (b,g), track and field (b,g), volleyball (b,g); coed interscholastic: physical fitness, physical training, roller hockey, strength & conditioning, surfing, water polo, weight lifting, weight training; coed intramural: dance team, outdoor education, snowboarding. 8 PE instructors, 63 coaches, 1 trainer.

Computers Computers are regularly used in art, English, French, history, mathematics, science, Spanish, technology classes. Computer network features include campus e-mail, on-campus library services, CD-ROMs, online commercial services, Internet access, file transfer, office computer access, DVD, wireless campus network, e-mail connection from home.

Contact Mr. Vincent Travaglione, Director of Admissions and Public Relations. 858-453-3440 Ext. 117. Fax: 858-453-8210. E-mail: vtravaglione@ljcds.org.

ANNOUNCEMENT FROM THE SCHOOL La Jolla Country Day School is an independent, coeducational, college-preparatory school achieving high academic standards in its comprehensive, multidimensional programs. Meeting the needs of more than 1,000 students from nursery through grade 12, Country Day balances a rigorous academic program with an abundance of offerings in the areas of athletics, visual and performing arts, and service learning. The 24-acre campus, located in the coastal community of La Jolla, houses an on-site observatory and state-of-the-art facilities for science, technology, fine and performing arts, and athletics. Country Day places a strong emphasis on character development, wellness, and service learning. The School strives to educate the whole child by enriching each individual intellectually, physically, creatively, socially, and emotionally. A low student-teacher ratio enables the dedicated faculty to genuinely know each child, enhancing innate talents and abilities within the framework of a supportive, dynamic, and educational environment.

LAKEFIELD COLLEGE SCHOOL

4391 County Road #29
Lakefield, Ontario K0L 2H0, Canada
Head of School: Mr. David J. Hadden

General Information Coeducational boarding and day college-preparatory, arts, technology, and distance learning, outdoor education program school, affiliated with Church of England (Anglican). Boarding grades 9–12, day grades 7–12. Founded: 1879. Setting: small town. Nearest major city is Toronto, Canada. Students are housed in single-sex dormitories. 155-acre campus. 23 buildings on campus. Approved or accredited by Canadian Association of Independent Schools, Canadian Educational Standards Institute, The Association of Boarding Schools, and Ontario Department of Education. Affiliate member of National Association of Independent Schools; member of Secondary School Admission Test Board. Language of instruction: English. Endowment: CAN$1 million. Total enrollment: 365. Upper school average class size: 17. Upper school faculty-student ratio: 1:7.

Upper School Student Profile Grade 7: 10 students (6 boys, 4 girls); Grade 8: 19 students (7 boys, 12 girls); Grade 9: 65 students (34 boys, 31 girls); Grade 10: 79 students (39 boys, 40 girls); Grade 11: 96 students (55 boys, 41 girls); Grade 12: 96 students (44 boys, 52 girls). 70% of students are boarding students. 80% are province residents. 17 provinces are represented in upper school student body. 14% are international students. International students from Barbados, Bermuda, Germany, Mexico, Saudi Arabia, and United States; 18 other countries represented in student body. 40% of students are members of Church of England (Anglican).

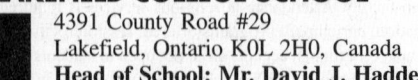

Faculty School total: 53. In upper school: 27 men, 26 women; 9 have advanced degrees; 28 reside on campus.

Subjects Offered Algebra, art, art history, biology, business, calculus, chemistry, computer programming, computer science, creative writing, drama, driver education, earth science, economics, English, English literature, environmental science, European history, fine arts, French, geography, geometry, German, government/civics, health, history, journalism, kinesiology, mathematics, music, physical education, physics, psychology, science, social studies, sociology, Spanish, speech, theater, trigonometry, vocal music, world history, world literature.

Graduation Requirements Arts and fine arts (art, music, dance, drama), computer science, English, foreign language, mathematics, physical education (includes health), science, social studies (includes history), two outdoor expeditions. Community service is required.

Special Academic Programs Advanced Placement exam preparation in 5 subject areas; honors section; accelerated programs; independent study; term-away projects; study at local college for college credit; study abroad; academic accommodation for the gifted, the musically talented, and the artistically talented.

College Placement 90 students graduated in 2005; 89 went to college, including Acadia University; Dalhousie University; Queen's University at Kingston; The University of Western Ontario; University of Guelph; University of Toronto. Other: 1 had other specific plans. 34% scored over 600 on SAT verbal, 41% scored over 600 on SAT math.

Student Life Upper grades have uniform requirement, student council, honor system. Discipline rests equally with students and faculty.

Tuition and Aid Day student tuition: CAN$21,625; 7-day tuition and room/board: CAN$36,595. Tuition installment plan (3-payment plan). Bursaries, merit scholarship grants, need-based scholarship grants available. In 2005–06, 35% of upper-school students received aid. Total amount of financial aid awarded in 2005–06: CAN$1,260,000.

Admissions Traditional secondary-level entrance grade is 9. For fall 2005, 275 students applied for upper-level admission, 160 were accepted, 121 enrolled. Otis-Lennon School Ability Test, SSAT or SSTS Placement Test required. Deadline for receipt of application materials: none. Application fee required: CAN$100. Interview required.

Athletics Interscholastic: alpine skiing (boys, girls), baseball (b), basketball (g), crew (g), cross-country running (b,g), field hockey (g), golf (b,g), hockey (b,g), ice hockey (b,g), nordic skiing (b,g), outdoor education (b,g), ropes courses (b,g), rowing (b,g), rugby (b,g), skiing (cross-country) (b,g), skiing (downhill) (b,g), snowboarding (b,g), soccer (b,g), softball (b); intramural: aerobics/dance (g), basketball (b,g), billiards (b,g), cross-country running (b,g), skiing (cross-country) (b,g); coed interscholastic: alpine skiing, cross-country running, equestrian sports, Frisbee, golf, hockey, horseback riding, ice hockey, nordic skiing, outdoor education, sailing, skiing (cross-country), skiing (downhill), snowboarding; coed intramural: aerobics/nautilus, baseball, basketball, bicycling, billiards, canoeing/kayaking, climbing, cross-country running, equestrian sports, fitness, ice hockey, kayaking, sailing, skiing (cross-country), skiing (downhill), softball. 10 coaches, 2 trainers.

Computers Computers are regularly used in art, English, foreign language, history, mathematics, music, science classes. Computer network features include campus e-mail, on-campus library services, CD-ROMs, online commercial services, Internet access, DVD.

Contact Mrs. Barbara M. Rutherford, Assistant Director of Admissions. 705-652-3324 Ext. 345. Fax: 705-652-6320. E-mail: admissions@lakefieldcs.on.ca. Web site: www.lakefieldcs.on.ca.

LAKE FOREST ACADEMY

1500 West Kennedy Road
Lake Forest, Illinois 60045
Head of School: Dr. John Strudwick

petersons.com

General Information Coeducational boarding and day college-preparatory school. Grades 9–12. Founded: 1857. Setting: suburban. Nearest major city is Chicago. Students are housed in single-sex dormitories. 160-acre campus. 22 buildings on campus. Approved or accredited by Independent Schools Association of the Central States, Midwest Association of Boarding Schools, The Association of Boarding Schools, and Illinois Department of Education. Member of National Association of Independent Schools and Secondary School Admission Test Board. Endowment: $17.5 million. Total enrollment: 349. Upper school average class size: 12. Upper school faculty-student ratio: 1:7.

Upper School Student Profile Grade 9: 72 students (41 boys, 31 girls); Grade 10: 101 students (55 boys, 46 girls); Grade 11: 95 students (53 boys, 42 girls); Grade 12: 81 students (44 boys, 37 girls). 51% of students are boarding students. 72% are state residents. 16 states are represented in upper school student body. 13% are international students. International students from Canada, Japan, Republic of Korea, Russian Federation, Saudi Arabia, and Taiwan; 12 other countries represented in student body.

Faculty School total: 54. In upper school: 26 men, 19 women; 36 have advanced degrees; 40 reside on campus.

Subjects Offered Algebra, American history, American literature, anthropology, art, art history, biology, calculus, chemistry, community service, computer programming, computer science, creative writing, drama, driver education, ecology, English, English literature, environmental science, ESL, fine arts, French, geometry, history, journal-

ism, Latin, mathematics, music, photography, physical education, physics, science, social studies, Spanish, speech, statistics, theater, world history.

Graduation Requirements Arts and fine arts (art, music, dance, drama), English, foreign language, mathematics, science, social studies (includes history). Community service is required.

Special Academic Programs Advanced Placement exam preparation in 19 subject areas; honors section; independent study; study abroad; ESL (20 students enrolled).

College Placement 77 students graduated in 2004; 76 went to college, including Northwestern University; University of Chicago; University of Illinois at Urbana–Champaign; University of Michigan; University of Wisconsin–Madison. Other: 1 had other specific plans. Mean SAT verbal: 587, mean SAT math: 627, mean composite ACT: 27. 44% scored over 600 on SAT verbal, 58% scored over 600 on SAT math, 41% scored over 26 on composite ACT.

Student Life Upper grades have specified standards of dress, student council. Discipline rests primarily with faculty.

Tuition and Aid Day student tuition: $20,750; 7-day tuition and room/board: $29,500. Tuition installment plan (FACTS Tuition Payment Plan). Merit scholarship grants, need-based scholarship grants available. In 2004–05, 31% of upper-school students received aid; total upper-school merit-scholarship money awarded: $80,000. Total amount of financial aid awarded in 2004–05: $1,940,000.

Admissions Traditional secondary-level entrance grade is 9. For fall 2005, 385 students applied for upper-level admission, 138 were accepted, 108 enrolled. SSAT and TOEFL required. Deadline for receipt of application materials: February 15. Application fee required: $50. Interview required.

Athletics Interscholastic: baseball (boys), basketball (b,g), cheering (g), cross-country running (b,g), diving (b,g), field hockey (g), football (b), golf (b,g), ice hockey (b,g), soccer (b,g), softball (g), tennis (b,g), track and field (b,g), volleyball (b,g), wrestling (b); intramural: indoor soccer (b,g); coed interscholastic: swimming and diving; coed intramural: aerobics, curling, martial arts, racquetball, soccer, weight lifting. 2 coaches, 1 trainer.

Computers Computers are regularly used in English, foreign language, mathematics, science classes. Computer network features include campus e-mail, on-campus library services, CD-ROMs, online commercial services, Internet access, file transfer, office computer access, DVD, wireless campus network.

Contact Admissions Office. 847-615-3267. Fax: 847-615-3202. E-mail: info@lfanet.org. Web site: www.lfanet.org.

See full description on page 866.

LAKE HIGHLAND PREPARATORY SCHOOL

901 North Highland Avenue
Orlando, Florida 32803
Head of School: Mr. Warren Hudson

General Information Coeducational day college-preparatory school, affiliated with Christian faith. Grades PK–12. Founded: 1970. Setting: urban. 30-acre campus. 8 buildings on campus. Approved or accredited by Florida Council of Independent Schools and Southern Association of Colleges and Schools. Member of National Association of Independent Schools and Secondary School Admission Test Board. Total enrollment: 1,931. Upper school average class size: 16. Upper school faculty-student ratio: 1:12.

Upper School Student Profile Grade 9: 182 students (91 boys, 91 girls); Grade 10: 179 students (85 boys, 94 girls); Grade 11: 158 students (80 boys, 78 girls); Grade 12: 152 students (79 boys, 73 girls).

Faculty School total: 183. In upper school: 18 men, 31 women; 26 have advanced degrees.

Subjects Offered Advanced chemistry, advanced computer applications, advanced studio art-AP, algebra, American literature, American literature-AP, anatomy, ancient world history, art, art-AP, band, Basic programming, biology, biology-AP, calculus, calculus-AP, chemistry, chemistry-AP, choir, chorus, composition, computer programming, computer programming-AP, computer science, computer science-AP, creative writing, debate, drama, earth science, economics, economics and history, English, English literature, English literature-AP, English-AP, environmental science, environmental science-AP, European history, European history-AP, fine arts, French, French language-AP, French-AP, geography, geometry, government and politics-AP, government/civics, health, history, history of mathematics, honors algebra, honors geometry, honors U.S. history, honors world history, humanities, jazz band, journalism, Latin, Latin-AP, leadership and service, leadership training, life management skills, literature, logic, rhetoric, and debate, Mandarin, marching band, mathematics, modern European history-AP, music, music theory-AP, personal fitness, photography, physical education, physical science, physics, physics-AP, physiology, pre-algebra, pre-calculus, psychology, research skills, SAT/ACT preparation, science, Shakespeare, social studies, Spanish, Spanish language-AP, Spanish-AP, speech, speech and debate, statistics and probability, statistics-AP, student government, studio art—AP, symphonic band, technology, theater, trigonometry, U.S. government, U.S. government-AP, U.S. history, U.S. history-AP, video, video film production, visual and performing arts, weight training, world cultures, world history, writing, yearbook.

Graduation Requirements Arts and fine arts (art, music, dance, drama), computer science, English, foreign language, humanities, mathematics, physical education (includes health), science, social studies (includes history), speech.

Lake Highland Preparatory School

Special Academic Programs Advanced Placement exam preparation in 20 subject areas; honors section; independent study; study abroad; academic accommodation for the gifted, the musically talented, and the artistically talented; special instructional classes for students needing additional support (Edison Program).

College Placement 138 students graduated in 2005; all went to college, including College of Charleston; New York University; Rollins College; Samford University; University of Florida; University of Miami. Mean SAT verbal: 609, mean SAT math: 613.

Student Life Upper grades have uniform requirement, student council, honor system. Discipline rests primarily with faculty.

Summer Programs Enrichment, advancement, sports, art/fine arts, computer instruction programs offered; session focuses on comprehensive enrichment; held both on and off campus; held at golf courses, Disney World, and Sea World; accepts boys and girls; open to students from other schools. 2100 students usually enrolled. 2006 schedule: June 10 to July 31. Application deadline: none.

Tuition and Aid Day student tuition: $12,500. Tuition installment plan (monthly payment plans, semester payment plan). Need-based scholarship grants available. In 2005–06, 4% of upper-school students received aid.

Admissions Traditional secondary-level entrance grade is 9. For fall 2005, 134 students applied for upper-level admission, 57 were accepted, 47 enrolled. Admissions testing, CTBS, Stanford Achievement Test, any other standardized test, SSAT, ERB, PSAT, SAT, PLAN or ACT or writing sample required. Deadline for receipt of application materials: none. Application fee required: $85. On-campus interview recommended.

Athletics Interscholastic: aerobics/dance (girls), aquatics (b,g), baseball (b), basketball (b,g), cheering (g), cross-country running (b,g), dance team (g), diving (b,g), fitness (b,g), football (b), golf (b,g), lacrosse (b,g), physical fitness (b,g), soccer (b,g), softball (g), strength & conditioning (b,g), swimming and diving (b,g), tennis (b,g), track and field (b,g), volleyball (g), weight lifting (b,g), weight training (b,g), wrestling (b). 2 PE instructors, 39 coaches, 2 trainers.

Computers Computers are regularly used in English, foreign language, history, keyboarding, library skills, mathematics, SAT preparation, science, video film production, Web site design, word processing, writing, writing classes. Computer network features include on-campus library services, CD-ROMs, online commercial services, Internet access, classroom E-Mates laptops, classroom white boards, wireless upper school library.

Contact Ann B. Mills, Director of Admissions. 407-206-1900 Ext. 1. Fax: 407-206-5042. E-mail: amills@lhps.org. Web site: www.lhps.org.

LAKEHILL PREPARATORY SCHOOL

2720 Hillside Drive
Dallas, Texas 75214
Head of School: Roger L. Perry

General Information Coeducational day college-preparatory school. Grades K–12. Founded: 1971. Setting: urban. 23-acre campus. 2 buildings on campus. Approved or accredited by Independent Schools Association of the Southwest, Southern Association of Colleges and Schools, Texas Private School Accreditation Commission, The College Board, and Texas Department of Education. Endowment: $200,000. Total enrollment: 391. Upper school average class size: 15. Upper school faculty-student ratio: 1:9.

Upper School Student Profile Grade 9: 26 students (14 boys, 12 girls); Grade 10: 32 students (16 boys, 16 girls); Grade 11: 27 students (15 boys, 12 girls); Grade 12: 25 students (15 boys, 10 girls).

Faculty School total: 44. In upper school: 9 men, 10 women; 14 have advanced degrees.

Subjects Offered Algebra, American history, American literature, art, art history, biology, calculus, chemistry, computer math, computer programming, computer science, drama, earth science, economics, English, English literature, European history, French, geography, geometry, government/civics, grammar, health, history, journalism, Latin, mathematics, music, physical education, physics, psychology, science, social science, social studies, Spanish, speech, statistics, theater, trigonometry, world history, world literature, writing.

Graduation Requirements Computer science, English, foreign language, mathematics, physical education (includes health), science, social science, social studies (includes history), senior projects and internships.

Special Academic Programs Advanced Placement exam preparation in 12 subject areas; honors section; independent study.

College Placement 31 students graduated in 2005; all went to college, including Southern Methodist University; The University of Texas at Austin. Median SAT verbal: 620, median SAT math: 660.

Student Life Upper grades have specified standards of dress, student council, honor system. Discipline rests primarily with faculty.

Summer Programs Enrichment, sports, art/fine arts programs offered; held on campus; accepts boys and girls; open to students from other schools.

Tuition and Aid Day student tuition: $11,639. Tuition installment plan (monthly payment plans). Tuition reduction for siblings, need-based scholarship grants available. In 2005–06, 15% of upper-school students received aid.

Admissions Traditional secondary-level entrance grade is 9. For fall 2005, 38 students applied for upper-level admission, 22 were accepted, 11 enrolled. Stanford Achievement Test required. Deadline for receipt of application materials: none. Application fee required: $100. On-campus interview required.

Athletics Interscholastic: baseball (boys), basketball (b,g), cheering (g), cross-country running (b,g), football (b), golf (b,g), jogging (b,g), softball (g), track and field (b,g), volleyball (g); coed interscholastic: tennis; coed intramural: bowling. 3 PE instructors, 6 coaches, 1 trainer.

Computers Computers are regularly used in college planning, creative writing, English, graphic design, journalism, mathematics, science, speech, Web site design, word processing, writing, yearbook classes. Computer network features include on-campus library services, CD-ROMs, online commercial services, Internet access, file transfer, DVD.

Contact Susanne Seitz, Director of Admissions. 214-826-2931. Fax: 214-826-4623. E-mail: sseitz@lakehillprep.org. Web site: www.lakehillprep.org.

LAKELAND CHRISTIAN ACADEMY

1093 South 250 East
Winona Lake, Indiana 46590
Head of School: Mrs. Joy Lavender

General Information Coeducational day college-preparatory, arts, religious studies, and technology school, affiliated with Christian faith. Grades 7–12. Founded: 1974. Setting: small town. Nearest major city is Ft. Wayne. 40-acre campus. 1 building on campus. Approved or accredited by North Central Association of Colleges and Schools and Indiana Department of Education. Endowment: $500,000. Total enrollment: 170. Upper school average class size: 22. Upper school faculty-student ratio: 1:15.

Upper School Student Profile Grade 9: 28 students (14 boys, 14 girls); Grade 10: 40 students (22 boys, 18 girls); Grade 11: 32 students (10 boys, 22 girls); Grade 12: 26 students (13 boys, 13 girls). 100% of students are Christian faith.

Faculty School total: 19. In upper school: 5 men, 14 women; 5 have advanced degrees.

Special Academic Programs Honors section; independent study; study at local college for college credit; remedial reading and/or remedial writing; remedial math; programs in English, mathematics for dyslexic students.

College Placement 48 students graduated in 2005; 40 went to college, including Wheaton College. Other: 7 went to work, 1 entered military service.

Student Life Upper grades have specified standards of dress, student council, honor system. Discipline rests primarily with faculty. Attendance at religious services is required.

Tuition and Aid Day student tuition: $4720. Tuition installment plan (monthly payment plans, individually arranged payment plans). Need-based scholarship grants available. In 2005–06, 22% of upper-school students received aid. Total amount of financial aid awarded in 2005–06: $76,000.

Admissions Traditional secondary-level entrance grade is 9. ACT required. Application fee required: $60. Interview required.

Athletics Interscholastic: basketball (boys, girls), soccer (b,g), volleyball (g); intramural: basketball (b,g); coed interscholastic: soccer. 2 PE instructors, 8 coaches.

Computers Computer resources include Internet access.

Contact Joy Lavender, Administrator. 574-267-7265. Fax: 574-267-5687. E-mail: jlavender@lcacougars.com. Web site: www.lcacougars.com.

LAKE RIDGE ACADEMY

37501 Center Ridge Road
North Ridgeville, Ohio 44039
Head of School: Mrs. Deborah M. Cook

General Information Coeducational day college-preparatory, arts, business, and technology school. Grades K–12. Founded: 1963. Setting: suburban. Nearest major city is Cleveland. 88-acre campus. 5 buildings on campus. Approved or accredited by Independent Schools Association of the Central States and Ohio Department of Education. Member of National Association of Independent Schools. Endowment: $3.2 million. Total enrollment: 435. Upper school average class size: 12. Upper school faculty-student ratio: 1:7.

Upper School Student Profile Grade 9: 45 students (24 boys, 21 girls); Grade 10: 37 students (23 boys, 14 girls); Grade 11: 44 students (19 boys, 25 girls); Grade 12: 38 students (17 boys, 21 girls).

Faculty School total: 60. In upper school: 12 men, 18 women; 22 have advanced degrees.

Subjects Offered Algebra, American history, American literature, art, biology, biology-AP, calculus, calculus-AP, Caribbean history, ceramics, chemistry, chemistry-AP, choir, computer applications, computer programming, computer science, creative writing, design, digital imaging, discrete math, drafting, ecology, environmental systems, economics, electronic publishing, English, English-AP, ethics, ethnic studies, expository writing, fiber arts, fine arts, French, French-AP, functions, geometry, graphic arts, health, humanities, instrumental music, interactive media, journalism, literature, mathematics, music composition, music theory, physical education, physics, physics-AP, play/screen writing, portfolio writing, pre-calculus, psychology, senior

seminar, Shakespeare, social studies, Spanish, Spanish-AP, statistics, theater, U.S. history-AP, video film production, world civilizations, world history, world literature, writing.

Graduation Requirements Arts and fine arts (art, music, dance, drama), English, ethics, foreign language, mathematics, physical education (includes health), science, social studies (includes history), U.S. history.

Special Academic Programs Advanced Placement exam preparation in 13 subject areas; honors section; independent study; term-away projects; study at local college for college credit; academic accommodation for the gifted and the musically talented; programs in general development for dyslexic students; special instructional classes for deaf students.

College Placement 37 students graduated in 2005; all went to college, including American University; Case Western Reserve University; Columbia College; Dartmouth College; Denison University; Kenyon College. Median SAT verbal: 630, median SAT math: 670, median composite ACT: 26. 63% scored over 600 on SAT verbal, 68% scored over 600 on SAT math, 70% scored over 26 on composite ACT.

Student Life Upper grades have specified standards of dress, student council, honor system. Discipline rests primarily with faculty.

Summer Programs Remediation, enrichment, advancement, sports, art/fine arts, computer instruction programs offered; session focuses on enrichment, learning, summer fun.; held both on and off campus; held at various locations (for field trips); accepts boys and girls; open to students from other schools. 300 students usually enrolled. 2006 schedule: June 12 to July 21. Application deadline: June.

Tuition and Aid Day student tuition: $20,725–$22,425. Tuition installment plan (The Tuition Plan, Insured Tuition Payment Plan, monthly payment plans, individually arranged payment plans). Merit scholarship grants, need-based scholarship grants available. In 2005–06, 45% of upper-school students received aid; total upper-school merit-scholarship money awarded: $10,000. Total amount of financial aid awarded in 2005–06: $912,743.

Admissions Traditional secondary-level entrance grade is 9. For fall 2005, 22 students applied for upper-level admission, 20 were accepted, 18 enrolled. CTBS, OLSAT, essay, ISEE, mathematics proficiency exam, school's own exam, SLEP for foreign students and writing sample required. Deadline for receipt of application materials: none. Application fee required: $30. Interview required.

Athletics Interscholastic: baseball (boys), basketball (b,g), cross-country running (b), golf (b,g), indoor track & field (b), soccer (b,g), softball (g), tennis (b,g), track and field (b,g), volleyball (g), winter (indoor) track (b), wrestling (b); intramural: indoor soccer (b,g), strength & conditioning (b,g), winter soccer (b,g); coed intramural: back packing, indoor soccer, outdoor adventure, outdoor recreation, physical fitness, physical training, strength & conditioning, ultimate Frisbee, weight lifting, weight training. 3 PE instructors, 12 coaches, 1 trainer.

Computers Computers are regularly used in college planning, creative writing, drawing and design, English, foreign language, history, journalism, mathematics, media production, psychology, research skills, science classes. Computer network features include campus e-mail, on-campus library services, CD-ROMs, online commercial services, Internet access, file transfer, DVD, wireless campus network, Intranet.

Contact Mrs. Alexa C. Hansen, Director of Admission & External Relations. 440-777-9434 Ext. 103. Fax: 440-327-3641. E-mail: admission@lakeridgeacadmy.org. Web site: www.lakeridgeacademy.org.

LAKESIDE SCHOOL

14050 First Avenue, NE
Seattle, Washington 98125-3099
Head of School: Mr. Bernard Noe

General Information Coeducational day college-preparatory, arts, and technology school. Grades 5–12. Founded: 1919. Setting: urban. 34-acre campus. 19 buildings on campus. Approved or accredited by Northwest Association of Schools and Colleges, Pacific Northwest Association of Independent Schools, and Washington Department of Education. Member of National Association of Independent Schools. Endowment: $56 million. Total enrollment: 778. Upper school average class size: 16. Upper school faculty-student ratio: 1:10.

Upper School Student Profile Grade 9: 132 students (67 boys, 65 girls); Grade 10: 129 students (57 boys, 72 girls); Grade 11: 133 students (67 boys, 66 girls); Grade 12: 127 students (65 boys, 62 girls).

Faculty School total: 89. In upper school: 30 men, 29 women; 47 have advanced degrees.

Subjects Offered Algebra, American history, American literature, art, biology, calculus, ceramics, chemistry, community service, computer programming, computer science, creative writing, drama, driver education, economics, English, English literature, environmental science, European history, expository writing, fine arts, French, geometry, government/civics, health, history, journalism, Latin, mathematics, music, outdoor education, philosophy, photography, physical education, physics, pre-calculus, science, social studies, Spanish, theater, trigonometry, world history, world literature, writing.

Graduation Requirements Arts, English, foreign language, history, mathematics, outdoor education, physical education (includes health), science. Community service is required.

Special Academic Programs Honors section; independent study; term-away projects; study abroad.

College Placement 113 students graduated in 2005; 107 went to college, including Santa Clara University; Stanford University; University of Pennsylvania; University of Southern California; Wesleyan University. Other: 1 went to work, 5 had other specific plans. Median SAT verbal: 694, median SAT math: 692. 86% scored over 600 on SAT verbal, 86% scored over 600 on SAT math.

Student Life Upper grades have student council. Discipline rests equally with students and faculty.

Summer Programs Enrichment, computer instruction programs offered; session focuses on enrichment for students from public middle schools; held on campus; accepts boys and girls; open to students from other schools. 85 students usually enrolled. 2006 schedule: June 26 to August 4. Application deadline: April 21.

Tuition and Aid Day student tuition: $20,100. Tuition installment plan (Key Tuition Payment Plan, monthly payment plans). Need-based scholarship grants, need-based loans, middle-income loans, CitiAssist K-12 Loans, prepGATE Loans available. In 2005–06, 23% of upper-school students received aid. Total amount of financial aid awarded in 2005–06: $1,904,666.

Admissions Traditional secondary-level entrance grade is 9. For fall 2005, 279 students applied for upper-level admission, 97 were accepted, 71 enrolled. ISEE or PSAT or SAT for applicants to grade 11 and 12 required. Deadline for receipt of application materials: January 26. Application fee required: $48. Interview required.

Athletics Interscholastic: baseball (boys), basketball (b,g), crew (b,g), football (b), lacrosse (b,g), soccer (b,g), softball (g), volleyball (g); coed interscholastic: cross-country running, golf, skiing (cross-country), swimming and diving, tennis, track and field. 49 coaches.

Computers Computers are regularly used in all academic classes. Computer network features include campus e-mail, on-campus library services, CD-ROMs, online commercial services, Internet access, file transfer, office computer access, DVD, wireless campus network.

Contact Ms. Karen Weslander, Admissions/Financial Aid Assistant. 206-368-3605. Fax: 206-440-2777. E-mail: admissions@lakesideschool.org. Web site: www.lakesideschool.org.

LAKEWOOD PREP

152 Lanes Mill Road
Howell, New Jersey 07731
Head of School: Mrs. Lois Hirshkowitz

General Information Coeducational day college-preparatory and arts school. Grades K–PG. Founded: 1972. Setting: small town. Nearest major city is New York, NY. 22-acre campus. 2 buildings on campus. Approved or accredited by Commission on Secondary Schools and Middle States Association of Colleges and Schools. Total enrollment: 167. Upper school average class size: 13. Upper school faculty-student ratio: 1:10.

Upper School Student Profile Grade 9: 23 students (19 boys, 4 girls); Grade 10: 20 students (14 boys, 6 girls); Grade 11: 19 students (12 boys, 7 girls); Grade 12: 13 students (8 boys, 5 girls); Postgraduate: 1 student (1 boy).

Faculty School total: 33. In upper school: 4 men, 9 women; 4 have advanced degrees.

Subjects Offered Algebra, American history, American literature, anatomy, art, art history, biology, calculus, career experience, chemistry, computer math, computer programming, computer science, creative writing, drama, economics, English, English literature, environmental science, ESL, European history, expository writing, fine arts, French, geography, geology, geometry, grammar, health, Hebrew, history, Latin, mathematics, music, mythology, philosophy, physical education, physics, physiology, poetry, science, social studies, Spanish, speech, theater, trigonometry, world history, world literature, writing.

Graduation Requirements Arts and fine arts (art, music, dance, drama), career experience, English, foreign language, mathematics, physical education (includes health), science, social studies (includes history).

Special Academic Programs Advanced Placement exam preparation in 5 subject areas; honors section; accelerated programs; independent study; study at local college for college credit; academic accommodation for the gifted and the artistically talented; remedial reading and/or remedial writing; remedial math.

College Placement 19 students graduated in 2005; all went to college, including Emory University; Hofstra University; New York University; State University of New York at Binghamton; The Pennsylvania State University University Park Campus. Median SAT verbal: 570, median SAT math: 570. 20% scored over 600 on SAT verbal, 25% scored over 600 on SAT math.

Student Life Upper grades have student council, honor system. Discipline rests primarily with faculty.

Tuition and Aid Day student tuition: $10,000–$15,500. Tuition installment plan (SMART Tuition Payment Plan, monthly payment plans, individually arranged payment plans, 3-payment plan). Tuition reduction for siblings, merit scholarship grants, need-based scholarship grants available. Total upper-school merit-scholarship money awarded for 2005–06: $20,000.

Admissions Traditional secondary-level entrance grade is 9. For fall 2005, 25 students applied for upper-level admission, 16 were accepted, 15 enrolled. Wechsler Intelligence Scale for Children required. Deadline for receipt of application materials: none. Application fee required: $125. On-campus interview required.

Athletics Interscholastic: baseball (boys), basketball (b,g), cross-country running (b,g), golf (b), soccer (b), softball (g), tennis (g), wrestling (b); intramural: baseball (b), basketball (b,g), bowling (b,g), cross-country running (b,g), skydiving (g), soccer (b,g), tennis (b,g), volleyball (b,g), weight lifting (b,g); coed interscholastic: golf, track and field. 2 PE instructors, 4 coaches.

Computers Computers are regularly used in English, mathematics, science classes. Computer network features include on-campus library services, CD-ROMs, online commercial services, Internet access, file transfer, wireless campus network.

Contact Mr. Timothy L. Costello, Dean of Admissions. 732-364-2812. Fax: 732-364-4004. E-mail: tcostello@lakewoodprep.org.

LA LUMIERE SCHOOL

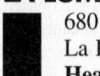

6801 North Wilhelm Road
La Porte, Indiana 46350
Head of School: Michael H. Kennedy

petersons.com

General Information Coeducational boarding and day college-preparatory, arts, and science and mathematics school. Grades 9–12. Founded: 1963. Setting: rural. Nearest major city is Chicago, IL. Students are housed in single-sex dormitories. 155-acre campus. 12 buildings on campus. Approved or accredited by Independent Schools Association of the Central States, Midwest Association of Boarding Schools, North Central Association of Colleges and Schools, and The Association of Boarding Schools. Member of National Association of Independent Schools. Endowment: $1.3 million. Total enrollment: 122. Upper school average class size: 12. Upper school faculty-student ratio: 1:5.

Upper School Student Profile Grade 9: 29 students (15 boys, 14 girls); Grade 10: 32 students (21 boys, 11 girls); Grade 11: 31 students (16 boys, 15 girls); Grade 12: 26 students (12 boys, 14 girls); Postgraduate: 1 student (1 boy). 41% of students are boarding students. 54% are state residents. 10 states are represented in upper school student body. 17% are international students. International students from Burundi, China, India, Japan, Republic of Korea, and Taiwan.

Faculty School total: 19. In upper school: 8 men, 11 women; 7 have advanced degrees; 10 reside on campus.

Subjects Offered Advanced Placement courses, algebra, American history-AP, American literature, art, art history, biology, biology-AP, British literature, calculus, chemistry, Christian and Hebrew scripture, college counseling, computer programming, conceptual physics, creative writing, drama, economics, English, English literature, English-AP, ESL, ethics, French, geography, geometry, government/civics, graphic design, health, physics, pre-calculus, SAT/ACT preparation, Spanish, study skills, trigonometry, U.S. history, U.S. history-AP, Web site design, world history, world literature.

Graduation Requirements Arts and fine arts (art, music, dance, drama), computer science, English, ethics, foreign language, mathematics, religion (includes Bible studies and theology), science, social studies (includes history). Community service is required.

Special Academic Programs Advanced Placement exam preparation in 2 subject areas; honors section; independent study; ESL (10 students enrolled).

College Placement 27 students graduated in 2005; all went to college, including DePauw University; Indiana University Bloomington; John Carroll University; Purdue University; University of Michigan; Valparaiso University. Median SAT verbal: 550, median SAT math: 580, median composite ACT: 24. 37% scored over 600 on SAT verbal, 41% scored over 600 on SAT math, 44% scored over 26 on composite ACT.

Student Life Upper grades have uniform requirement, student council, honor system. Discipline rests primarily with faculty.

Tuition and Aid Day student tuition: $6905; 7-day tuition and room/board: $21,885. Tuition installment plan (Academic Management Services Plan, Key Tuition Payment Plan, individually arranged payment plans). Tuition reduction for siblings, merit scholarship grants, need-based scholarship grants available. In 2005–06, 25% of upper-school students received aid; total upper-school merit-scholarship money awarded: $39,700. Total amount of financial aid awarded in 2005–06: $84,740.

Admissions Traditional secondary-level entrance grade is 9. For fall 2005, 111 students applied for upper-level admission, 67 were accepted, 33 enrolled. Achievement tests, admissions testing, any standardized test, English proficiency, ERB or ISEE required. Deadline for receipt of application materials: none. Application fee required: $50. Interview required.

Athletics Interscholastic: basketball (boys, girls), football (b), lacrosse (b), rugby (g), tennis (g), track and field (b,g), volleyball (g); intramural: aerobics (g), aerobics/dance (g), dance squad (g), volleyball (b,g); coed interscholastic: baseball, running, soccer; coed intramural: basketball, billiards, bowling, canoeing/kayaking, cooperative games, cross-country running, flag football, floor hockey, Frisbee, golf, jogging, martial arts, outdoor activities, outdoor skills, paddle tennis, paint ball, physical training, ropes courses, skateboarding, softball, table tennis, touch football, weight lifting, weight training, yoga. 3 coaches.

Computers Computers are regularly used in all academic, college planning, creative writing, programming, yearbook classes. Computer network features include on-campus library services, CD-ROMs, Internet access, file transfer, office computer access, DVD.

Contact Miss Annie G. Marcucci, Associate Director of Admissions. 219-326-7450. Fax: 219-325-3185. E-mail: amarcucci@lalumiere.org. Web site: www.lalumiere.org/.

See full description on page 868.

LANCASTER COUNTRY DAY SCHOOL

725 Hamilton Road
Lancaster, Pennsylvania 17603
Head of School: Michael J. Mersky

General Information Coeducational day college-preparatory school. Grades PS–12. Founded: 1943. Setting: suburban. Nearest major city is Philadelphia. 26-acre campus. 1 building on campus. Approved or accredited by Middle States Association of Colleges and Schools, Pennsylvania Association of Private Academic Schools, and Pennsylvania Department of Education. Member of National Association of Independent Schools. Endowment: $13 million. Total enrollment: 495. Upper school average class size: 12. Upper school faculty-student ratio: 1:5.

Upper School Student Profile Grade 9: 37 students (17 boys, 20 girls); Grade 10: 56 students (21 boys, 35 girls); Grade 11: 37 students (15 boys, 22 girls); Grade 12: 47 students (25 boys, 22 girls).

Faculty School total: 76. In upper school: 11 men, 25 women; 20 have advanced degrees.

Subjects Offered Algebra, Asian studies, athletic training, Basic programming, bioethics, DNA and culture, biology, biology-AP, calculus, calculus-AP, ceramics, chamber groups, chemistry, chemistry-AP, China/Japan history, chorus, computer art, computer graphics, computer programming, computer programming-AP, computer science, computer science-AP, conceptual physics, contemporary history, contemporary issues, contemporary issues in science, creative writing, critical thinking, critical writing, dance, desktop publishing, digital imaging, drama, drawing, driver education, economics, economics and history, English literature, English-AP, ensembles, environmental science, environmental science-AP, European civilization, European history, European literature, fine arts, French, French-AP, geometry, guitar, honors geometry, instrumental music, journalism, Latin, math applications, mathematics, model United Nations, music, music history, painting, photography, physical education, physics, pre-calculus, printmaking, programming, psychology, research seminar, senior project, service learning/internship, Spanish, Spanish-AP, sports medicine, statistics, statistics-AP, theater, trigonometry, U.S. history, U.S. history-AP, U.S. literature, United Nations and international issues, weight training, women in world history, world affairs, world civilizations, world history, world literature, writing skills, yearbook.

Graduation Requirements Algebra, arts, biology, chemistry, computer science, English, foreign language, geometry, history, Latin, mathematics, physical education (includes health), science, trigonometry, one-week off-campus senior project.

Special Academic Programs Advanced Placement exam preparation in 11 subject areas; independent study; study at local college for college credit; academic accommodation for the gifted, the musically talented, and the artistically talented.

College Placement 35 students graduated in 2005; 34 went to college, including Cornell University; Hamilton College; The College of William and Mary; The Johns Hopkins University; The Pennsylvania State University University Park Campus; University of Pittsburgh. Other: 1 had other specific plans. Median SAT verbal: 620, median SAT math: 599. 54% scored over 600 on SAT verbal, 60% scored over 600 on SAT math.

Student Life Upper grades have specified standards of dress, student council, honor system. Discipline rests equally with students and faculty.

Tuition and Aid Day student tuition: $15,400. Tuition installment plan (monthly payment plans, 2-installment plan). Need-based scholarship grants available. In 2005–06, 20% of upper-school students received aid. Total amount of financial aid awarded in 2005–06: $360,000.

Admissions Traditional secondary-level entrance grade is 9. For fall 2005, 13 students applied for upper-level admission, 11 were accepted, 9 enrolled. ERB CTP III required. Deadline for receipt of application materials: none. Application fee required: $75. Interview required.

Athletics Interscholastic: baseball (boys), basketball (b,g), field hockey (g), football (b), lacrosse (b,g), soccer (b,g), softball (g), swimming and diving (b,g), tennis (b,g); coed interscholastic: cross-country running, golf, squash, track and field; coed intramural: squash. 2 PE instructors, 9 coaches, 2 trainers.

Computers Computers are regularly used in desktop publishing, ESL, English, graphic arts, history, information technology, journalism, literary magazine, newspaper, programming, psychology, research skills, science, technology, Web site design, word processing, writing, yearbook classes. Computer network features include campus e-mail, on-campus library services, CD-ROMs, online commercial services, Internet access, office computer access, DVD, technology-rich environment with SmartBoards in every classroom.

Contact Beth Townsend, Assistant Director of Admission. 717-392-2916 Ext. 228. Fax: 717-392-0425. E-mail: admiss@e-lcds.org. Web site: www.lancastercountryday.org.

LANDMARK EAST SCHOOL
Wolfville, Nova Scotia, Canada
See Special Needs Schools section.

LANDMARK SCHOOL
Prides Crossing, Massachusetts
See Special Needs Schools section.

LANDON SCHOOL
6101 Wilson Lane
Bethesda, Maryland 20817
Head of School: Mr. David M. Armstrong

General Information Boys' day college-preparatory, arts, and music school. Grades 3–12. Founded: 1929. Setting: suburban. Nearest major city is Washington, DC. 75-acre campus. 13 buildings on campus. Approved or accredited by Association of Independent Maryland Schools, Middle States Association of Colleges and Schools, and Maryland Department of Education. Member of National Association of Independent Schools. Endowment: $16 million. Total enrollment: 675. Upper school average class size: 15. Upper school faculty-student ratio: 1:10.

Upper School Student Profile Grade 9: 87 students (87 boys); Grade 10: 81 students (81 boys); Grade 11: 81 students (81 boys); Grade 12: 84 students (84 boys).

Faculty School total: 110. In upper school: 50 men, 14 women; 49 have advanced degrees.

Subjects Offered Algebra, American history, American literature, art, art history, biology, calculus, ceramics, chemistry, Chinese, computer science, creative writing, drama, earth science, ecology, English, English literature, environmental science, ethics, European history, expository writing, fine arts, French, geography, geology, geometry, government/civics, grammar, health, history, humanities, Latin, mathematics, meteorology, Middle Eastern history, music, oceanography, photography, physical education, physics, religion, science, social studies, Spanish, statistics, technological applications, theater, trigonometry, typing, world history, world literature, writing.

Graduation Requirements Advanced Placement courses, American Civil War, American government, American government-AP, American history-AP, arts and fine arts (art, music, dance, drama), biology, biology-AP, calculus, calculus-AP, chemistry, chemistry-AP, civil war history, economics, English, ethics, foreign language, government, government-AP, humanities, mathematics, physical education (includes health), political science, science, social studies (includes history).

Special Academic Programs Advanced Placement exam preparation in 12 subject areas; honors section; independent study; term-away projects; study abroad.

College Placement 83 students graduated in 2005; all went to college, including Amherst College; Duke University; Emory University; Georgetown University; University of Maryland, College Park; University of Virginia. Mean SAT verbal: 625, mean SAT math: 644, mean combined SAT: 1898, mean composite ACT: 26.

Student Life Upper grades have specified standards of dress, student council, honor system. Discipline rests equally with students and faculty.

Summer Programs Remediation, enrichment, advancement, sports, art/fine arts, rigorous outdoor training, computer instruction programs offered; held both on and off campus; held at locations in France, China, and Spain; accepts boys and girls; open to students from other schools. 1500 students usually enrolled. 2006 schedule: June 19 to July 28. Application deadline: May 1.

Tuition and Aid Day student tuition: $24,500. Tuition installment plan (FACTS Tuition Payment Plan). Need-based scholarship grants, need-based loans available. In 2005–06, 15% of upper-school students received aid. Total amount of financial aid awarded in 2005–06: $772,665.

Admissions Traditional secondary-level entrance grade is 9. For fall 2005, 100 students applied for upper-level admission, 22 enrolled. ISEE and school's own exam required. Deadline for receipt of application materials: January 15. Application fee required: $65. On-campus interview required.

Athletics Interscholastic: baseball (boys), basketball (b), cross-country running (b), diving (b), football (b), golf (b), ice hockey (b), indoor track (b), lacrosse (b), riflery (b), soccer (b), swimming and diving (b), tennis (b), track and field (b), winter (indoor) track (b), wrestling (b); intramural: fencing (b), floor hockey (b), football (b), Frisbee (b), rugby (b), soccer (b), softball (b), squash (b), street hockey (b), tennis (b), touch football (b), ultimate Frisbee (b), volleyball (b), weight lifting (b). 2 PE instructors, 20 coaches, 1 trainer.

Computers Computers are regularly used in all classes. Computer network features include campus e-mail, on-campus library services, CD-ROMs, online commercial services, Internet access, file transfer, DVD.

Contact Mr. Russell L. Gagarin, Director of Admissions and Financial Aid. 301-320-1067. Fax: 301-320-1133. E-mail: russ_gagarin@landon.net. Web site: www.landon.net.

LANSDALE CATHOLIC HIGH SCHOOL
700 Lansdale Avenue
Lansdale, Pennsylvania 19446-2995
Head of School: Mrs. Linda Robinson

General Information Coeducational day college-preparatory, general academic, and religious studies school, affiliated with Roman Catholic Church. Grades 9–12. Founded: 1949. Setting: suburban. Nearest major city is Philadelphia. 1 building on campus. Approved or accredited by Middle States Association of Colleges and Schools and Pennsylvania Department of Education. Total enrollment: 800.

Upper School Student Profile Grade 9: 198 students (102 boys, 96 girls); Grade 10: 202 students (100 boys, 102 girls); Grade 11: 205 students (101 boys, 104 girls); Grade 12: 195 students (95 boys, 100 girls). 99% of students are Roman Catholic.

Faculty School total: 37. In upper school: 18 men, 17 women; 23 have advanced degrees.

Subjects Offered Algebra, American government, American government-AP, American history, American history-AP, American literature, analytic geometry, Basic programming, business law, calculus, calculus-AP, career education, career planning, career/college preparation, Catholic belief and practice, chemistry, chorus, church history, classical language, college counseling, college placement, college planning, computer education, computer programming, drama, English literature-AP, environmental science, European history, French, government and politics-AP, government-AP, Greek, health education, Italian, Latin, physical fitness, physical science, physics, pre-calculus, SAT/ACT preparation, Spanish, student government, trigonometry, U.S. government and politics-AP, Western civilization.

Special Academic Programs Advanced Placement exam preparation in 6 subject areas; honors section; study at local college for college credit; remedial reading and/or remedial writing; remedial math.

College Placement 191 students graduated in 2005; 185 went to college, including Saint Joseph's University; Shippensburg University of Pennsylvania; Temple University; The Pennsylvania State University University Park Campus; West Chester University of Pennsylvania. Other: 2 went to work, 2 entered military service, 1 had other specific plans.

Student Life Upper grades have uniform requirement, student council, honor system. Discipline rests primarily with faculty. Attendance at religious services is required.

Summer Programs Remediation, enrichment, advancement, sports, art/fine arts programs offered; held on campus; accepts boys and girls; not open to students from other schools.

Tuition and Aid Day student tuition: $4200. Tuition installment plan (monthly payment plans, individually arranged payment plans). Tuition reduction for siblings, merit scholarship grants, need-based scholarship grants available.

Admissions Traditional secondary-level entrance grade is 9. Deadline for receipt of application materials: none. Application fee required.

Athletics Interscholastic: baseball (boys), basketball (b,g), cheering (g), cross-country running (b,g), dance (b,g), field hockey (g), football (b), golf (b,g), ice skating (b,g), lacrosse (g), rugby (b,g), soccer (b,g), softball (g), swimming and diving (b,g), tennis (b,g), track and field (b,g), volleyball (g), weight lifting (b), winter (indoor) track (b,g), wrestling (b); intramural: ice hockey (b,g); coed interscholastic: bowling, diving. 1 PE instructor, 1 trainer.

Computers Computers are regularly used in all classes. Computer network features include on-campus library services, CD-ROMs, online commercial services, Internet access, office computer access, DVD, wireless campus network.

Contact Rev. Joseph Rymdeika, President. 215-362-6160 Ext. 133. Fax: 215-362-5746. E-mail: jrymdeika@lansdalecatholic.com. Web site: www.lansdalecatholic.com.

LA PIETRA–HAWAII SCHOOL FOR GIRLS
2933 Poni Moi Road
Honolulu, Hawaii 96815
Head of School: Mrs. Nancy D. White

General Information Girls' day college-preparatory, arts, bilingual studies, and technology school. Grades 6–12. Founded: 1962. Setting: suburban. 6-acre campus. 15 buildings on campus. Approved or accredited by Western Association of Schools and Colleges and Hawaii Department of Education. Member of National Association of Independent Schools and Secondary School Admission Test Board. Endowment: $3 million. Total enrollment: 240. Upper school average class size: 6. Upper school faculty-student ratio: 1:10.

Upper School Student Profile Grade 9: 38 students (38 girls); Grade 10: 30 students (30 girls); Grade 11: 30 students (30 girls); Grade 12: 34 students (34 girls).

Faculty School total: 36. In upper school: 8 men, 28 women; 23 have advanced degrees.

Subjects Offered Advanced Placement courses, algebra, American history, American literature, art, art history, biology, calculus, ceramics, chemistry, creative writing, drama, earth science, ecology, English, English literature, European history, expository writing, fine arts, French, geography, geometry, grammar, health, history, Japanese, marine biology, mathematics, music, oceanography, photography, physical education, physics, physiology, psychology, science, social studies, Spanish, theater, trigonometry, world history, writing.

La Pietra–Hawaii School for Girls

Graduation Requirements Arts and fine arts (art, music, dance, drama), English, foreign language, mathematics, physical education (includes health), science, social studies (includes history), independent project.

Special Academic Programs Advanced Placement exam preparation in 5 subject areas; honors section; accelerated programs; independent study; study at local college for college credit; remedial reading and/or remedial writing; remedial math.

College Placement 28 students graduated in 2005; 24 went to college, including United States Naval Academy; University of Hawaii at Manoa. Other: 2 went to work. 22% scored over 600 on SAT verbal, 19% scored over 600 on SAT math.

Student Life Upper grades have uniform requirement, student council. Discipline rests primarily with faculty.

Tuition and Aid Day student tuition: $11,925. Guaranteed tuition plan. Tuition installment plan (monthly payment plans, individually arranged payment plans, tuition insurance). Need-based scholarship grants available. In 2005–06, 43% of upper-school students received aid. Total amount of financial aid awarded in 2005–06: $253,300.

Admissions Traditional secondary-level entrance grade is 9. For fall 2005, 64 students applied for upper-level admission, 42 were accepted, 20 enrolled. SSAT required. Deadline for receipt of application materials: none. Application fee required: $40. Interview required.

Athletics Interscholastic: aerobics/nautilus, baseball, basketball, bowling, canoeing/kayaking, cross-country running, diving, equestrian sports, golf, gymnastics, judo, kayaking, ocean paddling, outdoor activities, paddling, sailing, soccer, softball, surfing, swimming and diving, tennis, track and field, volleyball, water polo, wrestling. 3 PE instructors, 10 coaches.

Computers Computers are regularly used in all academic, art classes. Computer network features include campus e-mail, on-campus library services, CD-ROMs, online commercial services, Internet access, DVD, LavaNet.

Contact Mrs. Sandra Robinson, Director of Admissions. 808-922-2744. Fax: 808-923-4514. E-mail: info@lapietra.edu. Web site: www.lapietra.edu.

LA SALLE ACADEMY

612 Academy Avenue
Providence, Rhode Island 02908
Head of School: Br. Michael McKenery, FSC

General Information Coeducational day college-preparatory, arts, religious studies, and technology school, affiliated with Roman Catholic Church. Grades 7–12. Founded: 1874. Setting: urban. 60-acre campus. 5 buildings on campus. Approved or accredited by New England Association of Schools and Colleges. Member of National Association of Independent Schools. Total enrollment: 1,379. Upper school average class size: 20. Upper school faculty-student ratio: 1:13.

Upper School Student Profile Grade 9: 353 students (172 boys, 181 girls); Grade 10: 346 students (170 boys, 176 girls); Grade 11: 304 students (158 boys, 146 girls); Grade 12: 292 students (144 boys, 148 girls). 85% of students are Roman Catholic.

Faculty School total: 104. In upper school: 58 men, 46 women; 76 have advanced degrees.

Subjects Offered Algebra, American history, American literature, anatomy, art, astronomy, biology, business, calculus, ceramics, chemistry, community service, computer programming, computer science, creative writing, dance, drama, drawing, economics, electronics, engineering, English, English literature, environmental science, ESL, film, fine arts, French, geology, geometry, history, Italian, journalism, law, mathematics, microbiology, music, painting, photography, physical education, physical science, physics, physiology, psychology, religion, science, social studies, sociology, Spanish, statistics, theater, trigonometry, world history, world literature, writing.

Graduation Requirements Arts and fine arts (art, music, dance, drama), computer science, English, foreign language, mathematics, physical education (includes health), religion (includes Bible studies and theology), science, social studies (includes history). Community service is required.

Special Academic Programs Advanced Placement exam preparation in 10 subject areas; honors section; study at local college for college credit; academic accommodation for the gifted, the musically talented, and the artistically talented.

College Placement 292 students graduated in 2005; 285 went to college, including Boston College; Brown University; Harvard University; United States Military Academy; University of Rhode Island; Yale University. Other: 6 went to work, 1 entered military service.

Student Life Upper grades have uniform requirement, student council, honor system. Discipline rests equally with students and faculty.

Tuition and Aid Day student tuition: $9300. Tuition installment plan (FACTS Tuition Payment Plan). Merit scholarship grants, need-based scholarship grants available. In 2005–06, 35% of upper-school students received aid; total upper-school merit-scholarship money awarded: $600,000. Total amount of financial aid awarded in 2005–06: $1,000,000.

Admissions Traditional secondary-level entrance grade is 9. For fall 2005, 850 students applied for upper-level admission, 400 were accepted, 350 enrolled. STS, Diocese Test required. Deadline for receipt of application materials: December 31. Application fee required: $25.

Athletics Interscholastic: baseball (boys), basketball (b,g), cross-country running (b,g), football (b), golf (b,g), gymnastics (b,g), ice hockey (b,g), lacrosse (b,g), sailing (b,g), soccer (b,g), softball (g), swimming and diving (b,g), tennis (b,g), track and field (b,g), volleyball (b,g), wrestling (b,g); coed intramural: fencing, modern dance, physical fitness, physical training, table tennis, touch football, volleyball, walking, whiffle ball. 5 PE instructors, 61 coaches, 4 trainers.

Computers Computers are regularly used in English, foreign language, history, mathematics, music, science classes. Computer network features include campus e-mail, CD-ROMs, online commercial services, Internet access.

Contact Mr. George Aldrich, Director of Admissions and Public Relations. 401-351-7750. Fax: 401-453-6315. E-mail: galdrich@lasalle-academy.org. Web site: www.lasalle-academy.org.

LA SALLE COLLEGE HIGH SCHOOL

8605 Cheltenham Avenue
Wyndmoor, Pennsylvania 19038
Head of School: Br. Richard Kestler, FSC

General Information Boys' day college-preparatory, arts, and technology school, affiliated with Roman Catholic Church. Grades 9–12. Founded: 1858. Setting: suburban. Nearest major city is Philadelphia. 52-acre campus. 7 buildings on campus. Approved or accredited by Christian Brothers Association, Middle States Association of Colleges and Schools, National Catholic Education Association, Pennsylvania Association of Private Academic Schools, and Pennsylvania Department of Education. Member of National Association of Independent Schools. Endowment: $12.6 million. Total enrollment: 1,080. Upper school average class size: 20. Upper school faculty-student ratio: 1:11.

Upper School Student Profile Grade 9: 267 students (267 boys); Grade 10: 281 students (281 boys); Grade 11: 270 students (270 boys); Grade 12: 262 students (262 boys). 95% of students are Roman Catholic.

Faculty School total: 94. In upper school: 74 men, 20 women; 66 have advanced degrees.

Subjects Offered Algebra, American history, American literature, anatomy, art, art history, astronomy, band, Bible studies, biology, business, business skills, calculus, ceramics, chemistry, chorus, computer programming, computer science, creative writing, drama, economics, English, English language and composition-AP, English literature, English literature and composition-AP, ensembles, environmental science, environmental science-AP, ethics, European history, European history-AP, fine arts, French, French language-AP, geometry, German, German-AP, government and politics-AP, government/civics, health, history, Holocaust studies, HTML design, instrumental music, integrated science, Italian, jazz, jazz band, jazz ensemble, jazz theory, Latin, Latin-AP, mathematics, Microsoft, moral and social development, moral reasoning, moral theology, music, music appreciation, music performance, music technology, oral communications, peer ministry, performing arts, physical education, physics, physics-AP, physiology, prayer/spirituality, psychology, public service, public speaking, religion, science, sculpture, social science, social studies, Spanish, Spanish literature-AP, speech, speech and debate, statistics, statistics-AP, swimming, swimming competency, technological applications, theater, theology, trigonometry, U.S. government-AP, U.S. history, U.S. history-AP, Vietnam, visual arts, vocal ensemble, Web authoring, Web site design, world civilizations, world history, world literature, writing.

Graduation Requirements Arts and fine arts (art, music, dance, drama), computer science, English, foreign language, mathematics, physical education (includes health), religion (includes Bible studies and theology), science, social studies (includes history), attendance at off-campus class retreat.

Special Academic Programs Advanced Placement exam preparation in 17 subject areas; honors section; independent study; study at local college for college credit; academic accommodation for the gifted, the musically talented, and the artistically talented; programs in general development for dyslexic students; special instructional classes for wheelchair-bound students.

College Placement 252 students graduated in 2005; 250 went to college, including Drexel University; La Salle University; Saint Joseph's University; The Pennsylvania State University University Park Campus; University of Pennsylvania; Villanova University. Other: 1 went to work, 1 entered military service. Mean SAT verbal: 579, mean SAT math: 625. 30% scored over 600 on SAT verbal, 32% scored over 600 on SAT math.

Student Life Upper grades have specified standards of dress, student council, honor system. Discipline rests primarily with faculty. Attendance at religious services is required.

Summer Programs Remediation, enrichment, sports, art/fine arts, computer instruction programs offered; session focuses on enrichment and secondary school transition; held on campus; accepts boys and girls; open to students from other schools. 1150 students usually enrolled. 2006 schedule: June 19 to August 2. Application deadline: June 1.

Tuition and Aid Day student tuition: $11,700. Tuition installment plan (Academic Management Services Plan, monthly payment plans, Higher Education Service, Inc). Merit scholarship grants, need-based scholarship grants, paying campus jobs available. In 2005–06, 33% of upper-school students received aid; total upper-school merit-scholarship money awarded: $35,600. Total amount of financial aid awarded in 2005–06: $1,200,000.

Admissions Traditional secondary-level entrance grade is 9. For fall 2005, 732 students applied for upper-level admission, 375 were accepted, 267 enrolled.

Scholastic Testing Service High School Placement Test required. Deadline for receipt of application materials: December 1. Application fee required: $40. On-campus interview required.

Athletics Interscholastic: baseball, basketball, bicycling, bowling, crew, cross-country running, diving, football, golf, ice hockey, indoor track, indoor track & field, lacrosse, rowing, running, swimming and diving, track and field, water polo, winter (indoor) track, wrestling; intramural: baseball, basketball, bicycling, bowling, cross-country running, football, independent competitive sports, lacrosse, outdoor adventure, swimming and diving, volleyball, weight lifting, weight training. 2 PE instructors, 2 trainers.

Computers Computers are regularly used in business, English, foreign language, history, Latin, mathematics, religion, science, Spanish, writing classes. Computer network features include campus e-mail, on-campus library services, CD-ROMs, online commercial services, Internet access, file transfer, office computer access, networking certification.

Contact Br. James Rieck, FSC, Director of Admissions. 215-233-2911. Fax: 215-233-1418. E-mail: rieck@lschs.org. Web site: www.lschs.org.

LA SALLE HIGH SCHOOL

3880 East Sierra Madre Boulevard
Pasadena, California 91107-1996
Head of School: Mr. Patrick Bonacci

General Information Coeducational day college-preparatory, arts, and religious studies school, affiliated with Roman Catholic Church. Grades 9–12. Founded: 1956. Setting: suburban. 10-acre campus. 3 buildings on campus. Approved or accredited by Christian Brothers Association, Western Association of Schools and Colleges, Western Catholic Education Association, and California Department of Education. Total enrollment: 735. Upper school average class size: 25. Upper school faculty-student ratio: 1:12.

Upper School Student Profile Grade 9: 187 students (90 boys, 97 girls); Grade 10: 180 students (94 boys, 86 girls); Grade 11: 197 students (107 boys, 90 girls); Grade 12: 171 students (84 boys, 87 girls). 66% of students are Roman Catholic.

Faculty School total: 64. In upper school: 37 men, 25 women; 33 have advanced degrees.

Subjects Offered 20th century history, acting, advanced computer applications, Advanced Placement courses, advanced studio art-AP, algebra, American Civil War, American government, American government-AP, American legal systems, American literature-AP, ancient world history, art, art-AP, ASB Leadership, band, biology-AP, business law, calculus, calculus-AP, campus ministry, Catholic belief and practice, chemistry-AP, chorus, Christian and Hebrew scripture, church history, cinematography, civics, Civil War, classical civilization, community service, comparative religion, composition, composition-AP, computer applications, computer education, computer graphics, computer literacy, computer programming, concert choir, constitutional history of U.S., creative writing, dance, dance performance, digital photography, drama, dramatic arts, drawing, ecology, environmental systems, economics, economics-AP, education, electives, English, English composition, English language-AP, English literature, English literature and composition-AP, English-AP, fiction, film, fine arts, foreign language, French, general math, general science, geometry, government, government/civics, government/civics-AP, health and safety, health education, Hispanic literature, history, history-AP, honors algebra, honors English, honors U.S. history, honors world history, integrated mathematics, introduction to theater, jazz, jazz band, jazz dance, jazz ensemble, journalism, keyboarding, lab science, lab/keyboard, Latin, Latin-AP, law and the legal system, leadership and service, leadership skills, mathematics, mathematics-AP, microbiology, modern European history-AP, musical productions, newspaper, photo shop, photography, physics, physics-AP, play production, pottery, pre-calculus, religion, religion and culture, religious studies, Roman civilization, science, social justice, Spanish, Spanish-AP, statistics, student government, studio art, studio art—AP, study skills, tap dance, technical theater, television, theater, theater arts, theater design and production, theater production, trigonometry, U.S. government, U.S. government and politics-AP, U.S. history, U.S. history-AP, U.S. literature, video communication, visual and performing arts, visual arts, Web authoring, wind instruments, world history, writing, yearbook.

Graduation Requirements Algebra, arts and fine arts (art, music, dance, drama), biology, British literature, campus ministry, chemistry, Christian and Hebrew scripture, Christian doctrine, church history, civics, computer literacy, economics, English, English composition, English literature, foreign language, geometry, integrated mathematics, physical education (includes health), physics, religious studies, U.S. history.

Special Academic Programs Advanced Placement exam preparation in 6 subject areas; honors section.

College Placement 174 students graduated in 2005; 173 went to college, including California State Polytechnic University, Pomona; Saint Mary's College of California; University of California, Irvine; University of California, San Diego; University of Southern California. Other: 1 had other specific plans. Median SAT verbal: 577, median SAT math: 564, median composite ACT: 25. 41% scored over 600 on SAT verbal, 42% scored over 600 on SAT math.

Student Life Upper grades have uniform requirement, student council, honor system. Discipline rests primarily with faculty. Attendance at religious services is required.

Summer Programs Remediation, enrichment, sports, art/fine arts, computer instruction programs offered; session focuses on academics and sports camp; held on campus; accepts boys and girls; open to students from other schools. 300 students usually enrolled. 2006 schedule: June 19 to July 21. Application deadline: May 1.

Tuition and Aid Day student tuition: $10,260. Tuition installment plan (monthly payment plans). Merit scholarship grants, need-based scholarship grants available. In 2005–06, 16% of upper-school students received aid; total upper-school merit-scholarship money awarded: $50,000. Total amount of financial aid awarded in 2005–06: $550,000.

Admissions Traditional secondary-level entrance grade is 9. For fall 2005, 622 students applied for upper-level admission, 287 were accepted, 187 enrolled. Scholastic Testing Service High School Placement Test required. Deadline for receipt of application materials: January 13. Application fee required: $70. Interview required.

Athletics Interscholastic: baseball (boys), basketball (b,g), cross-country running (b,g), football (b), soccer (b,g), softball (g), swimming and diving (b,g), tennis (b,g), track and field (b,g), volleyball (b,g), water polo (b,g); intramural: basketball (b,g), flag football (b); coed interscholastic: aerobics, cheering, equestrian sports, golf, physical fitness, weight training. 2 PE instructors, 40 coaches, 1 trainer.

Computers Computers are regularly used in all academic classes. Computer resources include on-campus library services, CD-ROMs, online commercial services, Internet access.

Contact Mrs. Norma J. Wong, Admissions Secretary. 626-351-8951. Fax: 626-696-4411. E-mail: nwong@lasallehs.org. Web site: www.lasallehs.org.

THE LATIN SCHOOL OF CHICAGO

59 West North Boulevard
Chicago, Illinois 60610-1492
Head of School: Donald W. Firke

General Information Coeducational day college-preparatory school. Grades JK–12. Founded: 1888. Setting: urban. 1-acre campus. 1 building on campus. Approved or accredited by Independent Schools Association of the Central States. Member of National Association of Independent Schools and Secondary School Admission Test Board. Endowment: $13.5 million. Total enrollment: 1,079. Upper school average class size: 15. Upper school faculty-student ratio: 1:8.

Upper School Student Profile Grade 9: 107 students (49 boys, 58 girls); Grade 10: 107 students (53 boys, 54 girls); Grade 11: 102 students (43 boys, 59 girls); Grade 12: 101 students (51 boys, 50 girls).

Faculty School total: 132. In upper school: 31 men, 32 women; 51 have advanced degrees.

Subjects Offered Advanced Placement courses, advanced studio art-AP, African studies, African-American literature, algebra, American history, American history-AP, American literature, anatomy, animal behavior, art, art history, Asian studies, astronomy, biochemistry, biology, biology-AP, calculus, calculus-AP, chemistry, chemistry-AP, chorus, community service, composition, computer graphics, computer programming, computer science, creative writing, dance, drama, ecology, electives, electronics, English, English literature, environmental science, environmental science-AP, ethics, European civilization, European history, fine arts, French, French language-AP, French literature-AP, geography, geometry, history, history of ideas, honors U.S. history, human relations, human sexuality, humanities, independent study, instrumental music, Latin, Latin American history, Latin American literature, Latin-AP, literature by women, Mandarin, mathematical modeling, mathematics, mathematics-AP, Middle East, Middle Eastern history, music theory, photography, physical education, physics, physics-AP, physiology, poetry, psychology, religion, science, social studies, Spanish, Spanish language-AP, Spanish literature, Spanish literature-AP, speech, stage design, statistics and probability, studio art—AP, theater, trigonometry, women's literature, world history, world literature, writing.

Graduation Requirements Arts and fine arts (art, music, dance, drama), English, ethics, foreign language, human relations, human sexuality, humanities, mathematics, performing arts, physical education (includes health), science, social studies (includes history), technology, one-week non-credit course each year, participation in an interdisciplinary humanities program. Community service is required.

Special Academic Programs Advanced Placement exam preparation in 17 subject areas; honors section; independent study; study abroad; academic accommodation for the gifted; remedial reading and/or remedial writing; remedial math; programs in general development for dyslexic students.

College Placement 102 students graduated in 2005; 101 went to college, including Dartmouth College; Georgetown University; Princeton University; University of Illinois at Urbana–Champaign; University of Southern California; University of Wisconsin–Madison. Other: 1 entered a postgraduate year. Median SAT verbal: 660, median SAT math: 650, median composite ACT: 28. 74% scored over 600 on SAT verbal, 64% scored over 600 on SAT math, 55% scored over 26 on composite ACT.

Student Life Upper grades have specified standards of dress, student council, honor system. Discipline rests equally with students and faculty.

Summer Programs Remediation, enrichment, advancement, sports, art/fine arts, rigorous outdoor training, computer instruction programs offered; session focuses on enrichment, remediation, sports, travel, and adventure; held both on and off campus; held at lakefront, city parks, wilderness experiences in the United States and abroad

The Latin School of Chicago

and trips abroad including Ecuador; accepts boys and girls; open to students from other schools. 180 students usually enrolled. 2006 schedule: June 12 to August 4. Application deadline: none.

Tuition and Aid Day student tuition: $20,675. Tuition installment plan (Insured Tuition Payment Plan, Key Tuition Payment Plan, monthly payment plans, individually arranged payment plans). Need-based scholarship grants, need-based loans, middle-income loans, Key Education Achiever Loans available. In 2005–06, 18% of upper-school students received aid. Total amount of financial aid awarded in 2005–06: $1,571,463.

Admissions Traditional secondary-level entrance grade is 9. For fall 2005, 234 students applied for upper-level admission, 100 were accepted, 46 enrolled. ISEE required. Deadline for receipt of application materials: February 1. Application fee required: $80. On-campus interview required.

Athletics Interscholastic: aquatics (boys, girls), badminton (g), baseball (b), basketball (b,g), cross-country running (b,g), field hockey (g), golf (b,g), ice hockey (b,g), soccer (b,g), softball (g), swimming and diving (b,g), tennis (b,g), track and field (b,g), volleyball (b,g), water polo (b,g); intramural: life saving (b,g); coed intramural: dance, kayaking, outdoor activities, outdoor adventure, outdoor education, outdoor recreation, physical fitness, physical training, skiing (downhill). 6 PE instructors, 12 coaches, 2 trainers.

Computers Computers are regularly used in art, English, foreign language, mathematics, science classes. Computer network features include campus e-mail, on-campus library services, CD-ROMs, online commercial services, Internet access, file transfer, office computer access, DVD, wireless campus network, password-protected Intranet Website.

Contact Anne Frame, Director of Admissions and Financial Aid. 312-582-6060. Fax: 312-582-6061. E-mail: aframe@latinschool.org. Web site: www.latinschool.org.

LAUREL SCHOOL

One Lyman Circle
Shaker Heights, Ohio 44122
Head of School: Ann V. Klotz

General Information Coeducational day (boys' only in lower grades) college-preparatory school. Boys grades PS–PK, girls grades PS–12. Founded: 1896. Setting: suburban. Nearest major city is Cleveland. 12-acre campus. 1 building on campus. Approved or accredited by Independent Schools Association of the Central States and Ohio Department of Education. Member of National Association of Independent Schools. Endowment: $33.9 million. Total enrollment: 644. Upper school average class size: 14. Upper school faculty-student ratio: 1:8.

Upper School Student Profile Grade 9: 43 students (43 girls); Grade 10: 55 students (55 girls); Grade 11: 47 students (47 girls); Grade 12: 55 students (55 girls).

Faculty School total: 91. In upper school: 14 men, 21 women; 29 have advanced degrees.

Subjects Offered Algebra, American history, American literature, American literature-AP, anatomy and physiology, art, art history-AP, astronomy, biology, biology-AP, biotechnology, calculus, calculus-AP, ceramics, chemistry, chemistry-AP, choir, choreography, classical studies, classics, community service, computer art, computer multimedia, computer science, creative writing, discrete mathematics, drama, drawing, driver education, earth science, engineering, English, English literature, English-AP, environmental science, European history, European history-AP, experiential education, expository writing, fine arts, forensics, French, French-AP, geography, geology, geometry, government-AP, grammar, health, history, honors algebra, honors English, honors geometry, honors U.S. history, independent study, Latin, Latin-AP, mathematics, music, music theory, orchestra, painting, photography, physical education, physics, physics-AP, pre-calculus, probability and statistics, science, sculpture, senior project, social studies, Spanish, Spanish language-AP, Spanish literature, Spanish literature-AP, Spanish-AP, speech, studio art, studio art-AP, technical theater, theater, trigonometry, U.S. history-AP, world history, writing.

Graduation Requirements Arts and fine arts (art, music, dance, drama), English, foreign language, history, mathematics, physical education (includes health), science, speech, 10-minute speech on a subject of choice to the entire Upper School student body and faculty. Community service is required.

Special Academic Programs Advanced Placement exam preparation in 16 subject areas; honors section; independent study; term-away projects; study at local college for college credit; study abroad; academic accommodation for the gifted, the musically talented, and the artistically talented.

College Placement 44 students graduated in 2005; all went to college, including Dartmouth College; Georgetown University; Miami University; The Johns Hopkins University; The Ohio State University; Wellesley College. Mean SAT verbal: 647, mean SAT math: 630, mean composite ACT: 28.

Student Life Upper grades have uniform requirement, student council, honor system. Discipline rests primarily with faculty.

Tuition and Aid Day student tuition: $19,300. Tuition installment plan (Key Tuition Payment Plan, monthly payment plans, individually arranged payment plans). Merit scholarship grants, need-based scholarship grants available. In 2005–06, 50% of upper-school students received aid. Total amount of financial aid awarded in 2005–06: $1,114,035.

Admissions Traditional secondary-level entrance grade is 9. For fall 2005, 56 students applied for upper-level admission, 43 were accepted, 21 enrolled. ISEE required. Deadline for receipt of application materials: none. Application fee required: $25. On-campus interview required.

Athletics Interscholastic: basketball (girls), cross-country running (g), field hockey (g), golf (g), lacrosse (g), soccer (g), softball (g), strength & conditioning (g), swimming and diving (g), tennis (g), track and field (g), volleyball (g); intramural: basketball (g), field hockey (g), lacrosse (g), soccer (g), softball (g), swimming and diving (g), tennis (g), volleyball (g). 15 coaches, 1 trainer.

Computers Computers are regularly used in all academic classes. Computer network features include campus e-mail, on-campus library services, CD-ROMs, Internet access, wireless campus network.

Contact Mary Lisa Geppert, Associate Director of Admissions. 216-464-0946. Fax: 216-464-8996. E-mail: mlgeppert@laurelschool.org. Web site: www.laurelschool.org.

LAUSANNE COLLEGIATE SCHOOL

1381 West Massey Road
Memphis, Tennessee 38120
Head of School: Mr. Stuart McCathie

General Information Coeducational day college-preparatory, arts, bilingual studies, and technology school. Grades PK–12. Founded: 1926. Setting: suburban. 28-acre campus. 5 buildings on campus. Approved or accredited by National Independent Private Schools Association, Southern Association of Colleges and Schools, Southern Association of Independent Schools, Tennessee Association of Independent Schools, and Tennessee Department of Education. Member of National Association of Independent Schools. Endowment: $700,000. Total enrollment: 742. Upper school average class size: 18. Upper school faculty-student ratio: 1:9.

Upper School Student Profile Grade 9: 55 students (29 boys, 26 girls); Grade 10: 51 students (22 boys, 29 girls); Grade 11: 56 students (36 boys, 20 girls); Grade 12: 55 students (25 boys, 30 girls).

Faculty School total: 92. In upper school: 9 men, 18 women; 13 have advanced degrees.

Subjects Offered Acting, algebra, American government, ancient world history, art, art-AP, biology, biology-AP, calculus, chemistry, choir, college admission preparation, comparative government and politics-AP, computer programming, creative writing, discrete mathematics, economics, English, English-AP, French, French-AP, geometry, health and wellness, honors algebra, honors English, honors geometry, humanities, instrumental music, international studies, journalism, Latin, Latin-AP, modern world history, photography, physical education, physical science, physics, physics-AP, play production, pre-calculus, public policy, short story, Spanish, Spanish-AP, statistics, U.S. history, U.S. history-AP, World War II, writing workshop.

Graduation Requirements Arts and fine arts (art, music, dance, drama), comparative government and politics-AP, computer science, English, foreign language, mathematics, physical education (includes health), science, social studies (includes history).

Special Academic Programs Advanced Placement exam preparation in 14 subject areas; honors section; academic accommodation for the gifted, the musically talented, and the artistically talented.

College Placement 52 students graduated in 2005; all went to college, including Southern Methodist University; The University of Tennessee; University of Colorado at Boulder; University of Miami; University of Mississippi; Vanderbilt University. 50% scored over 600 on SAT verbal, 55% scored over 600 on SAT math, 40% scored over 26 on composite ACT.

Student Life Upper grades have specified standards of dress, student council, honor system. Discipline rests primarily with faculty.

Summer Programs Remediation, enrichment, advancement, sports, art/fine arts, computer instruction programs offered; session focuses on academics, athletics and fun; held on campus; accepts boys and girls; open to students from other schools. 600 students usually enrolled. 2006 schedule: June 1 to August 7.

Tuition and Aid Day student tuition: $10,975. Tuition installment plan (monthly payment plans, Tuition Refund Plan). Merit scholarship grants, need-based scholarship grants, tuition remission for children of faculty, Lausanne Educators Scholarship Program available. In 2005–06, 15% of upper-school students received aid; total upper-school merit-scholarship money awarded: $37,161. Total amount of financial aid awarded in 2005–06: $110,125.

Admissions Traditional secondary-level entrance grade is 9. For fall 2005, 356 students applied for upper-level admission, 212 were accepted, 172 enrolled. ISEE or Kaufman Test of Educational Achievement required. Deadline for receipt of application materials: none. Application fee required: $75. On-campus interview required.

Athletics Interscholastic: back packing (boys, girls), basketball (b,g), cheering (g), cross-country running (b,g), dance squad (g), dance team (g), golf (b,g), gymnastics (g), lacrosse (b,g), soccer (b,g), swimming and diving (b,g), tennis (b,g), track and field (b,g), volleyball (g); intramural: back packing (b,g), ballet (b,g), basketball (b,g), bowling (b,g), canoeing/kayaking (b,g), climbing (b,g), dance team (g), flag football (b,g), floor hockey (b,g), football (b,g), Frisbee (b,g), hiking/backpacking (b,g), indoor soccer (b,g), kayaking (b,g), lacrosse (b,g), mountain biking (b,g), mountaineering (b,g), outdoor activities (b,g), outdoor adventure (b,g), outdoor education (b,g),

outdoor recreation (b,g), outdoor skills (b,g), rafting (b,g), rappelling (b,g), rock climbing (b,g), ropes courses (b,g), soccer (b,g), tennis (b,g), track and field (b,g), ultimate Frisbee (b,g), volleyball (b,g), wall climbing (b,g), weight lifting (b,g), wilderness (b,g); coed interscholastic: swimming and diving; coed intramural: back packing, basketball, bowling, canoeing/kayaking, climbing, fishing, flag football, floor hockey, football, Frisbee, hiking/backpacking, indoor soccer, kayaking, lacrosse, martial arts, mountain biking, mountaineering, outdoor activities, outdoor adventure, outdoor education, outdoor recreation, outdoor skills, rafting, rappelling, rock climbing, ropes courses, soccer, tennis, track and field, ultimate Frisbee, volleyball, wall climbing, weight lifting, wilderness. 3 PE instructors, 6 coaches.

Computers Computers are regularly used in all academic, technology classes. Computer network features include campus e-mail, on-campus library services, CD-ROMs, online commercial services, Internet access, file transfer, office computer access, wireless campus network, homework assignments available online.

Contact Ms. Melanie Cook, Assistant to the Director of Admissions. 901-474-1030. Fax: 901-474-1010. E-mail: melaniecook@lausanneschool.com. Web site: www.lausanneschool.com.

LAWRENCE ACADEMY

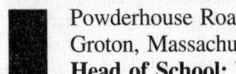

Powderhouse Road
Groton, Massachusetts 01450
Head of School: D. Scott Wiggins, Esq.

General Information Coeducational boarding and day college-preparatory school. Grades 9–12. Founded: 1793. Setting: small town. Nearest major city is Boston. Students are housed in single-sex dormitories. 100-acre campus. 31 buildings on campus. Approved or accredited by Association of Independent Schools in New England, New England Association of Schools and Colleges, The Association of Boarding Schools, and Massachusetts Department of Education. Member of National Association of Independent Schools and Secondary School Admission Test Board. Language of instruction: English. Endowment: $11 million. Total enrollment: 391. Upper school average class size: 15. Upper school faculty-student ratio: 1:8.

Upper School Student Profile Grade 9: 83 students (47 boys, 36 girls); Grade 10: 108 students (56 boys, 52 girls); Grade 11: 108 students (54 boys, 54 girls); Grade 12: 92 students (51 boys, 41 girls). 50% of students are boarding students. 58% are state residents. 15 states are represented in upper school student body. 10% are international students. International students from Germany, Hong Kong, Japan, Republic of Korea, Spain, and Taiwan; 14 other countries represented in student body.

Faculty School total: 55. In upper school: 34 men, 21 women; 35 have advanced degrees; 39 reside on campus.

Subjects Offered Advanced Placement courses, African-American literature, algebra, American government-AP, American history, anatomy, art, astronomy, biology, biology-AP, botany, calculus, calculus-AP, ceramics, chemistry, composition, creative writing, criminal justice, dance, drawing, ecology, electronics, English, English literature, entomology, environmental science-AP, ESL, European history, female experience in America, fine arts, finite math, fractals, French, French-AP, government/civics, history, Irish studies, John F. Kennedy, Latin, Latin American literature, limnology, marine science, mathematics, microbiology, music, music composition, Native American studies, ornithology, painting, pharoahs to mummies, photography, physics, physics-AP, playwriting, pre-calculus, psychology, scene study, science, Shakespeare, social psychology, Spanish, Spanish-AP, studio art, theater, tropical biology, writing.

Graduation Requirements Arts and fine arts (art, music, dance, drama), English, foreign language, mathematics, science, social studies (includes history), Winterim participation.

Special Academic Programs Advanced Placement exam preparation in 8 subject areas; honors section; independent study; study abroad; academic accommodation for the musically talented and the artistically talented; special instructional classes for deaf students, blind students; ESL (19 students enrolled).

College Placement 96 students graduated in 2004; 90 went to college, including Babson College; Bates College; Boston College; Carnegie Mellon University; The George Washington University; Tufts University. Other: 6 had other specific plans.

Student Life Upper grades have specified standards of dress, student council, honor system. Discipline rests primarily with faculty.

Tuition and Aid Day student tuition: $26,400; 7-day tuition and room/board: $34,800. Tuition installment plan (Key Tuition Payment Plan, monthly payment plans). Need-based scholarship grants, need-based loans, prepGATE Loans available. In 2004–05, 33% of upper-school students received aid. Total amount of financial aid awarded in 2004–05: $2,000,000.

Admissions Traditional secondary-level entrance grade is 9. For fall 2005, 602 students applied for upper-level admission, 269 were accepted, 132 enrolled. ISEE, PSAT or SAT, SSAT or TOEFL required. Deadline for receipt of application materials: February 1. Application fee required: $50. Interview required.

Athletics Interscholastic: baseball (boys), basketball (b,g), cross-country running (b,g), field hockey (g), football (b), golf (b,g), ice hockey (b,g), lacrosse (b,g), soccer (b,g), softball (g), tennis (b,g), volleyball (g), wrestling (b); intramural: badminton (b), tennis (b,g); coed interscholastic: alpine skiing, independent competitive sports, skiing (downhill); coed intramural: dance, independent competitive sports, modern dance, outdoors, physical fitness, physical training, rappelling, skiing (downhill), strength & conditioning, volleyball, weight training, yoga. 1 trainer.

Computers Computers are regularly used in art, English, foreign language, mathematics, science classes. Computer network features include campus e-mail, on-campus library services, CD-ROMs, online commercial services, Internet access, file transfer, office computer access.

Contact Andi C. O'Hearn, Director of Admissions. 978-448-6535. Fax: 978-448-9208. E-mail: admiss@lacademy.edu. Web site: www.lacademy.edu.

ANNOUNCEMENT FROM THE SCHOOL An academically demanding curriculum combines traditional teaching with student-centered learning through seminars, projects, and independent study opportunities. Signature programs, which encourage hands-on learning, include the Ninth Grade Program, Combined Studies Course, Winterim, and the Independent Immersion Program. Extensive arts offerings in dance, drama, music, and visual arts, as well as a competitive sports program, are available. A warm community environment, international diversity, daily adviser meetings, dorm e-mail and Internet, radio station, and recording studio enhance the program.

See full description on page 870.

LAWRENCE SCHOOL

Broadview Heights, Ohio
See Special Needs Schools section.

THE LAWRENCEVILLE SCHOOL

PO Box 6008
2500 Main Street
Lawrenceville, New Jersey 08648
Head of School: Elizabeth A. Duffy

General Information Coeducational boarding and day college-preparatory, arts, religious studies, and technology school. Grades 9–PG. Founded: 1810. Setting: small town. Nearest major city is Philadelphia, PA. Students are housed in single-sex dormitories. 700-acre campus. 31 buildings on campus. Approved or accredited by Middle States Association of Colleges and Schools, New Jersey Association of Independent Schools, The Association of Boarding Schools, and New Jersey Department of Education. Member of National Association of Independent Schools and Secondary School Admission Test Board. Endowment: $201.2 million. Total enrollment: 807. Upper school average class size: 11. Upper school faculty-student ratio: 1:8.

Upper School Student Profile Grade 9: 152 students (79 boys, 73 girls); Grade 10: 204 students (111 boys, 93 girls); Grade 11: 221 students (121 boys, 100 girls); Grade 12: 210 students (115 boys, 95 girls); Postgraduate: 20 students (14 boys, 6 girls). 72% of students are boarding students. 30% are state residents. 33 states are represented in upper school student body. 10% are international students. International students from Canada, Hong Kong, Ireland, Republic of Korea, Taiwan, and United Kingdom; 14 other countries represented in student body.

Faculty School total: 141. In upper school: 91 men, 50 women; 108 have advanced degrees; 125 reside on campus.

Subjects Offered Acting, advanced chemistry, advanced computer applications, advanced studio art-AP, African-American literature, algebra, American history-AP, American studies, art, art history, art history-AP, art-AP, astronomy, Bible, bioethics, DNA and culture, biology, biology-AP, Buddhism, calculus-AP, chemistry, chemistry-AP, Chinese, Chinese studies, choir, chorus, data analysis, design, digital art, drama, drawing, economics, English literature, English literature and composition-AP, English literature-AP, English/composition-AP, environmental science, European history, European history-AP, field ecology, film appreciation, filmmaking, French, French language-AP, French literature-AP, French-AP, geometry, global science, Hindi, history of China and Japan, human biology, Irish studies, Japanese, Jewish studies, journalism, Judaic studies, literature, organic chemistry, personal development, photography, physics, physics-AP, poetry, Southern literature, Spanish, Spanish language-AP, U.S. government, visual arts, water color painting, women in world history, world religions, writing.

Graduation Requirements Arts and fine arts (art, music, dance, drama), English, foreign language, interdisciplinary studies, mathematics, religion (includes Bible studies and theology), science, social science, social studies (includes history). Community service is required.

Special Academic Programs Advanced Placement exam preparation in 11 subject areas; honors section; independent study; term-away projects; study abroad.

College Placement 217 students graduated in 2005; all went to college, including Brown University; Duke University; Harvard University; New York University; Princeton University. Mean SAT verbal: 680, mean SAT math: 680.

Student Life Upper grades have specified standards of dress, student council, honor system. Discipline rests primarily with faculty. Attendance at religious services is required.

Tuition and Aid Day student tuition: $28,180; 7-day tuition and room/board: $34,570. Tuition installment plan (Insured Tuition Payment Plan, Academic Management Services Plan, Key Tuition Payment Plan). Need-based scholarship grants

The Lawrenceville School

available. In 2005–06, 29% of upper-school students received aid. Total amount of financial aid awarded in 2005–06: $600,000.

Admissions Traditional secondary-level entrance grade is 9. For fall 2005, 1,612 students applied for upper-level admission, 399 were accepted, 251 enrolled. ISEE, PSAT and SAT for applicants to grade 11 and 12, SSAT or TOEFL or SLEP required. Deadline for receipt of application materials: January 31. Application fee required: $50. Interview required.

Athletics Interscholastic: baseball (boys), basketball (b,g), crew (b,g), cross-country running (b,g), fencing (b,g), field hockey (g), football (b), golf (b,g), ice hockey (b,g), indoor track (b,g), indoor track & field (b,g), lacrosse (b,g), soccer (b,g), softball (g), squash (b,g), swimming and diving (b,g), tennis (b,g), track and field (b,g), volleyball (g), water polo (b,g), winter (indoor) track (b,g), wrestling (b); intramural: basketball (b,g), football (b), Frisbee (g), indoor track (b,g), indoor track & field (b,g), soccer (b,g), softball (b,g), tennis (b,g), track and field (b,g), ultimate Frisbee (b,g), volleyball (b,g), winter (indoor) track (b,g); coed interscholastic: golf, winter (indoor) track; coed intramural: back packing, canoeing/kayaking, cricket, dance, ice skating, kayaking, martial arts, modern dance, outdoor education, rock climbing, ropes courses, squash, strength & conditioning, tennis, ultimate Frisbee, weight lifting, winter (indoor) track, yoga.

Computers Computers are regularly used in art, English, mathematics, music, science, technology classes. Computer network features include campus e-mail, on-campus library services, CD-ROMs, online commercial services, Internet access, wireless campus network.

Contact Gregg W. M. Malaberti, Dean of Admission. 800-735-2030. Fax: 609-895-2217. E-mail: admissions@lawrenceville.org. Web site: www.lawrenceville.org.

ANNOUNCEMENT FROM THE SCHOOL New Serengeti Course will examine the Serengeti ecosystem and the behavior of Serengeti animals from a scientific perspective. The course will culminate in a 2-week trip during Spring Break to the Serengeti itself, where students will carry out individual projects with both scientific and documentary components.

See full description on page 872.

LAWRENCE WOODMERE ACADEMY

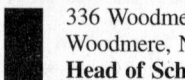

336 Woodmere Boulevard
Woodmere, New York 11598-2066
Head of School: Mr. Alan Bernstein

General Information Coeducational day college-preparatory, arts, and technology school. Grades PK–12. Founded: 1894. Setting: suburban. Nearest major city is New York. 7-acre campus. 3 buildings on campus. Approved or accredited by New York State Association of Independent Schools and New York Department of Education. Member of National Association of Independent Schools and Secondary School Admission Test Board. Total enrollment: 356. Upper school average class size: 12. Upper school faculty-student ratio: 1:6.

Faculty School total: 75. In upper school: 14 men, 16 women; 30 have advanced degrees.

Subjects Offered Advanced Placement courses, college admission preparation, community service, computer applications, drama, health education, humanities, interdisciplinary studies, mathematics, modern languages, physical education, science, science research, social science, visual and performing arts.

Graduation Requirements Arts, computer science, English, foreign language, mathematics, physical education (includes health), science, social science, social studies (includes history), college seminars, fine arts rotation (creative writing, drama, studio art). Community service is required.

Special Academic Programs Advanced Placement exam preparation in 14 subject areas; honors section; independent study; ESL (25 students enrolled).

College Placement 51 students graduated in 2005; all went to college, including Brandeis University; Cornell University; Georgetown University; New York University; Princeton University; Wesleyan University. Median SAT verbal: 580, median SAT math: 600. 50% scored over 600 on SAT verbal, 56% scored over 600 on SAT math.

Student Life Upper grades have specified standards of dress, student council, honor system. Discipline rests primarily with faculty.

Tuition and Aid Day student tuition: $23,000. Tuition installment plan (Insured Tuition Payment Plan, Academic Management Services Plan, monthly payment plans, individually arranged payment plans). Tuition reduction for siblings, merit scholarship grants, need-based scholarship grants, need-based loans available. In 2005–06, 22% of upper-school students received aid.

Admissions Traditional secondary-level entrance grade is 9. SSAT and writing sample required. Deadline for receipt of application materials: February 3. Application fee required: $50. Interview required.

Athletics Interscholastic: baseball (boys), basketball (b,g), cheering (g), cross-country running (b,g), golf (b,g), soccer (b,g), softball (g), tennis (b,g), volleyball (g); intramural: basketball (b,g), soccer (b,g), softball (b,g), volleyball (b,g); coed interscholastic: cross-country running, golf. 4 PE instructors, 8 coaches.

Computers Computers are regularly used in art, English, foreign language, history, mathematics, SAT preparation, science, technical drawing, word processing, yearbook classes. Computer network features include campus e-mail, on-campus library services, CD-ROMs, Internet access, file transfer, wireless campus network.

Contact Lisa Bellinzoni, Admissions Coordinator. 516-374-9000 Ext. 827. Fax: 516-374-4707. E-mail: lwa@lwa.ny.k12us.com. Web site: www.lawo.com.

LEBANON CATHOLIC JUNIOR / SENIOR HIGH SCHOOL

1400 Chestnut Street
Lebanon, Pennsylvania 17042
Head of School: Mr. David Chauvette

General Information Coeducational day college-preparatory, general academic, arts, and religious studies school, affiliated with Roman Catholic Church. Grades K4–12. Founded: 1859. Setting: small town. Nearest major city is Harrisburg. 1 building on campus. Approved or accredited by Middle States Association of Colleges and Schools and Pennsylvania Department of Education. Total enrollment: 458. Upper school average class size: 20. Upper school faculty-student ratio: 1:20.

Upper School Student Profile Grade 9: 37 students (19 boys, 18 girls); Grade 10: 37 students (15 boys, 22 girls); Grade 11: 43 students (18 boys, 25 girls); Grade 12: 33 students (17 boys, 16 girls). 90% of students are Roman Catholic.

Faculty School total: 36. In upper school: 4 men, 32 women; 4 have advanced degrees.

Special Academic Programs Advanced Placement exam preparation in 5 subject areas; honors section; independent study; study at local college for college credit; remedial reading and/or remedial writing; remedial math; special instructional classes for students with learning disabilities, ADD.

Student Life Upper grades have uniform requirement, student council, honor system. Discipline rests primarily with faculty. Attendance at religious services is required.

Tuition and Aid Day student tuition: $3000. Tuition installment plan (Key Tuition Payment Plan). Tuition reduction for siblings, need-based scholarship grants available. In 2005–06, 50% of upper-school students received aid. Total amount of financial aid awarded in 2005–06: $126,000.

Admissions Traditional secondary-level entrance grade is 9. For fall 2005, 10 students applied for upper-level admission, 7 were accepted, 7 enrolled. Deadline for receipt of application materials: June 1. No application fee required. Interview required.

Athletics Interscholastic: baseball (boys, girls), basketball (b,g), cheering (g), soccer (b,g), softball (g), volleyball (g), weight training (b,g); coed interscholastic: golf. 2 PE instructors, 15 coaches.

Computers Computers are regularly used in all academic classes. Computer network features include campus e-mail, on-campus library services, CD-ROMs, online commercial services, Internet access, DVD.

Contact Mrs. Rose M. Kury, Director of Studies. 717-273-3731 Ext. 305. Fax: 717-275-5167. E-mail: rosekury@lebanoncatholicschool.org.

THE LEELANAU SCHOOL

Glen Arbor, Michigan
See Special Needs Schools section.

LEE-SCOTT ACADEMY

1601 Academy Drive
Auburn, Alabama 36830
Head of School: Dr. Don Roberts

General Information Coeducational day college-preparatory school, affiliated with Christian faith. Grades PK–12. Founded: 1967. Setting: small town. Nearest major city is Montgomery. 70-acre campus. 4 buildings on campus. Approved or accredited by Southern Association of Colleges and Schools and Alabama Department of Education. Endowment: $800,000. Total enrollment: 653. Upper school average class size: 15. Upper school faculty-student ratio: 1:12.

Upper School Student Profile 97% of students are Christian.

Faculty School total: 56. In upper school: 12 men, 16 women; 12 have advanced degrees.

Subjects Offered Algebra, anatomy, art, band, Bible studies, biology, calculus-AP, chemistry, chorus, computer applications, drama, driver education, economics, English, English literature and composition-AP, French, geometry, government, health, history-AP, honors English, HTML design, jazz band, keyboarding, Latin, macroeconomics-AP, physical education, physical science, physics-AP, pre-calculus, Spanish, speech, trigonometry, U.S. history, U.S. history-AP, world history.

Graduation Requirements Arts and fine arts (art, music, dance, drama), computer science, English, foreign language, mathematics, physical education (includes health), science, social studies (includes history).

Special Academic Programs Advanced Placement exam preparation in 5 subject areas; honors section; study at local college for college credit.

College Placement 30 students graduated in 2005; all went to college, including Auburn University; Georgia Institute of Technology; Southern Union State Community College; The University of Alabama; Troy University; University of Mississippi.
Student Life Upper grades have specified standards of dress, student council, honor system. Discipline rests primarily with faculty.
Tuition and Aid Day student tuition: $4980. Tuition installment plan (monthly payment plans, quarterly, bi-annual, and annual payment plans). Tuition reduction for siblings available.
Admissions Traditional secondary-level entrance grade is 7. Stanford Achievement Test required. Deadline for receipt of application materials: none. Application fee required: $250. On-campus interview required.
Athletics Interscholastic: baseball (boys), basketball (b,g), cheering (g), football (b), pom squad (g), softball (g), tennis (b,g), track and field (b,g), volleyball (g); coed interscholastic: golf. 4 PE instructors, 6 coaches, 1 trainer.
Computers Computers are regularly used in English, history, mathematics, science classes. Computer network features include campus e-mail, on-campus library services, CD-ROMs, Internet access, file transfer, DVD.
Contact Sylvia Kirk, Receptionist/Secretary. 334-821-2430. Fax: 334-821-0876. E-mail: info@lee-scott.org. Web site: www.lee-scott.org.

LEHIGH VALLEY CHRISTIAN HIGH SCHOOL

1414 East Cedar Street
Allentown, Pennsylvania 18109
Head of School: Mr. Charles A. Bloomfield

General Information Coeducational day college-preparatory, general academic, and business school, affiliated with Evangelical/Fundamental faith. Grades 9–12. Founded: 1988. Setting: urban. 4-acre campus. 2 buildings on campus. Approved or accredited by Association of Christian Schools International, Middle States Association of Colleges and Schools, and Pennsylvania Department of Education. Endowment: $200,000. Total enrollment: 184. Upper school average class size: 20. Upper school faculty-student ratio: 1:10.
Upper School Student Profile Grade 9: 42 students (23 boys, 19 girls); Grade 10: 58 students (27 boys, 31 girls); Grade 11: 42 students (20 boys, 22 girls); Grade 12: 42 students (19 boys, 23 girls). 95% of students are Evangelical/Fundamental faith.
Faculty School total: 18. In upper school: 8 men, 9 women; 5 have advanced degrees.
Subjects Offered Accounting, advanced math, Advanced Placement courses, Alabama history and geography, algebra, American history, American literature, ancient world history, art, Bible, biology, calculus-AP, chemistry, chorus, civics, clayworking, computer applications, computer keyboarding, consumer mathematics, economics, English, English literature, environmental science, geometry, German, government, graphic design, health, history, physical education, physical science, physics, pre-algebra, Spanish, state history, U.S. history, Western civilization.
Graduation Requirements Algebra, American history, American literature, art, Bible, Bible studies, biology, British literature, chemistry, choir, civics, computer applications, English, foreign language, geometry, mathematics, physical education (includes health), physical science, science, social sciences, Western civilization, general lifestyle not harmful to the testimony of the school as a Christian institution, minimum one year of full-time enrollment in LVCH or another Christian high school.
Special Academic Programs Advanced Placement exam preparation in 3 subject areas; honors section; accelerated programs; independent study; study at local college for college credit; academic accommodation for the gifted; programs in English, mathematics, general development for dyslexic students; special instructional classes for students needing learning support.
College Placement 39 students graduated in 2005; 31 went to college, including Grove City College; Lehigh University; Liberty University; Moravian College; Philadelphia Biblical University; The Pennsylvania State University University Park Campus. Other: 3 went to work, 5 entered military service.
Student Life Upper grades have uniform requirement, student council. Discipline rests primarily with faculty.
Summer Programs Remediation, advancement programs offered; session focuses on make-up; held both on and off campus; held at students' homes (for independent credit); accepts boys and girls; not open to students from other schools. 12 students usually enrolled. 2006 schedule: June 19 to August 13.
Tuition and Aid Day student tuition: $5460. Tuition installment plan (SMART Tuition Payment Plan). Tuition reduction for siblings, need-based scholarship grants available. In 2005–06, 12% of upper-school students received aid. Total amount of financial aid awarded in 2005–06: $42,000.
Admissions Traditional secondary-level entrance grade is 9. For fall 2005, 65 students applied for upper-level admission, 65 were accepted, 64 enrolled. Achievement tests, Gates MacGinite Reading Tests or Wide Range Achievement Test required. Deadline for receipt of application materials: none. Application fee required: $120. On-campus interview required.
Athletics Interscholastic: baseball (boys), basketball (b,g), cheering (g), field hockey (g), soccer (b,g), volleyball (g); coed interscholastic: track and field; coed intramural: skiing (downhill). 1 PE instructor, 11 coaches.
Computers Computers are regularly used in graphic arts, library, life skills, science, technology, writing fundamentals, yearbook classes. Computer network features include on-campus library services, CD-ROMs, Internet access.

Contact Ms. Karen Carolan, Director of Admissions. 610-821-9443. Fax: 610-821-5527. E-mail: k.carolan@lvchs.com. Web site: www.lvchs.com.

LEHMAN HIGH SCHOOL

2400 Saint Mary Avenue
Sidney, Ohio 45365
Head of School: Mr. David Michael Barhorst

General Information Coeducational day college-preparatory school, affiliated with Roman Catholic Church. Grades 9–12. Founded: 1970. Setting: small town. Nearest major city is Dayton. 50-acre campus. 1 building on campus. Approved or accredited by North Central Association of Colleges and Schools, Ohio Catholic Schools Accreditation Association (OCSAA), and Ohio Department of Education. Endowment: $840,000. Upper school average class size: 15. Upper school faculty-student ratio: 1:12.
Upper School Student Profile Grade 9: 67 students (43 boys, 24 girls); Grade 10: 78 students (37 boys, 41 girls); Grade 11: 71 students (32 boys, 39 girls); Grade 12: 68 students (29 boys, 39 girls). 91% of students are Roman Catholic.
Faculty School total: 27. In upper school: 14 men, 13 women; 17 have advanced degrees.
Subjects Offered Accounting, advanced computer applications, algebra, American government, American government-AP, American literature, anatomy and physiology, architectural drawing, art, art history, Basic programming, biology, biology-AP, British literature, British literature (honors), business, calculus, calculus-AP, career and personal planning, ceramics, chemistry, chemistry-AP, child development, choir, church history, computer applications, computer programming, concert band, earth science, economics, English, English literature and composition-AP, environmental science, family and consumer science, French, general math, geography, geometry, government, health education, history of the Catholic Church, integrated science, international foods, intro to computers, keyboarding, moral theology, music theory, newspaper, painting, peace and justice, physical education, physics, pre-algebra, pre-calculus, psychology, reading/study skills, religious education, sociology, Spanish, studio art, U.S. history, vocal music, world history, yearbook.
Graduation Requirements Advanced Placement courses, foreign language, religion (includes Bible studies and theology), U.S. government.
Special Academic Programs Advanced Placement exam preparation in 5 subject areas; honors section; independent study; remedial reading and/or remedial writing.
College Placement 74 students graduated in 2005; 71 went to college, including Bowling Green State University; The Ohio State University; University of Cincinnati; University of Dayton; University of Notre Dame; Wright State University. Other: 2 went to work, 1 entered military service. Mean composite ACT: 23.
Student Life Upper grades have uniform requirement, student council. Discipline rests primarily with faculty. Attendance at religious services is required.
Tuition and Aid Day student tuition: $5350. Guaranteed tuition plan. Tuition installment plan (FACTS Tuition Payment Plan). Need-based scholarship grants available. In 2005–06, 36% of upper-school students received aid. Total amount of financial aid awarded in 2005–06: $283,030.
Admissions Traditional secondary-level entrance grade is 11. For fall 2005, 3 students applied for upper-level admission, 3 were accepted, 3 enrolled. Achievement tests, ACT or Cognitive Abilities Test required. Deadline for receipt of application materials: none. No application fee required. Interview recommended.
Athletics Interscholastic: aquatics (boys, girls), baseball (b), basketball (b,g), cheering (g), cross-country running (b,g), diving (b,g), football (b), golf (b), soccer (b,g), softball (g), swimming and diving (b,g), tennis (b,g), track and field (b,g), volleyball (g), wrestling (b); intramural: strength & conditioning (b,g), weight lifting (b), weight training (g). 30 coaches.
Computers Computers are regularly used in accounting, architecture, computer applications, desktop publishing, drafting, French, newspaper, yearbook classes. Computer resources include campus e-mail, on-campus library services, Internet access.
Contact Mr. Charles Hoying, Guidance Counselor. 937-498-1161 Ext. 119. Fax: 937-492-9877. E-mail: le_honing@woco-k12.org.

LE LYCEE FRANCAIS DE LOS ANGELES

3261 Overland Avenue
Los Angeles, California 90034
Head of School: Mrs. Clara-Lisa Kabbaz

General Information Coeducational day college-preparatory, general academic, arts, and bilingual studies school. Grades K–12. Founded: 1964. Setting: suburban. Nearest major city is West Los Angeles. 12-acre campus. 7 buildings on campus. Approved or accredited by French Ministry of Education and Western Association of Schools and Colleges. Member of European Council of International Schools. Languages of instruction: English and French. Endowment: $4.8 million. Total enrollment: 808. Upper school average class size: 16. Upper school faculty-student ratio: 1:15.

Le Lycee Francais de Los Angeles

Upper School Student Profile Grade 9: 51 students (29 boys, 22 girls); Grade 10: 24 students (8 boys, 16 girls); Grade 11: 36 students (13 boys, 23 girls); Grade 12: 39 students (20 boys, 19 girls).

Faculty School total: 85. In upper school: 16 men, 26 women; 31 have advanced degrees.

Subjects Offered 20th century history, algebra, American history, American literature, anatomy, art, biology, calculus, ceramics, chemistry, computer programming, computer science, creative writing, dance, drama, earth science, economics, English, English literature, environmental science, ESL, European history, expository writing, fine arts, French, geography, geology, geometry, German, government/civics, grammar, history, Latin, mathematics, music, philosophy, photography, physical education, physics, science, social science, social studies, Spanish, statistics, theater, trigonometry, typing, world history, world literature, writing.

Graduation Requirements Arts and fine arts (art, music, dance, drama), English, foreign language, mathematics, physical education (includes health), science, social science, social studies (includes history).

Special Academic Programs Advanced Placement exam preparation in 10 subject areas; honors section; study abroad; remedial reading and/or remedial writing; remedial math; ESL (25 students enrolled).

College Placement 36 students graduated in 2005; all went to college, including University of California, Berkeley; University of California, Los Angeles; University of California, San Diego; University of California, Santa Barbara. Mean SAT verbal: 528, mean SAT math: 585.

Student Life Upper grades have uniform requirement, student council, honor system. Discipline rests primarily with faculty.

Summer Programs Advancement, ESL, sports, art/fine arts, computer instruction programs offered; session focuses on academic and sports; held both on and off campus; held at various field trip locations; accepts boys and girls; open to students from other schools. 72 students usually enrolled. 2006 schedule: June 21 to July 30. Application deadline: May 15.

Tuition and Aid Day student tuition: $13,500. Tuition installment plan (The Tuition Plan, Insured Tuition Payment Plan, monthly payment plans, individually arranged payment plans, Dewar Tuition Refund Plan). Bursaries, need-based scholarship grants available. In 2005–06, 12% of upper-school students received aid. Total amount of financial aid awarded in 2005–06: $62,412.

Admissions Traditional secondary-level entrance grade is 9. For fall 2005, 45 students applied for upper-level admission, 32 were accepted, 28 enrolled. School's own exam required. Deadline for receipt of application materials: February 1. Application fee required: $400. Interview required.

Athletics Interscholastic: basketball (boys); intramural: ballet (g), baseball (g), fencing (b,g), outdoor activities (b,g), outdoor recreation (b,g), physical fitness (b,g), volleyball (b,g); coed interscholastic: soccer; coed intramural: martial arts, swimming and diving, table tennis, tennis, yoga. 6 PE instructors, 5 coaches, 4 trainers.

Computers Computers are regularly used in English, foreign language, mathematics, science classes. Computer resources include on-campus library services, CD-ROMs, Internet access.

Contact Mme. Léna Lagorce, Admissions. 310-836-3464 Ext. 315. Fax: 310-558-8069. E-mail: lfla@mindspring.com. Web site: www.mindspring.com/~lfla.

LEXINGTON CATHOLIC HIGH SCHOOL

2250 Clays Mill Road
Lexington, Kentucky 40503-1797
Head of School: Ms. Sally W. Stevens

General Information Coeducational day college-preparatory school, affiliated with Roman Catholic Church. Grades 9–12. Founded: 1823. Setting: urban. 6-acre campus. 3 buildings on campus. Approved or accredited by Southern Association of Colleges and Schools and Kentucky Department of Education. Endowment: $500,000. Total enrollment: 869. Upper school average class size: 22. Upper school faculty-student ratio: 1:15.

Upper School Student Profile Grade 9: 228 students (105 boys, 123 girls); Grade 10: 225 students (126 boys, 99 girls); Grade 11: 204 students (102 boys, 102 girls); Grade 12: 212 students (115 boys, 97 girls). 75% of students are Roman Catholic.

Faculty School total: 59. In upper school: 29 men, 30 women; 45 have advanced degrees.

Subjects Offered Accounting, advanced chemistry, Advanced Placement courses, advanced studio art-AP, algebra, American government, American government-AP, American history, American history-AP, American literature, anatomy and physiology, art, astronomy, band, Bible as literature, biology, biology-AP, British literature, British literature (honors), calculus, calculus-AP, Catholic belief and practice, ceramics, chemistry, chemistry-AP, choral music, Christian and Hebrew scripture, church history, comparative religion, computer applications, computer programming, creative writing, drama, economics, English-AP, ethics, film, French, French-AP, geography, geology, geometry, government and politics-AP, graphic design, health, history of the Catholic Church, honors English, honors geometry, honors U.S. history, honors world history, humanities, introduction to literature, Latin, Latin-AP, physics, physics-AP, psychology, religious studies, sociology, Spanish, Spanish language-AP, U.S. government, U.S. government-AP, U.S. history, U.S. history-AP, world history, world literature.

Special Academic Programs Advanced Placement exam preparation in 12 subject areas; honors section.

College Placement 214 students graduated in 2005; 212 went to college, including University of Kentucky. Other: 2 went to work. Mean SAT verbal: 581, mean SAT math: 568, mean composite ACT: 24. 41% scored over 600 on SAT verbal, 43% scored over 600 on SAT math, 33% scored over 26 on composite ACT.

Student Life Upper grades have specified standards of dress, student council. Discipline rests primarily with faculty. Attendance at religious services is required.

Tuition and Aid Day student tuition: $5230. Tuition installment plan (monthly payment plans, individually arranged payment plans). Need-based scholarship grants available. In 2005–06, 10% of upper-school students received aid. Total amount of financial aid awarded in 2005–06: $325,000.

Admissions Traditional secondary-level entrance grade is 9. For fall 2005, 267 students applied for upper-level admission, 267 were accepted, 227 enrolled. Scholastic Testing Service High School Placement Test required. Deadline for receipt of application materials: none. Application fee required: $150.

Athletics Interscholastic: baseball (boys), basketball (b,g), cheering (g), cross-country running (b,g), dance team (g), diving (b,g), football (b), golf (b,g), power lifting (b), soccer (b,g), softball (g), swimming and diving (b,g), tennis (b,g), track and field (b,g), volleyball (g); intramural: basketball (b,g), flag football (g), physical training (b,g); coed interscholastic: ice hockey, ultimate Frisbee; coed intramural: outdoor activities. 2 trainers.

Computers Computer network features include on-campus library services, Internet access.

Contact Ms. Susie Fryer, Admissions Director. 859-277-7183 Ext. 231. Fax: 859-276-5086. E-mail: sfryer@lexingtoncatholic.com. Web site: www. lexingtoncatholic.com.

LEXINGTON CHRISTIAN ACADEMY

48 Bartlett Avenue
Lexington, Massachusetts 02420
Head of School: Dr. J. Barry Koops

General Information Coeducational day college-preparatory, arts, religious studies, and technology school, affiliated with Christian faith. Grades 6–12. Founded: 1946. Setting: suburban. Nearest major city is Boston. 30-acre campus. 1 building on campus. Approved or accredited by Association of Christian Schools International, Association of Independent Schools in New England, New England Association of Schools and Colleges, and Massachusetts Department of Education. Member of National Association of Independent Schools. Endowment: $2.3 million. Total enrollment: 343. Upper school average class size: 16. Upper school faculty-student ratio: 1:11.

Upper School Student Profile Grade 9: 61 students (30 boys, 31 girls); Grade 10: 56 students (25 boys, 31 girls); Grade 11: 51 students (25 boys, 26 girls); Grade 12: 62 students (24 boys, 38 girls). 98% of students are Christian faith.

Faculty School total: 38. In upper school: 17 men, 13 women; 23 have advanced degrees.

Subjects Offered Algebra, American history-AP, anatomy, ancient history, art, Bible studies, biology, calculus-AP, chemistry, community service, computers, drama, English, English literature, English literature-AP, French, general science, geography, geometry, health, history, jazz ensemble, journalism, Latin, mathematics, music, physical education, physical science, physics, physiology, psychology, religion, science, social studies, Spanish, theater, trigonometry, world history, world literature, writing.

Graduation Requirements Algebra, American history, American literature, Bible, British literature, classics, college planning, computer literacy, creative thinking, English, English literature, ethics, European history, European literature, foreign language, health education, lab science, mathematics, physical education (includes health), religion (includes Bible studies and theology), science, senior internship, social studies (includes history), U.S. history, senior internship (3-week work experience in career of student's choice, including a journal of the experience), Interim (participation each year in one week of special Interim courses). Community service is required.

Special Academic Programs Advanced Placement exam preparation in 9 subject areas; honors section; independent study; term-away projects; study at local college for college credit.

College Placement 60 students graduated in 2005; 58 went to college, including Boston University; Calvin College; Georgia Institute of Technology; Gordon College; Grove City College; Massachusetts Institute of Technology. Other: 2 went to work. Mean SAT verbal: 585, mean SAT math: 597.

Student Life Upper grades have specified standards of dress, student council. Discipline rests primarily with faculty. Attendance at religious services is required.

Tuition and Aid Day student tuition: $16,500. Tuition installment plan (FACTS Tuition Payment Plan). Merit scholarship grants, need-based scholarship grants available. In 2005–06, 40% of upper-school students received aid; total upper-school merit-scholarship money awarded: $72,000. Total amount of financial aid awarded in 2005–06: $400,000.

Admissions Traditional secondary-level entrance grade is 9. For fall 2005, 89 students applied for upper-level admission, 59 were accepted, 35 enrolled. ERB CTP,

ISEE or SSAT required. Deadline for receipt of application materials: February 15. Application fee required: $50. Interview required.

Athletics Interscholastic: baseball (boys), basketball (b,g), cheering (g), cross-country running (b,g), field hockey (g), lacrosse (b,g), soccer (b,g), softball (g), wrestling (b); intramural: basketball (b,g), cheering (g), gymnastics (b,g), lacrosse (b), physical training (b,g), soccer (b,g), tennis (b,g), volleyball (b,g), wrestling (b); coed interscholastic: golf; coed intramural: climbing, fitness, outdoor activities, rock climbing, ropes courses, skiing (downhill), snowboarding, strength & conditioning, swimming and diving, ultimate Frisbee, volleyball, wall climbing, weight training. 10 coaches, 1 trainer.

Computers Computers are regularly used in library science, literary magazine, mathematics, media arts, music, photography, publications, science, word processing, yearbook classes. Computer network features include campus e-mail, on-campus library services, CD-ROMs, online commercial services, Internet access, DVD, wireless campus network.

Contact Jill C. Schuhmacher, Director of Admissions. 781-862-7850 Ext. 123. Fax: 781-863-8503. E-mail: jill.schuhmacher@lca.edu. Web site: www.lca.edu.

ANNOUNCEMENT FROM THE SCHOOL Interim week offers various minicourses on subjects that have not found a place in the regular curriculum. Long daily sessions and small classes allow extended, relaxed interaction between students and teachers; concentration on one topic; and exploration at depths not allowed in the press of yearlong college-prep courses.

LEYSIN AMERICAN SCHOOL IN SWITZERLAND

Admissions Office
Beau Site
Leysin 1854, Switzerland
Head of School: Dr. K. Steven Ott

General Information Coeducational boarding college-preparatory school. Grades 9–PG. Founded: 1961. Setting: small town. Nearest major city is Lausanne. Students are housed in single-sex dormitories. 12 buildings on campus. Approved or accredited by European Council of International Schools, International Baccalaureate Organization, Middle States Association of Colleges and Schools, Swiss Federation of Private Schools, and The Association of Boarding Schools. Member of Secondary School Admission Test Board. Language of instruction: English. Total enrollment: 345. Upper school average class size: 13. Upper school faculty-student ratio: 1:5.

Upper School Student Profile 100% of students are boarding students. 98% are international students. International students from Bulgaria, Japan, Kazakhstan, Mexico, Saudi Arabia, and United States; 41 other countries represented in student body.

Faculty School total: 72. In upper school: 40 men, 32 women; 42 have advanced degrees; 67 reside on campus.

Subjects Offered Algebra, American history, American literature, ancient history, art, band, biology, business, business studies, calculus, calculus-AP, chemistry, chorus, college counseling, computer programming, computer science, computer technologies, creative arts, current events, dance, drama, ecology, environmental systems, economics, English, English literature, ensembles, ESL, European history, fine arts, fitness, French, French studies, geometry, German, health education, history, history of the Americas, humanities, information technology, International Baccalaureate courses, intro to computers, journalism, language arts, math analysis, math methods, mathematics, mathematics-AP, model United Nations, modern languages, music, music appreciation, performing arts, physical education, physical science, physics, piano, pre-algebra, pre-calculus, psychology, SAT preparation, science, social sciences, social studies, Spanish, Spanish literature, stagecraft, studio art, study skills, theater, theory of knowledge, TOEFL preparation, trigonometry, United Nations and international issues, weightlifting, world history, yearbook.

Graduation Requirements Arts and fine arts (art, music, dance, drama), computer science, English, foreign language, mathematics, physical education (includes health), science, senior humanities, social studies (includes history), Swiss and European cultural trip reports.

Special Academic Programs International Baccalaureate program; honors section; study abroad; academic accommodation for the gifted, the musically talented, and the artistically talented; ESL (110 students enrolled).

College Placement 84 students graduated in 2005; 83 went to college, including Boston University; Marymount College, Palos Verdes, California; Mount Holyoke College; New York University; The University of Texas at Austin; University of Virginia. Other: 1 had other specific plans. Mean SAT verbal: 454, mean SAT math: 532.

Student Life Upper grades have specified standards of dress, student council, honor system. Discipline rests equally with students and faculty.

Summer Programs Remediation, enrichment, advancement, ESL, sports, art/fine arts, rigorous outdoor training, computer instruction programs offered; session focuses on enrichment, theatre, chamber music, leadership, dyslexia, and European travel; held on campus; accepts boys and girls; open to students from other schools. 250 students usually enrolled. 2006 schedule: June 24 to August 11. Application deadline: none.

Tuition and Aid 7-day tuition and room/board: €33,500. Tuition installment plan (corporate payment plan). Merit scholarship grants, need-based scholarship grants, paying campus jobs available. In 2005–06, 37% of upper-school students received aid; total upper-school merit-scholarship money awarded: €80,000. Total amount of financial aid awarded in 2005–06: €410,000.

Admissions Traditional secondary-level entrance grade is 10. Essay required. Deadline for receipt of application materials: none. Application fee required: €100. Interview recommended.

Athletics Interscholastic: alpine skiing (boys, girls), basketball (b,g), hockey (b), ice hockey (b), soccer (b,g), tennis (b,g), volleyball (b,g); intramural: basketball (b,g), soccer (b,g), tennis (b,g), volleyball (b,g); coed interscholastic: bicycling, cross-country running, equestrian sports, golf, skiing (cross-country), skiing (downhill), snowboarding, squash, swimming and diving, track and field; coed intramural: aerobics, aerobics/dance, alpine skiing, back packing, ball hockey, ballet, bicycling, canoeing/kayaking, climbing, cross-country running, curling, dance, dance team, equestrian sports, figure skating, fitness, flag football, floor hockey, freestyle skiing, golf, hiking/backpacking, horseback riding, ice skating, indoor hockey, indoor soccer, jogging, juggling, martial arts, mountain biking, mountaineering, nordic skiing, outdoor activities, outdoor adventure, outdoor education, outdoor recreation, paddle tennis, paint ball, physical fitness, physical training, rafting, rappelling, rock climbing, ropes courses, running, sailing, skiing (cross-country), skiing (downhill), snowboarding, snowshoeing, squash, street hockey, strength & conditioning, swimming and diving, table tennis, track and field, unicycling, walking, wall climbing, weight lifting, weight training, yoga. 1 PE instructor, 2 trainers.

Computers Computers are regularly used in all classes. Computer network features include campus e-mail, on-campus library services, CD-ROMs, Internet access, file transfer, DVD, wireless campus network.

Contact Ms. Colleen Lauriol, Admissions Office Manager. 603-431-7654. Fax: 41-24-494-1585. E-mail: admissions@las.ch. Web site: www.las.ch.

See full description on page 874.

LICK-WILMERDING HIGH SCHOOL

755 Ocean Avenue
San Francisco, California 94112
Head of School: Dr. Albert M. Adams II

General Information Coeducational day college-preparatory, technology, performing arts, and visual arts school. Grades 9–12. Founded: 1895. Setting: urban. 4-acre campus. 6 buildings on campus. Approved or accredited by California Association of Independent Schools, Western Association of Schools and Colleges, and California Department of Education. Member of National Association of Independent Schools and Secondary School Admission Test Board. Endowment: $37 million. Total enrollment: 418. Upper school average class size: 15. Upper school faculty-student ratio: 1:9.

Upper School Student Profile Grade 9: 110 students (57 boys, 53 girls); Grade 10: 105 students (50 boys, 55 girls); Grade 11: 103 students (53 boys, 50 girls); Grade 12: 100 students (48 boys, 52 girls).

Faculty School total: 51. In upper school: 23 men, 28 women; 38 have advanced degrees.

Subjects Offered Acting, adolescent issues, advanced chemistry, advanced computer applications, advanced math, Advanced Placement courses, advanced studio art-AP, African-American literature, algebra, American history, American literature, anatomy and physiology, architectural drawing, architecture, art, biology, biology-AP, calculus, calculus-AP, chemistry, choral music, computer applications, computer music, computer programming, computer science, concert choir, creative writing, critical thinking, dance, digital imaging, drafting, drama, electronics, English, English literature, European history, fine arts, French, French language-AP, French literature-AP, geometry, history, industrial arts, jazz band, jewelry making, journalism, mathematics, mechanical drawing, music, music theory-AP, peer counseling, photography, physical education, physics, psychology, psychology-AP, science, social studies, Spanish, Spanish literature, Spanish-AP, stagecraft, statistics-AP, studio art—AP, technical arts, theater, trigonometry, U.S. history, woodworking, word processing, world history, world literature, writing, yoga.

Graduation Requirements Adolescent issues, arts and fine arts (art, music, dance, drama), English, foreign language, mathematics, physical education (includes health), science, social studies (includes history), technical arts, technology/design, junior project with technical arts.

Special Academic Programs Advanced Placement exam preparation in 17 subject areas; honors section; independent study.

College Placement 91 students graduated in 2005; all went to college, including California Polytechnic State University, San Luis Obispo; Reed College; Stanford University; University of California, Berkeley; University of California, Davis; Vassar College. Mean SAT verbal: 683, mean SAT math: 669. 89% scored over 600 on SAT verbal, 89% scored over 600 on SAT math.

Student Life Upper grades have student council. Discipline rests primarily with faculty.

Lick-Wilmerding High School

Tuition and Aid Day student tuition: $25,700. Tuition installment plan (3- or 10-installment plans). Need-based scholarship grants available. In 2005–06, 42% of upper-school students received aid. Total amount of financial aid awarded in 2005–06: $3,049,000.

Admissions Traditional secondary-level entrance grade is 9. For fall 2005, 718 students applied for upper-level admission, 145 were accepted, 110 enrolled. ISEE or SSAT required. Deadline for receipt of application materials: January 10. Application fee required: $90. Interview required.

Athletics Interscholastic: baseball (boys), basketball (b,g), cross-country running (b,g), lacrosse (b), soccer (b,g), swimming and diving (b,g), tennis (b,g), track and field (b,g), volleyball (b,g); coed interscholastic: badminton; coed intramural: dance, fitness, modern dance, physical fitness, yoga. 2 PE instructors.

Computers Computers are regularly used in architecture, history, journalism, library, literary magazine, media, science, writing, yearbook classes. Computer network features include campus e-mail, on-campus library services, CD-ROMs, online commercial services, Internet access.

Contact Jane W. Faller, Director of Admissions. 415-337-9990. Fax: 415-239-1230. E-mail: lwadmit@lwhs.org. Web site: www.lwhs.org.

LIFEGATE SCHOOL

1052 Fairfield Avenue
Eugene, Oregon 97402-2053
Head of School: Mr. Tom Gregersen

General Information Coeducational day college-preparatory, general academic, and religious studies school, affiliated with Christian faith. Grades P3–12. Founded: 1994. Setting: suburban. 1-acre campus. 1 building on campus. Approved or accredited by Northwest Association of Schools and Colleges and Oregon Department of Education. Total enrollment: 102. Upper school average class size: 8. Upper school faculty-student ratio: 1:8.

Upper School Student Profile Grade 9: 8 students (6 boys, 2 girls); Grade 10: 11 students (4 boys, 7 girls); Grade 11: 13 students (9 boys, 4 girls); Grade 12: 6 students (3 boys, 3 girls). 95% of students are Christian faith.

Faculty School total: 13. In upper school: 5 men, 3 women; 1 has an advanced degree.

Subjects Offered Advanced math, algebra, American government, American government-AP, American history, ancient world history, art, audio visual/media, band, Bible, biology, biology-AP, career and personal planning, chemistry, computer applications, computer graphics, computer keyboarding, computer processing, cultural geography, drama, economics, English, English composition, English language and composition-AP, English literature-AP, environmental systems, geometry, health education, independent study, jazz band, journalism, physical education, physical science, physics, pre-algebra, pre-calculus, reading/study skills, Spanish, speech, world history, writing, yearbook.

Graduation Requirements Bible, computer keyboarding, English, government, history, life skills, mathematics, physical education (includes health), 25 hours of volunteer work per year.

Special Academic Programs Advanced Placement exam preparation in 2 subject areas; honors section; accelerated programs; independent study.

College Placement 10 students graduated in 2005; 7 went to college, including Lane Community College. Other: 3 went to work.

Student Life Upper grades have specified standards of dress, student council. Discipline rests primarily with faculty. Attendance at religious services is required.

Tuition and Aid Day student tuition: $4980. Tuition installment plan (SMART Tuition Payment Plan). Tuition reduction for siblings, need-based scholarship grants available.

Admissions Traditional secondary-level entrance grade is 9. Deadline for receipt of application materials: none. No application fee required. Interview required.

Athletics Interscholastic: basketball (boys, girls); intramural: golf (b,g); coed interscholastic: track and field, volleyball. 2 PE instructors, 2 coaches.

Computers Computers are regularly used in desktop publishing, English, freshman foundations, lab/keyboard, media arts, video film production, writing, yearbook classes. Computer network features include on-campus library services, Internet access, DVD.

Contact Ms. Anna Fanger, Administrative Assistant. 541-689-5847. Fax: 541-689-6028. E-mail: office@lifegatechristian.org. Web site: www.lifegatechristian.org.

LINDEN CHRISTIAN SCHOOL

877 Wilkes Avenue
Winnipeg, Manitoba R3P 1B8, Canada
Head of School: Mr. Robert Williams

General Information Coeducational day college-preparatory, arts, religious studies, and technology school, affiliated with Baptist Church. Grades 9–12. Founded: 1987. Setting: suburban. 1 building on campus. Approved or accredited by Association of Christian Schools International and Manitoba Department of Education. Language of instruction: English. Total enrollment: 777. Upper school average class size: 25. Upper school faculty-student ratio: 1:13.

Upper School Student Profile Grade 9: 67 students (23 boys, 44 girls); Grade 10: 51 students (29 boys, 22 girls); Grade 11: 46 students (25 boys, 21 girls); Grade 12: 38 students (12 boys, 26 girls).

Faculty School total: 61. In upper school: 14 men, 9 women.

Subjects Offered Choir, choral music, computer applications, computer information systems, computer science, computer studies, computer technologies, concert band, drama, dramatic arts, independent study, jazz band, jazz ensemble, leadership, leadership and service, music theater, religious studies, vocal jazz, voice ensemble.

Graduation Requirements Bible studies, English, mathematics, physical education (includes health), science, social studies (includes history).

College Placement 43 students graduated in 2005; 33 went to college, including Providence College; The University of Winnipeg; University of Manitoba; Wilfrid Laurier University. Other: 10 went to work.

Student Life Upper grades have specified standards of dress, student council, honor system. Discipline rests primarily with faculty. Attendance at religious services is required.

Tuition and Aid Day student tuition: CAN$2940. Tuition installment plan (monthly payment plans). Tuition reduction for siblings, bursaries available. In 2005–06, 8% of upper-school students received aid.

Admissions Traditional secondary-level entrance grade is 9. PSAT required. Application fee required: CAN$25. Interview required.

Athletics Interscholastic: badminton (boys, girls), basketball (b,g), broomball (b,g), cooperative games (b,g), cross-country running (b,g), fitness (b,g), flag football (b,g), floor hockey (b,g), football (b,g), golf (b,g), physical fitness (b,g), volleyball (b,g); intramural: badminton (b,g), basketball (b,g), cross-country running (b,g), soccer (b,g), volleyball (b,g). 3 PE instructors.

Computers Computers are regularly used in all classes. Computer network features include CD-ROMs, Internet access, file transfer, office computer access, DVD.

Contact Mrs. Terrie Bell, Registrar. 204-989-6739. Fax: 204-487-7068. E-mail: tbell@lindenchristian.org.

LINDEN HALL SCHOOL FOR GIRLS

212 East Main Street
Lititz, Pennsylvania 17543
Head of School: Shaaron H. Lavery

petersons.com

General Information Girls' boarding and day college-preparatory, arts, bilingual studies, and technology school. Grades 6–PG. Founded: 1746. Setting: small town. Nearest major city is Philadelphia. Students are housed in single-sex dormitories. 47-acre campus. 12 buildings on campus. Approved or accredited by Junior Boarding Schools Association, Middle States Association of Colleges and Schools, The Association of Boarding Schools, and Pennsylvania Department of Education. Member of National Association of Independent Schools and Secondary School Admission Test Board. Endowment: $2.2 million. Total enrollment: 121. Upper school average class size: 8. Upper school faculty-student ratio: 1:4.

Upper School Student Profile Grade 9: 16 students (16 girls); Grade 10: 28 students (28 girls); Grade 11: 22 students (22 girls); Grade 12: 23 students (23 girls); Postgraduate: 2 students (2 girls). 73% of students are boarding students. 47% are state residents. 14 states are represented in upper school student body. 20% are international students. International students from China, El Salvador, Germany, Japan, Mexico, and Republic of Korea; 4 other countries represented in student body.

Faculty School total: 41. In upper school: 6 men, 29 women; 20 have advanced degrees; 14 reside on campus.

Subjects Offered 20th century physics, 20th century world history, 3-dimensional art, acting, aesthetics, algebra, American history, American history-AP, American literature, American literature-AP, art, art history, bell choir, biology, botany, calculus, calculus-AP, career/college preparation, cell biology, ceramics, chemistry, choir, chorus, college admission preparation, college planning, composition, computer applications, computer literacy, computer processing, computer programming, computer science, computer skills, CPR, creative writing, critical writing, dance, dance performance, drama performance, drawing and design, driver education, earth science, electives, English, English composition, English literature, English literature-AP, environmental science, equine studies, ESL, European history, European literature, fine arts, French, genetics, geometry, grammar, history, Latin, library skills, marine biology, mathematics, music, photography, photojournalism, physical education, physics, psychology, reading, social studies, Spanish, speech, study skills, theater arts, TOEFL preparation, world culture, world literature, writing, zoology.

Graduation Requirements Aesthetics, arts and fine arts (art, music, dance, drama), composition, computer science, critical writing, English, foreign language, mathematics, physical education (includes health), SAT preparation, science, social studies (includes history), speech, study skills, TOEFL review (for ESL students), 40 hours of community service per year.

Special Academic Programs Advanced Placement exam preparation in 10 subject areas; honors section; independent study; study at local college for college credit; study abroad; academic accommodation for the gifted, the musically talented, and the artistically talented; ESL (7 students enrolled).

College Placement 28 students graduated in 2005; all went to college, including Bryn Mawr College; Carnegie Mellon University; Kenyon College; Massachusetts Institute

of Technology; New York University; University of Michigan. Mean SAT verbal: 578, mean SAT math: 521. 32% scored over 600 on SAT verbal, 29% scored over 600 on SAT math.

Student Life Upper grades have uniform requirement, student council, honor system. Discipline rests equally with students and faculty. Attendance at religious services is required.

Tuition and Aid Day student tuition: $15,530; 5-day tuition and room/board: $32,690; 7-day tuition and room/board: $34,720. Tuition installment plan (Key Tuition Payment Plan, monthly payment plans, individually arranged payment plans). Tuition reduction for siblings, need-based scholarship grants, paying campus jobs available. In 2005–06, 30% of upper-school students received aid. Total amount of financial aid awarded in 2005–06: $360,000.

Admissions Traditional secondary-level entrance grade is 9. For fall 2005, 71 students applied for upper-level admission, 48 were accepted, 29 enrolled. ACT, any standardized test, Individual IQ, ISEE, TOEFL or writing sample required. Deadline for receipt of application materials: none. Application fee required: $75. On-campus interview required.

Athletics Interscholastic: basketball, equestrian sports, field hockey, lacrosse, soccer, swimming and diving, tennis, volleyball; intramural: aerobics, aerobics/dance, cross-country running, fitness, fitness walking, self defense. 1 PE instructor, 4 coaches, 1 trainer.

Computers Computers are regularly used in all academic, business skills, career exploration, college planning, commercial art, desktop publishing, drawing and design, ESL, graphic arts, keyboarding, library skills, literary magazine, media production, newspaper, photojournalism, publications, SAT preparation, speech, theater arts, typing, Web site design, yearbook classes. Computer network features include campus e-mail, on-campus library services, CD-ROMs, online commercial services, Internet access, file transfer, office computer access, DVD, wireless campus network.

Contact Director of Admissions. 717-626-8512. Fax: 717-627-1384. E-mail: admissions@lindenhall.com. Web site: www.lindenhall.org.

ANNOUNCEMENT FROM THE SCHOOL New to the Linden Hall campus are the Anne Brossman Sweigart Sports and Fitness Center, which provides a regulation-size gymnasium, an exercise room, a dance studio, classrooms, and locker rooms, and the Steinman Arts Center, which houses a theater, a gallery, and the art and photography departments.

See full description on page 876.

LINDEN HILL SCHOOL

Northfield, Massachusetts
See Junior Boarding Schools section.

LINFIELD CHRISTIAN SCHOOL

31950 Pauba Road
Temecula, California 92592
Head of School: Karen Raftery

General Information Coeducational day college-preparatory, arts, religious studies, and technology school, affiliated with Christian faith. Grades K–12. Founded: 1936. Setting: suburban. Nearest major city is San Diego. 105-acre campus. 8 buildings on campus. Approved or accredited by Association of Christian Schools International, Western Association of Schools and Colleges, and California Department of Education. Total enrollment: 924. Upper school average class size: 20. Upper school faculty-student ratio: 1:19.

Upper School Student Profile Grade 9: 115 students (53 boys, 62 girls); Grade 10: 99 students (47 boys, 52 girls); Grade 11: 103 students (43 boys, 60 girls); Grade 12: 93 students (42 boys, 51 girls). 70% of students are Christian faith.

Faculty School total: 56. In upper school: 15 men, 13 women; 9 have advanced degrees.

Subjects Offered Advanced math, algebra, American sign language, anatomy and physiology, art, band, Bible, biology, calculus-AP, chemistry, choir, computers, economics, English, English-AP, European history-AP, freshman foundations, general science, geometry, government, government-AP, health, physical education, physics, pre-calculus, senior seminar, service learning/internship, Spanish, Spanish-AP, speech and debate, theater, U.S. history, U.S. history-AP, world history, world religions, yearbook.

Graduation Requirements Arts and fine arts (art, music, dance, drama), computer science, economics, English, foreign language, freshman foundations, government, mathematics, physical education (includes health), religion (includes Bible studies and theology), science, senior seminar, social science, social studies (includes history), speech and debate. Community service is required.

Special Academic Programs Advanced Placement exam preparation in 5 subject areas; honors section; study at local college for college credit.

College Placement 67 students graduated in 2005; all went to college, including Azusa Pacific University; California State University, San Marcos; Palomar College;

University of California, Riverside; University of California, San Diego. Median SAT verbal: 575, median SAT math: 580, median composite ACT: 24. 45% scored over 600 on SAT verbal, 34% scored over 600 on SAT math.

Student Life Upper grades have specified standards of dress, student council, honor system. Discipline rests primarily with faculty. Attendance at religious services is required.

Tuition and Aid Day student tuition: $7200. Tuition installment plan (monthly payment plans). Need-based scholarship grants available.

Admissions Traditional secondary-level entrance grade is 9. For fall 2005, 125 students applied for upper-level admission, 115 were accepted, 95 enrolled. 3-R Achievement Test and USC/UC Math Diagnostic Test required. Deadline for receipt of application materials: none. Application fee required: $50. On-campus interview required.

Athletics Interscholastic: baseball (boys), basketball (b,g), cheering (g), cross-country running (b,g), football (b), soccer (b,g), softball (g), tennis (g), track and field (b,g), volleyball (g), weight training (b); intramural: volleyball (g); coed interscholastic: golf; coed intramural: cross-country running. 2 PE instructors, 14 coaches, 1 trainer.

Computers Computers are regularly used in computer applications, keyboarding, science, senior seminar, yearbook classes. Computer network features include campus e-mail, on-campus library services, CD-ROMs, Internet access.

Contact Mrs. Becky Swanson, Admissions Assistant. 951-676-8111 Ext. 1402. Fax: 951-695-1291. E-mail: bswanson@linfield.com. Web site: www.linfield.com.

THE LINSLY SCHOOL
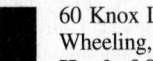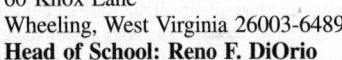
60 Knox Lane
Wheeling, West Virginia 26003-6489
Head of School: Reno F. DiOrio

petersons.com

General Information Coeducational boarding and day college-preparatory, arts, technology, and science, mathematics, humanities, foreign language school. Boarding grades 7–12, day grades 5–12. Founded: 1814. Setting: suburban. Nearest major city is Pittsburgh, PA. Students are housed in single-sex dormitories. 60-acre campus. 19 buildings on campus. Approved or accredited by Independent Schools Association of the Central States, North Central Association of Colleges and Schools, The Association of Boarding Schools, and West Virginia Department of Education. Member of National Association of Independent Schools. Endowment: $14 million. Total enrollment: 425. Upper school average class size: 15. Upper school faculty-student ratio: 1:9.

Upper School Student Profile Grade 9: 67 students (37 boys, 30 girls); Grade 10: 69 students (38 boys, 31 girls); Grade 11: 71 students (38 boys, 33 girls); Grade 12: 47 students (30 boys, 17 girls). 32% of students are boarding students. 60% are state residents. 10 states are represented in upper school student body. 5% are international students. International students from China, Germany, Republic of Korea, Saudi Arabia, and Thailand.

Faculty School total: 43. In upper school: 21 men, 8 women; 17 have advanced degrees; 21 reside on campus.

Subjects Offered Algebra, American history, American literature, art, art history, biology, calculus, chemistry, computer programming, computer science, creative writing, drama, earth science, economics, English, English literature, expository writing, fine arts, French, geometry, German, government/civics, health, history, humanities, Latin, mathematics, music, physical education, physics, psychology, science, social studies, Spanish, speech, statistics, theater, typing, world history, writing.

Graduation Requirements Arts and fine arts (art, music, dance, drama), computer science, English, foreign language, mathematics, physical education (includes health), science, social studies (includes history).

Special Academic Programs Advanced Placement exam preparation in 7 subject areas; honors section; academic accommodation for the gifted.

College Placement 84 students graduated in 2005; all went to college, including Boston College; New York University; The Ohio State University; West Virginia University. Mean SAT verbal: 560, mean SAT math: 560.

Student Life Upper grades have uniform requirement, student council. Discipline rests primarily with faculty.

Summer Programs Enrichment, advancement, computer instruction programs offered; held on campus; accepts boys and girls; open to students from other schools. 100 students usually enrolled. 2006 schedule: June 12 to July 12. Application deadline: June 12.

Tuition and Aid Day student tuition: $10,820; 5-day tuition and room/board: $21,950; 7-day tuition and room/board: $21,950. Tuition installment plan (Academic Management Services Plan). Need-based scholarship grants available. In 2005–06, 40% of upper-school students received aid. Total amount of financial aid awarded in 2005–06: $900,000.

Admissions Traditional secondary-level entrance grade is 9. For fall 2005, 143 students applied for upper-level admission, 68 were accepted, 37 enrolled. Otis-Lennon, Stanford Achievement Test required. Deadline for receipt of application materials: none. No application fee required. On-campus interview required.

Athletics Interscholastic: baseball (boys), basketball (b,g), cheering (g), cross-country running (b,g), diving (b,g), football (b), golf (b,g), ice hockey (b,g), soccer (b,g), softball (g), wrestling (b); intramural: flag football (b,g), floor hockey (b),

football (b), hiking/backpacking (b,g), indoor soccer (b,g), indoor track (b,g), indoor track & field (b,g), life saving (b,g), mountain biking (b,g), outdoor activities (b,g), outdoor adventure (b,g), outdoor education (b,g), outdoor recreation (b,g), outdoor skills (b,g), physical fitness (b,g), power lifting (b), rappelling (b,g), rock climbing (b,g), roller blading (b,g), ropes courses (b,g), running (b,g), street hockey (b); coed intramural: back packing, badminton, bowling, canoeing/kayaking, climbing, combined training, cooperative games, cross-country running, fitness, Frisbee, ice skating, in-line skating, jogging, kayaking, kickball, life saving, mountain biking, nautilus, outdoors, physical fitness, physical training, rafting, rock climbing, ropes courses, running, scuba diving, soccer, softball. 2 PE instructors, 4 coaches, 1 trainer.

Computers Computers are regularly used in economics, English, foreign language, humanities, mathematics, music, psychology, science classes. Computer network features include campus e-mail, on-campus library services, CD-ROMs, Internet access, file transfer, office computer access.

Contact Chad Barnett, Director of Admissions. 304-233-1436. Fax: 304-234-4614. E-mail: admit@linsly.org. Web site: www.linsly.org.

ANNOUNCEMENT FROM THE SCHOOL Located on a beautiful campus in Wheeling, West Virginia, The Linsly School is a coeducational, college-preparatory school, founded in 1814 by former Wheeling mayor, Noah Linsly. Linsly's traditional, values-based curriculum is supported by a warm, community-spirited environment. Linsly combines the values of hard work, respect, honor, honesty, and self-discipline within a rigorous academic program that challenges students to reach their highest potential physically, socially, and morally. With a student to teacher ratio of 15:1, Linsly offers small classes and individual attention for each student. Faculty members work closely with students and serve as role models and mentors in all areas of school activities. The Lower School, grades 5–8, develops sound work habits as well as academic preparation for the transition to the Upper School, grades 9–12. Students in the Upper School carry at least 5 core courses per semester, following a challenging college-preparatory curriculum. Advanced Placement instruction is offered in numerous disciplines. College counseling begins during the sophomore year, allowing each student the opportunity to arrive at an understanding of his or her academic and personal priorities when selecting a college. Students can choose from a variety of campus clubs, community service activities, and interscholastic athletics. Weekend activities for boarding students may include school dances, informal parties, recreational sports, and supervised off-campus trips to the mall or nearby Oglebay Park. An outdoor educational program unique to Linsly, The Linsly Outdoor Center, located in Pennsylvania's Raccoon Creek State Park, challenges students physically and mentally, builds self-esteem, and strengthens camaraderie among classmates. Linsly's 65-acre campus includes a central academic complex, a new visual arts center, music facilities, science/computer laboratories, a bookstore, the Coudon-Ogden Library, an athletic field house, and The Hess Center, a woodworking facility. Linsly is located 1 hour west of Pittsburgh and 2 hours east of Columbus.

LITTLE KESWICK SCHOOL

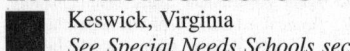

Keswick, Virginia
See Special Needs Schools section.

LITTLE RED SCHOOL HOUSE AND ELISABETH IRWIN HIGH SCHOOL

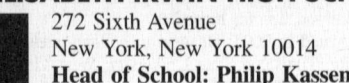

272 Sixth Avenue
New York, New York 10014
Head of School: Philip Kassen

petersons.com

General Information Coeducational day college-preparatory, arts, and technology school. Grades N–12. Founded: 1921. Setting: urban. 1 building on campus. Approved or accredited by New York State Association of Independent Schools and New York Department of Education. Member of National Association of Independent Schools. Total enrollment: 561. Upper school average class size: 15. Upper school faculty-student ratio: 1:6.

Faculty In upper school: 16 men, 16 women; 22 have advanced degrees.

Subjects Offered Adolescent issues, American history, American literature, ancient history, art, astronomy, biology, calculus, chemistry, choir, chorus, college counseling, computer applications, computer graphics, contemporary math, creative dance, dance, data analysis, drama, drawing, environmental science, environmental studies, film and literature, filmmaking, French, global studies, Hispanic literature, introduction to literature, introduction to technology, jazz band, Latin American literature, library research, life issues, life science, Mandarin, media studies, Middle Eastern history, modern dance, modern European history, multimedia design, music, music technology, painting, photography, physical science, physics, play production, pre-calculus, printmaking, psychology, research, research skills, sculpture, Spanish, Spanish literature, theater, U.S. history, urban studies, weight fitness, world literature.

Graduation Requirements Arts and fine arts (art, music, dance, drama), English, foreign language, history, mathematics, physical education (includes health), science, senior project, urban studies, 25 hours of community service per year.

Special Academic Programs Honors section; independent study; study at local college for college credit; study abroad.

College Placement 34 students graduated in 2005; all went to college, including Bard College; New York University; Northeastern University; Skidmore College; The Pennsylvania State University University Park Campus; Wesleyan University.

Student Life Upper grades have student council, honor system. Discipline rests equally with students and faculty.

Tuition and Aid Day student tuition: $25,745. Tuition installment plan (Insured Tuition Payment Plan, SMART Tuition Payment Plan, monthly payment plans). Need-based scholarship grants available. In 2005–06, 22% of upper-school students received aid.

Admissions Traditional secondary-level entrance grade is 9. For fall 2005, 176 students applied for upper-level admission, 55 were accepted, 23 enrolled. ISEE required. Deadline for receipt of application materials: November 30. Application fee required: $50. On-campus interview required.

Athletics Interscholastic: basketball (boys, girls), softball (b,g), track and field (b,g), volleyball (g); intramural: dance squad (g); coed interscholastic: cross-country running, dance team, golf, indoor track, soccer, tennis; coed intramural: aerobics, aerobics/dance, fitness, wall climbing, yoga. 8 PE instructors, 6 coaches, 1 trainer.

Computers Computers are regularly used in art, design, English, French, history, mathematics, media arts, music, photography, programming, science, Spanish, technology classes. Computer network features include campus e-mail, Internet access, DVD, wireless campus network.

Contact Admissions Office. 212-477-5316 Ext. 210. E-mail: admissions@lrei.org. Web site: www.lrei.org.

See full description on page 878.

LIVING WORD ACADEMY

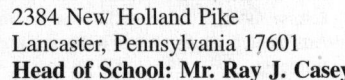

2384 New Holland Pike
Lancaster, Pennsylvania 17601
Head of School: Mr. Ray J. Casey

General Information Coeducational day college-preparatory, general academic, arts, religious studies, and technology school, affiliated with Christian faith, Protestant faith. Grades K–12. Founded: 1981. Setting: rural. 134-acre campus. 1 building on campus. Approved or accredited by Association of Christian Schools International, Middle States Association of Colleges and Schools, and Pennsylvania Department of Education. Endowment: $50,000. Total enrollment: 339. Upper school average class size: 22. Upper school faculty-student ratio: 1:14.

Upper School Student Profile Grade 9: 30 students (13 boys, 17 girls); Grade 10: 46 students (25 boys, 21 girls); Grade 11: 39 students (19 boys, 20 girls); Grade 12: 33 students (20 boys, 13 girls). 100% of students are Christian faith, Protestant.

Faculty School total: 38. In upper school: 7 men, 8 women; 6 have advanced degrees.

Special Academic Programs Advanced Placement exam preparation in 3 subject areas; honors section.

College Placement 39 students graduated in 2005; 21 went to college, including Eastern University; Messiah College; Millersville University of Pennsylvania; The Pennsylvania State University University Park Campus. Other: 16 went to work, 2 had other specific plans. Mean SAT verbal: 560, mean SAT math: 554. 34% scored over 600 on SAT verbal, 43% scored over 600 on SAT math.

Student Life Upper grades have specified standards of dress, student council, honor system. Discipline rests primarily with faculty. Attendance at religious services is required.

Summer Programs Sports programs offered; session focuses on fundamentals and team-building; held both on and off campus; held at Ponderosa Lodge (Williamsport, PA) and Lock Haven University; accepts boys and girls; open to students from other schools. 30 students usually enrolled.

Tuition and Aid Day student tuition: $5484. Tuition installment plan (monthly payment plans). Tuition reduction for siblings, need-based scholarship grants available. In 2005–06, 25% of upper-school students received aid. Total amount of financial aid awarded in 2005–06: $54,793.

Admissions Traditional secondary-level entrance grade is 9. For fall 2005, 30 students applied for upper-level admission, 30 were accepted, 23 enrolled. Admissions testing required. Deadline for receipt of application materials: none. Application fee required: $90. On-campus interview required.

Athletics Interscholastic: baseball (boys), basketball (b,g), field hockey (g), soccer (b,g), track and field (b,g); intramural: indoor hockey (g); coed interscholastic: golf; coed intramural: ropes courses. 2 PE instructors, 8 coaches.

Computers Computers are regularly used in desktop publishing, drafting, multimedia, technology, yearbook classes. Computer network features include campus e-mail, on-campus library services, CD-ROMs, Internet access, file transfer, wireless campus network.

Contact Mrs. Becky F. Smoker, Administrative Assistant. 717-556-0711 Ext. 224. Fax: 717-656-4868. E-mail: bfsmoker@livingwordacademy.org. Web site: www. livingwordacademy.org.

LONG ISLAND LUTHERAN MIDDLE AND HIGH SCHOOL

131 Brookville Road
Brookville, New York 11545-3399
Head of School: Dr. David Hahn

petersons.com

General Information Coeducational day college-preparatory, arts, business, and religious studies school, affiliated with Lutheran Church. Grades 6–12. Founded: 1960. Setting: suburban. Nearest major city is New York. 32-acre campus. 6 buildings on campus. Approved or accredited by Evangelical Lutheran Church in America, Middle States Association of Colleges and Schools, New York State Association of Independent Schools, US Department of State, and New York Department of Education. Endowment: $4.2 million. Total enrollment: 609. Upper school average class size: 18. Upper school faculty-student ratio: 1:11.

Upper School Student Profile Grade 9: 105 students (50 boys, 55 girls); Grade 10: 105 students (52 boys, 53 girls); Grade 11: 105 students (57 boys, 48 girls); Grade 12: 95 students (43 boys, 52 girls). 40% of students are Lutheran.

Faculty School total: 52. In upper school: 16 men, 26 women; 36 have advanced degrees.

Subjects Offered Accounting, algebra, American history, American literature, anatomy, art, band, biology, business, business communications, business skills, calculus, ceramics, choir, communication skills, computer programming, computer science, creative writing, driver education, earth science, economics, English, English literature, environmental science, European history, fine arts, French, geography, geometry, government/civics, grammar, health, history, marketing, mathematics, music, physical education, physics, physiology, psychology, religion, science, social studies, Spanish, Spanish language-AP, trigonometry, word processing, world history, writing.

Graduation Requirements Arts and fine arts (art, music, dance, drama), business skills (includes word processing), computer science, English, foreign language, mathematics, physical education (includes health), religion (includes Bible studies and theology), science, social studies (includes history).

Special Academic Programs Advanced Placement exam preparation in 10 subject areas; honors section; term-away projects; study at local college for college credit.

College Placement 92 students graduated in 2005; all went to college, including Georgetown University; Hofstra University; Loyola College in Maryland; New York University; Quinnipiac University; Stony Brook University, State University of New York. Mean SAT verbal: 556, mean SAT math: 608, mean composite ACT: 23. 40% scored over 600 on SAT verbal, 40% scored over 600 on SAT math, 25% scored over 26 on composite ACT.

Student Life Upper grades have uniform requirement, student council, honor system. Discipline rests primarily with faculty. Attendance at religious services is required.

Summer Programs Sports, art/fine arts, computer instruction programs offered; session focuses on sports, recreation, and education; held both on and off campus; held at local satellite facilities; accepts boys and girls; open to students from other schools. 6800 students usually enrolled. 2006 schedule: June 26 to August 18. Application deadline: January.

Tuition and Aid Day student tuition: $7700–$8975. Tuition installment plan (monthly payment plans, school's own payment plan). Tuition reduction for siblings, merit scholarship grants, need-based scholarship grants, principal's scholarship available. In 2005–06, 20% of upper-school students received aid; total upper-school merit-scholarship money awarded: $17,000. Total amount of financial aid awarded in 2005–06: $170,000.

Admissions Traditional secondary-level entrance grade is 9. For fall 2005, 122 students applied for upper-level admission, 74 were accepted, 53 enrolled. Cognitive Abilities Test, Math Placement Exam and writing sample required. Deadline for receipt of application materials: none. Application fee required: $100. On-campus interview required.

Athletics Interscholastic: baseball (boys, girls), basketball (b,g), cheering (g), dance team (g), football (b), lacrosse (b,g), roller hockey (b), soccer (b,g), softball (g), tennis (b,g), volleyball (g), wrestling (b); intramural: dance team (g); coed interscholastic: cross-country running, golf, running, track and field, winter (indoor) track; coed intramural: bowling, skiing (downhill). 3 PE instructors, 30 coaches.

Computers Computers are regularly used in accounting, art, business, business skills, college planning, design, English, graphic design, history, library skills, mathematics, science classes. Computer network features include campus e-mail, on-campus library services, CD-ROMs, Internet access, DVD, wireless campus network.

Contact Barbara Ward, Director of Admissions. 516-626-1700. Fax: 516-622-7459. E-mail: barbara.ward@luhi.org. Web site: www.luhi.org.

ANNOUNCEMENT FROM THE SCHOOL Located on a 32-acre estate on Long Island's North Shore, the School's college-preparatory climate is characterized by Christian care and individual attention for each student. LuHi's mission is to assist students of average to superior ability to develop intellectually, emotionally, physically, and socially.

THE LOOMIS CHAFFEE SCHOOL

4 Batchelder Road
Windsor, Connecticut 06095
Head of School: Dr. Russell H. Weigel

petersons.com

General Information Coeducational boarding and day college-preparatory school. Grades 9–PG. Founded: 1914. Setting: suburban. Nearest major city is Hartford. Students are housed in single-sex dormitories. 300-acre campus. 65 buildings on campus. Approved or accredited by New England Association of Schools and Colleges, The Association of Boarding Schools, and Connecticut Department of Education. Member of National Association of Independent Schools and Secondary School Admission Test Board. Endowment: $115 million. Total enrollment: 723. Upper school average class size: 14. Upper school faculty-student ratio: 1:5.

Upper School Student Profile Grade 9: 141 students (67 boys, 74 girls); Grade 10: 176 students (92 boys, 84 girls); Grade 11: 194 students (98 boys, 96 girls); Grade 12: 187 students (93 boys, 94 girls); Postgraduate: 25 students (24 boys, 1 girl). 60% of students are boarding students. 59% are state residents. 30 states are represented in upper school student body. 10% are international students. International students from Canada, China, Jamaica, Republic of Korea, Saudi Arabia, and Thailand; 9 other countries represented in student body.

Faculty School total: 150. In upper school: 72 men, 78 women; 123 have advanced degrees; 70 reside on campus.

Subjects Offered Algebra, American history, American literature, anatomy, art, art history, astronomy, biology, calculus, ceramics, chemistry, computer math, computer programming, computer science, creative writing, dance, drama, ecology, economics, English, English literature, environmental science, ethics, European history, expository writing, fine arts, French, geology, geometry, German, history, history of ideas, history of science, journalism, Latin, library studies, logic, Mandarin, mathematics, music, philosophy, photography, physical education, physics, physiology, religion, Russian, science, social studies, Spanish, speech, statistics, theater, trigonometry, video film production, world history, world literature, writing.

Graduation Requirements Arts and fine arts (art, music, dance, drama), English, foreign language, history, mathematics, philosophy, physical education (includes health), religion (includes Bible studies and theology), science.

Special Academic Programs Advanced Placement exam preparation in 13 subject areas; honors section; independent study; term-away projects; study at local college for college credit; study abroad; academic accommodation for the gifted, the musically talented, and the artistically talented.

College Placement 200 students graduated in 2005; 197 went to college, including Skidmore College. 68% scored over 600 on SAT verbal, 76% scored over 600 on SAT math.

Student Life Upper grades have specified standards of dress, student council. Discipline rests primarily with faculty.

Tuition and Aid Day student tuition: $26,200; 7-day tuition and room/board: $34,800. Guaranteed tuition plan. Tuition installment plan (Insured Tuition Payment Plan, Key Tuition Payment Plan, monthly payment plans). Need-based scholarship grants, need-based loans available. In 2005–06, 30% of upper-school students received aid. Total amount of financial aid awarded in 2005–06: $4,600,000.

Admissions Traditional secondary-level entrance grade is 9. For fall 2005, 1,247 students applied for upper-level admission, 507 were accepted, 246 enrolled. ISEE, PSAT, SAT, SSAT or TOEFL required. Deadline for receipt of application materials: January 15. Application fee required: $65. Interview required.

Athletics Interscholastic: baseball (boys), basketball (b,g), cross-country running (b,g), field hockey (g), football (b), golf (b,g), ice hockey (b,g), lacrosse (b,g), soccer (b,g), softball (g), squash (b,g), swimming and diving (b,g), tennis (b,g), track and field (b,g), volleyball (b,g), water polo (b,g), wrestling (b); intramural: ice hockey (b,g), soccer (b,g), volleyball (b,g), yoga (b,g); coed interscholastic: alpine skiing, diving, riflery, skiing (downhill); coed intramural: aerobics, aerobics/dance, aerobics/nautilus, back packing, basketball, bicycling, canoeing/kayaking, climbing, dance, fencing, figure skating, fitness, Frisbee, hiking/backpacking, ice skating, jogging, kayaking, life saving, mountain biking, nautilus, outdoor activities, outdoor adventure, physical fitness, physical training, ropes courses, running, skiing (downhill), soccer, softball, squash, strength & conditioning, ultimate Frisbee, weight training. 5 PE instructors, 2 trainers.

Computers Computers are regularly used in English, foreign language, history, library skills, mathematics, science classes. Computer network features include campus e-mail, on-campus library services, CD-ROMs, online commercial services, Internet access, wireless campus network.

Contact Thomas D. Southworth, Director of Admission. 860-687-6400. Fax: 860-298-8756. E-mail: tom_southworth@loomis.org. Web site: www.loomis.org.

ANNOUNCEMENT FROM THE SCHOOL Both traditional and innovative, the Loomis Chaffee School is an independent, coeducational, college-preparatory boarding and day school with 700 students from more than 15 countries and 30 states. Academically and athletically rigorous, the School promotes active learning, moral values, and close faculty-student bonds within a community of respect and civility. Students enjoy up-to-date facilities, numerous extracurricular activities, community service opportunities, and

individual guidance from a dedicated faculty of 150. Thirty percent of the students receive financial aid.

See full description on page 880.

LORETTO ACADEMY

1300 Hardaway Street
El Paso, Texas 79903
Head of School: Sr. Mary E. (Buffy) Boesen, SL

General Information Coeducational day (boys' only in lower grades) college-preparatory, arts, religious studies, and technology school, affiliated with Roman Catholic Church. Boys grades PK–5, girls grades PK–12. Founded: 1923. Setting: urban. 17-acre campus. 3 buildings on campus. Approved or accredited by Southern Association of Colleges and Schools and Texas Catholic Conference. Endowment: $1.3 million. Total enrollment: 698. Upper school average class size: 18. Upper school faculty-student ratio: 1:18.

Upper School Student Profile Grade 9: 98 students (98 girls); Grade 10: 112 students (112 girls); Grade 11: 118 students (118 girls); Grade 12: 101 students (101 girls). 85% of students are Roman Catholic.

Faculty School total: 28. In upper school: 7 men, 21 women; 15 have advanced degrees.

Subjects Offered Acting, advanced computer applications, advanced math, Advanced Placement courses, algebra, American government, American history, art, art appreciation, art-AP, arts, arts and crafts, Bible, biology, body human, business mathematics, calculus, calculus-AP, Catholic belief and practice, chemistry, choir, choral music, Christian and Hebrew scripture, Christian ethics, college writing, computer applications, computer keyboarding, computer programming, computer science, English, English/composition-AP, fine arts, French, French as a second language, geometry, government, government-AP, health, honors algebra, honors English, honors geometry, integrated science, Internet, jewelry making, journalism, keyboarding, life issues, literary magazine, literature, literature-AP, mathematics, modern dance, moral theology, music appreciation, photo shop, physical education, physics, physics-AP, religion, science, social studies, Spanish, Spanish language-AP, Spanish literature-AP, Spanish-AP, speech, speech and debate, student government, study skills, technical writing, theater production, U.S. government-AP, world geography, world history, world religions, yearbook, zoology.

Graduation Requirements Algebra, American government, arts and fine arts (art, music, dance, drama), biology, Christian and Hebrew scripture, Christian ethics, Christian studies, computer science, economics, English, English composition, English literature, foreign language, lab/keyboard, life issues, mathematics, moral reasoning, physical education (includes health), physical science, psychology, religion (includes Bible studies and theology), science, social studies (includes history), speech communications, world geography, world religions.

Special Academic Programs Advanced Placement exam preparation in 6 subject areas.

College Placement 67 students graduated in 2005; 66 went to college, including New Mexico State University; St. Edward's University; St. Mary's University of San Antonio; The University of Texas at El Paso; The University of Texas at San Antonio. Other: 1 had other specific plans. Mean SAT verbal: 522, mean SAT math: 480. 27% scored over 600 on SAT verbal, 8% scored over 600 on SAT math.

Student Life Upper grades have uniform requirement, student council, honor system. Discipline rests primarily with faculty.

Summer Programs Remediation programs offered; session focuses on remediation; held on campus; accepts girls; not open to students from other schools. 25 students usually enrolled. 2006 schedule: June 2 to July 3.

Tuition and Aid Day student tuition: $5275. Tuition installment plan (FACTS Tuition Payment Plan). Tuition reduction for siblings, need-based scholarship grants available. In 2005–06, 18% of upper-school students received aid. Total amount of financial aid awarded in 2005–06: $90,000.

Admissions Traditional secondary-level entrance grade is 9. For fall 2005, 145 students applied for upper-level admission, 143 were accepted, 98 enrolled. High School Placement Test (closed version) from Scholastic Testing Service required. Deadline for receipt of application materials: none. Application fee required: $30. On-campus interview required.

Athletics Interscholastic: aquatics, basketball, cheering, cross-country running, dance squad, dance team, soccer, softball, swimming and diving, tennis, track and field, volleyball. 10 coaches, 2 trainers.

Computers Computers are regularly used in all academic classes. Computer network features include campus e-mail, CD-ROMs, Internet access, office computer access.

Contact Mrs. Lily Miranda, Director of Admissions. 915-566-8400. Fax: 915-566-0636. E-mail: lmiranda@loretto.org. Web site: www.loretto.org.

LORETTO HIGH SCHOOL

2360 El Camino Avenue
Sacramento, California 95821
Head of School: Sr. Barbara Nelson

petersons.com

General Information Girls' day college-preparatory, arts, religious studies, and technology school, affiliated with Roman Catholic Church. Grades 9–12. Founded: 1955. Setting: suburban. 10-acre campus. 12 buildings on campus. Approved or accredited by Western Association of Schools and Colleges, Western Catholic Education Association, and California Department of Education. Total enrollment: 550. Upper school average class size: 23. Upper school faculty-student ratio: 1:14.

Upper School Student Profile Grade 9: 145 students (145 girls); Grade 10: 145 students (145 girls); Grade 11: 120 students (120 girls); Grade 12: 140 students (140 girls). 80% of students are Roman Catholic.

Faculty School total: 38. In upper school: 9 men, 29 women; all have advanced degrees.

Subjects Offered 3-dimensional art, advanced chemistry, advanced computer applications, advanced math, Advanced Placement courses, advanced studio art-AP, algebra, alternative physical education, American government, American history, American history-AP, American legal systems, American literature, art, art history, astronomy, athletics, Basic programming, basketball, Bible, biology, British literature, Broadway dance, calculus-AP, campus ministry, Catholic belief and practice, ceramics, chemistry, choir, Christian scripture, church history, college counseling, community service, computer applications, computer literacy, computer multimedia, computer programming, computer science, computer skills, computer technologies, conceptual physics, concert choir, critical studies in film, dance, dance performance, desktop publishing, drama, drama workshop, drawing, earth science, economics, electives, English, English composition, English language and composition-AP, English literature, English-AP, expository writing, film and literature, fine arts, fitness, foreign language, French, French-AP, geology, geometry, global issues, global studies, golf, government, Greek, health, health and wellness, health education, history of the Catholic Church, honors English, intro to computers, introduction to theater, Life of Christ, mathematics, music appreciation, music history, music theory, mythology, novel, oceanography, painting, participation in sports, peace and justice, peer ministry, performing arts, philosophy, physical education, physical fitness, physics, poetry, pre-calculus, psychology, religion, religious studies, SAT preparation, SAT/ACT preparation, Shakespeare, short story, Spanish, Spanish language-AP, stage design, stagecraft, stained glass, statistics and probability, student government, swimming, theater, theology, topics in dramatic literature, U.S. government, U.S. history, U.S. history-AP, visual and performing arts, volleyball, water color painting, water polo, Western civilization, Western philosophy, Western religions, women in literature, work-study, world history, world history-AP, world literature, writing, writing fundamentals, writing skills, yearbook.

Graduation Requirements Arts and fine arts (art, music, dance, drama), computer science, English, foreign language, mathematics, physical education (includes health), religion (includes Bible studies and theology), science, social science, social studies (includes history). Community service is required.

Special Academic Programs Advanced Placement exam preparation in 6 subject areas; honors section; study at local college for college credit; academic accommodation for the gifted, the musically talented, and the artistically talented.

College Placement 120 students graduated in 2005; all went to college, including California Polytechnic State University, San Luis Obispo; California State University, Sacramento; Loyola Marymount University; Seattle University; University of California, Davis; University of California, Los Angeles. 3% scored over 600 on SAT verbal, 3% scored over 600 on SAT math.

Student Life Upper grades have uniform requirement, student council, honor system. Discipline rests primarily with faculty. Attendance at religious services is required.

Tuition and Aid Day student tuition: $9490. Tuition installment plan (monthly payment plans, individually arranged payment plans). Merit scholarship grants, need-based scholarship grants available. In 2005–06, 18% of upper-school students received aid; total upper-school merit-scholarship money awarded: $5000. Total amount of financial aid awarded in 2005–06: $250,000.

Admissions Traditional secondary-level entrance grade is 9. For fall 2005, 255 students applied for upper-level admission, 170 were accepted, 145 enrolled. High School Placement Test or writing sample required. Deadline for receipt of application materials: January 31. No application fee required. On-campus interview required.

Athletics Interscholastic: aerobics/dance, aquatics, basketball, cross-country running, diving, golf, physical training, running, soccer, softball, swimming and diving, tennis, track and field, volleyball, water polo; intramural: basketball, field hockey, soccer, softball, volleyball. 2 PE instructors, 9 coaches, 9 trainers.

Computers Computers are regularly used in all academic classes. Computer network features include on-campus library services, CD-ROMs, online commercial services, Internet access, wireless campus network.

Contact Mrs. Antoinette A. Perez, Director of Admission. 916-482-7793 Ext. 103. Fax: 916-482-3621. E-mail: aperez@loretto.net. Web site: www.loretto.net.

ANNOUNCEMENT FROM THE SCHOOL Loretto, a small, independent Catholic school for young women, strives to develop the whole person—spirit, mind, and body—through a college-preparatory curriculum in an exhilarating and supportive atmosphere. The recently expanded campus provides a new

performing arts center and science center. An aquatic complex is planned for the near future.

LOS ANGELES BAPTIST JUNIOR/SENIOR HIGH SCHOOL

9825 Woodley Avenue
North Hills, California 91343
Head of School: Tim Piatt

General Information Coeducational day college-preparatory, arts, religious studies, and technology school, affiliated with Baptist Church. Grades 7–12. Founded: 1962. Setting: suburban. Nearest major city is Los Angeles. 11-acre campus. 5 buildings on campus. Approved or accredited by Association of Christian Schools International and Western Association of Schools and Colleges. Total enrollment: 963. Upper school average class size: 30. Upper school faculty-student ratio: 1:22.

Upper School Student Profile Grade 9: 174 students (78 boys, 96 girls); Grade 10: 159 students (82 boys, 77 girls); Grade 11: 166 students (92 boys, 74 girls); Grade 12: 160 students (75 boys, 85 girls).

Faculty School total: 43. In upper school: 24 men, 19 women; 21 have advanced degrees.

Subjects Offered Advanced computer applications, algebra, American history, American literature, American literature-AP, analysis and differential calculus, anatomy and physiology, art, art appreciation, ASB Leadership, band, Bible studies, biology, biology-AP, calculus-AP, chemistry, chemistry-AP, choir, choral music, Christian doctrine, Christian education, Christian ethics, computer applications, computer education, computer graphics, computer keyboarding, computer programming, computer science, computer skills, computer technologies, drama, drama performance, earth science, economics, English, English literature, English-AP, European history-AP, expository writing, fine arts, French, French-AP, geography, geometry, government/civics, health, home economics, HTML design, intro to computers, jazz band, mathematics, music, photography, physical education, physics, physics-AP, practical arts, pre-calculus, psychology, psychology-AP, religion, science, social studies, Spanish, Spanish-AP, speech, statistics-AP, trigonometry, typing, U.S. history-AP, world history, world history-AP.

Graduation Requirements Arts and fine arts (art, music, dance, drama), English, foreign language, mathematics, physical education (includes health), practical arts, religion (includes Bible studies and theology), science, social studies (includes history).

Special Academic Programs Advanced Placement exam preparation in 10 subject areas; honors section.

College Placement 134 students graduated in 2005; 132 went to college, including California State University, Northridge; University of California, Berkeley; University of California, Irvine; University of California, Los Angeles; University of California, Riverside; University of California, Santa Barbara. Other: 2 went to work. Median SAT verbal: 560, median SAT math: 550, median composite ACT: 24. 28.6% scored over 600 on SAT verbal, 29.8% scored over 600 on SAT math, 23.1% scored over 26 on composite ACT.

Student Life Upper grades have specified standards of dress, student council, honor system. Discipline rests primarily with faculty. Attendance at religious services is required.

Summer Programs Remediation, advancement, sports, computer instruction programs offered; session focuses on remediation and enrichment; held on campus; accepts boys and girls; open to students from other schools. 300 students usually enrolled. 2006 schedule: June 21 to August 3.

Tuition and Aid Day student tuition: $5950. Tuition installment plan (FACTS Tuition Payment Plan, monthly payment plans, 2-semester payment plan, annual payment plan). Merit scholarship grants, need-based scholarship grants available. In 2005–06, 24% of upper-school students received aid; total upper-school merit-scholarship money awarded: $2000. Total amount of financial aid awarded in 2005–06: $386,950.

Admissions Traditional secondary-level entrance grade is 9. For fall 2005, 216 students applied for upper-level admission, 73 were accepted, 63 enrolled. QUIC required. Deadline for receipt of application materials: November 21. Application fee required: $50. On-campus interview required.

Athletics Interscholastic: baseball (boys), basketball (b,g), cheering (g), cross-country running (b,g), drill team (g), football (b), soccer (b,g), softball (g), track and field (b,g), volleyball (b,g); coed interscholastic: golf. 2 PE instructors, 32 coaches.

Computers Computers are regularly used in animation, business applications, career technology, French, graphic design, graphics, introduction to technology, keyboarding, lab/keyboard, library, programming, Spanish, technology, typing, Web site design, word processing classes. Computer network features include campus e-mail, on-campus library services, CD-ROMs, Internet access, office computer access, DVD, CD-ROM Tower (Spanish and French programs), Accelerated Reader, Biblesoft.

Contact Laurie Minter, Admission Secretary. 818-894-5742 Ext. 322. Fax: 818-892-5018. E-mail: lminter@labaptist.org. Web site: www.labaptist.org/.

LOS ANGELES LUTHERAN HIGH SCHOOL

13570 Eldridge Avenue
Sylmar, California 91342
Head of School: Mr. Dale Wolfgram

General Information Coeducational day college-preparatory, arts, and religious studies school, affiliated with Lutheran Church. Grades 7–12. Founded: 1953. Setting: urban. Nearest major city is Los Angeles. 4-acre campus. 1 building on campus. Approved or accredited by Western Association of Schools and Colleges and California Department of Education. Endowment: $450,000. Total enrollment: 246. Upper school average class size: 25. Upper school faculty-student ratio: 1:16.

Upper School Student Profile Grade 9: 56 students (31 boys, 25 girls); Grade 10: 43 students (24 boys, 19 girls); Grade 11: 39 students (25 boys, 14 girls); Grade 12: 36 students (17 boys, 19 girls). 30% of students are Lutheran.

Faculty School total: 17. In upper school: 6 men, 4 women; 4 have advanced degrees.

Subjects Offered 3-dimensional art, algebra, American literature, anatomy and physiology, band, Bible, biology, biology-AP, business applications, business law, business mathematics, calculus, choir, composition, drawing, economics, English literature, English-AP, ethics, family studies, German, government, jazz band, Life of Christ, math analysis, music theory, painting, physics, psychology, sociology, Spanish, U.S. history, world history, yearbook.

Graduation Requirements Advanced math, algebra, American government, American history, American literature, analytic geometry, ancient world history, biology, British literature, calculus, career education, chemistry, Christian doctrine, Christian testament, comparative religion, composition, computer keyboarding, economics, English composition, English literature, geometry, government, physical education (includes health), pre-calculus, religious education, Spanish, U.S. government, U.S. history, world history.

Special Academic Programs Advanced Placement exam preparation; honors section; study at local college for college credit; academic accommodation for the gifted, the musically talented, and the artistically talented; ESL (5 students enrolled).

College Placement 36 students graduated in 2005; 32 went to college, including California State University, Long Beach; California State University, Northridge; College of the Canyons; Concordia University; Loyola Marymount University; University of Southern California. Other: 2 went to work.

Student Life Upper grades have specified standards of dress, student council. Discipline rests primarily with faculty. Attendance at religious services is required.

Summer Programs Remediation programs offered; session focuses on mathematics and English; held on campus; accepts boys and girls; not open to students from other schools. 2006 schedule: July 10 to July 28. Application deadline: June 15.

Tuition and Aid Day student tuition: $5275. Tuition installment plan (monthly payment plans). Merit scholarship grants, need-based scholarship grants available. In 2005–06, 15% of upper-school students received aid; total upper-school merit-scholarship money awarded: $10,000. Total amount of financial aid awarded in 2005–06: $25,000.

Admissions Traditional secondary-level entrance grade is 9. For fall 2005, 30 students applied for upper-level admission, 25 were accepted, 25 enrolled. Placement test required. Deadline for receipt of application materials: May. Application fee required: $300. Interview required.

Athletics Interscholastic: baseball (boys), basketball (b,g), cheering (g), drill team (g), flag football (b), football (b), ropes courses (b,g), track and field (b,g), volleyball (g), weight training (b,g); coed interscholastic: soccer. 2 PE instructors, 8 coaches.

Computers Computers are regularly used in business, business applications, computer applications, desktop publishing, digital applications, keyboarding, lab/keyboard, media production classes. Computer network features include on-campus library services, CD-ROMs, online commercial services, Internet access, DVD.

Contact Ms. Leslie Petit, Administrative Assistant. 818-362-5861. Fax: 818-367-0043. E-mail: leslie.anne.petit@lalhs.org. Web site: www.lalhs.org.

LOUISVILLE HIGH SCHOOL

22300 Mulholland Drive
Woodland Hills, California 91364
Head of School: Mrs. Kathleen Vercillo

General Information Girls' day college-preparatory, arts, religious studies, and technology school, affiliated with Roman Catholic Church. Grades 9–12. Founded: 1960. Setting: suburban. Nearest major city is Encino. 17-acre campus. 7 buildings on campus. Approved or accredited by National Catholic Education Association, Western Association of Schools and Colleges, Western Catholic Education Association, and California Department of Education. Total enrollment: 498. Upper school average class size: 25. Upper school faculty-student ratio: 1:25.

Upper School Student Profile Grade 9: 138 students (138 girls); Grade 10: 119 students (119 girls); Grade 11: 121 students (121 girls); Grade 12: 120 students (120 girls). 87% of students are Roman Catholic.

Faculty School total: 49. In upper school: 10 men, 34 women; 27 have advanced degrees.

Subjects Offered Advanced Placement courses, advanced studio art-AP, algebra, American history, American literature, anatomy, anthropology, art, Bible studies, biology, calculus, calculus-AP, campus ministry, ceramics, chemistry, computer science, creative writing, dance, drama, driver education, earth science, economics,

Louisville High School

English, English literature, European history, fine arts, French, geography, geometry, government/civics, grammar, history, journalism, law, mathematics, music, photography, physical education, physics, physiology, psychology, religion, science, social science, social studies, Spanish, speech, statistics, theater, trigonometry, video film production, Web site design, world history, world literature.

Graduation Requirements Arts and fine arts (art, music, dance, drama), computer science, English, foreign language, mathematics, performing arts, physical education (includes health), religion (includes Bible studies and theology), science, social science, social studies (includes history), visual arts. Community service is required.

Special Academic Programs Advanced Placement exam preparation in 15 subject areas; honors section.

College Placement 124 students graduated in 2005; 120 went to college, including California State University, Northridge; Loyola Marymount University; University of California, Santa Barbara; University of San Diego; University of Southern California. Other: 1 went to work, 2 entered a postgraduate year, 1 had other specific plans.

Student Life Upper grades have uniform requirement, student council, honor system. Discipline rests equally with students and faculty. Attendance at religious services is required.

Summer Programs Sports programs offered; session focuses on skill development; held both on and off campus; held at Los Angeles Pierce Community College and Balboa Park; accepts girls; open to students from other schools. 200 students usually enrolled. 2006 schedule: June 20 to August 20. Application deadline: May 27.

Tuition and Aid Day student tuition: $8500. Tuition installment plan (FACTS Tuition Payment Plan). Merit scholarship grants, need-based scholarship grants, paying campus jobs available. In 2005–06, 12% of upper-school students received aid; total upper-school merit-scholarship money awarded: $32,000. Total amount of financial aid awarded in 2005–06: $125,000.

Admissions Traditional secondary-level entrance grade is 9. For fall 2005, 236 students applied for upper-level admission, 150 were accepted, 138 enrolled. High School Placement Test required. Deadline for receipt of application materials: January 20. Application fee required: $50. On-campus interview recommended.

Athletics Interscholastic: basketball, bowling, cross-country running, equestrian sports, field hockey, golf, soccer, softball, swimming and diving, tennis, track and field, volleyball, water polo. 2 PE instructors, 25 coaches, 1 trainer.

Computers Computers are regularly used in all academic, journalism, library, media, religious studies, Web site design, yearbook classes. Computer network features include campus e-mail, on-campus library services, CD-ROMs, online commercial services, Internet access.

Contact Mrs. Linda Klarin, Secretary. 818-346-8812. Fax: 818-346-9483. E-mail: lklarin@louisvillehs.org. Web site: louisvillehs.org.

LOURDES CATHOLIC HIGH SCHOOL

PO Box 1865
Nogales, Arizona 85628
Head of School: Barbara Lorene Monsegur

General Information Coeducational day college-preparatory school, affiliated with Roman Catholic Church. Grades PK–12. Founded: 1934. Setting: rural. Nearest major city is Phoenix. 1 building on campus. Approved or accredited by North Central Association of Colleges and Schools, Western Catholic Education Association, and Arizona Department of Education. Languages of instruction: English and Spanish. Total enrollment: 429. Upper school average class size: 25. Upper school faculty-student ratio: 1:12.

Upper School Student Profile Grade 9: 28 students (11 boys, 17 girls); Grade 10: 33 students (14 boys, 19 girls); Grade 11: 17 students (6 boys, 11 girls); Grade 12: 21 students (9 boys, 12 girls). 99% of students are Roman Catholic.

Faculty School total: 25. In upper school: 3 men, 5 women; 3 have advanced degrees.

Subjects Offered Algebra, American government, American history, American literature, art, athletics, basketball, Bible, biology, British literature, calculus, campus ministry, character education, chemistry, choir, Christian and Hebrew scripture, Christian doctrine, Christian scripture, church history, college counseling, computer literacy, computer skills, computers, dance, economics, electives, English, English literature, ESL, folk dance, foreign language, geometry, government, Hebrew scripture, history, honors algebra, honors English, independent study, journalism, Life of Christ, Mexican history, Mexican literature, moral theology, photojournalism, religious studies, Shakespeare, social justice, Spanish, Spanish literature, student government, tennis, theology, U.S. government, U.S. history, world religions, yearbook.

Graduation Requirements Art, Bible studies, career/college preparation, computer education, economics, English, English literature, mathematics, physical education (includes health), religion (includes Bible studies and theology), science, social studies (includes history), student government, U.S. government, yearbook.

Special Academic Programs Independent study; remedial reading and/or remedial writing; remedial math; ESL (32 students enrolled).

College Placement 15 students graduated in 2005; all went to college, including Arizona State University; Northern Arizona University; Pima Community College; The University of Arizona. 1% scored over 600 on SAT verbal, 1% scored over 600 on SAT math.

Student Life Upper grades have uniform requirement, student council, honor system. Attendance at religious services is required.

Tuition and Aid Day student tuition: $5000. Guaranteed tuition plan. Tuition installment plan (monthly payment plans, individually arranged payment plans). Tuition reduction for siblings, merit scholarship grants, paying campus jobs available. In 2005–06, 2% of upper-school students received aid; total upper-school merit-scholarship money awarded: $500. Total amount of financial aid awarded in 2005–06: $2310.

Admissions Traditional secondary-level entrance grade is 9. For fall 2005, 6 students applied for upper-level admission, 4 were accepted, 4 enrolled. SSTS Placement Test required. Deadline for receipt of application materials: July 31. No application fee required. Interview recommended.

Athletics Interscholastic: baseball (boys, girls), basketball (b,g), volleyball (b,g). 1 PE instructor.

Computers Computer resources include CD-ROMs, Internet access.

Contact Mrs. Bertha P. Ramirez, Registrar. 520-287-5659. Fax: 520-287-2910. E-mail: registrar@lourdescatholicschool.org.

THE LOVETT SCHOOL

4075 Paces Ferry Road, NW
Atlanta, Georgia 30327
Head of School: William S. Peebles

General Information Coeducational day college-preparatory school. Grades K–12. Founded: 1926. Setting: suburban. 100-acre campus. 8 buildings on campus. Approved or accredited by Southern Association of Colleges and Schools and Georgia Department of Education. Member of National Association of Independent Schools and Secondary School Admission Test Board. Endowment: $30 million. Total enrollment: 1,555. Upper school average class size: 18. Upper school faculty-student ratio: 1:8.

Upper School Student Profile Grade 9: 146 students (70 boys, 76 girls); Grade 10: 168 students (87 boys, 81 girls); Grade 11: 152 students (71 boys, 81 girls); Grade 12: 146 students (72 boys, 74 girls).

Faculty School total: 229. In upper school: 30 men, 30 women.

Subjects Offered Advanced chemistry, advanced computer applications, advanced math, Advanced Placement courses, African American history, African history, African literature, African-American literature, algebra, American government, American history, American history-AP, American legal systems, American literature, ancient history, ancient world history, architecture, art, art history, Asian history, Asian studies, band, biology, botany, calculus, calculus-AP, career and personal planning, career/college preparation, ceramics, character education, chemistry, chorus, computer art, computer education, computer graphics, computer programming, computer science, creative writing, dance, debate, drama, driver education, earth science, ecology, economics, electronic music, English, English literature, English-AP, environmental science, ethics, European history, fiction, film history, fine arts, French, French language-AP, French literature-AP, French studies, French-AP, genetics, geometry, German, German-AP, history, human development, jazz dance, journalism, Latin, Latin-AP, leadership, marine biology, mathematics, medieval history, music theory, music theory-AP, newspaper, orchestra, painting, philosophy, photography, physical education, physics, portfolio art, pre-calculus, public speaking, religion, robotics, science, sculpture, social studies, Spanish, Spanish language-AP, Spanish literature-AP, speech, statistics, technical theater, theater, theater arts, trigonometry, U.S. government and politics-AP, video, Western civilization, Western philosophy, world cultures, world history, world literature, world religions, writing workshop, yearbook, zoology.

Graduation Requirements Algebra, American studies, arts and fine arts (art, music, dance, drama), biology, English, foreign language, geometry, history, mathematics, physical education (includes health), religion (includes Bible studies and theology), science, Western civilization.

Special Academic Programs Advanced Placement exam preparation in 16 subject areas; honors section; independent study; term-away projects; study abroad; academic accommodation for the gifted, the musically talented, and the artistically talented.

College Placement 136 students graduated in 2005; all went to college, including Auburn University; Georgia Institute of Technology; Southern Methodist University; University of Georgia; University of Mississippi; University of Virginia. 81% scored over 600 on SAT verbal, 80% scored over 600 on SAT math, 79% scored over 1800 on combined SAT, 65% scored over 26 on composite ACT.

Student Life Upper grades have uniform requirement, student council, honor system. Discipline rests primarily with faculty. Attendance at religious services is required.

Summer Programs Remediation, enrichment, advancement programs offered; session focuses on academic course work; held on campus; accepts boys and girls; open to students from other schools. 35 students usually enrolled. 2006 schedule: June 6 to July 20. Application deadline: none.

Tuition and Aid Day student tuition: $15,460. Tuition installment plan (The Tuition Plan, Key Tuition Payment Plan). Need-based scholarship grants, local bank loans available. In 2005–06, 10% of upper-school students received aid. Total amount of financial aid awarded in 2005–06: $620,700.

Admissions Traditional secondary-level entrance grade is 9. For fall 2005, 90 students applied for upper-level admission, 47 were accepted, 27 enrolled. SSAT required. Deadline for receipt of application materials: February 3. Application fee required: $65. On-campus interview required.

Athletics Interscholastic: baseball (boys), basketball (b,g), cheering (g), cross-country running (b,g), diving (b,g), football (b), golf (b,g), gymnastics (g), lacrosse (b,g), soccer (b,g), softball (g), swimming and diving (b,g), tennis (b,g), track and field (b,g), volleyball (g), wrestling (b); intramural: aerobics/dance (g), dance (g), modern dance (g), roller hockey (b); coed intramural: back packing, bicycling, bowling, canoeing/kayaking, climbing, flag football, Frisbee, hiking/backpacking, kayaking, mountain biking, outdoor activities, outdoor adventure, outdoor education, outdoor recreation, outdoor skills, outdoors, rappelling, rock climbing, ropes courses, strength & conditioning, ultimate Frisbee, wall climbing, weight lifting, weight training. 2 PE instructors, 40 coaches, 2 trainers.

Computers Computers are regularly used in all academic classes. Computer network features include campus e-mail, on-campus library services, CD-ROMs, online commercial services, Internet access, file transfer, DVD, wireless campus network, central file storage.

Contact Ms. Debbie Lange, Director of Admission. 404-262-3032. Fax: 404-479-8463. E-mail: dlange@lovett.org. Web site: www.lovett.org.

THE LOWELL WHITEMAN SCHOOL

42605 RCR 36
Steamboat Springs, Colorado 80487
Head of School: Walter Daub

petersons.com

General Information Coeducational boarding and day college-preparatory school. Grades 9–12. Founded: 1957. Setting: rural. Nearest major city is Denver. Students are housed in single-sex dormitories. 180-acre campus. 10 buildings on campus. Approved or accredited by Association of Colorado Independent Schools, The Association of Boarding Schools, and Colorado Department of Education. Member of National Association of Independent Schools and Secondary School Admission Test Board. Endowment: $750,000. Total enrollment: 95. Upper school average class size: 8. Upper school faculty-student ratio: 1:7.

Upper School Student Profile Grade 9: 24 students (13 boys, 11 girls); Grade 10: 17 students (8 boys, 9 girls); Grade 11: 26 students (14 boys, 12 girls); Grade 12: 28 students (15 boys, 13 girls). 45% of students are boarding students. 60% are state residents. 24 states are represented in upper school student body. 5% are international students. International students from Canada, Croatia, Germany, Mexico, Sweden, and United Kingdom; 1 other country represented in student body.

Faculty School total: 22. In upper school: 11 men, 11 women; 12 have advanced degrees; 17 reside on campus.

Subjects Offered 20th century history, algebra, American history, American literature, American studies, anatomy, art, art history, biology, calculus, chemistry, computer math, computer programming, computer science, creative writing, drama, economics, English, English literature, expository writing, film, fine arts, French, geography, geology, geometry, government/civics, grammar, mathematics, physical education, physics, science, social science, social studies, Spanish, theater, trigonometry, typing, world history, writing.

Graduation Requirements Algebra, arts and fine arts (art, music, dance, drama), business skills (includes word processing), chemistry, computer science, English, foreign language, geography, geometry, mathematics, physical education (includes health), science, social science, social studies (includes history), Western civilization, foreign travel program, competitive ski/snowboarding program.

Special Academic Programs Advanced Placement exam preparation in 5 subject areas; honors section; independent study; study abroad.

College Placement 18 students graduated in 2004; 17 went to college, including California State University, Fresno; Cornell University; Mount Holyoke College; The Colorado College; University of Denver. Other: 1 had other specific plans.

Student Life Upper grades have student council, honor system. Discipline rests equally with students and faculty.

Tuition and Aid Day student tuition: $15,535; 7-day tuition and room/board: $29,245. Tuition installment plan (Key Tuition Payment Plan, individually arranged payment plans, school's own payment plan). Merit scholarship grants, need-based scholarship grants available. In 2004–05, 30% of upper-school students received aid. Total amount of financial aid awarded in 2004–05: $222,533.

Admissions Traditional secondary-level entrance grade is 9. For fall 2005, 65 students applied for upper-level admission, 60 were accepted, 41 enrolled. Deadline for receipt of application materials: none. Application fee required: $40. On-campus interview required.

Athletics Interscholastic: alpine skiing (boys, girls), cross-country running (b,g), dance team (g), freestyle skiing (b,g), golf (b,g), hockey (b,g), ice hockey (b,g), indoor hockey (b,g), mountain biking (b,g), mountaineering (b,g), nordic skiing (b,g), outdoor adventure (b,g), outdoor education (b,g), ski jumping (b,g), skiing (cross-country) (b,g), skiing (downhill) (b,g), snowboarding (b,g), soccer (b,g), tennis (b,g), wrestling (b); intramural: back packing (b,g), basketball (b,g), bicycling (b,g), ice hockey (b,g), ice skating (b,g), independent competitive sports (b,g), indoor hockey (b,g), indoor soccer (b,g), judo (b,g), lacrosse (g), mountain biking (b,g), mountaineering (b,g), outdoor adventure (b,g), outdoor education (b,g), outdoor recreation (b,g), outdoor skills (b,g), outdoors (b,g), rock climbing (b,g), skiing (cross-country) (b,g), skiing (downhill) (b,g), snowboarding (b,g), soccer (b,g); coed interscholastic: alpine skiing, cross-country running, freestyle skiing, golf, ice hockey, indoor hockey, mountain biking, mountaineering, outdoor adventure, outdoor education, outdoor skills, outdoors, rock climbing, skiing (cross-country), skiing (downhill), snowboarding,

snowshoeing, soccer; coed intramural: aerobics, back packing, badminton, bicycling, billiards, canoeing/kayaking, climbing, combined training, equestrian sports, figure skating, flag football, golf, hiking/backpacking, horseback riding, ice hockey, ice skating, independent competitive sports, indoor hockey, indoor soccer, judo, kayaking, lacrosse, martial arts, mountain biking, mountaineering, outdoor adventure, outdoor education, outdoor recreation, outdoor skills, outdoors, physical fitness, physical training, rafting, rock climbing, running, self defense, skateboarding, skiing (cross-country), skiing (downhill), snowboarding, snowshoeing, soccer, strength & conditioning, swimming and diving, table tennis, telemark skiing, tennis, volleyball, weight lifting, weight training, wilderness, wilderness survival, wildernessways, winter soccer, winter walking, yoga.

Computers Computers are regularly used in all academic classes. Computer network features include campus e-mail, on-campus library services, CD-ROMs, online commercial services, Internet access, file transfer, DVD.

Contact Mike Whitacre, Director of Admission. 970-879-1350 Ext. 15. Fax: 970-879-0506. E-mail: admissions@whiteman.edu. Web site: www.whiteman.edu.

See full description on page 882.

LOWER BRULE HIGH SCHOOL

PO Box 245
Lower Brule, South Dakota 57548
Head of School: Cody Russell

General Information Coeducational day college-preparatory, general academic, arts, vocational, and bilingual studies school; primarily serves underachievers. Grades 7–12. Founded: 1978. Setting: rural. Nearest major city is Pierre. 25-acre campus. 1 building on campus. Approved or accredited by South Dakota Department of Education. Total enrollment: 281.

Upper School Student Profile Grade 9: 25 students (14 boys, 11 girls); Grade 10: 19 students (12 boys, 7 girls); Grade 11: 16 students (9 boys, 7 girls); Grade 12: 15 students (8 boys, 7 girls).

Faculty School total: 21. In upper school: 14 men, 7 women.

Subjects Offered Advanced computer applications, advanced math, algebra, American government, American history, American literature, ancient world history, art, athletics, basketball, biology, career experience, careers, carpentry, cheerleading, chemistry, college admission preparation, college awareness, college planning, composition, computer applications, computer keyboarding, computer literacy, computer studies, construction, creative writing, current events, drawing, driver education, English literature, general math, geography, geometry, government, grammar, health, health and wellness, human anatomy, human biology, independent living, JROTC, JROTC or LEAD (Leadership Education and Development), keyboarding/computer, lab science, language arts, library, literature, mathematics, metalworking, Native American arts and crafts, Native American history, Native American studies, newspaper, painting, photography, physical education, physical science, physics, pre-algebra, pre-college orientation, psychology, reading, reading/study skills, SAT/ACT preparation, short story, social science, social sciences, sociology, speech, sports, state history, study skills, substance abuse, track and field, U.S. government, U.S. history, vocational-technical courses, volleyball, welding, woodworking, world geography, world history, writing skills, yearbook.

Graduation Requirements Advanced math, algebra, American history, American literature, anatomy and physiology, arts, biology, British literature, chemistry, composition, computer keyboarding, computer science, computer skills, computer studies, electives, English, English composition, English-AP, geography, government, Internet, JROTC, keyboarding/computer, Native American studies, research and reference, short story, speech, U.S. government, U.S. history, world geography.

Special Academic Programs Accelerated programs; study at local college for college credit; remedial reading and/or remedial writing; programs in English for dyslexic students; special instructional classes for students with learning disabilities, ADD, emotional and behavioral problems.

College Placement 13 students graduated in 2005; 1 went to college. Other: 2 entered military service, 10 had other specific plans.

Student Life Upper grades have student council. Discipline rests primarily with faculty.

Admissions CTBS, Stanford Achievement Test, any other standardized test required. Deadline for receipt of application materials: none. No application fee required.

Athletics Interscholastic: basketball (boys, girls), cheering (g), cross-country running (b,g), football (b), JROTC drill (b,g), physical fitness (b,g), rodeo (b,g), running (b,g), track and field (b,g), volleyball (g); coed interscholastic: running. 2 PE instructors, 5 coaches.

Computers Computers are regularly used in accounting, career exploration, college planning, creative writing, current events, desktop publishing, history, library, mathematics, photography, social sciences, social studies, typing, yearbook classes. Computer network features include campus e-mail, on-campus library services, CD-ROMs, Internet access, office computer access, DVD.

Contact Cody Russell, Principal. 605-473-5510. Fax: 605-473-5207. E-mail: codyrussell@brule.bia.edu.

LOWER CANADA COLLEGE

4090 Royal Avenue
Montreal, Quebec H4A 2M5, Canada
Head of School: Mr. Christopher Shannon

General Information Coeducational day college-preparatory, arts, bilingual studies, technology, and mathematics and science school. Grades K–12. Founded: 1861. Setting: urban. 7-acre campus. 4 buildings on campus. Approved or accredited by Canadian Association of Independent Schools, Canadian Educational Standards Institute, European Council of International Schools, National Independent Private Schools Association, Quebec Association of Independent Schools, and Quebec Department of Education. Affiliate member of National Association of Independent Schools; member of Secondary School Admission Test Board. Languages of instruction: English and French. Endowment: CAN$4.4 million. Total enrollment: 744. Upper school average class size: 22. Upper school faculty-student ratio: 1:22.
Upper School Student Profile Grade 9: 89 students (51 boys, 38 girls); Grade 10: 86 students (52 boys, 34 girls); Grade 11: 90 students (53 boys, 37 girls); Grade 12: 46 students (24 boys, 22 girls).
Faculty School total: 87. In upper school: 31 men, 17 women; 20 have advanced degrees.
Subjects Offered Accounting, advanced chemistry, advanced computer applications, advanced math, Advanced Placement courses, algebra, American history, ancient history, ancient world history, ancient/medieval philosophy, art, art history, biology, biology-AP, broadcast journalism, calculus, calculus-AP, Canadian geography, Canadian history, Canadian literature, career/college preparation, chemistry, chemistry-AP, cinematography, college admission preparation, college counseling, community service, computer graphics, computer math, computer multimedia, computer science, computer studies, concert band, creative writing, current events, desktop publishing, drama, earth science, ecology, economics, English, English literature, English-AP, environmental science, ethics, European history, expository writing, filmmaking, fine arts, finite math, French, French language-AP, general science, geography, health, health education, history, independent study, leadership, linear algebra, mathematics, media, music, North American literature, philosophy, physical education, physical fitness, physical science, physics, political science, pre-calculus, psychology, public speaking, robotics, SAT preparation, science, Shakespeare, social science, social studies, Spanish, Spanish-AP, theater, video film production, world geography, world history.
Graduation Requirements English, French, mathematics, science, social studies (includes history), overall average of 70%. Community service is required.
Special Academic Programs Advanced Placement exam preparation in 13 subject areas; honors section; independent study; remedial reading and/or remedial writing; remedial math.
College Placement 138 students graduated in 2005; all went to college, including Acadia University; Mount Allison University; Queen's University at Kingston; The University of British Columbia; The University of Western Ontario; University of Toronto.
Student Life Upper grades have uniform requirement, student council, honor system. Discipline rests equally with students and faculty.
Tuition and Aid Day student tuition: CAN$14,045. Tuition installment plan (monthly payment plans, individually arranged payment plans). Bursaries, merit scholarship grants, need-based scholarship grants, need-based loans available. In 2005–06, 15% of upper-school students received aid; total upper-school merit-scholarship money awarded: CAN$145,500. Total amount of financial aid awarded in 2005–06: CAN$327,845.
Admissions Traditional secondary-level entrance grade is 12. For fall 2005, 284 students applied for upper-level admission, 149 were accepted, 99 enrolled. Otis-Lennon School Ability Test, school's own exam, SLEP, SSAT or TOEFL required. Deadline for receipt of application materials: none. Application fee required: CAN$125. On-campus interview required.
Athletics Interscholastic: badminton (boys, girls), baseball (b), basketball (b,g), cross-country running (b,g), football (b,g), hockey (b,g), ice hockey (b,g), indoor track & field (b,g), rugby (b,g), running (b,g), skiing (cross-country) (b,g), soccer (b,g), swimming and diving (b,g), tennis (b,g), touch football (g), track and field (b,g), volleyball (b,g); intramural: dance (g), football (b,g); coed interscholastic: aquatics, baseball, cross-country running, curling, football, golf, hockey, ice hockey, martial arts, skiing (cross-country), table tennis; coed intramural: aerobics, aerobics/dance, aerobics/nautilus, aquatics, archery, back packing, badminton, baseball, basketball, bowling, broomball, climbing, cooperative games, Cosom hockey, cross-country running, curling, fencing, field hockey, fitness, fitness walking, floor hockey, Frisbee, golf, gymnastics, handball, hiking/backpacking, hockey, ice hockey, ice skating, indoor track & field, judo, life saving, martial arts, outdoor activities, outdoor education, physical fitness, physical training, rappelling, rock climbing, rugby, running, self defense, skiing (cross-country), snowshoeing, soccer, softball, strength & conditioning, swimming and diving, table tennis, tennis, touch football, track and field, ultimate Frisbee, volleyball, wall climbing, weight training. 5 PE instructors, 8 coaches.
Computers Computers are regularly used in animation, basic skills, creative writing, current events, data processing, design, English, French, French as a second language, geography, graphic arts, graphic design, graphics, independent study, mathematics,

multimedia, science, technology classes. Computer network features include campus e-mail, on-campus library services, CD-ROMs, Internet access, DVD, audio/video production, DVD production.
Contact Mr. Martin Betts, Director of Admission. 514-482-0951. Fax: 514-482-0195. E-mail: mbetts@lcc.ca. Web site: www.lcc.ca.

LOYOLA ACADEMY

1100 Laramie Avenue
Wilmette, Illinois 60091
Head of School: Rev. Theodore G. Munz, SJ

General Information Coeducational day college-preparatory school, affiliated with Roman Catholic Church (Jesuit order); primarily serves mild learning disabilities. Grades 9–12. Founded: 1909. Setting: suburban. Nearest major city is Chicago. 26-acre campus. 1 building on campus. Approved or accredited by Jesuit Secondary Education Association, North Central Association of Colleges and Schools, and Illinois Department of Education. Endowment: $35 million. Total enrollment: 2,000. Upper school average class size: 24. Upper school faculty-student ratio: 1:17.
Upper School Student Profile 88% of students are Roman Catholic Church (Jesuit order).
Faculty School total: 160. In upper school: 80 men, 70 women; 130 have advanced degrees.
Subjects Offered Advanced Placement courses, algebra, American history, American history-AP, American literature, American literature-AP, anatomy, Ancient Greek, art, art history, Asian history, band, biology, biology-AP, calculus, chemistry, chemistry-AP, chorus, communications, computer math, computer programming, computer science, creative writing, dance, design, drama, drawing, earth science, economics, English, English literature, ethics, European history-AP, expository writing, fine arts, finite math, French, general science, genetics, geography, geometry, German, government and politics-AP, health, history, history-AP, humanities, instrumental music, justice seminar, keyboarding, Latin, literature, mathematics, music, musicianship, painting, physical education, physics, physics-AP, physiology, political science, psychology, psychology-AP, religious studies, science, sculpture, social studies, Spanish, Spanish-AP, speech, statistics, statistics-AP, theater, theology, theology and the arts, trigonometry, typing, word processing, world history, world literature, writing.
Graduation Requirements Arts and fine arts (art, music, dance, drama), English, foreign language, mathematics, physical education (includes health), religion (includes Bible studies and theology), science, social studies (includes history), attendance at Freshman and Junior Retreats.
Special Academic Programs Advanced Placement exam preparation in 18 subject areas; honors section; independent study; study abroad; academic accommodation for the gifted; remedial reading and/or remedial writing; remedial math; programs in English, mathematics, general development for dyslexic students; special instructional classes for students with mild learning challenges.
College Placement 500 students graduated in 2005; 490 went to college, including Boston College; DePaul University; Loyola University Chicago; Marquette University; University of Illinois; University of Notre Dame. Other: 4 went to work, 3 entered military service, 3 had other specific plans. Mean SAT verbal: 554, mean SAT math: 552, mean composite ACT: 24. 27% scored over 600 on SAT verbal, 29% scored over 600 on SAT math, 25% scored over 26 on composite ACT.
Student Life Upper grades have specified standards of dress, student council, honor system. Discipline rests primarily with faculty. Attendance at religious services is required.
Summer Programs Remediation, enrichment, advancement, sports, art/fine arts, computer instruction programs offered; session focuses on enrichment; held both on and off campus; held at 60-acre state-of-the-art Athletic Campus in Glenview (3.1 miles away); accepts boys and girls; open to students from other schools. 850 students usually enrolled. 2006 schedule: June 19 to July 28. Application deadline: none.
Tuition and Aid Day student tuition: $9650. Tuition installment plan (monthly payment plans, 1-, 2-, 4- monthly payment plans). Need-based scholarship grants available. In 2005–06, 20% of upper-school students received aid. Total amount of financial aid awarded in 2005–06: $1,750,000.
Admissions For fall 2005, 800 students applied for upper-level admission, 725 were accepted, 535 enrolled. STS Examination required. Deadline for receipt of application materials: none. Application fee required: $25. On-campus interview required.
Athletics Interscholastic: baseball (boys), basketball (b,g), crew (b,g), cross-country running (b,g), diving (b,g), field hockey (g), football (b), golf (b,g), ice hockey (b,g), indoor track & field (b,g), lacrosse (b,g), rowing (b,g), soccer (b,g), softball (g), swimming and diving (b,g), tennis (b,g), track and field (b,g), volleyball (b,g), water polo (b,g), wrestling (b); intramural: cheering (g), dance (b,g), dance squad (g), dance team (g), drill team (g), modern dance (b,g), pom squad (g); coed interscholastic: bowling, sailing; coed intramural: aerobics, aerobics/dance, ballet, basketball, bicycling, billiards, bowling, canoeing/kayaking, climbing, fitness, Frisbee, golf, hiking/backpacking, kayaking, martial arts, mountain biking, outdoor education, physical fitness, scuba diving, skateboarding, skiing (downhill), snowboarding, strength & conditioning, table tennis, ultimate Frisbee, wall climbing, weight lifting, weight training, yoga. 6 PE instructors, 2 trainers.

Computers Computers are regularly used in all academic classes. Computer network features include on-campus library services, CD-ROMs, Internet access, office computer access, DVD.

Contact Mr. Les Seitzinger, Director of Admissions. 847-256-1100 Ext. 2480. Fax: 847-920-2552. E-mail: lseitzinger@loy.org. Web site: www.goramblers.org.

LOYOLA-BLAKEFIELD

PO Box 6819
Baltimore, Maryland 21285-6819
Head of School: Mr. Christopher J. Post

General Information Boys' day college-preparatory, arts, and religious studies school, affiliated with Roman Catholic Church. Grades 6–12. Founded: 1852. Setting: suburban. 60-acre campus. 7 buildings on campus. Approved or accredited by Association of Independent Maryland Schools, Jesuit Secondary Education Association, and National Catholic Education Association. Endowment: $10.6 million. Total enrollment: 1,009. Upper school average class size: 19. Upper school faculty-student ratio: 1:12.

Upper School Student Profile Grade 9: 216 students (216 boys); Grade 10: 188 students (188 boys); Grade 11: 188 students (188 boys); Grade 12: 180 students (180 boys). 80% of students are Roman Catholic.

Faculty School total: 80. In upper school: 46 men, 15 women; 42 have advanced degrees.

Subjects Offered Advanced studio art-AP, algebra, American government, American government-AP, American literature, American literature-AP, art, art history, band, biology, biology-AP, biotechnology, British literature, British literature (honors), calculus, calculus-AP, ceramics, chemistry, chemistry-AP, Chesapeake Bay studies, chorus, composition, composition-AP, computer graphics, computer science, concert band, driver education, English, English language-AP, English literature-AP, European history-AP, film studies, fine arts, forensic science, French, French language-AP, German, German-AP, government and politics-AP, Greek, history, history of music, honors algebra, honors English, honors geometry, honors U.S. history, honors world history, instrumental music, jazz ensemble, journalism, Latin, Latin-AP, mathematics, Middle Eastern history, music history, oil painting, painting, photography, physical education, physics, physics-AP, poetry, pre-calculus, public speaking, religion, science, Spanish, Spanish language-AP, stagecraft, statistics-AP, U.S. government and politics-AP, U.S. history, U.S. history-AP, yearbook.

Graduation Requirements Arts and fine arts (art, music, dance, drama), computer science, English, foreign language, mathematics, physical education (includes health), religion (includes Bible studies and theology), science, social studies (includes history), 40 hours of Christian service.

Special Academic Programs Advanced Placement exam preparation in 16 subject areas; honors section.

College Placement 163 students graduated in 2005; 162 went to college, including Clemson University; James Madison University; Loyola College in Maryland; Towson University; University of Maryland, College Park; Virginia Polytechnic Institute and State University. Other: 1 went to work. Mean SAT verbal: 618, mean SAT math: 617.

Student Life Upper grades have specified standards of dress, student council, honor system. Discipline rests primarily with faculty. Attendance at religious services is required.

Summer Programs Remediation, enrichment, advancement, sports programs offered; held on campus; accepts boys and girls; open to students from other schools. 350 students usually enrolled. 2006 schedule: June 26 to July 28. Application deadline: none.

Tuition and Aid Day student tuition: $11,535. Tuition installment plan (Key Tuition Payment Plan). Merit scholarship grants, need-based scholarship grants available. In 2005–06, 32% of upper-school students received aid; total upper-school merit-scholarship money awarded: $210,780. Total amount of financial aid awarded in 2005–06: $1,262,480.

Admissions Traditional secondary-level entrance grade is 9. For fall 2005, 390 students applied for upper-level admission, 229 were accepted, 138 enrolled. ISEE or Scholastic Testing Service required. Deadline for receipt of application materials: December 31. Application fee required: $25. On-campus interview required.

Athletics Interscholastic: baseball, basketball, cross-country running, diving, football, golf, ice hockey, indoor track & field, lacrosse, rugby, soccer, swimming and diving, tennis, track and field, volleyball, water polo, winter (indoor) track, wrestling; intramural: badminton, basketball, boxing, fencing, flag football, football, indoor soccer, lacrosse, martial arts, tennis, ultimate Frisbee, volleyball. 4 PE instructors, 20 coaches, 1 trainer.

Computers Computers are regularly used in all classes. Computer network features include campus e-mail, on-campus library services, CD-ROMs, online commercial services, Internet access, file transfer, office computer access, DVD, wireless campus network.

Contact Ms. Paddy M. Sachse, Admissions Assistant. 443-841-3680. Fax: 443-841-3105. E-mail: pmsachse@blakefield.loyola.edu. Web site: www.blakefield.loyola.edu.

LOYOLA HIGH SCHOOL, JESUIT COLLEGE PREPARATORY

1901 Venice Boulevard
Los Angeles, California 90006-4496
Head of School: William R. Thomason

General Information Boys' day college-preparatory, arts, religious studies, bilingual studies, and technology school, affiliated with Roman Catholic Church. Grades 9–12. Founded: 1865. Setting: urban. 18-acre campus. 12 buildings on campus. Approved or accredited by California Association of Independent Schools and Western Association of Schools and Colleges. Endowment: $25 million. Total enrollment: 1,210. Upper school average class size: 26. Upper school faculty-student ratio: 1:15.

Upper School Student Profile Grade 9: 309 students (309 boys); Grade 10: 311 students (311 boys); Grade 11: 298 students (298 boys); Grade 12: 292 students (292 boys). 85% of students are Roman Catholic.

Faculty School total: 75. In upper school: 53 men, 22 women; 58 have advanced degrees.

Subjects Offered African-American studies, algebra, American history, American history-AP, American literature, anatomy and physiology, art, art history, Bible studies, biology, biology-AP, calculus, calculus-AP, ceramics, chemistry, chemistry-AP, community service, composition, computer math, computer programming, computer science, computer science-AP, creative writing, drama, earth science, economics-AP, English, English literature, English-AP, environmental science-AP, ethics, European history, European history-AP, expository writing, fine arts, French, French-AP, geometry, German, German-AP, government/civics, grammar, health, history, Latin, Latin-AP, mathematics, Mexican history, music, music theory-AP, oceanography, philosophy, photography, physical education, physics, physics-AP, pre-calculus, psychology-AP, religion, rhetoric, science, Shakespeare, social studies, Spanish, Spanish language-AP, Spanish literature-AP, theater, theology, trigonometry, typing, Western civilization, world history, world literature, writing.

Graduation Requirements Arts and fine arts (art, music, dance, drama), English, foreign language, mathematics, physical education (includes health), religion (includes Bible studies and theology), science, social science, social studies (includes history), three-week internship in senior year. Community service is required.

Special Academic Programs Advanced Placement exam preparation in 20 subject areas; honors section; independent study.

College Placement 292 students graduated in 2005; all went to college, including Loyola Marymount University; University of California, Berkeley; University of California, Irvine; University of California, Los Angeles; University of California, Santa Barbara; University of Southern California. Mean SAT verbal: 620, mean SAT math: 616. 54% scored over 600 on SAT verbal, 52% scored over 600 on SAT math.

Student Life Upper grades have specified standards of dress, student council, honor system. Discipline rests primarily with faculty. Attendance at religious services is required.

Summer Programs Remediation, enrichment, advancement, sports, art/fine arts, computer instruction programs offered; held on campus; accepts boys and girls; open to students from other schools. 1400 students usually enrolled. 2006 schedule: June 26 to July 28. Application deadline: June 5.

Tuition and Aid Day student tuition: $8300. Tuition installment plan (monthly payment plans, semester payment plan). Merit scholarship grants, need-based scholarship grants available. In 2005–06, 18% of upper-school students received aid; total upper-school merit-scholarship money awarded: $212,000. Total amount of financial aid awarded in 2005–06: $900,000.

Admissions Traditional secondary-level entrance grade is 9. For fall 2005, 782 students applied for upper-level admission, 345 were accepted, 309 enrolled. High School Placement Test required. Deadline for receipt of application materials: January 11. Application fee required: $70.

Athletics Interscholastic: baseball, basketball, cross-country running, diving, football, golf, lacrosse, soccer, swimming and diving, tennis, track and field, volleyball, water polo; intramural: baseball, basketball, diving, football, paddle tennis, soccer, swimming and diving, tennis, volleyball, water polo. 2 PE instructors, 3 coaches, 1 trainer.

Computers Computers are regularly used in English, history, journalism, keyboarding, mathematics, science, yearbook classes. Computer network features include campus e-mail, on-campus library services, CD-ROMs, Internet access, DVD.

Contact Heath B. Utley, Director of Admissions. 213-381-5121 Ext. 219. Fax: 213-368-3819. E-mail: hutley@loyolahs.edu. Web site: www.loyolahs.edu.

LOYOLA SCHOOL

980 Park Avenue
New York, New York 10028-0020
Head of School: Mr. James F. X. Lyness Jr.

General Information Coeducational day college-preparatory school, affiliated with Roman Catholic Church (Jesuit order). Grades 9–12. Founded: 1900. Setting: urban. 2 buildings on campus. Approved or accredited by Jesuit Secondary Education Association, Middle States Association of Colleges and Schools, National Catholic Education Association, New York State Association of Independent Schools, New York State Board of Regents, and New York Department of Education. Member of

Loyola School

National Association of Independent Schools. Endowment: $5 million. Total enrollment: 203. Upper school average class size: 16. Upper school faculty-student ratio: 1:8.

Upper School Student Profile Grade 9: 52 students (23 boys, 29 girls); Grade 10: 51 students (35 boys, 16 girls); Grade 11: 57 students (32 boys, 25 girls); Grade 12: 43 students (25 boys, 18 girls). 85% of students are Roman Catholic Church (Jesuit order).

Faculty School total: 30. In upper school: 16 men, 14 women; 24 have advanced degrees.

Subjects Offered Advanced Placement courses, algebra, American government, American history, American literature, art, art history, biology, calculus, chemistry, chorus, college counseling, community service, comparative religion, computer programming, computer science, creative writing, death and loss, discrete mathematics, drama, economics, English, English literature, ethics, European history, expository writing, film, film history, fine arts, French, geometry, grammar, health, history, instrumental music, Italian, journalism, language-AP, Latin, mathematics, music history, philosophy, photography, physical education, physics, political science, pre-calculus, religion, science, social studies, Spanish, speech, statistics-AP, student government, student publications, theater, theology, trigonometry, world history, writing.

Graduation Requirements Art history, computer literacy, English, foreign language, guidance, mathematics, music history, physical education (includes health), science, social studies (includes history), speech, theology, writing skills, Christian Service Program in each year.

Special Academic Programs Advanced Placement exam preparation in 9 subject areas; honors section; independent study; study at local college for college credit; study abroad.

College Placement 56 students graduated in 2005; all went to college, including Boston College; College of the Holy Cross; Cornell University; Georgetown University; New York University; University of Notre Dame. Median SAT verbal: 600, median SAT math: 600. 50% scored over 600 on SAT verbal, 50% scored over 600 on SAT math.

Student Life Upper grades have specified standards of dress, student council, honor system. Discipline rests primarily with faculty. Attendance at religious services is required.

Tuition and Aid Day student tuition: $20,450. Tuition installment plan (Academic Management Services Plan). Merit scholarship grants, need-based scholarship grants available. In 2005–06, 32% of upper-school students received aid; total upper-school merit-scholarship money awarded: $140,000. Total amount of financial aid awarded in 2005–06: $500,000.

Admissions Traditional secondary-level entrance grade is 9. ISEE, school's own exam or SSAT required. Deadline for receipt of application materials: December 2. Application fee required: $55. On-campus interview recommended.

Athletics Interscholastic: baseball (boys), basketball (b,g), cross-country running (b,g), soccer (b), softball (g), track and field (b,g), volleyball (g); intramural: basketball (b,g); coed interscholastic: golf; coed intramural: cross-country running, Frisbee, outdoor activities, paddle tennis, physical fitness, physical training, track and field. 1 PE instructor, 9 coaches.

Computers Computers are regularly used in all academic classes. Computer network features include on-campus library services, CD-ROMs, online commercial services, Internet access, DVD, wireless campus network.

Contact Ms. Lillian Diaz-Imbelli, Director of Admissions. 212-288-3522 Ext. 132. Fax: 212-861-1021. E-mail: limbelli@loyola-nyc.org. Web site: www.loyola-nyc.org.

LUSTRE CHRISTIAN HIGH SCHOOL

HC 66 Box 57
Lustre, Montana 59225
Head of School: Al Leland

General Information Coeducational boarding and day college-preparatory, general academic, and religious studies school, affiliated with Mennonite Brethren Church. Grades 9–12. Founded: 1948. Setting: rural. Nearest major city is Glasgow. Students are housed in single-sex by floor dormitories. 20-acre campus. 1 building on campus. Approved or accredited by Association of Christian Schools International and Montana Department of Education. Endowment: $220,000. Total enrollment: 24. Upper school average class size: 6. Upper school faculty-student ratio: 1:4.

Upper School Student Profile Grade 9: 2 students (2 boys); Grade 10: 11 students (6 boys, 5 girls); Grade 11: 6 students (1 boy, 5 girls); Grade 12: 5 students (2 boys, 3 girls). 67% of students are boarding students. 58% are state residents. 6 states are represented in upper school student body. 17% are international students. 33% of students are members of Mennonite Brethren Church.

Faculty School total: 6. In upper school: 3 men, 3 women; 2 have advanced degrees; 4 reside on campus.

Subjects Offered Algebra, band, Bible studies, biology, British literature, chemistry, choir, computer science, computers, English, fine arts, foreign language, geometry, health, journalism, mathematics, physical education, physical science, physics, pre-algebra, pre-calculus, religion, science, social science, social studies, U.S. government, U.S. history, world history.

Graduation Requirements Arts and fine arts (art, music, dance, drama), computer science, English, mathematics, physical education (includes health), religion (includes Bible studies and theology), science, social studies (includes history), senior chapel message (as part of senior Bible program).

Special Academic Programs Independent study.

College Placement 8 students graduated in 2005; all went to college, including Concordia College; Montana State University; Montana State University–Billings; Tabor College. Median composite ACT: 24. 13% scored over 26 on composite ACT.

Student Life Upper grades have specified standards of dress, student council. Discipline rests primarily with faculty. Attendance at religious services is required.

Tuition and Aid Day student tuition: $1000; 7-day tuition and room/board: $3500. Tuition installment plan (monthly payment plans, individually arranged payment plans). Need-based scholarship grants available.

Admissions Traditional secondary-level entrance grade is 9. For fall 2005, 24 students applied for upper-level admission, 24 were accepted, 24 enrolled. ITBS achievement test, PSAT or Stanford Achievement Test, Otis-Lennon School Ability Test required. Deadline for receipt of application materials: none. No application fee required. Interview required.

Athletics Interscholastic: basketball (boys, girls), football (b), track and field (b,g), volleyball (g). 3 coaches.

Computers Computers are regularly used in English, history, journalism, religious studies, science, yearbook classes. Computer resources include campus e-mail, CD-ROMs, Internet access.

Contact Al Leland, Supervising Teacher. 406-392-5735. Fax: 406-392-5765. E-mail: 2lchs@nemontel.net.

LUTHERAN HIGH NORTH

1130 West 34th Street
Houston, Texas 77018
Head of School: Mr. Bruce Schaller

General Information Coeducational day college-preparatory, arts, religious studies, bilingual studies, and technology school, affiliated with Lutheran Church–Missouri Synod. Grades 9–12. Founded: 1982. Setting: urban. 10-acre campus. 2 buildings on campus. Approved or accredited by Southern Association of Colleges and Schools, Texas Education Agency, Texas Private School Accreditation Commission, and Texas Department of Education. Endowment: $1 million. Total enrollment: 313. Upper school average class size: 18. Upper school faculty-student ratio: 1:17.

Upper School Student Profile Grade 9: 84 students (50 boys, 34 girls); Grade 10: 75 students (42 boys, 33 girls); Grade 11: 80 students (39 boys, 41 girls); Grade 12: 74 students (30 boys, 44 girls). 60% of students are Lutheran Church–Missouri Synod.

Faculty School total: 26. In upper school: 13 men, 12 women; 10 have advanced degrees.

Subjects Offered 20th century American writers, 20th century history, 20th century physics, 20th century world history, 3-dimensional art, 3-dimensional design, ACT preparation, acting, advanced chemistry, advanced computer applications, advanced math, Advanced Placement courses, algebra, American Civil War, American government, American history, American literature, anatomy and physiology, ancient world history, applied arts, applied music, art, athletic training, athletics, band, baseball, Basic programming, basketball, Bible, Bible studies, biology, British literature, British literature (honors), business technology, cabinet making, calculus, calculus-AP, ceramics, cheerleading, chemistry, choir, choral music, chorus, Christian doctrine, Christian education, Christian scripture, Christian testament, civil war history, college counseling, college placement, college planning, college writing, computer applications, computer information systems, computer keyboarding, computer multimedia, computer programming, concert band, concert choir, digital imaging, digital photography, drafting, drama, drama performance, economics, English, English composition, English literature, environmental science, foreign language, geometry, golf, government, health, history, honors algebra, honors English, honors geometry, human anatomy, human biology, instrumental music, jazz band, journalism, keyboarding, keyboarding/computer, language, marching band, musical productions, oil painting, photojournalism, physical education, physics, pre-calculus, public speaking, SAT preparation, SAT/ACT preparation, senior career experience, softball, Spanish, swimming, travel, U.S. government, volleyball, weight training, weightlifting, woodworking, world history, yearbook.

Graduation Requirements Algebra, art education, arts and fine arts (art, music, dance, drama), computer science, economics, electives, English, foreign language, geography, geometry, government, mathematics, physical education (includes health), public speaking, religion (includes Bible studies and theology), science, social studies (includes history), U.S. history, world history.

Special Academic Programs Honors section; study at local college for college credit.

College Placement 82 students graduated in 2005; 75 went to college, including Texas A&M University; Texas Christian University; The University of Texas at Austin; The University of Texas at San Antonio; University of Houston. Other: 2 went to work, 2 entered military service, 3 had other specific plans. Median combined SAT: 1136, median composite ACT: 25.

Student Life Upper grades have uniform requirement, student council, honor system. Discipline rests primarily with faculty. Attendance at religious services is required.

Summer Programs Sports, art/fine arts, computer instruction programs offered; session focuses on sports and band; held on campus; accepts boys and girls; open to students from other schools. 125 students usually enrolled. 2006 schedule: June 1 to July 31. Application deadline: May 31.

Tuition and Aid Day student tuition: $7900. Tuition installment plan (individually arranged payment plans, special tuition arrangements—full, 1/2 or monthly). Tuition reduction for siblings, need-based scholarship grants available. In 2005–06, 25% of upper-school students received aid. Total amount of financial aid awarded in 2005–06: $200,000.

Admissions Traditional secondary-level entrance grade is 9. For fall 2005, 130 students applied for upper-level admission, 110 were accepted, 94 enrolled. Admissions testing and High School Placement Test (closed version) from Scholastic Testing Service required. Deadline for receipt of application materials: none. Application fee required: $300. Interview required.

Athletics Interscholastic: aquatics (boys, girls), baseball (b), basketball (b,g), football (b), soccer (b,g), softball (g), volleyball (g), winter soccer (b,g); coed interscholastic: cheering, cross-country running, golf, physical fitness, physical training, power lifting, swimming and diving, track and field, weight lifting, weight training. 2 PE instructors, 7 coaches, 2 trainers.

Computers Computers are regularly used in all academic classes. Computer network features include on-campus library services, CD-ROMs, Internet access, DVD.

Contact LouAnn Webber, Director of Admissions. 713-880-3131 Ext. 322. Fax: 713-880-5447. E-mail: louannwebber@lea-hou.org. Web site: www.lutheranhighnorth.org/default.htm.

LUTHERAN HIGH SCHOOL
3960 Fruit Street
La Verne, California 91750
Head of School: Jeremy R. Lowe

General Information Coeducational day college-preparatory, general academic, religious studies, and technology school, affiliated with Lutheran Church–Missouri Synod. Grades 9–12. Founded: 1973. Setting: suburban. Nearest major city is Los Angeles. 10-acre campus. 7 buildings on campus. Approved or accredited by Lutheran School Accreditation Commission and Western Association of Schools and Colleges. Total enrollment: 131. Upper school average class size: 20. Upper school faculty-student ratio: 1:12.

Upper School Student Profile Grade 9: 36 students (16 boys, 20 girls); Grade 10: 36 students (18 boys, 18 girls); Grade 11: 24 students (12 boys, 12 girls); Grade 12: 35 students (18 boys, 17 girls). 40% of students are Lutheran Church–Missouri Synod.

Faculty School total: 15. In upper school: 6 men, 8 women; 4 have advanced degrees.

Subjects Offered Advanced math, algebra, American history, American history-AP, American literature, anatomy and physiology, art, biology, British literature, calculus-AP, chemistry, community service, comparative religion, composition, computer keyboarding, computer literacy, computer programming, computer science, drama, economics, English, English literature and composition-AP, fine arts, geography, geometry, government, honors English, mathematics, naval science, NJROTC, physical education, physical science, physics, pre-algebra, pre-calculus, psychology, religion, science, social science, social studies, Spanish, word processing, world history, world literature.

Graduation Requirements Arts and fine arts (art, music, dance, drama), business skills (includes word processing), computer science, English, foreign language, mathematics, physical education (includes health), religion (includes Bible studies and theology), science, social science, social studies (includes history). Community service is required.

Special Academic Programs Advanced Placement exam preparation in 4 subject areas; honors section; accelerated programs; independent study; study at local college for college credit.

College Placement 35 students graduated in 2005; all went to college, including California State University, Fullerton; California State University, San Bernardino; Concordia University; University of California, Riverside. Median SAT verbal: 558, median SAT math: 488.

Student Life Upper grades have specified standards of dress, student council, honor system. Discipline rests primarily with faculty. Attendance at religious services is required.

Tuition and Aid Day student tuition: $5900–$6000. Tuition installment plan (SMART Tuition Payment Plan, monthly payment plans, individually arranged payment plans, advance payment discounts). Tuition reduction for siblings, merit scholarship grants, need-based scholarship grants available. In 2005–06, 25% of upper-school students received aid; total upper-school merit-scholarship money awarded: $1200. Total amount of financial aid awarded in 2005–06: $10,000.

Admissions Traditional secondary-level entrance grade is 9. For fall 2005, 160 students applied for upper-level admission, 148 were accepted, 144 enrolled. Stanford Achievement Test required. Deadline for receipt of application materials: none. Application fee required: $75. Interview required.

Athletics Interscholastic: aerobics/dance (girls), baseball (b), basketball (b,g), cheering (g), cross-country running (b,g), dance squad (g), dance team (g), football (b), golf (b,g), softball (g), volleyball (g), wrestling (b); coed interscholastic: JROTC drill, soccer, track and field. 2 coaches.

Computers Computers are regularly used in English, geography, history, information technology, mathematics, NJROTC, programming, science, Spanish, yearbook classes. Computer resources include campus e-mail, CD-ROMs, online commercial services, Internet access.

Contact Diana Beckett, Administrative Assistant. 909-593-4494 Ext. 21. Fax: 909-596-3744. E-mail: dbeckett@lhslv.org. Web site: www.lhslv.org.

LUTHERAN HIGH SCHOOL
5555 South Arlington Avenue
Indianapolis, Indiana 46237-2366
Head of School: Mr. Gary St. Clair

General Information Coeducational day college-preparatory and general academic school, affiliated with Lutheran Church–Missouri Synod. Grades 9–12. Founded: 1975. Setting: suburban. 18-acre campus. 1 building on campus. Approved or accredited by National Lutheran School Accreditation, North Central Association of Colleges and Schools, and Indiana Department of Education. Endowment: $160,000. Total enrollment: 291. Upper school average class size: 23. Upper school faculty-student ratio: 1:13.

Upper School Student Profile Grade 9: 70 students (41 boys, 29 girls); Grade 10: 98 students (63 boys, 35 girls); Grade 11: 60 students (27 boys, 33 girls); Grade 12: 63 students (32 boys, 31 girls). 60% of students are Lutheran Church–Missouri Synod.

Faculty School total: 21. In upper school: 13 men, 7 women; 14 have advanced degrees.

Subjects Offered Accounting, algebra, American sign language, anatomy and physiology, art appreciation, band, Basic programming, Bible studies, biology, biology-AP, business applications, ceramics, chemistry, chemistry-AP, choir, death and loss, drama, drawing, economics, English, ethics, etymology, geometry, German, German literature, humanities, Japanese, music theory, painting, physics, pre-calculus, printmaking, probability and statistics, programming, psychology, sculpture, sociology, Spanish, speech, student publications, student teaching, trigonometry, U.S. government, U.S. history, world geography, world history, world religions.

Graduation Requirements Biology, computer applications, English, health and safety, mathematics, physical education (includes health), religious studies, science, social studies (includes history), U.S. government, U.S. history.

Special Academic Programs Advanced Placement exam preparation in 3 subject areas; honors section; independent study; remedial reading and/or remedial writing; remedial math.

College Placement 61 students graduated in 2005; 53 went to college, including Ball State University; Indiana University Bloomington; Purdue University; University of Indianapolis; Valparaiso University. Other: 3 went to work, 2 entered military service, 3 had other specific plans. Mean SAT verbal: 506, mean SAT math: 536, mean composite ACT: 23. 1% scored over 600 on SAT verbal, 1% scored over 600 on SAT math.

Student Life Upper grades have uniform requirement, student council, honor system. Discipline rests primarily with faculty. Attendance at religious services is required.

Admissions Traditional secondary-level entrance grade is 9. Scholastic Testing Service High School Placement Test required. Deadline for receipt of application materials: none. Application fee required: $150. On-campus interview required.

Athletics Interscholastic: baseball (boys), basketball (b,g), cheering (g), cross-country running (b,g), football (b), golf (b,g), soccer (b,g), softball (g), tennis (b,g), track and field (b,g), volleyball (g), wrestling (b); coed interscholastic: physical fitness, weight training; coed intramural: bowling. 3 PE instructors, 22 coaches.

Computers Computers are regularly used in accounting, art, Bible studies, business applications, career exploration, current events, design, desktop publishing, drawing and design, economics, English, foreign language, graphic design, historical foundations for arts, history, independent study, keyboarding, library skills, media production, publications, science, social sciences, yearbook classes. Computer network features include on-campus library services, CD-ROMs, online commercial services, Internet access, shared library catalog and Internet databases with Indianapolis-Marion County Public Library.

Contact Mrs. Evelyn Benning, Administrative Assistant. 317-787-5474 Ext. 211. Fax: 317-787-2794. E-mail: ebenning@lhsi.org. Web site: www.lhsi.org.

LUTHERAN HIGH SCHOOL
8201 Park Avenue South
Bloomington, Minnesota 55420
Head of School: Lynn Henry

General Information Coeducational day college-preparatory and religious studies school, affiliated with Lutheran Church–Missouri Synod; primarily serves individuals with Attention Deficit Disorder. Grades 9–12. Founded: 1966. Setting: suburban. Nearest major city is Minneapolis. 8-acre campus. 1 building on campus. Approved or accredited by North Central Association of Colleges and Schools and Minnesota Department of Education. Total enrollment: 86. Upper school average class size: 15. Upper school faculty-student ratio: 1:15.

Lutheran High School

Upper School Student Profile Grade 9: 18 students (11 boys, 7 girls); Grade 10: 25 students (14 boys, 11 girls); Grade 11: 14 students (3 boys, 11 girls); Grade 12: 29 students (11 boys, 18 girls). 70% of students are Lutheran Church–Missouri Synod.
Faculty School total: 12. In upper school: 7 men, 4 women; 8 have advanced degrees.
Subjects Offered Algebra, American government, American history, American history-AP, American literature, anatomy, art, Bible studies, biology, biology-AP, business, calculus-AP, career/college preparation, chemistry, communication skills, computer science, concert choir, consumer mathematics, driver education, earth science, economics, English, English literature, environmental science, ethics, fine arts, geography, geometry, government/civics, grammar, health, history, humanities, journalism, mathematics, music, physical education, physics, physiology, pre-calculus, psychology, religion, SAT/ACT preparation, science, social science, social studies, sociology, Spanish, theology, world history, world literature, writing.
Graduation Requirements Arts and fine arts (art, music, dance, drama), computer science, English, foreign language, mathematics, physical education (includes health), religion (includes Bible studies and theology), science, social science, social studies (includes history).
Special Academic Programs Advanced Placement exam preparation in 5 subject areas; honors section; accelerated programs; independent study; study at local college for college credit; special instructional classes for students with Attention Deficit Disorder.
College Placement 36 students graduated in 2005; 34 went to college, including Concordia College; Gustavus Adolphus College; Normandale Community College; University of Minnesota, Twin Cities Campus. Other: 1 went to work, 1 entered military service. Mean composite ACT: 25.
Student Life Upper grades have specified standards of dress, student council, honor system. Discipline rests primarily with faculty. Attendance at religious services is required.
Summer Programs Sports programs offered; session focuses on conditioning, weight lifting, athletic skills; held on campus; accepts boys and girls; not open to students from other schools. 35 students usually enrolled. 2006 schedule: June to August.
Tuition and Aid Day student tuition: $6700. Tuition installment plan (SMART Tuition Payment Plan, individually arranged payment plans). Tuition reduction for siblings, merit scholarship grants, need-based scholarship grants available. In 2005–06, 40% of upper-school students received aid. Total amount of financial aid awarded in 2005–06: $40,000.
Admissions Traditional secondary-level entrance grade is 9. For fall 2005, 86 students applied for upper-level admission, 86 were accepted, 86 enrolled. ACT-Explore, admissions testing, Cognitive Abilities Test, Iowa Tests of Basic Skills or PSAT required. Deadline for receipt of application materials: none. Application fee required. On-campus interview required.
Athletics Interscholastic: baseball (boys), basketball (b,g), cheering (g), football (b), soccer (b,g), softball (g), volleyball (g), wrestling (b); coed interscholastic: cross-country running, track and field. 1 PE instructor, 6 coaches.
Computers Computers are regularly used in data processing, English, journalism, mathematics, publications, science, social studies, technology, yearbook classes. Computer network features include CD-ROMs, Internet access.
Contact Chris Roth, Director of Recruitment. 612-854-0224. Fax: 612-854-8527.

LUTHERAN HIGH SCHOOL NORTH

5401 Lucas Hunt Road
St. Louis, Missouri 63121
Head of School: Mr. Tim Hipenbecker

General Information Coeducational day college-preparatory, arts, business, religious studies, and bilingual studies school, affiliated with Lutheran Church. Grades 9–12. Founded: 1946. Setting: urban. 47-acre campus. 1 building on campus. Approved or accredited by Lutheran School Accreditation Commission, National Lutheran School Accreditation, North Central Association of Colleges and Schools, and Missouri Department of Education. Endowment: $7 million. Total enrollment: 376. Upper school average class size: 21. Upper school faculty-student ratio: 1:12.
Upper School Student Profile Grade 9: 96 students (41 boys, 55 girls); Grade 10: 102 students (45 boys, 57 girls); Grade 11: 95 students (47 boys, 48 girls); Grade 12: 83 students (36 boys, 47 girls). 44% of students are Lutheran.
Faculty School total: 32. In upper school: 19 men, 13 women; 24 have advanced degrees.
Subjects Offered Accounting, advanced chemistry, Advanced Placement courses, algebra, American history, American history-AP, American literature, anatomy, art, art history, Bible studies, biology, business, business education, business law, business skills, business studies, calculus, calculus-AP, ceramics, chemistry, child development, choir, Christian doctrine, Christian education, Christian ethics, Christian scripture, Christian studies, Christian testament, Christianity, church history, computer applications, computer keyboarding, computer multimedia, computer science, concert band, concert choir, data analysis, design, drawing, drawing and design, economics, English, English composition, English literature, English literature-AP, entrepreneurship, European history, family and consumer science, family and consumer sciences, fashion, fine arts, finite math, food and nutrition, foods, French, geography, geometry, government, government/civics, health, health education, history, home economics, human anatomy, keyboarding, literature-AP, marketing, mathematics, media studies, multimedia design, music, newspaper, organic chemistry, painting, physical education, physics, physiology, play production, practical arts, pre-calculus, printmaking, probability and statistics, psychology, religion, research, science, social studies, Spanish, speech, statistics, student publications, theology, U.S. government, U.S. history-AP, world geography, world history, world literature, world religions, writing.
Graduation Requirements Arts and fine arts (art, music, dance, drama), English, mathematics, physical education (includes health), practical arts, religion (includes Bible studies and theology), science, social studies (includes history), Saved to Serve (community service hours).
Special Academic Programs Advanced Placement exam preparation in 3 subject areas; honors section; independent study; study at local college for college credit.
College Placement 84 students graduated in 2005; 79 went to college, including Saint Louis University; St. Louis Community College at Florissant Valley; Truman State University; University of Missouri–Columbia; University of Missouri–St. Louis; Valparaiso University. Other: 4 went to work, 1 entered military service. Mean composite ACT: 17.
Student Life Upper grades have uniform requirement, student council, honor system. Discipline rests equally with students and faculty. Attendance at religious services is required.
Tuition and Aid Day student tuition: $6809–$7985. Tuition installment plan (FACTS Tuition Payment Plan, monthly payment plans, individually arranged payment plans, semester payment plan, full-year payment plan with discount). Tuition reduction for siblings, merit scholarship grants, need-based scholarship grants available. In 2005–06, 65% of upper-school students received aid; total upper-school merit-scholarship money awarded: $18,000. Total amount of financial aid awarded in 2005–06: $440,135.
Admissions Traditional secondary-level entrance grade is 9. For fall 2005, 15 students applied for upper-level admission, 15 were accepted, 15 enrolled. ACT-Explore required. Deadline for receipt of application materials: none. Application fee required: $250. Interview recommended.
Athletics Interscholastic: baseball (boys), basketball (b,g), cheering (g), cross-country running (b,g), football (b), golf (b), pom squad (g), soccer (b,g), softball (g), tennis (b,g), track and field (b,g), volleyball (g). 2 PE instructors.
Computers Computers are regularly used in art, business education, English, history, mathematics, science, social studies, yearbook classes. Computer network features include on-campus library services, CD-ROMs, Internet access, office computer access, wireless campus network.
Contact Judy Knight, Records Clerk. 314-389-3100 Ext. 420. Fax: 314-389-3103. E-mail: jknight@lhsn.org. Web site: www.lhsn.org.

LUTHERAN HIGH SCHOOL OF DALLAS

8494 Stults Road
Dallas, Texas 75243

ANNOUNCEMENT FROM THE SCHOOL Lutheran High School of Dallas offers middle school students and high school students a strong academic program, while ministering to the whole child. Complementing the academic program are competitive athletics, drama and art, computer club, band, choir, small-group Bible studies, and more. With the help of a strong college counseling program, 96% of the School's students continue their education at the university level. For more information, call or visit the School's Web site (telephone: 214-349-8912; Web site: http://www.lhsdfw.com).

LUTHERAN HIGH SCHOOL OF HAWAII

1404 University Avenue
Honolulu, Hawaii 96822-2494
Head of School: Arthur Gundell

General Information Coeducational day college-preparatory school, affiliated with Lutheran Church. Grades 9–12. Founded: 1988. Setting: urban. 1-acre campus. 3 buildings on campus. Approved or accredited by Lutheran School Accreditation Commission, The Hawaii Council of Private Schools, Western Association of Schools and Colleges, and Hawaii Department of Education. Member of Secondary School Admission Test Board. Endowment: $15,000. Total enrollment: 131. Upper school average class size: 12. Upper school faculty-student ratio: 1:10.
Upper School Student Profile Grade 9: 41 students (26 boys, 15 girls); Grade 10: 36 students (19 boys, 17 girls); Grade 11: 21 students (15 boys, 6 girls); Grade 12: 33 students (13 boys, 20 girls). 13% of students are Lutheran.
Faculty School total: 16. In upper school: 10 men, 6 women; 9 have advanced degrees.
Subjects Offered 20th century history, 3-dimensional art, advanced math, Advanced Placement courses, algebra, American government, American history, American literature, analytic geometry, art, Bible studies, biology, calculus, calculus-AP, chemistry, choir, computer programming, computer science, concert band, drama, earth science, economics, English, English literature, European history, expository writing, fine arts, food and nutrition, geometry, government/civics, grammar, health,

history, home economics, Japanese, journalism, keyboarding, life skills, marine biology, mathematics, music, oceanography, photography, physical education, physics, psychology, religion, science, social science, social studies, Spanish, speech, theater, world history, world literature, writing.

Graduation Requirements Arts and fine arts (art, music, dance, drama), computer science, English, mathematics, physical education (includes health), religion (includes Bible studies and theology), science, social science, social studies (includes history).

Special Academic Programs Advanced Placement exam preparation in 2 subject areas; honors section.

College Placement 31 students graduated in 2005; all went to college, including Kapiolani Community College; University of Hawaii at Manoa. Median SAT verbal: 550, median SAT math: 600, median composite ACT: 26.

Student Life Upper grades have specified standards of dress, student council, honor system. Discipline rests primarily with faculty. Attendance at religious services is required.

Tuition and Aid Day student tuition: $5615–$6015. Tuition installment plan (Insured Tuition Payment Plan). Tuition reduction for siblings, merit scholarship grants, need-based scholarship grants available. In 2005–06, 10% of upper-school students received aid; total upper-school merit-scholarship money awarded: $30,075. Total amount of financial aid awarded in 2005–06: $42,125.

Admissions Traditional secondary-level entrance grade is 9. For fall 2005, 92 students applied for upper-level admission, 77 were accepted, 53 enrolled. SSAT required. Deadline for receipt of application materials: none. Application fee required: $30. Interview recommended.

Athletics Interscholastic: baseball (boys), basketball (b,g), bowling (b,g), cheering (b,g), cross-country running (b,g), diving (b,g), golf (b,g), gymnastics (b,g), kayaking (b,g), soccer (b,g), softball (g), swimming and diving (b,g), tennis (b,g), track and field (b,g), volleyball (b,g), water polo (b,g), wrestling (b,g); coed interscholastic: football. 1 PE instructor, 5 coaches, 1 trainer.

Computers Computers are regularly used in mathematics, science classes. Computer network features include on-campus library services.

Contact Arthur Gundell, Principal. 808-949-5302. Fax: 808-947-3701.

LUTHERAN HIGH SCHOOL SOUTH

9515 Tesson Ferry Road
St. Louis, Missouri 63123-4317
Head of School: Mr. Paul Buetow

General Information Coeducational day college-preparatory, arts, religious studies, and technology school, affiliated with Lutheran Church. Grades 9–12. Founded: 1957. Setting: suburban. 35-acre campus. 1 building on campus. Approved or accredited by North Central Association of Colleges and Schools and Missouri Department of Education. Endowment: $6.9 million. Total enrollment: 605. Upper school average class size: 22. Upper school faculty-student ratio: 1:13.

Upper School Student Profile Grade 9: 148 students (79 boys, 69 girls); Grade 10: 161 students (89 boys, 72 girls); Grade 11: 144 students (79 boys, 65 girls); Grade 12: 152 students (74 boys, 78 girls). 89% of students are Lutheran.

Faculty School total: 54. In upper school: 32 men, 18 women; 38 have advanced degrees.

Subjects Offered Accounting, algebra, American history, American history-AP, American literature, anatomy, art, art history, band, biology, biology-AP, business, business skills, calculus, calculus-AP, ceramics, chemistry, chorus, community service, composition, composition-AP, computer programming, computer science, consumer economics, creative writing, current events, drafting, drama, drawing, earth science, economics, English, English literature, English literature-AP, family studies, fine arts, food science, French, geography, geometry, German, government/civics, health, jazz, journalism, keyboarding, literature, mathematics, music history, music theory, nutrition, physical education, physics, physiology, psychology, reading, religion, robotics, science, sculpture, social science, sociology, Spanish, speech, technology, theater, theology, trigonometry, woodworking, world history, world literature, writing, yearbook.

Graduation Requirements Arts and fine arts (art, music, dance, drama), business skills (includes word processing), English, mathematics, physical education (includes health), religion (includes Bible studies and theology), science, social science, social studies (includes history), service component (20 hours per year).

Special Academic Programs Advanced Placement exam preparation in 6 subject areas; independent study; study at local college for college credit; remedial reading and/or remedial writing; remedial math; programs in English, mathematics, general development for dyslexic students.

College Placement 151 students graduated in 2005; 148 went to college, including Missouri State University; Saint Louis University; Truman State University; University of Missouri–Columbia; University of Missouri–St. Louis; Valparaiso University. Other: 3 went to work. 40% scored over 600 on SAT verbal, 40% scored over 600 on SAT math, 34% scored over 26 on composite ACT.

Student Life Upper grades have specified standards of dress, student council. Discipline rests primarily with faculty. Attendance at religious services is required.

Tuition and Aid Day student tuition: $6809–$7985. Tuition installment plan (FACTS Tuition Payment Plan, monthly payment plans, individually arranged payment plans, 3% discount for paying in full by July 1 prior to the start of school). Tuition reduction for siblings, merit scholarship grants, need-based scholarship grants available. In

2005–06, 29% of upper-school students received aid; total upper-school merit-scholarship money awarded: $12,000. Total amount of financial aid awarded in 2005–06: $450,000.

Admissions Traditional secondary-level entrance grade is 9. For fall 2005, 170 students applied for upper-level admission, 161 were accepted, 148 enrolled. Explore required. Deadline for receipt of application materials: none. Application fee required: $200. On-campus interview required.

Athletics Interscholastic: baseball (boys), basketball (b,g), cheering (g), cross-country running (b,g), dance squad (g), diving (g), field hockey (g), football (b), golf (b,g), ice hockey (b), soccer (b,g), softball (g), swimming and diving (g), tennis (b,g), track and field (b,g), volleyball (g); coed intramural: bowling, table tennis, tennis. 4 PE instructors, 8 coaches, 1 trainer.

Computers Computers are regularly used in accounting, drafting, drawing and design, English, industrial technology, journalism, keyboarding, mathematics, religion, science, social science classes. Computer network features include campus e-mail, on-campus library services, CD-ROMs, online commercial services, Internet access, DVD.

Contact Mrs. Jayne Lauer, Director of Recruitment and Public Relations. 314-631-1400 Ext. 426. Fax: 314-631-7762. E-mail: jlauer@lhssonline.org. Web site: www.lhssonline.org.

LUTHER COLLEGE HIGH SCHOOL

1500 Royal Street
Regina, Saskatchewan S4T 5A5, Canada
Head of School: Dr. Richard Hordern

General Information Coeducational boarding and day college-preparatory, general academic, arts, religious studies, International Baccalaureate, and English as a Second language school, affiliated with Lutheran Church. Grades 9–12. Founded: 1913. Setting: urban. Nearest major city is Winnipeg, MB, Canada. Students are housed in single-sex dormitories. 27-acre campus. 5 buildings on campus. Approved or accredited by Canadian Association of Independent Schools and Saskatchewan Department of Education. Language of instruction: English. Endowment: CAN$600,000. Total enrollment: 441. Upper school average class size: 22. Upper school faculty-student ratio: 1:22.

Upper School Student Profile Grade 9: 107 students (58 boys, 49 girls); Grade 10: 113 students (52 boys, 61 girls); Grade 11: 127 students (60 boys, 67 girls); Grade 12: 94 students (43 boys, 51 girls). 24% of students are boarding students. 81% are province residents. 5 provinces are represented in upper school student body. 19% are international students. International students from Germany, Hong Kong, Japan, Mexico, Republic of Korea, and Thailand; 5 other countries represented in student body. 22% of students are Lutheran.

Faculty School total: 32. In upper school: 20 men, 12 women; 5 have advanced degrees.

Subjects Offered Accounting, art-AP, biology, calculus, chemistry, choir, chorus, Christian ethics, computer science, drama, dramatic arts, English, entrepreneurship, ESL, film, French, German, handbells, information processing, International Baccalaureate courses, Latin, mathematics, music, physical fitness, physics, psychology, science, social science, video film production.

Graduation Requirements English, mathematics, science, social studies (includes history).

Special Academic Programs International Baccalaureate program; study at local college for college credit; study abroad; academic accommodation for the gifted; special instructional classes for deaf students; ESL (19 students enrolled).

College Placement 95 students graduated in 2004; 76 went to college, including McGill University; Queen's University at Kingston; University of Calgary; University of Regina; University of Saskatchewan. Other: 13 went to work, 6 had other specific plans.

Student Life Upper grades have specified standards of dress, student council. Discipline rests primarily with faculty. Attendance at religious services is required.

Tuition and Aid Day student tuition: CAN$3350; 7-day tuition and room/board: CAN$9390. Tuition installment plan (monthly payment plans, individually arranged payment plans). Tuition reduction for siblings, bursaries, merit scholarship grants, need-based scholarship grants available. In 2004–05, 20% of upper-school students received aid; total upper-school merit-scholarship money awarded: CAN$30,000. Total amount of financial aid awarded in 2004–05: CAN$163,000.

Admissions Traditional secondary-level entrance grade is 9. For fall 2005, 170 students applied for upper-level admission, 161 were accepted, 158 enrolled. Deadline for receipt of application materials: none. Application fee required: CAN$300. Interview recommended.

Athletics Interscholastic: badminton (boys, girls), baseball (b), basketball (b,g), bicycling (b,g), cheering (g), cross-country running (b,g), curling (b,g), football (b), golf (b,g), hockey (b,g), soccer (b,g), volleyball (g); intramural: basketball (b,g), floor hockey (b,g), soccer (b,g), volleyball (g); coed interscholastic: badminton, track and field; coed intramural: aerobics, basketball, floor hockey, football. 4 PE instructors, 28 coaches, 2 trainers.

Computers Computers are regularly used in all academic classes. Computer network features include campus e-mail, CD-ROMs, Internet access.

Luther College High School

Contact Mrs. Jan Schmidt, Registrar. 306-791-9154. Fax: 306-359-6962. E-mail: lutherhs@luthercollege.edu. Web site: www.luthercollege.edu.

See full description on page 884.

LYCEE FRANÇAIS DE NEW YORK

505 East 75th Street
New York, New York 10021
Head of School: Yves Theze

General Information Coeducational day college-preparatory and bilingual studies school. Grades N–12. Founded: 1935. Setting: urban. 1 building on campus. Approved or accredited by French Ministry of Education, New York State Association of Independent Schools, and New York Department of Education. Languages of instruction: English and French. Endowment: $40 million. Total enrollment: 1,263. Upper school average class size: 18. Upper school faculty-student ratio: 1:9.

Upper School Student Profile Grade 6: 95 students (50 boys, 45 girls); Grade 7: 87 students (45 boys, 42 girls); Grade 8: 87 students (42 boys, 45 girls); Grade 9: 70 students (33 boys, 37 girls); Grade 10: 64 students (30 boys, 34 girls); Grade 11: 73 students (37 boys, 36 girls); Grade 12: 82 students (39 boys, 43 girls).

Faculty School total: 124. In upper school: 20 men, 40 women; 56 have advanced degrees.

Subjects Offered Algebra, American history, American literature, art, art history, biology, calculus, chemistry, computer science, creative writing, earth science, economics, English, English literature, English literature-AP, European history, fine arts, French, French language-AP, French literature-AP, geography, geometry, German, German-AP, government/civics, Greek, health, history, Italian, Latin, mathematics, music, philosophy, physical education, physics, science, social science, social studies, Spanish, Spanish language-AP, Spanish literature-AP, trigonometry, world history, world literature, writing.

Graduation Requirements Arts and fine arts (art, music, dance, drama), computer science, English, foreign language, French, Latin, mathematics, physical education (includes health), physical fitness, science, social science, requirements for the French baccalaureate differ.

Special Academic Programs International Baccalaureate program; Advanced Placement exam preparation in 6 subject areas; honors section; accelerated programs; independent study; term-away projects; study abroad; ESL (57 students enrolled).

College Placement 64 students graduated in 2005; all went to college, including Brown University; Cornell University; McGill University; University of Pennsylvania; Wesleyan University; Yale University. Median SAT verbal: 601, median SAT math: 620.

Student Life Upper grades have specified standards of dress, student council, honor system. Discipline rests primarily with faculty.

Tuition and Aid Day student tuition: $12,300–$18,600. Tuition installment plan (Academic Management Services Plan, individually arranged payment plans). Need-based scholarship grants, French government financial assistance available. In 2005–06, 22% of upper-school students received aid. Total amount of financial aid awarded in 2005–06: $246,742.

Admissions Traditional secondary-level entrance grade is 10. For fall 2005, 66 students applied for upper-level admission, 61 were accepted, 50 enrolled. Deadline for receipt of application materials: none. Application fee required: $150. On-campus interview recommended.

Athletics Interscholastic: basketball (boys, girls), cross-country running (b,g), soccer (b,g), volleyball (g), winter soccer (b,g); intramural: badminton (b,g), ballet (g), dance (b,g), indoor soccer (b,g), tennis (b,g); coed interscholastic: running; coed intramural: basketball, cross-country running, fencing, gymnastics, judo, running, soccer, softball, swimming and diving, table tennis, track and field, volleyball, yoga. 4 PE instructors.

Computers Computers are regularly used in all academic, yearbook classes. Computer network features include campus e-mail, on-campus library services, CD-ROMs, online commercial services, Internet access, office computer access, DVD.

Contact Martine Lala, Director of Admissions. 212-439-3827. Fax: 212-439-4215. E-mail: mlala@lfny.org. Web site: www.lfny.org.

THE LYCEE INTERNATIONAL, AMERICAN SECTION

rue du Fer-a-Cheval
BP 5230
Saint-Germain-en-Laye Cedex 78175, France
Head of School: Dr. Theodore Faunce

General Information Coeducational day college-preparatory and bilingual studies school. Grades PK–12. Founded: 1952. Setting: suburban. Nearest major city is Paris. 10-acre campus. 6 buildings on campus. Member of European Council of International Schools. Languages of instruction: English and French. Total enrollment: 680. Upper school average class size: 18. Upper school faculty-student ratio: 1:18.

Upper School Student Profile Grade 10: 60 students (30 boys, 30 girls); Grade 11: 63 students (31 boys, 32 girls); Grade 12: 56 students (25 boys, 31 girls).

Faculty School total: 20. In upper school: 3 men, 5 women; 2 have advanced degrees.

Subjects Offered Algebra, American history, American literature, art, biology, botany, calculus, chemistry, computer math, computer programming, computer science, drama, Dutch, economics, English, English literature, English-AP, European history, French, geography, geometry, German, grammar, Greek, health, history, Italian, Latin, mathematics, music, philosophy, physical education, physics, Russian, science, social science, social studies, Spanish, statistics, theater, trigonometry, world history, world literature, writing, zoology.

Graduation Requirements English, foreign language, mathematics, physical education (includes health), science, social science, social studies (includes history), examination (French Baccalaureate with international option).

Special Academic Programs Advanced Placement exam preparation in 1 subject area; honors section.

College Placement 56 students graduated in 2005; all went to college, including Harvard University; McGill University; New York University; Stanford University; University of Pennsylvania. 73.4% scored over 600 on SAT verbal, 73.4% scored over 600 on SAT math.

Student Life Upper grades have student council. Discipline rests primarily with faculty.

Tuition and Aid Day student tuition: €15,400–€25,000. Tuition installment plan (monthly payment plans). Tuition reduction for siblings, need-based scholarship grants available.

Admissions Traditional secondary-level entrance grade is 10. For fall 2005, 47 students applied for upper-level admission, 23 were accepted, 14 enrolled. Admissions testing required. Deadline for receipt of application materials: none. Application fee required: $160. On-campus interview recommended.

Athletics Intramural: basketball (boys, girls), fencing (b), field hockey (g), martial arts (b), rugby (b), soccer (b), tennis (b,g), track and field (b,g), volleyball (b,g); coed intramural: baseball, equestrian sports, golf, gymnastics, softball, swimming and diving, table tennis, water polo. 9 PE instructors.

Computers Computers are regularly used in mathematics classes. Computer network features include on-campus library services, CD-ROMs, Internet access, file transfer.

Contact Mrs. Mary Friel, Director of Admissions. 33-1-34-51-90-92. Fax: 33-1-30-87-00-49. E-mail: admissions.american@wanadoo.fr. Web site: www.lycee-intl-american.org.

LYCEE INTERNATIONAL DE LOS ANGELES

4155 Russell Avenue
Los Angeles, California 90027
Head of School: Dr. John Larner

General Information Coeducational day college-preparatory, general academic, and bilingual studies school. Grades PK–12. Founded: 1978. Setting: urban. 6-acre campus. 6 buildings on campus. Approved or accredited by French Ministry of Education, International Baccalaureate Organization, Western Association of Schools and Colleges, and California Department of Education. Member of European Council of International Schools. Languages of instruction: English and French. Endowment: $150,000. Total enrollment: 461. Upper school average class size: 17. Upper school faculty-student ratio: 1:8.

Upper School Student Profile Grade 9: 23 students (12 boys, 11 girls); Grade 10: 33 students (20 boys, 13 girls); Grade 11: 19 students (11 boys, 8 girls); Grade 12: 18 students (12 boys, 6 girls).

Faculty School total: 30. In upper school: 10 men, 16 women; 14 have advanced degrees.

Subjects Offered Art, biology, chemistry, computer science, economics, English, fine arts, French, geography, government/civics, history, mathematics, physical education, physics, science, social studies, Spanish.

Graduation Requirements Arts and fine arts (art, music, dance, drama), computer science, English, foreign language, mathematics, physical education (includes health), science, social studies (includes history).

Special Academic Programs International Baccalaureate program; Advanced Placement exam preparation in 3 subject areas; honors section; remedial math; ESL (18 students enrolled).

College Placement 9 students graduated in 2005; all went to college, including University of California, Berkeley; University of Southern California. 20% scored over 600 on SAT verbal, 31% scored over 600 on SAT math, 22% scored over 26 on composite ACT.

Student Life Upper grades have specified standards of dress. Discipline rests primarily with students.

Summer Programs Enrichment, ESL, sports, art/fine arts, computer instruction programs offered; session focuses on speaking French; held on campus; accepts boys and girls; open to students from other schools. 2006 schedule: June 26 to July 31. Application deadline: May.

Tuition and Aid Day student tuition: $10,840. Tuition installment plan (SMART Tuition Payment Plan). Tuition reduction for siblings available.

Admissions Traditional secondary-level entrance grade is 9. For fall 2005, 10 students applied for upper-level admission, 10 were accepted, 9 enrolled. Admissions testing and math and English placement tests required. Deadline for receipt of application materials: none. Application fee required: $50. On-campus interview required.

Athletics Interscholastic: basketball (boys, girls), cross-country running (b,g), flag football (b), paddle tennis (b,g), soccer (b,g), volleyball (b,g); intramural: basketball (b,g), volleyball (b,g); coed interscholastic: basketball, cheering, ice skating, soccer; coed intramural: basketball, cheering. 3 PE instructors, 4 coaches.

Computers Computers are regularly used in art, computer applications, science classes. Computer resources include campus e-mail, on-campus library services, CD-ROMs, Internet access, office computer access, DVD, homework assignments available online.

Contact Valerie Lesure, Director of Admissions. 323-665-4526 Ext. 12. Fax: 323-665-2607. E-mail: valerie.lesure@lilaschool.com.

LYDIA PATTERSON INSTITUTE

517 South Florence Street
El Paso, Texas 79901-2998
Head of School: Mr. Hector Lachica

General Information Coeducational day college-preparatory and religious studies school, affiliated with United Methodist Church. Grades 9–12. Founded: 1913. Setting: urban. 1-acre campus. 5 buildings on campus. Approved or accredited by Southern Association of Colleges and Schools, University Senate of United Methodist Church, and Texas Department of Education. Language of instruction: Spanish. Endowment: $5 million. Total enrollment: 439. Upper school average class size: 21. Upper school faculty-student ratio: 1:20.

Upper School Student Profile Grade 9: 45 students (23 boys, 22 girls); Grade 10: 92 students (48 boys, 44 girls); Grade 11: 78 students (45 boys, 33 girls); Grade 12: 64 students (37 boys, 27 girls). 0.3% of students are United Methodist Church.

Faculty School total: 25. In upper school: 14 men, 7 women; 4 have advanced degrees.

Subjects Offered Computer science, economics, English, fine arts, foreign language, health, mathematics, physical education, religion, U.S. government, U.S. history, world geography, world history.

Graduation Requirements Arts and fine arts (art, music, dance, drama), computer science, economics, English, foreign language, mathematics, physical education (includes health), religion (includes Bible studies and theology), science, U.S. government, U.S. history, world history or world geography.

Special Academic Programs Honors section; study at local college for college credit; academic accommodation for the gifted; ESL (160 students enrolled).

College Placement 65 students graduated in 2005; 61 went to college, including El Paso Community College; MacMurray College; Oklahoma City University; Simpson University; Texas Wesleyan University; The University of Texas at El Paso. Other: 4 went to work. Median SAT verbal: 360, median SAT math: 380.

Student Life Upper grades have uniform requirement, student council, honor system. Discipline rests equally with students and faculty. Attendance at religious services is required.

Summer Programs Remediation, advancement, ESL programs offered; session focuses on advancement; held on campus; accepts boys and girls; not open to students from other schools. 180 students usually enrolled. 2006 schedule: May 30 to August 4. Application deadline: May 27.

Tuition and Aid Day student tuition: $1980. Tuition installment plan (monthly payment plans). Need-based scholarship grants available. In 2005–06, 25% of upper-school students received aid. Total amount of financial aid awarded in 2005–06: $89,100.

Admissions Traditional secondary-level entrance grade is 9. For fall 2005, 279 students applied for upper-level admission, 279 were accepted, 279 enrolled. Deadline for receipt of application materials: none. Application fee required: $220. On-campus interview required.

Athletics Interscholastic: basketball (boys, girls), cheering (g), cross-country running (b,g), soccer (b,g), volleyball (b,g); intramural: basketball (b,g); coed interscholastic: dance team. 2 PE instructors, 3 coaches.

Computers Computers are regularly used in yearbook classes. Computer resources include campus e-mail, on-campus library services, CD-ROMs, online commercial services, Internet access, office computer access.

Contact Mr. Hector Lachica, Vice President for Academic Affairs. 915-533-8286 Ext. 20. Fax: 915-533-5236. E-mail: lasshika@yahoo.com. Web site: www.lydiapattersoninstitute.org.

LYNDON INSTITUTE

PO Box 127
College Road
Lyndon Center, Vermont 05850-0127
Head of School: Richard D. Hilton

petersons.com

General Information Coeducational boarding and day college-preparatory, general academic, arts, business, vocational, technology, and ESL school. Boarding grades 8–12, day grades 9–12. Founded: 1867. Setting: small town. Nearest major city is Burlington. Students are housed in single-sex dormitories. 150-acre campus. 27 buildings on campus. Approved or accredited by Independent Schools of Northern New England, New England Association of Schools and Colleges, The Association

of Boarding Schools, and Vermont Department of Education. Endowment: $7.9 million. Total enrollment: 658. Upper school average class size: 15. Upper school faculty-student ratio: 1:10.

Upper School Student Profile Grade 9: 157 students (90 boys, 67 girls); Grade 10: 173 students (85 boys, 88 girls); Grade 11: 160 students (80 boys, 80 girls); Grade 12: 168 students (92 boys, 76 girls). 5% of students are boarding students. 96% are state residents. 2 states are represented in upper school student body. 3% are international students. International students from Germany, Japan, Republic of Korea, and Taiwan.

Faculty School total: 66. In upper school: 34 men, 31 women; 20 have advanced degrees; 3 reside on campus.

Subjects Offered 3-dimensional art, accounting, advanced chemistry, advanced math, algebra, American literature, ancient world history, art, auto mechanics, band, Basic programming, biology, bookmaking, business, business communications, business education, business mathematics, business technology, calculus, chemistry, chemistry-AP, chorus, college counseling, communications, computer applications, computer graphics, computer information systems, computer keyboarding, computer science, computer skills, computer technologies, computer-aided design, concert band, consumer economics, creative writing, data processing, desktop publishing, drafting, drawing, driver education, earth science, economics, engineering, English, English language and composition-AP, English literature, entrepreneurship, environmental science, European history, family and consumer science, fashion, fine arts, French, general math, geography, geometry, government/civics, graphic design, health, history, home economics, honors algebra, honors English, honors U.S. history, honors world history, industrial arts, information processing, information technology, instrumental music, jazz ensemble, Latin, literary magazine, mathematics, metalworking, music, music theory, photography, physical education, physics, printmaking, science, social studies, Spanish, speech, street law, studio art, studio art-AP, theater, theater arts, trigonometry, U.S. history, woodworking, word processing, world culture, world history, writing.

Graduation Requirements Arts and fine arts (art, music, dance, drama), electives, English, mathematics, physical education (includes health), science, social studies (includes history).

Special Academic Programs Advanced Placement exam preparation in 5 subject areas; honors section; independent study; study at local college for college credit; remedial reading and/or remedial writing; remedial math; ESL (18 students enrolled).

College Placement 57 went to college, including Mount Ida College; Saint Michael's College; University of Vermont. Other: 31 went to work, 2 entered military service, 10 had other specific plans. Mean SAT verbal: 520, mean SAT math: 490.

Student Life Upper grades have specified standards of dress, student council. Discipline rests primarily with faculty.

Summer Programs ESL programs offered; session focuses on ESL; held on campus; accepts boys and girls; open to students from other schools. 40 students usually enrolled. 2006 schedule: July 24 to August 18. Application deadline: May 31.

Tuition and Aid Day student tuition: $10,124; 5-day tuition and room/board: $18,900; 7-day tuition and room/board: $26,795. Tuition installment plan (monthly payment plans, individually arranged payment plans). Need-based scholarship grants, prepGATE Loans available.

Admissions Traditional secondary-level entrance grade is 9. SSAT, SSAT, ERB, PSAT, SAT, PLAN or ACT or TOEFL or SLEP required. Deadline for receipt of application materials: none. Application fee required: $50. Interview recommended.

Athletics Interscholastic: alpine skiing (boys, girls), baseball (b), basketball (b,g), cross-country running (b,g), field hockey (g), golf (b,g), ice hockey (b,g), nordic skiing (b,g), running (b,g), skiing (cross-country) (b,g), skiing (downhill) (b,g), soccer (b,g), softball (g), track and field (b,g); intramural: ballet (g), dance (b,g); coed interscholastic: cheering, football, ice hockey, outdoor activities; coed intramural: aerobics/dance, dance, dance team, fitness walking, marksmanship, modern dance, riflery, weight lifting. 2 PE instructors, 18 coaches, 2 trainers.

Computers Computers are regularly used in architecture, Bible studies, business, business applications, business education, business skills, desktop publishing, drafting, engineering, graphic design, information technology, literary magazine, publishing, SAT preparation, science, technical drawing, technology, yearbook classes. Computer resources include on-campus library services, CD-ROMs, Internet access, office computer access, Big Chalk eLibrary, Vermont Online Library, NewsBank.

Contact Mary B. Thomas, Assistant Head for Admissions. 802-626-5232. Fax: 802-626-6138. E-mail: mthomas@lyndon.k12.vt.us. Web site: www.LyndonInstitute.org.

See full description on page 886.

THE MACDUFFIE SCHOOL

petersons.com

1 Ames Hill Drive
Springfield, Massachusetts 01105
Head of School: Kathryn P. Gibson

General Information Coeducational boarding and day college-preparatory, arts, and technology school. Boarding grades 9–12, day grades 6–12. Founded: 1890. Setting: urban. Students are housed in single-sex dormitories. 14-acre campus. 15 buildings on campus. Approved or accredited by Association of Independent Schools in New England, New England Association of Schools and Colleges, The Association of

Boarding Schools, and Massachusetts Department of Education. Member of National Association of Independent Schools and Secondary School Admission Test Board. Total enrollment: 228. Upper school average class size: 11. Upper school faculty-student ratio: 1:7.

Upper School Student Profile Grade 9: 42 students (19 boys, 23 girls); Grade 10: 44 students (19 boys, 25 girls); Grade 11: 46 students (20 boys, 26 girls); Grade 12: 35 students (16 boys, 19 girls). 17% of students are boarding students. 80% are state residents. 3 states are represented in upper school student body. 14% are international students. International students from Germany, Hong Kong, Japan, Nigeria, Republic of Korea, and Spain; 4 other countries represented in student body.

Faculty School total: 36. In upper school: 15 men, 21 women; 20 have advanced degrees; 4 reside on campus.

Subjects Offered Acting, Advanced Placement courses, African-American history, algebra, American literature, architecture, art, astronomy, biology, British literature, calculus, calculus-AP, chemistry, choreography, computer programming, conceptual physics, creative writing, dance, earth science, East European studies, English, English-AP, environmental science, ESL, European history, film studies, French, geometry, global studies, graphic design, health, journalism, Latin, modern dance, modern European history, modern European history-AP, music, painting, peace studies, physical education, physics, physiology, portfolio art, pre-calculus, psychology, SAT/ACT preparation, sculpture, Spanish, theater, U.S. history, U.S. history-AP, visual arts, Web site design, Western philosophy, women in literature, world literature, yearbook.

Graduation Requirements Algebra, arts and fine arts (art, music, dance, drama), English, foreign language, geometry, history, mathematics, physical education (includes health), science.

Special Academic Programs Advanced Placement exam preparation in 10 subject areas; honors section; independent study; study at local college for college credit; academic accommodation for the gifted; ESL (14 students enrolled).

College Placement 35 students graduated in 2005; all went to college, including Assumption College; Brown University; University of Connecticut; University of Illinois at Chicago; University of Massachusetts Amherst; Wheaton College. Mean SAT verbal: 560, mean SAT math: 623.

Student Life Upper grades have specified standards of dress, student council, honor system. Discipline rests equally with students and faculty.

Summer Programs Enrichment, ESL, computer instruction programs offered; held on campus; accepts boys and girls; open to students from other schools. 150 students usually enrolled. 2006 schedule: July 5 to August 15. Application deadline: May 1.

Tuition and Aid Day student tuition: $17,775; 7-day tuition and room/board: $30,075. Tuition installment plan (Academic Management Services Plan, monthly payment plans, individually arranged payment plans). Merit scholarship grants, need-based scholarship grants, tuition remission for children of faculty available. In 2005–06, 42% of upper-school students received aid; total upper-school merit-scholarship money awarded: $6000. Total amount of financial aid awarded in 2005–06: $411,065.

Admissions Traditional secondary-level entrance grade is 9. For fall 2005, 89 students applied for upper-level admission, 50 were accepted, 31 enrolled. SSAT or TOEFL or SLEP required. Deadline for receipt of application materials: none. Application fee required: $50. Interview required.

Athletics Interscholastic: baseball (boys), basketball (b,g), cross-country running (b,g), field hockey (g), lacrosse (g), soccer (b), softball (g), tennis (b,g), volleyball (g); coed interscholastic: ballet, soccer; coed intramural: aerobics/dance, badminton, blading, cooperative games, cricket, dance, fitness, fitness walking, flag football, football, Frisbee, handball, in-line skating, jogging, modern dance, physical fitness, pillo polo. 2 PE instructors, 10 coaches, 2 trainers.

Computers Computers are regularly used in all academic, yearbook classes. Computer network features include on-campus library services, Internet access, campus computer labs.

Contact Ms. Linda Keating, Director of Admissions. 413-734-4971 Ext. 140. Fax: 413-734-6693. E-mail: lkeating@macduffie.com. Web site: www.macduffie.com.

See full description on page 888.

MADISON ACADEMY

325 Slaughter Road
Madison, Alabama 35758
Head of School: Robert F. Burton

General Information Coeducational day college-preparatory and religious studies school, affiliated with Church of Christ. Grades PS–12. Founded: 1955. Setting: suburban. Nearest major city is Huntsville. 160-acre campus. 5 buildings on campus. Approved or accredited by Southern Association of Colleges and Schools. Endowment: $800,000. Total enrollment: 800. Upper school average class size: 20. Upper school faculty-student ratio: 1:15.

Upper School Student Profile 46% of students are members of Church of Christ.

Faculty School total: 70. In upper school: 14 men, 20 women; 14 have advanced degrees.

Subjects Offered Accounting, advanced math, Alabama history and geography, algebra, American literature, anatomy, art, art history, arts, band, Bible studies, biology, calculus, calculus-AP, chemistry, choral music, chorus, Christian education,

Christian ethics, Christian scripture, Christian studies, church history, community service, computer science, concert choir, consumer mathematics, creative writing, drama, earth science, economics, English, English literature, English/composition-AP, environmental science, European history, expository writing, French, general math, geography, geology, geometry, government/civics, health, human anatomy, journalism, keyboarding/computer, music, photography, physical education, physical science, physics, physics-AP, physiology, pre-algebra, religion, Spanish, speech, studio art, trigonometry, U.S. government, U.S. government and politics, U.S. history, world geography, world history, world literature.

Graduation Requirements English, foreign language, mathematics, religion (includes Bible studies and theology), science, social science.

Special Academic Programs Honors section; accelerated programs; study at local college for college credit.

College Placement 50 students graduated in 2005; all went to college, including Abilene Christian University; Auburn University; Freed-Hardeman University; Lipscomb University; The University of Alabama. Mean composite ACT: 23.

Student Life Upper grades have uniform requirement, student council, honor system. Discipline rests primarily with faculty. Attendance at religious services is required.

Tuition and Aid Day student tuition: $4450. Tuition installment plan (monthly payment plans). Tuition reduction for siblings, need-based scholarship grants available. In 2005–06, 10% of upper-school students received aid. Total amount of financial aid awarded in 2005–06: $100,000.

Admissions Traditional secondary-level entrance grade is 9. For fall 2005, 100 students applied for upper-level admission, 50 were accepted, 41 enrolled. Stanford Achievement Test required. Deadline for receipt of application materials: none. Application fee required: $150. On-campus interview required.

Athletics Interscholastic: baseball (boys), basketball (b,g), cheering (g), football (b), golf (b), softball (g), volleyball (g), wrestling (b); coed interscholastic: weight training. 3 PE instructors, 36 coaches.

Computers Computers are regularly used in art, foreign language, science classes. Computer network features include on-campus library services, CD-ROMs, Internet access.

Contact Mrs. Tereasa Rollings, High School Principal. 256-971-1624. Fax: 256-971-1436. E-mail: trollings@macademy.org. Web site: www.macademy.org.

MADISON-RIDGELAND ACADEMY

7601 Old Canton Road
Madison, Mississippi 39110
Head of School: Mr. Tommy Thompson

General Information Coeducational day college-preparatory school. Grades 1–12. Founded: 1969. Setting: suburban. Nearest major city is Jackson. 25-acre campus. 5 buildings on campus. Approved or accredited by Mississippi Private School Association, Southern Association of Colleges and Schools, and Mississippi Department of Education. Endowment: $350,000. Total enrollment: 921. Upper school average class size: 20. Upper school faculty-student ratio: 1:13.

Upper School Student Profile Grade 9: 57 students (26 boys, 31 girls); Grade 10: 66 students (30 boys, 36 girls); Grade 11: 66 students (34 boys, 32 girls); Grade 12: 57 students (26 boys, 31 girls).

Faculty School total: 61. In upper school: 12 men, 20 women; 10 have advanced degrees.

Subjects Offered Accounting, algebra, American government, American government-AP, American history, American history-AP, anatomy and physiology, art, Bible, biology, biology-AP, chemistry, chemistry-AP, chorus, civics, communications, computer applications, computer programming, creative writing, debate, drama, driver education, economics, English, European history-AP, forensics, French, French-AP, geography, geometry, German, global studies, government, graphic arts, health, journalism, keyboarding, music, newspaper, physical fitness, physics, physics-AP, pre-calculus, probability and statistics, psychology, sociology, Spanish, Spanish-AP, speech, trigonometry, world history, yearbook.

Graduation Requirements ACT preparation, advanced math, algebra, American government, biology, chemistry, civics, computer applications, computer keyboarding, economics, electives, English, foreign language, geometry, health, science, social studies (includes history).

Special Academic Programs Advanced Placement exam preparation in 12 subject areas; honors section; study at local college for college credit; academic accommodation for the gifted.

College Placement 49 students graduated in 2005; all went to college, including Belhaven College; Millsaps College; Mississippi College; Mississippi State University; University of Mississippi; University of Southern Mississippi. Median SAT verbal: 705, median SAT math: 620, median composite ACT: 24. 100% scored over 600 on SAT verbal, 100% scored over 600 on SAT math, 25% scored over 26 on composite ACT.

Student Life Upper grades have specified standards of dress, student council. Discipline rests primarily with faculty. Attendance at religious services is required.

Summer Programs Enrichment, sports programs offered; held on campus; accepts boys and girls; open to students from other schools. 300 students usually enrolled. 2006 schedule: June to July. Application deadline: May.

Tuition and Aid Day student tuition: $5520. Tuition installment plan (monthly payment plans, semi-annual payment plan). Tuition reduction for siblings, need-based

scholarship grants available. In 2005–06, 2% of upper-school students received aid. Total amount of financial aid awarded in 2005–06: $70,000.

Admissions Traditional secondary-level entrance grade is 9. For fall 2005, 63 students applied for upper-level admission, 55 were accepted, 52 enrolled. BASIS or Otis-Lennon Ability or Stanford Achievement Test required. Deadline for receipt of application materials: none. Application fee required: $35. On-campus interview required.

Athletics Interscholastic: aquatics (boys, girls), baseball (b), basketball (b,g), cheering (g), cross-country running (b,g), dance team (b,g), football (b), golf (b), soccer (b,g), softball (g), strength & conditioning (b,g), tennis (b,g), track and field (b,g); coed interscholastic: aquatics, golf, tennis. 2 PE instructors, 10 coaches, 1 trainer.

Computers Computers are regularly used in accounting, art, journalism, media, media services classes. Computer resources include on-campus library services, CD-ROMs, Internet access.

Contact Mrs. Cheryl Hendrix, Registrar. 601-856-4455. Fax: 601-853-3835. Web site: www.mrapats.com.

MAHARISHI SCHOOL OF THE AGE

804 Dr. Robert Keith Wallace Drive
Fairfield, Iowa 52556-2200
Head of School: Dr. Ashley Deans

General Information Coeducational day college-preparatory school. Grades PS–12. Founded: 1972. Setting: small town. Nearest major city is Iowa City. 10-acre campus. 3 buildings on campus. Approved or accredited by Independent Schools Association of the Central States and Iowa Department of Education. Member of National Association of Independent Schools. Endowment: $98,000. Total enrollment: 240. Upper school average class size: 15. Upper school faculty-student ratio: 1:8.

Upper School Student Profile Grade 10: 29 students (13 boys, 16 girls); Grade 11: 33 students (16 boys, 17 girls); Grade 12: 31 students (18 boys, 13 girls).

Faculty School total: 54. In upper school: 7 men, 9 women; 7 have advanced degrees.

Subjects Offered Algebra, American government, American history, American literature, art history, biology, British literature, chemistry, discrete math, economics, English, expository writing, geology, geometry, physical science, physics, physiology, Sanskrit, senior thesis, trigonometry, world history, world literature, writing.

Graduation Requirements Electives, English, foreign language, mathematics, physical education (includes health), science, social studies (includes history), Science of Creative Intelligence course, citizenship credits, acceptance to at least one 4-year college.

Special Academic Programs Honors section.

College Placement 42 students graduated in 2005; 38 went to college, including Chapman University; Maharishi University of Management; The University of Iowa. Other: 1 went to work, 3 had other specific plans. Median SAT verbal: 630, median SAT math: 630, median composite ACT: 24. 55% scored over 600 on SAT verbal, 59% scored over 600 on SAT math, 37% scored over 26 on composite ACT.

Student Life Upper grades have uniform requirement, student council. Discipline rests primarily with faculty.

Tuition and Aid Day student tuition: $12,980. Tuition installment plan (tuition loan from local banks). Tuition reduction for siblings, need-based scholarship grants available. In 2005–06, 22% of upper-school students received aid. Total amount of financial aid awarded in 2005–06: $101,709.

Admissions Traditional secondary-level entrance grade is 10. For fall 2005, 7 students applied for upper-level admission, 7 were accepted, 5 enrolled. Deadline for receipt of application materials: none. No application fee required. Interview required.

Athletics Interscholastic: basketball (boys, girls), cross-country running (b), golf (b), soccer (b), tennis (b,g), volleyball (g). 5 PE instructors, 14 coaches.

Computers Computers are regularly used in desktop publishing, economics, geography, library skills, mathematics classes. Computer network features include on-campus library services, CD-ROMs, online commercial services, Internet access, file transfer, DVD.

Contact Mr. Rod Falk, Director of Admissions. 641-472-9400 Ext. 5064. Fax: 641-472-1211. E-mail: registrar@msae.edu. Web site: www.maharishischooliowa.org.

MAINE CENTRAL INSTITUTE

125 South Main Street
Pittsfield, Maine 04967
Head of School: Ms. Joanne Szadkowski

petersons.com

General Information Coeducational boarding and day college-preparatory, general academic, arts, vocational, bilingual studies, technology, and humanities school. Grades 9–PG. Founded: 1866. Setting: small town. Nearest major city is Bangor. Students are housed in single-sex dormitories. 23-acre campus. 13 buildings on campus. Approved or accredited by Independent Schools of Northern New England, New England Association of Schools and Colleges, The Association of Boarding Schools, and Maine Department of Education. Member of National Association of

Independent Schools and Secondary School Admission Test Board. Endowment: $3 million. Total enrollment: 522. Upper school average class size: 15. Upper school faculty-student ratio: 1:15.

Upper School Student Profile Grade 9: 127 students (62 boys, 65 girls); Grade 10: 118 students (58 boys, 60 girls); Grade 11: 135 students (71 boys, 64 girls); Grade 12: 135 students (80 boys, 55 girls); Postgraduate: 7 students (7 boys). 20% of students are boarding students. 83% are state residents. 13 states are represented in upper school student body. 13% are international students. International students from Jamaica, Mexico, Republic of Korea, Taiwan, Thailand, and Viet Nam; 9 other countries represented in student body.

Faculty School total: 51. In upper school: 22 men, 26 women; 13 have advanced degrees; 11 reside on campus.

Subjects Offered Algebra, American history, American literature, anatomy, Arabic, art, art-AP, Asian studies, astronomy, audio visual/media, ballet, biology, biology-AP, botany, calculus, calculus-AP, career exploration, chemistry, child development, civil rights, computer science, concert band, concert choir, contemporary issues, creative writing, drafting, drama, earth science, ecology, economics, electronic publishing, English, English literature, environmental science, ESL, ethics, fine arts, French, geology, geometry, government/civics, health, history, humanities, integrated science, jazz band, jazz dance, jazz ensemble, Latin, life management skills, literature-AP, mathematics, meteorology, music, music appreciation, music composition, music theory, personal finance, philosophy, photography, physical education, physics, physics-AP, piano, psychology, reading/study skills, SAT preparation, science, social science, social studies, sociology, Spanish, statistics, theater, trigonometry, video film production, Web site design, world history.

Graduation Requirements Arts and fine arts (art, music, dance, drama), computer skills, English, mathematics, physical education (includes health), science, senior project, social studies (includes history), Manson Essay.

Special Academic Programs Advanced Placement exam preparation in 4 subject areas; honors section; accelerated programs; independent study; study at local college for college credit; study abroad; academic accommodation for the musically talented; remedial reading and/or remedial writing; remedial math; programs in English, mathematics, general development for dyslexic students; ESL (26 students enrolled).

College Placement 98 students graduated in 2005; 68 went to college, including Michigan State University; Syracuse University; University of Indianapolis; University of Maine. Other: 26 went to work, 1 entered military service, 1 entered a postgraduate year, 2 had other specific plans. Median SAT verbal: 471, median SAT math: 516, median composite ACT: 22. 7% scored over 600 on SAT verbal, 17% scored over 600 on SAT math.

Student Life Upper grades have specified standards of dress, student council, honor system. Discipline rests primarily with faculty.

Summer Programs ESL programs offered; session focuses on intensive ESL program to strengthen the understanding of the English vocabulary; held both on and off campus; held at local area sites; accepts boys and girls; open to students from other schools. 20 students usually enrolled. 2006 schedule: July 24 to August 20. Application deadline: June 1.

Tuition and Aid Day student tuition: $9000; 7-day tuition and room/board: $31,000. Tuition installment plan (Key Tuition Payment Plan, SMART Tuition Payment Plan, school's own payment plan). Merit scholarship grants, need-based scholarship grants available. In 2005–06, 12% of upper-school students received aid; total upper-school merit-scholarship money awarded: $40,000. Total amount of financial aid awarded in 2005–06: $1,004,395.

Admissions Traditional secondary-level entrance grade is 9. For fall 2005, 169 students applied for upper-level admission, 118 were accepted, 56 enrolled. Deadline for receipt of application materials: none. Application fee required: $50. Interview recommended.

Athletics Interscholastic: baseball (boys), basketball (b,g), cheering (g), field hockey (g), football (b), golf (b,g), riflery (b,g), skiing (downhill) (b,g), soccer (b,g), softball (g), tennis (b,g), track and field (b,g); intramural: billiards (b,g), football (b), table tennis (b,g), volleyball (b,g); coed interscholastic: aerobics/dance, ballet, wrestling; coed intramural: fencing, floor hockey, outdoor activities, paddle tennis, snowboarding. 1 PE instructor, 30 coaches, 1 trainer.

Computers Computers are regularly used in humanities, mathematics, science classes. Computer network features include on-campus library services, Internet access.

Contact Mr. Clint M. Williams, Director of Admission. 207-487-2282 Ext. 128. Fax: 207-487-3512. E-mail: cwilliams@mci-school.org. Web site: www.mci-school.org.

See full description on page 890.

MALASPINA INTERNATIONAL HIGH SCHOOL

900 Fifth Street
Nanaimo, British Columbia V9R 5S5, Canada
Head of School: Mr. Tom Lewis

General Information Coeducational boarding and day college-preparatory, general academic, arts, and business school. Grades 10–12. Founded: 1996. Setting: small town. Nearest major city is Vancouver, Canada. Students are housed in host family homes. 110-acre campus. 6 buildings on campus. Approved or accredited by British

Columbia Department of Education. Language of instruction: English. Total enrollment: 130. Upper school average class size: 12. Upper school faculty-student ratio: 1:8.

Upper School Student Profile Grade 10: 17 students (9 boys, 8 girls); Grade 11: 43 students (25 boys, 18 girls); Grade 12: 70 students (36 boys, 34 girls). 98% of students are boarding students. 4% are province residents. 90% are international students. International students from China, Hong Kong, Japan, Taiwan, and Turkey; 12 other countries represented in student body.

Faculty School total: 12. In upper school: 3 men, 9 women; 2 have advanced degrees.

Subjects Offered 20th century history, accounting, advanced chemistry, advanced math, art, biology, biology-AP, Canadian geography, chemistry, chemistry-AP, communication skills, communications, composition, composition-AP, computer studies, developmental math, drawing, English, English/composition-AP, ESL, European history, French, geography, Japanese, Mandarin, mathematics, physical science, physics, SAT preparation, yearbook.

Graduation Requirements Applied skills, career and personal planning, English, mathematics, science, social studies (includes history).

Special Academic Programs Advanced Placement exam preparation in 5 subject areas; accelerated programs; independent study; study at local college for college credit; academic accommodation for the gifted; remedial reading and/or remedial writing; ESL (70 students enrolled).

College Placement 43 students graduated in 2005; 39 went to college, including Simon Fraser University; The University of British Columbia; University of Victoria. Other: 2 went to work, 2 had other specific plans.

Student Life Upper grades have specified standards of dress, student council, honor system. Discipline rests equally with students and faculty.

Summer Programs Remediation, enrichment, advancement, ESL, art/fine arts, computer instruction programs offered; session focuses on ESL and recreational activities; held both on and off campus; held at community facilities; accepts boys and girls; open to students from other schools. 55 students usually enrolled. 2006 schedule: July 4 to August 26. Application deadline: May 1.

Tuition and Aid Day student tuition: CAN$12,000; 7-day tuition and room/board: CAN$21,000. Tuition installment plan (individually arranged payment plans). Tuition reduction for siblings, bursaries, merit scholarship grants, need-based scholarship grants available.

Admissions For fall 2005, 56 students applied for upper-level admission, 52 were accepted, 48 enrolled. Achievement tests and math and English placement tests required. Deadline for receipt of application materials: none. Application fee required: CAN$150.

Athletics Interscholastic: basketball (girls), soccer (g); intramural: ice hockey (b); coed interscholastic: aerobics/dance, alpine skiing, badminton, ball hockey, basketball, bowling, canoeing/kayaking, dance, floor hockey, golf, gymnastics, modern dance, physical fitness, physical training, rock climbing, roller blading, skateboarding, skiing (cross-country), skiing (downhill), surfing, swimming and diving, table tennis, tennis, volleyball, walking, weight training, winter soccer; coed intramural: aerobics, aerobics/dance, alpine skiing, aquatics, badminton, basketball, bicycling, bowling, canoeing/kayaking, climbing, cross-country running, fitness, golf, kayaking, outdoor skills, paint ball, rock climbing, skiing (cross-country), skiing (downhill), snowboarding, soccer, swimming and diving, walking.

Computers Computers are regularly used in all classes. Computer resources include campus e-mail, on-campus library services, CD-ROMs, Internet access, office computer access.

Contact Mr. Tom Lewis, Principal. 604-740-6317. Fax: 604-740-6470. E-mail: lewist@mala.bc.ca. Web site: www.mala.bc.ca/www/discover/intercol/index.htm.

MALDEN CATHOLIC HIGH SCHOOL

99 Crystal Street
Malden, Massachusetts 02148
Head of School: Mr. Thomas Arria Jr.

General Information Boys' day college-preparatory, arts, religious studies, and bilingual studies school, affiliated with Roman Catholic Church. Grades 9–12. Founded: 1932. Setting: urban. Nearest major city is Boston. 15-acre campus. 1 building on campus. Approved or accredited by New England Association of Schools and Colleges and Massachusetts Department of Education. Endowment: $2 million. Total enrollment: 700. Upper school average class size: 23. Upper school faculty-student ratio: 1:14.

Upper School Student Profile Grade 9: 175 students (175 boys); Grade 10: 170 students (170 boys); Grade 11: 195 students (195 boys); Grade 12: 160 students (160 boys). 85% of students are Roman Catholic.

Faculty School total: 52. In upper school: 40 men, 12 women; 43 have advanced degrees.

Subjects Offered 20th century history, 3-dimensional art, accounting, advanced chemistry, advanced math, Advanced Placement courses, algebra, American government, American history-AP, American literature, ancient world history, applied music, art, art appreciation, art history, Asian history, athletics, basic language skills, Bible studies, biology, British literature, British literature (honors), British literature-AP, business, calculus-AP, campus ministry, Chinese history, choral music, Christian and Hebrew scripture, Christian testament, college admission preparation, community service, computer programming, computer skills, desktop publishing, English

language and composition-AP, English-AP, European history, European history-AP, fine arts, foreign language, French, French language-AP, genetics, geometry, global studies, government, guitar, health and safety, honors algebra, honors English, honors geometry, honors U.S. history, honors world history, independent study, integrated science, language arts, leadership and service, library studies, marine biology, marine science, math analysis, modern European history, music appreciation, physical education, psychology, religion, SAT preparation, Spanish, Spanish language-AP, studio art, the Sixties, U.S. history, U.S. history-AP, world history, world history-AP.

Graduation Requirements Algebra, American literature, arts and fine arts (art, music, dance, drama), biology, British literature, Catholic belief and practice, chemistry, computer skills, foreign language, geometry, global studies, mathematics, physical education (includes health), religion (includes Bible studies and theology), science, social studies (includes history), Christian service.

Special Academic Programs Advanced Placement exam preparation in 9 subject areas; honors section; independent study.

College Placement 149 students graduated in 2005; 145 went to college, including Boston College; Northeastern University; Salem State College; University of Massachusetts Lowell. Other: 2 went to work, 2 entered military service.

Student Life Upper grades have specified standards of dress, student council, honor system. Discipline rests primarily with faculty. Attendance at religious services is required.

Summer Programs Session focuses on academic preparation/college prep; held on campus; accepts boys and girls; open to students from other schools. 100 students usually enrolled. 2006 schedule: July 6 to July 28. Application deadline: July 1.

Tuition and Aid Day student tuition: $8600. Tuition installment plan (FACTS Tuition Payment Plan, monthly payment plans). Merit scholarship grants, need-based scholarship grants, paying campus jobs available. In 2005–06, 40% of upper-school students received aid; total upper-school merit-scholarship money awarded: $300,000. Total amount of financial aid awarded in 2005–06: $300,000.

Admissions Traditional secondary-level entrance grade is 9. For fall 2005, 500 students applied for upper-level admission, 300 were accepted, 175 enrolled. Archdiocese of Boston High School entrance exam provided by STS required. Deadline for receipt of application materials: December 15. No application fee required.

Athletics Interscholastic: baseball, basketball, cross-country running, football, golf, hockey, ice hockey, indoor track & field, lacrosse, swimming and diving, tennis, wrestling; intramural: ball hockey, basketball, fitness, flag football, floor hockey, jogging, lacrosse, snowboarding. 2 PE instructors, 15 coaches, 1 trainer.

Computers Computers are regularly used in all academic, basic skills, business applications, business studies, design, desktop publishing, graphic arts, graphic design, graphics, information technology, journalism, library, library skills, multimedia, news writing, photography, photojournalism, religion, study skills, technology, theology, Web site design, word processing classes. Computer network features include campus e-mail, on-campus library services, CD-ROMs, online commercial services, Internet access, file transfer, DVD, wireless campus network.

Contact Mr. Richard Mazzei, Director of Admissions. 781-322-3098 Ext. 308. Fax: 781-397-0573. E-mail: admissions@maldencatholic.org. Web site: www. maldencatholic.org.

MANHATTAN CHRISTIAN HIGH SCHOOL

8000 Churchill Road
Manhattan, Montana 59741
Head of School: Randy Van Dyk

General Information Coeducational day college-preparatory and religious studies school, affiliated with Christian Reformed Church, Christian faith. Grades PK–12. Founded: 1907. Setting: rural. Nearest major city is Bozeman. 20-acre campus. 1 building on campus. Approved or accredited by Christian Schools International and Montana Department of Education. Endowment: $2.8 million. Total enrollment: 320. Upper school average class size: 15. Upper school faculty-student ratio: 1:10.

Upper School Student Profile Grade 9: 20 students (10 boys, 10 girls); Grade 10: 39 students (27 boys, 12 girls); Grade 11: 38 students (15 boys, 23 girls); Grade 12: 25 students (12 boys, 13 girls). 52% of students are members of Christian Reformed Church, Christian faith.

Faculty School total: 16. In upper school: 7 men, 8 women; 2 have advanced degrees.

Subjects Offered Art, Bible studies, business, community service, English, general science, internship, mathematics, music, physical education, senior project, social studies, Spanish.

Graduation Requirements Arts and fine arts (art, music, dance, drama), business skills (includes word processing), English, mathematics, physical education (includes health), religion (includes Bible studies and theology), science, senior project, social studies (includes history). Community service is required.

Special Academic Programs Advanced Placement exam preparation in 3 subject areas; study at local college for college credit; remedial reading and/or remedial writing; remedial math.

College Placement 33 students graduated in 2005; 31 went to college, including Calvin College; Carroll College; Dordt College; George Fox University; Gonzaga University; Montana State University. Other: 2 went to work. Mean composite ACT: 23.

Student Life Upper grades have specified standards of dress, student council, honor system. Discipline rests primarily with faculty. Attendance at religious services is required.

Tuition and Aid Day student tuition: $5200. Tuition installment plan (monthly payment plans, individually arranged payment plans). Tuition reduction for siblings, need-based scholarship grants available. In 2005–06, 80% of upper-school students received aid.

Admissions Traditional secondary-level entrance grade is 9. For fall 2005, 7 students applied for upper-level admission, 7 were accepted, 6 enrolled. Any standardized test required. Deadline for receipt of application materials: none. No application fee required. Interview required.

Athletics Interscholastic: basketball (boys, girls), cheering (g), cross-country running (b,g), football (b), golf (b,g), track and field (b,g), volleyball (g). 1 PE instructor, 19 coaches.

Computers Computers are regularly used in business, English, science, senior seminar, social studies classes. Computer network features include on-campus library services, CD-ROMs, online commercial services, Internet access, DVD.

Contact Randy Van Dyk, Administrator. 406-282-7261. Fax: 406-282-7701. E-mail: admin@manhattanchristian.org. Web site: www.manhattanchristian.org.

MANLIUS PEBBLE HILL SCHOOL

5300 Jamesville Road
DeWitt, New York 13214
Head of School: Baxter F. Ball

General Information Coeducational day college-preparatory school. Grades PK–PG. Founded: 1869. Setting: suburban. Nearest major city is Syracuse. 25-acre campus. 9 buildings on campus. Approved or accredited by Middle States Association of Colleges and Schools. Member of National Association of Independent Schools. Endowment: $2 million. Total enrollment: 584. Upper school average class size: 16. Upper school faculty-student ratio: 1:8.

Upper School Student Profile Grade 9: 54 students (25 boys, 29 girls); Grade 10: 71 students (41 boys, 30 girls); Grade 11: 71 students (39 boys, 32 girls); Grade 12: 63 students (35 boys, 28 girls).

Faculty School total: 91. In upper school: 37 men, 54 women; 50 have advanced degrees.

Subjects Offered 3-dimensional design, advanced chemistry, advanced math, Advanced Placement courses, advanced studio art-AP, algebra, American history, American history-AP, American literature, American literature-AP, ancient world history, art history, ballet, Basic programming, biology, biology-AP, calculus, calculus-AP, ceramics, chemistry, chemistry-AP, college counseling, comedy, computer math, computer science, creative writing, drama, driver education, earth science, English, English literature, environmental science, European history, expository writing, fine arts, French, geometry, government/civics, health, information technology, Latin, literature, marketing, mathematics, music, philosophy, photography, physical education, physics, science, social studies, sociology, Spanish, statistics, theater, trigonometry, world history.

Graduation Requirements Arts and fine arts (art, music, dance, drama), computer science, electives, English, foreign language, health and wellness, history, mathematics, performing arts, physical education (includes health), science.

Special Academic Programs Advanced Placement exam preparation in 20 subject areas; honors section; independent study; term-away projects; study at local college for college credit; study abroad; academic accommodation for the gifted; ESL (5 students enrolled).

College Placement 72 students graduated in 2005; all went to college, including Colgate University; Cornell University; Syracuse University; University of Michigan; University of Rochester; Wellesley College. Mean SAT verbal: 627, mean SAT math: 616.

Student Life Upper grades have specified standards of dress, student council, honor system. Discipline rests primarily with faculty.

Summer Programs Remediation, enrichment, advancement, sports, art/fine arts, computer instruction programs offered; held on campus; accepts boys and girls; open to students from other schools. 900 students usually enrolled. 2006 schedule: June 26 to August 22. Application deadline: none.

Tuition and Aid Day student tuition: $13,690–$14,840; 5-day tuition and room/board: $19,690–$20,840; 7-day tuition and room/board: $21,690–$22,840. Tuition installment plan (Insured Tuition Payment Plan, FACTS Tuition Payment Plan). Merit scholarship grants, need-based scholarship grants available. In 2005–06, 36% of upper-school students received aid; total upper-school merit-scholarship money awarded: $529,120. Total amount of financial aid awarded in 2005–06: $721,190.

Admissions Traditional secondary-level entrance grade is 9. For fall 2005, 61 students applied for upper-level admission, 51 were accepted, 32 enrolled. ERB or PSAT or SAT for applicants to grade 11 and 12 required. Deadline for receipt of application materials: none. Application fee required: $50. On-campus interview required.

Athletics Interscholastic: basketball (boys), diving (g), lacrosse (b,g), soccer (b,g), softball (g), swimming and diving (g), tennis (b,g), volleyball (g); intramural: lacrosse (g); coed interscholastic: alpine skiing, ballet, cheering, cross-country running, dance, equestrian sports, fitness, golf, indoor track, modern dance, outdoor education, skiing (downhill), snowboarding, strength & conditioning, track and field, winter (indoor) track; coed intramural: outdoor education, trap and skeet. 4 PE instructors, 4 coaches, 1 trainer.

Computers Computers are regularly used in English, foreign language, graphic design, history, information technology, library skills, literary magazine, mathematics, newspaper, science, Web site design, yearbook classes. Computer network features include campus e-mail, on-campus library services, CD-ROMs, online commercial services, Internet access.

Contact Lynne E. Allard, Director of Admission. 315-446-2452 Ext. 131. Fax: 315-446-2620. E-mail: lallard@mph.net. Web site: www.mph.net.

MAPLEBROOK SCHOOL

Amenia, New York
See Special Needs Schools section.

MARET SCHOOL

3000 Cathedral Avenue, NW
Washington, District of Columbia 20008
Head of School: Marjo Talbott

General Information Coeducational day college-preparatory, arts, and technology school. Grades K–12. Founded: 1911. Setting: urban. 7-acre campus. 6 buildings on campus. Approved or accredited by Association of Independent Maryland Schools, Association of Independent Schools of Greater Washington, Middle States Association of Colleges and Schools, and District of Columbia Department of Education. Member of National Association of Independent Schools and Secondary School Admission Test Board. Endowment: $5.1 million. Total enrollment: 600. Upper school average class size: 14. Upper school faculty-student ratio: 1:6.

Upper School Student Profile Grade 9: 76 students (37 boys, 39 girls); Grade 10: 69 students (33 boys, 36 girls); Grade 11: 78 students (38 boys, 40 girls); Grade 12: 77 students (39 boys, 38 girls).

Faculty School total: 100. In upper school: 35 men, 65 women; 62 have advanced degrees.

Subjects Offered Acting, advanced computer applications, advanced studio art-AP, African-American literature, algebra, American history, American literature, anatomy, art, astronomy, biology, calculus-AP, ceramics, chemistry, civil rights, classical civilization, classical Greek literature, classical language, classics, computer graphics, computer math, computer programming, computer science, creative writing, drama, earth science, ecology, English, English literature, European history, film history, fine arts, French, gender issues, geometry, government/civics, history, humanities, Latin, marine biology, mathematics, music, philosophy, photography, physical education, physics, physiology, psychology, science, Spanish, statistics, technology, trigonometry, women in world history, world history, world literature, writing.

Graduation Requirements Arts and fine arts (art, music, dance, drama), English, foreign language, history, mathematics, performing arts, physical education (includes health), science, 15 hours of community service in grades 9 and 10; additional hours in grades 11 and 12.

Special Academic Programs Advanced Placement exam preparation in 16 subject areas; honors section; independent study; study at local college for college credit; study abroad; academic accommodation for the gifted, the musically talented, and the artistically talented.

College Placement 75 students graduated in 2005; all went to college, including Brown University; Cornell University; Haverford College; Trinity College; Yale University.

Student Life Upper grades have student council. Discipline rests primarily with faculty.

Summer Programs Remediation, enrichment, advancement, sports, art/fine arts, computer instruction programs offered; session focuses on academics and athletics; held both on and off campus; held at locations in Costa Rica and Florida; accepts boys and girls; open to students from other schools. 100 students usually enrolled. 2006 schedule: June 15 to August 15. Application deadline: June 1.

Tuition and Aid Day student tuition: $23,865. Tuition installment plan (Key Tuition Payment Plan, monthly payment plans, individually arranged payment plans). Need-based scholarship grants available. In 2005–06, 16% of upper-school students received aid. Total amount of financial aid awarded in 2005–06: $849,635.

Admissions Traditional secondary-level entrance grade is 9. ISEE, PSAT or SSAT required. Deadline for receipt of application materials: January 6. Application fee required: $60. On-campus interview required.

Athletics Interscholastic: baseball (boys), basketball (b,g), cross-country running (b,g), football (b), lacrosse (b,g), soccer (b,g), softball (g), tennis (b,g), volleyball (g), wrestling (b); coed interscholastic: aerobics, dance, golf, independent competitive sports, martial arts, skateboarding, ultimate Frisbee, weight training; coed intramural: weight lifting. 6 PE instructors, 2 coaches, 1 trainer.

Computers Computer network features include campus e-mail, on-campus library services, CD-ROMs, online commercial services, Internet access, DVD, wireless campus network.

Contact Annie M. Farquhar, Director of Admission and Financial Aid. 202-939-8814. Fax: 202-939-8845. E-mail: admissions@maret.org. Web site: www.maret.org.

MARIANAPOLIS PREPARATORY SCHOOL

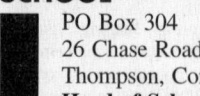

PO Box 304
26 Chase Road
Thompson, Connecticut 06277-0304
Head of School: Mrs. Marilyn S. Ebbitt

General Information Coeducational boarding and day college-preparatory, religious studies, and ESL school, affiliated with Roman Catholic Church. Grades 9–PG. Founded: 1926. Setting: small town. Nearest major city is Boston, MA. Students are housed in single-sex dormitories. 300-acre campus. 11 buildings on campus. Approved or accredited by Connecticut Association of Independent Schools, New England Association of Schools and Colleges, The Association of Boarding Schools, and Connecticut Department of Education. Member of Secondary School Admission Test Board. Total enrollment: 280. Upper school average class size: 15. Upper school faculty-student ratio: 1:10.

Upper School Student Profile Grade 9: 65 students (30 boys, 35 girls); Grade 10: 70 students (35 boys, 35 girls); Grade 11: 70 students (35 boys, 35 girls); Grade 12: 70 students (35 boys, 35 girls); Postgraduate: 5 students (3 boys, 2 girls). 38% of students are boarding students. 1% are state residents. 5 states are represented in upper school student body. 25% are international students. International students from Cameroon, Kazakhstan, Mexico, Republic of Korea, Spain, and Taiwan; 19 other countries represented in student body. 60% of students are Roman Catholic.

Faculty School total: 29. In upper school: 17 men, 12 women; 10 have advanced degrees; 14 reside on campus.

Subjects Offered Algebra, American government, American literature, art, Bible studies, biology, calculus, calculus-AP, chemistry, chemistry-AP, chorus, Christian and Hebrew scripture, Christian doctrine, Christian ethics, church history, comparative religion, computer programming, computer science, contemporary studies, drawing, English, English literature, English literature-AP, English-AP, ensembles, environmental science, ESL, fine arts, French, geometry, government/civics, guitar, history, honors algebra, honors English, honors geometry, mathematics, modern European history, moral theology, music, physics, physics-AP, piano, pre-calculus, probability and statistics, psychology, religion, science, social studies, Spanish, theology, trigonometry, U.S. history, world literature.

Graduation Requirements Arts and fine arts (art, music, dance, drama), computer science, electives, English, foreign language, mathematics, religion (includes Bible studies and theology), science, social studies (includes history). Community service is required.

Special Academic Programs Advanced Placement exam preparation in 9 subject areas; honors section; independent study; academic accommodation for the musically talented and the artistically talented; ESL (60 students enrolled).

College Placement 59 students graduated in 2005; all went to college, including College of the Holy Cross; Middlebury College; Providence College; Purdue University; Syracuse University; University of Connecticut.

Student Life Upper grades have specified standards of dress, student council, honor system. Discipline rests equally with students and faculty. Attendance at religious services is required.

Summer Programs Remediation, advancement, ESL, art/fine arts, computer instruction programs offered; session focuses on ESL; held on campus; accepts boys and girls; open to students from other schools. 45 students usually enrolled. 2006 schedule: June 10 to July 29. Application deadline: none.

Tuition and Aid Day student tuition: $8915; 5-day tuition and room/board: $26,770; 7-day tuition and room/board: $26,770. Tuition installment plan (Key Tuition Payment Plan, monthly payment plans, individually arranged payment plans). Tuition reduction for siblings, merit scholarship grants, need-based scholarship grants, paying campus jobs, tuition reduction for Diocese of Norwich affiliation available. In 2005–06, 67% of upper-school students received aid; total upper-school merit-scholarship money awarded: $100,000. Total amount of financial aid awarded in 2005–06: $600,000.

Admissions Traditional secondary-level entrance grade is 9. Common entrance examinations, SLEP, SSAT or TOEFL required. Deadline for receipt of application materials: none. Application fee required: $80. Interview required.

Athletics Interscholastic: baseball (boys), basketball (b,g), cross-country running (b,g), lacrosse (b,g), soccer (b,g), softball (g), tennis (b,g), winter (indoor) track (b,g); intramural: basketball (b,g), dance (g), modern dance (g); coed interscholastic: golf, running, wrestling; coed intramural: aerobics/dance, alpine skiing, bicycling, billiards, cross-country running, dance, flag football, Frisbee, independent competitive sports, jogging, judo, martial arts, mountain biking, skiing (cross-country), skiing (downhill), snowboarding, snowshoeing, swimming and diving, table tennis, tai chi, tennis, ultimate Frisbee, volleyball, weight lifting, yoga. 8 coaches.

Computers Computers are regularly used in all academic classes. Computer network features include campus e-mail, CD-ROMs, online commercial services, Internet access, file transfer, office computer access, DVD, wireless campus network.

Contact Mr. Daniel M. Harrop, Director of Admissions and Financial Aid. 860-923-9565 Ext. 233. Fax: 860-923-3730. E-mail: dharrop@marianapolis.org. Web site: www.marianapolis.org.

See full description on page 892.

MARIAN CENTRAL CATHOLIC HIGH SCHOOL

1001 McHenry Avenue
Woodstock, Illinois 60098
Head of School: Mr. Charles D. Rakers

General Information Coeducational day college-preparatory, arts, business, religious studies, bilingual studies, and technology school, affiliated with Roman Catholic Church. Grades 9–12. Founded: 1959. Setting: suburban. 42-acre campus. 1 building on campus. Approved or accredited by National Catholic Education Association, North Central Association of Colleges and Schools, and Illinois Department of Education. Endowment: $911,619. Total enrollment: 725. Upper school average class size: 25. Upper school faculty-student ratio: 1:15.

Upper School Student Profile Grade 9: 206 students (106 boys, 100 girls); Grade 10: 195 students (92 boys, 103 girls); Grade 11: 177 students (83 boys, 94 girls); Grade 12: 147 students (71 boys, 76 girls). 83% of students are Roman Catholic.

Faculty School total: 43. In upper school: 23 men, 20 women; 36 have advanced degrees.

Subjects Offered Accounting, advanced math, Advanced Placement courses, algebra, American government, art, band, biology, calculus, calculus-AP, chemistry, chorus, composition, consumer economics, English, English composition, English literature-AP, first aid, French, general science, geography, geometry, global issues, government, health, honors algebra, honors English, honors geometry, honors world history, humanities, information processing, integrated science, physical education, physical fitness, physical science, physics, pre-calculus, psychology, publications, religious studies, sociology, Spanish, speech, U.S. history, U.S. history-AP.

Graduation Requirements Art, biology, consumer economics, electives, English, foreign language, government, mathematics, music, physical education (includes health), religious studies, science, social studies (includes history), U.S. history.

Special Academic Programs Advanced Placement exam preparation in 3 subject areas; honors section; remedial reading and/or remedial writing; remedial math.

College Placement 180 students graduated in 2005; 176 went to college, including Illinois State University; Loyola University Chicago; Marquette University; Northern Illinois University; University of Illinois at Urbana–Champaign; University of Wisconsin–Madison. Other: 1 went to work, 1 entered a postgraduate year, 2 had other specific plans. Mean composite ACT: 23. 24% scored over 26 on composite ACT.

Student Life Upper grades have uniform requirement, student council. Discipline rests primarily with faculty. Attendance at religious services is required.

Summer Programs Sports programs offered; session focuses on sports camps; held on campus; accepts boys and girls; open to students from other schools. 2006 schedule: June to August.

Tuition and Aid Day student tuition: $4715–$6375. Tuition installment plan (monthly payment plans, quarterly payment plan, yearly payment plans). Tuition reduction for siblings, need-based scholarship grants, paying campus jobs available. In 2005–06, 14% of upper-school students received aid. Total amount of financial aid awarded in 2005–06: $152,387.

Admissions Traditional secondary-level entrance grade is 9. Latest standardized score from previous school required. Deadline for receipt of application materials: none. No application fee required.

Athletics Interscholastic: baseball (boys), basketball (b,g), cheering (g), cross-country running (b,g), dance team (g), football (b), golf (b,g), pom squad (g), soccer (b,g), softball (g), tennis (b,g), track and field (b,g), volleyball (g), wrestling (b); intramural: fencing (b,g), floor hockey (b,g). 4 PE instructors, 30 coaches, 1 trainer.

Computers Computers are regularly used in information technology, publications classes. Computer resources include on-campus library services, CD-ROMs, online commercial services, Internet access, DVD.

Contact Ms. Jacqueline Hyzy, Curriculum Assistant. 815-338-4220 Ext. 105. Fax: 815-338-4253. E-mail: jhyzy@marian.com. Web site: www.marian.com.

MARIAN HIGH SCHOOL

1311 South Logan Street
Mishawaka, Indiana 46544
Head of School: Carl Loesch

General Information Coeducational day college-preparatory, arts, business, vocational, religious studies, and technology school, affiliated with Roman Catholic Church. Grades 9–12. Founded: 1965. Setting: suburban. 46-acre campus. 1 building on campus. Approved or accredited by North Central Association of Colleges and Schools, The College Board, and Indiana Department of Education. Total enrollment: 816. Upper school average class size: 25. Upper school faculty-student ratio: 1:18.

Upper School Student Profile Grade 9: 193 students (94 boys, 99 girls); Grade 10: 219 students (110 boys, 109 girls); Grade 11: 195 students (91 boys, 104 girls); Grade 12: 209 students (109 boys, 100 girls). 82% of students are Roman Catholic.

Faculty School total: 53. In upper school: 20 men, 33 women; 18 have advanced degrees.

Subjects Offered 20th century history, 20th century physics, 20th century world history, 3-dimensional art, 3-dimensional design, accounting, advanced chemistry, advanced computer applications, advanced math, algebra, alternative physical education, American government, American literature, analysis and differential calculus, analytic geometry, anatomy, ancient world history, art, art history, arts and crafts, arts appreciation, business law, calculus, Catholic belief and practice, chemistry,

drama, drawing, drawing and design, economics, English composition, English literature-AP, environmental science, environmental studies, environmental systems, family and consumer science, family living, fashion, fine arts, food and nutrition, foods, French, French language-AP, general business, general math, geography, geometry, German, government and politics-AP, government-AP, government/civics, guidance, health, histology, honors world history, independent living, integrated science, keyboarding/computer, Latin, Life of Christ, media, media arts, moral theology, music, music appreciation, music theory-AP, nutrition, physics, physics-AP, pre-algebra, pre-calculus, psychology, religion, scripture, senior project, sewing, sociology, Spanish, Spanish language-AP, Spanish-AP, study skills, theology, U.S. government-AP, U.S. history, U.S. history-AP, visual arts, vocal music, Western civilization.

Graduation Requirements Algebra, American government, American history, analytic geometry, arts and fine arts (art, music, dance, drama), Bible studies, biology, chemistry, computer information systems, computer keyboarding, computer skills, economics, English, English composition, English literature, French, languages, mathematics, science, scripture, theology, writing skills, four years of theology.

Special Academic Programs Advanced Placement exam preparation in 2 subject areas; honors section; remedial math.

College Placement 150 students graduated in 2005; 140 went to college, including Ball State University; Indiana University Bloomington; Purdue University; Saint Mary's College; University of Notre Dame; Xavier University. Other: 4 went to work, 2 entered military service, 4 had other specific plans. Mean SAT verbal: 545, mean SAT math: 534.

Student Life Upper grades have specified standards of dress, student council, honor system. Discipline rests equally with students and faculty. Attendance at religious services is required.

Tuition and Aid Day student tuition: $5000–$6000. Tuition installment plan (The Tuition Plan, FACTS Tuition Payment Plan, individually arranged payment plans). Tuition reduction for siblings, need-based scholarship grants available. In 2005–06, 40% of upper-school students received aid. Total amount of financial aid awarded in 2005–06: $350,000.

Admissions Traditional secondary-level entrance grade is 9. For fall 2005, 200 students applied for upper-level admission, 198 were accepted, 193 enrolled. High School Placement Test, Math Placement Exam or placement test required. Deadline for receipt of application materials: August 21. Application fee required: $100. Interview required.

Athletics Interscholastic: aerobics/dance (girls), aquatics (b,g), baseball (b), basketball (b,g), cheering (b,g), Cosom hockey (b), cross-country running (b,g), dance team (g), flag football (g), football (b), golf (b,g), gymnastics (g), hockey (b), indoor hockey (b), lacrosse (b), power lifting (b,g), rugby (b), soccer (b,g), softball (g), swimming and diving (b,g), tennis (b,g), track and field (b,g), volleyball (g), weight training (b,g), wrestling (b,g); intramural: basketball (b), flag football (g), pom squad (g); coed interscholastic: wrestling; coed intramural: alpine skiing, bowling. 3 PE instructors, 39 coaches, 1 trainer.

Computers Computers are regularly used in business education, business skills, career education, career exploration, commercial art, economics, foreign language, graphic arts, history, library, media arts, occupational education, publications, religion, yearbook classes. Computer network features include on-campus library services, CD-ROMs, online commercial services, Internet access, DVD.

Contact Janet M. Hatfield, Dean. 574-259-5257. Fax: 574-258-7668. E-mail: jhatfield@marianhs.org. Web site: www.marianhs.org/.

MARIN ACADEMY

1600 Mission Avenue
San Rafael, California 94901-1859
Head of School: Ellanor Brizendine

General Information Coeducational day college-preparatory, arts, and technology school. Grades 9–12. Founded: 1971. Setting: suburban. Nearest major city is San Francisco. 10-acre campus. 11 buildings on campus. Approved or accredited by California Association of Independent Schools, The College Board, and Western Association of Schools and Colleges. Member of National Association of Independent Schools and Secondary School Admission Test Board. Endowment: $1.9 million. Total enrollment: 413. Upper school average class size: 15. Upper school faculty-student ratio: 1:9.

Upper School Student Profile Grade 9: 106 students (51 boys, 55 girls); Grade 10: 102 students (50 boys, 52 girls); Grade 11: 103 students (50 boys, 53 girls); Grade 12: 102 students (46 boys, 56 girls).

Faculty School total: 52. In upper school: 25 men, 27 women; 33 have advanced degrees.

Subjects Offered 20th century history, 20th century world history, 3-dimensional art, acting, adolescent issues, advanced computer applications, Advanced Placement courses, African history, algebra, American culture, American government, American history, American literature, American minority experience, American studies, ancient world history, art, art history, Asian history, Asian literature, astronomy, biology, biology-AP, British literature (honors), calculus, ceramics, chemistry, chemistry-AP, chorus, community service, computer programming, computer science, creative writing, dance, digital imaging, digital photography, English, English literature, environmental science, European history, fine arts, French, French language-AP,

French literature-AP, geology, geometry, government-AP, government/civics, health, history, honors U.S. history, human development, Islamic studies, Japanese, journalism, mathematics, music, oceanography, philosophy, photography, physical education, physics, physics-AP, pre-calculus, psychology, science, social studies, Spanish, studio art—AP, theater, trigonometry, world culture.

Graduation Requirements Arts and fine arts (art, music, dance, drama), English, foreign language, health and wellness, health education, mathematics, physical education (includes health), science, social studies (includes history), annual one-week experiential education course. Community service is required.

Special Academic Programs Advanced Placement exam preparation in 17 subject areas; honors section; independent study; term-away projects; study at local college for college credit; domestic exchange program (with The Masters School); study abroad; academic accommodation for the gifted, the musically talented, and the artistically talented.

College Placement 109 students graduated in 2005; 102 went to college, including Boston University; Brown University; New York University; University of California, Berkeley; University of California, Davis; University of Southern California. Other: 1 entered a postgraduate year, 6 had other specific plans. Mean SAT verbal: 657, mean SAT math: 645.

Student Life Upper grades have student council, honor system. Discipline rests equally with students and faculty.

Tuition and Aid Day student tuition: $25,785. Tuition installment plan (Key Tuition Payment Plan). Need-based scholarship grants, need-based loans available. In 2005–06, 20% of upper-school students received aid. Total amount of financial aid awarded in 2005–06: $1,542,763.

Admissions Traditional secondary-level entrance grade is 9. For fall 2005, 549 students applied for upper-level admission, 188 were accepted, 119 enrolled. CTBS or ERB, ISEE, SSAT or Star-9 required. Deadline for receipt of application materials: January 10. Application fee required: $75. On-campus interview required.

Athletics Interscholastic: aquatics (boys, girls), baseball (b), basketball (b,g), cross-country running (b,g), dance (b,g), fencing (b,g), fitness (b,g), golf (b,g), independent competitive sports (b,g), lacrosse (b,g), martial arts (b,g), nautilus (b,g), outdoor activities (b,g), outdoor education (b,g), outdoor skills (b,g), outdoors (b,g), sailing (b,g), soccer (b,g), softball (g), swimming and diving (b,g), tennis (b,g), track and field (b,g), volleyball (b,g), water polo (b,g); intramural: bicycling (b,g), climbing (b,g), crew (b,g), flag football (b,g); coed intramural: scuba diving. 22 coaches, 1 trainer.

Computers Computers are regularly used in English, foreign language, history, mathematics, music, photography, science classes. Computer network features include campus e-mail, on-campus library services, CD-ROMs, online commercial services, Internet access, file transfer, multimedia hardware and production applications.

Contact Dan Babior, Director of Admissions and Financial Aid. 415-453-4550 Ext. 216. Fax: 415-453-8905. E-mail: dbabior@ma.org. Web site: www.ma.org.

ANNOUNCEMENT FROM THE SCHOOL Marin Academy, an independent, coeducational, college-preparatory high school, enrolls a diversely talented student body of 400. The campus is located in San Rafael, a community of 57,000 residents, 12 miles north of San Francisco. Facilities on the 10-acre campus include 10 buildings, 2 playing fields, 2 athletic centers, a swimming pool, 3 computer labs, a multimedia lab, a science center, the Performing Arts Center, and the Visual Arts Center. The curriculum features 28 honors and AP courses, 63 electives, and outstanding opportunities in performing and visual arts as part of an extensive academic program. More than 40 interscholastic athletic teams are fielded annually. Many trips are offered through a highly developed Outdoor Education Program. Independent study and study-abroad programs are available. Graduates of the school attend leading colleges and universities throughout the country.

MARION ACADEMY

2002 Prier Drive
Marion, Alabama 36756
Head of School: Mrs. Myla Walworth

General Information Coeducational day college-preparatory, arts, bilingual studies, and technology school, affiliated with Christian faith. Grades K4–12. Founded: 1987. Setting: small town. Nearest major city is Tuscaloosa. 5-acre campus. 1 building on campus. Approved or accredited by Alabama Department of Education. Total enrollment: 110. Upper school average class size: 9. Upper school faculty-student ratio: 1:9.

Upper School Student Profile Grade 7: 7 students (4 boys, 3 girls); Grade 8: 7 students (2 boys, 5 girls); Grade 9: 9 students (2 boys, 7 girls); Grade 10: 3 students (1 boy, 2 girls); Grade 11: 9 students (2 boys, 7 girls); Grade 12: 8 students (4 boys, 4 girls). 98% of students are Christian.

Faculty School total: 16. In upper school: 4 men, 5 women; 5 have advanced degrees.

Subjects Offered 20th century history, 20th century world history, ACT preparation, advanced math, Alabama history and geography, algebra, American government, anatomy and physiology, art, athletics, basic language skills, biology, cheerleading, college planning, creative writing, drama, earth science, economics, English language and composition-AP, English language-AP, English literature, English literature and

composition-AP, English/composition-AP, foreign language, general math, geography, German, German-AP, government, grammar, health education, history, honors algebra, honors English, honors geometry, honors U.S. history, honors world history, human anatomy, Internet, language, language and composition, language arts, library, math applications, math methods, math review, mathematics, mathematics-AP, physical education, SAT/ACT preparation, speech, U.S. government, U.S. history.

College Placement 9 students graduated in 2005; 8 went to college, including Samford University. Other: 1 went to work.

Student Life Upper grades have specified standards of dress, student council, honor system. Discipline rests primarily with faculty.

Tuition and Aid Guaranteed tuition plan.

Admissions Traditional secondary-level entrance grade is 9. For fall 2005, 43 students applied for upper-level admission, 43 were accepted, 43 enrolled. Deadline for receipt of application materials: none. No application fee required. Interview recommended.

Athletics Interscholastic: baseball (boys), basketball (b,g), cheering (g), football (b), softball (g), track and field (b,g), volleyball (g); coed interscholastic: track and field. 1 PE instructor, 15 coaches.

Computers Computers are regularly used in career education classes. Computer network features include CD-ROMs, Internet access, DVD.

Contact Mrs. Jennifer W. Hughey. 334-683-8204. Fax: 334-683-4938. Web site: www.marionacademy.com.

MARIST HIGH SCHOOL

4200 West 115th Street
Chicago, Illinois 60655-4306
Head of School: Br. Richard Carey, FMS

General Information Coeducational day college-preparatory school, affiliated with Roman Catholic Church. Grades 9–12. Founded: 1963. Setting: suburban. 55-acre campus. 1 building on campus. Approved or accredited by National Catholic Education Association and Illinois Department of Education. Total enrollment: 1,830. Upper school average class size: 29. Upper school faculty-student ratio: 1:19.

Faculty School total: 112.

Subjects Offered Accounting, algebra, American legal systems, anatomy, architecture, art, band, biology, biology-AP, business mathematics, calculus, calculus-AP, chemistry, chemistry-AP, chorus, computer graphics, computer science, computer science-AP, creative writing, drawing, economics, English, English-AP, environmental science, film and literature, film studies, forensic science, French, French language-AP, geometry, information technology, journalism, painting, peer counseling, philosophy, physics, physics-AP, pottery, psychology, reading, religious studies, rhetoric, senior humanities, Spanish, Spanish-AP, studio art, U.S. history, U.S. history-AP, Web site design, wellness, Western civilization, world geography.

Graduation Requirements Electives, English, foreign language, mathematics, performing arts, physical education (includes health), religion (includes Bible studies and theology), science, social studies (includes history), technology, visual arts.

Special Academic Programs Honors section; study at local college for college credit.

College Placement 262 students graduated in 2005; 255 went to college, including DePaul University; Loyola University Chicago; Purdue University; University of Illinois at Chicago; University of Illinois at Urbana–Champaign; University of Notre Dame. Other: 7 went to work. Median composite ACT: 22.

Student Life Upper grades have uniform requirement, student council, honor system. Attendance at religious services is required.

Summer Programs Session focuses on academics; held on campus; accepts boys and girls; open to students from other schools.

Tuition and Aid Day student tuition: $6850. Merit scholarship grants, need-based scholarship grants, paying campus jobs available.

Admissions High School Placement Test required. Application fee required: $25.

Athletics Interscholastic: baseball (boys), basketball (b,g), cheering (b), cross-country running (b,g), football (b), golf (b,g), hockey (b), ice hockey (b), pom squad (b), soccer (b,g), softball (g), swimming and diving (g), tennis (b,g), track and field (b,g), volleyball (b,g), wrestling (b); intramural: boxing (b); coed intramural: bicycling, bowling, skiing (downhill).

Computers Computers are regularly used in architecture, drafting, graphic design classes. Computer resources include campus e-mail, CD-ROMs, Internet access, file transfer, DVD.

Contact Mrs. Alex Brown, Director of Admissions. 773-881-5300 Ext. 5330. Fax: 773-881-0595. E-mail: alex@marist.net. Web site: www.marist.net.

MARIST HIGH SCHOOL

1241 Kennedy Boulevard
Bayonne, New Jersey 07002
Head of School: Br. Steve Schlitte, FMS

General Information Coeducational day college-preparatory, religious studies, and technology school, affiliated with Roman Catholic Church. Grades 9–12. Founded: 1954. Setting: urban. 1 building on campus. Approved or accredited by Middle States

Association of Colleges and Schools, National Catholic Education Association, and New Jersey Department of Education. Total enrollment: 485. Upper school average class size: 22. Upper school faculty-student ratio: 1:20.

Upper School Student Profile 35% of students are Roman Catholic.

Faculty School total: 55. In upper school: 30 men, 25 women; 20 have advanced degrees.

Subjects Offered Advanced Placement courses, algebra, American history, American history-AP, art education, art history-AP, athletics, baseball, basketball, biology, biology-AP, bowling, British literature (honors), business education, calculus-AP, campus ministry, career/college preparation, character education, college awareness, college counseling, college placement, college planning, college writing, composition-AP, computer education, computer graphics, computer programming, computer skills, economics, English, geometry, health, history, history-AP, independent study, Internet, mathematics, mathematics-AP, programming, social sciences, Spanish, Spanish language-AP.

Graduation Requirements Art, computer skills, driver education, English, foreign language, mathematics, physical education (includes health), religion (includes Bible studies and theology), SAT preparation, science, social studies (includes history), writing workshop.

Special Academic Programs Honors section; independent study; study at local college for college credit; academic accommodation for the gifted; remedial reading and/or remedial writing; remedial math; special instructional classes for students with learning disabilities.

College Placement 85 students graduated in 2005; 81 went to college, including John Jay College of Criminal Justice of the City University of New York; Kean University; Saint Joseph's University; Saint Peter's College; Seton Hall University; Temple University. Other: 2 went to work, 2 entered military service.

Student Life Upper grades have uniform requirement, student council, honor system. Discipline rests primarily with faculty. Attendance at religious services is required.

Tuition and Aid Day student tuition: $5500. Tuition installment plan (FACTS Tuition Payment Plan). Merit scholarship grants, need-based scholarship grants available.

Admissions Traditional secondary-level entrance grade is 9. For fall 2005, 700 students applied for upper-level admission, 132 enrolled. Cooperative Entrance Exam (McGraw-Hill) or Terra Nova-CTB required. Deadline for receipt of application materials: none. Application fee required: $250. On-campus interview recommended.

Athletics Interscholastic: baseball (boys), basketball (b,g), football (b), soccer (b,g), softball (g), tennis (b,g); coed interscholastic: bowling, cheering, cross-country running, track and field, weight lifting; coed intramural: weight lifting, whiffle ball. 1 PE instructor.

Computers Computers are regularly used in all academic classes. Computer network features include on-campus library services, Internet access, wireless campus network.

Contact Mr. John A. Taormina, Director of Marketing and Admissions. 201-437-4544 Ext. 40. Fax: 201-437-6013. E-mail: admissions@marist.org. Web site: www.marist.org.

MARIST SCHOOL

3790 Ashford-Dunwoody Road, NE
Atlanta, Georgia 30319-1899
Head of School: Rev. Joel M. Konzen, SM

petersons.com

General Information Coeducational day college-preparatory, arts, religious studies, and technology school, affiliated with Roman Catholic Church. Grades 7–12. Founded: 1901. Setting: suburban. 57-acre campus. 18 buildings on campus. Approved or accredited by Georgia Independent School Association, Southern Association of Colleges and Schools, Southern Association of Independent Schools, and Georgia Department of Education. Member of National Association of Independent Schools and Secondary School Admission Test Board. Endowment: $12 million. Total enrollment: 1,042. Upper school average class size: 19. Upper school faculty-student ratio: 1:10.

Upper School Student Profile Grade 7: 132 students (66 boys, 66 girls); Grade 8: 131 students (66 boys, 65 girls); Grade 9: 201 students (102 boys, 99 girls); Grade 10: 189 students (91 boys, 98 girls); Grade 11: 194 students (89 boys, 105 girls); Grade 12: 195 students (104 boys, 91 girls). 75% of students are Roman Catholic.

Faculty School total: 96. In upper school: 51 men, 45 women; 84 have advanced degrees.

Subjects Offered Algebra, American history, American literature, ancient history, art, art history, astronomy, biology, business skills, calculus, ceramics, chemistry, community service, computer programming, computer science, creative writing, dance, drama, driver education, economics, English, English literature, European history, fine arts, French, general science, geography, geology, geometry, German, government/civics, health, history, humanities, journalism, keyboarding, Latin, mathematics, mechanical drawing, music, peace and justice, philosophy, photography, physical education, physics, religion, science, social studies, Spanish, speech, statistics, studio art, theater, theology, world history, world literature, world religions, writing.

Graduation Requirements Arts and fine arts (art, music, dance, drama), business skills (includes word processing), computer science, English, foreign language, mathematics, physical education (includes health), religion (includes Bible studies and theology), science, social studies (includes history). Community service is required.

Special Academic Programs Advanced Placement exam preparation in 19 subject areas; honors section; independent study.

College Placement 191 students graduated in 2005; all went to college, including Boston College; Emory University; Georgia Institute of Technology; University of Georgia; University of Notre Dame; University of Virginia. Mean SAT verbal: 597, mean SAT math: 622.

Student Life Upper grades have uniform requirement, student council, honor system. Discipline rests primarily with faculty. Attendance at religious services is required.

Tuition and Aid Day student tuition: $13,500. Tuition installment plan (The Tuition Plan, Insured Tuition Payment Plan). Need-based scholarship grants available. In 2005–06, 12% of upper-school students received aid. Total amount of financial aid awarded in 2005–06: $762,000.

Admissions Traditional secondary-level entrance grade is 9. For fall 2005, 521 students applied for upper-level admission, 242 were accepted, 212 enrolled. SSAT required. Deadline for receipt of application materials: February 1. Application fee required: $75. On-campus interview required.

Athletics Interscholastic: baseball (boys), basketball (b,g), cross-country running (b,g), diving (b,g), football (b), golf (b,g), soccer (b,g), softball (g), swimming and diving (b,g), tennis (b,g), track and field (b,g), volleyball (g), weight lifting (b,g), wrestling (b); intramural: lacrosse (b,g); coed interscholastic: drill team; coed intramural: outdoor education, ultimate Frisbee. 4 PE instructors, 17 coaches, 2 trainers.

Computers Computers are regularly used in accounting, English, foreign language, mathematics, music, science classes. Computer network features include campus e-mail, on-campus library services, CD-ROMs, online commercial services, Internet access.

Contact Rev. Patrick Scully, SM, Director of Admissions. 770-457-7201 Ext. 2227. Fax: 770-457-8402. E-mail: admissions@marist.com. Web site: www.marist.com.

ANNOUNCEMENT FROM THE SCHOOL Marist School is an independent Catholic school of the Marist Fathers and Brothers and delivers a principle-based education to students in grades 7–12. A close-knit and academically challenging community, Marist School gives students the tools for achievement and lifelong excellence in academics, the arts, and athletics in an environment that nurtures each student in the image of Christ.

MARLBOROUGH SCHOOL

250 South Rossmore Avenue
Los Angeles, California 90004
Head of School: Ms. Barbara E. Wagner

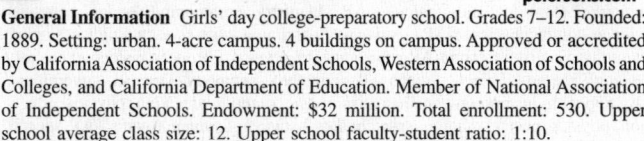

General Information Girls' day college-preparatory school. Grades 7–12. Founded: 1889. Setting: urban. 4-acre campus. 4 buildings on campus. Approved or accredited by California Association of Independent Schools, Western Association of Schools and Colleges, and California Department of Education. Member of National Association of Independent Schools. Endowment: $32 million. Total enrollment: 530. Upper school average class size: 12. Upper school faculty-student ratio: 1:10.

Upper School Student Profile Grade 10: 90 students (90 girls); Grade 11: 85 students (85 girls); Grade 12: 87 students (87 girls).

Faculty School total: 64. In upper school: 10 men, 16 women; 26 have advanced degrees.

Subjects Offered Algebra, American history, American literature, anatomy, art, art history, astronomy, biology, calculus, ceramics, chemistry, computer science, creative writing, dance, drama, economics, English, English literature, environmental science, European history, expository writing, fine arts, French, genetics, geometry, government/civics, health, history, journalism, Latin, mathematics, music, photography, physical education, physics, physiology, psychology, science, sculpture, social science, social studies, Spanish, Spanish language-AP, Spanish literature-AP, statistics, theater, trigonometry, world history, world literature, writing.

Graduation Requirements Arts and fine arts (art, music, dance, drama), computer science, English, foreign language, mathematics, physical education (includes health), science, social science, social studies (includes history).

Special Academic Programs Advanced Placement exam preparation in 19 subject areas; honors section; independent study.

College Placement 87 students graduated in 2005; 86 went to college, including Cornell University; New York University; Stanford University; University of California, Los Angeles; University of Pennsylvania; University of Southern California. Other: 1 had other specific plans. Mean SAT verbal: 674, mean SAT math: 663.

Student Life Upper grades have uniform requirement, student council, honor system. Discipline rests primarily with faculty.

Summer Programs Enrichment, advancement, sports, art/fine arts, computer instruction programs offered; session focuses on academic and recreational classes; held on campus; accepts boys and girls; open to students from other schools. 500 students usually enrolled. 2006 schedule: June 19 to July 28. Application deadline: none.

Tuition and Aid Day student tuition: $23,750. Tuition installment plan (Insured Tuition Payment Plan, FACTS Tuition Payment Plan, monthly payment plans). Merit

scholarship grants, need-based scholarship grants available. In 2005–06, 8% of upper-school students received aid. Total amount of financial aid awarded in 2005–06: $551,241.

Admissions For fall 2005, 10 students applied for upper-level admission. ISEE required. Deadline for receipt of application materials: January 14. Application fee required: $100. On-campus interview required.

Athletics Interscholastic: aquatics, basketball, cross-country running, dressage, equestrian sports, golf, independent competitive sports, soccer, softball, swimming and diving, tennis, track and field, volleyball. 7 PE instructors, 24 coaches.

Computers Computers are regularly used in all academic classes. Computer network features include campus e-mail, on-campus library services, CD-ROMs, online commercial services, Internet access, file transfer, DVD, wireless campus network, videoconferencing.

Contact Ms. Jeanette Woo Chitjian, Director of Admissions. 323-935-1147 Ext. 451. Fax: 323-933-0542. E-mail: jeanette.woochitjian@marlboroughschool.org. Web site: www.marlboroughschool.org.

ANNOUNCEMENT FROM THE SCHOOL With 100% of its graduates accepted by top accredited colleges and universities every year, Marlborough provides a learning environment where young women develop self-confidence, creativity, a sense of responsibility, and moral decisiveness. Rigorous academics, state-of-the-art facilities, competitive athletic programs, outdoor educational experiences, and outstanding fine arts productions place Marlborough among the top independent schools in the country.

MARMION ACADEMY

1000 Butterfield Road
Aurora, Illinois 60502
Head of School: John Milroy

General Information Boys' day college-preparatory, business, religious studies, Junior ROTC, and LEAD (Leadership Education and Development) school, affiliated with Roman Catholic Church. Grades 9–12. Founded: 1933. Setting: suburban. Nearest major city is Chicago. 325-acre campus. 5 buildings on campus. Approved or accredited by National Catholic Education Association, North Central Association of Colleges and Schools, and Illinois Department of Education. Member of Secondary School Admission Test Board. Endowment: $9 million. Total enrollment: 482. Upper school average class size: 25. Upper school faculty-student ratio: 1:11.

Upper School Student Profile Grade 9: 152 students (152 boys); Grade 10: 129 students (129 boys); Grade 11: 105 students (105 boys); Grade 12: 96 students (96 boys). 85% of students are Roman Catholic.

Faculty School total: 48. In upper school: 40 men, 8 women; 29 have advanced degrees.

Subjects Offered 1½ elective credits, accounting, algebra, American history, American literature, anatomy, art, astronomy, band, biology, biology-AP, botany, calculus, calculus-AP, chemistry, community service, computer science, computer science-AP, computer-aided design, creative writing, driver education, ecology, economics, English, English literature, English-AP, fine arts, French, general science, geometry, government/civics, history, history-AP, JROTC, Latin, leadership education training, leadership training, mathematics, mathematics-AP, meteorology, music, philosophy, physical education, physics, physics-AP, physiology, psychology, religion, science, social science, social studies, sociology, Spanish, Spanish language-AP, theology, trigonometry, Western civilization, zoology.

Graduation Requirements Arts and fine arts (art, music, dance, drama), English, foreign language, JROTC, leadership education training, mathematics, music appreciation, physical education (includes health), religion (includes Bible studies and theology), science, social science, social studies (includes history). Community service is required.

Special Academic Programs Advanced Placement exam preparation in 8 subject areas; honors section; independent study; academic accommodation for the gifted.

College Placement 101 students graduated in 2005; 96 went to college, including Benedictine University; Loyola University Chicago; Marquette University; Northern Illinois University; Purdue University; University of Illinois. Other: 1 went to work, 2 entered military service, 2 had other specific plans. Mean composite ACT: 25.

Student Life Upper grades have uniform requirement, student council. Discipline rests primarily with faculty. Attendance at religious services is required.

Tuition and Aid Day student tuition: $6950. Tuition installment plan (SMART Tuition Payment Plan). Merit scholarship grants, need-based scholarship grants, paying campus jobs available. In 2005–06, 25% of upper-school students received aid; total upper-school merit-scholarship money awarded: $115,000. Total amount of financial aid awarded in 2005–06: $218,650.

Admissions Traditional secondary-level entrance grade is 9. For fall 2005, 230 students applied for upper-level admission, 190 were accepted, 152 enrolled. High School Placement Test (closed version) from Scholastic Testing Service required. Deadline for receipt of application materials: none. Application fee required: $50. On-campus interview required.

Athletics Interscholastic: baseball, basketball, cross-country running, diving, football, golf, riflery, soccer, swimming and diving, tennis, track and field, wrestling; intramural: baseball, basketball, floor hockey, football, JROTC drill, outdoor

activities, outdoors, soccer, swimming and diving, table tennis, tennis, volleyball, water polo, weight lifting. 2 PE instructors, 3 coaches, 1 trainer.

Computers Computers are regularly used in drafting, science classes. Computer network features include campus e-mail, on-campus library services, CD-ROMs, Internet access.

Contact William J. Dickson Jr., Director of Admissions. 630-897-6936. Fax: 630-897-7086. Web site: www.marmion.org.

ANNOUNCEMENT FROM THE SCHOOL Marmion Academy is a Catholic and Benedictine college-preparatory day high school for boys. The school is for average and above-average students whose goal is to attend college. Marmion was founded in 1933 and has been owned and operated ever since by the Benedictine Priests and Brothers of Marmion Abbey. Located on a scenic 325-acre campus just off Interstate 88 in the western Chicago suburb of Aurora, Illinois, the Academy is 35 miles west of downtown Chicago, along the Illinois "High Tech Corridor." The school's educational objective is to educate the whole man by establishing a climate conducive to spiritual growth, intellectual endeavors, and leadership training. This goal is based on a firm belief in the goodness of each individual as an image of God, graced with a unique spiritual, intellectual, and physical potential. Marmion has a history of challenging academics and strong leadership programs. These academic-based leadership programs include a Junior Officer Training (JROTC) Program and Marmion's own Leadership Education And Development (LEAD) Program. Approximately 50 percent of Marmion graduates receive merit-based scholarships, with an average of $3.1 million awarded during the past 3 years. Marmion is a nonprofit organization with a self-perpetuating advisory Board of Lay Trustees, 34 in number, that meets in full session quarterly. The Alumni Association, representing more than 7,000 graduates, organizes alumni events and aids in recruiting students, many of whom are the sons, grandsons, and brothers of alumni. Marmion Academy is fully accredited by the North Central Association of Colleges and Schools and the Illinois State Board of Education. Marmion is a member of the National Catholic Educational Association and the Secondary School Admission Test Board.

MARQUETTE UNIVERSITY HIGH SCHOOL

3401 West Wisconsin Avenue
Milwaukee, Wisconsin 53208
Head of School: Rev. John Belmonte, SJ

General Information Boys' day college-preparatory school, affiliated with Roman Catholic Church. Grades 9–12. Founded: 1857. Setting: urban. 4 buildings on campus. Approved or accredited by Jesuit Secondary Education Association, National Catholic Education Association, North Central Association of Colleges and Schools, and Wisconsin Department of Education. Total enrollment: 1,067. Upper school average class size: 24. Upper school faculty-student ratio: 1:15.

Upper School Student Profile Grade 9: 272 students (272 boys); Grade 10: 275 students (275 boys); Grade 11: 257 students (257 boys); Grade 12: 263 students (263 boys). 84% of students are Roman Catholic.

Faculty School total: 69. In upper school: 50 men, 19 women; 45 have advanced degrees.

Subjects Offered Algebra, American history, American literature, architectural drawing, architecture, art, art history, art-AP, Bible studies, biology, biology-AP, calculus, calculus-AP, ceramics, chemistry, chemistry-AP, choral music, computer math, computer programming, computer science, computer science-AP, creative writing, drama, driver education, economics, English, English language-AP, English literature, English literature-AP, ethics, European history, European history-AP, expository writing, French, French language-AP, geography, geometry, German, government/civics, grammar, graphic design, health, history, jazz band, Latin, Latin-AP, macroeconomics-AP, mathematics, microeconomics-AP, music, philosophy, photography, physical education, physics, psychology, psychology-AP, religion, social studies, sociology, Spanish, Spanish language-AP, speech, statistics-AP, studio art-AP, theology, trigonometry, U.S. government and politics-AP, U.S. history-AP, world history, world literature, World War I, World War II, writing.

Graduation Requirements Arts and fine arts (art, music, dance, drama), English, foreign language, mathematics, science, social studies (includes history), theology, retreats. Community service is required.

Special Academic Programs Advanced Placement exam preparation in 18 subject areas; honors section.

College Placement 239 students graduated in 2005; 235 went to college, including Creighton University; Marquette University; Saint Louis University; University of Minnesota, Twin Cities Campus; University of Wisconsin–Madison; University of Wisconsin–Milwaukee. Other: 1 went to work, 1 entered military service, 2 had other specific plans. Median SAT verbal: 600, median SAT math: 620, median composite ACT: 26. 44% scored over 600 on SAT verbal, 59% scored over 600 on SAT math, 48% scored over 26 on composite ACT.

Student Life Upper grades have specified standards of dress, student council, honor system. Discipline rests primarily with faculty. Attendance at religious services is required.

Tuition and Aid Day student tuition: $7740. Tuition installment plan (monthly payment plans, pre-paid tuition loan program). Need-based scholarship grants, paying campus jobs, state-sponsored voucher program available. In 2005–06, 27% of upper-school students received aid. Total amount of financial aid awarded in 2005–06: $1,140,000.

Admissions Traditional secondary-level entrance grade is 9. For fall 2005, 525 students applied for upper-level admission, 400 were accepted, 272 enrolled. Essay and STS—Educational Development Series required. Deadline for receipt of application materials: none. Application fee required: $20. On-campus interview recommended.

Athletics Interscholastic: baseball, basketball, cross-country running, diving, football, golf, ice hockey, lacrosse, rugby, sailing, skiing (downhill), soccer, swimming and diving, tennis, track and field, ultimate Frisbee, volleyball, wrestling; intramural: basketball, soccer, softball, volleyball.

Computers Computers are regularly used in architecture, college planning, creative writing, data processing, desktop publishing, economics, English, graphic design, literary magazine, mathematics, music, newspaper, research skills, stock market, Web site design, word processing, writing, yearbook classes. Computer network features include campus e-mail, on-campus library services, CD-ROMs, online commercial services, Internet access, file transfer, office computer access, DVD, university and county library systems link.

Contact Mr. Dan Quesnell, Director of Admissions. 414-933-7220 Ext. 3046. Fax: 414-937-6002. E-mail: admissions@muhs.edu. Web site: www.muhs.edu.

MARSHALL SCHOOL

1215 Rice Lake Road
Duluth, Minnesota 55811
Head of School: Mrs. Marlene M. David

General Information Coeducational day college-preparatory, arts, religious studies, and technology school. Grades 5–12. Founded: 1904. Setting: suburban. Nearest major city is Minneapolis. 40-acre campus. 1 building on campus. Approved or accredited by Independent Schools Association of the Central States and North Central Association of Colleges and Schools. Member of National Association of Independent Schools. Endowment: $1.8 million. Total enrollment: 498. Upper school average class size: 18. Upper school faculty-student ratio: 1:9.

Upper School Student Profile Grade 9: 74 students (38 boys, 36 girls); Grade 10: 88 students (53 boys, 35 girls); Grade 11: 86 students (47 boys, 39 girls); Grade 12: 77 students (33 boys, 44 girls).

Faculty School total: 51. In upper school: 18 men, 13 women; 12 have advanced degrees.

Subjects Offered Algebra, American history, American literature, anatomy, art, biology, botany, calculus, calculus-AP, chemistry, community service, computer science, computer science-AP, creative writing, drama, earth science, English, English literature, English literature-AP, environmental science, European history, expository writing, fine arts, French, French-AP, geography, geometry, German, government/civics, health, history, law, mathematics, music, outdoor education, physical education, physics, poetry, religion, science, social studies, Spanish, Spanish-AP, speech, theater, theology, trigonometry, world history, world literature, writing.

Graduation Requirements Arts and fine arts (art, music, dance, drama), computer science, English, foreign language, mathematics, outdoor education, physical education (includes health), religion (includes Bible studies and theology), science, social studies (includes history). Community service is required.

Special Academic Programs Advanced Placement exam preparation in 9 subject areas; honors section; independent study; academic accommodation for the gifted.

College Placement 90 students graduated in 2005; 84 went to college, including Saint John's University; University of Minnesota, Duluth; University of Minnesota, Twin Cities Campus. Other: 6 had other specific plans. Median SAT verbal: 630, median SAT math: 621, median composite ACT: 26.

Student Life Upper grades have student council. Discipline rests equally with students and faculty.

Summer Programs Remediation, enrichment, art/fine arts, computer instruction programs offered; session focuses on enrichment and study skills; held both on and off campus; held at local parks; accepts boys and girls; open to students from other schools. 170 students usually enrolled. 2006 schedule: June 15 to July 9. Application deadline: none.

Tuition and Aid Day student tuition: $8910. Tuition installment plan (Insured Tuition Payment Plan, Key Tuition Payment Plan, monthly payment plans). Need-based scholarship grants, paying campus jobs, Achiever Loans (Key Education Resources) available. In 2005–06, 23% of upper-school students received aid. Total amount of financial aid awarded in 2005–06: $449,000.

Admissions Traditional secondary-level entrance grade is 9. CTP and ERB required. Deadline for receipt of application materials: none. Application fee required: $50. On-campus interview required.

Athletics Interscholastic: baseball (boys), basketball (b,g), cheering (b,g), cross-country running (b,g), dance squad (g), danceline (b,g), football (b), golf (b,g), ice hockey (b,g), nordic skiing (b,g), skiing (cross-country) (b,g), skiing (downhill) (b,g), soccer (b,g), softball (g), tennis (b,g), track and field (b,g), volleyball (g); coed intramural: outdoor education. 4 PE instructors, 43 coaches, 1 trainer.

Computers Computers are regularly used in English, foreign language, history, mathematics, science classes. Computer network features include on-campus library services, CD-ROMs, online commercial services, Internet access.

Contact Ms. Amy L. Arntson, Director of Admissions, Public Relations and Financial Aid. 218-727-7266 Ext. 111. Fax: 218-727-1569. E-mail: aarntson@marshallschool.org. Web site: MarshallSchool.org.

MARS HILL BIBLE SCHOOL
698 Cox Creek Parkway
Florence, Alabama 35630
Head of School: Dr. Kenny Barfield

General Information Coeducational day college-preparatory, arts, and religious studies school, affiliated with Church of Christ. Grades K–12. Founded: 1947. Setting: suburban. Nearest major city is Huntsville. 80-acre campus. 5 buildings on campus. Approved or accredited by National Christian School Association and Southern Association of Colleges and Schools. Endowment: $1 million. Total enrollment: 605. Upper school average class size: 20. Upper school faculty-student ratio: 1:14.

Upper School Student Profile Grade 9: 39 students (14 boys, 25 girls); Grade 10: 47 students (25 boys, 22 girls); Grade 11: 47 students (23 boys, 24 girls); Grade 12: 52 students (28 boys, 24 girls). 81% of students are members of Church of Christ.

Faculty School total: 44. In upper school: 10 men, 12 women; 17 have advanced degrees.

Subjects Offered ACT preparation, algebra, American government, American literature, American literature-AP, anatomy and physiology, ancient world history, band, Bible studies, biology, biology-AP, calculus, calculus-AP, chemistry, chemistry-AP, chorus, computer keyboarding, computer literacy, computer programming, computer science, concert band, concert choir, criminal justice, current events, debate, drama, drama performance, driver education, ecology, economics, English, English composition, English literature, English literature and composition-AP, English literature-AP, ensembles, environmental systems, forensics, geometry, government-AP, Greek, health, honors English, human anatomy, Internet research, jazz band, Life of Christ, marine biology, musical productions, physical education, physical science, physics, pre-algebra, pre-calculus, probability and statistics, psychology, psychology-AP, Spanish, speech, speech and debate, statistics-AP, student government, student publications, U.S. government-AP, U.S. history, U.S. history-AP, word processing, world geography, world history, yearbook.

Graduation Requirements Ancient world history, computer science, English, foreign language, mathematics, physical education (includes health), religion (includes Bible studies and theology), science, social studies (includes history). Community service is required.

Special Academic Programs Advanced Placement exam preparation in 5 subject areas; honors section; study at local college for college credit; special instructional classes for students with learning disabilities, Attention Deficit Disorder, and dyslexia.

College Placement 42 students graduated in 2005; all went to college, including Auburn University; Freed-Hardeman University; Harding University; The University of Alabama; University of North Alabama. Median composite ACT: 25. 45% scored over 26 on composite ACT.

Student Life Upper grades have specified standards of dress, student council. Discipline rests primarily with faculty. Attendance at religious services is required.

Summer Programs Enrichment, advancement, sports, art/fine arts programs offered; session focuses on driver's education, debate, show choir, sports camps; held on campus; accepts boys and girls; open to students from other schools. 100 students usually enrolled. 2006 schedule: June 1 to June 30. Application deadline: June 1.

Tuition and Aid Day student tuition: $4200. Tuition installment plan (FACTS Tuition Payment Plan, monthly payment plans). Tuition reduction for siblings, need-based scholarship grants available. In 2005–06, 25% of upper-school students received aid. Total amount of financial aid awarded in 2005–06: $120,000.

Admissions Traditional secondary-level entrance grade is 9. For fall 2005, 30 students applied for upper-level admission, 25 were accepted, 25 enrolled. Achievement tests, ACT, PSAT or Stanford Achievement Test required. Deadline for receipt of application materials: none. Application fee required: $50. Interview required.

Athletics Interscholastic: baseball (boys), basketball (b,g), cheering (g), cross-country running (b,g), golf (b,g), soccer (b,g), softball (g), tennis (b,g), track and field (b,g); intramural: aerobics (g), basketball (b,g), bowling (b,g), fitness (b,g), independent competitive sports (b,g), jogging (b,g), jump rope (b,g), outdoor activities (b,g), outdoor skills (b,g), physical fitness (b,g), running (b,g), strength & conditioning (b,g), table tennis (b,g), tennis (b,g), volleyball (b,g), walking (b,g), whiffle ball (b,g); coed interscholastic: Special Olympics; coed intramural: badminton, bowling, cooperative games, fitness, independent competitive sports, jogging, kickball, paddle tennis, physical fitness, running, soccer, softball, strength & conditioning, table tennis, tennis, volleyball, walking, wallyball, weight lifting, whiffle ball. 4 PE instructors, 6 coaches.

Computers Computers are regularly used in Bible studies, English, history, yearbook classes. Computer resources include on-campus library services, CD-ROMs, online commercial services, Internet access, DVD.

Contact Mr. David Willingham, Vice President. 256-767-1203 Ext. 203. Fax: 256-767-6304. E-mail: dwillingham@mhbs.org. Web site: www.mhbs.org.

THE MARVELWOOD SCHOOL
476 Skiff Mountain Road
PO Box 3001
Kent, Connecticut 06757-3001
Head of School: Mr. Scott E. Pottbecker

General Information Coeducational boarding and day college-preparatory, arts, field science, and community service school; primarily serves underachievers. Grades 9–12. Founded: 1957. Setting: rural. Nearest major city is Hartford. Students are housed in single-sex dormitories. 75-acre campus. 9 buildings on campus. Approved or accredited by Association of Independent Schools in New England, Connecticut Association of Independent Schools, National Independent Private Schools Association, New England Association of Schools and Colleges, The Association of Boarding Schools, and Connecticut Department of Education. Member of National Association of Independent Schools. Endowment: $1.4 million. Total enrollment: 150. Upper school average class size: 11. Upper school faculty-student ratio: 1:4.

Upper School Student Profile Grade 9: 22 students (16 boys, 6 girls); Grade 10: 49 students (29 boys, 20 girls); Grade 11: 38 students (28 boys, 10 girls); Grade 12: 41 students (34 boys, 7 girls). 97% of students are boarding students. 27% are state residents. 14 states are represented in upper school student body. 21% are international students. International students from Jamaica, Japan, Republic of Korea, Spain, Taiwan, and Turkey; 3 other countries represented in student body.

Faculty School total: 47. In upper school: 18 men, 29 women; 20 have advanced degrees; 30 reside on campus.

Subjects Offered Algebra, American history, American literature, anatomy and physiology, art, biology, business mathematics, calculus, ceramics, chemistry, chorus, community service, creative writing, design, drama, driver education, ecology, English, English literature, environmental science, ESL, European history, film, fine arts, French, geography, geometry, mathematics, music, photography, physics, psychology, religion, science, Shakespeare, social studies, Spanish, women's studies, world culture, world history, world literature.

Graduation Requirements Arts and fine arts (art, music, dance, drama), English, foreign language, mathematics, science, social studies (includes history), senior service project, daily participation in sports, weekly community service program.

Special Academic Programs Honors section; independent study; remedial reading and/or remedial writing; remedial math; ESL (12 students enrolled).

College Placement 41 students graduated in 2005; 39 went to college, including Hamilton College; Michigan State University; New York University; Purdue University; Syracuse University; University of Connecticut. Other: 2 went to work. Median SAT verbal: 410, median SAT math: 490.

Student Life Upper grades have specified standards of dress, student council. Discipline rests primarily with faculty.

Summer Programs Remediation, enrichment, ESL, art/fine arts programs offered; session focuses on study skills; held on campus; accepts boys and girls; open to students from other schools. 30 students usually enrolled. 2006 schedule: June 25 to July 31. Application deadline: none.

Tuition and Aid Day student tuition: $20,700; 7-day tuition and room/board: $32,500. Tuition installment plan (Insured Tuition Payment Plan, Academic Management Services Plan, Key Tuition Payment Plan, individually arranged payment plans). Merit scholarship grants, need-based scholarship grants available. In 2005–06, 22% of upper-school students received aid; total upper-school merit-scholarship money awarded: $5000. Total amount of financial aid awarded in 2005–06: $671,325.

Admissions Traditional secondary-level entrance grade is 9. For fall 2005, 165 students applied for upper-level admission, 98 were accepted, 74 enrolled. Deadline for receipt of application materials: none. Application fee required: $50. Interview required.

Athletics Interscholastic: baseball (boys), basketball (b,g), cross-country running (b,g), horseback riding (g), lacrosse (b), soccer (b,g), softball (g), tennis (b,g), volleyball (g), wrestling (b); intramural: lacrosse (g); coed interscholastic: alpine skiing, golf, skiing (downhill); coed intramural: bicycling, canoeing/kayaking, fishing, fly fishing, hiking/backpacking, horseback riding, mountain biking, mountaineering, outdoor activities, outdoor adventure, outdoor education, outdoor skills, physical training, ropes courses, skiing (downhill), snowboarding, strength & conditioning, weight training, wilderness, wildernessways, yoga. 1 trainer.

Computers Computers are regularly used in graphic design, mathematics, media, newspaper, photography, science, writing classes. Computer network features include CD-ROMs, Internet access, DVD, wireless campus network.

Contact Mr. Todd Holt, Director of Admissions. 860-927-0047 Ext. 26. Fax: 860-927-0021. E-mail: admissions@marvelwood.org. Web site: www.marvelwood.org.

ANNOUNCEMENT FROM THE SCHOOL For 45 years, the Marvelwood Summer Program has offered rigorous yet individualized academic challenge for students at all ability levels. Small classes, experienced faculty, and a dedication to each student's individual success distinguish Marvelwood's Summer Program and provide a solid foundation for academic success. A wide variety of interesting elective courses, structured study time, and daily opportunities for recreation keep all students engaged. Students return to their winter school confident in their

abilities and eager to apply what they've learned. Full-day boarding program for students entering grades 7–10.

See full description on page 894.

MARY HELP OF CHRISTIANS ACADEMY

659 Belmont Avenue
North Haledon, New Jersey 07508
Head of School: Sr. Margaret M. Wilhelm, FMA

General Information Girls' day college-preparatory, business, and religious studies school, affiliated with Roman Catholic Church. Grades 9–12. Founded: 1940. Setting: suburban. Nearest major city is Paterson. 21-acre campus. 6 buildings on campus. Approved or accredited by Middle States Association of Colleges and Schools and New Jersey Department of Education. Total enrollment: 238. Upper school average class size: 17. Upper school faculty-student ratio: 1:10.

Upper School Student Profile Grade 9: 70 students (70 girls); Grade 10: 52 students (52 girls); Grade 11: 57 students (57 girls); Grade 12: 59 students (59 girls). 80% of students are Roman Catholic.

Faculty School total: 30. In upper school: 7 men, 23 women; 22 have advanced degrees.

Subjects Offered Accounting, advanced chemistry, advanced math, Advanced Placement courses, advertising design, algebra, American literature, anatomy and physiology, art, art appreciation, art history, Bible studies, biology, biology-AP, British literature, British literature (honors), business, business studies, career/college preparation, Catholic belief and practice, chemistry, choral music, Christian and Hebrew scripture, Christian ethics, communication skills, computer applications, computer graphics, computer literacy, consumer mathematics, driver education, English, English literature-AP, environmental science, fashion, first aid, forensics, French, geometry, gymnastics, health science, history of the Catholic Church, home economics, honors English, human anatomy, instrumental music, journalism, marketing, music appreciation, music theory, photo shop, physical education, physical science, physics, political science, political systems, pre-algebra, pre-calculus, psychology, publications, SAT preparation, science and technology, social justice, sociology, Spanish, Spanish language-AP, student government, studio art, study skills, television, theology, trigonometry, U.S. history, video film production, vocal music, Web site design, world history, writing, yearbook.

Graduation Requirements Algebra, American history, American literature, art, art appreciation, biology, British literature, career/college preparation, Catholic belief and practice, Christian and Hebrew scripture, Christian doctrine, computer applications, computers, driver education, electives, English, first aid, foreign language, general science, geometry, health and safety, history of the Catholic Church, moral theology, music appreciation, physical education (includes health), science, study skills, world history, 80 hours of service performed with a nonprofit community organization.

Special Academic Programs Advanced Placement exam preparation in 4 subject areas; honors section; independent study; study at local college for college credit; remedial reading and/or remedial writing; remedial math; special instructional classes for students with moderate learning disabilities; ESL (3 students enrolled).

College Placement 69 students graduated in 2005; 68 went to college, including Fairleigh Dickinson University, College at Florham; Pace University; Rutgers, The State University of New Jersey, New Brunswick/Piscataway; Seton Hall University; St. John's University; William Paterson University of New Jersey. Other: 1 went to work.

Student Life Upper grades have uniform requirement, student council, honor system. Discipline rests primarily with faculty. Attendance at religious services is required.

Summer Programs Remediation, enrichment, advancement programs offered; session focuses on mathematics advancement, remediation in mathematics, language arts for incoming freshmen, honors biology; held on campus; accepts girls; not open to students from other schools. 30 students usually enrolled. 2006 schedule: June 26 to July 28. Application deadline: May 15.

Tuition and Aid Day student tuition: $5250. Tuition installment plan (monthly payment plans, individually arranged payment plans). Tuition reduction for siblings, merit scholarship grants, need-based scholarship grants, paying campus jobs available. In 2005–06, 43% of upper-school students received aid; total upper-school merit-scholarship money awarded: $64,995. Total amount of financial aid awarded in 2005–06: $283,081.

Admissions Traditional secondary-level entrance grade is 9. For fall 2005, 258 students applied for upper-level admission, 140 were accepted, 70 enrolled. Cooperative Entrance Exam (McGraw-Hill) and school placement exam required. Deadline for receipt of application materials: none. No application fee required. Interview required.

Athletics Interscholastic: basketball, cheering, soccer, softball, tennis, track and field, volleyball; intramural: basketball, cheering, gymnastics, skiing (downhill), volleyball. 2 PE instructors, 7 coaches.

Computers Computers are regularly used in accounting, English, graphic arts, graphics, journalism, publications, religion, SAT preparation, science, Spanish, video film production, Web site design, word processing, yearbook classes. Computer network features include on-campus library services, CD-ROMs, online commercial services, Internet access, wireless campus network, EBSCOhost[00ae], Kurzweil 3000 (assistive reading software).

Contact Sr. Maryann Schaefer, FMA, Admissions Director. 973-790-6200 Ext. 140. Fax: 973-790-6125. E-mail: admissions@maryhelp.org. Web site: www.maryhelp.org.

MARY INSTITUTE AND ST. LOUIS COUNTRY DAY SCHOOL (MICDS)

101 North Warson Road
St. Louis, Missouri 63124
Head of School: Matthew E. Gossage

General Information Coeducational day college-preparatory, arts, and technology school. Grades JK–12. Founded: 1859. Setting: suburban. 100-acre campus. 5 buildings on campus. Approved or accredited by Independent Schools Association of the Central States and Missouri Department of Education. Member of National Association of Independent Schools and Secondary School Admission Test Board. Endowment: $70 million. Total enrollment: 1,223. Upper school average class size: 15. Upper school faculty-student ratio: 1:8.

Upper School Student Profile Grade 9: 145 students (78 boys, 67 girls); Grade 10: 149 students (71 boys, 78 girls); Grade 11: 147 students (73 boys, 74 girls); Grade 12: 137 students (63 boys, 74 girls).

Faculty School total: 149. In upper school: 34 men, 39 women; 61 have advanced degrees.

Subjects Offered Acting, advanced chemistry, algebra, American literature, animal behavior, architecture, art history-AP, band, biology, biology-AP, calculus, calculus-AP, chemistry, chemistry-AP, chorus, civil rights, composition, creative writing, digital art, directing, economics, economics-AP, English language-AP, English literature and composition-AP, ethics, European history-AP, French, geometry, German, global studies, government-AP, Latin, literature, music theory-AP, painting, photography, physics, physics-AP, physiology, playwriting and directing, political science, pre-calculus, psychology, sculpture, Shakespeare, Spanish, Spanish language-AP, statistics, statistics-AP, studio art, studio art—AP, trigonometry, U.S. history, U.S. history-AP, utopia, Web site design, world history.

Graduation Requirements Arts and fine arts (art, music, dance, drama), English, foreign language, mathematics, physical education (includes health), science, social studies (includes history). Community service is required.

Special Academic Programs Advanced Placement exam preparation in 18 subject areas; honors section; independent study; term-away projects; study abroad.

College Placement 143 students graduated in 2005; all went to college, including Emory University; Saint Louis University; Southern Methodist University; Syracuse University; University of Colorado at Boulder; University of Southern California. Mean SAT verbal: 624, mean SAT math: 646, mean composite ACT: 28.

Student Life Upper grades have specified standards of dress, student council, honor system. Discipline rests equally with students and faculty.

Summer Programs Sports, rigorous outdoor training programs offered; session focuses on conditioning/training; held on campus; accepts boys and girls; open to students from other schools. 200 students usually enrolled. 2006 schedule: June 19 to July 28.

Tuition and Aid Day student tuition: $17,145. Tuition installment plan (The Tuition Plan, Insured Tuition Payment Plan, individually arranged payment plans). Need-based scholarship grants available. In 2005–06, 21% of upper-school students received aid. Total amount of financial aid awarded in 2005–06: $1,267,540.

Admissions Traditional secondary-level entrance grade is 9. For fall 2005, 56 students applied for upper-level admission, 39 were accepted, 27 enrolled. ISEE or SSAT, ERB, PSAT, SAT, PLAN or ACT required. Deadline for receipt of application materials: January 13. Application fee required: $40. Interview required.

Athletics Interscholastic: aerobics/dance (girls), baseball (b,g), basketball (b,g), bowling (b), cheering (g), crew (b,g), cross-country running (b,g), dance (b,g), diving (b,g), field hockey (g), fitness (b,g), fitness walking (b,g), football (b), golf (b,g), hockey (b), ice hockey (b), independent competitive sports (b,g), indoor track & field (b,g), jogging (b,g), lacrosse (b,g), modern dance (g), physical fitness (b,g), physical training (b,g), racquetball (b,g), rowing (b,g), soccer (b,g), swimming and diving (b,g), tennis (b,g), track and field (b,g), volleyball (g), water polo (b), wrestling (b). 45 coaches.

Computers Computers are regularly used in art, English, foreign language, history, mathematics, music, science classes. Computer network features include campus e-mail, on-campus library services, CD-ROMs, online commercial services, Internet access, DVD.

Contact Peggy B. Laramie, Director of Admission and Financial Aid. 314-995-7367. Fax: 314-872-3257. E-mail: plaramie@micds.org.

ANNOUNCEMENT FROM THE SCHOOL Founded in 1859, MICDS is today considered to be one of the nation's preeminent independent schools. MICDS is a coed, college-preparatory school serving 1,220 students. Junior kindergarten through 4th grade and 9th–12th grades are coed, while Middle School students, grades 5–8, learn within a framework of single-sex and coed classes. MICDS is committed to its mission of preparing young people for higher learning and lives of purpose and service. The School's outstanding education balances strong academics, an innovative arts program, service learning, and an athletics program that has claimed 23 team state championships, 4 individual/

relay team state championships, 52 appearances in the state semifinals, and 41 district championships over the past decade. Teachers and students benefit from a strong mission, a caring and diverse community, and exceptional facilities for learning. MICDS welcomes students from all backgrounds. New students represent 82 different public/parochial/independent schools. Student-to-teacher ratio is 8:1 and the average class size is 15. More than 21 percent of the student body receives financial aid. Nearly two-thirds of the School's faculty hold advanced degrees. The 143 graduates of the class of 2005 attend 80 four-year colleges. Tuition for the 2005–06 school year ranged from $14,170 to $17,145.

MARYKNOLL SCHOOL

petersons.com

1526 Alexander Street
Honolulu, Hawaii 96822
Head of School: Michael E. Baker

General Information Coeducational day college-preparatory school, affiliated with Roman Catholic Church. Grades PK–12. Founded: 1927. Setting: urban. 3-acre campus. 3 buildings on campus. Approved or accredited by National Catholic Education Association, Western Association of Schools and Colleges, Western Catholic Education Association, and Hawaii Department of Education. Member of National Association of Independent Schools and Secondary School Admission Test Board. Endowment: $3.5 million. Total enrollment: 1,399. Upper school average class size: 18. Upper school faculty-student ratio: 1:11.

Upper School Student Profile Grade 9: 150 students (69 boys, 81 girls); Grade 10: 157 students (77 boys, 80 girls); Grade 11: 142 students (79 boys, 63 girls); Grade 12: 132 students (58 boys, 74 girls). 50% of students are Roman Catholic.

Faculty School total: 104. In upper school: 26 men, 28 women; 30 have advanced degrees.

Subjects Offered Adolescent issues, algebra, American literature, art, art history-AP, biology, biology-AP, biotechnology, British literature, calculus-AP, chemistry, chemistry-AP, college counseling, college placement, computer programming, creative writing, drawing, economics, English language and composition-AP, English literature and composition-AP, ethics, European history-AP, French, geography, geometry, global science, golf, government, government-AP, guitar, Hawaiian history, Hawaiian language, human development, Japanese, journalism, library assistant, marine science, media, mythology, novels, Pacific art, painting, philosophy, physical education, physics, physics-AP, poetry, pre-calculus, psychology, psychology-AP, religion, religious studies, research, Russian history, science fiction, senior project, Shakespeare, sociology, Spanish, speech, statistics, studio art-AP, theater, U.S. history, U.S. history-AP, Web site design, weight training, world history, world literature, yearbook.

Graduation Requirements Arts and fine arts (art, music, dance, drama), English, foreign language, mathematics, physical education (includes health), religion (includes Bible studies and theology), science, senior project, social science, social studies (includes history), portfolio of student works. Community service is required.

Special Academic Programs Advanced Placement exam preparation in 12 subject areas; honors section; independent study.

College Placement 141 students graduated in 2005; all went to college, including Loyola Marymount University; Santa Clara University; University of Hawaii at Manoa; University of San Francisco; University of Southern California; University of Washington.

Student Life Upper grades have uniform requirement, student council. Discipline rests equally with students and faculty. Attendance at religious services is required.

Summer Programs Remediation, enrichment, advancement, sports, art/fine arts, computer instruction programs offered; session focuses on advancement and enrichment; held on campus; accepts boys and girls; open to students from other schools. 800 students usually enrolled. 2006 schedule: June 16 to July 28. Application deadline: May 15.

Tuition and Aid Day student tuition: $10,100. Tuition installment plan (Insured Tuition Payment Plan, monthly payment plans). Merit scholarship grants, need-based scholarship grants, paying campus jobs available. In 2005–06, 23% of upper-school students received aid; total upper-school merit-scholarship money awarded: $76,000. Total amount of financial aid awarded in 2005–06: $360,000.

Admissions Traditional secondary-level entrance grade is 9. For fall 2005, 230 students applied for upper-level admission, 137 were accepted, 69 enrolled. PSAT or SSAT required. Deadline for receipt of application materials: January 8. Application fee required: $65. On-campus interview required.

Athletics Interscholastic: aerobics/dance (girls), baseball (b), basketball (b,g), bowling (b,g), canoeing/kayaking (b,g), cross-country running (b,g), dance (g), diving (b,g), football (b), golf (b,g), gymnastics (b,g), judo (b,g), karate (b,g), martial arts (b,g), ocean paddling (b,g), paddling (b,g), power lifting (b,g), riflery (b,g), sailing (b,g), soccer (b,g), softball (g), strength & conditioning (b,g), swimming and diving (b,g), tennis (b,g), track and field (b,g), volleyball (b,g), water polo (b,g), weight lifting (b,g), weight training (b,g), wrestling (b,g); intramural: basketball (b,g), volleyball (b,g); coed interscholastic: canoeing/kayaking, cheering, football, ocean paddling, paddling, strength & conditioning, weight training, wrestling; coed intramural: basketball, bowling, floor hockey. 3 PE instructors, 50 coaches, 1 trainer.

Computers Computers are regularly used in English, foreign language, history, mathematics, science classes. Computer network features include campus e-mail, on-campus library services, CD-ROMs, online commercial services, Internet access, file transfer, DVD, wireless campus network.

Contact Mr. Scott C. Siegfried, Director of Admission. 808-952-7330. Fax: 808-952-7331. E-mail: admission@maryknollschool.org. Web site: www. maryknollschool.org.

ANNOUNCEMENT FROM THE SCHOOL Unique among Hawaii's private schools as the only private, coeducational, Catholic school for grades PK–12. With an enrollment of nearly 1,400, the School welcomes students from diverse backgrounds because personal growth is as valued as academic achievement. With a dedicated faculty to provide guidance and support, Maryknoll School is committed to providing each student with a well-rounded and high-quality education. Recognizing the importance of developing good citizens of character, Maryknoll strives to foster values of integrity and personal responsibility through emphasis on moral excellence. Maryknoll students develop into creative and critical thinkers and problem solvers who accept responsibility for their learning and personal choices and who value learning as a lifelong process. Students come to appreciate human diversity and can demonstrate understanding of other languages, cultures, and experiences. They learn the importance of physical well-being, while respecting themselves and others. On the Grade School campus, traditional teachings are blended with innovative practices, including the integration of technology in the Early Childhood, Elementary, and Middle School Programs. The fundamentals of learning are the focus of the lower grades, with an exceptional reading and writing program across the curriculum. During the Middle School years, youngsters build on these early skills, while exploring interdisciplinary studies and service learning. Emphasis is also placed on supporting the values, discipline, and sense of service of Maryknoll families. By high school, young teens build on the interdisciplinary studies in a unique learning format in which they are expected to demonstrate mastery of their subjects, as well as an understanding of the relationship across subjects. The high school's heralded and challenging college-prep curriculum, known as the Essential Schools Program, includes Advanced Placement courses in all core subjects. For information, call the Office of Admission at 808-952-7330.

MARYLAWN OF THE ORANGES

445 Scotland Road
South Orange, New Jersey 07079
Head of School: Mrs. Delores Thompson

General Information Girls' day college-preparatory, arts, religious studies, and technology school, affiliated with Roman Catholic Church. Grades 9–12. Founded: 1935. Setting: suburban. Nearest major city is Newark. 2 buildings on campus. Approved or accredited by Middle States Association of Colleges and Schools and New Jersey Department of Education. Total enrollment: 210. Upper school average class size: 15. Upper school faculty-student ratio: 1:15.

Upper School Student Profile Grade 9: 58 students (58 girls); Grade 10: 51 students (51 girls); Grade 11: 47 students (47 girls); Grade 12: 54 students (54 girls). 25% of students are Roman Catholic.

Faculty School total: 23. In upper school: 7 men, 16 women; 13 have advanced degrees.

Subjects Offered Advanced chemistry, advanced computer applications, advanced math, African-American literature, algebra, American literature, anatomy and physiology, art, art history, athletics, biology, British literature (honors), calculus, campus ministry, career/college preparation, Catholic belief and practice, cheerleading, chemistry, choir, choral music, Christian ethics, Christian scripture, civics, classical studies, community service, constitutional law, English, English-AP, environmental science, fine arts, French, geometry, global studies, grammar, guidance, handbells, health education, honors algebra, honors English, honors geometry, honors U.S. history, humanities, integrated math, Internet research, journalism, language arts, Latin, mathematics, mentorship program, moral theology, music theory, physical education, physics, pre-calculus, psychology, SAT/ACT preparation, social studies, Spanish, Spanish-AP, trigonometry, U.S. history, women in literature, world cultures, world religions, writing workshop, yearbook.

Graduation Requirements Arts and fine arts (art, music, dance, drama), English, foreign language, mathematics, physical education (includes health), religious studies, science, social studies (includes history), 25 hours of community service (junior year), 40 hours of community service (senior year).

Special Academic Programs Advanced Placement exam preparation in 5 subject areas; honors section; independent study; academic accommodation for the gifted, the musically talented, and the artistically talented; remedial reading and/or remedial writing; remedial math.

College Placement 28 students graduated in 2005; 25 went to college, including Kean University; Montclair State University; Rutgers, The State University of New Jersey, New Brunswick/Piscataway; Seton Hall University; Temple University. Other: 3 went to work. 7% scored over 600 on SAT verbal, 3% scored over 600 on SAT math.

Marylawn of the Oranges

Student Life Upper grades have uniform requirement, student council. Discipline rests primarily with faculty. Attendance at religious services is required.

Summer Programs Remediation, enrichment, advancement, computer instruction programs offered; session focuses on prep and advancement for secondary school courses; make-up for failed classes; held on campus; accepts girls; not open to students from other schools. 80 students usually enrolled. 2006 schedule: June 26 to July 25. Application deadline: none.

Tuition and Aid Day student tuition: $4900. Tuition installment plan (monthly payment plans). Tuition reduction for siblings, merit scholarship grants, need-based scholarship grants available. In 2005–06, 32% of upper-school students received aid; total upper-school merit-scholarship money awarded: $26,000. Total amount of financial aid awarded in 2005–06: $116,790.

Admissions Traditional secondary-level entrance grade is 9. Cooperative Entrance Exam (McGraw-Hill) required. Deadline for receipt of application materials: none. Application fee required: $125. On-campus interview required.

Athletics Interscholastic: basketball, cheering, dance team, drill team, softball, track and field, volleyball; intramural: basketball, physical fitness, soccer, tennis, volleyball. 1 PE instructor, 1 coach.

Computers Computers are regularly used in all classes. Computer resources include CD-ROMs, Internet access, file transfer, office computer access, DVD.

Contact Mrs. Tanya Craig, Admissions Officer. 973-762-9222 Ext. 15. Fax: 973-378-7975. E-mail: admissions@marylawn.net. Web site: www.marylawn.net.

THE MARY LOUIS ACADEMY

176-21 Wexford Terrace
Jamaica Estates, New York 11432-2926
Head of School: Kathleen M. McKinney, CSJ

General Information Girls' day college-preparatory, arts, religious studies, and technology school, affiliated with Roman Catholic Church. Grades 9–12. Founded: 1936. Setting: urban. Nearest major city is New York. 2 buildings on campus. Approved or accredited by Middle States Association of Colleges and Schools, New York State Board of Regents, and New York Department of Education. Endowment: $1.5 million. Total enrollment: 1,036. Upper school average class size: 28. Upper school faculty-student ratio: 1:13.

Upper School Student Profile Grade 9: 257 students (257 girls); Grade 10: 259 students (259 girls); Grade 11: 262 students (262 girls); Grade 12: 258 students (258 girls). 78.2% of students are Roman Catholic.

Faculty School total: 77. In upper school: 16 men, 61 women; 60 have advanced degrees.

Subjects Offered Advanced Placement courses, American history, art, astronomy, biology, calculus, career exploration, ceramics, chemistry, college planning, composition, computer science, current events, drawing, driver education, earth science, economics, English, English literature, European history, family studies, fine arts, first aid, French, government/civics, history, human development, Italian, Latin, law, leadership training, literature, mathematics, microbiology, music, music theory, nutrition, painting, physical education, physics, political science, religion, science, sculpture, social studies, Spanish, vocal music, world history, world literature.

Graduation Requirements Arts and fine arts (art, music, dance, drama), English, foreign language, mathematics, music, physical education (includes health), religion (includes Bible studies and theology), science, social studies (includes history), technology, service project.

Special Academic Programs Advanced Placement exam preparation in 7 subject areas; honors section; independent study; term-away projects; study at local college for college credit; study abroad; academic accommodation for the musically talented and the artistically talented.

College Placement 221 students graduated in 2005; all went to college, including Fordham University; New York University; Queens College of the City University of New York; St. John's University; Stony Brook University, State University of New York; The George Washington University. Mean SAT verbal: 535, mean SAT math: 527. 22% scored over 600 on SAT verbal, 11% scored over 600 on SAT math.

Student Life Upper grades have uniform requirement, student council. Discipline rests primarily with faculty. Attendance at religious services is required.

Summer Programs Remediation, enrichment programs offered; session focuses on Regents Competency Test preparation only; held on campus; accepts girls; open to students from other schools. 55 students usually enrolled. 2006 schedule: August 1 to August 15. Application deadline: June 30.

Tuition and Aid Day student tuition: $5900. Tuition installment plan (SMART Tuition Payment Plan, monthly payment plans, individually arranged payment plans). Tuition reduction for siblings, merit scholarship grants, need-based scholarship grants available. In 2005–06, 7% of upper-school students received aid; total upper-school merit-scholarship money awarded: $489,525. Total amount of financial aid awarded in 2005–06: $530,225.

Admissions Traditional secondary-level entrance grade is 9. For fall 2005, 1,167 students applied for upper-level admission, 608 were accepted, 257 enrolled. Cooperative Entrance Exam (McGraw-Hill) required. Deadline for receipt of application materials: February 6. Application fee required: $250.

Athletics Interscholastic: basketball, cross-country running, dance, golf, indoor track, indoor track & field, running, soccer, softball, swimming and diving, tennis, track and field, volleyball, winter (indoor) track; intramural: basketball, fitness, self defense, soccer. 4 PE instructors, 17 coaches.

Computers Computers are regularly used in career exploration, college planning, English, foreign language, history, mathematics, music, science classes. Computer network features include on-campus library services, CD-ROMs, online commercial services, Internet access.

Contact Sr. Lorraine O'Neill, CSJ, Administrative Secretary. 718-297-2120. Fax: 718-739-0037. Web site: www.tmla.org.

MARYMOUNT HIGH SCHOOL

10643 Sunset Boulevard
Los Angeles, California 90077
Head of School: Dr. Mary Ellen Gozdecki

General Information Girls' day college-preparatory and religious studies school, affiliated with Roman Catholic Church. Grades 9–12. Founded: 1923. Setting: suburban. 5-acre campus. 6 buildings on campus. Approved or accredited by California Association of Independent Schools, National Catholic Education Association, National Independent Private Schools Association, The College Board, Western Association of Schools and Colleges, and California Department of Education. Member of National Association of Independent Schools and Secondary School Admission Test Board. Endowment: $3.5 million. Total enrollment: 400. Upper school average class size: 15. Upper school faculty-student ratio: 1:8.

Upper School Student Profile Grade 9: 105 students (105 girls); Grade 10: 106 students (106 girls); Grade 11: 101 students (101 girls); Grade 12: 88 students (88 girls). 68% of students are Roman Catholic.

Faculty School total: 53. In upper school: 17 men, 36 women; 33 have advanced degrees.

Subjects Offered Acting, aerobics, African literature, algebra, American history, American legal systems, American literature, anatomy, art, art history, art-AP, biology, biology-AP, British literature, calculus, calculus-AP, ceramics, chemistry, choir, Christian testament, community service, computer literacy, computer science, contemporary issues, dance, death and loss, design, drama, drawing, ecology, economics, English, English literature, environmental science, environmental science-AP, ethics, fencing, fine arts, French, French-AP, gender and religion, geography, geometry, government/civics, Hebrew scripture, human development, Japanese literature, jazz ensemble, journalism, language and composition, literary magazine, literature, literature-AP, music, musical productions, painting, peace studies, performing arts, photography, physical education, physics, physiology, pre-calculus, printmaking, psychology, religion, religious studies, robotics, science, self-defense, social justice, social studies, softball, Spanish, Spanish language-AP, Spanish literature-AP, speech, swimming, theology, trigonometry, U.S. government-AP, U.S. history, U.S. history-AP, vocal music, volleyball, women's studies, world religions, writing.

Graduation Requirements Arts and fine arts (art, music, dance, drama), computer science, English, foreign language, mathematics, physical education (includes health), religion (includes Bible studies and theology), science, social studies (includes history). Community service is required.

Special Academic Programs Advanced Placement exam preparation in 17 subject areas; honors section; independent study.

College Placement 101 students graduated in 2005; all went to college, including Georgetown University; University of California, Los Angeles; University of California, Santa Barbara; University of Southern California; University of Washington; University of Wisconsin–Madison. Mean SAT verbal: 627, mean SAT math: 604. 63% scored over 600 on SAT verbal, 58% scored over 600 on SAT math.

Student Life Upper grades have uniform requirement, student council, honor system. Discipline rests primarily with faculty. Attendance at religious services is required.

Summer Programs Remediation, enrichment, advancement, sports, art/fine arts, computer instruction programs offered; session focuses on enrichment, advancement; held on campus; accepts boys and girls; open to students from other schools. 165 students usually enrolled. 2006 schedule: June 19 to July 21. Application deadline: May 15.

Tuition and Aid Day student tuition: $19,600. Tuition installment plan (Insured Tuition Payment Plan, FACTS Tuition Payment Plan). Merit scholarship grants, need-based scholarship grants available. In 2005–06, 22% of upper-school students received aid; total upper-school merit-scholarship money awarded: $20,000. Total amount of financial aid awarded in 2005–06: $824,130.

Admissions Traditional secondary-level entrance grade is 9. For fall 2005, 229 students applied for upper-level admission, 151 were accepted, 105 enrolled. ISEE required. Deadline for receipt of application materials: January 15. Application fee required: $100. Interview required.

Athletics Interscholastic: aerobics, basketball, cross-country running, equestrian sports, fencing, golf, soccer, softball, swimming and diving, tennis, track and field, volleyball, water polo; intramural: aerobics/dance, archery, crew, dance, physical fitness, self defense, strength & conditioning. 4 PE instructors, 21 coaches, 1 trainer.

Computers Computers are regularly used in all academic, yearbook classes. Computer network features include campus e-mail, on-campus library services, CD-ROMs, online commercial services, Internet access, file transfer, office computer

access, DVD, access to UCLA Library, Loyola Marymount University Library, 14 independent high school libraries, Intranet.

Contact Sally Helin, Associate Director of Admission. 310-472-1205 Ext. 306. Fax: 310-440-4316. E-mail: shelin@mhs-la.org. Web site: www.mhs-la.org.

ANNOUNCEMENT FROM THE SCHOOL Marymount High School, a Catholic, independent, college-preparatory day school established in 1923 by the Religious of the Sacred Heart of Mary (RSHM), shares the tradition of an international network of schools dedicated to the education of young women. Marymount maintains a philosophy deeply rooted in the RSHM mission of educating the heart and mind to prepare young women to make a better world. A hallmark of a Marymount education is a highly personalized, student-centered program. Each year, 100% of Marymount graduates are admitted to selective colleges and universities.

MARYMOUNT INTERNATIONAL SCHOOL

Via di Villa Lauchli, 180
Rome 00191, Italy
Head of School: Dr. Yvonne Hennigan

General Information Coeducational day college-preparatory school, affiliated with Roman Catholic Church. Grades PK–12. Founded: 1946. Setting: suburban. 16-acre campus. 3 buildings on campus. Approved or accredited by European Council of International Schools and New England Association of Schools and Colleges. Language of instruction: English. Total enrollment: 753. Upper school average class size: 18. Upper school faculty-student ratio: 1:15.

Upper School Student Profile Grade 9: 63 students (30 boys, 33 girls); Grade 10: 46 students (25 boys, 21 girls); Grade 11: 43 students (15 boys, 28 girls); Grade 12: 58 students (32 boys, 26 girls). 75% of students are Roman Catholic.

Faculty School total: 98. In upper school: 14 men, 28 women; 32 have advanced degrees.

Subjects Offered Algebra, American history, American literature, art, art history, art history-AP, arts, biology, calculus, ceramics, chemistry, computer programming, computer science, drama, English, English literature, environmental science, ESL, European history, fine arts, French, geometry, health, history, International Baccalaureate courses, international relations, Italian, mathematics, music, photography, physical education, physics, pre-calculus, religion, science, social studies, Spanish, study skills, theology, theory of knowledge, trigonometry, world history.

Graduation Requirements Arts and fine arts (art, music, dance, drama), English, foreign language, mathematics, physical education (includes health), religion (includes Bible studies and theology), science, social studies (includes history).

Special Academic Programs International Baccalaureate program; Advanced Placement exam preparation in 1 subject area); ESL (20 students enrolled).

College Placement 48 students graduated in 2005; 46 went to college, including Indiana University of Pennsylvania; New York University; Reed College; The College of William and Mary; Wheaton College. Other: 1 went to work, 1 entered a postgraduate year. Median SAT verbal: 500, median SAT math: 550. 8% scored over 600 on SAT verbal, 10% scored over 600 on SAT math.

Student Life Upper grades have specified standards of dress, student council, honor system. Discipline rests primarily with faculty. Attendance at religious services is required.

Tuition and Aid Day student tuition: €14,000.

Admissions Traditional secondary-level entrance grade is 9. For fall 2005, 40 students applied for upper-level admission, 35 were accepted, 29 enrolled. Deadline for receipt of application materials: none. Application fee required: €350. On-campus interview recommended.

Athletics Interscholastic: basketball (boys, girls), cheering (g), cross-country running (b,g), soccer (b,g), tennis (b,g), track and field (b,g), volleyball (b,g); intramural: basketball (b,g), soccer (b,g), table tennis (b,g), volleyball (b,g). 2 PE instructors, 9 coaches.

Computers Computers are regularly used in graphic arts classes. Computer network features include campus e-mail, on-campus library services, CD-ROMs, Internet access, DVD, wireless campus network.

Contact Ms. Deborah Woods, Admissions Director. 39-063629101 Ext. 212. Fax: 39-36301738. E-mail: admissions@marymountrome.org. Web site: www.marymountrome.org.

MARYMOUNT INTERNATIONAL SCHOOL

George Road
Kingston upon Thames
Surrey KT2 7PE, United Kingdom
Head of School: Sr. Kathleen Fagan, RSHM

General Information Girls' boarding and day college-preparatory, general academic, arts, religious studies, and International Baccalaureate school, affiliated with Roman Catholic Church. Grades 6–12. Founded: 1955. Setting: suburban. Nearest major city is London. Students are housed in single-sex dormitories. 7-acre campus.

9 buildings on campus. Approved or accredited by European Council of International Schools, Independent Schools Council (UK), International Baccalaureate Organization, and Middle States Association of Colleges and Schools. Member of Secondary School Admission Test Board. Language of instruction: English. Total enrollment: 217. Upper school average class size: 12. Upper school faculty-student ratio: 1:7.

Upper School Student Profile Grade 9: 27 students (27 girls); Grade 10: 47 students (47 girls); Grade 11: 47 students (47 girls); Grade 12: 46 students (46 girls). 68% of students are boarding students. 60% are international students. International students from China, Germany, Japan, Republic of Korea, Spain, and United States; 42 other countries represented in student body. 30% of students are Roman Catholic.

Faculty School total: 37. In upper school: 10 men, 27 women; 12 have advanced degrees; 1 resides on campus.

Subjects Offered Algebra, art, biology, chemistry, Chinese literature, creative writing, drama, economics, English, English literature, ESL, European history, French, general science, geography, German, German literature, history, information technology, Japanese as Second Language, Japanese literature, mathematics, music, personal and social education, physical education, physics, religion, Spanish, theater, theory of knowledge, world history, world literature.

Graduation Requirements English, foreign language, mathematics, physical education (includes health), religion (includes Bible studies and theology), science, social studies (includes history).

Special Academic Programs International Baccalaureate program; independent study; ESL (26 students enrolled).

College Placement 48 students graduated in 2005; 43 went to college, including Parsons The New School for Design. Other: 5 had other specific plans. Mean SAT verbal: 503, mean SAT math: 541. 7% scored over 600 on SAT verbal, 27% scored over 600 on SAT math.

Student Life Upper grades have uniform requirement, student council, honor system. Discipline rests primarily with faculty. Attendance at religious services is required.

Tuition and Aid Day student tuition: £12,350–£13,750; 5-day tuition and room/board: £20,650–£22,050; 7-day tuition and room/board: £21,750–£23,150. Tuition installment plan (2 semester payments). Tuition reduction for siblings, merit scholarship grants, need-based scholarship grants available. In 2005–06, 5% of upper-school students received aid.

Admissions Traditional secondary-level entrance grade is 10. For fall 2005, 64 students applied for upper-level admission, 50 were accepted, 48 enrolled. English proficiency required. Deadline for receipt of application materials: none. Application fee required: £100. Interview recommended.

Athletics Interscholastic: badminton, basketball, cross-country running, football, softball, tennis, volleyball; intramural: badminton, tennis. 2 PE instructors.

Computers Computers are regularly used in all academic, information technology classes. Computer network features include campus e-mail, CD-ROMs, Internet access, wireless campus network.

Contact Sr. Kathleen Fagan, RSHM, Headmistress. 44-(0) 20 8949 0571. Fax: 44-(0) 20 8336 2485. E-mail: headmistress@marymountlondon.com. Web site: www.marymountlondon.com.

MARYMOUNT SCHOOL

1026 Fifth Avenue
New York, New York 10028
Head of School: Concepcion Alvar, EdD

General Information Coeducational day (boys' only in lower grades) college-preparatory, arts, religious studies, and technology school, affiliated with Roman Catholic Church. Boys grades N–PK, girls grades N–12. Founded: 1926. Setting: urban. 3 buildings on campus. Approved or accredited by New York State Association of Independent Schools. Member of National Association of Independent Schools. Endowment: $4.6 million. Total enrollment: 544. Upper school average class size: 15. Upper school faculty-student ratio: 1:16.

Upper School Student Profile Grade 8: 38 students (38 girls); Grade 9: 50 students (50 girls); Grade 10: 48 students (48 girls); Grade 11: 47 students (47 girls); Grade 12: 43 students (43 girls). 65% of students are Roman Catholic.

Faculty School total: 80. In upper school: 6 men, 40 women; 37 have advanced degrees.

Subjects Offered Algebra, American history, American literature, art, art history, astronomy, Bible studies, biology, calculus, chemistry, chorus, community service, computer science, economics, English, English literature, ethics, European history, fine arts, French, geometry, Greek, health, Latin, mathematics, music, physics, political science, religion, science, Spanish, speech, statistics, trigonometry, world history, world literature, writing.

Graduation Requirements Arts and fine arts (art, music, dance, drama), computer science, English, foreign language, history, mathematics, physical education (includes health), religion (includes Bible studies and theology), science, speech, senior internships, senior seminars, Class XII Retreat. Community service is required.

Special Academic Programs Advanced Placement exam preparation in 18 subject areas; honors section; study abroad; academic accommodation for the gifted.

College Placement 48 students graduated in 2005; all went to college, including Boston University; Cornell University; Fordham University; Harvard University; Vanderbilt University. Median SAT verbal: 630, median SAT math: 600. 73% scored over 600 on SAT verbal, 54% scored over 600 on SAT math.

Marymount School

Student Life Upper grades have uniform requirement, student council, honor system. Discipline rests primarily with faculty. Attendance at religious services is required.
Summer Programs Advancement, art/fine arts programs offered; session focuses on middle school performing arts and middle school science and technology; held on campus; accepts boys and girls; open to students from other schools. 2006 schedule: June 19 to July 21. Application deadline: April 14.
Tuition and Aid Day student tuition: $24,100. Tuition installment plan (Key Tuition Payment Plan). Need-based scholarship grants available. In 2005–06, 19% of upper-school students received aid. Total amount of financial aid awarded in 2005–06: $1,360,000.
Admissions Traditional secondary-level entrance grade is 9. ISEE or SSAT required. Deadline for receipt of application materials: December 15. Application fee required: $60. On-campus interview required.
Athletics Interscholastic: badminton, basketball, cross-country running, fencing, field hockey, soccer, softball, swimming and diving, tennis, track and field, volleyball; intramural: aerobics, badminton, basketball, bicycling, cross-country running, dance, fitness, gymnastics, lacrosse, martial arts, modern dance, outdoor adventure, physical fitness, soccer, softball, volleyball, yoga. 3 PE instructors, 28 coaches, 1 trainer.
Computers Computers are regularly used in all classes. Computer network features include campus e-mail, on-campus library services, CD-ROMs, Internet access.
Contact Lillian Issa, Director of Admissions. 212-744-4486 Ext. 152. Fax: 212-744-0163. E-mail: lillian_issa@marymount.k12.ny.us. Web site: www.marymount.k12.ny.us.

See full description on page 896.

MARYVALE PREPARATORY SCHOOL

11300 Falls Road
Brooklandville, Maryland 21022
Head of School: Sr. Shawn Marie Maguire, SND

General Information Girls' day college-preparatory school, affiliated with Roman Catholic Church. Grades 6–12. Founded: 1945. Setting: suburban. Nearest major city is Baltimore. 113-acre campus. 3 buildings on campus. Approved or accredited by Association of Independent Maryland Schools, Middle States Association of Colleges and Schools, National Catholic Education Association, and Maryland Department of Education. Member of National Association of Independent Schools. Endowment: $1 million. Total enrollment: 371. Upper school average class size: 15. Upper school faculty-student ratio: 1:9.
Upper School Student Profile Grade 9: 77 students (77 girls); Grade 10: 61 students (61 girls); Grade 11: 69 students (69 girls); Grade 12: 59 students (59 girls). 80% of students are Roman Catholic.
Faculty School total: 41. In upper school: 4 men, 27 women; 25 have advanced degrees.
Subjects Offered Algebra, American history, American literature, anatomy and physiology, art, art history, band, biology, biology-AP, British literature (honors), calculus, calculus-AP, chemistry, chorus, college writing, community service, computer math, computer programming, computer science, current events, digital photography, drama, economics, English, English literature, English literature-AP, forensic science, French, French-AP, geography, geometry, grammar, health, history, Holocaust, honors algebra, honors English, honors U.S. history, honors world history, journalism, keyboarding, Latin, literary magazine, marine biology, mathematics, model United Nations, music, newspaper, physical education, physics, pre-algebra, pre-calculus, public speaking, religion, research, science, Shakespeare, social studies, Spanish, Spanish-AP, speech, statistics, theater, theology, trigonometry, U.S. history-AP, Web site design, world history, world literature, writing, yearbook.
Graduation Requirements Arts and fine arts (art, music, dance, drama), computer science, English, foreign language, mathematics, physical education (includes health), religion (includes Bible studies and theology), science, social studies (includes history). Community service is required.
Special Academic Programs Advanced Placement exam preparation in 6 subject areas; honors section; accelerated programs.
College Placement 62 students graduated in 2005; all went to college, including James Madison University; Loyola College in Maryland; Saint Joseph's University; University of Maryland, College Park; Virginia Polytechnic Institute and State University. Mean SAT verbal: 615, mean SAT math: 579. 55% scored over 600 on SAT verbal, 55% scored over 600 on SAT math, 23% scored over 26 on composite ACT.
Student Life Upper grades have uniform requirement, student council, honor system. Discipline rests equally with students and faculty. Attendance at religious services is required.
Tuition and Aid Day student tuition: $12,400. Tuition installment plan (Academic Management Services Plan). Bursaries, need-based scholarship grants available. In 2005–06, 18% of upper-school students received aid. Total amount of financial aid awarded in 2005–06: $247,100.
Admissions Traditional secondary-level entrance grade is 9. For fall 2005, 174 students applied for upper-level admission, 113 were accepted, 51 enrolled. High School Placement Test and ISEE required. Deadline for receipt of application materials: January 6. Application fee required: $50. On-campus interview required.

Athletics Interscholastic: basketball, cross-country running, field hockey, indoor soccer, indoor track, indoor track & field, lacrosse, physical fitness, soccer, softball, volleyball, winter soccer, yoga. 3 PE instructors, 9 coaches.
Computers Computers are regularly used in all academic classes. Computer network features include campus e-mail, on-campus library services, CD-ROMs, online commercial services, Internet access, file transfer, office computer access, DVD, wireless campus network.
Contact Monica C. Graham, Director of Admissions. 410-560-3243. Fax: 410-561-1826. E-mail: grahamm@maryvale.com. Web site: www.maryvale.com.

MASSANUTTEN MILITARY ACADEMY

614 South Main Street
Woodstock, Virginia 22664
Head of School: Col. Roy F. Zinser Jr.

General Information Coeducational boarding and day college-preparatory and arts school, affiliated with Christian faith. Grades 7–PG. Founded: 1899. Setting: small town. Nearest major city is Washington, DC. Students are housed in single-sex dormitories. 44-acre campus. 11 buildings on campus. Approved or accredited by Southern Association of Colleges and Schools, The Association of Boarding Schools, Virginia Association of Independent Schools, and Virginia Department of Education. Endowment: $11 million. Total enrollment: 194. Upper school average class size: 10. Upper school faculty-student ratio: 1:8.
Upper School Student Profile Grade 9: 29 students (19 boys, 10 girls); Grade 10: 33 students (25 boys, 8 girls); Grade 11: 51 students (38 boys, 13 girls); Grade 12: 47 students (33 boys, 14 girls); Postgraduate: 9 students (9 boys). 99% of students are boarding students. 41% are state residents. 23 states are represented in upper school student body. 11% are international students. International students from Cameroon, Netherlands, and Republic of Korea; 3 other countries represented in student body.
Faculty School total: 27. In upper school: 19 men, 8 women; 8 have advanced degrees; 6 reside on campus.
Subjects Offered Algebra, American history, American literature, art, art appreciation, band, biology, calculus, character education, chemistry, computer applications, criminal justice, earth science, English, English literature, equestrian sports, ESL, French, geometry, government/civics, grammar, health, history, Internet research, intro to computers, introduction to literature, JROTC, leadership training, mathematics, music, news writing, physical education, physical science, physics, pre-calculus, science, social science, social studies, Spanish, U.S. history, world history, world literature, writing.
Graduation Requirements Arts and fine arts (art, music, dance, drama), computer applications, English, foreign language, JROTC, mathematics, physical education (includes health), science, social studies (includes history).
Special Academic Programs Advanced Placement exam preparation in 1 subject area; independent study; study at local college for college credit; remedial reading and/or remedial writing; remedial math; ESL (6 students enrolled).
College Placement 36 students graduated in 2005; all went to college, including George Mason University; Mary Baldwin College; Radford University; The Citadel, The Military College of South Carolina; University of Georgia; Virginia Polytechnic Institute and State University. Median SAT verbal: 470, median SAT math: 520, median composite ACT: 20. 10% scored over 600 on SAT verbal, 7% scored over 600 on SAT math, 10% scored over 26 on composite ACT.
Student Life Upper grades have uniform requirement, student council, honor system. Discipline rests equally with students and faculty. Attendance at religious services is required.
Summer Programs Remediation, advancement, ESL, sports, computer instruction programs offered; session focuses on academics; only summer JROTC program in nation; held on campus; accepts boys and girls; open to students from other schools. 175 students usually enrolled. 2006 schedule: June 24 to July 29. Application deadline: June 21.
Tuition and Aid Day student tuition: $12,750; 7-day tuition and room/board: $20,710. Tuition installment plan (SMART Tuition Payment Plan, FACTS Tuition Payment Plan, monthly payment plans, individually arranged payment plans). Tuition reduction for siblings, need-based scholarship grants, need-based loans, USS Education Loan Program, PLATO Loans, legacy discounts available. In 2005–06, 50% of upper-school students received aid. Total amount of financial aid awarded in 2005–06: $46,000.
Admissions Traditional secondary-level entrance grade is 11. For fall 2005, 109 students applied for upper-level admission, 90 were accepted, 81 enrolled. Deadline for receipt of application materials: none. Application fee required: $50. Interview required.
Athletics Interscholastic: baseball (boys), basketball (b,g), cross-country running (b,g), fitness (b,g), football (b), independent competitive sports (b,g), lacrosse (b), softball (g), strength & conditioning (b), swimming and diving (b,g), tennis (b,g), track and field (b,g), volleyball (g), wrestling (b); intramural: aerobics (g), aerobics/nautilus (g), strength & conditioning (g); coed interscholastic: golf, JROTC drill, marksmanship, pistol, riflery, soccer; coed intramural: aquatics, back packing, billiards, canoeing/kayaking, climbing, cross-country running, dressage, drill team, equestrian sports, hiking/backpacking, horseback riding, jogging, kickball, marksmanship, mountaineering, outdoor activities, outdoor adventure, outdoor education, outdoor recreation, outdoor skills, outdoors, paddle tennis, paint ball, physical fitness, physical

training, pistol, power lifting, project adventure, rafting, rappelling, riflery, running, skiing (downhill), snowboarding, snowshoeing, soccer, swimming and diving, table tennis, tennis, walking, water polo, weight lifting, weight training, whiffle ball, wilderness, wilderness survival, winter walking. 2 PE instructors, 5 coaches, 1 trainer.
Computers Computers are regularly used in business applications, business skills, business studies, computer applications, journalism, JROTC, SAT preparation, yearbook classes. Computer network features include campus e-mail, on-campus library services, CD-ROMs, Internet access, office computer access, DVD, wireless campus network.
Contact Mr. Murray Sinnathamby, Director of Admissions. 540-459-2167 Ext. 262. Fax: 540-459-5421. E-mail: admissions@militaryschool.com. Web site: www.militaryschool.com.

ANNOUNCEMENT FROM THE SCHOOL MMA was founded in 1899 in Woodstock, Virginia. Massanutten attracts students from all over the world who desire advanced preparation for college in a structured environment. Situated in a small town on 40 acres in the heart of the Shenandoah Valley, the Academy is only 90 minutes from downtown Washington, DC.

See full description on page 898.

THE MASTERS SCHOOL

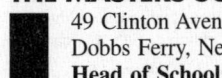

49 Clinton Avenue
Dobbs Ferry, New York 10522
Head of School: Dr. Maureen Fonseca

petersons.com

General Information Coeducational boarding and day college-preparatory and arts school. Boarding grades 9–12, day grades 5–12. Founded: 1877. Setting: suburban. Nearest major city is New York. Students are housed in single-sex dormitories. 96-acre campus. 10 buildings on campus. Approved or accredited by Middle States Association of Colleges and Schools, New York State Association of Independent Schools, The Association of Boarding Schools, and New York Department of Education. Member of National Association of Independent Schools and Secondary School Admission Test Board. Endowment: $20 million. Total enrollment: 540. Upper school average class size: 14. Upper school faculty-student ratio: 1:6.
Upper School Student Profile Grade 9: 85 students (37 boys, 48 girls); Grade 10: 91 students (45 boys, 46 girls); Grade 11: 123 students (51 boys, 72 girls); Grade 12: 103 students (54 boys, 49 girls). 36% of students are boarding students. 75% are state residents. 15 states are represented in upper school student body. 17% are international students. International students from China, Germany, Jamaica, Japan, Republic of Korea, and Taiwan; 11 other countries represented in student body.
Faculty School total: 70. In upper school: 28 men, 42 women; 49 have advanced degrees; 47 reside on campus.
Subjects Offered Acting, algebra, American history, American literature, art, art history, biology, biology-AP, calculus, calculus-AP, ceramics, chemistry, chemistry-AP, computer math, computer programming, computer science, creative writing, dance, drama, driver education, earth science, electronics, English, English language-AP, English literature, English literature-AP, environmental science, ESL, ethics, European history, European history-AP, expository writing, fine arts, French, French language-AP, French literature-AP, geography, geometry, grammar, health, health and wellness, health education, jazz, jazz band, journalism, Latin, Latin-AP, mathematics, meteorology, music, music theory-AP, performing arts, photography, physical education, physics, physics-AP, pre-calculus, religion, science, senior thesis, social studies, Spanish, Spanish language-AP, Spanish literature-AP, speech, statistics, statistics-AP, studio art, studio art—AP, theater, trigonometry, U.S. history, U.S. history-AP, world history, world literature, world religions, writing, writing, yearbook.
Graduation Requirements Arts, arts and fine arts (art, music, dance, drama), computer science, English, foreign language, mathematics, physical education (includes health), science, speech, U.S. history, world history, world religions.
Special Academic Programs Advanced Placement exam preparation in 17 subject areas; honors section; independent study; term-away projects; study abroad; academic accommodation for the gifted, the musically talented, and the artistically talented; ESL (29 students enrolled).
College Placement 80 students graduated in 2005; 77 went to college, including Barnard College; Franklin and Marshall College; New York University; Northeastern University; The Johns Hopkins University; Wesleyan University. Other: 2 went to work, 1 had other specific plans. Mean SAT verbal: 625, mean SAT math: 610. 59% scored over 600 on SAT verbal, 53% scored over 600 on SAT math.
Student Life Upper grades have specified standards of dress, student council. Discipline rests equally with students and faculty.
Tuition and Aid Day student tuition: $24,650; 7-day tuition and room/board: $33,950. Tuition installment plan (Key Tuition Payment Plan). Need-based scholarship grants available. In 2005–06, 28% of upper-school students received aid. Total amount of financial aid awarded in 2005–06: $2,336,800.
Admissions Traditional secondary-level entrance grade is 9. For fall 2005, 441 students applied for upper-level admission, 185 were accepted, 100 enrolled. ISEE or SSAT required. Deadline for receipt of application materials: January 5. Application fee required: $50. Interview required.

Athletics Interscholastic: baseball (boys), basketball (b,g), cross-country running (b,g), fencing (b,g), field hockey (g), lacrosse (b,g), soccer (b,g), softball (g), tennis (b,g), volleyball (g); coed interscholastic: dance, nautilus; coed intramural: aerobics, aerobics/dance, aerobics/nautilus, ballet, fitness, Frisbee, martial arts, modern dance, outdoor activities, physical fitness, physical training, strength & conditioning, ultimate Frisbee, yoga. 2 PE instructors, 13 coaches, 1 trainer.
Computers Computers are regularly used in English, foreign language, history, mathematics, science classes. Computer network features include campus e-mail, on-campus library services, CD-ROMs, online commercial services, Internet access.
Contact Office of Admission. 914-479-6420. Fax: 914-693-7295. E-mail: admission@themastersschool.com. Web site: www.themastersschool.com.

ANNOUNCEMENT FROM THE SCHOOL With nearly half boarding and half day in the Upper School, The Masters School opened in fall 2005 with a record enrollment of 540 students. The School continues its commitment to character, athletics, service, academic rigor, and the arts. These values permeate the academic day, the cocurricular activities, and the residential program.

See full description on page 900.

MATER DEI HIGH SCHOOL

1300 Harmony Way
Evansville, Indiana 47720-6199
Head of School: Anne Marie Williams, PhD

General Information Coeducational day college-preparatory, arts, business, religious studies, and technology school, affiliated with Roman Catholic Church. Grades 9–12. Founded: 1948. Setting: urban. 25-acre campus. 2 buildings on campus. Approved or accredited by National Christian School Association, North Central Association of Colleges and Schools, and Indiana Department of Education. Total enrollment: 598. Upper school average class size: 25. Upper school faculty-student ratio: 1:15.
Upper School Student Profile Grade 9: 147 students (79 boys, 68 girls); Grade 10: 151 students (86 boys, 65 girls); Grade 11: 131 students (72 boys, 59 girls); Grade 12: 169 students (87 boys, 82 girls). 98% of students are Roman Catholic.
Faculty School total: 40. In upper school: 18 men, 21 women; 28 have advanced degrees.
Graduation Requirements Service hours to church and community.
Special Academic Programs Advanced Placement exam preparation in 3 subject areas; honors section; study at local college for college credit; programs in English, mathematics for dyslexic students; special instructional classes for students with LD, ADD, emotional and behavioral problems.
College Placement 130 students graduated in 2005; 118 went to college, including Western Kentucky University. Other: 12 went to work. Median SAT math: 514, median combined SAT: 1023, median composite ACT: 23.
Student Life Upper grades have uniform requirement, student council, honor system. Discipline rests primarily with faculty. Attendance at religious services is required.
Tuition and Aid Need-based scholarship grants available. In 2005–06, 25% of upper-school students received aid.
Admissions Traditional secondary-level entrance grade is 9. For fall 2005, 598 students applied for upper-level admission, 598 were accepted, 598 enrolled. Deadline for receipt of application materials: none. Application fee required: $140. Interview recommended.
Athletics Interscholastic: baseball (boys), basketball (b,g), cheering (g), cross-country running (b,g), dance squad (g), football (b), golf (b,g), soccer (b,g), softball (g), swimming and diving (b,g), tennis (b,g), track and field (b,g), volleyball (g), weight training (b,g), wrestling (b); coed interscholastic: bowling.
Computers Computer network features include campus e-mail, on-campus library services, CD-ROMs, Internet access, file transfer, DVD, wireless campus network.
Contact Admissions. 812-426-2258. Fax: 812-421-5717. E-mail: materdeiwildcats@evansville.net.

MATIGNON HIGH SCHOOL

1 Matignon Road
Cambridge, Massachusetts 02140
Head of School: Donald Dabenigno

General Information Coeducational day college-preparatory, arts, business, religious studies, and technology school, affiliated with Roman Catholic Church. Grades 9–12. Founded: 1945. Setting: urban. Nearest major city is Boston. 10-acre campus. 3 buildings on campus. Approved or accredited by Association of Independent Schools in New England, National Catholic Education Association, New England Association of Schools and Colleges, and Massachusetts Department of Education. Endowment: $250,000. Total enrollment: 345. Upper school average class size: 20. Upper school faculty-student ratio: 1:15.
Upper School Student Profile Grade 9: 95 students (35 boys, 60 girls); Grade 10: 55 students (20 boys, 35 girls); Grade 11: 80 students (35 boys, 45 girls); Grade 12: 115 students (55 boys, 60 girls). 75% of students are Roman Catholic.

Matignon High School

Faculty School total: 28. In upper school: 10 men, 15 women; 10 have advanced degrees.

Subjects Offered 3-dimensional art, 3-dimensional design, accounting, adolescent issues, Advanced Placement courses, algebra, American history, American literature, anatomy and physiology, art, art history, Bible studies, biology, business, calculus, chemistry, community service, computer programming, computer science, desktop publishing, drawing and design, economics, English, English literature, environmental science, fine arts, French, geography, geology, geometry, government/civics, grammar, health, history, keyboarding, Latin, mathematics, microeconomics, photography, physical education, physics, programming, psychology, religion, science, social science, social studies, Spanish, theology, trigonometry, world history, writing.

Graduation Requirements Arts and fine arts (art, music, dance, drama), computer science, English, foreign language, mathematics, physical education (includes health), religion (includes Bible studies and theology), science, social science, social studies (includes history), Christian service, thirty hours of community service (before junior year).

Special Academic Programs Advanced Placement exam preparation in 6 subject areas; honors section; independent study; study at local college for college credit; study abroad.

College Placement 121 students graduated in 2005; 114 went to college, including Curry College; Merrimack College; Providence College; Suffolk University; Tufts University; University of Massachusetts Amherst. Other: 4 went to work, 2 entered military service, 1 had other specific plans. 10% scored over 600 on SAT verbal, 10% scored over 600 on SAT math.

Student Life Upper grades have uniform requirement, student council, honor system. Discipline rests primarily with faculty. Attendance at religious services is required.

Summer Programs Remediation, enrichment programs offered; held on campus; accepts boys and girls; open to students from other schools. 80 students usually enrolled. 2006 schedule: June 26 to July 26. Application deadline: June 23.

Tuition and Aid Day student tuition: $7300. Tuition installment plan (FACTS Tuition Payment Plan, monthly payment plans). Merit scholarship grants, need-based scholarship grants available. In 2005–06, 50% of upper-school students received aid; total upper-school merit-scholarship money awarded: $150,000. Total amount of financial aid awarded in 2005–06: $200,000.

Admissions Traditional secondary-level entrance grade is 9. For fall 2005, 450 students applied for upper-level admission, 270 were accepted, 95 enrolled. Archdiocese of Boston High School entrance exam provided by STS, Catholic High School Entrance Examination, English proficiency, SSAT or TOEFL or SLEP required. Deadline for receipt of application materials: none. Application fee required: $25. On-campus interview recommended.

Athletics Interscholastic: baseball (boys), basketball (b,g), cheering (g), cross-country running (b,g), football (b), golf (b,g), ice hockey (b,g), lacrosse (b,g), physical training (b,g), soccer (b,g), softball (g), swimming and diving (b,g), track and field (b,g), volleyball (g); intramural: aerobics/dance (b,g), dance squad (g). 2 PE instructors, 15 coaches, 1 trainer.

Computers Computers are regularly used in all academic classes. Computer network features include campus e-mail, on-campus library services, CD-ROMs, Internet access.

Contact Mr. Kevin J. Driscoll, Director of Admissions. 617-876-1212 Ext. 11. Fax: 617-491-0290. E-mail: admissions@matignon-hs.org. Web site: www.matignon-hs.org.

MAUMEE VALLEY COUNTRY DAY SCHOOL

1715 South Reynolds Road
Toledo, Ohio 43614-1499
Head of School: Hiram Goza

General Information Coeducational day college-preparatory and arts school. Grades N–12. Founded: 1884. Setting: suburban. 70-acre campus. 4 buildings on campus. Approved or accredited by Independent Schools Association of the Central States and Ohio Department of Education. Member of National Association of Independent Schools. Endowment: $7.2 million. Total enrollment: 465. Upper school average class size: 10. Upper school faculty-student ratio: 1:10.

Upper School Student Profile Grade 9: 43 students (18 boys, 25 girls); Grade 10: 46 students (15 boys, 31 girls); Grade 11: 38 students (19 boys, 19 girls); Grade 12: 44 students (24 boys, 20 girls).

Faculty School total: 55. In upper school: 14 men, 8 women; 17 have advanced degrees.

Subjects Offered Algebra, American government, American history, anthropology, art, biology, biology-AP, calculus-AP, chemistry, choir, computer graphics, computer science, creative writing, design, drama, earth science, ecology, English, environmental science, European history, expository writing, fine arts, French, geology, geometry, government/civics, grammar, health, history, human development, humanities, mathematics, microbiology, music, physical education, physics, science, social studies, Spanish, Spanish-AP, speech, statistics, statistics-AP, theater, trigonometry, women's studies, world history.

Graduation Requirements American government, arts and fine arts (art, music, dance, drama), English, foreign language, mathematics, physical education (includes health), science, social studies (includes history). Community service is required.

Special Academic Programs Advanced Placement exam preparation in 9 subject areas; honors section; independent study; term-away projects; study at local college for college credit; domestic exchange program (with The Athenian School, The Network Program Schools); study abroad; academic accommodation for the gifted, the musically talented, and the artistically talented; ESL (1 student enrolled).

College Placement 39 students graduated in 2005; all went to college, including Oberlin College; The Ohio State University; University of Michigan. Mean SAT verbal: 633, mean SAT math: 612. 50% scored over 600 on SAT verbal, 50% scored over 600 on SAT math.

Student Life Upper grades have specified standards of dress, student council, honor system. Discipline rests equally with students and faculty.

Summer Programs Enrichment, sports, art/fine arts, computer instruction programs offered; session focuses on day camp and sports camps; held on campus; accepts boys and girls; open to students from other schools. 350 students usually enrolled. 2006 schedule: June 14 to August 15. Application deadline: May 15.

Tuition and Aid Day student tuition: $9450–$12,450. Tuition installment plan (Key Tuition Payment Plan, SMART Tuition Payment Plan, monthly payment plans, individually arranged payment plans). Merit scholarship grants, need-based scholarship grants available. In 2005–06, 30% of upper-school students received aid; total upper-school merit-scholarship money awarded: $104,000. Total amount of financial aid awarded in 2005–06: $308,150.

Admissions Traditional secondary-level entrance grade is 9. For fall 2005, 43 students applied for upper-level admission, 28 were accepted, 20 enrolled. Brigance Test of Basic Skills, ERB—verbal abilities, reading comprehension, quantitative abilities (level F, form 1), Otis-Lennon Ability or Stanford Achievement Test, Otis-Lennon and 2 sections of ERB or Slosson Intelligence required. Deadline for receipt of application materials: none. Application fee required: $45. On-campus interview required.

Athletics Interscholastic: baseball (boys), basketball (b,g), cheering (b,g), cross-country running (b,g), field hockey (g), golf (b,g), soccer (b,g), swimming and diving (g), tennis (b,g), track and field (b,g); intramural: indoor soccer (g), lacrosse (g); coed intramural: strength & conditioning, weight training. 3 PE instructors, 10 coaches, 1 trainer.

Computers Computers are regularly used in English, foreign language, graphic design, history, information technology, library skills, literary magazine, mathematics, music, newspaper, science, yearbook classes. Computer network features include campus e-mail, on-campus library services, CD-ROMs, online commercial services, Internet access, DVD, wireless campus network.

Contact Nancy Linker, Admissions Officer, Director of Financial Aid. 419-381-1313 Ext. 3082. Fax: 419-381-9941. E-mail: nlinker@mvcds.net. Web site: www.mvcds.org.

MAUR HILL-MOUNT ACADEMY

1000 Green Street
Atchison, Kansas 66002
Head of School: Mr. Russell Norris

General Information Coeducational boarding and day college-preparatory, arts, religious studies, and English as a Second language school, affiliated with Roman Catholic Church. Grades 9–12. Founded: 1863. Setting: small town. Nearest major city is Kansas City, MO. Students are housed in single-sex dormitories. 150-acre campus. 7 buildings on campus. Approved or accredited by North Central Association of Colleges and Schools, The Association of Boarding Schools, and Kansas Department of Education. Member of Secondary School Admission Test Board. Endowment: $100,000. Total enrollment: 238. Upper school average class size: 22. Upper school faculty-student ratio: 1:8.

Upper School Student Profile Grade 9: 63 students (29 boys, 34 girls); Grade 10: 55 students (34 boys, 21 girls); Grade 11: 66 students (42 boys, 24 girls); Grade 12: 54 students (27 boys, 27 girls). 40% of students are boarding students. 50% are state residents. 12 states are represented in upper school student body. 25% are international students. International students from India, Japan, Mexico, Pakistan, Republic of Korea, and Taiwan; 7 other countries represented in student body. 82% of students are Roman Catholic.

Faculty School total: 24. In upper school: 10 men, 8 women; 5 have advanced degrees; 1 resides on campus.

Subjects Offered Algebra, American history, American literature, anatomy, art, basketball, Bible studies, biology, business, business skills, calculus, chemistry, computer math, computer programming, computer science, current events, drama, economics, English, English literature, ESL, ethics, fine arts, French, geography, geometry, government/civics, grammar, health, history, humanities, journalism, mathematics, music, photography, physical education, physics, physiology, psychology, religion, science, social science, social studies, sociology, Spanish, speech, theater, theology, trigonometry, typing, world history, world literature, writing.

Graduation Requirements Arts and fine arts (art, music, dance, drama), business skills (includes word processing), computer science, English, foreign language, mathematics, physical education (includes health), religion (includes Bible studies and theology), science, social science, social studies (includes history).

Special Academic Programs Honors section; study at local college for college credit; special instructional classes for students with Attention Deficit Disorder; ESL (15 students enrolled).

College Placement 48 students graduated in 2005; all went to college, including Benedictine College; Creighton University; Washburn University.

Student Life Upper grades have uniform requirement, student council, honor system. Discipline rests primarily with faculty.

Summer Programs Session focuses on activities camp/ESL program; held on campus; accepts boys and girls; open to students from other schools. 2006 schedule: July 10 to August 4. Application deadline: May 10.

Tuition and Aid Day student tuition: $4000; 5-day tuition and room/board: $14,500; 7-day tuition and room/board: $16,250. Tuition installment plan (Academic Management Services Plan). Tuition reduction for siblings, merit scholarship grants available. In 2005–06, 20% of upper-school students received aid; total upper-school merit-scholarship money awarded: $12,000. Total amount of financial aid awarded in 2005–06: $100,000.

Admissions Traditional secondary-level entrance grade is 10. For fall 2005, 134 students applied for upper-level admission, 65 were accepted, 45 enrolled. Deadline for receipt of application materials: September 12. Application fee required: $50. On-campus interview required.

Athletics Interscholastic: aquatics (girls), baseball (b), basketball (b), cheering (g), cross-country running (b), dance (g), dance squad (g), dance team (g), drill team (g), football (b), swimming and diving (g), tennis (b,g), track and field (b,g), volleyball (g); intramural: boxing (b), field hockey (b), fitness (b), flag football (b), floor hockey (b), football (b), running (b,g), skateboarding (b), skiing (downhill) (b,g), soccer (b,g), swimming and diving (b,g), touch football (b), track and field (b,g), weight lifting (b,g), weight training (b,g); coed interscholastic: golf, physical fitness, physical training, running, soccer, wrestling; coed intramural: baseball, basketball, nautilus, physical fitness, physical training, roller blading, table tennis, tennis, volleyball, walking. 2 PE instructors, 10 coaches, 2 trainers.

Computers Computer network features include campus e-mail, on-campus library services, Internet access, file transfer, office computer access, e-mail access in dorm rooms.

Contact Mr. Michael W. McGuire, Director of Admission. 913-367-5482 Ext. 237. Fax: 913-367-5096. E-mail: admissions@mh-ma.com. Web site: www.mhma.com.

MAYFIELD SENIOR SCHOOL

500 Bellefontaine Street
Pasadena, California 91105
Head of School: Mrs. Rita Curasi McBride

General Information Girls' day college-preparatory, arts, and religious studies school, affiliated with Roman Catholic Church. Grades 9–12. Founded: 1931. Setting: suburban. Nearest major city is Los Angeles. 8-acre campus. 4 buildings on campus. Approved or accredited by Western Association of Schools and Colleges. Member of National Association of Independent Schools. Endowment: $4.9 million. Total enrollment: 305. Upper school average class size: 17. Upper school faculty-student ratio: 1:8.

Upper School Student Profile Grade 9: 78 students (78 girls); Grade 10: 78 students (78 girls); Grade 11: 75 students (75 girls); Grade 12: 74 students (74 girls). 73% of students are Roman Catholic.

Faculty School total: 39. In upper school: 16 men, 23 women; 28 have advanced degrees.

Subjects Offered Algebra, American history, American history-AP, American literature, anatomy, art, art history-AP, bioethics, biology, biology-AP, British literature-AP, calculus, calculus-AP, ceramics, chemistry, community service, computer programming, computer science, creative writing, dance, drama, economics, English, English language-AP, English literature, English-AP, European history, European history-AP, fine arts, French, French language-AP, French literature-AP, French-AP, geography, geometry, government/civics, health, history, journalism, Latin, Latin-AP, marine biology, mathematics, music, music theory-AP, mythology, philosophy, photography, physical education, physics, physics-AP, physiology, psychology, psychology-AP, religion, science, social science, social studies, Spanish, Spanish language-AP, Spanish literature-AP, Spanish-AP, speech, studio art-AP, theater, theology, trigonometry, world history, writing.

Graduation Requirements Arts and fine arts (art, music, dance, drama), computer science, English, foreign language, mathematics, physical education (includes health), religion (includes Bible studies and theology), science, social science, social studies (includes history). Community service is required.

Special Academic Programs Advanced Placement exam preparation in 12 subject areas; academic accommodation for the gifted, the musically talented, and the artistically talented.

College Placement 78 students graduated in 2005; all went to college, including Loyola Marymount University; Stanford University; The University of Arizona; University of California, Berkeley; University of California, Los Angeles; University of Southern California. Mean SAT verbal: 632, mean SAT math: 617.

Student Life Upper grades have uniform requirement, student council, honor system. Discipline rests primarily with faculty. Attendance at religious services is required.

Summer Programs Remediation, enrichment, advancement, sports, art/fine arts, computer instruction programs offered; session focuses on arts and sciences; held on campus; accepts girls; open to students from other schools. 250 students usually enrolled. 2006 schedule: June 19 to July 19. Application deadline: May 12.

Tuition and Aid Day student tuition: $15,200. Tuition installment plan (monthly payment plans, 2-payment plan). Merit scholarship grants, need-based scholarship grants available. In 2005–06, 25% of upper-school students received aid; total upper-school merit-scholarship money awarded: $50,000. Total amount of financial aid awarded in 2005–06: $358,500.

Admissions Traditional secondary-level entrance grade is 9. For fall 2005, 272 students applied for upper-level admission, 110 were accepted, 78 enrolled. ISEE required. Deadline for receipt of application materials: January 17. Application fee required: $75. On-campus interview required.

Athletics Interscholastic: basketball, cross-country running, dance, diving, equestrian sports, fencing, fitness, fitness walking, jogging, jump rope, physical training, ropes courses, soccer, softball, swimming and diving, tennis, track and field, volleyball, water polo, winter soccer, yoga; intramural: fencing. 3 PE instructors, 17 coaches.

Computers Computers are regularly used in foreign language, history, mathematics, religious studies, science classes. Computer network features include campus e-mail, on-campus library services, CD-ROMs, online commercial services, Internet access, file transfer, office computer access.

Contact Brenda Castaneda, Administrative Assistant. 626-799-9121 Ext. 222. Fax: 626-799-8576. E-mail: brenda.castaneda@mayfieldsenior.org. Web site: www.mayfieldsenior.org.

MAZAPAN SCHOOL

Standard Fruit Company
Zona de Mazapan
La Ceiba, Honduras
Head of School: Ms. Martha Counsil

General Information Coeducational day college-preparatory and bilingual studies school. Grades 1–12. Founded: 1928. Setting: urban. Nearest major city is San Pedro Sula. 5-acre campus. 10 buildings on campus. Approved or accredited by European Council of International Schools, Southern Association of Colleges and Schools, The College Board, and state department of education. Languages of instruction: English and Spanish. Endowment: $1 million. Total enrollment: 311. Upper school average class size: 25. Upper school faculty-student ratio: 1:12.

Upper School Student Profile Grade 9: 25 students (14 boys, 11 girls); Grade 10: 25 students (8 boys, 17 girls); Grade 11: 26 students (10 boys, 16 girls); Grade 12: 35 students (10 boys, 25 girls).

Faculty School total: 26. In upper school: 5 men, 8 women; 3 have advanced degrees.

Subjects Offered Accounting, algebra, American history, American literature, art, band, biology, calculus, calculus-AP, chemistry, college counseling, computer science, earth science, economics, English, English literature, geometry, government/civics, grammar, health, history, Honduran history, mathematics, music, philosophy, physical education, physics, pre-calculus, psychology, science, social studies, sociology, Spanish, trigonometry, typing, world history.

Graduation Requirements Arts and fine arts (art, music, dance, drama), computer science, English, foreign language, mathematics, physical education (includes health), science, social science, social studies (includes history).

Special Academic Programs Independent study.

College Placement 25 students graduated in 2005; all went to college, including Louisiana State University and Agricultural and Mechanical College; Rochester Institute of Technology; Savannah College of Art and Design; University of Ottawa; University of the Ozarks; York University. Median SAT verbal: 570, median SAT math: 500, median composite ACT: 21.

Student Life Upper grades have uniform requirement, student council. Discipline rests primarily with faculty.

Tuition and Aid Day student tuition: $3756. Tuition installment plan (monthly payment plans). Merit scholarship grants, need-based scholarships/grants for children of Dole employees available. In 2005–06, 36% of upper-school students received aid; total upper-school merit-scholarship money awarded: $7700. Total amount of financial aid awarded in 2005–06: $210,204.

Admissions Traditional secondary-level entrance grade is 9. For fall 2005, 6 students applied for upper-level admission, 3 were accepted, 3 enrolled. Admissions testing and Stanford Achievement Test required. Deadline for receipt of application materials: none. Application fee required: $50. On-campus interview required.

Athletics Interscholastic: baseball (girls), basketball (b,g), cheering (g), soccer (b,g), volleyball (b,g); intramural: baseball (b,g), basketball (b,g), dance (g), paddle tennis (b,g), soccer (b,g), table tennis (b,g), volleyball (b,g), weight lifting (b,g); coed intramural: cheering, paddle tennis, soccer, swimming and diving. 1 PE instructor, 3 coaches.

Computers Computers are regularly used in all academic, journalism, library skills, music, newspaper classes. Computer resources include on-campus library services, CD-ROMs, Internet access, office computer access, DVD.

Contact Enma Nufio, Guidance Counselor. 504-443-2716 Ext. 14. Fax: 504-443-3559. E-mail: enufio@la.dole.com. Web site: www.mazapanschool.com.

THE MCCALLIE SCHOOL

500 Dodds Avenue
Chattanooga, Tennessee 37404
Head of School: Dr. R. Kirk Walker

petersons.com

General Information Boys' boarding and day college-preparatory school, affiliated with Christian faith. Boarding grades 9–12, day grades 6–12. Founded: 1905. Setting: suburban. Nearest major city is Atlanta, GA. Students are housed in single-sex dormitories. 100-acre campus. 16 buildings on campus. Approved or accredited by Southern Association of Colleges and Schools, Southern Association of Independent Schools, Tennessee Association of Independent Schools, The Association of Boarding Schools, and Tennessee Department of Education. Member of National Association of Independent Schools and Secondary School Admission Test Board. Endowment: $51 million. Total enrollment: 890. Upper school average class size: 14. Upper school faculty-student ratio: 1:8.

Upper School Student Profile Grade 9: 150 students (150 boys); Grade 10: 168 students (168 boys); Grade 11: 153 students (153 boys); Grade 12: 158 students (158 boys). 37% of students are boarding students. 16 states are represented in upper school student body. International students from Czech Republic, Germany, Republic of Korea, and Saudi Arabia.

Faculty School total: 123. In upper school: 81 men, 13 women; 41 have advanced degrees; 43 reside on campus.

Subjects Offered Algebra, American Civil War, American history, American literature, American studies, archaeology, art, Bible studies, bioethics, biology, calculus, ceramics, chemistry, computer science, creative writing, design, drama, economics, English, English literature, environmental science, European history, fine arts, French, geometry, government/civics, Greek, health, history, human development, Japanese, journalism, keyboarding, Latin, mathematics, music, music theory, photography, physical education, physical science, physics, poetry, political science, pottery, printmaking, public speaking, religion, rhetoric, science, social science, social studies, Spanish, speech, theater, trigonometry, world history, world literature, writing.

Graduation Requirements Arts and fine arts (art, music, dance, drama), English, foreign language, mathematics, physical education (includes health), public speaking, religion (includes Bible studies and theology), science, social science, social studies (includes history).

Special Academic Programs Advanced Placement exam preparation in 19 subject areas; honors section; study abroad; academic accommodation for the gifted, the musically talented, and the artistically talented.

College Placement 147 students graduated in 2005; all went to college, including Georgetown University; The University of North Carolina at Chapel Hill; The University of Tennessee; The University of Tennessee at Chattanooga; University of Georgia; University of Mississippi. 51% scored over 600 on SAT verbal, 54% scored over 600 on SAT math, 56% scored over 26 on composite ACT.

Student Life Upper grades have specified standards of dress, student council, honor system. Discipline rests equally with students and faculty. Attendance at religious services is required.

Summer Programs Enrichment, sports, rigorous outdoor training programs offered; session focuses on introduction to McCallie School with special emphasis on fun and participation; held on campus; accepts boys; open to students from other schools. 2000 students usually enrolled. 2006 schedule: June 1 to August 1.

Tuition and Aid Day student tuition: $16,410; 7-day tuition and room/board: $31,500. Tuition installment plan (Insured Tuition Payment Plan, monthly payment plans). Merit scholarship grants, need-based scholarship grants available. In 2005–06, 20% of upper-school students received aid; total upper-school merit-scholarship money awarded: $540,500. Total amount of financial aid awarded in 2005–06: $1,800,000.

Admissions Traditional secondary-level entrance grade is 9. ISEE or SSAT required. Deadline for receipt of application materials: none. Application fee required: $50. On-campus interview required.

Athletics Interscholastic: baseball, basketball, bowling, climbing, crew, cross-country running, diving, football, golf, indoor track, indoor track & field, lacrosse, rock climbing, rowing, skeet shooting, soccer, swimming and diving, tennis, track and field, trap and skeet, wall climbing, wrestling; intramural: back packing, baseball, basketball, billiards, bowling, canoeing/kayaking, climbing, fencing, fishing, fitness, flag football, football, Frisbee, golf, hiking/backpacking, indoor soccer, juggling, kayaking, lacrosse, martial arts, mountain biking, mountaineering, outdoor activities, outdoor adventure, outdoor education, outdoor recreation, outdoor skills, paint ball, physical training, power lifting, racquetball, rappelling, rock climbing, scuba diving, soccer, softball, strength & conditioning, swimming and diving, table tennis, tennis, touch football, ultimate Frisbee, volleyball, wall climbing, water polo, weight lifting, weight training, wrestling, yoga; coed interscholastic: cheering. 2 trainers.

Computers Computers are regularly used in Bible studies, English, foreign language, mathematics, science, writing classes. Computer network features include campus e-mail, on-campus library services, CD-ROMs, online commercial services, Internet access, DVD.

Contact Mr. David L. Hughes, Director of Boarding Admissions. 423-624-8300. Fax: 423-493-5426. E-mail: admissions@mccallie.org. Web site: www.mccallie.org.

See full description on page 902.

MCDONOGH SCHOOL

PO Box 380
Owings Mills, Maryland 21117-0380
Head of School: W. Boulton Dixon

petersons.com

General Information Coeducational boarding and day college-preparatory school. Boarding grades 9–12, day grades K–12. Founded: 1873. Setting: suburban. Nearest major city is Baltimore. Students are housed in single-sex dormitories. 800-acre campus. 44 buildings on campus. Approved or accredited by Association of Independent Maryland Schools. Member of National Association of Independent Schools. Endowment: $60 million. Total enrollment: 1,263. Upper school average class size: 15. Upper school faculty-student ratio: 1:9.

Upper School Student Profile Grade 9: 145 students (79 boys, 66 girls); Grade 10: 141 students (73 boys, 68 girls); Grade 11: 142 students (75 boys, 67 girls); Grade 12: 138 students (82 boys, 56 girls). 15% of students are boarding students. 99% are state residents. 2 states are represented in upper school student body.

Faculty School total: 176. In upper school: 39 men, 43 women; 58 have advanced degrees; 16 reside on campus.

Subjects Offered 20th century American writers, acting, advanced chemistry, Advanced Placement courses, African history, African literature, African-American studies, algebra, American government-AP, American history, American history-AP, American literature, American literature-AP, anatomy, area studies, art, art history, art-AP, Asian studies, band, bioethics, biology, biology-AP, botany, calculus, calculus-AP, ceramics, chemistry, chemistry-AP, Chesapeake Bay studies, classical Greek literature, composition-AP, computer animation, computer graphics, computer music, computer programming, computer science, computer science-AP, concert band, concert choir, creative writing, dance, drama, drawing, ecology, economics, economics-AP, electives, engineering, English, English composition, English literature, English literature and composition-AP, English literature-AP, English-AP, English/composition-AP, environmental science, environmental science-AP, ethics, European history, film, film and literature, fine arts, fitness, foreign language, French, French language-AP, French literature-AP, French-AP, genetics, geology, geometry, German, German-AP, government and politics-AP, government-AP, government/civics, health and wellness, history, history-AP, honors algebra, honors English, honors geometry, honors U.S. history, honors world history, Irish literature, jazz band, jazz dance, journalism, language-AP, languages, Latin American literature, linguistics, literature and composition-AP, literature by women, marine biology, mathematics, Middle Eastern history, music, music theory, music theory-AP, oceanography, photography, physical education, physical fitness, physics, poetry, pre-calculus, psychology, religion, Russian history, science, senior project, set design, Shakespeare, short story, Spanish, Spanish language-AP, Spanish literature, Spanish literature-AP, Spanish-AP, speech, speech communications, statistics-AP, tap dance, theater, trigonometry, tropical ecology, U.S. government and politics-AP, U.S. government-AP, U.S. history, U.S. history-AP, video, visual arts, Web site design, woodworking, world history, world history-AP, world religions, world wide web design, writing workshop, yearbook.

Graduation Requirements Arts and fine arts (art, music, dance, drama), English, foreign language, mathematics, physical education (includes health), science, senior project, social studies (includes history). Community service is required.

Special Academic Programs Advanced Placement exam preparation in 16 subject areas; honors section; independent study; term-away projects.

College Placement 131 students graduated in 2005; all went to college, including Bucknell University; Dickinson College; Harvard University; University of Maryland, College Park; University of Wisconsin–Madison; Vanderbilt University.

Student Life Upper grades have uniform requirement, student council, honor system. Discipline rests primarily with faculty.

Summer Programs Sports, art/fine arts, computer instruction programs offered; session focuses on recreation and sports camps; held on campus; accepts boys and girls; open to students from other schools. 2006 schedule: June 19 to July 28.

Tuition and Aid Day student tuition: $19,630; 5-day tuition and room/board: $26,420. Tuition installment plan (Key Tuition Payment Plan, monthly payment plans, individually arranged payment plans). Need-based scholarship grants, need-based loans, middle-income loans available. In 2005–06, 15% of upper-school students received aid. Total amount of financial aid awarded in 2005–06: $2,544,000.

Admissions Traditional secondary-level entrance grade is 9. For fall 2005, 294 students applied for upper-level admission, 80 were accepted, 53 enrolled. ISEE required. Deadline for receipt of application materials: December 15. Application fee required: $45. On-campus interview required.

Athletics Interscholastic: aquatics (boys, girls), baseball (b), basketball (b,g), cross-country running (b,g), equestrian sports (b,g), field hockey (g), football (b), golf (b,g), lacrosse (b,g), soccer (b,g), softball (g), swimming and diving (b,g), tennis (b,g), volleyball (g), water polo (b,g), winter (indoor) track (b,g), wrestling (b); coed interscholastic: cheering, equestrian sports, horseback riding; coed intramural: badminton, ballet, dance, fencing, fitness. 10 PE instructors, 22 coaches, 2 trainers.

Computers Computers are regularly used in all classes. Computer network features include campus e-mail, on-campus library services, CD-ROMs, online commercial services, Internet access, file transfer, office computer access, DVD, wireless campus network.

Contact Anita Hilson, Director of Admissions. 410-581-4719. Fax: 410-998-3537. E-mail: ahilson@mcdonogh.org. Web site: www.mcdonogh.org.

ANNOUNCEMENT FROM THE SCHOOL McDonogh School was established in 1873 with a bequest from philanthropist and merchant John McDonogh. Originally a free school for academically capable but economically disadvantaged boys, McDonogh has emerged as a nondenominational, college-preparatory, coeducational day and boarding school. John McDonogh's philosophy—to develop moral character, a sense of responsibility, and a capacity for leadership—still guides the School. There are 1,288 boys and girls in kindergarten through grade 12, including 90 students in grades 9–12 enrolled in the School's 5-day boarding program. McDonogh is set on nearly 800 picturesque acres in Owings Mills, a suburb of Baltimore. Bus transportation and hot lunches are included in tuition. Exemplary facilities include a 580-seat theater, computer labs and libraries for all levels, dance and art studios, 19 athletic fields, an outdoor stadium, a life fitness center, indoor multipurpose courts, a 50-meter swimming pool (new in 2006), and riding rings. In the Upper School, the college-preparatory program includes Advanced Placement courses and honors classes in all major subjects. With an average class size of 15, students are guaranteed individual attention. McDonogh also offers interscholastic competition in 26 different sports, and students are required to join teams or take physical education classes. Extracurriculars, which take place between the end of the academic day and athletic practices, include 50 clubs and activities. In addition, students must perform 40 hours of community service for graduation. One of McDonogh's strengths is its college counseling program. Experienced counselors serve as students' advocates through the process, and all graduates typically enroll in 4-year colleges.

MCGILL-TOOLEN CATHOLIC HIGH SCHOOL

1501 Old Shell Road
Mobile, Alabama 36604-2291
Head of School: Mrs. Michelle Tacon Haas

General Information Coeducational day college-preparatory, general academic, arts, religious studies, and technology school, affiliated with Roman Catholic Church. Grades 9–12. Founded: 1896. Setting: urban. 4 buildings on campus. Approved or accredited by Southern Association of Colleges and Schools and Alabama Department of Education. Total enrollment: 998. Upper school average class size: 21. Upper school faculty-student ratio: 1:13.

Upper School Student Profile Grade 9: 254 students (121 boys, 133 girls); Grade 10: 256 students (121 boys, 135 girls); Grade 11: 242 students (129 boys, 113 girls); Grade 12: 246 students (120 boys, 126 girls). 90.1% of students are Roman Catholic.

Faculty School total: 76. In upper school: 35 men, 41 women; 44 have advanced degrees.

Graduation Requirements Electives, English, keyboarding, mathematics, physical education (includes health), religion (includes Bible studies and theology), science, social studies (includes history).

Special Academic Programs Advanced Placement exam preparation in 9 subject areas; honors section; remedial reading and/or remedial writing.

College Placement 248 students graduated in 2005; 233 went to college, including Auburn University; Louisiana State University and Agricultural and Mechanical College; Spring Hill College; The University of Alabama; University of South Alabama; University of Southern Mississippi. Other: 15 went to work. Median composite ACT: 22. 17% scored over 26 on composite ACT.

Student Life Upper grades have uniform requirement, student council. Discipline rests primarily with faculty. Attendance at religious services is required.

Tuition and Aid Day student tuition: $4500–$5780. Tuition installment plan (FACTS Tuition Payment Plan). Tuition reduction for siblings, need-based scholarship grants available. In 2005–06, 25% of upper-school students received aid. Total amount of financial aid awarded in 2005–06: $332,450.

Admissions Traditional secondary-level entrance grade is 9. ACT-Explore required. Deadline for receipt of application materials: none. Application fee required: $100. On-campus interview recommended.

Athletics Interscholastic: baseball (boys), basketball (b,g), cheering (b,g), cross-country running (b,g), diving (b,g), football (b), golf (b,g), indoor track (b,g), soccer (b,g), softball (g), swimming and diving (b,g), tennis (b,g), track and field (b,g), volleyball (g), winter (indoor) track (b,g); coed intramural: hiking/backpacking. 3 PE instructors, 3 coaches, 1 trainer.

Computers Computers are regularly used in desktop publishing, keyboarding, lab/keyboard, life skills, technology, Web site design, word processing, yearbook classes. Computer resources include on-campus library services, CD-ROMs, Internet access.

Contact Wayne T. Merritt, Director of Admission and Records and Registrar. 251-432-0784 Ext. 138. Fax: 251-433-8356. E-mail: merritw@mcgill.pvt.k12.al.us.

MCNICHOLAS HIGH SCHOOL

6536 Beechmont Avenue
Cincinnati, Ohio 45230-2098
Head of School: Mr. Thomas R. Bill

General Information Coeducational day college-preparatory, general academic, and arts school, affiliated with Roman Catholic Church. Grades 9–12. Founded: 1951. Setting: suburban. 48-acre campus. 2 buildings on campus. Approved or accredited by North Central Association of Colleges and Schools, Ohio Catholic Schools Accreditation Association (OCSAA), The College Board, and Ohio Department of Education. Total enrollment: 810. Upper school average class size: 19. Upper school faculty-student ratio: 1:16.

Upper School Student Profile Grade 9: 193 students (103 boys, 90 girls); Grade 10: 205 students (101 boys, 104 girls); Grade 11: 220 students (100 boys, 120 girls); Grade 12: 192 students (102 boys, 90 girls). 93% of students are Roman Catholic.

Faculty School total: 58. In upper school: 21 men, 37 women; 30 have advanced degrees.

Subjects Offered Accounting, advanced computer applications, advanced math, Advanced Placement courses, advanced studio art-AP, algebra, American government-AP, American history, American history-AP, American legal systems, American literature, anatomy and physiology, architectural drawing, band, Basic programming, biology, biology-AP, British literature, British literature-AP, business applications, calculus-AP, Catholic belief and practice, ceramics, chemistry, choir, church history, civics, communication skills, comparative government and politics-AP, computer art, computer processing, computer programming, computer programming-AP, computer technologies, computer-aided design, concert band, concert choir, consumer economics, creative writing, death and loss, design, developmental math, digital photography, directing, drama, drawing and design, English, English literature and composition-AP, European history-AP, foreign language, French, French language-AP, government and politics-AP, guitar, health, honors algebra, honors English, honors geometry, integrated science, intro to computers, journalism, Latin, Latin-AP, Life of Christ, marching band, Microsoft, moral theology, music appreciation, music theory-AP, Native American studies, photography, physical education, physical science, physics, physics-AP, portfolio art, pottery, pre-algebra, pre-calculus, reading, reading/study skills, skills for success, Spanish, Spanish language-AP, Spanish literature-AP, speech and debate, statistics, street law, studio art, studio art-AP, theater, U.S. government and politics-AP, video film production, world history, world religions, writing.

Graduation Requirements Algebra, American government, American history, American literature, arts and fine arts (art, music, dance, drama), biology, British literature, Catholic belief and practice, civics, communication skills, computer applications, English, foreign language, geometry, mathematics, religion (includes Bible studies and theology), science, social justice, world history.

Special Academic Programs Advanced Placement exam preparation in 14 subject areas; honors section; academic accommodation for the gifted; remedial reading and/or remedial writing; remedial math; programs in English, mathematics for dyslexic students.

College Placement 213 students graduated in 2005; 205 went to college, including Ohio University; The Ohio State University; University of Cincinnati; University of Dayton. Other: 8 went to work.

Student Life Upper grades have uniform requirement. Discipline rests primarily with faculty. Attendance at religious services is required.

Summer Programs Remediation programs offered; session focuses on remediation of failed courses or new PE credit; held on campus; accepts boys and girls; not open to students from other schools. 40 students usually enrolled. 2006 schedule: June 12 to July 14. Application deadline: June 9.

Tuition and Aid Day student tuition: $6385. Tuition installment plan (FACTS Tuition Payment Plan). Tuition reduction for siblings, merit scholarship grants, need-based scholarship grants available. In 2005–06, 10% of upper-school students received aid; total upper-school merit-scholarship money awarded: $99,412. Total amount of financial aid awarded in 2005–06: $171,500.

Admissions Traditional secondary-level entrance grade is 9. High School Placement Test (closed version) from Scholastic Testing Service required. Deadline for receipt of application materials: none. No application fee required.

Athletics Interscholastic: baseball (boys), basketball (b,g), bowling (b,g), cheering (g), dance team (g), football (b), golf (b,g); coed interscholastic: cross-country running; coed intramural: bicycling, flag football. 22 coaches, 2 trainers.

Computers Computers are regularly used in computer applications, data processing, English, foreign language, French, graphic design, history, journalism, mathematics, multimedia, photography, programming, publications, reading, religion, science, Spanish, video film production, writing classes. Computer network features include on-campus library services, CD-ROMs, Internet access, file transfer, Blackboard, student files.

Contact Ms. Vicky Hausberger, Freshman Placement Coordinator. 513-231-3500 Ext. 5816. Fax: 513-231-1351. E-mail: vhausberger@mcnhs.org. Web site: www.mcnhs.org.

MCQUAID JESUIT HIGH SCHOOL

1800 South Clinton Avenue
Rochester, New York 14618
Head of School: Mr. William Hobbs

General Information Boys' day college-preparatory, arts, religious studies, and technology school, affiliated with Roman Catholic Church (Jesuit order). Grades 7–12. Founded: 1954. Setting: suburban. 33-acre campus. 1 building on campus. Approved or accredited by Jesuit Secondary Education Association, Middle States Association of Colleges and Schools, National Catholic Education Association, and New York Department of Education. Endowment: $6.1 million. Total enrollment: 878. Upper school average class size: 22. Upper school faculty-student ratio: 1:16.

Upper School Student Profile Grade 9: 161 students (161 boys); Grade 10: 181 students (181 boys); Grade 11: 156 students (156 boys); Grade 12: 174 students (174 boys). 79% of students are Roman Catholic Church (Jesuit order).

Faculty School total: 69. In upper school: 41 men, 15 women; 50 have advanced degrees.

Subjects Offered 3-dimensional art, advanced computer applications, advanced math, algebra, American government, American history, American literature, art, band, Bible studies, biology, biology-AP, biotechnology, calculus, calculus-AP, Catholic belief and practice, chemistry, chemistry-AP, choir, classical language, community service, computer keyboarding, computer literacy, computer math, computer programming, computer programming-AP, computer science, creative writing, drama, dramatic arts, driver education, earth science, economics, economics-AP, English, English literature, English literature and composition-AP, English literature-AP, environmental science, environmental science-AP, European history, European history-AP, expository writing, fine arts, foreign language, French, geography, geometry, global studies, government/civics, grammar, health, history, honors English, instrumental music, Italian, jazz band, Latin, mathematics, modern European history-AP, music, musical theater, novels, physical education, physics, physics-AP, poetry, portfolio writing, pre-calculus, psychology, psychology-AP, religion, religious studies, science, senior seminar, Shakespeare, social studies, Spanish, Spanish language-AP, speech and debate, statistics-AP, street law, studio art-AP, theology, U.S. history-AP, vocal ensemble, vocal music, word processing, world history-AP, writing.

Graduation Requirements Arts and fine arts (art, music, dance, drama), English, foreign language, health education, mathematics, physical education (includes health), religion (includes Bible studies and theology), science, social studies (includes history). Community service is required.

Special Academic Programs Advanced Placement exam preparation in 16 subject areas; honors section.

College Placement 144 students graduated in 2005; 142 went to college, including Boston College; Le Moyne College; Rochester Institute of Technology; State University of New York College at Geneseo; University of Rochester. Other: 2 went to work. Mean SAT verbal: 607, mean SAT math: 615.

Student Life Upper grades have specified standards of dress, student council, honor system. Discipline rests primarily with faculty. Attendance at religious services is required.

Tuition and Aid Day student tuition: $7775. Tuition installment plan (monthly payment plans, individually arranged payment plans). Merit scholarship grants, need-based scholarship grants available. In 2005–06, 25% of upper-school students received aid; total upper-school merit-scholarship money awarded: $20,000. Total amount of financial aid awarded in 2005–06: $684,000.

Admissions Traditional secondary-level entrance grade is 9. For fall 2005, 122 students applied for upper-level admission, 103 were accepted, 78 enrolled. STS required. Deadline for receipt of application materials: none. Application fee required: $10.

Athletics Interscholastic: alpine skiing, baseball, basketball, bowling, crew, cross-country running, football, golf, ice hockey, indoor track, lacrosse, rowing, rugby, sailing, skiing (downhill), soccer, swimming and diving, tennis, track and field, volleyball, winter (indoor) track, wrestling; intramural: baseball, basketball, bicycling, billiards, bocce, fencing, flag football, floor hockey, football, Frisbee, hiking/backpacking, martial arts, physical fitness, physical training, ropes courses, self defense, skiing (cross-country), soccer, softball, strength & conditioning, table tennis, tennis, touch football, ultimate Frisbee, volleyball, water polo, weight lifting, weight training, wrestling. 3 PE instructors, 22 coaches, 1 trainer.

Computers Computers are regularly used in art, English, foreign language, graphic design, history, journalism, lab/keyboard, library, literary magazine, mathematics, music, newspaper, religious studies, research skills, science, word processing, yearbook classes. Computer network features include campus e-mail, on-campus library services, CD-ROMs, online commercial services, Internet access, office computer access, DVD, wireless campus network.

Contact Mr. Christopher Parks, Director of Admissions. 585-256-6117. Fax: 585-256-6171. E-mail: cparks@mcquaid.org. Web site: www.mcquaid.org.

MEADOWRIDGE SENIOR SCHOOL

12224 240th Street
Maple Ridge, British Columbia V4R 1N1, Canada
Head of School: Mr. Hugh Burke

General Information Coeducational day college-preparatory, arts, and technology school. Grades JK–12. Founded: 1985. Setting: rural. Nearest major city is Vancouver, Canada. 17-acre campus. 1 building on campus. Approved or accredited by British Columbia Department of Education. Language of instruction: English. Total enrollment: 458. Upper school average class size: 18. Upper school faculty-student ratio: 1:9.

Upper School Student Profile Grade 8: 46 students (27 boys, 19 girls); Grade 9: 35 students (19 boys, 16 girls); Grade 10: 31 students (14 boys, 17 girls); Grade 11: 30 students (19 boys, 11 girls); Grade 12: 26 students (12 boys, 14 girls).

Faculty School total: 46. In upper school: 12 men, 7 women; 5 have advanced degrees.

Subjects Offered Accounting, Advanced Placement courses, art, biology, biology-AP, calculus, calculus-AP, career and personal planning, chemistry, comparative civilizations, computer science-AP, computer technologies, drama, English, English literature, English-AP, filmmaking, forensics, French, geography, history, humanities, marketing, mathematics, photography, physical education, physics, science, Spanish, weight training.

Graduation Requirements 3 other provincially examinable courses.

College Placement 26 students graduated in 2005; all went to college, including The University of British Columbia.

Student Life Upper grades have uniform requirement, student council, honor system. Discipline rests primarily with faculty.

Tuition and Aid Day student tuition: CAN$10,470. Tuition installment plan (Insured Tuition Payment Plan, monthly payment plans). Tuition reduction for siblings, bursaries, merit scholarship grants available. Total upper-school merit-scholarship money awarded for 2005–06: CAN$2000.

Admissions Traditional secondary-level entrance grade is 8. For fall 2005, 39 students applied for upper-level admission, 28 were accepted, 26 enrolled. Admissions testing required. Deadline for receipt of application materials: none. Application fee required: CAN$150. On-campus interview required.

Athletics Interscholastic: aerobics/dance (boys, girls), badminton (b,g), basketball (b,g), physical fitness (b,g), rugby (b,g), soccer (g), volleyball (b,g); intramural: aerobics/dance (b,g), basketball (b,g); coed interscholastic: aerobics/dance, cross-country running, flag football, outdoor activities, outdoor adventure, outdoor education, outdoor recreation, outdoor skills, outdoors, track and field; coed intramural: aerobics/dance. 1 PE instructor.

Computers Computer network features include campus e-mail, on-campus library services, CD-ROMs, Internet access, wireless campus network.

Contact Ms. Christine Bickle, Director of Admissions. 604-467-4444 Ext. 217. Fax: 604-467-4989. E-mail: christine.bickle@meadowridge.bc.ca. Web site: www.meadowridge.bc.ca.

THE MEADOWS SCHOOL

8601 Scholar Lane
Las Vegas, Nevada 89128-7302
Head of School: Mr. Robert M. Ryshke

General Information Coeducational day college-preparatory, arts, and technology school. Grades PK–12. Founded: 1981. Setting: suburban. Nearest major city is Los Angeles, CA. 42.6-acre campus. 10 buildings on campus. Approved or accredited by CITA (Commission on International and Trans-Regional Accreditation), Northwest Association of Schools and Colleges, Pacific Northwest Association of Independent Schools, and Nevada Department of Education. Member of National Association of Independent Schools and Secondary School Admission Test Board. Endowment: $1.4 million. Total enrollment: 898. Upper school average class size: 18. Upper school faculty-student ratio: 1:11.

Upper School Student Profile Grade 9: 66 students (32 boys, 34 girls); Grade 10: 73 students (36 boys, 37 girls); Grade 11: 54 students (20 boys, 34 girls); Grade 12: 57 students (31 boys, 26 girls).

Faculty School total: 89. In upper school: 24 men, 17 women; 33 have advanced degrees.

Subjects Offered 20th century American writers, acting, advanced chemistry, advanced computer applications, advanced math, advanced studio art-AP, American literature, anatomy and physiology, ancient history, anthropology, art, art history, band, Basic programming, biology, biology-AP, British literature, British literature (honors), British literature-AP, calculus, calculus-AP, ceramics, chemistry, chemistry-AP, chorus, comparative religion, composition, composition-AP, computer applications, computer keyboarding, computer literacy, computer programming, computer programming-AP, computer science, computer science-AP, concert choir, constitutional law, creative writing, dance, digital photography, drama, drama performance, drawing, drawing and design, economics, economics-AP, English, English composition, English language and composition-AP, English language-AP, English literature, English literature and composition-AP, English literature-AP, English-AP, English/composition-AP, environmental science-AP, European history, European history-AP, film studies, foreign language, forensics, French, French language-AP, French

literature-AP, genetics, geometry, government and politics-AP, health, honors English, honors geometry, honors U.S. history, honors world history, human anatomy, instrumental music, integrated mathematics, journalism, Latin, Latin-AP, law, literature and composition-AP, macroeconomics-AP, microeconomics-AP, music theater, painting, philosophy, photography, physics, physics-AP, pre-calculus, psychology, psychology-AP, SAT preparation, sculpture, Shakespeare, social justice, social sciences, Spanish, Spanish language-AP, Spanish literature, Spanish literature-AP, Spanish-AP, speech, speech and debate, speech and oral interpretations, statistics, statistics-AP, studio art, studio art-AP, technical theater, technology, trigonometry, U.S. government and politics-AP, U.S. government-AP, U.S. history, U.S. history-AP, yearbook.

Graduation Requirements American government, American literature, arts and fine arts (art, music, dance, drama), computer science, English, foreign language, mathematics, physical education (includes health), science, social science. Community service is required.

Special Academic Programs Advanced Placement exam preparation in 15 subject areas; honors section; independent study; academic accommodation for the gifted, the musically talented, and the artistically talented.

College Placement 57 students graduated in 2005; all went to college, including Babson College; The University of Arizona; University of Nevada, Las Vegas; University of Pennsylvania; University of San Diego; University of Southern California. Mean SAT verbal: 640, mean SAT math: 673, mean composite ACT: 28. 74% scored over 600 on SAT verbal, 86% scored over 600 on SAT math, 79% scored over 26 on composite ACT.

Student Life Upper grades have uniform requirement, student council, honor system. Discipline rests equally with students and faculty.

Summer Programs Enrichment, advancement, art/fine arts programs offered; session focuses on enrichment; held both on and off campus; held at Las Vegas Valley (for two weekly summer science program field trips for taking samples and of the environment to analyze in the school labs); accepts boys and girls; open to students from other schools. 50 students usually enrolled.

Tuition and Aid Day student tuition: $15,750. Tuition installment plan (Insured Tuition Payment Plan, monthly payment plans, individually arranged payment plans, 2-payment plan, 9-payment plan). Merit scholarship grants, need-based scholarship grants, need-based loans available. In 2005–06, 15% of upper-school students received aid. Total amount of financial aid awarded in 2005–06: $517,260.

Admissions Traditional secondary-level entrance grade is 9. For fall 2005, 76 students applied for upper-level admission, 32 were accepted, 26 enrolled. ERB, ISEE or SSAT required. Deadline for receipt of application materials: none. Application fee required: $100. On-campus interview required.

Athletics Interscholastic: baseball (boys), basketball (b,g), cheering (g), cross-country running (b,g), dance (g), diving (b,g), football (b), golf (b), soccer (b,g), softball (g), swimming and diving (b,g), tennis (b,g), track and field (b,g), volleyball (g), wrestling (b). 1 PE instructor, 14 coaches, 1 trainer.

Computers Computers are regularly used in college planning, desktop publishing, English, foreign language, graphic design, history, independent study, information technology, introduction to technology, library, mathematics, music, news writing, photography, photojournalism, programming, publications, publishing, science, technology, yearbook classes. Computer network features include campus e-mail, on-campus library services, CD-ROMs, online commercial services, Internet access, office computer access, DVD, Neon, two wireless mobile computer labs with notebook computers.

Contact Head of School. 702-254-1610. Fax: 702-254-3852. Web site: www.themeadowsschool.org.

THE MEETING SCHOOL

120 Thomas Road
Rindge, New Hampshire 03461
Head of School: Jacqueline Stillwell

petersons.com

General Information Coeducational boarding and day college-preparatory, general academic, arts, and experiential education school, affiliated with Society of Friends. Boarding grades 9–12, day grades 8–12. Founded: 1957. Setting: rural. Nearest major city is Keene. Students are housed in coed dormitories. 140-acre campus. 12 buildings on campus. Approved or accredited by Association of Independent Schools in New England, Friends Council on Education, Independent Schools of Northern New England, New England Association of Schools and Colleges, and New Hampshire Department of Education. Endowment: $51,000. Total enrollment: 24. Upper school average class size: 6. Upper school faculty-student ratio: 1:2.

Upper School Student Profile Grade 9: 2 students (2 boys); Grade 10: 2 students (1 boy, 1 girl); Grade 11: 6 students (2 boys, 4 girls); Grade 12: 14 students (7 boys, 7 girls). 90% of students are boarding students. 25% are state residents. 17 states are represented in upper school student body. International students from Canada. 30% of students are members of Society of Friends.

Faculty School total: 16. In upper school: 6 men, 8 women; 6 have advanced degrees; all reside on campus.

Subjects Offered Acting, algebra, art, biology, calculus, ceramics, computers, consumer mathematics, creative writing, English, environmental systems, fiber arts,

geology, geometry, literature, mathematics, music theory, peace studies, psychology, sexuality, Spanish, stained glass, statistics, trigonometry, U.S. history, weaving, woodworking, writing.

Graduation Requirements English, mathematics, oral communications, physical education (includes health), science, social studies (includes history), participation in writing program, community work program, and independent study projects.

Special Academic Programs Accelerated programs; independent study; term-away projects; study at local college for college credit; academic accommodation for the gifted and the artistically talented; remedial reading and/or remedial writing; remedial math; special instructional classes for students with learning disabilities.

College Placement 13 students graduated in 2005; 6 went to college, including Antioch College; Earlham College. Other: 4 went to work, 2 had other specific plans.

Student Life Upper grades have student council, honor system. Discipline rests equally with students and faculty.

Tuition and Aid Day student tuition: $18,500; 7-day tuition and room/board: $32,800. Tuition installment plan (monthly payment plans, individually arranged payment plans). Need-based scholarship grants, need-based loans, Sallie Mae Loans available. In 2005–06, 60% of upper-school students received aid. Total amount of financial aid awarded in 2005–06: $27,900.

Admissions Traditional secondary-level entrance grade is 10. For fall 2005, 9 students applied for upper-level admission, 8 were accepted, 8 enrolled. Deadline for receipt of application materials: none. Application fee required: $40. On-campus interview required.

Athletics Coed Intramural: aerobics, badminton, basketball, bicycling, bowling, canoeing/kayaking, cooperative games, fitness, fitness walking, flag football, Frisbee, hiking/backpacking, kickball, outdoor activities, outdoor education, skateboarding, skiing (cross-country), skiing (downhill), snowboarding, soccer, swimming and diving, tennis, ultimate Frisbee, walking, yoga.

Computers Computers are regularly used in English, mathematics, science classes. Computer resources include campus e-mail, on-campus library services, CD-ROMs, Internet access.

Contact Christine Smith, Administrative Assistant. 603-899-3366. Fax: 603-899-6216. E-mail: office@meetingschool.org. Web site: www.meetingschool.org.

ANNOUNCEMENT FROM THE SCHOOL This progressive Quaker school offers intellectual challenge and individual attention in small classes. The School's organic farm is integrated into the educational program. Homeschoolers and other self-motivated students often find hands-on, student-centered learning attractive. Intentional community living nurtures integrity, responsibility, tolerance, and compassion, as students learn good listening and decision-making skills.

See full description on page 904.

MEMPHIS UNIVERSITY SCHOOL

6191 Park Avenue
Memphis, Tennessee 38119-5399
Head of School: Mr. Ellis L. Haguewood

General Information Boys' day college-preparatory school. Grades 7–12. Founded: 1893. Setting: suburban. 94-acre campus. 8 buildings on campus. Approved or accredited by Southern Association of Colleges and Schools, Southern Association of Independent Schools, and Tennessee Association of Independent Schools. Member of National Association of Independent Schools. Endowment: $15.2 million. Total enrollment: 652. Upper school average class size: 15. Upper school faculty-student ratio: 1:15.

Upper School Student Profile Grade 9: 117 students (117 boys); Grade 10: 101 students (101 boys); Grade 11: 109 students (109 boys); Grade 12: 111 students (111 boys).

Faculty School total: 67. In upper school: 50 men, 17 women; 50 have advanced degrees.

Subjects Offered Algebra, American government, American literature, art, art history, art history-AP, arts and crafts, Bible, biology, biology-AP, British literature, calculus, calculus-AP, chemistry, chemistry-AP, choral music, college counseling, college placement, comparative government and politics-AP, comparative religion, composition-AP, computer education, computer programming, computer science, computer science-AP, driver education, earth science, economics, economics and history, English, English composition, English literature, English literature and composition-AP, environmental science, ethics, ethics and responsibility, European history, European history-AP, expository writing, fine arts, foreign language, French, geometry, German, global studies, government and politics-AP, government/civics, grammar, health, history, humanities, introduction to theater, keyboarding/computer, language and composition, Latin, library skills, literature, mathematics, music, music appreciation, music composition, music theory, physical education, physical science, physics, physics-AP, pre-algebra, pre-calculus, probability and statistics, psychology, religion, research skills, science, social science, social studies, Spanish, studio art, study skills, trigonometry, U.S. history, U.S. history-AP, United States government-AP, Western civilization, woodworking, world history, writing.

Memphis University School

Graduation Requirements Arts and fine arts (art, music, dance, drama), computer science, English, foreign language, mathematics, physical education (includes health), religion (includes Bible studies and theology), science, social science, social studies (includes history).

Special Academic Programs Advanced Placement exam preparation in 19 subject areas; honors section; study abroad.

College Placement 107 students graduated in 2005; all went to college, including Auburn University; Rhodes College; Southern Methodist University; The University of Tennessee; University of Mississippi; Vanderbilt University. 72% scored over 600 on SAT verbal, 75% scored over 600 on SAT math, 73% scored over 26 on composite ACT.

Student Life Upper grades have specified standards of dress, student council, honor system. Discipline rests primarily with faculty.

Summer Programs Remediation, enrichment, advancement, sports programs offered; session focuses on academics and athletics; held on campus; accepts boys and girls; open to students from other schools. 460 students usually enrolled. 2006 schedule: June 5 to July 21. Application deadline: none.

Tuition and Aid Day student tuition: $12,675. Tuition installment plan (monthly payment plans, individually arranged payment plans). Need-based scholarship grants available. In 2005–06, 20% of upper-school students received aid. Total amount of financial aid awarded in 2005–06: $900,000.

Admissions Traditional secondary-level entrance grade is 9. For fall 2005, 39 students applied for upper-level admission, 28 were accepted, 24 enrolled. ISEE required. Deadline for receipt of application materials: none. Application fee required: $15. On-campus interview recommended.

Athletics Interscholastic: baseball, basketball, cross-country running, football, golf, lacrosse, soccer, swimming and diving, tennis, track and field, wrestling. 5 PE instructors, 9 coaches, 1 trainer.

Computers Computers are regularly used in all academic, career exploration, college planning, library science, newspaper, publications, yearbook classes. Computer network features include campus e-mail, on-campus library services, CD-ROMs, online commercial services, Internet access, file transfer, office computer access, DVD, wireless campus network.

Contact Mr. Daniel H. Kahalley, Director of Admissions. 901-260-1349. Fax: 901-260-1301. E-mail: danny.kahalley@musowls.org. Web site: www.musowls.org.

MENAUL SCHOOL

301 Menaul Boulevard, NE
Albuquerque, New Mexico 87107
Head of School: Dr. Gloria G. Mallory

General Information Coeducational day college-preparatory, arts, and religious studies school, affiliated with Presbyterian Church. Grades 6–12. Founded: 1896. Setting: urban. 50-acre campus. 10 buildings on campus. Approved or accredited by North Central Association of Colleges and Schools, The College Board, and New Mexico Department of Education. Candidate for accreditation by Independent Schools Association of the Southwest. Endowment: $3 million. Total enrollment: 202. Upper school average class size: 15. Upper school faculty-student ratio: 1:10.

Upper School Student Profile Grade 9: 25 students (11 boys, 14 girls); Grade 10: 27 students (14 boys, 13 girls); Grade 11: 38 students (21 boys, 17 girls); Grade 12: 30 students (17 boys, 13 girls). 30% of students are Presbyterian.

Faculty School total: 24. In upper school: 14 men, 10 women; 14 have advanced degrees.

Subjects Offered Advanced Placement courses, algebra, American government, American government-AP, American history, American literature, art, arts and crafts, band, Bible studies, biology, calculus-AP, chemistry, clayworking, communications, computer graphics, computer programming, computer science, earth science, economics, English, English literature, English-AP, ethics, fine arts, French, geography, geometry, government/civics, history, Life of Christ, mathematics, metalworking, music, Native American arts and crafts, physical education, physics, psychology, religion, science, social science, social studies, sociology, Spanish, theology, trigonometry, typing, world history, world literature, writing, yearbook.

Graduation Requirements Arts and fine arts (art, music, dance, drama), communications, computer science, English, foreign language, mathematics, physical education (includes health), religion (includes Bible studies and theology), science, social science, social studies (includes history). Community service is required.

Special Academic Programs Advanced Placement exam preparation in 5 subject areas; honors section; study at local college for college credit; academic accommodation for the gifted and the artistically talented.

College Placement 45 students graduated in 2005; 43 went to college, including Colorado State University; Macalester College; New Mexico State University; The Evergreen State College; The University of Arizona; University of New Mexico. Other: 1 went to work, 1 entered military service. Median SAT verbal: 500, median SAT math: 450, median composite ACT: 21. 20% scored over 600 on SAT verbal, 15% scored over 600 on SAT math, 5% scored over 26 on composite ACT.

Student Life Upper grades have uniform requirement, student council. Discipline rests primarily with faculty. Attendance at religious services is required.

Summer Programs Remediation programs offered; session focuses on math; held on campus; accepts boys and girls; not open to students from other schools. 15 students usually enrolled. 2006 schedule: June 5 to July 10. Application deadline: none.

Tuition and Aid Day student tuition: $10,547. Tuition installment plan (FACTS Tuition Payment Plan). Need-based scholarship grants available. In 2005–06, 46% of upper-school students received aid. Total amount of financial aid awarded in 2005–06: $250,000.

Admissions Traditional secondary-level entrance grade is 9. For fall 2005, 76 students applied for upper-level admission, 42 were accepted, 35 enrolled. Achievement tests, ERB, Gates MacGinite Reading Tests, ISEE or SSAT required. Deadline for receipt of application materials: February 17. Application fee required: $30. Interview required.

Athletics Interscholastic: baseball (boys), basketball (b,g), flag football (b), football (b), soccer (g), softball (g), volleyball (g); coed interscholastic: outdoor education, running, track and field. 1 PE instructor, 6 coaches, 1 trainer.

Computers Computers are regularly used in art, college planning, English, graphics, history, mathematics, science, yearbook classes. Computer network features include campus e-mail, CD-ROMs, online commercial services, Internet access, file transfer, office computer access.

Contact Pamela J. Suazo, Director of Admissions. 505-341-7223. Fax: 505-344-2517. E-mail: psuazo@menaulschool.com. Web site: www.menaulschool.com.

MENLO SCHOOL

50 Valparaiso Avenue
Atherton, California 94027
Head of School: Norman M. Colb

General Information Coeducational day college-preparatory, arts, and technology school. Grades 6–12. Founded: 1915. Setting: suburban. Nearest major city is San Jose. 35-acre campus. 23 buildings on campus. Approved or accredited by California Association of Independent Schools, Western Association of Schools and Colleges, and California Department of Education. Member of National Association of Independent Schools. Endowment: $16.2 million. Total enrollment: 767. Upper school average class size: 16. Upper school faculty-student ratio: 1:11.

Upper School Student Profile Grade 9: 144 students (74 boys, 70 girls); Grade 10: 140 students (70 boys, 70 girls); Grade 11: 139 students (71 boys, 68 girls); Grade 12: 127 students (60 boys, 67 girls).

Faculty School total: 105. In upper school: 28 men, 40 women; 46 have advanced degrees.

Subjects Offered Advanced computer applications, algebra, American history, American history-AP, American literature, American literature-AP, analytic geometry, anatomy and physiology, ancient world history, art, art history, biology, biology-AP, calculus, calculus-AP, California writers, chemistry, chemistry-AP, chorus, computer graphics, computer literacy, computer multimedia, computer programming, computer science, computer science-AP, creative writing, dance, debate, drama, earth science, economics, English, English language and composition-AP, English literature, English literature-AP, English-AP, ethics, European history, European history-AP, fine arts, French, French language-AP, French literature-AP, French-AP, geometry, government, history, honors geometry, intro to computers, Japanese, Japanese as Second Language, jazz band, jazz dance, journalism, Latin, Latin-AP, macro/microeconomics-AP, martial arts, mathematics, mathematics-AP, methods of research, microeconomics-AP, multimedia, music, music theory-AP, music-AP, musical productions, newspaper, orchestra, performing arts, philosophy, photography, physical education, physics, physics-AP, play production, science, science research, senior internship, Shakespeare, society and culture, Spanish, Spanish language-AP, Spanish literature-AP, Spanish-AP, statistics-AP, student government, student publications, studio art, studio art-AP, swimming, U.S. government and politics-AP, United States government-AP, wellness, world history, world religions, writing.

Graduation Requirements Arts and fine arts (art, music, dance, drama), English, foreign language, mathematics, physical education (includes health), science, social studies (includes history). Community service is required.

Special Academic Programs Advanced Placement exam preparation in 19 subject areas; honors section; independent study; academic accommodation for the gifted, the musically talented, and the artistically talented.

College Placement 133 students graduated in 2005; all went to college, including Stanford University; University of California, Los Angeles; University of California, Santa Barbara; University of California, Santa Cruz; University of Colorado at Boulder; University of Southern California. Mean SAT verbal: 644, mean SAT math: 658. 71% scored over 600 on SAT verbal, 80% scored over 600 on SAT math.

Student Life Upper grades have student council. Discipline rests equally with students and faculty.

Tuition and Aid Day student tuition: $26,000. Tuition installment plan (Key Tuition Payment Plan). Need-based scholarship grants, paying campus jobs available. In 2005–06, 14% of upper-school students received aid. Total amount of financial aid awarded in 2005–06: $1,857,100.

Admissions Traditional secondary-level entrance grade is 9. For fall 2005, 362 students applied for upper-level admission, 135 were accepted, 78 enrolled. ISEE or SSAT required. Deadline for receipt of application materials: January 10. Application fee required: $75. On-campus interview required.

Athletics Interscholastic: aerobics/dance (girls), baseball (b), basketball (b,g), cross-country running (b,g), dance (g), football (b), golf (b,g), lacrosse (b,g), soccer (b,g),

softball (g), swimming and diving (b,g), tennis (b,g), track and field (b,g), volleyball (b,g), water polo (b,g); coed interscholastic: aerobics/dance, dance, martial arts. 67 coaches, 2 trainers.

Computers Computers are regularly used in English, history, journalism, mathematics, media arts, multimedia, newspaper, science, yearbook classes. Computer network features include campus e-mail, on-campus library services, CD-ROMs, online commercial services, Internet access, file transfer.

Contact Mary Emery, Admissions and Financial Aid Assistant. 650-330-2001 Ext. 2601. Fax: 650-330-2012. Web site: www.menloschool.org.

ANNOUNCEMENT FROM THE SCHOOL Menlo promotes the growth of mind, body, and spirit. In a framework of strong faculty and parent support, students are encouraged to fulfill their potential by engaging in a wide array of academic and extracurricular programs. Vital, energetic students of varied backgrounds and talents take ever-greater responsibility for their own learning and behavior. Graduates attend leading colleges and universities.

MENTOR COLLEGE

40 Forest Avenue
Mississauga, Ontario L5G 1L1, Canada
Head of School: Mr. Ken Philbrook

General Information Coeducational day college-preparatory school. Grades JK–12. Founded: 1984. Setting: urban. 20-hectare campus. Approved or accredited by Ontario Department of Education. Language of instruction: English. Total enrollment: 1,755. Upper school average class size: 16. Upper school faculty-student ratio: 1:14.

Faculty School total: 47. In upper school: 23 men, 20 women.

Subjects Offered Accounting, algebra, biology, business, calculus, Canadian geography, Canadian history, careers, chemistry, civics, computer multimedia, computer programming, data analysis, discrete mathematics, economics, English/composition-AP, environmental science, ESL, European history, exercise science, fine arts, French as a second language, history, law, literature, marine biology, mathematics, music, philosophy, physical education, physical science, physics, science, Spanish, visual arts, world issues.

Special Academic Programs ESL (70 students enrolled).

College Placement 131 students graduated in 2005; 130 went to college, including McGill University; McMaster University; The University of Western Ontario; University of Guelph; University of Toronto; University of Waterloo. Other: 1 had other specific plans.

Student Life Upper grades have uniform requirement, student council. Discipline rests primarily with faculty.

Summer Programs Remediation, enrichment, advancement, ESL programs offered; session focuses on advancement; held on campus; accepts boys and girls; open to students from other schools. 100 students usually enrolled. 2006 schedule: June 27 to July 31. Application deadline: June 15.

Tuition and Aid Day student tuition: CAN$12,500. Merit scholarship grants available. Total upper-school merit-scholarship money awarded for 2005–06: CAN$3002. Total amount of financial aid awarded in 2005–06: CAN$3002.

Admissions Traditional secondary-level entrance grade is 9. School's own exam required. Deadline for receipt of application materials: none. Application fee required: CAN$100. Interview required.

Athletics Interscholastic: alpine skiing (boys, girls), aquatics (b,g), badminton (b,g), basketball (b,g), cheering (b,g), cricket (b), cross-country running (b,g), golf (b,g), hockey (b), indoor soccer (b,g), rowing (b,g), rugby (b,g), skiing (downhill) (b,g), soccer (b,g), swimming and diving (b,g), table tennis (b,g), tennis (b,g), track and field (b,g), volleyball (b,g), wrestling (b,g); intramural: badminton (b,g), basketball (b,g), floor hockey (b,g), indoor hockey (b,g), indoor soccer (b,g), lacrosse (b,g), soccer (b,g), volleyball (b,g); coed interscholastic: archery, softball, ultimate Frisbee; coed intramural: cricket, dance, outdoor education, physical fitness, physical training, scuba diving, table tennis. 4 PE instructors.

Computers Computers are regularly used in business, geography, technology classes. Computer network features include CD-ROMs, online commercial services, Internet access, file transfer.

Contact Anna Penney, Registrar. 905-271-3393. Fax: 905-271-8367. E-mail: admin@mentorcollege.edu. Web site: www.mentorcollege.edu.

MERCEDES COLLEGE

540 Fullarton Road
Springfield 5062, Australia
Head of School: Mr. Peter Howard Daw

General Information Coeducational day college-preparatory, general academic, arts, business, vocational, religious studies, and bilingual studies school, affiliated with Roman Catholic Church. Grades 1–12. Founded: 1954. Setting: suburban. Nearest major city is Adelaide. 7-hectare campus. 10 buildings on campus. Member of European Council of International Schools. Language of instruction: English. Total enrollment: 1,168. Upper school average class size: 16.

Upper School Student Profile Grade 6: 80 students (37 boys, 43 girls); Grade 7: 77 students (38 boys, 39 girls); Grade 8: 141 students (68 boys, 73 girls); Grade 9: 139 students (66 boys, 73 girls); Grade 10: 142 students (81 boys, 61 girls); Grade 11: 162 students (103 boys, 59 girls); Grade 12: 138 students (68 boys, 70 girls). 90% of students are Roman Catholic.

Faculty School total: 100.

Special Academic Programs International Baccalaureate program; academic accommodation for the gifted; remedial reading and/or remedial writing; programs in general development for dyslexic students; ESL.

Student Life Upper grades have uniform requirement, student council, honor system. Discipline rests primarily with faculty. Attendance at religious services is required.

Admissions Deadline for receipt of application materials: none. Application fee required. Interview required.

Athletics Interscholastic: cricket (boys), football (b), netball (g), water polo (b); coed interscholastic: alpine skiing, badminton, basketball, canoeing/kayaking, climbing, cross-country running, equestrian sports, fitness, hiking/backpacking, hockey, outdoor education, physical fitness, physical training, rock climbing, soccer, swimming and diving, table tennis, tennis, track and field, volleyball, winter soccer.

Computers Computers are regularly used in all classes. Computer network features include campus e-mail, on-campus library services, CD-ROMs, Internet access, file transfer, office computer access, DVD, wireless campus network.

Contact Mrs. Shirley Smith, Registrar. 618-83723200. Fax: 618-83799540. E-mail: ssmith@mercedes.adl.catholic.edu.au. Web site: www.mercedes.adl.catholic.edu.au.

MERCERSBURG ACADEMY

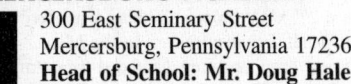

300 East Seminary Street
Mercersburg, Pennsylvania 17236
Head of School: Mr. Doug Hale

General Information Coeducational boarding and day college-preparatory school. Boarding grades 9–PG, day grades 9–11. Founded: 1893. Setting: small town. Nearest major city is Washington, DC. Students are housed in single-sex dormitories. 300-acre campus. 28 buildings on campus. Approved or accredited by Association of Independent Schools of Greater Washington, Middle States Association of Colleges and Schools, The Association of Boarding Schools, and Pennsylvania Department of Education. Member of National Association of Independent Schools and Secondary School Admission Test Board. Endowment: $160 million. Total enrollment: 442. Upper school average class size: 12. Upper school faculty-student ratio: 1:5.

Upper School Student Profile Grade 9: 83 students (41 boys, 42 girls); Grade 10: 107 students (55 boys, 52 girls); Grade 11: 122 students (66 boys, 56 girls); Grade 12: 111 students (54 boys, 57 girls); Postgraduate: 19 students (17 boys, 2 girls). 84% of students are boarding students. 33% are state residents. 29 states are represented in upper school student body. 12% are international students. International students from Ecuador, Germany, Jamaica, Republic of Korea, Saudi Arabia, and Taiwan; 16 other countries represented in student body.

Faculty School total: 89. In upper school: 36 men, 34 women; 59 have advanced degrees; 29 reside on campus.

Subjects Offered Advanced Placement courses, African history, algebra, American history, American literature, art, art history, art history-AP, Asian history, biology, biology-AP, botany, calculus, calculus-AP, ceramics, chemistry, chemistry-AP, Chinese, computer graphics, computer math, computer science, computer science-AP, creative writing, drama, economics-AP, English, English literature, English literature and composition-AP, environmental science-AP, ethics, European history, European history-AP, fine arts, French, French language-AP, French literature-AP, genetics, geometry, German, German-AP, health, history, humanities, Latin, Latin-AP, mathematics, music, physical education, physics, physics-AP, public speaking, religion, science, social studies, Spanish, Spanish language-AP, statistics-AP, theater, trigonometry, U.S. history-AP, United States government-AP.

Graduation Requirements Arts and fine arts (art, music, dance, drama), English, foreign language, history, mathematics, physical education (includes health), religion (includes Bible studies and theology), science, participation in sports, performing arts, or other activities.

Special Academic Programs Advanced Placement exam preparation in 20 subject areas; honors section; independent study; term-away projects; study abroad; academic accommodation for the gifted.

College Placement 132 students graduated in 2005; 131 went to college, including Bryn Mawr College; Bucknell University; Georgetown University; United States Naval Academy; University of Pennsylvania; University of the South. Other: 1 went to work. Mean SAT verbal: 612, mean SAT math: 612.

Student Life Upper grades have specified standards of dress, student council, honor system. Discipline rests primarily with faculty.

Summer Programs Enrichment, ESL, sports, art/fine arts, rigorous outdoor training programs offered; session focuses on enrichment ; held both on and off campus; held at various locations; accepts boys and girls; open to students from other schools. 1000 students usually enrolled. 2006 schedule: June 12 to August 19. Application deadline: none.

Tuition and Aid Day student tuition: $26,500; 7-day tuition and room/board: $34,700. Tuition installment plan (Insured Tuition Payment Plan, Key Tuition Payment Plan, monthly payment plans). Merit scholarship grants, need-based scholarship grants, need-based loans available. In 2005–06, 42% of upper-school

students received aid; total upper-school merit-scholarship money awarded: $243,600. Total amount of financial aid awarded in 2005–06: $3,730,000.

Admissions Traditional secondary-level entrance grade is 9. For fall 2005, 653 students applied for upper-level admission, 255 were accepted, 165 enrolled. ISEE, PSAT and SAT for applicants to grade 11 and 12, SSAT or TOEFL required. Deadline for receipt of application materials: February 1. Application fee required: $50. On-campus interview required.

Athletics Interscholastic: baseball (boys), basketball (b,g), cross-country running (b,g), diving (b,g), field hockey (g), football (b), lacrosse (b,g), skiing (downhill) (b,g), soccer (b,g), softball (g), squash (b,g), swimming and diving (b,g), tennis (b,g), track and field (b,g), volleyball (g), winter (indoor) track (b,g), wrestling (b); coed interscholastic: alpine skiing, golf; coed intramural: aerobics/dance, back packing, ballet, bicycling, canoeing/kayaking, climbing, dance, freestyle skiing, Frisbee, golf, hiking/backpacking, kayaking, martial arts, modern dance, outdoor adventure, outdoor education, outdoor recreation, skiing (downhill), snowboarding, strength & conditioning, ultimate Frisbee, weight training, yoga. 4 PE instructors, 20 coaches, 2 trainers.

Computers Computers are regularly used in art, English, foreign language, history, mathematics, music, science classes. Computer network features include campus e-mail, on-campus library services, CD-ROMs, Internet access, file transfer, DVD, wireless campus network.

Contact Mr. Christopher R. Tompkins, Director of Admission and Financial Aid. 717-328-6173. Fax: 717-328-6319. E-mail: admission@mercersburg.edu. Web site: www.mercersburg.edu.

ANNOUNCEMENT FROM THE SCHOOL The new Masinter Outdoor Education Center, which includes a 27' x 45' indoor climbing wall, has been dedicated and is the staging area for all activities related to the Mercersburg Outdoor Education Program. The new program offers extended trips (to Zion National Park in '05), a leadership development course, specific outdoor programs such as rock climbing and white-water kayaking, and weekend trips.

See full description on page 906.

MERCY HIGH SCHOOL

1740 Randolph Road
Middletown, Connecticut 06457-5155
Head of School: Sr. Mary McCarthy, RSM

General Information Girls' day college-preparatory, arts, and religious studies school, affiliated with Roman Catholic Church. Grades 9–12. Founded: 1963. Setting: rural. Nearest major city is Hartford. 26-acre campus. 1 building on campus. Approved or accredited by Mercy Secondary Education Association, National Catholic Education Association, New England Association of Schools and Colleges, and Connecticut Department of Education. Endowment: $393,000. Total enrollment: 667. Upper school average class size: 21. Upper school faculty-student ratio: 1:14.

Upper School Student Profile Grade 9: 167 students (167 girls); Grade 10: 167 students (167 girls); Grade 11: 158 students (158 girls); Grade 12: 175 students (175 girls). 79.5% of students are Roman Catholic.

Faculty School total: 55. In upper school: 7 men, 47 women; 41 have advanced degrees.

Subjects Offered Accounting, advanced math, algebra, American government, American literature, American literature-AP, anatomy and physiology, art, art appreciation, arts and crafts, biology, biology-AP, business, calculus, calculus-AP, Catholic belief and practice, ceramics, chamber groups, chemistry, chemistry-AP, choir, chorus, civics, comparative government and politics, computer applications, concert band, concert choir, creative writing, drama workshop, drawing and design, English, English literature, English-AP, environmental science, European history, expository writing, French, French language-AP, French literature-AP, French-AP, geometry, government/civics, grammar, health, history, honors algebra, honors English, honors geometry, honors U.S. history, honors world history, humanities, independent study, journalism, keyboarding/computer, Latin, Latin-AP, law, literature-AP, mathematics, modern history, music, music theory, neuroscience, photography, physical education, physical science, physics, physics-AP, pottery, pre-algebra, pre-calculus, psychology, reading/study skills, religious studies, science, social studies, sociology, Spanish, Spanish language-AP, Spanish-AP, statistics, statistics-AP, theater arts, trigonometry, U.S. history, U.S. history-AP, wind ensemble, word processing, world history, world literature, writing, writing workshop.

Graduation Requirements Civics, computer applications, English, foreign language, mathematics, physical education (includes health), religion (includes Bible studies and theology), science, social studies (includes history), 50 hours of community service.

Special Academic Programs Advanced Placement exam preparation in 11 subject areas; honors section; independent study; study at local college for college credit.

College Placement 170 students graduated in 2005; 167 went to college, including Central Connecticut State University; Roger Williams University; Southern Connecticut State University; University of Connecticut; University of New Hampshire. Other: 3 went to work. Median SAT verbal: 540, median SAT math: 510, median

composite ACT: 22. 26.8% scored over 600 on SAT verbal, 20.2% scored over 600 on SAT math, 19.2% scored over 26 on composite ACT.

Student Life Upper grades have uniform requirement, student council. Discipline rests primarily with faculty. Attendance at religious services is required.

Tuition and Aid Day student tuition: $7400–$7900. Tuition installment plan (FACTS Tuition Payment Plan, individually arranged payment plans). Tuition reduction for siblings, merit scholarship grants, need-based scholarship grants available. In 2005–06, 30% of upper-school students received aid; total upper-school merit-scholarship money awarded: $47,500. Total amount of financial aid awarded in 2005–06: $350,275.

Admissions Traditional secondary-level entrance grade is 9. For fall 2005, 353 students applied for upper-level admission, 321 were accepted, 186 enrolled. High School Placement Test (closed version) from Scholastic Testing Service required. Deadline for receipt of application materials: none. Application fee required: $50.

Athletics Interscholastic: basketball, cheering, cross-country running, diving, field hockey, golf, gymnastics, indoor track, lacrosse, soccer, softball, swimming and diving, tennis, track and field, volleyball; intramural: alpine skiing, golf, skiing (downhill), snowboarding, volleyball. 2 PE instructors, 23 coaches, 1 trainer.

Computers Computers are regularly used in accounting, all academic, journalism, word processing classes. Computer network features include on-campus library services, CD-ROMs, Internet access, DVD.

Contact Ms. Jo-Ellen Narstis, Admissions Director. 860-346-6659. Fax: 860-344-9887. E-mail: jnarstis@mercyhigh.com. Web site: www.mercyhigh.com.

MERCY HIGH SCHOOL

1501 South 48th Street
Omaha, Nebraska 68106-2598
Head of School: Ms. Carolyn Jaworski

General Information Girls' day college-preparatory, general academic, arts, business, religious studies, and technology school, affiliated with Roman Catholic Church. Grades 9–12. Founded: 1955. Setting: urban. 1-acre campus. 1 building on campus. Approved or accredited by Mercy Secondary Education Association, National Catholic Education Association, North Central Association of Colleges and Schools, and Nebraska Department of Education. Total enrollment: 335. Upper school average class size: 22. Upper school faculty-student ratio: 1:11.

Upper School Student Profile Grade 9: 97 students (97 girls); Grade 10: 83 students (83 girls); Grade 11: 94 students (94 girls); Grade 12: 61 students (61 girls). 89% of students are Roman Catholic.

Faculty School total: 32. In upper school: 4 men, 28 women; 18 have advanced degrees.

Subjects Offered Accounting, algebra, American government, American history, American history-AP, American literature, anatomy and physiology, art, ballet, biology, British literature, British literature-AP, business applications, calculus, calculus-AP, chemistry, chemistry-AP, child development, choir, computer education, computer keyboarding, consumer mathematics, culinary arts, debate, drama, drawing, ecology, English, French, general math, geometry, health, honors English, honors geometry, journalism, keyboarding/computer, math review, moral theology, painting, participation in sports, peace and justice, physics, physics-AP, play production, pottery, pre-algebra, pre-calculus, psychology, social justice, Spanish, Spanish-AP, speech, speech and debate, sports medicine, stagecraft, statistics, theology, theology and the arts, trigonometry, U.S. government, U.S. history, U.S. history-AP, vocal music, world history, yearbook.

Graduation Requirements Advanced math, algebra, American government, anatomy and physiology, arts and fine arts (art, music, dance, drama), biology, chemistry, computer applications, debate, English, foreign language, geometry, mathematics, physical education (includes health), physics, social studies (includes history), speech, theology, U.S. history, world history, service hours.

Special Academic Programs Advanced Placement exam preparation in 5 subject areas; honors section; remedial math; programs in general development for dyslexic students; special instructional classes for students with LD, ADD, emotional and behavioral problems.

College Placement 74 students graduated in 2005; 68 went to college, including Creighton University; Rockhurst University; University of Nebraska–Lincoln; University of Nebraska at Kearney; University of Nebraska at Omaha. Other: 4 went to work, 2 had other specific plans.

Student Life Upper grades have uniform requirement, student council, honor system. Discipline rests primarily with faculty. Attendance at religious services is required.

Tuition and Aid Day student tuition: $6300. Tuition installment plan (individually arranged payment plans, school's own payment plan). Tuition reduction for siblings, merit scholarship grants, need-based scholarship grants, paying campus jobs available. In 2005–06, 85% of upper-school students received aid; total upper-school merit-scholarship money awarded: $60,000. Total amount of financial aid awarded in 2005–06: $375,000.

Admissions Traditional secondary-level entrance grade is 9. For fall 2005, 99 students applied for upper-level admission, 99 were accepted, 97 enrolled. STS Examination required. Deadline for receipt of application materials: March 31. Application fee required: $100. Interview required.

Athletics Interscholastic: aerobics, archery, badminton, ballet, basketball, bowling, cheering, cross-country running, dance squad, dance team, diving, fitness walking,

golf, independent competitive sports, outdoor activities, physical fitness, pom squad, self defense, soccer, softball, swimming and diving, tennis, track and field, volleyball, weight training; intramural: indoor soccer. 1 PE instructor, 15 coaches, 1 trainer.

Computers Computers are regularly used in accounting, business, business applications, business education, business studies, history, journalism, keyboarding, lab/keyboard, library, library skills, mathematics, music, photojournalism, publications, religion, science, yearbook classes. Computer network features include campus e-mail, on-campus library services, CD-ROMs, Internet access, file transfer, office computer access, DVD.

Contact Mrs. Trisha Steele, Recruitment Director. 402-553-9424. Fax: 402-553-0394. E-mail: steelet@mercyhigh.org. Web site: www.mercyhigh.org.

MERCY HIGH SCHOOL COLLEGE PREPARATORY

3250 19th Avenue
San Francisco, California 94132-2000
Head of School: Dr. Dorothy McCrea

General Information Girls' day college-preparatory school, affiliated with Roman Catholic Church. Grades 9–12. Founded: 1952. Setting: urban. 6-acre campus. 2 buildings on campus. Approved or accredited by Western Association of Schools and Colleges and California Department of Education. Total enrollment: 530. Upper school average class size: 26. Upper school faculty-student ratio: 1:15.

Upper School Student Profile Grade 9: 116 students (116 girls); Grade 10: 135 students (135 girls); Grade 11: 148 students (148 girls); Grade 12: 131 students (131 girls). 62% of students are Roman Catholic.

Faculty School total: 44. In upper school: 8 men, 36 women; 29 have advanced degrees.

Subjects Offered Algebra, American history, American literature, art, biology, business, calculus, ceramics, chemistry, chorus, computer applications, computer programming, creative writing, dance, drama, English, English literature, environmental science, ethics, ethnic studies, expository writing, French, geometry, government/civics, keyboarding, mathematics, physical education, physics, religion, social studies, Spanish, speech, theater, trigonometry, world history.

Graduation Requirements 200 community service hours.

Special Academic Programs Advanced Placement exam preparation in 11 subject areas; honors section.

College Placement 142 students graduated in 2005; 141 went to college, including San Francisco State University; University of California, Berkeley; University of California, Davis; University of San Francisco. Other: 1 went to work.

Student Life Upper grades have uniform requirement, student council. Discipline rests primarily with faculty. Attendance at religious services is required.

Summer Programs Enrichment programs offered; session focuses on enrichment; held on campus; accepts boys and girls; open to students from other schools. 400 students usually enrolled. 2006 schedule: June 19 to July 14. Application deadline: June 19.

Tuition and Aid Day student tuition: $10,175. Guaranteed tuition plan. Tuition installment plan (monthly payment plans). Need-based scholarship grants available. In 2005–06, 45% of upper-school students received aid.

Admissions Traditional secondary-level entrance grade is 9. For fall 2005, 250 students applied for upper-level admission, 116 were accepted, 116 enrolled. High School Placement Test required. Deadline for receipt of application materials: March 1. Application fee required: $80. On-campus interview required.

Athletics Interscholastic: basketball, cross-country running, dance, soccer, softball, tennis, track and field, volleyball. 3 PE instructors, 11 coaches.

Computers Computers are regularly used in accounting, Bible studies, business education, business skills, English, religion, science classes. Computer network features include campus e-mail, on-campus library services, CD-ROMs, Internet access, office computer access, SASI system, Hunter Systems, Blackbaud.

Contact Mrs. Elizabeth Belonogoff, Admissions Director. 415-584-5929. Fax: 415-334-9726. E-mail: admissionsmercysf@mercyhs.org. Web site: www.mercyhs.org.

MERCYHURST PREPARATORY SCHOOL

538 East Grandview Boulevard
Erie, Pennsylvania 16504-2697
Head of School: Ms. Margaret Aste

General Information Coeducational day college-preparatory, arts, religious studies, and technology school, affiliated with Roman Catholic Church. Grades 9–12. Founded: 1926. Setting: urban. 5-acre campus. 1 building on campus. Approved or accredited by International Baccalaureate Organization, Middle States Association of Colleges and Schools, and Pennsylvania Department of Education. Total enrollment: 641. Upper school average class size: 25. Upper school faculty-student ratio: 1:15.

Upper School Student Profile Grade 9: 145 students (40 boys, 105 girls); Grade 10: 163 students (44 boys, 119 girls); Grade 11: 168 students (76 boys, 92 girls); Grade 12: 165 students (67 boys, 98 girls). 85% of students are Roman Catholic.

Faculty School total: 56. In upper school: 17 men, 38 women; 15 have advanced degrees.

Subjects Offered Accounting, algebra, American Civil War, American government, American history, American literature, anatomy, art, art appreciation, art education, art history, biology, broadcasting, business skills, calculus, campus ministry, career exploration, ceramics, chemistry, Christian ethics, communications, community service, computer applications, computer keyboarding, computer programming, computer science, creative arts, creative writing, dance, drama, drama performance, drawing, drawing and design, earth science, English, English literature, environmental science, ethics, European history, expository writing, fiber arts, fine arts, first aid, French, geology, geometry, government/civics, guitar, health, Hebrew scripture, history, Holocaust, humanities, Internet, journalism, mathematics, multimedia, music, musical productions, orchestra, painting, photography, physical education, physics, physiology, psychology, public speaking, publications, reading/study skills, religion, SAT preparation, SAT/ACT preparation, science, senior internship, set design, sign language, social studies, Spanish, speech, speech and debate, study skills, tap dance, technical theater, technology/design, theater, theater arts, theology, theory of knowledge, trigonometry, typing, U.S. government, visual and performing arts, weight fitness, weightlifting, word processing, world cultures, world history, writing, writing skills, yearbook.

Graduation Requirements Arts and fine arts (art, music, dance, drama), arts appreciation, business skills (includes word processing), computer science, creative arts, English, foreign language, mathematics, physical education (includes health), public speaking, religion (includes Bible studies and theology), science, social studies (includes history), 100 hours of community service.

Special Academic Programs International Baccalaureate program; honors section; accelerated programs; independent study; study at local college for college credit; study abroad; academic accommodation for the gifted, the musically talented, and the artistically talented; remedial reading and/or remedial writing; remedial math.

College Placement 207 students graduated in 2005; 198 went to college, including Duquesne University; Edinboro University of Pennsylvania; Gannon University; Mercyhurst College; The Pennsylvania State University University Park Campus; University of Pittsburgh. Other: 7 went to work, 2 entered military service. Mean SAT verbal: 514, mean SAT math: 502, mean composite ACT: 22.

Student Life Upper grades have uniform requirement, student council, honor system. Discipline rests primarily with faculty. Attendance at religious services is required.

Summer Programs Remediation, enrichment, advancement, art/fine arts, rigorous outdoor training, computer instruction programs offered; session focuses on enrichment; held both on and off campus; held at educational field sites; accepts boys and girls; open to students from other schools. 150 students usually enrolled. 2006 schedule: June 21 to August 13. Application deadline: none.

Tuition and Aid Day student tuition: $4920. Tuition installment plan (FACTS Tuition Payment Plan). Merit scholarship grants, need-based scholarship grants, bank loans available. In 2005–06, 40% of upper-school students received aid; total upper-school merit-scholarship money awarded: $75,000. Total amount of financial aid awarded in 2005–06: $159,000.

Admissions Traditional secondary-level entrance grade is 9. For fall 2005, 266 students applied for upper-level admission, 253 were accepted, 145 enrolled. Achievement tests, Iowa Tests of Basic Skills or Math Placement Exam required. Deadline for receipt of application materials: none. Application fee required: $10. Interview recommended.

Athletics Interscholastic: baseball (boys), basketball (b,g), bowling (g), cheering (g), crew (b,g), cross-country running (b,g), football (b), golf (b,g), rowing (b,g), soccer (b,g), softball (g), swimming and diving (b,g), tennis (b,g), track and field (b,g), volleyball (g); intramural: baseball (b), indoor soccer (b,g); coed interscholastic: fencing, ice hockey, tennis, weight training; coed intramural: bowling, ice skating, weight lifting, weight training, winter soccer. 2 PE instructors, 39 coaches, 1 trainer.

Computers Computers are regularly used in college planning, English, foreign language, history, journalism, mathematics, media, music, newspaper, photography, photojournalism, publications, publishing, SAT preparation, science, typing, word processing, writing, yearbook classes. Computer network features include campus e-mail, on-campus library services, CD-ROMs, online commercial services, Internet access, wireless campus network.

Contact Mrs. Marcia E. DiTullio, Administrative Assistant. 814-824-2323. Fax: 814-824-2116. E-mail: mditullio@mpslakers.com. Web site: www.mpslakers.com.

METROPOLITAN PREPARATORY ACADEMY

49 Mobile Drive
Toronto, Ontario M4A 1H5, Canada
Head of School: Mr. William (Wayne) McKelvey

General Information Coeducational day college-preparatory, arts, and business school. Grades 6–12. Founded: 1982. Setting: urban. 3-acre campus. 3 buildings on campus. Approved or accredited by Ontario Department of Education. Language of instruction: English. Total enrollment: 435. Upper school faculty-student ratio: 1:18.

Upper School Student Profile Grade 9: 80 students (50 boys, 30 girls); Grade 10: 85 students (50 boys, 35 girls); Grade 11: 85 students (50 boys, 35 girls); Grade 12: 85 students (50 boys, 35 girls).

Faculty School total: 30. In upper school: 11 men, 13 women.

Special Academic Programs Honors section; accelerated programs.

College Placement 120 students graduated in 2005; 115 went to college. Other: 5 had other specific plans.

Student Life Upper grades have student council. Discipline rests primarily with faculty.

Tuition and Aid Day student tuition: CAN$12,900. Tuition installment plan (monthly payment plans).

Admissions Traditional secondary-level entrance grade is 9. For fall 2005, 295 students applied for upper-level admission, 165 were accepted, 120 enrolled. Admissions testing required. Deadline for receipt of application materials: none. No application fee required. Interview required.

Athletics Interscholastic: alpine skiing (boys, girls), ball hockey (b,g), baseball (b,g), basketball (b,g), golf (b,g), ice hockey (b), indoor soccer (b), mountain biking (b); intramural: badminton (b,g), ball hockey (b,g), baseball (b,g), basketball (b,g), floor hockey (b,g), golf (b,g), ice hockey (b,g), indoor soccer (b,g), lacrosse (b,g), mountain biking (b,g), outdoor adventure (b); coed interscholastic: ball hockey, cross-country running; coed intramural: badminton, ball hockey, climbing, cross-country running, fitness, golf, ice hockey, lacrosse, mountain biking. 4 PE instructors, 15 coaches, 5 trainers.

Computers Computer network features include on-campus library services, CD-ROMs, Internet access.

Contact Mr. Steven Andrew Redding, Director of Admission and Student Affairs. 416-285 0870. Fax: 416-285 0873. E-mail: sredding@metroprep.com. Web site: www.metroprep.com.

MIAMI COUNTRY DAY SCHOOL

601 Northeast 107th Street
Miami, Florida 33161
Head of School: Dr. John P. Davies

petersons.com

General Information Coeducational day college-preparatory school. Grades JK–12. Founded: 1938. Setting: suburban. 16-acre campus. 6 buildings on campus. Approved or accredited by Florida Council of Independent Schools, Southern Association of Colleges and Schools, The College Board, and Florida Department of Education. Member of National Association of Independent Schools and Secondary School Admission Test Board. Language of instruction: English. Endowment: $1.3 million. Total enrollment: 1,000. Upper school average class size: 20. Upper school faculty-student ratio: 1:9.

Upper School Student Profile Grade 9: 104 students (58 boys, 46 girls); Grade 10: 88 students (48 boys, 40 girls); Grade 11: 82 students (44 boys, 38 girls); Grade 12: 77 students (43 boys, 34 girls).

Faculty School total: 117. In upper school: 23 men, 21 women; 24 have advanced degrees.

Subjects Offered Advanced Placement courses, African-American studies, algebra, American history, American literature, ancient history, art, art history, backpacking, band, biology, calculus, ceramics, chemistry, community service, composition, computer programming, computer science, conflict resolution, creative writing, design, desktop publishing, drama, drawing, economics, English, English literature, ESL, European history, film, film and literature, fine arts, French, geography, geometry, government/civics, health, instrumental music, jewelry making, journalism, law, life management skills, literature, marine biology, mathematics, music theory, orchestra, painting, philosophy, photography, physical education, physical science, physics, psychology, public speaking, religion, science, sculpture, social science, social studies, Spanish, theater, trigonometry, video film production, world history, world literature, writing, yearbook.

Graduation Requirements Arts and fine arts (art, music, dance, drama), computer science, electives, English, foreign language, mathematics, physical education (includes health), religion (includes Bible studies and theology), research seminar, science, social studies (includes history), 120 hours of community service.

Special Academic Programs Advanced Placement exam preparation in 17 subject areas; honors section; independent study; study at local college for college credit; ESL (8 students enrolled).

College Placement 77 students graduated in 2004; all went to college, including Florida International University; Florida State University; University of Florida; University of Miami; Vassar College; Wellesley College. Median SAT verbal: 600, median SAT math: 640.

Student Life Upper grades have uniform requirement, student council, honor system. Discipline rests equally with students and faculty.

Tuition and Aid Day student tuition: $16,400–$16,800. Tuition installment plan (Academic Management Services Plan). Need-based scholarship grants available. In 2004–05, 17% of upper-school students received aid. Total amount of financial aid awarded in 2004–05: $565,250.

Admissions Traditional secondary-level entrance grade is 9. For fall 2005, 61 students applied for upper-level admission, 33 were accepted, 31 enrolled. ESOL English Proficiency Test, ISEE or writing sample required. Deadline for receipt of application materials: February 15. Application fee required: $85. On-campus interview required.

Athletics Interscholastic: baseball (boys), basketball (b,g), cheering (g), cross-country running (b,g), football (b), golf (b), lacrosse (b), soccer (b,g), softball (g), swimming and diving (b,g), tennis (b,g), track and field (b,g), volleyball (g), water polo (b); intramural: baseball (b), basketball (b,g), cheering (g), cross-country running (b,g), football (b), volleyball (b); coed intramural: crew, flag football, outdoor

education, outdoor skills, physical fitness, physical training, soccer, strength & conditioning, weight training. 5 PE instructors, 24 coaches, 1 trainer.

Computers Computers are regularly used in all academic, graphic design, journalism, media, research skills, Web site design, yearbook classes. Computer network features include campus e-mail, on-campus library services, CD-ROMs, online commercial services, Internet access, file transfer, The Homework Site, faculty access via the Web (faweb).

Contact Dr. J. Victor McGlone, Director of Admission and Financial Aid. 305-779-7230. Fax: 305-758-5107. E-mail: mcglonev@miamicountryday.org. Web site: www.miamicountryday.org.

See full description on page 908.

MIDDLESEX SCHOOL

1400 Lowell Road
Concord, Massachusetts 01742
Head of School: Kathleen C. Giles

petersons.com

General Information Coeducational boarding and day college-preparatory school. Grades 9–12. Founded: 1901. Setting: rural. Nearest major city is Boston. Students are housed in single-sex dormitories. 350-acre campus. 31 buildings on campus. Approved or accredited by Association of Independent Schools in New England, New England Association of Schools and Colleges, The Association of Boarding Schools, and The College Board. Member of National Association of Independent Schools and Secondary School Admission Test Board. Endowment: $78 million. Total enrollment: 355. Upper school average class size: 11. Upper school faculty-student ratio: 1:5.

Upper School Student Profile Grade 9: 68 students (35 boys, 33 girls); Grade 10: 101 students (53 boys, 48 girls); Grade 11: 92 students (46 boys, 46 girls); Grade 12: 94 students (50 boys, 44 girls). 75% of students are boarding students. 50% are state residents. 20 states are represented in upper school student body. 10% are international students. International students from Bermuda, Canada, France, Jamaica, Republic of Korea, and Thailand; 6 other countries represented in student body.

Faculty School total: 58. In upper school: 33 men, 25 women; 47 have advanced degrees; 51 reside on campus.

Subjects Offered Acting, advanced chemistry, advanced computer applications, Advanced Placement courses, advanced studio art-AP, African-American history, algebra, American government-AP, American literature, analytic geometry, art, art history, art history-AP, art-AP, Asian literature, astronomy, biology, biology-AP, British literature, calculus, calculus-AP, ceramics, chemistry, chemistry-AP, Chinese, computer programming, computer programming-AP, computer science, computer science-AP, creative writing, discrete math, DNA, drama, economics, economics-AP, English, English literature, English literature and composition-AP, environmental science, environmental science-AP, ethics, European history, European history-AP, finite math, French, French language-AP, French literature-AP, geometry, Greek, history, Holocaust, Holocaust studies, independent study, jazz band, Latin, Latin American history, Latin-AP, mathematics, Middle East, Middle Eastern history, model United Nations, music, music theory, music theory-AP, philosophy, photography, physics, physics-AP, political science, religion, Shakespeare, Spanish, Spanish language-AP, Spanish literature-AP, statistics, statistics-AP, studio art—AP, theater, trigonometry, U.S. government and politics-AP, U.S. history, U.S. history-AP, Vietnam history, Vietnam War, vocal ensemble, women in world history, woodworking, world history, writing.

Graduation Requirements Algebra, analytic geometry, arts, English, English literature and composition-AP, European history, foreign language, geometry, science, trigonometry, U.S. history, completion of a wooden plaque.

Special Academic Programs Advanced Placement exam preparation in 19 subject areas; honors section; independent study; academic accommodation for the gifted.

College Placement 80 students graduated in 2005; all went to college, including Boston College; Bowdoin College; Brown University; Harvard University; Trinity College; University of Pennsylvania. Median SAT verbal: 670, median SAT math: 680.

Student Life Upper grades have specified standards of dress, student council. Discipline rests primarily with faculty.

Summer Programs Art/fine arts programs offered; session focuses on arts; held on campus; accepts boys and girls; open to students from other schools. 280 students usually enrolled. 2006 schedule: June 27 to July 30.

Tuition and Aid Day student tuition: $29,450; 7-day tuition and room/board: $36,800. Tuition installment plan (Insured Tuition Payment Plan, Key Tuition Payment Plan, monthly payment plans, semi-annual payment plan). Need-based scholarship grants, need-based loans, paying campus jobs, Achiever Loans (Key Education Resources) available. In 2005–06, 28% of upper-school students received aid. Total amount of financial aid awarded in 2005–06: $2,800,000.

Admissions Traditional secondary-level entrance grade is 9. For fall 2005, 774 students applied for upper-level admission, 198 were accepted, 101 enrolled. ISEE or SSAT required. Deadline for receipt of application materials: January 31. Application fee required: $50. On-campus interview recommended.

Athletics Interscholastic: alpine skiing (boys, girls), baseball (b), basketball (b,g), crew (b,g), cross-country running (b,g), field hockey (g), football (b), ice hockey (b,g), lacrosse (b,g), skiing (downhill) (b,g), soccer (b,g), softball (g), squash (b,g), tennis

(b,g), wrestling (b); coed interscholastic: golf, track and field; coed intramural: dance, fitness, strength & conditioning, yoga. 19 coaches, 1 trainer.

Computers Computers are regularly used in economics, history, mathematics, science classes. Computer network features include campus e-mail, on-campus library services, CD-ROMs, online commercial services, Internet access, DVD.

Contact Sibyl F. Cohane, Director of Admissions. 978-371-6524. Fax: 978-402-1400. E-mail: scohane@middlesex.edu. Web site: www.middlesex.edu.

ANNOUNCEMENT FROM THE SCHOOL For more than a century, Middlesex School, located in historic Concord, Massachusetts, has embraced a timeless intellectual tradition. Critical thinking is the hallmark of its small, interactive classes, where students learn to express themselves articulately and solve problems creatively. Outstanding opportunities in athletics and the arts enrich the learning environment, while state-of-the-art technological and math/science facilities enlarge it.

See full description on page 910.

MIDLAND SCHOOL

PO Box 8
5100 Figueroa Mountain Road
Los Olivos, California 93441
Head of School: David Lourie

General Information Coeducational boarding college-preparatory school. Grades 9–12. Founded: 1932. Setting: rural. Nearest major city is Santa Barbara. Students are housed in single-sex cabins. 2,860-acre campus. Approved or accredited by California Association of Independent Schools, The Association of Boarding Schools, US Department of State, and Western Association of Schools and Colleges. Member of National Association of Independent Schools and Secondary School Admission Test Board. Endowment: $3.9 million. Total enrollment: 78. Upper school average class size: 12. Upper school faculty-student ratio: 1:5.

Upper School Student Profile 100% of students are boarding students. 70% are state residents. 7 states are represented in upper school student body. 7% are international students. International students from Republic of Korea.

Faculty School total: 22. In upper school: 12 men, 10 women; 5 have advanced degrees; 20 reside on campus.

Subjects Offered 3-dimensional art, adolescent issues, advanced chemistry, advanced math, agroecology, algebra, American history, American literature, American studies, anthropology, backpacking, biology, calculus-AP, ceramics, character education, chemistry, clayworking, community service, composition, creative writing, drama, economics, environmental education, environmental studies, equestrian sports, film and literature, foreign language, gardening, geology, geometry, health education, Holocaust studies, human sexuality, hydrology, integrated science, land and ranch management, leadership skills, literature by women, metalworking, music, painting, physics, physics-AP, pre-calculus, senior project, senior seminar, senior thesis, sex education, Spanish, Spanish literature, Spanish-AP, statistics, U.S. history, volleyball, wilderness camping, wilderness education, world studies.

Graduation Requirements Arts and fine arts (art, music, dance, drama), English, foreign language, history, mathematics, science, senior thesis.

Special Academic Programs Advanced Placement exam preparation in 2 subject areas; honors section; independent study.

College Placement 12 students graduated in 2005; 11 went to college. Other: 1 went to work.

Student Life Upper grades have specified standards of dress, student council. Discipline rests equally with students and faculty.

Tuition and Aid 7-day tuition and room/board: $29,500. Need-based scholarship grants, need-based loans available. In 2005–06, 51% of upper-school students received aid. Total amount of financial aid awarded in 2005–06: $603,000.

Admissions Traditional secondary-level entrance grade is 9. For fall 2005, 56 students applied for upper-level admission, 45 were accepted, 32 enrolled. SSAT required. Deadline for receipt of application materials: none. Application fee required: $30. On-campus interview required.

Athletics Interscholastic: cross-country running (boys, girls), lacrosse (b,g), soccer (b,g), volleyball (g); intramural: table tennis (b,g); coed intramural: back packing, basketball, bicycling, equestrian sports, hiking/backpacking, horseback riding, mountain biking, outdoor adventure, outdoor education, outdoor skills, surfing, touch football, ultimate Frisbee. 8 coaches.

Computers Computer network features include campus e-mail, on-campus library services, Internet access, wireless campus network.

Contact Derek Svennungsen, Director of Admissions. 805-688-5114 Ext. 14. Fax: 805-686-2470. E-mail: dsvennungsen@midland-school.org. Web site: www.midland-school.org.

MID-PACIFIC INSTITUTE

2445 Kaala Street
Honolulu, Hawaii 96822-2299
Head of School: Mr. Joe C. Rice

General Information Coeducational day college-preparatory, arts, bilingual studies, technology, and International Baccalaureate school, affiliated with Christian faith. Grades K–12. Founded: 1864. Setting: urban. 34-acre campus. 30 buildings on campus. Approved or accredited by Western Association of Schools and Colleges. Member of National Association of Independent Schools and Secondary School Admission Test Board. Endowment: $5 million. Total enrollment: 1,395. Upper school average class size: 20. Upper school faculty-student ratio: 1:19.

Faculty School total: 102. In upper school: 42 men, 54 women; 20 have advanced degrees.

Subjects Offered Algebra, American history, American literature, art, art history, astronomy, ballet, band, biology, business skills, calculus, career education, ceramics, chemistry, computer programming, computer science, creative writing, dance, debate, drama, drawing, economics, English, English literature, ESL, film, fine arts, first aid, French, general science, geography, geometry, Hawaiian history, health, history, instrumental music, Japanese, Latin, law, mathematics, oceanography, oral communications, painting, philosophy, photography, physical education, physics, printmaking, psychology, religion, science, sculpture, social science, social studies, Spanish, speech, swimming, swimming competency, technological applications, technology, theater, video, weight training, world history, world literature, writing.

Graduation Requirements Arts and fine arts (art, music, dance, drama), business skills (includes word processing), career education, computer science, English, foreign language, mathematics, oral communications, physical education (includes health), religion (includes Bible studies and theology), science, social science, social studies (includes history), speech, swimming competency.

Special Academic Programs International Baccalaureate program; Advanced Placement exam preparation in 7 subject areas; honors section; study at local college for college credit; academic accommodation for the gifted and the artistically talented; ESL (30 students enrolled).

College Placement 205 students graduated in 2005; all went to college, including Hawai'i Pacific University; Stanford University; University of Hawaii at Manoa; University of Southern California; University of Washington.

Student Life Upper grades have specified standards of dress, student council, honor system. Discipline rests primarily with faculty. Attendance at religious services is required.

Summer Programs Enrichment, advancement, ESL, art/fine arts, computer instruction programs offered; session focuses on physical fitness and skills; held on campus; accepts boys and girls; open to students from other schools. 950 students usually enrolled. 2006 schedule: June 3 to July 26. Application deadline: April 5.

Tuition and Aid Day student tuition: $12,185. Tuition installment plan (Insured Tuition Payment Plan, FACTS Tuition Payment Plan, monthly payment plans, semi-annual payment plan). Merit scholarship grants, need-based scholarship grants, paying campus jobs, tuition reduction for children of employees available. In 2005–06, 15% of upper-school students received aid; total upper-school merit-scholarship money awarded: $305,000. Total amount of financial aid awarded in 2005–06: $644,000.

Admissions Traditional secondary-level entrance grade is 9. For fall 2005, 340 students applied for upper-level admission, 122 were accepted, 95 enrolled. SAT, SSAT and TOEFL required. Deadline for receipt of application materials: January 15. Application fee required: $75. Interview required.

Athletics Interscholastic: aquatics (boys, girls), baseball (b), basketball (b,g), bowling (b,g), canoeing/kayaking (b,g), cheering (g), cross-country running (b,g), football (b), golf (b,g), gymnastics (g), independent competitive sports (b,g), kayaking (b,g), ocean paddling (b,g), physical fitness (b,g), physical training (b,g), riflery (b,g), soccer (b,g), softball (g), strength & conditioning (b,g), surfing (b,g), swimming and diving (b,g), tennis (b,g), track and field (b,g), volleyball (b,g), water polo (b,g), wrestling (b,g); intramural: badminton (b,g), weight lifting (b,g), weight training (b,g); coed interscholastic: fitness, modern dance; coed intramural: badminton. 6 PE instructors, 15 coaches, 2 trainers.

Computers Computers are regularly used in English, foreign language, mathematics, media arts, science classes. Computer network features include campus e-mail, on-campus library services, CD-ROMs, online commercial services, Internet access, file transfer, office computer access, DVD, wireless campus network.

Contact Mr. John Williamson, Director of Admissions. 808-973-5005. Fax: 808-973-5099. E-mail: jwilliamson@midpac.edu. Web site: www.midpac.edu.

MID-PENINSULA HIGH SCHOOL

1340 Willow Road
Menlo Park, California 94025-1516
Head of School: Douglas Thompson, PhD

General Information Coeducational day college-preparatory, general academic, and arts school; primarily serves underachievers. Grades 9–12. Founded: 1979. Setting: suburban. Nearest major city is San Jose. 2-acre campus. 1 building on campus. Approved or accredited by California Association of Independent Schools, Western

 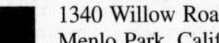

Association of Schools and Colleges, and California Department of Education. Endowment: $1.4 million. Total enrollment: 120. Upper school average class size: 12. Upper school faculty-student ratio: 1:8.

Upper School Student Profile Grade 9: 18 students (12 boys, 6 girls); Grade 10: 29 students (15 boys, 14 girls); Grade 11: 30 students (18 boys, 12 girls); Grade 12: 43 students (26 boys, 17 girls).

Faculty School total: 18. In upper school: 8 men, 8 women; 6 have advanced degrees.

Subjects Offered Algebra, art, biology, biology-AP, calculus, calculus-AP, chemistry, composition, contemporary issues, drama, driver education, English, English language-AP, English literature-AP, environmental science-AP, European history-AP, French language-AP, geometry, government, human relations, mathematics, microeconomics-AP, music performance, physical education, physics, SAT/ACT preparation, science, Spanish, Spanish language-AP, Spanish literature-AP, sports, statistics-AP, study skills, trigonometry, U.S. government and politics-AP, U.S. history, U.S. history-AP, world history-AP, world studies.

Graduation Requirements Government, human relations, mathematics, physical education (includes health), science, social science, U.S. history. Community service is required.

Special Academic Programs Accelerated programs; independent study; remedial reading and/or remedial writing; remedial math; special instructional classes for students wtih learning disabilities, ADD, dyslexia, emotional and behavioral problems.

College Placement 38 students graduated in 2005; 35 went to college, including American University; California State University, Monterey Bay; San Jose State University; University of California, Santa Cruz; University of Oregon; University of Redlands. Other: 3 went to work. Median SAT verbal: 569, median SAT math: 559, median combined SAT: 1695. 38% scored over 600 on SAT verbal, 44% scored over 600 on SAT math, 38% scored over 1800 on combined SAT.

Student Life Discipline rests primarily with faculty.

Summer Programs Remediation, enrichment, art/fine arts programs offered; session focuses on academic support for current students; held on campus; accepts boys and girls; open to students from other schools. 60 students usually enrolled. 2006 schedule: June 19 to July 21. Application deadline: June 9.

Tuition and Aid Day student tuition: $21,194. Tuition installment plan (monthly payment plans, individually arranged payment plans, 2-payment plan). Tuition reduction for siblings, need-based scholarship grants available. In 2005–06, 24% of upper-school students received aid.

Admissions Achievement/Aptitude/Writing or admissions testing required. Deadline for receipt of application materials: January 10. No application fee required. On-campus interview required.

Athletics Interscholastic: baseball (boys), basketball (b,g), soccer (b), softball (g), volleyball (b,g); coed interscholastic: cross-country running. 1 PE instructor, 2 coaches.

Contact Director of Admissions. 650-321-1991. Fax: 650-321-9921. E-mail: chloek@mid-pen.com. Web site: www.mid-pen.com.

MILKEN COMMUNITY HIGH SCHOOL OF STEPHEN WISE TEMPLE

15800 Zeldins' Way (at Mulholland Drive)
Los Angeles, California 90049
Head of School: Dr. Rennie R. Wrubel

petersons.com

General Information Coeducational day college-preparatory and Jewish Studies school, affiliated with Jewish faith. Grades 7–12. Founded: 1990. Setting: suburban. 6-acre campus. 4 buildings on campus. Approved or accredited by California Association of Independent Schools, Western Association of Schools and Colleges, and California Department of Education. Total enrollment: 787. Upper school average class size: 18. Upper school faculty-student ratio: 1:7.

Upper School Student Profile Grade 9: 149 students (74 boys, 75 girls); Grade 10: 150 students (69 boys, 81 girls); Grade 11: 153 students (82 boys, 71 girls); Grade 12: 132 students (65 boys, 67 girls). 100% of students are Jewish.

Faculty School total: 89. In upper school: 37 men, 52 women; 45 have advanced degrees.

Subjects Offered Acting, algebra, American government, American government-AP, American literature, architectural drawing, art, art history, art history-AP, astronomy, audio visual/media, Basic programming, Bible studies, biology, biology-AP, broadcasting, calculus, calculus-AP, career education internship, ceramics, chamber groups, chemistry, chemistry-AP, choir, classical music, college placement, community service, composition, computer applications, computer graphics, computer programming, computer technologies, creative writing, current events, dance performance, debate, drama performance, drawing, ecology, environmental systems, economics, electronics, English, English language and composition-AP, English literature and composition-AP, equestrian sports, European history-AP, French, French-AP, general math, general science, geometry, government and politics-AP, graphic design, guitar, health, Hebrew, Hebrew scripture, history, history-AP, Holocaust studies, honors algebra, honors English, honors geometry, honors U.S. history, honors world history, instrumental music, Israeli studies, jazz dance, jazz ensemble, Jewish studies, journalism, Latin, leadership training, life science, literary magazine, literature and composition-AP, macro/microeconomics-AP, marine biology, media arts, media production, model United Nations, modern dance, modern

world history, music appreciation, music composition, music performance, music theory, music theory-AP, musical theater, newspaper, oceanography, orchestra, painting, philosophy, physical science, physics, physics-AP, prayer/spirituality, pre-algebra, pre-calculus, pre-college orientation, psychology, psychology-AP, Rabbinic literature, religion, religion and culture, religious studies, science, science research, sculpture, senior career experience, senior seminar, set design, sex education, Spanish, Spanish-AP, speech and debate, stage design, statistics, statistics-AP, studio art, studio art-AP, study skills, Talmud, trigonometry, U.S. government and politics-AP, U.S. history, U.S. history-AP, video communication, video film production, water color painting, Web site design, world history, world history-AP.

Graduation Requirements Arts, electives, English, Hebrew, Jewish studies, mathematics, physical education (includes health), religion (includes Bible studies and theology), science, senior seminar, social science, senior sermon. Community service is required.

Special Academic Programs Advanced Placement exam preparation in 20 subject areas; honors section; independent study; study at local college for college credit; study abroad; academic accommodation for the gifted, the musically talented, and the artistically talented.

College Placement 137 students graduated in 2005; all went to college, including University of California, Irvine; University of California, Los Angeles; University of Michigan; University of Southern California; University of Wisconsin–Madison. Mean SAT math: 609.

Student Life Upper grades have specified standards of dress, student council, honor system. Discipline rests primarily with faculty. Attendance at religious services is required.

Summer Programs Remediation, enrichment, advancement, art/fine arts, computer instruction programs offered; session focuses on enrichment, advancement, remediation; held on campus; accepts boys and girls; open to students from other schools. 180 students usually enrolled. 2006 schedule: June 19 to July 28. Application deadline: June 12.

Tuition and Aid Day student tuition: $22,585. Tuition installment plan (Insured Tuition Payment Plan, Key Tuition Payment Plan, monthly payment plans, individually arranged payment plans). Need-based scholarship grants available. In 2005–06, 15% of upper-school students received aid. Total amount of financial aid awarded in 2005–06: $853,666.

Admissions Traditional secondary-level entrance grade is 9. For fall 2005, 110 students applied for upper-level admission, 82 were accepted, 40 enrolled. ISEE required. Deadline for receipt of application materials: January 27. Application fee required: $150. On-campus interview required.

Athletics Interscholastic: aquatics (boys, girls), baseball (b), basketball (b,g), cross-country running (b,g), dance (g), dance squad (g), dance team (g), equestrian sports (b,g), flag football (g), golf (b), soccer (b,g), softball (g), swimming and diving (b,g), tennis (b,g), volleyball (b,g), water polo (b,g); intramural: aerobics/dance (g), dance squad (g); coed interscholastic: badminton, physical fitness, physical training, running, track and field; coed intramural: aquatics, dance, soccer, softball, swimming and diving, volleyball, water polo, weight training. 8 PE instructors, 18 coaches.

Computers Computers are regularly used in architecture, art, design, drafting, drawing and design, economics, English, foreign language, graphic design, history, independent study, journalism, library, literary magazine, mathematics, multimedia, music, psychology, religious studies, research skills, science, video film production, Web site design, yearbook classes. Computer network features include campus e-mail, on-campus library services, CD-ROMs, online commercial services, Internet access, file transfer, DVD, wireless campus network.

Contact Muriel Green, Office of Admission. 310-440-3553. Fax: 310-471-5139. E-mail: admission@mchschool.org. Web site: www.mchschool.org.

ANNOUNCEMENT FROM THE SCHOOL Milken Community High School (MCHS) is the largest community Jewish Day School in the United States. The School's primary mission is to foster among its students a commitment to live according to the ethical and spiritual values of Judaism. Every student has an obligation to play a role in the Jewish practice of tikkun olam (repair of the world). The School provides a rigorous liberal arts college-preparatory program that is integrated with the highest ideals of Judaism, fostering a sense of intellectual curiosity, and spiritual growth. Milken embraces and fosters the individual talents and abilities of each student by providing a diverse selection of programs of study. The Mitchell Science & Technology Academy offers a select group of students an opportunity to participate in project-based scientific research. These students work with world-renowned scientists and assist graduate students at major universities in various scientific fields. The Advanced Jewish Studies Center, a program for students who desire a deeper immersion into Jewish learning, offers an intensive fellowship program of textual learning, spiritual practice, leadership, action, and service. MCHS also offers an integrated Advanced Placement English and High Honors Jewish Thought Course in which approximately 40% of the senior class participates. In 2005, 552 AP exams were administered to 259 students. Seventy-six percent scored 3 or higher; 47% scored 4 or higher. Approximately 97% of graduates attend 4-year colleges and universities, such as Amherst, Barnard, Wesleyan, Tufts, Yale, Emory, Harvard, Stanford, Michigan, Cornell, Caltech, and the Universities of Chicago and Pennsylvania. The college counseling office includes 3 full-time counselors. MCHS offers many unique programs, such as

study abroad in Israel and the Los Angeles Youth Orchestra, which is an academic conservatory dedicated to inspiring passion and inquiry in the study of music. In addition, there is the Wise Individual Senior Experience (WISE) program, an opportunity to enrich the academic experience by participating in a project that reflects a career and/or personal interest. The Spotlight Artist Series offers students in 11th and 12th grades the opportunity to submit 5 pieces of original art for selection to the Spotlight Artist exhibition. Milken Community High School provides a secure environment that challenges and enriches the lives of the students.

MILLBROOK SCHOOL

School Road
Millbrook, New York 12545
Head of School: Drew Casertano

General Information Coeducational boarding and day college-preparatory, general academic, arts, and scientific and environmental school. Grades 9–12. Founded: 1931. Setting: rural. Nearest major city is New York. Students are housed in single-sex dormitories. 800-acre campus. 69 buildings on campus. Approved or accredited by National Independent Private Schools Association, New York State Association of Independent Schools, and The Association of Boarding Schools. Member of National Association of Independent Schools and Secondary School Admission Test Board. Endowment: $15 million. Total enrollment: 262. Upper school average class size: 12. Upper school faculty-student ratio: 1:4.
Upper School Student Profile Grade 9: 44 students (24 boys, 20 girls); Grade 10: 81 students (42 boys, 39 girls); Grade 11: 69 students (37 boys, 32 girls); Grade 12: 68 students (38 boys, 30 girls). 80% of students are boarding students. 55% are state residents. 20 states are represented in upper school student body. 10% are international students. International students from Bermuda, Canada, Hong Kong, Macao, Netherlands, and Republic of Korea; 1 other country represented in student body.
Faculty School total: 40. In upper school: 21 men, 19 women; 27 have advanced degrees; 32 reside on campus.
Subjects Offered Advanced Placement courses, algebra, American history, American literature, animal behavior, art, art history, astronomy, biology, calculus, calculus-AP, ceramics, chemistry, choral music, choreography, constitutional law, creative writing, dance, dance performance, drama, drawing, ecology, English, English literature, English-AP, environmental science, ESL, European history, expository writing, fine arts, French, French language-AP, French-AP, geometry, health, history, honors English, honors U.S. history, human biology, independent study, jazz band, jazz ensemble, journalism, mathematics, Middle Eastern history, music, music appreciation, painting, philosophy, photography, physical education, physics, pre-calculus, psychology, science, social science, social studies, Spanish, Spanish-AP, studio art, theater, trigonometry, world history, zoology.
Graduation Requirements Arts and fine arts (art, music, dance, drama), biology, English, foreign language, mathematics, physical education (includes health), science, social science, social studies (includes history).
Special Academic Programs Advanced Placement exam preparation in 11 subject areas; honors section; independent study; study abroad.
College Placement 60 students graduated in 2005; 59 went to college, including Hamilton College; Hobart and William Smith Colleges; Savannah College of Art and Design; The Colorado College; University of Michigan; Wheaton College. Other: 1 had other specific plans. Mean composite ACT: 23.
Student Life Upper grades have specified standards of dress, student council. Discipline rests primarily with faculty.
Tuition and Aid Day student tuition: $25,240; 7-day tuition and room/board: $34,690. Tuition installment plan (Insured Tuition Payment Plan, Key Tuition Payment Plan, monthly payment plans, Tuition Management Systems Plan). Need-based scholarship grants, need-based loans available. In 2005–06, 25% of upper-school students received aid. Total amount of financial aid awarded in 2005–06: $1,474,668.
Admissions Traditional secondary-level entrance grade is 9. For fall 2005, 400 students applied for upper-level admission, 175 were accepted, 84 enrolled. ISEE, SSAT or TOEFL required. Deadline for receipt of application materials: January 31. Application fee required: $35. On-campus interview required.
Athletics Interscholastic: alpine skiing (boys, girls), baseball (b), basketball (b,g), cross-country running (b,g), dance (g), field hockey (g), ice hockey (b,g), lacrosse (b,g), skiing (downhill) (b,g), soccer (b,g), softball (g), squash (b,g), tennis (b,g); coed interscholastic: equestrian sports, golf, horseback riding, modern dance; coed intramural: bicycling, broomball. 1 coach, 1 trainer.
Computers Computers are regularly used in English, mathematics, science classes. Computer network features include campus e-mail, on-campus library services, CD-ROMs, online commercial services, Internet access, office computer access, DVD, wireless campus network.
Contact Cynthia S. McWilliams, Director of Admission. 845-677-8261. Fax: 845-677-1265. E-mail: admissions@millbrook.org. Web site: www.millbrook.org.

See full description on page 912.

MILLER SCHOOL

1000 Samuel Miller Loop
Charlottesville, Virginia 22903-9328
Head of School: Lindsay R. Barnes

General Information Coeducational boarding and day college-preparatory and arts school. Grades 7–12. Founded: 1878. Setting: rural. Students are housed in single-sex dormitories. 1,600-acre campus. 6 buildings on campus. Approved or accredited by The Association of Boarding Schools and Virginia Association of Independent Schools. Member of National Association of Independent Schools. Endowment: $14 million. Total enrollment: 140. Upper school average class size: 10. Upper school faculty-student ratio: 1:6.
Upper School Student Profile Grade 9: 21 students (12 boys, 9 girls); Grade 10: 38 students (27 boys, 11 girls); Grade 11: 34 students (18 boys, 16 girls); Grade 12: 26 students (19 boys, 7 girls). 66% of students are boarding students. 61% are state residents. 10 states are represented in upper school student body. 22% are international students. International students from Bolivia, Brazil, China, Kazakhstan, Lithuania, and Republic of Korea; 4 other countries represented in student body.
Faculty School total: 45. In upper school: 23 men, 22 women; 23 have advanced degrees; 23 reside on campus.
Subjects Offered Algebra, American government, American government-AP, American literature, ancient history, art, arts, biology, British literature, calculus, calculus-AP, carpentry, chemistry, civics, CPR, creative writing, drama performance, driver education, earth science, economics, economics and history, English, English language and composition-AP, English language-AP, English literature, English literature and composition-AP, English literature-AP, environmental science-AP, ESL, European history, European history-AP, fine arts, French, French-AP, geography, geometry, government, government-AP, instrumental music, Latin, modern European history, modern European history-AP, music, photography, physical education, physical science, physics, pre-algebra, pre-calculus, Spanish, Spanish-AP, studio art, studio art—AP, study skills, TOEFL preparation, trigonometry, U.S. history, U.S. history-AP, woodworking.
Graduation Requirements Arts and fine arts (art, music, dance, drama), English, foreign language, mathematics, physical education (includes health), science, social studies (includes history). Community service is required.
Special Academic Programs Advanced Placement exam preparation in 9 subject areas; honors section; accelerated programs; independent study; academic accommodation for the gifted, the musically talented, and the artistically talented; ESL (6 students enrolled).
College Placement 28 students graduated in 2005; 27 went to college, including James Madison University; Longwood University; Randolph-Macon College; University of Washington; Virginia Polytechnic Institute and State University; Washington and Lee University. Other: 1 went to work. Mean SAT verbal: 526, mean SAT math: 560. 23% scored over 600 on SAT verbal, 23% scored over 600 on SAT math.
Student Life Upper grades have specified standards of dress, student council, honor system. Discipline rests equally with students and faculty.
Summer Programs Sports programs offered; session focuses on cross-country camp; held on campus; accepts boys and girls; open to students from other schools. 75 students usually enrolled.
Tuition and Aid Day student tuition: $11,995; 5-day tuition and room/board: $21,135; 7-day tuition and room/board: $24,865. Tuition installment plan (Insured Tuition Payment Plan, individually arranged payment plans). Tuition reduction for siblings, need-based scholarship grants available. In 2005–06, 31% of upper-school students received aid. Total amount of financial aid awarded in 2005–06: $525,000.
Admissions Traditional secondary-level entrance grade is 9. For fall 2005, 82 students applied for upper-level admission, 55 were accepted, 36 enrolled. ACT, any standardized test, California Achievement Test, Iowa Tests of Basic Skills, PSAT or SAT, SSAT, Stanford Achievement Test or TOEFL or SLEP required. Deadline for receipt of application materials: none. Application fee required: $50. Interview required.
Athletics Interscholastic: baseball (boys), basketball (b,g), cross-country running (b,g), lacrosse (b), soccer (b,g), tennis (b,g), volleyball (g), wrestling (b); coed interscholastic: wrestling; coed intramural: basketball, bicycling, canoeing/kayaking, cross-country running, fishing, fitness, hiking/backpacking, in-line skating, mountain biking, mountaineering, outdoor activities, outdoor adventure, outdoor education, outdoor recreation, outdoor skills, paint ball, physical fitness, physical training, power lifting, rafting, roller blading, sailing, skateboarding, skiing (downhill), snowboarding, soccer, softball, street hockey, strength & conditioning, swimming and diving, table tennis, tennis, touch football, ultimate Frisbee, volleyball, walking, weight lifting, weight training, wilderness, wilderness survival. 3 coaches, 1 trainer.
Computers Computers are regularly used in English, foreign language, history, mathematics, science classes. Computer network features include campus e-mail, on-campus library services, CD-ROMs, online commercial services, Internet access.
Contact Jay Reeves, Director of Admissions. 434-823-4805. Fax: 434-823-6617. E-mail: jay@millerschool.org. Web site: www.millerschool.org.

See full description on page 914.

MILTON ACADEMY

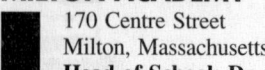

170 Centre Street
Milton, Massachusetts 02186
Head of School: Dr. Robin Robertson

petersons.com

General Information Coeducational boarding and day college-preparatory and arts school. Boarding grades 9–12, day grades K–12. Founded: 1798. Setting: suburban. Nearest major city is Boston. Students are housed in single-sex dormitories. 125-acre campus. 16 buildings on campus. Approved or accredited by Association of Independent Schools in New England, New England Association of Schools and Colleges, The Association of Boarding Schools, and Massachusetts Department of Education. Member of National Association of Independent Schools and Secondary School Admission Test Board. Language of instruction: English. Endowment: $140 million. Total enrollment: 989. Upper school average class size: 14. Upper school faculty-student ratio: 1:5.

Upper School Student Profile 50% of students are boarding students. 57% are state residents. 34 states are represented in upper school student body. 15% are international students. International students from Canada, Colombia, Hong Kong, Jamaica, Republic of Korea, and Thailand; 10 other countries represented in student body.

Faculty School total: 180. In upper school: 75 men, 64 women; 120 have advanced degrees; 80 reside on campus.

Subjects Offered Algebra, American history, American literature, anatomy, anthropology, archaeology, architecture, art, art history, arts, astronomy, biology, calculus, ceramics, chemistry, Chinese, computer math, computer programming, computer science, creative writing, current events, dance, drama, driver education, earth science, economics, English, English literature, ethics, European history, expository writing, fine arts, French, geography, geometry, German, government/civics, grammar, Greek, health, history, Italian, Latin, mathematics, music, philosophy, photography, physical education, physics, physiology, psychology, religion, science, social studies, sociology, Spanish, speech, statistics, theater, trigonometry, world history, world literature, writing.

Graduation Requirements Arts and fine arts (art, music, dance, drama), current events, English, foreign language, leadership skills, mathematics, physical education (includes health), public speaking, science, social studies (includes history).

Special Academic Programs Advanced Placement exam preparation in 11 subject areas; honors section; independent study; term-away projects; study abroad; academic accommodation for the gifted, the musically talented, and the artistically talented.

College Placement 179 students graduated in 2004; 175 went to college, including Brown University; Cornell University; Harvard University; Tufts University; Williams College; Yale University. Mean SAT verbal: 680, mean SAT math: 680.

Student Life Upper grades have student council. Discipline rests equally with students and faculty.

Tuition and Aid Day student tuition: $25,675; 7-day tuition and room/board: $32,725. Tuition installment plan (Key Tuition Payment Plan). Need-based scholarship grants available. In 2004–05, 26% of upper-school students received aid. Total amount of financial aid awarded in 2004–05: $4,500,000.

Admissions Traditional secondary-level entrance grade is 9. For fall 2005, 896 students applied for upper-level admission, 250 were accepted, 153 enrolled. ISEE, SSAT or TOEFL required. Deadline for receipt of application materials: January 15. Application fee required: $50. Interview required.

Athletics Interscholastic: baseball (boys), basketball (b,g), cross-country running (b,g), field hockey (g), football (b), ice hockey (b,g), lacrosse (b,g), running (b,g), soccer (b,g), softball (g), squash (b,g), tennis (b,g), track and field (b,g), volleyball (g), wrestling (b); intramural: basketball (b,g), soccer (b,g), volleyball (b); coed interscholastic: alpine skiing, bicycling, diving, golf, rock climbing, sailing, skiing (downhill), swimming and diving; coed intramural: climbing, martial arts, outdoor activities, rock climbing, skiing (downhill), squash, tennis, ultimate Frisbee, weight lifting. 6 PE instructors, 3 trainers.

Computers Computers are regularly used in mathematics, science classes. Computer network features include campus e-mail, on-campus library services, CD-ROMs, online commercial services, Internet access, file transfer, DVD.

Contact Mrs. Patricia Finn, Admission Assistant. 617-898-2227. Fax: 617-898-1701. E-mail: admissions@milton.edu. Web site: www.milton.edu.

ANNOUNCEMENT FROM THE SCHOOL Building on a 200-year tradition as a boarding and day school, Milton values honesty, energy, and compassion among students and faculty. Milton is an active and challenging academic community, supported by a deep respect for each individual and populated by committed learners, both young and old.

See full description on page 916.

MILTON HERSHEY SCHOOL

PO Box 830
Hershey, Pennsylvania 17033-0830
Head of School: Mr. John O'Brien

General Information Coeducational boarding college-preparatory, general academic, vocational, and technology school. Grades PK–12. Founded: 1909. Setting:

rural. Nearest major city is Harrisburg. Students are housed in student homes of 8 to 10 students. 2,640-acre campus. 9 buildings on campus. Approved or accredited by Middle States Association of Colleges and Schools, Pennsylvania Association of Private Academic Schools, and The Association of Boarding Schools. Member of National Association of Independent Schools. Endowment: $5.5 billion. Total enrollment: 1,301. Upper school average class size: 15. Upper school faculty-student ratio: 1:15.

Upper School Student Profile Grade 9: 163 students (79 boys, 84 girls); Grade 10: 146 students (62 boys, 84 girls); Grade 11: 137 students (72 boys, 65 girls); Grade 12: 112 students (60 boys, 52 girls). 100% of students are boarding students. 75% are state residents. 29 states are represented in upper school student body.

Faculty School total: 147. In upper school: 32 men, 27 women; 19 have advanced degrees.

Subjects Offered Agriculture, algebra, American history, American literature, art, art history, arts, auto mechanics, biology, business, business education, Canadian literature, carpentry, chemistry, communications, computer applications, computer education, computer graphics, computer information systems, computer keyboarding, computer literacy, computer math, computer music, computer science, computer technologies, computer-aided design, computers, construction, creative writing, drafting, drama, driver education, earth science, ecology, economics, English, English literature, environmental science, European history, fine arts, French, geography, geometry, German, government/civics, graphic arts, health, history, home economics, horticulture, journalism, mathematics, music, physical education, physics, science, social science, social studies, Spanish, speech, statistics, technology, theater, trigonometry, typing, vocational-technical courses, world history, writing.

Graduation Requirements Arts and fine arts (art, music, dance, drama), English, foreign language, mathematics, physical education (includes health), science, social science, social studies (includes history), technology.

Special Academic Programs Advanced Placement exam preparation in 5 subject areas; honors section; independent study; study at local college for college credit; study abroad; academic accommodation for the musically talented and the artistically talented; remedial reading and/or remedial writing; remedial math.

College Placement 112 students graduated in 2005; 102 went to college, including Indiana University of Pennsylvania; Pace University; St. John's University; Temple University; Towson University; University of Maryland, College Park. Other: 1 went to work, 2 entered military service. Median SAT verbal: 480, median SAT math: 480, median composite ACT: 22. 9% scored over 600 on SAT verbal, 8% scored over 600 on SAT math, 6% scored over 26 on composite ACT.

Student Life Upper grades have specified standards of dress, student council. Discipline rests primarily with faculty.

Summer Programs Remediation, enrichment, advancement, art/fine arts, computer instruction programs offered; session focuses on academics, career preparation, and life skills; held both on and off campus; held at numerous locations, usually in the Central Atlantic region; accepts boys and girls; not open to students from other schools. 486 students usually enrolled. 2006 schedule: June 12 to August 20. Application deadline: April.

Tuition and Aid School's endowment covers all costs for all students available. In 2005–06, 100% of upper-school students received aid.

Admissions Traditional secondary-level entrance grade is 9. For fall 2005, 109 students applied for upper-level admission, 41 were accepted, 26 enrolled. Comprehensive educational evaluation or Individual IQ required. Deadline for receipt of application materials: none. No application fee required. On-campus interview required.

Athletics Interscholastic: baseball (boys), basketball (b,g), cheering (g), cross-country running (b,g), diving (b,g), field hockey (g), football (b), soccer (b), softball (g), swimming and diving (b,g), track and field (b,g), wrestling (b); intramural: baseball (b,g), basketball (b,g), field hockey (g), football (b), ice hockey (b), soccer (b), softball (b,g), swimming and diving (b,g), track and field (b,g), wrestling (b). 4 PE instructors, 3 coaches, 1 trainer.

Computers Computers are regularly used in all classes. Computer network features include campus e-mail, on-campus library services, CD-ROMs, online commercial services, Internet access, file transfer, office computer access, Media on Demand, video conferencing, laptop computers (for all high school students).

Contact Mr. Danny Warner, Senior Officer, Admissions. 717-520-2100. Fax: 717-520-2117. E-mail: warnerd@mhs-pa.org. Web site: www.mhs-pa.org.

MISS EDGAR'S AND MISS CRAMP'S SCHOOL

525 Mount Pleasant Avenue
Montreal, Quebec H3Y 3H6, Canada
Head of School: Ms. Susyn Borer

General Information Girls' day college-preparatory, arts, bilingual studies, and technology school. Grades K–11. Founded: 1909. Setting: urban. 4-acre campus. 1 building on campus. Approved or accredited by Quebec Association of Independent Schools and Quebec Department of Education. Affiliate member of National Association of Independent Schools; member of Secondary School Admission Test Board. Languages of instruction: English and French. Total enrollment: 351. Upper school average class size: 19. Upper school faculty-student ratio: 1:9.

Upper School Student Profile Grade 9: 37 students (37 girls); Grade 10: 43 students (43 girls); Grade 11: 39 students (39 girls).

Faculty School total: 39. In upper school: 4 men, 20 women; 11 have advanced degrees.

Subjects Offered Art, art history, biology, calculus, career exploration, chemistry, computer science, creative writing, drama, ecology, economics, English, environmental science, European history, French, geography, history, mathematics, media, music, physical education, physics, science, social studies, Spanish, theater, women's studies, world history.

Graduation Requirements English, foreign language, mathematics, science, social studies (includes history).

Special Academic Programs Advanced Placement exam preparation in 2 subject areas; honors section.

College Placement 38 students graduated in 2005; all went to college, including College Brebeuf; John Abbott College; Lower Canada College; Marianopolis College.

Student Life Upper grades have uniform requirement, student council, honor system. Discipline rests equally with students and faculty.

Tuition and Aid Day student tuition: CAN$11,800. Tuition installment plan (individually arranged payment plans). Bursaries, merit scholarship grants available. In 2005–06, 10% of upper-school students received aid; total upper-school merit-scholarship money awarded: CAN$55,045. Total amount of financial aid awarded in 2005–06: CAN$87,910.

Admissions Traditional secondary-level entrance grade is 9. For fall 2005, 15 students applied for upper-level admission, 6 were accepted, 4 enrolled. CCAT, SSAT or writing sample required. Deadline for receipt of application materials: none. Application fee required: CAN$50. On-campus interview required.

Athletics Interscholastic: badminton, basketball, cross-country running, golf, soccer, swimming and diving, tennis, track and field, volleyball; intramural: archery, badminton, baseball, basketball, cross-country running, field hockey, gymnastics, ice hockey, rugby, skiing (cross-country), soccer, track and field, volleyball. 3 PE instructors, 11 coaches.

Computers Computers are regularly used in art, English, French, history, newspaper, writing, yearbook classes. Computer network features include campus e-mail, on-campus library services, CD-ROMs, Internet access.

Contact Ms. Diana Macdonald, Assistant to the Head of School. 514-935-6357 Ext. 225. Fax: 514-935-1099. E-mail: dmac@ecs.qc.ca. Web site: www.ecs.qc.ca.

MISS HALL'S SCHOOL

492 Holmes Road
Pittsfield, Massachusetts 01201
Head of School: Ms. Jeannie K. Norris

petersons.com

General Information Girls' boarding and day college-preparatory, arts, and technology school. Grades 9–12. Founded: 1898. Setting: suburban. Nearest major city is Albany, NY. Students are housed in single-sex dormitories. 80-acre campus. 9 buildings on campus. Approved or accredited by Association of Independent Schools in New England, New England Association of Schools and Colleges, The Association of Boarding Schools, and Massachusetts Department of Education. Member of National Association of Independent Schools and Secondary School Admission Test Board. Endowment: $7 million. Total enrollment: 172. Upper school average class size: 10. Upper school faculty-student ratio: 1:5.

Upper School Student Profile Grade 9: 44 students (44 girls); Grade 10: 47 students (47 girls); Grade 11: 43 students (43 girls); Grade 12: 38 students (38 girls). 75% of students are boarding students. 39% are state residents. 21 states are represented in upper school student body. 20% are international students. International students from Hong Kong, Japan, Mexico, Nigeria, Republic of Korea, and Taiwan; 8 other countries represented in student body.

Faculty School total: 30. In upper school: 8 men, 21 women; 26 have advanced degrees; 19 reside on campus.

Subjects Offered Advanced Placement courses, algebra, American government, American history, American literature, anatomy, art, art history, biology, business skills, calculus, ceramics, chemistry, community service, computer science, dance, drama, drawing, driver education, ecology, economics, English, English literature, environmental science, ESL, ethics, ethics and responsibility, European history, fine arts, forensic science, forensics, French, geometry, government/civics, health, history, Latin, mathematics, music, music history, painting, photography, physics, physiology, political science, psychology, science, social studies, Spanish, theater, trigonometry, world culture, world history.

Graduation Requirements Arts and fine arts (art, music, dance, drama), English, foreign language, mathematics, physical education (includes health), science, social studies (includes history). Community service is required.

Special Academic Programs Advanced Placement exam preparation in 19 subject areas; honors section; independent study; academic accommodation for the gifted, the musically talented, and the artistically talented; special instructional classes for students with mild learning disabilities and Attention Deficit Disorder; ESL (15 students enrolled).

College Placement 45 students graduated in 2005; all went to college, including Barnard College; Carnegie Mellon University; Georgetown University; Macalester College; Syracuse University; The George Washington University.

Student Life Upper grades have specified standards of dress, student council, honor system. Discipline rests equally with students and faculty.

Tuition and Aid Day student tuition: $21,000; 7-day tuition and room/board: $35,800. Tuition installment plan (Insured Tuition Payment Plan, Academic Management Services Plan, Key Tuition Payment Plan, monthly payment plans, individually arranged payment plans). Merit scholarship grants, need-based scholarship grants available. In 2005–06, 48% of upper-school students received aid; total upper-school merit-scholarship money awarded: $28,000. Total amount of financial aid awarded in 2005–06: $1,620,000.

Admissions Traditional secondary-level entrance grade is 9. For fall 2005, 180 students applied for upper-level admission, 110 were accepted, 66 enrolled. SSAT or TOEFL required. Deadline for receipt of application materials: February 15. Application fee required: $40. Interview required.

Athletics Interscholastic: alpine skiing, basketball, cross-country running, field hockey, lacrosse, skiing (downhill), soccer, softball, tennis, volleyball; intramural: aerobics, aerobics/dance, alpine skiing, dance, equestrian sports, fitness, horseback riding, jogging, modern dance, outdoor activities, outdoor education, outdoor skills, physical fitness, rock climbing, ropes courses, running, skiing (downhill), snowboarding, tennis, walking, wall climbing, wilderness. 3 coaches, 1 trainer.

Computers Computers are regularly used in English, foreign language, history, music, photography, science classes. Computer network features include campus e-mail, on-campus library services, CD-ROMs, online commercial services, Internet access.

Contact Ms. Kimberly B. Boland, Director of Admission. 413-499-1300. Fax: 413-448-2994. E-mail: info@misshalls.org. Web site: www.misshalls.org.

See full description on page 918.

MISSISSAUGA PRIVATE SCHOOL

30 Barrhead Crescent
Toronto, Ontario M9W 3Z7, Canada
Head of School: Mrs. Gabrielle Bush

General Information Coeducational day college-preparatory, arts, business, and technology school. Grades JK–12. Founded: 1977. Setting: urban. 1 building on campus. Approved or accredited by Ontario Department of Education. Language of instruction: English. Total enrollment: 312. Upper school average class size: 18. Upper school faculty-student ratio: 1:13.

Upper School Student Profile Grade 9: 25 students (12 boys, 13 girls); Grade 10: 31 students (20 boys, 11 girls); Grade 11: 26 students (22 boys, 4 girls); Grade 12: 20 students (9 boys, 11 girls).

Faculty School total: 30. In upper school: 7 men, 7 women; 5 have advanced degrees.

Subjects Offered Accounting, anthropology, biology, Canadian geography, Canadian history, Canadian law, chemistry, civics, communications, data processing, discrete math, dramatic arts, English, French, functions, geometry, healthful living, information technology, learning strategies, mathematics, organizational studies, personal finance, physics, psychology, reading, science, society challenge and change, sociology, visual arts, world history, writing.

Graduation Requirements Ontario Ministry of Education requirements.

Special Academic Programs ESL (30 students enrolled).

College Placement 27 students graduated in 2005; all went to college, including McMaster University; Queen's University at Kingston; University of Guelph; University of Toronto; University of Waterloo; York University.

Student Life Upper grades have uniform requirement, honor system. Discipline rests primarily with faculty.

Summer Programs Remediation, enrichment, advancement, ESL, sports, art/fine arts, computer instruction programs offered; session focuses on academics; held on campus; accepts boys and girls; open to students from other schools. 100 students usually enrolled. 2006 schedule: July 4 to August 28. Application deadline: June 25.

Tuition and Aid Day student tuition: CAN$11,000. Tuition installment plan (MPS Payment Plan). Tuition reduction for siblings available.

Admissions Admissions testing required. Deadline for receipt of application materials: August 30. No application fee required. Interview required.

Athletics Interscholastic: basketball (boys, girls), football (b), running (b,g), soccer (b,g), swimming and diving (b,g), track and field (b,g), volleyball (b,g); intramural: basketball (b,g), floor hockey (b,g), indoor hockey (b,g), physical fitness (b,g), rhythmic gymnastics (b,g), running (b,g), soccer (b,g), swimming and diving (b,g), track and field (b,g), volleyball (b,g), winter (indoor) track (b,g); coed interscholastic: aquatics; coed intramural: basketball, cooperative games, tennis. 4 PE instructors, 20 coaches.

Computers Computers are regularly used in art, business education, computer applications, graphic arts, media arts classes. Computer resources include CD-ROMs, Internet access, office computer access.

Contact Mrs. Gabrielle Bush, Head of School. 416-745-1328. Fax: 416-745-4168. E-mail: gbushmps@rogers.com. Web site: www.mpsontario.com.

MISSOURI MILITARY ACADEMY

204 Grand Avenue
Mexico, Missouri 65265
Head of School: Col. Ronald J. Kelly

General Information Boys' boarding college-preparatory, ESL, and military science school, affiliated with Christian faith. Grades 6–PG. Founded: 1889. Setting: small town. Nearest major city is St. Louis. Students are housed in single-sex dormitories. 288-acre campus. 19 buildings on campus. Approved or accredited by Independent Schools Association of the Central States and North Central Association of Colleges and Schools. Member of National Association of Independent Schools and Secondary School Admission Test Board. Endowment: $43 million. Total enrollment: 226. Upper school average class size: 11. Upper school faculty-student ratio: 1:11.

Upper School Student Profile Grade 9: 36 students (36 boys); Grade 10: 52 students (52 boys); Grade 11: 41 students (41 boys); Grade 12: 50 students (50 boys). 100% of students are boarding students. 21 states are represented in upper school student body. International students from Italy, Japan, Mexico, Republic of Korea, Russian Federation, and Taiwan; 10 other countries represented in student body.

Faculty School total: 47. In upper school: 27 men, 7 women; 27 have advanced degrees; 6 reside on campus.

Subjects Offered Algebra, American literature, art, biology, broadcasting, business, business skills, calculus, chemistry, computer science, drama, economics, English, ESL, fine arts, French, geography, geometry, government/civics, history, honors algebra, honors English, honors U.S. history, humanities, instrumental music, Internet, jazz band, journalism, JROTC or LEAD (Leadership Education and Development), keyboarding/computer, languages, Latin American studies, leadership, leadership skills, literary magazine, marching band, mathematics, military science, music, newspaper, physical education, physical science, physics, physics-AP, psychology, science, social studies, sociology, Spanish, speech, statistics, student government, student publications, swimming, theater, track and field, typing, U.S. government, U.S. history, vocal ensemble, vocal music, world history, wrestling, writing, yearbook.

Graduation Requirements Arts and fine arts (art, music, dance, drama), business skills (includes word processing), computer science, English, JROTC, mathematics, physical education (includes health), science, social studies (includes history). Community service is required.

Special Academic Programs Advanced Placement exam preparation in 5 subject areas; honors section; independent study; study at local college for college credit; academic accommodation for the musically talented and the artistically talented; remedial math; special instructional classes for students with Attention Deficit Disorder; ESL (50 students enrolled).

College Placement 52 students graduated in 2005; 50 went to college, including Illinois State University; Kansas State University; Texas A&M University; The University of Texas at Austin; University of Colorado at Boulder; University of Missouri–Columbia. Other: 2 entered military service. Median SAT verbal: 481, median SAT math: 489, median composite ACT: 20.

Student Life Upper grades have uniform requirement, student council, honor system. Discipline rests equally with students and faculty. Attendance at religious services is required.

Summer Programs Sports, rigorous outdoor training programs offered; session focuses on leadership; held both on and off campus; held at Water Park in Jefferson City, MO and Courtois River for float/canoe trips; accepts boys; open to students from other schools. 125 students usually enrolled. 2006 schedule: July 9 to July 22. Application deadline: July 3.

Tuition and Aid 7-day tuition and room/board: $19,690. Tuition installment plan (individually arranged payment plans, school's own payment plan). Need-based scholarship grants available. In 2005–06, 24% of upper-school students received aid. Total amount of financial aid awarded in 2005–06: $285,720.

Admissions Traditional secondary-level entrance grade is 9. For fall 2005, 143 students applied for upper-level admission, 124 were accepted, 108 enrolled. Deadline for receipt of application materials: none. Application fee required: $100. Interview recommended.

Athletics Interscholastic: aquatics (boys), baseball (b), basketball (b), cross-country running (b), diving (b), drill team (b), football (b), golf (b), JROTC drill (b), marksmanship (b), outdoor activities (b), riflery (b), soccer (b), swimming and diving (b), tennis (b), track and field (b), wrestling (b); intramural: aquatics (b), basketball (b), canoeing/kayaking (b), equestrian sports (b), fencing (b), fishing (b), fitness (b), fitness walking (b), flag football (b), horseback riding (b), indoor track (b), marksmanship (b), outdoor activities (b), outdoor skills (b), paint ball (b), physical fitness (b), physical training (b), rappelling (b), riflery (b), roller blading (b), ropes courses (b), running (b), skateboarding (b), soccer (b), softball (b), strength & conditioning (b), swimming and diving (b), table tennis (b), tennis (b), touch football (b), track and field (b), volleyball (b), weight lifting (b), weight training (b), winter (indoor) track (b), wrestling (b).

Computers Computers are regularly used in business, English, history, journalism, library, mathematics, newspaper, science, yearbook classes. Computer network features include campus e-mail, on-campus library services, CD-ROMs, online commercial services, Internet access, file transfer, office computer access, DVD.

Contact Maj. Dennis C. Diederich, Director of Admissions. 573-581-1776 Ext. 323. Fax: 573-581-0081. E-mail: ddie@mma.mexico.mo.us. Web site: mma-cadet.org.

MISS PORTER'S SCHOOL

60 Main Street
Farmington, Connecticut 06032
Head of School: Mrs. M. Burch Tracy Ford

General Information Girls' boarding and day college-preparatory and arts school. Grades 9–12. Founded: 1843. Setting: suburban. Nearest major city is Hartford. Students are housed in single-sex dormitories. 75-acre campus. 47 buildings on campus. Approved or accredited by Connecticut Association of Independent Schools, New England Association of Schools and Colleges, The Association of Boarding Schools, and Connecticut Department of Education. Member of National Association of Independent Schools and Secondary School Admission Test Board. Endowment: $77 million. Total enrollment: 325. Upper school average class size: 11. Upper school faculty-student ratio: 1:8.

Upper School Student Profile Grade 9: 74 students (74 girls); Grade 10: 79 students (79 girls); Grade 11: 79 students (79 girls); Grade 12: 93 students (93 girls). 66% of students are boarding students. 48% are state residents. 30 states are represented in upper school student body. 11% are international students. International students from China, Hong Kong, Panama, Republic of Korea, Thailand, and United Kingdom; 10 other countries represented in student body.

Faculty School total: 47. In upper school: 18 men, 29 women; 33 have advanced degrees; 34 reside on campus.

Subjects Offered Advanced Placement courses, algebra, American history, American literature, art, art history, astronomy, biology, botany, calculus, ceramics, chemistry, Chinese, community service, computer math, computer programming, computer science, conceptual physics, creative writing, dance, drama, driver education, economics, English, English literature, environmental science, ethics, European history, expository writing, fine arts, French, health, history, Latin, marine biology, mathematics, music, photography, physical education, physics, science, social studies, Spanish, speech, statistics, theater, trigonometry, word processing.

Graduation Requirements Arts and fine arts (art, music, dance, drama), computer science, English, foreign language, mathematics, science, social studies (includes history), participation in interscholastic athletics, 20 hours of community service, 80 hours of experiential learning.

Special Academic Programs Advanced Placement exam preparation in 18 subject areas; honors section; independent study; term-away projects; study abroad; ESL (10 students enrolled).

College Placement 74 students graduated in 2005; all went to college, including Brown University; Cornell University; Duke University; New York University; Trinity College. Mean SAT verbal: 642, mean SAT math: 624, mean composite ACT: 27.

Student Life Upper grades have specified standards of dress, student council, honor system. Discipline rests equally with students and faculty.

Summer Programs Enrichment, advancement, sports, art/fine arts, computer instruction programs offered; session focuses on mathematics and science, arts, leadership, athletics; held on campus; accepts girls; open to students from other schools. 60 students usually enrolled. 2006 schedule: June 25 to July 21. Application deadline: none.

Tuition and Aid Day student tuition: $26,625; 7-day tuition and room/board: $35,050. Tuition installment plan (Insured Tuition Payment Plan, Key Tuition Payment Plan, SMART Tuition Payment Plan, monthly payment plans, individually arranged payment plans). Merit scholarship grants, need-based scholarship grants, need-based loans available. In 2005–06, 38% of upper-school students received aid; total upper-school merit-scholarship money awarded: $164,138. Total amount of financial aid awarded in 2005–06: $2,300,000.

Admissions For fall 2005, 368 students applied for upper-level admission, 192 were accepted, 100 enrolled. ISEE, PSAT and SAT for applicants to grade 11 and 12 or SSAT required. Deadline for receipt of application materials: January 15. Application fee required: $50. Interview required.

Athletics Interscholastic: alpine skiing (girls), badminton (g), basketball (g), crew (g), cross-country running (g), dance (g), diving (g), field hockey (g), golf (g), ice hockey (g), independent competitive sports (g), lacrosse (g), modern dance (g), skiing (downhill) (g), soccer (g), softball (g), squash (g), swimming and diving (g), tennis (g), ultimate Frisbee (g), volleyball (g); intramural: aerobics (g), aerobics/nautilus (g), ballet (g), cross-country running (g), dance (g), equestrian sports (g), fitness (g), fitness walking (g), golf (g), hiking/backpacking (g), horseback riding (g), independent competitive sports (g), jogging (g), martial arts (g), modern dance (g), nautilus (g), outdoor activities (g), outdoor adventure (g), outdoor recreation (g), physical fitness (g), self defense (g), skiing (downhill) (g), snowboarding (g), squash (g), strength & conditioning (g), tennis (g), yoga (g). 2 coaches, 1 trainer.

Computers Computers are regularly used in art, English, foreign language, graphic design, history, mathematics, science, word processing classes. Computer network features include campus e-mail, on-campus library services, CD-ROMs, online commercial services, Internet access.

Contact Deborah Haskins, Director of Admission. 860-409-3530. Fax: 860-409-3531. E-mail: deborah_haskins@missporters.org. Web site: www.missporters.org.

ANNOUNCEMENT FROM THE SCHOOL A leader in preparing young women for competitive colleges since 1843, Miss Porter's offers a demanding curriculum, a collaborative environment, and a supportive community, which distinguish it as one of the best boarding schools in the nation. Miss Porter's boarding population is the largest among girls' boarding schools in the US. The

curriculum includes honors courses, AP course preparation, and elective courses. The Ann Whitney Olin Center for the Arts and Sciences houses classrooms with state-of-the-art equipment and technology for the instruction of math, science, and computer science. Art studios for photography, sculpture, printmaking, and jewelry making and a computer lab for graphic design are also located in Olin. Dance classes are held in the recently renovated Dance Barn. In addition, every classroom, dorm room, and office is wired for access to the campus network and the Internet. Each student has her own direct phone line as well as voice mail and an e-mail account. Recent changes to the 75-acre campus include a 22,000-square-foot library and state-of-the-art language laboratory in 2003 and 7 newly surfaced Deco-turf tennis courts in 2004.

See full description on page 920.

MMI PREPARATORY SCHOOL

154 Centre Street
Freeland, Pennsylvania 18224
Head of School: Dr. William A. Shergalis

General Information Coeducational day college-preparatory school. Grades 6–12. Founded: 1879. Setting: small town. Nearest major city is Wilkes-Barre. 20-acre campus. 1 building on campus. Approved or accredited by Middle States Association of Colleges and Schools and Pennsylvania Department of Education. Member of National Association of Independent Schools. Endowment: $10 million. Total enrollment: 190. Upper school average class size: 15. Upper school faculty-student ratio: 1:9.

Upper School Student Profile Grade 9: 40 students (22 boys, 18 girls); Grade 10: 29 students (15 boys, 14 girls); Grade 11: 25 students (12 boys, 13 girls); Grade 12: 24 students (12 boys, 12 girls).

Faculty School total: 21. In upper school: 10 men, 10 women; 13 have advanced degrees.

Subjects Offered Algebra, American history, American literature, anatomy, art, biology, calculus, chemistry, computer programming, computer science, consumer education, creative writing, earth science, economics, English, English literature, environmental science, European history, expository writing, fine arts, geography, geometry, German, government/civics, grammar, health, history, keyboarding, Latin, mathematics, music, physical education, physics, physiology, psychology, science, social studies, Spanish, speech, statistics, trigonometry, world history, world literature.

Graduation Requirements American history-AP, analysis and differential calculus, arts and fine arts (art, music, dance, drama), biology-AP, calculus-AP, chemistry-AP, college counseling, computer science, consumer education, economics, English, English language and composition-AP, English literature and composition-AP, English literature-AP, European history-AP, foreign language, mathematics, physical education (includes health), science, social studies (includes history), speech, independent research project presentation in the spring.

Special Academic Programs Advanced Placement exam preparation in 10 subject areas; honors section; academic accommodation for the gifted and the artistically talented.

College Placement 22 students graduated in 2005; all went to college, including Saint Joseph's University; Seton Hall University; Syracuse University; Temple University; The Pennsylvania State University University Park Campus; The University of Scranton. Mean SAT verbal: 614, mean SAT math: 629.

Student Life Upper grades have specified standards of dress, student council, honor system. Discipline rests primarily with faculty.

Summer Programs Remediation, enrichment, advancement programs offered; session focuses on academics; held on campus; accepts boys and girls; open to students from other schools. 20 students usually enrolled. 2006 schedule: June 18 to July 27. Application deadline: June 15.

Tuition and Aid Day student tuition: $9900. Tuition installment plan (monthly payment plans). Merit scholarship grants, need-based scholarship grants available. In 2005–06, 64% of upper-school students received aid; total upper-school merit-scholarship money awarded: $18,750. Total amount of financial aid awarded in 2005–06: $283,200.

Admissions Traditional secondary-level entrance grade is 9. For fall 2005, 38 students applied for upper-level admission, 32 were accepted, 24 enrolled. Iowa Silent Reading, Iowa Tests of Basic Skills and Otis-Lennon School Ability Test required. Deadline for receipt of application materials: none. Application fee required: $25. On-campus interview required.

Athletics Interscholastic: baseball (boys), basketball (b,g), cheering (g), cross-country running (b,g), softball (g), tennis (b,g), volleyball (g); intramural: basketball (b,g), bicycling (b,g), bowling (b,g), tennis (b,g), volleyball (b,g); coed interscholastic: golf; coed intramural: fencing, skiing (downhill), snowboarding. 2 PE instructors.

Computers Computers are regularly used in keyboarding, library science, programming, science, typing classes. Computer network features include on-campus library services, CD-ROMs, Internet access.

Contact Julie M. Lenio, Director of Admissions and Financial Aid. 570-636-1108. Fax: 570-636-0742. E-mail: jlenio@mmiprep.org. Web site: www.mmiprep.org.

MONTANA ACADEMY

Marion, Montana
See Special Needs Schools section.

MONTCALM SCHOOL

Albion, Michigan
See Special Needs Schools section.

MONTCLAIR COLLEGE PREPARATORY SCHOOL

8071 Sepulveda Boulevard
Van Nuys, California 91402-4420
Head of School: Dr. Vernon E. Simpson

petersons.com

General Information Coeducational boarding and day college-preparatory school. Grades 6–12. Founded: 1956. Setting: suburban. Nearest major city is Los Angeles. Students are housed in coed dormitories. 5-acre campus. 5 buildings on campus. Approved or accredited by Western Association of Schools and Colleges. Total enrollment: 439. Upper school average class size: 20. Upper school faculty-student ratio: 1:20.

Upper School Student Profile Grade 9: 58 students (36 boys, 22 girls); Grade 10: 73 students (43 boys, 30 girls); Grade 11: 108 students (64 boys, 44 girls); Grade 12: 80 students (40 boys, 40 girls). 5% of students are boarding students. 5% are international students. International students from Germany, Japan, Macedonia, Republic of Korea, and Taiwan; 1 other country represented in student body.

Faculty School total: 45. In upper school: 23 men, 22 women; 12 have advanced degrees; 5 reside on campus.

Graduation Requirements Arts and fine arts (art, music, dance, drama), computer science, English, foreign language, lab science, mathematics, U.S. government, U.S. history.

Special Academic Programs Advanced Placement exam preparation in 14 subject areas; ESL (50 students enrolled).

College Placement 93 students graduated in 2005; 92 went to college, including California State University, Northridge; Stanford University; University of California, Berkeley; University of California, Los Angeles. Other: 1 had other specific plans.

Student Life Upper grades have specified standards of dress, student council. Discipline rests primarily with faculty.

Summer Programs Remediation, sports, computer instruction programs offered; session focuses on review courses; held on campus; accepts boys and girls; open to students from other schools. 100 students usually enrolled. 2006 schedule: July 6 to August 13.

Tuition and Aid Day student tuition: $12,600; 7-day tuition and room/board: $27,700. Tuition installment plan (monthly payment plans, 1- and 2-payment plans). Limited need-based financial aid available. In 2005–06, 8% of upper-school students received aid. Total amount of financial aid awarded in 2005–06: $250,000.

Admissions Traditional secondary-level entrance grade is 9. For fall 2005, 150 students applied for upper-level admission, 100 were accepted, 50 enrolled. ISEE or school's own exam required. Deadline for receipt of application materials: none. Application fee required: $100.

Athletics Interscholastic: baseball (boys), basketball (b,g), football (b), soccer (b,g). 5 PE instructors, 5 coaches.

Computers Computers are regularly used in desktop publishing classes. Computer resources include campus e-mail, Internet access.

Contact Arlene Silverman, Director of Admissions. 818-787-5290. Fax: 818-786-3382.

See full description on page 922.

MONTCLAIR KIMBERLEY ACADEMY

201 Valley Road
Montclair, New Jersey 07042
Head of School: Mr. Thomas W. Nammack

General Information Coeducational day college-preparatory and arts school. Grades PK–12. Founded: 1887. Setting: suburban. Nearest major city is New York, NY. 28-acre campus. 1 building on campus. Approved or accredited by Middle States Association of Colleges and Schools. Member of National Association of Independent Schools and Secondary School Admission Test Board. Endowment: $12 million. Total enrollment: 1,038. Upper school average class size: 12. Upper school faculty-student ratio: 1:7.

Upper School Student Profile Grade 9: 119 students (54 boys, 65 girls); Grade 10: 112 students (58 boys, 54 girls); Grade 11: 102 students (53 boys, 49 girls); Grade 12: 107 students (49 boys, 58 girls).

Faculty School total: 64. In upper school: 35 men, 29 women; 49 have advanced degrees.

Subjects Offered Advanced chemistry, advanced math, algebra, American history, American literature, architecture, art, astronomy, biology, biology-AP, British literature, calculus, calculus-AP, chemistry, chemistry-AP, chorus, communications, computer programming, computer programming-AP, concert band, creative writing, dance, digital photography, drama, driver education, ecology, economics, economics-AP, English, English literature, environmental science, ethics, European history, expository writing, fine arts, French, French language-AP, French literature-AP, geometry, government/civics, health, history, Latin, mathematics, mechanical drawing, music, photography, physical education, physics, physics-AP, post-calculus, Spanish, Spanish language-AP, Spanish literature-AP, statistics-AP, theater, trigonometry, world history, world literature, world wide web design, writing.

Graduation Requirements Arts and fine arts (art, music, dance, drama), English, foreign language, history, mathematics, physical education (includes health), science, swimming, citizenship.

Special Academic Programs Advanced Placement exam preparation in 14 subject areas; honors section; independent study; academic accommodation for the gifted.

College Placement 105 students graduated in 2005; 103 went to college, including Boston University; Harvard University; Princeton University; University of Pennsylvania. Other: 2 entered a postgraduate year. Mean SAT verbal: 630, mean SAT math: 638. 60% scored over 600 on SAT verbal, 65% scored over 600 on SAT math.

Student Life Upper grades have specified standards of dress, student council, honor system. Discipline rests equally with students and faculty.

Summer Programs Remediation, enrichment, advancement, sports, art/fine arts, computer instruction programs offered; session focuses on academics; held on campus; accepts boys and girls; open to students from other schools. 150 students usually enrolled. 2006 schedule: June 27 to August 5. Application deadline: June.

Tuition and Aid Day student tuition: $23,200. Tuition installment plan (Insured Tuition Payment Plan, monthly payment plans, individually arranged payment plans). Need-based scholarship grants available. In 2005–06, 20% of upper-school students received aid. Total amount of financial aid awarded in 2005–06: $2,400,000.

Admissions Traditional secondary-level entrance grade is 9. For fall 2005, 120 students applied for upper-level admission, 50 were accepted, 33 enrolled. ISEE or SSAT required. Deadline for receipt of application materials: January 27. Application fee required: $50. On-campus interview required.

Athletics Interscholastic: baseball (boys), basketball (b,g), cheering (g), cross-country running (b,g), dance (b,g), dance team (b,g), fencing (b,g), field hockey (g), football (b), ice hockey (b), lacrosse (b,g), outdoor activities (b,g), soccer (b,g), softball (g), swimming and diving (b,g), tennis (b,g), track and field (b,g), volleyball (g), winter (indoor) track (b,g), wrestling (b); coed interscholastic: golf. 5 PE instructors, 5 coaches, 2 trainers.

Computers Computers are regularly used in all academic classes. Computer network features include campus e-mail, on-campus library services, CD-ROMs, online commercial services, Internet access, file transfer, office computer access, wireless campus network, Homework Hotline, community Intranet.

Contact John Zurcher, Director of Admissions and Financial Aid. 973-509-7930. Fax: 973-509-4526. E-mail: jzurcher@montclairkimberley.org. Web site: www.montclairkimberley.org.

MONTE VISTA CHRISTIAN SCHOOL

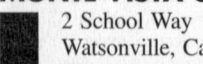

2 School Way
Watsonville, California 95076
Head of School: Mr. Stephen Sharp

General Information Coeducational boarding and day college-preparatory, arts, religious studies, technology, and ESL school, affiliated with Christian faith. Boarding grades 9–12, day grades 6–12. Founded: 1926. Setting: rural. Nearest major city is San Jose. Students are housed in single-sex dormitories. 100-acre campus. 27 buildings on campus. Approved or accredited by Association of Christian Schools International, The Association of Boarding Schools, Western Association of Schools and Colleges, and California Department of Education. Endowment: $1 million. Total enrollment: 866. Upper school average class size: 25. Upper school faculty-student ratio: 1:16.

Upper School Student Profile Grade 9: 166 students (84 boys, 82 girls); Grade 10: 167 students (69 boys, 98 girls); Grade 11: 190 students (95 boys, 95 girls); Grade 12: 153 students (83 boys, 70 girls). 12% of students are boarding students. 90% are state residents. 1 state is represented in upper school student body. 10% are international students. International students from China, Hong Kong, Panama, Republic of Korea, Taiwan, and Thailand; 1 other country represented in student body. 80% of students are Christian faith.

Faculty School total: 68. In upper school: 23 men, 25 women; 15 have advanced degrees; 15 reside on campus.

Subjects Offered 3-dimensional art, 3-dimensional design, advanced chemistry, advanced computer applications, advanced TOEFL/grammar, algebra, American government, American government-AP, American literature, anatomy, art, ASB Leadership, auto shop, band, basic skills, Bible studies, biology, biology-AP, calculus, calculus-AP, calligraphy, campus ministry, career/college preparation, carpentry, ceramics, chemistry, chemistry-AP, choir, choral music, Christian doctrine, Christian ethics, Christian scripture, Christian studies, Christianity, computer applications, computer education, computer graphics, computer keyboarding, computer literacy, computer science, computer skills, culinary arts, desktop publishing, digital imaging,

drafting, drama, drama performance, drawing, drawing and design, earth science, economics, English, English literature, English-AP, environmental science, equestrian sports, ESL, European history-AP, fine arts, French, geology, geometry, government/civics, grammar, guitar, health, history, honors algebra, honors English, honors geometry, honors world history, human anatomy, industrial arts, Japanese, keyboarding, learning lab, marine biology, mathematics, music, orchestra, photography, physical education, physics, physiology, pre-calculus, psychology, religion, SAT preparation, science, social studies, Spanish, statistics-AP, student government, trigonometry, U.S. history, U.S. history-AP, vocal music, Web site design, woodworking, world history, world literature, wrestling, yearbook.

Graduation Requirements American government, arts and fine arts (art, music, dance, drama), Bible, biology, computer keyboarding, computer science, economics, English, foreign language, geometry, health education, mathematics, physical education (includes health), science, U.S. history, world history.

Special Academic Programs Advanced Placement exam preparation in 7 subject areas; honors section; remedial reading and/or remedial writing; remedial math; special instructional classes for students with mild learning differences; ESL (30 students enrolled).

College Placement 173 students graduated in 2005; 154 went to college, including California Polytechnic State University, San Luis Obispo; Rensselaer Polytechnic Institute; Rhode Island School of Design; Santa Clara University; University of California, San Diego. Other: 13 went to work, 6 entered military service. Median SAT verbal: 514, median SAT math: 553, median composite ACT: 23.

Student Life Upper grades have specified standards of dress, student council, honor system. Discipline rests primarily with faculty. Attendance at religious services is required.

Summer Programs Remediation, enrichment, advancement, ESL, sports programs offered; session focuses on academics, ESL, and equestrian sports; held on campus; accepts boys and girls; open to students from other schools. 200 students usually enrolled. 2006 schedule: July 11 to August 19. Application deadline: June 15.

Tuition and Aid Day student tuition: $7100; 7-day tuition and room/board: $28,000–$31,000. Tuition installment plan (individually arranged payment plans, three payments (enrollment, 7/1 and 12/1)). Tuition reduction for siblings, need-based scholarship grants available. In 2005–06, 5% of upper-school students received aid. Total amount of financial aid awarded in 2005–06: $95,000.

Admissions Traditional secondary-level entrance grade is 9. SSAT or TOEFL or SLEP required. Deadline for receipt of application materials: none. Application fee required: $80. Interview recommended.

Athletics Interscholastic: baseball (boys), basketball (b,g), cheering (g), cross-country running (b,g), football (b), golf (b,g), soccer (b,g), softball (g), swimming and diving (b,g), tennis (b,g), track and field (b,g), volleyball (b,g), wrestling (b); intramural: baseball (b), basketball (b,g), cross-country running (b,g), equestrian sports (b,g), field hockey (b,g), football (b), golf (b,g); soccer (b,g), swimming and diving (b,g), tennis (b,g), track and field (b,g), volleyball (b,g), weight lifting (b,g), wrestling (b); coed interscholastic: aquatics, diving, drill team, horseback riding. 6 PE instructors, 14 coaches, 2 trainers.

Computers Computers are regularly used in desktop publishing, ESL, foreign language, mathematics, writing classes. Computer network features include campus e-mail, on-campus library services, Internet access, Homework Hotline.

Contact Ms. Susan S. Bernal, Director of Resident Admissions. 831-722-8178 Ext. 128. Fax: 831-722-6003. E-mail: susanbernal@mvcs.com. Web site: mvcs.org.

See full description on page 924.

MONTGOMERY BELL ACADEMY

4001 Harding Road
Nashville, Tennessee 37205
Head of School: Bradford Gioia

General Information Boys' day college-preparatory and arts school. Grades 7–12. Founded: 1867. Setting: urban. 40-acre campus. 9 buildings on campus. Approved or accredited by Southern Association of Colleges and Schools and Tennessee Association of Independent Schools. Member of National Association of Independent Schools and Secondary School Admission Test Board. Endowment: $49.3 million. Total enrollment: 662. Upper school average class size: 13. Upper school faculty-student ratio: 1:9.

Upper School Student Profile Grade 9: 107 students (107 boys); Grade 10: 113 students (113 boys); Grade 11: 117 students (117 boys); Grade 12: 108 students (108 boys).

Faculty School total: 85. In upper school: 60 men, 17 women; 50 have advanced degrees.

Subjects Offered Algebra, American history, American literature, art, art history, biology, calculus, chemistry, computer programming, computer science, drama, earth science, economics, English, English literature, environmental science-AP, European history, fine arts, French, geography, geology, geometry, German, government/civics, grammar, Greek, history, Latin, mathematics, music, music history, music theory, physical education, physics, science, social studies, Spanish, speech, statistics, theater, trigonometry, world history, writing.

Graduation Requirements Arts and fine arts (art, music, dance, drama), English, foreign language, mathematics, physical education (includes health), science, social studies (includes history).

Special Academic Programs Advanced Placement exam preparation in 16 subject areas; honors section; term-away projects; study abroad.

College Placement 119 students graduated in 2005; 114 went to college, including Auburn University; Southern Methodist University; University of Georgia; University of Virginia; Vanderbilt University; Wake Forest University. Other: 4 entered a postgraduate year, 1 had other specific plans. Median SAT verbal: 660, median SAT math: 660, median composite ACT: 28. 77% scored over 600 on SAT verbal, 86% scored over 600 on SAT math.

Student Life Upper grades have specified standards of dress, student council, honor system. Discipline rests primarily with faculty.

Summer Programs Remediation, enrichment, sports, art/fine arts, computer instruction programs offered; session focuses on academics and athletics; held on campus; accepts boys and girls; open to students from other schools. 250 students usually enrolled. 2006 schedule: June 18 to July 27. Application deadline: none.

Tuition and Aid Day student tuition: $15,700. Tuition installment plan (monthly payment plans, Dewar Tuition Refund Plan). Need-based scholarship grants available. In 2005–06, 15% of upper-school students received aid. Total amount of financial aid awarded in 2005–06: $525,750.

Admissions Traditional secondary-level entrance grade is 9. For fall 2005, 61 students applied for upper-level admission, 43 were accepted, 26 enrolled. ISEE required. Deadline for receipt of application materials: February 1. Application fee required: $50. On-campus interview required.

Athletics Interscholastic: baseball, basketball, bowling, cross-country running, diving, football, golf, hockey, ice hockey, lacrosse, riflery, soccer, swimming and diving, tennis, track and field, wrestling; intramural: back packing, baseball, basketball, cheering, flag football, football, Frisbee, hiking/backpacking, outdoor activities, outdoor adventure, outdoor education, outdoor recreation, paddle tennis, running, soccer, softball, strength & conditioning, table tennis, tennis, touch football, track and field, ultimate Frisbee, volleyball, weight lifting, weight training, wrestling. 5 PE instructors, 5 coaches, 2 trainers.

Computers Computers are regularly used in all academic classes. Computer network features include campus e-mail, on-campus library services, CD-ROMs, online commercial services, Internet access, office computer access, DVD, wireless campus network.

Contact Mr. Robert Black, Director, Admission and Financial Aid. 615-298-5514 Ext. 251. Fax: 615-297-0271. E-mail: blackr@montgomerybell.com. Web site: www.montgomerybell.com.

MONTGOMERY CATHOLIC PREPARATORY SCHOOL

5350 Vaughn Road
Montgomery, Alabama 36116
Head of School: Faustin N. Weber

General Information Coeducational day college-preparatory school, affiliated with Roman Catholic Church. Grades 9–12. Founded: 1873. Setting: suburban. 20-acre campus. 4 buildings on campus. Approved or accredited by European Council of International Schools, Southern Association of Colleges and Schools, and Alabama Department of Education. Endowment: $435,000. Total enrollment: 910. Upper school average class size: 19. Upper school faculty-student ratio: 1:13.

Upper School Student Profile Grade 9: 86 students (42 boys, 44 girls); Grade 10: 64 students (30 boys, 34 girls); Grade 11: 75 students (40 boys, 35 girls); Grade 12: 60 students (32 boys, 28 girls). 75% of students are Roman Catholic.

Faculty School total: 26. In upper school: 9 men, 12 women; 15 have advanced degrees.

Graduation Requirements Senior service.

College Placement 60 students graduated in 2005; 57 went to college, including Troy University. Other: 2 went to work, 1 entered military service.

Student Life Upper grades have uniform requirement, student council. Discipline rests primarily with faculty. Attendance at religious services is required.

Tuition and Aid Day student tuition: $4700–$5500. Need-based scholarship grants available. In 2005–06, 18% of upper-school students received aid.

Admissions Traditional secondary-level entrance grade is 9. Placement test required. Deadline for receipt of application materials: none. Application fee required: $25.

Athletics Interscholastic: baseball (boys), basketball (b,g), cheering (g), football (b), golf (b), soccer (b,g), softball (g), strength & conditioning (b,g), tennis (g), volleyball (g); coed interscholastic: physical fitness, physical training, track and field.

Computers Computer network features include campus e-mail, Internet access.

Contact Mary Kelley, Development Director. 334-272-7221 Ext. 15. Fax: 334-272-2440. E-mail: m_kelley@knights.pvt.k12.al.us. Web site: www.knights.pvt.k12.al.us.

MONT'KIARA INTERNATIONAL SCHOOL

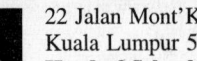

22 Jalan Mont'Kiara
Kuala Lumpur 50480, Malaysia
Head of School: Glenn Chapin

General Information Coeducational day college-preparatory school. Grades 1–12. Founded: 1994. Setting: suburban. 6-acre campus. 3 buildings on campus. Approved or accredited by International Baccalaureate Organization and Western Association of Schools and Colleges. Language of instruction: English. Total enrollment: 711. Upper school average class size: 12. Upper school faculty-student ratio: 1:7.

Faculty School total: 88. In upper school: 24 men, 23 women; 28 have advanced degrees.

Special Academic Programs International Baccalaureate program; ESL (14 students enrolled).

College Placement 34 students graduated in 2005; 33 went to college. Other: 1 had other specific plans. Mean SAT verbal: 569, mean SAT math: 603. 30% scored over 600 on SAT verbal, 41% scored over 600 on SAT math.

Student Life Upper grades have uniform requirement, student council. Discipline rests primarily with faculty.

Tuition and Aid Day student tuition: 51,000 Malaysian ringgits.

Admissions Traditional secondary-level entrance grade is 9. Deadline for receipt of application materials: none. Application fee required: 500 Malaysian ringgits. On-campus interview required.

Athletics Interscholastic: baseball (boys, girls), basketball (b,g), golf (b,g), rugby (g), soccer (b,g), softball (b,g), swimming and diving (b,g), track and field (b,g), volleyball (b,g); coed interscholastic: aquatics. 4 PE instructors.

Computers Computer network features include campus e-mail, on-campus library services, CD-ROMs, online commercial services, Internet access, file transfer, DVD, wireless campus network.

Contact Bridget Hall, Admissions Counselor. 60 3 2093 8604. Fax: 60 3 2903 6045. E-mail: b.hall@mkis.edu.my. Web site: www.mkis.edu.my.

MONTROSE SCHOOL

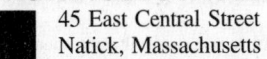

45 East Central Street
Natick, Massachusetts 01760
Head of School: Karen E. Bohlin, EdD

General Information Girls' day college-preparatory school, affiliated with Roman Catholic Church. Grades 6–12. Founded: 1979. Setting: suburban. Nearest major city is Boston. 1 building on campus. Approved or accredited by Massachusetts Department of Education. Languages of instruction: English, Spanish, and French. Total enrollment: 131. Upper school average class size: 13. Upper school faculty-student ratio: 1:10.

Upper School Student Profile Grade 9: 15 students (15 girls); Grade 10: 26 students (26 girls); Grade 11: 20 students (20 girls); Grade 12: 11 students (11 girls). 65% of students are Roman Catholic.

Faculty School total: 24. In upper school: 21 women; 13 have advanced degrees.

Subjects Offered 20th century history, algebra, American literature, biology, British literature, calculus-AP, chemistry, church history, computers, drama, English-AP, French, geometry, Life of Christ, medieval/Renaissance history, modern European history, moral theology, music, physical education, physics, pre-calculus, religion, social doctrine, Spanish, speech, studio art, trigonometry, U.S. history, world history, world literature.

Graduation Requirements Arts and fine arts (art, music, dance, drama), computer science, English, foreign language, mathematics, physical education (includes health), religion (includes Bible studies and theology), science, social studies (includes history).

Special Academic Programs Advanced Placement exam preparation in 2 subject areas; honors section; independent study.

College Placement 10 students graduated in 2005; all went to college, including Boston College; Brown University; Northeastern University; Providence College; Saint Michael's College; University of Notre Dame. Median SAT verbal: 660, median SAT math: 654. 53% scored over 600 on SAT verbal, 53% scored over 600 on SAT math.

Student Life Upper grades have uniform requirement, student council, honor system. Discipline rests primarily with faculty.

Tuition and Aid Day student tuition: $12,800. Tuition installment plan (SMART Tuition Payment Plan). Merit scholarship grants, need-based scholarship grants available. In 2005–06, 38% of upper-school students received aid; total upper-school merit-scholarship money awarded: $4000. Total amount of financial aid awarded in 2005–06: $75,000.

Admissions Traditional secondary-level entrance grade is 9. For fall 2005, 18 students applied for upper-level admission, 10 were accepted, 8 enrolled. Admissions testing, ERB Reading and Math, ERB verbal, ERB math, essay and SCAT required. Deadline for receipt of application materials: February 1. Application fee required: $50. Interview required.

Athletics Interscholastic: basketball, cross-country running, lacrosse, soccer; intramural: dance, fitness, volleyball. 1 PE instructor, 1 coach.

Computers Computers are regularly used in foreign language classes. Computer network features include campus e-mail, CD-ROMs, Internet access.

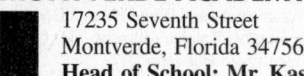

Contact Patricia Keefe, Office of Admissions. 508-650-6925 Ext. 15. Fax: 508-650-6926. E-mail: pkeefe@montroseschool.org. Web site: www.montroseschool. org.

MONTVERDE ACADEMY

17235 Seventh Street
Montverde, Florida 34756
Head of School: Mr. Kasey C. Kesselring

General Information Coeducational boarding and day college-preparatory and arts school. Boarding grades 7–PG, day grades PK–PG. Founded: 1912. Setting: small town. Nearest major city is Orlando. Students are housed in single-sex dormitories. 125-acre campus. 25 buildings on campus. Approved or accredited by Southern Association of Colleges and Schools, Southern Association of Independent Schools, and The Association of Boarding Schools. Member of National Association of Independent Schools. Endowment: $20 million. Total enrollment: 431. Upper school average class size: 20. Upper school faculty-student ratio: 1:8.

Upper School Student Profile 75% of students are boarding students. 30% are state residents. 9 states are represented in upper school student body. 70% are international students. International students from Germany, Puerto Rico, Republic of Korea, Taiwan, Turks and Caicos Islands, and Viet Nam; 36 other countries represented in student body.

Faculty School total: 43. In upper school: 15 men, 12 women; 17 have advanced degrees; 22 reside on campus.

Subjects Offered 20th century history, 3-dimensional art, accounting, advanced computer applications, algebra, American history, American literature, anatomy, ancient world history, art, art history, biology, British history, calculus, ceramics, chemistry, choral music, clayworking, computer applications, computer keyboarding, computer multimedia, computer science, desktop publishing, drama, economics, English, English literature, ESL, ethics, fitness, geography, geometry, government, history, history of music, honors algebra, honors English, mathematics, music appreciation, photo shop, photography, physical education, physics, physiology, pre-calculus, psychology, SAT/ACT preparation, science, Spanish, study skills, trigonometry, world history.

Graduation Requirements Arts and fine arts (art, music, dance, drama), computer science, electives, English, foreign language, mathematics, physical education (includes health), science, social studies (includes history), international students are not required to take a foreign language if their native language is not English.

Special Academic Programs Advanced Placement exam preparation in 10 subject areas; honors section; special instructional classes for students with Attention Deficit Disorder; ESL (62 students enrolled).

College Placement 41 students graduated in 2005; all went to college, including Dartmouth College; Florida State University; Michigan State University; Rollins College; The Pennsylvania State University University Park Campus. Mean SAT verbal: 422, mean SAT math: 520.

Student Life Upper grades have uniform requirement, student council, honor system. Discipline rests equally with students and faculty. Attendance at religious services is required.

Summer Programs Remediation, advancement, ESL programs offered; session focuses on academics; held on campus; accepts boys and girls; open to students from other schools. 50 students usually enrolled. 2006 schedule: June 26 to August 4. Application deadline: none.

Tuition and Aid Day student tuition: $9125; 7-day tuition and room/board: $23,500. Tuition installment plan (monthly payment plans). Tuition reduction for siblings, need-based scholarship grants available. In 2005–06, 30% of upper-school students received aid. Total amount of financial aid awarded in 2005–06: $843,540.

Admissions Traditional secondary-level entrance grade is 11. For fall 2005, 202 students applied for upper-level admission, 181 were accepted, 152 enrolled. SSAT, SSAT, ERB, PSAT, SAT, PLAN or ACT or TOEFL required. Deadline for receipt of application materials: none. Application fee required: $50. Interview recommended.

Athletics Interscholastic: baseball (boys), basketball (b,g), cheering (g), cross-country running (b,g), golf (b,g), soccer (b,g), tennis (b,g), track and field (b,g), volleyball (g); intramural: basketball (b,g), flag football (b), soccer (b,g), softball (b,g), table tennis (b,g), tennis (b,g); coed interscholastic: equestrian sports, horseback riding, track and field; coed intramural: aerobics, aquatics, bicycling, billiards, canoeing/kayaking, equestrian sports, fishing, fitness, fitness walking, Frisbee, horseback riding, jogging, kayaking, physical fitness, physical training, roller blading, ropes courses, running, skateboarding, soccer, strength & conditioning, swimming and diving, ultimate Frisbee, walking, whiffle ball. 2 PE instructors, 15 coaches.

Computers Computers are regularly used in all academic classes. Computer network features include campus e-mail, on-campus library services, CD-ROMs, Internet access, wireless campus network.

Contact Mr. Alan D. Whittemore, Dean of Admissions. 407-469-2561 Ext. 204. Fax: 407-469-3711. E-mail: awhittemore@montverde.org. Web site: www.montverde.org.

ANNOUNCEMENT FROM THE SCHOOL Founded in 1912, Montverde Academy serves 225 boarding and day students in grades 6–12 and 155 day students in PK3–grade 5. Internationally recognized as one of Florida's finest independent, coeducational, college-preparatory schools, the Academy hosts

students from many countries and all across the United States. Accredited by the Southern Association of Colleges and Schools, Montverde Academy holds membership in the Association of Boarding Schools (TABS) and the Secondary School Admission Testing Board (SSATB). The college-preparatory curriculum offers challenging courses in all major subject areas as well as many honors and Advanced Placement courses. English as a second language (ESL) is available at several different levels to international students who are learning to speak English. Students with study skills, time management, and organizational deficits are offered extra support through optional participation in the Discovery Program, a small-group tutorial program. Located on 125 beautiful acres only minutes from Orlando and its many world-class attractions, Montverde Academy has an exceptional facility that is valued at $24 million. Featured are 4 academic buildings; 3 dormitories (2 of which are new); a dining hall; a 450-seat fine arts center that includes a theater, music rooms, and an art and photography studio; a library/media center; 2 gymnasiums; a fitness center; a professional track; a swimming pool; 5 tennis courts; 2 athletic fields; two riding rings; and a lake for fishing. Golf, tennis, and equestrian studies are also available. A Lower Day School is also located on campus. Montverde Academy provides students with an excellent education, exciting recreational options, and a safe, structured environment where they can meet their academic potential and develop the character values that are necessary to become responsible and successful citizens of the community.

MOORESTOWN FRIENDS SCHOOL

110 East Main Street
Moorestown, New Jersey 08057
Head of School: Laurence Van Meter

General Information Coeducational day college-preparatory and arts school, affiliated with Society of Friends. Grades PS–12. Founded: 1785. Setting: suburban. Nearest major city is Philadelphia, PA. Students are housed in single-sex dormitories. 40-acre campus. 9 buildings on campus. Approved or accredited by Middle States Association of Colleges and Schools and New Jersey Department of Education. Member of National Association of Independent Schools. Endowment: $8.4 million. Total enrollment: 717. Upper school average class size: 18. Upper school faculty-student ratio: 1:9.

Upper School Student Profile Grade 9: 68 students (30 boys, 38 girls); Grade 10: 68 students (35 boys, 33 girls); Grade 11: 74 students (34 boys, 40 girls); Grade 12: 68 students (38 boys, 30 girls). 4% of students are members of Society of Friends.

Faculty School total: 83. In upper school: 21 men, 24 women; 28 have advanced degrees.

Subjects Offered Algebra, American history, American literature, art, art history, biology, calculus, ceramics, chemistry, community service, computer programming, computer science, creative writing, drama, driver education, earth science, economics, English, English literature, environmental science, ethics, European history, expository writing, fine arts, French, geometry, government/civics, grammar, health, history, mathematics, music, philosophy, photography, physical education, physics, psychology, religion, science, social studies, Spanish, theater, trigonometry, world history, writing.

Graduation Requirements Arts and fine arts (art, music, dance, drama), English, foreign language, mathematics, physical education (includes health), science, senior project, social studies (includes history). Community service is required.

Special Academic Programs Advanced Placement exam preparation in 12 subject areas; honors section; independent study; term-away projects; study at local college for college credit; study abroad.

College Placement 61 students graduated in 2005; all went to college, including Northwestern University; Rutgers, The State University of New Jersey, New Brunswick/Piscataway; The Johns Hopkins University; Tufts University; University of Delaware; University of Pennsylvania. Median SAT verbal: 620, median SAT math: 620.

Student Life Upper grades have specified standards of dress, student council, honor system. Discipline rests primarily with faculty. Attendance at religious services is required.

Tuition and Aid Day student tuition: $16,250. Tuition installment plan (Academic Management Services Plan, Tuition Refund Plan). Need-based scholarship grants, need-based loans, tuition reduction for children of faculty and staff available. In 2005–06, 27% of upper-school students received aid. Total amount of financial aid awarded in 2005–06: $484,320.

Admissions Traditional secondary-level entrance grade is 9. For fall 2005, 71 students applied for upper-level admission, 47 were accepted, 36 enrolled. ERB CTP required. Deadline for receipt of application materials: none. Application fee required: $45. On-campus interview required.

Athletics Interscholastic: baseball (boys), basketball (b,g), crew (b,g), cross-country running (b,g), field hockey (g), independent competitive sports (b,g), lacrosse (g), physical training (b,g), soccer (b,g), swimming and diving (b,g), tennis (b,g); intramural: floor hockey (b), roller hockey (b), street hockey (b), weight training (b,g); coed interscholastic: fencing, golf. 5 PE instructors, 23 coaches, 1 trainer.

Computers Computers are regularly used in English, foreign language, mathematics, music, science classes. Computer network features include campus e-mail, on-campus library services, CD-ROMs, Internet access, wireless campus network.

Contact Karin B. Miller, Director of Admission and Financial Aid. 856-235-2900 Ext. 227. Fax: 856-235-6684. E-mail: kmiller@mfriends.org. Web site: www.mfriends.org.

MOOSEHEART HIGH SCHOOL

255 James J. Davis Drive
Mooseheart, Illinois 60539
Head of School: Gary Lee Urwiler

General Information Coeducational boarding and day college-preparatory, general academic, arts, business, vocational, bilingual studies, technology, nursing, and cosmetology school, affiliated with Protestant faith, Roman Catholic Church; primarily serves underachievers and students in dysfunctional family situations. Grades K–12. Founded: 1913. Setting: small town. Nearest major city is Aurora. Students are housed in family homes. 1,100-acre campus. 40 buildings on campus. Approved or accredited by North Central Association of Colleges and Schools and Illinois Department of Education. Total enrollment: 216. Upper school faculty-student ratio: 1:6.

Upper School Student Profile Grade 9: 26 students (16 boys, 10 girls); Grade 10: 30 students (16 boys, 14 girls); Grade 11: 22 students (9 boys, 13 girls); Grade 12: 23 students (10 boys, 13 girls). 95% of students are Protestant, Roman Catholic.

Faculty School total: 45. In upper school: 5 men, 10 women; 6 have advanced degrees; 1 resides on campus.

College Placement 18 students graduated in 2005; 16 went to college. Other: 1 went to work, 1 entered military service.

Student Life Upper grades have specified standards of dress, student council, honor system. Discipline rests primarily with faculty. Attendance at religious services is required.

Summer Programs Remediation, sports programs offered; session focuses on recreation; held on campus; accepts boys and girls; not open to students from other schools. 225 students usually enrolled.

Admissions Mathematics proficiency exam required. No application fee required. Interview recommended.

Athletics Interscholastic: basketball (boys, girls), bowling (g), drill team (b,g), football (b), JROTC drill (b,g), track and field (b,g), volleyball (g). 2 PE instructors, 10 coaches.

Computers Computers are regularly used in word processing classes. Computer resources include on-campus library services, CD-ROMs, Internet access.

Contact Dale Jones, Director of Admission. 630-906-3631 Ext. 3631. Fax: 630-906-3634 Ext. 3634. E-mail: djones@mooseheart.org.

MORAVIAN ACADEMY

4313 Green Pond Road
Bethlehem, Pennsylvania 18020
Head of School: Barnaby J. Roberts

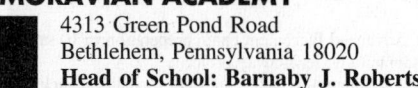 
petersons.com

General Information Coeducational day college-preparatory school, affiliated with Moravian Church. Grades PK–12. Founded: 1742. Setting: rural. Nearest major city is Philadelphia. 120-acre campus. 8 buildings on campus. Approved or accredited by Middle States Association of Colleges and Schools, Pennsylvania Association of Private Academic Schools, and Pennsylvania Department of Education. Member of National Association of Independent Schools and Secondary School Admission Test Board. Endowment: $10.5 million. Total enrollment: 793. Upper school average class size: 15. Upper school faculty-student ratio: 1:7.

Upper School Student Profile Grade 9: 74 students (39 boys, 35 girls); Grade 10: 72 students (36 boys, 36 girls); Grade 11: 70 students (30 boys, 40 girls); Grade 12: 69 students (33 boys, 36 girls).

Faculty School total: 95. In upper school: 21 men, 20 women; 29 have advanced degrees.

Subjects Offered Algebra, American history, American literature, anatomy, ancient history, art, biology, calculus, chemistry, community service, drama, driver education, ecology, economics, English, English literature, European history, fine arts, French, geometry, government, health, history, Japanese, Japanese studies, law, mathematics, music, photography, physical education, physics, poetry, religion, science, Spanish, statistics, theater, trigonometry, world history, world literature.

Graduation Requirements Arts and fine arts (art, music, dance, drama), English, foreign language, mathematics, physical education (includes health), religion (includes Bible studies and theology), science, social studies (includes history), service project.

Special Academic Programs Advanced Placement exam preparation in 9 subject areas; honors section; independent study; study at local college for college credit; remedial reading and/or remedial writing.

College Placement 64 students graduated in 2005; 62 went to college, including Franklin and Marshall College; Lafayette College; Lehigh University; New York University; University of Pennsylvania; University of Pittsburgh. Other: 2 had other

specific plans. Median SAT verbal: 670, median SAT math: 670. 83% scored over 600 on SAT verbal, 86% scored over 600 on SAT math.

Student Life Upper grades have specified standards of dress, student council. Discipline rests equally with students and faculty. Attendance at religious services is required.

Summer Programs Remediation, enrichment, art/fine arts programs offered; session focuses on enrichment; held on campus; accepts boys and girls; open to students from other schools. 2006 schedule: June 12 to July 21.

Tuition and Aid Day student tuition: $16,510. Tuition installment plan (monthly payment plans, individually arranged payment plans). Need-based scholarship grants, need-based loans available. In 2005–06, 18% of upper-school students received aid. Total amount of financial aid awarded in 2005–06: $480,950.

Admissions Traditional secondary-level entrance grade is 9. For fall 2005, 54 students applied for upper-level admission, 39 were accepted, 34 enrolled. ERB and Otis-Lennon School Ability Test required. Deadline for receipt of application materials: none. Application fee required: $65. On-campus interview required.

Athletics Interscholastic: baseball (boys), basketball (b,g), field hockey (g), lacrosse (b), soccer (b,g), softball (g), tennis (b,g); coed interscholastic: cross-country running, golf. 3 PE instructors, 9 coaches, 1 trainer.

Computers Computers are regularly used in art, English, foreign language, history, mathematics, music, science classes. Computer resources include on-campus library services, CD-ROMs, Internet access, wireless campus network.

Contact Suzanne H. Mason, Director of Admissions. 610-691-1600. Fax: 610-691-3354. E-mail: smason@moravian.k12.pa.us. Web site: www.moravianacademy.org.

See full description on page 926.

MOREAU CATHOLIC HIGH SCHOOL

27170 Mission Boulevard
Hayward, California 94544
Head of School: Mr. Terry Lee

General Information Coeducational day college-preparatory, arts, and religious studies school, affiliated with Roman Catholic Church. Grades 9–12. Founded: 1965. Setting: suburban. Nearest major city is Oakland. 14-acre campus. 6 buildings on campus. Approved or accredited by National Catholic Education Association, Western Association of Schools and Colleges, Western Catholic Education Association, and California Department of Education. Endowment: $2.5 million. Total enrollment: 930. Upper school average class size: 27. Upper school faculty-student ratio: 1:18.

Upper School Student Profile Grade 9: 227 students (104 boys, 123 girls); Grade 10: 227 students (107 boys, 120 girls); Grade 11: 242 students (124 boys, 118 girls); Grade 12: 234 students (124 boys, 110 girls). 75% of students are Roman Catholic.

Faculty School total: 60. In upper school: 25 men, 32 women; 34 have advanced degrees.

Subjects Offered Advanced Placement courses, aerobics, algebra, American Civil War, American government-AP, American history, American literature, anatomy, art, art history, ASB Leadership, astronomy, athletics, biology, biology-AP, business, business law, business skills, calculus, calculus-AP, campus ministry, ceramics, cheerleading, chemistry, choral music, Christian ethics, Christian scripture, Christianity, church history, community service, computer education, computer math, computer programming, computer science, concert band, creative writing, drafting, drama, drama performance, driver education, earth science, economics, electronics, engineering, English, English literature, English/composition-AP, ethics, ethics and responsibility, European history, expository writing, fine arts, French, French-AP, geometry, government-AP, government/civics, grammar, health, health education, history, history of the Catholic Church, home economics, honors algebra, honors English, honors geometry, honors U.S. history, honors world history, human biology, instrumental music, jazz band, jazz ensemble, journalism, marching band, mathematics, mechanical drawing, media studies, moral and social development, moral theology, music, music appreciation, newspaper, physical education, physics, physics-AP, physiology, psychology, religion, science, sculpture, social science, social studies, Spanish, Spanish language-AP, speech, sports medicine, sports science, student government, student publications, symphonic band, the Sixties, theater, theology, trigonometry, typing, U.S. government, U.S. government-AP, U.S. history, U.S. history-AP, weight training, world history, world literature, writing, yearbook.

Graduation Requirements Arts and fine arts (art, music, dance, drama), computer science, English, foreign language, mathematics, physical education (includes health), religion (includes Bible studies and theology), science, social science, social studies (includes history). Community service is required.

Special Academic Programs Advanced Placement exam preparation in 13 subject areas; honors section.

College Placement 232 students graduated in 2005; 230 went to college, including California State University; Saint Mary's College of California; Santa Clara University; Stanford University; University of California, Berkeley; University of San Francisco. Other: 2 entered military service. Mean SAT verbal: 555, mean SAT math: 559, mean composite ACT: 23.

Student Life Upper grades have specified standards of dress, student council. Discipline rests primarily with faculty. Attendance at religious services is required.

Summer Programs Remediation, enrichment, sports programs offered; session focuses on enrichment and remediation; held on campus; accepts boys and girls; open to students from other schools. 245 students usually enrolled. 2006 schedule: June 21 to July 30. Application deadline: May 31.

Tuition and Aid Day student tuition: $9980. Tuition installment plan (FACTS Tuition Payment Plan). Tuition reduction for siblings, merit scholarship grants, need-based scholarship grants, paying campus jobs available. In 2005–06, 25% of upper-school students received aid. Total amount of financial aid awarded in 2005–06: $665,000.

Admissions Traditional secondary-level entrance grade is 9. For fall 2005, 312 students applied for upper-level admission, 295 were accepted, 232 enrolled. Scholastic Testing Service High School Placement Test required. Deadline for receipt of application materials: January 10. Application fee required: $60. On-campus interview required.

Athletics Interscholastic: badminton (boys, girls), baseball (b), basketball (b,g), cheering (g), cross-country running (b,g), dance squad (g), football (b), golf (b,g), soccer (b,g), softball (g), swimming and diving (b,g), tennis (b,g), track and field (b,g), volleyball (b,g); intramural: lacrosse (g); coed interscholastic: modern dance; coed intramural: equestrian sports, skiing (downhill), strength & conditioning. 5 PE instructors, 50 coaches, 1 trainer.

Computers Computers are regularly used in career exploration, college planning, English, foreign language, history, journalism, keyboarding, mathematics, newspaper, religious studies, science, technology, theology, yearbook classes. Computer network features include on-campus library services, CD-ROMs, online commercial services, Internet access, office computer access, PowerSchool grade program.

Contact Chris Abdenour, Admissions Assistant. 510-881-4320. Fax: 510-581-5669. E-mail: apply@moreaucatholic.org. Web site: moreaucatholic.org.

MORGAN PARK ACADEMY

2153 West 111th Street
Chicago, Illinois 60643
Head of School: J. William Adams

General Information Coeducational day college-preparatory, arts, bilingual studies, and technology school. Grades PK–12. Founded: 1873. Setting: urban. 20-acre campus. 5 buildings on campus. Approved or accredited by Independent Schools Association of the Central States, North Central Association of Colleges and Schools, and Illinois Department of Education. Member of National Association of Independent Schools. Endowment: $905,450. Total enrollment: 520. Upper school average class size: 15. Upper school faculty-student ratio: 1:5.

Upper School Student Profile Grade 9: 48 students (26 boys, 22 girls); Grade 10: 35 students (14 boys, 21 girls); Grade 11: 50 students (16 boys, 34 girls); Grade 12: 48 students (25 boys, 23 girls).

Faculty School total: 58. In upper school: 12 men, 14 women; 20 have advanced degrees.

Subjects Offered Accounting, algebra, American history, American literature, art, art history, biology, calculus, chemistry, Coming of Age in the 20th Century, computer programming, computer science, creative writing, current events, drama, driver education, English, English literature, expository writing, fine arts, French, general science, geography, geometry, health, history, humanities, journalism, mathematics, music, physical education, physics, political science, science, social studies, Spanish, speech, studio art, trigonometry, word processing, world history, world literature, writing.

Graduation Requirements Arts and fine arts (art, music, dance, drama), English, foreign language, history, lab science, mathematics, physical education (includes health).

Special Academic Programs Advanced Placement exam preparation in 11 subject areas; honors section; independent study; study abroad; academic accommodation for the gifted, the musically talented, and the artistically talented.

College Placement 42 students graduated in 2005; all went to college, including Brown University; Northwestern University; University of Illinois; University of Michigan; Washington University in St. Louis. Median composite ACT: 27. 50% scored over 600 on SAT verbal, 80% scored over 600 on SAT math, 57% scored over 26 on composite ACT.

Student Life Upper grades have specified standards of dress, student council, honor system. Discipline rests primarily with faculty.

Summer Programs Remediation, enrichment, advancement, art/fine arts, computer instruction programs offered; session focuses on academics, sports and recreation; held on campus; accepts boys and girls; open to students from other schools. 300 students usually enrolled. 2006 schedule: June 24 to August 2. Application deadline: none.

Tuition and Aid Day student tuition: $12,890. Tuition installment plan (FACTS Tuition Payment Plan, 2-payment plus deposit plan). Tuition reduction for siblings, merit scholarship grants, need-based scholarship grants available. In 2005–06, 10% of upper-school students received aid; total upper-school merit-scholarship money awarded: $150,000. Total amount of financial aid awarded in 2005–06: $150,000.

Admissions Traditional secondary-level entrance grade is 9. Admissions testing, OLSAT, Stanford Achievement Test and writing sample required. Deadline for receipt of application materials: none. Application fee required: $50. On-campus interview required.

Athletics Interscholastic: baseball (boys), basketball (b,g), cheering (b,g), cross-country running (b,g), golf (b,g), soccer (b,g), softball (b,g), tennis (b,g), volleyball (g); coed interscholastic: golf, soccer, track and field; coed intramural: archery, badminton, bowling, football, golf, paddle tennis, skiing (cross-country), table tennis, weight lifting. 4 PE instructors, 4 coaches.

Computers Computers are regularly used in art, economics, English, foreign language, graphic arts, history, humanities, journalism, mathematics, news writing, newspaper, science, Spanish, yearbook classes. Computer network features include on-campus library services, CD-ROMs, online commercial services, Internet access.

Contact Melissa Harmening, Director of Admissions. 773-881-6700 Ext. 232. Fax: 773-881-8409. E-mail: mharmening@morganparkacademy.org.

MORRISTOWN-BEARD SCHOOL

70 Whippany Road
Morristown, New Jersey 07960
Head of School: Dr. Alex D. Curtis

petersons.com

General Information Coeducational day college-preparatory and arts school. Grades 6–12. Founded: 1891. Setting: suburban. Nearest major city is New York. 22-acre campus. 14 buildings on campus. Approved or accredited by Middle States Association of Colleges and Schools, New Jersey Association of Independent Schools, and New Jersey Department of Education. Member of National Association of Independent Schools and Secondary School Admission Test Board. Endowment: $8 million. Total enrollment: 491. Upper school average class size: 12. Upper school faculty-student ratio: 1:6.

Upper School Student Profile Grade 9: 100 students (51 boys, 49 girls); Grade 10: 93 students (47 boys, 46 girls); Grade 11: 81 students (44 boys, 37 girls); Grade 12: 94 students (45 boys, 49 girls).

Faculty School total: 80. In upper school: 22 men, 39 women; 34 have advanced degrees.

Subjects Offered 20th century history, acting, advanced chemistry, advanced math, Advanced Placement courses, African history, African studies, algebra, American history, American legal systems, American studies, ancient world history, architecture, art, art history, Asian studies, biology, biology-AP, calculus, calculus-AP, career exploration, chemistry, chemistry-AP, choir, chorus, community service, computer programming, computer science, computer science-AP, computer skills, computer studies, constitutional law, creative writing, dance, drama, drawing, earth science, ecology, engineering, English, English-AP, fine arts, French, geometry, health, instrumental music, journalism, Latin, Middle Eastern history, mythology, nature writers, painting, photography, physical education, physical science, physics, physics-AP, public speaking, regional literature, rite of passage, Russian history, Russian studies, Spanish, Spanish-AP, speech, statistics, statistics-AP, studio art—AP, the comic tradition, theater, trigonometry, U.S. history-AP, women in literature, world history.

Graduation Requirements Arts and fine arts (art, music, dance, drama), English, foreign language, mathematics, physical education (includes health), science, service learning/internship, social studies (includes history), senior projects. Community service is required.

Special Academic Programs Advanced Placement exam preparation in 10 subject areas; honors section; independent study; term-away projects.

College Placement 76 students graduated in 2005; 74 went to college, including Bucknell University; Dickinson College; Muhlenberg College; Skidmore College; St. Lawrence University. Other: 2 entered a postgraduate year. Median SAT verbal: 545, median SAT math: 565. 21% scored over 600 on SAT verbal, 31% scored over 600 on SAT math.

Student Life Upper grades have specified standards of dress, student council, honor system. Discipline rests equally with students and faculty.

Summer Programs Enrichment, advancement, sports, art/fine arts, computer instruction programs offered; session focuses on day camp; held on campus; accepts boys and girls; open to students from other schools. 500 students usually enrolled. 2006 schedule: June 15 to August 10.

Tuition and Aid Tuition installment plan (Key Tuition Payment Plan, individually arranged payment plans). Merit scholarship grants, need-based scholarship grants available. In 2005–06, 11% of upper-school students received aid; total upper-school merit-scholarship money awarded: $30,000. Total amount of financial aid awarded in 2005–06: $800,000.

Admissions Traditional secondary-level entrance grade is 9. For fall 2005, 219 students applied for upper-level admission, 130 were accepted, 70 enrolled. ISEE or SSAT required. Deadline for receipt of application materials: none. Application fee required: $55. On-campus interview required.

Athletics Interscholastic: baseball (boys), basketball (b,g), field hockey (g), football (b), golf (b,g), ice hockey (b,g), lacrosse (b,g), skiing (downhill) (b,g), soccer (b,g), softball (g), swimming and diving (b,g), tennis (b,g), track and field (b,g), volleyball (g); coed interscholastic: alpine skiing, cross-country running, swimming and diving, track and field; coed intramural: dance, figure skating, fitness, mountain biking, nautilus, physical fitness. 4 PE instructors, 3 coaches, 1 trainer.

Computers Computers are regularly used in architecture, art, English, foreign language, history, mathematics, music, science classes. Computer network features include campus e-mail, on-campus library services, CD-ROMs, online commercial services, Internet access, file transfer, DVD, wireless campus network.

Contact Mrs. Dana Murphy, Admission Assistant. 973-539-3032. Fax: 973-539-1590. E-mail: dmurphy@mobeard.org. Web site: www.mobeard.org.

See full description on page 928.

MOTHER MCAULEY HIGH SCHOOL

3737 West 99th Street
Chicago, Illinois 60655-3133
Head of School: Sr. Rose Wiorek

General Information Girls' day college-preparatory, arts, religious studies, and technology school, affiliated with Roman Catholic Church. Grades 9–12. Founded: 1846. Setting: urban. 21-acre campus. 2 buildings on campus. Approved or accredited by National Catholic Education Association, North Central Association of Colleges and Schools, and Illinois Department of Education. Endowment: $2 million. Total enrollment: 1,568. Upper school average class size: 28. Upper school faculty-student ratio: 1:15.

Upper School Student Profile Grade 9: 394 students (394 girls); Grade 10: 381 students (381 girls); Grade 11: 372 students (372 girls); Grade 12: 421 students (421 girls). 93% of students are Roman Catholic.

Faculty School total: 109. In upper school: 11 men, 98 women; 56 have advanced degrees.

Subjects Offered Anatomy and physiology, art history, art history-AP, calculus-AP, ceramics, chemistry-AP, English, English literature, English literature and composition-AP, European history-AP, first aid, French, French-AP, general science, geography, geometry, geometry with art applications, global issues, graphic design, history of the Catholic Church, honors algebra, honors English, honors geometry, honors U.S. history, honors world history, introduction to theater, journalism, Latin, Latin-AP, Life of Christ, marching band, media literacy, music appreciation, newspaper, orchestra, painting, photography, physical education, physics, play production, scripture, Spanish, Spanish-AP, speech, studio art, studio art-AP, theater, theology, U.S. history, U.S. history-AP, U.S. literature, Web site design, wind ensemble, world history, world history-AP, yearbook.

Graduation Requirements Art history, English, lab science, language, mathematics, music, physical education (includes health), social sciences, speech, theology.

Special Academic Programs Advanced Placement exam preparation in 12 subject areas; honors section; study at local college for college credit.

College Placement 410 students graduated in 2005; 405 went to college, including Eastern Illinois University; Illinois State University; Northern Illinois University; University of Illinois at Chicago; University of Illinois at Urbana–Champaign. Other: 3 went to work, 1 entered military service, 1 entered a postgraduate year. Median SAT verbal: 586, median SAT math: 581. Mean composite ACT: 22.

Student Life Upper grades have uniform requirement, student council. Discipline rests primarily with faculty. Attendance at religious services is required.

Summer Programs Remediation, advancement, sports, art/fine arts, computer instruction programs offered; held on campus; accepts girls; open to students from other schools. 200 students usually enrolled. 2006 schedule: June 12 to July 21. Application deadline: June 5.

Tuition and Aid Day student tuition: $6750. Tuition installment plan (monthly payment plans). Tuition reduction for siblings, merit scholarship grants, need-based scholarship grants, paying campus jobs available. In 2005–06, 18% of upper-school students received aid; total upper-school merit-scholarship money awarded: $1500. Total amount of financial aid awarded in 2005–06: $333,000.

Admissions Traditional secondary-level entrance grade is 9. For fall 2005, 484 students applied for upper-level admission, 445 were accepted, 394 enrolled. ACT-Explore or any standardized test required. Deadline for receipt of application materials: August 17. Application fee required: $150. On-campus interview required.

Athletics Interscholastic: basketball, cross-country running, diving, golf, independent competitive sports, soccer, softball, swimming and diving, tennis, track and field, volleyball, water polo; intramural: aerobics, basketball, bowling, softball, volleyball. 3 PE instructors, 21 coaches.

Computers Computers are regularly used in accounting, art, basic skills, business education, drafting, drawing and design, English, foreign language, French, graphics, journalism, Latin, mathematics, music, newspaper, photography, science, social sciences, Spanish, theater, Web site design, writing, yearbook classes. Computer network features include on-campus library services, CD-ROMs, Internet access.

Contact Mrs. LaToya M. Gutter, Administrative Assistant. 773-881-6527. Fax: 773-881-6562. E-mail: lgutter@mothermcauley.org. Web site: www.mothermcauley.org.

MOUNDS PARK ACADEMY

2051 Larpenteur Avenue East
St. Paul, Minnesota 55109
Head of School: Michael Downs

General Information Coeducational day college-preparatory, arts, bilingual studies, and technology school. Grades PK–12. Founded: 1982. Setting: suburban. 32-acre campus. 1 building on campus. Approved or accredited by Independent Schools Association of the Central States and Minnesota Department of Education. Member of National Association of Independent Schools. Languages of instruction: Spanish and French. Endowment: $1.8 million. Total enrollment: 703. Upper school average class size: 16. Upper school faculty-student ratio: 1:9.

Upper School Student Profile Grade 9: 72 students (41 boys, 31 girls); Grade 10: 64 students (28 boys, 36 girls); Grade 11: 68 students (35 boys, 33 girls); Grade 12: 54 students (24 boys, 30 girls).

Faculty School total: 83. In upper school: 13 men, 30 women; 22 have advanced degrees.

Subjects Offered Algebra, American history, American literature, anatomy, area studies, art, biology, calculus, ceramics, chemistry, chorus, contemporary women writers, creative writing, debate, design, drama, economics, English, English literature, fine arts, French, geometry, health, history, independent study, law, literature, mathematics, media, men's studies, multicultural literature, music, painting, photography, physical education, physical science, physics, physiology, printmaking, psychology, public policy issues and action, science, senior seminar, social science, social studies, Spanish, speech, statistics, theater, trigonometry, Western civilization, world literature, writing.

Graduation Requirements Arts and fine arts (art, music, dance, drama), English, foreign language, health education, mathematics, physical education (includes health), science, senior seminar, social studies (includes history), senior performance. Community service is required.

Special Academic Programs Advanced Placement exam preparation in 4 subject areas; honors section; independent study; study at local college for college credit.

College Placement 67 students graduated in 2005; all went to college, including Carleton College; Grinnell College; University of Minnesota, Twin Cities Campus; University of St. Thomas; Wellesley College. Median SAT verbal: 610, median SAT math: 600, median composite ACT: 27.

Student Life Upper grades have specified standards of dress, student council. Discipline rests equally with students and faculty.

Tuition and Aid Day student tuition: $15,600. Tuition installment plan (monthly payment plans, 2-payment plan, 3-payment plan, 8-payment plan). Need-based scholarship grants available. In 2005–06, 12% of upper-school students received aid. Total amount of financial aid awarded in 2005–06: $249,040.

Admissions Traditional secondary-level entrance grade is 9. For fall 2005, 43 students applied for upper-level admission, 30 were accepted, 23 enrolled. Writing sample required. Deadline for receipt of application materials: March 1. Application fee required: $50. Interview required.

Athletics Interscholastic: alpine skiing (boys, girls), baseball (b), basketball (b,g), cross-country running (b,g), football (b), golf (b,g), ice hockey (b), nordic skiing (b,g), skiing (cross-country) (b,g), skiing (downhill) (b,g), soccer (b,g), softball (g), swimming and diving (g), tennis (b,g), track and field (b,g), volleyball (g). 7 PE instructors.

Computers Computers are regularly used in English, foreign language, mathematics, science, social studies classes. Computer network features include campus e-mail, on-campus library services, CD-ROMs, online commercial services, Internet access, file transfer, DVD, wireless campus network.

Contact Mary M. Braun, Director of Admission Grades PK—12. 651-748-5577. Fax: 651-748-5534. E-mail: mbraun@moundsparkacademy.org. Web site: www.moundsparkacademy.org.

MOUNTAIN VIEW CHRISTIAN HIGH SCHOOL

3900 East Bonanza Road
Las Vegas, Nevada 89110
Head of School: Crystal Rae Van Kempen-McClanahan

General Information Coeducational day college-preparatory, arts, religious studies, and technology school, affiliated with Assemblies of God. Grades K–12. Founded: 1983. Setting: urban. 20-acre campus. 2 buildings on campus. Approved or accredited by Association of Christian Schools International. Total enrollment: 631. Upper school average class size: 25. Upper school faculty-student ratio: 1:8.

Upper School Student Profile Grade 9: 47 students (26 boys, 21 girls); Grade 10: 30 students (14 boys, 16 girls); Grade 11: 29 students (15 boys, 14 girls); Grade 12: 21 students (11 boys, 10 girls). 20% of students are Assemblies of God.

Faculty School total: 15. In upper school: 5 men, 10 women; 3 have advanced degrees.

Subjects Offered Algebra, American literature, anatomy and physiology, Bible, biology, British literature, chemistry, computers, concert band, early childhood, economics, English, French, geography, geometry, government, health, journalism, media arts, performing arts, physical education, physical science, physics-AP, pre-calculus, Spanish, symphonic band, U.S. history, world history.

Graduation Requirements American government, arts and fine arts (art, music, dance, drama), Bible, computers, English, foreign language, history, mathematics, physical education (includes health), science.

Special Academic Programs Honors section; study at local college for college credit; academic accommodation for the gifted and the musically talented.

College Placement 27 students graduated in 2005; 25 went to college, including Arizona State University; Azusa Pacific University; Biola University; University of Nevada, Las Vegas. Other: 2 went to work. Mean SAT verbal: 490, mean SAT math: 491, mean composite ACT: 24. 10% scored over 600 on SAT verbal, 10% scored over 600 on SAT math.

Student Life Upper grades have uniform requirement, student council, honor system. Discipline rests primarily with faculty. Attendance at religious services is required.
Summer Programs Remediation, advancement, computer instruction programs offered; session focuses on remediation and advancement; held on campus; accepts boys and girls; open to students from other schools. 30 students usually enrolled. 2006 schedule: June 20 to August 18. Application deadline: May 26.
Tuition and Aid Day student tuition: $5846. Tuition installment plan (monthly payment plans). Tuition reduction for siblings, need-based scholarship grants available. In 2005–06, 30% of upper-school students received aid. Total amount of financial aid awarded in 2005–06: $300,000.
Admissions Traditional secondary-level entrance grade is 9. Scholastic Achievement Test or school's own test required. Deadline for receipt of application materials: none. Application fee required: $195. Interview required.
Athletics Interscholastic: baseball (boys), basketball (b,g), football (b), golf (b), softball (g), volleyball (g); intramural: basketball (b,g), dance (g), dance squad (g), volleyball (g); coed interscholastic: cheering, physical fitness; coed intramural: aerobics, aerobics/dance, aerobics/nautilus, cheering, fitness, flag football, physical fitness, strength & conditioning, weight training.
Computers Computers are regularly used in Web site design, yearbook classes. Computer resources include campus e-mail, on-campus library services, CD-ROMs, Internet access, file transfer, office computer access, DVD.
Contact Cecelia Sacra, Registrar. 702-452-1300. Fax: 702-452-0499. E-mail: cisacra@mvcs.net. Web site: www.mvcs.net.

MOUNT ALVERNIA HIGH SCHOOL

146 Hawthorne Road
Pittsburgh, Pennsylvania 15209
Head of School: Mrs. Kimberly Minick

General Information Girls' day college-preparatory school, affiliated with Roman Catholic Church. Grades 9–12. Founded: 1942. Setting: suburban. 12-acre campus. 1 building on campus. Approved or accredited by Middle States Association of Colleges and Schools and Pennsylvania Department of Education. Total enrollment: 87. Upper school average class size: 15. Upper school faculty-student ratio: 1:7.
Upper School Student Profile Grade 9: 23 students (23 girls); Grade 10: 24 students (24 girls); Grade 11: 17 students (17 girls); Grade 12: 20 students (20 girls). 50% of students are Roman Catholic.
Faculty School total: 13. In upper school: 3 men, 10 women; 6 have advanced degrees.
Subjects Offered 20th century American writers, accounting, advanced math, algebra, art, art history, biology, business, calculus-AP, chemistry, comparative politics, comparative religion, computer applications, computer programming, computer science, consumer mathematics, creative writing, earth and space science, economics, English, English literature, environmental science, foreign language, French, geometry, graphic arts, health, honors English, Italian, keyboarding, Latin, mathematics, physical education, physics, pre-algebra, pre-calculus, psychology, publications, religious studies, science, social justice, social studies, Spanish, speech, street law, technology, theater, trigonometry, U.S. history, word processing, world cultures, world geography, world literature.
Special Academic Programs Advanced Placement exam preparation in 2 subject areas; honors section; independent study; study at local college for college credit; academic accommodation for the gifted; remedial math.
College Placement 22 students graduated in 2005; 21 went to college, including The Pennsylvania State University University Park Campus; University of Pittsburgh. Other: 1 went to work.
Student Life Upper grades have uniform requirement, student council, honor system. Discipline rests primarily with faculty. Attendance at religious services is required.
Tuition and Aid Day student tuition: $5850. Tuition installment plan (monthly payment plans, individually arranged payment plans). Need-based scholarship grants available.
Admissions Traditional secondary-level entrance grade is 9. For fall 2005, 35 students applied for upper-level admission, 30 were accepted, 25 enrolled. High School Placement Test required. Deadline for receipt of application materials: none. Application fee required: $50. Interview required.
Athletics Interscholastic: basketball, dance squad. 1 PE instructor.
Contact Mrs. Kimberly Minick, Principal. 412-821-3858. Fax: 412-821-2910. E-mail: k.minick@mtalvernia.com.

MOUNT BACHELOR ACADEMY

Prineville, Oregon
See Special Needs Schools section.

MOUNT CARMEL HIGH SCHOOL

6410 South Dante
Chicago, Illinois 60637
Head of School: Fr. Carl J. Markelz, OCARM

General Information Boys' day college-preparatory, arts, business, religious studies, and technology school, affiliated with Roman Catholic Church. Grades 9–12. Founded: 1900. Setting: urban. 3-acre campus. 5 buildings on campus. Approved or accredited by North Central Association of Colleges and Schools, The College Board, and Illinois Department of Education. Endowment: $5.4 million. Total enrollment: 805. Upper school average class size: 25. Upper school faculty-student ratio: 1:18.
Upper School Student Profile Grade 9: 268 students (268 boys); Grade 10: 188 students (188 boys); Grade 11: 196 students (196 boys); Grade 12: 153 students (153 boys). 89% of students are Roman Catholic.
Faculty School total: 56. In upper school: 37 men, 18 women; 32 have advanced degrees.
Subjects Offered Art history, business, computer science, economics, English, French, general science, geography, government/civics, health, history of music, Latin, mathematics, physical education, psychology, religion, science, social science, social studies, Spanish, speech, theology.
Graduation Requirements Computer science, English, foreign language, mathematics, physical education (includes health), religion (includes Bible studies and theology), science, social science, social studies (includes history). Community service is required.
Special Academic Programs Advanced Placement exam preparation in 10 subject areas; honors section; remedial reading and/or remedial writing; remedial math.
College Placement 162 students graduated in 2005; 149 went to college, including DePaul University; Eastern Illinois University; Marquette University; Northern Illinois University; University of Illinois; University of Illinois at Chicago. Other: 9 went to work, 4 entered military service. 15% scored over 26 on composite ACT.
Student Life Upper grades have specified standards of dress, student council. Discipline rests equally with students and faculty. Attendance at religious services is required.
Summer Programs Remediation programs offered; session focuses on earning credits to makeup for course failures; held on campus; accepts boys; open to students from other schools. 170 students usually enrolled. 2006 schedule: June 14 to July 2.
Tuition and Aid Day student tuition: $6400. Tuition installment plan (The Tuition Plan, FACTS Tuition Payment Plan). Tuition reduction for siblings, bursaries, merit scholarship grants, need-based scholarship grants, paying campus jobs available. In 2005–06, 35% of upper-school students received aid; total upper-school merit-scholarship money awarded: $100,000. Total amount of financial aid awarded in 2005–06: $325,000.
Admissions Traditional secondary-level entrance grade is 9. For fall 2005, 375 students applied for upper-level admission, 330 were accepted, 268 enrolled. ACT-Explore required. Deadline for receipt of application materials: none. Application fee required: $250. On-campus interview recommended.
Athletics Interscholastic: baseball, basketball, bowling, cross-country running, football, golf, ice hockey, rugby, soccer, swimming and diving, tennis, track and field, volleyball, water polo, wrestling; intramural: basketball, football, soccer, softball, volleyball, weight lifting. 3 PE instructors, 27 coaches, 1 trainer.
Computers Computers are regularly used in art, business, business education, college planning, data processing, desktop publishing, economics, English, foreign language, geography, graphic design, humanities, journalism, library, mathematics, psychology, science, technology classes. Computer network features include on-campus library services, CD-ROMs, Internet access, numerous databases, word processing, PowerPoint, spreadsheet training.
Contact John Haggerty, Assistant Principal. 773-324-1020 Ext. 252. Fax: 773-324-9235. E-mail: jhaggerty@mchs.org.

MOUNT MICHAEL BENEDICTINE HIGH SCHOOL

22520 Mount Michael Road
Elkhorn, Nebraska 68022-3400
Head of School: Rev. Raphael Walsh, OSB

General Information Boys' boarding and day college-preparatory, arts, religious studies, and technology school, affiliated with Roman Catholic Church. Grades 9–12. Founded: 1970. Setting: rural. Nearest major city is Omaha. Students are housed in single-sex dormitories. 440-acre campus. 1 building on campus. Approved or accredited by National Catholic Education Association, North Central Association of Colleges and Schools, and Nebraska Department of Education. Endowment: $1 million. Total enrollment: 170. Upper school average class size: 12. Upper school faculty-student ratio: 1:7.
Upper School Student Profile Grade 9: 44 students (44 boys); Grade 10: 34 students (34 boys); Grade 11: 46 students (46 boys); Grade 12: 46 students (46 boys). 88% of students are boarding students. 88% are state residents. 3 states are represented in upper school student body. 12% are international students. International students from Canada, China, and Republic of Korea. 85% are Roman Catholic.
Faculty School total: 24. In upper school: 18 men, 6 women; 17 have advanced degrees; 12 reside on campus.

Subjects Offered Accounting, Advanced Placement courses, algebra, American history, American history-AP, American literature, architectural drawing, art, band, Basic programming, basketball, bioethics, DNA and culture, biology, business, business skills, calculus-AP, ceramics, chemistry, chemistry-AP, chorus, Christian doctrine, Christian ethics, Christian scripture, Christianity, community service, computer programming, computer programming-AP, computer science, critical writing, drafting, drama, economics, English, English literature, English literature and composition-AP, European history, European history-AP, film studies, forensics, French, French language-AP, geography, geometry, government/civics, health education, Hebrew scripture, history of the Catholic Church, journalism, keyboarding/computer, math applications, mathematics, music, physical education, physics, physics-AP, reading, science, social science, social studies, Spanish, speech, theater, theology, trigonometry, weight training, Western civilization, world religions, wrestling, writing, yearbook.

Graduation Requirements Business skills (includes word processing), career/college preparation, Christian studies, computer science, economics, economics and history, English, ethics, foreign language, general math, government, languages, mathematics, physical education (includes health), religion (includes Bible studies and theology), science, social studies (includes history), speech. Community service is required.

Special Academic Programs Advanced Placement exam preparation in 9 subject areas; honors section; independent study; study at local college for college credit.

College Placement 30 students graduated in 2005; all went to college, including Creighton University; Kansas State University; Saint Louis University; University of Nebraska–Lincoln; University of Nebraska at Omaha; University of Notre Dame. Median SAT verbal: 690, median SAT math: 700, median composite ACT: 29. 84% scored over 600 on SAT verbal, 100% scored over 600 on SAT math, 63% scored over 26 on composite ACT.

Student Life Upper grades have specified standards of dress, student council, honor system. Discipline rests primarily with faculty. Attendance at religious services is required.

Tuition and Aid Day student tuition: $7000–$7250; 5-day tuition and room/board: $11,600–$11,850; 7-day tuition and room/board: $13,600–$13,850. Tuition installment plan (FACTS Tuition Payment Plan). Tuition reduction for siblings, merit scholarship grants, need-based scholarship grants, paying campus jobs available. In 2005–06, 49% of upper-school students received aid; total upper-school merit-scholarship money awarded: $105,000. Total amount of financial aid awarded in 2005–06: $250,000.

Admissions Traditional secondary-level entrance grade is 9. For fall 2005, 92 students applied for upper-level admission, 50 were accepted, 42 enrolled. High School Placement Test required. Deadline for receipt of application materials: February 15. Application fee required: $10. Interview required.

Athletics Interscholastic: baseball (boys), basketball (b), cheering (b), cross-country running (b), diving (b), football (b), golf (b), soccer (b), swimming and diving (b), tennis (b), wrestling (b); intramural: ball hockey (b), basketball (b), flag football (b), floor hockey (b), physical fitness (b), physical training (b), soccer (b), strength & conditioning (b), weight lifting (b), weight training (b). 1 PE instructor, 12 coaches, 2 trainers.

Computers Computers are regularly used in career education, career exploration, career technology, college planning, drafting, economics, geography, history, journalism, keyboarding, library, mathematics, occupational education, science, stock market, Web site design, yearbook classes. Computer network features include campus e-mail, on-campus library services, CD-ROMs, Internet access, file transfer, DVD.

Contact Mr. Eric Crawford, Director of Student Promotion. 402-289-2541 Ext. 1003. Fax: 402-289-4539. E-mail: ecrawford@muntmichael.org. Web site: www.mountmichaelhs.com.

MOUNT SAINT CHARLES ACADEMY

■ 800 Logee Street
Woonsocket, Rhode Island 02895-5599
Head of School: Br. Robert R. Croteau, SC

General Information Coeducational day college-preparatory, arts, and religious studies school, affiliated with Roman Catholic Church. Grades 7–12. Founded: 1924. Setting: suburban. Nearest major city is Providence. 22-acre campus. 2 buildings on campus. Approved or accredited by New England Association of Schools and Colleges and Rhode Island Department of Education. Total enrollment: 1,002. Upper school average class size: 25. Upper school faculty-student ratio: 1:14.

Upper School Student Profile Grade 7: 141 students (64 boys, 77 girls); Grade 8: 169 students (84 boys, 85 girls); Grade 9: 188 students (88 boys, 100 girls); Grade 10: 169 students (96 boys, 73 girls); Grade 11: 164 students (74 boys, 90 girls); Grade 12: 171 students (86 boys, 85 girls). 85% of students are Roman Catholic.

Faculty School total: 55. In upper school: 26 men, 26 women; 30 have advanced degrees.

Subjects Offered Advanced computer applications, algebra, American literature, architecture, art, art history, art-AP, band, biology, biology-AP, British literature, calculus, chemistry, chorus, computer science, creative writing, dance, drama, economics, English, English literature, English literature and composition-AP, environmental science, environmental science-AP, ethics, European history, European history-AP, expository writing, fine arts, French, geography, geometry, government,

government/civics, handbells, history, history of the Catholic Church, honors U.S. history, honors world history, jazz band, journalism, keyboarding, mathematics, mathematics-AP, modern European history, music, music theory-AP, physical education, physics, physiology, psychology, psychology-AP, religion, science, social studies, sociology, Spanish, theater, trigonometry, U.S. history, U.S. history-AP, world history, world literature, writing, yearbook.

Graduation Requirements Arts and fine arts (art, music, dance, drama), computer science, English, foreign language, mathematics, physical education (includes health), religion (includes Bible studies and theology), science, social studies (includes history).

Special Academic Programs Advanced Placement exam preparation in 10 subject areas; honors section; study at local college for college credit.

College Placement 161 students graduated in 2005; 156 went to college. Other: 1 went to work, 4 entered a postgraduate year.

Student Life Upper grades have uniform requirement, student council. Discipline rests primarily with faculty. Attendance at religious services is required.

Summer Programs Sports, art/fine arts programs offered; session focuses on fine arts, soccer, hockey, basketball ; held on campus; accepts boys and girls; open to students from other schools. 220 students usually enrolled. Application deadline: none.

Tuition and Aid Day student tuition: $7950. Tuition installment plan (FACTS Tuition Payment Plan, full-payment discount plan). Need-based scholarship grants available. In 2005–06, 20% of upper-school students received aid. Total amount of financial aid awarded in 2005–06: $300,000.

Admissions Traditional secondary-level entrance grade is 7. For fall 2005, 500 students applied for upper-level admission, 225 were accepted, 205 enrolled. STS required. Deadline for receipt of application materials: none. Application fee required: $25.

Athletics Interscholastic: baseball (boys), basketball (b,g), cheering (g), cross-country running (b,g), gymnastics (g), ice hockey (b,g), indoor track (b,g), soccer (b,g), softball (g), swimming and diving (b,g), tennis (b,g), track and field (b,g), volleyball (b,g); intramural: aerobics/dance (g), basketball (b,g); coed interscholastic: golf; coed intramural: billiards, bowling, dance team, flag football, indoor soccer, lacrosse, soccer. 4 PE instructors, 15 coaches, 1 trainer.

Computers Computers are regularly used in art, desktop publishing, graphic design, science, yearbook classes. Computer network features include on-campus library services, CD-ROMs, online commercial services, Internet access, DVD, college/financial aid searches.

Contact Joseph J. O'Neill Jr., Registrar/Director of Admissions. 401-769-0310. Fax: 401-762-2327. E-mail: mtstchrles@aol.com. Web site: www.mountsaintcharles.org.

MT. SAINT DOMINIC ACADEMY

■ 3 Ryerson Avenue
Caldwell, New Jersey 07006
Head of School: Sr. Frances Sullivan, OP

General Information Girls' day college-preparatory, arts, religious studies, and technology school, affiliated with Roman Catholic Church. Grades 9–12. Founded: 1892. Setting: suburban. Nearest major city is Newark. 100-acre campus. 2 buildings on campus. Approved or accredited by Commission on Secondary Schools, Middle States Association of Colleges and Schools, New Jersey Association of Independent Schools, and New Jersey Department of Education. Endowment: $200,000. Total enrollment: 360. Upper school average class size: 18. Upper school faculty-student ratio: 1:8.

Upper School Student Profile Grade 9: 90 students (90 girls); Grade 10: 90 students (90 girls); Grade 11: 90 students (90 girls); Grade 12: 90 students (90 girls). 70% of students are Roman Catholic.

Faculty School total: 68. In upper school: 3 men, 50 women; 46 have advanced degrees.

Subjects Offered Advanced math, algebra, American history, American history-AP, American legal systems, American literature, American literature-AP, art, art appreciation, art history-AP, Bible studies, biology, biology-AP, British literature, British literature (honors), British literature-AP, calculus, calculus-AP, Catholic belief and practice, chemistry, choir, college placement, communication skills, computer applications, computer keyboarding, computer programming, computer science, CPR, creative writing, dance, debate, desktop publishing, drama, driver education, ecology, environmental systems, economics and history, English, English literature, English literature and composition-AP, environmental science, forensics, French, geometry, health, history, Holocaust studies, literature, mathematics, music, photography, physical education, physics, pre-calculus, psychology, public speaking, religion, SAT preparation, science, Spanish, studio art-AP, word processing, world history, world literature, world wide web design, World-Wide-Web publishing.

Graduation Requirements 4 years of community service.

Special Academic Programs Advanced Placement exam preparation in 4 subject areas; honors section; independent study; academic accommodation for the gifted, the musically talented, and the artistically talented.

College Placement 81 students graduated in 2005; all went to college. 60% scored over 600 on SAT verbal, 60% scored over 600 on SAT math.

Student Life Upper grades have uniform requirement, student council, honor system. Discipline rests primarily with faculty. Attendance at religious services is required.

Summer Programs Advancement programs offered; session focuses on mathematics advancement; held on campus; accepts girls; not open to students from other schools. 2006 schedule: June to July. Application deadline: May.

Tuition and Aid Day student tuition: $10,650. Tuition installment plan (Key Tuition Payment Plan, SMART Tuition Payment Plan, individually arranged payment plans, one payment). Tuition reduction for siblings, merit scholarship grants, need-based scholarship grants available. In 2005–06, 15% of upper-school students received aid.

Admissions Traditional secondary-level entrance grade is 9. CTB/McGraw-Hill/Macmillan Co-op Test required. Deadline for receipt of application materials: December 15. Application fee required: $40.

Athletics Interscholastic: aerobics/dance, aquatics, basketball, cheering, cross-country running, golf, indoor track, soccer, softball, swimming and diving, tennis, track and field, volleyball; intramural: aerobics/dance, ballet, dance, dance squad, dance team, danceline, modern dance. 2 PE instructors, 20 coaches, 1 trainer.

Computers Computers are regularly used in English, foreign language, history, mathematics, music, science classes. Computer network features include campus e-mail, on-campus library services, CD-ROMs, online commercial services, Internet access, file transfer, DVD, wireless campus network.

Contact Laura Cristiano, Director of Admission. 973-226-0660 Ext. 14. Fax: 973-226-2135. E-mail: lcristiano@msdacademy.org. Web site: www.msdacademy.org.

MOUNT SAINT JOSEPH ACADEMY

120 West Wissahickon Avenue
Flourtown, Pennsylvania 19031
Head of School: Sr. Kathleen Brabson, SSJ

General Information Girls' day college-preparatory school, affiliated with Roman Catholic Church. Grades 9–12. Founded: 1858. Setting: suburban. Nearest major city is Philadelphia. 78-acre campus. 1 building on campus. Approved or accredited by Middle States Association of Colleges and Schools, Pennsylvania Association of Private Academic Schools, and Pennsylvania Department of Education. Member of National Association of Independent Schools. Endowment: $2 million. Total enrollment: 556. Upper school average class size: 19. Upper school faculty-student ratio: 1:10.

Upper School Student Profile Grade 9: 141 students (141 girls); Grade 10: 140 students (140 girls); Grade 11: 138 students (138 girls); Grade 12: 137 students (137 girls). 95% of students are Roman Catholic.

Faculty School total: 57. In upper school: 13 men, 44 women; 47 have advanced degrees.

Subjects Offered Accounting, algebra, American history, American history-AP, American literature, American studies, art, art history, astronomy, biochemistry, biology, calculus, calculus-AP, chemistry, chorus, communications, computer science, design, desktop publishing, drama, drawing, economics, English, English literature, English literature-AP, ethics, European history, film, fine arts, French, French-AP, geography, geometry, government/civics, health, history, human sexuality, instrumental music, journalism, keyboarding, Latin, literature, mathematics, music, music-AP, painting, physical education, physics, physics-AP, physiology, pre-calculus, psychology, religion, science, social studies, Spanish, Spanish-AP, speech, technology, theater, theology, trigonometry, word processing, world history, world literature, writing.

Graduation Requirements Arts and fine arts (art, music, dance, drama), computer science, English, foreign language, mathematics, physical education (includes health), religion (includes Bible studies and theology), science, social studies (includes history).

Special Academic Programs Advanced Placement exam preparation in 14 subject areas; honors section; independent study; study at local college for college credit; academic accommodation for the gifted, the musically talented, and the artistically talented.

College Placement 139 students graduated in 2005; all went to college, including Drexel University; Saint Joseph's University; The Pennsylvania State University University Park Campus; The University of Scranton; University of Pennsylvania; Villanova University. Mean SAT verbal: 621, mean SAT math: 594. 64% scored over 600 on SAT verbal, 51% scored over 600 on SAT math.

Student Life Upper grades have uniform requirement, student council, honor system. Discipline rests primarily with faculty. Attendance at religious services is required.

Tuition and Aid Day student tuition: $10,000. Tuition installment plan (Higher Education Service, Inc, semester payment plan). Tuition reduction for siblings, merit scholarship grants, need-based scholarship grants available. In 2005–06, 33% of upper-school students received aid; total upper-school merit-scholarship money awarded: $162,125. Total amount of financial aid awarded in 2005–06: $309,020.

Admissions Traditional secondary-level entrance grade is 9. For fall 2005, 380 students applied for upper-level admission, 141 were accepted, 141 enrolled. High School Placement Test, SAS, STS-HSPT or school's own test required. Deadline for receipt of application materials: October 28. Application fee required: $75.

Athletics Interscholastic: basketball, cheering, crew, cross-country running, diving, field hockey, golf, indoor track, lacrosse, soccer, softball, swimming and diving, tennis, track and field, volleyball. 2 PE instructors, 24 coaches, 1 trainer.

Computers Computers are regularly used in art, English, foreign language, history, mathematics, music, science classes. Computer network features include on-campus library services, CD-ROMs, online commercial services, Internet access, video conferencing, SmartBoards.

Contact Ms. Carol Finney, Director of Admissions. 215-233-9133. Fax: 215-233-5887. E-mail: cfinney@msjacad.org. Web site: www.msjacad.org.

MOUNT SAINT MARY ACADEMY

1645 Highway 22
Watchung, New Jersey 07069
Head of School: Sr. Lisa D. Gambacorto, Ed.S

General Information Girls' day college-preparatory and religious studies school, affiliated with Roman Catholic Church. Grades 9–12. Founded: 1908. Setting: suburban. Nearest major city is New York, NY. 84-acre campus. 5 buildings on campus. Approved or accredited by Mercy Secondary Education Association, Middle States Association of Colleges and Schools, National Catholic Education Association, New Jersey Association of Independent Schools, The College Board, and New Jersey Department of Education. Member of National Association of Independent Schools. Endowment: $1.3 million. Total enrollment: 353. Upper school average class size: 20. Upper school faculty-student ratio: 1:8.

Upper School Student Profile Grade 9: 98 students (98 girls); Grade 10: 84 students (84 girls); Grade 11: 78 students (78 girls); Grade 12: 93 students (93 girls). 90% of students are Roman Catholic.

Faculty School total: 45. In upper school: 4 men, 41 women; 33 have advanced degrees.

Subjects Offered Algebra, American history, American literature, art, art history, Bible studies, biology, business skills, calculus, career exploration, chemistry, computer programming, computer science, driver education, English, English literature, fine arts, French, geometry, government/civics, health, history, Italian, Latin, mathematics, music, physical education, physics, psychology, religion, science, social studies, Spanish, study skills, theology, trigonometry, world history, writing.

Graduation Requirements Arts and fine arts (art, music, dance, drama), business skills (includes word processing), computer science, English, foreign language, mathematics, physical education (includes health), religion (includes Bible studies and theology), science, self-defense, social science, social studies (includes history), 60 hours of community service.

Special Academic Programs Advanced Placement exam preparation in 9 subject areas; honors section; independent study; academic accommodation for the gifted.

College Placement 100 students graduated in 2005; all went to college, including Boston College; New York University; Rutgers, The State University of New Jersey, New Brunswick/Piscataway; Seton Hall University. Mean SAT verbal: 592, mean SAT math: 578.

Student Life Upper grades have uniform requirement, student council. Discipline rests primarily with faculty. Attendance at religious services is required.

Tuition and Aid Day student tuition: $13,650. Tuition installment plan (FACTS Tuition Payment Plan). Tuition reduction for siblings, merit scholarship grants, need-based scholarship grants, scholarships/grants for children of faculty available. In 2005–06, 23% of upper-school students received aid; total upper-school merit-scholarship money awarded: $60,000. Total amount of financial aid awarded in 2005–06: $165,000.

Admissions Traditional secondary-level entrance grade is 9. For fall 2005, 155 students applied for upper-level admission, 145 were accepted, 106 enrolled. ACT-Explore required. Deadline for receipt of application materials: June 1. Application fee required: $45. On-campus interview required.

Athletics Interscholastic: basketball, cheering, cross-country running, field hockey, indoor track, lacrosse, soccer, softball, swimming and diving, tennis, track and field; intramural: dance, golf, tai chi, volleyball. 2 PE instructors, 3 coaches.

Computers Computers are regularly used in all classes. Computer resources include campus e-mail, on-campus library services, CD-ROMs, online commercial services, Internet access, office computer access, DVD, wireless campus network.

Contact Ms. Donna Venezia Toryak, Director of Admissions. 908-757-0108 Ext. 4506. Fax: 908-756-8085. E-mail: dtoryak@mountsaintmary.org. Web site: www. mountsaintmary.org.

See full description on page 930.

MUNICH INTERNATIONAL SCHOOL

Schloss Buchhof
Starnberg D-82319, Germany
Head of School: Mary Seppala, EdD

General Information Coeducational day college-preparatory, arts, business, bilingual studies, and technology school. Grades PK–12. Founded: 1966. Setting: rural. Nearest major city is Munich. 26-acre campus. 5 buildings on campus. Approved or accredited by European Council of International Schools, International Baccalaureate Organization, and New England Association of Schools and Colleges. Affiliate

member of National Association of Independent Schools; member of Secondary School Admission Test Board. Language of instruction: English. Total enrollment: 1,255. Upper school average class size: 21. Upper school faculty-student ratio: 1:9.

Upper School Student Profile Grade 9: 108 students (51 boys, 57 girls); Grade 10: 99 students (47 boys, 52 girls); Grade 11: 107 students (47 boys, 60 girls); Grade 12: 97 students (43 boys, 54 girls).

Faculty School total: 161. In upper school: 28 men, 34 women; 35 have advanced degrees.

Subjects Offered Adolescent issues, algebra, art, biology, business, calculus, chemistry, community service, computer science, computer-aided design, design, drama, earth science, economics, English, English literature, ESL, European history, film studies, fine arts, French, geography, geometry, German, grammar, health, health education, history, home economics, information technology, instrumental music, integrated mathematics, International Baccalaureate courses, Japanese, journalism, lab/keyboard, library skills, math methods, mathematics, mathematics-AP, model United Nations, music, personal and social education, physical education, physics, SAT preparation, science, senior thesis, social science, social studies, Spanish, speech and debate, student government, technology/design, theater, theory of knowledge, trigonometry, world history, world literature, writing, yearbook.

Graduation Requirements Arts and fine arts (art, music, dance, drama), English, foreign language, mathematics, philosophy, physical education (includes health), science, social science, social studies (includes history), theory of knowledge, extended essay. Community service is required.

Special Academic Programs International Baccalaureate program; academic accommodation for the gifted; ESL (18 students enrolled).

College Placement 91 students graduated in 2005; they went to Boston University; Columbia College; Lewis & Clark College. Other: 1 entered military service, 20 had other specific plans. Mean SAT verbal: 587, mean SAT math: 606. 48% scored over 600 on SAT verbal, 55% scored over 600 on SAT math.

Student Life Upper grades have student council, honor system. Discipline rests equally with students and faculty.

Summer Programs Sports, rigorous outdoor training programs offered; held both on and off campus; held at Lake Garda (Italy); accepts boys and girls; open to students from other schools. 120 students usually enrolled. 2006 schedule: June 28 to July 9. Application deadline: May 31.

Tuition and Aid Day student tuition: €13,960. Tuition installment plan (monthly payment plans, individually arranged payment plans). Tuition reduction for siblings, merit scholarship grants, need-based tuition remission for current students available. In 2005–06, 3% of upper-school students received aid; total upper-school merit-scholarship money awarded: €39,000. Total amount of financial aid awarded in 2005–06: €52,000.

Admissions Traditional secondary-level entrance grade is 9. For fall 2005, 73 students applied for upper-level admission, 57 were accepted, 47 enrolled. English for Non-native Speakers or Secondary Level English Proficiency required. Deadline for receipt of application materials: none. Application fee required: €80. On-campus interview required.

Athletics Interscholastic: alpine skiing (boys, girls), basketball (b,g), canoeing/kayaking (b,g), cross-country running (b,g), dance (b,g), freestyle skiing (b,g), golf (b,g), gymnastics (b,g), indoor hockey (b,g), indoor soccer (b,g), kayaking (b,g), outdoor skills (b,g), skiing (downhill) (b,g), soccer (b,g), softball (g), strength & conditioning (b,g), swimming and diving (b,g), table tennis (b,g), tennis (b,g), track and field (b,g), volleyball (b,g); intramural: alpine skiing (b,g), badminton (b,g), basketball (b,g), cross-country running (b,g), freestyle skiing (b,g), skiing (downhill) (b,g), soccer (b,g), softball (g), swimming and diving (b,g), tennis (b,g), track and field (b,g), volleyball (b,g); coed interscholastic: alpine skiing, canoeing/kayaking, dance, golf, gymnastics, outdoor skills; coed intramural: alpine skiing. 7 PE instructors, 8 coaches, 11 trainers.

Computers Computers are regularly used in all academic, library skills, newspaper, research skills, yearbook classes. Computer network features include campus e-mail, on-campus library services, CD-ROMs, Internet access, file transfer, office computer access.

Contact Ms. Ola Schmidt, Director of Admissions. 49-8151-366 Ext. 120. Fax: 49-8151-366 Ext. 129. E-mail: admissions@mis-munich.de. Web site: www.mis-munich.de.

See full description on page 932.

NACEL INTERNATIONAL SCHOOL

1536 Hewitt Avenue
Box 268
Saint Paul, Minnesota 55104
Head of School: Dr. Frank Tarsitano

General Information Coeducational boarding and day college-preparatory, arts, business, bilingual studies, and liberal arts school. Grades 9–12. Founded: 2002. Setting: urban. Nearest major city is St. Paul. Students are housed in host family homes. 55-acre campus. 5 buildings on campus. Approved or accredited by National Association of Episcopal Schools, North Central Association of Colleges and Schools, and Minnesota Department of Education. Total enrollment: 80. Upper school faculty-student ratio: 1:15.

Upper School Student Profile 15% are state residents. 85% are international students.

Faculty School total: 16. In upper school: 5 men, 11 women; 10 have advanced degrees.

Subjects Offered Algebra, American government, American history, art, art history, biology, calculus, chemistry, Chinese, communications, computer science, earth science, ESL, French, geometry, German, Italian, life science, literature, modern European history, music, physical fitness, physical science, physics, pre-calculus, Russian, Spanish, theater, trigonometry, world civilizations, world cultures, writing fundamentals, writing workshop.

Special Academic Programs Advanced Placement exam preparation in 3 subject areas; study at local college for college credit; study abroad; academic accommodation for the gifted, the musically talented, and the artistically talented; ESL (30 students enrolled).

College Placement 20 students graduated in 2005; they went to Hamline University.

Student Life Upper grades have specified standards of dress, student council, honor system. Discipline rests equally with students and faculty.

Summer Programs Enrichment, advancement, ESL, sports programs offered; session focuses on language and culture; held both on and off campus; held at various countries abroad; accepts boys and girls; open to students from other schools.

Tuition and Aid Day student tuition: $9000; 7-day tuition and room/board: $17,000. Tuition installment plan (monthly payment plans). Tuition reduction for siblings, merit scholarship grants, paying campus jobs available. In 2005–06, 73% of upper-school students received aid.

Admissions Traditional secondary-level entrance grade is 11. Iowa Tests of Basic Skills, Stanford Achievement Test or TOEFL or SLEP required. Deadline for receipt of application materials: none. No application fee required. Interview required.

Athletics 1 PE instructor, 2 coaches.

Computers Computers are regularly used in creative writing, desktop publishing, English, ESL, foreign language, information technology, mathematics, science, social sciences, writing fundamentals, yearbook classes. Computer network features include on-campus library services, CD-ROMs, online commercial services, Internet access.

Contact Andrea Bitunjac, Director of Global Programming and Admissions. 651-288-4612. Fax: 651-288-4616. E-mail: abitunjac@nacelinternationalschool.org. Web site: www.nacelinternationalschool.org.

NATIONAL CATHEDRAL SCHOOL

Mount Saint Alban
Washington, District of Columbia 20016-5000
Head of School: Kathleen O'Neill Jamieson

General Information Girls' day college-preparatory school, affiliated with Episcopal Church. Grades 4–12. Founded: 1899. Setting: urban. 25-acre campus. 7 buildings on campus. Approved or accredited by Association of Independent Maryland Schools, Association of Independent Schools of Greater Washington, Middle States Association of Colleges and Schools, National Association of Episcopal Schools, The College Board, and District of Columbia Department of Education. Member of National Association of Independent Schools and Secondary School Admission Test Board. Endowment: $19.8 million. Total enrollment: 578. Upper school average class size: 15. Upper school faculty-student ratio: 1:6.

Upper School Student Profile Grade 9: 78 students (78 girls); Grade 10: 76 students (76 girls); Grade 11: 75 students (75 girls); Grade 12: 77 students (77 girls).

Faculty School total: 94. In upper school: 16 men, 40 women; 50 have advanced degrees.

Subjects Offered Advanced Placement courses, African American history, African-American literature, algebra, American history, American literature, art, art history, art history-AP, biology, calculus, ceramics, chemistry, Chinese, community service, computer programming, computer science, creative writing, dance, drama, earth science, economics, English, English literature, ethics, European history, expository writing, fine arts, French, geography, geometry, government/civics, Greek, history, Japanese, Latin, mathematics, music, photography, physical education, physics, political science, psychology, public speaking, religion, science, social studies, Spanish, statistics, theater, trigonometry, world history, writing.

Graduation Requirements Arts and fine arts (art, music, dance, drama), English, foreign language, mathematics, physical education (includes health), religion (includes Bible studies and theology), science, social studies (includes history). Community service is required.

Special Academic Programs Advanced Placement exam preparation in 17 subject areas; honors section; independent study; term-away projects; study abroad; academic accommodation for the gifted.

College Placement 68 students graduated in 2005; all went to college, including Brown University; Dartmouth College; Princeton University; Stanford University; University of Pennsylvania; Yale University. Mean SAT verbal: 718, mean SAT math: 698. 99% scored over 600 on SAT verbal, 96% scored over 600 on SAT math.

Student Life Upper grades have specified standards of dress, student council, honor system. Discipline rests equally with students and faculty. Attendance at religious services is required.

Summer Programs Enrichment, sports, art/fine arts programs offered; held on campus; accepts boys and girls; open to students from other schools.

Tuition and Aid Day student tuition: $24,724. Tuition installment plan (monthly payment plans). Need-based scholarship grants, need-based financial aid grants available. In 2005–06, 16% of upper-school students received aid. Total amount of financial aid awarded in 2005–06: $837,300.

Admissions Traditional secondary-level entrance grade is 9. For fall 2005, 105 students applied for upper-level admission, 32 were accepted, 19 enrolled. ERB CTP IV, ISEE, SSAT or Wechsler Intelligence Scale for Children required. Deadline for receipt of application materials: February 1. Application fee required: $60. On-campus interview required.

Athletics Interscholastic: aerobics, aerobics/dance, aerobics/nautilus, back packing, ballet, basketball, canoeing/kayaking, climbing, crew, dance, dance team, field hockey, fitness, hiking/backpacking, ice hockey, independent competitive sports, indoor soccer, indoor track, indoor track & field, kayaking, lacrosse, modern dance, mountain biking, nautilus, outdoor adventure, physical fitness, rafting, rappelling, rock climbing, rowing, soccer, softball, strength & conditioning, tennis, track and field, volleyball, wall climbing, weight lifting, weight training, winter (indoor) track; coed interscholastic: cross-country running, diving, swimming and diving. 11 PE instructors, 11 coaches, 1 trainer.

Computers Computers are regularly used in art, English, foreign language, mathematics, multimedia, science classes. Computer network features include campus e-mail, on-campus library services, CD-ROMs, online commercial services, Internet access, wireless campus network.

Contact Maureen V. Miller, Admission Coordinator. 202-537-6374. Fax: 202-537-2382. E-mail: ncs_admissions@cathedral.org. Web site: www.ncs.cathedral.org.

NATIONAL SPORTS ACADEMY AT LAKE PLACID

821 Mirror Lake Drive
Lake Placid, New York 12946
Head of School: David Wenn

General Information Coeducational boarding and day college-preparatory and student learning services school. Grades 8–PG. Founded: 1979. Setting: small town. Nearest major city is Albany. Students are housed in single-sex by floor dormitories. 2 buildings on campus. Approved or accredited by National Independent Private Schools Association, New York State Association of Independent Schools, New York State Board of Regents, and New York Department of Education. Member of National Association of Independent Schools. Total enrollment: 81. Upper school average class size: 8. Upper school faculty-student ratio: 1:6.

Upper School Student Profile Grade 9: 11 students (5 boys, 6 girls); Grade 10: 14 students (9 boys, 5 girls); Grade 11: 25 students (19 boys, 6 girls); Grade 12: 17 students (13 boys, 4 girls); Postgraduate: 11 students (9 boys, 2 girls). 75% of students are boarding students. 45% are state residents. 16 states are represented in upper school student body. 9% are international students. International students from Canada, Serbia and Montenegro, Sweden, and United Kingdom.

Faculty School total: 14. In upper school: 9 men, 5 women; 5 have advanced degrees; 6 reside on campus.

Subjects Offered Algebra, American history, American literature, biology, biology-AP, calculus, calculus-AP, chemistry, computers, earth science, English, English literature, English-AP, environmental science, European history, French, geometry, government, health, history, history-AP, mathematics, physical education, physics, pre-calculus, science, social studies, Spanish, sports science, world history.

Graduation Requirements Algebra, biology, calculus, chemistry, earth science, English, English literature, environmental science, European history, French, geometry, history, physical education (includes health), physics, pre-calculus, Spanish, sports science, U.S. government, U.S. history, world history. Community service is required.

Special Academic Programs Advanced Placement exam preparation in 4 subject areas; honors section; independent study.

College Placement 18 students graduated in 2005; 13 went to college, including Rochester Institute of Technology; St. Lawrence University; The George Washington University; Union College; University of New Hampshire. Other: 2 entered a postgraduate year, 3 had other specific plans. Mean SAT verbal: 534, mean SAT math: 528. 20% scored over 600 on SAT verbal, 20% scored over 600 on SAT math.

Student Life Upper grades have student council, honor system. Discipline rests primarily with faculty.

Summer Programs Sports programs offered; session focuses on sports-specific athletic training; held off campus; held at various sports venues; accepts boys and girls; open to students from other schools. 25 students usually enrolled. 2006 schedule: June to August.

Tuition and Aid Day student tuition: $10,725; 7-day tuition and room/board: $23,000. Tuition installment plan (Key Tuition Payment Plan, monthly payment plans). Tuition reduction for siblings, need-based scholarship grants, prepGATE Loans available. In 2005–06, 65% of upper-school students received aid.

Admissions Traditional secondary-level entrance grade is 10. For fall 2005, 115 students applied for upper-level admission, 58 were accepted, 37 enrolled. PSAT and SAT for applicants to grade 11 and 12 required. Deadline for receipt of application materials: March 31. Application fee required: $40. Interview required.

Athletics Interscholastic: alpine skiing (boys, girls), biathlon (b,g), bicycling (b,g), figure skating (b,g), freestyle skiing (b,g), ice hockey (b,g), ice skating (b,g), luge (b,g), nordic skiing (b,g), ski jumping (b,g), skiing (cross-country) (b,g), skiing (downhill)

(b,g), snowboarding (b,g), speedskating (b,g), strength & conditioning (b,g), weight training (b,g); coed interscholastic: physical training, soccer; coed intramural: golf, lacrosse, rappelling, rock climbing, tennis, weight training, yoga. 17 coaches, 1 trainer.

Computers Computers are regularly used in English, foreign language, history, mathematics, science classes. Computer network features include campus e-mail, CD-ROMs, Internet access, DVD, wireless campus network, E-Library.

Contact Gun Rand, Associate Director of Admissions. 518-523-3460 Ext. 22. Fax: 518-523-3488. E-mail: grand@nationalsportsacademy.com. Web site: www.nationalsportsacademy.com.

NAVAJO PREPARATORY SCHOOL, INC.

1220 West Apache Street
Farmington, New Mexico 87401
Head of School: Mrs. Wynora Bekis

General Information Coeducational boarding and day college-preparatory, arts, and bilingual studies school. Grades 9–12. Founded: 1991. Setting: suburban. Nearest major city is Albuquerque. Students are housed in single-sex dormitories. 84-acre campus. 17 buildings on campus. Approved or accredited by National Council for Nonpublic Schools, North Central Association of Colleges and Schools, and New Mexico Department of Education. Upper school faculty-student ratio: 1:15.

Upper School Student Profile Grade 9: 68 students (27 boys, 41 girls); Grade 10: 53 students (22 boys, 31 girls); Grade 11: 38 students (17 boys, 21 girls); Grade 12: 39 students (10 boys, 29 girls).

Faculty School total: 20. In upper school: 8 men, 10 women; 9 have advanced degrees.

Subjects Offered 3-dimensional art, algebra, biology, calculus, chemistry, communications, computers, creative arts, creative writing, design, digital photography, discrete math, drama, drawing, English, environmental science, first aid, geometry, guitar, health, honors English, journalism, music appreciation, Native American arts and crafts, Native American studies, Navajo, painting, physical education, physical science, physics, piano, pre-calculus, Spanish, statistics, U.S. government, U.S. history, video, world geography, world history.

Graduation Requirements Algebra, biology, communications, computers, English, environmental science, geometry, government, health, language, Navajo, science, social studies (includes history), Spanish, U.S. government, world history, Navajo language, Navajo history, Navajo culture.

Special Academic Programs Advanced Placement exam preparation; honors section; independent study; term-away projects; domestic exchange program; study abroad; academic accommodation for the gifted.

College Placement 35 students graduated in 2005; they went to Oberlin College; San Juan College; Swarthmore College; The University of Arizona; University of New Mexico; Whittier College. 6% scored over 26 on composite ACT.

Student Life Upper grades have specified standards of dress, student council, honor system. Discipline rests primarily with faculty.

Tuition and Aid Navajo Nation College Preparatory Scholarship Program available. In 2005–06, 3% of upper-school students received aid.

Admissions ACT-Explore required. Deadline for receipt of application materials: March 5. No application fee required. Interview required.

Athletics Interscholastic: baseball (boys, girls), basketball (b,g), cheering (b,g), cross-country running (b,g), football (b,g), golf (b,g), volleyball (b,g). 1 PE instructor, 19 coaches.

Computers Computer network features include campus e-mail, on-campus library services, CD-ROMs, Internet access, file transfer, office computer access, wireless campus network.

Contact Ms. Marilyn Harris, Director of Special Program/Admissions. 505-326-6571 Ext. 126. Fax: 505-564-8099. E-mail: mharris@opus.nps.bia.edu. Web site: www.nps.bia.edu.

NAWA ACADEMY

French Gulch, California
See Special Needs Schools section.

NAZARETH ACADEMY

1209 West Ogden Avenue
LaGrange Park, Illinois 60526
Head of School: Ms. Deborah A. Vondrasek

General Information Coeducational day college-preparatory school, affiliated with Roman Catholic Church. Grades 9–12. Founded: 1900. Setting: suburban. Nearest major city is Chicago. 15-acre campus. 3 buildings on campus. Approved or accredited by North Central Association of Colleges and Schools and Illinois Department of Education. Total enrollment: 772. Upper school average class size: 24. Upper school faculty-student ratio: 1:17.

Upper School Student Profile Grade 9: 205 students (89 boys, 116 girls); Grade 10: 203 students (80 boys, 123 girls); Grade 11: 168 students (82 boys, 86 girls); Grade 12: 196 students (90 boys, 106 girls). 90% of students are Roman Catholic.

Faculty School total: 45. In upper school: 17 men, 28 women; 36 have advanced degrees.

Subjects Offered Algebra, American government, American literature, art, band, biology, biology-AP, calculus-AP, chemistry, chorus, computer programming, computer science-AP, conceptual physics, creative writing, drama, economics, English, English language and composition-AP, English literature and composition-AP, fine arts, French, geography, geometry, German, health, humanities, Italian, journalism, photography, physical education, physics, pre-calculus, psychology, religion, Spanish, speech, studio art, theater, trigonometry, U.S. history, U.S. history-AP, Western civilization, world history, world literature.

Graduation Requirements Arts and fine arts (art, music, dance, drama), English, foreign language, mathematics, physical education (includes health), religion (includes Bible studies and theology), science, social studies (includes history). Community service is required.

Special Academic Programs Advanced Placement exam preparation in 11 subject areas; honors section.

College Placement 184 students graduated in 2005; all went to college, including DePaul University; Marquette University; Northwestern University; University of Illinois at Chicago; University of Illinois at Urbana–Champaign; University of Notre Dame. Median composite ACT: 25. 33% scored over 26 on composite ACT.

Student Life Upper grades have uniform requirement, student council. Discipline rests primarily with faculty. Attendance at religious services is required.

Tuition and Aid Day student tuition: $7800. Tuition installment plan (monthly payment plans). Tuition reduction for siblings, merit scholarship grants, need-based scholarship grants available. In 2005–06, 22% of upper-school students received aid; total upper-school merit-scholarship money awarded: $40,000. Total amount of financial aid awarded in 2005–06: $300,000.

Admissions Traditional secondary-level entrance grade is 9. For fall 2005, 350 students applied for upper-level admission, 205 enrolled. High School Placement Test (closed version) from Scholastic Testing Service required. Deadline for receipt of application materials: June 1. No application fee required. On-campus interview recommended.

Athletics Interscholastic: baseball (boys), basketball (b,g), cheering (g), cross-country running (b,g), football (b), golf (b,g), pom squad (g), soccer (b,g), softball (g), swimming and diving (b,g), tennis (b,g), track and field (b,g), volleyball (g); intramural: hockey (b), volleyball (b). 2 PE instructors, 1 coach, 1 trainer.

Computers Computers are regularly used in English, history, mathematics, science classes. Computer network features include on-campus library services, CD-ROMs, Internet access, office computer access, wireless campus network.

Contact Mr. Drew Carstens, Recruitment Director. 708-354-0061 Ext. 138. Fax: 708-354-0109. E-mail: dcarstens@nazarethacademy.com. Web site: www. nazarethacademy.com.

NBISIING EDUCATION CENTRE

469-B Couchie Memorial Drive
North Bay, Ontario P1B 8G5, Canada
Head of School: Mr. Chris Hachkowski

General Information Coeducational day college-preparatory, general academic, bilingual studies, technology, and First Nations Studies school; primarily serves underachievers. Grades 9–12. Founded: 1996. Setting: suburban. 1 building on campus. Approved or accredited by Ontario Ministry of Education and Ontario Department of Education. Language of instruction: English. Total enrollment: 79. Upper school average class size: 15. Upper school faculty-student ratio: 1:10.

Faculty School total: 8. In upper school: 3 men, 5 women; 1 has an advanced degree.

Subjects Offered Accounting, algebra, art, art and culture, basic skills, biology, business, business applications, business skills, calculus, Canadian geography, Canadian history, Canadian law, Canadian literature, career education, career education internship, career planning, careers, chemistry, civics, computer information systems, computer literacy, computer science, data analysis, drama, ecology, English, English literature, environmental geography, environmental science, family and consumer science, food and nutrition, functions, geography, health education, history, history of the Americas, integrated technology fundamentals, interdisciplinary studies, intro to computers, keyboarding/computer, law, literacy, mathematics, Native American arts and crafts, Native American history, Native American studies, outdoor education, physical education, physics, religions, science, social science, society challenge and change, woodworking, world religions.

Graduation Requirements Ontario Ministry of Education requirements.

Special Academic Programs Independent study; remedial reading and/or remedial writing; remedial math; special instructional classes for students with LD, ADD, emotional and behavioral problems.

College Placement 15 students graduated in 2005; 10 went to college. Other: 5 went to work.

Student Life Upper grades have specified standards of dress, student council. Discipline rests primarily with faculty. Attendance at religious services is required.

Summer Programs Remediation programs offered; session focuses on remediation and make-up; held on campus; accepts boys and girls; open to students from other schools. 15 students usually enrolled. 2006 schedule: July 3 to July 28.

Admissions Traditional secondary-level entrance grade is 9. For fall 2005, 79 students applied for upper-level admission, 79 were accepted, 79 enrolled. Deadline for receipt of application materials: none. No application fee required.

Athletics Intramural: badminton (boys, girls), ball hockey (b,g), baseball (b,g), basketball (b,g), floor hockey (b,g), golf (b,g), hockey (b,g); coed intramural: badminton, ball hockey, baseball, basketball, floor hockey, golf, hockey. 1 PE instructor.

Computers Computers are regularly used in all classes. Computer network features include on-campus library services, CD-ROMs, Internet access, DVD.

Contact Mr. Chris Hachkowski, Principal. 705-497-9938. Fax: 705-497-0389. E-mail: chrish@nbisiing.com. Web site: www.nbisiing.com.

NEBRASKA CHRISTIAN SCHOOLS

1847 Inskip Avenue
Central City, Nebraska 68826
Head of School: Dr. David J. Edgren

General Information Coeducational boarding and day college-preparatory school, affiliated with Protestant-Evangelical faith. Boarding grades 7–12, day grades K–12. Founded: 1959. Setting: rural. Nearest major city is Lincoln. Students are housed in single-sex dormitories. 27-acre campus. 6 buildings on campus. Approved or accredited by Association of Christian Schools International and Nebraska Department of Education. Endowment: $32,000. Total enrollment: 182. Upper school average class size: 20. Upper school faculty-student ratio: 1:10.

Upper School Student Profile Grade 9: 24 students (11 boys, 13 girls); Grade 10: 17 students (5 boys, 12 girls); Grade 11: 24 students (16 boys, 8 girls); Grade 12: 39 students (17 boys, 22 girls). 32% of students are boarding students. 78% are state residents. 2 states are represented in upper school student body. 21% are international students. International students from Hong Kong, Japan, Macao, Republic of Korea, Taiwan, and Viet Nam; 1 other country represented in student body. 90% of students are Protestant-Evangelical faith.

Faculty School total: 23. In upper school: 10 men, 8 women; 6 have advanced degrees.

Subjects Offered Accounting, advanced math, algebra, American government, American history, American literature, anatomy and physiology, ancient world history, art, band, Bible, biology, business, business law, chemistry, choir, Christian doctrine, Christian ethics, composition, computer applications, computer keyboarding, computer programming, concert band, consumer mathematics, creation science, desktop publishing, economics, English, English composition, ESL, family living, fitness, general math, geography, geometry, health and safety, history, lab science, language arts, Life of Christ, life science, literature, mathematics, music, music theory, physical education, physical fitness, physical science, physics, pre-calculus, science, science project, social studies, Spanish, speech, trigonometry, vocal ensemble, vocal music, Web site design, word processing, world geography, world history, writing, yearbook.

Graduation Requirements Algebra, American government, American history, American literature, art, Bible, biology, Christian doctrine, computer keyboarding, economics, English, family living, geometry, history, Life of Christ, physical education (includes health), physical science, world history.

Special Academic Programs Independent study; study at local college for college credit; ESL (18 students enrolled).

College Placement 34 students graduated in 2005; 25 went to college, including Hillsdale College; LeTourneau University; University of Nebraska–Lincoln. Other: 2 went to work, 2 entered military service, 2 had other specific plans. Median composite ACT: 24. 21% scored over 26 on composite ACT.

Student Life Upper grades have specified standards of dress, student council, honor system. Discipline rests primarily with faculty. Attendance at religious services is required.

Summer Programs ESL programs offered; held on campus; accepts boys and girls; open to students from other schools. 6 students usually enrolled. 2006 schedule: June to July. Application deadline: April.

Tuition and Aid Day student tuition: $5000; 5-day tuition and room/board: $7900; 7-day tuition and room/board: $18,000–$19,000. Tuition installment plan (FACTS Tuition Payment Plan, individually arranged payment plans). Tuition reduction for siblings, merit scholarship grants, need-based scholarship grants available. In 2005–06, 42% of upper-school students received aid. Total amount of financial aid awarded in 2005–06: $115,000.

Admissions Traditional secondary-level entrance grade is 9. For fall 2005, 30 students applied for upper-level admission, 30 were accepted, 30 enrolled. TOEFL or SLEP required. Deadline for receipt of application materials: none. Application fee required: $200. Interview recommended.

Athletics Interscholastic: basketball (boys, girls), cross-country running (b,g), football (b), track and field (b,g), volleyball (g), wrestling (b). 1 PE instructor, 7 coaches.

Computers Computers are regularly used in business applications, desktop publishing, programming, Web site design, yearbook classes. Computer network features include Internet access, wireless campus network.

Contact   Mr. Larry Hoff, Director, International Programs. 308-946-3836. Fax: 308-946-3837. E-mail: lhoff@nebraskachristian.org. Web site: www. nebraskachristian.org.

NERINX HALL
530 East Lockwood Avenue
Webster Groves, Missouri 63119
Head of School: Sr. Barbara Roche, SL

General Information Girls' day college-preparatory and arts school, affiliated with Roman Catholic Church. Grades 9–12. Founded: 1924. Setting: suburban. Nearest major city is St. Louis. 3 buildings on campus. Approved or accredited by North Central Association of Colleges and Schools and Missouri Department of Education. Endowment: $2.1 million. Total enrollment: 607. Upper school average class size: 20. Upper school faculty-student ratio: 1:11.

Upper School Student Profile Grade 9: 153 students (153 girls); Grade 10: 159 students (159 girls); Grade 11: 154 students (154 girls); Grade 12: 141 students (141 girls). 96% of students are Roman Catholic.

Faculty School total: 51. In upper school: 11 men, 40 women; 43 have advanced degrees.

Subjects Offered Acting, advanced math, American government, American history, American literature, anatomy, anthropology, art, astronomy, athletics, biology, business, calculus, ceramics, chemistry, computer applications, computer graphics, conceptual physics, creative writing, death and loss, desktop publishing, drawing and design, Eastern world civilizations, economics, English composition, English literature, film appreciation, French, geology, German, graphics, health, history, Holocaust, honors algebra, honors English, honors geometry, honors U.S. history, instrumental music, jazz band, keyboarding, lab science, Latin, media, Middle East, model United Nations, multimedia, orchestra, painting, performing arts, personal finance, physics, pre-calculus, psychology, public speaking, religious education, Spanish, stagecraft, theology, Web site design, Western civilization.

Graduation Requirements Algebra, arts and fine arts (art, music, dance, drama), biology, chemistry, foreign language, geometry, physical education (includes health), physics, theology, U.S. government and politics, U.S. history, U.S. literature, world history, writing.

Special Academic Programs Honors section; study at local college for college credit.

College Placement 142 students graduated in 2005; all went to college, including Missouri State University; Saint Louis University; Truman State University; University of Missouri–Columbia; University of Missouri–St. Louis; Xavier University. Median SAT verbal: 640, median SAT math: 630, median composite ACT: 26.

Student Life Upper grades have uniform requirement, student council, honor system. Discipline rests primarily with faculty. Attendance at religious services is required.

Summer Programs Advancement programs offered; session focuses on advancement; held on campus; accepts girls; not open to students from other schools. 175 students usually enrolled.

Tuition and Aid Day student tuition: $7900. Tuition installment plan (individually arranged payment plans). Tuition reduction for siblings, merit scholarship grants, need-based scholarship grants, paying campus jobs available. In 2005–06, 12% of upper-school students received aid. Total amount of financial aid awarded in 2005–06: $201,000.

Admissions Traditional secondary-level entrance grade is 9. For fall 2005, 177 students applied for upper-level admission, 157 were accepted, 153 enrolled. Any standardized test or CTBS (or similar from their school) required. Deadline for receipt of application materials: November 30. Application fee required: $10. Interview required.

Athletics Interscholastic: basketball, cross-country running, diving, field hockey, golf, lacrosse, racquetball, soccer, softball, swimming and diving, tennis, track and field, volleyball.

Computers Computers are regularly used in graphics, mathematics, science, speech, writing classes. Computer network features include on-campus library services, Internet access, file transfer, office computer access, wireless campus network.

Contact Mrs. Jane Kosash, Principal. 314-968-1505 Ext. 112. Fax: 314-968-0604. E-mail: jkosash@nerinxhs.org. Web site: www.nerinxhs.org.

NEUCHATEL JUNIOR COLLEGE
Cret-Taconnet 4
2002 Neuchâtel, Switzerland
Head of School: Mr. Norman Southward

General Information Coeducational boarding college-preparatory, arts, business, bilingual studies, and international development school. Grade 12. Founded: 1956. Setting: urban. Nearest major city is Berne. Students are housed in homes of host families. 1-acre campus. 3 buildings on campus. Approved or accredited by Canadian Association of Independent Schools and state department of education. Languages of instruction: English and French. Endowment: CAN$100,000. Total enrollment: 106. Upper school average class size: 14. Upper school faculty-student ratio: 1:10.

Upper School Student Profile Grade 12: 76 students (21 boys, 55 girls); Postgraduate: 30 students (8 boys, 22 girls). 100% of students are boarding students. 10% are international students. International students from Bangladesh, Barbados, Canada, United Arab Emirates, United Kingdom, and United States; 2 other countries represented in student body.

Faculty School total: 10. In upper school: 6 men, 4 women; 6 have advanced degrees; 2 reside on campus.

Graduation Requirements Minimum of 6 senior year university prep level courses.

Special Academic Programs Advanced Placement exam preparation in 11 subject areas; study abroad.

College Placement 103 students graduated in 2005; all went to college, including Dalhousie University; McGill University; McMaster University; Queen's University at Kingston; The University of Western Ontario; University of Toronto.

Student Life Upper grades have student council, honor system. Discipline rests primarily with faculty.

Tuition and Aid 7-day tuition and room/board: 36,200 Swiss francs. Bursaries, merit scholarship grants available. In 2005–06, 4% of upper-school students received aid; total upper-school merit-scholarship money awarded: 8000 Swiss francs. Total amount of financial aid awarded in 2005–06: 10,000 Swiss francs.

Admissions Traditional secondary-level entrance grade is 12. For fall 2005, 136 students applied for upper-level admission, 110 were accepted, 106 enrolled. Deadline for receipt of application materials: December 12. Application fee required: CAN$150. Interview recommended.

Athletics Interscholastic: field hockey (boys, girls), rugby (b,g), soccer (b,g); intramural: hockey (b,g), ice hockey (b,g), indoor hockey (b,g), rugby (b,g), soccer (b,g); coed interscholastic: alpine skiing, aquatics, snowboarding, swimming and diving; coed intramural: alpine skiing, aquatics, basketball, bicycling, cross-country running, curling, floor hockey, jogging, sailing, snowboarding, volleyball.

Computers Computer network features include on-campus library services, CD-ROMs, Internet access, DVD.

Contact Ms. Mandi Gerland, Admissions Counselor. 416-368-8169 Ext. 222. Fax: 416-368-0956. E-mail: admissions@neuchatel.org. Web site: www.njc.ch/school/.

NEWARK ACADEMY
91 South Orange Avenue
Livingston, New Jersey 07039-4989
Head of School: Ms. Elizabeth Penney Riegelman

General Information Coeducational day college-preparatory, arts, technology, and International Baccalaureate school. Grades 6–12. Founded: 1774. Setting: suburban. Nearest major city is Morristown. 68-acre campus. 1 building on campus. Approved or accredited by Middle States Association of Colleges and Schools, New Jersey Association of Independent Schools, and New Jersey Department of Education. Member of National Association of Independent Schools and Secondary School Admission Test Board. Endowment: $10 million. Total enrollment: 549. Upper school average class size: 13. Upper school faculty-student ratio: 1:12.

Upper School Student Profile Grade 9: 106 students (54 boys, 52 girls); Grade 10: 107 students (57 boys, 50 girls); Grade 11: 92 students (47 boys, 45 girls); Grade 12: 107 students (48 boys, 59 girls).

Faculty School total: 74. In upper school: 33 men, 34 women; 50 have advanced degrees.

Subjects Offered Algebra, American history, American literature, anatomy, art, art history, arts, biology, botany, calculus, ceramics, chemistry, chorus, communications, community service, computer programming, computer science, creative writing, drama, driver education, earth science, ecology, economics, English, English literature, European history, finance, fine arts, French, geometry, German, government/civics, grammar, health, history, humanities, Latin, leadership training, Mandarin, mathematics, music, philosophy, physical education, physics, religion, robotics, SAT/ACT preparation, science, social studies, Spanish, theater, theory of knowledge, trigonometry, typing, world history, world literature, writing.

Graduation Requirements Arts and fine arts (art, music, dance, drama), computer science, English, foreign language, mathematics, physical education (includes health), science, social studies (includes history), 40-hour senior service project.

Special Academic Programs International Baccalaureate program; Advanced Placement exam preparation in 19 subject areas; honors section; accelerated programs; independent study; term-away projects; study at local college for college credit; study abroad; academic accommodation for the gifted, the musically talented, and the artistically talented.

College Placement 98 students graduated in 2005; all went to college, including Barnard College; Carnegie Mellon University; Cornell University; Middlebury College; University of Pennsylvania; Wake Forest University. Median SAT math: 660, median composite ACT: 26. 83% scored over 600 on SAT math, 36% scored over 26 on composite ACT.

Student Life Upper grades have specified standards of dress, student council, honor system. Discipline rests equally with students and faculty.

Summer Programs Remediation, enrichment, advancement, ESL, sports, art/fine arts, computer instruction programs offered; session focuses on enrichment and

advancement; held on campus; accepts boys and girls; open to students from other schools. 850 students usually enrolled. 2006 schedule: June 19 to August 11. Application deadline: June 1.

Tuition and Aid Day student tuition: $22,100. Tuition installment plan (Insured Tuition Payment Plan, Key Tuition Payment Plan, monthly payment plans, individually arranged payment plans). Need-based scholarship grants available. In 2005–06, 13% of upper-school students received aid. Total amount of financial aid awarded in 2005–06: $1,120,800.

Admissions Traditional secondary-level entrance grade is 9. For fall 2005, 292 students applied for upper-level admission, 110 were accepted, 61 enrolled. ISEE or SSAT required. Deadline for receipt of application materials: January 31. Application fee required: $60. Interview required.

Athletics Interscholastic: baseball (boys), basketball (b,g), cross-country running (b,g), fencing (b,g), field hockey (g), football (b), golf (b,g), lacrosse (b,g), running (b,g), skiing (downhill) (b,g), soccer (b,g), softball (g), swimming and diving (b,g), tennis (b,g), track and field (b,g), volleyball (b); wrestling (b); intramural: aerobics/dance (b,g), aerobics/nautilus (b,g), baseball (b), basketball (b,g), bicycling (b,g), cross-country running (b,g), dance (b,g), dance team (b,g), field hockey (g), fitness (b,g), football (b), golf (b,g), hockey (b), ice hockey (b), lacrosse (b,g), modern dance (b,g), soccer (b,g), softball (g), swimming and diving (b,g), tennis (b,g), track and field (b,g), volleyball (g), weight lifting (b,g), wrestling (b), yoga (b,g); coed intramural: aerobics/dance, aerobics/nautilus, bicycling, dance, dance team, fitness, modern dance, mountain biking, skiing (downhill), table tennis, ultimate Frisbee, weight lifting, yoga. 5 PE instructors, 10 coaches, 1 trainer.

Computers Computers are regularly used in all academic classes. Computer network features include campus e-mail, on-campus library services, CD-ROMs, online commercial services, Internet access, file transfer, DVD, wireless campus network.

Contact Mr. Willard L. Taylor Jr., Director of Financial Aid and Associate Director of Admission. 973-992-7000 Ext. 341. Fax: 973-993-8962. E-mail: wtaylor@newarka.edu. Web site: www.newarka.edu.

ANNOUNCEMENT FROM THE SCHOOL Newark Academy's mission is to prepare young people for college and to assist them in reaching their full potential. Newark Academy offers the full AP program and the prestigious International Baccalaureate Diploma. The Academy offers a traditional college-preparatory program with a distinctive global orientation.

NEW COVENANT ACADEMY

3304 South Cox Road
Springfield, Missouri 65807
Head of School: Dr. Timothy Siebert

General Information Coeducational day college-preparatory, arts, business, religious studies, and technology school. Grades PK–12. Founded: 1979. Setting: urban. 24-acre campus. 1 building on campus. Approved or accredited by Academy of Orton-Gillingham Practitioners and Educators, North Central Association of Colleges and Schools, and Missouri Department of Education. Language of instruction: Spanish. Total enrollment: 377.

College Placement 50% scored over 26 on composite ACT.

Student Life Upper grades have specified standards of dress, student council. Discipline rests primarily with faculty. Attendance at religious services is required.

Admissions Application fee required. Interview required.

Athletics Interscholastic: basketball (boys, girls), cheering (g), golf (b), soccer (b), track and field (b,g), volleyball (g); coed interscholastic: golf, soccer, track and field.

Contact Mrs. Delana Reynolds, Admissions Officer. 417-887-9848 Ext. 3. Fax: 417-887-2419. E-mail: dreynolds@newcovenant.net. Web site: www.newcovenant.net.

NEW DOMINION SCHOOL

Oldtown, Maryland
See Special Needs Schools section.

NEW DOMINION SCHOOL

Dillwyn, Virginia
See Special Needs Schools section.

THE NEWGRANGE SCHOOL

Hamilton, New Jersey
See Special Needs Schools section.

petersons.com

NEW HAMPTON SCHOOL

70 Main Street
PO Box 579
New Hampton, New Hampshire 03256
Head of School: Andrew Menke

General Information Coeducational boarding and day college-preparatory, general academic, arts, and bilingual studies school. Grades 9–PG. Founded: 1821. Setting: small town. Nearest major city is Boston, MA. Students are housed in single-sex dormitories. 300-acre campus. 35 buildings on campus. Approved or accredited by Association of Independent Schools in New England, Independent Schools of Northern New England, New England Association of Schools and Colleges, The Association of Boarding Schools, and New Hampshire Department of Education. Member of National Association of Independent Schools and Secondary School Admission Test Board. Endowment: $7.7 million. Total enrollment: 330. Upper school average class size: 12. Upper school faculty-student ratio: 1:5.

Upper School Student Profile Grade 9: 55 students (35 boys, 20 girls); Grade 10: 70 students (40 boys, 30 girls); Grade 11: 95 students (55 boys, 40 girls); Grade 12: 95 students (55 boys, 40 girls); Postgraduate: 15 students (10 boys, 5 girls). 75% of students are boarding students. 50% are state residents. 28 states are represented in upper school student body. 14% are international students. International students from Brazil, Canada, France, Germany, Japan, and Republic of Korea; 6 other countries represented in student body.

Faculty School total: 82. In upper school: 38 men, 40 women; 34 have advanced degrees; 51 reside on campus.

Subjects Offered Algebra, American history, American literature, anatomy, art, art history, biology, broadcasting, calculus, ceramics, chemistry, community service, computer programming, computer science, creative writing, dance, drama, driver education, earth science, ecology, economics, electronics, English, English literature, environmental science, European history, expository writing, filmmaking, fine arts, French, geography, geometry, government/civics, grammar, health, history, human sexuality, journalism, Latin, logic, mathematics, music, music history, philosophy, photography, physical education, physics, physics-AP, physiology, psychology, science, senior seminar, social studies, sociology, Spanish, speech, statistics, theater, trigonometry, world history, world literature, writing.

Graduation Requirements Arts and fine arts (art, music, dance, drama), computer science, English, foreign language, mathematics, performing arts, science, social studies (includes history), speech. Community service is required.

Special Academic Programs Advanced Placement exam preparation in 5 subject areas; honors section; independent study; academic accommodation for the gifted, the musically talented, and the artistically talented; remedial reading and/or remedial writing; remedial math; programs in English for dyslexic students; ESL (15 students enrolled).

College Placement 112 students graduated in 2005; 109 went to college, including Colby College; Ithaca College; Northeastern University; St. Lawrence University; University of New Hampshire; University of Vermont. Other: 3 had other specific plans. Median SAT verbal: 500, median SAT math: 530. 15% scored over 600 on SAT verbal, 25% scored over 600 on SAT math.

Student Life Upper grades have student council, honor system. Discipline rests equally with students and faculty.

Summer Programs Enrichment, sports, art/fine arts programs offered; session focuses on performing arts and sports; held on campus; accepts boys and girls; open to students from other schools. 85 students usually enrolled. 2006 schedule: June 1 to August 31. Application deadline: none.

Tuition and Aid Day student tuition: $21,400; 7-day tuition and room/board: $34,900. Tuition installment plan (Insured Tuition Payment Plan, Academic Management Services Plan, Key Tuition Payment Plan, monthly payment plans, individually arranged payment plans). Need-based scholarship grants available. In 2005–06, 30% of upper-school students received aid. Total amount of financial aid awarded in 2005–06: $1,500,000.

Admissions Traditional secondary-level entrance grade is 9. For fall 2005, 470 students applied for upper-level admission, 250 were accepted, 130 enrolled. SSAT or TOEFL or SLEP required. Deadline for receipt of application materials: none. Application fee required: $50. Interview required.

Athletics Interscholastic: alpine skiing (boys, girls); baseball (b), basketball (b,g), cross-country running (b,g), field hockey (g), football (b), golf (b,g), ice hockey (b,g), lacrosse (b,g), skiing (downhill) (b,g), soccer (b,g), softball (g), tennis (b,g), volleyball (g); coed interscholastic: alpine skiing, canoeing/kayaking, equestrian sports, horseback riding, kayaking, mountain biking, snowboarding; coed intramural: aerobics/dance, ballet, bicycling, canoeing/kayaking, climbing, cross-country running, dance, equestrian sports, fishing, fitness, fly fishing, golf, hiking/backpacking, horseback riding, ice hockey, kayaking, modern dance, nordic skiing, outdoor activities, outdoor adventure, outdoor education, outdoor recreation, outdoor skills, physical training, project adventure, rock climbing, ropes courses, skiing (downhill), snowboarding, tai chi, tennis, wall climbing, weight lifting, weight training, yoga. 3 trainers.

Computers Computers are regularly used in English, graphic design, introduction to technology, journalism, mathematics, media production, music, science, video film production, yearbook classes. Computer resources include campus e-mail, on-campus library services, CD-ROMs, Internet access.

Contact Mrs. Alecia Farquhar, Admissions Administrative Assistant. 603-677-3407. Fax: 603-677-3481. E-mail: afarquhar@newhampton.org. Web site: www.newhampton.org.

ANNOUNCEMENT FROM THE SCHOOL New Hampton School educates young people differently. Following a nationally acclaimed model for experience-based education, our students and adults share their unique talents as we learn alongside each other how to be better students, teachers, and friends. Here you will be asked to take responsibility for your success by helping shape our community in ways that benefit us all.

See full description on page 934.

NEW HORIZON YOUTH MINISTRIES
Marion, Indiana
See Special Needs Schools section.

NEWMAN HIGH SCHOOL
1130 West Bridge
Wausau, Wisconsin 54401
Head of School: Mr. Lawrence P. Theiss

General Information Coeducational day college-preparatory and religious studies school, affiliated with Roman Catholic Church. Grades 9–12. Founded: 1951. Setting: urban. 80-acre campus. 1 building on campus. Approved or accredited by North Central Association of Colleges and Schools and Wisconsin Department of Education. Languages of instruction: Spanish and French. Upper school average class size: 15. Upper school faculty-student ratio: 1:15.

Upper School Student Profile Grade 9: 60 students (26 boys, 34 girls); Grade 10: 60 students (22 boys, 38 girls); Grade 11: 54 students (28 boys, 26 girls); Grade 12: 37 students (18 boys, 19 girls). 96% of students are Roman Catholic.

Faculty School total: 28. In upper school: 9 men, 18 women; 12 have advanced degrees.

Special Academic Programs Advanced Placement exam preparation in 8 subject areas; independent study.

College Placement 59 students graduated in 2005; 58 went to college, including Carroll College; Concordia University Wisconsin; University of Wisconsin–La Crosse; University of Wisconsin–Madison; University of Wisconsin–Milwaukee. Other: 1 entered a postgraduate year. Mean composite ACT: 23. 34% scored over 26 on composite ACT.

Student Life Upper grades have specified standards of dress, student council, honor system. Discipline rests primarily with faculty. Attendance at religious services is required.

Admissions Traditional secondary-level entrance grade is 9. For fall 2005, 211 students applied for upper-level admission, 211 were accepted, 211 enrolled. Deadline for receipt of application materials: none. No application fee required. On-campus interview required.

Athletics Interscholastic: baseball (boys), basketball (b,g), football (b), softball (g), track and field (b,g); intramural: ice hockey (b,g), soccer (g), swimming and diving (g); coed interscholastic: alpine skiing, soccer. 1 PE instructor, 19 coaches, 1 trainer.

Computers Computers are regularly used in accounting, basic skills, business applications, business education, business skills, photography, publications, publishing, research skills, senior seminar, stock market, technology, typing, word processing, writing, yearbook classes. Computer resources include on-campus library services, CD-ROMs, Internet access.

Contact Mr. Lawrence P. Theiss, Principal. 715-845-8274. Fax: 715-842-1302. E-mail: ltheiss@newmancatholicschools.com.

THE NEWMAN SCHOOL
247 Marlborough Street
Boston, Massachusetts 02116
Head of School: J. Harry Lynch

General Information Coeducational day college-preparatory and ESL school. Grades 9–PG. Founded: 1945. Setting: urban. 2 buildings on campus. Approved or accredited by Association of Independent Schools in New England, New England Association of Schools and Colleges, and Massachusetts Department of Education. Member of Secondary School Admission Test Board. Total enrollment: 230. Upper school average class size: 15. Upper school faculty-student ratio: 1:14.

Upper School Student Profile Grade 9: 45 students (20 boys, 25 girls); Grade 10: 51 students (25 boys, 26 girls); Grade 11: 69 students (32 boys, 37 girls); Grade 12: 65 students (27 boys, 38 girls).

Faculty School total: 23. In upper school: 11 men, 12 women; 9 have advanced degrees.

Subjects Offered Advanced chemistry, Advanced Placement courses, African-American history, algebra, American government-AP, American history, American history-AP, American literature, American literature-AP, anatomy and physiology, anthropology, art, art history, biology, biology-AP, British literature, calculus, calculus-AP, chemistry, computer programming, computer science, computer science-AP, creative writing, drama, earth science, English, English literature, environmental science, ESL, expository writing, fine arts, French, geography, geometry, government-AP, government/civics, grammar, international relations, journalism, Latin, marine biology, mathematics, moral reasoning, physics, psychology, religion, science, social studies, society, politics and law, sociology, Spanish, theater, trigonometry, word processing, world history, world literature, writing.

Graduation Requirements Arts and fine arts (art, music, dance, drama), computer science, English, foreign language, mathematics, science, senior project, social studies (includes history).

Special Academic Programs Advanced Placement exam preparation in 6 subject areas; honors section; accelerated programs; study at local college for college credit; ESL (25 students enrolled).

College Placement 60 students graduated in 2005; 56 went to college, including Boston College; Boston University; Northeastern University; Suffolk University; University of Massachusetts Amherst; Worcester Polytechnic Institute. Other: 2 went to work, 2 had other specific plans.

Student Life Upper grades have specified standards of dress, student council. Discipline rests primarily with faculty.

Summer Programs Remediation, enrichment, advancement, ESL, computer instruction programs offered; session focuses on high school credits for courses never before taken; held on campus; accepts boys and girls; open to students from other schools. 100 students usually enrolled. 2006 schedule: June 20 to August 19. Application deadline: none.

Tuition and Aid Day student tuition: $10,500–$16,000. Tuition installment plan (Academic Management Services Plan, monthly payment plans). Merit scholarship grants, need-based scholarship grants available. In 2005–06, 20% of upper-school students received aid; total upper-school merit-scholarship money awarded: $80,000. Total amount of financial aid awarded in 2005–06: $120,000.

Admissions Traditional secondary-level entrance grade is 9. For fall 2005, 165 students applied for upper-level admission, 95 were accepted, 60 enrolled. School's own exam or SSAT required. Deadline for receipt of application materials: none. Application fee required: $40. On-campus interview recommended.

Athletics Interscholastic: baseball (boys), basketball (b,g), cheering (g), dance (g), lacrosse (g), softball (g), tennis (b,g); coed interscholastic: crew, sailing, soccer; coed intramural: bicycling, fitness walking, flag football, hiking/backpacking, modern dance, outdoor activities, yoga.

Computers Computers are regularly used in English, ESL, history, library, mathematics, science classes. Computer network features include on-campus library services, CD-ROMs, Internet access, DVD, wireless campus network.

Contact Francis L. Donelan, Dean of Administration/Vice President. 617-267-4530. Fax: 617-267-7070. Web site: www.newmanboston.org.

See full description on page 936.

NEW MEXICO MILITARY INSTITUTE
101 West College Boulevard
Roswell, New Mexico 88201-5173
Head of School: David Ellison

General Information Coeducational boarding college-preparatory, arts, and business school. Grades 9–12. Founded: 1891. Setting: small town. Nearest major city is Albuquerque. Students are housed in coed dormitories. 42-acre campus. 17 buildings on campus. Approved or accredited by North Central Association of Colleges and Schools and New Mexico Department of Education. Member of Secondary School Admission Test Board. Endowment: $130 million. Total enrollment: 459. Upper school average class size: 15. Upper school faculty-student ratio: 1:15.

Upper School Student Profile Grade 9: 151 students (126 boys, 25 girls); Grade 10: 118 students (93 boys, 25 girls); Grade 11: 107 students (85 boys, 22 girls); Grade 12: 83 students (63 boys, 20 girls). 100% of students are boarding students. 35% are state residents. 44 states are represented in upper school student body. 8% are international students. International students from Australia, Canada, Fiji, Mexico, Republic of Korea, and Solomon Islands; 4 other countries represented in student body.

Faculty School total: 77. In upper school: 50 men, 25 women; 75 have advanced degrees.

Subjects Offered Algebra, American history, American literature, art, art history, biology, business, business skills, calculus, chemistry, computer programming, computer science, creative writing, drafting, drama, driver education, earth science, ecology, economics, English, English literature, European history, fine arts, French, geology, geometry, German, government/civics, grammar, health, history, journalism, JROTC, mathematics, mechanical drawing, music, physical education, physics, science, social science, social studies, sociology, Spanish, speech, theater, trigonometry, typing, world history, writing.

Graduation Requirements Arts and fine arts (art, music, dance, drama), business skills (includes word processing), computer science, English, foreign language, JROTC, mathematics, physical education (includes health), science, social science, social studies (includes history).

Special Academic Programs Honors section; study at local college for college credit.

College Placement 92 students graduated in 2005; 88 went to college, including New Mexico State University; Texas A&M University; United States Air Force Academy; United States Military Academy; United States Naval Academy; University of New Mexico. Other: 4 entered military service.

Student Life Upper grades have uniform requirement, student council, honor system. Discipline rests equally with students and faculty.

Summer Programs Remediation, enrichment, advancement, ESL, art/fine arts, rigorous outdoor training, computer instruction programs offered; session focuses on academics; held on campus; accepts boys and girls; open to students from other schools. 125 students usually enrolled. 2006 schedule: June 10 to July 15. Application deadline: June 9.

Tuition and Aid 7-day tuition and room/board: $10,100. Tuition installment plan (monthly payment plans, individually arranged payment plans). Merit scholarship grants, need-based scholarship grants available. In 2005–06, 52% of upper-school students received aid; total upper-school merit-scholarship money awarded: $250,000.

Admissions Traditional secondary-level entrance grade is 9. For fall 2005, 516 students applied for upper-level admission, 298 were accepted, 250 enrolled. Gates MacGinite Reading Tests and Math Placement Exam required. Deadline for receipt of application materials: none. Application fee required: $60. On-campus interview required.

Athletics Interscholastic: baseball (boys), basketball (b), cheering (b,g), football (b), softball (g), volleyball (g); coed interscholastic: cross-country running, drill team, fencing, golf, JROTC drill, life saving, marksmanship, riflery, soccer, swimming and diving, tennis, track and field; coed intramural: alpine skiing, archery, bicycling, bowling, fitness, flag football, martial arts, physical fitness, physical training, power lifting, racquetball, ropes courses, skiing (downhill), strength & conditioning, ultimate Frisbee, weight lifting, weight training. 6 PE instructors, 11 coaches, 1 trainer.

Computers Computers are regularly used in English, foreign language, mathematics classes. Computer network features include campus e-mail, on-campus library services, CD-ROMs, online commercial services, Internet access.

Contact Capt. Kerry J. Kiker, Associate Director of Admissions. 505-624-8050. Fax: 505-624-8058. E-mail: kerry@nmmi.edu. Web site: www.nmmi.edu.

THE NEWPORT SCHOOL

10914 Georgia Avenue
Silver Spring, Maryland 20902
Head of School: Mrs. Rachel Goldfarb

General Information Coeducational day college-preparatory school. Grades N–12. Founded: 1930. Setting: suburban. Nearest major city is Washington, DC. 1 building on campus. Approved or accredited by Association of Independent Maryland Schools, Association of Independent Schools of Greater Washington, and Maryland Department of Education. Candidate for accreditation by Middle States Association of Colleges and Schools. Member of National Association of Independent Schools. Total enrollment: 103. Upper school average class size: 5. Upper school faculty-student ratio: 1:4.

Upper School Student Profile Grade 9: 2 students (1 boy, 1 girl); Grade 10: 1 student (1 boy); Grade 11: 6 students (4 boys, 2 girls); Grade 12: 4 students (3 boys, 1 girl).

Faculty School total: 26. In upper school: 5 men, 4 women; 7 have advanced degrees.

Subjects Offered Advanced Placement courses, algebra, American history, American literature, art, art history, biology, calculus, chemistry, computer programming, computer science, creative writing, drama, economics, English, English literature, European history, fine arts, geometry, government/civics, history, mathematics, music, physics, science, Spanish, theater, trigonometry.

Graduation Requirements Arts and fine arts (art, music, dance, drama), English, foreign language, mathematics, science, social studies (includes history), demonstrated competency in computer skills.

Special Academic Programs Advanced Placement exam preparation in 2 subject areas; honors section.

College Placement Mean SAT verbal: 560, mean SAT math: 558.

Student Life Upper grades have uniform requirement. Discipline rests primarily with faculty.

Tuition and Aid Day student tuition: $16,770–$18,770. Tuition installment plan (SMART Tuition Payment Plan). Need-based scholarship grants available. In 2005–06, 28% of upper-school students received aid.

Admissions Traditional secondary-level entrance grade is 9. Deadline for receipt of application materials: none. Application fee required: $50. Interview recommended.

Athletics Interscholastic: soccer (boys, girls), softball (b,g); coed interscholastic: tennis. 1 PE instructor.

Computers Computer network features include online commercial services, Internet access.

Contact Mrs. Letty Rosen, Director of Admission. 301-942-4550. Fax: 301-949-2654. E-mail: lrosen@newportschool.org. Web site: www.newportschool.org.

NEW SUMMIT SCHOOL

Jackson, Mississippi
See Special Needs Schools section.

NEWTON COUNTRY DAY SCHOOL OF THE SACRED HEART

785 Centre Street
Newton, Massachusetts 02458
Head of School: Barbara Rogers, RSCJ

General Information Girls' day college-preparatory, arts, religious studies, and technology school, affiliated with Roman Catholic Church. Grades 5–12. Founded: 1880. Setting: suburban. Nearest major city is Boston. 20-acre campus. 3 buildings on campus. Approved or accredited by Association of Independent Schools in New England, Network of Sacred Heart Schools, New England Association of Schools and Colleges, and Massachusetts Department of Education. Member of National Association of Independent Schools and Secondary School Admission Test Board. Endowment: $11.5 million. Total enrollment: 365. Upper school average class size: 15. Upper school faculty-student ratio: 1:7.

Upper School Student Profile Grade 9: 51 students (51 girls); Grade 10: 54 students (54 girls); Grade 11: 49 students (49 girls); Grade 12: 53 students (53 girls). 70% of students are Roman Catholic.

Faculty School total: 70. In upper school: 19 men, 31 women; 40 have advanced degrees.

Subjects Offered Algebra, American history, American history-AP, American literature, anatomy, art, art history, art-AP, biology, biology-AP, calculus, calculus-AP, chemistry, chemistry-AP, community service, comparative government and politics, comparative government and politics-AP, creative writing, dance, drama, earth science, economics, English, English language-AP, English literature, English literature-AP, environmental science, environmental science-AP, European history-AP, expository writing, French, French language-AP, geography, geometry, government/civics, grammar, history, journalism, Latin, Latin-AP, mathematics, music, music theory, photography, physical education, physics, physics-AP, physiology, psychology, public speaking, religion, science, social science, social studies, Spanish, Spanish language-AP, Spanish literature-AP, statistics, statistics-AP, technology, theater, theology, trigonometry, U.S. government and politics-AP, world history, world literature, writing.

Graduation Requirements Arts and fine arts (art, music, dance, drama), English, foreign language, mathematics, physical education (includes health), religion (includes Bible studies and theology), science, senior project, social science, social studies (includes history). Community service is required.

Special Academic Programs Advanced Placement exam preparation in 14 subject areas; honors section; independent study; term-away projects; study at local college for college credit; domestic exchange program (with Network of Sacred Heart Schools); study abroad.

College Placement 54 students graduated in 2005; all went to college, including Amherst College; Boston College; College of the Holy Cross; Georgetown University; Harvard University; Trinity College.

Student Life Upper grades have specified standards of dress, student council, honor system. Discipline rests equally with students and faculty. Attendance at religious services is required.

Summer Programs Sports programs offered; session focuses on athletics; held on campus; accepts girls; open to students from other schools. 80 students usually enrolled. 2006 schedule: June to July. Application deadline: June 1.

Tuition and Aid Day student tuition: $26,450. Tuition installment plan (Insured Tuition Payment Plan, Academic Management Services Plan, monthly payment plans, individually arranged payment plans). Need-based scholarship grants available. In 2005–06, 31% of upper-school students received aid. Total amount of financial aid awarded in 2005–06: $1,177,245.

Admissions Traditional secondary-level entrance grade is 9. For fall 2005, 100 students applied for upper-level admission, 45 were accepted, 21 enrolled. ISEE or SSAT required. Deadline for receipt of application materials: February 1. Application fee required: $40. On-campus interview required.

Athletics Interscholastic: basketball, cross-country running, field hockey, golf, ice hockey, lacrosse, sailing, soccer, softball, squash, tennis, volleyball; intramural: aerobics, aerobics/dance, ballet, basketball, cooperative games, cross-country running, dance, dance team, fitness, flag football, modern dance, outdoor adventure, outdoor education, outdoor recreation, outdoor skills, physical fitness, physical training, soccer, softball, tennis, volleyball. 2 PE instructors, 13 coaches, 1 trainer.

Computers Computers are regularly used in all academic classes. Computer network features include campus e-mail, on-campus library services, CD-ROMs, online commercial services, Internet access, wireless campus network.

Contact Mary Delaney, Director of Admissions. 617-244-4246. Fax: 617-965-5313. E-mail: mdelaney@newtoncountryday.org. Web site: www.newtoncountryday.org.

NEW YORK MILITARY ACADEMY

78 Academy Avenue
Cornwall-on-Hudson, New York 12520
Head of School: Capt. Robert D. Watts

petersons.com

General Information Coeducational boarding and day college-preparatory, Junior ROTC, and ESL school. Grades 7–12. Founded: 1889. Setting: small town. Nearest major city is New York. Students are housed in single-sex dormitories. 165-acre campus. 11 buildings on campus. Approved or accredited by Middle States Association of Colleges and Schools, New York State Association of Independent Schools, The Association of Boarding Schools, and New York Department of Education. Member of National Association of Independent Schools and Secondary School Admission Test Board. Endowment: $2.6 million. Total enrollment: 240. Upper school average class size: 14. Upper school faculty-student ratio: 1:14.

Upper School Student Profile Grade 9: 37 students (33 boys, 4 girls); Grade 10: 47 students (41 boys, 6 girls); Grade 11: 80 students (72 boys, 8 girls); Grade 12: 58 students (49 boys, 9 girls). 86% of students are boarding students. 64% are state residents. 15 states are represented in upper school student body. 12% are international students. International students from Canada, Ethiopia, Hong Kong, Republic of Korea, Rwanda, and Zimbabwe; 6 other countries represented in student body.

Faculty School total: 43. In upper school: 27 men, 16 women; 18 have advanced degrees; 38 reside on campus.

Subjects Offered Algebra, American history, American history-AP, art, biology, business mathematics, chemistry, computer literacy, criminology, earth science, economics, English, English-AP, environmental science, French, geography, geometry, government, health, JROTC, Latin, physical science, physics, pre-calculus, social studies, Spanish, trigonometry, world history.

Graduation Requirements American history, art, biology, calculus, chemistry, computer science, economics, English, English composition, English literature, foreign language, global studies, government, JROTC or LEAD (Leadership Education and Development), mathematics, physical education (includes health), science, trigonometry. Community service is required.

Special Academic Programs Advanced Placement exam preparation in 3 subject areas; honors section; ESL (16 students enrolled).

College Placement 70 students graduated in 2005; all went to college, including Bucknell University; Mount Holyoke College; Norwich University; Rochester Institute of Technology; Stony Brook University, State University of New York; United States Military Academy. 10% scored over 600 on SAT verbal, 6% scored over 600 on SAT math.

Student Life Upper grades have uniform requirement, student council, honor system. Discipline rests equally with students and faculty. Attendance at religious services is required.

Summer Programs Remediation, enrichment, advancement, ESL, computer instruction programs offered; held on campus; accepts boys and girls; open to students from other schools. 100 students usually enrolled. 2006 schedule: July 5 to August 10. Application deadline: June 15.

Tuition and Aid Day student tuition: $5000; 7-day tuition and room/board: $20,000. Tuition installment plan (Academic Management Services Plan, individually arranged payment plans). Tuition reduction for siblings, need-based scholarship grants, TERI Loans, P.L.A.T.O. Junior Loans, Sallie Mae Loans, prepGATE Loans, CitiAssist Loans available. In 2005–06, 30% of upper-school students received aid. Total amount of financial aid awarded in 2005–06: $100,000.

Admissions Traditional secondary-level entrance grade is 10. For fall 2005, 160 students applied for upper-level admission, 123 were accepted, 90 enrolled. California Achievement Test, Cooperative Entrance Exam (McGraw-Hill), Iowa Tests of Basic Skills, Otis-Lennon School Ability Test, PSAT and SAT for applicants to grade 11 and 12, SLEP, SSAT, Stanford Achievement Test or TOEFL required. Deadline for receipt of application materials: September 15. Application fee required: $100. On-campus interview required.

Athletics Interscholastic: baseball (boys), basketball (b,g), football (b), ice hockey (b), lacrosse (b), soccer (b,g), softball (g), volleyball (g), wrestling (b); intramural: hockey (b); coed interscholastic: cross-country running, drill team, golf, JROTC drill, marksmanship, riflery, swimming and diving, tennis, track and field; coed intramural: equestrian sports, ice skating, martial arts, outdoor adventure, paint ball, physical fitness, physical training, ropes courses, skiing (downhill), snowboarding, strength & conditioning, swimming and diving, wall climbing, weight lifting, weight training. 1 PE instructor, 1 coach.

Computers Computers are regularly used in all academic, keyboarding, lab/keyboard, word processing classes. Computer network features include campus e-mail, on-campus library services, CD-ROMs, Internet access.

Contact Ms. Maureen T. Kelly, Director of Admissions. 845-534-3710 Ext. 4279. Fax: 845-534-7699. E-mail: mkelly@nyma.ouboces.org. Web site: www.nyma.org.

See full description on page 938.

NIAGARA CHRISTIAN COLLEGIATE

2619 Niagara Boulevard
Fort Erie, Ontario L2A 5M4, Canada
Head of School: Mr. Clare D. Lebold

General Information Coeducational boarding and day college-preparatory, general academic, arts, and business school, affiliated with Brethren in Christ Church. Boarding grades 9–12, day grades 7–12. Founded: 1932. Setting: rural. Nearest major city is Niagara Falls, Canada. Students are housed in single-sex dormitories. 121-acre campus. 15 buildings on campus. Approved or accredited by Association of Christian Schools International and Ontario Department of Education. Language of instruction: English. Total enrollment: 331. Upper school average class size: 18. Upper school faculty-student ratio: 1:17.

Upper School Student Profile Grade 9: 46 students (21 boys, 25 girls); Grade 10: 60 students (41 boys, 19 girls); Grade 11: 80 students (49 boys, 31 girls); Grade 12: 93 students (47 boys, 46 girls). 56% of students are boarding students. 65% are province residents. 7 provinces are represented in upper school student body. 35% are international students. International students from Hong Kong, Japan, Mexico, Republic of Korea, Taiwan, and Thailand; 6 other countries represented in student body. 17% of students are Brethren in Christ Church.

Faculty School total: 37. In upper school: 13 men, 15 women; 7 have advanced degrees.

Subjects Offered Accounting, advanced chemistry, advanced computer applications, advanced math, Advanced Placement courses, advanced TOEFL/grammar, algebra, American history, analysis and differential calculus, analytic geometry, anatomy, ancient history, art, art history, Bible, biology, biology-AP, business, business applications, business mathematics, calculus, calculus-AP, Canadian geography, Canadian history, Canadian literature, career education, chemistry, choir, civics, computer applications, computer keyboarding, data processing, discrete math, dramatic arts, early childhood, economics, English, ESL, European history, exercise science, family studies, French as a second language, general math, geography, geometry, guidance, health education, history, instrumental music, international affairs, keyboarding/computer, mathematics, medieval history, modern world history, music, parenting, physical education, physics, politics, science, Spanish, TOEFL preparation, world history, world history-AP, world issues.

Special Academic Programs Advanced Placement exam preparation in 3 subject areas; special instructional classes for students with learning disabilities; ESL (120 students enrolled).

College Placement 87 students graduated in 2005; 78 went to college, including Brock University; McMaster University; University of Guelph; University of Toronto; University of Waterloo; Wilfrid Laurier University. Other: 3 went to work, 6 had other specific plans.

Student Life Upper grades have uniform requirement, student council. Discipline rests primarily with faculty. Attendance at religious services is required.

Summer Programs ESL programs offered; session focuses on ESL; held both on and off campus; held at Toronto (3 days); accepts boys and girls; open to students from other schools. 30 students usually enrolled. 2006 schedule: July 2 to July 28. Application deadline: June 1.

Tuition and Aid Day student tuition: CAN$5995; 5-day tuition and room/board: CAN$13,270; 7-day tuition and room/board: CAN$19,145. Tuition installment plan (monthly payment plans, individually arranged payment plans, quarterly payment plan). Tuition reduction for siblings, bursaries, merit scholarship grants, need-based scholarship grants, paying campus jobs available. In 2005–06, 40% of upper-school students received aid; total upper-school merit-scholarship money awarded: CAN$5000. Total amount of financial aid awarded in 2005–06: CAN$200,000.

Admissions Traditional secondary-level entrance grade is 9. Admissions testing or TOEFL required. Deadline for receipt of application materials: none. No application fee required. Interview required.

Athletics Interscholastic: badminton (boys, girls), basketball (b,g), ice hockey (b,g), soccer (b,g), swimming and diving (b,g), track and field (b,g), volleyball (b,g); intramural: basketball (b,g), soccer (b,g), volleyball (b,g); coed interscholastic: badminton, baseball, swimming and diving, track and field, volleyball; coed intramural: badminton, baseball, bowling, canoeing/kayaking, cross-country running, floor hockey, golf, racquetball, skiing (downhill), snowboarding, volleyball. 1 PE instructor.

Computers Computers are regularly used in accounting, business, data processing, economics, ESL, keyboarding, mathematics, science, yearbook classes. Computer resources include on-campus library services, CD-ROMs, Internet access, DVD, wireless campus network.

Contact Mr. Marlin Reimer, Director of Student Life. 905-871-6980 Ext. 2280. Fax: 905-871-9260. E-mail: mreimer@niagaracc.com. Web site: www.niagaracc.com.

THE NICHOLS SCHOOL

1250 Amherst Street
Buffalo, New York 14216
Head of School: Richard C. Bryan Jr.

General Information Coeducational day college-preparatory, arts, and technology school. Grades 5–12. Founded: 1892. Setting: urban. 33-acre campus. 9 buildings on

campus. Member of National Association of Independent Schools. Endowment: $13 million. Total enrollment: 589. Upper school average class size: 15. Upper school faculty-student ratio: 1:9.

Upper School Student Profile Grade 9: 101 students (45 boys, 56 girls); Grade 10: 94 students (55 boys, 39 girls); Grade 11: 94 students (52 boys, 42 girls); Grade 12: 115 students (64 boys, 51 girls).

Faculty School total: 80. In upper school: 29 men, 23 women; 16 have advanced degrees.

Subjects Offered Algebra, American history, American literature, anatomy, art, art history, biology, calculus, chemistry, community service, computer graphics, computer math, computer programming, computer science, creative writing, dance, drama, driver education, earth science, economics, English, English literature, environmental science, European history, expository writing, fine arts, French, geometry, government/civics, history, Latin, mathematics, music, photography, physical education, physics, science, social studies, Spanish, speech, theater, trigonometry, world history, world literature.

Graduation Requirements Arts and fine arts (art, music, dance, drama), English, foreign language, mathematics, physical education (includes health), science, social studies (includes history).

Special Academic Programs Advanced Placement exam preparation in 19 subject areas; honors section; independent study.

College Placement 86 students graduated in 2005; all went to college, including American University; Buffalo State College, State University of New York; Canisius College; Hamilton College; The Johns Hopkins University; University of Rochester. 50% scored over 600 on SAT verbal, 56% scored over 600 on SAT math.

Student Life Upper grades have specified standards of dress, student council, honor system. Discipline rests equally with students and faculty.

Summer Programs Remediation, enrichment, advancement, art/fine arts, computer instruction programs offered; session focuses on academic enrichment; held on campus; accepts boys and girls; open to students from other schools. 75 students usually enrolled. 2006 schedule: June 15 to August 15. Application deadline: none.

Tuition and Aid Day student tuition: $14,100–$15,350. Tuition installment plan (Insured Tuition Payment Plan, Key Tuition Payment Plan, monthly payment plans). Need-based scholarship grants available. In 2005–06, 29% of upper-school students received aid. Total amount of financial aid awarded in 2005–06: $1,200,000.

Admissions Traditional secondary-level entrance grade is 9. For fall 2005, 181 students applied for upper-level admission, 172 were accepted, 110 enrolled. Otis-Lennon and 2 sections of ERB required. Deadline for receipt of application materials: none. Application fee required: $30. On-campus interview required.

Athletics Interscholastic: baseball (boys), basketball (b,g), crew (b,g), cross-country running (b,g), field hockey (g), football (b), golf (b), ice hockey (b,g), lacrosse (b,g), soccer (b,g), softball (g), squash (b,g), tennis (b,g), track and field (b,g), volleyball (g); coed interscholastic: bowling; coed intramural: aerobics/dance. 5 PE instructors, 12 coaches, 3 trainers.

Computers Computers are regularly used in art, library skills, newspaper, photography, science, technology, yearbook classes. Computer network features include campus e-mail, on-campus library services, CD-ROMs, online commercial services, Internet access.

Contact Jock Mitchell, Director of Admissions. 716-332-6325. Fax: 716-875-2169. E-mail: jmitchell@nicholsschool.org. Web site: www.nicholsschool.org.

THE NIGHTINGALE-BAMFORD SCHOOL

20 East 92nd Street
New York, New York 10128

ANNOUNCEMENT FROM THE SCHOOL The Nightingale-Bamford School provides a rigorous college-preparatory education for girls from kindergarten to class XII. The School features small classes, an extensive advisory system, many extracurricular opportunities, advanced technology, study-abroad options, and a diverse student body. One hundred percent of graduates attend 4-year, highly selective colleges.

NOBLE AND GREENOUGH SCHOOL

10 Campus Drive
Dedham, Massachusetts 02026-4099
Head of School: Mr. Robert P. Henderson Jr.

General Information Coeducational boarding and day college-preparatory school. Boarding grades 9–12, day grades 7–12. Founded: 1866. Setting: suburban. Nearest major city is Boston. Students are housed in single-sex dormitories. 187-acre campus. 11 buildings on campus. Approved or accredited by Association of Independent Schools in New England, New England Association of Schools and Colleges, The College Board, and Massachusetts Department of Education. Member of National Association of Independent Schools and Secondary School Admission Test Board. Endowment: $42 million. Total enrollment: 555. Upper school average class size: 14. Upper school faculty-student ratio: 1:7.

Upper School Student Profile Grade 9: 108 students (53 boys, 55 girls); Grade 10: 113 students (61 boys, 52 girls); Grade 11: 111 students (57 boys, 54 girls); Grade 12: 107 students (52 boys, 55 girls). 9% of students are boarding students. 99% are state residents. 2 states are represented in upper school student body.

Faculty School total: 80. In upper school: 43 men, 29 women; 40 have advanced degrees; 22 reside on campus.

Subjects Offered 20th century history, Advanced Placement courses, African-American literature, algebra, American history, American literature, anatomy, ancient history, art, art history, astronomy, biology, calculus, ceramics, chemistry, community service, computer programming, computer science, concert band, creative writing, drama, drawing, earth science, ecology, economics, English, English literature, environmental science, ethics, European history, expository writing, fine arts, French, genetics, geography, geometry, government/civics, grammar, health, history, independent study, Japanese, journalism, Latin, Latin American history, marine biology, mathematics, music, painting, philosophy, photography, physics, physiology, printmaking, psychology, Roman civilization, science, senior internship, senior project, social studies, Spanish, speech, statistics, theater, trigonometry, Vietnam, world history, world literature, writing.

Graduation Requirements Arts and fine arts (art, music, dance, drama), computer science, English, foreign language, mathematics, performing arts, physical education (includes health), science, social studies (includes history). Community service is required.

Special Academic Programs Advanced Placement exam preparation in 16 subject areas; honors section; independent study; term-away projects; study abroad; academic accommodation for the gifted, the musically talented, and the artistically talented.

College Placement 108 students graduated in 2005; all went to college, including Boston College; Brown University; Harvard University; Trinity College; University of Pennsylvania. 75% scored over 600 on SAT verbal, 83% scored over 600 on SAT math.

Student Life Upper grades have specified standards of dress, student council, honor system. Discipline rests equally with students and faculty.

Summer Programs Enrichment programs offered; session focuses on math and science; held both on and off campus; held at University of Massachusetts Boston; accepts boys and girls; open to students from other schools. 50 students usually enrolled. 2006 schedule: July 1 to August 10. Application deadline: February 2.

Tuition and Aid Day student tuition: $27,250; 5-day tuition and room/board: $31,600. Tuition installment plan (Key Tuition Payment Plan). Need-based scholarship grants, need-based loans, prepGATE Loans available. In 2005–06, 18% of upper-school students received aid. Total amount of financial aid awarded in 2005–06: $1,775,700.

Admissions Traditional secondary-level entrance grade is 9. For fall 2005, 520 students applied for upper-level admission, 134 were accepted, 70 enrolled. ISEE or SSAT required. Deadline for receipt of application materials: February 1. Application fee required: $50. On-campus interview required.

Athletics Interscholastic: baseball (boys), basketball (b,g), crew (b,g), cross-country running (b,g), field hockey (g), football (b), golf (b,g), ice hockey (b,g), lacrosse (b,g), skiing (downhill) (b,g), soccer (b,g), softball (g), squash (b,g), tennis (b,g); coed intramural: aerobics/dance, dance, outdoor adventure, strength & conditioning, tennis. 11 coaches, 2 trainers.

Computers Computers are regularly used in English, foreign language, history, journalism, Latin, mathematics, music, science classes. Computer network features include campus e-mail, on-campus library services, CD-ROMs, online commercial services, Internet access, file transfer, NoblesNet (first class e-mail and bulletin board with electronic conferencing capability), Wireless iBooks.

Contact Ms. Jennifer Hines, Director of Admission. 781-326-3700. Fax: 781-320-1329. E-mail: admission@nobles.edu. Web site: www.nobles.edu.

ANNOUNCEMENT FROM THE SCHOOL Located in Dedham, Massachusetts, Noble and Greenough School is a coeducational day and 5-day boarding school of 530 students in grades 7–12. The School believes that education at its best is relational, and the bonds that develop between students and faculty members are strong and lifelong. Every day is started with an all-school assembly, generating a sense of community that permeates the School and carries through the day. The School's core principles are "honesty" and "respect for self and others." The academic curriculum, coupled with a required afternoon program, not only keeps students engaged throughout the entire day, but also challenges them to stretch beyond their comfort zones and tackle new experiences. Many students participate in programs away from the campus, including School Year Abroad and City Term. In addition, the programs in arts, athletics, and community service have all received national recognition. The campus facilities are peerless. The School's mission statement reads: "Noble and Greenough School is a rigorous academic community that strives for excellence in its classroom teaching, intellectual growth in its students, and commitment to the arts, athletics, and service to others. Our diverse community draws together the range of experience from people of different backgrounds and promotes the principles of respect for self and for others in all its activities. Further, the School encourages students to develop within themselves qualities of curiosity, integrity, civility, and humor. Nobles believes in the educational benefit of a supportive environment. The caring relationships between faculty and students develop

confidence within young people and encourage them to work toward their highest potential."

THE NORA SCHOOL

955 Sligo Avenue
Silver Spring, Maryland 20910
Head of School: Mr. David E. Mullen

General Information Coeducational day college-preparatory, arts, and technology school. Grades 9–12. Founded: 1964. Setting: urban. Nearest major city is Washington, DC. 1-acre campus. 1 building on campus. Approved or accredited by Association of Independent Schools of Greater Washington, Middle States Association of Colleges and Schools, and Maryland Department of Education. Endowment: $190,000. Total enrollment: 60. Upper school average class size: 9. Upper school faculty-student ratio: 1:5.

Upper School Student Profile Grade 9: 15 students (8 boys, 7 girls); Grade 10: 15 students (6 boys, 9 girls); Grade 11: 15 students (8 boys, 7 girls); Grade 12: 15 students (7 boys, 8 girls).

Faculty School total: 16. In upper school: 8 men, 8 women; 13 have advanced degrees.

Subjects Offered Algebra, American history, American literature, art, biology, calculus, ceramics, chemistry, community service, computer education, computer graphics, computer science, crafts, creative writing, ecology, English, English literature, environmental science, ethics, expository writing, fine arts, French, geography, geometry, government/civics, grammar, history, history of ideas, leadership training, life skills, literature, mathematics, music, peer counseling, personal development, philosophy, photo shop, photography, physical education, physics, psychology, religion, science, social studies, Spanish, theater, trigonometry, wilderness education, women's studies, world history, world literature, writing.

Graduation Requirements Arts and fine arts (art, music, dance, drama), English, foreign language, mathematics, personal fitness, science, social studies (includes history), wilderness education, graduation portfolio. Community service is required.

Special Academic Programs Independent study; term-away projects; study at local college for college credit; academic accommodation for the gifted and the artistically talented; remedial reading and/or remedial writing; remedial math; programs in English, mathematics, general development for dyslexic students; special instructional classes for students with Attention Deficit Disorder and learning disabilities, students who have been unsuccessful in a traditional learning environment.

College Placement 15 students graduated in 2005; all went to college, including Guilford College; Hobart and William Smith Colleges; Hofstra University; Maryland College of Art and Design; Oberlin College. Median SAT verbal: 610, median SAT math: 600.

Student Life Upper grades have student council. Discipline rests primarily with faculty.

Summer Programs Remediation, enrichment, advancement, art/fine arts programs offered; held on campus; accepts boys and girls; open to students from other schools. 10 students usually enrolled. 2006 schedule: June 18 to July 21. Application deadline: April 10.

Tuition and Aid Day student tuition: $17,750. Tuition installment plan (Key Tuition Payment Plan, monthly payment plans, individually arranged payment plans). Need-based scholarship grants, Black student fund, Latino student fund, Washington Scholarship fund available. In 2005–06, 16% of upper-school students received aid. Total amount of financial aid awarded in 2005–06: $106,000.

Admissions Traditional secondary-level entrance grade is 9. For fall 2005, 122 students applied for upper-level admission, 21 were accepted, 17 enrolled. Deadline for receipt of application materials: none. Application fee required: $50. On-campus interview required.

Athletics Interscholastic: basketball (boys, girls); intramural: cheering (g); coed interscholastic: soccer, softball, volleyball; coed intramural: alpine skiing, back packing, bicycling, bowling, canoeing/kayaking, climbing, cooperative games, cross-country running, dance squad, flag football, freestyle skiing, golf, hiking/backpacking, ice skating, kayaking, outdoor activities, outdoor adventure, rafting, rock climbing, ropes courses, skiing (downhill), table tennis, tennis, touch football, triathlon, volleyball, weight lifting, wilderness. 3 coaches.

Computers Computers are regularly used in business applications, college planning, data processing, design, drawing and design, English, foreign language, graphic design, history, independent study, library skills, mathematics, SAT preparation, writing, yearbook classes. Computer network features include campus e-mail, on-campus library services, CD-ROMs, online commercial services, Internet access, file transfer, office computer access, DVD, wireless campus network.

Contact Elaine Mack, Director of Admissions. 301-495-6672. Fax: 301-495-7829. E-mail: elaine@nora-school.org. Web site: www.nora-school.org.

NORFOLK ACADEMY

1585 Wesleyan Drive
Norfolk, Virginia 23502
Head of School: Mr. Dennis G. Manning

petersons.com

General Information Coeducational day college-preparatory school. Grades 1–12. Founded: 1728. Setting: suburban. 63-acre campus. 14 buildings on campus. Approved or accredited by Southern Association of Colleges and Schools, Virginia Association of Independent Schools, and Virginia Department of Education. Member of National Association of Independent Schools. Endowment: $33 million. Total enrollment: 1,210. Upper school average class size: 20. Upper school faculty-student ratio: 1:10.

Upper School Student Profile Grade 10: 117 students (59 boys, 58 girls); Grade 11: 117 students (60 boys, 57 girls); Grade 12: 107 students (53 boys, 54 girls).

Faculty School total: 125. In upper school: 26 men, 18 women; 39 have advanced degrees.

Subjects Offered Advanced Placement courses, algebra, American history, American literature, art, art history, band, biology, calculus, chemistry, chorus, computer math, computer programming, computer science, dance, dramatic arts, driver education, economics, English, English literature, environmental science, European history, film studies, fine arts, French, geography, geometry, German, government/civics, health, history, instrumental music, Italian, Latin, mathematics, music, music history, music theory, physical education, physics, science, science project, social studies, Spanish, speech, statistics, studio art, theater arts, world history.

Graduation Requirements Arts and fine arts (art, music, dance, drama), computer science, English, foreign language, mathematics, physical education (includes health), science, social studies (includes history), 8-minute senior speech, Seminar Program. Community service is required.

Special Academic Programs Advanced Placement exam preparation in 17 subject areas; study abroad; academic accommodation for the gifted, the musically talented, and the artistically talented.

College Placement 107 students graduated in 2005; all went to college, including Hampden-Sydney College; James Madison University; The College of William and Mary; University of Virginia; Virginia Polytechnic Institute and State University. Mean SAT verbal: 636, mean SAT math: 642.

Student Life Upper grades have specified standards of dress, student council, honor system. Discipline rests primarily with faculty.

Summer Programs Enrichment, advancement, sports, art/fine arts programs offered; session focuses on academics and athletics; held on campus; accepts boys and girls; open to students from other schools. 500 students usually enrolled. 2006 schedule: June 19 to July 27.

Tuition and Aid Day student tuition: $13,700. Tuition installment plan (Key Tuition Payment Plan, monthly payment plans). Need-based scholarship grants, need-based loans available. In 2005–06, 15% of upper-school students received aid.

Admissions Traditional secondary-level entrance grade is 10. For fall 2005, 18 students applied for upper-level admission, 4 were accepted, 3 enrolled. ERB, ERB CTP III, Otis-Lennon School Ability Test and Stanford Test of Academic Skills required. Deadline for receipt of application materials: February 10. Application fee required: $35. On-campus interview required.

Athletics Interscholastic: baseball (boys), basketball (b,g), cheering (g), crew (b,g), cross-country running (b,g), diving (b,g), field hockey (g), football (b), golf (b,g), indoor track (b,g), lacrosse (b,g), sailing (b,g), soccer (b,g), softball (g), swimming and diving (b,g), tennis (b,g), volleyball (g), winter (indoor) track (b,g), wrestling (b); intramural: ballet (g), dance (g), dance team (g), modern dance (g), physical fitness (b,g), physical training (b,g), weight training (b,g). 2 PE instructors, 2 coaches, 2 trainers.

Computers Computers are regularly used in all academic classes. Computer network features include campus e-mail, on-campus library services, CD-ROMs, online commercial services, Internet access, DVD, online library resources, video production, curriculum-based software, desktop publishing, campus-wide media distribution system.

Contact Mrs. Linda Gorsline, Director of Upper School. 757-461-6236 Ext. 5362. Fax: 757-455-3186. E-mail: lgorsline@norfolkacademy.org. Web site: www.norfolkacademy.org.

ANNOUNCEMENT FROM THE SCHOOL Founded in 1728, Norfolk Academy is a coeducational, college-preparatory day school enrolling 1,200 students in grades 1–12. Committed to excellence in the classroom, on the athletic fields, in the arts, and in service to others, all members of the Norfolk Academy community are bound together by an honor code. Located on 63 acres in the heart of Hampton Roads, the campus now includes the new 50,000-square-foot Tucker Arts Center and the new Athletic Pavilion, in addition to 8 other school buildings, a 375-seat auditorium, 2 libraries, 2 gymnasiums, an aquatic center, 14 playing fields, 8 tennis courts, a football stadium, and a 400-meter track. The Lower School curriculum consists of language arts, mathematics, science, social studies, music, art, physical education, computers, library, Spanish, guidance and health, and problem-solving and thinking skills. The Middle and Upper Schools offer American and British literature; history; mathematics through Calculus BC; 4 years of French, German, and Spanish; 6 years of Latin; 3 years of Italian; science through advanced biology, chemistry,

and physics; public speaking; and a seminar program. A campuswide computer network includes 450 workstations and 7 computer labs. Internet access is available from each network computer. A campuswide media distribution system is available in all classrooms. Exchange programs to France, Germany, Spain, and South Africa are offered. There are 72 athletic teams and nearly 40 clubs. The faculty numbers 125: 80 women and 45 men; 101 hold advanced degrees. The combined SAT median of the class of 2005: 1311 (653 verbal, 658 math). Graduates (118 in 2005) entered such colleges and universities as Duke, Harvard, Stanford, Yale, William & Mary, and the Universities of Virginia and North Carolina.

NORFOLK COLLEGIATE SCHOOL

7336 Granby Street
Norfolk, Virginia 23505
Head of School: William W. King

General Information Coeducational day college-preparatory school. Grades K–12. Founded: 1948. Setting: urban. 10-acre campus. 1 building on campus. Approved or accredited by Southern Association of Colleges and Schools, Virginia Association of Independent Schools, and Virginia Department of Education. Member of National Association of Independent Schools. Total enrollment: 875. Upper school average class size: 18. Upper school faculty-student ratio: 1:10.

Upper School Student Profile Grade 9: 99 students (47 boys, 52 girls); Grade 10: 79 students (35 boys, 44 girls); Grade 11: 74 students (37 boys, 37 girls); Grade 12: 72 students (37 boys, 35 girls).

Faculty School total: 83. In upper school: 12 men, 27 women; 24 have advanced degrees.

Subjects Offered Algebra, American history, American literature, analysis, ancient world history, art, astronomy, band, bioethics, bioethics, DNA and culture, biology, biology-AP, calculus-AP, chemistry, chemistry-AP, chorus, computer science, concert band, creative writing, cultural geography, drawing, driver education, English, English literature, English literature-AP, environmental science-AP, European history-AP, expository writing, family life, film studies, first aid, French, French-AP, geology, geometry, German, global issues, government-AP, government/civics, graphic arts, history, independent study, jazz band, journalism, Latin, Latin American history, Latin-AP, marine biology, mathematics, music, oceanography, painting, physical education, physics, political science, pottery, pre-calculus, psychology-AP, publications, SAT preparation, science, social studies, Spanish, Spanish-AP, statistics-AP, trigonometry, U.S. and Virginia government-AP, U.S. government-AP, U.S. history-AP, video communication, video film production, world geography, world history-AP, yearbook.

Graduation Requirements Algebra, arts and fine arts (art, music, dance, drama), biology, chemistry, computer literacy, English, foreign language, geometry, health education, mathematics, physical education (includes health), science, senior project, social studies (includes history), U.S. and Virginia government, U.S. and Virginia history, Western civilization.

Special Academic Programs Advanced Placement exam preparation in 18 subject areas; honors section; independent study; academic accommodation for the gifted; remedial reading and/or remedial writing; remedial math; programs in English, mathematics, general development for dyslexic students.

College Placement 68 students graduated in 2005; all went to college, including Hampden-Sydney College; James Madison University; Old Dominion University; The College of William and Mary; The University of North Carolina Wilmington; University of Virginia. 45% scored over 600 on SAT verbal, 49% scored over 600 on SAT math, 45% scored over 1800 on combined SAT.

Student Life Upper grades have specified standards of dress, student council, honor system. Discipline rests primarily with faculty.

Summer Programs Remediation, enrichment, sports, art/fine arts, computer instruction programs offered; session focuses on academic review and enrichment; held on campus; accepts boys and girls; open to students from other schools. 30 students usually enrolled. 2006 schedule: June 19 to August 4. Application deadline: none.

Tuition and Aid Day student tuition: $10,800. Tuition installment plan (monthly payment plans, individually arranged payment plans, semi-annual payment plan, The Tuition Refund Plan). Merit scholarship grants, need-based scholarship grants available. In 2005–06, 37% of upper-school students received aid; total upper-school merit-scholarship money awarded: $10,725. Total amount of financial aid awarded in 2005–06: $400,072.

Admissions Traditional secondary-level entrance grade is 9. For fall 2005, 71 students applied for upper-level admission, 53 were accepted, 40 enrolled. ERB CTP (level F), ERB Reading and Math, essay and Otis-Lennon School Ability Test required. Deadline for receipt of application materials: February 11. Application fee required: $35. On-campus interview required.

Athletics Interscholastic: baseball (boys), basketball (b,g), cross-country running (b,g), field hockey (g), lacrosse (b,g), soccer (b,g), softball (g), swimming and diving (b,g), tennis (b,g), volleyball (b,g), wrestling (b); coed interscholastic: cheering, crew, golf, sailing. 3 PE instructors, 42 coaches, 1 trainer.

Computers Computers are regularly used in art, college planning, current events, desktop publishing, drawing and design, English, foreign language, health, humanities, independent study, journalism, keyboarding, library skills, literary magazine,

mathematics, music, newspaper, publications, publishing, research skills, SAT preparation, science, senior seminar, social science, stock market, video film production, Web site design, word processing, yearbook classes. Computer network features include on-campus library services, CD-ROMs, online commercial services, Internet access, ProQuest, Author's Service, InfoTrac.

Contact Brenda H. Waters, Director of Admissions. 757-480-1495. Fax: 757-588-8655. E-mail: bwaters@norfolkcollegiate.org. Web site: www.norfolkcollegiate.org.

THE NORTH BROWARD PREPARATORY UPPER SCHOOL

7600 Lyons Road
Coconut Creek, Florida 33073
Head of School: Dr. Michael Rossi

General Information Coeducational boarding and day college-preparatory school. Boarding grades 8–12, day grades PK–12. Founded: 1957. Setting: suburban. Nearest major city is Boca Raton. Students are housed in single-sex dormitories. 75-acre campus. 10 buildings on campus. Approved or accredited by Florida Council of Independent Schools and Southern Association of Colleges and Schools. Total enrollment: 1,900. Upper school average class size: 18. Upper school faculty-student ratio: 1:18.

Upper School Student Profile 1% of students are boarding students. 98% are state residents. 4 states are represented in upper school student body. 2% are international students. International students from Canada, Germany, and United Kingdom; 4 other countries represented in student body.

Faculty School total: 200. In upper school: 33 men, 86 women; 45 have advanced degrees; 3 reside on campus.

Subjects Offered Algebra, American history-AP, analysis and differential calculus, analytic geometry, ancient world history, art, art history, audio visual/media, Basic programming, biology, biology-AP, British literature, broadcast journalism, business, calculus, calculus-AP, chemistry, chemistry-AP, choir, choral music, college counseling, computer applications, computer graphics, computer keyboarding, computer programming, computer programming-AP, computers, concert band, concert choir, contemporary women writers, drama workshop, dramatic arts, ecology, environmental systems, economics, English, English composition, English literature, English literature and composition-AP, environmental science, environmental science-AP, European history, European history-AP, French, French language-AP, French literature-AP, geometry, German, Greek, guitar, honors algebra, honors English, honors geometry, honors U.S. history, honors world history, jazz band, jazz dance, jazz ensemble, model United Nations, modern European history, modern European history-AP, music, music appreciation, performing arts, physical education, physical fitness, physics-AP, psychology-AP, robotics, SAT preparation, Shakespeare, skills for success, sociology, Spanish, Spanish language-AP, Spanish literature, Spanish literature-AP, U.S. government, U.S. government-AP, U.S. history, U.S. literature, wind ensemble, wind instruments, women in literature, women's literature, world history-AP.

Graduation Requirements Algebra, American history, American literature, biology, calculus, chemistry, computer applications, electives, English, European history, foreign language, geometry, performing arts, physical education (includes health), physics, U.S. government, U.S. literature, world cultures. Community service is required.

Special Academic Programs Advanced Placement exam preparation in 14 subject areas; honors section; study at local college for college credit; academic accommodation for the gifted, the musically talented, and the artistically talented; remedial reading and/or remedial writing; remedial math; programs in English, mathematics for dyslexic students.

College Placement 140 students graduated in 2005; all went to college, including Boston University; Florida State University; Northwestern University; Tufts University; University of Florida; University of Miami. Median SAT verbal: 570, median SAT math: 590. 25% scored over 600 on SAT verbal, 25% scored over 600 on SAT math.

Student Life Upper grades have uniform requirement, student council, honor system. Discipline rests equally with students and faculty.

Summer Programs Remediation, enrichment, advancement, art/fine arts, computer instruction programs offered; session focuses on enrichment; held on campus; accepts boys and girls; open to students from other schools. 100 students usually enrolled. 2006 schedule: June 19 to August 11.

Tuition and Aid Day student tuition: $13,000–$20,000; 7-day tuition and room/board: $22,000–$29,000. Tuition installment plan (monthly payment plans). Tuition reduction for siblings, merit scholarship grants, need-based scholarship grants available. In 2005–06, 15% of upper-school students received aid; total upper-school merit-scholarship money awarded: $250,000. Total amount of financial aid awarded in 2005–06: $805,000.

Admissions Traditional secondary-level entrance grade is 9. For fall 2005, 300 students applied for upper-level admission, 250 were accepted, 200 enrolled. SSAT required. Deadline for receipt of application materials: none. Application fee required: $100. Interview required.

Athletics Interscholastic: aquatics (boys, girls), baseball (b,g), basketball (b,g), cheering (g), cross-country running (b,g), dance (g), dance squad (g), dance team (g),

flag football (b,g), football (b), golf (b,g), ice hockey (b), lacrosse (b,g), physical fitness (b,g), soccer (b,g), softball (g), tennis (b,g), track and field (b,g), volleyball (g), water polo (b,g), wrestling (b); coed interscholastic: aquatics, bowling, crew, cross-country running, dressage, golf, scuba diving, swimming and diving; coed intramural: basketball. 5 PE instructors, 17 coaches, 1 trainer.

Computers Computers are regularly used in all academic classes. Computer network features include campus e-mail, on-campus library services, CD-ROMs, online commercial services, Internet access, DVD, wireless campus network.

Contact Mrs. Jackie Fagan, Director of Admissions. 954-247-0011 Ext. 303. Fax: 954-247-0012. E-mail: faganj@nbps.org. Web site: www.nbps.org.

NORTH COBB CHRISTIAN SCHOOL

4500 Lakeview Drive
Kennesaw, Georgia 30144
Head of School: Dr. Gary Coker

General Information Coeducational day college-preparatory, arts, and vocational school, affiliated with Christian faith. Grades PK–12. Founded: 1983. Setting: suburban. Nearest major city is Atlanta. 16-acre campus. 3 buildings on campus. Approved or accredited by Association of Christian Schools International, Georgia Accrediting Commission, Southern Association of Colleges and Schools, and Georgia Department of Education. Endowment: $102,225. Total enrollment: 880. Upper school average class size: 20. Upper school faculty-student ratio: 1:9.

Upper School Student Profile Grade 9: 64 students (30 boys, 34 girls); Grade 10: 69 students (23 boys, 46 girls); Grade 11: 59 students (33 boys, 26 girls); Grade 12: 50 students (27 boys, 23 girls). 95% of students are Christian.

Faculty School total: 77. In upper school: 20 men, 22 women; 15 have advanced degrees.

Subjects Offered Acting, Advanced Placement courses, algebra, American government-AP, American literature, analysis, Bible, biology, British literature, calculus, calculus-AP, chemistry, choral music, composition, computer graphics, computer keyboarding, computers, dance, desktop publishing, ecology, economics, electives, English literature-AP, fine arts, French, geometry, government, health, leadership skills, literature, math analysis, physical education, physical science, physics, psychology, Spanish, Spanish-AP, statistics, trigonometry, world history, world literature.

Graduation Requirements Arts and fine arts (art, music, dance, drama), Bible, computers, electives, English, foreign language, mathematics, physical education (includes health), science, social studies (includes history), leadership practicum.

Special Academic Programs Honors section; study at local college for college credit; academic accommodation for the musically talented and the artistically talented; programs in general development for dyslexic students; special instructional classes for deaf students.

College Placement 55 students graduated in 2005; 47 went to college, including Colorado Christian University; Georgia College & State University; Georgia State University; Kennesaw State University; Savannah College of Art and Design; University of Georgia. Mean SAT verbal: 575, mean SAT math: 535, mean composite ACT: 25.

Student Life Upper grades have uniform requirement, student council, honor system. Discipline rests equally with students and faculty. Attendance at religious services is required.

Summer Programs Remediation, enrichment, sports, art/fine arts, computer instruction programs offered; session focuses on advancing skills and pleasure; held both on and off campus; held at other college campus for sports purposes; accepts boys and girls; open to students from other schools. 450 students usually enrolled. 2006 schedule: June 5 to July 28. Application deadline: May 8.

Tuition and Aid Day student tuition: $7645–$8025. Tuition installment plan (monthly payment plans). Tuition reduction for siblings, need-based scholarship grants available. In 2005–06, 10% of upper-school students received aid. Total amount of financial aid awarded in 2005–06: $100,025.

Admissions Traditional secondary-level entrance grade is 9. For fall 2005, 40 students applied for upper-level admission, 33 were accepted, 33 enrolled. Otis-Lennon, Stanford Achievement Test required. Deadline for receipt of application materials: none. Application fee required: $75. Interview required.

Athletics Interscholastic: aerobics (boys, girls), aerobics/dance (g), baseball (b), basketball (b,g), cheering (g), cross-country running (b,g), dance (g), physical fitness (b,g), soccer (b,g), softball (g), tennis (b,g), track and field (b,g), volleyball (g); coed interscholastic: aquatics, archery, golf, strength & conditioning, swimming and diving, weight training. 4 PE instructors, 4 coaches, 2 trainers.

Computers Computers are regularly used in art, basic skills, desktop publishing, drawing and design, graphic arts, graphic design, keyboarding, library skills, media production, video film production, word processing, yearbook classes. Computer network features include on-campus library services, CD-ROMs, Internet access, DVD, wireless campus network.

Contact Mrs. Kristin Cook, Admissions Assistant. 770-975-0252 Ext. 501. Fax: 770-975-9051. E-mail: kcook@ncchristian.org. Web site: www.ncchristian.org.

NORTH COUNTRY SCHOOL

Lake Placid, New York
See Junior Boarding Schools section.

NORTHFIELD MOUNT HERMON SCHOOL

206 Main Street
Northfield, Massachusetts 01360-1089
Head of School: Thomas K. Sturtevant

General Information Coeducational boarding and day college-preparatory, arts, and technology school. Grades 9–PG. Founded: 1879. Setting: rural. Nearest major city is Hartford, CT. Students are housed in single-sex dormitories. 1,100-acre campus. 73 buildings on campus. Approved or accredited by Association of Independent Schools in New England, New England Association of Schools and Colleges, The Association of Boarding Schools, and Massachusetts Department of Education. Member of National Association of Independent Schools and Secondary School Admission Test Board. Endowment: $124 million. Total enrollment: 717. Upper school average class size: 13. Upper school faculty-student ratio: 1:7.

Upper School Student Profile Grade 9: 86 students (45 boys, 41 girls); Grade 10: 152 students (76 boys, 76 girls); Grade 11: 219 students (106 boys, 113 girls); Grade 12: 235 students (129 boys, 106 girls); Postgraduate: 25 students (20 boys, 5 girls). 77% of students are boarding students. 31% are state residents. 33 states are represented in upper school student body. 25% are international students. International students from Germany, Hong Kong, Japan, Republic of Korea, Taiwan, and Thailand; 30 other countries represented in student body.

Faculty School total: 145. In upper school: 72 men, 73 women; 96 have advanced degrees; 121 reside on campus.

Subjects Offered Algebra, American history, American literature, anthropology, archaeology, art, art history, astronomy, athletics, Bible studies, biology, botany, calculus, ceramics, chemistry, Chinese, computer programming, computer science, creative writing, dance, drama, driver education, earth science, economics, English, English literature, environmental science, ethics, European history, expository writing, fine arts, French, geography, geology, geometry, German, government/civics, Greek, health, history, journalism, Latin, logic, mathematics, music, philosophy, photography, physical education, physics, physiology, psychology, religion, Russian, SAT/ACT preparation, science, social science, social studies, Spanish, speech, statistics, theater, trigonometry, typing, world history, world literature, writing.

Graduation Requirements Arts and fine arts (art, music, dance, drama), English, foreign language, mathematics, physical education (includes health), religion (includes Bible studies and theology), science, social studies (includes history), participation in work program.

Special Academic Programs Advanced Placement exam preparation in 15 subject areas; honors section; accelerated programs; independent study; term-away projects; study at local college for college credit; study abroad; academic accommodation for the gifted, the musically talented, and the artistically talented; ESL (32 students enrolled).

College Placement 330 students graduated in 2005; 313 went to college, including Boston University; Smith College; The George Washington University; United States Naval Academy; University of Illinois at Urbana–Champaign; University of Vermont. Other: 17 had other specific plans. Mean SAT verbal: 597, mean SAT math: 618, mean composite ACT: 24.

Student Life Upper grades have student council, honor system. Discipline rests primarily with faculty.

Summer Programs Enrichment, advancement, ESL, art/fine arts, computer instruction programs offered; session focuses on academic enrichment; held on campus; accepts boys and girls; open to students from other schools. 300 students usually enrolled. 2006 schedule: July 1 to August 5. Application deadline: none.

Tuition and Aid Day student tuition: $25,600; 7-day tuition and room/board: $35,000. Tuition installment plan (Academic Management Services Plan, monthly payment plans). Need-based scholarship grants, need-based loans, middle-income loans, Achiever Loans, prepGATE Loan Plan, SLM Financial loans available. In 2005–06, 44% of upper-school students received aid. Total amount of financial aid awarded in 2005–06: $5,500,000.

Admissions Traditional secondary-level entrance grade is 9. For fall 2005, 1,047 students applied for upper-level admission, 477 were accepted, 206 enrolled. ACT, CTP, ISEE, PSAT, SAT, SSAT or TOEFL required. Deadline for receipt of application materials: February 1. Application fee required: $50. Interview recommended.

Athletics Interscholastic: alpine skiing (boys, girls), baseball (b), basketball (b,g), crew (b,g), cross-country running (b,g), field hockey (g), football (b), hockey (b,g), ice hockey (b,g), lacrosse (b,g), nordic skiing (b,g), rowing (b,g), skiing (cross-country) (b,g), skiing (downhill) (b,g), soccer (b,g), softball (g), swimming and diving (b,g), tennis (b,g), track and field (b,g), volleyball (b,g), water polo (b,g), wrestling (b); coed interscholastic: dance, dance team, Frisbee, golf, modern dance, ultimate Frisbee; coed intramural: aerobics, aerobics/dance, alpine skiing, aquatics, badminton, ballet, basketball, bicycling, canoeing/kayaking, climbing, crew, cross-country running, dance, dance team, fencing, fitness, golf, jogging, lacrosse, martial arts, modern dance, mountain biking, nautilus, outdoor activities, outdoor education, outdoor skills, outdoors, physical fitness, physical training, rock climbing, roller blading, rowing,

running, sailing, scuba diving, skiing (downhill), snowboarding, soccer, strength & conditioning, swimming and diving, tennis, ultimate Frisbee, volleyball, weight lifting, weight training, yoga. 8 PE instructors, 42 coaches, 2 trainers.

Computers Computers are regularly used in desktop publishing, English, foreign language, mathematics, music, science classes. Computer network features include campus e-mail, on-campus library services, CD-ROMs, online commercial services, Internet access, file transfer, DVD, wireless campus network.

Contact Office of Admission. 413-498-3227. Fax: 413-498-3152. E-mail: admission@nmhschool.org. Web site: www.nmhschool.org.

ANNOUNCEMENT FROM THE SCHOOL The NMH academic program blends traditional values with the latest innovations in education. NMH provides focus (students take 2 or 3 major courses per term), individual attention (Moody system of advising, college counseling), opportunity (250 courses, 60 sports teams, more than 35 student groups, 11 study-abroad options), and values (work, service, spirituality programs).

See full description on page 940.

THE NORTH SHORE COUNTRY DAY SCHOOL

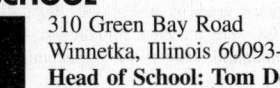

310 Green Bay Road
Winnetka, Illinois 60093-4094
Head of School: Tom Doar III

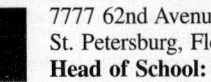 petersons.com

General Information Coeducational day college-preparatory, arts, and technology school. Grades PK–12. Founded: 1919. Setting: suburban. Nearest major city is Chicago. 16-acre campus. 6 buildings on campus. Approved or accredited by Independent Schools Association of the Central States and Illinois Department of Education. Member of National Association of Independent Schools and Secondary School Admission Test Board. Endowment: $17.5 million. Total enrollment: 454. Upper school average class size: 13. Upper school faculty-student ratio: 1:7.

Upper School Student Profile Grade 9: 43 students (28 boys, 15 girls); Grade 10: 39 students (19 boys, 20 girls); Grade 11: 45 students (20 boys, 25 girls); Grade 12: 44 students (24 boys, 20 girls).

Faculty School total: 76. In upper school: 15 men, 19 women; 26 have advanced degrees.

Subjects Offered Algebra, American history, American literature, anatomy, art, art history, Asian studies, biology, biology-AP, calculus, calculus-AP, ceramics, chemistry, chemistry-AP, computer math, computer programming, computer science, creative writing, drama, earth science, ecology, economics, English, English literature, English-AP, environmental science, European history, expository writing, fine arts, French, French-AP, geography, geometry, government/civics, grammar, industrial arts, journalism, Mandarin, marine biology, mathematics, music, photography, physical education, physics, physics-AP, science, social studies, Spanish, Spanish-AP, speech, statistics, statistics-AP, technology, theater, trigonometry, U.S. history-AP, world history, world literature, writing.

Graduation Requirements Arts and fine arts (art, music, dance, drama), computer science, English, foreign language, mathematics, physical education (includes health), physical fitness, science, social studies (includes history), technology, one stage performance in four years, completion of senior service project in May, completion of one-week community service project in four years.

Special Academic Programs Advanced Placement exam preparation in 10 subject areas; independent study; study at local college for college credit; study abroad; academic accommodation for the musically talented.

College Placement 45 students graduated in 2004; all went to college, including University of Michigan; University of Minnesota, Twin Cities Campus; University of Notre Dame; Washington University in St. Louis; Williams College. Median SAT verbal: 600, median SAT math: 600, median composite ACT: 28.

Student Life Upper grades have student council, honor system. Discipline rests primarily with faculty.

Tuition and Aid Day student tuition: $15,100–$16,100. Tuition installment plan (Insured Tuition Payment Plan, Key Tuition Payment Plan, monthly payment plans, individually arranged payment plans, trimester payment plan). Merit scholarship grants, need-based scholarship grants, need-based loans, middle-income loans available. In 2004–05, 28% of upper-school students received aid. Total amount of financial aid awarded in 2004–05: $600,000.

Admissions Traditional secondary-level entrance grade is 9. Deadline for receipt of application materials: none. Application fee required: $50. On-campus interview required.

Athletics Interscholastic: baseball (boys), basketball (b,g), cross-country running (b,g), field hockey (g), football (b), golf (b,g), indoor track & field (b,g), physical training (b,g), soccer (b,g), tennis (b,g), track and field (b,g), volleyball (g), yoga (b,g); intramural: weight lifting (b,g). 24 PE instructors, 24 coaches, 1 trainer.

Computers Computers are regularly used in all academic classes. Computer network features include campus e-mail, on-campus library services, CD-ROMs, online commercial services, Internet access, office computer access.

Contact Ms. Julie Schmidt, Admissions Associate. 847-441-3313. Fax: 847-446-0675. E-mail: juschmidt@nscds.org. Web site: www.nscds.org.

ANNOUNCEMENT FROM THE SCHOOL Committed to the academic, personal, and social development of its students, North Shore Country Day School offers a rigorous college-preparatory curriculum that includes Advanced Placement courses and strong arts and music programs. North Shore also requires participation in extracurricular activities. The School has developed unique programs in languages, global consciousness, humanities, math, science and technology. Call Admissions at 847-881-8517 or visit www.about.nscds.org.

NORTHSIDE CHRISTIAN SCHOOL

7777 62nd Avenue, North
St. Petersburg, Florida 33709
Head of School: Mrs. Mary Brandes

General Information Coeducational day college-preparatory, arts, religious studies, and technology school, affiliated with Baptist Church. Grades PS–12. Founded: 1971. Setting: urban. 32-acre campus. 3 buildings on campus. Approved or accredited by Association of Christian Schools International, Southern Association of Colleges and Schools, and Florida Department of Education. Endowment: $50,000. Total enrollment: 877. Upper school average class size: 20. Upper school faculty-student ratio: 1:11.

Upper School Student Profile 27% of students are Baptist.

Faculty School total: 65. In upper school: 10 men, 15 women; 10 have advanced degrees.

Subjects Offered 3-dimensional art, Advanced Placement courses, algebra, American government, American history, American history-AP, anatomy and physiology, band, Bible studies, biology, business mathematics, calculus-AP, chamber groups, chemistry, chemistry-AP, chorus, Christian education, communication skills, computer applications, computer information systems, computer keyboarding, computer multimedia, computers, drama, economics, economics and history, English, English literature and composition-AP, English-AP, eurythmics (guard), fine arts, fitness, foreign language, French, general science, geometry, health, health education, jazz band, journalism, keyboarding, language arts, marine biology, marine science, mathematics, mathematics-AP, music, music appreciation, music theory, physical education, physical science, physics, pre-algebra, pre-calculus, psychology, Spanish, Spanish literature, speech, sports, study skills, track and field, U.S. history, volleyball, weight fitness, weight training, world history, world religions, yearbook.

Graduation Requirements Arts and fine arts (art, music, dance, drama), business skills (includes word processing), computer science, English, foreign language, mathematics, physical education (includes health), religion (includes Bible studies and theology), science, social science, social studies (includes history), SAT and ACT testing. Community service is required.

Special Academic Programs Advanced Placement exam preparation in 5 subject areas; honors section; independent study; academic accommodation for the gifted; programs in English, mathematics, general development for dyslexic students.

College Placement 45 students graduated in 2005; all went to college, including Florida State University; St. Petersburg College; University of Central Florida; University of Florida; University of North Florida; University of South Florida. Mean SAT verbal: 538, mean SAT math: 529, mean composite ACT: 23. 25% scored over 600 on SAT verbal, 25% scored over 600 on SAT math.

Student Life Upper grades have specified standards of dress, student council, honor system. Discipline rests primarily with faculty. Attendance at religious services is required.

Summer Programs Enrichment, sports, art/fine arts, computer instruction programs offered; session focuses on enrichment; held on campus; accepts boys and girls; open to students from other schools. 70 students usually enrolled. 2006 schedule: June 1 to August 1. Application deadline: May 31.

Tuition and Aid Day student tuition: $6433. Tuition installment plan (monthly payment plans). Need-based scholarship grants available. In 2005–06, 10% of upper-school students received aid. Total amount of financial aid awarded in 2005–06: $20,000.

Admissions Traditional secondary-level entrance grade is 9. For fall 2005, 25 students applied for upper-level admission, 22 were accepted, 20 enrolled. PSAT or Stanford Achievement Test required. Deadline for receipt of application materials: none. Application fee required: $75. Interview required.

Athletics Interscholastic: baseball (boys), basketball (b,g), cheering (g), cross-country running (b,g), football (b), golf (b), soccer (g), softball (g), swimming and diving (b,g), track and field (b,g), volleyball (g), weight lifting (b), wrestling (b); intramural: basketball (b,g), fitness (b,g), flag football (b); coed interscholastic: cross-country running, track and field. 4 PE instructors, 4 coaches, 1 trainer.

Computers Computers are regularly used in business, desktop publishing, ESL, library, mathematics, newspaper, science, typing, word processing, yearbook classes. Computer network features include campus e-mail, on-campus library services, CD-ROMs, Internet access, file transfer, office computer access.

Contact Mrs. Joni McAlpin, Admissions /Registrar. 727-541-7593 Ext. 251. Fax: 727-546-5836. E-mail: joni.mcalpin@nck12.com. Web site: www.nck12.com.

NORTHWEST COMMUNITY CHRISTIAN SCHOOL

16401 North 43rd Avenue
Phoenix, Arizona 85053
Head of School: Mr. Bill Harbeck

General Information Coeducational day college-preparatory, general academic, arts, religious studies, and technology school, affiliated with Christian faith. Grades PK–12. Founded: 1982. Setting: urban. 20-acre campus. 6 buildings on campus. Approved or accredited by Association of Christian Schools International, North Central Association of Colleges and Schools, and Arizona Department of Education. Total enrollment: 1,350. Upper school average class size: 23. Upper school faculty-student ratio: 1:14.

Upper School Student Profile Grade 9: 124 students (58 boys, 66 girls); Grade 10: 115 students (55 boys, 60 girls); Grade 11: 66 students (27 boys, 39 girls); Grade 12: 82 students (44 boys, 38 girls). 100% of students are Christian faith.

Faculty School total: 74. In upper school: 14 men, 20 women; 9 have advanced degrees.

Subjects Offered American Civil War, American government, American history, anatomy and physiology, ancient history, art, arts, aviation, band, Bible, biology, British literature, British literature-AP, business applications, business law, calculus, career education, careers, ceramics, chemistry, choir, Christian and Hebrew scripture, Christian doctrine, Christian testament, church history, civil war history, computer education, computer keyboarding, computer multimedia, computer programming, drawing and design, driver education, economics, English literature-AP, English-AP, geometry, government, health, Hebrew, music, physics, science, Spanish, speech, U.S. history, yearbook.

Graduation Requirements Bible, English, mathematics, physical education (includes health), science, social studies (includes history). Community service is required.

Special Academic Programs Advanced Placement exam preparation in 1 subject area; honors section; special instructional classes for students with learning disabilities.

College Placement 73 students graduated in 2005; 71 went to college, including Arizona State University; Biola University; Grand Canyon University; Northern Arizona University; Point Loma Nazarene University; The University of Arizona. Other: 1 went to work, 1 entered military service.

Student Life Upper grades have specified standards of dress, student council, honor system. Discipline rests primarily with faculty.

Admissions Traditional secondary-level entrance grade is 9. For fall 2005, 409 students applied for upper-level admission, 398 were accepted. Scholastic Achievement Test required. Deadline for receipt of application materials: July 31. No application fee required. Interview required.

Athletics Interscholastic: baseball (boys), basketball (b,g), cheering (g). 2 PE instructors.

Computers Computer resources include on-campus library services, CD-ROMs, Internet access.

Contact Mrs. Deb Beckman, Admissions Officer. 602-978-5134. Fax: 602-978-5804. E-mail: dbeckman@nwccschool.org. Web site: www.nwccschool.org.

THE NORTHWEST SCHOOL

1415 Summit Avenue
Seattle, Washington 98122
Head of School: Ellen Taussig

General Information Coeducational boarding and day college-preparatory, arts, and ESL school. Boarding grades 9–12, day grades 6–12. Founded: 1978. Setting: urban. Students are housed in coed dormitories. 1-acre campus. 4 buildings on campus. Approved or accredited by Northwest Association of Schools and Colleges, Pacific Northwest Association of Independent Schools, and Washington Department of Education. Member of National Association of Independent Schools. Endowment: $243,249. Total enrollment: 446. Upper school average class size: 16. Upper school faculty-student ratio: 1:9.

Upper School Student Profile Grade 9: 71 students (38 boys, 33 girls); Grade 10: 74 students (36 boys, 38 girls); Grade 11: 88 students (41 boys, 47 girls); Grade 12: 84 students (45 boys, 39 girls). 14% of students are boarding students. 80% are state residents. 1 state is represented in upper school student body. 20% are international students. International students from Hong Kong, Japan, Republic of Korea, Taiwan, Thailand, and Viet Nam; 3 other countries represented in student body.

Faculty School total: 69. In upper school: 26 men, 31 women; 42 have advanced degrees.

Subjects Offered Advanced chemistry, algebra, astronomy, biology, calculus, cartooning, ceramics, chemistry, chorus, computer skills, dance, drama, drawing, driver education, earth science, English, ESL, evolution, fiber arts, film, fine arts, folk dance, French, geometry, health, history, humanities, illustration, improvisation, jazz dance, jazz ensemble, journalism, life science, Mandarin, math analysis, mathematics, mentorship program, musical theater, orchestra, outdoor education, painting, performing arts, philosophy, photography, physical education, physical science, physics, play production, pre-algebra, pre-calculus, printmaking, Spanish, statistics, strings,

textiles, theater, trigonometry, U.S. government and politics, U.S. history, visual arts, Washington State and Northwest History, water color painting, wilderness/outdoor program, world history, writing.

Graduation Requirements English, foreign language, humanities, mathematics, physical education (includes health), science, senior thesis, visual and performing arts, participation in environmental maintenance program.

Special Academic Programs Independent study; term-away projects; study abroad; academic accommodation for the gifted, the musically talented, and the artistically talented; ESL (47 students enrolled).

College Placement 87 students graduated in 2005; 86 went to college, including Bard College; Brown University; Sarah Lawrence College; University of Chicago; University of Southern California; University of Washington. Other: 1 had other specific plans.

Student Life Upper grades have honor system. Discipline rests primarily with faculty.

Summer Programs Enrichment, ESL, sports, art/fine arts, computer instruction programs offered; held on campus; accepts boys and girls; open to students from other schools. 325 students usually enrolled. 2006 schedule: July 3 to August 11. Application deadline: June 16.

Tuition and Aid Day student tuition: $21,475; 7-day tuition and room/board: $31,940. Tuition installment plan (school's own payment plan). Need-based scholarship grants available. In 2005–06, 14% of upper-school students received aid. Total amount of financial aid awarded in 2005–06: $617,255.

Admissions Traditional secondary-level entrance grade is 9. For fall 2005, 218 students applied for upper-level admission, 108 were accepted, 59 enrolled. ISEE required. Deadline for receipt of application materials: January 19. Application fee required: $50. On-campus interview required.

Athletics Interscholastic: basketball (boys, girls), crew (b,g), cross-country running (b,g), soccer (b,g), track and field (b,g), ultimate Frisbee (b,g), volleyball (g); coed interscholastic: ultimate Frisbee; coed intramural: fitness, hiking/backpacking, outdoor education, rock climbing, ropes courses, skiing (cross-country), skiing (downhill), ultimate Frisbee. 4 PE instructors, 4 coaches.

Computers Computers are regularly used in art, English, ESL, foreign language, health, humanities, journalism, mathematics, science, writing, yearbook classes. Computer network features include campus e-mail, on-campus library services, CD-ROMs, Internet access, DVD, wireless campus network, ProQuest, Big Chalk, and World Book Online databases.

Contact Anne Smith, Director of Admissions. 206-682-7309. Fax: 206-467-7353. E-mail: anne.smith@northwestschool.org. Web site: www.northwestschool.org.

NORTHWEST YESHIVA HIGH SCHOOL

5017 90th Avenue, Southeast
Mercer Island, Washington 98040
Head of School: Rabbi Bernie Fox

General Information Coeducational day college-preparatory and religious studies school, affiliated with Jewish faith. Grades 9–12. Founded: 1974. Setting: suburban. Nearest major city is Seattle. 2-acre campus. 3 buildings on campus. Approved or accredited by Northwest Association of Schools and Colleges and Washington Department of Education. Languages of instruction: English, Spanish, and Hebrew. Endowment: $841,000. Total enrollment: 108. Upper school average class size: 12. Upper school faculty-student ratio: 1:4.

Upper School Student Profile Grade 9: 32 students (19 boys, 13 girls); Grade 10: 26 students (12 boys, 14 girls); Grade 11: 35 students (20 boys, 15 girls); Grade 12: 15 students (5 boys, 10 girls). 100% of students are Jewish.

Faculty School total: 30. In upper school: 15 men, 15 women; 15 have advanced degrees.

Subjects Offered 20th century history, algebra, American legal systems, art, art history, biology, calculus, chemistry, college admission preparation, college counseling, drama, economics, English, film appreciation, fine arts, general math, geometry, Hebrew, Hebrew scripture, integrated mathematics, Jewish history, Judaic studies, lab science, language arts, modern Western civilization, newspaper, philosophy, physical education, physics, prayer/spirituality, pre-algebra, pre-calculus, psychology, Rabbinic literature, religious studies, Spanish, Talmud, U.S. government, U.S. history, U.S. literature, Western civilization, world history, writing, yearbook.

Graduation Requirements Advanced math, arts and fine arts (art, music, dance, drama), biology, conceptual physics, Hebrew, integrated mathematics, Judaic studies, language arts, physics, pre-calculus, Spanish, Talmud, U.S. government, U.S. history, world history. Community service is required.

Special Academic Programs Independent study; academic accommodation for the gifted; remedial reading and/or remedial writing; remedial math; special instructional classes for deaf students; ESL (2 students enrolled).

College Placement 32 students graduated in 2005; all went to college, including Boston University; University of Washington; Yeshiva University. Mean SAT verbal: 579, mean SAT math: 550. 47% scored over 600 on SAT verbal, 43% scored over 600 on SAT math.

Student Life Upper grades have specified standards of dress, student council, honor system. Discipline rests primarily with faculty. Attendance at religious services is required.

Summer Programs Sports programs offered; session focuses on softball; held off campus; held at ball parks on Mercer Island; accepts boys and girls; open to students from other schools. 30 students usually enrolled. 2006 schedule: May 16 to August 18. Application deadline: March 13.

Tuition and Aid Day student tuition: $6900. Tuition installment plan (monthly payment plans, individually arranged payment plans). Need-based scholarship grants available. In 2005–06, 37% of upper-school students received aid. Total amount of financial aid awarded in 2005–06: $153,680.

Admissions Traditional secondary-level entrance grade is 9. For fall 2005, 111 students applied for upper-level admission, 111 were accepted, 108 enrolled. Deadline for receipt of application materials: February 13. Application fee required: $225. Interview required.

Athletics Interscholastic: basketball (boys, girls), crew (b,g), cross-country running (b,g), golf (b,g), volleyball (g); coed interscholastic: cross-country running, softball. 5 PE instructors, 5 coaches.

Computers Computer network features include Internet access.

Contact Mr. Ian Weiner, Director of Student Services. 206-232-5272. Fax: 206-232-2711. E-mail: admin@nyhs.com. Web site: www.nyhs.net.

NORTHWOOD SCHOOL

PO Box 1070
Lake Placid, New York 12946
Head of School: Edward M. Good

General Information Coeducational boarding and day college-preparatory, arts, and technology school. Grades 9–PG. Founded: 1905. Setting: small town. Nearest major city is Albany. Students are housed in single-sex dormitories. 80-acre campus. 8 buildings on campus. Approved or accredited by Middle States Association of Colleges and Schools, New York State Association of Independent Schools, and The Association of Boarding Schools. Member of National Association of Independent Schools and Secondary School Admission Test Board. Endowment: $10 million. Total enrollment: 167. Upper school average class size: 8. Upper school faculty-student ratio: 1:8.

Upper School Student Profile Grade 9: 15 students (12 boys, 3 girls); Grade 10: 45 students (26 boys, 19 girls); Grade 11: 53 students (37 boys, 16 girls); Grade 12: 44 students (29 boys, 15 girls); Postgraduate: 10 students (7 boys, 3 girls). 75% of students are boarding students. 50% are state residents. 20 states are represented in upper school student body. 15% are international students. International students from Canada, Germany, Republic of Korea, Thailand, and United Kingdom; 3 other countries represented in student body.

Faculty School total: 28. In upper school: 19 men, 9 women; 15 have advanced degrees; 18 reside on campus.

Subjects Offered Algebra, American history, American literature, art, biology, calculus, ceramics, chemistry, computer science, drama, earth science, English, English literature, ensembles, environmental science, expository writing, fiber arts, French, geography, geology, geometry, government/civics, great issues, health, history, journalism, mathematics, music, photography, physical education, physics, psychology, SAT preparation, science, social studies, sociology, Spanish, theater, trigonometry, world history.

Graduation Requirements Arts and fine arts (art, music, dance, drama), English, foreign language, mathematics, physical education (includes health), science, social studies (includes history).

Special Academic Programs Advanced Placement exam preparation in 3 subject areas; honors section; independent study; remedial reading and/or remedial writing; ESL (18 students enrolled).

College Placement 57 students graduated in 2005; 49 went to college, including Boston College; Middlebury College; St. Lawrence University; Wesleyan College; Williams College. Other: 4 entered a postgraduate year, 1 had other specific plans. Median SAT verbal: 490, median SAT math: 480, median composite ACT: 21. 28% scored over 600 on SAT verbal, 45% scored over 600 on SAT math, 32% scored over 26 on composite ACT.

Student Life Upper grades have specified standards of dress, student council, honor system. Discipline rests primarily with faculty.

Tuition and Aid Day student tuition: $17,000; 7-day tuition and room/board: $32,000. Tuition installment plan (The Tuition Plan, Key Tuition Payment Plan, monthly payment plans, individually arranged payment plans, 3-payment plan). Need-based scholarship grants available. In 2005–06, 49% of upper-school students received aid. Total amount of financial aid awarded in 2005–06: $960,000.

Admissions Traditional secondary-level entrance grade is 11. For fall 2005, 165 students applied for upper-level admission, 125 were accepted, 82 enrolled. SSAT or TOEFL or SLEP required. Deadline for receipt of application materials: none. Application fee required: $35. On-campus interview required.

Athletics Interscholastic: crew (boys, girls), hockey (b,g), ice hockey (b,g), ice skating (b,g), lacrosse (b,g), nordic skiing (b,g), ski jumping (b,g), skiing (downhill) (b,g), soccer (b,g), telemark skiing (b,g), tennis (b,g); intramural: hockey (b,g), ice hockey (b,g), ice skating (b,g), skiing (downhill) (b,g), snowboarding (b,g); coed interscholastic: alpine skiing, figure skating, freestyle skiing, golf, nordic skiing, skiing (cross-country), snowboarding, telemark skiing; coed intramural: alpine skiing, back packing, bicycling, canoeing/kayaking, climbing, combined training, cross-country running, figure skating, fishing, fitness, fly fishing, freestyle skiing, golf,

hiking/backpacking, jogging, kayaking, luge, mountain biking, mountaineering, nordic skiing, outdoor adventure, physical training, rafting, rappelling, rock climbing, ropes courses, rowing, running, skiing (cross-country), skiing (downhill), snowboarding, street hockey, strength & conditioning, tennis, walking, wall climbing, weight training, wilderness, wilderness survival, wildernessways, winter walking. 1 coach, 1 trainer.

Computers Computers are regularly used in English, foreign language, history, mathematics, science classes. Computer network features include campus e-mail, on-campus library services, CD-ROMs, online commercial services, Internet access.

Contact Timothy Weaver, Director of Admissions. 518-523-3382. Fax: 518-523-3405. E-mail: weavert@northwoodschool.com. Web site: www.northwoodschool.com.

NORTH YARMOUTH ACADEMY

148 Main Street
Yarmouth, Maine 04096
Head of School: Peter W. Mertz

General Information Coeducational day college-preparatory, arts, and technology school. Grades 6–12. Founded: 1814. Setting: suburban. Nearest major city is Portland. 25-acre campus. 10 buildings on campus. Approved or accredited by Association of Independent Schools in New England, Independent Schools of Northern New England, New England Association of Schools and Colleges, and Maine Department of Education. Member of National Association of Independent Schools and Secondary School Admission Test Board. Endowment: $3 million. Total enrollment: 313. Upper school average class size: 14. Upper school faculty-student ratio: 1:8.

Upper School Student Profile Grade 9: 46 students (19 boys, 27 girls); Grade 10: 47 students (26 boys, 21 girls); Grade 11: 44 students (26 boys, 18 girls); Grade 12: 46 students (24 boys, 22 girls).

Faculty School total: 39. In upper school: 11 men, 14 women; 14 have advanced degrees.

Subjects Offered Algebra, American government, American history, American history-AP, ancient world history, art, art history-AP, biology-AP, calculus-AP, chemistry, chorus, composition-AP, computer graphics, contemporary issues, drama, drawing and design, earth science, English, English composition, English literature, English literature and composition-AP, environmental science-AP, European history, European history-AP, experiential education, fine arts, French, geometry, history, instrumental music, jazz, language-AP, Latin, Latin-AP, mathematics, music, music theory-AP, oceanography, painting, photography, physical education, physical science, physics, pottery, pre-calculus, science, social issues, social studies, society challenge and change, Spanish, statistics, studio art—AP, technology, theater, trigonometry, U.S. history, U.S. history-AP, world history.

Graduation Requirements Arts and fine arts (art, music, dance, drama), English, foreign language, history, mathematics, science, senior project, speech, two-week volunteer senior service project, senior speech, participation in athletics or performing arts program each trimester.

Special Academic Programs Advanced Placement exam preparation in 13 subject areas; honors section; study abroad.

College Placement 37 students graduated in 2005; 36 went to college, including Bentley College; Bowdoin College; Colby College; Franklin and Marshall College; University of Maine. Other: 1 entered military service. Median SAT verbal: 600, median SAT math: 600. 50% scored over 600 on SAT verbal, 50% scored over 600 on SAT math.

Student Life Upper grades have specified standards of dress, student council, honor system. Discipline rests primarily with faculty.

Summer Programs Enrichment, sports, art/fine arts programs offered; session focuses on sports and traditional recreation; held on campus; accepts boys and girls; open to students from other schools. 400 students usually enrolled. 2006 schedule: June 28 to August 13.

Tuition and Aid Day student tuition: $18,400. Tuition installment plan (Insured Tuition Payment Plan, Key Tuition Payment Plan, monthly payment plans). Need-based scholarship grants available. In 2005–06, 30% of upper-school students received aid. Total amount of financial aid awarded in 2005–06: $571,675.

Admissions Traditional secondary-level entrance grade is 9. For fall 2005, 58 students applied for upper-level admission, 23 were accepted, 14 enrolled. SSAT required. Deadline for receipt of application materials: February 10. Application fee required: $35. On-campus interview required.

Athletics Interscholastic: baseball (boys), basketball (b,g), cross-country running (b,g), field hockey (g), golf (b,g), ice hockey (b,g), indoor track (b,g), indoor track & field (b,g), lacrosse (b,g), nordic skiing (b,g), soccer (b,g), softball (g), swimming and diving (b,g), tennis (b,g), track and field (b,g), volleyball (g); coed interscholastic: tennis; coed intramural: outdoor activities, yoga. 1 PE instructor.

Computers Computers are regularly used in English, foreign language, graphic design, history, mathematics, science, technology classes. Computer network features include campus e-mail, on-campus library services, CD-ROMs, Internet access.

Contact Joseph P. Silvestri, Director of Admission. 207-846-2376. Fax: 207-846-2382. E-mail: admission@nya.org. Web site: www.nya.org.

THE NORWICH FREE ACADEMY

305 Broadway
Norwich, Connecticut 06360
Head of School: Mary Lou Bargnesi, PhD

General Information Coeducational day college-preparatory, general academic, arts, business, vocational, bilingual studies, and technology school. Grades 9–12. Founded: 1856. Setting: suburban. 15-acre campus. 11 buildings on campus. Approved or accredited by New England Association of Schools and Colleges and Connecticut Department of Education. Upper school average class size: 22. Upper school faculty-student ratio: 1:22.

Faculty School total: 85. In upper school: 30 men, 55 women; 75 have advanced degrees.

Special Academic Programs Advanced Placement exam preparation in 15 subject areas; honors section; remedial reading and/or remedial writing; remedial math; special instructional classes for students with learning disabilities, Attention Deficit Disorder, emotional and behavioral problems, and dyslexia; ESL (90 students enrolled).

College Placement 507 students graduated in 2005; 396 went to college. Other: 56 went to work, 45 entered military service, 3 had other specific plans.

Student Life Upper grades have specified standards of dress, honor system. Discipline rests equally with students and faculty.

Summer Programs Remediation, enrichment, ESL, sports programs offered; held on campus; accepts boys and girls; open to students from other schools. 250 students usually enrolled. 2006 schedule: July 1 to July 29. Application deadline: June 1.

Tuition and Aid Day student tuition: $9600.

Admissions Deadline for receipt of application materials: June 4. No application fee required. Interview required.

Athletics Interscholastic: baseball (boys), basketball (b,g), cheering (b,g), cross-country running (b,g), drill team (g), field hockey (g), football (b), golf (b), indoor track (b,g), lacrosse (b), physical fitness (b,g), running (b,g), soccer (b,g), softball (g), Special Olympics (b,g), swimming and diving (b,g), volleyball (b,g), weight lifting (b), winter (indoor) track (b,g), wrestling (b); intramural: fencing (b,g), hockey (b), ice hockey (b), ice skating (b,g), skiing (cross-country) (b,g), skiing (downhill) (b,g), table tennis (b,g). 8 PE instructors, 25 coaches, 5 trainers.

Computers Computer network features include on-campus library services, CD-ROMs, Internet access, DVD.

Contact Dr. Mary Lou Bargnesi, Superintendent/Principal. 860-425-5500. E-mail: bargnesim@norwichfreeacademy.com. Web site: www.norwichfreeacademy.com.

NOTRE DAME ACADEMY

425 Salisbury Street
Worcester, Massachusetts 01609
Head of School: Sr. Ann E. Morrison, SND

General Information Girls' day college-preparatory, arts, and religious studies school, affiliated with Roman Catholic Church. Grades 9–12. Founded: 1951. Setting: suburban. Nearest major city is Boston. 13-acre campus. 3 buildings on campus. Approved or accredited by Association of Independent Schools in New England. Member of National Association of Independent Schools. Total enrollment: 315. Upper school average class size: 18. Upper school faculty-student ratio: 1:11.

Upper School Student Profile 80% of students are Roman Catholic.

Faculty School total: 39. In upper school: 3 men, 36 women; 27 have advanced degrees.

Subjects Offered 20th century history, advanced chemistry, advanced math, advanced studio art-AP, algebra, American history, American literature, analysis and differential calculus, anatomy and physiology, ancient world history, art, art history, art history-AP, Bible studies, biology, British literature, British literature (honors), British literature-AP, calculus, calculus-AP, career exploration, Catholic belief and practice, chamber groups, chemistry, chemistry-AP, choral music, Christian and Hebrew scripture, Christian doctrine, college planning, communication skills, community service, computer skills, creative writing, dance, drama, drawing and design, economics and history, English, English composition, English literature, English literature and composition-AP, English-AP, ethics, European history, European history-AP, expository writing, fine arts, French, French language-AP, geometry, grammar, graphic design, health, history, honors geometry, keyboarding/computer, Latin, literature seminar, mathematics, mathematics-AP, music, music theory-AP, photography, physical education, physics, physiology-anatomy, pre-calculus, psychology, public service, religion, science, senior project, Shakespeare, social studies, sociology, Spanish, Spanish language-AP, studio art-AP, theater, theology, trigonometry, world history, world literature, world religions, writing.

Graduation Requirements Arts and fine arts (art, music, dance, drama), computer science, English, foreign language, mathematics, physical education (includes health), public service, religion (includes Bible studies and theology), science, social studies (includes history), guidance seminar. Community service is required.

Special Academic Programs Advanced Placement exam preparation in 12 subject areas; honors section; study abroad.

College Placement 72 students graduated in 2005; all went to college, including Boston College; Emerson College; Holy Cross College; Providence College; University of Massachusetts Amherst. Mean SAT verbal: 560, mean SAT math: 540.

Student Life Upper grades have specified standards of dress, student council. Discipline rests equally with students and faculty. Attendance at religious services is required.

Tuition and Aid Day student tuition: $8250. Tuition installment plan (Academic Management Services Plan). Need-based scholarship grants available. In 2005–06, 7% of upper-school students received aid.

Admissions Traditional secondary-level entrance grade is 9. For fall 2005, 163 students applied for upper-level admission, 120 were accepted, 78 enrolled. Admissions testing, California Achievement Test and CAT 5 required. Deadline for receipt of application materials: December 2. Application fee required: $40. On-campus interview recommended.

Athletics Interscholastic: alpine skiing, aquatics, basketball, cross-country running, diving, field hockey, fitness walking, freestyle skiing, golf, indoor track, indoor track & field, physical fitness, physical training, running, skiing (downhill), softball, swimming and diving, tennis, track and field, walking, winter (indoor) track. 1 PE instructor, 20 coaches.

Computers Computers are regularly used in English, foreign language, graphic design, history, library skills, literary magazine, mathematics, newspaper, psychology, religious studies, research skills, science, yearbook classes. Computer network features include on-campus library services, CD-ROMs, Internet access.

Contact Mrs. Mary F. Riordan, Admissions Director. 508-757-6200. Fax: 508-757-1800. E-mail: mriordan@nda-worc.org. Web site: www.nda-worc.org.

NOTRE DAME HIGH SCHOOL

petersons.com

1540 Ralston Avenue
Belmont, California 94002-1995
Head of School: Ms. Rita Gleason

General Information Girls' day college-preparatory, arts, religious studies, and technology school, affiliated with Roman Catholic Church. Grades 9–12. Founded: 1851. Setting: suburban. Nearest major city is San Francisco. 11-acre campus. 3 buildings on campus. Approved or accredited by Western Association of Schools and Colleges, Western Catholic Education Association, and California Department of Education. Endowment: $800,000. Total enrollment: 733. Upper school average class size: 25. Upper school faculty-student ratio: 1:17.

Upper School Student Profile Grade 9: 197 students (197 girls); Grade 10: 179 students (179 girls); Grade 11: 186 students (186 girls); Grade 12: 173 students (173 girls). 75% of students are Roman Catholic.

Faculty School total: 57. In upper school: 20 men, 37 women; 55 have advanced degrees.

Subjects Offered Algebra, American history, American literature, art, art history, art history-AP, band, bioethics, biology, biology-AP, British literature, British literature-AP, calculus, calculus-AP, chemistry, chemistry-AP, choral music, church history, computer literacy, computer science, creative writing, dance, digital photography, drama, driver education, economics, English, English literature, English literature-AP, ethics, European history, expository writing, fine arts, French, French language-AP, geometry, government-AP, history, integrated science, journalism, leadership and service, library skills, mathematics, moral reasoning, music history, orchestra, photography, physical education, physical science, physics, pre-calculus, psychology, religion, science, self-defense, social justice, social science, Spanish, Spanish language-AP, speech, studio art-AP, television, theater, theology, trigonometry, U.S. history-AP, world history, world literature, world religions, yearbook.

Graduation Requirements Arts and fine arts (art, music, dance, drama), English, foreign language, mathematics, physical education (includes health), religion (includes Bible studies and theology), science, social science, social studies (includes history). Community service is required.

Special Academic Programs Advanced Placement exam preparation in 10 subject areas; honors section; independent study; study at local college for college credit; special instructional classes for deaf students, blind students, students with learning disabilities, ADD.

College Placement 163 students graduated in 2005; all went to college, including San Jose State University; Santa Clara University; Sonoma State University; University of California, Berkeley; University of California, Davis; University of California, San Diego. Mean SAT verbal: 620, mean SAT math: 590.

Student Life Upper grades have uniform requirement, student council, honor system. Discipline rests primarily with faculty. Attendance at religious services is required.

Summer Programs Enrichment, advancement, sports, art/fine arts, computer instruction programs offered; session focuses on enrichment for grades 6-9; held on campus; accepts boys and girls; open to students from other schools. 100 students usually enrolled. 2006 schedule: June 19 to July 21. Application deadline: April 15.

Tuition and Aid Day student tuition: $13,600. Tuition installment plan (FACTS Tuition Payment Plan, individually arranged payment plans). Need-based scholarship grants available. In 2005–06, 25% of upper-school students received aid. Total amount of financial aid awarded in 2005–06: $600,000.

Admissions Traditional secondary-level entrance grade is 9. For fall 2005, 450 students applied for upper-level admission, 197 enrolled. High School Placement Test (closed version) from Scholastic Testing Service required. Deadline for receipt of application materials: December 9. Application fee required: $50. On-campus interview required.

Athletics Interscholastic: aquatics, basketball, cheering, cross-country running, golf, pom squad, soccer, softball, swimming and diving, tennis, track and field, volleyball, water polo; intramural: cheering, dance, dance squad, dance team, flag football, football, martial arts, modern dance, outdoor adventure, physical fitness, rock climbing, self defense, softball, strength & conditioning, swimming and diving, synchronized swimming, touch football, volleyball. 2 PE instructors, 20 coaches, 1 trainer.

Computers Computers are regularly used in college planning, English, foreign language, history, journalism, mathematics, media production, newspaper, photography, publishing, religious studies, science, social studies, theater arts, video film production, yearbook classes. Computer network features include campus e-mail, on-campus library services, CD-ROMs, Internet access, file transfer, DVD.

Contact Mrs. Lynn Stieren, Director of Admissions. 650-595-1913 Ext. 320. Fax: 650-595-2643. E-mail: lstieren@ndhsb.org. Web site: www.ndhsb.org.

ANNOUNCEMENT FROM THE SCHOOL Notre Dame High School is an independent, Catholic, college-preparatory school for young women dedicated to the educational mission of St. Julie Billiart and the Sisters of Notre Dame de Namur. Founded in 1851 by the Sisters of Notre Dame de Namur, the School moved from San Jose to the historic William Ralston estate in 1923. Notre Dame High School, with its sister schools Notre Dame Elementary School and Notre Dame de Namur University, is located in Belmont, California, a professional, suburban community located between San Francisco and San Jose in San Mateo County. The essence of Notre Dame High School lies in a strong college-preparatory curriculum within a caring, supportive environment that is committed to the development of young women of active faith, strong intellect, and Christian leadership. Notre Dame High School educates its students to master the foundational skills of learning necessary to become leaders of society and responsible citizens committed to justice and peace. Acknowledging that the development of the heart, mind, and body is essential and important to the growth of every young woman and seeking to educate the whole person, Notre Dame High School supports growth in 6 areas: spiritual, moral, intellectual, emotional, social, and physical. The Notre Dame High School curriculum is an excellent college-preparatory program designed to prepare all students to succeed in college. Graduation requirements fulfill the course requirements for admission to University of California campuses, California State University campuses, and other private, public, and Catholic colleges and universities. Historically, 99 to 100% of Notre Dame High School students enroll in colleges and universities throughout the country. A challenging 4-year sequence of college-preparatory and honors courses is available in all academic areas. Notre Dame High School also offers Advanced Placement classes to qualified students who wish to be challenged further. Balance and choice are important in a student's life; therefore, the required curriculum is supplemented by an extensive selection of elective courses in every department. Notre Dame High School provides numerous opportunities for self-expression through its comprehensive and award-winning Visual and Performing Arts Program, which enhances students' self-esteem in the classroom and on stage. An excellent cocurricular program is an integral part of the Notre Dame High School experience. Student-directed organizations and clubs offer opportunities for all students to become actively involved, make new friends, and assume leadership roles in a strong Christian community.

NOTRE DAME HIGH SCHOOL

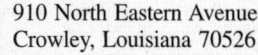

910 North Eastern Avenue
Crowley, Louisiana 70526
Head of School: Mrs. Cindy Istre

General Information Coeducational day college-preparatory school, affiliated with Roman Catholic Church. Grades 9–12. Founded: 1974. Setting: small town. Nearest major city is Lafayette. 10-acre campus. 7 buildings on campus. Approved or accredited by Louisiana Department of Education. Candidate for accreditation by Southern Association of Colleges and Schools. Total enrollment: 530. Upper school average class size: 25. Upper school faculty-student ratio: 1:25.

Upper School Student Profile 100% of students are Roman Catholic.

Faculty School total: 38. In upper school: 13 men, 25 women; 9 have advanced degrees.

Special Academic Programs Honors section; independent study; study at local college for college credit; academic accommodation for the gifted.

College Placement 127 students graduated in 2005; 120 went to college. Other: 7 went to work.

Student Life Upper grades have uniform requirement, student council. Discipline rests primarily with faculty. Attendance at religious services is required.

Tuition and Aid Tuition installment plan (The Tuition Plan, monthly payment plans). Tuition reduction for siblings available.

Admissions Deadline for receipt of application materials: January 30. Application fee required. Interview required.

Athletics Interscholastic: baseball (boys), basketball (b,g), cheering (g), cross-country running (b,g), dance squad (g), football (b), softball (g), tennis (b,g), track and field (b,g), volleyball (g); coed interscholastic: drill team, golf, soccer, swimming and diving. 12 coaches, 2 trainers.

Computers Computer network features include campus e-mail, on-campus library services, CD-ROMs, Internet access.

Contact Mr. Fred Menard, Dean of Students. 337-783-3519. Fax: 337-788-2115. Web site: www.ndpios.com.

NOTRE DAME HIGH SCHOOL

320 East Ripa Avenue
St. Louis, Missouri 63125-2897
Head of School: Sr. Michelle Emmerich, SSND

General Information Girls' day college-preparatory, arts, business, and religious studies school, affiliated with Roman Catholic Church. Grades 9–12. Founded: 1934. Setting: suburban. 40-acre campus. 3 buildings on campus. Approved or accredited by North Central Association of Colleges and Schools and Missouri Department of Education. Total enrollment: 425. Upper school faculty-student ratio: 1:10.

Upper School Student Profile Grade 9: 108 students (108 girls); Grade 10: 106 students (106 girls); Grade 11: 108 students (108 girls); Grade 12: 103 students (103 girls). 97% of students are Roman Catholic.

Faculty School total: 42. In upper school: 5 men, 37 women; 20 have advanced degrees.

Subjects Offered 3-dimensional art, ACT preparation, acting, advanced math, African-American literature, algebra, American history, American history-AP, American literature, analytic geometry, anatomy and physiology, applied music, art, arts, astronomy, basketball, Bible studies, biology, botany, British literature, business, calculus, calculus-AP, career/college preparation, ceramics, chemistry, chemistry-AP, choir, choral music, chorus, Christian and Hebrew scripture, Christian studies, communication skills, communications, community service, composition-AP, computer art, computer programming, computer science, concert choir, creative writing, culinary arts, dance, death and loss, debate, developmental language skills, developmental math, digital art, drama, early childhood, earth science, ecology, English, English literature, English literature and composition-AP, English literature-AP, ethics, expository writing, family and consumer science, family and consumer sciences, family life, fashion, film and literature, fine arts, food and nutrition, foreign language, French, French as a second language, French-AP, gardening, geography, geology, geometry, global studies, government and politics-AP, government/civics, grammar, graphic design, health, health education, history, history-AP, home economics, honors English, honors U.S. history, human sexuality, independent study, interdisciplinary studies, intro to computers, journalism, keyboarding/computer, leadership skills, literary genres, mathematics, media literacy, music, musical theater, newspaper, photography, physical education, physics, public speaking, religion, science, social studies, sociology, Spanish, Spanish-AP, speech, speech and debate, theater, trigonometry, typing, U.S. history-AP, volleyball, world history, world literature, writing, zoology.

Graduation Requirements Arts and fine arts (art, music, dance, drama), athletics, business skills (includes word processing), computer science, English, mathematics, physical education (includes health), religion (includes Bible studies and theology), science, social studies (includes history). Community service is required.

Special Academic Programs Advanced Placement exam preparation in 6 subject areas; honors section; accelerated programs; independent study; study at local college for college credit; academic accommodation for the gifted, the musically talented, and the artistically talented; remedial reading and/or remedial writing; remedial math.

College Placement 114 students graduated in 2005; all went to college, including Missouri State University; Saint Louis University; Southeast Missouri State University; St. Louis Community College at Meramec; University of Missouri–Columbia.

Student Life Upper grades have uniform requirement, student council, honor system. Discipline rests primarily with faculty.

Tuition and Aid Day student tuition: $7100. Tuition installment plan (monthly payment plans, individually arranged payment plans, quarterly payment plan). Tuition reduction for siblings, merit scholarship grants, need-based scholarship grants, paying campus jobs, tuition reduction for children of faculty and staff, reciprocal tuition agreement consortium available. In 2005–06, 20% of upper-school students received aid; total upper-school merit-scholarship money awarded: $10,000. Total amount of financial aid awarded in 2005–06: $155,000.

Admissions Traditional secondary-level entrance grade is 9. Any standardized test or Iowa Tests of Basic Skills required. Deadline for receipt of application materials: none. No application fee required.

Athletics Interscholastic: basketball, cross-country running, diving, racquetball, soccer, softball, swimming and diving, volleyball; intramural: cheering, dance. 2 PE instructors, 9 coaches.

Computers Computers are regularly used in business skills, English, journalism, mathematics, newspaper, writing, yearbook classes. Computer network features include campus e-mail, CD-ROMs, online commercial services, Internet access, DVD.

Contact Mrs. Sapna Jos Galloway, Director of Development. 314-544-1015 Ext. 308. Fax: 314-544-8003. E-mail: galls@ndhs.net. Web site: www.ndhs.net.

NOTRE DAME HIGH SCHOOL

601 Lawrence Road
Lawrenceville, New Jersey 08648
Head of School: Ms. Mary Liz Ivins

petersons.com

General Information Coeducational day college-preparatory school, affiliated with Roman Catholic Church. Grades 9–12. Founded: 1957. Setting: suburban. Nearest major city is Trenton. 100-acre campus. 1 building on campus. Approved or accredited by Middle States Association of Colleges and Schools, National Catholic Education Association, and New Jersey Department of Education. Total enrollment: 1,276. Upper school average class size: 24. Upper school faculty-student ratio: 1:24.

Upper School Student Profile Grade 9: 321 students (137 boys, 184 girls); Grade 10: 306 students (163 boys, 143 girls); Grade 11: 333 students (157 boys, 176 girls); Grade 12: 316 students (154 boys, 162 girls). 88% of students are Roman Catholic.

Faculty School total: 82. In upper school: 30 men, 48 women; 32 have advanced degrees.

Subjects Offered 20th century history, 3-dimensional art, 3-dimensional design, accounting, acting, advanced chemistry, advanced computer applications, advanced math, Advanced Placement courses, algebra, American history, American history-AP, American literature, ancient world history, applied music, art, art and culture, athletics, Basic programming, Bible studies, biology, biology-AP, bookkeeping, British literature, business, business applications, business studies, calculus, calculus-AP, Catholic belief and practice, ceramics, chemistry, chemistry-AP, choir, Christian doctrine, comparative religion, computer applications, computer keyboarding, concert band, concert choir, constitutional law, contemporary issues, creative writing, dance, dance performance, drama, driver education, ecology, environmental systems, economics, English, English composition, English literature-AP, environmental science-AP, European history-AP, first aid, French, geometry, German, German literature, health education, honors algebra, honors English, honors world history, journalism, Latin, law, leadership and service, leadership education training, literature-AP, madrigals, math review, philosophy, photography, physical education, physics, physics-AP, piano, portfolio art, pre-algebra, pre-calculus, psychology, psychology-AP, public speaking, reading/study skills, SAT preparation, scripture, senior project, sociology, Spanish, Spanish literature, speech and debate, sports medicine, theater design and production, U.S. history-AP, U.S. literature, world history, world literature, writing, yearbook.

Graduation Requirements Biology, computer applications, English, foreign language, lab science, mathematics, physical education (includes health), religion (includes Bible studies and theology), U.S. history, world history, Junior Interdisciplinary Portfolio. Community service is required.

Special Academic Programs Advanced Placement exam preparation in 10 subject areas; honors section; independent study; remedial reading and/or remedial writing; remedial math.

College Placement 304 students graduated in 2005; 295 went to college, including Drexel University; Loyola College in Maryland; Rutgers, The State University of New Jersey, New Brunswick/Piscataway; Saint Joseph's University; The Pennsylvania State University University Park Campus; The University of Scranton. Other: 2 went to work, 5 entered military service, 2 entered a postgraduate year. Mean SAT verbal: 555, mean SAT math: 546, mean combined SAT: 1626. 32% scored over 600 on SAT verbal, 33% scored over 600 on SAT math, 26% scored over 1800 on combined SAT.

Student Life Upper grades have uniform requirement, student council, honor system. Discipline rests primarily with faculty. Attendance at religious services is required.

Summer Programs Enrichment, sports, art/fine arts programs offered; session focuses on sports/arts/writing camps; held on campus; accepts boys and girls; open to students from other schools. 725 students usually enrolled. 2006 schedule: June 26 to August 4. Application deadline: June 26.

Tuition and Aid Day student tuition: $7800. Tuition installment plan (Tuition Management Systems Plan). Tuition reduction for siblings, need-based scholarship grants available. In 2005–06, 7% of upper-school students received aid. Total amount of financial aid awarded in 2005–06: $160,000.

Admissions Traditional secondary-level entrance grade is 9. For fall 2005, 500 students applied for upper-level admission, 400 were accepted, 320 enrolled. Scholastic Testing Service High School Placement Test required. Deadline for receipt of application materials: November 28. Application fee required: $50. On-campus interview required.

Athletics Interscholastic: baseball (boys), basketball (b,g), cheering (g), cross-country running (b,g), dance (b,g), field hockey (g), football (b), golf (b), hockey (b), ice hockey (b), indoor track (b,g), lacrosse (b,g), soccer (b,g), softball (g), swimming and diving (b,g), tennis (b,g), track and field (b,g), winter (indoor) track (b,g), wrestling (b); intramural: touch football (g), volleyball (b,g); coed interscholastic: ballet, cheering, diving, fitness, strength & conditioning; coed intramural: Frisbee, outdoor activities, outdoor recreation, physical fitness, ultimate Frisbee, volleyball, weight lifting, weight training. 8 PE instructors, 71 coaches, 1 trainer.

Computers Computers are regularly used in all academic classes. Computer network features include on-campus library services, CD-ROMs, online commercial services, Internet access, wireless campus network, wireless labs.

Contact Ms. Peggy Miller, Admissions Coordinator. 609-882-7900 Ext. 139. Fax: 609-882-6599. E-mail: miller@ndnj.org. Web site: www.ndnj.org.

ANNOUNCEMENT FROM THE SCHOOL Notre Dame High School, founded by the Sisters of Mercy in 1957, is a Catholic, college-preparatory, coeducational high school of 1270 students in grades 9–12. Located in suburban central New Jersey, Notre Dame is fully accredited by the Middle States Association of Colleges and Secondary Schools. Students attend from both Pennsylvania and New Jersey. Student-centered learning is an educational goal realized through block scheduling. The commitment to a teacher-student ratio that allows individualized instruction, active learning, and attention to a variety of learning styles is the key to Notre Dame's educational philosophy. Notre Dame High School, serving the local and worldwide community, is a National Service-learning Leader School, an honor awarded by the Corporation for National Service. The 100-acre campus includes a main building that houses classrooms, a media center, a 1200-seat auditorium, chapel, gymnasium, science labs, and mobile laptop labs. In addition, many students now use table PCs for note taking and research, utilizing the School's wireless network. The campus incorporates a football stadium and baseball, soccer, lacrosse, and softball fields as well as a cross-country course. Notre Dame is one of only 5 high schools in the country that offer a full-time Strength Training Program. The high school sponsors 49 athletic teams, including 25 varsity sports for boys and girls, as well as more than 40 clubs, 3 publications, and 7 performing arts opportunities. Ninety-nine percent of Notre Dame's 2005 graduates were accepted at more than 250 colleges and universities, including Princeton, Georgetown, Columbia, Johns Hopkins, and the University of Pennsylvania. The top 30 percent of SAT scores are 1200 and above. Notre Dame has 2 Merit Scholarship Semifinalists, 10 Merit Scholarship Commended Scholars, and 26 Edward J. Bloustein Distinguished Scholars.

NOTRE DAME HIGH SCHOOL

127 East Pike Street
Clarksburg, West Virginia 26301
Head of School: Dr. Carroll Kelly Morrison

General Information Coeducational day college-preparatory and religious studies school, affiliated with Roman Catholic Church. Grades 7–12. Founded: 1955. Setting: rural. Nearest major city is Wheeling. 1-acre campus. 1 building on campus. Approved or accredited by National Catholic Education Association, North Central Association of Colleges and Schools, and West Virginia Department of Education. Endowment: $150,000. Total enrollment: 136. Upper school average class size: 15. Upper school faculty-student ratio: 1:8.

Upper School Student Profile Grade 9: 24 students (17 boys, 7 girls); Grade 10: 18 students (9 boys, 9 girls); Grade 11: 22 students (14 boys, 8 girls); Grade 12: 31 students (21 boys, 10 girls). 75% of students are Roman Catholic.

Faculty School total: 17. In upper school: 8 men, 9 women; 7 have advanced degrees.

Subjects Offered Advanced math, Advanced Placement courses, algebra, American history-AP, American literature-AP, anatomy and physiology, art, band, biology-AP, British literature-AP, calculus, calculus-AP, Catholic belief and practice, chemistry, chemistry-AP, Christian and Hebrew scripture, Christian ethics, church history, civics, community service, computer programming, driver education, English, English-AP, French, geography, geometry, health, keyboarding/computer, language arts, music, newspaper, physical education, physics, pre-algebra, pre-calculus, religion, science, Spanish, state history, trigonometry, U.S. government, U.S. history, world history, yearbook.

Graduation Requirements Arts, computer literacy, English, foreign language, keyboarding, mathematics, physical education (includes health), religion (includes Bible studies and theology), science, social studies (includes history).

Special Academic Programs Advanced Placement exam preparation in 7 subject areas; honors section; accelerated programs; independent study; study at local college for college credit; academic accommodation for the gifted, the musically talented, and the artistically talented; remedial reading and/or remedial writing; programs in English for dyslexic students; special instructional classes for deaf students, blind students.

College Placement 36 students graduated in 2005; 34 went to college, including Fairmont State University; Marshall University; West Virginia University. Other: 1 entered military service, 1 entered a postgraduate year.

Student Life Upper grades have uniform requirement, student council, honor system. Discipline rests primarily with faculty. Attendance at religious services is required.

Summer Programs Remediation, advancement programs offered; held on campus; accepts boys and girls; open to students from other schools. 250 students usually enrolled. 2006 schedule: June 13 to July 9. Application deadline: June 13.

Tuition and Aid Day student tuition: $2850–$4050. Guaranteed tuition plan. Tuition installment plan (FACTS Tuition Payment Plan). Need-based scholarship grants, Diocese of Wheeling-Charleston assistance available. In 2005–06, 50% of upper-school students received aid.

Admissions Traditional secondary-level entrance grade is 9. For fall 2005, 95 students applied for upper-level admission, 95 were accepted, 95 enrolled. School's own exam required. Deadline for receipt of application materials: none. No application fee required. On-campus interview required.

Athletics Interscholastic: aquatics (boys, girls), baseball (b), basketball (b,g), cheering (g), danceline (g), football (b), softball (g), swimming and diving (b,g), tennis (b,g), track and field (b,g); intramural: badminton (b,g), fitness (b,g), fitness walking (b,g); coed interscholastic: golf. 1 PE instructor, 1 trainer.

Computers Computers are regularly used in all classes. Computer network features include CD-ROMs, Internet access, DVD.

Contact Dr. Carroll Kelly Morrison, Principal. 304-623-1026 Ext. 11. Fax: 304-623-1026. E-mail: ndhs@iolinc.net. Web site: www.notredamehighschool.net.

NOTRE DAME HIGH SCHOOL FOR GIRLS

3000 North Mango Avenue
Chicago, Illinois 60634
Head of School: Ms. Staci Viola

General Information Girls' day college-preparatory, arts, business, religious studies, and technology school, affiliated with Roman Catholic Church. Grades 9–12. Founded: 1938. Setting: urban. 3-acre campus. 1 building on campus. Approved or accredited by National Catholic Education Association, North Central Association of Colleges and Schools, and Illinois Department of Education. Total enrollment: 313. Upper school average class size: 18. Upper school faculty-student ratio: 1:14.

Upper School Student Profile Grade 9: 109 students (109 girls); Grade 10: 79 students (79 girls); Grade 11: 55 students (55 girls); Grade 12: 88 students (88 girls); Postgraduate: 313 students (313 girls). 65% of students are Roman Catholic.

Faculty School total: 26. In upper school: 8 men, 18 women; 16 have advanced degrees.

Subjects Offered Accounting, advanced math, algebra, American government, American government-AP, American literature, American studies, anatomy and physiology, art, band, Basic programming, biology, British literature, calculus, career and personal planning, chemistry, chemistry-AP, chorus, composition, computer applications, computer programming, computer-aided design, concert band, consumer economics, consumer education, consumer mathematics, drawing, driver education, English, English-AP, family living, family studies, first aid, French, French-AP, geography, geometry, government-AP, health education, honors algebra, honors English, honors geometry, honors U.S. history, humanities, internship, journalism, keyboarding, literature, mathematics, music theory, painting, peer ministry, physical education, physical science, physics, pre-algebra, pre-calculus, public speaking, reading, SAT/ACT preparation, scripture, sculpture, sociology, Spanish, Spanish-AP, theater arts, theology, U.S. history, word processing, world civilizations, world history, writing.

Graduation Requirements Arts and fine arts (art, music, dance, drama), electives, English, foreign language, mathematics, physical education (includes health), science, social studies (includes history), theology, word processing, 60 hours of Christian service per school year.

Special Academic Programs Advanced Placement exam preparation in 6 subject areas; honors section; remedial reading and/or remedial writing; remedial math; special instructional classes for students with IEPs.

College Placement 103 students graduated in 2005; 97 went to college, including DePaul University; Dominican University; Loyola University Chicago; Northeastern Illinois University; Northern Illinois University; University of Illinois at Chicago. Other: 2 entered military service, 1 entered a postgraduate year, 3 had other specific plans. Mean SAT verbal: 470, mean SAT math: 485. 2% scored over 26 on composite ACT.

Student Life Upper grades have uniform requirement, student council, honor system. Discipline rests equally with students and faculty. Attendance at religious services is required.

Summer Programs Enrichment, sports, computer instruction programs offered; session focuses on 9th grade reading, math, technology; held on campus; accepts girls; not open to students from other schools. 90 students usually enrolled. 2006 schedule: July 3 to July 31. Application deadline: none.

Tuition and Aid Day student tuition: $6500. Tuition installment plan (monthly payment plans, individually arranged payment plans). Tuition reduction for siblings, need-based scholarship grants, paying campus jobs available. In 2005–06, 79% of upper-school students received aid. Total amount of financial aid awarded in 2005–06: $990,000.

Admissions Traditional secondary-level entrance grade is 9. For fall 2005, 313 students applied for upper-level admission. TerraNova required. Deadline for receipt of application materials: none. Application fee required: $250. Interview required.

Athletics Interscholastic: basketball, bowling, cheering, soccer, softball, track and field, volleyball. 1 PE instructor, 12 coaches.

Computers Computers are regularly used in art, basic skills, business education, career exploration, college planning, data processing, desktop publishing, English, foreign language, geography, graphic arts, health, history, humanities, independent study, information technology, journalism, library skills, mathematics, publications, religious studies, research skills, social studies, study skills, technology, theater arts, vocational-technical courses, Web site design, word processing, writing, writing, yearbook classes. Computer network features include campus e-mail, on-campus library services, CD-ROMs, online commercial services, Internet access, office computer access, DVD, wireless campus network.

Contact Ms. Karen Booth, Director of Recruitment/Grade 9 Admissions. 773-622-9494 Ext. 25. Fax: 773-622-8511 Ext. 25. E-mail: kbooth@ndhs4girls.org. Web site: www.ndhs4girls.org.

NOTRE DAME JUNIOR/SENIOR HIGH SCHOOL

60 Spangenburg Avenue
East Stroudsburg, Pennsylvania 18301
Head of School: Mr. Jeffrey Neill Lyons Jr.

General Information Coeducational day college-preparatory, arts, and religious studies school, affiliated with Roman Catholic Church. Grades 9–12. Founded: 1967. Setting: suburban. 40-acre campus. 4 buildings on campus. Approved or accredited by Middle States Association of Colleges and Schools, National Catholic Education Association, and Pennsylvania Department of Education. Total enrollment: 247. Upper school average class size: 23. Upper school faculty-student ratio: 1:15.

Upper School Student Profile Grade 9: 69 students (32 boys, 37 girls); Grade 10: 59 students (24 boys, 35 girls); Grade 11: 52 students (29 boys, 23 girls); Grade 12: 67 students (34 boys, 33 girls). 87% of students are Roman Catholic.

Faculty School total: 27. In upper school: 8 men, 13 women; 10 have advanced degrees.

Graduation Requirements Lab/keyboard, mathematics, moral theology, physical education (includes health), physical science, religion (includes Bible studies and theology), senior project, theology, U.S. history, U.S. literature, Western civilization, word processing, world cultures, world religions.

Special Academic Programs Advanced Placement exam preparation in 4 subject areas; honors section; study at local college for college credit.

College Placement 50 students graduated in 2005; 49 went to college, including Marywood University; The University of Scranton. Other: 1 went to work.

Student Life Upper grades have uniform requirement, student council. Discipline rests primarily with faculty. Attendance at religious services is required.

Tuition and Aid Day student tuition: $4200. Tuition installment plan (FACTS Tuition Payment Plan). Tuition reduction for siblings, need-based scholarship grants available. In 2005–06, 30% of upper-school students received aid.

Admissions Traditional secondary-level entrance grade is 9. Achievement tests or TerraNova required. Deadline for receipt of application materials: May 1. No application fee required. Interview required.

Athletics Interscholastic: baseball (boys), basketball (b,g), cheering (g), field hockey (g), soccer (b,g), softball (g), swimming and diving (b,g), tennis (b,g), winter soccer (b,g); coed interscholastic: aerobics/dance, dance team, golf, soccer; coed intramural: cross-country running, indoor soccer, jogging, strength & conditioning, weight training. 2 PE instructors, 19 coaches, 1 trainer.

Computers Computer network features include campus e-mail, on-campus library services, CD-ROMs, Internet access, office computer access.

Contact Mr. Jeffrey Neill Lyons, Principal. 570-421-0466. Fax: 570-476-0629. E-mail: notredame@usnetway.com. Web site: www.notredamehigh.com.

NOTRE DAME PREPARATORY SCHOOL

815 Hampton Lane
Towson, Maryland 21286
Head of School: Sr. Patricia McCarron, SSND

General Information Girls' day college-preparatory school, affiliated with Roman Catholic Church. Grades 6–12. Founded: 1873. Setting: suburban. Nearest major city is Baltimore. 60-acre campus. 3 buildings on campus. Approved or accredited by Association of Independent Maryland Schools, Middle States Association of Colleges and Schools, National Catholic Education Association, and Maryland Department of Education. Member of National Association of Independent Schools. Endowment: $670,000. Total enrollment: 742. Upper school average class size: 16. Upper school faculty-student ratio: 1:9.

Upper School Student Profile Grade 9: 134 students (134 girls); Grade 10: 164 students (164 girls); Grade 11: 131 students (131 girls); Grade 12: 137 students (137 girls). 85% of students are Roman Catholic.

Faculty School total: 87. In upper school: 13 men, 67 women; 68 have advanced degrees.

Subjects Offered Algebra, American history, American literature, anatomy, architectural drawing, art, Bible studies, biology, calculus, calculus-AP, ceramics, chemistry, community service, creative writing, drama, economics, English, English literature, environmental science, European history, fine arts, French, geometry, government/civics, grammar, history, Japanese, journalism, Latin, marine biology, mathematics, music, philosophy, photography, physical education, physics, religion, science, social studies, Spanish, statistics, swimming, theater, trigonometry, world history, world literature, writing.

Graduation Requirements Arts and fine arts (art, music, dance, drama), English, foreign language, mathematics, physical education (includes health), religion (includes Bible studies and theology), science, social studies (includes history), swimming. Community service is required.

Special Academic Programs Advanced Placement exam preparation in 16 subject areas; honors section; independent study.

College Placement 133 students graduated in 2005; all went to college, including Clemson University; Gettysburg College; Loyola College in Maryland; University of Maryland, College Park; University of Notre Dame; Virginia Polytechnic Institute and State University. Median SAT verbal: 630, median SAT math: 610. 56% scored over 600 on SAT verbal, 52% scored over 600 on SAT math.

Student Life Upper grades have uniform requirement, student council, honor system. Discipline rests equally with students and faculty. Attendance at religious services is required.

Tuition and Aid Day student tuition: $12,600. Tuition installment plan (FACTS Tuition Payment Plan). Need-based scholarship grants available. In 2005–06, 25% of upper-school students received aid. Total amount of financial aid awarded in 2005–06: $884,988.

Admissions Traditional secondary-level entrance grade is 9. For fall 2005, 280 students applied for upper-level admission, 173 were accepted, 81 enrolled. High School Placement Test and ISEE required. Deadline for receipt of application materials: December 9. Application fee required: $75. On-campus interview required.

Athletics Interscholastic: badminton, basketball, cross-country running, field hockey, golf, indoor track, lacrosse, soccer, softball, swimming and diving, tennis, track and field, volleyball, winter (indoor) track, winter soccer; intramural: badminton, basketball, cheering, dance team, field hockey, soccer, tennis, volleyball, yoga. 6 PE instructors, 28 coaches, 1 trainer.

Computers Computers are regularly used in all classes. Computer network features include campus e-mail, on-campus library services, CD-ROMs, online commercial services, Internet access, file transfer, office computer access, wireless campus network, computer-based science, music, language and art labs, Microsoft Office, laptop program for freshmen, automated library research databases.

Contact Mrs. Katherine Goetz, Director of Admission. 410-825-0590. Fax: 410-825-0982. E-mail: goetzk@notredameprep.com. Web site: www.notredameprep.com.

ANNOUNCEMENT FROM THE SCHOOL Academic excellence, spiritual growth, and the practice of social justice are central to the School's mission. A new state-of-the-art sports and fitness center opened last spring and complements modern facilities. Technology remains central as the Upper Level transitions to a wireless laptop environment for all students by fall 2006.

NOTRE DAME REGIONAL SECONDARY

2855 Parker Street
Vancouver, British Columbia V5K 2T8, Canada
Head of School: Mr. Michael Cooke

General Information Coeducational day college-preparatory, general academic, arts, business, and religious studies school, affiliated with Roman Catholic Church. Grades 8–12. Founded: 1953. Setting: urban. 3-hectare campus. 1 building on campus. Approved or accredited by British Columbia Department of Education. Language of instruction: English. Total enrollment: 630. Upper school average class size: 27. Upper school faculty-student ratio: 1:15.

Upper School Student Profile Grade 8: 127 students (76 boys, 51 girls); Grade 9: 140 students (76 boys, 64 girls); Grade 10: 117 students (53 boys, 64 girls); Grade 11: 100 students (53 boys, 47 girls); Grade 12: 133 students (57 boys, 76 girls). 95% of students are Roman Catholic.

Faculty School total: 47. In upper school: 27 men, 20 women; 10 have advanced degrees.

Subjects Offered 20th century history, acting, art, band, biology, business communications, business education, calculus, Canadian history, Canadian law, career and personal planning, Catholic belief and practice, chemistry, choir, choreography, Christian education, comparative civilizations, computer education, concert choir, drama performance, dramatic arts, English, English literature, entrepreneurship, forestry, French as a second language, geography, history, history of the Catholic Church, independent study, information technology, Italian, journalism, leadership training, marketing, mathematics, performing arts, personal fitness, photography, physical education, physics, science, set design, social studies, Spanish, sports conditioning, stage design, stagecraft, work experience, writing.

Graduation Requirements Canadian history, career and personal planning, Catholic belief and practice, English, foreign language, mathematics, science, work experience.

Special Academic Programs Honors section; accelerated programs; independent study; academic accommodation for the gifted and the musically talented; remedial reading and/or remedial writing; remedial math; programs in English, mathematics, general development for dyslexic students; special instructional classes for deaf students, blind students.

College Placement 131 students graduated in 2005; 100 went to college, including Simon Fraser University; The University of British Columbia; University of Victoria. Other: 28 went to work, 3 had other specific plans.

Student Life Upper grades have uniform requirement, student council, honor system. Discipline rests primarily with faculty. Attendance at religious services is required.

Summer Programs ESL programs offered; held on campus; accepts boys and girls; open to students from other schools. 30 students usually enrolled. 2006 schedule: July 1 to July 31.

Tuition and Aid Day student tuition: CAN$12,500. Merit scholarship grants available. Total upper-school merit-scholarship money awarded for 2005–06: CAN$3200.

Admissions Traditional secondary-level entrance grade is 8. For fall 2005, 200 students applied for upper-level admission, 170 were accepted, 130 enrolled. Deadline for receipt of application materials: February. Application fee required: CAN$250. Interview required.

Athletics Interscholastic: basketball (boys, girls), dance squad (g), field hockey (g), football (b), mountain biking (b,g), soccer (b,g), track and field (b,g), volleyball (g), wrestling (b,g); intramural: basketball (b,g), floor hockey (b), weight training (b); coed interscholastic: golf, tennis, wilderness; coed intramural: hiking/backpacking, outdoor adventure, soccer, Special Olympics, volleyball. 4 PE instructors.

Computers Computers are regularly used in business education, independent study, information technology, remedial study skills, research skills, theater arts, Web site design, yearbook classes. Computer network features include on-campus library services, CD-ROMs, Internet access.

Contact Maureen Grant, Office Manager. 604-255-5454. Fax: 604-255-2115. E-mail: mgrant@ndrs.org. Web site: www.ndrs.org.

OAK CREEK RANCH SCHOOL

West Sedona, Arizona
See Special Needs Schools section.

OAK HILL ACADEMY

2635 Oak Hill Road
Mouth of Wilson, Virginia 24363
Head of School: Dr. Michael D. Groves

General Information Coeducational boarding and day college-preparatory and general academic school, affiliated with Baptist Church. Grades 8–12. Founded: 1878. Setting: rural. Nearest major city is Charlotte, NC. Students are housed in single-sex dormitories. 400-acre campus. 21 buildings on campus. Approved or accredited by Southern Association of Independent Schools, The Association of Boarding Schools, Virginia Association of Independent Schools, and Virginia Department of Education. Member of Secondary School Admission Test Board. Endowment: $704,144. Total enrollment: 109. Upper school average class size: 9. Upper school faculty-student ratio: 1:9.

Upper School Student Profile Grade 8: 7 students (2 boys, 5 girls); Grade 9: 12 students (8 boys, 4 girls); Grade 10: 15 students (10 boys, 5 girls); Grade 11: 24 students (14 boys, 10 girls); Grade 12: 51 students (28 boys, 23 girls). 95% of students are boarding students. 24% are state residents. 21 states are represented in upper school student body. 7% are international students. International students from India, Jamaica, Republic of Korea, and Switzerland. 27% of students are Baptist.

Faculty School total: 17. In upper school: 10 men, 7 women; 8 have advanced degrees; 14 reside on campus.

Subjects Offered 3-dimensional design, accounting, advanced math, Advanced Placement courses, algebra, American history, art, biology, business, business education, business mathematics, calculus, chemistry, computer science, creative writing, drama, earth science, English, equine studies, fine arts, geography, geometry, health, instrumental music, keyboarding, library studies, mathematics, Microsoft, photography, physical education, physics, psychology, religion, science, social science, social studies, Spanish, study skills, theater, trigonometry, U.S. government, U.S. history, world history, yearbook.

Graduation Requirements Arts and fine arts (art, music, dance, drama), computer science, English, foreign language, mathematics, physical education (includes health), religion (includes Bible studies and theology), science, social science, social studies (includes history).

Special Academic Programs Advanced Placement exam preparation in 2 subject areas; study at local college for college credit; remedial reading and/or remedial writing; special instructional classes for students with Attention Deficit Disorder.

College Placement 37 students graduated in 2005; 34 went to college, including Clemson University; East Carolina University; Marshall University; North Carolina State University; The College of William and Mary; Virginia Polytechnic Institute and State University. Other: 1 went to work, 2 had other specific plans. Median SAT verbal: 480, median SAT math: 470. 10% scored over 600 on SAT verbal, 5% scored over 600 on SAT math, 5% scored over 26 on composite ACT.

Student Life Upper grades have uniform requirement. Discipline rests primarily with faculty. Attendance at religious services is required.

Summer Programs Remediation, advancement programs offered; session focuses on advancement and remediation; held on campus; accepts boys and girls; open to students from other schools. 50 students usually enrolled. 2006 schedule: June 26 to July 29. Application deadline: none.

Tuition and Aid Day student tuition: $6000; 7-day tuition and room/board: $18,300. Tuition installment plan (monthly payment plans, individually arranged payment plans, 12-month interest free payment plan for those students accepted by June 1).

Tuition reduction for siblings, need-based scholarship grants available. In 2005–06, 32% of upper-school students received aid. Total amount of financial aid awarded in 2005–06: $335,000.

Admissions Traditional secondary-level entrance grade is 11. For fall 2005, 98 students applied for upper-level admission, 67 were accepted, 58 enrolled. Any standardized test required. Deadline for receipt of application materials: none. Application fee required: $50. On-campus interview recommended.

Athletics Interscholastic: baseball (boys), basketball (b,g), cheering (g), tennis (b,g), volleyball (g); intramural: back packing (g), baseball (b), basketball (b,g), billiards (b,g), bowling (b,g), canoeing/kayaking (b,g), equestrian sports (b,g), fishing (b), golf (b,g), hiking/backpacking (b,g), horseback riding (b,g), jogging (b,g), nautilus (b,g), outdoor recreation (b,g), running (b,g), softball (g), strength & conditioning (b,g), table tennis (b,g), tennis (b,g), walking (g), weight lifting (b,g); coed interscholastic: soccer, track and field; coed intramural: flag football, skiing (downhill), snowboarding, soccer, volleyball, yoga. 1 PE instructor, 1 coach, 1 trainer.

Computers Computers are regularly used in business education, English, mathematics, science classes. Computer resources include campus e-mail, on-campus library services, Internet access, wireless campus network.

Contact Dr. Michael D. Groves, President. 276-579-2619. Fax: 276-579-4722. E-mail: info@oak-hill.net. Web site: www.oak-hill.net.

See full description on page 942.

OAK KNOLL SCHOOL OF THE HOLY CHILD

44 Blackburn Road
Summit, New Jersey 07901
Head of School: Timothy J. Saburn

General Information Coeducational day college-preparatory, arts, and religious studies school, affiliated with Roman Catholic Church. Boys grades K–6, girls grades K–12. Founded: 1924. Setting: suburban. Nearest major city is New York, NY. 11-acre campus. 4 buildings on campus. Approved or accredited by Middle States Association of Colleges and Schools and New Jersey Department of Education. Member of National Association of Independent Schools and Secondary School Admission Test Board. Endowment: $8.8 million. Total enrollment: 549. Upper school average class size: 15. Upper school faculty-student ratio: 1:8.

Upper School Student Profile Grade 7: 36 students (36 girls); Grade 8: 37 students (37 girls); Grade 9: 59 students (59 girls); Grade 10: 64 students (64 girls); Grade 11: 55 students (55 girls); Grade 12: 59 students (59 girls). 88% of students are Roman Catholic.

Faculty School total: 68. In upper school: 11 men, 39 women; 29 have advanced degrees.

Subjects Offered Advanced studio art-AP, algebra, American history, American literature, anatomy, art, biology, biology-AP, calculus, calculus-AP, chemistry, chemistry-AP, Chinese, computer science, computer science-AP, creative writing, dance, digital photography, driver education, earth science, English, English literature, English-AP, environmental science, ethics, European history, European history-AP, expository writing, fine arts, French, French-AP, genetics, geography, geology, geometry, health, history, mathematics, music, oceanography, physical education, physics, science, social studies, Spanish, Spanish-AP, speech, studio art-AP, theology, trigonometry, U.S. history-AP, word processing, world history, world literature, writing.

Graduation Requirements Arts and fine arts (art, music, dance, drama), computer science, English, foreign language, mathematics, physical education (includes health), religion (includes Bible studies and theology), science, social studies (includes history).

Special Academic Programs Advanced Placement exam preparation in 11 subject areas; honors section.

College Placement 60 students graduated in 2005; 58 went to college, including Boston University; Cornell University; Georgetown University; Trinity College; University of Notre Dame; Villanova University. Mean SAT verbal: 630, mean SAT math: 620.

Student Life Upper grades have uniform requirement, student council. Discipline rests primarily with faculty. Attendance at religious services is required.

Tuition and Aid Day student tuition: $22,250. Tuition installment plan (Key Tuition Payment Plan). Merit scholarship grants, need-based scholarship grants available. In 2005–06, 16% of upper-school students received aid; total upper-school merit-scholarship money awarded: $41,375. Total amount of financial aid awarded in 2005–06: $915,000.

Admissions Traditional secondary-level entrance grade is 9. For fall 2005, 121 students applied for upper-level admission, 71 were accepted, 48 enrolled. SSAT required. Deadline for receipt of application materials: January 27. Application fee required: $50. Interview required.

Athletics Interscholastic: basketball, cross-country running, fencing, field hockey, lacrosse, soccer, softball, swimming and diving, tennis, track and field, volleyball; intramural: deck hockey. 3 PE instructors, 9 coaches, 1 trainer.

Computers Computers are regularly used in all classes. Computer network features include campus e-mail, on-campus library services, CD-ROMs, Internet access, wireless campus network, 9th grade laptop program.

Contact Suzanne Kimm Lewis, Admissions Director. 908-522-8109. Fax: 908-277-1838. E-mail: okadmissions@oakknoll.org. Web site: www.oakknoll.org.

See full description on page 944.

THE OAKLAND SCHOOL

362 McKee Place
Pittsburgh, Pennsylvania 15213
Head of School: Jack C. King

General Information Coeducational day college-preparatory school; primarily serves underachievers. Grades 8–12. Founded: 1982. Setting: urban. 1 building on campus. Approved or accredited by Pennsylvania Association of Private Academic Schools, United Private Schools Association of Pennsylvania, and Pennsylvania Department of Education. Total enrollment: 60. Upper school average class size: 6. Upper school faculty-student ratio: 1:6.

Upper School Student Profile Grade 8: 2 students (2 boys); Grade 9: 14 students (9 boys, 5 girls); Grade 10: 19 students (11 boys, 8 girls); Grade 11: 24 students (16 boys, 8 girls); Grade 12: 27 students (22 boys, 5 girls).

Faculty School total: 12. In upper school: 6 men, 4 women; 7 have advanced degrees.

Subjects Offered Advanced math, algebra, American history, American literature, art, art history, biology, business skills, calculus, chemistry, computer math, computer science, creative writing, drama, earth science, ecology, economics, English, English literature, environmental science, ESL, expository writing, fine arts, French, geography, geometry, government/civics, history, Latin, mathematics, physical education, physics, pre-calculus, psychology, SAT/ACT preparation, science, social studies, Spanish, speech, trigonometry, world history, world literature, writing.

Graduation Requirements Arts and fine arts (art, music, dance, drama), computer literacy, English, mathematics, physical education (includes health), science, social studies (includes history). Community service is required.

Special Academic Programs Advanced Placement exam preparation in 3 subject areas; honors section; accelerated programs; independent study; study at local college for college credit; academic accommodation for the gifted and the artistically talented; remedial reading and/or remedial writing; remedial math; ESL (2 students enrolled).

College Placement 18 students graduated in 2005; 16 went to college, including Chatham College; Indiana University of Pennsylvania; University of Pittsburgh. Other: 2 went to work. Mean SAT verbal: 580, mean SAT math: 504.

Student Life Upper grades have student council. Discipline rests primarily with faculty.

Tuition and Aid Day student tuition: $8900. Tuition installment plan (monthly payment plans, individually arranged payment plans, quarterly payment plan, semi-annual payment plan). Tuition reduction for siblings, merit scholarship grants, need-based scholarship grants available. In 2005–06, 30% of upper-school students received aid; total upper-school merit-scholarship money awarded: $10,000. Total amount of financial aid awarded in 2005–06: $51,000.

Admissions Traditional secondary-level entrance grade is 10. For fall 2005, 32 students applied for upper-level admission, 26 were accepted, 26 enrolled. WRAT required. Deadline for receipt of application materials: none. Application fee required: $100. On-campus interview required.

Athletics Intramural: aerobics/dance (girls), dance (g); coed intramural: baseball, basketball, bicycling, billiards, bowling, cooperative games, cross-country running, fitness, fitness walking, flag football, Frisbee, golf, hiking/backpacking, ice skating, jogging, jump rope, kickball, martial arts, racquetball, running, skateboarding, skiing (cross-country), skiing (downhill), snowboarding, softball, swimming and diving, tai chi, tennis, volleyball, walking.

Computers Computers are regularly used in all academic classes. Computer network features include campus e-mail, CD-ROMs, Internet access, office computer access, DVD, wireless campus network.

Contact Admissions Desk. 412-621-7878. Fax: 412-621-7881. E-mail: oschool@stargate.net. Web site: www.theoaklandschool.org.

See full description on page 946.

OAKLAND SCHOOL

Keswick, Virginia
See Special Needs Schools section.

OAKLEY SCHOOL

251 West Weber Canyon Road
Oakley, Utah 84055

See full description on page 948.

OAK MOUNTAIN ACADEMY

222 Cross Plains Road
Carrollton, Georgia 30116
Head of School: Mr. Ricky Parmer

General Information Coeducational day college-preparatory school, affiliated with Christian faith. Grades K–12. Founded: 1962. Setting: small town. Nearest major city is Atlanta. 88-acre campus. 2 buildings on campus. Approved or accredited by Georgia Accrediting Commission, Georgia Independent School Association, and Georgia Department of Education. Candidate for accreditation by Southern Association of Colleges and Schools. Endowment: $496,583. Total enrollment: 233. Upper school average class size: 9. Upper school faculty-student ratio: 1:4.

Upper School Student Profile Grade 9: 19 students (7 boys, 12 girls); Grade 10: 14 students (8 boys, 6 girls); Grade 11: 13 students (9 boys, 4 girls); Grade 12: 10 students (4 boys, 6 girls).

Faculty School total: 30. In upper school: 7 men, 6 women; 8 have advanced degrees.

Subjects Offered Advanced math, Advanced Placement courses, algebra, American government, American history, American literature, anatomy, ancient world history, art, athletic training, athletics, Bible, biology, biology-AP, calculus, calculus-AP, chemistry, chemistry-AP, chorus, college counseling, community service, computer graphics, computer science, discrete mathematics, drama, economics, electives, English composition, English language-AP, English literature, English literature-AP, English-AP, expository writing, film appreciation, French, geometry, government, graphic arts, guidance, independent study, Latin, modern civilization, music, physical fitness, physical science, physics, pre-calculus, public speaking, research skills, senior internship, senior project, Spanish, Spanish-AP, statistics, student government, U.S. history, U.S. history-AP, world literature, yearbook.

Graduation Requirements Algebra, ancient world history, Bible, biology, chemistry, computer science, economics, electives, English, foreign language, geometry, modern civilization, physical education (includes health), physical science, public speaking, U.S. government, U.S. history, Senior Project, including research paper, oral presentation, creating a product and 50-hour internship. Community service is required.

Special Academic Programs Advanced Placement exam preparation in 5 subject areas; honors section; independent study; study at local college for college credit.

College Placement 12 students graduated in 2005; all went to college, including Auburn University; Davidson College; The University of Alabama at Birmingham; University of Georgia. Mean SAT verbal: 576, mean SAT math: 580. 45% scored over 600 on SAT verbal, 45% scored over 600 on SAT math.

Student Life Upper grades have specified standards of dress, student council. Discipline rests primarily with faculty.

Tuition and Aid Day student tuition: $8120. Tuition installment plan (monthly payment plans, three-payment plan). Tuition reduction for siblings, need-based scholarship grants available. In 2005–06, 23% of upper-school students received aid. Total amount of financial aid awarded in 2005–06: $64,130.

Admissions Traditional secondary-level entrance grade is 9. School's own exam required. Deadline for receipt of application materials: none. Application fee required: $50. Interview required.

Athletics Interscholastic: baseball (boys), basketball (b,g), cheering (g), cross-country running (b,g), soccer (b,g), softball (g), swimming and diving (b,g), tennis (b,g), track and field (b,g); coed interscholastic: golf. 2 PE instructors, 4 coaches.

Computers Computers are regularly used in English, foreign language, graphic arts, independent study, lab/keyboard, programming, science, Spanish, yearbook classes. Computer network features include campus e-mail, on-campus library services, CD-ROMs, online commercial services, Internet access, DVD.

Contact Ms. Peggy Harmon, Director of Admissions and Development. 770-834-6651. Fax: 770-834-6785. E-mail: peggyharmon@oakmountain.us. Web site: www.oakmountain.us.

OAK RIDGE MILITARY ACADEMY

2309 Oak Ridge Road
PO Box 498
Oak Ridge, North Carolina 27310
Head of School: Lt. Col. James P. Flanigan

General Information Coeducational boarding and day college-preparatory and leadership school. Boarding grades 7–12, day grades 6–12. Founded: 1852. Setting: rural. Nearest major city is Greensboro. Students are housed in single-sex dormitories. 101-acre campus. 22 buildings on campus. Approved or accredited by Southern Association of Colleges and Schools and North Carolina Department of Education. Member of National Association of Independent Schools. Endowment: $2.7 million. Total enrollment: 146. Upper school average class size: 11. Upper school faculty-student ratio: 1:7.

Upper School Student Profile 84% of students are boarding students. 49% are state residents. 16 states are represented in upper school student body. 14% are international students. International students from Bermuda, China, Honduras, Mexico, Philippines, and Republic of Korea; 4 other countries represented in student body.

Faculty School total: 19. In upper school: 10 men, 9 women; 6 have advanced degrees; 14 reside on campus.

Subjects Offered Algebra, American government-AP, American history, American history-AP, American literature, biology, calculus, chemistry, college writing, computer math, computer science, creative writing, driver education, earth science, English, English literature, environmental science, environmental science-AP, ESL, French, geometry, German, government/civics, grammar, health, JROTC, JROTC or LEAD (Leadership Education and Development), mathematics, military science, music, physical education, physics, SAT preparation, science, social studies, Spanish, trigonometry, world history, writing.

Graduation Requirements Computer science, English, foreign language, mathematics, physical education (includes health), ROTC, science, social studies (includes history), letter of acceptance from a college, 20 hours of community service.

Special Academic Programs Advanced Placement exam preparation in 5 subject areas; honors section; accelerated programs; independent study; study at local college for college credit; academic accommodation for the gifted; special instructional classes for students with Attention Deficit Disorder and Attention Deficit Hyperactivity Disorder; ESL (6 students enrolled).

College Placement 41 students graduated in 2004; 40 went to college, including Appalachian State University; East Carolina University; North Carolina State University; The Citadel, The Military College of South Carolina; The University of North Carolina at Chapel Hill; The University of North Carolina at Charlotte. Other: 1 entered military service.

Student Life Upper grades have uniform requirement, student council, honor system. Discipline rests equally with students and faculty. Attendance at religious services is required.

Tuition and Aid Day student tuition: $11,325; 7-day tuition and room/board: $19,990. Tuition installment plan (Key Tuition Payment Plan, SMART Tuition Payment Plan, monthly payment plans). Tuition reduction for siblings, merit scholarship grants, USS Education Loan Program available. In 2004–05, 24% of upper-school students received aid; total upper-school merit-scholarship money awarded: $134,000.

Admissions For fall 2005, 162 students applied for upper-level admission, 141 were accepted, 129 enrolled. Deadline for receipt of application materials: none. Application fee required: $100. Interview recommended.

Athletics Interscholastic: baseball (boys), basketball (b,g), cross-country running (b,g), golf (b), JROTC drill (b,g), lacrosse (b), marksmanship (b,g), soccer (b,g), swimming and diving (b,g), tennis (b), track and field (b,g), volleyball (g), wrestling (b); intramural: baseball (b), basketball (b,g), flag football (b), outdoor adventure (b,g), paint ball (b,g), rappelling (b,g), scuba diving (b,g), skydiving (b,g), strength & conditioning (b,g), weight lifting (b,g); coed interscholastic: drill team, JROTC drill, marksmanship, riflery, swimming and diving, track and field; coed intramural: outdoor adventure, paint ball, pistol, rappelling, scuba diving, skydiving, softball, strength & conditioning, weight lifting. 1 PE instructor, 12 coaches, 1 trainer.

Computers Computers are regularly used in English, mathematics, science classes. Computer resources include on-campus library services, CD-ROMs, Internet access.

Contact Mr. John Campbell, Deputy Director of Admissions. 336-643-4131 Ext. 148. Fax: 336-643-1797. E-mail: jcampbell@ormila.com. Web site: www.oakridgemilitary.com.

See full description on page 950.

THE OAKRIDGE SCHOOL

5900 West Pioneer Parkway
Arlington, Texas 76013-2899
Head of School: Andy J. Broadus

General Information Coeducational day college-preparatory, arts, and technology school. Grades PS–12. Founded: 1979. Setting: suburban. 35-acre campus. 4 buildings on campus. Approved or accredited by Independent Schools Association of the Southwest and Texas Department of Education. Member of National Association of Independent Schools. Endowment: $220,000. Total enrollment: 765. Upper school average class size: 15. Upper school faculty-student ratio: 1:9.

Upper School Student Profile Grade 9: 59 students (29 boys, 30 girls); Grade 10: 68 students (32 boys, 36 girls); Grade 11: 70 students (35 boys, 35 girls); Grade 12: 53 students (24 boys, 29 girls).

Faculty School total: 94. In upper school: 10 men, 14 women; 16 have advanced degrees.

Subjects Offered Acting, Advanced Placement courses, algebra, American government-AP, American history, American history-AP, American literature, anatomy, anthropology, archaeology, art, athletics, biology, calculus, calculus-AP, chemistry, Chinese, choir, community service, computer science, computer science-AP, creative writing, drama, economics, English, European history, European history-AP, fine arts, French, French-AP, geography, geometry, government/civics, grammar, history, history of England, honors algebra, honors English, honors geometry, honors U.S. history, honors world history, independent study, language and composition, literature and composition-AP, mathematics, physics, physics-AP, physiology, pre-calculus, Spanish, Spanish-AP, strings, theater, trigonometry, world history.

Graduation Requirements Arts and fine arts (art, music, dance, drama), English, foreign language, mathematics, physical education (includes health), science, social studies (includes history), participation in five seasons of athletics. Community service is required.

Special Academic Programs Advanced Placement exam preparation in 17 subject areas; honors section; independent study; study abroad; academic accommodation for the gifted, the musically talented, and the artistically talented.

College Placement 70 students graduated in 2005; 69 went to college, including Baylor University; Southern Methodist University; Texas A&M University; Texas Christian University; Texas Tech University; The University of Texas at Austin. Other: 1 entered military service. Mean SAT verbal: 590, mean SAT math: 600, mean composite ACT: 25. 50% scored over 600 on SAT verbal, 50% scored over 600 on SAT math, 39% scored over 26 on composite ACT.

Student Life Upper grades have uniform requirement, student council, honor system. Discipline rests primarily with faculty.

Summer Programs Remediation, enrichment, advancement, sports, art/fine arts, computer instruction programs offered; session focuses on enrichment and remediation; held both on and off campus; held at museums, recreational facilities; accepts boys and girls; open to students from other schools. 200 students usually enrolled. 2006 schedule: June 13 to July 15. Application deadline: none.

Tuition and Aid Day student tuition: $11,370. Tuition installment plan (FACTS Tuition Payment Plan, early discount option). Need-based scholarship grants, tuition remission for faculty and staff available. In 2005–06, 38% of upper-school students received aid. Total amount of financial aid awarded in 2005–06: $300,000.

Admissions Traditional secondary-level entrance grade is 9. For fall 2005, 58 students applied for upper-level admission, 43 were accepted, 36 enrolled. ERB Reading and Math, ISEE or Otis-Lennon School Ability Test required. Deadline for receipt of application materials: none. Application fee required: $50. On-campus interview required.

Athletics Interscholastic: baseball (boys), basketball (b,g), cross-country running (b,g), field hockey (g), football (b), golf (b,g), soccer (b,g), softball (g), tennis (b,g), track and field (b,g), volleyball (g), winter soccer (b,g); intramural: weight training (b); coed interscholastic: cheering. 10 coaches, 1 trainer.

Computers Computers are regularly used in art, English, foreign language, history, mathematics, programming, science, yearbook classes. Computer network features include campus e-mail, on-campus library services, CD-ROMs, online commercial services, Internet access.

Contact Mrs. Linda H. Broadus, Director of Admissions. 817-451-4994 Ext. 704. Fax: 817-457-6681. E-mail: lbroadus@theoakridgeschool.org. Web site: www.theoakridgeschool.org.

ANNOUNCEMENT FROM THE SCHOOL The Oakridge School is an independent college-preparatory school founded in 1979. Serving students in preschool through 12th grade, the School encourages the students to develop a lifelong interest in learning, staying physically fit, and making contributions to their communities. At Oakridge, students experience a broad range of opportunities in a challenging academic environment. Athletics, the fine arts, and numerous extracurricular activities provide additional outlets for students' talents and interests. The School offers half-day and full-day programs for preschool and prekindergarten and a full-day program for kindergarten. In Lower School, grades 1 and 2 are self-contained classrooms; grades 3 and 4 rotate among the 3 teachers at each level. In addition, children also work with specialists in Spanish, computer, art, music, and P.E. Middle and Upper School offer honors courses, and all disciplines in Upper School offer Advanced Placement courses. The college adviser supports Upper School students and their parents in their search for the right colleges or universities and then becomes the students' advocate in the college admissions process. The arts at Oakridge flourish in the 32,000-square-foot fine arts center. The center includes a 400-seat performance hall. Oakridge students receive outstanding recognition throughout the state for their accomplishments in choral music, strings, art, and drama. In athletics, Oakridge students participate in interscholastic sports beginning in 7th grade. The School offers 10 different sports during the fall, winter, and spring seasons. The full range of opportunities for students means that "everybody can be somebody at Oakridge."

OAKWOOD FRIENDS SCHOOL

22 Spackenkill Road
Poughkeepsie, New York 12603
Head of School: Peter F. Baily

General Information Coeducational boarding and day college-preparatory and arts school, affiliated with Society of Friends. Boarding grades 9–12, day grades 6–12. Founded: 1858. Setting: suburban. Nearest major city is New York. Students are housed in single-sex by floor dormitories. 63-acre campus. 22 buildings on campus. Approved or accredited by Friends Council on Education, New York State Association of Independent Schools, The Association of Boarding Schools, and New York Department of Education. Member of National Association of Independent Schools

and Secondary School Admission Test Board. Endowment: $1.8 million. Total enrollment: 176. Upper school average class size: 15. Upper school faculty-student ratio: 1:8.

Upper School Student Profile Grade 9: 31 students (21 boys, 10 girls); Grade 10: 38 students (19 boys, 19 girls); Grade 11: 43 students (25 boys, 18 girls); Grade 12: 33 students (13 boys, 20 girls). 39% of students are boarding students. 81% are state residents. 10 states are represented in upper school student body. 12% are international students. International students from China, Jamaica, Republic of Korea, and U.S. Virgin Islands. 4% of students are members of Society of Friends.

Faculty School total: 35. In upper school: 14 men, 15 women; 21 have advanced degrees; 21 reside on campus.

Subjects Offered Acting, algebra, American history, American literature, anthropology, art, art history, biology, calculus, ceramics, chemistry, community service, computer programming, computer science, creative writing, dance, directing, drama, drawing, earth science, ecology, English, English literature, environmental science, ESL, European history, expository writing, fine arts, French, geometry, government/civics, health, history, interdisciplinary studies, mathematics, music, painting, photography, physical education, physics, printmaking, Quakerism and ethics, science, social studies, Spanish, technology, theater, world history, writing.

Graduation Requirements American history, arts and fine arts (art, music, dance, drama), computer literacy, English, foreign language, interdisciplinary studies, mathematics, physical education (includes health), Quakerism and ethics, science, world history. Community service is required.

Special Academic Programs Advanced Placement exam preparation in 8 subject areas; independent study; academic accommodation for the gifted; special instructional classes for students with mild learning differences; ESL (12 students enrolled).

College Placement 25 students graduated in 2005; all went to college, including American University; Boston University; Goucher College; Manhattanville College; Sarah Lawrence College; Vassar College. Median SAT verbal: 650, median SAT math: 550. 52% scored over 600 on SAT verbal, 28% scored over 600 on SAT math.

Student Life Upper grades have specified standards of dress, student council, honor system. Discipline rests equally with students and faculty. Attendance at religious services is required.

Tuition and Aid Day student tuition: $18,300; 5-day tuition and room/board: $27,560; 7-day tuition and room/board: $31,720. Tuition installment plan (Academic Management Services Plan, Key Tuition Payment Plan, monthly payment plans, individually arranged payment plans). Need-based scholarship grants, need-based loans available. In 2005–06, 39% of upper-school students received aid. Total amount of financial aid awarded in 2005–06: $420,000.

Admissions Traditional secondary-level entrance grade is 9. For fall 2005, 89 students applied for upper-level admission, 76 were accepted, 31 enrolled. SLEP for foreign students, TOEFL or writing sample required. Deadline for receipt of application materials: none. Application fee required: $40. On-campus interview required.

Athletics Interscholastic: baseball (boys), basketball (b,g), cross-country running (b,g), soccer (b,g), softball (g), tennis (b,g), volleyball (g); coed interscholastic: independent competitive sports, swimming and diving, ultimate Frisbee; coed intramural: fitness, fitness walking, martial arts, table tennis, ultimate Frisbee, walking, yoga. 1 coach.

Computers Computers are regularly used in basic skills, English, foreign language, mathematics, music, science classes. Computer network features include campus e-mail, on-campus library services, CD-ROMs, online commercial services, Internet access.

Contact Robert J. Suphan, Director of Admissions. 845-462-4200. Fax: 845-462-4251. E-mail: bsuphan@oakwoodfriends.org. Web site: www.oakwoodfriends.org.

See full description on page 952.

OAKWOOD SCHOOL

11600 Magnolia Boulevard
North Hollywood, California 91601-3098
Head of School: Dr. James Alan Astman

General Information Coeducational day college-preparatory and arts school. Grades K–12. Founded: 1951. Setting: urban. Nearest major city is Los Angeles. 5-acre campus. 6 buildings on campus. Approved or accredited by California Association of Independent Schools and Western Association of Schools and Colleges. Member of National Association of Independent Schools and Secondary School Admission Test Board. Endowment: $6.3 million. Total enrollment: 764. Upper school average class size: 18. Upper school faculty-student ratio: 1:10.

Upper School Student Profile Grade 7: 80 students (40 boys, 40 girls); Grade 8: 81 students (37 boys, 44 girls); Grade 9: 80 students (42 boys, 38 girls); Grade 10: 79 students (46 boys, 33 girls); Grade 11: 78 students (37 boys, 41 girls); Grade 12: 78 students (40 boys, 38 girls).

Faculty School total: 58. In upper school: 28 men, 28 women; 36 have advanced degrees.

Subjects Offered Algebra, American history, American literature, art, art history-AP, astronomy, ballet, Basic programming, biology, biology-AP, botany, calculus, calculus-AP, ceramics, chemistry, chemistry-AP, choir, community service, comparative religion, composition, computer keyboarding, computer literacy, computer math,

computer programming, computer programming-AP, computer science, computer science-AP, computer skills, conceptual physics, constitutional law, creative writing, critical studies in film, dance, discrete math, drama, earth and space science, earth science, ecology, economics, English, English language and composition-AP, English literature, English literature and composition-AP, environmental science, ethics, European civilization, European history, expository writing, film studies, fine arts, French, French language-AP, geography, geology, geometry, government and politics-AP, government/civics, grammar, health, health and wellness, history, history of jazz, honors English, honors algebra, honors geometry, honors U.S. history, HTML design, human development, human sexuality, independent study, introduction to theater, Japanese, jazz band, jazz ensemble, lab science, Latin, life science, marine biology, mathematics, medieval/Renaissance history, modern dance, music, music composition, music theory, music theory-AP, musical theater, philosophy, photography, physical education, physics, physics-AP, pre-algebra, pre-calculus, psychology, psychology-AP, science, science fiction, senior project, Shakespeare, social studies, Spanish, Spanish language-AP, statistics, statistics-AP, theater, trigonometry, U.S. government and politics-AP, world history, world literature, writing.

Graduation Requirements Arts and fine arts (art, music, dance, drama), computer science, English, foreign language, mathematics, physical education (includes health), science, senior project, social studies (includes history), class trips. Community service is required.

Special Academic Programs Advanced Placement exam preparation in 17 subject areas; honors section; independent study; term-away projects; academic accommodation for the gifted.

College Placement 75 students graduated in 2005; all went to college, including Bard College; Brown University; New York University; University of California, Berkeley; University of Miami; University of Wisconsin–Madison. Mean SAT verbal: 667, mean SAT math: 660. 80% scored over 600 on SAT verbal, 75% scored over 600 on SAT math.

Student Life Upper grades have student council. Discipline rests primarily with faculty.

Summer Programs Enrichment, sports, art/fine arts programs offered; held on campus; accepts boys and girls; open to students from other schools.

Tuition and Aid Day student tuition: $22,000. Tuition installment plan (Key Tuition Payment Plan, monthly payment plans, individually arranged payment plans, 2- and 10-payment plans). Need-based scholarship grants, Key Education Resources Achiever Loans available. In 2005–06, 13% of upper-school students received aid. Total amount of financial aid awarded in 2005–06: $789,050.

Admissions Traditional secondary-level entrance grade is 7. For fall 2005, 317 students applied for upper-level admission, 138 were accepted, 51 enrolled. ISEE required. Deadline for receipt of application materials: January 21. Application fee required: $100. On-campus interview required.

Athletics Interscholastic: baseball (boys), basketball (b,g), cross-country running (b,g), soccer (b,g), softball (g), track and field (b,g), volleyball (b,g); coed interscholastic: equestrian sports, tennis, track and field; coed intramural: aerobics, aerobics/dance, aerobics/nautilus, badminton, basketball, bowling, cooperative games, Cosom hockey, cricket, dance, fitness, fitness walking, flag football, floor hockey, fly fishing, football, physical fitness, physical training, racquetball, rugby, softball, speedball, street hockey, strength & conditioning, table tennis, team handball, tennis, touch football, ultimate Frisbee, volleyball, walking, wallyball, weight training, winter (indoor) track. 3 PE instructors, 6 coaches.

Computers Computers are regularly used in humanities, programming, science classes. Computer network features include campus e-mail, on-campus library services, CD-ROMs, online commercial services, Internet access.

Contact Margie Llinas, Assistant to Director of Admission 7-12. 818-752-5277. Fax: 818-766-1285. E-mail: mllinas@oakwoodschool.org. Web site: www.oakwoodschool.org.

ANNOUNCEMENT FROM THE SCHOOL Oakwood School is an educational community that provides children with an educational experience that is rich in the arts, sciences, and humanities. The School is characterized by individual attention, creative and intellectual challenge, a love of learning and, above all, humanity. (www.oakwoodschool.org)

THE OAKWOOD SCHOOL
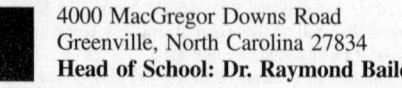
4000 MacGregor Downs Road
Greenville, North Carolina 27834
Head of School: Dr. Raymond Bailey

petersons.com

General Information Coeducational day college-preparatory and arts school. Grades K–9. Founded: 1996. Setting: small town. Nearest major city is Raleigh. 34-acre campus. 1 building on campus. Approved or accredited by North Carolina Association of Independent Schools, Southern Association of Colleges and Schools, and North Carolina Department of Education. Total enrollment: 260. Upper school faculty-student ratio: 1:4.

Upper School Student Profile Grade 9: 15 students (8 boys, 7 girls).

Faculty School total: 34. In upper school: 2 men, 2 women; 3 have advanced degrees.

Special Academic Programs Honors section.

Student Life Upper grades have specified standards of dress, student council, honor system. Discipline rests equally with students and faculty.

Tuition and Aid Day student tuition: $8600. Tuition installment plan (Insured Tuition Payment Plan, monthly payment plans, individually arranged payment plans). Need-based scholarship grants available. In 2005–06, 9% of upper-school students received aid. Total amount of financial aid awarded in 2005–06: $91,500.

Admissions Traditional secondary-level entrance grade is 9. For fall 2005, 2 students applied for upper-level admission, 2 were accepted, 2 enrolled. Writing sample required. Deadline for receipt of application materials: none. Application fee required. On-campus interview required.

Athletics Interscholastic: baseball (boys), basketball (b,g), softball (g), volleyball (g); coed interscholastic: physical fitness. 2 PE instructors, 3 coaches.

Computers Computers are regularly used in writing classes. Computer network features include on-campus library services, CD-ROMs, Internet access, office computer access, wireless campus network.

Contact Ms. Myra Bowen, Director of Admissions. 252-931-0760 Ext. 223. Fax: 252-931-0964. E-mail: mbowen@theoakwoodschool.org. Web site: theoakwoodschool.org.

ANNOUNCEMENT FROM THE SCHOOL The Oakwood School, an independent, coeducational entity in Greenville, North Carolina, was founded by a group of parents who sought a college-preparatory education for their children in a diverse community with small classes in a safe and secure setting. The School has encountered remarkable growth since its founding in 1996 and is currently comprised of 268 students in kindergarten–grade 9. (The Upper School began with grade 9 in August 2005.) The School owns 34 acres and is comprised of 3 buildings; the first section of the new Upper School will be ready for occupation in 2006. The Lower School offers a full-day program in kindergarten through grade 5. Classes are taught by an experienced and enthusiastic faculty, 68% of whom have earned an advanced degree. Interdisciplinary courses that combine the study of literature and history or mathematics and science allow students to realize that subject matter is not limited by subject name or the confines of a time period. Students are taught to think critically and creatively and to express themselves well orally and in writing. Students are introduced to elementary algebra in grades 4 and 5. The Middle School is seen as an effective bridge between the Lower and Upper Schools, and students are challenged to be ready for demanding Upper School courses that will engage and excite them. The goal is to prepare students for life by providing access to directions and interests that will serve them throughout their lives, in addition to preparing them for entry into and success within the colleges and universities of their choice. Upper School courses are available in the Middle School in mathematics and Spanish. Students in the Upper School encounter a full panoply of Advanced Placement classes and will be assisted in their college applications by the counseling staff. In addition, students throughout the School have access to the arts, clubs, and athletics as a means of ensuring a well-rounded education. Upper School students will move to their new building in summer 2006 and will graduate in 2009, at which point they will be prepared to be successful in any and all of the challenges that colleges and universities present.

O'DEA HIGH SCHOOL

802 Terry Avenue
Seattle, Washington 98104-2018
Head of School: Br. D. D. Murray

General Information Boys' day college-preparatory, general academic, and religious studies school, affiliated with Roman Catholic Church. Grades 9–12. Founded: 1923. Setting: urban. 1-acre campus. 1 building on campus. Approved or accredited by National Catholic Education Association, Northwest Association of Schools and Colleges, and Washington Department of Education. Endowment: $3.7 million. Total enrollment: 480. Upper school average class size: 25. Upper school faculty-student ratio: 1:13.

Upper School Student Profile Grade 9: 140 students (140 boys); Grade 10: 120 students (120 boys); Grade 11: 118 students (118 boys); Grade 12: 102 students (102 boys). 81% of students are Roman Catholic.

Faculty School total: 39. In upper school: 32 men, 7 women; 23 have advanced degrees.

Subjects Offered Advanced chemistry, Advanced Placement courses, African-American history, algebra, American history, American literature, art, art appreciation, arts, band, biology, calculus, chemistry, Christian doctrine, Christian ethics, Christian scripture, church history, civics, college counseling, community service, computer music, computer programming, computer-aided design, contemporary problems, drama performance, driver education, economics, English, fine arts, geometry, health, history, humanities, independent study, Japanese, jazz band, Latin, leadership training, math analysis, mathematics, mathematics-AP, physical education, physics, science, social science, Spanish, trigonometry, world literature, writing.

Graduation Requirements Arts and fine arts (art, music, dance, drama), English, foreign language, mathematics, physical education (includes health), religion (includes Bible studies and theology), science, social studies (includes history). Community service is required.

Special Academic Programs Advanced Placement exam preparation in 2 subject areas; honors section; study at local college for college credit; academic accommodation for the gifted; remedial reading and/or remedial writing.

College Placement 117 students graduated in 2005; 114 went to college, including Gonzaga University; Seattle University; University of Portland; University of Washington; Washington State University; Western Washington University. Other: 3 went to work.

Student Life Upper grades have specified standards of dress, student council, honor system. Discipline rests primarily with faculty. Attendance at religious services is required.

Tuition and Aid Day student tuition: $6038–$6944. Tuition reduction for siblings, need-based scholarship grants available. In 2005–06, 28% of upper-school students received aid. Total amount of financial aid awarded in 2005–06: $260,000.

Admissions Traditional secondary-level entrance grade is 9. For fall 2005, 300 students applied for upper-level admission, 160 were accepted, 140 enrolled. Metropolitan Achievement Test required. Deadline for receipt of application materials: January 22. No application fee required. Interview recommended.

Athletics Interscholastic: baseball, basketball, cross-country running, football, golf, soccer, swimming and diving, tennis, track and field, weight training, wrestling; intramural: basketball, bicycling, flag football, indoor soccer, physical training, soccer, touch football, volleyball, weight training. 1 PE instructor.

Computers Computers are regularly used in accounting, desktop publishing, ESL, English, graphic design, mathematics, publications, SAT preparation, science, study skills, technical drawing, yearbook classes. Computer network features include on-campus library services, CD-ROMs, Internet access, DVD.

Contact Mrs. Linda Thornton, Director of Admissions. 206-622-1308. E-mail: admissions@odea.org. Web site: www.odea.org.

OJAI VALLEY SCHOOL

723 El Paseo Road
Ojai, California 93023
Head of School: M. D. Hermes

petersons.com

General Information Coeducational boarding and day college-preparatory school. Boarding grades 3–12, day grades PK–12. Founded: 1911. Setting: rural. Nearest major city is Los Angeles. Students are housed in single-sex dormitories. 200-acre campus. 13 buildings on campus. Approved or accredited by California Association of Independent Schools, The Association of Boarding Schools, Western Association of Schools and Colleges, and California Department of Education. Member of National Association of Independent Schools and Secondary School Admission Test Board. Endowment: $1 million. Total enrollment: 339. Upper school average class size: 12. Upper school faculty-student ratio: 1:5.

Upper School Student Profile Grade 9: 30 students (20 boys, 10 girls); Grade 10: 26 students (13 boys, 13 girls); Grade 11: 38 students (15 boys, 23 girls); Grade 12: 24 students (9 boys, 15 girls). 72% of students are boarding students. 65% are state residents. 6 states are represented in upper school student body. 30% are international students. International students from Germany, Japan, Mexico, Republic of Korea, Russian Federation, and Taiwan; 6 other countries represented in student body.

Faculty School total: 54. In upper school: 11 men, 12 women; 10 have advanced degrees; 8 reside on campus.

Subjects Offered 20th century history, algebra, American history, American literature, art, art history, biology, biology-AP, calculus, chemistry, chemistry-AP, community service, computer science, conceptual physics, creative writing, drama, driver education, ecology, economics, English, English literature, English-AP, environmental science, equestrian sports, ESL, European history, fine arts, French, French-AP, geography, geometry, government/civics, grammar, health, history, honors English, humanities, independent study, Latin, mathematics, mathematics-AP, music, music theory-AP, philosophy, photography, physical education, physics, psychology, science, social studies, Spanish, speech, statistics, studio art, studio art-AP, theater, trigonometry, typing, wilderness/outdoor program, world history, writing.

Graduation Requirements Arts and fine arts (art, music, dance, drama), English, foreign language, geography, health, mathematics, science, social studies (includes history), speech.

Special Academic Programs Advanced Placement exam preparation in 10 subject areas; honors section; accelerated programs; independent study; study abroad; academic accommodation for the gifted and the artistically talented; remedial reading and/or remedial writing; remedial math; ESL (12 students enrolled).

College Placement 27 students graduated in 2005; 26 went to college, including Georgetown University; The Johns Hopkins University; University of California, Berkeley; University of California, Davis; University of California, Santa Barbara. Other: 1 had other specific plans. Median SAT verbal: 537, median SAT math: 599, median combined SAT: 1136. 25% scored over 600 on SAT math.

Student Life Upper grades have specified standards of dress, student council, honor system. Discipline rests equally with students and faculty.

Summer Programs Remediation, enrichment, advancement, ESL, art/fine arts, computer instruction programs offered; session focuses on academic and course credit;

held on campus; accepts boys and girls; open to students from other schools. 65 students usually enrolled. 2006 schedule: June 28 to July 28. Application deadline: none.

Tuition and Aid Day student tuition: $16,330; 7-day tuition and room/board: $35,900. Tuition installment plan (individually arranged payment plans). Need-based scholarship grants, need-based loans available. In 2005–06, 10% of upper-school students received aid. Total amount of financial aid awarded in 2005–06: $92,830.

Admissions Traditional secondary-level entrance grade is 9. For fall 2005, 118 students applied for upper-level admission, 64 were accepted, 27 enrolled. Any standardized test, SSAT or TOEFL required. Deadline for receipt of application materials: none. Application fee required: $50. Interview required.

Athletics Interscholastic: baseball (boys), basketball (b,g), cross-country running (b,g), dressage (b,g), lacrosse (b,g), soccer (b,g), volleyball (b,g); intramural: archery (b,g); coed interscholastic: equestrian sports, flag football, golf, track and field; coed intramural: aerobics, aerobics/dance, back packing, basketball, bicycling, canoeing/kayaking, climbing, cross-country running, equestrian sports, fencing, fitness, fitness walking, golf, hiking/backpacking, horseback riding, kayaking, martial arts, mountain biking, outdoor education, paddle tennis, rafting, rappelling, rock climbing, ropes courses, scuba diving, surfing, swimming and diving, wall climbing, weight training, yoga.

Computers Computers are regularly used in English, introduction to technology, mathematics, music, SAT preparation, science, yearbook classes. Computer resources include campus e-mail, on-campus library services, CD-ROMs, online commercial services, Internet access.

Contact Mr. John H. Williamson, Director of Admission. 805-646-1423. Fax: 805-646-0362. E-mail: admission@ovs.org. Web site: www.ovs.org.

See full description on page 954.

OKANAGAN ADVENTIST ACADEMY

1035 Hollywood Road
Kelowna, British Columbia V1X 4N3, Canada
Head of School: Mr. Dan Self

General Information Coeducational day college-preparatory, arts, religious studies, and technology school, affiliated with Seventh-day Adventist Church. Grades K–12. Founded: 1920. Setting: small town. Nearest major city is Vancouver, Canada. 10-acre campus. Approved or accredited by British Columbia Department of Education. Language of instruction: English. Total enrollment: 133. Upper school average class size: 15.

Upper School Student Profile 85% of students are Seventh-day Adventists.

Faculty School total: 12. In upper school: 7 men, 1 woman; 3 have advanced degrees.

Subjects Offered Art, biology, chemistry, choir, drama, English, family studies, French, health education, home economics, mathematics, physical education, physics, religion, science, social studies.

Graduation Requirements Applied skills, arts and fine arts (art, music, dance, drama), career planning, careers, English, mathematics, religion (includes Bible studies and theology), science, social studies (includes history).

College Placement 15 students graduated in 2005; 11 went to college.

Student Life Upper grades have specified standards of dress, student council, honor system. Discipline rests primarily with faculty.

Tuition and Aid Day student tuition: CAN$2100–CAN$3500. Church-based financial aid available.

Admissions Deadline for receipt of application materials: none. Application fee required: CAN$160. Interview required.

Athletics Coed Interscholastic: flag football, volleyball; coed intramural: badminton, flag football, floor hockey, independent competitive sports, soccer, volleyball.

Computers Computer resources include campus e-mail, on-campus library services, CD-ROMs, Internet access, DVD.

Contact Mr. Dan Self, Principal. 250-860-5305. Fax: 250-868-9703. E-mail: okaaprincipal@shaw.ca.

OLDENBURG ACADEMY

1 Twister Circle
Oldenburg, Indiana 47036
Head of School: Sr. Therese Gillman, OSF

General Information Coeducational day college-preparatory, arts, and religious studies school, affiliated with Roman Catholic Church. Grades 9–12. Founded: 1852. Setting: small town. Nearest major city is Indianapolis. 23-acre campus. 3 buildings on campus. Approved or accredited by Association of Colorado Independent Schools, North Central Association of Colleges and Schools, and Indiana Department of Education. Total enrollment: 205. Upper school average class size: 13.

Upper School Student Profile Grade 9: 53 students (23 boys, 30 girls); Grade 10: 63 students (22 boys, 41 girls); Grade 11: 47 students (20 boys, 27 girls); Grade 12: 42 students (18 boys, 24 girls). 80% of students are Roman Catholic.

Faculty School total: 20. In upper school: 1 man, 19 women; 16 have advanced degrees.

Graduation Requirements 40 hours of community service.

Oldenburg Academy

Special Academic Programs Advanced Placement exam preparation in 9 subject areas.

College Placement Colleges students went to include Indiana University Bloomington; Purdue University.

Student Life Upper grades have uniform requirement, student council, honor system. Discipline rests primarily with faculty. Attendance at religious services is required.

Tuition and Aid Day student tuition: $5700. Tuition installment plan (FACTS Tuition Payment Plan). Tuition reduction for siblings, merit scholarship grants, need-based scholarship grants available.

Admissions Traditional secondary-level entrance grade is 9. High School Placement Test (closed version) from Scholastic Testing Service required. Deadline for receipt of application materials: none. Application fee required: $350. Interview recommended.

Athletics Interscholastic: baseball (boys), basketball (b,g), cheering (g), cross-country running (b,g), golf (b,g), soccer (b,g), softball (g), swimming and diving (b,g), tennis (b,g), track and field (b,g), volleyball (g). 1 PE instructor, 9 coaches.

Computers Computers are regularly used in all academic classes. Computer network features include campus e-mail, Internet access, DVD.

Contact Mrs. Connie Deardoff, Principal. 812-934-4440 Ext. 223. Fax: 812-934-4838. E-mail: deardorff@oldenburgacademy.org.

OLDFIELDS SCHOOL

1500 Glencoe Road
Glencoe, Maryland 21152
Head of School: Mr. George Swope Jr.

General Information Girls' boarding and day college-preparatory, arts, and technology school. Grades 8–PG. Founded: 1867. Setting: rural. Nearest major city is Baltimore. Students are housed in single-sex dormitories. 225-acre campus. 14 buildings on campus. Approved or accredited by Association of Independent Maryland Schools, Middle States Association of Colleges and Schools, and The Association of Boarding Schools. Member of National Association of Independent Schools and Secondary School Admission Test Board. Endowment: $10 million. Total enrollment: 174. Upper school average class size: 14. Upper school faculty-student ratio: 1:6.

Upper School Student Profile Grade 8: 13 students (13 girls); Grade 9: 29 students (29 girls); Grade 10: 49 students (49 girls); Grade 11: 39 students (39 girls); Grade 12: 48 students (48 girls). 65% of students are boarding students. 20% are state residents. 24 states are represented in upper school student body. 10% are international students. International students from Brazil, Bulgaria, El Salvador, Mexico, Republic of Korea, and Saudi Arabia; 1 other country represented in student body.

Faculty School total: 31. In upper school: 8 men, 23 women; 20 have advanced degrees; 24 reside on campus.

Subjects Offered 20th century history, 3-dimensional design, acting, advanced chemistry, algebra, American history, anatomy and physiology, art history, astronomy, biology, calculus, ceramics, chemistry, choreography, college counseling, computer science, dance, directing, drawing, English, equine science, ethics, French, geometry, government, graphic design, health, honors algebra, honors English, honors geometry, honors U.S. history, honors world history, HTML design, international relations, Latin, painting, photography, physics, pre-algebra, pre-calculus, psychology, publications, science, sociology, Spanish, technical theater, theater, trigonometry, voice, world history.

Graduation Requirements Arts and fine arts (art, music, dance, drama), computer literacy, English, foreign language, mathematics, physical education (includes health), science, social studies (includes history), participation in May Program, senior presentation.

Special Academic Programs Advanced Placement exam preparation in 8 subject areas; honors section; independent study; study abroad.

College Placement 42 students graduated in 2005; all went to college, including Agnes Scott College; Syracuse University; The Johns Hopkins University; University of Maryland, College Park; University of Michigan; Washington College.

Student Life Upper grades have specified standards of dress, student council, honor system. Discipline rests equally with students and faculty.

Tuition and Aid Day student tuition: $22,600; 7-day tuition and room/board: $35,900. Tuition installment plan (Key Tuition Payment Plan). Need-based scholarship grants available. In 2005–06, 27% of upper-school students received aid. Total amount of financial aid awarded in 2005–06: $1,200,000.

Admissions Traditional secondary-level entrance grade is 9. For fall 2005, 205 students applied for upper-level admission, 123 were accepted, 51 enrolled. ISEE, PSAT and SAT for applicants to grade 11 and 12, SSAT, TOEFL or SLEP or Wechsler Intelligence Scale for Children required. Deadline for receipt of application materials: February 1. Application fee required: $50. Interview required.

Athletics Interscholastic: badminton, basketball, equestrian sports, field hockey, horseback riding, indoor soccer, lacrosse, soccer, softball, tennis, volleyball, winter soccer; intramural: aerobics, aerobics/dance, dance, dressage, equestrian sports, fitness, horseback riding, modern dance, outdoor activities, outdoor adventure, outdoor education, outdoor recreation, outdoor skills, outdoors, physical fitness, sailing, surfing, ultimate Frisbee, walking, weight lifting, weight training, yoga. 3 PE instructors, 5 coaches.

Computers Computers are regularly used in all classes. Computer network features include campus e-mail, on-campus library services, CD-ROMs, online commercial services, Internet access, file transfer, office computer access, DVD.

Contact Mrs. Kimberly Loughlin, Director of Admission and Financial Aid. 410-472-4800. Fax: 410-472-6839. E-mail: loughlink@oldfieldsschool.org. Web site: www.oldfieldsschool.org.

See full description on page 956.

OLNEY FRIENDS SCHOOL

61830 Sandy Ridge Road
Barnesville, Ohio 43713
Head of School: Richard F. Sidwell

General Information Coeducational boarding and day college-preparatory and religious studies school, affiliated with Society of Friends. Grades 9–12. Founded: 1837. Setting: rural. Nearest major city is Pittsburgh, PA. Students are housed in single-sex dormitories. 350-acre campus. 10 buildings on campus. Approved or accredited by Friends Council on Education, Independent Schools Association of the Central States, Midwest Association of Boarding Schools, Ohio Association of Independent Schools, The Association of Boarding Schools, and Ohio Department of Education. Member of National Association of Independent Schools. Endowment: $510,000. Total enrollment: 58. Upper school average class size: 10. Upper school faculty-student ratio: 1:4.

Upper School Student Profile Grade 9: 8 students (4 boys, 4 girls); Grade 10: 19 students (11 boys, 8 girls); Grade 11: 17 students (9 boys, 8 girls); Grade 12: 14 students (6 boys, 8 girls). 95% of students are boarding students. 19% are state residents. 18 states are represented in upper school student body. 28% are international students. International students from China, Japan, Republic of Korea, Rwanda, Serbia and Montenegro, and Viet Nam; 3 other countries represented in student body. 39% of students are members of Society of Friends.

Faculty School total: 17. In upper school: 8 men, 9 women; 8 have advanced degrees; 9 reside on campus.

Subjects Offered Advanced math, agriculture, agroecology, algebra, alternative physical education, American studies, ancient history, art, astronomy, biology, calculus, calculus-AP, ceramics, chemistry, chorus, clayworking, college counseling, community service, drawing, English, English literature, English literature-AP, environmental science, ESL, fine arts, folk art, gardening, general science, geometry, global issues, government/civics, health, history, library research, library skills, mathematics, photography, physical education, physics, religion, social studies, Spanish, Western civilization, women in society, woodworking, world literature.

Graduation Requirements Arts and fine arts (art, music, dance, drama), English, foreign language, mathematics, physical education (includes health), religion (includes Bible studies and theology), science, social studies (includes history), research graduation essay. Community service is required.

Special Academic Programs Advanced Placement exam preparation in 5 subject areas; independent study; term-away projects; ESL (7 students enrolled).

College Placement 18 students graduated in 2005; 16 went to college, including Earlham College; Guilford College; Haverford College. Other: 2 went to work. Median SAT verbal: 500, median SAT math: 560. 33% scored over 600 on SAT verbal, 33% scored over 600 on SAT math.

Student Life Upper grades have student council, honor system. Discipline rests equally with students and faculty. Attendance at religious services is required.

Tuition and Aid Day student tuition: $11,975; 7-day tuition and room/board: $23,950. Tuition installment plan (monthly payment plans, individually arranged payment plans). Need-based scholarship grants, tuition discounts for children of faculty and members of Ohio Yearly Meeting available. In 2005–06, 62% of upper-school students received aid. Total amount of financial aid awarded in 2005–06: $571,450.

Admissions Traditional secondary-level entrance grade is 9. For fall 2005, 47 students applied for upper-level admission, 39 were accepted, 30 enrolled. Deadline for receipt of application materials: none. Application fee required: $50. On-campus interview required.

Athletics Interscholastic: basketball (boys); intramural: basketball (b,g), volleyball (b,g); coed interscholastic: soccer; coed intramural: aerobics, aerobics/dance, artistic gym, back packing, bicycling, cooperative games, cross-country running, field hockey, fitness, fitness walking, Frisbee, gymnastics, hiking/backpacking, jump rope, outdoor activities, outdoor education, outdoor skills, running, soccer, softball, tennis, ultimate Frisbee, walking, wall climbing.

Computers Computers are regularly used in college planning, English, history, music classes. Computer network features include campus e-mail, on-campus library services, CD-ROMs, online commercial services, Internet access, DVD, PC computer classroom with a multimedia presentation system, Mac Lab.

Contact Meg Short, Director of Admissions. 740-425-3655. Fax: 740-425-3202. E-mail: admissions@olneyfriends.org. Web site: www.olneyfriends.org.

ANNOUNCEMENT FROM THE SCHOOL An intellectually challenging college-preparatory high school within a supportive Quaker community. With a small, diverse student body made up of students from 9 countries, Olney is a

418 *www.petersons.com*

Peterson's Private Secondary Schools 2007

coeducational boarding school on a scenic campus in rural Ohio, offering a safe environment for students from all backgrounds.

See full description on page 958.

THE O'NEAL SCHOOL

3300 Airport Road
PO Box 290
Southern Pines, North Carolina 28388-0290
Head of School: Mr. John Neiswender

General Information Coeducational day college-preparatory school. Grades PK–12. Founded: 1971. Setting: small town. Nearest major city is Raleigh. 40-acre campus. 3 buildings on campus. Approved or accredited by North Carolina Association of Independent Schools, Southern Association of Colleges and Schools, and North Carolina Department of Education. Member of National Association of Independent Schools. Endowment: $1.3 million. Total enrollment: 445. Upper school average class size: 15. Upper school faculty-student ratio: 1:10.

Upper School Student Profile Grade 9: 44 students (20 boys, 24 girls); Grade 10: 44 students (24 boys, 20 girls); Grade 11: 44 students (16 boys, 28 girls); Grade 12: 29 students (16 boys, 13 girls).

Faculty School total: 55. In upper school: 9 men, 6 women; 7 have advanced degrees.

Subjects Offered Advanced studio art-AP, algebra, American history, American literature, art, art history, biology, biology-AP, calculus-AP, chemistry, community service, computer science, creative writing, economics, English, English literature, English literature and composition-AP, environmental science, environmental science-AP, ethics, European history, European history-AP, expository writing, film appreciation, fine arts, French, French-AP, geometry, journalism, Latin, logic, mathematics, music, philosophy, photography, physical education, physics-AP, political science, pottery, public speaking, science, social studies, Spanish, speech, statistics-AP, U.S. history-AP, world history, world literature.

Graduation Requirements Arts and fine arts (art, music, dance, drama), computer science, English, foreign language, mathematics, physical education (includes health), science, social studies (includes history), speech, 36 hours of community service.

Special Academic Programs Advanced Placement exam preparation in 10 subject areas; independent study; study at local college for college credit; remedial reading and/or remedial writing; remedial math; programs in English, mathematics, general development for dyslexic students.

College Placement 36 students graduated in 2005; all went to college, including Appalachian State University; North Carolina State University; Rice University; The University of North Carolina at Chapel Hill; The University of North Carolina at Charlotte; Tulane University. Median SAT verbal: 595, median SAT math: 605. 49% scored over 600 on SAT verbal, 55% scored over 600 on SAT math.

Student Life Upper grades have specified standards of dress, student council, honor system. Discipline rests primarily with faculty.

Tuition and Aid Day student tuition: $11,640. Tuition installment plan (Insured Tuition Payment Plan, monthly payment plans, individually arranged payment plans). Merit scholarship grants, need-based scholarship grants available. In 2005–06, 24% of upper-school students received aid; total upper-school merit-scholarship money awarded: $53,430. Total amount of financial aid awarded in 2005–06: $278,920.

Admissions Traditional secondary-level entrance grade is 9. For fall 2005, 31 students applied for upper-level admission, 25 were accepted, 22 enrolled. Otis-Lennon School Ability Test/writing sample and writing sample required. Deadline for receipt of application materials: none. Application fee required: $50. On-campus interview required.

Athletics Interscholastic: baseball (boys), basketball (b,g), cross-country running (b,g), soccer (b,g), swimming and diving (b,g), tennis (b,g), volleyball (g); intramural: cheering (g); coed interscholastic: golf; coed intramural: fencing, martial arts. 3 PE instructors, 4 coaches.

Computers Computers are regularly used in all academic classes. Computer network features include campus e-mail, on-campus library services, CD-ROMs, Internet access, file transfer, DVD, wireless campus network, EBSCO, World Book Online.

Contact Mrs. Missy Quis, Director of Admissions. 910-692-6920 Ext. 103. Fax: 910-692-6930. E-mail: mquis@onealschool.org.

ANNOUNCEMENT FROM THE SCHOOL O'Neal is a college-preparatory school dedicated to the development of academic excellence, strength of character, and physical well-being of its students in an environment where integrity, self-discipline, and consideration for others are fundamental. O'Neal enrolls approximately 450 students from prekindergarten through grade 12. Community service, athletics, and extracurricular activities are integral to O'Neal's mission. O'Neal also has a program for students with learning differences. Financial aid is available. John Neiswender is Headmaster.

ONEIDA BAPTIST INSTITUTE

11 Mulberry Street
Oneida, Kentucky 40972
Head of School: Dr. W. F. Underwood

General Information Coeducational boarding and day college-preparatory, general academic, arts, business, vocational, religious studies, bilingual studies, and agriculture school, affiliated with Southern Baptist Convention. Grades 6–12. Founded: 1899. Setting: rural. Nearest major city is Lexington. Students are housed in single-sex dormitories. 200-acre campus. 15 buildings on campus. Approved or accredited by Kentucky Department of Education. Endowment: $15 million. Total enrollment: 350. Upper school average class size: 11. Upper school faculty-student ratio: 1:11.

Upper School Student Profile Grade 9: 49 students (29 boys, 20 girls); Grade 10: 72 students (33 boys, 39 girls); Grade 11: 74 students (37 boys, 37 girls); Grade 12: 55 students (28 boys, 27 girls). 88% of students are boarding students. 39% are state residents. 21 states are represented in upper school student body. 13% are international students. International students from China, Ethiopia, Japan, Kenya, Republic of Korea, and Saudi Arabia; 2 other countries represented in student body. 25% of students are Southern Baptist Convention.

Faculty School total: 54. In upper school: 22 men, 15 women; 10 have advanced degrees; 53 reside on campus.

Subjects Offered Agriculture, algebra, anatomy, animal science, art, auto mechanics, band, Bible, biology, biology-AP, calculus, calculus-AP, chemistry, child development, choir, commercial art, computers, drafting, drama, English, English-AP, ESL, family and consumer science, foods, geography, geometry, German, guitar, health, journalism, language arts, life skills, literature, mathematics, physical education, piano, political science, pre-calculus, psychology, science, social studies, sociology, Spanish, Spanish-AP, sports medicine, stagecraft, U.S. history, U.S. history-AP, weight training, welding, world history.

Graduation Requirements Arts and fine arts (art, music, dance, drama), Bible, computer literacy, English, foreign language, mathematics, physical education (includes health), science, social studies (includes history), field placement.

Special Academic Programs Advanced Placement exam preparation in 5 subject areas; honors section; accelerated programs; independent study; academic accommodation for the gifted and the musically talented; remedial reading and/or remedial writing; remedial math; programs in English, mathematics, general development for dyslexic students; ESL (14 students enrolled).

College Placement 51 students graduated in 2005; 34 went to college, including Eastern Kentucky University; Kentucky State University; Lindsey Wilson College; Union College; University of Kentucky; University of Louisville. Other: 2 went to work, 3 entered military service, 6 entered a postgraduate year, 6 had other specific plans. 12% scored over 26 on composite ACT.

Student Life Upper grades have specified standards of dress. Discipline rests primarily with faculty. Attendance at religious services is required.

Summer Programs Remediation, enrichment, advancement, ESL programs offered; session focuses on remediation and make-up courses; held on campus; accepts boys and girls; open to students from other schools. 125 students usually enrolled. 2006 schedule: June 4 to July 21. Application deadline: none.

Tuition and Aid 7-day tuition and room/board: $4550–$9000. Tuition installment plan (monthly payment plans). Need-based scholarship grants available. In 2005–06, 100% of upper-school students received aid.

Admissions Traditional secondary-level entrance grade is 9. Deadline for receipt of application materials: none. Application fee required: $25. On-campus interview required.

Athletics Interscholastic: baseball (boys), basketball (b,g), cheering (g), cross-country running (b,g), softball (g), swimming and diving (b,g), tennis (b,g), track and field (b,g), volleyball (g); intramural: baseball (b), basketball (b,g), cheering (g), cross-country running (b,g), fishing (b,g), softball (g), swimming and diving (b,g), tennis (b,g), track and field (b,g), volleyball (b,g), walking (g), weight training (b); coed interscholastic: soccer; coed intramural: soccer, table tennis.

Computers Computers are regularly used in commercial art, drafting, English, journalism classes. Computer resources include Internet access.

Contact Admissions. 606-847-4111 Ext. 233. Fax: 606-847-4496. E-mail: admissions@oneidaschool.org. Web site: www.oneidaschool.org.

ORANGEWOOD ADVENTIST ACADEMY

13732 Clinton Street
Garden Grove, California 92843
Head of School: Mr. Ruben A. Escalante

General Information Coeducational day college-preparatory and religious studies school, affiliated with Seventh-day Adventist Church. Grades PK–12. Founded: 1956. Setting: urban. Nearest major city is Anaheim. 11-acre campus. 6 buildings on campus. Approved or accredited by Western Association of Schools and Colleges and California Department of Education. Total enrollment: 274. Upper school average class size: 22. Upper school faculty-student ratio: 1:10.

Upper School Student Profile 80% of students are Seventh-day Adventists.

Faculty School total: 20. In upper school: 9 men, 5 women; 4 have advanced degrees.

Subjects Offered Algebra, arts, biology, calculus, career education, chemistry, choir, computer science, computers, drama, English, family studies, fine arts, geometry,

government, health, journalism, life skills, mathematics, photography, physical education, physical science, physics, pre-calculus, religion, science, silk screening, social studies, Spanish, technical arts, typing, U.S. history, world history, yearbook.

Graduation Requirements Arts and fine arts (art, music, dance, drama), business skills (includes word processing), computer science, English, foreign language, mathematics, physical education (includes health), religion (includes Bible studies and theology), science, social studies (includes history), work experience.

Special Academic Programs Honors section.

College Placement 28 students graduated in 2005; 24 went to college, including California State University; La Sierra University; Loma Linda University; Pacific Union College. Other: 1 went to work, 2 entered military service. 4% scored over 600 on SAT verbal, 3% scored over 600 on SAT math, 2% scored over 26 on composite ACT.

Student Life Upper grades have uniform requirement, student council, honor system. Discipline rests primarily with faculty. Attendance at religious services is required.

Summer Programs Enrichment programs offered; session focuses on math and reading; held on campus; accepts boys and girls; open to students from other schools.

Tuition and Aid Day student tuition: $4680. Tuition installment plan (monthly payment plans). Tuition reduction for siblings, need-based scholarship grants, paying campus jobs available. Total amount of financial aid awarded in 2005–06: $7000.

Admissions Deadline for receipt of application materials: none. No application fee required. Interview required.

Athletics Interscholastic: basketball (boys, girls), cheering (g), flag football (b), soccer (b), softball (g), volleyball (b,g); intramural: basketball (b,g), flag football (b), volleyball (b,g); coed interscholastic: soccer; coed intramural: gymnastics. 2 PE instructors, 5 coaches.

Computers Computer network features include campus e-mail, on-campus library services, CD-ROMs, online commercial services, Internet access.

Contact Mrs. Martha Machado, Director of Admissions and Records. 714-534-4694 Ext. 214. Fax: 714-534-5931. E-mail: mrsmach57@aol.com. Web site: www.orangewoodacademy.com.

OREGON EPISCOPAL SCHOOL

6300 Southwest Nicol Road
Portland, Oregon 97223-7566
Head of School: Dr. Dulany O. Bennett

General Information Coeducational boarding and day college-preparatory, arts, religious studies, technology, and science school, affiliated with Episcopal Church. Boarding grades 9–12, day grades PK–12. Founded: 1869. Setting: suburban. Students are housed in single-sex dormitories. 59-acre campus. 9 buildings on campus. Approved or accredited by National Association of Episcopal Schools, Northwest Association of Schools and Colleges, Pacific Northwest Association of Independent Schools, and Oregon Department of Education. Member of National Association of Independent Schools and Secondary School Admission Test Board. Endowment: $15.3 million. Total enrollment: 768. Upper school average class size: 14. Upper school faculty-student ratio: 1:7.

Upper School Student Profile Grade 9: 69 students (37 boys, 32 girls); Grade 10: 53 students (27 boys, 26 girls); Grade 11: 58 students (37 boys, 21 girls); Grade 12: 55 students (23 boys, 32 girls). 19% of students are boarding students. 82% are state residents. 4 states are represented in upper school student body. 13% are international students. International students from China, Japan, Republic of Korea, and Taiwan; 11 other countries represented in student body. 14% of students are members of Episcopal Church.

Faculty School total: 113. In upper school: 19 men, 20 women; 26 have advanced degrees; 13 reside on campus.

Subjects Offered Algebra, American history, American literature, anatomy, art, Asian history, band, Basic programming, biology, Buddhism, calculus, ceramics, chemistry, Chinese, chorus, Christianity, community service, computer animation, computer graphics, computer science, creative writing, drama, drawing, driver education, ecology, English, English literature, environmental science, ESL, European history, filmmaking, fine arts, French, French language-AP, French literature-AP, geology, geometry, graphic arts, history, history of ideas, humanities, international relations, Japanese, literature, mathematics, music, painting, philosophy, photography, physical education, physics, physiology, poetry, religion, Russian literature, science, Shakespeare, social studies, Spanish, Spanish language-AP, Spanish literature-AP, speech, stagecraft, statistics, theater, theology, trigonometry, U.S. history-AP, world history, world literature, writing.

Graduation Requirements Arts and fine arts (art, music, dance, drama), computer science, electives, English, foreign language, humanities, mathematics, philosophy, physical education (includes health), religion (includes Bible studies and theology), science, U.S. history, Winterim, College Decisions (for juniors), Senior Discovery Program, 120 hours of service learning.

Special Academic Programs Advanced Placement exam preparation in 8 subject areas; honors section; independent study; term-away projects; study at local college for college credit; study abroad; academic accommodation for the gifted; ESL (13 students enrolled).

College Placement 57 students graduated in 2005; 56 went to college, including Duke University; Oregon State University; Pepperdine University; Pitzer College;

University of Oregon; University of Washington. Other: 1 had other specific plans. Median SAT verbal: 630, median SAT math: 650. 65% scored over 600 on SAT verbal, 75% scored over 600 on SAT math.

Student Life Upper grades have specified standards of dress, student council. Discipline rests equally with students and faculty. Attendance at religious services is required.

Summer Programs Remediation, enrichment, advancement, sports, art/fine arts programs offered; session focuses on variety of academic and artistic enrichment programs; held on campus; accepts boys and girls; open to students from other schools. 75 students usually enrolled. 2006 schedule: June 13 to August 12. Application deadline: June.

Tuition and Aid Day student tuition: $18,415; 7-day tuition and room/board: $33,445. Tuition installment plan (Insured Tuition Payment Plan, monthly payment plans). Need-based scholarship grants available. In 2005–06, 13% of upper-school students received aid. Total amount of financial aid awarded in 2005–06: $598,978.

Admissions Traditional secondary-level entrance grade is 9. For fall 2005, 163 students applied for upper-level admission, 89 were accepted, 52 enrolled. SSAT or TOEFL required. Deadline for receipt of application materials: January 27. Application fee required: $75. Interview required.

Athletics Interscholastic: basketball (boys, girls), cross-country running (b,g), fencing (b,g), lacrosse (b,g), skiing (downhill) (b,g), soccer (b,g), tennis (b,g), track and field (b,g), volleyball (g). 2 PE instructors, 22 coaches, 1 trainer.

Computers Computers are regularly used in art, English, foreign language, history, mathematics, music, science classes. Computer network features include campus e-mail, on-campus library services, CD-ROMs, online commercial services, Internet access, file transfer, office computer access, wireless campus network.

Contact Marge Benedict, Admissions Assistant. 503-768-3115. Fax: 503-768-3140. E-mail: admit@oes.edu. Web site: www.oes.edu.

See full description on page 960.

ORINDA ACADEMY

19 Altarinda Road
Orinda, California 94563-2602
Head of School: Ron Graydon

General Information Coeducational day college-preparatory and general academic school. Grades 7–12. Founded: 1982. Setting: suburban. Nearest major city is Walnut Creek. 1-acre campus. 3 buildings on campus. Approved or accredited by East Bay Independent Schools Association, The College Board, and Western Association of Schools and Colleges. Total enrollment: 129. Upper school average class size: 9. Upper school faculty-student ratio: 1:9.

Upper School Student Profile Grade 9: 30 students (21 boys, 9 girls); Grade 10: 34 students (22 boys, 12 girls); Grade 11: 24 students (16 boys, 8 girls); Grade 12: 27 students (14 boys, 13 girls).

Faculty School total: 19. In upper school: 10 men, 8 women; 10 have advanced degrees.

Subjects Offered Algebra, American history, American literature, art, basketball, biology, British literature, British literature (honors), calculus, chemistry, chorus, community service, computer graphics, computer keyboarding, computer literacy, computer multimedia, computer music, computer processing, computer programming, contemporary issues, creative writing, dance, drama, earth science, economics, English, English literature, English literature and composition-AP, English literature-AP, ensembles, environmental science, ESL, European history, film history, fine arts, French, geography, geometry, government/civics, health, history, history of music, introduction to theater, journalism, mathematics, music, music performance, musical productions, performing arts, physical education, physics, psychology, SAT preparation, science, social studies, Spanish, Spanish language-AP, theater, trigonometry, visual arts, women's literature, yearbook.

Graduation Requirements Algebra, biology, civics, composition, economics, English, foreign language, geometry, physical education (includes health), science, trigonometry, U.S. history, visual and performing arts. Community service is required.

Special Academic Programs Advanced Placement exam preparation in 2 subject areas; honors section; accelerated programs; academic accommodation for the gifted; ESL (2 students enrolled).

College Placement 28 students graduated in 2005; 24 went to college, including Carnegie Mellon University; Saint Mary's College of California; The George Washington University; University of California, Davis; University of Oregon; University of Washington. Other: 4 had other specific plans. Median SAT verbal: 600, median SAT math: 570, median combined SAT: 1710, median composite ACT: 24. 50% scored over 600 on SAT verbal, 39% scored over 600 on SAT math, 50% scored over 1800 on combined SAT, 20% scored over 26 on composite ACT.

Student Life Upper grades have specified standards of dress, student council, honor system. Discipline rests primarily with faculty.

Summer Programs Remediation, enrichment, advancement, sports programs offered; held on campus; accepts boys and girls; open to students from other schools. 70 students usually enrolled. 2006 schedule: June 19 to July 28. Application deadline: none.

Tuition and Aid Day student tuition: $19,500. Tuition installment plan (FACTS Tuition Payment Plan, monthly payment plans). Tuition reduction for siblings,

need-based scholarship grants available. In 2005–06, 20% of upper-school students received aid. Total amount of financial aid awarded in 2005–06: $270,000.

Admissions Traditional secondary-level entrance grade is 9. For fall 2005, 120 students applied for upper-level admission, 50 were accepted, 42 enrolled. ISEE required. Deadline for receipt of application materials: January 10. Application fee required: $50. On-campus interview required.

Athletics Interscholastic: baseball (boys), basketball (b,g), softball (g); coed interscholastic: soccer; coed intramural: fitness walking, soccer, softball, ultimate Frisbee, volleyball, weight training, yoga.

Computers Computers are regularly used in English, journalism, social sciences, typing, writing, yearbook classes. Computer network features include CD-ROMs, Internet access, file transfer, office computer access.

Contact Paul Greenwood, Director of Admission. 925-250-7659. Fax: 925-254-4768. E-mail: admission@orindaacademy.org. Web site: orindaacademy.org.

ANNOUNCEMENT FROM THE SCHOOL Orinda Academy is an independent, coeducational, college-preparatory school located in a beautiful suburban setting. Orinda Academy is fully accredited with 23 years of success. Orinda students are successful, confident, and responsible and they work to potential. The small classes and excellent faculty provide a quality learning environment.

THE ORME SCHOOL

HC 63 Box 3040
Mayer, Arizona 86333
Head of School: Dr. Stephen Robinson

petersons.com

General Information Coeducational boarding and day college-preparatory school. Boarding grades 8–PG, day grades 7–PG. Founded: 1929. Setting: rural. Nearest major city is Phoenix. Students are housed in single-sex dormitories. 300-acre campus. 30 buildings on campus. Approved or accredited by Arizona Association of Independent Schools, North Central Association of Colleges and Schools, The Association of Boarding Schools, and Arizona Department of Education. Member of National Association of Independent Schools and Secondary School Admission Test Board. Endowment: $9 million. Total enrollment: 154. Upper school average class size: 12. Upper school faculty-student ratio: 1:6.

Upper School Student Profile Grade 9: 38 students (16 boys, 22 girls); Grade 10: 30 students (16 boys, 14 girls); Grade 11: 30 students (11 boys, 19 girls); Grade 12: 30 students (17 boys, 13 girls). 90% of students are boarding students. 54% are state residents. 18 states are represented in upper school student body. 16% are international students. International students from Bahamas, Germany, Hong Kong, Japan, Republic of Korea, and Taiwan; 2 other countries represented in student body.

Faculty School total: 38. In upper school: 15 men, 19 women; 23 have advanced degrees; 30 reside on campus.

Subjects Offered Advanced Placement courses, algebra, American history, American literature, art, art history, astronomy, biology, calculus, ceramics, chemistry, community service, computer programming, computer science, creative writing, dance, drama, ecology, English, English literature, European history, fine arts, French, geography, geology, geometry, grammar, history, humanities, Latin, mathematics, music, photography, physical education, physics, psychology, science, social science, social studies, Spanish, theater, trigonometry, typing, world history, world literature, writing.

Graduation Requirements Arts and fine arts (art, music, dance, drama), computer science, English, foreign language, humanities, mathematics, science, social science, social studies (includes history). Community service is required.

Special Academic Programs Advanced Placement exam preparation in 5 subject areas; honors section; independent study; remedial reading and/or remedial writing; remedial math; ESL (10 students enrolled).

College Placement 30 students graduated in 2005; 26 went to college, including Arizona State University; Northern Arizona University; Santa Clara University; The University of Arizona; University of Rochester. Other: 1 entered military service, 1 entered a postgraduate year, 2 had other specific plans. Mean SAT verbal: 524, mean SAT math: 523, mean composite ACT: 21.

Student Life Upper grades have specified standards of dress, student council, honor system. Discipline rests equally with students and faculty.

Summer Programs Remediation, ESL programs offered; session focuses on remediation; held on campus; accepts boys and girls; open to students from other schools. 12 students usually enrolled. 2006 schedule: June 13 to July 22. Application deadline: none.

Tuition and Aid Day student tuition: $14,910; 7-day tuition and room/board: $29,190. Tuition installment plan (monthly payment plans, individually arranged payment plans). Need-based scholarship grants, need-based loans, middle-income loans available. In 2005–06, 37% of upper-school students received aid. Total amount of financial aid awarded in 2005–06: $695,000.

Admissions Traditional secondary-level entrance grade is 9. For fall 2005, 100 students applied for upper-level admission, 83 were accepted, 65 enrolled. PSAT and SAT for applicants to grade 11 and 12, SAT for students entering as juniors, SSAT or TOEFL or SLEP required. Deadline for receipt of application materials: February 15. Application fee required: $50. Interview required.

Athletics Interscholastic: baseball (boys), basketball (b,g), cheering (g), cross-country running (b,g), equestrian sports (b,g), football (b), pom squad (g), rodeo (b,g), soccer (b,g), softball (g), tennis (b,g), track and field (b,g), volleyball (g); intramural: aerobics/dance (g), back packing (b,g), climbing (b,g), dressage (b,g), fitness (b,g), outdoor adventure (b,g), outdoor education (b,g), outdoor recreation (b,g), outdoor skills (b,g), outdoors (b,g), physical training (b,g), rappelling (b,g), rock climbing (b,g), rodeo (b,g), strength & conditioning (b,g), tennis (b,g), wall climbing (b,g), weight lifting (b,g), weight training (b,g), wilderness (b,g), wilderness survival (b,g), wrestling (b); coed interscholastic: equestrian sports, horseback riding, rodeo, soccer; coed intramural: back packing, climbing, dressage, fitness, fitness walking, hiking/backpacking, horseback riding, mountain biking, mountaineering, outdoor activities, outdoor adventure, outdoor education, outdoor recreation, outdoor skills, outdoors, physical training, power lifting, rappelling, rock climbing, rodeo, soccer, strength & conditioning, walking, wall climbing, weight lifting, weight training, wilderness, wilderness survival.

Computers Computers are regularly used in all academic classes. Computer network features include campus e-mail, on-campus library services, CD-ROMs, Internet access, DVD, wireless campus network.

Contact Ms. Paige Bekins Kaltsas, Assistant Director of Admissions. 928-632-7601 Ext. 2350. Fax: 928-632-7605. E-mail: pkaltsas@ormeschool.org. Web site: www.ormeschool.org.

ANNOUNCEMENT FROM THE SCHOOL Founded in 1929 and built upon tradition, excellence, and character, The Orme School is located on a lush and green 300-acre campus in central Arizona's high country. Orme's college-preparatory academic program provides its students with the background for admission to a competitive university. Yet, an Orme education is much broader; it is designed to help students achieve greater awareness, clearer perspectives, better decision-making capabilities, self-discipline, and wise use of leisure time. Baseball, basketball, football, softball, tennis, cross-country, track, and volleyball teams compete in the Arizona Interscholastic Association. Orme is one of the few boarding schools in the nation that competes against public rather than private schools. A diverse horsemanship program offers Western and English riding, hunter-jumper, dressage, gymkhana, roping, and rodeo. During the annual Fine Arts Festival, students participate in weeklong workshops under the leadership of professional artists. The annual Caravan offers a choice of several weeklong experiential learning adventures.

See full description on page 962.

OUR LADY OF FATIMA HIGH SCHOOL

360 Market Street
Warren, Rhode Island 02885
Head of School: Sr. Mary Margaret Souza

General Information Coeducational day college-preparatory, arts, religious studies, and technology school, affiliated with Roman Catholic Church. Grades 7–12. Founded: 1965. Setting: small town. Nearest major city is Providence. 33-acre campus. 1 building on campus. Approved or accredited by National Catholic Education Association, New England Association of Schools and Colleges, and Rhode Island Department of Education. Total enrollment: 162. Upper school average class size: 17. Upper school faculty-student ratio: 1:8.

Upper School Student Profile Grade 9: 43 students (18 boys, 25 girls); Grade 10: 35 students (18 boys, 17 girls); Grade 11: 32 students (13 boys, 19 girls); Grade 12: 30 students (15 boys, 15 girls). 85% of students are Roman Catholic.

Faculty School total: 22. In upper school: 10 men, 11 women; 16 have advanced degrees.

Student Life Upper grades have uniform requirement, student council, honor system. Discipline rests equally with students and faculty. Attendance at religious services is required.

Tuition and Aid Day student tuition: $7800. Tuition installment plan (SMART Tuition Payment Plan, monthly payment plans).

Admissions Traditional secondary-level entrance grade is 9. Catholic High School Entrance Examination required. Deadline for receipt of application materials: none. Application fee required: $25. Interview recommended.

Athletics Interscholastic: baseball (boys), basketball (b,g), dance squad (g), dance team (g), gymnastics (b,g), soccer (b,g), softball (g), swimming and diving (b,g), tennis (b,g), volleyball (b,g). 1 PE instructor, 12 coaches.

Contact Sr. Lisa Palazio, Admissions Director. 401-245-4960 Ext. 205. Fax: 401-245-1380. E-mail: admissions@fatimahs.org. Web site: www.fatimahs.org.

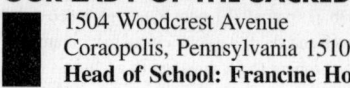

OUR LADY OF THE SACRED HEART

1504 Woodcrest Avenue
Coraopolis, Pennsylvania 15108
Head of School: Francine Horos

General Information Coeducational day college-preparatory, arts, and vocational school, affiliated with Roman Catholic Church. Grades 9–12. Founded: 1932. Setting: suburban. Nearest major city is Pittsburgh. 75-acre campus. 2 buildings on campus. Approved or accredited by Middle States Association of Colleges and Schools, National Catholic Education Association, and Pennsylvania Department of Education. Endowment: $20,600. Total enrollment: 331. Upper school average class size: 20. Upper school faculty-student ratio: 1:12.

Upper School Student Profile Grade 9: 86 students (37 boys, 49 girls); Grade 10: 75 students (27 boys, 48 girls); Grade 11: 95 students (41 boys, 54 girls); Grade 12: 75 students (31 boys, 44 girls). 94% of students are Roman Catholic.

Faculty School total: 29. In upper school: 12 men, 16 women; 13 have advanced degrees.

Subjects Offered Advanced chemistry, algebra, American history, American literature, anatomy and physiology, art appreciation, band, Basic programming, biology, communications, economics-AP, environmental science, world history.

Graduation Requirements Arts and fine arts (art, music, dance, drama), computers, electives, English, grammar, language, mathematics, physical education (includes health), reading, religion (includes Bible studies and theology), science, social studies (includes history).

Special Academic Programs Advanced Placement exam preparation in 1 subject area; honors section; study at local college for college credit; remedial reading and/or remedial writing.

College Placement 78 students graduated in 2005; 73 went to college, including Duquesne University; Edinboro University of Pennsylvania; John Carroll University; The Pennsylvania State University University Park Campus; University of Pittsburgh. Other: 5 went to work. Mean SAT verbal: 532, mean SAT math: 485. 19% scored over 600 on SAT verbal, 10% scored over 600 on SAT math.

Student Life Upper grades have uniform requirement, student council. Discipline rests primarily with faculty. Attendance at religious services is required.

Tuition and Aid Day student tuition: $5995. Tuition installment plan (SMART Tuition Payment Plan, monthly payment plans, individually arranged payment plans, quarterly payment plan). Tuition reduction for siblings, need-based scholarship grants, paying campus jobs available. In 2005–06, 57% of upper-school students received aid. Total amount of financial aid awarded in 2005–06: $660,476.

Admissions Traditional secondary-level entrance grade is 9. For fall 2005, 120 students applied for upper-level admission, 120 were accepted, 86 enrolled. High School Placement Test (closed version) from Scholastic Testing Service required. Deadline for receipt of application materials: December 1. Application fee required: $10.

Athletics Interscholastic: baseball (boys), basketball (b,g), bowling (b,g), cheering (g), cross-country running (b,g), football (b), golf (b,g), horseback riding (g), soccer (b,g), softball (g), swimming and diving (b,g), track and field (b,g), volleyball (b,g); intramural: basketball (b,g), flag football (b,g), floor hockey (b,g), horseshoes (b,g), soccer (b,g), volleyball (b,g). 1 PE instructor, 7 coaches.

Computers Computer network features include on-campus library services, CD-ROMs, Internet access, wireless campus network.

Contact Francine Horos, Principal. 412-264-5140. Fax: 412-264-4143. E-mail: smfhoros@olsh.org. Web site: www.olsh.org.

OUR SAVIOUR LUTHERAN SCHOOL

1734 Williamsbridge Road
Bronx, New York 10461
Head of School: Lewis E. Williams

General Information Coeducational day college-preparatory, arts, religious studies, and technology school, affiliated with Lutheran Church–Missouri Synod. Grades PK–12. Founded: 1942. Setting: urban. Nearest major city is New York. 2-acre campus. 1 building on campus. Approved or accredited by Middle States Association of Colleges and Schools, New York Department of Education, and New York Department of Education. Endowment: $100,000. Total enrollment: 340. Upper school average class size: 20. Upper school faculty-student ratio: 1:14.

Upper School Student Profile Grade 7: 30 students (14 boys, 16 girls); Grade 8: 37 students (16 boys, 21 girls); Grade 9: 30 students (15 boys, 15 girls); Grade 10: 37 students (21 boys, 16 girls); Grade 11: 38 students (26 boys, 12 girls); Grade 12: 28 students (14 boys, 14 girls). 5% of students are Lutheran Church–Missouri Synod.

Faculty School total: 30. In upper school: 10 men, 4 women; 13 have advanced degrees.

Subjects Offered Algebra, American history, American literature, art, art history, Bible studies, biology, chemistry, computer programming, computer science, drama, earth science, economics, English, English literature, English-AP, environmental science, ethics, European history, French, geography, geometry, government/civics, grammar, health, history, history-AP, Latin, mathematics, mathematics-AP, music, physical education, physics, psychology, religion, social studies, Spanish, theology, trigonometry, world history, world literature, writing.

Graduation Requirements Arts and fine arts (art, music, dance, drama), Bible studies, biology, British literature, chemistry, Christian doctrine, Christian ethics, Christian scripture, Christian testament, church history, computer education, computer science, English, English composition, English-AP, European civilization, foreign language, geometry, government, Latin, mathematics, music, physical education (includes health), physical fitness, physics, religion (includes Bible studies and theology), science, Shakespeare, social studies (includes history), Spanish, theology, trigonometry, U.S. history-AP, Western civilization.

Special Academic Programs Advanced Placement exam preparation in 3 subject areas.

College Placement 16 students graduated in 2005; 13 went to college, including Concordia College; Fordham University; Hofstra University; Howard University; Morgan State University; University at Albany, State University of New York. Other: 2 went to work, 1 entered military service. Median SAT verbal: 520, median SAT math: 480, median combined SAT: 1560, median composite ACT: 22. 5% scored over 600 on SAT verbal, 3% scored over 600 on SAT math, 3% scored over 1800 on combined SAT, 3% scored over 26 on composite ACT.

Student Life Upper grades have uniform requirement, student council. Discipline rests primarily with faculty. Attendance at religious services is required.

Summer Programs Remediation, enrichment programs offered; session focuses on remediation; held on campus; accepts boys and girls; open to students from other schools. 200 students usually enrolled. 2006 schedule: July 1 to August 15. Application deadline: none.

Tuition and Aid Day student tuition: $5200. Tuition installment plan (FACTS Tuition Payment Plan). Tuition reduction for siblings, merit scholarship grants, need-based scholarship grants available. In 2005–06, 10% of upper-school students received aid; total upper-school merit-scholarship money awarded: $10,000. Total amount of financial aid awarded in 2005–06: $30,000.

Admissions Traditional secondary-level entrance grade is 7. For fall 2005, 200 students applied for upper-level admission, 150 were accepted, 100 enrolled. Any standardized test or Stanford Achievement Test required. Deadline for receipt of application materials: none. Application fee required: $30.

Athletics Interscholastic: baseball (boys), basketball (b,g), softball (g), volleyball (g); intramural: basketball (b,g); coed interscholastic: soccer, track and field. 1 PE instructor, 6 coaches.

Computers Computers are regularly used in English, foreign language, history, Latin, mathematics, programming, SAT preparation, science, word processing classes. Computer resources include Internet access.

Contact Paulette Brown, Secretary. 718-792-5665. Fax: 718-409-3877. E-mail: ousalubn@aol.com.

OUT-OF-DOOR-ACADEMY

5950 Deer Drive
Sarasota, Florida 34240
Head of School: Mr. David Mahler

General Information Coeducational day college-preparatory school. Grades PK–12. Founded: 1924. Setting: suburban. Nearest major city is Tampa. 94-acre campus. 8 buildings on campus. Approved or accredited by Florida Council of Independent Schools. Member of National Association of Independent Schools. Endowment: $801,000. Total enrollment: 593. Upper school average class size: 16. Upper school faculty-student ratio: 1:10.

Upper School Student Profile Grade 9: 49 students (26 boys, 23 girls); Grade 10: 43 students (14 boys, 29 girls); Grade 11: 48 students (21 boys, 27 girls); Grade 12: 36 students (23 boys, 13 girls).

Faculty School total: 66. In upper school: 13 men, 13 women; 14 have advanced degrees.

Subjects Offered Advanced Placement courses, advanced studio art-AP, algebra, American history-AP, art history, biology, biology-AP, British literature, calculus, calculus-AP, chemistry, chemistry-AP, college counseling, computers, drama, drama performance, dramatic arts, English, English composition, English language and composition-AP, English literature, English literature and composition-AP, English-AP, European history-AP, expository writing, French, French language-AP, geometry, graphic design, health and wellness, history-AP, honors algebra, honors geometry, Latin, Latin-AP, literature, literature and composition-AP, music, newspaper, photography, portfolio art, Spanish, Spanish language-AP, studio art, studio art-AP, U.S. government, U.S. history, U.S. history-AP, women's studies, world culture, world literature, world studies, yearbook, zoology.

Graduation Requirements Arts and fine arts (art, music, dance, drama), electives, English, foreign language, health, history, mathematics, performing arts, personal fitness, science, senior seminar. Community service is required.

Special Academic Programs Advanced Placement exam preparation in 13 subject areas; honors section; independent study.

College Placement 47 students graduated in 2005; all went to college, including Davidson College; Florida State University; Swarthmore College; University of Florida; University of Richmond; Vanderbilt University. Mean SAT verbal: 591, mean SAT math: 625, mean combined SAT: 1803. 53% scored over 600 on SAT verbal, 64% scored over 600 on SAT math, 56% scored over 1800 on combined SAT.

Student Life Upper grades have specified standards of dress, student council, honor system. Discipline rests equally with students and faculty.

Summer Programs Enrichment, sports, art/fine arts programs offered; held on campus; accepts boys and girls; open to students from other schools. 100 students usually enrolled. 2006 schedule: June to August. Application deadline: May.

Tuition and Aid Day student tuition: $13,800. Tuition installment plan (monthly payment plans). Need-based scholarship grants, faculty/staff tuition remission available. In 2005–06, 19% of upper-school students received aid. Total amount of financial aid awarded in 2005–06: $450,000.

Admissions Traditional secondary-level entrance grade is 9. For fall 2005, 27 students applied for upper-level admission, 23 were accepted, 15 enrolled. ACT, ERB, ISEE, PSAT, SAT or SSAT required. Deadline for receipt of application materials: March 3. Application fee required: $75. Interview required.

Athletics Interscholastic: baseball (boys), basketball (b,g), cheering (g), cross-country running (b,g), football (b), golf (b,g), independent competitive sports (b,g), soccer (b,g), softball (g), swimming and diving (b,g), tennis (b,g), track and field (b,g), volleyball (g); intramural: strength & conditioning (b,g), weight training (b,g). 3 PE instructors, 20 coaches.

Computers Computers are regularly used in computer applications, English, foreign language, French, graphic design, history, Latin, mathematics, newspaper, science, senior seminar, social studies, Spanish, yearbook classes. Computer network features include on-campus library services, online commercial services, Internet access, office computer access, wireless campus network, digital video production, Blackboard.

Contact Ms. Molly Hareid, Associate Director of Admissions. 941-554-5954. Fax: 941-907-1251. E-mail: mhareid@oda.edu. Web site: www.oda.edu.

THE OVERLAKE SCHOOL

20301 Northeast 108th Street
Redmond, Washington 98053
Head of School: Francisco J. Grijalva, EdD

General Information Coeducational day college-preparatory, arts, and technology school. Grades 5–12. Founded: 1967. Setting: rural. Nearest major city is Seattle. 75-acre campus. 22 buildings on campus. Approved or accredited by Northwest Association of Schools and Colleges, Pacific Northwest Association of Independent Schools, and Washington Department of Education. Member of National Association of Independent Schools. Endowment: $6.5 million. Total enrollment: 492. Upper school average class size: 13. Upper school faculty-student ratio: 1:9.

Upper School Student Profile Grade 9: 78 students (38 boys, 40 girls); Grade 10: 67 students (33 boys, 34 girls); Grade 11: 70 students (37 boys, 33 girls); Grade 12: 67 students (36 boys, 31 girls).

Faculty School total: 55. In upper school: 19 men, 33 women; 37 have advanced degrees.

Subjects Offered Algebra, American history, American history-AP, American literature, art-AP, biology-AP, botany, calculus, calculus-AP, ceramics, chemistry-AP, chorus, community service, computer programming, computer science, concert band, creative writing, drama, driver education, economics, English, English literature, English-AP, environmental science, ethics, European history-AP, European literature, film, fine arts, French, French-AP, geology, geometry, industrial arts, integrated science, Islamic history, Japanese, jazz band, journalism, Latin, Latin American literature, Latin-AP, life skills, literature, math review, mathematics, music, outdoor education, philosophy, photography, physical education, physics, physics-AP, precalculus, science, social studies, Spanish, Spanish-AP, statistics, studio art, study skills, theater, Vietnam War, woodworking, world history, world literature, World-Wide-Web publishing, yearbook, zoology.

Graduation Requirements Arts and fine arts (art, music, dance, drama), English, foreign language, mathematics, physical education (includes health), science, senior project, social studies (includes history), annual project week, 3 co-curricular activities, 15 hours of community service per year (60 total).

Special Academic Programs Advanced Placement exam preparation in 14 subject areas; honors section; independent study; term-away projects; study abroad; academic accommodation for the gifted, the musically talented, and the artistically talented.

College Placement 64 students graduated in 2005; all went to college, including Santa Clara University; Stanford University; University of Washington. Median SAT verbal: 650, median SAT math: 640. 72% scored over 600 on SAT verbal, 71% scored over 600 on SAT math.

Student Life Upper grades have student council, honor system. Discipline rests equally with students and faculty.

Summer Programs Sports programs offered; session focuses on skill building sports camps; held on campus; accepts boys and girls; not open to students from other schools. 75 students usually enrolled. 2006 schedule: August 1 to August 15. Application deadline: June 30.

Tuition and Aid Day student tuition: $19,600. Tuition installment plan (Insured Tuition Payment Plan, monthly payment plans). Need-based scholarship grants, 50% tuition remission for faculty and staff available. In 2005–06, 15% of upper-school students received aid. Total amount of financial aid awarded in 2005–06: $389,400.

Admissions Traditional secondary-level entrance grade is 9. For fall 2005, 55 students applied for upper-level admission, 28 were accepted, 22 enrolled. ISEE required. Deadline for receipt of application materials: January 19. Application fee required: $50. Interview required.

Athletics Interscholastic: baseball (boys), basketball (b,g), cross-country running (b,g), golf (b,g), lacrosse (b,g), outdoor education (b,g), physical fitness (b,g), rock

climbing (b,g), ropes courses (b,g), soccer (b,g), tennis (b,g), track and field (b,g), volleyball (g); intramural: baseball (b), basketball (b,g), cross-country running (b,g), lacrosse (b,g), outdoor education (b,g), physical fitness (b,g), rock climbing (b,g), ropes courses (b,g), skiing (cross-country) (b,g), skiing (downhill) (b,g), soccer (b,g), strength & conditioning (b,g), tennis (b,g), track and field (b,g), ultimate Frisbee (b,g), volleyball (b,g), weight lifting (b,g), weight training (b,g); coed interscholastic: outdoor education, rock climbing, ropes courses, squash, tennis; coed intramural: basketball, bicycling, cross-country running, fencing, golf, outdoor education, rock climbing, ropes courses, skiing (cross-country), skiing (downhill), table tennis, tennis. 4 PE instructors, 22 coaches.

Computers Computers are regularly used in all classes. Computer network features include campus e-mail, on-campus library services, CD-ROMs, online commercial services, Internet access, DVD.

Contact Lori Maughan, Director of Admission. 425-868-1000. Fax: 425-868-5771. E-mail: lmaughan@overlake.org. Web site: www.overlake.org.

OVERSEAS FAMILY SCHOOL

25F Paterson Road
Singapore 238515, Singapore
Head of School: Irene Chee

General Information Coeducational day college-preparatory, arts, business, bilingual studies, and technology school. Grades PK–12. Founded: 1991. Setting: urban. 11-acre campus. 11 buildings on campus. Approved or accredited by International Baccalaureate Organization and Western Association of Schools and Colleges. Member of European Council of International Schools. Language of instruction: English. Total enrollment: 1,950. Upper school faculty-student ratio: 1:8.

Upper School Student Profile Grade 9: 98 students (43 boys, 55 girls); Grade 10: 117 students (68 boys, 49 girls); Grade 11: 96 students (51 boys, 45 girls); Grade 12: 96 students (53 boys, 43 girls).

Faculty School total: 180. In upper school: 29 men, 26 women; 20 have advanced degrees.

Special Academic Programs International Baccalaureate program; ESL (62 students enrolled).

College Placement 84 students graduated in 2005; 77 went to college, including University of Massachusetts Amherst; University of Massachusetts Boston; University of Massachusetts Dartmouth. Other: 1 went to work, 4 entered military service, 2 had other specific plans.

Student Life Upper grades have uniform requirement, student council. Discipline rests primarily with faculty.

Tuition and Aid Day student tuition: 10,200 Singapore dollars.

Admissions Deadline for receipt of application materials: none. No application fee required. Interview recommended.

Athletics Interscholastic: basketball (boys, girls), cricket (b), netball (b); intramural: basketball (b,g); coed interscholastic: aquatics, ball hockey, climbing, cross-country running; coed intramural: aquatics, ball hockey, climbing, cross-country running, deck hockey. 6 PE instructors.

Computers Computer network features include campus e-mail, on-campus library services, CD-ROMs, online commercial services, Internet access, file transfer.

Contact Mrs. Soma Mathews, Academic Registrar. 65-6738-0211. Fax: 65-6733-8825. E-mail: soma_mathews@ofs.edu.sg. Web site: www.ofs.edu.sg.

See full description on page 964.

THE OXFORD ACADEMY

1393 Boston Post Road
Westbrook, Connecticut 06498-0685
Head of School: Philip H. Davis

General Information Boys' boarding college-preparatory, arts, bilingual studies, and ESL school; primarily serves underachievers. Grades 9–PG. Founded: 1906. Setting: small town. Nearest major city is New Haven. Students are housed in single-sex dormitories. 13-acre campus. 8 buildings on campus. Approved or accredited by Connecticut Association of Independent Schools, European Council of International Schools, New England Association of Schools and Colleges, The Association of Boarding Schools, and Connecticut Department of Education. Member of National Association of Independent Schools and Secondary School Admission Test Board. Endowment: $250,000. Total enrollment: 38. Upper school average class size: 1. Upper school faculty-student ratio: 1:1.

Upper School Student Profile 100% of students are boarding students. 35% are state residents. 8 states are represented in upper school student body. 33% are international students. International students from Bahamas, Bermuda, Japan, Mexico, Republic of Korea, and Saudi Arabia.

Faculty School total: 22. In upper school: 15 men, 7 women; 8 have advanced degrees; 12 reside on campus.

Subjects Offered Algebra, American history, American literature, anatomy, astronomy, biology, botany, calculus, chemistry, creative writing, earth science, ecology, economics, English, English literature, environmental science, ESL, European history, expository writing, French, geography, geology, geometry, German, government/

civics, grammar, history, Latin, marine biology, mathematics, oceanography, paleontology, philosophy, physical education, physics, physiology, psychology, science, social studies, sociology, Spanish, study skills, trigonometry, world history, world literature, writing, zoology.

Graduation Requirements English, foreign language, mathematics, science, social studies (includes history). Community service is required.

Special Academic Programs Advanced Placement exam preparation in 8 subject areas; honors section; accelerated programs; independent study; academic accommodation for the gifted; remedial reading and/or remedial writing; remedial math; ESL (6 students enrolled).

College Placement 26 students graduated in 2005; all went to college, including Bucknell University; Georgia Southern University; Lynn University; Rhode Island School of Design; Suffolk University; Wheaton College.

Student Life Upper grades have specified standards of dress, student council, honor system. Discipline rests equally with students and faculty.

Summer Programs Remediation, enrichment, advancement, ESL programs offered; session focuses on acceleration of academics, study skills; held on campus; accepts boys; open to students from other schools. 25 students usually enrolled. 2006 schedule: June 18 to July 21. Application deadline: none.

Tuition and Aid 7-day tuition and room/board: $45,700. Tuition installment plan (monthly payment plans, individually arranged payment plans). Tuition reduction for siblings, paying campus jobs available.

Admissions For fall 2005, 22 students applied for upper-level admission, 19 were accepted, 13 enrolled. SLEP for foreign students, Stanford Achievement Test, Otis-Lennon School Ability Test, TOEFL, WISC or WAIS or Woodcock-Johnson required. Deadline for receipt of application materials: none. Application fee required: $65. On-campus interview required.

Athletics Interscholastic: basketball, soccer, tennis; intramural: alpine skiing, basketball, cricket, flag football, Frisbee, hiking/backpacking, hockey, paint ball, power lifting, roller blading, strength & conditioning, table tennis, weight lifting, weight training.

Computers Computers are regularly used in mathematics classes. Computer network features include campus e-mail, CD-ROMs, Internet access, file transfer, DVD.

Contact Mrs. Michele M. Deane, Assistant Admissions Director. 860-399-6247 Ext. 100. Fax: 860-399-6805. E-mail: admissions@oxfordacademy.net. Web site: www.oxfordacademy.net.

ANNOUNCEMENT FROM THE SCHOOL Oxford Academy's exclusive one-on-one teaching method ensures academic success in most cases. Hidden abilities surface in boys ages 14–20 with average/superior intelligence who have experienced learning difficulties, lost time due to illness or other reasons, or who wish to accelerate. Admission decisions within 48 hours accommodate the urgent mid-year entry. International students in the ESL program prepare for American universities. There are rolling admissions. Graduates have attended Loyola University of New Orleans, Southern Methodist University, Virginia Military Institute, Wheaton College, Bucknell University, and Hartwick College.

See full description on page 966.

OXFORD SCHOOL

18760 East Colima Road
Rowland Heights, California 91748
Head of School: Peter Nichols

General Information Coeducational day college-preparatory and ESL school. Grades 7–12. Founded: 1980. Setting: suburban. Nearest major city is Los Angeles. 2-acre campus. 3 buildings on campus. Approved or accredited by Western Association of Schools and Colleges and California Department of Education. Endowment: $350,000. Total enrollment: 60. Upper school average class size: 15. Upper school faculty-student ratio: 1:14.

Upper School Student Profile Grade 9: 1 student (1 girl); Grade 10: 14 students (6 boys, 8 girls); Grade 11: 10 students (5 boys, 5 girls); Grade 12: 28 students (16 boys, 12 girls).

Faculty School total: 9. In upper school: 4 men, 4 women; 4 have advanced degrees.

Subjects Offered Art, biology, biology-AP, British literature, calculus, chemistry, choir, civics, college counseling, college writing, composition, computers, earth science, English, English as a foreign language, English composition, English literature, geography, history, independent study, instrumental music, lab science, language and composition, language arts, language development, mathematics, music performance, news writing, newspaper, physical education, physics, piano, pre-algebra, pre-calculus, pre-college orientation, public speaking, reading/study skills, remedial/makeup course work, research techniques, science, senior project, speech, student publications, substance abuse, TOEFL preparation, U.S. government and politics, U.S. history, U.S. literature, Western literature, world civilizations, world history, writing, yearbook.

Graduation Requirements Arts and fine arts (art, music, dance, drama), English, foreign language, mathematics, physical education (includes health), portfolio writing, science, social studies (includes history), portfolio and oral presentation, Creativity, Action, Service Program.

Special Academic Programs Advanced Placement exam preparation in 1 subject area; honors section; accelerated programs; independent study; study at local college for college credit; domestic exchange program; study abroad; remedial reading and/or remedial writing; remedial math; special instructional classes for students with limited English proficiency; ESL (50 students enrolled).

College Placement 23 students graduated in 2005; all went to college, including California State Polytechnic University, Pomona; California State University, Fullerton; California State University, Long Beach; California State University, San Bernardino; Mt. San Antonio College; University of California, Riverside. Median SAT verbal: 400, median SAT math: 600. 12% scored over 600 on SAT verbal, 33% scored over 600 on SAT math.

Student Life Upper grades have uniform requirement, student council, honor system. Discipline rests equally with students and faculty.

Summer Programs Enrichment programs offered; session focuses on English improvement; held both on and off campus; held at various locations (museums, field trips); accepts boys and girls; not open to students from other schools. 40 students usually enrolled. 2006 schedule: July 5 to August 27. Application deadline: January 2.

Tuition and Aid Day student tuition: $7548. Guaranteed tuition plan.

Admissions Traditional secondary-level entrance grade is 10. For fall 2005, 22 students applied for upper-level admission, 22 were accepted, 22 enrolled. ESOL English Proficiency Test required. Deadline for receipt of application materials: none. Application fee required: $160. Interview recommended.

Athletics Interscholastic: basketball (boys, girls); intramural: badminton (b,g), basketball (b,g); coed interscholastic: basketball; coed intramural: basketball. 1 PE instructor, 1 coach.

Computers Computers are regularly used in art, desktop publishing, ESL, English, ESL, foreign language, French, French as a second language, geography, history, independent study, language development, literacy, mathematics, newspaper, reading, religious studies, research skills, SAT preparation, science, Spanish, stock market, writing, writing, yearbook classes. Computer network features include campus e-mail, on-campus library services, CD-ROMs, Internet access.

Contact George Wang, Director of Admissions. 626-964-9588 Ext. 101. Fax: 626-913-3919. E-mail: george_w@oxfordschool.org. Web site: www.oxfordschool.org.

PACE ACADEMY

966 West Paces Ferry Road, NW
Atlanta, Georgia 30327
Head of School: Mr. Frederick G. Assaf

General Information Coeducational day college-preparatory, arts, and technology school. Grades K–12. Founded: 1958. Setting: suburban. 27-acre campus. 7 buildings on campus. Approved or accredited by Southern Association of Colleges and Schools and Southern Association of Independent Schools. Member of National Association of Independent Schools and Secondary School Admission Test Board. Endowment: $20 million. Total enrollment: 922. Upper school average class size: 15. Upper school faculty-student ratio: 1:8.

Upper School Student Profile Grade 9: 98 students (53 boys, 45 girls); Grade 10: 90 students (41 boys, 49 girls); Grade 11: 98 students (53 boys, 45 girls); Grade 12: 94 students (48 boys, 46 girls).

Faculty School total: 100. In upper school: 26 men, 27 women; 41 have advanced degrees.

Subjects Offered Adolescent issues, advanced math, advanced studio art-AP, algebra, American history, American history-AP, American literature, ancient world history, architectural drawing, art, art history, art history-AP, arts, band, biology, biology-AP, British literature, British literature (honors), calculus, calculus-AP, ceramics, chemistry, chemistry-AP, Chinese history, chorus, community service, comparative government and politics-AP, comparative politics, computer keyboarding, computer skills, creative writing, debate, digital imaging, digital photography, drawing, earth science, economics, English, English literature, English-AP, environmental science-AP, European history, fine arts, French, French language-AP, geometry, history, honors algebra, honors English, honors geometry, honors U.S. history, honors world history, Japanese history, Latin, Latin-AP, leadership education training, mathematics, modern European history-AP, music history, music theory-AP, painting, photography, physical education, physics, physics-AP, political science, pre-algebra, psychology, public speaking, religion, science, social science, Spanish, Spanish language-AP, stagecraft, statistics-AP, student publications, trigonometry, world history, world literature, yearbook.

Graduation Requirements Arts and fine arts (art, music, dance, drama), English, foreign language, mathematics, physical education (includes health), science, social science, social studies (includes history), 40 hours of community service, one semester of public speaking.

Special Academic Programs Advanced Placement exam preparation in 16 subject areas; honors section; independent study; term-away projects; study abroad; academic accommodation for the gifted, the musically talented, and the artistically talented; remedial reading and/or remedial writing.

College Placement 88 students graduated in 2005; all went to college, including Auburn University; Georgia Institute of Technology; Southern Methodist University; University of Georgia; University of Virginia; Vanderbilt University. Mean SAT verbal: 653, mean SAT math: 659.

Student Life Upper grades have specified standards of dress, student council, honor system. Discipline rests primarily with faculty.

Summer Programs Remediation, enrichment, advancement, sports, art/fine arts, computer instruction programs offered; session focuses on traditional day camp (primarily younger children attend); held on campus; accepts boys and girls; open to students from other schools. 900 students usually enrolled. 2006 schedule: June 15 to August 10.

Tuition and Aid Day student tuition: $16,635. Tuition installment plan (FACTS Tuition Payment Plan). Need-based scholarship grants available. In 2005–06, 15% of upper-school students received aid. Total amount of financial aid awarded in 2005–06: $850,000.

Admissions Traditional secondary-level entrance grade is 9. For fall 2005, 102 students applied for upper-level admission, 54 were accepted, 27 enrolled. SSAT required. Deadline for receipt of application materials: February 21. Application fee required: $65. On-campus interview required.

Athletics Interscholastic: baseball (boys), basketball (b,g), cheering (g), cross-country running (b,g), diving (b,g), fitness (b,g), golf (b,g), gymnastics (g), lacrosse (b,g), soccer (b,g), softball (g), swimming and diving (b,g), tennis (b,g), track and field (b,g), volleyball (g), wrestling (b); intramural: squash (b,g); coed interscholastic: ultimate Frisbee; coed intramural: squash. 6 PE instructors, 6 coaches, 1 trainer.

Computers Computers are regularly used in all academic classes. Computer network features include campus e-mail, on-campus library services, CD-ROMs, online commercial services, Internet access, file transfer, office computer access, DVD, wireless campus network, classroom SmartBoards.

Contact Mrs. Claire Drummond Strowd, Assistant Director of Admissions. 404-240-9109. Fax: 404-240-9124. E-mail: cstrowd@paceacademy.org. Web site: www.paceacademy.org.

PACIFIC HILLS SCHOOL

8628 Holloway Drive
West Hollywood, California 90069
Head of School: Mr. Richard S. Makoff

General Information Coeducational day college-preparatory school. Grades 6–12. Founded: 1983. Setting: urban. Nearest major city is Beverly Hills. 2-acre campus. 2 buildings on campus. Approved or accredited by California Association of Independent Schools, Western Association of Schools and Colleges, and California Department of Education. Member of National Association of Independent Schools. Total enrollment: 289. Upper school average class size: 18. Upper school faculty-student ratio: 1:15.

Upper School Student Profile Grade 9: 40 students (22 boys, 18 girls); Grade 10: 55 students (28 boys, 27 girls); Grade 11: 53 students (26 boys, 27 girls); Grade 12: 50 students (23 boys, 27 girls).

Faculty School total: 36. In upper school: 21 men, 15 women; 12 have advanced degrees.

Subjects Offered Advanced Placement courses, aerobics, algebra, American history, American literature, anatomy, art, biology, calculus-AP, cheerleading, chemistry, computers, economics, English, English literature, film, French, geometry, government, human development, independent study, music, newspaper, photography, physical education, physics, pre-calculus, Spanish, speech, theater arts, yearbook.

Graduation Requirements Arts and fine arts (art, music, dance, drama), computer science, English, foreign language, mathematics, physical education (includes health), science, social science, social studies (includes history). Community service is required.

Special Academic Programs Honors section.

College Placement 47 students graduated in 2005; 46 went to college, including California State University, Long Beach; California State University, Northridge; University of California, San Diego; University of California, Santa Barbara; University of Southern California. Other: 1 had other specific plans. Median SAT verbal: 505, median SAT math: 490. 17% scored over 600 on SAT verbal, 15% scored over 600 on SAT math.

Student Life Upper grades have specified standards of dress, student council, honor system. Discipline rests primarily with faculty.

Summer Programs Remediation, enrichment programs offered; held on campus; accepts boys and girls; open to students from other schools. 110 students usually enrolled. 2006 schedule: June 26 to August 5. Application deadline: none.

Tuition and Aid Day student tuition: $16,900. Tuition installment plan (Insured Tuition Payment Plan, SMART Tuition Payment Plan, monthly payment plans, individually arranged payment plans). Tuition reduction for siblings, need-based scholarship grants, need-based loans available. In 2005–06, 33% of upper-school students received aid. Total amount of financial aid awarded in 2005–06: $1,327,190.

Admissions Traditional secondary-level entrance grade is 9. For fall 2005, 330 students applied for upper-level admission, 100 were accepted, 46 enrolled. CTBS (or similar from their school) or ISEE required. Deadline for receipt of application materials: none. Application fee required: $100. On-campus interview required.

Athletics Interscholastic: baseball (boys), basketball (b,g), cheering (g), softball (g), tennis (b,g), volleyball (b,g); coed interscholastic: aerobics, cross-country running, golf, outdoor education, soccer, track and field, yoga. 6 PE instructors, 7 coaches.

Computers Computers are regularly used in graphic design, journalism, yearbook classes. Computer network features include CD-ROMs, Internet access, DVD.

Contact Ms. Lynne Bradshaw, Admissions Assistant. 310-276-3068 Ext. 112. Fax: 310-657-3831. E-mail: lbradshaw@phschool.org. Web site: www.phschool.org.

PACIFIC NORTHERN ACADEMY

550 Bragaw Street
Anchorage, Alaska 99508
Head of School: Bob Christal

General Information Coeducational day college-preparatory, arts, and bilingual studies school. Grades K–12. Founded: 1996. Setting: urban. 9-acre campus. 1 building on campus. Candidate for accreditation by Pacific Northwest Association of Independent Schools. Total enrollment: 115. Upper school average class size: 7. Upper school faculty-student ratio: 1:2.

Upper School Student Profile Grade 9: 4 students (1 boy, 3 girls); Grade 10: 3 students (1 boy, 2 girls); Grade 11: 3 students (1 boy, 2 girls); Grade 12: 6 students (4 boys, 2 girls).

Faculty School total: 20. In upper school: 2 men, 6 women; 4 have advanced degrees.

Subjects Offered Algebra, American history, American literature, art, biology, biology-AP, British literature, business communications, calculus, career education internship, character education, choir, composition, drama, economics, electives, English, English composition, English language and composition-AP, English literature, English literature and composition-AP, humanities, Spanish, world history.

Special Academic Programs Accelerated programs; independent study; study at local college for college credit; academic accommodation for the gifted.

College Placement 5 students graduated in 2005; all went to college, including University of Alaska Anchorage.

Student Life Upper grades have specified standards of dress, student council, honor system. Discipline rests primarily with faculty.

Tuition and Aid Day student tuition: $13,300. Tuition installment plan (monthly payment plans, individually arranged payment plans). Tuition reduction for siblings, need-based scholarship grants available. In 2005–06, 15% of upper-school students received aid.

Admissions Traditional secondary-level entrance grade is 9. For fall 2005, 3 students applied for upper-level admission, 3 were accepted, 2 enrolled. Deadline for receipt of application materials: none. Application fee required: $50. Interview required.

Athletics Interscholastic: basketball (boys), volleyball (g); coed interscholastic: diving, nordic skiing, swimming and diving; coed intramural: climbing, rock climbing, running. 1 PE instructor.

Computers Computer network features include Internet access.

Contact Shannon Tetlow, Director of Admissions and Marketing. 907-333-1080. Fax: 907-333-1652. E-mail: stetlow@pacificnorthern.org. Web site: www. pacificnorthern.org.

PADUA FRANCISCAN HIGH SCHOOL

6740 State Road
Parma, Ohio 44134-4598
Head of School: Mr. Chris Keavy

General Information Coeducational day college-preparatory, arts, business, religious studies, and technology school, affiliated with Roman Catholic Church. Grades 9–12. Founded: 1961. Setting: suburban. Nearest major city is Cleveland. 40-acre campus. 1 building on campus. Approved or accredited by North Central Association of Colleges and Schools, Ohio Catholic Schools Accreditation Association (OCSAA), and Ohio Department of Education. Endowment: $1.5 million. Total enrollment: 995. Upper school average class size: 25. Upper school faculty-student ratio: 1:18.

Upper School Student Profile Grade 9: 245 students (123 boys, 122 girls); Grade 10: 228 students (117 boys, 111 girls); Grade 11: 264 students (124 boys, 140 girls); Grade 12: 258 students (130 boys, 128 girls). 90% of students are Roman Catholic.

Faculty School total: 79. In upper school: 39 men, 40 women; 40 have advanced degrees.

Subjects Offered Accounting, algebra, American government, art appreciation, biology-AP, business, calculus-AP, chemistry, child development, Christian ethics, church history, computers, concert band, concert choir, consumer economics, current events, design, drawing, earth science, economics, English, English language-AP, ensembles, fitness, food and nutrition, French, French-AP, geography, geometry, German, German-AP, honors algebra, honors English, honors geometry, honors U.S. history, integrated science, interior design, Italian, Latin, Latin-AP, marching band, marketing, math analysis, music appreciation, music theory, orchestra, painting, photography, physics, pre-calculus, programming, psychology, social issues, social justice, sociology, Spanish, Spanish-AP, stagecraft, symphonic band, theater, trigonometry, U.S. history, U.S. history-AP, world cultures, world history.

Graduation Requirements Arts and fine arts (art, music, dance, drama), computer science, English, foreign language, lab science, mathematics, physical education (includes health), social studies (includes history), theology, four years of service.

Special Academic Programs Advanced Placement exam preparation in 6 subject areas; honors section; accelerated programs; study at local college for college credit; study abroad; special instructional classes for students with learning disabilities.

College Placement 257 students graduated in 2005; 253 went to college, including Bowling Green State University; Kent State University; Miami University; The

Padua Franciscan High School

University of Akron; The University of Toledo; University of Dayton. Other: 2 went to work, 2 entered military service. Median SAT verbal: 530, median SAT math: 519, median composite ACT: 23.

Student Life Upper grades have uniform requirement, student council, honor system. Discipline rests primarily with faculty. Attendance at religious services is required.

Summer Programs Enrichment, sports, art/fine arts, computer instruction programs offered; session focuses on introducing students to school, programs, coaches and other students; held on campus; accepts boys and girls; open to students from other schools. 500 students usually enrolled. 2006 schedule: June 15 to July 31. Application deadline: May 31.

Tuition and Aid Day student tuition: $6950. Tuition installment plan (monthly payment plans, individually arranged payment plans). Tuition reduction for siblings, merit scholarship grants, need-based scholarship grants, paying campus jobs available. In 2005–06, 48% of upper-school students received aid; total upper-school merit-scholarship money awarded: $181,000. Total amount of financial aid awarded in 2005–06: $777,980.

Admissions Traditional secondary-level entrance grade is 9. For fall 2005, 300 students applied for upper-level admission, 275 were accepted, 263 enrolled. STS required. Deadline for receipt of application materials: January 29. Application fee required: $100.

Athletics Interscholastic: aquatics (boys, girls), baseball (b), basketball (b,g), cheering (g), combined training (b,g), cross-country running (b,g), dance team (g), diving (b,g), football (b), golf (b,g), hockey (b), ice hockey (b), physical fitness (b,g), soccer (b,g), softball (g), strength & conditioning (b,g), swimming and diving (b,g), tennis (g), track and field (b,g), volleyball (g), wrestling (b); intramural: flag football (b), freestyle skiing (b,g), golf (g), gymnastics (g), power lifting (b), touch football (b), weight lifting (b), weight training (b,g), winter soccer (b); coed intramural: alpine skiing, back packing, canoeing/kayaking, fishing, hiking/backpacking, skiing (downhill), snowboarding, wilderness, wilderness survival, wildernessways. 3 PE instructors, 30 coaches, 5 trainers.

Computers Computers are regularly used in all academic classes. Computer network features include campus e-mail, on-campus library services, CD-ROMs, online commercial services, Internet access, office computer access.

Contact Mrs. Nancy Hodas, Admissions Coordinator. 440-845-2444 Ext. 112. Fax: 440-845-5710. E-mail: nhodas@paduafranciscan.com. Web site: www.paduafranciscan.com.

THE PAIDEIA SCHOOL

1509 Ponce de Leon Avenue
Atlanta, Georgia 30307
Head of School: Paul F. Bianchi

petersons.com

General Information Coeducational day college-preparatory, arts, and technology school. Grades N–12. Founded: 1971. Setting: urban. 21-acre campus. 13 buildings on campus. Approved or accredited by Georgia Independent School Association, Southern Association of Colleges and Schools, Southern Association of Independent Schools, and Georgia Department of Education. Endowment: $14.5 million. Total enrollment: 915. Upper school average class size: 14. Upper school faculty-student ratio: 1:10.

Upper School Student Profile Grade 9: 98 students (45 boys, 53 girls); Grade 10: 103 students (50 boys, 53 girls); Grade 11: 93 students (42 boys, 51 girls); Grade 12: 93 students (43 boys, 50 girls).

Faculty School total: 133. In upper school: 29 men, 35 women; 49 have advanced degrees.

Subjects Offered African-American history, algebra, American culture, American government, American history, American literature, anatomy, archaeology, art, art history, Asian history, auto mechanics, bioethics, biology, biology-AP, calculus, ceramics, chemistry, chemistry-AP, chorus, community service, comparative religion, computer programming, creative writing, drama, drawing, ecology, environmental systems, economics, English, English literature, environmental science, ethics, European history, European history-AP, expository writing, fine arts, forensics, French, French literature-AP, geography, geology, geometry, government/civics, health, history, humanities, jazz, journalism, literature, mathematics, medieval history, organic chemistry, photography, physical education, physics, physics-AP, physiology, poetry, pre-calculus, psychology, psychology-AP, Shakespeare, social studies, sociology, Spanish, Spanish-AP, speech, statistics, statistics-AP, theater, trigonometry, typing, Web site design, weight training, women's health, women's studies, world history, world literature, writing.

Graduation Requirements Arts and fine arts (art, music, dance, drama), English, foreign language, mathematics, physical education (includes health), science, social science, social studies (includes history). Community service is required.

Special Academic Programs Advanced Placement exam preparation in 8 subject areas; honors section; independent study.

College Placement 90 students graduated in 2005; 88 went to college, including Emory University, Oxford College; Morehouse College; Pomona College; Savannah College of Art and Design; University of Georgia; University of Miami. Other: 2 had other specific plans.

Student Life Upper grades have student council, honor system. Discipline rests equally with students and faculty.

Tuition and Aid Day student tuition: $15,150. Need-based tuition assistance, bank-arranged tuition loan program available. In 2005–06, 12% of upper-school students received aid. Total amount of financial aid awarded in 2005–06: $642,263.

Admissions Traditional secondary-level entrance grade is 9. Deadline for receipt of application materials: February 8. Application fee required: $75. On-campus interview required.

Athletics Interscholastic: baseball (boys), basketball (b,g), cross-country running (b,g), diving (b,g), soccer (b,g), softball (g), swimming and diving (b,g), tennis (b,g), track and field (b,g), ultimate Frisbee (b,g), volleyball (b,g); coed interscholastic: ultimate Frisbee; coed intramural: basketball, bicycling, bowling, flag football, soccer, softball, ultimate Frisbee. 2 PE instructors, 1 trainer.

Computers Computers are regularly used in art, English, foreign language, graphic arts, mathematics, music, science classes. Computer network features include campus e-mail, on-campus library services, CD-ROMs, Internet access.

Contact Florence Henry, Assistant to Director of Admissions. 404-270-2312. Fax: 404-377-0032. E-mail: henry.flo@paideiaschool.org. Web site: www.paideiaschool.org.

ANNOUNCEMENT FROM THE SCHOOL The Paideia School is committed to a racial, socioeconomic, and cultural cross-section of students and faculty. Students balance a rigorous academic program with independent projects, community service, the arts, and athletics. The philosophy is based on the belief that schools can be informal and individualized, yet still educate well.

PALMA HIGH SCHOOL

919 Iverson Street
Salinas, California 93901
Head of School: Br. Patrick D. Dunne, CFC

General Information Boys' day college-preparatory and religious studies school, affiliated with Roman Catholic Church. Grades 7–12. Founded: 1951. Setting: suburban. Nearest major city is San Jose. 25-acre campus. 15 buildings on campus. Approved or accredited by Western Association of Schools and Colleges, Western Catholic Education Association, and California Department of Education. Total enrollment: 642. Upper school average class size: 25. Upper school faculty-student ratio: 1:16.

Upper School Student Profile Grade 9: 123 students (123 boys); Grade 10: 107 students (107 boys); Grade 11: 113 students (113 boys); Grade 12: 111 students (111 boys). 69% of students are Roman Catholic.

Faculty School total: 40. In upper school: 32 men, 8 women; 18 have advanced degrees.

Subjects Offered Algebra, American history, American literature, anatomy, art, art history, band, biology, business, calculus, calculus-AP, chemistry, Christian and Hebrew scripture, church history, civics, community service, computer applications, computer art, computer math, computer multimedia, computer programming, computer programming-AP, computer science, computer-aided design, creative writing, debate, digital art, driver education, earth science, economics, English, English language and composition-AP, English literature, English literature-AP, ethics, European history, European history-AP, expository writing, film, film studies, fine arts, French, geography, geometry, government/civics, grammar, health, health education, history, honors algebra, honors geometry, Japanese, jazz ensemble, journalism, Latin, mathematics, music, participation in sports, physical education, physical science, physics, pre-calculus, psychology, religion, Russian, Russian literature, science, social studies, Spanish, Spanish language-AP, speech, statistics-AP, student government, theology, trigonometry, typing, U.S. government and politics-AP, U.S. history-AP, video film production, world history, world literature, world religions, writing.

Graduation Requirements Arts and fine arts (art, music, dance, drama), English, foreign language, mathematics, physical education (includes health), religion (includes Bible studies and theology), science, social studies (includes history), religious retreat (8th, 9th, 10th grades), 60 hours of community service.

Special Academic Programs Advanced Placement exam preparation in 11 subject areas; honors section; study at local college for college credit.

College Placement 105 students graduated in 2005; all went to college, including California Polytechnic State University, San Luis Obispo; Saint Mary's College of California; Santa Clara University; Stanford University; University of California, Berkeley; University of California, Davis. 26% scored over 600 on SAT verbal, 34% scored over 600 on SAT math, 43% scored over 26 on composite ACT.

Student Life Upper grades have specified standards of dress, student council, honor system. Discipline rests primarily with faculty. Attendance at religious services is required.

Summer Programs Remediation, enrichment, advancement programs offered; session focuses on remediation and advancement; held on campus; accepts boys and girls; open to students from other schools. 200 students usually enrolled. 2006 schedule: June to July. Application deadline: March 1.

Tuition and Aid Day student tuition: $7980. Tuition installment plan (monthly payment plans, 2-payment plan). Merit scholarship grants, need-based scholarship grants available. In 2005–06, 15% of upper-school students received aid.

Admissions Traditional secondary-level entrance grade is 9. For fall 2005, 327 students applied for upper-level admission, 229 were accepted, 186 enrolled. ETS high school placement exam required. Deadline for receipt of application materials: January 14. Application fee required: $50. On-campus interview required.

Athletics Interscholastic: baseball, basketball, cross-country running, diving, football, golf, soccer, swimming and diving, track and field, volleyball, water polo, wrestling; intramural: basketball, indoor soccer. 4 PE instructors, 15 coaches, 1 trainer.

Computers Computers are regularly used in art, English, foreign language, history, mathematics, music, science, writing, yearbook classes. Computer network features include campus e-mail, on-campus library services, CD-ROMs, online commercial services, Internet access.

Contact Kevin Rawson, Vice Principal. 831-422-6391. Fax: 831-422-5065: E-mail: rawson@palmahs.org. Web site: palmahs.org.

PALMER TRINITY SCHOOL

7900 Southwest 176th Street
Miami, Florida 33157
Head of School: Sean Murphy

petersons.com

General Information Coeducational day college-preparatory, arts, technology, and ESL school, affiliated with Episcopal Church. Grades 6–12. Founded: 1973. Setting: suburban. 58-acre campus. 10 buildings on campus. Approved or accredited by Association of Independent Schools of Florida, Florida Council of Independent Schools, National Association of Episcopal Schools, Southern Association of Colleges and Schools, and Florida Department of Education. Member of National Association of Independent Schools and Secondary School Admission Test Board. Endowment: $4.3 million. Total enrollment: 600. Upper school average class size: 15. Upper school faculty-student ratio: 1:14.

Upper School Student Profile Grade 9: 83 students (36 boys, 47 girls); Grade 10: 88 students (42 boys, 46 girls); Grade 11: 90 students (46 boys, 44 girls). 10% of students are members of Episcopal Church.

Faculty School total: 65. In upper school: 21 men, 25 women; 38 have advanced degrees.

Subjects Offered Advanced studio art-AP, advanced TOEFL/grammar, algebra, American culture, American government, anatomy, area studies, art, art history, art history-AP, Asian studies, Basic programming, Bible studies, biology, biology-AP, British literature, British literature (honors), calculus, calculus-AP, ceramics, chemistry, chemistry-AP, choir, civics, classics, college admission preparation, college counseling, community service, comparative government and politics, comparative government and politics-AP, comparative religion, composition-AP, computer graphics, computer keyboarding, computer science, computer science-AP, conceptual physics, concert band, concert choir, creative writing, dance, debate, drama, earth science, economics, economics-AP, English, English composition, English language and composition-AP, English literature, English literature and composition-AP, environmental science, ESL, ethics and responsibility, European history, European history-AP, expository writing, film, fine arts, French, French language-AP, French literature-AP, genetics, geography, geometry, global studies, government/civics, guitar, health and wellness, history, honors algebra, honors English, honors geometry, honors U.S. history, honors world history, humanities, journalism, Latin, Latin American history, Latin American studies, law, literature, logic, marine biology, marine science, mathematics, Middle Eastern history, model United Nations, modern European history-AP, music, musical theater, newspaper, oral communications, philosophy, photography, physical education, physical science, physics, physics-AP, physiology, pre-algebra, pre-calculus, psychology, religion, religion and culture, Russian studies, SAT preparation, science, sculpture, social science, social studies, sociology, Spanish, Spanish language-AP, Spanish literature-AP, speech, statistics, studio art-AP, telecommunications and the Internet, theater, theology, TOEFL preparation, trigonometry, U.S. history, U.S. history-AP, U.S. literature, United States government-AP, world history, world history-AP, world literature, world religions, writing, yearbook.

Graduation Requirements Arts and fine arts (art, music, dance, drama), business skills (includes word processing), computer science, English, ethics, foreign language, humanities, mathematics, physical education (includes health), science, social science, social studies (includes history), theology, minimum 20 hours of community service per year.

Special Academic Programs Advanced Placement exam preparation in 16 subject areas; honors section; accelerated programs; independent study; term-away projects; study at local college for college credit; study abroad; academic accommodation for the gifted, the musically talented, and the artistically talented; ESL (30 students enrolled).

College Placement Colleges students went to include Boston College; Florida International University; Southern Methodist University; University of Miami; University of Notre Dame; Vanderbilt University.

Student Life Upper grades have uniform requirement, student council, honor system. Discipline rests equally with students and faculty.

Tuition and Aid Day student tuition: $15,400–$16,000. Tuition installment plan (monthly payment plans). Merit scholarship grants, need-based scholarship grants, one merit-based scholarship for freshmen available. In 2004–05, 20% of upper-school students received aid; total upper-school merit-scholarship money awarded: $5000. Total amount of financial aid awarded in 2004–05: $800,000.

Admissions ACT, ISEE, PSAT and SAT for applicants to grade 11 and 12 or SLEP for foreign students required. Deadline for receipt of application materials: February 1. Application fee required: $100. On-campus interview required.

Athletics Interscholastic: baseball (boys), basketball (b,g), cheering (g), cross-country running (b,g), football (b), golf (b,g), lacrosse (b), soccer (b,g), softball (g), swimming and diving (b,g), tennis (b,g), track and field (b,g), volleyball (g), wrestling (b); intramural: basketball (b), canoeing/kayaking (b), dance team (g), floor hockey (b), hockey (b), in-line hockey (b), in-line skating (b), rugby (b), volleyball (g), weight training (b,g); coed intramural: climbing, ice hockey, outdoor education, physical training, rock climbing, strength & conditioning, weight training. 7 PE instructors, 25 coaches, 2 trainers.

Computers Computers are regularly used in all classes. Computer network features include campus e-mail, on-campus library services, CD-ROMs, online commercial services, Internet access, file transfer, office computer access, DVD, wireless campus network, laptop program in all academic areas.

Contact Danny Reynolds, Director of Admissions and Financial Aid. 305-969-4208. Fax: 305-251-0607. E-mail: reynolds@palmertrinity.org. Web site: www.palmertrinity.org.

ANNOUNCEMENT FROM THE SCHOOL Palmer Trinity School is an independent, college-preparatory, coeducational Episcopal day school located on 54 acres of tropical hammock in southwest Miami. Established in 1991, Palmer Trinity School enrolls 600 students in grades 6–12. Palmer Trinity School balances a rigorous college-prep program with the development of the spiritual and moral life of students. The core values of the School include academic excellence, spiritual growth, and service to others. When students graduate, they are prepared for the challenges and course work they will experience at the university level. In addition, the Palmer Trinity School program includes opportunities for leadership, experiences in the arts and athletics, and participation in a wide variety of extracurricular and social activities. Students are prepared to live in a diverse, multicultural world, and the highest ideals of tolerance, personal integrity, and social responsibility are encouraged. The best environment for young people is a school where they feel valued, affirmed, and supported while they explore their interests and develop their special gifts. Palmer Trinity School is a community of caring, talented faculty and staff who work in partnership with parents and families to help young people develop into competent and compassionate adults. Students are expected to participate in and contribute to the life of the School and the greater community. Palmer Trinity School demands much of its students, challenging them to actualize their potential as individual scholars in an atmosphere of love, acceptance, and support. Admission to Palmer Trinity School is competitive. The early admission deadline is November 15 and regular admission deadline is February 1. For more information about Palmer Trinity School or to apply online, please visit the Web site at www.palmertrinity.org.

PARACLETE HIGH SCHOOL

42145 North 30th Street West
Lancaster, California 93536
Head of School: Mr. John Anson

General Information Coeducational day college-preparatory, arts, religious studies, and technology school, affiliated with Roman Catholic Church. Grades 9–12. Founded: 1963. Setting: urban. Nearest major city is Los Angeles. 17-acre campus. 7 buildings on campus. Approved or accredited by National Catholic Education Association, Western Association of Schools and Colleges, and California Department of Education. Total enrollment: 783. Upper school average class size: 25. Upper school faculty-student ratio: 1:18.

Upper School Student Profile Grade 9: 224 students (98 boys, 126 girls); Grade 10: 189 students (86 boys, 103 girls); Grade 11: 195 students (95 boys, 100 girls); Grade 12: 175 students (77 boys, 98 girls). 65% of students are Roman Catholic.

Faculty School total: 47. In upper school: 22 men, 22 women; 24 have advanced degrees.

Subjects Offered Advanced Placement courses, algebra, American history, American literature, anatomy, anthropology, art, art history, Bible studies, biology, biology-AP, calculus, calculus-AP, Catholic belief and practice, character education, chemistry, choir, computer graphics, computer science, computer technologies, computer-aided design, concert band, constitutional history of U.S., creative writing, current events, drafting, drama, drawing, earth science, economics, English, English literature, ethics, European history, expository writing, fine arts, French, geometry, government/civics, grammar, graphic design, health, history, jazz band, journalism, leadership, mathematics, media production, music, peer ministry, performing arts, physical education, physics, pre-algebra, pre-calculus, psychology, religion, science, social studies, sociology, Spanish, Spanish language-AP, speech, sports, statistics, technical theater, theater, theology, trigonometry, world history, world literature, writing.

Graduation Requirements Arts and fine arts (art, music, dance, drama), computer science, English, foreign language, mathematics, physical education (includes health), religion (includes Bible studies and theology), science, social studies (includes history).

Special Academic Programs Advanced Placement exam preparation in 5 subject areas; honors section.

College Placement 174 students graduated in 2005; 171 went to college, including California State University; Loyola Marymount University; Mount St. Mary's College; University of California, Santa Barbara; University of San Diego. Other: 2 entered military service, 1 had other specific plans.

Student Life Upper grades have uniform requirement, student council, honor system. Discipline rests equally with students and faculty. Attendance at religious services is required.

Summer Programs Remediation, enrichment, advancement, sports, art/fine arts, computer instruction programs offered; session focuses on Algebra I and English review; incoming freshmen study skills; held on campus; accepts boys and girls; not open to students from other schools. 250 students usually enrolled. 2006 schedule: June 19 to July 28. Application deadline: June 12.

Tuition and Aid Day student tuition: $4840–$6380. Tuition installment plan (monthly payment plans). Tuition reduction for siblings, merit scholarship grants, need-based scholarship grants, Archdiocese of Los Angeles grants, alumni foundation grants, Knights of Columbus grants available. In 2005–06, 12% of upper-school students received aid.

Admissions Traditional secondary-level entrance grade is 9. For fall 2005, 300 students applied for upper-level admission, 225 were accepted, 224 enrolled. Catholic High School Entrance Examination and SSAT required. Deadline for receipt of application materials: July 1. Application fee required: $50. On-campus interview required.

Athletics Interscholastic: baseball (boys), basketball (b,g), cheering (b,g), cross-country running (b,g), dance team (g), football (b), golf (b,g), soccer (b,g), softball (g), track and field (b,g), volleyball (g), weight training (b,g); coed interscholastic: cheering. 5 PE instructors, 27 coaches, 2 trainers.

Computers Computers are regularly used in English, foreign language, history, information technology, library skills, mathematics, media arts, media production, multimedia, newspaper, photojournalism, SAT preparation, science, technical drawing, yearbook classes. Computer network features include campus e-mail, on-campus library services, CD-ROMs, online commercial services, Internet access, office computer access, DVD.

Contact Mrs. Denise Vallejos, Admissions Officer. 661-943-3255 Ext. 106. Fax: 661-722-9455. E-mail: dvallejos@paraclete.pvt.k12.ca.us. Web site: www.paraclete.pvt.k12.ca.us.

THE PARKER SCHOOL

65-1224 Lindsey Road
Kamuela, Hawaii 96743
Head of School: Dr. Carl Sturges

General Information Coeducational day college-preparatory, arts, and technology school. Grades K–12. Founded: 1976. Setting: rural. Nearest major city is Kona. 6-acre campus. 6 buildings on campus. Approved or accredited by Western Association of Schools and Colleges and Hawaii Department of Education. Member of National Association of Independent Schools. Endowment: $3 million. Total enrollment: 269. Upper school average class size: 12. Upper school faculty-student ratio: 1:8.

Upper School Student Profile Grade 9: 35 students (16 boys, 19 girls); Grade 10: 25 students (11 boys, 14 girls); Grade 11: 28 students (13 boys, 15 girls); Grade 12: 19 students (6 boys, 13 girls).

Faculty School total: 24. In upper school: 3 men, 9 women; 7 have advanced degrees.

Subjects Offered Advanced math, Advanced Placement courses, algebra, American literature, art, art and culture, biology, chemistry, college planning, computer programming, computer science, computer technologies, creative writing, drama, earth science, English, English literature, European history, film studies, fine arts, geography, geometry, government/civics, grammar, Hawaiian history, health, history, mathematics, music, Pacific Island studies, physical education, physics, pre-algebra, pre-calculus, science, senior seminar, social science, social studies, sociology, Spanish, theater, trigonometry, U.S. history, weight training, world history, world literature, writing.

Graduation Requirements Arts and fine arts (art, music, dance, drama), English, foreign language, mathematics, physical education (includes health), science, social studies (includes history).

Special Academic Programs Advanced Placement exam preparation in 5 subject areas; honors section; independent study.

College Placement 16 students graduated in 2005; all went to college, including University of Hawaii at Manoa. Median SAT verbal: 593, median SAT math: 563.

Student Life Upper grades have specified standards of dress, student council, honor system. Discipline rests equally with students and faculty.

Summer Programs Remediation, enrichment programs offered; session focuses on remediation and enrichment; held on campus; accepts boys and girls; open to students from other schools. 20 students usually enrolled. 2006 schedule: June 9 to July 11. Application deadline: none.

Tuition and Aid Day student tuition: $9900. Tuition installment plan (Key Tuition Payment Plan, monthly payment plans, individually arranged payment plans). Merit scholarship grants, need-based scholarship grants, paying campus jobs available. In 2005–06, 46% of upper-school students received aid; total upper-school merit-scholarship money awarded: $59,500. Total amount of financial aid awarded in 2005–06: $117,000.

Admissions Traditional secondary-level entrance grade is 9. For fall 2005, 26 students applied for upper-level admission, 21 were accepted, 21 enrolled. Admissions testing required. Deadline for receipt of application materials: none. Application fee required: $50. Interview required.

Athletics Interscholastic: basketball (boys, girls), canoeing/kayaking (b,g), cross-country running (b,g), golf (b,g), ocean paddling (b,g), soccer (b,g), swimming and diving (b,g), tennis (b,g), track and field (b,g), volleyball (b,g); coed intramural: cooperative games. 13 coaches.

Computers Computers are regularly used in drafting, English, graphics, independent study, science classes. Computer network features include campus e-mail, CD-ROMs, Internet access.

Contact Mr. Mike Fischer, Admission Director. 808-885-7933. Fax: 808-885-6233. E-mail: mfischer@parkerschool.net. Web site: www.parkerschool.net/.

PARKLANE ACADEMY

1115 Parklane Road
McComb, Mississippi 39648
Head of School: Mr. Billy L. Swindle

General Information Coeducational day college-preparatory school. Grades PK–12. Founded: 1970. Setting: small town. Nearest major city is Jackson. 44-acre campus. 3 buildings on campus. Approved or accredited by Southern Association of Colleges and Schools and Mississippi Department of Education. Total enrollment: 843. Upper school average class size: 27. Upper school faculty-student ratio: 1:27.

Upper School Student Profile Grade 7: 58 students (40 boys, 18 girls); Grade 8: 92 students (43 boys, 49 girls); Grade 9: 58 students (38 boys, 20 girls); Grade 10: 67 students (31 boys, 36 girls); Grade 11: 40 students (19 boys, 21 girls); Grade 12: 63 students (31 boys, 32 girls).

Faculty School total: 48. In upper school: 9 men, 18 women; 7 have advanced degrees.

Subjects Offered 20th century world history, accounting, advanced chemistry, algebra, ancient world history, art, band, basic language skills, Bible, biology, bookkeeping, business mathematics, calculus, career/college preparation, choral music, choreography, civics, composition, computer applications, computer keyboarding, computer science, concert band, consumer economics, creative writing, driver education, economics, economics and history, English composition, English language-AP, English literature and composition-AP, English-AP, French, geography, government, government and politics-AP, government-AP, grammar, health, history-AP, honors geometry, honors U.S. history, human anatomy, lab science, library, literature, literature and composition-AP, literature-AP, media services, musical productions, physical science, physics, public speaking, reading, SAT/ACT preparation, science, Spanish, speech, state government, U.S. history, U.S. literature, world history, world literature.

Special Academic Programs Advanced Placement exam preparation in 4 subject areas; honors section; study at local college for college credit.

College Placement 60 students graduated in 2005; all went to college.

Student Life Upper grades have specified standards of dress, student council, honor system. Discipline rests primarily with faculty.

Summer Programs Remediation, computer instruction programs offered; session focuses on making up credits, keyboarding, and driver education; held on campus; accepts boys and girls; not open to students from other schools. 15 students usually enrolled. 2006 schedule: June 1 to July 30. Application deadline: May 10.

Tuition and Aid Day student tuition: $2700. Tuition installment plan (monthly payment plans). Tuition reduction for siblings available. In 2005–06, 1% of upper-school students received aid. Total amount of financial aid awarded in 2005–06: $2700.

Admissions Traditional secondary-level entrance grade is 10. Deadline for receipt of application materials: none. Application fee required: $150. On-campus interview required.

Athletics Interscholastic: baseball (boys), basketball (b,g), cheering (b,g), danceline (g), football (b), golf (b), soccer (b), softball (g), track and field (b,g), weight training (b,g). 1 PE instructor, 6 coaches.

Computers Computers are regularly used in yearbook classes. Computer resources include on-campus library services, CD-ROMs, Internet access.

Contact Mrs. Lisa Alexander, Registrar/Technology Coordinator. 601-684-8113 Ext. 223. Fax: 601-684-4166 Ext. 256. E-mail: parklane@cableone.net. Web site: www.parklaneacademy.com.

THE PARK SCHOOL

2425 Old Court Road
PO Box 8200
Brooklandville, Maryland 21022
Head of School: Dr. David E. Jackson

General Information Coeducational day college-preparatory school. Grades PK–12. Founded: 1912. Setting: suburban. Nearest major city is Baltimore. 100-acre campus. 4 buildings on campus. Approved or accredited by Association of Independent Maryland Schools and Maryland Department of Education. Member of National Association of Independent Schools. Endowment: $21.7 million. Total enrollment: 865. Upper school average class size: 15. Upper school faculty-student ratio: 1:8.

Upper School Student Profile Grade 9: 78 students (39 boys, 39 girls); Grade 10: 82 students (46 boys, 36 girls); Grade 11: 81 students (36 boys, 45 girls); Grade 12: 84 students (43 boys, 41 girls).

Faculty School total: 112. In upper school: 26 men, 19 women; 32 have advanced degrees.

Subjects Offered 3-dimensional art, 3-dimensional design, acting, advanced computer applications, advanced math, Advanced Placement courses, advanced studio art-AP, algebra, American history, American literature, animal behavior, art, art history, astronomy, biology, calculus, calculus-AP, ceramics, chemistry, choral music, chorus, computer graphics, computer math, computer science, creative writing, design, drama, earth science, ecology, economics, English, English literature, environmental science, European history, expository writing, fine arts, French, genetics, geometry, government/civics, health, history, history of science, marine biology, mathematics, mechanical drawing, music, philosophy, photography, physical education, physics, science, sculpture, social studies, Spanish, trigonometry, world history, world literature, writing.

Graduation Requirements Arts and fine arts (art, music, dance, drama), electives, English, foreign language, history, mathematics, physical education (includes health), science.

Special Academic Programs Advanced Placement exam preparation in 7 subject areas; independent study; term-away projects; academic accommodation for the gifted, the musically talented, and the artistically talented.

College Placement 75 students graduated in 2005; all went to college, including Columbia College; Oberlin College; The George Washington University; Washington University in St. Louis; Wesleyan University; Yale University. Mean SAT verbal: 660, mean SAT math: 640. 72% scored over 600 on SAT verbal, 65% scored over 600 on SAT math.

Student Life Upper grades have student council. Discipline rests equally with students and faculty.

Summer Programs Sports, art/fine arts, rigorous outdoor training programs offered; session focuses on arts, outdoors; held both on and off campus; held at Appalachian Trail and various wilderness areas on the East Coast; accepts boys and girls; open to students from other schools. 300 students usually enrolled. 2006 schedule: June 19 to August 11. Application deadline: May 15.

Tuition and Aid Day student tuition: $19,150. Tuition installment plan (monthly payment plans, 12-month interest free payment plan). Need-based scholarship grants available. In 2005–06, 15% of upper-school students received aid. Total amount of financial aid awarded in 2005–06: $596,615.

Admissions Traditional secondary-level entrance grade is 9. For fall 2005, 98 students applied for upper-level admission, 41 were accepted, 18 enrolled. ISEE required. Deadline for receipt of application materials: January 2. Application fee required: $50. On-campus interview required.

Athletics Interscholastic: baseball (boys), basketball (b,g), cross-country running (b,g), field hockey (g), indoor soccer (g), lacrosse (b,g), soccer (b,g), softball (g), tennis (b,g), winter soccer (g); intramural: ultimate Frisbee (b,g). 6 PE instructors, 16 coaches, 1 trainer.

Computers Computers are regularly used in art, creative writing, English, graphic design, mathematics, media production, music, programming, publications, science, theater arts, video film production, writing, yearbook classes. Computer network features include campus e-mail, on-campus library services, CD-ROMs, online commercial services, Internet access, DVD.

Contact Valerie Brice, Admission Administrative Assistant. 410-339-4130. Fax: 410-339-4127. E-mail: admission@parkschool.net. Web site: www.parkschool.net.

THE PARK SCHOOL OF BUFFALO

4625 Harlem Road
Snyder, New York 14226
Head of School: Donald H. Grace

General Information Coeducational day college-preparatory and arts school. Grades N–12. Founded: 1912. Setting: suburban. Nearest major city is Buffalo. 34-acre campus. 15 buildings on campus. Approved or accredited by New York State Association of Independent Schools and New York Department of Education. Member of National Association of Independent Schools. Endowment: $1.5 million. Total enrollment: 264. Upper school average class size: 15. Upper school faculty-student ratio: 1:9.

Upper School Student Profile Grade 9: 21 students (13 boys, 8 girls); Grade 10: 28 students (18 boys, 10 girls); Grade 11: 28 students (8 boys, 20 girls); Grade 12: 26 students (15 boys, 11 girls).

Faculty School total: 40. In upper school: 13 men, 27 women; 19 have advanced degrees.

Subjects Offered Algebra, American history, American literature, anthropology, archaeology, art, biology, calculus, ceramics, chemistry, community service, computer math, computer programming, computer science, creative writing, drama, economics, English, English literature, environmental science, ethics, European history, expository writing, fine arts, French, geography, geology, geometry, government/civics, grammar, history, mathematics, media production, microbiology, music, organic chemistry, philosophy, photography, physical education, physics, physiology, science, social science, social studies, Spanish, speech, statistics, theater, trigonometry, world history, world literature, writing.

Graduation Requirements Arts and fine arts (art, music, dance, drama), computer science, English, foreign language, mathematics, physical education (includes health), science, senior project, senior thesis, social science, social studies (includes history). Community service is required.

Special Academic Programs Advanced Placement exam preparation in 11 subject areas; honors section; accelerated programs; independent study; study at local college for college credit; academic accommodation for the gifted; ESL (8 students enrolled).

College Placement 32 students graduated in 2005; 31 went to college, including Berklee College of Music; Boston University; Howard University; Rochester Institute of Technology; State University of New York at Buffalo; University of Michigan. Other: 1 had other specific plans. Median SAT verbal: 610, median SAT math: 610. 50% scored over 600 on SAT verbal, 58% scored over 600 on SAT math.

Student Life Upper grades have specified standards of dress, student council. Discipline rests primarily with faculty.

Tuition and Aid Day student tuition: $14,000. Tuition installment plan (Insured Tuition Payment Plan, FACTS Tuition Payment Plan). Tuition reduction for siblings, merit scholarship grants, need-based scholarship grants available. In 2005–06, 60% of upper-school students received aid; total upper-school merit-scholarship money awarded: $10,500. Total amount of financial aid awarded in 2005–06: $525,000.

Admissions Traditional secondary-level entrance grade is 9. For fall 2005, 108 students applied for upper-level admission, 101 were accepted, 54 enrolled. ERB Reading and Math and Otis-Lennon School Ability Test required. Deadline for receipt of application materials: none. Application fee required: $25. On-campus interview required.

Athletics Interscholastic: baseball (boys), basketball (b,g), golf (b,g), lacrosse (b), soccer (b,g), softball (g), track and field (b,g); coed interscholastic: tennis. 2 PE instructors, 5 coaches.

Computers Computers are regularly used in creative writing, current events, data processing, English, graphic arts, independent study, mathematics, media, media services, newspaper, photography, science, word processing, yearbook classes. Computer network features include campus e-mail, on-campus library services, CD-ROMs, online commercial services, Internet access, office computer access, DVD, wireless campus network.

Contact Anthony Billoni, Director of Admissions. 716-839-1242 Ext. 107. Fax: 716-839-2014. E-mail: abilloni@theparkschool.org. Web site: www.theparkschool.org.

PARK TUDOR SCHOOL

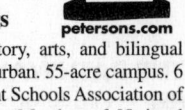

7200 North College Avenue
Indianapolis, Indiana 46240-3016
Head of School: Mr. Douglas S. Jennings

General Information Coeducational day college-preparatory, arts, and bilingual studies school. Grades PK–12. Founded: 1902. Setting: suburban. 55-acre campus. 6 buildings on campus. Approved or accredited by Independent Schools Association of the Central States and Indiana Department of Education. Member of National Association of Independent Schools and Secondary School Admission Test Board. Endowment: $89.6 million. Total enrollment: 984. Upper school average class size: 14. Upper school faculty-student ratio: 1:9.

Upper School Student Profile Grade 9: 109 students (60 boys, 49 girls); Grade 10: 105 students (58 boys, 47 girls); Grade 11: 95 students (50 boys, 45 girls); Grade 12: 107 students (52 boys, 55 girls).

Faculty School total: 152. In upper school: 23 men, 32 women; 40 have advanced degrees.

Subjects Offered 3-dimensional design, acting, advanced chemistry, advanced computer applications, advanced math, Advanced Placement courses, advanced studio art-AP, algebra, American history, American history-AP, American literature, American literature-AP, Ancient Greek, art, art history, art history-AP, athletics, ballet, biology, biology-AP, calculus, calculus-AP, Canadian history, ceramics, chemistry, chemistry-AP, choir, classics, computer math, computer programming-AP, computer science, computer science-AP, creative writing, critical studies in film, dance, drama, earth science, economics, economics-AP, electives, English, English language-AP, English literature, English literature-AP, English-AP, English/composition-AP, environmental science, environmental science-AP, ethics, etymology, European history, expository writing, film history, fine arts, French, French language-AP, French literature-AP, geography, geometry, German, government/civics, grammar, health,

history, history-AP, jazz band, jazz ensemble, journalism, Latin, Latin-AP, madrigals, mathematics, music, music history, music theory, music theory-AP, philosophy, photography, physical education, physics, physics-AP, physiology, printmaking, science, social science, social studies, sociology, Spanish, Spanish language-AP, speech, speech and debate, statistics, statistics-AP, studio art, studio art—AP, theater, theater design and production, theater history, trigonometry, U.S. government, U.S. history, U.S. history-AP, world history, world history-AP, world literature, world wide web design, writing.

Graduation Requirements Arts and fine arts (art, music, dance, drama), English, foreign language, mathematics, physical education (includes health), science, social science, social studies (includes history).

Special Academic Programs Advanced Placement exam preparation in 14 subject areas; honors section; accelerated programs; independent study; academic accommodation for the gifted, the musically talented, and the artistically talented.

College Placement 95 students graduated in 2005; all went to college, including Carleton College; DePauw University; Indiana University Bloomington; Purdue University; Washington University in St. Louis. Mean SAT verbal: 619, mean SAT math: 624, mean composite ACT: 28.

Student Life Upper grades have specified standards of dress, student council, honor system. Discipline rests equally with students and faculty.

Summer Programs Remediation, enrichment, advancement, sports, art/fine arts, rigorous outdoor training, computer instruction programs offered; session focuses on academics, fine arts, and athletics; held both on and off campus; held at Bradford Woods, Martinsville IN; accepts boys and girls; open to students from other schools. 275 students usually enrolled. 2006 schedule: June 5 to August 4. Application deadline: none.

Tuition and Aid Day student tuition: $14,805. Tuition installment plan (annual, biannual or quarterly payment plans). Merit scholarship grants, need-based scholarship grants available. In 2005–06, 25% of upper-school students received aid; total upper-school merit-scholarship money awarded: $524,257. Total amount of financial aid awarded in 2005–06: $1,028,521.

Admissions Traditional secondary-level entrance grade is 9. For fall 2005, 100 students applied for upper-level admission, 58 enrolled. ERB CTP IV required. Deadline for receipt of application materials: December 16. Application fee required: $50. On-campus interview required.

Athletics Interscholastic: baseball (boys), basketball (b,g), crew (b,g), cross-country running (b,g), football (b), golf (b,g), ice hockey (b), lacrosse (b,g), soccer (b,g), softball (g), swimming and diving (b,g), tennis (b,g), track and field (b,g), volleyball (g), wrestling (b); coed interscholastic: cheering; coed intramural: soccer. 3 PE instructors, 29 coaches, 1 trainer.

Computers Computers are regularly used in all classes. Computer network features include campus e-mail, on-campus library services, CD-ROMs, online commercial services, Internet access, file transfer, office computer access, DVD, wireless campus network.

Contact Mr. David Amstutz, Director of Admissions. 317-415-2777. Fax: 317-254-2714. E-mail: damstutz@parktudor.org. Web site: www.parktudor.org.

ANNOUNCEMENT FROM THE SCHOOL Park Tudor School helps average- to high-ability children (3K–12) of good character develop and achieve their potential, preparing them for an increasingly complex and diverse world. The comprehensive college-preparatory curriculum includes foreign language study, 21 Advanced Placement classes, complete arts and athletics offerings, and Extended Day and After School Programs.

See full description on page 968.

THE PATHWAY SCHOOL

Norristown, Pennsylvania
See Special Needs Schools section.

PEDDIE SCHOOL

South Main Street
Hightstown, New Jersey 08520
Head of School: John F. Green

petersons.com

General Information Coeducational boarding and day college-preparatory, arts, and technology school. Grades 9–PG. Founded: 1864. Setting: small town. Nearest major city is Princeton. Students are housed in single-sex dormitories. 230-acre campus. 53 buildings on campus. Approved or accredited by Middle States Association of Colleges and Schools, New Jersey Association of Independent Schools, The Association of Boarding Schools, and New Jersey Department of Education. Member of National Association of Independent Schools and Secondary School Admission Test Board. Endowment: $249 million. Total enrollment: 514. Upper school average class size: 12. Upper school faculty-student ratio: 1:6.

Upper School Student Profile Grade 9: 116 students (58 boys, 58 girls); Grade 10: 136 students (77 boys, 59 girls); Grade 11: 130 students (64 boys, 66 girls); Grade 12: 117 students (63 boys, 54 girls); Postgraduate: 15 students (13 boys, 2 girls). 63%

---

of students are boarding students. 20 states are represented in upper school student body. 11% are international students. International students from Canada, China, France, Hong Kong, Jamaica, and Republic of Korea; 22 other countries represented in student body.

Faculty School total: 94. In upper school: 50 men, 35 women; 64 have advanced degrees; 76 reside on campus.

Subjects Offered Acting, African studies, algebra, American history, American literature, American studies, anatomy, art, art history, astronomy, Bible studies, biology, calculus, chemistry, Chinese, comparative religion, computer programming, computer science, creative writing, debate, digital imaging, DNA, drama, earth science, ecology, economics, English, English literature, environmental science, European history, expository writing, film history, fine arts, French, geometry, government/civics, health, history, information technology, Latin, mathematics, music, philosophy, photography, physical education, physics, psychology, science, Shakespeare, social studies, Spanish, speech, statistics, theater, trigonometry, video film production, world history, world literature, writing.

Graduation Requirements Arts and fine arts (art, music, dance, drama), computer science, English, foreign language, history, mathematics, physical education (includes health), science. Community service is required.

Special Academic Programs Advanced Placement exam preparation in 10 subject areas; honors section; independent study; term-away projects; study abroad.

College Placement 135 students graduated in 2005; all went to college, including Boston College; Carnegie Mellon University; Columbia University; Cornell University; The George Washington University; University of Pennsylvania.

Student Life Upper grades have specified standards of dress, student council. Discipline rests primarily with faculty.

Summer Programs Enrichment, advancement programs offered; session focuses on enrichment; held on campus; accepts boys and girls; open to students from other schools. 175 students usually enrolled. 2006 schedule: June 26 to August 4. Application deadline: none.

Tuition and Aid Day student tuition: $25,250; 7-day tuition and room/board: $33,900. Tuition installment plan (Academic Management Services Plan, monthly payment plans, individually arranged payment plans). Merit scholarship grants, need-based scholarship grants, need-based loans available. In 2005–06, 42% of upper-school students received aid; total upper-school merit-scholarship money awarded: $86,350. Total amount of financial aid awarded in 2005–06: $4,500,000.

Admissions Traditional secondary-level entrance grade is 9. For fall 2005, 1,093 students applied for upper-level admission, 269 were accepted, 151 enrolled. ISEE or SSAT required. Deadline for receipt of application materials: January 17. Application fee required: $50. Interview required.

Athletics Interscholastic: baseball (boys), basketball (b,g), crew (b,g), cross-country running (b,g), diving (b,g), field hockey (g), fitness (b,g), football (b), golf (b,g), indoor track & field (b,g), lacrosse (b,g), soccer (b,g), softball (g), swimming and diving (b,g), tennis (b,g), track and field (b,g), volleyball (g), winter (indoor) track (b,g), wrestling (b); intramural: volleyball (b), weight lifting (b,g), weight training (b,g); coed intramural: bicycling, softball. 9 coaches, 3 trainers.

Computers Computers are regularly used in English, foreign language, history, mathematics, science classes. Computer network features include campus e-mail, on-campus library services, CD-ROMs, online commercial services, Internet access, file transfer, DVD, wireless campus network, NewsBank, Britannica, GaleNet, Electric Library.

Contact Edward A. deVillafranca, Dean of Admission and College Counseling. 609-490-7501. Fax: 609-944-7901. E-mail: edevilla@peddie.org. Web site: www.peddie.org.

ANNOUNCEMENT FROM THE SCHOOL Peddie School's extraordinary new Walter and Leonore Annenberg Science Center features state-of-the-art classrooms equipped with multimedia stations, DVD players, ceiling projectors, electronic whiteboards, special project rooms for long-term experimentation, a DNA laboratory, and a two-story greenhouse! All Peddie students receive laptop computers as part of tuition.

See full description on page 970.

THE PEMBROKE HILL SCHOOL

400 West 51st Street
Kansas City, Missouri 64112
Head of School: Dr. Richard Hibschman

petersons.com

General Information Coeducational day college-preparatory and arts school. Grades PS–12. Founded: 1910. Setting: urban. 36-acre campus. 8 buildings on campus. Approved or accredited by Independent Schools Association of the Central States, The College Board, and Missouri Department of Education. Member of National Association of Independent Schools. Endowment: $17 million. Total enrollment: 1,193. Upper school average class size: 14. Upper school faculty-student ratio: 1:11.

Upper School Student Profile Grade 9: 110 students (61 boys, 49 girls); Grade 10: 110 students (46 boys, 64 girls); Grade 11: 96 students (52 boys, 44 girls); Grade 12: 96 students (34 boys, 62 girls).

Faculty School total: 129. In upper school: 25 men, 37 women; 42 have advanced degrees.

Subjects Offered 20th century American writers, advanced studio art-AP, algebra, American history, American literature, art, art history, biology, calculus, ceramics, chemistry, choir, computer programming, computer science-AP, creative writing, debate, drama, driver education, economics, electronic imagery, English, English literature, European history, fine arts, French, geometry, government/civics, Holocaust, Holocaust studies, independent study, Irish literature, journalism, Latin, mathematics, metalworking, microbiology, music, photography, physical education, physics, physiology, poetry, programming, psychology, science, social studies, Spanish, speech, statistics, theater, Web site design, world history, world literature, writing, yearbook.

Graduation Requirements Arts and fine arts (art, music, dance, drama), English, foreign language, mathematics, physical education (includes health), science, social studies (includes history). Community service is required.

Special Academic Programs Advanced Placement exam preparation in 15 subject areas; honors section; independent study; term-away projects; study abroad; academic accommodation for the gifted and the artistically talented.

College Placement 93 students graduated in 2005; all went to college, including Harvard University; Southern Methodist University; University of Kansas; University of Missouri–Columbia; Vanderbilt University. Mean SAT verbal: 658, mean SAT math: 656, mean composite ACT: 28. 77% scored over 600 on SAT verbal, 70% scored over 600 on SAT math, 66% scored over 26 on composite ACT.

Student Life Upper grades have specified standards of dress, student council. Discipline rests primarily with faculty.

Summer Programs Enrichment, advancement, sports, art/fine arts, computer instruction programs offered; session focuses on enrichment; held on campus; accepts boys and girls; open to students from other schools. 764 students usually enrolled. 2006 schedule: June 13 to August 26. Application deadline: none.

Tuition and Aid Day student tuition: $14,105. Tuition installment plan (monthly payment plans, 2-payment plan, 1-payment plan). Merit scholarship grants, need-based scholarship grants, need-based loans available. In 2005–06, 15% of upper-school students received aid; total upper-school merit-scholarship money awarded: $23,500. Total amount of financial aid awarded in 2005–06: $466,410.

Admissions Traditional secondary-level entrance grade is 9. For fall 2005, 67 students applied for upper-level admission, 44 were accepted, 29 enrolled. ITBS achievement test and Otis-Lennon School Ability Test required. Deadline for receipt of application materials: January 12. Application fee required: $40. Interview required.

Athletics Interscholastic: baseball (boys), basketball (b,g), cheering (g), cross-country running (b,g), dance (g), dance team (g), diving (b,g), field hockey (g), football (b), golf (b,g), independent competitive sports (b,g), indoor track & field (b,g), soccer (b,g), swimming and diving (b,g), tennis (b,g), track and field (b,g), volleyball (g), wrestling (b); coed interscholastic: cheering. 4 PE instructors, 20 coaches, 1 trainer.

Computers Computers are regularly used in all academic classes. Computer network features include on-campus library services, CD-ROMs, online commercial services, Internet access, file transfer, DVD.

Contact Carolyn Sullivan, Assistant Head of School-Admissions and Financial Aid. 816-936-1230. Fax: 816-936-1238. E-mail: csullivan@pembrokehill.org. Web site: www.pembrokehill.org.

ANNOUNCEMENT FROM THE SCHOOL The Pembroke Hill School enrolls 599 boys and 594 girls in early years through grade 12. The facilities accommodate a broad academic program plus extended-day. The curriculum is enriched by Advanced Placement courses, the arts, publications, community service, and sports. Summer offerings include enrichment courses.

THE PENNINGTON SCHOOL

112 West Delaware Avenue
Pennington, New Jersey 08534-1601
Head of School: Mr. Lyle D. Rigg

General Information Coeducational boarding and day college-preparatory school, affiliated with Methodist Church. Boarding grades 7–12, day grades 6–12. Founded: 1838. Setting: small town. Nearest major city is Philadelphia, PA. Students are housed in single-sex by floor dormitories and single-sex dormitories. 54-acre campus. 17 buildings on campus. Approved or accredited by Middle States Association of Colleges and Schools, National Independent Private Schools Association, New Jersey Association of Independent Schools, The Association of Boarding Schools, The College Board, University Senate of United Methodist Church, and New Jersey Department of Education. Member of National Association of Independent Schools and Secondary School Admission Test Board. Endowment: $20 million. Total enrollment: 451. Upper school average class size: 13. Upper school faculty-student ratio: 1:8.

Upper School Student Profile Grade 9: 86 students (50 boys, 36 girls); Grade 10: 94 students (53 boys, 41 girls); Grade 11: 101 students (45 boys, 56 girls); Grade 12: 77 students (39 boys, 38 girls). 27% of students are boarding students. 68% are state residents. 12 states are represented in upper school student body. 12% are international

students. International students from Japan, Nigeria, Republic of Korea, Russian Federation, Taiwan, and Thailand; 8 other countries represented in student body. 5% of students are Methodist.

Faculty School total: 79. In upper school: 29 men, 35 women; 38 have advanced degrees; 49 reside on campus.

Subjects Offered African-American history, algebra, American history, American literature, anatomy and physiology, art, biology, British literature-AP, calculus, chemistry, chemistry-AP, computer applications, computer skills, creative writing, drama, driver education, economics, English, English literature, English literature-AP, English-AP, environmental science, ESL, fine arts, French, French language-AP, geometry, German, government and politics-AP, Greek, Greek culture, health, history-AP, honors algebra, honors English, honors geometry, honors U.S. history, jazz ensemble, Latin, macroeconomics-AP, marine biology, music, music history, music theory, photography, physics, physics-AP, pottery, pre-calculus, public speaking, religion, robotics, senior internship, Spanish, Spanish literature, Spanish-AP, stagecraft, U.S. government and politics-AP, world history, world history-AP, world literature.

Graduation Requirements Algebra, American history, arts and fine arts (art, music, dance, drama), athletics, chemistry, computer education, English, foreign language, geometry, health education, religion (includes Bible studies and theology), world history.

Special Academic Programs Advanced Placement exam preparation in 14 subject areas; honors section; independent study; study at local college for college credit; academic accommodation for the gifted; programs in English for dyslexic students; ESL (42 students enrolled).

College Placement 93 students graduated in 2005; all went to college, including Carnegie Mellon University. Mean SAT verbal: 541, mean SAT math: 570.

Student Life Upper grades have specified standards of dress, student council. Discipline rests equally with students and faculty. Attendance at religious services is required.

Tuition and Aid Day student tuition: $22,900; 7-day tuition and room/board: $34,100. Tuition installment plan (Key Tuition Payment Plan). Merit scholarship grants, need-based scholarship grants available. In 2005–06, 22% of upper-school students received aid; total upper-school merit-scholarship money awarded: $160,300. Total amount of financial aid awarded in 2005–06: $1,100,000.

Admissions Traditional secondary-level entrance grade is 9. For fall 2005, 499 students applied for upper-level admission, 224 were accepted, 117 enrolled. Secondary Level English Proficiency or SSAT required. Deadline for receipt of application materials: February 10. Application fee required: $50. On-campus interview required.

Athletics Interscholastic: baseball (boys), basketball (b,g), field hockey (g), football (b), ice hockey (b), lacrosse (b,g), soccer (b,g), softball (g), tennis (b,g); intramural: aerobics (g); coed interscholastic: cheering, cross-country running, golf, indoor track, swimming and diving, track and field, winter (indoor) track; coed intramural: fitness, strength & conditioning, weight training. 1 coach, 1 trainer.

Computers Computers are regularly used in college planning, creative writing, desktop publishing, literary magazine, mathematics, music, newspaper, science, yearbook classes. Computer network features include campus e-mail, on-campus library services, CD-ROMs, online commercial services, Internet access, office computer access, wireless campus network, The Homework Site.

Contact Ms. Diane P. Monteleone, Director of Admission. 609-737-6128. Fax: 609-730-1405. E-mail: admiss@pennington.org. Web site: www.pennington.org.

See full description on page 972.

PERKIOMEN SCHOOL

200 Seminary Street
Pennsburg, Pennsylvania 18073
Head of School: Mr. George K. Allison

General Information Coeducational boarding and day college-preparatory school, affiliated with Schwenkfelder Church. Boarding grades 7–PG, day grades 5–PG. Founded: 1875. Setting: small town. Nearest major city is Philadelphia. Students are housed in single-sex dormitories. 165-acre campus. 22 buildings on campus. Approved or accredited by Middle States Association of Colleges and Schools, Pennsylvania Association of Private Academic Schools, The Association of Boarding Schools, The College Board, and Pennsylvania Department of Education. Member of National Association of Independent Schools and Secondary School Admission Test Board. Endowment: $4 million. Total enrollment: 249. Upper school average class size: 12. Upper school faculty-student ratio: 1:7.

Upper School Student Profile Grade 9: 34 students (28 boys, 6 girls); Grade 10: 43 students (28 boys, 15 girls); Grade 11: 59 students (34 boys, 25 girls); Grade 12: 58 students (30 boys, 28 girls); Postgraduate: 4 students (4 boys). 60% of students are boarding students. 65% are state residents. 15 states are represented in upper school student body. 18% are international students. International students from Bahamas, China, Japan, Republic of Korea, Spain, and Taiwan; 10 other countries represented in student body.

Faculty School total: 49. In upper school: 26 men, 23 women; 31 have advanced degrees; 36 reside on campus.

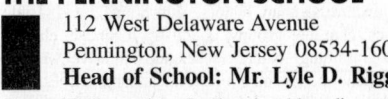

Subjects Offered African history, algebra, American history, American literature, art, art history, astronomy, Bible studies, biology, calculus, ceramics, chemistry, computer graphics, computer programming, computer science, creative writing, current events, dance, developmental language skills, drama, driver education, earth science, economics, English, English literature, environmental science, ESL, ethics, European history, fine arts, French, gender issues, geography, geology, geometry, government/civics, grammar, health, history, humanities, journalism, Latin, library studies, mathematics, music, painting, philosophy, photography, physical education, physics, physics-AP, psychology, religion, science, social studies, sociology, Spanish, speech, statistics, textiles, theater, trigonometry, world history, world literature.

Graduation Requirements Arts and fine arts (art, music, dance, drama), computer studies, English, foreign language, mathematics, physical education (includes health), religion (includes Bible studies and theology), science, social studies (includes history). Community service is required.

Special Academic Programs Advanced Placement exam preparation in 12 subject areas; honors section; independent study; academic accommodation for the gifted, the musically talented, and the artistically talented; programs in English, general development for dyslexic students; ESL (36 students enrolled).

College Placement 72 students graduated in 2005; all went to college, including Bryn Mawr College; Emory University; Haverford College; Lehigh University; Northwestern University; University of Chicago.

Student Life Upper grades have specified standards of dress, student council. Discipline rests primarily with faculty. Attendance at religious services is required.

Tuition and Aid Day student tuition: $19,100; 7-day tuition and room/board: $32,800. Tuition installment plan (monthly payment plans). Need-based scholarship grants available. In 2005–06, 32% of upper-school students received aid. Total amount of financial aid awarded in 2005–06: $1,200,000.

Admissions Traditional secondary-level entrance grade is 10. For fall 2005, 227 students applied for upper-level admission, 188 were accepted, 67 enrolled. SLEP or SSAT required. Deadline for receipt of application materials: none. Application fee required: $45. Interview required.

Athletics Interscholastic: baseball (boys), basketball (b,g), field hockey (g), football (b), golf (b), lacrosse (b,g), power lifting (b), soccer (b), softball (g), tennis (b,g), weight lifting (b), wrestling (b); coed interscholastic: cheering, cross-country running, dance, martial arts, swimming and diving; coed intramural: dance, skateboarding. 1 PE instructor, 7 coaches, 1 trainer.

Computers Computers are regularly used in all academic classes. Computer network features include campus e-mail, on-campus library services, CD-ROMs, online commercial services, Internet access, file transfer, DVD.

Contact Carol Dougherty, Assistant Head of School. 215-679-9511. Fax: 215-679-1146. E-mail: cdougherty@perkiomen.org. Web site: www.perkiomen.org.

See full description on page 974.

THE PHELPS SCHOOL

583 Sugartown Road
Malvern, Pennsylvania 19355
Head of School: Mr. Norman T. Phelps Jr.

petersons.com

General Information Boys' boarding and day college-preparatory and general academic school; primarily serves underachievers. Grades 7–PG. Founded: 1946. Setting: suburban. Nearest major city is Philadelphia. Students are housed in single-sex dormitories. 70-acre campus. 18 buildings on campus. Approved or accredited by Middle States Association of Colleges and Schools, Pennsylvania Association of Private Academic Schools, The Association of Boarding Schools, and Pennsylvania Department of Education. Endowment: $643,000. Total enrollment: 138. Upper school average class size: 7. Upper school faculty-student ratio: 1:5.

Upper School Student Profile Grade 9: 17 students (17 boys); Grade 10: 31 students (31 boys); Grade 11: 39 students (39 boys); Grade 12: 35 students (35 boys); Postgraduate: 5 students (5 boys). 81% of students are boarding students. 33% are state residents. 21 states are represented in upper school student body. 16% are international students. International students from China, Puerto Rico, Republic of Korea, Saudi Arabia, Spain, and Switzerland; 4 other countries represented in student body.

Faculty School total: 26. In upper school: 18 men, 8 women; 13 have advanced degrees; 20 reside on campus.

Subjects Offered Algebra, American history, American literature, art, biology, calculus, chemistry, earth science, English, English literature, environmental science, ESL, European history, geography, geometry, government/civics, health, mathematics, physical education, physics, psychology, reading, Spanish, study skills, trigonometry, world history.

Graduation Requirements English, mathematics, physical education (includes health), science, social studies (includes history).

Special Academic Programs Remedial reading and/or remedial writing; remedial math; programs in English, mathematics, general development for dyslexic students; special instructional classes for learning disabled students, students with Attention Deficit Disorder and dyslexia; ESL (5 students enrolled).

College Placement 49 students graduated in 2005; 47 went to college, including Curry College; Drexel University; Lynn University; Northern Arizona University; The Pennsylvania State University University Park Campus; Villanova University. Other: 1 entered military service, 1 entered a postgraduate year.

Student Life Upper grades have specified standards of dress, student council. Discipline rests primarily with faculty.

Summer Programs Remediation, enrichment, ESL, art/fine arts, computer instruction programs offered; session focuses on remediation; held on campus; accepts boys; open to students from other schools. 40 students usually enrolled. 2006 schedule: June 29 to August 1. Application deadline: none.

Tuition and Aid Day student tuition: $17,000; 7-day tuition and room/board: $27,500. Tuition installment plan (monthly payment plans, individually arranged payment plans). Tuition reduction for siblings, need-based scholarship grants, Key Education Resources Achiever Loan Plan available. In 2005–06, 16% of upper-school students received aid. Total amount of financial aid awarded in 2005–06: $201,500.

Admissions Traditional secondary-level entrance grade is 10. Deadline for receipt of application materials: none. Application fee required: $50. Interview required.

Athletics Interscholastic: baseball, basketball, cross-country running, golf, lacrosse, soccer, tennis; intramural: aerobics, aerobics/nautilus, basketball, bowling, equestrian sports, fitness, golf, lacrosse, martial arts, nautilus, physical fitness, physical training, rock climbing, softball, strength & conditioning, table tennis, ultimate Frisbee, volleyball, weight lifting, weight training. 2 PE instructors, 15 coaches.

Computers Computers are regularly used in college planning, English, ESL, remedial study skills, research skills, yearbook classes. Computer resources include on-campus library services, CD-ROMs, online commercial services, Internet access, online bibliographic services.

Contact Mr. F. Christopher Chirieleison, Assistant Headmaster for Enrollment. 610-644-1754. Fax: 610-644-6679. E-mail: admis@thephelpsschool.org. Web site: www.thephelpsschool.org.

ANNOUNCEMENT FROM THE SCHOOL The Phelps School is now in its 60th year of providing a caring, structured environment for boys. Emphasis is placed on helping boys achieve more of their academic potential via small classes, nurturing support, and daily tutorial sessions. "Access, Accommodation, and Accountability" are the hallmarks of a Phelps School education. In addition to the basic program, a 5-week summer program is also available.

See full description on page 976.

PHILLIPS ACADEMY (ANDOVER)

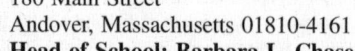

180 Main Street
Andover, Massachusetts 01810-4161
Head of School: Barbara L. Chase

petersons.com

General Information Coeducational boarding and day college-preparatory school. Grades 9–PG. Founded: 1778. Setting: suburban. Nearest major city is Boston. Students are housed in single-sex dormitories and with 9th graders housed separately from others. 500-acre campus. 160 buildings on campus. Approved or accredited by New England Association of Schools and Colleges and The Association of Boarding Schools. Member of National Association of Independent Schools and Secondary School Admission Test Board. Endowment: $622.8 million. Total enrollment: 1,083. Upper school average class size: 13. Upper school faculty-student ratio: 1:5.

Upper School Student Profile Grade 9: 196 students (93 boys, 103 girls); Grade 10: 287 students (142 boys, 145 girls); Grade 11: 285 students (144 boys, 141 girls); Grade 12: 288 students (140 boys, 148 girls); Postgraduate: 27 students (16 boys, 11 girls). 72% of students are boarding students. 42% are state residents. 47 states are represented in upper school student body. 9% are international students. International students from Canada, China, Hong Kong, Japan, Republic of Korea, and Saudi Arabia; 20 other countries represented in student body.

Faculty School total: 219. In upper school: 114 men, 105 women; 159 have advanced degrees; 196 reside on campus.

Subjects Offered Algebra, American history, American literature, ancient history, animal behavior, animation, architecture, art, art history, astronomy, band, Bible studies, biology, calculus, ceramics, chamber groups, chemistry, Chinese, chorus, computer graphics, computer programming, computer science, creative writing, dance, drama, drawing, driver education, ecology, economics, English, English literature, environmental science, ethics, European history, expository writing, film, fine arts, French, geology, geometry, German, government/civics, grammar, Greek, health, history, international relations, Japanese, jazz, Latin, Latin American studies, life issues, literature, mathematics, Middle Eastern history, music, mythology, oceanography, painting, philosophy, photography, physical education, physics, physiology, printmaking, psychology, religion, Russian, Russian studies, science, sculpture, social science, social studies, sociology, Spanish, speech, swimming, theater, trigonometry, video, world history, writing.

Graduation Requirements Arts and fine arts (art, music, dance, drama), English, foreign language, history, life issues, mathematics, philosophy, physical education (includes health), religion (includes Bible studies and theology), science, social science, swimming test.

Special Academic Programs Advanced Placement exam preparation in 14 subject areas; honors section; independent study; term-away projects; study abroad.

College Placement 308 students graduated in 2005; 297 went to college, including Columbia College; Cornell University; Georgetown University; Harvard University;

University of Pennsylvania; Vanderbilt University. Other: 9 had other specific plans. Mean SAT verbal: 697, mean SAT math: 691. 85% scored over 600 on SAT verbal, 89% scored over 600 on SAT math.

Student Life Upper grades have student council, honor system. Discipline rests primarily with faculty.

Summer Programs Enrichment, advancement, ESL, art/fine arts, computer instruction programs offered; session focuses on academics; held on campus; accepts boys and girls; open to students from other schools. 550 students usually enrolled. 2006 schedule: June 27 to August 2. Application deadline: none.

Tuition and Aid Day student tuition: $25,700; 7-day tuition and room/board: $33,000. Tuition installment plan (The Andover Plan). Need-based scholarship grants, need-based loans, middle-income loans available. In 2005–06, 40% of upper-school students received aid. Total amount of financial aid awarded in 2005–06: $11,321,000.

Admissions For fall 2005, 2,229 students applied for upper-level admission, 469 were accepted, 347 enrolled. Iowa Test of Educational Development, ISEE, PSAT, SAT, SSAT or TOEFL required. Deadline for receipt of application materials: February 1. Application fee required: $40. Interview required.

Athletics Interscholastic: baseball (boys), basketball (b,g), bicycling (b,g), crew (b,g), cross-country running (b,g), diving (b,g), field hockey (g), football (b), golf (b,g), ice hockey (b,g), indoor track & field (b,g), lacrosse (b,g), nordic skiing (b,g), skiing (cross-country) (b,g), soccer (b,g), softball (g), squash (b,g), swimming and diving (b,g), tennis (b,g), track and field (b,g), volleyball (b,g), water polo (b,g), wrestling (b); intramural: aerobics/dance (b,g), back packing (b,g), basketball (b,g), crew (b,g), martial arts (b,g), physical fitness (b,g), physical training (b,g); coed interscholastic: bicycling, Frisbee, golf, wrestling; coed intramural: ballet, canoeing/kayaking, cheering, cross-country running, dance, fencing, fitness, fitness walking, hiking/backpacking, martial arts, modern dance, outdoor adventure, outdoor education, physical fitness, physical training, rappelling, rock climbing, ropes courses, soccer, softball, strength & conditioning, tennis. 7 PE instructors, 25 coaches, 3 trainers.

Computers Computers are regularly used in animation, architecture, art, classics, computer applications, digital applications, English, foreign language, history, mathematics, music, photography; psychology, religious studies, science, theater, video film production classes. Computer network features include campus e-mail, on-campus library services, CD-ROMs, Internet access.

Contact Jane F. Fried, Dean of Admission. 978-749-4050. Fax: 978-749-4068. E-mail: admissions@andover.edu. Web site: www.andover.edu.

See full description on page 978.

PHILLIPS EXETER ACADEMY

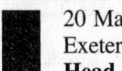

20 Main Street
Exeter, New Hampshire 03833-2460
Head of School: Mr. Tyler C. Tingley

petersons.com

General Information Coeducational boarding and day college-preparatory school. Grades 9–PG. Founded: 1781. Setting: small town. Nearest major city is Boston, MA. Students are housed in single-sex dormitories. 471-acre campus. 126 buildings on campus. Approved or accredited by Association of Independent Schools in New England, New England Association of Schools and Colleges, and The Association of Boarding Schools. Member of National Association of Independent Schools and Secondary School Admission Test Board. Endowment: $706 million. Total enrollment: 1,050. Upper school average class size: 12. Upper school faculty-student ratio: 1:5.

Upper School Student Profile Grade 9: 190 students (97 boys, 93 girls); Grade 10: 246 students (118 boys, 128 girls); Grade 11: 294 students (158 boys, 136 girls); Grade 12: 292 students (142 boys, 150 girls); Postgraduate: 28 students (23 boys, 5 girls). 80% of students are boarding students. 23% are state residents. 46 states are represented in upper school student body. 9% are international students. International students from Canada, China, Philippines, Republic of Korea, Singapore, and United Kingdom; 23 other countries represented in student body.

Faculty School total: 194. In upper school: 105 men, 89 women; 157 have advanced degrees; 103 reside on campus.

Subjects Offered Algebra, American history, American literature, anatomy, anthropology, Arabic, archaeology, architecture, art, art history, astronomy, biology, botany, calculus, ceramics, chemistry, Chinese, classics, computer programming, computer science, creative writing, dance, discrete math, drama, driver education, ecology, economics, electronics, English, English literature, environmental science, ethics, European history, evolution, existentialism, expository writing, film, fine arts, French, genetics, geology, geometry, German, Greek, health, history, Italian, Japanese, Latin, linear algebra, logic, marine biology, mathematics, music, music composition, ornithology, philosophy, photography, physical education, physics, physiology, psychology, religion, Russian, science, sculpture, Spanish, statistics, theater, trigonometry, world literature, writing, Zen Buddhism.

Graduation Requirements American history, art, biology, computer science, English, foreign language, mathematics, physical education (includes health), physical science, religion (includes Bible studies and theology), science.

Special Academic Programs Advanced Placement exam preparation in 19 subject areas; honors section; independent study; term-away projects; study abroad; academic accommodation for the gifted, the musically talented, and the artistically talented.

College Placement 306 students graduated in 2005; all went to college, including Harvard University; New York University; Stanford University; The George Washington University; The Johns Hopkins University; University of Pennsylvania. Mean SAT verbal: 693, mean SAT math: 698.

Student Life Upper grades have specified standards of dress, student council, honor system. Discipline rests primarily with faculty.

Summer Programs Remediation, enrichment, advancement, ESL, sports, art/fine arts, computer instruction programs offered; session focuses on academic and social enrichment; held on campus; accepts boys and girls; open to students from other schools. 650 students usually enrolled. 2006 schedule: July 2 to August 5. Application deadline: none.

Tuition and Aid Day student tuition: $25,500; 7-day tuition and room/board: $33,000. Tuition installment plan (Academic Management Services Plan, Tuition Management Systems Plan). Need-based scholarship grants, need-based loans available. In 2005–06, 33% of upper-school students received aid. Total amount of financial aid awarded in 2005–06: $8,200,000.

Admissions Traditional secondary-level entrance grade is 9. For fall 2005, 2,142 students applied for upper-level admission, 518 were accepted, 328 enrolled. PSAT or SAT, SSAT or TOEFL required. Deadline for receipt of application materials: January 16. Application fee required: $50. Interview required.

Athletics Interscholastic: baseball (boys), basketball (b,g), crew (b,g), cross-country running (b,g), diving (b,g), field hockey (g), football (b), ice hockey (b,g), indoor track & field (b,g), lacrosse (b,g), soccer (b,g), softball (g), squash (b,g), swimming and diving (b,g), tennis (b,g), track and field (b,g), volleyball (g), water polo (b,g), winter (indoor) track (b,g), wrestling (b); intramural: crew (b,g), ice hockey (b,g), rugby (b,g); coed interscholastic: bicycling, golf; coed intramural: aerobics/dance, ballet, basketball, bicycling, dance, fencing, fitness, golf, lacrosse, life saving, martial arts, modern dance, outdoor activities, outdoor recreation, physical fitness, physical training, skiing (cross-country), skiing (downhill), soccer, softball, squash, strength & conditioning, tennis, ultimate Frisbee, volleyball, weight lifting, weight training, yoga. 12 PE instructors, 12 coaches, 3 trainers.

Computers Computers are regularly used in computer applications, foreign language, mathematics, science classes. Computer network features include campus e-mail, on-campus library services, CD-ROMs, Internet access, file transfer.

Contact Mr. Michael Gary, Director of Admissions. 603-777-3437. Fax: 603-777-4399. E-mail: admit@exeter.edu. Web site: www.exeter.edu.

See full description on page 980.

PHOENIX CHRISTIAN UNIFIED SCHOOLS

1751 West Indian School Road
Phoenix, Arizona 85015
Head of School: Mr. Robert L. Byrd

General Information Coeducational day college-preparatory, general academic, and religious studies school, affiliated with Christian faith. Grades 7–12. Founded: 1949. Setting: urban. 12-acre campus. 10 buildings on campus. Approved or accredited by Association of Christian Schools International, North Central Association of Colleges and Schools, and Arizona Department of Education. Total enrollment: 717. Upper school average class size: 20. Upper school faculty-student ratio: 1:20.

Upper School Student Profile Grade 9: 97 students (49 boys, 48 girls); Grade 10: 74 students (41 boys, 33 girls); Grade 11: 93 students (45 boys, 48 girls); Grade 12: 109 students (59 boys, 50 girls).

Faculty School total: 52. In upper school: 16 men, 13 women; 14 have advanced degrees.

Subjects Offered Advanced computer applications, algebra, American literature, American literature-AP, anatomy, art, band, Bible, biology, calculus, career and personal planning, chemistry, choir, choral music, computer applications, computers, drama, drama performance, drawing, earth science, economics, English, English literature, English literature-AP, English-AP, fine arts, French, geometry, government, instrumental music, integrated science, intro to computers, library, literature, literature-AP, marching band, physical education, physics, pre-algebra, pre-calculus, psychology, social studies, Spanish, Spanish language-AP, speech, student government, study skills, U.S. government, U.S. history, U.S. history-AP, Web site design, world history, yearbook.

Graduation Requirements Advanced math, algebra, arts and fine arts (art, music, dance, drama), biology, chemistry, computer education, earth and space science, economics, English, English composition, English literature, foreign language, geography, geometry, government, pre-calculus, religious studies, speech, U.S. history, world history, world literature, one year of Bible for each year of attendance.

Special Academic Programs Advanced Placement exam preparation in 5 subject areas; honors section; study at local college for college credit; ESL (12 students enrolled).

College Placement 104 students graduated in 2005; 101 went to college, including Arizona State University; Glendale Community College; Northern Arizona University; Paradise Valley Community College; The University of Arizona. Other: 1 went to work, 2 entered a postgraduate year. Median SAT verbal: 546, median SAT math: 533.

Student Life Upper grades have uniform requirement, student council. Discipline rests primarily with faculty. Attendance at religious services is required.

Summer Programs Remediation, enrichment programs offered; session focuses on academics; held on campus; accepts boys and girls; open to students from other schools. 18 students usually enrolled. 2006 schedule: May 31 to July 12. Application deadline: May 17.

Tuition and Aid Day student tuition: $5975. Tuition installment plan (monthly payment plans). Tuition reduction for siblings, need-based scholarship grants available. In 2005–06, 9% of upper-school students received aid. Total amount of financial aid awarded in 2005–06: $73,000.

Admissions Traditional secondary-level entrance grade is 9. For fall 2005, 132 students applied for upper-level admission, 126 were accepted, 126 enrolled. Achievement tests or any standardized test required. Deadline for receipt of application materials: none. Application fee required: $150. On-campus interview required.

Athletics Interscholastic: baseball (boys), basketball (b,g), cheering (g), drill team (g), football (b), softball (g), volleyball (g), wrestling (b); coed interscholastic: cross-country running, golf, soccer, swimming and diving, tennis, track and field, weight lifting, weight training. 1 PE instructor, 30 coaches, 1 trainer.

Computers Computers are regularly used in newspaper, Web site design, yearbook classes. Computer resources include on-campus library services, CD-ROMs, Internet access, file transfer, office computer access.

Contact Mr. Robert L. Byrd, Superintendent. 602-265-4707. Fax: 602-277-7170. E-mail: bbyrd@phoenixchristian.org.

PHOENIX COUNTRY DAY SCHOOL

3901 East Stanford Drive
Paradise Valley, Arizona 85253
Head of School: Geoff Campbell

petersons.com

General Information Coeducational day college-preparatory, arts, and music school. Grades PK–12. Founded: 1961. Setting: suburban. Nearest major city is Phoenix. 40-acre campus. 8 buildings on campus. Approved or accredited by Independent Schools Association of the Southwest and North Central Association of Colleges and Schools. Member of National Association of Independent Schools. Endowment: $15 million. Total enrollment: 738. Upper school average class size: 16. Upper school faculty-student ratio: 1:9.

Upper School Student Profile Grade 9: 61 students (36 boys, 25 girls); Grade 10: 67 students (30 boys, 37 girls); Grade 11: 60 students (29 boys, 31 girls); Grade 12: 67 students (33 boys, 34 girls).

Faculty School total: 90. In upper school: 18 men, 12 women; 25 have advanced degrees.

Subjects Offered Algebra, American history, American literature, anatomy, anthropology, art, art history, biology, calculus, ceramics, chemistry, computer programming, computer science, creative writing, ecology, economics, English, English literature, environmental science, ethics, European history, fine arts, French, geography, geology, geometry, government/civics, history, journalism, Latin, marine biology, mathematics, music, oceanography, philosophy, photography, physical education, physics, physiology, psychology, science, social science, social studies, Spanish, speech, statistics, theater, trigonometry, world history.

Graduation Requirements American history, American literature, ancient world history, arts and fine arts (art, music, dance, drama), biology, English, foreign language, mathematics, physical education (includes health), science.

Special Academic Programs Advanced Placement exam preparation in 15 subject areas; honors section; independent study.

College Placement 60 students graduated in 2005; 57 went to college, including Arizona State University; Stanford University; The George Washington University; The University of Arizona; University of Pennsylvania; University of Southern California. Other: 2 went to work, 1 had other specific plans. Median SAT verbal: 690, median SAT math: 690.

Student Life Upper grades have specified standards of dress, student council, honor system. Discipline rests primarily with faculty.

Summer Programs Enrichment, advancement, sports, art/fine arts, computer instruction programs offered; session focuses on academics/sports camp/arts program; held on campus; accepts boys and girls; open to students from other schools. 450 students usually enrolled. 2006 schedule: June 12 to July 21. Application deadline: none.

Tuition and Aid Day student tuition: $18,700. Tuition installment plan (monthly payment plans, individually arranged payment plans, quarterly, semi-annual, and yearly payment plans). Need-based scholarship grants available. In 2005–06, 20% of upper-school students received aid. Total amount of financial aid awarded in 2005–06: $1,272,000.

Admissions Traditional secondary-level entrance grade is 9. For fall 2005, 76 students applied for upper-level admission, 37 were accepted, 27 enrolled. Achievement/Aptitude/Writing, ERB CTP IV and Otis-Lennon IQ required. Deadline for receipt of application materials: March 1. Application fee required: $100. On-campus interview required.

Athletics Interscholastic: baseball (boys), basketball (b,g), cross-country running (b,g), diving (b,g), golf (b,g), lacrosse (b,g), soccer (b,g), softball (g), swimming and diving (b,g), tennis (b,g), volleyball (g); intramural: badminton (b,g), field hockey (b,g). 5 PE instructors, 50 coaches.

Computers Computers are regularly used in art, college planning, creative writing, data processing, desktop publishing, economics, engineering, English, foreign language, French, history, humanities, independent study, information technology, keyboarding, library, library skills, literary magazine, mathematics, news writing, newspaper, photography, programming, publications, research skills, science, social sciences, social studies, Spanish, stock market, typing, Web site design, word processing, writing, yearbook classes. Computer resources include campus e-mail, on-campus library services, CD-ROMs, online commercial services, Internet access, DVD, wireless campus network, Intranet.

Contact Michelle Parciak, Admissions. 602-955-8200 Ext. 2255. Fax: 602-381-4554. E-mail: michelle.parciak@pcds.org.

ANNOUNCEMENT FROM THE SCHOOL Founded in 1961 on the principles of traditional independent education, Phoenix Country Day School, PK–12, emphasizes the development of the whole student and the acquisition of thinking skills and cooperative behaviors within the framework of an exceptional college-preparatory program. The School seeks students with talent and good character and prepares them to be responsible leaders who use their educational advantage for the greater good.

PICKENS ACADEMY

225 Ray Bass Road
Carrollton, Alabama 35447
Head of School: Mr. Louis McBride

General Information Coeducational day college-preparatory and general academic school. Grades K4–12. Founded: 1970. Setting: rural. Nearest major city is Tuscaloosa. 2 buildings on campus. Approved or accredited by Southern Association of Colleges and Schools and Alabama Department of Education. Total enrollment: 386. Upper school average class size: 25. Upper school faculty-student ratio: 1:20.

Upper School Student Profile Grade 7: 24 students (14 boys, 10 girls); Grade 8: 31 students (14 boys, 17 girls); Grade 9: 33 students (12 boys, 21 girls); Grade 10: 26 students (17 boys, 9 girls); Grade 11: 26 students (15 boys, 11 girls); Grade 12: 27 students (15 boys, 12 girls).

Faculty School total: 20. In upper school: 4 men, 16 women; 8 have advanced degrees.

Special Academic Programs Honors section; study at local college for college credit.

College Placement 25 students graduated in 2005; 24 went to college, including The University of Alabama. Other: 1 went to work.

Student Life Upper grades have specified standards of dress, student council. Discipline rests primarily with faculty.

Summer Programs Remediation programs offered; session focuses on remediation; held on campus; accepts boys and girls; not open to students from other schools. 5 students usually enrolled. 2006 schedule: May 1 to July 30. Application deadline: May 15.

Tuition and Aid Day student tuition: $2800. Guaranteed tuition plan. Tuition installment plan (Insured Tuition Payment Plan, monthly payment plans).

Admissions Traditional secondary-level entrance grade is 9. Deadline for receipt of application materials: none. Application fee required: $100. On-campus interview required.

Athletics Interscholastic: baseball (boys), basketball (b,g), cheering (g), danceline (g), football (b), golf (b,g), softball (g), volleyball (g); coed interscholastic: tennis, track and field.

Computers Computers are regularly used in all academic classes. Computer network features include on-campus library services, Internet access, office computer access.

Contact Admissions. 205-367-8144. Fax: 205-367-8145. Web site: www.pickensacademy.com.

PICKERING COLLEGE

16945 Bayview Avenue
Newmarket, Ontario L3Y 4X2, Canada
Head of School: Peter C. Sturrup

General Information Coeducational boarding and day college-preparatory and arts school. Boarding grades 7–12, day grades JK–12. Founded: 1842. Setting: suburban. Nearest major city is Toronto, Canada. Students are housed in single-sex dormitories. 42-acre campus. 4 buildings on campus. Approved or accredited by Canadian Association of Independent Schools, Canadian Educational Standards Institute, National Independent Private Schools Association, The Association of Boarding Schools, and Ontario Department of Education. Affiliate member of National Association of Independent Schools. Language of instruction: English. Total enrollment: 402. Upper school average class size: 18. Upper school faculty-student ratio: 1:9.

Upper School Student Profile Grade 9: 52 students (31 boys, 21 girls); Grade 10: 57 students (31 boys, 26 girls); Grade 11: 66 students (32 boys, 34 girls); Grade 12: 55 students (29 boys, 26 girls). 40% of students are boarding students. 70% are

province residents. 2 provinces are represented in upper school student body. 25% are international students. International students from China, Mexico, and Republic of Korea; 14 other countries represented in student body.

Faculty In upper school: 17 men, 12 women; 20 reside on campus.

Subjects Offered Algebra, art, art history, biology, business, business skills, business studies, calculus, Canadian geography, Canadian history, careers, chemistry, community service, computer applications, computer multimedia, computer programming, computer science, concert band, creative writing, drama, dramatic arts, economics, English, English composition, English literature, entrepreneurship, environmental science, ESL, experiential education, family studies, filmmaking, fine arts, finite math, French, geography, geometry, government/civics, guitar, health, health education, history, instrumental music, jazz band, law, leadership, literature, mathematics, media studies, music, physical education, physics, politics, science, social science, social studies, Spanish, theater, video film production, visual arts, vocal music, world history.

Graduation Requirements 60 hours of community service completed over 4 years before graduation.

Special Academic Programs Independent study; ESL.

College Placement 53 students graduated in 2005; 52 went to college, including McMaster University; Queen's University at Kingston; Ryerson University; The University of Western Ontario; University of Toronto; Wilfrid Laurier University. Other: 1 had other specific plans.

Student Life Upper grades have uniform requirement, student council, honor system. Discipline rests equally with students and faculty.

Summer Programs ESL programs offered; session focuses on ESL; held on campus; accepts boys and girls; open to students from other schools. 2006 schedule: July to August. Application deadline: none.

Tuition and Aid Day student tuition: CAN$16,310; 7-day tuition and room/board: CAN$35,000. Tuition installment plan (Insured Tuition Payment Plan, monthly payment plans). Tuition reduction for siblings, bursaries, merit scholarship grants available.

Admissions Traditional secondary-level entrance grade is 9. SSAT, ERB, PSAT, SAT, PLAN or ACT and TOEFL required. Deadline for receipt of application materials: none. Application fee required: CAN$200. Interview required.

Athletics Interscholastic: badminton (boys), basketball (b,g), cross-country running (b,g), hockey (b,g), horseback riding (b,g), ice hockey (b), ice skating (b,g), volleyball (b,g); intramural: badminton (b,g), ball hockey (b,g), basketball (b,g), floor hockey (b,g), hockey (b,g), ice hockey (b), ice skating (b,g), skiing (cross-country) (b,g), skiing (downhill) (b,g), snowboarding (b,g), soccer (b,g), softball (b,g), swimming and diving (b,g), table tennis (b,g), tai chi (b,g), tennis (b,g), track and field (b,g), volleyball (b,g); coed interscholastic: bicycling, cross-country running, equestrian sports, hockey, horseback riding, ice hockey, ice skating, snowboarding; coed intramural: ball hockey, bowling, equestrian sports, figure skating, floor hockey, Frisbee, golf, hockey, ice hockey, ice skating, mountain biking, skateboarding, skiing (cross-country), skiing (downhill), snowboarding, soccer, softball, swimming and diving, table tennis, tai chi, tennis, track and field, volleyball.

Computers Computers are regularly used in all classes. Computer network features include campus e-mail, on-campus library services, CD-ROMs, Internet access, DVD, wireless campus network.

Contact Jayne Fillman, Director of Admissions. 905-895-1700. Fax: 905-895-1306. E-mail: admissions@pickeringcollege.on.ca. Web site: www.pickeringcollege.on.ca.

PIEDMONT ACADEMY

PO Box 231
126 Highway 212 West
Monticello, Georgia 31064
Head of School: Mr. James P. Champion, IV

General Information Coeducational day college-preparatory, arts, business, vocational, religious studies, bilingual studies, and technology school, affiliated with Protestant faith. Grades K4–12. Founded: 1970. Setting: small town. Nearest major city is Atlanta. 25-acre campus. 5 buildings on campus. Approved or accredited by Georgia Accrediting Commission, Georgia Independent School Association, and Georgia Department of Education. Languages of instruction: English and Spanish. Total enrollment: 313. Upper school average class size: 25. Upper school faculty-student ratio: 1:13.

Upper School Student Profile Grade 9: 28 students (15 boys, 13 girls); Grade 10: 30 students (15 boys, 15 girls); Grade 11: 19 students (15 boys, 4 girls); Grade 12: 11 students (6 boys, 5 girls). 98% of students are Protestant.

Faculty School total: 35. In upper school: 4 men, 17 women; 15 have advanced degrees.

Subjects Offered Advanced chemistry, advanced computer applications, advanced math, algebra, American government, American history, American history-AP, anatomy and physiology, band, biology, business law, calculus, calculus-AP, chemistry, chemistry-AP, civics, computer science, computer science-AP, computers, concert band, concert choir, consumer economics, consumer law, economics, English, English-AP, geometry, government and politics-AP, government-AP, government/civics, grammar, health education, honors algebra, honors English, honors geometry, Internet, intro to computers, keyboarding/computer, language arts, leadership and service, literature, mathematics, performing arts, personal finance, physical fitness,

physical science, physics, pre-calculus, science, sociology, Spanish, student government, typing, wind instruments, world history, yearbook.

Graduation Requirements Algebra, American government, American literature, biology, calculus, chemistry, civics, computer keyboarding, English composition, English literature, geometry, government, grammar, history, mathematics, physical education (includes health), physical science, science, Spanish.

Special Academic Programs Advanced Placement exam preparation; honors section; study at local college for college credit.

College Placement 18 students graduated in 2005; 17 went to college, including Georgia Institute of Technology; Georgia Southern University; University of Georgia; Valdosta State University. Other: 1 entered military service.

Student Life Upper grades have uniform requirement, student council, honor system. Discipline rests primarily with faculty.

Summer Programs Sports, art/fine arts programs offered; session focuses on preparation for school year competition; held both on and off campus; held at various colleges/recreation areas; accepts boys and girls; not open to students from other schools. 130 students usually enrolled. 2006 schedule: June 1 to August 2.

Tuition and Aid Day student tuition: $4920. Guaranteed tuition plan. Tuition installment plan (monthly payment plans, individually arranged payment plans). Tuition reduction for siblings, need-based scholarship grants, prepGATE Loans available. In 2005–06, 7% of upper-school students received aid. Total amount of financial aid awarded in 2005–06: $15,000.

Admissions Traditional secondary-level entrance grade is 9. For fall 2005, 12 students applied for upper-level admission, 10 were accepted, 10 enrolled. OLSAT, Stanford Achievement Test required. Deadline for receipt of application materials: none. Application fee required: $75. Interview required.

Athletics Interscholastic: baseball (boys), basketball (b,g), cheering (b,g), fitness (b,g), flag football (b,g), football (b), golf (b,g), softball (b,g), tennis (b,g), weight lifting (b,g), weight training (b,g), wrestling (b,g); coed interscholastic: track and field; coed intramural: flag football. 2 PE instructors, 5 coaches.

Computers Computers are regularly used in all academic classes. Computer network features include campus e-mail, on-campus library services, CD-ROMs, Internet access, file transfer, office computer access, DVD.

Contact Judy M. Nelson, Director of Admissions and Public and Alumni Relations. 706-468-8818 Ext. 19. Fax: 706-468-2409. E-mail: judy_nelson@piedmontacademy.com. Web site: www.piedmontacademy.com/.

PINE CREST SCHOOL

1501 Northeast 62nd Street
Fort Lauderdale, Florida 33334-5116
Head of School: Dr. Lourdes Cowgill

General Information Coeducational day college-preparatory school. Grades PK–12. Founded: 1934. Setting: urban. 49-acre campus. 22 buildings on campus. Approved or accredited by Association of Independent Schools of Florida, Florida Council of Independent Schools, and Southern Association of Colleges and Schools. Member of National Association of Independent Schools and Secondary School Admission Test Board. Endowment: $30 million. Total enrollment: 1,675. Upper school average class size: 17. Upper school faculty-student ratio: 1:9.

Upper School Student Profile Grade 9: 199 students (94 boys, 105 girls); Grade 10: 177 students (73 boys, 104 girls); Grade 11: 204 students (107 boys, 97 girls); Grade 12: 190 students (96 boys, 94 girls).

Faculty School total: 129. In upper school: 27 men, 38 women; 35 have advanced degrees.

Subjects Offered Algebra, American history, art, art history, band, biology, calculus, ceramics, chemistry, chorus, computer graphics, computer programming, computer science, dance, drama, economics, English, environmental science, ethics, European history, fine arts, forensics, French, geometry, German, government/civics, history, marine biology, marine studies, mathematics, music, orchestra, photography, physical education, physics, psychology, Spanish, speech, statistics.

Graduation Requirements Arts and fine arts (art, music, dance, drama), computer science, English, ethics, foreign language, mathematics, physical education (includes health), science, social studies (includes history), speech.

Special Academic Programs Advanced Placement exam preparation in 19 subject areas; honors section.

College Placement 178 students graduated in 2005; all went to college, including Boston University; Harvard University; Northwestern University; University of Florida; University of Pennsylvania; Washington University in St. Louis. Median SAT verbal: 660, median SAT math: 666. 78% scored over 600 on SAT verbal, 81% scored over 600 on SAT math.

Student Life Upper grades have uniform requirement, student council, honor system. Discipline rests primarily with faculty.

Summer Programs Enrichment, advancement, sports programs offered; session focuses on competitive learning, summer camp (ages 5-11), summer school (grades 9-12); held on campus; accepts boys and girls; open to students from other schools. 300 students usually enrolled. 2006 schedule: June 5 to August 11. Application deadline: none.

Pine Crest School

Tuition and Aid Day student tuition: $16,980. Tuition installment plan (Key Tuition Payment Plan). Need-based scholarship grants available. In 2005–06, 11% of upper-school students received aid. Total amount of financial aid awarded in 2005–06: $850,000.

Admissions Traditional secondary-level entrance grade is 9. For fall 2005, 175 students applied for upper-level admission, 77 were accepted, 64 enrolled. SSAT required. Deadline for receipt of application materials: none. Application fee required: $100. Interview required.

Athletics Interscholastic: aquatics (boys, girls), baseball (b), basketball (b,g), crew (b,g), cross-country running (b,g), diving (b,g), fitness (b,g), flag football (b), football (b), golf (b,g), lacrosse (b,g), physical fitness (b,g), soccer (b,g), softball (g), strength & conditioning (b,g), swimming and diving (b,g), tennis (b,g), track and field (b,g), volleyball (b,g), weight lifting (b,g); intramural: aquatics (b,g), swimming and diving (b,g); coed interscholastic: ballet, cheering; coed intramural: ballet, physical training, strength & conditioning. 8 PE instructors, 1 trainer.

Computers Computers are regularly used in all classes. Computer network features include campus e-mail, on-campus library services, CD-ROMs, Internet access, file transfer, wireless campus network, laptop program (grades 6-12).

Contact Mrs. Elena Del Alamo, Director of Admission. 954-492-4103. Fax: 954-492-4188. E-mail: pcadmit@pinecrest.edu. Web site: www.pinecrest.edu.

PINE FORGE ACADEMY

PO Box 338
Pine Forge, Pennsylvania 19548
Head of School: Prof. Cynthia Poole-Gibson

General Information Coeducational boarding and day college-preparatory, arts, business, vocational, religious studies, bilingual studies, and technology school, affiliated with Seventh-day Adventist Church. Grades 9–12. Founded: 1946. Setting: rural. Nearest major city is Philadelphia. Students are housed in single-sex dormitories. 595-acre campus. 6 buildings on campus. Approved or accredited by Middle States Association of Colleges and Schools, National Council for Private School Accreditation, and Pennsylvania Department of Education. Endowment: $400,000. Total enrollment: 186. Upper school average class size: 25. Upper school faculty-student ratio: 1:15.

Upper School Student Profile Grade 9: 31 students (18 boys, 13 girls); Grade 10: 46 students (25 boys, 21 girls); Grade 11: 60 students (28 boys, 32 girls); Grade 12: 49 students (26 boys, 23 girls). 90% of students are boarding students. 14% are state residents. 21 states are represented in upper school student body. 1% are international students. International students from Bermuda, Canada, Haiti, Jamaica, Panama, and Trinidad and Tobago. 85% of students are Seventh-day Adventists.

Faculty School total: 16. In upper school: 8 men, 8 women; 10 have advanced degrees; 7 reside on campus.

Subjects Offered Accounting, African-American studies, algebra, American history, anatomy, biology, business skills, calculus, chemistry, computer applications, computer programming, computer science, English, fine arts, French, general science, geography, geometry, government/civics, health, home economics, industrial arts, instrumental music, keyboarding, mathematics, music, physical education, physics, physiology, pre-calculus, reading, religion, science, social science, social studies, Spanish, statistics, U.S. history-AP, vocal music, world history, writing.

Graduation Requirements Arts and fine arts (art, music, dance, drama), business skills (includes word processing), computer science, English, foreign language, mathematics, physical education (includes health), religion (includes Bible studies and theology), science, social science, social studies (includes history).

Special Academic Programs Honors section; independent study; remedial math; programs in English, mathematics for dyslexic students.

College Placement 45 students graduated in 2005; 42 went to college, including Andrews University; Duke University; Howard University; Oakwood College; Southern Adventist University. Other: 2 went to work, 1 had other specific plans. Median SAT verbal: 460, median SAT math: 430. 4% scored over 600 on SAT verbal, 4% scored over 600 on SAT math.

Student Life Upper grades have uniform requirement, student council, honor system. Discipline rests primarily with faculty. Attendance at religious services is required.

Tuition and Aid Day student tuition: $8000; 7-day tuition and room/board: $14,000. Tuition installment plan (monthly payment plans, individually arranged payment plans). Tuition reduction for siblings, merit scholarship grants, paying campus jobs available. In 2005–06, 15% of upper-school students received aid. Total amount of financial aid awarded in 2005–06: $140,000.

Admissions Traditional secondary-level entrance grade is 11. For fall 2005, 250 students applied for upper-level admission, 194 were accepted, 186 enrolled. Deadline for receipt of application materials: none. Application fee required: $25. Interview recommended.

Athletics Interscholastic: baseball (boys), basketball (b,g), soccer (b,g), softball (g), tennis (b,g); intramural: basketball (b,g), soccer (b,g), softball (b,g); coed interscholastic: cross-country running; coed intramural: cross-country running. 2 PE instructors, 3 coaches, 1 trainer.

Computers Computers are regularly used in all academic classes. Computer network features include campus e-mail, on-campus library services, CD-ROMs, online commercial services, Internet access, office computer access, DVD.

Contact Karen Y. Christmas, Executive Administrative Assistant. 610-326-5800 Ext. 10. Fax: 610-326-4260. E-mail: kchristmas@pineforgeacademy.org. Web site: www.pineforgeacademy.org.

PINEHURST SCHOOL

St. Catharines, Ontario, Canada
See Special Needs Schools section.

PINE RIDGE SCHOOL

Williston, Vermont
See Special Needs Schools section.

THE PINGREE SCHOOL

537 Highland Street
South Hamilton, Massachusetts 01982
Head of School: Mr. Peter M. Cowen

General Information Coeducational day college-preparatory school. Grades 9–12. Founded: 1961. Setting: suburban. Nearest major city is Boston. 100-acre campus. 2 buildings on campus. Approved or accredited by Association of Independent Schools in New England, National Independent Private Schools Association, and New England Association of Schools and Colleges. Member of National Association of Independent Schools and Secondary School Admission Test Board. Endowment: $2.5 million. Total enrollment: 311. Upper school average class size: 15. Upper school faculty-student ratio: 1:7.

Upper School Student Profile Grade 9: 74 students (35 boys, 39 girls); Grade 10: 81 students (41 boys, 40 girls); Grade 11: 79 students (38 boys, 41 girls); Grade 12: 77 students (31 boys, 46 girls).

Faculty School total: 43. In upper school: 17 men, 23 women; 26 have advanced degrees.

Subjects Offered Algebra, American history, American literature, American studies, art, art history, astronomy, biology, calculus, ceramics, chemistry, computer programming, computer science, creative writing, dance, drama, driver education, earth science, ecology, economics, English, English literature, European history, fine arts, French, geometry, history, Latin, mathematics, music, oceanography, philosophy, photography, physics, psychology, Russian literature, science, social studies, Spanish, theater, trigonometry, writing.

Graduation Requirements Arts and fine arts (art, music, dance, drama), English, foreign language, mathematics, science, social studies (includes history), 50 hours of community service.

Special Academic Programs Advanced Placement exam preparation in 10 subject areas; honors section; independent study; term-away projects.

College Placement 74 students graduated in 2005; 72 went to college, including Boston College; Bowdoin College; Colby College; Connecticut College; Union College; University of Pennsylvania. Other: 2 entered a postgraduate year.

Student Life Upper grades have specified standards of dress, student council, honor system. Discipline rests equally with students and faculty.

Tuition and Aid Day student tuition: $26,300. Tuition installment plan (Academic Management Services Plan). Merit scholarship grants, need-based scholarship grants, need-based loans available. In 2005–06, 25% of upper-school students received aid; total upper-school merit-scholarship money awarded: $52,000. Total amount of financial aid awarded in 2005–06: $775,000.

Admissions Traditional secondary-level entrance grade is 9. For fall 2005, 354 students applied for upper-level admission, 150 were accepted, 78 enrolled. ISEE or SSAT required. Deadline for receipt of application materials: January 15. Application fee required: $50. On-campus interview required.

Athletics Interscholastic: baseball (boys), basketball (b,g), cross-country running (b,g), dance (g), field hockey (g), football (b), golf (b,g), ice hockey (b,g), lacrosse (b,g), soccer (b,g), softball (g), swimming and diving (b,g), tennis (b,g), volleyball (g), wrestling (b); coed interscholastic: outdoor adventure, outdoor education, weight lifting, weight training; coed intramural: fitness, hiking/backpacking, outdoor adventure, outdoor education, outdoor skills, skiing (downhill), strength & conditioning. 24 coaches, 2 trainers.

Computers Computers are regularly used in English, foreign language classes. Computer network features include campus e-mail, on-campus library services, CD-ROMs, online commercial services, Internet access, DVD.

Contact Eric Stacey, Director of Admission. 978-468-4415 Ext. 239. Fax: 978-468-3758. E-mail: estacey@pingree.org. Web site: www.pingree.org.

THE PINGRY SCHOOL

Martinsville Road
PO Box 366
Martinsville, New Jersey 08836
Head of School: Mr. Nathaniel Conard

General Information Coeducational day college-preparatory and arts school. Grades K–12. Founded: 1861. Setting: suburban. Nearest major city is New York, NY. 240-acre campus. 1 building on campus. Approved or accredited by Middle States Association of Colleges and Schools, New Jersey Association of Independent Schools, and New Jersey Department of Education. Member of National Association of Independent Schools. Endowment: $51 million. Total enrollment: 1,017. Upper school average class size: 14. Upper school faculty-student ratio: 1:8.

Upper School Student Profile Grade 9: 135 students (69 boys, 66 girls); Grade 10: 128 students (63 boys, 65 girls); Grade 11: 129 students (64 boys, 65 girls); Grade 12: 124 students (67 boys, 57 girls).

Faculty School total: 140. In upper school: 45 men, 37 women; 50 have advanced degrees.

Subjects Offered Algebra, American literature, analysis, analysis and differential calculus, anatomy, architecture, art, art history-AP, biology, biology-AP, brass choir, calculus, chemistry, chemistry-AP, clayworking, comparative cultures, computer science-AP, creative writing, drafting, drama, driver education, English, ethics, European literature, filmmaking, French, French-AP, geometry, German, German-AP, Greek drama, health, jazz band, jewelry making, Latin, literature by women, macro/microeconomics-AP, macroeconomics-AP, modern European history, music theory, mythology, orchestra, painting, peer counseling, photography, physics, physics-AP, physiology, psychology, psychology-AP, sculpture, Shakespeare, Spanish, Spanish-AP, studio art-AP, trigonometry, U.S. government-AP, U.S. history-AP, wind ensemble, world literature, yearbook.

Graduation Requirements Arts and fine arts (art, music, dance, drama), English, foreign language, mathematics, physical education (includes health), science, social studies (includes history). Community service is required.

Special Academic Programs Advanced Placement exam preparation in 17 subject areas; honors section; independent study.

College Placement 122 students graduated in 2005; all went to college, including Boston College; Colgate University; Cornell University; Duke University; Harvard University; University of Pennsylvania.

Student Life Upper grades have specified standards of dress, student council, honor system. Discipline rests equally with students and faculty.

Summer Programs Enrichment programs offered; session focuses on enrichment/writing and study skills; held on campus; accepts boys and girls; open to students from other schools. 2006 schedule: June 26 to August 4.

Tuition and Aid Day student tuition: $18,435–$23,575. Tuition installment plan (Key Tuition Payment Plan). Need-based scholarship grants available. In 2005–06, 8% of upper-school students received aid. Total amount of financial aid awarded in 2005–06: $1,159,638.

Admissions Traditional secondary-level entrance grade is 9. For fall 2005, 224 students applied for upper-level admission, 87 were accepted, 50 enrolled. ERB, ISEE, SSAT or Wechsler Intelligence Scale for Children required. Deadline for receipt of application materials: January 23. Application fee required: $75. Interview required.

Athletics Interscholastic: baseball (boys), basketball (b,g), cheering (g), cross-country running (b,g), fencing (b,g), field hockey (g), football (b), golf (b,g), ice hockey (b,g), lacrosse (b,g), skiing (downhill) (b,g), soccer (b,g), softball (g), swimming and diving (b,g), tennis (b,g), track and field (b,g), wrestling (b); coed interscholastic: dance, physical fitness, physical training, squash, water polo. 2 PE instructors, 15 coaches.

Computers Computers are regularly used in all academic classes. Computer network features include campus e-mail, on-campus library services, CD-ROMs, online commercial services, Internet access, DVD, wireless campus network.

Contact Ms. Sara Boisvert, Director of Admission. 908-647-6419. Fax: 908-647-4395. E-mail: sboisvert@pingry.org. Web site: www.pingry.org.

ANNOUNCEMENT FROM THE SCHOOL Since its founding in 1861 by Dr. John F. Pingry, the Pingry School has stood for excellence in teaching, high moral standards, and the development of integrity and character among its students. Pingry is a coeducational, college-preparatory, country day school that enrolls approximately 1,000 students from 90 communities in New Jersey. The School serves its students through two campuses. Situated on 28 acres, the Short Hills campus (316 students in grades K–6) houses 28 classrooms, 3 science labs, a computer lab, a newly renovated media center, a gym, and 2 music rooms. The 230-acre Martinsville campus (692 students in grades 7–12) houses more than 50 classrooms; science laboratories; a 732-seat auditorium; a 60-seat attic theater; music practice rooms; 3 computer labs; a multimedia library; world-class athletic facilities that support 28 different sports at the varsity, junior varsity, and middle school levels; and a new 41,000-square-foot Academic Arts Center. The School, accredited by the Middle States Association, the New Jersey Association of Independent Schools, and the State of New Jersey, is nationally recognized for its outstanding academic program—a solid liberal arts curriculum enriched by extracurricular activities and athletics. Pingry offers 16 Advanced Placement courses, and any student may sit for AP exams. Class sizes in all grades average

16 students. Pingry's 147 full- and part-time faculty members have 15 doctoral and 78 master's degrees, with an average tenure of 12 years at Pingry. The School strongly upholds the student-initiated Honor System from 1925, and encourages the students to give back to the community by requiring 10 hours of community service. In 11th grade, each student chooses a college counselor to help with the college admission process. The counselors work closely with students to select the most appropriate institution for them. The top 6 schools that Pingry graduates currently attend are the University of Pennsylvania, Brown, Georgetown, Cornell, Columbia, and Princeton. Tuition ranges from $18,435 for K–grade 2 to $23,575 for grades 9–12.

PIUS X HIGH SCHOOL

6000 A Street
Lincoln, Nebraska 68510
Head of School: Fr. Michael J. Morin

General Information Coeducational day college-preparatory and religious studies school, affiliated with Roman Catholic Church. Grades 9–12. Founded: 1956. Setting: urban. 30-acre campus. 1 building on campus. Approved or accredited by North Central Association of Colleges and Schools and Nebraska Department of Education. Endowment: $6 million. Total enrollment: 976. Upper school average class size: 26. Upper school faculty-student ratio: 1:16.

Upper School Student Profile Grade 9: 256 students (136 boys, 120 girls); Grade 10: 247 students (130 boys, 117 girls); Grade 11: 239 students (125 boys, 114 girls); Grade 12: 234 students (120 boys, 114 girls). 98% of students are Roman Catholic.

Faculty School total: 62. In upper school: 32 men, 30 women; 24 have advanced degrees.

Subjects Offered Accounting, acting, advanced chemistry, advanced computer applications, advanced math, advanced studio art-AP, algebra, American government, American government-AP, American literature, anatomy, applied arts, applied music, architectural drawing, art, art appreciation, art history, Bible studies, biology, biology-AP, bookkeeping, British literature, business, business law, calculus, calculus-AP, campus ministry, carpentry, Catholic belief and practice, chemistry, chemistry-AP, choir, choral music, civics, comparative government and politics-AP, comparative religion, composition, computer applications, computer graphics, computer keyboarding, computer literacy, concert band, concert choir, drafting, drama, drawing, drawing and design, driver education, English, English composition, English literature, English literature-AP, family living, Farsi, fitness, food and nutrition, French, general math, geography, government and politics-AP, government-AP, graphic design, health, history of music, history of the Catholic Church, human anatomy, industrial arts, instrumental music, integrated science, interior design, jazz band, journalism, literature-AP, marching band, marketing, mechanical drawing, moral theology, music appreciation, personal money management, photography, physical education, physical science, physics, physics-AP, play production, pre-algebra, pre-calculus, psychology, religion, small engine repair, social justice, Spanish, speech and debate, stage design, student publications, studio art, symphonic band, U.S. history, U.S. history-AP, vocal music, world geography, world history, yearbook.

Graduation Requirements Arts and fine arts (art, music, dance, drama), civics, computer literacy, electives, English, geography, mathematics, physical education (includes health), religion (includes Bible studies and theology), science, speech communications, U.S. history, world history.

Special Academic Programs Advanced Placement exam preparation in 5 subject areas; independent study.

College Placement 256 students graduated in 2005; 240 went to college, including Creighton University; University of Nebraska–Lincoln; University of Nebraska at Kearney; University of Nebraska at Omaha; Wesleyan University. Other: 13 went to work, 3 entered military service.

Student Life Upper grades have uniform requirement, student council, honor system. Discipline rests primarily with faculty. Attendance at religious services is required.

Tuition and Aid Day student tuition: $1500. Guaranteed tuition plan. Tuition installment plan (monthly payment plans, individually arranged payment plans). Need-based scholarship grants available. In 2005–06, 5% of upper-school students received aid. Total amount of financial aid awarded in 2005–06: $10,000.

Admissions Traditional secondary-level entrance grade is 9. Deadline for receipt of application materials: none. Application fee required: $35. Interview recommended.

Athletics Interscholastic: baseball (boys), basketball (b,g), cheering (g), cross-country running (b,g), dance squad (g), drill team (g), football (b), golf (b,g), soccer (b,g), softball (g), tennis (b,g), track and field (b,g), volleyball (g); intramural: running (g); coed intramural: basketball, bowling, running. 4 PE instructors, 18 coaches.

Computers Computers are regularly used in accounting, business, business applications, business education, business skills, business studies, creative writing, drafting, journalism, yearbook classes. Computer network features include campus e-mail, on-campus library services, CD-ROMs, Internet access, office computer access.

Contact Mrs. Jan Frayser, Director of Guidance. 402-488-0931. Fax: 402-488-1061. E-mail: jan.frayser@piusx.net. Web site: www.piusx.net.

POLYTECHNIC PREPARATORY COUNTRY DAY SCHOOL

9216 Seventh Avenue
Brooklyn, New York 11228
Head of School: David B. Harman

General Information Coeducational day college-preparatory school. Grades N–12. Founded: 1854. Setting: urban. 24-acre campus. 3 buildings on campus. Approved or accredited by Middle States Association of Colleges and Schools and New York State Association of Independent Schools. Member of National Association of Independent Schools and Secondary School Admission Test Board. Endowment: $15 million. Total enrollment: 976. Upper school average class size: 17. Upper school faculty-student ratio: 1:7.

Upper School Student Profile Grade 9: 123 students (59 boys, 64 girls); Grade 10: 115 students (69 boys, 46 girls); Grade 11: 111 students (58 boys, 53 girls); Grade 12: 121 students (65 boys, 56 girls).

Faculty School total: 140. In upper school: 58 men, 82 women; 96 have advanced degrees.

Subjects Offered 20th century world history, Advanced Placement courses, African American history, algebra, American history, American literature, art, art history, art history-AP, astronomy, bioethics, biology, biology-AP, biotechnology, calculus, calculus-AP, Caribbean history, ceramics, chemistry, chemistry-AP, choral music, classics, computer programming, computer programming-AP, computer science, computer-aided design, creative writing, DNA research, drama, drawing, earth science, ecology, economics, English, English literature-AP, environmental science, European history, European history-AP, filmmaking, fine arts, forensic science, forensics, French, French language-AP, French literature-AP, geology, geometry, history, international relations, jazz band, Latin, Latin-AP, mathematics, music, music theory-AP, paleontology, philosophy, physical education, physics, physics-AP, psychology, science, senior project, Shakespeare, social studies, Spanish, Spanish language-AP, Spanish literature-AP, speech, theater, theater arts, trigonometry, U.S. history-AP, world history, world history-AP, writing.

Graduation Requirements Arts and fine arts (art, music, dance, drama), English, foreign language, history, mathematics, music, physical education (includes health), science, speech, senior thesis with oral presentation. Community service is required.

Special Academic Programs Advanced Placement exam preparation in 20 subject areas; honors section; independent study; term-away projects; academic accommodation for the gifted and the artistically talented.

College Placement 116 students graduated in 2005; all went to college, including American University; Harvard University; Lehigh University; New York University; The George Washington University; Yale University. Mean SAT verbal: 630, mean SAT math: 640.

Student Life Upper grades have specified standards of dress, student council, honor system. Discipline rests equally with students and faculty.

Summer Programs Remediation, enrichment, advancement, sports, art/fine arts, computer instruction programs offered; session focuses on recreational and sports camps and some academic programs; held on campus; accepts boys and girls; open to students from other schools. 700 students usually enrolled. 2006 schedule: June 12 to August 25. Application deadline: June 1.

Tuition and Aid Day student tuition: $7100–$24,650. Tuition installment plan (Academic Management Services Plan, Key Tuition Payment Plan). Need-based scholarship grants available. In 2005–06, 27% of upper-school students received aid. Total amount of financial aid awarded in 2005–06: $3,600,000.

Admissions Traditional secondary-level entrance grade is 9. For fall 2005, 364 students applied for upper-level admission, 133 were accepted, 50 enrolled. ERB, ISEE or SSAT required. Deadline for receipt of application materials: December 9. Application fee required: $50. On-campus interview required.

Athletics Interscholastic: baseball (boys), basketball (b,g), cross-country running (b,g), football (b), lacrosse (b,g), soccer (b,g), softball (g), squash (b,g), swimming and diving (b,g), tennis (b,g), track and field (b,g), volleyball (g), wrestling (b); intramural: gymnastics (g); coed interscholastic: golf; coed intramural: ballet, cheering, dance, dance team, fitness, water polo, yoga. 12 PE instructors, 25 coaches, 2 trainers.

Computers Computers are regularly used in all academic, publications, yearbook classes. Computer network features include campus e-mail, on-campus library services, CD-ROMs, Internet access, file transfer, office computer access, DVD, wireless campus network.

Contact Lori W. Redell, Assistant Head for Admissions and Financial Aid. 718-836-9800 Ext. 306. Fax: 718-238-3393. E-mail: lwredell@polyprep.org. Web site: www.polyprep.brooklyn.ny.us.

POLYTECHNIC SCHOOL

1030 East California Boulevard
Pasadena, California 91106-4099
Head of School: Mrs. Deborah E. Reed

General Information Coeducational day college-preparatory school. Grades K–12. Founded: 1907. Setting: suburban. 15-acre campus. 7 buildings on campus. Approved or accredited by The College Board, Western Association of Schools and Colleges, and California Department of Education. Member of National Association of

Independent Schools. Endowment: $45 million. Total enrollment: 834. Upper school average class size: 17. Upper school faculty-student ratio: 1:17.

Upper School Student Profile Grade 9: 97 students (54 boys, 43 girls); Grade 10: 88 students (45 boys, 43 girls); Grade 11: 89 students (49 boys, 40 girls); Grade 12: 83 students (42 boys, 41 girls).

Faculty School total: 105. In upper school: 17 men, 31 women; 30 have advanced degrees.

Subjects Offered Acting, algebra, analytic geometry, art history, Basic programming, batik, biology, biology-AP, calculus-AP, ceramics, chamber groups, chemistry, chemistry-AP, choral music, communications, computer art, computer science, constitutional law, data analysis, drama, drama performance, drawing, East Asian history, economics, English, English language and composition-AP, English literature and composition-AP, ensembles, ethics, filmmaking, French, French literature-AP, functions, geometry, German, German-AP, guitar, improvisation, jazz dance, jazz ensemble, Latin, Latin-AP, madrigals, math analysis, mathematical modeling, music history, music theory, musical productions, musical theater, orchestra, painting, photography, physical science, physics, physics-AP, Roman civilization, sculpture, silk screening, society, Spanish, Spanish literature-AP, statistics, tap dance, technical theater, theater, theater design and production, theater history, trigonometry, U.S. government and politics, U.S. history-AP, Vietnam War, visual arts, Western civilization, woodworking, world cultures, world religions.

Special Academic Programs Honors section; independent study.

College Placement 85 students graduated in 2005; all went to college, including Brown University; New York University; Princeton University; Stanford University; University of California, Berkeley; University of Southern California.

Student Life Upper grades have specified standards of dress, student council, honor system. Discipline rests equally with students and faculty.

Summer Programs Enrichment, advancement, sports, art/fine arts, computer instruction programs offered; session focuses on academics, enrichment, and arts; held on campus; accepts boys and girls; open to students from other schools. 900 students usually enrolled. 2006 schedule: June 27 to July 28. Application deadline: March 6.

Tuition and Aid Day student tuition: $20,700. Tuition installment plan (monthly payment plans). Need-based scholarship grants available. In 2005–06, 18% of upper-school students received aid. Total amount of financial aid awarded in 2005–06: $1,039,000.

Admissions Traditional secondary-level entrance grade is 9. For fall 2005, 200 students applied for upper-level admission, 26 enrolled. ISEE required. Deadline for receipt of application materials: January 6. Application fee required: $100. On-campus interview required.

Athletics Interscholastic: baseball (boys), basketball (b,g), cheering (g), cross-country running (b,g), diving (b,g), equestrian sports (g), football (b), golf (b,g), soccer (b,g), softball (g), swimming and diving (b,g), tennis (b,g), track and field (b,g), volleyball (b,g), water polo (b,g); coed interscholastic: badminton. 7 PE instructors, 15 coaches, 2 trainers.

Computers Computers are regularly used in all classes. Computer network features include on-campus library services, CD-ROMs, Internet access.

Contact Ms. Sally Jeanne McKenna, Director of Admissions. 626-792-2147. Fax: 626-449-5727. E-mail: sjmckenna@polytechnic.org. Web site: www.polytechnic.org.

POMFRET SCHOOL

PO Box 128
398 Pomfret Street
Pomfret, Connecticut 06258-0128
Head of School: Mr. Bradford Hastings

General Information Coeducational boarding and day college-preparatory, arts, and technology school, affiliated with Episcopal Church. Grades 9–PG. Founded: 1894. Setting: small town. Nearest major city is Hartford. Students are housed in single-sex dormitories. 500-acre campus. 63 buildings on campus. Approved or accredited by Connecticut Association of Independent Schools, New England Association of Schools and Colleges, The Association of Boarding Schools, and Connecticut Department of Education. Member of National Association of Independent Schools and Secondary School Admission Test Board. Endowment: $30 million. Total enrollment: 353. Upper school average class size: 10. Upper school faculty-student ratio: 1:5.

Upper School Student Profile Grade 9: 68 students (34 boys, 34 girls); Grade 10: 84 students (40 boys, 44 girls); Grade 11: 101 students (60 boys, 41 girls); Grade 12: 100 students (50 boys, 50 girls); Postgraduate: 7 students (6 boys, 1 girl). 80% of students are boarding students. 35% are state residents. 25 states are represented in upper school student body. 14% are international students. International students from Bermuda, Canada, Germany, and Republic of Korea; 7 other countries represented in student body. 22% of students are members of Episcopal Church.

Faculty School total: 57. In upper school: 35 men, 22 women; 36 have advanced degrees; all reside on campus.

Subjects Offered Advanced Placement courses, algebra, American history, American literature, anatomy, art, art history, astronomy, biology, botany, calculus, ceramics, chemistry, computer programming, computer science, creative writing, drama, driver education, earth science, ecology, economics, English, English literature, environmental science, ethics, European history, expository writing, fine arts, French, geometry, government/civics, history, Latin, marine biology, mathematics, music,

photography, physics, psychology, religion, science, social studies, Spanish, statistics, theater, trigonometry, world history, writing.

Graduation Requirements Arts and fine arts (art, music, dance, drama), computer science, English, foreign language, mathematics, religion (includes Bible studies and theology), science, social studies (includes history).

Special Academic Programs Advanced Placement exam preparation in 19 subject areas; honors section; independent study; term-away projects; academic accommodation for the gifted, the musically talented, and the artistically talented.

College Placement 91 students graduated in 2005; all went to college, including Bates College; Colby College; Hamilton College; Hobart and William Smith Colleges; Trinity College; Wesleyan University. Median SAT verbal: 580, median SAT math: 595.

Student Life Upper grades have specified standards of dress, student council. Discipline rests equally with students and faculty. Attendance at religious services is required.

Summer Programs Art/fine arts programs offered; session focuses on creative writing; held on campus; accepts boys and girls; open to students from other schools. 25 students usually enrolled. 2006 schedule: June 24 to July 2. Application deadline: June 1.

Tuition and Aid Day student tuition: $23,400; 7-day tuition and room/board: $36,200. Tuition installment plan (The Tuition Plan, Insured Tuition Payment Plan, Academic Management Services Plan, monthly payment plans). Need-based scholarship grants available. In 2005–06, 28% of upper-school students received aid. Total amount of financial aid awarded in 2005–06: $2,362,450.

Admissions Traditional secondary-level entrance grade is 9. For fall 2005, 565 students applied for upper-level admission, 380 were accepted, 122 enrolled. SSAT and TOEFL required. Deadline for receipt of application materials: January 15. Application fee required: $50. On-campus interview required.

Athletics Interscholastic: baseball (boys), basketball (b,g), crew (b,g), cross-country running (b,g), field hockey (g), football (b), golf (b,g), ice hockey (b,g), lacrosse (b,g), soccer (b,g), softball (g), squash (b,g), tennis (b,g); coed interscholastic: wrestling; coed intramural: aerobics, aerobics/dance, dance, hiking/backpacking, skiing (cross-country), skiing (downhill), snowboarding, weight training, wilderness, yoga. 1 coach, 1 trainer.

Computers Computers are regularly used in foreign language, history, mathematics, science classes. Computer network features include campus e-mail, on-campus library services, CD-ROMs, Internet access, wireless campus network.

Contact Mr. Erik Bertelsen, Assistant Head for Enrollment. 860-963-6121. Fax: 860-963-2042. E-mail: bertelse@pomfretschool.org. Web site: www.pomfretschool.org.

ANNOUNCEMENT FROM THE SCHOOL In 2004–05, students worked with Schwartz Fellow Christine Todd Whitman, former Administrator of the US Environmental Protection Agency and former Governor of New Jersey. Overall, the athletic teams had terrific seasons, and the chorus is planning to tour Austria in spring 2006. Pomfret's magnificent new athletic and student center, ice rink, and boat house are now open for students and families to enjoy.

See full description on page 982.

POPE JOHN PAUL II HIGH SCHOOL

4001 North Military Trail
Boca Raton, Florida 33431
Head of School: Rev. Fr. Guy Stephen Fiano, OCARM

General Information Coeducational day college-preparatory and religious studies school, affiliated with Roman Catholic Church. Grades 9–12. Setting: suburban. Nearest major city is West Palm Beach. 33-acre campus. 10 buildings on campus. Approved or accredited by National Catholic Education Association, Southern Association of Colleges and Schools, The College Board, and Florida Department of Education. Total enrollment: 871. Upper school average class size: 28. Upper school faculty-student ratio: 1:28.

Upper School Student Profile Grade 9: 200 students (103 boys, 97 girls); Grade 10: 214 students (95 boys, 119 girls); Grade 11: 229 students (108 boys, 121 girls); Grade 12: 228 students (100 boys, 128 girls). 85% of students are Roman Catholic.

Faculty School total: 69. In upper school: 29 men, 40 women; 36 have advanced degrees.

Subjects Offered Acting, adolescent issues, advanced computer applications, algebra, American government-AP, American history, American literature, anatomy, art, art history, band, Basic programming, Bible studies, biology, biology-AP, broadcasting, business, business law, business skills, calculus, calculus-AP, campus ministry, career/college preparation, Catholic belief and practice, character education, chemistry, chemistry-AP, choral music, chorus, Christian and Hebrew scripture, Christian ethics, Christian scripture, Christian testament, college counseling, college placement, communications, community service, computer applications, computer graphics, computer programming, computer technologies, creative writing, debate, desktop publishing, drama, drawing, earth science, economics, English, English language-AP, English literature, English literature and composition-AP, English literature-AP, European history, finance, fine arts, first aid, French, geometry, government-AP,

government/civics, health, health education, history, history of the Catholic Church, honors English, honors U.S. history, honors world history, integrated math, Italian, jazz band, jazz ensemble, journalism, keyboarding/computer, leadership and service, life management skills, Life of Christ, marine biology, marine science, mathematics, media production, moral theology, music appreciation, music theory, newspaper, peer ministry, personal finance, personal fitness, physical education, physical fitness, physical science, physics, pre-algebra, pre-calculus, psychology, religion, SAT/ACT preparation, science, social studies, Spanish, Spanish language-AP, speech, speech and debate, theater, theology, trigonometry, typing, U.S. government, U.S. history-AP, video, video film production, weight training, Western civilization, world history, yearbook.

Graduation Requirements Arts and fine arts (art, music, dance, drama), English, foreign language, mathematics, physical education (includes health), religion (includes Bible studies and theology), science, social studies (includes history), 100 hours of community service.

Special Academic Programs Advanced Placement exam preparation in 6 subject areas; honors section; study at local college for college credit; remedial reading and/or remedial writing; remedial math; special instructional classes for students with learning disabilities and Attention Deficit Disorder.

College Placement 233 students graduated in 2005; all went to college, including Florida Atlantic University; Florida State University; Palm Beach Community College; University of Central Florida; University of Florida; University of Miami. Mean SAT verbal: 533, mean SAT math: 520, mean composite ACT: 23.

Student Life Upper grades have uniform requirement, student council. Discipline rests primarily with faculty. Attendance at religious services is required.

Summer Programs Remediation, enrichment, sports programs offered; session focuses on enrichment for incoming 9th-grade students; held on campus; accepts boys and girls; not open to students from other schools. 40 students usually enrolled. 2006 schedule: June 15 to July 15. Application deadline: May 23.

Tuition and Aid Day student tuition: $6500–$8000. Tuition installment plan (FACTS Tuition Payment Plan). Tuition reduction for siblings, need-based scholarship grants, need-based loans available. In 2005–06, 20% of upper-school students received aid. Total amount of financial aid awarded in 2005–06: $370,000.

Admissions Traditional secondary-level entrance grade is 9. For fall 2005, 400 students applied for upper-level admission, 305 were accepted, 200 enrolled. High School Placement Test required. Deadline for receipt of application materials: none. Application fee required: $50. Interview recommended.

Athletics Interscholastic: baseball (boys), basketball (b,g), cheering (g), cross-country running (b,g), diving (b,g), football (b), golf (b,g), ice hockey (b), lacrosse (b), soccer (b,g), softball (g), strength & conditioning (b,g), swimming and diving (b,g), tennis (b,g), track and field (b,g), volleyball (g), weight lifting (b); coed intramural: basketball, floor hockey, soccer, volleyball. 4 PE instructors, 10 coaches, 1 trainer.

Computers Computers are regularly used in English, foreign language, history, mathematics, music, science classes. Computer network features include campus e-mail, on-campus library services, CD-ROMs, online commercial services, Internet access.

Contact Sr. Eileen Sullivan, OP, Principal. 561-314-2108. Fax: 561-989-8582. E-mail: esullivan@pjpii.org. Web site: www.pjpii.org.

PORTLAND CHRISTIAN SCHOOLS

12425 NE San Rafael Street
Portland, Oregon 97230
Head of School: Mr. Bruce Reinhardt

General Information Coeducational day college-preparatory, arts, religious studies, bilingual studies, and technology school, affiliated with Christian faith. Grades PS–12. Founded: 1947. Setting: suburban. 36-acre campus. 2 buildings on campus. Approved or accredited by Association of Christian Schools International and Oregon Department of Education. Endowment: $60,000. Total enrollment: 950. Upper school average class size: 18. Upper school faculty-student ratio: 1:10.

Upper School Student Profile 100% of students are Christian faith.

Faculty School total: 40. In upper school: 16 men, 16 women; 4 have advanced degrees.

Subjects Offered Arts, band, Bible studies, community service, computer science, English, fine arts, health, history, home economics, Japanese, journalism, mathematics, philosophy, photography, physical education, religion, science, social science, social studies, Spanish, U.S. history, vocal music, yearbook.

Graduation Requirements Arts and fine arts (art, music, dance, drama), computer science, English, foreign language, mathematics, physical education (includes health), religion (includes Bible studies and theology), science, social science, social studies (includes history). Community service is required.

Special Academic Programs Advanced Placement exam preparation in 5 subject areas; honors section; independent study; academic accommodation for the gifted; remedial reading and/or remedial writing; remedial math; ESL (30 students enrolled).

College Placement 72 students graduated in 2005; 70 went to college. Other: 2 went to work. 12% scored over 600 on SAT verbal, 13% scored over 600 on SAT math.

Student Life Upper grades have specified standards of dress, student council, honor system. Discipline rests primarily with faculty. Attendance at religious services is required.

Portland Christian Schools

Summer Programs Enrichment, ESL, art/fine arts, computer instruction programs offered; session focuses on ESL; held both on and off campus; held at Mt. Hood; accepts boys and girls; open to students from other schools. 15 students usually enrolled. 2006 schedule: June 13 to July 22. Application deadline: June 3.

Tuition and Aid Day student tuition: $7390. Tuition installment plan (FACTS Tuition Payment Plan). Tuition reduction for siblings, need-based scholarship grants available. In 2005–06, 20% of upper-school students received aid. Total amount of financial aid awarded in 2005–06: $82,000.

Admissions Traditional secondary-level entrance grade is 9. For fall 2005, 10 students applied for upper-level admission, 8 were accepted, 8 enrolled. Otis-Lennon School Ability Test required. Deadline for receipt of application materials: none. Application fee required: $150. On-campus interview required.

Athletics Interscholastic: baseball (boys), basketball (b,g), cheering (g), cross-country running (b,g), football (b), soccer (b,g), softball (g), track and field (b,g), volleyball (g). 4 PE instructors, 40 coaches.

Computers Computers are regularly used in English, science classes. Computer network features include on-campus library services, CD-ROMs, Internet access, DVD.

Contact Mr. Kevin Barrows, Junior—Senior High School Principal. 503-256-3960. Fax: 503-256-2773. E-mail: kevin.barrows@pcschools.org. Web site: www.pcschools.org.

PORTLAND LUTHERAN SCHOOL

740 Southeast 182nd Avenue
Portland, Oregon 97233-4960
Head of School: Mr. Donn Maier

General Information Coeducational boarding and day college-preparatory and religious studies school, affiliated with Lutheran Church. Boarding grades 9–12, day grades PK–12. Founded: 1905. Setting: urban. Students are housed in homes of school families (international students). 16-acre campus. 5 buildings on campus. Approved or accredited by National Lutheran School Accreditation, Northwest Association of Schools and Colleges, and Oregon Department of Education. Endowment: $328,562. Total enrollment: 278. Upper school average class size: 17. Upper school faculty-student ratio: 1:8.

Upper School Student Profile Grade 9: 26 students (18 boys, 8 girls); Grade 10: 33 students (18 boys, 15 girls); Grade 11: 30 students (17 boys, 13 girls); Grade 12: 23 students (14 boys, 9 girls). 32% of students are boarding students. 63% are state residents. 2 states are represented in upper school student body. 32% are international students. International students from Hong Kong, Japan, Macao, Republic of Korea, Spain, and Taiwan; 2 other countries represented in student body. 30% of students are Lutheran.

Faculty School total: 25. In upper school: 8 men, 6 women; 7 have advanced degrees.

Subjects Offered Algebra, art, astronomy, band, Bible studies, biology, calculus, choir, computer applications, dance, drama performance, economics, English, English literature, ESL, expository writing, finite math, geology, geometry, government/civics, health, integrated science, Japanese, physical education, physics, pre-algebra, pre-calculus, psychology, religion, Spanish, trigonometry, typing, weight training, world geography, world history, world literature, yearbook.

Graduation Requirements Arts and fine arts (art, music, dance, drama), computer science, English, foreign language, mathematics, physical education (includes health), religion (includes Bible studies and theology), science, social science. Community service is required.

Special Academic Programs Advanced Placement exam preparation in 1 subject area; honors section; independent study; ESL (31 students enrolled).

College Placement 30 students graduated in 2005; 29 went to college, including Concordia University; Mt. Hood Community College; Pacific Lutheran University; University of Portland. Other: 1 entered military service. Mean SAT verbal: 478, mean SAT math: 569, mean composite ACT: 19. 14% scored over 600 on SAT verbal, 41% scored over 600 on SAT math.

Student Life Upper grades have specified standards of dress, honor system. Discipline rests primarily with faculty. Attendance at religious services is required.

Tuition and Aid Day student tuition: $6500; 7-day tuition and room/board: $15,300. Tuition installment plan (monthly payment plans, individually arranged payment plans, quarterly, semi-annual, and annual payment plans, Simply Giving). Tuition reduction for siblings, merit scholarship grants, need-based scholarship grants, tuition reduction for members of association congregations available. In 2005–06, 11% of upper-school students received aid; total upper-school merit-scholarship money awarded: $3000. Total amount of financial aid awarded in 2005–06: $19,620.

Admissions Traditional secondary-level entrance grade is 9. For fall 2005, 35 students applied for upper-level admission, 35 were accepted, 35 enrolled. Deadline for receipt of application materials: none. No application fee required. On-campus interview required.

Athletics Interscholastic: baseball (boys), basketball (b,g), cheering (g), cross-country running (b,g), dance team (g), football (b), softball (g), volleyball (g); coed interscholastic: golf, soccer, track and field; coed intramural: skiing (downhill). 1 PE instructor, 5 coaches.

Computers Computers are regularly used in data processing, publications, publishing, typing, Web site design, word processing, yearbook classes. Computer network features include on-campus library services, CD-ROMs, Internet access.

Contact Ms. Vicki Stephenson, Administrative Assistant. 503-667-3199 Ext. 301. Fax: 503-405-5002. E-mail: vstephenson@portland-lutheran.org. Web site: www.portland-lutheran.org.

PORTLEDGE SCHOOL

355 Duck Pond Road
Locust Valley, New York 11560
Head of School: Huson R. Gregory

General Information Coeducational day college-preparatory school. Grades N–12. Founded: 1965. Setting: suburban. Nearest major city is New York. 62-acre campus. 4 buildings on campus. Approved or accredited by New York State Association of Independent Schools and New York Department of Education. Member of National Association of Independent Schools and Secondary School Admission Test Board. Endowment: $1.5 million. Total enrollment: 420. Upper school average class size: 12. Upper school faculty-student ratio: 1:8.

Upper School Student Profile Grade 9: 34 students (20 boys, 14 girls); Grade 10: 41 students (22 boys, 19 girls); Grade 11: 45 students (16 boys, 29 girls); Grade 12: 31 students (18 boys, 13 girls).

Faculty School total: 80. In upper school: 22 men, 20 women; 28 have advanced degrees.

Subjects Offered 3-dimensional art, advanced chemistry, advanced computer applications, advanced math, Advanced Placement courses, advanced studio art-AP, algebra, American history, American history-AP, American literature, American literature-AP, ancient history, architectural drawing, architecture, art, art appreciation, art history, art-AP, Basic programming, biology, calculus, calculus-AP, ceramics, chemistry, chemistry-AP, Chinese history, chorus, communications, community service, computer programming, computer science, computers, creative writing, digital music, drama, drama workshop, driver education, earth science, economics, English, English language-AP, English literature, English literature-AP, environmental science, European history, expository writing, fine arts, foreign language, French, French-AP, geography, geometry, government/civics, grammar, graphic design, health, health education, history, honors English, honors geometry, honors U.S. history, independent study, instrumental music, introduction to digital multitrack recording techniques, jazz ensemble, journalism, keyboarding, mathematics, music, music theory-AP, Native American history, photography, physical education, physics, psychology, public policy, public service, public speaking, Russian history, science, senior project, social science, social studies, Spanish, Spanish-AP, theater, trigonometry, U.S. history-AP, world history.

Graduation Requirements Arts and fine arts (art, music, dance, drama), computer science, English, foreign language, mathematics, performing arts, physical education (includes health), public speaking, science, senior project, social science, social studies (includes history). Community service is required.

Special Academic Programs Advanced Placement exam preparation in 10 subject areas; honors section; independent study; academic accommodation for the gifted, the musically talented, and the artistically talented.

College Placement 24 students graduated in 2005; all went to college. Median SAT verbal: 610, median SAT math: 640. 55% scored over 600 on SAT verbal, 55% scored over 600 on SAT math.

Student Life Upper grades have specified standards of dress, student council, honor system. Discipline rests primarily with faculty.

Summer Programs Enrichment, sports, art/fine arts, computer instruction programs offered; session focuses on chess, computers, tennis, field hockey, lacrosse, and soccer; held on campus; accepts boys and girls; open to students from other schools. 300 students usually enrolled. 2006 schedule: June 26 to August 25.

Tuition and Aid Day student tuition: $5500–$22,200. Tuition installment plan (Key Tuition Payment Plan). Tuition reduction for siblings, need-based scholarship grants available. In 2005–06, 28% of upper-school students received aid. Total amount of financial aid awarded in 2005–06: $600,000.

Admissions Traditional secondary-level entrance grade is 9. For fall 2005, 71 students applied for upper-level admission, 36 were accepted, 20 enrolled. SSAT required. Deadline for receipt of application materials: none. Application fee required: $50. On-campus interview required.

Athletics Interscholastic: baseball (boys), basketball (b,g), fencing (b,g), ice hockey (b,g), lacrosse (b,g), soccer (b,g), tennis (b,g); coed interscholastic: cross-country running, golf, squash. 3 PE instructors, 2 coaches.

Computers Computers are regularly used in art, English, foreign language, history, mathematics, music, science classes. Computer network features include on-campus library services, CD-ROMs, online commercial services, Internet access, file transfer, office computer access, DVD, wireless campus network.

Contact Susan Simon, Director of Admissions. 516-750-3203. Fax: 516-674-7063. E-mail: ssimon@portledge.org. Web site: www.portledge.org.

ANNOUNCEMENT FROM THE SCHOOL Portledge is a coed college-preparatory day school for prenursery–grade 12. In addition to a traditional curriculum, the Lower School features classes in French, computer, lab science, the arts, and physical education. These programs continue in the Middle School and lead to demanding courses and Advanced Placement options in the Upper School.

PORTSMOUTH ABBEY SCHOOL

285 Cory's Lane
Portsmouth, Rhode Island 02871
Head of School: Dr. James De Vecchi

petersons.com

General Information Coeducational boarding and day college-preparatory, arts, and religious studies school, affiliated with Roman Catholic Church. Grades 9–12. Founded: 1926. Setting: small town. Nearest major city is Providence. Students are housed in single-sex dormitories. 550-acre campus. 34 buildings on campus. Approved or accredited by Association of Independent Schools in New England, New England Association of Schools and Colleges, and The Association of Boarding Schools. Member of National Association of Independent Schools and Secondary School Admission Test Board. Endowment: $32 million. Total enrollment: 354. Upper school average class size: 13. Upper school faculty-student ratio: 1:7.

Upper School Student Profile Grade 9: 73 students (39 boys, 34 girls); Grade 10: 88 students (46 boys, 42 girls); Grade 11: 105 students (57 boys, 48 girls); Grade 12: 88 students (47 boys, 41 girls). 66% of students are boarding students. 55% are state residents. 20 states are represented in upper school student body. 11% are international students. International students from Bermuda, El Salvador, Germany, Guatemala, Mexico, and Republic of Korea; 16 other countries represented in student body. 62% of students are Roman Catholic.

Faculty School total: 50. In upper school: 32 men, 18 women; 32 have advanced degrees; 34 reside on campus.

Subjects Offered Algebra, American literature, art, art history, art history-AP, art-AP, Bible studies, biology, biology-AP, calculus, calculus-AP, Catholic belief and practice, chemistry, chemistry-AP, Christian doctrine, Christian ethics, Christian scripture, church history, computer programming, computer programming-AP, computer science, computer science-AP, constitutional law, drama, economics, English, English language and composition-AP, English literature, English literature and composition-AP, ethics, European history, European history-AP, fine arts, French, French language-AP, French literature-AP, geometry, government/civics, Greek, health, history, history-AP, humanities, international relations, Latin, Latin-AP, marine biology, mathematics, mathematics-AP, modern European history, modern European history-AP, music, music appreciation, music composition, music history, music theory, music theory-AP, philosophy, photography, physical education, physics, physics-AP, physiology, political science, religion, Russian history, science, scripture, social science, Spanish, Spanish language-AP, Spanish literature-AP, statistics and probability, statistics-AP, studio art-AP, theater, theology, trigonometry, U.S. history, U.S. history-AP, world history, writing workshop.

Graduation Requirements Arts and fine arts (art, music, dance, drama), English, foreign language, history, Latin, mathematics, religion (includes Bible studies and theology), science.

Special Academic Programs Advanced Placement exam preparation in 14 subject areas; honors section; independent study; academic accommodation for the gifted, the musically talented, and the artistically talented.

College Placement 85 students graduated in 2005; 84 went to college, including Bates College; Boston College; Boston University; Georgetown University; Providence College; University of Richmond. Other: 1 entered a postgraduate year. Median SAT verbal: 615, median SAT math: 610. 55% scored over 600 on SAT verbal, 49% scored over 600 on SAT math.

Student Life Upper grades have specified standards of dress, student council, honor system. Discipline rests primarily with faculty. Attendance at religious services is required.

Summer Programs Enrichment, advancement, ESL, sports, art/fine arts, computer instruction programs offered; session focuses on enrichment and advancement; held on campus; accepts boys and girls; open to students from other schools. 80 students usually enrolled. 2006 schedule: June 25 to July 30. Application deadline: none.

Tuition and Aid Day student tuition: $23,325; 7-day tuition and room/board: $33,450. Tuition installment plan (monthly payment plans, individually arranged payment plans, Tuition Management Systems Plan). Merit scholarship grants, need-based scholarship grants available. In 2005–06, 33% of upper-school students received aid; total upper-school merit-scholarship money awarded: $250,000. Total amount of financial aid awarded in 2005–06: $1,900,000.

Admissions Traditional secondary-level entrance grade is 9. For fall 2005, 324 students applied for upper-level admission, 209 were accepted, 112 enrolled. SSAT required. Deadline for receipt of application materials: January 31. Application fee required: $50. Interview required.

Athletics Interscholastic: baseball (boys), basketball (b,g), cross-country running (b,g), field hockey (g), football (b), golf (b,g), ice hockey (b,g), lacrosse (b,g), soccer (b,g), softball (g), squash (b,g), swimming and diving (b,g), track and field (b,g); coed interscholastic: sailing, tennis, weight training; coed intramural: equestrian sports, fitness, horseback riding. 1 trainer.

Computers Computers are regularly used in English, mathematics, music, science classes. Computer network features include campus e-mail, on-campus library services, CD-ROMs, Internet access, file transfer, office computer access, wireless campus network.

Contact Mrs. Ann Motta, Admissions Coordinator. 401-643-1248. Fax: 401-683-6766. E-mail: admissions@portsmouthabbey.org. Web site: www.portsmouthabbey.org.

See full description on page 984.

PORTSMOUTH CHRISTIAN ACADEMY

20 Seaborne Drive
Dover, New Hampshire 03820
Head of School: Dr. David Thompson

General Information Coeducational day college-preparatory, arts, and religious studies school, affiliated with Christian faith. Grades K–12. Founded: 1993. Setting: small town. 50-acre campus. 3 buildings on campus. Approved or accredited by Association of Christian Schools International and New Hampshire Department of Education. Candidate for accreditation by New England Association of Schools and Colleges. Endowment: $2 million. Total enrollment: 797. Upper school average class size: 18. Upper school faculty-student ratio: 1:18.

Upper School Student Profile Grade 9: 57 students (32 boys, 25 girls); Grade 10: 59 students (22 boys, 37 girls); Grade 11: 72 students (30 boys, 42 girls); Grade 12: 56 students (33 boys, 23 girls). 80% of students are Christian faith.

Faculty School total: 21. In upper school: 9 men, 11 women; 13 have advanced degrees.

Subjects Offered 20th century American writers, 20th century history, art history, band, baseball, basketball, Bible studies, biochemistry, biology, British literature, calculus, calculus-AP, chemistry, choir, chorus, Christian doctrine, Christian studies, Christian testament, church history, college placement, comparative religion, computer graphics, computer processing, contemporary issues, drama, drama performance, drawing, English, English language and composition-AP, environmental science, European history, French, French language-AP, guitar, health and wellness, honors algebra, honors English, honors geometry, jazz band, law studies, microbiology, musical productions, musical theater, novels, physics, physics-AP, political economics, pre-calculus, Shakespeare, Spanish, Spanish language-AP, student government, theology, U.S. history, world history, World War II, yearbook.

Graduation Requirements 20th century history, algebra, arts and fine arts (art, music, dance, drama), biology, chemistry, comparative cultures, composition, computer skills, foreign language, geometry, physical education (includes health), physical science, U.S. history, writing, one Bible course for each year of Upper School attendance.

Special Academic Programs Advanced Placement exam preparation in 4 subject areas; honors section; accelerated programs; independent study; academic accommodation for the gifted; special instructional classes for students with Attention Deficit Disorder and dyslexia.

College Placement 57 students graduated in 2005; they went to Georgetown University; Gordon College; Palm Beach Atlantic University; University of New Hampshire; University of Southern Maine. Median SAT verbal: 590, median SAT math: 570. 48% scored over 600 on SAT verbal, 40% scored over 600 on SAT math.

Student Life Upper grades have specified standards of dress, student council, honor system. Discipline rests primarily with faculty. Attendance at religious services is required.

Summer Programs Remediation, enrichment, sports programs offered; session focuses on soccer, basketball and volleyball; held on campus; accepts boys and girls; open to students from other schools. 40 students usually enrolled. 2006 schedule: July 10 to August 10. Application deadline: June 1.

Tuition and Aid Day student tuition: $7280. Tuition installment plan (FACTS Tuition Payment Plan). Tuition reduction for siblings, merit scholarship grants, need-based scholarship grants available. In 2005–06, 20% of upper-school students received aid; total upper-school merit-scholarship money awarded: $25,000. Total amount of financial aid awarded in 2005–06: $76,000.

Admissions Traditional secondary-level entrance grade is 9. Stanford Achievement Test required. Deadline for receipt of application materials: none. Application fee required: $75. On-campus interview required.

Athletics Interscholastic: baseball (boys), basketball (b,g), cross-country running (b,g), indoor track & field (b,g), soccer (b,g), softball (g), track and field (b,g), volleyball (g); intramural: golf (b,g), skiing (cross-country) (b,g); coed interscholastic: alpine skiing. 1 PE instructor, 8 coaches.

Computers Computers are regularly used in art, Bible studies, career education, Christian doctrine, classics, college planning, desktop publishing, economics, English, foreign language, graphic design, history, humanities, independent study, library, library skills, mathematics, media arts, religion, religious studies, SAT preparation, science, social studies, writing classes. Computer network features include on-campus library services, CD-ROMs, online commercial services, Internet access, office computer access.

Contact Mrs. Kathy Deame, Director of Admissions. 603-742-3617 Ext. 116. Fax: 603-750-0490. E-mail: kathy.deame@pcaschool.us. Web site: www.pcaschool.org.

THE POTOMAC SCHOOL

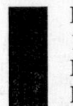

Box 430
1301 Potomac School Road
McLean, Virginia 22101
Head of School: Geoffrey Jones

General Information Coeducational day college-preparatory, arts, and technology school. Grades K–12. Founded: 1904. Setting: suburban. Nearest major city is Washington, DC. 87-acre campus. 5 buildings on campus. Approved or accredited by

The Potomac School

Virginia Association of Independent Schools. Member of National Association of Independent Schools and Secondary School Admission Test Board. Endowment: $23.3 million. Total enrollment: 875. Upper school average class size: 14. Upper school faculty-student ratio: 1:6.

Upper School Student Profile Grade 9: 79 students (41 boys, 38 girls); Grade 10: 82 students (38 boys, 44 girls); Grade 11: 77 students (39 boys, 38 girls); Grade 12: 71 students (33 boys, 38 girls).

Faculty School total: 145. In upper school: 27 men, 25 women; 40 have advanced degrees.

Subjects Offered 20th century American writers, 20th century history, 20th century world history, 3-dimensional art, acting, advanced computer applications, advanced math, African-American literature, African-American studies, algebra, American literature, anatomy and physiology, ancient history, art, art history, Asian studies, band, bell choir, Bible as literature, biology, British literature, calculus, calculus-AP, cell biology, ceramics, chamber groups, chemistry, chemistry-AP, China/Japan history, choral music, community service, comparative religion, computer programming, computer programming-AP, computer science, conceptual physics, concert band, creative writing, debate, directing, drama, drama performance, drawing and design, economics and history, electives, engineering, English, English literature, environmental science, ethics, European history, expository writing, film and literature, fine arts, French, French language-AP, French literature-AP, functions, geometry, global studies, government/civics, handbells, Harlem Renaissance, health education, historical research, history of jazz, history of music, international relations, Japanese, Japanese literature, jazz band, Latin, Latin American literature, Latin-AP, literary magazine, madrigals, mathematics, medieval history, Middle Eastern history, model United Nations, modern European history, music, music composition, music theory-AP, newspaper, painting, performing arts, photography, physical education, physics, physics-AP, portfolio art, pre-calculus, robotics, science, science and technology, sculpture, senior project, Shakespeare, short story, Spanish, Spanish language-AP, Spanish literature-AP, stagecraft, statistics-AP, strings, student government, studio art-AP, theater arts, trigonometry, U.S. history-AP, vocal music, World War II, yearbook.

Graduation Requirements Arts and fine arts (art, music, dance, drama), English, ethics, foreign language, history, mathematics, physical education (includes health), science, senior project, month-long senior project.

Special Academic Programs Advanced Placement exam preparation in 15 subject areas; honors section; independent study.

College Placement 83 students graduated in 2005; all went to college, including Georgetown University; Princeton University; University of Pennsylvania; University of Virginia; Wesleyan University. Median SAT verbal: 675, median SAT math: 687. 84% scored over 600 on SAT verbal, 89% scored over 600 on SAT math.

Student Life Upper grades have specified standards of dress, student council. Discipline rests equally with students and faculty.

Summer Programs Enrichment, advancement, sports, art/fine arts programs offered; session focuses on academics and enrichment; held on campus; accepts boys and girls; open to students from other schools. 26 students usually enrolled. 2006 schedule: June 19 to August 18. Application deadline: none.

Tuition and Aid Day student tuition: $22,670. Tuition installment plan (Insured Tuition Payment Plan, Key Tuition Payment Plan, monthly payment plans). Need-based scholarship grants available. In 2005–06, 12% of upper-school students received aid. Total amount of financial aid awarded in 2005–06: $630,839.

Admissions Traditional secondary-level entrance grade is 9. ISEE or SSAT required. Deadline for receipt of application materials: January 15. Application fee required: $60. Interview required.

Athletics Interscholastic: baseball (boys), basketball (b,g), cross-country running (b,g), field hockey (g), football (b), lacrosse (b,g), soccer (b,g), softball (g), squash (b,g), tennis (b,g), track and field (b,g), wrestling (b); intramural: weight lifting (b,g); coed interscholastic: fitness, golf, outdoor education, physical fitness, physical training, strength & conditioning, swimming and diving, weight training, winter (indoor) track; coed intramural: martial arts, outdoor education. 1 PE instructor, 65 coaches, 1 trainer.

Computers Computers are regularly used in art, English, foreign language, history, mathematics, music, science classes. Computer network features include on-campus library services, CD-ROMs, online commercial services, Internet access, DVD, wireless campus network.

Contact Liza Hodskins, Admission Services Coordinator. 703-749-6313. Fax: 703-356-1764. Web site: www.potomacschool.org.

POUGHKEEPSIE DAY SCHOOL

260 Boardman Road
Poughkeepsie, New York 12603
Head of School: Liz Vinogradov

General Information Coeducational day college-preparatory and arts school. Grades PK–12. Founded: 1934. Setting: suburban. Nearest major city is New York. 35-acre campus. 2 buildings on campus. Approved or accredited by New York State Association of Independent Schools and New York Department of Education. Member of National Association of Independent Schools. Endowment: $2.3 million. Total enrollment: 324. Upper school average class size: 12. Upper school faculty-student ratio: 1:6.

Upper School Student Profile Grade 9: 16 students (2 boys, 14 girls); Grade 10: 32 students (15 boys, 17 girls); Grade 11: 29 students (17 boys, 12 girls); Grade 12: 33 students (15 boys, 18 girls).

Faculty School total: 51. In upper school: 6 men, 11 women; 9 have advanced degrees.

Subjects Offered 3-dimensional art, Advanced Placement courses, advanced studio art-AP, African drumming, algebra, American literature, ancient history, art history, arts, biology, calculus, calculus-AP, chamber groups, chemistry, collage and assemblage, college admission preparation, community service, computer programming, computer science, conflict resolution, contemporary art, creative arts, creative writing, current events, decision making skills, drama, drawing, ecology, English, English literature, English-AP, ensembles, environmental science, European civilization, European history, European literature, expository writing, film appreciation, fine arts, French, French-AP, geography, geology, geometry, guitar, history, independent study, instrumental music, integrated arts, Internet research, jazz ensemble, keyboarding/computer, lab science, leadership skills, life saving, life skills, literary magazine, literature, literature-AP, mathematics, modern European history, multicultural literature, multicultural studies, music, music appreciation, music composition, music performance, music theory, music theory-AP, musical productions, musical theater, oil painting, painting, peer counseling, performing arts, photography, physical education, physical science, physics, physiology, piano, play production, playwriting, poetry, pre-algebra, printmaking, religion and culture, Russian, SAT preparation, science, senior internship, service learning/internship, Shakespeare, social issues, social studies, Spanish, Spanish-AP, stained glass, strings, studio art, studio art—AP, technical theater, theater arts, theater production, trigonometry, U.S. history, video film production, visual arts, voice ensemble, Web site design, Western civilization, wind ensemble, wind instruments, writing workshop, yearbook.

Graduation Requirements Algebra, arts, biology, calculus, chemistry, classical Greek literature, college planning, electives, English, English literature, foreign language, geometry, interdisciplinary studies, life skills, mathematics, music, performing arts, physical education (includes health), physics, physiology, pre-calculus, SAT preparation, senior internship, senior thesis, trigonometry, visual arts, four-week off-campus senior internship. Community service is required.

Special Academic Programs Advanced Placement exam preparation in 6 subject areas; independent study; term-away projects; academic accommodation for the gifted, the musically talented, and the artistically talented.

College Placement 25 students graduated in 2005; all went to college, including Barnard College; Brown University; Cornell University; Ithaca College; Vassar College; Yale University. Mean SAT verbal: 648, mean SAT math: 590. 65% scored over 600 on SAT verbal, 50% scored over 600 on SAT math.

Student Life Upper grades have student council, honor system. Discipline rests equally with students and faculty.

Summer Programs Art/fine arts programs offered; session focuses on drama; held on campus; accepts boys and girls; open to students from other schools. 24 students usually enrolled. 2006 schedule: June 26 to August 5. Application deadline: May.

Tuition and Aid Day student tuition: $17,810. Tuition installment plan (monthly payment plans, individually arranged payment plans, The Tuition Refund Plan). Need-based scholarship grants, tuition reduction for children of full-time faculty and staff available. In 2005–06, 25% of upper-school students received aid. Total amount of financial aid awarded in 2005–06: $302,031.

Admissions Traditional secondary-level entrance grade is 9. For fall 2005, 21 students applied for upper-level admission, 15 were accepted, 7 enrolled. School's own exam required. Deadline for receipt of application materials: January 15. Application fee required: $50. On-campus interview required.

Athletics Interscholastic: baseball (boys); basketball (b,g), soccer (b,g), softball (g); intramural: baseball (b), basketball (b,g), softball (g); coed interscholastic: soccer, ultimate Frisbee; coed intramural: alpine skiing, basketball, bicycling, cooperative games, cross-country running, dance, figure skating, fitness walking, Frisbee, hiking/backpacking, ice skating, jogging, life saving, outdoor education, outdoor skills, skiing (downhill), snowboarding, soccer, swimming and diving, tennis, ultimate Frisbee, volleyball, walking, yoga. 2 PE instructors, 5 coaches.

Computers Computers are regularly used in all academic, college planning, desktop publishing, journalism, library skills, literary magazine, media, music, newspaper, photography, photojournalism, SAT preparation, video film production, Web site design, yearbook classes. Computer network features include campus e-mail, on-campus library services, CD-ROMs, Internet access, file transfer, office computer access, DVD, wireless campus network, EBSCOhost[00ae], Maps101, Web Feet Guides Gale databases, ProQuest, unitedstreaming¿, Britannica Online, World Book Online, Grolier Online.

Contact Tammy Reilly, Admissions Assistant. 845-462-7600 Ext. 201. Fax: 845-462-7602. E-mail: treilly@poughkeepsieday.org. Web site: www.poughkeepsieday.org/.

POWERS CATHOLIC HIGH SCHOOL

G-2040 West Carpenter Road
Flint, Michigan 48505-1028
Head of School: Mr. Thomas H. Furnas

General Information Coeducational day college-preparatory, arts, and religious studies school, affiliated with Roman Catholic Church. Grades 9–12. Founded: 1970.

Setting: urban. 1 building on campus. Approved or accredited by North Central Association of Colleges and Schools and Michigan Department of Education. Total enrollment: 692. Upper school average class size: 25. Upper school faculty-student ratio: 1:18.

Upper School Student Profile Grade 10: 198 students (100 boys, 98 girls); Grade 11: 158 students (91 boys, 67 girls); Grade 12: 183 students (92 boys, 91 girls). 75% of students are Roman Catholic.

Faculty School total: 46. In upper school: 37 have advanced degrees.

Subjects Offered Government, government-AP, health, honors algebra, honors English, honors geometry, interdisciplinary studies, macroeconomics-AP, marching band, math analysis, math applications, mechanical drawing, mythology, physics, pre-algebra, pre-calculus, psychology-AP, public speaking, religion, social justice, sociology, Spanish, state history, studio art—AP, theology, trigonometry, wind ensemble, world geography, world history, world issues, world religions, yearbook.

Graduation Requirements American history, English, government, health, mathematics, science, theology, world history.

Special Academic Programs Advanced Placement exam preparation in 8 subject areas; honors section; remedial reading and/or remedial writing; remedial math.

College Placement 189 students graduated in 2005; 184 went to college, including Central Michigan University; Grand Valley State University; Michigan State University; University of Michigan; Western Michigan University. Other: 5 had other specific plans. Mean SAT verbal: 587, mean SAT math: 582, mean composite ACT: 23.

Student Life Upper grades have specified standards of dress, student council. Discipline rests primarily with faculty. Attendance at religious services is required.

Tuition and Aid Day student tuition: $5300. Tuition installment plan (monthly payment plans). Need-based scholarship grants available.

Admissions Traditional secondary-level entrance grade is 9. ACT-Explore required. Deadline for receipt of application materials: none. Application fee required: $50. Interview required.

Athletics Interscholastic: alpine skiing (boys, girls), baseball (b), basketball (b,g), dance team (g), diving (b,g), football (b), golf (b,g), ice hockey (b), lacrosse (b,g), nautilus (b,g), soccer (b,g), swimming and diving (b,g), track and field (b,g), volleyball (g), wrestling (b); coed interscholastic: cheering, indoor track, power lifting, strength & conditioning; coed intramural: ultimate Frisbee, weight training. 1 PE instructor.

Computers Computers are regularly used in accounting, business applications, drafting, graphic design, keyboarding, yearbook classes. Computer resources include on-campus library services, Internet access.

Contact Ms. Sally Bartos, Assistant Principal for Instruction. 810-591-4741. Fax: 810-591-0383. E-mail: sbartos@powerscatholic.org. Web site: www.powerscatholic.org.

THE PRAIRIE SCHOOL
4050 Lighthouse Drive
Racine, Wisconsin 53402
Head of School: Mr. Wm. Mark H. Murphy

petersons.com

General Information Coeducational day college-preparatory and arts school. Grades PK–12. Founded: 1965. Setting: small town. Nearest major city is Milwaukee. 33-acre campus. 1 building on campus. Approved or accredited by Independent Schools Association of the Central States and Wisconsin Department of Education. Member of National Association of Independent Schools. Endowment: $36 million. Total enrollment: 662. Upper school average class size: 15. Upper school faculty-student ratio: 1:15.

Upper School Student Profile Grade 9: 74 students (40 boys, 34 girls); Grade 10: 55 students (23 boys, 32 girls); Grade 11: 53 students (21 boys, 32 girls); Grade 12: 63 students (32 boys, 31 girls).

Faculty School total: 76. In upper school: 14 men, 14 women; 18 have advanced degrees.

Subjects Offered Algebra, American history, American history-AP, American literature, art, biology, biology-AP, calculus, calculus-AP, ceramics, chemistry, chemistry-AP, choir, community service, comparative religion, computer science, digital imaging, drama, drawing and design, earth and space science, earth science, ecology, economics, English, English literature, English-AP, environmental science, environmental science-AP, European history, European history-AP, fine arts, French, French language-AP, geometry, glassblowing, government/civics, health, history, international relations, jazz ensemble, mathematics, multicultural literature, music, music theory-AP, orchestra, photography, physical education, physics, physics-AP, pre-calculus, probability and statistics, public speaking, science, social studies, Spanish, Spanish language-AP, speech, study skills, theater, trigonometry, Western literature, world history, world literature.

Graduation Requirements Arts and fine arts (art, music, dance, drama), English, foreign language, mathematics, physical education (includes health), science, social studies (includes history), study skills, Spring Interim Program (including on-campus seminars, community service, off-campus internships), 100-hour service requirement.

Special Academic Programs Advanced Placement exam preparation in 11 subject areas; honors section; independent study; term-away projects; academic accommodation for the gifted, the musically talented, and the artistically talented; remedial reading and/or remedial writing; ESL (2 students enrolled).

College Placement 51 students graduated in 2005; all went to college, including Montana State University; Northwestern University; Tulane University; University of Wisconsin–Madison; University of Wisconsin–Milwaukee. Median SAT math: 600, median combined SAT: 1230, median composite ACT: 26.

Student Life Upper grades have specified standards of dress, student council, honor system. Discipline rests primarily with faculty.

Summer Programs Enrichment, advancement, ESL, art/fine arts, computer instruction programs offered; session focuses on enrichment and athletics; held on campus; accepts boys and girls; open to students from other schools. 200 students usually enrolled. 2006 schedule: June 19 to August 18. Application deadline: none.

Tuition and Aid Day student tuition: $11,050. Tuition installment plan (FACTS Tuition Payment Plan). Tuition reduction for siblings, merit scholarship grants, need-based scholarship grants available. In 2005–06, 43% of upper-school students received aid; total upper-school merit-scholarship money awarded: $135,400. Total amount of financial aid awarded in 2005–06: $528,450.

Admissions Traditional secondary-level entrance grade is 9. For fall 2005, 28 students applied for upper-level admission, 24 were accepted, 18 enrolled. Admissions testing, school's own exam or TerraNova required. Deadline for receipt of application materials: none. Application fee required: $50. On-campus interview required.

Athletics Interscholastic: baseball (boys), basketball (b,g), soccer (b,g), tennis (b,g), volleyball (g); coed interscholastic: cross-country running, golf, outdoor activities, track and field. 7 PE instructors, 13 coaches, 1 trainer.

Computers Computers are regularly used in all academic classes. Computer network features include on-campus library services, CD-ROMs, Internet access, file transfer, wireless campus network.

Contact Mrs. Molly Lofquist, Director of Admissions. 262-260-4393. Fax: 262-260-3790. E-mail: mlofquist@prairieschool.com. Web site: www.prairieschool.com.

ANNOUNCEMENT FROM THE SCHOOL Serving 663 students in early school through grade 12, Prairie provides a college-preparatory curriculum combining challenging academics, comprehensive fine and creative arts, and a strong athletic program. Courses include film production, glass blowing, and Junior/Senior Interim, a career exploration program. The campus houses the Student Research Center, the Samuel C. Johnson Upper School, computer labs with more than 400 computers, and the new Johnson Athletic Center, which opened in fall 2005.

PRESTON HIGH SCHOOL
2780 Schurz Avenue
Bronx, New York 10465
Head of School: Sr. Lucille M. Coldrick

General Information Girls' day college-preparatory, arts, religious studies, and technology school, affiliated with Roman Catholic Church. Grades 9–12. Founded: 1947. Setting: urban. Nearest major city is New York. 5-acre campus. 2 buildings on campus. Approved or accredited by Middle States Association of Colleges and Schools and New York Department of Education. Total enrollment: 600. Upper school average class size: 25. Upper school faculty-student ratio: 1:12.

Upper School Student Profile Grade 9: 190 students (190 girls); Grade 10: 151 students (151 girls); Grade 11: 137 students (137 girls); Grade 12: 122 students (122 girls). 87% of students are Roman Catholic.

Faculty School total: 45. In upper school: 12 men, 33 women; 33 have advanced degrees.

Subjects Offered Advanced computer applications, advanced math, Advanced Placement courses, algebra, American government-AP, American history, American history-AP, anatomy and physiology, art, biology, biology-AP, British literature, British literature (honors), calculus-AP, Catholic belief and practice, chemistry, chorus, communication skills, computer education, computer graphics, computer programming, creative writing, earth science, economics and history, English, English literature and composition-AP, film history, foreign language, geometry, global studies, government-AP, graphic design, health, honors algebra, honors English, honors geometry, honors U.S. history, honors world history, Italian, Latin, law, media studies, moral theology, music, peer counseling, philosophy, physical education, physics, play/screen writing, religious studies, service learning/internship, Spanish, Spanish language-AP, Spanish literature-AP, women in world history, world literature.

Special Academic Programs Advanced Placement exam preparation in 6 subject areas; honors section; independent study; study at local college for college credit.

College Placement 122 students graduated in 2005; 121 went to college, including Fordham University; Iona College; Manhattan College; New York University; State University of New York at Binghamton; University at Albany, State University of New York. Other: 1 went to work. Mean SAT verbal: 523; mean SAT math: 506.

Student Life Upper grades have uniform requirement, student council, honor system. Discipline rests equally with students and faculty. Attendance at religious services is required.

Summer Programs Remediation, enrichment programs offered; session focuses on enrichment for incoming freshmen; held on campus; accepts girls; not open to students from other schools. 30 students usually enrolled.

Preston High School

Tuition and Aid Day student tuition: $5590. Tuition reduction for siblings, merit scholarship grants, need-based scholarship grants available. In 2005–06, 25% of upper-school students received aid.

Admissions Traditional secondary-level entrance grade is 9. New York Archdiocesan Cooperative Entrance Examination required. Deadline for receipt of application materials: March 8. Application fee required: $75.

Athletics Interscholastic: basketball, cheering, soccer, softball, swimming and diving, track and field, volleyball. 2 PE instructors, 7 coaches.

Computers Computers are regularly used in desktop publishing, graphic design, language development, mathematics classes. Computer network features include on-campus library services, CD-ROMs, Internet access, office computer access, DVD.

Contact Ms. Julia Wall, Director of Freshman Admissions. 718-863-9134 Ext. 132. Fax: 718-863-6125. E-mail: jwall@prestonhs.org. Web site: www.prestonhs.org.

PRESTONWOOD CHRISTIAN ACADEMY

6801 West Park Boulevard
Plano, Texas 75093
Head of School: Mr. Larry Taylor

General Information Coeducational day college-preparatory school, affiliated with Southern Baptist Convention. Grades PK–12. Founded: 1997. Setting: suburban. Nearest major city is Dallas. 44-acre campus. 2 buildings on campus. Approved or accredited by Association of Christian Schools International, Southern Association of Colleges and Schools, and Texas Department of Education. Total enrollment: 1,434. Upper school average class size: 17. Upper school faculty-student ratio: 1:10.

Upper School Student Profile Grade 9: 98 students (49 boys, 49 girls); Grade 10: 102 students (54 boys, 48 girls); Grade 11: 97 students (47 boys, 50 girls); Grade 12: 89 students (37 boys, 52 girls). 71% of students are Southern Baptist Convention.

Faculty School total: 112. In upper school: 16 men, 22 women; 18 have advanced degrees.

Subjects Offered 20th century history, advanced math, Advanced Placement courses, algebra, American government-AP, American history-AP, American literature, American literature-AP, anatomy and physiology, art, art-AP, athletics, band, baseball, basketball, Bible, biology, biology-AP, British literature, British literature-AP, calculus-AP, ceramics, cheerleading, chemistry, choir, Christian doctrine, computer applications, conceptual physics, debate, drama, drawing, economics, English language-AP, ethics, fine arts, foreign language, geometry, golf, government, government-AP, health, honors algebra, honors English, honors geometry, honors U.S. history, honors world history, internship, introduction to theater, leadership education training, learning lab, logic, multimedia, multimedia design, news writing, newspaper, painting, participation in sports, performing arts, personal fitness, philosophy, photo shop, physical fitness, physics, pre-calculus, printmaking, sculpture, service learning/internship, softball, Spanish, Spanish-AP, speech, sports, statistics, student government, studio art, swimming, tennis, theater, theater arts, track and field, U.S. history, volleyball, Web site design, Western literature, world history, world religions, yearbook.

Graduation Requirements 1½ elective credits, algebra, arts and fine arts (art, music, dance, drama), Bible, biology, British literature, chemistry, Christian doctrine, computer applications, computers, economics, English, English literature, ethics, foreign language, geometry, government, literature, philosophy, physical education (includes health), physics, speech, U.S. history, Western literature, world history.

Special Academic Programs Advanced Placement exam preparation in 7 subject areas; honors section; academic accommodation for the gifted.

College Placement 68 students graduated in 2005; 67 went to college, including Baylor University; Dallas Baptist University; Hardin-Simmons University; Ouachita Baptist University; Texas A&M University; University of Oklahoma. Other: 1 entered a postgraduate year. Median SAT verbal: 600, median SAT math: 540, median combined SAT: 1680, median composite ACT: 23. 50% scored over 600 on SAT verbal, 25% scored over 600 on SAT math, 25% scored over 1800 on combined SAT, 21% scored over 26 on composite ACT.

Student Life Upper grades have uniform requirement, student council, honor system. Discipline rests primarily with faculty.

Summer Programs Remediation, enrichment, sports, art/fine arts, computer instruction programs offered; session focuses on enrichment, advancement, sports and fine arts; held on campus; accepts boys and girls; open to students from other schools. 350 students usually enrolled. 2006 schedule: June 1 to August 1. Application deadline: April 1.

Tuition and Aid Day student tuition: $11,158–$11,709. Tuition installment plan (FACTS Tuition Payment Plan, monthly payment plans, individually arranged payment plans). Tuition reduction for siblings, need-based scholarship grants available. In 2005–06, 14% of upper-school students received aid. Total amount of financial aid awarded in 2005–06: $217,328.

Admissions For fall 2005, 111 students applied for upper-level admission, 86 were accepted, 75 enrolled. ISEE or Stanford Achievement Test required. Deadline for receipt of application materials: none. Application fee required: $100. Interview required.

Athletics Interscholastic: baseball (boys), basketball (b,g), cheering (g), cross-country running (b,g), drill team (g), football (b), golf (b,g), soccer (b,g), softball (g), swimming and diving (b,g), tennis (b,g), track and field (b,g), volleyball (g). 2 PE instructors, 23 coaches, 1 trainer.

Computers Computers are regularly used in all academic, technology classes. Computer network features include on-campus library services, CD-ROMs, Internet access, file transfer, office computer access, DVD, wireless campus network.

Contact Ms. Marsha Backof, Admissions Assistant. 972-930-4010. Fax: 972-930-4008. E-mail: mbackof@prestonwoodchristian.org. Web site: www.prestonwoodchristian.org.

PRINCETON DAY SCHOOL

PO Box 75
The Great Road
Princeton, New Jersey 08542
Head of School: Dr. Judith R. Fox

General Information Coeducational day college-preparatory and arts school. Grades JK–12. Founded: 1899. Setting: suburban. Nearest major city is Trenton. 105-acre campus. 14 buildings on campus. Approved or accredited by Middle States Association of Colleges and Schools and New Jersey Association of Independent Schools. Member of National Association of Independent Schools and Secondary School Admission Test Board. Endowment: $25 million. Total enrollment: 895. Upper school average class size: 13. Upper school faculty-student ratio: 1:8.

Upper School Student Profile Grade 9: 94 students (49 boys, 45 girls); Grade 10: 94 students (53 boys, 41 girls); Grade 11: 90 students (46 boys, 44 girls); Grade 12: 94 students (53 boys, 41 girls).

Faculty School total: 124. In upper school: 32 men, 20 women.

Subjects Offered 3-dimensional design, algebra, American government, American government-AP, American history, American history-AP, American literature, ancient history, architectural drawing, architecture, art, art history, art history-AP, Bible studies, biology, biology-AP, calculus, calculus-AP, ceramics, chemistry, chemistry-AP, choir, community service, comparative government and politics-AP, computer math, computer programming, computer science, creative writing, debate, drafting, drama, economics, English, English literature, environmental science, ethics, European history, film, fine arts, forensic science, French, French language-AP, French literature-AP, geometry, health, history, industrial arts, jazz ensemble, Latin, Latin-AP, leadership training, mathematics, music history, music theory, philosophy, photography, physical education, physics, physics-AP, physiology, religion, science, social studies, Spanish, Spanish language-AP, Spanish literature-AP, speech, statistics, theater, trigonometry, world history, world literature, writing.

Graduation Requirements Art, English, foreign language, mathematics, physical education (includes health), religion (includes Bible studies and theology), science, social studies (includes history), senior project (six-week off-campus assignment). Community service is required.

Special Academic Programs Advanced Placement exam preparation in 13 subject areas; honors section; accelerated programs; independent study; term-away projects; study at local college for college credit; domestic exchange program; study abroad; academic accommodation for the gifted, the musically talented, and the artistically talented.

College Placement 80 students graduated in 2005; all went to college, including Boston University; Carnegie Mellon University; Columbia College; Princeton University; The George Washington University; University of Pennsylvania. Mean SAT verbal: 660, mean SAT math: 680.

Student Life Upper grades have specified standards of dress, student council, honor system. Discipline rests equally with students and faculty.

Summer Programs Remediation, enrichment, sports, art/fine arts, computer instruction programs offered; held on campus; accepts boys and girls; open to students from other schools. 1300 students usually enrolled. 2006 schedule: June 7 to August 4. Application deadline: none.

Tuition and Aid Day student tuition: $23,600. Tuition installment plan (Key Tuition Payment Plan, monthly payment plans, individually arranged payment plans). Need-based scholarship grants available. In 2005–06, 19% of upper-school students received aid. Total amount of financial aid awarded in 2005–06: $2,290,100.

Admissions Traditional secondary-level entrance grade is 9. SSAT and writing sample required. Deadline for receipt of application materials: January 6. Application fee required: $50. Interview required.

Athletics Interscholastic: baseball (boys), basketball (b,g), cross-country running (b,g), fencing (b,g), field hockey (g), football (b), ice hockey (b,g), lacrosse (b,g), soccer (b,g), softball (g), tennis (b,g), volleyball (g); coed interscholastic: figure skating, golf, independent competitive sports, squash, weight training; coed intramural: cricket, ropes courses, ultimate Frisbee, weight lifting, yoga. 7 PE instructors, 19 coaches, 1 trainer.

Computers Computers are regularly used in all classes. Computer network features include campus e-mail, on-campus library services, CD-ROMs, online commercial services, Internet access, file transfer, wireless campus network.

Contact Mrs. Lisa Smoots, Office Manager. 609-924-6700 Ext. 1200. Fax: 609-924-8944. E-mail: lsmoots@pds.org. Web site: www.pds.org.

ANNOUNCEMENT FROM THE SCHOOL Headed by Dr. Judith Fox since 2001, the School complex is bright, modern, and comfortable. It offers exceptional educational resources, including 3 libraries, computers in every grade level linked through PDS Net, a newly renovated campus center, and a

400-seat theater. Beyond the buildings lie 105 acres that offer excellent sports facilities, including 4 new playing fields, a synthetic-turf field, and a skating rink. Over the past 5 years, more than 90% of Princeton Day School graduates have been accepted by colleges and universities that rate themselves "most difficult" according to Thomson Peterson's.

See full description on page 986.

PROCTOR ACADEMY

PO Box 500
204 Main Street
Andover, New Hampshire 03216
Head of School: Mr. Michael Henriques

General Information Coeducational boarding and day college-preparatory, arts, technology, and environmental studies school. Grades 9–12. Founded: 1848. Setting: rural. Nearest major city is Concord. Students are housed in single-sex dormitories. 3,000-acre campus. 45 buildings on campus. Approved or accredited by Association for Experiential Education, Association of Independent Schools in New England, Independent Schools of Northern New England, New England Association of Schools and Colleges, The Association of Boarding Schools, and New Hampshire Department of Education. Member of National Association of Independent Schools and Secondary School Admission Test Board. Endowment: $25 million. Total enrollment: 345. Upper school average class size: 12. Upper school faculty-student ratio: 1:4.

Upper School Student Profile Grade 9: 66 students (34 boys, 32 girls); Grade 10: 89 students (46 boys, 43 girls); Grade 11: 108 students (61 boys, 47 girls); Grade 12: 82 students (46 boys, 36 girls); Postgraduate: 5 students (4 boys, 1 girl). 80% of students are boarding students. 34% are state residents. 27 states are represented in upper school student body. 4% are international students. International students from Bermuda, Cameroon, Germany, Israel, Republic of Korea, and United Kingdom; 4 other countries represented in student body.

Faculty School total: 88. In upper school: 39 men, 49 women; 44 have advanced degrees; 35 reside on campus.

Subjects Offered Algebra, American history, American literature, art, art history, biology, boat building, calculus, ceramics, chemistry, computer math, computer programming, creative writing, drama, economics, English, English literature, environmental science, European history, fine arts, finite math, forestry, French, geometry, health, history, industrial arts, mathematics, Middle Eastern history, music, music history, music technology, Native American history, performing arts, photography, physical education, physics, piano, play/screen writing, poetry, political thought, probability and statistics, psychology, public speaking, publications, robotics, science, senior project, social science, Spanish, sports medicine, studio art, study skills, the Web, theater, theater history, U.S. government and politics-AP, U.S. history-AP, Vietnam history, voice, voice ensemble, wilderness experience, woodworking, world literature, writing, writing workshop.

Graduation Requirements Arts and fine arts (art, music, dance, drama), English, foreign language, mathematics, science, social science, social sciences.

Special Academic Programs Advanced Placement exam preparation in 11 subject areas; honors section; term-away projects; study at local college for college credit; study abroad; academic accommodation for the gifted; programs in general development for dyslexic students.

College Placement 90 students graduated in 2005; 87 went to college, including Bates College; Skidmore College; The Colorado College; University of Colorado at Boulder; University of New Hampshire. Other: 3 had other specific plans. Mean SAT verbal: 555, mean SAT math: 565. 20% scored over 600 on SAT verbal, 24% scored over 600 on SAT math.

Student Life Upper grades have student council, honor system. Discipline rests equally with students and faculty.

Tuition and Aid Day student tuition: $21,900; 7-day tuition and room/board: $36,000. Tuition installment plan (Academic Management Services Plan, monthly payment plans, individually arranged payment plans). Need-based scholarship grants available. In 2005–06, 26% of upper-school students received aid. Total amount of financial aid awarded in 2005–06: $1,771,800.

Admissions Traditional secondary-level entrance grade is 9. For fall 2005, 485 students applied for upper-level admission, 220 were accepted, 120 enrolled. PSAT or SAT for applicants to grade 11 and 12, SSAT, TOEFL or SLEP, WISC/Woodcock-Johnson or writing sample required. Deadline for receipt of application materials: February 1. Application fee required: $40. On-campus interview required.

Athletics Interscholastic: alpine skiing (boys, girls), baseball (b), basketball (b,g), cross-country running (b,g), field hockey (g), football (b), hockey (b,g), ice hockey (b,g), lacrosse (b,g), nordic skiing (b,g), skiing (downhill) (b,g), snowboarding (b,g), soccer (b,g), softball (g), tennis (b,g), wrestling (b); intramural: alpine skiing (b,g), snowboarding (b,g); coed interscholastic: bicycling, canoeing/kayaking, dance, freestyle skiing, golf, horseback riding, kayaking, ski jumping, skiing (cross-country); coed intramural: aerobics/dance, aerobics/nautilus, back packing, broomball, canoeing/kayaking, climbing, combined training, dance, equestrian sports, fencing, fitness, Frisbee, hiking/backpacking, horseback riding, kayaking, martial arts, modern dance, mountain biking, mountaineering, outdoor activities, outdoor adventure, outdoor education, outdoor recreation, outdoor skills, outdoors, paint ball, rock climbing, running, skiing (downhill), snowshoeing, strength & conditioning, ultimate Frisbee, wall climbing, weight lifting, weight training, wilderness, yoga. 3 coaches, 2 trainers.

Computers Computers are regularly used in all academic classes. Computer network features include campus e-mail, on-campus library services, CD-ROMs, online commercial services, Internet access, file transfer, wireless campus network.

Contact Charlie Durell, Admissions Coordinator. 603-735-6312. Fax: 603-735-6284. E-mail: charlie_durell@proctornet.com. Web site: www.proctoracademy.org.

ANNOUNCEMENT FROM THE SCHOOL Proctor has completed the renovations that transform the Holland Auditorium into the Wise Community Center, which houses the snack bar, game loft, juke box, and wide-screen television. Located at the center of the village campus, the Wise Community Center reflects the school's commitment to community values.

See full description on page 988.

PROFESSIONAL CHILDREN'S SCHOOL

132 West 60th Street
New York, New York 10023
Head of School: Dr. James Dawson

General Information Coeducational boarding and day college-preparatory school. Grades 4–12. Founded: 1914. Setting: urban. 1 building on campus. Approved or accredited by New York State Association of Independent Schools. Member of National Association of Independent Schools. Total enrollment: 201. Upper school average class size: 10. Upper school faculty-student ratio: 1:8.

Upper School Student Profile Grade 9: 27 students (7 boys, 20 girls); Grade 10: 38 students (5 boys, 33 girls); Grade 11: 58 students (12 boys, 46 girls); Grade 12: 41 students (14 boys, 27 girls). 52% are state residents. 18 states are represented in upper school student body. 20% are international students.

Faculty School total: 25. In upper school: 10 men, 12 women; 21 have advanced degrees.

Subjects Offered Advanced math, algebra, American government, American history, biology, calculus, chemistry, chorus, computer education, constitutional history of U.S., constitutional law, creative writing, drama, English, English literature, environmental science, ESL, foreign language, French, general math, geometry, health education, introduction to literature, keyboarding/computer, library research, library skills, physical education, physics, physics-AP, pre-algebra, pre-calculus, Spanish, studio art, studio art-AP, U.S. government, U.S. history.

Graduation Requirements Art, English, foreign language, health, history, mathematics, science.

Special Academic Programs Advanced Placement exam preparation in 1 subject area; ESL (10 students enrolled).

College Placement 50 students graduated in 2005; 30 went to college, including Columbia University; Fordham University; Harvard University; New York University; Stanford University. Other: 10 went to work, 10 had other specific plans.

Student Life Upper grades have student council, honor system. Discipline rests primarily with faculty.

Tuition and Aid Day student tuition: $23,500–$26,000. Tuition installment plan (Academic Management Services Plan). Need-based financial assistance available. In 2005–06, 24% of upper-school students received aid. Total amount of financial aid awarded in 2005–06: $416,262.

Admissions Traditional secondary-level entrance grade is 9. For fall 2005, 123 students applied for upper-level admission, 77 were accepted, 56 enrolled. ERB, ISEE or Stanford Achievement Test required. Deadline for receipt of application materials: none. Application fee required: $50. On-campus interview recommended.

Athletics 1 PE instructor.

Computers Computer network features include on-campus library services, CD-ROMs, Internet access.

Contact Sherrie A. Hinkle, Director of Admissions. 212-582-3116 Ext. 112. Fax: 212-307-6542. E-mail: admit@pcs-nyc.org. Web site: www.pcs-nyc.org.

ANNOUNCEMENT FROM THE SCHOOL Professional Children's School (PCS) provides a college-preparatory curriculum for young people engaged in professional training and/or performance in the arts or sports. Current PCS students include dancers with the New York City Ballet; actors from movies, TV, and Broadway shows; models at such agencies as Ford and Elite; and athletes and musicians who study at institutions such as the Juilliard School.

See full description on page 990.

PROVIDENCE COUNTRY DAY SCHOOL

660 Waterman Avenue
East Providence, Rhode Island 02914-1724
Head of School: Mrs. Susan M. Haberlandt

petersons.com

General Information Coeducational day college-preparatory, arts, and technology school. Grades 5–12. Founded: 1923. Setting: suburban. Nearest major city is Providence. 42-acre campus. 6 buildings on campus. Approved or accredited by Association of Independent Schools in New England, New England Association of Schools and Colleges, and The College Board. Member of National Association of Independent Schools and Secondary School Admission Test Board. Endowment: $800,000. Total enrollment: 311. Upper school average class size: 12. Upper school faculty-student ratio: 1:6.

Upper School Student Profile Grade 9: 69 students (44 boys, 25 girls); Grade 10: 50 students (31 boys, 19 girls); Grade 11: 51 students (24 boys, 27 girls); Grade 12: 41 students (23 boys, 18 girls).

Faculty School total: 49. In upper school: 13 men, 18 women; 31 have advanced degrees.

Subjects Offered Advanced Placement courses, algebra, American government, American history, American history-AP, American literature, art, art history, biology, biology-AP, calculus, calculus-AP, ceramics, chemistry, choir, civics, computer graphics, computer math, computer programming, computer science, conceptual physics, creative writing, drama, earth science, ecology, economics, English, English literature, English literature-AP, English-AP, environmental science, European civilization, European history, expository writing, fine arts, foreign language, French, geography, geometry, government/civics, health, history, journalism, Latin, marine biology, mathematics, modern European history, music, music theory, performing arts, photography, physical education, physics, pre-algebra, pre-calculus, psychology, public speaking, SAT preparation, science, senior internship, social studies, Spanish, studio art, the Sixties, theater, trigonometry, visual arts, women in literature, world history, writing.

Graduation Requirements Arts and fine arts (art, music, dance, drama), English, foreign language, mathematics, physical education (includes health), science, social studies (includes history), senior independent project.

Special Academic Programs Advanced Placement exam preparation in 11 subject areas; honors section; independent study; term-away projects; study at local college for college credit; study abroad; academic accommodation for the gifted and the artistically talented; programs in English, mathematics, general development for dyslexic students; special instructional classes for deaf students.

College Placement 50 students graduated in 2005; 48 went to college, including Furman University; Hampden-Sydney College; The University of North Carolina at Chapel Hill; University of Florida; University of Georgia; Virginia Polytechnic Institute and State University. Other: 2 entered a postgraduate year.

Student Life Upper grades have specified standards of dress, student council, honor system. Discipline rests equally with students and faculty.

Tuition and Aid Day student tuition: $17,700. Tuition installment plan (monthly payment plans). Need-based scholarship grants available. In 2005–06, 30% of upper-school students received aid. Total amount of financial aid awarded in 2005–06: $820,000.

Admissions Traditional secondary-level entrance grade is 9. For fall 2005, 130 students applied for upper-level admission, 90 were accepted, 38 enrolled. ISEE or SSAT required. Deadline for receipt of application materials: February 1. Application fee required: $50. On-campus interview required.

Athletics Interscholastic: baseball (boys, girls), basketball (b,g), cross-country running (g), football (b,g), ice hockey (g), lacrosse (b,g), soccer (b,g), tennis (b,g), wrestling (b); coed interscholastic: crew, golf, sailing; coed intramural: volleyball, weight lifting. 2 PE instructors, 5 coaches, 1 trainer.

Computers Computers are regularly used in art, English, foreign language, history, mathematics, music, science classes. Computer network features include campus e-mail, on-campus library services, CD-ROMs, online commercial services, Internet access, file transfer, office computer access.

Contact Ms. Suzanne L. Bailey, Director of Admissions. 401-438-5170 Ext. 137. Fax: 401-435-4514. E-mail: bailey@providencecountryday.org. Web site: www.providencecountryday.org.

ANNOUNCEMENT FROM THE SCHOOL Providence Country Day School is pleased to announce that it is the recipient of the Champlin Foundations grant for the establishment of The Shurman Center for Global Understanding and Language Studies. Using state-of-the-art technology, the center will enrich students' ability to learn about all aspects of foreign language study as well as different cultures throughout the world.

See full description on page 992.

PROVIDENCE HIGH SCHOOL

511 South Buena Vista Street
Burbank, California 91505-4865
Head of School: Mrs. Michele Schulte

General Information Coeducational day college-preparatory, arts, religious studies, and technology school, affiliated with Roman Catholic Church. Grades 9–12. Founded: 1955. Setting: urban. Nearest major city is Los Angeles. 4-acre campus. 6 buildings on campus. Approved or accredited by National Catholic Education Association, Western Association of Schools and Colleges, and California Department of Education. Total enrollment: 580. Upper school average class size: 25. Upper school faculty-student ratio: 1:20.

Upper School Student Profile Grade 9: 178 students (78 boys, 100 girls); Grade 10: 158 students (73 boys, 85 girls); Grade 11: 115 students (45 boys, 70 girls); Grade 12: 129 students (57 boys, 72 girls). 61.1% of students are Roman Catholic.

Faculty School total: 38. In upper school: 15 men, 22 women; 23 have advanced degrees.

Subjects Offered Accounting, algebra, American government-AP, American history, American literature, Bible studies, biology, biology-AP, calculus, ceramics, chemistry, chorus, communications, community service, computer science, drama, economics, economics-AP, English, English literature, English literature and composition-AP, environmental science, ethics, film, fine arts, French, French-AP, geography, geometry, graphic arts, health, history, journalism, law, mathematics, media studies, music, photography, physical education, physics, pre-calculus, psychology, religion, science, social studies, Spanish, Spanish-AP, theater, trigonometry, U.S. government, U.S. government-AP, U.S. history-AP, United States government-AP, video, video and animation, video film production, visual and performing arts, volleyball, weight fitness, weight training, world cultures, world geography, world history, world religions, world religions, writing, writing fundamentals, yearbook.

Graduation Requirements Art, computer science, economics, English, ethics, foreign language, humanities, mathematics, philosophy, physical education (includes health), religion (includes Bible studies and theology), science, social studies (includes history), sociology, speech, completion of Christian Service hours.

Special Academic Programs Advanced Placement exam preparation in 11 subject areas; honors section; academic accommodation for the musically talented and the artistically talented.

College Placement 129 students graduated in 2005; 120 went to college, including California State University, Northridge; Loyola Marymount University; Pasadena City College; University of California, Irvine; University of California, Riverside; University of Southern California. Other: 9 had other specific plans. Mean SAT verbal: 538, mean SAT math: 541. 26% scored over 600 on SAT verbal, 25% scored over 600 on SAT math.

Student Life Upper grades have uniform requirement, student council. Discipline rests equally with students and faculty. Attendance at religious services is required.

Summer Programs Remediation, enrichment, advancement, sports, art/fine arts, computer instruction programs offered; session focuses on remediation and extra-curricular activities; held on campus; accepts boys and girls; open to students from other schools. 252 students usually enrolled. 2006 schedule: June 26 to July 27. Application deadline: June 22.

Tuition and Aid Day student tuition: $7700. Tuition installment plan (The Tuition Plan, 1-payment plan: payment in full due July 1st, 2-payment plan: 60% due July 1st—40% January 1st, 5-payment plan: 20% due July 1, September 1, November 1, January 1 and April 1). Tuition reduction for siblings, bursaries, merit scholarship grants, need-based scholarship grants, need-based loans, middle-income loans, paying campus jobs available. In 2005–06, 36% of upper-school students received aid; total upper-school merit-scholarship money awarded: $16,050. Total amount of financial aid awarded in 2005–06: $192,830.

Admissions Traditional secondary-level entrance grade is 9. For fall 2005, 244 students applied for upper-level admission, 181 were accepted, 174 enrolled. Admissions testing required. Deadline for receipt of application materials: January 22. Application fee required: $50. On-campus interview required.

Athletics Interscholastic: aerobics (boys, girls), baseball (b), basketball (b,g), cross-country running (b,g), fitness (b,g), physical fitness (b,g), soccer (b,g), softball (g), strength & conditioning (b,g), volleyball (b,g), weight training (b,g); coed interscholastic: cheering, cross-country running, dance team, track and field. 4 PE instructors, 10 coaches.

Computers Computers are regularly used in yearbook classes. Computer network features include campus e-mail, on-campus library services, CD-ROMs, online commercial services, Internet access, file transfer, office computer access, DVD, wireless campus network, Microsoft Office Suite XP Professional, Extranet portal.

Contact Sr. Renate Hayum SP, Associate Administrator. 818-846-8141 Ext. 109. Fax: 818-846-6510. E-mail: renate.hayumsp@providencehigh.org. Web site: www.providencehigh.org.

PROVIDENCE HIGH SCHOOL

1215 North St. Mary's
San Antonio, Texas 78215-1787
Head of School: Mrs. Bristol

General Information Girls' day college-preparatory, arts, and religious studies school, affiliated with Roman Catholic Church. Grades 6–12. Founded: 1951. Setting: urban. 3-acre campus. 4 buildings on campus. Approved or accredited by Independent Schools Association of the Southwest, Southern Association of Colleges and Schools, Texas Catholic Conference, and Texas Department of Education. Total enrollment: 348. Upper school average class size: 22. Upper school faculty-student ratio: 1:10.
Upper School Student Profile Grade 9: 66 students (66 girls); Grade 10: 71 students (71 girls); Grade 11: 62 students (62 girls); Grade 12: 85 students (85 girls). 75% of students are Roman Catholic.
Faculty School total: 34. In upper school: 4 men, 26 women; 28 have advanced degrees.
Subjects Offered 3-dimensional art, acting, advanced chemistry, advanced computer applications, advanced math, Advanced Placement courses, aerobics, algebra, American government-AP, American history, American history-AP, American literature, American literature-AP, analysis and differential calculus, anatomy, ancient world history, art, athletics, audio visual/media, band, biology, biology-AP, British literature, British literature-AP, broadcast journalism, broadcasting, calculus-AP, career education internship, Catholic belief and practice, cheerleading, chemistry, choir, choral music, chorus, church history, composition-AP, computer information systems, computer programming, computer technology certification, concert band, concert choir, conflict resolution, creative writing, dance, dance performance, death and loss, desktop publishing, drama, drama performance, drama workshop, economics, English, English composition, English language and composition-AP, English language-AP, English literature, English literature and composition-AP, English literature-AP, English-AP, English/composition-AP, film, fitness, foreign language, French, geography, government, government and politics-AP, history, history-AP, human anatomy, integrated physics, jazz band, journalism, JROTC, JROTC or LEAD (Leadership Education and Development), justice seminar, Latin, Latin-AP, law, leadership, literature and composition-AP, music theory, newspaper, peer ministry, personal fitness, photography, photojournalism, physical education, physical fitness, physical science, physics, play production, portfolio art, probability and statistics, psychology, social justice, sociology, softball, Spanish, Spanish language-AP, Spanish-AP, speech, sports, statistics-AP, street law, student government, student publications, tennis, the Web, theater, theater arts, theater design and production, theater history, theater production, theology, U.S. government and politics, U.S. government and politics-AP, U.S. history, U.S. history-AP, volleyball, Web site design, weight fitness, world civilizations, world geography, world history, yearbook.
Special Academic Programs Advanced Placement exam preparation in 9 subject areas; honors section; independent study; study at local college for college credit; academic accommodation for the gifted, the musically talented, and the artistically talented; remedial reading and/or remedial writing; remedial math.
College Placement 92 students graduated in 2005; all went to college, including St. Mary's University of San Antonio; Texas A&M University; The University of Texas at Austin; The University of Texas at San Antonio.
Student Life Upper grades have uniform requirement, student council. Discipline rests primarily with faculty. Attendance at religious services is required.
Summer Programs Remediation, enrichment, advancement, sports, art/fine arts programs offered; held on campus; accepts boys and girls; open to students from other schools. 100 students usually enrolled. 2006 schedule: June 6 to July 1.
Tuition and Aid Merit scholarship grants available.
Admissions Traditional secondary-level entrance grade is 9. High School Placement Test required. Deadline for receipt of application materials: none. No application fee required.
Athletics Interscholastic: basketball, cheering, cross-country running, dance, dance squad, dance team, golf, JROTC drill, soccer, softball, tennis. 2 PE instructors, 7 coaches, 1 trainer.
Computers Computers are regularly used in desktop publishing, journalism, newspaper, Web site design, writing, yearbook classes. Computer resources include on-campus library services, CD-ROMs, online commercial services, Internet access, DVD, online classrooms.
Contact Ms. Farwell, Marketing and Admissions Director. 210-224-6651 Ext. 203. Fax: 210-224-6214. E-mail: kfarwell@providencehs.net. Web site: www.providencehs.net.

PROVIDENCE SCHOOL

2701 Hodges Boulevard
Jacksonville, Florida 32224
Head of School: Mr. Christopher E. Begley

General Information Coeducational day college-preparatory, arts, religious studies, and technology school, affiliated with Church of Christ, Scientist. Grades K–12. Founded: 1997. Setting: suburban. 1 building on campus. Approved or accredited by Association of Christian Schools International, Southern Association of Colleges and Schools, and Florida Department of Education. Total enrollment: 1,170. Upper school average class size: 25. Upper school faculty-student ratio: 1:14.

Faculty School total: 49. In upper school: 20 men, 29 women; 26 have advanced degrees.
Subjects Offered 3-dimensional art, 3-dimensional design, ACT preparation, acting, advanced chemistry, advanced computer applications, advanced math, Advanced Placement courses, advanced studio art-AP, algebra, American government, American history, American history-AP, American legal systems, American literature, American literature-AP, analysis and differential calculus, anatomy and physiology, art, art-AP, athletic training, athletics, ballet, ballet technique, band, baseball, Basic programming, basketball, Bible, biology, biology-AP, British literature, British literature-AP, calculus-AP, career and personal planning, ceramics, character education, cheerleading, chemistry, chemistry-AP, choir, choral music, chorus, Christian education, Christian ethics, civics, civics/free enterprise, college admission preparation, college awareness, college counseling, college placement, college planning, college writing, composition, composition-AP, computer information systems, computer programming, computer-aided design, conceptual physics, concert band, concert bell choir, concert choir, constitutional history of U.S., constitutional law, CPR, dance, dance performance, death and loss, debate, digital imaging, digital photography, drama, dramatic arts, drawing, drawing and design, earth science, economics, English composition, English language and composition-AP, English literature and composition-AP, English-AP, English/composition-AP, European history-AP, first aid, fitness, foreign language, French, geography, geometry, government, government/civics, grammar, guidance, health, health and safety, health and wellness, health education, history, honors algebra, honors English, honors geometry, honors U.S. history, honors world history, human anatomy, human biology, intro to computers, jazz band, jazz dance, jazz ensemble, junior and senior seminars, language and composition, Latin, law and the legal system, law studies, leadership education training, Life of Christ, mathematics-AP, music theory, musical theater, musical theater dance, mythology, newspaper, novels, oceanography, oral expression, painting, peer counseling, performing arts, physical fitness, physical science, physics, physics-AP, physiology-anatomy, poetry, portfolio art, pre-algebra, pre-calculus, probability and statistics, psychology, psychology-AP, reading, reading/study skills, religious studies, research, research and reference, research skills, robotics, SAT/ACT preparation, science, science project, science research, set design, Shakespeare, social skills, social studies, society, politics and law, sociology, Spanish, Spanish literature-AP, speech and debate, speech and oral interpretations, sports, stage design, stagecraft, statistics, student government, student publications, studio art—AP, study skills, tap dance, theater arts, theater design and production, track and field, U.S. government, U.S. history-AP, visual and performing arts, vocal music, Web authoring, Web site design, weight fitness, weight training, Western civilization-AP, wind ensemble, world geography, world history-AP, wrestling, yearbook.
Special Academic Programs Advanced Placement exam preparation in 12 subject areas; honors section; study at local college for college credit.
College Placement 76 students graduated in 2005; 74 went to college, including Florida Atlantic University; Florida Institute of Technology; Florida State University; Samford University; University of Central Florida; University of Florida. Other: 1 went to work, 1 entered military service. Mean SAT verbal: 620, mean SAT math: 590, mean composite ACT: 24.
Student Life Upper grades have uniform requirement, honor system. Discipline rests primarily with faculty. Attendance at religious services is required.
Summer Programs Remediation programs offered; held on campus; accepts boys and girls; not open to students from other schools. 25 students usually enrolled.
Tuition and Aid Tuition installment plan (FACTS Tuition Payment Plan). Tuition reduction for siblings, H.E.R.O.E.S. Scholarships through State of Florida available.
Admissions Traditional secondary-level entrance grade is 9. Achievement tests, OLSAT and English Exam and placement test required. Deadline for receipt of application materials: none. Application fee required: $100. On-campus interview required.
Athletics Interscholastic: aquatics (boys, girls), baseball (b), basketball (b,g), cheering (g), cross-country running (b,g), dance (b,g), dance team (b,g), football (b), golf (b,g), physical fitness (b,g), soccer (b,g), softball (g), strength & conditioning (b,g), tennis (b,g), volleyball (g).
Computers Computer resources include campus e-mail, on-campus library services, CD-ROMs, online commercial services, Internet access, DVD.
Contact Mrs. Linda Gullakson, Admissions. 904-223-5270 Ext. 2117. Fax: 904-223-3028. E-mail: lgullakson@prov.org. Web site: www.prov.org.

PROVO CANYON SCHOOL

Provo, Utah
See Special Needs Schools section.

PULASKI ACADEMY

12701 Hinson Road
Little Rock, Arkansas 72212
Head of School: Mr. Ellis Arnold III

General Information Coeducational day college-preparatory school. Grades PK–12. Founded: 1971. Setting: urban. 16-acre campus. 4 buildings on campus. Approved or accredited by Independent Schools Association of the Central States. Member of

National Association of Independent Schools and Secondary School Admission Test Board. Endowment: $550,000. Total enrollment: 1,292. Upper school average class size: 13. Upper school faculty-student ratio: 1:13.

Upper School Student Profile Grade 9: 110 students (63 boys, 47 girls); Grade 10: 100 students (52 boys, 48 girls); Grade 11: 87 students (39 boys, 48 girls); Grade 12: 97 students (47 boys, 50 girls).

Faculty School total: 112. In upper school: 19 men, 42 women; 14 have advanced degrees.

Subjects Offered Algebra, American government-AP, American history-AP, American literature, anatomy, art, art history, band, biology, biology-AP, calculus, calculus-AP, chemistry, chemistry-AP, chorus, community service, composition-AP, creative writing, debate, design, desktop publishing, drama, drawing, English, English literature, English literature-AP, European history-AP, fine arts, French, French-AP, geometry, German, government and politics-AP, grammar, health, humanities, journalism, Latin, Latin-AP, mathematics, music, music history, music theory, physical education, physical science, physics, physics-AP, physiology, pre-calculus, reading, science, social studies, Spanish, Spanish-AP, speech, statistics, theater, trigonometry, world civilizations, world history, yearbook.

Graduation Requirements Arts and fine arts (art, music, dance, drama), English, foreign language, history, mathematics, physical education (includes health), science. Community service is required.

Special Academic Programs Advanced Placement exam preparation in 16 subject areas; honors section; independent study; study abroad.

College Placement 102 students graduated in 2005; all went to college, including Baylor University; Southern Methodist University; University of Arkansas; University of Mississippi; Vanderbilt University.

Student Life Upper grades have specified standards of dress, student council, honor system. Discipline rests primarily with faculty.

Summer Programs Enrichment, art/fine arts, computer instruction programs offered; session focuses on enrichment opportunities; held on campus; accepts boys and girls; open to students from other schools. 700 students usually enrolled. 2006 schedule: June 15 to August 4. Application deadline: none.

Tuition and Aid Day student tuition: $7085. Tuition installment plan (monthly payment plans, school's own payment plan). Tuition reduction for siblings, need-based scholarship grants available. In 2005–06, 10% of upper-school students received aid. Total amount of financial aid awarded in 2005–06: $450,000.

Admissions Traditional secondary-level entrance grade is 9. For fall 2005, 23 students applied for upper-level admission, 18 were accepted, 13 enrolled. Stanford Achievement Test required. Deadline for receipt of application materials: none. Application fee required: $50. On-campus interview recommended.

Athletics Interscholastic: aerobics/dance (girls), aerobics/nautilus (b), aquatics (b,g), baseball (b), basketball (b,g), cheering (g), cross-country running (b,g), dance (g), dance squad (g), dance team (g), diving (b,g), drill team (g), football (b), golf (b,g), pom squad (g), soccer (b,g), softball (g), swimming and diving (b,g), tennis (b,g); intramural: fitness (b,g); coed interscholastic: aerobics. 4 PE instructors, 10 coaches, 1 trainer.

Computers Computers are regularly used in business, career exploration, college planning, creative writing, current events, data processing, economics, English, foreign language, geography, human geography—AP, information technology, introduction to technology, mathematics, newspaper, publications, SAT preparation, science, yearbook classes. Computer network features include campus e-mail, on-campus library services, CD-ROMs, Internet access, file transfer.

Contact Gregg R. Ledbetter Sr., Director of Admissions and Financial Assistance. 501-604-1923. Fax: 501-225-1974. E-mail: gregg@pulaskiacademy.org. Web site: www.pulaskiacademy.org.

PUNAHOU SCHOOL
1601 Punahou Street
Honolulu, Hawaii 96822
Head of School: Dr. James K. Scott

General Information Coeducational day college-preparatory school. Grades K–12. Founded: 1841. Setting: urban. 76-acre campus. 15 buildings on campus. Approved or accredited by Western Association of Schools and Colleges and Hawaii Department of Education. Member of National Association of Independent Schools and Secondary School Admission Test Board. Endowment: $131.3 million. Total enrollment: 3,768. Upper school average class size: 25. Upper school faculty-student ratio: 1:12.

Upper School Student Profile Grade 9: 439 students (224 boys, 215 girls); Grade 10: 438 students (220 boys, 218 girls); Grade 11: 435 students (208 boys, 227 girls); Grade 12: 432 students (215 boys, 217 girls).

Faculty School total: 285. In upper school: 64 men, 77 women; 107 have advanced degrees.

Subjects Offered 20th century history, acting, algebra, American culture, American literature, American studies, anatomy and physiology, anthropology, art history-AP, Asian history, Asian literature, astronomy, bioethics, biology, biology-AP, British literature, calculus-AP, calligraphy, ceramics, character education, chemistry, chemistry-AP, child development, Chinese history, chorus, composition, computer science, computer science-AP, conceptual physics, concert band, contemporary issues, creative writing, drawing, economics, English, environmental science-AP, European history, European history-AP, film and literature, French, French language-AP,

genetics, geometry, glassblowing, global issues, government and politics-AP, guidance, Hawaiian history, Hawaiian language, humanities, independent study, integrated science, Japanese, Japanese history, jewelry making, JROTC or LEAD (Leadership Education and Development), keyboarding/computer, law, Mandarin, marching band, marine biology, mechanical drawing, media arts, medieval history, money management, music technology, music theory, oceanography, painting, peer counseling, photography, physical education, physics, physics-AP, pre-calculus, psychology, psychology-AP, religions, science research, sculpture, Shakespeare, social studies, Spanish, Spanish-AP, sports psychology, statistics-AP, studio art, studio art-AP, symphonic band, technical theater, the Sixties, theater design and production, trigonometry, U.S. history, U.S. history-AP, video, video film production, Vietnam, Vietnam history, Western literature, wind ensemble, world civilizations, world literature, writing.

Graduation Requirements English, foreign language, mathematics, physical education (includes health), science, social studies (includes history), visual and performing arts, credits in ethical, spiritual, community responsibility and critical thinking.

Special Academic Programs Advanced Placement exam preparation in 14 subject areas; honors section; accelerated programs; independent study; study abroad.

College Placement 422 students graduated in 2005; 414 went to college, including Loyola Marymount University; New York University; Santa Clara University; University of Hawaii at Manoa; University of Southern California; University of Washington. Other: 2 went to work, 6 had other specific plans. Mean SAT verbal: 623, mean SAT math: 670. 64% scored over 600 on SAT verbal, 87% scored over 600 on SAT math.

Student Life Upper grades have specified standards of dress, student council, honor system. Discipline rests primarily with faculty. Attendance at religious services is required.

Summer Programs Enrichment, advancement, sports, art/fine arts, computer instruction programs offered; session focuses on enrichment and graduation credit; held both on and off campus; held at France, Spain, China, Japan, Italy; accepts boys and girls; open to students from other schools. 4200 students usually enrolled. 2006 schedule: June 13 to July 21. Application deadline: none.

Tuition and Aid Day student tuition: $13,775. Tuition installment plan (monthly payment plans, semester payment plan). Merit scholarship grants, need-based scholarship grants available. In 2005–06, 6% of upper-school students received aid; total upper-school merit-scholarship money awarded: $186,500. Total amount of financial aid awarded in 2005–06: $1,343,000.

Admissions Traditional secondary-level entrance grade is 9. For fall 2005, 407 students applied for upper-level admission, 124 were accepted, 85 enrolled. SAT or SSAT required. Deadline for receipt of application materials: January 31. Application fee required: $75. On-campus interview required.

Athletics Interscholastic: baseball (boys), basketball (b,g), bowling (b,g), canoeing/kayaking (b,g), cross-country running (b,g), diving (b,g), football (b), golf (b,g), gymnastics (b,g), judo (b,g), kayaking (b,g), ocean paddling (b,g), riflery (b,g), soccer (b,g), softball (g), swimming and diving (b,g), tennis (b,g), track and field (b,g), volleyball (b,g), water polo (b,g), wrestling (b,g); coed interscholastic: cheering, sailing. 6 PE instructors, 150 coaches, 3 trainers.

Computers Computers are regularly used in English, foreign language, mathematics, music, science classes. Computer network features include campus e-mail, on-campus library services, CD-ROMs, online commercial services, Internet access, DVD, wireless campus network.

Contact Mrs. Betsy S. Hata, Director of Admission and Financial Aid. 808-944-5714. Fax: 808-943-3602. E-mail: admission@punahou.edu. Web site: www.punahou.edu.

PURCELL MARIAN HIGH SCHOOL
2935 Hackberry Street
Cincinnati, Ohio 45206
Head of School: Mr. Al Early

General Information Coeducational day college-preparatory, general academic, arts, business, religious studies, bilingual studies, and technology school, affiliated with Roman Catholic Church. Grades 9–12. Founded: 1928. Setting: urban. 4-acre campus. 2 buildings on campus. Approved or accredited by National Catholic Education Association and Ohio Department of Education. Total enrollment: 425. Upper school average class size: 15. Upper school faculty-student ratio: 1:11.

Upper School Student Profile 63% of students are Roman Catholic.

Subjects Offered Art, business, calculus-AP, chemistry-AP, computer science-AP, English, English literature-AP, English-AP, fine arts, government-AP, health, mathematics, mathematics-AP, music, physics-AP, religion, science, social studies, technology.

Graduation Requirements Electives, English, mathematics, physical education (includes health), religion (includes Bible studies and theology), science, social studies (includes history), service hours.

Special Academic Programs Advanced Placement exam preparation in 6 subject areas; honors section; study abroad; academic accommodation for the musically talented and the artistically talented; remedial reading and/or remedial writing; remedial math; special instructional classes for students with special needs.

Student Life Upper grades have uniform requirement, student council. Discipline rests equally with students and faculty. Attendance at religious services is required.

Summer Programs Remediation, sports programs offered; session focuses on summer school, basketball camps, volleyball camps; held on campus; accepts boys and girls; open to students from other schools. 2006 schedule: June to August. Application deadline: May.

Tuition and Aid Day student tuition: $6600. Tuition installment plan (monthly payment plans). Tuition reduction for siblings, merit scholarship grants, need-based scholarship grants, paying campus jobs available.

Admissions Traditional secondary-level entrance grade is 9. Placement test required. Deadline for receipt of application materials: March. Application fee required: $195.

Athletics Interscholastic: aquatics (boys, girls), baseball (b), basketball (b,g), bowling (b,g), cheering (b,g), cross-country running (b,g), dance team (g), diving (b,g), football (b), golf (b,g), gymnastics (g), soccer (b,g), softball (g), swimming and diving (b,g), track and field (b,g), ultimate Frisbee (b,g), volleyball (b,g), weight training (b,g), wrestling (b). 1 PE instructor, 64 coaches, 1 trainer.

Computers Computers are regularly used in all academic classes. Computer network features include campus e-mail, on-campus library services, CD-ROMs, Internet access, office computer access, DVD, video editing software.

Contact Director of Marketing and Recruitment. 513-487-3133. Fax: 513-487-3141. Web site: www.purcellmarian.org.

PURNELL SCHOOL

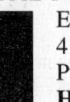

Pottersville, New Jersey
See Special Needs Schools section.

THE PUTNEY SCHOOL

Elm Lea Farm
418 Houghton Brook Road
Putney, Vermont 05346-8675
Head of School: Brian Morgan

General Information Coeducational boarding and day college-preparatory, arts, environmental science, and ESL school. Grades 9–12. Founded: 1935. Setting: rural. Nearest major city is Boston, MA. Students are housed in single-sex dormitories. 500-acre campus. 37 buildings on campus. Approved or accredited by Association of Independent Schools in New England, Independent Schools of Northern New England, New England Association of Schools and Colleges, The Association of Boarding Schools, and Vermont Department of Education. Member of National Association of Independent Schools and Secondary School Admission Test Board. Endowment: $10.9 million. Total enrollment: 226. Upper school average class size: 12. Upper school faculty-student ratio: 1:5.

Upper School Student Profile Grade 9: 39 students (18 boys, 21 girls); Grade 10: 58 students (21 boys, 37 girls); Grade 11: 65 students (32 boys, 33 girls); Grade 12: 64 students (31 boys, 33 girls). 74% of students are boarding students. 30% are state residents. 22 states are represented in upper school student body. 19% are international students. International students from China, France, Germany, Japan, and Republic of Korea; 8 other countries represented in student body.

Faculty School total: 42. In upper school: 20 men, 22 women; 29 have advanced degrees; 22 reside on campus.

Subjects Offered Advanced chemistry, African dance, African drumming, agroecology, algebra, American history, American literature, anatomy, ancient history, art, art history, astronomy, biology, calculus, cartooning, ceramics, chamber groups, chemistry, chorus, college placement, comparative religion, computer science, conservation, creative writing, dance, design, digital photography, drama, drawing, ecology, economics, English, English literature, ensembles, environmental science, environmental systems, ESL, European history, expository writing, fabric arts, fiber arts, fine arts, foods, French, genetics, geometry, history, human development, instruments, jazz, jazz ensemble, Latin American history, literature, mathematics, music, music appreciation, music composition, music history, music theory, musical theater, orchestra, painting, philosophy, photography, physical education, physics, physiology, post-calculus, printmaking, Russian, science, sculpture, sewing, Shakespeare, social studies, Spanish, stained glass, statistics, theater, U.S. history, video film production, vocal jazz, voice, weaving, women's studies, woodworking, work experience, world history, world literature, writing, yearbook, yoga.

Graduation Requirements Arts and fine arts (art, music, dance, drama), electives, English, foreign language, history, human development, lab science, mathematics, physical education (includes health), science, one trimester each of 6 required jobs, including lunch, dinner, barn, dishwashing, general substitute, and a land-use activity, Project Week: two projects each semester of dedicated work, one academic and one non-academic, participation in annual Long Spring camping/backpacking trips.

Special Academic Programs Advanced Placement exam preparation in 2 subject areas; independent study; term-away projects; study abroad; academic accommodation for the gifted, the musically talented, and the artistically talented; ESL (17 students enrolled).

College Placement 62 students graduated in 2005; 60 went to college, including Columbia College; Dartmouth College; Earlham College; Hampshire College; Mount Holyoke College; New York University. Other: 2 had other specific plans. Mean SAT verbal: 632, mean SAT math: 570, mean composite ACT: 25. 59% scored over 600 on SAT verbal, 33% scored over 600 on SAT math, 50% scored over 26 on composite ACT.

Student Life Upper grades have student council, honor system. Discipline rests equally with students and faculty.

Summer Programs Enrichment, ESL, art/fine arts programs offered; session focuses on arts, music, theater, writing, ESL; held on campus; accepts boys and girls; open to students from other schools. 200 students usually enrolled. 2006 schedule: June 26 to August 6. Application deadline: none.

Tuition and Aid Day student tuition: $21,600; 7-day tuition and room/board: $34,300. Tuition installment plan (Academic Management Services Plan, Key Tuition Payment Plan, monthly payment plans, Tuition Management Systems Plan, discount for prepayment). Need-based scholarship grants available. In 2005–06, 38% of upper-school students received aid. Total amount of financial aid awarded in 2005–06: $1,205,820.

Admissions Traditional secondary-level entrance grade is 9. For fall 2005, 157 students applied for upper-level admission, 137 were accepted, 81 enrolled. SSAT required. Deadline for receipt of application materials: January 31. Application fee required: $40. Interview required.

Athletics Interscholastic: bicycling (boys, girls), crew (b,g), cross-country running (b,g), lacrosse (b,g), nordic skiing (b,g), rowing (b,g), running (b,g), skiing (cross-country) (b,g), soccer (b,g); coed interscholastic: alpine skiing, basketball, Frisbee, skiing (downhill), ultimate Frisbee; coed intramural: alpine skiing, back packing, badminton, ballet, basketball, bicycling, broomball, canoeing/kayaking, climbing, crew, cross-country running, dance, equestrian sports, fencing, fitness, fitness walking, Frisbee, hiking/backpacking, horseback riding, jogging, kayaking, lacrosse, modern dance, mountain biking, nordic skiing, outdoor activities, outdoor adventure, outdoor education, outdoor recreation, outdoor skills, outdoors, paddling, physical fitness, rappelling, rock climbing, running, sailboarding, skiing (cross-country), skiing (downhill), snowboarding, snowshoeing, soccer, strength & conditioning, table tennis, tennis, ultimate Frisbee, volleyball, walking, wall climbing, weight training, wilderness, windsurfing, winter walking, yoga. 3 coaches.

Computers Computers are regularly used in English, foreign language, history, mathematics, music, science classes. Computer network features include campus e-mail, on-campus library services, CD-ROMs, online commercial services, Internet access, DVD, wireless campus network.

Contact Ann McBroom, Admission Assistant. 802-387-6219. Fax: 802-387-6278. E-mail: admission@putneyschool.org. Web site: www.putneyschool.org.

QUEEN ANNE SCHOOL

14111 Oak Grove Road
Upper Marlboro, Maryland 20774
Head of School: Mr. J. Temple Blackwood

General Information Coeducational day college-preparatory, arts, religious studies, and technology school, affiliated with Episcopal Church. Grades 6–12. Founded: 1964. Setting: rural. Nearest major city is Washington, DC. 60-acre campus. 8 buildings on campus. Approved or accredited by Accreditation Commission of the Texas Association of Baptist Schools, Middle States Association of Colleges and Schools, and Maryland Department of Education. Member of National Association of Independent Schools and Secondary School Admission Test Board. Total enrollment: 249. Upper school average class size: 15. Upper school faculty-student ratio: 1:8.

Upper School Student Profile Grade 9: 39 students (18 boys, 21 girls); Grade 10: 37 students (15 boys, 22 girls); Grade 11: 36 students (15 boys, 21 girls); Grade 12: 29 students (12 boys, 17 girls). 15% of students are members of Episcopal Church.

Faculty School total: 40. In upper school: 12 men, 22 women; 15 have advanced degrees.

Subjects Offered Algebra, American history, American history-AP, art, art history, arts, biology, biology-AP, calculus, calculus-AP, ceramics, chemistry, chemistry-AP, computer programming, computer science, creative writing, drama, earth science, economics, English, English literature, English literature and composition-AP, environmental science, ethics, fine arts, French, geography, geometry, government/civics, grammar, history, journalism, mathematics, music, philosophy, physical education, physics, physiology, psychology, religion, science, social studies, Spanish, theater, theory of knowledge, trigonometry, world history, world literature.

Graduation Requirements Arts and fine arts (art, music, dance, drama), English, foreign language, mathematics, physical education (includes health), religion (includes Bible studies and theology), science, social studies (includes history).

Special Academic Programs Advanced Placement exam preparation in 7 subject areas; honors section; independent study; study at local college for college credit.

College Placement 29 students graduated in 2005; 28 went to college, including Boston University; Randolph-Macon College. Other: 1 went to work. Mean SAT verbal: 585, mean SAT math: 558.

Student Life Upper grades have specified standards of dress, student council, honor system. Discipline rests equally with students and faculty.

Summer Programs Enrichment, sports, computer instruction programs offered; session focuses on enrichment and sports; held on campus; accepts boys and girls; open to students from other schools. 200 students usually enrolled. 2006 schedule: June 16 to August 20. Application deadline: June 16.

Queen Anne School

Tuition and Aid Day student tuition: $17,700. Tuition installment plan (FACTS Tuition Payment Plan, monthly payment plans, full-payment discount plan, 2- and 10-payment plans). Need-based scholarship grants available. In 2005–06, 36% of upper-school students received aid. Total amount of financial aid awarded in 2005–06: $200,000.

Admissions Traditional secondary-level entrance grade is 9. For fall 2005, 116 students applied for upper-level admission, 76 were accepted, 67 enrolled. ISEE required. Deadline for receipt of application materials: none. Application fee required: $50. On-campus interview required.

Athletics Interscholastic: aerobics/dance (girls), baseball (b), basketball (b,g), cheering (g), dance (g), dance squad (g), dance team (g), lacrosse (b,g), soccer (b,g), softball (g), swimming and diving (b,g), tennis (b,g), volleyball (b,g), wrestling (b); intramural: aerobics/dance (g), archery (b,g), dance (g), dance team (g), volleyball (b,g); coed interscholastic: cross-country running, outdoor education, tennis, track and field. 2 PE instructors, 2 coaches.

Computers Computers are regularly used in English, foreign language, mathematics, music, science classes. Computer network features include campus e-mail, on-campus library services, CD-ROMs, online commercial services, Internet access, DVD, wireless campus network.

Contact Brenda B. Walker, Director of Admissions. 301-249-5000 Ext. 310. Fax: 301-249-3838. E-mail: bwalker@queenanne.org. Web site: www.queenanne.org.

QUEEN MARGARET'S SCHOOL

660 Brownsey Avenue
Duncan, British Columbia V9L 1C2, Canada
Head of School: Pat Rowantree

General Information Girls' boarding and coeducational day college-preparatory and general academic school. Boarding girls grades 6–12, day boys grades K–7, day girls grades K–12. Founded: 1921. Setting: small town. Nearest major city is Victoria, Canada. Students are housed in single-sex dormitories. 27-acre campus. 13 buildings on campus. Approved or accredited by Canadian Association of Independent Schools, Canadian Educational Standards Institute, Pacific Northwest Association of Independent Schools, and British Columbia Department of Education. Member of Canadian Association of Independent Schools. Language of instruction: English. Endowment: CAN$500,000. Total enrollment: 260. Upper school average class size: 18. Upper school faculty-student ratio: 1:7.

Upper School Student Profile 60% of students are boarding students. 35% are province residents. 11 provinces are represented in upper school student body. 50% are international students. International students from Hong Kong, Japan, Mexico, Republic of Korea, Taiwan, and United States; 4 other countries represented in student body.

Faculty School total: 36. In upper school: 8 men, 12 women; 8 have advanced degrees; 2 reside on campus.

Subjects Offered Advanced math, algebra, animal husbandry, animal science, applied skills, art, art-AP, biology, business education, business skills, calculus, calculus-AP, Canadian history, career and personal planning, career exploration, chemistry, chemistry-AP, chorus, college planning, computer science, creative writing, drama, English, English literature, English-AP, equine science, ESL, fine arts, French, French-AP, geography, geometry, grammar, health, history, home economics, instrumental music, Japanese, journalism, mathematics, mathematics-AP, photography, physical education, physics, SAT preparation, science, social studies, Spanish, speech, sports, sports psychology, theater, TOEFL preparation, trigonometry, visual arts, world history, writing.

Graduation Requirements Arts and fine arts (art, music, dance, drama), career and personal planning, computer science, English, foreign language, mathematics, physical education (includes health), science, social studies (includes history). Community service is required.

Special Academic Programs Advanced Placement exam preparation in 7 subject areas; independent study; academic accommodation for the gifted, the musically talented, and the artistically talented; remedial reading and/or remedial writing; remedial math; ESL (30 students enrolled).

College Placement 20 students graduated in 2005; 17 went to college, including McGill University; Queen's University at Kingston; The University of British Columbia; University of Alberta; University of Victoria; Washington State University. Other: 3 had other specific plans.

Student Life Upper grades have uniform requirement, student council. Discipline rests primarily with faculty. Attendance at religious services is required.

Summer Programs ESL programs offered; session focuses on equestrian sports; held on campus; accepts boys and girls; open to students from other schools. 50 students usually enrolled. 2006 schedule: July 6 to August 29. Application deadline: June 15.

Tuition and Aid Day student tuition: CAN$6980–CAN$10,500; 5-day tuition and room/board: CAN$25,000; 7-day tuition and room/board: CAN$25,000–CAN$34,500. Tuition installment plan (Insured Tuition Payment Plan, monthly payment plans). Tuition reduction for siblings, bursaries, merit scholarship grants, tuition reduction for children of staff available. In 2005–06, 30% of upper-school students received aid; total upper-school merit-scholarship money awarded: CAN$50,000. Total amount of financial aid awarded in 2005–06: CAN$76,000.

Admissions Traditional secondary-level entrance grade is 8. Otis-Lennon School Ability Test, SLEP or Stanford Achievement Test required. Deadline for receipt of application materials: none. Application fee required: CAN$75. Interview required.

Athletics Interscholastic: badminton (girls), basketball (g), canoeing/kayaking (g), cooperative games (g), cross-country running (g), dressage (g), equestrian sports (g), field hockey (g), golf (g), horseback riding (g), ocean paddling (g), outdoor activities (g), outdoor recreation (g), paddling (g), rugby (g), soccer (g), tennis (g), track and field (g), volleyball (g); intramural: aerobics (g), aerobics/dance (g), alpine skiing (g), aquatics (g), back packing (g), badminton (g), ball hockey (g), basketball (g), canoeing/kayaking (g), cooperative games (g), Cosom hockey (g), cross-country running (g), dressage (g), equestrian sports (g), field hockey (g), floor hockey (g), Frisbee (g), golf (g), horseback riding (g), indoor hockey (g), indoor soccer (g), jogging (g), nordic skiing (g), ocean paddling (g), outdoor activities (g), outdoor recreation (g), paddling (g), physical fitness (g), physical training (g), rugby (g), skiing (downhill) (g), snowboarding (g), soccer (g), tennis (g), track and field (g), ultimate Frisbee (g), volleyball (g). 2 PE instructors, 2 coaches, 2 trainers.

Computers Computers are regularly used in career education, career exploration, college planning, creative writing, English, ESL, French, information technology, introduction to technology, journalism, mathematics, media arts, science, social science, technology, typing classes. Computer network features include campus e-mail, on-campus library services, CD-ROMs, Internet access, file transfer, office computer access.

Contact Chad Holtum, Director of Admissions, Marketing and Communications. 250-746-4185. Fax: 250-746-4187. E-mail: admissions@qms.bc.ca. Web site: www. qms.bc.ca.

QUEENSWAY CHRISTIAN COLLEGE

1536 The Queensway
Etobicoke, Ontario M8Z 1T5, Canada
Head of School: Mr. John Allardyce

General Information Coeducational day college-preparatory, arts, religious studies, and technology school, affiliated with Pentecostal Assemblies of Canada, Bible Fellowship Church. Grades JK–12. Founded: 1978. Setting: urban. Nearest major city is Toronto, Canada. 1 building on campus. Approved or accredited by Association of Christian Schools International and Ontario Department of Education. Language of instruction: English. Total enrollment: 183. Upper school average class size: 18. Upper school faculty-student ratio: 1:10.

Upper School Student Profile Grade 9: 14 students (8 boys, 6 girls); Grade 10: 14 students (9 boys, 5 girls); Grade 11: 22 students (18 boys, 4 girls); Grade 12: 23 students (10 boys, 13 girls).

Faculty School total: 20. In upper school: 6 men, 4 women; 3 have advanced degrees.

Subjects Offered Algebra, biology, calculus, Canadian geography, Canadian history, career exploration, chemistry, Christian education, civics, computers, dramatic arts, English, family studies, finite math, French, geometry, health education, law, music, physical education, physics, politics, visual arts, work experience, world history, world issues.

Graduation Requirements Arts, Canadian geography, Canadian history, career exploration, civics, English, French, mathematics, physical education (includes health), science, either business or technology, senior survey.

Special Academic Programs Accelerated programs; independent study; study at local college for college credit; domestic exchange program; academic accommodation for the gifted; remedial reading and/or remedial writing; ESL (16 students enrolled).

College Placement 17 students graduated in 2005; 16 went to college, including McMaster University; Queen's University at Kingston; University of Toronto; University of Waterloo; Wilfrid Laurier University. Other: 1 went to work.

Student Life Upper grades have uniform requirement, student council, honor system. Discipline rests primarily with faculty. Attendance at religious services is required.

Tuition and Aid Day student tuition: CAN$7320. Tuition installment plan (monthly payment plans, individually arranged payment plans). Tuition reduction for siblings, merit scholarship grants, need-based scholarship grants available. In 2005–06, 1% of upper-school students received aid.

Admissions Traditional secondary-level entrance grade is 9. For fall 2005, 18 students applied for upper-level admission, 13 were accepted, 13 enrolled. CTBS (or similar from their school) required. Deadline for receipt of application materials: none. Application fee required: CAN$400. On-campus interview required.

Athletics Interscholastic: basketball (boys, girls), cross-country running (b,g), flag football (b), floor hockey (b,g), golf (b), indoor track & field (b,g), running (b,g), softball (b), track and field (b,g), winter (indoor) track (b,g), wrestling (b); intramural: badminton (b,g), ball hockey (b,g), ballet (b,g), baseball (b,g), fitness (b,g), hockey (b), ice hockey (b), in-line hockey (b,g), paddle tennis (b,g), physical fitness (b,g), physical training (b,g), rugby (b), strength & conditioning (b,g); coed interscholastic: aerobics, alpine skiing, aquatics, badminton, baseball, cross-country running, running, softball, swimming and diving, track and field, triathlon, winter (indoor) track; coed intramural: badminton, ball hockey, ballet, baseball, canoeing/kayaking, climbing, combined training, cooperative games, Cosom hockey, curling, fitness, floor hockey, football, gymnastics, independent competitive sports, indoor soccer, life saving, outdoor activities, outdoor recreation, outdoor skills, paddle tennis, physical fitness, physical training, rappelling, rock climbing, ropes courses, skateboarding, snow-

boarding, squash, strength & conditioning, swimming and diving, ultimate Frisbee, wall climbing, whiffle ball. 2 PE instructors, 2 coaches.

Computers Computers are regularly used in all classes. Computer network features include campus e-mail, on-campus library services, CD-ROMs, online commercial services, Internet access, file transfer, office computer access.

Contact Mrs. Sue Broomer. 416-255-6033. Fax: 416-255-7389. E-mail: qcc@ qccollege.com. Web site: www.qccollege.com.

QUIGLEY CATHOLIC HIGH SCHOOL

200 Quigley Drive
Baden, Pennsylvania 15005-1295
Head of School: Dr. Madonna J. Helbling

General Information Coeducational day college-preparatory and religious studies school, affiliated with Roman Catholic Church. Grades 9–12. Founded: 1967. Setting: suburban. Nearest major city is Pittsburgh. 19-acre campus. 1 building on campus. Approved or accredited by National Catholic Education Association and Pennsylvania Department of Education. Endowment: $2.5 million. Total enrollment: 154. Upper school faculty-student ratio: 1:12.

Upper School Student Profile Grade 9: 37 students (14 boys, 23 girls); Grade 10: 41 students (20 boys, 21 girls); Grade 11: 38 students (24 boys, 14 girls); Grade 12: 38 students (17 boys, 21 girls). 95% of students are Roman Catholic.

Faculty School total: 18. In upper school: 10 men, 6 women; 14 have advanced degrees.

Subjects Offered Advanced Placement courses, algebra, American government, American history-AP, American literature, anatomy and physiology, art, athletics, band, baseball, Basic programming, basketball, biology, bookbinding, bowling, British literature, British literature (honors), calculus, calculus-AP, campus ministry, ceramics, cheerleading, chemistry, choir, chorus, church history, composition-AP, computer programming, computer science, concert choir, debate, drawing, ecology, English-AP, European history-AP, French language-AP, geometry, government, guitar, health education, honors algebra, honors world history, library, physical education, physical science, physics, piano, play production, pottery, pre-algebra, pre-calculus, printmaking, religious education, SAT preparation, Spanish, speech and debate, sports, student government, studio art, trigonometry, wrestling, yearbook.

Graduation Requirements Algebra, American government, American history, American history-AP, British literature, British literature (honors), chemistry, church history, computer science, English, English literature, European history, European history-AP, French, geometry, government, health, math review, music, physical science, physics, religion (includes Bible studies and theology), Spanish, U.S. history, 125 hours of service completed by end of senior year.

Special Academic Programs Advanced Placement exam preparation in 3 subject areas; honors section; study at local college for college credit.

College Placement 47 students graduated in 2005; 45 went to college, including Duquesne University; John Carroll University; The Pennsylvania State University University Park Campus; University of Pittsburgh. Other: 2 went to work. Mean SAT verbal: 554, mean SAT math: 545. 32% scored over 600 on SAT verbal, 26% scored over 600 on SAT math, 58% scored over 1800 on combined SAT.

Student Life Upper grades have uniform requirement, student council, honor system. Discipline rests primarily with faculty. Attendance at religious services is required.

Tuition and Aid Day student tuition: $7050. Tuition installment plan (SMART Tuition Payment Plan, individually arranged payment plans, full-payment discount plan). Tuition reduction for siblings, merit scholarship grants, need-based scholarship grants, paying campus jobs available. In 2005–06, 56% of upper-school students received aid; total upper-school merit-scholarship money awarded: $33,594. Total amount of financial aid awarded in 2005–06: $279,953.

Admissions Traditional secondary-level entrance grade is 9. For fall 2005, 13 students applied for upper-level admission, 13 were accepted, 11 enrolled. Iowa Test, CTBS, or TAP, Math Placement Exam or PSAT required. Deadline for receipt of application materials: none. Application fee required: $25. Interview required.

Athletics Interscholastic: aquatics (girls), baseball (b), basketball (b,g), bowling (b,g), cheering (g), cross-country running (b,g), dance team (g), golf (b), gymnastics (g), ice hockey (b), soccer (b,g), softball (g), swimming and diving (g), tennis (g), volleyball (g), wrestling (b); intramural: aerobics (g). 2 PE instructors, 11 coaches, 1 trainer.

Computers Computers are regularly used in newspaper, programming, yearbook classes. Computer resources include on-campus library services, Internet access, office computer access.

Contact Sr. Bridget Reilly, Guidance Counselor. 724-869-2188. Fax: 724-869-2188. E-mail: reilly@qchs.org. Web site: www.qchs.org.

QUINCY NOTRE DAME HIGH SCHOOL

1400 South 11th Street
Quincy, Illinois 62301-7299
Head of School: Mr. Raymond Edward Heilmann

General Information Coeducational day college-preparatory, arts, business, religious studies, and technology school, affiliated with Roman Catholic Church. Grades

9–12. Founded: 1866. Setting: small town. Nearest major city is Springfield. 12-acre campus. 1 building on campus. Approved or accredited by North Central Association of Colleges and Schools and Illinois Department of Education. Endowment: $1 million. Total enrollment: 490. Upper school average class size: 23. Upper school faculty-student ratio: 1:23.

Upper School Student Profile Grade 9: 118 students (64 boys, 54 girls); Grade 10: 132 students (66 boys, 66 girls); Grade 11: 124 students (53 boys, 71 girls); Grade 12: 116 students (66 boys, 50 girls). 98% of students are Roman Catholic.

Faculty School total: 32. In upper school: 15 men, 17 women; 14 have advanced degrees.

Subjects Offered Accounting, algebra, American history, American history-AP, analysis, art, band, biology, business law, business mathematics, calculus-AP, chemistry, choir, chorus, Christian ethics, church history, computer applications, computer skills, consumer economics, design, drawing, geography, geometry, German, government, health education, Hebrew scripture, jazz band, life skills, modern civilization, multimedia, painting, physical education, physical science, physics, physiology, portfolio art, pottery, prayer/spirituality, pre-algebra, print-making, social justice, sociology, Spanish.

Graduation Requirements Arts and fine arts (art, music, dance, drama), computer skills, consumer economics, driver education, English, mathematics, physical education (includes health), religion (includes Bible studies and theology), science, U.S. constitutional history, U.S. government.

Special Academic Programs Advanced Placement exam preparation in 3 subject areas; study at local college for college credit; remedial reading and/or remedial writing; remedial math; special instructional classes for students with Attention Deficit Disorder.

College Placement 131 students graduated in 2005; 127 went to college, including Illinois State University; John Wood Community College; Millikin University; University of Illinois at Urbana–Champaign; Western Illinois University. Other: 2 went to work, 2 entered military service. Mean composite ACT: 22.

Student Life Upper grades have specified standards of dress, student council, honor system. Discipline rests primarily with faculty. Attendance at religious services is required.

Tuition and Aid Tuition installment plan (Private School Aid Service). Tuition reduction for siblings, merit scholarship grants, need-based scholarship grants, middle-income loans, paying campus jobs available. In 2005–06, 35% of upper-school students received aid; total upper-school merit-scholarship money awarded: $3900. Total amount of financial aid awarded in 2005–06: $80,000.

Admissions Traditional secondary-level entrance grade is 9. For fall 2005, 128 students applied for upper-level admission, 128 were accepted, 118 enrolled. Deadline for receipt of application materials: none. Application fee required: $50. Interview recommended.

Athletics Interscholastic: baseball (boys), basketball (b,g), cheering (g), cross-country running (b,g), dance squad (g), drill team (g), football (b), golf (b,g), physical fitness (b,g), soccer (b,g), softball (g), strength & conditioning (b,g), tennis (b,g), volleyball (g), weight training (b,g), wrestling (b). 2 PE instructors, 12 coaches, 1 trainer.

Computers Computer network features include campus e-mail, Internet access.

Contact Mr. Raymond Edward Heilmann, Principal. 217-223-2479. Fax: 217-223-0023. E-mail: rayjudy@dstream.net. Web site: www.quincynotredame.org.

QUINTE CHRISTIAN HIGH SCHOOL

289 Pinnacle Street
Belleville, Ontario K8N 3B3, Canada
Head of School: Mr. Johan Cooke

General Information Coeducational day college-preparatory, general academic, arts, business, vocational, religious studies, bilingual studies, and technology school, affiliated with Evangelical Friends. Grades 9–12. Founded: 1977. Setting: small town. Nearest major city is Toronto, Canada. 5-acre campus. 1 building on campus. Approved or accredited by Christian Schools International, Ontario Ministry of Education, and Ontario Department of Education. Language of instruction: English. Total enrollment: 135. Upper school average class size: 15. Upper school faculty-student ratio: 1:15.

Upper School Student Profile Grade 9: 32 students (13 boys, 19 girls); Grade 10: 30 students (21 boys, 9 girls); Grade 11: 45 students (26 boys, 19 girls); Grade 12: 28 students (16 boys, 12 girls). 100% of students are Evangelical Friends.

Faculty School total: 15. In upper school: 8 men, 7 women; 2 have advanced degrees.

Subjects Offered Accounting, art, Bible, biology, calculus, careers, chemistry, Christian education, civics, computers, drama, English, English literature, ESL, French, geography, history, law, leadership education training, mathematics, mathematics-AP, media, music, peer counseling, physical education, physics, religious education, science, shop, society challenge and change, technical education, transportation technology, world issues, world religions.

Graduation Requirements Accounting, applied arts, careers, Christian education, civics, computers, English, French, geography, mathematics, physical education (includes health), religious education, science, social studies (includes history), world religions.

Special Academic Programs Independent study; programs in English, mathematics, general development for dyslexic students; special instructional classes for students with learning disabilities.

College Placement 31 students graduated in 2005; 26 went to college, including Calvin College; Carleton University; Redeemer University College; Trinity Western University; University of Guelph; University of Waterloo. Other: 1 went to work, 3 had other specific plans. 100% scored over 26 on composite ACT.

Student Life Upper grades have specified standards of dress, student council, honor system. Discipline rests primarily with faculty. Attendance at religious services is required.

Tuition and Aid Day student tuition: CAN$10,900. Tuition installment plan (monthly payment plans, individually arranged payment plans). Tuition reduction for siblings, need-based scholarship grants available. In 2005–06, 14% of upper-school students received aid.

Admissions Traditional secondary-level entrance grade is 9. For fall 2005, 33 students applied for upper-level admission, 33 were accepted, 32 enrolled. Deadline for receipt of application materials: March 31. Application fee required: CAN$250. Interview required.

Athletics Interscholastic: badminton (boys, girls), basketball (b,g), cross-country running (b,g), golf (b,g), rowing (g), track and field (b,g), volleyball (b,g); intramural: basketball (b,g); coed interscholastic: badminton; coed intramural: badminton, fitness walking, indoor soccer, volleyball. 3 PE instructors, 14 coaches.

Computers Computers are regularly used in all classes. Computer network features include CD-ROMs, Internet access, DVD.

Contact Mrs. Hermien Hogewoning, Administrative Assistant. 613-968-7870. Fax: 613-968-7970. E-mail: admin@qchs.ca. Web site: www.qchs.ca.

RABBI ALEXANDER S. GROSS HEBREW ACADEMY

2400 Pine Tree Drive
Miami Beach, Florida 33140
Head of School: Rabbi Mordechai Shifman

General Information Coeducational day college-preparatory, general academic, religious studies, and technology school, affiliated with Jewish faith. Grades N–12. Founded: 1948. Setting: urban. 4-acre campus. 1 building on campus. Approved or accredited by Massachusetts Office of Child Care Services, Southern Association of Colleges and Schools, and Florida Department of Education. Member of Secondary School Admission Test Board. Languages of instruction: English, Spanish, and Hebrew. Endowment: $650,000. Total enrollment: 589. Upper school average class size: 18. Upper school faculty-student ratio: 1:4.

Upper School Student Profile Grade 9: 41 students (22 boys, 19 girls); Grade 10: 34 students (19 boys, 15 girls); Grade 11: 34 students (23 boys, 11 girls); Grade 12: 34 students (16 boys, 18 girls). 100% of students are Jewish.

Faculty School total: 70. In upper school: 14 men, 15 women; 23 have advanced degrees.

Subjects Offered Algebra, audio visual/media, Bible studies, biology, biology-AP, calculus, calculus-AP, chemistry, chemistry-AP, computers, driver education, ecology, economics, English, English-AP, environmental science, geometry, Jewish studies, life science, physical education, physics, political science, pre-calculus, SAT preparation, social studies, statistics-AP, Talmud, technology.

Graduation Requirements Arts and fine arts (art, music, dance, drama), business skills (includes word processing), computer science, English, foreign language, mathematics, physical education (includes health), religion (includes Bible studies and theology), science, social science, social studies (includes history). Community service is required.

Special Academic Programs Advanced Placement exam preparation in 8 subject areas; honors section; independent study; study at local college for college credit; academic accommodation for the gifted; ESL (3 students enrolled).

College Placement 30 students graduated in 2005; 29 went to college, including Columbia College; Florida International University; New York University; University of Maryland, College Park; Yeshiva University. Other: 1 went to work. Mean SAT verbal: 585, mean SAT math: 585. 36% scored over 600 on SAT verbal, 43% scored over 600 on SAT math.

Student Life Upper grades have specified standards of dress, student council, honor system. Discipline rests equally with students and faculty. Attendance at religious services is required.

Tuition and Aid Day student tuition: $12,000. Tuition installment plan (monthly payment plans, individually arranged payment plans). Tuition reduction for siblings, need-based scholarship grants available. In 2005–06, 46% of upper-school students received aid. Total amount of financial aid awarded in 2005–06: $300,000.

Admissions Traditional secondary-level entrance grade is 9. For fall 2005, 35 students applied for upper-level admission, 27 were accepted, 24 enrolled. School's own test required. Deadline for receipt of application materials: none. No application fee required. On-campus interview required.

Athletics Interscholastic: basketball (boys, girls), soccer (b), tennis (b,g), volleyball (g); intramural: basketball (b,g), soccer (b), tennis (b,g), volleyball (g). 2 PE instructors, 3 coaches.

Computers Computers are regularly used in English, mathematics, religion, science classes. Computer network features include campus e-mail, CD-ROMs, Internet access.

Contact Rabbi Mordechai Shifman, Principal of Judaic Studies. 305-532-6421. Fax: 305-535-5670. E-mail: mshifman@rasg.org. Web site: www.rasg.org.

RABUN GAP-NACOOCHEE SCHOOL

339 Nacoochee Drive
Rabun Gap, Georgia 30568
Head of School: Mr. John D. Marshall

General Information Coeducational boarding and day college-preparatory, arts, ESL, and performing arts school, affiliated with Presbyterian Church. Boarding grades 7–12, day grades 6–12. Founded: 1903. Setting: rural. Nearest major city is Atlanta. Students are housed in single-sex dormitories. 1,400-acre campus. 14 buildings on campus. Approved or accredited by Georgia Independent School Association, Southern Association of Colleges and Schools, Southern Association of Independent Schools, The Association of Boarding Schools, and Georgia Department of Education. Member of National Association of Independent Schools and Secondary School Admission Test Board. Endowment: $78 million. Total enrollment: 314. Upper school average class size: 15. Upper school faculty-student ratio: 1:14.

Upper School Student Profile Grade 9: 45 students (24 boys, 21 girls); Grade 10: 64 students (33 boys, 31 girls); Grade 11: 65 students (32 boys, 33 girls); Grade 12: 52 students (18 boys, 34 girls). 47% of students are boarding students. 44% are state residents. 15 states are represented in upper school student body. 16% are international students. International students from Germany, Mexico, Republic of Korea, Saudi Arabia, Taiwan, and Turks and Caicos Islands; 7 other countries represented in student body. 10% of students are Presbyterian.

Faculty School total: 55. In upper school: 24 men, 15 women; 29 have advanced degrees; 36 reside on campus.

Subjects Offered Advanced Placement courses, algebra, American literature, anatomy, ancient world history, art, art history-AP, band, Bible studies, biology, biology-AP, botany, calculus-AP, chemistry, chorus, computer-aided design, creative writing, economics, English literature-AP, environmental science, ESL, European history-AP, finite math, French, French-AP, genetics, geography, geometry, government, health, health education, honors algebra, honors English, honors U.S. history, honors world history, industrial arts, journalism, Latin, life science, mathematics, modern world history, music, orchestra, physical education, physical science, physics, pre-algebra, pre-calculus, psychology, science, Spanish, Spanish-AP, studio art-AP, theater, U.S. history, U.S. history-AP, wind ensemble, world geography, world history, world literature, yearbook.

Graduation Requirements Arts and fine arts (art, music, dance, drama), computer science, English, foreign language, mathematics, physical education (includes health), religion (includes Bible studies and theology), science, senior project, social studies (includes history).

Special Academic Programs Advanced Placement exam preparation in 8 subject areas; honors section; independent study; ESL (34 students enrolled).

College Placement 45 students graduated in 2005; all went to college, including Georgia Southern University; Princeton University; Savannah College of Art and Design; The University of North Carolina at Chapel Hill; University of Georgia; Valdosta State University. Mean SAT verbal: 535, mean SAT math: 575, mean composite ACT: 23. 40% scored over 600 on SAT verbal, 40% scored over 600 on SAT math, 37% scored over 26 on composite ACT.

Student Life Upper grades have uniform requirement, student council, honor system. Discipline rests primarily with faculty. Attendance at religious services is required.

Summer Programs Remediation, advancement, art/fine arts programs offered; session focuses on fine and performing arts; held on campus; accepts boys and girls; open to students from other schools. 25 students usually enrolled. 2006 schedule: June.

Tuition and Aid Day student tuition: $11,250; 7-day tuition and room/board: $23,950. Tuition installment plan (monthly payment plans, semester payment plan, discount for full pay in August). Merit scholarship grants, need-based scholarship grants, tuition remission for children of faculty and staff available. In 2005–06, 73% of upper-school students received aid; total upper-school merit-scholarship money awarded: $400,000. Total amount of financial aid awarded in 2005–06: $2,200,000.

Admissions Traditional secondary-level entrance grade is 9. For fall 2005, 214 students applied for upper-level admission, 87 were accepted, 61 enrolled. ACT, ISEE, PSAT, SAT, SLEP for foreign students, SSAT or TOEFL required. Deadline for receipt of application materials: none. Application fee required: $50. Interview required.

Athletics Interscholastic: baseball (boys), basketball (b,g), cross-country running (b,g); coed interscholastic: aquatics, cheering, Circus, golf; coed intramural: aerobics/dance, aerobics/nautilus, back packing, ballet, bicycling, billiards, canoeing/kayaking, climbing, dance, dance team, fitness, fitness walking, hiking/backpacking, kayaking, modern dance, mountain biking, nautilus, outdoor activities, outdoor adventure, outdoor recreation, outdoor skills, outdoors, physical training. 1 PE instructor, 2 coaches, 1 trainer.

Computers Computers are regularly used in all academic, technical drawing classes. Computer network features include campus e-mail, on-campus library services, CD-ROMs, online commercial services, Internet access, DVD, application and re-enrollment online services.

Contact Mrs. Kathy Watts, Admission Assistant. 706-746-7467 Ext. 202. Fax: 706-746-2594. E-mail: kwatts@rabungap.org. Web site: www.rabungap.org.

See full description on page 994.

RAMONA CONVENT SECONDARY SCHOOL

1701 West Ramona Road
Alhambra, California 91803-3080
Head of School: Ms. Kathleen Pillon

General Information Girls' day college-preparatory, arts, business, religious studies, and bilingual studies school, affiliated with Roman Catholic Church. Grades 7–12. Founded: 1889. Setting: suburban. Nearest major city is Los Angeles. 15-acre campus. 9 buildings on campus. Approved or accredited by Western Association of Schools and Colleges, Western Catholic Education Association, and California Department of Education. Endowment: $2 million. Total enrollment: 497. Upper school average class size: 22. Upper school faculty-student ratio: 1:10.

Upper School Student Profile Grade 9: 121 students (121 girls); Grade 10: 125 students (125 girls); Grade 11: 117 students (117 girls); Grade 12: 100 students (100 girls). 81% of students are Roman Catholic.

Faculty School total: 44. In upper school: 17 men, 27 women; 21 have advanced degrees.

Subjects Offered Accounting, Advanced Placement courses, advanced studio art-AP, algebra, American government-AP, American history, American literature, art history, Bible studies, biology, biology-AP, calculus, calculus-AP, ceramics, chemistry, chemistry-AP, computer programming, computer science, dance, drama, economics, English, English literature, environmental science, European history, European history-AP, fine arts, French, French-AP, geography, geometry, government/civics, grammar, graphic arts, health, history, honors English, honors geometry, Latin, mathematics, music, photography, physical education, physics, pre-calculus, religion, science, social science, social studies, Spanish, Spanish language-AP, Spanish literature-AP, speech, theater, theology, trigonometry, visual arts, word processing, world history, world literature.

Graduation Requirements Arts and fine arts (art, music, dance, drama), business skills (includes word processing), computer science, English, foreign language, mathematics, physical education (includes health), religion (includes Bible studies and theology), science, social studies (includes history), speech, passing grade in the Ramona Arithmetic Proficiency Test.

Special Academic Programs Advanced Placement exam preparation in 13 subject areas; honors section; independent study; study abroad; academic accommodation for the gifted, the musically talented, and the artistically talented.

College Placement 104 students graduated in 2005; all went to college, including California State Polytechnic University, Pomona; California State University, Fullerton; California State University, Long Beach; Loyola Marymount University; University of California, Irvine; University of California, Los Angeles. Mean SAT verbal: 534, mean SAT math: 518.

Student Life Upper grades have uniform requirement, student council, honor system. Discipline rests primarily with faculty. Attendance at religious services is required.

Summer Programs Remediation, enrichment, advancement, art/fine arts, computer instruction programs offered; session focuses on academics; held on campus; accepts boys and girls; open to students from other schools. 250 students usually enrolled. 2006 schedule: June 19 to July 20. Application deadline: May 26.

Tuition and Aid Day student tuition: $7500. Tuition installment plan (monthly payment plans, quarterly and semester payment plans). Merit scholarship grants, need-based scholarship grants, paying campus jobs available. In 2005–06, 19% of upper-school students received aid; total upper-school merit-scholarship money awarded: $10,000. Total amount of financial aid awarded in 2005–06: $225,000.

Admissions Traditional secondary-level entrance grade is 9. For fall 2005, 190 students applied for upper-level admission, 163 were accepted, 121 enrolled. High School Placement Test required. Deadline for receipt of application materials: January 11. Application fee required: $55. On-campus interview required.

Athletics Interscholastic: basketball, cross-country running, soccer, softball, swimming and diving, track and field, volleyball. 2 PE instructors, 9 coaches, 1 trainer.

Computers Computers are regularly used in all academic classes. Computer network features include on-campus library services, CD-ROMs, online commercial services, Internet access, DVD.

Contact Laura Dumas, Recruitment. 626-282-4151 Ext. 145. Fax: 626-281-0797. Web site: www.ramona.pvt.k12.ca.us.

RANCHO VALMORA

Valmora, New Mexico
See Special Needs Schools section.

RANDOLPH-MACON ACADEMY

200 Academy Drive
Front Royal, Virginia 22630
Head of School: Maj. Gen. Henry M. Hobgood

General Information Coeducational boarding and day college-preparatory, religious studies, technology, Air Force Junior ROTC, and ESL school, affiliated with Methodist Church. Grades 6–PG. Founded: 1892. Setting: small town. Nearest major city is Washington, DC. Students are housed in single-sex dormitories. 135-acre campus. 8 buildings on campus. Approved or accredited by Southern Association of Colleges and Schools, The Association of Boarding Schools, University Senate of United Methodist Church, Virginia Association of Independent Schools, and Virginia Department of Education. Member of National Association of Independent Schools. Total enrollment: 397. Upper school average class size: 13. Upper school faculty-student ratio: 1:9.

Upper School Student Profile Grade 9: 66 students (47 boys, 19 girls); Grade 10: 72 students (53 boys, 19 girls); Grade 11: 106 students (74 boys, 32 girls); Grade 12: 80 students (58 boys, 22 girls). 84% of students are boarding students. 51% are state residents. 25 states are represented in upper school student body. 18% are international students. International students from China and Republic of Korea; 10 other countries represented in student body. 11% of students are Methodist.

Faculty School total: 43. In upper school: 26 men, 13 women; 24 have advanced degrees; 17 reside on campus.

Subjects Offered Advanced math, aerospace education, aerospace science, algebra, American government, American government-AP, American history, American history-AP, American literature-AP, Bible studies, biology, biology-AP, calculus, calculus-AP, chemistry, chorus, comparative religion, composition-AP, computer applications, computer keyboarding, computer skills, concert band, concert choir, drama, English, English literature, English-AP, environmental science, ESL, flight instruction, French, geometry, German, German-AP, government/civics, history, honors algebra, honors English, honors geometry, honors U.S. history, JROTC, Latin, Latin-AP, mathematics, music, music appreciation, personal finance, physical education, physics, physics-AP, pre-calculus, religion, science, senior seminar, social studies, Spanish, speech and debate, TOEFL preparation, trigonometry, world history, yearbook.

Graduation Requirements Aerospace science, computer science, English, foreign language, mathematics, physical education (includes health), religion (includes Bible studies and theology), science, social studies (includes history), Air Force Junior ROTC for each year student is enrolled.

Special Academic Programs Advanced Placement exam preparation in 9 subject areas; honors section; accelerated programs; independent study; study at local college for college credit; study abroad; academic accommodation for the gifted; ESL (24 students enrolled).

College Placement 84 students graduated in 2005; 82 went to college, including Brigham Young University; Embry-Riddle Aeronautical University; George Mason University; Purdue University; Roanoke College; Virginia Polytechnic Institute and State University. Other: 1 went to work, 1 entered military service. 13% scored over 600 on SAT verbal, 22% scored over 600 on SAT math, 7% scored over 26 on composite ACT.

Student Life Upper grades have uniform requirement, student council, honor system. Discipline rests equally with students and faculty. Attendance at religious services is required.

Summer Programs Remediation, enrichment, advancement, ESL programs offered; session focuses on remediation, new courses, ESL, flight; held on campus; accepts boys and girls; open to students from other schools. 184 students usually enrolled. 2006 schedule: June 25 to July 21. Application deadline: June 23.

Tuition and Aid Day student tuition: $9266; 7-day tuition and room/board: $20,097. Tuition installment plan (monthly payment plans, 2-payment plan). Tuition reduction for siblings, merit scholarship grants, need-based scholarship grants, paying campus jobs, Methodist Church scholarships available. In 2005–06, 10% of upper-school students received aid; total upper-school merit-scholarship money awarded: $25,000. Total amount of financial aid awarded in 2005–06: $119,574.

Admissions Traditional secondary-level entrance grade is 9. For fall 2005, 191 students applied for upper-level admission, 162 were accepted, 119 enrolled. Any standardized test required. Deadline for receipt of application materials: none. Application fee required: $75. Interview recommended.

Athletics Interscholastic: baseball (boys), basketball (b,g), cross-country running (b,g), football (b), indoor track (b,g), lacrosse (b), soccer (b,g), softball (g), swimming and diving (b,g), tennis (b,g), track and field (b,g), volleyball (b,g), wrestling (b); intramural: basketball (b,g), horseback riding (g), independent competitive sports (b,g), soccer (b,g), strength & conditioning (b,g), swimming and diving (b,g), tennis (b,g), track and field (b,g), volleyball (b,g); coed interscholastic: cheering, cross-country running, drill team, golf, indoor track, JROTC drill, marksmanship, riflery, wrestling; coed intramural: indoor soccer, jogging, JROTC drill, marksmanship, nautilus, outdoor activities, outdoor recreation, outdoors, physical fitness, riflery, soccer, strength & conditioning, swimming and diving, volleyball, weight lifting, weight training. 2 PE instructors, 1 trainer.

Computers Computers are regularly used in aerospace science, aviation, English, ESL, foreign language, independent study, Latin, SAT preparation, science, yearbook classes. Computer network features include campus e-mail, on-campus library services, CD-ROMs, online commercial services, Internet access.

Contact Mrs. Paula Brady, Admissions Coordinator. 540-636-5200 Ext. 5484. Fax: 540-636-5419. E-mail: paulab@rma.edu. Web site: www.rma.edu.

ANNOUNCEMENT FROM THE SCHOOL Randolph-Macon Academy was the first coeducational college-prep boarding school in America to offer Air Force Junior ROTC. An optional flight training program offers ground school and flying lessons from FAA-certified staff flight instructors in school-owned

aircraft. The Middle School offers a structured environment with a separate campus and uniform.

See full description on page 996.

RANDOLPH SCHOOL

1005 Drake Avenue, SE
Huntsville, Alabama 35802
Head of School: David E. Wood

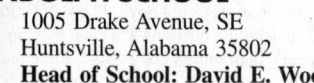

General Information Coeducational day college-preparatory, arts, and technology school. Grades K–12. Founded: 1959. Setting: suburban. 67-acre campus. 8 buildings on campus. Approved or accredited by Southern Association of Colleges and Schools and The College Board. Member of National Association of Independent Schools. Endowment: $2.5 million. Total enrollment: 804. Upper school average class size: 12. Upper school faculty-student ratio: 1:12.

Upper School Student Profile Grade 9: 67 students (32 boys, 35 girls); Grade 10: 63 students (33 boys, 30 girls); Grade 11: 67 students (25 boys, 42 girls); Grade 12: 71 students (39 boys, 32 girls).

Faculty School total: 82. In upper school: 8 men, 24 women; 30 have advanced degrees.

Subjects Offered Algebra, American literature, anatomy, art, biology, calculus, ceramics, chemistry, computer math, computer programming, computer science, creative writing, drama, economics, English, English literature, environmental science, European history, film appreciation, fine arts, forensics, French, geometry, government/civics, grammar, history, journalism, Latin, marine biology, mathematics, music, physical education, physics, physiology, psychology, science, social studies, society, politics and law, Southern literature, Spanish, speech, theater, trigonometry, world history, world literature, writing.

Graduation Requirements Algebra, American literature, arts and fine arts (art, music, dance, drama), biology, British literature, chemistry, computer science, English, European history, foreign language, geometry, literature, mathematics, science, social studies (includes history), world literature.

Special Academic Programs Advanced Placement exam preparation in 17 subject areas; honors section; independent study; study at local college for college credit.

College Placement 53 students graduated in 2005; all went to college, including Auburn University; Birmingham-Southern College; Emory University; Furman University; Rhodes College; Vanderbilt University. Median SAT verbal: 640, median SAT math: 640, median composite ACT: 25. 66% scored over 600 on SAT verbal, 62% scored over 600 on SAT math, 44% scored over 26 on composite ACT.

Student Life Upper grades have specified standards of dress, student council, honor system. Discipline rests primarily with faculty.

Summer Programs Enrichment, sports, art/fine arts, computer instruction programs offered; session focuses on science, art, foreign language, technology; held on campus; accepts boys and girls; open to students from other schools. 100 students usually enrolled. 2006 schedule: June 1 to July 31. Application deadline: April 30.

Tuition and Aid Day student tuition: $9205–$11,425. Tuition installment plan (Insured Tuition Payment Plan, 2- or 10-payment plans). Merit scholarship grants, need-based scholarship grants available. In 2005–06, 13% of upper-school students received aid; total upper-school merit-scholarship money awarded: $3528. Total amount of financial aid awarded in 2005–06: $112,500.

Admissions Traditional secondary-level entrance grade is 9. For fall 2005, 25 students applied for upper-level admission, 19 were accepted, 15 enrolled. ISEE and writing sample required. Deadline for receipt of application materials: none. Application fee required: $40. On-campus interview required.

Athletics Interscholastic: baseball (boys), basketball (b,g), cheering (g), cross-country running (b,g), diving (b,g), football (b), golf (b,g), indoor track & field (b,g), soccer (b,g), softball (g), swimming and diving (b,g), tennis (b,g), track and field (b,g), volleyball (g), winter (indoor) track (b,g); coed interscholastic: diving; coed intramural: flag football. 6 PE instructors, 5 coaches.

Computers Computers are regularly used in all academic classes. Computer network features include campus e-mail, on-campus library services, CD-ROMs, online commercial services, Internet access, file transfer, wireless campus network, laptops.

Contact Nancy Hodges, Director of Admissions. 256-881-1701 Ext. 103. Fax: 256-881-1784. E-mail: nhodges@randolphschool.net. Web site: www.randolphschool.net.

ANNOUNCEMENT FROM THE SCHOOL Randolph's K–12 faculty members and Upper School students have successfully integrated laptop computers and a wireless network into the curriculum. Each student in grades 9–12 is required to bring a School-approved laptop to class. Randolph also offers a weeklong Interim program for students in grades 7–12 that includes on-campus enrichment activities and a selection of trips. Travel varies from year to year and may include a fine arts trip to Chicago, kayaking and camping on the Gulf Coast, and cultural and historical explorations of Europe, Latin America, and Washington, DC. The week also offers career-search internships with area employers.

RANNEY SCHOOL

235 Hope Road
Tinton Falls, New Jersey 07724
Head of School: Dr. Lawrence S. Sykoff

General Information Coeducational day college-preparatory school. Grades N–12. Founded: 1960. Setting: suburban. Nearest major city is New York, NY. 60-acre campus. 3 buildings on campus. Approved or accredited by Middle States Association of Colleges and Schools and New Jersey Department of Education. Member of National Association of Independent Schools. Total enrollment: 785. Upper school average class size: 15.

Upper School Student Profile Grade 9: 64 students (27 boys, 37 girls); Grade 10: 61 students (25 boys, 36 girls); Grade 11: 55 students (25 boys, 30 girls); Grade 12: 46 students (27 boys, 19 girls).

Faculty School total: 85. In upper school: 10 men, 16 women; 12 have advanced degrees.

Subjects Offered Advanced Placement courses, algebra, American history, American literature, art, art history, art history-AP, biology, biology-AP, calculus, calculus-AP, ceramics, chemistry, chemistry-AP, computer programming, computer science, computer science-AP, economics, economics-AP, English, English language-AP, English literature, English literature-AP, European history, European history-AP, fine arts, French, French-AP, geometry, grammar, health, history, journalism, Latin, mathematics, music, physical education, physics, psychology, science, social studies, Spanish, Spanish language-AP, world history, world literature, writing.

Graduation Requirements Arts and fine arts (art, music, dance, drama), English, foreign language, history, mathematics, physical education (includes health), science.

Special Academic Programs Advanced Placement exam preparation in 17 subject areas; honors section.

College Placement 48 students graduated in 2005; all went to college, including Cornell University; Drew University; New York University; Rutgers, The State University of New Jersey, New Brunswick/Piscataway; University of Pennsylvania. Median SAT verbal: 632, median SAT math: 646.

Student Life Upper grades have specified standards of dress, student council, honor system. Discipline rests equally with students and faculty.

Summer Programs Enrichment, computer instruction programs offered; session focuses on mathematics and English; held on campus; accepts boys and girls; open to students from other schools. 2006 schedule: July 1 to August 23. Application deadline: March 30.

Tuition and Aid Day student tuition: $18,700–$19,850. Tuition installment plan (Key Tuition Payment Plan). Tuition reduction for siblings, need-based scholarship grants, reduced tuition for children of employees available. In 2005–06, 5% of upper-school students received aid. Total amount of financial aid awarded in 2005–06: $17,500.

Admissions Traditional secondary-level entrance grade is 9. For fall 2005, 48 students applied for upper-level admission, 35 were accepted, 27 enrolled. ERB required. Deadline for receipt of application materials: none. Application fee required: $75. On-campus interview required.

Athletics Interscholastic: baseball (boys), basketball (b,g), cheering (g), field hockey (g), lacrosse (b), soccer (b,g), softball (g), tennis (b,g); coed interscholastic: aquatics, cross-country running, golf, swimming and diving, track and field; coed intramural: fencing, fitness, weight training. 6 PE instructors, 16 coaches, 1 trainer.

Computers Computer resources include CD-ROMs, Internet access.

Contact Heather Rudisi, Associate Head for Admission and Marketing. 732-542-4777 Ext. 107. Fax: 732-460-1078. E-mail: hrudisi@ranneyschool.com. Web site: www.ranneyschool.com.

See full description on page 998.

RANSOM EVERGLADES SCHOOL

3575 Main Highway
Miami, Florida 33133
Head of School: Mrs. Ellen Y. Moceri

General Information Coeducational day college-preparatory school. Grades 6–12. Founded: 1903. Setting: urban. 11-acre campus. 21 buildings on campus. Approved or accredited by Florida Council of Independent Schools, Southern Association of Colleges and Schools, and Florida Department of Education. Member of National Association of Independent Schools and Secondary School Admission Test Board. Endowment: $13.1 million. Total enrollment: 991. Upper school average class size: 14. Upper school faculty-student ratio: 1:14.

Upper School Student Profile Grade 9: 151 students (72 boys, 79 girls); Grade 10: 138 students (65 boys, 73 girls); Grade 11: 132 students (62 boys, 70 girls); Grade 12: 141 students (68 boys, 73 girls).

Faculty School total: 95. In upper school: 25 men, 31 women; 41 have advanced degrees.

Subjects Offered Advanced Placement courses, algebra, American government-AP, American history, American history-AP, American literature, anatomy and physiology, art, art history, art history-AP, astronomy, band, biology, calculus, calculus-AP, ceramics, chemistry, chemistry-AP, chorus, college counseling, computer math, computer programming, computer science, creative writing, dance, debate, drama,

earth science, ecology, economics, English, English literature, English literature and composition-AP, environmental science, environmental science-AP, ethics, ethics and responsibility, European history, European history-AP, fine arts, French, French language-AP, geography, geology, geometry, government and politics-AP, government/civics, grammar, guitar, health, history, history-AP, journalism, Latin-AP, macro/microeconomics-AP, Mandarin, marine biology, mathematics, music, music theory-AP, mythology, philosophy, photography, physical education, physics, physics-AP, psychology, psychology-AP, science, social studies, sociology, Spanish, speech, statistics, statistics-AP, theater, theory of knowledge, trigonometry, typing, U.S. government-AP, U.S. history-AP, world history, world literature, writing.

Graduation Requirements Arts and fine arts (art, music, dance, drama), computer science, English, foreign language, mathematics, physical education (includes health), science, social studies (includes history).

Special Academic Programs Advanced Placement exam preparation in 20 subject areas; honors section.

College Placement 133 students graduated in 2005; all went to college, including Boston College; Brown University; The George Washington University; University of Florida; University of Pennsylvania; Washington University in St. Louis. Median SAT verbal: 670, median SAT math: 672.

Student Life Upper grades have specified standards of dress, student council, honor system. Discipline rests primarily with faculty.

Summer Programs Enrichment, advancement, computer instruction programs offered; session focuses on enrichment to reinforce basic skills and advancement for credit; held on campus; accepts boys and girls; open to students from other schools. 130 students usually enrolled. 2006 schedule: June 12 to July 21. Application deadline: June 9.

Tuition and Aid Day student tuition: $19,010. Tuition installment plan (monthly payment plans, 60%/40% payment plan). Need-based scholarship grants available. In 2005–06, 14% of upper-school students received aid. Total amount of financial aid awarded in 2005–06: $2,050,995.

Admissions Traditional secondary-level entrance grade is 9. For fall 2005, 124 students applied for upper-level admission, 60 were accepted, 34 enrolled. SSAT required. Deadline for receipt of application materials: February 15. Application fee required: $100. On-campus interview required.

Athletics Interscholastic: baseball (boys), basketball (b,g), canoeing/kayaking (b,g), cheering (g), crew (b,g), cross-country running (b,g), dance (g), dance team (g), football (b), golf (b,g), kayaking (b,g), lacrosse (b), physical training (b,g), sailing (b,g), soccer (b,g), softball (g), swimming and diving (b,g), tennis (b,g), track and field (b,g), volleyball (b,g), water polo (b,g), wrestling (b); coed interscholastic: crew, kayaking, sailing. 9 PE instructors, 91 coaches, 2 trainers.

Computers Computers are regularly used in all classes. Computer network features include campus e-mail, on-campus library services, CD-ROMs, online commercial services, Internet access, DVD, wireless campus network.

Contact Elaine J. Mijalis-Kahn, Director of Admission. 305-250-6875. Fax: 305-854-1846. E-mail: admission@ransomeverglades.org. Web site: www.ransomeverglades.org.

RAVENSCROFT SCHOOL

7409 Falls of the Neuse Road
Raleigh, North Carolina 27615
Head of School: Mrs. Doreen C. Kelly

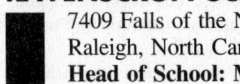

General Information Coeducational day college-preparatory, arts, and technology school. Grades PK–12. Founded: 1862. Setting: suburban. 127-acre campus. 10 buildings on campus. Approved or accredited by Southern Association of Colleges and Schools, Southern Association of Independent Schools, and North Carolina Department of Education. Member of National Association of Independent Schools. Endowment: $10 million. Total enrollment: 1,119. Upper school average class size: 12. Upper school faculty-student ratio: 1:6.

Upper School Student Profile Grade 9: 106 students (60 boys, 46 girls); Grade 10: 100 students (45 boys, 55 girls); Grade 11: 79 students (49 boys, 30 girls); Grade 12: 89 students (43 boys, 46 girls).

Faculty School total: 130. In upper school: 27 men, 28 women; 35 have advanced degrees.

Subjects Offered Algebra, American history, American literature, anatomy, art, art history, biology, calculus, chemistry, computer programming, computer science, drama, economics, English, English literature, environmental science, European history, expository writing, fine arts, French, geometry, government/civics, health, history, journalism, Latin, mathematics, music, photography, physical education, physics, science, social science, social studies, Spanish, speech, theater, trigonometry, typing, world history, writing.

Graduation Requirements Arts and fine arts (art, music, dance, drama), composition, English, foreign language, mathematics, physical education (includes health), science, social science, social studies (includes history). Community service is required.

Special Academic Programs Advanced Placement exam preparation in 17 subject areas; honors section; independent study; term-away projects; study at local college for college credit; study abroad; academic accommodation for the gifted, the musically talented, and the artistically talented.

College Placement 86 students graduated in 2005; all went to college, including Duke University; Elon University; North Carolina State University; The University of North Carolina at Chapel Hill; The University of North Carolina Wilmington; Wake Forest University. Median SAT verbal: 640, median SAT math: 650, median composite ACT: 26. 67% scored over 600 on SAT verbal, 72% scored over 600 on SAT math.

Student Life Upper grades have specified standards of dress, student council, honor system. Discipline rests equally with students and faculty.

Summer Programs Enrichment, advancement, sports, art/fine arts, computer instruction programs offered; session focuses on enrichment ; held on campus; accepts boys and girls; open to students from other schools. 2000 students usually enrolled. 2006 schedule: June 5 to August 11. Application deadline: none.

Tuition and Aid Day student tuition: $13,730. Tuition installment plan (individually arranged payment plans). Merit scholarship grants, need-based scholarship grants, need-based loans available. In 2005–06, 13% of upper-school students received aid; total upper-school merit-scholarship money awarded: $75,082. Total amount of financial aid awarded in 2005–06: $395,858.

Admissions Traditional secondary-level entrance grade is 9. For fall 2005, 103 students applied for upper-level admission, 72 were accepted, 47 enrolled. ERB required. Deadline for receipt of application materials: none. Application fee required: $110. On-campus interview required.

Athletics Interscholastic: baseball (boys), basketball (b,g), cheering (g), cross-country running (b,g), dance squad (g), field hockey (g), fitness (b,g), football (b), golf (b,g), lacrosse (b), physical training (b,g), soccer (b,g), softball (g), strength & conditioning (b,g), swimming and diving (b,g), tennis (b,g), track and field (b,g), volleyball (g), weight training (b,g), wrestling (b); intramural: baseball (b), basketball (b,g), cheering (g), football (b,g), lacrosse (b), soccer (b,g), softball (g), strength & conditioning (b,g), swimming and diving (b,g), tennis (b,g), track and field (b,g), volleyball (g), wrestling (b); coed interscholastic: life saving. 8 PE instructors, 30 coaches, 2 trainers.

Computers Computers are regularly used in economics, English, foreign language, history, mathematics, science, social studies, writing classes. Computer network features include on-campus library services, CD-ROMs, online commercial services, Internet access, file transfer, office computer access, DVD.

Contact Mrs. Pamela J. Jamison, Director of Admissions. 919-847-0900 Ext. 2226. Fax: 919-846-2371. E-mail: pjamison@ravenscroft.org. Web site: www.ravenscroft.org.

ANNOUNCEMENT FROM THE SCHOOL Located on a 125-acre campus in North Raleigh, Ravenscroft School is a coeducational, college-preparatory day school enrolling 1,100 students in prekindergarten through grade 12. The purpose of Ravenscroft School is to promote the development of the total child: academically, through a balanced college-preparatory curriculum with numerous AP offerings; socially, through leadership opportunities, extracurricular activities, and community service; aesthetically, through a comprehensive program of visual and performing arts; physically, through complete physical education and interscholastic athletics programs; and spiritually, through affirmation of the Judeo-Christian tradition and the American ideals of freedom, democracy, and tolerance. The School's campus features 3 academic classroom buildings, including a new Upper School, a dining room, a fine arts center with a 450-seat capacity theater, an athletic center with weight-training facilities, gymnasiums, an indoor pool, and several playing fields, and a new library-technology center. A wide range of summer programs and off-campus learning experiences are offered. Need-based financial aid and academic scholarships are available.

THE RECTORY SCHOOL

Pomfret, Connecticut
See Junior Boarding Schools section.

REGINA HIGH SCHOOL

1857 South Green Road
South Euclid, Ohio 44121
Head of School: Sr. Maureen Burke, SND

General Information Girls' day college-preparatory, arts, religious studies, and technology school, affiliated with Roman Catholic Church. Grades 9–12. Founded: 1953. Setting: suburban. Nearest major city is Cleveland. 40-acre campus. 1 building on campus. Approved or accredited by National Catholic Education Association, North Central Association of Colleges and Schools, Ohio Catholic Schools Accreditation Association (OCSAA), and Ohio Department of Education. Endowment: $1 million. Total enrollment: 267. Upper school average class size: 20. Upper school faculty-student ratio: 1:14.

Upper School Student Profile Grade 9: 62 students (62 girls); Grade 10: 67 students (67 girls); Grade 11: 81 students (81 girls); Grade 12: 57 students (57 girls). 80% of students are Roman Catholic.

Faculty School total: 31. In upper school: 6 men, 25 women; 18 have advanced degrees.

Regina High School

Subjects Offered ACT preparation, advanced chemistry, Advanced Placement courses, African dance, algebra, American history-AP, American literature-AP, anatomy, art, arts, British literature, business, career/college preparation, chemistry, Christian and Hebrew scripture, college counseling, college planning, communications, computer math, computer science, dance, drama, earth science, engineering, English, English literature-AP, environmental science, fine arts, French studies, German literature, government/civics, health, home economics, Internet, Japanese, library skills, music, peace education, performing arts, physical science, prayer/spirituality, pre-calculus, SAT/ACT preparation, science, social issues, social studies, Spanish literature, telecommunications and the Internet, theater arts, trigonometry, world cultures, world literature, yearbook.

Graduation Requirements Portfolio.

Special Academic Programs Advanced Placement exam preparation in 5 subject areas; honors section; independent study; study at local college for college credit; study abroad; academic accommodation for the gifted, the musically talented, and the artistically talented; remedial reading and/or remedial writing; remedial math; programs in English, mathematics, general development for dyslexic students; special instructional classes for students with learning disabilities, Attention Deficit Disorder, and dyslexia.

College Placement 58 students graduated in 2005; 57 went to college, including John Carroll University; Kent State University; Lake Forest Academy; Xavier University. Other: 1 entered military service.

Student Life Upper grades have uniform requirement, student council, honor system. Discipline rests primarily with faculty. Attendance at religious services is required.

Summer Programs Remediation, enrichment, advancement, sports, art/fine arts programs offered; session focuses on drama; held on campus; accepts girls; open to students from other schools. 20 students usually enrolled. 2006 schedule: July.

Tuition and Aid Day student tuition: $7450. Tuition installment plan (monthly payment plans). Tuition reduction for siblings, merit scholarship grants, need-based scholarship grants available. In 2005–06, 30% of upper-school students received aid; total upper-school merit-scholarship money awarded: $25,000. Total amount of financial aid awarded in 2005–06: $125,000.

Admissions Traditional secondary-level entrance grade is 9. For fall 2005, 100 students applied for upper-level admission, 81 were accepted, 61 enrolled. Scholastic Testing Service High School Placement Test required. Deadline for receipt of application materials: none. Application fee required: $100. Interview required.

Athletics Interscholastic: basketball, cheering, cross-country running, diving, softball, swimming and diving, tennis, track and field, volleyball, winter (indoor) track. 1 PE instructor, 15 coaches, 1 trainer.

Computers Computers are regularly used in all classes. Computer network features include campus e-mail, on-campus library services, CD-ROMs, online commercial services, Internet access, file transfer, office computer access, DVD.

Contact Hillary Fox, Director of Admissions. 216-382-2110 Ext. 225. Fax: 216-382-3555. E-mail: foxh@reginahigh.com. Web site: www.reginahigh.com.

REGIS HIGH SCHOOL

55 East 84th Street
New York, New York 10028-0884
Head of School: Rev. Vincent L. Biagi, SJ

General Information Boys' day college-preparatory school, affiliated with Roman Catholic Church. Grades 9–12. Founded: 1914. Setting: urban. 3-acre campus. 1 building on campus. Approved or accredited by Jesuit Secondary Education Association, Middle States Association of Colleges and Schools, New York State Association of Independent Schools, and New York Department of Education. Total enrollment: 533. Upper school average class size: 15. Upper school faculty-student ratio: 1:12.

Upper School Student Profile Grade 9: 139 students (139 boys); Grade 10: 143 students (143 boys); Grade 11: 127 students (127 boys); Grade 12: 124 students (124 boys). 100% of students are Roman Catholic.

Faculty School total: 64. In upper school: 36 men, 28 women; 49 have advanced degrees.

Subjects Offered Algebra, American history, American literature, architecture, art, art history, biology, calculus, chemistry, Chinese, computer programming, computer science, creative writing, drama, driver education, economics, English, English literature, ethics, European history, expository writing, film, French, geometry, German, history, Italian, Latin, mathematics, music, physical education, physics, psychology, social studies, Spanish, speech, statistics, theater, theology, trigonometry, writing.

Graduation Requirements Art, computer literacy, English, foreign language, history, mathematics, music, physical education (includes health), science, theology, Christian Service Program.

Special Academic Programs Advanced Placement exam preparation; independent study; study abroad.

College Placement 128 students graduated in 2005; all went to college, including Boston University; Fordham University; Georgetown University; Harvard University; Loyola College in Maryland; New York University. Mean SAT verbal: 716, mean SAT math: 698. 96% scored over 600 on SAT verbal, 96% scored over 600 on SAT math.

Student Life Upper grades have specified standards of dress, student council. Discipline rests primarily with faculty. Attendance at religious services is required.

Summer Programs Remediation programs offered; session focuses on remediation; held on campus; accepts boys; not open to students from other schools. 20 students usually enrolled. 2006 schedule: July 6 to August 15.

Tuition and Aid Tuition-free school available.

Admissions Traditional secondary-level entrance grade is 9. For fall 2005, 739 students applied for upper-level admission, 150 were accepted, 139 enrolled. Admissions testing required. Deadline for receipt of application materials: October 28. Application fee required: $40. On-campus interview required.

Athletics Interscholastic: baseball, basketball, bowling, cross-country running, golf, indoor track & field, soccer, tennis, track and field; intramural: basketball, floor hockey, indoor hockey, soccer. 2 PE instructors, 14 coaches.

Computers Computer network features include campus e-mail, on-campus library services, CD-ROMs, Internet access, DVD.

Contact Mr. Eric P. DiMichele, Director of Admissions. 212-288-1100 Ext. 101. Fax: 212-794-1221. E-mail: edimiche@regis-nyc.org. Web site: www.regis-nyc.org.

REGIS HIGH SCHOOL

550 West Regis Street
Stayton, Oregon 97383
Head of School: Mr. Tony Guevara

General Information Coeducational day college-preparatory, general academic, and religious studies school, affiliated with Roman Catholic Church. Grades 9–12. Founded: 1963. Setting: small town. Nearest major city is Salem. 45-acre campus. 4 buildings on campus. Approved or accredited by Northwest Association of Schools and Colleges, Western Catholic Education Association, and Oregon Department of Education. Endowment: $2.7 million. Total enrollment: 189. Upper school average class size: 23. Upper school faculty-student ratio: 1:15.

Upper School Student Profile Grade 9: 53 students (23 boys, 30 girls); Grade 10: 47 students (27 boys, 20 girls); Grade 11: 51 students (24 boys, 27 girls); Grade 12: 38 students (23 boys, 15 girls). 96% of students are Roman Catholic.

Faculty School total: 15. In upper school: 10 men, 5 women; 10 have advanced degrees.

Subjects Offered Accounting, algebra, athletics, biology, business, Catholic belief and practice, chemistry, composition, computer science, English, fine arts, geometry, journalism, mathematics, music, physical education, physical science, physics, psychology, religion, science, social science, yearbook.

Graduation Requirements Arts and fine arts (art, music, dance, drama), business skills (includes word processing), computer science, English, mathematics, physical education (includes health), religion (includes Bible studies and theology), science, social science, social studies (includes history), 60 hours of Christian service.

Special Academic Programs Advanced Placement exam preparation in 1 subject area; study at local college for college credit; programs in general development for dyslexic students.

College Placement 42 students graduated in 2005; 41 went to college, including Chemeketa Community College; Oregon State University; University of Oregon; University of Portland; Western Oregon University. Other: 1 went to work. 64% scored over 600 on SAT verbal, 40% scored over 600 on SAT math.

Student Life Upper grades have specified standards of dress, student council, honor system. Discipline rests primarily with faculty. Attendance at religious services is required.

Summer Programs Sports programs offered; held on campus; accepts boys and girls; open to students from other schools. 50 students usually enrolled. 2006 schedule: June 15 to August 20.

Tuition and Aid Day student tuition: $4375–$5175. Tuition installment plan (FACTS Tuition Payment Plan). Tuition reduction for siblings, merit scholarship grants, need-based scholarship grants available. In 2005–06, 24% of upper-school students received aid; total upper-school merit-scholarship money awarded: $8000. Total amount of financial aid awarded in 2005–06: $53,000.

Admissions Traditional secondary-level entrance grade is 9. For fall 2005, 192 students applied for upper-level admission, 192 were accepted, 189 enrolled. STS required. Deadline for receipt of application materials: April 25. Application fee required: $175. Interview required.

Athletics Interscholastic: baseball (boys), basketball (b,g), cross-country running (b,g), football (b), golf (b), softball (g), track and field (b,g), volleyball (g), wrestling (b); intramural: cheering (b), tennis (b); coed interscholastic: swimming and diving, tennis; coed intramural: basketball, bowling, skiing (downhill), volleyball, weight lifting. 1 PE instructor, 5 coaches.

Computers Computers are regularly used in business, economics, English, history, journalism, keyboarding, library, mathematics, multimedia, newspaper, occupational education, publications, research skills, science, stock market, word processing, yearbook classes. Computer network features include on-campus library services, CD-ROMs, online commercial services, Internet access, DVD.

Contact Jan Harpole, Office Manager. 503-769-2159. Fax: 503-769-1706. E-mail: busofc@regishighschool.net. Web site: www.regishighschool.net.

RESURRECTION HIGH SCHOOL

7500 West Talcott Avenue
Chicago, Illinois 60631-3742
Head of School: Mrs. Jo Marie Yonkus

General Information Girls' day college-preparatory, arts, business, religious studies, and technology school, affiliated with Roman Catholic Church. Grades 9–12. Founded: 1922. Setting: urban. 6-acre campus. 1 building on campus. Approved or accredited by North Central Association of Colleges and Schools and Illinois Department of Education. Total enrollment: 921. Upper school average class size: 28. Upper school faculty-student ratio: 1:14.

Upper School Student Profile Grade 9: 218 students (218 girls); Grade 10: 246 students (246 girls); Grade 11: 238 students (238 girls); Grade 12: 219 students (219 girls). 80% of students are Roman Catholic.

Faculty School total: 55. In upper school: 11 men, 44 women; 30 have advanced degrees.

Subjects Offered 3-dimensional art, acting, advanced math, Advanced Placement courses, algebra, American government, American history, American literature, anatomy and physiology, art, calculus, calculus-AP, chamber groups, chemistry, child development, chorus, Christian and Hebrew scripture, Christian education, Christian scripture, Christian studies, Christian testament, computer applications, dance, dance performance, death and loss, drama, drama performance, earth science, English, English-AP, environmental science, finite math, fitness, foreign language, French, geometry, health education, honors algebra, honors English, honors geometry, honors U.S. history, honors world history, Italian, journalism, law, mathematics, modern history, music, peace and justice, physical fitness, physical science, physics, physics-AP, practicum, prayer/spirituality, pre-calculus, psychology, publications, scripture, sociology, Spanish, Spanish-AP, sports, student government, student publications, studio art, study skills, trigonometry, U.S. government and politics, U.S. history-AP, U.S. literature, world history, writing.

Special Academic Programs Advanced Placement exam preparation in 9 subject areas; honors section; study at local college for college credit; remedial reading and/or remedial writing; remedial math.

College Placement 188 students graduated in 2005.

Student Life Upper grades have uniform requirement, student council, honor system. Discipline rests primarily with faculty. Attendance at religious services is required.

Summer Programs Enrichment, sports, computer instruction programs offered; session focuses on taking computer graduation requirement; held on campus; accepts boys and girls; open to students from other schools. 150 students usually enrolled. 2006 schedule: June 12 to June 29. Application deadline: March 24.

Tuition and Aid Day student tuition: $6525. Tuition installment plan (Insured Tuition Payment Plan, monthly payment plans). Tuition reduction for siblings, need-based scholarship grants available. In 2005–06, 20% of upper-school students received aid. Total amount of financial aid awarded in 2005–06: $90,000.

Admissions Traditional secondary-level entrance grade is 9. For fall 2005, 311 students applied for upper-level admission, 282 were accepted, 256 enrolled. Stanford Achievement Test, Otis-Lennon required. Deadline for receipt of application materials: July 10. No application fee required. On-campus interview required.

Athletics Interscholastic: ballet, basketball, cross-country running, dance, dance squad, dance team, golf, soccer, softball, swimming and diving, tennis, track and field, volleyball. 3 PE instructors, 6 coaches, 1 trainer.

Computers Computer network features include on-campus library services, CD-ROMs, Internet access, file transfer.

Contact Mrs. Patricia Lawrence, College Counselor. 773-775-6616 Ext. 119. Fax: 773-775-0611. E-mail: plawrence@reshs.org. Web site: www.reshs.org.

RIBET ACADEMY

2911 San Fernando Road
Los Angeles, California 90065
Head of School: Mr. Ronald L. Sires

General Information Coeducational boarding and day college-preparatory, arts, and technology school. Boarding grades 9–12, day grades 1–12. Founded: 1982. Setting: urban. Nearest major city is Glendale. 9-acre campus. 3 buildings on campus. Approved or accredited by Western Association of Schools and Colleges and California Department of Education. Total enrollment: 442. Upper school average class size: 18. Upper school faculty-student ratio: 1:8.

Upper School Student Profile Grade 9: 44 students (32 boys, 12 girls); Grade 10: 60 students (43 boys, 17 girls); Grade 11: 65 students (38 boys, 27 girls); Grade 12: 54 students (33 boys, 21 girls).

Faculty School total: 53. In upper school: 12 men, 17 women; 14 have advanced degrees.

Subjects Offered ACT preparation, advanced chemistry, advanced math, advanced studio art-AP, African-American history, algebra, American history-AP, American literature, art-AP, ballet, band, Basic programming, basic skills, biology, biology-AP, British literature, business law, calculus, calculus-AP, chemistry, chemistry-AP, choir, civics, Civil War, college planning, composition-AP, computer literacy, concert band, creative writing, English, European history-AP, French, French-AP, geometry, oral communications, physics, physics-AP, pre-calculus, Spanish, Spanish-AP.

Graduation Requirements Arts and fine arts (art, music, dance, drama), computers, electives, English, foreign language, mathematics, physical education (includes health), science, social studies (includes history). Community service is required.

Special Academic Programs Advanced Placement exam preparation in 13 subject areas; honors section; accelerated programs; independent study; study abroad; academic accommodation for the musically talented and the artistically talented; ESL (40 students enrolled).

College Placement 45 students graduated in 2005; 40 went to college, including University of California, Berkeley; University of California, Los Angeles; University of California, Riverside; University of California, San Diego; University of California, Santa Barbara; University of Southern California. Other: 2 went to work, 1 entered military service, 2 had other specific plans. Median SAT verbal: 600, median SAT math: 600. 5% scored over 600 on SAT verbal, 5% scored over 600 on SAT math.

Student Life Upper grades have uniform requirement, student council, honor system. Discipline rests equally with students and faculty.

Summer Programs Remediation, enrichment, advancement, ESL, sports, art/fine arts, computer instruction programs offered; session focuses on advancement and remediation; held on campus; accepts boys and girls; open to students from other schools. 150 students usually enrolled. 2006 schedule: July 5 to August 11. Application deadline: May 30.

Tuition and Aid Day student tuition: $12,900; 7-day tuition and room/board: $20,900. Guaranteed tuition plan. Tuition installment plan (SMART Tuition Payment Plan, individually arranged payment plans). Tuition reduction for siblings, need-based scholarship grants, Reduction In Tuition Exchange (RITE) available. In 2005–06, 33% of upper-school students received aid. Total amount of financial aid awarded in 2005–06: $100,000.

Admissions Traditional secondary-level entrance grade is 9. For fall 2005, 75 students applied for upper-level admission, 60 were accepted, 50 enrolled. Essay, ISEE or latest standardized score from previous school required. Deadline for receipt of application materials: February 1. Application fee required: $100. Interview required.

Athletics Interscholastic: baseball (boys), basketball (b,g), flag football (b), football (b), physical fitness (b,g), softball (g), strength & conditioning (b,g), volleyball (b,g); intramural: paint ball (b), physical fitness (b,g), strength & conditioning (b,g), volleyball (b,g); coed interscholastic: aerobics/dance, cheering, dance squad, dance team, golf, physical fitness; coed intramural: aerobics/dance, basketball, cheering, cooperative games, dance, dance squad, dance team, flag football, football, golf, jogging, jump rope, kickball, martial arts, outdoor activities, outdoor adventure, paddle tennis, physical fitness, power lifting, rock climbing, running, soccer, softball, strength & conditioning, table tennis, touch football, track and field, volleyball, walking. 3 PE instructors, 12 coaches, 1 trainer.

Computers Computer network features include campus e-mail, on-campus library services, Internet access, wireless campus network.

Contact Mrs. Vicky Schleifstein, Director of International Admissions. 323-344-4330 Ext. 108. Fax: 323-344-4339. E-mail: vschleifstein@ribetacademy.com. Web site: www.ribetacademy.com.

RIDGEWOOD PREPARATORY SCHOOL

201 Pasadena Avenue
Metairie, Louisiana 70001
Head of School: Mr. M.J. Montgomery Jr.

General Information Coeducational day college-preparatory school. Grades PK–12. Founded: 1948. Setting: suburban. 4-acre campus. 3 buildings on campus. Approved or accredited by Southern Association of Colleges and Schools and Louisiana Department of Education. Endowment: $45,000. Total enrollment: 281. Upper school average class size: 25. Upper school faculty-student ratio: 1:25.

Faculty School total: 45. In upper school: 11 men, 23 women; 10 have advanced degrees.

Graduation Requirements Computer science, English, foreign language, mathematics, physical education (includes health), science, social studies (includes history).

College Placement 65 students graduated in 2005; all went to college, including Louisiana State University and Agricultural and Mechanical College; Loyola University New Orleans; Tulane University; University of Louisiana at Lafayette; University of Mississippi; University of New Orleans.

Student Life Upper grades have specified standards of dress, student council, honor system. Discipline rests primarily with faculty.

Tuition and Aid Day student tuition: $4450.

Admissions School's own exam required. Deadline for receipt of application materials: none. No application fee required. Interview required.

Athletics Interscholastic: baseball (boys), basketball (b,g), football (b), softball (g), volleyball (g); coed interscholastic: soccer.

Contact Mr. M. J. Montgomery Jr., Headmaster. 504-835-2545. Fax: 504-837-1864. E-mail: mjmontgomery@ridgewoodprep.com. Web site: www.ridgewoodprep.com.

RIDLEY COLLEGE

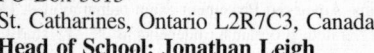

2 Ridley Road
PO Box 3013
St. Catharines, Ontario L2R7C3, Canada
Head of School: Jonathan Leigh

petersons.com

General Information Coeducational boarding and day college-preparatory, arts, and technology school, affiliated with Church of England (Anglican). Grades 5–PG. Founded: 1889. Setting: suburban. Nearest major city is Buffalo, NY. Students are housed in single-sex dormitories. 100-acre campus. 11 buildings on campus. Approved or accredited by Canadian Association of Independent Schools, Canadian Educational Standards Institute, Conference of Independent Schools of Ontario, European Council of International Schools, The Association of Boarding Schools, and Ontario Department of Education. Affiliate member of National Association of Independent Schools; member of Secondary School Admission Test Board. Language of instruction: English. Endowment: CAN$25 million. Total enrollment: 607. Upper school average class size: 17. Upper school faculty-student ratio: 1:9.

Upper School Student Profile Grade 9: 81 students (56 boys, 25 girls); Grade 10: 134 students (80 boys, 54 girls); Grade 11: 127 students (71 boys, 56 girls); Grade 12: 153 students (84 boys, 69 girls); Postgraduate: 8 students (5 boys, 3 girls). 67% of students are boarding students. 70% are province residents. 15 provinces are represented in upper school student body. 25% are international students. International students from Bahamas, Bermuda, Hong Kong, Mexico, Republic of Korea, and United States; 30 other countries represented in student body. 20% of students are members of Church of England (Anglican).

Faculty School total: 102. In upper school: 55 men, 46 women; 34 have advanced degrees; 39 reside on campus.

Subjects Offered Advanced Placement courses, algebra, American history, art, art history, biology, business mathematics, business skills, calculus, Canadian history, Canadian law, chemistry, computer programming, computer science, creative writing, drafting, drama, dramatic arts, driver education, economics, English, English literature, ESL, fine arts, French, geography, German, kinesiology, Latin, mathematics, music, physical education, physics, science, social science, social studies, Spanish, theater, world history.

Graduation Requirements Arts and fine arts (art, music, dance, drama), business skills (includes word processing), English, foreign language, mathematics, physical education (includes health), science, social science, social studies (includes history).

Special Academic Programs Advanced Placement exam preparation in 10 subject areas; honors section; independent study; domestic exchange program; study abroad; academic accommodation for the musically talented and the artistically talented; ESL (21 students enrolled).

College Placement 139 students graduated in 2005; 130 went to college, including McGill University; Queen's University at Kingston; The University of Western Ontario; University of Toronto; Wilfrid Laurier University. Other: 3 went to work, 6 entered a postgraduate year. Mean SAT verbal: 570, mean SAT math: 590.

Student Life Upper grades have uniform requirement, student council, honor system. Discipline rests primarily with faculty. Attendance at religious services is required.

Summer Programs Advancement programs offered; session focuses on academics; held on campus; accepts boys and girls; open to students from other schools. 50 students usually enrolled. 2006 schedule: July 1 to August 7. Application deadline: May 31.

Tuition and Aid Day student tuition: CAN$21,090; 7-day tuition and room/board: CAN$34,990. Tuition installment plan (monthly payment plans, individually arranged payment plans). Tuition reduction for siblings, bursaries, merit scholarship grants, need-based loans available. In 2005–06, 30% of upper-school students received aid; total upper-school merit-scholarship money awarded: CAN$400,000. Total amount of financial aid awarded in 2005–06: CAN$1,700,000.

Admissions Traditional secondary-level entrance grade is 9. For fall 2005, 352 students applied for upper-level admission, 298 were accepted, 216 enrolled. Differential Aptitude Test or SSAT required. Deadline for receipt of application materials: none. Application fee required: CAN$150. Interview recommended.

Athletics Interscholastic: artistic gym (girls), baseball (b,g), basketball (b,g), crew (b,g), cross-country running (b,g), dance (g), dance squad (g), field hockey (g), football (b), golf (b), gymnastics (g), hockey (b,g), ice hockey (b,g), lacrosse (b), modern dance (g), rowing (b,g), rugby (b,g), soccer (b,g), softball (b,g), squash (b,g), swimming and diving (b,g), tennis (b,g), track and field (b,g), volleyball (g); intramural: aerobics (g), aerobics/dance (g), ballet (g), Cosom hockey (g), ice hockey (b), modern dance (b); coed interscholastic: tennis; coed intramural: alpine skiing, aquatics, back packing, badminton, baseball, basketball, bicycling, canoeing/kayaking, climbing, drill team, equestrian sports, fitness, Frisbee, hiking/backpacking, horseback riding, ice skating, life saving, martial arts, outdoor activities, outdoor adventure, outdoor education, outdoor recreation, outdoor skills, outdoors, physical fitness, ropes courses, scuba diving, skeet shooting, skiing (downhill), snowboarding, soccer, softball, squash, swimming and diving, table tennis, tennis, track and field, trap and skeet, ultimate Frisbee, volleyball, weight training, windsurfing, yoga. 5 PE instructors, 6 coaches, 3 trainers.

Computers Computers are regularly used in all academic classes. Computer network features include campus e-mail, on-campus library services, CD-ROMs, online commercial services, Internet access, file transfer, DVD, wireless campus network.

Contact Don Rickers, Director of Admission. 905-684-1889 Ext. 2255. Fax: 905-684-8875. E-mail: admission@ridley.on.ca. Web site: www.ridley.on.ca.

ANNOUNCEMENT FROM THE SCHOOL Located only 20 minutes from Niagara Falls, Ridley attracts boys and girls from more than 30 countries, including many from the USA. SAT, AP, and ESL instruction are offered. Students have campuswide, wireless Internet access; Macintosh laptop computers are curriculum integrated.

RIO LINDO ADVENTIST ACADEMY

3200 Rio Lindo Avenue
Healdsburg, California 95448
Head of School: Mr. Douglas Schmidt

General Information Coeducational boarding and day college-preparatory, general academic, arts, religious studies, technology, music, and sports school, affiliated with Seventh-day Adventist Church. Grades 9–12. Founded: 1962. Setting: rural. Nearest major city is Santa Rosa. Students are housed in single-sex dormitories. 368-acre campus. 10 buildings on campus. Approved or accredited by Western Association of Schools and Colleges and California Department of Education. Endowment: $1.5 million. Total enrollment: 145. Upper school average class size: 20. Upper school faculty-student ratio: 1:10.

Upper School Student Profile Grade 9: 23 students (14 boys, 9 girls); Grade 10: 30 students (14 boys, 16 girls); Grade 11: 47 students (18 boys, 29 girls); Grade 12: 45 students (23 boys, 22 girls). 87% of students are boarding students. 76% are state residents. 5 states are represented in upper school student body. 18% are international students. International students from Haiti, Hong Kong, Japan, Macao, Republic of Korea, and Taiwan. 74% of students are Seventh-day Adventists.

Faculty School total: 22. In upper school: 12 men, 10 women; 8 have advanced degrees; all reside on campus.

Subjects Offered Algebra, alternative physical education, anatomy and physiology, auto body, auto mechanics, biology, calculus, ceramics, chemistry, choir, chorus, community service, computer keyboarding, computer literacy, concert bell choir, consumer mathematics, drama, driver education, economics, English, ESL, fitness, geometry, handbells, health science, home economics, honors English, honors U.S. history, keyboarding/computer, mathematics, media production, photo shop, physical education, physical science, physics, piano, pre-algebra, publications, religion, shop, Spanish, U.S. government, U.S. history, welding, woodworking, world history.

Graduation Requirements Algebra, American government, arts and fine arts (art, music, dance, drama), biology, chemistry, computer keyboarding, computer literacy, economics, electives, English, geometry, health education, life skills, modern languages, physical education (includes health), physics, religion (includes Bible studies and theology), U.S. history, world history, 25 community service hours per year.

Special Academic Programs Advanced Placement exam preparation in 1 subject area; honors section; remedial reading and/or remedial writing; ESL (5 students enrolled).

College Placement 53 students graduated in 2005; 46 went to college, including De Anza College; La Sierra University; Pacific Union College; Southern Adventist University; Walla Walla College. Other: 7 went to work. Median SAT verbal: 440, median SAT math: 520, median composite ACT: 20. 6% scored over 600 on SAT verbal, 28% scored over 600 on SAT math, 9% scored over 26 on composite ACT.

Student Life Upper grades have specified standards of dress. Discipline rests primarily with faculty. Attendance at religious services is required.

Tuition and Aid Day student tuition: $9540; 7-day tuition and room/board: $17,874. Tuition installment plan (monthly payment plans). Tuition reduction for siblings, merit scholarship grants, need-based scholarship grants, paying campus jobs, Pathways to Success Scholarships available. In 2005–06, 40% of upper-school students received aid; total upper-school merit-scholarship money awarded: $27,000. Total amount of financial aid awarded in 2005–06: $240,000.

Admissions Traditional secondary-level entrance grade is 9. For fall 2005, 170 students applied for upper-level admission, 167 were accepted, 145 enrolled. Any standardized test required. Deadline for receipt of application materials: none. Application fee required: $25. Interview recommended.

Athletics Interscholastic: baseball (girls), basketball (b,g), flag football (b,g), golf (b), soccer (b), softball (g), volleyball (g); intramural: baseball (b,g), basketball (b,g), flag football (b,g), floor hockey (b), softball (b,g); coed interscholastic: back packing; coed intramural: back packing, baseball, canoeing/kayaking, fitness, flag football, jogging, ropes courses, skiing (downhill), snowboarding, softball, tennis. 1 PE instructor, 1 coach.

Computers Computers are regularly used in computer applications, English, ESL, history, keyboarding, media production, publications, religion, writing, yearbook classes. Computer network features include CD-ROMs, Internet access.

Contact Mrs. Karen Nicola, Recruiting and Marketing Coordinator. 707-431-5100 Ext. 132. Fax: 707-431-5115. E-mail: knicola@riolindo.org. Web site: www.riolindo.org.

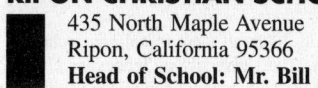

RIPON CHRISTIAN SCHOOLS

435 North Maple Avenue
Ripon, California 95366
Head of School: Mr. Bill Finley

General Information Coeducational day college-preparatory, arts, business, religious studies, and technology school, affiliated with Calvinist faith. Grades 9–12. Founded: 1946. Setting: small town. Nearest major city is San Francisco. 34-acre campus. 3 buildings on campus. Approved or accredited by Christian Schools International, Western Association of Schools and Colleges, and California Department of Education. Endowment: $2.5 million. Total enrollment: 780. Upper school average class size: 22. Upper school faculty-student ratio: 1:18.

Upper School Student Profile 60% of students are Calvinist.

Faculty School total: 51. In upper school: 9 men, 11 women; 8 have advanced degrees.

Subjects Offered Algebra, American history, anatomy, art, Bible studies, biology, business, calculus, chemistry, computer applications, computer math, computer programming, computer science, creative writing, drafting, English, environmental science, ethics, fine arts, geography, geometry, government/civics, grammar, health, history, logic, mathematics, music, physical education, physics, physiology, psychology, science, social science, social studies, Spanish, trigonometry, world history.

Graduation Requirements Arts and fine arts (art, music, dance, drama), computer science, English, foreign language, mathematics, physical education (includes health), religion (includes Bible studies and theology), science, social science, social studies (includes history).

Special Academic Programs Advanced Placement exam preparation in 3 subject areas; independent study; academic accommodation for the musically talented and the artistically talented.

College Placement 45 students graduated in 2005; 42 went to college, including Azusa Pacific University; California Polytechnic State University, San Luis Obispo; California State University, Stanislaus; Calvin College; Dordt College; Modesto Junior College. Other: 1 went to work, 2 entered military service.

Student Life Upper grades have specified standards of dress, student council. Discipline rests primarily with faculty. Attendance at religious services is required.

Tuition and Aid Day student tuition: $6000. Tuition installment plan (FACTS Tuition Payment Plan, individually arranged payment plans). Tuition reduction for siblings, need-based scholarship grants, need-based financial assistance available. In 2005–06, 10% of upper-school students received aid. Total amount of financial aid awarded in 2005–06: $20,000.

Admissions Traditional secondary-level entrance grade is 9. For fall 2005, 24 students applied for upper-level admission, 20 were accepted, 20 enrolled. Deadline for receipt of application materials: none. No application fee required. On-campus interview required.

Athletics Interscholastic: baseball (boys), basketball (b,g), cheering (g), football (b), golf (b,g), physical fitness (b,g), physical training (b,g), soccer (b,g), softball (g), volleyball (b,g), weight training (b,g); intramural: indoor soccer (b); coed interscholastic: tennis; coed intramural: tennis. 2 PE instructors, 8 coaches.

Computers Computers are regularly used in business skills classes. Computer network features include on-campus library services, CD-ROMs, Internet access, DVD, wireless campus network.

Contact Mr. Bill Finley, Principal. 209-599-2155. Fax: 209-599-2170. E-mail: bfinley@rcschools.com. Web site: www.rcschools.com.

RIVERDALE COUNTRY SCHOOL

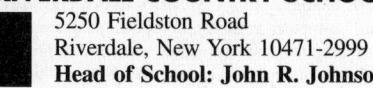

5250 Fieldston Road
Riverdale, New York 10471-2999
Head of School: John R. Johnson

petersons.com

General Information Coeducational day college-preparatory school. Grades PK–12. Founded: 1907. Setting: suburban. Nearest major city is New York. 27-acre campus. 9 buildings on campus. Approved or accredited by New York State Association of Independent Schools and New York Department of Education. Member of National Association of Independent Schools and Secondary School Admission Test Board. Total enrollment: 1,060. Upper school average class size: 16. Upper school faculty-student ratio: 1:8.

Upper School Student Profile Grade 7: 85 students (45 boys, 40 girls); Grade 8: 71 students (40 boys, 31 girls); Grade 9: 118 students (68 boys, 50 girls); Grade 10: 119 students (58 boys, 61 girls); Grade 11: 119 students (51 boys, 68 girls); Grade 12: 113 students (54 boys, 59 girls).

Faculty School total: 141. In upper school: 36 men, 41 women; 53 have advanced degrees.

Subjects Offered Algebra, American literature, anatomy, art, art history, biology, calculus, ceramics, chemistry, community service, computer math, computer programming, computer science, creative writing, drama, driver education, earth science, ecology, economics, English, English literature, environmental science, European history, expository writing, fine arts, French, geology, geometry, government/civics, grammar, health, history, history of science, introduction to liberal studies, Japanese, journalism, Latin, marine biology, mathematics, music, oceanography, philosophy,

photography, physical education, physics, psychology, science, social studies, Spanish, speech, statistics, theater, theory of knowledge, trigonometry, world history, writing.

Graduation Requirements American studies, arts and fine arts (art, music, dance, drama), computer science, English, foreign language, mathematics, physical education (includes health), science, social studies (includes history), integrated liberal studies. Community service is required.

Special Academic Programs Advanced Placement exam preparation in 8 subject areas; honors section; independent study; term-away projects; study abroad; academic accommodation for the gifted, the musically talented, and the artistically talented.

College Placement 107 students graduated in 2004; all went to college, including Brown University; Columbia University; Harvard University; New York University; University of Pennsylvania; Yale University. Median SAT verbal: 660, median SAT math: 670.

Student Life Upper grades have student council, honor system. Discipline rests primarily with faculty.

Tuition and Aid Day student tuition: $27,175. Tuition installment plan (Key Tuition Payment Plan, monthly payment plans). Need-based scholarship grants available. In 2004–05, 20% of upper-school students received aid. Total amount of financial aid awarded in 2004–05: $3,100,000.

Admissions Traditional secondary-level entrance grade is 9. For fall 2005, 577 students applied for upper-level admission, 80 enrolled. ISEE or SSAT required. Deadline for receipt of application materials: December 3. Application fee required: $50. On-campus interview required.

Athletics Interscholastic: baseball (boys), basketball (b,g), field hockey (g), football (b), gymnastics (g), lacrosse (b,g), soccer (b,g), softball (g), tennis (b,g), volleyball (g), wrestling (b); intramural: baseball (b), basketball (b,g), field hockey (g), football (b), gymnastics (g), lacrosse (b,g), soccer (b,g), softball (b,g), tennis (b,g), volleyball (g), wrestling (b); coed interscholastic: cross-country running, fencing, golf, indoor track, swimming and diving, track and field; coed intramural: cross-country running, dance, fencing, fitness, indoor track, physical fitness, swimming and diving, tennis, track and field, yoga. 7 PE instructors, 31 coaches, 1 trainer.

Computers Computers are regularly used in art, English, foreign language, history, mathematics, music, science classes. Computer network features include campus e-mail, on-campus library services, CD-ROMs, online commercial services, Internet access, file transfer, DVD, off-campus e-mail, off-campus library services.

Contact Ridie L. Markenson, Director of Middle and Upper School Admission. 718-519-2715. Fax: 718-519-2793. E-mail: rmarkenson@riverdale.edu. Web site: www.riverdale.edu.

ANNOUNCEMENT FROM THE SCHOOL Riverdale draws students from Manhattan, the Bronx, Westchester County, Rockland County, and northern New Jersey. It combines the academic and cultural stimulation of the city with country surroundings on a 27.5-acre campus. Its rigorous academic program, emphasis on social issues, and diverse opportunities in the arts, athletics, and extracurricular activities prepare students to study in the most demanding colleges and universities.

RIVERMONT COLLEGIATE

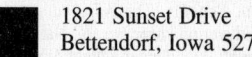

1821 Sunset Drive
Bettendorf, Iowa 52722
Head of School: Mr. Richard E. St. Laurent

General Information Coeducational day college-preparatory, arts, and technology school. Grades PS–12. Founded: 1884. Setting: suburban. Nearest major city is Davenport. 16-acre campus. 6 buildings on campus. Approved or accredited by Independent Schools Association of the Central States and Iowa Department of Education. Member of National Association of Independent Schools and Secondary School Admission Test Board. Endowment: $1.9 million. Total enrollment: 207. Upper school average class size: 10. Upper school faculty-student ratio: 1:4.

Upper School Student Profile Grade 9: 16 students (9 boys, 7 girls); Grade 10: 7 students (5 boys, 2 girls); Grade 11: 8 students (5 boys, 3 girls); Grade 12: 11 students (5 boys, 6 girls).

Faculty School total: 36. In upper school: 7 men, 15 women; 7 have advanced degrees.

Subjects Offered Acting, advanced chemistry, advanced math, algebra, anatomy and physiology, ancient world history, art, arts, band, biology, business law, calculus, calculus-AP, chemistry, chemistry-AP, Chinese, computer multimedia, computer programming, computer science, creative writing, drama, earth science, economics, English, English literature, English-AP, European history, fine arts, French, French language-AP, French literature-AP, French-AP, geography, geometry, global science, government/civics, grammar, health, health education, history, history-AP, Holocaust studies, honors algebra, honors English, HTML design, humanities, independent study, jazz band, Latin, Latin American history, life science, mathematics, music, photography, physical education, physical fitness, physics, piano, psychology, public speaking, science, senior project, social studies, Spanish, Spanish literature-AP, Spanish-AP, speech, speech and debate, theater, theater arts, theater design and production, U.S. government, U.S. history, U.S. history-AP, vocal ensemble, Web site design, writing.

Rivermont Collegiate

Graduation Requirements Arts and fine arts (art, music, dance, drama), computer science, English, foreign language, mathematics, physical education (includes health), science, senior project, social studies (includes history).

Special Academic Programs Advanced Placement exam preparation in 8 subject areas; honors section; independent study; study at local college for college credit; academic accommodation for the gifted and the musically talented.

College Placement 15 students graduated in 2005; all went to college, including Augustana College; The George Washington University; The University of Iowa; University of Chicago; University of Notre Dame; Washington University in St. Louis. Median SAT verbal: 670, median SAT math: 640, median composite ACT: 28.

Student Life Upper grades have specified standards of dress, student council. Discipline rests primarily with faculty.

Summer Programs Enrichment, sports programs offered; session focuses on Enrichment; held on campus; accepts boys and girls; open to students from other schools. 75 students usually enrolled. 2006 schedule: June 21 to August 6. Application deadline: May 28.

Tuition and Aid Day student tuition: $9255. Tuition installment plan (Insured Tuition Payment Plan, Key Tuition Payment Plan, monthly payment plans). Tuition reduction for siblings, merit scholarship grants, need-based scholarship grants available. In 2005–06, 45% of upper-school students received aid; total upper-school merit-scholarship money awarded: $13,240. Total amount of financial aid awarded in 2005–06: $309,755.

Admissions Traditional secondary-level entrance grade is 11. For fall 2005, 8 students applied for upper-level admission, 6 were accepted, 5 enrolled. Any standardized test, Iowa Tests of Basic Skills or Wide Range Achievement Test required. Deadline for receipt of application materials: none. Application fee required: $50. Interview recommended.

Athletics Interscholastic: basketball (boys, girls), cheering (g), cross-country running (b,g), golf (b,g), soccer (b), swimming and diving (g), track and field (b,g), volleyball (g); intramural: basketball (b,g), cheering (g), table tennis (b,g); coed interscholastic: soccer; coed intramural: bowling, floor hockey, indoor soccer, table tennis, volleyball. 1 PE instructor, 3 coaches.

Computers Computers are regularly used in English, foreign language, history, independent study, mathematics classes. Computer network features include campus e-mail, on-campus library services, CD-ROMs, Internet access, file transfer, wireless campus network.

Contact Mrs. Heidi J. Herman, Director of Admission and Financial Aid. 563-359-1366 Ext. 302. Fax: 563-359-7576. E-mail: herman@rvmt.org. Web site: www.rivermontcollegiate.org.

Special Academic Programs Advanced Placement exam preparation in 6 subject areas; honors section; ESL.

College Placement 86 students graduated in 2005; all went to college, including Auburn University; Florida State University; The University of Tennessee; United States Military Academy; University of Florida; University of Georgia. 11% scored over 600 on SAT verbal, 17% scored over 600 on SAT math.

Student Life Upper grades have uniform requirement, student council, honor system. Discipline rests equally with students and faculty. Attendance at religious services is required.

Summer Programs Remediation, enrichment, advancement, ESL, sports, art/fine arts, rigorous outdoor training, computer instruction programs offered; session focuses on academics; held on campus; accepts boys; open to students from other schools. 170 students usually enrolled. 2006 schedule: June 25 to July 26. Application deadline: none.

Tuition and Aid Day student tuition: $15,000; 7-day tuition and room/board: $23,950. Tuition installment plan (Key Tuition Payment Plan, FACTS Tuition Payment Plan). Tuition reduction for siblings available.

Admissions Traditional secondary-level entrance grade is 9. Any standardized test and writing sample required. Deadline for receipt of application materials: none. Application fee required: $100. On-campus interview required.

Athletics Interscholastic: baseball, basketball, crew, cross-country running, drill team, football, golf, JROTC drill, lacrosse, marksmanship, riflery, soccer, swimming and diving, tennis, track and field, wrestling; intramural: aquatics, back packing, baseball, basketball, billiards, canoeing/kayaking, climbing, cross-country running, fitness, flag football, football, hiking/backpacking, indoor track, jogging, kayaking, marksmanship, mountaineering, outdoor activities, outdoor adventure, outdoor recreation, outdoor skills, outdoors, paddle tennis, physical training, rappelling, rock climbing, ropes courses, running, skateboarding, soccer, strength & conditioning, swimming and diving, table tennis, tennis, volleyball, water polo, water volleyball, weight lifting, weight training. 3 PE instructors, 6 coaches, 1 trainer.

Computers Computers are regularly used in college planning, desktop publishing, English, foreign language, journalism, library, mathematics, photography, SAT preparation, science, technology, yearbook classes. Computer network features include campus e-mail, on-campus library services, CD-ROMs, Internet access.

Contact Mr. Matt Gifford, Director of Admissions. 770-532-6251 Ext. 2122. Fax: 678-291-3364. E-mail: mgifford@cadet.com. Web site: www.cadet.com.

See full description on page 1000.

RIVERSIDE MILITARY ACADEMY

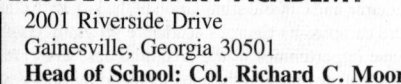

2001 Riverside Drive
Gainesville, Georgia 30501
Head of School: Col. Richard C. Moore

General Information Boys' boarding and day college-preparatory, arts, and technology school. Grades 7–12. Founded: 1907. Setting: suburban. Nearest major city is Atlanta. Students are housed in single-sex dormitories. 236-acre campus. 9 buildings on campus. Approved or accredited by Georgia Independent School Association, National Independent Private Schools Association, Southern Association of Colleges and Schools, Southern Association of Independent Schools, The Association of Boarding Schools, and Georgia Department of Education. Member of National Association of Independent Schools. Total enrollment: 412. Upper school average class size: 10. Upper school faculty-student ratio: 1:10.

Upper School Student Profile Grade 9: 77 students (77 boys); Grade 10: 78 students (78 boys); Grade 11: 99 students (99 boys); Grade 12: 99 students (99 boys). 91% of students are boarding students. 58% are state residents. 22 states are represented in upper school student body. 4% are international students. International students from China, Colombia, Dominican Republic, Republic of Korea, Spain, and Taiwan; 1 other country represented in student body.

Faculty School total: 63. In upper school: 48 men, 12 women; 39 have advanced degrees; 30 reside on campus.

Subjects Offered Advanced chemistry, algebra, American literature, art, art appreciation, band, biology, biology-AP, British literature-AP, calculus, calculus-AP, chemistry, chemistry-AP, computer applications, computer education, computer keyboarding, computer math, computer programming, computer science, computer skills, computer studies, creative writing, desktop publishing, drama, driver education, earth science, ecology, economics, English, English language and composition-AP, English language-AP, English literature, ESL, ethics, European history, fine arts, French, French language-AP, geography, geometry, German, government-AP, government/civics, grammar, health, history-AP, honors English, honors geometry, honors U.S. history, honors world history, journalism, JROTC, Latin, leadership, mathematics, military science, modern world history, music, music theory, physical education, physics, political science, pre-algebra, pre-calculus, science, social science, social studies, Spanish, speech, statistics, theater, typing, U.S. government, U.S. government-AP, U.S. history, U.S. history-AP, weight training, world history, world history-AP, world literature.

Graduation Requirements Arts and fine arts (art, music, dance, drama), computer science, English, foreign language, JROTC, mathematics, physical education (includes health), science, social studies (includes history).

RIVERSIDE SCHOOL

Artherstrasse 55
Zug 6300, Switzerland
Head of School: Dominic Currer

General Information Coeducational day college-preparatory, International Baccalaureate Middle Years Program, and Advanced Placement school. Ungraded, ages 12–19. Founded: 1990. Setting: small town. Nearest major city is Zurich. 5-hectare campus. 1 building on campus. Approved or accredited by International Baccalaureate Organization. Member of European Council of International Schools. Language of instruction: English. Total enrollment: 112. Upper school average class size: 12. Upper school faculty-student ratio: 1:6.

Faculty School total: 20. In upper school: 8 men, 12 women; 7 have advanced degrees.

Subjects Offered Art, art history-AP, biology, biology-AP, calculus-AP, chemistry, chemistry-AP, computer applications, computer graphics, computer programming, computer science-AP, dance, drama, English, environmental science-AP, French, French language-AP, German, German literature, German-AP, history, human geography—AP, humanities, integrated mathematics, integrated science, Latin, macro/microeconomics-AP, modern European history-AP, music, music theory-AP, photography, physical education, physics, physics-AP, pre-calculus, studio art-AP, technology/design, U.S. history.

Graduation Requirements Art, computers, English, foreign language, lab science, mathematics, physical education (includes health), social sciences.

Special Academic Programs Advanced Placement exam preparation in 16 subject areas; accelerated programs; independent study; ESL (9 students enrolled).

College Placement 20 students graduated in 2005; 14 went to college, including Boston University; Parsons The New School for Design; Rhode Island College; The University of Tennessee; University of Colorado at Boulder. Other: 3 went to work, 3 had other specific plans. Median SAT verbal: 568, median SAT math: 540, median combined SAT: 1676. 38% scored over 600 on SAT verbal, 25% scored over 600 on SAT math, 38% scored over 1800 on combined SAT.

Student Life Discipline rests primarily with faculty.

Tuition and Aid Day student tuition: 27,000 Swiss francs. Tuition installment plan (monthly payment plans, individually arranged payment plans, semester payment plan). Bursaries, discounts for children of staff available. In 2005–06, 19% of upper-school students received aid. Total amount of financial aid awarded in 2005–06: 300,000 Swiss francs.

Admissions Traditional secondary-level entrance age is 12. For fall 2005, 12 students applied for upper-level admission, 12 were accepted, 10 enrolled. Writing sample required. Deadline for receipt of application materials: none. No application fee required. Interview recommended.

Athletics Interscholastic: alpine skiing (boys, girls), basketball (b,g), cross-country running (b,g), indoor soccer (b,g), skiing (downhill) (b,g), soccer (b,g), track and field (b,g), volleyball (b,g); intramural: alpine skiing (b,g), basketball (b,g), cross-country running (b,g), indoor soccer (b,g), soccer (b,g), track and field (b,g); coed interscholastic: softball; coed intramural: aerobics/dance, back packing, badminton, bicycling, canoeing/kayaking, dance, golf, hiking/backpacking, ice skating, kayaking, martial arts, mountain biking, outdoor activities, outdoor education, rowing, running, sailing, skiing (downhill), snowboarding, soccer, softball, swimming and diving, tennis, walking, winter walking. 1 PE instructor.

Computers Computers are regularly used in human geography—AP, humanities, information technology classes. Computer network features include campus e-mail, CD-ROMs, Internet access.

Contact Jelena Vasak, Financial Director. 41-41-726-0450. Fax: 41-41-726-0452. E-mail: jelena.vasak@riverside.ch. Web site: www.riverside.ch.

THE RIVERS SCHOOL

333 Winter Street
Weston, Massachusetts 02493-1040
Head of School: Thomas P. Olverson

petersons.com

General Information Coeducational day college-preparatory and arts school. Grades 6–12. Founded: 1915. Setting: suburban. Nearest major city is Boston. 60-acre campus. 8 buildings on campus. Approved or accredited by Association of Independent Schools in New England and New England Association of Schools and Colleges. Member of National Association of Independent Schools and Secondary School Admission Test Board. Endowment: $14.8 million. Total enrollment: 418. Upper school average class size: 14. Upper school faculty-student ratio: 1:7.

Upper School Student Profile Grade 9: 80 students (40 boys, 40 girls); Grade 10: 76 students (44 boys, 32 girls); Grade 11: 81 students (38 boys, 43 girls); Grade 12: 41 students (41 boys).

Faculty School total: 86. In upper school: 31 men, 27 women; 36 have advanced degrees.

Subjects Offered Advanced Placement courses, algebra, American history, American literature, art, art history, art history-AP, biology, biology-AP, calculus, calculus-AP, ceramics, chamber groups, chemistry, chorus, civil rights, Civil War, computer graphics, computer science, computer science-AP, creative writing, drama, earth science, English, English language and composition-AP, English literature, English literature and composition-AP, environmental science-AP, European history, expository writing, film studies, filmmaking, fine arts, French, French-AP, geography, geometry, history, jazz band, journalism, Latin, Latin-AP, mathematics, modern European history-AP, music, photography, physics, physics-AP, science, social studies, Spanish, Spanish-AP, statistics-AP, theater, trigonometry, U.S. history-AP, world history, world literature.

Graduation Requirements Algebra, athletics, English, foreign language, geometry, history, mathematics, modern European history, science, U.S. history, visual and performing arts, participation in athletics. Community service is required.

Special Academic Programs Advanced Placement exam preparation in 15 subject areas; honors section; independent study; study at local college for college credit.

College Placement 71 students graduated in 2005; 70 went to college, including Boston University; Colgate University; New York University; The Johns Hopkins University; Trinity College; Union College. Other: 1 entered a postgraduate year. Median SAT verbal: 620, median SAT math: 610. 60% scored over 600 on SAT verbal, 58% scored over 600 on SAT math.

Student Life Upper grades have specified standards of dress, student council, honor system. Discipline rests primarily with faculty.

Tuition and Aid Day student tuition: $27,250. Tuition installment plan (Academic Management Services Plan, Key Tuition Payment Plan, monthly payment plans). Need-based scholarship grants available. In 2005–06, 19% of upper-school students received aid. Total amount of financial aid awarded in 2005–06: $1,346,950.

Admissions Traditional secondary-level entrance grade is 9. For fall 2005, 293 students applied for upper-level admission, 99 were accepted, 40 enrolled. ISEE or SSAT required. Deadline for receipt of application materials: February 1. Application fee required: $40. On-campus interview required.

Athletics Interscholastic: alpine skiing (boys, girls), baseball (b), basketball (b,g), cross-country running (b,g), field hockey (g), football (b), golf (b), ice hockey (b,g), lacrosse (b,g), skiing (downhill) (b,g), soccer (b,g), softball (g), strength & conditioning (b,g), tennis (b,g); intramural: basketball (b,g), tennis (g); coed interscholastic: fitness, physical training, track and field, weight lifting, weight training; coed intramural: strength & conditioning. 4 coaches, 2 trainers.

Computers Computers are regularly used in art, aviation, history, humanities, language development, mathematics, newspaper, publications, science, writing, yearbook classes. Computer network features include campus e-mail, on-campus library services, CD-ROMs, online commercial services, Internet access, file transfer, office computer access, DVD, wireless campus network, language lab.

Contact Gillian Lloyd, Director of Admissions. 781-235-9300. Fax: 781-239-3614. E-mail: g.lloyd@rivers.org. Web site: www.rivers.org.

ANNOUNCEMENT FROM THE SCHOOL Originally located in Brookline, Massachusetts, The Rivers School was founded in 1915 by Robert W. Rivers. The School grew rapidly and moved to a larger site to accommodate its increased enrollment. The School's final move occurred in 1960 when it settled on the banks of Nonesuch Pond in Weston, just 15 miles west of Boston. In 1975, the School's program was enhanced with the opening of The Rivers Music School, a community conservatory offering classes for Rivers students as well as children and adults in the wider community. The recently renovated MacDowell Library and the Lewis Math and Science Center, among others, provide state-of-the-art facilities. Over a dozen acres of playing fields, 6 tennis courts, and the 77,000-square-foot MacDowell Athletic Center provide the setting for the School's strong athletic program. Rivers also offers ample facilities in support of its extensive visual and performing arts programs. The Rivers School Conservatory Program offers extraordinary opportunities for the serious musician. The middle school, encompassing grades 6–8, is a model of innovation, challenge, and collaboration. Structured yet creative, the program provides a foundation upon which students build when they enter the rigorous college-preparatory program in the Upper School. The Upper School (9–12) challenges students to explore new areas and become independent in their academic and cocurricular activities. Rivers offers honors and Advanced Placement courses in all disciplines. Teachers at Rivers have a talent for discovering a student's potential and then challenging and motivating the student to excel. The philosophy of the college counseling office at Rivers is simple: match the right student with the right college. The highly experienced college counselors lead students through a 2-year process of workshops and self-evaluation to help determine the best college choices for individual students. Last year, all 76 graduating seniors matriculated at 52 different colleges and universities, including Brown, Yale, Tufts, Dartmouth, Middlebury, Vanderbilt, Wellesley, Colby, Bowdoin, Emory, and Boston College.

RIVERSTONE COMMUNITY SCHOOL

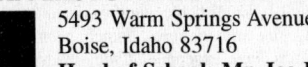

5493 Warm Springs Avenue
Boise, Idaho 83716
Head of School: Mr. Joe Kennedy

General Information Coeducational day college-preparatory school. Grades K–12. Founded: 1997. Setting: suburban. 13-acre campus. 4 buildings on campus. Approved or accredited by International Baccalaureate Organization, Northwest Association of Accredited Schools, Northwest Association of Schools and Colleges, Pacific Northwest Association of Independent Schools, and Idaho Department of Education. Total enrollment: 252. Upper school average class size: 15. Upper school faculty-student ratio: 1:4.

Upper School Student Profile Grade 9: 29 students (18 boys, 11 girls); Grade 10: 17 students (7 boys, 10 girls); Grade 11: 22 students (11 boys, 11 girls); Grade 12: 9 students (5 boys, 4 girls).

Faculty School total: 37. In upper school: 8 men, 9 women; 9 have advanced degrees.

Subjects Offered International Baccalaureate courses.

Graduation Requirements International Baccalaureate courses.

Special Academic Programs International Baccalaureate program; ESL (25 students enrolled).

College Placement 12 students graduated in 2005; all went to college, including American University; Middlebury College; Savannah College of Art and Design; University of Pennsylvania; Wellesley College; Williams College. Median SAT verbal: 590, median SAT math: 570.

Student Life Upper grades have specified standards of dress, honor system. Discipline rests primarily with faculty.

Summer Programs Enrichment, art/fine arts programs offered; session focuses on camps and outdoor education; held both on and off campus; held at Boise River; accepts boys and girls; open to students from other schools. 100 students usually enrolled. 2006 schedule: July 10 to August 11.

Tuition and Aid Day student tuition: $9394. Tuition installment plan (monthly payment plans). Tuition reduction for siblings, need-based scholarship grants available.

Admissions Traditional secondary-level entrance grade is 9. Application fee required: $50. Interview required.

Athletics Intramural: fitness (girls); coed interscholastic: aquatics, cross-country running, indoor soccer; coed intramural: back packing, fitness walking, golf, ice skating, kayaking, lacrosse, nordic skiing, outdoor activities, outdoor adventure, outdoor education, outdoor recreation, outdoor skills, outdoors, physical fitness, rafting, ropes courses, running, skiing (cross-country), skiing (downhill), snowboarding.

Computers Computer network features include CD-ROMs, Internet access, DVD, wireless campus network.

Contact Ms. Rachel Pusch, Admissions Director. 208-424-5000 Ext. 2104. Fax: 208-424-0033. E-mail: rpusch@riverstonecs.org. Web site: www.riverstonecs.org.

RIVERVIEW SCHOOL

East Sandwich, Massachusetts
See Special Needs Schools section.

ROBERT LAND ACADEMY

Wellandport, Ontario, Canada
See Special Needs Schools section.

ROBERT LOUIS STEVENSON SCHOOL
New York, New York
See Special Needs Schools section.

THE ROCKLAND COUNTRY DAY SCHOOL
34 Kings Highway
Congers, New York 10920-2199
Head of School: Dr. James P. Handlin

General Information Coeducational day college-preparatory, arts, and technology school. Grades PK–12. Founded: 1959. Setting: suburban. Nearest major city is New York. 20-acre campus. 5 buildings on campus. Approved or accredited by New York State Association of Independent Schools and New York State Department of Education. Member of National Association of Independent Schools. Languages of instruction: Spanish and French. Total enrollment: 169. Upper school average class size: 15. Upper school faculty-student ratio: 1:3.

Upper School Student Profile Grade 9: 23 students (11 boys, 12 girls); Grade 10: 8 students (4 boys, 4 girls); Grade 11: 15 students (9 boys, 6 girls); Grade 12: 14 students (6 boys, 8 girls).

Faculty School total: 37. In upper school: 9 men, 9 women; 7 have advanced degrees.

Subjects Offered Algebra, American history, American literature, art, art history, band, biology, calculus, ceramics, chemistry, chorus, community service, computer math, creative writing, drama, drawing, English, English literature, environmental science, European history, expository writing, fine arts, forensics, French, geometry, government/civics, health, history, humanities, jazz ensemble, Latin, madrigals, mathematics, music, orchestra, painting, philosophy, photography, photojournalism, physical education, physics, psychology, science, social studies, sociology, Spanish, theater, world history, world literature, writing.

Graduation Requirements Arts and fine arts (art, music, dance, drama), computer science, English, foreign language, mathematics, music, physical education (includes health), science, social studies (includes history), off-campus senior internship. Community service is required.

Special Academic Programs Advanced Placement exam preparation in 14 subject areas; honors section; accelerated programs; independent study; term-away projects; study at local college for college credit; academic accommodation for the gifted, the musically talented, and the artistically talented.

College Placement 14 students graduated in 2005; all went to college, including Chapman University; James Madison University; Siena College; University of Vermont; University of Wisconsin–Madison. Median SAT verbal: 585, median SAT math: 610. Mean composite ACT: 24.

Student Life Upper grades have specified standards of dress, student council, honor system. Discipline rests equally with students and faculty.

Tuition and Aid Day student tuition: $22,500. Guaranteed tuition plan. Tuition installment plan (Insured Tuition Payment Plan, Key Tuition Payment Plan, monthly payment plans, individually arranged payment plans). Need-based scholarship grants available. In 2005–06, 20% of upper-school students received aid. Total amount of financial aid awarded in 2005–06: $126,665.

Admissions Traditional secondary-level entrance grade is 9. For fall 2005, 21 students applied for upper-level admission, 11 were accepted, 8 enrolled. Admissions testing, English entrance exam, English proficiency, ERB and writing sample required. Deadline for receipt of application materials: none. Application fee required: $50. On-campus interview required.

Athletics Interscholastic: aerobics/dance (girls), baseball (b), basketball (b,g), cheering (g), golf (b,g), modern dance (g), softball (g); intramural: cheering (g); coed interscholastic: cross-country running, dance, golf, paddle tennis, skiing (downhill), soccer, tennis, volleyball; coed intramural: alpine skiing, dance, flag football, Frisbee, martial arts, skateboarding, skiing (downhill), snowboarding, soccer, softball, table tennis, tennis, ultimate Frisbee, volleyball, yoga. 2 PE instructors, 8 coaches.

Computers Computers are regularly used in art, desktop publishing, English, history, humanities, keyboarding, lab/keyboard, newspaper, photography, research skills, science, video film production, word processing, yearbook classes. Computer network features include campus e-mail, CD-ROMs, online commercial services, Internet access, file transfer, office computer access, DVD, wireless campus network, E-Library.

Contact Mr. Jim Fyfe, Director of Admissions. 845-268-6802 Ext. 213. Fax: 845-268-4644. E-mail: jfyfe@rocklandcds.org. Web site: www.rocklandcds.org.

ROCKLYN ACADEMY

Meaford, Ontario, Canada
See Special Needs Schools section.

ROCK POINT SCHOOL

1 Rock Point Road
Burlington, Vermont 05401
Head of School: John Rouleau

General Information Coeducational boarding and day college-preparatory and arts school, affiliated with Episcopal Church. Grades 9–12. Founded: 1928. Setting: small town. Students are housed in single-sex by floor dormitories. 150-acre campus. 1 building on campus. Approved or accredited by Independent Schools of Northern New England, National Association of Episcopal Schools, New England Association of Schools and Colleges, The Association of Boarding Schools, and Vermont Department of Education. Endowment: $2.7 million. Total enrollment: 38. Upper school average class size: 11. Upper school faculty-student ratio: 1:5.

Upper School Student Profile Grade 9: 4 students (2 boys, 2 girls); Grade 10: 11 students (8 boys, 3 girls); Grade 11: 13 students (5 boys, 8 girls); Grade 12: 10 students (5 boys, 5 girls). 85% of students are boarding students. 39% are state residents. 15 states are represented in upper school student body. 1% are international students. International students from Canada and Japan. 12% of students are members of Episcopal Church.

Faculty School total: 9. In upper school: 3 men, 5 women; 1 has an advanced degree.

Subjects Offered Algebra, American history, American literature, ancient history, art, art history, biology, calculus, chemistry, drawing, earth science, English, geometry, health, historical foundations for arts, history, mathematics, painting, photography, physical education, poetry, pottery, pre-calculus, science, sculpture, stained glass, trigonometry, Western civilization, world history, world literature.

Graduation Requirements Art, art history, English, history, mathematics, physical education (includes health), science.

Special Academic Programs Independent study; term-away projects; study at local college for college credit; special instructional classes for students who need structure and personal attention.

College Placement 11 students graduated in 2005; 7 went to college, including Ball State University; Bridgewater State College; Knox College; Mount Ida College; St. John's College; University of Vermont. Other: 3 went to work, 1 had other specific plans. Median SAT verbal: 565, median SAT math: 535, median combined SAT: 1633. 30% scored over 600 on SAT verbal, 30% scored over 600 on SAT math, 20% scored over 1800 on combined SAT.

Student Life Upper grades have specified standards of dress. Discipline rests primarily with faculty.

Tuition and Aid Day student tuition: $20,700; 7-day tuition and room/board: $37,600. Tuition installment plan (A typical contract has a deposit, and the balance is paid in 2 installments—September 1 and December 1). Need-based scholarship grants, need-based loans available. In 2005–06, 22% of upper-school students received aid. Total amount of financial aid awarded in 2005–06: $150,000.

Admissions Traditional secondary-level entrance grade is 10. For fall 2005, 64 students applied for upper-level admission, 26 were accepted, 22 enrolled. Writing sample required. Deadline for receipt of application materials: none. Application fee required: $45. On-campus interview required.

Athletics Coed Intramural: alpine skiing, back packing, ball hockey, baseball, basketball, bicycling, boxing, canoeing/kayaking, climbing, cooperative games, fitness, fitness walking, Frisbee, hiking/backpacking, jogging, kickball, martial arts, outdoor activities, outdoor adventure, outdoor recreation, physical fitness, physical training, rock climbing, running, skateboarding, skiing (downhill), snowboarding, soccer, softball, walking, weight training. 4 PE instructors.

Computers Computers are regularly used in all academic, art, college planning, music, video film production, word processing classes. Computer network features include Internet access.

Contact Hillary Kramer, Director of Admissions. 802-863-1104 Ext. 12. Fax: 802-863-6628. E-mail: hkramer@rockpoint.org. Web site: www.rockpoint.org.

ANNOUNCEMENT FROM THE SCHOOL Rock Point School is a small, coeducational, boarding/day, college-preparatory school, located in Burlington, Vermont. The program, accredited by the New England Association of School and Colleges and approved by the Vermont State Board of Education, is designed to meet the needs of average to above-average students who have found themselves off-track academically or socially/emotionally and who want the structure and support of a close-knit community of 42 students and 20 staff. Rock Point students are typically creative, bright, free-thinking individuals who have struggled in other school settings. Rock Point School was founded in 1928 by Bishop Booth of the Episcopal Diocese, replacing an earlier school located on the same grounds since 1889. The School is located on 150 acres bordering Lake Champlain, within minutes of downtown Burlington. Students come from across the country, with the largest percentage coming from New England. All students enroll in a core curriculum of English, history, science, math, art, and physical education. The academic program emphasizes writing across the curriculum. The

art program includes art history, painting, sculpture, stained glass, photography, and song writing/recording. Classes range from 6 to 12 students in size. Students attend 2 supervised study halls each day, and they have access to tutoring and organizational support. A senior seminar helps with college application. Rock Point recognizes the equally important roles that the dormitory and academic programs play in a student's ability to get back on track and experience success and satisfaction. Students are offered a rich after-school and weekend program that includes community service (with local and international opportunities), skiing and snowboarding, hiking, camping, and many art and cultural activities. As needed, students can access community-based services, such as counseling and AA/NA meetings. They have the opportunity to explore downtown Burlington, as well as many locations throughout Vermont. Some students earn the privilege of taking an outside class, getting a job, or participating in an internship.

ROCKWAY MENNONITE COLLEGIATE

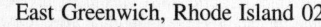

110 Doon Road
Kitchener, Ontario N2G 3C8, Canada
Head of School: Mr. Terry Schellenberg

General Information Coeducational boarding and day college-preparatory, arts, religious studies, and technology school, affiliated with Mennonite Church USA. Grades 6–12. Founded: 1945. Setting: suburban. Nearest major city is Toronto, Canada. Students are housed in host family homes. 14-acre campus. 7 buildings on campus. Approved or accredited by Mennonite Schools Council and Ontario Department of Education. Language of instruction: English. Endowment: CAN$350,000. Total enrollment: 422. Upper school average class size: 17. Upper school faculty-student ratio: 1:10.
Upper School Student Profile Grade 9: 81 students (31 boys, 50 girls); Grade 10: 72 students (40 boys, 32 girls); Grade 11: 76 students (41 boys, 35 girls); Grade 12: 79 students (45 boys, 34 girls). 9% of students are boarding students. 91% are province residents. 2 provinces are represented in upper school student body. 9% are international students. International students from China, Germany, Hong Kong, Japan, Republic of Korea, and Taiwan; 4 other countries represented in student body. 51% of students are Mennonite Church USA.
Faculty School total: 50. In upper school: 22 men, 23 women; 8 have advanced degrees.
Subjects Offered Algebra, auto mechanics, Bible, biology, calculus, Canadian history, career education, chemistry, choral music, civics, computer science, computer studies, construction, dramatic arts, English, entrepreneurship, ESL, family studies, finite math, food and nutrition, French, functions, geography, geometry, German, guidance, health, healthful living, history, information technology, instrumental music, integrated technology fundamentals, Mandarin, mathematics, music, orchestra, parenting, personal finance, philosophy, physical education, physics, religious studies, science, strings, technology/design, transportation technology, visual arts, vocal music, wind instruments, world history, world religions.
Graduation Requirements Ontario Ministry of Education requirements.
Special Academic Programs Independent study; academic accommodation for the gifted and the musically talented; ESL (28 students enrolled).
College Placement 85 students graduated in 2005; 52 went to college, including Carleton University; The University of Western Ontario; University of Guelph; University of Toronto; University of Waterloo; Wilfrid Laurier University. Other: 24 went to work, 9 had other specific plans.
Student Life Upper grades have specified standards of dress, student council. Discipline rests primarily with faculty. Attendance at religious services is required.
Tuition and Aid Day student tuition: CAN$9420; 7-day tuition and room/board: CAN$18,990. Tuition installment plan (monthly payment plans, individually arranged payment plans). Tuition reduction for siblings, bursaries, need-based scholarship grants, paying campus jobs available. In 2005–06, 15% of upper-school students received aid. Total amount of financial aid awarded in 2005–06: CAN$100,000.
Admissions Traditional secondary-level entrance grade is 9. For fall 2005, 48 students applied for upper-level admission, 45 were accepted, 44 enrolled. Deadline for receipt of application materials: none. Application fee required: CAN$100.
Athletics Interscholastic: badminton (boys, girls), baseball (b,g), basketball (b,g), cross-country running (b,g), soccer (b), softball (b,g), track and field (b,g), volleyball (b,g), wrestling (b,g); intramural: ball hockey (b,g), baseball (b,g), basketball (b,g), cooperative games (b,g), dance (b,g), field hockey (b,g), flag football (b,g), flagball (b,g), floor hockey (b,g), football (b,g), indoor soccer (b,g), nordic skiing (b,g), outdoor education (b,g), physical training (b,g), power lifting (b,g), rock climbing (b,g), rugby (b,g), skiing (downhill) (b,g), soccer (b,g), strength & conditioning (b,g), volleyball (b,g); coed interscholastic: soccer; coed intramural: baseball, canoeing/kayaking, cooperative games, outdoor education, roller skating, skiing (downhill), street hockey, table tennis, track and field. 2 PE instructors.
Computers Computers are regularly used in Bible studies, business, career technology, college planning, construction, drafting, English, geography, library, mathematics, religious studies, science, typing, Web site design classes. Computer network features include on-campus library services, CD-ROMs, Internet access.

Contact Mr. Tom Bileski, Director of Community Relations. 519-743-5209 Ext. 3029. Fax: 519-743-5935. E-mail: admin@rockway.on.ca. Web site: www.rockway.on.ca.

ROCKY HILL SCHOOL

530 Ives Road
East Greenwich, Rhode Island 02818
Head of School: James J. Young III

General Information Coeducational day college-preparatory, arts, and technology school. Grades PS–12. Founded: 1934. Setting: rural. Nearest major city is Providence. 100-acre campus. 16 buildings on campus. Approved or accredited by Association of Independent Schools in New England, New England Association of Schools and Colleges, and Rhode Island Department of Education. Member of National Association of Independent Schools and Secondary School Admission Test Board. Endowment: $984,000. Total enrollment: 333. Upper school average class size: 12. Upper school faculty-student ratio: 1:5.
Upper School Student Profile Grade 9: 43 students (23 boys, 20 girls); Grade 10: 32 students (18 boys, 14 girls); Grade 11: 40 students (22 boys, 18 girls); Grade 12: 36 students (14 boys, 22 girls).
Faculty School total: 60. In upper school: 18 men, 20 women; 15 have advanced degrees.
Subjects Offered African-American history, algebra, American foreign policy, American history, American literature, anatomy, ancient history, anthropology, art, art history, biology, calculus, chemistry, computer math, computer programming, computer science, constitutional history of U.S., creative writing, drama, earth science, ecology, English, English literature, environmental science, European history, expository writing, fine arts, French, geography, geometry, government/civics, history, Latin, marine science, mathematics, medieval history, music, oceanography, physical education, physics, psychology, science, social studies, sociology, Spanish, speech, statistics, theater, trigonometry, typing, world history, world literature, writing.
Graduation Requirements Arts and fine arts (art, music, dance, drama), computer science, English, environmental science, foreign language, history, mathematics, physical education (includes health), science. Community service is required.
Special Academic Programs Advanced Placement exam preparation in 8 subject areas; honors section; independent study; term-away projects; study abroad; academic accommodation for the gifted, the musically talented, and the artistically talented; ESL (4 students enrolled).
College Placement 35 students graduated in 2005; all went to college, including Brown University; Carnegie Mellon University; The Johns Hopkins University; University of Pennsylvania; University of Rhode Island; Vanderbilt University.
Student Life Upper grades have specified standards of dress, student council. Discipline rests primarily with faculty.
Summer Programs Enrichment, sports programs offered; session focuses on sports and enrichment activities; held on campus; accepts boys and girls; open to students from other schools. 400 students usually enrolled. 2006 schedule: June 19 to August 4. Application deadline: none.
Tuition and Aid Day student tuition: $20,500. Tuition installment plan (Tuition Management Service (TMS)). Need-based scholarship grants available. In 2005–06, 31% of upper-school students received aid. Total amount of financial aid awarded in 2005–06: $522,000.
Admissions Traditional secondary-level entrance grade is 9. For fall 2005, 59 students applied for upper-level admission, 39 were accepted, 25 enrolled. ISEE or SSAT required. Deadline for receipt of application materials: none. Application fee required: $50. Interview required.
Athletics Interscholastic: basketball (boys, girls), field hockey (g), lacrosse (b,g), soccer (b,g); coed interscholastic: golf, sailing, tennis; coed intramural: canoeing/kayaking, climbing, fitness, kayaking, mountain biking, outdoor adventure, rock climbing, sailing, tennis, wall climbing. 2 PE instructors, 15 coaches.
Computers Computers are regularly used in all classes. Computer network features include campus e-mail, on-campus library services, CD-ROMs, Internet access, DVD, wireless campus network, laptop program integrated into the curriculum.
Contact Maria T. Emmons, Admission Associate. 401-884-9070 Ext. 107. Fax: 401-885-4985. E-mail: memmons@rockyhill.org. Web site: www.rockyhill.org.

ROCKY MOUNT ACADEMY

1313 Avondale Avenue
Rocky Mount, North Carolina 27803
Head of School: Mr. Thomas R. Stevens

General Information Coeducational day college-preparatory school. Grades PK–12. Founded: 1968. Setting: small town. Nearest major city is Raleigh. 44-acre campus. 9 buildings on campus. Approved or accredited by North Carolina Association of Independent Schools and Southern Association of Colleges and Schools. Member of National Association of Independent Schools. Endowment: $428,895. Total enrollment: 446. Upper school average class size: 12. Upper school faculty-student ratio: 1:12.

Upper School Student Profile Grade 9: 39 students (20 boys, 19 girls); Grade 10: 34 students (11 boys, 23 girls); Grade 11: 35 students (19 boys, 16 girls); Grade 12: 41 students (19 boys, 22 girls).

Faculty School total: 52. In upper school: 8 men, 13 women; 6 have advanced degrees.

Subjects Offered Adolescent issues, advanced computer applications, Advanced Placement courses, algebra, American history, American history-AP, American literature, anatomy, art, art appreciation, art history, astronomy, athletics, biology, biology-AP, calculus, calculus-AP, ceramics, cheerleading, chemistry, civics, community service, composition, computer education, creative writing, criminal justice, drama, earth science, English, English literature, English literature-AP, European history, fine arts, French, French-AP, geography, geology, geometry, government/ civics, grammar, history, honors English, honors U.S. history, HTML design, human sexuality, keyboarding/computer, Latin, mathematics, music appreciation, newspaper, North Carolina history, novels, participation in sports, photography, photojournalism, physical education, physics, pottery, pre-algebra, pre-calculus, psychology, psychology-AP, public speaking, publications, research skills, SAT preparation, science, social studies, Spanish, student government, studio art-AP, technology, theater, trigonometry, visual arts, Web site design, women in world history, word processing, world history, world literature, yearbook.

Graduation Requirements Arts and fine arts (art, music, dance, drama), computer science, English, foreign language, mathematics, physical education (includes health), public speaking, science, social studies (includes history). Community service is required.

Special Academic Programs Advanced Placement exam preparation in 9 subject areas; honors section; independent study.

College Placement 32 students graduated in 2005; all went to college, including Appalachian State University; East Carolina University; North Carolina State University; The University of North Carolina at Chapel Hill; The University of North Carolina Wilmington. Mean SAT verbal: 559, mean SAT math: 549. 28% scored over 600 on SAT verbal, 18% scored over 600 on SAT math.

Student Life Upper grades have specified standards of dress, student council, honor system. Discipline rests primarily with faculty.

Summer Programs Enrichment, sports, art/fine arts, computer instruction programs offered; session focuses on enrichment; held on campus; accepts boys and girls; open to students from other schools. 150 students usually enrolled. 2006 schedule: June 10 to August 15.

Tuition and Aid Day student tuition: $7235–$8665. Tuition installment plan (monthly payment plans, 3-payment plan, full-year payment plan). Merit scholarship grants, need-based scholarship grants available. In 2005–06, 36% of upper-school students received aid; total upper-school merit-scholarship money awarded: $33,860. Total amount of financial aid awarded in 2005–06: $144,960.

Admissions Traditional secondary-level entrance grade is 9. For fall 2005, 13 students applied for upper-level admission, 13 were accepted, 12 enrolled. Essay and school's own exam required. Deadline for receipt of application materials: none. Application fee required: $75. On-campus interview required.

Athletics Interscholastic: baseball (boys), basketball (b,g), cross-country running (b,g), football (b), physical fitness (b,g), soccer (b,g), softball (g), tennis (b,g), volleyball (g); coed interscholastic: cheering, golf, physical fitness, swimming and diving. 4 PE instructors, 4 coaches.

Computers Computers are regularly used in English, foreign language, graphics, health, history, independent study, library, mathematics, news writing, photojournalism, reading, remedial study skills, research skills, SAT preparation, science, speech, technology, writing fundamentals, yearbook classes. Computer resources include CD-ROMs, Internet access, file transfer, office computer access, INET Library.

Contact Mrs. Millie Harris Walker, Director of Enrollment Management. 252-443-4126 Ext. 224. Fax: 252-937-7922. E-mail: mwalker@rmacademy.com. Web site: www.rmacademy.com.

THE ROEPER SCHOOL

41190 Woodward Avenue
Bloomfield Hills, Michigan 48304
Head of School: Randall C. Dunn

petersons.com

General Information Coeducational day college-preparatory school. Grades PK–12. Founded: 1941. Setting: urban. Nearest major city is Birmingham. 1-acre campus. 1 building on campus. Approved or accredited by Independent Schools Association of the Central States. Member of National Association of Independent Schools. Endowment: $3.9 million. Total enrollment: 609. Upper school average class size: 13. Upper school faculty-student ratio: 1:10.

Upper School Student Profile Grade 9: 48 students (25 boys, 23 girls); Grade 10: 47 students (23 boys, 24 girls); Grade 11: 51 students (19 boys, 32 girls); Grade 12: 49 students (26 boys, 23 girls).

Faculty School total: 86. In upper school: 15 men, 28 women; 21 have advanced degrees.

Subjects Offered Algebra, American history, American literature, art, art history, biology, calculus, chemistry, computer programming, computer science, creative writing, dance, drama, English, English literature, European history, fine arts, French, geometry, government/civics, health, history, journalism, Latin, mathematics, music,

philosophy, photography, physical education, physics, science, social studies, Spanish, speech, statistics, theater, trigonometry, world history, world literature, writing.

Graduation Requirements Arts and fine arts (art, music, dance, drama), computer science, English, foreign language, government, health, mathematics, science, social studies (includes history).

Special Academic Programs Advanced Placement exam preparation in 14 subject areas; independent study; academic accommodation for the gifted, the musically talented, and the artistically talented; programs in English, mathematics, general development for dyslexic students.

College Placement 45 students graduated in 2005; 44 went to college, including Albion College; Kalamazoo College; Michigan State University; Northwestern University; Oakland University; University of Michigan. Other: 1 went to work.

Student Life Upper grades have student council, honor system. Discipline rests primarily with faculty.

Summer Programs Art/fine arts programs offered; session focuses on theater; held on campus; accepts boys and girls; open to students from other schools. 40 students usually enrolled. 2006 schedule: June 19 to August 11.

Tuition and Aid Day student tuition: $18,200. Tuition installment plan (FACTS Tuition Payment Plan, individually arranged payment plans, Tuition Management Systems Plan). Need-based scholarship grants available. In 2005–06, 37% of upper-school students received aid. Total amount of financial aid awarded in 2005–06: $810,042.

Admissions Traditional secondary-level entrance grade is 9. For fall 2005, 47 students applied for upper-level admission, 31 were accepted, 22 enrolled. Individual IQ required. Deadline for receipt of application materials: none. Application fee required: $70. On-campus interview required.

Athletics Interscholastic: baseball (boys), basketball (b,g), cross-country running (b,g), nautilus (b,g), physical training (b,g), soccer (b,g), strength & conditioning (b,g), track and field (b,g), volleyball (g), weight lifting (b,g); intramural: indoor soccer (b,g); coed intramural: physical training, strength & conditioning, weight lifting.

Computers Computers are regularly used in English, journalism, library, mathematics, publishing, science, yearbook classes. Computer network features include campus e-mail, on-campus library services, CD-ROMs, online commercial services, Internet access.

Contact Lori Zinser, Director of Admissions. 248-203-7302. Fax: 248-203-7310. E-mail: lori.zinser@roeper.org.

ANNOUNCEMENT FROM THE SCHOOL The Roeper School is an independent coeducational day school for gifted students, prekindergarten through grade 12. Roeper provides a solid educational background in all academic disciplines and offers many Advanced Placement courses. While Roeper is a college-preparatory school, students are prepared, more important, for life. Roeper provides a personalized education in which teachers innovate and adapt to meet the needs of each student at each stage of development. Respect, trust, fairness, and integrity are the core values that direct each child's development. Decision making, problem solving, social responsibility, and leadership are taught throughout the School's curriculum.

ROLAND PARK COUNTRY SCHOOL

5204 Roland Avenue
Baltimore, Maryland 21210
Head of School: Mrs. Jean Waller Brune

General Information Girls' day college-preparatory and arts school. Grades K–12. Founded: 1901. Setting: suburban. 21-acre campus. 1 building on campus. Approved or accredited by Association of Independent Maryland Schools and Maryland Department of Education. Member of National Association of Independent Schools and Secondary School Admission Test Board. Endowment: $43.4 million. Total enrollment: 709. Upper school average class size: 16. Upper school faculty-student ratio: 1:7.

Upper School Student Profile Grade 9: 75 students (75 girls); Grade 10: 63 students (63 girls); Grade 11: 76 students (76 girls); Grade 12: 75 students (75 girls).

Faculty School total: 107. In upper school: 7 men, 37 women; 41 have advanced degrees.

Subjects Offered Algebra, American literature, anatomy, Arabic, architectural drawing, art, art history, astronomy, biology, calculus, ceramics, chemistry, Chinese, community service, computer programming, computer science, creative writing, dance, drama, ecology, economics, engineering, English, English literature, environmental science, European history, French, geometry, German, government/civics, Greek, health, Latin, mechanical drawing, music, philosophy, photography, physical education, physics, physiology, religion, Russian, science, social studies, Spanish, speech, statistics, theater, trigonometry, world history.

Graduation Requirements Adolescent issues, arts and fine arts (art, music, dance, drama), biology, chemistry, English, foreign language, history, mathematics, physical education (includes health), physics, public speaking, science. Community service is required.

Special Academic Programs Advanced Placement exam preparation in 19 subject areas; honors section; independent study; term-away projects; study abroad.

College Placement 66 students graduated in 2005; 65 went to college, including Duke University. Other: 1 had other specific plans. Mean SAT verbal: 631, mean SAT math: 614, mean composite ACT: 25. 62% scored over 600 on SAT verbal, 55% scored over 600 on SAT math, 29% scored over 26 on composite ACT.

Student Life Upper grades have uniform requirement, student council, honor system. Discipline rests equally with students and faculty.

Summer Programs Remediation, enrichment, advancement, sports, art/fine arts programs offered; session focuses on summer camp, arts, some academics; held both on and off campus; held at off-site pool and venues for outdoor education programs and various sites around Baltimore for art projects; accepts boys and girls; open to students from other schools. 90 students usually enrolled. 2006 schedule: June 19 to September 1. Application deadline: none.

Tuition and Aid Day student tuition: $17,975. Tuition installment plan (Academic Management Services Plan). Need-based scholarship grants, paying campus jobs available. In 2005–06, 24% of upper-school students received aid. Total amount of financial aid awarded in 2005–06: $606,475.

Admissions Traditional secondary-level entrance grade is 9. For fall 2005, 90 students applied for upper-level admission, 48 were accepted, 17 enrolled. CTP or ISEE required. Deadline for receipt of application materials: January 15. Application fee required: $40. On-campus interview required.

Athletics Interscholastic: badminton, basketball, crew, cross-country running, field hockey, golf, indoor soccer, indoor track, lacrosse, soccer, softball, squash, swimming and diving, tennis, volleyball, winter soccer; intramural: dance, fitness, modern dance, outdoor education, strength & conditioning. 5 PE instructors, 1 trainer.

Computers Computers are regularly used in all classes. Computer network features include campus e-mail, on-campus library services, CD-ROMs, online commercial services, Internet access, office computer access, wireless campus network, online database.

Contact Peggy Wolf, Director of Admissions. 410-323-5500. Fax: 410-323-2164. E-mail: admissions@rpcs.org. Web site: www.rpcs.org.

ROLLING HILLS PREPARATORY SCHOOL

300 A Paseo Del Mar
Palos Verdes Estates, California 90274
Head of School: Peter McCormack

General Information Coeducational day college-preparatory, arts, and technology school. Grades 6–12. Founded: 1981. Setting: suburban. Nearest major city is Los Angeles. 14-acre campus. 5 buildings on campus. Approved or accredited by California Association of Independent Schools, Western Association of Schools and Colleges, and California Department of Education. Member of National Association of Independent Schools. Endowment: $2,000. Total enrollment: 256. Upper school average class size: 16. Upper school faculty-student ratio: 1:9.

Upper School Student Profile Grade 9: 37 students (20 boys, 17 girls); Grade 10: 38 students (20 boys, 18 girls); Grade 11: 38 students (20 boys, 18 girls); Grade 12: 43 students (23 boys, 20 girls).

Faculty School total: 36. In upper school: 7 men, 21 women; 17 have advanced degrees.

Subjects Offered Algebra, American history, American literature, American sign language, anatomy, art, biology, calculus, ceramics, chemistry, computer science, creative writing, drama, economics, English, English literature, European history, fine arts, French, geography, geometry, government/civics, history, mathematics, music, photography, physical education, physics, pre-calculus, robotics, science, social studies, Spanish, speech, statistics, theater, trigonometry, world history.

Graduation Requirements Arts and fine arts (art, music, dance, drama), English, foreign language, mathematics, outdoor education, physical education (includes health), science, social studies (includes history), two-week senior internship, senior speech.

Special Academic Programs Advanced Placement exam preparation in 8 subject areas; honors section; independent study; academic accommodation for the gifted; programs in general development for dyslexic students; ESL (18 students enrolled).

College Placement 35 students graduated in 2005; 34 went to college, including The University of Arizona; University of California, Berkeley; University of California, Irvine; University of California, Los Angeles; University of California, Santa Barbara; University of Southern California. Other: 1 entered military service. Mean SAT verbal: 580, mean SAT math: 610. 42% scored over 600 on SAT verbal, 49% scored over 600 on SAT math.

Student Life Upper grades have specified standards of dress, student council. Discipline rests primarily with faculty.

Summer Programs Remediation, enrichment, art/fine arts programs offered; session focuses on academics and arts; held on campus; accepts boys and girls; open to students from other schools. 30 students usually enrolled. 2006 schedule: June 26 to August 28. Application deadline: June 1.

Tuition and Aid Day student tuition: $17,400. Tuition installment plan (Insured Tuition Payment Plan, Key Tuition Payment Plan, monthly payment plans). Merit scholarship grants, need-based scholarship grants available. In 2005–06, 30% of upper-school students received aid; total upper-school merit-scholarship money awarded: $20,000. Total amount of financial aid awarded in 2005–06: $650,000.

Admissions Traditional secondary-level entrance grade is 9. For fall 2005, 36 students applied for upper-level admission, 21 were accepted, 16 enrolled. ISEE required. Deadline for receipt of application materials: none. Application fee required: $150. On-campus interview required.

Athletics Interscholastic: baseball (boys), basketball (b,g), cheering (g), football (b), soccer (g), softball (g), volleyball (b,g); intramural: cheering (g), dance (g); coed interscholastic: cross-country running, golf, roller hockey, running, soccer; coed intramural: back packing, climbing, hiking/backpacking, outdoor education, rock climbing, ropes courses. 4 PE instructors, 9 coaches, 1 trainer.

Computers Computers are regularly used in English, foreign language, mathematics, science classes. Computer network features include campus e-mail, on-campus library services, CD-ROMs, Internet access, file transfer, office computer access.

Contact Renee Bischoff, Director of Admission. 310-791-1101 Ext. 118. Fax: 310-373-4931. E-mail: rbischoff@rhps-k12.com. Web site: www.rollinghillsprep.org.

RONCALLI HIGH SCHOOL

3300 Prague Road
Indianapolis, Indiana 46227
Head of School: Mr. Chuck Weisenbach

General Information Coeducational day college-preparatory and religious studies school, affiliated with Roman Catholic Church. Grades 9–12. Founded: 1969. Setting: suburban. 38-acre campus. 1 building on campus. Approved or accredited by North Central Association of Colleges and Schools and Indiana Department of Education. Total enrollment: 1,062. Upper school average class size: 26. Upper school faculty-student ratio: 1:15.

Upper School Student Profile Grade 9: 270 students (145 boys, 125 girls); Grade 10: 299 students (146 boys, 153 girls); Grade 11: 255 students (130 boys, 125 girls); Grade 12: 238 students (111 boys, 127 girls). 95% of students are Roman Catholic.

Faculty School total: 77. In upper school: 41 have advanced degrees.

Graduation Requirements Biology, computer applications, English, mathematics, physical education (includes health), physical science, religious studies, U.S. government, U.S. history, service requirements each year of school.

Special Academic Programs Advanced Placement exam preparation in 9 subject areas; honors section; independent study; academic accommodation for the gifted; remedial math; programs in English, mathematics, general development for dyslexic students; special instructional classes for blind students, students with autism, learning disabilities, Attention Deficit Disorder.

College Placement 226 students graduated in 2005; 215 went to college, including Ball State University; Indiana University Bloomington; Purdue University. Other: 5 went to work, 3 entered military service, 3 had other specific plans. Median SAT verbal: 520, median SAT math: 536, median combined SAT: 1056, median composite ACT: 22. 20% scored over 600 on SAT verbal, 28% scored over 600 on SAT math, 36% scored over 26 on composite ACT.

Student Life Upper grades have uniform requirement, student council. Discipline rests primarily with faculty. Attendance at religious services is required.

Tuition and Aid Tuition reduction for siblings, need-based scholarship grants, paying campus jobs available. In 2005–06, 16% of upper-school students received aid. Total amount of financial aid awarded in 2005–06: $450,000.

Admissions Traditional secondary-level entrance grade is 9. High School Placement Test or High School Placement Test (closed version) from Scholastic Testing Service required. Deadline for receipt of application materials: none. Application fee required: $100. On-campus interview required.

Athletics Interscholastic: baseball (boys), basketball (b,g), bowling (b,g), cheering (g), cross-country running (b,g), diving (b,g), football (b), golf (b,g), gymnastics (g), soccer (b,g), softball (g), strength & conditioning (b), swimming and diving (b,g), tennis (b,g), track and field (b,g), volleyball (b,g), wrestling (b,g); intramural: ice hockey (b), power lifting (b). 3 PE instructors, 1 trainer.

Computers Computers are regularly used in all academic, business, career education, religious studies, yearbook classes. Computer network features include on-campus library services, Internet access, office computer access, wireless campus network.

Contact Mr. Kevin Stanton, Assistant Principal for academic affairs. 317-787-8277 Ext. 222. Fax: 317-788-4095. E-mail: kstanton@roncallihs.org. Web site: www. roncalli.org.

RON PETTIGREW CHRISTIAN SCHOOL

1761-110th Avenue
Dawson Creek, British Columbia V1G 4X4, Canada
Head of School: Phyllis L. Roch

General Information Coeducational day college-preparatory and general academic school, affiliated with Christian faith. Grades K–12. Founded: 1989. Setting: small town. Nearest major city is Prince George, Canada. 1-acre campus. 1 building on campus. Approved or accredited by Association of Christian Schools International and British Columbia Department of Education. Language of instruction: English. Total enrollment: 78. Upper school faculty-student ratio: 1:5.

Upper School Student Profile Grade 9: 10 students (8 boys, 2 girls); Grade 10: 6 students (2 boys, 4 girls); Grade 11: 3 students (3 girls); Grade 12: 2 students (1 boy, 1 girl). 76% of students are Christian faith.
Faculty School total: 6. In upper school: 2 men, 4 women.
College Placement 5 students graduated in 2005. Other: 5 went to work.
Student Life Upper grades have uniform requirement, student council, honor system. Discipline rests primarily with faculty. Attendance at religious services is required.
Admissions No application fee required. Interview required.
Computers Computer network features include Internet access, wireless campus network.
Contact Phyllis L. Roch, Head of School. 250-782-4580. Fax: 250-782-9805. E-mail: rpcs@pris.ca.

ROSARY HIGH SCHOOL

901 North Edgelawn Drive
Aurora, Illinois 60506
Head of School: Sr. Patricia Burke, OP

General Information Girls' day college-preparatory, arts, and religious studies school, affiliated with Roman Catholic Church. Grades 9–12. Founded: 1962. Setting: suburban. Nearest major city is Chicago. 20-acre campus. 1 building on campus. Approved or accredited by National Catholic Education Association, North Central Association of Colleges and Schools, and Illinois Department of Education. Endowment: $1.7 million. Total enrollment: 472. Upper school average class size: 20. Upper school faculty-student ratio: 1:14.
Upper School Student Profile Grade 9: 130 students (130 girls); Grade 10: 123 students (123 girls); Grade 11: 112 students (112 girls); Grade 12: 107 students (107 girls). 90% of students are Roman Catholic.
Faculty School total: 35. In upper school: 5 men, 24 women; 20 have advanced degrees.
Subjects Offered Accounting, algebra, American history, art, art appreciation, biology, calculus, chemistry, chorus, community service, computer science, consumer economics, creative writing, desktop publishing, English, English-AP, French, geometry, government/civics, graphic design, health, human development, interior design, keyboarding, Latin, mathematics, music, orchestra, painting, physical education, physical science, physics, psychology, religion, science, social science, social studies, sociology, Spanish, speech, theology, trigonometry, world history.
Graduation Requirements Arts and fine arts (art, music, dance, drama), English, mathematics, physical education (includes health), religion (includes Bible studies and theology), science, social science, social studies (includes history). Community service is required.
Special Academic Programs Advanced Placement exam preparation in 2 subject areas; honors section; study at local college for college credit.
College Placement 100 students graduated in 2005; all went to college, including DePaul University; Illinois State University; Marquette University; Northern Illinois University; University of Illinois at Urbana–Champaign; Waubonsee Community College. Mean SAT verbal: 608, mean SAT math: 587, mean composite ACT: 25. 28% scored over 600 on SAT verbal, 45% scored over 600 on SAT math, 21% scored over 26 on composite ACT.
Student Life Upper grades have uniform requirement, student council. Discipline rests primarily with faculty. Attendance at religious services is required.
Tuition and Aid Day student tuition: $5100–$5800. Tuition installment plan (FACTS Tuition Payment Plan, monthly payment plans, individually arranged payment plans, quarterly and semester payment plans). Tuition reduction for siblings, merit scholarship grants, need-based scholarship grants available. In 2005–06, 25% of upper-school students received aid; total upper-school merit-scholarship money awarded: $11,600. Total amount of financial aid awarded in 2005–06: $133,000.
Admissions Traditional secondary-level entrance grade is 9. STS required. Deadline for receipt of application materials: none. Application fee required: $50. On-campus interview required.
Athletics Interscholastic: basketball, cross-country running, diving, golf, pom squad, soccer, softball, swimming and diving, tennis, track and field. 2 PE instructors, 20 coaches, 1 trainer.
Computers Computers are regularly used in accounting, keyboarding, library, science classes. Computer network features include on-campus library services, CD-ROMs, online commercial services, Internet access.
Contact Sr. Patricia Burke, OP, Principal. 630-896-0831 Ext. 222. Fax: 630-896-8372. E-mail: spbop@rosaryhs.com. Web site: www.rosaryhs.com.

ROTHESAY NETHERWOOD SCHOOL

40 College Hill Road
Rothesay, New Brunswick E2E 5H1, Canada
Head of School: Paul G. Kitchen

General Information Coeducational boarding and day college-preparatory, arts, and technology school, affiliated with Anglican Church of Canada. Grades 6–12. Founded: 1877. Setting: small town. Nearest major city is Saint John, Canada. Students are housed in single-sex dormitories. 180-acre campus. 24 buildings on campus.

Approved or accredited by Canadian Association of Independent Schools, Canadian Educational Standards Institute, Conference of Independent Schools of Ontario, The Association of Boarding Schools, and New Brunswick Department of Education. Languages of instruction: English and French. Endowment: CAN$3.5 million. Total enrollment: 230. Upper school average class size: 15. Upper school faculty-student ratio: 1:7.
Upper School Student Profile Grade 9: 35 students (15 boys, 20 girls); Grade 10: 33 students (19 boys, 14 girls); Grade 11: 58 students (28 boys, 30 girls); Grade 12: 48 students (30 boys, 18 girls). 54% of students are boarding students. 42% are province residents. 8 provinces are represented in upper school student body. 24% are international students. International students from Bahamas, Bermuda, Japan, Mexico, Republic of Korea, and United States; 5 other countries represented in student body. 30% of students are members of Anglican Church of Canada.
Faculty School total: 40. In upper school: 16 men, 15 women; 10 have advanced degrees; 24 reside on campus.
Subjects Offered Advanced chemistry, art, art history, biology, biology-AP, calculus, calculus-AP, Canadian history, chemistry, chemistry-AP, computer programming, computer science, CPR, digital art, discrete mathematics, drama, driver education, English, English literature, English-AP, ESL, European history, fine arts, finite math, French, geography, geometry, health, history, human geography—AP, information technology, language-AP, leadership, macroeconomics-AP, mathematical modeling, mathematics, microeconomics-AP, music, music-AP, outdoor education, physical education, physics, physics-AP, science, social studies, Spanish, Spanish-AP, theater arts, world history, writing.
Graduation Requirements Arts and fine arts (art, music, dance, drama), computer science, English, foreign language, mathematics, physical education (includes health), science, social science, social studies (includes history).
Special Academic Programs Advanced Placement exam preparation in 11 subject areas; honors section; independent study; term-away projects; study at local college for college credit; academic accommodation for the gifted, the musically talented, and the artistically talented; ESL (28 students enrolled).
College Placement 49 students graduated in 2005; all went to college, including Acadia University; Carleton University; Dalhousie University; McMaster University; Saint Mary's University; University of Toronto.
Student Life Upper grades have uniform requirement, student council, honor system. Discipline rests primarily with faculty. Attendance at religious services is required.
Tuition and Aid Day student tuition: CAN$15,000; 7-day tuition and room/board: CAN$31,000. Tuition installment plan (monthly payment plans, individually arranged payment plans). Tuition reduction for siblings, bursaries, merit scholarship grants, need-based scholarship grants, need-based loans available. In 2005–06, 30% of upper-school students received aid; total upper-school merit-scholarship money awarded: CAN$37,000. Total amount of financial aid awarded in 2005–06: CAN$490,000.
Admissions Traditional secondary-level entrance grade is 9. For fall 2005, 62 students applied for upper-level admission, 54 were accepted, 45 enrolled. CAT 2 or school's own exam required. Deadline for receipt of application materials: none. Application fee required: CAN$200. Interview required.
Athletics Interscholastic: badminton (boys, girls), basketball (b,g), crew (b,g), cross-country running (b,g), golf (b,g), ice hockey (b,g), rowing (b,g), rugby (b,g), running (b,g), soccer (b,g), squash (b,g), tennis (b,g), track and field (b,g), volleyball (g); intramural: aerobics/dance (g), badminton (b,g), bicycling (b), cross-country running (b,g), golf (b,g), ice hockey (b,g), indoor soccer (b), squash (b,g), tennis (b,g), track and field (b,g), yoga (g); coed interscholastic: badminton, crew, cross-country running, golf, rowing, tennis, track and field; coed intramural: aerobics, back packing, badminton, bicycling, billiards, bowling, broomball, canoeing/kayaking, climbing, cooperative games, cross-country running, fitness, fitness walking, floor hockey, Frisbee, golf, hiking/backpacking, ice hockey, ice skating, indoor soccer, jogging, kayaking, mountain biking, outdoor activities, outdoor adventure, outdoor education, outdoor recreation, outdoor skills, paddle tennis, paint ball, physical fitness, physical training, roller blading, roller hockey, running, skiing (downhill), snowboarding, squash, street hockey, strength & conditioning, swimming and diving, table tennis, tennis, track and field, ultimate Frisbee, volleyball, walking, wall climbing, weight training. 3 PE instructors.
Computers Computers are regularly used in all classes. Computer network features include campus e-mail, on-campus library services, CD-ROMs, Internet access, file transfer, office computer access, DVD, wireless campus network, Intranet, informative, interactive online community for parents, teachers and students, Website for each academic course.
Contact Mr. Peter Davidson, Co-Director of Admission. 506-847-8224. Fax: 506-848-0851. E-mail: admissions@rns.cc. Web site: www.rns.cc.

ROTTERDAM INTERNATIONAL SECONDARY SCHOOL, WOLFERT VAN BORSELEN

Bentincklaan 294
Rotterdam 3039 KK, Netherlands
Head of School: Aidan Campbell

General Information Coeducational day college-preparatory, bilingual studies, and languages school. Grades 6–12. Founded: 1988. Setting: urban. 2-hectare campus. 2

buildings on campus. Approved or accredited by International Baccalaureate Organization and state department of education. Member of European Council of International Schools. Language of instruction: English. Total enrollment: 162. Upper school average class size: 15. Upper school faculty-student ratio: 1:10.

Upper School Student Profile Grade 6: 15 students (10 boys, 5 girls); Grade 7: 24 students (11 boys, 13 girls); Grade 8: 22 students (16 boys, 6 girls); Grade 9: 17 students (11 boys, 6 girls); Grade 10: 31 students (17 boys, 14 girls); Grade 11: 28 students (15 boys, 13 girls); Grade 12: 25 students (13 boys, 12 girls).

Faculty School total: 35. In upper school: 6 men, 25 women; 3 have advanced degrees.

Subjects Offered International Baccalaureate courses.

Special Academic Programs International Baccalaureate program; ESL.

College Placement 19 students graduated in 2005; 18 went to college.

Student Life Upper grades have student council. Discipline rests primarily with faculty.

Tuition and Aid Day student tuition: €5800–€6800. Tuition installment plan (eight yearly payments).

Admissions Traditional secondary-level entrance grade is 11. For fall 2005, 40 students applied for upper-level admission, 40 were accepted, 40 enrolled. Admissions testing required. Deadline for receipt of application materials: none. Application fee required: €250. On-campus interview required.

Athletics Coed Interscholastic: basketball, soccer; coed intramural: baseball, basketball, bicycling, rowing, soccer, tai chi, track and field, volleyball. 4 PE instructors.

Computers Computers are regularly used in all academic classes. Computer network features include campus e-mail, Internet access.

Contact Alexa Nijpels, Development Director. 31-10 890 7745. Fax: 31-10 8907755. E-mail: info.riss@wolfert.nl. Web site: www.wolfert.nl/riss/.

ROUTT HIGH SCHOOL

500 East College
Jacksonville, Illinois 62650
Head of School: Randy Verticchio

General Information Coeducational day college-preparatory, arts, business, and religious studies school, affiliated with Roman Catholic Church. Grades 9–12. Founded: 1902. Setting: small town. Nearest major city is Springfield. 3-acre campus. 1 building on campus. Approved or accredited by North Central Association of Colleges and Schools and Illinois Department of Education. Total enrollment: 135. Upper school average class size: 15. Upper school faculty-student ratio: 1:8.

Upper School Student Profile Grade 9: 36 students (20 boys, 16 girls); Grade 10: 44 students (23 boys, 21 girls); Grade 11: 28 students (14 boys, 14 girls); Grade 12: 27 students (11 boys, 16 girls). 90% of students are Roman Catholic.

Faculty School total: 16. In upper school: 5 men, 11 women; 4 have advanced degrees.

Graduation Requirements 15 community service hours per year (60 total).

Special Academic Programs Advanced Placement exam preparation in 2 subject areas; honors section; remedial reading and/or remedial writing; remedial math.

College Placement 33 went to college, including University of Illinois at Urbana–Champaign; Villanova University. Other: 32 entered a postgraduate year, 1 had other specific plans. Median composite ACT: 23. 25% scored over 26 on composite ACT.

Student Life Upper grades have uniform requirement, student council, honor system. Discipline rests primarily with faculty. Attendance at religious services is required.

Tuition and Aid Day student tuition: $3500. Tuition installment plan (FACTS Tuition Payment Plan). Tuition reduction for siblings, merit scholarship grants, need-based scholarship grants available. In 2005–06, 7% of upper-school students received aid; total upper-school merit-scholarship money awarded: $3500. Total amount of financial aid awarded in 2005–06: $26,000.

Admissions Traditional secondary-level entrance grade is 9. ACT-Explore required. Deadline for receipt of application materials: none. No application fee required. Interview required.

Athletics Interscholastic: baseball (boys), basketball (b,g), cheering (g), cross-country running (g), football (b), golf (b), softball (g), swimming and diving (g), track and field (b,g), volleyball (g), wrestling (b); intramural: pom squad (g); coed intramural: bocce. 1 PE instructor, 10 coaches.

Computers Computer network features include CD-ROMs, Internet access, office computer access.

Contact Mr. Dude Wildrick, Counselor. 217-243-5323. Fax: 217-243-3138. E-mail: dwildrick@routtcatholic.com. Web site: www.csj.net/~routt/.

ROWLAND HALL-ST. MARK'S SCHOOL

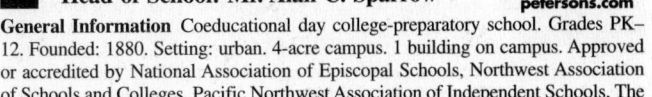

843 South Lincoln Street
Salt Lake City, Utah 84102
Head of School: Mr. Alan C. Sparrow

General Information Coeducational day college-preparatory school. Grades PK–12. Founded: 1880. Setting: urban. 4-acre campus. 1 building on campus. Approved or accredited by National Association of Episcopal Schools, Northwest Association of Schools and Colleges, Pacific Northwest Association of Independent Schools, The

College Board, and Utah Department of Education. Member of National Association of Independent Schools. Endowment: $4 million. Total enrollment: 949. Upper school average class size: 16. Upper school faculty-student ratio: 1:14.

Upper School Student Profile Grade 9: 67 students (27 boys, 40 girls); Grade 10: 77 students (36 boys, 41 girls); Grade 11: 70 students (28 boys, 42 girls); Grade 12: 61 students (37 boys, 24 girls).

Faculty School total: 39. In upper school: 21 men, 18 women; 22 have advanced degrees.

Subjects Offered Adolescent issues, advanced studio art-AP, algebra, band, biology, biology-AP, calculus, calculus-AP, ceramics, chemistry, chemistry-AP, chorus, computer graphics, computer programming, creative writing, dance, debate, drama, English, English language and composition-AP, English literature and composition-AP, environmental science, ethics, European history-AP, filmmaking, French, French language-AP, French literature-AP, geology, geometry, graphic design, history, human development, intro to computers, jazz band, Latin, Latin-AP, math applications, modern European history-AP, music theory-AP, newspaper, photography, physical education, physics, physics-AP, political science, pre-calculus, psychology-AP, Spanish, Spanish-AP, speech and debate, statistics-AP, studio art, studio art-AP, theater, trigonometry, U.S. history, U.S. history-AP, Web site design, weight training, Western civilization, world cultures, world religions, yearbook.

Graduation Requirements American history, arts and fine arts (art, music, dance, drama), biology, chemistry, computer skills, English, ethics, foreign language, mathematics, physical education (includes health), physics, science, social studies (includes history), world religions.

Special Academic Programs Advanced Placement exam preparation in 15 subject areas; honors section; independent study.

College Placement 83 students graduated in 2005; 82 went to college, including The Colorado College; University of Pennsylvania; University of Puget Sound; University of Southern California; University of Utah; Vassar College. Other: 1 had other specific plans. Mean SAT verbal: 608, mean SAT math: 590, mean composite ACT: 26. 58% scored over 600 on SAT verbal, 43% scored over 600 on SAT math, 51% scored over 26 on composite ACT.

Student Life Upper grades have specified standards of dress, student council, honor system. Discipline rests equally with students and faculty.

Summer Programs Enrichment, advancement programs offered; session focuses on advancement; held on campus; accepts boys and girls; open to students from other schools. 60 students usually enrolled. 2006 schedule: June 19 to July 28. Application deadline: none.

Tuition and Aid Day student tuition: $13,500. Tuition installment plan (monthly payment plans, individually arranged payment plans, 2-installment plan). Merit scholarship grants, need-based scholarship grants, diversity scholarship grants available. In 2005–06, 25% of upper-school students received aid; total upper-school merit-scholarship money awarded: $42,800. Total amount of financial aid awarded in 2005–06: $549,295.

Admissions Traditional secondary-level entrance grade is 9. For fall 2005, 54 students applied for upper-level admission, 42 were accepted, 35 enrolled. ERB CTP IV or ISEE required. Deadline for receipt of application materials: none. Application fee required: $50. Interview recommended.

Athletics Interscholastic: alpine skiing (boys, girls), baseball (b), basketball (b,g), diving (b,g), skiing (downhill) (b,g), soccer (b,g), softball (g), swimming and diving (b,g), tennis (b,g), track and field (b,g), volleyball (g); intramural: skiing (downhill) (b,g), soccer (b,g); coed interscholastic: crew, cross-country running, dance, golf, modern dance, skiing (downhill), swimming and diving, track and field; coed intramural: alpine skiing, archery, bowling, climbing, deck hockey, hiking/backpacking, ice hockey, ice skating, outdoor activities, outdoor education, physical fitness, skiing (cross-country), snowboarding, strength & conditioning, swimming and diving, telemark skiing, weight training, yoga. 4 PE instructors, 12 coaches, 1 trainer.

Computers Computers are regularly used in drawing and design, graphic design, mathematics, newspaper, science, yearbook classes. Computer network features include campus e-mail, on-campus library services, CD-ROMs, Internet access, office computer access, wireless campus network.

Contact Karen Hyde, Director of Admission. 801-355-7494. Fax: 801-355-0474. E-mail: karenhyde@rhsm.org. Web site: www.rhsm.org.

See full description on page 1002.

THE ROXBURY LATIN SCHOOL

101 St. Theresa Avenue
West Roxbury, Massachusetts 02132
Head of School: Mr. Kerry Paul Brennan

General Information Boys' day college-preparatory school. Grades 7–12. Founded: 1645. Setting: urban. Nearest major city is Boston. 65-acre campus. 1 building on campus. Approved or accredited by Association of Independent Schools in New England, Headmasters' Conference, and New England Association of Schools and Colleges. Member of National Association of Independent Schools and Secondary School Admission Test Board. Endowment: $120 million. Total enrollment: 290. Upper school average class size: 14. Upper school faculty-student ratio: 1:8.

The Roxbury Latin School

Upper School Student Profile Grade 7: 42 students (42 boys); Grade 8: 44 students (44 boys); Grade 9: 54 students (54 boys); Grade 10: 51 students (51 boys); Grade 11: 49 students (49 boys); Grade 12: 50 students (50 boys).

Faculty School total: 36. In upper school: 31 men, 5 women; 23 have advanced degrees.

Subjects Offered Advanced chemistry, advanced math, advanced studio art-AP, algebra, American Civil War, American government, American government-AP, American history, American literature, analytic geometry, Ancient Greek, ancient history, ancient world history, art, art history, art history-AP, arts, biology, calculus, calculus-AP, chemistry, classical Greek literature, classical language, college counseling, college placement, computer science, computer science-AP, creative writing, drama, earth science, economics, economics-AP, English, English language and composition-AP, English literature, English literature and composition-AP, European history, expository writing, fine arts, French, geometry, government/civics, grammar, Greek, history, history-AP, Latin, life science, macro/microeconomics-AP, mathematics, mathematics-AP, microeconomics-AP, music, personal development, photography, physical education, physical science, physics, science, senior project, statistics-AP, studio art, studio art-AP, theater, trigonometry, U.S. history-AP, Western civilization, world history, writing.

Graduation Requirements Arts and fine arts (art, music, dance, drama), computer science, English, foreign language, mathematics, physical education (includes health), science, social studies (includes history), independent senior project.

Special Academic Programs Advanced Placement exam preparation in 11 subject areas; honors section; independent study; academic accommodation for the gifted, the musically talented, and the artistically talented.

College Placement 51 students graduated in 2005; 49 went to college, including Bowdoin College; Georgetown University; Harvard University; Massachusetts Institute of Technology; Princeton University; Yale University. Other: 2 entered a postgraduate year. Median SAT verbal: 720, median SAT math: 725, median combined SAT: 2180. 92% scored over 600 on SAT verbal, 96% scored over 600 on SAT math.

Student Life Upper grades have specified standards of dress, student council. Discipline rests equally with students and faculty.

Tuition and Aid Day student tuition: $16,800. Tuition installment plan (Insured Tuition Payment Plan, Key Tuition Payment Plan, 2-payment plan). Need-based scholarship grants, need-based loans available. In 2005–06, 33% of upper-school students received aid. Total amount of financial aid awarded in 2005–06: $12,511.

Admissions Traditional secondary-level entrance grade is 7. For fall 2005, 393 students applied for upper-level admission, 57 were accepted, 51 enrolled. ISEE or SSAT required. Deadline for receipt of application materials: January 6. No application fee required. On-campus interview required.

Athletics Interscholastic: baseball, basketball, cross-country running, football, ice hockey, lacrosse, soccer, tennis, track and field, wrestling; intramural: Frisbee. 1 PE instructor, 4 coaches, 1 trainer.

Computers Computers are regularly used in all academic, desktop publishing, literary magazine, newspaper, yearbook classes. Computer network features include campus e-mail, on-campus library services, CD-ROMs, online commercial services, Internet access, file transfer, DVD, wireless campus network.

Contact Michael C. Obel-Omia, Director of Admission. 617-325-4920. Fax: 617-325-3585. E-mail: michael.obel-omia@roxburylatin.org. Web site: www.roxburylatin.org.

ANNOUNCEMENT FROM THE SCHOOL Roxbury Latin is a small, diverse community, unified by a common purpose and shared values. It instills in its students a capacity for rigorous analysis, disciplined reflection, and lucid expression. Students come to experience the excitement and joy that result from hard and deep thinking. The School stresses standards of honesty, simplicity, respect, and concern for others, and it tries to practice these values in life as a community.

ROYAL CANADIAN COLLEGE

8610 Ash Street
Vancouver, British Columbia V6P 3M2, Canada
Head of School: Mr. Howard H. Jiang

General Information Coeducational day college-preparatory and general academic school. Grades 9–12. Founded: 1989. Setting: suburban. 1-acre campus. 1 building on campus. Approved or accredited by British Columbia Department of Education. Language of instruction: English. Total enrollment: 90. Upper school average class size: 20. Upper school faculty-student ratio: 1:15.

Upper School Student Profile Grade 11: 19 students (11 boys, 8 girls); Grade 12: 51 students (32 boys, 19 girls).

Faculty School total: 6. In upper school: 5 men, 1 woman; 1 has an advanced degree.

Subjects Offered 20th century world history, accounting, applied skills, biology, calculus, Canadian geography, Canadian history, career and personal planning, career planning, chemistry, communications, comparative civilizations, computer science, computer science-AP, drama, economics, English, ESL, fine arts, general science, history, information technology, Mandarin, mathematics, physical education, physics, social sciences, world history, writing.

Graduation Requirements Applied skills, arts and fine arts (art, music, dance, drama), career and personal planning, language arts, mathematics, science, social studies (includes history).

Special Academic Programs ESL (10 students enrolled).

College Placement 57 students graduated in 2005; 55 went to college, including McGill University; Simon Fraser University; The University of British Columbia; The University of Western Ontario; University of Manitoba; University of Toronto. Other: 2 had other specific plans.

Student Life Upper grades have honor system. Discipline rests primarily with faculty.

Summer Programs ESL programs offered; session focuses on learning survival English conversational skills and Canadian cultural experience; held on campus; accepts boys and girls; open to students from other schools. 30 students usually enrolled. 2006 schedule: July 3 to August 27. Application deadline: May 31.

Tuition and Aid Day student tuition: CAN$11,000. Merit scholarship grants available. Total upper-school merit-scholarship money awarded for 2005–06: CAN$10,000.

Admissions Traditional secondary-level entrance grade is 11. For fall 2005, 42 students applied for upper-level admission, 34 were accepted, 33 enrolled. English language required. Deadline for receipt of application materials: none. Application fee required: CAN$150.

Athletics Intramural: badminton (boys, girls), baseball (b,g), basketball (b,g), soccer (b,g), ultimate Frisbee (b,g); coed intramural: badminton, baseball, ultimate Frisbee. 2 PE instructors.

Computers Computers are regularly used in accounting, career exploration, information technology classes. Computer network features include CD-ROMs, Internet access.

Contact Mr. Jeffry Yip, Senior Administrator. 604-738-2221. Fax: 604-738-2282. E-mail: info@royalcanadiancollege.com. Web site: www.royalcanadiancollege.com.

ROYCEMORE SCHOOL

640 Lincoln Street
Evanston, Illinois 60201
Head of School: Mr. Joseph A. Becker

General Information Coeducational day college-preparatory and arts school. Grades PK–12. Founded: 1915. Setting: suburban. Nearest major city is Chicago. 1-acre campus. 1 building on campus. Approved or accredited by Independent Schools Association of the Central States, Independent Schools Joint Council, and Illinois Department of Education. Member of National Association of Independent Schools. Endowment: $1 million. Total enrollment: 238. Upper school average class size: 9. Upper school faculty-student ratio: 1:8.

Upper School Student Profile Grade 9: 12 students (5 boys, 7 girls); Grade 10: 17 students (13 boys, 4 girls); Grade 11: 19 students (13 boys, 6 girls); Grade 12: 25 students (12 boys, 13 girls).

Faculty School total: 37. In upper school: 5 men, 12 women; 12 have advanced degrees.

Subjects Offered Advanced Placement courses, advanced studio art-AP, algebra, American history, American literature, art, biology, ceramics, chemistry, creative writing, drama, ecology, English, English literature, environmental science, European history, expository writing, French, geography, geometry, government/civics, grammar, history, keyboarding/computer, mathematics, music, physical education, physics, science, social studies, Spanish, speech, trigonometry, world history, world literature, writing, yearbook.

Graduation Requirements English, foreign language, mathematics, physical education (includes health), science, social studies (includes history), participation in a January short-term project each year.

Special Academic Programs Advanced Placement exam preparation in 12 subject areas; honors section; accelerated programs; independent study; study at local college for college credit.

College Placement 18 students graduated in 2005; all went to college, including DePaul University; Northwestern University; Oberlin College; Occidental College; University of Connecticut; University of Illinois at Urbana–Champaign. Mean SAT verbal: 640, mean SAT math: 630, mean composite ACT: 26. 63% scored over 600 on SAT verbal, 56% scored over 600 on SAT math, 50% scored over 26 on composite ACT.

Student Life Upper grades have specified standards of dress, student council, honor system. Discipline rests primarily with faculty.

Summer Programs Enrichment, art/fine arts programs offered; session focuses on enrichment for gifted students; held both on and off campus; held at museums, theaters, and other educational locations in and around Chicago; accepts boys and girls; open to students from other schools. 7 students usually enrolled. 2006 schedule: June 19 to July 21. Application deadline: June 1.

Tuition and Aid Day student tuition: $17,125. Tuition installment plan (monthly payment plans, semi-annual payment plan, 9-month payment plan). Merit scholarship grants, need-based scholarship grants, discounts for children of Northwestern University employees available. In 2005–06, 55% of upper-school students received aid; total upper-school merit-scholarship money awarded: $102,800. Total amount of financial aid awarded in 2005–06: $358,000.

Admissions Traditional secondary-level entrance grade is 9. For fall 2005, 38 students applied for upper-level admission, 21 were accepted, 8 enrolled. Any standardized test required. Deadline for receipt of application materials: none. Application fee required: $50. On-campus interview required.

Athletics Interscholastic: baseball (boys), basketball (b,g), soccer (b,g), volleyball (g); intramural: basketball (b,g), soccer (b,g); coed intramural: dance, gymnastics, softball, volleyball. 3 PE instructors.

Computers Computers are regularly used in all classes. Computer network features include on-campus library services, CD-ROMs, Internet access, office computer access, DVD.

Contact Ms. Barbara B. Turnbull, Director of Admissions. 847-866-6055. Fax: 847-866-6545. E-mail: bturnbull@roycemoreschool.org. Web site: www.roycemoreschool.org.

RUMSEY HALL SCHOOL

Washington Depot, Connecticut
See Junior Boarding Schools section.

RUTGERS PREPARATORY SCHOOL

1345 Easton Avenue
Somerset, New Jersey 08873
Head of School: Dr. Steven A. Loy

General Information Coeducational day college-preparatory and arts school. Grades PK–12. Founded: 1766. Setting: suburban. Nearest major city is New York, NY. 35-acre campus. 8 buildings on campus. Approved or accredited by Middle States Association of Colleges and Schools and New Jersey Association of Independent Schools. Member of National Association of Independent Schools and Secondary School Admission Test Board. Endowment: $3 million. Total enrollment: 726. Upper school average class size: 14. Upper school faculty-student ratio: 1:6.

Upper School Student Profile Grade 9: 72 students (33 boys, 39 girls); Grade 10: 87 students (43 boys, 44 girls); Grade 11: 87 students (46 boys, 41 girls); Grade 12: 82 students (39 boys, 43 girls).

Faculty School total: 105. In upper school: 29 men, 27 women; 43 have advanced degrees.

Subjects Offered Algebra, American history, American literature, architecture, art, art history, astronomy, biology, calculus, ceramics, chemistry, classics, community service, comparative religion, computer programming, computer science, creative writing, discrete math, drama, driver education, economics, English, English literature, environmental science, European history, fine arts, foundations of civilization, French, geometry, government/civics, health, history, Japanese, Latin, literature, mathematics, media, multimedia, music, photography, physical education, physical science, physics, poetry, psychology, psychology-AP, science, Shakespeare, social studies, Spanish, statistics, theater, word processing, world history, writing.

Graduation Requirements Arts and fine arts (art, music, dance, drama), computer science, English, foreign language, mathematics, physical education (includes health), science, social studies (includes history). Community service is required.

Special Academic Programs Advanced Placement exam preparation in 19 subject areas; honors section; independent study; term-away projects; academic accommodation for the gifted, the musically talented, and the artistically talented.

College Placement 78 students graduated in 2005; all went to college, including Boston University; Lehigh University; New York University; Princeton University; Rutgers, The State University of New Jersey, Rutgers College; The George Washington University. Mean SAT verbal: 626, mean SAT math: 641. 63% scored over 600 on SAT verbal, 70% scored over 600 on SAT math.

Student Life Upper grades have specified standards of dress, student council, honor system. Discipline rests primarily with faculty.

Summer Programs Remediation, enrichment, advancement, computer instruction programs offered; session focuses on academics and sports; held on campus; accepts boys and girls; open to students from other schools. 500 students usually enrolled. 2006 schedule: June 26 to August 4. Application deadline: June 23.

Tuition and Aid Day student tuition: $20,780. Tuition installment plan (Key Tuition Payment Plan). Need-based scholarship grants, need-based financial aid, Key Education Resources available. In 2005–06, 28% of upper-school students received aid. Total amount of financial aid awarded in 2005–06: $867,902.

Admissions Traditional secondary-level entrance grade is 9. For fall 2005, 134 students applied for upper-level admission, 77 were accepted, 47 enrolled. Iowa Tests of Basic Skills and SSAT required. Deadline for receipt of application materials: none. Application fee required: $75. On-campus interview required.

Athletics Interscholastic: baseball (boys), basketball (b,g), lacrosse (b,g), soccer (b,g), softball (g), tennis (b,g), volleyball (g), wrestling (b); intramural: dance team (g); coed interscholastic: cross-country running, golf, swimming and diving. 6 PE instructors, 8 coaches, 1 trainer.

Computers Computers are regularly used in English, foreign language, history, mathematics, music, science classes. Computer network features include on-campus library services, CD-ROMs, online commercial services, Internet access, DVD, laptops.

Contact Judy Iannacone, Admissions Assistant. 732-545-5600 Ext. 261. Fax: 732-214-1819. Web site: www.rutgersprep.org.

RYE COUNTRY DAY SCHOOL

Cedar Street
Rye, New York 10580-2034
Head of School: Mr. Scott A. Nelson

General Information Coeducational day college-preparatory, arts, and technology school. Grades PK–12. Founded: 1869. Setting: suburban. Nearest major city is New York. 30-acre campus. 7 buildings on campus. Approved or accredited by Middle States Association of Colleges and Schools, New York State Association of Independent Schools, and New York Department of Education. Member of National Association of Independent Schools and Secondary School Admission Test Board. Endowment: $14 million. Total enrollment: 848. Upper school average class size: 13. Upper school faculty-student ratio: 1:7.

Upper School Student Profile Grade 9: 88 students (47 boys, 41 girls); Grade 10: 97 students (53 boys, 44 girls); Grade 11: 94 students (48 boys, 46 girls); Grade 12: 89 students (49 boys, 40 girls).

Faculty School total: 108. In upper school: 29 men, 26 women; 41 have advanced degrees.

Subjects Offered 20th century history, algebra, American history, American history-AP, American literature, American literature-AP, Ancient Greek, art, art history, art history-AP, art-AP, astronomy, biology, biology-AP, calculus, calculus-AP, ceramics, chemistry, chemistry-AP, chorus, classics, computer music, computer programming, computer science-AP, computer-aided design, CPR, creative writing, dance, drama, driver education, economics, English, English literature, English literature-AP, English-AP, environmental science, environmental science-AP, European history, European history-AP, expository writing, fencing, fine arts, forensic science, French, French-AP, geometry, government, government and politics-AP, government-AP, Greek, health, history, honors English, honors geometry, independent study, instrumental music, interdisciplinary studies, jazz band, Latin, Latin-AP, mathematics, mechanical drawing, modern European history-AP, music, music theory-AP, oceanography, philosophy, photography, physical education, physics, physics-AP, psychology, psychology-AP, science, social studies, Spanish, Spanish-AP, speech, squash, statistics-AP, studio art-AP, The 20th Century, the Sixties, theater, theater arts, trigonometry, U.S. government-AP, U.S. history, U.S. history-AP, U.S. literature, weight training, wind ensemble, world civilizations, writing.

Graduation Requirements Arts and fine arts (art, music, dance, drama), English, foreign language, life management skills, mathematics, physical education (includes health), science, social studies (includes history), senior interdisciplinary humanities course.

Special Academic Programs Advanced Placement exam preparation in 15 subject areas; honors section; independent study; academic accommodation for the gifted; special instructional classes for deaf students.

College Placement 83 students graduated in 2005; 79 went to college, including Duke University; Harvard University; New York University; The George Washington University; Trinity College; University of Pennsylvania. Other: 2 entered military service, 2 entered a postgraduate year. Median SAT verbal: 660, median SAT math: 665. 80% scored over 600 on SAT verbal, 89% scored over 600 on SAT math.

Student Life Upper grades have student council. Discipline rests primarily with faculty.

Summer Programs Remediation, enrichment, advancement, ESL, art/fine arts, computer instruction programs offered; session focuses on remediation; held on campus; accepts boys and girls; open to students from other schools. 200 students usually enrolled. 2006 schedule: June 26 to August 4. Application deadline: June 23.

Tuition and Aid Day student tuition: $24,100–$24,300. Tuition installment plan (monthly payment plans). Need-based scholarship grants available. In 2005–06, 15% of upper-school students received aid. Total amount of financial aid awarded in 2005–06: $1,218,100.

Admissions Traditional secondary-level entrance grade is 9. For fall 2005, 216 students applied for upper-level admission, 65 were accepted, 46 enrolled. ISEE or SSAT required. Deadline for receipt of application materials: January 31. Application fee required: $50. On-campus interview required.

Athletics Interscholastic: baseball (boys), basketball (b,g), cross-country running (b,g), fencing (b,g), field hockey (g), football (b), golf (b,g), ice hockey (b,g), lacrosse (b,g), soccer (b,g), softball (g), squash (b,g), tennis (b,g), wrestling (b); intramural: aerobics/dance (g), basketball (b), dance (g), figure skating (b,g), fitness (b,g), physical fitness (b,g), physical training (b,g), squash (b,g), tennis (b,g), weight training (b,g), wrestling (b); coed intramural: fitness, ice skating, squash. 4 PE instructors, 14 coaches, 1 trainer.

Computers Computers are regularly used in art, classics, English, foreign language, history, mathematics, music, photography, publishing, science, technology, yearbook classes. Computer network features include campus e-mail, on-campus library services, CD-ROMs, online commercial services, Internet access, file transfer, office computer access, DVD, wireless campus network, schedules online.

Contact Mr. Matthew J.M. Suzuki, Director of Admissions. 914-925-4513. Fax: 914-921-2147. E-mail: matt_suzuki@rcds.rye.ny.us. Web site: www.rcds.rye.ny.us.

See full description on page 1004.

SACRAMENTO COUNTRY DAY SCHOOL

2636 Latham Drive
Sacramento, California 95864-7198
Head of School: Stephen T. Repsher

General Information Coeducational day college-preparatory, arts, and technology school. Grades PK–12. Founded: 1964. Setting: urban. 12-acre campus. 8 buildings on campus. Approved or accredited by California Association of Independent Schools and Western Association of Schools and Colleges. Member of National Association of Independent Schools. Total enrollment: 539. Upper school average class size: 12. Upper school faculty-student ratio: 1:10.

Upper School Student Profile Grade 9: 44 students (26 boys, 18 girls); Grade 10: 30 students (18 boys, 12 girls); Grade 11: 28 students (15 boys, 13 girls); Grade 12: 40 students (19 boys, 21 girls).

Faculty School total: 60. In upper school: 11 men, 9 women; 12 have advanced degrees.

Subjects Offered Algebra, American history, American literature, art, art history, band, biology, calculus, chemistry, computer science, creative writing, drama, earth science, ecology, economics, English, English literature, European history, fine arts, French, geography, geometry, government/civics, grammar, history, international relations, journalism, Latin, mathematics, model United Nations, physical education, physics, science, social studies, Spanish, speech, technology/design, theater, trigonometry, world history, world literature, writing.

Graduation Requirements Arts and fine arts (art, music, dance, drama), computer science, English, foreign language, history, mathematics, physical education (includes health), science, 40-hour senior project. Community service is required.

Special Academic Programs Advanced Placement exam preparation in 12 subject areas; independent study; study at local college for college credit; academic accommodation for the gifted and the artistically talented.

College Placement 30 students graduated in 2005; all went to college, including Colgate University; Occidental College; Stanford University; University of California, Berkeley; University of California, Los Angeles.

Student Life Upper grades have specified standards of dress, student council, honor system. Discipline rests primarily with faculty.

Tuition and Aid Day student tuition: $1390. Tuition installment plan (Insured Tuition Payment Plan, monthly payment plans, individually arranged payment plans). Need-based scholarship grants available. In 2005–06, 18% of upper-school students received aid. Total amount of financial aid awarded in 2005–06: $269,950.

Admissions Traditional secondary-level entrance grade is 9. For fall 2005, 35 students applied for upper-level admission, 20 were accepted, 15 enrolled. ERB, Otis-Lennon Mental Ability Test and writing sample required. Deadline for receipt of application materials: none. Application fee required: $25. Interview required.

Athletics Interscholastic: baseball (boys), basketball (b,g), cross-country running (b,g), flag football (b), soccer (b,g), swimming and diving (b,g), track and field (b,g), volleyball (b,g); coed interscholastic: golf, paint ball, skiing (downhill), tennis. 5 PE instructors, 14 coaches.

Computers Computers are regularly used in all classes. Computer network features include campus e-mail, on-campus library services, CD-ROMs, Internet access, file transfer, DVD.

Contact Lonna Bloedau, Director of Admission. 916-481-8811. Fax: 916-481-6016. E-mail: lbloedau@saccds.org. Web site: www.saccds.org.

SACRED HEART ACADEMY

200 Strawberry Hill Avenue
Stamford, Connecticut 06902
Head of School: Sr. Jeanne Paulella

General Information Girls' day college-preparatory, arts, and religious studies school, affiliated with Roman Catholic Church. Grades 9–12. Founded: 1922. Setting: suburban. 10-acre campus. 1 building on campus. Approved or accredited by Connecticut Association of Independent Schools, New England Association of Schools and Colleges, and Connecticut Department of Education. Total enrollment: 125. Upper school average class size: 15. Upper school faculty-student ratio: 1:10.

Upper School Student Profile Grade 9: 30 students (30 girls); Grade 10: 25 students (25 girls); Grade 11: 35 students (35 girls); Grade 12: 35 students (35 girls). 85% of students are Roman Catholic.

Faculty School total: 20. In upper school: 4 men, 16 women; 15 have advanced degrees.

Subjects Offered Algebra, American history, American history-AP, American literature, anatomy and physiology, art, Bible studies, biology, calculus, calculus-AP, chemistry, computer programming, English, English literature, English-AP, fine arts, French, geometry, health, history, literature, mathematics, physical education, physical science, physics, pre-calculus, psychology, religion, science, social studies, Spanish, Spanish language-AP, trigonometry, world history, world literature.

Graduation Requirements Arts and fine arts (art, music, dance, drama), English, foreign language, mathematics, physical education (includes health), religion (includes Bible studies and theology), science, social studies (includes history), zoology, 20 hours of community service per year.

Special Academic Programs Advanced Placement exam preparation in 5 subject areas; honors section; independent study; study at local college for college credit; academic accommodation for the artistically talented.

College Placement 28 students graduated in 2005; all went to college, including Sacred Heart University; University of Connecticut.

Student Life Upper grades have uniform requirement, student council. Discipline rests primarily with faculty. Attendance at religious services is required.

Tuition and Aid Day student tuition: $8750. Tuition installment plan (monthly payment plans). Tuition reduction for siblings, merit scholarship grants, need-based scholarship grants available.

Admissions Traditional secondary-level entrance grade is 9. For fall 2005, 40 students applied for upper-level admission, 37 were accepted, 30 enrolled. STS required. Deadline for receipt of application materials: none. Application fee required: $35. Interview recommended.

Athletics Interscholastic: basketball, cross-country running, soccer, softball, tennis, volleyball. 1 PE instructor, 2 coaches.

Computers Computers are regularly used in accounting, creative writing, English, history, mathematics, photojournalism, SAT preparation, science, yearbook classes. Computer resources include CD-ROMs, Internet access, office computer access, DVD.

Contact Mrs. Diana E. Pietrangelo, Director of Admissions. 203-323-3173. Fax: 203-975-7804. E-mail: sha200adm@aol.com. Web site: www.shastamford.org.

SACRED HEART HIGH SCHOOL

2111 Griffin Avenue
Los Angeles, California 90031
Head of School: Sr. Mary Diane Scott, OP

General Information Girls' day college-preparatory, general academic, arts, and religious studies school, affiliated with Roman Catholic Church. Grades 9–12. Founded: 1907. Setting: urban. 1-acre campus. 2 buildings on campus. Approved or accredited by Western Association of Schools and Colleges, Western Catholic Education Association, and California Department of Education. Total enrollment: 370. Upper school average class size: 30. Upper school faculty-student ratio: 1:15.

Upper School Student Profile Grade 9: 114 students (114 girls); Grade 10: 98 students (98 girls); Grade 11: 82 students (82 girls); Grade 12: 76 students (76 girls). 95% of students are Roman Catholic.

Faculty School total: 26. In upper school: 3 men, 23 women.

Graduation Requirements Arts and fine arts (art, music, dance, drama), business skills (includes word processing), computer science, English, foreign language, mathematics, physical education (includes health), religion (includes Bible studies and theology), science, social studies (includes history). Community service is required.

College Placement 86 students graduated in 2005; 80 went to college, including California State University, Los Angeles; California State University, Northridge; Loyola Marymount University; University of California, Irvine; University of California, Los Angeles; University of Southern California. Median composite ACT: 18.

Student Life Upper grades have uniform requirement, student council, honor system. Discipline rests equally with students and faculty. Attendance at religious services is required.

Summer Programs Remediation programs offered; held on campus; accepts girls; not open to students from other schools. 60 students usually enrolled. 2006 schedule: June 21 to July 23. Application deadline: June 1.

Tuition and Aid Day student tuition: $3000. Tuition installment plan (monthly payment plans, individually arranged payment plans). Tuition reduction for siblings, merit scholarship grants, need-based scholarship grants, paying campus jobs available. Total upper-school merit-scholarship money awarded for 2005–06: $3800. Total amount of financial aid awarded in 2005–06: $105,000.

Admissions Traditional secondary-level entrance grade is 9. For fall 2005, 115 students applied for upper-level admission, 111 were accepted, 99 enrolled. High School Placement Test required. Deadline for receipt of application materials: August 15. Application fee required: $25. Interview required.

Athletics Interscholastic: basketball, cross-country running, soccer, softball, track and field, volleyball. 1 PE instructor, 6 coaches.

Computers Computers are regularly used in remedial study skills classes. Computer resources include campus e-mail, on-campus library services, Internet access.

Contact Ms. Jeannie Stone, Administrative Assistant. 323-225-2209. Fax: 323-225-5046. E-mail: jstoneshhs72@yahoo.com. Web site: www.shhsla.org.

SACRED HEART PREPARATORY

150 Valparaiso Avenue
Atherton, California 94027
Head of School: Mr. Richard A. Dioli

General Information Coeducational day college-preparatory, arts, religious studies, and technology school, affiliated with Roman Catholic Church. Grades 9–12. Founded: 1898. Setting: suburban. Nearest major city is San Francisco. 63-acre campus. 5 buildings on campus. Approved or accredited by California Association of

Independent Schools, Western Association of Schools and Colleges, and California Department of Education. Member of National Association of Independent Schools. Total enrollment: 485. Upper school average class size: 15. Upper school faculty-student ratio: 1:8.

Upper School Student Profile Grade 9: 127 students (61 boys, 66 girls); Grade 10: 125 students (63 boys, 62 girls); Grade 11: 114 students (57 boys, 57 girls); Grade 12: 119 students (59 boys, 60 girls). 55% of students are Roman Catholic.

Faculty School total: 61. In upper school: 31 men, 30 women; 33 have advanced degrees.

Subjects Offered 3-dimensional art, advanced chemistry, African history, algebra, American foreign policy, American government-AP, American history, American history-AP, American literature, American literature-AP, anatomy and physiology, applied music, art, art-AP, biology, biology-AP, British literature-AP, calculus, calculus-AP, ceramics, chemistry, China/Japan history, chorus, Christian scripture, church history, community service, computer science, computer science-AP, contemporary women writers, creative dance, dance, digital imaging, drama, drama performance, economics, English, English language-AP, English literature-AP, English-AP, ethics, fine arts, French, French language-AP, French-AP, geography, geometry, history, history of China and Japan, jazz band, Latin, Latin-AP, mathematics, modern Chinese history, photography, physical education, physics, physics-AP, political science, pre-calculus, religion, science, sculpture, senior project, Shakespeare, social science, social studies, Spanish, Spanish-AP, statistics-AP, theater, theater production, trigonometry, video and animation, world civilizations, world religions, yearbook.

Graduation Requirements Arts and fine arts (art, music, dance, drama), English, foreign language, mathematics, physical education (includes health), religion (includes Bible studies and theology), science, social science. Community service is required.

Special Academic Programs Advanced Placement exam preparation in 13 subject areas; honors section; accelerated programs; independent study; term-away projects; domestic exchange program (with Network of Sacred Heart Schools); programs in English, mathematics, general development for dyslexic students.

College Placement 109 students graduated in 2005; all went to college, including Loyola Marymount University; Princeton University; Santa Clara University; Stanford University; University of California, Los Angeles; University of Southern California.

Student Life Upper grades have specified standards of dress, student council, honor system. Discipline rests primarily with faculty. Attendance at religious services is required.

Summer Programs Sports, art/fine arts, computer instruction programs offered; held on campus; accepts boys and girls; open to students from other schools. 2006 schedule: June to August.

Tuition and Aid Day student tuition: $21,870. Tuition installment plan (monthly payment plans). Merit scholarship grants, need-based scholarship grants available. In 2005–06, 32% of upper-school students received aid.

Admissions Traditional secondary-level entrance grade is 9. For fall 2005, 327 students applied for upper-level admission, 160 were accepted, 89 enrolled. High School Placement Test required. Deadline for receipt of application materials: January 5. Application fee required: $50. On-campus interview required.

Athletics Interscholastic: aquatics (boys, girls), baseball (b), basketball (b,g), football (b), soccer (b,g), softball (g), swimming and diving (b,g), tennis (b,g), track and field (b,g), volleyball (b,g), water polo (b,g); coed interscholastic: cross-country running, diving, fitness, golf, lacrosse; coed intramural: bicycling. 1 PE instructor, 48 coaches, 2 trainers.

Computers Computers are regularly used in art, college planning, English, French, history, Latin, mathematics, newspaper, religious studies, science, Spanish, technology, yearbook classes. Computer network features include campus e-mail, on-campus library services, CD-ROMs, online commercial services, Internet access, file transfer, office computer access, DVD, wireless campus network.

Contact Mrs. Wendy Quattlebaum, Admission Assistant. 650-473-4006. Fax: 650-322-7151. E-mail: wendyq@shschools.org. Web site: www.shschools.org.

SACRED HEART SCHOOL OF HALIFAX

5820 Spring Garden Road
Halifax, Nova Scotia B3H 1X8, Canada
Head of School: Ms. Patricia Donnelly

General Information Coeducational day college-preparatory and religious studies school, affiliated with Roman Catholic Church. Boys grades K–6, girls grades K–12. Founded: 1849. Setting: urban. 1 building on campus. Approved or accredited by Canadian Association of Independent Schools and Nova Scotia Department of Education. Language of instruction: English. Total enrollment: 429. Upper school average class size: 20. Upper school faculty-student ratio: 1:18.

Upper School Student Profile Grade 7: 33 students (33 girls); Grade 8: 36 students (36 girls); Grade 9: 44 students (44 girls); Grade 10: 34 students (34 girls); Grade 11: 31 students (31 girls); Grade 12: 38 students (38 girls). 60% of students are Roman Catholic.

Faculty School total: 53. In upper school: 26 women; 9 have advanced degrees.

Subjects Offered 20th century history, 20th century world history, algebra, art, Bible studies, biology, calculus, Canadian history, chemistry, creative writing, earth science,

economics, English, English literature, environmental science, European history, expository writing, French, geography, geometry, government/civics, grammar, health, history, mathematics, music, physical education, physics, religion, science, social studies, sociology, Spanish, theater, trigonometry, world history, writing.

Graduation Requirements Arts and fine arts (art, music, dance, drama), English, foreign language, history, mathematics, physical education (includes health), religion (includes Bible studies and theology), science. Community service is required.

Special Academic Programs Advanced Placement exam preparation in 6 subject areas; honors section; domestic exchange program (with Network of Sacred Heart Schools); study abroad.

College Placement 31 students graduated in 2005; 30 went to college, including Acadia University; Dalhousie University; Mount Allison University; Saint Mary's University; St. Francis Xavier University. Other: 1 had other specific plans.

Student Life Upper grades have uniform requirement, student council, honor system. Discipline rests primarily with faculty. Attendance at religious services is required.

Summer Programs Remediation programs offered; session focuses on French remediation; held on campus; accepts girls; not open to students from other schools. 15 students usually enrolled. Application deadline: none.

Tuition and Aid Day student tuition: CAN$8420. Tuition installment plan (monthly payment plans, individually arranged payment plans). Tuition reduction for siblings, bursaries, merit scholarship grants, need-based scholarship grants available. In 2005–06, 15% of upper-school students received aid; total upper-school merit-scholarship money awarded: CAN$63,150. Total amount of financial aid awarded in 2005–06: CAN$63,150.

Admissions Traditional secondary-level entrance grade is 7. For fall 2005, 35 students applied for upper-level admission, 32 were accepted, 31 enrolled. SCAT and school's own test required. Deadline for receipt of application materials: none. Application fee required: CAN$100. On-campus interview required.

Athletics Interscholastic: aquatics, badminton (b), basketball (b), cross-country running (b), field hockey, soccer (b), swimming and diving (b), tennis, volleyball; intramural: alpine skiing (b), badminton (b), basketball (b), cross-country running (b), fitness walking, jogging (b), running (b), skiing (downhill) (b), soccer (b), swimming and diving (b), tennis, track and field, volleyball. 2 PE instructors.

Computers Computers are regularly used in all academic classes. Computer network features include campus e-mail, on-campus library services, CD-ROMs, Internet access, wireless campus network.

Contact Pauline Scott, Principal, Girls' High School. 902-422-4459. Fax: 902-423-7691. E-mail: pscott@sacredheartschool.ns.ca. Web site: www.sacredheartschool.ns.ca.

SADDLEBACK VALLEY CHRISTIAN SCHOOL

26333 Oso Road
San Juan Capistrano, California 92675
Head of School: Mr. Edward Carney

General Information Coeducational day college-preparatory, general academic, religious studies, and technology school, affiliated with Christian faith. Grades PK–12. Founded: 1997. Setting: suburban. Nearest major city is Irvine/Anaheim. 69-acre campus. 8 buildings on campus. Approved or accredited by Western Association of Schools and Colleges and California Department of Education. Total enrollment: 643. Upper school average class size: 15. Upper school faculty-student ratio: 1:12.

Upper School Student Profile Grade 9: 42 students (23 boys, 19 girls); Grade 10: 54 students (21 boys, 33 girls); Grade 11: 48 students (23 boys, 25 girls); Grade 12: 32 students (19 boys, 13 girls). 75% of students are Christian faith.

Faculty School total: 52. In upper school: 9 men, 15 women; 12 have advanced degrees.

Subjects Offered 1½ elective credits, algebra, American government-AP, American history, American history-AP, American literature, American literature-AP, anatomy and physiology, applied arts, Bible, Bible as literature, biology, biology-AP, British literature, computers, drama, English-AP, ESL, geography, geometry, history, music, science, Spanish, Spanish language-AP, sports, trigonometry, U.S. history, U.S. history-AP, world history, world literature, world religions.

Graduation Requirements Algebra, American history, American literature, anatomy and physiology, art, Bible, biology, British literature, earth science, English, English literature, foreign language, geometry, history, life science, performing arts, physical education (includes health), physical science, science, senior project, Spanish, speech, trigonometry, U.S. history, world history.

Special Academic Programs Advanced Placement exam preparation; honors section; independent study; study at local college for college credit; study abroad; remedial reading and/or remedial writing; remedial math; programs in English, mathematics, general development for dyslexic students; special instructional classes for students with learning disabilities; ESL (5 students enrolled).

College Placement 41 students graduated in 2005; 40 went to college, including Azusa Pacific University; Biola University; California State Polytechnic University, Pomona; Pepperdine University; University of California, Los Angeles; Westmont College. Other: 1 went to work.

Student Life Upper grades have uniform requirement, student council, honor system. Discipline rests primarily with faculty. Attendance at religious services is required.

Saddleback Valley Christian School

Summer Programs Remediation, enrichment, ESL programs offered; session focuses on make-up; held on campus; accepts boys and girls; open to students from other schools. 50 students usually enrolled. 2006 schedule: June 21 to July 31. Application deadline: May 20.

Tuition and Aid Day student tuition: $6650. Tuition installment plan (monthly payment plans). Tuition reduction for siblings, merit scholarship grants, need-based scholarship grants available. In 2005–06, 25% of upper-school students received aid; total upper-school merit-scholarship money awarded: $175,000. Total amount of financial aid awarded in 2005–06: $175,000.

Admissions Traditional secondary-level entrance grade is 9. Placement test required. Deadline for receipt of application materials: none. Application fee required: $200. Interview required.

Athletics Interscholastic: baseball (boys), cheering (g), flagball (b), football (b), softball (g), volleyball (g); coed interscholastic: basketball, cross-country running, golf, soccer, track and field. 2 PE instructors, 3 coaches, 3 trainers.

Computers Computers are regularly used in computer applications classes. Computer network features include campus e-mail, CD-ROMs, Internet access, DVD.

Contact Mrs. Denise Carlson, Registrar. 949-443-4050. Fax: 949-443-3941. E-mail: dcarlson@svcschools.org. Web site: www.svcschools.org/.

SADDLE RIVER DAY SCHOOL

147 Chestnut Ridge Road
Saddle River, New Jersey 07458
Head of School: John T. O'Brien

petersons.com

General Information Coeducational day college-preparatory, arts, bilingual studies, and technology school. Grades K–12. Founded: 1957. Setting: suburban. Nearest major city is New York, NY. 26-acre campus. 3 buildings on campus. Approved or accredited by Middle States Association of Colleges and Schools, New Jersey Association of Independent Schools, and New Jersey Department of Education. Member of National Association of Independent Schools and Secondary School Admission Test Board. Total enrollment: 314. Upper school average class size: 14. Upper school faculty-student ratio: 1:8.

Upper School Student Profile Grade 9: 29 students (16 boys, 13 girls); Grade 10: 53 students (24 boys, 29 girls); Grade 11: 36 students (19 boys, 17 girls); Grade 12: 32 students (17 boys, 15 girls).

Faculty School total: 52. In upper school: 17 men, 19 women; 23 have advanced degrees.

Subjects Offered Advanced Placement courses, algebra, American history, American literature, anatomy, art, astronomy, bell choir, biology, calculus, chemistry, computer programming, computer science, concert choir, creative writing, desktop publishing, drama, driver education, earth science, economics, English, English literature, European history, finance, fine arts, French, geography, geometry, government/civics, grammar, history, Latin, mathematics, music, photography, physical education, physics, psychology, public speaking, science, social science, social studies, Spanish, theater, trigonometry, world history, writing.

Graduation Requirements Arts and fine arts (art, music, dance, drama), computer science, English, foreign language, mathematics, physical education (includes health), science, social science, social studies (includes history).

Special Academic Programs Advanced Placement exam preparation in 13 subject areas; honors section; independent study; term-away projects; study abroad; academic accommodation for the gifted, the musically talented, and the artistically talented.

College Placement 38 students graduated in 2005; all went to college, including Cornell University; Haverford College; New York University; The Johns Hopkins University; Yale University. Median SAT verbal: 602, median SAT math: 604.

Student Life Upper grades have specified standards of dress, student council, honor system. Discipline rests equally with students and faculty.

Summer Programs Enrichment, advancement, sports, art/fine arts programs offered; session focuses on enrichment; held on campus; accepts boys and girls; open to students from other schools. 50 students usually enrolled. 2006 schedule: June 19 to August 4. Application deadline: May 15.

Tuition and Aid Day student tuition: $20,787. Tuition installment plan (The Tuition Plan, Insured Tuition Payment Plan, Academic Management Services Plan, monthly payment plans). Tuition reduction for siblings, merit scholarship grants, need-based scholarship grants available. In 2005–06, 18% of upper-school students received aid; total upper-school merit-scholarship money awarded: $298,500. Total amount of financial aid awarded in 2005–06: $437,000.

Admissions Traditional secondary-level entrance grade is 9. For fall 2005, 61 students applied for upper-level admission, 48 were accepted, 34 enrolled. ISEE, placement test, SSAT or writing sample required. Deadline for receipt of application materials: none. Application fee required: $50. On-campus interview required.

Athletics Interscholastic: baseball (boys), basketball (b,g), golf (b,g), soccer (b,g), softball (g), tennis (b,g), volleyball (g); intramural: baseball (b), basketball (b,g), tennis (b,g); coed interscholastic: cross-country running; coed intramural: cross-country running, fitness, fly fishing, Frisbee, lacrosse, skiing (cross-country), skiing (downhill), snowboarding, weight training. 3 PE instructors, 15 coaches, 2 trainers.

Computers Computers are regularly used in English, foreign language, mathematics, science, social studies classes. Computer network features include campus e-mail, on-campus library services, CD-ROMs, Internet access, DVD, wireless campus network.

Contact Gretchen Lee, Assistant to the Director of Admissions. 201-327-4050 Ext. 1105. Fax: 201-327-6161. E-mail: glee@saddleriverday.org. Web site: saddleriverday.org.

ANNOUNCEMENT FROM THE SCHOOL Saddle River Day School (SRDS) in Saddle River, New Jersey, is a coeducational, college-preparatory day school enrolling students in kindergarten through grade 12. Located in the northeastern corner of the state, SRDS is 18 miles from New York City and benefits from the cultural opportunities available in the metropolitan area. Founded in 1957 by John and Diane Alford and Headmaster Douglas Olgilvie, Saddle River Day was created to provide families with school choice and to create lasting educational value for the community. SRDS seeks to provide a safe, intellectually challenging environment where children are encouraged to learn, to question, and to grow as individuals while being part of a community. With its goal of helping students become caring, competent adults able to succeed in and contribute to society, the School best serves those who have the ability to thrive in a traditional college-preparatory curriculum. The 26-acre campus provides a view of the Ramapo Mountains and includes 2 soccer fields, a softball field, a baseball diamond, 6 tennis courts, 2 playgrounds, 3 academic buildings, and the Headmaster's house as well as formal gardens, lawns, and woods. Grades K–5 combine classroom learning with hands-on experiences in an integrated curriculum. Students are engaged in reading/language arts, mathematics, science, and social studies. Art, music, world languages, physical education, and computer lab supplement the core curriculum. Middle School students follow a fully departmentalized curriculum. Core courses include literature, composition, research skills, mathematics, laboratory science, calculator skills, history and world cultures, and world languages, including Latin, French, and Spanish. Upper School students follow a rigorous, traditional, college-preparatory curriculum that may include honors and AP-level courses in all subject areas. College counseling is a 4-year process. Typically, 100% of the senior class matriculates at colleges and universities such as Amherst, Boston College, Brown, Brandeis, Carnegie Mellon, Cornell, Hamilton, Ithaca, Johns Hopkins, Princeton, Union, University of Chicago, Wesleyan, Williams, and Yale.

ST. AGNES ACADEMY

9000 Bellaire Boulevard
Houston, Texas 77036
Head of School: Sr. Jane Meyer

petersons.com

General Information Girls' day college-preparatory, arts, business, religious studies, and technology school, affiliated with Roman Catholic Church. Grades 9–12. Founded: 1906. Setting: urban. 15-acre campus. 2 buildings on campus. Approved or accredited by Southern Association of Colleges and Schools, Texas Education Agency, and Texas Department of Education. Endowment: $4 million. Total enrollment: 822. Upper school average class size: 20. Upper school faculty-student ratio: 1:15.

Upper School Student Profile Grade 9: 216 students (216 girls); Grade 10: 200 students (200 girls); Grade 11: 211 students (211 girls); Grade 12: 195 students (195 girls). 85% of students are Roman Catholic.

Faculty School total: 63. In upper school: 16 men, 46 women; 48 have advanced degrees.

Subjects Offered Accounting, acting, algebra, American history, American literature, art, art history, biology, business law, business skills, calculus, chemistry, community service, computer programming, computer science, creative writing, dance, drama, economics, English, English literature, European history, fine arts, French, geology, geometry, government/civics, health, history, integrated physics, journalism, keyboarding, Latin, marine biology, mathematics, music, philosophy, photography, physical education, physics, physiology, psychology, religion, science, social science, social studies, Spanish, speech, theater, theology, trigonometry, video film production, world history, world literature.

Graduation Requirements Arts and fine arts (art, music, dance, drama), computer science, electives, English, foreign language, mathematics, physical education (includes health), religion (includes Bible studies and theology), science, social science, social studies (includes history), speech, 100 hours of community service.

Special Academic Programs Advanced Placement exam preparation in 12 subject areas; honors section; independent study.

College Placement 183 students graduated in 2005; 180 went to college, including Louisiana State University and Agricultural and Mechanical College; St. Edward's University; Texas A&M University; The University of Texas at Austin; University of Houston. Other: 3 had other specific plans. Mean SAT verbal: 620, mean SAT math: 620, mean composite ACT: 26. 56% scored over 600 on SAT verbal, 58% scored over 600 on SAT math, 50% scored over 26 on composite ACT.

Student Life Upper grades have uniform requirement, student council, honor system. Discipline rests primarily with faculty. Attendance at religious services is required.

Summer Programs Remediation, art/fine arts, computer instruction programs offered; session focuses on remediation and elective credit; held on campus; accepts girls; not open to students from other schools. 100 students usually enrolled.

Tuition and Aid Day student tuition: $9100. Tuition installment plan (plans arranged through local bank). Merit scholarship grants, need-based scholarship grants available.

In 2005–06, 25% of upper-school students received aid; total upper-school merit-scholarship money awarded: $24,000. Total amount of financial aid awarded in 2005–06: $300,000.

Admissions Traditional secondary-level entrance grade is 9. For fall 2005, 448 students applied for upper-level admission, 311 were accepted, 224 enrolled. ISEE required. Deadline for receipt of application materials: February 1. Application fee required: $25. On-campus interview required.

Athletics Interscholastic: aquatics, basketball, cheering, cross-country running, dance team, diving, golf, soccer, softball, swimming and diving, tennis, track and field, volleyball, water polo, winter soccer; intramural: badminton, floor hockey, volleyball. 4 PE instructors, 6 coaches.

Computers Computers are regularly used in all classes. Computer network features include campus e-mail, on-campus library services, CD-ROMs, online commercial services, Internet access, file transfer, office computer access, DVD, wireless campus network.

Contact Deborah Whalen, Director of Admission. 713-219-5400. Fax: 713-219-5499. E-mail: dwhalen@st-agnes.org. Web site: www.st-agnes.org.

ANNOUNCEMENT FROM THE SCHOOL St. Agnes Academy is very proud of the 27 members of the class of 2006 named by the National Merit Corporation for awards in the NMSQT competition. In addition, the College Board has recognized 11 National Hispanic Scholars and 3 honorable mentions.

SAINT AGNES BOYS HIGH SCHOOL

555 West End Avenue
New York, New York 10024
Head of School: Br. Emil Denworth, FMS

General Information Boys' day college-preparatory and religious studies school, affiliated with Roman Catholic Church. Grades 9–12. Founded: 1892. Setting: urban. 1 building on campus. Approved or accredited by Middle States Association of Colleges and Schools, New York State Board of Regents, New York State University, and New York Department of Education. Language of instruction: Spanish. Total enrollment: 350. Upper school average class size: 25. Upper school faculty-student ratio: 1:16.

Upper School Student Profile Grade 9: 95 students (95 boys); Grade 10: 90 students (90 boys); Grade 11: 90 students (90 boys); Grade 12: 75 students (75 boys). 85% of students are Roman Catholic.

Faculty School total: 25. In upper school: 18 men, 7 women; 20 have advanced degrees.

Special Academic Programs Advanced Placement exam preparation in 4 subject areas; honors section.

College Placement 92 students graduated in 2005; 90 went to college, including Hunter College of the City University of New York; Manhattan College; St. John's University; State University of New York at Binghamton. Other: 1 went to work, 1 entered military service. Mean SAT verbal: 450, mean SAT math: 450.

Student Life Upper grades have specified standards of dress. Discipline rests primarily with faculty. Attendance at religious services is required.

Summer Programs Remediation programs offered; session focuses on remediation; held on campus; accepts boys and girls; open to students from other schools. 200 students usually enrolled. 2006 schedule: July 5 to August 15.

Tuition and Aid Day student tuition: $5350. Tuition installment plan (monthly payment plans). Need-based scholarship grants available. In 2005–06, 60% of upper-school students received aid.

Admissions Traditional secondary-level entrance grade is 9. For fall 2005, 390 students applied for upper-level admission, 280 were accepted, 100 enrolled. Cooperative Entrance Exam (McGraw-Hill) required. Deadline for receipt of application materials: none. No application fee required. Interview recommended.

Athletics Interscholastic: baseball, basketball, bowling, cross-country running, soccer; intramural: basketball, floor hockey, table tennis, volleyball. 1 PE instructor, 5 coaches.

Computers Computer network features include campus e-mail, on-campus library services, CD-ROMs, Internet access.

Contact Mr. David J. Dianora, Director of Admissions. 212-873-9100. Fax: 212-873-9292. E-mail: admissions@staghs.org. Web site: www.staghs.org.

ST. AGNES HIGH SCHOOL

530 Lafond Avenue
St. Paul, Minnesota 55103
Head of School: Mr. Jeff Brengman

General Information Coeducational day college-preparatory school, affiliated with Roman Catholic Church. Grades K–12. Founded: 1938. Setting: urban. 2 buildings on campus. Approved or accredited by North Central Association of Colleges and Schools and Minnesota Department of Education. Endowment: $160,000. Total enrollment: 472. Upper school average class size: 15. Upper school faculty-student ratio: 1:10.

Upper School Student Profile Grade 9: 68 students (38 boys, 30 girls); Grade 10: 42 students (17 boys, 25 girls); Grade 11: 56 students (30 boys, 26 girls); Grade 12: 61 students (31 boys, 30 girls). 68% of students are Roman Catholic.

Faculty School total: 39. In upper school: 12 men, 11 women; 13 have advanced degrees.

Subjects Offered Algebra, American history, American history-AP, American literature, arts, biology, biology-AP, British literature, British literature (honors), calculus, Catholic belief and practice, chemistry, choir, choral music, church history, civics, composition, computer education, economics, English, English literature, English literature-AP, environmental science, exercise science, family and consumer sciences, family living, family studies, foreign language, French, geography, geometry, health education, history, history of the Catholic Church, honors algebra, honors English, honors geometry, independent living, Latin, leadership, Life of Christ, literature, literature-AP, moral and social development, newspaper, physical education, physical science, physics, pre-algebra, pre-calculus, psychology, religion, religious studies, sewing, Spanish, speech, theater, trigonometry, U.S. history, U.S. literature, world history, writing, yearbook.

Graduation Requirements Advanced math, algebra, American history, American literature, arts and fine arts (art, music, dance, drama), biology, British literature, Catholic belief and practice, chemistry, church history, civics, economics, geometry, health education, physical education (includes health), physical science, religion (includes Bible studies and theology), world geography, world history, world literature.

Special Academic Programs Advanced Placement exam preparation in 3 subject areas; honors section; independent study.

College Placement 51 students graduated in 2005; 45 went to college, including Hamline University; Loras College; Saint Mary's University of Minnesota; University of Dallas; University of Minnesota, Twin Cities Campus; University of St. Thomas. Other: 4 went to work, 2 entered military service. Median SAT verbal: 570, median SAT math: 550, median combined SAT: 1606, median composite ACT: 22. 41% scored over 600 on SAT verbal, 41% scored over 600 on SAT math, 45% scored over 1800 on combined SAT, 21% scored over 26 on composite ACT.

Student Life Upper grades have uniform requirement, student council. Discipline rests primarily with students. Attendance at religious services is required.

Tuition and Aid Day student tuition: $6400. Tuition installment plan (FACTS Tuition Payment Plan). Tuition reduction for siblings, merit scholarship grants, need-based scholarship grants, paying campus jobs available. In 2005–06, 59% of upper-school students received aid; total upper-school merit-scholarship money awarded: $11,000. Total amount of financial aid awarded in 2005–06: $514,976.

Admissions Traditional secondary-level entrance grade is 9. For fall 2005, 29 students applied for upper-level admission, 29 were accepted, 29 enrolled. ACT-Explore required. Deadline for receipt of application materials: none. No application fee required. Interview recommended.

Athletics Interscholastic: baseball (boys), basketball (b,g), football (b), golf (b,g), ice hockey (b,g), pom squad (g), soccer (b,g), softball (g), swimming and diving (g), track and field (b,g), volleyball (g); intramural: strength & conditioning (b,g), weight lifting (b,g), weight training (b,g); coed interscholastic: cheering. 2 PE instructors, 19 coaches.

Computers Computers are regularly used in all classes. Computer network features include on-campus library services, CD-ROMs, online commercial services, Internet access, office computer access.

Contact Mr. Ronald Rice, Admission Director. 651-228-1161 Ext. 315. Fax: 651-228-1158. E-mail: rrice@stagnesschools.org. Web site: www.stagnesschools.org.

ST. ANDREW'S COLLEGE

15800 Yonge Street
Aurora, Ontario L4G 3H7, Canada
Head of School: E. G. Staunton

General Information Boys' boarding and day college-preparatory, arts, business, and technology school. Grades 6–12. Founded: 1899. Setting: small town. Nearest major city is Toronto, Canada. Students are housed in single-sex dormitories. 110-acre campus. 24 buildings on campus. Approved or accredited by Canadian Association of Independent Schools, Canadian Educational Standards Institute, Conference of Independent Schools of Ontario, The Association of Boarding Schools, and Ontario Department of Education. Affiliate member of National Association of Independent Schools; member of Secondary School Admission Test Board. Language of instruction: English. Endowment: CAN$183 million. Total enrollment: 538. Upper school average class size: 17. Upper school faculty-student ratio: 1:10.

Upper School Student Profile Grade 9: 95 students (95 boys); Grade 10: 88 students (88 boys); Grade 11: 124 students (124 boys); Grade 12: 97 students (97 boys). 54% of students are boarding students. 45% are province residents. 9 provinces are represented in upper school student body. 55% are international students. International students from Bahamas, Hong Kong, Jamaica, Mexico, Republic of Korea, and United States; 20 other countries represented in student body.

Faculty School total: 62. In upper school: 42 men, 7 women; 13 have advanced degrees; 25 reside on campus.

Subjects Offered Accounting, Advanced Placement courses, algebra, American history, art, biology, business, calculus, chemistry, communications, community service, computer science, creative writing, drama, economics, English, English

literature, environmental science, European history, fine arts, French, geography, geometry, health, history, mathematics, music, physical education, physics, physiology, science, social science, social studies, sociology, Spanish, statistics, world history, world religions.

Graduation Requirements Arts, arts and fine arts (art, music, dance, drama), business, careers, civics, computer science, dance, drama, English, foreign language, French, geography, health education, history, mathematics, physical education (includes health), science, science and technology, social science. Community service is required.

Special Academic Programs Advanced Placement exam preparation in 5 subject areas; honors section; accelerated programs; independent study; term-away projects; study abroad; ESL (11 students enrolled).

College Placement 94 students graduated in 2005; 89 went to college, including Acadia University; Dalhousie University; McGill University; Queen's University at Kingston; The University of Western Ontario; University of Toronto. Other: 3 entered a postgraduate year, 2 had other specific plans. Median SAT verbal: 540, median SAT math: 650, median combined SAT: 1890. 25% scored over 600 on SAT verbal, 55% scored over 600 on SAT math, 80% scored over 1800 on combined SAT.

Student Life Upper grades have uniform requirement, student council, honor system. Discipline rests equally with students and faculty. Attendance at religious services is required.

Summer Programs ESL, sports, art/fine arts programs offered; session focuses on Scottish music (piping and drumming), sports/arts camps, leadership camps, academics; held on campus; accepts boys and girls; open to students from other schools. 75 students usually enrolled. 2006 schedule: June 28 to August 13. Application deadline: none.

Tuition and Aid Day student tuition: CAN$21,900; 5-day tuition and room/board: CAN$35,270; 7-day tuition and room/board: CAN$35,270. Tuition installment plan (monthly payment plans, individually arranged payment plans). Bursaries, merit scholarship grants, need-based scholarship grants available. In 2005–06, 15% of upper-school students received aid; total upper-school merit-scholarship money awarded: CAN$150,000. Total amount of financial aid awarded in 2005–06: CAN$858,250.

Admissions Traditional secondary-level entrance grade is 9. For fall 2005, 195 students applied for upper-level admission, 131 were accepted, 97 enrolled. SLEP, SSAT or TOEFL required. Deadline for receipt of application materials: none. Application fee required: CAN$100. Interview required.

Athletics Interscholastic: alpine skiing, aquatics, badminton, baseball, basketball, biathlon, cricket, cross-country running, fencing, football, golf, ice hockey, indoor track, indoor track & field, lacrosse, marksmanship, nordic skiing, rugby, running, skiing (cross-country), skiing (downhill), soccer, squash, swimming and diving, table tennis, tennis, track and field, volleyball, winter (indoor) track; intramural: aquatics, archery, back packing, badminton, ball hockey, baseball, basketball, canoeing/kayaking, climbing, cooperative games, cross-country running, fencing, fitness, flag football, floor hockey, football, Frisbee, golf, hiking/backpacking, ice hockey, ice skating, jogging, lacrosse, marksmanship, mountain biking, nordic skiing, outdoor activities, outdoor education, outdoor skills, physical fitness, rock climbing, ropes courses, running, scuba diving, self defense, skiing (cross-country), skiing (downhill), snowboarding, soccer, softball, squash, strength & conditioning, swimming and diving, table tennis, tennis, touch football, track and field, ultimate Frisbee, volleyball, wall climbing, water polo, weight training, wilderness survival. 5 coaches, 3 trainers.

Computers Computers are regularly used in all academic classes. Computer network features include campus e-mail, on-campus library services, CD-ROMs, online commercial services, Internet access, wireless campus network.

Contact Mrs. Dolly Moffat-Lynch, Associate Director of Admission. 905-727-3178 Ext. 224. Fax: 905-727-9032. E-mail: admission@sac.on.ca. Web site: www.sac.on.ca.

ST. ANDREW'S COLLEGE, DUBLIN

Booterstown Avenue, Blackrock
County Dublin, Ireland
Head of School: Arthur Godsil

General Information Coeducational day college-preparatory, general academic, arts, business, religious studies, bilingual studies, and technology school, affiliated with Presbyterian Church. Grades 8–13. Founded: 1894. Setting: suburban. Nearest major city is Dublin. 15-acre campus. 2 buildings on campus. Approved or accredited by European Council of International Schools, International Baccalaureate Organization, Irish department of education, and New England Association of Schools and Colleges. Language of instruction: English. Total enrollment: 950. Upper school average class size: 24.

Subjects Offered Accounting, American history, art, biology, business, business studies, career education, chemistry, Chinese, choir, civics, classical studies, computer applications, computer studies, computer-aided design, economics, electronics, English, English as a foreign language, European history, film studies, French, German, history, Italian, Japanese, Korean, Latin, math methods, mathematics, music, navigation, personal and social education, personal development, physical education, physics, Portuguese, religion, religious education, Russian, SAT preparation, science, social skills, Spanish, technical drawing, theory of knowledge, U.S. history.

Special Academic Programs International Baccalaureate program; honors section; remedial reading and/or remedial writing; remedial math; programs in English, mathematics, general development for dyslexic students.

College Placement 138 students graduated in 2005; 130 went to college, including Harvard University; Seattle University; University of Oxford. Other: 8 went to work.

Student Life Upper grades have uniform requirement. Discipline rests primarily with faculty.

Tuition and Aid Day student tuition: €4015. Tuition installment plan (monthly payment plans, individually arranged payment plans). Tuition reduction for siblings, bursaries, merit scholarship grants, need-based scholarship grants available. Total upper-school merit-scholarship money awarded for 2005–06: €8500.

Admissions Placement test and school's own test required. Deadline for receipt of application materials: none. Application fee required: €300. Interview required.

Athletics Interscholastic: aerobics/dance (girls), back packing (b,g), badminton (b,g), ballet (g), basketball (b,g), cricket (b,g), cross-country running (b,g), field hockey (b,g), football (b), golf (b,g), hockey (b,g), indoor hockey (b,g), indoor soccer (b,g), judo (b,g), life saving (b,g), martial arts (b,g), netball (g), outdoor education (b,g), outdoor recreation (b,g), outdoor skills (b,g), racquetball (b,g), rounders (g), rugby (b), sailing (b,g), self defense (b,g), soccer (b), squash (b,g), swimming and diving (b,g), tennis (b,g), water polo (b,g); coed interscholastic: archery, gymnastics. 4 PE instructors.

Computers Computers are regularly used in all academic classes. Computer network features include on-campus library services, CD-ROMs, Internet access, file transfer, office computer access, DVD.

Contact Mr. Ronnie Hay, Vice Principal. 353-1-288-2785. Fax: 353-1-283-1627. E-mail: information@st-andrews.ie. Web site: www.st-andrews.ie.

ST. ANDREW'S EPISCOPAL SCHOOL

8804 Postoak Road
Potomac, Maryland 20854
Head of School: Mr. Robert Kosasky

General Information Coeducational day college-preparatory, arts, religious studies, and technology school, affiliated with Episcopal Church. Grades 6–12. Founded: 1978. Setting: suburban. Nearest major city is Washington, DC. 19-acre campus. 5 buildings on campus. Approved or accredited by Association of Independent Maryland Schools, Association of Independent Schools of Greater Washington, Middle States Association of Colleges and Schools, National Association of Episcopal Schools, and National Association of Private Schools for Exceptional Children. Member of National Association of Independent Schools and Secondary School Admission Test Board. Endowment: $1 million. Total enrollment: 454. Upper school average class size: 15. Upper school faculty-student ratio: 1:8.

Upper School Student Profile Grade 9: 87 students (41 boys, 46 girls); Grade 10: 73 students (35 boys, 38 girls); Grade 11: 85 students (42 boys, 43 girls); Grade 12: 71 students (33 boys, 38 girls). 30% of students are members of Episcopal Church.

Faculty School total: 58. In upper school: 26 men, 32 women.

Subjects Offered 20th century American writers, 20th century history, 20th century world history, 3-dimensional art, 3-dimensional design, acting, Advanced Placement courses, advanced studio art-AP, algebra, alternative physical education, American history, American literature, animation, art, art history, art history-AP, art-AP, Asian studies, band, Bible, Bible studies, biology, biology-AP, British literature, calculus, calculus-AP, ceramics, chemistry, chorus, college counseling, composition-AP, computer animation, computer art, computer graphics, creative writing, dance, digital photography, drama, dramatic arts, earth science, English, English literature, English literature-AP, English-AP, ethics, European history, fine arts, French, geography, geometry, government, government/civics, grammar, guitar, health, health education, history, journalism, Latin, Latin American studies, Latin-AP, mathematics, music, musical theater, newspaper, orchestra, photography, physical education, physical science, physics, physics-AP, pre-algebra, pre-calculus, public speaking, religion, robotics, science, social studies, Spanish, Spanish language-AP, Spanish literature, Spanish literature-AP, Spanish-AP, sports, stage design, statistics, student publications, The 20th Century, theater, theater arts, theology, trigonometry, U.S. history, U.S. history-AP, video, world cultures, world history, world religions, writing, yearbook.

Graduation Requirements Algebra, arts and fine arts (art, music, dance, drama), biology, English, foreign language, geometry, mathematics, physical education (includes health), religion (includes Bible studies and theology), science, social studies (includes history), community service (one service learning course in the 9th grade, 20 hours per year in 10th and 11th grade, 60 hours senior year).

Special Academic Programs Advanced Placement exam preparation in 8 subject areas; independent study.

College Placement 81 students graduated in 2005; 80 went to college, including Dickinson College; Reed College; Tufts University; Wake Forest University; Washington and Lee University. Other: 1 entered military service. 63% scored over 600 on SAT verbal, 66% scored over 600 on SAT math.

Student Life Upper grades have specified standards of dress, student council, honor system. Discipline rests primarily with faculty. Attendance at religious services is required.

Summer Programs Enrichment, advancement, sports, art/fine arts programs offered; session focuses on advancement and enrichment; held on campus; accepts boys and

girls; open to students from other schools. 400 students usually enrolled. 2006 schedule: June 19 to July 28. Application deadline: none.

Tuition and Aid Day student tuition: $24,975. Tuition installment plan (Key Tuition Payment Plan, monthly payment plans). Need-based scholarship grants, Achiever Loan Program available. In 2005–06, 17% of upper-school students received aid. Total amount of financial aid awarded in 2005–06: $626,510.

Admissions Traditional secondary-level entrance grade is 9. For fall 2005, 167 students applied for upper-level admission, 100 were accepted, 32 enrolled. SSAT required. Deadline for receipt of application materials: February 1. Application fee required: $50. On-campus interview required.

Athletics Interscholastic: baseball (boys), basketball (b,g), fitness (b,g), lacrosse (b,g), soccer (b,g), softball (g), tennis (b,g), volleyball (g), wrestling (b); intramural: physical fitness (b,g); coed interscholastic: cross-country running, equestrian sports, golf, track and field; coed intramural: dance, weight training. 2 PE instructors, 38 coaches, 1 trainer.

Computers Computers are regularly used in English, foreign language, graphic arts, history, journalism, mathematics, music, science classes. Computer network features include campus e-mail, on-campus library services, Internet access, wireless campus network.

Contact Mrs. Aileen Moodie, Admission Coordinator. 301-983-5200 Ext. 236. Fax: 301-983-4620. E-mail: admission@saes.org. Web site: www.saes.org.

ST. ANDREW'S EPISCOPAL SCHOOL

370 Old Agency Road
Ridgeland, Mississippi 39157
Head of School: Mr. Stephen R. Blanchard

General Information Coeducational day college-preparatory, arts, and technology school, affiliated with Episcopal Church. Grades PK–12. Founded: 1947. Setting: suburban. Nearest major city is Jackson. 56-acre campus. 12 buildings on campus. Approved or accredited by National Association of Episcopal Schools and Southern Association of Colleges and Schools. Member of National Association of Independent Schools. Total enrollment: 1,153. Upper school average class size: 15. Upper school faculty-student ratio: 1:9.

Upper School Student Profile Grade 9: 90 students (44 boys, 46 girls); Grade 10: 74 students (38 boys, 36 girls); Grade 11: 78 students (37 boys, 41 girls); Grade 12: 68 students (28 boys, 40 girls). 31% of students are members of Episcopal Church.

Faculty School total: 104. In upper school: 13 men, 18 women; 18 have advanced degrees.

Subjects Offered Algebra, American government-AP, American history, American literature, art, art history, art history-AP, astronomy, biology, biology-AP, calculus, calculus-AP, chemistry, chemistry-AP, community service, computers, creative writing, drama, driver education, English, English literature, English literature-AP, English-AP, European history, European literature, film, fine arts, French, French language-AP, freshman seminar, geometry, government-AP, government/civics, grammar, history-AP, honors algebra, honors English, honors geometry, honors U.S. history, Latin, Latin-AP, literature-AP, mathematics, modern European history, music, physics, physics-AP, probability and statistics, psychology, Spanish, Spanish language-AP, speech, speech and debate, studio art-AP, theater, U.S. history-AP, visual arts, world history, world literature.

Graduation Requirements Arts and fine arts (art, music, dance, drama), English, foreign language, mathematics, science, social studies (includes history), speech. Community service is required.

Special Academic Programs Advanced Placement exam preparation in 15 subject areas; honors section; study abroad; academic accommodation for the gifted, the musically talented, and the artistically talented.

College Placement 59 students graduated in 2005; 55 went to college, including Belmont University; Millsaps College; Mississippi State University; Rhodes College; University of Mississippi; University of the South. Other: 2 went to work, 1 entered military service, 1 had other specific plans. Mean SAT verbal: 631, mean SAT math: 604, mean composite ACT: 27.

Student Life Upper grades have specified standards of dress, student council, honor system. Discipline rests primarily with faculty. Attendance at religious services is required.

Tuition and Aid Day student tuition: $9100. Tuition installment plan (monthly payment plans, semester payment plan). Merit scholarship grants, need-based scholarship grants available. In 2005–06, 18% of upper-school students received aid; total upper-school merit-scholarship money awarded: $4500. Total amount of financial aid awarded in 2005–06: $176,170.

Admissions Traditional secondary-level entrance grade is 9. For fall 2005, 20 students applied for upper-level admission, 19 were accepted, 15 enrolled. ACT, ERB Reading and Math or writing sample required. Deadline for receipt of application materials: none. Application fee required: $35. On-campus interview required.

Athletics Interscholastic: baseball (boys), basketball (b,g), cross-country running (b,g), fitness (b,g), football (b), golf (b), power lifting (b), soccer (b,g), softball (g), tennis (b,g), track and field (b,g), volleyball (g); coed interscholastic: cheering, lacrosse, physical fitness, sailing, swimming and diving, tennis; coed intramural: bowling, equestrian sports. 1 coach.

Computers Computers are regularly used in all academic classes. Computer network features include campus e-mail, on-campus library services, CD-ROMs, online

commercial services, Internet access, file transfer, office computer access, DVD, wireless campus network, laptop requirement for all students in grades 9 through 12.

Contact Kay H. Mortimer, Middle and Upper School Admissions. 601-853-6042. Fax: 601-853-6001. E-mail: mortimerk@gosaints.org. Web site: www.gosaints.org.

ST. ANDREW'S ON THE MARSH SCHOOL

PO Box 30639
601 Penn Waller Road
Savannah, Georgia 31410-0639
Head of School: Mr. E. C. Hubbard Jr.

General Information Coeducational day college-preparatory, arts, and bilingual studies school. Grades PK–12. Founded: 1947. Setting: suburban. 30-acre campus. 6 buildings on campus. Approved or accredited by Georgia Independent School Association, South Carolina Independent School Association, Southern Association of Colleges and Schools, and Georgia Department of Education. Member of National Association of Independent Schools. Endowment: $3 million. Total enrollment: 469. Upper school average class size: 20. Upper school faculty-student ratio: 1:9.

Upper School Student Profile Grade 9: 38 students (15 boys, 23 girls); Grade 10: 31 students (16 boys, 15 girls); Grade 11: 30 students (17 boys, 13 girls); Grade 12: 36 students (20 boys, 16 girls).

Faculty School total: 60. In upper school: 11 men, 12 women; 10 have advanced degrees.

Subjects Offered Algebra, American history, American literature, anatomy, art, art history, biology, calculus, chemistry, classical studies, community service, computer programming, computer science, creative writing, drama, earth science, economics, English, English literature, environmental science, ethics, European history, fine arts, French, geography, geometry, government/civics, health, history, mathematics, music, physical education, physics, psychology, science, social studies, Spanish, theater, trigonometry, world history.

Graduation Requirements Arts and fine arts (art, music, dance, drama), computer science, English, foreign language, mathematics, physical education (includes health), science, social studies (includes history), senior work project. Community service is required.

Special Academic Programs Advanced Placement exam preparation in 7 subject areas; honors section; independent study; study at local college for college credit; study abroad.

College Placement 29 students graduated in 2005; all went to college, including Appalachian State University; Georgia Southern University; Hampden-Sydney College; The University of North Carolina at Asheville; Tulane University; University of Georgia.

Student Life Upper grades have specified standards of dress, student council, honor system. Discipline rests equally with students and faculty.

Summer Programs Enrichment, sports, art/fine arts programs offered; session focuses on enrichment; held on campus; accepts boys and girls; open to students from other schools. 100 students usually enrolled. 2006 schedule: June 7 to August 6.

Tuition and Aid Day student tuition: $7950–$8950. Tuition installment plan (monthly payment plans, individually arranged payment plans). Need-based financial aid grants available. In 2005–06, 25% of upper-school students received aid. Total amount of financial aid awarded in 2005–06: $70,000.

Admissions Traditional secondary-level entrance grade is 9. For fall 2005, 35 students applied for upper-level admission, 30 were accepted, 26 enrolled. ERB, Iowa Tests of Basic Skills, SSAT or Stanford Achievement Test required. Deadline for receipt of application materials: none. Application fee required: $100. Interview required.

Athletics Interscholastic: basketball (boys, girls), cheering (g), cross-country running (b,g), football (b), golf (b,g), physical fitness (b,g), soccer (b,g), softball (g), strength & conditioning (b,g), tennis (b,g), track and field (b,g), volleyball (g); intramural: basketball (b,g), soccer (b,g), softball (g), volleyball (b,g), weight lifting (b,g), weight training (b,g); coed interscholastic: cheering, physical fitness. 4 PE instructors, 2 coaches, 1 trainer.

Computers Computers are regularly used in English, history, science, Spanish classes. Computer network features include on-campus library services, CD-ROMs, Internet access, office computer access.

Contact Mrs. Kelley Waldron, Director of Admissions. 912-897-4941 Ext. 303. Fax: 912-897-4943. E-mail: waldronk@saintschool.com. Web site: www.saintschool.com.

ST. ANDREW'S PRIORY SCHOOL

224 Queen Emma Square
Honolulu, Hawaii 96813
Head of School: Marilyn A. Matsunaga

General Information Girls' day college-preparatory, arts, and technology school, affiliated with Episcopal Church. Grades K–12. Founded: 1867. Setting: urban. 3-acre campus. 7 buildings on campus. Approved or accredited by National Association of Episcopal Schools, The College Board, The Hawaii Council of Private Schools, Western Association of Schools and Colleges, and Hawaii Department of Education. Member of National Association of Independent Schools and Secondary School

St. Andrew's Priory School

Admission Test Board. Endowment: $3.2 million. Total enrollment: 538. Upper school average class size: 12. Upper school faculty-student ratio: 1:4.

Upper School Student Profile Grade 9: 51 students (51 girls); Grade 10: 46 students (46 girls); Grade 11: 51 students (51 girls); Grade 12: 41 students (41 girls). 15% of students are members of Episcopal Church.

Faculty School total: 63. In upper school: 10 men, 24 women; 20 have advanced degrees.

Subjects Offered Algebra, American government, American history, American literature, ancient history, applied arts, applied music, art, art history, Asian studies, Bible studies, biology, biology-AP, British literature, British literature-AP, calculus, calculus-AP, ceramics, chemistry, chemistry-AP, choir, college counseling, college placement, community service, competitive science projects, computer art, computer education, computer graphics, computer keyboarding, computer literacy, computer multimedia, computer programming, computer science, computer technology certification, creative writing, drama, economics, economics and history, English, English literature, English literature-AP, ESL, European history, expository writing, fine arts, French, geography, geometry, government/civics, grammar, guidance, handbells, Hawaiian history, Hawaiian language, health, history, honors U.S. history, humanities, Japanese, journalism, Latin, leadership training, life skills, mathematics, mechanical drawing, medieval history, microbiology, modern world history, music, Pacific Island studies, photography, physical education, physics, physics-AP, physiology, Polynesian dance, pre-algebra, pre-calculus, psychology, religion, science, science research, social science, social studies, sociology, Spanish, Spanish-AP, speech, speech communications, theater, theology, trigonometry, U.S. history-AP, United States government-AP, video and animation, visual and performing arts, wind ensemble, world civilizations, world history, world literature, world wide web design, writing, writing workshop, yearbook.

Graduation Requirements Advanced Placement courses, arts and fine arts (art, music, dance, drama), computer science, English, foreign language, Hawaiian history, humanities, mathematics, physical education (includes health), religion (includes Bible studies and theology), science, science research, social science, social studies (includes history), speech. Community service is required.

Special Academic Programs Advanced Placement exam preparation in 8 subject areas; honors section; independent study; study at local college for college credit; academic accommodation for the musically talented and the artistically talented; ESL (5 students enrolled).

College Placement 28 students graduated in 2005; all went to college, including Boston University; Goucher College; University of Hawaii at Manoa; University of Notre Dame; University of San Francisco; University of Southern California.

Student Life Upper grades have uniform requirement, student council, honor system. Discipline rests primarily with faculty. Attendance at religious services is required.

Summer Programs Remediation, enrichment, advancement, ESL, sports, art/fine arts, rigorous outdoor training, computer instruction programs offered; session focuses on academics, arts, sports; held on campus; accepts boys and girls; open to students from other schools. 700 students usually enrolled. 2006 schedule: June 13 to July 21. Application deadline: March.

Tuition and Aid Day student tuition: $10,480. Tuition installment plan (FACTS Tuition Payment Plan, monthly payment plans, individually arranged payment plans). Tuition reduction for siblings, merit scholarship grants, need-based scholarship grants available. In 2005–06, 36% of upper-school students received aid; total upper-school merit-scholarship money awarded: $83,840. Total amount of financial aid awarded in 2005–06: $107,290.

Admissions Traditional secondary-level entrance grade is 9. SSAT required. Deadline for receipt of application materials: none. Application fee required: $50. On-campus interview required.

Athletics Interscholastic: basketball, bowling, canoeing/kayaking, cheering, cross-country running, dance team, diving, golf, gymnastics, martial arts, ocean paddling, soccer, softball, swimming and diving, tennis, track and field, volleyball, water polo, wrestling; intramural: aerobics/dance, dance squad, drill team, fitness, flag football, jogging, outdoor activities, outdoor adventure, physical fitness, ropes courses, self defense, strength & conditioning, tai chi, weight training, windsurfing. 4 PE instructors, 18 coaches.

Computers Computers are regularly used in animation, art, college planning, English, ESL, foreign language, graphic design, history, humanities, independent study, library, literary magazine, mathematics, media arts, music, newspaper, photojournalism, psychology, religion, science, speech, technology, writing, yearbook classes. Computer network features include on-campus library services, CD-ROMs, online commercial services, Internet access, file transfer, DVD, wireless campus network.

Contact Sue Ann Wargo, Director of Admissions. 808-532-2418. Fax: 808-531-8426. E-mail: sawargo@priory.net. Web site: www.priory.net.

ST. ANDREW'S SCHOOL

350 Noxontown Road
Middletown, Delaware 19709
Head of School: Daniel T. Roach

General Information Coeducational boarding college-preparatory, arts, and religious studies school, affiliated with Episcopal Church. Grades 9–12. Founded: 1929. Setting: rural. Nearest major city is Wilmington. Students are housed in single-sex

dormitories. 2,200-acre campus. 13 buildings on campus. Approved or accredited by Middle States Association of Colleges and Schools, National Association of Episcopal Schools, The Association of Boarding Schools, The College Board, and Delaware Department of Education. Member of National Association of Independent Schools and Secondary School Admission Test Board. Endowment: $170 million. Total enrollment: 270. Upper school average class size: 11. Upper school faculty-student ratio: 1:5.

Upper School Student Profile Grade 9: 53 students (31 boys, 22 girls); Grade 10: 74 students (36 boys, 38 girls); Grade 11: 68 students (37 boys, 31 girls); Grade 12: 75 students (38 boys, 37 girls). 100% of students are boarding students. 14% are state residents. 26 states are represented in upper school student body. 5% are international students. International students from France, Germany, Hong Kong, Mexico, Republic of Korea, and South Africa; 3 other countries represented in student body. 40% of students are members of Episcopal Church.

Faculty School total: 60. In upper school: 31 men, 29 women; 43 have advanced degrees; 59 reside on campus.

Subjects Offered Acting, algebra, American history, American literature, art, art history, biology, calculus, ceramics, chemistry, Chinese, computer programming, creative writing, drama, driver education, English, English literature, environmental science, ethics, European history, fine arts, French, geometry, history, Latin, mathematics, music, philosophy, photography, physics, religion, science, Spanish, speech, theater, trigonometry, western religions.

Graduation Requirements Arts and fine arts (art, music, dance, drama), English, foreign language, history, mathematics, religion (includes Bible studies and theology), science.

Special Academic Programs Advanced Placement exam preparation in 11 subject areas; honors section; independent study; academic accommodation for the gifted, the musically talented, and the artistically talented.

College Placement 78 students graduated in 2005; 76 went to college, including Davidson College; Georgetown University; Middlebury College; University of Virginia; Williams College. Other: 2 had other specific plans. Mean SAT verbal: 656, mean SAT math: 651.

Student Life Upper grades have specified standards of dress, student council, honor system. Discipline rests equally with students and faculty. Attendance at religious services is required.

Tuition and Aid 7-day tuition and room/board: $33,000. Tuition installment plan (Key Tuition Payment Plan, monthly payment plans). Need-based scholarship grants available. In 2005–06, 46% of upper-school students received aid. Total amount of financial aid awarded in 2005–06: $3,150,000.

Admissions Traditional secondary-level entrance grade is 9. For fall 2005, 430 students applied for upper-level admission, 132 were accepted, 81 enrolled. SSAT or TOEFL required. Deadline for receipt of application materials: January 15. Application fee required: $50. On-campus interview required.

Athletics Interscholastic: baseball (boys), basketball (b,g), crew (b,g), cross-country running (b,g), diving (b,g), field hockey (g), football (b), lacrosse (b,g), soccer (b,g), squash (b,g), swimming and diving (b,g), tennis (b,g), volleyball (g), wrestling (b); intramural: weight lifting (b,g); coed interscholastic: aerobics/dance, aquatics, dance; coed intramural: aerobics, aerobics/dance, dance, fishing, fitness, Frisbee, indoor soccer, kayaking, paddle tennis, physical training, rowing, sailing, weight lifting, weight training, yoga. 5 coaches, 1 trainer.

Computers Computers are regularly used in English, foreign language, history, mathematics, science classes. Computer network features include campus e-mail, on-campus library services, CD-ROMs, online commercial services, Internet access, file transfer, office computer access, DVD, wireless campus network.

Contact Louisa H. Zendt, Director of Admissions. 302-285-4230. Fax: 302-378-7120. E-mail: lzendt@standrews-de.org. Web site: www.standrews-de.org.

SAINT ANDREW'S SCHOOL

3900 Jog Road
Boca Raton, Florida 33434
Head of School: Rev. George E. Andrews II

petersons.com

General Information Coeducational boarding and day college-preparatory school, affiliated with Episcopal Church. Boarding grades 9–12, day grades K–12. Founded: 1961. Setting: suburban. Nearest major city is West Palm Beach. Students are housed in single-sex dormitories. 85-acre campus. 18 buildings on campus. Approved or accredited by Florida Council of Independent Schools, The Association of Boarding Schools, and Florida Department of Education. Member of National Association of Independent Schools and Secondary School Admission Test Board. Endowment: $6.5 million. Total enrollment: 1,135. Upper school average class size: 15. Upper school faculty-student ratio: 1:10.

Upper School Student Profile 17% of students are boarding students. 82% are state residents. 11 states are represented in upper school student body. 12% are international students. International students from Austria, Bahamas, Cayman Islands, Germany, Jamaica, and Republic of Korea; 17 other countries represented in student body. 15% of students are members of Episcopal Church.

Faculty School total: 210. In upper school: 55 men, 75 women; 80 have advanced degrees; 45 reside on campus.

Subjects Offered Advanced studio art-AP, algebra, American history, American literature, American studies, anatomy, archaeology, art, art history, Bible studies,

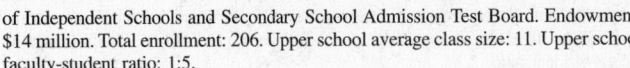

biology, biology-AP, calculus, calculus-AP, chemistry, chemistry-AP, community service, computer math, computer programming, computer science, computer science-AP, creative writing, drafting, drama, earth science, ecology, economics, English, English literature, English-AP, environmental science, ethics, European history, expository writing, fine arts, French, French-AP, geography, geometry, German, German-AP, government/civics, grammar, history, journalism, Latin, marine biology, mathematics, music, photography, physical education, physics, physics-AP, pre-calculus, psychology, science, social studies, Spanish, Spanish-AP, speech, statistics, theater, theology, trigonometry, U.S. history-AP, world history, world history-AP, world literature, writing.

Graduation Requirements Arts and fine arts (art, music, dance, drama), computer science, English, foreign language, mathematics, physical education (includes health), religion (includes Bible studies and theology), science, social studies (includes history), speech, participation in sports. Community service is required.

Special Academic Programs Advanced Placement exam preparation in 17 subject areas; honors section; academic accommodation for the gifted; ESL (20 students enrolled).

College Placement 146 students graduated in 2005; 145 went to college, including Boston University; Indiana University–Purdue University Fort Wayne; Northwestern University; The George Washington University; University of Florida; University of Miami. Mean SAT verbal: 603, mean SAT math: 622. 42% scored over 600 on SAT verbal, 52% scored over 600 on SAT math.

Student Life Upper grades have specified standards of dress, student council, honor system. Discipline rests primarily with faculty. Attendance at religious services is required.

Summer Programs Remediation, enrichment, advancement, ESL, art/fine arts, computer instruction programs offered; held on campus; accepts boys and girls; open to students from other schools. 225 students usually enrolled. 2006 schedule: June 10 to July 20. Application deadline: none.

Tuition and Aid Day student tuition: $18,400; 7-day tuition and room/board: $33,100. Tuition installment plan (Insured Tuition Payment Plan, Key Tuition Payment Plan, monthly payment plans, individually arranged payment plans). Need-based scholarship grants available. In 2005–06, 17% of upper-school students received aid. Total amount of financial aid awarded in 2005–06: $1,332,000.

Admissions Traditional secondary-level entrance grade is 9. SSAT required. Deadline for receipt of application materials: February 10. Application fee required: $75. Interview recommended.

Athletics Interscholastic: baseball (boys), basketball (b,g), cheering (g), cross-country running (b,g), danceline (g), diving (b,g), football (b), golf (b,g), lacrosse (b,g), soccer (b,g), softball (g), swimming and diving (b,g), tennis (b,g), track and field (b,g), volleyball (g), water polo (b,g), wrestling (b); intramural: weight lifting (b,g); coed interscholastic: water polo. 2 PE instructors, 4 coaches, 1 trainer.

Computers Computers are regularly used in college planning, English, foreign language, history, mathematics, science classes. Computer network features include campus e-mail, on-campus library services, CD-ROMs, online commercial services, Internet access.

Contact Kilian J. Forgus, Director of Admission. 561-210-2020. Fax: 561-210-2027. E-mail: admission@saintandrewsschool.net. Web site: www.saintandrewsschool.net.

ANNOUNCEMENT FROM THE SCHOOL Saint Andrew's School, situated on an 80-acre campus 5 miles from the Atlantic Ocean in south Florida, is an independent, college-preparatory school for grades K–12. The upper school curriculum is distinguished by a number of honors courses, along with over 20 Advanced Placement classes. Elective courses include anatomy and physiology, marine science, comparative government, expository writing, comparative religion, music appreciation, and art appreciation. Athletic programs are offered in 16 different interscholastic sports, with the swimming, tennis, golf, basketball, and lacrosse teams having recently received statewide recognition. Students have benefited from $18-million in new facilities over the last 3 years, including a state-of-the-art science center; an athletic and aquatics complex with 2 gymnasiums, a modern fitness center, and a 50-meter pool; and a center for the performing arts, which includes a 650-seat auditorium. Saint Andrew's offers a family-like community and distinguished, nurturing faculty members who help students develop in mind, body, and spirit.

ST. ANDREW'S SCHOOL
63 Federal Road
Barrington, Rhode Island 02806
Head of School: Mr. John D. Martin

General Information Coeducational boarding and day college-preparatory and arts school. Boarding grades 9–12, day grades 6–12. Founded: 1893. Setting: suburban. Nearest major city is Providence. Students are housed in single-sex dormitories. 83-acre campus. 32 buildings on campus. Approved or accredited by Association of Independent Schools in New England, National Association of Episcopal Schools, New England Association of Schools and Colleges, The Association of Boarding Schools, and Rhode Island Department of Education. Member of National Association

of Independent Schools and Secondary School Admission Test Board. Endowment: $14 million. Total enrollment: 206. Upper school average class size: 11. Upper school faculty-student ratio: 1:5.

Upper School Student Profile Grade 9: 37 students (28 boys, 9 girls); Grade 10: 52 students (33 boys, 19 girls); Grade 11: 44 students (28 boys, 16 girls); Grade 12: 35 students (27 boys, 8 girls). 32% of students are boarding students. 68% are state residents. 11 states are represented in upper school student body. 7% are international students. International students from Jamaica, Japan, and Republic of Korea.

Faculty School total: 42. In upper school: 16 men, 18 women; 23 have advanced degrees; 17 reside on campus.

Subjects Offered Algebra, American history, American literature, American studies, ancient history, art, biology, calculus, calculus-AP, ceramics, chemistry, chorus, college counseling, college placement, computer graphics, computer science, consumer mathematics, desktop publishing, digital photography, drama, drama workshop, drawing, English, environmental science, ESL, ethics, European history, fine arts, general math, geometry, graphic arts, graphic design, human anatomy, keyboarding, literature, mathematics, oceanography, photography, physical education, physics, physics-AP, portfolio art, pre-calculus, probability and statistics, remedial study skills, SAT preparation, science, social studies, Spanish, study skills, theater, theater arts, TOEFL preparation, word processing, yearbook.

Graduation Requirements Arts and fine arts (art, music, dance, drama), English, mathematics, physical education (includes health), science, social studies (includes history). Community service is required.

Special Academic Programs Advanced Placement exam preparation in 1 subject area; honors section; independent study; academic accommodation for the musically talented and the artistically talented; remedial reading and/or remedial writing; programs in English for dyslexic students; special instructional classes for students with mild language-based learning disabilities, students with attention/organizational issues (ADHD); ESL (5 students enrolled).

College Placement 31 students graduated in 2005; 29 went to college, including Curry College; Emory University; Pratt Institute; Providence College; Rhode Island College; University of Massachusetts Boston. Other: 1 went to work, 1 had other specific plans. Median SAT verbal: 433, median SAT math: 453.

Student Life Upper grades have specified standards of dress, student council. Discipline rests primarily with faculty.

Summer Programs Sports, art/fine arts programs offered; session focuses on skills development; held on campus; accepts boys and girls; open to students from other schools. 500 students usually enrolled. 2006 schedule: June 27 to August 18. Application deadline: June 15.

Tuition and Aid Day student tuition: $21,075; 7-day tuition and room/board: $33,600. Tuition installment plan (Academic Management Services Plan, Key Tuition Payment Plan). Need-based scholarship grants, need-based loans, paying campus jobs available. In 2005–06, 42% of upper-school students received aid. Total amount of financial aid awarded in 2005–06: $1,103,465.

Admissions Traditional secondary-level entrance grade is 9. For fall 2005, 192 students applied for upper-level admission, 126 were accepted, 58 enrolled. Any standardized test, psychoeducational evaluation or WISC-III and Woodcock-Johnson required. Deadline for receipt of application materials: February 6. Application fee required: $50. Interview required.

Athletics Interscholastic: basketball (boys, girls), cross-country running (b,g), lacrosse (b,g), soccer (b,g), tennis (b,g); coed interscholastic: Frisbee, golf, soccer; coed intramural: basketball, bicycling, bocce, cooperative games, croquet, fitness, fitness walking, Frisbee, horseshoes, jogging, physical fitness, project adventure, running, ultimate Frisbee, walking, weight lifting, weight training. 1 PE instructor, 1 coach, 1 trainer.

Computers Computers are regularly used in all academic, computer applications, engineering, library skills, multimedia, SAT preparation, yearbook classes. Computer network features include campus e-mail, on-campus library services, CD-ROMs, Internet access, office computer access, DVD, wireless campus network, local area network for students, including dorms.

Contact Mary Bishop, Admissions Assistant. 401-246-1230 Ext. 3025. Fax: 401-246-0510. E-mail: admissions@standrews-ri.org. Web site: www.standrews-ri.org.

See full description on page 1006.

ST. ANDREW'S–SEWANEE SCHOOL
290 Quintard Road
Sewanee, Tennessee 37375-3000
Head of School: Rev. William S. Wade

General Information Coeducational boarding and day college-preparatory, arts, and theater school, affiliated with Episcopal Church. Boarding grades 9–12, day grades 6–12. Founded: 1868. Setting: small town. Nearest major city is Chattanooga. Students are housed in single-sex dormitories. 550-acre campus. 18 buildings on campus. Approved or accredited by National Association of Episcopal Schools, Southern Association of Colleges and Schools, Tennessee Association of Independent Schools, The Association of Boarding Schools, and Tennessee Department of Education. Member of National Association of Independent Schools and Secondary School

St. Andrew's–Sewanee School

Admission Test Board. Languages of instruction: Spanish and French. Endowment: $8.5 million. Total enrollment: 254. Upper school average class size: 13. Upper school faculty-student ratio: 1:7.

Upper School Student Profile Grade 9: 46 students (27 boys, 19 girls); Grade 10: 51 students (27 boys, 24 girls); Grade 11: 48 students (25 boys, 23 girls); Grade 12: 54 students (33 boys, 21 girls). 48% of students are boarding students. 25% are state residents. 17 states are represented in upper school student body. 28% are international students. International students from Germany, Jamaica, Republic of Korea, Taiwan, and United Kingdom; 6 other countries represented in student body. 37% of students are members of Episcopal Church.

Faculty School total: 42. In upper school: 22 men, 20 women; 33 have advanced degrees; 21 reside on campus.

Subjects Offered 20th century history, acting, adolescent issues, advanced chemistry, algebra, American history, American literature, art, band, biology, calculus, chamber groups, chemistry, choir, college counseling, community service, drama, ecology, emergency medicine, English, English literature, environmental systems, ESL, fine arts, French, general science, geometry, history, Holocaust, humanities, Latin, mathematics, music, physical education, physics, pottery, pre-algebra, religion, science, social studies, Spanish, statistics, theater, trigonometry, world history, yearbook.

Graduation Requirements Arts and fine arts (art, music, dance, drama), English, foreign language, mathematics, physical education (includes health), religion (includes Bible studies and theology), science, social studies (includes history), junior essay, Senior Lecture Series, outreach, credal statement. Community service is required.

Special Academic Programs Advanced Placement exam preparation in 6 subject areas; independent study; term-away projects; study at local college for college credit; academic accommodation for the gifted, the musically talented, and the artistically talented; ESL (16 students enrolled).

College Placement 49 students graduated in 2005; 48 went to college, including Kenyon College; The University of Tennessee; The University of Tennessee at Chattanooga; University of Georgia; University of the South; Vanderbilt University. Other: 1 had other specific plans. Mean SAT verbal: 599, mean SAT math: 576. 53% scored over 600 on SAT verbal, 37% scored over 600 on SAT math, 44% scored over 26 on composite ACT.

Student Life Upper grades have specified standards of dress, student council, honor system. Discipline rests equally with students and faculty. Attendance at religious services is required.

Summer Programs Enrichment, rigorous outdoor training programs offered; session focuses on outdoor adventure; held both on and off campus; held at various locations for field trips and activities; accepts boys and girls; open to students from other schools. 24 students usually enrolled. 2006 schedule: June 7 to July 23. Application deadline: none.

Tuition and Aid Day student tuition: $12,420; 7-day tuition and room/board: $30,825. Tuition installment plan (monthly payment plans, Tuition Management Systems Plan). Merit scholarship grants, need-based scholarship grants available. In 2005–06, 39% of upper-school students received aid; total upper-school merit-scholarship money awarded: $45,000. Total amount of financial aid awarded in 2005–06: $1,248,000.

Admissions Traditional secondary-level entrance grade is 9. For fall 2005, 104 students applied for upper-level admission, 63 were accepted, 47 enrolled. ISEE, SLEP, SSAT, Stanford Achievement Test, Otis-Lennon, TOEFL or writing sample required. Deadline for receipt of application materials: none. Application fee required: $50. Interview required.

Athletics Interscholastic: baseball (boys), basketball (b,g), cross-country running (b,g), dance squad (g), football (b), modern dance (b), soccer (b,g), swimming and diving (b,g), tennis (b,g), track and field (b,g), volleyball (g), wrestling (b); intramural: cheering (g), dance team (g); coed interscholastic: equestrian sports, golf, mountain biking, outdoor skills, rock climbing, strength & conditioning; coed intramural: aerobics/dance, bicycling, canoeing/kayaking, climbing, fitness, outdoor adventure, outdoor education, physical training, rappelling, ropes courses, weight training. 10 coaches, 1 trainer.

Computers Computers are regularly used in art, English, foreign language, history, introduction to technology, mathematics, SAT preparation, science, yearbook classes. Computer network features include campus e-mail, on-campus library services, CD-ROMs, online commercial services, Internet access, access to University of the South technology facilities.

Contact Mr. Jim Tucker, Director of Admission and Financial Aid. 931-598-5651 Ext. 3217. Fax: 931-968-0208. E-mail: admissions@sasweb.org. Web site: www.sasweb.org.

ANNOUNCEMENT FROM THE SCHOOL St. Andrew's–Sewanee (SAS) School offers The Claiborne Scholars Program through which the School awards 4 merit scholarships, 2 for half tuition and 2 for quarter tuition, to new 9th and 10th grade boarding students who demonstrate both academic achievement and community involvement. These awards require a third-party nomination. Those interested should contact SAS for deadlines and other requirements.

See full description on page 1008.

ST. ANNE'S–BELFIELD SCHOOL

2132 Ivy Road
Charlottesville, Virginia 22903
Head of School: Rev. George E. Conway

General Information Coeducational boarding and day college-preparatory, arts, religious studies, and ESL school, affiliated with Christian faith, Jewish faith. Boarding grades 9–12, day grades PK–12. Founded: 1910. Setting: suburban. Nearest major city is Richmond. Students are housed in coed dormitories. 49-acre campus. 6 buildings on campus. Approved or accredited by The Association of Boarding Schools and Virginia Association of Independent Schools. Member of National Association of Independent Schools and Secondary School Admission Test Board. Endowment: $2.8 million. Total enrollment: 853. Upper school average class size: 12. Upper school faculty-student ratio: 1:12.

Upper School Student Profile Grade 9: 84 students (41 boys, 43 girls); Grade 10: 81 students (45 boys, 36 girls); Grade 11: 81 students (31 boys, 50 girls); Grade 12: 75 students (40 boys, 35 girls). 13% of students are boarding students. 93% are state residents. 7% are international students. International students from China, Hong Kong, Japan, Republic of Korea, South Africa, and Taiwan; 9 other countries represented in student body.

Faculty School total: 95. In upper school: 19 men, 19 women; 30 have advanced degrees; 2 reside on campus.

Subjects Offered Algebra, art, art history, biology, biology-AP, calculus-AP, ceramics, chemistry, chemistry-AP, chorus, Civil War, conceptual physics, discrete mathematics, drama, economics, English, ESL, French, French language-AP, French literature-AP, geometry, honors algebra, honors geometry, humanities, Latin, Latin-AP, modern world history, music theory, orchestra, photography, physics-AP, pre-calculus, science fiction, scripture, sculpture, Shakespeare, short story, Southern literature, Spanish, Spanish language-AP, statistics, statistics-AP, theology, trigonometry, U.S. history, U.S. history-AP, Vietnam, world history, World War II, writing workshop.

Graduation Requirements Arts and fine arts (art, music, dance, drama), English, foreign language, history, mathematics, physical education (includes health), religion (includes Bible studies and theology), science. Community service is required.

Special Academic Programs Advanced Placement exam preparation in 11 subject areas; honors section; independent study; study at local college for college credit; study abroad; academic accommodation for the gifted; ESL (12 students enrolled).

College Placement 89 students graduated in 2005; all went to college, including College of Charleston; Hampden-Sydney College; The College of William and Mary; The University of North Carolina at Chapel Hill; University of Mary Washington; University of Virginia. Median SAT verbal: 630, median SAT math: 620. 68% scored over 600 on SAT verbal, 60% scored over 600 on SAT math.

Student Life Upper grades have specified standards of dress, student council, honor system. Discipline rests primarily with faculty. Attendance at religious services is required.

Summer Programs Remediation, enrichment, advancement, sports, art/fine arts, computer instruction programs offered; session focuses on academic enrichment and remediation; held both on and off campus; held at Wintergreen on Thursday/Friday for summer camp only; accepts boys and girls; open to students from other schools. 1600 students usually enrolled. 2006 schedule: June 13 to August 5. Application deadline: none.

Tuition and Aid Day student tuition: $16,850–$17,100; 5-day tuition and room/board: $29,600–$29,850; 7-day tuition and room/board: $38,600–$38,850. Tuition installment plan (The Tuition Plan, Insured Tuition Payment Plan, monthly payment plans). Need-based scholarship grants available. In 2005–06, 26% of upper-school students received aid. Total amount of financial aid awarded in 2005–06: $975,650.

Admissions Traditional secondary-level entrance grade is 9. For fall 2005, 120 students applied for upper-level admission, 58 were accepted, 53 enrolled. ERB verbal, ERB math, school's own exam, SLEP, SSAT or TOEFL required. Deadline for receipt of application materials: none. Application fee required: $30. Interview required.

Athletics Interscholastic: baseball (boys), basketball (b,g), cross-country running (b,g), field hockey (g), football (b), golf (b,g), lacrosse (b,g), soccer (b,g), softball (g), tennis (b,g), volleyball (g), wrestling (b); coed interscholastic: cross-country running, golf, squash, track and field; coed intramural: fitness. 6 PE instructors, 14 coaches, 2 trainers.

Computers Computer network features include campus e-mail, on-campus library services, CD-ROMs, online commercial services, Internet access.

Contact Elizabeth W. Lewis, Associate Director of Admissions. 434-296-5106. Fax: 434-979-1486. E-mail: elewis@stab.org. Web site: www.stab.org.

See full description on page 1010.

ST. ANSELM'S ABBEY SCHOOL

4501 South Dakota Avenue, NE
Washington, District of Columbia 20017
Head of School: Rev. Peter Weigand, OSB

General Information Boys' day college-preparatory school, affiliated with Roman Catholic Church. Grades 6–12. Founded: 1942. Setting: urban. 40-acre campus. 4

buildings on campus. Approved or accredited by Association of Independent Maryland Schools, Association of Independent Schools of Greater Washington, Middle States Association of Colleges and Schools, and National Catholic Education Association. Member of National Association of Independent Schools. Endowment: $2 million. Total enrollment: 261. Upper school average class size: 14. Upper school faculty-student ratio: 1:6.

Upper School Student Profile Grade 9: 44 students (44 boys); Grade 10: 31 students (31 boys); Grade 11: 33 students (33 boys); Grade 12: 33 students (33 boys). 60% of students are Roman Catholic.

Faculty School total: 45. In upper school: 31 men, 14 women; 33 have advanced degrees.

Subjects Offered Algebra, American history, American literature, anatomy, anthropology, art, art history, Bible studies, biology, botany, calculus, ceramics, chemistry, computer math, computer programming, computer science, drama, earth science, economics, English, English literature, environmental science, ethics, European history, expository writing, fine arts, French, geography, geology, geometry, government/civics, grammar, Greek, history, history of science, journalism, Latin, mathematics, music, Native American studies, philosophy, physical education, physics, science, social studies, Spanish, speech, statistics, theater, theology, trigonometry, world history, world literature, writing.

Graduation Requirements Arts and fine arts (art, music, dance, drama), English, foreign language, mathematics, physical education (includes health), religion (includes Bible studies and theology), science, social studies (includes history), community service for 11th and 12th grade.

Special Academic Programs Advanced Placement exam preparation in 17 subject areas; academic accommodation for the gifted.

College Placement 38 students graduated in 2005; all went to college, including Boston College; Saint Mary's College; The College of William and Mary; University of Chicago; University of Maryland, College Park; University of Michigan. Median SAT verbal: 679, median SAT math: 658, median combined SAT: 1987.

Student Life Upper grades have specified standards of dress, student council. Discipline rests primarily with faculty.

Summer Programs Remediation, enrichment, advancement, sports, art/fine arts programs offered; session focuses on academic enrichment; held on campus; accepts boys and girls; open to students from other schools. 50 students usually enrolled. 2006 schedule: June 12 to July 14. Application deadline: June 12.

Tuition and Aid Day student tuition: $17,950. Tuition installment plan (monthly payment plans, individually arranged payment plans, two payments (one prior to each semester)). Need-based scholarship grants, Archdiocese of Washington financial aid program, Washington Scholarship Fund, Latino Student Fund available. In 2005–06, 25% of upper-school students received aid. Total amount of financial aid awarded in 2005–06: $500,000.

Admissions Traditional secondary-level entrance grade is 9. For fall 2005, 37 students applied for upper-level admission, 14 were accepted, 7 enrolled. Admissions testing required. Deadline for receipt of application materials: none. Application fee required: $35. Interview required.

Athletics Interscholastic: baseball, basketball, cross-country running, fencing, golf, soccer, tennis, track and field; intramural: baseball, basketball, flag football, football, outdoor activities, strength & conditioning, weight lifting, weight training. 3 PE instructors, 8 coaches.

Computers Computers are regularly used in art, college planning, creative writing, design, desktop publishing, drawing and design, foreign language, geography, graphics, history, humanities, Latin, library, mathematics, news writing, newspaper, photography, publications, science, social sciences, yearbook classes. Computer network features include on-campus library services, CD-ROMs, online commercial services, Internet access, office computer access, DVD.

Contact Mr. Patrick I. Parsons, Director of Admissions. 202-269-2379. Fax: 202-269-2373. E-mail: admissions@saintanselms.org. Web site: www.saintanselms.org.

ANNOUNCEMENT FROM THE SCHOOL Located on a wooded, 40-acre campus, St. Anselm's Abbey School, a Benedictine foundation, provides a traditional liberal arts education with maximum challenge to able and motivated young men, grades 6–12. The low pupil-teacher ratio, supportive faculty, and high academic standards result in excellent SAT scores and placements in America's top colleges and universities. The School supports a full competitive sports program. Music, drama, publications, visual arts, coed social activities, and transportation to subway are provided.

SAINT ANTHONY HIGH SCHOOL

304 East Roadway Avenue
Effingham, Illinois 62401
Head of School: Miss Marianne Larimer

General Information Coeducational day college-preparatory school, affiliated with Roman Catholic Church. Grades 9–12. Setting: small town. Nearest major city is St. Louis, MO. 1 building on campus. Approved or accredited by North Central Association of Colleges and Schools and Illinois Department of Education. Total enrollment: 209. Upper school average class size: 18. Upper school faculty-student ratio: 1:10.

Upper School Student Profile Grade 9: 52 students (21 boys, 31 girls); Grade 10: 59 students (34 boys, 25 girls); Grade 11: 52 students (27 boys, 25 girls); Grade 12: 46 students (18 boys, 28 girls). 95% of students are Roman Catholic.

Faculty School total: 25. In upper school: 7 men, 15 women; 5 have advanced degrees.

College Placement 51 students graduated in 2005; 49 went to college, including Eastern Illinois University; Southern Illinois University Edwardsville; University of Illinois at Urbana–Champaign. Other: 1 went to work, 1 entered military service. Median composite ACT: 21.

Student Life Upper grades have specified standards of dress, student council. Discipline rests primarily with faculty. Attendance at religious services is required.

Admissions Traditional secondary-level entrance grade is 9. No application fee required.

Athletics Interscholastic: baseball (boys), basketball (b,g), cheering (g), dance team (g), golf (b,g), softball (g), tennis (b,g), track and field (b,g), volleyball (g); coed interscholastic: cross-country running, soccer. 2 PE instructors, 19 coaches.

Computers Computers are regularly used in drafting, yearbook classes. Computer resources include Internet access, office computer access.

Contact Miss Marianne Larimer, Interim Principal. 217-342-6969. Fax: 217-342-6997. E-mail: mlarimer@stanthony.com. Web site: www.stanthony.com.

SAINT AUGUSTINE PREPARATORY SCHOOL

611 Cedar Avenue
PO Box 279
Richland, New Jersey 08350
Head of School: Rev. Francis J. Horn

General Information Boys' day college-preparatory and religious studies school, affiliated with Roman Catholic Church. Grades 9–12. Founded: 1959. Setting: rural. Nearest major city is Vineland. 125-acre campus. 3 buildings on campus. Approved or accredited by Middle States Association of Colleges and Schools, National Catholic Education Association, and New Jersey Department of Education. Endowment: $250,000. Total enrollment: 547. Upper school average class size: 18. Upper school faculty-student ratio: 1:12.

Upper School Student Profile Grade 9: 160 students (160 boys); Grade 10: 145 students (145 boys); Grade 11: 126 students (126 boys); Grade 12: 116 students (116 boys). 80% of students are Roman Catholic.

Faculty School total: 44. In upper school: 35 men, 9 women; 21 have advanced degrees.

Subjects Offered Accounting, Advanced Placement courses, American Civil War, American history-AP, American legal systems, American literature, anatomy, ancient world history, art appreciation, art history, band, Bible as literature, Bible studies, biology, biology-AP, British literature, British literature (honors), British literature-AP, business applications, calculus, calculus-AP, Catholic belief and practice, chemistry, chemistry-AP, choir, Christian and Hebrew scripture, Christian doctrine, Christian ethics, church history, classical language, comparative religion, computer applications, computer programming, computer science, computer-aided design, CPR, creative writing, culinary arts, drama, driver education, English composition, English literature, ethics and responsibility, European history, European history-AP, film, film studies, filmmaking, finance, French as a second language, French-AP, geology, geometry, grammar, history, history of the Catholic Church, honors algebra, honors English, honors geometry, honors U.S. history, Italian, jazz band, language-AP, Latin, Latin-AP, law and the legal system, marine biology, mathematics-AP, moral theology, music appreciation, music theory, music theory-AP, peer ministry, philosophy, physics, physics-AP, political science, pre-calculus, psychology-AP, religion, Spanish, Spanish language-AP, Spanish literature-AP, Spanish-AP, sports medicine, U.S. history-AP.

Graduation Requirements English, foreign language, history, lab science, mathematics, religion (includes Bible studies and theology), social service hours, retreat experiences, third semester experiences.

Special Academic Programs Advanced Placement exam preparation in 14 subject areas; honors section; independent study; study at local college for college credit.

College Placement 110 students graduated in 2005; all went to college, including Drexel University; Rutgers, The State University of New Jersey, New Brunswick/Piscataway; Saint Joseph's University; The College of New Jersey; University of Delaware; Villanova University. Mean SAT verbal: 595, mean SAT math: 623. 46% scored over 600 on SAT verbal, 57% scored over 600 on SAT math.

Student Life Upper grades have uniform requirement, student council, honor system. Discipline rests primarily with faculty. Attendance at religious services is required.

Summer Programs Enrichment, advancement, sports, art/fine arts, computer instruction programs offered; session focuses on community relations; held on campus; accepts boys and girls; open to students from other schools. 500 students usually enrolled. 2006 schedule: June 25 to August 10. Application deadline: May 15.

Tuition and Aid Day student tuition: $8900. Tuition installment plan (FACTS Tuition Payment Plan, individually arranged payment plans, credit card payment). Merit scholarship grants, need-based scholarship grants available. In 2005–06, 31% of

upper-school students received aid; total upper-school merit-scholarship money awarded: $84,000. Total amount of financial aid awarded in 2005–06: $487,000.

Admissions Traditional secondary-level entrance grade is 9. For fall 2005, 307 students applied for upper-level admission, 168 were accepted, 150 enrolled. High School Placement Test required. Deadline for receipt of application materials: January 30. Application fee required: $50. On-campus interview required.

Athletics Interscholastic: baseball, basketball, bowling, crew, cross-country running, fencing, football, golf, ice hockey, indoor track, lacrosse, rowing, sailing, soccer, swimming and diving, tennis, track and field, volleyball, winter (indoor) track, wrestling; intramural: bicycling, weight training. 3 PE instructors, 5 coaches, 1 trainer.

Computers Computers are regularly used in all classes. Computer network features include campus e-mail, on-campus library services, CD-ROMs, online commercial services, Internet access, file transfer, office computer access.

Contact Mrs. Linda Pine, Director of Admissions. 856-697-2600 Ext. 212. Fax: 856-697-8389. E-mail: mrs.pine@hermits.com. Web site: www.hermits.com.

SAINT BASIL ACADEMY

711 Fox Chase Road
Jenkintown, Pennsylvania 19046
Head of School: Sr. Carla Hernandez

petersons.com

General Information Girls' day college-preparatory, arts, business, religious studies, bilingual studies, and technology school, affiliated with Roman Catholic Church. Grades 9–12. Founded: 1931. Setting: suburban. Nearest major city is Philadelphia. 28-acre campus. 1 building on campus. Approved or accredited by Middle States Association of Colleges and Schools and Pennsylvania Department of Education. Endowment: $600,000. Total enrollment: 396. Upper school average class size: 24. Upper school faculty-student ratio: 1:9.

Upper School Student Profile Grade 9: 100 students (100 girls); Grade 10: 110 students (110 girls); Grade 11: 91 students (91 girls); Grade 12: 95 students (95 girls). 95% of students are Roman Catholic.

Faculty School total: 33. In upper school: 7 men, 23 women; 15 have advanced degrees.

Subjects Offered Accounting, algebra, American government-AP, American history, American history-AP, American literature, anatomy, art, biology, business, calculus, calculus-AP, chemistry, Christian and Hebrew scripture, Christian ethics, computer applications, computer literacy, concert choir, desktop publishing, digital applications, earth science, economics, English, English language-AP, English literature, English literature-AP, ensembles, environmental science, European history, fine arts, French, French literature-AP, geometry, German, German-AP, government/civics, history, honors algebra, honors English, honors geometry, journalism, keyboarding, keyboarding/computer, Latin, mathematics, music, physical education, physics, pre-calculus, religion, science, social studies, Spanish, Spanish literature-AP, statistics, trigonometry, Ukrainian, world history.

Graduation Requirements Arts and fine arts (art, music, dance, drama), English, foreign language, keyboarding, mathematics, physical education (includes health), religion (includes Bible studies and theology), science, social studies (includes history). Community service is required.

Special Academic Programs Advanced Placement exam preparation in 9 subject areas; honors section; study at local college for college credit.

College Placement 89 students graduated in 2005; all went to college, including Gwynedd-Mercy College; La Salle University; Manor College; Saint Joseph's University; Temple University; The Pennsylvania State University University Park Campus. Mean SAT verbal: 576, mean SAT math: 545, mean composite ACT: 21. 39% scored over 600 on SAT verbal, 21% scored over 600 on SAT math, 1% scored over 26 on composite ACT.

Student Life Upper grades have uniform requirement, student council. Discipline rests primarily with faculty. Attendance at religious services is required.

Tuition and Aid Day student tuition: $6800. Tuition installment plan (monthly payment plans, individually arranged payment plans, 2-month payment plan (pay 1/2 tuition July—1/2 tuition November), 10-month installment payment plan (July to April)). Tuition reduction for siblings, merit scholarship grants, need-based scholarship grants, Ellis Grant for children of single parents living in Philadelphia, BLOCS Scholarships and Foundations available. In 2005–06, 14% of upper-school students received aid; total upper-school merit-scholarship money awarded: $69,500. Total amount of financial aid awarded in 2005–06: $100,000.

Admissions Traditional secondary-level entrance grade is 9. For fall 2005, 262 students applied for upper-level admission, 102 enrolled. High School Placement Test (closed version) from Scholastic Testing Service required. Deadline for receipt of application materials: November 12. Application fee required: $40.

Athletics Interscholastic: basketball, cheering, cross-country running, field hockey, indoor track, soccer, softball, tennis, track and field, volleyball, winter (indoor) track. 1 PE instructor, 25 coaches.

Computers Computers are regularly used in accounting, business, creative writing, economics, English, journalism, keyboarding, mathematics, science classes. Computer network features include campus e-mail, on-campus library services, CD-ROMs, Internet access, file transfer, office computer access, DVD, wireless campus network.

Contact Mrs. Maureen Walsh, Director of Admissions. 215-885-6952. Fax: 215-885-0395. E-mail: mwalsh@stbasilacademy.org. Web site: www.stbasilacademy.org.

ANNOUNCEMENT FROM THE SCHOOL Saint Basil Academy offers each student a liberal arts education with the goal of deepening her powers of critical and analytical thinking, effective communication, and appreciation of aesthetic values. It encourages a student's thirst for knowledge, a positive outlook on life, and a confidence to help develop her unique talents and abilities.

ST. BENEDICT AT AUBURNDALE

8250 Varnavas Drive
Cordova, Tennessee 38016
Head of School: Mr. George D. Valadie

General Information Coeducational day college-preparatory, arts, religious studies, bilingual studies, and technology school, affiliated with Roman Catholic Church. Grades 9–12. Founded: 1966. Setting: suburban. Nearest major city is Memphis. 40-acre campus. 1 building on campus. Approved or accredited by National Catholic Education Association, Southern Association of Colleges and Schools, and Tennessee Department of Education. Endowment: $100,000. Total enrollment: 850. Upper school average class size: 24. Upper school faculty-student ratio: 1:9.

Upper School Student Profile Grade 9: 267 students (117 boys, 150 girls); Grade 10: 234 students (101 boys, 133 girls); Grade 11: 199 students (101 boys, 98 girls); Grade 12: 150 students (78 boys, 72 girls). 90% of students are Roman Catholic.

Faculty School total: 90. In upper school: 35 men, 55 women; 40 have advanced degrees.

Subjects Offered Accounting, algebra, American government-AP, American history-AP, American literature-AP, anatomy and physiology, applied music, art, art appreciation, art education, art history, art-AP, band, biology, calculus-AP, chemistry, chorus, cinematography, computer graphics, computer keyboarding, computer multimedia, computers, creative writing, dance, digital photography, drama, drama performance, ecology, economics, English, etymology, European history, forensics, French, general business, geometry, German, government, health and wellness, instrumental music, internship, jazz band, keyboarding/computer, Latin, marketing, modern history, music appreciation, music history, music theory, newspaper, performing arts, personal finance, photography, physical education, physical science, physics, play production, pre-algebra, pre-calculus, psychology, religion, sociology, Spanish, speech, sports conditioning, U.S. history-AP, world geography, world history, yearbook.

Graduation Requirements Arts and fine arts (art, music, dance, drama), English, foreign language, government, mathematics, physical education (includes health), religion (includes Bible studies and theology), science, social studies (includes history).

Special Academic Programs Advanced Placement exam preparation in 5 subject areas; honors section; independent study; academic accommodation for the gifted, the musically talented, and the artistically talented; remedial reading and/or remedial writing; remedial math; programs in English, mathematics, general development for dyslexic students; special instructional classes for students with diagnosed learning disabilities and Attention Deficit Disorder.

College Placement 130 students graduated in 2005; 129 went to college, including Christian Brothers University; Middle Tennessee State University; The University of Memphis; The University of Tennessee; The University of Tennessee at Martin; University of Mississippi. Other: 1 went to work. Mean SAT verbal: 570, mean SAT math: 560, mean composite ACT: 24. 38% scored over 600 on SAT verbal, 37% scored over 600 on SAT math, 30% scored over 26 on composite ACT.

Student Life Upper grades have uniform requirement, student council, honor system. Discipline rests primarily with faculty. Attendance at religious services is required.

Summer Programs Remediation, enrichment programs offered; session focuses on enrichment for math and language; held on campus; accepts boys and girls; open to students from other schools. 30 students usually enrolled. 2006 schedule: July 5 to July 31. Application deadline: none.

Tuition and Aid Day student tuition: $5700. Tuition installment plan (FACTS Tuition Payment Plan, monthly payment plans, individually arranged payment plans). Merit scholarship grants, need-based scholarship grants available. In 2005–06, 4% of upper-school students received aid; total upper-school merit-scholarship money awarded: $30,000. Total amount of financial aid awarded in 2005–06: $35,000.

Admissions Traditional secondary-level entrance grade is 9. High School Placement Test required. Deadline for receipt of application materials: none. Application fee required: $25. Interview required.

Athletics Interscholastic: baseball (boys), basketball (b,g), bowling (b,g), cheering (g), cross-country running (b,g), dance (g), dance team (g), football (b), golf (b,g), lacrosse (b,g), pom squad (g), soccer (b,g), softball (g), strength & conditioning (b,g), swimming and diving (b,g), tennis (b,g), track and field (b,g), volleyball (g), weight lifting (b), weight training (b), wrestling (b); coed intramural: Frisbee. 4 PE instructors, 17 coaches, 1 trainer.

Computers Computers are regularly used in art, mathematics, newspaper, science, yearbook classes. Computer network features include on-campus library services, CD-ROMs, Internet access, file transfer, DVD, wireless campus network.

Contact Mrs. Ann O'Leary, Director of Admissions. 901-260-2875. Fax: 901-260-2850. E-mail: olearya@sbaeagles.org. Web site: www.sbaeagles.org.

ST. BENEDICT'S PREPARATORY SCHOOL

520 Dr. Martin Luther King Jr. Boulevard
Newark, New Jersey 07102-1314
Head of School: Rev. Edwin D. Leahy, OSB

General Information Boys' day college-preparatory school, affiliated with Roman Catholic Church. Grades 7–12. Founded: 1868. Setting: urban. 12-acre campus. 14 buildings on campus. Approved or accredited by Middle States Association of Colleges and Schools and New Jersey Department of Education. Endowment: $20 million. Total enrollment: 551. Upper school average class size: 20. Upper school faculty-student ratio: 1:11.

Upper School Student Profile Grade 9: 135 students (135 boys); Grade 10: 129 students (129 boys); Grade 11: 112 students (112 boys); Grade 12: 104 students (104 boys). 40% of students are Roman Catholic.

Faculty School total: 57. In upper school: 46 men, 6 women; 34 have advanced degrees.

Subjects Offered Algebra, American history, American literature, architecture, art, astronomy, Bible studies, biology, Black history, calculus, chemistry, computer science, creative writing, drama, economics, English, English literature, ESL, European history, French, geometry, health, Hispanic literature, history, Latin, mathematics, mechanical drawing, music, physical education, physics, religion, social studies, sociology, Spanish, theater, trigonometry, world history.

Graduation Requirements English, foreign language, mathematics, physical education (includes health), religion (includes Bible studies and theology), science, social studies (includes history), spring projects.

Special Academic Programs Term-away projects; domestic exchange program (with The Network Program Schools); remedial reading and/or remedial writing; remedial math; ESL (18 students enrolled).

College Placement 105 students graduated in 2005; 102 went to college, including Boston College; Montclair State University; Mount St. Mary's University; New Jersey Institute of Technology; Rutgers, The State University of New Jersey, Newark; Saint Peter's College. Other: 2 went to work, 1 had other specific plans. Mean SAT verbal: 455, mean SAT math: 475.

Student Life Upper grades have uniform requirement, student council, honor system. Discipline rests equally with students and faculty. Attendance at religious services is required.

Summer Programs Remediation, enrichment, ESL, art/fine arts, computer instruction programs offered; session focuses on enrichment or remedial academic courses as appropriate; held on campus; accepts boys; not open to students from other schools. 500 students usually enrolled. 2006 schedule: June 26 to July 27.

Tuition and Aid Day student tuition: $7000. Need-based scholarship grants available. In 2005–06, 58% of upper-school students received aid. Total amount of financial aid awarded in 2005–06: $1,056,000.

Admissions Traditional secondary-level entrance grade is 9. For fall 2005, 281 students applied for upper-level admission, 172 were accepted, 111 enrolled. Deadline for receipt of application materials: December 31. No application fee required. On-campus interview required.

Athletics Interscholastic: baseball, basketball, cross-country running, fencing, golf, indoor track & field, lacrosse, soccer, swimming and diving, tennis, track and field, water polo, winter (indoor) track, wrestling; intramural: basketball, hiking/backpacking, life saving, outdoor adventure, outdoor skills, physical training, soccer, swimming and diving, weight lifting. 4 PE instructors, 7 coaches, 1 trainer.

Computers Computers are regularly used in English, information technology, journalism, science classes. Computer network features include campus e-mail, on-campus library services, CD-ROMs, online commercial services, Internet access, file transfer, office computer access, DVD, wireless campus network.

Contact Rev. Mark M. Payne, OSB, Director of Admissions. 973-792-5744. Fax: 973-643-6922. E-mail: mmpayne@sbp.org. Web site: www.sbp.org.

ST. BERNARD HIGH SCHOOL

9100 Falmouth Avenue
Playa del Rey, California 90293-8299
Head of School: Mr. James McClune

General Information Coeducational day college-preparatory, arts, and religious studies school, affiliated with Roman Catholic Church. Grades 9–12. Founded: 1957. Setting: suburban. Nearest major city is Los Angeles. 12-acre campus. 5 buildings on campus. Approved or accredited by National Catholic Education Association, Western Association of Schools and Colleges, Western Catholic Education Association, and California Department of Education. Endowment: $1.2 million. Total enrollment: 644. Upper school average class size: 24. Upper school faculty-student ratio: 1:24.

Upper School Student Profile Grade 9: 195 students (93 boys, 102 girls); Grade 10: 173 students (77 boys, 96 girls); Grade 11: 145 students (79 boys, 66 girls); Grade 12: 131 students (62 boys, 69 girls). 65% of students are Roman Catholic.

Faculty School total: 41. In upper school: 20 men, 21 women; 30 have advanced degrees.

Subjects Offered Advanced math, algebra, American literature, American minority experience, ancient history, applied music, band, Bible, biology, biology-AP, British literature, British literature (honors), broadcasting, business law, calculus, campus ministry, Catholic belief and practice, chemistry, chemistry-AP, choir, choral music, Christian and Hebrew scripture, church history, college counseling, comparative religion, competitive science projects, computer literacy, concert band, concert choir, CPR, dance, drama, drawing and design, driver education, earth science, economics, economics-AP, English, English composition, English language and composition-AP, English literature-AP, entrepreneurship, ethics, European history, European history-AP, first aid, French, government, health, history of the Catholic Church, honors algebra, honors English, honors geometry, honors U.S. history, honors world history, human biology, instrumental music, introduction to theater, Life of Christ, literary magazine, marine biology, modern European history-AP, music appreciation, physics, play production, psychology, social science, Spanish, Spanish language-AP, speech, study skills, U.S. government, U.S. government-AP, U.S. history, U.S. history-AP, yearbook.

Graduation Requirements 60 hours of community service.

Special Academic Programs Advanced Placement exam preparation in 14 subject areas; honors section; study at local college for college credit.

College Placement 163 students graduated in 2005; 160 went to college, including California State University, Dominguez Hills; California State University, Long Beach; California State University, Northridge; Loyola Marymount University; Santa Monica College; University of California, Los Angeles. Other: 1 went to work, 1 entered military service, 1 had other specific plans.

Student Life Upper grades have uniform requirement, student council, honor system. Discipline rests primarily with faculty. Attendance at religious services is required.

Summer Programs Remediation, enrichment, advancement, sports, art/fine arts, computer instruction programs offered; held on campus; accepts boys and girls; open to students from other schools. 300 students usually enrolled. 2006 schedule: June 16 to July 29. Application deadline: June 5.

Tuition and Aid Day student tuition: $5460. Tuition installment plan (FACTS Tuition Payment Plan, monthly payment plans, individually arranged payment plans). Tuition reduction for siblings, merit scholarship grants, need-based scholarship grants available. In 2005–06, 30% of upper-school students received aid; total upper-school merit-scholarship money awarded: $8000. Total amount of financial aid awarded in 2005–06: $200,000.

Admissions Traditional secondary-level entrance grade is 9. For fall 2005, 300 students applied for upper-level admission, 175 were accepted, 165 enrolled. Catholic High School Entrance Examination required. Deadline for receipt of application materials: January 19. Application fee required: $50. On-campus interview required.

Athletics Interscholastic: baseball (boys), basketball (b,g), cheering (g), cross-country running (b,g), dance team (g), football (b), soccer (b,g), softball (g), track and field (b,g), volleyball (b,g), wrestling (b); coed interscholastic: dance, golf, modern dance; coed intramural: aerobics/dance, bowling, dance, dance squad, jogging, physical fitness, strength & conditioning, surfing, weight training. 3 PE instructors, 18 coaches, 1 trainer.

Computers Computers are regularly used in all classes. Computer network features include campus e-mail, on-campus library services, CD-ROMs, Internet access, file transfer, DVD.

Contact Ms. Liz Remington, Registrar. 310-823-4651. Fax: 310-827-3365. Web site: www.stbernardhs.com.

ST. CATHERINE'S MILITARY ACADEMY

Anaheim, California
See Junior Boarding Schools section.

ST. CATHERINE'S SCHOOL

6001 Grove Avenue
Richmond, Virginia 23226
Head of School: Auguste Johns Bannard

General Information Girls' day college-preparatory school, affiliated with Episcopal Church. Grades PK–12. Founded: 1890. Setting: suburban. Nearest major city is Washington, DC. 17-acre campus. 19 buildings on campus. Approved or accredited by Virginia Association of Independent Schools and Virginia Department of Education. Member of National Association of Independent Schools and Secondary School Admission Test Board. Endowment: $52 million. Total enrollment: 820. Upper school average class size: 17. Upper school faculty-student ratio: 1:6.

Upper School Student Profile Grade 9: 59 students (59 girls); Grade 10: 65 students (65 girls); Grade 11: 83 students (83 girls); Grade 12: 85 students (85 girls).

Faculty School total: 125. In upper school: 16 men, 34 women; 30 have advanced degrees.

Subjects Offered Acting, adolescent issues, advanced chemistry, advanced computer applications, advanced math, African American history, African-American literature, algebra, American government, American history, American history-AP, American literature, ancient history, architecture, art, art and culture, art history, art history-AP,

astronomy, band, Bible, biology, British literature-AP, Broadway dance, business mathematics, calculus, calculus-AP, ceramics, chamber groups, chemistry, chemistry-AP, Chinese, Chinese history, choir, choral music, choreography, chorus, comparative government and politics-AP, comparative religion, computer applications, computer math, computer programming, computer science, computer science-AP, constitutional law, creative writing, dance, dance performance, desktop publishing, drama, driver education, economics, economics-AP, English, English language and composition-AP, English literature, English literature and composition-AP, environmental science, environmental science-AP, ethics, ethics and responsibility, European history, expository writing, film and literature, fine arts, French, French language-AP, French literature-AP, gender issues, geography, geology, geometry, government and politics-AP, government/civics, grammar, Greek, guitar, health and wellness, health education, history, history of jazz, honors algebra, honors English, honors geometry, independent study, Internet, Latin, Latin American studies, Latin-AP, macro/microeconomics-AP, mathematics, modern dance, modern European history, modern European history-AP, moral and social development, moral theology, music, music history, music theory, music theory-AP, orchestra, painting, performing arts, philosophy, photography, physical education, physical fitness, physics, physics-AP, playwriting and directing, portfolio art, post-calculus, pre-calculus, printmaking, regional literature, religion, rhetoric, science, sculpture, short story, social science, social studies, Southern literature, Spanish, Spanish language-AP, Spanish literature, Spanish literature-AP, speech, speech communications, statistics, statistics-AP, theater, theater arts, theology, trigonometry, typing, U.S. government and politics-AP, Vietnam, world cultures, world geography, world history, world literature, writing.

Graduation Requirements Arts and fine arts (art, music, dance, drama), computer science, English, foreign language, mathematics, physical education (includes health), religion (includes Bible studies and theology), science, social science, social studies (includes history).

Special Academic Programs Advanced Placement exam preparation in 17 subject areas; honors section; independent study; term-away projects; study abroad.

College Placement 72 students graduated in 2005; all went to college, including James Madison University; The College of William and Mary; University of Georgia; University of Virginia; Virginia Polytechnic Institute and State University. Median SAT verbal: 620, median SAT math: 620. 59% scored over 600 on SAT verbal, 59% scored over 600 on SAT math.

Student Life Upper grades have specified standards of dress, student council, honor system. Discipline rests equally with students and faculty. Attendance at religious services is required.

Summer Programs Sports, art/fine arts programs offered; session focuses on creative arts program and sports camps; held both on and off campus; held at James River (rafting); accepts boys and girls; open to students from other schools. 1200 students usually enrolled. 2006 schedule: June 19 to July 27.

Tuition and Aid Day student tuition: $12,430–$15,820. Tuition installment plan (Academic Management Services Plan, Key Tuition Payment Plan, monthly payment plans, individually arranged payment plans, Tuition Management Systems Plan). Need-based scholarship grants, need-based loans, middle-income loans, paying campus jobs available. In 2005–06, 10% of upper-school students received aid. Total amount of financial aid awarded in 2005–06: $1,052,800.

Admissions SSAT and TOEFL required. Deadline for receipt of application materials: none. Application fee required: $50. Interview required.

Athletics Interscholastic: aquatics, basketball, cross-country running, field hockey, indoor track & field, lacrosse, soccer, softball, swimming and diving, tennis, track and field, volleyball, whiffle ball, winter (indoor) track, winter soccer; intramural: aerobics, aerobics/dance, aerobics/nautilus, aquatics, ballet, basketball, canoeing/kayaking, climbing, dance, diving, equestrian sports, field hockey, lacrosse, martial arts, modern dance, physical fitness, physical training, strength & conditioning, swimming and diving, tennis, volleyball, weight lifting, weight training, whiffle ball, wilderness, yoga; coed interscholastic: indoor track & field, track and field; coed intramural: aerobics/dance, back packing, ballet, canoeing/kayaking, climbing, dance, diving, modern dance, outdoor adventure, wilderness. 7 PE instructors, 50 coaches, 2 trainers.

Computers Computers are regularly used in all classes. Computer network features include campus e-mail, on-campus library services, CD-ROMs, online commercial services, Internet access, file transfer, DVD, wireless campus network.

Contact Katherine S. Wallmeyer, Director of Admission. 804-288-2804. Fax: 804-285-8169. E-mail: kwallmeyer@st.catherines.org. Web site: www.st.catherines.org.

See full description on page 1012.

ST. CECILIA ACADEMY

4210 Harding Road
Nashville, Tennessee 37205
Head of School: Sr. Mary Thomas, OP

General Information Girls' day college-preparatory, arts, religious studies, and technology school, affiliated with Roman Catholic Church. Grades 9–12. Founded: 1860. Setting: suburban. 92-acre campus. 6 buildings on campus. Approved or accredited by National Catholic Education Association, Southern Association of Colleges and Schools, Southern Association of Independent Schools, Tennessee Association of Independent Schools, The College Board, and Tennessee Department of Education. Endowment: $600,000. Total enrollment: 236. Upper school average class size: 13. Upper school faculty-student ratio: 1:9.

Upper School Student Profile Grade 9: 48 students (48 girls); Grade 10: 65 students (65 girls); Grade 11: 64 students (64 girls); Grade 12: 59 students (59 girls). 71% of students are Roman Catholic.

Faculty School total: 27. In upper school: 4 men, 23 women; 20 have advanced degrees.

Subjects Offered Algebra, American history-AP, American literature, anatomy and physiology, biology, biology-AP, British literature, calculus, calculus-AP, chemistry, chemistry-AP, chorus, church history, computer programming, computer science, dance, drawing, economics, economics and history, English literature, English-AP, ethics, European civilization, European history, European history-AP, fine arts, French, French language-AP, geometry, German, German-AP, government, government/civics, Internet research, journalism, Latin, microcomputer technology applications, moral theology, music, music appreciation, music theory, natural history, photography, physical education, physics, physics-AP, religion, scripture, Spanish language-AP, Spanish-AP, speech, studio art-AP, tap dance, theology, trigonometry, U.S. history, U.S. history-AP, visual and performing arts, visual arts, world history, yearbook.

Graduation Requirements Arts and fine arts (art, music, dance, drama), computer science, English, foreign language, history, mathematics, physical education (includes health), religion (includes Bible studies and theology), science.

Special Academic Programs Advanced Placement exam preparation in 12 subject areas; honors section; study at local college for college credit; academic accommodation for the gifted, the musically talented, and the artistically talented.

College Placement 72 students graduated in 2005; all went to college, including Auburn University; Saint Louis University; The University of Tennessee. Median SAT verbal: 610, median SAT math: 540. Mean composite ACT: 23. 57% scored over 600 on SAT verbal, 27% scored over 600 on SAT math.

Student Life Upper grades have uniform requirement, student council, honor system. Discipline rests primarily with faculty. Attendance at religious services is required.

Summer Programs Sports, art/fine arts, computer instruction programs offered; session focuses on enrichment; held on campus; accepts girls; open to students from other schools. 2006 schedule: June 1 to June 30. Application deadline: May 15.

Tuition and Aid Day student tuition: $10,950. Tuition installment plan (Tuition Management Systems Plan). Need-based scholarship grants available. In 2005–06, 30% of upper-school students received aid. Total amount of financial aid awarded in 2005–06: $138,150.

Admissions Traditional secondary-level entrance grade is 9. For fall 2005, 60 students applied for upper-level admission, 48 enrolled. High School Placement Test and ISEE required. Deadline for receipt of application materials: January 12. Application fee required: $45. Interview required.

Athletics Interscholastic: aquatics, basketball, cross-country running, golf, running, soccer, softball, swimming and diving, tennis, track and field, volleyball; intramural: dance, modern dance, physical training, self defense, strength & conditioning, weight lifting, weight training. 1 PE instructor, 8 coaches, 1 trainer.

Computers Computers are regularly used in all classes. Computer network features include on-campus library services, CD-ROMs, online commercial services, Internet access, DVD.

Contact Ms. Susan Hansen, Director of Enrollment Management. 615-298-4525 Ext. 377. Fax: 615-783-0561. E-mail: hansens@stcecilia.edu. Web site: www.stcecilia.edu.

SAINT CECILIA HIGH SCHOOL

521 North Kansas Avenue
Hastings, Nebraska 68901-7594
Head of School: Rev. Fr. James J. Meysenburg

General Information Coeducational day college-preparatory, arts, business, religious studies, and technology school, affiliated with Roman Catholic Church. Grades 6–12. Founded: 1912. Setting: small town. Nearest major city is Lincoln. 1-acre campus. 2 buildings on campus. Approved or accredited by National Catholic Education Association, North Central Association of Colleges and Schools, and Nebraska Department of Education. Endowment: $3.5 million. Total enrollment: 371. Upper school average class size: 20. Upper school faculty-student ratio: 1:11.

Upper School Student Profile Grade 9: 55 students (27 boys, 28 girls); Grade 10: 52 students (24 boys, 28 girls); Grade 11: 43 students (19 boys, 24 girls); Grade 12: 50 students (26 boys, 24 girls). 97% of students are Roman Catholic.

Faculty School total: 36. In upper school: 19 men, 17 women; 12 have advanced degrees.

Subjects Offered Accounting, algebra, American history, art history, automated accounting, band, Basic programming, biology, business law, business mathematics, calculus-AP, career education, Catholic belief and practice, chemistry, chorus, computer applications, computer programming, computer technology certification, computer-aided design, consumer economics, drafting, drawing, driver education, economics, English, environmental science, ESL, family and consumer science, fashion, fine arts, foods, French, French studies, geometry, health, history of the Catholic Church, instrumental music, interior design, Internet, introduction to technology, jazz band, language arts, library skills, Life of Christ, marketing, music,

musical productions, newspaper, painting, peace and justice, physical education, physics, physiology, play production, portfolio art, pre-calculus, probability and statistics, psychology, religion, science, science project, sculpture, social science, social studies, sociology, Spanish, Spanish literature, speech, statistics, textiles, theater arts, TOEFL preparation, trigonometry, U.S. government, video film production, vocational arts, weight training, world history, yearbook.

Graduation Requirements American government, American history, American literature, arts and fine arts (art, music, dance, drama), British literature, career education, computer skills, English, foreign language, mathematics, physical education (includes health), practical arts, religion (includes Bible studies and theology), science, social studies (includes history), speech, vocational arts, vocational-technical courses, 40-45 volunteer service hours.

Special Academic Programs Honors section; independent study; study at local college for college credit; remedial reading and/or remedial writing; special instructional classes for students with learning disabilities and Attention Deficit Disorder; ESL (20 students enrolled).

College Placement 52 students graduated in 2005; 49 went to college, including Doane College; Kansas State University; University of Nebraska–Lincoln; University of Nebraska at Kearney; University of Nebraska at Omaha; Wesleyan University. Other: 2 went to work, 1 entered military service. Median SAT verbal: 590, median SAT math: 510, median composite ACT: 24. 16% scored over 600 on SAT verbal, 16% scored over 600 on SAT math, 10% scored over 26 on composite ACT.

Student Life Upper grades have uniform requirement, student council, honor system. Discipline rests primarily with faculty. Attendance at religious services is required.

Summer Programs Sports programs offered; session focuses on driver's education; held on campus; accepts boys and girls; open to students from other schools. 22 students usually enrolled. 2006 schedule: May 29 to July 25. Application deadline: April 1.

Tuition and Aid Day student tuition: $1175. Tuition installment plan (monthly payment plans, individually arranged payment plans). Tuition reduction for siblings, merit scholarship grants, scrip participation program, tuition assistance with parish pastors, Parish Pastor will pay or match family contribution to reach the total tuition available. In 2005–06, 3% of upper-school students received aid; total upper-school merit-scholarship money awarded: $5250. Total amount of financial aid awarded in 2005–06: $40,000.

Admissions Traditional secondary-level entrance grade is 9. For fall 2005, 6 students applied for upper-level admission, 5 were accepted, 5 enrolled. English proficiency, PSAT, Terra Nova-CTB or writing sample required. Deadline for receipt of application materials: none. No application fee required. Interview required.

Athletics Interscholastic: basketball (boys, girls), drill team (g), football (b), golf (b,g), running (b,g), tennis (g), volleyball (g), wrestling (b); intramural: dance team (g), drill team (g), power lifting (b); coed interscholastic: track and field; coed intramural: badminton, bowling, juggling, jump rope, life saving, physical fitness, physical training, weight lifting, weight training. 2 PE instructors, 2 trainers.

Computers Computers are regularly used in accounting, computer applications, desktop publishing, ESL, drafting, drawing and design, ESL, graphics, keyboarding, mathematics, media production, music, newspaper, reading, science, video film production, Web site design, writing, yearbook classes. Computer network features include CD-ROMs, online commercial services, Internet access, file transfer, office computer access, DVD, wireless campus network, SmartBoards.

Contact Mrs. Marie K. Butler, Principal. 402-462-2105. Fax: 402-462-2106. E-mail: mbutler@esu9.org. Web site: www.esu9.org/~hcs.

ST. CHRISTOPHER'S SCHOOL

711 St. Christopher's Road
Richmond, Virginia 23226
Head of School: Charles M. Stillwell

petersons.com

General Information Boys' day college-preparatory school, affiliated with Episcopal Church. Grades JK–12. Founded: 1911. Setting: suburban. 46-acre campus. 9 buildings on campus. Approved or accredited by Virginia Association of Independent Schools. Member of National Association of Independent Schools and Secondary School Admission Test Board. Endowment: $50 million. Total enrollment: 941. Upper school average class size: 15. Upper school faculty-student ratio: 1:8.

Upper School Student Profile Grade 9: 80 students (80 boys); Grade 10: 82 students (82 boys); Grade 11: 68 students (68 boys); Grade 12: 79 students (79 boys). 48% of students are members of Episcopal Church.

Faculty School total: 149. In upper school: 27 men, 17 women; 38 have advanced degrees.

Subjects Offered Algebra, American history, American literature, ancient history, architecture, art, art history, astronomy, Bible studies, biology, calculus, ceramics, chemistry, Chinese, community service, computer math, computer programming, computer science, creative writing, dance, drama, driver education, ecology, economics, English, English literature, environmental science, ethics, European history, expository writing, fine arts, French, geography, geology, geometry, government/civics, grammar, Greek, health, history, industrial arts, journalism, Latin, mathematics, music, philosophy, photography, physical education, physics, public speaking, religion, science, social studies, Spanish, speech, statistics, theater arts, theology, trigonometry, typing, woodworking, writing.

Graduation Requirements 1½ elective credits, algebra, American history, American literature, ancient history, arts and fine arts (art, music, dance, drama), Bible studies, biology, British literature, chemistry, church history, computer science, English, English literature, European history, foreign language, geometry, physical education (includes health), physics, public speaking, religion (includes Bible studies and theology), speech, U.S. history. Community service is required.

Special Academic Programs Advanced Placement exam preparation in 18 subject areas; honors section; independent study; academic accommodation for the gifted, the musically talented, and the artistically talented.

College Placement 66 students graduated in 2005; all went to college, including Hampden-Sydney College; University of Virginia; Virginia Polytechnic Institute and State University. 75% scored over 600 on SAT verbal, 75% scored over 600 on SAT math.

Student Life Upper grades have specified standards of dress, student council, honor system. Discipline rests equally with students and faculty. Attendance at religious services is required.

Summer Programs Advancement programs offered; session focuses on enrichment, sports, day camp, leadership; held on campus; accepts boys and girls; open to students from other schools. 750 students usually enrolled. 2006 schedule: June 19 to July 28. Application deadline: none.

Tuition and Aid Day student tuition: $15,925. Tuition installment plan (Academic Management Services Plan, Tuition Refund Plan). Merit scholarship grants, need-based scholarship grants available. In 2005–06, 19% of upper-school students received aid; total upper-school merit-scholarship money awarded: $14,000. Total amount of financial aid awarded in 2005–06: $1,423,063.

Admissions Traditional secondary-level entrance grade is 9. For fall 2005, 57 students applied for upper-level admission, 29 were accepted, 18 enrolled. SSAT and writing sample required. Deadline for receipt of application materials: none. Application fee required: $40. On-campus interview recommended.

Athletics Interscholastic: baseball, basketball, football, golf, indoor soccer, lacrosse, sailing, soccer, strength & conditioning, tennis, weight lifting, weight training, wrestling; intramural: martial arts; coed interscholastic: canoeing/kayaking, climbing, cross-country running, dance, indoor track & field, martial arts, rappelling, swimming and diving, track and field, winter (indoor) track; coed intramural: swimming and diving. 5 coaches, 2 trainers.

Computers Computers are regularly used in English, foreign language, history, mathematics, music, science classes. Computer network features include campus e-mail, on-campus library services, CD-ROMs, online commercial services, Internet access, file transfer.

Contact Anne D. Booker, Director of Admissions. 804-282-3185 Ext. 387. Fax: 804-673-6632. E-mail: bookera@stcva.org. Web site: www.stchristophers.com.

ANNOUNCEMENT FROM THE SCHOOL St. Christopher's is committed to educating the whole boy for college and for life. Academics, athletics, art, and student life are major components of the whole-boy development. Small classes and individual attention from caring and talented teachers influence college choices and provide life-shaping experiences. A coordinate program with St. Catherine's at the Upper School level provides a broad curriculum with a wide selection of electives and AP courses in a coeducational context.

ST. CLEMENT'S SCHOOL

21 St. Clements Avenue
Toronto, Ontario M4R 1G8, Canada
Head of School: Patricia D. Parisi

General Information Girls' day college-preparatory, arts, business, and technology school, affiliated with Anglican Church of Canada. Grades 1–12. Founded: 1901. Setting: urban. 1-acre campus. 1 building on campus. Approved or accredited by Canadian Association of Independent Schools, Canadian Educational Standards Institute, Conference of Independent Schools of Ontario, and Ontario Department of Education. Affiliate member of National Association of Independent Schools; member of Secondary School Admission Test Board. Language of instruction: English. Endowment: CAN$1 million. Total enrollment: 442. Upper school average class size: 16. Upper school faculty-student ratio: 1:9.

Upper School Student Profile Grade 10: 62 students (62 girls); Grade 11: 55 students (55 girls); Grade 12: 57 students (57 girls).

Faculty School total: 54. In upper school: 8 men, 39 women; 20 have advanced degrees.

Subjects Offered Algebra, American history, art, art history-AP, biology, biology-AP, business, business skills, calculus, calculus-AP, Canadian geography, Canadian history, Canadian law, career education, chemistry, chemistry-AP, civics, computer science, creative writing, data processing, drama, economics, economics-AP, English, English literature, English literature and composition-AP, environmental science, European history, fine arts, finite math, French, French-AP, geography, geometry, German, grammar, Greek, guidance, health, history, history-AP, instrumental music, jazz ensemble, keyboarding/computer, language and composition, language arts, Latin, Latin-AP, law, mathematics, modern Western civilization, music, philosophy, photography, physical education, physics, physics-AP, physiology, religion, science,

social science, social studies, Spanish, Spanish-AP, theater, trigonometry, Western civilization, world history, writing workshop.

Graduation Requirements Arts and fine arts (art, music, dance, drama), business skills (includes word processing), computer science, English, foreign language, mathematics, physical education (includes health), science, social science, social studies (includes history), OAC mathematics, OAC French.

Special Academic Programs Advanced Placement exam preparation in 15 subject areas; accelerated programs; independent study; academic accommodation for the gifted.

College Placement 56 students graduated in 2005; all went to college, including McGill University; McMaster University; Queen's University at Kingston; The University of Western Ontario; University of Toronto.

Student Life Upper grades have uniform requirement, student council, honor system. Discipline rests equally with students and faculty. Attendance at religious services is required.

Summer Programs Advancement programs offered; session focuses on cooperative program and summer school credit courses; held both on and off campus; held at Europe; accepts boys and girls; open to students from other schools. 10 students usually enrolled. 2006 schedule: July 1 to July 30. Application deadline: March.

Tuition and Aid Day student tuition: CAN$17,450. Tuition installment plan (monthly payment plans, individually arranged payment plans). Bursaries, merit scholarship grants, need-based scholarship grants available. In 2005–06, 11% of upper-school students received aid; total upper-school merit-scholarship money awarded: CAN$11,000. Total amount of financial aid awarded in 2005–06: CAN$200,000.

Admissions Traditional secondary-level entrance grade is 10. For fall 2005, 14 students applied for upper-level admission, 5 were accepted, 5 enrolled. SSAT required. Deadline for receipt of application materials: December 16. Application fee required: CAN$100. On-campus interview required.

Athletics Interscholastic: alpine skiing, badminton, basketball, cross-country running, curling, dance team, equestrian sports, field hockey, golf, hockey, ice hockey, skiing (downhill), soccer, softball, swimming and diving, tennis, track and field, volleyball; intramural: aerobics, back packing, badminton, basketball, bocce, cooperative games, cross-country running, dance, dance team, field hockey, fitness, floor hockey, hiking/backpacking, indoor soccer, jogging, life saving, outdoor education, paddle tennis, soccer, softball, swimming and diving, table tennis, tennis, track and field, ultimate Frisbee, volleyball, yoga. 5 PE instructors, 10 coaches.

Computers Computers are regularly used in economics, English, geography, history, independent study, science, social science, yearbook classes. Computer network features include campus e-mail, on-campus library services, CD-ROMs, online commercial services, Internet access, file transfer, office computer access, DVD.

Contact Martha Perry, Director of Admissions. 416-483-4414 Ext. 227. Fax: 416-483-8242. E-mail: mperry@scs.on.ca. Web site: scs.on.ca.

ST. CROIX COUNTRY DAY SCHOOL

RR#1, Box 6199
Kingshill, Virgin Islands 00850-9807
Head of School: Mr. James C. Sadler

General Information Coeducational day college-preparatory and technology school. Grades N–12. Founded: 1964. Setting: rural. Nearest major city is Christiansted. 25-acre campus. 6 buildings on campus. Approved or accredited by Middle States Association of Colleges and Schools and Virgin Islands Department of Education. Member of National Association of Independent Schools. Endowment: $574,000. Total enrollment: 488. Upper school average class size: 14. Upper school faculty-student ratio: 1:12.

Upper School Student Profile Grade 9: 44 students (20 boys, 24 girls); Grade 10: 44 students (19 boys, 25 girls); Grade 11: 41 students (22 boys, 19 girls); Grade 12: 36 students (21 boys, 15 girls).

Faculty School total: 45. In upper school: 9 men, 10 women; 10 have advanced degrees.

Subjects Offered Algebra, American history, American literature, art, art history, arts, band, biology, calculus, ceramics, chemistry, chorus, community service, computer programming, computer science, creative writing, current events, dance, drama, earth science, ecology, economics, electronics, English, English literature, film, fine arts, French, geometry, government/civics, health, history, journalism, keyboarding, marine biology, mathematics, music, Native American studies, photography, physical education, physical science, physics, pre-calculus, psychology, public speaking, science, social studies, sociology, Spanish, statistics, swimming, theater, trigonometry, world history.

Graduation Requirements Arts and fine arts (art, music, dance, drama), computer science, English, foreign language, mathematics, physical education (includes health), science, social studies (includes history), swimming, typing. Community service is required.

Special Academic Programs Advanced Placement exam preparation in 8 subject areas.

College Placement 36 students graduated in 2005; all went to college, including American University; Bucknell University; Jacksonville State University; Rice University; The University of North Carolina at Charlotte; University of Virginia.

Median SAT verbal: 520, median SAT math: 540, median composite ACT: 22. 35% scored over 600 on SAT verbal, 25% scored over 600 on SAT math, 19% scored over 26 on composite ACT.

Student Life Upper grades have specified standards of dress, student council, honor system. Discipline rests primarily with faculty.

Tuition and Aid Day student tuition: $9600. Tuition installment plan (monthly payment plans, individually arranged payment plans, semi-annual and annual payment plans). Merit scholarship grants, need-based scholarship grants available. In 2005–06, 37% of upper-school students received aid; total upper-school merit-scholarship money awarded: $22,000. Total amount of financial aid awarded in 2005–06: $227,700.

Admissions Traditional secondary-level entrance grade is 9. For fall 2005, 45 students applied for upper-level admission, 30 were accepted, 19 enrolled. Essay and Test of Achievement and Proficiency required. Deadline for receipt of application materials: none. Application fee required: $150. On-campus interview required.

Athletics Interscholastic: baseball (boys), basketball (b,g), cheering (g; cross-country running (b,g), football (b), softball (g), tennis (b,g), volleyball (b,g); intramural: basketball (b,g), volleyball (b,g); coed interscholastic: aquatics, golf, soccer; coed intramural: soccer. 3 PE instructors, 5 coaches.

Computers Computers are regularly used in mathematics, music, science, yearbook classes. Computer network features include campus e-mail, on-campus library services, CD-ROMs, online commercial services, Internet access.

Contact Mrs. Alma V. Castro-Nieves, Registrar. 340-778-1974 Ext. 2108. Fax: 340-779-3331. E-mail: anieves@stxcountryday.com. Web site: stxcountryday.com.

ST. CROIX LUTHERAN HIGH SCHOOL

1200 Oakdale Avenue
West St. Paul, Minnesota 55118
Head of School: Mr. Merlyn Kruse

General Information Coeducational boarding and day college-preparatory, general academic, arts, business, vocational, religious studies, bilingual studies, technology, and ESL school, affiliated with Wisconsin Evangelical Lutheran Synod, Christian faith. Grades 9–12. Founded: 1958. Setting: suburban. Nearest major city is St. Paul. Students are housed in single-sex dormitories. 30-acre campus. 3 buildings on campus. Approved or accredited by Minnesota Non-Public School Accrediting Association and Minnesota Department of Education. Endowment: $1.4 million. Total enrollment: 396. Upper school average class size: 23. Upper school faculty-student ratio: 1:14.

Upper School Student Profile Grade 9: 80 students (43 boys, 37 girls); Grade 10: 104 students (56 boys, 48 girls); Grade 11: 109 students (54 boys, 55 girls); Grade 12: 103 students (56 boys, 47 girls). 27% of students are boarding students. 78% are state residents. 2 states are represented in upper school student body. 15% are international students. International students from China, Hong Kong, Japan, Malaysia, Republic of Korea, and Taiwan. 73% of students are Wisconsin Evangelical Lutheran Synod, Christian.

Faculty School total: 28. In upper school: 18 men, 10 women; 12 have advanced degrees; 4 reside on campus.

Subjects Offered Accounting, algebra, American history, American literature, art, band, Bible studies, biology, business skills, calculus, chemistry, chorus, computer programming, computer science, drama, economics, English, English literature, environmental science, general science, geography, geology, geometry, German, home economics, keyboarding, Latin, literature, mathematics, music, physical education, physics, pre-algebra, reading, religion, science, social science, social studies, Spanish, speech, trigonometry, world history, writing.

Graduation Requirements Algebra, arts and fine arts (art, music, dance, drama), biology, chemistry, English, English composition, English literature, foreign language, geometry, government, grammar, literature, physical education (includes health), physics, religion (includes Bible studies and theology), science, social studies (includes history), speech, world geography.

Special Academic Programs Advanced Placement exam preparation in 3 subject areas; honors section; independent study; study at local college for college credit; academic accommodation for the gifted and the artistically talented; remedial reading and/or remedial writing; remedial math; programs in English for dyslexic students; special instructional classes for students with learning disabilities; ESL (28 students enrolled).

College Placement 93 students graduated in 2005; 83 went to college, including Bethany Lutheran College; Hamline University; Martin Luther College; Minnesota State University Mankato; University of Minnesota, Twin Cities Campus; University of Wisconsin–Madison. Other: 4 entered military service, 6 had other specific plans. 16% scored over 600 on SAT verbal, 54% scored over 600 on SAT math, 21% scored over 26 on composite ACT.

Student Life Upper grades have specified standards of dress, student council. Discipline rests primarily with faculty. Attendance at religious services is required.

Summer Programs ESL programs offered; session focuses on ESL; held on campus; accepts boys and girls; open to students from other schools. 25 students usually enrolled. 2006 schedule: July 10 to July 28. Application deadline: March 28.

Tuition and Aid 7-day tuition and room/board: $18,100. Need-based scholarship grants available.

Admissions Traditional secondary-level entrance grade is 9. Secondary Level English Proficiency and writing sample required. Deadline for receipt of application materials: none. Application fee required: $100. Interview recommended.

Athletics Interscholastic: baseball (boys), basketball (b,g), cheering (g), dance team (g), football (b), golf (b), soccer (b,g), softball (g), tennis (g), track and field (b,g), volleyball (g), wrestling (b); intramural: strength & conditioning (b,g), weight training (b,g); coed interscholastic: cross-country running; coed intramural: basketball, physical fitness.

Computers Computers are regularly used in accounting, computer applications, desktop publishing, keyboarding, yearbook classes. Computer network features include CD-ROMs, Internet access, interactive classroom/college courses for credit.

Contact Mrs. Beverly Leier, Assistant to President. 651-455-1521. Fax: 651-451-3968. E-mail: baleier@sclhs.org. Web site: www.sclhs.org.

ST. DAVID'S SCHOOL

3400 White Oak Road
Raleigh, North Carolina 27609
Head of School: John A. Murray

General Information Coeducational day college-preparatory, arts, religious studies, and technology school, affiliated with Episcopal Church, Christian faith. Grades K–12. Founded: 1972. Setting: suburban. 13-acre campus. 7 buildings on campus. Approved or accredited by National Association of Episcopal Schools, North Carolina Association of Independent Schools, Southern Association of Colleges and Schools, Southern Association of Independent Schools, and North Carolina Department of Education. Member of Secondary School Admission Test Board. Endowment: $50,000. Total enrollment: 513. Upper school average class size: 15. Upper school faculty-student ratio: 1:10.

Upper School Student Profile Grade 9: 55 students (22 boys, 33 girls); Grade 10: 57 students (30 boys, 27 girls); Grade 11: 42 students (23 boys, 19 girls); Grade 12: 47 students (25 boys, 22 girls). 11% of students are members of Episcopal Church, Christian.

Faculty School total: 50. In upper school: 13 men, 13 women; 15 have advanced degrees.

Subjects Offered Algebra, American history, American literature, art, art history, biology, calculus, ceramics, chemistry, community service, composition, computer science, drama, drawing, earth science, English, English literature, European history, film studies, French, geography, geometry, government/civics, Greek, Latin, mathematics, music, physical education, physical science, physics, religion, science, social studies, Spanish, speech, studio art, theater, world history, world literature.

Graduation Requirements English, foreign language, mathematics, physical education (includes health), religion (includes Bible studies and theology), science, social studies (includes history), 40 hours of community service.

Special Academic Programs Advanced Placement exam preparation in 15 subject areas; honors section; independent study.

College Placement 52 students graduated in 2005; all went to college, including Davidson College; Duke University; Elon University; North Carolina State University; The University of North Carolina at Chapel Hill; Wake Forest University.

Student Life Upper grades have specified standards of dress, student council, honor system. Discipline rests equally with students and faculty. Attendance at religious services is required.

Summer Programs Enrichment, advancement, sports, art/fine arts, computer instruction programs offered; held on campus; accepts boys and girls; open to students from other schools. 100 students usually enrolled. 2006 schedule: June 4 to August 10. Application deadline: May 15.

Tuition and Aid Day student tuition: $11,250. Tuition installment plan (Insured Tuition Payment Plan, monthly payment plans, 10-month payment plan). Tuition reduction for siblings, need-based scholarship grants available. In 2005–06, 18% of upper-school students received aid. Total amount of financial aid awarded in 2005–06: $430,000.

Admissions Traditional secondary-level entrance grade is 9. For fall 2005, 25 students applied for upper-level admission, 22 were accepted, 22 enrolled. ISEE and writing sample required. Deadline for receipt of application materials: none. Application fee required: $75. On-campus interview required.

Athletics Interscholastic: baseball (boys, girls), basketball (b,g), cheering (g), cross-country running (b,g), football (b), indoor track & field (b,g), lacrosse (b), soccer (b,g), softball (g), tennis (b,g), track and field (b,g), volleyball (g), winter (indoor) track (b,g), wrestling (b); intramural: basketball (b,g), soccer (b,g); coed interscholastic: golf, swimming and diving. 5 PE instructors, 5 coaches, 1 trainer.

Computers Computers are regularly used in all academic classes. Computer network features include on-campus library services, CD-ROMs, Internet access.

Contact Mr. Paul Arceneaux, Director of Admissions. 919-782-3331 Ext. 230. Fax: 919-571-3330. E-mail: parceneaux@sdsw.org. Web site: www.sdsw.org.

SAINT DOMINIC ACADEMY

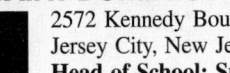

2572 Kennedy Boulevard
Jersey City, New Jersey 07304
Head of School: Sr. Vivien Jenings, OP

General Information Girls' day college-preparatory, arts, business, religious studies, and technology school, affiliated with Roman Catholic Church. Grades 9–12. Founded: 1878. Setting: urban. Nearest major city is New York, NY. 2-acre campus. 1 building on campus. Approved or accredited by Middle States Association of Colleges and Schools and National Catholic Education Association. Total enrollment: 509. Upper school average class size: 23. Upper school faculty-student ratio: 1:12.

Upper School Student Profile Grade 9: 142 students (142 girls); Grade 10: 130 students (130 girls); Grade 11: 120 students (120 girls); Grade 12: 117 students (117 girls). 77% of students are Roman Catholic.

Faculty School total: 47. In upper school: 15 men, 23 women; 22 have advanced degrees.

Subjects Offered Accounting, advanced chemistry, algebra, American history, American literature, anatomy, art, art appreciation, art history, art history-AP, Bible studies, biology, business, business applications, business education, business skills, calculus, calculus-AP, chemistry, collage and assemblage, college counseling, college placement, college writing, computer applications, computer education, computer keyboarding, computer literacy, computer math, computer processing, computer programming, computer science, CPR, creative writing, critical thinking, critical writing, drama, driver education, economics, English, English language and composition-AP, English literature, European history, fine arts, French, French language-AP, geometry, government/civics, health, history, history-AP, Italian, Latin, mathematics, music, music performance, music theory, peer counseling, peer ministry, physical education, physics, physiology, psychology, psychology-AP, religion, science, social studies, sociology, Spanish, Spanish language-AP, theater, theology, trigonometry, women in literature, women's studies, world history, world literature, writing.

Graduation Requirements Arts and fine arts (art, music, dance, drama), business skills (includes word processing), computer science, English, foreign language, mathematics, physical education (includes health), religion (includes Bible studies and theology), science, social studies (includes history), 40 hours of community service, term paper.

Special Academic Programs Advanced Placement exam preparation in 8 subject areas; honors section; remedial reading and/or remedial writing; remedial math.

College Placement 120 students graduated in 2005; 119 went to college, including Montclair State University; New Jersey City University; Rutgers, The State University of New Jersey, Rutgers College; Saint Peter's College; Seton Hall University; St. John's University. Other: 1 went to work. Mean SAT verbal: 500, mean SAT math: 500, mean composite ACT: 31. 9% scored over 600 on SAT verbal, 13% scored over 600 on SAT math, 9% scored over 26 on composite ACT.

Student Life Upper grades have uniform requirement, student council, honor system. Discipline rests primarily with faculty. Attendance at religious services is required.

Summer Programs Remediation, enrichment, advancement, computer instruction programs offered; session focuses on preparing students for a successful high school career; held on campus; accepts girls; open to students from other schools. 130 students usually enrolled. 2006 schedule: June 19 to August 3. Application deadline: June 13.

Tuition and Aid Day student tuition: $6600. Tuition installment plan (SMART Tuition Payment Plan, monthly payment plans, individually arranged payment plans, quarterly payment plan, semi-annual payment plan, pay in full in advance). Tuition reduction for siblings, merit scholarship grants, need-based scholarship grants, paying campus jobs available. In 2005–06, 25% of upper-school students received aid; total upper-school merit-scholarship money awarded: $100,000. Total amount of financial aid awarded in 2005–06: $100,000.

Admissions Traditional secondary-level entrance grade is 9. For fall 2005, 456 students applied for upper-level admission, 418 were accepted, 140 enrolled. Cooperative Entrance Exam (McGraw-Hill) required. Deadline for receipt of application materials: none. Application fee required: $100. On-campus interview required.

Athletics Interscholastic: basketball (girls), cross-country running (g), dance team (g), diving (g), indoor track & field (g), outdoor activities (g), soccer (g), softball (g), swimming and diving (g), tennis (g), track and field (g). 3 PE instructors, 13 coaches.

Computers Computers are regularly used in accounting, art, basic skills, business applications, business education, business skills, business studies, career education, career exploration, career technology, creative writing, introduction to technology, keyboarding, programming classes. Computer network features include on-campus library services, CD-ROMs, Internet access, office computer access, COIN.

Contact Ms. Carolyn Smith, Director of Public Relations/Admissions. 201-434-5938 Ext. 35. Fax: 201-434-2603. E-mail: csmith@stdominicacad.com. Web site: stdominicacad.com.

ST. DOMINIC'S INTERNATIONAL SCHOOL, PORTUGAL

Rua Maria Brown
Outeiro de Polima
Sao Domingos de Rana 2785-518, Portugal
Head of School: Dra. Maria do Rosário Empis

General Information Coeducational day college-preparatory and general academic school, affiliated with Roman Catholic Church. Grades 1–13. Founded: 1974. Setting: suburban. Nearest major city is Lisbon. 5-acre campus. 3 buildings on campus. Approved or accredited by International Baccalaureate Organization and New England Association of Schools and Colleges. Language of instruction: English. Endowment: €6.8 million. Total enrollment: 612. Upper school average class size: 18. Upper school faculty-student ratio: 1:7.

Upper School Student Profile Grade 7: 53 students (29 boys, 24 girls); Grade 8: 41 students (24 boys, 17 girls); Grade 9: 57 students (30 boys, 27 girls); Grade 10: 59 students (31 boys, 28 girls); Grade 11: 39 students (24 boys, 15 girls); Grade 12: 43 students (23 boys, 20 girls); Grade 13: 53 students (23 boys, 30 girls). 40% of students are Roman Catholic.

Faculty School total: 75. In upper school: 19 men, 30 women; 20 have advanced degrees.

Subjects Offered International Baccalaureate courses.

Graduation Requirements Arts, humanities, languages, mathematics, science.

Special Academic Programs International Baccalaureate program; academic accommodation for the gifted, the musically talented, and the artistically talented; remedial reading and/or remedial writing; remedial math; programs in English, mathematics, general development for dyslexic students; ESL (19 students enrolled).

College Placement 37 students graduated in 2005; all went to college. 1% scored over 600 on SAT verbal, 1% scored over 600 on SAT math.

Student Life Upper grades have uniform requirement, student council, honor system. Discipline rests equally with students and faculty.

Tuition and Aid Merit scholarship grants available. In 2005–06, 3% of upper-school students received aid; total upper-school merit-scholarship money awarded: €53,834. Total amount of financial aid awarded in 2005–06: €53,834.

Admissions For fall 2005, 46 students applied for upper-level admission, 46 were accepted, 46 enrolled. Math and English placement tests required. Deadline for receipt of application materials: none. No application fee required.

Athletics Interscholastic: badminton (boys, girls), basketball (b,g), fitness (b,g), floor hockey (b,g), gymnastics (b,g), independent competitive sports (b,g), judo (b,g), martial arts (b,g), outdoor adventure (b,g), physical training (b,g), soccer (b,g), table tennis (b,g), tennis (b,g), track and field (b,g), volleyball (b,g); intramural: badminton (b,g), basketball (b,g), fitness (b,g), floor hockey (b,g), gymnastics (b,g), independent competitive sports (b,g), judo (b,g), martial arts (b,g), outdoor adventure (b,g), physical training (b,g), soccer (b,g), table tennis (b,g), tennis (b,g), track and field (b,g), volleyball (b,g). 4 PE instructors.

Computers Computers are regularly used in all academic classes. Computer network features include campus e-mail, on-campus library services, CD-ROMs, Internet access, wireless campus network.

Contact Admissions. 351-214440434. E-mail: school@dominics-int.org. Web site: www.dominics-int.org.

SAINT EDWARD'S SCHOOL

1895 Saint Edward's Drive
Vero Beach, Florida 32963
Head of School: Dr. Charles F. Clark

petersons.com

General Information Coeducational day college-preparatory school, affiliated with Episcopal Church. Grades PK–12. Founded: 1965. Setting: small town. Nearest major city is West Palm Beach. 33-acre campus. 15 buildings on campus. Approved or accredited by Florida Council of Independent Schools, National Association of Episcopal Schools, and Southern Association of Colleges and Schools. Member of National Association of Independent Schools and Secondary School Admission Test Board. Endowment: $2.9 million. Total enrollment: 932. Upper school average class size: 16. Upper school faculty-student ratio: 1:16.

Upper School Student Profile Grade 9: 77 students (43 boys, 34 girls); Grade 10: 92 students (46 boys, 46 girls); Grade 11: 95 students (52 boys, 43 girls); Grade 12: 75 students (47 boys, 28 girls). 15% of students are members of Episcopal Church.

Faculty School total: 90. In upper school: 17 men, 20 women; 24 have advanced degrees.

Subjects Offered Algebra, American history, American literature, anatomy, art, art history, biology, biology-AP, calculus, calculus-AP, chemistry, chemistry-AP, drama, economics, English, English language and composition-AP, English literature and composition-AP, ethics, European history, fine arts, French, French language-AP, geography, geometry, government, government-AP, grammar, health, history, journalism, Latin American studies, macroeconomics-AP, Mandarin, marine biology, mathematics, Middle Eastern history, modern European history-AP, music, music appreciation, music theory, musical theater, oceanography, physical education, physics, physics-AP, physiology, physiology-anatomy, psychology, religion, science, social science, social studies, sociology, Spanish, Spanish language-AP, speech,

statistics, theater arts, U.S. government and politics-AP, U.S. history-AP, video film production, Western civilization-AP, world history, world history-AP.

Graduation Requirements Arts and fine arts (art, music, dance, drama), English, foreign language, mathematics, physical education (includes health), religion (includes Bible studies and theology), science, social science, social studies (includes history), 20 hours of community service each year of high school.

Special Academic Programs Advanced Placement exam preparation in 15 subject areas; honors section; independent study; study at local college for college credit; study abroad; academic accommodation for the gifted, the musically talented, and the artistically talented.

College Placement 73 students graduated in 2005; all went to college, including Florida State University; Massachusetts Institute of Technology; Southern Methodist University; University of Florida; University of Mississippi; Vanderbilt University.

Student Life Upper grades have specified standards of dress, student council, honor system. Discipline rests primarily with faculty. Attendance at religious services is required.

Tuition and Aid Day student tuition: $17,470. Tuition installment plan (1-, 2-, and 10-payment plans). Need-based scholarship grants available. In 2005–06, 20% of upper-school students received aid. Total amount of financial aid awarded in 2005–06: $1,486,527.

Admissions Traditional secondary-level entrance grade is 9. For fall 2005, 70 students applied for upper-level admission, 59 were accepted, 41 enrolled. SSAT required. Deadline for receipt of application materials: February 15. Application fee required: $50. Interview required.

Athletics Interscholastic: baseball (boys), basketball (b,g), cheering (g), crew (b,g), cross-country running (b,g), football (b), golf (b,g), lacrosse (b,g), sailing (b,g), soccer (b,g), softball (g), swimming and diving (b,g), tennis (b,g), volleyball (g), weight lifting (b); coed intramural: outdoor education. 6 coaches, 1 trainer.

Computers Computers are regularly used in all academic classes. Computer network features include campus e-mail, on-campus library services, CD-ROMs, online commercial services, Internet access, wireless campus network.

Contact Mr. Tom Eccleston, Director of Admission and Financial Aid. 772-231-4136 Ext. 2364. Fax: 772-231-2427. E-mail: teccleston@steds.org. Web site: www.steds.org.

ANNOUNCEMENT FROM THE SCHOOL Saint Edward's School is a pre-K–12, independent, coeducational, college-preparatory school with an enrollment of 935 students. Since its founding in 1965, Saint Edward's has been one of the leading independent schools in the state of Florida. Located 2 miles apart on 33 acres in Vero Beach, 2 campuses are situated between the Indian River lagoon and the Atlantic Ocean, providing a unique learning environment for students. The Lower School campus (pre-K–grade 5, 360 students) is located on Club Drive adjacent to the Riomar Country Club, while the Middle and Upper School campus (grades 6–12, 575 students) is located on Saint Edward's Drive off of A1A. Saint Edward's is committed to educational excellence through an environment of advocacy that promotes a lifelong passion for learning. Small class sizes, experienced faculty, and first-rate academic facilities offer Saint Edward's students an opportunity to excel in the classroom. The School offers numerous extracurricular opportunities in interscholastic athletics, fine and performing arts, music, student clubs, and community service. A strong Episcopal tradition cultivates moral courage and spiritual growth. Members of the class of 2005 were accepted at Amherst, Boston College, Bucknell, Clemson, Dartmouth, Elon, Florida State, Harvard, Lehigh, MIT, Princeton, Rollins, Skidmore, Stetson, Villanova, Williams, Wesleyan, and Yale and the Universities of Florida, Miami, Michigan, Notre Dame, and Virginia. The admission deadline is February 15, with applicant notification on March 15. Late applications for all grades are reviewed if space is available. Financial aid applications are due February 1. Financial aid is awarded on a need basis to 20% of the student body.

SAINT ELIZABETH HIGH SCHOOL

1530 34th Avenue
Oakland, California 94601
Head of School: Sr. Mary Liam Brock, OP

General Information Coeducational day college-preparatory, arts, and religious studies school, affiliated with Roman Catholic Church. Grades 9–12. Founded: 1921. Setting: urban. Nearest major city is Berkeley. 2-acre campus. 1 building on campus. Approved or accredited by National Catholic Education Association, Western Association of Schools and Colleges, and California Department of Education. Endowment: $350,000. Total enrollment: 265. Upper school average class size: 19. Upper school faculty-student ratio: 1:15.

Upper School Student Profile Grade 9: 70 students (38 boys, 32 girls); Grade 10: 65 students (37 boys, 28 girls); Grade 11: 64 students (33 boys, 31 girls); Grade 12: 66 students (32 boys, 34 girls). 60% of students are Roman Catholic.

Faculty School total: 22. In upper school: 9 men, 13 women; 15 have advanced degrees.

Subjects Offered Advanced math, algebra, American literature, American literature-AP, anatomy and physiology, art and culture, biology, British literature, business

mathematics, calculus-AP, Catholic belief and practice, chemistry, Christian and Hebrew scripture, Christian testament, civics, composition, computer applications, computer graphics, computer literacy, creative writing, desktop publishing, drama, drawing and design, economics, economics and history, English, English literature and composition-AP, geometry, journalism, learning strategies, moral and social development, physical education, physical science, physics, pre-algebra, pre-calculus, psychology, social justice, Spanish, Spanish language-AP, Spanish literature-AP, speech, speech communications, trigonometry, U.S. history, Web site design, world cultures, world geography, world history, world religions.

Graduation Requirements Arts and fine arts (art, music, dance, drama), electives, English, foreign language, mathematics, physical education (includes health), religious studies, science, social science, 100 hours of community service.

Special Academic Programs Advanced Placement exam preparation in 3 subject areas; honors section; remedial reading and/or remedial writing; remedial math; programs in English, mathematics for dyslexic students; special instructional classes for students with learning disabilities, Attention Deficit Disorder, dyslexia, and emotional and behavioral problems.

College Placement 56 students graduated in 2005; 51 went to college, including California State University, East Bay; San Francisco State University; University of California, Berkeley. Other: 2 went to work.

Student Life Upper grades have specified standards of dress, honor system. Discipline rests primarily with faculty. Attendance at religious services is required.

Tuition and Aid Day student tuition: $7650. Tuition reduction for siblings, merit scholarship grants, need-based scholarship grants available. In 2005–06, 71% of upper-school students received aid; total upper-school merit-scholarship money awarded: $42,000. Total amount of financial aid awarded in 2005–06: $380,000.

Admissions Traditional secondary-level entrance grade is 9. For fall 2005, 120 students applied for upper-level admission, 91 were accepted, 70 enrolled. High School Placement Test required. Deadline for receipt of application materials: none. Application fee required: $50. Interview required.

Athletics Interscholastic: baseball (boys), basketball (b,g), cross-country running (b,g), football (b), soccer (b,g), softball (g), track and field (b,g), volleyball (b,g). 3 PE instructors, 5 coaches.

Computers Computer network features include on-campus library services, CD-ROMs, Internet access, file transfer.

Contact Lillie Fitzpatrick, Secretary. 510-532-8947 Ext. 0. Fax: 510-532-9754. Web site: www.stliz-hs.org.

SAINT FRANCIS DE SALES HIGH SCHOOL

10155 South Ewing Avenue
Chicago, Illinois 60617-6022
Head of School: Mr. Richard D. Hawkins

General Information Coeducational day college-preparatory, arts, and business school, affiliated with Roman Catholic Church. Grades 9–12. Founded: 1937. Setting: urban. 1-acre campus. 1 building on campus. Approved or accredited by National Catholic Education Association, North Central Association of Colleges and Schools, and Illinois Department of Education. Total enrollment: 360. Upper school average class size: 22. Upper school faculty-student ratio: 1:16.

Upper School Student Profile Grade 9: 121 students (68 boys, 53 girls); Grade 10: 98 students (54 boys, 44 girls); Grade 11: 83 students (42 boys, 41 girls); Grade 12: 58 students (33 boys, 25 girls). 60% of students are Roman Catholic.

Faculty School total: 25. In upper school: 11 men, 11 women; 7 have advanced degrees.

Subjects Offered 3-dimensional art, ACT preparation, advanced math, American literature, analytic geometry, applied music, architectural drawing, art, art appreciation, art-AP, Basic programming, biology, British literature, British literature (honors), Catholic belief and practice, chemistry, computer graphics, drafting, English, English composition, English literature, French, general math, geography, geometry, government, history, history-AP, honors algebra, honors English, honors geometry, language-AP, Life of Christ, mechanical drawing, newspaper, physical education, physics, pre-calculus, religious studies, science, sociology, Spanish, Spanish-AP, speech, street law, technical drawing, U.S. history, U.S. history-AP, U.S. literature, world history, world literature.

Graduation Requirements Algebra, American literature, biology, chemistry, English literature, geography, geometry, health education, language, literature-AP, math analysis, physics, science, U.S. history, U.S. literature, world literature, world religions.

Special Academic Programs Advanced Placement exam preparation in 4 subject areas; honors section; independent study; remedial reading and/or remedial writing; remedial math.

College Placement 67 students graduated in 2005; 57 went to college, including Chicago State University; DePaul University; Northern Illinois University; Saint Xavier University; University of Illinois at Chicago; University of Illinois at Urbana–Champaign. Other: 5 went to work, 1 entered military service, 3 entered a postgraduate year, 1 had other specific plans.

Student Life Upper grades have uniform requirement, student council, honor system. Discipline rests primarily with faculty. Attendance at religious services is required.

Summer Programs Remediation, enrichment, sports programs offered; session focuses on remediation, enrichment, and training; held both on and off campus; held

at Calumet Park; accepts boys and girls; open to students from other schools. 200 students usually enrolled. 2006 schedule: June 19 to August 4. Application deadline: none.

Tuition and Aid Tuition installment plan (monthly payment plans, individually arranged payment plans). Tuition reduction for siblings, merit scholarship grants, need-based scholarship grants available. In 2005–06, 65% of upper-school students received aid; total upper-school merit-scholarship money awarded: $25,000. Total amount of financial aid awarded in 2005–06: $300,000.

Admissions Traditional secondary-level entrance grade is 9. For fall 2005, 244 students applied for upper-level admission, 223 were accepted, 121 enrolled. TerraNova required. Deadline for receipt of application materials: none. No application fee required. Interview recommended.

Athletics Interscholastic: baseball (boys), basketball (b,g), cheering (g), football (b), softball (g), volleyball (g), wrestling (b); coed interscholastic: dance squad. 1 PE instructor, 16 coaches.

Computers Computers are regularly used in basic skills, college planning, drafting, drawing and design, English, French, graphic arts, graphic design, history, industrial technology, mathematics, psychology, publications, science, social sciences, Spanish, stock market, theology classes. Computer network features include CD-ROMs, Internet access.

Contact Mr. Jeff Fiedler, Marketing Director. 773-731-7272 Ext. 239. Fax: 773-731-7888. E-mail: jfiedler@sfdshs.org. Web site: www.sfdshs.org.

ST. FRANCIS DE SALES HIGH SCHOOL

2323 West Bancroft Street
Toledo, Ohio 43607
Head of School: Mr. Andrew Hill

General Information Boys' day college-preparatory and religious studies school, affiliated with Roman Catholic Church. Grades 9–12. Founded: 1955. Setting: urban. Nearest major city is Cleveland. 25-acre campus. 1 building on campus. Approved or accredited by Ohio Catholic Schools Accreditation Association (OCSAA) and Ohio Department of Education. Endowment: $5.1 million. Total enrollment: 660. Upper school average class size: 24. Upper school faculty-student ratio: 1:14.

Upper School Student Profile Grade 9: 163 students (163 boys); Grade 10: 163 students (163 boys); Grade 11: 154 students (154 boys); Grade 12: 180 students (180 boys). 81% of students are Roman Catholic.

Faculty School total: 57. In upper school: 41 men, 16 women; 33 have advanced degrees.

Subjects Offered Algebra, American history, American literature, anatomy, art, art history-AP, astronomy, Bible studies, biology, calculus, chemistry, community service, computer programming, computer science, creative writing, criminal justice, drama, earth science, economics, English, English literature, ethics, European history, expository writing, French, geography, geometry, German, government/civics, grammar, Greek, health, history, journalism, Latin, mathematics, music, physical education, physics, physiology, psychology, religion, science, social science, social studies, Spanish, statistics, theater, theology, trigonometry, world history, world literature, yearbook.

Graduation Requirements Art, computer science, English, foreign language, mathematics, physical education (includes health), religion (includes Bible studies and theology), science, social science, social studies (includes history), participation in religious retreats 4 of 4 years. Community service is required.

Special Academic Programs Advanced Placement exam preparation in 18 subject areas; honors section; study at local college for college credit.

College Placement 143 students graduated in 2005; all went to college, including Bowling Green State University; Miami University; The University of Toledo; University of Dayton; Xavier University. Mean SAT verbal: 561, mean SAT math: 575, mean composite ACT: 26.

Student Life Upper grades have specified standards of dress, student council. Discipline rests primarily with faculty. Attendance at religious services is required.

Summer Programs Remediation, enrichment programs offered; session focuses on mathematics, English, reading; held on campus; accepts boys; not open to students from other schools. 60 students usually enrolled. 2006 schedule: June 12 to June 30. Application deadline: none.

Tuition and Aid Day student tuition: $6600. Tuition installment plan (monthly payment plans, quarterly payment plan). Tuition reduction for siblings, merit scholarship grants, need-based scholarship grants, paying campus jobs available. In 2005–06, 55% of upper-school students received aid; total upper-school merit-scholarship money awarded: $435,000. Total amount of financial aid awarded in 2005–06: $1,000,000.

Admissions Traditional secondary-level entrance grade is 9. For fall 2005, 198 students applied for upper-level admission, 192 were accepted, 163 enrolled. TerraNova required. Deadline for receipt of application materials: none. Application fee required: $200. Interview required.

Athletics Interscholastic: baseball, basketball, bowling, crew, cross-country running, diving, football, golf, ice hockey, lacrosse, soccer, swimming and diving, tennis, track and field, water polo, winter (indoor) track, wrestling; intramural: basketball, football. 3 PE instructors, 24 coaches, 2 trainers.

Computers Computers are regularly used in art, desktop publishing, English, mathematics, science classes. Computer network features include campus e-mail, on-campus library services, CD-ROMs, Internet access.
Contact Mrs. Jacqueline VanDemark, Administrative Assistant. 419-531-1618. Fax: 419-531-9740. E-mail: jvandemark@sfstoledo.org. Web site: www.sfstoledo.org.

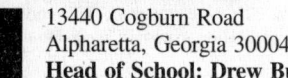

ST. FRANCIS SCHOOL

13440 Cogburn Road
Alpharetta, Georgia 30004
Head of School: Drew Buccellato

General Information Coeducational day college-preparatory and arts school. Grades K–12. Founded: 1976. Setting: suburban. Nearest major city is Atlanta. 43-acre campus. 5 buildings on campus. Approved or accredited by Georgia Accrediting Commission, Georgia Independent School Association, Southern Association of Colleges and Schools, Southern Association of Independent Schools, and Georgia Department of Education. Endowment: $2 million. Total enrollment: 830. Upper school average class size: 14. Upper school faculty-student ratio: 1:14.
Upper School Student Profile Grade 9: 74 students (36 boys, 38 girls); Grade 10: 88 students (42 boys, 46 girls); Grade 11: 82 students (36 boys, 46 girls); Grade 12: 70 students (21 boys, 49 girls).
Faculty School total: 57. In upper school: 19 men, 38 women; 36 have advanced degrees.
Subjects Offered Algebra, American literature, art-AP, biology, British literature, calculus, character education, cheerleading, chemistry, chorus, college counseling, computer processing, computer programming, drama, drawing, economics, English, English literature-AP, English-AP, geography, geometry, government, graphic design, health, history-AP, honors algebra, honors English, honors geometry, honors U.S. history, honors world history, instrumental music, journalism, keyboarding, Latin, mathematics, newspaper, painting, physical education, physical science, physics, play production, psychology, public speaking, SAT preparation, science, social studies, Spanish, studio art, study skills, trigonometry, U.S. government, U.S. government-AP, U.S. history, U.S. history-AP, word processing, world history, writing, yearbook.
Graduation Requirements Arts and fine arts (art, music, dance, drama), electives, English, foreign language, mathematics, physical education (includes health), science, social studies (includes history), technology, writing.
Special Academic Programs Honors section; study at local college for college credit; remedial reading and/or remedial writing; remedial math; special instructional classes for students with learning disabilities and Attention Deficit Disorder.
College Placement 65 students graduated in 2005; all went to college, including Auburn University; Elon University; Furman University; Georgia Institute of Technology; The University of Alabama; University of Georgia.
Student Life Upper grades have uniform requirement, student council, honor system. Discipline rests primarily with faculty.
Tuition and Aid Day student tuition: $15,900. Tuition installment plan (FACTS Tuition Payment Plan). Tuition reduction for siblings, need-based scholarship grants available. In 2005–06, 4% of upper-school students received aid. Total amount of financial aid awarded in 2005–06: $80,000.
Admissions Traditional secondary-level entrance grade is 9. For fall 2005, 115 students applied for upper-level admission, 65 were accepted, 55 enrolled. School placement exam required. Deadline for receipt of application materials: none. Application fee required: $100. On-campus interview required.
Athletics Interscholastic: baseball (boys), basketball (b,g), cheering (g), equestrian sports (g), golf (b), lacrosse (b), soccer (b,g), softball (g), swimming and diving (b,g), volleyball (g), wrestling (b); intramural: equestrian sports (g), horseback riding (g); coed interscholastic: cross-country running, swimming and diving, tennis, track and field, weight lifting. 3 PE instructors, 6 coaches, 1 trainer.
Computers Computers are regularly used in English, graphic design, journalism, keyboarding, newspaper, research skills, science, typing, word processing, writing, yearbook classes. Computer network features include campus e-mail, on-campus library services, CD-ROMs, Internet access, office computer access, DVD.
Contact Ellen V. Brown, Admissions Director. 770-641-8257 Ext. 24. Fax: 770-641-0283. E-mail: ebrown@stfranschool.com. Web site: www.stfranschool.com.

SAINT FRANCIS SCHOOL

2707 Pamoa Road
Honolulu, Hawaii 96822
Head of School: Sr. Joan of Arc Souza

General Information Girls' day college-preparatory, general academic, arts, business, religious studies, bilingual studies, technology, and ESL school, affiliated with Roman Catholic Church. Grades 6–12. Founded: 1924. Setting: suburban. 11-acre campus. 8 buildings on campus. Approved or accredited by Western Association of Schools and Colleges, Western Catholic Education Association, and Hawaii Department of Education. Languages of instruction: English, Spanish, and Japanese. Total enrollment: 387. Upper school average class size: 20. Upper school faculty-student ratio: 1:20.

Upper School Student Profile Grade 9: 79 students (79 girls); Grade 10: 78 students (78 girls); Grade 11: 83 students (83 girls); Grade 12: 76 students (76 girls). 85% of students are Roman Catholic.
Faculty School total: 32. In upper school: 7 men, 21 women; 10 have advanced degrees.
Subjects Offered Accounting, algebra, American history, American history-AP, American literature, ancient history, art, Asian history, band, Bible studies, biology, calculus, ceramics, chemistry, chemistry-AP, chorus, college admission preparation, college counseling, college planning, community service, computer literacy, computer programming, computer technologies, creative writing, drama, earth science, economics, English, English literature, English literature-AP, environmental science, ESL, European history, family life, fine arts, geography, geometry, government and politics-AP, government/civics, grammar, Hawaiian history, health, history, humanities, Japanese, journalism, keyboarding, marine biology, mathematics, medieval/Renaissance history, music, newspaper, photography, physical education, physical science, physics, psychology, religion, SAT/ACT preparation, science, social studies, sociology, Spanish, Spanish language-AP, speech, theater, trigonometry, women's studies, world history, world literature, writing, yearbook.
Graduation Requirements Arts and fine arts (art, music, dance, drama), business skills (includes word processing), computer keyboarding, computer literacy, English, foreign language, mathematics, physical education (includes health), religion (includes Bible studies and theology), science, social studies (includes history). Community service is required.
Special Academic Programs Advanced Placement exam preparation in 8 subject areas; honors section; independent study; study at local college for college credit; study abroad; ESL (6 students enrolled).
College Placement 58 students graduated in 2005; all went to college, including Chaminade University of Honolulu; Hawai'i Pacific University; Kapiolani Community College; University of Hawaii at Manoa; University of Portland; University of San Francisco. Median SAT verbal: 484, median SAT math: 484. 6% scored over 600 on SAT verbal, 12% scored over 600 on SAT math.
Student Life Upper grades have uniform requirement, student council, honor system. Discipline rests primarily with faculty. Attendance at religious services is required.
Summer Programs Enrichment, ESL programs offered; held on campus; accepts boys and girls; open to students from other schools. 80 students usually enrolled. 2006 schedule: June 14 to July 20.
Tuition and Aid Day student tuition: $7200. Tuition installment plan (FACTS Tuition Payment Plan, individually arranged payment plans, quarterly, semi-annual, and full payment plans, SFS/Damien discount plan). Tuition reduction for siblings, merit scholarship grants, need-based scholarship grants, paying campus jobs, alumni scholarships available. In 2005–06, 25% of upper-school students received aid; total upper-school merit-scholarship money awarded: $17,000. Total amount of financial aid awarded in 2005–06: $53,000.
Admissions Traditional secondary-level entrance grade is 9. For fall 2005, 186 students applied for upper-level admission, 166 were accepted, 102 enrolled. School placement exam or SSAT required. Deadline for receipt of application materials: none. Application fee required: $40. Interview required.
Athletics Interscholastic: archery, basketball, bowling, canoeing/kayaking, cheering, cross-country running, diving, golf, JROTC drill, kayaking, ocean paddling, paddling, riflery, running, soccer, softball, swimming and diving, tennis, track and field, volleyball, water polo, wrestling; intramural: basketball, soccer, softball, surfing. 1 PE instructor, 20 coaches.
Computers Computers are regularly used in English, foreign language, mathematics, music, newspaper, religion, science, yearbook classes. Computer network features include campus e-mail, on-campus library services, CD-ROMs, Internet access, office computer access, DVD, wireless campus network, database, word processing and spreadsheet applications, Web programming, Web design.
Contact Karen Curry, Director of Admissions. 808-988-4111 Ext. 112. Fax: 808-988-5497. E-mail: kcurry@stfrancis-oahu.org. Web site: www.stfrancis-oahu.org.

ST. GEORGE'S SCHOOL

372 Purgatory Road
Middletown, Rhode Island 02842-5984
Head of School: Eric F. Peterson

petersons.com

General Information Coeducational boarding and day college-preparatory, arts, technology, and marine sciences school, affiliated with Episcopal Church. Grades 9–12. Founded: 1896. Setting: suburban. Nearest major city is Providence. Students are housed in single-sex dormitories. 200-acre campus. 43 buildings on campus. Approved or accredited by Association of Independent Schools in New England, New England Association of Schools and Colleges, The Association of Boarding Schools, and Rhode Island Department of Education. Member of National Association of Independent Schools and Secondary School Admission Test Board. Endowment: $95 million. Total enrollment: 347. Upper school average class size: 11. Upper school faculty-student ratio: 1:5.
Upper School Student Profile Grade 9: 64 students (33 boys, 31 girls); Grade 10: 97 students (48 boys, 49 girls); Grade 11: 91 students (49 boys, 42 girls); Grade 12: 95 students (43 boys, 52 girls). 88% of students are boarding students. 18% are state residents. 30 states are represented in upper school student body. 13% are international

students. International students from Canada, Republic of Korea, and Saudi Arabia; 12 other countries represented in student body.

Faculty School total: 61. In upper school: 34 men, 27 women; 50 have advanced degrees; 55 reside on campus.

Subjects Offered Acting, algebra, American history, American literature, architecture, art, art history, Asian studies, astronomy, Bible studies, biology, calculus, ceramics, chemistry, computer graphics, computer math, computer programming, computer science, creative writing, dance, drama, driver education, ecology, economics, English, English literature, environmental science, ESL, ethics, European history, expository writing, fine arts, French, geometry, government/civics, grammar, health, history, journalism, Latin, law, logic, Mandarin, marine biology, mathematics, microbiology, music, navigation, oceanography, philosophy, photography, physical education, physics, psychology, public speaking, religion, science, sculpture, social studies, Spanish, statistics, theater, theology, trigonometry, veterinary science, world history, world literature, writing.

Graduation Requirements Arts and fine arts (art, music, dance, drama), computer science, English, foreign language, mathematics, physical education (includes health), religion (includes Bible studies and theology), science, social studies (includes history).

Special Academic Programs Advanced Placement exam preparation in 19 subject areas; honors section; independent study; term-away projects; study abroad; academic accommodation for the gifted, the musically talented, and the artistically talented.

College Placement 74 students graduated in 2005; 72 went to college, including Bowdoin College; College of Charleston; Davidson College; Georgetown University; Hamilton College; Vanderbilt University. Other: 2 had other specific plans. Mean SAT verbal: 646, mean SAT math: 645.

Student Life Upper grades have specified standards of dress, student council, honor system. Discipline rests primarily with faculty. Attendance at religious services is required.

Summer Programs Enrichment, advancement, ESL, sports, art/fine arts, computer instruction programs offered; session focuses on academic enrichment; held on campus; accepts boys and girls; open to students from other schools. 125 students usually enrolled. 2006 schedule: July 3 to August 5. Application deadline: none.

Tuition and Aid Day student tuition: $23,500; 7-day tuition and room/board: $34,500. Tuition installment plan (Insured Tuition Payment Plan, Academic Management Services Plan, Key Tuition Payment Plan, monthly payment plans, individually arranged payment plans). Need-based scholarship grants, need-based loans, middle-income loans available. In 2005–06, 27% of upper-school students received aid. Total amount of financial aid awarded in 2005–06: $2,100,000.

Admissions Traditional secondary-level entrance grade is 9. For fall 2005, 663 students applied for upper-level admission, 209 were accepted, 95 enrolled. PSAT, SSAT or TOEFL required. Deadline for receipt of application materials: February 1. Application fee required: $50. Interview required.

Athletics Interscholastic: baseball (boys), basketball (b,g), cross-country running (b,g), field hockey (g), football (b), ice hockey (b,g), lacrosse (b,g), sailing (b,g), soccer (b,g), softball (g), squash (b,g), swimming and diving (b,g), tennis (b,g), track and field (b,g); coed interscholastic: bicycling, sailing; coed intramural: aerobics/dance, dance, modern dance, mountain biking, nautilus, soccer, softball, squash, strength & conditioning. 2 coaches, 1 trainer.

Computers Computers are regularly used in art, English, foreign language, history, mathematics, music, religion, science, theater classes. Computer network features include campus e-mail, on-campus library services, CD-ROMs, online commercial services, Internet access, file transfer, wireless campus network, scanners, digital cameras, and access to printers.

Contact James A. Hamilton, Director of Admission. 401-842-6600. Fax: 401-842-6696. E-mail: admissions_office@stgeorges.edu. Web site: www.stgeorges.edu.

See full description on page 1014.

SAINT GEORGE'S SCHOOL

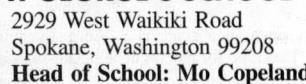

2929 West Waikiki Road
Spokane, Washington 99208
Head of School: Mo Copeland

General Information Coeducational day college-preparatory, arts, and technology school. Grades K–12. Founded: 1955. Setting: suburban. 120-acre campus. 10 buildings on campus. Approved or accredited by Northwest Association of Schools and Colleges, Pacific Northwest Association of Independent Schools, and Washington Department of Education. Member of National Association of Independent Schools. Endowment: $3 million. Total enrollment: 380. Upper school average class size: 15. Upper school faculty-student ratio: 1:6.

Upper School Student Profile Grade 9: 28 students (17 boys, 11 girls); Grade 10: 41 students (26 boys, 15 girls); Grade 11: 36 students (19 boys, 17 girls); Grade 12: 25 students (11 boys, 14 girls).

Faculty School total: 42. In upper school: 11 men, 7 women; 11 have advanced degrees.

Subjects Offered Algebra, American history, American literature, art, biology, calculus, ceramics, chemistry, computer science, creative writing, drama, earth science, ecology, economics, English, English literature, environmental science, European history, fine arts, French, geography, geometry, grammar, health, history,

humanities, journalism, mathematics, music, photography, physical education, physical science, physics, science, social studies, Spanish, theater, trigonometry, world history, writing.

Graduation Requirements Arts and fine arts (art, music, dance, drama), computer science, English, foreign language, history, mathematics, physical education (includes health), science.

Special Academic Programs Advanced Placement exam preparation in 12 subject areas; honors section; study at local college for college credit.

College Placement 27 students graduated in 2005; all went to college, including Reed College; Seattle University; Tufts University; University of Puget Sound; University of Washington; Whitworth College. Mean SAT verbal: 639, mean SAT math: 661.

Student Life Upper grades have student council, honor system. Discipline rests equally with students and faculty.

Tuition and Aid Day student tuition: $13,740. Tuition installment plan (Insured Tuition Payment Plan, monthly payment plans, individually arranged payment plans). Merit scholarship grants, need-based scholarship grants available. In 2005–06, 34% of upper-school students received aid; total upper-school merit-scholarship money awarded: $36,480. Total amount of financial aid awarded in 2005–06: $279,530.

Admissions Traditional secondary-level entrance grade is 9. School's own test or TOEFL required. Deadline for receipt of application materials: none. Application fee required: $50. On-campus interview required.

Athletics Interscholastic: baseball (boys), basketball (b,g), cross-country running (b,g), soccer (b), softball (g), tennis (b,g), track and field (b,g), volleyball (g); coed interscholastic: rock climbing. 2 PE instructors, 11 coaches.

Computers Computer network features include campus e-mail, on-campus library services, CD-ROMs, Internet access.

Contact Debra Duvoisin, Admissions Associate. 509-466-1636 Ext. 304. Fax: 509-467-3258. E-mail: debbie.duvoisin@sgs.org. Web site: www.sgs.org.

ST. GEORGE'S SCHOOL

4175 West 29th Avenue
Vancouver, British Columbia V6S 1V1, Canada
Head of School: Mr. Nigel R. L. Toy

General Information Boys' boarding and day college-preparatory, arts, bilingual studies, and technology school. Boarding grades 6–12, day grades 1–12. Founded: 1931. Setting: suburban. Students are housed in single-sex dormitories. 27-acre campus. 1 building on campus. Approved or accredited by Canadian Association of Independent Schools, The Association of Boarding Schools, and British Columbia Department of Education. Affiliate member of National Association of Independent Schools; member of Secondary School Admission Test Board. Language of instruction: English. Total enrollment: 1,127. Upper school average class size: 19. Upper school faculty-student ratio: 1:10.

Upper School Student Profile Grade 8: 146 students (146 boys); Grade 9: 148 students (148 boys); Grade 10: 156 students (156 boys); Grade 11: 155 students (155 boys); Grade 12: 143 students (143 boys). 18% of students are boarding students. 91% are province residents. 9 provinces are represented in upper school student body. 9% are international students. International students from Hong Kong, Mexico, Republic of Korea, Taiwan, United Arab Emirates, and United States; 4 other countries represented in student body.

Faculty School total: 119. In upper school: 63 men, 23 women; 35 have advanced degrees; 9 reside on campus.

Subjects Offered Advanced chemistry, advanced computer applications, advanced math, algebra, analysis and differential calculus, applied arts, applied music, applied skills, architecture, art, art history, art history-AP, biology, biology-AP, business, business skills, calculus, calculus-AP, Canadian geography, Canadian history, Canadian literature, career and personal planning, ceramics, chemistry, chemistry-AP, comparative government and politics-AP, computer graphics, computer programming, computer programming-AP, computer science, computer science-AP, creative writing, critical thinking, debate, drama, drama performance, dramatic arts, earth science, economics, economics-AP, English, English literature, English literature-AP, environmental science, European history, expository writing, film, fine arts, French, French-AP, geography, geology, geometry, German, German-AP, government/civics, grammar, history, industrial arts, introduction to theater, Japanese, journalism, Latin, Latin-AP, law, library, Mandarin, mathematics, mathematics-AP, music, music-AP, performing arts, photography, physical education, physical fitness, physics, physics-AP, psychology, psychology-AP, science, social studies, society, politics and law, Spanish, Spanish-AP, speech and debate, studio art, studio art-AP, technical theater, theater, trigonometry, typing, U.S. history-AP, United States government-AP, Western civilization, world history, world literature, writing.

Graduation Requirements Arts and fine arts (art, music, dance, drama), business skills (includes word processing), English, foreign language, mathematics, physical education (includes health), science, social studies (includes history).

Special Academic Programs Advanced Placement exam preparation in 13 subject areas; honors section; remedial reading and/or remedial writing.

College Placement 151 students graduated in 2005; all went to college, including McGill University; Queen's University at Kingston; The University of British Columbia; The University of Western Ontario; University of Toronto; University of Victoria.

St. George's School

Student Life Upper grades have uniform requirement, student council, honor system. Discipline rests primarily with faculty.

Summer Programs Advancement, ESL, sports, art/fine arts, computer instruction programs offered; session focuses on recreation and enrichment; held both on and off campus; held at other schools in area (outdoor education); accepts boys and girls; open to students from other schools. 1000 students usually enrolled. 2006 schedule: July 2 to August 15. Application deadline: none.

Tuition and Aid Day student tuition: CAN$13,825; 7-day tuition and room/board: CAN$36,000. Tuition installment plan (monthly payment plans, term payment plan, 1-time payment plan). Tuition reduction for siblings, bursaries, merit scholarship grants, need-based scholarship grants available. In 2005–06, 10% of upper-school students received aid; total upper-school merit-scholarship money awarded: CAN$75,000. Total amount of financial aid awarded in 2005–06: CAN$400,000.

Admissions Traditional secondary-level entrance grade is 8. For fall 2005, 250 students applied for upper-level admission, 90 were accepted, 50 enrolled. School's own exam and SSAT required. Deadline for receipt of application materials: February 10. Application fee required: CAN$200. Interview required.

Athletics Interscholastic: badminton, basketball, cricket, cross-country running, field hockey, golf, ice hockey, rowing, rugby, soccer, swimming and diving, tennis, track and field, triathlon, volleyball, water polo; intramural: badminton, ball hockey, basketball, bicycling, canoeing/kayaking, cross-country running, flag football, floor hockey, ice hockey, martial arts, outdoor education, outdoor recreation, physical fitness, rugby, running, sailing, skiing (downhill), soccer, softball, squash, swimming and diving, table tennis, tennis, track and field, ultimate Frisbee, volleyball, water polo, weight lifting. 4 PE instructors, 8 coaches.

Computers Computers are regularly used in desktop publishing, history, information technology, mathematics, media, publications, science, technology classes. Computer network features include campus e-mail, on-campus library services, CD-ROMs, online commercial services, Internet access.

Contact Mr. Gordon C. Allan, Associate Director of Admissions. 604-222-5817. Fax: 604-224-5820. E-mail: gallan@stgeorges.bc.ca. Web site: www.stgeorges.bc.ca.

ST. GEORGE'S SCHOOL IN SWITZERLAND

Chemin de St. Georges 19
1815 Clarens/Montreux 1815, Switzerland
Head of School: Mrs. C. S. Steinson

General Information Girls' boarding and coeducational day college-preparatory and general academic school. Boarding girls grades 6–12, day boys grades K–12, day girls grades K–12. Founded: 1927. Setting: small town. Nearest major city is Lausanne. Students are housed in single-sex by floor dormitories. 4-hectare campus. 1 building on campus. Member of European Council of International Schools. Language of instruction: English. Total enrollment: 313. Upper school average class size: 14. Upper school faculty-student ratio: 1:7.

Upper School Student Profile 32% of students are boarding students. 32% are international students. International students from United Kingdom; 25 other countries represented in student body.

Faculty School total: 31. In upper school: 13 men, 18 women; 18 have advanced degrees; 1 resides on campus.

Subjects Offered Algebra, art, art history, biology, business, calculus, chemistry, computer programming, computer science, creative writing, drama, economics, English, English literature, ESL, European history, foreign language, French, geography, geometry, German, history, Italian, mathematics, music, physical education, physics, psychology, science, social science, Spanish, theater, trigonometry, typing, word processing, world history.

Graduation Requirements English, foreign language, mathematics, physical education (includes health), science, social science, TOEFL score of 550/213 or C or better pass in GCSE English.

Special Academic Programs Remedial reading and/or remedial writing; remedial math; ESL.

College Placement 20 students graduated in 2005; all went to college, including Johnson & Wales University; Long Beach City College; Lynn University; San Diego State University; The George Washington University; The Pennsylvania State University University Park Campus.

Student Life Upper grades have uniform requirement. Discipline rests primarily with faculty.

Summer Programs ESL, sports, art/fine arts, rigorous outdoor training, computer instruction programs offered; session focuses on intensive French/English (mornings), activities and excursions (afternoons); held on campus; accepts boys and girls; open to students from other schools. 100 students usually enrolled. 2006 schedule: July 3 to July 29. Application deadline: May 31.

Tuition and Aid Day student tuition: 12,000 Swiss francs–30,000 Swiss francs; 5-day tuition and room/board: 43,700 Swiss francs–46,000 Swiss francs; 7-day tuition and room/board: 62,400 Swiss francs–65,000 Swiss francs. Tuition reduction for siblings, bursaries, merit scholarship grants available.

Admissions Deadline for receipt of application materials: none. Application fee required: 850 Swiss francs. On-campus interview recommended.

Athletics Interscholastic: basketball (boys, girls), climbing (b,g), cross-country running (b,g), equestrian sports (g), indoor hockey (b,g), skiing (downhill) (b,g); intramural: aerobics/dance (g), basketball (b,g), netball (b,g), rounders (b,g), skiing

(downhill) (b,g); coed interscholastic: alpine skiing, aquatics, archery, back packing, bowling, cricket, cross-country running, fencing, field hockey, football, gymnastics, indoor hockey, indoor track & field, jogging, outdoor activities, rounders, tennis, volleyball; coed intramural: badminton, basketball, cross-country running, field hockey, indoor hockey, skiing (downhill). 3 PE instructors, 3 coaches.

Computers Computers are regularly used in business, typing classes. Computer resources include campus e-mail, on-campus library services, CD-ROMs, Internet access, DVD.

Contact Ms. V. Perbos-Parsons, Head of Admissions. 41-21-9643411. Fax: 41-21-9644932. E-mail: office@st-georges.ch. Web site: www.st-georges.ch.

ST. GEORGE'S SCHOOL OF MONTREAL

3100 The Boulevard
Montreal, Quebec H3Y 1R9, Canada
Head of School: Mr. James A. Officer

General Information Coeducational day college-preparatory, arts, bilingual studies, and technology school. Grades PK–11. Founded: 1930. Setting: urban. 2-acre campus. 1 building on campus. Approved or accredited by Canadian Association of Independent Schools, Quebec Association of Independent Schools, and Quebec Department of Education. Affiliate member of National Association of Independent Schools. Languages of instruction: English and French. Total enrollment: 538. Upper school average class size: 17. Upper school faculty-student ratio: 1:17.

Upper School Student Profile Grade 7: 50 students (32 boys, 18 girls); Grade 8: 65 students (38 boys, 27 girls); Grade 9: 70 students (45 boys, 25 girls); Grade 10: 84 students (50 boys, 34 girls); Grade 11: 74 students (41 boys, 33 girls).

Faculty School total: 47. In upper school: 20 men, 27 women; 15 have advanced degrees.

Subjects Offered Advanced chemistry, advanced math, Advanced Placement courses, algebra, art, art history, art-AP, biology, biology-AP, calculus, Canadian history, chemistry, civics, computer art, computer math, computer programming, computer science, creative writing, dance, debate, drama, earth science, ecology, economics, English, English literature, English-AP, environmental science, European history-AP, expository writing, film, fine arts, French, French as a second language, French literature-AP, French studies, French-AP, general math, general science, geography, government/civics, Internet research, leadership, library research, mathematics, media, moral and social development, moral reasoning, music, music appreciation, musical productions, newspaper, outdoor education, performing arts, physical education, physics, pre-calculus, psychology, SAT preparation, science, science project, set design, social studies, theater, world history, world history-AP, writing.

Graduation Requirements Economics, English, French as a second language, mathematics, physical education (includes health), science, social studies (includes history), completion of two optional courses in grade 10 and three optional courses in grade 11, community service hours and project.

Special Academic Programs Advanced Placement exam preparation in 6 subject areas; honors section; independent study; academic accommodation for the gifted, the musically talented, and the artistically talented; remedial reading and/or remedial writing; remedial math; programs in English, mathematics, general development for dyslexic students; special instructional classes for deaf students; ESL (4 students enrolled).

College Placement 70 students graduated in 2005; all went to college, including Bishop's University; Carleton University; Cornell University; McGill University; University of Toronto; University of Waterloo.

Student Life Upper grades have specified standards of dress, student council. Discipline rests primarily with faculty.

Tuition and Aid Day student tuition: CAN$11,599. Tuition installment plan (individually arranged payment plans, one-payment, two-payment, and four-payment plans). Need-based scholarship grants available. In 2005–06, 8% of upper-school students received aid. Total amount of financial aid awarded in 2005–06: CAN$175,000.

Admissions Traditional secondary-level entrance grade is 7. Admissions testing, school's own exam or SSAT required. Deadline for receipt of application materials: none. Application fee required: CAN$125. Interview required.

Athletics Interscholastic: badminton (boys, girls), basketball (b,g), flag football (g), hockey (g), ice hockey (g), indoor track & field (b,g), rugby (b), soccer (b,g), tennis (b,g), volleyball (b,g); intramural: basketball (b,g); coed interscholastic: cross-country running, dance, Frisbee; coed intramural: aerobics, alpine skiing, badminton, ball hockey, baseball, basketball, canoeing/kayaking, climbing, cooperative games, Cosom hockey, fencing, fitness, flag football, floor hockey, Frisbee, golf, ice hockey, indoor track & field, outdoor education, rock climbing, skiing (downhill), squash, ultimate Frisbee, volleyball, wall climbing, wilderness survival, yoga. 3 PE instructors, 5 coaches.

Computers Computers are regularly used in all classes. Computer network features include campus e-mail, on-campus library services, CD-ROMs, online commercial services, Internet access, file transfer, office computer access, DVD, wireless campus network.

Contact Ms. Katherine S. Nikidis, Director of the High School. 514-937-9289 Ext. 212. Fax: 514-933-3621. E-mail: katherine.nikidis@stgeorges.qc.ca. Web site: www.stgeorges.qc.ca.

ANNOUNCEMENT FROM THE SCHOOL The School is a coeducational day school with an International Home-Stay Programme. It is dedicated to developing academic excellence within a caring and child-centered environment that is conducive to students' growth as responsible world citizens. The School's progressive and outstanding curriculum is supported by The Student Achievement Centre, which creates additional enrichment opportunities and offers support wherever necessary.

SAINT GERTRUDE HIGH SCHOOL

3215 Stuart Avenue
Richmond, Virginia 23221
Head of School: Mrs. Susan Walker

General Information Girls' day college-preparatory and religious studies school, affiliated with Roman Catholic Church. Grades 9–12. Founded: 1922. Setting: urban. Nearest major city is Norfolk. 1 building on campus. Approved or accredited by Southern Association of Colleges and Schools and Virginia Association of Independent Schools. Member of National Association of Independent Schools. Total enrollment: 253. Upper school average class size: 15. Upper school faculty-student ratio: 1:9.

Upper School Student Profile Grade 9: 62 students (62 girls); Grade 10: 74 students (74 girls); Grade 11: 60 students (60 girls); Grade 12: 57 students (57 girls). 62% of students are Roman Catholic.

Faculty School total: 33. In upper school: 3 men, 30 women; 23 have advanced degrees.

Subjects Offered Advanced Placement courses, algebra, American government-AP, American history, American history-AP, American literature, American literature-AP, anatomy, art, bell choir, Bible studies, biology, calculus, calculus-AP, ceramics, chemistry, chemistry-AP, chorus, church history, community service, computer keyboarding, computer science, drama, drawing, driver education, English, English language and composition-AP, English language-AP, English literature, English literature and composition-AP, environmental science, European history, expository writing, fine arts, French, geometry, government and politics-AP, government/civics, grammar, history, honors algebra, honors English, honors world history, humanities, keyboarding, Latin, mathematics, media, music, painting, physical education, physics, physics-AP, pre-calculus, probability and statistics, psychology, religion, science, social science, social studies, sociology, Spanish, Spanish literature, studio art—AP, theater, theology, trigonometry, world history, world literature, writing, yearbook.

Graduation Requirements Arts and fine arts (art, music, dance, drama), computer science, English, keyboarding, mathematics, physical education (includes health), religion (includes Bible studies and theology), science, social science, social studies (includes history). Community service is required.

Special Academic Programs Advanced Placement exam preparation in 7 subject areas; honors section.

College Placement 76 students graduated in 2005; 75 went to college, including James Madison University; The College of William and Mary; University of Richmond; University of Virginia; Virginia Commonwealth University; Virginia Polytechnic Institute and State University. Other: 1 went to work.

Student Life Upper grades have uniform requirement, student council, honor system. Discipline rests primarily with faculty. Attendance at religious services is required.

Tuition and Aid Day student tuition: $9500. Tuition installment plan (FACTS Tuition Payment Plan). Tuition reduction for siblings, merit scholarship grants, need-based scholarship grants available. In 2005–06, 18% of upper-school students received aid; total upper-school merit-scholarship money awarded: $11,000.

Admissions Traditional secondary-level entrance grade is 9. For fall 2005, 133 students applied for upper-level admission, 117 were accepted, 78 enrolled. Admissions testing, latest standardized score from previous school and Otis-Lennon School Ability Test required. Deadline for receipt of application materials: January 31. Application fee required: $40. On-campus interview required.

Athletics Interscholastic: basketball, cross-country running, diving, field hockey, golf, indoor track, lacrosse, soccer, softball, swimming and diving, tennis, track and field, volleyball. 1 PE instructor, 14 coaches.

Computers Computers are regularly used in all academic, Web site design classes. Computer network features include on-campus library services, CD-ROMs, Internet access, DVD.

Contact Margaret Shibley, Director of Admission. 804-358-9885 Ext. 341. Fax: 804-353-8929. E-mail: mshibley@saintgertrude.org. Web site: www.saintgertrude.org.

ST. GREGORY COLLEGE PREPARATORY SCHOOL

3231 North Craycroft Road
Tucson, Arizona 85712
Head of School: Mr. Bryn S. Roberts

General Information Coeducational day college-preparatory and arts school. Grades 6–PG. Founded: 1980. Setting: suburban. 40-acre campus. 9 buildings on campus. Approved or accredited by Independent Schools Association of the Southwest, The College Board, and Arizona Department of Education. Member of National Association of Independent Schools and Secondary School Admission Test Board. Total enrollment: 351. Upper school average class size: 16. Upper school faculty-student ratio: 1:16.

Upper School Student Profile Grade 9: 57 students (31 boys, 26 girls); Grade 10: 55 students (28 boys, 27 girls); Grade 11: 48 students (24 boys, 24 girls); Grade 12: 45 students (21 boys, 24 girls).

Faculty School total: 44. In upper school: 10 men, 16 women; 21 have advanced degrees.

Subjects Offered Advanced studio art-AP, algebra, American history, American literature, art, art history, band, biology, biology-AP, calculus, ceramics, chemistry, chemistry-AP, choir, chorus, college counseling, college placement, community service, comparative government and politics-AP, computer programming, creative writing, drama, earth science, ecology, English, English literature, English-AP, ethics, European history, European history-AP, expository writing, fine arts, finite math, French, French language-AP, French-AP, geography, geology, geometry, government and politics-AP, government/civics, government/civics-AP, grammar, history, history of drama, history of music, humanities, independent study, jazz band, journalism, Latin, literature, marine biology, mathematics, music, music theory, music theory-AP, newspaper, photography, physical education, physical science, physics, pre-calculus, religion, SAT preparation, science, social studies, Spanish, Spanish language-AP, Spanish-AP, speech, stage design, stagecraft, studio art-AP, theater, trigonometry, U.S. government-AP, U.S. history-AP, world history, writing.

Graduation Requirements Arts and fine arts (art, music, dance, drama), English, foreign language, history, humanities, mathematics, science, senior internships. Community service is required.

Special Academic Programs Advanced Placement exam preparation in 12 subject areas; honors section; accelerated programs; independent study; term-away projects; study at local college for college credit; academic accommodation for the gifted, the musically talented, and the artistically talented.

College Placement 61 students graduated in 2005; all went to college, including Brown University; Cornell University; Duke University; The University of Arizona; Tulane University; University of California, San Diego. Mean SAT verbal: 615, mean SAT math: 603, mean composite ACT: 24.

Student Life Upper grades have specified standards of dress, student council, honor system. Discipline rests primarily with faculty.

Summer Programs Remediation, enrichment, advancement, sports, art/fine arts, computer instruction programs offered; session focuses on academics, arts, sports; held on campus; accepts boys and girls; open to students from other schools. 75 students usually enrolled. 2006 schedule: June 10 to July 28. Application deadline: April 30.

Tuition and Aid Day student tuition: $12,980–$14,260. Tuition installment plan (Insured Tuition Payment Plan, individually arranged payment plans, 2- and 10-payment plans). Tuition reduction for siblings, need-based scholarship grants available. In 2005–06, 25% of upper-school students received aid. Total amount of financial aid awarded in 2005–06: $430,563.

Admissions Traditional secondary-level entrance grade is 9. For fall 2005, 40 students applied for upper-level admission, 37 were accepted, 29 enrolled. Any standardized test and writing sample required. Deadline for receipt of application materials: February 10. Application fee required: $45. Interview recommended.

Athletics Interscholastic: baseball (boys), basketball (b,g), soccer (b,g), softball (g), swimming and diving (b,g), tennis (b,g), volleyball (g); intramural: touch football (b); coed interscholastic: cross-country running, golf, hiking/backpacking, outdoor education, ropes courses, strength & conditioning; coed intramural: basketball, cooperative games, cross-country running, dance, flag football, football, hiking/backpacking, outdoor education, outdoor recreation, outdoor skills, physical training, ropes courses, strength & conditioning, volleyball, weight training, yoga. 2 PE instructors, 12 coaches.

Computers Computers are regularly used in foreign language, mathematics, science classes. Computer network features include campus e-mail, on-campus library services, CD-ROMs, online commercial services, Internet access, DVD.

Contact Debby R. Kennedy, Director of Admissions. 520-327-6395 Ext. 213. Fax: 520-327-8276. E-mail: debby_kennedy@stgregoryschool.org. Web site: www.stgregoryschool.org.

See full description on page 1016.

SAINT JAMES SCHOOL

6010 Vaughn Road
Montgomery, Alabama 36116
Head of School: Dr. John H. Lindsell

General Information Coeducational day college-preparatory, arts, and technology school. Grades PK–12. Founded: 1955. Setting: suburban. 80-acre campus. 9 buildings on campus. Approved or accredited by Southern Association of Colleges and Schools, Southern Association of Independent Schools, and The College Board. Endowment: $1.5 million. Total enrollment: 1,166. Upper school average class size: 20. Upper school faculty-student ratio: 1:20.

Saint James School

Upper School Student Profile Grade 9: 98 students (59 boys, 39 girls); Grade 10: 87 students (40 boys, 47 girls); Grade 11: 95 students (40 boys, 55 girls); Grade 12: 86 students (39 boys, 47 girls).

Faculty School total: 100. In upper school: 13 men, 22 women; 23 have advanced degrees.

Subjects Offered Advanced computer applications, advanced studio art-AP, algebra, American government, American government-AP, American history, American history-AP, American literature, American literature-AP, anatomy, art, art history-AP, art-AP, athletics, band, Basic programming, biology, biology-AP, British literature, British literature-AP, calculus, calculus-AP, chemistry, chemistry-AP, choir, choral music, chorus, community service, computer applications, computer information systems, computer keyboarding, computer multimedia, computer processing, computer programming, computer science, concert band, concert choir, creative writing, critical thinking, debate, drama, drama performance, dramatic arts, earth science, economics, economics-AP, English, English literature, English literature and composition-AP, English literature-AP, English-AP, environmental science, European history-AP, fine arts, foreign language, forensics, French, French language-AP, geography, geometry, government/civics, government/civics-AP, grammar, interpersonal skills, jazz band, journalism, Latin, Latin-AP, library assistant, marching band, mathematics, music, music theater, musical productions, newspaper, performing arts, personal development, philosophy, photography, physical education, physics, physiology, pre-algebra, psychology, publications, science, social studies, Spanish, Spanish-AP, speech, speech and debate, statistics, studio art—AP, technical theater, The 20th Century, theater, theater arts, theater design and production, theater production, trigonometry, U.S. government, U.S. government-AP, U.S. history, U.S. history-AP, visual arts, vocal music, world affairs, world history, world literature, world religions, writing, yearbook.

Graduation Requirements Biology, biology-AP, chemistry, chemistry-AP, computer science, concert band, critical thinking, debate, dramatic arts, English, English literature, English literature-AP, foreign language, mathematics, physical education (includes health), physical fitness, science, social studies (includes history), fine arts and community service (for honors diplomas).

Special Academic Programs Advanced Placement exam preparation in 13 subject areas; honors section; independent study; academic accommodation for the gifted and the artistically talented; remedial reading and/or remedial writing.

College Placement 90 students graduated in 2005; all went to college, including Auburn University; Auburn University Montgomery; Samford University; The University of Alabama; Tulane University; Vanderbilt University. Mean SAT verbal: 540, mean SAT math: 550, mean composite ACT: 24.

Student Life Upper grades have uniform requirement, student council, honor system. Discipline rests primarily with faculty.

Summer Programs Enrichment, advancement, sports, art/fine arts, computer instruction programs offered; held on campus; accepts boys and girls; open to students from other schools. 200 students usually enrolled. 2006 schedule: June 1 to August 6. Application deadline: none.

Tuition and Aid Day student tuition: $8064. Tuition installment plan (Insured Tuition Payment Plan, monthly payment plans, individually arranged payment plans). Tuition reduction for siblings, merit scholarship grants, need-based scholarship grants, need-based tuition reduction through SSS available. In 2005–06, 3% of upper-school students received aid; total upper-school merit-scholarship money awarded: $20,000. Total amount of financial aid awarded in 2005–06: $40,700.

Admissions Traditional secondary-level entrance grade is 9. For fall 2005, 17 students applied for upper-level admission, 15 were accepted, 15 enrolled. CTP III, ISEE, Otis-Lennon School Ability Test, Stanford Achievement Test, Wechsler Intelligence Scale for Children III or writing sample required. Deadline for receipt of application materials: none. Application fee required: $75. On-campus interview required.

Athletics Interscholastic: baseball (boys), basketball (b,g), cheering (g), cross-country running (b,g), dance team (g), football (b), golf (b,g), indoor track & field (b,g), power lifting (b), soccer (b,g), softball (g), strength & conditioning (b,g), tennis (b,g), track and field (b,g), volleyball (g), weight lifting (b), weight training (b,g), wrestling (b); coed intramural: physical fitness. 6 PE instructors, 10 coaches.

Computers Computers are regularly used in all academic classes. Computer network features include campus e-mail, on-campus library services, CD-ROMs, online commercial services, Internet access.

Contact Mrs. Aimee B. Steineker, Director of Admissions. 334-273-3000. Fax: 334-274-9097. E-mail: asteineker@stjweb.org. Web site: www.stjweb.org.

SAINT JAMES SCHOOL

17641 College Road
St. James, Maryland 21781-9999
Head of School: Rev. Dr. D. Stuart Dunnan

General Information Coeducational boarding and day college-preparatory school, affiliated with Episcopal Church. Grades 8–12. Founded: 1842. Setting: rural. Nearest major city is Washington, DC. Students are housed in single-sex dormitories. 700-acre campus. 36 buildings on campus. Approved or accredited by Association of Independent Maryland Schools, Association of Independent Schools of Greater Washington, Middle States Association of Colleges and Schools, National Association of Episcopal Schools, The Association of Boarding Schools, and Maryland Depart-

ment of Education. Member of National Association of Independent Schools and Secondary School Admission Test Board. Endowment: $12.7 million. Total enrollment: 222. Upper school average class size: 12. Upper school faculty-student ratio: 1:7.

Upper School Student Profile Grade 9: 49 students (32 boys, 17 girls); Grade 10: 48 students (33 boys, 15 girls); Grade 11: 58 students (37 boys, 21 girls); Grade 12: 41 students (20 boys, 21 girls). 75% of students are boarding students. 55% are state residents. 15 states are represented in upper school student body. 9% are international students. International students from Bermuda, Cote d'Ivoire, Japan, Nigeria, Republic of Korea, and Taiwan; 4 other countries represented in student body. 20% of students are members of Episcopal Church.

Faculty School total: 31. In upper school: 18 men, 13 women; 17 have advanced degrees; 29 reside on campus.

Subjects Offered Algebra, American history-AP, American literature, ancient history, art, art history, art-AP, biology-AP, calculus-AP, chemistry, chemistry-AP, choir, community service, economics, English, English literature, environmental science, European history-AP, fine arts, French-AP, geography, geometry, government-AP, keyboarding, Latin-AP, mathematics, modern European history, music, music history, physical science, physics, physics-AP, political science, science, Spanish-AP, theology, voice, world literature, writing workshop.

Graduation Requirements Arts and fine arts (art, music, dance, drama), English, foreign language, history, mathematics, science. Community service is required.

Special Academic Programs Advanced Placement exam preparation in 13 subject areas; independent study.

College Placement 41 students graduated in 2005; all went to college, including Amherst College; Hampden-Sydney College; The George Washington University; University of Maryland, College Park; University of the South; University of Virginia. Mean SAT verbal: 630, mean SAT math: 633. 51% scored over 600 on SAT verbal, 58% scored over 600 on SAT math.

Student Life Upper grades have specified standards of dress, student council, honor system. Discipline rests equally with students and faculty. Attendance at religious services is required.

Tuition and Aid Day student tuition: $19,000; 7-day tuition and room/board: $28,500. Tuition installment plan (Insured Tuition Payment Plan, Academic Management Services Plan). Tuition reduction for siblings, merit scholarship grants, need-based scholarship grants available. In 2005–06, 25% of upper-school students received aid; total upper-school merit-scholarship money awarded: $20,000. Total amount of financial aid awarded in 2005–06: $871,122.

Admissions Traditional secondary-level entrance grade is 9. For fall 2005, 204 students applied for upper-level admission, 107 were accepted, 70 enrolled. PSAT or SAT or SSAT required. Deadline for receipt of application materials: January 31. Application fee required: $50. Interview required.

Athletics Interscholastic: baseball (boys), basketball (b,g), cross-country running (b), field hockey (g), football (b), golf (b), lacrosse (b,g), soccer (b,g), softball (g), tennis (b,g), volleyball (g), wrestling (b); intramural: aerobics/dance (g), ballet (g), dance (g), modern dance (g), weight training (b,g); coed intramural: alpine skiing, indoor soccer, martial arts, skiing (downhill), strength & conditioning. 2 coaches, 1 trainer.

Computers Computers are regularly used in all academic classes. Computer network features include campus e-mail, on-campus library services, CD-ROMs, online commercial services, Internet access, DVD, wireless campus network.

Contact William W. Ellis, Director of Admission and Financial Aid. 301-733-9330. Fax: 301-739-1310. E-mail: admissions@stjames.edu. Web site: www.stjames.edu.

See full description on page 1018.

ST. JOHNSBURY ACADEMY

PO Box 906
1000 Main Street
St. Johnsbury, Vermont 05819
Head of School: Mr. Thomas W. Lovett

General Information Coeducational boarding and day college-preparatory, general academic, arts, business, vocational, and technology school. Grades 9–PG. Founded: 1842. Setting: small town. Nearest major city is Boston, MA. Students are housed in single-sex dormitories. 150-acre campus. 28 buildings on campus. Approved or accredited by Independent Schools of Northern New England, New England Association of Schools and Colleges, The Association of Boarding Schools, and Vermont Department of Education. Member of National Association of Independent Schools and Secondary School Admission Test Board. Endowment: $16.2 million. Total enrollment: 981. Upper school average class size: 15. Upper school faculty-student ratio: 1:8.

Upper School Student Profile Grade 9: 219 students (112 boys, 107 girls); Grade 10: 238 students (129 boys, 109 girls); Grade 11: 254 students (144 boys, 110 girls); Grade 12: 263 students (140 boys, 123 girls); Postgraduate: 7 students (5 boys, 2 girls). 20% of students are boarding students. 75% are state residents. 18 states are represented in upper school student body. 14% are international students. International students from Bermuda, Germany, Hong Kong, Mexico, Republic of Korea, and Taiwan; 15 other countries represented in student body.

Faculty School total: 119. In upper school: 76 men, 43 women; 75 have advanced degrees; 20 reside on campus.

Subjects Offered Accounting, acting, Advanced Placement courses, advanced studio art-AP, advanced TOEFL/grammar, algebra, American government, American government-AP, American history, American history-AP, American literature, analysis, anatomy and physiology, ancient world history, architectural drawing, architecture, art, astronomy, audio visual/media, auto body, auto mechanics, auto shop, automated accounting, band, basic skills, biology, biology-AP, British literature, business, business communications, business skills, calculus-AP, career education, career experience, carpentry, chemistry, chemistry-AP, chorus, civics, college writing, Coming of Age in the 20th Century, composition-AP, computer keyboarding, computer math, computer programming, computer science-AP, concert band, construction, CPR, culinary arts, dance, dance performance, desktop publishing, developmental math, digital art, directing, discrete math, drafting, drama, drama performance, drama workshop, dramatic arts, drawing and design, driver education, earth science, economics, electronics, engineering, English, English language and composition-AP, English literature, English literature and composition-AP, environmental education, environmental science, environmental science-AP, ESL, European history, European history-AP, expository writing, fashion, film studies, forest resources, forestry, French, French language-AP, French literature-AP, French-AP, geometry, government, government-AP, government/civics, guitar, health, health education, history, industrial arts, introduction to theater, Japanese, jazz band, journalism, land management, Latin, mathematics, mechanical drawing, media production, modern European history-AP, music, music appreciation, music theory, navigation, newspaper, oil painting, photography, physical education, physics, physics-AP, playwriting, playwriting and directing, portfolio art, pottery, pre-algebra, pre-calculus, pre-vocational education, psychology, psychology-AP, reading/study skills, science, sculpture, small engine repair, social science, social studies, sociology, Spanish, Spanish literature, sports medicine, sports science, stagecraft, statistics and probability, statistics-AP, studio art-AP, study skills, technical education, technical writing, technology, theater, theater design and production, TOEFL preparation, trigonometry, U.S. government-AP, U.S. history-AP, video communication, video film production, visual and performing arts, vocal ensemble, Web site design, welding, wilderness/outdoor program, wind ensemble, wind instruments, woodworking, word processing, world civilizations, world history, world literature, writing, yearbook.
Graduation Requirements Economics, English, keyboarding/computer, mathematics, physical education (includes health), science, U.S. government, U.S. history.
Special Academic Programs Advanced Placement exam preparation in 18 subject areas; honors section; term-away projects; academic accommodation for the gifted and the artistically talented; remedial reading and/or remedial writing; remedial math; programs in English, mathematics, general development for dyslexic students; ESL (77 students enrolled).
College Placement 249 students graduated in 2005; 192 went to college, including Mount Ida College; Northeastern University; Plymouth State University; Syracuse University; The George Washington University; University of Vermont. Other: 38 went to work, 8 entered military service, 11 had other specific plans. Mean SAT verbal: 522, mean SAT math: 550.
Student Life Upper grades have specified standards of dress, student council, honor system. Discipline rests primarily with faculty.
Summer Programs ESL programs offered; session focuses on English; held on campus; accepts boys and girls; open to students from other schools. 30 students usually enrolled. 2006 schedule: July 14 to August 25. Application deadline: none.
Tuition and Aid Day student tuition: $10,520; 7-day tuition and room/board: $29,920. Tuition installment plan (individually arranged payment plans, two payments (August 1 and November 25)). Need-based scholarship grants available. In 2005–06, 3% of upper-school students received aid. Total amount of financial aid awarded in 2005–06: $360,000.
Admissions Traditional secondary-level entrance grade is 9. For fall 2005, 221 students applied for upper-level admission, 176 were accepted, 115 enrolled. Deadline for receipt of application materials: none. Application fee required: $20. Interview recommended.
Athletics Interscholastic: alpine skiing (boys, girls), baseball (b), basketball (b,g), cross-country running (b,g), field hockey (g), football (b), golf (b,g), gymnastics (g), hockey (b,g), ice hockey (b), lacrosse (b,g), nordic skiing (b,g), skiing (cross-country) (b,g), skiing (downhill) (b,g), soccer (b,g), softball (g), tennis (b,g), track and field (b,g), wrestling (b); intramural: ice hockey (g), volleyball (b,g); coed interscholastic: cheering, ultimate Frisbee; coed intramural: badminton, basketball, bowling, flag football, floor hockey, Frisbee, martial arts, mountain biking, outdoor adventure, paddle tennis, swimming and diving, volleyball, weight lifting, wilderness. 3 PE instructors, 1 trainer.
Computers Computers are regularly used in business education, career education, drafting, English, foreign language, keyboarding, mathematics, science, technology, Web site design classes. Computer network features include campus e-mail, on-campus library services, CD-ROMs, online commercial services, Internet access, office computer access, wireless campus network.
Contact Mr. John J. Cummings, Director of Admission and Advancement. 802-751-2130. Fax: 802-748-5463. E-mail: admissions@stjacademy.org. Web site: www.stjohnsburyacademy.org.

ANNOUNCEMENT FROM THE SCHOOL Through a matching grant from the Edward E. Ford Foundation, St. Johnsbury Academy is implementing a STeM (Science, Technology and Math) initiative beginning fall 2006. The STeM program will create new curricula, facilities, extracurriculars, and faculty in these fields and provide a new lab, new equipment, and outreach opportunities for faculty and students.

See full description on page 1020.

ST. JOHN'S COLLEGE HIGH SCHOOL

2607 Military Road, NW
Washington, District of Columbia 20015
Head of School: Mr. Jeffrey W. Mancabelli

General Information Coeducational day college-preparatory, arts, religious studies, and technology school, affiliated with Roman Catholic Church. Grades 9–12. Founded: 1851. Setting: urban. 30-acre campus. 5 buildings on campus. Approved or accredited by Middle States Association of Colleges and Schools and District of Columbia Department of Education. Endowment: $5 million. Total enrollment: 1,074. Upper school average class size: 23. Upper school faculty-student ratio: 1:13.
Upper School Student Profile Grade 9: 292 students (192 boys, 100 girls); Grade 10: 282 students (188 boys, 94 girls); Grade 11: 245 students (174 boys, 71 girls); Grade 12: 255 students (164 boys, 91 girls). 70% of students are Roman Catholic.
Faculty School total: 72. In upper school: 42 men, 28 women; 50 have advanced degrees.
Subjects Offered Accounting, Advanced Placement courses, algebra, American history, American literature, anatomy, art, band, biology, business, calculus, ceramics, chemistry, chorus, community service, computer math, computer programming, computer science, creative writing, earth science, economics, English, English literature, European history, fine arts, French, genetics, geometry, government/civics, history, journalism, JROTC, leadership training, mathematics, military science, music, physical education, physics, physiology, religion, science, Shakespeare, social science, social studies, Spanish, trigonometry, typing, weight training, world history, world literature.
Graduation Requirements Arts and fine arts (art, music, dance, drama), computer science, English, foreign language, mathematics, physical education (includes health), religion (includes Bible studies and theology), science, social science, social studies (includes history). Community service is required.
Special Academic Programs Advanced Placement exam preparation in 12 subject areas; honors section; independent study; academic accommodation for the gifted.
College Placement 246 students graduated in 2005; 244 went to college, including St. Mary's College of Maryland; Temple University; The Catholic University of America; University of Maryland, College Park; University of Virginia. Other: 1 went to work, 1 entered military service. Mean SAT verbal: 610, mean SAT math: 600.
Student Life Upper grades have uniform requirement, student council. Discipline rests primarily with faculty. Attendance at religious services is required.
Summer Programs Remediation, enrichment, advancement, sports, computer instruction programs offered; session focuses on remediation and advancement; held on campus; accepts boys and girls; not open to students from other schools. 75 students usually enrolled. 2006 schedule: June 22 to July 22.
Tuition and Aid Day student tuition: $10,520. Tuition installment plan (FACTS Tuition Payment Plan). Merit scholarship grants, need-based scholarship grants available.
Admissions Traditional secondary-level entrance grade is 9. For fall 2005, 760 students applied for upper-level admission, 550 were accepted, 290 enrolled. High School Placement Test (closed version) from Scholastic Testing Service required. Deadline for receipt of application materials: December 15. Application fee required: $50.
Athletics Interscholastic: baseball (boys), basketball (b,g), cheering (g), cross-country running (b,g), field hockey (g), football (b), ice hockey (b), lacrosse (b,g), soccer (b,g), softball (g), tennis (b,g), track and field (b,g), volleyball (g), wrestling (b); intramural: dance (g), dance squad (g), pom squad (g); coed interscholastic: diving, drill team, golf, ice hockey, JROTC drill, marksmanship, physical fitness, riflery, rugby, swimming and diving. Other: coed intramural: alpine skiing, bowling, equestrian sports, fishing, Frisbee, martial arts, outdoor activities, riflery, skiing (downhill), snowboarding, strength & conditioning, ultimate Frisbee, weight training. 1 PE instructor, 26 coaches, 1 trainer.
Computers Computers are regularly used in all classes. Computer network features include on-campus library services, CD-ROMs, online commercial services, Internet access, wireless campus network.
Contact Mr. Christopher J. Themistos, Director of Admissions. 202-363-2316 Ext. 3016. Fax: 202-363-2916. E-mail: cthemistos@stjohns-chs.org. Web site: stjohns-chs.org.

ST. JOHNS COUNTRY DAY SCHOOL

3100 Doctors Lake Drive
Orange Park, Florida 32073
Head of School: Mr. Gregory L. Foster

petersons.com

General Information Coeducational day college-preparatory, arts, religious studies, and technology school. Grades PK–12. Founded: 1953. Setting: suburban. Nearest major city is Jacksonville. 26-acre campus. 11 buildings on campus. Approved or

accredited by Florida Council of Independent Schools, Southern Association of Colleges and Schools, and Florida Department of Education. Member of National Association of Independent Schools. Endowment: $3.4 million. Total enrollment: 754. Upper school average class size: 17. Upper school faculty-student ratio: 1:10.

Upper School Student Profile Grade 9: 56 students (28 boys, 28 girls); Grade 10: 54 students (22 boys, 32 girls); Grade 11: 58 students (26 boys, 32 girls); Grade 12: 64 students (37 boys, 27 girls).

Faculty School total: 86. In upper school: 14 men, 23 women; 34 have advanced degrees.

Subjects Offered Algebra, American history, American literature, anatomy, art, art history, biology, calculus, ceramics, chemistry, computer programming, computer science, creative writing, drama, drawing, earth science, economics, English, English literature, ethics, European history, fine arts, French, geometry, government/civics, grammar, health, history, Holocaust studies, journalism, Latin, marine biology, mathematics, music, oceanography, painting, physical education, physics, psychology, religion, science, social studies, sociology, Spanish, speech, statistics, theater, trigonometry, world history, world literature, writing.

Graduation Requirements Arts and fine arts (art, music, dance, drama), computer science, English, ethics, foreign language, government, history, lab science, mathematics, physical education (includes health), senior practicum.

Special Academic Programs Advanced Placement exam preparation in 17 subject areas; honors section; independent study; study at local college for college credit; academic accommodation for the gifted, the musically talented, and the artistically talented.

College Placement 47 students graduated in 2005; all went to college, including Rollins College; University of Central Florida; University of Florida; University of North Florida; University of Pennsylvania. Median SAT verbal: 630, median SAT math: 620, median composite ACT: 27. 60% scored over 600 on SAT verbal, 70% scored over 600 on SAT math, 45% scored over 26 on composite ACT.

Student Life Upper grades have specified standards of dress, student council, honor system. Discipline rests primarily with faculty.

Summer Programs Remediation, enrichment, advancement programs offered; session focuses on remediation; held on campus; accepts boys and girls; open to students from other schools. 65 students usually enrolled. 2006 schedule: June 12 to July 21. Application deadline: June 12.

Tuition and Aid Day student tuition: $10,385. Tuition installment plan (monthly payment plans, individually arranged payment plans). Need-based scholarship grants available. In 2005–06, 29% of upper-school students received aid. Total amount of financial aid awarded in 2005–06: $152,635.

Admissions Traditional secondary-level entrance grade is 9. For fall 2005, 29 students applied for upper-level admission, 27 were accepted, 20 enrolled. CTP III, ERB, independent norms and school's own exam required. Deadline for receipt of application materials: none. Application fee required: $150. Interview required.

Athletics Interscholastic: baseball (boys), basketball (b,g), cheering (g), crew (b,g), cross-country running (b,g), golf (b,g), rowing (b,g), soccer (b,g), softball (g), swimming and diving (b,g), tennis (b,g), track and field (b,g), volleyball (g); intramural: aerobics/dance (g), dance squad (g); coed interscholastic: aquatics; coed intramural: aquatics, cooperative games, cross-country running, fitness, fitness walking, flag football, floor hockey, golf, gymnastics, independent competitive sports, indoor soccer, jogging, jump rope, kickball, life saving, nautilus, Newcombe ball, outdoor activities, outdoor adventure, outdoor education, outdoor recreation, paddle tennis, physical fitness, racquetball, roller blading, running, soccer, softball, speedball, street hockey, strength & conditioning, swimming and diving, table tennis, team handball, tennis, touch football, track and field, triathlon, volleyball, walking, water polo, water volleyball, weight lifting, weight training, whiffle ball, winter soccer. 6 PE instructors, 22 coaches.

Computers Computers are regularly used in English, foreign language, mathematics, music, science, social studies classes. Computer network features include campus e-mail, on-campus library services, CD-ROMs, online commercial services, Internet access, wireless campus network.

Contact Mrs. Amy Weaver, Director of Admissions. 904-264-9572. Fax: 904-264-0375. E-mail: amy_weaver@stjohnscds.com. Web site: www.stjohnscds.com/.

ANNOUNCEMENT FROM THE SCHOOL St. Johns admission is competitive; academically qualified students are admitted without regard to race, creed, color, or national or ethnic origin. The teaching faculty numbers 86, providing a healthy student-teacher ratio, the small class size typically expected of independent schools, and an overall environment best described as challenging and caring. Situated on 26 wooded acres in Orange Park, a growing suburban community just south of Jacksonville, St. Johns attracts students from throughout the greater Jacksonville and Clay County area; the student body reflects many diverse social, ethnic, and professional backgrounds.

ST. JOHN'S-KILMARNOCK SCHOOL

2201 Shantz Station Road
Box 179
Breslau, Ontario N0B 1M0, Canada
Head of School: Mr. Gary Lukachko

General Information Coeducational day college-preparatory, arts, and business school, affiliated with Anglican Church of Canada. Grades JK–12. Founded: 1972. Setting: rural. Nearest major city is Kitchener, Canada. 36-acre campus. 3 buildings on campus. Approved or accredited by Canadian Association of Independent Schools, Canadian Educational Standards Institute, Conference of Independent Schools of Ontario, International Baccalaureate Organization, and Ontario Department of Education. Language of instruction: English. Total enrollment: 454. Upper school average class size: 18. Upper school faculty-student ratio: 1:12.

Upper School Student Profile Grade 9: 50 students (29 boys, 21 girls); Grade 10: 48 students (30 boys, 18 girls); Grade 11: 53 students (22 boys, 31 girls); Grade 12: 48 students (26 boys, 22 girls). 30% of students are members of Anglican Church of Canada.

Faculty School total: 51. In upper school: 11 men, 15 women; 7 have advanced degrees.

Special Academic Programs Advanced Placement exam preparation in 8 subject areas; independent study; study abroad; ESL.

College Placement 54 students graduated in 2005; 52 went to college, including McGill University. Other: 2 had other specific plans.

Student Life Upper grades have uniform requirement, student council, honor system. Discipline rests primarily with faculty. Attendance at religious services is required.

Tuition and Aid Tuition installment plan (The Tuition Plan).

Admissions Traditional secondary-level entrance grade is 9. For fall 2005, 65 students applied for upper-level admission, 54 were accepted, 52 enrolled. Brigance Test of Basic Skills, essay and mathematics proficiency exam required. Deadline for receipt of application materials: May 30. Application fee required: CAN$100. On-campus interview required.

Athletics Interscholastic: alpine skiing (boys, girls), badminton (b,g), basketball (b,g), cross-country running (b,g), field hockey (g), golf (b,g), outdoor education (b,g), rugby (b), skiing (cross-country) (b,g), skiing (downhill) (b,g), soccer (b,g), softball (g), strength & conditioning (b,g), track and field (b,g), volleyball (b,g), wrestling (b,g); intramural: ball hockey (b,g), basketball (b,g), broomball (b,g), cooperative games (b,g), fitness (b,g), Fives (b,g), handball (b,g), hockey (b,g), ice hockey (b,g), indoor soccer (b,g), mountain biking (b,g), nordic skiing (b,g), physical training (b,g), ropes courses (b,g), skiing (cross-country) (b,g), snowboarding (b,g), soccer (b,g), tennis (b,g), weight lifting (b,g), weight training (b,g); coed interscholastic: badminton, outdoor education, running, skiing (cross-country); coed intramural: basketball, broomball, cooperative games, fitness, Fives, handball, hockey, ice hockey, indoor soccer, mountain biking, nordic skiing, physical training, ropes courses, skiing (cross-country), snowboarding, soccer, softball, table tennis, tennis, weight lifting, weight training. 4 PE instructors.

Computers Computer network features include campus e-mail, on-campus library services, CD-ROMs, online commercial services, Internet access, DVD, wireless campus network.

Contact Ms. Kim Wakeford, Director of Admissions and Marketing. 519-648-3602 Ext. 25. Fax: 519-648-2186. E-mail: wakeford@sjkschool.org. Web site: www.sjkschool.org.

ST. JOHN'S LITERARY INSTITUTION AT PROSPECT HALL

889 Butterfly Lane
Frederick, Maryland 21703
Head of School: Dr. Robert Pastoor

General Information Coeducational day college-preparatory school, affiliated with Roman Catholic Church. Grades 9–12. Founded: 1829. Setting: suburban. 31-acre campus. 9 buildings on campus. Approved or accredited by Association of Independent Maryland Schools and Maryland Department of Education. Total enrollment: 300. Upper school average class size: 17. Upper school faculty-student ratio: 1:10.

Upper School Student Profile 75% of students are Roman Catholic.

Faculty School total: 41. In upper school: 15 men, 26 women.

Special Academic Programs Advanced Placement exam preparation; honors section; study at local college for college credit.

College Placement 68 students graduated in 2005; all went to college. Median SAT verbal: 577, median SAT math: 564.

Student Life Upper grades have uniform requirement, honor system. Discipline rests primarily with faculty. Attendance at religious services is required.

Summer Programs Sports, art/fine arts, computer instruction programs offered; held on campus; accepts boys and girls; open to students from other schools. 2006 schedule: June to August.

Tuition and Aid Day student tuition: $8250. Tuition installment plan (monthly payment plans). Tuition reduction for siblings, merit scholarship grants, need-based scholarship grants available. In 2005–06, 25% of upper-school students received aid. Total amount of financial aid awarded in 2005–06: $200,000.

Admissions Traditional secondary-level entrance grade is 9. High School Placement Test (closed version) from Scholastic Testing Service required. Deadline for receipt of application materials: none. Application fee required: $95. On-campus interview required.

Athletics Interscholastic: baseball (boys), basketball (b,g), cheering (g), cross-country running (b,g), football (b), golf (b,g), lacrosse (b,g), soccer (b,g), softball (g), swimming and diving (b,g), tennis (b,g), volleyball (g), wrestling (b); coed interscholastic: indoor track & field, track and field; coed intramural: equestrian sports, horseback riding, indoor hockey, skiing (downhill), snowboarding, strength & conditioning, weight training. 3 PE instructors, 13 coaches.

Computers Computer network features include campus e-mail, on-campus library services, CD-ROMs, Internet access, DVD.

Contact Mrs. Julie Doyle, Director of Admissions. 301-662-4210. Fax: 301-662-5166. E-mail: jdoyle@stjph.org.

ST. JOHN'S MILITARY SCHOOL

PO Box 827
Salina, Kansas 67402-0827
Head of School: Col. Jack R. Fox

General Information Boys' boarding college-preparatory, general academic, arts, religious studies, bilingual studies, and technology school, affiliated with Episcopal Church. Grades 7–12. Founded: 1887. Setting: small town. Nearest major city is Wichita. Students are housed in single-sex dormitories. 20-acre campus. 17 buildings on campus. Approved or accredited by North Central Association of Colleges and Schools, The Association of Boarding Schools, and Kansas Department of Education. Endowment: $9 million. Total enrollment: 184. Upper school average class size: 12. Upper school faculty-student ratio: 1:12.

Upper School Student Profile Grade 9: 38 students (38 boys); Grade 10: 42 students (42 boys); Grade 11: 44 students (44 boys); Grade 12: 33 students (33 boys). 100% of students are boarding students. 26% are state residents. 20 states are represented in upper school student body. 8% are international students. International students from Germany, Japan, Mexico, and Nigeria; 1 other country represented in student body. 33% of students are members of Episcopal Church.

Faculty School total: 24. In upper school: 15 men, 9 women; 3 have advanced degrees; 8 reside on campus.

Subjects Offered Aerospace science, algebra, American literature, anatomy, art, art history, band, Bible studies, biology, business, calculus, chemistry, computer science, consumer education, creative writing, debate, desktop publishing, drafting, driver education, earth science, ecology, economics, English, English literature, environmental science, ethics, family studies, geography, geometry, government/civics, grammar, health, history, industrial arts, instrumental music, JROTC, mathematics, military science, music, photography, physical education, physics, religion, science, social science, social studies, Spanish, speech, statistics, trigonometry, weight training, world literature, writing, yearbook.

Graduation Requirements American government, biology, computer science, English, foreign language, JROTC, mathematics, physical education (includes health), physical science, religion (includes Bible studies and theology), science, social science, social studies (includes history), world geography.

Special Academic Programs Honors section; accelerated programs; independent study; study at local college for college credit.

College Placement 27 students graduated in 2004; 18 went to college, including Norwich University; University of Colorado at Boulder. Other: 5 went to work, 1 entered military service, 3 had other specific plans. Median SAT verbal: 435, median SAT math: 475, median composite ACT: 22. 5% scored over 600 on SAT verbal, 5% scored over 600 on SAT math, 10% scored over 26 on composite ACT.

Student Life Upper grades have uniform requirement, honor system. Discipline rests equally with students and faculty. Attendance at religious services is required.

Tuition and Aid 7-day tuition and room/board: $21,686. Tuition installment plan (monthly payment plans, individually arranged payment plans). Tuition reduction for siblings, merit scholarship grants, educational loan programs available. In 2004–05, 33% of upper-school students received aid; total upper-school merit-scholarship money awarded: $150,000. Total amount of financial aid awarded in 2004–05: $150,000.

Admissions For fall 2005, 70 students applied for upper-level admission, 66 were accepted, 66 enrolled. Deadline for receipt of application materials: none. Application fee required: $75. Interview recommended.

Athletics Interscholastic: baseball, basketball, drill team, football, golf, JROTC drill, marksmanship, riflery, soccer, tennis, track and field, wrestling; intramural: baseball, basketball, bicycling, bowling, fitness, flag football, floor hockey, physical fitness, physical training, softball. 1 PE instructor, 2 coaches.

Computers Computers are regularly used in art, business applications, career technology, English, foreign language, mathematics, science, vocational-technical courses, yearbook classes. Computer resources include campus e-mail, on-campus library services, CD-ROMs, Internet access.

Contact Mrs. Judy C. Rutherford, Associate Director of Admissions. 785-823-7231 Ext. 7725. Fax: 785-823-7236. E-mail: judyr@sjms.org. Web site: www.sjms.org.

See full description on page 1022.

ST. JOHN'S NORTHWESTERN MILITARY ACADEMY

1101 North Genesee Street
Delafield, Wisconsin 53018-1498
Head of School: Mr. Jack H. Albert Jr.

General Information Boys' boarding and day college-preparatory and arts school, affiliated with Episcopal Church; primarily serves underachievers. Boarding grades 7–12, day grades 7–8. Founded: 1884. Setting: small town. Nearest major city is Milwaukee. Students are housed in single-sex dormitories. 150-acre campus. 15 buildings on campus. Approved or accredited by Independent Schools Association of the Central States, Midwest Association of Boarding Schools, North Central Association of Colleges and Schools, The Association of Boarding Schools, and Wisconsin Department of Education. Member of National Association of Independent Schools and Secondary School Admission Test Board. Endowment: $4.5 million. Total enrollment: 300. Upper school average class size: 12. Upper school faculty-student ratio: 1:12.

Upper School Student Profile Grade 9: 63 students (63 boys); Grade 10: 66 students (66 boys); Grade 11: 57 students (57 boys); Grade 12: 61 students (61 boys). 100% of students are boarding students. 22% are state residents. 22 states are represented in upper school student body. 21% are international students. International students from Australia, China, France, Germany, Mexico, and Republic of Korea; 5 other countries represented in student body. 4% of students are members of Episcopal Church.

Faculty School total: 40. In upper school: 34 men, 6 women; 16 have advanced degrees; 4 reside on campus.

Subjects Offered Advanced math, algebra, American government, American literature, art, aviation, band, biology, British literature, calculus, ceramics, chemistry, choir, Christianity, computer programming, computer science, current events, drama, driver education, earth science, economics, English, entrepreneurship, environmental science, ESL, geography, geometry, German, government/civics, grammar, health, history, honors English, honors U.S. history, journalism, JROTC, mathematics, music, physical science, physics, psychology, reading, science, social studies, sociology, Spanish, statistics, strings, trigonometry, U.S. history, world geography, world history, world literature.

Graduation Requirements Advanced math, algebra, American government, American literature, arts and fine arts (art, music, dance, drama), biology, British literature, chemistry, computer science, electives, foreign language, geometry, introduction to literature, JROTC, physical science, U.S. history, world history, world literature. Community service is required.

Special Academic Programs Honors section; independent study; study at local college for college credit; ESL (10 students enrolled).

College Placement 58 students graduated in 2005; all went to college, including DePaul University; Embry-Riddle Aeronautical University; Marquette University; Purdue University; University of Illinois at Urbana–Champaign.

Student Life Upper grades have uniform requirement, student council, honor system. Discipline rests equally with students and faculty. Attendance at religious services is required.

Summer Programs Remediation, ESL, rigorous outdoor training programs offered; session focuses on military adventure and leadership training and ESL; held both on and off campus; held at various venues for outdoor training; accepts boys; open to students from other schools. 200 students usually enrolled. 2006 schedule: June 25 to July 22. Application deadline: none.

Tuition and Aid Day student tuition: $11,000; 7-day tuition and room/board: $27,250. Tuition installment plan (Key Tuition Payment Plan, FACTS Tuition Payment Plan, TeriPlease Tuition Payment Plans). Tuition reduction for siblings, merit scholarship grants, need-based scholarship grants, tuition remission for children of employees, endowed scholarships, alumni scholarships available. In 2005–06, 41% of upper-school students received aid. Total amount of financial aid awarded in 2005–06: $404,606.

Admissions Traditional secondary-level entrance grade is 9. For fall 2005, 430 students applied for upper-level admission, 236 were accepted, 125 enrolled. Kuhlmann-Anderson, SSAT or TOEFL required. Deadline for receipt of application materials: none. Application fee required: $75. On-campus interview required.

Athletics Interscholastic: archery, baseball, basketball, cross-country running, football, golf, hockey, ice hockey, JROTC drill, marksmanship, riflery, rugby, soccer, softball, swimming and diving, tennis, track and field, wrestling; intramural: billiards, fishing, martial arts, outdoor adventure, paint ball, physical fitness, rappelling, scuba diving, skiing (downhill), snowboarding, volleyball, weight lifting. 4 coaches.

Computers Computers are regularly used in all academic classes. Computer network features include campus e-mail, on-campus library services, CD-ROMs, Internet access, file transfer.

Contact Maj. Charles E. Moore, Director of Marketing, Public Relations, and Enrollment Services. 262-646-7199. Fax: 262-646-7128. E-mail: admissions@sjnma.org. Web site: www.sjnma.org.

ANNOUNCEMENT FROM THE SCHOOL Since 1884, St. John's Northwestern Military Academy has had a history of excellence in preparing young boys for college, career, and life. Its dedicated faculty and staff members guide

cadets to challenge themselves academically, make the right decisions, set high standards, and become men of integrity.

See full description on page 1024.

ST. JOHN'S PREPARATORY SCHOOL

72 Spring Street
Danvers, Massachusetts 01923
Head of School: Albert J. Shannon, PhD

General Information Boys' day college-preparatory, arts, religious studies, and technology school, affiliated with Roman Catholic Church. Grades 9–12. Founded: 1907. Setting: suburban. Nearest major city is Boston. 175-acre campus. 9 buildings on campus. Approved or accredited by National Catholic Education Association and New England Association of Schools and Colleges. Endowment: $5.4 million. Total enrollment: 1,217. Upper school average class size: 19. Upper school faculty-student ratio: 1:13.

Upper School Student Profile Grade 9: 312 students (312 boys); Grade 10: 328 students (328 boys); Grade 11: 330 students (330 boys); Grade 12: 247 students (247 boys). 70% of students are Roman Catholic.

Faculty School total: 96. In upper school: 62 men, 34 women; 64 have advanced degrees.

Subjects Offered Accounting, acting, algebra, American government-AP, American history, American history-AP, American literature, anatomy and physiology, art, biology, biology-AP, business, calculus, calculus-AP, ceramics, chemistry, chemistry-AP, chorus, computer programming, computer science, computer science-AP, desktop publishing, drama, driver education, economics, economics-AP, English, English literature, English-AP, environmental science, environmental studies, ethics, European history, European history-AP, French, French-AP, geometry, German, German-AP, government/civics, Latin, Latin-AP, mathematics, music, neuroscience, physical education, physics, physics-AP, religion, science, sculpture, social studies, society, politics and law, Spanish, Spanish-AP, statistics, statistics-AP, studio art, technology, trigonometry, U.S. history-AP, world history, world religions.

Graduation Requirements Arts and fine arts (art, music, dance, drama), computer science, English, foreign language, mathematics, physical education (includes health), religion (includes Bible studies and theology), science, social studies (includes history).

Special Academic Programs Advanced Placement exam preparation in 16 subject areas; honors section; independent study; study abroad; academic accommodation for the gifted, the musically talented, and the artistically talented.

College Placement 288 students graduated in 2005; 282 went to college, including Boston College; Boston University; Northeastern University; Providence College; University of Massachusetts Amherst; University of New Hampshire. Other: 2 entered a postgraduate year, 4 had other specific plans. Mean SAT verbal: 603, mean SAT math: 626. 45% scored over 600 on SAT verbal, 58% scored over 600 on SAT math.

Student Life Upper grades have specified standards of dress, student council. Discipline rests primarily with faculty. Attendance at religious services is required.

Summer Programs Enrichment programs offered; session focuses on academic enrichment and study skills; held on campus; accepts boys; not open to students from other schools.

Tuition and Aid Day student tuition: $13,800. Tuition installment plan (monthly payment plans). Merit scholarship grants, need-based scholarship grants available. In 2005–06, 30% of upper-school students received aid; total upper-school merit-scholarship money awarded: $335,000. Total amount of financial aid awarded in 2005–06: $2,085,000.

Admissions Traditional secondary-level entrance grade is 9. SSAT or STS, Diocese Test required. Deadline for receipt of application materials: December 31. No application fee required.

Athletics Interscholastic: baseball, basketball, cross-country running, fencing, football, golf, hockey, lacrosse, rugby, sailing, skiing (downhill), soccer, swimming and diving, tennis, track and field, volleyball, water polo, winter (indoor) track, wrestling; intramural: baseball, basketball, bicycling, bocce, bowling, climbing, combined training, cooperative games, crew, flag football, floor hockey, Frisbee, golf, in-line hockey, martial arts, nautilus, physical fitness, sailing, skiing (downhill), snowboarding, strength & conditioning, surfing, table tennis, tennis, touch football, ultimate Frisbee, volleyball, weight lifting, weight training, whiffle ball. 3 PE instructors, 57 coaches, 2 trainers.

Computers Computers are regularly used in all academic, career exploration, college planning, research skills classes. Computer network features include campus e-mail, on-campus library services, CD-ROMs, Internet access, file transfer, DVD, wireless campus network, student access to 300 computer workstations.

Contact John Driscoll, Dean of Admissions and Freshmen Academy Programs. 978-774-1050 Ext. 301. Fax: 978-624-1315. E-mail: jdriscoll@stjohnsprep.org. Web site: www.stjohnsprep.org.

SAINT JOHN'S PREPARATORY SCHOOL

Box 4000
1857 Water Tower Road
Collegeville, Minnesota 56321
Head of School: Fr. Gordon Tavis, OSB

General Information Coeducational boarding and day college-preparatory school, affiliated with Roman Catholic Church. Boarding grades 9–PG, day grades 7–PG. Founded: 1857. Setting: rural. Nearest major city is St. Cloud. Students are housed in single-sex dormitories. 2,600-acre campus. 22 buildings on campus. Approved or accredited by Independent Schools Association of the Central States, The Association of Boarding Schools, and Minnesota Department of Education. Member of National Association of Independent Schools. Endowment: $6.9 million. Total enrollment: 317. Upper school average class size: 15. Upper school faculty-student ratio: 1:11.

Upper School Student Profile Grade 9: 44 students (24 boys, 20 girls); Grade 10: 71 students (39 boys, 32 girls); Grade 11: 61 students (35 boys, 26 girls); Grade 12: 62 students (31 boys, 31 girls); Postgraduate: 2 students (2 boys). 40% of students are boarding students. 66% are state residents. 10 states are represented in upper school student body. 27% are international students. International students from Austria, Japan, Mexico, Republic of Korea, and Taiwan; 6 other countries represented in student body.

Faculty School total: 27. In upper school: 18 men, 9 women; 17 have advanced degrees; 3 reside on campus.

Subjects Offered 3-dimensional design, advanced chemistry, Advanced Placement courses, algebra, American history, American literature, art, art history, band, Bible studies, biology, biology-AP, British literature, calculus, ceramics, chemistry, Chinese, choir, civics, conceptual physics, creative writing, current events, drawing, driver education, economics, English, English literature, English-AP, environmental science-AP, ESL, European history, fine arts, geometry, German, government/civics, grammar, health, history, mathematics, music, orchestra, photography, physical education, physics, pre-calculus, religion, science, social studies, Spanish, speech, statistics, theology, trigonometry, world history, world literature, writing.

Graduation Requirements Arts and fine arts (art, music, dance, drama), English, foreign language, mathematics, physical education (includes health), science, social studies (includes history), theology, U.S. history.

Special Academic Programs Advanced Placement exam preparation in 6 subject areas; honors section; independent study; term-away projects; study at local college for college credit; study abroad; academic accommodation for the gifted, the musically talented, and the artistically talented; ESL (43 students enrolled).

College Placement 65 students graduated in 2005; 62 went to college, including College of Saint Benedict; Loyola University Chicago; St. John's University; St. Thomas University; University of Minnesota, Twin Cities Campus; University of Wisconsin–Madison. Other: 2 went to work, 1 entered a postgraduate year. Median SAT verbal: 640, median SAT math: 634, median combined SAT: 1915, median composite ACT: 25. 61% scored over 600 on SAT verbal, 73% scored over 600 on SAT math, 65% scored over 1800 on combined SAT, 33% scored over 26 on composite ACT.

Student Life Upper grades have specified standards of dress, student council, honor system. Discipline rests primarily with faculty. Attendance at religious services is required.

Summer Programs Enrichment, advancement, art/fine arts programs offered; session focuses on fun camp experiences; held on campus; accepts boys and girls; open to students from other schools. 2006 schedule: June 13 to July 23. Application deadline: June 1.

Tuition and Aid Day student tuition: $10,817; 5-day tuition and room/board: $22,069; 7-day tuition and room/board: $24,800. Tuition installment plan (monthly payment plans, individually arranged payment plans, semester payment plan). Merit scholarship grants, need-based scholarship grants, paying campus jobs available. In 2005–06, 60% of upper-school students received aid; total upper-school merit-scholarship money awarded: $28,200. Total amount of financial aid awarded in 2005–06: $626,732.

Admissions Traditional secondary-level entrance grade is 9. For fall 2005, 114 students applied for upper-level admission, 91 were accepted, 70 enrolled. Differential Aptitude Test required. Deadline for receipt of application materials: none. Application fee required: $30. Interview required.

Athletics Interscholastic: baseball (boys), basketball (b,g), cross-country running (b,g), diving (g), football (b), golf (b,g), gymnastics (g), ice hockey (b,g), indoor track & field (b,g), nordic skiing (b,g), soccer (b,g), softball (g), swimming and diving (g), tennis (b,g), track and field (b,g); intramural: volleyball (g); coed intramural: aerobics/dance, canoeing/kayaking, cross-country running, dance, fitness, fitness walking, Frisbee, indoor soccer, nordic skiing, physical fitness, racquetball, skiing (cross-country), skiing (downhill), soccer, swimming and diving, ultimate Frisbee, walking, wall climbing, weight lifting, weight training. 1 PE instructor, 17 coaches.

Computers Computers are regularly used in English, mathematics, science classes. Computer network features include campus e-mail, on-campus library services, CD-ROMs, Internet access, file transfer, office computer access.

Contact Bryan Backes, Director of Admission. 320-363-3321. Fax: 320-363-3322. E-mail: bbackes@csbsju.edu. Web site: www.sjprep.net.

See full description on page 1026.

ST. JOHN'S-RAVENSCOURT SCHOOL

400 South Drive
Winnipeg, Manitoba R3T 3K5, Canada
Head of School: Dr. David Howie

General Information Coeducational boarding and day college-preparatory school. Boarding grades 9–12, day grades K–12. Founded: 1820. Setting: suburban. Students are housed in single-sex dormitories. 23-acre campus. 6 buildings on campus. Approved or accredited by Canadian Association of Independent Schools, The Association of Boarding Schools, and Manitoba Department of Education. Language of instruction: English. Endowment: CAN$7.7 million. Total enrollment: 780. Upper school average class size: 20. Upper school faculty-student ratio: 1:9.

Upper School Student Profile Grade 9: 84 students (50 boys, 34 girls); Grade 10: 85 students (46 boys, 39 girls); Grade 11: 92 students (55 boys, 37 girls); Grade 12: 88 students (54 boys, 34 girls). 13% of students are boarding students. 92% are province residents. 4 provinces are represented in upper school student body. 7% are international students. International students from China, Democratic People's Republic of Korea, Germany, Mexico, Netherlands, and South Africa; 1 other country represented in student body.

Faculty School total: 78. In upper school: 24 men, 14 women; 13 have advanced degrees; 12 reside on campus.

Subjects Offered Algebra, American history, art, band, biology, biology-AP, calculus, calculus-AP, chemistry, chemistry-AP, computer programming, computer science, creative writing, debate, drama, driver education, economics, English, English literature, English-AP, European history, fine arts, French, geography, geometry, history, human development, law, mathematics, music, physical education, physics, physics-AP, psychology, science, social science, social studies, Spanish, speech, statistics-AP, theater, trigonometry, world history, world history-AP.

Graduation Requirements Computer science, English, mathematics, physical education (includes health), science, social science, social studies (includes history).

Special Academic Programs Advanced Placement exam preparation in 10 subject areas; honors section; independent study; study at local college for college credit; ESL (15 students enrolled).

College Placement 80 students graduated in 2005; 78 went to college, including McGill University; Queen's University at Kingston; The University of Western Ontario; The University of Winnipeg; University of Manitoba; University of Toronto. Other: 1 went to work, 1 had other specific plans.

Student Life Upper grades have uniform requirement, student council, honor system. Discipline rests equally with students and faculty.

Tuition and Aid Day student tuition: CAN$12,090; 7-day tuition and room/board: CAN$22,850–CAN$30,550. Tuition installment plan (The Tuition Plan, FACTS Tuition Payment Plan, monthly payment plans, individually arranged payment plans). Bursaries, merit scholarship grants available. In 2005–06, 28% of upper-school students received aid; total upper-school merit-scholarship money awarded: CAN$119,300. Total amount of financial aid awarded in 2005–06: CAN$324,500.

Admissions Traditional secondary-level entrance grade is 9. For fall 2005, 242 students applied for upper-level admission, 43 were accepted, 33 enrolled. Otis-Lennon School Ability Test and school's own exam required. Deadline for receipt of application materials: none. Application fee required: CAN$100. Interview recommended.

Athletics Interscholastic: badminton (boys, girls), basketball (b,g), cross-country running (b,g), golf (b), hockey (b,g), ice hockey (b,g), rugby (b), soccer (b,g), track and field (b,g), ultimate Frisbee (b,g), volleyball (b,g); intramural: cross-country running (g), dance (g), self defense (g), ultimate Frisbee (b,g); coed interscholastic: badminton, physical fitness, running, skiing (cross-country), ultimate Frisbee; coed intramural: basketball, climbing, floor hockey, hockey, ice hockey, indoor soccer, physical fitness, running, soccer, ultimate Frisbee, wall climbing. 5 PE instructors.

Computers Computers are regularly used in business skills, career exploration, college planning, creative writing, English, history, library skills, newspaper, science, social studies, yearbook classes. Computer network features include campus e-mail, on-campus library services, CD-ROMs, Internet access, file transfer, office computer access, DVD, wireless campus network, EBSCO.

Contact Ms. Jane L. Baizley, Director of Admissions. 204-477-2400. Fax: 204-477-2429. E-mail: admissions@sjr.ca. Web site: www.sjr.mb.ca.

SAINT JOHN'S SCHOOL

911 North Marine Corps Drive
Tumon, Guam 96913
Head of School: Dr. Jorge O. Nelson

General Information Coeducational boarding and day college-preparatory, religious studies, and bilingual studies school, affiliated with Episcopal Church. Boarding grades 9–12, day grades PK–12. Founded: 1962. Setting: urban. Nearest major city is Manila. Students are housed in single-sex apartments. 17-acre campus. 7 buildings on campus. Approved or accredited by International Baccalaureate Organization, National Association of Episcopal Schools, The College Board, Western Association of Schools and Colleges, and Guam Department of Education. Language of instruction: English. Endowment: $3.5 million. Total enrollment: 520. Upper school average class size: 12. Upper school faculty-student ratio: 1:12.

Upper School Student Profile 3% of students are boarding students. 1 state is represented in upper school student body. 100% are international students. International students from Palau; 10 other countries represented in student body. 10% of students are members of Episcopal Church.

Faculty School total: 60. In upper school: 16 men, 13 women; 13 have advanced degrees; 7 reside on campus.

Subjects Offered Algebra, American government, American history, American literature, anatomy, ancient world history, art, art history, Asian history, biology, biotechnology, chemistry, Christian education, computer applications, computers, creative writing, current events, dance, drama, drawing and design, earth science, economics, English, environmental science, ethics, European history, film, geography, geometry, health, history of the Americas, honors algebra, honors geometry, human sexuality, International Baccalaureate courses, Japanese, journalism, language arts, library assistant, library skills, Life of Christ, life science, marine science, math methods, mathematics, modern languages, modern world history, music, mythology, nutrition, personal fitness, philosophy, physical education, physics, pre-algebra, reading, religion, science, social sciences, social studies, Spanish, speech, theory of knowledge, trigonometry, weight training, world history, yearbook.

Graduation Requirements Algebra, arts and fine arts (art, music, dance, drama), English, foreign language, geometry, mathematics, physical education (includes health), social science, theory of knowledge.

Special Academic Programs International Baccalaureate program; Advanced Placement exam preparation; honors section; ESL.

College Placement 31 students graduated in 2005; 30 went to college, including Hawai'i Pacific University; Santa Clara University; University of California, Santa Barbara; University of Pennsylvania; University of Portland; University of Southern California. Other: 1 entered a postgraduate year. Mean SAT verbal: 602, mean SAT math: 656. 44% scored over 600 on SAT verbal, 67% scored over 600 on SAT math.

Student Life Upper grades have uniform requirement, student council, honor system. Discipline rests primarily with faculty. Attendance at religious services is required.

Summer Programs Remediation, enrichment, advancement, ESL, sports, art/fine arts, computer instruction programs offered; session focuses on enrichment; held on campus; accepts boys and girls; open to students from other schools. 100 students usually enrolled. 2006 schedule: June 12 to July 21. Application deadline: May 30.

Tuition and Aid Day student tuition: $10,300–$12,900; 7-day tuition and room/board: $27,500. Tuition installment plan (Insured Tuition Payment Plan, monthly payment plans). Tuition reduction for siblings, merit scholarship grants, need-based scholarship grants available. In 2005–06, 23% of upper-school students received aid; total upper-school merit-scholarship money awarded: $261,200. Total amount of financial aid awarded in 2005–06: $500,000.

Admissions Admissions testing required. Deadline for receipt of application materials: none. Application fee required: $50. Interview required.

Athletics Interscholastic: basketball (boys, girls), cross-country running (b,g), golf (b,g), paddling (b,g), rugby (b,g), soccer (b,g), softball (g), tennis (b,g), track and field (b,g), volleyball (b,g); intramural: fitness (b,g), ocean paddling (b,g), physical fitness (b,g); coed intramural: basketball, kickball, ocean paddling, outdoor activities, outdoor recreation, physical fitness, soccer, softball, strength & conditioning, volleyball. 4 PE instructors, 12 coaches.

Computers Computers are regularly used in all classes. Computer network features include campus e-mail, on-campus library services, CD-ROMs, Internet access, DVD.

Contact Mrs. Emily Caseres, Registrar. 671-646-8080 Ext. 221. Fax: 671-649.6791. E-mail: ecaseres@stjohnsguam.com. Web site: www.stjohnsguam.com.

ST. JOHN'S SCHOOL

1466 Ashford Avenue
San Juan, Puerto Rico 00907-1560
Head of School: Dr. Barry Farnham

General Information Coeducational day college-preparatory school. Grades PK–12. Founded: 1915. Setting: urban. 2-acre campus. 2 buildings on campus. Approved or accredited by Middle States Association of Colleges and Schools and Puerto Rico Department of Education. Member of National Association of Independent Schools. Endowment: $138,000. Total enrollment: 760. Upper school average class size: 15. Upper school faculty-student ratio: 1:12.

Faculty School total: 90. In upper school: 10 men, 19 women; 3 have advanced degrees.

Subjects Offered Algebra, American history, American literature, art, biology, calculus, chemistry, computer math, computer programming, computer science, creative writing, drama, earth science, economics, English, English literature, environmental science, European history, French, geography, geometry, government/civics, grammar, history, journalism, marine biology, mathematics, physical education, physics, psychology, science, social studies, sociology, Spanish, theater, world history, world literature, writing.

Graduation Requirements Electives, English, mathematics, physical education (includes health), science, social studies (includes history), Spanish.

Special Academic Programs Advanced Placement exam preparation in 10 subject areas; independent study.

College Placement 47 students graduated in 2005; 45 went to college, including Columbia University; Duquesne University; Harvard University; The Johns Hopkins

University; Tufts University; Yale University. Median SAT verbal: 530, median SAT math: 560. 28% scored over 600 on SAT verbal, 33% scored over 600 on SAT math.
Student Life Upper grades have uniform requirement, student council, honor system. Discipline rests primarily with faculty.
Summer Programs Enrichment programs offered; session focuses on enrichment and learning skills; held on campus; accepts boys and girls; open to students from other schools. 2006 schedule: June 1 to June 30.
Tuition and Aid Day student tuition: $6500–$6900. Tuition installment plan (semester payment plan). Need-based scholarship grants, need-based loans available. Total amount of financial aid awarded in 2005–06: $29,394.
Admissions For fall 2005, 43 students applied for upper-level admission, 23 were accepted, 22 enrolled. Admissions testing required. Deadline for receipt of application materials: none. Application fee required: $100. On-campus interview required.
Athletics Interscholastic: basketball (boys, girls), indoor soccer (b,g), soccer (b,g), tennis (b,g), volleyball (b,g); intramural: soccer (b,g), volleyball (b,g). 3 PE instructors.
Computers Computers are regularly used in English, mathematics, science classes. Computer resources include on-campus library services, CD-ROMs, Internet access, office computer access.
Contact Annette Hequin, Director of Admissions. 787-728-5343 Ext. 2225. Fax: 787-728-0202. E-mail: ahequin@sjspr.org. Web site: www.sjspr.org.

ST. JOHN'S SCHOOL

2401 Claremont Lane
Houston, Texas 77019-5987
Head of School: John C. Allman

General Information Coeducational day college-preparatory, arts, and technology school. Grades K–12. Founded: 1946. Setting: urban. 28-acre campus. 6 buildings on campus. Approved or accredited by Independent Schools Association of the Southwest. Member of National Association of Independent Schools. Endowment: $51.8 million. Total enrollment: 1,217. Upper school average class size: 14. Upper school faculty-student ratio: 1:7.
Upper School Student Profile Grade 9: 142 students (69 boys, 73 girls); Grade 10: 139 students (68 boys, 71 girls); Grade 11: 123 students (62 boys, 61 girls); Grade 12: 136 students (64 boys, 72 girls).
Faculty School total: 165. In upper school: 31 men, 40 women; 53 have advanced degrees.
Subjects Offered Algebra, American literature, anatomy, architecture, art, biology, biology-AP, calculus, calculus-AP, ceramics, chemistry, chemistry-AP, computer programming, computer science, computer science-AP, creative writing, dance, drama, drawing, economics, English, English language-AP, English literature, English literature-AP, English-AP, European history, European history-AP, French, French language-AP, French literature-AP, French-AP, geometry, government-AP, history, Latin, Latin-AP, mathematics, music, music theory-AP, organic chemistry, painting, philosophy, photography, physical education, physics, physics-AP, physiology, pre-calculus, psychology, psychology-AP, Spanish, Spanish language-AP, Spanish literature-AP, Spanish-AP, statistics-AP, theater, trigonometry, U.S. history, U.S. history-AP, world history, world history-AP.
Graduation Requirements Arts and fine arts (art, music, dance, drama), English, foreign language, mathematics, physical education (includes health), science, social studies (includes history).
Special Academic Programs Advanced Placement exam preparation in 19 subject areas; honors section; independent study; term-away projects; study abroad; academic accommodation for the gifted.
College Placement 126 students graduated in 2005; all went to college, including Duke University; Rice University; Southern Methodist University; Stanford University; The University of Texas at Austin. Median SAT verbal: 700, median SAT math: 720, median combined SAT: 2140.
Student Life Upper grades have uniform requirement, student council, honor system. Discipline rests primarily with faculty.
Tuition and Aid Day student tuition: $15,050. Tuition installment plan (Key Tuition Payment Plan, semi-annual and quarterly payment plans). Need-based scholarship grants, need-based loans, Achiever Loans, prepGATE Loans available. In 2005–06, 10% of upper-school students received aid. Total amount of financial aid awarded in 2005–06: $548,000.
Admissions Traditional secondary-level entrance grade is 9. For fall 2005, 214 students applied for upper-level admission, 41 were accepted, 33 enrolled. ISEE, Otis-Lennon School Ability Test and writing sample required. Deadline for receipt of application materials: December 15. Application fee required: $100. On-campus interview required.
Athletics Interscholastic: baseball (boys), basketball (b,g), cheering (g), cross-country running (b,g), diving (b,g), field hockey (g), football (b), golf (b,g), lacrosse (b,g), soccer (b,g), softball (g), swimming and diving (b,g), tennis (b,g), track and field (b,g), volleyball (b,g), wrestling (b). 15 PE instructors, 25 coaches, 3 trainers.
Computers Computers are regularly used in English, history, mathematics, psychology, science classes. Computer network features include campus e-mail, on-campus library services, CD-ROMs, online commercial services, Internet access, DVD, wireless campus network.

Contact Myrtle Alice Sims, Director of Admissions. 713-850-0222 Ext. 313. Fax: 713-850-4089. Web site: www.sjs.org.

SAINT JOHN'S SCHOOL OF ALBERTA

RR 5
Stony Plain, Alberta T7Z 1X5, Canada
Head of School: Mr. Jason Coates

General Information Coeducational boarding college-preparatory, general academic, and religious studies school, affiliated with Anglican Church of Canada. Boys grades 7–12, girls grades 10–12. Founded: 1968. Setting: rural. Nearest major city is Edmonton, Canada. Students are housed in single-sex dormitories and with grade 12 students in houses. 230-acre campus. 5 buildings on campus. Approved or accredited by Alberta Department of Education. Language of instruction: English. Endowment: CAN$3 million. Total enrollment: 106. Upper school average class size: 16. Upper school faculty-student ratio: 1:10.
Upper School Student Profile Grade 10: 35 students (20 boys, 15 girls); Grade 11: 21 students (12 boys, 9 girls); Grade 12: 15 students (9 boys, 6 girls). 100% of students are boarding students. 81% are province residents. 6 provinces are represented in upper school student body. 8% are international students. International students from China, Japan, Mexico, Saudi Arabia, Taiwan, and United States; 2 other countries represented in student body. 15% of students are members of Anglican Church of Canada.
Faculty School total: 16. In upper school: 12 men, 4 women; 2 have advanced degrees; 6 reside on campus.
Subjects Offered Arts, career and technology systems, English, fine arts, information technology, mathematics, physical education, science, social studies, sports conditioning, student government, survival training, swimming competency, twentieth century ethnic conflicts, United Nations and international issues, weight training, Western civilization, wilderness experience, World War II.
Graduation Requirements Arts and fine arts (art, music, dance, drama), computer science, English, mathematics, physical education (includes health), science, social studies (includes history). Community service is required.
Special Academic Programs Honors section; remedial math; ESL (6 students enrolled).
College Placement 12 students graduated in 2005; 9 went to college, including Augustana College; University of Alberta; University of Calgary. Other: 3 went to work.
Student Life Upper grades have uniform requirement, student council, honor system. Discipline rests primarily with faculty. Attendance at religious services is required.
Summer Programs Remediation programs offered; session focuses on academics and remediation; held on campus; accepts boys and girls; open to students from other schools. 25 students usually enrolled. 2006 schedule: July 2 to July 28. Application deadline: May 5.
Tuition and Aid Day student tuition: CAN$8500; 5-day tuition and room/board: CAN$21,000; 7-day tuition and room/board: CAN$24,000. Tuition reduction for siblings, bursaries, merit scholarship grants available. In 2005–06, 25% of upper-school students received aid; total upper-school merit-scholarship money awarded: CAN$6000. Total amount of financial aid awarded in 2005–06: CAN$130,000.
Admissions Traditional secondary-level entrance grade is 10. For fall 2005, 258 students applied for upper-level admission, 49 were accepted, 46 enrolled. Canada Quick Individual Educational Test required. Deadline for receipt of application materials: August 21. Application fee required: CAN$100. Interview recommended.
Athletics Interscholastic: alpine skiing (boys), aquatics (b), back packing (b), basketball (b), bicycling (b), cross-country running (b), jogging (b), martial arts (b), volleyball (b); intramural: badminton (b), baseball (b), basketball (b), bicycling (b), canoeing/kayaking (b), cross-country running (b), fitness walking (b), floor hockey (b), football (b), hiking/backpacking (b), hockey (b), ice hockey (b), outdoor adventure (b), snowshoeing (b), wilderness survival (b). 4 PE instructors, 7 coaches.
Computers Computers are regularly used in basic skills, career technology, current events, English, ESL, history, independent study, information technology, mathematics, religious studies, remedial study skills, research skills, science, Web site design, wilderness education, writing, yearbook classes. Computer network features include campus e-mail, CD-ROMs, Internet access, DVD.
Contact Mrs. Deb McDonald, Admissions Contact. 780-789-4826 Ext. 127. Fax: 780-848-2395. E-mail: dmcdonald@sjsa.ab.ca. Web site: www.sjsa.ab.ca.

ST. JOSEPH ACADEMY

155 State Road 207
St. Augustine, Florida 32084
Head of School: Mr. Michael H. Heubeck

General Information Coeducational day college-preparatory, religious studies, and technology school, affiliated with Roman Catholic Church. Grades 9–12. Founded: 1866. Setting: suburban. 33-acre campus. 13 buildings on campus. Approved or accredited by Southern Association of Colleges and Schools and Florida Department of Education. Total enrollment: 350. Upper school average class size: 27. Upper school faculty-student ratio: 1:13.

Upper School Student Profile Grade 9: 107 students (53 boys, 54 girls); Grade 10: 92 students (43 boys, 49 girls); Grade 11: 76 students (35 boys, 41 girls); Grade 12: 75 students (36 boys, 39 girls). 72% of students are Roman Catholic.

Faculty School total: 28. In upper school: 12 men, 15 women; 17 have advanced degrees.

Subjects Offered Advanced computer applications, advanced math, Advanced Placement courses, advanced studio art-AP, algebra, American government, American history, American sign language, anatomy and physiology, ancient world history, applied arts, art, art history, Bible studies, biology, biology-AP, calculus-AP, career education, career exploration, career planning, Catholic belief and practice, chemistry, Christianity, church history, clayworking, college counseling, college placement, college planning, community service, computer applications, computer education, computer keyboarding, computer skills, costumes and make-up, creative drama, drama, drama performance, drama workshop, drawing, English, English composition, English language-AP, environmental science, French, government, history of the Catholic Church, honors algebra, honors English, honors geometry, honors U.S. history, honors world history, integrated math, Internet research, life management skills, marine biology, Microsoft, moral theology, peer ministry, personal fitness, physical education, physics, play production, playwriting and directing, portfolio art, pottery, pre-algebra, pre-calculus, psychology, religious education, senior career experience, Shakespeare, Spanish, Spanish language-AP, Spanish literature-AP, theology, U.S. history, weight training.

Special Academic Programs Advanced Placement exam preparation in 5 subject areas; honors section; accelerated programs; study at local college for college credit.

College Placement 56 students graduated in 2005; all went to college, including University of Florida; University of North Florida.

Student Life Upper grades have uniform requirement, student council, honor system. Discipline rests primarily with faculty. Attendance at religious services is required.

Tuition and Aid Day student tuition: $5960–$7460. Tuition installment plan (FACTS Tuition Payment Plan). Need-based scholarship grants available. In 2005–06, 22% of upper-school students received aid. Total amount of financial aid awarded in 2005–06: $70,000.

Admissions Traditional secondary-level entrance grade is 9. ACT-Explore, any standardized test, Gates MacGinite Reading Tests, Iowa Tests of Basic Skills, Iowa Tests of Basic Skills-Grades 7-8, Archdiocese HSEPT-Grade 9, PSAT or SAT required. Deadline for receipt of application materials: none. Application fee required: $440. Interview required.

Athletics Interscholastic: baseball (boys), basketball (b,g), cross-country running (b,g), flag football (g), football (b), golf (b), physical fitness (b,g), soccer (b,g), softball (g), swimming and diving (b,g), volleyball (g), winter soccer (b,g), wrestling (b). 2 coaches.

Computers Computers are regularly used in all classes. Computer network features include on-campus library services, CD-ROMs, Internet access, DVD.

Contact Mrs. Diane M. Albano, Director, Admissions and Development. 904-824-0431 Ext. 307. Fax: 904-824-4412. E-mail: admissions@sjaweb.org. Web site: www.sjaweb.org.

SAINT JOSEPH CENTRAL CATHOLIC HIGH SCHOOL

702 Croghan Street
Fremont, Ohio 43420
Head of School: Mr. Michael Gabel

General Information Coeducational day college-preparatory, arts, business, religious studies, bilingual studies, and technology school, affiliated with Roman Catholic Church. Grades 9–12. Founded: 1893. Setting: small town. Nearest major city is Toledo. 5-acre campus. 1 building on campus. Approved or accredited by Ohio Department of Education. Endowment: $380,000. Total enrollment: 276. Upper school average class size: 20. Upper school faculty-student ratio: 1:13.

Upper School Student Profile Grade 9: 71 students (28 boys, 43 girls); Grade 10: 62 students (36 boys, 26 girls); Grade 11: 70 students (35 boys, 35 girls); Grade 12: 73 students (39 boys, 34 girls). 97% of students are Roman Catholic.

Faculty School total: 27. In upper school: 9 men, 17 women; 5 have advanced degrees.

Subjects Offered Advanced computer applications, advanced math, American history, American literature, art, band, biology, biology-AP, bookkeeping, calculus, Catholic belief and practice, chemistry, choir, desktop publishing, drama, earth science, English, environmental science, family and consumer science, French, general business, graphic design, health education, honors English, human biology, integrated math, philosophy, physical education, physics, probability and statistics, programming, psychology, public speaking, reading/study skills, religion, senior project, social justice, social studies, Spanish, yearbook.

Graduation Requirements Computer literacy, English, government, humanities, mathematics, physical education (includes health), religion (includes Bible studies and theology), science, social studies (includes history), citizenship.

Special Academic Programs Advanced Placement exam preparation in 1 subject area; honors section; study at local college for college credit; remedial reading and/or remedial writing; remedial math.

College Placement 67 students graduated in 2005; 63 went to college, including Bowling Green State University; Miami University; Ohio University; The Ohio State University; University of Dayton. Other: 3 went to work, 1 entered military service.

Student Life Upper grades have uniform requirement, student council, honor system. Discipline rests primarily with faculty. Attendance at religious services is required.

Tuition and Aid Day student tuition: $4000. Tuition reduction for siblings, merit scholarship grants, need-based scholarship grants available. In 2005–06, 19% of upper-school students received aid; total upper-school merit-scholarship money awarded: $2000. Total amount of financial aid awarded in 2005–06: $20,000.

Admissions Traditional secondary-level entrance grade is 9. For fall 2005, 276 students applied for upper-level admission, 276 were accepted, 276 enrolled. High School Placement Test required. Deadline for receipt of application materials: none. Application fee required: $100.

Athletics Interscholastic: baseball (boys), basketball (b), bowling (b,g), cheering (g), cross-country running (b,g), football (b), golf (b), soccer (b,g), softball (g), swimming and diving (b,g), tennis (b,g), track and field (b,g), volleyball (g), wrestling (b); intramural: indoor track & field (b,g); coed intramural: basketball. 1 PE instructor, 10 coaches.

Computers Computers are regularly used in Spanish, yearbook classes. Computer network features include Internet access, file transfer, wireless campus network.

Contact Mrs. Kathy Bouskissen, Development Director. 419-332-9947. Fax: 419-332-4945. E-mail: kboukiss@fremontstjoe.org. Web site: www.fremontstjoe.org.

ST. JOSEPH HIGH SCHOOL

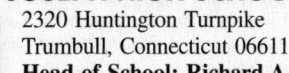

2320 Huntington Turnpike
Trumbull, Connecticut 06611
Head of School: Richard A. Bishop

General Information Coeducational day college-preparatory, business, and religious studies school, affiliated with Roman Catholic Church. Grades 9–12. Founded: 1962. Setting: suburban. Nearest major city is New Haven. 25-acre campus. 2 buildings on campus. Approved or accredited by New England Association of Schools and Colleges and Connecticut Department of Education. Total enrollment: 850. Upper school average class size: 23. Upper school faculty-student ratio: 1:14.

Upper School Student Profile 85% of students are Roman Catholic.

Faculty School total: 68. In upper school: 30 men, 38 women; 47 have advanced degrees.

Subjects Offered 1968, accounting, algebra, American history, American literature, art, art history, band, biology, business skills, calculus, chemistry, chorus, community service, computer applications, current events, design, drawing, driver education, earth science, ecology, economics, English, English literature, European history, finance, fine arts, French, geography, geometry, government/civics, health, history, international relations, Italian, journalism, Latin, law, mathematics, music, painting, philosophy, physical education, physics, poetry, pre-calculus, psychology, religion, science, sculpture, Shakespeare, social studies, sociology, Spanish, statistics, study skills, theology, trigonometry, word processing.

Graduation Requirements Arts and fine arts (art, music, dance, drama), business skills (includes word processing), English, foreign language, mathematics, physical education (includes health), religion (includes Bible studies and theology), science, social studies (includes history), study skills. Community service is required.

Special Academic Programs Advanced Placement exam preparation in 7 subject areas; honors section; study at local college for college credit; academic accommodation for the gifted; special instructional classes for students with learning disabilities and Attention Deficit Disorder.

College Placement 194 students graduated in 2005; 193 went to college, including Boston College; Boston University; Fairfield University; Providence College; Southern Connecticut State University; University of Connecticut. Other: 1 entered military service. Median SAT verbal: 542, median SAT math: 515. 25% scored over 600 on SAT verbal, 21% scored over 600 on SAT math.

Student Life Upper grades have uniform requirement, student council. Discipline rests primarily with faculty. Attendance at religious services is required.

Tuition and Aid Tuition installment plan (monthly payment plans, one lump sum payment with discount by June 1 or two payments by semester, payment plan through People's Bank). Tuition reduction for siblings, merit scholarship grants, need-based scholarship grants available.

Admissions Traditional secondary-level entrance grade is 9. For fall 2005, 407 students applied for upper-level admission, 379 were accepted, 223 enrolled. High School Placement Test and STS—Educational Development Series required. Deadline for receipt of application materials: December 1. Application fee required: $40.

Athletics Interscholastic: baseball (boys), basketball (b,g), cheering (g), cross-country running (b,g), dance team (g), football (b), lacrosse (b), soccer (b,g), softball (g), tennis (b,g), track and field (b,g), volleyball (b,g); coed interscholastic: bowling, golf, swimming and diving, winter (indoor) track; coed intramural: martial arts. 2 PE instructors, 51 coaches, 1 trainer.

Computers Computer network features include on-campus library services, CD-ROMs, online commercial services, Internet access, office computer access.

Contact Peggy Kuhar Marino, Director of Admission. 203-378-9378 Ext. 308. Fax: 203-378-7306. E-mail: pmarino@sjcadets.org. Web site: www.sjcadets.org.

SAINT JOSEPH HIGH SCHOOL

2401 69th Street
Kenosha, Wisconsin 53143
Head of School: Mr. Robert Freund

General Information Coeducational day college-preparatory, general academic, arts, religious studies, and technology school, affiliated with Roman Catholic Church. Grades 7–12. Founded: 1957. Setting: urban. Nearest major city is Milwaukee. 1 building on campus. Approved or accredited by National Catholic Education Association, North Central Association of Colleges and Schools, and Wisconsin Department of Education. Total enrollment: 495. Upper school average class size: 20. Upper school faculty-student ratio: 1:20.

Upper School Student Profile 80% of students are Roman Catholic.

Faculty School total: 34. In upper school: 12 men, 22 women; 16 have advanced degrees.

Subjects Offered Algebra, American government, anatomy and physiology, architecture, art, band, biology, biology-AP, calculus-AP, ceramics, chemistry, chemistry-AP, choir, Christian scripture, computer applications, computers, consumer mathematics, creative writing, critical writing, drafting, drama, drawing, economics, English, English-AP, film, French, geometry, health, Hebrew scripture, journalism, keyboarding, mathematics, newspaper, photography, physical education, physical science, physics-AP, pre-algebra, pre-calculus, psychology, reading/study skills, science, social studies, Spanish, speech, statistics, studio art, theater, theology, trigonometry, U.S. history, world history, world religions, yearbook.

Graduation Requirements Arts and fine arts (art, music, dance, drama), computers, electives, English, mathematics, physical education (includes health), religion (includes Bible studies and theology), science, social studies (includes history).

Special Academic Programs Advanced Placement exam preparation in 4 subject areas; honors section; special instructional classes for students with learning disabilities, Attention Deficit Disorder, and dyslexia.

College Placement 62 students graduated in 2005; 58 went to college, including Cardinal Stritch University; Marquette University; University of Notre Dame; University of Wisconsin–Madison; University of Wisconsin–Milwaukee. Other: 2 went to work, 2 entered military service. Mean composite ACT: 22. 21% scored over 26 on composite ACT.

Student Life Upper grades have uniform requirement, student council, honor system. Discipline rests primarily with faculty. Attendance at religious services is required.

Tuition and Aid Day student tuition: $5650. Tuition installment plan (FACTS Tuition Payment Plan, individually arranged payment plans). Tuition reduction for siblings, merit scholarship grants, need-based scholarship grants available. In 2005–06, 28% of upper-school students received aid; total upper-school merit-scholarship money awarded: $7500. Total amount of financial aid awarded in 2005–06: $48,450.

Admissions Traditional secondary-level entrance grade is 9. Admissions testing required. Deadline for receipt of application materials: none. Application fee required: $100.

Athletics Interscholastic: baseball (boys), basketball (b,g), cheering (b,g), cross-country running (b,g), football (b), golf (b,g), soccer (b,g), softball (g), tennis (b,g), track and field (b,g), volleyball (g), wrestling (b). 2 PE instructors.

Computers Computers are regularly used in all classes. Computer resources include campus e-mail, CD-ROMs, online commercial services, Internet access, file transfer, office computer access.

Contact Mrs. Molly Whyte, Recruitment Director. 262-654-8651 Ext. 108. Fax: 262-654-1615. E-mail: mwhyte@kenoshastjoseph.com. Web site: www.kenoshastjoseph.com.

ST. JOSEPH'S ACADEMY

3015 Broussard Street
Baton Rouge, Louisiana 70808
Head of School: Linda Fryoux Harvison

General Information Girls' day college-preparatory and technology school, affiliated with Roman Catholic Church. Grades 9–12. Founded: 1868. Setting: urban. 14-acre campus. 6 buildings on campus. Approved or accredited by National Catholic Education Association, Southern Association of Colleges and Schools, Southern Association of Independent Schools, and Louisiana Department of Education. Endowment: $3.6 million. Total enrollment: 872. Upper school average class size: 23. Upper school faculty-student ratio: 1:12.

Upper School Student Profile Grade 9: 221 students (221 girls); Grade 10: 224 students (224 girls); Grade 11: 202 students (202 girls); Grade 12: 225 students (225 girls). 96% of students are Roman Catholic.

Faculty School total: 62. In upper school: 5 men, 57 women; 41 have advanced degrees.

Subjects Offered Advanced chemistry, advanced computer applications, advanced math, Advanced Placement courses, algebra, American history-AP, American literature-AP, analysis, analysis and differential calculus, art, art appreciation, band, Basic programming, Bible, biology, biology-AP, calculus-AP, campus ministry, Catholic belief and practice, chemistry, child development, choir, choral music, chorus, Christian and Hebrew scripture, church history, civics, civics/free enterprise, computer applications, computer information systems, computer multimedia, computer programming, computer technologies, CPR, critical studies in film, desktop

publishing, economics, English, English literature-AP, English-AP, entrepreneurship, European history-AP, family and consumer science, family and consumer sciences, film and literature, foreign language, French, French as a second language, French-AP, geometry, grammar, health, health and safety, Hebrew scripture, honors algebra, honors English, honors geometry, human sexuality, independent study, information technology, Latin, marching band, media arts, media production, novels, physical education, physical fitness, physics, poetry, pre-calculus, public speaking, religion, research, social justice, Spanish, speech, speech communications, technology, the Web, transition mathematics, U.S. history, U.S. history-AP, U.S. literature, Web authoring, Web site design, world history-AP.

Graduation Requirements Advanced math, algebra, American history, arts and fine arts (art, music, dance, drama), biology, chemistry, civics, computer applications, English, foreign language, geometry, physical education (includes health), physical science, physics, religion (includes Bible studies and theology), world history, service hours.

Special Academic Programs Advanced Placement exam preparation in 7 subject areas; honors section; independent study.

College Placement 185 students graduated in 2005; 184 went to college, including Auburn University; Louisiana State University and Agricultural and Mechanical College; Louisiana Tech University; Loyola University New Orleans; University of Louisiana at Lafayette; University of Mississippi. Other: 1 went to work. 68% scored over 26 on composite ACT.

Student Life Upper grades have uniform requirement, student council, honor system. Discipline rests primarily with faculty. Attendance at religious services is required.

Summer Programs Computer instruction programs offered; session focuses on computer applications for incoming 9th grade students; held on campus; accepts girls; not open to students from other schools. 220 students usually enrolled. 2006 schedule: June 6 to July 19. Application deadline: March 17.

Tuition and Aid Day student tuition: $7200. Tuition installment plan (monthly debit plan). Need-based scholarship grants, need-based loans available. In 2005–06, 6% of upper-school students received aid. Total amount of financial aid awarded in 2005–06: $160,000.

Admissions Traditional secondary-level entrance grade is 9. For fall 2005, 248 students applied for upper-level admission, 236 were accepted, 220 enrolled. STS required. Deadline for receipt of application materials: November 18. Application fee required: $35. On-campus interview required.

Athletics Interscholastic: basketball, bowling, cheering, cross-country running, dance squad, golf, gymnastics, running, soccer, softball, strength & conditioning, swimming and diving, tennis, track and field, volleyball. 4 PE instructors, 7 coaches, 1 trainer.

Computers Computers are regularly used in all classes. Computer network features include campus e-mail, on-campus library services, CD-ROMs, online commercial services, Internet access, file transfer, office computer access, DVD, wireless campus network, administrative software/grading/scheduling.

Contact Kathy Meares, Assistant Principal of Records. 225-383-7207. Fax: 225-344-5714. E-mail: mearesk@sjabr.org. Web site: www.sjabr.org.

ST. JOSEPH'S CATHOLIC SCHOOL

100 St. Joseph's Drive
Greenville, South Carolina 29607
Head of School: Mr. Keith F. Kiser

General Information Coeducational day college-preparatory school, affiliated with Roman Catholic Church. Grades 6–12. Founded: 1993. Setting: suburban. 36-acre campus. 3 buildings on campus. Approved or accredited by South Carolina Independent School Association and South Carolina Department of Education. Total enrollment: 425. Upper school average class size: 16. Upper school faculty-student ratio: 1:11.

Upper School Student Profile Grade 9: 57 students (31 boys, 26 girls); Grade 10: 59 students (22 boys, 37 girls); Grade 11: 72 students (34 boys, 38 girls); Grade 12: 59 students (30 boys, 29 girls). 77% of students are Roman Catholic.

Faculty School total: 41. In upper school: 9 men, 19 women; 10 have advanced degrees.

Subjects Offered Algebra, American history, American literature, art, arts appreciation, bell choir, biology, biology-AP, calculus-AP, chemistry, chemistry-AP, chorus, Christian doctrine, church history, computer applications, computer graphics, dance, English literature and composition-AP, English-AP, ensembles, European history, European history-AP, European literature, fine arts, forensic science, French, geometry, government, government-AP, honors algebra, honors English, honors geometry, human movement and its application to health, Latin, literature, newspaper, physics, physics-AP, pre-calculus, Spanish, Spanish-AP, speech, theater arts, theater production, U.S. history, U.S. history-AP, yearbook.

Graduation Requirements 60 hours of community service.

Special Academic Programs Advanced Placement exam preparation in 13 subject areas; honors section.

College Placement 63 students graduated in 2005; all went to college, including Clemson University; College of Charleston; University of South Carolina. Median SAT verbal: 613, median SAT math: 599, median composite ACT: 26.

Student Life Upper grades have uniform requirement, student council, honor system. Discipline rests primarily with faculty. Attendance at religious services is required.

Tuition and Aid Tuition installment plan (monthly payment plans). Tuition reduction for siblings, merit scholarship grants, need-based scholarship grants available. In 2005–06, 24% of upper-school students received aid; total upper-school merit-scholarship money awarded: $26,000. Total amount of financial aid awarded in 2005–06: $100,000.

Admissions Traditional secondary-level entrance grade is 9. High School Placement Test (closed version) from Scholastic Testing Service required. Deadline for receipt of application materials: May 31. Application fee required: $125. On-campus interview required.

Athletics Interscholastic: baseball (boys), basketball (b,g), cheering (g), cross-country running (b,g), golf (b), soccer (b,g), softball (g), tennis (b,g), volleyball (g), wrestling (b); intramural: field hockey (g), flag football (b); coed interscholastic: swimming and diving; coed intramural: bowling, dance, weight training, yoga.

Computers Computer network features include campus e-mail, Internet access.

Contact Mrs. Barbara L. McGrath, Director of Admissions. 864-234-9009 Ext. 104. Fax: 864-234-5516. E-mail: bmcgrath@sjcatholicschool.org. Web site: www.sjcatholicschool.org.

SAINT JOSEPH'S HIGH SCHOOL

145 Plainfield Avenue
Metuchen, New Jersey 08840
Head of School: Mr. Lawrence N. Walsh

General Information Boys' day college-preparatory, arts, religious studies, and technology school, affiliated with Roman Catholic Church. Grades 9–12. Founded: 1961. Setting: suburban. Nearest major city is New York, NY. 80-acre campus. 8 buildings on campus. Approved or accredited by Middle States Association of Colleges and Schools, National Catholic Education Association, and New Jersey Department of Education. Endowment: $470,000. Total enrollment: 850. Upper school average class size: 23. Upper school faculty-student ratio: 1:18.

Upper School Student Profile Grade 9: 229 students (229 boys); Grade 10: 219 students (219 boys); Grade 11: 204 students (204 boys); Grade 12: 198 students (198 boys). 85% of students are Roman Catholic.

Faculty School total: 60. In upper school: 39 men, 21 women; 45 have advanced degrees.

Subjects Offered Accounting, acting, algebra, American history, American history-AP, American literature, art, arts, astronomy, biology, biology-AP, calculus, calculus-AP, chemistry, chemistry-AP, computer programming, computer science, discrete math, driver education, English, English literature, European history, European history-AP, French, geometry, German, history, journalism, Latin, mathematics, meteorology, music, photography, physical education, physics, physics-AP, public speaking, religion, social studies, Spanish, stagecraft, technical drawing, theology, world history, world literature, writing.

Graduation Requirements Arts and fine arts (art, music, dance, drama), computer science, English, foreign language, lab science, mathematics, physical education (includes health), religion (includes Bible studies and theology), science, social studies (includes history). Community service is required.

Special Academic Programs Advanced Placement exam preparation in 8 subject areas; honors section; independent study; study at local college for college credit.

College Placement 199 students graduated in 2005; 198 went to college, including New York University; Rutgers, The State University of New Jersey, Rutgers College; Villanova University. Mean SAT verbal: 551, mean SAT math: 570. 33% scored over 600 on SAT verbal, 43% scored over 600 on SAT math.

Student Life Upper grades have specified standards of dress, student council, honor system. Discipline rests primarily with faculty. Attendance at religious services is required.

Summer Programs Remediation, enrichment, advancement, sports, computer instruction programs offered; session focuses on remediation and enrichment; held on campus; accepts boys and girls; open to students from other schools. 205 students usually enrolled. 2006 schedule: June 27 to July 22. Application deadline: June 17.

Tuition and Aid Day student tuition: $8100. Tuition installment plan (FACTS Tuition Payment Plan, individually arranged payment plans). Merit scholarship grants, need-based scholarship grants available. In 2005–06, 10% of upper-school students received aid. Total amount of financial aid awarded in 2005–06: $85,200.

Admissions Traditional secondary-level entrance grade is 9. For fall 2005, 555 students applied for upper-level admission, 275 were accepted, 240 enrolled. High School Placement Test required. Deadline for receipt of application materials: none. No application fee required.

Athletics Interscholastic: baseball, basketball, bowling, cross-country running, golf, ice hockey, indoor track & field, lacrosse, soccer, swimming and diving, tennis, track and field, ultimate Frisbee, volleyball, winter (indoor) track; intramural: flag football, football, ultimate Frisbee. 2 PE instructors, 41 coaches, 1 trainer.

Computers Computers are regularly used in animation, desktop publishing, drawing and design, graphics, journalism, news writing, newspaper, photography, publications, publishing, science, technical drawing, Web site design, word processing, yearbook classes. Computer network features include campus e-mail, on-campus library services, CD-ROMs, online commercial services, Internet access, file transfer, office computer access.

Contact Mrs. Susan Kaloyerakis, Secretary. 732-549-7600 Ext. 221. Fax: 732-549-0664. Web site: www.stjoes.org.

ST. JOSEPH'S PREPARATORY SCHOOL

1733 Girard Avenue
Philadelphia, Pennsylvania 19130
Head of School: Rev. Bruce M. Bidinger, SJ

General Information Boys' day college-preparatory, arts, and religious studies school, affiliated with Roman Catholic Church. Grades 9–12. Founded: 1851. Setting: urban. 7-acre campus. 2 buildings on campus. Approved or accredited by Jesuit Secondary Education Association, Middle States Association of Colleges and Schools, National Catholic Education Association, and Pennsylvania Department of Education. Member of National Association of Independent Schools. Endowment: $3.5 million. Total enrollment: 976. Upper school average class size: 26. Upper school faculty-student ratio: 1:16.

Upper School Student Profile Grade 9: 230 students (230 boys); Grade 10: 259 students (259 boys); Grade 11: 236 students (236 boys); Grade 12: 251 students (251 boys). 95% of students are Roman Catholic.

Faculty School total: 65. In upper school: 49 men, 13 women; 40 have advanced degrees.

Subjects Offered Algebra, American history, American literature, anatomy, archaeology, art, biology, business, calculus, chemistry, classics, computer math, computer programming, computer science, driver education, earth science, English, English literature, environmental science, ethics, European history, fine arts, French, geometry, German, government/civics, Greek, history, Latin, Mandarin, marine biology, mathematics, photography, physical education, physics, physiology, religion, science, social science, social studies, Spanish, speech, trigonometry, world history, world literature.

Graduation Requirements Arts and fine arts (art, music, dance, drama), classics, computer science, English, foreign language, mathematics, physical education (includes health), religion (includes Bible studies and theology), science, social science, social studies (includes history), Christian service hours in junior and senior year.

Special Academic Programs Advanced Placement exam preparation in 14 subject areas; honors section; accelerated programs; independent study; study at local college for college credit; study abroad; academic accommodation for the gifted, the musically talented, and the artistically talented.

College Placement 251 students graduated in 2005; they went to Boston College; College of the Holy Cross; Fordham University; Georgetown University; Saint Joseph's University; University of Pennsylvania. Mean SAT verbal: 613, mean SAT math: 619. 55% scored over 600 on SAT verbal, 50% scored over 600 on SAT math.

Student Life Upper grades have specified standards of dress, student council. Discipline rests primarily with faculty. Attendance at religious services is required.

Summer Programs Remediation, enrichment, art/fine arts programs offered; session focuses on pre-8th grade enrichment; held on campus; accepts boys and girls; open to students from other schools. 500 students usually enrolled. 2006 schedule: June 27 to July 27. Application deadline: none.

Tuition and Aid Day student tuition: $13,600. Tuition installment plan (monthly payment plans). Tuition reduction for siblings, merit scholarship grants, need-based scholarship grants, need-based loans, middle-income loans, paying campus jobs available. In 2005–06, 66% of upper-school students received aid; total upper-school merit-scholarship money awarded: $260,000. Total amount of financial aid awarded in 2005–06: $1,300,000.

Admissions Traditional secondary-level entrance grade is 9. For fall 2005, 663 students applied for upper-level admission, 270 were accepted, 230 enrolled. 3-R Achievement Test required. Deadline for receipt of application materials: November 11. Application fee required: $50. On-campus interview recommended.

Athletics Interscholastic: baseball, basketball, bowling, crew, cross-country running, football, golf, ice hockey, indoor track & field, lacrosse, rowing, soccer, swimming and diving, tennis, track and field, ultimate Frisbee, wrestling; intramural: basketball, juggling, martial arts, rugby, table tennis, volleyball. 35 coaches, 1 trainer.

Computers Computers are regularly used in English, mathematics, science classes. Computer network features include campus e-mail, on-campus library services, CD-ROMs, Internet access, file transfer, DVD, wireless campus network.

Contact Jason M. Zazyczny, Director of Admission. 215-978-1958. Fax: 215-978-1920. E-mail: jzazyczny@sjprep.org. Web site: www.sjprep.org.

SAINT LAURENCE HIGH SCHOOL

5556 West 77th Street
Burbank, Illinois 60459-1398
Head of School: Mr. Tom Ondrla

General Information Boys' day college-preparatory school, affiliated with Roman Catholic Church. Grades 9–12. Founded: 1961. Setting: suburban. Nearest major city is Chicago. 26-acre campus. 1 building on campus. Approved or accredited by Christian Brothers Association, North Central Association of Colleges and Schools, and Illinois Department of Education. Total enrollment: 650. Upper school average class size: 23. Upper school faculty-student ratio: 1:18.

Upper School Student Profile 92% of students are Roman Catholic.

Faculty In upper school: 28 men, 8 women; 18 have advanced degrees.

Saint Laurence High School

Special Academic Programs Advanced Placement exam preparation in 12 subject areas; honors section; independent study; remedial reading and/or remedial writing; remedial math.

College Placement 147 students graduated in 2005; 140 went to college. Other: 1 went to work, 5 entered military service.

Student Life Upper grades have uniform requirement, student council. Discipline rests primarily with faculty.

Summer Programs Remediation, sports programs offered; held on campus; accepts boys and girls; open to students from other schools. 100 students usually enrolled. 2006 schedule: June 11 to July 28.

Tuition and Aid Day student tuition: $6500. Tuition installment plan (monthly payment plans). Tuition reduction for siblings, merit scholarship grants, need-based scholarship grants available. In 2005–06, 52% of upper-school students received aid. Total amount of financial aid awarded in 2005–06: $400,000.

Admissions Explore required. Deadline for receipt of application materials: none. Application fee required: $25. Interview required.

Athletics Interscholastic: ball hockey, baseball, basketball, bowling, cheering (g), combined training, cooperative games, cross-country running, fitness, flag football, floor hockey, football, golf, hockey, ice hockey, kickball, physical fitness, physical training, power lifting, soccer, strength & conditioning, tennis, track and field, volleyball, wallyball, weight lifting, weight training, wrestling. 3 PE instructors, 100 coaches, 1 trainer.

Computers Computer resources include on-campus library services, CD-ROMs, Internet access, file transfer, DVD.

Contact Mr. Dennis O'Connell, Admissions Director. 708-458-6900 Ext. 237. Fax: 708-458-6908. E-mail: doconnell@stlaurence.com. Web site: www.stlaurence.com.

ST. LEONARDS

St. Andrews
Fife, Scotland KY16 9QJ, United Kingdom
Head of School: Robert Tims

General Information Coeducational boarding and day college-preparatory, general academic, arts, business, bilingual studies, and technology school. Boarding grades 4–13, day grades N–13. Founded: 1877. Setting: small town. Nearest major city is Edinburgh. Students are housed in single-sex dormitories. 26-acre campus. 8 buildings on campus. Approved or accredited by Scottish Education Department. Language of instruction: English. Total enrollment: 390. Upper school average class size: 10. Upper school faculty-student ratio: 1:7.

Upper School Student Profile Grade 12: 55 students (19 boys, 36 girls); Grade 13: 44 students (20 boys, 24 girls). 72% of students are boarding students. 65% are international students. International students from China and Germany.

Faculty In upper school: 9 men, 29 women; 3 have advanced degrees; 5 reside on campus.

Subjects Offered 20th century physics, 20th century world history, 3-dimensional art, 3-dimensional design, acting, adolescent issues, advanced chemistry, advanced computer applications, advanced math, advanced TOEFL/grammar, Ancient Greek, art, art history, arts, biology, British history, business, career and personal planning, chemistry, classics, computer literacy, computer skills, creative arts, design, drama, economics, English, English as a foreign language, European history, geography, German, Greek, history, humanities, Latin, mathematics, modern history, modern languages, music, personal and social education, physics, politics, psychology, religious studies, science, theater design and production, vocal ensemble, voice, wind ensemble, wind instruments, word processing, work experience, world geography, world history.

Special Academic Programs International Baccalaureate program; study at local college for college credit; academic accommodation for the gifted, the musically talented, and the artistically talented; remedial reading and/or remedial writing; programs in English, mathematics, general development for dyslexic students; ESL (25 students enrolled).

College Placement Colleges students went to include Yale University.

Student Life Upper grades have specified standards of dress, student council, honor system. Discipline rests equally with students and faculty.

Tuition and Aid Day student tuition: £8271; 7-day tuition and room/board: £20,262. Tuition installment plan (monthly payment plans, individually arranged payment plans). Merit scholarship grants available.

Admissions Traditional secondary-level entrance grade is 12. For fall 2005, 33 students applied for upper-level admission, 33 were accepted, 33 enrolled. School's own exam required. Deadline for receipt of application materials: none. Application fee required: £100. Interview recommended.

Athletics Interscholastic: equestrian sports (girls); intramural: aerobics (g), aerobics/dance (g), ballet (g), cricket (b), netball (g), rugby (b), soccer (b), yoga (g); coed interscholastic: alpine skiing, cross-country running, freestyle skiing, golf, horseback riding, lacrosse, skiing (downhill), squash, swimming and diving, tennis, track and field, winter soccer; coed intramural: archery, back packing, badminton, ball hockey, basketball, bicycling, canoeing/kayaking, cross-country running, dance, equestrian sports, fencing, field hockey, fitness, freestyle skiing, golf, gymnastics, hiking/backpacking, hockey, horseback riding, indoor hockey, indoor soccer, judo, lacrosse, life saving, outdoor activities, outdoors, physical fitness, rock climbing, running, sailing, self defense, skiing (downhill), squash, swimming and diving, table tennis,

tennis, track and field, volleyball, wall climbing, weight training, wilderness survival, winter soccer. 3 PE instructors, 13 coaches.

Computers Computers are regularly used in art, career exploration, English, French, geography, history, information technology, language development, library skills, mathematics, music, research skills, Spanish, technical drawing classes. Computer network features include campus e-mail, on-campus library services, CD-ROMs, Internet access, file transfer.

Contact Jennifer Wylie, Registrar. 44-1334-472126. Fax: 44-1334 476152. E-mail: info@stleonards-fife.org. Web site: www.stleonards-fife.org/.

SAINT LOUIS PRIORY SCHOOL

500 South Mason Road
St. Louis, Missouri 63141
Head of School: Rev. Michael Brunner, OSB

General Information Boys' day college-preparatory and religious studies school, affiliated with Roman Catholic Church. Grades 7–12. Founded: 1955. Setting: suburban. 155-acre campus. 9 buildings on campus. Approved or accredited by Independent Schools Association of the Central States. Member of National Association of Independent Schools and Educational Records Bureau. Endowment: $14 million. Total enrollment: 392. Upper school average class size: 17. Upper school faculty-student ratio: 1:8.

Upper School Student Profile Grade 9: 65 students (65 boys); Grade 10: 64 students (64 boys); Grade 11: 61 students (61 boys); Grade 12: 65 students (65 boys). 85% of students are Roman Catholic.

Faculty School total: 54. In upper school: 40 men, 14 women; 38 have advanced degrees.

Subjects Offered Accounting, Advanced Placement courses, algebra, American history, American literature, art, art history, Bible studies, biology, calculus, calligraphy, chemistry, Chinese studies, Civil War, community service, computer math, computer programming, computer science, creative writing, drama, earth science, ecology, economics, English, English literature, environmental science, ethics, European history, expository writing, film series, fine arts, French, general science, geography, geometry, government/civics, grammar, Greek, health, history, Japanese studies, Latin, mathematics, music, philosophy, photography, physical education, physics, religion, science, social studies, Spanish, speech, theater, theology, trigonometry, world history, world literature.

Graduation Requirements Arts and fine arts (art, music, dance, drama), computer science, English, foreign language, mathematics, physical education (includes health), religion (includes Bible studies and theology), science, senior thesis, social studies (includes history); service projects, sports requirements (every season of every year).

Special Academic Programs Advanced Placement exam preparation in 14 subject areas; honors section; independent study; study at local college for college credit; academic accommodation for the gifted.

College Placement 60 students graduated in 2005; all went to college, including Duke University; Georgetown University; United States Naval Academy; University of Notre Dame; University of Pennsylvania; Washington University in St. Louis. Mean SAT verbal: 656, mean SAT math: 661, mean composite ACT: 29. 70% scored over 600 on SAT verbal, 80% scored over 600 on SAT math, 70% scored over 26 on composite ACT.

Student Life Upper grades have specified standards of dress, student council, honor system. Discipline rests primarily with faculty. Attendance at religious services is required.

Summer Programs Remediation, enrichment, art/fine arts, computer instruction programs offered; session focuses on academics and athletics; held on campus; accepts boys and girls; open to students from other schools. 120 students usually enrolled. 2006 schedule: June 12 to July 21. Application deadline: none.

Tuition and Aid Day student tuition: $13,800. Tuition installment plan (monthly payment plans, individually arranged payment plans). Need-based scholarship grants available. In 2005–06, 25% of upper-school students received aid. Total amount of financial aid awarded in 2005–06: $650,000.

Admissions For fall 2005, 154 students applied for upper-level admission, 96 were accepted, 69 enrolled. ISEE or SSAT required. Deadline for receipt of application materials: January 30. Application fee required: $35. Interview required.

Athletics Interscholastic: baseball, basketball, cross-country running, football, golf, ice hockey, rugby, soccer, tennis, track and field; intramural: baseball, basketball, cross-country running, football, physical fitness, racquetball, soccer, softball, tennis, track and field, volleyball, weight lifting. 2 coaches, 1 trainer.

Computers Computers are regularly used in English, foreign language, mathematics, science classes. Computer network features include campus e-mail, on-campus library services, CD-ROMs, online commercial services, Internet access, DVD, wireless campus network.

Contact Dennis P. Guilliams, Director of Admission. 314-434-3690 Ext. 151. Fax: 314-576-7088. E-mail: admissions@priory.org. Web site: www.priory.org/.

SAINT LUCY'S PRIORY HIGH SCHOOL

655 West Sierra Madre Avenue
Glendora, California 91741-1997
Head of School: Sr. Monica Collins

General Information Girls' day college-preparatory, arts, and religious studies school, affiliated with Roman Catholic Church. Grades 9–12. Founded: 1962. Setting: suburban. Nearest major city is Pomona. 20-acre campus. 3 buildings on campus. Approved or accredited by Western Association of Schools and Colleges and California Department of Education. Endowment: $2 million. Total enrollment: 871. Upper school average class size: 26. Upper school faculty-student ratio: 1:22.

Upper School Student Profile Grade 9: 244 students (244 girls); Grade 10: 236 students (236 girls); Grade 11: 208 students (208 girls); Grade 12: 183 students (183 girls). 82% of students are Roman Catholic.

Faculty School total: 43. In upper school: 7 men, 36 women; 11 have advanced degrees.

Subjects Offered Adolescent issues, algebra, art, art appreciation, Bible studies, biology, biology-AP, calculus, calculus-AP, calligraphy, chemistry, commercial art, creative writing, drama, drawing, early childhood, earth science, economics, English, English literature-AP, ethics, European history-AP, French, geometry, health, journalism, kinesiology, painting, physical education, physical science, physics, physics-AP, physiology, psychology, religion, sculpture, sewing, Spanish, Spanish-AP, theater production, trigonometry, U.S. government, U.S. government-AP, U.S. history, U.S. history-AP, voice, world history, world literature, yearbook.

Graduation Requirements Arts and fine arts (art, music, dance, drama), English, foreign language, mathematics, physical education (includes health), religion (includes Bible studies and theology), science, social science, social studies (includes history).

Special Academic Programs Advanced Placement exam preparation in 10 subject areas; honors section.

College Placement 213 students graduated in 2005; all went to college, including California State Polytechnic University, Pomona; California State University, Fullerton; Loyola Marymount University; University of California, Irvine; University of California, Los Angeles; University of California, Riverside. Median SAT verbal: 520, median SAT math: 480. Mean composite ACT: 24. 16.6% scored over 600 on SAT verbal, 11.2% scored over 600 on SAT math.

Student Life Upper grades have uniform requirement, student council. Discipline rests primarily with faculty. Attendance at religious services is required.

Summer Programs Remediation programs offered; session focuses on remediation; held on campus; accepts girls; not open to students from other schools. 115 students usually enrolled. 2006 schedule: June 19 to July 14. Application deadline: June 1.

Tuition and Aid Day student tuition: $5300. Tuition installment plan (quarterly payment plan). Tuition reduction for siblings, merit scholarship grants, need-based scholarship grants available. In 2005–06, 5% of upper-school students received aid; total upper-school merit-scholarship money awarded: $25,000. Total amount of financial aid awarded in 2005–06: $95,000.

Admissions Traditional secondary-level entrance grade is 9. For fall 2005, 375 students applied for upper-level admission, 270 were accepted, 244 enrolled. STS required. Deadline for receipt of application materials: January 21. Application fee required: $125. On-campus interview required.

Athletics Interscholastic: basketball, cross-country running, diving, soccer, softball, swimming and diving, tennis, track and field, water polo; intramural: badminton, basketball, cheering, dance squad, soccer, softball. 2 PE instructors, 36 coaches.

Computers Computers are regularly used in English, foreign language, history, mathematics, music, science classes. Computer resources include CD-ROMs, Internet access, DVD, wireless campus network.

Contact Mrs. Irma Esparza, Secretary. 626-335-3322. Fax: 626-335-4373.

ST. LUKE'S SCHOOL

PO Box 1148
377 North Wilton Road
New Canaan, Connecticut 06840
Head of School: Mr. Mark C. Davis

General Information Coeducational day college-preparatory, arts, and technology school. Grades 5–12. Founded: 1927. Setting: suburban. Nearest major city is New York, NY. 40-acre campus. 5 buildings on campus. Approved or accredited by Connecticut Association of Independent Schools and New England Association of Schools and Colleges. Member of National Association of Independent Schools. Endowment: $7.5 million. Total enrollment: 485. Upper school average class size: 11. Upper school faculty-student ratio: 1:8.

Upper School Student Profile Grade 9: 64 students (32 boys, 32 girls); Grade 10: 63 students (36 boys, 27 girls); Grade 11: 59 students (31 boys, 28 girls); Grade 12: 61 students (34 boys, 27 girls).

Faculty School total: 63. In upper school: 34 men, 28 women; 50 have advanced degrees.

Subjects Offered Algebra, American history, American literature, art, art history, astronomy, biology, calculus, ceramics, chemistry, community service, computer math, computer programming, computer science, creative writing, drama, earth science, English, English literature, environmental science, European history, expository writing, fine arts, forensics, French, geography, geology, geometry, government/civics, grammar, humanities, journalism, marine biology, mathematics, music, oceanography, photography, physical education, physics, psychology, science, social science, social studies, Spanish, statistics, theater, trigonometry, world history, writing.

Graduation Requirements Arts and fine arts (art, music, dance, drama), computer science, English, foreign language, mathematics, physical education (includes health), science, social science, social studies (includes history), 20 hours of community service.

Special Academic Programs Advanced Placement exam preparation in 19 subject areas; honors section; independent study; term-away projects; study at local college for college credit; study abroad; academic accommodation for the gifted.

College Placement 60 students graduated in 2005; all went to college, including Boston College; Brown University; Carnegie Mellon University; The Johns Hopkins University; University of Chicago. Median SAT verbal: 600, median SAT math: 600, median composite ACT: 26.

Student Life Upper grades have specified standards of dress, student council, honor system. Discipline rests equally with students and faculty.

Summer Programs Enrichment, advancement, sports, art/fine arts, computer instruction programs offered; session focuses on enrichment; held on campus; accepts boys and girls; open to students from other schools. 2006 schedule: June 19 to August 12. Application deadline: April 1.

Tuition and Aid Day student tuition: $24,130–$24,635. Tuition installment plan (The Tuition Plan, Insured Tuition Payment Plan, monthly payment plans). Merit scholarship grants, need-based scholarship grants available. In 2005–06, 16% of upper-school students received aid; total upper-school merit-scholarship money awarded: $90,000. Total amount of financial aid awarded in 2005–06: $896,805.

Admissions Traditional secondary-level entrance grade is 9. For fall 2005, 125 students applied for upper-level admission, 44 were accepted, 35 enrolled. ISEE required. Deadline for receipt of application materials: February 1. Application fee required: $75. On-campus interview required.

Athletics Interscholastic: baseball (boys), basketball (b,g), crew (b,g), cross-country running (b,g), field hockey (g), fitness (b,g), football (b), golf (b,g), lacrosse (b,g), soccer (b,g), softball (g), squash (b,g), tennis (b,g), volleyball (g); intramural: aerobics/dance (g), equestrian sports (g), physical training (b,g); coed interscholastic: crew, cross-country running, golf, squash, weight lifting, weight training; coed intramural: physical training. 4 PE instructors, 2 coaches, 1 trainer.

Computers Computers are regularly used in art, college planning, design, English, foreign language, graphic design, library, mathematics, science, social sciences, technology, yearbook classes. Computer network features include campus e-mail, on-campus library services, CD-ROMs, online commercial services, Internet access, file transfer, DVD, wireless campus network.

Contact Mr. David M. Suter, Director of Admissions. 203-966-5612. Fax: 203-972-5353. E-mail: suterd@stlukesct.org. Web site: www.stlukesct.org.

ST. MARGARET'S EPISCOPAL SCHOOL

31641 La Novia Avenue
San Juan Capistrano, California 92675
Head of School: Marcus D. Hurlbut

General Information Coeducational day college-preparatory, arts, and technology school, affiliated with Episcopal Church. Grades N–12. Founded: 1979. Setting: suburban. Nearest major city is Los Angeles. 19-acre campus. 6 buildings on campus. Approved or accredited by California Association of Independent Schools, Western Association of Schools and Colleges, and California Department of Education. Member of National Association of Independent Schools. Endowment: $1.5 million. Total enrollment: 1,221. Upper school average class size: 16. Upper school faculty-student ratio: 1:14.

Upper School Student Profile Grade 9: 96 students (45 boys, 51 girls); Grade 10: 106 students (47 boys, 59 girls); Grade 11: 91 students (43 boys, 48 girls); Grade 12: 97 students (41 boys, 56 girls). 15% of students are members of Episcopal Church.

Faculty School total: 113. In upper school: 21 men, 16 women; 28 have advanced degrees.

Subjects Offered Algebra, American history, American literature, anatomy and physiology, anthropology, art, art history, Bible studies, biology, calculus, chemistry, community service, computer math, computer programming, computer science, creative writing, drama, economics, English, English literature, environmental science, ethics, European history, expository writing, fine arts, French, geography, geometry, government/civics, history, human development, Japanese, journalism, Latin, mathematics, music, philosophy, physical education, physics, religion, science, social science, social studies, Spanish, speech, theater, trigonometry, world history, world literature, writing.

Graduation Requirements Arts and fine arts (art, music, dance, drama), computer science, English, foreign language, mathematics, physical education (includes health), religion (includes Bible studies and theology), science, social science, social studies (includes history). Community service is required.

Special Academic Programs Advanced Placement exam preparation in 19 subject areas; honors section; independent study; study at local college for college credit; academic accommodation for the gifted, the musically talented, and the artistically talented.

St. Margaret's Episcopal School

College Placement 94 students graduated in 2005; all went to college, including Boston College; University of California, Berkeley; University of California, Los Angeles; University of Pennsylvania; University of Southern California. Median SAT verbal: 609, median SAT math: 630.

Student Life Upper grades have specified standards of dress, student council, honor system. Discipline rests equally with students and faculty. Attendance at religious services is required.

Summer Programs Enrichment, advancement, sports programs offered; session focuses on academic enrichment; held on campus; accepts boys and girls; open to students from other schools. 250 students usually enrolled. 2006 schedule: June 30 to August 15.

Tuition and Aid Day student tuition: $15,000. Tuition installment plan (monthly payment plans, individually arranged payment plans). Need-based scholarship grants available. In 2005–06, 17% of upper-school students received aid. Total amount of financial aid awarded in 2005–06: $902,000.

Admissions Traditional secondary-level entrance grade is 9. For fall 2005, 179 students applied for upper-level admission, 66 were accepted, 38 enrolled. ISEE or SSAT required. Deadline for receipt of application materials: February 15. Application fee required: $50. On-campus interview recommended.

Athletics Interscholastic: baseball (boys), basketball (b,g), cheering (g), dance (b,g), football (b), golf (b,g), lacrosse (b,g), modern dance (g), soccer (b,g), softball (g), strength & conditioning (b,g), tennis (b,g), track and field (b,g), volleyball (b,g), wrestling (g); intramural: aerobics/dance (b,g), badminton (g), lacrosse (b,g), paint ball (b); coed interscholastic: cross-country running, diving, dressage, equestrian sports, independent competitive sports, swimming and diving; coed intramural: badminton, physical fitness. 3 PE instructors, 10 coaches, 1 trainer.

Computers Computers are regularly used in English, foreign language, history, mathematics, science, technology classes. Computer network features include campus e-mail, on-campus library services, CD-ROMs, Internet access, wireless campus network.

Contact Judy Haidinger, Admissions Director. 949-661-0108. Fax: 949-661-8637. E-mail: jhaiding@smes.org. Web site: www.smes.org.

ST. MARGARET'S SCHOOL

444 Water Lane
PO Box 158
Tappahannock, Virginia 22560
Head of School: Margaret R. Broad

petersons.com

General Information Girls' boarding and day college-preparatory and religious studies school, affiliated with Episcopal Church. Grades 8–12. Founded: 1921. Setting: small town. Nearest major city is Richmond. Students are housed in single-sex dormitories. 51-acre campus. 9 buildings on campus. Approved or accredited by Southern Association of Colleges and Schools, The Association of Boarding Schools, Virginia Association of Independent Schools, and Virginia Department of Education. Member of National Association of Independent Schools and Secondary School Admission Test Board. Endowment: $6 million. Total enrollment: 149. Upper school average class size: 12. Upper school faculty-student ratio: 1:6.

Upper School Student Profile Grade 8: 8 students (8 girls); Grade 9: 37 students (37 girls); Grade 10: 29 students (29 girls); Grade 11: 35 students (35 girls); Grade 12: 39 students (39 girls). 78% of students are boarding students. 48% are state residents. 17 states are represented in upper school student body. 17% are international students. International students from British Virgin Islands, Japan, Mexico, Republic of Korea, Taiwan, and Thailand; 5 other countries represented in student body. 25% of students are members of Episcopal Church.

Faculty School total: 34. In upper school: 6 men, 28 women; 18 have advanced degrees; 21 reside on campus.

Subjects Offered Algebra, American literature, anatomy and physiology, ancient history, art, art history, biology, biology-AP, British literature, calculus, calculus-AP, ceramics, chemistry, chorus, community service, computer science, conceptual physics, creative writing, drama, driver education, ecology, English, English-AP, ESL, European history, finance, fine arts, French, French-AP, geography, geometry, government/civics, health, history, history-AP, illustration, journalism, Latin, leadership, mathematics, music, music history, painting, photography, physical education, physics, piano, pre-algebra, religion, science, social studies, Spanish, U.S. government, world history, world literature, writing.

Graduation Requirements Arts and fine arts (art, music, dance, drama), computer science, English, foreign language, history, mathematics, physical education (includes health), religion (includes Bible studies and theology), science. Community service is required.

Special Academic Programs Advanced Placement exam preparation in 5 subject areas; honors section; independent study; study abroad; ESL (15 students enrolled).

College Placement 29 students graduated in 2005; all went to college, including Rensselaer Polytechnic Institute; Roanoke College; The College of William and Mary; The University of Alabama; University of Virginia; Virginia Polytechnic Institute and State University.

Student Life Upper grades have uniform requirement, student council, honor system. Discipline rests equally with students and faculty. Attendance at religious services is required.

Tuition and Aid Day student tuition: $12,400; 7-day tuition and room/board: $32,800. Tuition installment plan (monthly payment plans). Need-based scholarship grants available. In 2005–06, 32% of upper-school students received aid. Total amount of financial aid awarded in 2005–06: $776,700.

Admissions Traditional secondary-level entrance grade is 9. For fall 2005, 107 students applied for upper-level admission, 86 were accepted, 58 enrolled. SSAT required. Deadline for receipt of application materials: none. Application fee required: $40. On-campus interview required.

Athletics Interscholastic: basketball, crew, cross-country running, field hockey, soccer, softball, swimming and diving, tennis, volleyball; intramural: ballet, canoeing/kayaking, crew, dance, fitness, fitness walking, golf, horseback riding, kayaking, modern dance, outdoor activities, sailing, self defense, strength & conditioning, tennis, walking, weight lifting, yoga. 1 PE instructor, 2 coaches.

Computers Computers are regularly used in English, foreign language, history, journalism, science, yearbook classes. Computer network features include campus e-mail, on-campus library services, CD-ROMs, online commercial services, Internet access, file transfer.

Contact Kimberly McDowell, Assistant Head, External Affairs, Director of Admission. 804-443-3357. Fax: 804-443-6781. E-mail: admit@sms.com. Web site: www.sms.org.

ANNOUNCEMENT FROM THE SCHOOL It's an exciting time to be at St. Margaret's School. A new 24-student dorm opened for the 2005–06 academic year, and 42 acres near campus have been purchased in order to develop a multifield athletic complex. St. Margaret's programs are growing, too, from student leadership to the life-skills cocurriculum. Come join us!

See full description on page 1028.

ST. MARGARET'S SCHOOL

1080 Lucas Avenue
Victoria, British Columbia V8X 3P7, Canada
Head of School: S. Victor Clayton

General Information Girls' boarding and day college-preparatory, general academic, arts, technology, and ESL school. Boarding grades 7–12, day grades JK–12. Founded: 1908. Setting: suburban. Students are housed in single-sex dormitories. 22-acre campus. 10 buildings on campus. Approved or accredited by Canadian Association of Independent Schools, The Association of Boarding Schools, and British Columbia Department of Education. Language of instruction: English. Total enrollment: 438. Upper school average class size: 18. Upper school faculty-student ratio: 1:8.

Upper School Student Profile Grade 7: 25 students (25 girls); Grade 8: 42 students (42 girls); Grade 9: 35 students (35 girls); Grade 10: 54 students (54 girls); Grade 11: 43 students (43 girls); Grade 12: 51 students (51 girls). 30% of students are boarding students. 70% are province residents. 6 provinces are represented in upper school student body. 30% are international students. International students from Hong Kong, Japan, Mexico, Republic of Korea, and Taiwan; 6 other countries represented in student body.

Faculty School total: 38. In upper school: 7 men, 30 women; 12 have advanced degrees.

Subjects Offered Advanced Placement courses, algebra, applied skills, art, biology, calculus, Canadian geography, Canadian history, career and personal planning, chemistry, Chinese, choir, communications, comparative civilizations, computer science, creative writing, dance, drama, English, English literature, ESL, fine arts, French, geography, history, information technology, Japanese, journalism, law, leadership training, Mandarin, mathematics, music, music appreciation, outdoor education, performing arts, photography, physical education, physics, science, social studies, Spanish, theater, Western civilization, writing.

Graduation Requirements Applied skills, arts and fine arts (art, music, dance, drama), English, foreign language, mathematics, science, social studies (includes history).

Special Academic Programs Advanced Placement exam preparation in 5 subject areas; honors section; academic accommodation for the gifted, the musically talented, and the artistically talented; ESL (38 students enrolled).

College Placement 51 students graduated in 2005; 49 went to college, including McGill University; Queen's University at Kingston; Simon Fraser University; The University of British Columbia; University of Victoria. Other: 2 had other specific plans.

Student Life Upper grades have uniform requirement, student council. Discipline rests primarily with faculty.

Summer Programs ESL programs offered; session focuses on ESL combined with recreational activities and sightseeing; held both on and off campus; held at various locations for the local home stay program; accepts girls; open to students from other schools. 20 students usually enrolled. 2006 schedule: July 5 to July 31. Application deadline: May 1.

Tuition and Aid Day student tuition: CAN$8233–CAN$13,278; 7-day tuition and room/board: CAN$26,880–CAN$36,398. Tuition installment plan (Insured Tuition Payment Plan, monthly payment plans). Tuition reduction for siblings, bursaries, merit

scholarship grants, need-based scholarship grants available. In 2005–06, 17% of upper-school students received aid; total upper-school merit-scholarship money awarded: CAN$30,000. Total amount of financial aid awarded in 2005–06: CAN$70,000.

Admissions For fall 2005, 115 students applied for upper-level admission, 97 were accepted, 92 enrolled. School's own exam required. Deadline for receipt of application materials: none. No application fee required. Interview required.

Athletics Interscholastic: aquatics, badminton, basketball, crew, cross-country running, field hockey, rowing, running, soccer, swimming and diving, synchronized swimming, track and field, volleyball; intramural: aerobics, aerobics/dance, alpine skiing, aquatics, back packing, badminton, baseball, basketball, bicycling, canoeing/kayaking, climbing, cooperative games, cross-country running, dance, equestrian sports, field hockey, figure skating, fitness, floor hockey, Frisbee, golf, gymnastics, hiking/backpacking, horseback riding, ice skating, indoor soccer, jogging, jump rope, kayaking, martial arts, modern dance, mountain biking, ocean paddling, outdoor activities, outdoor adventure, outdoor education, outdoor recreation, outdoor skills, paddle tennis, physical fitness, rock climbing, ropes courses, rugby, running, sailing, skiing (cross-country), skiing (downhill), snowboarding, soccer, softball, squash, strength & conditioning, surfing, swimming and diving, table tennis, tennis, track and field, ultimate Frisbee, volleyball, wallyball, weight training, wilderness, wilderness survival. 4 PE instructors, 3 coaches, 1 trainer.

Computers Computers are regularly used in career exploration, English, ESL, foreign language, French, history, journalism, mathematics, science classes. Computer network features include campus e-mail, on-campus library services, CD-ROMs, online commercial services, Internet access.

Contact Mr. Vic Clayton, Head of School. 250-479-7171. Fax: 250-479-8976. E-mail: stmarg@stmarg.ca. Web site: www.stmarg.ca.

ST. MARK'S HIGH SCHOOL

2501 Pike Creek Road
Wilmington, Delaware 19808
Head of School: Mark J. Freund

General Information Coeducational day college-preparatory, arts, business, religious studies, and technology school, affiliated with Roman Catholic Church. Grades 9–12. Founded: 1969. Setting: suburban. Nearest major city is Philadelphia, PA. 45-acre campus. 3 buildings on campus. Approved or accredited by Middle States Association of Colleges and Schools, National Catholic Education Association, and Delaware Department of Education. Endowment: $3 million. Total enrollment: 1,585. Upper school average class size: 24. Upper school faculty-student ratio: 1:15.

Upper School Student Profile Grade 9: 415 students (200 boys, 215 girls); Grade 10: 395 students (188 boys, 207 girls); Grade 11: 400 students (177 boys, 223 girls); Grade 12: 375 students (173 boys, 202 girls). 80% of students are Roman Catholic.

Faculty School total: 110. In upper school: 40 men, 70 women; 60 have advanced degrees.

Subjects Offered Advanced Placement courses, art, business, computer science, drama, driver education, English, family and consumer sciences, fine arts, French, general science, German, history, Italian, mathematics, media, music, physical education, reading, religion, science, social studies, Spanish, theater.

Graduation Requirements Arts and fine arts (art, music, dance, drama), English, mathematics, physical education (includes health), religion (includes Bible studies and theology), science, social studies (includes history).

Special Academic Programs Advanced Placement exam preparation in 18 subject areas; honors section; study at local college for college credit; study abroad; academic accommodation for the gifted; remedial reading and/or remedial writing.

College Placement 380 students graduated in 2005; 360 went to college, including Saint Joseph's University; The Pennsylvania State University University Park Campus; University of Delaware; University of Maryland, College Park; Virginia Polytechnic Institute and State University; West Chester University of Pennsylvania. Mean SAT verbal: 585, mean SAT math: 575. 33% scored over 600 on SAT verbal, 33% scored over 600 on SAT math.

Student Life Upper grades have uniform requirement, student council. Discipline rests primarily with faculty. Attendance at religious services is required.

Summer Programs Remediation programs offered; session focuses on skill development and remediation; held on campus; accepts boys and girls; open to students from other schools. 30 students usually enrolled. 2006 schedule: June to July. Application deadline: none.

Tuition and Aid Day student tuition: $7200. Tuition installment plan (monthly payment plans). Merit scholarship grants, need-based scholarship grants, full academic scholarships for gifted students available. In 2005–06, 30% of upper-school students received aid; total upper-school merit-scholarship money awarded: $250,000. Total amount of financial aid awarded in 2005–06: $750,000.

Admissions Traditional secondary-level entrance grade is 9. For fall 2005, 520 students applied for upper-level admission, 475 were accepted, 415 enrolled. STS required. Deadline for receipt of application materials: none. Application fee required: $50.

Athletics Interscholastic: baseball (boys), basketball (b,g), cross-country running (b,g), diving (b,g), field hockey (g), football (b), ice hockey (b), indoor track & field (b,g), lacrosse (b,g), soccer (b,g), softball (g), swimming and diving (b,g), tennis (b,g),

track and field (b,g), volleyball (g), wrestling (b); coed interscholastic: golf, indoor hockey. 4 PE instructors, 10 coaches, 1 trainer.

Computers Computers are regularly used in all academic classes. Computer network features include campus e-mail, on-campus library services, CD-ROMs, online commercial services, Internet access, file transfer, DVD, wireless campus network, PowerSchool system for parents to monitor child's progress.

Contact Thomas J. Lemon, Director of Admissions. 302-738-3300 Ext. 3065. Fax: 302-738-5132. E-mail: tl@stmarkshs.net. Web site: www.stmarkshs.net.

SAINT MARK'S SCHOOL

25 Marlborough Road
Southborough, Massachusetts 01772
Head of School: Elsa N. and Antony J. Hill

General Information Coeducational boarding and day college-preparatory, arts, religious studies, and classics, math school, affiliated with Episcopal Church. Grades 9–12. Founded: 1865. Setting: suburban. Nearest major city is Boston. Students are housed in single-sex dormitories. 250-acre campus. 15 buildings on campus. Approved or accredited by New England Association of Schools and Colleges and Massachusetts Department of Education. Member of National Association of Independent Schools and Secondary School Admission Test Board. Endowment: $101 million. Total enrollment: 333. Upper school average class size: 10. Upper school faculty-student ratio: 1:5.

Upper School Student Profile Grade 9: 76 students (39 boys, 37 girls); Grade 10: 94 students (54 boys, 40 girls); Grade 11: 90 students (48 boys, 42 girls); Grade 12: 73 students (34 boys, 39 girls). 77% of students are boarding students. 42% are state residents. 21 states are represented in upper school student body. 10% are international students. International students from Antigua and Barbuda, Canada, China, Republic of Korea, Taiwan, and Thailand; 6 other countries represented in student body. 30% of students are members of Episcopal Church.

Faculty School total: 66. In upper school: 28 men, 28 women; 36 have advanced degrees; 60 reside on campus.

Subjects Offered 20th century history, Advanced Placement courses, algebra, American history, American literature, art, art history, biology, calculus, ceramics, chemistry, civil war history, computer math, computer science, constitutional history of U.S., creative writing, drama, drama workshop, driver education, earth science, Eastern religion and philosophy, ecology, economics, English, English literature, environmental science, ethics, European history, expository writing, fine arts, French, geography, geometry, German, government/civics, Greek, history, Latin, Latin-AP, logic, mathematics, music, music history, music theory, music theory-AP, music-AP, photography, physics, physiology, psychology, religion, science, scripture, social studies, Spanish, Spanish language-AP, Spanish literature, Spanish literature-AP, statistics, studio art, studio art—AP, theater, trigonometry, world history, world literature.

Graduation Requirements Arts and fine arts (art, music, dance, drama), English, foreign language, mathematics, religion (includes Bible studies and theology), science, social studies (includes history).

Special Academic Programs Advanced Placement exam preparation in 14 subject areas; honors section; independent study; term-away projects; study abroad; academic accommodation for the gifted, the musically talented, and the artistically talented.

College Placement 87 students graduated in 2005; 85 went to college, including Boston College; Dickinson College; Hamilton College; Middlebury College; The George Washington University; Trinity College. Other: 2 had other specific plans. Mean SAT verbal: 649, mean SAT math: 656.

Student Life Upper grades have specified standards of dress, student council, honor system. Discipline rests equally with students and faculty.

Tuition and Aid Day student tuition: $27,400; 7-day tuition and room/board: $35,350. Tuition installment plan (Key Tuition Payment Plan). Need-based scholarship grants, need-based loans available. In 2005–06, 32% of upper-school students received aid. Total amount of financial aid awarded in 2005–06: $2,200,000.

Admissions Traditional secondary-level entrance grade is 9. For fall 2005, 571 students applied for upper-level admission, 260 were accepted, 106 enrolled. SSAT and TOEFL required. Deadline for receipt of application materials: January 31. Application fee required: $50. Interview required.

Athletics Interscholastic: baseball (boys), basketball (b,g), crew (b,g), cross-country running (b,g), field hockey (g), Fives (b), football (b), golf (b,g), ice hockey (b,g), lacrosse (b,g), soccer (b,g), softball (g), squash (b,g), tennis (b,g), volleyball (g), wrestling (b); intramural: aerobics/dance (g), volleyball (b,g), weight lifting (b,g); coed interscholastic: dance; coed intramural: aerobics, aerobics/nautilus, billiards, outdoor activities, yoga. 13 coaches, 1 trainer.

Computers Computers are regularly used in English, foreign language, mathematics, science classes. Computer network features include campus e-mail, on-campus library services, Internet access, wireless campus network.

Contact Anne E. Behnke, Director of Admission. 508-786-6000. Fax: 508-786-6120. E-mail: annebehnke@stmarksschool.org. Web site: www.stmarksschool.org.

See full description on page 1030.

ST. MARK'S SCHOOL OF TEXAS

10600 Preston Road
Dallas, Texas 75230-4000
Head of School: Mr. Arnold E. Holtberg

petersons.com

General Information Boys' day college-preparatory, arts, technology, and Advanced Placement school. Grades 1–12. Founded: 1906. Setting: urban. 40-acre campus. 13 buildings on campus. Approved or accredited by Independent Schools Association of the Southwest. Member of National Association of Independent Schools. Endowment: $98.5 million. Total enrollment: 817. Upper school average class size: 15. Upper school faculty-student ratio: 1:8.

Upper School Student Profile Grade 9: 94 students (94 boys); Grade 10: 79 students (79 boys); Grade 11: 90 students (90 boys); Grade 12: 87 students (87 boys).

Faculty School total: 120. In upper school: 46 men, 27 women; 55 have advanced degrees.

Subjects Offered 3-dimensional art, acting, algebra, ancient world history, art, art history, astronomy, Basic programming, biology, biology-AP, calculus, calculus-AP, ceramics, chemistry, chemistry-AP, choir, community service, computer programming, computer science, computer science-AP, concert band, creative writing, digital art, digital photography, DNA, DNA science lab, drama, drama workshop, economics, economics-AP, English, English literature and composition-AP, English literature-AP, environmental science-AP, European history, European history-AP, fine arts, geology, geometry, German-AP, history, honors English, honors geometry, independent study, Japanese, journalism, Latin, Latin-AP, macroeconomics-AP, mathematics, microeconomics-AP, modern European history-AP, modern world history, music, photography, physical education, physics, physics-AP, psychology, science, senior project, Spanish, Spanish language-AP, Spanish literature-AP, statistics-AP, studio art-AP, theater, trigonometry, U.S. history, video film production, woodworking, world history.

Graduation Requirements Arts and fine arts (art, music, dance, drama), English, foreign language, mathematics, physical education (includes health), science, social studies (includes history), senior exhibition. Community service is required.

Special Academic Programs Advanced Placement exam preparation in 17 subject areas; honors section; independent study; term-away projects.

College Placement 80 students graduated in 2005; 79 went to college, including New York University; Princeton University; The University of Texas at Austin; University of Pennsylvania; Vanderbilt University; Washington University in St. Louis. Other: 1 had other specific plans. Median SAT verbal: 670, median SAT math: 720, median combined SAT: 2050. Mean composite ACT: 30. 79% scored over 600 on SAT verbal, 98% scored over 600 on SAT math, 83% scored over 1800 on combined SAT.

Student Life Upper grades have uniform requirement, student council, honor system. Discipline rests primarily with faculty. Attendance at religious services is required.

Tuition and Aid Day student tuition: $19,216–$19,812. Tuition installment plan (Insured Tuition Payment Plan, SMART Tuition Payment Plan, financial aid student monthly payment plan). Need-based scholarship grants, tuition remission for sons of faculty and staff, need-based middle-income financial aid available. In 2005–06, 18% of upper-school students received aid. Total amount of financial aid awarded in 2005–06: $850,245.

Admissions Traditional secondary-level entrance grade is 9. For fall 2005, 83 students applied for upper-level admission, 27 were accepted, 22 enrolled. ISEE required. Deadline for receipt of application materials: January 6. Application fee required: $175. On-campus interview required.

Athletics Interscholastic: back packing, baseball, basketball, cheering, climbing, crew, cross-country running, diving, fencing, fitness, football, golf, hiking/backpacking, hockey, ice hockey, lacrosse, outdoor education, outdoor skills, outdoors, physical fitness, rugby, soccer, strength & conditioning, swimming and diving, team handball, tennis, track and field, volleyball, wall climbing, water polo, weight training, wilderness, winter soccer, wrestling. 5 PE instructors, 6 coaches, 1 trainer.

Computers Computers are regularly used in English, foreign language, humanities, mathematics, science classes. Computer network features include campus e-mail, on-campus library services, CD-ROMs, online commercial services, Internet access, file transfer, office computer access, DVD, wireless campus network.

Contact Mr. David P. Baker, Director of Admission. 214-346-8700. Fax: 214-346-8701. E-mail: admission@smtexas.org. Web site: www.smtexas.org.

See full description on page 1032.

ST. MARY'S ACADEMY

4545 South University Boulevard
Englewood, Colorado 80113-6059
Head of School: Judith Baenen

General Information Coeducational day college-preparatory, arts, religious studies, and technology school, affiliated with Roman Catholic Church. Boys grades K–8, girls grades K–12. Founded: 1864. Setting: suburban. Nearest major city is Denver. 24-acre campus. 5 buildings on campus. Approved or accredited by Association of Colorado Independent Schools, National Independent Private Schools Association, North Central Association of Colleges and Schools, and Colorado Department of Education.

Member of National Association of Independent Schools. Endowment: $2 million. Total enrollment: 751. Upper school average class size: 16. Upper school faculty-student ratio: 1:10.

Upper School Student Profile Grade 9: 71 students (71 girls); Grade 10: 57 students (57 girls); Grade 11: 68 students (68 girls); Grade 12: 81 students (81 girls). 52% of students are Roman Catholic.

Faculty School total: 79. In upper school: 9 men, 28 women; 27 have advanced degrees.

Subjects Offered Algebra, American history, American literature, anatomy, art, art history, astronomy, biology, calculus, ceramics, chemistry, community service, creative writing, cultural criticism, dance, drama, ecology, economics, English, English literature, European history, expository writing, fine arts, French, genetics, geography, geometry, government/civics, grammar, history, mathematics, music, philosophy, philosophy of government, photography, physical education, physics, physiology, psychology, religion, science, social studies, Spanish, theater, theology, trigonometry, women's studies, world history, world literature, writing, zoology.

Graduation Requirements Arts and fine arts (art, music, dance, drama), English, foreign language, mathematics, physical education (includes health), religion (includes Bible studies and theology), science, social studies (includes history). Community service is required.

Special Academic Programs Advanced Placement exam preparation in 11 subject areas; honors section; independent study.

College Placement 65 students graduated in 2005; all went to college, including Boston University; Creighton University; University of Colorado at Boulder; University of Denver; University of Notre Dame. Median SAT math: 559.

Student Life Upper grades have specified standards of dress, student council. Discipline rests primarily with faculty.

Tuition and Aid Day student tuition: $9990. Tuition installment plan (FACTS Tuition Payment Plan, monthly payment plans). Merit scholarship grants, need-based scholarship grants available. In 2005–06, 34% of upper-school students received aid; total upper-school merit-scholarship money awarded: $67,200. Total amount of financial aid awarded in 2005–06: $346,885.

Admissions Traditional secondary-level entrance grade is 9. High School Placement Test (closed version) from Scholastic Testing Service required. Deadline for receipt of application materials: January 11. Application fee required: $60. Interview required.

Athletics Interscholastic: basketball, cross-country running, dance team, diving, field hockey, independent competitive sports, lacrosse, running, soccer, softball, swimming and diving, tennis, volleyball. 3 PE instructors, 18 coaches, 1 trainer.

Computers Computers are regularly used in art, college planning, drawing and design, English, foreign language, history, journalism, mathematics, science, technology, writing classes. Computer network features include campus e-mail, on-campus library services, CD-ROMs, online commercial services, Internet access, DVD, wireless campus network.

Contact Linda Ticer, Director of Admissions. 303-762-8300. Fax: 303-783-6201. E-mail: linda_ticer@smanet.org. Web site: www.smanet.org.

ST. MARY'S BUNDSCHU MEMORIAL HIGH SCHOOL

622 North Main Street
Independence, Missouri 64050
Head of School: Trudy Jonas

General Information Coeducational day college-preparatory and general academic school, affiliated with Roman Catholic Church. Grades 9–12. Founded: 1853. Setting: urban. Nearest major city is Kansas City. 1-acre campus. 3 buildings on campus. Approved or accredited by National Catholic Education Association and North Central Association of Colleges and Schools. Endowment: $18,000. Total enrollment: 207. Upper school average class size: 16. Upper school faculty-student ratio: 1:11.

Upper School Student Profile Grade 9: 65 students (40 boys, 25 girls); Grade 10: 36 students (13 boys, 23 girls); Grade 11: 49 students (23 boys, 26 girls); Grade 12: 57 students (29 boys, 28 girls). 80% of students are Roman Catholic.

Faculty School total: 18. In upper school: 6 men, 12 women; 10 have advanced degrees.

Subjects Offered Accounting, ACT preparation, advanced chemistry, advanced math, algebra, American government, American government-AP, American history, anatomy, art, athletics, biology, biology-AP, business skills, calculus, calligraphy, career education, Catholic belief and practice, chemistry, choir, choral music, computer applications, computer keyboarding, desktop publishing, drafting, drama, drama performance, English, English composition, English literature, English-AP, ethics, fiber arts, fine arts, folk art, foreign language, geography, geometry, government, government-AP, graphic design, health, history of the Catholic Church, Holocaust, honors English, independent study, Internet, intro to computers, jewelry making, keyboarding/computer, lab science, leadership and service, library, mathematics, meditation, mythology, newspaper, oil painting, peace and justice, physical education, physical science, poetry, pottery, pre-algebra, pre-calculus, religion, social justice, social studies, Spanish, speech and debate, street law, student government, studio art-AP, trigonometry, U.S. government, water color painting, weight training, world geography, world history, yearbook.

Graduation Requirements Algebra, American government, American history, American literature, art, biology, Catholic belief and practice, chemistry, computer applications, English, English composition, English literature, geography, geometry, government, physical education (includes health), physical science, Spanish, world history.

Special Academic Programs Advanced Placement exam preparation in 4 subject areas; honors section; accelerated programs; independent study; remedial math.

College Placement 55 students graduated in 2005; 48 went to college, including Benedictine College; Missouri State University; Rockhurst University; University of Kansas; University of Missouri–Columbia. Other: 6 went to work, 1 entered military service. Mean composite ACT: 22. 12% scored over 26 on composite ACT.

Student Life Upper grades have uniform requirement, student council, honor system. Discipline rests equally with students and faculty. Attendance at religious services is required.

Summer Programs Remediation, enrichment programs offered; session focuses on make-up and enrichment; held on campus; accepts boys and girls; open to students from other schools. 120 students usually enrolled. 2006 schedule: June 1 to July 31.

Tuition and Aid Day student tuition: $4700. Tuition installment plan (monthly payment plans). Tuition reduction for siblings, merit scholarship grants, need-based scholarship grants available. In 2005–06, 60% of upper-school students received aid; total upper-school merit-scholarship money awarded: $5000. Total amount of financial aid awarded in 2005–06: $182,000.

Admissions Traditional secondary-level entrance grade is 9. For fall 2005, 66 students applied for upper-level admission, 66 were accepted, 65 enrolled. ACT-Explore required. Deadline for receipt of application materials: none. No application fee required. On-campus interview required.

Athletics Interscholastic: baseball (boys), basketball (b,g), cheering (g), cross-country running (b,g), drill team (g), football (b), golf (b), pom squad (g), softball (g), tennis (b,g), track and field (b,g), volleyball (g), wrestling (b); intramural: flag football (b,g), physical fitness (b,g); coed intramural: physical fitness, physical training, weight training. 1 PE instructor, 24 coaches.

Computers Computers are regularly used in business education, career education, English, mathematics, newspaper, yearbook classes. Computer network features include campus e-mail, CD-ROMs, Internet access.

Contact Lori Jonas, Development Assistant. 816-252-8733. Fax: 816-252-2780. E-mail: ljonas@stmhs.org. Web site: www.stmhs.org.

SAINT MARY'S COLLEGE HIGH SCHOOL

1294 Albina Avenue
Peralta Park
Berkeley, California 94706
Head of School: Peter Imperial

General Information Coeducational day college-preparatory school, affiliated with Roman Catholic Church. Grades 9–12. Founded: 1863. Setting: urban. Nearest major city is Oakland. 13-acre campus. 9 buildings on campus. Approved or accredited by National Catholic Education Association, Western Association of Schools and Colleges, and Western Catholic Education Association. Endowment: $638,000. Total enrollment: 629. Upper school average class size: 28. Upper school faculty-student ratio: 1:17.

Upper School Student Profile Grade 9: 179 students (79 boys, 100 girls); Grade 10: 160 students (87 boys, 73 girls); Grade 11: 159 students (73 boys, 86 girls); Grade 12: 131 students (69 boys, 62 girls). 55% of students are Roman Catholic.

Faculty School total: 42. In upper school: 25 men, 16 women; 20 have advanced degrees.

Subjects Offered Algebra, American history, American literature, art, band, biology, calculus, calculus-AP, chemistry, chorus, conceptual physics, concert band, constitutional law, dance, diversity studies, economics, English, English literature, English literature-AP, French, French language-AP, geometry, government/civics, health education, jazz band, mathematics, philosophy, photography, physical education, physics, physics-AP, psychology, religion, sociology, Spanish, Spanish language-AP, studio art-AP, theater, trigonometry, U.S. history-AP, world history, world religions, yearbook.

Graduation Requirements Electives, English, foreign language, health and wellness, lab science, mathematics, physical education (includes health), religious studies, U.S. history, visual and performing arts, world history, service learning, enrichment week mini-course (once a year).

Special Academic Programs Advanced Placement exam preparation in 7 subject areas; honors section.

College Placement 148 students graduated in 2005; 147 went to college, including San Diego State University; San Francisco State University; University of California, Berkeley; University of California, Irvine; University of California, Santa Cruz; University of Southern California. Other: 1 went to work. Mean SAT verbal: 547, mean SAT math: 544, mean composite ACT: 22.

Student Life Upper grades have specified standards of dress, student council. Discipline rests primarily with faculty. Attendance at religious services is required.

Summer Programs Remediation, advancement programs offered; held on campus; accepts boys and girls; not open to students from other schools. 75 students usually enrolled. 2006 schedule: June 19 to July 28. Application deadline: January 5.

Tuition and Aid Day student tuition: $10,680. Tuition installment plan (monthly payment plans). Need-based scholarship grants available. In 2005–06, 30% of upper-school students received aid. Total amount of financial aid awarded in 2005–06: $800,000.

Admissions Traditional secondary-level entrance grade is 9. For fall 2005, 500 students applied for upper-level admission, 240 were accepted, 179 enrolled. High School Placement Test and writing sample required. Deadline for receipt of application materials: January 4. Application fee required: $60. Interview required.

Athletics Interscholastic: baseball (boys), basketball (b,g), cheering (g), cross-country running (b,g), dance squad (g), football (b), golf (b,g), lacrosse (b), soccer (b,g), softball (g), tennis (b,g), track and field (b,g), volleyball (b,g); coed interscholastic: diving, swimming and diving; coed intramural: ball hockey, basketball, flag football, indoor soccer, table tennis, volleyball. 1 PE instructor.

Computers Computers are regularly used in all academic, art, college planning, graphic arts, newspaper, yearbook classes. Computer network features include CD-ROMs, online commercial services, Internet access.

Contact Lawrence Puck, Director of Admissions. 510-559-6235. Fax: 510-559-6277. E-mail: lpuck@stmchs.org. Web site: www.saintmaryschs.org.

ST. MARY'S DOMINICAN HIGH SCHOOL

7701 Walmsley Avenue
New Orleans, Louisiana 70125-0000
Head of School: Ms. Cynthia A. Thomas

General Information Girls' day college-preparatory school. Grades 8–12. Founded: 1860. Setting: urban. 3 buildings on campus. Approved or accredited by Southern Association of Colleges and Schools and Louisiana Department of Education. Total enrollment: 1,068.

Faculty School total: 76. In upper school: 11 men, 57 women; 29 have advanced degrees.

Special Academic Programs Advanced Placement exam preparation; honors section.

College Placement 225 students graduated in 2005; 100 went to college.

Student Life Upper grades have uniform requirement, student council, honor system. Discipline rests primarily with faculty. Attendance at religious services is required.

Tuition and Aid Merit scholarship grants, need-based scholarship grants, paying campus jobs available.

Admissions Traditional secondary-level entrance grade is 8. High School Placement Test required. No application fee required. On-campus interview required.

Athletics Interscholastic: basketball (girls), bowling (g), cheering (g), dance squad (g), dance team (g), danceline (g), golf (g), gymnastics (g), indoor track (g), indoor track & field (g), soccer (g), softball (g), swimming and diving (g), tennis (g), track and field (g), volleyball (g); intramural: flag football (g), kickball (g). 4 PE instructors, 18 coaches, 1 trainer.

Computers Computer network features include on-campus library services, CD-ROMs, Internet access, DVD.

Contact Mrs. Cathy Rice. 504-865-9401. Fax: 504-866-5958.

ST. MARY'S EPISCOPAL SCHOOL

60 Perkins Extension
Memphis, Tennessee 38117-3199
Head of School: Ms. Marlene R. Shaw

General Information Girls' day college-preparatory, arts, and technology school, affiliated with Episcopal Church. Grades PK–12. Founded: 1847. Setting: urban. 25-acre campus. 7 buildings on campus. Approved or accredited by National Association of Episcopal Schools, National Independent Private Schools Association, Southern Association of Colleges and Schools, Southern Association of Independent Schools, Tennessee Association of Independent Schools, The College Board, and Tennessee Department of Education. Member of National Association of Independent Schools. Endowment: $11.5 million. Total enrollment: 812. Upper school average class size: 19. Upper school faculty-student ratio: 1:19.

Upper School Student Profile Grade 9: 51 students (51 girls); Grade 10: 66 students (66 girls); Grade 11: 59 students (59 girls); Grade 12: 61 students (61 girls). 19% of students are members of Episcopal Church.

Faculty School total: 106. In upper school: 6 men, 28 women; 24 have advanced degrees.

Subjects Offered Algebra, art, art history, art history-AP, biology, biology-AP, calculus, calculus-AP, chemistry, chemistry-AP, choir, chorus, composition, computers, contemporary history, creative writing, drama, English, English language and composition-AP, English literature and composition-AP, European history-AP, French, French-AP, geometry, global issues, health, humanities, instrumental music, Latin, Latin-AP, microbiology, music, music history, music theory-AP, physical education, physics, physics-AP, pre-calculus, psychology, religion, Spanish, Spanish-AP, speech, statistics, studio art-AP, technology, theater, U.S. history, U.S. history-AP, world history.

Graduation Requirements Algebra, arts and fine arts (art, music, dance, drama), biology, chemistry, English, foreign language, geometry, physical education (includes

health), physics, pre-calculus, religion (includes Bible studies and theology), social studies (includes history), U.S. history, world history.

Special Academic Programs Advanced Placement exam preparation in 16 subject areas; honors section.

College Placement 56 students graduated in 2005; all went to college, including Auburn University; Furman University; The University of Tennessee; University of Mississippi; University of Richmond; Washington University in St. Louis. Mean SAT verbal: 657, mean SAT math: 641, mean composite ACT: 28. 88% scored over 600 on SAT verbal, 73% scored over 600 on SAT math, 80% scored over 26 on composite ACT.

Student Life Upper grades have specified standards of dress, student council, honor system. Discipline rests equally with students and faculty. Attendance at religious services is required.

Summer Programs Enrichment, sports programs offered; session focuses on summer enrichment; held both on and off campus; held at Pinecrest Retreat Center for overnight camp and swimming at a nearby residence; accepts boys and girls; open to students from other schools. 600 students usually enrolled. 2006 schedule: June 12 to July 28. Application deadline: May 5.

Tuition and Aid Day student tuition: $12,875. Tuition installment plan (Insured Tuition Payment Plan, Key Tuition Payment Plan, monthly payment plans, credit card payment). Need-based scholarship grants, discounts for children of faculty, staff, and clergy, Key Education Resources Loan Program available. In 2005–06, 11% of upper-school students received aid. Total amount of financial aid awarded in 2005–06: $149,153.

Admissions Traditional secondary-level entrance grade is 9. For fall 2005, 21 students applied for upper-level admission, 17 were accepted, 12 enrolled. ISEE, Otis-Lennon School Ability Test, ERB CPT III, school's own test or writing sample required. Deadline for receipt of application materials: none. Application fee required: $50. On-campus interview required.

Athletics Interscholastic: basketball, bowling, cross-country running, dance team, golf, lacrosse, soccer, softball, swimming and diving, tennis, track and field, volleyball; intramural: Frisbee. 2 PE instructors, 10 coaches.

Computers Computers are regularly used in career exploration, college planning, creative writing, English, foreign language, history, Latin, library, literary magazine, mathematics, music, newspaper, psychology, religious studies, research skills, SAT preparation, science, speech, theater arts, yearbook classes. Computer network features include campus e-mail, on-campus library services, CD-ROMs, online commercial services, Internet access, file transfer, office computer access, DVD, wireless campus network, full-text databases.

Contact Ms. Mandy Yandell, Director of Admission and Financial Aid. 901-537-1405. Fax: 901-685-1098. E-mail: myandell@stmarysschool.org. Web site: www.stmarysschool.org.

SAINT MARY'S HALL

9401 Starcrest Drive
San Antonio, Texas 78217
Head of School: Bob Windham

petersons.com

General Information Coeducational day college-preparatory and arts school. Grades PK–12. Founded: 1879. Setting: suburban. 60-acre campus. 6 buildings on campus. Approved or accredited by Independent Schools Association of the Southwest and Southern Association of Independent Schools. Member of National Association of Independent Schools and Secondary School Admission Test Board. Endowment: $32.7 million. Total enrollment: 918. Upper school average class size: 12. Upper school faculty-student ratio: 1:12.

Upper School Student Profile Grade 9: 69 students (39 boys, 30 girls); Grade 10: 86 students (41 boys, 45 girls); Grade 11: 90 students (47 boys, 43 girls); Grade 12: 67 students (35 boys, 32 girls).

Faculty School total: 94. In upper school: 17 men, 25 women; 22 have advanced degrees.

Subjects Offered 3-dimensional art, Advanced Placement courses, African history, algebra, American government-AP, American history, American history-AP, American literature, anatomy and physiology, art, art history, art history-AP, athletic training, ballet, basketball, biology, biology-AP, British literature, calculus, calculus-AP, cell biology, ceramics, chemistry, chemistry-AP, choir, college counseling, composition, computer programming, computer science, computer science-AP, concert choir, creative writing, dance, digital photography, drama, drawing and design, economics, English language and composition-AP, English literature and composition-AP, environmental science-AP, European history, fitness, French, French language-AP, genetics, geography, geometry, golf, government/civics, guitar, history, Japanese, jazz band, journalism, Latin, Latin American history, literary magazine, marine biology, mathematics, mathematics-AP, model United Nations, modern European history-AP, music, music theory, music theory-AP, photography, physical education, physics, physics-AP, pre-calculus, psychology, religious studies, SAT preparation, science, science research, sculpture, set design, sociology, softball, Spanish, Spanish language-AP, Spanish literature-AP, speech, statistics-AP, studio art-AP, swimming, technical theater, tennis, theater, theology, trigonometry, U.S. history, U.S. history-AP, voice, volleyball, Web site design, world geography, world history, world history-AP, world literature, world wide web design, yearbook, zoology.

Graduation Requirements Arts and fine arts (art, music, dance, drama), electives, English, foreign language, mathematics, physical education (includes health), science, social studies (includes history), theology.

Special Academic Programs Advanced Placement exam preparation in 19 subject areas; honors section; independent study; study abroad; academic accommodation for the gifted; ESL (5 students enrolled).

College Placement 61 students graduated in 2005; all went to college, including New York University; Southern Methodist University; The University of Texas at San Antonio; Trinity University; University of the South; Wake Forest University. Median SAT verbal: 619, median SAT math: 625.

Student Life Upper grades have uniform requirement, student council, honor system. Discipline rests primarily with faculty. Attendance at religious services is required.

Summer Programs Enrichment, sports, art/fine arts, computer instruction programs offered; held on campus; accepts boys and girls; open to students from other schools. 550 students usually enrolled. 2006 schedule: June 1 to August 13. Application deadline: none.

Tuition and Aid Day student tuition: $15,495. Tuition installment plan (monthly payment plans, individually arranged payment plans, full-year payment plan, 2-payment plan). Merit scholarship grants, need-based scholarship grants, Achiever Loans available. In 2005–06, 19% of upper-school students received aid; total upper-school merit-scholarship money awarded: $342,380. Total amount of financial aid awarded in 2005–06: $577,747.

Admissions Traditional secondary-level entrance grade is 9. For fall 2005, 152 students applied for upper-level admission, 40 were accepted, 27 enrolled. ISEE required. Deadline for receipt of application materials: February 15. Application fee required: $50. Interview required.

Athletics Interscholastic: ballet (boys, girls), baseball (b), basketball (b,g), cross-country running (b,g), dance (b,g), field hockey (g), fitness (b,g), golf (b,g), independent competitive sports (b,g), lacrosse (b), physical fitness (b,g), physical training (b,g), soccer (b,g), softball (g), strength & conditioning (b,g), swimming and diving (b,g), tennis (b,g), track and field (b,g), volleyball (b,g), weight training (b,g). 5 PE instructors, 35 coaches, 1 trainer.

Computers Computers are regularly used in art, newspaper, photography, yearbook classes. Computer network features include campus e-mail, on-campus library services, CD-ROMs, Internet access, wireless campus network.

Contact Ms. Elena D. Hicks, Director of Admission. 210-483-9234. Fax: 210-655-5211. E-mail: admissions@smhall.org. Web site: www.smhall.org.

See full description on page 1034.

ST. MARY'S HALL–DOANE ACADEMY

350 Riverbank
Burlington, New Jersey 08016-2199
Head of School: Mr. John F. McGee

General Information Coeducational day college-preparatory, arts, and technology school, affiliated with Episcopal Church. Grades PK–12. Founded: 1837. Setting: suburban. Nearest major city is Philadelphia, PA. 14-acre campus. 5 buildings on campus. Approved or accredited by Middle States Association of Colleges and Schools and National Association of Episcopal Schools. Member of National Association of Independent Schools. Endowment: $250,000. Total enrollment: 197. Upper school average class size: 15. Upper school faculty-student ratio: 1:6.

Upper School Student Profile Grade 7: 16 students (7 boys, 9 girls); Grade 8: 19 students (9 boys, 10 girls); Grade 9: 21 students (10 boys, 11 girls); Grade 10: 25 students (13 boys, 12 girls); Grade 11: 21 students (9 boys, 12 girls); Grade 12: 13 students (5 boys, 8 girls). 10% of students are members of Episcopal Church.

Faculty School total: 32. In upper school: 9 men, 12 women; 9 have advanced degrees.

Subjects Offered African American history, algebra, American Civil War, American literature, ancient world history, arts and crafts, band, biology, biology-AP, British literature, calculus, calculus-AP, chemistry, chemistry-AP, choir, Civil War, computer graphics, computer literacy, computer programming, computer science, computer science-AP, creative writing, cultural geography, digital photography, drama, drawing, economics, English literature and composition-AP, environmental science, ethics, European history, European history-AP, French, French-AP, geometry, graphic design, health and wellness, honors algebra, instrumental music, Latin, Latin-AP, library skills, life science, music, novel, painting, physical education, physical science, physics, piano, poetry, pre-algebra, psychology, psychology-AP, research skills, SAT preparation, sculpture, Shakespeare, short story, Spanish, Spanish-AP, speech and debate, studio art—AP, trigonometry, U.S. history, U.S. history-AP, Web site design, world history, world literature, world religions, writing skills.

Graduation Requirements Arts and fine arts (art, music, dance, drama), computer science, English, foreign language, mathematics, physical education (includes health), science, social studies (includes history), world religions.

Special Academic Programs Advanced Placement exam preparation in 9 subject areas; honors section; independent study; academic accommodation for the gifted, the musically talented, and the artistically talented.

College Placement 16 students graduated in 2005; 15 went to college, including Brown University; Duke University; Manhattan College; Temple University; Xavier

University of Louisiana. Other: 1 had other specific plans. Median SAT verbal: 565, median SAT math: 536, median combined SAT: 1646.

Student Life Upper grades have uniform requirement, student council, honor system. Discipline rests primarily with faculty. Attendance at religious services is required.

Tuition and Aid Day student tuition: $7982–$10,335. Tuition installment plan (SMART Tuition Payment Plan). Tuition reduction for siblings, need-based scholarship grants, tuition remission for children of faculty/staff available. In 2005–06, 50% of upper-school students received aid. Total amount of financial aid awarded in 2005–06: $226,000.

Admissions Traditional secondary-level entrance grade is 9. For fall 2005, 43 students applied for upper-level admission, 31 were accepted, 28 enrolled. ISEE or SSAT required. Deadline for receipt of application materials: none. Application fee required: $35. On-campus interview required.

Athletics Interscholastic: baseball (boys), basketball (b,g), crew (b,g), cross-country running (b,g), golf (b,g), soccer (b,g), softball (g); coed interscholastic: soccer, strength & conditioning; coed intramural: basketball, kickball, outdoor activities, soccer, softball, table tennis, volleyball. 1 PE instructor, 8 coaches.

Computers Computers are regularly used in graphic design, lab/keyboard, mathematics, newspaper, photography, programming, research skills, SAT preparation, science, Web site design, yearbook classes. Computer resources include campus e-mail, on-campus library services, CD-ROMs, Internet access.

Contact Mrs. Nancy Naftulin, Dean of Admission. 609-386-3500 Ext. 15. Fax: 609-386-5878. E-mail: nnaftulin@thehall.org. Web site: www.thehall.org.

SAINT MARY'S HIGH SCHOOL

2525 North Third Street
Phoenix, Arizona 85004
Head of School: Mr. Mark A. Mauro

General Information Coeducational day college-preparatory, general academic, and religious studies school, affiliated with Roman Catholic Church. Grades 9–12. Founded: 1917. Setting: urban. 6-acre campus. 4 buildings on campus. Approved or accredited by North Central Association of Colleges and Schools and Western Catholic Education Association. Endowment: $1 million. Total enrollment: 818. Upper school average class size: 25. Upper school faculty-student ratio: 1:20.

Upper School Student Profile Grade 9: 227 students (114 boys, 113 girls); Grade 10: 186 students (98 boys, 88 girls); Grade 11: 209 students (92 boys, 117 girls); Grade 12: 196 students (109 boys, 87 girls). 89% of students are Roman Catholic.

Faculty School total: 40. In upper school: 23 men, 17 women; 16 have advanced degrees.

Subjects Offered Advanced Placement courses, algebra, American government, American government-AP, American history, American history-AP, American literature, art, band, biology, British literature, British literature (honors), calculus-AP, Catholic belief and practice, chemistry, chorus, Christian and Hebrew scripture, composition, computer graphics, computer keyboarding, conceptual physics, dance, drama, economics, electives, English, English composition, English language and composition-AP, English literature, English literature and composition-AP, fine arts, foreign language, French, geometry, health, history, history of the Catholic Church, honors algebra, honors English, honors geometry, honors U.S. history, intro to computers, journalism, keyboarding/computer, language and composition, Life of Christ, literature, mathematics, peace and justice, personal finance, physical education, physical science, physics, prayer/spirituality, pre-algebra, pre-calculus, religious education, religious studies, remedial study skills, science, social studies, Spanish, Spanish language-AP, standard curriculum, state government, state history, theology, trigonometry, world geography, world history, world religions, yearbook.

Graduation Requirements Algebra, American government, American history, American literature, arts and fine arts (art, music, dance, drama), biology, British literature, British literature (honors), Catholic belief and practice, chemistry, Christian and Hebrew scripture, church history, composition, computer skills, economics, electives, geometry, honors algebra, honors English, honors geometry, honors U.S. history, modern languages, physics, pre-calculus, science, world history, 90 hours of Christian community service.

Special Academic Programs Advanced Placement exam preparation in 6 subject areas; honors section; study at local college for college credit; remedial reading and/or remedial writing; remedial math.

College Placement 194 students graduated in 2005; 184 went to college, including Arizona State University; Gonzaga University; Northern Arizona University; Santa Clara University; The University of Arizona; University of San Diego. Other: 2 went to work, 2 entered military service, 6 had other specific plans. Median composite ACT: 28. Mean SAT verbal: 529, mean SAT math: 526. 14% scored over 600 on SAT verbal, 20% scored over 600 on SAT math, 13% scored over 26 on composite ACT.

Student Life Upper grades have uniform requirement, student council. Discipline rests primarily with faculty. Attendance at religious services is required.

Summer Programs Remediation, advancement, sports, art/fine arts programs offered; session focuses on high school preparation for incoming freshmen; held on campus; accepts boys and girls; not open to students from other schools. 250 students usually enrolled. 2006 schedule: June 6 to July 14. Application deadline: May 15.

Tuition and Aid Day student tuition: $6295–$8460. Tuition installment plan (FACTS Tuition Payment Plan, monthly payment plans, individually arranged payment plans, quarterly and semester payment plans). Need-based scholarship grants, paying campus

jobs available. In 2005–06, 46% of upper-school students received aid. Total amount of financial aid awarded in 2005–06: $1,100,000.

Admissions Traditional secondary-level entrance grade is 9. For fall 2005, 320 students applied for upper-level admission, 299 were accepted, 284 enrolled. High School Placement Test required. Deadline for receipt of application materials: none. Application fee required: $200. Interview required.

Athletics Interscholastic: baseball (boys), basketball (b,g), cheering (g), cross-country running (b,g), football (b), golf (b,g), softball (g), swimming and diving (b,g), tennis (b,g), track and field (b,g), volleyball (b,g), winter soccer (b,g); coed interscholastic: cross-country running; coed intramural: bowling, racquetball. 2 PE instructors, 20 coaches, 1 trainer.

Computers Computers are regularly used in graphics, journalism, keyboarding, newspaper, yearbook classes. Computer resources include on-campus library services, CD-ROMs, Internet access.

Contact Mrs. Linda Schmaltz, Office Manager. 602-251-2500. Fax: 602-253-0337. E-mail: lschmaltz@smknights.org. Web site: www.smknights.org.

SAINT MARY'S HIGH SCHOOL

2501 East Yampa Street
Colorado Springs, Colorado 80909
Head of School: Ms. Patty Beckert

General Information Coeducational day college-preparatory and religious studies school, affiliated with Roman Catholic Church. Grades 9–12. Founded: 1885. Setting: urban. 5-acre campus. 3 buildings on campus. Approved or accredited by National Catholic Education Association, North Central Association of Colleges and Schools, and Colorado Department of Education. Total enrollment: 380. Upper school average class size: 18. Upper school faculty-student ratio: 1:11.

Upper School Student Profile 70% of students are Roman Catholic.

Faculty School total: 31. In upper school: 16 men, 15 women; 16 have advanced degrees.

Special Academic Programs Advanced Placement exam preparation in 7 subject areas; honors section; independent study.

College Placement 79 students graduated in 2005; 75 went to college. Other: 1 went to work, 3 entered military service.

Student Life Upper grades have specified standards of dress, student council. Discipline rests primarily with faculty. Attendance at religious services is required.

Summer Programs Advancement, computer instruction programs offered; held on campus; accepts boys and girls; not open to students from other schools. 220 students usually enrolled. 2006 schedule: June 5 to June 30.

Tuition and Aid Day student tuition: $5650. Tuition installment plan (SMART Tuition Payment Plan). Need-based scholarship grants available. In 2005–06, 30% of upper-school students received aid. Total amount of financial aid awarded in 2005–06: $150,000.

Admissions Traditional secondary-level entrance grade is 9. Deadline for receipt of application materials: January 4. Application fee required: $300.

Athletics Interscholastic: baseball (boys), basketball (b,g), cheering (b,g), cross-country running (b,g), football (b), golf (b), soccer (b,g), softball (g), swimming and diving (g), tennis (g), track and field (b,g), volleyball (g), wrestling (b). 2 PE instructors, 25 coaches, 2 trainers.

Contact Mrs. Leah Ramzy, Director of Admissions. 719-635-7540 Ext. 16. Fax: 719-471-7623. E-mail: lramzy@smhscs.org. Web site: smhscs.org.

ST. MARY'S INTERNATIONAL SCHOOL

1-6-19 Seta, Setagaya-ku
Tokyo 158-8668, Japan
Head of School: Br. Michel Jutras

General Information Boys' day college-preparatory school, affiliated with Roman Catholic Church. Grades K–12. Founded: 1954. Setting: urban. 9-acre campus. 1 building on campus. Approved or accredited by East Asia Regional Council of Schools, European Council of International Schools, International Baccalaureate Organization, The College Board, and Western Association of Schools and Colleges. Language of instruction: English. Total enrollment: 963. Upper school average class size: 15. Upper school faculty-student ratio: 1:10.

Upper School Student Profile Grade 9: 78 students (78 boys); Grade 10: 76 students (76 boys); Grade 11: 56 students (56 boys); Grade 12: 57 students (57 boys). 20% of students are Roman Catholic.

Faculty School total: 102. In upper school: 40 men, 20 women; 45 have advanced degrees.

Subjects Offered Algebra, American history, architecture, art, Asian studies, band, biology, calculus, ceramics, chemistry, Chinese, computer programming, computer science, earth science, economics, English, English literature, ESL, ethics, fine arts, French, geometry, German, health, history, Italian, Japanese, journalism, Latin, mathematics, mechanical drawing, music, photography, physical education, physics, religion, science, social science, social studies, Spanish, statistics, Swedish, television, theory of knowledge, trigonometry, video, world history, world literature, writing.

St. Mary's International School

Graduation Requirements Arts and fine arts (art, music, dance, drama), English, foreign language, mathematics, physical education (includes health), religion (includes Bible studies and theology), science, social science, social studies (includes history), community service (for IB students).

Special Academic Programs International Baccalaureate program; honors section; ESL (10 students enrolled).

College Placement 63 students graduated in 2005; all went to college, including Boston University; Brown University; Cornell University; New York University; University of Notre Dame; University of Southern California. Mean SAT verbal: 539, mean SAT math: 632.

Student Life Upper grades have uniform requirement, student council. Discipline rests primarily with faculty.

Summer Programs Remediation, enrichment, art/fine arts, computer instruction programs offered; session focuses on English and math remediation; held on campus; accepts boys and girls; open to students from other schools. 30 students usually enrolled. 2006 schedule: June 13 to June 25. Application deadline: none.

Tuition and Aid Day student tuition: ¥1,930,000. Need-based scholarship grants available.

Admissions Deadline for receipt of application materials: none. No application fee required. Interview recommended.

Athletics Interscholastic: baseball, basketball, cross-country running, soccer, swimming and diving, tennis, track and field, wrestling; intramural: badminton, baseball, cricket, golf, ice hockey, indoor soccer, judo, martial arts, table tennis, volleyball, water polo, weight lifting, weight training. 6 PE instructors.

Computers Computers are regularly used in architecture, art, career exploration, college planning, literary magazine, mathematics, music, newspaper, science, yearbook classes. Computer network features include on-campus library services, CD-ROMs, online commercial services, Internet access, office computer access.

Contact Mrs. Bedos Santos, Admissions Office. 81-3-3709-3411. Fax: 81-3-3707-1950. E-mail: admissions@smis.ac.jp. Web site: www.smis.ac.jp.

ST. MARY'S PREPARATORY SCHOOL
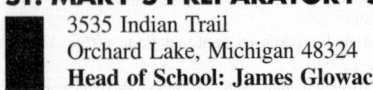

3535 Indian Trail
Orchard Lake, Michigan 48324
Head of School: James Glowacki

petersons.com

General Information Boys' boarding and day college-preparatory school, affiliated with Roman Catholic Church. Grades 9–12. Founded: 1885. Setting: suburban. Nearest major city is Detroit. Students are housed in single-sex dormitories. 80-acre campus. 12 buildings on campus. Approved or accredited by Michigan Association of Non-Public Schools and Michigan Department of Education. Total enrollment: 530. Upper school average class size: 18. Upper school faculty-student ratio: 1:10.

Upper School Student Profile Grade 9: 140 students (140 boys); Grade 10: 140 students (140 boys); Grade 11: 130 students (130 boys); Grade 12: 120 students (120 boys). 15% of students are boarding students. 90% are state residents. 5 states are represented in upper school student body. 5% are international students. International students from Brazil, Japan, Mexico, Poland, Republic of Korea, and Taiwan. 80% of students are Roman Catholic.

Faculty School total: 51. In upper school: 33 men, 18 women; 16 have advanced degrees; 11 reside on campus.

Subjects Offered Algebra, American history, American literature, art, Bible studies, biology, business, business skills, calculus, chemistry, computer programming, computer science, creative writing, drafting, driver education, earth science, ecology, economics, English, English literature, expository writing, fine arts, French, geometry, government/civics, grammar, health, history, journalism, law, mathematics, mythology, physical education, physics, Polish, psychology, religion, science, social science, social studies, Spanish, speech, theology, trigonometry, world history, writing.

Graduation Requirements Arts and fine arts (art, music, dance, drama), business skills (includes word processing), computer science, English, foreign language, mathematics, physical education (includes health), religion (includes Bible studies and theology), science, social science, social studies (includes history).

Special Academic Programs Advanced Placement exam preparation in 8 subject areas; honors section; study at local college for college credit; programs in general development for dyslexic students; special instructional classes for students with learning disabilities, Attention Deficit Disorder, and dyslexia; ESL (15 students enrolled).

College Placement 118 students graduated in 2005; 115 went to college, including Michigan State University; Oakland University; University of Detroit Mercy; University of Michigan; Wayne State University; Western Michigan University. Other: 3 went to work. Median SAT verbal: 486, median SAT math: 659, median composite ACT: 24. 5% scored over 600 on SAT verbal, 15% scored over 600 on SAT math, 30% scored over 26 on composite ACT.

Student Life Upper grades have specified standards of dress, student council, honor system. Discipline rests primarily with faculty. Attendance at religious services is required.

Summer Programs Sports programs offered; session focuses on football, basketball, and lacrosse; held on campus; accepts boys and girls; open to students from other schools. 400 students usually enrolled. 2006 schedule: June to August. Application deadline: June.

Tuition and Aid Day student tuition: $8300; 5-day tuition and room/board: $15,535; 7-day tuition and room/board: $18,600. Tuition installment plan (FACTS Tuition Payment Plan, individually arranged payment plans). Tuition reduction for siblings, merit scholarship grants, need-based scholarship grants available. In 2005–06, 50% of upper-school students received aid.

Admissions Traditional secondary-level entrance grade is 9. For fall 2005, 200 students applied for upper-level admission, 160 were accepted, 140 enrolled. STS and TOEFL required. Deadline for receipt of application materials: none. Application fee required: $30. Interview recommended.

Athletics Interscholastic: alpine skiing, baseball, basketball, crew, cross-country running, football, golf, hockey, ice hockey, indoor track, indoor track & field, jogging, lacrosse, rowing, skiing (downhill), track and field, wrestling; intramural: basketball, bicycling, billiards, bowling, fitness, ice hockey, indoor hockey, indoor track, jogging, lacrosse, mountain biking, nautilus, physical fitness, physical training, running, skiing (downhill), snowboarding, strength & conditioning, swimming and diving, table tennis, weight lifting, weight training, whiffle ball. 2 PE instructors, 25 coaches, 1 trainer.

Computers Computers are regularly used in desktop publishing, drafting, engineering, yearbook classes. Computer network features include campus e-mail, Internet access.

Contact Kevin Kosco, Dean of Admissions. 248-683-0532. Fax: 248-683-1740. E-mail: kkosco@stmarysprep.com. Web site: www.stmarysprep.com/.

See full description on page 1036.

ST. MARY'S RYKEN HIGH SCHOOL

22600 Camp Calvert Road
Leonardtown, Maryland 20650
Head of School: Mrs. Mary Joy Hurlburt

General Information Coeducational day college-preparatory, arts, religious studies, and technology school, affiliated with Roman Catholic Church. Grades 9–12. Founded: 1885. Setting: rural. Nearest major city is Washington, DC. 105-acre campus. 5 buildings on campus. Approved or accredited by Middle States Association of Colleges and Schools, National Catholic Education Association, The College Board, and Maryland Department of Education. Endowment: $240,000. Total enrollment: 670. Upper school average class size: 22. Upper school faculty-student ratio: 1:13.

Upper School Student Profile Grade 9: 180 students (65 boys, 115 girls); Grade 10: 164 students (90 boys, 74 girls); Grade 11: 176 students (84 boys, 92 girls); Grade 12: 150 students (76 boys, 74 girls). 85% of students are Roman Catholic.

Faculty School total: 45. In upper school: 16 men, 29 women; 25 have advanced degrees.

Subjects Offered Algebra, American government, American government-AP, American literature, anatomy, ancient world history, architecture, art, art appreciation, art-AP, biology, biology-AP, British literature, calculus, calculus-AP, chemistry, chemistry-AP, chorus, computer science-AP, conceptual physics, concert band, dance, drama, English composition, environmental science, environmental science-AP, French, French-AP, geometry, history of the Catholic Church, honors algebra, honors English, honors geometry, honors U.S. history, honors world history, Italian, jazz band, journalism, Latin, Microsoft, modern world history, music appreciation, music theory, music theory-AP, orchestra, peace and justice, philosophy, physical education, physics, physics-AP, psychology, psychology-AP, religion, Spanish, Spanish-AP, studio art, trigonometry, U.S. history, U.S. history-AP, Web site design, world history, world history-AP, world religions, yearbook.

Graduation Requirements Algebra, American government, American literature, arts and fine arts (art, music, dance, drama), biology, British literature, chemistry, Christian scripture, Christianity, computer applications, conceptual physics, English composition, English literature, foreign language, geometry, history of the Catholic Church, peace and justice, physical education (includes health), U.S. history, U.S. literature, world history, world literature, world religions, Christian Service Project.

Special Academic Programs Advanced Placement exam preparation in 17 subject areas; honors section; study at local college for college credit; ESL (8 students enrolled).

College Placement 134 students graduated in 2005; 122 went to college, including Clemson University; Frostburg State University; St. Mary's College of Maryland; The Catholic University of America; Towson University; University of Maryland, College Park. Other: 1 went to work, 11 had other specific plans. Mean SAT verbal: 548, mean SAT math: 515. 26% scored over 600 on SAT verbal, 19% scored over 600 on SAT math.

Student Life Upper grades have uniform requirement, student council, honor system. Discipline rests equally with students and faculty. Attendance at religious services is required.

Tuition and Aid Day student tuition: $7700. Tuition installment plan (FACTS Tuition Payment Plan). Tuition reduction for siblings, merit scholarship grants, need-based scholarship grants available. In 2005–06, 40% of upper-school students received aid; total upper-school merit-scholarship money awarded: $143,950. Total amount of financial aid awarded in 2005–06: $450,000.

Admissions Traditional secondary-level entrance grade is 9. For fall 2005, 282 students applied for upper-level admission, 275 were accepted, 180 enrolled. High

School Placement Test (closed version) from Scholastic Testing Service required. Deadline for receipt of application materials: none. Application fee required: $25.
Athletics Interscholastic: baseball (boys), basketball (b,g), cheering (g), cross-country running (b,g), field hockey (g), lacrosse (b,g), soccer (b,g), softball (g), tennis (b,g), track and field (b,g), volleyball (g), wrestling (b); coed interscholastic: golf, ice hockey, sailing. 2 PE instructors, 30 coaches, 1 trainer.
Computers Computers are regularly used in mathematics, religious studies, science, social sciences classes. Computer resources include campus e-mail, on-campus library services, Internet access.
Contact Mrs. Dawn Simpson, Director of Admissions. 301-373-4183. Fax: 301-373-4185. E-mail: admissions@smrhs.org. Web site: www.smrhs.org.

SAINT MARY'S SCHOOL

900 Hillsborough Street
Raleigh, North Carolina 27603-1689
Head of School: Ms. Theo W. Coonrod

petersons.com

General Information Girls' boarding and day college-preparatory, arts, religious studies, and technology school, affiliated with Episcopal Church. Grades 9–12. Founded: 1842. Setting: urban. Students are housed in single-sex dormitories. 23-acre campus. 27 buildings on campus. Approved or accredited by National Association of Episcopal Schools, North Carolina Association of Independent Schools, Southern Association of Colleges and Schools, and The Association of Boarding Schools. Member of National Association of Independent Schools and Secondary School Admission Test Board. Total enrollment: 268. Upper school average class size: 12. Upper school faculty-student ratio: 1:7.
Upper School Student Profile Grade 9: 61 students (61 girls); Grade 10: 75 students (75 girls); Grade 11: 75 students (75 girls); Grade 12: 57 students (57 girls). 45% of students are boarding students. 88% are state residents. 11 states are represented in upper school student body. 2% are international students. International students from Hong Kong, Republic of Korea, and United Arab Emirates.
Faculty School total: 45. In upper school: 14 men, 31 women; 33 have advanced degrees; 25 reside on campus.
Subjects Offered Algebra, American literature, anatomy, art, biology, calculus, calculus-AP, ceramics, chemistry, chemistry-AP, choral music, computer science, dance, drama, English, English literature, English literature-AP, European history, French, geometry, government/civics, Latin, mathematics, philosophy, physical education, physics, psychology, psychology-AP, religion, senior project, social studies, Spanish, speech, studio art-AP, U.S. history, U.S. history-AP, Western civilization, world literature, yearbook.
Graduation Requirements Algebra, arts and fine arts (art, music, dance, drama), biology, electives, English, foreign language, geography, geometry, government, physical education (includes health), physical science, religion (includes Bible studies and theology), social sciences, U.S. history, Western civilization.
Special Academic Programs Advanced Placement exam preparation in 9 subject areas; honors section; independent study; study at local college for college credit; special instructional classes for students with learning disabilities, Attention Deficit Disorder, and dyslexia.
College Placement 63 students graduated in 2005; all went to college, including Appalachian State University; College of Charleston; East Carolina University; North Carolina State University; The University of North Carolina at Chapel Hill; The University of North Carolina Wilmington.
Student Life Upper grades have student council, honor system. Discipline rests equally with students and faculty. Attendance at religious services is required.
Summer Programs Enrichment, sports, art/fine arts, computer instruction programs offered; session focuses on sports, fine arts, and technology day camps; held on campus; accepts girls; open to students from other schools. 2006 schedule: June to July.
Tuition and Aid Day student tuition: $13,900; 7-day tuition and room/board: $28,515. Tuition installment plan (FACTS Tuition Payment Plan, monthly payment plans, individually arranged payment plans). Merit scholarship grants, need-based scholarship grants available. In 2005–06, 51% of upper-school students received aid. Total amount of financial aid awarded in 2005–06: $1,000,000.
Admissions Traditional secondary-level entrance grade is 9. SSAT required. Deadline for receipt of application materials: none. Application fee required: $50. Interview required.
Athletics Interscholastic: basketball, cross-country running, field hockey, golf, modern dance, soccer, softball, swimming and diving, tennis, track and field, volleyball; intramural: aerobics, aerobics/dance, ballet, dance, weight training. 2 PE instructors, 7 coaches, 1 trainer.
Computers Computers are regularly used in dance, English, introduction to technology, mathematics, newspaper, publications, science, senior seminar, writing, yearbook classes. Computer network features include campus e-mail, on-campus library services, CD-ROMs, online commercial services, Internet access, wireless campus network.
Contact Mr. Matthew R. Crane, Director of Admissions. 800-948-2557. Fax: 919-424-4122. E-mail: admiss@saint-marys.edu. Web site: www.saint-marys.edu.

ST. MARY'S SCHOOL

816 Black Oak Drive
Medford, Oregon 97504-8504
Head of School: Mr. Frank Phillips

General Information Coeducational day college-preparatory, arts, and religious studies school, affiliated with Roman Catholic Church. Grades 6–12. Founded: 1865. Setting: small town. Nearest major city is Eugene. 23-acre campus. 9 buildings on campus. Approved or accredited by National Catholic Education Association, Northwest Association of Schools and Colleges, Pacific Northwest Association of Independent Schools, and Oregon Department of Education. Member of National Association of Independent Schools. Total enrollment: 317. Upper school average class size: 14. Upper school faculty-student ratio: 1:10.
Upper School Student Profile Grade 9: 58 students (26 boys, 32 girls); Grade 10: 45 students (23 boys, 22 girls); Grade 11: 42 students (19 boys, 23 girls); Grade 12: 42 students (26 boys, 16 girls). 45% of students are Roman Catholic.
Faculty School total: 31. In upper school: 12 men, 18 women; 16 have advanced degrees.
Subjects Offered Advanced Placement courses, algebra, American history, American history-AP, American literature, ancient history, art, art history-AP, biology, biology-AP, calculus-AP, ceramics, chamber groups, chemistry, chemistry-AP, chorus, community service, computer programming-AP, computer science, creative writing, drama, earth science, economics-AP, English, English-AP, environmental science-AP, ethics, European history, European history-AP, expository writing, fine arts, general science, geometry, German, government/civics, government/civics-AP, grammar, health, history, human geography—AP, instrumental music, jazz band, Latin, Latin-AP, mathematics, music theory-AP, physical education, physics, physics-AP, religion, science, social science, social studies, Spanish, Spanish-AP, speech, studio art-AP, theater, trigonometry, world history, world literature, writing.
Graduation Requirements Arts and fine arts (art, music, dance, drama), electives, English, foreign language, mathematics, physical education (includes health), religion (includes Bible studies and theology), science, social science, social studies (includes history), 100 hours of community service (25 each year in upper school).
Special Academic Programs Advanced Placement exam preparation in 20 subject areas; independent study; academic accommodation for the gifted, the musically talented, and the artistically talented.
College Placement 45 students graduated in 2005; all went to college. Mean SAT verbal: 610, mean SAT math: 620. 50% scored over 600 on SAT verbal, 58% scored over 600 on SAT math.
Student Life Upper grades have specified standards of dress, student council, honor system. Discipline rests equally with students and faculty. Attendance at religious services is required.
Summer Programs Remediation, enrichment, advancement, sports, art/fine arts programs offered; session focuses on skill building in mathematics, writing, SAT and ACT preparation, basketball, and volleyball; held on campus; accepts boys and girls; open to students from other schools. 75 students usually enrolled. 2006 schedule: June 7 to August 13. Application deadline: none.
Tuition and Aid Day student tuition: $8500. Tuition installment plan (monthly payment plans, semi-annual and annual payment plans). Tuition reduction for siblings, need-based scholarship grants available. In 2005–06, 24% of upper-school students received aid. Total amount of financial aid awarded in 2005–06: $200,000.
Admissions Traditional secondary-level entrance grade is 9. Deadline for receipt of application materials: none. Application fee required: $50. On-campus interview required.
Athletics Interscholastic: baseball (boys), basketball (b,g), cross-country running (b,g), football (b), golf (b,g), independent competitive sports (b,g), soccer (b,g), softball (g), tennis (b,g), track and field (b,g), volleyball (g); intramural: alpine skiing (b,g), baseball (b), equestrian sports (b,g), flag football (g), football (b); coed intramural: back packing, bicycling, canoeing/kayaking, equestrian sports, fitness, floor hockey, golf, hiking/backpacking, outdoor activities, outdoor recreation, skiing (cross-country), strength & conditioning, tennis, volleyball, weight lifting. 2 PE instructors.
Computers Computers are regularly used in English, history, mathematics, science, speech classes. Computer network features include campus e-mail, on-campus library services, CD-ROMs, online commercial services, Internet access, file transfer, access to homework, daily bulletins and teachers via e-mail.
Contact Michelle Tresemer, Director of Admissions. 541-773-7877 Ext. 3108. Fax: 541-772-8973. E-mail: admissions@stmarysschool.us. Web site: www. stmarysschool.us.

ST. MAUR INTERNATIONAL SCHOOL

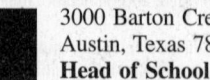

83 Yamate-cho, Naka-ku
Yokohama 231-8654, Japan
Head of School: Jeanette K. Thomas

General Information Coeducational day college-preparatory, general academic, and arts school, affiliated with Roman Catholic Church. Grades PK–12. Founded: 1872. Setting: urban. 1-hectare campus. 5 buildings on campus. Approved or accredited by European Council of International Schools and New England Association of Schools and Colleges. Language of instruction: English. Total enrollment: 467. Upper school average class size: 15. Upper school faculty-student ratio: 1:4.

Upper School Student Profile Grade 9: 31 students (12 boys, 19 girls); Grade 10: 33 students (17 boys, 16 girls); Grade 11: 36 students (19 boys, 17 girls); Grade 12: 31 students (11 boys, 20 girls). 20% of students are Roman Catholic.

Faculty School total: 62. In upper school: 15 men, 20 women; 20 have advanced degrees.

Subjects Offered Art, Asian studies, biology, chemistry, computer science, creative writing, drama, drama performance, economics, English, fine arts, French, geography, information technology, Japanese, Japanese history, Korean, mathematics, music, physical education, physics, psychology, religious education, science, social studies, Spanish, visual arts, world history.

Graduation Requirements Arts and fine arts (art, music, dance, drama), English, foreign language, mathematics, physical education (includes health), religion (includes Bible studies and theology), science, social studies (includes history), graduation requirements for IB diploma differ.

Special Academic Programs International Baccalaureate program; Advanced Placement exam preparation in 10 subject areas; honors section; independent study; academic accommodation for the gifted, the musically talented, and the artistically talented; ESL (42 students enrolled).

College Placement 30 students graduated in 2005; all went to college, including Brown University; Embry-Riddle Aeronautical University; Ohio Wesleyan University; Rochester Institute of Technology; University of Notre Dame; University of Rochester. Mean SAT math: 622. 60% scored over 600 on SAT math.

Student Life Upper grades have uniform requirement, student council. Discipline rests primarily with faculty. Attendance at religious services is required.

Summer Programs Enrichment, advancement, ESL, sports, art/fine arts, computer instruction programs offered; session focuses on TOEFL and SAT preparation ; held both on and off campus; held at nearby public athletic facilities; accepts boys and girls; open to students from other schools. 60 students usually enrolled. 2006 schedule: June 19 to July 7. Application deadline: May 21.

Tuition and Aid Day student tuition: ¥1,975,000. Tuition installment plan (monthly payment plans, individually arranged payment plans).

Admissions For fall 2005, 57 students applied for upper-level admission, 23 were accepted, 17 enrolled. School's own test required. Deadline for receipt of application materials: none. Application fee required: ¥10,000. On-campus interview required.

Athletics Interscholastic: baseball (boys), basketball (b,g), cross-country running (b,g), field hockey (g), soccer (b,g), volleyball (b,g); intramural: baseball (b), basketball (b,g), soccer (b), tennis (b,g), volleyball (b,g). 2 PE instructors.

Computers Computers are regularly used in computer applications, English, foreign language, French, information technology, mathematics, SAT preparation, science, writing, yearbook classes. Computer network features include campus e-mail, on-campus library services, CD-ROMs, Internet access, office computer access.

Contact Jeanette K. Thomas, School Head. 81-45-641-5751. Fax: 81-45-641-6688. E-mail: jthomas@stmaur.ac.jp. Web site: www.stmaur.ac.jp.

ST. MICHAEL'S CATHOLIC ACADEMY

3000 Barton Creek Boulevard
Austin, Texas 78735
Head of School: Dr. Michael J. Coury

General Information Coeducational day college-preparatory, arts, religious studies, and technology school, affiliated with Roman Catholic Church. Grades 9–12. Founded: 1984. Setting: suburban. 50-acre campus. 6 buildings on campus. Approved or accredited by National Catholic Education Association, Texas Catholic Conference, and The College Board. Total enrollment: 442. Upper school average class size: 17. Upper school faculty-student ratio: 1:11.

Upper School Student Profile Grade 9: 131 students (63 boys, 68 girls); Grade 10: 96 students (46 boys, 50 girls); Grade 11: 101 students (62 boys, 39 girls); Grade 12: 114 students (42 boys, 72 girls). 80% of students are Roman Catholic.

Faculty School total: 48. In upper school: 21 men, 27 women; 23 have advanced degrees.

Subjects Offered Algebra, American history, American literature, art, art history, biology, calculus, chemistry, computer programming, computer science, drama, economics, English, English literature, European history, fine arts, French, geography, geometry, government/civics, health, history, journalism, Latin, mathematics, music, physical education, physics, public speaking, science, social studies, Spanish, statistics, statistics-AP, theater, theology, trigonometry, world history, world literature.

Graduation Requirements Arts and fine arts (art, music, dance, drama), computer science, English, foreign language, mathematics, physical education (includes health), science, social studies (includes history), theology, 65 service hours over 4 years.

Special Academic Programs Advanced Placement exam preparation in 20 subject areas; honors section; programs in English, mathematics, general development for dyslexic students.

College Placement Colleges students went to include Baylor University; Southern Methodist University; St. Edward's University; The University of Texas at Austin. Mean SAT verbal: 607, mean SAT math: 611.

Student Life Upper grades have specified standards of dress, student council, honor system. Discipline rests primarily with faculty. Attendance at religious services is required.

Summer Programs Enrichment, advancement, computer instruction programs offered; held on campus; accepts boys and girls; open to students from other schools.

Tuition and Aid Day student tuition: $10,100. Tuition installment plan (monthly payment plans). Need-based scholarship grants available. In 2005–06, 30% of upper-school students received aid. Total amount of financial aid awarded in 2005–06: $60,000.

Admissions Traditional secondary-level entrance grade is 9. ACT-Explore or ISEE required. Deadline for receipt of application materials: none. Application fee required: $60.

Athletics Interscholastic: baseball (boys), basketball (b,g), cheering (b,g), cross-country running (b,g), football (b), golf (b,g), lacrosse (b,g), soccer (b,g), softball (g), swimming and diving (b,g), tennis (b,g), track and field (b,g), volleyball (g). 3 PE instructors, 32 coaches, 1 trainer.

Computers Computer resources include Internet access.

Contact Ms. Christyana Ramirez, Admissions Director. 512-328-0984. Fax: 512-328-2327. E-mail: cramirez@smca.com. Web site: www.smca.com.

ST. MICHAEL'S PREPARATORY SCHOOL OF THE NORBERTINE FATHERS

19292 El Toro Road
Silverado, California 92676-9710
Head of School: Rev. Gabriel D. Stack, OPRAEM

General Information Boys' boarding college-preparatory and religious studies school, affiliated with Roman Catholic Church. Grades 9–12. Founded: 1961. Setting: suburban. Nearest major city is Los Angeles. Students are housed in single-sex dormitories. 35-acre campus. 2 buildings on campus. Approved or accredited by Western Association of Schools and Colleges and California Department of Education. Total enrollment: 64. Upper school average class size: 6. Upper school faculty-student ratio: 1:3.

Upper School Student Profile Grade 9: 24 students (24 boys); Grade 10: 15 students (15 boys); Grade 11: 14 students (14 boys); Grade 12: 11 students (11 boys). 100% of students are boarding students. 90% are state residents. 4 states are represented in upper school student body. 4% are international students. International students from Mexico and Republic of Korea; 2 other countries represented in student body. 98% of students are Roman Catholic.

Faculty School total: 20. In upper school: 20 men; 18 have advanced degrees; 13 reside on campus.

Subjects Offered Algebra, American history, American history-AP, American literature, ancient history, art history, Bible studies, calculus-AP, chemistry, chorus, economics, economics-AP, English, English literature, ethics, fine arts, geography, geometry, government-AP, government/civics, health, history, Latin, Latin-AP, mathematics, philosophy, physical education, physical science, physics, pre-calculus, religion, science, social studies, Spanish, Spanish-AP, theology, trigonometry, world literature.

Graduation Requirements Arts and fine arts (art, music, dance, drama), English, foreign language, mathematics, physical education (includes health), religion (includes Bible studies and theology), science, social studies (includes history), Senior Matura.

Special Academic Programs Advanced Placement exam preparation in 6 subject areas; honors section; independent study.

College Placement 17 students graduated in 2005; all went to college, including California State Polytechnic University, Pomona; California State University, Fullerton; California State University, Long Beach; Gonzaga University; Johnson & Wales University; University of California, Davis. Mean SAT verbal: 514, mean SAT math: 530.

Student Life Upper grades have uniform requirement, student council, honor system. Discipline rests equally with students and faculty. Attendance at religious services is required.

Tuition and Aid 5-day tuition and room/board: $12,500; 7-day tuition and room/board: $14,600. Tuition installment plan (FACTS Tuition Payment Plan, monthly payment plans, individually arranged payment plans). Need-based scholarship grants available. Total amount of financial aid awarded in 2005–06: $350,000.

Admissions Traditional secondary-level entrance grade is 9. High School Placement Test required. Deadline for receipt of application materials: June 30. Application fee required: $50. Interview required.

Athletics Interscholastic: baseball, cross-country running, football, soccer; intramural: basketball, field hockey, outdoor activities, swimming and diving, table tennis, volleyball, weight lifting. 1 PE instructor, 2 coaches.

Computers Computers are regularly used in English, mathematics, science classes. Computer resources include on-campus library services, Internet access.

Contact Rev. Gabriel D. Stack, OPRAEM, Headmaster. 949-858-0222 Ext. 237. Fax: 949-858-7365. E-mail: admissions@stmichaelsprep.org. Web site: www.stmichaelsprep.org.

ST. MICHAELS UNIVERSITY SCHOOL

3400 Richmond Road
Victoria, British Columbia V8P 4P5, Canada
Head of School: Robert T. Snowden

General Information Coeducational boarding and day college-preparatory and arts school, affiliated with Church of England (Anglican). Boarding grades 8–12, day grades K–12. Founded: 1906. Setting: suburban. Students are housed in single-sex dormitories. 20-acre campus. 12 buildings on campus. Approved or accredited by Canadian Association of Independent Schools, Canadian Educational Standards Institute, Pacific Northwest Association of Independent Schools, The Association of Boarding Schools, and British Columbia Department of Education. Language of instruction: English. Endowment: CAN$2.1 million. Total enrollment: 914. Upper school average class size: 20. Upper school faculty-student ratio: 1:10.

Upper School Student Profile Grade 9: 124 students (67 boys, 57 girls); Grade 10: 134 students (60 boys, 74 girls); Grade 11: 150 students (76 boys, 74 girls); Grade 12: 142 students (76 boys, 66 girls). 42% of students are boarding students. 78% are province residents. 9 provinces are represented in upper school student body. 20% are international students. International students from Germany, Hong Kong, Japan, Mexico, Taiwan, and United States; 12 other countries represented in student body. 15% of students are members of Church of England (Anglican).

Faculty School total: 87. In upper school: 40 men, 20 women; 23 have advanced degrees; 15 reside on campus.

Subjects Offered Advanced Placement courses, algebra, art, art history, biology, calculus, career and personal planning, chemistry, computer programming, computer science, creative writing, drama, earth science, economics, English, English literature, environmental science, ESL, European history, fine arts, French, geography, geology, geometry, history, Japanese, mathematics, music, physical education, physics, science, social studies, Spanish, theater, trigonometry.

Graduation Requirements Arts and fine arts (art, music, dance, drama), career and personal planning, computer science, English, foreign language, mathematics, physical education (includes health), science, social studies (includes history), 30 hours of work experience.

Special Academic Programs Advanced Placement exam preparation in 16 subject areas; honors section; accelerated programs; term-away projects; study abroad; ESL (40 students enrolled).

College Placement 143 students graduated in 2005; 140 went to college, including McGill University; Queen's University at Kingston; Simon Fraser University; The University of British Columbia; University of Toronto; University of Victoria. Other: 1 went to work, 1 entered military service, 1 had other specific plans. Mean SAT verbal: 574, mean SAT math: 653.

Student Life Upper grades have uniform requirement, student council. Discipline rests primarily with faculty. Attendance at religious services is required.

Summer Programs Enrichment, advancement, ESL, sports, art/fine arts, computer instruction programs offered; session focuses on ESL; held both on and off campus; held at locations in local community; accepts boys and girls; open to students from other schools. 80 students usually enrolled. 2006 schedule: July to August.

Tuition and Aid Day student tuition: CAN$10,460–CAN$13,000; 7-day tuition and room/board: CAN$28,650–CAN$45,240. Tuition installment plan (Insured Tuition Payment Plan, monthly payment plans, 2-payment plan). Tuition reduction for siblings, bursaries, merit scholarship grants, need-based scholarship grants available. In 2005–06, 10% of upper-school students received aid; total upper-school merit-scholarship money awarded: CAN$100,000. Total amount of financial aid awarded in 2005–06: CAN$620,000.

Admissions Traditional secondary-level entrance grade is 9. For fall 2005, 257 students applied for upper-level admission, 120 were accepted, 120 enrolled. Naglieri Nonverbal School Ability Test, OLSAT, Stanford Achievement Test, SLEP, SSAT, Stanford Achievement Test, Otis-Lennon School Ability Test, Stanford Achievement Test, Otis-Lennon School Ability Test, school's own exam or writing sample required. Deadline for receipt of application materials: none. Application fee required: CAN$250. On-campus interview required.

Athletics Interscholastic: badminton (boys, girls), basketball (b,g), bicycling (b,g), crew (b,g), cricket (b,g), cross-country running (b,g), field hockey (g), rowing (b,g), rugby (b), running (b,g), soccer (b,g), swimming and diving (b,g), tennis (b,g), track and field (b,g), volleyball (b,g); intramural: rugby (b,g); coed interscholastic: badminton, golf, rowing, running; coed intramural: aerobics, aerobics/nautilus, alpine skiing, aquatics, back packing, badminton, ball hockey, basketball, bowling, canoeing/kayaking, climbing, cricket, cross-country running, dance, dance team, equestrian sports, fitness, floor hockey, fly fishing, hiking/backpacking, ice skating, indoor soccer, kayaking, martial arts, mountain biking, nautilus, outdoor activities, outdoor education, outdoor skills, physical training, rock climbing, sailing, skiing (downhill), snowboarding, soccer, softball, squash, swimming and diving, triathlon, ultimate Frisbee, volleyball, wall climbing, weight lifting, weight training, yoga. 5 PE instructors.

Computers Computers are regularly used in English, foreign language, humanities, library, mathematics, science, social science, writing, yearbook classes. Computer network features include campus e-mail, on-campus library services, CD-ROMs, Internet access, file transfer, office computer access.

Contact Ms. Tammy Fowler, Admissions Assistant. 250-370-6170. Fax: 250-519 7502. E-mail: admit@smus.bc.ca. Web site: www.smus.bc.ca.

SAINT PATRICK HIGH SCHOOL

5900 West Belmont Avenue
Chicago, Illinois 60634
Head of School: Br. Konrad Diebold

General Information Boys' day college-preparatory, arts, and religious studies school, affiliated with Roman Catholic Church. Grades 9–12. Founded: 1861. Setting: urban. 1 building on campus. Approved or accredited by Christian Brothers Association, North Central Association of Colleges and Schools, and Illinois Department of Education. Endowment: $200,000. Total enrollment: 1,016. Upper school average class size: 24. Upper school faculty-student ratio: 1:24.

Upper School Student Profile Grade 9: 288 students (288 boys); Grade 10: 280 students (280 boys); Grade 11: 232 students (232 boys); Grade 12: 216 students (216 boys). 90% of students are Roman Catholic.

Faculty School total: 68. In upper school: 52 men, 16 women; 42 have advanced degrees.

Subjects Offered Accounting, algebra, American history, American literature, anatomy, art, art history, biology, broadcasting, business, business skills, calculus, chemistry, chorus, computer graphics, computer science, creative writing, drama, driver education, ecology, economics, English, English literature, ESL, ethics, European history, fine arts, French, geography, geometry, German, government/civics, grammar, health, history, journalism, keyboarding, mathematics, music, physical education, physics, psychology, religion, science, social science, social studies, sociology, Spanish, speech, theater, trigonometry, word processing, world history, writing.

Graduation Requirements Arts and fine arts (art, music, dance, drama), business skills (includes word processing), computer science, English, mathematics, physical education (includes health), religion (includes Bible studies and theology), science, social science, social studies (includes history), participation in a retreat program. Community service is required.

Special Academic Programs Advanced Placement exam preparation in 8 subject areas; honors section; study at local college for college credit; remedial reading and/or remedial writing; ESL (3 students enrolled).

College Placement 215 students graduated in 2005; 199 went to college, including DePaul University; Dominican University; Northeastern Illinois University; Northern Illinois University; University of Illinois at Chicago; University of Illinois at Urbana–Champaign. Other: 6 went to work, 2 entered military service, 8 had other specific plans. Mean composite ACT: 22. 16% scored over 26 on composite ACT.

Student Life Upper grades have specified standards of dress, student council, honor system. Discipline rests primarily with faculty. Attendance at religious services is required.

Summer Programs Remediation, enrichment, sports, art/fine arts, computer instruction programs offered; session focuses on remediation; held on campus; accepts boys and girls; open to students from other schools. 625 students usually enrolled. 2006 schedule: June 19 to August 11. Application deadline: June 12.

Tuition and Aid Day student tuition: $6800. Tuition installment plan (monthly payment plans, quarterly payment plan). Need-based scholarship grants, paying campus jobs available. In 2005–06, 24% of upper-school students received aid. Total amount of financial aid awarded in 2005–06: $500,000.

Admissions Traditional secondary-level entrance grade is 9. For fall 2005, 361 students applied for upper-level admission, 356 were accepted, 288 enrolled. ACT-Explore or any standardized test required. Deadline for receipt of application materials: none. Application fee required: $250. On-campus interview required.

Athletics Interscholastic: baseball, basketball, bowling, cross-country running, diving, football, golf, soccer, swimming and diving, tennis, track and field, volleyball, water polo, wrestling; intramural: basketball, football, volleyball. 6 PE instructors, 31 coaches, 1 trainer.

Computers Computers are regularly used in business, English, foreign language, geography, graphic arts, graphic design, graphics, history, information technology, introduction to technology, library skills, mathematics, media arts, media production, media services, newspaper, photojournalism, religion, remedial study skills, research skills, science, typing, word processing, yearbook classes. Computer network features include on-campus library services, CD-ROMs, online commercial services, Internet access, DVD.

Contact Jeffrey R. Troxell, Director of Curriculum. 773-282-8844. Fax: 773-282-2361. E-mail: jtroxell@stpatrick.org. Web site: www.stpatrick.org.

SAINT PATRICK—SAINT VINCENT HIGH SCHOOL

1500 Benicia Road
Vallejo, California 94591
Head of School: Ms. Mary Ellen Ryan

General Information Coeducational day college-preparatory, arts, business, and religious studies school, affiliated with Roman Catholic Church. Grades 9–12. Founded: 1870. Setting: suburban. 31-acre campus. 8 buildings on campus. Approved or accredited by Western Association of Schools and Colleges, Western Catholic Education Association, and California Department of Education. Total enrollment: 665. Upper school average class size: 30. Upper school faculty-student ratio: 1:30.
Upper School Student Profile Grade 9: 182 students (90 boys, 92 girls); Grade 10: 172 students (76 boys, 96 girls); Grade 11: 149 students (77 boys, 72 girls); Grade 12: 162 students (69 boys, 93 girls). 80% of students are Roman Catholic.
Faculty School total: 49. In upper school: 19 men, 30 women; 20 have advanced degrees.
Subjects Offered Algebra, art, biology, calculus, calculus-AP, campus ministry, Catholic belief and practice, chemistry, chemistry-AP, choir, civics, college counseling, college planning, computer keyboarding, computer multimedia, concert bell choir, concert choir, economics, English, English language-AP, English-AP, environmental science, environmental studies, ethnic studies, film appreciation, French, French language-AP, geometry, government-AP, health, history-AP, honors algebra, honors English, honors geometry, honors U.S. history, honors world history, human biology, leadership training, organic chemistry, physical education, physics, psychology, religion, science, Spanish, Spanish language-AP, statistics, theater arts, U.S. history, vocal jazz, world history.
Graduation Requirements English, foreign language, mathematics, physical education (includes health), religion (includes Bible studies and theology), science, social studies (includes history), Christian service.
Special Academic Programs Advanced Placement exam preparation in 7 subject areas; honors section; academic accommodation for the gifted, the musically talented, and the artistically talented; remedial reading and/or remedial writing; remedial math.
College Placement 163 students graduated in 2005; 161 went to college, including California State University, Sacramento; San Francisco State University; San Jose State University; Sonoma State University; University of California, Davis; University of California, Santa Cruz. Other: 1 went to work, 1 entered military service. Mean SAT verbal: 512, mean SAT math: 510. 19% scored over 600 on SAT verbal, 19% scored over 600 on SAT math.
Student Life Upper grades have uniform requirement, student council, honor system. Discipline rests primarily with faculty. Attendance at religious services is required.
Tuition and Aid Day student tuition: $7600. Tuition installment plan (FACTS Tuition Payment Plan). Need-based scholarship grants available.
Admissions Traditional secondary-level entrance grade is 9. For fall 2005, 240 students applied for upper-level admission, 200 were accepted, 183 enrolled. High School Placement Test required. Deadline for receipt of application materials: June 30. Application fee required: $30.
Athletics Interscholastic: baseball (boys), basketball (b,g), football (b), golf (b,g), soccer (b,g), softball (g), water polo (b,g), wrestling (b); coed interscholastic: cross-country running, swimming and diving, tennis, track and field, volleyball. 4 PE instructors, 44 coaches, 1 trainer.
Computers Computers are regularly used in Web site design, yearbook classes. Computer resources include on-campus library services, CD-ROMs, Internet access.
Contact Mrs. Sheila Williams, Director of Admissions. 707-644-4425 Ext. 448. Fax: 707-644-3107. Web site: spsv.org.

SAINT PATRICK'S SCHOOL

318 Limestone Street
Maysville, Kentucky 41056
Head of School: Mr. William Hauke

General Information Coeducational day college-preparatory school, affiliated with Roman Catholic Church. Grades 1–12. Founded: 1926. Setting: small town. Nearest major city is Cincinnati, OH. 1-acre campus. 1 building on campus. Approved or accredited by Southern Association of Colleges and Schools and Kentucky Department of Education. Total enrollment: 295. Upper school average class size: 25. Upper school faculty-student ratio: 1:13.
Upper School Student Profile Grade 9: 27 students (17 boys, 10 girls); Grade 10: 25 students (10 boys, 15 girls); Grade 11: 30 students (18 boys, 12 girls); Grade 12: 18 students (7 boys, 11 girls). 75% of students are Roman Catholic.
Faculty School total: 13. In upper school: 4 men, 9 women; 11 have advanced degrees.
Subjects Offered Accounting, algebra, analytic geometry, art, art appreciation, biology, bookkeeping, calculus, chemistry, computer applications, computer keyboarding, computer literacy, drama, earth and space science, economics, English, English composition, English literature, general science, government/civics, guidance, health, health education, language arts, library, library assistant, mathematics, music, music appreciation, physical education, physical science, physics, pre-algebra, pre-calculus, psychology, religion, senior composition, senior humanities, social studies, sociology, Spanish, student government, U.S. government, U.S. history, vocal music, world geography, world history, yearbook.

Graduation Requirements Computer applications, electives, English, foreign language, mathematics, physical education (includes health), religion (includes Bible studies and theology), science, social studies (includes history). Community service is required.
Special Academic Programs Independent study.
College Placement 24 students graduated in 2005; 22 went to college, including Canisius College; Eastern Kentucky University; Northern Kentucky University; Saint Louis University; University of Kentucky; University of Louisville. Other: 2 went to work.
Student Life Upper grades have uniform requirement, student council. Discipline rests primarily with faculty. Attendance at religious services is required.
Tuition and Aid Day student tuition: $3456. Tuition installment plan (The Tuition Plan). Tuition reduction for siblings available.
Admissions Traditional secondary-level entrance grade is 9. For fall 2005, 6 students applied for upper-level admission, 5 were accepted, 5 enrolled. No application fee required. Interview required.
Athletics Interscholastic: baseball (boys, girls), basketball (b,g), cheering (g), cross-country running (b,g), golf (b), soccer (b,g), swimming and diving (b,g), tennis (b,g), track and field (b,g), volleyball (g); coed interscholastic: tennis, track and field. 1 PE instructor, 2 coaches, 2 trainers.
Computers Computers are regularly used in accounting, business applications, data processing, economics, newspaper classes. Computer network features include CD-ROMs, Internet access.
Contact Mr. Douglas K. Calland, Counselor. 606-564-5949 Ext. 238. Fax: 606-564-8795. E-mail: dcalland@stpatschool.com.

ST. PAUL ACADEMY AND SUMMIT SCHOOL

1712 Randolph
St. Paul, Minnesota 55105
Head of School: Thomas J. Rodd

General Information Coeducational day college-preparatory school. Grades K–12. Founded: 1900. Setting: urban. 32-acre campus. 4 buildings on campus. Approved or accredited by Independent Schools Association of the Central States and Minnesota Department of Education. Member of National Association of Independent Schools. Endowment: $37,893. Total enrollment: 894. Upper school average class size: 16. Upper school faculty-student ratio: 1:7.
Upper School Student Profile Grade 9: 90 students (47 boys, 43 girls); Grade 10: 83 students (44 boys, 39 girls); Grade 11: 93 students (42 boys, 51 girls); Grade 12: 93 students (41 boys, 52 girls).
Faculty School total: 104. In upper school: 20 men, 36 women; 44 have advanced degrees.
Subjects Offered Algebra, American literature, art, biology, calculus, ceramics, chemistry, Chinese, creative writing, criminal justice, current events, debate, drama, earth science, economics, English, English literature, European history, expository writing, fine arts, French, geometry, German, journalism, law and the legal system, marine biology, mathematics, multicultural studies, music, music theory, newspaper, photography, physical education, physics, psychology, science, senior project, Shakespeare, social psychology, social studies, sociology, space and physical sciences, Spanish, trigonometry, world history, world literature, world religions, yearbook.
Graduation Requirements Arts and fine arts (art, music, dance, drama), English, foreign language, mathematics, physical education (includes health), science, social studies (includes history), participation in athletics, month-long senior project, senior speech.
Special Academic Programs Honors section; independent study; term-away projects; study abroad.
College Placement 100 students graduated in 2005; 99 went to college, including Carleton College; St. Olaf College; The George Washington University; University of Minnesota, Twin Cities Campus; University of Pennsylvania; University of Wisconsin–Madison. Other: 1 went to work. Mean SAT verbal: 644, mean SAT math: 653, mean composite ACT: 28. 69% scored over 600 on SAT verbal, 74% scored over 600 on SAT math, 75% scored over 26 on composite ACT.
Student Life Upper grades have specified standards of dress, student council. Discipline rests equally with students and faculty.
Summer Programs Remediation, enrichment, sports, art/fine arts programs offered; session focuses on academic enrichment and the arts; held on campus; accepts boys and girls; open to students from other schools. 900 students usually enrolled. 2006 schedule: June 19 to July 28. Application deadline: none.
Tuition and Aid Day student tuition: $19,400. Tuition installment plan (Insured Tuition Payment Plan, monthly payment plans). Need-based scholarship grants, need-based loans available. In 2005–06, 14% of upper-school students received aid. Total amount of financial aid awarded in 2005–06: $1,624,860.
Admissions Traditional secondary-level entrance grade is 9. For fall 2005, 60 students applied for upper-level admission, 39 were accepted, 24 enrolled. SSAT, ERB, PSAT, SAT, PLAN or ACT or writing sample required. Deadline for receipt of application materials: February 16. Application fee required: $80. Interview required.
Athletics Interscholastic: alpine skiing (boys, girls), baseball (b), basketball (b,g), cross-country running (b,g), danceline (g), diving (b,g), fencing (b,g), football (b), golf (b,g), ice hockey (b,g), skiing (cross-country) (b,g), skiing (downhill) (b,g), swimming and diving (b,g), tennis (b,g), track and field (b,g); intramural: outdoor adventure (b,g),

weight training (b,g), wilderness survival (b,g); coed intramural: hiking/backpacking, physical fitness, snowboarding, table tennis. 3 PE instructors, 78 coaches, 1 trainer.

Computers Computers are regularly used in all academic classes. Computer network features include campus e-mail, on-campus library services, CD-ROMs, online commercial services, Internet access, file transfer, office computer access, DVD, wireless campus network, laptop program (beginning in grade 7).

Contact Sally Foster, Director of Admissions. 651-698-2451. Fax: 651-698-6787. E-mail: sfoster@spa.edu. Web site: www.spa.edu.

SAINT PAUL LUTHERAN HIGH SCHOOL

petersons.com

205 South Main Street
PO Box 719
Concordia, Missouri 64020
Head of School: Rev. Paul M. Mehl

General Information Coeducational boarding and day college-preparatory, general academic, arts, and religious studies school, affiliated with Lutheran Church–Missouri Synod. Grades 9–12. Founded: 1883. Setting: small town. Nearest major city is Kansas City. Students are housed in single-sex dormitories. 50-acre campus. 9 buildings on campus. Approved or accredited by Lutheran School Accreditation Commission, Midwest Association of Boarding Schools, North Central Association of Colleges and Schools, and Missouri Department of Education. Endowment: $1.5 million. Total enrollment: 169. Upper school average class size: 20. Upper school faculty-student ratio: 1:9.

Upper School Student Profile Grade 9: 24 students (8 boys, 16 girls); Grade 10: 38 students (14 boys, 24 girls); Grade 11: 67 students (30 boys, 37 girls); Grade 12: 40 students (17 boys, 23 girls). 59% of students are boarding students. 49% are state residents. 13 states are represented in upper school student body. 33% are international students. International students from Hong Kong, Japan, Norway, Republic of Korea, Taiwan, and Viet Nam; 2 other countries represented in student body. 70% of students are Lutheran Church–Missouri Synod.

Faculty School total: 19. In upper school: 12 men, 5 women; 13 have advanced degrees; 11 reside on campus.

Subjects Offered Accounting, algebra, American history, American literature, art, band, Bible studies, biology, business law, business skills, ceramics, chemistry, child development, chorus, community service, composition, computer programming, computer science, consumer mathematics, creative writing, drawing, driver education, economics, English, English literature, family studies, fine arts, first aid, general science, geography, geometry, German, government/civics, health, keyboarding, math analysis, mathematics, music appreciation, music theory, novels, painting, physical education, physical science, physics, poetry, psychology, religion, science, Shakespeare, social studies, Spanish, speech, statistics, theology, trigonometry, world history, world literature, writing.

Graduation Requirements Arts and fine arts (art, music, dance, drama), computer science, English, foreign language, mathematics, physical education (includes health), practical arts, religion (includes Bible studies and theology), science, social studies (includes history), 3.0 grade point average on a 4.0 scale for college preparatory students, above (national) average score on ACT or SAT. Community service is required.

Special Academic Programs International Baccalaureate program; independent study; study at local college for college credit.

College Placement 36 students graduated in 2005; 33 went to college, including Central Missouri State University; Concordia University; State Fair Community College; University of Missouri–Columbia. Other: 2 went to work, 1 entered military service. 25% scored over 26 on composite ACT.

Student Life Upper grades have specified standards of dress, student council, honor system. Discipline rests primarily with faculty. Attendance at religious services is required.

Tuition and Aid Day student tuition: $6900; 7-day tuition and room/board: $11,000. Guaranteed tuition plan. Tuition installment plan (monthly payment plans; individually arranged payment plans, lump sum payment discount plan). Tuition reduction for siblings, need-based scholarship grants, paying campus jobs, LCMS Grants for church vocation students, early bird tuition grants available. In 2005–06, 52% of upper-school students received aid. Total amount of financial aid awarded in 2005–06: $337,311.

Admissions Traditional secondary-level entrance grade is 9. For fall 2005, 100 students applied for upper-level admission, 90 were accepted, 74 enrolled. School placement exam required. Deadline for receipt of application materials: none. Application fee required: $100. On-campus interview recommended.

Athletics Interscholastic: baseball (boys), basketball (b,g), cheering (g), cross-country running (b,g), football (b), soccer (b,g), softball (g), track and field (b,g), volleyball (g); intramural: baseball (b), basketball (b,g), football (b), golf (b,g), jogging (b,g), roller blading (b,g), running (b,g), soccer (b,g), softball (g), strength & conditioning (b,g), tennis (b,g), volleyball (b,g), weight lifting (b,g); coed interscholastic: cross-country running, track and field; coed intramural: jogging, roller blading, running, soccer, table tennis. 1 PE instructor, 1 coach.

Computers Computers are regularly used in Christian doctrine, creative writing, data processing, English, freshman foundations, history, keyboarding, lab/keyboard, library skills, religious studies, speech, study skills, word processing, writing, writing, yearbook classes. Computer resources include CD-ROMs, Internet access.

Contact Mrs. Gloria A. Burrow, Director of Admissions. 660-463-2238 Ext. 231. Fax: 660-463-7621. E-mail: gburrow@splhs.org. Web site: www.GoSaintPaul.org.

ANNOUNCEMENT FROM THE SCHOOL Saint Paul's campus in a quiet Midwest city offers residential and day students a unique learning environment that is drug-, tobacco-, and alcohol-free. A pervasive Christian atmosphere combined with a student-faculty ratio of 17:1, general and college-preparatory curriculums, and courses for college credit offer excellence in education and well-being. Saint Paul's is a Christus Award–winning school. Web site: http://www.GoSaintPaul.org.

ST. PAUL'S EPISCOPAL SCHOOL

161 Dogwood Lane
Mobile, Alabama 36608
Head of School: Mr. Robert H. Rutledge

General Information Coeducational day college-preparatory, arts, and technology school, affiliated with Episcopal Church. Grades PK–12. Founded: 1947. Setting: suburban. 35-acre campus. 10 buildings on campus. Approved or accredited by National Association of Episcopal Schools, Southern Association of Colleges and Schools, Southern Association of Independent Schools, and Alabama Department of Education. Member of National Association of Independent Schools and Secondary School Admission Test Board. Endowment: $1 million. Total enrollment: 1,577. Upper school average class size: 21. Upper school faculty-student ratio: 1:16.

Upper School Student Profile Grade 9: 153 students (74 boys, 79 girls); Grade 10: 147 students (82 boys, 65 girls); Grade 11: 154 students (70 boys, 84 girls); Grade 12: 156 students (81 boys, 75 girls). 23% of students are members of Episcopal Church.

Faculty School total: 140. In upper school: 11 men, 32 women; 35 have advanced degrees.

Subjects Offered Algebra, American history, American literature, art, band, biology, British literature-AP, calculus, chemistry, composition, computer science, drama, driver education, economics, English, English literature, English-AP, European history, fine arts, French, geometry, government/civics, grammar, history, human anatomy, instrumental music, journalism, Latin, marine biology, mathematics, music, photography, physical education, physics, pre-calculus, Spanish, speech, theater, trigonometry, world history.

Graduation Requirements Arts and fine arts (art, music, dance, drama), English, foreign language, history, mathematics, physical education (includes health), science. Community service is required.

Special Academic Programs Advanced Placement exam preparation in 6 subject areas; honors section; study at local college for college credit; special instructional classes for students with diagnosed learning disabilities.

College Placement 135 students graduated in 2005; all went to college, including Auburn University; Birmingham-Southern College; The University of Alabama; University of Mississippi; University of South Alabama; University of Southern Mississippi.

Student Life Upper grades have uniform requirement, student council, honor system. Discipline rests primarily with faculty. Attendance at religious services is required.

Summer Programs Remediation, enrichment, advancement, sports, art/fine arts, computer instruction programs offered; session focuses on enrichment; held both on and off campus; held at various sites in Europe and around the world; accepts boys and girls; open to students from other schools. 175 students usually enrolled. 2006 schedule: June to August. Application deadline: May.

Tuition and Aid Day student tuition: $6920. Tuition installment plan (monthly payment plans, semi-annual payment plan). Need-based scholarship grants available. In 2005–06, 6% of upper-school students received aid. Total amount of financial aid awarded in 2005–06: $326,000.

Admissions Traditional secondary-level entrance grade is 9. For fall 2005, 38 students applied for upper-level admission, 30 were accepted, 24 enrolled. ERB CTP IV, Otis-Lennon and 2 sections of ERB or writing sample required. Deadline for receipt of application materials: none. No application fee required. On-campus interview required.

Athletics Interscholastic: baseball (boys), basketball (b,g), cheering (g), cross-country running (b,g), football (b), golf (b,g), indoor track & field (b,g), soccer (b,g), softball (g), swimming and diving (b,g), tennis (b,g), track and field (b,g), volleyball (g), weight lifting (b), winter (indoor) track (b,g); intramural: basketball (b,g), cheering (g), soccer (b,g), volleyball (g), weight lifting (b). 9 PE instructors, 18 coaches, 4 trainers.

Computers Computers are regularly used in college planning, economics, English, history, journalism, keyboarding, newspaper, science, video film production, yearbook classes. Computer network features include campus e-mail, on-campus library services, CD-ROMs, online commercial services, Internet access, file transfer, office computer access, DVD, wireless campus network.

Contact Mrs. Julie L. Taylor, Admissions Office. 251-461-2129. Fax: 251-342-1844. E-mail: jtaylor@stpaulsmobile.net. Web site: www.stpaulsmobile.net.

ST. PAUL'S HIGH SCHOOL

2200 Grant Avenue
Winnipeg, Manitoba R3P 0P8, Canada
Head of School: Fr. Joe Mroz, SJ

General Information Boys' day college-preparatory, arts, religious studies, and technology school, affiliated with Roman Catholic Church. Grades 9–12. Founded: 1926. Setting: suburban. 18-acre campus. 1 building on campus. Approved or accredited by Jesuit Secondary Education Association and Manitoba Department of Education. Language of instruction: English. Endowment: CAN$3.5 million. Total enrollment: 589. Upper school average class size: 26. Upper school faculty-student ratio: 1:14.

Upper School Student Profile Grade 9: 144 students (144 boys); Grade 10: 143 students (143 boys); Grade 11: 154 students (154 boys); Grade 12: 148 students (148 boys). 70% of students are Roman Catholic.

Faculty School total: 40. In upper school: 37 men, 3 women; 10 have advanced degrees.

Subjects Offered Algebra, American history, art, biology, calculus, chemistry, classics, computer science, current events, economics, English, ethics, French, geography, geometry, history, law, mathematics, media, multimedia, multimedia design, music, physical education, physics, political science, psychology, religion, science, social studies, speech, theology.

Graduation Requirements English, mathematics, physical education (includes health), religion (includes Bible studies and theology), science, social studies (includes history), completion of Christian service program.

Special Academic Programs Advanced Placement exam preparation in 3 subject areas; honors section; remedial math.

College Placement 124 students graduated in 2005; 117 went to college, including McGill University; The University of Winnipeg; University of Manitoba; University of North Dakota; University of Toronto. Other: 4 went to work, 3 had other specific plans.

Student Life Upper grades have specified standards of dress, student council, honor system. Discipline rests primarily with faculty. Attendance at religious services is required.

Summer Programs Sports programs offered; held on campus; accepts boys; not open to students from other schools. 2006 schedule: August 15 to August 29.

Tuition and Aid Day student tuition: CAN$4400. Tuition installment plan (Insured Tuition Payment Plan, monthly payment plans, individually arranged payment plans). Bursaries, merit scholarship grants, need-based loans available. In 2005–06, 13% of upper-school students received aid; total upper-school merit-scholarship money awarded: CAN$20,000. Total amount of financial aid awarded in 2005–06: CAN$140,000.

Admissions Traditional secondary-level entrance grade is 9. For fall 2005, 350 students applied for upper-level admission, 150 were accepted, 150 enrolled. Achievement tests and STS required. Deadline for receipt of application materials: February 28. Application fee required: CAN$50. On-campus interview required.

Athletics Interscholastic: badminton, basketball, cross-country running, curling, football, golf, ice hockey, indoor track, indoor track & field, rugby, soccer, track and field, volleyball, wrestling; intramural: basketball, curling, football, golf, physical fitness, physical training, skiing (downhill), strength & conditioning, table tennis, volleyball, weight training. 3 PE instructors.

Computers Computers are regularly used in French, French as a second language, mathematics, multimedia, religious studies, science classes. Computer network features include on-campus library services, CD-ROMs, online commercial services, Internet access, DVD.

Contact Mr. Tom Lussier, Principal. 204-831-2300. Fax: 204-831-2340. E-mail: tlussier@merlin.mb.ca. Web site: www.stpauls.mb.ca.

ST. PAUL'S PREPARATORY ACADEMY

Phoenix, Arizona
See Special Needs Schools section.

ST. PAUL'S SCHOOL

11152 Falls Road
PO Box 8100
Brooklandville, Maryland 21022-8100
Head of School: Mr. Thomas J. Reid

General Information Coeducational day (girls' only in lower grades) college-preparatory school, affiliated with Episcopal Church. Boys grades P1–12, girls grades P1–4. Founded: 1849. Setting: suburban. Nearest major city is Baltimore. 95-acre campus. 23 buildings on campus. Approved or accredited by Association of Independent Maryland Schools and Maryland Department of Education. Member of National Association of Independent Schools. Endowment: $23 million. Total enrollment: 872. Upper school average class size: 17. Upper school faculty-student ratio: 1:9.

Upper School Student Profile Grade 9: 78 students (78 boys); Grade 10: 76 students (76 boys); Grade 11: 82 students (82 boys); Grade 12: 76 students (76 boys).

Faculty School total: 119. In upper school: 27 men, 7 women; 28 have advanced degrees.

Subjects Offered Acting, algebra, American history, American literature, anatomy, art, art history, biology, biology-AP, calculus, calculus-AP, chemistry, Civil War, community service, design, drama, drawing, driver education, economics, English, ethics, forensics, French, French-AP, geometry, German, German-AP, health, instrumental music, Japanese, Latin American studies, mathematics, music, oceanography, painting, philosophy, photography, physical education, physics, physics-AP, physiology, psychology, religion, SAT/ACT preparation, Spanish, Spanish-AP, statistics, statistics-AP, theater, trigonometry, U.S. Presidents, urban studies, world history, world literature.

Graduation Requirements Arts and fine arts (art, music, dance, drama), English, foreign language, mathematics, physical education (includes health), religion (includes Bible studies and theology), science, social science, social studies (includes history). Community service is required.

Special Academic Programs International Baccalaureate program; Advanced Placement exam preparation in 12 subject areas; honors section; independent study; term-away projects; study abroad; academic accommodation for the gifted; programs in general development for dyslexic students.

College Placement 77 students graduated in 2005; 76 went to college, including University of Delaware; University of Maryland, College Park; University of Pennsylvania. Other: 1 entered a postgraduate year.

Student Life Upper grades have specified standards of dress, student council, honor system. Discipline rests equally with students and faculty. Attendance at religious services is required.

Tuition and Aid Day student tuition: $17,450. Tuition installment plan (Key Tuition Payment Plan). Need-based scholarship grants available. In 2005–06, 20% of upper-school students received aid. Total amount of financial aid awarded in 2005–06: $638,425.

Admissions Traditional secondary-level entrance grade is 9. For fall 2005, 96 students applied for upper-level admission, 60 were accepted, 26 enrolled. CTP III, ERB, ISEE or SSAT required. Deadline for receipt of application materials: January 15. Application fee required: $50. On-campus interview required.

Athletics Interscholastic: baseball, basketball, crew, cross-country running, football, golf, ice hockey, independent competitive sports, lacrosse, soccer, squash, tennis, volleyball, wrestling; intramural: bicycling, combined training, Frisbee, mountain biking, outdoor activities, physical fitness, physical training, ropes courses, running, soccer, softball, strength & conditioning, ultimate Frisbee, weight training. 3 PE instructors, 3 coaches, 2 trainers.

Computers Computers are regularly used in all classes. Computer network features include campus e-mail, on-campus library services, CD-ROMs, online commercial services, Internet access, file transfer, DVD, wireless campus network.

Contact Ms. Cassie Andrzejewski, Director of Admissions and Financial Aid. 410-821-3034. Fax: 410-427-0380. E-mail: admissions@stpaulsschool.org. Web site: www.stpaulsschool.org.

ST. PAUL'S SCHOOL

325 Pleasant Street
Concord, New Hampshire 03301-2591
Head of School: Mr. William R. Matthews Jr.

General Information Coeducational boarding college-preparatory and arts school, affiliated with Episcopal Church. Grades 9–12. Founded: 1856. Setting: rural. Nearest major city is Manchester. Students are housed in single-sex dormitories. 2,000-acre campus. 75 buildings on campus. Approved or accredited by Association of Independent Schools in New England, National Association of Episcopal Schools, New England Association of Schools and Colleges, The Association of Boarding Schools, and New Hampshire Department of Education. Member of National Association of Independent Schools and Secondary School Admission Test Board. Endowment: $334 million. Total enrollment: 533. Upper school average class size: 10. Upper school faculty-student ratio: 1:5.

Upper School Student Profile Grade 9: 108 students (55 boys, 53 girls); Grade 10: 141 students (79 boys, 62 girls); Grade 11: 151 students (70 boys, 81 girls); Grade 12: 133 students (69 boys, 64 girls). 100% of students are boarding students. 15% are state residents. 37 states are represented in upper school student body. 17% are international students. International students from Canada, Democratic People's Republic of Korea, Hong Kong, Jamaica, Japan, and United Kingdom; 15 other countries represented in student body. 33% of students are members of Episcopal Church.

Faculty School total: 104. In upper school: 55 men, 45 women; 76 have advanced degrees; 100 reside on campus.

Subjects Offered Algebra, American history, American literature, applied arts, applied music, architecture, art, art history, astronomy, biology, calculus, ceramics, chemistry, Chinese, classical civilization, classical Greek literature, classical language, computer math, computer programming, computer science, creative writing, dance, drama, driver education, ecology, English, English literature, environmental science, ethics, European history, fine arts, French, geometry, German, government/civics,

grammar, Greek, health, history, humanities, instrumental music, Japanese, Latin, mathematics, music, photography, physical education, physics, religion, science, social studies, Spanish, speech, statistics, theater, trigonometry, writing.

Graduation Requirements Art, athletics, humanities, language, mathematics, religion (includes Bible studies and theology), science, residential life. Community service is required.

Special Academic Programs Advanced Placement exam preparation in 19 subject areas; honors section; accelerated programs; independent study; term-away projects; study abroad; academic accommodation for the gifted, the musically talented, and the artistically talented.

College Placement 131 students graduated in 2005; 130 went to college, including Brown University; Dartmouth College; Georgetown University; Harvard University; University of Pennsylvania; Yale University. Other: 1 had other specific plans.

Student Life Upper grades have specified standards of dress, student council, honor system. Discipline rests primarily with faculty. Attendance at religious services is required.

Summer Programs Enrichment programs offered; session focuses on enrichment for New Hampshire public high school juniors only; held on campus; accepts boys and girls; open to students from other schools. 245 students usually enrolled. 2006 schedule: June 23 to July 30. Application deadline: December 1.

Tuition and Aid 7-day tuition and room/board: $34,965. Tuition installment plan (Academic Management Services Plan, monthly payment plans). Merit scholarship grants, need-based scholarship grants, need-based loans, tuition remission for children of faculty and staff available. In 2005–06, 33% of upper-school students received aid; total upper-school merit-scholarship money awarded: $548,570. Total amount of financial aid awarded in 2005–06: $5,300,000.

Admissions Traditional secondary-level entrance grade is 9. For fall 2005, 1,082 students applied for upper-level admission, 241 were accepted, 164 enrolled. SSAT and TOEFL required. Deadline for receipt of application materials: January 15. Application fee required: $50. Interview required.

Athletics Interscholastic: alpine skiing (boys, girls), baseball (b), basketball (b,g), crew (b,g), cross-country running (b,g), field hockey (g), football (b), ice hockey (b,g), lacrosse (b,g), rowing (b,g), skiing (cross-country) (b,g), skiing (downhill) (b,g), soccer (b,g), softball (g), squash (b,g), tennis (b,g), track and field (b,g), volleyball (g), wrestling (b); intramural: crew (b,g), ice hockey (b,g), rowing (b,g), soccer (b,g); coed interscholastic: ballet; coed intramural: aerobics, aerobics/nautilus, alpine skiing, back packing, baseball, basketball, crew, equestrian sports, fitness, fly fishing, horseback riding, ice hockey, rowing, skeet shooting, skiing (cross-country), skiing (downhill), snowboarding, soccer, squash, tai chi, tennis, weight training. 4 coaches, 2 trainers.

Computers Computers are regularly used in English, foreign language, humanities, mathematics, science classes. Computer network features include campus e-mail, on-campus library services, CD-ROMs, online commercial services, Internet access.

Contact Ms. Holly Foote, Office Coordinator. 603-229-4700. Fax: 603-229-4771. E-mail: admissions@sps.edu. Web site: www.sps.edu.

See full description on page 1038.

ST. PAUL'S SCHOOL FOR GIRLS

11232 Falls Road
Brooklandville, Maryland 21022
Head of School: Mr. Michael N. Eanes

General Information Girls' day college-preparatory, arts, religious studies, and technology school, affiliated with Episcopal Church. Grades 5–12. Founded: 1959. Setting: suburban. Nearest major city is Baltimore. 38-acre campus. 4 buildings on campus. Approved or accredited by Association of Independent Maryland Schools, National Association of Episcopal Schools, and Maryland Department of Education. Member of National Association of Independent Schools. Endowment: $7.1 million. Total enrollment: 477. Upper school average class size: 15. Upper school faculty-student ratio: 1:7.

Upper School Student Profile Grade 9: 82 students (82 girls); Grade 10: 67 students (67 girls); Grade 11: 72 students (72 girls); Grade 12: 63 students (63 girls).

Faculty School total: 63. In upper school: 7 men, 28 women; 24 have advanced degrees.

Subjects Offered Algebra, American history, American literature, anatomy, ancient history, art, biology, biology-AP, biotechnology, calculus, calculus-AP, chemistry, chemistry-AP, chorus, community service, computer science, dance, drama, economics, economics-AP, English, English language and composition-AP, English literature and composition-AP, English-AP, environmental science, environmental science-AP, ethics, fine arts, forensics, French, French-AP, genetics, geography, geometry, German, German-AP, health, history, Japanese, journalism, literary magazine, literature, mathematics, mechanics, medieval history, modern history, music, newspaper, optics, photography, physical education, physics, physics-AP, physiology, pre-calculus, psychology-AP, religion, research skills, science, social studies, Spanish, Spanish language-AP, speech, sports medicine, statistics, studio art-AP, theater, trigonometry, U.S. history-AP, world culture, world history.

Graduation Requirements Arts and fine arts (art, music, dance, drama), English, foreign language, mathematics, physical education (includes health), religion (includes Bible studies and theology), science, social studies (includes history), senior work project. Community service is required.

Special Academic Programs Advanced Placement exam preparation in 16 subject areas; honors section; accelerated programs; independent study; term-away projects; domestic exchange program; study abroad; academic accommodation for the gifted, the musically talented, and the artistically talented.

College Placement 62 students graduated in 2005; all went to college, including Bucknell University; Dickinson College; University of Pennsylvania; Vanderbilt University. Mean SAT verbal: 600, mean SAT math: 600.

Student Life Upper grades have uniform requirement, student council, honor system. Discipline rests equally with students and faculty.

Tuition and Aid Day student tuition: $18,295. Tuition installment plan (Key Tuition Payment Plan). Merit scholarship grants, need-based scholarship grants available. In 2005–06, 18% of upper-school students received aid; total upper-school merit-scholarship money awarded: $18,295. Total amount of financial aid awarded in 2005–06: $575,033.

Admissions Traditional secondary-level entrance grade is 9. ISEE required. Deadline for receipt of application materials: January 15. Application fee required: $50. On-campus interview required.

Athletics Interscholastic: badminton, basketball, crew, cross-country running, field hockey, golf, indoor soccer, lacrosse, modern dance, physical fitness, rowing, soccer, softball, squash, swimming and diving, tennis, volleyball; coed intramural: sailing. 4 PE instructors, 12 coaches, 1 trainer.

Computers Computers are regularly used in college planning, creative writing, current events, English, French, geography, history, introduction to technology, journalism, language development, library science, literary magazine, mathematics, newspaper, photography, psychology, religious studies, research skills, SAT preparation, science, Spanish, study skills, technology, yearbook classes. Computer network features include campus e-mail, on-campus library services, CD-ROMs, online commercial services, Internet access, file transfer, office computer access, wireless campus network, Moodle, Senior Systems, Blackbaud.

Contact Sheri Reynolds, Admission Administrative Assistant. 443-632-1002. Fax: 410-828-7238. E-mail: sreynolds@spsfg.org. Web site: www.spsfg.org.

ST. PETER'S PREPARATORY SCHOOL

144 Grand Street
Jersey City, New Jersey 07302
Head of School: Rev. James F. Keenan, SJ

General Information Boys' day college-preparatory, arts, technology, and music school, affiliated with Roman Catholic Church. Grades 9–12. Founded: 1872. Setting: urban. Nearest major city is New York, NY. 5-acre campus. 6 buildings on campus. Approved or accredited by Jesuit Secondary Education Association, Middle States Association of Colleges and Schools, and New Jersey Department of Education. Languages of instruction: Spanish, French, and Italian. Endowment: $10 million. Total enrollment: 930. Upper school average class size: 22. Upper school faculty-student ratio: 1:10.

Upper School Student Profile Grade 9: 248 students (248 boys); Grade 10: 232 students (232 boys); Grade 11: 222 students (222 boys); Grade 12: 228 students (228 boys). 80% of students are Roman Catholic.

Faculty School total: 77. In upper school: 54 men, 21 women; 65 have advanced degrees.

Subjects Offered Advanced Placement courses, algebra, American history, American history-AP, American literature, art, art history, Bible studies, biology, biology-AP, calculus, calculus-AP, chemistry, chemistry-AP, choral music, Christian ethics, computer programming, computer science, computer science-AP, concert band, creative writing, drawing, driver education, economics, economics-AP, English, English language-AP, English literature, English-AP, European history, French, French-AP, geometry, German, Greek, history, HTML design, Irish studies, Italian, journalism, Latin, Latin-AP, mathematics, music, music theory, physical education, physics, religion, sculpture, Shakespeare, social justice, Spanish, Spanish language-AP, Spanish literature-AP, statistics, statistics-AP, studio art, theology, trigonometry, Web site design, world civilizations, world history, world literature, writing.

Graduation Requirements 60 hours of community service in the third (junior) year.

Special Academic Programs Advanced Placement exam preparation in 10 subject areas; honors section; study abroad.

College Placement 226 students graduated in 2005; 220 went to college, including Fordham University; Georgetown University; Rutgers, The State University of New Jersey, Rutgers College; Saint Joseph's University; Saint Peter's College; The University of Scranton. Other: 1 went to work, 2 entered military service, 3 had other specific plans. Median SAT verbal: 570, median SAT math: 590. 40% scored over 600 on SAT verbal, 49% scored over 600 on SAT math.

Student Life Upper grades have specified standards of dress, student council, honor system. Discipline rests primarily with faculty.

Summer Programs Remediation, art/fine arts programs offered; held on campus; accepts boys and girls; open to students from other schools. 20 students usually enrolled. 2006 schedule: June 26 to July 28. Application deadline: June 20.

Tuition and Aid Day student tuition: $6750. Tuition installment plan (monthly payment plans, individually arranged payment plans). Merit scholarship grants, need-based scholarship grants, paying campus jobs available. In 2005–06, 45% of upper-school students received aid; total upper-school merit-scholarship money awarded: $160,000. Total amount of financial aid awarded in 2005–06: $700,000.

St. Peter's Preparatory School

Admissions Traditional secondary-level entrance grade is 9. For fall 2005, 850 students applied for upper-level admission, 350 were accepted, 248 enrolled. Cooperative Entrance Exam (McGraw-Hill) required. Deadline for receipt of application materials: November 15. No application fee required.

Athletics Interscholastic: baseball, basketball, bowling, cross-country running, diving, football, golf, ice hockey, indoor track, indoor track & field, lacrosse, rugby, soccer, swimming and diving, tennis, track and field, volleyball, winter (indoor) track, wrestling; intramural: basketball, cricket, fencing, fishing, flag football, football, Frisbee, handball, indoor soccer, outdoor adventure, skiing (downhill), snowboarding, table tennis, tennis, touch football, ultimate Frisbee, weight lifting, whiffle ball. 15 coaches, 1 trainer.

Computers Computers are regularly used in all academic classes. Computer network features include campus e-mail, on-campus library services, CD-ROMs, online commercial services, Internet access, wireless campus network.

Contact Mr. John T. Irvine, Director of Admissions. 201-547-6389. Fax: 201-547-6421. E-mail: irvinej@spprep.org. Web site: www.spprep.org.

ST. PIUS X CATHOLIC HIGH SCHOOL

2674 Johnson Road, NE
Atlanta, Georgia 30345
Head of School: Mr. Steve Spellman

General Information Coeducational day college-preparatory school, affiliated with Roman Catholic Church. Grades 9–12. Founded: 1958. Setting: suburban. 22-acre campus. 8 buildings on campus. Approved or accredited by National Catholic Education Association, Southern Association of Colleges and Schools, and Georgia Department of Education. Member of Secondary School Admission Test Board. Total enrollment: 1,000. Upper school average class size: 21. Upper school faculty-student ratio: 1:15.

Upper School Student Profile Grade 9: 260 students (130 boys, 130 girls); Grade 10: 250 students (125 boys, 125 girls); Grade 11: 250 students (125 boys, 125 girls); Grade 12: 240 students (120 boys, 120 girls). 83% of students are Roman Catholic.

Faculty School total: 84. In upper school: 38 men, 46 women; 54 have advanced degrees.

Subjects Offered Accounting, algebra, American history, American literature, anatomy, art, band, biology, business, business law, calculus, ceramics, chemistry, chorus, computer programming, computer science, creative writing, current events, dance, drama, driver education, economics, English, English literature, European history, expository writing, French, geography, geometry, German, government/civics, health, history, instrumental music, journalism, Latin, mathematics, music, physical education, physical science, physics, physiology, psychology, religion, science, social studies, sociology, Spanish, speech, statistics, theater, trigonometry, word processing, world history, world literature.

Graduation Requirements Computer science, English, foreign language, mathematics, physical education (includes health), religion (includes Bible studies and theology), religious studies, science, social studies (includes history).

Special Academic Programs Advanced Placement exam preparation in 19 subject areas; honors section; special instructional classes for students with learning disabilities and Attention Deficit Disorder.

College Placement 240 students graduated in 2005; 238 went to college, including Emory University; Furman University; Georgia Institute of Technology; Georgia State University; University of Georgia; University of Notre Dame. Other: 2 had other specific plans. 50% scored over 600 on SAT verbal, 50% scored over 600 on SAT math, 40% scored over 26 on composite ACT.

Student Life Upper grades have uniform requirement, student council, honor system. Discipline rests equally with students and faculty. Attendance at religious services is required.

Tuition and Aid Day student tuition: $9000. Tuition installment plan (FACTS Tuition Payment Plan, monthly payment plans). Tuition reduction for siblings, need-based scholarship grants, paying campus jobs available. In 2005–06, 28% of upper-school students received aid.

Admissions Traditional secondary-level entrance grade is 9. For fall 2005, 420 students applied for upper-level admission, 310 were accepted, 270 enrolled. SSAT required. Deadline for receipt of application materials: February 4. Application fee required: $75.

Athletics Interscholastic: baseball (boys), basketball (b,g), cheering (g), cross-country running (b,g), dance squad (g), dance team (g), diving (b,g), dressage (g), football (b), golf (b,g), lacrosse (b,g), soccer (b,g), softball (g), strength & conditioning (b,g), swimming and diving (b,g), tennis (b,g), track and field (b,g), volleyball (g), weight training (b,g), wrestling (b). 4 PE instructors, 32 coaches, 1 trainer.

Computers Computers are regularly used in science classes. Computer network features include campus e-mail, on-campus library services, CD-ROMs, online commercial services, Internet access.

Contact Stephanie Dunn, Coordinator of Admissions. 404-636-0323 Ext. 291. Fax: 404-636-2118. E-mail: sdunn@spx.org. Web site: www.spx.org.

ST. PIUS X HIGH SCHOOL

811 West Donovan
Houston, Texas 77091-5699
Head of School: Sr. Donna Pollard, OP

General Information Coeducational day college-preparatory, arts, business, religious studies, and technology school, affiliated with Roman Catholic Church. Grades 9–12. Founded: 1956. Setting: urban. 25-acre campus. 1 building on campus. Approved or accredited by Southern Association of Colleges and Schools, Texas Catholic Conference, Texas Education Agency, and Texas Department of Education. Total enrollment: 630. Upper school average class size: 22. Upper school faculty-student ratio: 1:13.

Upper School Student Profile Grade 9: 148 students (67 boys, 81 girls); Grade 10: 173 students (87 boys, 86 girls); Grade 11: 139 students (70 boys, 69 girls); Grade 12: 170 students (75 boys, 95 girls). 85% of students are Roman Catholic.

Faculty School total: 52. In upper school: 23 men, 29 women; 29 have advanced degrees.

Subjects Offered Advanced chemistry, advanced computer applications, advanced math, Advanced Placement courses, advanced studio art-AP, algebra, American literature, American literature-AP, anatomy and physiology, art, band, biology, business law, calculus, calculus-AP, campus ministry, Catholic belief and practice, chemistry, choir, chorus, Christian ethics, church history, college counseling, community service, computer applications, computer multimedia, computer programming, dance, death and loss, desktop publishing, economics, English language-AP, English literature-AP, environmental science, fine arts, foreign language, French, geography, geometry, graphic design, health, honors geometry, honors world history, human sexuality, introduction to theater, Italian, jewelry making, language arts, Latin, library assistant, marching band, moral and social development, moral theology, musical productions, painting, philosophy, photography, physical education, physics, psychology, reading/study skills, SAT/ACT preparation, Shakespeare, social justice, sociology, Spanish, Spanish language-AP, speech, stagecraft, student government, student publications, theology, U.S. government, U.S. government and politics-AP, U.S. history, U.S. history-AP, Web site design, world history, world religions, yearbook.

Graduation Requirements Electives, English, mathematics, physical education (includes health), science, social studies (includes history), speech, theology, foreign language or reading development, Christian Service Learning.

Special Academic Programs Advanced Placement exam preparation in 6 subject areas; honors section; remedial reading and/or remedial writing; programs in English for dyslexic students.

College Placement 186 students graduated in 2005; 183 went to college, including Sam Houston State University; Texas A&M University; Texas State University-San Marcos; Texas Tech University; The University of Texas at San Antonio; University of Houston. Other: 2 entered military service. Mean SAT verbal: 545, mean SAT math: 540, mean composite ACT: 22. 27% scored over 600 on SAT verbal, 26% scored over 600 on SAT math, 19% scored over 26 on composite ACT.

Student Life Upper grades have uniform requirement, student council, honor system. Discipline rests primarily with faculty. Attendance at religious services is required.

Summer Programs Enrichment, sports, computer instruction programs offered; session focuses on conditioning and strengthening; held on campus; accepts boys and girls; not open to students from other schools. 100 students usually enrolled. 2006 schedule: June 6 to July 30. Application deadline: May 1.

Tuition and Aid Day student tuition: $7650. Tuition installment plan (monthly payment plans, individually arranged payment plans). Merit scholarship grants, need-based scholarship grants available. In 2005–06, 14% of upper-school students received aid; total upper-school merit-scholarship money awarded: $19,000. Total amount of financial aid awarded in 2005–06: $253,024.

Admissions Traditional secondary-level entrance grade is 9. For fall 2005, 264 students applied for upper-level admission, 230 were accepted, 186 enrolled. High School Placement Test (closed version) from Scholastic Testing Service required. Deadline for receipt of application materials: February 3. Application fee required: $25. Interview required.

Athletics Interscholastic: baseball (boys), basketball (b,g), cheering (g), cross-country running (b,g), dance squad (g), dance team (b,g), drill team (g), football (b), golf (b,g), soccer (b,g), softball (g), swimming and diving (b,g), tennis (b,g), track and field (b,g), volleyball (g). 3 PE instructors, 6 coaches, 1 trainer.

Computers Computers are regularly used in all academic classes. Computer network features include campus e-mail, on-campus library services, CD-ROMs, Internet access, DVD, faculty Web pages for courses.

Contact Ms. Susie Kramer, Admissions Director. 713-692-3581 Ext. 137. Fax: 713-692-5725. E-mail: kramers@stpiusx.org. Web site: www.stpiusx.org.

SAINT RAYMOND HIGH SCHOOL FOR BOYS

2151 Saint Raymond Avenue
Bronx, New York 10462
Head of School: Br. Daniel J. Brenner, FSC

General Information Boys' day college-preparatory, general academic, arts, business, vocational, religious studies, and technology school, affiliated with Roman Catholic Church. Grades 9–12. Founded: 1959. Setting: urban. Nearest major city is

New York. 3-acre campus. 1 building on campus. Approved or accredited by Middle States Association of Colleges and Schools, National Catholic Education Association, and New York Department of Education. Total enrollment: 806. Upper school average class size: 25. Upper school faculty-student ratio: 1:24.

Upper School Student Profile 65% of students are Roman Catholic.

Faculty School total: 66. In upper school: 42 men, 24 women; 40 have advanced degrees.

Special Academic Programs Honors section; remedial reading and/or remedial writing; programs in English, mathematics for dyslexic students.

College Placement 165 students graduated in 2005; 158 went to college. Other: 3 went to work, 4 entered military service. 2% scored over 600 on SAT verbal, 2% scored over 600 on SAT math, 2% scored over 26 on composite ACT.

Student Life Upper grades have specified standards of dress, honor system. Discipline rests primarily with faculty. Attendance at religious services is required.

Tuition and Aid Tuition reduction for siblings, merit scholarship grants, need-based scholarship grants available. In 2005–06, 68% of upper-school students received aid; total upper-school merit-scholarship money awarded: $256,000.

Admissions Traditional secondary-level entrance grade is 9. Deadline for receipt of application materials: June 30. No application fee required. Interview required.

Athletics Interscholastic: baseball, basketball, cross-country running, golf, ice hockey, indoor track, softball; intramural: baseball, basketball, flagball, football, golf, physical fitness, physical training, tennis. 4 PE instructors, 13 coaches.

Computers Computer resources include campus e-mail, on-campus library services.

Contact Ms. Cynthia McDonald, Administrative Assistant. 718-824-5050 Ext. 12. Fax: 718-863-8808. E-mail: cmcdonald@straymondhighschool.org. Web site: straymondhighschool.org.

ST. SEBASTIAN'S SCHOOL

1191 Greendale Avenue
Needham, Massachusetts 02492
Head of School: William L. Burke III

General Information Boys' day college-preparatory school, affiliated with Roman Catholic Church. Grades 7–12. Founded: 1941. Setting: suburban. Nearest major city is Boston. 23-acre campus. 5 buildings on campus. Approved or accredited by New England Association of Schools and Colleges and Massachusetts Department of Education. Member of National Association of Independent Schools and Secondary School Admission Test Board. Endowment: $9 million. Total enrollment: 354. Upper school average class size: 11. Upper school faculty-student ratio: 1:7.

Upper School Student Profile Grade 9: 68 students (68 boys); Grade 10: 63 students (63 boys); Grade 11: 62 students (62 boys); Grade 12: 54 students (54 boys). 80% of students are Roman Catholic.

Faculty School total: 61. In upper school: 50 men, 11 women; 39 have advanced degrees.

Subjects Offered Algebra, American history, American literature, art, art history, biology, calculus, chemistry, computer science, drama, economics, English, English literature, ethics, European history, fine arts, geography, geometry, government/civics, Greek, history, Latin, mathematics, music, philosophy, photography, physical education, physics, religion, science, social studies, Spanish, speech, theater, trigonometry, world history, world literature, writing.

Graduation Requirements Arts and fine arts (art, music, dance, drama), English, foreign language, mathematics, physical education (includes health), religion (includes Bible studies and theology), science, social studies (includes history), senior service, chapel speaking program.

Special Academic Programs Advanced Placement exam preparation in 17 subject areas; honors section; independent study; academic accommodation for the gifted, the musically talented, and the artistically talented.

College Placement 51 students graduated in 2005; all went to college, including Boston College; Fairfield University; Harvard University; Middlebury College; Syracuse University; Yale University. Median SAT verbal: 640, median SAT math: 640.

Student Life Upper grades have specified standards of dress, student council, honor system. Discipline rests primarily with faculty. Attendance at religious services is required.

Tuition and Aid Day student tuition: $25,500. Tuition installment plan (Academic Management Services Plan, Key Tuition Payment Plan). Need-based scholarship grants, need-based loans available. In 2005–06, 26% of upper-school students received aid. Total amount of financial aid awarded in 2005–06: $1,401,000.

Admissions Traditional secondary-level entrance grade is 9. For fall 2005, 94 students applied for upper-level admission, 32 were accepted, 18 enrolled. ISEE or SSAT required. Deadline for receipt of application materials: February 3. Application fee required: $40. On-campus interview required.

Athletics Interscholastic: baseball, basketball, cross-country running, football, golf, ice hockey, lacrosse, sailing, skiing (downhill), soccer, squash, tennis; intramural: strength & conditioning, ultimate Frisbee, weight lifting, whiffle ball. 1 trainer.

Computers Computers are regularly used in English, foreign language, mathematics, science, social studies, writing classes. Computer network features include on-campus library services, CD-ROMs, Internet access, file transfer, DVD, wireless campus network.

SAINTS PETER AND PAUL HIGH SCHOOL

900 High Street
Easton, Maryland 21601
Head of School: Mr. James Edward Nemeth

General Information Coeducational day college-preparatory school, affiliated with Roman Catholic Church. Grades 9–12. Founded: 1958. Setting: small town. Nearest major city is Baltimore. 4-acre campus. 4 buildings on campus. Approved or accredited by Middle States Association of Colleges and Schools, National Catholic Education Association, and Maryland Department of Education. Total enrollment: 210. Upper school average class size: 15. Upper school faculty-student ratio: 1:8.

Upper School Student Profile Grade 9: 67 students (31 boys, 36 girls); Grade 10: 58 students (30 boys, 28 girls); Grade 11: 52 students (26 boys, 26 girls); Grade 12: 33 students (18 boys, 15 girls). 70% of students are Roman Catholic.

Faculty School total: 26. In upper school: 12 men, 14 women; 14 have advanced degrees.

Subjects Offered Advanced computer applications, algebra, American government, American literature, anatomy and physiology, art and culture, biology, biology-AP, British literature, British literature (honors), calculus, calculus-AP, campus ministry, Catholic belief and practice, chemistry, chemistry-AP, Christian and Hebrew scripture, Christian ethics, Christianity, church history, computer multimedia, computer programming, computer science, conceptual physics, creative writing, drama, earth science, economics, English literature and composition-AP, environmental science, French, geography, geometry, health and wellness, Hebrew scripture, honors algebra, honors English, honors geometry, honors U.S. history, honors world history, Microsoft, moral theology, music appreciation, music theory, philosophy, physical education, physics, pre-calculus, probability and statistics, Spanish, speech, studio art-AP, theology, U.S. government and politics-AP, U.S. history, U.S. history-AP, Web site design, world history, yearbook.

Graduation Requirements Algebra, American literature, arts and fine arts (art, music, dance, drama), biology, British literature, Catholic belief and practice, chemistry, Christian and Hebrew scripture, Christianity, computer applications, computer science, English, foreign language, geometry, history of the Catholic Church, mathematics, moral theology, physical education (includes health), physics, social justice, U.S. government, U.S. history, world history.

Special Academic Programs Advanced Placement exam preparation in 8 subject areas; honors section; independent study.

College Placement 48 students graduated in 2005; 47 went to college, including Drexel University; Loyola College in Maryland; Saint Joseph's University; University of Maryland, College Park. Other: 1 went to work. Mean SAT verbal: 560, mean SAT math: 530. 25% scored over 600 on SAT verbal, 25% scored over 600 on SAT math.

Student Life Upper grades have uniform requirement. Discipline rests primarily with faculty. Attendance at religious services is required.

Summer Programs Remediation programs offered; session focuses on math and Spanish; held on campus; accepts boys and girls; not open to students from other schools. 12 students usually enrolled.

Tuition and Aid Day student tuition: $6200. Tuition installment plan (FACTS Tuition Payment Plan). Tuition reduction for siblings, need-based scholarship grants, parish subsidies available. In 2005–06, 2% of upper-school students received aid. Total amount of financial aid awarded in 2005–06: $6000.

Admissions Traditional secondary-level entrance grade is 9. For fall 2005, 82 students applied for upper-level admission, 75 were accepted, 67 enrolled. High School Placement Test (closed version) from Scholastic Testing Service required. Deadline for receipt of application materials: February 15. Application fee required: $40. On-campus interview required.

Athletics Interscholastic: baseball (boys), basketball (b,g), field hockey (g), ice hockey (b), lacrosse (b,g), soccer (b,g), softball (g), swimming and diving (b,g); coed interscholastic: golf, tennis. 1 PE instructor, 31 coaches.

Computers Computers are regularly used in all academic classes. Computer network features include campus e-mail, on-campus library services, CD-ROMs, Internet access, office computer access, wireless campus network.

Contact Mr. James Edward Nemeth, Principal. 410-822-2275 Ext. 152. Fax: 410-822-1767. E-mail: jnemeth@ssppeaston.org. Web site: www.ssppeaston.org.

ST. STANISLAUS COLLEGE

304 South Beach Boulevard
Bay St. Louis, Mississippi 39520
Head of School: Br. Ronald Talbot, SC

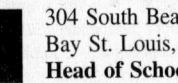

petersons.com

General Information Boys' boarding and day college-preparatory, general academic, and religious studies school, affiliated with Roman Catholic Church. Boarding grades 6–12, day grades 7–12. Founded: 1854. Setting: small town. Nearest major city is New Orleans, LA. Students are housed in single-sex dormitories. 30-acre campus. 8 buildings on campus. Approved or accredited by Southern Association of Colleges

Contact Mrs. Deborah Sewall, Assistant to Director of Admissions. 781-449-5200 Ext. 125. Fax: 781-449-5630. E-mail: admissions@stsebs.org. Web site: www.stsebs.org.

St. Stanislaus College

and Schools, The Association of Boarding Schools, and Mississippi Department of Education. Member of Secondary School Admission Test Board. Endowment: $7 million. Total enrollment: 530. Upper school average class size: 23. Upper school faculty-student ratio: 1:11.

Upper School Student Profile Grade 9: 85 students (85 boys); Grade 10: 85 students (85 boys); Grade 11: 97 students (97 boys); Grade 12: 85 students (85 boys). 45% of students are boarding students. 85% are state residents. 10 states are represented in upper school student body. 10% are international students. International students from Cameroon, Guatemala, Guinea-Bissau, Mexico, Republic of Korea, and Viet Nam; 6 other countries represented in student body. 70% of students are Roman Catholic.

Faculty School total: 66. In upper school: 44 men, 19 women; 38 have advanced degrees; 9 reside on campus.

Subjects Offered Accounting, algebra, American history, American literature, art, astronomy, biology, business, business law, calculus, chemistry, computer programming, computer science, creative writing, drama, economics, English, English literature, finance, French, geography, geometry, government/civics, grammar, health, history, journalism, marine biology, marine science, mathematics, minority studies, music, physical education, physics, psychology, religion, science, short story, social science, social studies, Spanish, speech, theater, theology, trigonometry, typing, world history, world literature.

Graduation Requirements Arts and fine arts (art, music, dance, drama), computer science, English, foreign language, mathematics, physical education (includes health), religion (includes Bible studies and theology), science, social science, social studies (includes history).

Special Academic Programs Advanced Placement exam preparation in 3 subject areas; honors section; remedial reading and/or remedial writing; remedial math; programs in English, mathematics, general development for dyslexic students; special instructional classes for students with Attention Deficit Disorder; ESL (15 students enrolled).

College Placement 85 students graduated in 2005; 80 went to college, including Louisiana State University and Agricultural and Mechanical College; Mississippi State University; University of Mississippi; University of New Orleans; University of South Alabama; University of Southern Mississippi. Other: 2 entered military service, 3 had other specific plans. Mean SAT verbal: 550, mean SAT math: 580, mean composite ACT: 22. 43% scored over 600 on SAT verbal, 50% scored over 600 on SAT math, 18% scored over 26 on composite ACT.

Student Life Upper grades have uniform requirement, student council. Discipline rests primarily with faculty. Attendance at religious services is required.

Summer Programs Enrichment programs offered; session focuses on traditional camp for boys with academic reinforcement ; held on campus; accepts boys; open to students from other schools. 150 students usually enrolled. 2006 schedule: June 12 to July 22. Application deadline: none.

Tuition and Aid Day student tuition: $4400; 7-day tuition and room/board: $17,500. Tuition installment plan (monthly payment plans). Need-based scholarship grants available. Total amount of financial aid awarded in 2005–06: $185,000.

Admissions Traditional secondary-level entrance grade is 10. For fall 2005, 200 students applied for upper-level admission, 175 were accepted, 175 enrolled. Deadline for receipt of application materials: none. Application fee required: $100. On-campus interview required.

Athletics Interscholastic: baseball, basketball, cross-country running, football, golf, physical fitness, sailing, soccer, swimming and diving, tennis, track and field, weight training; intramural: baseball, basketball, billiards, fishing, fitness walking, flag football, outdoor recreation, soccer, swimming and diving, table tennis, volleyball, walking. 3 PE instructors, 16 coaches, 1 trainer.

Computers Computers are regularly used in accounting, English, mathematics, religion, SAT preparation, science, typing classes. Computer network features include campus e-mail, on-campus library services, CD-ROMs, online commercial services, Internet access.

Contact Mrs. Dolores Richmond, Director of Admissions. 228-467-9057 Ext. 226. Fax: 228-466-2972. E-mail: admissions@ststan.com. Web site: www.ststan.com.

See full description on page 1040.

ST. STEPHEN'S & ST. AGNES SCHOOL

1000 St. Stephen's Road
Alexandria, Virginia 22304
Head of School: Joan G. Ogilvy Holden

General Information Coeducational day college-preparatory, arts, religious studies, and technology school, affiliated with Episcopal Church. Grades JK–12. Founded: 1924. Setting: suburban. Nearest major city is Washington, DC. 35-acre campus. 5 buildings on campus. Approved or accredited by Association of Independent Schools of Greater Washington and Virginia Association of Independent Schools. Member of National Association of Independent Schools and Secondary School Admission Test Board. Endowment: $15.9 million. Total enrollment: 1,155. Upper school average class size: 15. Upper school faculty-student ratio: 1:8.

Upper School Student Profile 32% of students are members of Episcopal Church.

Faculty School total: 145. In upper school: 27 men, 28 women; 39 have advanced degrees.

Subjects Offered Advanced computer applications, Advanced Placement courses, algebra, American government-AP, American history, American history-AP, American literature, art, art history, art history-AP, bioethics, biology, biology-AP, calculus, calculus-AP, ceramics, chemistry, chemistry-AP, choir, choral music, Christian and Hebrew scripture, Christian education, Christian ethics, Christian scripture, Christian studies, Christian testament, college counseling, community service, comparative government and politics-AP, computer graphics, computer programming, computer programming-AP, computer science, concert choir, creative writing, debate, drama, drawing, driver education, economics, electronic publishing, English, English literature, English-AP, ensembles, environmental science, environmental science-AP, European history, European history-AP, fine arts, finite math, forensics, French, French language-AP, French literature-AP, geology, geometry, government-AP, government/civics, graphic design, Hebrew scripture, history, honors algebra, honors English, honors geometry, honors U.S. history, honors world history, instrumental music, jazz, journalism, Latin, Latin-AP, mathematics, medieval history, medieval/ Renaissance history, microcomputer technology applications, music, music composition, music theory, music theory-AP, newspaper, painting, physical education, physics, physics-AP, playwriting and directing, pre-calculus, printmaking, religion, robotics, SAT preparation, science, sculpture, senior internship, senior project, Spanish, Spanish language-AP, Spanish literature-AP, speech, speech and debate, sports, sports medicine, statistics-AP, studio art, studio art-AP, technical theater, The 20th Century, the Sixties, theater, theater arts, theater design and production, theology, theology and the arts, trigonometry, U.S. history-AP, world history, world literature, writing, yearbook.

Graduation Requirements Arts and fine arts (art, music, dance, drama), English, family studies, foreign language, history, mathematics, physical education (includes health), religion (includes Bible studies and theology), science, technological applications, senior year independent off-campus project, 40 hours of community service.

Special Academic Programs Advanced Placement exam preparation in 19 subject areas; honors section; independent study; term-away projects; study abroad; academic accommodation for the gifted, the musically talented, and the artistically talented.

College Placement 106 students graduated in 2005; 103 went to college, including Boston College; Emory University; The College of William and Mary; University of Virginia; Virginia Polytechnic Institute and State University; Wake Forest University. Other: 1 entered military service, 1 entered a postgraduate year, 1 had other specific plans. Mean SAT verbal: 627, mean SAT math: 637. 66% scored over 600 on SAT verbal, 80% scored over 600 on SAT math.

Student Life Upper grades have specified standards of dress, student council, honor system. Discipline rests equally with students and faculty. Attendance at religious services is required.

Summer Programs Enrichment, advancement, art/fine arts, computer instruction programs offered; session focuses on enrichment; held both on and off campus; held at Chesapeake Bay, DC, VA and MD area; accepts boys and girls; open to students from other schools. 1500 students usually enrolled. 2006 schedule: June 12 to August 25. Application deadline: none.

Tuition and Aid Day student tuition: $21,975. Tuition installment plan (FACTS Tuition Payment Plan). Need-based scholarship grants available. In 2005–06, 22% of upper-school students received aid. Total amount of financial aid awarded in 2005–06: $1,267,192.

Admissions Traditional secondary-level entrance grade is 9. ISEE or SSAT required. Deadline for receipt of application materials: January 15. Application fee required: $60. Interview required.

Athletics Interscholastic: baseball (boys), basketball (b,g), cross-country running (b,g), diving (b,g), field hockey (g), football (b), ice hockey (b), indoor track & field (b,g), lacrosse (b,g), soccer (b,g), softball (g), swimming and diving (b,g), tennis (b,g), track and field (b,g), volleyball (g), wrestling (b); intramural: dance team (g), field hockey (g); coed interscholastic: dance team, golf; coed intramural: nautilus, physical fitness, physical training, weight training. 8 PE instructors, 2 trainers.

Computers Computers are regularly used in all academic classes. Computer network features include on-campus library services, CD-ROMs, online commercial services, Internet access, file transfer, DVD, wireless campus network, computer labs for foreign language, math, tech ed, library, newspaper, physics, and chemistry; mobile wireless laptop cart.

Contact Len Armstrong, Director of Middle and Upper School Admission. 703-212-2706. Fax: 703-751-7142. E-mail: larmstrong@sssas.org. Web site: www.sssas.org.

SAINT STEPHEN'S EPISCOPAL SCHOOL

315 41st Street West
Bradenton, Florida 34209
Head of School: Janet S. Pullen

General Information Coeducational day college-preparatory, arts, and religious studies school, affiliated with Episcopal Church. Grades PK–12. Founded: 1970. Setting: small town. Nearest major city is Tampa. 35-acre campus. 5 buildings on campus. Approved or accredited by Florida Council of Independent Schools, National Association of Episcopal Schools, and Southern Association of Independent Schools.

Member of National Association of Independent Schools. Endowment: $350,000. Total enrollment: 801. Upper school average class size: 15. Upper school faculty-student ratio: 1:11.

Upper School Student Profile Grade 9: 84 students (42 boys, 42 girls); Grade 10: 70 students (37 boys, 33 girls); Grade 11: 75 students (38 boys, 37 girls); Grade 12: 71 students (41 boys, 30 girls). 21% of students are members of Episcopal Church.

Faculty School total: 97. In upper school: 15 men, 20 women; 22 have advanced degrees.

Subjects Offered Advanced studio art-AP, algebra, art, art history, art history-AP, band, biology, biology-AP, broadcast journalism, calculus, calculus-AP, ceramics, chemistry, chemistry-AP, choir, community service, composition, computer programming, computer programming-AP, conceptual physics, dance, debate, discrete math, drama, economics, English, English literature-AP, European history-AP, filmmaking, French, geometry, humanities, journalism, Latin, marine science, music, newspaper, painting, personal fitness, photography, physical education, physics, physics-AP, pre-calculus, probability and statistics, science research, Spanish, studio art, trigonometry, U.S. government and politics, U.S. history, U.S. history-AP, Western civilization, world culture, world history.

Graduation Requirements Arts and fine arts (art, music, dance, drama), electives, English, foreign language, mathematics, physical education (includes health), science, social studies (includes history), senior speech. Community service is required.

Special Academic Programs Advanced Placement exam preparation in 14 subject areas; honors section.

College Placement 66 students graduated in 2005; 62 went to college, including Davidson College; Florida State University; Rutgers, The State University of New Jersey, New Brunswick/Piscataway; University of Central Florida; University of Florida; Wake Forest University. Other: 2 entered a postgraduate year, 2 had other specific plans. Mean SAT verbal: 576, mean SAT math: 613, mean composite ACT: 25.

Student Life Upper grades have specified standards of dress, student council, honor system. Discipline rests primarily with faculty. Attendance at religious services is required.

Summer Programs Enrichment, advancement, sports programs offered; session focuses on academic enrichment; held on campus; accepts boys and girls; open to students from other schools. 100 students usually enrolled. 2006 schedule: June 10 to August 16. Application deadline: May 1.

Tuition and Aid Day student tuition: $11,650. Tuition installment plan (monthly payment plans). Need-based scholarship grants available. In 2005–06, 13% of upper-school students received aid. Total amount of financial aid awarded in 2005–06: $218,514.

Admissions Traditional secondary-level entrance grade is 9. For fall 2005, 100 students applied for upper-level admission, 74 were accepted, 55 enrolled. School's own exam required. Deadline for receipt of application materials: none. Application fee required: $200. Interview recommended.

Athletics Interscholastic: aerobics/dance (girls), aquatics (b,g), baseball (b), basketball (b,g), cheering (g), cross-country running (b,g), dance (g), dance team (g), diving (b,g), golf (b,g), independent competitive sports (b,g), soccer (b,g), softball (g), swimming and diving (b,g), tennis (b,g), track and field (b,g), volleyball (g), winter soccer (b,g); intramural: aerobics/dance (g), ballet (g), basketball (b,g), cheering (g), cross-country running (b,g), dance (g), fitness (b,g), horseback riding (b,g), jogging (b,g), lacrosse (b), physical fitness (b,g), physical training (b,g), running (b,g), soccer (b,g), softball (b,g), strength & conditioning (b,g), track and field (b,g), weight training (b,g). 9 PE instructors, 14 coaches, 2 trainers.

Computers Computers are regularly used in art, economics, foreign language, history, library, mathematics, science, social science, word processing, writing, yearbook classes. Computer network features include on-campus library services, CD-ROMs, online commercial services, Internet access, office computer access, DVD, wireless campus network, Microsoft Office.

Contact Judith C. Southerland, Director of Admissions. 941-746-2121. Fax: 941-746-5699. E-mail: jsoutherland@saintstephens.org. Web site: www.saintstephens.org.

ANNOUNCEMENT FROM THE SCHOOL Saint Stephen's is a coeducational independent day school located in Bradenton, Florida. The 35-acre campus serves students of all faiths in prekindergarten through grade 12. The curriculum is based on traditional goals of university preparation enriched with programs in the fine arts, athletics, and civic affairs. With a student to faculty ratio of 11:1, Saint Stephen's provides an educational environment that holds high, yet attainable, standards for all students.

ST. STEPHEN'S EPISCOPAL SCHOOL

2900 Bunny Run
Austin, Texas 78746
Head of School: Rev. Roger Bowen

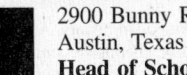

General Information Coeducational boarding and day college-preparatory and Theatre Focus Program school, affiliated with Episcopal Church. Boarding grades 8–12, day grades 6–12. Founded: 1950. Setting: suburban. Students are housed in single-sex dormitories. 400-acre campus. 40 buildings on campus. Approved or accredited by Independent Schools Association of the Southwest, National Association of Episcopal Schools, Southwest Association of Episcopal Schools, The Association of Boarding Schools, Western Catholic Education Association, and Texas Department of Education. Member of National Association of Independent Schools. Endowment: $6 million. Total enrollment: 656. Upper school average class size: 16. Upper school faculty-student ratio: 1:8.

Upper School Student Profile Grade 9: 102 students (57 boys, 45 girls); Grade 10: 115 students (51 boys, 64 girls); Grade 11: 122 students (60 boys, 62 girls); Grade 12: 114 students (60 boys, 54 girls). 35% of students are boarding students. 82% are state residents. 16 states are represented in upper school student body. 13% are international students. International students from Germany, Japan, Mexico, Republic of Korea, Saudi Arabia, and Taiwan; 9 other countries represented in student body. 18% of students are members of Episcopal Church.

Faculty School total: 100. In upper school: 46 men, 37 women; 62 have advanced degrees; 50 reside on campus.

Subjects Offered 20th century world history, 3-dimensional design, acting, algebra, American history, American history-AP, American literature, anthropology, applied music, art, art history, art history-AP, astrophysics, ballet, band, biology, biology-AP, calculus, calculus-AP, ceramics, chamber groups, chemistry, chemistry-AP, Chinese, choreography, classics, computer math, computer science, computer studies, creative writing, directing, drama, earth science, English, English literature, environmental science, ESL, European history, European history-AP, fine arts, French, French-AP, geometry, government/civics, Greek culture, history, improvisation, jazz band, Latin, literature and composition-AP, mathematics, music, music theory-AP, musical theater, photography, physical education, physics, physics-AP, play/screen writing, pre-calculus, psychology, public policy issues and action, public speaking, religion, religions, science, social studies, Spanish, Spanish-AP, statistics-AP, studio art-AP, theater arts, theology, trigonometry, video, world history, world literature.

Graduation Requirements Arts and fine arts (art, music, dance, drama), electives, English, foreign language, mathematics, physical education (includes health), religion (includes Bible studies and theology), science, social studies (includes history), community service requirement in middle and upper schools.

Special Academic Programs Advanced Placement exam preparation in 17 subject areas; honors section; independent study; study abroad; ESL (21 students enrolled).

College Placement 115 students graduated in 2005; all went to college, including Boston University; Pomona College; Rhodes College; Stanford University; The University of Texas at Austin; Wesleyan University. Median SAT verbal: 600, median SAT math: 630.

Student Life Upper grades have specified standards of dress, student council. Discipline rests equally with students and faculty. Attendance at religious services is required.

Summer Programs Enrichment, advancement, sports, art/fine arts, rigorous outdoor training programs offered; session focuses on soccer, tennis, academic credit, travel abroad, foreign language/culture, fine arts, community service; held both on and off campus; held at locations in Europe, El Salvador, Nicaragua, Costa Rica, American wilderness areas; accepts boys and girls; open to students from other schools. 120 students usually enrolled. 2006 schedule: June 1 to July 31. Application deadline: none.

Tuition and Aid Day student tuition: $17,300; 7-day tuition and room/board: $19,150. Tuition installment plan (Insured Tuition Payment Plan, Key Tuition Payment Plan, Compass Bank 12-month payment plan or local bank 12-month payment plan). Need-based scholarship grants, partial tuition remission for children of faculty and staff available. In 2005–06, 18% of upper-school students received aid. Total amount of financial aid awarded in 2005–06: $1,168,094.

Admissions Traditional secondary-level entrance grade is 9. For fall 2005, 393 students applied for upper-level admission, 217 were accepted, 167 enrolled. ISEE required. Deadline for receipt of application materials: February 1. Application fee required: $50. Interview required.

Athletics Interscholastic: baseball (boys), basketball (b,g), crew (b,g), cross-country running (b,g), dance (g), field hockey (g), football (b), golf (b,g), lacrosse (b,g), soccer (b,g), softball (g), swimming and diving (b,g), tennis (b,g), track and field (b,g), volleyball (g). 5 PE instructors, 7 coaches, 1 trainer.

Computers Computers are regularly used in all academic classes. Computer network features include campus e-mail, on-campus library services, CD-ROMs, online commercial services, Internet access, file transfer, DVD, wireless campus network, online schedules, syllabi, homework, examples, and links to information sources.

Contact Lawrence Sampleton, Director of Admission. 512-327-1213 Ext. 210. Fax: 512-327-6771. E-mail: admission@sstx.org. Web site: www.sstx.org.

ANNOUNCEMENT FROM THE SCHOOL St. Stephen's Episcopal School offers boarding and day students exceptional academic opportunity in an inclusive, international community. The School provides 17 Advanced Placement courses and distinguished, dedicated, and accessible faculty members who are passionate about their subjects. The scenic 400-acre campus, overlooking Lake Austin, is ideal for outdoor activities and study.

See full description on page 1042.

ST. STEPHEN'S SCHOOL, ROME

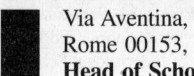

Via Aventina, 3
Rome 00153, Italy
Head of School: Philip Allen

General Information Coeducational boarding and day college-preparatory, arts, and bilingual studies school. Grades 9–PG. Founded: 1964. Setting: urban. Students are housed in single-sex by floor dormitories. 2-acre campus. 1 building on campus. Approved or accredited by European Council of International Schools, International Baccalaureate Organization, New England Association of Schools and Colleges, and US Department of State. Affiliate member of National Association of Independent Schools. Language of instruction: English. Endowment: €1.1 million. Total enrollment: 211. Upper school average class size: 13. Upper school faculty-student ratio: 1:6.

Upper School Student Profile Grade 9: 40 students (22 boys, 18 girls); Grade 10: 46 students (19 boys, 27 girls); Grade 11: 68 students (33 boys, 35 girls); Grade 12: 54 students (19 boys, 35 girls); Postgraduate: 3 students (1 boy, 2 girls). 16% of students are boarding students. 13% are international students. International students from Australia, France, Germany, India, United Kingdom, and United States; 26 other countries represented in student body.

Faculty School total: 39. In upper school: 14 men, 25 women; 25 have advanced degrees; 7 reside on campus.

Subjects Offered Algebra, American literature, art, art history, biology, calculus, chemistry, chorus, classical studies, dance, drama, economics, English, English literature, European history, French, geometry, health, Islamic studies, Italian, Italian history, Latin, music appreciation, physical education, physics, pre-calculus, Roman civilization, sculpture, theory of knowledge, trigonometry, U.S. history, world literature.

Graduation Requirements Arts and fine arts (art, music, dance, drama), English, foreign language, mathematics, physical education (includes health), science, social studies (includes history), senior essay.

Special Academic Programs International Baccalaureate program; Advanced Placement exam preparation in 11 subject areas; domestic exchange program (with Buckingham Browne & Nichols School, Friends Seminary, Choate Rosemary Hall); ESL (8 students enrolled).

College Placement 51 students graduated in 2005; 47 went to college, including Boston University; Columbia College; Georgetown University; Haverford College; University of Chicago; Vassar College. Other: 3 went to work, 1 entered a postgraduate year. Median SAT verbal: 600, median SAT math: 600. 55% scored over 600 on SAT verbal, 50% scored over 600 on SAT math.

Student Life Upper grades have student council. Discipline rests equally with students and faculty.

Tuition and Aid Day student tuition: €16,070–€16,440; 7-day tuition and room/board: €26,870–€27,240. Tuition installment plan (individually arranged payment plans). Tuition reduction for siblings, need-based scholarship grants available. In 2005–06, 29% of upper-school students received aid. Total amount of financial aid awarded in 2005–06: €269,000.

Admissions Traditional secondary-level entrance grade is 9. For fall 2005, 167 students applied for upper-level admission, 117 were accepted, 91 enrolled. School's own exam required. Deadline for receipt of application materials: February 25. Application fee required: €100. Interview recommended.

Athletics Interscholastic: basketball (boys, girls), soccer (b,g), volleyball (b,g); intramural: basketball (b,g), dance (b,g), soccer (b,g), softball (b,g), tennis (b,g), track and field (b,g), volleyball (b,g), yoga (b,g); coed interscholastic: tennis; coed intramural: dance, tennis, track and field, volleyball. 7 coaches.

Computers Computers are regularly used in English, foreign language, mathematics, science, social studies classes. Computer network features include campus e-mail, on-campus library services, CD-ROMs, Internet access, file transfer, office computer access, DVD, wireless campus network.

Contact Suzanne Fusi, Admissions Coordinator. 39-06-575-0605. Fax: 39-06-574-1941. E-mail: ststephens@ststephens-rome.com. Web site: www.ststephens-rome.com.

SAINT TERESA'S ACADEMY

5600 Main Street
Kansas City, Missouri 64113
Head of School: Dr. Faith P. Wilson

General Information Girls' day college-preparatory school, affiliated with Roman Catholic Church. Grades 9–12. Founded: 1866. Setting: urban. 20-acre campus. 3 buildings on campus. Approved or accredited by North Central Association of Colleges and Schools and Missouri Department of Education. Endowment: $2 million. Total enrollment: 528. Upper school average class size: 21. Upper school faculty-student ratio: 1:12.

Upper School Student Profile Grade 9: 148 students (148 girls); Grade 10: 129 students (129 girls); Grade 11: 123 students (123 girls); Grade 12: 128 students (128 girls). 86% of students are Roman Catholic.

Faculty School total: 46. In upper school: 11 men, 35 women; 34 have advanced degrees.

Subjects Offered Advanced chemistry, advanced math, algebra, American government, American history, American history-AP, American literature, American literature-AP, analysis, anatomy and physiology, art, athletics, basketball, biology, biology-AP, botany, British literature, calculus, career/college preparation, chamber groups, chemistry, chemistry-AP, choir, chorus, Christian studies, computer graphics, computer programming, computer science-AP, current events, dance, directing, drama, drawing, ecology, English, English literature, fiber arts, fitness, foreign language, forensics, French, French language-AP, French-AP, freshman seminar, geometry, golf, graphic design, health, independent study, journalism, keyboarding/computer, language arts, Latin, Latin History, music-AP, newspaper, painting, physical education, portfolio art, psychology, Shakespeare, social issues, social studies, sociology, softball, Spanish, Spanish language-AP, Spanish-AP, speech, sports conditioning, sports performance development, stagecraft, swimming, tennis, theater, theology and the arts, track and field, trigonometry, U.S. government, U.S. history, volleyball, Western civilization, women spirituality and faith, world geography, world religions, writing, yearbook.

Graduation Requirements Arts and fine arts (art, music, dance, drama), computer science, electives, English, foreign language, mathematics, physical education (includes health), science, social studies (includes history), theology. Community service is required.

Special Academic Programs Advanced Placement exam preparation; honors section.

College Placement 125 students graduated in 2005; 124 went to college, including Kansas State University; Loyola University Chicago; Rockhurst University; Truman State University; University of Kansas; University of Missouri–Columbia. Other: 1 had other specific plans. Median SAT verbal: 569, median SAT math: 537, median combined SAT: 1210, median composite ACT: 24.

Student Life Upper grades have uniform requirement. Discipline rests primarily with faculty. Attendance at religious services is required.

Summer Programs Sports, art/fine arts, computer instruction programs offered; session focuses on fine arts and sports; held on campus; accepts girls; open to students from other schools. 100 students usually enrolled. 2006 schedule: June 25 to July 8. Application deadline: May 1.

Tuition and Aid Day student tuition: $7950. Tuition installment plan (SMART Tuition Payment Plan). Tuition reduction for siblings, merit scholarship grants, need-based scholarship grants, paying campus jobs available. In 2005–06, 20% of upper-school students received aid; total upper-school merit-scholarship money awarded: $90,000. Total amount of financial aid awarded in 2005–06: $125,000.

Admissions Traditional secondary-level entrance grade is 9. For fall 2005, 204 students applied for upper-level admission, 173 were accepted, 148 enrolled. Placement test required. Deadline for receipt of application materials: February 28. No application fee required.

Athletics Interscholastic: aerobics/dance, basketball, cross-country running, diving, drill team, golf, soccer, softball, swimming and diving, tennis, track and field, volleyball; intramural: aerobics/dance, badminton, basketball, fitness, fitness walking, jogging, physical fitness, physical training, running, strength & conditioning, table tennis, volleyball, walking, weight lifting, weight training. 2 PE instructors, 19 coaches, 1 trainer.

Computers Computers are regularly used in business education, creative writing, graphics, journalism, library, newspaper, research skills, science, writing, yearbook classes. Computer resources include campus e-mail, on-campus library services, CD-ROMs, online commercial services, Internet access.

Contact Mrs. Mary N. Casey, Admissions Director. 816-501-0011 Ext. 135. Fax: 816-523-0232. E-mail: mcasey@stteresasacademy.org. Web site: www.stteresasacademy.org.

SAINT THOMAS ACADEMY

949 Mendota Heights Road
Mendota Heights, Minnesota 55120
Head of School: Thomas B. Mich, PhD

General Information Boys' day college-preparatory and religious studies school, affiliated with Roman Catholic Church. Grades 7–12. Founded: 1885. Setting: suburban. Nearest major city is St. Paul. 72-acre campus. 8 buildings on campus. Approved or accredited by Independent Schools Association of the Central States. Endowment: $13.1 million. Total enrollment: 670. Upper school average class size: 18. Upper school faculty-student ratio: 1:10.

Upper School Student Profile Grade 9: 131 students (131 boys); Grade 10: 138 students (138 boys); Grade 11: 136 students (136 boys); Grade 12: 106 students (106 boys). 75% of students are Roman Catholic.

Faculty School total: 60. In upper school: 32 men, 18 women; 42 have advanced degrees.

Subjects Offered Advanced Placement courses, algebra, American history, American literature, art, art history, biology, calculus, campus ministry, chemistry, computer science, creative writing, earth science, economics, English, English literature, environmental studies, European history, fine arts, French, geometry, government/civics, health, history, JROTC, Latin, mathematics, military science, music, physical education, physics, psychology, religion, science, social studies, Spanish, trigonometry, world history, world literature, writing.

Graduation Requirements Arts and fine arts (art, music, dance, drama), English, foreign language, JROTC or LEAD (Leadership Education and Development), math applications, mathematics, physical education (includes health), religion (includes Bible studies and theology), religions, science, social studies (includes history).

Special Academic Programs Advanced Placement exam preparation in 7 subject areas; honors section; independent study.

College Placement 110 students graduated in 2005; all went to college, including Creighton University; University of Minnesota, Twin Cities Campus; University of North Dakota; University of St. Thomas; University of Wisconsin–Madison. Mean SAT verbal: 586, mean SAT math: 619, mean composite ACT: 25. 48% scored over 600 on SAT verbal, 56% scored over 600 on SAT math, 39% scored over 26 on composite ACT.

Student Life Upper grades have uniform requirement, student council, honor system. Discipline rests primarily with faculty. Attendance at religious services is required.

Summer Programs Remediation, enrichment programs offered; session focuses on study skills and remediation/make-up; held on campus; accepts boys; not open to students from other schools. 12 students usually enrolled. 2006 schedule: June 19 to July 21. Application deadline: April 30.

Tuition and Aid Day student tuition: $13,125. Tuition installment plan (monthly payment plans, individually arranged payment plans, quarterly payment plan). Merit scholarship grants, need-based scholarship grants available. In 2005–06, 30% of upper-school students received aid; total upper-school merit-scholarship money awarded: $30,000. Total amount of financial aid awarded in 2005–06: $1,300,000.

Admissions Traditional secondary-level entrance grade is 9. For fall 2005, 65 students applied for upper-level admission, 60 were accepted, 50 enrolled. Cognitive Abilities Test required. Deadline for receipt of application materials: none. No application fee required. On-campus interview recommended.

Athletics Interscholastic: alpine skiing, baseball, basketball, cross-country running, diving, drill team, football, golf, ice hockey, JROTC drill, marksmanship, nordic skiing, riflery, soccer, swimming and diving, tennis, track and field, wrestling; intramural: basketball, football, lacrosse, physical training, strength & conditioning, table tennis, weight training. 4 PE instructors, 1 trainer.

Computers Computers are regularly used in art, English, foreign language, mathematics, music, science classes. Computer network features include on-campus library services, CD-ROMs, online commercial services, Internet access, file transfer, office computer access.

Contact Peggy Mansur, Admissions Assistant. 651-683-1515. Fax: 651-454-4574. E-mail: pmansur@cadets.com. Web site: www.cadets.com.

ST. THOMAS AQUINAS HIGH SCHOOL

2801 Southwest 12th Street
Fort Lauderdale, Florida 33312-2999
Head of School: Mrs. Tina Jones

General Information Coeducational day college-preparatory, arts, religious studies, and technology school, affiliated with Roman Catholic Church. Grades 9–12. Founded: 1936. Setting: suburban. 20-acre campus. 17 buildings on campus. Approved or accredited by National Catholic Education Association, Southern Association of Colleges and Schools, and Florida Department of Education. Total enrollment: 2,141. Upper school average class size: 25. Upper school faculty-student ratio: 1:18.

Upper School Student Profile Grade 9: 543 students (254 boys, 289 girls); Grade 10: 534 students (273 boys, 261 girls); Grade 11: 555 students (269 boys, 286 girls); Grade 12: 509 students (246 boys, 263 girls). 90% of students are Roman Catholic.

Faculty School total: 116. In upper school: 50 men, 66 women; 58 have advanced degrees.

Subjects Offered 20th century history, 20th century world history, 3-dimensional art, acting, advanced chemistry, advanced computer applications, advanced math, Advanced Placement courses, algebra, American government, American government-AP, American history, American history-AP, American literature, anatomy and physiology, art, art appreciation, art history-AP, athletics, biology, biology-AP, British literature, British literature (honors), British literature-AP, broadcast journalism, calculus, calculus-AP, chemistry, chemistry-AP, Chinese, choir, choral music, chorus, Christianity, church history, comparative government and politics-AP, comparative political systems-AP, composition-AP, computer art, computer graphics, computer keyboarding, computer programming-AP, computer science-AP, debate, desktop publishing, digital art, digital imaging, directing, drama, drama performance, drawing, economics-AP, electives, English, English language and composition-AP, English literature, English literature and composition-AP, English literature-AP, English-AP, English/composition-AP, environmental science, environmental science-AP, European history, European history-AP, film and literature, film and new technologies, fitness, food science, forensics, French, French language-AP, French literature-AP, French-AP, general science, geometry, government, government and politics-AP, government-AP, government/civics-AP, grammar, graphic arts, graphic design, health, health and safety, health and wellness, health education, health enhancement, health science, healthful living, Hispanic literature, history, history of drama, history-AP, Holocaust, honors algebra, honors English, honors geometry, honors U.S. history, honors world history, human anatomy, human geography—AP, jazz, jazz band, journalism, keyboarding, keyboarding/computer, lab science, language, language and composition, language arts, language-AP, Latin, Latin-AP, leadership, leadership and

service, leadership education training, leadership skills, leadership training, Life of Christ, literature, literature and composition-AP, literature-AP, macro/microeconomics-AP, macroeconomics-AP, marine biology, marine studies, mathematics-AP, media, microeconomics, microeconomics-AP, model United Nations, modern European history, modern European history-AP, news writing, newspaper, nutrition, oral expression, orchestra, peace and justice, peace education, peace studies, performing arts, photography, photojournalism, physical education, physical fitness, physics, physics-AP, physiology-anatomy, play production, play/screen writing, playwriting, playwriting and directing, poetry, political systems, pottery, pre-algebra, pre-calculus, psychology, psychology-AP, public speaking, reading, SAT preparation, SAT/ACT preparation, Spanish, Spanish language-AP, Spanish literature, Spanish literature-AP, Spanish-AP, speech, speech and debate, speech and oral interpretations, speech communications, sports team management, stage design, stagecraft, statistics, statistics and probability, statistics-AP, student government, student publications, studio art, technical theater, television, trigonometry, U.S. government and politics-AP, U.S. government-AP, U.S. history, U.S. history-AP, United States government-AP, world history, world history-AP.

Graduation Requirements Arts and fine arts (art, music, dance, drama), computer science, electives, English, foreign language, health, mathematics, personal fitness, science, social science, theology.

Special Academic Programs Advanced Placement exam preparation in 18 subject areas; honors section; study at local college for college credit; remedial reading and/or remedial writing; remedial math.

College Placement 487 students graduated in 2005; 485 went to college, including Florida Atlantic University; Florida International University; Florida State University; University of Central Florida; University of Florida; University of Miami. Other: 2 entered military service. Mean SAT verbal: 599, mean SAT math: 590, mean composite ACT: 23. 43% scored over 600 on SAT verbal, 40% scored over 600 on SAT math, 5% scored over 26 on composite ACT.

Student Life Upper grades have uniform requirement, student council, honor system. Discipline rests primarily with faculty. Attendance at religious services is required.

Summer Programs Remediation, enrichment, advancement, art/fine arts programs offered; session focuses on enrichment; held on campus; accepts boys and girls; not open to students from other schools. 1000 students usually enrolled. 2006 schedule: May 30 to June 15. Application deadline: May 16.

Tuition and Aid Day student tuition: $5900. Need-based scholarship grants available.

Admissions Traditional secondary-level entrance grade is 9. For fall 2005, 875 students applied for upper-level admission, 560 were accepted, 543 enrolled. High School Placement Test required. Deadline for receipt of application materials: January 17. Application fee required: $45.

Athletics Interscholastic: baseball (boys), basketball (b,g), cheering (g), cross-country running (b,g), dance team (g), danceline (g), diving (b,g), drill team (g), football (g), golf (b,g), running (b,g), soccer (b,g), softball (g), swimming and diving (b,g), tennis (b,g), track and field (b,g), volleyball (b,g), water polo (g), weight training (b,g); coed interscholastic: ice hockey, indoor hockey, physical training. 3 PE instructors, 12 coaches, 1 trainer.

Computers Computers are regularly used in all academic, data processing, desktop publishing, graphic arts, graphic design, graphics, journalism, keyboarding, lab/keyboard, media, media arts, media production, media services, news writing, newspaper, programming, publications, publishing, technology, video film production, Web site design, word processing classes. Computer network features include campus e-mail, on-campus library services, CD-ROMs, online commercial services, Internet access, DVD.

Contact Mrs. Tina Jones, Principal. 954-581-2127 Ext. 2220. Fax: 954-581-8263. E-mail: tjones@aquinas-sta.org. Web site: www.aquinas-sta.org.

SAINT THOMAS AQUINAS HIGH SCHOOL

11411 Pflumm Road
Overland Park, Kansas 66215-4816
Head of School: Dr. William P. Ford

General Information Coeducational day college-preparatory, religious studies, and technology school, affiliated with Roman Catholic Church. Grades 9–12. Founded: 1988. Setting: suburban. Nearest major city is Kansas City, MO. 44-acre campus. 2 buildings on campus. Approved or accredited by National Catholic Education Association, North Central Association of Colleges and Schools, and Kansas Department of Education. Total enrollment: 1,275. Upper school average class size: 25. Upper school faculty-student ratio: 1:16.

Upper School Student Profile Grade 9: 294 students (142 boys, 152 girls); Grade 10: 351 students (156 boys, 195 girls); Grade 11: 341 students (157 boys, 184 girls); Grade 12: 289 students (132 boys, 157 girls). 97% of students are Roman Catholic.

Faculty School total: 84. In upper school: 37 men, 47 women; 50 have advanced degrees.

Graduation Requirements Arts and fine arts (art, music, dance, drama), computer technologies, electives, English, Latin, mathematics, modern languages, physical education (includes health), science, social studies (includes history), speech, theology.

Special Academic Programs Advanced Placement exam preparation; honors section; study at local college for college credit; academic accommodation for the gifted; remedial reading and/or remedial writing; remedial math.

College Placement 304 students graduated in 2005; 298 went to college, including Benedictine College; Creighton University; Kansas State University; Saint Louis University; University of Kansas; University of Missouri–Columbia. Other: 6 had other specific plans. Mean SAT verbal: 573, mean SAT math: 591, mean composite ACT: 23. 40% scored over 600 on SAT verbal, 42% scored over 600 on SAT math, 22% scored over 26 on composite ACT.

Student Life Upper grades have uniform requirement, student council. Discipline rests primarily with faculty. Attendance at religious services is required.

Summer Programs Advancement, sports programs offered; session focuses on sports; held on campus; accepts boys and girls; open to students from other schools.

Tuition and Aid Day student tuition: $5950–$6950. Tuition installment plan (SMART Tuition Payment Plan). Need-based scholarship grants available.

Admissions Traditional secondary-level entrance grade is 9. Placement test required. Deadline for receipt of application materials: none. Application fee required: $125. Interview required.

Athletics Interscholastic: baseball (boys), basketball (b,g), bowling (b,g), diving (b,g), drill team (g), football (b), golf (b,g), soccer (b,g), softball (g), swimming and diving (b,g), tennis (b,g), track and field (b,g), volleyball (g), wrestling (b); coed interscholastic: cheering, cross-country running; coed intramural: table tennis, ultimate Frisbee. 3 PE instructors.

Computers Computers are regularly used in all academic, computer applications, desktop publishing, programming, video film production, Web site design classes. Computer network features include campus e-mail, on-campus library services, CD-ROMs, Internet access, office computer access, wireless campus network, computer labs and laptop carts.

Contact Mrs. Diane Pyle, Director of Admissions. 913-319-2423. Fax: 913-345-2319. E-mail: dpyle@stasaints.net. Web site: www.stasaints.net.

ST. THOMAS AQUINAS HIGH SCHOOL

197 Dover Point Road
Dover, New Hampshire 03820
Head of School: Mr. Jeffrey Andrew Quinn

General Information Coeducational day college-preparatory and religious studies school, affiliated with Roman Catholic Church. Grades 9–12. Founded: 1960. Setting: small town. Nearest major city is Boston, MA. 11-acre campus. 2 buildings on campus. Approved or accredited by New England Association of Schools and Colleges and New Hampshire Department of Education. Endowment: $121,000. Total enrollment: 716. Upper school average class size: 21. Upper school faculty-student ratio: 1:15.

Upper School Student Profile Grade 9: 190 students (89 boys, 101 girls); Grade 10: 183 students (78 boys, 105 girls); Grade 11: 170 students (81 boys, 89 girls); Grade 12: 173 students (77 boys, 96 girls). 75% of students are Roman Catholic.

Faculty School total: 46. In upper school: 24 men, 22 women; 22 have advanced degrees.

Subjects Offered Algebra, anatomy and physiology, biology, biology-AP, calculus, calculus-AP, chemistry, chorus, Christian ethics, concert band, contemporary studies, drawing, economics, English, French, geography, geometry, honors algebra, honors English, honors geometry, humanities, introduction to technology, Latin, marine biology, math applications, media arts, music appreciation, music theory, painting, physics, prayer/spirituality, pre-calculus, psychology, science, scripture, sculpture, social justice, sociology, Spanish, studio art, theology, U.S. government and politics-AP, U.S. history, U.S. history-AP, wellness, Western civilization, world religions.

Graduation Requirements Arts and fine arts (art, music, dance, drama), Christian ethics, electives, English, foreign language, freshman seminar, mathematics, prayer/spirituality, science, scripture, social justice, social studies (includes history), theology, world religions. Community service is required.

Special Academic Programs Advanced Placement exam preparation in 8 subject areas; honors section.

College Placement 171 students graduated in 2005; 165 went to college, including Bentley College; Brandeis University; Northeastern University; Saint Anselm College; Saint Michael's College; University of New Hampshire. Other: 1 went to work, 1 entered military service, 1 entered a postgraduate year, 3 had other specific plans. Mean SAT verbal: 587, mean SAT math: 576.

Student Life Upper grades have specified standards of dress, student council. Discipline rests primarily with faculty. Attendance at religious services is required.

Tuition and Aid Day student tuition: $7400. Tuition installment plan (annual, semi-annual, and 10-month payment plans). Need-based scholarship grants available. In 2005–06, 10% of upper-school students received aid. Total amount of financial aid awarded in 2005–06: $215,000.

Admissions Traditional secondary-level entrance grade is 9. For fall 2005, 267 students applied for upper-level admission, 244 were accepted, 192 enrolled. Scholastic Testing Service High School Placement Test required. Deadline for receipt of application materials: December 31. Application fee required: $40.

Athletics Interscholastic: baseball (boys), basketball (b,g), cheering (g), cross-country running (b,g), field hockey (g), football (b), golf (b,g), gymnastics (g), ice hockey (b,g), lacrosse (b,g), skiing (downhill) (b,g), soccer (b,g), softball (g),

swimming and diving (b,g), tennis (b,g), track and field (b,g), volleyball (g), winter (indoor) track (b,g), wrestling (b). 47 coaches, 1 trainer.

Computers Computers are regularly used in introduction to technology, media arts classes. Computer network features include on-campus library services, Internet access.

Contact Mr. Gary Finley, Admissions Coordinator. 603-742-3206. Fax: 603-749-7822. E-mail: gfinley@stalux.org. Web site: www.stalux.org.

ST. THOMAS CHOIR SCHOOL

New York, New York
See Junior Boarding Schools section.

ST. THOMAS HIGH SCHOOL

4500 Memorial Drive
Houston, Texas 77007-7332
Head of School: Rev. Ronald Schwenzer, CSB

General Information Boys' day college-preparatory and religious studies school, affiliated with Roman Catholic Church. Grades 9–12. Founded: 1900. Setting: urban. 37-acre campus. 6 buildings on campus. Approved or accredited by Southern Association of Colleges and Schools, Texas Catholic Conference, Texas Education Agency, and Texas Department of Education. Endowment: $9 million. Total enrollment: 643. Upper school average class size: 22. Upper school faculty-student ratio: 1:13.

Upper School Student Profile Grade 9: 173 students (173 boys); Grade 10: 178 students (178 boys); Grade 11: 146 students (146 boys); Grade 12: 146 students (146 boys). 83% of students are Roman Catholic.

Faculty School total: 49. In upper school: 35 men, 14 women; 30 have advanced degrees.

Subjects Offered Algebra, American government, American government-AP, American history, American history-AP, American literature, ancient history, art, arts, Basic programming, Bible studies, bioethics, biology, biology-AP, British literature, calculus, calculus-AP, ceramics, chemistry, chemistry-AP, civics/free enterprise, classical civilization, college counseling, comparative government and politics-AP, computer applications, computer information systems, computer programming, computer studies, creative writing, critical thinking, critical writing, decision making, drama, drawing, ecology, environmental systems, economics, economics-AP, English, English language-AP, English literature, English literature-AP, environmental science, ethics, European history, fine arts, forensics, French, geography, geology, geometry, government and politics-AP, government/civics, grammar, guidance, health, health education, history of the Catholic Church, Holocaust studies, instrumental music, jazz band, journalism, Latin, marine biology, mathematics, oceanography, oral communications, orchestra, painting, photography, physical education, physics, physics-AP, pre-calculus, programming, public speaking, publications, religion, social studies, Spanish, Spanish language-AP, speech, student government, student publications, theater, theology, trigonometry, world history, world literature.

Graduation Requirements Arts and fine arts (art, music, dance, drama), computer applications, English, foreign language, mathematics, physical education (includes health), religion (includes Bible studies and theology), science, social studies (includes history).

Special Academic Programs Advanced Placement exam preparation in 10 subject areas; honors section.

College Placement 151 students graduated in 2005; 145 went to college, including Texas A&M University; Texas Tech University; The University of Texas at Austin; University of Houston; University of Notre Dame; University of St. Thomas. Other: 1 entered military service, 2 had other specific plans. Mean SAT verbal: 591, mean SAT math: 577. 44% scored over 600 on SAT verbal, 42% scored over 600 on SAT math.

Student Life Upper grades have specified standards of dress, student council. Discipline rests primarily with faculty. Attendance at religious services is required.

Summer Programs Remediation programs offered; session focuses on remediation classes for original credit courses; held on campus; accepts boys and girls; open to students from other schools. 300 students usually enrolled. 2006 schedule: June 6 to July 15. Application deadline: June 1.

Tuition and Aid Day student tuition: $9100. Tuition installment plan (monthly payment plans). Merit scholarship grants, need-based scholarship grants, paying campus jobs available. In 2005–06, 34% of upper-school students received aid; total upper-school merit-scholarship money awarded: $40,000. Total amount of financial aid awarded in 2005–06: $634,000.

Admissions Traditional secondary-level entrance grade is 9. For fall 2005, 400 students applied for upper-level admission, 250 were accepted, 185 enrolled. High School Placement Test required. Deadline for receipt of application materials: February 3. Application fee required: $25.

Athletics Interscholastic: baseball, basketball, cross-country running, football, golf, roller hockey, soccer, swimming and diving, tennis, track and field, wrestling; intramural: basketball, bowling, flag football, rugby, table tennis. 2 PE instructors, 2 coaches, 1 trainer.

Computers Computers are regularly used in data processing, desktop publishing, multimedia, newspaper, programming, publications, word processing classes. Computer network features include on-campus library services, CD-ROMs, online commercial services, Internet access, DVD.
Contact Ms. Christine Westman, Assistant Principal. 713-864-6348. Fax: 713-864-5750. E-mail: chris.westman@sths.org. Web site: www.sths.org.

SAINT THOMAS MORE SCHOOL

45 Cottage Road
Oakdale, Connecticut 06370
Head of School: James F. Hanrahan Jr.

petersons.com

General Information Boys' boarding college-preparatory, arts, and religious studies school, affiliated with Roman Catholic Church; primarily serves underachievers. Grades 8–PG. Founded: 1962. Setting: rural. Nearest major city is Hartford. Students are housed in single-sex dormitories. 100-acre campus. 14 buildings on campus. Approved or accredited by Connecticut Association of Independent Schools, New England Association of Schools and Colleges, The Association of Boarding Schools, and Connecticut Department of Education. Member of National Association of Independent Schools and Secondary School Admission Test Board. Endowment: $7 million. Total enrollment: 210. Upper school average class size: 15. Upper school faculty-student ratio: 1:7.
Upper School Student Profile Grade 9: 21 students (21 boys); Grade 10: 32 students (32 boys); Grade 11: 55 students (55 boys); Grade 12: 60 students (60 boys); Postgraduate: 26 students (26 boys). 100% of students are boarding students. 16% are state residents. 14 states are represented in upper school student body. 28% are international students. International students from Japan, Latvia, Mexico, Republic of Korea, Spain, and Taiwan; 8 other countries represented in student body. 65% of students are Roman Catholic.
Faculty School total: 30. In upper school: 22 men, 7 women; 17 have advanced degrees; 27 reside on campus.
Subjects Offered Algebra, American literature, ancient history, arts appreciation, biology, British literature, calculus, chemistry, comparative religion, death and loss, earth science, economics, English, environmental science, ESL, geometry, global studies, grammar, intro to computers, language arts, life science, medieval history, moral theology, mythology, physics, political thought, pre-algebra, pre-calculus, programming, reading, Spanish, speech, studio art, U.S. history, world history, world literature, writing.
Graduation Requirements Arts and fine arts (art, music, dance, drama), English, foreign language, mathematics, religion (includes Bible studies and theology), science, social studies (includes history).
Special Academic Programs Remedial reading and/or remedial writing; remedial math; programs in general development for dyslexic students; special instructional classes for students with learning disabilities and Attention Deficit Disorder; ESL (23 students enrolled).
College Placement 50 students graduated in 2005; 49 went to college, including Fordham University; Plymouth State University; Quinnipiac University; Temple University; University of Connecticut. Other: 1 entered a postgraduate year. Median SAT verbal: 480, median SAT math: 550. 15% scored over 600 on SAT verbal, 15% scored over 600 on SAT math.
Student Life Upper grades have uniform requirement, student council, honor system. Discipline rests primarily with faculty. Attendance at religious services is required.
Summer Programs Remediation, enrichment, ESL, art/fine arts, computer instruction programs offered; session focuses on study skills, make-up credits, enrichment; held on campus; accepts boys; open to students from other schools. 90 students usually enrolled. 2006 schedule: July 2 to August 4. Application deadline: none.
Tuition and Aid 7-day tuition and room/board: $29,250–$32,250. Tuition installment plan (monthly payment plans, individually arranged payment plans). Merit scholarship grants, need-based scholarship grants available. In 2005–06, 20% of upper-school students received aid. Total amount of financial aid awarded in 2005–06: $662,000.
Admissions Traditional secondary-level entrance grade is 10. For fall 2005, 274 students applied for upper-level admission, 195 were accepted, 99 enrolled. Otis-Lennon School Ability Test, SAT, SLEP, SSAT or TOEFL required. Deadline for receipt of application materials: none. Application fee required: $50. Interview required.
Athletics Interscholastic: baseball, basketball, crew, cross-country running, football, golf, hockey, ice hockey, lacrosse, sailing, soccer, tennis, track and field; intramural: alpine skiing, baseball, basketball, billiards, canoeing/kayaking, fishing, flag football, Frisbee, jogging, kickball, martial arts, nordic skiing, outdoor activities, paddle tennis, physical fitness, physical training, roller blading, sailing, skateboarding, skiing (downhill), snowboarding, soccer, strength & conditioning, swimming and diving, table tennis, tennis, ultimate Frisbee, volleyball, weight lifting, weight training.
Computers Computers are regularly used in college planning, newspaper, research skills, yearbook classes. Computer resources include on-campus library services, CD-ROMs, Internet access.
Contact Timothy P. Riordan, Director of Admissions. 860-823-3861. Fax: 860-823-3863. E-mail: stmadmit@stthomasmoreschool.com. Web site: www.stthomasmoreschool.com.

See full description on page 1044.

ST. TIMOTHY'S SCHOOL

8400 Greenspring Avenue
Stevenson, Maryland 21153
Head of School: Randy S. Stevens

petersons.com

General Information Girls' boarding and day college-preparatory, arts, and Cambridge (UK) General Certificate of Secondary Education school, affiliated with Episcopal Church. Grades 9–PG. Founded: 1882. Setting: rural. Nearest major city is Baltimore. Students are housed in single-sex dormitories. 145-acre campus. 23 buildings on campus. Approved or accredited by Association of Independent Maryland Schools, Middle States Association of Colleges and Schools, National Association of Episcopal Schools, The Association of Boarding Schools, and Maryland Department of Education. Member of National Association of Independent Schools and Secondary School Admission Test Board. Endowment: $12 million. Total enrollment: 133. Upper school average class size: 10. Upper school faculty-student ratio: 1:5.
Upper School Student Profile Grade 9: 32 students (32 girls); Grade 10: 42 students (42 girls); Grade 11: 31 students (31 girls); Grade 12: 28 students (28 girls). 55% of students are boarding students. 50% are state residents. 13 states are represented in upper school student body. 17% are international students. International students from Bahamas, Cote d'Ivoire, Hong Kong, Japan, Mexico, and Republic of Korea; 3 other countries represented in student body.
Faculty School total: 28. In upper school: 14 men, 14 women; 22 have advanced degrees; 21 reside on campus.
Subjects Offered Algebra, American literature, art, art history, art history-AP, biology, biology-AP, British literature, calculus, calculus-AP, chemistry, community service, creative writing, dance, drama, drama performance, drama workshop, economics, English, English composition, English literature, European history, expository writing, fine arts, French, French-AP, geometry, grammar, history, Latin, Latin-AP, law, mathematics, modern dance, music, music theory, photography, physical education, physical science, physics, piano, politics, religion, science, social studies, Spanish, Spanish-AP, U.S. history, U.S. history-AP, world history, world literature, writing.
Graduation Requirements Arts and fine arts (art, music, dance, drama), English, foreign language, history, mathematics, physical education (includes health), religion (includes Bible studies and theology), science, independent senior project. Community service is required.
Special Academic Programs Advanced Placement exam preparation in 12 subject areas; honors section; independent study; ESL (12 students enrolled).
College Placement 28 students graduated in 2005; 27 went to college, including Gettysburg College; New York University; Princeton University; University of Maryland, College Park; University of Pennsylvania; University of Virginia. Other: 1 had other specific plans. Mean SAT verbal: 600, mean SAT math: 550.
Student Life Upper grades have uniform requirement, student council, honor system. Discipline rests equally with students and faculty. Attendance at religious services is required.
Tuition and Aid Day student tuition: $19,600; 5-day tuition and room/board: $34,500; 7-day tuition and room/board: $34,500. Tuition installment plan (FACTS Tuition Payment Plan). Merit scholarship grants, need-based scholarship grants, need-based loans available. In 2005–06, 43% of upper-school students received aid; total upper-school merit-scholarship money awarded: $30,000. Total amount of financial aid awarded in 2005–06: $1,250,000.
Admissions Traditional secondary-level entrance grade is 9. For fall 2005, 162 students applied for upper-level admission, 111 were accepted, 60 enrolled. ISEE, SLEP for foreign students, SSAT or TOEFL required. Deadline for receipt of application materials: February 10. Application fee required: $40. Interview required.
Athletics Interscholastic: basketball, dressage, equestrian sports, field hockey, golf, horseback riding, ice hockey, indoor soccer, lacrosse, soccer, softball, squash, tennis, volleyball; intramural: ballet, cross-country running, dance, dance squad, equestrian sports, fitness, horseback riding, modern dance, physical fitness, weight training, yoga. 3 coaches, 1 trainer.
Computers Computers are regularly used in art, college planning, English, mathematics, publications, SAT preparation, science, yearbook classes. Computer network features include campus e-mail, on-campus library services, CD-ROMs, online commercial services, Internet access, file transfer, DVD, wireless campus network.
Contact Patrick M. Finn, Director of Admissions and Assistant Head of School. 410-486-7401. Fax: 410-486-1167. E-mail: admis@sttims-school.org. Web site: www.sttims-school.org.

ANNOUNCEMENT FROM THE SCHOOL Established in 1882 as the Episcopal college-preparatory boarding and day school for girls (grades 9–12 and PG), the School offers small class size, rigorous academics, excellent fine arts, and athletics. St. Timothy's is located on a large, rural campus near Baltimore, Maryland, and includes an equestrian center, a dance studio, and a 350-seat theater. For more information, contact the Admission Office (telephone: 410-486-7401; Web site: http://www.sttims-school.org).

See full description on page 1046.

SAINT VIATOR HIGH SCHOOL

1213 East Oakton Street
Arlington Heights, Illinois 60004
Head of School: Rev. Robert M. Egan, CSV

General Information Coeducational day college-preparatory, arts, religious studies, bilingual studies, and technology school, affiliated with Roman Catholic Church. Grades 9–12. Founded: 1961. Setting: suburban. Approved or accredited by Illinois Department of Education. Upper school average class size: 25. Upper school faculty-student ratio: 1:13.
College Placement Mean composite ACT: 24.
Tuition and Aid Day student tuition: $8100. Financial aid available to upper-school students. In 2005–06, 16% of upper-school students received aid. Total amount of financial aid awarded in 2005–06: $650,000.
Admissions No application fee required.
Contact Mrs. Eileen Manno, Assistant Principal. 847-392-4050 Ext. 229. Fax: 847-392-8305. E-mail: emanno@saintviator.com. Web site: www.saintviator.com.

SAINT VINCENT FERRER HIGH SCHOOL

151 East 65th Street
New York, New York 10021
Head of School: Sr. Gail Morgan

General Information Girls' day college-preparatory school, affiliated with Roman Catholic Church. Grades 9–12. Founded: 1888. Setting: urban. 1 building on campus. Approved or accredited by Middle States Association of Colleges and Schools. Total enrollment: 501. Upper school average class size: 22. Upper school faculty-student ratio: 1:16.
Upper School Student Profile Grade 9: 135 students (135 girls); Grade 10: 134 students (134 girls); Grade 11: 115 students (115 girls); Grade 12: 117 students (117 girls). 85% of students are Roman Catholic.
Faculty School total: 33. In upper school: 9 men, 24 women.
Graduation Requirements Regents Diploma requirements.
Special Academic Programs Advanced Placement exam preparation; honors section; independent study.
College Placement 115 students graduated in 2005; 113 went to college. Other: 1 entered military service, 1 had other specific plans.
Student Life Upper grades have uniform requirement, student council, honor system. Discipline rests primarily with faculty. Attendance at religious services is required.
Summer Programs Remediation, enrichment programs offered; held on campus; accepts girls; open to students from other schools. 50 students usually enrolled. 2006 schedule: July 5 to July 26. Application deadline: June 25.
Tuition and Aid Day student tuition: $5850. Tuition installment plan (monthly payment plans, individually arranged payment plans). Merit scholarship grants, need-based scholarship grants available. In 2005–06, 25% of upper-school students received aid.
Admissions Traditional secondary-level entrance grade is 9. For fall 2005, 700 students applied for upper-level admission, 250 were accepted, 135 enrolled. Diocesan Entrance Exam required. Deadline for receipt of application materials: January 1. No application fee required. Interview required.
Athletics Intramural: basketball, cheering, fitness walking, kickball, martial arts, outdoor activities, soccer, softball, volleyball. 1 PE instructor.
Computers Computer resources include on-campus library services, CD-ROMs, Internet access, office computer access, DVD.
Contact Julie Ferenc, Admissions Director. 212-535-4680 Ext. 102. Fax: 212-988-3455. E-mail: julief@saintvincentferrer.com. Web site: www.saintvincentferrer.com.

ST. VINCENT PALLOTTI HIGH SCHOOL

113 St. Mary's Place
Laurel, Maryland 20707
Head of School: Mr. Stephen J. Edmonds

General Information Coeducational day college-preparatory school, affiliated with Roman Catholic Church. Grades 9–12. Founded: 1921. Setting: suburban. Nearest major city is Washington, DC. 5 buildings on campus. Approved or accredited by Association of Independent Maryland Schools and Maryland Department of Education. Total enrollment: 510. Upper school average class size: 20. Upper school faculty-student ratio: 1:20.
Upper School Student Profile 70% of students are Roman Catholic.
Faculty School total: 65.
Special Academic Programs Advanced Placement exam preparation; honors section; independent study; study at local college for college credit; programs in English, mathematics, general development for dyslexic students.
Student Life Upper grades have uniform requirement, student council, honor system. Discipline rests primarily with faculty. Attendance at religious services is required.
Summer Programs Remediation, sports programs offered; held on campus; accepts boys and girls; open to students from other schools.

Tuition and Aid Day student tuition: $10,025. Tuition installment plan (FACTS Tuition Payment Plan). Tuition reduction for siblings, merit scholarship grants, need-based scholarship grants available.
Admissions Traditional secondary-level entrance grade is 9. For fall 2005, 285 students applied for upper-level admission, 200 were accepted, 121 enrolled. High School Placement Test required. Deadline for receipt of application materials: December 15. Application fee required: $50. On-campus interview required.
Athletics Interscholastic: baseball (boys), basketball (b,g), cross-country running (b,g), dance squad (g), football (b), lacrosse (b,g), pom squad (g), soccer (b,g), softball (g), volleyball (g), wrestling (b); coed interscholastic: cheering, golf, swimming and diving; coed intramural: mountain biking, skiing (downhill), snowboarding.
Contact Mrs. Tina M. Hyatt, Director of Admissions. 301-725-3228 Ext. 202. Fax: 301-725-0493. E-mail: thyatt@pallottihs.org. Web site: www.pallottihs.org/.

SAINT VINCENT'S ACADEMY

207 East Liberty Street
Savannah, Georgia 31401
Head of School: Sr. Helen Marie Buttimer, RSM

General Information Girls' day college-preparatory school, affiliated with Roman Catholic Church. Grades 9–12. Founded: 1845. Setting: urban. 5 buildings on campus. Approved or accredited by Southern Association of Colleges and Schools and Georgia Department of Education. Endowment: $200,000. Total enrollment: 346. Upper school average class size: 18. Upper school faculty-student ratio: 1:12.
Upper School Student Profile Grade 9: 87 students (87 girls); Grade 10: 90 students (90 girls); Grade 11: 75 students (75 girls); Grade 12: 94 students (94 girls). 70% of students are Roman Catholic.
Faculty School total: 27. In upper school: 5 men, 22 women; 13 have advanced degrees.
Graduation Requirements Adolescent issues, algebra, American government, American history, American literature, applied music, art, Bible studies, biology, British literature, Catholic belief and practice, chemistry, Christian studies, composition, computer education, economics, electives, foreign language, four units of summer reading, geometry, guidance, health, history, history of the Catholic Church, trigonometry, word processing, world geography.
Special Academic Programs Advanced Placement exam preparation in 5 subject areas; honors section; independent study.
College Placement 93 students graduated in 2005; 90 went to college, including University of Georgia. Other: 2 went to work, 1 had other specific plans.
Student Life Upper grades have uniform requirement, student council. Discipline rests primarily with faculty. Attendance at religious services is required.
Admissions Traditional secondary-level entrance grade is 9. For fall 2005, 346 students applied for upper-level admission, 346 were accepted, 346 enrolled. High School Placement Test required. Deadline for receipt of application materials: none. Application fee required: $100. Interview required.
Athletics Interscholastic: basketball, bowling, cheering, cross-country running, riflery, sailing, soccer, softball, swimming and diving, tennis, track and field, volleyball. 1 PE instructor, 1 coach, 1 trainer.
Computers Computer network features include on-campus library services, CD-ROMs, Internet access.
Contact Mrs. Kathryn K. Grayson, Administrative Assistant. 912-236-5508. Fax: 912-236-7877. E-mail: kgrayson@stvincentsacademy.com. Web site: www. stvincentsacademy.com.

SAINT XAVIER HIGH SCHOOL

1609 Poplar Level Road
Louisville, Kentucky 40217
Head of School: Perry Sangalli, EdD

General Information Boys' day college-preparatory, arts, business, religious studies, bilingual studies, and technology school, affiliated with Roman Catholic Church. Grades 9–12. Founded: 1864. Setting: suburban. 72-acre campus. 6 buildings on campus. Approved or accredited by Southern Association of Colleges and Schools and Kentucky Department of Education. Endowment: $10 million. Total enrollment: 1,402. Upper school average class size: 23. Upper school faculty-student ratio: 1:12.
Upper School Student Profile Grade 9: 381 students (381 boys); Grade 10: 362 students (362 boys); Grade 11: 317 students (317 boys); Grade 12: 342 students (342 boys). 75% of students are Roman Catholic.
Faculty School total: 117. In upper school: 93 men, 24 women; 98 have advanced degrees.
Subjects Offered Accounting, acting, Advanced Placement courses, algebra, American government, anatomy and physiology, band, biology, business law, ceramics, chemistry, chorus, computer applications, computer programming, computer-aided design, creative writing, desktop publishing, drafting, economics, English, environmental science, fitness, French, geometry, German, global issues, health, humanities, journalism, keyboarding, mathematics, mechanical drawing, music, music history, music theory, philosophy, photography, physical education, physics, probability and

statistics, psychology, reading, sculpture, sociology, Spanish, speech, theology, trigonometry, U.S. history, world civilizations, world geography, yearbook.

Graduation Requirements Arts and fine arts (art, music, dance, drama), electives, English, foreign language, mathematics, physical education (includes health), science, social studies (includes history), theology, U.S. history.

Special Academic Programs Advanced Placement exam preparation in 18 subject areas; honors section; study at local college for college credit; academic accommodation for the gifted, the musically talented, and the artistically talented; remedial reading and/or remedial writing; remedial math; programs in English, mathematics, general development for dyslexic students; special instructional classes for students with Attention Deficit Disorder, Attention Deficit Hyperactivity Disorder, dyslexia, and central auditory processing disorder.

College Placement 326 students graduated in 2005; 218 went to college, including Bellarmine University; Saint Louis University; University of Dayton; University of Kentucky; University of Louisville; Xavier University. Other: 8 went to work, 4 entered military service. Mean SAT verbal: 579, mean SAT math: 585, mean composite ACT: 23.

Student Life Upper grades have specified standards of dress, student council, honor system. Discipline rests primarily with faculty. Attendance at religious services is required.

Tuition and Aid Day student tuition: $7875. Tuition installment plan (FACTS Tuition Payment Plan). Merit scholarship grants, need-based scholarship grants, paying campus jobs available. In 2005–06, 30% of upper-school students received aid; total upper-school merit-scholarship money awarded: $73,000. Total amount of financial aid awarded in 2005–06: $950,000.

Admissions Traditional secondary-level entrance grade is 9. For fall 2005, 475 students applied for upper-level admission, 475 were accepted, 381 enrolled. STS required. Deadline for receipt of application materials: none. Application fee required: $100. On-campus interview recommended.

Athletics Interscholastic: baseball, basketball, bowling, cheering, cross-country running, diving, fishing, fly fishing, football, golf, ice hockey, indoor track, indoor track & field, lacrosse, power lifting, running, soccer, strength & conditioning, swimming and diving, tennis, track and field, volleyball, weight lifting, weight training, wrestling; intramural: alpine skiing, basketball, billiards, bowling, cooperative games, fishing, flag football, football, Frisbee, golf, ice hockey, kickball, mountain biking, outdoor activities, skiing (downhill), snowboarding, soccer, table tennis, tennis, touch football, ultimate Frisbee, weight training. 3 PE instructors, 63 coaches, 1 trainer.

Computers Computers are regularly used in all classes. Computer network features include campus e-mail, on-campus library services, CD-ROMs, online commercial services, Internet access, office computer access, DVD.

Contact Mr. Nelson C. Nunn, Principal. 502-637-4712 Ext. 124. Fax: 502-634-2171. E-mail: nnunn@saintx.com. Web site: www.saintx.com.

SAINT XAVIER HIGH SCHOOL

600 North Bend Road
Cincinnati, Ohio 45224
Head of School: Rev. Walter C. Deye, SJ

General Information Boys' day college-preparatory, religious studies, technology, and service learning school, affiliated with Roman Catholic Church. Grades 9–12. Founded: 1831. Setting: suburban. 100-acre campus. 1 building on campus. Approved or accredited by Jesuit Secondary Education Association, North Central Association of Colleges and Schools, Ohio Catholic Schools Accreditation Association (OCSAA), and Ohio Department of Education. Endowment: $20 million. Total enrollment: 1,498. Upper school average class size: 28. Upper school faculty-student ratio: 1:13.

Upper School Student Profile Grade 9: 380 students (380 boys); Grade 10: 402 students (402 boys); Grade 11: 338 students (338 boys); Grade 12: 378 students (378 boys). 85% of students are Roman Catholic.

Faculty School total: 100. In upper school: 72 men, 28 women; 80 have advanced degrees.

Subjects Offered Arts, biology, chemistry, computer science, English, fine arts, French, German, Greek, health, Latin, mathematics, physical education, physics, religion, Russian, science, social studies, Spanish.

Graduation Requirements Arts and fine arts (art, music, dance, drama), computer science, English, foreign language, forensics, mathematics, physical education (includes health), religion (includes Bible studies and theology), science, social studies (includes history).

Special Academic Programs Advanced Placement exam preparation in 19 subject areas; independent study; term-away projects; study at local college for college credit.

College Placement 333 students graduated in 2005; 330 went to college, including Miami University; Saint Louis University; The Ohio State University; University of Cincinnati; University of Notre Dame; Xavier University. Other: 2 entered military service, 1 had other specific plans. Median SAT verbal: 630, median SAT math: 640, median composite ACT: 27. 64% scored over 600 on SAT verbal, 72% scored over 600 on SAT math, 60% scored over 26 on composite ACT.

Student Life Upper grades have specified standards of dress, student council. Discipline rests primarily with faculty. Attendance at religious services is required.

Tuition and Aid Day student tuition: $8995. Merit scholarship grants, need-based scholarship grants available. In 2005–06, 26% of upper-school students received aid;

total upper-school merit-scholarship money awarded: $24,975. Total amount of financial aid awarded in 2005–06: $1,500,000.

Admissions Traditional secondary-level entrance grade is 9. For fall 2005, 865 students applied for upper-level admission, 475 were accepted, 380 enrolled. High School Placement Test required. Deadline for receipt of application materials: December 1. Application fee required: $20.

Athletics Interscholastic: baseball, basketball, bowling, crew, cross-country running, diving, football, golf, ice hockey, lacrosse, soccer, swimming and diving, tennis, track and field, volleyball, wrestling; intramural: basketball, football, golf, soccer, table tennis, tennis, volleyball. 3 PE instructors, 1 trainer.

Computers Computers are regularly used in art, design, drawing and design, foreign language, graphic arts, graphic design, graphics, keyboarding, lab/keyboard, language development, library, programming, research skills, science classes. Computer network features include campus e-mail, on-campus library services, CD-ROMs, online commercial services, Internet access, DVD.

Contact Mr. Roderick D. Hinton, Director of Admissions. 513-761-7815 Ext. 106. Fax: 513-761-3811. E-mail: rhinton@stxavier.org. Web site: www.stxavier.org.

SALEM ACADEMY

500 Salem Avenue
Winston-Salem, North Carolina 27108-0578
Head of School: Dr. Wayne Burkette

General Information Girls' boarding and day college-preparatory and arts school, affiliated with Moravian Church. Grades 9–12. Founded: 1772. Setting: urban. Students are housed in single-sex dormitories. 60-acre campus. 4 buildings on campus. Approved or accredited by North Carolina Association of Independent Schools, Southern Association of Colleges and Schools, and The Association of Boarding Schools. Member of National Association of Independent Schools and Secondary School Admission Test Board. Endowment: $7 million. Total enrollment: 183. Upper school average class size: 13. Upper school faculty-student ratio: 1:9.

Upper School Student Profile Grade 9: 37 students (37 girls); Grade 10: 52 students (52 girls); Grade 11: 49 students (49 girls); Grade 12: 45 students (45 girls). 50% of students are boarding students. 75% are state residents. 14 states are represented in upper school student body. 18% are international students. International students from China, Democratic People's Republic of Korea, Germany, Hungary, Macao, and Saudi Arabia; 6 other countries represented in student body. 7% of students are Moravian.

Faculty School total: 25. In upper school: 25 women; 17 have advanced degrees; 1 resides on campus.

Subjects Offered Algebra, American history, art, biology, calculus, chemistry, dance, drama, economics, English, European history, fine arts, French, geometry, government/civics, Latin, mathematics, music, physical education, physics, precalculus, psychology, religion, science, social science, social studies, Spanish, theater, trigonometry, world history.

Graduation Requirements Arts and fine arts (art, music, dance, drama), English, foreign language, mathematics, physical education (includes health), religion (includes Bible studies and theology), science, social science, social studies (includes history), 2 years of Latin.

Special Academic Programs Advanced Placement exam preparation in 10 subject areas; honors section; term-away projects; study at local college for college credit; study abroad; ESL (8 students enrolled).

College Placement 52 students graduated in 2005; 51 went to college, including Duke University; North Carolina State University; The University of North Carolina at Chapel Hill; Wake Forest University. Other: 1 had other specific plans. Mean SAT verbal: 635, mean SAT math: 618.

Student Life Upper grades have specified standards of dress, student council, honor system. Discipline rests equally with students and faculty. Attendance at religious services is required.

Tuition and Aid Day student tuition: $14,750; 7-day tuition and room/board: $26,941. Tuition installment plan (Key Tuition Payment Plan, monthly payment plans). Merit scholarship grants, need-based scholarship grants available. In 2005–06, 43% of upper-school students received aid; total upper-school merit-scholarship money awarded: $50,000. Total amount of financial aid awarded in 2005–06: $1,098,143.

Admissions Traditional secondary-level entrance grade is 9. For fall 2005, 149 students applied for upper-level admission, 107 were accepted, 71 enrolled. ACT, PSAT, SAT, SSAT or TOEFL required. Deadline for receipt of application materials: none. Application fee required: $50. Interview required.

Athletics Interscholastic: basketball, cross-country running, field hockey, golf, soccer, softball, swimming and diving, tennis, track and field, volleyball; intramural: aerobics/dance, archery, badminton, dance, fitness, flag football, floor hockey, golf, horseback riding, indoor hockey, indoor soccer, self defense. 2 PE instructors, 15 coaches, 1 trainer.

Computers Computers are regularly used in all academic classes. Computer network features include campus e-mail, on-campus library services, CD-ROMs, online commercial services, Internet access.

Contact C. Lucia Uldrick, Director of Admissions. 336-721-2643. Fax: 336-917-5340. E-mail: academy@salem.edu. Web site: www.salemacademy.com.

See full description on page 1048.

Salem Academy

SALEM ACADEMY

942 Lancaster Drive, NE
Salem, Oregon 97301
Head of School: Dr. Benjamin V. Potloff

General Information Coeducational day college-preparatory, general academic, arts, vocational, religious studies, bilingual studies, and technology school, affiliated with Protestant Church. Grades K–12. Founded: 1945. Setting: suburban. 34-acre campus. 5 buildings on campus. Approved or accredited by Association of Christian Schools International, Northwest Association of Schools and Colleges, and Oregon Department of Education. Total enrollment: 576. Upper school average class size: 20. Upper school faculty-student ratio: 1:17.

Upper School Student Profile 90% of students are Protestant.

Faculty School total: 48. In upper school: 13 men, 11 women; 4 have advanced degrees.

Subjects Offered Advanced chemistry, Advanced Placement courses, algebra, American history, American literature, anatomy and physiology, art, athletics, auto mechanics, auto shop, baseball, Bible, Bible studies, biology, business, calculus, ceramics, cheerleading, chemistry, choir, college counseling, college writing, computer programming, computer science, consumer mathematics, drama, drama performance, Eastern world civilizations, economics, English, English literature, English literature and composition-AP, English literature-AP, ESL, European history-AP, foods, geography, geometry, government/civics, grammar, health, history, history-AP, home economics, honors English, industrial arts, Japanese, jazz ensemble, Life of Christ, mathematics, music, physical education, physical science, physics, psychology, radio broadcasting, religion, SAT preparation, science, shop, social science, social studies, softball, Spanish, speech, sports, track and field, typing, U.S. history-AP, vocal music, volleyball, weight training, woodworking, world history, world literature, writing.

Graduation Requirements English, foreign language, mathematics, physical education (includes health), religion (includes Bible studies and theology), science, social science, social studies (includes history), 1 credit in biblical studies for each year attended.

Special Academic Programs Advanced Placement exam preparation in 4 subject areas; honors section; independent study; study at local college for college credit; academic accommodation for the gifted, the musically talented, and the artistically talented; ESL (18 students enrolled).

College Placement 37 students graduated in 2005; 34 went to college, including Corban College; George Fox University; Northwest Nazarene University; Oregon State University; Point Loma Nazarene University; University of Oregon. Other: 1 entered military service.

Student Life Upper grades have specified standards of dress, student council. Discipline rests primarily with faculty.

Tuition and Aid Tuition reduction for siblings, need-based scholarship grants available.

Admissions Traditional secondary-level entrance grade is 9. Deadline for receipt of application materials: none. Application fee required: $50. On-campus interview required.

Athletics Interscholastic: baseball (boys), basketball (b,g), cheering (g), football (b), softball (g), track and field (b,g), volleyball (g), wrestling (b); coed interscholastic: equestrian sports, weight training. 2 PE instructors.

Computers Computers are regularly used in yearbook classes. Computer network features include on-campus library services, CD-ROMs, Internet access, office computer access, wireless campus network.

Contact Sharon Whitbeck, Administrative Assistant to the Superintendent. 503-378-1219. Fax: 503-375-3522. Web site: www.salemacademy.org.

SALESIAN HIGH SCHOOL

148 Main Street
New Rochelle, New York 10801
Head of School: John P. Flaherty

General Information Boys' day college-preparatory, general academic, technology, and American Studies school, affiliated with Roman Catholic Church. Grades 9–12. Founded: 1920. Setting: suburban. Nearest major city is New York. 17-acre campus. 4 buildings on campus. Approved or accredited by Middle States Association of Colleges and Schools and New York Department of Education. Endowment: $350,000. Total enrollment: 430. Upper school faculty-student ratio: 1:11.

Upper School Student Profile 80% of students are Roman Catholic.

Faculty School total: 37. In upper school: 13 men, 24 women; 28 have advanced degrees.

Subjects Offered Algebra, American history, American history-AP, American literature, art, arts, Bible studies, biology, British literature, business, calculus, chemistry, community service, computer math, computer science, creative writing, driver education, earth science, economics, English, English literature, environmental science, ethics, European history, fine arts, geography, geometry, government/civics, grammar, health, history, Italian, law, mathematics, music, physical education, physics, physiology, psychology, religion, science, social studies, sociology, Spanish, theology, trigonometry, world affairs, world history, world literature, writing.

Graduation Requirements Arts and fine arts (art, music, dance, drama), computer science, English, foreign language, mathematics, physical education (includes health), religion (includes Bible studies and theology), science, social studies (includes history). Community service is required.

Special Academic Programs Advanced Placement exam preparation in 6 subject areas; honors section; study at local college for college credit.

College Placement 90 students graduated in 2005; 87 went to college, including Fordham University; Iona College; Manhattan College; St. John's University; The Catholic University of America; University at Albany, State University of New York. Other: 1 went to work, 2 entered military service.

Student Life Upper grades have uniform requirement, student council. Discipline rests equally with students and faculty. Attendance at religious services is required.

Summer Programs Remediation, enrichment programs offered; held on campus; accepts boys and girls; open to students from other schools. 150 students usually enrolled. 2006 schedule: July 5 to July 30.

Tuition and Aid Day student tuition: $5675. Tuition installment plan (FACTS Tuition Payment Plan). Tuition reduction for siblings, merit scholarship grants available. Total amount of financial aid awarded in 2005–06: $100,000.

Admissions School's own exam or coop required. Deadline for receipt of application materials: none. No application fee required. On-campus interview required.

Athletics Interscholastic: baseball, basketball, bowling, cross-country running, golf, ice hockey, soccer, tennis, volleyball, wrestling; intramural: back packing, baseball, basketball, blading, bocce, bowling, flag football, floor hockey, football, hiking/backpacking, martial arts, physical fitness, softball, volleyball, weight training. 2 coaches.

Computers Computers are regularly used in yearbook classes. Computer network features include campus e-mail, on-campus library services, CD-ROMs, Internet access, DVD.

Contact Sr. Barbara Wright, Assistant Principal. 914-632-0248. Fax: 914-632-1362. Web site: www.salesianhigh.org.

SALESIANUM SCHOOL

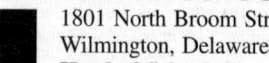

1801 North Broom Street
Wilmington, Delaware 19802-3891
Head of School: Rev. William T. McCandless

General Information Boys' day college-preparatory school, affiliated with Roman Catholic Church. Grades 9–12. Founded: 1903. Setting: suburban. 26-acre campus. 1 building on campus. Approved or accredited by Commission on Secondary Schools and Delaware Department of Education. Total enrollment: 1,032. Upper school average class size: 20.

Upper School Student Profile Grade 9: 269 students (269 boys); Grade 10: 231 students (231 boys); Grade 11: 272 students (272 boys); Grade 12: 260 students (260 boys). 83% of students are Roman Catholic.

Faculty School total: 85. In upper school: 64 men, 21 women; 47 have advanced degrees.

Subjects Offered Algebra, American history, American history-AP, American literature, anatomy, art, band, biology, biology-AP, business, business law, business mathematics, calculus, calculus-AP, chemistry, chemistry-AP, chorus, community service, computer applications, computer programming, computer science, computer science-AP, consumer economics, drafting, driver education, ecology, economics, English, English literature, English-AP, ensembles, environmental science-AP, European history-AP, fine arts, foreign policy, French, French-AP, geometry, German, German-AP, government/civics, health, Italian, journalism, keyboarding, Latin, law, literature, marketing, mathematics, physical education, physical science, physics, physics-AP, pre-calculus, psychology, religion, science, social science, social studies, Spanish, Spanish-AP, statistics, statistics-AP, television, trigonometry, U.S. government-AP, video, Western literature, word processing, world affairs, world history, world literature.

Graduation Requirements Business skills (includes word processing), computer science, driver education, English, foreign language, mathematics, physical education (includes health), religion (includes Bible studies and theology), science, social science, social studies (includes history). Community service is required.

Special Academic Programs Advanced Placement exam preparation in 15 subject areas; honors section; independent study; study at local college for college credit; domestic exchange program (with Ursuline Academy, Padua Academy); academic accommodation for the gifted; remedial reading and/or remedial writing; remedial math.

College Placement 234 students graduated in 2005; all went to college, including Saint Joseph's University; The Pennsylvania State University University Park Campus; University of Delaware; University of Maryland, College Park; Villanova University. Mean SAT verbal: 559, mean SAT math: 563. 35% scored over 600 on SAT verbal, 37% scored over 600 on SAT math.

Student Life Upper grades have specified standards of dress, student council. Discipline rests primarily with faculty. Attendance at religious services is required.

Tuition and Aid Day student tuition: $8445. Tuition installment plan (monthly payment plans, semester payments, annual payment). Merit scholarship grants, need-based scholarship grants, paying campus jobs, minority grants available. In

2005–06, 16% of upper-school students received aid; total upper-school merit-scholarship money awarded: $244,905. Total amount of financial aid awarded in 2005–06: $462,000.

Admissions Traditional secondary-level entrance grade is 9. ACT, High School Placement Test (closed version) from Scholastic Testing Service, PSAT or SAT required. Deadline for receipt of application materials: December 1. Application fee required: $55.

Athletics Interscholastic: baseball (boys), basketball (b), cross-country running (b), diving (b), football (b), golf (b), ice hockey (b), lacrosse (b), soccer (b), swimming and diving (b), tennis (b), track and field (b), volleyball (b), wrestling (b); intramural: basketball (b), bowling (b), lacrosse (b), roller hockey (b), skateboarding (b), ultimate Frisbee (b), weight lifting (b). 3 PE instructors, 18 coaches, 1 trainer.

Computers Computers are regularly used in college planning, drafting, English, foreign language, mathematics, science, social studies, yearbook classes. Computer network features include on-campus library services, CD-ROMs, online commercial services, Internet access.

Contact Mr. Dennis R. Harris Jr., Director of Admissions. 302-654-2495 Ext. 158. Fax: 302-654-7767. E-mail: dharris@salesianum.org. Web site: www.salesianum.org.

SALISBURY SCHOOL

251 Canaan Road
Salisbury, Connecticut 06068
Head of School: Mr. Chisholm S. Chandler

General Information Boys' boarding and day college-preparatory and technology school, affiliated with Episcopal Church. Grades 9–PG. Founded: 1901. Setting: rural. Nearest major city is Hartford. Students are housed in single-sex dormitories. 750-acre campus. 31 buildings on campus. Approved or accredited by Connecticut Association of Independent Schools, New England Association of Schools and Colleges, and The Association of Boarding Schools. Member of National Association of Independent Schools and Secondary School Admission Test Board. Endowment: $25 million. Total enrollment: 285. Upper school average class size: 9. Upper school faculty-student ratio: 1:4.

Upper School Student Profile Grade 9: 42 students (42 boys); Grade 10: 78 students (78 boys); Grade 11: 83 students (83 boys); Grade 12: 66 students (66 boys); Postgraduate: 20 students (20 boys). 92% of students are boarding students. 26% are state residents. 28 states are represented in upper school student body. 10% are international students. International students from Canada, Democratic People's Republic of Korea, Germany, Hong Kong, and Taiwan; 7 other countries represented in student body.

Faculty School total: 65. In upper school: 50 men, 15 women; 27 have advanced degrees; 55 reside on campus.

Subjects Offered Algebra, American history, American literature, anatomy, art, art history, Bible studies, biology, calculus, chemistry, computer science, creative writing, drama, driver education, English, English literature, environmental science, ethics, European history, fine arts, French, geometry, history, journalism, Latin, mathematics, mechanical drawing, philosophy, photography, physics, religion, science, social science, social studies, Spanish, theater, theology, trigonometry.

Graduation Requirements Arts and fine arts (art, music, dance, drama), English, foreign language, mathematics, philosophy, religion (includes Bible studies and theology), science, social studies (includes history). Community service is required.

Special Academic Programs Advanced Placement exam preparation in 10 subject areas; honors section; study abroad.

College Placement 75 students graduated in 2005; 73 went to college, including Boston College; Bowdoin College; Brown University; Colgate University; Hobart and William Smith Colleges; Trinity College. Other: 2 had other specific plans. Mean SAT verbal: 590, mean SAT math: 590.

Student Life Upper grades have specified standards of dress, student council, honor system. Discipline rests primarily with faculty. Attendance at religious services is required.

Summer Programs Remediation, enrichment, advancement, sports programs offered; session focuses on reading, writing, study skills, organization, mathematics; held on campus; accepts boys and girls; open to students from other schools. 105 students usually enrolled. 2006 schedule: July 1 to August 5. Application deadline: none.

Tuition and Aid Day student tuition: $26,000; 7-day tuition and room/board: $35,750.

Admissions Traditional secondary-level entrance grade is 9. For fall 2005, 500 students applied for upper-level admission, 244 were accepted, 125 enrolled. ISEE, PSAT and SAT for applicants to grade 11 and 12, SSAT or TOEFL or SLEP required. Deadline for receipt of application materials: February 1. Application fee required: $40. Interview required.

Athletics Interscholastic: alpine skiing, baseball, basketball, crew, cross-country running, football, golf, ice hockey, kayaking, lacrosse, mountain biking, nautilus, outdoor education, skiing (downhill), soccer, squash, tennis, weight training, wilderness, wrestling; intramural: aerobics/nautilus, basketball, bicycling, canoeing/kayaking, climbing, fitness, paddle tennis, paint ball, racquetball, rock climbing, ropes courses, sailing, snowboarding, squash, volleyball. 50 coaches, 2 trainers.

Computers Computers are regularly used in all classes. Computer network features include campus e-mail, on-campus library services, CD-ROMs, online commercial services, Internet access, office computer access, DVD, wireless campus network.

Contact Mr. Peter B. Gilbert, Director of Admissions and Financial Aid. 860-435-5700. Fax: 860-435-5750. E-mail: pgilbert@salisburyschool.org. Web site: www.salisburyschool.org.

ANNOUNCEMENT FROM THE SCHOOL For fall 2004, the School completed a new 40-student dormitory and increased its boarding population by 12% to 92%. In addition, the student center/snack bar has been fully remodeled. The Belin Lodge Student Center now has a full grill, a game room, 8 televisions, and a deck.

See full description on page 1050.

SALPOINTE CATHOLIC HIGH SCHOOL

1545 East Copper Street
Tucson, Arizona 85719-3199
Head of School: Rev. Frederick J. Tillotson, OCARM

General Information Coeducational day college-preparatory, arts, and religious studies school, affiliated with Roman Catholic Church. Grades 9–12. Founded: 1950. Setting: urban. 40-acre campus. 5 buildings on campus. Approved or accredited by National Catholic Education Association, North Central Association of Colleges and Schools, Western Catholic Education Association, and Arizona Department of Education. Endowment: $3 million. Total enrollment: 1,245. Upper school average class size: 22. Upper school faculty-student ratio: 1:22.

Upper School Student Profile Grade 9: 316 students (179 boys, 137 girls); Grade 10: 285 students (144 boys, 141 girls); Grade 11: 336 students (175 boys, 161 girls); Grade 12: 308 students (145 boys, 163 girls). 75% of students are Roman Catholic.

Faculty School total: 89. In upper school: 43 men, 46 women; 55 have advanced degrees.

Subjects Offered Algebra, American history, American literature, art, art history, Bible studies, biology, business, calculus, ceramics, chemistry, computer programming, computer science, creative writing, drama, driver education, economics, English, English literature, ethics, European history, expository writing, French, geography, geometry, government/civics, grammar, history, history of ideas, home economics, journalism, logic, mathematics, music, philosophy, photography, physical education, physics, psychology, religion, science, social studies, Spanish, speech, theater, theology, trigonometry, typing, world history, world literature, writing.

Graduation Requirements English, humanities, mathematics, modern languages, religion (includes Bible studies and theology), science, social studies (includes history).

Special Academic Programs Advanced Placement exam preparation in 11 subject areas; honors section; study at local college for college credit; remedial reading and/or remedial writing; remedial math; programs in English, mathematics, general development for dyslexic students.

College Placement 301 students graduated in 2005; 294 went to college, including Arizona State University; Northern Arizona University; Pima Community College; Santa Clara University; The University of Arizona; University of San Diego. Other: 4 went to work, 3 entered military service. Median SAT verbal: 542, median SAT math: 526, median composite ACT: 23.

Student Life Upper grades have specified standards of dress, student council, honor system. Discipline rests equally with students and faculty. Attendance at religious services is required.

Summer Programs Remediation, enrichment, advancement, sports, art/fine arts, rigorous outdoor training, computer instruction programs offered; session focuses on advancement and remediation; held on campus; accepts boys and girls; not open to students from other schools. 100 students usually enrolled. 2006 schedule: June 1 to June 25. Application deadline: June 1.

Tuition and Aid Day student tuition: $5130–$5930. Tuition installment plan (monthly payment plans, individually arranged payment plans). Tuition reduction for siblings, need-based scholarship grants, USS Education Loan Program available. In 2005–06, 23% of upper-school students received aid. Total amount of financial aid awarded in 2005–06: $500,000.

Admissions Traditional secondary-level entrance grade is 9. For fall 2005, 384 students applied for upper-level admission, 368 were accepted, 316 enrolled. High School Placement Test required. Deadline for receipt of application materials: none. Application fee required: $45. On-campus interview required.

Athletics Interscholastic: aerobics/dance (girls), baseball (b), basketball (b,g), cheering (g), cross-country running (b,g), dance team (g), diving (b,g), football (b), golf (b,g), soccer (b,g), softball (g), swimming and diving (b,g), tennis (b,g), track and field (b,g), volleyball (b,g), weight lifting (b,g), wrestling (b); intramural: bicycling (b,g), ice hockey (b); coed interscholastic: cheering; coed intramural: basketball, bowling, outdoor adventure, ultimate Frisbee, volleyball. 2 PE instructors, 75 coaches, 1 trainer.

Computers Computers are regularly used in English, mathematics, science classes. Computer network features include on-campus library services, CD-ROMs, Internet access.

Salpointe Catholic High School

Contact Ms. Meg Gossmann, Registrar. 520-547-4460. Fax: 520-327-8477. E-mail: mgossmann@salpointe.org. Web site: www.salpointe.org.

SALTUS GRAMMAR SCHOOL

PO Box HM 2224
Hamilton HMJX, Bermuda
Head of School: Mr. Nigel J.G. Kermode

General Information Coeducational day college-preparatory, general academic, arts, business, and technology school, affiliated with Church of England (Anglican). Grades K–12. Founded: 1888. Setting: small town. Nearest major city is Hamilton. 6 buildings on campus. Approved or accredited by Christian Brothers Association. Affiliate member of National Association of Independent Schools. Language of instruction: English. Endowment: 3 million Bermuda dollars. Total enrollment: 994. Upper school average class size: 18. Upper school faculty-student ratio: 1:13.

Upper School Student Profile Grade 9: 70 students (43 boys, 27 girls); Grade 10: 45 students (25 boys, 20 girls); Grade 11: 57 students (34 boys, 23 girls); Grade 12: 68 students (35 boys, 33 girls). 55% of students are members of Church of England (Anglican).

Faculty School total: 90. In upper school: 19 men, 16 women; 20 have advanced degrees.

Subjects Offered American history, art, art history, biology, business, chemistry, computer programming, computer science, design, drama, earth science, economics, electronics, English, English literature, environmental science, European history, French, geography, health, history, mathematics, music, photography, physical education, physics, psychology, social studies, sociology, Spanish, speech, statistics, theater, trigonometry, world history.

Special Academic Programs Advanced Placement exam preparation in 12 subject areas.

College Placement 64 students graduated in 2005; 62 went to college, including Acadia University; Brock University; Dalhousie University; McGill University; Queen's University at Kingston; University of Guelph. Other: 2 went to work.

Student Life Upper grades have uniform requirement, student council. Discipline rests primarily with faculty.

Tuition and Aid Day student tuition: 12,670 Bermuda dollars. Tuition installment plan (monthly payment plans). Bursaries, merit scholarship grants, need-based scholarship grants available. In 2005–06, 15% of upper-school students received aid; total upper-school merit-scholarship money awarded: 130,000 Bermuda dollars. Total amount of financial aid awarded in 2005–06: 350,000 Bermuda dollars.

Admissions Traditional secondary-level entrance grade is 9. Grade equivalent tests or Saltus Achievement Test required. Deadline for receipt of application materials: none. Application fee required: 50 Bermuda dollars. On-campus interview required.

Athletics Interscholastic: badminton (boys, girls), basketball (b,g), cricket (b), cross-country running (b,g), field hockey (g), football (b,g), golf (b), rugby (b), running (b,g), soccer (b,g), softball (b,g), swimming and diving (b,g), track and field (b,g), volleyball (b,g); intramural: badminton (b,g), basketball (b,g), cricket (b), cross-country running (b,g), field hockey (b,g), football (b,g), golf (b), rugby (b), running (b,g), soccer (b,g), softball (b,g), swimming and diving (b,g), table tennis (b,g), track and field (b,g), volleyball (b,g); coed interscholastic: badminton, basketball, field hockey, football, running, swimming and diving, water polo; coed intramural: badminton, field hockey, running, swimming and diving, table tennis, water polo. 3 PE instructors.

Computers Computers are regularly used in art, business education, economics, English, foreign language, geography, history, mathematics, music, science, technology classes. Computer network features include campus e-mail, on-campus library services, CD-ROMs, Internet access, DVD, wireless campus network.

Contact Mr. Malcolm J. Durrant, Deputy Headmaster. 441-292-6177. Fax: 441-295-4977. E-mail: mdurrant@saltus.bm. Web site: www.saltus.bm.

SAN DIEGO JEWISH ACADEMY

11860 Carmel Creek Road
San Diego, California 92130
Head of School: Larry Acheatel

General Information Coeducational day college-preparatory, arts, and religious studies school, affiliated with Jewish faith. Grades K–12. Founded: 1979. Setting: suburban. 52-acre campus. 3 buildings on campus. Approved or accredited by California Association of Independent Schools, Western Association of Schools and Colleges, and California Department of Education. Languages of instruction: English, Spanish, and Hebrew. Endowment: $2.5 million. Total enrollment: 687. Upper school average class size: 20. Upper school faculty-student ratio: 1:20.

Upper School Student Profile Grade 9: 53 students (27 boys, 26 girls); Grade 10: 59 students (31 boys, 28 girls); Grade 11: 42 students (20 boys, 22 girls); Grade 12: 32 students (16 boys, 16 girls). 99% of students are Jewish.

Faculty School total: 60. In upper school: 12 men, 20 women; 15 have advanced degrees.

Subjects Offered 20th century American writers, 20th century history, 20th century physics, 20th century world history, advanced chemistry, advanced math, Advanced Placement courses, algebra, American government, American history, American history-AP, American literature, American literature-AP, American studies, analytic geometry, art, art history-AP, arts, athletics, baseball, basketball, Bible, Bible studies, biology, biology-AP, British history, British literature, British literature (honors), British literature-AP, calculus-AP, chemistry, chemistry-AP, Christian and Hebrew scripture, civil rights, Civil War, classical Greek literature, classical studies, college admission preparation, college counseling, community service, competitive science projects, composition, composition-AP, conceptual physics, creative drama, digital photography, dramatic arts, economics, economics and history, electives, English, English composition, English language and composition-AP, English language-AP, English literature, English literature and composition-AP, English literature-AP, English-AP, English/composition-AP, European history, European literature, fitness, foreign language, four units of summer reading, golf, government, government/civics, guitar, Hebrew, Hebrew scripture, history, history-AP, Holocaust, Holocaust studies, honors algebra, honors English, honors geometry, honors world history, humanities, independent study, instrumental music, instruments, Jewish history, Jewish studies, Judaic studies, language, language and composition, language-AP, languages, literature and composition-AP, literature-AP, Middle Eastern history, music, musical theater dance, photography, physical education, physics, physics-AP, prayer/spirituality, pre-algebra, pre-calculus, pre-college orientation, psychology, Rabbinic literature, religious education, religious studies, social science, Spanish, standard curriculum, state government, statistics-AP, student government, theater, trigonometry, U.S. government, U.S. history, U.S. history-AP, U.S. literature, video film production, visual arts, volleyball, weight fitness, weightlifting, world history, world literature, world studies, writing workshop, yearbook.

Special Academic Programs Advanced Placement exam preparation in 12 subject areas; honors section; independent study.

College Placement 24 students graduated in 2005; 22 went to college, including The University of Arizona; University of San Diego; University of Southern California. Other: 2 had other specific plans. Mean SAT verbal: 576, mean SAT math: 598. 50% scored over 600 on SAT verbal, 58% scored over 600 on SAT math.

Student Life Upper grades have specified standards of dress, student council, honor system. Discipline rests primarily with faculty. Attendance at religious services is required.

Tuition and Aid Day student tuition: $12,050–$13,750. Tuition installment plan (FACTS Tuition Payment Plan). Tuition reduction for siblings, need-based scholarship grants available. In 2005–06, 30% of upper-school students received aid. Total amount of financial aid awarded in 2005–06: $496,204.

Admissions Traditional secondary-level entrance grade is 9. For fall 2005, 52 students applied for upper-level admission, 45 were accepted, 38 enrolled. ERB verbal, ERB math required. Deadline for receipt of application materials: none. Application fee required.

Athletics Interscholastic: baseball (boys), basketball (b,g), cross-country running (b,g), flag football (b), football (b), golf (b,g), soccer (b,g), softball (g), tennis (b,g), volleyball (g); coed interscholastic: in-line hockey, roller hockey; coed intramural: biathlon, bicycling, fitness, physical fitness, physical training, surfing, weight lifting, weight training. 3 PE instructors, 15 coaches, 1 trainer.

Computers Computers are regularly used in college planning, English, foreign language, history, humanities, mathematics, psychology, religious studies, science, video film production, writing, yearbook classes. Computer network features include campus e-mail, on-campus library services, Internet access.

Contact Judith Gross, Admissions Director. 858-704-3716. Fax: 858-704-3850. E-mail: jgross@sdja.com. Web site: www.sdja.com.

SAN DOMENICO SCHOOL

1500 Butterfield Road
San Anselmo, California 94960
Head of School: Dr. Mathew Heersche

General Information Girls' boarding and coeducational day college-preparatory, arts, religious studies, music, and theater arts school, affiliated with Roman Catholic Church. Boarding girls grades 9–12, day boys grades PK–8, day girls grades PK–12. Founded: 1850. Setting: suburban. Nearest major city is San Francisco. Students are housed in single-sex dormitories. 515-acre campus. 10 buildings on campus. Approved or accredited by California Association of Independent Schools, Western Association of Schools and Colleges, and Western Catholic Education Association. Member of National Association of Independent Schools. Endowment: $5.5 million. Total enrollment: 582. Upper school average class size: 12. Upper school faculty-student ratio: 1:9.

Upper School Student Profile Grade 9: 40 students (40 girls); Grade 10: 46 students (46 girls); Grade 11: 39 students (39 girls); Grade 12: 43 students (43 girls). 38% of students are boarding students. 76% are state residents. 1 state is represented in upper school student body. 24% are international students. International students from China, Hong Kong, Republic of Korea, and Taiwan; 8 other countries represented in student body. 30% of students are Roman Catholic.

Faculty School total: 46. In upper school: 12 men, 34 women; 29 have advanced degrees; 7 reside on campus.

Subjects Offered Acting, algebra, American history, American literature, art, art history, biology, biology-AP, calculus, ceramics, chemistry, community service, drama, English, English literature, environmental science, ESL, ethics, European

history, expository writing, fine arts, French, freshman foundations, geometry, government/civics, grammar, history, mathematics, modern world history, music, music composition, music theater, music theory, musical productions, musicianship, photography, physical education, physics, religion, science, social studies, sociology, Spanish, studio art—AP, theater, theology, trigonometry, world history, world literature.

Graduation Requirements Arts and fine arts (art, music, dance, drama), English, foreign language, mathematics, physical education (includes health), religion (includes Bible studies and theology), science, social studies (includes history). Community service is required.

Special Academic Programs Advanced Placement exam preparation in 14 subject areas; honors section; independent study; academic accommodation for the musically talented and the artistically talented; ESL (6 students enrolled).

College Placement 31 students graduated in 2005; all went to college, including Carnegie Mellon University; University of California, Santa Cruz; Wellesley College. Mean SAT verbal: 617, mean SAT math: 597, mean composite ACT: 25. 57% scored over 600 on SAT verbal, 50% scored over 600 on SAT math, 37% scored over 26 on composite ACT.

Student Life Upper grades have uniform requirement, student council, honor system. Discipline rests primarily with faculty. Attendance at religious services is required.

Summer Programs Enrichment, sports, art/fine arts, computer instruction programs offered; session focuses on coed K–12 activities; held both on and off campus; held at various locations (different each year); accepts boys and girls; open to students from other schools. 300 students usually enrolled. 2006 schedule: June 12 to August 18. Application deadline: May 31.

Tuition and Aid Day student tuition: $23,157; 5-day tuition and room/board: $38,717; 7-day tuition and room/board: $38,717. Tuition installment plan (Insured Tuition Payment Plan, monthly payment plans). Need-based scholarship grants available. In 2005–06, 30% of upper-school students received aid. Total amount of financial aid awarded in 2005–06: $1,000,000.

Admissions Traditional secondary-level entrance grade is 9. High School Placement Test, ISEE or SSAT required. Deadline for receipt of application materials: January 10. Application fee required: $100. Interview required.

Athletics Interscholastic: badminton, basketball, cross-country running, soccer, softball, swimming and diving, tennis, volleyball; intramural: dance, equestrian sports, horseback riding, modern dance, strength & conditioning, tennis, weight lifting, yoga. 8 coaches.

Computers Computers are regularly used in freshman foundations, mathematics, science, social studies, technology, yearbook classes. Computer network features include campus e-mail, on-campus library services, CD-ROMs, Internet access, office computer access, DVD, wireless campus network.

Contact Ms. Risa Oganesoff Heersche, Associate Director of Admissions. 415-258-1905 Ext. 1124. Fax: 415-258-1906. E-mail: rheersche@sandomenico.org. Web site: www.sandomenico.org/.

ANNOUNCEMENT FROM THE SCHOOL San Domenico School, the oldest independent Catholic school in California, is dedicated to empowering young women. San Domenico explores and develops the unique gifts of each individual with a rigorous and innovative college-preparatory program for day and boarding students. San Domenico celebrates diversity and welcomes students from the greater San Francisco Bay Area and around the world. San Domenico's spectacular 515-acre campus is set in a lovely natural environment of hills, trees, and creeks in beautiful Marin County. San Domenico features a state-of-the-art Athletic Center, a brand new Hall of the Arts, an Equestrian Center, a spacious library, 3 dormitories, organic gardens, and outdoor facilities for swimming, basketball, soccer, softball, and tennis. Public and school transportation provides access to the greater San Francisco Bay Area. San Domenico's individualized academic program promotes intellectual curiosity, independent thinking, and a values-based perspective. San Domenico students thrive in honors and Advanced Placement courses and flourish with extensive opportunities for athletics and the performing arts. Freshmen, sophomores, and juniors are challenged by an innovative, team-taught, humanities-based curriculum. Talented faculty members integrate courses in literature, world history, world religions, art, and performance. A select group of high school students excel in San Domenico's nationally recognized Music Conservatory's voice and music training. The Performing Arts Department engages theater and dance students in dance recitals, acting, and production and technical design, with 6 full-length drama productions each year. Professional artists design visual arts classes in drawing, painting, printmaking, ceramics, photography, and advanced studio art. San Domenico sports teams successfully compete in the Bay Counties League in volleyball, tennis, cross country, basketball, soccer, swimming, softball, badminton, and track and field. Recent San Domenico graduates attend colleges and universities such as Amherst, Barnard, Brown, Carnegie Mellon, Columbia, Cornell, Lewis and Clark, Loyola, Peabody Conservatory, Vassar, and Wellesley and the University of California at Berkeley.

SANDY SPRING FRIENDS SCHOOL

16923 Norwood Road
Sandy Spring, Maryland 20860
Head of School: Kenneth W. Smith

General Information Coeducational boarding and day college-preparatory, arts, and ESL school, affiliated with Society of Friends. Boarding grades 9–12, day grades PK–12. Founded: 1961. Setting: suburban. Nearest major city is Washington, DC. Students are housed in single-sex by floor dormitories. 140-acre campus. 15 buildings on campus. Approved or accredited by Association of Independent Maryland Schools, The Association of Boarding Schools, and Maryland Department of Education. Member of National Association of Independent Schools and Secondary School Admission Test Board. Endowment: $700,000. Total enrollment: 547. Upper school average class size: 12. Upper school faculty-student ratio: 1:7.

Upper School Student Profile Grade 9: 54 students (31 boys, 23 girls); Grade 10: 61 students (26 boys, 35 girls); Grade 11: 57 students (24 boys, 33 girls); Grade 12: 60 students (24 boys, 36 girls). 18% of students are boarding students. 44% are state residents. 8 states are represented in upper school student body. 56% are international students. International students from China, Republic of Korea, Saudi Arabia, Taiwan, and Thailand. 15% of students are members of Society of Friends.

Faculty School total: 62. In upper school: 17 men, 14 women; 14 have advanced degrees; 14 reside on campus.

Subjects Offered African literature, algebra, American history, American literature, anatomy, animation, art, art history, astronomy, biology, British literature-AP, calculus, calculus-AP, ceramics, chemistry, chemistry-AP, choral music, choreography, computer math, computer programming, computer science, computer skills, creative writing, dance, dance performance, drama, earth science, English, English as a foreign language, English literature, English literature and composition-AP, English literature-AP, environmental science, environmental science-AP, ESL, ethics, European history, expository writing, fine arts, French, French language-AP, geography, geology, geometry, government and politics-AP, government/civics, grammar, history, history of science, journalism, mathematics, music, music theory-AP, Native American history, orchestra, photography, physical education, physics, physics-AP, psychology, Quakerism and ethics, religion, Russian literature, science, social studies, Spanish, Spanish language-AP, statistics-AP, study skills, theater, trigonometry, U.S. history-AP, Western civilization, world history, world literature, writing.

Graduation Requirements Art, English, foreign language, history, mathematics, physical education (includes health), religion (includes Bible studies and theology), science. Community service is required.

Special Academic Programs Advanced Placement exam preparation in 10 subject areas; honors section; independent study; ESL (26 students enrolled).

College Placement 52 students graduated in 2005; all went to college, including Carleton College; Guilford College; Haverford College; The George Washington University; University of Maryland; Wesleyan University.

Student Life Upper grades have student council. Discipline rests equally with students and faculty. Attendance at religious services is required.

Tuition and Aid Day student tuition: $20,100; 5-day tuition and room/board: $28,600; 7-day tuition and room/board: $34,700. Tuition installment plan (Insured Tuition Payment Plan, Key Tuition Payment Plan). Need-based scholarship grants available. In 2005–06, 28% of upper-school students received aid. Total amount of financial aid awarded in 2005–06: $900,000.

Admissions Traditional secondary-level entrance grade is 9. For fall 2005, 149 students applied for upper-level admission, 85 were accepted, 47 enrolled. SSAT or TOEFL or SLEP required. Deadline for receipt of application materials: January 15. Application fee required: $60. Interview required.

Athletics Interscholastic: baseball (boys), basketball (b,g), cross-country running (b,g), lacrosse (b,g), soccer (b,g), softball (g), tennis (b,g), volleyball (g); coed interscholastic: cooperative games, golf, modern dance, track and field; coed intramural: dance, flag football, Frisbee, table tennis, track and field, ultimate Frisbee, walking, weight lifting, yoga. 3 PE instructors, 5 coaches, 1 trainer.

Computers Computers are regularly used in all academic classes. Computer network features include campus e-mail, on-campus library services, CD-ROMs, Internet access.

Contact Robert Jones, Upper School Admissions. 301-774-7455 Ext. 203. Fax: 301-924-1115. E-mail: robert.jones@ssfs.org. Web site: www.ssfs.org.

See full description on page 1052.

SANFORD SCHOOL

6900 Lancaster Pike
PO Box 888
Hockessin, Delaware 19707-0888
Head of School: Douglas MacKelcan

General Information Coeducational day college-preparatory school. Grades PK–12. Founded: 1930. Setting: suburban. Nearest major city is Wilmington. 100-acre campus. 6 buildings on campus. Approved or accredited by Arizona Association of Independent Schools, Middle States Association of Colleges and Schools, and Delaware Department of Education. Member of National Association of Independent

Schools and Secondary School Admission Test Board. Endowment: $5 million. Total enrollment: 711. Upper school average class size: 14. Upper school faculty-student ratio: 1:7.

Upper School Student Profile Grade 9: 64 students (30 boys, 34 girls); Grade 10: 61 students (32 boys, 29 girls); Grade 11: 64 students (39 boys, 25 girls); Grade 12: 56 students (24 boys, 32 girls).

Faculty School total: 95. In upper school: 12 men, 22 women; 24 have advanced degrees.

Subjects Offered Algebra, American history, American history-AP, American literature, American literature-AP, anatomy and physiology, art, biology, calculus, calculus-AP, ceramics, chemistry, chemistry-AP, computer programming, computer science, computer science-AP, drawing, driver education, ecology, economics, engineering, English, English language-AP, English literature, English literature-AP, environmental science, European history, European history-AP, fine arts, French, geometry, German, health, history, journalism, Latin, mathematics, music, painting, photography, physics, physics-AP, pre-calculus, psychology, social studies, Spanish, Spanish-AP, statistics, statistics-AP, studio art-AP, technology, trigonometry, U.S. history, U.S. history-AP, visual arts, vocal ensemble, voice, world civilizations, world history, world history-AP, world literature, writing.

Graduation Requirements Arts and fine arts (art, music, dance, drama), athletics, computer science, electives, English, foreign language, health, lab science, mathematics, music, senior project, social science.

Special Academic Programs Advanced Placement exam preparation in 16 subject areas; honors section.

College Placement 58 students graduated in 2005; all went to college, including Boston University; Franklin and Marshall College; Hobart and William Smith Colleges; The Johns Hopkins University; University of Delaware; Virginia Polytechnic Institute and State University.

Student Life Upper grades have specified standards of dress, student council, honor system. Discipline rests equally with students and faculty.

Summer Programs Remediation, enrichment, advancement, art/fine arts, computer instruction programs offered; session focuses on enrichment; held on campus; accepts boys and girls; open to students from other schools. 2006 schedule: June 26 to August 4. Application deadline: none.

Tuition and Aid Day student tuition: $17,530. Tuition installment plan (Key Tuition Payment Plan). Need-based scholarship grants available. In 2005–06, 25% of upper-school students received aid. Total amount of financial aid awarded in 2005–06: $586,780.

Admissions Traditional secondary-level entrance grade is 9. For fall 2005, 82 students applied for upper-level admission, 54 were accepted, 38 enrolled. ERB CTP IV, ISEE or SSAT required. Deadline for receipt of application materials: January 8. Application fee required: $40. On-campus interview required.

Athletics Interscholastic: baseball (boys), basketball (b,g), cross-country running (b,g), field hockey (g), golf (b,g), lacrosse (b,g), soccer (b,g), swimming and diving (b,g), tennis (b,g), volleyball (g), wrestling (b). 37 coaches, 2 trainers.

Computers Computers are regularly used in English, foreign language, history, mathematics, science classes. Computer network features include on-campus library services, CD-ROMs, Internet access, Blackboard.

Contact Ceil Baum, Admission Administrative Assistant. 302-239-5263 Ext. 265. Fax: 302-239-1912. E-mail: admission@sanfordschool.org. Web site: www.sanfordschool.org.

ANNOUNCEMENT FROM THE SCHOOL Sanford graduates are successful in college because they advocate for themselves, get involved in their community, and stretch themselves. A recent graduate attending an Ivy League school said that Sanford prepared her especially well for the academic writing and time-management demands of college. Families choose Sanford because of what they describe as its friendly, welcoming, inclusive, and unpretentious community in which the teachers are passionate, fun, and accessible and the students are actively engaged in their learning and like school.

SAN MARCOS BAPTIST ACADEMY

2801 Ranch Road Twelve
San Marcos, Texas 78666-9406
Head of School: Mr. Victor H. Schmidt

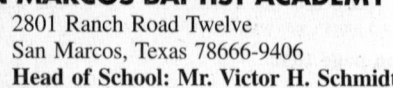
petersons.com

General Information Coeducational boarding and day college-preparatory, general academic, arts, religious studies, and technology school, affiliated with Baptist Church. Grades 7–12. Founded: 1907. Setting: small town. Nearest major city is Austin. Students are housed in single-sex dormitories. 200-acre campus. 8 buildings on campus. Approved or accredited by Accreditation Commission of the Texas Association of Baptist Schools, Southern Association of Colleges and Schools, Texas Education Agency, The Association of Boarding Schools, and Texas Department of Education. Member of National Association of Independent Schools. Endowment: $5 million. Total enrollment: 219. Upper school average class size: 11. Upper school faculty-student ratio: 1:11.

Upper School Student Profile Grade 9: 39 students (26 boys, 13 girls); Grade 10: 54 students (39 boys, 15 girls); Grade 11: 50 students (33 boys, 17 girls); Grade 12: 35 students (24 boys, 11 girls). 72% of students are boarding students. 64% are state residents. 10 states are represented in upper school student body. 24% are international students. International students from Hong Kong, Japan, Mexico, Republic of Korea, Saudi Arabia, and Taiwan; 12 other countries represented in student body. 25% of students are Baptist.

Faculty School total: 33. In upper school: 18 men, 13 women; 16 have advanced degrees; 5 reside on campus.

Subjects Offered Advanced math, Advanced Placement courses, algebra, American government, American history, American literature, analysis and differential calculus, analytic geometry, anatomy and physiology, ancient world history, applied arts, applied music, art, astronomy, athletics, baseball, basketball, Bible, Bible studies, biology, biology-AP, British literature, British literature-AP, business, business applications, calculus, calculus-AP, character education, cheerleading, chemistry, choir, civics, clayworking, communication skills, comparative religion, computer keyboarding, computer science, critical thinking, desktop publishing, digital photography, drama, drama performance, drawing, driver education, earth and space science, earth science, economics, economics and history, English, English composition, English literature, English literature-AP, ESL, fine arts, geography, geometry, golf, government/civics, grammar, guidance, health, health education, history, history of the Americas, honors algebra, honors geometry, honors U.S. history, honors world history, HTML design, jazz band, journalism, JROTC or LEAD (Leadership Education and Development), keyboarding, library skills, Life of Christ, logic, mathematics, military science, music, photography, physical education, physics, pottery, pre-calculus, psychology, reading, religion, science, social studies, sociology, softball, Spanish, speech, speech communications, sports, student government, student publications, study skills, swimming, tennis, Texas history, theater, theater arts, theology, U.S. government, U.S. history, visual arts, weight training, world geography, world history.

Graduation Requirements Arts and fine arts (art, music, dance, drama), computer science, economics, English, foreign language, mathematics, physical education (includes health), religion (includes Bible studies and theology), ROTC (for boys), science, social studies (includes history), speech.

Special Academic Programs Advanced Placement exam preparation in 3 subject areas; honors section; accelerated programs; independent study; study at local college for college credit; academic accommodation for the gifted; remedial reading and/or remedial writing; remedial math; programs in general development for dyslexic students; special instructional classes for students with Section 504 learning disabilities, Attention Deficit Disorder, and dyslexia; ESL (32 students enrolled).

College Placement 44 students graduated in 2005; 41 went to college, including Baylor University; Purdue University; Texas Tech University; The University of Texas at Austin; The University of Texas at San Antonio; University of Houston. Other: 2 went to work, 1 entered military service. Median SAT verbal: 530, median SAT math: 640, median combined SAT: 1640.

Student Life Upper grades have uniform requirement, student council, honor system. Discipline rests primarily with faculty. Attendance at religious services is required.

Tuition and Aid Day student tuition: $7199; 7-day tuition and room/board: $22,275. Tuition installment plan (individually arranged payment plans). Need-based scholarship grants available. In 2005–06, 25% of upper-school students received aid. Total amount of financial aid awarded in 2005–06: $400,000.

Admissions Traditional secondary-level entrance grade is 9. For fall 2005, 140 students applied for upper-level admission, 131 were accepted, 99 enrolled. Deadline for receipt of application materials: none. Application fee required: $75. Interview required.

Athletics Interscholastic: baseball (boys), basketball (b,g), cheering (g), cross-country running (b,g), drill team (b), equestrian sports (b,g), football (b), golf (b,g), JROTC drill (b,g), marksmanship (b), power lifting (b,g), softball (g), swimming and diving (b,g), tennis (b,g), track and field (b,g), volleyball (g); intramural: aerobics/dance (g), riflery (b), weight training (b); coed interscholastic: soccer, weight lifting, winter soccer; coed intramural: horseback riding, soccer, weight lifting, winter soccer. 2 PE instructors, 8 coaches, 1 trainer.

Computers Computers are regularly used in desktop publishing, keyboarding, newspaper, photojournalism, technology, typing, Web site design, yearbook classes. Computer network features include campus e-mail, on-campus library services, CD-ROMs, Internet access.

Contact Mr. Jeffrey D. Baergen, Director of Admissions. 800-428-5120. Fax: 512-753-8031. E-mail: admissions@smba.org. Web site: www.smba.org.

ANNOUNCEMENT FROM THE SCHOOL Located 45 miles northeast of San Antonio and 30 miles south of Austin, San Marcos Baptist Academy is a coeducational college-preparatory school with a boarding and day program for boys and girls in grades 7–12. Founded in 1907, San Marcos is about to celebrate its 100th anniversary. The school is accredited by the Southern Association of Colleges and Schools and the Accreditation Committee of the Texas Association of Baptist Schools and is recognized by the Texas Education Agency. The Academy seeks to provide for the intellectual, physical, and spiritual development of each student. The highly structured residential life program provides dormitory supervision in a 1:8 staff-to-student ratio. A school-wide program for Leadership Education and Development (LEAD) offers training in key life skills and includes a Junior Reserve Officers' Training Corps unit. Male high school students who are U.S. citizens are required to participate in JROTC during their first semester at the Academy. Additional participation is voluntary. SMBA seeks to meet each student's individual needs. Although the primary emphasis is

college preparation, the curriculum provides assistance for students needing academic reinforcement in basic subjects or specialized instruction for learning differences. The Learning Skills Program, staffed by 3 full-time learning specialists, provides individual assistance for students with documented mild to moderate learning differences. Opportunities exist for more advanced students to take up to 28 hours of dual-credit college courses. The Academy's English as a Second Language program helps assimilate international students from 9 different countries. Rounding out the academic program are fine arts opportunities in visual arts, music and theater, vocal ensembles, and a concert/marching and a jazz band. With a full complement of sports and student activities offered, the Academy is a wonderful place for young people to grow and mature as they prepare for college and life afterward.

SANTA CATALINA SCHOOL

1500 Mark Thomas Drive
Monterey, California 93940-5291
Head of School: Sr. Claire Barone

General Information Girls' boarding and coeducational day college-preparatory and liberal arts school, affiliated with Roman Catholic Church. Boarding girls grades 9–12, day boys grades PK–8, day girls grades PK–12. Founded: 1950. Setting: small town. Nearest major city is San Francisco. Students are housed in single-sex dormitories. 36-acre campus. 21 buildings on campus. Approved or accredited by California Association of Independent Schools, The Association of Boarding Schools, Western Association of Schools and Colleges, and California Department of Education. Member of National Association of Independent Schools and Secondary School Admission Test Board. Languages of instruction: English, Spanish, and French. Endowment: $219,000. Total enrollment: 551. Upper school average class size: 12. Upper school faculty-student ratio: 1:7.
Upper School Student Profile Grade 9: 68 students (68 girls); Grade 10: 78 students (78 girls); Grade 11: 78 students (78 girls); Grade 12: 65 students (65 girls). 55% of students are boarding students. 80% are state residents. 14 states are represented in upper school student body. 10% are international students. International students from Hong Kong, Indonesia, Mexico, Saudi Arabia, Singapore, and Taiwan; 6 other countries represented in student body. 40% of students are Roman Catholic.
Faculty School total: 39. In upper school: 18 men, 21 women; 33 have advanced degrees; 37 reside on campus.
Subjects Offered African-American history, algebra, American literature, art, art history, biology, biology-AP, calculus, calculus-AP, ceramics, chemistry, computer science, conceptual physics, creative writing, dance, drama, driver education, economics, English, English language and composition-AP, English literature, English literature and composition-AP, environmental science-AP, ethics, European history, expository writing, fine arts, French, French language-AP, French literature-AP, geography, geometry, grammar, health, history, humanities, information processing, Latin, Latin-AP, marine science, mathematics, music, philosophy, photography, physical education, physics, religion, science, Spanish, Spanish language-AP, Spanish literature-AP, theater, theology, U.S. history, U.S. history-AP, world history, world literature, world religions, writing.
Graduation Requirements Arts and fine arts (art, music, dance, drama), computer science, English, foreign language, humanities, mathematics, physical education (includes health), religion (includes Bible studies and theology), science, social studies (includes history).
Special Academic Programs Advanced Placement exam preparation in 19 subject areas; honors section; independent study; academic accommodation for the gifted, the musically talented, and the artistically talented.
College Placement 69 students graduated in 2005; all went to college, including Boston University; Loyola Marymount University; New York University; University of California, Davis; University of California, Los Angeles; Willamette University. Mean SAT verbal: 598, mean SAT math: 611.
Student Life Upper grades have uniform requirement, student council, honor system. Discipline rests equally with students and faculty. Attendance at religious services is required.
Tuition and Aid Day student tuition: $21,500; 7-day tuition and room/board: $34,500. Tuition installment plan (Key Tuition Payment Plan, monthly payment plans). Merit scholarship grants, need-based scholarship grants, need-based loans available. In 2005–06, 30% of upper-school students received aid; total upper-school merit-scholarship money awarded: $5800. Total amount of financial aid awarded in 2005–06: $1,508,275.
Admissions Traditional secondary-level entrance grade is 9. For fall 2005, 190 students applied for upper-level admission, 141 were accepted, 91 enrolled. ISEE or SSAT required. Deadline for receipt of application materials: February 1. Application fee required: $75. Interview required.
Athletics Interscholastic: basketball, cross-country running, diving, equestrian sports, field hockey, golf, lacrosse, soccer, softball, swimming and diving, tennis, track and field, volleyball, water polo; intramural: aerobics/dance, aerobics/nautilus, ballet, canoeing/kayaking, climbing, dance, fitness, hiking/backpacking, horseback riding, kayaking, modern dance, nautilus, outdoor activities, outdoor adventure, outdoor

education, outdoor recreation, outdoor skills, physical fitness, rafting, rock climbing, ropes courses, self defense, strength & conditioning, surfing, weight training. 6 PE instructors, 26 coaches.
Computers Computers are regularly used in English, foreign language, science classes. Computer network features include campus e-mail, on-campus library services, CD-ROMs, Internet access.
Contact Marian Donovan Corrigan, Director of Admission. 831-655-9329. Fax: 831-655-7535. E-mail: marian_corrigan@santacatalina.org. Web site: www.santacatalina.org.

ANNOUNCEMENT FROM THE SCHOOL Santa Catalina is an all-girls, college-preparatory, independent, Catholic school. Rigorous academics, including Advanced Placement and honors courses in all disciplines, are complemented by superb art, music, dance, and drama programs, as well as community service and exceptional leadership opportunities. Santa Catalina also fields competitive athletic teams in 13 sports and offers an established riding program. Advanced computer technology is utilized in all aspects of student life. State-of-the-art facilities include a 25-yard by 30-meter pool, wireless Internet access in the dorms, and a music center, which includes a 150-seat recital hall, a dance studio, and soundproof practice rooms.

See full description on page 1054.

SANTA FE PREPARATORY SCHOOL

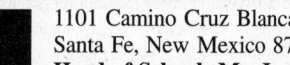

1101 Camino Cruz Blanca
Santa Fe, New Mexico 87505
Head of School: Mr. James W. Leonard

General Information Coeducational day college-preparatory, arts, and community service school. Grades 7–12. Founded: 1961. Setting: suburban. 13-acre campus. 4 buildings on campus. Approved or accredited by Independent Schools Association of the Southwest and New Mexico Department of Education. Member of National Association of Independent Schools. Endowment: $2.1 million. Total enrollment: 345. Upper school average class size: 13. Upper school faculty-student ratio: 1:7.
Faculty School total: 76. In upper school: 26 men, 19 women; 35 have advanced degrees.
Subjects Offered Acting, advanced chemistry, advanced computer applications, advanced math, algebra, American Civil War, American culture, American democracy, American government, American history, American history-AP, American literature, analytic geometry, art, art appreciation, art history, art history-AP, arts, athletics, basketball, biology, calculus, calculus-AP, ceramics, chemistry, chemistry-AP, chorus, clayworking, college counseling, community service, computer applications, computer graphics, computer keyboarding, computer literacy, computer programming, computer science, conceptual physics, creative writing, drama, drama performance, dramatic arts, driver education, earth science, English, English literature, European history, fine arts, French, geography, geometry, health, history, humanities, journalism, Latin, mathematics, music, photography, physical education, physics, psychology, science, social studies, Spanish, theater, trigonometry, world history, world literature, writing.
Graduation Requirements Arts and fine arts (art, music, dance, drama), computer science, English, foreign language, humanities, mathematics, music appreciation, physical education (includes health), science, social studies (includes history), Senior Seminar Program. Community service is required.
Special Academic Programs Advanced Placement exam preparation in 4 subject areas; honors section; independent study; study at local college for college credit; study abroad.
College Placement 49 students graduated in 2005; 48 went to college, including Georgetown University; New York University; The George Washington University; University of Colorado at Boulder; University of New Mexico. Other: 1 had other specific plans. Mean SAT verbal: 633, mean SAT math: 594, mean composite ACT: 26.
Student Life Upper grades have specified standards of dress, student council. Discipline rests equally with students and faculty.
Tuition and Aid Day student tuition: $14,500. Tuition installment plan (Tuition Management Systems Plan). Need-based scholarship grants available. In 2005–06, 22% of upper-school students received aid. Total amount of financial aid awarded in 2005–06: $348,000.
Admissions Traditional secondary-level entrance grade is 9. School's own exam required. Deadline for receipt of application materials: March 1. Application fee required: $35. On-campus interview required.
Athletics Interscholastic: basketball (boys, girls), cross-country running (b,g), diving (b,g), lacrosse (b,g), soccer (b,g), softball (g), swimming and diving (b,g), tennis (b,g), track and field (b,g), volleyball (g); intramural: basketball (b,g), cross-country running (b,g), football (b,g), soccer (b,g), tennis (b,g), track and field (b,g), volleyball (g); coed interscholastic: field hockey; coed intramural: basketball, bowling, field hockey, skiing (downhill), swimming and diving. 1 PE instructor, 16 coaches.
Computers Computers are regularly used in current events, English, French, freshman foundations, geography, graphic arts, history, humanities, journalism, library, literary magazine, mathematics, newspaper, photography, photojournalism,

science, social science, writing, yearbook classes. Computer network features include campus e-mail, on-campus library services, CD-ROMs, Internet access.

Contact Marta M. Miskolczy, Director of Admissions. 505-982-1829 Ext. 212. Fax: 505-982-2897. E-mail: admissions@sfprep.org. Web site: www.santafeprep.org.

SANTIAM CHRISTIAN SCHOOL

7220 Northeast Arnold Avenue
Corvallis, Oregon 97330-9498
Head of School: Mr. Stan Baker

General Information Coeducational day college-preparatory, arts, business, vocational, religious studies, bilingual studies, and technology school, affiliated with Christian faith. Grades PS–12. Founded: 1978. Setting: small town. Nearest major city is Salem. 18-acre campus. 13 buildings on campus. Approved or accredited by Association of Christian Schools International, Northwest Association of Schools and Colleges, and Oregon Department of Education. Total enrollment: 810. Upper school average class size: 22. Upper school faculty-student ratio: 1:17.

Upper School Student Profile 95% of students are Christian faith.

Faculty School total: 41. In upper school: 16 men, 16 women; 11 have advanced degrees.

Subjects Offered 20th century American writers, 20th century physics, 20th century world history, 3-dimensional art, 3-dimensional design, acting, advanced computer applications, advanced math, advanced studio art-AP, algebra, American biography, American Civil War, American culture, American democracy, American foreign policy, American literature, anatomy and physiology, ancient world history, animal science, art, art appreciation, band, Bible studies, biology, body human, British history, business applications, calculus, career and personal planning, career education, carpentry, character education, chemistry, child development, choir, choral music, Christian doctrine, Christian education, Christian ethics, Christian testament, Christianity, church history, civics, Civil War, college counseling, college writing, comparative government and politics, computer applications, computer education, computer graphics, computer keyboarding, computer programming, concert band, concert choir, drama, drama performance, drawing, early childhood, earth science, economics, English, English composition, English literature, ethics, family living, fine arts, first aid, fitness, food and nutrition, foods, French, general math, general science, geography, geometry, global studies, government, grammar, graphic arts, guidance, health and wellness, health education, human anatomy, instrumental music, Internet, intro to computers, introduction to literature, journalism, language arts, leadership, library, Life of Christ, literature, marine biology, marketing, mathematics, moral and social development, music, music appreciation, music composition, music performance, occupational education, oral expression, physics, play production, playwriting and directing, poetry, pre-algebra, pre-calculus, public speaking, science, sewing, Spanish, speech, stage design, studio art-AP, theater, theater arts, theater production, U.S. government, U.S. history, vocal music, Western civilization, woodworking, world history, world literature, writing.

Graduation Requirements Arts and fine arts (art, music, dance, drama), computer science, English, mathematics, physical education (includes health), religion (includes Bible studies and theology), science, social science, social studies (includes history).

Special Academic Programs Independent study; study at local college for college credit.

College Placement 67 students graduated in 2005; 65 went to college, including Corban College; George Fox University; Linn-Benton Community College; Oregon State University; Western Oregon University. Other: 1 went to work, 1 entered military service. Mean SAT verbal: 586, mean SAT math: 535. 47.9% scored over 600 on SAT verbal, 25% scored over 600 on SAT math.

Student Life Upper grades have specified standards of dress, student council. Discipline rests primarily with faculty. Attendance at religious services is required.

Tuition and Aid Day student tuition: $4235. Tuition installment plan (monthly payment plans, individually arranged payment plans, prepayment discount plan). Tuition reduction for siblings, need-based scholarship grants, paying campus jobs available. Total amount of financial aid awarded in 2005–06: $128,000.

Admissions Traditional secondary-level entrance grade is 9. For fall 2005, 90 students applied for upper-level admission, 75 were accepted, 70 enrolled. Deadline for receipt of application materials: none. Application fee required: $25. Interview required.

Athletics Interscholastic: baseball (boys), basketball (b,g), cross-country running (b,g), equestrian sports (g), football (b), golf (b), soccer (b), softball (g), track and field (b,g), volleyball (g), wrestling (b). 4 PE instructors, 3 coaches.

Computers Computer network features include campus e-mail, on-campus library services, CD-ROMs, Internet access.

Contact Mrs. Teri Dueyer, Registrar. 541-745-5524. Fax: 541-745-6338. E-mail: duevert@santiam.org.

SAVANNAH CHRISTIAN PREPARATORY SCHOOL

PO Box 2848
Savannah, Georgia 31402-2848
Head of School: Mr. Roger L. Yancey

General Information Coeducational day college-preparatory school, affiliated with Christian faith. Grades PK–12. Founded: 1951. Setting: suburban. 254-acre campus. 5 buildings on campus. Approved or accredited by Southern Association of Colleges and Schools and Georgia Department of Education. Total enrollment: 1,516. Upper school average class size: 23. Upper school faculty-student ratio: 1:23.

Upper School Student Profile Grade 9: 129 students (65 boys, 64 girls); Grade 10: 111 students (55 boys, 56 girls); Grade 11: 105 students (54 boys, 51 girls); Grade 12: 110 students (53 boys, 57 girls). 95% of students are Christian faith.

Faculty School total: 125. In upper school: 11 men, 22 women; 18 have advanced degrees.

Subjects Offered 20th century history, accounting, algebra, American Civil War, American history, American history-AP, art, astronomy, band, Bible, biology, botany, business law, calculus-AP, chemistry, chemistry-AP, chorus, computer applications, creative writing, design, drama, driver education, earth science, ecology, economics, English, English-AP, European history-AP, French, geometry, government/civics, graphic arts, health, marine biology, mathematics, mechanical drawing, music appreciation, physical education, physics, probability and statistics, psychology, science, social studies, sociology, Spanish, speech, theater, trigonometry, typing, world history, yearbook.

Graduation Requirements Accounting, algebra, biology, chemistry, economics, English, foreign language, geometry, mathematics, physical education (includes health), religion (includes Bible studies and theology), science, social studies (includes history).

Special Academic Programs Advanced Placement exam preparation in 4 subject areas; honors section; study at local college for college credit.

College Placement 109 students graduated in 2005; 104 went to college, including Armstrong Atlantic State University; Georgia College & State University; Georgia Institute of Technology; Georgia Southern University; University of Georgia; Valdosta State University. Other: 1 went to work, 1 entered military service, 3 had other specific plans. Mean SAT verbal: 558, mean SAT math: 558, mean composite ACT: 23.

Student Life Upper grades have uniform requirement, student council, honor system. Discipline rests primarily with faculty.

Tuition and Aid Day student tuition: $5205. Tuition installment plan (monthly payment plans). Merit scholarship grants, need-based scholarship grants available.

Admissions Traditional secondary-level entrance grade is 9. For fall 2005, 54 students applied for upper-level admission, 49 were accepted, 44 enrolled. Stanford Achievement Test and writing sample required. Deadline for receipt of application materials: January. Application fee required: $160. On-campus interview required.

Athletics Interscholastic: baseball (boys), basketball (b,g), cheering (g), cross-country running (b,g), danceline (g), football (b), golf (b,g), soccer (b,g), softball (g), tennis (b,g), track and field (b,g), volleyball (g); coed intramural: sailing. 3 PE instructors, 3 coaches, 1 trainer.

Computers Computers are regularly used in accounting, business applications, English, graphic arts, history, science, word processing, yearbook classes. Computer network features include on-campus library services, CD-ROMs, Internet access, DVD.

Contact Mrs. Debbie Fairbanks, Director of Admissions and Alumni Relations. 912-234-1653 Ext. 106. Fax: 912-234-0491. E-mail: dfairbanks@savcps.com. Web site: www.savcps.com.

THE SAVANNAH COUNTRY DAY SCHOOL

824 Stillwood Drive
Savannah, Georgia 31419-2643
Head of School: Mr. Thomas C. Bonnell

General Information Coeducational day college-preparatory and arts school. Grades PK–12. Founded: 1955. Setting: suburban. 65-acre campus. 11 buildings on campus. Approved or accredited by Southern Association of Colleges and Schools. Member of National Association of Independent Schools. Endowment: $7.6 million. Total enrollment: 989. Upper school average class size: 15. Upper school faculty-student ratio: 1:10.

Upper School Student Profile Grade 9: 85 students (37 boys, 48 girls); Grade 10: 78 students (43 boys, 35 girls); Grade 11: 79 students (46 boys, 33 girls); Grade 12: 67 students (43 boys, 24 girls).

Faculty School total: 95. In upper school: 15 men, 24 women; 31 have advanced degrees.

Subjects Offered Algebra, American history, American literature, analysis and differential calculus, analysis of data, anatomy and physiology, art, art history, art history-AP, biology, biology-AP, British literature-AP, calculus, calculus-AP, ceramics, chemistry, chemistry-AP, computer education, computer science, dance, drama, drama performance, economics, economics and history, English, English literature, English-AP, environmental science, environmental science-AP, European history, European history-AP, fine arts, French, geometry, government-AP, government/civics,

guidance, health, honors algebra, honors English, honors geometry, honors U.S. history, honors world history, independent study, instrumental music, intro to computers, jazz band, language-AP, Latin, Latin-AP, music, photography, physical education, physics, physics-AP, pre-calculus, public speaking, robotics, senior project, Spanish, Spanish language-AP, statistics, studio art—AP, theater, U.S. history-AP, world history, world history-AP, yearbook.

Graduation Requirements Arts and fine arts (art, music, dance, drama), English, foreign language, health education, history, mathematics, physical education (includes health), science, speech, four years of foreign language.

Special Academic Programs Advanced Placement exam preparation in 16 subject areas; honors section; independent study; study at local college for college credit.

College Placement 67 students graduated in 2005; 66 went to college, including Boston University; Chicago State University; College of Charleston; Georgia Institute of Technology; University of Georgia; Washington and Lee University. Other: 1 entered a postgraduate year. Mean SAT verbal: 664, mean SAT math: 649. 71% scored over 600 on SAT verbal, 74% scored over 600 on SAT math.

Student Life Upper grades have specified standards of dress, student council, honor system. Discipline rests equally with students and faculty.

Summer Programs Enrichment, advancement, sports, art/fine arts, computer instruction programs offered; session focuses on recreation and enrichment; held on campus; accepts boys and girls; open to students from other schools. 1000 students usually enrolled. 2006 schedule: May 31 to August 14. Application deadline: May 1.

Tuition and Aid Day student tuition: $13,360. Tuition installment plan (Insured Tuition Payment Plan, monthly payment plans, individually arranged payment plans, plans arranged through local bank). Merit scholarship grants, need-based scholarship grants available. In 2005–06, 16% of upper-school students received aid; total upper-school merit-scholarship money awarded: $2000. Total amount of financial aid awarded in 2005–06: $306,807.

Admissions Traditional secondary-level entrance grade is 9. For fall 2005, 37 students applied for upper-level admission, 20 were accepted, 15 enrolled. ERB Reading and Math, Otis-Lennon Mental Ability Test or writing sample required. Deadline for receipt of application materials: none. Application fee required: $50. Interview required.

Athletics Interscholastic: baseball (boys), basketball (b,g), cheering (g), crew (b,g), cross-country running (b,g), football (b), golf (b,g), soccer (b,g), softball (g), tennis (b,g), track and field (b,g), volleyball (g); intramural: basketball (b,g), bocce (b,g), cheering (g), climbing (b,g), cooperative games (b,g), dance (b,g), outdoor adventure (b,g), outdoor education (b,g), physical training (b,g), power lifting (b,g), project adventure (b,g), ropes courses (b,g), strength & conditioning (b,g), water polo (g), weight lifting (b,g), weight training (b,g). 1 coach, 1 trainer.

Computers Computers are regularly used in college planning, creative writing, economics, English, foreign language, history, library skills, mathematics, publications, publishing, research skills, SAT preparation, science, yearbook classes. Computer network features include campus e-mail, on-campus library services, CD-ROMs, online commercial services, Internet access, DVD, wireless campus network.

Contact Mrs. Josceline Reardon, Assistant Director of Admissions and Financial Aid Officer. 912-961-8807. Fax: 912-920-7800. E-mail: reardon@savcds.org. Web site: www.savcds.org.

ANNOUNCEMENT FROM THE SCHOOL In 1955, Savannah Country Day School was established as a college-preparatory school (preK–12) to assist young people in development of superior scholarship, wisdom, and moral commitment. The original trustees purchased the Pape School, founded in 1905, with its tradition of academic excellence and concern for community service. Drawing on the principles of the Judeo-Christian faiths, Savannah Country Day School seeks to prepare students of academic and personal promise to meet the challenges of college and of life with confidence, imagination, and integrity. In partnership with supportive families, the School strives to cultivate in each student the desire and the discipline to grow in wisdom, to lead lives of personal honor, to appreciate beauty, to pursue physical well-being, and to serve others with a generous and compassionate spirit. In fulfilling this mission, the School subscribes to the following core beliefs: that the ultimate goal of education is to cultivate in each student a lifelong passion for learning; each student's academic potential is most fully realized through a challenging and varied curriculum that has appropriate support; students learn best in a respectful, supportive community of trust where each student's learning needs and abilities are understood and accommodated as fully as possible; intellectual growth requires not only the acquisition of knowledge but also its application in analytical, creative, and expressive ways that make learning meaningful to the student; physical and emotional health is critical to the development of each student's personal potential; each student's life is enriched in a diverse community where differences among people are affirmed and celebrated; the School shares with families the responsibility for fostering in each student strength of character, a sense of personal responsibility, and an attitude of faith, reverence, and tolerance; and the development of leadership in each student should include instilling a commitment to use one's knowledge, skills, and resources in service to others.

SAYRE SCHOOL

194 North Limestone Street
Lexington, Kentucky 40507
Head of School: Mr. Clayton G. Chambliss

General Information Coeducational day college-preparatory, arts, and technology school. Grades PK–12. Founded: 1854. Setting: urban. 9-acre campus. 10 buildings on campus. Approved or accredited by Independent Schools Association of the Central States and Kentucky Department of Education. Member of National Association of Independent Schools and Secondary School Admission Test Board. Endowment: $6 million. Total enrollment: 669. Upper school average class size: 15. Upper school faculty-student ratio: 1:10.

Upper School Student Profile Grade 9: 64 students (34 boys, 30 girls); Grade 10: 60 students (32 boys, 28 girls); Grade 11: 53 students (25 boys, 28 girls); Grade 12: 67 students (37 boys, 30 girls).

Faculty School total: 137. In upper school: 12 men, 15 women; 20 have advanced degrees.

Subjects Offered Algebra, American history, American literature, art, art history, biology, calculus, chemistry, community service, computer science, creative writing, drama, earth science, English, English literature, fine arts, French, geometry, government/civics, health, history, journalism, mathematics, music, photography, physical education, physics, public speaking, science, social studies, Spanish, speech, statistics, theater, U.S. constitutional history, world history, writing.

Graduation Requirements Arts and fine arts (art, music, dance, drama), computer science, creative writing, English, foreign language, mathematics, physical education (includes health), public speaking, science, social studies (includes history), senior project internship. Community service is required.

Special Academic Programs Advanced Placement exam preparation in 11 subject areas; honors section; independent study; term-away projects; study at local college for college credit; academic accommodation for the gifted and the artistically talented.

College Placement 45 students graduated in 2005; all went to college, including Columbia College; University of Kentucky. Mean SAT verbal: 590, mean SAT math: 595, mean composite ACT: 25. 58% scored over 600 on SAT verbal, 58% scored over 600 on SAT math, 50% scored over 26 on composite ACT.

Student Life Upper grades have specified standards of dress, student council, honor system. Discipline rests equally with students and faculty.

Tuition and Aid Day student tuition: $13,100–$13,700. Tuition installment plan (Insured Tuition Payment Plan, monthly payment plans, individually arranged payment plans). Merit scholarship grants, need-based scholarship grants available. In 2005–06, 12% of upper-school students received aid; total upper-school merit-scholarship money awarded: $9000. Total amount of financial aid awarded in 2005–06: $250,000.

Admissions Traditional secondary-level entrance grade is 9. For fall 2005, 39 students applied for upper-level admission, 24 were accepted, 24 enrolled. Admissions testing and Stanford Binet required. Deadline for receipt of application materials: none. Application fee required: $75. On-campus interview required.

Athletics Interscholastic: baseball (boys), basketball (b,g), cheering (g), diving (b,g), golf (b,g), lacrosse (b), physical fitness (b), physical training (b,g), soccer (b,g), softball (g), swimming and diving (b,g), tennis (b,g). 5 PE instructors, 4 coaches, 1 trainer.

Computers Computers are regularly used in English, foreign language, mathematics, music, science classes. Computer network features include campus e-mail, on-campus library services, CD-ROMs, online commercial services, Internet access, office computer access, DVD, wireless campus network.

Contact Mrs. Barbara N. Parsons, Assistant Head of School and Director of Admission. 859-254-1361. Fax: 859-254-5627. E-mail: bparsons@sayreschool.org. Web site: www.sayreschool.org.

SCARBOROUGH CHRISTIAN SCHOOL

95 Jonesville Crescent
North York, Ontario M4A 1H2, Canada
Head of School: Mr. Martin D. Sandford

General Information Coeducational day college-preparatory and business school, affiliated with Christian faith. Grades JK–12. Founded: 1975. Setting: urban. Nearest major city is Toronto, Canada. 1 building on campus. Approved or accredited by Ontario Department of Education. Language of instruction: English. Total enrollment: 120. Upper school average class size: 12. Upper school faculty-student ratio: 1:12.

Upper School Student Profile Grade 9: 11 students (7 boys, 4 girls); Grade 10: 1 student (1 boy); Grade 11: 4 students (3 boys, 1 girl); Grade 12: 5 students (2 boys, 3 girls). 50% of students are Christian.

Faculty School total: 18. In upper school: 4 men, 4 women; 2 have advanced degrees.

Subjects Offered Business studies, calculus, Canadian geography, Canadian history, career education, chemistry, civics, English, ESL, math analysis, math applications, physics, science, visual arts.

Graduation Requirements Ontario Ministry of Education requirements.

Special Academic Programs Independent study; ESL (10 students enrolled).

Student Life Upper grades have uniform requirement. Discipline rests primarily with faculty. Attendance at religious services is required.

Scarborough Christian School

Summer Programs Remediation, advancement, ESL programs offered; session focuses on academic courses as regular credits; held on campus; accepts boys and girls; open to students from other schools. 12 students usually enrolled.

Tuition and Aid Day student tuition: CAN$6400. Tuition installment plan (individually arranged payment plans). Tuition reduction for siblings available. In 2005–06, 20% of upper-school students received aid.

Admissions Traditional secondary-level entrance grade is 12. For fall 2005, 14 students applied for upper-level admission, 13 were accepted, 10 enrolled. SLEP required. Deadline for receipt of application materials: none. No application fee required.

Computers Computers are regularly used in mathematics classes. Computer resources include CD-ROMs, Internet access, office computer access.

Contact Admissions. 416-750-7515. Fax: 416-750-7720. E-mail: scs@titan.tcn.net. Web site: www.scarboroughchristianschool.com.

SCATTERGOOD FRIENDS SCHOOL

1951 Delta Avenue
West Branch, Iowa 52358-8507
Head of School: Ms. Jan Luchini

General Information Coeducational boarding and day college-preparatory and arts school, affiliated with Society of Friends. Boarding grades 9–PG, day grades 9–12. Founded: 1890. Setting: rural. Nearest major city is Iowa City. Students are housed in single-sex dormitories. 120-acre campus. 15 buildings on campus. Approved or accredited by Friends Council on Education, Independent Schools Association of the Central States, Midwest Association of Boarding Schools, The Association of Boarding Schools, and Iowa Department of Education. Member of National Association of Independent Schools. Endowment: $1.1 million. Total enrollment: 47. Upper school average class size: 12. Upper school faculty-student ratio: 1:2.

Upper School Student Profile Grade 9: 6 students (4 boys, 2 girls); Grade 10: 16 students (6 boys, 10 girls); Grade 11: 12 students (8 boys, 4 girls); Grade 12: 13 students (4 boys, 9 girls). 90% of students are boarding students. 50% are state residents. 11 states are represented in upper school student body. 15% are international students. International students from Brazil, China, Japan, Mexico, Republic of Korea, and Rwanda; 1 other country represented in student body. 20% of students are members of Society of Friends.

Faculty School total: 23. In upper school: 8 men, 10 women; 5 have advanced degrees; all reside on campus.

Subjects Offered 20th century American writers, 3-dimensional art, advanced TOEFL/grammar, agriculture, algebra, alternative physical education, American government, American history, ancient history, art, biology, calculus, career/college preparation, ceramics, chemistry, choreography, college admission preparation, community service, conflict resolution, contemporary women writers, creative writing, critical thinking, dance, dance performance, digital art, drama, drama performance, drawing and design, ecology, environmental systems, economics, electronic music, environmental science, ESL, ethics, expository writing, fencing, film and literature, filmmaking, fine arts, gardening, geometry, glassblowing, government/civics, grammar, history, horticulture, independent study, industrial arts, Internet research, library research, martial arts, mathematics, organic gardening, physics, portfolio writing, pottery, Quakerism and ethics, religion, research seminar, SAT/ACT preparation, science, senior seminar, set design, social studies, Spanish, stained glass, studio art, swimming, U.S. history, wilderness/outdoor program, woodworking, writing, writing workshop, yearbook, yoga.

Graduation Requirements Algebra, art, biology, chemistry, earth science, English, foreign language, geometry, government, history, humanities, junior and senior seminars, physical education (includes health), physics, portfolio writing, precalculus, Quakerism and ethics, SAT/ACT preparation, U.S. history, world history, 30 hours of community service per year in attendance, 20-page research paper with a thesis defense presentation, acceptance at 4-year college or university.

Special Academic Programs Honors section; accelerated programs; independent study; term-away projects; study at local college for college credit; study abroad; ESL (11 students enrolled).

College Placement 10 students graduated in 2005; 8 went to college, including Beloit College; Cornell College; Earlham College; Knox College; Reed College; University of Chicago. Other: 1 went to work, 1 had other specific plans. Median SAT verbal: 530, median SAT math: 590. 29% scored over 600 on SAT verbal, 43% scored over 600 on SAT math.

Student Life Upper grades have student council. Discipline rests equally with students and faculty. Attendance at religious services is required.

Tuition and Aid Day student tuition: $11,000; 5-day tuition and room/board: $18,500; 7-day tuition and room/board: $20,000. Tuition installment plan (Academic Management Services Plan, monthly payment plans, individually arranged payment plans). Merit scholarship grants, need-based scholarship grants, paying campus jobs, scholarships for Quaker students available. In 2005–06, 74% of upper-school students received aid; total upper-school merit-scholarship money awarded: $1000. Total amount of financial aid awarded in 2005–06: $360,000.

Admissions Traditional secondary-level entrance grade is 9. For fall 2005, 40 students applied for upper-level admission, 30 were accepted, 25 enrolled. Deadline for receipt of application materials: April 1. Application fee required: $50. Interview recommended.

Athletics Coed Interscholastic: indoor soccer; coed intramural: archery, back packing, basketball, bicycling, canoeing/kayaking, dance, fencing, field hockey, fitness, hiking/backpacking, in-line hockey, indoor soccer, juggling, martial arts, physical fitness, roller hockey, skateboarding, soccer, softball, strength & conditioning, ultimate Frisbee, volleyball, yoga.

Computers Computers are regularly used in all classes. Computer network features include campus e-mail, on-campus library services, CD-ROMs, online commercial services, Internet access, file transfer, DVD, wireless campus network, laptop computers (for each student).

Contact Ms. Rachel Thomson, Director of Admissions. 319-643-7628. Fax: 319-643-7638. E-mail: admissions@scattergood.org. Web site: www.scattergood.org.

ANNOUNCEMENT FROM THE SCHOOL To further enhance students' learning capabilities, Scattergood has issued each student a personal laptop computer to use while attending Scattergood. A portion of their tuition is applied toward the optional purchase of the student's computer at the time the student graduates or leaves Scattergood. Each laptop is linked to the wireless, high-speed data network that spans all of the academic buildings on campus, as well as both dorms. The School has its own file server, allowing students and staff members the flexibility of working on their laptop or any of the desktops on campus while saving work to a central location. Scattergood offers free e-mail accounts to all community members for both personal and academic use. Scattergood has also added a portfolio program to its academic curriculum. The portfolios will be used to showcase both academic and nonacademic work when applying to colleges. Portfolio assignments are occasionally given in classes as an assessment tool for teachers in lieu of tests.

See full description on page 1056.

SCHOOL FOR YOUNG PERFORMERS

175 West 92nd Street
Suite 1D
New York, New York 10025
Head of School: Mr. Alan Simon

General Information Coeducational day college-preparatory, general academic, and arts school. Grades K–12. Founded: 1995. Setting: urban. Approved or accredited by New York Department of Education. Total enrollment: 12. Upper school average class size: 1. Upper school faculty-student ratio: 1:1.

Upper School Student Profile Grade 9: 1 student (1 girl); Grade 10: 2 students (1 boy, 1 girl); Grade 11: 1 student (1 girl); Grade 12: 2 students (1 boy, 1 girl).

Faculty School total: 15. In upper school: 5 men, 10 women; all have advanced degrees.

Graduation Requirements English, mathematics, science, social studies (includes history).

Special Academic Programs Advanced Placement exam preparation in 19 subject areas; honors section; accelerated programs; independent study; term-away projects; study abroad; academic accommodation for the gifted, the musically talented, and the artistically talented; remedial reading and/or remedial writing; remedial math; programs in English, mathematics, general development for dyslexic students; special instructional classes for deaf students, blind students.

College Placement 2 students graduated in 2005; all went to college.

Student Life Upper grades have honor system. Discipline rests equally with students and faculty.

Summer Programs Remediation, enrichment, advancement, art/fine arts programs offered; session focuses on academics; held off campus; held at local agencies; accepts boys and girls; open to students from other schools. 2 students usually enrolled.

Tuition and Aid Day student tuition: $4250.

Admissions For fall 2005, 2 students applied for upper-level admission, 2 were accepted, 2 enrolled. Deadline for receipt of application materials: none. No application fee required. Interview recommended.

Computers Computer resources include CD-ROMs.

Contact Mr. Alan Simon, Principal. 212-663-3921. Fax: 914-666-3810. E-mail: alan@onlocationeducation.com. Web site: www.onlocationeducation.com/syp/.

ANNOUNCEMENT FROM THE SCHOOL The School for Young Performers offers high-quality schooling to students who want to balance an education with a career in the performing arts or athletics. As a "school without walls," SYP delivers its college-preparatory curriculum directly to its students, wherever their careers take them, by means of highly qualified and dynamic private tutors.

SCHOOL OF THE HOLY CHILD

2225 Westchester Avenue
Rye, New York 10580
Head of School: Ann F. Sullivan

General Information Girls' day college-preparatory school, affiliated with Roman Catholic Church. Grades 5–12. Founded: 1904. Setting: suburban. Nearest major city is White Plains. 17-acre campus. 1 building on campus. Approved or accredited by Middle States Association of Colleges and Schools, New York State Association of Independent Schools, The College Board, and New York Department of Education. Member of National Association of Independent Schools and Secondary School Admission Test Board. Endowment: $990,000. Total enrollment: 324. Upper school average class size: 17. Upper school faculty-student ratio: 1:9.

Upper School Student Profile Grade 9: 64 students (64 girls); Grade 10: 53 students (53 girls); Grade 11: 54 students (54 girls); Grade 12: 48 students (48 girls). 81% of students are Roman Catholic.

Faculty School total: 47. In upper school: 3 men, 26 women; 22 have advanced degrees.

Subjects Offered Algebra, American history, American literature, anatomy, art, art history, art history-AP, arts, arts and crafts, astronomy, Bible studies, bioethics, biology, biology-AP, calculus, ceramics, chamber groups, chemistry, chorus, community service, computer programming, computer science, creative writing, design, drama, drawing, driver education, English, English literature, ethics, European history, expository writing, film, fine arts, French, French-AP, geometry, government/civics, grammar, health, history, illustration, Latin, Latin-AP, mathematics, music, music theory-AP, physical education, physics, psychology, religion, science, Shakespeare, social studies, Spanish, Spanish-AP, speech, statistics, studio art-AP, theater, trigonometry, world history, writing.

Graduation Requirements Arts and fine arts (art, music, dance, drama), English, foreign language, independent study, mathematics, physical education (includes health), religion (includes Bible studies and theology), science, social studies (includes history), senior internship project, life skills for 9th and 10th grades, guidance for 11th and 12th grades, 100 hours of community service.

Special Academic Programs Advanced Placement exam preparation in 14 subject areas; independent study; term-away projects; domestic exchange program (with The Network Program Schools).

College Placement 44 students graduated in 2005; all went to college, including Boston College; Bucknell University; Georgetown University; Lafayette College; New York University; Villanova University. Mean SAT verbal: 590, mean SAT math: 585.

Student Life Upper grades have uniform requirement, student council, honor system. Discipline rests primarily with faculty. Attendance at religious services is required.

Tuition and Aid Day student tuition: $18,600–$18,975. Tuition installment plan (Key Tuition Payment Plan). Tuition reduction for siblings, merit scholarship grants, need-based scholarship grants available. In 2005–06, 30% of upper-school students received aid; total upper-school merit-scholarship money awarded: $120,975. Total amount of financial aid awarded in 2005–06: $500,300.

Admissions Traditional secondary-level entrance grade is 9. For fall 2005, 164 students applied for upper-level admission, 50 were accepted, 34 enrolled. Catholic High School Entrance Examination, ISEE or SSAT required. Deadline for receipt of application materials: January 21. Application fee required: $50. On-campus interview required.

Athletics Interscholastic: basketball, cross-country running, field hockey, golf, indoor track & field, lacrosse, soccer, softball, squash, swimming and diving, tennis, track and field, volleyball, winter (indoor) track; intramural: basketball, dance, dance squad, dance team, fitness, fitness walking, modern dance, volleyball, winter (indoor) track. 2 PE instructors, 12 coaches.

Computers Computers are regularly used in all academic classes. Computer network features include campus e-mail, on-campus library services, CD-ROMs, Internet access.

Contact Admission Office. 914-967-5622 Ext. 227. Fax: 914-967-6476. E-mail: admissions@holychildrye.org. Web site: www.holychildrye.org.

SCHULE SCHLOSS SALEM

Salem D88682, Germany

Head of School: Ms. Ingrid Sund

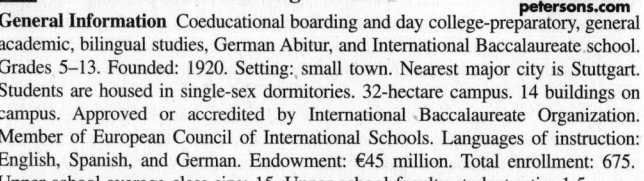

General Information Coeducational boarding and day college-preparatory, general academic, bilingual studies, German Abitur, and International Baccalaureate school. Grades 5–13. Founded: 1920. Setting: small town. Nearest major city is Stuttgart. Students are housed in single-sex dormitories. 32-hectare campus. 14 buildings on campus. Approved or accredited by International Baccalaureate Organization. Member of European Council of International Schools. Languages of instruction: English, Spanish, and German. Endowment: €45 million. Total enrollment: 675. Upper school average class size: 15. Upper school faculty-student ratio: 1:5.

Upper School Student Profile Grade 11: 130 students (67 boys, 63 girls); Grade 12: 157 students (81 boys, 76 girls); Grade 13: 161 students (86 boys, 75 girls). 95% of students are boarding students. 21% are international students. International students from Austria, China, Russian Federation, Spain, and Switzerland; 15 other countries represented in student body.

Faculty School total: 125. In upper school: 35 men, 30 women; 60 have advanced degrees; 40 reside on campus.

Subjects Offered Art history, biology, chemistry, computer science, economics, English, ethics, French, geography, German, Greek, history, Latin, mathematics, music, philosophy, physical education, physics, political science, religion, Russian, science, Spanish, theater arts, visual arts.

Graduation Requirements Arts and fine arts (art, music, dance, drama), English, foreign language, German, mathematics, physical education (includes health), science, social science, theory of knowledge, 2 hours of community service per week, academic requirements vary depending upon academic program pursued.

Special Academic Programs International Baccalaureate program; independent study; term-away projects; domestic exchange program (with Bishop's College School, Sedbergh School, The Athenian School, Choate Rosemary Hall); study abroad; academic accommodation for the gifted, the musically talented, and the artistically talented; ESL.

College Placement 150 students graduated in 2005; 146 went to college, including Harvard University; London School of Economics and Political Science; University of Chicago; University of Oxford; University of St. Andrews.

Student Life Upper grades have student council. Discipline rests equally with students and faculty.

Summer Programs Enrichment, advancement, ESL, sports, art/fine arts programs offered; session focuses on language training in English and German; held on campus; accepts boys and girls; open to students from other schools. 65 students usually enrolled. 2006 schedule: July 27 to August 13. Application deadline: none.

Tuition and Aid Day student tuition: €12,000; 7-day tuition and room/board: €28,000. Guaranteed tuition plan. Tuition installment plan (monthly payment plans, individually arranged payment plans, trimester payment plan, annual payment plan). Tuition reduction for siblings, merit scholarship grants, need-based scholarship grants, need-based loans available. In 2005–06, 30% of upper-school students received aid; total upper-school merit-scholarship money awarded: €2,000,000.

Admissions School's own exam or school's own test required. Deadline for receipt of application materials: none. Application fee required: €1200. Interview required.

Athletics Interscholastic: basketball (boys, girls), field hockey (b,g), gymnastics (b,g), indoor hockey (b,g), rugby (b), volleyball (b,g); intramural: aerobics/dance (g), basketball (b,g), field hockey (b,g), gymnastics (b,g), indoor hockey (b,g), rowing (b,g), rugby (b), soccer (b), softball (b,g), track and field (b,g), ultimate Frisbee (b,g), volleyball (b,g); coed interscholastic: sailing, volleyball; coed intramural: alpine skiing, back packing, badminton, bicycling, canoeing/kayaking, Circus, climbing, cross-country running, equestrian sports, fitness, golf, handball, hiking/backpacking, horseback riding, independent competitive sports, jogging, kayaking, life saving, mountain biking, nordic skiing, outdoor activities, rock climbing, running, sailing, sea rescue, skiing (cross-country), skiing (downhill), snowboarding, snowshoeing, squash, strength & conditioning, swimming and diving, table tennis, tennis, volleyball, wall climbing, water polo, weight training, windsurfing, yoga. 7 PE instructors, 7 coaches.

Computers Computers are regularly used in economics classes. Computer network features include campus e-mail, on-campus library services, CD-ROMs, Internet access, file transfer, DVD.

Contact Ms. Margaret Tzanakakis, Director of Admissions. 49-7553-919 Ext. 337. Fax: 49-7553-919-303. E-mail: margaret.tzanakakis@salem-net.de. Web site: www.salemcollege.de.

ANNOUNCEMENT FROM THE SCHOOL Salem, Germany's most prominent school, is located on the northern shore of Lake Constance. It is the only boarding school in Germany that offers pupils from all countries of the world a comprehensive education leading to either the International Baccalaureate Diploma or the German Abitur.

SCRANTON PREPARATORY SCHOOL

1000 Wyoming Avenue
Scranton, Pennsylvania 18509-2993
Head of School: Rev. Herbert Keller, SJ

General Information Coeducational day college-preparatory and religious studies school, affiliated with Roman Catholic Church (Jesuit order). Grades 9–12. Founded: 1944. Setting: urban. Nearest major city is New York, NY. 1 building on campus. Approved or accredited by Jesuit Secondary Education Association, Middle States Association of Colleges and Schools, National Catholic Education Association, and Pennsylvania Department of Education. Member of National Association of Independent Schools. Total enrollment: 800.

Upper School Student Profile 85% of students are Roman Catholic Church (Jesuit order).

Faculty School total: 57. In upper school: 26 men, 31 women; 4 have advanced degrees.

Subjects Offered Algebra, American culture, American history, analytic geometry, art, biology, biology-AP, calculus, calculus-AP, chemistry, chemistry-AP, computer

Scranton Preparatory School

science, creative writing, English, English language and composition-AP, English literature-AP, ethics, fine arts, French, geometry, German, Greek, Greek drama, health, health education, history, honors English, international affairs, intro to computers, Latin, Latin-AP, mathematics, music, mythology, physical education, physics, physics-AP, probability and statistics, religious education, science, social studies, Spanish, speech, statistics, trigonometry, world cultures.

Graduation Requirements Arts and fine arts (art, music, dance, drama), computer science, English, foreign language, Latin, mathematics, physical education (includes health), religion (includes Bible studies and theology), science, social studies (includes history). Community service is required.

Special Academic Programs Honors section; study at local college for college credit.

College Placement 189 students graduated in 2005; 188 went to college, including Georgetown University; Marywood University; Saint Joseph's University; The University of Scranton; Villanova University. Other: 1 had other specific plans. Median SAT verbal: 560, median SAT math: 540. 33% scored over 600 on SAT verbal, 30% scored over 600 on SAT math.

Student Life Upper grades have specified standards of dress, student council. Discipline rests primarily with faculty.

Summer Programs Enrichment programs offered; session focuses on enrichment and make-up courses; held on campus; accepts boys and girls; open to students from other schools. 2006 schedule: June 25 to July 31. Application deadline: none.

Tuition and Aid Day student tuition: $7800. Tuition installment plan (SMART Tuition Payment Plan, monthly payment plans). Need-based scholarship grants available. In 2005–06, 33% of upper-school students received aid. Total amount of financial aid awarded in 2005–06: $646,300.

Admissions For fall 2005, 405 students applied for upper-level admission. School's own exam required. Deadline for receipt of application materials: none. No application fee required. Interview required.

Athletics Interscholastic: baseball (boys), basketball (b,g), cheering (g), cross-country running (b,g), football (b), golf (b,g), softball (g), swimming and diving (b,g), tennis (b,g), track and field (b,g), wrestling (b); coed interscholastic: soccer; coed intramural: bowling, golf.

Computers Computers are regularly used in foreign language, science classes. Computer resources include CD-ROMs, Internet access.

Contact Mr. Henry Hewitt, Director of Admissions. 717-941-7737 Ext. 112. Fax: 717-941-6318. E-mail: hhewitt@scrantonprep.com. Web site: www.scrantonprep.com.

SEABURY HALL

480 Olinda Road
Makawao, Hawaii 96768-9399
Head of School: Mr. Joseph J. Schmidt

General Information Coeducational day college-preparatory, arts, religious studies, bilingual studies, and technology school, affiliated with Episcopal Church. Grades 6–12. Founded: 1964. Setting: rural. Nearest major city is Kahului. 52-acre campus. 8 buildings on campus. Approved or accredited by Accrediting Commission for Schools, National Association of Episcopal Schools, Western Association of Schools and Colleges, and Hawaii Department of Education. Member of National Association of Independent Schools and Secondary School Admission Test Board. Endowment: $22 million. Total enrollment: 406. Upper school average class size: 18. Upper school faculty-student ratio: 1:12.

Upper School Student Profile Grade 9: 78 students (31 boys, 47 girls); Grade 10: 77 students (35 boys, 42 girls); Grade 11: 58 students (27 boys, 31 girls); Grade 12: 53 students (25 boys, 28 girls). 10% of students are members of Episcopal Church.

Faculty School total: 52. In upper school: 15 men, 18 women; 16 have advanced degrees.

Subjects Offered Acting, algebra, American history, American literature, art, band, biology, biology-AP, calculus-AP, ceramics, chemistry, chorus, community service, comparative religion, computer programming, dance, drawing, economics, English, English literature, ethics, European history-AP, expository writing, fine arts, geometry, global studies, government, history, Japanese, keyboarding, mathematics, mythology, painting, philosophy, physical education, physical science, physics, physics-AP, political science, pre-algebra, pre-calculus, religion, science, set design, social studies, Spanish, Spanish-AP, speech, studio art-AP, yearbook.

Graduation Requirements Arts and fine arts (art, music, dance, drama), English, foreign language, mathematics, physical education (includes health), religion (includes Bible studies and theology), science, social studies (includes history), speech. Community service is required.

Special Academic Programs Advanced Placement exam preparation in 12 subject areas; honors section; independent study.

College Placement 63 students graduated in 2005; all went to college, including Chapman University; Loyola Marymount University; Santa Barbara City College; Santa Clara University; University of San Diego; Yale University. Mean SAT verbal: 588, mean SAT math: 603. 42% scored over 600 on SAT verbal, 48% scored over 600 on SAT math.

Student Life Upper grades have specified standards of dress, student council, honor system. Discipline rests primarily with faculty.

Summer Programs Sports, art/fine arts programs offered; held on campus; accepts boys and girls; open to students from other schools. 110 students usually enrolled. 2006 schedule: June 19 to July 14. Application deadline: June 17.

Tuition and Aid Day student tuition: $13,625. Tuition installment plan (FACTS Tuition Payment Plan). Need-based scholarship grants available. In 2005–06, 27% of upper-school students received aid. Total amount of financial aid awarded in 2005–06: $499,125.

Admissions Traditional secondary-level entrance grade is 9. For fall 2005, 78 students applied for upper-level admission, 63 were accepted, 49 enrolled. ERB CTP III, ISEE or SSAT required. Deadline for receipt of application materials: March 9. Application fee required: $55. Interview required.

Athletics Interscholastic: basketball (boys, girls), cross-country running (b,g), dance (g), football (b), golf (b,g), soccer (b,g), swimming and diving (b,g), tennis (b,g), track and field (b,g), volleyball (b,g); intramural: basketball (b,g), dance (g), fitness (b,g), strength & conditioning (b,g); coed interscholastic: baseball, dance; coed intramural: ballet, baseball, cross-country running, dance, fitness, track and field, volleyball. 4 PE instructors, 12 coaches, 1 trainer.

Computers Computers are regularly used in art, English, foreign language, history, mathematics, science classes. Computer network features include campus e-mail, on-campus library services, CD-ROMs, online commercial services, Internet access, DVD, wireless campus network.

Contact Elaine V. Nelson, Director of Admissions. 808-572-0807. Fax: 808-572-2042. E-mail: enelson@seaburyhall.org. Web site: www.seaburyhall.org.

SEATTLE ACADEMY OF ARTS AND SCIENCES

1201 East Union Street
Seattle, Washington 98122
Head of School: Jean Marie Orvis

General Information Coeducational day college-preparatory, arts, and technology school. Grades 6–12. Founded: 1983. Setting: urban. 4 buildings on campus. Approved or accredited by Northwest Association of Schools and Colleges, Pacific Northwest Association of Independent Schools, and Washington Department of Education. Member of National Association of Independent Schools. Total enrollment: 547. Upper school average class size: 18. Upper school faculty-student ratio: 1:7.

Upper School Student Profile Grade 9: 97 students (50 boys, 47 girls); Grade 10: 78 students (35 boys, 43 girls); Grade 11: 80 students (39 boys, 41 girls); Grade 12: 75 students (40 boys, 35 girls).

Faculty School total: 65. In upper school: 28 men, 25 women; 25 have advanced degrees.

Subjects Offered Acting, advanced chemistry, algebra, American history, American literature, biology, biotechnology, calculus, chemistry, civics, dance, debate, drawing, economics, English, French, geometry, health, history, humanities, independent study, instrumental music, lab science, literature, marine science, math analysis, musical productions, painting, physical education, physics, printmaking, sculpture, Spanish, speech, stagecraft, statistics, visual arts, vocal music, world literature, yearbook.

Graduation Requirements Arts and fine arts (art, music, dance, drama), English, foreign language, mathematics, physical education (includes health), science, social studies (includes history). Community service is required.

Special Academic Programs Honors section; independent study; study abroad; programs in English for dyslexic students.

College Placement 76 students graduated in 2005; they went to New York University; The George Washington University; Western Washington University; Willamette University. Mean SAT verbal: 594, mean SAT math: 565, mean composite ACT: 25.

Student Life Upper grades have student council. Discipline rests equally with students and faculty.

Summer Programs Enrichment, sports, art/fine arts programs offered; held on campus; accepts boys and girls; not open to students from other schools. 2006 schedule: June 19 to August 11.

Tuition and Aid Day student tuition: $19,690. Tuition installment plan (Academic Management Services Plan, monthly payment plans). Need-based scholarship grants available. In 2005–06, 20% of upper-school students received aid.

Admissions Traditional secondary-level entrance grade is 9. ISEE required. Deadline for receipt of application materials: January 19. Application fee required: $50. Interview required.

Athletics Interscholastic: basketball (boys, girls), cross-country running (b,g), golf (b,g), soccer (b,g), tennis (b,g), track and field (b,g), ultimate Frisbee (b,g); intramural: physical training (b,g); coed interscholastic: dance; coed intramural: Frisbee, in-line skating, outdoor activities, roller blading, skateboarding, squash. 5 PE instructors, 1 trainer.

Computers Computers are regularly used in English, foreign language, history, mathematics, science, speech, video film production, yearbook classes. Computer network features include campus e-mail, on-campus library services, CD-ROMs, online commercial services, Internet access, wireless campus network.

Contact Jim Rupp, Admission Director. 206-324-7227. Fax: 206-323-6618. E-mail: jrupp@seattleacademy.org. Web site: www.seattleacademy.org.

SEATTLE CHRISTIAN SCHOOLS

18301 Military Road South
Seattle, Washington 98188
Head of School: Dr. Greg Johnson

General Information Coeducational day college-preparatory, arts, religious studies, bilingual studies, and technology school, affiliated with Christian faith. Grades K–12. Founded: 1946. Setting: suburban. 13-acre campus. 1 building on campus. Approved or accredited by Association of Christian Schools International, CITA (Commission on International and Trans-Regional Accreditation), Northwest Association of Accredited Schools, and Washington Department of Education. Endowment: $635,328. Total enrollment: 695. Upper school average class size: 22. Upper school faculty-student ratio: 1:12.

Upper School Student Profile Grade 9: 87 students (33 boys, 54 girls); Grade 10: 61 students (28 boys, 33 girls); Grade 11: 65 students (28 boys, 37 girls); Grade 12: 62 students (23 boys, 39 girls). 100% of students are Christian faith.

Faculty School total: 51. In upper school: 12 men, 11 women; 14 have advanced degrees.

Subjects Offered Advanced Placement courses, algebra, American literature, American sign language, art, band, Bible, biology, business mathematics, calculus, calculus-AP, chemistry, Christian education, Christian studies, civics, computer applications, computer education, computer skills, current events, desktop publishing, drama, English, English-AP, ensembles, foreign language, French, geometry, health, keyboarding, math analysis, multimedia, music, Pacific Northwest seminar, photography, physical education, physical science, physics, physics-AP, physiology, pre-algebra, psychology, Spanish, U.S. history, U.S. history-AP, weight training, world history, yearbook.

Graduation Requirements Algebra, arts and fine arts (art, music, dance, drama), Bible, biology, chemistry, civics, English, English composition, English literature, foreign language, geometry, Life of Christ, mathematics, occupational education, physical education (includes health), physics, science, social studies (includes history), U.S. history, Washington State and Northwest History, world history.

Special Academic Programs Advanced Placement exam preparation in 5 subject areas; honors section; independent study; study at local college for college credit; remedial reading and/or remedial writing; programs in English, general development for dyslexic students.

College Placement 47 students graduated in 2005; all went to college, including Bellevue Community College; Highline Community College; Pepperdine University; Seattle Pacific University; University of Washington; Washington State University. Mean SAT verbal: 593, mean SAT math: 565, mean composite ACT: 22. 59% scored over 600 on SAT verbal, 33% scored over 600 on SAT math, 38% scored over 26 on composite ACT.

Student Life Upper grades have specified standards of dress, student council, honor system. Discipline rests primarily with faculty. Attendance at religious services is required.

Tuition and Aid Day student tuition: $7400. Tuition installment plan (FACTS Tuition Payment Plan, monthly payment plans, individually arranged payment plans). Tuition reduction for siblings, need-based scholarship grants available. In 2005–06, 11% of upper-school students received aid. Total amount of financial aid awarded in 2005–06: $72,601.

Admissions Traditional secondary-level entrance grade is 9. For fall 2005, 28 students applied for upper-level admission, 26 were accepted, 24 enrolled. Admissions testing required. Deadline for receipt of application materials: none. Application fee required: $25. On-campus interview required.

Athletics Interscholastic: baseball (boys), basketball (b,g), cheering (g), cross-country running (b,g), golf (b,g), soccer (b,g), softball (g), track and field (b,g), volleyball (g); coed interscholastic: cross-country running; coed intramural: archery, badminton, ball hockey, baseball, basketball, combined training, field hockey, floor hockey, juggling, lacrosse, softball, strength & conditioning, touch football, weight training, whiffle ball. 1 PE instructor, 11 coaches.

Computers Computers are regularly used in art, computer applications, desktop publishing, keyboarding, library, multimedia, science, social studies, yearbook classes. Computer network features include campus e-mail, on-campus library services, CD-ROMs, online commercial services, Internet access, DVD.

Contact Fran Hubeek, Admissions Coordinator. 206-246-8241 Ext. 1301. Fax: 206-246-9066. E-mail: admissions@seattlechristian.org. Web site: www.seattlechristian.org.

SECOND BAPTIST SCHOOL

6410 Woodway Drive
Houston, Texas 77057
Head of School: Dr. J. Brett Jacobsen

General Information Coeducational day college-preparatory and religious studies school, affiliated with Baptist Church. Grades PK–12. Founded: 1946. Setting: suburban. 42-acre campus. 4 buildings on campus. Approved or accredited by Accreditation Commission of the Texas Association of Baptist Schools, Southern Association of Colleges and Schools, Texas Education Agency, and Texas Department of Education. Upper school average class size: 15.

Upper School Student Profile 65% of students are Baptist.

Faculty In upper school: 49 have advanced degrees.

Subjects Offered 3-dimensional art, Advanced Placement courses, algebra, American literature, anatomy and physiology, art, art-AP, band, Bible, biology, biology-AP, British literature, British literature-AP, broadcasting, calculus, calculus-AP, chemistry, chemistry-AP, choir, computer programming, computer programming-AP, computer science, computer science-AP, concert band, concert choir, debate, desktop publishing, drama, economics, English, English-AP, European history-AP, French, French language-AP, French literature-AP, geometry, government, health, honors algebra, honors geometry, jazz ensemble, journalism, Latin, marching band, music theory-AP, photography, physical education, physics, physics-AP, pre-calculus, Spanish, Spanish language-AP, Spanish literature-AP, speech, statistics-AP, U.S. history, U.S. history-AP, world geography, world history.

Graduation Requirements Arts and fine arts (art, music, dance, drama), Bible, computer science, economics, electives, English, foreign language, government, mathematics, physical education (includes health), science, social studies (includes history), speech.

Special Academic Programs Advanced Placement exam preparation in 17 subject areas; honors section; accelerated programs; independent study; term-away projects; study at local college for college credit; study abroad.

College Placement 76 students graduated in 2005; all went to college, including Baylor University; Rice University; Texas A&M University; Texas Christian University; The University of Texas at Austin; Washington State University. Mean SAT verbal: 592, mean SAT math: 612, mean composite ACT: 24. 47% scored over 600 on SAT verbal, 53% scored over 600 on SAT math, 31% scored over 26 on composite ACT.

Student Life Upper grades have specified standards of dress, student council. Discipline rests primarily with faculty. Attendance at religious services is required.

Tuition and Aid Day student tuition: $11,892. Tuition installment plan (monthly payment plans). Tuition reduction for siblings, merit scholarship grants, need-based scholarship grants available. In 2005–06, 20% of upper-school students received aid; total upper-school merit-scholarship money awarded: $15,000. Total amount of financial aid awarded in 2005–06: $200,000.

Admissions Traditional secondary-level entrance grade is 9. For fall 2005, 80 students applied for upper-level admission, 48 were accepted, 22 enrolled. ISEE and writing sample required. Deadline for receipt of application materials: none. Application fee required: $50. Interview required.

Athletics Interscholastic: baseball (boys), basketball (b,g), cross-country running (b,g), diving (b,g), drill team (g), fitness (b,g), football (b), golf (b,g); coed interscholastic: cheering. 9 PE instructors, 37 coaches, 2 trainers.

Computers Computers are regularly used in all academic classes. Computer network features include campus e-mail, on-campus library services, CD-ROMs, online commercial services, Internet access, file transfer, office computer access, DVD, wireless campus network, science student interactive programs and computer-based labs.

Contact Mrs. Diane VanZandt, Director of Admissions. 713-365-2314. Fax: 713-365-2445. E-mail: dvanzandt@sbseagles.org. Web site: www.sbseagles.org.

SEDBERGH SCHOOL

810 côte Azélie
Montebello, Quebec J0V 1L0, Canada
Head of School: Jeremy McLean

petersons.com

General Information Coeducational boarding and day college-preparatory and outdoor education school. Grades 7–12. Founded: 1939. Setting: rural. Nearest major city is Ottawa, ON, Canada. Students are housed in single-sex dormitories. 1,200-acre campus. 3 buildings on campus. Approved or accredited by Canadian Association of Independent Schools, Canadian Educational Standards Institute, Québec Association of Independent Schools, The Association of Boarding Schools, and Quebec Department of Education. Language of instruction: English. Total enrollment: 83. Upper school average class size: 12. Upper school faculty-student ratio: 1:5.

Upper School Student Profile Grade 9: 14 students (8 boys, 6 girls); Grade 10: 19 students (11 boys, 8 girls); Grade 11: 17 students (12 boys, 5 girls); Grade 12: 13 students (6 boys, 7 girls). 87% of students are boarding students. 30% are province residents. 7 provinces are represented in upper school student body. 35% are international students. International students from Bahamas, Hong Kong, Japan, Mexico, Senegal, and Taiwan; 6 other countries represented in student body.

Faculty School total: 25. In upper school: 10 men, 9 women; 6 have advanced degrees; 15 reside on campus.

Subjects Offered Algebra, art, biology, calculus, Canadian literature, character education, chemistry, communication skills, conflict resolution, contemporary issues, creative writing, decision making skills, earth science, economics, economics and history, English, English literature, environmental education, environmental geography, environmental science, environmental studies, ESL, ethics, expository writing, French, geography, geology, geometry, grammar, health and wellness, history, home economics, linear algebra, marine biology, mathematics, outdoor education, physical education, physics, physiology, science, senior thesis, social science, social studies, trigonometry, world history.

Graduation Requirements English, environmental studies, French, history, mathematics, physical education (includes health), science, province-wide exams.

Special Academic Programs Independent study; term-away projects; study abroad; remedial reading and/or remedial writing; remedial math; programs in English, mathematics, general development for dyslexic students; ESL (10 students enrolled).

College Placement 14 students graduated in 2005; 13 went to college, including Ottawa University; Queen's University at Kingston; St. Francis Xavier University; The University of Western Ontario; University of Calgary; University of Toronto. Other: 1 went to work.

Student Life Upper grades have uniform requirement, student council, honor system. Discipline rests equally with students and faculty.

Tuition and Aid Day student tuition: CAN$13,500; 5-day tuition and room/board: CAN$31,950; 7-day tuition and room/board: CAN$31,950. Tuition installment plan (monthly payment plans). Tuition reduction for siblings, bursaries, merit scholarship grants, need-based scholarship grants available. In 2005–06, 25% of upper-school students received aid; total upper-school merit-scholarship money awarded: CAN$50,000. Total amount of financial aid awarded in 2005–06: CAN$250,000.

Admissions Traditional secondary-level entrance grade is 9. For fall 2005, 35 students applied for upper-level admission, 25 were accepted, 20 enrolled. Secondary Level English Proficiency and SLEP for foreign students required. Deadline for receipt of application materials: none. No application fee required. Interview required.

Athletics Coed Interscholastic: canoeing/kayaking, kayaking, mountain biking, nordic skiing, rugby, running, skiing (cross-country), soccer; coed intramural: alpine skiing, back packing, badminton, ball hockey, baseball, basketball, bicycling, billiards, broomball, canoeing/kayaking, climbing, combined training, cross-country running, fishing, fitness, flag football, floor hockey, Frisbee, hiking/backpacking, hockey, ice hockey, ice skating, jogging, kayaking, mountain biking, nordic skiing, outdoor activities, outdoor adventure, outdoor education, outdoor recreation, outdoor skills, outdoors, paddling, physical fitness, power lifting, rock climbing, rugby, running, skateboarding, skiing (cross-country), skiing (downhill), snowboarding, snowshoeing, soccer, softball, strength & conditioning, swimming and diving, tennis, touch football, ultimate Frisbee, volleyball, wall climbing, weight lifting, weight training, wilderness survival, yoga.

Computers Computers are regularly used in all academic classes. Computer network features include campus e-mail, CD-ROMs, online commercial services, Internet access, file transfer, wireless campus network.

Contact Ms. Joanna A. A. Hoad, Assistant Headmaster, Enrollment and Advancement. 819-423-5523. Fax: 819-423-5769. E-mail: jhoad@sedbergh.com. Web site: www.sedbergh.com.

ANNOUNCEMENT FROM THE SCHOOL Sedbergh is a coeducational, university-preparatory boarding and day school for students in grades 7–12. Situated on 1,200 acres of woodlands and fields, Sedbergh's location provides unique opportunities for educational success and personal growth. Sedbergh offers an education that expands beyond the classroom to challenge students academically, socially, and physically. To ensure that all students are engaged in their own learning, Sedbergh teachers use traditional and experiential methods to deliver instruction. The integrated curriculum enables students to study major themes across more than one discipline. This student-directed approach also teaches individuals responsibility and teamwork as they progress through projects and assignments. The cocurricular program at Sedbergh School focuses heavily on outdoor skills, wilderness trips, and activities that incorporate teamwork, physical activity, and environmental awareness. Mountain biking, canoeing, kayaking, rock climbing, boarding, and downhill and cross-country skiing all take place within walking distance of the main school building. Arts activities, including nature photography, pottery, woodworking, and painting, are also available. Team skills and sportsmanship are developed by playing soccer and rugby. Volleyball, basketball, badminton, and squash are also available in the newly built gymnasium and student activity center. The qualified, caring, and experienced faculty provides Sedbergh's 90 students with a family atmosphere in a pristine outdoor environment. With a 100% university entrance success rate, Sedbergh graduates are not only academically well prepared but they also possess the necessary life skills to make an effective and positive contribution to the global society. Students discover a school of textbooks and tents, pens and paddles, computers and Canadian wilderness. Learning is everywhere.

SEISEN INTERNATIONAL SCHOOL

12-15 Yoga 1-chome, Setagaya-ku
Tokyo 158-0097, Japan
Head of School: Ms. Virginia Villegas

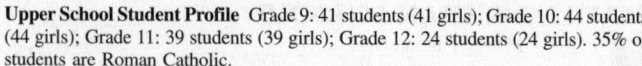

General Information Coeducational day (boys' only in lower grades) college-preparatory school, affiliated with Roman Catholic Church. Boys grade K, girls grades K–12. Founded: 1962. Setting: urban. 1-hectare campus. 3 buildings on campus. Approved or accredited by East Asia Regional Council of Schools, European Council of International Schools, International Baccalaureate Organization, Ministry of Education, Japan, National Catholic Education Association, and New England Association of Schools and Colleges. Member of Secondary School Admission Test Board. Language of instruction: English. Total enrollment: 693. Upper school average class size: 20. Upper school faculty-student ratio: 1:6.

Upper School Student Profile Grade 9: 41 students (41 girls); Grade 10: 44 students (44 girls); Grade 11: 39 students (39 girls); Grade 12: 24 students (24 girls). 35% of students are Roman Catholic.

Faculty School total: 81. In upper school: 12 men, 32 women; 29 have advanced degrees.

Subjects Offered 3-dimensional art, algebra, American literature, art, biology, business, calculus, chemistry, choir, computer graphics, computer science, dance, drama, English, English literature, environmental science, ESL, European history, French, geography, geometry, history, information technology, integrated math, integrated science, Japanese, journalism, library assistant, math methods, mathematics, model United Nations, music, music performance, physical education, physics, pottery, psychology, religion, science, social science, social studies, Spanish, speech, theory of knowledge, trigonometry, visual arts, world history, world literature, yearbook.

Graduation Requirements Arts and fine arts (art, music, dance, drama), computers, English, foreign language, mathematics, physical education (includes health), religion (includes Bible studies and theology), science, social studies (includes history).

Special Academic Programs International Baccalaureate program; honors section; independent study; ESL (20 students enrolled).

College Placement 32 students graduated in 2005; all went to college, including Boston University; Brown University; Parsons The New School for Design; Stanford University; University of California, Los Angeles; University of California, Santa Barbara. Mean SAT verbal: 479, mean SAT math: 616. 23% scored over 600 on SAT verbal, 51% scored over 600 on SAT math.

Student Life Upper grades have uniform requirement, student council. Discipline rests primarily with faculty.

Summer Programs Remediation, ESL programs offered; session focuses on high school remedial work only; held on campus; accepts girls; not open to students from other schools. 15 students usually enrolled. 2006 schedule: June 12 to June 30. Application deadline: May.

Tuition and Aid Day student tuition: ¥1,940,000. Need-based scholarship grants available. In 2005–06, 3% of upper-school students received aid.

Admissions Traditional secondary-level entrance grade is 9. For fall 2005, 65 students applied for upper-level admission, 33 were accepted, 30 enrolled. Admissions testing required. Deadline for receipt of application materials: none. No application fee required. On-campus interview required.

Athletics Interscholastic: badminton, basketball, cross-country running, netball, running, softball, swimming and diving, tennis, track and field, volleyball; intramural: badminton, ballet, basketball, dance, modern dance, running, self defense, swimming and diving, table tennis, volleyball, yoga.

Computers Computers are regularly used in art, business studies, design, English, graphic design, journalism, mathematics, music, science, social studies, yearbook classes. Computer network features include campus e-mail, on-campus library services, CD-ROMs, online commercial services, Internet access, file transfer, DVD, wireless campus network.

Contact Ms. Virginia Villegas, School Head. 81-3-3704-2661. Fax: 81-3-3701-1033. E-mail: sisadmissions@seisen.com. Web site: www.seisen.com.

See full description on page 1058.

SELWYN HOUSE SCHOOL

95 chemin Côte St-Antoine
Westmount, Quebec H3Y 2H8, Canada
Head of School: William Mitchell

General Information Boys' day college-preparatory, bilingual studies, and technology school. Grades K–11. Founded: 1908. Setting: urban. Nearest major city is Montreal, Canada. 21-acre campus. 3 buildings on campus. Approved or accredited by Canadian Association of Independent Schools, Canadian Educational Standards Institute, Quebec Association of Independent Schools, and Quebec Department of Education. Affiliate member of National Association of Independent Schools; member of Secondary School Admission Test Board. Languages of instruction: English and French. Endowment: CAN$2.7 million. Total enrollment: 570. Upper school average class size: 15. Upper school faculty-student ratio: 1:9.

Upper School Student Profile Grade 9: 68 students (68 boys); Grade 10: 61 students (61 boys); Grade 11: 54 students (54 boys).

Faculty School total: 65. In upper school: 22 men, 13 women; 19 have advanced degrees.

Subjects Offered Algebra, art, art appreciation, art history, biology, calculus, Canadian geography, Canadian history, Canadian literature, chemistry, computer applications, computer education, computer graphics, computer information systems, computer keyboarding, computer literacy, computer multimedia, computer programming, computer science, computer skills, debate, earth science, ecology, economics, English, English literature, European history, expository writing, film, French, French as a second language, geography, geometry, golf, health, history, integrated science, introduction to technology, Japanese, jazz band, jazz ensemble, keyboarding, law, mathematics, media, music, music appreciation, outdoor education, photography, physical education, physical fitness, physics, public speaking, robotics, self-defense, social studies, Spanish, theater, world geography, world history, world issues, writing, yearbook.

Graduation Requirements English, French, history, mathematics, physical science.
Special Academic Programs Honors section.
College Placement 54 students graduated in 2005; all went to college, including Choate Rosemary Hall; Kent School; Phillips Exeter Academy; St. Paul's School; The Hotchkiss School.
Student Life Upper grades have uniform requirement, student council, honor system. Discipline rests primarily with faculty.
Summer Programs Sports programs offered; session focuses on basketball, football, and rock-climbing camps, hockey school, and cycling trip; held both on and off campus; held at Quebec, Canada; accepts boys; open to students from other schools. 2006 schedule: June 20 to August 30. Application deadline: May 1.
Tuition and Aid Day student tuition: CAN$14,360. Guaranteed tuition plan. Tuition installment plan (monthly payment plans, individually arranged payment plans, 2- or 4-installment plans, credit card payment). Bursaries, merit scholarship grants, need-based scholarship grants, full (three-year) merit-based scholarship to a new grade 9 student, staff benefits available. In 2005–06, 22% of upper-school students received aid; total upper-school merit-scholarship money awarded: CAN$34,300. Total amount of financial aid awarded in 2005–06: CAN$141,140.
Admissions For fall 2005, 20 students applied for upper-level admission, 9 were accepted, 8 enrolled. English, French, and math proficiency required. Deadline for receipt of application materials: October 15. Application fee required: CAN$125. On-campus interview required.
Athletics Interscholastic: baseball, basketball, cross-country running, curling, football, golf, ice hockey, rock climbing, rugby, skiing (cross-country), soccer, tennis, track and field, wrestling; intramural: badminton, ball hockey, fitness, golf, ice hockey, rowing, rugby, skiing (cross-country), soccer, tennis, track and field, weight lifting. 6 PE instructors, 6 coaches.
Computers Computers are regularly used in all classes. Computer network features include campus e-mail, on-campus library services, CD-ROMs, online commercial services, Internet access, file transfer, office computer access, DVD, wireless campus network, laptop program.
Contact Sylvie Bastien-Doss, Director of Admission. 514-931-2775. Fax: 514-932-8776. E-mail: admission@selwyn.ca. Web site: www.selwyn.ca/.

ANNOUNCEMENT FROM THE SCHOOL Selwyn House School, an independent day school for boys (kindergarten–grade 11), provides a thorough academic curriculum in preparation for university entrance, as well as challenging athletic and extracurricular programmes. Elementary school (K–6) offers a bilingual and a French immersion programme. Each student is encouraged to work to the best of his ability and to develop a strong sense of responsibility toward the school community and his studies. The new ACCESS Laptop Programme ensures that secondary school students have their own laptop for use in school and at home. The programme also provides in-school use of laptops for K–6 students. Scholarships and financial aid are available.

SEOUL FOREIGN SCHOOL

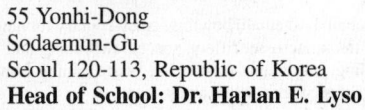 

55 Yonhi-Dong
Sodaemun-Gu
Seoul 120-113, Republic of Korea
Head of School: Dr. Harlan E. Lyso

General Information Coeducational day college-preparatory and International Baccalaureate school, affiliated with Christian faith. Grades PK–12. Founded: 1912. Setting: urban. 25-acre campus. 8 buildings on campus. Approved or accredited by International Baccalaureate Organization and Western Association of Schools and Colleges. Affiliate member of National Association of Independent Schools; member of European Council of International Schools. Language of instruction: English. Endowment: $2.7 million. Total enrollment: 1,338. Upper school average class size: 18. Upper school faculty-student ratio: 1:10.
Upper School Student Profile Grade 9: 96 students (51 boys, 45 girls); Grade 10: 91 students (50 boys, 41 girls); Grade 11: 84 students (39 boys, 45 girls); Grade 12: 80 students (35 boys, 45 girls). 80% of students are Christian faith.
Faculty School total: 125. In upper school: 14 men, 22 women; 29 have advanced degrees.
Subjects Offered Algebra, American history, American literature, art, art history, Bible studies, biology, calculus, chemistry, computer science, creative writing, drama, earth science, economics, English, English literature, ESL, ethics, European history, expository writing, French, geography, health, integrated mathematics, Korean, Korean culture, mathematics, music, philosophy, photography, physical education, physics, psychology, religion, Spanish, speech, theology, theory of knowledge, world history, world literature.
Graduation Requirements Arts and fine arts (art, music, dance, drama), biology, English, foreign language, Korean culture, mathematics, physical education (includes health), physical science, religion (includes Bible studies and theology), social studies (includes history).
Special Academic Programs International Baccalaureate program; Advanced Placement exam preparation in 2 subject areas; honors section; academic accommodation for the gifted, the musically talented, and the artistically talented; ESL (16 students enrolled).

College Placement 85 students graduated in 2005; 81 went to college, including Boston College; New York University; Parsons The New School for Design; University of Michigan; University of Pennsylvania; Wellesley College. Other: 1 went to work, 1 entered military service, 2 entered a postgraduate year. Mean SAT verbal: 600, mean SAT math: 640. 59% scored over 600 on SAT verbal, 73% scored over 600 on SAT math.
Student Life Upper grades have specified standards of dress, student council. Discipline rests primarily with faculty.
Tuition and Aid Day student tuition: $20,380. Tuition installment plan (2-payment plan with final payment due in January). Need-based scholarship grants available. In 2005–06, 3% of upper-school students received aid. Total amount of financial aid awarded in 2005–06: $60,000.
Admissions Traditional secondary-level entrance grade is 9. For fall 2005, 91 students applied for upper-level admission, 71 were accepted, 66 enrolled. Deadline for receipt of application materials: none. Application fee required: $230. On-campus interview required.
Athletics Interscholastic: basketball (boys, girls), cheering (b,g), cross-country running (b,g), soccer (b,g), swimming and diving (b,g), tennis (b,g), volleyball (b,g); coed intramural: badminton, lacrosse, weight lifting. 2 PE instructors.
Computers Computers are regularly used in English, history, mathematics, music, science classes. Computer network features include on-campus library services, CD-ROMs, Internet access, wireless campus network.
Contact Mrs. Esther Myong, Admissions Director. 822-330-3100 Ext. 121. Fax: 822-335-2045. E-mail: admissions@sfs.or.kr. Web site: www.sfs.or.kr.

ANNOUNCEMENT FROM THE SCHOOL Seoul Foreign School provides programs and an atmosphere that develop the body, mind, and spirit. The academically challenging curriculum includes a program that leads to the International Baccalaureate diploma and incorporates advanced educational technological resources. Faculty members are certified, caring, and experienced. The 24-acre campus is located adjacent to a greenbelt near the heart of Seoul.

SEOUL INTERNATIONAL SCHOOL

Songpa, PO Box 47
Seoul 138-600, Republic of Korea
Head of School: Mr. Hyung Shik Kim

General Information Coeducational day college-preparatory and arts school. Grades PK–12. Founded: 1973. Setting: urban. 8-acre campus. 1 building on campus. Approved or accredited by Western Association of Schools and Colleges. Language of instruction: English. Total enrollment: 1,101. Upper school average class size: 19. Upper school faculty-student ratio: 1:13.
Upper School Student Profile Grade 9: 86 students (44 boys, 42 girls); Grade 10: 77 students (41 boys, 36 girls); Grade 11: 86 students (41 boys, 45 girls); Grade 12: 75 students (38 boys, 37 girls).
Faculty School total: 100. In upper school: 22 men, 10 women; 8 have advanced degrees.
Subjects Offered 3-dimensional art, algebra, American history, American literature, art, Asian studies, biology, biology-AP, calculus, chemistry, communications, computer programming, computer science, drama, drawing, earth science, economics, English, English literature, environmental science-AP, ESL, European history, French, general science, geometry, health, history, journalism, mathematics, music, musical theater, physical education, physical science, physics, psychology, science, social science, social studies, Spanish, world history, world literature, writing.
Graduation Requirements English, mathematics, physical education (includes health), science, social studies (includes history).
Special Academic Programs Advanced Placement exam preparation in 13 subject areas; academic accommodation for the musically talented and the artistically talented; remedial reading and/or remedial writing; ESL (64 students enrolled).
College Placement 78 students graduated in 2005; all went to college, including Carnegie Mellon University; New York University; Syracuse University; University of Pennsylvania; Wellesley College. Mean SAT verbal: 642, mean SAT math: 741.
Student Life Upper grades have specified standards of dress, student council, honor system. Discipline rests primarily with faculty.
Tuition and Aid Day student tuition: $15,700. Tuition installment plan (individually arranged payment plans). Need-based scholarship grants available. In 2005–06, 1% of upper-school students received aid. Total amount of financial aid awarded in 2005–06: $45,000.
Admissions Traditional secondary-level entrance grade is 9. For fall 2005, 42 students applied for upper-level admission, 37 were accepted, 32 enrolled. Gates MacGinite Reading Tests, Math Placement Exam and Oral and Written Language Scales required. Deadline for receipt of application materials: April 30. Application fee required: $350. On-campus interview required.
Athletics Interscholastic: basketball (boys, girls), cross-country running (b,g), soccer (b,g), swimming and diving (b,g), tennis (b,g), volleyball (b,g); coed interscholastic: cheering; coed intramural: basketball, indoor soccer, soccer. 3 PE instructors.
Computers Computers are regularly used in English, history, mathematics, science classes. Computer network features include on-campus library services, CD-ROMs, online commercial services, Internet access, online registration.

Contact Mrs. Kyoung Ai Kim, Director of Admissions. 82-31- 750 1200 Ext. 310. Fax: 82-31-759 5133. E-mail: kimka@siskorea.or.kr. Web site: www.siskorea.or.kr.

SETON CATHOLIC CENTRAL HIGH SCHOOL

70 Seminary Avenue
Binghamton, New York 13905
Head of School: Miss Kathleen M. Dwyer

General Information Coeducational day college-preparatory, arts, business, vocational, religious studies, and technology school, affiliated with Roman Catholic Church. Grades 9–12. Founded: 1963. Setting: suburban. Nearest major city is Syracuse. 4-acre campus. 1 building on campus. Approved or accredited by Middle States Association of Colleges and Schools, National Catholic Education Association, New York State Board of Regents, and New York Department of Education. Total enrollment: 380. Upper school average class size: 23. Upper school faculty-student ratio: 1:23.

Upper School Student Profile 90% of students are Roman Catholic.

Faculty School total: 35. In upper school: 19 men, 13 women; 27 have advanced degrees.

Subjects Offered 3-dimensional design, accounting, advanced computer applications, Advanced Placement courses, advertising design, algebra, alternative physical education, American government, American history-AP, American legal systems, American literature, American literature-AP, ancient world history, applied music, architectural drawing, art-AP, band, Bible, biology, biology-AP, business, business law, business mathematics, calculus, calculus-AP, chemistry, chemistry-AP, chorus, Christian scripture, church history, comparative religion, computer applications, computer programming, computer programming-AP, creative drama, criminal justice, dramatic arts, economics, English, English language and composition-AP, English literature and composition-AP, entrepreneurship, environmental science, ethical decision making, ethics and responsibility, European history-AP, food and nutrition, foreign language, forensic science, French, government/civics, guitar, health, honors English, honors geometry, instrumental music, integrated mathematics, keyboarding/computer, Latin, Latin-AP, law and the legal system, literature and composition-AP, math applications, mathematics-AP, music theater, music theory, performing arts, photography, physical education, physics, physics-AP, pre-algebra, religions, social psychology, Spanish, Spanish-AP, studio art-AP, theater arts, theology, U.S. history, U.S. history-AP, wood processing, work-study, world history-AP, world religions.

Graduation Requirements Arts and fine arts (art, music, dance, drama), English, foreign language, mathematics, physical education (includes health), science, social studies (includes history), theology.

Special Academic Programs Advanced Placement exam preparation in 12 subject areas; honors section; study at local college for college credit; academic accommodation for the gifted; remedial reading and/or remedial writing; remedial math.

College Placement 101 students graduated in 2005; 99 went to college, including Nazareth College of Rochester; Rochester Institute of Technology; St. Bonaventure University; State University of New York at Binghamton; The University of Scranton. Other: 2 entered military service. Mean SAT verbal: 557, mean SAT math: 542.

Student Life Upper grades have specified standards of dress, student council, honor system. Discipline rests primarily with faculty.

Summer Programs Enrichment, sports programs offered; held on campus; accepts boys and girls; open to students from other schools. 200 students usually enrolled.

Tuition and Aid Tuition installment plan (FACTS Tuition Payment Plan). Tuition reduction for siblings, merit scholarship grants, need-based scholarship grants available. In 2005–06, 40% of upper-school students received aid.

Admissions Traditional secondary-level entrance grade is 9. High School Placement Test required. Application fee required: $25. Interview required.

Athletics Interscholastic: baseball (boys), basketball (b,g), cross-country running (b,g), football (b), ice hockey (b), indoor track & field (b,g), lacrosse (b,g), soccer (b,g), tennis (b,g), track and field (b,g), winter (indoor) track (b,g); intramural: snowboarding (b,g), strength & conditioning (b,g), weight training (b,g); coed interscholastic: cheering; coed intramural: alpine skiing. 2 PE instructors, 25 coaches, 1 trainer.

Computers Computers are regularly used in all academic, desktop publishing, keyboarding, yearbook classes. Computer network features include on-campus library services, CD-ROMs, online commercial services, Internet access, office computer access, DVD, wireless campus network.

Contact Guidance Office. 607-723-5307. Fax: 607-723-4811. E-mail: SeCathB@syrdiocese.org. Web site: www.setoncchs.com.

SETON HALL PREPARATORY SCHOOL

120 Northfield Avenue
West Orange, New Jersey 07052
Head of School: Rev. Msgr. Michael Kelly

General Information Boys' day college-preparatory and religious studies school, affiliated with Roman Catholic Church. Grades 9–12. Founded: 1856. Setting: suburban. Nearest major city is Newark. 55-acre campus. 2 buildings on campus.

Approved or accredited by Middle States Association of Colleges and Schools. Endowment: $9.5 million. Total enrollment: 970. Upper school average class size: 18. Upper school faculty-student ratio: 1:14.

Upper School Student Profile Grade 9: 261 students (261 boys); Grade 10: 252 students (252 boys); Grade 11: 235 students (235 boys); Grade 12: 222 students (222 boys). 82% of students are Roman Catholic.

Faculty School total: 80. In upper school: 65 men, 15 women; 67 have advanced degrees.

Subjects Offered Algebra, American literature, band, Bible studies, biology, biology-AP, calculus, calculus-AP, Catholic belief and practice, chemistry, chemistry-AP, church history, classical studies, computer programming, computer science, computer science-AP, creative writing, drawing, driver education, ecology, economics, English, English language and composition-AP, English literature, English literature and composition-AP, environmental science, environmental science-AP, epic literature, film, French, geometry, global studies, health, honors algebra, honors English, honors geometry, honors U.S. history, honors world history, Italian, Latin, leadership training, literature, macro/microeconomics-AP, mathematics, modern European history, modern European history-AP, music, music history, music theory, music theory-AP, organic chemistry, photography, physical education, physics, science, Spanish, Spanish language-AP, Spanish-AP, speech, statistics-AP, studio art-AP, theater arts, theology, U.S. history, U.S. history-AP, video film production, world history.

Graduation Requirements Arts and fine arts (art, music, dance, drama), English, foreign language, mathematics, physical education (includes health), religion (includes Bible studies and theology), science, social studies (includes history). Community service is required.

Special Academic Programs Advanced Placement exam preparation in 16 subject areas; honors section; independent study.

College Placement 194 students graduated in 2005; all went to college, including Rutgers, The State University of New Jersey, Rutgers College; Seton Hall University; The Pennsylvania State University University Park Campus; The University of Scranton; University of Maryland, College Park; Villanova University. Median SAT verbal: 570, median SAT math: 600. 75% scored over 600 on SAT verbal, 90% scored over 600 on SAT math.

Student Life Upper grades have specified standards of dress, student council. Discipline rests primarily with faculty. Attendance at religious services is required.

Summer Programs Remediation, enrichment, computer instruction programs offered; session focuses on enrichment; held on campus; accepts boys; not open to students from other schools. 130 students usually enrolled. 2006 schedule: June 12 to July 21. Application deadline: May 5.

Tuition and Aid Day student tuition: $9700. Tuition installment plan (monthly payment plans, 3 in-house plans). Merit scholarship grants, need-based scholarship grants available. In 2005–06, 40% of upper-school students received aid; total upper-school merit-scholarship money awarded: $330,000. Total amount of financial aid awarded in 2005–06: $1,100,000.

Admissions Traditional secondary-level entrance grade is 9. For fall 2005, 558 students applied for upper-level admission, 404 were accepted, 261 enrolled. SHP Entrance Test required. Deadline for receipt of application materials: January 7. Application fee required: $40.

Athletics Interscholastic: baseball, basketball, bowling, cross-country running, football, golf, ice hockey, indoor track, lacrosse, riflery, soccer, swimming and diving, tennis, track and field, wrestling; intramural: basketball, bocce, skiing (downhill), volleyball, weight lifting. 5 PE instructors, 48 coaches, 1 trainer.

Computers Computers are regularly used in art, economics, English, history, mathematics, music, science, Spanish, speech, theater arts classes. Computer network features include on-campus library services, CD-ROMs, online commercial services, Internet access, DVD, interlibrary loan program, online newspaper, magazine, and encyclopedia services.

Contact Mr. Matthew F. Cannizzo, Director of Admission. 973-325-6632. Fax: 973-325-6652. E-mail: mcannizzo@shp.org. Web site: www.shp.org.

THE SEVEN HILLS SCHOOL

5400 Red Bank Road
Cincinnati, Ohio 45227
Head of School: Ms. Sandra J. Theunick

petersons.com

General Information Coeducational day college-preparatory, arts, and technology school. Grades PK–12. Founded: 1974. Setting: suburban. 35-acre campus. 16 buildings on campus. Approved or accredited by Independent Schools Association of the Central States. Member of National Association of Independent Schools and Secondary School Admission Test Board. Endowment: $14 million. Total enrollment: 1,070. Upper school average class size: 15. Upper school faculty-student ratio: 1:9.

Upper School Student Profile Grade 9: 76 students (38 boys, 38 girls); Grade 10: 80 students (40 boys, 40 girls); Grade 11: 78 students (38 boys, 40 girls); Grade 12: 81 students (38 boys, 43 girls).

Faculty School total: 130. In upper school: 23 men, 28 women; 32 have advanced degrees.

Subjects Offered Acting, advanced computer applications, Advanced Placement courses, African-American studies, algebra, American history, American literature, ancient history, art, art history, biology, British literature, calculus, ceramics,

chemistry, comparative religion, computer programming, computer science, economics, English, European history, fine arts, French, geometry, journalism, Latin, linear algebra, medieval/Renaissance history, Middle Eastern history, modern political theory, music, physical education, physics, pre-calculus, psychology, Spanish, speech, theater, world history, world literature, writing.

Graduation Requirements Algebra, arts and fine arts (art, music, dance, drama), biology, chemistry, computer science, English, foreign language, geometry, performing arts, physical education (includes health), physics, U.S. history, U.S. literature, completion of a personal challenge project, successfully pass writing competency exam, 30 hours of community service.

Special Academic Programs Advanced Placement exam preparation in 14 subject areas; honors section; independent study; term-away projects; academic accommodation for the gifted.

College Placement 82 students graduated in 2005; all went to college, including Boston College; Kenyon College; Northwestern University; Princeton University; Stanford University; University of Michigan. Median SAT verbal: 650, median SAT math: 665. 76% scored over 600 on SAT verbal, 76% scored over 600 on SAT math.

Student Life Upper grades have specified standards of dress, student council. Discipline rests primarily with faculty.

Summer Programs Session focuses on SAT review, sports clinics, and acting workshop; held on campus; accepts boys and girls; open to students from other schools. 470 students usually enrolled. 2006 schedule: June 14 to August 4. Application deadline: none.

Tuition and Aid Day student tuition: $15,490. Tuition installment plan (monthly payment plans, individually arranged payment plans). Need-based scholarship grants available. In 2005–06, 20% of upper-school students received aid. Total amount of financial aid awarded in 2005–06: $570,000.

Admissions Traditional secondary-level entrance grade is 9. For fall 2005, 50 students applied for upper-level admission, 25 were accepted, 18 enrolled. ISEE required. Deadline for receipt of application materials: December 1. Application fee required: $50. On-campus interview required.

Athletics Interscholastic: baseball (boys), basketball (b,g), cheering (g), cross-country running (b,g), golf (b), gymnastics (g), lacrosse (b,g), soccer (b,g), softball (g), swimming and diving (b,g), tennis (b,g), volleyball (g); coed interscholastic: track and field. 3 PE instructors, 9 coaches.

Computers Computers are regularly used in foreign language, mathematics, science classes. Computer network features include on-campus library services, CD-ROMs, online commercial services, Internet access.

Contact Mr. Peter C. Egan, Director of Admission. 513-271-9027. Fax: 513-271-2471. E-mail: peter.egan@7hills.org. Web site: www.7hills.org.

ANNOUNCEMENT FROM THE SCHOOL Seven Hills School is a nonprofit school with 1,070 students in PK–12 from 65 greater Cincinnati zip codes. The Upper School combines academic rigor, freedom, and accountability. Honors and AP courses are offered in all disciplines along with a wide selection of electives. The School is also widely recognized for its excellence in the fine and performing arts. The 74,000-square-foot Upper School building features 24 classrooms that support wired and wireless technologies, 6 state-of-the-art science labs, and a library/media center for grades 6–12. Highly individualized counseling is provided by 3 college counselors, and each student has a faculty adviser. Graduation requirements include community service and the completion of a personal challenge, which is an independent project of each student's own design. Challenge projects foster creative thinking and decision making, encourage students to persevere and go beyond perceived limitations, and give them the satisfaction of personal accomplishment. The 82 members of the class of 2005 received 308 offers from 154 colleges and universities in 35 states. SAT scores for the class of 2005 at the mid-50% were 644 verbal and 658 math. Ninety-two percent of 140 students taking 264 AP exams earned a score of 3 or better, qualifying them for advanced standing in college. Twenty-two percent of the class of 2006 qualified for National Merit/National Achievement recognition. Approximately 85% of those in the Upper School play at least one interscholastic sport. Miami Valley Conference teams include boys' and girls' soccer, basketball, cross-country, swimming, track, and tennis; boys' golf, lacrosse, and baseball; and girls' volleyball, gymnastics, softball, lacrosse, and cheerleading. The School's athletes are consistently selected for All-State, All-City, and All-League honors. Facilities include 2 gyms, an all-weather track, and a weight training area.

SEVERN SCHOOL

201 Water Street
Severna Park, Maryland 21146
Head of School: William Creeden

General Information Coeducational day college-preparatory, arts, and technology school. Grades 6–12. Founded: 1914. Setting: suburban. Nearest major city is Annapolis. 19-acre campus. 8 buildings on campus. Approved or accredited by Association of Independent Maryland Schools, Middle States Association of Colleges and Schools, and Maryland Department of Education. Member of National Asso-

ciation of Independent Schools and Secondary School Admission Test Board. Endowment: $4 million. Total enrollment: 592. Upper school average class size: 15. Upper school faculty-student ratio: 1:12.

Upper School Student Profile Grade 6: 109 students (47 boys, 62 girls); Grade 9: 109 students (47 boys, 62 girls); Grade 10: 96 students (49 boys, 47 girls); Grade 11: 91 students (48 boys, 43 girls); Grade 12: 101 students (42 boys, 59 girls).

Faculty School total: 72. In upper school: 24 men, 23 women; 27 have advanced degrees.

Subjects Offered Algebra, American history, American literature, art, biology, calculus, ceramics, chemistry, community service, computer programming, computer science, CPR, creative writing, dance, desktop publishing, digital art, digital imaging, digital photography, discrete math, drama, drama performance, dramatic arts, drawing, drawing and design, earth science, ecology, economics, economics-AP, English, English literature, environmental science, environmental systems, European civilization, European history, European history-AP, expository writing, fine arts, forensics, French, French language-AP, French literature-AP, geometry, government/civics, grammar, graphic arts, health, history, journalism, Latin, marine biology, mathematics, multimedia, music, photography, physical education, physics, psychology, science, social studies, Spanish, speech, theater, trigonometry, world history, world literature, writing.

Graduation Requirements Arts and fine arts (art, music, dance, drama), computer science, CPR, English, foreign language, mathematics, physical education (includes health), science, social studies (includes history). Community service is required.

Special Academic Programs Advanced Placement exam preparation in 11 subject areas; honors section; independent study; study abroad; academic accommodation for the gifted, the musically talented, and the artistically talented.

College Placement 85 students graduated in 2005; all went to college, including College of Charleston; Elon University; Gettysburg College; Loyola College in Maryland; University of Maryland, College Park; University of Pennsylvania.

Student Life Upper grades have uniform requirement, student council, honor system. Discipline rests equally with students and faculty.

Summer Programs Advancement, sports programs offered; session focuses on advanced math, day camp, and sports camps; held on campus; accepts boys and girls; open to students from other schools. 1000 students usually enrolled. 2006 schedule: June 23 to August 1.

Tuition and Aid Day student tuition: $17,600. Tuition installment plan (Academic Management Services Plan). Need-based scholarship grants available. In 2005–06, 15% of upper-school students received aid. Total amount of financial aid awarded in 2005–06: $904,000.

Admissions Traditional secondary-level entrance grade is 9. For fall 2005, 105 students applied for upper-level admission, 55 were accepted, 44 enrolled. ISEE required. Deadline for receipt of application materials: February 1. Application fee required: $55. On-campus interview required.

Athletics Interscholastic: baseball (boys), basketball (b,g), combined training (b,g), dance team (g), field hockey (g), football (b), lacrosse (b,g), soccer (b,g), tennis (b,g); coed interscholastic: cross-country running, dance, golf, sailing, strength & conditioning, swimming and diving, track and field, weight training; coed intramural: aerobics/dance. 56 coaches, 1 trainer.

Computers Computers are regularly used in all academic classes. Computer network features include campus e-mail, on-campus library services, CD-ROMs, online commercial services, Internet access, office computer access, DVD.

Contact Ellen Murray, Associate Director of Admissions. 410-647-7701 Ext. 266. Fax: 410-544-9451. E-mail: e.murray@severnschool.com. Web site: www. severnschool.com.

ANNOUNCEMENT FROM THE SCHOOL Severn School, a coed day school for grades 6–12 founded in 1914, emphasizes rigorous academics, athletics, and character development. Current enrollment is 586 students. In addition to a strong fine arts program, the Upper School offers lab spaces, opportunities for technological applications, and facilities for library research and independent study. Summer academic, day, and sports camps.

SEWICKLEY ACADEMY

315 Academy Avenue
Sewickley, Pennsylvania 15143
Head of School: Kolia J. O'Connor

General Information Coeducational day college-preparatory, arts, and technology school. Grades PK–12. Founded: 1838. Setting: suburban. Nearest major city is Pittsburgh. 30-acre campus. 10 buildings on campus. Approved or accredited by Middle States Association of Colleges and Schools, Pennsylvania Association of Private Academic Schools, and Pennsylvania Department of Education. Member of National Association of Independent Schools. Endowment: $20 million. Total enrollment: 795. Upper school average class size: 15. Upper school faculty-student ratio: 1:6.

Upper School Student Profile Grade 9: 79 students (41 boys, 38 girls); Grade 10: 78 students (48 boys, 30 girls); Grade 11: 72 students (42 boys, 30 girls); Grade 12: 79 students (41 boys, 38 girls).

Sewickley Academy

Faculty School total: 102. In upper school: 25 men, 26 women; 30 have advanced degrees.

Subjects Offered Accounting, advanced chemistry, Advanced Placement courses, advanced studio art-AP, algebra, American history, American history-AP, American literature, American literature-AP, art, art-AP, astronomy, band, biology, biology-AP, British literature, British literature-AP, calculus, calculus-AP, ceramics, chemistry, chemistry-AP, choral music, chorus, clayworking, computer applications, computer art, computer keyboarding, computer programming, computer science, computer science-AP, concert band, concert choir, contemporary issues, creative writing, dance, dance performance, digital art, drama, drama performance, drama workshop, drawing, driver education, economics, English, English language-AP, English literature, English literature-AP, environmental science, ethics, European history, European history-AP, expository writing, fine arts, French, French language-AP, French literature-AP, geometry, German, German-AP, government/civics, health, health education, history, Italian, keyboarding/computer, literature-AP, music, musical theater, performing arts, philosophy, photography, physical education, physics, physics-AP, pre-calculus, psychology, psychology-AP, senior project, Spanish, Spanish literature, Spanish-AP, speech, speech and debate, statistics, statistics-AP, studio art, theater, trigonometry, U.S. history-AP, U.S. literature, Vietnam War, world history, world literature, writing.

Graduation Requirements Arts and fine arts (art, music, dance, drama), English, foreign language, mathematics, physical education (includes health), science, social studies (includes history), U.S. history, world cultures, world studies. Community service is required.

Special Academic Programs Advanced Placement exam preparation in 17 subject areas; honors section; accelerated programs; independent study; term-away projects; study at local college for college credit; study abroad.

College Placement 76 students graduated in 2005; all went to college, including Carnegie Mellon University; Colby College; Stanford University; The George Washington University; The Pennsylvania State University University Park Campus; Vassar College. Median SAT verbal: 630, median SAT math: 650. 50% scored over 600 on SAT verbal, 50% scored over 600 on SAT math.

Student Life Upper grades have specified standards of dress, student council, honor system. Discipline rests equally with students and faculty.

Summer Programs Remediation, enrichment, sports, art/fine arts, computer instruction programs offered; session focuses on academics, athletics, and musical theater; held on campus; accepts boys and girls; open to students from other schools. 150 students usually enrolled. 2006 schedule: June 17 to July 12. Application deadline: none.

Tuition and Aid Day student tuition: $17,600. Tuition installment plan (monthly payment plans). Need-based scholarship grants available. In 2005–06, 25% of upper-school students received aid. Total amount of financial aid awarded in 2005–06: $700,000.

Admissions Traditional secondary-level entrance grade is 9. For fall 2005, 55 students applied for upper-level admission, 29 were accepted, 19 enrolled. ISEE required. Deadline for receipt of application materials: February 3. Application fee required: $45. On-campus interview required.

Athletics Interscholastic: baseball (boys), basketball (b,g), cheering (g), cross-country running (b,g), diving (b,g), field hockey (g), fitness (b,g), golf (b,g), ice hockey (b,g), indoor track (b,g), jogging (b,g), lacrosse (b,g), modern dance (g), nautilus (b,g), outdoor adventure (b,g), physical fitness (b,g), running (b,g), soccer (b,g), softball (g), tennis (b,g), track and field (b,g); coed interscholastic: cross-country running, fitness, golf, indoor track, jogging, modern dance, nautilus, outdoor adventure, physical fitness, running, swimming and diving; coed intramural: skiing (downhill), volleyball. 4 PE instructors, 2 coaches, 1 trainer.

Computers Computers are regularly used in all academic classes. Computer network features include campus e-mail, on-campus library services, CD-ROMs, Internet access, file transfer, office computer access, wireless campus network.

Contact Priscilla Henry, Admissions Office Assistant. 412-741-2230. Fax: 412-741-1411. E-mail: phenry@sewickley.org. Web site: www.sewickley.org.

SHADY SIDE ACADEMY

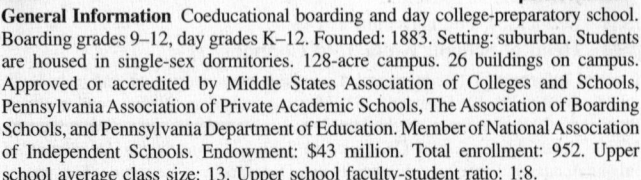

423 Fox Chapel Road
Pittsburgh, Pennsylvania 15238
Head of School: Mr. Thomas N. Southard

General Information Coeducational boarding and day college-preparatory school. Boarding grades 9–12, day grades K–12. Founded: 1883. Setting: suburban. Students are housed in single-sex dormitories. 128-acre campus. 26 buildings on campus. Approved or accredited by Middle States Association of Colleges and Schools, Pennsylvania Association of Private Academic Schools, The Association of Boarding Schools, and Pennsylvania Department of Education. Member of National Association of Independent Schools. Endowment: $43 million. Total enrollment: 952. Upper school average class size: 13. Upper school faculty-student ratio: 1:8.

Upper School Student Profile Grade 9: 124 students (71 boys, 53 girls); Grade 10: 125 students (65 boys, 60 girls); Grade 11: 124 students (59 boys, 65 girls); Grade 12: 126 students (64 boys, 62 girls). 10% of students are boarding students. 99% are state residents. 4 states are represented in upper student body.

Faculty School total: 111. In upper school: 33 men, 27 women; 39 have advanced degrees; 15 reside on campus.

Subjects Offered Advanced Placement courses, algebra, American history, American literature, architectural drawing, architecture, art, art history, Asian studies, biology, calculus, calculus-AP, ceramics, chemistry, Chinese, computer graphics, computer math, computer programming, computer science, computer science-AP, creative writing, drama, driver education, economics, English, English literature, ethics, European history, expository writing, fine arts, French, French-AP, geography, geometry, German, German-AP, health, history, holography, Latin, logic, mathematics, music, philosophy, photography, physical education, physics, science, social studies, Spanish, Spanish-AP, speech, statistics, theater, trigonometry, world history, world literature, writing.

Graduation Requirements Arts and fine arts (art, music, dance, drama), athletics, computer science, English, foreign language, mathematics, physical education (includes health), science, social studies (includes history), CPR certification, participation in five seasons of athletics.

Special Academic Programs Advanced Placement exam preparation in 6 subject areas; honors section; accelerated programs; independent study; term-away projects; study abroad; academic accommodation for the gifted, the musically talented, and the artistically talented.

College Placement 134 students graduated in 2005; all went to college, including Carnegie Mellon University; Columbia College; Denison University; Rensselaer Polytechnic Institute; The George Washington University; The Pennsylvania State University University Park Campus. Mean SAT verbal: 630, mean SAT math: 645.

Student Life Upper grades have specified standards of dress, student council. Discipline rests primarily with faculty.

Summer Programs Remediation, enrichment, advancement, art/fine arts, computer instruction programs offered; session focuses on academic and nonacademic enrichment; held on campus; accepts boys and girls; open to students from other schools. 85 students usually enrolled. 2006 schedule: June 19 to July 28. Application deadline: none.

Tuition and Aid Day student tuition: $19,825; 5-day tuition and room/board: $28,075. Tuition installment plan (Academic Management Services Plan). Tuition reduction for siblings, need-based scholarship grants, merit-based aid (some need required), FAME awards, partial tuition remission for children of full-time employees available. In 2005–06, 15% of upper-school students received aid. Total amount of financial aid awarded in 2005–06: $1,133,636.

Admissions Traditional secondary-level entrance grade is 9. For fall 2005, 149 students applied for upper-level admission, 107 were accepted, 70 enrolled. ISEE, SSAT or TOEFL required. Deadline for receipt of application materials: February 4. Application fee required: $50. On-campus interview required.

Athletics Interscholastic: baseball (boys), basketball (b,g), cross-country running (b,g), field hockey (g), football (b), golf (b,g), ice hockey (b,g), lacrosse (b,g), soccer (b,g), softball (g), squash (b,g), swimming and diving (b,g), tennis (b,g), track and field (b,g), wrestling (b); intramural: cheering (g); coed intramural: back packing, badminton, bowling, cricket, ultimate Frisbee, volleyball, weight lifting. 39 coaches, 2 trainers.

Computers Computers are regularly used in all classes. Computer network features include campus e-mail, on-campus library services, CD-ROMs, online commercial services, Internet access, DVD.

Contact Ms. Katherine H. Mihm, Academy Director of Admission. 412-968-3179. Fax: 412-968-3213. E-mail: kmihm@shadysideacademy.org. Web site: www.shadysideacademy.org.

ANNOUNCEMENT FROM THE SCHOOL Shady Side Academy is Pittsburgh's largest, coeducational, college-preparatory independent school, serving 950 students. Located on 3 campuses in the Pittsburgh region, this community fosters the joy of learning and close student-teacher relationships. The Academy grounds feature a 650-seat theater, blackbox performance space, playing fields, and indoor swimming and hockey centers. Faculty members average 18 years of teaching experience and 66% hold advanced degrees. At the Academy's Junior School (grades K–5), located in Pittsburgh's East End, the curriculum offers broad themes to help children make meaningful connections between subject areas in a stimulating and structured but flexible environment. Children learn basic skills and concepts in an integrated approach. The Middle School (grades 6–8), located in the Pittsburgh suburb of Fox Chapel, is dedicated to the principle that 10- to 14-year-olds thrive in an environment that recognizes their uniqueness as a group and as individuals. With its own faculty and campus, the Middle School addresses students' readiness and needs in a supportive, student-centered environment. At the Senior School (grades 9–12), also located in Fox Chapel, students experience a traditional liberal arts program that helps deepen their understanding of the humanities, math and science, and the arts while they learn to think critically and creatively. In addition, a range of opportunities exists for students to discover talents and experience successes, including 40+ clubs, a strong service-learning program, numerous visual and performing arts options, 26 different sports teams, international exchange partnerships, and independent study. A 5-day boarding program is also available for grades 9–12, offering the best of home and school. Average SAT scores for the class of 2005 were 626 verbal and 641 math. Shady Side Academy has traditionally enjoyed 100 percent college placement among its graduating seniors. The Academy's goal is the balanced development of students' analytical, artistic, and physical abilities; their

ability to reason ethically and to listen carefully; and their ability to speak, write, and read with clarity and precision.

SHANNON FOREST CHRISTIAN SCHOOL

829 Garlington Road
Greenville, South Carolina 29615
Head of School: Ms. Brenda K. Hillman

General Information Coeducational day college-preparatory, religious studies, and technology school, affiliated with Presbyterian Church. Grades PK–12. Founded: 1968. Setting: suburban. 50-acre campus. 3 buildings on campus. Approved or accredited by Association of Christian Schools International and Southern Association of Colleges and Schools. Endowment: $30,600. Total enrollment: 545. Upper school average class size: 17. Upper school faculty-student ratio: 1:17.

Upper School Student Profile Grade 6: 41 students (24 boys, 17 girls); Grade 7: 48 students (26 boys, 22 girls); Grade 8: 36 students (20 boys, 16 girls); Grade 9: 41 students (16 boys, 25 girls); Grade 10: 28 students (17 boys, 11 girls); Grade 11: 22 students (12 boys, 10 girls); Grade 12: 30 students (15 boys, 15 girls). 3% of students are Presbyterian.

Faculty School total: 49. In upper school: 7 men, 14 women; 12 have advanced degrees.

Subjects Offered Algebra, American literature, art, Bible, Bible studies, biology, biology-AP, calculus, calculus-AP, career/college preparation, chemistry, choir, college planning, computer keyboarding, computer science, drama, economics, English, English literature-AP, English-AP, European history-AP, French, geometry, government, health, journalism, literature, music, physical education, physical science, physics, pre-algebra, pre-calculus, psychology, SAT preparation, sociology, Spanish, theater arts, U.S. history, U.S. history-AP, world geography, world history, yearbook.

Graduation Requirements Computer science, English, foreign language, mathematics, physical education (includes health), religion (includes Bible studies and theology), SAT preparation, science, social science, social studies (includes history), annual attendance at two fine arts programs (grades 9—12), 30 hours of community service per year.

Special Academic Programs Advanced Placement exam preparation in 5 subject areas; honors section; programs in English, mathematics, general development for dyslexic students; special instructional classes for students with emotional/behavioral problems, learning disabilities, Attention Deficit Hyperactivity Disorder.

College Placement 20 students graduated in 2005; all went to college, including Anderson University; Clemson University; Converse College; Furman University; United States Naval Academy; University of South Carolina.

Student Life Upper grades have specified standards of dress, student council, honor system. Discipline rests primarily with faculty. Attendance at religious services is required.

Summer Programs Remediation, enrichment programs offered; session focuses on remediation; held on campus; accepts boys and girls; not open to students from other schools. 33 students usually enrolled. 2006 schedule: June 1 to July 31. Application deadline: none.

Tuition and Aid Day student tuition: $7200. Tuition installment plan (FACTS Tuition Payment Plan). Need-based scholarship grants, Scholar Loans available. In 2005–06, 19% of upper-school students received aid. Total amount of financial aid awarded in 2005–06: $32,734.

Admissions Traditional secondary-level entrance grade is 7. For fall 2005, 13 students applied for upper-level admission, 10 were accepted, 10 enrolled. Stanford Achievement Test required. Deadline for receipt of application materials: none. Application fee required: $100. Interview required.

Athletics Interscholastic: baseball (boys), basketball (b,g), cheering (g), cross-country running (b,g), golf (b), soccer (b,g), softball (g), swimming and diving (b,g), volleyball (g); coed interscholastic: physical fitness; coed intramural: tennis. 2 PE instructors, 18 coaches, 1 trainer.

Computers Computers are regularly used in English, journalism, keyboarding, yearbook classes. Computer network features include on-campus library services, CD-ROMs, online commercial services, Internet access, DVD.

Contact Mrs. Elizabeth Sipe, Administrative Assistant. 864-678-5119. Fax: 864-281-9372. E-mail: esipe@shannonforest.com. Web site: www.shannonforest.com.

SHATTUCK-ST. MARY'S SCHOOL

1000 Shumway Avenue
PO Box 218
Faribault, Minnesota 55021
Head of School: Nick J.B. Stoneman

General Information Coeducational boarding and day college-preparatory and arts school, affiliated with Episcopal Church. Grades 6–12. Founded: 1858. Setting: small town. Nearest major city is Minneapolis. Students are housed in single-sex dormitories. 250-acre campus. 10 buildings on campus. Approved or accredited by Independent Schools Association of the Central States, Midwest Association of Boarding Schools, National Association of Episcopal Schools, The Association of

Boarding Schools, and Minnesota Department of Education. Member of National Association of Independent Schools and Secondary School Admission Test Board. Endowment: $10 million. Total enrollment: 334. Upper school average class size: 12. Upper school faculty-student ratio: 1:7.

Upper School Student Profile Grade 9: 77 students (53 boys, 24 girls); Grade 10: 93 students (59 boys, 34 girls); Grade 11: 59 students (37 boys, 22 girls); Grade 12: 46 students (27 boys, 19 girls). 70% of students are boarding students. 30% are state residents. 30 states are represented in upper school student body. 15% are international students. International students from Canada, China, Japan, Republic of Korea, Saudi Arabia, and Taiwan; 9 other countries represented in student body. 10% of students are members of Episcopal Church.

Faculty School total: 56. In upper school: 25 men, 12 women; 24 have advanced degrees; 38 reside on campus.

Subjects Offered 20th century world history, Advanced Placement courses, advanced studio art-AP, advanced TOEFL/grammar, African literature, algebra, American Civil War, American history, American history-AP, American literature, American sign language, art, art history, Asian literature, Asian studies, athletic training, ballet, band, Bible studies, biology, biology-AP, British literature, calculus, calculus-AP, ceramics, chamber groups, chemistry, chemistry-AP, China/Japan history, choir, choral music, community service, composition, composition-AP, computer programming, computer science, dance, digital photography, drama, drawing, economics, English, English language and composition-AP, English literature, English literature and composition-AP, ESL, ethics, European history, expository writing, fine arts, French, French language-AP, geography, geometry, grammar, high adventure outdoor program, history, instrumental music, Latin, Latin American history, linguistics, literary magazine, Mandarin, mathematics, Middle Eastern history, music, Native American history, oil painting, painting, photography, physics, physics-AP, pottery, pre-algebra, pre-calculus, public speaking, religion, robotics, science, social studies, Spanish, Spanish-AP, speech, statistics-AP, theater, trigonometry, U.S. history-AP, world history, writing.

Graduation Requirements Arts and fine arts (art, music, dance, drama), computer science, English, foreign language, mathematics, religion (includes Bible studies and theology), science, social studies (includes history), 20 hours of community service per year.

Special Academic Programs Advanced Placement exam preparation in 14 subject areas; honors section; independent study; study at local college for college credit; academic accommodation for the gifted, the musically talented, and the artistically talented; remedial reading and/or remedial writing; remedial math; programs in English, mathematics, general development for dyslexic students; ESL (20 students enrolled).

College Placement 63 students graduated in 2005; 40 went to college. Other: 1 entered a postgraduate year, 22 had other specific plans. Mean SAT verbal: 539, mean SAT math: 591, mean composite ACT: 24.

Student Life Upper grades have specified standards of dress. Discipline rests primarily with faculty. Attendance at religious services is required.

Summer Programs Remediation, enrichment, advancement, ESL, sports, art/fine arts, computer instruction programs offered; session focuses on reading, writing, mathematics, and study skills; held on campus; accepts boys and girls; open to students from other schools. 75 students usually enrolled.

Tuition and Aid Day student tuition: $19,600; 7-day tuition and room/board: $29,900. Tuition installment plan (monthly payment plans). Merit scholarship grants, need-based scholarship grants, performing arts scholarships, Episcopal clergy discounts, Headmaster's Scholarships available. In 2005–06, 33% of upper-school students received aid; total upper-school merit-scholarship money awarded: $126,000. Total amount of financial aid awarded in 2005–06: $1,300,000.

Admissions Traditional secondary-level entrance grade is 9. For fall 2005, 396 students applied for upper-level admission, 216 were accepted, 148 enrolled. SLEP, SSAT, ERB, PSAT, SAT, PLAN or ACT or TOEFL required. Deadline for receipt of application materials: none. Application fee required: $50. Interview required.

Athletics Interscholastic: baseball (boys), basketball (b,g), golf (b,g), hockey (b,g), ice hockey (b,g), lacrosse (b,g), soccer (b,g), softball (g), tennis (b,g), track and field (b,g), volleyball (g); intramural: golf (b,g), soccer (b,g), weight lifting (b,g); coed interscholastic: fencing, figure skating, ice skating; coed intramural: bicycling, climbing, dance, fitness, ice skating, jogging, martial arts, modern dance, outdoor activities, outdoor recreation, physical fitness, rock climbing, ropes courses, strength & conditioning, table tennis. 10 coaches, 2 trainers.

Computers Computers are regularly used in English, foreign language, history, mathematics, science classes. Computer network features include campus e-mail, on-campus library services, CD-ROMs, Internet access, file transfer, DVD, wireless campus network, Gateway National Model Notebook Program.

Contact Amy D. Wolf, Director of Admissions. 507-333-1655. Fax: 507-333-1661. E-mail: awolf@s-sm.org. Web site: www.s-sm.org.

ANNOUNCEMENT FROM THE SCHOOL This year, SSM launched a full-time, elite-level soccer program for boys and girls. Players train and compete on a daily basis September–May and receive technical, tactical, and physical training from a staff of professional coaches. In addition, SSM now offers a figure skating program with daily ice times, national-caliber coaching, and access to dance and weight training.

See full description on page 1060.

THE SHIPLEY SCHOOL

814 Yarrow Street
Bryn Mawr, Pennsylvania 19010-3598
Head of School: Dr. Steven S. Piltch

petersons.com

General Information Coeducational day college-preparatory school. Grades PK–12. Founded: 1894. Setting: suburban. Nearest major city is Philadelphia. 36-acre campus. 4 buildings on campus. Approved or accredited by Middle States Association of Colleges and Schools and Pennsylvania Association of Private Academic Schools. Member of National Association of Independent Schools and Secondary School Admission Test Board. Endowment: $14 million. Total enrollment: 857. Upper school average class size: 15. Upper school faculty-student ratio: 1:8.

Upper School Student Profile Grade 9: 86 students (41 boys, 45 girls); Grade 10: 83 students (40 boys, 43 girls); Grade 11: 84 students (42 boys, 42 girls); Grade 12: 81 students (44 boys, 37 girls).

Faculty School total: 129. In upper school: 22 men, 28 women; 35 have advanced degrees.

Subjects Offered Advanced chemistry, Advanced Placement courses, advanced studio art-AP, algebra, American history, American history-AP, American literature, American studies, ancient history, ancient world history, art, art history, art history-AP, band, biology, biology-AP, calculus, calculus-AP, chemistry, chemistry-AP, China/Japan history, choir, chorus, college counseling, computer keyboarding, computer literacy, computer programming, computer science, computer science-AP, concert bell choir, CPR, creative writing, desktop publishing, drama, drama performance, dramatic arts, driver education, economics, English, English literature, English-AP, European history, European history-AP, expository writing, fine arts, finite math, French, French language-AP, geometry, government/civics, grammar, health education, history of religion, honors English, honors geometry, honors U.S. history, honors world history, humanities, jazz band, Latin, Latin American literature, Latin-AP, library skills, mathematics, mathematics-AP, medieval history, modern European history-AP, music, music theory, music theory-AP, musical productions, orchestra, philosophy, photography, physical education, physics, physics-AP, pre-calculus, Russia and contemporary Europe, science, sex education, social studies, Spanish, Spanish language-AP, statistics, studio art-AP, theater, trigonometry, word processing, world affairs, world history, world literature.

Graduation Requirements Arts and fine arts (art, music, dance, drama), computer science, English, foreign language, mathematics, physical education (includes health), science, social studies (includes history), 40 hours of community service.

Special Academic Programs Advanced Placement exam preparation in 17 subject areas; honors section; accelerated programs; independent study; term-away projects; study at local college for college credit; domestic exchange program (with The Masters School); study abroad; academic accommodation for the gifted.

College Placement 78 students graduated in 2005; all went to college, including Boston University; Bowdoin College; Columbia University; Trinity College; University of Pennsylvania; Wesleyan University. Mean SAT verbal: 658, mean SAT math: 658.

Student Life Upper grades have specified standards of dress, student council, honor system. Discipline rests equally with students and faculty.

Summer Programs Remediation, enrichment, advancement, sports, art/fine arts, computer instruction programs offered; session focuses on academic enrichment, sports, and theater; held on campus; accepts boys and girls; open to students from other schools. 60 students usually enrolled. 2006 schedule: June 27 to August 5. Application deadline: none.

Tuition and Aid Day student tuition: $21,225–$21,675. Tuition installment plan (monthly payment plans). Need-based scholarship grants, Centennial Scholarships (grade 9 need- and merit-based), prepGATE Loans available. Total amount of financial aid awarded in 2005–06: $1,909,000.

Admissions Traditional secondary-level entrance grade is 9. For fall 2005, 114 students applied for upper-level admission, 51 were accepted, 30 enrolled. ISEE, SSAT or WISC-R or WISC-III required. Deadline for receipt of application materials: January 15. Application fee required: $50. On-campus interview required.

Athletics Interscholastic: baseball (boys), basketball (b,g), crew (b,g), cross-country running (b,g), field hockey (g), independent competitive sports (b,g), lacrosse (b,g), rowing (b,g), soccer (b,g), softball (g), squash (b,g), tennis (b,g), volleyball (g), weight training (b,g); intramural: aerobics (b,g), aerobics/nautilus (b,g), dance (g), modern dance (g), nautilus (b,g); coed interscholastic: diving, golf, independent competitive sports, swimming and diving, weight training; coed intramural: aerobics, aerobics/nautilus, fitness, nautilus, physical fitness, yoga. 6 PE instructors, 51 coaches, 2 trainers.

Computers Computers are regularly used in all academic classes. Computer network features include campus e-mail, on-campus library services, CD-ROMs, Internet access, file transfer, office computer access, DVD.

Contact Mr. Gregory W. Coleman, Director of Admissions. 610-525-4300 Ext. 4118. Fax: 610-525-5082. E-mail: gcoleman@shipleyschool.org. Web site: www.shipleyschool.org.

See full description on page 1062.

SHORECREST PREPARATORY SCHOOL

5101 First Street NE
Saint Petersburg, Florida 33703
Head of School: Mr. Michael A. Murphy

petersons.com

General Information Coeducational day college-preparatory, arts, and technology school. Grades PK–12. Founded: 1923. Setting: suburban. Nearest major city is Tampa. 28-acre campus. 11 buildings on campus. Approved or accredited by Florida Council of Independent Schools, Southern Association of Colleges and Schools, Southern Association of Independent Schools, The College Board, and Florida Department of Education. Member of National Association of Independent Schools and Secondary School Admission Test Board. Endowment: $500,000. Total enrollment: 991. Upper school average class size: 15. Upper school faculty-student ratio: 1:6.

Upper School Student Profile Grade 9: 53 students (24 boys, 29 girls); Grade 10: 71 students (40 boys, 31 girls); Grade 11: 54 students (32 boys, 22 girls); Grade 12: 59 students (30 boys, 29 girls).

Faculty School total: 104. In upper school: 18 men, 13 women; 19 have advanced degrees.

Subjects Offered Algebra, American literature, ancient history, art, art history, art history-AP, band, biology, biology-AP, calculus, calculus-AP, chemistry, chemistry-AP, computer graphics, computer keyboarding, computer music, computer programming-AP, computer science-AP, conceptual physics, creative writing, drama, economics, economics-AP, English, English language and composition-AP, English literature-AP, European history, European history-AP, fine arts, French language-AP, French literature-AP, geometry, government/civics, guitar, health, history of ideas, humanities, Internet, journalism, macroeconomics-AP, marine biology, mathematics, microeconomics-AP, music, music theory-AP, musical theater, photography, physical education, physics, physics-AP, play/screen writing, political science, portfolio art, pre-calculus, psychology, psychology-AP, social studies, Spanish language-AP, statistics and probability, studio art-AP, telecommunications, theater, trigonometry, U.S. history, U.S. history-AP, video, Web site design, Western civilization, world history, world history-AP, world literature, yearbook.

Graduation Requirements Arts and fine arts (art, music, dance, drama), computer science, English, foreign language, health education, mathematics, science, social studies (includes history).

Special Academic Programs Advanced Placement exam preparation in 19 subject areas; honors section; independent study; academic accommodation for the gifted.

College Placement 52 students graduated in 2005; all went to college, including Duke University; Florida State University; University of Central Florida; University of Florida; University of Pennsylvania; Vanderbilt University. Mean SAT verbal: 608, mean SAT math: 647, mean composite ACT: 26.

Student Life Upper grades have specified standards of dress, student council, honor system. Discipline rests primarily with faculty.

Tuition and Aid Day student tuition: $14,190. Tuition installment plan (monthly payment plans, semi-annual payment plan). Tuition reduction for siblings, need-based scholarship grants available. In 2005–06, 15% of upper-school students received aid. Total amount of financial aid awarded in 2005–06: $256,160.

Admissions Traditional secondary-level entrance grade is 9. For fall 2005, 37 students applied for upper-level admission, 29 were accepted, 23 enrolled. ERB, ISEE, PSAT or SAT or school's own test required. Deadline for receipt of application materials: none. Application fee required: $75. On-campus interview required.

Athletics Interscholastic: baseball (boys), basketball (b,g), cheering (g), cross-country running (b,g), diving (b,g), football (b), golf (b,g), soccer (b,g), softball (g), swimming and diving (b,g), tennis (b,g), track and field (b,g), volleyball (g); coed interscholastic: sailing. 4 PE instructors, 27 coaches.

Computers Computers are regularly used in all academic classes. Computer network features include campus e-mail, on-campus library services, CD-ROMs, online commercial services, Internet access, office computer access, DVD.

Contact Mrs. Diana Craig, Director of Admissions. 727-522-2111 Ext. 106. Fax: 727-527-4191. E-mail: admissions@shorecrest.org. Web site: www.shorecrest.org.

See full description on page 1064.

SHORELINE CHRISTIAN

2400 Northeast 147th Street
Shoreline, Washington 98155
Head of School: Mr. Timothy E. Visser

General Information Coeducational day college-preparatory and general academic school, affiliated with Christian faith. Grades PS–12. Founded: 1952. Setting: suburban. Nearest major city is Seattle. 7-acre campus. 2 buildings on campus. Approved or accredited by Christian Schools International, Northwest Association of Accredited Schools, Northwest Association of Schools and Colleges, and Washington Department of Education. Endowment: $380,000. Total enrollment: 287. Upper school average class size: 25. Upper school faculty-student ratio: 1:7.

Upper School Student Profile Grade 9: 30 students (13 boys, 17 girls); Grade 10: 25 students (13 boys, 12 girls); Grade 11: 25 students (11 boys, 14 girls); Grade 12: 32 students (18 boys, 14 girls). 100% of students are Christian.

Faculty School total: 27. In upper school: 8 men, 10 women; 6 have advanced degrees.

Subjects Offered Advanced computer applications, advanced math, algebra, American history, art, band, Bible, biology, British literature, chemistry, choir, Christian doctrine, college writing, composition, computer applications, consumer education, creative writing, current events, current history, drama, English, film, film appreciation, geometry, global studies, government, health, human anatomy, keyboarding/computer, life science, life skills, literature, mechanical drawing, media, music appreciation, physical education, physical science, physics, sociology, Spanish, speech, study skills, Washington State and Northwest History, Western civilization, world literature, world religions, yearbook.

Graduation Requirements American government, American literature, Bible, British literature, college writing, composition, electives, English, foreign language, global issues, keyboarding/computer, life skills, mathematics, occupational education, physical education (includes health), science, social science, speech, U.S. history, Washington State and Northwest History, Western civilization, world literature.

Special Academic Programs Independent study; study at local college for college credit; remedial reading and/or remedial writing.

College Placement 37 students graduated in 2005; 36 went to college, including Azusa Pacific University; Calvin College; Dordt College; Seattle Pacific University; Trinity Western University; University of Washington. Other: 1 went to work. Median SAT verbal: 600, median SAT math: 620, median composite ACT: 28. 38% scored over 600 on SAT verbal, 44% scored over 600 on SAT math, 60% scored over 26 on composite ACT.

Student Life Upper grades have specified standards of dress, student council. Discipline rests primarily with faculty. Attendance at religious services is required.

Tuition and Aid Day student tuition: $7425–$7725. Tuition installment plan (monthly payment plans, individually arranged payment plans, prepaid cash tuition discount, quarterly or semi-annual payment plans). Tuition reduction for siblings, need-based scholarship grants, discount for qualifying Pastor families available. In 2005–06, 25% of upper-school students received aid. Total amount of financial aid awarded in 2005–06: $100,000.

Admissions Traditional secondary-level entrance grade is 9. For fall 2005, 13 students applied for upper-level admission, 9 were accepted, 9 enrolled. Deadline for receipt of application materials: none. Application fee required: $100. Interview required.

Athletics Interscholastic: baseball (boys), basketball (b,g), soccer (b), softball (g), volleyball (g); coed interscholastic: cheering, golf, soccer, track and field. 1 PE instructor.

Computers Computers are regularly used in all academic, art, library, media, music, occupational education, research skills, yearbook classes. Computer network features include campus e-mail, on-campus library services, CD-ROMs, Internet access.

Contact Mrs. Laurie Ann Dykstra, Director of Development. 206-364-7777 Ext. 308. Fax: 206-364-0349. E-mail: ldykstra@shorelinechristian.org. Web site: www.shorelinechristian.org.

SICES INTERNATIONAL ACADEMY

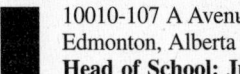

10010-107 A Avenue
Edmonton, Alberta T5H 4H8, Canada
Head of School: Julie V. Kallal

General Information Coeducational boarding college-preparatory, general academic, vocational, and caregiving and ESL school. Grades 7–12. Founded: 1999. Setting: urban. Students are housed in private homes. 3-acre campus. 3 buildings on campus. Approved or accredited by Canadian Association of Independent Schools and Alberta Department of Education. Language of instruction: English. Endowment: CAN$57,000. Total enrollment: 102. Upper school average class size: 15. Upper school faculty-student ratio: 1:20.

Faculty School total: 5. In upper school: 1 man, 2 women; 2 have advanced degrees.

Special Academic Programs Independent study; study abroad; ESL (27 students enrolled).

College Placement 227 students graduated in 2005. Other: 12 went to work, 3 entered a postgraduate year, 8 had other specific plans.

Student Life Discipline rests equally with students and faculty.

Tuition and Aid Day student tuition: CAN$5000. Guaranteed tuition plan. Tuition installment plan (The Tuition Plan, monthly payment plans, individually arranged payment plans, tuition fee must be paid in six (6) months).

Admissions Deadline for receipt of application materials: none. Application fee required: CAN$250. On-campus interview required.

Athletics Interscholastic: archery (boys, girls); coed interscholastic: archery, indoor soccer, modern dance; coed intramural: archery, modern dance.

Computers Computers are regularly used in accounting classes. Computer network features include campus e-mail, CD-ROMs, Internet access.

Contact Julie V. Kallal, Principal. 780-451-0752. Fax: 780-489-9669. E-mail: jvkallal@shaw.ca. Web site: sices.net.

SIDWELL FRIENDS SCHOOL

3825 Wisconsin Avenue, NW
Washington, District of Columbia 20016
Head of School: Bruce B. Stewart

General Information Coeducational day college-preparatory and arts school, affiliated with Society of Friends. Grades PK–12. Founded: 1883. Setting: urban. 15-acre campus. 8 buildings on campus. Approved or accredited by Association of Independent Maryland Schools, Association of Independent Schools of Greater Washington, and District of Columbia Department of Education. Member of National Association of Independent Schools and Secondary School Admission Test Board. Endowment: $37.1 million. Total enrollment: 1,091. Upper school average class size: 15. Upper school faculty-student ratio: 1:9.

Upper School Student Profile Grade 9: 117 students (57 boys, 60 girls); Grade 10: 128 students (62 boys, 66 girls); Grade 11: 110 students (59 boys, 51 girls); Grade 12: 111 students (58 boys, 53 girls). 7% of students are members of Society of Friends.

Faculty School total: 147. In upper school: 28 men, 28 women; 42 have advanced degrees.

Subjects Offered Algebra, American history, American literature, architecture, art, art history, biology, calculus, ceramics, chemistry, Chinese, community service, computer science, dance, drama, English, English literature, environmental science, European history, expository writing, fine arts, French, geometry, German, Greek, history, instrumental music, Japanese, jazz, Latin, mathematics, music, philosophy, photography, physical education, physical science, physics, religion, Russian, science, social studies, Spanish, statistics, theater, trigonometry, world history, world literature, writing.

Graduation Requirements Arts and fine arts (art, music, dance, drama), English, foreign language, mathematics, physical education (includes health), science, social studies (includes history). Community service is required.

Special Academic Programs Advanced Placement exam preparation in 11 subject areas; independent study; study abroad.

College Placement 113 students graduated in 2005; all went to college, including Columbia University; Harvard University; Haverford College; University of Pennsylvania; Washington University in St. Louis; Yale University. 89% scored over 600 on SAT verbal, 86% scored over 600 on SAT math.

Student Life Upper grades have specified standards of dress, student council, honor system. Discipline rests equally with students and faculty. Attendance at religious services is required.

Summer Programs Remediation, enrichment, advancement, sports, art/fine arts, computer instruction programs offered; held both on and off campus; held at Camp Corsica (Centreville, MD), Hawaii, and Costa Rica; accepts boys and girls; open to students from other schools. 700 students usually enrolled. 2006 schedule: June 12 to August 25. Application deadline: none.

Tuition and Aid Day student tuition: $23,545–$24,545. Tuition installment plan (Insured Tuition Payment Plan, Key Tuition Payment Plan, monthly payment plans). Need-based scholarship grants, Achiever Loan Program available. In 2005–06, 21% of upper-school students received aid. Total amount of financial aid awarded in 2005–06: $3,704,000.

Admissions Traditional secondary-level entrance grade is 9. For fall 2005, 245 students applied for upper-level admission, 33 were accepted, 25 enrolled. ISEE, SSAT or WISC III or other aptitude measures; standardized achievement test required. Deadline for receipt of application materials: January 6. Application fee required: $50. Interview required.

Athletics Interscholastic: baseball (boys), basketball (b,g), crew (g), cross-country running (b,g), diving (b,g), field hockey (g), football (b), indoor soccer (b), lacrosse (b,g), soccer (b,g), softball (g), swimming and diving (b,g), tennis (b,g), track and field (b,g), volleyball (g), wrestling (b); coed interscholastic: aquatics, golf, running, wrestling; coed intramural: aerobics, aerobics/dance, aerobics/nautilus, ball hockey, basketball, climbing, combined training, cross-country running, dance, Frisbee, indoor soccer, outdoor activities, physical fitness, squash, tennis, volleyball, weight lifting, yoga. 15 PE instructors, 28 coaches, 1 trainer.

Computers Computers are regularly used in English, foreign language, mathematics, science classes. Computer network features include campus e-mail, on-campus library services, CD-ROMs, online commercial services, Internet access, wireless campus network.

Contact Joshua P. Wolman, Assistant Head of School for Admissions and Financial Aid. 202-537-8111. Fax: 202-537-2401. Web site: www.sidwell.edu.

SMITH SCHOOL

New York, New York
See Special Needs Schools section.

SMITHVILLE DISTRICT CHRISTIAN HIGH SCHOOL

6488 Smithville Road
Smithville, Ontario L0R 2A0, Canada
Head of School: Mr. Ted W. Harris

General Information Coeducational day college-preparatory, general academic, arts, business, religious studies, bilingual studies, and technology school, affiliated with Christian faith, Reformed Church. Grades 9–12. Founded: 1980. Setting: rural. Nearest major city is Hamilton, Canada. 4-acre campus. 1 building on campus. Approved or accredited by Christian Schools International and Ontario Department of Education. Language of instruction: English. Total enrollment: 232. Upper school average class size: 20. Upper school faculty-student ratio: 1:11.

Upper School Student Profile 100% of students are Christian, Reformed.

Faculty School total: 21. In upper school: 13 men, 8 women; 3 have advanced degrees.

Subjects Offered 20th century history, accounting, advanced math, arts, Bible, biology, business, calculus, Canadian geography, Canadian history, careers, chemistry, civics, computer applications, computer information systems, construction, data analysis, discrete math, drama, dramatic arts, English, finance, fitness, food and nutrition, French, French as a second language, functions, general math, geography, geometry, health, health education, healthful living, instrumental music, integrated technology fundamentals, mathematics, media, parenting, physical education, physics, science, society challenge and change, transportation technology, urban studies, visual arts, vocal music, world geography, world history, writing fundamentals.

Graduation Requirements Arts, Bible, Canadian geography, Canadian history, careers, civics, electives, English, French, mathematics, physical education (includes health), science, society challenge and change.

Special Academic Programs Independent study; remedial reading and/or remedial writing; remedial math; programs in English for dyslexic students; special instructional classes for students with learning disabilities, Attention Deficit Disorder, emotional and behavioral problems.

College Placement 60 students graduated in 2005; 45 went to college, including Calvin College; Dordt College; Redeemer University College. Other: 15 went to work.

Student Life Upper grades have specified standards of dress, student council, honor system. Discipline rests primarily with faculty. Attendance at religious services is required.

Tuition and Aid Day student tuition: CAN$7670. Bursaries available.

Admissions Traditional secondary-level entrance grade is 9. Deadline for receipt of application materials: none. No application fee required. Interview required.

Athletics Interscholastic: badminton (boys, girls), basketball (b,g), cross-country running (b,g), soccer (b,g), track and field (b,g), volleyball (b,g); coed interscholastic: badminton; coed intramural: ball hockey, basketball, field hockey, hockey, winter soccer.

Computers Computers are regularly used in writing classes. Computer network features include CD-ROMs, Internet access, DVD.

Contact Mr. Al Korvemaker, Vice Principal. 905-957-3255. Fax: 905-957-3431. E-mail: akorvemaker@sdch.on.ca. Web site: www.sdch.on.ca.

SOLEBURY SCHOOL

6820 Phillips Mill Road
PO Box 429
New Hope, Pennsylvania 18938-0429
Head of School: Mr. John D. Brown

General Information Coeducational boarding and day college-preparatory and arts school. Boarding grades 9–PG, day grades 7–PG. Founded: 1925. Setting: small town. Nearest major city is Philadelphia. Students are housed in single-sex dormitories. 90-acre campus. 22 buildings on campus. Approved or accredited by Middle States Association of Colleges and Schools, Pennsylvania Association of Private Academic Schools, The Association of Boarding Schools, and Pennsylvania Department of Education. Member of National Association of Independent Schools and Secondary School Admission Test Board. Endowment: $2.6 million. Total enrollment: 222. Upper school average class size: 11. Upper school faculty-student ratio: 1:6.

Upper School Student Profile Grade 9: 49 students (28 boys, 21 girls); Grade 10: 43 students (30 boys, 13 girls); Grade 11: 49 students (24 boys, 25 girls); Grade 12: 52 students (22 boys, 30 girls); Postgraduate: 2 students (2 boys). 28% of students are boarding students. 45% are state residents. 9 states are represented in upper school student body. 15% are international students. International students from Brazil, Croatia, Germany, Japan, Republic of Korea, and Taiwan; 2 other countries represented in student body.

Faculty School total: 53. In upper school: 24 men, 29 women; 20 have advanced degrees; 29 reside on campus.

Subjects Offered Acting, advanced chemistry, advanced computer applications, Advanced Placement courses, advanced TOEFL/grammar, algebra, American history-AP, American studies, anatomy and physiology, ancient history, art, art history, batik, biology, calculus, calculus-AP, ceramics, chemistry, chorus, computer graphics, computer music, computer programming, conceptual physics, creative writing, drama, drawing, English, English-AP, environmental science-AP, ESL, ethics, fine arts, forensics, French, French-AP, geometry, government and politics-AP, health, honors

geometry, Latin American literature, music, painting, performing arts, photography, physical education, playwriting, pre-algebra, pre-calculus, printmaking, psychology, sculpture, senior project, Shakespeare, Spanish, Spanish-AP, statistics-AP, studio art, theater, theater design and production, trigonometry, U.S. history, world history, writing.

Graduation Requirements Art, computers, electives, English, foreign language, health, mathematics, science, social studies (includes history), 10 hours of community service per year.

Special Academic Programs Advanced Placement exam preparation in 9 subject areas; honors section; independent study; term-away projects; academic accommodation for the gifted, the musically talented, and the artistically talented; remedial reading and/or remedial writing; programs in English, general development for dyslexic students; ESL (23 students enrolled).

College Placement 42 students graduated in 2005; 40 went to college, including Bryn Mawr College; Cornell University; Dickinson College; Oberlin College; The George Washington University; Vassar College. Other: 2 had other specific plans. Mean SAT verbal: 540, mean SAT math: 560. 28% scored over 600 on SAT verbal, 33% scored over 600 on SAT math.

Student Life Upper grades have student council. Discipline rests equally with students and faculty.

Summer Programs ESL programs offered; session focuses on ESL; held both on and off campus; held at Washington, DC; Philadelphia, PA; New York, NY; Baltimore, MD; accepts boys and girls; open to students from other schools. 34 students usually enrolled. 2006 schedule: July 10 to August 18. Application deadline: April 30.

Tuition and Aid Day student tuition: $20,700; 7-day tuition and room/board: $31,200. Tuition installment plan (Key Tuition Payment Plan, monthly payment plans). Merit scholarship grants, need-based scholarship grants available. In 2005–06, 34% of upper-school students received aid; total upper-school merit-scholarship money awarded: $57,000. Total amount of financial aid awarded in 2005–06: $1,134,000.

Admissions Traditional secondary-level entrance grade is 9. For fall 2005, 163 students applied for upper-level admission, 123 were accepted, 68 enrolled. Any standardized test, SSAT or TOEFL or SLEP required. Deadline for receipt of application materials: January 15. Application fee required: $50. Interview required.

Athletics Interscholastic: baseball (boys), basketball (b,g), field hockey (g), lacrosse (g), soccer (b,g), softball (g); coed interscholastic: cross-country running, tennis, track and field; coed intramural: bicycling, canoeing/kayaking, dance, fitness, fitness walking, golf, hiking/backpacking, horseback riding, independent competitive sports, rock climbing, skiing (downhill), tennis, volleyball, walking, weight training, wrestling, yoga. 1 PE instructor, 1 coach.

Computers Computers are regularly used in art, college planning, English, ESL, foreign language, independent study, language development, literary magazine, mathematics, music, news writing, newspaper, research skills, science, social studies, theater, yearbook classes. Computer network features include campus e-mail, on-campus library services, CD-ROMs, online commercial services, Internet access, DVD, wireless campus network.

Contact Ms. Denise DiFiglia, Director of Admission. 215-862-5261. Fax: 215-862-3366. E-mail: admissions@solebury.org. Web site: www.solebury.org.

See full description on page 1066.

SORENSON'S RANCH SCHOOL

Koosharem, Utah
See Special Needs Schools section.

SOUNDVIEW PREPARATORY SCHOOL

272 North Bedford Road
Mount Kisco, New York 10549
Head of School: W. Glyn Hearn

General Information Coeducational day college-preparatory, arts, and technology school. Grades 6–PG. Founded: 1989. Setting: suburban. Nearest major city is New York. 1-acre campus. 1 building on campus. Approved or accredited by New York State Association of Independent Schools and New York Department of Education. Language of instruction: English. Endowment: $679,700. Total enrollment: 75. Upper school average class size: 7. Upper school faculty-student ratio: 1:4.

Upper School Student Profile Grade 9: 13 students (8 boys, 5 girls); Grade 10: 18 students (13 boys, 5 girls); Grade 11: 20 students (12 boys, 8 girls); Grade 12: 7 students (6 boys, 1 girl).

Faculty School total: 19. In upper school: 8 men, 11 women; 11 have advanced degrees.

Subjects Offered Algebra, American history, American literature, architecture, art, art history, biology, calculus, chemistry, creative writing, drama, earth science, ecology, English, English literature, European history, expository writing, fine arts, French, geometry, grammar, health, history, Italian, Latin, mathematics, philosophy, physical education, physics, science, social studies, Spanish, trigonometry, world history.

Graduation Requirements Arts and fine arts (art, music, dance, drama), English, foreign language, mathematics, physical education (includes health), science, social studies (includes history).

Special Academic Programs Advanced Placement exam preparation in 5 subject areas; honors section; accelerated programs; independent study; study at local college for college credit; academic accommodation for the gifted, the musically talented, and the artistically talented; special instructional classes for students needing wheelchair accessibility.

College Placement 9 students graduated in 2004; 8 went to college, including Clark University; Drexel University; Sarah Lawrence College; University of Hartford. Other: 1 had other specific plans. Median SAT verbal: 610, median SAT math: 640, median composite ACT: 24.

Student Life Discipline rests primarily with faculty.

Tuition and Aid Day student tuition: $22,750–$24,250. Need-based scholarship grants available. In 2004–05, 10% of upper-school students received aid. Total amount of financial aid awarded in 2004–05: $210,000.

Admissions Traditional secondary-level entrance grade is 9. For fall 2005, 38 students applied for upper-level admission, 18 were accepted, 17 enrolled. ERB (CTP-Verbal, Quantitative) or ERB Mathematics required. Deadline for receipt of application materials: none. Application fee required: $50. On-campus interview required.

Athletics Interscholastic: basketball (girls); intramural: dance (g); coed interscholastic: basketball, soccer; coed intramural: fencing, golf. 1 coach.

Computers Computers are regularly used in all academic, mathematics classes. Computer network features include campus e-mail, CD-ROMs, Internet access, DVD, wireless campus network.

Contact Mary E. Ivanyi, Assistant Head. 914-242-9693. Fax: 914-242-9658. E-mail: mivanyi@soundviewprep.org. Web site: www.soundviewprep.org.

See full description on page 1068.

SOUTHAMPTON ACADEMY

26495 Old Plank Road
Courtland, Virginia 23837
Head of School: Richard Craig Jones

General Information Coeducational day college-preparatory, arts, and technology school. Grades PK–12. Founded: 1969. Setting: small town. Nearest major city is Richmond. 25-acre campus. 7 buildings on campus. Approved or accredited by Southern Association of Colleges and Schools. Endowment: $1.8 million. Total enrollment: 432. Upper school average class size: 12. Upper school faculty-student ratio: 1:12.

Upper School Student Profile Grade 9: 24 students (16 boys, 8 girls); Grade 10: 20 students (10 boys, 10 girls); Grade 11: 24 students (12 boys, 12 girls); Grade 12: 16 students (7 boys, 9 girls).

Faculty School total: 40. In upper school: 3 men, 7 women; 3 have advanced degrees.

Subjects Offered Algebra, band, biology, business mathematics, chemistry, computers, English, English-AP, fine arts, geometry, physical education, physical science, physics, pre-calculus, psychology, Spanish, studio art, U.S. government, U.S. history, world geography, world history.

Graduation Requirements Arts and fine arts (art, music, dance, drama), computer science, English, foreign language, mathematics, physical education (includes health), science, social science, social studies (includes history).

Special Academic Programs Advanced Placement exam preparation in 2 subject areas; independent study; study at local college for college credit.

College Placement 12 students graduated in 2005; 11 went to college, including Christopher Newport University. Mean SAT verbal: 550, mean SAT math: 530. 25% scored over 600 on SAT verbal, 33% scored over 600 on SAT math.

Student Life Upper grades have specified standards of dress, student council, honor system. Discipline rests primarily with faculty.

Tuition and Aid Day student tuition: $5013. Guaranteed tuition plan. Tuition installment plan (monthly payment plans, individually arranged payment plans, quarterly and semi-annual payment plans). Tuition reduction for siblings, need-based scholarship grants, minority scholarships available. In 2005–06, 10% of upper-school students received aid. Total amount of financial aid awarded in 2005–06: $85,000.

Admissions Traditional secondary-level entrance grade is 9. ERB required. Deadline for receipt of application materials: none. No application fee required. On-campus interview required.

Athletics Interscholastic: baseball (boys), basketball (b,g), cheering (g), dance squad (g), football (b), softball (g), volleyball (g); intramural: baseball (b), basketball (b,g), football (b), softball (g), volleyball (g), weight lifting (b,g); coed interscholastic: golf; coed intramural: martial arts. 2 PE instructors, 2 coaches.

Computers Computers are regularly used in English, history, science classes. Computer network features include campus e-mail, CD-ROMs, Internet access.

Contact Richard Craig Jones, Head of School. 757-653-2512 Ext. 302. Fax: 757-653-0011. E-mail: cjones@southamptonacademy.org.

SOUTH KENT SCHOOL

40 Bull's Bridge Road
South Kent, Connecticut 06785
Head of School: Mr. Andrew J. Vadnais

General Information Boys' boarding and day college-preparatory, arts, and technology school, affiliated with Episcopal Church. Grades 9–PG. Founded: 1923. Setting: rural. Nearest major city is New York, NY. Students are housed in single-sex dormitories. 320-acre campus. 30 buildings on campus. Approved or accredited by National Association of Episcopal Schools, New England Association of Schools and Colleges, The Association of Boarding Schools, and Connecticut Department of Education. Member of National Association of Independent Schools and Secondary School Admission Test Board. Endowment: $4 million. Total enrollment: 142. Upper school average class size: 7. Upper school faculty-student ratio: 1:4.

Upper School Student Profile Grade 9: 25 students (25 boys); Grade 10: 36 students (36 boys); Grade 11: 45 students (45 boys); Grade 12: 33 students (33 boys); Postgraduate: 3 students (3 boys). 88% of students are boarding students. 28% are state residents. 17 states are represented in upper school student body. 17% are international students. International students from Croatia, Japan, Morocco, Republic of Korea, Russian Federation, and Thailand; 2 other countries represented in student body. 35% of students are members of Episcopal Church.

Faculty School total: 34. In upper school: 23 men, 11 women; 11 have advanced degrees; 25 reside on campus.

Subjects Offered Algebra, American history, American literature, art, art history, biology, calculus, ceramics, chemistry, creative writing, driver education, English, English literature, ESL, European history, expository writing, fine arts, French, geometry, grammar, health, history, mathematics, Native American history, photography, physics, physiology, psychology, science, Spanish, world history, writing.

Graduation Requirements Art, English, foreign language, lab science, mathematics, U.S. history.

Special Academic Programs Advanced Placement exam preparation in 5 subject areas; honors section; independent study; ESL (9 students enrolled).

College Placement 28 students graduated in 2005; 27 went to college, including Charleston Southern University; Clemson University; Hobart and William Smith Colleges; Lafayette College; Northeastern University; Purdue University. Other: 1 went to work. Median SAT verbal: 520, median SAT math: 500. 18% scored over 600 on SAT verbal, 24% scored over 600 on SAT math.

Student Life Upper grades have specified standards of dress, student council, honor system. Discipline rests primarily with faculty. Attendance at religious services is required.

Tuition and Aid Day student tuition: $21,000; 7-day tuition and room/board: $32,000. Tuition installment plan (SMART Tuition Payment Plan, monthly payment plans, individually arranged payment plans). Merit scholarship grants, need-based scholarship grants, need-based loans, middle-income loans available. In 2005–06, 27% of upper-school students received aid. Total amount of financial aid awarded in 2005–06: $1,370,000.

Admissions Traditional secondary-level entrance grade is 9. For fall 2005, 185 students applied for upper-level admission, 120 were accepted, 67 enrolled. SSAT and writing sample required. Deadline for receipt of application materials: none. Application fee required: $40. Interview required.

Athletics Interscholastic: baseball, basketball, crew, cross-country running, football, golf, ice hockey, lacrosse, ropes courses, soccer, tennis; intramural: alpine skiing, baseball, basketball, bicycling, canoeing/kayaking, climbing, crew, golf, hiking/backpacking, ice hockey, outdoor activities, skiing (cross-country), skiing (downhill), snowboarding, soccer, strength & conditioning, ultimate Frisbee, wall climbing, weight lifting, weight training. 28 coaches, 2 trainers.

Computers Computers are regularly used in art classes. Computer network features include campus e-mail, on-campus library services, online commercial services, Internet access, file transfer, DVD, wireless campus network.

Contact Mr. Richard A. Brande, Director of Admissions and Financial Aid. 860-927-3539 Ext. 202. Fax: 860-927-0024. E-mail: brander@southkentschool.net. Web site: www.southkentschool.net.

See full description on page 1070.

SOUTHRIDGE SCHOOL

2656 160th Street
Surrey, British Columbia V3S 0B7, Canada
Head of School: Mr. William Jones

General Information Coeducational day college-preparatory and arts school. Grades K–12. Founded: 1994. Setting: rural. Nearest major city is Vancouver, Canada. 17-acre campus. 1 building on campus. Approved or accredited by Canadian Association of Independent Schools and British Columbia Department of Education. Language of instruction: English. Total enrollment: 674. Upper school average class size: 20. Upper school faculty-student ratio: 1:10.

Upper School Student Profile Grade 8: 66 students (29 boys, 37 girls); Grade 9: 65 students (29 boys, 36 girls); Grade 10: 68 students (35 boys, 33 girls); Grade 11: 65 students (32 boys, 33 girls); Grade 12: 58 students (30 boys, 28 girls).

Southridge School

Faculty School total: 56. In upper school: 13 men, 20 women; 18 have advanced degrees.

Subjects Offered Biology, biology-AP, calculus-AP, chemistry, chemistry-AP, computer science-AP, drama, economics, English, English language-AP, English literature-AP, French, geography, history-AP, information technology, jazz band, mathematics, media arts, physical education, physics, physics-AP, science, social studies, Spanish, studio art, studio art—AP, world civilizations.

Graduation Requirements Applied skills, arts and fine arts (art, music, dance, drama), athletics, career planning, language arts, mathematics, science, social studies or BC First Nations studies, 30 hours of service per year.

Special Academic Programs Advanced Placement exam preparation in 9 subject areas; honors section; term-away projects; study abroad.

College Placement 65 students graduated in 2005; 63 went to college, including Queen's University at Kingston; The University of British Columbia; The University of Western Ontario; University of Alberta; University of Victoria. Other: 1 went to work, 1 had other specific plans. Mean SAT verbal: 636, mean SAT math: 651. 80% scored over 600 on SAT verbal, 90% scored over 600 on SAT math.

Student Life Upper grades have uniform requirement, student council, honor system. Discipline rests primarily with faculty.

Summer Programs Enrichment, ESL, sports, art/fine arts, computer instruction programs offered; session focuses on K-12 academic and extracurricular; held both on and off campus; held at various nearby locations especially relating to outdoor education; accepts boys and girls; open to students from other schools. 300 students usually enrolled. 2006 schedule: July to August. Application deadline: May.

Tuition and Aid Day student tuition: CAN$7000–CAN$10,000. Tuition installment plan (individually arranged payment plans, quarterly payment plan). Tuition reduction for siblings, bursaries available. In 2005–06, 1% of upper-school students received aid.

Admissions Traditional secondary-level entrance grade is 8. For fall 2005, 129 students applied for upper-level admission, 49 were accepted, 41 enrolled. Achievement/Aptitude/Writing, CCAT, PSAT and SAT for applicants to grade 11 and 12 or SSAT required. Deadline for receipt of application materials: January 15. Application fee required: CAN$200. On-campus interview required.

Athletics Interscholastic: field hockey (girls), rugby (b), soccer (b,g), swimming and diving (b,g), synchronized swimming (g), track and field (b,g), volleyball (g); coed interscholastic: aquatics, basketball, cross-country running, golf, tennis; coed intramural: aerobics/nautilus, alpine skiing, back packing, badminton, ball hockey, bicycling, canoeing/kayaking, Circus, cross-country running, floor hockey, kayaking, ocean paddling, outdoor education, running, skiing (cross-country), skiing (downhill), snowboarding, snowshoeing, ultimate Frisbee, wall climbing, weight training. 2 PE instructors.

Computers Computers are regularly used in all academic classes. Computer network features include campus e-mail, on-campus library services, CD-ROMs, Internet access, file transfer, wireless campus network, Grades 5-12 laptop program (in 05-06, first year of roll-out, for grades 5 and 8 only).

Contact Ms. Hilary R. Lehn, Director of Admissions. 604-542-5391. Fax: 604-535-3676. E-mail: hlehn@southridge.bc.ca. Web site: www.southridge.bc.ca.

SOUTHWEST CHRISTIAN SCHOOL, INC.

7001 Benbrook Lake Drive
Fort Worth, Texas 76132
Head of School: Mr. Scott Edward Barron

General Information Coeducational day college-preparatory and religious studies school. Grades PK–12. Founded: 1969. Setting: suburban. 24-acre campus. 3 buildings on campus. Approved or accredited by Association of Christian Schools International, Southern Association of Colleges and Schools, Texas Education Agency, and Texas Department of Education. Languages of instruction: Spanish and French. Total enrollment: 757. Upper school average class size: 16. Upper school faculty-student ratio: 1:11.

Faculty School total: 36. In upper school: 12 men, 22 women; 10 have advanced degrees.

Subjects Offered 1½ elective credits, adolescent issues, advanced math, algebra, American government, American literature, American literature-AP, anatomy and physiology, art, Bible studies, biology, biology-AP, British literature, British literature-AP, calculus, calculus-AP, chemistry, chemistry-AP, choir, drama, English, English literature-AP, English-AP, foreign language, French, geometry, government, health, history, honors algebra, honors English, honors geometry, honors U.S. history, honors world history, journalism, keyboarding/computer, lab science, leadership, literature and composition-AP, physics, physics-AP, pre-algebra, pre-calculus, Spanish, speech, technology, U.S. history, U.S. history-AP, Web authoring, Web site design.

Special Academic Programs Advanced Placement exam preparation in 7 subject areas; honors section; study at local college for college credit; academic accommodation for the gifted.

College Placement 43 students graduated in 2005; all went to college, including Abilene Christian University; Baylor University; Texas A&M University; Texas Christian University; Texas Tech University. Median SAT verbal: 564, median SAT math: 565, median composite ACT: 24. 35% scored over 600 on SAT verbal, 37% scored over 600 on SAT math.

Student Life Upper grades have uniform requirement, student council. Discipline rests primarily with faculty. Attendance at religious services is required.

Summer Programs Enrichment, sports programs offered; held on campus; accepts boys and girls; open to students from other schools.

Tuition and Aid Day student tuition: $6950–$8800. Tuition installment plan (FACTS Tuition Payment Plan). Need-based scholarship grants available. In 2005–06, 24% of upper-school students received aid.

Admissions Traditional secondary-level entrance grade is 9. Stanford 9 required. Deadline for receipt of application materials: March 27. No application fee required. Interview required.

Athletics Interscholastic: baseball (boys), basketball (b,g), cheering (g), crew (b), equestrian sports (b,g), football (b), soccer (b,g), softball (g), track and field (b,g), volleyball (g); coed interscholastic: aquatics, golf; coed intramural: aquatics, fitness, weight training. 2 PE instructors, 8 coaches, 1 trainer.

Computers Computers are regularly used in all academic classes. Computer network features include campus e-mail, on-campus library services, CD-ROMs, online commercial services, Internet access, file transfer, office computer access, DVD.

Contact Mrs. Kathy Severson, Admissions Director. 817-294-9596 Ext. 242. Fax: 817-292-3644. E-mail: kseverson@southwestchristian.org. Web site: www.southwestchristian.org.

SOUTHWESTERN ACADEMY

Beaver Creek Ranch Campus
Rimrock, Arizona 86335
Head of School: Mr. Kenneth Veronda

petersons.com

General Information Coeducational boarding and day college-preparatory and general academic school. Grades 8–PG. Founded: 1963. Setting: rural. Nearest major city is Sedona. Students are housed in single-sex dormitories. 180-acre campus. 19 buildings on campus. Approved or accredited by The Association of Boarding Schools and Arizona Department of Education. Endowment: $7.9 million. Total enrollment: 25. Upper school average class size: 6. Upper school faculty-student ratio: 1:4.

Upper School Student Profile Grade 9: 6 students (3 boys, 3 girls); Grade 10: 6 students (3 boys, 3 girls); Grade 11: 7 students (3 boys, 4 girls); Grade 12: 5 students (2 boys, 3 girls). 95% of students are boarding students. 3 states are represented in upper school student body. 65% are international students. International students from China, Hong Kong, Macedonia, Nepal, Republic of Korea, and Thailand; 2 other countries represented in student body.

Faculty School total: 10. In upper school: 6 men, 4 women; 4 have advanced degrees; 6 reside on campus.

Subjects Offered Advanced math, Advanced Placement courses, algebra, American history, American literature, American literature-AP, Arabic, art, art appreciation, art history, biology, biology-AP, British literature, calculus, chemistry, computer literacy, drama, earth science, ecology, economics, English, English composition, environmental education, environmental science, environmental studies, ESL, fine arts, general math, geology, geometry, health, integrated science, journalism, Latin, math review, mathematics, music, music appreciation, outdoor education, physics, pre-algebra, Spanish, studio art, U.S. government, world cultures, yearbook.

Graduation Requirements Algebra, American government, American history, American literature, British literature, computer literacy, economics, electives, English, foreign language, geometry, lab science, mathematics, physical education (includes health), visual and performing arts, world cultures. Community service is required.

Special Academic Programs Advanced Placement exam preparation in 2 subject areas; honors section; accelerated programs; independent study; term-away projects; ESL (5 students enrolled).

College Placement 6 students graduated in 2005; 4 went to college, including Arizona State University; Northern Arizona University; Occidental College. Other: 2 entered a postgraduate year. Median SAT verbal: 400, median SAT math: 600.

Student Life Upper grades have specified standards of dress, student council, honor system. Discipline rests primarily with faculty.

Summer Programs Remediation, enrichment, advancement, ESL, art/fine arts, rigorous outdoor training programs offered; session focuses on academics and outdoor/environmental education; held on campus; accepts boys and girls; open to students from other schools. 30 students usually enrolled. 2006 schedule: June 26 to August 4. Application deadline: none.

Tuition and Aid Day student tuition: $13,800; 7-day tuition and room/board: $29,500. Tuition installment plan (monthly payment plans, individually arranged payment plans). Need-based scholarship grants available. In 2005–06, 45% of upper-school students received aid. Total amount of financial aid awarded in 2005–06: $316,600.

Admissions Traditional secondary-level entrance grade is 9. For fall 2005, 20 students applied for upper-level admission, 12 were accepted, 11 enrolled. Any standardized test required. Deadline for receipt of application materials: none. Application fee required: $100. Interview recommended.

Athletics Coed Intramural: archery, back packing, baseball, basketball, bicycling, billiards, cross-country running, fishing, fitness, golf, hiking/backpacking, horseback riding, horseshoes, ice skating, mountain biking, outdoor education, outdoor recreation, outdoor skills, paint ball, rock climbing, ropes courses, skiing (cross-country), skiing (downhill), snowboarding, soccer, softball, swimming and diving, table tennis, tennis, track and field, volleyball. 1 PE instructor, 1 coach.

Computers Computers are regularly used in all classes. Computer network features include campus e-mail, on-campus library services, CD-ROMs, Internet access, office computer access, wireless campus network.

Contact Ms. Lauren Brunjes, Admissions Director. 626-799-5010 Ext. 1204. Fax: 626-799-0407. E-mail: admissions@southwesternacademy.edu. Web site: www. southwesternacademy.edu.

See full description on page 1072.

SOUTHWESTERN ACADEMY

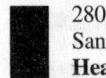

2800 Monterey Road
San Marino, California 91108
Head of School: Kenneth R. Veronda

petersons.com

General Information Coeducational boarding and day college-preparatory, general academic, and ESL school. Grades 6–PG. Founded: 1924. Setting: suburban. Nearest major city is Pasadena. Students are housed in single-sex dormitories. 8-acre campus. 8 buildings on campus. Approved or accredited by The Association of Boarding Schools, Western Association of Schools and Colleges, and California Department of Education. Member of Secondary School Admission Test Board. Endowment: $15.5 million. Total enrollment: 111. Upper school average class size: 9. Upper school faculty-student ratio: 1:6.

Upper School Student Profile Grade 9: 14 students (9 boys, 5 girls); Grade 10: 23 students (17 boys, 6 girls); Grade 11: 23 students (15 boys, 8 girls); Grade 12: 27 students (16 boys, 11 girls); Postgraduate: 3 students (2 boys, 1 girl). 66% of students are boarding students. 49% are state residents. 3 states are represented in upper school student body. 47% are international students. International students from China, Hong Kong, Japan, Republic of Korea, Taiwan, and Thailand; 9 other countries represented in student body.

Faculty School total: 25. In upper school: 18 men, 7 women; 7 have advanced degrees; 7 reside on campus.

Subjects Offered Algebra, American history, American literature, anthropology, art, art history, biology, calculus, ceramics, chemistry, computer math, computer programming, computer science, creative writing, drama, driver education, earth science, ecology, economics, English, English literature, ESL, European history, expository writing, film appreciation, fine arts, geography, geology, geometry, government/civics, grammar, health, history, history of science, journalism, library studies, mathematics, music, photography, physical education, physics, psychology, science, social science, social studies, Spanish, speech, world culture, world history, world literature, writing.

Graduation Requirements Algebra, American government, American history, American literature, British literature, computer literacy, economics, electives, English, foreign language, geometry, lab science, mathematics, physical education (includes health), visual and performing arts, world cultures. Community service is required.

Special Academic Programs Advanced Placement exam preparation in 3 subject areas; honors section; accelerated programs; independent study; study at local college for college credit; ESL (22 students enrolled).

College Placement 29 students graduated in 2005; 28 went to college, including Boston University; California State University; Pasadena City College; University of California, Los Angeles; University of San Francisco; University of Southern California. Other: 1 entered a postgraduate year. Median SAT verbal: 440, median SAT math: 650.

Student Life Upper grades have specified standards of dress, student council, honor system. Discipline rests primarily with faculty.

Summer Programs Remediation, enrichment, advancement, ESL, art/fine arts, computer instruction programs offered; session focuses on academics; held on campus; accepts boys and girls; open to students from other schools. 60 students usually enrolled. 2006 schedule: June 12 to September 15. Application deadline: none.

Tuition and Aid Day student tuition: $13,800; 7-day tuition and room/board: $29,500. Tuition installment plan (monthly payment plans, individually arranged payment plans). Need-based scholarship grants available. In 2005–06, 32% of upper-school students received aid. Total amount of financial aid awarded in 2005–06: $229,500.

Admissions Traditional secondary-level entrance grade is 9. For fall 2005, 175 students applied for upper-level admission, 70 were accepted, 45 enrolled. Any standardized test required. Deadline for receipt of application materials: none. Application fee required: $100. Interview recommended.

Athletics Interscholastic: baseball (boys), basketball (b,g), track and field (b,g), volleyball (b,g); intramural: baseball (b), basketball (b,g), track and field (b,g), volleyball (b,g); coed interscholastic: baseball, cross-country running, soccer, tennis; coed intramural: baseball, bicycling, cross-country running, flag football, golf, hiking/backpacking, outdoor activities, physical fitness, skiing (downhill), snowboarding, soccer, table tennis, tennis, weight training. 4 PE instructors, 9 coaches, 1 trainer.

Computers Computers are regularly used in art, English, ESL, foreign language, history, mathematics, music, science, yearbook classes. Computer network features include campus e-mail, on-campus library services, CD-ROMs, online commercial services, Internet access, file transfer, office computer access, wireless campus network.

Contact Ms. Lauren Brunjes, Admissions Director. 626-799-5010 Ext. 1204. Fax: 626-799-0407. E-mail: admissions@southwesternacademy.edu. Web site: www. southwesternacademy.edu.

See full description on page 1072.

SPAR HAWK SCHOOL

18 Maple Street
Salisbury, Massachusetts 01952
Head of School: Louise Stilphen

General Information Coeducational day college-preparatory school. Grades K–12. Setting: rural. 7-acre campus. 1 building on campus. Approved or accredited by Massachusetts Department of Education.

Faculty School total: 44. In upper school: 5 men, 9 women.

Tuition and Aid Day student tuition: $16,000.

Admissions Deadline for receipt of application materials: none. No application fee required.

Contact Danielle Shylit, Dean of Students (Upper School). 978-388-5354. Web site: www.sparhawkschool.com/home.html.

SPARTANBURG DAY SCHOOL

1701 Skylyn Drive
Spartanburg, South Carolina 29307
Head of School: Mr. Christopher A. Dorrance

General Information Coeducational day college-preparatory and arts school. Grades PK–12. Founded: 1957. Setting: suburban. Nearest major city is Charlotte. 40-acre campus. 9 buildings on campus. Approved or accredited by Southern Association of Colleges and Schools and Southern Association of Independent Schools. Member of National Association of Independent Schools. Endowment: $1.8 million. Total enrollment: 472. Upper school average class size: 12. Upper school faculty-student ratio: 1:11.

Upper School Student Profile Grade 9: 25 students (14 boys, 11 girls); Grade 10: 39 students (18 boys, 21 girls); Grade 11: 30 students (14 boys, 16 girls); Grade 12: 32 students (13 boys, 19 girls).

Faculty School total: 59. In upper school: 9 men, 7 women; 11 have advanced degrees.

Subjects Offered Advanced chemistry, advanced computer applications, advanced math, algebra, American government, American government-AP, American history, American history-AP, American literature, applied music, art, art history, art history-AP, art in New York, arts appreciation, band, biochemistry, biology, biology-AP, calculus, calculus-AP, career/college preparation, character education, chemistry, chemistry-AP, chorus, college counseling, college placement, college writing, communications, community service, comparative government and politics-AP, competitive science projects, composition, composition-AP, computer education, computer keyboarding, computer math, computer multimedia, computer processing, computer programming, computer programming-AP, computer science, computer science-AP, concert band, concert choir, creative drama, creative writing, critical thinking, critical writing, cultural arts, debate, decision making skills, drama performance, drawing, drawing and design, earth science, economics, economics-AP, English, English composition, English literature, English literature-AP, ESL, European history, fine arts, French, French language-AP, geometry, German, German-AP, government/civics, grammar, history, HTML design, intro to computers, jazz band, Latin, Latin American literature, Latin-AP, macroeconomics-AP, mathematics, modern European history-AP, music, music theory, philosophy, physical education, physics, physics-AP, science, Spanish, Spanish language-AP, speech, statistics, statistics-AP, studio art-AP, trigonometry, world history.

Graduation Requirements Algebra, arts and fine arts (art, music, dance, drama), biology, chemistry, English, foreign language, geometry, ancient or European history, one additional lab science, participation in one sport per year.

Special Academic Programs Advanced Placement exam preparation in 16 subject areas; honors section; study at local college for college credit; academic accommodation for the gifted and the artistically talented; programs in English, mathematics, general development for dyslexic students; ESL.

College Placement 24 students graduated in 2005; all went to college, including Clemson University; Furman University; Hampshire College; University of Mississippi; University of Virginia; Wofford College. Mean SAT verbal: 622, mean SAT math: 590. 59% scored over 600 on SAT verbal, 46% scored over 600 on SAT math.

Student Life Upper grades have specified standards of dress, student council, honor system. Discipline rests primarily with faculty.

Summer Programs Enrichment, sports, art/fine arts programs offered; session focuses on enrichment; held on campus; accepts boys and girls; open to students from other schools. 10 students usually enrolled. 2006 schedule: June 16 to August 9. Application deadline: May 1.

Tuition and Aid Day student tuition: $10,600. Tuition installment plan (monthly payment plans, tuition insurance). Merit scholarship grants, need-based scholarship

Spartanburg Day School

grants, tuition reduction for children of faculty/staff available. In 2005–06, 22% of upper-school students received aid. Total amount of financial aid awarded in 2005–06: $110,170.

Admissions Traditional secondary-level entrance grade is 9. For fall 2005, 16 students applied for upper-level admission, 12 were accepted, 9 enrolled. ERB, Kaufman Test of Educational Achievement, Metropolitan Test, ITBS, Otis-Lennon School Ability Test, Stanford Achievement Test or writing sample required. Deadline for receipt of application materials: none. Application fee required: $50. On-campus interview recommended.

Athletics Interscholastic: baseball (boys), basketball (b,g), cheering (g), cross-country running (b,g), field hockey (g), soccer (b,g), swimming and diving (b,g); coed interscholastic: golf, martial arts, physical fitness, weight lifting. 4 PE instructors, 8 coaches.

Computers Computers are regularly used in art, English, history, mathematics classes. Computer network features include on-campus library services, CD-ROMs, Internet access, multimedia presentation stations.

Contact Mrs. Robbie Richards, Director of Admissions. 864-582-7539 Ext. 202. Fax: 864-948-0026. E-mail: robbie.richards@sdsgriffin.org. Web site: www.sdsgriffin.org.

THE SPENCE SCHOOL

22 East 91st Street
New York, New York 10128-0657
Head of School: Arlene J. Gibson

General Information Girls' day college-preparatory school. Grades K–12. Founded: 1892. Setting: urban. 1 building on campus. Approved or accredited by New York State Association of Independent Schools. Member of National Association of Independent Schools and Secondary School Admission Test Board. Endowment: $58.5 million. Total enrollment: 644. Upper school average class size: 14. Upper school faculty-student ratio: 1:7.

Upper School Student Profile Grade 9: 57 students (57 girls); Grade 10: 56 students (56 girls); Grade 11: 45 students (45 girls); Grade 12: 42 students (42 girls).

Faculty School total: 93. In upper school: 17 men, 29 women; 32 have advanced degrees.

Subjects Offered Acting, advanced math, African history, African literature, African-American literature, algebra, American literature, art, art history, art-AP, Asian literature, astronomy, bioethics, biology, calculus, ceramics, chemistry, Chinese history, computer science, critical writing, design, drama, dramatic arts, earth science, English, European history, exercise science, fiber arts, French, French literature-AP, geometry, health, history, Indian studies, Japanese history, Latin, Latin American literature, Latin American studies, mathematics, Middle East, music, music composition, Native American studies, novel, nutrition, painting, photo shop, photography, physical education, physics, poetry, pre-algebra, robotics, science, sculpture, Shakespeare, Spanish, Spanish literature, speech, statistics, technology, theater production, U.S. history, women's studies, world religions, world studies.

Graduation Requirements Advanced math, algebra, American literature, art, biology, chemistry, computer science, dance, drama, English, European history, foreign language, geometry, history, music, non-Western societies, physical education (includes health), physics, pre-algebra, science, Shakespeare, speech, technology, U.S. history, visual and performing arts, world religions, world studies.

Special Academic Programs Advanced Placement exam preparation in 2 subject areas; honors section; independent study; term-away projects; study abroad.

College Placement 38 students graduated in 2005; all went to college, including Columbia College; Cornell University; Lehigh University; Tufts University; University of Pennsylvania; Wellesley College. Mean SAT verbal: 729, mean SAT math: 711. 97% scored over 600 on SAT verbal, 97% scored over 600 on SAT math.

Student Life Upper grades have uniform requirement, student council. Discipline rests primarily with faculty.

Tuition and Aid Day student tuition: $27,000. Tuition installment plan (Academic Management Services Plan). Need-based scholarship grants, prepGATE Private School Loan Program, Academic Management Services Private Loans available. In 2005–06, 24% of upper-school students received aid. Total amount of financial aid awarded in 2005–06: $987,010.

Admissions Traditional secondary-level entrance grade is 9. ERB, ISEE and school's own test required. Deadline for receipt of application materials: January 1. Application fee required: $65. On-campus interview required.

Athletics Interscholastic: badminton, basketball, field hockey, soccer, softball, swimming and diving, tennis, track and field, volleyball. 8 PE instructors, 12 coaches, 1 trainer.

Computers Computers are regularly used in art, basic skills, design, independent study, library, library skills, literary magazine, mathematics, news writing, newspaper, photojournalism, programming, publications, research skills, science, Web site design, yearbook classes. Computer network features include campus e-mail, on-campus library services, CD-ROMs, online commercial services, Internet access.

Contact Susan Parker, Director of Admissions. 212-289-5940. Fax: 212-289-6025. E-mail: sparker@spenceschool.org.

SPRING CREEK LODGE ACADEMY

Thompson Falls, Montana
See Special Needs Schools section.

SPRING RIDGE ACADEMY

Spring Valley, Arizona
See Special Needs Schools section.

SPRINGSIDE SCHOOL

8000 Cherokee Street
Philadelphia, Pennsylvania 19118
Head of School: Ms. Priscilla Sands

petersons.com

General Information Girls' day college-preparatory, arts, and technology school. Grades PK–12. Founded: 1879. Setting: suburban. 30-acre campus. 1 building on campus. Approved or accredited by Pennsylvania Association of Private Academic Schools and Pennsylvania Department of Education. Member of National Association of Independent Schools and Secondary School Admission Test Board. Endowment: $16 million. Total enrollment: 639. Upper school average class size: 16. Upper school faculty-student ratio: 1:7.

Upper School Student Profile Grade 9: 46 students (46 girls); Grade 10: 51 students (51 girls); Grade 11: 47 students (47 girls); Grade 12: 41 students (41 girls).

Faculty School total: 94. In upper school: 8 men, 22 women; 23 have advanced degrees.

Subjects Offered Adolescent issues, Advanced Placement courses, African studies, algebra, American history, American literature, architecture, art, art history, biology, biology-AP, botany, calculus, calculus-AP, chemistry, choral music, community service, comparative government and politics-AP, computer math, computer programming, computer science, creative writing, dance, dance performance, drama, earth science, economics, English, English literature, English-AP, environmental science, European history, European history-AP, expository writing, fine arts, forensics, French, French language-AP, geology, geometry, handbells, jazz ensemble, Latin, Latin-AP, logic, mathematics, Middle Eastern history, music, orchestra, photography, physical education, physics, physics-AP, physiology, science, Shakespeare, social studies, Spanish, Spanish-AP, speech, statistics, statistics-AP, theater, trigonometry, U.S. government-AP, world history-AP, writing, yearbook, yoga.

Graduation Requirements Arts and fine arts (art, music, dance, drama), computer science, English, foreign language, history, mathematics, music, physical education (includes health), science. Community service is required.

Special Academic Programs Advanced Placement exam preparation in 18 subject areas; honors section; independent study; term-away projects; study abroad.

College Placement 41 students graduated in 2005; all went to college, including American University; Bucknell University; Drexel University; Georgetown University; Gettysburg College; University of Pennsylvania. Mean SAT verbal: 630, mean SAT math: 630.

Student Life Upper grades have uniform requirement, student council, honor system. Discipline rests equally with students and faculty.

Tuition and Aid Day student tuition: $19,850. Tuition installment plan (monthly payment plans, Higher Education Service, Inc). Merit scholarship grants, need-based scholarship grants available. In 2005–06, 23% of upper-school students received aid; total upper-school merit-scholarship money awarded: $5000. Total amount of financial aid awarded in 2005–06: $474,100.

Admissions Traditional secondary-level entrance grade is 9. For fall 2005, 51 students applied for upper-level admission, 17 were accepted, 6 enrolled. ISEE or SSAT required. Deadline for receipt of application materials: January 15. Application fee required: $35. On-campus interview required.

Athletics Interscholastic: basketball, crew, field hockey, golf, independent competitive sports, lacrosse, soccer, softball, squash, tennis, track and field, volleyball; intramural: aerobics, aerobics/dance, badminton, ballet, basketball, dance, fitness, fitness walking, flag football, Frisbee, golf, martial arts, physical fitness, physical training, soccer, softball, ultimate Frisbee, volleyball, weight training. 4 PE instructors, 6 coaches, 1 trainer.

Computers Computers are regularly used in all academic classes. Computer network features include campus e-mail, on-campus library services, CD-ROMs, online commercial services, Internet access, DVD, wireless campus network.

Contact Ms. Murielle Telemaque, Admissions Assistant. 215-247-7007. Fax: 215-247-7308. E-mail: mtelemaque@springside.org. Web site: www.springside.org.

ANNOUNCEMENT FROM THE SCHOOL Springside School, founded in 1879 and the oldest school for girls in Philadelphia, enrolls 639 students in prekindergarten through grade 12, drawing students and faculty members from over 65 Zip codes throughout the city and its suburbs. Springside offers a comprehensive and rigorous college-preparatory curriculum that includes opportunities in visual and performing arts, athletics, service, and technology and extensive leadership and extracurricular activities. The 30-acre campus includes playing fields, tennis courts, and land in the Wissahickon watershed, which is

used by the fully integrated environmental education program as an outdoor classroom to combine science, technology, and environmental stewardship for this urban forest. In 2004, Springside opened a new academic wing with 12 classrooms, 5 science laboratories, art studios and gallery space, commons space for students, and a library with dedicated reading and study areas and a technology suite. The Vare Field House, an athletic facility that will house 3 full basketball/volleyball courts, 4 squash courts, a crew tank, a dance studio, and a weight and fitness center, is scheduled to open in February 2006. From Springside's Mission Statement: "All college preparatory schools expect their students to excel in a rigorous academic program. Springside asks more: that girls discover how they learn, that they take intellectual delight in their education, and that they gain the courage and integrity to negotiate the breadth of their complex futures. In every way, Springside School educates girls and young women to develop their capacities for leadership in the 21st century." For more information, please visit www.springside.org.

SQUAW VALLEY ACADEMY

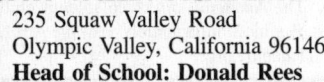

235 Squaw Valley Road
Olympic Valley, California 96146
Head of School: Donald Rees

petersons.com

General Information Coeducational boarding and day college-preparatory and arts school. Grades 6–12. Founded: 1978. Setting: small town. Nearest major city is Sacramento. Students are housed in single-sex dormitories. 3-acre campus. 3 buildings on campus. Approved or accredited by Western Association of Schools and Colleges. Total enrollment: 75. Upper school average class size: 9. Upper school faculty-student ratio: 1:7.

Upper School Student Profile Grade 9: 7 students (5 boys, 2 girls); Grade 10: 12 students (8 boys, 4 girls); Grade 11: 24 students (15 boys, 9 girls); Grade 12: 25 students (21 boys, 4 girls). 85% of students are boarding students. 68% are state residents. 12 states are represented in upper school student body. 12% are international students. International students from Brazil, Germany, Republic of Korea, and Saudi Arabia.

Faculty School total: 11. In upper school: 6 men, 4 women; 2 have advanced degrees; 1 resides on campus.

Subjects Offered Algebra, American history, American literature, anatomy, art, biology, calculus, ceramics, chemistry, computer programming, computer science, creative writing, drama, English, English literature, environmental science, expository writing, fine arts, French, geography, geometry, government/civics, grammar, health, history, mathematics, music appreciation, outdoor education, photography, physical education, physics, psychology, publications, science, social science, social studies, Spanish, trigonometry, typing, video, world history, writing.

Graduation Requirements Arts and fine arts (art, music, dance, drama), English, foreign language, mathematics, outdoor education, physical education (includes health), science, social science, social studies (includes history), participation in skiing and snowboarding.

Special Academic Programs Advanced Placement exam preparation in 4 subject areas; honors section; independent study; academic accommodation for the gifted and the artistically talented; ESL (4 students enrolled).

College Placement 14 students graduated in 2005; 12 went to college, including California Polytechnic State University, San Luis Obispo; California State University, Los Angeles; Southern Oregon University; The Pennsylvania State University University Park Campus; University of Colorado at Boulder; University of Nevada, Reno. Other: 1 entered military service, 1 had other specific plans. Median SAT verbal: 560, median SAT math: 515, median combined SAT: 1555. 23% scored over 600 on SAT verbal, 23% scored over 600 on SAT math, 15% scored over 1800 on combined SAT.

Student Life Upper grades have specified standards of dress, student council, honor system. Discipline rests primarily with faculty.

Summer Programs Remediation, enrichment, advancement, ESL, sports programs offered; session focuses on academics and outdoor recreation; held both on and off campus; held at Lake Tahoe; accepts boys and girls; open to students from other schools. 60 students usually enrolled. 2006 schedule: June 25 to August 4. Application deadline: none.

Tuition and Aid Day student tuition: $11,916; 5-day tuition and room/board: $24,876; 7-day tuition and room/board: $31,914. Tuition installment plan (individually arranged payment plans). Tuition reduction for siblings, need-based scholarship grants available.

Admissions Traditional secondary-level entrance grade is 9. For fall 2005, 83 students applied for upper-level admission, 75 were accepted, 70 enrolled. School's own exam required. Deadline for receipt of application materials: none. Application fee required: $50. Interview required.

Athletics Interscholastic: golf (boys), skiing (downhill) (b,g), snowboarding (b,g); intramural: skiing (downhill) (b,g), snowboarding (b,g); coed interscholastic: bowling, skiing (downhill), snowboarding, soccer; coed intramural: alpine skiing, back packing, baseball, bicycling, canoeing/kayaking, climbing, cross-country running, fishing, fitness, fitness walking, fly fishing, freestyle skiing, Frisbee, golf, hiking/backpacking, ice skating, jogging, kayaking, martial arts, mountain biking, mountaineering, nordic skiing, outdoor activities, outdoor adventure, outdoor education, outdoor recreation,

outdoor skills, physical fitness, physical training, rafting, rock climbing, ropes courses, skateboarding, skiing (cross-country), skiing (downhill), snowboarding, soccer, softball, strength & conditioning, swimming and diving, telemark skiing, ultimate Frisbee, walking, weight lifting, weight training, yoga.

Computers Computers are regularly used in English, graphic arts, health, history, journalism, publications, SAT preparation, science, typing, wilderness education, word processing, writing classes. Computer network features include CD-ROMs, online commercial services, Internet access, office computer access, DVD, wireless campus network.

Contact Amye Cole, Admissions Director. 530-583-9393 Ext. 21. Fax: 530-581-1111. E-mail: enroll@sva.org. Web site: www.sva.org.

See full description on page 1074.

STANBRIDGE ACADEMY

San Mateo, California
See Special Needs Schools section.

STANSTEAD COLLEGE

450 Dufferin Street
Stanstead, Quebec J0B 3E0, Canada
Head of School: Mr. Michael Wolfe

petersons.com

General Information Coeducational boarding and day college-preparatory and bilingual studies school. Grades 7–12. Founded: 1872. Setting: rural. Nearest major city is Montreal, Canada. Students are housed in single-sex dormitories. 720-acre campus. 10 buildings on campus. Approved or accredited by New England Association of Schools and Colleges, Quebec Association of Independent Schools, The Association of Boarding Schools, and Quebec Department of Education. Affiliate member of National Association of Independent Schools. Language of instruction: English. Endowment: CAN$4.2 million. Total enrollment: 205. Upper school average class size: 12. Upper school faculty-student ratio: 1:8.

Upper School Student Profile Grade 10: 38 students (23 boys, 15 girls); Grade 11: 60 students (36 boys, 24 girls); Grade 12: 36 students (21 boys, 15 girls). 74% of students are boarding students. 38% are province residents. 11 provinces are represented in upper school student body. 42% are international students. International students from Germany, Japan, Mexico, Republic of Korea, Taiwan, and United States; 10 other countries represented in student body.

Faculty School total: 32. In upper school: 15 men, 17 women; 5 have advanced degrees; 18 reside on campus.

Subjects Offered Algebra, art, biology, calculus, career planning, chemistry, computer programming, computer science, drama, ecology, economics, English, English literature, environmental science, ESL, ethics, French, geography, geometry, history, home economics, mathematics, music, physics, political science, psychology, science, social studies, sociology, Spanish, statistics, technology, theater, trigonometry, world history.

Graduation Requirements English, foreign language, mathematics, science, social studies (includes history).

Special Academic Programs Advanced Placement exam preparation in 13 subject areas; honors section; independent study; study abroad; special instructional classes for students with mild learning disorders; ESL (10 students enrolled).

College Placement 39 students graduated in 2005; 37 went to college, including Boston College; Queen's University at Kingston; University of Toronto. Other: 1 went to work, 1 had other specific plans.

Student Life Upper grades have uniform requirement, student council, honor system. Discipline rests primarily with faculty.

Summer Programs ESL, sports programs offered; session focuses on second-language training; held both on and off campus; held at nearby lakes, mountains, local attractions; accepts boys and girls; open to students from other schools. 130 students usually enrolled. 2006 schedule: July 3 to July 23. Application deadline: none.

Tuition and Aid Day student tuition: CAN$15,590; 7-day tuition and room/board: CAN$34,660. Tuition installment plan (monthly payment plans). Tuition reduction for siblings, merit scholarship grants, need-based scholarship grants, need-based loans available. In 2005–06, 35% of upper-school students received aid; total upper-school merit-scholarship money awarded: CAN$800,000. Total amount of financial aid awarded in 2005–06: CAN$800,000.

Admissions Traditional secondary-level entrance grade is 10. For fall 2005, 130 students applied for upper-level admission, 123 were accepted, 94 enrolled. OLSAT, Stanford Achievement Test required. Deadline for receipt of application materials: none. Application fee required: CAN$100. Interview required.

Athletics Interscholastic: basketball (boys, girls), football (b,g), ice hockey (b,g), rugby (b,g), soccer (b,g), squash (b,g), tennis (b,g), track and field (b,g); coed interscholastic: aquatics, cross-country running, golf, skiing (cross-country), swimming and diving; coed intramural: aerobics, alpine skiing, back packing, badminton, basketball, broomball, canoeing/kayaking, curling, dance, equestrian sports, figure skating, fitness, hiking/backpacking, horseback riding, kayaking, life saving, martial arts, outdoor education, outdoor recreation, outdoor skills, scuba diving, skiing

(cross-country), skiing (downhill), snowboarding, softball, swimming and diving, track and field, volleyball, water polo, weight lifting. 3 PE instructors, 2 coaches, 1 trainer.

Computers Computers are regularly used in English, mathematics, science classes. Computer network features include on-campus library services, CD-ROMs, Internet access, wireless campus network.

Contact Joanne Tracy Carruthers, Director of Admissions. 819-876-2223. Fax: 819-876-5891. E-mail: admissions@stansteadcollege.com. Web site: www. stansteadcollege.com.

See full description on page 1076.

STATEN ISLAND ACADEMY

715 Todt Hill Road
Staten Island, New York 10304
Head of School: Mrs. Diane J. Hulse

petersons.com

General Information Coeducational day college-preparatory, arts, and technology school. Grades PK–12. Founded: 1886. Setting: urban. Nearest major city is New York. 12-acre campus. 7 buildings on campus. Approved or accredited by Middle States Association of Colleges and Schools and New York State Association of Independent Schools. Member of National Association of Independent Schools. Endowment: $4.5 million. Total enrollment: 402. Upper school average class size: 17. Upper school faculty-student ratio: 1:5.

Upper School Student Profile Grade 9: 27 students (16 boys, 11 girls); Grade 10: 31 students (18 boys, 13 girls); Grade 11: 33 students (23 boys, 10 girls); Grade 12: 35 students (22 boys, 13 girls).

Faculty School total: 75. In upper school: 15 men, 17 women; 30 have advanced degrees.

Subjects Offered Algebra, American history, American literature, anatomy, art, art history, astronomy, biology, calculus, ceramics, chemistry, community service, computer science, creative writing, dance, drama, economics, English, English literature, European history, expository writing, fine arts, French, geometry, grammar, health, human relations, journalism, Latin, law, mathematics, meteorology, music, oceanography, photography, physical education, physical science, physics, psychology, public speaking, robotics, science, social science, social studies, Spanish, speech, statistics, theater, trigonometry, visual and performing arts, Web site design, world history, writing.

Graduation Requirements Arts and fine arts (art, music, dance, drama), computer science, English, foreign language, human relations, mathematics, physical education (includes health), public speaking, science, science and technology, social science, social studies (includes history), Senior Year Internship Program. Community service is required.

Special Academic Programs Advanced Placement exam preparation in 12 subject areas; honors section; independent study; study at local college for college credit; study abroad; academic accommodation for the gifted, the musically talented, and the artistically talented; ESL.

College Placement 34 students graduated in 2005; all went to college, including Brown University; Hamilton College; Harvard University; New York University; Princeton University. Mean SAT verbal: 594, mean SAT math: 592.

Student Life Upper grades have specified standards of dress, student council, honor system. Discipline rests primarily with faculty.

Tuition and Aid Day student tuition: $20,220. Tuition installment plan (monthly payment plans, individually arranged payment plans). Tuition reduction for siblings, merit scholarship grants, need-based scholarship grants, need-based loans available. In 2005–06, 26% of upper-school students received aid. Total amount of financial aid awarded in 2005–06: $1,000,000.

Admissions Traditional secondary-level entrance grade is 9. For fall 2005, 110 students applied for upper-level admission, 80 were accepted, 20 enrolled. ERB or ISEE required. Deadline for receipt of application materials: January 15. Application fee required: $50. On-campus interview required.

Athletics Interscholastic: baseball (boys), basketball (b,g), lacrosse (g), soccer (b,g), softball (g), tennis (b,g), volleyball (b,g); coed interscholastic: cheering, cross-country running, dance, golf. 7 PE instructors, 19 coaches.

Computers Computers are regularly used in art, data processing, English, graphic design, independent study, journalism, keyboarding, library, mathematics, newspaper, publications, research skills, SAT preparation, science, social sciences, word processing, writing, yearbook classes. Computer network features include campus e-mail, on-campus library services, CD-ROMs, online commercial services, Internet access, file transfer, DVD, wireless campus network.

Contact Mrs. Linda Shuffman, Director of Admission. 718-303-7803. Fax: 718-979-7641. E-mail: lshuffman@statenislandacademy.org. Web site: www. statenislandacademy.org.

ANNOUNCEMENT FROM THE SCHOOL Staten Island Academy was founded in 1884 as a nonsectarian, coeducational, college-preparatory day school for students in prekindergarten through grade 12. The only independent school on Staten Island, the Academy is a beacon of educational excellence for students from throughout the metropolitan area. The Academy's seven-building, 12-acre campus includes a 6,000-square-foot Science and Technology Center, complete with computer labs and classrooms; a recently renovated library with a CD-ROM index and Dialog; a gym and fitness center; 3 tennis courts; soccer, lacrosse, and baseball fields; 2 outdoor, in-ground pools; and 2 playgrounds. "To educate the whole child" is the underlying principle of the Academy's philosophy of education. Academy students are critical thinkers and thoughtful critics, and they respect the differences among people, societies, and cultures. The Academy encourages its students to achieve their best by providing a supportive environment that cultivates intellectual and personal growth. The broad curriculum is designed to prepare students to reach their goals as well as to meet the challenges and opportunities of a complex future. At the high school level, honors and Advanced Placement courses are offered in every major discipline. Faculty members are dedicated to promoting intellectual rigor, imagination, and curiosity. The Academy welcomes and encourages parental cooperation and communication. There is an adviser system for grades 5–12 and a college guidance program with a 1:8 adviser-student ratio. The Academy integrates performing arts, visual arts, computer education, and physical education within the academic program throughout all grade levels. Students further develop their talents and interests by actively participating in community service, after-school clubs, and academic competitions. The Academy offers 26 student clubs and organizations and 30 athletic teams. For more information, visit the Academy's Web site at http://www.statenislandacademy.org.

STELLA MARIS HIGH SCHOOL AND THE MAURA CLARKE JUNIOR HIGH PROGRAM

Beach 112 Street
Rockaway Park, New York 11694
Head of School: Miss Geri Martinez

General Information Coeducational day college-preparatory school, affiliated with Roman Catholic Church. Boys grades 6–8, girls grades 6–12. Founded: 1943. Setting: urban. Nearest major city is New York. 3-acre campus. 1 building on campus. Approved or accredited by Middle States Association of Colleges and Schools, National Catholic Education Association, New York State Board of Regents, and New York Department of Education. Total enrollment: 440. Upper school average class size: 22. Upper school faculty-student ratio: 1:11.

Upper School Student Profile 85% of students are Roman Catholic.

Faculty School total: 41. In upper school: 7 men, 33 women; 25 have advanced degrees.

Subjects Offered Accounting, American literature, art, bioethics, biology-AP, British literature, British literature (honors), calculus, career/college preparation, chemistry, child development, chorus, Christian ethics, college planning, crafts, desktop publishing, earth science, economics, English, English literature, environmental science, family and consumer science, French, health, honors English, human anatomy, interior design, Italian, keyboarding, library, marketing, mathematics, music appreciation, painting, parent/child development, parenting, peer counseling, physical education, portfolio art, pre-calculus, psychology, SAT preparation, scripture, Spanish, technology, U.S. government, U.S. history, U.S. history-AP, word processing, world geography, world history.

Graduation Requirements Arts and fine arts (art, music, dance, drama), English, foreign language, health education, mathematics, physical education (includes health), religious studies, science, social studies (includes history), passing grade in required NY State Regents examinations.

Special Academic Programs Advanced Placement exam preparation in 2 subject areas; honors section; study at local college for college credit; academic accommodation for the gifted.

College Placement Colleges students went to include City College of the City University of New York; Nassau Community College; St. John's University; St. Joseph's College, New York.

Student Life Upper grades have uniform requirement, student council. Discipline rests primarily with faculty. Attendance at religious services is required.

Summer Programs Remediation programs offered; session focuses on remediation and make-up (courses and state exams); held on campus; accepts boys and girls; open to students from other schools. 175 students usually enrolled. 2006 schedule: July 12 to August 16. Application deadline: June 26.

Tuition and Aid Day student tuition: $6100. Tuition installment plan (SMART Tuition Payment Plan). Merit scholarship grants, need-based scholarship grants available. In 2005–06, 13% of upper-school students received aid; total upper-school merit-scholarship money awarded: $55,000. Total amount of financial aid awarded in 2005–06: $67,200.

Admissions Diocesan Entrance Exam or TerraNova required. Deadline for receipt of application materials: none. Application fee required: $25. Interview required.

Athletics Interscholastic: basketball (girls), cheering (g), dance squad (g), soccer (g), softball (g), swimming and diving (g), volleyball (g); intramural: aerobics (g), aerobics/dance (g), dance (g), fitness (g), golf (g), gymnastics (g). 2 PE instructors, 9 coaches.

Computers Computers are regularly used in business education, career exploration, college planning, data processing, foreign language, mathematics, religious studies,

science, social studies, word processing classes. Computer network features include on-campus library services, CD-ROMs, Internet access, office computer access, homework assignments available online.

Contact Sr. Barbara Buckbee, CSJ, Assistant Principal. 718-634-4994. Fax: 718-634-5267. E-mail: sbbuckbee@stellamarishigh.org. Web site: www.stellamarishs.org.

STEVENSON SCHOOL

3152 Forest Lake Road
Pebble Beach, California 93953
Head of School: Joseph E. Wandke

General Information Coeducational boarding and day college-preparatory and arts school. Boarding grades 9–12, day grades PK–12. Founded: 1952. Setting: suburban. Nearest major city is San Francisco. Students are housed in single-sex by floor dormitories. 60-acre campus. 22 buildings on campus. Approved or accredited by The Association of Boarding Schools, Western Association of Schools and Colleges, and California Department of Education. Member of National Association of Independent Schools and Secondary School Admission Test Board. Endowment: $15 million. Total enrollment: 750. Upper school average class size: 14. Upper school faculty-student ratio: 1:10.

Upper School Student Profile Grade 9: 130 students (68 boys, 62 girls); Grade 10: 146 students (74 boys, 72 girls); Grade 11: 147 students (72 boys, 75 girls); Grade 12: 126 students (71 boys, 55 girls). 49% of students are boarding students. 77% are state residents. 21 states are represented in upper school student body. 15% are international students. International students from Germany, Hong Kong, Republic of Korea, Saudi Arabia, Taiwan, and Thailand; 6 other countries represented in student body.

Faculty School total: 65. In upper school: 35 men, 22 women; 45 have advanced degrees; 28 reside on campus.

Subjects Offered 3-dimensional art, advanced chemistry, Advanced Placement courses, algebra, American history, American literature, American literature-AP, architecture, art, art history, art-AP, biology, biology-AP, broadcasting, calculus, calculus-AP, ceramics, chemistry, chemistry-AP, computer programming, computer science, concert band, creative writing, dance, dance performance, drama, drama performance, drama workshop, dramatic arts, drawing, drawing and design, driver education, economics, economics-AP, English, English literature, English-AP, environmental science, environmental science-AP, ethics, European civilization, European history, expository writing, fine arts, French, French-AP, geometry, German-AP, government/civics, grammar, history of ideas, history-AP, honors algebra, honors English, honors geometry, honors U.S. history, Japanese, jazz, jazz band, jazz ensemble, jazz theory, journalism, Latin, Latin-AP, macroeconomics-AP, marine biology, mathematics, mathematics-AP, microbiology, music, musical productions, musical theater, ornithology, photography, physical education, physics, physics-AP, portfolio art, pre-calculus, psychology, science, social studies, Spanish, Spanish-AP, speech, stage design, stagecraft, studio art—AP, tap dance, theater, trigonometry, U.S. history-AP, visual and performing arts, visual arts, vocal ensemble, wilderness experience, wilderness/outdoor program, wind ensemble, world cultures, world history, world literature, writing, yearbook.

Graduation Requirements Arts and fine arts (art, music, dance, drama), English, foreign language, mathematics, physical education (includes health), science, social studies (includes history).

Special Academic Programs Advanced Placement exam preparation in 18 subject areas; honors section; independent study; term-away projects; domestic exchange program; study abroad; academic accommodation for the gifted, the musically talented, and the artistically talented.

College Placement 125 students graduated in 2005; 122 went to college, including Boston University; Stanford University; United States Military Academy; University of California, Berkeley; University of California, Los Angeles; University of Southern California. Other: 1 entered military service, 2 entered a postgraduate year. Mean SAT verbal: 603, mean SAT math: 636. 46% scored over 600 on SAT verbal, 60% scored over 600 on SAT math.

Student Life Upper grades have student council, honor system. Discipline rests equally with students and faculty.

Summer Programs Enrichment programs offered; held on campus; accepts boys and girls; open to students from other schools. 100 students usually enrolled. 2006 schedule: June 26 to July 28. Application deadline: none.

Tuition and Aid Day student tuition: $21,400; 7-day tuition and room/board: $35,700. Tuition installment plan (Insured Tuition Payment Plan). Need-based scholarship grants available. In 2005–06, 15% of upper-school students received aid. Total amount of financial aid awarded in 2005–06: $1,600,000.

Admissions Traditional secondary-level entrance grade is 9. For fall 2005, 510 students applied for upper-level admission, 239 were accepted, 147 enrolled. SSAT required. Deadline for receipt of application materials: February 15. Application fee required: $75. Interview required.

Athletics Interscholastic: baseball (boys), basketball (b,g), cross-country running (b,g), diving (b,g), field hockey (g), football (b), golf (b,g), lacrosse (b,g), sailing (b,g), soccer (b,g), softball (g), swimming and diving (b,g), tennis (b,g), track and field (b,g), volleyball (g), water polo (b,g); intramural: dance (b,g), golf (b,g), horseback riding (b,g), kayaking (b,g), modern dance (b,g), mountaineering (b,g), outdoor education

(b,g), outdoors (b,g), power lifting (b,g), rock climbing (b,g), strength & conditioning (b,g), table tennis (b,g), weight lifting (b,g), wilderness (b,g), yoga (b,g); coed interscholastic: sailing; coed intramural: basketball, bicycling, climbing, dance, equestrian sports, fencing, horseback riding, kayaking, modern dance, mountaineering, outdoor education, outdoors, rock climbing, sailing, softball, strength & conditioning, table tennis, weight lifting, wilderness, yoga. 22 coaches.

Computers Computers are regularly used in all classes. Computer network features include campus e-mail, on-campus library services, CD-ROMs, online commercial services, Internet access, file transfer, wireless campus network.

Contact Thomas W. Sheppard, Director of Admission. 831-625-8309. Fax: 831-625-5208. E-mail: info@rlstevenson.org. Web site: www.rlstevenson.org.

STONELEIGH–BURNHAM SCHOOL

574 Bernardston Road
Greenfield, Massachusetts 01301
Head of School: Ms. Martha W. Shepardson-Killam

General Information Girls' boarding and day college-preparatory and arts school. Grades 6–PG. Founded: 1869. Setting: small town. Nearest major city is Springfield. Students are housed in single-sex dormitories. 100-acre campus. 7 buildings on campus. Approved or accredited by Georgia Accrediting Commission, Independent Schools of Northern New England, New England Association of Schools and Colleges, The Association of Boarding Schools, and Massachusetts Department of Education. Member of National Association of Independent Schools. Endowment: $2 million. Total enrollment: 159. Upper school average class size: 11. Upper school faculty-student ratio: 1:5.

Upper School Student Profile Grade 9: 22 students (22 girls); Grade 10: 37 students (37 girls); Grade 11: 38 students (38 girls); Grade 12: 40 students (40 girls); Postgraduate: 3 students (3 girls). 63% of students are boarding students. 42% are state residents. 17 states are represented in upper school student body. 14% are international students. International students from El Salvador, Hong Kong, Mexico, Republic of Korea, Rwanda, and Taiwan; 5 other countries represented in student body.

Faculty School total: 43. In upper school: 10 men, 33 women; 28 have advanced degrees; 16 reside on campus.

Subjects Offered Accounting, acting, Advanced Placement courses, algebra, American history, anatomy, art, band, biology, calculus, ceramics, chemistry, Chinese, dance, desktop publishing, drama, drawing, ecology, English, equine studies, ESL, European history, fine arts, French, gender issues, geometry, graphic arts, health, history, mathematics, music, music theory, nutrition, photography, physics, poetry, political science, psychology, science, social studies, Spanish, sports medicine, theater, water color painting, weaving, Web site design, yearbook.

Graduation Requirements Arts and fine arts (art, music, dance, drama), English, foreign language, history, mathematics, physical education (includes health), science, U.S. history.

Special Academic Programs Advanced Placement exam preparation in 9 subject areas; honors section; independent study; ESL (11 students enrolled).

College Placement 44 students graduated in 2005; all went to college, including Georgetown University; Hamilton College; Mount Holyoke College; Smith College; The George Washington University; Tufts University.

Student Life Upper grades have specified standards of dress, student council, honor system. Discipline rests primarily with faculty.

Summer Programs Enrichment, ESL, sports, art/fine arts programs offered; session focuses on debate, softball, dance, riding, financial literacy, volleyball, soccer; held on campus; accepts girls; open to students from other schools. 210 students usually enrolled. 2006 schedule: July 3 to August 13. Application deadline: none.

Tuition and Aid Day student tuition: $21,520; 7-day tuition and room/board: $34,350. Tuition installment plan (Academic Management Services Plan). Merit scholarship grants, need-based scholarship grants available. In 2005–06, 39% of upper-school students received aid; total upper-school merit-scholarship money awarded: $2500. Total amount of financial aid awarded in 2005–06: $904,000.

Admissions Traditional secondary-level entrance grade is 9. For fall 2005, 161 students applied for upper-level admission, 132 were accepted, 68 enrolled. SAT, SSAT or TOEFL or SLEP required. Deadline for receipt of application materials: February 18. Application fee required: $40. Interview required.

Athletics Interscholastic: aerobics/dance, ballet, basketball, cross-country running, dance, dressage, equestrian sports, field hockey, horseback riding, lacrosse, modern dance, soccer, softball, tennis, volleyball; intramural: alpine skiing, fitness, golf, skiing (downhill), snowboarding. 1 PE instructor, 2 trainers.

Computers Computers are regularly used in all classes. Computer network features include campus e-mail, on-campus library services, CD-ROMs, online commercial services, Internet access, DVD, wireless campus network.

Contact Ms. Sharon L. Pleasant, Director of Admissions. 413-774-2711 Ext. 257. Fax: 413-772-2602. E-mail: admissions@sbschool.org. Web site: www.sbschool.org.

STONE MOUNTAIN SCHOOL

Black Mountain, North Carolina
See Special Needs Schools section.

THE STONY BROOK SCHOOL

1 Chapman Parkway
Stony Brook, New York 11790
Head of School: Mr. Robert E. Gustafson Jr.

petersons.com

General Information Coeducational boarding and day college-preparatory and arts school, affiliated with Christian faith. Grades 7–12. Founded: 1922. Setting: suburban. Nearest major city is New York. Students are housed in single-sex dormitories. 52-acre campus. 14 buildings on campus. Approved or accredited by Middle States Association of Colleges and Schools, New York State Association of Independent Schools, New York State Board of Regents, The Association of Boarding Schools, and New York Department of Education. Member of National Association of Independent Schools and Secondary School Admission Test Board. Endowment: $10.5 million. Total enrollment: 336. Upper school average class size: 14. Upper school faculty-student ratio: 1:7.

Upper School Student Profile Grade 9: 58 students (40 boys, 18 girls); Grade 10: 69 students (39 boys, 30 girls); Grade 11: 68 students (41 boys, 27 girls); Grade 12: 70 students (39 boys, 31 girls). 67% of students are boarding students. 77% are state residents. 17 states are represented in upper school student body. 23% are international students. International students from Bahamas, China, Germany, Republic of Korea, Saudi Arabia, and Taiwan; 20 other countries represented in student body.

Faculty School total: 45. In upper school: 23 men, 18 women; 29 have advanced degrees; 38 reside on campus.

Subjects Offered Algebra, American history, American history-AP, ancient history, art, art-AP, Bible, Bible studies, biology, biology-AP, calculus, calculus-AP, ceramics, chamber groups, character education, chemistry, chemistry-AP, chorus, comparative government and politics, concert choir, creative writing, drama, earth science, English, English literature, English-AP, ESL, European history, European history-AP, fine arts, French, French-AP, geometry, health, history, jazz, Jewish studies, Latin, Latin-AP, marine science, mathematics, music, orchestra, philosophy, photography, physical education, physics, physics-AP, political science, psychology, psychology-AP, science, social studies, Spanish, Spanish-AP, study skills, theater, U.S. government and politics-AP, world history, writing.

Graduation Requirements Arts and fine arts (art, music, dance, drama), Bible, English, European history, foreign language, mathematics, physical education (includes health), science, social studies (includes history), U.S. history.

Special Academic Programs Advanced Placement exam preparation in 17 subject areas; honors section; independent study; study at local college for college credit; ESL (26 students enrolled).

College Placement 66 students graduated in 2005; 64 went to college, including Boston College; Emory University; Georgetown University; Gordon College; State University of New York at Binghamton; University of Virginia. Other: 2 had other specific plans. Mean SAT verbal: 603, mean SAT math: 612.

Student Life Upper grades have specified standards of dress, student council, honor system. Discipline rests equally with students and faculty. Attendance at religious services is required.

Summer Programs Enrichment programs offered; session focuses on athletics, recreation and/or writing; held on campus; accepts boys and girls; open to students from other schools. 2006 schedule: July 3 to August 11.

Tuition and Aid Day student tuition: $17,800; 5-day tuition and room/board: $24,000; 7-day tuition and room/board: $29,600. Tuition installment plan (Key Tuition Payment Plan, monthly payment plans). Need-based scholarship grants available. In 2005–06, 30% of upper-school students received aid.

Admissions For fall 2005, 287 students applied for upper-level admission, 133 were accepted, 97 enrolled. SSAT required. Deadline for receipt of application materials: none. Application fee required: $50. Interview required.

Athletics Interscholastic: basketball (boys, girls), cross-country running (b,g), football (b), lacrosse (b,g), soccer (b,g), softball (g), tennis (b,g), track and field (b,g), volleyball (g), winter (indoor) track (b), wrestling (b); intramural: basketball (b,g), weight lifting (b,g); coed interscholastic: golf, sailing; coed intramural: flag football, outdoor adventure, physical fitness, soccer. 13 coaches, 1 trainer.

Computers Computers are regularly used in mathematics, science classes. Computer network features include campus e-mail, CD-ROMs, Internet access.

Contact Mr. Kevin M. Kunst, Director of Admissions. 631-751-1800 Ext. 1. Fax: 631-751-4211. E-mail: admissions@stonybrookschool.org. Web site: www.stonybrookschool.org.

See full description on page 1078.

STORM KING SCHOOL

314 Mountain Road
Cornwall-on-Hudson, New York 12520-1899
Head of School: Helen S. Chinitz

petersons.com

General Information Coeducational boarding and day college-preparatory, arts, and technology school. Boarding grades 9–12, day grades 7–12. Founded: 1867. Setting: small town. Nearest major city is New York. Students are housed in single-sex dormitories. 40-acre campus. 24 buildings on campus. Approved or accredited by Middle States Association of Colleges and Schools, New York State Association of Independent Schools, The Association of Boarding Schools, and New York Depart-

---

ment of Education. Member of National Association of Independent Schools and Secondary School Admission Test Board. Endowment: $600,000. Total enrollment: 128. Upper school average class size: 8. Upper school faculty-student ratio: 1:6.

Upper School Student Profile Grade 9: 15 students (15 boys); Grade 10: 38 students (25 boys, 13 girls); Grade 11: 34 students (26 boys, 8 girls); Grade 12: 37 students (26 boys, 11 girls). 71% of students are boarding students. 48% are state residents. 16 states are represented in upper school student body. 25% are international students. International students from China, Hong Kong, Republic of Korea, Russian Federation, Taiwan, and U.S. Virgin Islands; 4 other countries represented in student body.

Faculty School total: 31. In upper school: 19 men, 12 women; 22 have advanced degrees; 26 reside on campus.

Subjects Offered Acting, Advanced Placement courses, advanced studio art-AP, advanced TOEFL/grammar, algebra, American history, American sign language, art, art history-AP, biology, calculus, calculus-AP, ceramics, chemistry, choral music, college counseling, community service, creative writing, dance, drama, drawing, economics, English, English literature, English literature-AP, environmental science, ESL, expository writing, fine arts, foreign language, geometry, government/civics, guitar, health, history, Japanese, mathematics, mechanical drawing, music, painting, performing arts, photography, physical education, physics, piano, playwriting, psychology, SAT preparation, science, social studies, Spanish, stagecraft, studio art—AP, theater, theater history, U.S. history-AP, wilderness/outdoor program, world history, writing.

Graduation Requirements Arts and fine arts (art, music, dance, drama), English, foreign language, mathematics, physical education (includes health), science, senior career experience, social studies (includes history). Community service is required.

Special Academic Programs Advanced Placement exam preparation in 5 subject areas; independent study; remedial reading and/or remedial writing; remedial math; ESL (30 students enrolled).

College Placement 43 students graduated in 2005; all went to college, including Boston College; Bucknell University; New York University; Rensselaer Polytechnic Institute; University of Vermont; Virginia Polytechnic Institute and State University. Median SAT verbal: 488, median SAT math: 510. 7% scored over 600 on SAT verbal, 11% scored over 600 on SAT math.

Student Life Upper grades have specified standards of dress, student council, honor system. Discipline rests equally with students and faculty.

Summer Programs ESL programs offered; session focuses on ESL; held on campus; accepts boys and girls; open to students from other schools. 10 students usually enrolled.

Tuition and Aid Day student tuition: $16,900; 7-day tuition and room/board: $31,750. Tuition installment plan (individually arranged payment plans). Tuition reduction for siblings, merit scholarship grants, need-based scholarship grants available. In 2005–06, 25% of upper-school students received aid; total upper-school merit-scholarship money awarded: $321,000. Total amount of financial aid awarded in 2005–06: $400,000.

Admissions Traditional secondary-level entrance grade is 9. For fall 2005, 120 students applied for upper-level admission, 55 were accepted, 45 enrolled. Admissions testing, OLSAT/Stanford, Otis-Lennon School Ability Test, SLEP for foreign students and TOEFL or SLEP required. Deadline for receipt of application materials: January 1. Application fee required: $85. Interview required.

Athletics Interscholastic: baseball (boys), basketball (b,g), lacrosse (b), soccer (b,g), softball (g), volleyball (b,g), wrestling (b); coed interscholastic: cross-country running, fitness walking, freestyle skiing, hiking/backpacking, jogging, skiing (downhill), tennis, track and field, ultimate Frisbee; coed intramural: aerobics/dance, aerobics/nautilus, alpine skiing, back packing, bicycling, billiards, blading, bocce, bowling, canoeing/kayaking, climbing, fitness, flag football, freestyle skiing, golf, hiking/backpacking, ice skating, jogging, martial arts, mountain biking, nautilus, outdoor adventure, outdoor education, outdoor recreation, outdoor skills, paddle tennis, physical fitness, power lifting, rappelling, rock climbing, ropes courses, running, skiing (cross-country), strength & conditioning, table tennis, tennis, touch football, track and field, ultimate Frisbee, volleyball, weight lifting, wilderness, yoga. 2 PE instructors, 12 coaches, 1 trainer.

Computers Computers are regularly used in art, ESL, science, theater, theater arts classes. Computer network features include on-campus library services, CD-ROMs, Internet access, office computer access, DVD, wireless campus network.

Contact Mrs. Caroline A. Petro, Admissions and Communications Coordinator. 845-534-9860 Ext. 210. Fax: 845-534-4128. E-mail: cpetro@sks.org. Web site: www.sks.org.

See full description on page 1080.

STRAKE JESUIT COLLEGE PREPARATORY

8900 Bellaire Boulevard
Houston, Texas 77036
Head of School: Fr. Dan Lahart, SJ

General Information Boys' day college-preparatory school, affiliated with Roman Catholic Church (Jesuit order). Grades 9–12. Founded: 1960. Setting: suburban. 44-acre campus. 13 buildings on campus. Approved or accredited by Jesuit Secondary Education Association, Southern Association of Colleges and Schools, Texas Catholic

Conference, Texas Education Agency, and Texas Department of Education. Endowment: $6 million. Total enrollment: 869. Upper school average class size: 20. Upper school faculty-student ratio: 1:12.

Upper School Student Profile Grade 9: 230 students (230 boys); Grade 10: 221 students (221 boys); Grade 11: 215 students (215 boys); Grade 12: 203 students (203 boys). 76% of students are Roman Catholic Church (Jesuit order).

Faculty School total: 79. In upper school: 64 men, 15 women; 26 have advanced degrees.

Subjects Offered Accounting, algebra, American history, American literature, art, art history, band, biology, broadcasting, calculus, chemistry, chorus, community service, computer science, debate, drama, drawing, economics, English, English literature, French, geometry, government/civics, health, journalism, Latin, mathematics, music, music theory, oceanography, orchestra, painting, physical education, physical science, physics, physiology, pre-calculus, reading, religion, science, social studies, Spanish, speech, television, theater, theology, trigonometry, video, word processing, world history, world literature.

Graduation Requirements Arts and fine arts (art, music, dance, drama), business skills (includes word processing), computer science, English, foreign language, mathematics, physical education (includes health), religion (includes Bible studies and theology), science, social studies (includes history), speech. Community service is required.

Special Academic Programs Advanced Placement exam preparation in 10 subject areas; honors section; study at local college for college credit.

College Placement 215 students graduated in 2005; all went to college, including Loyola University New Orleans; Texas A&M University; Texas Tech University; The University of Texas at Austin; University of Dallas; University of Notre Dame. Median SAT verbal: 650, median SAT math: 670, median composite ACT: 27. 76% scored over 600 on SAT verbal, 81% scored over 600 on SAT math, 62% scored over 26 on composite ACT.

Student Life Upper grades have specified standards of dress, student council, honor system. Discipline rests primarily with faculty. Attendance at religious services is required.

Tuition and Aid Need-based scholarship grants available. In 2005–06, 12% of upper-school students received aid. Total amount of financial aid awarded in 2005–06: $750,000.

Admissions Traditional secondary-level entrance grade is 9. For fall 2005, 465 students applied for upper-level admission, 304 were accepted, 230 enrolled. STS required. Deadline for receipt of application materials: February 8. Application fee required: $25.

Athletics Interscholastic: baseball, basketball, cross-country running, football, golf, lacrosse, soccer, swimming and diving, track and field, water polo. 33 coaches, 1 trainer.

Computers Computer resources include on-campus library services, online commercial services, Internet access.

Contact Ms. Marian Harper, Assistant to the Director of Admissions. 713-490-8113. Fax: 713-774-6427. E-mail: mharper@strakejesuit.org. Web site: www.strakejesuit.org.

STRATFORD ACADEMY

6010 Peake Road
Macon, Georgia 31220-3903
Head of School: David M. Wahl

General Information Coeducational day college-preparatory, arts, and technology school. Grades PK–12. Founded: 1960. Setting: suburban. Nearest major city is Atlanta. 65-acre campus. 3 buildings on campus. Approved or accredited by Georgia Independent School Association, Southern Association of Colleges and Schools, Southern Association of Independent Schools, and Georgia Department of Education. Member of National Association of Independent Schools. Endowment: $1 million. Total enrollment: 931. Upper school average class size: 17. Upper school faculty-student ratio: 1:13.

Upper School Student Profile Grade 9: 79 students (41 boys, 38 girls); Grade 10: 69 students (40 boys, 29 girls); Grade 11: 91 students (54 boys, 37 girls); Grade 12: 63 students (26 boys, 37 girls).

Faculty School total: 87. In upper school: 22 men, 18 women; 24 have advanced degrees.

Subjects Offered Advanced Placement courses, algebra, American history, American literature, anatomy, art, art history, art-AP, athletics, baseball, basketball, biology, biology-AP, calculus, calculus-AP, chemistry, chemistry-AP, community service, comparative government and politics-AP, computer keyboarding, computer programming, computer science, creative writing, drama, drama performance, driver education, earth science, economics, English, English literature, English literature-AP, English-AP, European history, European history-AP, expository writing, French, French-AP, geography, geometry, government/civics, grammar, history, history-AP, humanities, journalism, Latin, Latin-AP, madrigals, mathematics, mathematics-AP, music, physical education, physical science, physics, pre-calculus, science, social science, social studies, sociology, Spanish, Spanish-AP, speech, theater, trigonometry, U.S. government and politics-AP, world history, world literature, writing.

Graduation Requirements English, foreign language, math applications, mathematics, science, senior seminar, social science, social studies (includes history). Community service is required.

Special Academic Programs Advanced Placement exam preparation in 16 subject areas; independent study; special instructional classes for students with learning disabilities, Attention Deficit Disorder, and dyslexia.

College Placement 57 students graduated in 2005; all went to college, including Georgia Institute of Technology; Georgia Southern University; Harvard University; University of Georgia; University of Mississippi; Wake Forest University.

Student Life Upper grades have specified standards of dress, student council, honor system. Discipline rests primarily with faculty.

Tuition and Aid Day student tuition: $9571. Tuition installment plan (Insured Tuition Payment Plan, monthly payment plans, individually arranged payment plans). Merit scholarship grants, need-based scholarship grants available. In 2005–06, 10% of upper-school students received aid; total upper-school merit-scholarship money awarded: $9571. Total amount of financial aid awarded in 2005–06: $205,000.

Admissions Traditional secondary-level entrance grade is 9. For fall 2005, 12 students applied for upper-level admission, 9 were accepted, 9 enrolled. ERB required. Deadline for receipt of application materials: none. Application fee required: $50. On-campus interview required.

Athletics Interscholastic: aquatics (boys, girls), baseball (b), basketball (b,g), cheering (g), cross-country running (b,g), dance team (g), drill team (g), football (b); coed interscholastic: badminton, golf. 8 PE instructors, 2 coaches, 1 trainer.

Computers Computers are regularly used in art, creative writing, English, French, information technology, Spanish classes. Computer network features include campus e-mail, on-campus library services, CD-ROMs, Internet access, DVD.

Contact Ms. Marilyn Holton-Walker, Registrar/Admissions Assistant. 478-477-8073 Ext. 205. Fax: 478-477-0299. E-mail: mwalker@stratford.org. Web site: www.stratford.org.

STRATHCONA-TWEEDSMUIR SCHOOL

RR #2
Okotoks, Alberta T1S 1A2, Canada
Head of School: Dr. Catherine Raaflaub

General Information Coeducational day college-preparatory, arts, and technology school. Grades 1–12. Founded: 1905. Setting: rural. Nearest major city is Calgary, Canada. 160-acre campus. 1 building on campus. Approved or accredited by Canadian Association of Independent Schools, Canadian Educational Standards Institute, International Baccalaureate Organization, and Alberta Department of Education. Affiliate member of National Association of Independent Schools. Language of instruction: English. Endowment: CAN$2 million. Total enrollment: 752. Upper school average class size: 20. Upper school faculty-student ratio: 1:20.

Upper School Student Profile Grade 10: 106 students (45 boys, 61 girls); Grade 11: 85 students (43 boys, 42 girls); Grade 12: 100 students (59 boys, 41 girls).

Faculty School total: 82. In upper school: 25 men, 18 women; 14 have advanced degrees.

Subjects Offered Art, band, biology, calculus, chemistry, computer science, drama, English, fine arts, French, Latin, mathematics, music, outdoor education, physical education, physics, science, social science, social studies, Spanish, theater.

Graduation Requirements Arts and fine arts (art, music, dance, drama), business skills (includes word processing), English, foreign language, mathematics, physical education (includes health), science, social science, social studies (includes history).

Special Academic Programs International Baccalaureate program; term-away projects.

College Placement 88 students graduated in 2005; 83 went to college, including Dalhousie University; Queen's University at Kingston; The University of Western Ontario; University of Alberta; University of Calgary; University of Victoria. Other: 5 had other specific plans.

Student Life Upper grades have uniform requirement, student council, honor system. Discipline rests primarily with faculty.

Tuition and Aid Day student tuition: CAN$10,890–CAN$13,480. Tuition installment plan (monthly payment plans). Bursaries, need-based scholarship grants available. In 2005–06, 2% of upper-school students received aid. Total amount of financial aid awarded in 2005–06: CAN$50,000.

Admissions Traditional secondary-level entrance grade is 10. For fall 2005, 69 students applied for upper-level admission, 44 were accepted, 44 enrolled. CTBS, OLSAT, Henmon-Nelson or SSAT required. Deadline for receipt of application materials: none. Application fee required: CAN$100. Interview required.

Athletics Interscholastic: badminton (boys, girls), basketball (b,g), cross-country running (b,g), field hockey (g), golf (b,g), outdoor education (b,g), rugby (b), soccer (g), telemark skiing (b,g), track and field (b,g), triathlon (b,g), volleyball (b,g), wall climbing (b,g); coed interscholastic: back packing, badminton, climbing, outdoor education; coed intramural: basketball, volleyball. 10 PE instructors, 38 coaches, 2 trainers.

Computers Computers are regularly used in all classes. Computer network features include campus e-mail, on-campus library services, CD-ROMs, online commercial services, Internet access, DVD, wireless campus network.

Contact Ms. Tina Ierakidis, Director of Admissions. 403-938-8303. Fax: 403-938-4492. E-mail: ierakit@sts.ab.ca. Web site: www.sts.ab.ca.

STRATTON MOUNTAIN SCHOOL

World Cup Circle
Stratton Mountain, Vermont 05155
Head of School: Christopher G. Kaltsas

General Information Coeducational boarding and day college-preparatory, arts, bilingual studies, and technology school. Grades 7–PG. Founded: 1972. Setting: rural. Nearest major city is Albany, NY. Students are housed in single-sex by floor dormitories. 12-acre campus. 7 buildings on campus, Approved or accredited by Independent Schools of Northern New England, New England Association of Schools and Colleges, and Vermont Department of Education. Member of National Association of Independent Schools. Total enrollment: 129. Upper school average class size: 8. Upper school faculty-student ratio: 1:6.

Upper School Student Profile Grade 9: 19 students (6 boys, 13 girls); Grade 10: 23 students (13 boys, 10 girls); Grade 11: 32 students (22 boys, 10 girls); Grade 12: 25 students (17 boys, 8 girls); Postgraduate: 9 students (6 boys, 3 girls). 65% of students are boarding students. 45% are state residents. 17 states are represented in upper school student body. 7% are international students. International students from Australia, Bulgaria, Canada, Czech Republic, and Republic of Korea.

Faculty School total: 30. In upper school: 10 men, 8 women; 9 have advanced degrees; 13 reside on campus.

Subjects Offered Algebra, American history, American literature, art, astronomy, biology, calculus, chemistry, computer science, creative writing, earth science, economics, English, English literature, environmental science, European history, fine arts, French, geography, geometry, government/civics, grammar, health, history, journalism, mathematics, music, nutrition, photography, physical education, physics, psychology, science, social studies, Spanish, speech, speech and oral interpretations, trigonometry, world history, writing.

Graduation Requirements Arts and fine arts (art, music, dance, drama), computer education, English, foreign language, mathematics, science, social studies (includes history), superior competence in winter sports (skiing/snowboarding). Community service is required.

Special Academic Programs Independent study; term-away projects; ESL (4 students enrolled).

College Placement 27 students graduated in 2005; 18 went to college, including Bates College; Middlebury College; St. Lawrence University; University of Colorado at Boulder; University of Vermont. Other: 8 entered a postgraduate year. Mean SAT verbal: 520, mean SAT math: 580. 30% scored over 600 on SAT verbal, 40% scored over 600 on SAT math.

Student Life Upper grades have specified standards of dress, student council, honor system. Discipline rests primarily with faculty.

Summer Programs Rigorous outdoor training programs offered; session focuses on cross-country ski training and ski race training ; held both on and off campus; held at Sass-Fee (Switzerland) and Mt. Hood (Oregon); accepts boys and girls; open to students from other schools. 80 students usually enrolled. 2006 schedule: June 25 to July 10. Application deadline: May 15.

Tuition and Aid Day student tuition: $21,750; 7-day tuition and room/board: $31,800. Tuition installment plan (Insured Tuition Payment Plan, Key Tuition Payment Plan, individually arranged payment plans). Need-based scholarship grants, need-based loans available. In 2005–06, 40% of upper-school students received aid. Total amount of financial aid awarded in 2005–06: $425,000.

Admissions Traditional secondary-level entrance grade is 9. For fall 2005, 70 students applied for upper-level admission, 53 were accepted, 47 enrolled. Deadline for receipt of application materials: none. Application fee required: $40. On-campus interview recommended.

Athletics Interscholastic: golf (boys, girls), lacrosse (b,g), skiing (cross-country) (b,g), skiing (downhill) (b,g), snowboarding (b,g), soccer (b,g), track and field (b,g); coed interscholastic: alpine skiing, cross-country running, nordic skiing; coed intramural: bicycling, golf, rock climbing. 16 coaches, 1 trainer.

Computers Computers are regularly used in computer applications, graphic design, mathematics, media production, research skills, science, Web site design, yearbook classes. Computer network features include campus e-mail, on-campus library services, CD-ROMs, online commercial services, Internet access, DVD.

Contact Mr. Todd G. Ormiston, Director of Admissions. 802-856-1111. Fax: 802-297-0020. E-mail: todd@gosms.org. Web site: www.gosms.org.

STUART COUNTRY DAY SCHOOL OF THE SACRED HEART

1200 Stuart Road
Princeton, New Jersey 08540-1219
Head of School: Frances de la Chapelle, RSCJ

petersons.com

General Information Coeducational day (boys' only in lower grades) college-preparatory, arts, religious studies, and technology school, affiliated with Roman Catholic Church. Boys grade PS, girls grades PS–12. Founded: 1963. Setting: suburban. 55-acre campus. 1 building on campus. Approved or accredited by Middle States Association of Colleges and Schools, Network of Sacred Heart Schools, New Jersey Association of Independent Schools, and New Jersey Department of Education.

Member of National Association of Independent Schools and Secondary School Admission Test Board. Endowment: $590,000. Total enrollment: 551. Upper school average class size: 15. Upper school faculty-student ratio: 1:12.

Upper School Student Profile Grade 9: 43 students (43 girls); Grade 10: 41 students (41 girls); Grade 11: 40 students (40 girls); Grade 12: 41 students (41 girls). 56% of students are Roman Catholic.

Faculty School total: 92. In upper school: 3 men, 30 women; 27 have advanced degrees.

Subjects Offered African studies, algebra, American culture, American literature, anatomy, art, art history, Bible studies, biology, biology-AP, calculus, calculus-AP, ceramics, chemistry, college counseling, communications, community service, computer programming, computer science, conceptual physics, creative writing, dance, drama, drawing and design, English, English literature, English-AP, environmental science, environmental science-AP, ethics, European history, European history-AP, expository writing, film, fine arts, French, French-AP, geometry, government/civics, handbells, health education, independent study, Latin, Latin-AP, mathematics, music, music history, music theory, philosophy, photography, physical education, physical fitness, physics, physiology, portfolio art, pre-calculus, probability and statistics, religion, religious studies, science, senior project, social studies, Spanish, Spanish-AP, speech, stagecraft, studio art, studio art—AP, theater, theology, trigonometry, U.S. history, U.S. history-AP, visual arts, vocal ensemble, world culture, world cultures, world literature, world religions, writing.

Graduation Requirements Arts and fine arts (art, music, dance, drama), computer science, English, foreign language, history, lab science, mathematics, physical education (includes health), religious studies, 50 hours of community service per year for each year of high school.

Special Academic Programs Advanced Placement exam preparation in 15 subject areas; honors section; accelerated programs; independent study; term-away projects; study at local college for college credit; study abroad; academic accommodation for the gifted, the musically talented, and the artistically talented.

College Placement 36 students graduated in 2005; 35 went to college, including Boston College; Massachusetts Institute of Technology; The Johns Hopkins University; University of Pennsylvania; Villanova University. Other: 1 entered a postgraduate year. Mean SAT verbal: 602, mean SAT math: 627, mean composite ACT: 27. 60% scored over 600 on SAT verbal, 60% scored over 600 on SAT math, 64% scored over 26 on composite ACT.

Student Life Upper grades have specified standards of dress, student council, honor system. Discipline rests equally with students and faculty. Attendance at religious services is required.

Summer Programs Enrichment, art/fine arts programs offered; session focuses on various course selections for enrichment, remediation and athletic development; held on campus; accepts boys and girls; open to students from other schools. 65 students usually enrolled. 2006 schedule: July 3 to August 18. Application deadline: May 15.

Tuition and Aid Day student tuition: $23,150. Tuition installment plan (Academic Management Services Plan, Key Tuition Payment Plan, SMART Tuition Payment Plan, FACTS Tuition Payment Plan). Merit scholarship grants, need-based scholarship grants, prepGATE Loans available. In 2005–06, 25% of upper-school students received aid; total upper-school merit-scholarship money awarded: $54,981. Total amount of financial aid awarded in 2005–06: $544,175.

Admissions Traditional secondary-level entrance grade is 9. For fall 2005, 48 students applied for upper-level admission, 21 were accepted, 14 enrolled. SSAT required. Deadline for receipt of application materials: January 9. Application fee required: $50. On-campus interview required.

Athletics Interscholastic: aerobics, aerobics/dance, basketball, cross-country running, dance, field hockey, fitness, ice hockey, lacrosse, squash, tennis, track and field; intramural: dance, fitness. 2 PE instructors, 16 coaches, 1 trainer.

Computers Computer network features include campus e-mail, on-campus library services, CD-ROMs, Internet access.

Contact Stephanie Lupero, Director of Admissions. 609-921-2330 Ext. 235. Fax: 609-497-0784. E-mail: slupero@stuartschool.org. Web site: stuartschool.org.

See full description on page 1082.

STUART HALL

235 West Frederick Street
Staunton, Virginia 24401
Head of School: Mr. Mark Eastham

petersons.com

General Information Girls' boarding and coeducational day college-preparatory and arts school, affiliated with Episcopal Church. Boarding girls grades 8–12, day boys grades 5–12, day girls grades 5–12. Founded: 1844. Setting: small town. Nearest major city is Richmond. Students are housed in single-sex dormitories. 8-acre campus. 6 buildings on campus. Approved or accredited by National Association of Episcopal Schools, Virginia Association of Independent Schools, and Virginia Department of Education. Member of National Association of Independent Schools and Secondary School Admission Test Board. Endowment: $900,000. Total enrollment: 156. Upper school average class size: 9. Upper school faculty-student ratio: 1:7.

Upper School Student Profile Grade 9: 20 students (1 boy, 19 girls); Grade 10: 15 students (3 boys, 12 girls); Grade 11: 20 students (4 boys, 16 girls); Grade 12: 16 students (6 boys, 10 girls). 45% of students are boarding students. 77% are state

residents. 9 states are represented in upper school student body. 14% are international students. International students from Republic of Korea. 25% of students are members of Episcopal Church.

Faculty School total: 27. In upper school: 5 men, 17 women; 14 have advanced degrees; 6 reside on campus.

Subjects Offered Algebra, American literature, ancient world history, applied arts, applied music, art appreciation, art history, biology, biology-AP, British literature, calculus-AP, career and personal planning, career education, career/college preparation, ceramics, chamber groups, chemistry, choir, choral music, chorus, civics, college counseling, college placement, community service, composition, creative writing, drama, drama performance, dramatic arts, driver education, English, English composition, English language and composition-AP, English literature-AP, English-AP, environmental science, environmental science-AP, ESL, fine arts, French, French language-AP, geometry, grammar, guitar, health education, history of drama, history of music, history-AP, honors algebra, honors English, honors geometry, honors world history, instrumental music, lab science, language and composition, learning lab, mathematics, modern world history, music, music composition, music history, music performance, music theater, music theory, philosophy, photography, physical education, physical fitness, physics, piano, playwriting and directing, portfolio art, pre-algebra, pre-calculus, religion, SAT preparation, science, social studies, Spanish, Spanish language-AP, Spanish-AP, stage and body movement, stage design, statistics and probability, strings, student government, student publications, study skills, theater, theater arts, theater history, theater production, trigonometry, U.S. government, U.S. government-AP, U.S. history, U.S. history-AP, visual and performing arts, visual arts, vocal ensemble, vocal music, voice, voice ensemble, world geography, world history, world history-AP, world literature, yearbook.

Graduation Requirements Arts and fine arts (art, music, dance, drama), English, foreign language, mathematics, philosophy, physical education (includes health), religion (includes Bible studies and theology), SAT preparation, science, social studies (includes history).

Special Academic Programs Advanced Placement exam preparation; honors section; study at local college for college credit; academic accommodation for the artistically talented; ESL (8 students enrolled).

College Placement 30 students graduated in 2005; all went to college, including Duke University; Michigan State University; Roanoke College; Temple University; University of Virginia; Virginia Polytechnic Institute and State University. Mean SAT verbal: 587, mean SAT math: 587.

Student Life Upper grades have specified standards of dress, student council, honor system. Discipline rests equally with students and faculty. Attendance at religious services is required.

Tuition and Aid Day student tuition: $10,500; 5-day tuition and room/board: $29,500; 7-day tuition and room/board: $32,000. Tuition installment plan (Academic Management Services Plan, monthly payment plans, individually arranged payment plans). Merit scholarship grants, need-based scholarship grants available. In 2005–06, 30% of upper-school students received aid; total upper-school merit-scholarship money awarded: $150,000. Total amount of financial aid awarded in 2005–06: $800,000.

Admissions Traditional secondary-level entrance grade is 10. For fall 2005, 47 students applied for upper-level admission, 38 were accepted, 23 enrolled. TOEFL or SLEP required. Deadline for receipt of application materials: none. Application fee required: $45. Interview required.

Athletics Interscholastic: basketball (boys, girls), lacrosse (b,g), soccer (g), swimming and diving (g), tennis (b,g), volleyball (g); intramural: cheering (g), skiing (downhill) (b,g), snowboarding (b,g); coed interscholastic: cross-country running, lacrosse, running, soccer. 1 PE instructor, 7 coaches.

Computers Computers are regularly used in all classes. Computer network features include campus e-mail, CD-ROMs, Internet access.

Contact Ms. Jessica L. Hyde, Director of Admissions. 888-306-8926. Fax: 540-886-2275. E-mail: jhyde@stuart-hall.org. Web site: www.stuart-hall.org.

See full description on page 1084.

THE STUDY SCHOOL

3233 The Boulevard
Westmount, Quebec H3Y 1S4, Canada
Head of School: Elizabeth Falco

General Information Girls' day college-preparatory, arts, bilingual studies, technology, and science school. Grades K–11. Founded: 1915. Setting: urban. Nearest major city is Montreal, Canada. 2 buildings on campus. Approved or accredited by Canadian Association of Independent Schools and Quebec Department of Education. Affiliate member of National Association of Independent Schools. Languages of instruction: English and French. Endowment: CAN$25 million. Total enrollment: 421. Upper school average class size: 18. Upper school faculty-student ratio: 1:8.

Upper School Student Profile Grade 7: 38 students (38 girls); Grade 8: 36 students (36 girls); Grade 9: 38 students (38 girls); Grade 10: 37 students (37 girls); Grade 11: 41 students (41 girls).

Faculty School total: 55. In upper school: 7 men, 25 women; 5 have advanced degrees.

Subjects Offered Algebra, art, art history, biology, chemistry, computer science, ecology, economics, English, environmental science, European history, film, French, gender issues, geography, geometry, history, Mandarin, mathematics, music, philosophy, physical education, physics, science, social studies, Spanish, stagecraft, technology, theater, world history.

Graduation Requirements English, foreign language, French, mathematics, physical education (includes health), science, social studies (includes history), technology. Community service is required.

Special Academic Programs Honors section; independent study; study at local college for college credit; domestic exchange program.

College Placement 34 students graduated in 2005; all went to college.

Student Life Upper grades have uniform requirement, student council, honor system. Discipline rests primarily with faculty.

Tuition and Aid Day student tuition: CAN$12,000. Tuition installment plan (monthly payment plans, individually arranged payment plans, 2-payment plan). Bursaries, merit scholarship grants, need-based scholarship grants available. In 2005–06, 11% of upper-school students received aid; total upper-school merit-scholarship money awarded: CAN$40,000. Total amount of financial aid awarded in 2005–06: CAN$145,000.

Admissions Traditional secondary-level entrance grade is 7. For fall 2005, 13 students applied for upper-level admission. SSAT required. Deadline for receipt of application materials: none. Application fee required: CAN$125. On-campus interview required.

Athletics Interscholastic: alpine skiing, aquatics, badminton, basketball, crew, cross-country running, Fives, football, golf, hockey, ice hockey, rowing, running, skiing (cross-country), soccer, swimming and diving, tennis, touch football, track and field, volleyball; intramural: aerobics, aerobics/dance, aerobics/nautilus, badminton, ballet, basketball, bicycling, cooperative games, dance, field hockey, football, handball, ice hockey, jump rope, martial arts, outdoor activities, outdoor skills, soccer, touch football, track and field, ultimate Frisbee, volleyball. 3 PE instructors, 8 coaches.

Computers Computers are regularly used in art, English, history, mathematics, science classes. Computer network features include campus e-mail, on-campus library services, CD-ROMs, Internet access, file transfer, office computer access, DVD, wireless campus network.

Contact Marie-Françoise Jothy, Director of Admissions. 514-935-9352. Fax: 514-935-1721. E-mail: admissions@thestudy.qc.ca.

SUBIACO ACADEMY
405 North Subiaco Avenue
Subiaco, Arkansas 72865
Head of School: Mr. Michael Berry

General Information Boys' boarding and day college-preparatory, arts, religious studies, bilingual studies, and technology school, affiliated with Roman Catholic Church. Grades 9–12. Founded: 1887. Setting: rural. Nearest major city is Little Rock. Students are housed in single-sex dormitories. 100-acre campus. 8 buildings on campus. Approved or accredited by Headmasters' Conference, Independent Schools Association of the Central States, Midwest Association of Boarding Schools, National Catholic Education Association, The Association of Boarding Schools, and Arkansas Department of Education. Member of National Association of Independent Schools. Endowment: $1.5 million. Total enrollment: 157. Upper school average class size: 17. Upper school faculty-student ratio: 1:9.

Upper School Student Profile Grade 9: 35 students (35 boys); Grade 10: 45 students (45 boys); Grade 11: 45 students (45 boys); Grade 12: 32 students (32 boys). 75% of students are boarding students. 45% are state residents. 16 states are represented in upper school student body. 18% are international students. International students from China, Mexico, Republic of Korea, and Taiwan. 75% of students are Roman Catholic.

Faculty School total: 24. In upper school: 16 men, 8 women; 18 have advanced degrees; 10 reside on campus.

Subjects Offered Algebra, American history, American history-AP, anthropology, art, art-AP, band, biology, biology-AP, calculus, chemistry, chemistry-AP, chorus, Christian doctrine, communications, computer science, drama, earth science, economics, English, English literature, English-AP, European history, finance, fine arts, geography, geometry, government/civics, international relations, journalism, Latin, music, physical education, physics, piano, psychology, religion, sociology, Spanish, speech, Western civilization, world history.

Graduation Requirements Arts and fine arts (art, music, dance, drama), computer science, English, foreign language, mathematics, physical education (includes health), religion (includes Bible studies and theology), science, social studies (includes history), Western civilization. Community service is required.

Special Academic Programs Advanced Placement exam preparation in 10 subject areas; honors section; independent study; academic accommodation for the gifted, the musically talented, and the artistically talented; ESL (15 students enrolled).

College Placement 40 students graduated in 2005; all went to college, including Truman State University; University of Arkansas. Median combined SAT: 1077, median composite ACT: 25.

Student Life Upper grades have uniform requirement, student council, honor system. Discipline rests equally with students and faculty. Attendance at religious services is required.

Subiaco Academy

Tuition and Aid Day student tuition: $4450; 7-day tuition and room/board: $14,500. Tuition installment plan (Key Tuition Payment Plan, monthly payment plans). Tuition reduction for siblings, merit scholarship grants, need-based scholarship grants available. In 2005–06, 40% of upper-school students received aid; total upper-school merit-scholarship money awarded: $5000. Total amount of financial aid awarded in 2005–06: $300,000.

Admissions Traditional secondary-level entrance grade is 9. For fall 2005, 99 students applied for upper-level admission, 80 were accepted, 59 enrolled. Catholic High School Entrance Examination, ISEE, PSAT, PSAT and SAT for applicants to grade 11 and 12, Scholastic Testing Service High School Placement Test (open version), SSAT and TOEFL or SLEP required. Deadline for receipt of application materials: August 1. Application fee required: $50. Interview required.

Athletics Interscholastic: baseball, basketball, cross-country running, football, golf, soccer, tennis, track and field; intramural: archery, back packing, baseball, basketball, bicycling, billiards, boxing, canoeing/kayaking, cheering, climbing, cross-country running, diving, fishing, flag football, fly fishing, football, Frisbee, golf, handball, hiking/backpacking, horseshoes, in-line hockey, indoor soccer, jogging, marksmanship, mountain biking, mountaineering, outdoor activities, outdoor adventure, outdoor education, outdoor recreation, outdoor skills, outdoors, paint ball, physical fitness, physical training, power lifting, project adventure, racquetball, riflery, rock climbing, roller blading, running, skateboarding, skeet shooting, soccer, softball, swimming and diving, table tennis, tennis, touch football, volleyball, water skiing, weight lifting, wilderness, winter soccer. 1 PE instructor, 5 coaches.

Computers Computers are regularly used in art, Christian doctrine, commercial art, desktop publishing, digital applications, English, graphic arts, history, journalism, keyboarding, literary magazine, mathematics, newspaper, photography, photojournalism, publications, SAT preparation, word processing, writing, yearbook classes. Computer network features include campus e-mail, on-campus library services, CD-ROMs, Internet access, office computer access, DVD.

Contact Br. Ephrem P. O'Bryan, OSB, Director of Admission. 800-364-7824. Fax: 479-934-1033. E-mail: brephrem@subi.org. Web site: www.subi.org.

THE SUDBURY VALLEY SCHOOL

2 Winch Street
Framingham, Massachusetts 01701
Head of School: Michael Sadofsky

General Information Coeducational day college-preparatory, general academic, arts, business, and vocational school. Ungraded, ages 4–19. Founded: 1968. Setting: suburban. Nearest major city is Boston. 10-acre campus. 2 buildings on campus. Approved or accredited by Massachusetts Department of Education. Total enrollment: 160. Upper school faculty-student ratio: 1:16.

Faculty School total: 10. In upper school: 5 men, 5 women; 3 have advanced degrees.

Subjects Offered Algebra, American history, American literature, anatomy, anthropology, archaeology, art, art history, Bible studies, biology, botany, business, calculus, ceramics, chemistry, computer programming, computer science, creative writing, dance, drama, economics, English, English literature, ethics, European history, expository writing, French, geography, geometry, German, government/civics, grammar, Hebrew, history, history of ideas, history of science, home economics, Latin, mathematics, music, philosophy, photography, physical education, physics, physiology, psychology, religion, social studies, Spanish, speech, theater, trigonometry, typing, world history, world literature, writing.

Graduation Requirements Students must successfully defend the thesis that they have taken responsibility for preparing themselves to be an effective adult in the community.

Special Academic Programs Independent study.

College Placement 21 students graduated in 2005; 15 went to college. Other: 6 went to work.

Student Life Upper grades have student council, honor system. Discipline rests equally with students and faculty.

Tuition and Aid Day student tuition: $5635.

Admissions Deadline for receipt of application materials: none. Application fee required: $30. On-campus interview required.

Computers Computer resources include campus e-mail, on-campus library services, CD-ROMs, Internet access, file transfer, office computer access.

Contact Hanna Greenberg, Admissions Clerk. 508-877-3030. Fax: 508-788-0674. E-mail: sudval@aol.com. Web site: www.sudval.org.

SUFFIELD ACADEMY

185 North Main Street
Suffield, Connecticut 06078
Head of School: Charles Cahn III

General Information Coeducational boarding and day college-preparatory, arts, technology, and leadership school. Grades 9–PG. Founded: 1833. Setting: small town. Nearest major city is Hartford. Students are housed in single-sex dormitories. 340-acre campus. 49 buildings on campus. Approved or accredited by Connecticut Association of Independent Schools, New England Association of Schools and Colleges, and The

Association of Boarding Schools. Member of National Association of Independent Schools and Secondary School Admission Test Board. Endowment: $21 million. Total enrollment: 404. Upper school average class size: 10. Upper school faculty-student ratio: 1:6.

Upper School Student Profile Grade 9: 78 students (42 boys, 36 girls); Grade 10: 107 students (58 boys, 49 girls); Grade 11: 109 students (58 boys, 51 girls); Grade 12: 99 students (46 boys, 53 girls); Postgraduate: 11 students (10 boys, 1 girl). 58% of students are boarding students. 45% are state residents. 16 states are represented in upper school student body. 14% are international students. International students from Bermuda, China, Germany, Republic of Korea, Taiwan, and Thailand; 10 other countries represented in student body.

Faculty School total: 68. In upper school: 36 men, 29 women; 52 have advanced degrees; all reside on campus.

Subjects Offered Acting, Advanced Placement courses, algebra, American history, American literature, anatomy and physiology, archaeology, art, art history, biology, calculus, ceramics, chemistry, Chinese, computer math, computer programming, computer science, constitutional law, dance, drama, economics, economics-AP, English, English literature, environmental science, ESL, ethics, European history, expository writing, fine arts, French, geometry, government/civics, grammar, great books, health, history, jazz band, Latin, leadership skills, leadership training, mathematics, mechanical drawing, music, music theory, news writing, philosophy, photography, physical education, physics, religion, science, senior seminar, short story, social studies, sociology, Spanish, Spanish-AP, statistics, statistics and probability, statistics-AP, technology, theater, theater arts, trigonometry, U.S. history, U.S. history-AP, visual and performing arts, visual arts, voice ensemble, wilderness/outdoor program, wind ensemble, wind instruments, woodworking, world history, writing.

Graduation Requirements Arts and fine arts (art, music, dance, drama), English, foreign language, leadership, mathematics, physical education (includes health), religion (includes Bible studies and theology), science, social studies (includes history), technology portfolio.

Special Academic Programs Advanced Placement exam preparation in 11 subject areas; honors section; independent study; academic accommodation for the gifted, the musically talented, and the artistically talented; programs in English for dyslexic students; ESL (35 students enrolled).

College Placement 115 students graduated in 2005; 114 went to college, including Bentley College; Emory University; Northeastern University; Trinity College; University of Connecticut; University of Vermont. Other: 1 entered a postgraduate year.

Student Life Upper grades have specified standards of dress, student council, honor system. Discipline rests primarily with faculty.

Summer Programs Enrichment, advancement, ESL, art/fine arts, computer instruction programs offered; held on campus; accepts boys and girls; open to students from other schools. 100 students usually enrolled. 2006 schedule: July 1 to August 4. Application deadline: none.

Tuition and Aid Day student tuition: $24,800; 7-day tuition and room/board: $35,500. Tuition installment plan (Key Tuition Payment Plan, monthly payment plans). Merit scholarship grants, need-based scholarship grants, need-based loans, middle-income loans, tuition remission for children of faculty available. In 2005–06, 31% of upper-school students received aid; total upper-school merit-scholarship money awarded: $173,000. Total amount of financial aid awarded in 2005–06: $1,972,930.

Admissions Traditional secondary-level entrance grade is 9. For fall 2005, 770 students applied for upper-level admission, 307 were accepted, 149 enrolled. PSAT or SAT or SSAT required. Deadline for receipt of application materials: February 1. Application fee required: $50. Interview required.

Athletics Interscholastic: alpine skiing (boys, girls), aquatics (b,g), baseball (b), basketball (b,g), cross-country running (b,g), field hockey (g), football (b), lacrosse (b,g), skiing (downhill) (b,g), soccer (b,g), softball (g), squash (b,g), swimming and diving (b,g), tennis (b,g), track and field (b,g), volleyball (g), water polo (b,g), wrestling (b); coed interscholastic: alpine skiing, back packing, dance, diving, fitness, golf, outdoors, riflery, snowboarding; coed intramural: weight lifting. 2 trainers.

Computers Computers are regularly used in English, foreign language, history, mathematics, science classes. Computer network features include campus e-mail, on-campus library services, CD-ROMs, Internet access, file transfer, DVD, wireless campus network.

Contact Terry Breault, Director of Admissions & Financial Aid. 860-386-4440. Fax: 860-668-2966. E-mail: saadmit@suffieldacademy.org. Web site: www. suffieldacademy.org.

See full description on page 1086.

SUMITON CHRISTIAN SCHOOL

PO Box 40
Sumiton, Alabama 35148
Head of School: Mrs. Becky C. Potts

General Information Coeducational day college-preparatory, arts, business, and religious studies school, affiliated with Church of God. Grades K–12. Founded: 1976. Setting: small town. Nearest major city is Birmingham. 30-acre campus. 1 building

on campus. Approved or accredited by Southern Association of Colleges and Schools and Alabama Department of Education. Total enrollment: 637. Upper school average class size: 20. Upper school faculty-student ratio: 1:12.

Upper School Student Profile Grade 9: 65 students (35 boys, 30 girls); Grade 10: 53 students (29 boys, 24 girls); Grade 11: 52 students (30 boys, 22 girls); Grade 12: 61 students (37 boys, 24 girls). 30% of students are Church of God.

Faculty School total: 42. In upper school: 11 men, 9 women; 9 have advanced degrees.

Subjects Offered ACT preparation, advanced computer applications, algebra, American history, American literature, analytic geometry, anatomy and physiology, ancient world history, art appreciation, art history, athletic training, athletics, band, baseball, Basic programming, basketball, Bible, biology, British literature, broadcasting, business mathematics, calculus, career/college preparation, cheerleading, chemistry, chorus, Christian education, college admission preparation, computer applications, computer education, computer keyboarding, computer literacy, computer programming, computer science, consumer economics, drama, economics, English, English literature, environmental science, fine arts, foreign language, general business, general math, geography, geometry, golf, government, guitar, gymnastics, health, honors English, instrumental music, marching band, media communications, modern Western civilization, music appreciation, music history, physical education, physical science, physics, pre-calculus, psychology, public speaking, religious education, research skills, Spanish, speech communications, student government, swimming, trigonometry, U.S. government, video film production, vocal music, weight training, yearbook.

Graduation Requirements 1½ elective credits, algebra, analytic geometry, anatomy and physiology, art, Bible, biology, chemistry, computer keyboarding, computer literacy, computer programming, English literature, foreign language, government, history, honors English, language arts, physical education (includes health), physical science, physics, political economics, pre-calculus, psychology, public speaking, research techniques, trigonometry, 75 hours of community service (for Honors Diploma students).

Special Academic Programs Honors section; study at local college for college credit; academic accommodation for the gifted and the artistically talented.

College Placement 59 students graduated in 2005; 54 went to college, including Auburn University; Bevill State Community College; Birmingham-Southern College; Mississippi State University; The University of Alabama; The University of Alabama at Birmingham. Other: 3 went to work, 2 entered military service. Mean composite ACT: 20. 9% scored over 26 on composite ACT.

Student Life Upper grades have uniform requirement, student council, honor system. Discipline rests primarily with faculty. Attendance at religious services is required.

Summer Programs Remediation, enrichment, sports programs offered; session focuses on summer sport camps; held on campus; accepts boys and girls; open to students from other schools. 30 students usually enrolled.

Tuition and Aid Guaranteed tuition plan. Tuition installment plan (Key Tuition Payment Plan, monthly payment plans). Tuition reduction for siblings available.

Admissions Deadline for receipt of application materials: none. No application fee required. Interview required.

Athletics Interscholastic: baseball (boys), basketball (b,g), cheering (g), cross-country running (b,g), dance team (g), football (b), golf (b), power lifting (b), running (b,g), softball (g), swimming and diving (b,g), volleyball (g), wrestling (b); intramural: flag football (g), gymnastics (g), jump rope (b,g), kickball (b,g), physical training (b,g), softball (g), strength & conditioning (b,g), volleyball (g), weight training (b,g). 3 PE instructors, 6 coaches, 2 trainers.

Computers Computers are regularly used in computer applications, data processing, desktop publishing, drafting, graphic arts, graphic design, journalism, keyboarding, media production, technical drawing, video film production, Web site design classes. Computer network features include campus e-mail, on-campus library services, CD-ROMs, Internet access, DVD.

Contact Mrs. Maria Vines, High School Office. 205-648-6648 Ext. 100. Fax: 205-648-0047. Web site: www.scs-eagles.org.

SUMMERFIELD WALDORF SCHOOL

655 Willowside Road
Santa Rosa, California 95472
Head of School: Mrs. Terri Hobart

General Information Coeducational day college-preparatory, general academic, and arts school. Grades 1–12. Founded: 1974. Setting: rural. 38-acre campus. 5 buildings on campus. Approved or accredited by Association of Waldorf Schools of North America, Western Association of Schools and Colleges, and California Department of Education. Endowment: $25,000. Total enrollment: 365. Upper school average class size: 25. Upper school faculty-student ratio: 1:4.

Upper School Student Profile Grade 9: 26 students (10 boys, 16 girls); Grade 10: 20 students (10 boys, 10 girls); Grade 11: 30 students (14 boys, 16 girls); Grade 12: 20 students (11 boys, 9 girls).

Faculty School total: 60. In upper school: 16 men, 10 women; 18 have advanced degrees.

Subjects Offered Arts, history, humanities, literature, mathematics, music, science.

Special Academic Programs Advanced Placement exam preparation in 3 subject areas.

College Placement 14 students graduated in 2005; 13 went to college. Other: 1 went to work.

Student Life Upper grades have specified standards of dress, student council, honor system. Discipline rests primarily with faculty.

Tuition and Aid Tuition installment plan (FACTS Tuition Payment Plan). Tuition reduction for siblings, need-based scholarship grants available. In 2005–06, 25% of upper-school students received aid.

Admissions Traditional secondary-level entrance grade is 9. 3-R Achievement Test required. Deadline for receipt of application materials: none. Application fee required: $75. On-campus interview required.

Athletics Intramural: basketball (boys, girls), rowing (b,g), volleyball (b,g); coed interscholastic: tennis. 1 PE instructor, 4 coaches.

Computers Computers are regularly used in accounting classes.

Contact Ms. Pamela Sonn, High School Secretary. 707-575-7194 Ext. 15. Fax: 707-575-3217. E-mail: psonn@summerfieldwaldorf.org. Web site: www.summerfieldwaldorf.org.

THE SUMMIT COUNTRY DAY SCHOOL

2161 Grandin Road
Cincinnati, Ohio 45208-3300
Head of School: Mr. Joseph T. Devlin

General Information Coeducational day college-preparatory school, affiliated with Roman Catholic Church. Grades PK–12. Founded: 1890. Setting: suburban. 24-acre campus. 2 buildings on campus. Approved or accredited by Independent Schools Association of the Central States, Ohio Association of Independent Schools, The College Board, and Ohio Department of Education. Member of Secondary School Admission Test Board. Endowment: $9 million. Total enrollment: 1,087. Upper school average class size: 16. Upper school faculty-student ratio: 1:9.

Upper School Student Profile Grade 9: 89 students (35 boys, 54 girls); Grade 10: 67 students (27 boys, 40 girls); Grade 11: 85 students (39 boys, 46 girls); Grade 12: 82 students (43 boys, 39 girls). 65% of students are Roman Catholic.

Faculty School total: 136. In upper school: 18 men, 19 women; 31 have advanced degrees.

Subjects Offered 1968, Advanced Placement courses, algebra, American government-AP, American history, American history-AP, American literature, anatomy and physiology, archaeology, area studies, art, Basic programming, Bible studies, biology, biology-AP, business, business law, calculus, calculus-AP, ceramics, chemistry, chemistry-AP, chorus, college admission preparation, college placement, community service, computer applications, computer programming, computer science, computer science-AP, concert choir, creative writing, critical studies in film, critical thinking, drama, earth science, economics, English, English literature, English-AP, environmental science, European history, European history-AP, expository writing, fine arts, French, French-AP, geometry, government-AP, government/civics, grammar, graphic design, health, history, history of science, history-AP, Holocaust studies, language-AP, Latin, Latin-AP, leadership and service, leadership education training, leadership training, literary magazine, mathematics, music, music theory-AP, music-AP, philosophy, physical education, physics, physics-AP, pre-calculus, psychology, psychology-AP, public speaking, religion, religious studies, science, senior career experience, service learning/internship, social studies, Spanish, Spanish language-AP, Spanish-AP, speech, speech communications, statistics-AP, student government, studio art, studio art—AP, study skills, theater, theology, trigonometry, world history, world history-AP, world literature, world religions, writing.

Graduation Requirements Arts and fine arts (art, music, dance, drama), computer applications, computer science, English, foreign language, mathematics, physical education (includes health), religion (includes Bible studies and theology), science, social science, social studies (includes history), speech communications, junior year leadership course (one semester), junior year speech course, 40 hours of Christian service, senior search (2 week field experience in career of interest area).

Special Academic Programs Advanced Placement exam preparation in 18 subject areas; honors section; independent study; study abroad; academic accommodation for the gifted.

College Placement 79 students graduated in 2005; all went to college, including Boston University; Clemson University; DePauw University; Saint Louis University; Savannah College of Art and Design; University of Notre Dame.

Student Life Upper grades have uniform requirement, student council, honor system. Discipline rests equally with students and faculty. Attendance at religious services is required.

Summer Programs Enrichment, advancement, sports, art/fine arts, computer instruction programs offered; session focuses on enrichment/academic advancement; held on campus; accepts boys and girls; open to students from other schools. 2006 schedule: June 8 to August 16. Application deadline: none.

Tuition and Aid Day student tuition: $13,150. Tuition installment plan (monthly payment plans, individually arranged payment plans). Merit scholarship grants, need-based scholarship grants, need-based loans available. In 2005–06, 50% of upper-school students received aid; total upper-school merit-scholarship money awarded: $126,000. Total amount of financial aid awarded in 2005–06: $600,000.

Admissions Traditional secondary-level entrance grade is 9. For fall 2005, 117 students applied for upper-level admission, 87 were accepted, 37 enrolled. High

The Summit Country Day School

School Placement Test or ISEE required. Deadline for receipt of application materials: December 19. Application fee required: $50. On-campus interview recommended.

Athletics Interscholastic: baseball (boys, girls), basketball (b,g), cheering (g), cross-country running (b,g), dance team (g), diving (b,g), field hockey (g), football (b), golf (b,g), lacrosse (b), soccer (b,g), softball (g), swimming and diving (b,g), tennis (b,g), track and field (b,g), volleyball (g), wrestling (b); intramural: dance team (g); coed interscholastic: weight lifting. 13 coaches, 1 trainer.

Computers Computers are regularly used in all classes. Computer network features include campus e-mail, on-campus library services, CD-ROMs, online commercial services, Internet access, file transfer, office computer access, DVD, wireless campus network, mobile laptop computer lab, Basmati Grades, Blackboard, Sketchpad, 8 full-text databases including Big Chalk, World Book, Children's Lit, SIRS, Biography Resource Center, Wilson Web, INFOhio, JSTOR.

Contact Kelley Schiess, Director of Admission. 513-533-5350. Fax: 513-533-5373. E-mail: schiess_k@summitcds.org. Web site: www.summitcds.org.

ANNOUNCEMENT FROM THE SCHOOL Founded in 1890, the Summit Country Day School is Cincinnati's only Catholic, independent, college-preparatory school for preschool through grade 12 students. The School is situated in Hyde Park, on a beautiful 23-acre campus, with a separate 16-acre Athletic Complex, offering 4 sports fields, 5 tennis courts, and a 20,000-square-foot gymnasium. The Summit has three contiguous divisions: Lower School includes a Montessori preK–kindergarten program and grades 1–4; Middle School, grades 5–8; and Upper School, grades 9–12. The Summit is a Christian learning environment in which values are fostered and students are challenged to bring forth their best efforts spiritually, academically, physically, socially, and artistically. Paramount to The Summit's education is its nationally recognized Educating for Character program, *CREDO,* which instills those qualities that define good character: respect, responsibility, and honesty. The educational environment is complimented by the religious and ethnic diversity of the 1,060 student population, of whom 15% are students of color. Students in all grades participate in field trips, leadership workshops, performing arts, academic and artistic competitions, and extensive athletic programs. As part of The Summit technology initiative, keyboarding begins in grade 1 and wireless laptops are used in grades 4–12 to enhance learning in all areas of study. This, along with access to more than 700 computers and leading-edge hardware, software, and Web resources, makes The Summit one of the most technologically advanced independent schools in the country. Through scholarship, service, creativity, and physical drive, Summit graduates have distinguished themselves nationally among other graduating seniors. Annually, over 20% of Summit seniors are recognized by the National Merit Scholarship Corporation, 60% receive college scholarships, and 100% of graduating students successfully pursue college degrees. Tuition ranges from $4860 to $13,150, depending upon grade level. Financial aid is available to qualifying families in grades 7–12, and merit-based scholarships are available to Upper School students. For more information, visit www.summitcds.org.

SUMMIT PREPARATORY SCHOOL

Kalispell, Montana
See Special Needs Schools section.

SURABAYA INTERNATIONAL SCHOOL

Citra Raya International Village
Tromol Pos 2/SBDK
Surabaya 60225, Indonesia
Head of School: Mr. Larry Jones

General Information Coeducational day college-preparatory, arts, and technology school. Grades PK–12. Founded: 1971. Setting: suburban. 5-hectare campus. 4 buildings on campus. Approved or accredited by Western Association of Schools and Colleges. Language of instruction: English. Total enrollment: 242. Upper school average class size: 15. Upper school faculty-student ratio: 1:8.

Upper School Student Profile Grade 9: 14 students (8 boys, 6 girls); Grade 10: 22 students (10 boys, 12 girls); Grade 11: 19 students (10 boys, 9 girls); Grade 12: 21 students (11 boys, 10 girls).

Faculty School total: 30. In upper school: 11 men, 8 women; 11 have advanced degrees.

Subjects Offered Algebra, art, biology, calculus-AP, chemistry-AP, computer applications, computer science, drama, economics, economics-AP, English, English literature-AP, fine arts, French, French-AP, geometry, health, journalism, music, physical education, physical science, pre-calculus, social studies, speech, trigonometry, world civilizations, world geography, world history, world literature, yearbook.

Graduation Requirements Arts and fine arts (art, music, dance, drama), computer science, English, mathematics, physical education (includes health), science, social studies (includes history).

Special Academic Programs Advanced Placement exam preparation in 7 subject areas; accelerated programs; independent study; ESL (60 students enrolled).

College Placement 15 students graduated in 2005; all went to college, including Cornell University; Purdue University; University of San Francisco. Mean SAT verbal: 430, mean SAT math: 640, mean composite ACT: 22. 50% scored over 600 on SAT math.

Student Life Upper grades have student council. Discipline rests primarily with faculty.

Tuition and Aid Day student tuition: $10,666. Tuition installment plan (individually arranged payment plans, quarterly payment plan). Need-based scholarship grants available. In 2005–06, 6% of upper-school students received aid. Total amount of financial aid awarded in 2005–06: $30,000.

Admissions Traditional secondary-level entrance grade is 9. For fall 2005, 19 students applied for upper-level admission, 18 were accepted, 18 enrolled. Deadline for receipt of application materials: none. No application fee required. On-campus interview required.

Athletics Interscholastic: aquatics (boys, girls), badminton (b,g), basketball (b,g), soccer (b,g), swimming and diving (b,g), table tennis (b,g), tennis (b,g), volleyball (b,g); intramural: aquatics (b,g), badminton (b,g), basketball (b,g), soccer (b,g), softball (b,g), table tennis (b,g), tennis (b,g), volleyball (b,g), wall climbing (b,g); coed interscholastic: aquatics, golf, martial arts; coed intramural: golf, martial arts, soccer, swimming and diving, volleyball. 2 PE instructors.

Computers Computers are regularly used in English, mathematics, science, social science classes. Computer network features include campus e-mail, on-campus library services, CD-ROMs, online commercial services, Internet access.

Contact Mrs. Maya Moeried, Administrative Assistant. 62-31-741-4300. Fax: 62-31-741-4334. E-mail: sisadmin@sisedu.net. Web site: w3.sisedu.net.

SWEDISH LANGUAGE SCHOOL

739-20 Avenue, NW
Calgary, Alberta T2M 1E2, Canada
Head of School: Markus Jagrelius

General Information Coeducational day college-preparatory, general academic, bilingual studies, and Swedish language and culture school. Grades K–12. Founded: 1975. Approved or accredited by Alberta Department of Education. Total enrollment: 35.

Upper School Student Profile Grade 12: 7 students (4 boys, 3 girls).

Faculty School total: 5.

Admissions Deadline for receipt of application materials: none. No application fee required. Interview required.

Contact Markus Jagrelius. 403-284-2610. Fax: 403-284-2675. E-mail: jagrelius@yahoo.com. Web site: www.swedishschool.com/.

TABOR ACADEMY

66 Spring Street
Marion, Massachusetts 02738
Head of School: Mr. Jay S. Stroud

General Information Coeducational boarding and day college-preparatory and arts school. Grades 9–12. Founded: 1876. Setting: rural. Nearest major city is Boston. Students are housed in single-sex dormitories. 80-acre campus. 42 buildings on campus. Approved or accredited by Association of Independent Schools in New England, New England Association of Schools and Colleges, and The Association of Boarding Schools. Member of National Association of Independent Schools and Secondary School Admission Test Board. Endowment: $34.6 million. Total enrollment: 486. Upper school average class size: 12. Upper school faculty-student ratio: 1:6.

Upper School Student Profile Grade 9: 100 students (47 boys, 53 girls); Grade 10: 136 students (71 boys, 65 girls); Grade 11: 115 students (63 boys, 52 girls); Grade 12: 135 students (73 boys, 62 girls). 70% of students are boarding students. 63% are state residents. 27 states are represented in upper school student body. 12% are international students. International students from Bermuda, China, Germany, Republic of Korea, Taiwan, and Thailand; 9 other countries represented in student body.

Faculty School total: 82. In upper school: 55 men, 27 women; 48 have advanced degrees; 59 reside on campus.

Subjects Offered Algebra, American history, American literature, ancient history, architecture, art, art history, astronomy, biology, calculus, celestial navigation, ceramics, chemistry, creative writing, drama, ecology, economics, English, English literature, European history, fine arts, French, geology, geometry, German, Greek, health, history, Latin, maritime history, mathematics, meteorology, microbiology, music, navigation, oceanography, photography, physics, physiology, science, social science, social studies, Spanish, speech, statistics, theater, trigonometry, world history, world literature.

Graduation Requirements Algebra, arts and fine arts (art, music, dance, drama), biology, English, foreign language, geometry, mathematics, science, social science, social studies (includes history).

Special Academic Programs Advanced Placement exam preparation in 19 subject areas; honors section; independent study; term-away projects; academic accommodation for the gifted, the musically talented, and the artistically talented; ESL (7 students enrolled).

College Placement 132 students graduated in 2005; all went to college, including Boston College; Boston University; Brown University; Connecticut College; New York University; University of Vermont. Mean SAT verbal: 593, mean SAT math: 607.

Student Life Upper grades have specified standards of dress, student council. Discipline rests equally with students and faculty.

Tuition and Aid Day student tuition: $24,700; 7-day tuition and room/board: $35,000. Tuition installment plan (Academic Management Services Plan, Key Tuition Payment Plan, monthly payment plans, Tuition Management Systems Plan). Need-based scholarship grants available. In 2005–06, 34% of upper-school students received aid. Total amount of financial aid awarded in 2005–06: $2,894,600.

Admissions Traditional secondary-level entrance grade is 9. For fall 2005, 622 students applied for upper-level admission, 411 were accepted, 166 enrolled. ISEE, PSAT or SSAT required. Deadline for receipt of application materials: January 31. Application fee required: $50. Interview required.

Athletics Interscholastic: baseball (boys), basketball (b,g), crew (b,g), cross-country running (b,g), field hockey (g), football (b), ice hockey (b,g), lacrosse (b,g), soccer (b,g), softball (g), squash (b,g), tennis (b,g), track and field (b,g), wrestling (b); intramural: crew (b,g), ice hockey (g), squash (b,g), tennis (b,g); coed interscholastic: golf, sailing; coed intramural: aerobics, dance, fitness, sailing, strength & conditioning, weight training. 2 trainers.

Computers Computers are regularly used in English, foreign language, history, literary magazine, mathematics, newspaper, photography, publications, science, yearbook classes. Computer network features include campus e-mail, on-campus library services, CD-ROMs, online commercial services, Internet access, DVD, wireless campus network, digital media labs.

Contact Andrew L. McCain, Director of Admissions. 508-748-2000 Ext. 2219. Fax: 508-748-0353. E-mail: admissions@taboracademy.org. Web site: www.taboracademy.org.

ANNOUNCEMENT FROM THE SCHOOL Tabor, the school by the sea, combines a big school's program with a small school's humanity. Tabor offers 70 individualized courses, including 24 AP courses. Dorms average 14 students per faculty member; standard class size is 12 students. Cocurricular programs include 49 different athletics, art, and music offerings. The newest facility is the Marine and Nautical Sciences Center, located right on Sippican Harbor, with direct access to the ocean, expanded wet lab for tanks and research, and waterfront classrooms.

See full description on page 1088.

THE TAFT SCHOOL

110 Woodbury Road
Watertown, Connecticut 06795
Head of School: Mr. William R. MacMullen

General Information Coeducational boarding and day college-preparatory, arts, and humanities school. Grades 9–PG. Founded: 1890. Setting: small town. Nearest major city is Waterbury. Students are housed in single-sex dormitories. 220-acre campus. 20 buildings on campus. Approved or accredited by Association of Independent Schools in New England, Connecticut Association of Independent Schools, New England Association of Schools and Colleges, The Association of Boarding Schools, The College Board, and Connecticut Department of Education. Member of National Association of Independent Schools and Secondary School Admission Test Board. Endowment: $159 million. Total enrollment: 566. Upper school average class size: 12. Upper school faculty-student ratio: 1:6.

Upper School Student Profile Grade 9: 103 students (55 boys, 48 girls); Grade 10: 147 students (72 boys, 75 girls); Grade 11: 151 students (76 boys, 75 girls); Grade 12: 156 students (81 boys, 75 girls); Postgraduate: 9 students (8 boys, 1 girl). 81% of students are boarding students. 38% are state residents. 34 states are represented in upper school student body. 12% are international students. International students from China, Hong Kong, Japan, Republic of Korea, Taiwan, and Thailand; 13 other countries represented in student body.

Faculty School total: 84. In upper school: 52 men, 32 women; 58 have advanced degrees; 73 reside on campus.

Subjects Offered Algebra, American history, American literature, American studies, anatomy, art, art history, biology, calculus, ceramics, chemistry, Chinese, computer math, computer programming, computer science, creative writing, dance, drama, earth science, ecology, economics, electronics, English, English literature, environmental science, ethics, European history, expository writing, fine arts, French, geography, geology, geometry, government/civics, grammar, Greek, history, history of ideas, history of science, humanities, Japanese, Latin, marine biology, mathematics, music, philosophy, photography, physical education, physics, physiology, psychology, religion, science, social studies, Spanish, speech, statistics, theater, theology, trigonometry, world history, world literature, writing, zoology.

Graduation Requirements American history, arts and fine arts (art, music, dance, drama), English, foreign language, mathematics, science, social studies (includes history), three semesters of arts.

Special Academic Programs Advanced Placement exam preparation in 19 subject areas; honors section; independent study; term-away projects; study abroad; academic accommodation for the gifted, the musically talented, and the artistically talented.

College Placement 165 students graduated in 2005; all went to college, including Boston College; Brown University; Davidson College; Georgetown University; Middlebury College; Trinity College. Mean SAT verbal: 651, mean SAT math: 655. 75% scored over 600 on SAT verbal, 81% scored over 600 on SAT math.

Student Life Upper grades have specified standards of dress, student council, honor system. Discipline rests equally with students and faculty.

Summer Programs Enrichment, ESL, sports, art/fine arts, computer instruction programs offered; session focuses on academic enrichment; held on campus; accepts boys and girls; open to students from other schools. 150 students usually enrolled. 2006 schedule: June 25 to July 29. Application deadline: May 15.

Tuition and Aid Day student tuition: $26,000; 7-day tuition and room/board: $35,000. Guaranteed tuition plan. Tuition installment plan (Key Tuition Payment Plan). Need-based scholarship grants, need-based loans, prepGATE Loans available. In 2005–06, 34% of upper-school students received aid. Total amount of financial aid awarded in 2005–06: $4,400,000.

Admissions Traditional secondary-level entrance grade is 9. For fall 2005, 1,371 students applied for upper-level admission, 371 were accepted, 193 enrolled. SSAT required. Deadline for receipt of application materials: January 31. Application fee required: $40. Interview required.

Athletics Interscholastic: alpine skiing (boys, girls), baseball (b), basketball (b,g), crew (b,g), cross-country running (b,g), field hockey (g), football (b), golf (b,g), hockey (b,g), ice hockey (b,g), lacrosse (b,g), rowing (b,g), soccer (b,g), softball (g), squash (b,g), tennis (b,g), track and field (b,g), ultimate Frisbee (b,g), volleyball (g), wrestling (b); coed interscholastic: dressage, equestrian sports, horseback riding; coed intramural: aerobics, aerobics/dance, ballet, basketball, climbing, cross-country running, dance, dressage, equestrian sports, figure skating, fitness, fitness walking, Frisbee, hockey, horseback riding, ice hockey, ice skating, jogging, martial arts, modern dance, rowing, running, soccer, squash, strength & conditioning, tennis, track and field, ultimate Frisbee, walking, wall climbing, weight lifting, weight training, yoga. 2 trainers.

Computers Computers are regularly used in art, English, foreign language, geography, history, mathematics, music, science classes. Computer network features include campus e-mail, on-campus library services, CD-ROMs, online commercial services, Internet access, file transfer, DVD, wireless campus network.

Contact Mr. Frederick H. Wandelt III, Director of Admissions. 860-945-7700. Fax: 860-945-7808. E-mail: admissions@taftschool.org. Web site: www.taftschool.org.

ANNOUNCEMENT FROM THE SCHOOL Known for close faculty-student relationships and academic rigor, the Taft School seeks students who are intellectually curious, who will become involved, and who will commit themselves to the highest standard of academic and personal growth. Taft emphasizes individual development through rigorous academic, athletic, and extracurricular programs. In 2005, 201 Taft students took 464 Advanced Placement examinations and achieved an average score of 4.0. This achievement places Taft among the finest secondary schools in the country.

See full description on page 1090.

TAIPEI AMERICAN SCHOOL

800 Chung Shan North Road, Section 6
Taipei 111, Taiwan
Head of School: Mr. Charles Chris Hanna

General Information Coeducational day college-preparatory school. Grades PK–12. Founded: 1949. Setting: urban. 14-acre campus. 4 buildings on campus. Approved or accredited by Western Association of Schools and Colleges. Affiliate member of National Association of Independent Schools; member of European Council of International Schools. Language of instruction: English. Endowment: 900 million Taiwan dollars. Total enrollment: 2,235. Upper school average class size: 22. Upper school faculty-student ratio: 1:9.

Upper School Student Profile Grade 9: 208 students (104 boys, 104 girls); Grade 10: 220 students (95 boys, 125 girls); Grade 11: 215 students (118 boys, 97 girls); Grade 12: 200 students (115 boys, 85 girls).

Faculty School total: 243. In upper school: 56 men, 35 women; 77 have advanced degrees.

Subjects Offered Advanced Placement courses, algebra, American history, American literature, art, art history, Asian studies, biology, British literature, business, calculus, ceramics, chemistry, Chinese, choir, comedy, computer programming, computer science, creative writing, cultural criticism, current events, current history, dance, drafting, drama, drawing, Dutch, earth science, economics, English, English literature, English literature and composition-AP, ESL, European history, fine arts, French, geography, geology, geometry, German, health, history, International Baccalaureate courses, Japanese, journalism, mathematics, mechanical drawing, music,

mythology, orchestra, philosophy, photography, physical education, physics, psychology, rhetoric, science, social science, social studies, Spanish, speech, theater, theory of knowledge, trigonometry, Western civilization, world culture, world history, writing, yearbook.

Graduation Requirements Arts and fine arts (art, music, dance, drama), English, mathematics, physical education (includes health), science, social science, social studies (includes history).

Special Academic Programs International Baccalaureate program; Advanced Placement exam preparation in 17 subject areas; honors section; accelerated programs; remedial reading and/or remedial writing; remedial math; ESL (69 students enrolled).

College Placement 201 students graduated in 2005; all went to college, including Carnegie Mellon University; New York University; University of California, San Diego; University of Illinois at Urbana–Champaign; University of Washington. Mean SAT verbal: 576, mean SAT math: 681.

Student Life Upper grades have student council, honor system. Discipline rests primarily with faculty.

Summer Programs Enrichment programs offered; session focuses on English enrichment; held on campus; accepts boys and girls; open to students from other schools. 35 students usually enrolled. 2006 schedule: June 7 to July 2. Application deadline: May 30.

Tuition and Aid Day student tuition: 389,700 Taiwan dollars. Need-based scholarship grants available.

Admissions Traditional secondary-level entrance grade is 9. English for Non-native Speakers required. Deadline for receipt of application materials: none. Application fee required: 10,000 Taiwan dollars. Interview required.

Athletics Interscholastic: aquatics (boys, girls), badminton (b,g), basketball (b,g), cross-country running (b,g), dance (b,g), rugby (b,g), soccer (b,g), softball (b,g), swimming and diving (b,g), tennis (b,g), volleyball (b,g); intramural: aquatics (b,g), badminton (b,g), basketball (b,g), martial arts (b), volleyball (b,g). 4 PE instructors.

Computers Computers are regularly used in all academic classes. Computer network features include campus e-mail, on-campus library services, CD-ROMs, online commercial services, Internet access, file transfer, office computer access.

Contact Alec Aspinwall, Director of Advancement/Admissions. 886-22-873-9900 Ext. 328. Fax: 886-22-873-1641. E-mail: admissns@tas.edu.tw. Web site: www.tas.edu.tw.

TALLULAH FALLS SCHOOL

PO Box 249
Tallulah Falls, Georgia 30573
Head of School: Dr. Kent Anglin

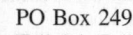

General Information Coeducational boarding and day college-preparatory, general academic, arts, and technology school, affiliated with Christian faith. Grades 7–12. Founded: 1909. Setting: rural. Nearest major city is Atlanta. Students are housed in single-sex dormitories. 600-acre campus. 16 buildings on campus. Approved or accredited by Georgia Accrediting Commission, Georgia Independent School Association, Southern Association of Colleges and Schools, The Association of Boarding Schools, and Georgia Department of Education. Languages of instruction: English, Spanish, and French. Endowment: $32 million. Total enrollment: 157. Upper school average class size: 12. Upper school faculty-student ratio: 1:8.

Upper School Student Profile Grade 9: 30 students (18 boys, 12 girls); Grade 10: 29 students (14 boys, 15 girls); Grade 11: 40 students (12 boys, 28 girls); Grade 12: 20 students (9 boys, 11 girls). 82% of students are boarding students. 80% are state residents. 12 states are represented in upper school student body. 15% are international students. International students from Japan, Mexico, Republic of Korea, Rwanda, Thailand, and Uganda; 4 other countries represented in student body. 75% of students are Christian faith.

Faculty School total: 22. In upper school: 8 men, 10 women; 17 have advanced degrees; 8 reside on campus.

Subjects Offered Algebra, American culture, American history, American literature, American literature-AP, anatomy, art, biology, calculus, chemistry, chorus, computer animation, computer applications, computer education, computer graphics, computer information systems, computer literacy, computer multimedia, computer processing, computer programming, computer science, computer studies, computer technologies, computer-aided design, creative writing, earth science, English literature, English literature and composition-AP, French, geometry, government/civics, health, history, home economics, industrial arts, journalism, keyboarding, mathematics, music, physical education, physical science, physics, physiology, Spanish, technology, trigonometry, world literature, world religions.

Graduation Requirements Algebra, American government, American literature, biology, British literature, chemistry, computer science, English, foreign language, geometry, government, mathematics, physical education (includes health), physical fitness, physical science, physics, political science, pre-calculus, science, social science, social studies (includes history).

Special Academic Programs Advanced Placement exam preparation in 6 subject areas; honors section; independent study; study at local college for college credit; academic accommodation for the gifted, the musically talented, and the artistically talented; ESL (14 students enrolled).

College Placement 27 students graduated in 2005; 25 went to college, including Dartmouth College; Georgia Institute of Technology; North Georgia College & State

University; The University of Tennessee; University of Georgia; University of Southern California. Other: 2 went to work. Median SAT verbal: 520, median SAT math: 530. 40% scored over 600 on SAT verbal, 50% scored over 600 on SAT math.

Student Life Upper grades have uniform requirement, student council, honor system. Discipline rests primarily with faculty. Attendance at religious services is required.

Summer Programs ESL, sports programs offered; session focuses on baseball, cross-country, volleyball, basketball; held on campus; accepts boys and girls; open to students from other schools. 50 students usually enrolled. 2006 schedule: June 10 to July 7. Application deadline: April 1.

Tuition and Aid Day student tuition: $7875; 7-day tuition and room/board: $17,850. Tuition installment plan (Key Tuition Payment Plan, monthly payment plans, individually arranged payment plans, tuition freeze if paid in full by June 1). Tuition reduction for siblings, need-based scholarship grants, need-based loans available. In 2005–06, 50% of upper-school students received aid. Total amount of financial aid awarded in 2005–06: $1,000,000.

Admissions Traditional secondary-level entrance grade is 10. For fall 2005, 161 students applied for upper-level admission, 125 were accepted, 100 enrolled. Admissions testing, any standardized test and Comprehensive Test of Basic Skills required. Deadline for receipt of application materials: May 15. Application fee required: $30. Interview required.

Athletics Interscholastic: basketball (boys, girls), cheering (g), cross-country running (b,g), soccer (b), tennis (b,g), track and field (b,g), volleyball (g); coed interscholastic: golf, running; coed intramural: aquatics, back packing, badminton, basketball, biathlon, bicycling, billiards, canoeing/kayaking, climbing, combined training, dance squad, dance team, fishing, fitness, flag football, floor hockey, fly fishing, football, Frisbee, golf, hiking/backpacking, kayaking, mountain biking, nautilus, outdoor activities, outdoor adventure, outdoor education, outdoor recreation, outdoor skills, paddle tennis, paint ball, physical fitness, physical training, power lifting, rafting, rappelling, rock climbing, ropes courses, running, skiing (downhill), snowboarding, soccer, softball, strength & conditioning, swimming and diving, table tennis, tennis, touch football, track and field, ultimate Frisbee, volleyball, walking, water polo, weight lifting, weight training. 2 PE instructors, 8 coaches, 1 trainer.

Computers Computers are regularly used in all classes. Computer network features include campus e-mail, on-campus library services, CD-ROMs, online commercial services, Internet access, wireless campus network.

Contact Ms. Jessica L. Robinson, Assistant Director of Admissions. 706-754-0400 Ext. 5150. Fax: 706-754-3595. E-mail: admissions@tallulahfalls.org. Web site: www.tallulahfalls.org.

See full description on page 1092.

TAPPLY BINET COLLEGE

245 Garner Road West
Ancaster, Ontario L9G 3K9, Canada
Head of School: Ms. Sue Davidson

General Information Coeducational day college-preparatory and general academic school. Grades 7–12. Founded: 1997. Setting: small town. Nearest major city is Hamilton, Canada. 1 building on campus. Approved or accredited by Ontario Department of Education. Language of instruction: English. Total enrollment: 13. Upper school average class size: 5. Upper school faculty-student ratio: 1:3.

Upper School Student Profile Grade 9: 1 student (1 girl); Grade 10: 1 student (1 boy); Grade 11: 2 students (1 boy, 1 girl); Grade 12: 9 students (7 boys, 2 girls).

Faculty School total: 5. In upper school: 2 men, 3 women; 1 has an advanced degree.

College Placement Colleges students went to include Brock University.

Student Life Upper grades have uniform requirement, student council, honor system. Discipline rests primarily with faculty.

Admissions Battery of testing done through outside agency required. Deadline for receipt of application materials: none. No application fee required.

Athletics Coed Interscholastic: aerobics/nautilus. 1 PE instructor.

Contact Ms. Sue Davidson, Principal. 905-648-2737. Fax: 905-648-8762. E-mail: tapply@bellnet.ca. Web site: www.tapplybinetcollege.com.

TASIS THE AMERICAN SCHOOL IN ENGLAND

Coldharbour Lane
Thorpe, Surrey TW20 8TE, United Kingdom
Head of School: Dr. James A. Doran

General Information Coeducational boarding and day college-preparatory and arts school. Boarding grades 9–13, day grades N–13. Founded: 1976. Setting: rural. Nearest major city is London. Students are housed in single-sex dormitories. 35-acre campus. 23 buildings on campus. Approved or accredited by European Council of International Schools, New England Association of Schools and Colleges, and The Association of Boarding Schools. Affiliate member of National Association of Independent Schools; member of Secondary School Admission Test Board. Language of instruction: English. Total enrollment: 705. Upper school average class size: 15. Upper school faculty-student ratio: 1:8.

Upper School Student Profile 46% of students are boarding students. 47% are international students. International students from Germany, Japan, Nigeria, Republic of Korea, Spain, and United States; 28 other countries represented in student body.
Faculty School total: 105. In upper school: 20 men, 25 women; 33 have advanced degrees; 16 reside on campus.
Subjects Offered Algebra, American history, American literature, art, art history, biology, calculus, ceramics, chemistry, computer science, drama, earth science, economics, English, English literature, environmental science, ESL, European history, fine arts, French, geometry, government/civics, history, humanities, international relations, keyboarding, Latin, mathematics, music, photography, physical education, physical science, physics, science, sculpture, senior humanities, social studies, Spanish, statistics, theater, world history.
Graduation Requirements Arts and fine arts (art, music, dance, drama), English, foreign language, history, lab science, mathematics, senior humanities. Community service is required.
Special Academic Programs International Baccalaureate program; Advanced Placement exam preparation in 19 subject areas; independent study; academic accommodation for the gifted; remedial reading and/or remedial writing; ESL (78 students enrolled).
College Placement 89 students graduated in 2005; 85 went to college, including The George Washington University; The University of Texas at Austin; Trinity University; Tufts University. Other: 2 entered a postgraduate year, 2 had other specific plans.
Student Life Upper grades have specified standards of dress, student council. Discipline rests primarily with faculty.
Summer Programs Remediation, enrichment, advancement, ESL, sports, art/fine arts, computer instruction programs offered; session focuses on ESL, academics, enrichment, theater, International Baccalaureate preparation; held on campus; accepts boys and girls; open to students from other schools. 260 students usually enrolled. 2006 schedule: June 24 to August 13. Application deadline: none.
Tuition and Aid Day student tuition: £15,300; 7-day tuition and room/board: £23,600. Tuition installment plan (monthly payment plans, individually arranged payment plans). Merit scholarship grants, need-based scholarship grants available.
Admissions Deadline for receipt of application materials: none. Application fee required: £75. Interview recommended.
Athletics Interscholastic: baseball (boys), basketball (b,g), cross-country running (b,g), rugby (b), soccer (b,g), softball (g), tennis (b,g), volleyball (b,g); intramural: aerobics (g), aerobics/dance (g), badminton (b,g), ballet (g), cricket (b,g), dance (g), dance team (g), equestrian sports (g), field hockey (b,g), fitness (b,g), floor hockey (b,g), gymnastics (b,g), handball (b,g), indoor soccer (b,g), jump rope (b,g), lacrosse (b,g), modern dance (b,g), outdoor activities (b,g), outdoor adventure (b,g), physical fitness (b,g), physical training (b,g), rhythmic gymnastics (b,g), rugby (b), running (b,g), scooter football (b,g), soccer (b,g), softball (b,g), strength & conditioning (b,g), team handball (b,g), weight training (b,g), winter soccer (b,g); coed interscholastic: cheering, golf; coed intramural: basketball, bicycling, equestrian sports, golf, gymnastics, handball, horseback riding, indoor soccer, lacrosse, martial arts, outdoor activities, outdoor adventure, squash, strength & conditioning, swimming and diving, table tennis, team handball, tennis, track and field, volleyball, weight training, winter soccer. 3 PE instructors, 12 coaches, 1 trainer.
Computers Computers are regularly used in all academic classes. Computer network features include campus e-mail, on-campus library services, CD-ROMs, online commercial services, Internet access, office computer access, DVD, wireless campus network.
Contact Ms. Bronwyn Thorburn, Director of Admissions. 44-1932-565252. Fax: 44-1932-564644. E-mail: ukadmissions@tasis.com. Web site: www.tasis.com/England/.

See full description on page 1094.

TASIS, THE AMERICAN SCHOOL IN SWITZERLAND

Montagnola-Lugano CH-6926, Switzerland

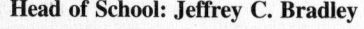

Head of School: Jeffrey C. Bradley

General Information Coeducational boarding and day college-preparatory school. Grades 7–PG. Founded: 1956. Setting: small town. Nearest major city is Lugano. Students are housed in single-sex dormitories. 9-acre campus. 17 buildings on campus. Approved or accredited by European Council of International Schools, New England Association of Schools and Colleges, and Swiss Federation of Private Schools. Affiliate member of National Association of Independent Schools; member of Secondary School Admission Test Board. Language of instruction: English. Total enrollment: 337. Upper school average class size: 12. Upper school faculty-student ratio: 1:5.
Upper School Student Profile Grade 9: 42 students (23 boys, 19 girls); Grade 10: 75 students (40 boys, 35 girls); Grade 11: 118 students (57 boys, 61 girls); Grade 12: 58 students (27 boys, 31 girls); Postgraduate: 5 students (1 boy, 4 girls). 83% of students are boarding students. 83% are international students. International students from Brazil, Germany, Italy, Mexico, Turkey, and United States; 46 other countries represented in student body.

Faculty School total: 73. In upper school: 32 men, 35 women; 37 have advanced degrees; 40 reside on campus.
Subjects Offered Advanced Placement courses, algebra, American history, American literature, ancient history, art, art history, art history-AP, biology, biology-AP, calculus, calculus-AP, ceramics, chemistry, chemistry-AP, digital photography, drama, ecology, economics, economics-AP, English, English language and composition-AP, English literature, English literature and composition-AP, environmental science, ESL, European history, European history-AP, fine arts, French, French language-AP, French literature-AP, geography, geometry, German literature, German-AP, graphic design, health, history, information technology, international relations, Italian, Latin, mathematics, medieval/Renaissance history, music, photography, physical education, physics, science, social studies, Spanish, Spanish language-AP, studio art—AP, theater, theory of knowledge, U.S. government, U.S. history-AP, world culture, world history, world literature.
Graduation Requirements Arts, English, European history, foreign language, mathematics, science, senior humanities, sports, U.S. history.
Special Academic Programs International Baccalaureate program; Advanced Placement exam preparation in 15 subject areas; honors section; independent study; ESL (145 students enrolled).
College Placement 92 students graduated in 2005; 90 went to college, including Boston College; Georgetown University; Hamilton College; Maryland College of Art and Design; Middlebury College; The George Washington University. Other: 1 entered a postgraduate year. Median SAT verbal: 540, median SAT math: 540. 30% scored over 600 on SAT verbal, 33% scored over 600 on SAT math.
Student Life Upper grades have specified standards of dress, student council, honor system. Discipline rests equally with students and faculty.
Summer Programs ESL, sports, art/fine arts programs offered; session focuses on languages, sports, and arts; held both on and off campus; held at TASIS Lugano Campus and Chateau d'Oex; accepts boys and girls; open to students from other schools. 300 students usually enrolled. 2006 schedule: June 23 to August 12. Application deadline: none.
Tuition and Aid Day student tuition: 33,800 Swiss francs; 7-day tuition and room/board: 59,000 Swiss francs. Tuition installment plan (individually arranged payment plans). Need-based scholarship grants available. In 2005–06, 15% of upper-school students received aid.
Admissions Traditional secondary-level entrance grade is 11. For fall 2005, 222 students applied for upper-level admission, 148 were accepted, 148 enrolled. TOEFL or SLEP required. Deadline for receipt of application materials: none. Application fee required: 250 Swiss francs. Interview recommended.
Athletics Interscholastic: basketball (boys, girls), golf (b), rugby (b), soccer (b,g), swimming and diving (b,g), tennis (b,g), track and field (b,g), volleyball (b,g); intramural: basketball (b,g), rugby (b); coed interscholastic: softball, swimming and diving, track and field; coed intramural: aerobics, aerobics/dance, aerobics/nautilus, basketball, climbing, combined training, cross-country running, dance, fitness, flag football, floor hockey, golf, horseback riding, indoor soccer, jogging, martial arts, modern dance, physical fitness, physical training, rock climbing, running, sailing, soccer, softball, squash, strength & conditioning, swimming and diving, tennis, ultimate Frisbee, volleyball, weight lifting, weight training. 2 PE instructors.
Computers Computers are regularly used in art, English, ESL, foreign language, history, information technology, photography, science classes. Computer network features include campus e-mail, on-campus library services, CD-ROMs, Internet access, DVD, wireless campus network.
Contact William E. Eichner, Director of Admissions. 41-91-960-5151. Fax: 41-91-993-2979. E-mail: admissions@tasis.ch. Web site: www.tasis.com/Switzerland/.

See full description on page 1096.

THE TATNALL SCHOOL

1501 Barley Mill Road
Wilmington, Delaware 19807
Head of School: Eric G. Ruoss

General Information Coeducational day college-preparatory school. Grades N–12. Founded: 1930. Setting: suburban. 110-acre campus. 5 buildings on campus. Approved or accredited by Middle States Association of Colleges and Schools and Delaware Department of Education. Member of National Association of Independent Schools. Endowment: $21 million. Total enrollment: 722. Upper school average class size: 13. Upper school faculty-student ratio: 1:8.
Upper School Student Profile Grade 9: 64 students (28 boys, 36 girls); Grade 10: 69 students (40 boys, 29 girls); Grade 11: 64 students (33 boys, 31 girls); Grade 12: 61 students (39 boys, 22 girls).
Faculty School total: 108. In upper school: 18 men, 24 women; 26 have advanced degrees.
Subjects Offered 20th century American writers, 20th century world history, 3-dimensional art, 3-dimensional design, acting, advanced chemistry, advanced computer applications, advanced math, Advanced Placement courses, advanced studio art-AP, African-American literature, algebra, American Civil War, American government, American history, American history-AP, American literature, analysis and differential calculus, anatomy, art, athletic training, athletics, baseball, biology,

biology-AP, botany, calculus, calculus-AP, ceramics, chemistry, chemistry-AP, college counseling, community service, computer programming, computer science, concert band, concert choir, drama, driver education, ecology, economics, English, English literature, English literature-AP, environmental science, environmental science-AP, European history, European history-AP, film, fine arts, French, French language-AP, geometry, health, history, Holocaust, Latin, Latin-AP, literature and composition-AP, marine biology, mathematics, modern European history-AP, music, newspaper, physical education, physics, physics-AP, psychology, psychology-AP, science, service learning/internship, social studies, Spanish, Spanish-AP, statistics, statistics-AP, theater, theater arts, theater production, trigonometry, U.S. history-AP, video, Vietnam War, world history, world literature, writing, yearbook.

Graduation Requirements Arts and fine arts (art, music, dance, drama), computer literacy, English, foreign language, mathematics, physical education (includes health), science, social studies (includes history). Community service is required.

Special Academic Programs Advanced Placement exam preparation in 15 subject areas; honors section; accelerated programs; independent study; term-away projects; study abroad; academic accommodation for the gifted, the musically talented, and the artistically talented.

College Placement 67 students graduated in 2005; all went to college, including Cornell University; Duke University; Swarthmore College; The College of William and Mary; University of Delaware; University of Richmond. Median SAT verbal: 610, median SAT math: 640. 53% scored over 600 on SAT verbal, 71% scored over 600 on SAT math.

Student Life Upper grades have specified standards of dress, student council. Discipline rests primarily with faculty.

Summer Programs Enrichment, advancement, art/fine arts programs offered; session focuses on sports, the arts; held on campus; accepts boys and girls; open to students from other schools. 250 students usually enrolled. 2006 schedule: June to August.

Tuition and Aid Day student tuition: $17,900. Tuition installment plan (Key Tuition Payment Plan). Need-based scholarship grants, need-based loans available. In 2005–06, 17% of upper-school students received aid. Total amount of financial aid awarded in 2005–06: $935,000.

Admissions Traditional secondary-level entrance grade is 9. For fall 2005, 88 students applied for upper-level admission, 45 were accepted, 28 enrolled. ERB CTP IV required. Deadline for receipt of application materials: January 15. Application fee required: $40. On-campus interview required.

Athletics Interscholastic: baseball (boys), basketball (b,g), cheering (g), cross-country running (b,g), field hockey (g), football (b), ice hockey (b), indoor track & field (b,g), lacrosse (b,g), soccer (b,g), swimming and diving (b,g), tennis (b,g), track and field (b,g), volleyball (g), winter (indoor) track (b,g), wrestling (b); coed interscholastic: golf; coed intramural: ultimate Frisbee. 3 PE instructors, 1 trainer.

Computers Computers are regularly used in all classes. Computer network features include campus e-mail, on-campus library services, CD-ROMs, online commercial services, Internet access, DVD, wireless campus network.

Contact Judith M. Bagdon, Admissions Coordinator. 302-892-4285. Fax: 302-892-4387. E-mail: bagdon@tatnall.org. Web site: www.tatnall.org.

THE TENNEY SCHOOL

2055 South Gessner
Houston, Texas 77063
Head of School: George Edward Tenney

General Information Coeducational day college-preparatory school. Grades 6–12. Founded: 1973. Setting: urban. 1-acre campus. 1 building on campus. Approved or accredited by Southern Association of Colleges and Schools and Texas Department of Education. Total enrollment: 55. Upper school average class size: 1. Upper school faculty-student ratio: 1:1.

Upper School Student Profile Grade 9: 8 students (6 boys, 2 girls); Grade 10: 11 students (5 boys, 6 girls); Grade 11: 15 students (6 boys, 9 girls); Grade 12: 9 students (2 boys, 7 girls).

Faculty School total: 25. In upper school: 2 men, 23 women; 8 have advanced degrees.

Subjects Offered Accounting, algebra, American history, American literature, biology, British literature, business law, calculus, chemistry, computer programming, computer studies, creative writing, economics, English, fine arts, geometry, government, health, independent study, journalism, keyboarding, mathematics, microcomputer technology applications, physical education, physical science, physics, pre-calculus, psychology, science, social studies, sociology, Spanish, studio art, theater arts, world geography, world history, world literature, yearbook.

Special Academic Programs Advanced Placement exam preparation in 2 subject areas; honors section; academic accommodation for the gifted; remedial reading and/or remedial writing; remedial math.

College Placement 20 students graduated in 2005; 18 went to college. Other: 2 went to work.

Student Life Upper grades have specified standards of dress. Discipline rests primarily with faculty.

Summer Programs Remediation, enrichment, advancement, computer instruction programs offered; session focuses on academic course work; held on campus; accepts boys and girls; open to students from other schools. 25 students usually enrolled. 2006 schedule: June 1 to July 3. Application deadline: May 25.

Admissions Scholastic Achievement Test required. Deadline for receipt of application materials: none. No application fee required. On-campus interview required.

Athletics 1 PE instructor.

Computers Computers are regularly used in computer applications, creative writing, desktop publishing, English, foreign language, journalism, keyboarding, speech, word processing, yearbook classes. Computer network features include campus e-mail, CD-ROMs, Internet access, DVD.

Contact George E. Tenney, Director. 713-783-6990. Fax: 713-783-6992. E-mail: gtenney@tenneyschool.com. Web site: tenneyschool.com.

TEURLINGS CATHOLIC HIGH SCHOOL

139 Teurlings Drive
Lafayette, Louisiana 70501-0000
Head of School: Mr. Michael Harrison Boyer

General Information Coeducational day college-preparatory and religious studies school, affiliated with Roman Catholic Church. Grades 9–12. Founded: 1955. Setting: urban. Nearest major city is Baton Rouge. 25-acre campus. 12 buildings on campus. Approved or accredited by National Catholic Education Association, Southern Association of Colleges and Schools, and Louisiana Department of Education. Endowment: $755,400. Total enrollment: 674. Upper school average class size: 26. Upper school faculty-student ratio: 1:26.

Upper School Student Profile Grade 9: 187 students (103 boys, 84 girls); Grade 10: 168 students (98 boys, 70 girls); Grade 11: 176 students (78 boys, 98 girls); Grade 12: 143 students (80 boys, 63 girls). 93% of students are Roman Catholic.

Faculty School total: 39. In upper school: 13 men, 26 women; 7 have advanced degrees.

Subjects Offered Accounting, acting, advanced chemistry, advanced computer applications, advanced math, algebra, American history, American history-AP, American literature, anatomy and physiology, art, art-AP, biology, British literature, business applications, calculus, campus ministry, chemistry, civics/free enterprise, computer keyboarding, computer science, drama, earth science, English, environmental science, fine arts, French, geography, geometry, health, honors algebra, honors English, honors geometry, honors U.S. history, honors world history, interpersonal skills, Latin, newspaper, physical education, physical science, physics, psychology, public speaking, publications, SAT/ACT preparation, Spanish, speech, theology, Web site design, world history, world history-AP.

Graduation Requirements Advanced math, algebra, American history, American literature, biology, chemistry, civics, civics/free enterprise, computer applications, computer literacy, electives, English, geometry, literature, physical education (includes health), physical science, public speaking, theology, world geography, world history.

Special Academic Programs Advanced Placement exam preparation in 2 subject areas; honors section; programs in English, mathematics, general development for dyslexic students; special instructional classes for students with learning disabilities, Attention Deficit Disorder, and dyslexia.

College Placement 126 students graduated in 2005; 119 went to college, including Centenary College of Louisiana; Louisiana State University and Agricultural and Mechanical College; Louisiana State University at Eunice; Loyola University New Orleans; Northwestern State University of Louisiana; University of Louisiana at Lafayette. Other: 4 went to work, 3 entered military service. Median composite ACT: 21. 10% scored over 26 on composite ACT.

Student Life Upper grades have uniform requirement, student council, honor system. Discipline rests equally with students and faculty. Attendance at religious services is required.

Tuition and Aid Day student tuition: $3800. Tuition installment plan (monthly payment plans). Tuition reduction for siblings, need-based scholarship grants, paying campus jobs available. In 2005–06, 8% of upper-school students received aid. Total amount of financial aid awarded in 2005–06: $32,513.

Admissions Traditional secondary-level entrance grade is 9. For fall 2005, 202 students applied for upper-level admission, 176 were accepted, 176 enrolled. Any standardized test required. Deadline for receipt of application materials: none. No application fee required. On-campus interview recommended.

Athletics Interscholastic: baseball (boys), basketball (b,g), bowling (b,g), cheering (g), cross-country running (b,g), dance team (g), football (b), golf (b,g), indoor track & field (b,g), power lifting (b,g), soccer (b,g), softball (g), strength & conditioning (b,g), swimming and diving (b,g), tennis (b,g), track and field (b,g), volleyball (g), winter (indoor) track (b,g), wrestling (b); intramural: cheering (g), skeet shooting (b); coed interscholastic: archery, riflery, skeet shooting, trap and skeet. 2 coaches.

Computers Computers are regularly used in business applications, English, foreign language, history, mathematics, newspaper, science, social studies, theology, yearbook classes. Computer network features include CD-ROMs, Internet access, office computer access, DVD, wireless campus network.

Contact Mrs. Kathy Dodson, Administrative Secretary. 337-235-5711 Ext. 101. Fax: 337-234-8057. E-mail: kdodson@tchs.net. Web site: www.tchs.net.

TEXAS NEROREHAB CENTER

■ Austin, Texas
See Special Needs Schools section.

THE THACHER SCHOOL

■ 5025 Thacher Road
Ojai, California 93023
Head of School: Michael K. Mulligan

General Information Coeducational boarding and day college-preparatory, arts, and technology school. Grades 9–12. Founded: 1889. Setting: small town. Nearest major city is Santa Barbara. Students are housed in single-sex dormitories. 450-acre campus. 89 buildings on campus. Approved or accredited by The Association of Boarding Schools, Western Association of Schools and Colleges, and California Department of Education. Member of National Association of Independent Schools and Secondary School Admission Test Board. Endowment: $80 million. Total enrollment: 245. Upper school average class size: 11. Upper school faculty-student ratio: 1:5.

Upper School Student Profile Grade 9: 59 students (28 boys, 31 girls); Grade 10: 62 students (29 boys, 33 girls); Grade 11: 62 students (29 boys, 33 girls); Grade 12: 62 students (31 boys, 31 girls). 90% of students are boarding students. 60% are state residents. 24 states are represented in upper school student body. 7% are international students. International students from Canada, Hong Kong, Japan, Saudi Arabia, and Taiwan; 5 other countries represented in student body.

Faculty School total: 46. In upper school: 22 men, 20 women; 37 have advanced degrees; 42 reside on campus.

Subjects Offered 3-dimensional art, ACT preparation, acting, advanced chemistry, advanced math, Advanced Placement courses, advanced studio art-AP, algebra, American history, American history-AP, American literature, art, art history, art history-AP, astronomy, biology, biology-AP, calculus, calculus-AP, ceramics, chemistry, chemistry-AP, Chinese, computer math, computer science, computer science-AP, conceptual physics, creative writing, dance, drama, ecology, economics, economics and history, electronic music, English, English literature, English literature-AP, English/composition-AP, environmental science, environmental science-AP, European history, European history-AP, film, fine arts, French, French language-AP, French literature-AP, geography, geometry, health, history, journalism, Latin, logic, marine biology, mathematics, music, music theory-AP, philosophy, photography, physical education, physics, physics-AP, psychology, religion, science, social studies, Spanish, Spanish language-AP, Spanish literature-AP, statistics, studio art-AP, theater, trigonometry, U.S. history-AP, world history, world literature, writing.

Graduation Requirements Arts and fine arts (art, music, dance, drama), English, foreign language, mathematics, physical education (includes health), science, social studies (includes history), Senior Exhibition Program (students choose an academic topic of interest and study it for one year, culminating in a schoolwide presentation).

Special Academic Programs Advanced Placement exam preparation in 17 subject areas; honors section; independent study; study abroad; academic accommodation for the gifted, the musically talented, and the artistically talented.

College Placement 63 students graduated in 2005; all went to college, including Brown University; Columbia College; Dartmouth College; Stanford University; The Colorado College; University of California, Berkeley. Mean SAT verbal: 690, mean SAT math: 670.

Student Life Upper grades have specified standards of dress, student council, honor system. Discipline rests equally with students and faculty.

Tuition and Aid Day student tuition: $22,950; 7-day tuition and room/board: $34,600. Tuition installment plan (Key Tuition Payment Plan, monthly payment plans). Need-based scholarship grants available. In 2005–06, 29% of upper-school students received aid. Total amount of financial aid awarded in 2005–06: $1,300,000.

Admissions Traditional secondary-level entrance grade is 9. For fall 2005, 415 students applied for upper-level admission, 102 were accepted, 74 enrolled. ISEE or SSAT required. Deadline for receipt of application materials: February 1. Application fee required: $75. Interview required.

Athletics Interscholastic: baseball (boys), basketball (b,g), cross-country running (b,g), dance (b,g), football (b), lacrosse (b,g), soccer (b,g), tennis (b,g), track and field (b,g), volleyball (g); intramural: back packing (b,g), canoeing/kayaking (b,g), climbing (b,g), dance (b,g), horseback riding (b,g), outdoor activities (b,g), yoga (b,g); coed interscholastic: dance, equestrian sports; coed intramural: back packing, bowling, canoeing/kayaking, climbing, dance, equestrian sports, fencing, golf, handball, hiking/backpacking, horseback riding, modern dance, outdoor activities, outdoor education, outdoor skills, pistol, Polocrosse, riflery, rock climbing, rodeo, skiing (downhill), surfing, trap and skeet, wall climbing, weight lifting, yoga. 4 coaches.

Computers Computers are regularly used in English, foreign language, history, mathematics, science classes. Computer network features include campus e-mail, on-campus library services, CD-ROMs, online commercial services, Internet access, office computer access, DVD, wireless campus network.

Contact Mr. William P. McMahon, Director of Admission. 805-640-3210. Fax: 805-640-9377. E-mail: admission@thacher.org. Web site: www.thacher.org.

See full description on page 1098.

THAYER ACADEMY

■ 745 Washington Street
Braintree, Massachusetts 02184
Head of School: William (Ted) Koskores

General Information Coeducational day college-preparatory, arts, and technology school. Grades 6–12. Founded: 1877. Setting: suburban. Nearest major city is Boston. 38-acre campus. 7 buildings on campus. Approved or accredited by New England Association of Schools and Colleges and Massachusetts Department of Education. Member of National Association of Independent Schools and Secondary School Admission Test Board. Endowment: $36 million. Total enrollment: 663. Upper school average class size: 15. Upper school faculty-student ratio: 1:7.

Upper School Student Profile Grade 9: 106 students (53 boys, 53 girls); Grade 10: 116 students (49 boys, 67 girls); Grade 11: 119 students (65 boys, 54 girls); Grade 12: 109 students (46 boys, 63 girls).

Faculty School total: 102. In upper school: 36 men, 33 women; 51 have advanced degrees.

Subjects Offered Acting, African American history, algebra, American history, American literature, anatomy, architecture, art, art history, astronomy, biology, calculus, ceramics, chemistry, computer programming, computer science, creative writing, current events, dance, directing, drama, driver education, economics, English, English literature, environmental science, European history, expository writing, fine arts, French, geology, geometry, health, history, journalism, Latin, mathematics, music, oceanography, performing arts, philosophy, photography, physical education, physics, physiology, poetry, pottery, pre-calculus, psychology, science, Spanish, theater, trigonometry, world history, world literature, writing.

Graduation Requirements Arts and fine arts (art, music, dance, drama), English, foreign language, mathematics, physical education (includes health), science, social studies (includes history).

Special Academic Programs Advanced Placement exam preparation in 13 subject areas; honors section; independent study; term-away projects; study abroad; academic accommodation for the gifted, the musically talented, and the artistically talented.

College Placement 108 students graduated in 2005; 106 went to college, including Boston College; Boston University; Connecticut College; Merrimack College; Providence College; Tufts University. Other: 2 entered a postgraduate year. 48% scored over 600 on SAT verbal, 56% scored over 600 on SAT math.

Student Life Upper grades have specified standards of dress, student council, honor system. Discipline rests primarily with faculty.

Summer Programs Remediation, enrichment, advancement, sports, art/fine arts, rigorous outdoor training, computer instruction programs offered; session focuses on recreation and enrichment; held both on and off campus; held at various sites (field trips) and lakefront; accepts boys and girls; open to students from other schools. 400 students usually enrolled. 2006 schedule: June 26 to August 25.

Admissions Traditional secondary-level entrance grade is 9. For fall 2005, 257 students applied for upper-level admission, 107 were accepted, 49 enrolled. ISEE or SSAT required. Deadline for receipt of application materials: February 1. Application fee required: $40. On-campus interview required.

Athletics Interscholastic: baseball (boys), basketball (b,g), cross-country running (b,g), field hockey (g), football (b), gymnastics (g), hockey (b,g), ice hockey (b,g), lacrosse (b,g), soccer (b,g), softball (g), tennis (b,g), track and field (b,g), wrestling (b); coed interscholastic: alpine skiing, aquatics, diving, golf, skiing (downhill), swimming and diving; coed intramural: back packing, badminton, climbing, crew, fitness, fitness walking, physical fitness, physical training, ropes courses, strength & conditioning, weight training. 7 PE instructors, 26 coaches, 4 trainers.

Computers Computers are regularly used in architecture, art, college planning, current events, drawing and design, English, foreign language, French, graphic arts, history, introduction to technology, journalism, library, mathematics, music, photography, publications, science, study skills, writing, yearbook classes. Computer network features include campus e-mail, on-campus library services, CD-ROMs, online commercial services, Internet access, file transfer, office computer access, wireless campus network, DVD-R, CD-R.

Contact Jonathan R. White, Director of Admissions. 781-664-2221. Fax: 781-843-2916. E-mail: admissions@thayer.org. Web site: www.thayer.org.

ANNOUNCEMENT FROM THE SCHOOL William T. Koskores, '70, Thayer Academy's 9th Headmaster since the school's founding in 1877, has announced a capital campaign to support endowment growth and build a new performing arts and meeting center, additional state-of-the-art science laboratories, a 2-story life fitness facility, and 4 artificial turf athletic fields. Significant upgrades to the library and visual arts facilities are also planned.

THOMAS A. EDISON HIGH SCHOOL

■ Portland, Oregon
See Special Needs Schools section.

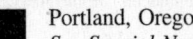

THOMAS JEFFERSON SCHOOL

4100 South Lindbergh Boulevard
St. Louis, Missouri 63127
Head of School: Mr. William C. Rowe

General Information Coeducational boarding and day college-preparatory school. Grades 7–PG. Founded: 1946. Setting: suburban. Students are housed in single-sex dormitories. 20-acre campus. 12 buildings on campus. Approved or accredited by Independent Schools Association of the Central States, Midwest Association of Boarding Schools, and The Association of Boarding Schools. Member of National Association of Independent Schools and Secondary School Admission Test Board. Endowment: $800,000. Total enrollment: 86. Upper school average class size: 10. Upper school faculty-student ratio: 1:7.

Upper School Student Profile Grade 9: 10 students (8 boys, 2 girls); Grade 10: 18 students (11 boys, 7 girls); Grade 11: 17 students (6 boys, 11 girls); Grade 12: 17 students (9 boys, 8 girls). 42% of students are boarding students. 68% are state residents. 7 states are represented in upper school student body. 20% are international students. International students from China, Hungary, Japan, Mexico, Poland, and Republic of Korea.

Faculty School total: 18. In upper school: 6 men, 6 women; 6 have advanced degrees; 6 reside on campus.

Subjects Offered 3-dimensional art, Advanced Placement courses, algebra, American history-AP, ancient history, ancient world history, art, art history, biology, biology-AP, calculus, calculus-AP, ceramics, chemistry, chemistry-AP, dance, earth science, English, English language-AP, English literature-AP, ESL, European history-AP, fine arts, French, geography, geometry, government/civics, Greek, history, Homeric Greek, Italian, Latin, life science, mathematics, music, physical science, physics, physics-AP, science, social studies, trigonometry, U.S. history-AP, world history, world history-AP.

Graduation Requirements Arts and fine arts (art, music, dance, drama), English, foreign language, mathematics, science, social studies (includes history). Community service is required.

Special Academic Programs Advanced Placement exam preparation in 12 subject areas; honors section; academic accommodation for the gifted; ESL (7 students enrolled).

College Placement 13 students graduated in 2005; all went to college, including Duke University; Harvard University; Northwestern University; Stanford University; Vanderbilt University; Washington University in St. Louis. Median SAT verbal: 710, median SAT math: 710.

Student Life Upper grades have specified standards of dress, student council, honor system. Discipline rests equally with students and faculty.

Tuition and Aid Day student tuition: $17,800; 5-day tuition and room/board: $27,500; 7-day tuition and room/board: $29,200. Tuition installment plan (Academic Management Services Plan, monthly payment plans, individually arranged payment plans). Merit scholarship grants, need-based scholarship grants, paying campus jobs available. In 2005–06, 40% of upper-school students received aid.

Admissions Traditional secondary-level entrance grade is 9. For fall 2005, 21 students applied for upper-level admission, 18 were accepted, 12 enrolled. ISEE, school's own exam, SSAT or TOEFL or SLEP required. Deadline for receipt of application materials: February 15. Application fee required: $40. On-campus interview required.

Athletics Interscholastic: basketball (boys, girls), soccer (b,g), volleyball (b,g); intramural: basketball (b,g), soccer (b,g), volleyball (b,g), weight lifting (b); coed interscholastic: soccer; coed intramural: dance, martial arts, tai chi, tennis, volleyball, weight training, yoga. 5 coaches.

Computers Computers are regularly used in mathematics, science classes. Computer network features include campus e-mail, CD-ROMs, online commercial services, Internet access.

Contact Ms. Marie De Jesus, Director of Admissions. 314-843-4151 Ext. 128. Fax: 314-843-3527. E-mail: admissions@tjs.org. Web site: www.tjs.org.

See full description on page 1100.

THORNTON FRIENDS SCHOOL

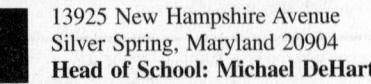

13925 New Hampshire Avenue
Silver Spring, Maryland 20904
Head of School: Michael DeHart

General Information Coeducational day college-preparatory, general academic, and arts school, affiliated with Society of Friends; primarily serves underachievers. Grades 9–12. Founded: 1973. Setting: suburban. Nearest major city is Washington, DC. 2-acre campus. 2 buildings on campus. Approved or accredited by Association of Independent Schools of Greater Washington, Friends Council on Education, and Maryland Department of Education. Endowment: $33,528. Total enrollment: 84. Upper school average class size: 9. Upper school faculty-student ratio: 1:6.

Upper School Student Profile Grade 9: 9 students (7 boys, 2 girls); Grade 10: 14 students (9 boys, 5 girls); Grade 11: 18 students (9 boys, 9 girls); Grade 12: 9 students (6 boys, 3 girls); Postgraduate: 1 student (1 girl). 1% of students are members of Society of Friends.

Faculty School total: 9. In upper school: 6 men, 3 women; 4 have advanced degrees.

Subjects Offered Algebra, American literature, American politics in film, art, biology, calculus, chemistry, community service, computer multimedia, creative writing, current events, drama, English, English literature, environmental science, expository writing, geography, geometry, history, journalism, Latin, logic, mathematics, philosophy, physical education, physics, pre-calculus, Quakerism and ethics, science, social studies, Spanish, stained glass, theater, trigonometry, world culture, world history, world literature, writing, yearbook.

Graduation Requirements English, mathematics, science, social studies (includes history). Community service is required.

Special Academic Programs Accelerated programs; term-away projects; academic accommodation for the gifted.

College Placement 16 students graduated in 2005; 7 went to college, including Beloit College; Guilford College; Pratt Institute; Warren Wilson College. Other: 7 went to work, 1 entered military service, 1 entered a postgraduate year.

Student Life Upper grades have specified standards of dress, student council. Discipline rests primarily with faculty. Attendance at religious services is required.

Tuition and Aid Day student tuition: $17,995. Tuition installment plan (FACTS Tuition Payment Plan, prepayment discount plan, 60%/40% option (due August 1 and December 1)). Tuition reduction for siblings, need-based scholarship grants, tuition reduction for children of employees available. In 2005–06, 24% of upper-school students received aid. Total amount of financial aid awarded in 2005–06: $105,035.

Admissions Traditional secondary-level entrance grade is 9. Deadline for receipt of application materials: none. Application fee required: $50. On-campus interview required.

Athletics Interscholastic: basketball (boys, girls); coed interscholastic: soccer, softball; coed intramural: basketball, bowling, cooperative games, Frisbee, rafting, rock climbing, ropes courses, soccer, softball, touch football, ultimate Frisbee.

Computers Computers are regularly used in English, foreign language, geography, history, journalism, literary magazine, mathematics, science, social science, yearbook classes. Computer network features include CD-ROMs, Internet access.

Contact Norman Maynard, Principal. 301-384-0320. Fax: 301-236-9481. E-mail: nmaynard@thorntonfriends.org. Web site: www.thorntonfriends.org.

ANNOUNCEMENT FROM THE SCHOOL Thornton Friends School, founded in 1974, is a small, independent college-preparatory Quaker school serving middle and high school students in suburban Maryland and Virginia. Thornton seeks to inspire and engage students in a process of inquiry and reflection in community with one another. Thornton celebrates each student and his or her academic and human potential. Thornton Friends School believes each student has unique and inherent insight, motivation, and ability to learn. Faculty members at Thornton nurture the spiritual, intellectual, artistic, social, and physical aspects of the students within a college-preparatory curriculum rooted in progressive Quaker educational theory and practice. Students and teachers enter into relationships marked by trust, respect, and collegiality that is crucial to success in the classroom and beyond. Thornton Friends School's student-centered classes are active, inquiry-based, and rich in discussion and participation. Ample use is made of many resources outside of the school building. High expectations are combined with flexibility to meet all students where they are and challenge them to extend their perceived limits. Thornton's teachers and its curriculum respect differing styles of learning and multiple intelligences, mixing traditional and innovative approaches. Thornton works best for students who will thrive in a very small school setting, in classrooms in which they are well known and understood by their teachers. Young people with curiosity, a gentle spirit, and above-average intelligence tend to do well at Thornton, even if they have found success hard to come by and need to reengage in the educational process. Thornton graduates tend go to small colleges, though some defer enrollment while working or participating in programs such as Americorps. Recent graduates have attended colleges such as Goucher, Guilford, and Reed. Thornton's Virginia Upper School has 32 students, while the Middle and Upper Schools in Maryland have 33 and 54 students, respectively.

THORNTON FRIENDS SCHOOL/N.V.A.

3830 Seminary Road
Alexandria, Virginia 22304
Head of School: Michael DeHart

General Information Coeducational day college-preparatory, general academic, and arts school, affiliated with Society of Friends; primarily serves underachievers. Grades 9–12. Founded: 1973. Setting: suburban. Nearest major city is Washington, DC. 5-acre campus. 1 building on campus. Approved or accredited by Association of Independent Schools of Greater Washington, Friends Council on Education, and Virginia Department of Education. Endowment: $33,528. Total enrollment: 30. Upper school average class size: 7. Upper school faculty-student ratio: 1:6.

Upper School Student Profile Grade 9: 5 students (3 boys, 2 girls); Grade 10: 7 students (4 boys, 3 girls); Grade 11: 5 students (2 boys, 3 girls); Grade 12: 13 students (10 boys, 3 girls). 1% of students are members of Society of Friends.

Faculty School total: 8. In upper school: 6 men, 2 women; 3 have advanced degrees.

Subjects Offered Algebra, American history, art, biology, calculus, chemistry, composition, current events, English, English literature, environmental science, fine arts, geometry, government, mathematics, physical education, physics, pre-calculus, social science, social studies, Spanish, world history, yearbook.

Graduation Requirements English, mathematics, science, social studies (includes history). Community service is required.

Special Academic Programs Accelerated programs; term-away projects; academic accommodation for the gifted.

College Placement 8 students graduated in 2005; 7 went to college, including George Mason University; Ohio Wesleyan University; Old Dominion University; The Evergreen State College. Other: 1 went to work.

Student Life Discipline rests primarily with faculty. Attendance at religious services is required.

Tuition and Aid Day student tuition: $17,995. Tuition installment plan (FACTS Tuition Payment Plan, prepayment discount plan, 60%/40% option (due August 1 and December 1)). Tuition reduction for siblings, need-based scholarship grants, tuition reduction for children of employees available. In 2005–06, 27% of upper-school students received aid. Total amount of financial aid awarded in 2005–06: $63,490.

Admissions Traditional secondary-level entrance grade is 9. For fall 2005, 17 students applied for upper-level admission, 15 were accepted, 11 enrolled. Deadline for receipt of application materials: none. Application fee required: $50. On-campus interview required.

Athletics Coed Interscholastic: basketball, bowling, soccer, softball; coed intramural: basketball, bowling, flag football, Frisbee, golf, rock climbing, ropes courses, soccer, softball, touch football, ultimate Frisbee, yoga.

Computers Computers are regularly used in college planning, English, foreign language, journalism, literary magazine, mathematics, science, yearbook classes. Computer network features include CD-ROMs, Internet access, wireless campus network.

Contact Eric Goldman, Principal. 703-461-8880. Fax: 703-461-3697. E-mail: eric@thorntonfriends.org. Web site: www.thorntonfriends.org.

ANNOUNCEMENT FROM THE SCHOOL Thornton Friends School, founded in 1974, is a small, independent college-preparatory Quaker school serving middle and high school students in suburban Maryland and Virginia. Thornton seeks to inspire and engage students in a process of inquiry and reflection in community with one another. Thornton celebrates each student and his or her academic and human potential. Thornton Friends School believes each student has unique and inherent insight, motivation, and ability to learn. Faculty members at Thornton nurture the spiritual, intellectual, artistic, social, and physical aspects of the students within a college-preparatory curriculum rooted in progressive Quaker educational theory and practice. Students and teachers enter into relationships marked by trust, respect, and collegiality that is crucial to success in the classroom and beyond. Thornton Friends School's student-centered classes are active, inquiry-based, and rich in discussion and participation. Ample use is made of many resources outside of the school building. High expectations are combined with flexibility to meet all students where they are and challenge them to extend their perceived limits. Thornton's teachers and its curriculum respect differing styles of learning and multiple intelligences, mixing traditional and innovative approaches. Thornton works best for students who will thrive in a very small school setting, in classrooms in which they are well known and understood by their teachers. Young people with curiosity, a gentle spirit, and above-average intelligence tend to do well at Thornton, even if they have found success hard to come by and need to reengage in the educational process. Thornton graduates tend go to small colleges, though some defer enrollment while working or participating in programs such as Americorps. Recent graduates have attended colleges such as Goucher, Guilford, and Reed. Thornton's Virginia Upper School has 32 students, while the Middle and Upper Schools in Maryland have 33 and 54 students, respectively.

THREE SPRINGS

Huntsville, Alabama
See Special Needs Schools section.

THREE SPRINGS/PRINCE MOUNTAIN ACADEMY

Blue Ridge, Georgia
See Special Needs Schools section.

TILTON SCHOOL

30 School Street
Tilton, New Hampshire 03276
Head of School: James R. Clements

General Information Coeducational boarding and day college-preparatory school, affiliated with Methodist Church. Grades 9–PG. Founded: 1845. Setting: small town. Nearest major city is Concord. Students are housed in single-sex dormitories. 146-acre campus. 27 buildings on campus. Approved or accredited by Association of Independent Schools in New England, Independent Schools of Northern New England, New England Association of Schools and Colleges, The Association of Boarding Schools, and New Hampshire Department of Education. Member of National Association of Independent Schools and Secondary School Admission Test Board. Endowment: $11 million. Total enrollment: 215. Upper school average class size: 10. Upper school faculty-student ratio: 1:5.

Upper School Student Profile Grade 9: 27 students (17 boys, 10 girls); Grade 10: 47 students (34 boys, 13 girls); Grade 11: 62 students (39 boys, 23 girls); Grade 12: 58 students (37 boys, 21 girls); Postgraduate: 21 students (17 boys, 4 girls). 80% of students are boarding students. 27% are state residents. 25 states are represented in upper school student body. 19% are international students. International students from Cameroon, Germany, Japan, Republic of Korea, Taiwan, and Turkey; 9 other countries represented in student body. 2% of students are Methodist.

Faculty School total: 40. In upper school: 25 men, 15 women; 15 have advanced degrees; 36 reside on campus.

Subjects Offered Advanced chemistry, advanced math, advanced studio art-AP, algebra, American history, anatomy and physiology, art, band, biology, biology-AP, calculus, calculus-AP, ceramics, chemistry, chemistry-AP, chorus, college counseling, community service, computer graphics, creative writing, criminal justice, critical writing, debate, drama, ecology, economics, English, English language and composition-AP, English literature-AP, ESL, European history-AP, fiction, fine arts, forensic science, French, French-AP, geometry, health, honors algebra, honors English, honors geometry, independent study, integrated mathematics, integrated science, leadership training, music, music composition, music theory, musical productions, newspaper, painting, photography, physics, physics-AP, poetry, politics, pre-calculus, psychology, SAT preparation, Shakespeare, short story, sociology, Spanish, Spanish-AP, statistics, studio art, studio art-AP, theater, trigonometry, wilderness/outdoor program, world cultures, world religions, writing, yearbook.

Graduation Requirements American history, arts and fine arts (art, music, dance, drama), English, foreign language, history, lab science, mathematics, science, annual participation in Plus/5 (including activities in art and culture, athletics, community service, leadership, and outdoor experience).

Special Academic Programs Advanced Placement exam preparation in 11 subject areas; honors section; independent study; remedial reading and/or remedial writing; remedial math; ESL (12 students enrolled).

College Placement 80 students graduated in 2005; 78 went to college, including Bentley College; Merrimack College; Sacred Heart University; Saint Michael's College; Stonehill College; University of New Hampshire. Other: 1 entered military service, 1 had other specific plans. Median SAT verbal: 501, median SAT math: 527, median composite ACT: 20. 16% scored over 600 on SAT verbal, 23% scored over 600 on SAT math, 10% scored over 26 on composite ACT.

Student Life Upper grades have specified standards of dress, student council, honor system. Discipline rests primarily with faculty.

Tuition and Aid Day student tuition: $20,150; 7-day tuition and room/board: $34,975. Tuition installment plan (FACTS Tuition Payment Plan, individually arranged payment plans). Merit scholarship grants, need-based scholarship grants, need-based loans available. In 2005–06, 36% of upper-school students received aid; total upper-school merit-scholarship money awarded: $45,150. Total amount of financial aid awarded in 2005–06: $1,424,100.

Admissions Traditional secondary-level entrance grade is 9. For fall 2005, 396 students applied for upper-level admission, 221 were accepted, 104 enrolled. PSAT or SAT for applicants to grade 11 and 12, SSAT or writing sample required. Deadline for receipt of application materials: February 1. Application fee required: $45. Interview required.

Athletics Interscholastic: baseball (boys), basketball (b,g), field hockey (g), football (b), ice hockey (b,g), lacrosse (b,g), soccer (b,g), softball (g), tennis (b,g), wrestling (b); coed interscholastic: alpine skiing, cross-country running, golf, skiing (downhill), snowboarding; coed intramural: canoeing/kayaking, hiking/backpacking, outdoor adventure, outdoor education, outdoor skills, rock climbing, snowshoeing, squash, strength & conditioning, wall climbing, weight training, wilderness survival. 1 trainer.

Computers Computers are regularly used in English, foreign language, graphic arts, history, mathematics, newspaper, science, yearbook classes. Computer network features include campus e-mail, on-campus library services, CD-ROMs, online commercial services, Internet access, file transfer, DVD, USB Ports, Smart Media Readers.

Contact Katherine E. Saunders, Director of Admission. 603-286-1733. Fax: 603-286-1705. E-mail: ksaunders@tiltonschool.org. Web site: www.tiltonschool.org.

See full description on page 1102.

TIMBER RIDGE SCHOOL

Cross Junction, Virginia
See Special Needs Schools section.

TIMOTHY CHRISTIAN HIGH SCHOOL

1061 South Prospect Avenue
Elmhurst, Illinois 60126
Head of School: Mr. Clyde Rinsema

General Information Coeducational day college-preparatory, general academic, arts, business, vocational, religious studies, and technology school, affiliated with Christian faith. Grades K–12. Founded: 1911. Setting: suburban. Nearest major city is Chicago. 26-acre campus. 1 building on campus. Approved or accredited by Christian Schools International, North Central Association of Colleges and Schools, and Illinois Department of Education. Endowment: $2.5 million. Total enrollment: 1,092. Upper school faculty-student ratio: 1:13.

Upper School Student Profile Grade 9: 91 students (51 boys, 40 girls); Grade 10: 93 students (53 boys, 40 girls); Grade 11: 115 students (60 boys, 55 girls); Grade 12: 97 students (55 boys, 42 girls).

Faculty School total: 30. In upper school: 22 men, 8 women.

Subjects Offered Advanced math, algebra, American literature, anatomy and physiology, art, band, Bible, biology, British literature, British literature-AP, calculus, calculus-AP, ceramics, chemistry, choir, Christian ethics, communication skills, community service, computer applications, computer graphics, concert choir, creative writing, drafting, drama, economics, electives, English, European history, expository writing, family living, food and nutrition, French, geometry, German, health, home economics, independent living, industrial arts, instrumental music, music, oil painting, parent/child development, photography, physical education, physical science, physics, physics-AP, pre-algebra, psychology, sewing, sociology, Spanish, Spanish literature-AP, strings, study skills, theater, theater production, trigonometry, U.S. government, U.S. history, U.S. history-AP, United States government-AP, Western civilization, world history, world literature.

Graduation Requirements English, mathematics, music, physical education (includes health), religious studies, science, social science, social studies (includes history), technological applications, senior service retreat at end of 12th grade, service requirement in grades 9-11(10 hours per year).

Special Academic Programs Advanced Placement exam preparation in 7 subject areas; honors section; remedial reading and/or remedial writing; remedial math.

College Placement 117 students graduated in 2005; 113 went to college, including Calvin College; Hope College; Illinois State University; Taylor University; Trinity Christian College. Other: 4 had other specific plans. Mean composite ACT: 25.

Student Life Upper grades have specified standards of dress, student council, honor system. Discipline rests primarily with faculty. Attendance at religious services is required.

Summer Programs Enrichment, sports, art/fine arts programs offered; session focuses on athletics; held on campus; accepts boys and girls; not open to students from other schools. 2006 schedule: June to July. Application deadline: May.

Tuition and Aid Day student tuition: $6950. Tuition installment plan (monthly payment plans). Some financial assistance through the school foundation available. In 2005–06, 4% of upper-school students received aid.

Admissions Traditional secondary-level entrance grade is 9. Scholastic Testing Service High School Placement Test and school's own exam required. Deadline for receipt of application materials: none. Application fee required: $100. On-campus interview required.

Athletics Interscholastic: baseball (boys), basketball (b,g), cheering (g), cross-country running (b,g), golf (b,g), pom squad (g), soccer (b,g), softball (g), tennis (b,g), track and field (b,g), volleyball (g); intramural: basketball (b), flag football (b); coed interscholastic: golf; coed intramural: volleyball. 2 PE instructors, 1 trainer.

Computers Computers are regularly used in art, business applications, English, science classes. Computer network features include on-campus library services, CD-ROMs, Internet access, office computer access, DVD, wireless campus network.

Contact Mrs. Ann Raley, K-12 Admissions Coordinator—High School Registrar. 630-833-7575 Ext. 202. Fax: 630-833-9821. E-mail: raley@timothychristian.com. Web site: www.timothychristian.com.

TMI—THE EPISCOPAL SCHOOL OF TEXAS

20955 West Tejas Trail
San Antonio, Texas 78257
Head of School: Dr. James A. Freeman

petersons.com

General Information Coeducational boarding and day college-preparatory, arts, and religious studies school, affiliated with Episcopal Church. Boarding grades 9–12, day grades 6–12. Founded: 1893. Setting: suburban. Students are housed in single-sex dormitories. 80-acre campus. 16 buildings on campus. Approved or accredited by Independent Schools Association of the Southwest, National Association of Episcopal Schools, Southwest Association of Episcopal Schools, The Association of Boarding Schools, and Texas Department of Education. Endowment: $1.3 million. Total enrollment: 311. Upper school average class size: 15. Upper school faculty-student ratio: 1:8.

Upper School Student Profile Grade 9: 57 students (35 boys, 22 girls); Grade 10: 60 students (30 boys, 30 girls); Grade 11: 53 students (33 boys, 20 girls); Grade 12: 57 students (31 boys, 26 girls). 10% of students are boarding students. 98% are state residents. 4 states are represented in upper school student body. 1% are international students. International students from Mexico, Nigeria, and U.S. Virgin Islands. 16% of students are members of Episcopal Church.

Faculty School total: 40. In upper school: 12 men, 16 women; 24 have advanced degrees; 13 reside on campus.

Subjects Offered 20th century history, acting, Advanced Placement courses, advanced studio art-AP, algebra, American Civil War, American history, American literature, anatomy and physiology, astronomy, athletics, biology, British literature, calculus, ceramics, chemistry, choir, computer programming, conceptual physics, earth science, economics, English, English literature, environmental science, fine arts, geometry, government, Greek, history, JROTC, Latin, meteorology, military history, philosophy, photography, physics, playwriting, religion, Spanish, statistics, studio art, theater arts, theater design and production, world history, writing.

Graduation Requirements Arts and fine arts (art, music, dance, drama), electives, English, foreign language, history, mathematics, philosophy, physical education (includes health), religion (includes Bible studies and theology), science.

Special Academic Programs Advanced Placement exam preparation in 14 subject areas; honors section; independent study.

College Placement 43 students graduated in 2005; all went to college, including Baylor University; Texas A&M University; Texas Christian University; The University of Texas at Austin; Tulane University; Westmont College. Median SAT verbal: 610, median SAT math: 600.

Student Life Upper grades have uniform requirement, student council, honor system. Discipline rests equally with students and faculty. Attendance at religious services is required.

Summer Programs Enrichment, advancement, sports programs offered; session focuses on academics and enrichment ; held on campus; accepts boys and girls; open to students from other schools. 30 students usually enrolled. 2006 schedule: June 6 to July 8. Application deadline: May 28.

Tuition and Aid Day student tuition: $15,150; 5-day tuition and room/board: $23,000; 7-day tuition and room/board: $29,460. Tuition installment plan (Academic Management Services Plan). Merit scholarship grants, need-based scholarship grants, tuition remission for children of faculty available. In 2005–06, 32% of upper-school students received aid; total upper-school merit-scholarship money awarded: $177,710. Total amount of financial aid awarded in 2005–06: $703,457.

Admissions Traditional secondary-level entrance grade is 9. For fall 2005, 92 students applied for upper-level admission, 62 were accepted, 43 enrolled. ISEE required. Deadline for receipt of application materials: February 10. Application fee required: $50. Interview required.

Athletics Interscholastic: baseball (boys), basketball (b,g), cheering (g), cross-country running (b,g), diving (b,g), football (b), golf (b,g), lacrosse (b,g), soccer (b,g), softball (g), swimming and diving (b,g), tennis (b,g), volleyball (g); coed interscholastic: JROTC drill, marksmanship, physical training, riflery, strength & conditioning. 10 coaches, 1 trainer.

Computers Computers are regularly used in programming, science classes. Computer network features include campus e-mail, on-campus library services, CD-ROMs, online commercial services, Internet access, file transfer.

Contact Mr. Krishna Perkins, Admission Counselor. 210-698-7175 Ext. 233. Fax: 210-698-0715. E-mail: k.perkins@tmi-sa.org. Web site: www.tmi-sa.org.

See full description on page 1104.

TORONTO DISTRICT CHRISTIAN HIGH SCHOOL

366 Woodbridge Avenue
Woodbridge, Ontario L4L 2V7, Canada
Head of School: Ren Siebenga

General Information Coeducational day college-preparatory, general academic, arts, business, religious studies, bilingual studies, and technology school, affiliated with Christian Reformed Church, Christian faith. Grades 9–12. Founded: 1963. Setting: urban. Nearest major city is Toronto, Canada. 16-acre campus. 1 building on campus. Approved or accredited by Christian Schools International, Ontario Ministry of Education, and Ontario Department of Education. Language of instruction: English. Endowment: CAN$100,000. Total enrollment: 453. Upper school average class size: 25. Upper school faculty-student ratio: 1:13.

Upper School Student Profile 99% of students are members of Christian Reformed Church, Christian.

Faculty School total: 33. In upper school: 17 men, 16 women; 8 have advanced degrees.

Subjects Offered 20th century history, advanced math, art, Bible, biology, bookkeeping, business applications, business law, business mathematics, business technology, cabinet making, calculus, Canadian geography, Canadian history, career and personal planning, chemistry, choir, civics, computer applications, computer keyboarding, computer multimedia, computer programming, discrete math, economics,

English, English literature, ESL, family studies, French, geography, global issues, health, history, law, modern Western civilization, music, philosophy, physical education, physics, political science, remedial study skills, science, theater arts, visual arts, Western civilization, world religions.

Graduation Requirements Ontario Ministry of Education requirements, family studies or philosophy.

Special Academic Programs Honors section; remedial reading and/or remedial writing; remedial math; programs in English, mathematics, general development for dyslexic students; ESL (10 students enrolled).

College Placement Colleges students went to include McMaster University; Redeemer University College; University of Guelph; University of Toronto; University of Waterloo; York University.

Student Life Upper grades have specified standards of dress, student council, honor system. Discipline rests equally with students and faculty. Attendance at religious services is required.

Tuition and Aid Day student tuition: CAN$8580–CAN$11,160. Tuition installment plan (monthly payment plans, individually arranged payment plans). Tuition reduction for siblings available.

Admissions Traditional secondary-level entrance grade is 9. Deadline for receipt of application materials: February 1. Application fee required: CAN$400. Interview required.

Athletics Interscholastic: badminton (boys, girls), basketball (b,g), ice hockey (b), soccer (b,g), volleyball (b,g); intramural: ice hockey (b); coed interscholastic: cross-country running, track and field.

Computers Computers are regularly used in accounting, all academic, business applications, yearbook classes. Computer network features include campus e-mail, on-campus library services, CD-ROMs, Internet access, file transfer, wireless campus network.

Contact Mrs. Jennie Das, Vice President, Finance and Admissions. 905-851-1772 Ext. 4. Fax: 905-851-9992. E-mail: das@tdchristian.ca. Web site: www.tdchristian.ca.

TORONTO WALDORF SCHOOL

9100 Bathurst Street
Thornhill, Ontario L4J 8C7, Canada
Head of School: Mr. Todd Royer

General Information Coeducational day college-preparatory, general academic, arts, business, vocational, bilingual studies, and technology school; primarily serves underachievers. Grades N–12. Founded: 1974. Setting: suburban. Nearest major city is Toronto, Canada. 24-acre campus. 2 buildings on campus. Approved or accredited by Association of Waldorf Schools of North America and Ontario Department of Education. Language of instruction: English. Total enrollment: 294. Upper school average class size: 25. Upper school faculty-student ratio: 1:5.

Upper School Student Profile Grade 9: 29 students (14 boys, 15 girls); Grade 10: 25 students (12 boys, 13 girls); Grade 11: 23 students (10 boys, 13 girls); Grade 12: 18 students (7 boys, 11 girls).

Faculty School total: 55. In upper school: 8 men, 12 women.

Subjects Offered Acting, advanced computer applications, algebra, American history, ancient history, art, art history, astronomy, atomic theory, biochemistry, botany, business mathematics, business studies, Canadian geography, Canadian history, careers, chemistry, choir, civics, clayworking, composition, computer science, crafts, drama, drawing, English composition, English literature, ESL, eurythmy, evolution, family studies, French, gardening, genetics, geography, geology, geometry, German, grammar, health, history, history of architecture, history of drama, history of music, human anatomy, inorganic chemistry, literature, mathematics, mechanics, medieval/ Renaissance history, meteorology, microbiology, modeling, modern history, music, mythology, novel, nutrition, optics, orchestra, organic chemistry, painting, performing arts, philosophy, physical education, physics, physiology, practical arts, reading, Shakespeare, trigonometry, visual arts, water color painting, woodworking, writing, zoology.

Special Academic Programs Study abroad; ESL (10 students enrolled).

Student Life Upper grades have specified standards of dress, student council. Discipline rests primarily with faculty.

Tuition and Aid Day student tuition: CAN$12,500. Tuition installment plan (monthly payment plans). Tuition reduction for siblings, bursaries available.

Admissions Traditional secondary-level entrance grade is 11. Deadline for receipt of application materials: none. Application fee required: CAN$100. On-campus interview required.

Athletics Intramural: badminton (boys, girls), basketball (b,g), cross-country running (b,g), mountain biking (b,g); coed interscholastic: artistic gym, badminton, basketball, canoeing/kayaking, Circus, cooperative games, cross-country running, fitness, indoor track & field, juggling, outdoor adventure, outdoor education, outdoor recreation, outdoor skills, physical fitness, physical training, rhythmic gymnastics, running, skiing (cross-country), skiing (downhill), strength & conditioning, track and field, unicycling, wallyball, wilderness survival, wildernessways, yoga. 1 PE instructor.

Computers Computers are regularly used in yearbook classes.

Contact Ms. Aileen Stewart, Admissions Coordinator. 905-881-1611 Ext. 314. Fax: 905-881-6710. E-mail: astewart@torontowaldorfschool.com. Web site: www.torontowaldorfschool.com.

TOWER HILL SCHOOL

2813 West 17th Street
Wilmington, Delaware 19806
Head of School: Christopher D. Wheeler

General Information Coeducational day college-preparatory school. Grades PK–12. Founded: 1919. Setting: suburban. Nearest major city is Philadelphia, PA. 40-acre campus. 4 buildings on campus. Approved or accredited by Middle States Association of Colleges and Schools and Delaware Department of Education. Member of National Association of Independent Schools and Secondary School Admission Test Board. Endowment: $26.1 million. Total enrollment: 755. Upper school average class size: 12. Upper school faculty-student ratio: 1:7.

Upper School Student Profile Grade 9: 59 students (24 boys, 35 girls); Grade 10: 59 students (32 boys, 27 girls); Grade 11: 54 students (25 boys, 29 girls); Grade 12: 58 students (21 boys, 37 girls).

Faculty School total: 88. In upper school: 25 men, 10 women; 24 have advanced degrees.

Subjects Offered Acting, algebra, American history, American literature, analysis, art, art history, band, biology, biology-AP, calculus, calculus-AP, ceramics, chemistry, chorus, community service, computer science, creative writing, drama, drawing, driver education, English, English literature, European history, European history-AP, film, fine arts, French, French language-AP, geometry, historical research, history, human anatomy, Internet, jazz band, Latin, Latin-AP, mathematics, music, music theory, organic chemistry, painting, photography, physical science, physics, physics-AP, poetry, pre-calculus, psychology, science, sculpture, Shakespeare, shop, sociology, Spanish, Spanish language-AP, stagecraft, statistics-AP, strings, theater, trigonometry, urban studies, woodworking, world history, writing.

Graduation Requirements Arts and fine arts (art, music, dance, drama), athletics, English, foreign language, mathematics, science, social studies (includes history). Community service is required.

Special Academic Programs Advanced Placement exam preparation in 17 subject areas; honors section; independent study.

College Placement 52 students graduated in 2004; all went to college, including Middlebury College; University of Delaware; University of Pennsylvania; University of Virginia; Vanderbilt University. Mean SAT verbal: 648, mean SAT math: 663. 76% scored over 600 on SAT verbal, 77% scored over 600 on SAT math.

Student Life Upper grades have specified standards of dress, student council, honor system. Discipline rests equally with students and faculty.

Tuition and Aid Day student tuition: $17,595–$18,040. Guaranteed tuition plan. Tuition installment plan (Key Tuition Payment Plan, monthly payment plans, individually arranged payment plans). Need-based scholarship grants available. In 2004–05, 14% of upper-school students received aid.

Admissions Traditional secondary-level entrance grade is 9. For fall 2005, 57 students applied for upper-level admission, 27 were accepted, 11 enrolled. ERB CTP IV, PSAT or SAT for applicants to grade 11 and 12, SSAT or writing sample required. Deadline for receipt of application materials: January 5. Application fee required: $40. On-campus interview required.

Athletics Interscholastic: baseball (boys), basketball (b,g), cross-country running (b,g), field hockey (g), football (b), indoor track (b,g), lacrosse (b,g), soccer (b,g), swimming and diving (b,g), tennis (b,g), track and field (b,g), volleyball (g), winter (indoor) track (b,g), wrestling (b); intramural: tennis (g); coed interscholastic: aerobics, aerobics/nautilus, crew, golf, nautilus, speedball; coed intramural: speedball, weight lifting. 21 coaches, 1 trainer.

Computers Computers are regularly used in all academic classes. Computer network features include campus e-mail, on-campus library services, CD-ROMs, Internet access, file transfer.

Contact Michelle K Coulter, Assistant Director of Admission. 302-657-8350. Fax: 302-657-8377. E-mail: thsadmit@towerhill.org. Web site: www.towerhill.org.

ANNOUNCEMENT FROM THE SCHOOL Located in Wilmington, Delaware, Tower Hill is a challenging, supportive community devoted to promoting growth in its students by helping them develop inquisitive, discerning, and critical minds, the capacity to be creative and aesthetically sensitive, the appreciation of physical well-being, and the courage to live with integrity.

TOWN CENTRE MONTESSORI SCHOOL

155 Clayton Drive
Markham, Ontario L3R 7P3, Canada
Head of School: Mrs. Marianne Vanderlugt

General Information Coeducational day college-preparatory school. Grades PK–12. Founded: 1986. Setting: suburban. Nearest major city is Toronto, Canada. Approved or accredited by Canadian Council of Montessori Administrators and Ontario Department of Education. Language of instruction: English. Total enrollment: 1,400. Upper school average class size: 15. Upper school faculty-student ratio: 1:15. **Faculty** School total: 15. In upper school: 7 men, 8 women.

Special Academic Programs ESL (25 students enrolled).

College Placement 34 students graduated in 2005; they went to McMaster University; Queen's University at Kingston; The University of Western Ontario; University of Toronto; University of Waterloo; York University.

Student Life Upper grades have uniform requirement, student council, honor system.

Tuition and Aid Tuition installment plan (monthly payment plans, individually arranged payment plans, 2 installments and full payment). Tuition reduction for siblings available.

Admissions High School Placement Test (closed version) from Scholastic Testing Service required. Deadline for receipt of application materials: none. Application fee required: CAN$200. Interview required.

Athletics Intramural: ball hockey (boys), ballet (g), basketball (b,g), soccer (b,g), volleyball (b,g); coed interscholastic: badminton, ball hockey, basketball, cooperative games, fitness, floor hockey, physical fitness, soccer, volleyball; coed intramural: badminton, baseball, bowling, cross-country running, flag football, golf, softball, table tennis, tennis, ultimate Frisbee. 4 PE instructors, 6 coaches.

Contact Mrs. Elrethe van Rooyen, Dean of Student Life. 905-470-1200. Fax: 905-470-1721. E-mail: admin@tcmps.com. Web site: tcmps.com.

TRADITIONAL LEARNING ACADEMY

1189 Rochester Avenue
Coquitlam, British Columbia V3K 2X3, Canada
Head of School: Mr. Martin Dale

General Information Coeducational day college-preparatory and general academic school, affiliated with Roman Catholic Church. Grades K–12. Founded: 1991. Setting: suburban. Nearest major city is Vancouver, Canada. 4-acre campus. 1 building on campus. Approved or accredited by British Columbia Department of Education. Language of instruction: English. Total enrollment: 195. Upper school average class size: 15. Upper school faculty-student ratio: 1:15.

Upper School Student Profile Grade 8: 11 students (8 boys, 3 girls); Grade 9: 16 students (3 boys, 13 girls); Grade 10: 13 students (8 boys, 5 girls); Grade 11: 6 students (3 boys, 3 girls); Grade 12: 5 students (1 boy, 4 girls). 85% of students are Roman Catholic.

Faculty School total: 16. In upper school: 4 men, 3 women; 2 have advanced degrees.

Subjects Offered Art, choral music, English literature, French, grammar, history, Latin, mathematics, physical education, religion, science, social studies.

Special Academic Programs Programs in general development for dyslexic students; special instructional classes for students with learning disabilities (Arrowsmith Learning Program).

College Placement 7 students graduated in 2005; 6 went to college, including Simon Fraser University; The University of British Columbia; Trinity Western University. Other: 1 went to work. Mean SAT verbal: 800, mean SAT math: 720. 100% scored over 600 on SAT verbal, 100% scored over 600 on SAT math.

Student Life Upper grades have uniform requirement, honor system. Discipline rests primarily with faculty.

Tuition and Aid Day student tuition: CAN$3300. Tuition installment plan (monthly payment plans, individually arranged payment plans).

Admissions Traditional secondary-level entrance grade is 8. For fall 2005, 24 students applied for upper-level admission, 12 were accepted, 12 enrolled. English entrance exam required. Deadline for receipt of application materials: none. Application fee required: CAN$75. On-campus interview recommended.

Athletics Interscholastic: basketball (boys, girls), soccer (b,g), softball (b,g), volleyball (b,g); intramural: basketball (b,g); coed interscholastic: curling, ultimate Frisbee; coed intramural: badminton. 1 PE instructor.

Computers Computer resources include CD-ROMs, Internet access.

Contact Mr. Allan Garneau, Administrator. 604-931-7265. Fax: 604-931-3432. E-mail: admin@traditionallearning.org. Web site: www.traditionallearning.com.

TRAFALGAR CASTLE SCHOOL

401 Reynolds Street
Whitby, Ontario L1N 3W9, Canada
Head of School: Ms. Pamela McInroy

General Information Girls' boarding and day college-preparatory, arts, business, and technology school. Boarding grades 7–12, day grades 6–12. Founded: 1874. Setting: small town. Nearest major city is Toronto, Canada. Students are housed in single-sex dormitories. 28-acre campus. 2 buildings on campus. Approved or accredited by Canadian Association of Independent Schools, Canadian Educational Standards Institute, Conference of Independent Schools of Ontario, Ontario Ministry of Education, The Association of Boarding Schools, and Ontario Department of Education. Language of instruction: English. Endowment: CAN$153,000. Total enrollment: 232. Upper school average class size: 15. Upper school faculty-student ratio: 1:9.

Upper School Student Profile Grade 6: 12 students (12 girls); Grade 7: 33 students (33 girls); Grade 8: 36 students (36 girls); Grade 9: 32 students (32 girls); Grade 10: 40 students (40 girls); Grade 11: 42 students (42 girls); Grade 12: 37 students (37 girls). 30% of students are boarding students. 75% are province residents. 2 provinces are represented in upper school student body. 25% are international students. International

students from China, Hong Kong, Mexico, Republic of Korea, Saint Lucia, and Spain; 6 other countries represented in student body.

Faculty School total: 28. In upper school: 5 men, 23 women; 6 have advanced degrees; 5 reside on campus.

Subjects Offered Algebra, art, art history, biology, business skills, calculus, ceramics, chemistry, computer math, computer science, creative writing, drama, earth science, economics, English, English literature, environmental science, ESL, European history, fine arts, French, geography, geometry, grammar, law, mathematics, music, photography, physical education, physics, science, social studies, theater, typing, world history, world literature, writing.

Graduation Requirements Arts and fine arts (art, music, dance, drama), business skills (includes word processing), computer science, English, foreign language, mathematics, physical education (includes health), science, social studies (includes history).

Special Academic Programs Advanced Placement exam preparation in 2 subject areas; honors section; term-away projects; domestic exchange program (with Sedbergh School); special instructional classes for students with slight learning disabilities; ESL (18 students enrolled).

College Placement 49 students graduated in 2005; 46 went to college, including McMaster University; Queen's University at Kingston; The University of Western Ontario; University of Toronto; University of Waterloo; Wilfrid Laurier University. Other: 1 entered military service, 2 entered a postgraduate year.

Student Life Upper grades have uniform requirement, student council. Discipline rests primarily with faculty.

Tuition and Aid Day student tuition: CAN$15,500–CAN$17,600; 7-day tuition and room/board: CAN$32,950–CAN$36,600. Tuition installment plan (monthly payment plans, individually arranged payment plans, early payment discounts). Tuition reduction for siblings, bursaries, merit scholarship grants, need-based scholarship grants available. In 2005–06, 5% of upper-school students received aid; total upper-school merit-scholarship money awarded: CAN$14,000. Total amount of financial aid awarded in 2005–06: CAN$43,000.

Admissions Traditional secondary-level entrance grade is 9. For fall 2005, 93 students applied for upper-level admission, 89 were accepted, 77 enrolled. Cognitive Abilities Test required. Deadline for receipt of application materials: none. Application fee required: CAN$500. Interview required.

Athletics Interscholastic: badminton, baseball, basketball, cross-country running, field hockey, fitness, fitness walking, golf, gymnastics, horseback riding, ice hockey, outdoor adventure, outdoor recreation, outdoor skills, physical fitness, physical training, rowing, running, skiing (cross-country), skiing (downhill), snowboarding, soccer, softball, swimming and diving, tennis, track and field, volleyball, wall climbing, weight training, wilderness survival; intramural: badminton, baseball, basketball, cross-country running, field hockey, golf, gymnastics, ice hockey, rowing, soccer, softball, swimming and diving, tennis, track and field, volleyball. 3 PE instructors.

Computers Computers are regularly used in all academic classes. Computer network features include campus e-mail, on-campus library services, CD-ROMs, Internet access, file transfer, DVD, wireless campus network.

Contact Irene Talent, Admissions Officer. 905-668-3358 Ext. 227. Fax: 905-668-4136. E-mail: talenti@castle-ed.com. Web site: www.castle-ed.com.

TREVOR DAY SCHOOL

1 West 88th Street
New York, New York 10024
Head of School: Pamela J. Clarke

General Information Coeducational day college-preparatory, arts, and technology school. Grades N–12. Founded: 1930. Setting: urban. 1 building on campus. Approved or accredited by New York State Association of Independent Schools and New York Department of Education. Member of National Association of Independent Schools and Secondary School Admission Test Board. Endowment: $8 million. Total enrollment: 785. Upper school average class size: 15. Upper school faculty-student ratio: 1:6.

Upper School Student Profile Grade 9: 68 students (31 boys, 37 girls); Grade 10: 65 students (29 boys, 36 girls); Grade 11: 61 students (31 boys, 30 girls); Grade 12: 49 students (25 boys, 24 girls).

Faculty School total: 138. In upper school: 37 men, 38 women; 53 have advanced degrees.

Subjects Offered Advanced chemistry, advanced computer applications, advanced math, African-American literature, algebra, American history, American literature, ancient world history, animation, architectural drawing, art, art history, Asian literature, Basic programming, biology, British literature, calculus, calculus-AP, ceramics, chemistry, choreography, chorus, college counseling, community service, computer programming, computer science, computer studies, concert band, creative writing, dance, discrete math, drama, drama performance, drawing, economics, English, English literature, environmental science, ethics, European history, expository writing, film and literature, filmmaking, fine arts, foreign language, French, French language-AP, genetics, geometry, grammar, Harlem Renaissance, health, Hispanic literature, history, honors English, independent study, intro to computers, Italian, jazz ensemble, literary magazine, madrigals, mathematics, model United Nations, music, musical productions, newspaper, peer counseling, performing arts,

photography, photojournalism, physical education, physics, play production, playwriting, poetry, pottery, pre-calculus, Russian literature, science, senior internship, Shakespeare, Shakespearean histories, social studies, Spanish, Spanish language-AP, stained glass, statistics, statistics-AP, student government, studio art, technical theater, theater, U.S. history-AP, video, Web site design, wilderness/outdoor program, world history, world literature, writing, yearbook.

Graduation Requirements Arts and fine arts (art, music, dance, drama), computer science, English, ethics, foreign language, mathematics, physical education (includes health), science, social studies (includes history), 80 hours of community service.

Special Academic Programs Advanced Placement exam preparation in 6 subject areas; honors section; independent study; term-away projects.

College Placement 61 students graduated in 2005; all went to college, including Brown University; Cornell University; New York University; Oberlin College; University of Michigan; Vassar College.

Student Life Upper grades have student council. Discipline rests equally with students and faculty.

Tuition and Aid Day student tuition: $26,590–$28,275. Tuition installment plan (FACTS Tuition Payment Plan, plan A: balance (85%) due August 15, plan B: 45% due May 30—balance due December 28, plan C: 9-monthly installments). Need-based scholarship grants available. In 2005–06, 40% of upper-school students received aid. Total amount of financial aid awarded in 2005–06: $2,305,279.

Admissions Traditional secondary-level entrance grade is 9. ERB, ISEE or SSAT required. Deadline for receipt of application materials: January 15. Application fee required: $50. On-campus interview required.

Athletics Interscholastic: baseball (boys), basketball (b,g), soccer (b,g), softball (g), tennis (b,g), volleyball (g); coed interscholastic: cross-country running, dance, modern dance, outdoor education, project adventure, track and field. 4 PE instructors, 6 coaches.

Computers Computers are regularly used in art, English, foreign language, history, mathematics, music, science classes. Computer network features include campus e-mail, on-campus library services, CD-ROMs, online commercial services, Internet access, file transfer, office computer access, DVD, wireless campus network, personal portals with homework and schedules for each student.

Contact Libby Macartney, Interim Director of Admissions, grades 6-12. 212-426-3389. Fax: 646-672-5579. E-mail: lmacartney@admin.trevornet.org. Web site: www.trevor.org.

TRI-CITY CHRISTIAN SCHOOLS

1737 West Vista Way
Vista, California 92083
Head of School: Mrs. Sharon Privett

General Information Coeducational day college-preparatory, arts, vocational, religious studies, bilingual studies, and technology school, affiliated with Baptist Church. Grades PK–12. Founded: 1971. Setting: suburban. Nearest major city is San Diego. 4-acre campus. 4 buildings on campus. Approved or accredited by Association of Christian Schools International and Western Association of Schools and Colleges. Endowment: $100,000. Total enrollment: 1,132. Upper school average class size: 22. Upper school faculty-student ratio: 1:10.

Upper School Student Profile Grade 9: 72 students (23 boys, 49 girls); Grade 10: 90 students (46 boys, 44 girls); Grade 11: 77 students (32 boys, 45 girls); Grade 12: 59 students (32 boys, 27 girls). 25% of students are Baptist.

Faculty School total: 61. In upper school: 14 men, 21 women; 11 have advanced degrees.

Subjects Offered Algebra, American literature, American sign language, art, auto shop, band, Bible studies, biology, biology-AP, British literature (honors), business communications, business mathematics, calculus, calculus-AP, chemistry, civics, computer science, dance, drama, economics, English, English language-AP, English literature, English literature-AP, ensembles, environmental science, European history, geometry, government/civics, guitar, health education, history, honors English, honors U.S. history, honors world history, jazz band, journalism, library studies, mathematics, music, philosophy, physical education, physical science, physiology, religion, science, social studies, Spanish, Spanish language-AP, speech, trigonometry, typing, U.S. history, world history, world literature.

Graduation Requirements Arts and fine arts (art, music, dance, drama), computer studies, English, foreign language, mathematics, physical education (includes health), religion (includes Bible studies and theology), science, social studies (includes history), speech. Community service is required.

Special Academic Programs Advanced Placement exam preparation in 4 subject areas; honors section; accelerated programs; study at local college for college credit.

College Placement 46 students graduated in 2005; 45 went to college, including Azusa Pacific University; Biola University; MiraCosta College; Palomar College; Point Loma Nazarene University; San Diego State University. Other: 1 went to work. Mean SAT verbal: 559, mean SAT math: 526.

Student Life Upper grades have specified standards of dress, student council. Discipline rests primarily with faculty. Attendance at religious services is required.

Summer Programs Remediation, advancement, sports programs offered; session focuses on development; held both on and off campus; held at other area schools; accepts boys and girls; open to students from other schools. 60 students usually enrolled. 2006 schedule: June 15 to July 30.

Tuition and Aid Day student tuition: $6100. Tuition installment plan (monthly payment plans, individually arranged payment plans). Tuition reduction for siblings, need-based scholarship grants, paying campus jobs, church affiliation grants available. In 2005–06, 56% of upper-school students received aid. Total amount of financial aid awarded in 2005–06: $371,256.

Admissions Traditional secondary-level entrance grade is 9. Any standardized test required. Deadline for receipt of application materials: September 21. Application fee required: $100. On-campus interview required.

Athletics Interscholastic: baseball (boys), basketball (b,g), cheering (g), cross-country running (b,g), flag football (b), football (b), soccer (b,g), softball (g), tennis (g), touch football (b), track and field (b,g), volleyball (b,g), weight training (b,g); intramural: dance (g), physical fitness (b,g); coed interscholastic: golf. 2 PE instructors, 20 coaches, 1 trainer.

Computers Computers are regularly used in business applications, English, journalism, science, yearbook classes. Computer network features include campus e-mail, on-campus library services, CD-ROMs, Internet access.

Contact Mrs. Mary Panos, Registrar. 760-806-8247 Ext. 200. Fax: 760-906-9002. E-mail: mary.panos@tccs.org. Web site: www.tccs.org.

TRIDENT ACADEMY

Mt. Pleasant, South Carolina
See Special Needs Schools section.

TRINITY ACADEMY

12345 East 21st Street North
Wichita, Kansas 67206
Head of School: Mr. David Swank

General Information Coeducational day college-preparatory and religious studies school, affiliated with Christian faith, Christian faith. Grades 9–12. Founded: 1994. Setting: suburban. 70-acre campus. 1 building on campus. Approved or accredited by Association of Christian Schools International, North Central Association of Colleges and Schools, and The College Board. Endowment: $30,000. Total enrollment: 242. Upper school average class size: 18. Upper school faculty-student ratio: 1:12.

Upper School Student Profile Grade 9: 70 students (27 boys, 43 girls); Grade 10: 61 students (35 boys, 26 girls); Grade 11: 68 students (33 boys, 35 girls); Grade 12: 43 students (25 boys, 18 girls). 100% of students are Christian faith, Christian.

Faculty School total: 25. In upper school: 12 men, 13 women; 19 have advanced degrees.

Subjects Offered Advanced chemistry, advanced math, algebra, art, band, Bible, biology, business, calculus, chemistry, choir, computer information systems, creative writing, debate, desktop publishing, economics, electives, English, environmental science, environmental studies, ethics, forensics, geometry, honors algebra, honors English, honors geometry, lab science, madrigals, newspaper, physics, pottery, pre-calculus, psychology, SAT/ACT preparation, sociology, sophomore skills, Spanish, speech, sports conditioning, theater arts, U.S. government, U.S. history, Web site design, world history, yearbook.

Graduation Requirements Advanced math, algebra, American government, American history, Bible, biology, chemistry, computer technology certification, English, geometry, mathematics, physics, Spanish, world history.

Special Academic Programs Honors section; study at local college for college credit; academic accommodation for the gifted.

College Placement 58 students graduated in 2005; 57 went to college, including John Brown University; Kansas State University; Texas A&M University; The University of Texas at Austin; United States Naval Academy; University of Kansas. Other: 1 entered military service. Median SAT verbal: 620, median SAT math: 590, median composite ACT: 25. 62% scored over 600 on SAT verbal, 38% scored over 600 on SAT math, 33% scored over 26 on composite ACT.

Student Life Upper grades have uniform requirement, student council, honor system. Discipline rests primarily with faculty. Attendance at religious services is required.

Summer Programs Computer instruction programs offered; session focuses on computer skills; held on campus; accepts boys and girls; not open to students from other schools. 25 students usually enrolled. 2006 schedule: June 1 to June 30.

Tuition and Aid Day student tuition: $6900. Tuition installment plan (monthly payment plans, individually arranged payment plans). Need-based scholarship grants available. In 2005–06, 30% of upper-school students received aid.

Admissions Traditional secondary-level entrance grade is 9. For fall 2005, 105 students applied for upper-level admission, 98 were accepted, 82 enrolled. OLSAT, Stanford Achievement Test and writing sample required. Deadline for receipt of application materials: none. Application fee required: $100. Interview required.

Athletics Interscholastic: baseball (boys), basketball (b,g), cheering (g), cross-country running (b,g), drill team (g), golf (b), soccer (b,g), swimming and diving (b,g), tennis (b,g), volleyball (g); intramural: football (b).

Computers Computers are regularly used in all classes. Computer network features include campus e-mail, on-campus library services, CD-ROMs, Internet access, office computer access, DVD.

Contact Mrs. Amy Bankston, Admissions Coordinator. 316-634-0909. Fax: 316-634-0928. E-mail: bankstoa@trinityacademy.org. Web site: www.trinityacademy.org.

TRINITY CATHOLIC HIGH SCHOOL

926 Newfield Avenue
Stamford, Connecticut 06905
Head of School: Mr. Robert D'Aquila

General Information Coeducational day college-preparatory school, affiliated with Roman Catholic Church. Grades 9–12. Founded: 1956. Setting: suburban. 27-acre campus. 1 building on campus. Approved or accredited by New England Association of Schools and Colleges and Connecticut Department of Education. Total enrollment: 483. Upper school average class size: 21. Upper school faculty-student ratio: 1:15.
Upper School Student Profile Grade 9: 147 students (68 boys, 79 girls); Grade 10: 113 students (50 boys, 63 girls); Grade 11: 129 students (64 boys, 65 girls); Grade 12: 94 students (50 boys, 44 girls). 85% of students are Roman Catholic.
Faculty School total: 38. In upper school: 17 men, 19 women; 32 have advanced degrees.
Subjects Offered Algebra, American history, American literature, analysis, anatomy, art, art history, Bible studies, biology, business, calculus, calculus-AP, chemistry, chemistry-AP, computer programming, computer science, economics, English, English language-AP, English literature, English literature-AP, environmental science, ethics, European civilization, European history, European history-AP, French, geography, geometry, government, government/civics, mathematics, music, physical education, physical science, physics, physics-AP, pre-calculus, psychology, religion, social studies, Spanish, speech, trigonometry, word processing, world history, world literature, writing.
Graduation Requirements Arts and fine arts (art, music, dance, drama), business skills (includes word processing), computer science, English, foreign language, mathematics, physical education (includes health), religion (includes Bible studies and theology), science, social science, social studies (includes history). Community service is required.
Special Academic Programs Advanced Placement exam preparation in 8 subject areas; honors section; study at local college for college credit.
College Placement 68 students graduated in 2005; 66 went to college, including Boston College; Fairfield University; James Madison University; Providence College; University of Connecticut; Villanova University. Other: 2 went to work. Mean SAT verbal: 518, mean SAT math: 518. 25% scored over 600 on SAT verbal, 20% scored over 600 on SAT math.
Student Life Upper grades have specified standards of dress, student council. Discipline rests primarily with faculty. Attendance at religious services is required.
Summer Programs Remediation programs offered; held on campus; accepts boys and girls; open to students from other schools. 60 students usually enrolled. 2006 schedule: June 25 to August 2. Application deadline: June 25.
Tuition and Aid Day student tuition: $7800. Tuition installment plan (FACTS Tuition Payment Plan, monthly payment plans). Tuition reduction for siblings, merit scholarship grants, need-based scholarship grants, middle-income loans available. In 2005–06, 15% of upper-school students received aid; total upper-school merit-scholarship money awarded: $62,000. Total amount of financial aid awarded in 2005–06: $62,000.
Admissions Traditional secondary-level entrance grade is 9. For fall 2005, 205 students applied for upper-level admission, 200 were accepted, 148 enrolled. High School Placement Test required. Deadline for receipt of application materials: none. Application fee required: $50. On-campus interview recommended.
Athletics Interscholastic: baseball (boys), basketball (b,g), cheering (g), cross-country running (b,g), football (b), golf (b), hockey (b), ice hockey (b), lacrosse (b,g), soccer (b,g), softball (g), tennis (b,g), track and field (b,g), volleyball (g); intramural: bicycling (b,g), drill team (g), ice hockey (g), skiing (downhill) (b,g), weight lifting (b,g); coed interscholastic: indoor track & field. 2 PE instructors, 1 trainer.
Computers Computers are regularly used in all classes. Computer network features include CD-ROMs, online commercial services, Internet access, file transfer, DVD, wireless campus network.
Contact Mrs. Connie McGoldrick, Director of Admissions. 203-322-3401 Ext. 32. Fax: 203-322-5330. E-mail: cmcgoldrick.tchs@juno.com. Web site: www.trinitycatholic.org.

TRINITY CATHOLIC HIGH SCHOOL

575 Washington Street
Newton, Massachusetts 02458-1493
Head of School: Mrs. Kelly Ann Surapaneni

General Information Coeducational day college-preparatory and arts school, affiliated with Roman Catholic Church. Grades 9–12. Founded: 1894. Setting: suburban. Nearest major city is Boston. 14-acre campus. 2 buildings on campus. Approved or accredited by New England Association of Schools and Colleges and Massachusetts Department of Education. Languages of instruction: English, Spanish, and French. Endowment: $43,000. Total enrollment: 270. Upper school average class size: 25. Upper school faculty-student ratio: 1:15.
Upper School Student Profile Grade 9: 84 students (41 boys, 43 girls); Grade 10: 64 students (39 boys, 25 girls); Grade 11: 78 students (40 boys, 38 girls); Grade 12: 44 students (25 boys, 19 girls). 80% of students are Roman Catholic.
Faculty School total: 22. In upper school: 13 men, 9 women; 9 have advanced degrees.

Subjects Offered 20th century history, advanced computer applications, advanced math, algebra, American history, American history-AP, art, British literature, British literature-AP, calculus, chemistry, choir, Christianity, civics, computer applications, debate, drama, earth science, English, English-AP, French as a second language, freshman seminar, global studies, government, health, history, honors algebra, honors English, honors geometry, honors U.S. history, honors world history, human biology, introduction to literature, language, mathematics, media, physics, pre-algebra, pre-calculus, religion, Spanish, writing, yearbook.
Graduation Requirements Art, computers, English, foreign language, mathematics, science, social studies (includes history), theology, senior service. Community service is required.
Special Academic Programs Advanced Placement exam preparation in 3 subject areas; honors section; independent study.
College Placement 45 students graduated in 2005; 42 went to college, including Boston College; Northeastern University; Saint Anselm College; Suffolk University; University of Massachusetts Amherst; University of Massachusetts Boston. Other: 3 went to work. Median SAT verbal: 511, median SAT math: 521.
Student Life Upper grades have uniform requirement, student council, honor system. Discipline rests primarily with faculty. Attendance at religious services is required.
Tuition and Aid Day student tuition: $7195. Tuition installment plan (FACTS Tuition Payment Plan). Tuition reduction for siblings, merit scholarship grants, need-based scholarship grants available. In 2005–06, 50% of upper-school students received aid; total upper-school merit-scholarship money awarded: $25,000. Total amount of financial aid awarded in 2005–06: $90,000.
Admissions Traditional secondary-level entrance grade is 9. For fall 2005, 240 students applied for upper-level admission, 135 were accepted, 85 enrolled. Catholic High School Entrance Examination required. Deadline for receipt of application materials: January 7. Application fee required: $20. On-campus interview required.
Athletics Interscholastic: baseball (boys), basketball (b,g), football (b), hockey (g), ice hockey (b), soccer (b,g), softball (g), volleyball (g); coed interscholastic: cheering, cross-country running, golf, track and field; coed intramural: dance, lacrosse, weight lifting, whiffle ball. 1 PE instructor, 2 coaches.
Computers Computers are regularly used in basic skills, publications classes. Computer network features include on-campus library services, CD-ROMs, Internet access, DVD, wireless campus network, student server accounts.
Contact Ms. Leilani Fortin Bowie, Director of Admissions and Development. 617-244-1841 Ext. 312. Fax: 617-796-9175. E-mail: lbowie@trinitycatholic.com. Web site: www.trinitycatholic.com/.

TRINITY CHRISTIAN ACADEMY

17001 Addison Road
Addison, Texas 75001-5096
Head of School: Mr. David Delph

General Information Coeducational day college-preparatory, arts, religious studies, bilingual studies, and technology school, affiliated with Christian faith. Grades K–12. Founded: 1970. Setting: suburban. Nearest major city is Dallas. 40-acre campus. 7 buildings on campus. Approved or accredited by Association of Christian Schools International, Christian Schools International, Southern Association of Colleges and Schools, The College Board, and Texas Department of Education. Languages of instruction: English, Spanish, and French. Endowment: $6.1 million. Total enrollment: 1,459. Upper school average class size: 18. Upper school faculty-student ratio: 1:10.
Upper School Student Profile Grade 9: 122 students (58 boys, 64 girls); Grade 10: 117 students (59 boys, 58 girls); Grade 11: 114 students (56 boys, 58 girls); Grade 12: 115 students (57 boys, 58 girls).
Faculty School total: 132. In upper school: 20 men, 24 women; 32 have advanced degrees.
Subjects Offered Algebra, American history, American history-AP, American literature, art, Bible studies, biology, business skills, calculus, chemistry, community service, computer programming, creative writing, drama, economics, English, English language and composition-AP, English literature, European history, expository writing, fine arts, French, geography, geology, geometry, government, government/civics, health, history, history of ideas, keyboarding, Latin, mathematics, music, philosophy, photography, physical education, physics, religion, science, social science, social studies, Spanish, speech, theater, theology, trigonometry, world history, world literature.
Graduation Requirements Arts and fine arts (art, music, dance, drama), business skills (includes word processing), economics, English, foreign language, government, mathematics, physical education (includes health), religion (includes Bible studies and theology), science, social science, social studies (includes history), speech communications, technology. Community service is required.
Special Academic Programs Advanced Placement exam preparation in 14 subject areas; honors section; independent study; study abroad.
College Placement 114 students graduated in 2005; all went to college, including Baylor University; Southern Methodist University; Texas A&M University; The University of Texas at Austin; Wake Forest University; Wheaton College. Mean SAT verbal: 622, mean SAT math: 630, mean composite ACT: 27. 63% scored over 600 on SAT verbal, 59% scored over 600 on SAT math, 44% scored over 26 on composite ACT.

Student Life Upper grades have uniform requirement, student council, honor system. Discipline rests equally with students and faculty. Attendance at religious services is required.
Summer Programs Enrichment, advancement, sports, art/fine arts, computer instruction programs offered; session focuses on enhancement ; held on campus; accepts boys and girls; open to students from other schools. 700 students usually enrolled. 2006 schedule: June 15 to July 31. Application deadline: January 15.
Tuition and Aid Day student tuition: $7780–$8200. Tuition installment plan (monthly payment plans). Need-based scholarship grants available. In 2005–06, 15% of upper-school students received aid. Total amount of financial aid awarded in 2005–06: $250,000.
Admissions Traditional secondary-level entrance grade is 9. For fall 2005, 135 students applied for upper-level admission, 28 were accepted, 26 enrolled. ERB and ISEE required. Deadline for receipt of application materials: February 1. Application fee required: $75. On-campus interview required.
Athletics Interscholastic: baseball (boys), basketball (b,g), cheering (g), cross-country running (b,g), drill team (g), football (b), golf (b,g), running (b,g), soccer (b,g), softball (g), strength & conditioning (b,g), swimming and diving (b,g), tennis (b,g), track and field (b,g), volleyball (g), weight lifting (b), weight training (b), winter soccer (b,g), wrestling (b); coed interscholastic: cross-country running, golf, swimming and diving, tennis. 6 PE instructors, 15 coaches, 1 trainer.
Computers Computers are regularly used in animation, art, Bible studies, career exploration, college planning, desktop publishing, digital applications, English, foreign language, mathematics, multimedia, photojournalism, publications, science, technology, video film production, Web site design, word processing, yearbook classes. Computer network features include campus e-mail, on-campus library services, CD-ROMs, Internet access.
Contact Mary Helen Noland, Admission Director. 972-931-8325. Fax: 972-931-8923. E-mail: mhnoland@trinitychristian.org. Web site: www.trinitychristian.org.

TRINITY CHRISTIAN SCHOOL

200 Trinity Road
Dublin, Georgia 31021
Head of School: Mr. Rick Johnson

General Information Coeducational day college-preparatory, vocational, religious studies, and technology school, affiliated with Baptist Church, United Methodist Church. Grades K4–12. Founded: 1970. Setting: small town. Nearest major city is Macon. 47-acre campus. 9 buildings on campus. Approved or accredited by Georgia Accrediting Commission, Georgia Independent School Association, Southern Association of Colleges and Schools, Southern Association of Independent Schools, and Georgia Department of Education. Total enrollment: 389. Upper school average class size: 20. Upper school faculty-student ratio: 1:12.
Upper School Student Profile Grade 9: 21 students (12 boys, 9 girls); Grade 10: 37 students (18 boys, 19 girls); Grade 11: 33 students (12 boys, 21 girls); Grade 12: 19 students (11 boys, 8 girls). 90% of students are Baptist, United Methodist Church.
Faculty School total: 34. In upper school: 7 men, 9 women; 7 have advanced degrees.
Subjects Offered Algebra, American government, American history, American literature, analytic geometry, anatomy and physiology, ancient world history, band, Bible, biology, British literature, British literature (honors), business mathematics, calculus-AP, chemistry, chorus, Christian education, composition, computer applications, computer math, computer processing, constitutional history of U.S., creative writing, desktop publishing, earth science, English composition, English literature, English literature and composition-AP, ensembles, geometry, government/civics, grammar, guidance, health education, history, honors algebra, honors English, honors geometry, human biology, intro to computers, keyboarding/computer, language and composition, literature, music, physical education, physical science, physics, social studies, Spanish, state government, state history, student government, trigonometry, weight training, world geography, writing, yearbook.
Special Academic Programs Advanced Placement exam preparation in 2 subject areas; honors section; study at local college for college credit; academic accommodation for the gifted.
College Placement 28 students graduated in 2005; 27 went to college, including Georgia College & State University; Georgia Southern University; Middle Georgia College; University of Georgia. Other: 1 had other specific plans. Median SAT verbal: 515, median SAT math: 496. 25% scored over 600 on SAT verbal, 18% scored over 600 on SAT math.
Student Life Upper grades have specified standards of dress, student council, honor system. Discipline rests primarily with faculty. Attendance at religious services is required.
Tuition and Aid Day student tuition: $4890. Tuition installment plan (monthly payment plans, individually arranged payment plans). Tuition reduction for siblings, need-based scholarship grants available. In 2005–06, 10% of upper-school students received aid. Total amount of financial aid awarded in 2005–06: $25,000.
Admissions Traditional secondary-level entrance grade is 9. For fall 2005, 7 students applied for upper-level admission, 6 were accepted, 6 enrolled. School's own exam required. Deadline for receipt of application materials: none. Application fee required: $50. On-campus interview required.
Athletics Interscholastic: baseball (boys), basketball (b,g), cheering (g), cross-country running (b,g), football (b), golf (b,g), running (b,g), soccer (b,g), softball (g), tennis (b,g), track and field (b,g), wrestling (b); intramural: basketball (b,g). 3 PE instructors, 1 coach.
Computers Computers are regularly used in business skills, computer applications, creative writing, mathematics, reading, yearbook classes. Computer network features include on-campus library services, CD-ROMs, Internet access, file transfer.
Contact Mr. Jon Martin, Director of Admissions. 478-272-7699. Fax: 478-272-7685. E-mail: jmartin@tcsweb.org. Web site: www.tcsweb.org.

TRINITY COLLEGE SCHOOL

55 Deblaquire Street North
Port Hope, Ontario L1A 4K7, Canada
Head of School: Mr. Stuart K. C. Grainger

General Information Coeducational boarding and day college-preparatory school, affiliated with Church of England (Anglican). Boarding grades 9–12, day grades 5–12. Founded: 1865. Setting: small town. Nearest major city is Toronto, Canada. Students are housed in single-sex dormitories. 100-acre campus. 15 buildings on campus. Approved or accredited by Canadian Association of Independent Schools, Canadian Educational Standards Institute, Conference of Independent Schools of Ontario, The Association of Boarding Schools, and Ontario Department of Education. Affiliate member of National Association of Independent Schools; member of Secondary School Admission Test Board. Language of instruction: English. Endowment: CAN$23 million. Total enrollment: 602. Upper school average class size: 16. Upper school faculty-student ratio: 1:8.
Upper School Student Profile Grade 9: 97 students (58 boys, 39 girls); Grade 10: 106 students (53 boys, 53 girls); Grade 11: 164 students (103 boys, 61 girls); Grade 12: 135 students (68 boys, 67 girls). 60% of students are boarding students. 61% are province residents. 18 provinces are represented in upper school student body. 33% are international students. International students from Bahamas, Barbados, Bermuda, Cayman Islands, China, and United States; 20 other countries represented in student body. 30% of students are members of Church of England (Anglican).
Faculty School total: 74. In upper school: 40 men, 24 women; 17 have advanced degrees; 22 reside on campus.
Subjects Offered Algebra, art, art history-AP, astronomy, biology, biology-AP, calculus, calculus-AP, Canadian geography, Canadian history, career education, career/college preparation, chemistry, chemistry-AP, civics, classical civilization, classics, community service, computer programming, computer science, creative writing, dramatic arts, earth science, economics, English, English literature, English-AP, environmental science, environmental studies, ESL, European history, fine arts, finite math, French, French-AP, general science, geography, geometry, German, guidance, health, history, independent study, Latin, law, mathematics, modern Western civilization, music, philosophy, physical education, physics, physics-AP, political science, science, social science, social studies, Spanish.
Graduation Requirements Arts and fine arts (art, music, dance, drama), Canadian geography, Canadian history, civics, English, French, guidance, mathematics, physical education (includes health), science, social science, technology.
Special Academic Programs Advanced Placement exam preparation in 9 subject areas; accelerated programs; independent study; term-away projects; study abroad; ESL (15 students enrolled).
College Placement 140 students graduated in 2005; all went to college, including Dalhousie University; McGill University; Queen's University at Kingston; The University of Western Ontario; University of Guelph; University of Toronto.
Student Life Upper grades have specified standards of dress, student council, honor system. Discipline rests primarily with faculty. Attendance at religious services is required.
Summer Programs Advancement, art/fine arts, computer instruction programs offered; session focuses on advancement through cultural enrichment; held off campus; held at France, Banff (Canada); accepts boys and girls; open to students from other schools. 30 students usually enrolled. 2006 schedule: June 26 to July 26. Application deadline: April 14.
Tuition and Aid Day student tuition: CAN$20,860; 5-day tuition and room/board: CAN$37,050; 7-day tuition and room/board: CAN$37,050. Tuition installment plan (monthly payment plans, quarterly payment plan). Bursaries, need-based scholarship grants available. In 2005–06, 30% of upper-school students received aid. Total amount of financial aid awarded in 2005–06: CAN$1,000,000.
Admissions Traditional secondary-level entrance grade is 9. For fall 2005, 500 students applied for upper-level admission, 338 were accepted, 256 enrolled. CCAT, SAT, SSAT or TOEFL required. Deadline for receipt of application materials: none. Application fee required: CAN$200. Interview required.
Athletics Interscholastic: baseball (boys), basketball (b,g), field hockey (g), football (b), ice hockey (b,g), rugby (b,g), soccer (b,g), softball (g), squash (b,g), tennis (b,g), volleyball (b,g); coed interscholastic: badminton, cricket, cross-country running, dressage, equestrian sports, golf, nordic skiing, outdoor education, rowing, skiing (cross-country), swimming and diving, track and field; coed intramural: aerobics, aerobics/dance, alpine skiing, badminton, basketball, bicycling, cricket, cross-country running, dance, equestrian sports, fitness, golf, horseback riding, ice hockey, mountain biking, paddling, skiing (downhill), snowboarding, soccer, softball, squash, strength

& conditioning, swimming and diving, table tennis, tennis, water polo, weight lifting, weight training. 4 PE instructors, 5 coaches, 2 trainers.

Computers Computers are regularly used in career education, college planning, English, ESL, foreign language, French, geography, history, humanities, independent study, information technology, mathematics, music, science, technology classes. Computer network features include campus e-mail, on-campus library services, CD-ROMs, Internet access, file transfer.

Contact Ms. Kathryn A. LaBranche, Director of Admissions. 905-885-3209. Fax: 905-885-7444. E-mail: admissions@tcs.on.ca. Web site: www.tcs.on.ca.

See full description on page 1106.

TRINITY EPISCOPAL SCHOOL

3850 Pittaway Drive
Richmond, Virginia 23235
Head of School: Dr. Thomas G. Aycock

General Information Coeducational day college-preparatory, arts, and International Baccalaureate school, affiliated with Episcopal Church. Grades 8–12. Founded: 1972. Setting: suburban. 40-acre campus. 6 buildings on campus. Approved or accredited by National Association of Episcopal Schools, Virginia Association of Independent Schools, and Virginia Department of Education. Member of National Association of Independent Schools. Endowment: $75,000. Total enrollment: 402. Upper school average class size: 13. Upper school faculty-student ratio: 1:10.

Upper School Student Profile Grade 8: 21 students (12 boys, 9 girls); Grade 9: 112 students (50 boys, 62 girls); Grade 10: 101 students (59 boys, 42 girls); Grade 11: 94 students (49 boys, 45 girls); Grade 12: 34 students (34 girls).

Faculty School total: 44. In upper school: 22 men, 22 women; 25 have advanced degrees.

Subjects Offered 20th century history, 20th century world history, 3-dimensional art, Advanced Placement courses, advanced studio art-AP, algebra, American government, American government-AP, American history, American history-AP, American literature, American politics in film, anatomy, art, astronomy, band, Bible studies, biology, biology-AP, calculus, calculus-AP, chemistry, chemistry-AP, chorus, computer graphics, computer keyboarding, computer programming, computer science, concert band, concert choir, creative writing, digital music, drama, driver education, earth science, economics, English, English literature, English-AP, environmental science, European history, European history-AP, foreign policy, French, French-AP, geography, geology, geometry, German, German-AP, government-AP, government/civics, International Baccalaureate courses, jazz band, keyboarding, Latin, math analysis, mathematics, music, physics, physics-AP, pre-calculus, religion, science, social science, social studies, Southern literature, Spanish, studio art-AP, theater, theology, theory of knowledge, trigonometry, U.S. history-AP, Web site design, word processing, world history, world literature, world religions, writing.

Graduation Requirements Arts and fine arts (art, music, dance, drama), computer science, English, foreign language, mathematics, religion (includes Bible studies and theology), science, social science, social studies (includes history). Community service is required.

Special Academic Programs International Baccalaureate program; Advanced Placement exam preparation in 14 subject areas; honors section; independent study; study at local college for college credit; academic accommodation for the gifted, the musically talented, and the artistically talented.

College Placement 82 students graduated in 2005; all went to college, including Hampden-Sydney College; James Madison University; University of Virginia; Virginia Commonwealth University; Virginia Polytechnic Institute and State University; West Virginia University.

Student Life Upper grades have specified standards of dress, student council, honor system. Discipline rests equally with students and faculty. Attendance at religious services is required.

Tuition and Aid Day student tuition: $13,650. Tuition installment plan (Key Tuition Payment Plan, monthly payment plans). Merit scholarship grants, need-based scholarship grants available. In 2005–06, 23% of upper-school students received aid; total upper-school merit-scholarship money awarded: $109,200. Total amount of financial aid awarded in 2005–06: $660,800.

Admissions Traditional secondary-level entrance grade is 9. For fall 2005, 200 students applied for upper-level admission, 174 were accepted, 130 enrolled. English entrance exam and Otis-Lennon School Ability Test required. Deadline for receipt of application materials: February 24. Application fee required: $50. On-campus interview required.

Athletics Interscholastic: baseball (boys), basketball (b,g), field hockey (g), football (b), indoor soccer (b,g), lacrosse (b,g), soccer (b,g), softball (g), tennis (b,g), track and field (b,g), volleyball (b,g); coed interscholastic: aquatics, cross-country running, diving, fitness, golf, indoor track, running, swimming and diving, winter (indoor) track; coed intramural: canoeing/kayaking, physical fitness, physical training, rock climbing, scuba diving, strength & conditioning, wall climbing, weight training. 14 coaches, 1 trainer.

Computers Computers are regularly used in all academic classes. Computer resources include on-campus library services, CD-ROMs, online commercial services, Internet access, DVD.

Contact Mrs. Emily H. McLeod, Director of Admission. 804-327-3156. Fax: 804-272-4652. E-mail: emilymcleod@trinityes.org. Web site: www.trinityes.org.

TRINITY HIGH SCHOOL

7574 West Division Street
River Forest, Illinois 60305
Head of School: Mrs. Michele Kathryn Whitehead

General Information Girls' day college-preparatory, arts, and religious studies school, affiliated with Roman Catholic Church. Grades 9–12. Founded: 1918. Setting: suburban. Nearest major city is Chicago. 1-acre campus. 2 buildings on campus. Approved or accredited by International Baccalaureate Organization, National Catholic Education Association, North Central Association of Colleges and Schools, The College Board, and Illinois Department of Education. Endowment: $2 million. Total enrollment: 469. Upper school average class size: 20. Upper school faculty-student ratio: 1:12.

Upper School Student Profile Grade 9: 133 students (133 girls); Grade 10: 100 students (100 girls); Grade 11: 120 students (120 girls); Grade 12: 116 students (116 girls). 80% of students are Roman Catholic.

Faculty School total: 38. In upper school: 6 men, 32 women; 31 have advanced degrees.

Subjects Offered Algebra, British literature, choir, comparative religion, computer art, computer graphics, computer keyboarding, creative dance, creative drama, dance, desktop publishing, digital art, ecology, environmental systems, economics, English, environmental science, European history, film studies, French, geometry, government, graphic design, health, honors algebra, honors English, honors geometry, honors U.S. history, honors world history, integrated mathematics, Italian, math methods, moral theology, newspaper, painting, physical education, physics, pre-calculus, pre-college orientation, probability and statistics, psychology, religious studies, scripture, Spanish, speech, speech and debate, theater, theology, theory of knowledge, U.S. government, U.S. government and politics, U.S. history, vocal music, women in society, word processing, world civilizations, world geography, world governments, world history, world religions, world studies, yearbook.

Graduation Requirements Algebra, arts and fine arts (art, music, dance, drama), biology, British literature, Catholic belief and practice, chemistry, Christian ethics, Christian scripture, church history, computer applications, computer keyboarding, English composition, English literature, geometry, health education, physical education (includes health), speech, theology, world history, world literature, world religions, world studies.

Special Academic Programs International Baccalaureate program; honors section; independent study; academic accommodation for the gifted.

College Placement 109 students graduated in 2005; all went to college, including DePaul University; Illinois State University; Loyola University Chicago; Marquette University; Northern Illinois University; University of Illinois at Urbana–Champaign. Median composite ACT: 23. 25% scored over 26 on composite ACT.

Student Life Upper grades have uniform requirement, student council. Discipline rests primarily with faculty. Attendance at religious services is required.

Summer Programs Enrichment, advancement, sports, art/fine arts, computer instruction programs offered; session focuses on enrichment; held on campus; accepts girls; not open to students from other schools. 20 students usually enrolled. 2006 schedule: June 19 to July 28. Application deadline: May 1.

Tuition and Aid Day student tuition: $7650. Tuition installment plan (monthly payment plans, individually arranged payment plans). Tuition reduction for siblings, merit scholarship grants, need-based scholarship grants, paying campus jobs available. In 2005–06, 30% of upper-school students received aid; total upper-school merit-scholarship money awarded: $23,100. Total amount of financial aid awarded in 2005–06: $41,600.

Admissions Traditional secondary-level entrance grade is 9. For fall 2005, 217 students applied for upper-level admission, 197 were accepted, 133 enrolled. ACT-Explore required. Deadline for receipt of application materials: none. No application fee required. On-campus interview recommended.

Athletics Interscholastic: basketball, bowling, cross-country running, golf, soccer, softball, swimming and diving, tennis, track and field, volleyball, water polo. 1 PE instructor, 19 coaches, 1 trainer.

Computers Computers are regularly used in all classes. Computer network features include campus e-mail, on-campus library services, CD-ROMs, online commercial services, Internet access, DVD, wireless campus network.

Contact Miss Meg Bigane, Assistant Principal. 708-771-8383. Fax: 708-488-2014. E-mail: mbigane@trinityhs.org. Web site: www.trinityhs.org.

TRINITY HIGH SCHOOL

4011 Shelbyville Road
Louisville, Kentucky 40207-9427
Head of School: Robert J. Mullen, EdD

General Information Boys' day college-preparatory, arts, business, religious studies, and technology school, affiliated with Roman Catholic Church. Grades 9–12. Founded: 1953. Setting: suburban. 110-acre campus. 11 buildings on campus.

Approved or accredited by National Catholic Education Association, Southern Association of Colleges and Schools, and Kentucky Department of Education. Endowment: $2.4 million. Total enrollment: 1,400. Upper school average class size: 21. Upper school faculty-student ratio: 1:12.

Upper School Student Profile Grade 9: 320 students (320 boys); Grade 10: 355 students (355 boys); Grade 11: 347 students (347 boys); Grade 12: 332 students (332 boys). 84% of students are Roman Catholic.

Faculty School total: 110. In upper school: 81 men, 29 women; 99 have advanced degrees.

Subjects Offered Accounting, algebra, art, band, banking, biology, broadcasting, business, business law, calculus, chemistry, choral music, civics, communication skills, computers, creative writing, economics, English, European history, film studies, finite math, first aid, forensics, French, geography, geometry, German, health, humanities, instrumental music, keyboarding, language arts, mathematics, newspaper, philosophy, photography, physical education, physical fitness, physics, pre-calculus, psychology, religion, science, social studies, sociology, Spanish, technology, trigonometry, U.S. history, world civilizations, yearbook.

Graduation Requirements Communication arts, English, foreign language, humanities, mathematics, physical education (includes health), religion (includes Bible studies and theology), science, social studies (includes history). Community service is required.

Special Academic Programs Advanced Placement exam preparation; honors section; independent study; study at local college for college credit; study abroad; academic accommodation for the gifted, the musically talented, and the artistically talented; remedial reading and/or remedial writing; remedial math; programs in English, mathematics, general development for dyslexic students.

College Placement 312 students graduated in 2005; 300 went to college, including Bellarmine University; Eastern Kentucky University; Indiana University Bloomington; University of Dayton; University of Kentucky; University of Louisville. Other: 2 went to work, 10 entered military service. Mean composite ACT: 23.

Student Life Upper grades have specified standards of dress, student council, honor system. Discipline rests equally with students and faculty. Attendance at religious services is required.

Summer Programs Remediation, enrichment, advancement, sports, computer instruction programs offered; held on campus; accepts boys; not open to students from other schools. 1000 students usually enrolled. 2006 schedule: June 4 to July 15. Application deadline: May 15.

Tuition and Aid Day student tuition: $7825. Guaranteed tuition plan. Tuition installment plan (monthly payment plans, individually arranged payment plans). Merit scholarship grants, need-based scholarship grants, paying campus jobs available. In 2005–06, 40% of upper-school students received aid. Total amount of financial aid awarded in 2005–06: $925,000.

Admissions Traditional secondary-level entrance grade is 9. Placement test required. Deadline for receipt of application materials: none. Application fee required: $75. Interview required.

Athletics Interscholastic: baseball, basketball, bowling, cheering, crew, cross-country running, diving, football, golf, hockey, ice hockey, lacrosse, power lifting, soccer, swimming and diving, tennis, track and field, volleyball, wrestling; intramural: alpine skiing, basketball, bicycling, bocce, bowling, fencing, fishing, flag football, freestyle skiing, Frisbee, golf, hiking/backpacking, indoor soccer, life saving, mountain biking, paddle tennis, skiing (downhill), snowboarding, soccer, softball, strength & conditioning, table tennis, ultimate Frisbee, volleyball, weight lifting, weight training. 5 PE instructors, 30 coaches, 3 trainers.

Computers Computers are regularly used in all classes. Computer network features include campus e-mail, on-campus library services, CD-ROMs, online commercial services, Internet access, file transfer, office computer access, DVD.

Contact Mr. Joseph M. Porter Jr., Vice President for Advancement. 502-736-2119. Fax: 502-899-2052. E-mail: porter@thsrock.net. Web site: www.thsrock.net.

TRINITY HIGH SCHOOL

581 Bridge Street
Manchester, New Hampshire 03104
Head of School: Mr. Denis Mailloux

General Information Coeducational day college-preparatory, arts, religious studies, and technology school, affiliated with Roman Catholic Church. Grades 9–12. Founded: 1886. Setting: urban. Nearest major city is Boston, MA. 5-acre campus. 2 buildings on campus. Approved or accredited by New England Association of Schools and Colleges and New Hampshire Department of Education. Total enrollment: 535. Upper school average class size: 20. Upper school faculty-student ratio: 1:16.

Upper School Student Profile Grade 9: 146 students (73 boys, 73 girls); Grade 10: 139 students (76 boys, 63 girls); Grade 11: 126 students (66 boys, 60 girls); Grade 12: 124 students (50 boys, 74 girls). 75% of students are Roman Catholic.

Faculty School total: 36. In upper school: 18 men, 18 women; 21 have advanced degrees.

Subjects Offered Advanced Placement courses, algebra, American history, American literature, art, Bible studies, biology, calculus, chemistry, computer science, driver education, English, English literature, ethics, French, geometry, German, grammar,

health, history, human development, Latin, mathematics, physical education, physics, psychology, religion, science, social studies, sociology, Spanish, theology, trigonometry, world history, world literature.

Special Academic Programs Advanced Placement exam preparation in 4 subject areas; honors section; study at local college for college credit.

College Placement 117 students graduated in 2005; 113 went to college, including Saint Anselm College; University of New Hampshire. Other: 3 went to work, 1 entered a postgraduate year. Mean SAT verbal: 569, mean SAT math: 551. 41% scored over 600 on SAT verbal, 29% scored over 600 on SAT math.

Student Life Upper grades have specified standards of dress, student council, honor system. Discipline rests primarily with faculty. Attendance at religious services is required.

Tuition and Aid Day student tuition: $6560. Tuition installment plan (FACTS Tuition Payment Plan). Need-based scholarship grants available. In 2005–06, 10% of upper-school students received aid.

Admissions Traditional secondary-level entrance grade is 9. For fall 2005, 350 students applied for upper-level admission, 250 were accepted, 145 enrolled. STS required. Deadline for receipt of application materials: none. Application fee required: $50. On-campus interview recommended.

Athletics Interscholastic: baseball (boys), basketball (b,g), cheering (g), cross-country running (b,g), football (b), hockey (b), ice hockey (b), indoor soccer (g), indoor track & field (b,g), lacrosse (b), nordic skiing (b,g), skiing (cross-country) (b,g), skiing (downhill) (b,g), soccer (b,g), softball (g), tennis (b,g), volleyball (g), winter (indoor) track (b,g), wrestling (b); coed interscholastic: alpine skiing, golf, track and field; coed intramural: gymnastics. 1 PE instructor, 25 coaches, 1 trainer.

Computers Computers are regularly used in desktop publishing, science, social science, yearbook classes. Computer network features include campus e-mail, CD-ROMs, Internet access.

Contact Mrs. Carol Hurley, Admissions Director. 603-668-1779. Fax: 603-668-2913. E-mail: churley@trinity-hs.org. Web site: www.trinity-hs.org.

TRINITY-PAWLING SCHOOL

700 Route 22
Pawling, New York 12564
Head of School: Mr. Archibald A. Smith III

General Information Boys' boarding and day college-preparatory, arts, religious studies, technology, and ESL school, affiliated with Episcopal Church. Boarding grades 9–PG, day grades 7–PG. Founded: 1907. Setting: small town. Nearest major city is New York. Students are housed in single-sex dormitories. 140-acre campus. 20 buildings on campus. Approved or accredited by New York State Association of Independent Schools, New York State Board of Regents, and The Association of Boarding Schools. Member of National Association of Independent Schools and Secondary School Admission Test Board. Endowment: $25 million. Total enrollment: 318. Upper school average class size: 13. Upper school faculty-student ratio: 1:7.

Upper School Student Profile Grade 9: 46 students (46 boys); Grade 10: 70 students (70 boys); Grade 11: 87 students (87 boys); Grade 12: 78 students (78 boys); Postgraduate: 9 students (9 boys). 75% of students are boarding students. 20% are state residents. 33 states are represented in upper school student body. 20% are international students. International students from Australia, China, Germany, Republic of Korea, Saudi Arabia, and Ukraine; 10 other countries represented in student body. 20% of students are members of Episcopal Church.

Faculty School total: 53. In upper school: 40 men, 13 women; 23 have advanced degrees; all reside on campus.

Subjects Offered Advanced Placement courses, algebra, American history, American literature, anatomy, art, art history, biology, calculus, ceramics, chemistry, computer information systems, computer math, computer programming, computer science, computer technologies, data analysis, drafting, drama, earth science, ecology, economics, English, English literature, environmental science, ethics, European history, fine arts, French, geology, geometry, government/civics, grammar, history, Latin, literature, mathematics, mechanical drawing, music, philosophy, photography, physical education, physics, physiology, psychology, religion, science, social studies, Spanish, theater, theology, trigonometry, word processing, world history.

Graduation Requirements Arts and fine arts (art, music, dance, drama), English, foreign language, mathematics, physical education (includes health), religion (includes Bible studies and theology), science, social studies (includes history).

Special Academic Programs Advanced Placement exam preparation in 17 subject areas; honors section; remedial reading and/or remedial writing; programs in English for dyslexic students; ESL (19 students enrolled).

College Placement 89 students graduated in 2005; all went to college, including Hobart and William Smith Colleges; Providence College; Purdue University; Sacred Heart University; The George Washington University. Mean SAT verbal: 580, mean SAT math: 570.

Student Life Upper grades have specified standards of dress, student council, honor system. Discipline rests equally with students and faculty. Attendance at religious services is required.

Tuition and Aid Day student tuition: $24,300; 7-day tuition and room/board: $35,000–$41,800. Guaranteed tuition plan. Tuition installment plan (Insured Tuition Payment Plan, Key Tuition Payment Plan, monthly payment plans). Need-based

scholarship grants, need-based loans available. In 2005–06, 35% of upper-school students received aid. Total amount of financial aid awarded in 2005–06: $1,600,000.

Admissions Traditional secondary-level entrance grade is 9. For fall 2005, 342 students applied for upper-level admission, 234 were accepted, 120 enrolled. PSAT or SAT, SLEP, SSAT, TOEFL, Wechsler Intelligence Scale for Children III or WISC-R required. Deadline for receipt of application materials: February 1. Application fee required: $40. On-campus interview required.

Athletics Interscholastic: alpine skiing (boys), baseball (b), basketball (b), crew (b), cross-country running (b), football (b), golf (b), ice hockey (b), lacrosse (b), ropes courses (b), skiing (downhill) (b), soccer (b), squash (b), strength & conditioning (b), tennis (b), track and field (b), weight lifting (b), weight training (b), wrestling (b); intramural: alpine skiing (b), basketball (b), climbing (b), cross-country running (b), fishing (b), golf (b), hiking/backpacking (b), ice skating (b), mountain biking (b), outdoor recreation (b), physical training (b), rock climbing (b), skiing (downhill) (b), snowboarding (b), soccer (b), softball (b), squash (b), strength & conditioning (b), tennis (b), ultimate Frisbee (b). 2 trainers.

Computers Computers are regularly used in English, mathematics, remedial study skills, science classes. Computer network features include campus e-mail, on-campus library services, CD-ROMs, online commercial services, Internet access, file transfer, office computer access, wireless campus network.

Contact Mr. MacGregor Robinson, Director of Admission. 845-855-4825. Fax: 845-855-3816. E-mail: grobinson@trinitypawling.org. Web site: www.trinitypawling. org.

See full description on page 1108.

TRINITY PREPARATORY SCHOOL

5700 Trinity Prep Lane
Winter Park, Florida 32792
Head of School: Craig S. Maughan

General Information Coeducational day college-preparatory, arts, and technology school, affiliated with Episcopal Church. Grades 6–12. Founded: 1966. Setting: suburban. Nearest major city is Orlando. 100-acre campus. 12 buildings on campus. Approved or accredited by Florida Council of Independent Schools, National Association of Episcopal Schools, The College Board, and Florida Department of Education. Member of National Association of Independent Schools and Secondary School Admission Test Board. Languages of instruction: Spanish and French. Endowment: $4.9 million. Total enrollment: 822. Upper school average class size: 17. Upper school faculty-student ratio: 1:12.

Upper School Student Profile Grade 9: 139 students (67 boys, 72 girls); Grade 10: 129 students (66 boys, 63 girls); Grade 11: 110 students (53 boys, 57 girls); Grade 12: 112 students (60 boys, 52 girls). 12.2% of students are members of Episcopal Church.

Faculty School total: 77. In upper school: 28 men, 30 women; 34 have advanced degrees.

Subjects Offered Algebra, American government-AP, American history, American literature, anatomy, art, audio visual/media, biology, biology-AP, calculus, calculus-AP, character education, chemistry, chemistry-AP, choral music, computer multimedia, computer processing, computer programming, computer programming-AP, computer science-AP, concert band, concert choir, creative writing, drama, economics, economics-AP, English, English language and composition-AP, English literature, English literature and composition-AP, environmental science, ethics, European history, European history-AP, fine arts, forensics, French, French language-AP, French literature-AP, geography, geometry, government and politics-AP, government/civics, health, history, honors algebra, honors English, honors geometry, journalism, Latin, Latin-AP, life management skills, mathematics, music, music theory-AP, newspaper, painting, photography, physical education, physics, physics-AP, portfolio art, pre-algebra, pre-calculus, probability and statistics, psychology, psychology-AP, science, sculpture, social science, social studies, Spanish, Spanish language-AP, Spanish literature-AP, speech, strings, studio art-AP, theater, trigonometry, U.S. government and politics-AP, U.S. history-AP, weight training, world history, world literature, world religions, world wide web design, writing, yearbook.

Graduation Requirements Arts and fine arts (art, music, dance, drama), computer science, English, foreign language, mathematics, physical education (includes health), science, social sciences.

Special Academic Programs Advanced Placement exam preparation in 16 subject areas; honors section; academic accommodation for the gifted, the musically talented, and the artistically talented.

College Placement 118 students graduated in 2005; all went to college, including Duke University; Florida State University; New York University; University of Central Florida; University of Florida; Washington University in St. Louis. Mean SAT verbal: 690, mean SAT math: 690, mean composite ACT: 30. 63% scored over 600 on SAT verbal, 69% scored over 600 on SAT math, 50% scored over 26 on composite ACT.

Student Life Upper grades have specified standards of dress, student council, honor system. Discipline rests primarily with faculty. Attendance at religious services is required.

Summer Programs Remediation, enrichment, advancement, sports, art/fine arts, computer instruction programs offered; session focuses on enrichment; held on

campus; accepts boys and girls; open to students from other schools. 300 students usually enrolled. 2006 schedule: June 5 to August 8. Application deadline: none.

Tuition and Aid Day student tuition: $12,800. Tuition installment plan (Insured Tuition Payment Plan, FACTS Tuition Payment Plan, semi-annual and annual payment plans). Need-based scholarship grants, middle-income loans available. In 2005–06, 13% of upper-school students received aid. Total amount of financial aid awarded in 2005–06: $760,180.

Admissions Traditional secondary-level entrance grade is 9. For fall 2005, 87 students applied for upper-level admission, 46 were accepted, 40 enrolled. CTP, ISEE, PSAT, SAT or SSAT required. Deadline for receipt of application materials: none. Application fee required: $50. On-campus interview recommended.

Athletics Interscholastic: baseball (boys), basketball (b,g), bowling (b,g), cheering (g), cross-country running (b,g), diving (b,g), football (b), golf (b,g), physical fitness (b,g), soccer (b,g), softball (g), swimming and diving (b,g), tennis (b,g), track and field (b,g), volleyball (g), weight lifting (b,g); intramural: ropes courses (b,g), sailing (b,g), strength & conditioning (b,g). 3 PE instructors, 47 coaches, 1 trainer.

Computers Computers are regularly used in art, creative writing, English, foreign language, keyboarding, literary magazine, mathematics, multimedia, music, newspaper, photography, programming, psychology, science, social studies, technology, video film production, Web site design, writing, yearbook classes. Computer network features include campus e-mail, on-campus library services, CD-ROMs, online commercial services, Internet access, office computer access, DVD, wireless campus network.

Contact Katie G. Seymour, Assistant Director of Admission. 407-671-4140 Ext. 515. Fax: 407-671-6935. E-mail: seymourk@trinityprep.org. Web site: www.trinityprep. org.

TRINITY SCHOOL

139 West 91st Street
New York, New York 10024
Head of School: Henry C. Moses

General Information Coeducational day college-preparatory school, affiliated with Episcopal Church. Grades K–12. Founded: 1709. Setting: urban. 1 building on campus. Approved or accredited by National Association of Private Schools for Exceptional Children, New York State Association of Independent Schools, and New York Department of Education. Member of National Association of Independent Schools. Endowment: $34 million. Total enrollment: 961. Upper school average class size: 15. Upper school faculty-student ratio: 1:7.

Upper School Student Profile Grade 9: 117 students (59 boys, 58 girls); Grade 10: 105 students (55 boys, 50 girls); Grade 11: 116 students (53 boys, 63 girls); Grade 12: 84 students (44 boys, 40 girls).

Faculty School total: 161. In upper school: 48 men, 40 women; 70 have advanced degrees.

Subjects Offered Algebra, American history, American literature, art, art history, biology, calculus, ceramics, chemistry, computer math, computer programming, computer science, creative writing, dance, drama, driver education, economics, English, English literature, environmental science, ethics, European history, expository writing, fine arts, French, geometry, German, government/civics, Greek, history, Latin, marine biology, mathematics, music, photography, physical education, physics, psychology, religion, science, social studies, Spanish, speech, statistics, theater, trigonometry.

Graduation Requirements Arts and fine arts (art, music, dance, drama), English, foreign language, mathematics, physical education (includes health), religion (includes Bible studies and theology), science, social studies (includes history).

Special Academic Programs Advanced Placement exam preparation in 11 subject areas; honors section; independent study.

College Placement 120 students graduated in 2005; 106 went to college, including Brown University; Columbia College; Harvard University; University of Pennsylvania; Yale University. Other: 1 had other specific plans. Median SAT verbal: 690, median SAT math: 680.

Student Life Upper grades have specified standards of dress, student council. Discipline rests primarily with faculty. Attendance at religious services is required.

Tuition and Aid Day student tuition: $27,990. Need-based scholarship grants available. In 2005–06, 20% of upper-school students received aid. Total amount of financial aid awarded in 2005–06: $1,656,360.

Admissions Traditional secondary-level entrance grade is 9. For fall 2005, 400 students applied for upper-level admission, 115 were accepted, 65 enrolled. ISEE or SSAT required. Deadline for receipt of application materials: January 15. Application fee required: $60. On-campus interview required.

Athletics Interscholastic: baseball (boys), basketball (b,g), cross-country running (b,g), golf (b,g), indoor track & field (b,g), lacrosse (b,g), soccer (b,g), softball (g), swimming and diving (b,g), tennis (b,g), track and field (b,g), volleyball (g), winter (indoor) track (b,g), wrestling (b); coed interscholastic: water polo. 16 PE instructors, 43 coaches, 1 trainer.

Computers Computers are regularly used in art, mathematics, science classes. Computer network features include campus e-mail, on-campus library services, CD-ROMs, Internet access.

Contact Sandy O'Shea, Admissions Coordinator. 212-932-6819. Fax: 212-932-6812. E-mail: so'shea@trinity.nyc.ny.us. Web site: www.trinityschoolnyc.org.

TRINITY VALLEY SCHOOL

7500 Dutch Branch Road
Fort Worth, Texas 76132
Head of School: Dr. Ned Fox

General Information Coeducational day college-preparatory school. Grades K–12. Founded: 1959. Setting: urban. 75-acre campus. 7 buildings on campus. Approved or accredited by Independent Schools Association of the Southwest and Texas Department of Education. Member of National Association of Independent Schools. Endowment: $18 million. Total enrollment: 946. Upper school average class size: 16. Upper school faculty-student ratio: 1:10.

Upper School Student Profile Grade 9: 85 students (37 boys, 48 girls); Grade 10: 83 students (43 boys, 40 girls); Grade 11: 75 students (51 boys, 24 girls); Grade 12: 83 students (44 boys, 39 girls).

Faculty School total: 90. In upper school: 18 men, 18 women; 28 have advanced degrees.

Subjects Offered Algebra, American history, American history-AP, ancient history, art, Asian history, biology, biology-AP, calculus, calculus-AP, ceramics, chemistry, chemistry-AP, chorus, computer science, computer science-AP, creative writing, debate, drama, economics, economics-AP, English, English language-AP, English literature-AP, French, French-AP, geometry, government-AP, government/civics, humanities, Latin, Latin-AP, medieval/Renaissance history, music theory, photography, physical education, physics, physics-AP, psychology-AP, Spanish, Spanish-AP, speech, video film production, yearbook.

Graduation Requirements Algebra, American government, American history, arts and fine arts (art, music, dance, drama), biology, chemistry, economics, English, foreign language, geometry, physical education (includes health), physics, pre-calculus, Western civilization. Community service is required.

Special Academic Programs Advanced Placement exam preparation in 15 subject areas; honors section; academic accommodation for the gifted, the musically talented, and the artistically talented.

College Placement 70 students graduated in 2005; all went to college, including Baylor University; Southern Methodist University; Texas Christian University; The University of Texas at Austin; University of Oklahoma; Vanderbilt University. Mean SAT verbal: 628, mean SAT math: 650. 55% scored over 600 on SAT verbal, 64% scored over 600 on SAT math.

Student Life Upper grades have uniform requirement, student council, honor system. Discipline rests equally with students and faculty.

Summer Programs Enrichment, sports, art/fine arts, rigorous outdoor training programs offered; session focuses on enrichment; held both on and off campus; held at New Mexico and Colorado (backpacking); accepts boys and girls; open to students from other schools. 200 students usually enrolled. 2006 schedule: June 5 to June 16. Application deadline: May 1.

Tuition and Aid Day student tuition: $12,320. Tuition installment plan (monthly payment plans). Need-based scholarship grants, loans from bank associated with school available. In 2005–06, 9% of upper-school students received aid. Total amount of financial aid awarded in 2005–06: $230,540.

Admissions Traditional secondary-level entrance grade is 9. For fall 2005, 54 students applied for upper-level admission, 39 were accepted, 27 enrolled. CTP or ISEE required. Deadline for receipt of application materials: March 4. Application fee required: $75. Interview recommended.

Athletics Interscholastic: baseball (boys), basketball (b,g), cross-country running (b,g), field hockey (g), football (b), golf (b,g), soccer (b,g), softball (g), tennis (b,g), track and field (b,g), volleyball (b,g). 10 PE instructors, 2 trainers.

Computers Computers are regularly used in all academic classes. Computer network features include campus e-mail, on-campus library services, CD-ROMs, online commercial services, Internet access, DVD.

Contact Judith Kinser, Director of Admissions and Financial Aid. 817-321-0100. Fax: 817-321-0105. E-mail: kinserj@trinityvalleyschool.org. Web site: www.trinityvalleyschool.org.

TYLER STREET CHRISTIAN ACADEMY

915 West 9th Street
Dallas, Texas 75208
Head of School: Mrs. Karen J. Egger

General Information Coeducational day college-preparatory, general academic, arts, religious studies, and technology school, affiliated with Christian faith. Grades P3–12. Founded: 1972. Setting: urban. 5-acre campus. 2 buildings on campus. Approved or accredited by Association of Christian Schools International, Southern Association of Colleges and Schools, Texas Education Agency, Texas Private School Accreditation Commission, and Texas Department of Education. Endowment: $50,000. Total enrollment: 211. Upper school average class size: 13. Upper school faculty-student ratio: 1:10.

Upper School Student Profile Grade 9: 19 students (13 boys, 6 girls); Grade 10: 13 students (5 boys, 8 girls); Grade 11: 11 students (5 boys, 6 girls); Grade 12: 18 students (7 boys, 11 girls). 82% of students are Christian faith.

Faculty School total: 23. In upper school: 6 men, 6 women; 6 have advanced degrees.

Subjects Offered Algebra, American government, American history, art, art appreciation, art history, band, bell choir, Bible studies, biology, British literature, British

literature (honors), calculus, calculus-AP, chemistry, choir, college counseling, community service, composition, computer applications, computer keyboarding, computer literacy, concert band, CPR, economics, English literature, family living, freshman seminar, geometry, grammar, guidance, health, Holocaust studies, honors algebra, honors English, honors geometry, lab science, literature, physical education, physical science, physics, pre-calculus, Spanish, speech communications, student government, U.S. literature, world geography, world history, world literature, yearbook.

Graduation Requirements Algebra, American government, arts and fine arts (art, music, dance, drama), Bible, biology, calculus, chemistry, computer science, economics, English, geometry, physical education (includes health), physical science, physics, Spanish, speech communications, U.S. history, world geography, world history.

Special Academic Programs Advanced Placement exam preparation in 1 subject area; honors section; study at local college for college credit.

College Placement 12 students graduated in 2005; all went to college, including Baylor University; Prairie View A&M University; Texas A&M University; Texas A&M University–Commerce; University of North Texas. Mean SAT verbal: 555, mean SAT math: 515, mean composite ACT: 22.

Student Life Upper grades have uniform requirement, student council, honor system. Discipline rests primarily with faculty. Attendance at religious services is required.

Tuition and Aid Day student tuition: $5800. Tuition installment plan (FACTS Tuition Payment Plan). Merit scholarship grants, need-based scholarship grants available. In 2005–06, 66% of upper-school students received aid; total upper-school merit-scholarship money awarded: $7500. Total amount of financial aid awarded in 2005–06: $120,008.

Admissions Traditional secondary-level entrance grade is 9. For fall 2005, 32 students applied for upper-level admission, 20 were accepted, 15 enrolled. Mathematics proficiency exam, Stanford Diagnostic Test and writing sample required. Deadline for receipt of application materials: none. Application fee required: $50. On-campus interview required.

Athletics Interscholastic: basketball (boys, girls), cheering (g), football (b), track and field (b,g), volleyball (g). 1 PE instructor, 4 coaches.

Computers Computers are regularly used in desktop publishing, introduction to technology, yearbook classes. Computer network features include CD-ROMs, Internet access, office computer access.

Contact Mrs. Shirley Allen, Registrar. 214-941-9717. Fax: 214-941-0324. E-mail: info@tsca.org. Web site: www.tsca.org.

UNITED MENNONITE EDUCATIONAL INSTITUTE

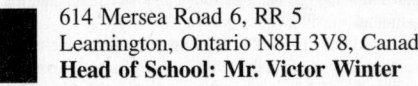

614 Mersea Road 6, RR 5
Leamington, Ontario N8H 3V8, Canada
Head of School: Mr. Victor Winter

General Information Coeducational day college-preparatory, arts, and religious studies school, affiliated with Mennonite Church USA. Grades 9–12. Founded: 1945. Setting: rural. Nearest major city is Windsor, Canada. 12-acre campus. 3 buildings on campus. Approved or accredited by Ontario Department of Education. Language of instruction: English. Total enrollment: 80. Upper school average class size: 18. Upper school faculty-student ratio: 1:15.

Upper School Student Profile Grade 9: 23 students (11 boys, 12 girls); Grade 10: 16 students (8 boys, 8 girls); Grade 11: 18 students (8 boys, 10 girls); Grade 12: 23 students (13 boys, 10 girls). 65% of students are Mennonite Church USA.

Faculty School total: 10. In upper school: 5 men, 5 women; 1 has an advanced degree.

Subjects Offered 20th century physics, advanced chemistry, advanced math, algebra, American history, ancient world history, art, Bible, biology, business studies, career exploration, chemistry, choir, choral music, Christian ethics, church history, civics, communication arts, computer applications, computer studies, computer technologies, English, environmental geography, family studies, film and new technologies, foreign language, French as a second language, German, instrumental music, introduction to theater, mathematics, orchestra, parenting, religious studies, society challenge and change, theater arts.

Graduation Requirements Arts, Canadian geography, Canadian history, careers, civics, English, French, mathematics, physical education (includes health), science.

College Placement 19 students graduated in 2005; 16 went to college. Other: 2 went to work, 1 had other specific plans.

Student Life Upper grades have specified standards of dress, student council. Discipline rests equally with students and faculty. Attendance at religious services is required.

Tuition and Aid Day student tuition: CAN$5300. Tuition installment plan (monthly payment plans). Tuition reduction for siblings, need-based scholarship grants, need-based loans available. In 2005–06, 5% of upper-school students received aid. Total amount of financial aid awarded in 2005–06: CAN$4000.

Admissions Traditional secondary-level entrance grade is 9. For fall 2005, 20 students applied for upper-level admission, 20 were accepted, 20 enrolled. Deadline for receipt of application materials: none. No application fee required.

Athletics Interscholastic: badminton (boys, girls), baseball (b,g), basketball (b,g), cross-country running (b,g), floor hockey (b,g), golf (b), softball (g), volleyball (b,g);

intramural: badminton (b,g), baseball (b,g), basketball (b,g), bicycling (b), football (b), indoor soccer (b,g), volleyball (b,g); coed intramural: skiing (downhill), ultimate Frisbee. 1 PE instructor.

Computers Computers are regularly used in all classes. Computer network features include campus e-mail, on-campus library services, CD-ROMs, Internet access, file transfer.

Contact Mr. Victor J. Winter, Principal. 519-326 7448. Fax: 519-326-0278. E-mail: umeiadmi@mnsi.net. Web site: www.umei.on.ca.

UNITED NATIONS INTERNATIONAL SCHOOL

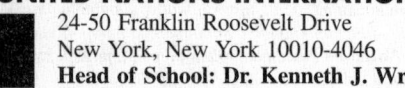

24-50 Franklin Roosevelt Drive
New York, New York 10010-4046
Head of School: Dr. Kenneth J. Wrye

General Information Coeducational day college-preparatory, ESL, and International Baccalaureate school, affiliated with United Church of Christ. Grades K–12. Founded: 1947. Setting: urban. 3-acre campus. 1 building on campus. Approved or accredited by European Council of International Schools, New York State Association of Independent Schools, and New York Department of Education. Member of National Association of Independent Schools. Languages of instruction: English, Spanish, and French. Endowment: $14.7 million. Total enrollment: 1,460. Upper school average class size: 17. Upper school faculty-student ratio: 1:10.

Upper School Student Profile Grade 9: 107 students (54 boys, 53 girls); Grade 10: 111 students (47 boys, 64 girls); Grade 11: 111 students (56 boys, 55 girls); Grade 12: 103 students (50 boys, 53 girls).

Faculty School total: 200. In upper school: 52 men, 45 women; 70 have advanced degrees.

Subjects Offered Algebra, American history, American literature, anthropology, Arabic, art, biology, calculus, chemistry, Chinese, community service, computer applications, computer science, creative writing, drama, economics, English, English literature, ESL, European history, expository writing, fine arts, French, geometry, German, history, humanities, Italian, Japanese, journalism, languages, library, mathematics, media production, modern languages, music, philosophy, photography, physical education, physics, psychology, Russian, science, social science, social studies, Spanish, theater arts, theory of knowledge, United Nations and international issues, world history, world literature, writing.

Graduation Requirements Art, electives, English, health and wellness, humanities, mathematics, modern languages, music, physical education (includes health), science, United Nations and international issues, individual project. Community service is required.

Special Academic Programs International Baccalaureate program; independent study; academic accommodation for the gifted, the musically talented, and the artistically talented; ESL (17 students enrolled).

College Placement 106 students graduated in 2005; all went to college, including Barnard College; Boston University; Duke University; McGill University; University of Virginia; Wellesley College. Median SAT verbal: 600, median SAT math: 620. 58.9% scored over 600 on SAT verbal, 68.7% scored over 600 on SAT math.

Student Life Upper grades have student council. Discipline rests primarily with faculty.

Summer Programs Enrichment, ESL, sports programs offered; session focuses on providing recreational enrichment in an international environment; held on campus; accepts boys and girls; open to students from other schools. 300 students usually enrolled. 2006 schedule: June 27 to July 29. Application deadline: May 30.

Tuition and Aid Day student tuition: $18,000–$20,000. Tuition installment plan (Key Tuition Payment Plan, monthly payment plans). Bursaries available. In 2005–06, 10% of upper-school students received aid. Total amount of financial aid awarded in 2005–06: $236,872.

Admissions Traditional secondary-level entrance grade is 9. For fall 2005, 136 students applied for upper-level admission, 52 were accepted, 38 enrolled. ISEE or SSAT required. Deadline for receipt of application materials: November 15. Application fee required: $50. On-campus interview required.

Athletics Interscholastic: baseball (boys), basketball (b,g), rhythmic gymnastics (g), soccer (b,g), softball (g), track and field (b,g), volleyball (b,g); intramural: baseball (b), rhythmic gymnastics (g), volleyball (b,g); coed interscholastic: basketball; coed intramural: aerobics, aerobics/dance, aerobics/nautilus, alpine skiing, aquatics, back packing, badminton, ballet, basketball, bicycling, canoeing/kayaking, climbing, cooperative games, dance, fencing, fitness, flag football, floor hockey, hiking/backpacking, indoor soccer, jogging, life saving, martial arts, modern dance, nautilus, outdoor activities, outdoor adventure, outdoor education, outdoor skills, outdoors, paddling, physical fitness, rock climbing, ropes courses, running, self defense, snowshoeing, soccer, softball, strength & conditioning, swimming and diving, table tennis, team handball, tennis, track and field, volleyball, weight training, wilderness, wilderness survival. 9 PE instructors, 12 coaches.

Computers Computers are regularly used in art, English, ESL, foreign language, library skills, mathematics, music, science classes. Computer network features include campus e-mail, on-campus library services, CD-ROMs, online commercial services, Internet access, file transfer, DVD, wireless campus network, media lab, TV studio, digital video streaming, digital video editing.

Contact Admissions Office. 212-584-3071. Fax: 212-685-5023. E-mail: admissions@unis.org. Web site: www.unis.org.

THE UNITED WORLD COLLEGE—USA

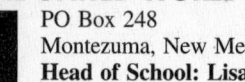

PO Box 248
Montezuma, New Mexico 87731
Head of School: Lisa Darling

General Information Coeducational boarding college-preparatory school. Grades 11–12. Founded: 1982. Setting: rural. Nearest major city is Santa Fe. Students are housed in single-sex dormitories. 100-acre campus. 20 buildings on campus. Approved or accredited by Independent Schools Association of the Southwest and New Mexico Department of Education. Endowment: $85 million. Total enrollment: 200. Upper school average class size: 12. Upper school faculty-student ratio: 1:8.

Upper School Student Profile Grade 11: 100 students (50 boys, 50 girls); Grade 12: 100 students (50 boys, 50 girls). 100% of students are boarding students. 1% are state residents. 54 states are represented in upper school student body. 75% are international students. International students from Canada, China, Italy, Mexico, Norway, and United Kingdom; 90 other countries represented in student body.

Faculty School total: 30. In upper school: 17 men, 12 women; 25 have advanced degrees; 21 reside on campus.

Subjects Offered Anthropology, art, biology, calculus, chemistry, community service, conflict resolution, economics, English, English literature, environmental science, ESL, fine arts, French, German, history, information technology, International Baccalaureate courses, mathematics, music, physics, science, social science, social studies, Spanish, theater arts, theory of knowledge, world history, world literature, world religions.

Graduation Requirements Arts and fine arts (art, music, dance, drama), foreign language, International Baccalaureate courses, literature, mathematics, science, social science, theory of knowledge, extended essay, independent research. Community service is required.

Special Academic Programs International Baccalaureate program; ESL (40 students enrolled).

College Placement 100 students graduated in 2005; 91 went to college, including Colby College; Harvard University; Macalester College; Middlebury College; Princeton University; Wellesley College. Other: 3 entered military service, 6 had other specific plans. 25% scored over 600 on SAT verbal, 75% scored over 600 on SAT math, 95% scored over 26 on composite ACT.

Student Life Upper grades have student council, honor system. Discipline rests equally with students and faculty.

Tuition and Aid 7-day tuition and room/board: $18,000. Guaranteed tuition plan. Merit scholarship grants, need-based scholarship grants, full-tuition merit scholarships to all admitted U.S. citizens available. In 2005–06, 90% of upper-school students received aid; total upper-school merit-scholarship money awarded: $1,600,000. Total amount of financial aid awarded in 2005–06: $1,600,000.

Admissions For fall 2005, 300 students applied for upper-level admission, 50 were accepted, 50 enrolled. ACT or PSAT or SAT required. Deadline for receipt of application materials: January 20. No application fee required. Interview required.

Athletics Coed Intramural: aerobics, aerobics/dance, aerobics/nautilus, alpine skiing, aquatics, back packing, badminton, ballet, basketball, billiards, canoeing/kayaking, climbing, combined training, cross-country running, dance, fitness, Frisbee, hiking/backpacking, jogging, modern dance, mountaineering, nordic skiing, outdoor activities, outdoor adventure, outdoor education, outdoor recreation, outdoor skills, outdoors, physical training, racquetball, ropes courses, running, sailing, skiing (cross-country), skiing (downhill), snowboarding, snowshoeing, soccer, softball, squash, strength & conditioning, swimming and diving, table tennis, tennis, volleyball, walking, weight lifting, weight training, wilderness, wilderness survival, yoga. 1 PE instructor, 12 trainers.

Computers Computers are regularly used in art, foreign language, mathematics, music, science classes. Computer network features include campus e-mail, on-campus library services, CD-ROMs, Internet access, file transfer, DVD.

Contact Tim Smith, Director of Admissions and University Advising. 505-454-4201. Fax: 505-454-4294. E-mail: tim.smith@uwc.net. Web site: www.uwc-usa.org.

See full description on page 1110.

UNIVERSAL ACADEMY OF FLORIDA

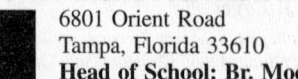

6801 Orient Road
Tampa, Florida 33610
Head of School: Br. Moosa Yahya

General Information Coeducational day college-preparatory, general academic, and religious studies school, affiliated with Muslim faith. Grades K–12. Founded: 1992. Setting: suburban. 1 building on campus. Approved or accredited by French Ministry of Education and Florida Department of Education. Languages of instruction: English and Arabic. Total enrollment: 288. Upper school average class size: 12. Upper school faculty-student ratio: 1:16.

Upper School Student Profile Grade 9: 11 students (1 boy, 10 girls); Grade 10: 6 students (3 boys, 3 girls); Grade 11: 11 students (6 boys, 5 girls); Grade 12: 20 students (9 boys, 11 girls). 100% of students are Muslim.

Faculty School total: 28. In upper school: 5 men, 11 women; 2 have advanced degrees.

Special Academic Programs Honors section; study at local college for college credit.

College Placement 14 students graduated in 2005; all went to college.

Student Life Upper grades have uniform requirement, student council, honor system. Discipline rests primarily with faculty. Attendance at religious services is required.

Tuition and Aid Guaranteed tuition plan. Tuition installment plan (SMART Tuition Payment Plan, monthly payment plans). Tuition reduction for siblings, need-based scholarship grants available. In 2005–06, 3% of upper-school students received aid.

Admissions Traditional secondary-level entrance grade is 9. For fall 2005, 3 students applied for upper-level admission, 3 were accepted, 3 enrolled. Deadline for receipt of application materials: none. Application fee required: $50. Interview required.

Athletics Interscholastic: aerobics (girls), archery (b,g), basketball (b,g), field hockey (b,g), fitness walking (b,g), flag football (b), marksmanship (b,g), physical fitness (b,g), soccer (b,g), track and field (b,g), volleyball (b,g), walking (b,g), yoga (g). 2 PE instructors.

Computers Computer network features include on-campus library services, CD-ROMs, online commercial services, Internet access, DVD.

Contact Sr. Nafeesah Abdurrashid, Registrar. 813-664-0695 Ext. 108. Fax: 813-664-4506. E-mail: nafeesah.abdurrashid@uaftampa.org. Web site: www.uaftampa.org/home.asp.

UNIVERSITY LAKE SCHOOL

4024 Nagawicka Road
Hartland, Wisconsin 53029
Head of School: Mr. Bradley F. Ashley

General Information Coeducational day college-preparatory, arts, business, and technology school. Grades JK–12. Founded: 1956. Setting: small town. Nearest major city is Milwaukee. 180-acre campus. 5 buildings on campus. Approved or accredited by Independent Schools Association of the Central States. Member of National Association of Independent Schools. Endowment: $12.2 million. Total enrollment: 349. Upper school average class size: 12. Upper school faculty-student ratio: 1:9.

Upper School Student Profile Grade 9: 25 students (14 boys, 11 girls); Grade 10: 17 students (10 boys, 7 girls); Grade 11: 36 students (19 boys, 17 girls); Grade 12: 18 students (9 boys, 9 girls).

Faculty School total: 44. In upper school: 11 men, 10 women; 11 have advanced degrees.

Subjects Offered Algebra, American history, American literature, art, biology, business skills, calculus, chemistry, cinematography, computer science, creative writing, design, drama, English, English literature, environmental science, fine arts, French, geometry, government/civics, journalism, mathematics, music, photography, physical education, physics, science, social studies, Spanish, speech, statistics, theater, video film production, Web site design, world history, world literature, writing.

Graduation Requirements Art, arts and fine arts (art, music, dance, drama), computer science, English, foreign language, literature, mathematics, physical education (includes health), science, social studies (includes history), speech.

Special Academic Programs Advanced Placement exam preparation in 9 subject areas; honors section; accelerated programs; independent study; study at local college for college credit; academic accommodation for the gifted; remedial reading and/or remedial writing.

College Placement 25 students graduated in 2005; 24 went to college, including Boston University; Colby College; Cornell University; Dartmouth College; The George Washington University; University of Wisconsin–Madison. Other: 1 went to work. Mean SAT verbal: 585, mean SAT math: 551, mean composite ACT: 24.

Student Life Upper grades have specified standards of dress, student council, honor system. Discipline rests equally with students and faculty.

Summer Programs Remediation, enrichment, sports, art/fine arts, computer instruction programs offered; session focuses on academics, arts, and athletics; held on campus; accepts boys and girls; open to students from other schools. 500 students usually enrolled. 2006 schedule: June 12 to August 5. Application deadline: May 31.

Tuition and Aid Day student tuition: $12,670. Tuition installment plan (FACTS Tuition Payment Plan, monthly payment plans). Merit scholarship grants, need-based scholarship grants available. In 2005–06, 31% of upper-school students received aid; total upper-school merit-scholarship money awarded: $38,000. Total amount of financial aid awarded in 2005–06: $322,395.

Admissions Traditional secondary-level entrance grade is 9. For fall 2005, 19 students applied for upper-level admission, 17 were accepted, 15 enrolled. Admissions testing, Kuhlmann-Anderson and Kuhlmann-Anderson Level G (for grades 7-9) or Level H (for grades 10-12) required. Deadline for receipt of application materials: none. Application fee required: $25. On-campus interview recommended.

Athletics Interscholastic: basketball (boys, girls), field hockey (g), skiing (downhill) (b,g), soccer (b,g), softball (b,g), tennis (b,g), volleyball (g); coed interscholastic: cross-country running, golf; coed intramural: alpine skiing, volleyball. 2 PE instructors, 7 coaches.

Computers Computers are regularly used in all classes. Computer network features include campus e-mail, on-campus library services, CD-ROMs, Internet access, wireless campus network.

Contact Mrs. Debra H. Smith, Director of Admissions. 262-367-6011 Ext. 1455. Fax: 262-367-3146. E-mail: dsmith@universitylake.org. Web site: www.universitylake.org.

UNIVERSITY LIGGETT SCHOOL

1045 Cook Road
Grosse Pointe Woods, Michigan 48236
Head of School: Mr. Matthew H. Hanly

General Information Coeducational day college-preparatory, arts, and technology school. Grades PK–12. Founded: 1878. Setting: suburban. Nearest major city is Detroit. 50-acre campus. 4 buildings on campus. Approved or accredited by Association of Christian Schools International and Independent Schools Association of the Central States. Member of National Association of Independent Schools. Endowment: $43 million. Total enrollment: 624. Upper school average class size: 16. Upper school faculty-student ratio: 1:9.

Upper School Student Profile Grade 9: 63 students (31 boys, 32 girls); Grade 10: 64 students (28 boys, 36 girls); Grade 11: 65 students (34 boys, 31 girls); Grade 12: 43 students (26 boys, 17 girls).

Faculty School total: 94. In upper school: 24 men, 12 women; 36 have advanced degrees.

Subjects Offered Algebra, American history, American literature, art, art history, biology, calculus, ceramics, chemistry, creative writing, drama, engineering, English, English literature, European history, fine arts, French, geology, geometry, government/civics, Latin, mathematics, photography, physical education, physics, physiology, science, social studies, Spanish, technology, theater, world history.

Graduation Requirements Algebra, arts and fine arts (art, music, dance, drama), biology, chemistry, computer science, English, foreign language, geometry, government, mathematics, physical education (includes health), science, U.S. history, world history. Community service is required.

Special Academic Programs Advanced Placement exam preparation in 14 subject areas; honors section; independent study; term-away projects; study abroad; academic accommodation for the gifted, the musically talented, and the artistically talented.

College Placement 61 students graduated in 2005; all went to college, including Albion College; Kalamazoo College; Michigan State University; University of Michigan. Mean SAT verbal: 600, mean SAT math: 567, mean composite ACT: 25. 51% scored over 600 on SAT verbal, 44% scored over 600 on SAT math.

Student Life Upper grades have specified standards of dress, student council, honor system. Discipline rests primarily with faculty.

Summer Programs Remediation, enrichment programs offered; session focuses on SAT preparation ; held on campus; accepts boys and girls; open to students from other schools. 30 students usually enrolled. 2006 schedule: June 26 to August 4. Application deadline: May 31.

Tuition and Aid Day student tuition: $16,990–$17,610. Tuition installment plan (Insured Tuition Payment Plan, monthly payment plans, individually arranged payment plans, 2- and 4-payment plans). Merit scholarship grants, need-based scholarship grants, scholarships for children of alumni available. In 2005–06, 30% of upper-school students received aid; total upper-school merit-scholarship money awarded: $108,500. Total amount of financial aid awarded in 2005–06: $790,430.

Admissions Traditional secondary-level entrance grade is 9. For fall 2005, 47 students applied for upper-level admission, 34 were accepted, 24 enrolled. ERB CTP III or SSAT required. Deadline for receipt of application materials: none. Application fee required: $50. Interview required.

Athletics Interscholastic: aerobics/dance (girls), baseball (b), basketball (b,g), field hockey (g), football (b), golf (b), ice hockey (b,g), lacrosse (b,g), soccer (b,g), softball (g), tennis (b,g), volleyball (g); coed interscholastic: swimming and diving; coed intramural: ultimate Frisbee, weight lifting. 4 PE instructors, 15 coaches, 1 trainer.

Computers Computers are regularly used in all academic classes. Computer network features include campus e-mail, on-campus library services, CD-ROMs, online commercial services, Internet access.

Contact Mrs. Denise Deane, Associate Director of Admissions. 313-884-4444 Ext. 216. Fax: 313-884-1775. E-mail: ddeane@uls.org. Web site: www.uls.org.

UNIVERSITY OF CHICAGO LABORATORY SCHOOLS

1362 East 59th Street
Chicago, Illinois 60637
Head of School: Dr. David W. Magill

petersons.com

General Information Coeducational day college-preparatory school. Grades N–12. Founded: 1896. Setting: urban. 11-acre campus. 3 buildings on campus. Approved or accredited by Independent Schools Association of the Central States, North Central Association of Colleges and Schools, and Illinois Department of Education. Member of National Association of Independent Schools. Endowment: $10.1 million. Total enrollment: 1,731. Upper school average class size: 20. Upper school faculty-student ratio: 1:10.

Upper School Student Profile Grade 9: 131 students (63 boys, 68 girls); Grade 10: 129 students (53 boys, 76 girls); Grade 11: 115 students (57 boys, 58 girls); Grade 12: 129 students (54 boys, 75 girls).

Faculty School total: 216. In upper school: 26 men, 35 women; 42 have advanced degrees.

Subjects Offered Acting, African-American history, algebra, American history, art, art history-AP, biology, biology-AP, calculus, calculus-AP, chemistry, chemistry-AP,

community service, computer science, creative writing, drama, drawing, driver education, economics-AP, English, English literature, European history, European history-AP, expository writing, fine arts, French, French-AP, geometry, German, German-AP, government/civics, history, journalism, Latin, mathematics, music, music theory-AP, photography, physical education, physics, physics-AP, science, sculpture, social studies, Spanish, Spanish-AP, statistics, statistics-AP, theater, trigonometry, U.S. history-AP, world history, writing.

Graduation Requirements Arts and fine arts (art, music, dance, drama), English, foreign language, mathematics, music, physical education (includes health), science, social studies (includes history). Community service is required.

Special Academic Programs Advanced Placement exam preparation in 15 subject areas; accelerated programs; independent study; study at local college for college credit.

College Placement 113 students graduated in 2005; 112 went to college, including Harvard University; New York University; Northwestern University; The George Washington University; University of Illinois at Urbana–Champaign; University of Michigan. Other: 1 entered military service. Median SAT verbal: 672, median SAT math: 684, median composite ACT: 29. 80% scored over 600 on SAT verbal, 75% scored over 600 on SAT math, 75% scored over 26 on composite ACT.

Student Life Upper grades have student council. Discipline rests primarily with faculty.

Summer Programs Enrichment, advancement programs offered; session focuses on advancement of placement in courses; held on campus; accepts boys and girls; open to students from other schools. 200 students usually enrolled. 2006 schedule: June 19 to July 28. Application deadline: May 15.

Tuition and Aid Day student tuition: $18,393. Tuition installment plan (monthly payment plans, quarterly payment plan). Need-based scholarship grants available. In 2005–06, 12% of upper-school students received aid. Total amount of financial aid awarded in 2005–06: $465,760.

Admissions Traditional secondary-level entrance grade is 9. For fall 2005, 161 students applied for upper-level admission, 69 were accepted, 50 enrolled. ISEE required. Deadline for receipt of application materials: December 1. Application fee required: $75. On-campus interview required.

Athletics Interscholastic: baseball (boys), basketball (b,g), cross-country running (b,g), indoor track & field (b,g), soccer (b,g), swimming and diving (b,g), tennis (b,g), track and field (b,g), volleyball (g), winter (indoor) track (b,g); intramural: dance squad (g), weight training (b,g); coed interscholastic: cross-country running, golf; coed intramural: fencing, life saving. 12 PE instructors, 25 coaches, 1 trainer.

Computers Computers are regularly used in mathematics, music, newspaper, science, yearbook classes. Computer network features include on-campus library services, CD-ROMs, Internet access, office computer access, DVD, wireless campus network.

Contact D. Michael Veitch, Director of Admissions. 773-702-9451. Fax: 773-702-7455. E-mail: mveitch@ucls.uchicago.edu. Web site: www.ucls.uchicago.edu/.

ANNOUNCEMENT FROM THE SCHOOL Students at the University of Chicago Laboratory Schools take advantage of many opportunities available at the University of Chicago, where they may study world history with museum materials, receive library privileges at the University libraries, work with professors on research, and enroll as high school students in University courses.

UNIVERSITY OF DETROIT JESUIT HIGH SCHOOL AND ACADEMY

8400 South Cambridge Avenue
Detroit, Michigan 48221
Head of School: Mrs. Susan Rowe

General Information Boys' day college-preparatory school, affiliated with Roman Catholic Church (Jesuit order). Grades 7–12. Founded: 1877. Setting: urban. 14-acre campus. 1 building on campus. Approved or accredited by Jesuit Secondary Education Association, North Central Association of Colleges and Schools, and Michigan Department of Education. Endowment: $8 million. Total enrollment: 908. Upper school average class size: 23. Upper school faculty-student ratio: 1:15.

Upper School Student Profile Grade 9: 208 students (208 boys); Grade 10: 187 students (187 boys); Grade 11: 190 students (190 boys); Grade 12: 203 students (203 boys). 70% of students are Roman Catholic Church (Jesuit order).

Faculty School total: 51. In upper school: 37 men, 14 women; 32 have advanced degrees.

Subjects Offered Acting, African-American history, algebra, American history, American literature, art, Bible studies, biology, calculus, ceramics, chemistry, comparative religion, computer applications, computer programming, earth science, English, English literature, environmental science, ethics, European history, expository writing, French, geography, geometry, government/civics, history, Latin, mathematics, music, physical education, physics, psychology, public speaking, religion, science, social studies, sociology, Spanish, speech, theology, trigonometry, world history, world literature, writing.

Graduation Requirements Arts and fine arts (art, music, dance, drama), business skills (includes word processing), English, foreign language, mathematics, physical

education (includes health), public speaking, religion (includes Bible studies and theology), science, social studies (includes history), Senior Community Service Program.

Special Academic Programs Advanced Placement exam preparation in 7 subject areas; honors section; independent study.

College Placement 193 students graduated in 2005; 192 went to college, including Loyola University Chicago; Michigan State University; University of Dayton; University of Michigan; University of Notre Dame. Other: 1 had other specific plans. Mean SAT verbal: 594, mean SAT math: 590, mean composite ACT: 25.

Student Life Upper grades have specified standards of dress, student council. Discipline rests primarily with faculty. Attendance at religious services is required.

Summer Programs Remediation programs offered; held on campus; accepts boys and girls; open to students from other schools. 130 students usually enrolled. 2006 schedule: June 21 to July 23.

Tuition and Aid Day student tuition: $8300. Tuition installment plan (FACTS Tuition Payment Plan). Merit scholarship grants, need-based scholarship grants available. In 2005–06, 32% of upper-school students received aid; total upper-school merit-scholarship money awarded: $43,750. Total amount of financial aid awarded in 2005–06: $1,100,000.

Admissions Traditional secondary-level entrance grade is 9. For fall 2005, 600 students applied for upper-level admission, 400 were accepted, 208 enrolled. Catholic High School Entrance Examination required. Deadline for receipt of application materials: none. No application fee required.

Athletics Interscholastic: baseball, basketball, bowling, cross-country running, diving, football, golf, ice hockey, lacrosse, skiing (downhill), soccer, swimming and diving, tennis, track and field, wrestling; intramural: basketball, flag football, soccer. 2 PE instructors, 15 coaches, 2 trainers.

Computers Computers are regularly used in history, mathematics, science, speech classes. Computer network features include campus e-mail, on-campus library services, CD-ROMs, online commercial services, Internet access.

Contact Mr. Patrick T. Cleary, Director of Admissions. 313-862-5400 Ext. 2309. Fax: 313-862-3299. E-mail: patrick.cleary@uofdhigh.k12.mi.us. Web site: www.uofdjesuit.org/.

UNIVERSITY OF MIAMI ONLINE HIGH SCHOOL

16614 Saddleclub Road
Weston, Florida 33326
Head of School: Howard Adam Liebman, PhD

General Information Coeducational day college-preparatory school. Grades 8–12. Founded: 2001. Setting: suburban. Approved or accredited by CITA (Commission on International and Trans-Regional Accreditation), Southern Association of Colleges and Schools, and Florida Department of Education. Total enrollment: 450. Upper school average class size: 25. Upper school faculty-student ratio: 1:14.

Faculty School total: 22. In upper school: 6 men, 16 women; 14 have advanced degrees.

Subjects Offered Advanced Placement courses, algebra, American government, American government-AP, American history, American history-AP, American literature, American literature-AP, art history, biology, biology-AP, British literature, British literature (honors), British literature-AP, business technology, chemistry, chemistry-AP, computer applications, earth and space science, economics, emerging technology, English, English language and composition-AP, English literature and composition-AP, English literature-AP, French, geometry, health, honors algebra, language, life management skills, marine science, mathematics, mathematics-AP, physical education, physical fitness, physics, pre-algebra, pre-calculus, psychology, SAT preparation, science, Spanish, U.S. history, world history.

Graduation Requirements American government, American history, American literature, biology, British literature, chemistry, economics, electives, English literature, foreign language, general science, life management skills, performing arts, personal fitness, physical education (includes health), world history, world literature.

Special Academic Programs Advanced Placement exam preparation; honors section; accelerated programs; independent study; term-away projects.

College Placement 34 students graduated in 2005; 23 went to college, including University of Miami; University of Michigan; University of Oregon; University of South Carolina; University of Virginia; Wake Forest University. Other: 11 had other specific plans.

Student Life Upper grades have honor system. Discipline rests primarily with faculty.

Summer Programs Enrichment, ESL, sports, art/fine arts, computer instruction programs offered; held on campus; accepts boys and girls; open to students from other schools. 450 students usually enrolled. 2006 schedule: May 1 to July 15.

Tuition and Aid Day student tuition: $6250. Tuition installment plan (monthly payment plans, individually arranged payment plans). Need-based scholarship grants available.

Admissions Traditional secondary-level entrance grade is 9. For fall 2005, 457 students applied for upper-level admission, 364 were accepted, 304 enrolled. Deadline for receipt of application materials: none. Application fee required: $100. Interview recommended.

Athletics Interscholastic: baseball (boys), basketball (b,g), flag football (b), golf (b,g), softball (g), tennis (b,g), volleyball (g); coed intramural: aerobics, aquatics. 1 PE instructor.

Computers Computers are regularly used in all classes.

Contact Mrs. Wendy Kauffman, Admissions Coordinator. 305-689-8641. Fax: 954-349-3490. E-mail: wkauffman@umohs.org. Web site: www.umohs.org.

UNIVERSITY OF MISSOURI—COLUMBIA HIGH SCHOOL

136 Clark Hall
Columbia, Missouri 65211
Head of School: Ms. Kristi D. Smalley

General Information Coeducational day college-preparatory, general academic, and distance learning school. Grades 9–12. Founded: 1999. Setting: small town. Nearest major city is St. Louis. Approved or accredited by Missouri Independent School Association and North Central Association of Colleges and Schools.

Subjects Offered 20th century American writers, 20th century physics, 20th century world history, 3-dimensional art, accounting, adolescent issues, advanced math, Advanced Placement courses, aerospace science, African-American literature, algebra, American history, ancient world history, art, art appreciation, astronomy, basic language skills, Basic programming, biology, business applications, business mathematics, business skills, business studies, career exploration, career planning, career/college preparation, careers, character education, chemistry, child development, civics, college planning, communication arts, comparative politics, comparative religion, computer applications, computer literacy, computer programming, conservation, consumer education, consumer mathematics, contemporary history, contemporary issues, contemporary math, creative writing, decision making skills, economics, English, English literature and composition-AP, entrepreneurship, environmental science, European literature, family and consumer sciences, family living, family studies, female experience in America, fiction, film and literature, fitness, food and nutrition, French, general science, geography, geology, geometry, German, government, grammar, health and wellness, history, independent study, integrated mathematics, interpersonal skills, Japanese, keyboarding, language, language arts, Latin, law and the legal system, literature, literature by women, math applications, mathematics, media studies, medieval history, modern history, modern world history, music appreciation, mythology, newspaper, North American literature, novels, parent/child development, personal and social education, personal development, personal fitness, personal money management, photography, poetry, political science, pre-algebra, pre-calculus, psychology, reading/study skills, religious studies, science fiction, Shakespeare, short story, skills for success, social studies, sociology, Spanish, state history, statistics, study skills, trigonometry, U.S. constitutional history, U.S. government and politics, U.S. literature, women's literature, world geography, world religions, writing skills.

Graduation Requirements Missouri Department of Elementary & Secondary Education requirements.

Special Academic Programs Advanced Placement exam preparation in 1 subject area; accelerated programs; independent study; academic accommodation for the gifted; remedial reading and/or remedial writing.

College Placement 69 students graduated in 2005.

Admissions Deadline for receipt of application materials: none. Application fee required: $25.

Computers Computers are regularly used in accounting, aerospace science, art, business, business applications, business education, business skills, business studies, career education, career exploration, classics, college planning, computer applications, creative writing, current events, digital applications, economics, English, foreign language, French, French as a second language, geography, health, historical foundations for arts, history, humanities, independent study, information technology, journalism, keyboarding, language development, Latin, life skills, mathematics, media, music, news writing, occupational education, photography, programming, psychology, reading, religious studies, research skills, science, social sciences, social studies, Spanish, study skills, theater, theater arts, typing, writing, writing classes. Computer resources include INET Library, Britannica Online School Edition.

Contact Alicia Bixby, Counselor. 800-609-3727. Fax: 573-882-6808. E-mail: cdis@missouri.edu. Web site: cdis.missouri.edu/.

UNIVERSITY OF TORONTO SCHOOLS

371 Bloor Street West
Toronto, Ontario M5S 2R8, Canada
Head of School: Mr. Ron Mintz

General Information Coeducational day college-preparatory, arts, bilingual studies, and liberal arts and sciences school. Grades 7–12. Founded: 1910. Setting: urban. 3-acre campus. 1 building on campus. Approved or accredited by National Independent Private Schools Association, Ontario Ministry of Education, and Ontario Department of Education. Candidate for accreditation by North Central Association

of Colleges and Schools. Language of instruction: English. Endowment: CAN$700,000. Total enrollment: 619. Upper school average class size: 24. Upper school faculty-student ratio: 1:11.

Upper School Student Profile Grade 9: 105 students (55 boys, 50 girls); Grade 10: 108 students (57 boys, 51 girls); Grade 11: 100 students (50 boys, 50 girls); Grade 12: 90 students (46 boys, 44 girls).

Faculty School total: 60. In upper school: 28 men, 32 women; 38 have advanced degrees.

Subjects Offered 20th century history, Advanced Placement courses, American history, ancient world history, art, biology, calculus, Canadian geography, Canadian history, Canadian literature, career education, chemistry, chemistry-AP, civics, economics, English, English literature, European history, French, general science, geometry, German, history, Latin, law, mathematics, philosophy, physical education, physics, science, Spanish, studio art, visual arts, world history, world issues.

Graduation Requirements Arts, business studies, Canadian geography, Canadian history, career education, civics, computer studies, English, French, mathematics, physical education (includes health), science, 40 hours of community service, literacy test, additional language and physical education courses.

Special Academic Programs Advanced Placement exam preparation in 1 subject area; honors section; independent study; study abroad; academic accommodation for the gifted.

College Placement 94 students graduated in 2005; they went to McGill University; McMaster University; Queen's University at Kingston; The University of Western Ontario; University of Toronto; University of Waterloo. Other: 91 entered a postgraduate year, 3 had other specific plans.

Student Life Upper grades have student council, honor system. Discipline rests primarily with faculty.

Tuition and Aid Day student tuition: CAN$11,375. Tuition installment plan (monthly payment plans, 2-installment plan). Bursaries available. In 2005–06, 15% of upper-school students received aid. Total amount of financial aid awarded in 2005–06: CAN$700,000.

Admissions Traditional secondary-level entrance grade is 9. School's own test and SSAT required. Deadline for receipt of application materials: March 1. Application fee required: CAN$100. Interview required.

Athletics Interscholastic: aerobics (boys, girls), aerobics/dance (b,g), aquatics (b,g), badminton (b,g), ball hockey (b,g), baseball (b,g), basketball (b,g), broomball (b,g), combined training (b,g), cooperative games (b,g), cross-country running (b,g), curling (b,g), field hockey (g), fitness (b,g), flag football (b,g), floor hockey (b,g), football (b,g), Frisbee (b,g), golf (b,g), handball (b,g), hockey (b), ice hockey (b), independent competitive sports (b,g), indoor hockey (b,g), indoor track (b,g), indoor track & field (b,g), jogging (b,g), jump rope (b,g), lacrosse (b,g), life saving (b,g), outdoor activities (b,g), outdoor adventure (b,g), outdoor education (b,g), outdoor recreation (b,g), outdoor skills (b,g), outdoors (b,g), physical fitness (b,g), physical training (b,g), rugby (b,g), running (b,g), skiing (cross-country) (b,g), soccer (b,g), softball (g), strength & conditioning (b,g), swimming and diving (b,g), table tennis (b,g), tennis (b,g), touch football (b,g), track and field (b,g), ultimate Frisbee (b,g), volleyball (b,g), walking (b,g), water polo (b,g), weight lifting (b,g), weight training (b,g), wilderness (b,g), wilderness survival (b,g), wrestling (b,g), yoga (b,g); intramural: aerobics/nautilus (b,g), aquatics (b,g), badminton (b,g), ball hockey (b,g), basketball (b,g), cross-country running (b,g), fitness (b,g), floor hockey (b,g), nautilus (b,g), outdoor activities (b,g), outdoor adventure (b,g), outdoor education (b,g), outdoor recreation (b,g), outdoor skills (b,g), outdoors (b,g), physical fitness (b,g), physical training (b,g), power lifting (b,g), strength & conditioning (b,g), swimming and diving (b,g), table tennis (b,g), volleyball (b,g), weight lifting (b,g), weight training (b,g), wilderness (b,g), wilderness survival (b,g), wildernessways (b,g); coed interscholastic: aerobics, aerobics/dance, aquatics, badminton, ball hockey, basketball, broomball, combined training, cooperative games, cross-country running, curling, fitness, flag football, floor hockey, football, Frisbee, golf, handball, independent competitive sports, indoor hockey, indoor track, indoor track & field, jogging, jump rope, lacrosse, life saving, outdoor activities, outdoor adventure, outdoor education, outdoor recreation, outdoor skills, outdoors, physical fitness, physical training, rugby, running, skiing (cross-country), soccer, strength & conditioning, swimming and diving, table tennis, tennis, touch football, track and field, ultimate Frisbee, volleyball, walking, water polo, weight lifting, weight training, wilderness, wilderness survival, wrestling, yoga; coed intramural: aerobics/nautilus, aquatics, badminton, ball hockey, basketball, climbing, cross-country running, fitness, floor hockey, hiking/backpacking, nautilus, outdoor activities, outdoor adventure, outdoor education, outdoor recreation, outdoor skills, outdoors, physical fitness, physical training, power lifting, strength & conditioning, swimming and diving, table tennis, volleyball, weight lifting, weight training, wilderness, wilderness survival, wildernessways. 5 PE instructors, 30 coaches.

Computers Computers are regularly used in all academic classes. Computer resources include campus e-mail, on-campus library services, CD-ROMs, Internet access, file transfer, DVD.

Contact Ms. Kristine Maitland, Admissions Secretary. 416-946-7995. Fax: 416-978-6775. E-mail: kmaitland@uts.utoronto.ca. Web site: www.uts.utoronto.ca.

UNIVERSITY PREP

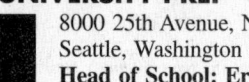

8000 25th Avenue, NE
Seattle, Washington 98115
Head of School: Erica L. Hamlin

petersons.com

General Information Coeducational day college-preparatory school. Grades 6–12. Founded: 1976. Setting: urban. 6-acre campus. 5 buildings on campus. Approved or accredited by Northwest Association of Schools and Colleges, Pacific Northwest Association of Independent Schools, and Washington Department of Education. Member of National Association of Independent Schools. Endowment: $2.3 million. Total enrollment: 462. Upper school average class size: 16. Upper school faculty-student ratio: 1:9.

Upper School Student Profile Grade 9: 81 students (41 boys, 40 girls); Grade 10: 60 students (30 boys, 30 girls); Grade 11: 61 students (34 boys, 27 girls); Grade 12: 63 students (34 boys, 29 girls).

Faculty School total: 58. In upper school: 13 men, 15 women; 28 have advanced degrees.

Subjects Offered 3-dimensional art, advanced chemistry, advanced math, algebra, American history, American literature, art, art history, Asian literature, astronomy, band, biology, British literature, calculus, chemistry, civil rights, classical civilization, community service, comparative religion, computer art, computer science, conceptual physics, creative writing, dance, decision making skills, digital art, drafting, drama, drama performance, dramatic arts, drawing, ecology, economics, English, English literature, ensembles, European history, expository writing, film studies, fine arts, French, geography, geometry, government/civics, history, history of religion, independent study, information technology, introduction to technology, Japanese, Japanese history, Japanese studies, jazz ensemble, jewelry making, journalism, Latin American studies, life skills, literary magazine, mathematics, medieval/Renaissance history, minority studies, music, music theory, Pacific Northwest seminar, painting, philosophy, photography, physical education, physics, poetry, programming, psychology, public policy, Russian studies, science, senior thesis, social justice, Spanish, stagecraft, student publications, theater, trigonometry, vocal ensemble, Web site design, women in society, world literature, yearbook.

Graduation Requirements American history, arts and fine arts (art, music, dance, drama), biology, chemistry, English, foreign language, life skills, mathematics, Pacific Northwest seminar, physical education (includes health), physics, science, senior thesis, social studies (includes history). Community service is required.

Special Academic Programs Advanced Placement exam preparation in 7 subject areas; independent study; study abroad; special instructional classes for college-bound students with high intellectual potential who have diagnosed specific learning disability.

College Placement 58 students graduated in 2005; all went to college, including Kenyon College; Pomona College; Santa Clara University; Trinity College; University of Washington; Western Washington University.

Student Life Upper grades have student council, honor system. Discipline rests equally with students and faculty.

Tuition and Aid Day student tuition: $19,911. Tuition installment plan (Key Tuition Payment Plan, Dewar Tuition Insurance Plan). Need-based scholarship grants available. In 2005–06, 18% of upper-school students received aid. Total amount of financial aid awarded in 2005–06: $631,254.

Admissions Traditional secondary-level entrance grade is 9. For fall 2005, 182 students applied for upper-level admission, 84 were accepted, 26 enrolled. ISEE required. Deadline for receipt of application materials: January 19. Application fee required: $60. On-campus interview required.

Athletics Interscholastic: baseball (boys), basketball (b,g), cross-country running (b,g), soccer (b,g), softball (g), tennis (b,g), track and field (b,g), volleyball (g); intramural: ultimate Frisbee (b,g); coed intramural: skiing (downhill), ultimate Frisbee. 5 PE instructors, 38 coaches.

Computers Computers are regularly used in English, foreign language, history, information technology, journalism, mathematics, music, science, technology, Web site design, yearbook classes. Computer network features include campus e-mail, on-campus library services, CD-ROMs, online commercial services, Internet access, file transfer.

Contact Roger D. Cibella, Director of Admission. 206-523-6407. Fax: 206-525-5320. E-mail: rcibella@universityprep.org. Web site: www.universityprep.org.

ANNOUNCEMENT FROM THE SCHOOL University Prep is committed to developing each student's potential to become an intellectually courageous, socially responsible citizen of the world. The curriculum is designed to inspire students' natural curiosity and to instill within them the desire for lifelong learning. Small classes, exceptional teachers, and innovative course work challenge students to develop creativity and critical-thinking skills. University Prep students learn to solve problems and make mature decisions, as well as learn the value of diversity and the importance of giving back to their community.

UNIVERSITY SCHOOL

2785 SOM Center Road
Hunting Valley, Ohio 44022
Head of School: Mr. Stephen S. Murray

General Information Boys' day college-preparatory, arts, business, and technology school. Grades K–12. Founded: 1890. Setting: suburban. Nearest major city is Cleveland. 220-acre campus. 1 building on campus. Approved or accredited by Independent Schools Association of the Central States and Ohio Association of Independent Schools. Member of National Association of Independent Schools. Endowment: $54 million. Total enrollment: 869. Upper school average class size: 14. Upper school faculty-student ratio: 1:15.

Upper School Student Profile Grade 9: 109 students (109 boys); Grade 10: 97 students (97 boys); Grade 11: 99 students (99 boys); Grade 12: 99 students (99 boys).

Faculty School total: 137. In upper school: 54 men, 15 women; 53 have advanced degrees.

Subjects Offered Advanced math, algebra, American history, American literature, art, art history, biology, calculus, ceramics, chemistry, computer animation, computer graphics, computer programming, computer science, computer-aided design, CPR, digital photography, drama, earth science, ecology, economics, engineering, English, English language-AP, English literature, English literature-AP, environmental science, ethics, European history, filmmaking, fine arts, French, geometry, government/civics, Greek, health, history, history-AP, Latin, mathematics, mathematics-AP, music, orchestra, philosophy, photography, physical education, physics, psychology, science, social studies, Spanish, theater, trigonometry, woodworking, world history, writing.

Graduation Requirements Arts and fine arts (art, music, dance, drama), English, foreign language, history, mathematics, physical education (includes health), science.

Special Academic Programs Advanced Placement exam preparation in 13 subject areas; honors section; independent study; term-away projects; study at local college for college credit; study abroad; academic accommodation for the gifted, the musically talented, and the artistically talented.

College Placement 89 students graduated in 2005; all went to college, including Boston College; Case Western Reserve University; Elon University; Miami University; Ohio University; Yale University. Mean SAT verbal: 642, mean SAT math: 654, mean composite ACT: 27. 42% scored over 600 on SAT verbal, 42% scored over 600 on SAT math, 50% scored over 26 on composite ACT.

Student Life Upper grades have specified standards of dress, student council, honor system. Discipline rests equally with students and faculty.

Summer Programs Remediation, enrichment, computer instruction programs offered; session focuses on academic enrichment; held on campus; accepts boys and girls; open to students from other schools. 200 students usually enrolled. 2006 schedule: June 12 to July 21. Application deadline: none.

Tuition and Aid Day student tuition: $17,740–$19,165. Tuition installment plan (Academic Management Services Plan, Key Tuition Payment Plan). Need-based scholarship grants available. In 2005–06, 28% of upper-school students received aid. Total amount of financial aid awarded in 2005–06: $1,424,300.

Admissions Traditional secondary-level entrance grade is 9. For fall 2005, 79 students applied for upper-level admission, 61 were accepted, 34 enrolled. ISEE required. Deadline for receipt of application materials: none. No application fee required. On-campus interview required.

Athletics Interscholastic: baseball, basketball, cross-country running, football, golf, ice hockey, lacrosse, soccer, swimming and diving, tennis, track and field, wrestling; intramural: skiing (downhill), soccer, swimming and diving, tennis, volleyball. 5 coaches, 1 trainer.

Computers Computers are regularly used in animation, art, drafting, engineering, graphics, photography, science, yearbook classes. Computer network features include campus e-mail, on-campus library services, CD-ROMs, Internet access, file transfer, office computer access, DVD, wireless campus network.

Contact Mr. David V. Stewart, Director of Admissions, Upper School. 216-831-2200 Ext. 7350. Fax: 216-292-7810. E-mail: dstewart@us.edu. Web site: www.us.edu.

UNIVERSITY SCHOOL OF MILWAUKEE

2100 West Fairy Chasm Road
Milwaukee, Wisconsin 53217
Head of School: Ward J. Ghory, EdD

petersons.com

General Information Coeducational day college-preparatory, arts, and technology school. Grades PK–12. Founded: 1851. Setting: suburban. 127-acre campus. 2 buildings on campus. Approved or accredited by Independent Schools Association of the Central States and Wisconsin Department of Education. Member of National Association of Independent Schools and Secondary School Admission Test Board. Endowment: $48 million. Total enrollment: 1,046. Upper school average class size: 17. Upper school faculty-student ratio: 1:9.

Upper School Student Profile Grade 9: 88 students (54 boys, 34 girls); Grade 10: 85 students (45 boys, 40 girls); Grade 11: 91 students (43 boys, 48 girls); Grade 12: 89 students (49 boys, 40 girls).

Faculty School total: 104. In upper school: 21 men, 15 women; 28 have advanced degrees.

Subjects Offered Algebra, American history, American literature, art, art history, band, biology, calculus, chemistry, computer programming, computer science, concert

choir, discrete math, drama, drawing, economics, English, English literature, European history, expository writing, French, geometry, health, Latin, mathematics, music, orchestra, painting, photography, physical education, physics, printmaking, psychology, SAT/ACT preparation, sculpture, Spanish, statistics, theater, world history, world literature.

Graduation Requirements Arts and fine arts (art, music, dance, drama), English, foreign language, history, mathematics, physical education (includes health), science, 40 hours of community service.

Special Academic Programs Advanced Placement exam preparation in 19 subject areas; honors section; independent study; study at local college for college credit.

College Placement 85 students graduated in 2005; 84 went to college, including Boston College; Georgetown University; Lawrence University; Miami University; University of Wisconsin–Madison; Washington University in St. Louis. Other: 1 had other specific plans. Mean SAT verbal: 645, mean SAT math: 649, mean composite ACT: 28. 63% scored over 600 on SAT verbal, 67% scored over 600 on SAT math, 67% scored over 26 on composite ACT.

Student Life Upper grades have specified standards of dress, student council, honor system. Discipline rests equally with students and faculty.

Summer Programs Remediation, enrichment, sports, art/fine arts, computer instruction programs offered; session focuses on enrichment; August preparation for school, sports, and developmental writing; held on campus; accepts boys and girls; open to students from other schools. 1500 students usually enrolled. 2006 schedule: June 6 to August 26. Application deadline: none.

Tuition and Aid Day student tuition: $16,650. Tuition installment plan (Key Tuition Payment Plan, FACTS Tuition Payment Plan, monthly payment plans). Need-based scholarship grants available. In 2005–06, 21% of upper-school students received aid. Total amount of financial aid awarded in 2005–06: $761,040.

Admissions Traditional secondary-level entrance grade is 9. For fall 2005, 48 students applied for upper-level admission, 37 were accepted, 29 enrolled. ERB Achievement Test required. Deadline for receipt of application materials: none. Application fee required: $50. On-campus interview required.

Athletics Interscholastic: baseball (boys), basketball (b,g), cross-country running (b,g), field hockey (g), football (b), golf (b), ice hockey (b,g), physical training (b,g), skiing (downhill) (b,g), soccer (b,g), strength & conditioning (b,g), swimming and diving (b,g), tennis (b,g), track and field (b,g), volleyball (g); intramural: cricket (b), dance team (g), lacrosse (b,g), volleyball (g); coed interscholastic: diving; coed intramural: figure skating, flag football, strength & conditioning, ultimate Frisbee. 7 PE instructors, 15 coaches, 1 trainer.

Computers Computers are regularly used in college planning, creative writing, English, foreign language, history, journalism, mathematics, science, yearbook classes. Computer network features include campus e-mail, on-campus library services, CD-ROMs, online commercial services, Internet access, DVD, wireless campus network.

Contact Kathleen Friedman, Director of Admissions. 414-540-3321. Fax: 414-352-8076. E-mail: kfriedman@usmk12.org. Web site: www.usmk12.org.

ANNOUNCEMENT FROM THE SCHOOL USM is a prekindergarten (age 3) through grade 12, coeducational, college-preparatory school. A diverse student body of 1,050 benefits from an outstanding faculty, small classes, and challenging curriculum in an atmosphere of mutual respect. Features of the School include foreign language instruction (prekindergarten-grade 12), a focus on writing, technology education, a successful Advanced Placement program, competitive sports, and a variety of visual and performing arts opportunities.

UNIVERSITY SCHOOL OF NASHVILLE

2000 Edgehill Avenue
Nashville, Tennessee 37212-2198
Head of School: Mr. Vincent W. Durnan

General Information Coeducational day college-preparatory, arts, and technology school. Grades K–12. Founded: 1915. Setting: urban. 7-acre campus. 4 buildings on campus. Approved or accredited by Southern Association of Colleges and Schools. Member of National Association of Independent Schools. Endowment: $1.7 million. Total enrollment: 995. Upper school average class size: 15. Upper school faculty-student ratio: 1:12.

Upper School Student Profile Grade 9: 87 students (44 boys, 43 girls); Grade 10: 94 students (46 boys, 48 girls); Grade 11: 79 students (40 boys, 39 girls); Grade 12: 87 students (36 boys, 51 girls).

Faculty School total: 110. In upper school: 22 men, 34 women; 37 have advanced degrees.

Subjects Offered 3-dimensional art, acting, algebra, American history, American literature, analysis and differential calculus, ancient world history, art history, art history-AP, astronomy, band, biology, biology-AP, British literature, calculus, calculus-AP, ceramics, chemistry, chemistry-AP, college planning, community service, comparative religion, computer multimedia, computer programming, computer tools, concert choir, contemporary issues in science, creative dance, creative writing, dance, debate, desktop publishing, drama, drawing, economics, English, English composition, English literature, English literature-AP, environmental science, ethics, filmmaking, French, French-AP, functions, geology, geometry, government and

politics-AP, government/civics, Harlem Renaissance, history, history-AP, jazz band, journalism, Latin, Latin-AP, literary magazine, modern dance, music appreciation, music theory, newspaper, painting, peer counseling, performing arts, photography, physical education, physics, pre-calculus, psychology, science research, sculpture, social issues, Spanish, Spanish language-AP, sports nutrition, statistics, statistics-AP, studio art, theater, theater arts, theater production, trigonometry, U.S. history-AP, visual literacy, Western civilization, wilderness/outdoor program, world history, yearbook.

Graduation Requirements Algebra, American history, American literature, ancient world history, arts and fine arts (art, music, dance, drama), biology, British literature, chemistry, English, foreign language, geometry, history, physical education (includes health), physics, Western civilization.

Special Academic Programs Advanced Placement exam preparation in 19 subject areas; honors section; independent study; term-away projects; study at local college for college credit; academic accommodation for the gifted, the musically talented, and the artistically talented; ESL (4 students enrolled).

College Placement 87 students graduated in 2005; 86 went to college, including Indiana University Bloomington; Kenyon College; The George Washington University; The University of Tennessee; Vanderbilt University; Washington University in St. Louis. Other: 1 had other specific plans. Mean SAT verbal: 646, mean SAT math: 646. 46% scored over 600 on SAT verbal, 44% scored over 600 on SAT math.

Student Life Upper grades have specified standards of dress, student council, honor system. Discipline rests equally with students and faculty.

Tuition and Aid Day student tuition: $12,655. Tuition installment plan (Insured Tuition Payment Plan, monthly payment plans). Need-based scholarship grants available. In 2005–06, 7% of upper-school students received aid. Total amount of financial aid awarded in 2005–06: $204,075.

Admissions Traditional secondary-level entrance grade is 9. For fall 2005, 101 students applied for upper-level admission, 50 were accepted, 33 enrolled. Deadline for receipt of application materials: none. Application fee required: $50. Interview required.

Athletics Interscholastic: baseball (boys), basketball (b,g), cross-country running (b,g), golf (b,g), lacrosse (b,g), soccer (b,g), softball (g), swimming and diving (b,g), tennis (b,g), track and field (b,g), volleyball (g), weight training (b,g); coed interscholastic: ultimate Frisbee; coed intramural: back packing, canoeing/kayaking, climbing, fitness walking, Frisbee, hiking/backpacking. 7 PE instructors, 2 coaches, 1 trainer.

Computers Computers are regularly used in all classes. Computer network features include campus e-mail, on-campus library services, CD-ROMs, online commercial services, Internet access, file transfer.

Contact Ms. Juliet Douglas, Director of Admissions and Financial Aid. 615-327-3812. Fax: 615-321-0889. E-mail: jdouglas@usn.org. Web site: www.usn.org.

ANNOUNCEMENT FROM THE SCHOOL USN is an independent, college-preparatory, coeducational day school of 985 students in grades K–12, located in Nashville, Tennessee. The School seeks academically oriented and curious students who are eager to explore the outstanding artistic, athletic, and cocurricular opportunities offered by USN. Founded in 1915 as the demonstration school for Peabody College, USN was the first independent school in the Southeast to integrate. Its mission is to serve the diverse religious, racial, and socioeconomic populations that constitute the Nashville metropolitan area. World Wide Web: http://www.usn.org

---

UNIVERSITY SCHOOL OF NOVA SOUTHEASTERN UNIVERSITY

3301 College Avenue
Sonken Building
Fort Lauderdale, Florida 33314
Head of School: Dr. Jerome S. Chermak

General Information Coeducational day college-preparatory school. Grades PK–12. Founded: 1970. Setting: suburban. 300-acre campus. 2 buildings on campus. Approved or accredited by Association of Independent Schools of Florida, Florida Council of Independent Schools, Southern Association of Colleges and Schools, and Florida Department of Education. Member of National Association of Independent Schools. Endowment: $500,000. Total enrollment: 1,681. Upper school average class size: 20. Upper school faculty-student ratio: 1:11.

Upper School Student Profile Grade 9: 141 students (57 boys, 84 girls); Grade 10: 158 students (91 boys, 67 girls); Grade 11: 123 students (62 boys, 61 girls); Grade 12: 104 students (51 boys, 53 girls).

Faculty School total: 157. In upper school: 22 men, 34 women; 36 have advanced degrees.

Subjects Offered Advanced Placement courses, advanced studio art-AP, algebra, American government, American history, American literature, anatomy, art, band, biology, calculus, ceramics, chemistry, chorus, community service, computer programming, computer science, concert choir, creative writing, debate, directing, drawing and design, economics, English, English literature, environmental science, expository writing, fine arts, forensics, French, geometry, grammar, guitar, Internet,

University School of Nova Southeastern University

journalism, keyboarding, Latin, media production, music, music appreciation, music theory, orchestra, performing arts, personal fitness, physical education, physics, physiology, portfolio art, pre-calculus, psychology, public speaking, Spanish, speech, theater, trigonometry, video film production, Web site design, wilderness experience, world geography, world history, world literature, writing.

Graduation Requirements Art, computer science, electives, English, expository writing, foreign language, health education, journalism, mathematics, music, personal fitness, physical education (includes health), public speaking, science, social studies (includes history), speech and debate, Senior Capstone Project-internship. Community service is required.

Special Academic Programs Advanced Placement exam preparation in 20 subject areas; honors section; accelerated programs; term-away projects; study at local college for college credit; study abroad; academic accommodation for the gifted, the musically talented, and the artistically talented; remedial reading and/or remedial writing.

College Placement 93 students graduated in 2005; all went to college, including Cornell University; Florida State University; Indiana University Bloomington; University of Central Florida; University of Florida; University of Miami. Mean SAT verbal: 602, mean SAT math: 590, mean composite ACT: 24. 55% scored over 600 on SAT verbal, 48% scored over 600 on SAT math, 45% scored over 26 on composite ACT.

Student Life Upper grades have uniform requirement, student council, honor system. Discipline rests primarily with faculty.

Summer Programs Enrichment, art/fine arts programs offered; session focuses on sports and the arts; held on campus; accepts boys and girls; open to students from other schools. 300 students usually enrolled. 2006 schedule: June 5 to August 12. Application deadline: none.

Tuition and Aid Day student tuition: $12,870–$13,500. Tuition installment plan (Key Tuition Payment Plan). Tuition reduction for siblings, need-based scholarship grants available. In 2005–06, 11% of upper-school students received aid. Total amount of financial aid awarded in 2005–06: $500,000.

Admissions Traditional secondary-level entrance grade is 9. For fall 2005, 96 students applied for upper-level admission, 63 were accepted, 47 enrolled. Gates MacGinite Reading Tests, Metropolitan Achievement Short Form and Metropolitan Achievement Test required. Deadline for receipt of application materials: none. Application fee required: $100. On-campus interview required.

Athletics Interscholastic: baseball (boys), basketball (b,g), cheering (g), crew (b,g), cross-country running (b,g), dance team (g), diving (b,g), golf (b,g), ice hockey (b), lacrosse (g), roller hockey (b), soccer (b,g), softball (g), swimming and diving (b,g), tennis (b,g), track and field (b,g), volleyball (b,g), wrestling (b). 1 PE instructor, 19 coaches, 1 trainer.

Computers Computers are regularly used in English, foreign language, mathematics, science, social science classes. Computer network features include campus e-mail, on-campus library services, CD-ROMs, Internet access, DVD, wireless campus network.

Contact Mrs. Janet Goldstein, Coordinator of Admission. 954-262-4405. Fax: 954-262-3535. E-mail: goldjan@nova.edu. Web site: uschool.nova.edu.

UPPER CANADA COLLEGE

200 Lonsdale Road
Toronto, Ontario M4V 1W6, Canada
Head of School: Dr. Jim Power

General Information Boys' boarding and day college-preparatory, arts, and technology school. Boarding grades 8–13, day grades K–13. Founded: 1829. Setting: urban. Students are housed in single-sex dormitories. 40-acre campus. 15 buildings on campus. Approved or accredited by Canadian Educational Standards Institute, International Baccalaureate Organization, The Association of Boarding Schools, and Ontario Department of Education. Affiliate member of National Association of Independent Schools; member of Secondary School Admission Test Board. Language of instruction: English. Endowment: CAN$30 million. Total enrollment: 1,116. Upper school average class size: 19. Upper school faculty-student ratio: 1:9.

Upper School Student Profile 15% of students are boarding students. 89% are province residents. 6 provinces are represented in upper school student body. 6% are international students. International students from Hong Kong, Hungary, Saudi Arabia, and United States; 11 other countries represented in student body.

Faculty School total: 72. In upper school: 52 men, 12 women; 26 have advanced degrees; 10 reside on campus.

Subjects Offered Algebra, American history, art, biology, business skills, calculus, chemistry, community service, computer programming, computer science, creative writing, drama, economics, English, English literature, environmental science, European history, expository writing, fine arts, French, geography, geometry, German, Greek, health, history, history of science, Latin, mathematics, music, physical education, physics, science, social science, social studies, Spanish, theater, theory of knowledge, trigonometry, world history, writing.

Graduation Requirements Arts and fine arts (art, music, dance, drama), computer science, English, foreign language, geography, mathematics, physical education (includes health), science, social science, social studies (includes history). Community service is required.

Special Academic Programs International Baccalaureate program; honors section; independent study; study abroad; academic accommodation for the gifted, the musically talented, and the artistically talented.

College Placement 252 students graduated in 2005; 149 went to college, including McGill University; Queen's University at Kingston; The University of Western Ontario; University of Toronto. Other: 1 entered a postgraduate year, 3 had other specific plans.

Student Life Upper grades have uniform requirement, student council. Discipline rests primarily with faculty.

Summer Programs Remediation, enrichment, art/fine arts, computer instruction programs offered; session focuses on earning extra credits; held both on and off campus; held at various venues in Toronto and Norval Country Property; accepts boys and girls; open to students from other schools. 300 students usually enrolled. 2006 schedule: July 1 to August 15. Application deadline: none.

Tuition and Aid Day student tuition: CAN$21,725–CAN$23,474; 7-day tuition and room/board: CAN$38,675–CAN$40,425. Tuition installment plan (Insured Tuition Payment Plan, monthly payment plans, term payment plan, full-payment discount plan). Need-based scholarship grants available. In 2005–06, 10% of upper-school students received aid. Total amount of financial aid awarded in 2005–06: CAN$1,600,000.

Admissions Traditional secondary-level entrance grade is 8. For fall 2005, 225 students applied for upper-level admission, 59 enrolled. ISEE, SAT or SSAT required. Deadline for receipt of application materials: none. Application fee required: CAN$250. Interview required.

Athletics Interscholastic: badminton, baseball, basketball, crew, cricket, cross-country running, football, Frisbee, golf, ice hockey, in-line hockey, lacrosse, mountain biking, outdoor education, rowing, rugby, running, sailing, skiing (cross-country), skiing (downhill), soccer, softball, squash, swimming and diving, tennis, track and field, ultimate Frisbee, volleyball; intramural: badminton, baseball, basketball, bicycling, canoeing/kayaking, climbing, cooperative games, flag football, floor hockey, Frisbee, hiking/backpacking, ice hockey, in-line hockey, indoor hockey, kayaking, life saving, martial arts, mountain biking, outdoor activities, outdoor adventure, physical fitness, physical training, rock climbing, ropes courses, soccer, softball, swimming and diving, table tennis, tennis, touch football, track and field, volleyball, wilderness. 4 PE instructors, 5 coaches, 2 trainers.

Computers Computers are regularly used in art, geography, music, science classes. Computer network features include campus e-mail, on-campus library services, CD-ROMs, online commercial services, Internet access, office computer access.

Contact Connie Carmichael, Coordinator, Upper School Admission. 416-488-1125 Ext. 4020. Fax: 416-484-8618. E-mail: ccarmichael@ucc.on.ca. Web site: www.ucc. on.ca.

THE URBAN SCHOOL OF SAN FRANCISCO

1563 Page Street
San Francisco, California 94117
Head of School: Mark Salkind

General Information Coeducational day college-preparatory, arts, technology, and service learning (community service) school. Grades 9–12. Founded: 1966. Setting: urban. 2 buildings on campus. Approved or accredited by California Association of Independent Schools, Western Association of Schools and Colleges, and California Department of Education. Member of National Association of Independent Schools and Secondary School Admission Test Board. Endowment: $1 million. Total enrollment: 295. Upper school average class size: 13. Upper school faculty-student ratio: 1:9.

Upper School Student Profile Grade 9: 95 students (44 boys, 51 girls); Grade 10: 75 students (41 boys, 34 girls); Grade 11: 70 students (28 boys, 42 girls); Grade 12: 55 students (25 boys, 30 girls).

Faculty School total: 46. In upper school: 24 men, 22 women; 23 have advanced degrees.

Subjects Offered 20th century history, advanced chemistry, advanced math, African American history, African history, algebra, American Civil War, American culture, American history, American literature, animal behavior, art, art history, art-AP, Asian history, Asian literature, astronomy, audio visual/media, Bible studies, biochemistry, biology, bookmaking, British literature, calculus, calculus-AP, cell biology, ceramics, chemistry, chemistry-AP, Chinese history, chorus, circus acts, classical Greek literature, college counseling, community service, comparative religion, computer literacy, computer multimedia, computer programming, conflict resolution, constitutional law, creative writing, current events, dance, digital photography, diversity studies, drama, drama performance, drawing, drawing and design, English, English literature, environmental science, European history, expository writing, female experience in America, field ecology, fine arts, French, French-AP, genetics, geometry, health, history, Holocaust seminar, improvisation, independent study, instrumental music, jazz band, Latin American literature, literature, logic, Mandarin, marine biology, mathematics, medieval literature, music, music theory, neurobiology, ornithology, painting, peer counseling, photography, physics, play production, play/screen writing, playwriting and directing, printmaking, religion, science, sex education, Shakespeare, social studies, sophomore skills, Spanish, speech, statistics,

stone carving, studio art-AP, theater, trigonometry, video, water color painting, Web site design, women in world history, women's literature, women's studies, woodworking, world history, writing.

Graduation Requirements Arts and fine arts (art, music, dance, drama), English, foreign language, history, mathematics, science. Community service is required.

Special Academic Programs Advanced Placement exam preparation in 8 subject areas; honors section; independent study; term-away projects; domestic exchange program; study abroad; academic accommodation for the gifted and the artistically talented.

College Placement 65 students graduated in 2005; 64 went to college, including Brown University; Oberlin College; The Johns Hopkins University; University of California, Berkeley; University of California, Los Angeles; University of Southern California. Other: 1 had other specific plans. Median SAT verbal: 660, median SAT math: 634.

Student Life Upper grades have student council, honor system. Discipline rests equally with students and faculty.

Summer Programs Enrichment, sports, art/fine arts, computer instruction programs offered; session focuses on academic enrichment for middle school students from disadvantaged backgrounds; held both on and off campus; held at several schools in San Francisco and Oakland; accepts boys and girls; open to students from other schools. 500 students usually enrolled. 2006 schedule: June 26 to July 29. Application deadline: May 1.

Tuition and Aid Day student tuition: $25,300. Tuition installment plan (monthly payment plans, 2-payment plan). Need-based scholarship grants, Achiever Loans (Key Education Resources) available. In 2005–06, 24% of upper-school students received aid. Total amount of financial aid awarded in 2005–06: $1,100,000.

Admissions Traditional secondary-level entrance grade is 9. For fall 2005, 440 students applied for upper-level admission, 102 enrolled. SSAT required. Deadline for receipt of application materials: January 10. Application fee required: $75. On-campus interview recommended.

Athletics Interscholastic: baseball (boys), basketball (b,g), cross-country running (b,g), golf (b), soccer (b,g), softball (g), tennis (b,g), volleyball (b,g); intramural: golf (g); coed interscholastic: fencing; coed intramural: aerobics/dance, back packing, bowling, canoeing/kayaking, Circus, climbing, fencing, fitness, gatorball, hiking/backpacking, jogging, juggling, kayaking, martial arts, outdoor activities, outdoor education, physical fitness, physical training, rafting, rock climbing, skiing (cross-country), skiing (downhill), strength & conditioning, ultimate Frisbee, weight training, yoga. 28 coaches.

Computers Computers are regularly used in all classes. Computer network features include campus e-mail, on-campus library services, CD-ROMs, online commercial services, Internet access, file transfer, office computer access, DVD, wireless campus network, laptop program (for all incoming students).

Contact Abigail Munn, Admissions Associate. 415-593-9555. Fax: 415-626-1125. E-mail: amunn@urbanschool.org. Web site: www.urbanschool.org.

ANNOUNCEMENT FROM THE SCHOOL The Urban School seeks to ignite a passion for learning. With an imaginative academic program that combines a college-preparatory curriculum with community service, fieldwork, and internships, Urban inspires its students to become self-motivated, enthusiastic participants in their education.

URSULINE ACADEMY

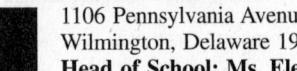

1106 Pennsylvania Avenue
Wilmington, Delaware 19806
Head of School: Ms. Elena M.P. Bingham

General Information Coeducational day (boys' only in lower grades) college-preparatory, arts, religious studies, and technology school, affiliated with Roman Catholic Church. Boys grades PK–3, girls grades PK–12. Founded: 1893. Setting: urban. 5-acre campus. 2 buildings on campus. Approved or accredited by Middle States Association of Colleges and Schools and Delaware Department of Education. Member of National Association of Independent Schools. Endowment: $3 million. Total enrollment: 653. Upper school average class size: 17. Upper school faculty-student ratio: 1:7.

Upper School Student Profile Grade 9: 61 students (61 girls); Grade 10: 45 students (45 girls); Grade 11: 64 students (64 girls); Grade 12: 54 students (54 girls). 75% of students are Roman Catholic.

Faculty School total: 75. In upper school: 8 men, 36 women; 28 have advanced degrees.

Subjects Offered Algebra, American history, American literature, anthropology, archaeology, art, art history, biology, business law, calculus, chemistry, chorus, computer programming, computer science, creative writing, drafting, drama, driver education, earth science, economics, English, English literature, environmental science, European history, European history-AP, fine arts, French, geometry, government/civics, grammar, health, history, journalism, keyboarding, mathematics, music appreciation, painting, photography, physical education, physical science, physics, psychology, religion, science, social studies, Spanish, statistics, theater, theology, trigonometry, word processing, world history, world literature.

Graduation Requirements Arts and fine arts (art, music, dance, drama), computer science, English, foreign language, mathematics, physical education (includes health), religion (includes Bible studies and theology), science, social studies (includes history), 40-hour service project.

Special Academic Programs Advanced Placement exam preparation in 11 subject areas; honors section; academic accommodation for the gifted.

College Placement 57 students graduated in 2005; all went to college, including Boston College; Saint Joseph's University; University of Delaware; University of Notre Dame; Villanova University.

Student Life Upper grades have uniform requirement, student council, honor system. Discipline rests primarily with faculty. Attendance at religious services is required.

Tuition and Aid Day student tuition: $11,750. Tuition installment plan (monthly payment plans, 2-payment plan, 1-payment plan). Merit scholarship grants, need-based scholarship grants available. In 2005–06, 24% of upper-school students received aid; total upper-school merit-scholarship money awarded: $96,000. Total amount of financial aid awarded in 2005–06: $497,000.

Admissions Traditional secondary-level entrance grade is 9. For fall 2005, 224 students applied for upper-level admission, 224 were accepted, 224 enrolled. CTP III required. Deadline for receipt of application materials: none. Application fee required: $35. On-campus interview required.

Athletics Interscholastic: basketball (girls), cross-country running (g), diving (g), field hockey (g), golf (g), indoor track & field (g), lacrosse (g), soccer (g), softball (g), swimming and diving (g), tennis (g), track and field (g), volleyball (g), winter (indoor) track (g); intramural: basketball (g), field hockey (g), golf (g), indoor soccer (g), volleyball (g). 3 PE instructors, 25 coaches, 1 trainer.

Computers Computers are regularly used in art, English, foreign language, history, mathematics, religion, science classes. Computer network features include campus e-mail, on-campus library services, CD-ROMs, online commercial services, Internet access, office computer access.

Contact Jennifer Callahan, Assistant Director of Admission. 302-658-7158 Ext. 210. Fax: 302-658-4297. Web site: www.ursuline.org.

URSULINE HIGH SCHOOL

90 Ursuline Road
Santa Rosa, California 95403
Head of School: Mrs. Barbara Johannes

General Information Girls' day college-preparatory, arts, business, religious studies, and technology school, affiliated with Roman Catholic Church. Grades 9–12. Founded: 1880. Setting: suburban. 51-acre campus. 5 buildings on campus. Approved or accredited by Western Association of Schools and Colleges, Western Catholic Education Association, and California Department of Education. Endowment: $700,000. Total enrollment: 336. Upper school average class size: 25. Upper school faculty-student ratio: 1:12.

Upper School Student Profile Grade 9: 83 students (83 girls); Grade 10: 78 students (78 girls); Grade 11: 91 students (91 girls); Grade 12: 84 students (84 girls). 69% of students are Roman Catholic.

Faculty School total: 29. In upper school: 9 men, 20 women; 14 have advanced degrees.

Subjects Offered 20th century world history, algebra, art, ASB Leadership, biology, biology-AP, calculus, calculus-AP, chemistry, choir, Christian and Hebrew scripture, communication skills, communications, computers, conceptual physics, creative writing, cultural geography, dance, design, desktop publishing, drama, drawing, economics, English, English literature-AP, ensembles, ethics, film, fine arts, French, geometry, health, honors English, journalism, Latin, literature-AP, photography, physical education, physical science, physics-AP, pre-algebra, pre-calculus, psychology, public speaking, social justice, Spanish, Spanish language-AP, studio art—AP, trigonometry, U.S. government, U.S. history-AP, water color painting, word processing, world history, world religions, yearbook.

Graduation Requirements Bible studies, biology, Christian ethics, church history, cultural geography, economics, English, foreign language, government, mathematics, physical education (includes health), physical science, public speaking, social justice, visual and performing arts, world history, world religions, 25 hours of student service per year, cumulative 2.0 GPA (8 semesters).

Special Academic Programs Advanced Placement exam preparation in 4 subject areas; honors section; study at local college for college credit.

College Placement 87 students graduated in 2005; 86 went to college, including California Polytechnic State University, San Luis Obispo; California State University, Chico; Saint Mary's College of California; Santa Clara University; University of California, Davis; University of California, Santa Cruz. Other: 1 had other specific plans. Median SAT verbal: 550, median SAT math: 520, median composite ACT: 23. 30% scored over 600 on SAT verbal, 26% scored over 600 on SAT math, 33% scored over 26 on composite ACT.

Student Life Upper grades have uniform requirement, student council, honor system. Discipline rests primarily with faculty. Attendance at religious services is required.

Summer Programs Remediation, enrichment, advancement programs offered; session focuses on enrichment, advancement, math make-up; held on campus; accepts girls; not open to students from other schools. 80 students usually enrolled. 2006 schedule: June 12 to July 14. Application deadline: May 20.

Tuition and Aid Day student tuition: $9480. Tuition installment plan (monthly payment plans, individually arranged payment plans). Merit scholarship grants, need-based scholarship grants, paying campus jobs available. In 2005–06, 24% of upper-school students received aid; total upper-school merit-scholarship money awarded: $53,000. Total amount of financial aid awarded in 2005–06: $104,000.

Admissions Traditional secondary-level entrance grade is 9. For fall 2005, 118 students applied for upper-level admission, 109 were accepted, 90 enrolled. STS required. Deadline for receipt of application materials: none. Application fee required: $80. On-campus interview required.

Athletics Interscholastic: basketball, cross-country running, diving, golf, soccer, softball, swimming and diving, tennis, track and field, volleyball, water polo. 3 PE instructors, 33 coaches.

Computers Computers are regularly used in business applications, Web site design, word processing classes. Computer network features include campus e-mail, on-campus library services, CD-ROMs, Internet access.

Contact Mrs. Debbie Lamela, Admissions Director. 707-524-1133 Ext. 15. Fax: 707-542-0131. E-mail: dlamela@ursulinehs.org. Web site: www.ursulinehs.org.

VAIL MOUNTAIN SCHOOL

3000 Booth Falls Road
Vail, Colorado 81657
Head of School: Peter M. Abuisi

General Information Coeducational day college-preparatory school. Grades K–12. Founded: 1962. Setting: small town. Nearest major city is Denver. 9-acre campus. 3 buildings on campus. Approved or accredited by Association of Colorado Independent Schools, National Independent Private Schools Association, and Colorado Department of Education. Member of National Association of Independent Schools. Endowment: $2 million. Total enrollment: 330. Upper school average class size: 16. Upper school faculty-student ratio: 1:10.

Upper School Student Profile Grade 9: 32 students (17 boys, 15 girls); Grade 10: 34 students (16 boys, 18 girls); Grade 11: 22 students (8 boys, 14 girls); Grade 12: 14 students (6 boys, 8 girls).

Faculty School total: 42. In upper school: 6 have advanced degrees.

Subjects Offered Advanced Placement courses, algebra, American history, American literature, art, arts, biology, calculus, chemistry, computer math, computer science, creative writing, drama, earth science, English, English literature, environmental science, ethics, European history, expository writing, fine arts, geography, geometry, government/civics, grammar, history, Latin, Latin American literature, mathematics, photography, physical education, physics, poetry, psychology, science, Shakespeare, social science, social studies, Spanish, theater, trigonometry, world history, writing.

Graduation Requirements Arts and fine arts (art, music, dance, drama), English, foreign language, mathematics, physical education (includes health), psychology, science, social science, social studies (includes history), Spanish, acceptance into a four-year college or university.

Special Academic Programs Advanced Placement exam preparation in 6 subject areas; honors section; independent study; ESL (4 students enrolled).

College Placement 26 students graduated in 2005; all went to college, including Bowdoin College; University of Colorado at Boulder.

Student Life Upper grades have specified standards of dress, honor system. Discipline rests primarily with faculty.

Tuition and Aid Day student tuition: $12,700–$15,200. Tuition installment plan (monthly payment plans, individually arranged payment plans). Need-based scholarship grants, need-based loans available. In 2005–06, 30% of upper-school students received aid. Total amount of financial aid awarded in 2005–06: $227,460.

Admissions Traditional secondary-level entrance grade is 9. For fall 2005, 30 students applied for upper-level admission, 15 were accepted, 7 enrolled. Any standardized test required. Deadline for receipt of application materials: February 17. Application fee required: $30. Interview required.

Athletics Interscholastic: alpine skiing (boys, girls), golf (b,g), skiing (cross-country) (b,g), skiing (downhill) (b,g), soccer (b,g); intramural: back packing (b,g), basketball (b,g), dance team (g), ice hockey (b), independent competitive sports (b,g), indoor soccer (b,g), jogging (b,g), skiing (cross-country) (b,g), skiing (downhill) (b,g), strength & conditioning (b,g), volleyball (g), weight lifting (b,g); coed interscholastic: freestyle skiing, nordic skiing, snowboarding; coed intramural: back packing, basketball, canoeing/kayaking, climbing, fitness, Fives, fly fishing, Frisbee, hiking/backpacking, indoor soccer, jogging, jump rope, kayaking, mountain biking, mountaineering, outdoor activities, outdoor adventure, outdoor education, physical fitness, physical training, rock climbing, snowshoeing, strength & conditioning, telemark skiing, touch football, ultimate Frisbee, weight lifting, wilderness survival, yoga. 1 PE instructor, 15 coaches, 1 trainer.

Computers Computers are regularly used in all academic, independent study, library, photography, senior seminar, yearbook classes. Computer network features include campus e-mail, on-campus library services, CD-ROMs, online commercial services, Internet access, file transfer, DVD, wireless campus network.

Contact Ms. Laurie M. Geromini, Director of Admission. 970-477-7164. Fax: 970-476-3860. E-mail: admissions@vms.edu.

VALLEY CHRISTIAN SCHOOL

100 Skyway Drive
San Jose, California 95111-3636
Head of School: Jeanie Stephenson

General Information Coeducational day college-preparatory, general academic, arts, religious studies, bilingual studies, and technology school, affiliated with Christian faith. Grades K–12. Founded: 1960. Setting: suburban. 50-acre campus. 2 buildings on campus. Approved or accredited by Association of Christian Schools International, Western Association of Schools and Colleges, and California Department of Education. Endowment: $15 million. Total enrollment: 2,135. Upper school average class size: 30. Upper school faculty-student ratio: 1:17.

Upper School Student Profile Grade 9: 289 students (149 boys, 140 girls); Grade 10: 318 students (173 boys, 145 girls); Grade 11: 282 students (142 boys, 140 girls); Grade 12: 272 students (131 boys, 141 girls). 80% of students are Christian faith.

Faculty School total: 65. In upper school: 33 men, 32 women.

Subjects Offered 20th century American writers, acting, advanced chemistry, advanced computer applications, advanced math, Advanced Placement courses, advanced studio art-AP, algebra, American history, American literature, American sign language, anatomy and physiology, ancient world history, applied music, art, athletics, audio visual/media, baseball, Basic programming, basketball, Bible, biology, calculus-AP, career and personal planning, cheerleading, chemistry, chemistry-AP, choir, choral music, choreography, Christian education, computer art, computer education, computer keyboarding, computer literacy, concert choir, dance, dance performance, digital art, drama, drama performance, dramatic arts, driver education, earth science, English, English language-AP, foreign language, French, geometry, government, health science, history, honors algebra, honors English, honors U.S. history, honors world history, human anatomy, instrumental music, introduction to theater, Japanese, jazz band, jazz dance, jazz ensemble, journalism, land and ranch management, leadership and service, marching band, mathematics, mathematics-AP, Microsoft, musical productions, musical theater, photo shop, physics-AP, physiology-anatomy, pre-algebra, radio broadcasting, SAT preparation, Spanish, Spanish-AP, stage design, student government, symphonic band, telecommunications, theater arts, theater production, track and field, trigonometry, typing, U.S. history, weight training, world history, wrestling, yearbook.

Special Academic Programs Advanced Placement exam preparation in 14 subject areas; honors section.

College Placement 272 students graduated in 2005.

Student Life Upper grades have specified standards of dress, student council, honor system. Discipline rests primarily with faculty.

Summer Programs Remediation, enrichment, advancement, sports, art/fine arts programs offered; held on campus; accepts boys and girls; open to students from other schools. 2006 schedule: June 13 to July 30. Application deadline: none.

Tuition and Aid Day student tuition: $10,500. Tuition installment plan (FACTS Tuition Payment Plan). Tuition reduction for siblings, need-based scholarship grants available.

Admissions Traditional secondary-level entrance grade is 9. Deadline for receipt of application materials: none. Application fee required: $55. Interview required.

Athletics Interscholastic: aquatics (boys, girls), baseball (b), basketball (b,g), cheering (g), cross-country running (b,g), dance (b,g), dance squad (b,g), diving (b,g), football (b), golf (b,g), rugby (b), soccer (b,g), softball (g), swimming and diving (b,g), tennis (b,g), track and field (b,g), volleyball (b,g), water polo (b,g), wrestling (b); intramural: weight training (b,g). 2 trainers.

Computers Computers are regularly used in digital applications, foreign language, graphic design, journalism, keyboarding, library, music, newspaper, photojournalism, video film production, Web site design, word processing classes. Computer network features include on-campus library services, Internet access.

Contact Admissions. 408-513-2400. Fax: 408-513-2424. Web site: www.valleychristian.net.

VALLEY CHRISTIAN SCHOOL

2526 Sunset Lane
Missoula, Montana 59804
Head of School: Mr. Earle Reimer

General Information Coeducational day college-preparatory, general academic, business, and religious studies school, affiliated with Christian faith. Grades K–12. Founded: 1978. Setting: small town. Nearest major city is Spokane, WA. 5-acre campus. 2 buildings on campus. Approved or accredited by Montana Department of Education. Total enrollment: 434. Upper school average class size: 22. Upper school faculty-student ratio: 1:8.

Upper School Student Profile Grade 9: 44 students (22 boys, 22 girls); Grade 10: 29 students (13 boys, 16 girls); Grade 11: 42 students (20 boys, 22 girls); Grade 12: 28 students (13 boys, 15 girls). 100% of students are Christian faith.

Faculty School total: 23. In upper school: 14 men, 9 women; 5 have advanced degrees.

Subjects Offered Accounting, algebra, American history, American literature, art, arts, band, Bible studies, biology, biology-AP, business, business skills, chemistry, chorus, computer science, economics, English, English literature, environmental science, fine arts, geometry, German, government/civics, health, keyboarding,

literature, mathematics, music theory, physical education, physics, religion, science, social studies, Spanish, world affairs, world history.

College Placement 30 students graduated in 2005; 24 went to college, including Montana State University; University of Nebraska at Kearney. Other: 6 went to work. Mean SAT verbal: 523, mean SAT math: 505, mean composite ACT: 21. 10% scored over 600 on SAT verbal, 10% scored over 600 on SAT math, 14% scored over 26 on composite ACT.

Student Life Upper grades have specified standards of dress, student council, honor system. Discipline rests primarily with faculty. Attendance at religious services is required.

Tuition and Aid Day student tuition: $3425. Tuition installment plan (FACTS Tuition Payment Plan, monthly payment plans, individually arranged payment plans). Tuition reduction for siblings, need-based scholarship grants, paying campus jobs available.

Admissions Traditional secondary-level entrance grade is 9. Deadline for receipt of application materials: none. Application fee required: $75. Interview required.

Athletics Interscholastic: basketball (boys, girls), cross-country running (b,g), independent competitive sports (b,g), soccer (b), tennis (b,g), track and field (b,g), volleyball (g). 2 PE instructors, 5 coaches, 1 trainer.

Contact Dawn Kinzle, Office Manager. 406-549-0482 Ext. 227. Fax: 406-549-5047. E-mail: dawn.kinzle@valleychristian.org. Web site: www.valleychristian.org.

VALLEY FORGE MILITARY ACADEMY AND COLLEGE

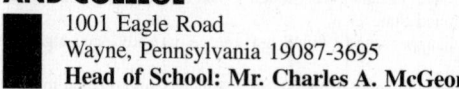

1001 Eagle Road
Wayne, Pennsylvania 19087-3695
Head of School: Mr. Charles A. McGeorge

petersons.com

General Information Boys' boarding and day college-preparatory, arts, business, religious studies, and music school. Boarding grades 7–PG, day grades 7–8. Founded: 1928. Setting: suburban. Nearest major city is Philadelphia. Students are housed in single-sex dormitories. 120-acre campus. 83 buildings on campus. Approved or accredited by Middle States Association of Colleges and Schools, The Association of Boarding Schools, and Pennsylvania Department of Education. Member of National Association of Independent Schools and Secondary School Admission Test Board. Endowment: $8 million. Total enrollment: 328. Upper school average class size: 12. Upper school faculty-student ratio: 1:12.

Upper School Student Profile Grade 9: 38 students (38 boys); Grade 10: 68 students (68 boys); Grade 11: 83 students (83 boys); Grade 12: 90 students (90 boys); Postgraduate: 14 students (14 boys). 100% of students are boarding students. 27% are state residents. 32 states are represented in upper school student body. 15% are international students. International students from Canada, Dominican Republic, Ecuador, Mexico, and Republic of Korea; 31 other countries represented in student body.

Faculty School total: 50. In upper school: 36 men, 14 women; 24 have advanced degrees; 30 reside on campus.

Subjects Offered ACT preparation, advanced computer applications, algebra, American foreign policy, American government, American history, American history-AP, ancient world history, applied music, art, art education, band, biology, business, business law, business studies, calculus, character education, chemistry, choir, comparative religion, computer keyboarding, computer math, computer programming, computer science, concert band, drama, driver education, earth science, ecology, economics, English, English literature and composition-AP, ESL, ethics, European history, fencing, fine arts, flight instruction, foreign language, French, French studies, geometry, German, government/civics, grammar, health, health education, honors algebra, honors English, honors geometry, honors U.S. history, honors world history, journalism, JROTC, lab science, Latin, leadership, leadership and service, leadership education training, leadership skills, leadership training, marching band, mathematics, mathematics-AP, military science, modern world history, music, music theory, newspaper, official social customs, personal growth, physical education, physics, physics-AP, pre-algebra, reading, reading/study skills, ROTC (for boys), Russian, science, social science, social studies, sociology, Spanish, speech, sports, statistics and probability, swimming, theater, therapeutic horseback riding, TOEFL preparation, trigonometry, typing, U.S. government, U.S. history, U.S. history-AP, video communication, video film production, Web site design, world history, world religions, world religions, world wide web design, writing, writing, writing fundamentals, writing skills.

Special Academic Programs Advanced Placement exam preparation in 6 subject areas; honors section; independent study; study at local college for college credit; study abroad; academic accommodation for the musically talented and the artistically talented; remedial reading and/or remedial writing; remedial math; ESL (15 students enrolled).

College Placement 110 students graduated in 2005; 108 went to college, including Drexel University; Duke University; Harvard University; Tulane University; United States Air Force Academy; United States Naval Academy. Other: 1 went to work, 1 entered a postgraduate year. Median SAT verbal: 495, median SAT math: 525. 12% scored over 600 on SAT verbal, 26% scored over 600 on SAT math.

Student Life Upper grades have uniform requirement, student council, honor system. Discipline rests equally with students and faculty. Attendance at religious services is required.

Summer Programs Enrichment, ESL, sports, art/fine arts, rigorous outdoor training programs offered; session focuses on outdoor adventure, fitness, aviation, band music, ; held on campus; accepts boys and girls; open to students from other schools. 330 students usually enrolled. 2006 schedule: June 24 to July 21. Application deadline: April.

Tuition and Aid Day student tuition: $20,000; 7-day tuition and room/board: $28,550. Tuition installment plan (monthly payment plans). Tuition reduction for siblings, merit scholarship grants, need-based scholarship grants, middle-income loans, paying campus jobs available. In 2005–06, 25% of upper-school students received aid; total upper-school merit-scholarship money awarded: $550,142. Total amount of financial aid awarded in 2005–06: $550,142.

Admissions Traditional secondary-level entrance grade is 9. For fall 2005, 427 students applied for upper-level admission, 302 were accepted, 178 enrolled. Iowa Test, CTBS, or TAP, ISEE, OLSAT and English Exam, SSAT, ERB, PSAT, SAT, PLAN or ACT or TOEFL or SLEP required. Deadline for receipt of application materials: none. Application fee required: $100. Interview required.

Athletics Interscholastic: baseball, basketball, climbing, cross-country running, dressage, drill team, equestrian sports, fitness, football, golf, horseback riding, indoor track, JROTC drill, judo, lacrosse, marksmanship, outdoor activities, outdoor recreation, paint ball, physical fitness, physical training, polo, rappelling, riflery, ropes courses, running, soccer, swimming and diving, tennis, track and field, winter (indoor) track, wrestling; intramural: blading, fencing, martial arts, physical training, rappelling, rock climbing, scuba diving, skateboarding, strength & conditioning, table tennis, volleyball, wall climbing, water polo, weight lifting, weight training. 3 PE instructors, 5 coaches, 1 trainer.

Computers Computers are regularly used in accounting, aerospace science, basic skills, business applications, business education, business skills, business studies, college planning, data processing, English, journalism, keyboarding, lab/keyboard, library, library skills, mathematics, music, news writing, newspaper, photography, photojournalism, SAT preparation, science, video film production, Web site design classes. Computer network features include campus e-mail, on-campus library services, online commercial services, Internet access, wireless campus network.

Contact Maj. Greg W. Potts, Director of Admissions and Financial Aid. 610-989-1300. Fax: 610-688-1545. E-mail: admissions@vfmac.edu. Web site: www.vfmac.edu.

See full description on page 1112.

VALLEY VIEW SCHOOL

North Brookfield, Massachusetts
See Special Needs Schools section.

VANDEBILT CATHOLIC HIGH SCHOOL

209 South Hollywood Road
Houma, Louisiana 70360
Head of School: Mr. James Reiss

General Information Coeducational day college-preparatory, arts, business, religious studies, bilingual studies, and technology school, affiliated with Roman Catholic Church. Grades 8–12. Founded: 1965. Setting: suburban. Nearest major city is New Orleans. 29-acre campus. 7 buildings on campus. Approved or accredited by Southern Association of Colleges and Schools and Louisiana Department of Education. Endowment: $355,000. Total enrollment: 915. Upper school average class size: 25. Upper school faculty-student ratio: 1:25.

Upper School Student Profile Grade 8: 207 students (95 boys, 112 girls); Grade 9: 192 students (107 boys, 85 girls); Grade 10: 192 students (96 boys, 96 girls); Grade 11: 215 students (111 boys, 104 girls); Grade 12: 154 students (78 boys, 76 girls). 85% of students are Roman Catholic.

Faculty School total: 63. In upper school: 23 men, 40 women; 20 have advanced degrees.

Subjects Offered 20th century physics, 20th century world history, 3-dimensional art, accounting, advanced chemistry, advanced math, algebra, American history, art, band, biology, bookkeeping, business education, business law, calculus, chemistry, choir, Christian education, civics, civics/free enterprise, computer applications, computer keyboarding, computer science, driver education, earth science, English, English literature, French, general business, geography, history of music, honors algebra, honors English, honors geometry, honors U.S. history, Latin, leadership, mathematics, media, music appreciation, physical education, physical science, physics, pre-algebra, reading, reading/study skills, religion, Spanish, speech, world history.

Graduation Requirements Algebra, American history, biology, chemistry, civics, computer applications, English, geometry, physical education (includes health), religion (includes Bible studies and theology), science, social studies (includes history).

Special Academic Programs Honors section; programs in English for dyslexic students; special instructional classes for students with Attention Deficit Disorder and dyslexia.

Vandebilt Catholic High School

College Placement 163 students graduated in 2005; 161 went to college, including Louisiana State University and Agricultural and Mechanical College; Louisiana Tech University; Loyola University New Orleans; Nicholls State University; Tulane University; University of Louisiana at Lafayette. Other: 1 went to work, 1 entered military service. Mean composite ACT: 23. 21% scored over 26 on composite ACT.
Student Life Upper grades have uniform requirement, student council. Discipline rests primarily with faculty. Attendance at religious services is required.
Tuition and Aid Day student tuition: $4530. Tuition reduction for siblings, need-based scholarship grants, middle-income loans available. In 2005–06, 10% of upper-school students received aid. Total amount of financial aid awarded in 2005–06: $75,000.
Admissions Traditional secondary-level entrance grade is 8. For fall 2005, 918 students applied for upper-level admission, 915 were accepted, 915 enrolled. Admissions testing required. Deadline for receipt of application materials: none. No application fee required. On-campus interview required.
Athletics Interscholastic: baseball (boys), basketball (b,g), cheering (g), cross-country running (b,g), dance squad (g), football (b), golf (b), gymnastics (b,g), soccer (b,g), softball (g), swimming and diving (b,g), tennis (b,g), track and field (b,g), volleyball (g). 5 PE instructors, 15 coaches.
Computers Computers are regularly used in all classes. Computer network features include CD-ROMs, Internet access.
Contact Mr. Quinn Moreaux, Assistant Principal. 985-876-2551. Fax: 985-868-9774. E-mail: qmoreaux@htdiocese.org.

VANGUARD COLLEGE PREPARATORY SCHOOL

2517 Mt. Carmel
Waco, Texas 76710
Head of School: Mrs. Fred M. Niell, EdD

General Information Coeducational day college-preparatory school. Grades 7–12. Founded: 1973. Setting: small town. 8-acre campus. 6 buildings on campus. Approved or accredited by Southern Association of Colleges and Schools and Texas Education Agency. Member of National Association of Independent Schools. Endowment: $590,000. Total enrollment: 181. Upper school average class size: 16. Upper school faculty-student ratio: 1:7.
Upper School Student Profile Grade 9: 32 students (16 boys, 16 girls); Grade 10: 31 students (15 boys, 16 girls); Grade 11: 29 students (15 boys, 14 girls); Grade 12: 30 students (15 boys, 15 girls).
Faculty School total: 32. In upper school: 11 men, 18 women; 12 have advanced degrees.
Subjects Offered Algebra, American history, art, arts, band, biology, biology-AP, calculus, calculus-AP, chemistry, chemistry-AP, choir, college admission preparation, computer science, contemporary math, creative writing, economics, English, English-AP, environmental science, fine arts, French, geometry, German, government, journalism, mathematics, orchestra, physical education, physics, pre-calculus, psychology, psychology-AP, science, social science, social studies, sociology, Spanish, Spanish-AP, Western civilization, yearbook.
Graduation Requirements Arts and fine arts (art, music, dance, drama), college admission preparation, computer science, English, foreign language, mathematics, physical education (includes health), science, social science, social studies (includes history).
Special Academic Programs Advanced Placement exam preparation in 6 subject areas; honors section; independent study; term-away projects; study at local college for college credit; study abroad; academic accommodation for the artistically talented.
College Placement 42 students graduated in 2005; all went to college, including Baylor University; Southern Methodist University; Texas Christian University; Trinity University; University of Arkansas; University of the South. Median SAT verbal: 625, median SAT math: 615, median combined SAT: 1890. 47% scored over 600 on SAT verbal, 44% scored over 600 on SAT math.
Student Life Upper grades have student council, honor system. Discipline rests primarily with faculty.
Summer Programs Advancement programs offered; held on campus; accepts boys and girls; not open to students from other schools. 20 students usually enrolled. 2006 schedule: July 6 to August 15. Application deadline: June 1.
Tuition and Aid Day student tuition: $9300. Tuition installment plan (The Tuition Plan, monthly payment plans). Tuition reduction for siblings, need-based scholarship grants, faculty remission available. In 2005–06, 17% of upper-school students received aid. Total amount of financial aid awarded in 2005–06: $97,000.
Admissions Traditional secondary-level entrance grade is 9. For fall 2005, 37 students applied for upper-level admission, 37 were accepted, 33 enrolled. Otis-Lennon School Ability Test required. Deadline for receipt of application materials: none. Application fee required: $50. Interview required.
Athletics Interscholastic: baseball (boys), basketball (b,g), cheering (g), cross-country running (b,g), golf (b,g), independent competitive sports (b,g), softball (g), tennis (b,g), track and field (b,g); coed intramural: power lifting. 3 PE instructors, 7 coaches.
Computers Computers are regularly used in English classes. Computer network features include campus e-mail, on-campus library services, CD-ROMs, online commercial services, Internet access, wireless campus network.

Contact Mrs. MaryHelen George, Director of Admissions. 254-772-8111. Fax: 254-772-8263. E-mail: fred_niell@vanguard.org. Web site: www.vanguard.org.

THE VANGUARD SCHOOL

Lake Wales, Florida
See Special Needs Schools section.

VENTA PREPARATORY SCHOOL

2013 Old Carp Road
Ottawa, Ontario K0A 1L0, Canada
Head of School: Ms. Marilyn Mansfield

General Information Coeducational boarding and day college-preparatory, arts, and music school. Grades 1–10. Founded: 1981. Setting: rural. Students are housed in single-sex by floor dormitories. 50-acre campus. 8 buildings on campus. Approved or accredited by Ontario Ministry of Education and Ontario Department of Education. Language of instruction: English. Total enrollment: 85. Upper school average class size: 10. Upper school faculty-student ratio: 1:6.
Upper School Student Profile Grade 8: 13 students (7 boys, 6 girls); Grade 9: 8 students (4 boys, 4 girls); Grade 10: 7 students (5 boys, 2 girls). 40% of students are boarding students. 90% are province residents. 5 provinces are represented in upper school student body. 2% are international students. International students from Bermuda, Mexico, and United States.
Faculty School total: 14. In upper school: 4 men, 5 women; 3 have advanced degrees; 6 reside on campus.
Special Academic Programs Independent study; academic accommodation for the gifted; remedial reading and/or remedial writing; remedial math; programs in English, mathematics, general development for dyslexic students.
Student Life Upper grades have uniform requirement. Discipline rests primarily with faculty.
Summer Programs Remediation, enrichment, advancement, sports, rigorous outdoor training programs offered; session focuses on academics, sports, and outdoor education; held on campus; accepts boys and girls; not open to students from other schools. 70 students usually enrolled. 2006 schedule: July 7 to August 1.
Tuition and Aid Day student tuition: CAN$13,622; 5-day tuition and room/board: CAN$24,290; 7-day tuition and room/board: CAN$25,680. Tuition installment plan (monthly payment plans, individually arranged payment plans). Tuition reduction for siblings, merit scholarship grants available. In 2005–06, 10% of upper-school students received aid.
Admissions Traditional secondary-level entrance grade is 9. Psychoeducational evaluation required. Deadline for receipt of application materials: none. Application fee required: CAN$50. On-campus interview required.
Athletics 4 PE instructors.
Computers Computers are regularly used in current events, geography, keyboarding, mathematics, research skills, science, Web site design classes. Computer network features include CD-ROMs, Internet access, office computer access, wireless campus network.
Contact Mrs. Tracey H. Quinn, Director of Public Relations and Enrollment. 613-839-2175 Ext. 240. Fax: 613-839-1956. E-mail: info@ventapreparatoryschool.com. Web site: www.ventapreparatoryschool.com.

VERMONT ACADEMY

20 Pleasant Street
PO Box 500
Saxtons River, Vermont 05154
Head of School: James C. Mooney

General Information Coeducational boarding and day college-preparatory, arts, and technology school. Grades 9–PG. Founded: 1876. Setting: small town. Nearest major city is Boston, MA. Students are housed in single-sex dormitories. 515-acre campus. 21 buildings on campus. Approved or accredited by Association of Independent Schools in New England, Independent Schools of Northern New England, National Independent Private Schools Association, New England Association of Schools and Colleges, The Association of Boarding Schools, and Vermont Department of Education. Member of National Association of Independent Schools and Secondary School Admission Test Board. Endowment: $6 million. Total enrollment: 267. Upper school average class size: 11. Upper school faculty-student ratio: 1:7.
Upper School Student Profile Grade 9: 30 students (18 boys, 12 girls); Grade 10: 72 students (48 boys, 24 girls); Grade 11: 85 students (59 boys, 26 girls); Grade 12: 69 students (47 boys, 22 girls); Postgraduate: 11 students (8 boys, 3 girls). 71% of students are boarding students. 31% are state residents. 20 states are represented in upper school student body. 12% are international students. International students from Brazil, Canada, Germany, Japan, Mexico, and Republic of Korea; 6 other countries represented in student body.
Faculty School total: 52. In upper school: 31 men, 21 women; 25 have advanced degrees; 30 reside on campus.

Subjects Offered 20th century American writers, 3-dimensional art, acting, advanced chemistry, advanced computer applications, Advanced Placement courses, advanced studio art-AP, algebra, American government, American history, American history-AP, American literature, American literature-AP, architecture, art, art history, art history-AP, art-AP, astronomy, Basic programming, biochemistry, bioethics, DNA and culture, biology, biology-AP, calculus, calculus-AP, ceramics, chemistry, chemistry-AP, Chinese history, Chinese studies, choral music, chorus, computer programming-AP, computers, conflict resolution, contemporary issues, current events, drama, drawing and design, driver education, ecology, environmental systems, economics, electives, electronic music, electronic publishing, English, English literature, English literature-AP, English-AP, environmental science, environmental studies, ESL, ethics, filmmaking, French, French as a second language, French-AP, functions, geography, geology, geometry, government, health, heritage of American Women, Holocaust, Holocaust studies, honors English, honors U.S. history, honors world history, instrumental music, Internet, jazz band, keyboarding, literary magazine, modern world history, music, music theory, organic biochemistry, photo shop, photography, physics, physics-AP, poetry, pre-calculus, psychology, reading/study skills, Russian, Russian history, Russian studies, SAT preparation, sculpture, senior internship, senior project, Spanish, Spanish-AP, speech communications, sports science, statistics, studio art—AP, theater, theater arts, TOEFL preparation, trigonometry, U.S. history, U.S. history-AP, visual and performing arts, vocal ensemble, women in literature, women in society, world history, World-Wide-Web publishing, writing, writing fundamentals.

Graduation Requirements Arts, English, foreign language, mathematics, science, social studies (includes history).

Special Academic Programs Advanced Placement exam preparation in 11 subject areas; honors section; independent study; study abroad; ESL (16 students enrolled).

College Placement 68 students graduated in 2005; 67 went to college, including Gettysburg College; Saint Michael's College; Skidmore College; St. Lawrence University; United States Naval Academy; University of Vermont. Other: 1 had other specific plans. Mean SAT verbal: 545, mean SAT math: 545.

Student Life Upper grades have specified standards of dress, student council, honor system. Discipline rests primarily with faculty.

Tuition and Aid Day student tuition: $20,800; 7-day tuition and room/board: $35,300. Tuition installment plan (Academic Management Services Plan, FACTS Tuition Payment Plan, monthly payment plans, individually arranged payment plans). Need-based scholarship grants available. In 2005–06, 37% of upper-school students received aid. Total amount of financial aid awarded in 2005–06: $1,300,000.

Admissions Traditional secondary-level entrance grade is 9. For fall 2005, 367 students applied for upper-level admission, 241 were accepted, 108 enrolled. Any standardized test, SSAT, ERB, PSAT, SAT, PLAN or ACT, TOEFL or SLEP, Wechsler Intelligence Scale for Children III, WISC/Woodcock-Johnson, Woodcock-Johnson/ Reading Inventory, WRAT or writing sample required. Deadline for receipt of application materials: February 1. Application fee required: $50. Interview required.

Athletics Interscholastic: alpine skiing (boys, girls), baseball (b), basketball (b,g), cross-country running (b,g), field hockey (g), football (b), golf (b,g), hockey (b,g), ice hockey (b,g), lacrosse (b,g), nordic skiing (b,g), running (b,g), ski jumping (b,g), skiing (cross-country) (b,g), skiing (downhill) (b,g), snowboarding (b,g), soccer (b,g), softball (g), tennis (b,g), track and field (b,g); coed interscholastic: aerobics/dance, back packing, ballet, bicycling, canoeing/kayaking, dance, dressage, equestrian sports, fishing, freestyle skiing, horseback riding, independent competitive sports, mountain biking, trap and skeet; coed intramural: bicycling, billiards, blading, canoeing/ kayaking, climbing, combined training, figure skating, fishing, fitness, fly fishing, freestyle skiing, Frisbee, hiking/backpacking, ice skating, in-line skating, jogging, kayaking, mountain biking, mountaineering, outdoor activities, outdoor adventure, outdoor education, outdoor recreation, outdoor skills, outdoors, physical fitness, physical training, rappelling, rock climbing, ropes courses, skateboarding, skiing (downhill), snowboarding, snowshoeing, strength & conditioning, telemark skiing, touch football, ultimate Frisbee, volleyball, walking, wall climbing, weight lifting, weight training, wilderness survival, winter walking, yoga. 5 coaches, 2 trainers.

Computers Computers are regularly used in all academic classes. Computer network features include campus e-mail, on-campus library services, CD-ROMs, online commercial services, Internet access, office computer access, DVD, wireless campus network, Tablet PCs.

Contact William J. Newman, Dean of Admissions. 802-869-6229. Fax: 802-869-6242. E-mail: admissions@vermontacademy.org. Web site: www.vermontacademy. org.

ANNOUNCEMENT FROM THE SCHOOL Vermont Academy offers an exciting college-preparatory curriculum designed for the development of confident and independent learners. Small classes and personal attention put each student in the front row. Everyone makes the team in 18 sports offerings. Students discover their talents in visual and performing arts classes. Highlights include a Tablet PC program with wireless Internet access and new on-campus facilities: Winter Sports Park for skiing, jumping, and snowboarding; 20-student dormitory; renovated gym with new locker rooms, fitness center, and dance studio; an observatory with high-powered telescope; and a Performing Arts Center with a 350-seat state-of-the-art theater.

See full description on page 1114.

VIANNEY HIGH SCHOOL

1311 South Kirkwood Road
St. Louis, Missouri 63122
Head of School: Mr. Lawrence D. Keller

General Information Boys' day college-preparatory, arts, business, religious studies, and technology school, affiliated with Roman Catholic Church. Grades 9–12. Founded: 1960. Setting: suburban. Nearest major city is Saint Louis. 37-acre campus. 6 buildings on campus. Approved or accredited by National Catholic Education Association, North Central Association of Colleges and Schools, The College Board, and Missouri Department of Education. Endowment: $659,000. Total enrollment: 734. Upper school average class size: 22. Upper school faculty-student ratio: 1:22.

Upper School Student Profile Grade 9: 172 students (172 boys); Grade 10: 190 students (190 boys); Grade 11: 181 students (181 boys); Grade 12: 181 students (181 boys). 98% of students are Roman Catholic.

Faculty School total: 49. In upper school: 35 men, 6 women; 29 have advanced degrees.

Subjects Offered Accounting, advanced chemistry, advanced math, Advanced Placement courses, algebra, American government, American history, American history-AP, American literature-AP, analysis, analysis and differential calculus, analytic geometry, ancient world history, architectural drawing, Basic programming, biology, biology-AP, British literature (honors), business law, business mathematics, calculus, calculus-AP, Catholic belief and practice, chemistry, choir, Christian and Hebrew scripture, Christian doctrine, Christian ethics, Christian scripture, church history, communication skills, composition, computer applications, computer programming, conceptual physics, concert band, contemporary history, contemporary issues, creative writing, critical studies in film, drafting, drama, drama performance, drawing, economics, English, English composition, English literature, English-AP, environmental science, film studies, fine arts, foreign language, fractals, French, German, German literature, government, health and safety, health and wellness, history of the Catholic Church, honors algebra, honors English, honors geometry, honors U.S. history, HTML design, introduction to theater, jazz band, journalism, keyboarding/computer, lab science, leadership skills, leadership training, literature, math analysis, music performance, music theory, physics, physics-AP, practical arts, pre-calculus, probability and statistics, set design, speech communications, stage design, studio art, trigonometry, U.S. government, U.S. history, U.S. history-AP, Web site design, weight training, weightlifting, world geography, yearbook.

Graduation Requirements 100 hours of community service.

Special Academic Programs Advanced Placement exam preparation in 8 subject areas; honors section; study at local college for college credit; remedial reading and/or remedial writing; remedial math; special instructional classes for students with learning disabilities, Attention Deficit Disorder, dyslexia, emotional and behavioral problems.

College Placement 194 students graduated in 2005; 184 went to college, including Missouri State University; Rockhurst University; Saint Louis University; Southeast Missouri State University; St. Louis Community College at Meramec; University of Missouri–Columbia. Other: 5 went to work, 3 entered military service, 2 had other specific plans. Median composite ACT: 23. 25% scored over 26 on composite ACT.

Student Life Upper grades have specified standards of dress, student council, honor system. Discipline rests equally with students and faculty. Attendance at religious services is required.

Tuition and Aid Day student tuition: $7800. Tuition installment plan (The Tuition Plan, SMART Tuition Payment Plan, FACTS Tuition Payment Plan, monthly payment plans, individually arranged payment plans). Tuition reduction for siblings, merit scholarship grants, need-based scholarship grants, paying campus jobs available.

Admissions Traditional secondary-level entrance grade is 9. For fall 2005, 761 students applied for upper-level admission, 751 were accepted, 734 enrolled. High School Placement Test (closed version) from Scholastic Testing Service required. Deadline for receipt of application materials: none. Application fee required: $7. On-campus interview recommended.

Athletics Interscholastic: aquatics, baseball, basketball, bowling, cross-country running, diving, football, golf, ice hockey, in-line hockey, lacrosse, racquetball, roller hockey, soccer, swimming and diving, tennis, track and field, volleyball, wrestling; intramural: flag football, paint ball, touch football. 3 PE instructors, 35 coaches, 1 trainer.

Computers Computers are regularly used in computer applications, creative writing, design, drafting, drawing and design, engineering, English, journalism, keyboarding, lab/keyboard, media, news writing, newspaper, photojournalism, programming, publications, publishing, research skills, technical drawing, technology, typing, Web site design, word processing, writing, writing, writing fundamentals, yearbook classes. Computer network features include campus e-mail, on-campus library services, CD-ROMs, online commercial services, Internet access, file transfer, office computer access, DVD, wireless campus network.

Contact Dennis A. Matreci, Assistant Principal. 314-965-4853 Ext. 116. Fax: 314-965-1950. E-mail: dmatreci@vianney.com. Web site: www.vianney.com.

Vicksburg Catholic School

VICKSBURG CATHOLIC SCHOOL

1900 Grove Street
Vicksburg, Mississippi 39183
Head of School: Mrs. Michele Townsend

General Information Coeducational day college-preparatory and religious studies school, affiliated with Roman Catholic Church. Grades PK–12. Founded: 1860. Setting: rural. Nearest major city is Jackson. 8-acre campus. 3 buildings on campus. Approved or accredited by Southern Association of Colleges and Schools and Mississippi Department of Education. Endowment: $350,000. Total enrollment: 602. Upper school average class size: 25. Upper school faculty-student ratio: 1:12.

Upper School Student Profile Grade 9: 50 students (27 boys, 23 girls); Grade 10: 38 students (12 boys, 26 girls); Grade 11: 38 students (22 boys, 16 girls); Grade 12: 41 students (21 boys, 20 girls). 50% of students are Roman Catholic.

Faculty School total: 50. In upper school: 9 men, 15 women; 4 have advanced degrees.

Subjects Offered Algebra, American government, American history, American literature, anatomy and physiology, art, band, biology, British literature, calculus-AP, cartooning/animation, Catholic belief and practice, celestial navigation, chemistry, choir, computer applications, desktop publishing, environmental science, foreign language, geometry, health, honors algebra, honors English, honors geometry, honors U.S. history, keyboarding, law, law and the legal system, learning lab, mathematics, pre-algebra, pre-calculus, psychology, religion, Spanish, statistics, theology, trigonometry, U.S. government, U.S. history, weight training, world geography, world history.

Graduation Requirements Mississippi state requirements.

Special Academic Programs Advanced Placement exam preparation in 1 subject area; honors section; special instructional classes for students with learning disabilities, Attention Deficit Disorder, dyslexia, emotional and behavioral problems.

College Placement 46 students graduated in 2005; 44 went to college, including Hinds Community College; Mississippi State University; University of Mississippi. Other: 1 entered military service, 1 had other specific plans. Median composite ACT: 24. 27% scored over 26 on composite ACT.

Student Life Upper grades have specified standards of dress, student council, honor system. Discipline rests primarily with faculty. Attendance at religious services is required.

Tuition and Aid Day student tuition: $3500. Tuition installment plan (monthly payment plans, bank draft). Tuition reduction for siblings, need-based scholarship grants available. In 2005–06, 2% of upper-school students received aid. Total amount of financial aid awarded in 2005–06: $20,000.

Admissions Traditional secondary-level entrance grade is 9. For fall 2005, 67 students applied for upper-level admission, 67 were accepted, 59 enrolled. Deadline for receipt of application materials: none. Application fee required: $100. Interview required.

Athletics Interscholastic: baseball (boys), basketball (b,g), cheering (g), cross-country running (b,g), dance (g), dance squad (g), dance team (g), football (b), golf (b), soccer (b,g), softball (g), swimming and diving (b,g), track and field (b,g); intramural: bowling (b,g); coed interscholastic: swimming and diving; coed intramural: bowling. 2 PE instructors, 5 coaches, 1 trainer.

Computers Computers are regularly used in accounting, desktop publishing, keyboarding classes. Computer network features include on-campus library services, CD-ROMs, Internet access.

Contact Mrs. Patricia Rabalais, Admission. 601-636-2256. Fax: 601-631-0430. E-mail: patricia.rabalais@vicksburgcatholic.org.

VIEWPOINT SCHOOL

23620 Mulholland Highway
Calabasas, California 91302
Head of School: Dr. Robert J. Dworkoski

petersons.com

General Information Coeducational day college-preparatory and arts school. Grades K–12. Founded: 1961. Setting: suburban. Nearest major city is Los Angeles. 25-acre campus. 4 buildings on campus. Approved or accredited by California Association of Independent Schools and Western Association of Schools and Colleges. Member of National Association of Independent Schools. Endowment: $4.4 million. Total enrollment: 1,185. Upper school average class size: 18. Upper school faculty-student ratio: 1:10.

Upper School Student Profile Grade 9: 120 students (60 boys, 60 girls); Grade 10: 112 students (60 boys, 52 girls); Grade 11: 108 students (60 boys, 48 girls); Grade 12: 92 students (48 boys, 44 girls).

Faculty School total: 142. In upper school: 28 men, 38 women; 48 have advanced degrees.

Subjects Offered Adolescent issues, advanced chemistry, advanced computer applications, advanced studio art-AP, African literature, algebra, American history, American history-AP, American literature, ancient history, ancient world history, animation, art, art appreciation, art history, art history-AP, Asian history, Asian studies, ballet, Basic programming, basic skills, Bible as literature, biology, biology-AP, British literature, business skills, calculus, calculus-AP, California writers, ceramics, character education, chemistry, chemistry-AP, Chinese, Chinese studies, choir, choreography, chorus, clayworking, college admission preparation, community

service, comparative government and politics, comparative government and politics-AP, comparative politics, computer animation, computer keyboarding, computer programming, computer science, computer science-AP, concert band, contemporary women writers, creative writing, critical studies in film, dance, debate, decision making skills, diversity studies, drama, drama performance, dramatic arts, drawing and design, earth science, economics, English, English language-AP, English literature, English literature-AP, ensembles, environmental education, environmental science, environmental science-AP, European history, European history-AP, film, film appreciation, filmmaking, fine arts, French, French language-AP, French literature-AP, geometry, global science, government/civics, history, history-AP, Holocaust and other genocides, honors algebra, honors English, honors geometry, human development, humanities, instrumental music, international relations, jazz, jazz band, jazz dance, jazz ensemble, journalism, Latin, Latin American history, Latin History, library skills, literary magazine, literature by women, mathematics, medieval history, multicultural literature, music, music composition, music history, music theory-AP, newspaper, oceanography, outdoor education, performing arts, photography, physical education, physics, physics-AP, physiology, poetry, psychology, psychology-AP, public speaking, robotics, science, sculpture, senior project, Shakespeare, short story, social studies, sociology, Spanish, Spanish language-AP, Spanish literature-AP, speech and debate, statistics and probability, student publications, studio art-AP, study skills, swimming, theater, trigonometry, U.S. government-AP, video, vocal jazz, women's literature, word processing, world history, yearbook.

Graduation Requirements Arts and fine arts (art, music, dance, drama), computer science, English, foreign language, mathematics, physical education (includes health), science, social studies (includes history). Community service is required.

Special Academic Programs Advanced Placement exam preparation in 20 subject areas; honors section; independent study; study abroad.

College Placement 106 students graduated in 2005; all went to college, including Loyola Marymount University; University of California, Berkeley; University of California, Davis; University of California, San Diego; University of California, Santa Barbara; University of Southern California. Mean SAT verbal: 637, mean SAT math: 661, mean composite ACT: 26.

Student Life Upper grades have specified standards of dress, student council. Discipline rests primarily with faculty.

Summer Programs Remediation, enrichment, advancement, sports, art/fine arts, computer instruction programs offered; session focuses on academics, arts, sports, and recreation; held on campus; accepts boys and girls; open to students from other schools. 315 students usually enrolled. 2006 schedule: June 20 to July 28. Application deadline: none.

Tuition and Aid Day student tuition: $19,100. Tuition installment plan (monthly payment plans). Tuition reduction for siblings, need-based scholarship grants available. In 2005–06, 14% of upper-school students received aid. Total amount of financial aid awarded in 2005–06: $856,885.

Admissions Traditional secondary-level entrance grade is 9. For fall 2005, 115 students applied for upper-level admission, 78 were accepted, 42 enrolled. ISEE required. Deadline for receipt of application materials: January 14. Application fee required: $100. Interview required.

Athletics Interscholastic: baseball (boys), basketball (b,g), football (b), soccer (b,g), softball (g), volleyball (b,g); intramural: back packing (b,g), ball hockey (b,g), ballet (b,g), baseball (b), basketball (b,g), soccer (b,g), volleyball (b,g); coed interscholastic: cross-country running, equestrian sports, golf, swimming and diving, tennis; coed intramural: cheering, dance, dance team, fencing, hiking/backpacking, modern dance, outdoor education, physical fitness, strength & conditioning, weight training. 15 PE instructors, 15 coaches, 1 trainer.

Computers Computers are regularly used in animation, basic skills, college planning, English, foreign language, history, keyboarding, library skills, mathematics, multimedia, music, newspaper, publications, science, video film production, Web site design, word processing, yearbook classes. Computer network features include campus e-mail, on-campus library services, CD-ROMs, online commercial services, Internet access, wireless campus network.

Contact Mrs. Julie Montgomery, Coordinator of Admission and Financial Aid Offices. 818-591-6560. Fax: 818-591-0834. E-mail: admission@viewpoint.org. Web site: www.viewpoint.org.

ANNOUNCEMENT FROM THE SCHOOL Viewpoint is an independent, nonprofit, coeducational college-preparatory day school for grades K–12. Viewpoint is located in the foothills of the Santa Monica Mountains on a 25-acre campus with scenic vistas, rolling hillsides, and large heritage oaks. For 46 years, families have been attracted to Viewpoint's excellent academic programs, its tranquil and nurturing environment, and its extensive facilities for academics, athletics, film, computer science, arts, and music.

See full description on page 1116.

See full description on page 1116.

592 *www.petersons.com*

Peterson's Private Secondary Schools 2007

VILLAGE CHRISTIAN SCHOOLS

8930 Village Avenue
Sun Valley, California 91352
Head of School: Dr. Ronald G. Sipus

General Information Coeducational day college-preparatory, general academic, arts, religious studies, and technology school, affiliated with Christian faith. Grades K–12. Founded: 1949. Setting: suburban. Nearest major city is Los Angeles. 110-acre campus. 7 buildings on campus. Approved or accredited by Association of Christian Schools International, Western Association of Schools and Colleges, and California Department of Education. Total enrollment: 1,735. Upper school average class size: 24. Upper school faculty-student ratio: 1:17.

Upper School Student Profile Grade 9: 180 students (100 boys, 80 girls); Grade 10: 140 students (60 boys, 80 girls); Grade 11: 146 students (70 boys, 76 girls); Grade 12; 144 students (72 boys, 72 girls). 75% of students are Christian faith.

Faculty School total: 87. In upper school: 20 men, 15 women; 10 have advanced degrees.

Subjects Offered Algebra, American government-AP, American history-AP, American literature, anatomy, art, ASB Leadership, band, Bible studies, biology, biology-AP, British literature, calculus-AP, career education, careers, ceramics, chemistry, choir, choral music, church history, clayworking, computer graphics, computer literacy, drama, earth science, economics, English, English language and composition-AP, English literature and composition-AP, English-AP, geometry, health education, history-AP, honors English, jazz band, leadership training, library assistant, Life of Christ, marching band, mathematics, painting, physical education, physics, physiology, pre-calculus, Spanish, Spanish language-AP, Spanish literature-AP, statistics, statistics-AP, strings, theater arts, trigonometry, U.S. government, U.S. history, world history, world religions, yearbook.

Graduation Requirements Arts and fine arts (art, music, dance, drama), computer science, English, foreign language, mathematics, physical education (includes health), religion (includes Bible studies and theology), science, social science, social studies (includes history).

Special Academic Programs Advanced Placement exam preparation in 9 subject areas; honors section; study at local college for college credit; study abroad.

College Placement 141 students graduated in 2005; 135 went to college, including Azusa Pacific University; California State University, Northridge; San Diego State University; University of California, Irvine; University of California, Los Angeles; University of Southern California. Other: 1 went to work, 2 entered military service, 3 had other specific plans. Median SAT verbal: 510, median SAT math: 520. 23% scored over 600 on SAT verbal, 25% scored over 600 on SAT math.

Student Life Upper grades have uniform requirement, student council. Discipline rests equally with students and faculty.

Summer Programs Remediation, enrichment, advancement, art/fine arts, computer instruction programs offered; session focuses on academic advancement and remediation; held on campus; accepts boys and girls; open to students from other schools. 590 students usually enrolled. 2006 schedule: June 19 to July 28. Application deadline: June 9.

Tuition and Aid Day student tuition: $6692. Tuition installment plan (monthly payment plans, individually arranged payment plans). Tuition reduction for siblings, merit scholarship grants, need-based scholarship grants, short-term emergency help for continuing families available. In 2005–06, 5% of upper-school students received aid; total upper-school merit-scholarship money awarded: $2500.

Admissions Traditional secondary-level entrance grade is 9. For fall 2005, 90 students applied for upper-level admission, 61 were accepted, 60 enrolled. ISEE required. Deadline for receipt of application materials: none. Application fee required: $100. On-campus interview required.

Athletics Interscholastic: baseball (boys), basketball (b,g), cheering (g), cross-country running (b,g), dance team (g), football (b), physical fitness (b,g), physical training (b,g), soccer (b,g), softball (g), tennis (b,g), track and field (b,g), volleyball (b,g); intramural: basketball (b,g), cross-country running (b,g), flag football (b,g), physical fitness (b,g), physical training (b,g); coed interscholastic: golf; coed intramural: equestrian sports. 4 PE instructors, 15 coaches, 1 trainer.

Computers Computers are regularly used in English, graphic arts, history, mathematics, science, Spanish, technology, yearbook classes. Computer network features include campus e-mail, on-campus library services, CD-ROMs, online commercial services, Internet access, file transfer, office computer access.

Contact Mrs. Lorraine Carter, Admissions Administrative Assistant. 818-767-8382 Ext. 209. Fax: 818-768-2006. E-mail: lorrainec@villagechristian.org. Web site: www.villagechristian.org.

VILLA MARIA ACADEMY

2403 West Eighth Street
Erie, Pennsylvania 16505-4492
Head of School: Ms. Geri Cicchetti

General Information Coeducational day college-preparatory and general academic school, affiliated with Roman Catholic Church. Grades 9–12. Founded: 1892. Setting: suburban. 3 buildings on campus. Approved or accredited by Middle States Association of Colleges and Schools. Total enrollment: 390. Upper school average class size: 14. Upper school faculty-student ratio: 1:11.

Upper School Student Profile Grade 9: 84 students (13 boys, 71 girls); Grade 10: 96 students (20 boys, 76 girls); Grade 11: 95 students (16 boys, 79 girls); Grade 12: 115 students (22 boys, 93 girls). 88% of students are Roman Catholic.

Faculty School total: 47. In upper school: 13 men, 34 women; 13 have advanced degrees.

Subjects Offered Arts, community service, computer science, English, fine arts, French, health, keyboarding, Latin, mathematics, newspaper, physical education, practical arts, science, social studies, Spanish, theology, word processing, yearbook.

Graduation Requirements Arts and fine arts (art, music, dance, drama), English, foreign language, mathematics, physical education (includes health), religion (includes Bible studies and theology), science, social studies (includes history). Community service is required.

Special Academic Programs Advanced Placement exam preparation in 5 subject areas; honors section; study at local college for college credit.

College Placement 117 students graduated in 2005; 109 went to college, including Edinboro University of Pennsylvania; Gannon University; George Mason University; The Pennsylvania State University University Park Campus. Other: 8 went to work.

Student Life Upper grades have uniform requirement, student council, honor system. Discipline rests primarily with faculty.

Tuition and Aid Day student tuition: $4475–$4725. Tuition installment plan (FACTS Tuition Payment Plan). Tuition reduction for siblings, merit scholarship grants, need-based scholarship grants available.

Admissions Traditional secondary-level entrance grade is 9. Deadline for receipt of application materials: January 27. Application fee required: $10.

Athletics Interscholastic: baseball (boys), basketball (b,g), bowling (g), cheering (g), golf (b,g), soccer (b,g), softball (g), swimming and diving (g), tennis (b,g), volleyball (g), water polo (g); coed interscholastic: cross-country running, track and field. 1 PE instructor.

Computers Computers are regularly used in computer applications, French, graphic design, keyboarding, literary magazine, newspaper, Spanish, yearbook classes. Computer network features include on-campus library services, CD-ROMs, Internet access, file transfer, DVD, wireless campus network.

Contact Mrs. Kathleen DiNicola, Assistant Principal. 814-838-2061 Ext. 233. Fax: 814-836-0881. E-mail: kdinicola@villamaria.com. Web site: www.villamaria.com.

VILLA MARIA ACADEMY

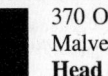

370 Old Lincoln Highway
Malvern, Pennsylvania 19355
Head of School: Sr. Marita Carmel McCarthy, IHM

General Information Girls' day college-preparatory, religious studies, and technology school, affiliated with Roman Catholic Church. Grades 9–12. Founded: 1872. Setting: suburban. Nearest major city is Philadelphia. 28-acre campus. 4 buildings on campus. Approved or accredited by Middle States Association of Colleges and Schools, The College Board, and Pennsylvania Department of Education. Total enrollment: 465. Upper school average class size: 15. Upper school faculty-student ratio: 1:9.

Upper School Student Profile Grade 9: 116 students (116 girls); Grade 10: 115 students (115 girls); Grade 11: 124 students (124 girls); Grade 12: 110 students (110 girls). 95% of students are Roman Catholic.

Faculty School total: 51. In upper school: 6 men, 45 women; 38 have advanced degrees.

Subjects Offered Accounting, advanced chemistry, advanced math, algebra, American government, American literature, analysis, art, Bible, biology, biology-AP, British literature, British literature (honors), calculus, calculus-AP, Catholic belief and practice, chemistry, chemistry-AP, choral music, church history, college counseling, computer applications, computer keyboarding, computer literacy, discrete mathematics, English, English composition, English language-AP, English literature, English literature-AP, environmental science, European history, European history-AP, first aid, French, French-AP, geometry, government-AP, grammar, guidance, health education, history of the Catholic Church, honors algebra, honors English, honors geometry, honors U.S. history, honors world history, information design technology, Latin, library skills, literary magazine, modern European history, modern European history-AP, music performance, music theory, music-AP, orchestra, physical education, physics, physics-AP, piano, religious studies, social studies, Spanish, Spanish language-AP, statistics, statistics-AP, studio art, studio art-AP, trigonometry, U.S. history, U.S. history-AP, vocal ensemble, voice, Western civilization, world issues.

Graduation Requirements Catholic belief and practice, college admission preparation, computer applications, English, foreign language, keyboarding/computer, mathematics, physical education (includes health), science, social studies (includes history), theology.

Special Academic Programs Advanced Placement exam preparation in 14 subject areas; honors section; study at local college for college credit.

College Placement 99 students graduated in 2005; all went to college, including Lehigh University; Saint Joseph's University; The Pennsylvania State University University Park Campus; University of Delaware; Villanova University. Mean SAT verbal: 590, mean SAT math: 590.

Student Life Upper grades have uniform requirement, student council. Discipline rests equally with students and faculty. Attendance at religious services is required.

Villa Maria Academy

Tuition and Aid Day student tuition: $10,500. Tuition reduction for siblings, merit scholarship grants, need-based scholarship grants available. In 2005–06, 12% of upper-school students received aid; total upper-school merit-scholarship money awarded: $125,000. Total amount of financial aid awarded in 2005–06: $410,900.

Admissions Traditional secondary-level entrance grade is 9. For fall 2005, 255 students applied for upper-level admission, 145 were accepted, 116 enrolled. High School Placement Test (closed version) from Scholastic Testing Service required. Deadline for receipt of application materials: January 31. Application fee required: $50. On-campus interview required.

Athletics Interscholastic: basketball, cheering, cross-country running, dance team, field hockey, golf, indoor track, indoor track & field, lacrosse, soccer, softball, swimming and diving, tennis, track and field, volleyball, winter (indoor) track. 2 PE instructors, 12 coaches, 1 trainer.

Computers Computers are regularly used in accounting, art, Bible studies, Christian doctrine, college planning, economics, English, French, health, history, humanities, journalism, Latin, library skills, mathematics, music, publications, religious studies, science, social studies, Spanish, theology, writing, yearbook classes. Computer network features include campus e-mail, on-campus library services, CD-ROMs, online commercial services, Internet access, file transfer, office computer access.

Contact Mrs. Mary Kay D. Napoli, Director of Admissions. 610-644-2551 Ext. 40. Fax: 610-644-2866. E-mail: mknapoli@vmahs.org.

VILLA VICTORIA ACADEMY

376 West Upper Ferry Road
Ewing, New Jersey 08628
Head of School: Sr. Lillian Harrington, MPF

General Information Girls' day college-preparatory, arts, religious studies, and technology school, affiliated with Roman Catholic Church. Grades PK–12. Founded: 1933. Setting: suburban. Nearest major city is Trenton. 44-acre campus. 7 buildings on campus. Approved or accredited by British Accreditation Council, Middle States Association of Colleges and Schools, National Catholic Education Association, New Jersey Association of Independent Schools, and New Jersey Department of Education. Member of Secondary School Admission Test Board. Endowment: $375,000. Total enrollment: 246. Upper school average class size: 12. Upper school faculty-student ratio: 1:6.

Upper School Student Profile Grade 9: 33 students (33 girls); Grade 10: 22 students (22 girls); Grade 11: 14 students (14 girls); Grade 12: 23 students (23 girls). 79% of students are Roman Catholic.

Faculty School total: 43. In upper school: 5 men, 21 women; 14 have advanced degrees.

Subjects Offered Algebra, American literature, art, art history, art-AP, astronomy, Bible studies, biology, calculus, calculus-AP, campus ministry, Catholic belief and practice, ceramics, chemistry, chemistry-AP, choral music, chorus, college planning, community service, computer programming, computer science, creative writing, drama, driver education, earth science, electronics, English, English literature, English-AP, environmental science, European history, fine arts, French, geography, geometry, health, history, humanities, Latin, mathematics, microbiology, multimedia, music, peer ministry, personal development, photography, physical education, physics, psychology, religion, SAT preparation, science, social studies, Spanish, theater, trigonometry, world history, world literature.

Graduation Requirements American literature, art history, arts and fine arts (art, music, dance, drama), biology, British literature, chemistry, computer science, English, foreign language, mathematics, physical education (includes health), physics, religion (includes Bible studies and theology), SAT/ACT preparation, science, social studies (includes history), world cultures, world literature, interdisciplinary humanities. Community service is required.

Special Academic Programs Advanced Placement exam preparation in 6 subject areas; honors section; independent study; academic accommodation for the gifted, the musically talented, and the artistically talented.

College Placement 22 students graduated in 2005; all went to college, including Saint Joseph's University; University of Delaware; University of Pittsburgh; University of Richmond; University of Rochester; Villanova University.

Student Life Upper grades have uniform requirement, student council, honor system. Discipline rests primarily with faculty. Attendance at religious services is required.

Tuition and Aid Day student tuition: $7600–$8375. Tuition installment plan (FACTS Tuition Payment Plan, individually arranged payment plans, 2-payment plan). Merit scholarship grants, need-based scholarship grants available. In 2005–06, 20% of upper-school students received aid.

Admissions Traditional secondary-level entrance grade is 9. For fall 2005, 62 students applied for upper-level admission, 49 were accepted, 20 enrolled. Brigance Test of Basic Skills, Gates MacGinite (vocab) and Stanford Achievement Test (math), Gates MacGinite Reading Tests, SSAT or Wechsler Intelligence Scale for Children III required. Deadline for receipt of application materials: none. Application fee required: $50. On-campus interview required.

Athletics Interscholastic: basketball, cross-country running, soccer, softball, tennis; intramural: aerobics, aerobics/dance. 1 PE instructor, 6 coaches.

Computers Computers are regularly used in art, English, foreign language, history, mathematics, music, SAT preparation, science, theater classes. Computer network features include campus e-mail, on-campus library services, CD-ROMs, Internet access.

Contact Ms. Marcie Sandleben, Director of Admission. 609-882-1700 Ext. 19. Fax: 609-882-8421. E-mail: msandleben@villavictoria.org. Web site: www.villavictoria.org.

VILLA WALSH ACADEMY

455 Western Avenue
Morristown, New Jersey 07960
Head of School: Sr. Patricia Pompa

General Information Girls' day college-preparatory, arts, religious studies, and technology school, affiliated with Roman Catholic Church. Grades 7–12. Founded: 1967. Setting: suburban. Nearest major city is New York, NY. 130-acre campus. 3 buildings on campus. Approved or accredited by Middle States Association of Colleges and Schools, New Jersey Association of Independent Schools, and New Jersey Department of Education. Endowment: $4 million. Total enrollment: 234. Upper school average class size: 12. Upper school faculty-student ratio: 1:8.

Upper School Student Profile Grade 9: 49 students (49 girls); Grade 10: 52 students (52 girls); Grade 11: 55 students (55 girls); Grade 12: 46 students (46 girls). 90% of students are Roman Catholic.

Faculty School total: 35. In upper school: 5 men, 30 women; 23 have advanced degrees.

Subjects Offered Advanced Placement courses, algebra, American history, American literature, anatomy and physiology, art, Bible as literature, biology, biology-AP, British literature, British literature (honors), calculus, calculus-AP, career education, career/college preparation, chemistry, chemistry-AP, choral music, chorus, church history, college admission preparation, computer applications, computer graphics, computer keyboarding, computer literacy, computer processing, computer programming, computer science, computer skills, CPR, creative writing, desktop publishing, driver education, economics, economics and history, English, English language and composition-AP, English literature, environmental science, environmental science-AP, ethics, European civilization, family life, finite math, first aid, French, French-AP, geometry, health education, honors English, honors geometry, honors U.S. history, Italian, life science, mathematics, modern European history, modern European history-AP, moral theology, philosophy, physical education, physics, physics-AP, pre-algebra, pre-calculus, psychology, psychology-AP, religion, social studies, Spanish, Spanish-AP, studio art, theology, U.S. government and politics, U.S. government and politics-AP, U.S. history, U.S. history-AP, voice ensemble, Web site design, world history, world literature.

Graduation Requirements Arts and fine arts (art, music, dance, drama), English, foreign language, mathematics, physical education (includes health), science, social studies (includes history), theology.

Special Academic Programs Advanced Placement exam preparation in 11 subject areas; honors section; independent study; academic accommodation for the gifted, the musically talented, and the artistically talented.

College Placement 48 students graduated in 2005; all went to college, including Colgate University; Fairfield University; Lehigh University; New York University; University of Pennsylvania; Villanova University. Mean SAT verbal: 680, mean SAT math: 660. 65% scored over 600 on SAT verbal, 65% scored over 600 on SAT math.

Student Life Upper grades have uniform requirement, student council, honor system. Discipline rests primarily with faculty. Attendance at religious services is required.

Tuition and Aid Day student tuition: $11,500. Tuition installment plan (Insured Tuition Payment Plan, Key Tuition Payment Plan, individually arranged payment plans). Merit scholarship grants, need-based scholarship grants available. In 2005–06, 12% of upper-school students received aid; total upper-school merit-scholarship money awarded: $15,000. Total amount of financial aid awarded in 2005–06: $89,000.

Admissions Traditional secondary-level entrance grade is 9. For fall 2005, 160 students applied for upper-level admission, 68 were accepted, 65 enrolled. Math, reading, and mental ability tests required. Deadline for receipt of application materials: none. Application fee required: $50. On-campus interview required.

Athletics Interscholastic: basketball, cross-country running, indoor track, lacrosse, soccer, softball, swimming and diving, tennis, track and field, winter (indoor) track. 2 PE instructors, 22 coaches.

Computers Computers are regularly used in college planning, desktop publishing, independent study, keyboarding, library science, mathematics, newspaper, programming, SAT preparation, science, technology, Web site design, word processing classes. Computer network features include campus e-mail, on-campus library services, CD-ROMs, Internet access, DVD, wireless campus network.

Contact Sr. Doris Lavinthal, Director. 973-538-3680 Ext. 175. Fax: 973-538-6733. E-mail: lavinthald@aol.com. Web site: www.villawalsh.org.

VIRGINIA BEACH FRIENDS SCHOOL

1537 Laskin Road
Virginia Beach, Virginia 23451
Head of School: Mr. Jonathan K. Alden

General Information Coeducational day college-preparatory, general academic, arts, and religious studies school, affiliated with Society of Friends. Grades PK–12. Founded: 1955. Setting: suburban. Nearest major city is Norfolk. 11-acre campus. 3 buildings on campus. Approved or accredited by Friends Council on Education, Virginia Association of Independent Schools, and Virginia Department of Education. Endowment: $109,000. Total enrollment: 210. Upper school average class size: 12. Upper school faculty-student ratio: 1:5.

Upper School Student Profile Grade 9: 8 students (4 boys, 4 girls); Grade 10: 17 students (12 boys, 5 girls); Grade 11: 9 students (6 boys, 3 girls); Grade 12: 21 students (11 boys, 10 girls). 5% of students are members of Society of Friends.

Faculty School total: 32. In upper school: 3 men, 9 women; 4 have advanced degrees.

Graduation Requirements Peace studies, physical education (includes health), practical arts, Quakerism and ethics, science, senior internship, senior project, U.S. history, Quaker Studies. Community service is required.

Special Academic Programs Advanced Placement exam preparation in 5 subject areas; honors section; accelerated programs.

College Placement 22 students graduated in 2005; 18 went to college, including Hampshire College; Old Dominion University; Savannah College of Art and Design. Other: 4 went to work. Median SAT verbal: 600, median SAT math: 500, median composite ACT: 22. 14% scored over 600 on SAT verbal, 10% scored over 600 on SAT math, 10% scored over 26 on composite ACT.

Student Life Upper grades have specified standards of dress, student council, honor system. Discipline rests equally with students and faculty. Attendance at religious services is required.

Tuition and Aid Day student tuition: $10,200. Tuition installment plan (monthly payment plans). Merit scholarship grants, need-based scholarship grants available. In 2005–06, 12% of upper-school students received aid.

Admissions Traditional secondary-level entrance grade is 9. For fall 2005, 22 students applied for upper-level admission, 21 were accepted, 16 enrolled. Achievement tests or admissions testing required. Deadline for receipt of application materials: none. Application fee required: $50. Interview required.

Athletics Interscholastic: basketball (boys, girls), lacrosse (b); coed interscholastic: soccer, softball; coed intramural: fitness, hiking/backpacking, indoor soccer, physical fitness. 2 PE instructors, 8 coaches.

Computers Computer network features include on-campus library services, online commercial services, Internet access.

Contact Ms. Karen Wilson Forget, Director of Admissions. 757-428-7534 Ext. 104. Fax: 757-428-7511. E-mail: tkaren@friends-school.org. Web site: www.friends-school.org.

VIRGINIA EPISCOPAL SCHOOL

400 VES Road
Lynchburg, Virginia 24503
Head of School: Dr. Phillip L. Hadley

General Information Coeducational boarding and day college-preparatory, arts, religious studies, and technology school, affiliated with Episcopal Church. Grades 9–12. Founded: 1916. Setting: suburban. Nearest major city is Richmond. Students are housed in single-sex dormitories. 160-acre campus. 14 buildings on campus. Approved or accredited by National Association of Episcopal Schools, The Association of Boarding Schools, Virginia Association of Independent Schools, and Virginia Department of Education. Member of National Association of Independent Schools and Secondary School Admission Test Board. Endowment: $15 million. Total enrollment: 273. Upper school average class size: 14. Upper school faculty-student ratio: 1:8.

Upper School Student Profile Grade 9: 37 students (25 boys, 12 girls); Grade 10: 87 students (56 boys, 31 girls); Grade 11: 72 students (37 boys, 35 girls); Grade 12: 77 students (42 boys, 35 girls); Grade 13: 1 student (1 boy). 65% of students are boarding students. 56% are state residents. 17 states are represented in upper school student body. 10% are international students. International students from Cameroon, China, Finland, Germany, Greece, and Republic of Korea; 7 other countries represented in student body. 50% of students are members of Episcopal Church.

Faculty School total: 44. In upper school: 28 men, 14 women; 26 have advanced degrees; 24 reside on campus.

Subjects Offered Advanced math, algebra, American history, American history-AP, American literature, analysis, ancient history, art, art history, Bible studies, biology, biology-AP, calculus, calculus-AP, chemistry, choir, computer graphics, computer keyboarding, computer math, computer programming, computer programming-AP, computer science, computer science-AP, creative writing, drama, driver education, economics, English, English literature, English-AP, environmental science, environmental studies, ethics, ethics and responsibility, European history, European history-AP, fine arts, French, French language-AP, geometry, government/civics, grammar, graphic design, health education, history, honors algebra, honors English, honors geometry, honors U.S. history, honors world history, instrumental music, Latin, Latin American history, life issues, mathematics, medieval history, modern European

history-AP, music, music history, music theory-AP, musical theater, physical education, physics, pre-calculus, religion, SAT preparation, science, social studies, Spanish, Spanish language-AP, sports medicine, theater, theater history, theology, trigonometry, Web site design, world history, world literature, writing.

Graduation Requirements Arts and fine arts (art, music, dance, drama), computer science, English, foreign language, life issues, mathematics, physical education (includes health), religion (includes Bible studies and theology), science, social studies (includes history).

Special Academic Programs Advanced Placement exam preparation in 16 subject areas; honors section; independent study; study abroad.

College Placement 62 students graduated in 2005; all went to college, including North Carolina State University; The University of North Carolina at Chapel Hill; University of Virginia.

Student Life Upper grades have specified standards of dress, student council, honor system. Discipline rests equally with students and faculty. Attendance at religious services is required.

Tuition and Aid Day student tuition: $14,950; 5-day tuition and room/board: $22,950; 7-day tuition and room/board: $30,100. Tuition installment plan (FACTS Tuition Payment Plan, individually arranged payment plans). Tuition reduction for siblings, merit scholarship grants, need-based scholarship grants available. In 2005–06, 26% of upper-school students received aid; total upper-school merit-scholarship money awarded: $66,000. Total amount of financial aid awarded in 2005–06: $725,000.

Admissions Traditional secondary-level entrance grade is 9. For fall 2005, 199 students applied for upper-level admission, 142 were accepted, 96 enrolled. SSAT required. Deadline for receipt of application materials: none. Application fee required: $45. Interview required.

Athletics Interscholastic: baseball (boys), basketball (b,g), field hockey (g), football (b), indoor soccer (b), lacrosse (b,g), soccer (b,g), softball (g), tennis (b,g), volleyball (g), winter soccer (g), wrestling (b); intramural: weight lifting (b); coed interscholastic: cross-country running, equestrian sports, fitness, golf, horseback riding, indoor track, indoor track & field, swimming and diving, track and field, winter (indoor) track; coed intramural: paint ball, physical fitness, physical training, strength & conditioning. 1 coach, 1 trainer.

Computers Computers are regularly used in all classes. Computer network features include campus e-mail, on-campus library services, CD-ROMs, online commercial services, off-campus e-mail, Internet connections in each dorm room.

Contact Mrs. Pamela D. Barile, Director of Admission. 434-385-3605. Fax: 434-385-3603. E-mail: pbarile@ves.org. Web site: www.ves.org.

VISITATION ACADEMY OF ST. LOUIS COUNTY

3020 North Ballas Road
St. Louis, Missouri 63131
Head of School: Mrs. Rosalie Henry

General Information Coeducational day (boys' only in lower grades) college-preparatory, arts, and technology school, affiliated with Roman Catholic Church. Boys grades PK–K, girls grades PK–12. Founded: 1833. Setting: suburban. 30-acre campus. 1 building on campus. Approved or accredited by Independent Schools Association of the Central States, North Central Association of Colleges and Schools, and Missouri Department of Education. Member of National Association of Independent Schools. Endowment: $6 million. Total enrollment: 692. Upper school average class size: 18. Upper school faculty-student ratio: 1:9.

Upper School Student Profile Grade 7: 73 students (73 girls); Grade 8: 69 students (69 girls); Grade 9: 72 students (72 girls); Grade 10: 85 students (85 girls); Grade 11: 74 students (74 girls); Grade 12: 74 students (74 girls). 85% of students are Roman Catholic.

Faculty School total: 62. In upper school: 8 men, 37 women; 29 have advanced degrees.

Subjects Offered Algebra, American history, American literature, anatomy, art, art history, Bible studies, biology, calculus, ceramics, chemistry, computer art, computer math, computer programming, computer science, creative writing, drama, earth science, economics, English, English literature, European history, expository writing, fine arts, French, geography, geometry, government/civics, grammar, health, history, journalism, keyboarding, Latin, mathematics, music, photography, physical education, physical science, physics, psychology, science, social studies, Spanish, speech, theater, theology, trigonometry, world literature.

Special Academic Programs Advanced Placement exam preparation in 11 subject areas; honors section; study at local college for college credit.

College Placement 65 students graduated in 2005; all went to college, including Saint Louis University; Santa Clara University; Southern Methodist University; University of Kansas; University of Missouri–Columbia; Washington University in St. Louis. Median SAT verbal: 644, median SAT math: 630, median composite ACT: 27. 67% scored over 600 on SAT verbal, 60% scored over 600 on SAT math, 66% scored over 26 on composite ACT.

Student Life Upper grades have uniform requirement, student council. Discipline rests primarily with faculty. Attendance at religious services is required.

Summer Programs Sports programs offered; session focuses on sport camps; held on campus; accepts girls; open to students from other schools. 100 students usually enrolled.

Visitation Academy of St. Louis County

Tuition and Aid Day student tuition: $12,600. Tuition installment plan (FACTS Tuition Payment Plan). Need-based scholarship grants, need-based loans available. In 2005–06, 10% of upper-school students received aid. Total amount of financial aid awarded in 2005–06: $249,000.

Admissions Traditional secondary-level entrance grade is 7. For fall 2005, 114 students applied for upper-level admission, 87 were accepted, 49 enrolled. ISEE required. Deadline for receipt of application materials: January 29. Application fee required: $75. Interview required.

Athletics Interscholastic: basketball, cheering, cross-country running, diving, field hockey, golf, soccer, softball, swimming and diving, tennis, volleyball; intramural: basketball, field hockey, soccer, softball, volleyball. 3 PE instructors, 17 coaches, 1 trainer.

Computers Computers are regularly used in art, English, history, mathematics, science, theology classes. Computer network features include campus e-mail, on-campus library services, CD-ROMs, Internet access, file transfer, office computer access, wireless campus network.

Contact Mrs. Ingrid Bremer, Director of Admission. 314-625-9102. Fax: 314-432-7210. E-mail: ibremer@visitationacademy.org. Web site: www.visitationacademy.org.

WAKEFIELD SCHOOL

4439 Old Tavern Road
PO Box 107
The Plains, Virginia 20198
Head of School: Mr. Peter A. Quinn

petersons.com

General Information Coeducational day college-preparatory and arts school. Grades PK–12. Founded: 1972. Setting: rural. Nearest major city is Washington, DC. 50-acre campus. 4 buildings on campus. Approved or accredited by Virginia Association of Independent Schools. Endowment: $65,925. Total enrollment: 471. Upper school average class size: 9. Upper school faculty-student ratio: 1:9.

Upper School Student Profile Grade 9: 44 students (17 boys, 27 girls); Grade 10: 43 students (17 boys, 26 girls); Grade 11: 27 students (12 boys, 15 girls); Grade 12: 19 students (8 boys, 11 girls).

Faculty School total: 60. In upper school: 13 men, 15 women; 16 have advanced degrees.

Subjects Offered Algebra, American government, American history-AP, American literature, art, art history, bell choir, biology, biology-AP, British history, British literature, calculus, calculus-AP, chemistry, chemistry-AP, chorus, classical language, composition, computer applications, computer programming, drama, dramatic arts, earth science, Eastern world civilizations, English language and composition-AP, English literature and composition-AP, environmental science, environmental science-AP, European history-AP, forensics, French, French language-AP, geometry, geopolitics, government and politics-AP, government/civics, Latin, Latin-AP, model United Nations, music, music composition, music history, music theory, music theory-AP, physical fitness, physics, physics-AP, political science, psychology, publications, Spanish, Spanish language-AP, statistics, statistics-AP, studio art, studio art-AP, U.S. history, world civilizations.

Graduation Requirements Advanced math, algebra, American history, American literature, arts, biology, British literature, chemistry, computer literacy, English, geometry, government/civics, grammar, language, physical education (includes health), physics, pre-calculus, world civilizations, 2 interdisciplinary compositions, 2 thesis and portfolio projects.

Special Academic Programs Advanced Placement exam preparation in 19 subject areas; honors section; independent study.

College Placement 25 students graduated in 2005; 24 went to college, including Brigham Young University; Lynchburg College; Middlebury College; The College of William and Mary; The University of North Carolina at Chapel Hill; Washington and Lee University. Other: 1 had other specific plans. Median SAT verbal: 658, median SAT math: 616.

Student Life Upper grades have uniform requirement, student council. Discipline rests equally with students and faculty.

Summer Programs Enrichment, sports, art/fine arts programs offered; session focuses on academics/athletics/fine arts; held on campus; accepts boys and girls; open to students from other schools. 200 students usually enrolled. 2006 schedule: June 23 to August 22.

Tuition and Aid Day student tuition: $14,650. Tuition installment plan (FACTS Tuition Payment Plan, monthly payment plans, The Tuition Refund Plan). Need-based scholarship grants available. In 2005–06, 10% of upper-school students received aid. Total amount of financial aid awarded in 2005–06: $83,000.

Admissions Traditional secondary-level entrance grade is 9. For fall 2005, 32 students applied for upper-level admission, 28 were accepted, 26 enrolled. Admissions testing, SSAT or writing sample required. Deadline for receipt of application materials: none. Application fee required: $50. Interview required.

Athletics Interscholastic: basketball (boys, girls), cross-country running (b,g), field hockey (g), golf (b,g), lacrosse (b,g), soccer (b,g), squash (b,g), swimming and diving (b,g), tennis (b,g), volleyball (b,g); intramural: field hockey (g); coed interscholastic: cross-country running, fencing, golf, swimming and diving; coed intramural: alpine skiing. 4 PE instructors, 7 coaches.

Computers Computers are regularly used in computer applications, English, independent study, publications, writing, yearbook classes. Computer network features include CD-ROMs, Internet access, DVD.

Contact Ms. Victoria M. Jann-Lewis, Director of Admission and Financial Aid. 540-253-9972. Fax: 540-253-5422. E-mail: vjannlewis@wakefieldschool.org. Web site: www.wakefieldschool.org.

ANNOUNCEMENT FROM THE SCHOOL Wakefield School, an independent, coeducational day school in The Plains, Virginia, serves students in prekindergarten through 12th grade. Wakefield School is a community committed to helping students become ethical, capable, articulate citizens seeking a challenge, making a difference, and living extraordinary lives. The Wakefield Student Strengths Program promotes understanding of a student's learning style and successful navigation of all learning environments. In addition, this program helps foster students' resiliency against choices that may distract them from their goals. The Wakefield Courtesies, Honor Pledge, and Virtues Project establish standards for considerate, honest behavior. The School supports 16 AP courses, 20 athletic teams, an active Student Government, and a wide range of extracurricular activities, all designed to support the School's fundamental mission. Seniors design a year-long thesis project according to their passions and strengths. A content-rich curriculum is offered because critical-thinking skills cannot be taught effectively without content to challenge and discipline the mind. A new Arts and Music Building provides opportunities for drama, music, drawing, painting, and photography, and ground breaking has begun on a new Science and Technology Building that will bring new laboratories and a state-of-the-art library. The results of Wakefield's traditional approach to education are evident in the joy students find in learning, their active role in the community, their outstanding college preparation (86% say they are better prepared than their peers, 98% say they are better at writing), and their success as citizens. College matriculations include College of William and Mary, Cornell University, Corcoran College of Art, Emory University, James Madison University, Middlebury College, New York University, Princeton University, United States Air Force Academy, United States Military Academy, University of North Carolina at Chapel Hill, University of Virginia, Washington University in St. Louis, and Yale University.

WALDEN PREPARATORY SCHOOL

Dallas, Texas
See Special Needs Schools section.

THE WALDORF HIGH SCHOOL OF MASSACHUSETTS BAY

132 Lexington Street
Belmont, Massachusetts 02478
Head of School: Mara D. White

petersons.com

General Information Coeducational day college-preparatory and arts school. Grades 9–12. Founded: 1996. Setting: suburban. Nearest major city is Boston. 1 building on campus. Approved or accredited by Association of Waldorf Schools of North America, New England Association of Schools and Colleges, and Massachusetts Department of Education. Total enrollment: 41. Upper school average class size: 11. Upper school faculty-student ratio: 1:4.

Upper School Student Profile Grade 9; 11 students (2 boys, 9 girls); Grade 10: 11 students (3 boys, 8 girls); Grade 11: 8 students (4 boys, 4 girls); Grade 12: 11 students (7 boys, 4 girls).

Faculty School total: 19. In upper school: 9 men, 10 women; 10 have advanced degrees.

Subjects Offered Algebra, American history, American literature, American studies, analysis and differential calculus, anatomy and physiology, ancient history, ancient world history, art, art history, astronomy, athletics, Bible as literature, biology, bookbinding, bookmaking, botany, calculus, calligraphy, chamber groups, chemistry, child development, chorus, classical Greek literature, college admission preparation, college counseling, college placement, community service, computer applications, computer resources, creative writing, current events, drama, drama performance, earth science, electives, English, English literature, epic literature, European history, expository writing, fine arts, fitness, geography, geometry, German, global studies, grammar, guitar, history of architecture, history of music, Internet research, jazz ensemble, mathematics, medieval/Renaissance history, model United Nations, modern history, music, Native American history, orchestra, painting, physical education, physics, play production, poetry, projective geometry, Russian literature, SAT preparation, senior internship, senior seminar, Spanish, stone carving, swimming, theory of knowledge, trigonometry, U.S. government, woodworking, world history, world literature, writing, yearbook, zoology.

Graduation Requirements Algebra, arts and fine arts (art, music, dance, drama), chemistry, English, English literature, foreign language, geometry, global studies,

mathematics, music, performing arts, physical education (includes health), physics, practical arts, science, social studies (includes history). Community service is required.

Special Academic Programs Study abroad.

College Placement 12 students graduated in 2005; 9 went to college, including Bentley College; Bowdoin College; Earlham College; Hampshire College; University of Massachusetts Amherst; University of Massachusetts Boston. Other: 3 had other specific plans.

Student Life Upper grades have specified standards of dress, student council. Discipline rests primarily with faculty.

Tuition and Aid Day student tuition: $18,600. Tuition installment plan (Insured Tuition Payment Plan, monthly payment plans). Tuition reduction for siblings, need-based scholarship grants available. In 2005–06, 31% of upper-school students received aid. Total amount of financial aid awarded in 2005–06: $146,000.

Admissions Traditional secondary-level entrance grade is 9. For fall 2005, 21 students applied for upper-level admission, 20 were accepted, 14 enrolled. Grade equivalent tests, math and English placement tests or writing sample required. Deadline for receipt of application materials: none. Application fee required: $50. On-campus interview required.

Athletics Interscholastic: basketball (boys, girls), soccer (b,g); coed intramural: running. 1 PE instructor, 3 coaches.

Computers Computers are regularly used in college planning, creative writing, current events, independent study, mathematics, research skills, SAT preparation, Spanish, yearbook classes. Computer network features include CD-ROMs, Internet access.

Contact Susan Morris, Admissions. 617-489-6600 Ext. 10. Fax: 617-489-6619. E-mail: s.morris@waldorfhighschool.org. Web site: www.waldorfhighschool.org.

ANNOUNCEMENT FROM THE SCHOOL Waldorf High School of Massachusetts Bay, one of approximately 800 Waldorf schools worldwide, offers a secondary school education to students in the greater Boston area. The program serves students who wish to continue their Waldorf education and students who are new to Waldorf. Each Waldorf school is independent and directed by its faculty. The School is based on the educational principles of Dr. Rudolf Steiner (Austrian scientist, educator, and founder of the first Waldorf School in 1919) and his insights into human development and social forms. The high school curriculum is interdisciplinary and rigorous. Intellect, imagination, and the capacity to carry out initiatives are nurtured in a balanced curriculum that comprises academic disciplines, artistic expression, and practical work. Required academic courses in science, literature, history, and mathematics are taught intensively in a double academic period at the beginning of each day (the Main Lesson). Main Lessons are taught in blocks that last from 3 to 4 weeks each. Students create Main Lesson books that are a record and a culmination of each block of study and filled with references, research, essays, scientific observations, and artistic work. Students also attend nineteen 45-minute skill classes each week that cover foreign languages, English, history, mathematics, civics, current events, and music. In addition, each student takes three 90-minute classes per week in physical education, fine arts, and practical arts in which students discover that artistic and practical work demands intelligence and conceptualization both in planning and implementation. All students take all courses and must complete community service requirements. They participate in a variety of committees, student council, and team sports. A foreign exchange program enlivens the School environment. High faculty-student ratios, mentors, and small classes create an environment where each student is valued and given the opportunity to maximize his or her potential. Graduates attend Wellesley, Bowdoin, London School of Economics, Oberlin, RISD, Boston College, and other fine colleges and universities.

THE WALDORF SCHOOL OF GARDEN CITY

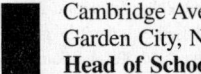

Cambridge Avenue
Garden City, New York 11530
Head of School: Mrs. Roxanne Murphy

petersons.com

General Information Coeducational day college-preparatory, arts, and liberal arts school. Grades N–12. Founded: 1947. Setting: suburban. Nearest major city is New York. 10-acre campus. 1 building on campus. Approved or accredited by Association of Waldorf Schools of North America, New York State Association of Independent Schools, and New York Department of Education. Member of National Association of Independent Schools and Secondary School Admission Test Board. Total enrollment: 354. Upper school average class size: 23. Upper school faculty-student ratio: 1:7.

Upper School Student Profile Grade 9: 21 students (12 boys, 9 girls); Grade 10: 23 students (7 boys, 16 girls); Grade 11: 24 students (9 boys, 15 girls); Grade 12: 19 students (8 boys, 11 girls).

Faculty School total: 50. In upper school: 9 men, 12 women; 14 have advanced degrees.

Subjects Offered Algebra, American history, American literature, anatomy, art, art history, biology, botany, calculus, cartography, chemistry, computer science, creative writing, dance, drama, earth science, economics, English, English literature, European history, expository writing, fine arts, French, geography, geology, geometry, German, government/civics, grammar, health, history, mathematics, music, physical education, physics, physiology, science, sculpture, social studies, speech, trigonometry, woodworking, world history, world literature, writing, zoology.

Graduation Requirements Applied arts, arts and fine arts (art, music, dance, drama), English, French, German, history of architecture, history of drama, history of music, history of science, literature, medieval history, medieval/Renaissance history, music, organic chemistry, physical education (includes health), science, social studies (includes history), 4 years of math, 4 years of foreign language.

Special Academic Programs Advanced Placement exam preparation in 4 subject areas; independent study; study abroad.

College Placement 25 students graduated in 2005; 23 went to college, including Boston University; Cornell University; Goucher College; Oberlin College; University of Chicago. Other: 1 entered military service, 1 had other specific plans. Median composite ACT: 25. 55% scored over 26 on composite ACT.

Student Life Upper grades have specified standards of dress, student council, honor system. Discipline rests equally with students and faculty.

Summer Programs Enrichment programs offered; session focuses on music, drama, field trips, tennis, painting, crafts, puppetry, swimming, athletics ; held both on and off campus; held at Camp Glen Brook (programs in summer and winter); accepts boys and girls; open to students from other schools. 80 students usually enrolled. 2006 schedule: June 26 to August 4. Application deadline: none.

Tuition and Aid Day student tuition: $15,500. Tuition installment plan (SMART Tuition Payment Plan, individually arranged payment plans). Merit scholarship grants, need-based scholarship grants available. In 2005–06, 35% of upper-school students received aid; total upper-school merit-scholarship money awarded: $30,000. Total amount of financial aid awarded in 2005–06: $140,000.

Admissions Traditional secondary-level entrance grade is 9. For fall 2005, 25 students applied for upper-level admission, 14 were accepted, 10 enrolled. SSAT required. Deadline for receipt of application materials: none. Application fee required: $50. On-campus interview required.

Athletics Interscholastic: basketball (boys, girls), cross-country running (b,g), independent competitive sports (b,g), lacrosse (b), physical fitness (b,g), soccer (b,g), softball (g), volleyball (g); intramural: artistic gym (b,g), dance (b,g), fitness (b,g), volleyball (b,g); coed interscholastic: outdoor education, ropes courses, soccer; coed intramural: artistic gym, dance, fitness, volleyball. 2 PE instructors, 6 coaches.

Computers Computers are regularly used in research skills, science, yearbook classes. Computer network features include CD-ROMs, Internet access, office computer access.

Contact Ms. Sara Walsh, Director of Admissions. 516-742-3434 Ext. 116. Fax: 516-742-3457. E-mail: walshs@waldorfgarden.org. Web site: www.waldorfgarden.org.

ANNOUNCEMENT FROM THE SCHOOL Established in 1947 and located on a beautiful 10-acre campus adjacent to Adelphi University, The Waldorf School of Garden City is a college-preparatory, coeducational, independent day school for nursery through grade 12. A before- and after-school care program, as well as a Parent-Toddler program for ages 2 to 3, is offered. Facilities include a gymnasium, full-service kitchen and cafeteria, two auditoriums, and an outdoor athletic complex for soccer, lacrosse, softball, and track. The School is bordered by a nature trail and preserve and offers lovely secluded play areas for the early childhood program. Students enjoy well-equipped physics, biology, and chemistry labs, a computer center, and library. High school students also have access to the Adelphi University library. A veteran career and educational counselor guides students in decisions about colleges and careers. The Waldorf School strives to balance academic, practical, creative, and physical endeavors in an interdisciplinary manner based on the educational philosophy of Dr. Rudolf Steiner. Teachers foster genuine enthusiasm for learning, respect for the world, and a healthy sense of self. Students in all grades master practical skills and explore diverse areas of interest and academic disciplines. In 11th grade, for example, the curriculum for the Middle Ages includes studying medieval history and literature, learning the techniques of stone sculpture, practicing Gregorian Chants, visiting the Cloisters in New York City, becoming adept at calligraphy, and creating an original illuminated manuscript. High school electives include Model UN, improvisational theater, ethics and social criticism, chorus, guitar, world music, open art studio, orchestra, jazz band, and woodworking. Beginning in grade 3, each class takes an annual class trip to the School's extension campus at Camp Glen Brook in southern New Hampshire. College acceptances among recent graduates include Amherst, Brandeis, Brown, Carnegie Mellon, Columbia, Cornell, Duke, Emory, Georgetown, Harvard, MIT, NYU, Swarthmore, and Wellesley.

THE WALKER SCHOOL

700 Cobb Parkway North
Marietta, Georgia 30062
Head of School: Donald B. Robertson

petersons.com

General Information Coeducational day college-preparatory, arts, bilingual studies, and technology school. Grades PK–12. Founded: 1957. Setting: suburban. Nearest major city is Atlanta. 32-acre campus. 7 buildings on campus. Approved or accredited by Southern Association of Colleges and Schools, Southern Association of Independent Schools, and Georgia Department of Education. Member of National Association of Independent Schools and Secondary School Admission Test Board. Endowment: $1 million. Total enrollment: 1,075. Upper school average class size: 14. Upper school faculty-student ratio: 1:14.

Upper School Student Profile Grade 9: 102 students (50 boys, 52 girls); Grade 10: 97 students (51 boys, 46 girls); Grade 11: 106 students (54 boys, 52 girls); Grade 12: 77 students (35 boys, 42 girls).

Faculty School total: 127. In upper school: 21 men, 15 women; 34 have advanced degrees.

Subjects Offered Acting, advanced chemistry, advanced computer applications, algebra, American history, American literature, anatomy, art, art education, art history, art-AP, astronomy, athletics, band, Bible, biology, biology-AP, botany, calculus, calculus-AP, ceramics, chemistry, chemistry-AP, computer programming, computer science, computer science-AP, computer technologies, creative writing, drama, driver education, economics, economics-AP, English, English-AP, ethics, European history, expository writing, film history, fine arts, fitness, French, French language-AP, French literature-AP, geometry, German, German-AP, government and politics-AP, government-AP, government/civics, grammar, history, history-AP, Latin, Latin-AP, literature and composition-AP, mathematics, music, musical theater, newspaper, orchestra, personal finance, physical education, physics, physics-AP, play production, psychology, public speaking, science, social studies, Spanish, Spanish-AP, statistics, statistics-AP, trigonometry, U.S. history-AP, Web site design, world history, world history-AP, world literature, writing, zoology.

Graduation Requirements American government, arts and fine arts (art, music, dance, drama), computer science, economics, English, English composition, English literature, foreign language, mathematics, physical education (includes health), science, social studies (includes history).

Special Academic Programs Honors section; independent study; academic accommodation for the gifted and the artistically talented.

College Placement 85 students graduated in 2005; all went to college, including Davidson College; Furman University; Georgia Institute of Technology; University of Georgia; Vanderbilt University. Mean SAT verbal: 660, mean SAT math: 658, mean composite ACT: 28. 80% scored over 600 on SAT verbal, 80% scored over 600 on SAT math, 69% scored over 26 on composite ACT.

Student Life Upper grades have specified standards of dress, student council, honor system. Discipline rests equally with students and faculty.

Summer Programs Enrichment, sports, computer instruction programs offered; session focuses on sports, writing, study skills; held on campus; accepts boys and girls; open to students from other schools. 80 students usually enrolled. 2006 schedule: June 10 to July 26. Application deadline: none.

Tuition and Aid Day student tuition: $13,600. Tuition installment plan (school's own payment plan). Need-based scholarship grants available. In 2005–06, 10% of upper-school students received aid. Total amount of financial aid awarded in 2005–06: $75,000.

Admissions Traditional secondary-level entrance grade is 9. For fall 2005, 105 students applied for upper-level admission, 50 were accepted, 42 enrolled. Otis-Lennon School Ability Test, SSAT, SSAT or WISC III or Stanford Achievement Test required. Deadline for receipt of application materials: February 22. Application fee required: $75. On-campus interview required.

Athletics Interscholastic: aerobics/dance (girls), aquatics (b,g), baseball (b), basketball (b,g), cheering (g), dance (g), dance squad (g), dance team (g), football (b), golf (b,g), soccer (b,g), softball (g), tennis (b,g), touch football (g), volleyball (g), wrestling (b); intramural: aerobics (g), bowling (b,g), golf (b,g), softball (g), tennis (b,g); coed interscholastic: cricket, cross-country running, diving, fitness, golf, indoor track & field, physical fitness, physical training, power lifting, rugby, swimming and diving, track and field, weight lifting, weight training; coed intramural: bowling, cricket, fencing, fishing, golf, ultimate Frisbee, weight lifting. 7 PE instructors, 8 coaches, 1 trainer.

Computers Computers are regularly used in art, drawing and design, English, foreign language, history, information technology, introduction to technology, literary magazine, mathematics, news writing, newspaper, science classes. Computer network features include campus e-mail, on-campus library services, CD-ROMs, online commercial services, Internet access, DVD.

Contact Patricia H. Mozley, Director of Admission. 678-581-6921. Fax: 770-514-8122. E-mail: mozleyp@thewalkerschool.org. Web site: www.thewalkerschool.org.

ANNOUNCEMENT FROM THE SCHOOL Walker's traditional curriculum, master teachers, and incorporation of current technology work together to prepare students for success in the 21st century. Students are encouraged to explore opportunities for academic challenge and self-expression through art, literature, music, drama, and sports. Twenty-two advanced-placement courses

are available. For more information, students should visit the School's Web site at http://www.thewalkerschool.org.

WALNUT HILL SCHOOL

12 Highland Street
Natick, Massachusetts 01760-2199
Head of School: Stephanie B. Perrin

petersons.com

General Information Coeducational boarding and day college-preparatory and arts school. Grades 9–12. Founded: 1893. Setting: suburban. Nearest major city is Boston. Students are housed in single-sex dormitories. 46-acre campus. 18 buildings on campus. Approved or accredited by Association of Independent Schools in New England, New England Association of Schools and Colleges, and Massachusetts Department of Education. Member of National Association of Independent Schools and Secondary School Admission Test Board. Endowment: $12 million. Total enrollment: 277. Upper school average class size: 14. Upper school faculty-student ratio: 1:6.

Upper School Student Profile Grade 9: 35 students (8 boys, 27 girls); Grade 10: 71 students (26 boys, 45 girls); Grade 11: 86 students (21 boys, 65 girls); Grade 12: 85 students (19 boys, 66 girls). 75% of students are boarding students. 40% are state residents. 38 states are represented in upper school student body. 26% are international students. International students from Canada, Germany, Ireland, Japan, Republic of Korea, and Taiwan; 5 other countries represented in student body.

Faculty School total: 51. In upper school: 25 men, 26 women; 47 have advanced degrees; 18 reside on campus.

Subjects Offered 20th century world history, 3-dimensional art, acting, advanced chemistry, advanced math, algebra, American history, American literature, art history, arts, ballet, ballet technique, biology, calculus, ceramics, chemistry, choral music, choreography, chorus, classical music, college counseling, community service, creative writing, dance, directing, drama, drawing, English, English literature, environmental science, ESL, fine arts, French, geometry, health, history, history of dance, jazz dance, mathematics, modern dance, music history, music theory, musical theater, musical theater dance, opera, orchestra, painting, photography, physics, piano, poetry, pre-calculus, research seminar, science, sculpture, set design, Shakespeare, social studies, Spanish, stage design, technical theater, theater, theater design and production, theater production, U.S. history, visual and performing arts, visual arts, vocal music, voice, voice ensemble, world history, writing, writing.

Graduation Requirements Arts, English, foreign language, mathematics, science, social studies (includes history), completion of arts portfolio, body of writing, or participation in performing arts ensembles and/or solo recital.

Special Academic Programs Advanced Placement exam preparation in 6 subject areas; honors section; academic accommodation for the gifted, the musically talented, and the artistically talented; ESL (35 students enrolled).

College Placement 91 students graduated in 2005; 86 went to college, including Carnegie Mellon University; Maryland Institute College of Art; New England Conservatory of Music; School of the Art Institute of Chicago; The Juilliard School; University of Southern California. Other: 5 had other specific plans. Median SAT verbal: 580, median SAT math: 570, median composite ACT: 26.

Student Life Upper grades have student council. Discipline rests equally with students and faculty.

Summer Programs Art/fine arts programs offered; session focuses on theater, ballet, writing, visual art, and music ; held both on and off campus; held at Italy (visual art), England (writing), and France (music); accepts boys and girls; open to students from other schools. 240 students usually enrolled. 2006 schedule: June to August. Application deadline: none.

Tuition and Aid Day student tuition: $28,150; 7-day tuition and room/board: $35,350. Tuition installment plan (Insured Tuition Payment Plan, Academic Management Services Plan). Merit scholarship grants, need-based scholarship grants available. In 2005–06, 45% of upper-school students received aid. Total amount of financial aid awarded in 2005–06: $2,200,000.

Admissions For fall 2005, 323 students applied for upper-level admission, 165 were accepted, 111 enrolled. Any standardized test, TOEFL or writing sample required. Deadline for receipt of application materials: February 6. Application fee required: $65. Interview recommended.

Athletics Coed Intramural: ballet, dance, modern dance, yoga.

Computers Computer network features include on-campus library services, Internet access, office computer access, wireless campus network.

Contact Matthew Allen Derr, Dean for Admission and Placement. 508-650-5020. Fax: 508-655-3726. E-mail: admissions@walnuthillarts.org. Web site: www.walnuthillarts.org.

See full description on page 1118.

THE WARDLAW-HARTRIDGE SCHOOL

1295 Inman Avenue
Edison, New Jersey 08820
Head of School: Andrew Webster

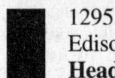

General Information Coeducational day college-preparatory and arts school. Grades PK–12. Founded: 1882. Setting: suburban. Nearest major city is New York, NY. 36-acre campus. 1 building on campus. Approved or accredited by Middle States Association of Colleges and Schools, New Jersey Association of Independent Schools, and New Jersey Department of Education. Member of National Association of Independent Schools. Endowment: $1.4 million. Total enrollment: 415. Upper school average class size: 16. Upper school faculty-student ratio: 1:4.

Upper School Student Profile Grade 9: 36 students (18 boys, 18 girls); Grade 10: 44 students (23 boys, 21 girls); Grade 11: 50 students (32 boys, 18 girls); Grade 12: 25 students (18 boys, 7 girls).

Faculty School total: 65. In upper school: 15 men, 17 women; 15 have advanced degrees.

Subjects Offered Algebra, American history, American history-AP, American literature, ancient history, art, art history, astronomy, band, biology, biology-AP, calculus, calculus-AP, chemistry, computer programming, computer science, computer science-AP, discrete math, drama, driver education, economics, English, English literature, English-AP, environmental science, ESL, European history, film, fine arts, French, French-AP, geometry, government/civics, health, history, independent study, journalism, Latin, Latin-AP, macroeconomics-AP, marine biology, math analysis, mathematics, modern European history-AP, music, music theory-AP, peer counseling, physical education, physical science, physics, physics-AP, pre-calculus, science, senior project, senior thesis, Shakespeare, short story, Spanish, Spanish-AP, studio art-AP, TOEFL preparation, U.S. government and politics-AP, world history.

Graduation Requirements Arts and fine arts (art, music, dance, drama), computer science, English, foreign language, history, mathematics, physical education (includes health), public speaking, science.

Special Academic Programs Advanced Placement exam preparation in 19 subject areas; honors section; accelerated programs; independent study; study abroad; academic accommodation for the gifted, the musically talented, and the artistically talented; ESL (8 students enrolled).

College Placement 31 students graduated in 2005; all went to college, including Duke University; Mount Holyoke College; Muhlenberg College; Princeton University; Rutgers, The State University of New Jersey, New Brunswick/Piscataway. Median SAT verbal: 590, median SAT math: 620.

Student Life Upper grades have specified standards of dress, student council, honor system. Discipline rests equally with students and faculty.

Summer Programs Remediation, enrichment, advancement, ESL programs offered; session focuses on academics; held on campus; accepts boys and girls; open to students from other schools. 350 students usually enrolled. 2006 schedule: June 27 to August 5. Application deadline: June 21.

Tuition and Aid Day student tuition: $20,600. Tuition installment plan (Insured Tuition Payment Plan, Key Tuition Payment Plan, monthly payment plans, variable tuition (50%-100%) in 10% steps). Merit scholarship grants, need-based scholarship grants available. In 2005–06, 33% of upper-school students received aid; total upper-school merit-scholarship money awarded: $55,275. Total amount of financial aid awarded in 2005–06: $418,050.

Admissions Traditional secondary-level entrance grade is 9. For fall 2005, 53 students applied for upper-level admission, 35 were accepted, 19 enrolled. ERB CTP III, ISEE or SSAT required. Deadline for receipt of application materials: February 17. Application fee required: $60. On-campus interview required.

Athletics Interscholastic: baseball (boys), basketball (b,g), cheering (g), soccer (b,g), softball (g), tennis (b,g), track and field (b,g), volleyball (g); coed interscholastic: golf, swimming and diving; coed intramural: outdoor activities, table tennis. 4 PE instructors, 8 coaches, 2 trainers.

Computers Computers are regularly used in all academic classes. Computer network features include campus e-mail, on-campus library services, CD-ROMs, Internet access, office computer access, wireless campus network.

Contact Ms. Charlotte Davis, Director of Admission. 908-754-1882 Ext. 110. Fax: 908-754-9678. E-mail: cdavis@whschool.org. Web site: www.whschool.org.

ANNOUNCEMENT FROM THE SCHOOL The Wardlaw-Hartridge School, a coeducational and college-preparatory community, provides an enriching educational program for students in PK–grade 12. The School cultivates a deep respect for diversity of talents, interests, and backgrounds. It is united by a shared commitment to an environment that encourages the personal growth of all in the community. Between the teachers and students, among the students themselves, and in participation with parents, Wardlaw-Hartridge encourages relationships built on mutual trust and esteem. These relationships foster a learning culture that is both secure and challenging. In addition to its comprehensive and rigorous academic preparation, the School seeks to instill in its students the intellectual open-mindedness, love of learning, and courage needed to sustain personal integrity in their daily lives. The Wardlaw-Hartridge School graduates young men and women who are as intellectually curious about what is unknown to them as they are confident in their understanding of the traditional arts and sciences. Trained in critical thinking, they are capable of both independent and collaborative learning. They begin their collegiate studies able to articulate ideas and opinions persuasively and accurately, both orally and in writing. They have developed an appreciation for the fine and performing arts. They have become competent in both electronic and traditional research methods and enjoy a firm grasp of scientific and quantitative skills. Indeed, Wardlaw-Hartridge graduates, reflecting the motto of the School, are committed "to learn and to achieve" and to provide leadership and service in a rapidly changing world.

WARING SCHOOL

35 Standley Street
Beverly, Massachusetts 01915
Head of School: Mr. Peter L. Smick

General Information Coeducational day college-preparatory, bilingual studies, and liberal arts, French school. Grades 6–12. Founded: 1972. Setting: suburban. Nearest major city is Boston. 32-acre campus. 8 buildings on campus. Approved or accredited by New England Association of Schools and Colleges. Languages of instruction: English and French. Endowment: $4.6 million. Total enrollment: 150. Upper school average class size: 14. Upper school faculty-student ratio: 1:8.

Upper School Student Profile Grade 9: 20 students (9 boys, 11 girls); Grade 10: 26 students (13 boys, 13 girls); Grade 11: 27 students (11 boys, 16 girls); Grade 12: 26 students (10 boys, 16 girls).

Faculty School total: 52. In upper school: 16 men, 17 women; 17 have advanced degrees.

Subjects Offered Algebra, American history, art history, biology, calculus, chemistry, computer science, drama, ecology, European history, fine arts, French, history of science, music, physics, theater, trigonometry, U.S. history, world history, world literature, writing.

Graduation Requirements Arts and fine arts (art, music, dance, drama), English, foreign language, mathematics, physical education (includes health), science, social science.

Special Academic Programs Advanced Placement exam preparation in 5 subject areas; honors section; independent study; term-away projects; study at local college for college credit; study abroad; academic accommodation for the gifted, the musically talented, and the artistically talented.

College Placement 26 students graduated in 2005; 23 went to college, including Brown University; University of Vermont; Yale University. Other: 3 had other specific plans. Median SAT verbal: 610, median SAT math: 620. 56% scored over 600 on SAT verbal, 60% scored over 600 on SAT math.

Student Life Upper grades have specified standards of dress, honor system. Discipline rests equally with students and faculty.

Summer Programs Art/fine arts programs offered; session focuses on French, reading and music; held on campus; accepts boys and girls; open to students from other schools. 30 students usually enrolled. 2006 schedule: July 1 to August 1.

Tuition and Aid Day student tuition: $18,000. Tuition installment plan (monthly payment plans, individually arranged payment plans). Merit scholarship grants, need-based scholarship grants available. In 2005–06, 40% of upper-school students received aid. Total amount of financial aid awarded in 2005–06: $150,000.

Admissions Traditional secondary-level entrance grade is 9. For fall 2005, 40 students applied for upper-level admission, 7 were accepted, 6 enrolled. Deadline for receipt of application materials: February 1. Application fee required: $30. On-campus interview required.

Athletics Interscholastic: basketball (boys, girls), cross-country running (g), lacrosse (b,g), soccer (b,g); coed interscholastic: aerobics/dance, combined training, cross-country running, running, yoga; coed intramural: dance, fitness, fitness walking, running. 1 PE instructor, 12 coaches.

Computers Computers are regularly used in literary magazine, mathematics, music, publications, science, technical drawing, video film production, Web site design, writing, yearbook classes. Computer network features include campus e-mail, CD-ROMs, Internet access, file transfer, office computer access.

Contact Mrs. Dorothy Wang, Dean of Admissions and Student Affairs. 978-927-8793 Ext. 226. Fax: 978-921-2107. E-mail: dwang@waringschool.org. Web site: www.waringschool.org.

ANNOUNCEMENT FROM THE SCHOOL Waring's principal mission is to establish, sustain, and strengthen a community of lifelong learners who are working and learning together for the common as well as the individual good. Located on 32 acres in Beverly, the Waring School offers a highly demanding college-preparatory education in liberal arts. Humanities is the fulcrum of an integrated core curriculum encompassing math, science, French (language and culture), English, literature, history, music, and studio art, with a special emphasis on writing and discussion. Interscholastic sports include soccer, basketball, and lacrosse. Students may participate in various theater, instrumental, or choral ensembles. Student-teacher ratio is 7.5:1. Dorothy Wang is Dean of Student Affairs and Admissions.

WASATCH ACADEMY

120 South 100 West
Mt. Pleasant, Utah 84647
Head of School: Mr. Joseph Loftin

General Information Coeducational boarding and day college-preparatory, arts, bilingual studies, and technology school. Grades 9–12. Founded: 1875. Setting: small town. Nearest major city is Provo. Students are housed in single-sex dormitories. 30-acre campus. 19 buildings on campus. Approved or accredited by Northwest Association of Schools and Colleges, Pacific Northwest Association of Independent Schools, The Association of Boarding Schools, and Utah Department of Education. Member of National Association of Independent Schools. Endowment: $1.3 million. Total enrollment: 155. Upper school average class size: 10. Upper school faculty-student ratio: 1:6.

Upper School Student Profile Grade 9: 24 students (14 boys, 10 girls); Grade 10: 29 students (16 boys, 13 girls); Grade 11: 52 students (40 boys, 12 girls); Grade 12: 49 students (30 boys, 19 girls); Postgraduate: 1 student (1 boy). 95% of students are boarding students. 19% are state residents. 23 states are represented in upper school student body. 32% are international students. International students from El Salvador, Hong Kong, Japan, Nepal, Rwanda, and Taiwan; 14 other countries represented in student body.

Faculty School total: 53. In upper school: 25 men, 26 women; 19 have advanced degrees; 48 reside on campus.

Subjects Offered Acting, advanced studio art-AP, advanced TOEFL/grammar, algebra, anatomy, ballet, biology, biology-AP, calculus-AP, ceramics, chemistry, chemistry-AP, choir, college counseling, college placement, comedy, community garden, community service, dance, design, drama, drawing, drawing and design, driver education, earth science, electronic music, English, English-AP, equine studies, ESL, European history-AP, fencing, film, filmmaking, fine arts, forensic science, French, geography, geology, global issues, golf, guitar, honors algebra, honors English, honors U.S. history, Japanese, jewelry making, Latin, learning strategies, math applications, music, music theory, outdoor education, painting, performing arts, philosophy, photography, physical education, physical science, physics, piano, play production, pottery, pre-calculus, reading, SAT/ACT preparation, Spanish, Spanish-AP, speech and debate, stained glass, statistics-AP, study skills, theater, TOEFL preparation, U.S. history, U.S. history-AP, weightlifting, Western civilization, woodworking, world religions, yoga.

Graduation Requirements Arts and fine arts (art, music, dance, drama), computer literacy, English, foreign language, mathematics, physical education (includes health), science, social science, social studies (includes history), U.S. history, outdoor, cultural, and recreational requirements. Community service is required.

Special Academic Programs Advanced Placement exam preparation in 8 subject areas; honors section; accelerated programs; independent study; term-away projects; academic accommodation for the gifted, the musically talented, and the artistically talented; programs in English, mathematics, general development for dyslexic students; ESL (29 students enrolled).

College Placement 39 students graduated in 2005; all went to college, including Boston University; Lewis & Clark College; University of California, Berkeley; University of Pennsylvania; University of San Diego; University of Utah. Median SAT verbal: 500, median SAT math: 480, median composite ACT: 22. 13% scored over 600 on SAT verbal, 9% scored over 600 on SAT math, 27% scored over 26 on composite ACT.

Student Life Upper grades have specified standards of dress, student council, honor system. Discipline rests primarily with faculty. Attendance at religious services is required.

Summer Programs Remediation, enrichment, advancement, ESL programs offered; session focuses on boarding program transition; held both on and off campus; held at Utah's beautiful outdoor areas; accepts boys and girls; open to students from other schools. 25 students usually enrolled. 2006 schedule: June 25 to August 5. Application deadline: none.

Tuition and Aid Day student tuition: $18,300; 5-day tuition and room/board: $28,800; 7-day tuition and room/board: $31,800. Tuition installment plan (Key Tuition Payment Plan, monthly payment plans, individually arranged payment plans). Merit scholarship grants, need-based scholarship grants, need-based loans available. In 2005–06, 33% of upper-school students received aid; total upper-school merit-scholarship money awarded: $55,000. Total amount of financial aid awarded in 2005–06: $580,000.

Admissions Traditional secondary-level entrance grade is 9. For fall 2005, 185 students applied for upper-level admission, 78 were accepted, 62 enrolled. ISEE, SSAT, Stanford Achievement Test, TOEFL or SLEP or WISC III or other aptitude measures; standardized achievement test required. Deadline for receipt of application materials: none. Application fee required: $50. Interview required.

Athletics Interscholastic: alpine skiing (boys, girls), baseball (b), basketball (b,g), climbing (b,g), cross-country running (b,g), dance (b,g), dressage (b,g), fencing (b,g), fishing (b,g), fly fishing (b,g), golf (b,g), horseback riding (b,g), outdoor activities (b,g), outdoor adventure (b,g), outdoor education (b,g), outdoor recreation (b,g), outdoor skills (b,g), paint ball (b,g), physical training (b,g), rodeo (b,g), running (b,g), skiing (cross-country) (b,g), snowboarding (b,g), soccer (b,g), tennis (b,g), track and field (b,g), volleyball (g); intramural: dance (g), skiing (downhill) (b,g), soccer (b,g), table tennis (b,g); coed interscholastic: cheering, dance, equestrian sports, fencing, fishing, fly fishing, golf, horseback riding, martial arts, paint ball, physical training, rock climbing, rodeo, running, snowboarding, tennis, track and field; coed intramural: aerobics/dance, aquatics, archery, back packing, badminton, ballet, bicycling, billiards, blading, bowling, canoeing/kayaking, climbing, combined training, cooperative games, dance team, equestrian sports, fishing, fitness, flag football, fly fishing, freestyle skiing, Frisbee, golf, hiking/backpacking, horseback riding, horseshoes, jogging, lacrosse, life saving, modern dance, mountain biking, nordic skiing, outdoor activities, outdoor adventure, outdoor education, outdoor recreation, outdoor skills, paint ball, physical training, power lifting, rafting, rappelling, rock climbing, running, skateboarding, skiing (downhill), snowshoeing, swimming and diving, table tennis, telemark skiing, ultimate Frisbee, volleyball, weight lifting, weight training, yoga. 2 coaches, 1 trainer.

Computers Computers are regularly used in all academic classes. Computer network features include campus e-mail, on-campus library services, CD-ROMs, online commercial services, Internet access, wireless campus network.

Contact Mrs. Kim Stephens, Director of Admissions. 800-634-4690 Ext. 143. Fax: 435-462-1450. E-mail: admissions@wacad.org. Web site: www.wacad.org.

ANNOUNCEMENT FROM THE SCHOOL Wasatch Academy provides a nurturing community that empowers young men and women to develop academically, socially, and morally, while preparing them for college and the challenges of living in the 21st century.

See full description on page 1120.

WASHINGTON ACADEMY

PO Box 190
East Machias, Maine 04630
Head of School: Judson McBrine

General Information Coeducational boarding and day college-preparatory, general academic, arts, business, and vocational school. Grades 9–12. Founded: 1792. Setting: small town. Nearest major city is Bangor. Students are housed in single-sex dormitories and host family homes. 45-acre campus. 7 buildings on campus. Approved or accredited by New England Association of Schools and Colleges, The Association of Boarding Schools, and Maine Department of Education. Endowment: $1 million. Total enrollment: 359. Upper school average class size: 14. Upper school faculty-student ratio: 1:14.

Upper School Student Profile Grade 9: 95 students (48 boys, 47 girls); Grade 10: 93 students (47 boys, 46 girls); Grade 11: 95 students (41 boys, 54 girls); Grade 12: 76 students (36 boys, 40 girls). 10% of students are boarding students. 90% are state residents. 1 state is represented in upper school student body. 10% are international students. International students from Bermuda, Japan, Republic of Korea, Spain, Taiwan, and Viet Nam; 3 other countries represented in student body.

Faculty School total: 30. In upper school: 13 men, 15 women; 15 have advanced degrees; 2 reside on campus.

Subjects Offered Accounting, Advanced Placement courses, algebra, American culture, American history-AP, architectural drawing, art, art history, art-AP, band, basic language skills, Basic programming, biology, biology-AP, business, calculus, calculus-AP, career education internship, carpentry, chemistry, chorus, computer programming, computer science, computer-aided design, consumer mathematics, creative writing, desktop publishing, drama, earth science, ecology, economics, English, English-AP, environmental science, environmental systems, ESL, field ecology, film, film studies, foreign language, French, geography, geometry, government/civics, guitar, honors algebra, HTML design, industrial technology, jazz band, journalism, keyboarding, Latin, literature, marine studies, mathematics, metalworking, Microsoft, music, music appreciation, music history, music theory, photography, physical education, physical science, physics, pre-calculus, psychology, sociology, Spanish, speech, technical drawing, theater, TOEFL preparation, U.S. history, U.S. history-AP, video, video film production, vocational-technical courses, welding, woodworking, world history, writing.

Graduation Requirements Arts and fine arts (art, music, dance, drama), English, mathematics, physical education (includes health), science, social studies (includes history), 1 credit of advisor/advisee.

Special Academic Programs Advanced Placement exam preparation in 9 subject areas; honors section; independent study; term-away projects; study at local college for college credit; study abroad; remedial reading and/or remedial writing; remedial math; programs in general development for dyslexic students; special instructional classes for students with learning disabilities; ESL (17 students enrolled).

College Placement 72 students graduated in 2005; 56 went to college, including Bates College; Maine Maritime Academy; Roger Williams University; University of Maine; Vassar College. Other: 14 went to work, 2 entered military service. Median SAT verbal: 500, median SAT math: 530. 23% scored over 600 on SAT verbal, 24% scored over 600 on SAT math.

Student Life Upper grades have specified standards of dress, student council. Discipline rests primarily with faculty.

Summer Programs ESL programs offered; session focuses on beginning, intermediate and advanced ESL; held on campus; accepts boys and girls; open to students from other schools. 25 students usually enrolled. 2006 schedule: July 3 to August 11. Application deadline: April 1.

Tuition and Aid Day student tuition: $8000; 7-day tuition and room/board: $27,400. Tuition installment plan (Insured Tuition Payment Plan). Merit scholarship grants available. In 2005–06, 12% of upper-school students received aid; total upper-school merit-scholarship money awarded: $184,700. Total amount of financial aid awarded in 2005–06: $273,762.

Admissions Traditional secondary-level entrance grade is 9. SLEP or TOEFL required. Deadline for receipt of application materials: none. Application fee required: $50. Interview recommended.

Athletics Interscholastic: baseball (boys), basketball (b,g), cross-country running (b,g), golf (b,g), soccer (b,g), softball (g), tennis (b,g), volleyball (g); coed interscholastic: cheering; coed intramural: flag football. 2 PE instructors, 17 coaches.

Computers Computers are regularly used in all classes. Computer network features include campus e-mail, on-campus library services, CD-ROMs, online commercial services, Internet access, T3 Internet access throughout school.

Contact Kim Gardner, Director of Admissions. 207-255-8301 Ext. 207. Fax: 207-255-8303. E-mail: admissions@washingtonacademy.org. Web site: www.washingtonacademy.org.

See full description on page 1122.

WASHINGTON COUNTY DAY SCHOOL

1605 East Reed Road
Greenville, Mississippi 38703-7297
Head of School: Mr. Rodney Brown

General Information Coeducational day college-preparatory, arts, bilingual studies, and technology school. Boys grades PK–9, girls grades PK–7. Founded: 1970. Setting: suburban. Nearest major city is Jackson. 30-acre campus. 1 building on campus. Approved or accredited by Mississippi Private School Association, Southern Association of Colleges and Schools, and Southern Association of Independent Schools. Total enrollment: 769. Upper school average class size: 20. Upper school faculty-student ratio: 1:20.

Upper School Student Profile Grade 9: 72 students (38 boys, 34 girls); Grade 10: 61 students (30 boys, 31 girls); Grade 11: 61 students (31 boys, 30 girls); Grade 12: 62 students (30 boys, 32 girls).

Faculty School total: 65. In upper school: 9 men, 27 women; 17 have advanced degrees.

Subjects Offered Advanced chemistry, algebra, American history-AP, American literature, anatomy and physiology, art, band, biology, business skills, calculus, calculus-AP, chemistry, chemistry-AP, computer keyboarding, computer multimedia, computer science, computers, concert band, creative writing, drama, drama performance, driver education, economics, English, English literature, English-AP, French, French studies, geography, geometry, government, government/civics, history, honors U.S. history, journalism, marching band, mathematics, music, physical education, physics, political systems, pre-algebra, pre-calculus, psychology, publications, science, social science, social studies, Spanish, speech, speech and debate, world history, yearbook.

Graduation Requirements Algebra, American government, arts, biology, chemistry, computer science, economics, English, English composition, foreign language, mathematics, physics, science, social science, social studies (includes history), speech, student government.

Special Academic Programs Honors section.

College Placement 68 students graduated in 2005; all went to college, including Delta State University; Millsaps College; Mississippi College; Mississippi State University; The University of Alabama; University of Mississippi.

Student Life Upper grades have specified standards of dress, student council. Discipline rests primarily with faculty.

Tuition and Aid Day student tuition: $3870. Tuition installment plan (monthly payment plans). Need-based scholarship grants available. In 2005–06, 2% of upper-school students received aid. Total amount of financial aid awarded in 2005–06: $18,000.

Admissions Traditional secondary-level entrance grade is 9. For fall 2005, 15 students applied for upper-level admission, 15 were accepted, 15 enrolled. Deadline for receipt of application materials: none. Application fee required: $80. On-campus interview required.

Athletics Interscholastic: baseball (boys), basketball (b,g), cheering (g), cross-country running (b,g), drill team (g), football (b), soccer (b,g), softball (g), tennis (b,g), track and field (b,g); coed interscholastic: golf. 2 PE instructors, 1 trainer.

Computers Computers are regularly used in data processing, graphic design, typing classes. Computer network features include on-campus library services, CD-ROMs, Internet access.

Contact Mrs. Ruth Vowell, Administrative Assistant. 662-332-0786. Fax: 662-332-0434. E-mail: generals@wschool.greenville.ms.us. Web site: wschool.greenville.ms.us.

WASHINGTON INTERNATIONAL SCHOOL

3100 Macomb Street, NW
Washington, District of Columbia 20008
Head of School: Richard P. Hall

General Information Coeducational day college-preparatory, bilingual studies, and International Baccalaureate school. Grades PK–12. Founded: 1966. Setting: urban. 6-acre campus. 7 buildings on campus. Approved or accredited by Association of Independent Schools of Greater Washington, European Council of International Schools, International Baccalaureate Organization, Middle States Association of Colleges and Schools, and District of Columbia Department of Education. Member of National Association of Independent Schools and Secondary School Admission Test Board. Languages of instruction: English, Spanish, and French. Endowment: $750,000. Total enrollment: 820. Upper school average class size: 15. Upper school faculty-student ratio: 1:8.

Upper School Student Profile Grade 9: 54 students (28 boys, 26 girls); Grade 10: 67 students (30 boys, 37 girls); Grade 11: 52 students (24 boys, 28 girls); Grade 12: 73 students (38 boys, 35 girls).

Faculty School total: 117. In upper school: 22 men, 27 women; 20 have advanced degrees.

Subjects Offered Advanced chemistry, advanced math, art, arts, biology, calculus, chemistry, chorus, community service, comparative government and politics, contemporary history, drama, Dutch, economics, English, English literature, environmental science, ESL, fine arts, French, geography, history, information technology, integrated mathematics, International Baccalaureate courses, Italian, Japanese, literature seminar, music, musical productions, physical education, physics, science, social science, Spanish, theater, theory of knowledge, world history.

Graduation Requirements Algebra, arts and fine arts (art, music, dance, drama), biology, chemistry, computer science, English, foreign language, geography, geometry, physical education (includes health), physics, trigonometry, world history, world literature. Community service is required.

Special Academic Programs International Baccalaureate program; ESL (8 students enrolled).

College Placement 58 students graduated in 2005; all went to college, including McGill University; New York University; The College of William and Mary; The Johns Hopkins University; University of Toronto; University of Virginia. Median SAT verbal: 600, median SAT math: 610.

Student Life Upper grades have specified standards of dress, student council, honor system. Discipline rests primarily with faculty.

Summer Programs Remediation, enrichment, ESL programs offered; held on campus; accepts boys and girls; open to students from other schools. 50 students usually enrolled. 2006 schedule: June 24 to July 26. Application deadline: April 30.

Tuition and Aid Day student tuition: $22,115. Tuition installment plan (Key Tuition Payment Plan, monthly payment plans, 2-payment plan). Need-based scholarship grants available. In 2005–06, 15% of upper-school students received aid. Total amount of financial aid awarded in 2005–06: $556,600.

Admissions Traditional secondary-level entrance grade is 9. For fall 2005, 69 students applied for upper-level admission, 29 were accepted, 13 enrolled. School's own exam required. Deadline for receipt of application materials: January 10. Application fee required: $50. On-campus interview required.

Athletics Interscholastic: baseball (boys), basketball (b,g), soccer (b,g), softball (g), tennis (b,g), track and field (b,g), volleyball (g); coed interscholastic: cross-country running, golf; coed intramural: equestrian sports, ice hockey. 3 PE instructors.

Computers Computers are regularly used in all classes. Computer network features include campus e-mail, on-campus library services, CD-ROMs, online commercial services, Internet access, file transfer, office computer access, DVD, wireless campus network.

Contact Mrs. Debra Von Bargen, Associate Director for Middle and Upper School Admissions. 202-243-1815. Fax: 202-243-1807. E-mail: vonbargen@wis.edu. Web site: www.wis.edu.

WASHINGTON WALDORF SCHOOL

4800 Sangamore Road
Bethesda, Maryland 20816
Head of School: Mrs. Natalie Adams

General Information Coeducational day college-preparatory and arts school. Grades PS–12. Founded: 1984. Setting: suburban. Nearest major city is Washington, DC. 6-acre campus. 1 building on campus. Approved or accredited by Association of Independent Schools of Greater Washington, Association of Waldorf Schools of North America, Middle States Association of Colleges and Schools, and Maryland Department of Education. Total enrollment: 280. Upper school average class size: 20. Upper school faculty-student ratio: 1:8.

Upper School Student Profile Grade 9: 18 students (4 boys, 14 girls); Grade 10: 16 students (4 boys, 12 girls); Grade 11: 17 students (7 boys, 10 girls); Grade 12: 11 students (6 boys, 5 girls).

Faculty School total: 34. In upper school: 8 men, 4 women; 8 have advanced degrees.

Subjects Offered 3-dimensional art, African-American history, algebra, American Civil War, American literature, anatomy and physiology, ancient world history, art, art and culture, art history, biochemistry, biology, bookbinding, botany, British literature,

calculus, calculus-AP, chamber groups, chemistry, choir, chorus, civil rights, classical civilization, crafts, critical thinking, critical writing, drama performance, ecology, epic literature, eurythmy, fine arts, general math, general science, geology, geometry, German, grammar, history of architecture, history of music, human anatomy, human development, lab science, medieval literature, metalworking, modern history, modern world history, mythology, oil painting, optics, physical education, pre-calculus, printmaking, research skills, sculpture, Shakespeare, Spanish, stone carving, trigonometry, U.S. constitutional history, weaving, Western literature, writing, zoology.

Graduation Requirements Arts and fine arts (art, music, dance, drama), crafts, English, eurythmy, foreign language, mathematics, physical education (includes health), science, social studies (includes history).

Special Academic Programs Advanced Placement exam preparation in 1 subject area; study abroad; academic accommodation for the musically talented and the artistically talented.

College Placement 21 students graduated in 2005; all went to college, including Georgetown University; Kenyon College; The College of Wooster; University of Michigan; University of Vermont; Vassar College. Mean SAT verbal: 639, mean SAT math: 559, mean combined SAT: 1824.

Student Life Upper grades have student council. Discipline rests primarily with faculty.

Summer Programs Sports programs offered; session focuses on basketball and baseball camps; held on campus; accepts boys and girls; open to students from other schools. 18 students usually enrolled.

Tuition and Aid Day student tuition: $17,140. Tuition installment plan (FACTS Tuition Payment Plan, monthly payment plans, individually arranged payment plans, self-insured tuition insurance). Tuition reduction for siblings, need-based scholarship grants, need-based assistance grants, tuition remission for children of faculty, one full scholarship for inner-city student available. In 2005–06, 20% of upper-school students received aid. Total amount of financial aid awarded in 2005–06: $125,000.

Admissions Traditional secondary-level entrance grade is 9. For fall 2005, 19 students applied for upper-level admission, 10 were accepted, 7 enrolled. Math and English placement tests required. Deadline for receipt of application materials: none. Application fee required: $40. On-campus interview required.

Athletics Interscholastic: baseball (boys), basketball (b,g), cross-country running (b,g), soccer (b,g), softball (g); coed intramural: volleyball. 1 PE instructor.

Computers Computers are regularly used in graphic design classes. Computer resources include Internet access.

Contact Mr. Edward J. Buckley, Admissions/Enrollment Director. 301-229-6107 Ext. 154. Fax: 301-229-9379. E-mail: ebuckley@washingtonwaldorf.org. Web site: www.washingtonwaldorf.org.

THE WATERFORD SCHOOL

1480 East 9400 South
Sandy, Utah 84093
Head of School: Mrs. Nancy M. Heuston

petersons.com

General Information Coeducational day college-preparatory, arts, technology, and visual arts, music, photography, dance, and theater school. Grades PK–12. Founded: 1981. Setting: suburban. Nearest major city is Salt Lake City. 50-acre campus. 10 buildings on campus. Approved or accredited by Northwest Association of Schools and Colleges, Pacific Northwest Association of Independent Schools, and Utah Department of Education. Member of National Association of Independent Schools. Total enrollment: 973. Upper school average class size: 15. Upper school faculty-student ratio: 1:5.

Upper School Student Profile Grade 9: 78 students (40 boys, 38 girls); Grade 10: 74 students (37 boys, 37 girls); Grade 11: 72 students (34 boys, 38 girls); Grade 12: 69 students (29 boys, 40 girls).

Faculty School total: 121. In upper school: 44 men, 36 women; 55 have advanced degrees.

Subjects Offered 20th century history, 3-dimensional design, acting, advanced math, Advanced Placement courses, aerobics, algebra, American history, American history-AP, American literature, art, Asian history, baseball, basketball, biology, biology-AP, British literature, calculus, calculus-AP, ceramics, chemistry, chemistry-AP, chorus, computer applications, computer art, computer graphics, computer programming, computer science, computer science-AP, creative writing, debate, drama, drama performance, drama workshop, drawing, ecology, economics, English-AP, European history, European history-AP, French, French-AP, geology, geometry, German, German-AP, Japanese, jazz ensemble, Latin, Latin American literature, music history, music performance, music theater, newspaper, outdoor education, painting, philosophy, photography, physical education, physics, physics-AP, pre-calculus, psychology, sculpture, Spanish, Spanish-AP, statistics and probability, statistics-AP, strings, studio art—AP, trigonometry, voice ensemble, volleyball, weight training, wind ensemble, world literature, writing workshop, yearbook, zoology.

Graduation Requirements 20th century world history, algebra, American history, American literature, biology, British literature, calculus, chemistry, computer science, English, European history, foreign language, geometry, music performance, physics, pre-calculus, trigonometry, visual arts, world history, writing workshop, six terms of physical education or participation on athletic teams, twelve terms in art, music, theater and/or dance (combination of courses).

Special Academic Programs Advanced Placement exam preparation in 14 subject areas; honors section; independent study; term-away projects; academic accommodation for the gifted, the musically talented, and the artistically talented.

College Placement 65 students graduated in 2005; all went to college. Mean SAT verbal: 620, mean SAT math: 625, mean combined SAT: 1836, mean composite ACT: 26.

Student Life Upper grades have uniform requirement, student council, honor system. Discipline rests equally with students and faculty.

Summer Programs Enrichment, advancement, sports, art/fine arts, computer instruction programs offered; session focuses on enrichment and advancement; held both on and off campus; held at various locations in Utah and abroad; accepts boys and girls; not open to students from other schools. 100 students usually enrolled. 2006 schedule: June 10 to August 10. Application deadline: March 15.

Tuition and Aid Day student tuition: $14,800. Guaranteed tuition plan. Tuition installment plan (Insured Tuition Payment Plan, monthly payment plans). Tuition reduction for siblings, need-based scholarship grants available. In 2005–06, 10% of upper-school students received aid. Total amount of financial aid awarded in 2005–06: $375,000.

Admissions Traditional secondary-level entrance grade is 9. For fall 2005, 36 students applied for upper-level admission, 27 were accepted, 25 enrolled. ERB CTP IV required. Deadline for receipt of application materials: none. Application fee required: $35. On-campus interview required.

Athletics Interscholastic: basketball (boys, girls), cross-country running (b,g), golf (b,g), lacrosse (b,g), soccer (b,g), swimming and diving (b,g), tennis (b,g), track and field (b,g), volleyball (g); intramural: indoor soccer (b,g); coed interscholastic: alpine skiing, ballet, crew, dance, Frisbee, outdoor education, racquetball, skiing (downhill); coed intramural: aerobics, alpine skiing, back packing, climbing, crew, mountain biking, nordic skiing, outdoor recreation, rock climbing, wall climbing, weight training. 7 PE instructors, 6 coaches.

Computers Computers are regularly used in animation, college planning, graphic design, library, literary magazine, newspaper, photography, publications, yearbook classes. Computer network features include campus e-mail, on-campus library services, CD-ROMs, Internet access.

Contact Mr. Todd Winters, Director of Admissions. 801-816-2213. Fax: 801-572-1787. E-mail: toddwinters@waterfordschool.org. Web site: www.waterfordschool.org.

ANNOUNCEMENT FROM THE SCHOOL Nestled near the base of Utah's majestic Wasatch mountains, Waterford, which sits on 50 acres, reflects the grandeur of its dramatic setting. The School's tradition is liberal arts. The focus is on each student learning. Here, expectations are high, the curriculum rich, and the scholarship engaging and renewing. Founded in 1981, Waterford has quickly established a tradition of excellence in education. At Waterford, the process of learning—no matter the discipline—engages its students. They are immersed in the liberal arts, personally applying that focus with progressive involvement in science labs, history and English seminars, foreign language discussion groups, art and music courses, and computer labs and on the playing field. This intensity of purpose prompted the US Office of Education to name the Waterford School "one of the top twelve schools in the country for academic and technological excellence." Upper School students are taught to be self-reflective in their learning and to acquire a repertoire of learning styles, which may be used across subject matter that varies widely and is freshly challenging. In the process, students learn the merits of primary sources, class discussions, and personal discipline. A majority of students in grades 10–12 take honors classes; many enroll in AP courses, which culminate in the AP examinations. The fine arts also receive strong emphasis. Students may sample widely or focus on a particular specialty in the arts. In every case, the teachers are specialists in the fields they teach, from choral music to strings or band, watercolor to oil painting and ceramics, photography to drama and dance. This much is certain: When they graduate, Waterford students are primed for lifelong learning and are ready to contribute that learning to the common good.

WATKINSON SCHOOL

180 Bloomfield Avenue
Hartford, Connecticut 06105
Head of School: Mr. John W. Bracker

petersons.com

General Information Coeducational day college-preparatory, arts, technology, and athletics school. Grades 6–PG. Founded: 1881. Setting: suburban. 40-acre campus. 5 buildings on campus. Approved or accredited by Association of Independent Schools in New England, Connecticut Association of Independent Schools, New England Association of Schools and Colleges, and Connecticut Department of Education. Member of National Association of Independent Schools and Secondary School Admission Test Board. Endowment: $2.3 million. Total enrollment: 272. Upper school average class size: 13. Upper school faculty-student ratio: 1:5.

Upper School Student Profile Grade 9: 34 students (20 boys, 14 girls); Grade 10: 39 students (24 boys, 15 girls); Grade 11: 57 students (23 boys, 34 girls); Grade 12: 43 students (24 boys, 19 girls); Postgraduate: 2 students (1 boy, 1 girl).

Faculty School total: 60. In upper school: 19 men, 41 women; 35 have advanced degrees.

Subjects Offered African history, algebra, American history, American literature, American sign language, anatomy, ancient world history, art, Asian history, athletics, biology, calculus, ceramics, chemistry, creative writing, dance, drama, drawing, earth science, English, English literature, environmental science, environmental studies, European history, expository writing, fine arts, French, geography, geometry, health, history, internship, life skills, mathematics, modern European history, painting, photography, physical education, physics, pottery, science, social studies, Spanish, theater, U.S. history, world history, world literature, writing.

Graduation Requirements Arts and fine arts (art, music, dance, drama), English, foreign language, mathematics, science, social studies (includes history).

Special Academic Programs Accelerated programs; independent study; term-away projects; study at local college for college credit; academic accommodation for the gifted, the musically talented, and the artistically talented.

College Placement 49 students graduated in 2005; 46 went to college. Other: 2 entered a postgraduate year, 1 had other specific plans.

Student Life Upper grades have specified standards of dress, student council, honor system. Discipline rests equally with students and faculty.

Summer Programs Remediation, enrichment, computer instruction programs offered; session focuses on enrichment and tutorial support; held on campus; accepts boys and girls; open to students from other schools. 30 students usually enrolled. 2006 schedule: June 20 to August 15. Application deadline: none.

Tuition and Aid Day student tuition: $23,475. Tuition installment plan (Insured Tuition Payment Plan, Academic Management Services Plan, prepayment discount plan). Need-based scholarship grants, paying campus jobs available. In 2005–06, 29% of upper-school students received aid. Total amount of financial aid awarded in 2005–06: $766,893.

Admissions Traditional secondary-level entrance grade is 9. For fall 2005, 97 students applied for upper-level admission, 55 were accepted, 41 enrolled. ISEE or SSAT required. Deadline for receipt of application materials: February 10. Application fee required: $50. On-campus interview required.

Athletics Interscholastic: basketball (boys, girls), cross-country running (b,g), lacrosse (b,g), soccer (b,g), softball (g), volleyball (g); coed interscholastic: golf, ice hockey, tennis, track and field; coed intramural: alpine skiing, ballet, baseball, boxing, climbing, combined training, crew, dance, dance squad, fencing, fitness, Frisbee, golf, outdoor adventure, physical fitness, project adventure, strength & conditioning, tennis, volleyball, weight lifting, yoga. 2 PE instructors, 2 coaches, 1 trainer.

Computers Computers are regularly used in all classes. Computer network features include campus e-mail, on-campus library services, CD-ROMs, online commercial services, Internet access, file transfer, wireless campus network, T1 connection to University of Hartford library services.

Contact Mrs. Cathy Batson, Admissions Office Assistant, 860-236-5618 Ext. 136. Fax: 860-233-8295. E-mail: cathy_batson@watkinson.org. Web site: www. watkinson.org.

ANNOUNCEMENT FROM THE SCHOOL A member of the Coalition of Essential Schools, Watkinson's award-winning college-preparatory curriculum serves grades 6–PG. Emphasis is on mastery of essential skills and concepts. Ninety-minute classes allow for in-depth study. Special programs include creative arts, learning skills, and technology. College credits are available at the adjacent University of Hartford.

THE WAVERLY SCHOOL

67 West Bellevue Drive
Pasadena, California 91105
Head of School: Ms. Heidi Johnson

General Information Coeducational day college-preparatory and arts school. Grades PK–12. Founded: 1993. Setting: urban. Nearest major city is Los Angeles. 1-acre campus. 2 buildings on campus. Approved or accredited by Western Association of Schools and Colleges and California Department of Education. Total enrollment: 289. Upper school average class size: 15. Upper school faculty-student ratio: 1:8.

Upper School Student Profile Grade 9: 25 students (16 boys, 9 girls); Grade 10: 18 students (11 boys, 7 girls); Grade 11: 21 students (13 boys, 8 girls); Grade 12: 16 students (7 boys, 9 girls).

Faculty School total: 49. In upper school: 5 men, 9 women; 9 have advanced degrees.

Subjects Offered 20th century history, algebra, American history-AP, American literature, ancient history, art, biology, biology-AP, calculus-AP, chemistry-AP, Chinese history, college counseling, composition, contemporary issues, English language-AP, English-AP, environmental science-AP, ethics, European history-AP, filmmaking, French-AP, geometry, history, modern civilization, performing arts, physical science, physics-AP, physiology, pre-calculus, Spanish-AP, statistics, world religions, yearbook.

Graduation Requirements Algebra, American history, American literature, ancient history, art, biology, chemistry, foreign language, geometry, performing arts, physical science, pre-calculus, ancient literature, interactive mathematics program. Community service is required.

Special Academic Programs Advanced Placement exam preparation in 10 subject areas; independent study.

College Placement 12 students graduated in 2005; all went to college, including California Polytechnic State University, San Luis Obispo; Occidental College; Pepperdine University; Pitzer College; University of California, Santa Barbara; University of California, Santa Cruz. Median SAT verbal: 640, median SAT math: 610. 57% scored over 600 on SAT verbal, 71% scored over 600 on SAT math.

Student Life Upper grades have student council, honor system. Discipline rests primarily with faculty.

Tuition and Aid Day student tuition: $14,438. Tuition installment plan (monthly payment plans). Need-based scholarship grants available. In 2005–06, 8% of upper-school students received aid. Total amount of financial aid awarded in 2005–06: $17,000.

Admissions Traditional secondary-level entrance grade is 9. For fall 2005, 35 students applied for upper-level admission, 25 were accepted, 14 enrolled. Non-standardized placement tests required. Deadline for receipt of application materials: February 1. Application fee required: $75. On-campus interview required.

Athletics Interscholastic: basketball (boys, girls), cheering (g), cross-country running (b,g), fencing (b); intramural: basketball (b,g), cooperative games (b,g), fitness (b,g), flag football (b,g), yoga (b,g); coed intramural: basketball, cooperative games, fitness, yoga. 2 PE instructors.

Computers Computers are regularly used in science classes. Computer network features include CD-ROMs, Internet access, office computer access.

Contact Ms. Joanne Kesten, Admissions Director. 626-792-5940. Fax: 626-683-5460. E-mail: admissions@thewaverlyschool.org. Web site: www.thewaverlyschool.org.

WAYLAND ACADEMY

101 North University Avenue
Beaver Dam, Wisconsin 53916-2253
Head of School: Mr. Robert L. Esten '64

General Information Coeducational boarding and day college-preparatory school. Grades 9–12. Founded: 1855. Setting: small town. Nearest major city is Milwaukee. Students are housed in single-sex dormitories. 55-acre campus. 20 buildings on campus. Approved or accredited by Independent Schools Association of the Central States, North Central Association of Colleges and Schools, and The Association of Boarding Schools. Member of National Association of Independent Schools and Secondary School Admission Test Board. Endowment: $9 million. Total enrollment: 190. Upper school average class size: 12. Upper school faculty-student ratio: 1:6.

Upper School Student Profile Grade 9: 58 students (35 boys, 23 girls); Grade 10: 52 students (26 boys, 26 girls); Grade 11: 45 students (25 boys, 20 girls); Grade 12: 35 students (17 boys, 18 girls). 75% of students are boarding students. 52% are state residents. 15 states are represented in upper school student body. 17% are international students. International students from China, Germany, Ghana, Japan, Republic of Korea, and Saudi Arabia; 5 other countries represented in student body.

Faculty School total: 35. In upper school: 19 men, 16 women; 28 have advanced degrees; 24 reside on campus.

Subjects Offered Advanced Placement courses, algebra, American history, American literature, art, art history, astronomy, biology, calculus, ceramics, chemistry, computer programming, computer science, creative writing, drama, dramatic arts, economics, English, English literature, ESL, European history, expository writing, fine arts, French studies, functions, geometry, German, government/civics, grammar, Greek, health, history, Latin, mathematics, music, music history, photography, physics, political science, science, social studies, Spanish, speech, statistics, theater, trigonometry, world civilizations, world history, world literature, writing, yearbook.

Graduation Requirements Arts and fine arts (art, music, dance, drama), English, foreign language, Latin, mathematics, physical education (includes health), science, social studies (includes history), acceptance to at least one four-year college or university. Community service is required.

Special Academic Programs Advanced Placement exam preparation in 12 subject areas; honors section; independent study; study abroad; ESL (4 students enrolled).

College Placement 45 students graduated in 2005; all went to college, including Brown University; California Institute of Technology; Northwestern University; University of Illinois at Urbana–Champaign; University of Wisconsin–Madison. Mean composite ACT: 24.

Student Life Upper grades have specified standards of dress, student council, honor system. Discipline rests primarily with faculty.

Tuition and Aid Day student tuition: $13,700; 7-day tuition and room/board: $29,720. Tuition installment plan (Academic Management Services Plan, Key Tuition Payment Plan). Tuition reduction for siblings, merit scholarship grants, need-based scholarship grants, paying campus jobs available. In 2005–06, 51% of upper-school students received aid; total upper-school merit-scholarship money awarded: $305,540. Total amount of financial aid awarded in 2005–06: $1,108,000.

Admissions Traditional secondary-level entrance grade is 9. For fall 2005, 151 students applied for upper-level admission, 127 were accepted, 89 enrolled. Any standardized test, SLEP or TOEFL required. Deadline for receipt of application materials: none. Application fee required: $35. Interview required.

Athletics Interscholastic: alpine skiing (boys, girls), baseball (b), basketball (b,g), cheering (g), cross-country running (b,g), dance squad (g), field hockey (g), football

(b), pom squad (g), skiing (downhill) (b,g), soccer (b,g), softball (g), tennis (b,g), track and field (b,g), volleyball (g); coed interscholastic: golf, swimming and diving; coed intramural: aerobics/dance, bicycling, billiards, bowling, combined training, figure skating, fitness, flag football, Frisbee, horseback riding, independent competitive sports, martial arts, outdoor activities, outdoor recreation, paint ball, power lifting, rock climbing, scuba diving, self defense, skiing (downhill), squash, strength & conditioning, swimming and diving, table tennis, tennis, ultimate Frisbee, wall climbing, weight training. 1 PE instructor, 2 coaches, 2 trainers.

Computers Computers are regularly used in English, mathematics, science classes. Computer network features include campus e-mail, CD-ROMs, online commercial services, Internet access, wireless campus network.

Contact Mr. Eric S. Peters, Dean of Admission and College Counseling. 920-885-3373 Ext. 241. Fax: 920-887-3373. E-mail: epeters@wayland.org. Web site: www.wayland.org.

See full description on page 1124.

WAYNE COUNTRY DAY SCHOOL

480 Country Day Road
Goldsboro, North Carolina 27530
Head of School: Mr. Todd Anderson

General Information Coeducational day college-preparatory school. Grades PK–12. Founded: 1968. Setting: rural. Nearest major city is Raleigh. 40-acre campus. 5 buildings on campus. Approved or accredited by Southern Association of Colleges and Schools and North Carolina Department of Education. Total enrollment: 227. Upper school average class size: 19. Upper school faculty-student ratio: 1:15.

Upper School Student Profile Grade 7: 11 students (5 boys, 6 girls); Grade 8: 13 students (7 boys, 6 girls); Grade 9: 12 students (3 boys, 9 girls); Grade 10: 29 students (16 boys, 13 girls); Grade 11: 20 students (11 boys, 9 girls); Grade 12: 15 students (11 boys, 4 girls).

Faculty School total: 42. In upper school: 3 men, 12 women; 6 have advanced degrees.

Subjects Offered Algebra, art, biology, calculus, chemistry, civics, composition, computers, earth science, English, French, geography, geometry, health, keyboarding, life science, music, North Carolina history, physical education, physical science, physics, pre-algebra, pre-calculus, Spanish, study skills, theater, theater production, U.S. history, Western civilization.

Graduation Requirements Arts and fine arts (art, music, dance, drama), composition, computer science, English, foreign language, mathematics, physical education (includes health), science, social studies (includes history). Community service is required.

Special Academic Programs Advanced Placement exam preparation in 5 subject areas; honors section; independent study; study at local college for college credit; academic accommodation for the gifted.

College Placement 18 students graduated in 2005; all went to college, including Duke University; East Carolina University; Meredith College; North Carolina State University; The University of North Carolina at Greensboro; The University of North Carolina Wilmington.

Student Life Upper grades have specified standards of dress, student council, honor system. Discipline rests equally with students and faculty.

Tuition and Aid Day student tuition: $6650. Tuition installment plan (monthly payment plans). Need-based scholarship grants available. In 2005–06, 5% of upper-school students received aid.

Admissions Traditional secondary-level entrance grade is 9. For fall 2005, 10 students applied for upper-level admission, 8 were accepted, 5 enrolled. Admissions testing required. Deadline for receipt of application materials: none. Application fee required: $60. Interview required.

Athletics Interscholastic: baseball (boys), basketball (b,g), cheering (g), soccer (b,g), softball (g), tennis (b,g), volleyball (g); coed interscholastic: cross-country running, golf, strength & conditioning; coed intramural: soccer. 2 PE instructors.

Computers Computers are regularly used in English, foreign language, history, science classes. Computer network features include CD-ROMs, online commercial services, Internet access.

Contact Ms. Elidia M. Eason, Director of Admissions. 919-736-1045 Ext. 233. Fax: 919-583-9493. E-mail: wcdsadmissions@waynecountryday.com. Web site: www.waynecountryday.com.

WAYNFLETE SCHOOL

360 Spring Street
Portland, Maine 04102
Head of School: Dr. Mark Segar

General Information Coeducational day college-preparatory school. Grades PK–12. Founded: 1898. Setting: urban. Nearest major city is Boston, MA. 45-acre campus. 8 buildings on campus. Approved or accredited by Association of Independent Schools in New England, Independent Schools of Northern New England, New England Association of Schools and Colleges, The College Board, and Maine Department of Education. Member of National Association of Independent Schools. Endowment: $7.5 million. Total enrollment: 553. Upper school average class size: 12. Upper school faculty-student ratio: 1:7.

Upper School Student Profile Grade 9: 66 students (24 boys, 42 girls); Grade 10: 68 students (29 boys, 39 girls); Grade 11: 56 students (31 boys, 25 girls); Grade 12: 60 students (30 boys, 30 girls).

Faculty School total: 87. In upper school: 18 men, 43 women; 24 have advanced degrees.

Subjects Offered Algebra, American history, American literature, anthropology, art history, biology, calculus, ceramics, chemistry, computer science, creative writing, dance, drama, earth science, ecology, English, English literature, environmental science, ethics, European history, expository writing, film, fine arts, French, geography, geometry, government/civics, grammar, health, history of ideas, Latin, marine biology, mathematics, music, physical education, physics, psychology, social studies, Spanish, studio art, theater, trigonometry, world history, world literature, writing.

Graduation Requirements Arts, biology, English, foreign language, geometry, sports, U.S. history. Community service is required.

Special Academic Programs Independent study; term-away projects; study abroad.

College Placement 56 students graduated in 2005; all went to college, including Bates College; Boston University; Colby College; The Johns Hopkins University; University of Vermont; Yale University. Median SAT verbal: 660, median SAT math: 650. 75.9% scored over 600 on SAT verbal, 68.5% scored over 600 on SAT math.

Student Life Upper grades have student council. Discipline rests primarily with faculty.

Summer Programs Enrichment, sports, art/fine arts programs offered; session focuses on fine arts, sports camps, performing arts, and science; held on campus; accepts boys and girls; open to students from other schools. 625 students usually enrolled. 2006 schedule: June 26 to August 4. Application deadline: April 1.

Tuition and Aid Day student tuition: $18,490. Tuition installment plan (Insured Tuition Payment Plan, Key Tuition Payment Plan, monthly payment plans). Need-based scholarship grants available. In 2005–06, 20% of upper-school students received aid. Total amount of financial aid awarded in 2005–06: $639,821.

Admissions Traditional secondary-level entrance grade is 9. For fall 2005, 43 students applied for upper-level admission, 35 were accepted, 23 enrolled. Deadline for receipt of application materials: February 10. Application fee required: $35. Interview required.

Athletics Interscholastic: baseball (boys), basketball (b,g), cross-country running (b,g), field hockey (g), lacrosse (b,g), skiing (cross-country) (b,g), soccer (b,g), softball (g), tennis (b,g); intramural: back packing (b,g), handball (b); coed interscholastic: crew, fitness walking, nordic skiing, rowing; coed intramural: alpine skiing, bowling, combined training, dance, fitness walking, Frisbee, modern dance, physical fitness, sailing, tennis, ultimate Frisbee, weight lifting, weight training, yoga. 4 PE instructors, 15 coaches, 1 trainer.

Computers Computers are regularly used in mathematics, science classes. Computer network features include campus e-mail, on-campus library services, CD-ROMs, online commercial services, Internet access, DVD.

Contact Admission Office. 207-774-5721 Ext. 224. Fax: 207-772-4782. E-mail: admission_office@waynflete.org. Web site: www.waynflete.org.

WEBBER ACADEMY

1515—93 Street SW
Calgary, Alberta T3H 4A8, Canada
Head of School: Dr. Neil Webber

General Information Coeducational day college-preparatory school. Grades K–12. Founded: 1997. Setting: urban. 47-acre campus. 1 building on campus. Approved or accredited by Alberta Department of Education. Language of instruction: English. Total enrollment: 699. Upper school average class size: 22. Upper school faculty-student ratio: 1:18.

Faculty School total: 60. In upper school: 7 men, 9 women; 6 have advanced degrees.

Subjects Offered 20th century American writers, 20th century physics, 20th century world history, 3-dimensional design, advanced chemistry, advanced math, aerospace education, algebra, analysis and differential calculus, analytic geometry, art, band, biology, biology-AP, British literature, calculus, calculus-AP, Canadian geography, Canadian history, Canadian literature, career/college preparation, chemistry, chemistry-AP, choir, choral music, Christianity, college counseling, computer programming, computer studies, computer technologies, computers, concert band, current history, debate, directing, drama, drama performance, dramatic arts, English, English language and composition-AP, English language-AP, English literature, English literature-AP, English-AP, English/composition-AP, European history, European history-AP, film studies, fine arts, first aid, fitness, folk music, foreign policy, French, French as a second language, general math, general science, geography, geometry, global science, government and politics-AP, grammar, guidance, handbells, health and safety, health education, history, history-AP, human geography-AP, information design technology, information technology, inorganic chemistry, intro to computers, introduction to technology, jazz, jazz band, keyboarding, language and composition, language-AP, leadership skills, library, linear algebra, literature and composition-AP, literature-AP, logarithms, logic, rhetoric, and debate, Mandarin, math applications, math review, mathematics, mathematics-AP, modern civilization, mod-

ern history, music, music performance, newspaper, novels, nutrition, oil painting, optics, organic chemistry, outdoor education, painting, performing arts, physical education, physical fitness, physics, practical living, prayer/spirituality, pre-algebra, pre-calculus, public speaking, reading/study skills, research skills, research techniques, SAT/ACT preparation, science, science and technology, science project, sex education, sexuality, social skills, space and physical sciences, Spanish, speech, speech and debate, statistics and probability, stock market, swimming competency, technology, trigonometry, vocal music, weight training, Western civilization, wind instruments, word processing, work-study, world geography, world history, world issues, world studies, writing, yearbook.

Graduation Requirements Alberta Learning requirements.

Special Academic Programs Advanced Placement exam preparation in 5 subject areas; honors section; academic accommodation for the gifted, the musically talented, and the artistically talented.

College Placement 20 students graduated in 2005; all went to college, including University of Alberta.

Student Life Upper grades have uniform requirement, student council, honor system. Discipline rests primarily with faculty.

Tuition and Aid Day student tuition: CAN$10,000. Tuition installment plan (The Tuition Plan). Bursaries, merit scholarship grants available. In 2005–06, 5% of upper-school students received aid; total upper-school merit-scholarship money awarded: CAN$10,000. Total amount of financial aid awarded in 2005–06: CAN$90,000.

Admissions Traditional secondary-level entrance grade is 10. Admissions testing or SSAT required. Deadline for receipt of application materials: none. Application fee required: CAN$100. On-campus interview required.

Athletics Interscholastic: basketball (boys, girls), cross-country running (b,g), indoor soccer (b,g), soccer (b,g), volleyball (b,g); intramural: basketball (b,g), cross-country running (b,g), field hockey (b,g), floor hockey (b,g), indoor soccer (b,g), soccer (b,g), volleyball (b,g); coed interscholastic: badminton, golf, indoor soccer, running, soccer, volleyball; coed intramural: badminton, field hockey, fitness, fitness walking, floor hockey, golf, indoor soccer, jogging, modern dance, outdoor activities, outdoor education, outdoor recreation, outdoor skills, physical fitness, physical training, running, skiing (cross-country), skiing (downhill), soccer, swimming and diving, track and field, volleyball. 5 PE instructors, 8 coaches.

Computers Computers are regularly used in all classes. Computer network features include campus e-mail, on-campus library services, CD-ROMs, Internet access, office computer access.

Contact Dr. Neil Webber, Head of School. 403-277-4700. Fax: 403-277-2770. E-mail: nwebber@webberacademy.ca.

THE WEBB SCHOOL

319 Webb Road East
PO Box 488
Bell Buckle, Tennessee 37020
Head of School: Mr. Albert Cauz

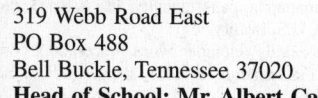

General Information Coeducational boarding and day college-preparatory and arts school. Boarding grades 7–12, day grades 6–12. Founded: 1870. Setting: rural. Nearest major city is Nashville. Students are housed in single-sex dormitories. 150-acre campus. 15 buildings on campus. Approved or accredited by Southern Association of Colleges and Schools, Tennessee Association of Independent Schools, The Association of Boarding Schools, and Tennessee Department of Education. Member of National Association of Independent Schools and Secondary School Admission Test Board. Endowment: $21 million. Total enrollment: 272. Upper school average class size: 12. Upper school faculty-student ratio: 1:7.

Upper School Student Profile Grade 9: 37 students (25 boys, 12 girls); Grade 10: 43 students (21 boys, 22 girls); Grade 11: 50 students (28 boys, 22 girls); Grade 12: 47 students (21 boys, 26 girls). 33% of students are boarding students. 70% are state residents. 11 states are represented in upper school student body. 10% are international students. International students from China, Germany, Jamaica, Republic of Korea, Slovakia, and Taiwan; 1 other country represented in student body.

Faculty School total: 42. In upper school: 17 men, 19 women; 25 have advanced degrees; 16 reside on campus.

Subjects Offered Advanced Placement courses, algebra, American Civil War, American government, American history, American literature, American literature-AP, anatomy, art, art history, biology, business skills, calculus, ceramics, chemistry, chemistry-AP, computer programming, computer science, creative writing, drama, driver education, earth science, ecology, economics, English, English literature, ESL, ethics, European history, fine arts, French, geography, geometry, German, government/civics, grammar, health, history, history-AP, journalism, Latin, mathematics, physical education, physics, physics-AP, physiology, poetry, psychology, religion, Russian history, science, Shakespeare, social science, social studies, Spanish, speech, statistics, theater, trigonometry, Western civilization, wilderness education, world history, world literature.

Graduation Requirements Arts and fine arts (art, music, dance, drama), computer science, economics, English, ethics, foreign language, mathematics, physical education (includes health), science, senior thesis, social science, social studies (includes history), speech, declamation.

Special Academic Programs Advanced Placement exam preparation in 6 subject areas; honors section; academic accommodation for the gifted; special instructional classes for deaf students; ESL (9 students enrolled).

College Placement 53 students graduated in 2005; all went to college, including Oberlin College; The University of Tennessee; Tufts University; Vanderbilt University; Wake Forest University. Mean SAT verbal: 625, mean SAT math: 610.

Student Life Upper grades have uniform requirement, student council, honor system. Discipline rests equally with students and faculty.

Summer Programs Remediation, enrichment, advancement, ESL, art/fine arts, computer instruction programs offered; session focuses on academics; held on campus; accepts boys and girls; open to students from other schools. 35 students usually enrolled. 2006 schedule: June 18 to August 1. Application deadline: none.

Tuition and Aid Day student tuition: $12,600; 5-day tuition and room/board: $22,000; 7-day tuition and room/board: $30,500–$36,500. Tuition installment plan (Key Tuition Payment Plan, monthly payment plans, individually arranged payment plans, Tuition Management Systems Plan). Merit scholarship grants, need-based scholarship grants available. In 2005–06, 40% of upper-school students received aid. Total amount of financial aid awarded in 2005–06: $900,000.

Admissions Traditional secondary-level entrance grade is 9. For fall 2005, 108 students applied for upper-level admission, 94 were accepted, 70 enrolled. ISEE or SSAT required. Deadline for receipt of application materials: none. Application fee required: $35. Interview required.

Athletics Interscholastic: baseball (boys), basketball (b,g), golf (b,g), lacrosse (b), soccer (b,g), softball (g), tennis (b,g), volleyball (g); intramural: aerobics (g), aerobics/dance (g), aerobics/nautilus (b,g), lacrosse (b), tennis (b,g); coed interscholastic: bowling, cross-country running, trap and skeet, ultimate Frisbee; coed intramural: aquatics, back packing, ballet, bicycling, canoeing/kayaking, climbing, combined training, equestrian sports, fishing, fitness, fitness walking, flag football, fly fishing, Frisbee, hiking/backpacking, horseback riding, jogging, kayaking, kickball, marksmanship, martial arts, mountain biking, nautilus, outdoor activities, outdoor adventure, outdoor education, outdoor recreation, outdoor skills, paddle tennis, paddling, paint ball, physical fitness, physical training, rafting, riflery, rock climbing, ropes courses, running, scuba diving, skeet shooting, softball, strength & conditioning, table tennis, trap and skeet, walking, wall climbing, weight training, wilderness, wilderness survival, yoga. 3 PE instructors, 15 coaches, 1 trainer.

Computers Computers are regularly used in English, foreign language, history, journalism, mathematics, science classes. Computer network features include campus e-mail, on-campus library services, CD-ROMs, Internet access, office computer access.

Contact Mr. Chad C. Sartini, Director of Admissions. 931-389-6003. Fax: 931-389-6657. E-mail: admissions@webbschool.com. Web site: www.thewebbschool.com.

See full description on page 1126.

WEBB SCHOOL OF KNOXVILLE

9800 Webb School Drive
Knoxville, Tennessee 37923-3399
Head of School: Mr. Scott L. Hutchinson

General Information Coeducational day college-preparatory, arts, and religious studies school. Grades K–12. Founded: 1955. Setting: urban. Nearest major city is Chattanooga. 108-acre campus. 8 buildings on campus. Approved or accredited by Southern Association of Colleges and Schools, Southern Association of Independent Schools, and Tennessee Department of Education. Member of National Association of Independent Schools and Secondary School Admission Test Board. Endowment: $55 million. Total enrollment: 1,052. Upper school average class size: 15. Upper school faculty-student ratio: 1:11.

Upper School Student Profile Grade 9: 123 students (63 boys, 60 girls); Grade 10: 120 students (68 boys, 52 girls); Grade 11: 120 students (60 boys, 60 girls); Grade 12: 108 students (69 boys, 39 girls).

Faculty School total: 102. In upper school: 21 men, 20 women; 34 have advanced degrees.

Subjects Offered 3-dimensional design, acting, algebra, American literature, art history-AP, biology, biology-AP, calculus, calculus-AP, ceramics, chamber groups, chemistry, chemistry-AP, computer science, computer science-AP, concert choir, digital imaging, drama, dramatic arts, drawing, driver education, economics, economics-AP, English composition, English language and composition-AP, English literature, English literature and composition-AP, English-AP, environmental science-AP, ethics, film, French, French-AP, geometry, German, German-AP, honors English, honors geometry, honors world history, human biology, independent study, Irish literature, journalism, Latin, Latin-AP, macroeconomics-AP, math applications, modern European history-AP, music theory-AP, painting, photography, physics, physics-AP, pre-calculus, probability and statistics, psychology-AP, religious education, Spanish, Spanish-AP, speech communications, statistics-AP, strings, studio art-AP, theater, trigonometry, U.S. government and politics, U.S. government and politics-AP, U.S. history, U.S. history-AP, wind ensemble, world history, world history-AP, world religions, yearbook.

Graduation Requirements Algebra, American history, arts and fine arts (art, music, dance, drama), biology, chemistry, electives, English, foreign language, geometry,

mathematics, physical education (includes health), religion (includes Bible studies and theology), science, world history, public speaking (two chapel talks), 25 hours of service learning per year.

Special Academic Programs Advanced Placement exam preparation in 20 subject areas; honors section; independent study.

College Placement 105 students graduated in 2005; all went to college, including Auburn University; Furman University; Middle Tennessee State University; The University of North Carolina at Chapel Hill; The University of Tennessee; University of Georgia. Mean SAT verbal: 600, mean SAT math: 590, mean composite ACT: 26. 56% scored over 600 on SAT verbal, 44% scored over 600 on SAT math.

Student Life Upper grades have uniform requirement, student council, honor system. Discipline rests equally with students and faculty.

Summer Programs Remediation, enrichment, advancement, sports, art/fine arts programs offered; session focuses on camp and sports-oriented fun; held on campus; accepts boys and girls; open to students from other schools. 2094 students usually enrolled. 2006 schedule: June 5 to August 4. Application deadline: June 5.

Tuition and Aid Day student tuition: $13,220. Tuition installment plan (Key Tuition Payment Plan, monthly payment plans, individually arranged payment plans). Need-based scholarship grants available. In 2005–06, 14% of upper-school students received aid. Total amount of financial aid awarded in 2005–06: $560,104.

Admissions Traditional secondary-level entrance grade is 9. For fall 2005, 54 students applied for upper-level admission, 40 were accepted, 31 enrolled. SSAT required. Deadline for receipt of application materials: June 1. Application fee required: $40. On-campus interview required.

Athletics Interscholastic: baseball (boys), basketball (b,g), bowling (b,g), cheering (g), cross-country running (b,g), diving (b,g), field hockey (g), football (b), golf (b,g), lacrosse (b), soccer (b,g), softball (g), swimming and diving (b,g), tennis (b,g), track and field (b,g), volleyball (g), wrestling (b); coed interscholastic: sailing; coed intramural: weight training. 20 coaches, 1 trainer.

Computers Computers are regularly used in art, English, foreign language, history, journalism, mathematics, science, technology, yearbook classes. Computer network features include campus e-mail, on-campus library services, CD-ROMs, Internet access, office computer access, DVD, wireless campus network.

Contact Mrs. Sarah Lowe, Admissions Administrative Assistant. 865-291-3830. Fax: 865-291-1532. E-mail: sarah_lowe@webbschool.org. Web site: www. webbschool.org.

THE WELLINGTON SCHOOL

3650 Reed Road
Columbus, Ohio 43220
Head of School: Mr. Richard J. O'Hara

General Information Coeducational day college-preparatory, arts, and bilingual studies school. Grades PK–12. Founded: 1982. Setting: suburban. 21-acre campus. 1 building on campus. Approved or accredited by Independent Schools Association of the Central States and Ohio Department of Education. Member of National Association of Independent Schools. Total enrollment: 616. Upper school average class size: 12. Upper school faculty-student ratio: 1:12.

Upper School Student Profile Grade 9: 60 students (29 boys, 31 girls); Grade 10: 47 students (21 boys, 26 girls); Grade 11: 34 students (17 boys, 17 girls); Grade 12: 48 students (29 boys, 19 girls).

Faculty School total: 56. In upper school: 14 men, 11 women; 16 have advanced degrees.

Subjects Offered Algebra, art and culture, band, biology, biology-AP, calculus-AP, ceramics, chemistry, chemistry-AP, choir, chorus, computer graphics, creative arts, drama, drawing, earth and space science, economics, English, English-AP, European history-AP, film, finite math, French, French-AP, geometry, government, issues of the 90's, journalism, Latin, Latin-AP, mathematics, modern history, music appreciation, music theory-AP, painting, photography, physical education, physics, physics-AP, printmaking, Spanish, Spanish-AP, speech, strings, studio art-AP, U.S. history, U.S. history-AP, visual arts, voice, Western civilization, word processing, writing, yearbook.

Graduation Requirements 3-dimensional art, arts and fine arts (art, music, dance, drama), English, foreign language, government, lab science, mathematics, physical education (includes health), science, social science, social studies (includes history), speech, senior independent project. Community service is required.

Special Academic Programs Advanced Placement exam preparation in 13 subject areas; honors section; accelerated programs; independent study; study at local college for college credit; study abroad; academic accommodation for the gifted, the musically talented, and the artistically talented.

College Placement 46 students graduated in 2005; all went to college, including Boston University; Miami University; Ohio Wesleyan University; The Ohio State University; University of Kentucky.

Student Life Upper grades have specified standards of dress, student council. Discipline rests equally with students and faculty.

Summer Programs Enrichment, advancement, sports programs offered; session focuses on advancement; held on campus; accepts boys and girls; open to students from other schools. 50 students usually enrolled. 2006 schedule: June 10 to August 18. Application deadline: none.

Tuition and Aid Day student tuition: $14,400. Tuition installment plan (Key Tuition Payment Plan, monthly payment plans, individually arranged payment plans, 2-, 6-, and 10-month payment plans). Merit scholarship grants, need-based scholarship grants, need-based loans available.

Admissions Traditional secondary-level entrance grade is 9. Admissions testing or ERB required. Deadline for receipt of application materials: none. Application fee required: $50. On-campus interview required.

Athletics Interscholastic: baseball (boys), basketball (b,g), crew (b,g), fencing (b,g), golf (b,g), lacrosse (b,g), soccer (b,g), softball (g), tennis (b,g); intramural: basketball (b,g), lacrosse (g); coed interscholastic: crew, fencing, swimming and diving; coed intramural: climbing, flag football, martial arts. 2 PE instructors, 1 coach, 1 trainer.

Computers Computers are regularly used in English, foreign language, library, mathematics, music, newspaper, research skills, science, senior seminar, theater arts, typing, yearbook classes. Computer network features include campus e-mail, on-campus library services, CD-ROMs, online commercial services, Internet access, file transfer, office computer access, DVD, wireless campus network, SmartBoards.

Contact Ms. Lynne Steger, Assistant Director of Admission. 614-324-1647. Fax: 614-442-3286. E-mail: steger@wellington.org. Web site: www.wellington.org.

WELLSPRING FOUNDATION

Bethlehem, Connecticut
See Special Needs Schools section.

WELLSPRINGS FRIENDS SCHOOL

3590 West 18th Avenue
Eugene, Oregon 97402
Head of School: Dennis Hoerner

General Information Coeducational day college-preparatory and general academic school, affiliated with Society of Friends; primarily serves underachievers. Grades 9–12. Founded: 1994. Setting: small town. Nearest major city is Portland. 4-acre campus. 2 buildings on campus. Approved or accredited by Northwest Association of Schools and Colleges and Oregon Department of Education. Endowment: $18,000. Total enrollment: 60. Upper school average class size: 10. Upper school faculty-student ratio: 1:6.

Upper School Student Profile Grade 9: 8 students (6 boys, 2 girls); Grade 10: 18 students (11 boys, 7 girls); Grade 11: 9 students (3 boys, 6 girls); Grade 12: 25 students (13 boys, 12 girls).

Faculty School total: 8. In upper school: 4 men, 4 women; 2 have advanced degrees.

Subjects Offered 20th century world history, advanced math, algebra, English, film, finance, fine arts, geometry, government, human sexuality, life science, physical science, poetry, pre-algebra, Spanish, U.S. history.

Graduation Requirements Business skills (includes word processing), computer science, English, foreign language, mathematics, science, social studies (includes history). Community service is required.

Special Academic Programs Independent study; remedial reading and/or remedial writing; remedial math.

College Placement 8 students graduated in 2005; 4 went to college, including Lane Community College; University of Oregon. Other: 3 went to work, 1 had other specific plans.

Student Life Upper grades have student council, honor system. Discipline rests equally with students and faculty.

Tuition and Aid Day student tuition: $6000. Tuition installment plan (monthly payment plans, individually arranged payment plans). Need-based scholarship grants available.

Admissions Traditional secondary-level entrance grade is 9. For fall 2005, 15 students applied for upper-level admission, 15 were accepted, 14 enrolled. Deadline for receipt of application materials: none. No application fee required. Interview required.

Athletics Interscholastic: soccer (boys, girls), track and field (b,g), volleyball (g); coed intramural: basketball, bocce, Frisbee, yoga. 1 PE instructor.

Computers Computer network features include CD-ROMs, Internet access.

Contact Office Manager. 541-686-1223. Fax: 541-687-1493. E-mail: info@ wellspringsfriends.org.

WENTWORTH MILITARY ACADEMY AND JUNIOR COLLEGE

1880 Washington Avenue
Lexington, Missouri 64067-1799
Head of School: Maj. Gen. John H. Little

General Information Coeducational boarding and day college-preparatory and general academic school. Grades 9–12. Founded: 1880. Setting: small town. Nearest major city is Kansas City. Students are housed in coed-by-floor dorms. 137-acre campus. 9 buildings on campus. Approved or accredited by North Central Association

of Colleges and Schools and Missouri Department of Education. Endowment: $1.2 million. Total enrollment: 122. Upper school average class size: 14. Upper school faculty-student ratio: 1:8.

Upper School Student Profile Grade 9: 21 students (19 boys, 2 girls); Grade 10: 28 students (21 boys, 7 girls); Grade 11: 35 students (24 boys, 11 girls); Grade 12: 27 students (25 boys, 2 girls). 99% of students are boarding students. 20% are state residents. 24 states are represented in upper school student body. 3% are international students. International students from Canada, France, Guatemala, Mexico, Republic of Korea, and Spain.

Faculty School total: 27. In upper school: 13 men, 3 women; 8 have advanced degrees; 4 reside on campus.

Subjects Offered ACT preparation, algebra, American history, American literature, art, biology, business, calculus, chemistry, computer science, economics, English, ESL, fine arts, geography, geometry, German, government/civics, health, journalism, JROTC, mathematics, music, physical education, physics, science, Spanish, speech, trigonometry, typing, world history.

Graduation Requirements Arts and fine arts (art, music, dance, drama), computer science, English, foreign language, JROTC, mathematics, physical education (includes health), science, social studies (includes history), community service (hours vary by grade level).

Special Academic Programs Honors section; study at local college for college credit; special instructional classes for students with Attention Deficit Disorder; ESL.

College Placement 26 students graduated in 2005; 23 went to college, including Central Missouri State University; Kansas State University; The University of Iowa; United States Air Force Academy; University of Missouri–Columbia; University of Missouri–St. Louis. Other: 1 went to work, 1 entered military service, 1 had other specific plans. Mean composite ACT: 20.

Student Life Upper grades have uniform requirement, student council, honor system. Discipline rests equally with students and faculty. Attendance at religious services is required.

Summer Programs Remediation, enrichment, sports, rigorous outdoor training programs offered; session focuses on academics and adventure/leadership camp; held both on and off campus; held at locations of interest within a 100-mile radius (day and night trips); accepts boys and girls; open to students from other schools. 85 students usually enrolled. 2006 schedule: June 12 to July 14. Application deadline: May 31.

Tuition and Aid 7-day tuition and room/board: $25,990. Guaranteed tuition plan. Tuition installment plan (Key Tuition Payment Plan, FACTS Tuition Payment Plan, individually arranged payment plans, monthly payment plans using ACH withdrawals). Tuition reduction for siblings, merit scholarship grants, need-based scholarship grants available. In 2005–06, 30% of upper-school students received aid. Total amount of financial aid awarded in 2005–06: $375,000.

Admissions Traditional secondary-level entrance grade is 10. Deadline for receipt of application materials: none. Application fee required: $75. Interview recommended.

Athletics Interscholastic: football (boys), golf (b), soccer (b), volleyball (g); intramural: archery (b,g); coed interscholastic: basketball, cross-country running, drill team, indoor track & field, JROTC drill, marksmanship, riflery, track and field, wrestling; coed intramural: aerobics/nautilus, aquatics, basketball, cross-country running, diving, fitness, outdoor activities, outdoor adventure, outdoor recreation, paint ball, physical fitness, physical training, riflery, scuba diving, swimming and diving, water polo. 2 PE instructors, 4 coaches.

Computers Computers are regularly used in career exploration, college planning, science classes. Computer network features include CD-ROMs, Internet access.

Contact Director of Admissions. 660-259-2221 Ext. 211. Fax: 660-259-2677. E-mail: admissions@wma1880.org. Web site: www.wma.edu.

WESLEYAN SCHOOL

5405 Spalding Drive
Norcross, Georgia 30092
Head of School: Mr. Zach Young

petersons.com

General Information Coeducational day college-preparatory, arts, religious studies, bilingual studies, and technology school, affiliated with Christian faith. Grades K–12. Founded: 1963. Setting: suburban. Nearest major city is Atlanta. 70-acre campus. 5 buildings on campus. Approved or accredited by Georgia Independent School Association, National Independent Private Schools Association, Southern Association of Colleges and Schools, and Georgia Department of Education. Endowment: $700,000. Total enrollment: 1,071. Upper school average class size: 18. Upper school faculty-student ratio: 1:7.

Upper School Student Profile Grade 9: 104 students (57 boys, 47 girls); Grade 10: 107 students (56 boys, 51 girls); Grade 11: 100 students (50 boys, 50 girls); Grade 12: 103 students (52 boys, 51 girls).

Faculty School total: 126. In upper school: 26 men, 32 women; 43 have advanced degrees.

Subjects Offered 20th century history, 20th century physics, 20th century world history, 3-dimensional art, acting, advanced chemistry, advanced computer applications, advanced math, algebra, American government, American literature, art, art history, band, Basic programming, Bible, biology, biology-AP, British literature, British literature (honors), calculus, calculus-AP, chemistry, chemistry-AP, choral music, chorus, Christian doctrine, Christian education, Christian ethics, Christian

studies, classical language, college placement, English literature-AP, U.S. history, U.S. history-AP, vocal ensemble, weight training, word processing, world literature.

Graduation Requirements Algebra, American history, American literature, analysis, Bible, biology, British literature, chemistry, economics, environmental science, foreign language, geometry, modern world history, physical education (includes health), physics, pre-calculus, statistics.

Special Academic Programs Advanced Placement exam preparation in 16 subject areas; honors section; independent study; remedial reading and/or remedial writing; remedial math.

College Placement 95 students graduated in 2005; all went to college, including Auburn University; Georgia Institute of Technology; Georgia Southern University; The University of Alabama; University of Georgia; Vanderbilt University. Mean SAT verbal: 597, mean SAT math: 606. 54% scored over 600 on SAT verbal, 55% scored over 600 on SAT math.

Student Life Upper grades have uniform requirement, student council, honor system. Discipline rests equally with students and faculty. Attendance at religious services is required.

Summer Programs Enrichment, sports, art/fine arts, computer instruction programs offered; session focuses on sports, arts, and academics; held on campus; accepts boys and girls; open to students from other schools. 640 students usually enrolled. 2006 schedule: June 1 to August 6.

Tuition and Aid Day student tuition: $14,420. Tuition installment plan (Insured Tuition Payment Plan). Need-based scholarship grants available. In 2005–06, 6% of upper-school students received aid. Total amount of financial aid awarded in 2005–06: $240,000.

Admissions Traditional secondary-level entrance grade is 9. For fall 2005, 71 students applied for upper-level admission, 42 were accepted, 27 enrolled. SSAT and writing sample required. Deadline for receipt of application materials: February 17. Application fee required: $75. On-campus interview required.

Athletics Interscholastic: baseball (boys, girls), basketball (b,g), cheering (g), cross-country running (b,g), diving (b,g), football (b), golf (b,g), lacrosse (b,g), soccer (b,g), softball (g), strength & conditioning (b,g), swimming and diving (b,g), tennis (b,g), track and field (b,g), volleyball (g), weight training (b,g), wrestling (b); intramural: basketball (b,g), cheering (g), cross-country running (b,g), football (b), soccer (b,g), softball (g), swimming and diving (b,g), tennis (b,g), track and field (b,g), volleyball (g), wrestling (b); coed interscholastic: fitness. 2 coaches, 1 trainer.

Computers Computers are regularly used in all classes. Computer network features include on-campus library services, CD-ROMs, Internet access, file transfer.

Contact Ms. Sylvia Pryor, Admissions Assistant. 770-448-7640 Ext. 2267. Fax: 770-448-3699. E-mail: spryor@wesleyanschool.org. Web site: www.wesleyanschool.org.

ANNOUNCEMENT FROM THE SCHOOL Wesleyan's mission is to be a Christian school of academic excellence by providing each student with a diverse college-preparatory education guided by Christian principles and beliefs; challenging and nurturing the mind, body, and spirit of each student; and developing responsible stewardship in a changing world. Believing that all children are uniquely gifted, the School offers a learning environment that challenges, nurtures, and strengthens students intellectually, spiritually, and physically. Wesleyan is fully accredited by the Southern Association of Colleges and Schools and the Georgia Accreditation Commission. The School is also affiliated with the Atlanta Area Association of Independent Schools, The College Board, Educational Records Bureau, Georgia High School Association, Georgia Independent School Association, and the National Association of College Admission Counseling. The enrollment for the 2005-06 academic year for kindergarten through grade 12 is 1,071 students. Total school population is limited in order to maintain rigorous academic standards in the context of a close-knit school community that welcomes students of diverse racial, cultural, and religious backgrounds. The Wesleyan faculty is made up of 125 professional staff members, 74 of whom hold advanced degrees. Administrators teach classes in addition to performing administrative duties. A competitive athletics program is designed to provide quality experiences through preparation and competition; goals include enhancing physical fitness and promoting sportsmanship and team play. Interscholastic sports are available throughout the school year for both boys and girls at the varsity, junior varsity, and 7th and 8th grade levels. Wesleyan offers comprehensive performing and visual arts programs in theater, music, band, chorus, dance, and the visual arts. Students have the opportunity to participate in a wide spectrum of extracurricular activities: Honor Council, National Honor Society, Student Council, yearbook, newspaper, literary magazine, Environmental Awareness Club, Fellowship of Christian Athletes, Young Life, Bible Fellowship, and Serve-His League, as well as numerous other service activities.

WESTBURY CHRISTIAN SCHOOL

10420 Hillcroft
Houston, Texas 77096
Head of School: Mr. Robert O. McCloy

General Information Coeducational day college-preparatory and religious studies school, affiliated with Church of Christ. Grades PK–12. Founded: 1975. Setting: urban. 13-acre campus. 1 building on campus. Approved or accredited by National Christian School Association, Southern Association of Colleges and Schools, Texas Private School Accreditation Commission, and Texas Department of Education. Endowment: $300,000. Total enrollment: 500. Upper school average class size: 18. Upper school faculty-student ratio: 1:10.

Upper School Student Profile Grade 9: 73 students (39 boys, 34 girls); Grade 10: 51 students (26 boys, 25 girls); Grade 11: 63 students (44 boys, 19 girls); Grade 12: 48 students (26 boys, 22 girls). 20% of students are members of Church of Christ.

Faculty School total: 50. In upper school: 18 men, 12 women; 8 have advanced degrees.

Subjects Offered Advanced math, algebra, American history, art, athletics, band, basketball, Bible, biology, biology-AP, calculus, calculus-AP, cheerleading, chemistry, chemistry-AP, chorus, community service, computer animation, computer applications, computer graphics, computer programming-AP, concert band, drama, economics, economics-AP, English, English language and composition-AP, English literature and composition-AP, European history-AP, geography, geometry, government, government-AP, human geography—AP, humanities, instrumental music, jazz band, marching band, physical education, physics, pre-calculus, Spanish, Spanish-AP, speech, statistics-AP, studio art-AP, trigonometry, U.S. history, vocal ensemble, vocal music, world history, yearbook.

Graduation Requirements Arts and fine arts (art, music, dance, drama), Bible, computer science, electives, English, foreign language, mathematics, physical education (includes health), science, social studies (includes history), speech, continuous participation in student activities programs, community service each semester.

Special Academic Programs Advanced Placement exam preparation in 13 subject areas.

College Placement 40 students graduated in 2005; all went to college, including Abilene Christian University; Baylor University; Harding University; The University of Texas at Austin; The University of Texas at San Antonio; University of Houston. Median SAT verbal: 490, median SAT math: 480, median composite ACT: 22. 9% scored over 600 on SAT verbal, 20% scored over 600 on SAT math.

Student Life Upper grades have uniform requirement, student council, honor system. Discipline rests primarily with faculty. Attendance at religious services is required.

Summer Programs Sports programs offered; session focuses on basketball instruction (camps); held on campus; accepts boys and girls; open to students from other schools. 320 students usually enrolled. 2006 schedule: June 6 to July 8. Application deadline: May 27.

Tuition and Aid Day student tuition: $6100. Tuition installment plan (SMART Tuition Payment Plan, tuition discount if entire year paid by June 1). Tuition reduction for siblings, merit scholarship grants, need-based scholarship grants available. In 2005–06, 5% of upper-school students received aid; total upper-school merit-scholarship money awarded: $20,000. Total amount of financial aid awarded in 2005–06: $48,000.

Admissions Traditional secondary-level entrance grade is 9. For fall 2005, 95 students applied for upper-level admission, 71 were accepted, 59 enrolled. Secondary Level English Proficiency or Stanford Achievement Test, Otis-Lennon required. Deadline for receipt of application materials: none. Application fee required: $65. Interview required.

Athletics Interscholastic: baseball (boys), basketball (b,g), cross-country running (b,g), football (b), golf (b), running (b,g), soccer (b,g), softball (g), strength & conditioning (b,g), swimming and diving (b,g), tennis (b,g), track and field (b,g), volleyball (g); intramural: weight training (b); coed interscholastic: cheering, running. 1 PE instructor, 3 coaches.

Computers Computers are regularly used in English, human geography—AP, library, publications, social sciences, yearbook classes. Computer network features include on-campus library services, CD-ROMs, online commercial services, Internet access.

Contact Mrs. Ann Arnold, Director of Admissions. 713-551-8100 Ext. 1015. Fax: 713-551-8117. E-mail: admissions@westburychristian.org. Web site: www.westburychristian.org.

WEST CATHOLIC HIGH SCHOOL

1801 Bristol Avenue, NW
Grand Rapids, Michigan 49504
Head of School: Mr. Stan Spetoskey

General Information Coeducational day college-preparatory, arts, and religious studies school, affiliated with Roman Catholic Church. Grades 9–12. Founded: 1962. Setting: urban. 20-acre campus. 1 building on campus. Approved or accredited by National Catholic Education Association, North Central Association of Colleges and Schools, and Michigan Department of Education. Endowment: $1 million. Total enrollment: 630. Upper school average class size: 25. Upper school faculty-student ratio: 1:16.

Upper School Student Profile Grade 9: 162 students (84 boys, 78 girls); Grade 10: 174 students (96 boys, 78 girls); Grade 11: 147 students (69 boys, 78 girls); Grade 12: 147 students (79 boys, 68 girls). 95% of students are Roman Catholic.

Faculty School total: 41. In upper school: 17 men, 24 women; 20 have advanced degrees.

Subjects Offered 20th century world history, 3-dimensional art, accounting, acting, advanced chemistry, advanced computer applications, advanced math, American government, American government-AP, American history-AP, American literature, American literature-AP, analytic geometry, anatomy, art, band, basic language skills, Basic programming, Bible studies, biology, biology-AP, British literature, British literature (honors), British literature-AP, business studies, calculus, calculus-AP, career planning, chemistry, chemistry-AP, choir, Christian and Hebrew scripture, Christian doctrine, college writing, composition, composition-AP, computer applications, computer programming, concert band, culinary arts, debate, desktop publishing, drama, drawing, earth science, economics, economics-AP, English, English language and composition-AP, English language-AP, English literature, English literature and composition-AP, English literature-AP, English-AP, environmental science, family life, French, general business, general math, genetics, geometry, government, government and politics-AP, government-AP, government/civics, history, history of the Catholic Church, honors algebra, honors English, honors geometry, honors world history, human anatomy, Internet, intro to computers, jazz band, journalism, keyboarding/computer, Latin, marching band, physics, physics-AP, pre-algebra, pre-calculus, printmaking, psychology, public speaking, sex education, sexuality, social justice, sociology, Spanish, Spanish language-AP, speech, survival training, U.S. history, Web site design, world history, world history-AP, yearbook.

Graduation Requirements Economics, English composition, foreign language, government, health, mathematics, religion (includes Bible studies and theology), science.

Special Academic Programs Advanced Placement exam preparation in 6 subject areas; honors section; independent study; study at local college for college credit; remedial reading and/or remedial writing.

College Placement 142 students graduated in 2005; 135 went to college, including Central Michigan University; Grand Valley State University; Michigan State University; University of Michigan; Western Michigan University. Other: 5 went to work, 2 entered military service. Mean composite ACT: 22.

Student Life Upper grades have specified standards of dress, student council, honor system. Discipline rests primarily with faculty. Attendance at religious services is required.

Summer Programs Sports programs offered; session focuses on weight lifting; held on campus; accepts boys and girls; not open to students from other schools. 100 students usually enrolled. 2006 schedule: June 10 to August 21. Application deadline: June 1.

Tuition and Aid Day student tuition: $6200. Tuition installment plan (The Tuition Plan, monthly payment plans, individually arranged payment plans). Need-based scholarship grants available. In 2005–06, 20% of upper-school students received aid. Total amount of financial aid awarded in 2005–06: $330,000.

Admissions Traditional secondary-level entrance grade is 9. For fall 2005, 162 students applied for upper-level admission, 162 were accepted, 162 enrolled. CTBS (or similar from their school) and High School Placement Test required. Deadline for receipt of application materials: none. No application fee required. Interview required.

Athletics Interscholastic: baseball (boys), basketball (b,g), bowling (b,g), cheering (g), cross-country running (b,g), diving (b,g), football (b), golf (b,g), gymnastics (g), hockey (b), ice hockey (b), pom squad (g), skiing (downhill) (b,g), soccer (b,g), softball (g), swimming and diving (b,g), tennis (b,g), track and field (b,g), volleyball (g), wrestling (b); intramural: bowling (b,g), equestrian sports (b,g), lacrosse (b,g), physical training (b,g), pom squad (g), rugby (b,g), weight lifting (b,g). 1 PE instructor, 66 coaches, 1 trainer.

Computers Computers are regularly used in all academic classes. Computer network features include CD-ROMs, Internet access.

Contact Mrs. Marzi Johnson, Guidance Secretary. 616-233-5909. Fax: 616-453-8470. E-mail: marzijohnson@grcss.org. Web site: www.grwestcatholic.org.

WESTCHESTER ACADEMY

2045 North Old Greensboro Road
High Point, North Carolina 27265
Head of School: Mr. Thomas P. Hudgins Jr.

General Information Coeducational day college-preparatory and arts school. Grades K–12. Founded: 1967. Setting: rural. Nearest major city is Greensboro. 52-acre campus. 6 buildings on campus. Approved or accredited by North Carolina Association of Independent Schools, Southern Association of Colleges and Schools, and Southern Association of Independent Schools. Member of National Association of Independent Schools. Endowment: $2.4 million. Total enrollment: 410. Upper school average class size: 15. Upper school faculty-student ratio: 1:7.

Upper School Student Profile Grade 9: 26 students (14 boys, 12 girls); Grade 10: 39 students (20 boys, 19 girls); Grade 11: 34 students (17 boys, 17 girls); Grade 12: 37 students (20 boys, 17 girls).

Faculty School total: 48. In upper school: 6 men, 15 women; 12 have advanced degrees.

Subjects Offered Algebra, American history, American literature, art, biology, calculus, chemistry, community service, computer science, creative writing, earth science, economics, English, English literature, European history, fine arts, French, geography, geology, geometry, government/civics, grammar, health, history, mathematics, music, physical education, physics, science, social studies, Spanish, speech, theater, world history, world literature, writing.

Graduation Requirements Arts and fine arts (art, music, dance, drama), civics, English, foreign language, mathematics, physical education (includes health), science, social studies (includes history). Community service is required.

Special Academic Programs Advanced Placement exam preparation in 14 subject areas; honors section.

College Placement 48 students graduated in 2005; all went to college, including Appalachian State University; Elon University; North Carolina State University; The University of North Carolina at Chapel Hill; The University of North Carolina Wilmington; Wake Forest University. Mean SAT verbal: 601, mean SAT math: 606.

Student Life Upper grades have specified standards of dress, student council, honor system. Discipline rests primarily with faculty.

Summer Programs Sports, art/fine arts programs offered; session focuses on sports; held on campus; accepts boys and girls; open to students from other schools. 200 students usually enrolled. 2006 schedule: June 12 to August 12. Application deadline: May.

Tuition and Aid Day student tuition: $6740–$10,545. Tuition installment plan (Key Tuition Payment Plan, FACTS Tuition Payment Plan, monthly payment plans). Merit scholarship grants, need-based scholarship grants available. In 2005–06, 27% of upper-school students received aid; total upper-school merit-scholarship money awarded: $34,000. Total amount of financial aid awarded in 2005–06: $59,100.

Admissions Traditional secondary-level entrance grade is 9. For fall 2005, 30 students applied for upper-level admission, 19 were accepted, 13 enrolled. Brigance Test of Basic Skills, ERB CTP IV, Kaufman Test of Educational Achievement, Wide Range Achievement Test or Woodcock-Johnson Revised Achievement Test required. Deadline for receipt of application materials: none. Application fee required: $75. On-campus interview required.

Athletics Interscholastic: baseball (boys), basketball (b,g), cheering (g), soccer (b,g), tennis (b,g); coed interscholastic: cross-country running, golf, physical fitness, swimming and diving, track and field. 1 PE instructor, 11 coaches.

Computers Computers are regularly used in English, foreign language, history, library science, mathematics, science, yearbook classes. Computer network features include on-campus library services, CD-ROMs, Internet access, DVD, wireless campus network.

Contact Mrs. Kerie Beth Scott, Director of Admissions. 336-822-4005. Fax: 336-869-6685. E-mail: keriebethscott@westchesteracademy.org. Web site: www.westchesteracademy.org.

ANNOUNCEMENT FROM THE SCHOOL Founded in 1967, Westchester Academy is an independent, coeducational day school. The Academy is a nonsectarian institution established to provide a college-preparatory education for students in grades K–12. An intellectually exciting environment enables students to excel in all areas associated with the classical liberal arts tradition—academics, athletics, and the arts—while simultaneously developing strong moral and ethical values. The school's low student-teacher ratio and family-like atmosphere enhance the learning process. Located in a country setting, the school's 52-acre campus is in Davidson County. The school has 6 buildings and is accredited by the Southern Association of Colleges and Schools. The Academy serves the Piedmont Triad (High Point, Greensboro, and Winston-Salem) and neighboring communities of North Carolina. AP courses are offered in 13 disciplines.

WESTERN MENNONITE SCHOOL

9045 Wallace Road NW
Salem, Oregon 97304-9716
Head of School: Darrel Camp

General Information Coeducational boarding and day college-preparatory, general academic, and religious studies school, affiliated with Mennonite Church USA. Boarding grades 9–12, day grades 6–12. Founded: 1945. Setting: rural. Students are housed in single-sex dormitories. 45-acre campus. 10 buildings on campus. Approved or accredited by Mennonite Education Agency, Mennonite Schools Council, Northwest Association of Schools and Colleges, and Oregon Department of Education. Endowment: $739,000. Total enrollment: 231. Upper school average class size: 14. Upper school faculty-student ratio: 1:14.

Upper School Student Profile Grade 9: 34 students (24 boys, 10 girls); Grade 10: 28 students (16 boys, 12 girls); Grade 11: 37 students (22 boys, 15 girls); Grade 12: 33 students (16 boys, 17 girls). 22% of students are boarding students. 85% are state residents. 4 states are represented in upper school student body. 13% are international students. International students from Canada, Eritrea, Ethiopia, Hong Kong, Japan, and Republic of Korea. 24% of students are Mennonite Church USA.

Faculty School total: 29. In upper school: 10 men, 11 women; 8 have advanced degrees; 1 resides on campus.

Subjects Offered Accounting, advanced math, algebra, art, Bible studies, biology, business law, calculus, career and personal planning, career education, chemistry, choral music, Christian education, Christian scripture, church history, computer applications, computer keyboarding, computer programming, drawing and design, economics, English, English composition, English literature, family living, general math, geography, geometry, government, health education, human anatomy, instrumental music, intro to computers, mathematics, music, music performance, novels, peace and justice, personal finance, physical education, physical fitness, physical science, physics, physiology-anatomy, piano, pre-algebra, pre-calculus, psychology, religious education, religious studies, research, science, Shakespeare, Spanish, speech, speech and debate, U.S. government, U.S. history, U.S. literature, woodworking, yearbook.

Graduation Requirements Algebra, applied arts, Bible studies, biology, career education, chemistry, choir, economics, English, English literature, geometry, global studies, music, physical education (includes health), Spanish, U.S. government, U.S. history, U.S. literature, world geography, Mini-Term—one week of co-curricular activity at end of academic year (sophomore through senior year).

Special Academic Programs Advanced Placement exam preparation in 1 subject area; independent study; term-away projects; study at local college for college credit.

College Placement 31 students graduated in 2005; 24 went to college, including Chemeketa Community College; Columbia Bible College; Corban College; Eastern Mennonite University; Hesston College; Oregon State University. Other: 1 went to work, 6 had other specific plans. Median SAT math: 520, median composite ACT: 27. 11% scored over 600 on SAT math, 50% scored over 26 on composite ACT.

Student Life Upper grades have specified standards of dress, student council, honor system. Discipline rests primarily with faculty. Attendance at religious services is required.

Summer Programs Sports programs offered; session focuses on soccer, volleyball, basketball; held on campus; accepts boys and girls; open to students from other schools. 25 students usually enrolled. 2006 schedule: June to August. Application deadline: June.

Tuition and Aid Day student tuition: $5795; 5-day tuition and room/board: $8770; 7-day tuition and room/board: $9960–$18,500. Tuition installment plan (monthly payment plans, individually arranged payment plans). Tuition reduction for siblings, merit scholarship grants, need-based scholarship grants, paying campus jobs available. In 2005–06, 39% of upper-school students received aid; total upper-school merit-scholarship money awarded: $2400. Total amount of financial aid awarded in 2005–06: $195,460.

Admissions Traditional secondary-level entrance grade is 9. For fall 2005, 49 students applied for upper-level admission, 42 were accepted, 35 enrolled. Deadline for receipt of application materials: none. Application fee required: $50. Interview recommended.

Athletics Interscholastic: baseball (boys, girls), basketball (b,g), cross-country running (b,g), soccer (b,g), volleyball (g); coed intramural: softball. 8 coaches.

Computers Computers are regularly used in independent study, introduction to technology, keyboarding, yearbook classes. Computer network features include campus e-mail, on-campus library services, CD-ROMs, online commercial services, Internet access, file transfer, office computer access.

Contact Mr. Paul Schultz, Director of Admissions. 503-363-2000. Fax: 503-370-9455. E-mail: pschultz@westrnmennoniteschool.org. Web site: www.westernmennoniteschool.org.

WESTERN RESERVE ACADEMY

115 College Street
Hudson, Ohio 44236
Head of School: Henry E. Flanagan

General Information Coeducational boarding and day college-preparatory and arts school. Grades 9–PG. Founded: 1826. Setting: small town. Nearest major city is Cleveland. Students are housed in single-sex dormitories. 190-acre campus. 49 buildings on campus. Approved or accredited by Independent Schools Association of the Central States, North Central Association of Colleges and Schools, Ohio Association of Independent Schools, The Association of Boarding Schools, and Ohio Department of Education. Member of National Association of Independent Schools and Secondary School Admission Test Board. Endowment: $81 million. Total enrollment: 401. Upper school average class size: 12. Upper school faculty-student ratio: 1:6.

Upper School Student Profile Grade 9: 87 students (50 boys, 37 girls); Grade 10: 84 students (49 boys, 35 girls); Grade 11: 113 students (61 boys, 52 girls); Grade 12: 117 students (66 boys, 51 girls). 65% of students are boarding students. 70% are state residents. 29 states are represented in upper school student body. 14% are international students. International students from Canada, Germany, Jamaica, Republic of Korea, Thailand, and United Kingdom; 15 other countries represented in student body.

Faculty School total: 68. In upper school: 38 men, 30 women; 39 have advanced degrees; 55 reside on campus.

Subjects Offered Algebra, American history, American literature, architecture, art, art history, Asian history, astronomy, band, biology, calculus, ceramics, chemistry, chorus, computer programming, creative writing, dance, drafting, drama, economics,

engineering, English, English literature, environmental science, European history, fine arts, French, geometry, German, health, history, humanities, independent study, industrial arts, Latin, mathematics, mechanical drawing, music, music history, music theory, orchestra, photography, physical education, physics, science, social studies, Spanish, speech, statistics, theater, trigonometry, world history, zoology.

Graduation Requirements Arts and fine arts (art, music, dance, drama), English, foreign language, history, mathematics, physical education (includes health), science, senior seminar, senior thesis.

Special Academic Programs Advanced Placement exam preparation in 19 subject areas; honors section; independent study; study at local college for college credit; study abroad; academic accommodation for the gifted, the musically talented, and the artistically talented.

College Placement 102 students graduated in 2005; all went to college, including Cornell University; Kenyon College; The George Washington University; The Johns Hopkins University; United States Naval Academy; Vanderbilt University.

Student Life Upper grades have specified standards of dress, student council. Discipline rests equally with students and faculty.

Tuition and Aid Day student tuition: $23,000; 7-day tuition and room/board: $32,000. Tuition installment plan (The Tuition Plan, Insured Tuition Payment Plan, Key Tuition Payment Plan, monthly payment plans, individually arranged payment plans). Merit scholarship grants, need-based scholarship grants, need-based loans available. In 2005–06, 33% of upper-school students received aid; total upper-school merit-scholarship money awarded: $102,000. Total amount of financial aid awarded in 2005–06: $3,100,000.

Admissions Traditional secondary-level entrance grade is 9. For fall 2005, 364 students applied for upper-level admission, 229 were accepted, 154 enrolled. ISEE, SSAT or TOEFL required. Deadline for receipt of application materials: February 1. Application fee required: $50. Interview required.

Athletics Interscholastic: baseball (boys), basketball (b,g), cross-country running (b,g), diving (b,g), field hockey (g), football (b), golf (b), hockey (b), ice hockey (b), lacrosse (b,g), riflery (b,g), soccer (b,g), softball (g), swimming and diving (b,g), tennis (b,g), track and field (b,g), volleyball (g), wrestling (b); intramural: basketball (b); coed interscholastic: marksmanship; coed intramural: aerobics, aerobics/dance, aerobics/nautilus, back packing, bicycling, cricket, dance, fitness, fly fishing, hiking/backpacking, jogging, juggling, martial arts, nautilus, outdoor recreation, paddle tennis, physical fitness, physical training, rock climbing, running, sailing, skiing (downhill), snowboarding, soccer, strength & conditioning, weight lifting, weight training, wilderness, winter (indoor) track. 1 coach, 2 trainers.

Computers Computers are regularly used in architecture, drawing and design, engineering, English, foreign language, history, mathematics, science, technical drawing classes. Computer network features include campus e-mail, on-campus library services, CD-ROMs, online commercial services, Internet access, DVD, wireless campus network.

Contact Mrs. Gayle Kish, Admission Office Coordinator. 330-650-9717. Fax: 330-650-5858. E-mail: admission@wra.net. Web site: www.wra.net.

ANNOUNCEMENT FROM THE SCHOOL As one of the oldest and most respected independent boarding schools, WRA offers an academically challenging, affordable secondary education. A large endowment supports a significantly generous financial aid program. Honors, AP, independent study, and college-credit courses provide students with an academic profile demanding notice at the college level. Annual college placement speaks to the strength of this experience.

See full description on page 1128.

THE WESTFIELD SCHOOLS

PO Box 2300
Perry, Georgia 31069
Head of School: Michael C. Franklin

General Information Coeducational day college-preparatory school, affiliated with Christian faith. Grades PK–12. Founded: 1969. Setting: rural. Nearest major city is Macon. 28-acre campus. 7 buildings on campus. Approved or accredited by Southern Association of Colleges and Schools, Southern Association of Independent Schools, and Georgia Department of Education. Endowment: $100,000. Total enrollment: 637. Upper school average class size: 14. Upper school faculty-student ratio: 1:14.

Upper School Student Profile Grade 6: 46 students (20 boys, 26 girls); Grade 7: 37 students (23 boys, 14 girls); Grade 8: 62 students (30 boys, 32 girls); Grade 9: 56 students (32 boys, 24 girls); Grade 10: 53 students (28 boys, 25 girls); Grade 11: 38 students (19 boys, 19 girls); Grade 12: 45 students (17 boys, 28 girls). 98% of students are Christian faith.

Faculty School total: 53. In upper school: 7 men, 18 women; 14 have advanced degrees.

Subjects Offered Advanced computer applications, Advanced Placement courses, algebra, American history-AP, American literature-AP, Bible studies, biology, calculus, calculus-AP, chemistry, chorus, Christian ethics, computer education, computer science, drama, economics, English, English language-AP, French, geometry, government, humanities, Japanese, modern European history, physical science, physics,

physiology, physiology-anatomy, pre-calculus, psychology-AP, sociology, Spanish, speech, statistics, statistics-AP, studio art, U.S. history, weightlifting, world history.

Special Academic Programs Advanced Placement exam preparation in 5 subject areas; independent study.

College Placement 37 students graduated in 2005; all went to college, including Georgia College & State University; Georgia Institute of Technology; Georgia Southern University; Mercer University; University of Georgia; Valdosta State University. Median SAT verbal: 530, median SAT math: 530. 24% scored over 600 on SAT verbal, 32% scored over 600 on SAT math.

Student Life Upper grades have specified standards of dress, student council, honor system. Discipline rests primarily with faculty.

Summer Programs Remediation, enrichment, sports programs offered; session focuses on science; held on campus; accepts boys and girls; not open to students from other schools. 2006 schedule: June 3 to June 30. Application deadline: June 3.

Tuition and Aid Day student tuition: $6960. Tuition installment plan (monthly payment plans, individually arranged payment plans). Need-based scholarship grants available. In 2005–06, 2% of upper-school students received aid. Total amount of financial aid awarded in 2005–06: $39,500.

Admissions For fall 2005, 28 students applied for upper-level admission, 26 were accepted, 21 enrolled. Admissions testing, Comprehensive Test of Basic Skills, Otis-Lennon School Ability Test, school placement exam and writing sample required. Deadline for receipt of application materials: none. Application fee required: $50. On-campus interview required.

Athletics Interscholastic: aerobics/dance (girls), baseball (b), basketball (b,g), cheering (g), cross-country running (b,g), dance team (g), fitness (b,g), football (b), outdoor recreation (b,g), softball (g), strength & conditioning (b,g), swimming and diving (b,g), tennis (b,g), track and field (b,g), weight training (b,g), wrestling (b); coed interscholastic: golf. 4 PE instructors, 4 coaches, 1 trainer.

Computers Computers are regularly used in all academic, business education, desktop publishing, journalism, library, research skills, SAT preparation, science, yearbook classes. Computer network features include campus e-mail, CD-ROMs, Internet access, office computer access.

Contact Janette J. Anderson, Director of Admissions and Academic Affairs. 478-987-0547. Fax: 478-987-7379. E-mail: janderson@westfieldschools.net. Web site: www.westfieldschools.net.

WESTGATE MENNONITE COLLEGIATE

86 West Gate
Winnipeg, Manitoba R3C 2E1, Canada
Head of School: Ms. Gail Schellenberg

General Information Coeducational day college-preparatory, general academic, arts, religious studies, technology, and music, German, and French school, affiliated with Mennonite Church USA. Grades 7–12. Founded: 1957. Setting: urban. 3-acre campus. 1 building on campus. Approved or accredited by Canadian Association of Independent Schools and Manitoba Department of Education. Language of instruction: English. Total enrollment: 318. Upper school average class size: 25. Upper school faculty-student ratio: 1:15.

Upper School Student Profile Grade 10: 57 students (23 boys, 34 girls); Grade 11: 54 students (24 boys, 30 girls); Grade 12: 51 students (31 boys, 20 girls). 55% of students are Mennonite Church USA.

Faculty School total: 25. In upper school: 9 men, 9 women; 4 have advanced degrees.

Special Academic Programs Advanced Placement exam preparation in 5 subject areas; independent study; term-away projects; ESL (11 students enrolled).

College Placement 48 students graduated in 2005; 43 went to college, including The University of Winnipeg; University of Manitoba. Other: 2 went to work, 3 had other specific plans.

Student Life Upper grades have specified standards of dress, student council. Discipline rests primarily with faculty. Attendance at religious services is required.

Tuition and Aid Day student tuition: CAN$4000. Tuition installment plan (monthly payment plans, individually arranged payment plans). Tuition reduction for siblings, bursaries, merit scholarship grants, need-based scholarship grants available. In 2005–06, 10% of upper-school students received aid; total upper-school merit-scholarship money awarded: CAN$5000. Total amount of financial aid awarded in 2005–06: CAN$36,000.

Admissions Traditional secondary-level entrance grade is 10. Deadline for receipt of application materials: March 10. Application fee required: CAN$50. Interview required.

Athletics Interscholastic: badminton (boys, girls), baseball (b,g), basketball (b,g), bowling (b,g), cheering (b,g), cross-country running (b,g), curling (b,g), floor hockey (b,g), golf (b,g), gymnastics (b,g), outdoor education (b,g), outdoor skills (b,g), rock climbing (b,g), running (b,g), soccer (b,g), strength & conditioning (b,g), volleyball (b,g); intramural: aerobics/dance (b,g), back packing (b,g), badminton (b,g), basketball (b,g), bicycling (b,g), broomball (b,g), canoeing/kayaking (b,g), cross-country running (b,g), curling (b,g), field hockey (b,g), floor hockey (b,g), football (b,g), golf (b,g), gymnastics (b,g), hiking/backpacking (b,g), ice hockey (b,g), ice skating (b,g), outdoor education (b,g), paddle tennis (b,g), racquetball (b,g), rock climbing (b,g), running (b,g), soccer (b,g), strength & conditioning (b,g), swimming and diving (b,g), volleyball (b,g), wall climbing (b,g); coed interscholastic: badminton, baseball, basketball, bowling, cheering, cross-country running, curling, floor hockey, golf,

gymnastics, outdoor education, outdoor skills, rock climbing, running, soccer, strength & conditioning, volleyball; coed intramural: aerobics/dance, back packing, badminton, basketball, bicycling, broomball, canoeing/kayaking, cross-country running, curling, field hockey, floor hockey, football, golf, gymnastics, hiking/backpacking, ice hockey, ice skating, outdoor education, paddle tennis, racquetball, rock climbing, running, soccer, strength & conditioning, swimming and diving, volleyball, wall climbing. 3 PE instructors, 7 coaches, 4 trainers.

Computers Computer network features include campus e-mail, on-campus library services, CD-ROMs, online commercial services, Internet access.

Contact Ms. C. Gail Schellenberg, Principal. 204-775-7111 Ext. 202. Fax: 204-786-1651. E-mail: westgate@westgate.mb.ca. Web site: westgatemcol.mennonite.net/.

WESTHILL INSTITUTE

Domingo Garcia Ramos No. 56
Prados de la Montana
Santa Fe Cuajimalpa
Mexico City, DF 05610, Mexico
Head of School: Andrew Neil Sherman

General Information Coeducational day college-preparatory, general academic, and bilingual studies school. Grades PK–12. Founded: 1992. Setting: urban. Nearest major city is Mexico City. 3-hectare campus. 1 building on campus. Approved or accredited by Southern Association of Colleges and Schools and Texas Private School Accreditation Commission. Languages of instruction: English, Spanish, and French. Total enrollment: 718. Upper school average class size: 18. Upper school faculty-student ratio: 1:9.

Upper School Student Profile Grade 10: 41 students (28 boys, 13 girls); Grade 11: 33 students (20 boys, 13 girls); Grade 12: 33 students (24 boys, 9 girls).

Faculty School total: 27. In upper school: 13 men, 14 women; 5 have advanced degrees.

Subjects Offered 20th century history, 20th century world history, advanced chemistry, advanced math, American culture, American history, American literature, applied music, art appreciation, arts, biology, British literature, business mathematics, calculus, calculus-AP, career and personal planning, chemistry, chemistry-AP, civics/free enterprise, college counseling, composition, computer literacy, computer science, debate, drama, economics, economics and history, English, English composition, ESL, ethics, ethics and responsibility, ethnic studies, French, general math, geography, geometry, global issues, global studies, government, health, health education, history, lab science, math analysis, math applications, math methods, math review, mathematics, Mexican history, Mexican literature, music, music appreciation, music history, philosophy, physics, physics-AP, social studies, Spanish, Spanish language-AP, Spanish literature, Spanish literature-AP, student government, trigonometry, U.S. government and politics, world cultures, world geography, world governments, world history.

Graduation Requirements Arts and fine arts (art, music, dance, drama), computer science, English, foreign language, mathematics, physical education (includes health), science, social studies (includes history), 60 community service hours.

Special Academic Programs Advanced Placement exam preparation in 6 subject areas; honors section; independent study; remedial reading and/or remedial writing; remedial math; special instructional classes for deaf students, blind students, students with learning disabilities and Attention Deficit Disorder; ESL (17 students enrolled).

College Placement 28 students graduated in 2005; 27 went to college, including Columbia College; McGill University; Savannah College of Art and Design; The American University of Paris; University of Pittsburgh. Other: 1 went to work. Median SAT math: 508, median combined SAT: 1033. Mean SAT verbal: 525. 10% scored over 600 on SAT verbal, 5% scored over 600 on SAT math.

Student Life Upper grades have uniform requirement, student council, honor system. Discipline rests equally with students and faculty.

Summer Programs Remediation, enrichment, ESL programs offered; session focuses on enrichment of general educational program; held on campus; accepts boys and girls; not open to students from other schools. 25 students usually enrolled. 2006 schedule: July 10 to August 4. Application deadline: May 28.

Tuition and Aid Day student tuition: $12,000. Tuition installment plan (monthly payment plans, annual plan with 10% discount). Tuition reduction for siblings, merit scholarship grants, need-based scholarship grants available. In 2005–06, 10% of upper-school students received aid.

Admissions Traditional secondary-level entrance grade is 10. For fall 2005, 62 students applied for upper-level admission, 38 were accepted, 33 enrolled. School's own exam required. Deadline for receipt of application materials: none. Application fee required. Interview required.

Athletics Interscholastic: basketball (boys, girls), soccer (b,g), volleyball (b,g); intramural: basketball (b,g), floor hockey (b,g), soccer (b,g), volleyball (b,g); coed intramural: floor hockey, soccer. 1 PE instructor, 6 coaches.

Computers Computers are regularly used in all academic classes. Computer network features include campus e-mail, on-campus library services, CD-ROMs, Internet access, EBSCO.

Contact Andrew Neil Sherman, Headmaster. 525-55292 6627. Fax: 525-55292 6628 Ext. 105. E-mail: headmaster@westhill.edu.mx. Web site: www.wi.edu.mx.

WEST ISLAND COLLEGE

7410 Blackfoot Trail, SE
Calgary, Alberta T2H IM5, Canada
Head of School: Mr. Jack A. Grant

General Information Coeducational day college-preparatory, arts, business, bilingual studies, technology, and Advanced Placement school. Grades 7–12. Founded: 1982. Setting: urban. 18-acre campus. 2 buildings on campus. Approved or accredited by Alberta Department of Education. Languages of instruction: English and French. Total enrollment: 437. Upper school average class size: 18. Upper school faculty-student ratio: 1:17.

Upper School Student Profile Grade 10: 76 students (46 boys, 30 girls); Grade 11: 71 students (35 boys, 36 girls); Grade 12: 59 students (29 boys, 30 girls).

Faculty School total: 38. In upper school: 20 men, 18 women; 13 have advanced degrees.

Subjects Offered Advanced Placement courses, anthropology, art, arts, biology, chemistry, choral music, communications, debate, drama, English, European history, experiential education, French, French studies, health, information processing, information technology, leadership, literature, mathematics, modern languages, outdoor education, philosophy, physical education, physics, political thought, politics, psychology, public speaking, science, social science, social studies, sociology, Spanish, standard curriculum, study skills, world geography, world history, world religions.

Graduation Requirements Alberta Education requirements.

Special Academic Programs Advanced Placement exam preparation in 9 subject areas; honors section; independent study; study abroad.

College Placement 62 students graduated in 2005; 61 went to college, including McGill University; Queen's University at Kingston; The University of British Columbia; University of Alberta; University of Calgary; University of Victoria. Other: 1 had other specific plans.

Student Life Upper grades have uniform requirement, student council, honor system. Discipline rests equally with students and faculty.

Summer Programs Enrichment, advancement, sports, computer instruction programs offered; session focuses on study skills; held both on and off campus; held at various public parks in the city; accepts boys and girls; open to students from other schools. 20 students usually enrolled. 2006 schedule: July 5 to July 9. Application deadline: March 31.

Tuition and Aid Day student tuition: CAN$8900. Tuition installment plan (monthly payment plans).

Admissions 3-R Achievement Test required. Deadline for receipt of application materials: none. Application fee required: CAN$50. Interview required.

Athletics Interscholastic: basketball (boys, girls), field hockey (g), rugby (b), volleyball (b,g); intramural: aquatics (b,g), basketball (b,g), floor hockey (b,g), volleyball (b,g); coed interscholastic: badminton, climbing, cross-country running, soccer; coed intramural: alpine skiing, back packing, badminton, bicycling, bowling, canoeing/kayaking, climbing, cross-country running, curling, dance, fitness, golf, hiking/backpacking, kayaking, mountaineering, nordic skiing, outdoor activities, outdoor adventure, outdoor education, outdoor recreation, outdoor skills, physical fitness, physical training, rock climbing, sailing, skiing (cross-country), skiing (downhill), snowboarding, soccer, swimming and diving, touch football, wilderness survival, wildernessways. 4 PE instructors, 10 coaches, 2 trainers.

Computers Computers are regularly used in all academic classes. Computer network features include campus e-mail, CD-ROMs, online commercial services, Internet access.

Contact Mr. Murray J. Marran, Director of Admissions. 403-444-0023. Fax: 403-444-2820. E-mail: admissions@westislandcollege.ab.ca. Web site: www. westislandcollege.ab.ca.

WESTMINSTER CHRISTIAN ACADEMY

1400 Evangel Drive
Huntsville, Alabama 35816
Head of School: Dr. Robert Illman

General Information Coeducational day college-preparatory, general academic, arts, religious studies, and technology school, affiliated with Presbyterian Church. Grades K4–12. Founded: 1964. Setting: suburban. Nearest major city is Birmingham. 15-acre campus. 4 buildings on campus. Approved or accredited by Christian Schools International, Southern Association of Colleges and Schools, and Alabama Department of Education. Member of Secondary School Admission Test Board. Endowment: $275,000. Total enrollment: 750. Upper school average class size: 18. Upper school faculty-student ratio: 1:12.

Upper School Student Profile 14% of students are Presbyterian.

Faculty School total: 78. In upper school: 11 men, 22 women; 20 have advanced degrees.

Subjects Offered Advanced computer applications, algebra, American history, American history-AP, art, band, Bible studies, biology, botany, calculus, calculus-AP, chemistry, choir, civics, computer programming, computer programming-AP, concert choir, consumer mathematics, CPR, drama, drama performance, economics-AP, English, English-AP, ensembles, environmental science, first aid, fitness, French, geography, geometry, government, government-AP, health education, home econom-

ics, journalism, keyboarding, Latin, modern dance, painting, photography, physical education, physical science, physics, physiology, pre-calculus, psychology, Spanish, Web site design, world history, yearbook.

Graduation Requirements Arts and fine arts (art, music, dance, drama), computer applications, electives, English, foreign language, mathematics, physical education (includes health), religion (includes Bible studies and theology), science, social studies (includes history).

Special Academic Programs Advanced Placement exam preparation in 5 subject areas; honors section; independent study; study at local college for college credit; academic accommodation for the gifted, the musically talented, and the artistically talented.

College Placement 47 students graduated in 2005; 45 went to college, including Auburn University; Calhoun Community College; Covenant College; The University of Alabama; The University of Alabama in Huntsville. Other: 1 went to work, 1 entered military service. 35% scored over 600 on SAT verbal, 50% scored over 600 on SAT math.

Student Life Upper grades have specified standards of dress, student council. Discipline rests primarily with faculty. Attendance at religious services is required.

Tuition and Aid Day student tuition: $5750. Guaranteed tuition plan. Tuition installment plan (monthly payment plans, individually arranged payment plans). Tuition reduction for siblings, need-based scholarship grants, free tuition for children of faculty available. In 2005–06, 15% of upper-school students received aid. Total amount of financial aid awarded in 2005–06: $200,000.

Admissions Traditional secondary-level entrance grade is 9. Any standardized test, school's own test or writing sample required. Deadline for receipt of application materials: none. Application fee required: $25. Interview required.

Athletics Interscholastic: baseball (boys), basketball (b,g), cheering (g), cross-country running (b,g), dance (g), golf (b,g), modern dance (g), soccer (b,g), softball (g), swimming and diving (b,g), track and field (b,g), volleyball (g); intramural: physical fitness (b,g), physical training (b,g), strength & conditioning (b,g), weight training (b,g); coed interscholastic: cheering; coed intramural: weight training. 6 coaches, 1 trainer.

Computers Computers are regularly used in all academic classes. Computer network features include campus e-mail, on-campus library services, CD-ROMs, Internet access, file transfer, DVD, wireless campus network, school-issued PDAs (for 10th & 11th grade students).

Contact Angie Johnson, Admissions Coordinator. 256-705-8000 Ext. 212. Fax: 256-705-8001. E-mail: angie.johnson@wca-hsv.org. Web site: www.wcahsv.org.

WESTMINSTER CHRISTIAN ACADEMY

186 Westminster Drive
Opelousas, Louisiana 70570
Head of School: Mr. Bill Thompson

General Information Coeducational day college-preparatory and religious studies school, affiliated with Protestant-Evangelical faith. Grades PK–12. Founded: 1978. Setting: rural. Nearest major city is Lafayette. 30-acre campus. 6 buildings on campus. Approved or accredited by Association of Christian Schools International and Louisiana Department of Education. Total enrollment: 974. Upper school average class size: 20. Upper school faculty-student ratio: 1:13.

Upper School Student Profile Grade 9: 66 students (28 boys, 38 girls); Grade 10: 72 students (36 boys, 36 girls); Grade 11: 62 students (29 boys, 33 girls); Grade 12: 53 students (23 boys, 30 girls). 80% of students are Protestant-Evangelical faith.

Faculty School total: 66. In upper school: 10 men, 9 women; 5 have advanced degrees.

Subjects Offered Advanced math, algebra, American history, art, biology, calculus, calculus-AP, ceramics, chemistry, chemistry-AP, civics, concert choir, creative writing, drama, economics, English, English-AP, ensembles, fine arts, French, geometry, guitar, history-AP, Latin, linguistics, mathematics, music, physics, religion, Spanish, world history, yearbook.

Graduation Requirements Arts and fine arts (art, music, dance, drama), computer literacy, English, foreign language, mathematics, physical education (includes health), religion (includes Bible studies and theology), science, social studies (includes history).

Special Academic Programs Advanced Placement exam preparation in 4 subject areas; honors section; accelerated programs; programs in English, mathematics for dyslexic students; special instructional classes for students with learning disabilities and Attention Deficit Disorder.

College Placement 59 students graduated in 2005; 53 went to college, including Louisiana State University and Agricultural and Mechanical College; Louisiana Tech University; Loyola University New Orleans; Texas A&M University; University of Louisiana at Lafayette; Wheaton College. Other: 6 had other specific plans. Mean composite ACT: 24.

Student Life Upper grades have uniform requirement, student council. Discipline rests primarily with faculty. Attendance at religious services is required.

Summer Programs Remediation programs offered; held on campus; accepts boys and girls; not open to students from other schools. 10 students usually enrolled. 2006 schedule: June 1 to June 30. Application deadline: May 30.

Tuition and Aid Day student tuition: $4890. Guaranteed tuition plan. Tuition installment plan (monthly payment plans, annual and biannual payment plans).

Need-based scholarship grants, pastor discounts available. In 2005–06, 9% of upper-school students received aid. Total amount of financial aid awarded in 2005–06: $41,395.

Admissions Traditional secondary-level entrance grade is 9. For fall 2005, 54 students applied for upper-level admission, 44 were accepted, 42 enrolled. School's own exam and Stanford Achievement Test required. Deadline for receipt of application materials: none. Application fee required: $50. On-campus interview required.

Athletics Interscholastic: baseball (boys), basketball (b,g), cheering (g), football (b), golf (b,g), hiking/backpacking (b,g), soccer (b), softball (g), swimming and diving (b,g), tennis (b,g), track and field (b,g), volleyball (g). 1 coach, 1 trainer.

Computers Computers are regularly used in literacy classes. Computer network features include on-campus library services, CD-ROMs, Internet access.

Contact Rachael B. Patin, Admissions Coordinator. 337-948-4623 Ext. 117. Fax: 337-948-4090. E-mail: rpatin@wcala.org. Web site: www.wcala.org.

WESTMINSTER CHRISTIAN SCHOOL

6855 Southwest 152nd Street
Miami, Florida 33157
Head of School: Mr. George J.W. Lawrence Jr.

General Information Coeducational day college-preparatory, general academic, arts, and religious studies school, affiliated with Christian faith. Grades PK–12. Founded: 1961. Setting: suburban. 26-acre campus. 9 buildings on campus. Approved or accredited by Christian Schools of Florida, Florida Council of Independent Schools, Southern Association of Colleges and Schools, and Florida Department of Education. Endowment: $2.1 million. Total enrollment: 1,094. Upper school average class size: 11. Upper school faculty-student ratio: 1:12.

Upper School Student Profile Grade 9: 122 students (58 boys, 64 girls); Grade 10: 102 students (42 boys, 60 girls); Grade 11: 91 students (48 boys, 43 girls); Grade 12: 103 students (48 boys, 55 girls). 100% of students are Christian.

Faculty School total: 102. In upper school: 15 men, 19 women; 16 have advanced degrees.

Subjects Offered Advanced Placement courses, algebra, American history, American literature, anatomy, art, Bible studies, biology, biology-AP, business law, business skills, calculus, ceramics, chemistry, chemistry-AP, community service, computer programming, computer science, creative writing, drama, driver education, economics, English, English literature, fine arts, French, French-AP, general science, geometry, government-AP, government/civics, grammar, health, history, macroeconomics-AP, marine biology, mathematics, music, organic chemistry, photography, physical education, physics, physiology, psychology, religion, SAT preparation, science, scripture, sculpture, sex education, social studies, sociology, softball, Spanish, Spanish language-AP, Spanish literature-AP, Spanish-AP, speech, sports, statistics-AP, strings, study skills, swimming, theater, track and field, trigonometry, typing, U.S. government, U.S. government-AP, U.S. history, U.S. history-AP, vocal ensemble, volleyball, weightlifting, wind ensemble, world history, world literature, wrestling, writing, yearbook.

Graduation Requirements Arts and fine arts (art, music, dance, drama), Bible, computer science, electives, English, foreign language, health science, keyboarding, lab science, mathematics, physical education (includes health), science, social studies (includes history), speech. Community service is required.

Special Academic Programs Advanced Placement exam preparation in 13 subject areas; honors section; accelerated programs; independent study; study at local college for college credit; academic accommodation for the gifted, the musically talented, and the artistically talented; programs in English, mathematics for dyslexic students.

College Placement 121 students graduated in 2005; 119 went to college, including Auburn University; Florida International University; Florida State University; University of Central Florida; University of Florida; University of Miami. Other: 2 went to work. Mean SAT verbal: 554, mean SAT math: 558, mean composite ACT: 21. 33% scored over 600 on SAT verbal, 32% scored over 600 on SAT math, 24% scored over 26 on composite ACT.

Student Life Upper grades have uniform requirement, student council, honor system. Discipline rests primarily with faculty. Attendance at religious services is required.

Summer Programs Remediation, advancement, computer instruction programs offered; session focuses on academics and athletics; held on campus; accepts boys and girls; open to students from other schools. 50 students usually enrolled. 2006 schedule: June 7 to July 7.

Tuition and Aid Day student tuition: $11,900. Tuition installment plan (monthly payment plans, individually arranged payment plans, semi-annual and annual payment plans). Need-based scholarship grants available. In 2005–06, 10% of upper-school students received aid. Total amount of financial aid awarded in 2005–06: $197,324.

Admissions Traditional secondary-level entrance grade is 9. For fall 2005, 69 students applied for upper-level admission, 52 were accepted, 49 enrolled. Iowa Tests of Basic Skills and writing sample required. Deadline for receipt of application materials: none. Application fee required: $125. On-campus interview required.

Athletics Interscholastic: baseball (boys), basketball (b,g), cheering (g), cross-country running (b,g), football (b), golf (b), soccer (b,g), softball (g), swimming and diving (b,g), tennis (b,g), track and field (b,g), volleyball (b,g), wrestling (b). 8 PE instructors, 63 coaches, 1 trainer.

Computers Computers are regularly used in accounting, art, Bible studies, business applications, career exploration, college planning, computer applications, creative

writing, economics, English, foreign language, keyboarding, mathematics, music, photography, programming, science, word processing, writing, writing, yearbook classes. Computer network features include campus e-mail, on-campus library services, CD-ROMs, Internet access.

Contact Mrs. Caroline H. Stone, Director of Admissions. 305-233-2030 Ext. 246. Fax: 305-253-9623. E-mail: cstone@wcsmiami.org. Web site: www.wcsmiami.org.

WESTMINSTER SCHOOL
995 Hopmeadow Street
Simsbury, Connecticut 06070
Head of School: Mr. W. Graham Cole Jr.

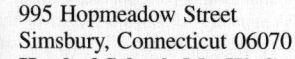

General Information Coeducational boarding and day college-preparatory, arts, and technology school. Grades 9–PG. Founded: 1888. Setting: suburban. Nearest major city is Hartford. Students are housed in single-sex dormitories. 230-acre campus. 38 buildings on campus. Approved or accredited by Connecticut Association of Independent Schools, New England Association of Schools and Colleges, The Association of Boarding Schools, and Connecticut Department of Education. Member of National Association of Independent Schools and Secondary School Admission Test Board. Endowment: $68 million. Total enrollment: 375. Upper school average class size: 12. Upper school faculty-student ratio: 1:5.

Upper School Student Profile Grade 9: 75 students (38 boys, 37 girls); Grade 10: 94 students (50 boys, 44 girls); Grade 11: 100 students (55 boys, 45 girls); Grade 12: 97 students (49 boys, 48 girls); Postgraduate: 9 students (9 boys). 69% of students are boarding students. 43% are state residents. 24 states are represented in upper school student body. 9% are international students. International students from Bahamas, Bermuda, Canada, China, Republic of Korea, and Saudi Arabia; 10 other countries represented in student body.

Faculty School total: 79. In upper school: 47 men, 32 women; 49 have advanced degrees; 58 reside on campus.

Subjects Offered Algebra, American history, American literature, architecture, art, art history, astronomy, biology, calculus, chemistry, computer programming, creative writing, dance, drama, driver education, ecology, economics, English, English literature, ethics, European history, fine arts, French, geology, geometry, health, history, Latin, mathematics, mechanical drawing, music, philosophy, photography, physics, SAT/ACT preparation, science, social studies, Spanish, statistics, theater, trigonometry, world history, writing.

Graduation Requirements Arts, English, foreign language, history, mathematics, science.

Special Academic Programs Advanced Placement exam preparation in 19 subject areas; honors section; independent study; term-away projects; study at local college for college credit; study abroad.

College Placement 105 students graduated in 2005; all went to college, including Boston College; Bowdoin College; Columbia College; Duke University; Trinity College; Tufts University. Median SAT verbal: 603, median SAT math: 626, median combined SAT: 1826.

Student Life Upper grades have specified standards of dress, student council. Discipline rests primarily with faculty.

Summer Programs Sports programs offered; session focuses on soccer, football; held on campus; accepts boys and girls; open to students from other schools. 350 students usually enrolled. 2006 schedule: July 10 to August 4.

Tuition and Aid Day student tuition: $26,000; 7-day tuition and room/board: $35,400. Tuition installment plan (Academic Management Services Plan, Key Tuition Payment Plan). Merit scholarship grants, need-based scholarship grants, need-based loans available. In 2005–06, 29% of upper-school students received aid; total upper-school merit-scholarship money awarded: $50,500. Total amount of financial aid awarded in 2005–06: $2,676,000.

Admissions Traditional secondary-level entrance grade is 9. For fall 2005, 792 students applied for upper-level admission, 315 were accepted, 132 enrolled. PSAT and SAT for applicants to grade 11 and 12 or SSAT, ERB, PSAT, SAT, PLAN or ACT required. Deadline for receipt of application materials: January 15. Application fee required: $50. On-campus interview required.

Athletics Interscholastic: baseball (boys), basketball (b,g), cross-country running (b,g), diving (b,g), field hockey (g), football (b), golf (b,g), ice hockey (b,g), lacrosse (b,g), soccer (b,g), softball (g), squash (b,g), swimming and diving (b,g), tennis (b,g), track and field (b,g), volleyball (g); intramural: strength & conditioning (b,g); coed interscholastic: paddle tennis; coed intramural: aerobics/dance, ballet, dance, modern dance. 2 trainers.

Computers Computers are regularly used in English, foreign language, history, mathematics, science classes. Computer network features include campus e-mail, on-campus library services, CD-ROMs, online commercial services, Internet access, file transfer, DVD, wireless campus network.

Contact Mr. Jon C. Deveaux, Director of Admissions. 860-408-3060. Fax: 860-408-3042. E-mail: admit@westminster-school.org. Web site: www.westminster-school.org.

See full description on page 1130.

THE WESTMINSTER SCHOOLS
1424 West Paces Ferry Road, NW
Atlanta, Georgia 30327
Head of School: Dr. William Clarkson, IV

General Information Coeducational day college-preparatory, arts, business, religious studies, bilingual studies, and technology school, affiliated with Christian faith. Grades K–12. Founded: 1951. Setting: suburban. 176-acre campus. 7 buildings on campus. Approved or accredited by Georgia Independent School Association, Southern Association of Colleges and Schools, and Southern Association of Independent Schools. Member of National Association of Independent Schools and Secondary School Admission Test Board. Endowment: $180 million. Total enrollment: 1,804. Upper school average class size: 14. Upper school faculty-student ratio: 1:14.

Upper School Student Profile Grade 9: 196 students (102 boys, 94 girls); Grade 10: 201 students (97 boys, 104 girls); Grade 11: 185 students (99 boys, 86 girls); Grade 12: 200 students (97 boys, 103 girls). 85% of students are Christian.

Faculty School total: 264. In upper school: 54 men, 50 women; 89 have advanced degrees.

Subjects Offered Advanced Placement courses, advanced studio art-AP, algebra, American history, art, art history, Bible studies, biology, calculus, ceramics, chemistry, choral music, computer math, computer programming, computer science, drama, driver education, earth science, economics, English, English literature, ethics, European history, fine arts, French, geometry, German, grammar, health, history, Latin, leadership education training, mathematics, music, natural history, outdoor education, philosophy, photography, physical education, physics, psychology, religion, science, social studies, sociology, Spanish, speech, statistics, studio art—AP, theater, theater arts, trigonometry, visual and performing arts, world history, writing.

Graduation Requirements Arts and fine arts (art, music, dance, drama), English, experiential education, foreign language, history, mathematics, physical education (includes health), religion (includes Bible studies and theology), science.

Special Academic Programs Advanced Placement exam preparation in 17 subject areas; honors section; independent study; term-away projects; study abroad; academic accommodation for the gifted, the musically talented, and the artistically talented.

College Placement 189 students graduated in 2005; all went to college, including Auburn University; Georgia Institute of Technology; Princeton University; University of Georgia; University of Virginia; Vanderbilt University. 77% scored over 600 on SAT verbal, 78% scored over 600 on SAT math.

Student Life Upper grades have specified standards of dress, student council, honor system. Discipline rests equally with students and faculty. Attendance at religious services is required.

Summer Programs Remediation, enrichment, advancement, sports, art/fine arts, rigorous outdoor training, computer instruction programs offered; session focuses on academics and sports/arts camps; held on campus; accepts boys and girls; open to students from other schools. 190 students usually enrolled. 2006 schedule: June 5 to July 14. Application deadline: February 28.

Tuition and Aid Day student tuition: $15,717. Need-based scholarship grants available. In 2005–06, 14% of upper-school students received aid. Total amount of financial aid awarded in 2005–06: $1,024,591.

Admissions Traditional secondary-level entrance grade is 9. For fall 2005, 85 students applied for upper-level admission, 37 were accepted, 29 enrolled. Individual IQ, SAT for students entering as juniors and SSAT required. Deadline for receipt of application materials: February 13. Application fee required: $75. On-campus interview required.

Athletics Interscholastic: baseball (boys), basketball (b,g), cheering (g), crew (g), cross-country running (b,g), dance (g), diving (b,g), football (b), golf (b,g), gymnastics (g), lacrosse (b,g), soccer (b,g), softball (g), swimming and diving (b,g), tennis (b,g), track and field (b,g), volleyball (g), water polo (b), wrestling (b); intramural: climbing (b,g), crew (b,g), physical fitness (b,g), squash (b,g), strength & conditioning (b,g); coed intramural: back packing, cross-country running, flag football, hiking/backpacking, paddle tennis, rappelling, rock climbing, ropes courses, table tennis, tennis, ultimate Frisbee. 2 PE instructors, 4 coaches, 4 trainers.

Computers Computers are regularly used in art, Bible studies, desktop publishing, economics, English, foreign language, keyboarding, mathematics, multimedia, music, science, technology, video film production, writing classes. Computer network features include campus e-mail, on-campus library services, CD-ROMs, online commercial services, Internet access, file transfer, DVD, wireless campus network.

Contact Mrs. Julie Williams, Assistant Director of Admissions. 404-609-6202. Fax: 404-367-7894. E-mail: admissions@westminster.net. Web site: www.westminster.net.

WESTMINSTER SCHOOLS OF AUGUSTA
3067 Wheeler Road
Augusta, Georgia 30909
Head of School: Mr. James A. Adare

General Information Coeducational day college-preparatory, arts, religious studies, and music, debate and drama school, affiliated with Presbyterian Church in America. Grades PK–12. Founded: 1972. Setting: suburban. 30-acre campus. 7 buildings on campus. Approved or accredited by Southern Association of Colleges and Schools and Southern Association of Independent Schools. Member of National Association of

Westminster Schools of Augusta

Independent Schools. Endowment: $304,000. Total enrollment: 511. Upper school average class size: 14. Upper school faculty-student ratio: 1:6.

Upper School Student Profile Grade 9: 36 students (19 boys, 17 girls); Grade 10: 47 students (21 boys, 26 girls); Grade 11: 30 students (14 boys, 16 girls); Grade 12: 38 students (17 boys, 21 girls). 30% of students are Presbyterian Church in America.

Faculty School total: 30. In upper school: 18 men, 12 women; 18 have advanced degrees.

Subjects Offered Algebra, analysis and differential calculus, analysis of data, analytic geometry, anatomy and physiology, Ancient Greek, art, arts, band, Bible studies, biology, biology-AP, British literature (honors), calculus, calculus-AP, chemistry, chemistry-AP, choir, chorus, Christian scripture, classical Greek literature, community service, computer keyboarding, computer programming, computer skills, computers, conceptual physics, concert band, concert choir, drama, drama performance, dramatic arts, earth science, economics, English, English language and composition-AP, English language-AP, English literature, English literature and composition-AP, English literature-AP, European history, family life, French, French language-AP, French-AP, geography, geometry, government/civics, Greek, guidance, health, health education, history, history-AP, honors algebra, honors English, honors geometry, honors U.S. history, lab science, Latin, Latin-AP, mathematics, modern European history, modern European history-AP, modern history, modern world history, music, physical education, physical science, physics, physics-AP, physiology-anatomy, pre-algebra, pre-calculus, psychology, religion, SAT preparation, science, social studies, Spanish, Spanish language-AP, Spanish-AP, speech, studio art, study skills, swimming, theater, trigonometry, U.S. government and politics-AP, U.S. history, U.S. history-AP, U.S. literature, United States government-AP, weight training, word processing, world history, world literature, writing, yearbook.

Graduation Requirements Arts and fine arts (art, music, dance, drama), electives, English, foreign language, mathematics, physical education (includes health), religion (includes Bible studies and theology), science, social studies (includes history).

Special Academic Programs Advanced Placement exam preparation in 11 subject areas; honors section; academic accommodation for the gifted; programs in general development for dyslexic students.

College Placement 44 students graduated in 2005; all went to college, including Georgia Institute of Technology; Georgia Southern University; Samford University; University of Georgia; University of South Carolina. Median SAT verbal: 620, median SAT math: 630. 66% scored over 600 on SAT verbal, 76% scored over 600 on SAT math.

Student Life Upper grades have specified standards of dress, honor system. Discipline rests primarily with faculty.

Summer Programs Sports programs offered; session focuses on sports; held on campus; accepts boys and girls; open to students from other schools. 76 students usually enrolled. 2006 schedule: June 2 to August 1. Application deadline: May 1.

Tuition and Aid Day student tuition: $8043–$8659. Tuition installment plan (monthly payment plans). Tuition reduction for siblings, need-based scholarship grants available. In 2005–06, 40% of upper-school students received aid. Total amount of financial aid awarded in 2005–06: $375,000.

Admissions Traditional secondary-level entrance grade is 9. For fall 2005, 24 students applied for upper-level admission, 24 were accepted, 22 enrolled. ERB—verbal abilities, reading comprehension, quantitative abilities (level F, form 1) required. Deadline for receipt of application materials: none. Application fee required: $75. Interview required.

Athletics Interscholastic: baseball (boys), basketball (b,g), cheering (g), cross-country running (b,g), golf (b), soccer (b,g), swimming and diving (b,g), tennis (b,g), track and field (b,g). 3 PE instructors, 4 coaches, 1 trainer.

Computers Computers are regularly used in college planning, keyboarding, programming, SAT preparation, technology, yearbook classes. Computer network features include campus e-mail, CD-ROMs, Internet access, file transfer, office computer access.

Contact W. Alexander McCallie, Director of Admissions. 706-731-5260 Ext. 2201. Fax: 706-261-7786. E-mail: amccallie@wsa.net. Web site: www.wsa.net.

student body. 16% are international students. International students from Hong Kong, Japan, Republic of Korea, Taiwan, and Thailand.

Faculty School total: 45. In upper school: 24 men, 21 women; 16 have advanced degrees; 36 reside on campus.

Subjects Offered Advanced chemistry, advanced math, advanced TOEFL/grammar, African-American history, algebra, American literature, anatomy, ancient world history, applied arts, art, art history, Asian history, astronomy, basic language skills, biology, biology-AP, body human, British literature, British literature (honors), calculus, calculus-AP, ceramics, chemistry, chemistry-AP, choir, chorus, clayworking, college counseling, comparative religion, computer education, computer keyboarding, computer processing, diversity studies, drama, drama performance, drawing, earth science, English, English literature, English literature-AP, English-AP, environmental science, equestrian sports, ESL, ethics, ethics and responsibility, ethnic studies, European history, European history-AP, film, fine arts, French, French-AP, geography, geometry, government/civics, guitar, health, health and wellness, history, history-AP, honors algebra, honors English, honors geometry, honors U.S. history, human anatomy, human biology, humanities, independent study, instrumental music, intro to computers, Latin, Latin-AP, mathematics, model United Nations, modern European history, modern European history-AP, multicultural studies, music, music appreciation, photography, physical education, physics, physics-AP, piano, play production, pottery, pre-calculus, psychology, religion, SAT preparation, science, senior humanities, senior project, senior thesis, social studies, Spanish, Spanish-AP, sports, stage design, student government, student publications, studio art, studio art-AP, U.S. history, U.S. history-AP, visual and performing arts, voice, voice ensemble, weight training, wellness, world history, world literature, world religions, wrestling, writing fundamentals, yearbook.

Special Academic Programs Advanced Placement exam preparation in 9 subject areas; honors section; independent study; study at local college for college credit; academic accommodation for the gifted, the musically talented, and the artistically talented; remedial reading and/or remedial writing; remedial math; programs in English, mathematics, general development for dyslexic students; ESL (10 students enrolled).

College Placement 37 students graduated in 2004; all went to college, including Drexel University; St. Mary's College of Maryland; Syracuse University; The Pennsylvania State University University Park Campus; University of Maryland; Washington College.

Student Life Upper grades have specified standards of dress, student council. Discipline rests primarily with faculty.

Tuition and Aid Day student tuition: $15,540–$22,060; 7-day tuition and room/board: $30,200–$36,720. Tuition installment plan (monthly payment plans, individually arranged payment plans). Need-based scholarship grants available. In 2004–05, 30% of upper-school students received aid. Total amount of financial aid awarded in 2004–05: $340,000.

Admissions Traditional secondary-level entrance grade is 9. For fall 2005, 166 students applied for upper-level admission, 121 were accepted, 73 enrolled. SSAT, TOEFL or WISC-III and Woodcock-Johnson required. Deadline for receipt of application materials: none. Application fee required: $50. On-campus interview required.

Athletics Interscholastic: baseball (boys), basketball (b,g), cheering (g), cross-country running (b,g), field hockey (g), football (b), golf (b), lacrosse (b), soccer (b,g), tennis (b,g), track and field (b,g), volleyball (g), wrestling (b); intramural: bicycling (b); coed interscholastic: cross-country running, power lifting, tennis, track and field, weight training; coed intramural: equestrian sports, horseback riding, strength & conditioning, weight training. 2 coaches, 1 trainer.

Computers Computers are regularly used in all academic, introduction to technology classes. Computer network features include campus e-mail, on-campus library services, CD-ROMs, Internet access, office computer access.

Contact Heidi K. L. Sprinkle, Director of Admission and Financial Aid. 410-658-5556 Ext. 9224. Fax: 410-658-9264. E-mail: admissions@wna.org. Web site: www.wna.org.

ANNOUNCEMENT FROM THE SCHOOL In November 2005, 15 students used their 7-day Thanksgiving break to participate in the hurricane relief efforts in Ocean Springs, Mississippi. They had an unforgettable experience and came back with memories of people and circumstances that will stay with them forever. West Nottingham Academy is very proud of its community service programs and its student volunteers.

See full description on page 1132.

WEST NOTTINGHAM ACADEMY

1079 Firetower Road
Colora, Maryland 21917-1599
Head of School: Dr. D. John Watson

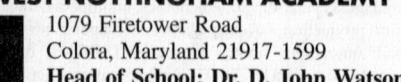

General Information Coeducational boarding and day college-preparatory, arts, and ESL school. Boarding grades 9–PG, day grades 6–PG. Founded: 1744. Setting: rural. Nearest major city is Baltimore. Students are housed in single-sex dormitories. 120-acre campus. 12 buildings on campus. Approved or accredited by Association of Independent Maryland Schools, Middle States Association of Colleges and Schools, National Commission of Accreditation of Special Education Services, The Association of Boarding Schools, and Maryland Department of Education. Member of National Association of Independent Schools and Secondary School Admission Test Board. Language of instruction: English. Total enrollment: 190. Upper school average class size: 10. Upper school faculty-student ratio: 1:6.

Upper School Student Profile Grade 9: 39 students (29 boys, 10 girls); Grade 10: 40 students (29 boys, 11 girls); Grade 11: 46 students (30 boys, 16 girls); Grade 12: 39 students (22 boys, 17 girls); Postgraduate: 1 student (1 girl). 64% of students are boarding students. 22% are state residents. 15 states are represented in upper school

WESTOVER SCHOOL

1237 Whittemore Road
Middlebury, Connecticut 06762
Head of School: Mrs. Ann S. Pollina

General Information Girls' boarding and day college-preparatory, arts, technology, and mathematics and science school. Grades 9–12. Founded: 1909. Setting: small town. Nearest major city is New York, NY. Students are housed in single-sex dormitories. 100-acre campus. 11 buildings on campus. Approved or accredited by

Association of Independent Schools in New England, Connecticut Association of Independent Schools, New England Association of Schools and Colleges, The Association of Boarding Schools, and Connecticut Department of Education. Member of National Association of Independent Schools and Secondary School Admission Test Board. Endowment: $38.2 million. Total enrollment: 205. Upper school average class size: 11. Upper school faculty-student ratio: 1:8.

Upper School Student Profile Grade 9: 47 students (47 girls); Grade 10: 57 students (57 girls); Grade 11: 51 students (51 girls); Grade 12: 50 students (50 girls). 61% of students are boarding students. 43% are state residents. 21 states are represented in upper school student body. 11% are international students. International students from Bermuda, Germany, Hong Kong, Japan, Mongolia, and Republic of Korea; 8 other countries represented in student body.

Faculty School total: 36. In upper school: 12 men, 24 women; 19 have advanced degrees; all reside on campus.

Subjects Offered Advanced chemistry, Advanced Placement courses, African-American studies, algebra, American government, American history, American history-AP, American literature, art, art history, art-AP, astronomy, athletic training, ballet technique, bell choir, biology, biology-AP, calculus, calculus-AP, ceramics, chemistry, chemistry-AP, clayworking, community service, computer literacy, computer programming, computer science, computer science-AP, creative writing, dance, drama, drawing, English, English language and composition-AP, English literature, environmental science, ESL, etymology, European history, European history-AP, fabric arts, filmmaking, fine arts, French, French-AP, geography, geology, geometry, grammar, health and wellness, history of mathematics, honors algebra, journalism, Latin, Latin-AP, marine biology, mathematics, model United Nations, modern European history-AP, music, music theory-AP, musical productions, ornithology, painting, performing arts, photo shop, photography, physics, physics-AP, poetry, politics, portfolio art, pre-calculus, religion, robotics, science, sculpture, Shakespeare, short story, social studies, Spanish, Spanish-AP, speech, studio art-AP, theater, theology, trigonometry, wilderness/outdoor program, women's studies, world history, writing.

Graduation Requirements American history, art, arts and fine arts (art, music, dance, drama), athletics, computer skills, English, foreign language, library studies, mathematics, science, social studies (includes history), summer reading. Community service is required.

Special Academic Programs Advanced Placement exam preparation in 17 subject areas; honors section; independent study; term-away projects; study abroad; academic accommodation for the gifted, the musically talented, and the artistically talented; ESL (5 students enrolled).

College Placement 42 students graduated in 2005; all went to college, including Carnegie Mellon University; Columbia College; Cornell University; Dartmouth College; Skidmore College; University of Connecticut. Median composite ACT: 26. Mean SAT verbal: 637, mean SAT math: 613. 63% scored over 600 on SAT verbal, 61% scored over 600 on SAT math, 50% scored over 26 on composite ACT.

Student Life Upper grades have specified standards of dress, student council, honor system. Discipline rests equally with students and faculty.

Tuition and Aid Day student tuition: $23,450; 7-day tuition and room/board: $33,900. Tuition installment plan (The Tuition Plan, Insured Tuition Payment Plan, FACTS Tuition Payment Plan). Need-based scholarship grants, need-based loans, middle-income loans available. In 2005–06, 49% of upper-school students received aid. Total amount of financial aid awarded in 2005–06: $1,879,500.

Admissions Traditional secondary-level entrance grade is 9. For fall 2005, 192 students applied for upper-level admission, 118 were accepted, 63 enrolled. ISEE, SSAT or TOEFL required. Deadline for receipt of application materials: February 1. Application fee required: $45. On-campus interview required.

Athletics Interscholastic: ballet, basketball, cross-country running, dance, field hockey, independent competitive sports, lacrosse, modern dance, outdoor activities, paddle tennis, soccer, softball, squash, tennis, volleyball; intramural: aerobics, aerobics/dance, back packing, ballet, canoeing/kayaking, climbing, dance, fitness, fitness walking, hiking/backpacking, horseback riding, jogging, kayaking, modern dance, outdoor activities, outdoor adventure, outdoor education, outdoor recreation, outdoor skills, outdoors, physical fitness, physical training, rappelling, rock climbing, running, self defense, squash, strength & conditioning, tennis, volleyball, wall climbing, weight lifting, weight training, wilderness, yoga. 2 PE instructors, 5 coaches, 1 trainer.

Computers Computers are regularly used in art, English, foreign language, history, mathematics, music, science classes. Computer network features include campus e-mail, on-campus library services, CD-ROMs, online commercial services, Internet access, office computer access, DVD.

Contact Ms. Sara Lynn Renda, Director of Admission and Financial Aid. 203-758-2423. Fax: 203-577-4588. E-mail: admission@westoverschool.org. Web site: www.westoverschool.org.

ANNOUNCEMENT FROM THE SCHOOL A leader in girls' education, Westover is an academically rigorous school dedicated to challenging and encouraging young women to participate in all aspects of academic, community, and athletic life. The Westover community is diverse, with students representing 13 countries and 21 states. Westover offers excellent college placement and its students continue outstanding success in 17 AP programs, particularly in mathematics and science. A new performing arts center opened in fall 2004.

Three programs enhance the curriculum: Women in Science and Engineering (WISE), a joint, cocurricular program with Rensselaer Polytechnic Institute in Troy, New York; a joint program for preprofessional musicians with the Manhattan School of Music; and a program with the Brass City Ballet for talented dancers.

See full description on page 1134.

WESTPARK SCHOOL

Box 91
2375 Saskatchewan Avenue West
Portage la Prairie, Manitoba R1N 3B2, Canada
Head of School: Mrs. Shanon Lee Weselake

General Information Coeducational day college-preparatory, arts, and religious studies school, affiliated with The Christian and Missionary Alliance. Grades K–12. Founded: 1987. Setting: small town. Nearest major city is Winnipeg, Canada. 11-acre campus. 1 building on campus. Approved or accredited by Association of Christian Schools International and Manitoba Department of Education. Language of instruction: English. Total enrollment: 224. Upper school average class size: 13. Upper school faculty-student ratio: 1:10.

Upper School Student Profile Grade 9: 22 students (13 boys, 9 girls); Grade 10: 6 students (4 boys, 2 girls); Grade 11: 10 students (4 boys, 6 girls); Grade 12: 13 students (8 boys, 5 girls). 35% of students are The Christian and Missionary Alliance.

Faculty School total: 18. In upper school: 3 men, 2 women; 1 has an advanced degree.

Subjects Offered Band, biology, Canadian history, chemistry, chorus, computers, drama, expressive arts, geography, health, law, marketing, mathematics, music, physical education, religion, science, social studies, visual arts.

Graduation Requirements English, mathematics, physical education (includes health), religion (includes Bible studies and theology), science, social studies (includes history).

Special Academic Programs Independent study; remedial reading and/or remedial writing; remedial math.

College Placement 16 students graduated in 2005; 2 went to college, including University of Manitoba. Other: 8 went to work, 1 entered military service, 5 had other specific plans.

Student Life Upper grades have specified standards of dress, student council, honor system. Discipline rests equally with students and faculty.

Tuition and Aid Day student tuition: CAN$2069. Tuition installment plan (monthly payment plans, individually arranged payment plans). Tuition reduction for siblings, bursaries available. In 2005–06, 18% of upper-school students received aid. Total amount of financial aid awarded in 2005–06: CAN$11,634.

Admissions Traditional secondary-level entrance grade is 9. For fall 2005, 4 students applied for upper-level admission, 4 were accepted, 4 enrolled. CAT required. Deadline for receipt of application materials: none. Application fee required: CAN$50. Interview required.

Athletics Interscholastic: badminton (boys, girls), basketball (b), golf (b), volleyball (b,g); coed interscholastic: aerobics/dance, cross-country running, curling, dance; coed intramural: badminton, basketball, floor hockey, volleyball. 1 PE instructor, 2 coaches.

Computers Computers are regularly used in drafting, independent study, keyboarding classes. Computer network features include campus e-mail, CD-ROMs, Internet access.

Contact Mrs. Gayle G. Loewen, Administrative Assistant to the Principal. 204-857-3726. Fax: 204-239-6545. E-mail: gloewen@westpark.mb.ca. Web site: www.westpark.mb.ca.

WESTRIDGE SCHOOL

324 Madeline Drive
Pasadena, California 91105-3399
Head of School: Ms. Fran N. Scoble

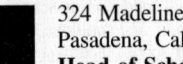

petersons.com

General Information Girls' day college-preparatory, arts, and technology school. Grades 4–12. Founded: 1913. Setting: suburban. Nearest major city is Los Angeles. 10-acre campus. 11 buildings on campus. Approved or accredited by California Association of Independent Schools, National Independent Private Schools Association, Western Association of Schools and Colleges, and California Department of Education. Member of National Association of Independent Schools. Endowment: $13.6 million. Total enrollment: 510. Upper school average class size: 18. Upper school faculty-student ratio: 1:9.

Upper School Student Profile Grade 9: 71 students (71 girls); Grade 10: 66 students (66 girls); Grade 11: 63 students (63 girls); Grade 12: 63 students (63 girls).

Faculty School total: 60. In upper school: 12 men, 24 women; 19 have advanced degrees.

Subjects Offered Acting, Advanced Placement courses, algebra, American history, American literature, art, art history, Asian history, biology, calculus, ceramics, chemistry, chorus, classical language, college counseling, computer applications, computer science, creative writing, dance, directing, drama, earth science, English,

English literature, environmental science, European history, fine arts, French, geometry, government/civics, history, Latin, life science, mathematics, modern languages, music, orchestra, photography, physical education, physical science, physics, physiology, pre-calculus, psychology, science, social science, social studies, Spanish, Spanish literature, statistics, studio art, theater, trigonometry, video, visual and performing arts, world history, world literature, writing.

Graduation Requirements Art, college counseling, cultural arts, English, foreign language, history, mathematics, music, physical education (includes health), science, senior project. Community service is required.

Special Academic Programs Advanced Placement exam preparation in 14 subject areas; honors section; independent study.

College Placement 67 students graduated in 2005; all went to college, including Barnard College; Boston College; Columbia College; University of California, Santa Barbara; University of California, Santa Cruz; University of Southern California. Median SAT verbal: 680, median SAT math: 660. 85% scored over 600 on SAT verbal, 79% scored over 600 on SAT math.

Student Life Upper grades have uniform requirement, student council. Discipline rests primarily with faculty.

Summer Programs Sports, art/fine arts programs offered; session focuses on non-academic activities; held on campus; accepts boys and girls; open to students from other schools. 150 students usually enrolled. 2006 schedule: June 19 to July 14. Application deadline: May 31.

Tuition and Aid Day student tuition: $20,600. Tuition installment plan (The Tuition Plan, monthly payment plans). Need-based scholarship grants available. In 2005–06, 37% of upper-school students received aid. Total amount of financial aid awarded in 2005–06: $900,550.

Admissions Traditional secondary-level entrance grade is 9. For fall 2005, 91 students applied for upper-level admission, 38 were accepted, 16 enrolled. ISEE, school's own exam or writing sample required. Deadline for receipt of application materials: February 1. Application fee required: $60. On-campus interview required.

Athletics Interscholastic: basketball, cross-country running, dance, diving, fencing, golf, soccer, softball, tennis, track and field, volleyball, water polo, yoga. 4 PE instructors, 26 coaches.

Computers Computers are regularly used in art, English, foreign language, history, mathematics, science classes. Computer network features include campus e-mail, on-campus library services, CD-ROMs, online commercial services, Internet access, file transfer, office computer access, DVD, wireless campus network.

Contact Ms. Helen V. Hopper, Director of Admissions. 626-799-1153 Ext. 213. Fax: 626-799-7068. E-mail: hhopper@westridge.org. Web site: www.westridge.org.

ANNOUNCEMENT FROM THE SCHOOL For 91 years, Westridge School has offered girls and young women an educational program rich in tradition, yet committed to innovation. The rigorous academic curriculum is enhanced by study of music, dance, drama, art, science, technology, and foreign language, as well as a full athletics program. Leadership training; academic, cocurricular, and community service opportunities; and international travel are also included.

WESTTOWN SCHOOL

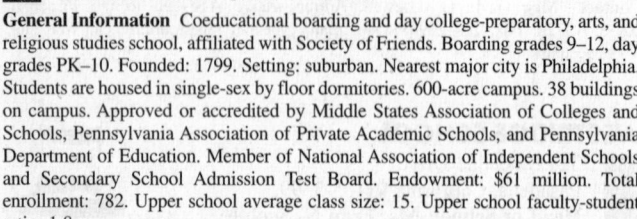

975 Westtown Road
PO Box 1799
Westtown, Pennsylvania 19395-1799
Head of School: John W. Baird

petersons.com

General Information Coeducational boarding and day college-preparatory, arts, and religious studies school, affiliated with Society of Friends. Boarding grades 9–12, day grades PK–10. Founded: 1799. Setting: suburban. Nearest major city is Philadelphia. Students are housed in single-sex by floor dormitories. 600-acre campus. 38 buildings on campus. Approved or accredited by Middle States Association of Colleges and Schools, Pennsylvania Association of Private Academic Schools, and Pennsylvania Department of Education. Member of National Association of Independent Schools and Secondary School Admission Test Board. Endowment: $61 million. Total enrollment: 782. Upper school average class size: 15. Upper school faculty-student ratio: 1:8.

Upper School Student Profile Grade 9: 71 students (35 boys, 36 girls); Grade 10: 110 students (54 boys, 56 girls); Grade 11: 103 students (46 boys, 57 girls); Grade 12: 110 students (49 boys, 61 girls). 74% of students are boarding students. 61% are state residents. 22 states are represented in upper school student body. 14% are international students. International students from Germany, Japan, Kenya, Nigeria, Republic of Korea, and Taiwan; 6 other countries represented in student body. 22% of students are members of Society of Friends.

Faculty School total: 113. In upper school: 36 men, 33 women; 45 have advanced degrees; 55 reside on campus.

Subjects Offered 3-dimensional art, acting, advanced math, Advanced Placement courses, African history, algebra, American history, ancient history, art, Asian studies, astrophysics, Bible studies, biology, biology-AP, calculus-AP, ceramics, chemistry, chemistry-AP, chorus, college planning, computer programming, computer science, concert choir, dance, discrete math, drama, driver education, ecology, English, English literature, environmental science, environmental studies, ESL, ethics, expository writing, fine arts, French, French language-AP, geometry, German, German-AP,

health, Holocaust, Holocaust studies, jazz, jazz ensemble, Latin, Latin American history, Latin-AP, mathematics, modern European history, music, music theory, orchestra, peace education, photography, physics, physics-AP, pre-calculus, Quakerism and ethics, religion, sculpture, Spanish, statistics-AP, theater, theater history, trigonometry, U.S. history-AP, woodworking, world history, world religions, writing.

Graduation Requirements Arts and fine arts (art, music, dance, drama), English, foreign language, mathematics, physical education (includes health), religion (includes Bible studies and theology), religious studies, science, senior project, social science.

Special Academic Programs Advanced Placement exam preparation in 10 subject areas; honors section; academic accommodation for the gifted, the musically talented, and the artistically talented; remedial math; ESL (18 students enrolled).

College Placement 101 students graduated in 2005; all went to college, including Brown University; Columbia College; Earlham College; The George Washington University; The Johns Hopkins University; University of Chicago. Median SAT verbal: 585, median SAT math: 615, median combined SAT: 1200. 51% scored over 600 on SAT verbal, 54% scored over 600 on SAT math.

Student Life Upper grades have specified standards of dress, student council. Discipline rests equally with students and faculty. Attendance at religious services is required.

Summer Programs Remediation, enrichment, advancement, art/fine arts programs offered; held on campus; accepts boys and girls; open to students from other schools.

Tuition and Aid Day student tuition: $20,100; 7-day tuition and room/board: $32,575. Tuition installment plan (Key Tuition Payment Plan). Need-based scholarship grants, need-based loans available. In 2005–06, 40% of upper-school students received aid. Total amount of financial aid awarded in 2005–06: $2,394,822.

Admissions Traditional secondary-level entrance grade is 9. For fall 2005, 301 students applied for upper-level admission, 152 were accepted, 82 enrolled. ISEE, SSAT or TOEFL required. Deadline for receipt of application materials: none. Application fee required: $50. On-campus interview required.

Athletics Interscholastic: baseball (boys), basketball (b,g), cross-country running (b,g), field hockey (g), lacrosse (b,g), soccer (b,g), softball (g), swimming and diving (b,g), tennis (b,g), track and field (b,g), volleyball (g), wrestling (b); coed interscholastic: golf, independent competitive sports; coed intramural: aquatics, canoeing/kayaking, combined training, dance, fitness, hiking/backpacking, indoor soccer, life saving, modern dance, outdoor activities, outdoor adventure, outdoor education, outdoor recreation, physical fitness, physical training, ropes courses, running, strength & conditioning, swimming and diving, tennis, weight lifting, weight training, winter soccer, yoga. 18 coaches, 1 trainer.

Computers Computers are regularly used in all academic, animation, art, career exploration, college planning, current events, desktop publishing, digital applications, graphic arts, introduction to technology, library, library skills, literary magazine, newspaper, publications, research skills, theater, yearbook classes. Computer network features include campus e-mail, on-campus library services, CD-ROMs, online commercial services, Internet access, wireless campus network.

Contact Kate Holz, Director of Admissions and Financial Aid. 610-399-7900. Fax: 610-399-7909. E-mail: admissions@westtown.edu. Web site: www.westtown.edu.

ANNOUNCEMENT FROM THE SCHOOL Westtown School is the Quaker preparatory school that, through its unique combination of 205-year-old Quaker heritage, unusually spacious and beautiful campus, academic strength, arts/athletics, and 2 year requisite boarding, invites students to participate in essential education: thoughtful, thorough preparation for college and university work; the discovery and use of individual voice and gifts; an active and informed sense of social responsibility; individual and shared exploration of Spirit; and the maturing experience of living, learning, and opening up with a diverse community of equals.

See full description on page 1136.

WESTVIEW SCHOOL

Los Angeles, California
See Special Needs Schools section.

WHEATON ACADEMY

900 Prince Crossing Road
West Chicago, Illinois 60185
Head of School: Dr. David L. Roth

General Information Coeducational day college-preparatory and religious studies school, affiliated with Christian faith. Grades 9–12. Founded: 1853. Setting: suburban. Nearest major city is Chicago. 43-acre campus. 7 buildings on campus. Approved or accredited by Association of Christian Schools International, North Central Association of Colleges and Schools, and Illinois Department of Education. Total enrollment: 565. Upper school average class size: 20. Upper school faculty-student ratio: 1:13.

Upper School Student Profile Grade 9: 146 students (79 boys, 67 girls); Grade 10: 138 students (66 boys, 72 girls); Grade 11: 137 students (64 boys, 73 girls); Grade 12: 144 students (68 boys, 76 girls). 99% of students are Christian faith.

Faculty School total: 44. In upper school: 22 men, 22 women; 34 have advanced degrees.

Subjects Offered 20th century history, ACT preparation, algebra, art, arts and crafts, band, Bible, Bible studies, biology, biology-AP, British literature, business, business applications, calculus, calculus-AP, ceramics, chemistry, child development, choir, Christian doctrine, Christian education, classics, computer art, computer education, computer graphics, computer keyboarding, computer multimedia, computer processing, computer programming-AP, computer science, concert choir, consumer economics, creative writing, debate, desktop publishing, drama, drama workshop, drawing, driver education, earth science, economics, English, English literature, environmental science, European history, family living, fiber arts, fine arts, foods, French, freshman seminar, geology, geometry, government/civics, graphic design, Greek, health, health and wellness, history, honors English, honors geometry, honors U.S. history, industrial arts, internship, journalism, leadership, literature, mathematics, multimedia design, music, music theory-AP, novels, orchestra, personal growth, physical education, physics, portfolio art, pre-algebra, psychology, publications, science, social science, social studies, sociology, Spanish, Spanish language-AP, speech, statistics, student publications, theater, theology, trigonometry, U.S. government, U.S. history, U.S. history-AP, U.S. literature, world history, world literature, writing.

Graduation Requirements Arts and fine arts (art, music, dance, drama), English, mathematics, physical education (includes health), religion (includes Bible studies and theology), science, social science, social studies (includes history), Winterim (3-week period during January allowing students to take two classes beyond the typical curriculum).

Special Academic Programs Advanced Placement exam preparation in 5 subject areas; honors section; independent study; term-away projects; study at local college for college credit; academic accommodation for the gifted, the musically talented, and the artistically talented; remedial reading and/or remedial writing; remedial math; special instructional classes for students with learning disabilities.

College Placement 127 students graduated in 2005; 124 went to college, including Bethel College; Calvin College; Hope College; Olivet Nazarene University; Taylor University; Wheaton College. Other: 2 went to work, 1 had other specific plans. Median composite ACT: 25. 44% scored over 26 on composite ACT.

Student Life Upper grades have specified standards of dress, student council, honor system. Discipline rests primarily with faculty. Attendance at religious services is required.

Summer Programs Advancement, sports, art/fine arts, computer instruction programs offered; held on campus; accepts boys and girls; open to students from other schools. 35 students usually enrolled. 2006 schedule: June 5 to June 23.

Tuition and Aid Day student tuition: $9900. Tuition installment plan (monthly payment plans, semester payment plan). Tuition reduction for siblings, merit scholarship grants, need-based scholarship grants, paying campus jobs available. In 2005–06, 30% of upper-school students received aid; total upper-school merit-scholarship money awarded: $12,000. Total amount of financial aid awarded in 2005–06: $520,000.

Admissions Traditional secondary-level entrance grade is 9. ACT-Explore or placement test required. Deadline for receipt of application materials: none. Application fee required: $50. On-campus interview required.

Athletics Interscholastic: baseball (boys), basketball (b,g), cheering (g), cross-country running (b,g), dance team (g), football (b), golf (b,g), ice hockey (b), pom squad (g), soccer (b,g), softball (g), tennis (b,g), track and field (b,g), volleyball (b,g); intramural: aerobics (g), flagball (g), ice hockey (b), wilderness survival (b); coed interscholastic: modern dance, physical training, running; coed intramural: climbing, floor hockey, hiking/backpacking, outdoor education, outdoor skills, power lifting, project adventure, rock climbing, skiing (cross-country), strength & conditioning, wall climbing, weight lifting, weight training. 2 PE instructors, 6 coaches.

Computers Computers are regularly used in Bible studies, graphic design, independent study, journalism, mathematics, multimedia, writing, yearbook classes. Computer network features include on-campus library services, CD-ROMs, online commercial services, Internet access.

Contact David Underwood, Assistant Principal/Director of Admissions. 630-562-7500 Ext. 7539. Fax: 630-231-0842. E-mail: dunderwood@wheatonacademy.org. Web site: www.wheatonacademy.org.

THE WHEELER SCHOOL

216 Hope Street
Providence, Rhode Island 02906
Head of School: Dan Miller, PhD

General Information Coeducational day college-preparatory and arts school. Grades N–12. Founded: 1889. Setting: urban. 7 buildings on campus. Approved or accredited by New England Association of Schools and Colleges and Rhode Island Department of Education. Member of National Association of Independent Schools. Endowment: $7.8 million. Total enrollment: 800. Upper school average class size: 15. Upper school faculty-student ratio: 1:13.

Upper School Student Profile Grade 9: 87 students (46 boys, 41 girls); Grade 10: 81 students (43 boys, 38 girls); Grade 11: 78 students (42 boys, 36 girls); Grade 12: 79 students (48 boys, 31 girls).

Faculty School total: 108. In upper school: 24 men, 32 women; 30 have advanced degrees.

Subjects Offered 20th century world history, acting, Advanced Placement courses, advanced studio art-AP, algebra, American history, anatomy, art, art history, biology, biology-AP, business skills, calculus, calculus-AP, ceramics, chemistry, Chinese, Chinese studies, computer programming, computer science, dance, drama, earth science, economics, English, English literature, English-AP, environmental science, environmental science-AP, European history, fine arts, French, geometry, Japanese, Latin, mathematics, music, photography, physical education, physics, physiology, psychology, science, social studies, Spanish, theater, trigonometry.

Graduation Requirements Arts and fine arts (art, music, dance, drama), computer science, English, foreign language, mathematics, physical education (includes health), science, social studies (includes history).

Special Academic Programs Advanced Placement exam preparation in 11 subject areas; honors section; accelerated programs; independent study; term-away projects; study at local college for college credit; study abroad.

College Placement 75 students graduated in 2005; 73 went to college, including Boston University; Brown University; Columbia College; Georgetown University; University of Rhode Island; Vassar College. Other: 1 entered a postgraduate year, 1 had other specific plans. Median SAT verbal: 570, median SAT math: 590.

Student Life Upper grades have specified standards of dress, student council. Discipline rests equally with students and faculty.

Tuition and Aid Day student tuition: $20,070. Tuition installment plan (Insured Tuition Payment Plan, Key Tuition Payment Plan, monthly payment plans). Need-based scholarship grants available. In 2005–06, 17% of upper-school students received aid. Total amount of financial aid awarded in 2005–06: $694,435.

Admissions Traditional secondary-level entrance grade is 9. For fall 2005, 174 students applied for upper-level admission, 64 were accepted, 31 enrolled. ISEE or SSAT required. Deadline for receipt of application materials: January 27. Application fee required: $50. On-campus interview required.

Athletics Interscholastic: baseball (boys), basketball (b,g), cross-country running (b,g), field hockey (g), football (b), ice hockey (b,g), lacrosse (b,g), soccer (b,g), softball (g), tennis (b,g), track and field (b,g), winter (indoor) track (b,g); intramural: field hockey (g), lacrosse (b,g), soccer (b,g), tennis (g), weight training (b,g); coed interscholastic: golf, sailing, squash; coed intramural: fencing, rock climbing. 7 PE instructors, 43 coaches, 1 trainer.

Computers Computers are regularly used in mathematics, science classes. Computer network features include on-campus library services, CD-ROMs, Internet access.

Contact Jeanette Epstein, Director of Admission. 401-421-8100. Fax: 401-751-7674. E-mail: wheeler@ids.net. Web site: www.wheelerschool.org.

ANNOUNCEMENT FROM THE SCHOOL The Wheeler School, established in 1889, is an N–12, coed, independent day school. The main campus houses all academic and administrative buildings, a field house, and a playground. Wheeler maintains a conference center, athletics fields, tennis courts, and a basketball court field house on 120 acres nearby.

WHITEFIELD ACADEMY

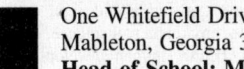

One Whitefield Drive
Mableton, Georgia 30126
Head of School: Mr. Timothy Hillen Jr.

General Information Coeducational day college-preparatory, arts, religious studies, and bilingual studies school, affiliated with Christian faith. Grades PK–12. Founded: 1996. Setting: suburban. Nearest major city is Atlanta. 78-acre campus. 2 buildings on campus. Approved or accredited by Association of Christian Schools International, Georgia Accrediting Commission, Southern Association of Colleges and Schools, and Georgia Department of Education. Member of Secondary School Admission Test Board. Total enrollment: 635. Upper school average class size: 18. Upper school faculty-student ratio: 1:10.

Upper School Student Profile Grade 9: 73 students (43 boys, 30 girls); Grade 10: 58 students (30 boys, 28 girls); Grade 11: 54 students (32 boys, 22 girls); Grade 12: 51 students (22 boys, 29 girls). 100% of students are Christian faith.

Faculty School total: 65. In upper school: 13 men, 18 women; 7 have advanced degrees.

Subjects Offered Advanced Placement courses, algebra, American history, American literature, art, band, biology, calculus, chemistry, choral music, Christian studies, English, English literature, European history, geometry, health education, mathematics, orchestra, physical education, physics, pre-calculus, Spanish, world civilizations.

Graduation Requirements Algebra, American history, American literature, arts and fine arts (art, music, dance, drama), biology, British literature, chemistry, Christian studies, English, foreign language, geometry, health education, modern European history, physical fitness, physics, pre-calculus, public speaking, Western civilization. Community service is required.

Special Academic Programs Advanced Placement exam preparation in 8 subject areas; honors section; independent study.

College Placement 38 students graduated in 2005; all went to college, including Auburn University; Furman University; University of Georgia.

Student Life Upper grades have uniform requirement, student council, honor system. Discipline rests equally with students and faculty. Attendance at religious services is required.

Summer Programs Remediation, enrichment, sports programs offered; session focuses on skills improvement; held on campus; accepts boys and girls; open to students from other schools. 150 students usually enrolled.

Tuition and Aid Day student tuition: $15,000. Need-based financial assistance (through SSS application), PLEASE Loan Program, AchieverLoans, and PrepGATE Loans available.

Admissions Traditional secondary-level entrance grade is 9. SSAT required. Deadline for receipt of application materials: February 14. Application fee required: $65. On-campus interview required.

Athletics Interscholastic: baseball (boys), basketball (b,g), cheering (g), cross-country running (b,g), football (b), golf (b), physical fitness (b,g), soccer (b,g), softball (g), strength & conditioning (b), tennis (b,g), track and field (b,g), volleyball (g), weight lifting (b), wrestling (b); coed interscholastic: cross-country running, physical fitness, tennis, track and field; coed intramural: golf. 2 PE instructors, 5 coaches, 1 trainer.

Computers Computer network features include on-campus library services, CD-ROMs, online commercial services, Internet access, DVD, wireless campus network.

Contact Mrs. Linda J. Simpson, Admission Director. 678-305-3027. Fax: 678-305-3010. E-mail: lindas@whitefieldacademy.com.

THE WHITE MOUNTAIN SCHOOL

West Farm Road
Bethlehem, New Hampshire 03574
Head of School: Alan Popp

petersons.com

General Information Coeducational boarding and day college-preparatory, arts, and sustainability studies school, affiliated with Episcopal Church. Grades 9–PG. Founded: 1886. Setting: rural. Nearest major city is Concord. Students are housed in single-sex dormitories. 250-acre campus. 13 buildings on campus. Approved or accredited by National Association of Episcopal Schools, New England Association of Schools and Colleges, The Association of Boarding Schools, and New Hampshire Department of Education. Member of National Association of Independent Schools and Secondary School Admission Test Board. Endowment: $1 million. Total enrollment: 108. Upper school average class size: 8. Upper school faculty-student ratio: 1:4.

Upper School Student Profile Grade 9: 13 students (7 boys, 6 girls); Grade 10: 27 students (17 boys, 10 girls); Grade 11: 30 students (19 boys, 11 girls); Grade 12: 38 students (20 boys, 18 girls). 85% of students are boarding students. 25% are state residents. 22 states are represented in upper school student body. 10% are international students. International students from Austria, Germany, India, Japan, Kenya, and Saint Lucia; 3 other countries represented in student body. 5% of students are members of Episcopal Church.

Faculty School total: 36. In upper school: 19 men, 17 women; 13 have advanced degrees; 29 reside on campus.

Subjects Offered Algebra, American literature, American studies, biology, calculus, Caribbean history, ceramics, chemistry, Chinese history, college counseling, community garden, community service, creative writing, drawing and design, earth science, economics, English, environmental education, environmental science, environmental studies, ESL, ethics, French, geometry, health, human development, independent study, Japanese history, jazz theory, learning strategies, literature, Middle Eastern history, music history, painting, philosophy, photography, physics, physiology-anatomy, pre-calculus, printmaking, senior project, social justice, Spanish, studio art, theater arts, theater production, U.S. history, Vietnam, world history, writing.

Graduation Requirements Algebra, American history, arts and fine arts (art, music, dance, drama), English, geometry, health, literature, non-Western societies, physical science, theology, Western civilization, writing, wilderness skills and outdoor learning expeditions, sustainability studies, residential curriculum. Community service is required.

Special Academic Programs Honors section; independent study; term-away projects; academic accommodation for the gifted and the artistically talented; remedial reading and/or remedial writing; remedial math; programs in English, mathematics, general development for dyslexic students; special instructional classes for students with dysgraphia and other learning differences; ESL.

College Placement 28 students graduated in 2005; 22 went to college, including Eckerd College; Eugene Lang College The New School for Liberal Arts; Hampshire College; Temple University; University of Colorado at Boulder; University of Pittsburgh. Other: 6 had other specific plans. 10% scored over 600 on SAT verbal, 24% scored over 600 on SAT math.

Student Life Upper grades have specified standards of dress, student council, honor system. Discipline rests primarily with faculty.

Tuition and Aid Day student tuition: $15,300; 7-day tuition and room/board: $35,500. Tuition installment plan (Insured Tuition Payment Plan, Academic Management Services Plan, 2-payment plan). Merit scholarship grants, need-based

scholarship grants available. In 2005–06, 37% of upper-school students received aid. Total amount of financial aid awarded in 2005–06: $828,600.

Admissions Traditional secondary-level entrance grade is 10. For fall 2005, 144 students applied for upper-level admission, 90 were accepted, 63 enrolled. TOEFL or SLEP, WISC III or other aptitude measures; standardized achievement test or writing sample required. Deadline for receipt of application materials: none. Application fee required: $50. Interview required.

Athletics Interscholastic: lacrosse (boys, girls), soccer (b,g); intramural: dance (g); coed interscholastic: mountain biking; coed intramural: aerobics/nautilus, alpine skiing, back packing, bicycling, canoeing/kayaking, climbing, combined training, fitness, freestyle skiing, hiking/backpacking, kayaking, martial arts, mountain biking, mountaineering, nautilus, nordic skiing, outdoor activities, outdoor adventure, outdoor education, outdoor recreation, outdoor skills, outdoors, paddling, rappelling, rock climbing, running, skiing (cross-country), skiing (downhill), snowboarding, snowshoeing, squash, strength & conditioning, telemark skiing, tennis, ultimate Frisbee, wall climbing, wilderness, wilderness survival. 1 trainer.

Computers Computers are regularly used in college planning, foreign language, library skills, mathematics, yearbook classes. Computer network features include campus e-mail, on-campus library services, CD-ROMs, online commercial services, Internet access, office computer access, DVD, wireless campus network.

Contact Amy Broberg, Director of Admissions. 603-444-2928 Ext. 16. Fax: 603-444-5568. E-mail: amy.broberg@whitemountain.org. Web site: www.whitemountain.org.

ANNOUNCEMENT FROM THE SCHOOL Small school. Big outdoors. More than 100 students and 29 faculty members engage in a traditional college-preparatory program. Outdoor sports include backpacking, rock climbing, biking, paddling, skiing, and snow boarding. The 250-acre campus borders a 600,000-acre national forest. Art, music, theater, and international community service are integral parts of the School's program.

See full description on page 1138.

WHITE ROCK CHRISTIAN ACADEMY

2265 152nd Street
Surrey, British Columbia V4A 4P1, Canada
Head of School: Mrs. Lorna J. Baerg

General Information Coeducational day college-preparatory school, affiliated with Christian faith. Grades K–12. Founded: 1981. Setting: urban. Nearest major city is Vancouver, Canada. 5-acre campus. 1 building on campus. Approved or accredited by British Columbia Department of Education. Language of instruction: English. Total enrollment: 308. Upper school average class size: 25. Upper school faculty-student ratio: 1:12.

Upper School Student Profile Grade 9: 26 students (14 boys, 12 girls); Grade 10: 30 students (10 boys, 20 girls); Grade 11: 18 students (13 boys, 5 girls); Grade 12: 19 students (9 boys, 10 girls). 90% of students are Christian faith.

Faculty School total: 24. In upper school: 4 men, 5 women.

Subjects Offered Art, band, Bible, biology, calculus, career and personal planning, character education, chemistry, choir, choral music, Christian education, Christian ethics, computer applications, computer keyboarding, computer literacy, computer processing, computer-aided design, concert band, concert choir, English, English literature, fitness, French, French as a second language, geography, history, jazz band, jazz ensemble, math applications, mathematics, music, physics, science, social studies, vocal ensemble, vocal jazz.

Graduation Requirements British Columbia Ministry of Education requirements.

Special Academic Programs Special instructional classes for students with learning disabilities.

College Placement 17 students graduated in 2005; 7 went to college, including Simon Fraser University; The University of British Columbia; Trinity Western University. Other: 10 went to work.

Student Life Upper grades have uniform requirement, student council, honor system. Discipline rests primarily with faculty. Attendance at religious services is required.

Tuition and Aid Day student tuition: CAN$3500. Tuition installment plan (monthly payment plans). Tuition reduction for siblings available. In 2005–06, 3% of upper-school students received aid.

Admissions Traditional secondary-level entrance grade is 9. For fall 2005, 100 students applied for upper-level admission, 94 were accepted, 94 enrolled. 3-R Achievement Test required. Deadline for receipt of application materials: June 15. Application fee required: CAN$50. On-campus interview required.

Athletics Interscholastic: basketball (boys), cheering (b,g), floor hockey (b,g), lacrosse (b,g), physical fitness (b,g), soccer (b), softball (b,g), volleyball (g); intramural: soccer (b), volleyball (g); coed interscholastic: cross-country running; coed intramural: ball hockey. 2 PE instructors, 2 coaches.

Computers Computer resources include on-campus library services, Internet access.

Contact Admissions. 604-531-9186. Fax: 604-531-1727. E-mail: wrca@wrca.bc.ca. Web site: www.wrca.bc.ca.

WHITFIELD SCHOOL

175 South Mason Road
St. Louis, Missouri 63141
Head of School: Mr. Mark Anderson

General Information Coeducational day college-preparatory school. Grades 6–12. Founded: 1952. Setting: suburban. 25-acre campus. 3 buildings on campus. Approved or accredited by Independent Schools Association of the Central States. Member of National Association of Independent Schools. Endowment: $5 million. Total enrollment: 470. Upper school average class size: 12. Upper school faculty-student ratio: 1:8.

Upper School Student Profile Grade 6: 32 students (21 boys, 11 girls); Grade 7: 70 students (40 boys, 30 girls); Grade 8: 76 students (47 boys, 29 girls); Grade 9: 76 students (28 boys, 48 girls); Grade 10: 72 students (40 boys, 32 girls); Grade 11: 70 students (33 boys, 37 girls); Grade 12: 74 students (32 boys, 42 girls).

Faculty School total: 68. In upper school: 24 men, 44 women; 34 have advanced degrees.

Subjects Offered Advanced chemistry, algebra, American history, American literature, art, biochemistry, biology, calculus, calculus-AP, ceramics, chemistry, chemistry-AP, choir, college counseling, college placement, college planning, community service, concert band, DNA, earth science, English, European history, fine arts, French, French-AP, geometry, German, German-AP, health, history, junior and senior seminars, Latin, mathematics, modern world history, music, painting, photography, physical education, physics, pre-algebra, pre-calculus, science, senior internship, social studies, Spanish, Spanish-AP, symphonic band, theater, trigonometry, visual and performing arts, Western civilization, world cultures, world history, world literature.

Graduation Requirements Arts and fine arts (art, music, dance, drama), English, foreign language, mathematics, physical education (includes health), science, social studies (includes history), sophomore, junior and senior seminars.

Special Academic Programs Advanced Placement exam preparation in 7 subject areas; honors section; independent study; academic accommodation for the gifted, the musically talented, and the artistically talented.

College Placement 68 students graduated in 2005; all went to college, including Davidson College; Elon University; Southern Methodist University; Texas Christian University; University of Missouri–Columbia; University of San Diego. Mean SAT verbal: 620, mean SAT math: 610, mean composite ACT: 27.

Student Life Upper grades have specified standards of dress, student council, honor system. Discipline rests primarily with faculty.

Summer Programs Sports, art/fine arts, computer instruction programs offered; session focuses on recreational and athletic programs; held on campus; accepts boys and girls; open to students from other schools. 150 students usually enrolled. 2006 schedule: June 12 to August 4. Application deadline: June 1.

Tuition and Aid Day student tuition: $17,725. Tuition installment plan (Insured Tuition Payment Plan, Key Tuition Payment Plan, monthly payment plans, 1-, 2-, and 10-payment plans). Need-based scholarship grants available. In 2005–06, 11% of upper-school students received aid. Total amount of financial aid awarded in 2005–06: $756,000.

Admissions Traditional secondary-level entrance grade is 7. For fall 2005, 188 students applied for upper-level admission, 127 were accepted, 90 enrolled. School's own exam required. Deadline for receipt of application materials: January 15. Application fee required: $60. On-campus interview required.

Athletics Interscholastic: baseball (boys), basketball (b,g), cheering (g), cross-country running (b,g), dance squad (g), field hockey (g), lacrosse (g), soccer (b,g), track and field (b,g), volleyball (g), wrestling (b); intramural: basketball (b,g), cheering (g), cross-country running (b,g), dance squad (g), field hockey (g), soccer (b,g), volleyball (g), wrestling (b); coed interscholastic: golf, ice hockey, tennis; coed intramural: baseball, ice hockey. 3 PE instructors, 9 coaches, 2 trainers.

Computers Computers are regularly used in all classes. Computer network features include campus e-mail, on-campus library services, CD-ROMs, online commercial services, Internet access, file transfer, DVD, wireless campus network, off-campus library and database searches, limited IBM ThinkPad laptop program.

Contact Ms. Cynthia Crum Alverson, Director of Admission and College Counseling. 314-434-5141. Fax: 314-434-6193. E-mail: cyndy.alverson@whitfieldschool.org. Web site: www.whitfieldschool.org.

ANNOUNCEMENT FROM THE SCHOOL Whitfield School's demanding academic program challenges students while teaching them to work both independently and collaboratively. Technological media enhance thinking, reading, and writing skills, while the demanding academic program and the support of a dedicated faculty prepare graduates for college and life beyond. With an average class size of 12 and a School size of 475 in grades 6–12, Whitfield seeks to develop and maintain a community that values mutual respect and personal responsibility. Students are encouraged to take part in activities that include visual and performing arts, community service, and 42 athletic teams, clubs, and organizations. Tuition: $17,725. Financial aid is available. Cynthia Crum Alverson is Admission Director and Mark J. Anderson is President.

WHITTIER CHRISTIAN HIGH SCHOOL

501 North Beach Boulevard
La Habra, California 90631
Head of School: Robert D. Brown

General Information Coeducational day college-preparatory, general academic, and religious studies school, affiliated with Christian faith. Grades 9–12. Founded: 1958. Setting: suburban. Nearest major city is Los Angeles. 19-acre campus. 10 buildings on campus. Approved or accredited by Association of Christian Schools International and Western Association of Schools and Colleges. Endowment: $200,000. Total enrollment: 585. Upper school average class size: 21. Upper school faculty-student ratio: 1:10.

Upper School Student Profile Grade 9: 171 students (84 boys, 87 girls); Grade 10: 149 students (73 boys, 76 girls); Grade 11: 144 students (74 boys, 70 girls); Grade 12: 121 students (46 boys, 75 girls). 95% of students are Christian.

Faculty School total: 42. In upper school: 20 men, 22 women; 20 have advanced degrees.

Subjects Offered Accounting, Advanced Placement courses, advanced studio art-AP, algebra, American history, American literature, art, arts, band, biology, business, business law, business skills, calculus, chemistry, chorus, Christian doctrine, Christian scripture, Christianity, community service, computer applications, computer education, computer keyboarding, computer science, computer skills, dance, drama, driver education, economics, English, English literature, fine arts, French, geography, geometry, German, government/civics, grammar, graphic arts, home economics, mathematics, music, photography, physical education, physics, physiology, publications, religion, science, social science, social studies, Spanish, speech, statistics, theater, trigonometry, Web site design, world literature.

Graduation Requirements Arts and fine arts (art, music, dance, drama), business skills (includes word processing), English, first aid, foreign language, mathematics, physical education (includes health), religion (includes Bible studies and theology), science, social science, social studies (includes history), speech, Bible class during each semester of attendance. Community service is required.

Special Academic Programs Advanced Placement exam preparation in 5 subject areas; honors section; study at local college for college credit; academic accommodation for the gifted, the musically talented, and the artistically talented; remedial reading and/or remedial writing; programs in general development for dyslexic students; special instructional classes for students with learning disabilities and Attention Deficit Disorder; ESL (40 students enrolled).

College Placement 98 students graduated in 2005; 92 went to college, including Azusa Pacific University; Biola University; California State University, Fullerton; California State University, Long Beach; Fullerton College; University of California, Irvine. Other: 5 went to work, 1 entered military service. Mean SAT verbal: 524, mean SAT math: 536. 26% scored over 600 on SAT verbal, 29% scored over 600 on SAT math.

Student Life Upper grades have specified standards of dress, student council. Discipline rests primarily with faculty. Attendance at religious services is required.

Summer Programs Remediation, advancement, ESL, art/fine arts, computer instruction programs offered; session focuses on advancement and make-up courses; held on campus; accepts boys and girls; open to students from other schools. 300 students usually enrolled. 2006 schedule: June 19 to July 28. Application deadline: June 19.

Tuition and Aid Day student tuition: $7300. Tuition installment plan (monthly payment plans, full-payment and 2-payment discount plans). Merit scholarship grants, need-based scholarship grants available. In 2005–06, 20% of upper-school students received aid; total upper-school merit-scholarship money awarded: $8000. Total amount of financial aid awarded in 2005–06: $265,000.

Admissions Traditional secondary-level entrance grade is 9. For fall 2005, 205 students applied for upper-level admission, 180 were accepted, 171 enrolled. ACT-Explore, SLEP or TOEFL required. Deadline for receipt of application materials: none. Application fee required: $50. On-campus interview required.

Athletics Interscholastic: baseball (boys), basketball (b,g), cross-country running (b,g), dance squad (g), football (b), golf (b), soccer (b,g), softball (g), tennis (b,g), track and field (b,g), volleyball (b,g), weight training (b,g), wrestling (b). 2 PE instructors, 29 coaches, 1 trainer.

Computers Computers are regularly used in business skills, English, foreign language, graphic arts, keyboarding, mathematics, publications, science, yearbook classes. Computer network features include campus e-mail, on-campus library services, CD-ROMs, Internet access, DVD, wireless campus network.

Contact Steve Benke, Director of Admission. 562-694-3803. Fax: 562-697-1673. E-mail: sbenke@wchs.com. Web site: www.wchs.com.

WICHITA COLLEGIATE SCHOOL

9115 East 13th Street
Wichita, Kansas 67206
Head of School: Mr. Jonathan Eades

General Information Coeducational day college-preparatory, arts, and technology school. Grades PS–12. Founded: 1963. Setting: urban. 42-acre campus. 1 building on campus. Approved or accredited by Independent Schools Association of the

Southwest. Member of National Association of Independent Schools. Endowment: $1.5 million. Total enrollment: 964. Upper school average class size: 15. Upper school faculty-ratio: 1:15.

Upper School Student Profile Grade 9: 61 students (31 boys, 30 girls); Grade 10: 66 students (32 boys, 34 girls); Grade 11: 70 students (36 boys, 34 girls); Grade 12: 71 students (40 boys, 31 girls).

Faculty School total: 99. In upper school: 10 men, 13 women; 18 have advanced degrees.

Subjects Offered Algebra, American history, American literature, art, biology, calculus, chemistry, computer programming, computer science, drama, economics, English, English literature, European history, fine arts, French, geometry, government/civics, history, humanities, journalism, Latin, mathematics, medieval/Renaissance history, music, photography, physical education, physics, science, social studies, Spanish, statistics, theater, trigonometry, video, video film production, world history, world literature, writing, yearbook.

Graduation Requirements Arts and fine arts (art, music, dance, drama), computer science, economics, English, foreign language, humanities, mathematics, physical education (includes health), science, social studies (includes history).

Special Academic Programs Advanced Placement exam preparation in 17 subject areas; study at local college for college credit; academic accommodation for the gifted.

College Placement 79 students graduated in 2005; all went to college, including Georgetown University; Southern Methodist University; University of Kansas; University of Pennsylvania; University of Tulsa. Median SAT verbal: 630, median SAT math: 620, median composite ACT: 26. 56% scored over 600 on SAT verbal, 75% scored over 600 on SAT math, 56% scored over 26 on composite ACT.

Student Life Upper grades have specified standards of dress, student council, honor system. Discipline rests equally with students and faculty.

Summer Programs Remediation, enrichment, sports, art/fine arts, computer instruction programs offered; held on campus; accepts boys and girls; open to students from other schools. 700 students usually enrolled. 2006 schedule: June 13 to July 29. Application deadline: none.

Tuition and Aid Day student tuition: $10,995. Tuition installment plan (monthly payment plans, individually arranged payment plans, 3-payment plan). Need-based scholarship grants available. In 2005–06, 23% of upper-school students received aid. Total amount of financial aid awarded in 2005–06: $327,347.

Admissions Traditional secondary-level entrance grade is 9. For fall 2005, 31 students applied for upper-level admission, 22 were accepted, 20 enrolled. Otis-Lennon, Stanford Achievement Test required. Deadline for receipt of application materials: none. Application fee required: $35. Interview recommended.

Athletics Interscholastic: baseball (boys), basketball (b,g), cheering (b,g), cross-country running (b,g), dance team (b,g), football (b), golf (b), softball (g), strength & conditioning (b,g), tennis (b,g), track and field (b,g), volleyball (g); coed interscholastic: bowling, cross-country running, track and field. 2 PE instructors, 1 coach, 1 trainer.

Computers Computers are regularly used in all classes. Computer network features include campus e-mail, on-campus library services, CD-ROMs, Internet access, file transfer, DVD, wireless campus network.

Contact Ms. Susie Steed, Director of Admission and Communication. 316-634-0433 Ext. 203. Fax: 316-634-0598. E-mail: ssteed@wcsks.com. Web site: www.wcsks.com.

ANNOUNCEMENT FROM THE SCHOOL Wichita Collegiate School is a student-centered, coeducational, college-preparatory day school for age 2 through grade 12. The School offers individual attention in small classes, a dynamic faculty, strong academics, and opportunities to participate in cocurricular programs in the arts, athletics, debate, and other areas for a balanced educational experience. WCS is accredited by ISAS and is a member of NAIS. More information may be obtained on the World Wide Web (http://www.wcsks.com).

WILBRAHAM & MONSON ACADEMY

423 Main Street
Wilbraham, Massachusetts 01095
Head of School: Rodney LaBrecque

General Information Coeducational boarding and day college-preparatory, arts, business, and technology school. Boarding grades 9–PG, day grades 6–PG. Founded: 1804. Setting: suburban. Nearest major city is Springfield. Students are housed in single-sex by floor dormitories and single-sex dormitories. 300-acre campus. 24 buildings on campus. Approved or accredited by Association of Independent Schools in New England, New England Association of Schools and Colleges, The Association of Boarding Schools, and Massachusetts Department of Education. Member of National Association of Independent Schools and Secondary School Admission Test Board. Endowment: $4.2 million. Total enrollment: 315. Upper school average class size: 14. Upper school faculty-student ratio: 1:7.

Upper School Student Profile Grade 9: 41 students (25 boys, 16 girls); Grade 10: 68 students (38 boys, 30 girls); Grade 11: 67 students (41 boys, 26 girls); Grade 12: 79 students (51 boys, 28 girls); Postgraduate: 13 students (13 boys). 49% of students are boarding students. 61% are state residents. 11 states are represented in upper school

student body. 24% are international students. International students from Germany, Japan, Republic of Korea, Russian Federation, Taiwan, and Thailand; 10 other countries represented in student body.

Faculty School total: 52. In upper school: 25 men, 22 women; 28 have advanced degrees; 41 reside on campus.

Subjects Offered Advanced Placement courses, algebra, American history, American literature, art, art history, biology, biology-AP, bookmaking, calculus, calculus-AP, ceramics, chemistry, chemistry-AP, college admission preparation, computer programming, computer science, computer-aided design, conceptual physics, creative writing, critical studies in film, decision making skills, desktop publishing, drama, driver education, economics, economics-AP, English, English literature, English-AP, entrepreneurship, environmental science, environmental science-AP, ESL, ethical decision making, European history, European history-AP, finance, fine arts, French, French-AP, geometry, global studies, honors algebra, honors geometry, honors U.S. history, honors world history, humanities, instrumental music, instruments, Internet research, Irish literature, Latin, Latin-AP, leadership training, mathematics, modern European history, modern European history-AP, music-AP, painting, performing arts, personal finance, photography, physical education, physics, play/screen writing, poetry, pre-algebra, pre-calculus, pre-college orientation, probability and statistics, public speaking, research and reference, SAT preparation, science, sculpture, Shakespeare, short story, social studies, sociology, Spanish, Spanish-AP, statistics-AP, studio art, studio art-AP, the Web, theater, U.S. history, U.S. history-AP, Vietnam War, visual arts, vocal ensemble, Web site design, world history, world literature, writing, writing workshop.

Graduation Requirements Algebra, American history, arts and fine arts (art, music, dance, drama), English, foreign language, geometry, lab science, physical education (includes health).

Special Academic Programs Advanced Placement exam preparation in 18 subject areas; honors section; independent study; study abroad; academic accommodation for the musically talented and the artistically talented; ESL (17 students enrolled).

College Placement 84 students graduated in 2005; 83 went to college, including Babson College; Clark University; Roger Williams University; Smith College.

Student Life Upper grades have specified standards of dress, student council, honor system. Discipline rests equally with students and faculty.

Tuition and Aid Day student tuition: $22,250; 7-day tuition and room/board: $34,600. Tuition installment plan (The Tuition Plan, Academic Management Services Plan, monthly payment plans, Tuition Management Systems Plan, Key Bank). Merit scholarship grants, need-based scholarship grants, need-based loans available. In 2005–06, 41% of upper-school students received aid; total upper-school merit-scholarship money awarded: $258,000. Total amount of financial aid awarded in 2005–06: $1,498,433.

Admissions Traditional secondary-level entrance grade is 9. For fall 2005, 392 students applied for upper-level admission, 225 were accepted, 103 enrolled. PSAT or SAT for applicants to grade 11 and 12, SSAT, TOEFL or Wechsler Intelligence Scale for Children III required. Deadline for receipt of application materials: February 1. Application fee required: $50. Interview required.

Athletics Interscholastic: baseball (boys), basketball (b,g), cross-country running (b,g), field hockey (g), football (b), independent competitive sports (b,g), lacrosse (b,g), soccer (b,g), softball (g), swimming and diving (b,g), tennis (b,g), track and field (b,g), volleyball (g), wrestling (b); intramural: basketball (b,g); coed interscholastic: alpine skiing, dance, golf, independent competitive sports, modern dance, riflery, skiing (downhill), water polo, winter (indoor) track; coed intramural: aerobics, aerobics/dance, aerobics/nautilus, back packing, canoeing/kayaking, climbing, fitness, hiking/backpacking, jogging, kayaking, life saving, outdoor adventure, physical fitness, rock climbing, running, snowboarding, strength & conditioning, tai chi, tennis, weight lifting, weight training, yoga. 11 coaches.

Computers Computers are regularly used in architecture, art, college planning, drawing and design, English, graphic design, library skills, literary magazine, mathematics, music, newspaper, research skills, science, Web site design, yearbook classes. Computer network features include campus e-mail, on-campus library services, CD-ROMs, online commercial services, Internet access, file transfer, office computer access, DVD.

Contact Christopher Moore, Director of Admission and Financial Aid. 413-596-6811 Ext. 109. Fax: 413-599-1749. E-mail: cmoore@wmanet.org. Web site: WMAcademy.org.

See full description on page 1140.

WILDWOOD CATHOLIC HIGH SCHOOL

1500 Central Avenue
North Wildwood, New Jersey 08260
Head of School: Mr. Richard John Turco

General Information Coeducational day college-preparatory school, affiliated with Roman Catholic Church. Grades 9–12. Founded: 1948. Setting: small town. Nearest major city is Philadelphia, PA. 2-acre campus. 1 building on campus. Approved or accredited by Middle States Association of Colleges and Schools and New Jersey Department of Education. Total enrollment: 316. Upper school average class size: 18. Upper school faculty-student ratio: 1:20.

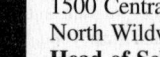

Upper School Student Profile Grade 9: 69 students (30 boys, 39 girls); Grade 10: 83 students (43 boys, 40 girls); Grade 11: 96 students (50 boys, 46 girls); Grade 12: 68 students (38 boys, 30 girls). 80% of students are Roman Catholic.

Faculty School total: 23. In upper school: 14 men, 9 women; 10 have advanced degrees.

Special Academic Programs Advanced Placement exam preparation in 5 subject areas; honors section.

College Placement 82 students graduated in 2005; 80 went to college, including Seton Hall University. Other: 2 went to work.

Student Life Upper grades have uniform requirement, student council. Discipline rests primarily with faculty. Attendance at religious services is required.

Tuition and Aid Day student tuition: $4995. Tuition installment plan (The Tuition Plan, SMART Tuition Payment Plan). Financial aid available to upper-school students. In 2005–06, 20% of upper-school students received aid.

Admissions Traditional secondary-level entrance grade is 9. For fall 2005, 96 students applied for upper-level admission, 93 were accepted, 69 enrolled. Deadline for receipt of application materials: April 5. Application fee required: $175. Interview required.

Athletics Interscholastic: ball hockey (girls), baseball (b), basketball (b,g), cross-country running (b,g), field hockey (g), softball (g), swimming and diving (b,g), tennis (b,g); coed interscholastic: golf, running, surfing, track and field. 1 PE instructor, 30 coaches.

Computers Computer network features include CD-ROMs, Internet access, DVD.

Contact Mr. Richard John Turco, Principal. 609-522-7257. Fax: 609-522-7214. E-mail: richard.turco@verizon.net.

WILLIAM PENN CHARTER SCHOOL

3000 West School House Lane
Philadelphia, Pennsylvania 19144
Head of School: Earl J. Ball

General Information Coeducational day college-preparatory school, affiliated with Society of Friends. Grades K–12. Founded: 1689. Setting: urban. 44-acre campus. 5 buildings on campus. Approved or accredited by Middle States Association of Colleges and Schools and Pennsylvania Association of Private Academic Schools. Member of National Association of Independent Schools. Endowment: $44 million. Total enrollment: 896. Upper school average class size: 15. Upper school faculty-student ratio: 1:9.

Upper School Student Profile Grade 9: 111 students (66 boys, 45 girls); Grade 10: 109 students (70 boys, 39 girls); Grade 11: 105 students (62 boys, 43 girls); Grade 12: 96 students (50 boys, 46 girls). 3% of students are members of Society of Friends.

Faculty School total: 131. In upper school: 38 men, 26 women; 57 have advanced degrees.

Subjects Offered Algebra, American history, American literature, architectural drawing, art, art history-AP, Asian studies, band, Bible studies, bioethics, biology, biology-AP, botany, British literature, calculus, calculus-AP, calligraphy, ceramics, chemistry, chemistry-AP, choral music, chorus, college counseling, computer math, computer programming, computer science, creative writing, design, drama, drawing, earth science, Eastern religion and philosophy, ecology, economics, electronic music, English, English literature, environmental science, environmental science-AP, ethics, European history, European history-AP, film, filmmaking, fine arts, French, French-AP, genetics, geology, geometry, government and politics-AP, health, Hebrew scripture, history, history of rock and roll, history of science, human anatomy, independent study, Irish literature, jazz band, junior and senior seminars, Latin, learning cognition classes, learning strategies, marine biology, mathematics, Middle East, model United Nations, modern European history-AP, music, music performance, oceanography, organic chemistry, painting, peace and justice, photography, physical education, physics, physics-AP, pottery, pre-calculus, public speaking, Quakerism and ethics, religion, science, sculpture, senior project, service learning/internship, Shakespeare, social studies, Spanish, Spanish-AP, speech, statistics-AP, symphonic band, theater, theater arts, theater design and production, theater production, trigonometry, U.S. history-AP, United States government-AP, video, visual and performing arts, world history, world literature, world religions, writing.

Graduation Requirements Computer science, English, foreign language, mathematics, music, physical education (includes health), religious studies, science, social studies (includes history), theater, visual arts.

Special Academic Programs Advanced Placement exam preparation in 14 subject areas; honors section; independent study; study at local college for college credit; academic accommodation for the gifted, the musically talented, and the artistically talented.

College Placement 101 students graduated in 2005; 100 went to college, including Brown University; Princeton University; The George Washington University; The Pennsylvania State University University Park Campus; Tufts University; University of Pennsylvania. Mean SAT verbal: 658, mean SAT math: 650. 88% scored over 600 on SAT verbal, 71% scored over 600 on SAT math.

Student Life Upper grades have specified standards of dress, student council, honor system. Discipline rests primarily with faculty. Attendance at religious services is required.

Tuition and Aid Day student tuition: $19,400. Tuition installment plan (Academic Management Services Plan, Key Tuition Payment Plan). Need-based scholarship grants available. In 2005–06, 28% of upper-school students received aid. Total amount of financial aid awarded in 2005–06: $1,369,200.

Admissions Traditional secondary-level entrance grade is 9. For fall 2005, 246 students applied for upper-level admission, 84 were accepted, 49 enrolled. ISEE or SSAT required. Deadline for receipt of application materials: none. Application fee required: $30. On-campus interview required.

Athletics Interscholastic: baseball (boys), basketball (b,g), cross-country running (b,g), diving (b,g), field hockey (g), football (b), golf (b,g), lacrosse (b,g), soccer (b,g), softball (g), squash (b,g), swimming and diving (b,g), tennis (b,g), track and field (b,g), water polo (b,g), wrestling (b); intramural: basketball (b,g). 7 PE instructors, 40 coaches, 2 trainers.

Computers Computers are regularly used in all academic classes. Computer network features include campus e-mail, on-campus library services, CD-ROMs, online commercial services, Internet access, file transfer, DVD, wireless campus network.

Contact Stephen A. Bonnie, Director of Admissions. 215-844-3460. Fax: 215-844-5537. E-mail: sbonnie@penncharter.com. Web site: www.penncharter.com.

THE WILLIAMS SCHOOL

182 Mohegan Avenue
New London, Connecticut 06320-4110
Head of School: Charlotte Rea

General Information Coeducational day college-preparatory school. Grades 7–12. Founded: 1891. Setting: small town. Nearest major city is Providence, RI. 25-acre campus. 1 building on campus. Approved or accredited by Connecticut Association of Independent Schools, New England Association of Schools and Colleges, The College Board, and Connecticut Department of Education. Member of National Association of Independent Schools and Secondary School Admission Test Board. Endowment: $3 million. Total enrollment: 321. Upper school average class size: 15. Upper school faculty-student ratio: 1:8.

Upper School Student Profile Grade 9: 62 students (27 boys, 35 girls); Grade 10: 68 students (36 boys, 32 girls); Grade 11: 53 students (29 boys, 24 girls); Grade 12: 56 students (32 boys, 24 girls).

Faculty School total: 36. In upper school: 16 men, 20 women; 30 have advanced degrees.

Subjects Offered Algebra, American history, art, art-AP, band, biology, biology-AP, calculus, calculus-AP, chemistry, chemistry-AP, Chinese history, chorus, dance, digital art, drama, earth science, economics, English, English literature, English-AP, European history, expository writing, fine arts, French, French-AP, geography, geometry, Greek, history, Japanese history, jazz, Latin-AP, mathematics, modern European history, music, music composition, music history, physical education, physics, physics-AP, pre-calculus, Russian history, science, social studies, Spanish, Spanish-AP, theater, trigonometry, world history, world literature.

Graduation Requirements Arts and fine arts (art, music, dance, drama), English, foreign language, mathematics, physical education (includes health), science, senior project, social studies (includes history).

Special Academic Programs Advanced Placement exam preparation in 7 subject areas; honors section; independent study; study at local college for college credit.

College Placement 55 students graduated in 2005; all went to college, including Boston University; Cornell University; Northeastern University; University of Colorado at Boulder; University of Vermont; Yale University. Mean SAT verbal: 625, mean SAT math: 625.

Student Life Upper grades have specified standards of dress, student council, honor system. Discipline rests primarily with faculty.

Summer Programs Sports programs offered; session focuses on lacrosse; held on campus; accepts boys and girls; open to students from other schools.

Tuition and Aid Day student tuition: $19,000. Tuition installment plan (Insured Tuition Payment Plan, FACTS Tuition Payment Plan, monthly payment plans, individually arranged payment plans). Need-based scholarship grants available. In 2005–06, 20% of upper-school students received aid. Total amount of financial aid awarded in 2005–06: $800,000.

Admissions Traditional secondary-level entrance grade is 9. SSAT required. Deadline for receipt of application materials: February 2. Application fee required: $50. On-campus interview required.

Athletics Interscholastic: baseball (boys), basketball (b,g), cross-country running (b,g), diving (b,g), field hockey (g), indoor soccer (b,g), lacrosse (b,g), sailing (b,g), soccer (b,g), softball (g), swimming and diving (b,g), tennis (b,g); coed interscholastic: cross-country running, golf, sailing, swimming and diving; coed intramural: fishing, golf. 2 PE instructors, 6 coaches, 1 trainer.

Computers Computers are regularly used in English, foreign language, history, mathematics, music, science classes. Computer network features include campus e-mail, on-campus library services, CD-ROMs, online commercial services, Internet access.

Contact Beatrice Fratoni, Admission Office Counselor. 860-439-2756. Fax: 860-439-2796. E-mail: bfratoni@williamsschool.org. Web site: www.williamsschool.org.

See full description on page 1142.

THE WILLISTON NORTHAMPTON SCHOOL

19 Payson Avenue
Easthampton, Massachusetts 01027
Head of School: Dr. Brian R. Wright

General Information Coeducational boarding and day college-preparatory school. Boarding grades 9–PG, day grades 7–12. Founded: 1841. Setting: small town. Nearest major city is Northampton. Students are housed in single-sex dormitories. 125-acre campus. 57 buildings on campus. Approved or accredited by Association of Independent Schools in New England, New England Association of Schools and Colleges, and The Association of Boarding Schools. Member of National Association of Independent Schools and Secondary School Admission Test Board. Endowment: $33 million. Total enrollment: 568. Upper school average class size: 13. Upper school faculty-student ratio: 1:7.

Upper School Student Profile Grade 9: 93 students (47 boys, 46 girls); Grade 10: 126 students (60 boys, 66 girls); Grade 11: 120 students (62 boys, 58 girls); Grade 12: 149 students (72 boys, 77 girls); Postgraduate: 20 students (15 boys, 5 girls). 60% of students are boarding students. 48% are state residents. 26 states are represented in upper school student body. 10% are international students. International students from Bermuda, Hong Kong, Japan, Republic of Korea, Taiwan, and Thailand; 7 other countries represented in student body.

Faculty School total: 90. In upper school: 41 men, 40 women; 60 have advanced degrees; 59 reside on campus.

Subjects Offered African-American history, algebra, American history, American literature, animal behavior, art, art history, astronomy, Bible as literature, biology, biology-AP, calculus, calculus-AP, chemistry, chemistry-AP, China/Japan history, choral music, choreography, Christian and Hebrew scripture, comparative government and politics-AP, comparative politics, computer math, computer programming, computer science, computer science-AP, constitutional law, creative writing, dance, discrete mathematics, drama, earth science, economics, economics and history, economics-AP, English, English language-AP, English literature, English literature-AP, environmental science, ESL, ethics, European history, expository writing, fine arts, French, French language-AP, French literature-AP, French-AP, genetics, geography, geometry, global studies, government/civics, health, history, history of jazz, Holocaust studies, honors algebra, honors English, honors geometry, Islamic studies, Latin, Latin American history, Latin-AP, marine biology, mathematics, music, music theory, oceanography, organic biochemistry, organic chemistry, philosophy, photography, photojournalism, physics, physics-AP, play production, playwriting, poetry, psychology, psychology-AP, religion, religion and culture, Russian history, science, sculpture, social studies, Spanish, Spanish language-AP, Spanish literature-AP, statistics-AP, theater, theology, trigonometry, U.S. history-AP, world history, world literature, writing, writing workshop.

Graduation Requirements Arts and fine arts (art, music, dance, drama), English, foreign language, mathematics, philosophy, religion (includes Bible studies and theology), science, social studies (includes history).

Special Academic Programs Advanced Placement exam preparation in 12 subject areas; honors section; independent study; term-away projects; study at local college for college credit; study abroad; academic accommodation for the gifted, the musically talented, and the artistically talented; special instructional classes for deaf students; ESL (6 students enrolled).

College Placement 120 students graduated in 2005; all went to college, including Brown University; Carnegie Mellon University; Mount Holyoke College; Smith College; The George Washington University; Wesleyan University.

Student Life Upper grades have specified standards of dress, student council, honor system. Discipline rests equally with students and faculty.

Summer Programs Sports, art/fine arts programs offered; session focuses on sports camps and summer stock theater; held on campus; accepts boys and girls; open to students from other schools. 2006 schedule: June 19 to August 19.

Tuition and Aid Day student tuition: $24,500; 7-day tuition and room/board: $34,500. Tuition installment plan (Academic Management Services Plan, Key Tuition Payment Plan). Need-based scholarship grants, need-based loans available. In 2005–06, 42% of upper-school students received aid. Total amount of financial aid awarded in 2005–06: $4,000,000.

Admissions Traditional secondary-level entrance grade is 9. For fall 2005, 618 students applied for upper-level admission, 271 were accepted, 140 enrolled. PSAT or SAT for applicants to grade 11 and 12, SSAT or TOEFL required. Deadline for receipt of application materials: February 1. Application fee required: $40. Interview required.

Athletics Interscholastic: alpine skiing (boys, girls), baseball (b), basketball (b,g), cross-country running (b,g), field hockey (g), football (b), ice hockey (b,g), lacrosse (b,g), soccer (b,g), softball (g), squash (b,g), swimming and diving (b,g), tennis (b,g), track and field (b,g), volleyball (b), water polo (b,g), wrestling (b); coed interscholastic: dance, diving, golf; coed intramural: aerobics, aerobics/dance, crew, dance, equestrian sports, fitness, fly fishing, Frisbee, horseback riding, judo, martial arts, modern dance, mountain biking, snowboarding, yoga. 1 PE instructor, 5 coaches, 2 trainers.

Computers Computers are regularly used in college planning, geography, graphic design, history, library, mathematics, newspaper, photography, photojournalism, programming, science, yearbook classes. Computer network features include campus e-mail, on-campus library services, CD-ROMs, online commercial services, Internet access, file transfer, office computer access, DVD, wireless campus network.

Contact Ann C. Pickrell, Director of Admission and Financial Aid. 413-529-3241. Fax: 413-527-9494. E-mail: admission@williston.com. Web site: www.williston.com.

See full description on page 1144.

WILLOW HILL SCHOOL

Sudbury, Massachusetts
See Special Needs Schools section.

THE WILLOWS ACADEMY

1012 Thacker Street
Des Plaines, Illinois 60016
Head of School: Christine Verhelst

General Information Girls' day college-preparatory school, affiliated with Roman Catholic Church. Grades 6–12. Founded: 1974. Setting: suburban. Nearest major city is Chicago. 4-acre campus. 1 building on campus. Approved or accredited by Independent Schools Association of the Central States and Illinois Department of Education. Total enrollment: 226. Upper school average class size: 18. Upper school faculty-student ratio: 1:10.

Upper School Student Profile Grade 9: 45 students (45 girls); Grade 10: 49 students (49 girls); Grade 11: 27 students (27 girls); Grade 12: 32 students (32 girls). 85% of students are Roman Catholic.

Faculty School total: 35. In upper school: 1 man, 17 women; 13 have advanced degrees.

Subjects Offered Algebra, American history, American literature, art, biology, calculus, chemistry, computer science, creative writing, economics, English, English literature, ethics, European history, expository writing, fine arts, four units of summer reading, French, geography, geometry, government/civics, grammar, health, history, Latin, mathematics, music, philosophy, physical education, physics, pre-calculus, science, social studies, Spanish, speech, statistics, theology, world history, world literature, writing.

Graduation Requirements Arts and fine arts (art, music, dance, drama), English, foreign language, four units of summer reading, mathematics, physical education (includes health), religion (includes Bible studies and theology), science, social studies (includes history), 40 hours of service work per year.

Special Academic Programs Advanced Placement exam preparation in 7 subject areas; honors section.

College Placement 32 students graduated in 2005; all went to college, including Marquette University; Northwestern University; Purdue University; University of Dallas; University of Illinois at Chicago; University of Illinois at Urbana–Champaign. Mean SAT verbal: 595, mean SAT math: 571, mean composite ACT: 25.

Student Life Upper grades have uniform requirement, student council, honor system. Discipline rests primarily with faculty.

Tuition and Aid Day student tuition: $8998. Tuition installment plan (Insured Tuition Payment Plan, monthly payment plans, quarterly, semi-annual, and annual payment plans). Tuition reduction for siblings, need-based scholarship grants available. In 2005–06, 30% of upper-school students received aid.

Admissions Traditional secondary-level entrance grade is 9. For fall 2005, 17 students applied for upper-level admission, 17 were accepted, 12 enrolled. Achievement tests and school's own exam required. Deadline for receipt of application materials: none. Application fee required: $50. On-campus interview required.

Athletics Interscholastic: basketball, cross-country running, soccer, softball, track and field, volleyball. 1 PE instructor, 3 coaches.

Computers Computers are regularly used in mathematics, science classes. Computer network features include campus e-mail, CD-ROMs, Internet access.

Contact Angela Reiter, Director of Admission and Marketing. 847-824-6927. Fax: 847-824-7089. E-mail: reiter@willows.org. Web site: www.willows.org.

WILMINGTON CHRISTIAN SCHOOL

825 Loveville Road
Hockessin, Delaware 19707
Head of School: Mr. William F. Stevens Jr.

General Information Coeducational day college-preparatory, arts, religious studies, and technology school, affiliated with Protestant faith. Grades PK–12. Founded: 1946. Setting: suburban. Nearest major city is Wilmington. 15-acre campus. 1 building on campus. Approved or accredited by Association of Christian Schools International, Middle States Association of Colleges and Schools, and Delaware Department of Education. Endowment: $360,000. Total enrollment: 549. Upper school average class size: 25. Upper school faculty-student ratio: 1:15.

Upper School Student Profile Grade 7: 50 students (22 boys, 28 girls); Grade 8: 44 students (15 boys, 29 girls); Grade 9: 45 students (19 boys, 26 girls); Grade 10: 48

students (26 boys, 22 girls); Grade 11: 59 students (25 boys, 34 girls); Grade 12: 44 students (22 boys, 22 girls). 98% of students are Protestant.

Faculty School total: 28. In upper school: 10 men, 18 women; 14 have advanced degrees.

Subjects Offered Accounting, advanced math, algebra, American history, American history-AP, American minority experience, anatomy and physiology, art, band, biology, calculus, calculus-AP, chemistry, chorus, Christian doctrine, Christian ethics, church history, civics, computer applications, consumer mathematics, creative writing, democracy in America, driver education, ecology, economics, English, geometry, German, health, honors algebra, honors English, honors geometry, information processing, journalism, lab science, library assistant, marine biology, modern history, music theory, novel, physical education, physical science, physics, pre-calculus, Spanish, speech, study skills, trigonometry, world civilizations, world religions, yearbook.

Graduation Requirements Bible studies, English, foreign language, health education, mathematics, physical education (includes health), science, social studies (includes history), 40 hours of community service.

Special Academic Programs Advanced Placement exam preparation in 3 subject areas; honors section; study at local college for college credit; remedial reading and/or remedial writing; remedial math.

College Placement 44 students graduated in 2005; 43 went to college, including Calvin College; Eastern University; Gordon College; Liberty University; Messiah College; University of Delaware. Other: 1 entered military service. Median SAT verbal: 580, median SAT math: 590.

Student Life Upper grades have specified standards of dress, student council, honor system. Discipline rests primarily with faculty. Attendance at religious services is required.

Tuition and Aid Day student tuition: $8290. Tuition installment plan (STEP Plan (monthly deduction from a checking account)). Tuition reduction for siblings, need-based scholarship grants available. In 2005–06, 15% of upper-school students received aid. Total amount of financial aid awarded in 2005–06: $200,270.

Admissions Traditional secondary-level entrance grade is 9. For fall 2005, 48 students applied for upper-level admission, 25 were accepted, 16 enrolled. Stanford Achievement Test required. Deadline for receipt of application materials: August 1. Application fee required: $125. On-campus interview required.

Athletics Interscholastic: baseball (boys), basketball (b,g), field hockey (g), lacrosse (b), soccer (b,g), softball (g), volleyball (g); coed interscholastic: cross-country running, golf, running. 2 PE instructors, 16 coaches.

Computers Computers are regularly used in accounting, business education, data processing, information technology, newspaper, yearbook classes. Computer network features include campus e-mail, on-campus library services, CD-ROMs, Internet access.

Contact Mrs. Kim Connell, Admissions/Headmaster's Assistant. 302-239-2121 Ext. 3205. Fax: 302-239-2778. E-mail: kconnell@wilmingtonchristian.org.

WILMINGTON FRIENDS SCHOOL

101 School Road
Wilmington, Delaware 19803
Head of School: Leo P. Dressel

General Information Coeducational day college-preparatory school, affiliated with Society of Friends. Grades PS–12. Founded: 1748. Setting: suburban. Nearest major city is Philadelphia, PA. 57-acre campus. 4 buildings on campus. Approved or accredited by Friends Council on Education, International Baccalaureate Organization, Middle States Association of Colleges and Schools, and Delaware Department of Education. Member of National Association of Independent Schools. Language of instruction: English. Endowment: $16 million. Total enrollment: 847. Upper school average class size: 15. Upper school faculty-student ratio: 1:9.

Upper School Student Profile Grade 9: 72 students (36 boys, 36 girls); Grade 10: 55 students (27 boys, 28 girls); Grade 11: 69 students (28 boys, 41 girls); Grade 12: 58 students (35 boys, 23 girls). 6% of students are members of Society of Friends.

Faculty School total: 100. In upper school: 15 men, 16 women; 28 have advanced degrees.

Subjects Offered 3-dimensional art, advanced chemistry, algebra, American history, art, art history, astronomy, Bible as literature, biology, calculus, chemistry, community service, computer art, computer programming, drama, driver education, earth science, economics, English, environmental science, ethics, European history, French, geology, geometry, global science, history, history of the Americas, improvisation, independent study, Internet, jazz ensemble, journalism, mathematics, media studies, music, music theory, physical education, physics, pre-calculus, Quakerism and ethics, religion, science, social science, Spanish, studio art, theater, theater arts, Web site design, wellness, wind ensemble, world history, writing.

Graduation Requirements Computer science, English, foreign language, mathematics, participation in sports, peace studies, performing arts, physical education (includes health), religion (includes Bible studies and theology), science, senior thesis, social science, social studies (includes history), visual arts, wellness, 50 hours of community service (single location) before senior year.

Special Academic Programs International Baccalaureate program; Advanced Placement exam preparation in 4 subject areas; honors section; independent study;

term-away projects; study abroad; academic accommodation for the gifted, the musically talented, and the artistically talented.

College Placement 55 students graduated in 2005; 54 went to college, including University of Delaware; University of Miami. Other: 1 had other specific plans. Median SAT verbal: 563, median SAT math: 615. 54% scored over 600 on SAT verbal, 63% scored over 600 on SAT math.

Student Life Upper grades have specified standards of dress, student council. Discipline rests primarily with faculty. Attendance at religious services is required.

Summer Programs Enrichment, computer instruction programs offered; session focuses on leadership; held on campus; accepts boys and girls; open to students from other schools. 20 students usually enrolled. 2006 schedule: July 31 to August 18.

Tuition and Aid Day student tuition: $16,700. Tuition installment plan (Key Tuition Payment Plan). Need-based scholarship grants available. In 2005–06, 19% of upper-school students received aid. Total amount of financial aid awarded in 2005–06: $495,600.

Admissions Traditional secondary-level entrance grade is 9. For fall 2005, 62 students applied for upper-level admission, 25 were accepted, 21 enrolled. CTP and ERB required. Deadline for receipt of application materials: none. Application fee required: $40. On-campus interview required.

Athletics Interscholastic: baseball (boys), basketball (b,g), cross-country running (b,g), field hockey (g), football (b), lacrosse (b,g), soccer (b,g), swimming and diving (g), tennis (b,g), volleyball (g), winter (indoor) track (b,g), wrestling (b); coed intramural: aerobics/nautilus. 2 PE instructors, 21 coaches, 1 trainer.

Computers Computers are regularly used in art, English, library skills, literary magazine, mathematics, music, newspaper, science, social studies, yearbook classes. Computer network features include on-campus library services, CD-ROMs, Internet access, document storage, backup, and security, off-campus library services (catalog and book request).

Contact Ms. Kathleen Hopkins, Director of Admissions and Financial Aid. 302-576-2930. Fax: 302-576-2939. E-mail: khopkins@wilmingtonfriends.org. Web site: wilmingtonfriends.org.

WILSON HALL

2801 South Wise Drive
Sumter, South Carolina 29150
Head of School: Mr. Frederick B. Moulton

General Information Coeducational day college-preparatory, arts, and technology school. Grades PS–12. Founded: 1966. Setting: small town. Nearest major city is Columbia. 17-acre campus. 7 buildings on campus. Approved or accredited by South Carolina Independent School Association, Southern Association of Colleges and Schools, Southern Association of Independent Schools, and South Carolina Department of Education. Endowment: $280,000. Total enrollment: 779. Upper school average class size: 20. Upper school faculty-student ratio: 1:12.

Upper School Student Profile Grade 9: 62 students (30 boys, 32 girls); Grade 10: 49 students (24 boys, 25 girls); Grade 11: 54 students (27 boys, 27 girls); Grade 12: 44 students (21 boys, 23 girls).

Faculty School total: 74. In upper school: 10 men, 20 women; 18 have advanced degrees.

Subjects Offered 3-dimensional design, algebra, anatomy, biology-AP, calculus-AP, chemistry-AP, computer applications, computer programming, economics, English, English language-AP, English literature-AP, environmental science, European history-AP, French, government, government-AP, Latin, multimedia, music theory-AP, philosophy, physical education, physical science, physics-AP, pottery, Spanish, studio art-AP, trigonometry, U.S. history-AP, world history.

Graduation Requirements Arts and fine arts (art, music, dance, drama), business skills (includes word processing), computer science, English, foreign language, mathematics, physical education (includes health), science, social studies (includes history), acceptance into four-year college or university, 20 hours community service.

Special Academic Programs Advanced Placement exam preparation in 14 subject areas; honors section.

College Placement 46 students graduated in 2005; all went to college, including Clemson University; College of Charleston; The Citadel, The Military College of South Carolina; University of South Carolina; University of Virginia; Wofford College. Mean SAT verbal: 600, mean SAT math: 579.

Student Life Upper grades have specified standards of dress, honor system. Discipline rests primarily with faculty.

Summer Programs Enrichment, sports, art/fine arts, computer instruction programs offered; session focuses on enrichment; held on campus; accepts boys and girls; not open to students from other schools. 100 students usually enrolled. 2006 schedule: June 1 to July 31.

Tuition and Aid Day student tuition: $4030–$4540. Tuition installment plan (monthly payment plans). Need-based scholarship grants available. In 2005–06, 8% of upper-school students received aid. Total amount of financial aid awarded in 2005–06: $100,000.

Admissions Traditional secondary-level entrance grade is 9. For fall 2005, 43 students applied for upper-level admission, 19 were accepted, 19 enrolled. ACT, CTBS, OLSAT, Iowa Tests of Basic Skills, PSAT and SAT for applicants to grade 11 and 12, school's own test or Stanford Achievement Test, Otis-Lennon School Ability

Test required. Deadline for receipt of application materials: none. Application fee required: $150. On-campus interview required.

Athletics Interscholastic: baseball (boys), basketball (b,g), cheering (g), cross-country running (b,g), football (b), golf (b), softball (g), strength & conditioning (b,g), swimming and diving (b,g), tennis (b,g), track and field (b,g), volleyball (g), weight lifting (b,g), wrestling (b); intramural: weight training (b,g); coed interscholastic: climbing, hiking/backpacking, mountain biking, rock climbing, soccer; coed intramural: outdoor adventure. 2 PE instructors, 12 coaches, 1 trainer.

Computers Computers are regularly used in English, technology, yearbook classes. Computer network features include campus e-mail, on-campus library services, CD-ROMs, online commercial services, Internet access, file transfer.

Contact Sean Hoskins, Director of Admissions and Public Relations. 803-469-3475 Ext. 107. Fax: 803-469-3477. E-mail: sean_hoskins@hotmail.com. Web site: www.wilsonhall.org.

THE WINCHENDON SCHOOL

172 Ash Street
Winchendon, Massachusetts 01475
Head of School: J. William LaBelle

General Information Coeducational boarding and day college-preparatory, general academic, arts, and technology school; primarily serves underachievers. Grades 8–PG. Founded: 1926. Setting: small town. Nearest major city is Boston. Students are housed in single-sex by floor dormitories. 375-acre campus. 23 buildings on campus. Approved or accredited by Association of Independent Schools in New England, New England Association of Schools and Colleges, and The Association of Boarding Schools. Member of National Association of Independent Schools and Secondary School Admission Test Board. Endowment: $15 million. Total enrollment: 209. Upper school average class size: 6. Upper school faculty-student ratio: 1:6.

Upper School Student Profile Grade 8: 9 students (9 boys); Grade 9: 21 students (13 boys, 8 girls); Grade 10: 44 students (37 boys, 7 girls); Grade 11: 38 students (31 boys, 7 girls); Grade 12: 56 students (46 boys, 10 girls); Postgraduate: 41 students (40 boys, 1 girl). 87% of students are boarding students. 35% are state residents. 21 states are represented in upper school student body. 50% are international students. International students from Brazil, Hong Kong, Japan, Republic of Korea, Spain, and Taiwan; 13 other countries represented in student body.

Faculty School total: 31. In upper school: 25 men, 6 women; 12 have advanced degrees; 26 reside on campus.

Subjects Offered Algebra, American history, American literature, anatomy, art, art history, biology, calculus, ceramics, chemistry, chorus, computer programming, computer science, creative writing, dance, drama, driver education, earth science, ecology, economics, English, English literature, environmental science, ESL, European history, expository writing, French, geography, geometry, government/civics, grammar, health, history, instrumental music, Latin, mathematics, music appreciation, music history, photography, physical education, physics, physiology, psychology, science, social science, social studies, sociology, Spanish, speech, theater, trigonometry, typing, world history, writing.

Graduation Requirements Computer science, English, mathematics, physical education (includes health), science, social science, social studies (includes history).

Special Academic Programs Advanced Placement exam preparation in 5 subject areas; academic accommodation for the gifted; remedial reading and/or remedial writing; remedial math; programs in English, mathematics for dyslexic students; special instructional classes for students with learning disabilities and Attention Deficit Disorder; ESL (35 students enrolled).

College Placement 98 students graduated in 2005; 93 went to college, including American University; Boston University; Northeastern University; University of Massachusetts Amherst; University of Rhode Island. Other: 3 entered a postgraduate year, 2 had other specific plans. Median SAT verbal: 510, median SAT math: 550. 3% scored over 600 on SAT verbal, 5% scored over 600 on SAT math.

Student Life Upper grades have specified standards of dress, student council. Discipline rests primarily with faculty.

Summer Programs Remediation, enrichment, advancement, ESL, sports, art/fine arts, rigorous outdoor training, computer instruction programs offered; session focuses on structured learning experience; held on campus; accepts boys and girls; open to students from other schools. 60 students usually enrolled. 2006 schedule: July 2 to August 12.

Tuition and Aid Day student tuition: $21,250; 7-day tuition and room/board: $33,850. Tuition installment plan (SMART Tuition Payment Plan). Need-based scholarship grants available. In 2005–06, 37% of upper-school students received aid. Total amount of financial aid awarded in 2005–06: $1,250,000.

Admissions Traditional secondary-level entrance grade is 10. For fall 2005, 437 students applied for upper-level admission, 382 were accepted, 209 enrolled. Deadline for receipt of application materials: none. Application fee required: $50. Interview recommended.

Athletics Interscholastic: baseball (boys), basketball (b,g), cross-country running (b), dance (g), golf (b,g), hockey (b), ice hockey (b), lacrosse (b), running (b,g), soccer (b), tennis (b,g), volleyball (b,g); intramural: aerobics/dance (g), basketball (b,g), nautilus (b,g), power lifting (b,g), running (b,g); coed interscholastic: alpine skiing, bicycling, cross-country running, golf, running; coed intramural: aerobics, aerobics/dance, alpine skiing, bicycling, bowling, cross-country running, equestrian sports,

fishing, fitness, fitness walking, flagball, floor hockey, freestyle skiing, Frisbee, golf, horseback riding, ice skating, in-line skating, indoor soccer, jogging, jump rope, mountain biking, nordic skiing, outdoor activities, outdoor adventure, paint ball, physical fitness, power lifting, running, skateboarding, skiing (cross-country), skiing (downhill), snowboarding, strength & conditioning, swimming and diving, synchronized swimming, tennis, ultimate Frisbee, volleyball, walking, weight lifting, weight training, winter walking.

Computers Computers are regularly used in art, English, science, writing classes. Computer network features include campus e-mail, on-campus library services, CD-ROMs, Internet access, DVD, wireless campus network.

Contact J. William LaBelle, Headmaster. 800-622-1119. Fax: 978-297-0911. E-mail: admissions@winchendon.org. Web site: www.winchendon.org.

See full description on page 1146.

WINCHESTER THURSTON SCHOOL

555 Morewood Avenue
Pittsburgh, Pennsylvania 15213-2899
Head of School: Mr. Gary J. Niels

General Information Coeducational day college-preparatory and arts school. Grades PK–12. Founded: 1887. Setting: urban. 5-acre campus. 1 building on campus. Approved or accredited by Middle States Association of Colleges and Schools, Pennsylvania Association of Private Academic Schools, The College Board, and Pennsylvania Department of Education. Member of National Association of Independent Schools. Endowment: $6.7 million. Total enrollment: 580. Upper school average class size: 14. Upper school faculty-student ratio: 1:7.

Upper School Student Profile Grade 9: 34 students (22 boys, 12 girls); Grade 10: 42 students (21 boys, 21 girls); Grade 11: 47 students (19 boys, 28 girls); Grade 12: 45 students (27 boys, 18 girls).

Faculty School total: 86. In upper school: 11 men, 17 women; 17 have advanced degrees.

Subjects Offered Algebra, American history, American literature, art, art history, biology, calculus, ceramics, chemistry, choir, chorus, classics, composition-AP, computer programming, computer science, creative writing, dance, drama, drawing, economics, English, English literature, English literature-AP, English-AP, European history, European history-AP, expository writing, filmmaking, French, French-AP, geometry, government/civics, health, history, journalism, Latin, mathematics, music, music theory, philosophy, photography, physical education, physics, psychology, SAT preparation, science, social studies, Spanish, Spanish-AP, speech, visual arts, world history, world literature, writing, yearbook.

Graduation Requirements Arts and fine arts (art, music, dance, drama), computer science, English, foreign language, mathematics, physical education (includes health), science, social studies (includes history), speech.

Special Academic Programs Advanced Placement exam preparation in 17 subject areas; independent study; term-away projects; study at local college for college credit; study abroad; academic accommodation for the gifted, the musically talented, and the artistically talented.

College Placement 37 students graduated in 2005; 36 went to college, including Carnegie Mellon University; University of Pittsburgh. Other: 1 had other specific plans. Median SAT verbal: 650, median SAT math: 590. 67% scored over 600 on SAT verbal, 51% scored over 600 on SAT math.

Student Life Upper grades have specified standards of dress, student council. Discipline rests equally with students and faculty.

Summer Programs Enrichment, sports programs offered; held on campus; accepts boys and girls; open to students from other schools. 40 students usually enrolled.

Tuition and Aid Day student tuition: $18,500. Tuition installment plan (10-month payment plan managed by the school's business office). Need-based scholarship grants available. In 2005–06, 37% of upper-school students received aid. Total amount of financial aid awarded in 2005–06: $845,350.

Admissions Traditional secondary-level entrance grade is 9. For fall 2005, 63 students applied for upper-level admission, 38 were accepted, 27 enrolled. CTP III, ISEE or writing sample required. Deadline for receipt of application materials: December 15. Application fee required: $50. On-campus interview required.

Athletics Interscholastic: basketball (boys, girls), cross-country running (b,g), drill team (g), field hockey (g), golf (b), lacrosse (b,g), rowing (b,g), running (b,g), tennis (g); coed interscholastic: crew, fencing, nautilus, soccer; coed intramural: basketball, dance, Frisbee, golf, independent competitive sports, nautilus, outdoor activities, physical fitness, physical training, soccer, strength & conditioning, weight training, winter soccer, yoga. 4 PE instructors, 12 coaches, 1 trainer.

Computers Computers are regularly used in art, English, history, mathematics, music, science, writing classes. Computer network features include campus e-mail, on-campus library services, CD-ROMs, online commercial services, Internet access, file transfer, office computer access, DVD.

Contact Rebecca King, Director of Admission. 412-578-7518. Fax: 412-578-7504. E-mail: kingr@winchesterthurston.org. Web site: www.winchesterthurston.org.

ANNOUNCEMENT FROM THE SCHOOL Winchester Thurston offers a student-centered, rigorous, college-preparatory program in a coeducational environment. WT engages each student in a challenging, responsive learning

process and a connected, accessible educational community. Together, these elements foster strong student-teacher relationships, motivation to pursue individual interests and talents, and participation in the larger world around WT's campuses.

WINDERMERE ST. ANNE'S SCHOOL

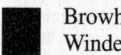

Browhead
Windermere LA23 1NW, United Kingdom
Head of School: Miss W.A. Ellis

General Information Coeducational boarding and day college-preparatory, arts, and business school. Grades 1–13. Founded: 1863. Setting: rural. Nearest major city is Manchester. Students are housed in student apartments. 84-acre campus. 20 buildings on campus. Approved or accredited by Boarding Schools Association (UK), Department for Education and Skills (UK), and Independent Schools Council (UK). Language of instruction: English. Endowment: £4 million. Total enrollment: 375. Upper school average class size: 10. Upper school faculty-student ratio: 1:6.

Upper School Student Profile Grade 7: 36 students (15 boys, 21 girls); Grade 8: 34 students (15 boys, 19 girls); Grade 9: 37 students (10 boys, 27 girls); Grade 10: 37 students (19 boys, 18 girls); Grade 11: 35 students (7 boys, 28 girls); Grade 12: 25 students (6 boys, 19 girls); Grade 13: 28 students (8 boys, 20 girls). 50% of students are boarding students. 10% are international students. International students from China, Germany, Malaysia, Saudi Arabia, and United States; 13 other countries represented in student body.

Faculty School total: 66. In upper school: 10 men, 31 women; 2 have advanced degrees; 12 reside on campus.

Subjects Offered Art, biology, ceramics, chemistry, computer programming, dance, drama, English, English literature, fabric arts, French, geography, German, government/civics, history, home economics, information technology, Latin, mathematics, music, physical education, physics, psychology, religion, science, Spanish, speech, theater.

Special Academic Programs Term-away projects; domestic exchange program (with The Athenian School, Bishop's College School, Sedbergh School); study abroad; programs in English for dyslexic students; ESL (10 students enrolled).

College Placement 29 students graduated in 2005. Other: 26 entered a postgraduate year, 3 had other specific plans.

Student Life Upper grades have uniform requirement, student council. Discipline rests primarily with faculty.

Tuition and Aid Day student tuition: £6648–£7347; 5-day tuition and room/board: £11,898–£12,597; 7-day tuition and room/board: £12,597–£13,296. Tuition installment plan (monthly payment plans, individually arranged payment plans). Tuition reduction for siblings, bursaries, merit scholarship grants available.

Admissions Traditional secondary-level entrance grade is 7. Admissions testing and school's own exam required. Deadline for receipt of application materials: none. Application fee required: £50. Interview required.

Athletics Interscholastic: ballet (girls), football (b,g), netball (g), sailing (g), soccer (b,g); intramural: ballet (g), basketball (g), martial arts (g), netball (g), riflery (g), sailing (g), skiing (downhill) (g), soccer (g), softball (g), squash (g); coed interscholastic: aerobics, aerobics/dance, aquatics, artistic gym, back packing, ball hockey, basketball, canoeing/kayaking, climbing, cricket, cross-country running, dance, equestrian sports, field hockey, fitness, football, golf, gymnastics, hiking/backpacking, hockey, horseback riding, kayaking, martial arts, modern dance, mountaineering, outdoor adventure, outdoor education, outdoor recreation, physical training, rafting, rock climbing, roller blading, rounders, sailboarding, skiing (downhill), soccer, speleology, squash, swimming and diving, table tennis, tennis, track and field, walking, wall climbing, windsurfing, winter soccer, winter walking. 5 PE instructors, 3 coaches.

Computers Computers are regularly used in creative writing, design, English, information technology, music, science classes. Computer network features include campus e-mail, Internet access, wireless campus network.

Contact Mrs. Harriet Pethica, Registrar. 44-153-944-6164. Fax: 44-153-948-8414. E-mail: admissions@wsaschool.com. Web site: www.wsaschool.com.

WINDHOEK INTERNATIONAL SCHOOL

Private Bag 16007
Windhoek, Namibia
Head of School: Ms. Helen Mary Birkbeck

General Information Coeducational day college-preparatory, general academic, and arts school. Grades K–13. Founded: 1991. Setting: suburban. 4-hectare campus. 10 buildings on campus. Approved or accredited by European Council of International Schools and New England Association of Schools and Colleges. Language of instruction: English. Upper school average class size: 15. Upper school faculty-student ratio: 1:7.

Faculty School total: 55. In upper school: 6 men, 17 women; 7 have advanced degrees.

Subjects Offered Art, biology, chemistry, computers, drama, economics, English, ESL, French, German, health and safety, history, International Baccalaureate courses, mathematics, music, physics, Portuguese, science, sports, theater arts.

Special Academic Programs International Baccalaureate program; remedial reading and/or remedial writing; remedial math; ESL (50 students enrolled).

Student Life Upper grades have specified standards of dress, student council. Discipline rests primarily with faculty.

Tuition and Aid Day student tuition: 118,050 Namibian dollars. Tuition installment plan (monthly payment plans, three installments).

Admissions School's own exam required. Deadline for receipt of application materials: none. No application fee required. Interview required.

Athletics Interscholastic: basketball (boys, girls), cricket (b), rugby (b), soccer (b,g); intramural: basketball (b,g), indoor track & field (b,g), netball (g), rugby (b), soccer (b,g); coed interscholastic: table tennis; coed intramural: baseball, fitness, hockey. 2 PE instructors, 4 coaches.

Computers Computers are regularly used in business studies, English, geography, history, mathematics, science, social studies classes. Computer network features include campus e-mail, on-campus library services, CD-ROMs, Internet access, DVD.

Contact Ms. Carol Heimstadt, Admissions Officer. 26461241783. Fax: 26461243127. E-mail: cheimstadt@wis.edu.na. Web site: www.wis.edu.na.

WINDSOR CHRISTIAN FELLOWSHIP ACADEMY

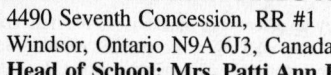

4490 Seventh Concession, RR #1
Windsor, Ontario N9A 6J3, Canada
Head of School: Mrs. Patti Ann Banks

General Information Coeducational day college-preparatory and religious studies school, affiliated with Christian faith. Grades K–12. Founded: 1992. Setting: suburban. 50-acre campus. 1 building on campus. Approved or accredited by National Christian School Association. Language of instruction: English. Total enrollment: 66. Upper school faculty-student ratio: 1:12.

Upper School Student Profile Grade 8: 5 students (1 boy, 4 girls); Grade 9: 7 students (5 boys, 2 girls); Grade 10: 5 students (2 boys, 3 girls); Grade 11: 4 students (1 boy, 3 girls); Grade 12: 3 students (1 boy, 2 girls). 100% of students are Christian faith.

Faculty School total: 11. In upper school: 1 man, 5 women; 3 have advanced degrees.

Special Academic Programs Honors section; accelerated programs; independent study; academic accommodation for the gifted; remedial reading and/or remedial writing; remedial math.

College Placement 4 students graduated in 2005; 3 went to college, including University of Windsor. Other: 1 went to work.

Student Life Upper grades have uniform requirement, honor system. Discipline rests primarily with faculty. Attendance at religious services is required.

Tuition and Aid Day student tuition: CAN$4100. Tuition installment plan (monthly payment plans).

Admissions Traditional secondary-level entrance grade is 8. CAT required. Deadline for receipt of application materials: none. Application fee required: CAN$100. On-campus interview required.

Athletics Interscholastic: ball hockey (boys, girls), football (b,g), track and field (b,g); intramural: ball hockey (b,g); coed interscholastic: badminton, baseball, cross-country running, volleyball; coed intramural: badminton, baseball, cross-country running, track and field, volleyball. 1 PE instructor.

Computers Computers are regularly used in all academic classes. Computer resources include CD-ROMs, office computer access.

Contact Mrs. Patti Ann Banks, Principal/Head of Guidance. 519-972-5986 Ext. 246. Fax: 519-972-5643. E-mail: wcfa@windsorchristianfellowship.com. Web site: windsorchristianfellowship.com.

THE WINDSOR SCHOOL

Administration Building
136-23 Sanford Avenue
Flushing, New York 11355
Head of School: Mr. James Seery

General Information Coeducational day college-preparatory and arts school. Grades 6–PG. Founded: 1968. Setting: urban. Nearest major city is New York. 2-acre campus. 3 buildings on campus. Approved or accredited by Middle States Association of Colleges and Schools and New York Department of Education. Total enrollment: 100. Upper school average class size: 14. Upper school faculty-student ratio: 1:14.

Upper School Student Profile Grade 9: 10 students (6 boys, 4 girls); Grade 10: 21 students (14 boys, 7 girls); Grade 11: 20 students (17 boys, 3 girls); Grade 12: 39 students (25 boys, 14 girls).

Faculty School total: 14. In upper school: 8 men, 5 women; 13 have advanced degrees.

Subjects Offered Advanced Placement courses, algebra, American history, American literature, art, basic skills, biology, business, business applications, calculus, ceramics, chemistry, computer programming, computer science, computer skills, computer studies, creative writing, driver education, economics, English, English

The Windsor School

literature, environmental science, ESL, European history, fine arts, French, geometry, government/civics, grammar, health, keyboarding, marketing, mathematics, music, physical education, physics, pre-calculus, psychology, science, social science, social studies, Spanish, trigonometry, typing, world affairs, world history.

Graduation Requirements Arts and fine arts (art, music, dance, drama), English, foreign language, mathematics, physical education (includes health), science, social science, social studies (includes history).

Special Academic Programs Advanced Placement exam preparation in 5 subject areas; honors section; accelerated programs; independent study; academic accommodation for the gifted, the musically talented, and the artistically talented; remedial reading and/or remedial writing; remedial math; ESL (21 students enrolled).

College Placement 41 students graduated in 2005; all went to college, including St. John's University; State University of New York at Binghamton. Median SAT verbal: 450, median SAT math: 530. 18% scored over 600 on SAT verbal, 20% scored over 600 on SAT math.

Student Life Upper grades have specified standards of dress. Discipline rests primarily with faculty.

Summer Programs Remediation, enrichment, advancement, ESL, art/fine arts, computer instruction programs offered; session focuses on advancement, enrichment, remediation; held on campus; accepts boys and girls; open to students from other schools. 435 students usually enrolled. 2006 schedule: July 1 to August 18. Application deadline: June 30.

Tuition and Aid Day student tuition: $14,800. Tuition installment plan (individually arranged payment plans).

Admissions Traditional secondary-level entrance grade is 9. For fall 2005, 61 students applied for upper-level admission, 53 were accepted, 38 enrolled. School's own exam required. Deadline for receipt of application materials: none. No application fee required. On-campus interview required.

Athletics Interscholastic: basketball (boys, girls), soccer (b,g), softball (b,g); intramural: aerobics (b,g), basketball (b,g), cooperative games (b,g), fitness (b,g), jump rope (g), physical fitness (b,g), soccer (b,g), softball (b,g), tennis (b,g), volleyball (b,g); coed interscholastic: basketball, soccer, softball; coed intramural: basketball, fitness, jump rope, physical fitness, soccer, softball, table tennis, tennis, volleyball. 2 PE instructors, 2 coaches.

Computers Computers are regularly used in art, business applications, mathematics, research skills, typing, yearbook classes. Computer resources include CD-ROMs, Internet access.

Contact Dr. Philip A. Stewart, Director of Admissions. 718-359-8300. Fax: 718-359-1876. E-mail: admin@thewindsorschool.com. Web site: www.windsorschool.com.

WINDWARD SCHOOL

11350 Palms Boulevard
Los Angeles, California 90066
Head of School: Tom Gilder

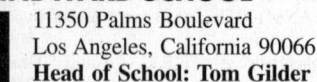

General Information Coeducational day college-preparatory school. Grades 7–12. Founded: 1971. Setting: urban. 9-acre campus. 9 buildings on campus. Approved or accredited by California Association of Independent Schools and Western Association of Schools and Colleges. Member of National Association of Independent Schools. Total enrollment: 474. Upper school average class size: 16. Upper school faculty-student ratio: 1:7.

Upper School Student Profile Grade 9: 86 students (45 boys, 41 girls); Grade 10: 87 students (46 boys, 41 girls); Grade 11: 79 students (38 boys, 41 girls); Grade 12: 73 students (35 boys, 38 girls).

Faculty School total: 63. In upper school: 32 men, 27 women; 37 have advanced degrees.

Subjects Offered Algebra, American history, American literature, art, art history, biology, calculus, ceramics, chemistry, chorus, computer science, creative writing, dance, drama, English, English literature, environmental science, European history, fine arts, French, geometry, government/civics, health, history, Japanese, journalism, Latin, marine biology, mathematics, music, photography, physical education, physiology, science, social studies, Spanish, theater, trigonometry, world history.

Graduation Requirements Arts and fine arts (art, music, dance, drama), English, foreign language, mathematics, physical education (includes health), science, social studies (includes history).

Special Academic Programs Advanced Placement exam preparation in 10 subject areas; honors section; independent study; study at local college for college credit.

College Placement 73 students graduated in 2005; all went to college, including Boston College; New York University; Stanford University; University of California, Berkeley; University of Pennsylvania. Mean SAT verbal: 619, mean SAT math: 619, mean combined SAT: 1867.

Student Life Upper grades have specified standards of dress, student council, honor system. Discipline rests primarily with faculty.

Summer Programs Sports programs offered; session focuses on skill development and team play; held on campus; accepts boys and girls; open to students from other schools. 75 students usually enrolled. 2006 schedule: June 15 to July 31.

Tuition and Aid Day student tuition: $24,884. Tuition installment plan (Key Tuition Payment Plan, monthly payment plans). Need-based scholarship grants, need-based

loans available. In 2005–06, 12% of upper-school students received aid. Total amount of financial aid awarded in 2005–06: $720,963.

Admissions Traditional secondary-level entrance grade is 9. For fall 2005, 138 students applied for upper-level admission, 26 were accepted, 19 enrolled. ISEE required. Deadline for receipt of application materials: December 15. Application fee required: $100. On-campus interview required.

Athletics Interscholastic: baseball (boys), basketball (b,g), football (b); coed interscholastic: cross-country running, flag football, lacrosse. 5 PE instructors, 15 coaches, 2 trainers.

Computers Computers are regularly used in art, English, history, mathematics, science classes. Computer network features include campus e-mail, on-campus library services, CD-ROMs, online commercial services, Internet access.

Contact Sharon Pearline, Director of Admissions. 310-391-7127. Fax: 310-397-5655.

See full description on page 1148.

THE WINSOR SCHOOL

Pilgrim Road
Boston, Massachusetts 02215
Head of School: Mrs. Rachel Friis Stettler

General Information Girls' day college-preparatory school. Grades 5–12. Founded: 1886. Setting: urban. 8-acre campus. 2 buildings on campus. Approved or accredited by Association of Independent Schools in New England, New England Association of Schools and Colleges, and Massachusetts Department of Education. Member of National Association of Independent Schools. Endowment: $36.4 million. Total enrollment: 428. Upper school average class size: 12. Upper school faculty-student ratio: 1:5.

Upper School Student Profile Grade 9: 64 students (64 girls); Grade 10: 64 students (64 girls); Grade 11: 57 students (57 girls); Grade 12: 59 students (59 girls).

Faculty School total: 78. In upper school: 14 men, 37 women; 41 have advanced degrees.

Subjects Offered African history, algebra, American history, art, art history, astronomy, biology, calculus, ceramics, chemistry, Chinese, Chinese history, computer programming, creative writing, drama, English, environmental science, European history, expository writing, fine arts, French, geometry, health, Latin, Latin American history, literature, marine biology, music, photography, physical education, physics, pre-calculus, psychology, Russian history, Spanish, speech, theater, world literature.

Graduation Requirements Algebra, art, biology, English, European history, French, geometry, Latin, physical education (includes health), Spanish, U.S. history.

Special Academic Programs Advanced Placement exam preparation in 8 subject areas; honors section.

College Placement 57 students graduated in 2005; all went to college, including Brown University; Columbia College; Duke University; Harvard University; Massachusetts Institute of Technology; University of Pennsylvania. Median SAT verbal: 710, median SAT math: 700. 96% scored over 600 on SAT verbal, 93% scored over 600 on SAT math.

Student Life Upper grades have specified standards of dress, student council, honor system. Discipline rests primarily with faculty.

Tuition and Aid Day student tuition: $26,500. Tuition installment plan (Academic Management Services Plan, FACTS Tuition Payment Plan, individually arranged payment plans). Need-based scholarship grants available. In 2005–06, 22% of upper-school students received aid. Total amount of financial aid awarded in 2005–06: $1,126,000.

Admissions Traditional secondary-level entrance grade is 9. For fall 2005, 148 students applied for upper-level admission, 19 were accepted, 9 enrolled. ISEE and SSAT required. Deadline for receipt of application materials: January 15. Application fee required: $45. On-campus interview required.

Athletics Interscholastic: basketball, crew, cross-country running, field hockey, ice hockey, lacrosse, sailing, soccer, softball, squash, swimming and diving, tennis, track and field. 5 PE instructors, 5 coaches, 1 trainer.

Computers Computers are regularly used in art, English, foreign language, history, mathematics, music, science classes. Computer network features include campus e-mail, on-campus library services, Internet access.

Contact Mrs. Pamela D. McLaurin, Director of Admission. 617-735-9503. Fax: 617-739-5519. Web site: www.winsor.edu/.

ANNOUNCEMENT FROM THE SCHOOL Founded in 1886 by Mary Pickard Winsor, the Winsor School is an independent day school for academically motivated and promising girls in grades 5–12. Winsor offers a rigorous academic program balanced by the arts and physical education in an environment of warmth and personal attention. Winsor is set on a 7-acre campus in Boston, and makes frequent use of the city's resources. Facilities include a renovated library with 27,000 volumes plus access to 850 periodicals, a multimedia language lab, 3 computer labs, 3 art studios, 8 science laboratories, acres of playing fields, tennis courts, and a gymnasium. The Lower School comprises grades 5 through 8. In this supportive environment, teachers foster natural curiosity through active, hands-on lessons. The Upper School is an energetic

learning community of 9th through 12th graders. The faculty encourages girls to think logically, creatively, and compassionately and to take increasing responsibility for their own learning. At all levels, students enjoy dedicated, caring teachers who know their subjects intimately. Beyond the classroom, clubs, the arts, and sports offer ways for girls to explore interests. Winsor offers teams in 14 sports and has more than 30 clubs. Girls approach extracurriculars passionately, and have won national honors in crew, debate, engineering, and choral competitions. Girls also work with boys from Belmont Hill and The Roxbury Latin Schools on coordinated drama, music, and newspaper activities. The majority of students go on to attend the most selective colleges and universities. An experienced College Counselor guides and supports girls through the process. In the last 5 years, the students' most common college choices were Brown, Columbia, Dartmouth, Harvard, MIT, Penn, Princeton, and Yale. As a community, Winsor cherishes respect and generosity of spirit and its mission underscores a commitment to diversity. Its size means girls build lasting friendships, and it encourages each girl to realize her own uniqueness and promise.

WINSTON PREPARATORY SCHOOL

New York, New York
See Special Needs Schools section.

THE WINSTON SCHOOL

Dallas, Texas
See Special Needs Schools section.

THE WINSTON SCHOOL SAN ANTONIO

San Antonio, Texas
See Special Needs Schools section.

WISCONSIN ACADEMY

N2355 DuBorg Road
Columbus, Wisconsin 53925
Head of School: Mr. Derral W. Reeve

General Information Coeducational boarding and day college-preparatory, general academic, and religious studies school, affiliated with Seventh-day Adventist Church. Grades 9–12. Founded: 1950. Setting: rural. Nearest major city is Madison. Students are housed in single-sex dormitories. 50-acre campus. 7 buildings on campus. Approved or accredited by North Central Association of Colleges and Wisconsin Department of Education. Endowment: $100,000. Total enrollment: 102. Upper school faculty-student ratio: 1:6.

Upper School Student Profile Grade 9: 27 students (15 boys, 12 girls); Grade 10: 21 students (5 boys, 16 girls); Grade 11: 27 students (9 boys, 18 girls); Grade 12: 27 students (11 boys, 16 girls). 87% of students are boarding students. 88% are state residents. 5 states are represented in upper school student body. 1% are international students. International students from Canada; 1 other country represented in student body. 85% of students are Seventh-day Adventists.

Faculty School total: 21. In upper school: 9 men, 5 women; 5 have advanced degrees; 20 reside on campus.

Subjects Offered Advanced math, algebra, American government, American history, American literature, anatomy and physiology, art, bell choir, Bible, biology, chemistry, choir, chorus, composition, computer applications, computer graphics, computer keyboarding, computer literacy, driver education, economics, English, English-AP, general math, geography, geometry, guitar, gymnastics, handbells, health, home economics, newspaper, photo shop, physical education, physical science, physics, piano, pre-algebra, pre-calculus, religion, Spanish, work-study.

Graduation Requirements Algebra, American government, American history, American literature, Bible, biology, computer literacy, computer skills, English, foreign language, geometry, lab/keyboard, physical education (includes health), science, social studies (includes history), U.S. government.

College Placement 27 students graduated in 2005; 18 went to college, including Andrews University; Southern Adventist University. Other: 6 went to work, 3 had other specific plans.

Student Life Upper grades have specified standards of dress, student council, honor system. Discipline rests primarily with faculty. Attendance at religious services is required.

Tuition and Aid Day student tuition: $7400; 7-day tuition and room/board: $11,700. Tuition installment plan (monthly payment plans, individually arranged payment plans). Tuition reduction for siblings, need-based scholarship grants, paying campus jobs available. In 2005–06, 55% of upper-school students received aid. Total amount of financial aid awarded in 2005–06: $190,000.

Admissions Traditional secondary-level entrance grade is 9. For fall 2005, 115 students applied for upper-level admission, 107 were accepted. Iowa Test, CTBS, or TAP or TOEFL required. Deadline for receipt of application materials: none. Application fee required: $10. Interview recommended.

Athletics Intramural: basketball (boys, girls), flag football (b,g), flagball (b,g), floor hockey (b,g), softball (b,g), volleyball (b,g); coed intramural: gymnastics, volleyball. 1 PE instructor.

Computers Computers are regularly used in all academic classes. Computer resources include campus e-mail, on-campus library services, CD-ROMs, Internet access, office computer access, DVD.

Contact Mrs. Holly Roy, Registrar. 920-623-3300 Ext. 13. Fax: 920-623-3318. E-mail: registrar@wisacad.org. Web site: www.wisacad.org.

WOODBERRY FOREST SCHOOL

10 Woodberry Station
Woodberry Forest, Virginia 22989
Head of School: Dr. Dennis M. Campbell

General Information Boys' boarding college-preparatory school, affiliated with Christian faith. Grades 9–12. Founded: 1889. Setting: rural. Nearest major city is Charlottesville. Students are housed in single-sex dormitories. 1,200-acre campus. 38 buildings on campus. Approved or accredited by Southern Association of Colleges and Schools, The Association of Boarding Schools, Virginia Association of Independent Schools, and Virginia Department of Education. Member of National Association of Independent Schools and Secondary School Admission Test Board. Endowment: $165 million. Total enrollment: 386. Upper school average class size: 11. Upper school faculty-student ratio: 1:8.

Upper School Student Profile Grade 9: 80 students (80 boys); Grade 10: 110 students (110 boys); Grade 11: 99 students (99 boys); Grade 12: 113 students (113 boys). 100% of students are boarding students. 30% are state residents. 24 states are represented in upper school student body. 5% are international students. International students from Bahamas, Croatia, Germany, Hong Kong, Republic of Korea, and Saudi Arabia; 4 other countries represented in student body.

Faculty School total: 69. In upper school: 54 men, 15 women; 54 have advanced degrees; 64 reside on campus.

Subjects Offered Algebra, American history, American literature, art, art history, biology, calculus, chemistry, Chinese, community service, computer math, computer science, creative writing, drama, économics, English, English literature, environmental science, European history, expository writing, fine arts, French, geology, geometry, German, government/civics, health, Latin, mathematics, music, photography, physics, psychology, religion, science, social studies, Spanish, speech, theater, trigonometry, world history, world literature.

Graduation Requirements Arts and fine arts (art, music, dance, drama), English, foreign language, mathematics, physical education (includes health), religion (includes Bible studies and theology), science, social studies (includes history). Community service is required.

Special Academic Programs Advanced Placement exam preparation in 19 subject areas; honors section; independent study; study abroad; academic accommodation for the gifted, the musically talented, and the artistically talented.

College Placement 113 students graduated in 2004; all went to college, including Davidson College; The College of William and Mary; The University of North Carolina at Chapel Hill; University of Virginia; Vanderbilt University; Washington and Lee University. Median SAT verbal: 640, median SAT math: 650. 64% scored over 600 on SAT verbal, 76% scored over 600 on SAT math.

Student Life Upper grades have specified standards of dress, student council, honor system. Discipline rests equally with students and faculty. Attendance at religious services is required.

Tuition and Aid 7-day tuition and room/board: $30,000. Tuition installment plan (Key Tuition Payment Plan). Need-based scholarship grants, need-based loans available. In 2004–05, 30% of upper-school students received aid. Total amount of financial aid awarded in 2004–05: $2,500,000.

Admissions Traditional secondary-level entrance grade is 9. SSAT required. Deadline for receipt of application materials: February 1. Application fee required: $50. On-campus interview required.

Athletics Interscholastic: baseball, basketball, cross-country running, diving, football, golf, indoor track, indoor track & field, lacrosse, running, skeet shooting, soccer, squash, swimming and diving, tennis, track and field, winter (indoor) track, wrestling; intramural: archery, back packing, basketball, bicycling, billiards, boxing, canoeing/kayaking, climbing, combined training, cross-country running, fencing, fishing, fitness, fitness walking, flag football, golf, hiking/backpacking, jump rope, kayaking, lacrosse, mountaineering, outdoor activities, outdoor adventure, outdoor education, outdoor recreation, outdoor skills, outdoors, paint ball, physical fitness, physical training, power lifting, riflery, ropes courses, running, skeet shooting, skiing (cross-country), skiing (downhill), softball, squash, strength & conditioning, swimming and diving, tennis, track and field, trap and skeet, walking, wall climbing, weight lifting, weight training, wilderness, wilderness survival, winter walking. 1 trainer.

Computers Computers are regularly used in art, English, foreign language, history, mathematics, science classes. Computer network features include campus e-mail, on-campus library services, CD-ROMs, online commercial services, Internet access, file transfer, office computer access, DVD.

Woodberry Forest School

Contact Mr. Joseph G. Coleman, Director of Admissions. 540-672-6023. Fax: 540-672-6471. E-mail: joe_coleman@woodberry.org. Web site: www.woodberry.org.

ANNOUNCEMENT FROM THE SCHOOL Woodberry Forest is an all-male boarding school with an enrollment of approximately 390 boys in grades 9–12. Woodberry has a long history of academic excellence and is highly selective in admissions. The School recently completed expansion of the Walker Fine Arts Center, the Leonard W. Dick Gymnasium, and Terry House, a new dorm.

See full description on page 1150.

WOODBRIDGE ACADEMY

Lexington, Kentucky
See Special Needs Schools section.

WOODCLIFF ACADEMY

Wall, New Jersey
See Special Needs Schools section.

THE WOODHALL SCHOOL

58 Harrison Lane
Bethlehem, Connecticut 06751
Head of School: Sally Campbell Woodhall

General Information Boys' boarding and day college-preparatory, arts, and ESL school. Grades 9–PG. Founded: 1982. Setting: rural. Nearest major city is Hartford. Students are housed in single-sex dormitories. 30-acre campus. 10 buildings on campus. Approved or accredited by Association of Independent Schools in New England, Connecticut Association of Independent Schools, New England Association of Schools and Colleges, and Connecticut Department of Education. Member of National Association of Independent Schools. Endowment: $120,000. Total enrollment: 44. Upper school average class size: 4. Upper school faculty-student ratio: 1:3.
Upper School Student Profile Grade 9: 8 students (8 boys); Grade 10: 8 students (8 boys); Grade 11: 15 students (15 boys); Grade 12: 13 students (13 boys). 95% of students are boarding students. 20% are state residents. 19 states are represented in upper school student body. 7% are international students. International students from Bermuda, Canada, and El Salvador.
Faculty School total: 16. In upper school: 13 men, 3 women; 12 have advanced degrees; 12 reside on campus.
Subjects Offered Algebra, American history, American literature, anatomy, art, biology, calculus, chemistry, English, English literature, ESL, European history, government/civics, Greek, history, Latin, mathematics, physics, social studies, Spanish, trigonometry, Western civilization, world history.
Graduation Requirements Arts and fine arts (art, music, dance, drama), communication skills, English, foreign language, mathematics, physical education (includes health), science, social studies (includes history).
Special Academic Programs Independent study; special instructional classes for students with Attention Deficit Disorder and non-verbal learning disabilities; ESL.
College Placement 10 students graduated in 2005; all went to college, including Florida Institute of Technology; Franklin Pierce College; Hartwick College; New England College; Ohio Wesleyan University; Washington College. Median SAT verbal: 600, median SAT math: 540, median combined SAT: 560. 50% scored over 600 on SAT verbal, 28% scored over 600 on SAT math.
Student Life Upper grades have specified standards of dress, student council, honor system. Discipline rests primarily with faculty.
Tuition and Aid Day student tuition: $36,000; 7-day tuition and room/board: $47,000. Tuition installment plan (individually arranged payment plans).
Admissions Traditional secondary-level entrance grade is 10. For fall 2005, 60 students applied for upper-level admission, 19 were accepted, 17 enrolled. Deadline for receipt of application materials: none. Application fee required: $75. On-campus interview required.
Athletics Interscholastic: basketball, cross-country running, lacrosse, soccer; intramural: alpine skiing, basketball, bicycling, billiards, bowling, canoeing/kayaking, cross-country running, fishing, fitness, fitness walking, Frisbee, hiking/backpacking, ice skating, jogging, lacrosse, mountain biking, outdoor activities, outdoor education, outdoor recreation, physical fitness, rafting, running, skiing (cross-country), skiing (downhill), snowboarding, soccer, street hockey, strength & conditioning, table tennis, volleyball, walking, weight lifting, winter walking.
Computers Computers are regularly used in art, English, foreign language, history, mathematics, science, social science classes. Computer network features include Internet access.
Contact Sally Campbell Woodhall, Head of School. 203-266-7788. Fax: 203-266-5896. E-mail: woodhallschool@lycos.com. Web site: woodhallschool.org.

ANNOUNCEMENT FROM THE SCHOOL The Woodhall program of individualized education has an interpersonal component that recognizes the psychological dimensions of education that permeate all aspects of school life—academics, communications, student life, and athletics. The program's goal is to open the door to success by meeting each student where he is and helping him move beyond to realize his potential. Woodhall offers an integrated college-preparatory curriculum with small classes, ESL, a Communications Program to develop skills of self-expression with accountability, daily athletics, a full residential life program, community service, and social and recreational activities with nearby prep schools.

See full description on page 1152.

WOODLANDS ACADEMY OF THE SACRED HEART

760 East Westleigh Road
Lake Forest, Illinois 60045-3298
Head of School: Mr. Gerald Grossman

General Information Girls' boarding and day college-preparatory, arts, technology, and music school, affiliated with Roman Catholic Church. Grades 9–12. Founded: 1858. Setting: suburban. Nearest major city is Chicago. Students are housed in single-sex dormitories. 20-acre campus. 1 building on campus. Approved or accredited by Independent Schools Association of the Central States, Network of Sacred Heart Schools, North Central Association of Colleges and Schools, The Association of Boarding Schools, and Illinois Department of Education. Language of instruction: English. Endowment: $6 million. Total enrollment: 180. Upper school average class size: 15. Upper school faculty-student ratio: 1:9.
Upper School Student Profile Grade 9: 45 students (45 girls); Grade 10: 45 students (45 girls); Grade 11: 45 students (45 girls); Grade 12: 45 students (45 girls). 30% of students are boarding students. 58% are state residents. 6 states are represented in upper school student body. 30% are international students. International students from Canada, Japan, Mexico, Republic of Korea, Taiwan, and Thailand; 9 other countries represented in student body. 62% of students are Roman Catholic.
Faculty School total: 40. In upper school: 5 men, 35 women; 20 have advanced degrees; 5 reside on campus.
Subjects Offered Algebra, American history, American literature, anatomy, art, art history, Bible studies, biology, calculus, ceramics, chemistry, chorus, computer math, computer programming, computer science, creative writing, drama, drawing, driver education, earth science, English, English literature, ESL, ethics, European history, expository writing, fine arts, French, geometry, government/civics, grammar, health, history, Japanese, Latin, Mandarin, mathematics, music, painting, philosophy, photography, physical education, physical science, physics, physiology, psychology, religion, Russian, Russian history, science, social studies, sociology, Spanish, speech, theater, theology, trigonometry, world history, world literature, writing.
Graduation Requirements Arts and fine arts (art, music, dance, drama), English, foreign language, mathematics, physical education (includes health), religion (includes Bible studies and theology), science, social studies (includes history). Community service is required.
Special Academic Programs Advanced Placement exam preparation in 6 subject areas; honors section; study at local college for college credit; domestic exchange program; study abroad; academic accommodation for the gifted; ESL (15 students enrolled).
College Placement 50 students graduated in 2004; all went to college, including Boston College; Georgetown University; Princeton University; University of Notre Dame; University of Pennsylvania; Washington University in St. Louis.
Student Life Upper grades have uniform requirement, student council. Discipline rests equally with students and faculty. Attendance at religious services is required.
Tuition and Aid Day student tuition: $14,900; 7-day tuition and room/board: $30,000. Tuition installment plan (Academic Management Services Plan, monthly payment plans, individually arranged payment plans). Merit scholarship grants, need-based scholarship grants, need-based loans available. In 2004–05, 27% of upper-school students received aid.
Admissions Traditional secondary-level entrance grade is 9. For fall 2005, 95 students applied for upper-level admission, 72 were accepted, 60 enrolled. STS required. Deadline for receipt of application materials: none. Application fee required: $50. Interview required.
Athletics Interscholastic: basketball, crew, field hockey, golf, soccer, softball, tennis, volleyball. 2 PE instructors, 5 coaches.
Computers Computers are regularly used in English, foreign language, mathematics, science classes. Computer network features include campus e-mail, on-campus library services, CD-ROMs, online commercial services, Internet access.
Contact Kathleen Creed, Director of Admission and Financial Aid. 847-234-4300 Ext. 213. Fax: 847-234-0865. E-mail: admissions@woodlands.lfc.edu. Web site: www.woodlands.lfc.edu.

See full description on page 1154.

THE WOODLYNDE SCHOOL

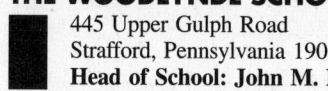

445 Upper Gulph Road
Strafford, Pennsylvania 19087
Head of School: John M. Murray

General Information Coeducational day college-preparatory and technology school. Grades 1–12. Founded: 1976. Setting: suburban. Nearest major city is Philadelphia. 8-acre campus. 2 buildings on campus. Approved or accredited by Pennsylvania Association of Private Academic Schools and Pennsylvania Department of Education. Member of National Association of Independent Schools. Endowment: $795,000. Total enrollment: 309. Upper school average class size: 11. Upper school faculty-student ratio: 1:6.

Faculty School total: 62. In upper school: 14 men, 17 women; 25 have advanced degrees.

Subjects Offered Algebra, American history, American literature, art, art history, art-AP, arts, biology, botany, chemistry, creative writing, drama, earth science, ecology, English, English literature, English-AP, environmental science, European history, fine arts, French, geometry, government/civics, health, history, journalism, keyboarding, Latin, mathematics, music, photography, physical education, physics, political science, psychology, science, social studies, sociology, Spanish, studio art, theater, world history, world literature, writing.

Graduation Requirements Arts and fine arts (art, music, dance, drama), English, foreign language, mathematics, physical education (includes health), science, social studies (includes history).

Special Academic Programs Advanced Placement exam preparation in 2 subject areas; honors section.

College Placement 34 students graduated in 2005; 32 went to college, including Albright College; Drexel University; Elon University; Saint Joseph's University; Temple University. Other: 2 had other specific plans.

Student Life Upper grades have specified standards of dress, student council. Discipline rests primarily with faculty.

Summer Programs Remediation, enrichment programs offered; session focuses on mathematics and reading enrichment; held on campus; accepts boys and girls; open to students from other schools. 100 students usually enrolled. 2006 schedule: June 27 to July 22. Application deadline: May 30.

Tuition and Aid Day student tuition: $20,000. Tuition installment plan (FACTS Tuition Payment Plan). Need-based scholarship grants available. In 2005–06, 24% of upper-school students received aid. Total amount of financial aid awarded in 2005–06: $214,660.

Admissions Traditional secondary-level entrance grade is 10. For fall 2005, 72 students applied for upper-level admission, 28 were accepted, 22 enrolled. Individual IQ required. Deadline for receipt of application materials: none. Application fee required: $100. On-campus interview required.

Athletics Interscholastic: basketball (boys, girls), cross-country running (b), field hockey (g), lacrosse (b,g), soccer (b), softball (g), tennis (b), volleyball (g), wrestling (b); coed intramural: weight lifting. 4 PE instructors, 10 coaches, 1 trainer.

Computers Computers are regularly used in creative writing, English, history, newspaper, publications, social studies, study skills, technology, word processing, writing, yearbook classes. Computer network features include campus e-mail, CD-ROMs, Internet access, DVD.

Contact Barbara A. Zbrzeznj, Director of Middle and Upper School Admissions. 610-687-9660. Fax: 610-687-4752. E-mail: zbrzeznj@woodlynde.org. Web site: www.woodlynde.org.

WOODSIDE INTERNATIONAL SCHOOL

1555 Irving Street
San Francisco, California 94122-1908
Head of School: Mr. John S. Edwards

General Information Coeducational day college-preparatory and arts school. Grades 6–12. Founded: 1976. Setting: urban. 2 buildings on campus. Approved or accredited by Western Association of Schools and Colleges, Western Catholic Education Association, and California Department of Education. Total enrollment: 85. Upper school average class size: 16. Upper school faculty-student ratio: 1:10.

Faculty School total: 19. In upper school: 10 men, 9 women; 3 have advanced degrees.

Subjects Offered Art, art history, biology, calculus, calculus-AP, chemistry, chemistry-AP, civics, community service, creative writing, culinary arts, current events, economics, English, English as a foreign language, ESL, film appreciation, French, gardening, general science, geography, guitar, health, high adventure outdoor program, Japanese, Latin, Mandarin, music, music history, music performance, music theory, outdoor education, parenting, philosophy, photography, physical education, physics, physics-AP, physiology-anatomy, portfolio art, pre-calculus, Russian, science, Spanish, U.S. history, work experience, world history, writing.

Graduation Requirements Arts and fine arts (art, music, dance, drama), current events, English, foreign language, mathematics, parenting, philosophy, physical education (includes health), science, social studies (includes history), work experience. Community service is required.

Special Academic Programs Advanced Placement exam preparation in 4 subject areas; honors section; accelerated programs; independent study; academic accommodation for the gifted, the musically talented, and the artistically talented; ESL (20 students enrolled).

College Placement 25 students graduated in 2005; all went to college, including Academy of Art University; California State University; City College of San Francisco; San Francisco State University; University of California System; University of San Francisco.

Student Life Discipline rests primarily with faculty.

Summer Programs Remediation, advancement, ESL programs offered; session focuses on extra work, make-up work, advancement; held on campus; accepts boys and girls; open to students from other schools. 45 students usually enrolled. 2006 schedule: July 1 to July 29. Application deadline: none.

Tuition and Aid Day student tuition: $14,940. Tuition installment plan (monthly payment plans, individually arranged payment plans). Tuition reduction for siblings, need-based scholarship grants, need-based loans, middle-income loans, prepGATE Loans available.

Admissions Any standardized test required. Deadline for receipt of application materials: none. Application fee required: $50. On-campus interview required.

Athletics Coed Intramural: basketball. 2 PE instructors.

Computers Computer resources include CD-ROMs, Internet access, online weekly homework assignments.

Contact Ms. Janet McClelland, Admissions Counselor. 415-564-1063. Fax: 415-564-2511. E-mail: jmcclelland@wissf.com. Web site: www.wissf.com.

WOODSIDE PARK INTERNATIONAL SCHOOL

Friern Barnet Lane
London N11 3LX, United Kingdom
Head of School: Mr. David Rose

General Information Coeducational boarding and day college-preparatory, general academic, arts, business, and technology school. Boarding grades 12–13, day grades K–13. Setting: suburban. 2 buildings on campus. Approved or accredited by Independent Schools Council (UK). Member of European Council of International Schools. Languages of instruction: English, Spanish, and French. Total enrollment: 404. Upper school average class size: 15. Upper school faculty-student ratio: 1:10.

Upper School Student Profile Grade 7: 25 students (15 boys, 10 girls); Grade 8: 29 students (20 boys, 9 girls); Grade 9: 34 students (23 boys, 11 girls); Grade 10: 36 students (23 boys, 13 girls); Grade 11: 33 students (28 boys, 5 girls); Grade 12: 10 students (6 boys, 4 girls); Grade 13: 15 students (9 boys, 6 girls).

Faculty School total: 81. In upper school: 16 men, 20 women; 10 have advanced degrees.

Subjects Offered Arts, creative arts, ESL, language, mathematics, physical education, science and technology, social studies, Spanish, technology, visual arts.

Special Academic Programs International Baccalaureate program; programs in English, general development for dyslexic students; special instructional classes for students with dyslexia; ESL (16 students enrolled).

College Placement 14 students graduated in 2005; all went to college.

Student Life Upper grades have uniform requirement, student council, honor system. Discipline rests equally with students and faculty.

Admissions Traditional secondary-level entrance grade is 7. No application fee required. On-campus interview required.

Athletics 4 PE instructors.

Computers Computers are regularly used in drawing and design classes. Computer network features include campus e-mail, on-campus library services, CD-ROMs, Internet access.

Contact Ms. Fran Henthorn, Admissions Officer. 44-20-8920-0600. Fax: 44-20-8368-3220. E-mail: admissions@wpis.org. Web site: www.wpis.org.

WOODSIDE PRIORY SCHOOL

302 Portola Road
Founders Hall
Portola Valley, California 94028
Head of School: Mr. Tim J. Molak

petersons.com

General Information Coeducational boarding and day college-preparatory, arts, religious studies, and technology school, affiliated with Roman Catholic Church. Boarding grades 9–12, day grades 6–12. Founded: 1957. Setting: suburban. Nearest major city is San Francisco. Students are housed in single-sex dormitories. 60-acre campus. 25 buildings on campus. Approved or accredited by California Association of Independent Schools, National Catholic Education Association, The Association of Boarding Schools, The College Board, Western Association of Schools and Colleges, Western Catholic Education Association, and California Department of Education. Member of National Association of Independent Schools and Secondary School Admission Test Board. Endowment: $2 million. Total enrollment: 350. Upper school average class size: 18. Upper school faculty-student ratio: 1:10.

Upper School Student Profile Grade 9: 64 students (35 boys, 29 girls); Grade 10: 63 students (34 boys, 29 girls); Grade 11: 69 students (34 boys, 35 girls); Grade 12:

50 students (30 boys, 20 girls). 7% of students are boarding students. 85% are state residents. 4 states are represented in upper school student body. 10% are international students. International students from Hong Kong, Hungary, India, Japan, Republic of Korea, and Taiwan; 4 other countries represented in student body. 40% of students are Roman Catholic.

Faculty School total: 64. In upper school: 28 men, 27 women; 25 reside on campus.

Subjects Offered 20th century physics, 3-dimensional art, acting, advanced chemistry, advanced computer applications, advanced math, algebra, American democracy, American foreign policy, American government, American history, American literature, analysis and differential calculus, animation, anthropology, architecture, art, art history, art-AP, ASB Leadership, astronomy, Basic programming, Bible studies, biology, biology-AP, British literature, calculus, calculus-AP, ceramics, chemistry, chemistry-AP, choir, choral music, Christian and Hebrew scripture, Christian doctrine, church history, classics, college admission preparation, college counseling, community garden, community service, comparative cultures, computer applications, computer art, computer graphics, computer keyboarding, computer math, computer programming, computer science, computer science-AP, computer technologies, computers, constitutional history of U.S., contemporary issues, creative arts, creative writing, desktop publishing, drama, drama performance, earth and space science, earth science, ecology, economics, economics-AP, English, English composition, English literature, English literature-AP, English-AP, environmental science-AP, ethics, European history, European history-AP, expository writing, fine arts, French, French-AP, geography, geometry, government/civics, grammar, health and wellness, history of ideas, honors English, humanities, Japanese, journalism, Latin, life science, mathematics, music, music appreciation, music performance, peer counseling, personal fitness, philosophy, photography, physical education, physics, physics-AP, play production, portfolio art, pre-algebra, pre-calculus, probability and statistics, psychology, religion, science, social science, social studies, sociology, Spanish, Spanish language-AP, Spanish literature-AP, speech, studio art-AP, theater, theology, trigonometry, typing, U.S. history-AP, world history, world literature, writing.

Graduation Requirements Algebra, arts and fine arts (art, music, dance, drama), biology, British literature, calculus, chemistry, Christian and Hebrew scripture, comparative religion, computer science, earth science, English, environmental science, expository writing, foreign language, geometry, mathematics, physical education (includes health), physics, science, social science, social studies (includes history), theology. Community service is required.

Special Academic Programs Advanced Placement exam preparation in 18 subject areas; honors section; independent study; academic accommodation for the gifted, the musically talented, and the artistically talented.

College Placement 50 students graduated in 2005; all went to college, including Harvard University; Princeton University; Santa Clara University; Stanford University; University of California, Berkeley; University of Pennsylvania. Median SAT verbal: 659, median SAT math: 668. 85% scored over 600 on SAT verbal, 82% scored over 600 on SAT math.

Student Life Upper grades have specified standards of dress, student council, honor system. Discipline rests primarily with faculty. Attendance at religious services is required.

Tuition and Aid Day student tuition: $25,617; 7-day tuition and room/board: $35,632. Tuition installment plan (monthly payment plans, individually arranged payment plans). Need-based scholarship grants, paying campus jobs available. In 2005–06, 20% of upper-school students received aid. Total amount of financial aid awarded in 2005–06: $1,087,000.

Admissions Traditional secondary-level entrance grade is 9. For fall 2005, 178 students applied for upper-level admission, 63 were accepted, 37 enrolled. High School Placement Test (closed version) from Scholastic Testing Service, ISEE, PSAT or SAT for applicants to grade 11 and 12, SLEP for foreign students, SSAT, TOEFL or writing sample required. Deadline for receipt of application materials: January 10. Application fee required: $50. On-campus interview required.

Athletics Interscholastic: baseball (boys), basketball (b,g), cross-country running (g), flag football (b), soccer (b,g), softball (g), swimming and diving (g), track and field (b,g), volleyball (g); intramural: alpine skiing (b,g); coed interscholastic: golf, outdoor education, tennis; coed intramural: alpine skiing, bowling, canoeing/kayaking, cross-country running, fitness, ropes courses. 4 PE instructors, 10 coaches, 1 trainer.

Computers Computers are regularly used in all academic, animation, art, college planning, drafting, library, literary magazine, media arts, research skills, senior seminar, study skills, technology, yearbook classes. Computer network features include campus e-mail, on-campus library services, CD-ROMs, online commercial services, Internet access, file transfer, office computer access, DVD, wireless campus network.

Contact Mr. Al D. Zappelli, Director of Admissions and Financial Aid. 650-851-8223 Ext. 101. Fax: 650-851-2839. E-mail: azappelli@woodsidepriory.com. Web site: www.woodsidepriory.com.

See full description on page 1156.

WOODSTOCK SCHOOL

Mussoorie
Uttaranchal 248 179, India
Head of School: Mr. David Jeffery

General Information Coeducational boarding and day college-preparatory, music, and science school, affiliated with Christian faith. Boarding grades 2–12, day grades K–12. Founded: 1854. Setting: rural. Nearest major city is New Delhi. Students are housed in single-sex dormitories. 290-acre campus. 6 buildings on campus. Approved or accredited by Middle States Association of Colleges and Schools. Member of European Council of International Schools. Language of instruction: English. Total enrollment: 467. Upper school average class size: 15. Upper school faculty-student ratio: 1:15.

Upper School Student Profile Grade 9: 63 students (35 boys, 28 girls); Grade 10: 62 students (36 boys, 26 girls); Grade 11: 72 students (33 boys, 39 girls); Grade 12: 78 students (31 boys, 47 girls). 93% of students are boarding students. 55% are international students. International students from Bhutan, Democratic People's Republic of Korea, Japan, Nepal, United Kingdom, and United States; 20 other countries represented in student body. 44% of students are Christian.

Faculty School total: 68. In upper school: 18 men, 15 women; 13 have advanced degrees; 55 reside on campus.

Subjects Offered Algebra, American history, American history-AP, American literature, American studies, art, art history, Asian studies, Bible, Bible studies, biology, biology-AP, business, calculus, calculus-AP, ceramics, chemistry, chemistry-AP, choir, choral music, Christianity, community service, comparative religion, computer programming, computer science, computer science-AP, concert band, dance, drama, economics, English, English language-AP, English literature, English-AP, environmental science, environmental science-AP, ethics, European history, fine arts, French, French-AP, geography, geometry, government, government and politics-AP, health education, Hindi, home economics, Indian studies, industrial arts, jazz band, journalism, macro/microeconomics-AP, macroeconomics-AP, mathematics, mathematics-AP, microeconomics-AP, music, philosophy, physical education, physics, physics-AP, religion, science, social studies, sociology, statistics, theater, trigonometry, U.S. government and politics-AP, vocal music, world history, world history-AP, world literature, world religions, writing, yearbook.

Graduation Requirements Arts and fine arts (art, music, dance, drama), Christian studies, computer literacy, English, foreign language, mathematics, physical education (includes health), science, social studies (includes history). Community service is required.

Special Academic Programs Advanced Placement exam preparation in 18 subject areas; independent study; study abroad; academic accommodation for the gifted, the musically talented, and the artistically talented; ESL (30 students enrolled).

College Placement 85 students graduated in 2005; 83 went to college, including Brandeis University; Calvin College; Gordon College; Indiana University Bloomington; University of Chicago; Wheaton College. Other: 2 had other specific plans. Mean SAT verbal: 531, mean SAT math: 589, mean composite ACT: 23. 29% scored over 600 on SAT verbal, 35% scored over 600 on SAT math, 30% scored over 26 on composite ACT.

Student Life Upper grades have specified standards of dress, student council. Discipline rests primarily with faculty. Attendance at religious services is required.

Tuition and Aid Day student tuition: $13,000; 7-day tuition and room/board: $13,000. Tuition installment plan (individually arranged payment plans). Need-based scholarship grants available. In 2005–06, 20% of upper-school students received aid.

Admissions Traditional secondary-level entrance grade is 11. For fall 2005, 420 students applied for upper-level admission, 76 were accepted, 60 enrolled. Deadline for receipt of application materials: none. Application fee required: $60. On-campus interview recommended.

Athletics Interscholastic: basketball (boys, girls), cricket (b), cross-country running (b,g), field hockey (b,g), track and field (b,g); intramural: back packing (b,g), badminton (b,g), basketball (b,g), climbing (b,g), cricket (b), cross-country running (b,g), field hockey (b,g), gymnastics (b,g), hiking/backpacking (b,g), hockey (b,g), outdoor activities (b,g), outdoor education (b,g), outdoor skills (b,g), running (b,g), soccer (b,g), table tennis (b,g), tennis (b,g), track and field (b,g); coed intramural: back packing, hiking/backpacking. 3 PE instructors.

Computers Computers are regularly used in all academic classes. Computer network features include campus e-mail, on-campus library services, CD-ROMs, Internet access.

Contact Ms. Cathy E. Holmes, Director of Admissions. 91-135-2632547 Ext. 2424. Fax: 91-135-2630897. E-mail: admissions@woodstock.ac.in. Web site: www.woodstock.ac.in.

THE WOODWARD SCHOOL

1102 Hancock Street
Quincy, Massachusetts 02169
Head of School: Thomas L. Wesner, JD

General Information Girls' day college-preparatory, arts, and technology school. Grades 6–12. Founded: 1869. Setting: urban. Nearest major city is Boston. 1-acre campus. 1 building on campus. Approved or accredited by Association of Independent Schools in New England, New England Association of Schools and Colleges, and

Massachusetts Department of Education. Endowment: $231,000. Total enrollment: 158. Upper school average class size: 15. Upper school faculty-student ratio: 1:8.
Upper School Student Profile Grade 9: 25 students (25 girls); Grade 10: 25 students (25 girls); Grade 11: 25 students (25 girls); Grade 12: 29 students (29 girls).
Faculty School total: 24. In upper school: 6 men, 18 women; 12 have advanced degrees.
Subjects Offered Advanced computer applications, algebra, American history, American literature, anatomy, art, arts, biology, calculus, calculus-AP, chemistry, classical studies, classics, community service, computer graphics, computer science, constitutional law, drama, ecology, English, English language and composition-AP, environmental science, filmmaking, fine arts, French, health and wellness, health science, language arts, Latin, Latin-AP, law and the legal system, literature, literature and composition-AP, mathematics, media studies, physics, physics-AP, physiology, political science, portfolio art, pre-algebra, psychology, science, social science, social studies, Spanish, theater arts, U.S. government, U.S. history, Vietnam history, Web authoring, Web site design, world history, world literature, World War II, writing, writing.
Graduation Requirements Arts and fine arts (art, music, dance, drama), computer science, English, foreign language, mathematics, science, social studies (includes history). Community service is required.
Special Academic Programs Advanced Placement exam preparation in 4 subject areas; honors section; independent study; study at local college for college credit; academic accommodation for the artistically talented.
College Placement 24 students graduated in 2005; all went to college, including Boston College; Lesley University; Mount Ida College; University of Massachusetts Amherst; Wheaton College; Worcester Polytechnic Institute.
Student Life Upper grades have specified standards of dress, student council, honor system. Discipline rests primarily with faculty.
Tuition and Aid Day student tuition: $8820. Tuition installment plan (SMART Tuition Payment Plan, individually arranged payment plans). Tuition reduction for siblings, merit scholarship grants, need-based scholarship grants available. In 2005–06, 28% of upper-school students received aid; total upper-school merit-scholarship money awarded: $6500. Total amount of financial aid awarded in 2005–06: $61,590.
Admissions Traditional secondary-level entrance grade is 9. For fall 2005, 35 students applied for upper-level admission, 20 were accepted, 17 enrolled. School's own exam and writing sample required. Deadline for receipt of application materials: none. Application fee required: $40. On-campus interview required.
Athletics Interscholastic: basketball, lacrosse, soccer, softball. 6 coaches.
Computers Computers are regularly used in all academic classes. Computer network features include on-campus library services, CD-ROMs, Internet access, file transfer, office computer access, DVD.
Contact Barbara A. Segadelli, Director of Admissions. 617-773-5610. Fax: 617-770-1551. E-mail: wdwdschl@aol.com. Web site: www.thewoodwardschool.org.

WOOSTER SCHOOL

91 Miry Brook Road
Danbury, Connecticut 06810
Head of School: Mr. George N. King Jr.

petersons.com

General Information Coeducational day college-preparatory, arts, and technology school, affiliated with Episcopal Church. Grades K–12. Founded: 1926. Setting: suburban. 125-acre campus. 15 buildings on campus. Approved or accredited by Connecticut Association of Independent Schools, National Association of Episcopal Schools, New England Association of Schools and Colleges, and Connecticut Department of Education. Member of National Association of Independent Schools. Endowment: $5.5 million. Total enrollment: 426. Upper school average class size: 12. Upper school faculty-student ratio: 1:10.
Upper School Student Profile Grade 9: 36 students (21 boys, 15 girls); Grade 10: 41 students (22 boys, 19 girls); Grade 11: 32 students (16 boys, 16 girls); Grade 12: 35 students (15 boys, 20 girls). 8% of students are members of Episcopal Church.
Faculty School total: 97. In upper school: 13 men, 11 women; 14 have advanced degrees.
Subjects Offered Algebra, American government, American history, American history-AP, ancient history, art, art-AP, biology, biology-AP, calculus, calculus-AP, chemistry, community service, computer animation, computer science, computer science-AP, creative thinking, earth science, ecology, economics, electronics, English, English literature-AP, English/composition-AP, ESL, ethics, European history-AP, fine arts, French, French-AP, general science, geography, geometry, Japanese, mathematics, music, music-AP, Pacific art, photography, physical education, physics, political science, pottery, religion, science, social studies, Spanish, Spanish-AP, statistics, statistics-AP, U.S. history-AP.
Graduation Requirements 20th century history, arts and fine arts (art, music, dance, drama), computer science, English, foreign language, mathematics, physical education (includes health), religion (includes Bible studies and theology), science, social studies (includes history), 100 hours of community service, senior independent study and senior colloquium, Leadership in Self-help (jobs) Program.
Special Academic Programs Advanced Placement exam preparation in 12 subject areas; honors section; accelerated programs; independent study; term-away projects; study at local college for college credit; study abroad; ESL (5 students enrolled).

College Placement 35 students graduated in 2004; all went to college, including Columbia College; Cornell University; Dartmouth College; Hamilton College; Princeton University; Swarthmore College. Mean SAT verbal: 594, mean SAT math: 582. 50% scored over 600 on SAT verbal, 47% scored over 600 on SAT math.
Student Life Upper grades have specified standards of dress, student council, honor system. Discipline rests equally with students and faculty. Attendance at religious services is required.
Tuition and Aid Day student tuition: $13,950–$21,800. Tuition installment plan (The Tuition Plan, Insured Tuition Payment Plan, monthly payment plans, individually arranged payment plans, school's own payment plan). Need-based scholarship grants available. In 2004–05, 25% of upper-school students received aid. Total amount of financial aid awarded in 2004–05: $1,370,000.
Admissions Traditional secondary-level entrance grade is 9. For fall 2005, 47 students applied for upper-level admission, 35 were accepted, 18 enrolled. ISEE or SSAT required. Deadline for receipt of application materials: February 2. Application fee required: $50. On-campus interview required.
Athletics Interscholastic: baseball (boys), basketball (b,g), cross-country running (b,g), golf (b), lacrosse (b,g), soccer (b,g), softball (g), tennis (b,g), volleyball (g); intramural: dance (g), strength & conditioning (b,g); coed intramural: basketball, outdoor education, ropes courses, soccer, weight lifting, weight training. 3 PE instructors, 15 coaches, 1 trainer.
Computers Computers are regularly used in all classes. Computer network features include campus e-mail, on-campus library services, CD-ROMs, Internet access, file transfer, office computer access, DVD, wireless campus network.
Contact Samuel L. Gaudet, Director of Admissions. 203-830-3916. Fax: 203-790-7147. E-mail: sam.gaudet@woostersch.org. Web site: www.woosterschool.org.

ANNOUNCEMENT FROM THE SCHOOL Founded in 1926 by Reverend Aaron C. Coburn, Wooster School, an independent, coeducational, K–12 day school, is committed to its founding principles: Intellectual Excellence, Hard Work, Simplicity, and Religion. Wooster has a long tradition of diversity: 29% of students receive financial aid and 22% represent ethnic minorities. Benefiting from small classes and a 7:1 student-teacher ratio, 421 students from Fairfield and Westchester Counties learn life's lessons as they prepare for college and beyond, discovering joy in this journey along the rigorous road to becoming leaders for good in the world. The Upper School's (9–12) rigorous college-preparatory, liberal arts curriculum includes Honors and AP courses in the core curriculum and computer science, music, and art. A yearlong or semester-long study-abroad program in France or Spain allows sophomores and juniors to develop their fluency in foreign languages and cultures. By junior year, students meet weekly with College Guidance to explore personal, intellectual, and career aspirations and to customize a college search and application strategy. During senior year, students complete a culminating independent project. Wooster's K–12 curriculum is supplemented by a social and academic Honor Code, a weekly ecumenical chapel program, and a founding philosophy of self-help, manifested in a senior-administered program to teach personal responsibility through service and leadership. Anchoring the 125-acre hillside campus is Wooster's historic James Marshall Chapel, which is surrounded by 15 buildings, including a state-of-the-art Middle School building, library, computer lab, music and science buildings, an art center, and the Alumni and new Forever Young Gymnasiums. Providing students the opportunity to unearth hidden talents and passions, Wooster strives to balance academics, athletics, and the arts. Armed with the tools for success and an appreciation for all of life's opportunities, students are motivated to pursue with zeal their academic, physical, spiritual, moral, and aesthetic possibilities.

WORCESTER ACADEMY

81 Providence Street
Worcester, Massachusetts 01604
Head of School: Dexter Morse

petersons.com

General Information Coeducational boarding and day college-preparatory, arts, and ESL school. Boarding grades 9–PG, day grades 6–12. Founded: 1834. Setting: urban. Nearest major city is Boston. Students are housed in single-sex dormitories. 60-acre campus. 14 buildings on campus. Approved or accredited by Association of Independent Schools in New England, New England Association of Schools and Colleges, and The Association of Boarding Schools. Member of National Association of Independent Schools and Secondary School Admission Test Board. Endowment: $31.5 million. Total enrollment: 631. Upper school average class size: 13. Upper school faculty-student ratio: 1:7.
Upper School Student Profile Grade 9: 96 students (45 boys, 51 girls); Grade 10: 121 students (76 boys, 45 girls); Grade 11: 128 students (73 boys, 55 girls); Grade 12: 109 students (53 boys, 56 girls); Postgraduate: 26 students (23 boys, 3 girls). 30% of students are boarding students. 70% are state residents. 15 states are represented in upper school student body. 15% are international students. International students from China, Hong Kong, Japan, Republic of Korea, Taiwan, and Thailand; 8 other countries represented in student body.

Worcester Academy

Faculty School total: 100. In upper school: 45 men, 35 women; 50 have advanced degrees; 30 reside on campus.

Subjects Offered Algebra, American history, American literature, anatomy, art, biology, calculus, chemistry, community service, drama, earth science, English, English literature, environmental science, ESL, European history, fine arts, French, geography, geometry, health, history, Holocaust studies, human anatomy, Latin, mathematics, music, organic chemistry, photography, physical education, physics, Russia and contemporary Europe, Russian history, science, social studies, Spanish, theater, theater design and production, trigonometry, world history.

Graduation Requirements Arts and fine arts (art, music, dance, drama), English, foreign language, mathematics, physical education (includes health), science, social studies (includes history), senior projects. Community service is required.

Special Academic Programs Advanced Placement exam preparation in 14 subject areas; honors section; independent study; ESL (25 students enrolled).

College Placement 115 students graduated in 2005; all went to college, including Boston College; Holy Cross College; Trinity College; University of Massachusetts Amherst; University of Wisconsin–Madison; Yale University. 56% scored over 600 on SAT verbal, 63% scored over 600 on SAT math.

Student Life Upper grades have specified standards of dress, student council. Discipline rests equally with students and faculty.

Tuition and Aid Day student tuition: $19,800; 5-day tuition and room/board: $31,725; 7-day tuition and room/board: $35,525. Tuition installment plan (Academic Management Services Plan). Merit scholarship grants, need-based scholarship grants, paying campus jobs available. In 2005–06, 36% of upper-school students received aid; total upper-school merit-scholarship money awarded: $100,000. Total amount of financial aid awarded in 2005–06: $2,500,000.

Admissions Traditional secondary-level entrance grade is 9. For fall 2005, 370 students applied for upper-level admission, 185 were accepted, 114 enrolled. ACT, PSAT or SAT for applicants to grade 11 and 12, school's own test, SSAT or TOEFL or SLEP required. Deadline for receipt of application materials: February 1. Application fee required: $50. On-campus interview required.

Athletics Interscholastic: baseball (boys), basketball (b,g), cross-country running (b,g), field hockey (g), football (b), ice hockey (b), lacrosse (b,g), skiing (downhill) (b,g), soccer (b,g), softball (g), swimming and diving (b,g), tennis (b,g), track and field (b,g), volleyball (g); intramural: aerobics/dance (g), basketball (b,g), dance squad (g), dance team (g); coed interscholastic: golf, water polo; coed intramural: paddle tennis, softball, tennis, volleyball. 3 PE instructors, 5 coaches, 3 trainers.

Computers Computer network features include campus e-mail, on-campus library services, CD-ROMs, online commercial services, Internet access, DVD, wireless campus network.

Contact Jonathan G. Baker, Director of Admission and Financial Aid. 508-754-5302 Ext. 119. Fax: 508-752-2382. E-mail: jonathan.baker@worcesteracademy.org. Web site: www.worcesteracademy.org.

ANNOUNCEMENT FROM THE SCHOOL Worcester Academy, distinctive for its urban location, is a coeducational college-preparatory school for day students in grades 6–PG and resident students in grades 9–PG. Worcester Academy combines a traditional course of study with extensive offerings in athletics and the visual and performing arts. A special program is offered for international students.

See full description on page 1158.

WORCESTER PREPARATORY SCHOOL

508 South Main Street
PO Box 1006
Berlin, Maryland 21811
Head of School: Dr. Barry W. Tull

General Information Coeducational day college-preparatory, arts, and technology school. Grades PK–12. Founded: 1970. Setting: small town. Nearest major city is Ocean City. 45-acre campus. 6 buildings on campus. Approved or accredited by Association of Independent Maryland Schools, Middle States Association of Colleges and Schools, and Maryland Department of Education. Member of National Association of Independent Schools. Total enrollment: 563. Upper school average class size: 15. Upper school faculty-student ratio: 1:10.

Upper School Student Profile Grade 9: 58 students (29 boys, 29 girls); Grade 10: 44 students (22 boys, 22 girls); Grade 11: 43 students (22 boys, 21 girls); Grade 12: 29 students (16 boys, 13 girls).

Faculty School total: 59. In upper school: 12 men, 20 women; 26 have advanced degrees.

Subjects Offered Algebra, American history, American literature, art, art history, biology, biology-AP, calculus, calculus-AP, chemistry, chemistry-AP, computer programming, computer science, creative writing, dance, drama, earth science, economics, English, English literature, English literature and composition-AP, English-AP, European history, fine arts, French, geography, geometry, government/civics, Latin, literature and composition-AP, literature-AP, mathematics, military history, music, music theory, paleontology, physical education, physics, physics-AP, psychology, SAT preparation, science, social science, social studies, Spanish, speech,

statistics, technological applications, technology/design, theater, typing, U.S. history-AP, vocal music, world history, world history-AP, world literature, writing.

Graduation Requirements Arts and fine arts (art, music, dance, drama), computer science, English, foreign language, mathematics, physical education (includes health), science, social science, social studies (includes history).

Special Academic Programs Advanced Placement exam preparation in 9 subject areas; honors section; independent study; academic accommodation for the gifted.

College Placement 46 students graduated in 2005; all went to college, including Duke University; Furman University; University of Pennsylvania; University of Richmond; Villanova University; Washington College.

Student Life Upper grades have uniform requirement, student council, honor system. Discipline rests primarily with faculty.

Tuition and Aid Day student tuition: $9300. Tuition installment plan (Key Tuition Payment Plan, monthly payment plans, individually arranged payment plans). Need-based scholarship grants available. In 2005–06, 1% of upper-school students received aid.

Admissions Traditional secondary-level entrance grade is 9. For fall 2005, 29 students applied for upper-level admission, 17 were accepted, 14 enrolled. Achievement/Aptitude/Writing and writing sample required. Deadline for receipt of application materials: none. Application fee required: $50. On-campus interview required.

Athletics Interscholastic: basketball (boys, girls), field hockey (g), golf (b,g), lacrosse (b,g), soccer (b,g), tennis (b,g); intramural: basketball (b,g), dance (b,g), flag football (b,g), soccer (b,g); coed interscholastic: tennis. 3 PE instructors, 162 coaches, 1 trainer.

Computers Computers are regularly used in all classes. Computer network features include campus e-mail, on-campus library services, CD-ROMs, online commercial services, Internet access, file transfer, office computer access, DVD.

Contact Lisa B. Cook, Director of Admissions. 410-641-3575. Fax: 410-641-3586. E-mail: lcook@worcesterprep.org. Web site: www.worcesterprep.org.

WYOMING SEMINARY

201 North Sprague Avenue
Kingston, Pennsylvania 18704-3593
Head of School: H. Jeremy Packard

petersons.com

General Information Coeducational boarding and day college-preparatory school, affiliated with Methodist Church. Boarding grades 9–PG, day grades PK–PG. Founded: 1844. Setting: suburban. Nearest major city is Wilkes-Barre. Students are housed in single-sex dormitories. 18-acre campus. 12 buildings on campus. Approved or accredited by Middle States Association of Colleges and Schools, Pennsylvania Association of Private Academic Schools, The Association of Boarding Schools, The College Board, and Pennsylvania Department of Education. Member of National Association of Independent Schools and Secondary School Admission Test Board. Endowment: $47.5 million. Total enrollment: 793. Upper school average class size: 13. Upper school faculty-student ratio: 1:8.

Upper School Student Profile Grade 9: 77 students (40 boys, 37 girls); Grade 10: 132 students (66 boys, 66 girls); Grade 11: 110 students (59 boys, 51 girls); Grade 12: 108 students (56 boys, 52 girls); Postgraduate: 14 students (13 boys, 1 girl). 33% of students are boarding students. 74% are state residents. 10 states are represented in upper school student body. 10% are international students. International students from Germany, Japan, Republic of Korea, Saudi Arabia, Taiwan, and Thailand; 14 other countries represented in student body. 10% of students are Methodist.

Faculty School total: 122. In upper school: 39 men, 30 women; 46 have advanced degrees; 45 reside on campus.

Subjects Offered 20th century world history, 3-dimensional design, advanced computer applications, African history, algebra, alternative physical education, American Civil War, American government-AP, American history, American literature, analysis, analysis and differential calculus, analytic geometry, anatomy and physiology, ancient world history, animal behavior, art, art appreciation, art history, art history-AP, astronomy, Bible studies, biology, biology-AP, botany, British literature, calculus, calculus-AP, ceramics, chemistry, chemistry-AP, choral music, civil rights, college admission preparation, college counseling, community service, computer education, computer graphics, computer math, computer programming, computer science, conceptual physics, creative writing, critical writing, dance, desktop publishing, discrete math, drama, drawing and design, ecology, economics, economics and history, English, English literature, environmental science, environmental science-AP, ESL, European history, European history-AP, expository writing, fine arts, forensic science, French, French-AP, genetics, geography, geometry, health education, history, history of music, honors geometry, independent study, Irish literature, Judaic studies, Latin, Latin-AP, marine biology, mathematics, microeconomics, music, music theory, music theory-AP, oceanography, philosophy, photography, physical education, physics, poetry, pre-calculus, printmaking, psychology, psychology-AP, public speaking, religion, Russian, Russian literature, science, science research, Shakespeare, social studies, sociology, Spanish, Spanish-AP, statistics, statistics-AP, studio art-AP, theater, trigonometry, U.S. history-AP, women in literature, world civilizations, world geography, world history, world literature, world religions, World War II.

Graduation Requirements Arts and fine arts (art, music, dance, drama), computer science, English, foreign language, mathematics, physical education (includes health),

public speaking, religion (includes Bible studies and theology), science, social studies (includes history), 40 hours of community service.

Special Academic Programs Advanced Placement exam preparation in 19 subject areas; honors section; independent study; study at local college for college credit; study abroad; ESL (37 students enrolled).

College Placement 127 students graduated in 2005; 122 went to college, including Boston College; Cornell University; Duke University; Georgetown University; Hamilton College; Lafayette College. Other: 2 went to work, 1 entered a postgraduate year.

Student Life Upper grades have specified standards of dress, student council, honor system. Discipline rests equally with students and faculty.

Summer Programs Remediation, enrichment, advancement, ESL, sports, art/fine arts, computer instruction programs offered; session focuses on performing arts and ESL; held on campus; accepts boys and girls; open to students from other schools. 700 students usually enrolled. 2006 schedule: June 25 to August 24.

Tuition and Aid Day student tuition: $17,275; 7-day tuition and room/board: $33,725. Tuition installment plan (Key Tuition Payment Plan, monthly payment plans). Merit scholarship grants, need-based scholarship grants, need-based loans, prepGATE Loans available. In 2005–06, 45% of upper-school students received aid; total upper-school merit-scholarship money awarded: $126,175. Total amount of financial aid awarded in 2005–06: $4,400,000.

Admissions Traditional secondary-level entrance grade is 9. For fall 2005, 265 students applied for upper-level admission, 169 were accepted, 107 enrolled. ACT, PSAT or SAT for applicants to grade 11 and 12, SSAT or TOEFL or SLEP required. Deadline for receipt of application materials: none. Application fee required: $75. Interview required.

Athletics Interscholastic: baseball (boys), basketball (b,g), cross-country running (b,g), diving (b,g), field hockey (g), football (b), ice hockey (b,g), lacrosse (b,g), soccer (b,g), softball (b,g), swimming and diving (b,g), tennis (b,g), wrestling (b,g); coed interscholastic: golf; coed intramural: alpine skiing, back packing, ballet, bicycling, bowling, combined training, dance, fencing, fitness, modern dance, nautilus, outdoor activities, outdoor recreation, physical training, skiing (downhill), tai chi. 2 PE instructors, 4 coaches, 2 trainers.

Computers Computers are regularly used in art, history, mathematics, music, science classes. Computer network features include campus e-mail, on-campus library services, CD-ROMs, Internet access, DVD.

Contact Mr. Randolph I. Granger, Director of Admission. 570-270-2160. Fax: 570-270-2191. E-mail: admission@wyomingseminary.org. Web site: www.wyomingseminary.org.

See full description on page 1160.

XAVIER COLLEGE PREPARATORY

4710 North Fifth Street
Phoenix, Arizona 85012
Head of School: Sr. Joan Fitzgerald, BVM

General Information Girls' day college-preparatory school, affiliated with Roman Catholic Church. Grades 9–12. Founded: 1943. Setting: urban. 13-acre campus. 7 buildings on campus. Approved or accredited by National Catholic Education Association, North Central Association of Colleges and Schools, Western Catholic Education Association, and Arizona Department of Education. Endowment: $1 million. Total enrollment: 1,163. Upper school average class size: 25. Upper school faculty-student ratio: 1:22.

Upper School Student Profile Grade 9: 307 students (307 girls); Grade 10: 266 students (266 girls); Grade 11: 301 students (301 girls); Grade 12: 289 students (289 girls). 75% of students are Roman Catholic.

Faculty School total: 90. In upper school: 20 men, 70 women; 50 have advanced degrees.

Subjects Offered Accounting, algebra, American history, American literature, anatomy, art, art history, biology, calculus, chemistry, Chinese, choir, clayworking, community service, computer programming, computer science, concert choir, contemporary issues, creative arts, dance, drama, economics, English, English literature, environmental science, ethics, European history, expository writing, fine arts, French, geography, geometry, government/civics, Latin, mathematics, music, philosophy, physical education, physics, psychology, religion, science, social science, social studies, sociology, Spanish, studio art, theology, trigonometry, world literature, writing.

Graduation Requirements American literature, arts and fine arts (art, music, dance, drama), computer science, English, foreign language, mathematics, physical education (includes health), religion (includes Bible studies and theology), science, social studies (includes history), AZ History Free Enterprise Independent Study. Community service is required.

Special Academic Programs Advanced Placement exam preparation in 18 subject areas; honors section; independent study; study at local college for college credit; academic accommodation for the gifted.

College Placement 290 students graduated in 2005; all went to college, including Arizona State University; Northern Arizona University; The University of Arizona; University of San Diego; University of Southern California. Median SAT verbal: 592, median SAT math: 560.

Student Life Upper grades have uniform requirement, student council. Discipline rests primarily with faculty. Attendance at religious services is required.

Summer Programs Enrichment, advancement, sports, art/fine arts, computer instruction programs offered; session focuses on advancement and fitness; held both on and off campus; held at a variety of tracks and fields in Phoenix; accepts girls; not open to students from other schools. 180 students usually enrolled. 2006 schedule: May 30 to June 23. Application deadline: April 1.

Tuition and Aid Day student tuition: $7605–$9990. Tuition installment plan (monthly payment plans, semester payment plan). Need-based scholarship grants, reduced tuition rate for Catholic families registered in Catholic parishes of the Diocese of Phoenix available. In 2005–06, 22% of upper-school students received aid. Total amount of financial aid awarded in 2005–06: $660,000.

Admissions Traditional secondary-level entrance grade is 9. High School Placement Test (closed version) from Scholastic Testing Service required. Deadline for receipt of application materials: January 30. Application fee required: $35. On-campus interview required.

Athletics Interscholastic: aerobics/dance, badminton, basketball, cheering, crew, cross-country running, danceline, diving, golf, lacrosse, pom squad, soccer, softball, swimming and diving, tennis, track and field, volleyball; intramural: aerobics, basketball, crew, dance, modern dance, physical fitness, physical training; coed intramural: badminton, basketball, soccer, softball, tennis. 4 PE instructors, 21 coaches, 1 trainer.

Computers Computers are regularly used in all classes. Computer network features include campus e-mail, on-campus library services, CD-ROMs, Internet access.

Contact Paula Petrowski, Director of Admissions. 602-277-3772. Fax: 602-279-1346. E-mail: admissions@xcp.org. Web site: www.xcp.org.

YESHIVA ATLANTA

3130 Raymond Drive
Atlanta, Georgia 30340
Head of School: Rabbi Michael Berger

General Information Coeducational day college-preparatory, general academic, religious studies, bilingual studies, and technology school, affiliated with Jewish faith. Grades 9–12. Founded: 1970. Setting: urban. 19-acre campus. 1 building on campus. Approved or accredited by Southern Association of Colleges and Schools and Georgia Department of Education. Total enrollment: 80. Upper school average class size: 10. Upper school faculty-student ratio: 1:6.

Upper School Student Profile Grade 9: 23 students (8 boys, 15 girls); Grade 10: 15 students (8 boys, 7 girls); Grade 11: 22 students (16 boys, 6 girls); Grade 12: 20 students (10 boys, 10 girls). 100% of students are Jewish.

Faculty School total: 16. In upper school: 9 men, 7 women; 15 have advanced degrees.

Subjects Offered Algebra, American history, American literature, anatomy and physiology, Bible, biology, biology-AP, British literature, calculus, calculus-AP, chemistry, composition, computer applications, computer programming, drama, geometry, grammar, health, Hebrew, internship, Jewish history, Jewish studies, journalism, library assistant, literature, Middle East, physical education, physics, pre-calculus, Spanish, speech, Talmud, U.S. history-AP, Web site design, world history, world history-AP, yearbook.

Graduation Requirements Electives, English, foreign language, Judaic studies, mathematics, physical education (includes health), science, social studies (includes history).

Special Academic Programs Advanced Placement exam preparation in 6 subject areas; honors section; independent study.

College Placement 23 students graduated in 2005; all went to college, including Brandeis University; Dartmouth College; Georgia State University; Goucher College; University of Maryland, College Park; Yeshiva University. Median SAT verbal: 581, median SAT math: 568. 43% scored over 600 on SAT verbal, 35% scored over 600 on SAT math.

Student Life Upper grades have uniform requirement, student council, honor system. Discipline rests primarily with faculty. Attendance at religious services is required.

Tuition and Aid Day student tuition: $1600. Tuition installment plan (FACTS Tuition Payment Plan). Need-based scholarship grants available.

Admissions Traditional secondary-level entrance grade is 9. Achievement tests required. Deadline for receipt of application materials: none. Application fee required: $50. Interview required.

Athletics Interscholastic: baseball (boys), basketball (b,g), golf (b), soccer (b,g), volleyball (g), wrestling (b). 1 PE instructor, 5 coaches.

Computers Computers are regularly used in French, journalism, Spanish, video film production, Web site design, yearbook classes.

Contact Ms. Kim Bieniemy, Office Manager. 770-451-5299 Ext. 21. Fax: 770-451-5571. E-mail: kbieniemy.ya@atlchai.org.

YOKOHAMA INTERNATIONAL SCHOOL

258 Yamate-cho, Naka-ku
Yokohama 231-0862, Japan
Head of School: Mr. Neil M. Richards

General Information Coeducational day college-preparatory school. Grades N–12. Founded: 1924. Setting: urban. 3-acre campus. 8 buildings on campus. Approved or accredited by European Council of International Schools and New England Association of Schools and Colleges. Language of instruction: English. Total enrollment: 637. Upper school average class size: 13. Upper school faculty-student ratio: 1:10.
Upper School Student Profile Grade 9: 48 students (23 boys, 25 girls); Grade 10: 57 students (28 boys, 29 girls); Grade 11: 60 students (31 boys, 29 girls); Grade 12: 46 students (19 boys, 27 girls).
Faculty School total: 94. In upper school: 27 men, 20 women; 20 have advanced degrees.
Subjects Offered Advanced chemistry, advanced math, art, band, biology, ceramics, chemistry, choir, computer programming, drama, Dutch, economics, English, English literature, environmental science, European history, French, geography, German, horticulture, information technology, International Baccalaureate courses, Japanese, mathematics, modern languages, music composition, music theory, physical education, physics, Spanish, studio art, theater, theory of knowledge, world history, world literature.
Graduation Requirements Arts, English, foreign language, information technology, mathematics, physical education (includes health), science, senior thesis, social studies (includes history), theory of knowledge, 50 hours of community service.
Special Academic Programs International Baccalaureate program.
College Placement 33 students graduated in 2005; 30 went to college, including Middlebury College; State University of New York College at Geneseo; University of California, San Diego; University of Chicago; University of Hawaii at Manoa; Yale University. Other: 1 went to work, 2 had other specific plans. Mean SAT verbal: 537, mean SAT math: 577.
Student Life Upper grades have specified standards of dress, student council. Discipline rests primarily with faculty.
Summer Programs Remediation, enrichment, sports programs offered; session focuses on English, mathematics and basketball; held on campus; accepts boys and girls; open to students from other schools. 40 students usually enrolled. 2006 schedule: June 19 to July 7. Application deadline: May 15.
Tuition and Aid Day student tuition: ¥1,975,000. Tuition installment plan (individually arranged payment plans).
Admissions Traditional secondary-level entrance grade is 9. For fall 2005, 113 students applied for upper-level admission, 67 were accepted, 54 enrolled. Deadline for receipt of application materials: none. Application fee required: ¥20,000. Interview recommended.
Athletics Interscholastic: baseball (boys), basketball (b,g), cross-country running (b,g), field hockey (g), soccer (b), track and field (b,g), volleyball (g); coed intramural: back packing, bicycling, canoeing/kayaking, fitness walking, hiking/backpacking, kayaking, outdoor education, skiing (downhill), yoga. 4 PE instructors.
Computers Computers are regularly used in career education, career exploration, college planning, geography, graphic arts, graphic design, mathematics, media, music, newspaper, photography, publications, SAT preparation, science, senior seminar, social sciences, theater arts, video film production, Web site design, word processing, writing, yearbook classes. Computer network features include campus e-mail, on-campus library services, CD-ROMs, online commercial services, Internet access, wireless campus network.
Contact Ms. Susan Chen, Administrative Officer. 81-45-622-0084. Fax: 81-45-621-0379. E-mail: yis@yis.ac.jp. Web site: www.yis.ac.jp.

ANNOUNCEMENT FROM THE SCHOOL Yokohama International School is located opposite a park in the heart of the old foreign residential section of Yokohama. Founded in 1924 on the principles of internationalism, the School was the first nonsectarian, nonnational, coeducational school in Japan, and it was the second in the world to use the word "international" in its name.

YORK COUNTRY DAY SCHOOL

1071 Regents' Glen Boulevard
York, Pennsylvania 17403
Head of School: Robert W. Shanner

General Information Coeducational day college-preparatory school. Boys grades PS–11, girls grades PS–8. Founded: 1953. Setting: small town. Nearest major city is Baltimore, MD. 17-acre campus. 1 building on campus. Approved or accredited by Middle States Association of Colleges and Schools, Pennsylvania Association of Private Academic Schools, and Pennsylvania Department of Education. Member of National Association of Independent Schools. Endowment: $200,000. Total enrollment: 243. Upper school average class size: 13.
Faculty School total: 42.
Subjects Offered Algebra, American history, American literature, art, art history, biochemistry, biology, calculus, chemistry, community service, computer programming, computer science, creative writing, drama, English, English literature, European

history, fine arts, French, geography, geometry, government/civics, health, history, journalism, literature, mathematics, music, physical education, physics, psychology, public speaking, science, social studies, Spanish, speech, theater, world history.
Graduation Requirements English, foreign language, mathematics, physical education (includes health), public speaking, science, social studies (includes history). Community service is required.
Special Academic Programs Advanced Placement exam preparation in 8 subject areas; honors section; independent study; term-away projects; study at local college for college credit; study abroad; academic accommodation for the gifted.
College Placement 20 students graduated in 2005; all went to college, including Carnegie Mellon University; Connecticut College; Franklin and Marshall College. Median SAT verbal: 610, median SAT math: 610.
Student Life Upper grades have specified standards of dress, student council, honor system. Discipline rests primarily with faculty.
Tuition and Aid Day student tuition: $11,475. Tuition installment plan (Insured Tuition Payment Plan, monthly payment plans, semester payment plan). Need-based scholarship grants available. In 2005–06, 22% of upper-school students received aid. Total amount of financial aid awarded in 2005–06: $215,000.
Admissions Traditional secondary-level entrance grade is 9. 3-R Achievement Test, Academic Profile Tests, Archdiocese of Boston High School entrance exam provided by STS or Archdiocese of Boston or STS required. Deadline for receipt of application materials: none. Application fee required: $35. On-campus interview required.
Athletics Interscholastic: basketball (boys, girls), field hockey (g), soccer (b,g), softball (g), tennis (b,g); intramural: basketball (b,g); coed interscholastic: golf. 2 PE instructors, 6 coaches.
Computers Computer network features include campus e-mail, on-campus library services, CD-ROMs, online commercial services, Internet access, file transfer.
Contact Mr. William D. Diskin, Director of Admission and Marketing. 717-843-9805. Fax: 717-815-6769. E-mail: wdiskin@ycds.org. Web site: www.ycds.org.

YORK PREPARATORY SCHOOL

40 West 68th Street
New York, New York 10023-6092
Head of School: Ronald P. Stewart

General Information Coeducational day college-preparatory, arts, technology, music (practical and theory), and drama school. Grades 6–12. Founded: 1969. Setting: urban. 1 building on campus. Approved or accredited by Middle States Association of Colleges and Schools. Total enrollment: 316. Upper school average class size: 15. Upper school faculty-student ratio: 1:6.
Upper School Student Profile Grade 9: 63 students (25 boys, 38 girls); Grade 10: 53 students (24 boys, 29 girls); Grade 11: 61 students (22 boys, 39 girls); Grade 12: 42 students (16 boys, 26 girls).
Faculty School total: 49. In upper school: 18 men, 31 women; 28 have advanced degrees.
Subjects Offered 20th century history, 20th century world history, 3-dimensional art, advanced chemistry, advanced computer applications, Advanced Placement courses, advanced studio art-AP, algebra, American history, American history-AP, American literature, anatomy, anthropology, art, art appreciation, astronomy, biology, calculus, calculus-AP, ceramics, chemistry, chemistry-AP, community service, comparative religion, computer math, computer programming, computer science, computer skills, concert band, creative writing, current events, drama, drama performance, driver education, earth science, economics, English, English literature, English-AP, environmental science, ethics, European history, expository writing, filmmaking, fine arts, forensic science, French, genetics, geography, geology, geometry, government/civics, grammar, health education, Holocaust studies, law, literary magazine, mathematics, music, music history, philosophy, photography, physical education, physics, physiology, political science, politics, pre-calculus, psychology, reading/study skills, research skills, SAT preparation, science, science project, social studies, Spanish, speech, statistics, theater, trigonometry, typing, world history, world literature, writing, zoology.
Graduation Requirements Arts and fine arts (art, music, dance, drama), computer science, English, foreign language, mathematics, physical education (includes health), science, social studies (includes history). Community service is required.
Special Academic Programs Advanced Placement exam preparation in 3 subject areas; honors section; accelerated programs; independent study; study at local college for college credit; academic accommodation for the gifted, the musically talented, and the artistically talented; remedial reading and/or remedial writing; remedial math; programs in English, mathematics, general development for dyslexic students; special instructional classes for students with mild learning issues (extra tutoring program).
College Placement 61 students graduated in 2004; all went to college, including Amherst College; New York University; Syracuse University; University of Miami; University of Michigan; Vassar College.
Student Life Upper grades have specified standards of dress, student council, honor system. Discipline rests primarily with faculty.
Tuition and Aid Day student tuition: $24,000–$24,900. Tuition installment plan (The Tuition Plan, Insured Tuition Payment Plan, Academic Management Services Plan, Key Tuition Payment Plan, monthly payment plans, individually arranged payment plans). Tuition reduction for siblings, bursaries, merit scholarship grants, need-based

scholarship grants available. In 2004–05, 20% of upper-school students received aid; total upper-school merit-scholarship money awarded: $600,000.

Admissions Traditional secondary-level entrance grade is 9. ISEE required. Deadline for receipt of application materials: January 15. Application fee required: $50. On-campus interview required.

Athletics Interscholastic: basketball (boys, girls), softball (b,g), volleyball (g); intramural: dance squad (g), volleyball (g); coed interscholastic: baseball, basketball, cross-country running, fencing, golf, hockey, soccer, tennis, track and field; coed intramural: aerobics, aquatics, ball hockey, basketball, bicycling, billiards, bowling, climbing, cross-country running, dance, equestrian sports, fencing, Frisbee, golf, horseback riding, indoor hockey, judo, rock climbing, roller hockey, sailing, soccer, softball, swimming and diving, ultimate Frisbee. 4 PE instructors, 6 coaches, 3 trainers.

Computers Computers are regularly used in all academic classes. Computer network features include campus e-mail, on-campus library services, CD-ROMs, online commercial services, Internet access, file transfer, wireless campus network, T1 Internet connection in every class.

Contact Ms. Maryll E. Feild, Director of Admissions. 212-362-0400 Ext. 103. Fax: 212-362-7424. E-mail: admissions@yorkprep.org. Web site: www.yorkprep.org.

ANNOUNCEMENT FROM THE SCHOOL York Prep, founded in 1969, is a college-preparatory school, enrolling students in grades 6–12, where contemporary methods enliven a strong, academically challenging, and traditional curriculum. The School's approach emphasizes independent thought and builds confidence and graduates go on to the finest colleges and universities. York Prep offers state-of-the-art computer labs, varsity and junior varsity athletics, and many extracurricular activities.

See full description on page 1162.

THE YORK SCHOOL

1320 Yonge Street
Toronto, Ontario M4T 1X2, Canada
Head of School: Ms. Barbara Goodwin-Zeibots

General Information Coeducational day college-preparatory school. Grades 1–12. Founded: 1965. Setting: urban. 1 building on campus. Approved or accredited by Canadian Association of Independent Schools, Canadian Educational Standards Institute, Conference of Independent Schools of Ontario, International Baccalaureate Organization, and Ontario Department of Education. Language of instruction: English. Total enrollment: 520. Upper school average class size: 15. Upper school faculty-student ratio: 1:12.

Faculty School total: 70. In upper school: 14 men, 20 women.

Subjects Offered 20th century history, American history, biology, calculus, Canadian geography, Canadian history, Canadian law, careers, chemistry, civics, discrete mathematics, dramatic arts, economics, English, environmental systems, French, functions, geography, geometry, global issues, healthful living, instrumental music, physical education, physics, social science, society challenge and change, Spanish, theater arts, theory of knowledge, visual arts, vocal music, world history, world religions.

Graduation Requirements International Baccalaureate Diploma Exams.

Special Academic Programs International Baccalaureate program; honors section; term-away projects; study abroad; academic accommodation for the gifted, the musically talented, and the artistically talented.

College Placement 35 students graduated in 2005; all went to college, including McGill University; McMaster University; Queen's University at Kingston; University of Toronto; University of Waterloo; York University.

Student Life Upper grades have uniform requirement, student council, honor system. Discipline rests primarily with faculty.

Tuition and Aid Day student tuition: CAN$17,800. Tuition installment plan (monthly payment plans, individually arranged payment plans). Bursaries, merit scholarship grants, need-based scholarship grants available.

Admissions Traditional secondary-level entrance grade is 9. For fall 2005, 100 students applied for upper-level admission, 40 were accepted, 30 enrolled. Deadline for receipt of application materials: none. Application fee required: CAN$100. Interview required.

Athletics Interscholastic: aerobics/dance (boys, girls), aerobics/nautilus (b,g), alpine skiing (b,g), badminton (b,g), baseball (b,g), basketball (b,g), cooperative games (b,g), cross-country running (b,g), fitness (b,g), floor hockey (b,g), outdoor activities (b,g), outdoor education (b,g), running (b,g), soccer (b,g), softball (b,g), strength & conditioning (b,g), track and field (b,g); intramural: aerobics/nautilus (b,g), badminton (b,g), baseball (b,g), basketball (b,g), outdoor education (b,g), volleyball (b,g); coed interscholastic: badminton, cooperative games, cross-country running, floor hockey, ice skating, outdoor activities, outdoor education, running, strength & conditioning, track and field, ultimate Frisbee; coed intramural: back packing, badminton, curling, Frisbee, hiking/backpacking, outdoor adventure, outdoor education, outdoor skills, track and field, ultimate Frisbee. 4 PE instructors.

Computers Computer network features include campus e-mail, on-campus library services, CD-ROMs, Internet access, laptop program in upper school.

Contact Mrs. Marilyn Andrews, Director of Admissions. 416-926 1325 Ext. 107. Fax: 416-926 9592. E-mail: marilyn_andrews@tys.on.ca. Web site: www.yorkschool.com.

ZURICH INTERNATIONAL SCHOOL

Steinacherstrasse 140
Wädenswil 8820, Switzerland
Head of School: Peter C. Mott

General Information Coeducational day college-preparatory school. Grades PS–13. Founded: 1963. Setting: suburban. Nearest major city is Zurich. 10-acre campus. 1 building on campus. Approved or accredited by International Baccalaureate Organization and New England Association of Schools and Colleges. Language of instruction: English. Total enrollment: 931. Upper school average class size: 16. Upper school faculty-student ratio: 1:7.

Upper School Student Profile Grade 9: 91 students (55 boys, 36 girls); Grade 10: 70 students (42 boys, 28 girls); Grade 11: 71 students (40 boys, 31 girls); Grade 12: 63 students (39 boys, 24 girls); Grade 13: 6 students (4 boys, 2 girls).

Faculty School total: 156. In upper school: 27 men, 28 women; 42 have advanced degrees.

Subjects Offered Acting, advanced computer applications, advanced math, algebra, American history, art history, art history-AP, biology, biology-AP, business mathematics, calculus, calculus-AP, career/college preparation, ceramics, chemistry-AP, college counseling, community service, computer applications, computer programming, computer science, concert band, creative writing, drama, drama performance, earth science, economics, English, English literature, English literature and composition-AP, ESL, European history-AP, expository writing, fine arts, French, French language-AP, German, German-AP, global studies, health, health education, history, history-AP, International Baccalaureate courses, jazz band, journalism, math methods, mathematics, model United Nations, music, music theory-AP, philosophy, photography, physical education, physics-AP, pre-algebra, pre-calculus, science, social studies, sports, statistics and probability, statistics-AP, studio art, studio art-AP, theater, trigonometry, U.S. history-AP, visual arts, world history, world literature, writing, yearbook.

Graduation Requirements Arts and fine arts (art, music, dance, drama), computer science, English, foreign language, history, mathematics, physical education (includes health), science, theory of knowledge, CAS (with IB Diploma), extended essay (IB). Community service is required.

Special Academic Programs International Baccalaureate program; Advanced Placement exam preparation in 17 subject areas; honors section; independent study; academic accommodation for the gifted, the musically talented, and the artistically talented; programs in English, mathematics, general development for dyslexic students; ESL (99 students enrolled).

College Placement 60 students graduated in 2005; 48 went to college, including Northwestern University; Parsons The New School for Design; Princeton University; Tufts University; University of Massachusetts Amherst; University of Virginia. Other: 1 went to work, 1 entered military service, 5 entered a postgraduate year, 5 had other specific plans. Mean SAT math: 623. 65% scored over 600 on SAT math.

Student Life Upper grades have specified standards of dress, student council, honor system. Discipline rests primarily with faculty.

Tuition and Aid Day student tuition: 30,300 Swiss francs. Tuition installment plan (monthly payment plans, individually arranged payment plans). Need-based scholarship grants available. In 2005–06, 3% of upper-school students received aid. Total amount of financial aid awarded in 2005–06: 84,800 Swiss francs.

Admissions Traditional secondary-level entrance grade is 9. English for Non-native Speakers or writing sample required. Deadline for receipt of application materials: none. Application fee required: 4500 Swiss francs. Interview recommended.

Athletics Interscholastic: basketball (boys, girls), rugby (b), soccer (b,g), softball (g), tennis (b,g), volleyball (b,g); coed interscholastic: alpine skiing, cross-country running (cross-country), skiing (downhill), swimming and diving, track and field; coed intramural: climbing, golf, rock climbing. 2 PE instructors, 24 coaches.

Computers Computers are regularly used in art, English, foreign language, history, mathematics, science classes. Computer network features include campus e-mail, on-campus library services, CD-ROMs, online commercial services, Internet access, file transfer, office computer access.

Contact Dale Braunschweig, Director of Admissions. 41-76 337 05 50. Fax: 41-43 244 20 51. E-mail: dbraunschweig@zis.ch. Web site: www.zis.ch.

ANNOUNCEMENT FROM THE SCHOOL Zurich International School is the only internationally accredited independent school in Zurich spanning preschool through grade 12. ZIS offers the IB Primary Years Programme, the US Advanced Placement program, and the IB Diploma. Over 900 students from more than 45 countries attend ZIS at one of the School's 4 campuses.

ACADEMY FOR GLOBAL EXPLORATION

Ashland, Oregon

Academy for Global Exploration

Type: Coeducational boarding and traveling college-preparatory school
Grades: 9–12
Enrollment: 12
Head of School: Greg Guevara

THE ACADEMY

At the Academy for Global Exploration (AGE), the world is the classroom. AGE is a college-preparatory boarding school offering a unique international travel experience for students in grades 9 through 12. AGE combines a rigorous academic and cultural studies curriculum with an intensive outdoor-adventure sports program. In a typical school day, students might demonstrate a physics lesson through rock climbing, speak Spanish with native villagers, and camp under the stars at night. One of the most remarkable aspects of AGE is its student-teacher ratio of 3:1. The educational model allows for enrollment of up to 12 students per year. When in residence in the United States, AGE calls Ashland, Oregon, home. Students begin and end each semester there. Each semester, faculty members and students travel to one of various locations, such as Greece, Thailand, the American Southwest, or Costa Rica. On the road, students continue a complete academic curriculum. AGE is fully accredited by the Northwest Association of Accredited Schools. Each academic lesson is intimately connected to the natural environment in which students find themselves. An integral part of each day is outdoor adventure, such as rock climbing, kayaking, or skiing. Homestays with families, community service, and local experts provide students with the opportunity for cultural and social exploration far beyond the traditional classroom setting.

AGE's base camp in Ashland is nestled in the foothills of the Siskiyou Mountains just north of the California border. This picturesque small city is famous up and down the West Coast for its acclaimed Oregon Shakespeare Festival. The school's location reflects its strong emphasis on education and outdoor recreation. With Mt. Ashland Ski Area, several climbing areas, and the Rogue River only a short drive away, students have daily opportunities to rock climb, kayak, backpack, boulder, ski, and mountain bike.

The governing body of AGE consists of a 7–member Board of Directors, who work closely with the Head of School to provide support and direction.

ACADEMIC PROGRAMS

The Academy for Global Exploration organizes its curriculum on a hierarchy of educational priorities. Experiential education is the backbone of AGE. Cultural studies are integrated into all subjects of the academic program, and students spend the semester learning about and experiencing many aspects of the culture they have the privilege of visiting. Students actively learn their subjects through critical thinking, reading, writing, discussion, labs, group activities, debates, performances, presentations, and art.

The curriculum is built around the Oregon Content Standards and the guidelines set forth by the Northwest Association of Accredited Schools for each subject area. Teachers incorporate core disciplines with the natural environment of the chosen destination. Science classes explore the biology and geology of encountered landscapes. English classes study local literature. History classes explore regional and relevant international histories of the people and the land. Math classes demonstrate principles through physical activities, and Spanish classes benefit from immersion in a Spanish-speaking culture.

The academic experience for students at AGE is extremely challenging. Small classes require students to be accountable for their work both in terms of quality and completion. Collaborative learning takes place spontaneously, enhancing the students' understanding of course material while also allowing them to develop productive study habits. AGE students support one another; it is an environment where student peers celebrate each other's successes.

The core classes at AGE include English, 8 units; social studies (history, geography, and social sciences), 6 units; mathematics, 6 units; sciences, 6 units; foreign languages, 4 units; outdoor recreation/physical education, 8 units; and general electives, such as computers and videography, 4 units. Students must also enroll in the Cultural Studies and Fitness course during each semester they attend AGE. As a college-preparatory program, AGE models its distribution and graduation requirements around the general expectations of colleges and universities.

Every student, regardless of class or grade level, must enroll in a minimum of five classes per semester and cannot enroll in more than eight academic classes per semester. Each course is worth 1 credit, and full-year courses are worth 2 credits. By assigning credits in this way, AGE can grant those students transferring into and out of AGE full credit even after one semester of study. AGE requires a minimum of 50 credits for a standard diploma.

Students' grades are calculated quarterly, along with faculty evaluations, comments, and recommendations. The AGE grading system is numeric, with letter grade equivalents of A–D; averages below 60 percent earn a nonpassing grade. Due to the small class size, the school does not calculate class rank and does not weight grades when calculating GPA.

Students wishing to gain credit for Advanced Placement courses may set up an independent study course, and AGE administers any AP exam a student wishes to take.

FACULTY AND ADVISERS

AGE employs 4 full-time faculty members and a school administrator. All faculty members hold a master's degree in education and a state teaching license. Teachers are required to hold a bachelor's degree in the subject area(s) being taught or relevant teaching experience in a related field and one year of formal instructional experience in secondary or postsecondary education.

In such a small intellectual community, teachers are able to develop partnerships with each student, assessing their progress and ensuring their academic and personal success. Teachers employ a number of instructional methods to convey course material, including hands-on practical experience, interdisciplinary teaching and project work, Internet research, audiovisual resources, guest speakers, field projects, interactive lessons, collaborative work among students and between student and teacher pairs, student-directed points of inquiry, scaffolding, modeling, assigned reading from textbooks and other supplemental materials, lectures, cultural exchange, and community service.

The teachers' duties also include tutoring, advising, mentoring, and participation in teacher workshops and continuing education programs. In addition, all teachers assist in supervising athletics and outdoor education instruction.

Due to the nature of the international travel and outdoor adventure program, AGE's primary concern is the safety of its students. Each student is ensured adequate physical and emotional safety in the school's diverse learning environments and within the community of peers and teachers. All AGE students and staff members are, at a minimum, required to be certified in American Red Cross Standard First Aid and CPR. In compliance with its strong safety mission, Wilderness First Responder, EMT, Swift Water Rescue, and other outdoor recreation safety certifications are highly encouraged.

COLLEGE PLACEMENT

AGE aims to see 100 percent of its graduates enrolled in college. To that end, the course work is rigorous, the schedule is demanding, and the teachers are both challenging and supportive of the students. College applications range from small private colleges to large universities. There were 5 students in the 2003 graduating class, and all 5 students attended their first-choice college.

STUDENT BODY AND CONDUCT

The student body is roughly a 50-50 mix of girls and boys, representing all four corners of the United States. Due to the school's deep commitment to community building, students are very active in social, disciplinary, and policymaking functions at the school.

ACADEMIC FACILITIES

AGE's Southern Oregon base camp is about 10 minutes from downtown Ashland. The school is far enough from town to enjoy all the privacy and space needed yet close enough to take advantage of Ashland's many cultural and educational opportunities. The rest of the

academic year is spent on the road, either domestically or abroad. While traveling, the school's facilities vary from the shade of a palapa in Costa Rica to a campground in Zion National Park to apartments overlooking the Acropolis in Greece.

EXTRACURRICULAR OPPORTUNITIES
AGE facilitates personal growth and development through outdoor adventure. Each semester, students learn a variety of technical outdoor skills that allow them to move safely in natural environments. Individualized athletic programs are developed and maintained through daily workouts, cooperative sports, and outdoor challenges. Each semester, AGE students focus on a select number of outdoor activities tailored to their traveling destinations, including kayaking, mountaineering, trekking, rock climbing, bouldering, and surfing. Destinations include rock climbing in Rei Leh, Thailand; bouldering in Quantum Field, New Zealand; trekking in LaBuche, Nepal, or the region of Patagonia; canyoneering in Buckskin Gulch, Utah; kayaking on the Sarapiqui River in Costa Rica or the Kaituna River in New Zealand; or sea kayaking around Isla Espiritu Santo in Mexico.

DAILY LIFE
The academic calendar is based on a two-semester model; each semester is sixteen weeks. Students are in class five days each week, and AGE utilizes a block-style schedule. Classes are 75 minutes and meet every other day. When students are not in academic classes, their time is dedicated to cultural exchange, physical activity, designated study hall hours, and volunteer/community service projects. Weekends abroad sometimes involve travel from one site to another. A typical day of learning starts at 7 a.m. with a physical education workout, breakfast at 8:15, and classes from 9:15 to 3. Lunch is served at 11:45 and dinner is at 6. Activities, usually outdoor oriented, are scheduled from 3:30 to 5:30, Monday through Friday. Mandatory study hall begins at 8 p.m., with lights out at 11.

WEEKEND LIFE
Weekend life at AGE consists of many outdoor excursions, from day hikes to overnight treks in the surrounding parks and national forests. It may also include kayaking and paddling trips, rock-climbing adventures, or skiing and snowboarding in the winter. From time to time, staff members and students also travel to local area venues to attend concerts, speaking engagements, and community events. While traveling abroad, students and staff members partake in local offerings, such as rafting trips, island excursions, canopy tours, or volcano treks.

COSTS AND FINANCIAL AID
The cost of attending the Academy for Global Exploration for the 2005–06 calendar year was $13,500 per semester, which included tuition, room, board, and student activity fees. This comprehensive fee did not include the housing/security deposit, weekly spending allowance, or airfare. A $2500 deposit is required to secure a place at AGE after an application is accepted. This nonrefundable deposit is due June 1 for the fall term and October 1 for the spring term. The remaining balance is due August 15 and December 15, respectively. Installment plans can be made available on an as-needed basis.

ADMISSIONS INFORMATION
AGE operates on a rolling admissions basis. Completed application files are reviewed as they are received, and the Admissions Committee notifies candidates of its decision as soon as possible. The Admissions Committee devotes careful attention to each candidate, assessing academic potential and records as well as individual achievements and interests.

APPLICATION TIMETABLE
Although applications may be submitted throughout the year, early application is encouraged. It is recommended that students begin the application process four to six months before the semester in which they wish to enroll. Once the program is filled, a waiting list is established for all applicants deemed admissible but for whom a place in the program has not yet been reserved. Those on the waiting list are notified of their status on or before August 1 for the fall semester and December 15 for the spring semester. Campus tours can be arranged by appointment, and personal interviews are highly recommended.

ADMISSIONS CORRESPONDENCE
Greg Guevara, Head of School
P.O. Box 712
Ashland, Oregon 97520

Phone: 541-913-0660
E-mail: info@AGExplore.org
Web site: http://www.AGExplore.org

ACCELERATED SCHOOLS

Denver, Colorado

Type: Coeducational boarding and day college-preparatory school
Grades: K–16; Elementary School, Kindergarten–6; Middle School, 7–8; High School, 9–12; postgraduate years
Enrollment: School total: 150; High School: 111
Head of School: John Klieforth

THE SCHOOL

Accelerated Schools was established in 1920. The School has many winning systems in its design that benefit the instructional process. Its individualized and tutorial program is designed to quickly improve a student's performance in every academic and social area. Student progress is so rapid that most students starting below grade level are effectively doing superior work after one or two semesters. Gifted and talented students find maximum challenge in the high performance, Honors, Advanced Placement, and Accelerated Thinking curriculums.

With 1 teacher for every 7 students, teachers have time to counsel, advise, tutor, and manage a very effective motivation system. Students learn to write and speak fluently. The average student completes 2,000 to 3,000 pages of notetaking, writing, and word processing during one school year. The School measures its accountability with standardized testing, mastery tests, and extensive writing portfolios.

Accelerated Schools provides a computer-intensive education and heavily emphasizes thinking, speaking, and writing skills. All students have access to a microcomputer for at least 3 hours per day. More than 150 microcomputers are available. The School's library of more than 2,000 educational and business computer programs meets a wide range of skill needs. In addition, computers can be borrowed for the School year.

Students' academic progress averages a three-year grade-level gain on standardized tests every nine months. Students raise their scores an average of three times more rapidly than the average school program, as measured by standardized tests.

Accelerated Schools is highly successful in its mission of educating students of any age, race, or creed. Each student has a completely individualized program dealing with his or her particular needs. There is extensive coordination with the student's home to develop and maintain a positive educational environment.

Accelerated Schools headquarters is located on the grounds of the historic Fitzroy Place in Denver, Colorado. In reality, the School has few boundaries. Its ten vans crisscross the metro area and a 150-mile radius with hundreds of daylong tours and afternoon field trips scheduled each year. Trips include tours of factories, gold mines, museums, historical and geological sites, dinosaur nests, and early Indian dwellings. The School is within 1½ hours of several popular ski areas. Optional ski school trips are scheduled every Wednesday during the long ski season from November to June.

Denver is located on the plains at 5,280 feet, but half the School's trips are in the mountains 10 miles to the west at elevations of 8,000 to 12,000 feet. The Denver metro area is an ideal resource for a well-rounded education. The high academic standards of the community have supported an abundance of exceptional educational and cultural happenings.

The Denver metro area, with a population of 2 million, is noted for its abundance of mild, sunny days, water sports, and a wide range of recreational activities. Denver is a beautiful city, renowned for its tree-lined streets, 205 parks, and many miles of biking and hiking trails.

Accelerated Schools is a private nonprofit corporation operated by an 8-member Board of Trustees composed of education and business leaders from the Denver area. The School plant is valued at $2.5 million.

Accelerated Schools also has a similar facility in Kansas City, Missouri, which may be reached at 913-341-6666.

Accelerated Schools High School is fully accredited by the North Central Association of Colleges and Schools and accepted by the Colorado State Board of Education.

ACADEMIC PROGRAMS

Accelerated Schools offers highly accelerated programs for students who are gifted and talented as well as those students who need remedial help. All student enrollments are individualized; students may start any day of the year. Their school year ends when attendance and course mastery requirements have been met. Attendance and work on a subject are equivalent to 1 Carnegie unit.

To graduate High School, students must complete a minimum of 22 approved credits as follows: 5 credits in English (including a senior research paper); 3 credits in social studies (1 of which must be in U.S. history); 7 credits in math, science, and computer science; 1 credit in physical education or health; ½ credit in reading; ½ credit in study skills; and 5 in academic electives.

Advanced Placement courses are available in many areas; study in most AP subjects can be arranged on an individual basis. In addition, Accelerated offers a post–high school, advanced studies program.

An average student-teacher ratio of 7:1 allows substantial faculty-student interaction. Each student receives a report card at the close of every school day. This daily evaluation ensures a close and constant screening of the student's progress toward fulfilling identified needs.

Students are graded by letter grades, A through C. No failing grades are given. If a student has not mastered a subject adequately, an "incomplete" is given until the student meets the mastery requirements of the subject. Daily grades are based upon the average of the day's reports.

Fifteen percent of the students are from other countries. In 1989, the School pioneered the computer-based Accelerated Language courses for its international students. English language classroom results improved markedly. In 1990, the School added an ESL version of its Accelerated Thinking procedures (listening, memory, speaking, and writing), which has rapidly improved the speaking and writing fluency of its ESL students. Results have been documented by improved TOEFL, mastery, and standardized test scores and by the number of writing portfolios completed.

Accelerated Schools specializes in preparing all English as a second language students for more advanced college courses. It offers both regular and intensive tracks toward a certificate of completion from its International Student Department. Accelerated Thinking, Think Tank, and field trip procedures create many small conversation groups for practicing English.

Some students stay at the School after earning their diploma for more college prep, TOEFL prep, intensive English, or other college courses. The Accelerated Advanced Studies program is a great way to become more competitive in college while mastering more of the English language. Extra preparation for the demands of competitive college work gives students an additional edge over other students when applying to other colleges.

FACULTY AND ADVISERS

Accelerated Schools employs carefully screened professionals in every area of administration and instruction. All teachers are certified in the specific fields of their assignments, and all have a specialty that complements the backgrounds of their associates. Many teachers hold advanced degrees in education, special education, psychology, sociology, mathematics, and reading. Each teacher must also complete extensive independent study courses in behavior and computer classroom management.

In addition to the teaching staff, head teachers and educational counselors with special training in behavior management analyze the educational background and factors of psychological motivation affecting each student. They hold regular conferences with students and parents throughout the school year.

Because the faculty holds itself responsible for the student's education, weekly staff-training and review sessions are held. This allows the entire staff the opportunity to contribute to an individual's progress.

Of the 21 High School faculty members, 13 are women and 8 are men. Nine hold master's degrees, and 1 has a Ph.D. Accelerated selects and retains only those teachers who are willing to accept the level of responsibility required by young students.

Principal John Klieforth is noted in Colorado as an outstanding teacher and school administrator. Carl Peterson, the Director of the School and founder of Accelerated Schools concept, is the

author of the book *Winning Systems,* a guide for student motivation. More than 100,000 students and teachers have attended classes directed by Mr. Peterson.

COLLEGE PLACEMENT
College counseling is extensive for all students. The head teachers and educational counselors advise students on the college application process. All seniors are expected to take both the ACT and SAT. A complete library of college catalogs is available.

More than 75 percent of the graduates since 1980 enrolled in and were successful at the colleges or universities of their choice. Recent graduates are attending such schools as Arapahoe Community, Metropolitan State, and the Universities of Colorado, Denver, and Northern Colorado.

STUDENT BODY AND CONDUCT
The School's enrollment in 2004–05 was 150 students: 111 in High School, 26 in Middle School, and 13 in Elementary School. These students were predominantly from all over the United States, Canada, Russia, Europe, the Middle East, and Asia.

The School has one primary rule—no student has the right to interfere with the rights of another student to learn, to be comfortable, and to be safe.

The School works to create and develop in its students self-control and self-esteem through accelerated academic development. Each student is treated as a complete individual in terms of social behavior, educational accomplishment, and personal discipline. Disciplinary action is seldom necessary, but if it becomes necessary, the student's family, or the host family in the case of boarding students, is the final arbiter.

The School's location in Denver, Colorado, provides an international crossroads and rich multicultural experiences for students from both the Atlantic and Pacific basins.

ACADEMIC FACILITIES
The main buildings on campus are the Mansion and the science and art building. The library is located in the Mansion and contains more than 2,000 volumes and more than 100 CD-ROM computers are located in the classrooms.

By providing one computer for each student, the School is set apart from most education facilities. Many brands of computers are available for students, as is a large accumulation of educational software. Computers do not replace books, paper, and pencils as tools for learning,

but they are a very important part of the overall program for academic excellence.

BOARDING AND GENERAL FACILITIES
Room, board, and supervision for out-of-town students are provided by host families who can give students valuable attention and include them in social activities. The supportive family environment provided by host parents has proven most effective. The families whom the School recommends have been screened and trained to support the positive reinforcement program by awarding students extra privileges based on their work.

Students are treated as members of the host family and are responsible for the care of their own room. The host family's proximity to the School is not important—instructors pick up the students and take them home every day.

ATHLETICS
The School offers some sports on a noncompetitive basis. These include basketball, hiking, jogging, running, soccer, softball, snow skiing, swimming, tennis, and volleyball. Facilities for athletics are available locally.

EXTRACURRICULAR OPPORTUNITIES
There are frequent educational tours and trips for such activities as snow skiing, camping, and backpacking. All trips are well supervised by recreation professionals.

DAILY LIFE
The School is informal and nonstressful. It is a warm and friendly yet studious environment. Students quickly adapt to the high-level challenges being presented.

The student is picked up at the door of his or her residence and brought to school by 9 a.m. From 9 a.m. to 1:05 p.m. the student is under the supervision of one teacher for academics. This person does not teach all subjects but rather is responsible for the student's schedule, behavior, and progress.

The student has supervised breaks at 10:30 and 11:30 a.m. The balance of school time is spent working as directed on a teacher-monitored contract that results in a report card at the end of each day. Lunch is at 1:05 p.m. A student may bring a lunch or purchase a lunch from a catering truck that comes to the School. At 1:35, afternoon activities begin. Regularly scheduled activities are Accelerated Thinking, Accelerated Think Tank, computer lab, science lab, art, study hall, and library. Special activities such as swimming, jogging, and bowling may be scheduled by the staff. School ends at 3 p.m.

WEEKEND LIFE
Day students spend weekends with their families, and boarding students with their host families. Many of the host families organize activities and trips. There are optional escorted tours on some Saturdays, Sundays, and holidays.

SUMMER PROGRAMS
Accelerated Schools maintains a regular summer program that is just like that of the rest of the year. Features of the summer program include special trips and tours; supervised study in specific areas, particularly for gifted and talented students; special library and research programs; and many outdoor activities.

The summer program lasts from 40 hours to three months, depending on the student's progress, and is taught by regular faculty members. Students earn credit for their work.

COSTS AND FINANCIAL AID
Day student tuition in 2006–07 is $20,750 (meals not included). Boarding student tuition, room, and board costs $27,950. A monthly payment plan is available.

Some need-based scholarships are awarded. In 2005–06, 10 percent of the students received $90,000 in financial aid.

ADMISSIONS INFORMATION
Any student is eligible for admission. Placement within the program is determined by the student's needs and by free testing prior to admission. An application form should be submitted and an academic transcript forwarded to the School.

APPLICATION TIMETABLE
Accelerated is an individualized year-round school. A student may start any day of the year. Students take vacations when it is convenient for their parents or when they have met their course requirements. The year-round school allows fast track students to graduate from high school or the college within 36 months. Candidates are notified of the admission decision as soon as their applications have been reviewed.

ADMISSIONS CORRESPONDENCE
Jane Queen
Associate Director of Admissions
Accelerated Schools
2160 South Cook Street
Denver, Colorado 80210

Phone: 303-758-2003
Fax: 303-757-4336
E-mail: info@acceleratedschools.org
Web site: http://www.acceleratedschools.org

ACS INTERNATIONAL SCHOOLS

Cobham, Surrey; Egham, Surrey; and Hillingdon, Middlesex, England

Type: Coeducational boarding and day college-preparatory schools
Grades: Preschool (age 2½) to grade 12
Enrollment: School total: 2,300; Upper Schools: 456 (Cobham), 199 (Hillingdon), 108 (Egham)
Heads of Schools: Tom Lehman, Cobham; Moyra Hadley, Egham; Ginger Apple, Hillingdon

---

THE SCHOOLS

The three ACS International Schools (formerly American Community Schools) are nonsectarian and co-educational (with boarding at ACS Cobham), enrolling students from 2½ to 18 years of age from more than sixty countries. ACS International Schools offer the International Baccalaureate (IB) Diploma and an American curriculum, including Advanced Placement (AP) courses, leading to a U.S. high school diploma. ACS International Schools' excellent exam results have ensured that its graduates attend the world's finest universities.

ACS inspires its students to become successful lifelong learners and responsible global citizens. The Schools promote high standards of scholarship and challenge all members of the community to fulfill their potential.

ACS is accredited by the New England Association of Schools and Colleges and is authorized by the International Baccalaureate Organization to offer the IB Diploma. In addition, ACS Egham is one of only three schools in the U.K. to also offer the IB Primary Years Program (3–11) and the IB Middle Years Program (11–16). The Schools hold memberships in the U.S. College Board Advanced Placement (AP) Program, the European Council of International Schools, the Council of International Schools, and the Independent Schools Association.

The campuses are situated southwest of central London, offering families spacious suburban homes with direct public transportation links to central London. The Surrey campuses, ACS Cobham International School (23 miles south of London) and ACS Egham International School (25 miles southwest of London), are both served by direct rail links, while ACS Hillingdon International School (15 miles west of London) is served by London Underground and direct rail links.

The schools set the benchmark standard for high-quality facilities and grounds. Each campus is built around a spacious country estate, enhanced by modern, purpose-built classrooms, libraries, cafeterias, and sports facilities. Lower, Middle, and High Schools have designated computer rooms, libraries, science laboratories, and art studios. The organisation's robust program of development and renewal has invested more than £80 million into the campus facilities over the past ten years.

ACADEMIC PROGRAMS

All three campuses accept students from preschool through high school. ACS Cobham and ACS Egham accept students from age 2½; ACS Hillingdon accepts students from age 4. All students graduate with an American high school diploma and have the option of studying for the full IB diploma. In addition, ACS Cobham and ACS Hillingdon campuses offer American AP courses. ACS Egham offers the IB Primary Years and Middle Years Programs.

Specialized learning support is available in the Lower, Middle, and High Schools for students with mild learning differences. English as an Additional Language (EAL) is available on all three campuses. Students should be intermediate English speakers before entering high school. The Schools also offer strong native language support as needed.

To graduate, High School students must complete at least 20 credits, including 6 in social studies and foreign language, 6 in mathematics and science, 4 in English, 1 in fine arts, and physical education in grades 9–12.

While courses may vary slightly, the full-year courses offered are English I–IV, French I–V, German I–IV, Spanish I–IV, world history I–II, contemporary history, U.S. history, economics, algebra I–II, plane geometry, advanced algebra II, trigonometry/analytic geometry, biology, chemistry, physics, drawing and painting, crafts, ceramics and sculpture, advanced art, advanced music, advanced drama, and word processing. Depending on student interest, AP or IB courses may be offered in English, French, German, Spanish, U.S. history, European history, calculus, biology, chemistry, physics, computer science, art, psychology, economics, and government.

The full International Baccalaureate Diploma Program is offered on all three campuses. In 2005, the combined IB Diploma pass rate of 94 percent was well above the international average of 82 percent, and ACS International Schools' average IB Diploma score of 34 points clearly surpassed the international average of 30. These results continue to place ACS International among the highest achieving independent schools in the U.K.

Average class sizes range from 15 to 20 students. Teachers are available for extra help sessions during and after school. School reports are issued every quarter (approximately every nine weeks). Regular parent-teacher conferences are scheduled twice per year and on an occasional basis, as necessary. All schools have thriving parent communities, including parent-teacher organisations and associations, and families are made to feel welcome at the schools and are encouraged to be involved in school life.

FACULTY AND ADVISERS

There are 152 full-time teachers at ACS Cobham, 111 women and 41 men. At ACS Hillingdon, there are 82 full-time teachers, 55 women and 27 men. There are 69 full-time teachers, 49 women and 20 men, at ACS Egham. All teachers hold bachelor's degrees, and 141 have graduate degrees. There are 12 part-time instructors. Full-time nurses at all schools provide health care. Faculty benefits include a variety of options, such as health insurance, home leave, housing allowance, and a pension fund. Other benefits include a professional development allowance and bereavement fund.

COLLEGE PLACEMENT

Assisted by university placement counselors on the Cobham, Egham, and Hillingdon campuses, nearly all ACS students attend institutions of higher education. ACS graduates attend leading universities around the world, including Cambridge, Imperial College London, London School of Economics, and Oxford in the U.K.; Harvard, Princeton, Stanford, and Yale in the U.S.; and Delft University of Technology, Keio, McGill, Stockholm School of Economics, and the Universities of Oslo and Tokyo throughout the rest of the world.

STUDENT BODY AND CONDUCT

Fifty-one percent of the student body at ACS Cobham is American, with other major nationality groups being British, Canadian, Norwegian, Dutch, Swedish, Danish, and Australian. The total enrollment is approximately 1,308 students, consisting of 737 boys and 571 girls. The boarding school has 58 boys and 43 girls.

Approximately 43 percent of the student body at ACS Hillingdon is from the United States, with other main student populations from Japan, Britain, Canada, Norway, the Netherlands, and Sweden. The total enrollment at ACS Hillingdon is 493, 259 boys and 234 girls.

Approximately 48 percent of the student population at ACS Egham is American, with the other major nationality groups being Dutch, British, Canadian, Mexican, Belgian, and Danish. The Egham campus currently enrolls 476 students, 250 boys and 226 girls.

Approximately 50 percent of the total number of students at the ACS International Schools are American; 15 percent are British and Canadian. The remaining 35 percent represent more than sixty other nationalities. Most of the children are from families in business or government on assignment in London, and the Schools also attract a growing local British following.

ACADEMIC FACILITIES

Situated on a beautiful 128-acre country estate, ACS Cobham International School has purpose-built Lower, Middle, and High School buildings. In addition, the campus has premier sports facilities that include on-site soccer and rugby fields, softball and baseball diamonds, an all-weather Olympic-sized track, tennis courts, a six-hole golf course, and a new Sports Centre, which houses a basketball/volleyball show court, a 25-metre competition-class swimming pool, a dance studio, a fitness suite, and a cafeteria. The recently completed, purpose-built Early Child-

hood Village expansion project offers additional purpose-built classrooms and office space

Situated on a superbly kept 11-acre site, ACS Hillingdon International School has excellent facilities augmented by a new purpose-built music centre, complete with a digital recording studio, rehearsal rooms, practice studios, and a computer lab for music technology. There are on-site playing fields, tennis courts, and playgrounds, with additional off-site soccer, rugby, track, baseball, softball, swimming, and golf facilities available.

The 20-acre ACS Egham International School has superb teaching, sports, and extracurricular facilities and a newly refurbished cafeteria and kitchen. The campuswide wireless and cabled IT network makes working with laptop or desktop computers an effortless and integral part of the learning process.

BOARDING AND GENERAL FACILITIES
Staffed by teachers and full-time houseparents, the co-educational boarding house at ACS Cobham has separate-wing accommodation for 110 students ranging in age from 12 (grade 7) to 18 (grade 12). The ergonomically designed 2-person rooms have en-suite facilities and Internet connections. There are game and television rooms, kitchens, and common rooms for the students. A variety of weekend and afterschool trips and activities ensure a lively, active life for boarders.

Nurses at all schools provide health care in modern, purpose-built health centers. Each of the three schools has a Housing Department that offers a free house-finding service for parents wishing to relocate to an ACS catchment area. The Schools provide an extensive door-to-door bus service within their catchment areas, which is popular with families.

ATHLETICS
School teams compete with local American and British schools as well as with international schools. Boys' and girls' varsity teams compete in basketball, cross-country, soccer, swimming, tennis, track and field, and volleyball. There are also boys' rugby and baseball teams and girls' softball and cheerleading teams. Intramural sports and noncompetitive physical activities include badminton, basketball, dance, darts, "fun runs," gymnastics, soccer, tennis, and volleyball.

EXTRACURRICULAR OPPORTUNITIES
The three schools provide a variety of different after-school clubs, sports, and activities for Lower, Middle, and High School students. Optional Lower School activities may include various arts and crafts clubs, Scouts, music (additional choir or band), dance, chess, tennis,

bowling, golf, dance, or other sports. Middle School activities and clubs may include a similar variety but also cooking clubs, safe-sitter programs, and a Middle School musical production. Both the High Schools and Middle Schools also have student councils, peer counsellors, cheerleaders, student newspapers, literary magazines, and yearbooks as well as recycling and environmental clubs. High School students may participate in up to three drama productions per year, math teams, Model United Nations, National Honor Society, International Schools Thespian Association, choir, speech and debate competitions, quiz bowls, and various community service organizations, such as Habitat for Humanity, the Duke of Edinburgh Award scheme, and World Challenge projects.

In addition to extensive field trips that enliven classroom learning, students also participate in more extended trips. Typical examples include trips to Stratford-upon-Avon, environmental or history centers in England, and Outward Bound or pony-trekking trips in Wales; foreign language, skiing, and arts trips in Europe; and community-service activities in Africa or Asia. The Schools regularly host visiting artists, writers, and musicians and hold arts festivals, international celebrations, and a variety of community-service events.

DAILY LIFE
The school year, from the end of August to mid-June, is divided into two semesters. There are vacations in October, December, February, and April. The daily schedule for all grades extends from 8:30 a.m. to 3:10 p.m. each day. Middle and High School students have eight instructional periods each day, with extracurricular activities held after 3 p.m. Faculty members are available to provide individual help after school.

WEEKEND LIFE
Boarding students participate in planned trips to various cultural and sports events on weekends, virtually all of which are included in the basic fee. The prearranged programs for each weekend include attending concerts and plays in London, visiting such historic sites as the Naval Museum in Portsmouth, and attending ACS sports games.

SUMMER PROGRAMS
The ACS International Schools offer academic and recreational programs to fit the needs of participating students. Pioneered in 1996, the British Studies course is an interdisciplinary, three-week study and travel course for talented high school students 15–19 years old. The course offers enrichment in European history, English literature, art, and music.

COSTS AND FINANCIAL AID
For 2005–06, semester tuition for day students was between £7475 and £7825 for grades 9–12; semester fees were £3850 for five-day boarding students and £5275 for seven-day boarding students. Bus service is extra, with a reduced rate for siblings. In addition, all families must pay a one-time £500 debenture subscription for each student enrolled.

ADMISSIONS INFORMATION
The ACS International Schools seek to enroll motivated students of all nationalities with the potential to succeed in a challenging college-preparatory curriculum. New students are accepted in all grades throughout the year (except grade 12—first-semester entry only) on the basis of the completed application form, previous school records, standardized test results, a student questionnaire, and recommendations from the previous school. The Schools administer placement exams as necessary. High school students whose native language is not English must take a language test for entrance. Those interested should note that if students have mild learning disabilities, additional information is requested.

APPLICATION TIMETABLE
Students may apply at any time. Preregistration for returning families begins in April. There is a £95 registration fee.

ADMISSIONS CORRESPONDENCE
Admissions Office
ACS Cobham International School
Heywood, Portsmouth Road
Cobham, Surrey KT11 1BL

Phone: 44-1-932-869744
Fax: 44-1-932-869789
E-mail: cobhamadmissions@acs-england.co.uk
Web site: http://www.acs-england.co.uk

Admissions Office
ACS Hillingdon International School
Hillingdon Court, 108 Vine Lane
Hillingdon, Uxbridge
Middlesex UB10 0BE

Phone: 44-1-895-818402
Fax: 44-1-895-818404
E-mail: hillingdonadmissions@acs-england.co.uk
Web site: http://www.acs-england.co.uk

Admissions Office
ACS Egham International School
Woodlee, London Road (A30)
Egham, Surrey TW20 0HS

Phone: 44-1-784-430611
Fax: 44-1-784-430626
E-mail: eghamadmissions@acs-england.co.uk
Web site: http://www.acs-england.co.uk

ADMIRAL FARRAGUT ACADEMY

St. Petersburg, Florida

Type: Coeducational boarding and day college-preparatory military school
Grades: K–12: Lower Division, K–5; Middle Division, 6–8; Upper Division, 9–12
Enrollment: School total: 407; Lower Division, 68; Middle Division, 86; Upper Division: 253
Head of School: Capt. Robert J. Fine, Headmaster

THE ACADEMY

Admiral Farragut Academy (AFA) is America's only Honor Naval Academy by an act of Congress and is recognized as an NJROTC Distinguished Unit by the Department of Navy. In 1933, under the leadership of Adm. S. S. Robison, USN (Ret.), former Superintendent of the United States Naval Academy, and Brig. Gen. Cyrus S. Radford, USMC (Ret.), AFA was established in Pine Beach, New Jersey. The Academy opened the Florida campus in 1945. In 1990, both campuses broke a fifty-six year tradition of enrolling only boys and became coeducational. In 1994, the New Jersey campus consolidated with the Florida campus.

The Academy is authorized to nominate 22 graduates to the various service academies. The school is chartered as a nonprofit corporation directed by the headmaster and a self-perpetuating Board of Trustees that consists of active members, including alumni and parents of alumni. The Academy occupies 55 acres, and its physical plant is valued at $12 million, with a $1.5 million endowment.

Admiral Farragut Academy is accredited by the Southern Association of Colleges and Schools (SACS), the Florida Council of Independent Schools (FCIS), and the Florida Kindergarten Council (FKC). AFA holds membership in the Association of Military Colleges and Schools of the United States (AMSCUS), the Southeastern Association of Boarding Schools (SABS), the Florida High School Activities Associations (FHSAA), the National Association of College Admissions Counselors (NACAC), the Southern Association of College Admissions Counselors (SACAC), the Florida County Licensing for Children Centers, Family Day Care, and Coordinated Childcare of Pinellas, Inc.

ACADEMIC PROGRAMS

Minimum graduation requirements of 24 credits include the following: English, 4 units; fine arts, 1 unit; algebra, 2 units; science (including two labs), 3 units; geometry, 1 unit; foreign language, 2 units; U.S. history, 1 unit; physical education, ½ unit; health, ½ unit; government/economics, 1 unit; world history, 1 unit; geography/ethics, 1 unit; naval science, 1 unit; and academic electives, 5 units. All cadets must also earn their Qualified Boat Handler's Certificate (QBH) as a graduation requirement.

Dual-enrollment, Advanced Placement, and Honors classes are offered to students of advanced ability in grade 10 who have a minimum 3.0 GPA. Dual-enrollment courses enable a student to earn college credit through St. Petersburg College; high school credit is also granted for these courses. Seventy-two semester hours of Dual Enrollment credit were offered in 2005–06.

Upper Division students are normally scheduled for five academic courses plus naval science each year. The average class size is 16 to 22 students; the overall student-teacher ratio is 11:1. The ratio of boys to girls is 2:1. Courses are grouped by academic ability as much as possible. Each department is assigned test days to ensure that cadets are not overloaded with tests on any single day. Tutorials are held each morning before the first class of the day and each afternoon after class. Students may seek out teachers for extra help during these tutorial periods, or, on certain days, a teacher may require a student's attendance. Two hours of evening study is

required Monday through Thursday for all boarding students. The Upper Division college-preparatory academic curriculum is designed to ensure that a student graduates with a working knowledge of a foreign language, the ability to function comfortably and knowledgeably in a science laboratory, and the ability to read and write well. Science lab classes, field trips, foreign language, and a wide variety of reading and writing assignments across the academic curriculum enable students to achieve these goals.

All sections of grades 6–8 academics are ability-grouped according to math skills. The high level of structure and close teacher-student relationships prevail in the middle grades. Core academic classes are joined by a wide selection of electives, tutorials and academic remediation, afternoon outdoor activities, physical education classes, sports practices, guest speakers, and field trips. The academic program strives to prepare students for the rigors of the college-preparatory curriculum that they will encounter in grades 9–12. Students of high academic ability in the eighth grade may receive high school credit for algebra and foreign languages.

Lower Division students (K–5) follow a broad curriculum based on the Florida Council of Independent Schools (FCIS) and national standards, incorporating active learning and instruction. Math, science, social studies, reading, and writing are taught daily. Spanish, art, music, character education, drama workshops, library skills, computer technology, and physical education are offered a number of times per week, depending on the week's schedule. The average class size is 16 to 18 students. Individualized learning is enhanced through the Learning Center. Specials include Chess Club, Crafts of the Month, Fit and Flexible, Jewelry Club, Junior Service Club, Mad Science, and Spanish Club. Sports and related topics include soccer, Tae Kwon Do, tennis, and yoga. Students experience field trips, guest readers, guest speakers, and student mentors from the Middle and Upper Divisions. The library provides three reading programs: Florida Reading Association, Sunshine State Readers, and Reading Counts. Parents may view the Plan Of The Day (POD) on the school's Web site.

In the English Speakers of Other Languages (ESOL) program (grades 6–12), students receive extensive instruction in English proficiency skills and are fully integrated into AFA's wide selection of sports, extracurricular activities, and trips. International students are required to take the SLEP test upon entry.

FACULTY AND ADVISERS

There are 60 full-time and 8 part-time teachers, including 4 full-time naval science instructors. Twelve faculty members reside in the dormitory areas and at other locations on campus. Resident faculty members have various supervisory responsibilities, both in the evenings and on weekends. Thirty-eight faculty members have master's degrees, and 2 hold doctoral degrees.

Robert J. Fine (B.A., Carroll College; M.A., National-Louis University) is Headmaster. Robert Gibbons (B.A., Evansville; M.A., Ball State) is Chief Academic Officer; Commandant is Major General Robert M. Flanagan USMC (Ret.) (B.A., Michigan; M.A., Troy State). William Ford (B.S., James Madison; M.A., National-Louis) is Upper Division Head. Jennifer Vernine (B.S., Florida; M.A., National-Louis) is Middle

Division Head. Anita Hensley (B.A., Purdue; M.A., Argosy) is Lower Division Head.

COLLEGE PLACEMENT

A full-time college placement and guidance officer assists with scheduling, hosts numerous visits from college admissions representatives, and assists with college applications for all upperclass students. All students undergo yearly standardized testing. Beginning in the spring of the tenth-grade year, students receive regular individual academic counseling with the College Placement Director, at which time future schedules are discussed. Admiral Farragut Academy is a national test center for the SAT, ACT, PSAT, and California Achievement Test (CAT). Typically, AFA students exceed the national average on standardized tests. The class of 2005 (61 graduates) earned more than $5.3 million in college scholarships, with ten Academy appointments, seven ROTC scholarships, and seven athletic recruitments in baseball, basketball, football, and track and field.

Farragut graduates tend to enroll in eastern and southern colleges and universities; about one third go to schools inside the state of Florida. Other schools typically chosen by Farragut graduates include Auburn, The Citadel, Eckerd, Embry-Riddle, Florida State, Johnson and Wales, McDaniel, North Carolina State, Norwich, Savannah College of Art and Design, Stetson, St. Petersburg, the U.S. Air Force Academy, the U.S. Merchant Marine Academy, the U.S. Naval Academy, and the Universities of Central Florida, Florida, Maine, Miami (Florida), North Carolina, North Florida, South Florida, and West Florida. In 2005, 100 percent of Farragut graduates were accepted to colleges and universities.

STUDENT BODY AND CONDUCT

In 2005, the Upper Division student body opened with a total of 253 students: 64 students in grade 9, 77 in grade 10, 62 in grade 11, and 50 in grade 12. The Middle Division opened with 86 students, and the Lower Division opened with 68 students. Boarding students represent twenty-five states and 40 students represent twenty-two countries.

Farragut students are expected to conduct themselves as young ladies and gentlemen. Students who are not of good moral character or who have a history of defiance or severe discipline problems need not apply. Students are allowed certain numbers of demerits each week; as long as the total does not surpass the demerits allowed, their conduct is considered to be satisfactory. Restriction to the campus and loss of privileges may result for students who have unsatisfactory deportment. Corporal punishment and hazing practices are strictly forbidden.

ACADEMIC FACILITIES

Upper Division science classes meet in the newly renovated Charles M. Duke Science Center (four classrooms with adjoining labs) and the Russell Building (sixteen classrooms). The Mills Science Center serves the Middle Division population; others meet in the Michel Building (six classrooms). The Parrott Memorial Library contains 13,000 volumes, a media center, and several computer terminals. Two computer labs contain forty multimedia IBM terminals.

Farragut's waterfront facility includes a marine touch tank and a wet lab, both associated with the marine biology program. A newly installed weather

station on the rooftop provides access to weatherbug.com and helpful data for the meteorology class.

The newly renovated the Aviation Lab houses the Aeronautical Science department and includes an FAA-certified PCATD flight simulator. Students receive training in basic aerodynamics, aircraft performance, flight planning, weather data interpretation, and Federal Aviation Regulations (Private and Commercial Pilot Certification).

The Lower/Middle Division (K–8) consists of three buildings surrounded by tennis courts, basketball courts, three athletic fields, and the newly equipped playground that houses age-appropriate equipment for maximum safety. For grades K–5, there is a private area where parents can drop off or pick up their children without leaving their car, providing safety and convenience.

BOARDING AND GENERAL FACILITIES
A five-day boarding option for grades 6–12 was initiated to enable boarding students to profit from the weekly structured environment, while spending weekends with their families. Students may leave the campus following the close of school on Friday and return on Sunday evening by 9 p.m.

Farragut Hall, a former resort hotel, contains all dormitory facilities. Each dorm room normally houses 2 to 4 students. The facility is air conditioned with a new roof, new windows, and new furniture. All dormitory rooms are equipped with private or semiprivate bathrooms. The campus houses a mailroom, a laundry facility, a barber, and a school store. Faculty members occupy apartments throughout the dorm and have supervisory responsibilities. Returning students may select their rooms and roommates. Dorm rooms are equipped with wireless Internet service with firewalls against chat rooms and questionable Web sites.

Other facilities include a 350-seat assembly hall and a number of faculty apartments and quarters. Registered nurses staff the infirmary, and a physician is available by appointment.

ATHLETICS
AFA offers seventeen interscholastic sports. Each student is encouraged but not required to participate on an interscholastic sports team. Sports offerings include boys' teams in baseball, basketball, crosscountry, football, golf, soccer, swimming and diving, tennis, track and field, and wrestling and girls' teams in basketball, cheerleading, cross-country, golf, paintball, softball, swimming and diving, tennis, track and field, and volleyball. Basketball, diving, flag football, paintball, riflery, sailing, soccer, swimming, volleyball, and weight training are popular afternoon activities. AFA is a member of the Florida High School Activities Association (FHSAA). In 2004, Farragut's varsity boys' basketball team won the 2A Florida State Championship.

Athletic facilities include the waterfront facilities, a ¼-mile asphalt track, a baseball diamond, a softball field, an indoor rifle range, a wrestling building, a swimming pool, the Moyer Gymnasium, a weight room, a lighted football field with a new concession stand, and a soccer field.

EXTRACURRICULAR OPPORTUNITIES
Special-interest clubs are numerous and are held before and after school. Typically, the Aviation, Chess, Drama, Sailing, and SCUBA clubs are popular orga-

nizations, as are the National Honor Society, Key Club, and Leo Club. In 2005, other Upper Division clubs included the Arborist Club, Art Club, Bowling Club, Book Club, Debate Club, Bowling Club, Cake Club, Cosmetic Club, Debate Club, Fitness Club, Fellowship Christian Club, Guitar Club, Journalism Club, Multicultural Club, National Arborist Club, Prom Committee, Psychology Club, Role-Playing/Games Club, School Newspaper Committee, and SWAT Club. Lower Division students are offered numerous field trips and after-school sport programs, including soccer and tennis, and after-school care is available daily.

The SCUBA program is also taught on campus and culminates with open-water dives in the Gulf of Mexico and the Atlantic Ocean. Numerous dive trips follow throughout the year and are open to all students who have their certification. Optional summer cruises aboard U.S. Navy vessels are a favorite of AFA students. An on-campus indoor rifle range provides opportunity for cadets to complete their NRA safety requirements and qualify for the Academy's rifle team, listed amongst the top 10 percent in the nation. Students in Middle and Upper Divisions may participate in the Drill Team and Color Guard.

The yearbook, *The Buccaneer*, is produced through the Journalism Class. The high school creative-writing students produce *Ocean Currents* six times a year. *Making Waves* is produced monthly in the Middle Division. Student art shows, competitions, and dramatic productions occur on campus throughout the year. Each student must fulfill 80 hours of community service and may participate in either the Key or Leo Club in grades 9–12.

Students may receive flight training in Cessna aircraft during afternoon and weekend hours from the Albert Whitted Airport in St. Petersburg, only 5 miles from the Academy.

DAILY LIFE
Reveille begins the day at 6:20 a.m., and taps signals its end at 10 p.m. The day is structured carefully from breakfast through evening study hall to ensure that each cadet may participate in as many school functions as possible. Formation, room inspection, and uniform inspection take place during regularly scheduled school days.

There are eight 45-minute academic periods beginning at 8 a.m. each day, followed by an academic tutorial period, during which time students may seek a teacher's help; the teacher can require attendance at these tutorials.

WEEKEND LIFE
Because 35 percent of the students in grades 6–12 are either five- or seven-day boarders, much of AFA's program is designed with the boarding student in mind. A "day room" in the main building has cable TV, Foosball, air hockey, and pool and Ping-Pong tables for use during free time. Campus facilities are open throughout the weekend for student use, including the gym, pool, weight room, and waterfront sailing area. The school's canteen (snack bar) is open seven days a week. There are many weekend options for off-campus trips, both recreational and educational. Disney World, Busch Gardens, Adventure Island, Sea World, and other Florida theme parks; deep-sea fishing; professional sports games; and trips to museums, plays, and festivals are among the most popular weekend events. On-campus movies are fea-

tured on Friday and Saturday night. The school operates shuttles for students on weekends to the many area stores and theaters, as well as to and from Tampa International Airport.

COSTS AND FINANCIAL AID
In 2006–07, the tuition for grades 6–8 is $13,350 for day students and $28,600 for seven-day boarding students. For grades 9–12, the day-student tuition is $13,600, and the seven-day boarding tuition is $29,100. The five-day boarding tuition for grades 6–12 is $23,950. Extra costs for uniforms, books, and other miscellaneous expendables range from $1500 to $4000.

Tuition is $8350 for kindergarten and $9075 for grades 1–5. Extra costs for textbooks, field trips, and supplies (K–5) range from $800 to $1000. Used books and uniforms are available for grades 6–12.

Full-year program costs for ESOL boarding students (including tuition and all fees) are $33,600 (grades 9–12) and $33,100 (grades 6–8). ESOL classes are charged separately. Each ESOL class costs $1250.

Payment plans are offered. Requests for financial aid are considered after a student has been accepted and are processed through School and Student Service for Financial Aid, Princeton, New Jersey. Financial aid is available to students according to family need and the student's merit.

ADMISSIONS INFORMATION
Admiral Farragut Academy admits qualified students without regard to race, color, creed, or sex. Candidates must be capable of doing college-preparatory work in the grade for which they apply. When making application, students must include grades from the previous three years as well as the most recent standardized test score and two teacher references from the student's last school (preferably math and English teachers). A $150 nonrefundable application fee is required. Each family receives a one-on-one in-depth tour and interview prior to consideration. All acceptances are conditional upon completion of final grades. A student interview is required and may be conducted by phone if a student is out of the country.

APPLICATION TIMETABLE
Visitors are asked to make an appointment through the Admissions Office. Interview and campus tours are available throughout the year during weekday business hours. Shadow days are available for grades 6–12 and mandatory for grades K–5. Appointments are made with the Admissions Office. Application forms are available on the Web or by the online application process. Students are encouraged to apply by April 1, although later applications are considered on a first-come, first-served basis. AFA has a rolling admission policy, which permits new students to be admitted through the middle of October. In the spring semester, new students may be accepted through the middle of March.

ADMISSIONS CORRESPONDENCE
CDR David Graham
Director of Admissions
Admiral Farragut Academy
501 Park Street North
St. Petersburg, Florida 33710

Phone: 727-384-5500 Option 1
Fax: 727-347-5160
E-mail: admissions@farragut.org
Web site: http://www.farragut.org

THE AGNES IRWIN SCHOOL

Rosemont, Pennsylvania

The
Agnes Irwin
School

Type: Girls' day college-preparatory school
Grades: Pre-K–12
Enrollment: 663
Head of School: Martha M. Cutts

THE SCHOOL

At the entrance to the Admissions Office at Harvard University, there is a plaque honoring Miss Agnes Irwin, who was chosen by Harvard to be the first dean of Radcliffe College. Her selection was not surprising; she was highly regarded as a pioneering educator of women and the founder in 1869 of one of the first schools in the United States devoted to girls—The Agnes Irwin School. The School was at the forefront in developing academic opportunities for girls and continues today to be a nationally recognized leader in this field. The atmosphere is both nurturing and fortifying, with a faculty and program attuned specifically to the developmental strengths and needs of girls.

The School is located 12 miles west of Philadelphia on an 18-acre suburban campus. Twenty school districts provide bus transpiration, enabling girls to attend the School from more than seventy-five ZIP code areas in Philadelphia and suburban communities. Public transportation is within walking distance.

A 34-member Board of Trustees, including alumnae, parents, and members of local education and business communities, governs Agnes Irwin. There is an active Alumnae Association with more than 4,000 members and a supportive Parent Association. Sponsored programs in recent years have included a Science Symposium for Girls, a day of workshops with astronaut Sally Ride and Poet Laureate Billy Collins, and faculty and parents' workshops with Mel Levine, JoAnn Deak, Edward Hallowell, and Leonard Sax exploring the current research on gender and learning. This year's annual giving and fund-raising activities totaled more than $1 million and the endowment currently stands at $18 million.

Accreditations include Middle States Association of Colleges and Schools and Pennsylvania Association of Private Academic Schools. Memberships include National Association of Independent Schools, Pennsylvania Association of Independent Schools, the National Coalition of Girls' Schools, and the Cum Laude Society.

ACADEMIC PROGRAMS

Graduation requirements include 4 years of English; 3 years of French or Spanish or completion of Latin III; 3 years of mathematics; 3 years of history; 3 years of lab science, including physics, chemistry, and biology; 1 year of fine arts; and 4 years of physical education. Students are expected to take five subjects per year. Grading is on a trimester system.

Electives are available in all areas and include bioethics, economics, international politics, Middle Eastern history, media arts and graphic design, independent science research, craft of writing, financial literacy, banned books: censorship today, war and literature, and advanced topics in math. A consortium course with three local independent

schools is offered annually and this year's course is "Time: Clock Time, Time and Narrative, and the Natural Philosophy of Time."

Honors and Advanced Placement (AP) courses are available in English, U.S. history, European history, calculus, Latin, French, Spanish, physics, chemistry, biology, and environmental science. In the class of 2005, 44 percent were honored by the AP Scholars Program, and 30 percent took five or more AP courses. Ninety-eight percent of the class took a total of 210 AP tests in sixteen subjects, and 88 percent scored 3 or better.

Visual and Performing Arts courses include AP Photography, Studio Art, AP Drawing/Painting, AP Mixed Portfolio with 2-D Design, Computer Graphics, 3-D Design in Pottery and/or Sculpture, Drama, Communications and the Media, Dance, Glee Club, and the Bel Cantos.

A unique feature of an Agnes Irwin education is the Special Studies Program. For two weeks in February, sophomores and juniors leave the School to explore careers or special interests in the greater classroom of the "real world." Students choose one of the School-sponsored courses offered, an independent program, or a combination of the two. The goals of the program are to enrich the student's educational experience by expanding her understanding of the world beyond Agnes Irwin through internships, community service, cultural immersion, and wilderness exploration as well as provide opportunities to pursue special talents and interests. In 2006, 70 percent of the girls are involved with the following programs: Habitat for Humanity, Santa Fe Photography Workshop, Presidential Classroom, Marine Ecology, a homestay in France or Mexico, Theater Arts, Teton Science School, Philadelphia Exploration, Shakespeare Theater and Stage Combat, and community service programs, including a week at an orphanage in the Dominican Republic and a week at a women's shelter in Grand Coteau, Louisiana. The remainder of the girls pursued independent projects, such as working in a law firm, interning in an architect's office, shadowing a Division I women's basketball coach, assisting a molecular biologist conducting research, and interning at a radio station.

The Senior Assembly is another treasured tradition at Agnes Irwin. Each senior is required to present a 10-minute speech in the theater before her peers and faculty members on a topic of her choosing. Recent topics include Kent State, Autism, In Opposition to the Death Penalty, Ski Patrol, Taliban Women, and Dog Shows. This special feature emphasizes the School's belief that each and every girl has something important to say and the confidence and the ability to address an audience of 300 people.

FACULTY AND ADVISERS

Of the 44 faculty members in the Upper School, 75 percent hold advanced degrees and 25 percent are men. The average class size is 15, with a 7:1 student-teacher ratio.

In addition to teaching responsibilities, some faculty members also serve as advisers. Seven girls are grouped with 1 adviser and meet once a week for a school period and then individually as needed. In addition, girls receive guidance and assistance through Support Services, which includes guidance counselors, learning specialists, and academic tutors.

COLLEGE PLACEMENT

In January of their junior year, the girls meet with the College Guidance Director for twelve small-group seminars to learn how to conduct a successful college search. Topics include interview skills, effective college application essay writing, information regarding athletic recruitment, and financial aid. In March, the girls and their parents have individual meetings with their college guidance counselor to help them plan for school visits over the summer and for the more than 75 college reps who visit AIS in the fall. Each girl works closely with her guidance counselor throughout the fall of her senior year and into the spring until her choice has been made.

The average SAT scores for the class of 2005 were 645, verbal and 655, math. Typically, 20–25 percent of each graduating class is recognized by the National Merit Program. One hundred percent of the seniors attend college, and, in the last five years, they have matriculated at more than ninety different colleges and universities. Five or more members of the last five graduating classes have attended Pennsylvania (25), Georgetown (8), Delaware (8), Boston College (7), Virginia (7), Trinity College (7), Yale (6), Penn State (6), Columbia (5), Princeton (5), and NYU (5).

STUDENT BODY

The enrollment for 2005–06 was 663 and breaks down as follows: twelfth grade, 61; eleventh grade, 57; tenth grade, 65; ninth grade, 66; eighth grade, 47; seventh grade, 57; sixth grade, 59; fifth grade, 51; fourth grade, 44; third grade, 46; second grade, 38; first grade, 40; and kindergarten, 32.

Agnes Irwin fosters an environment where respect for the individual, appreciation of differences, and supportive, lasting friendships are developed and nurtured. The students represent an array of racial, ethnic, religious, socioeconomic, and geographic backgrounds. Students of color represent 17 percent of the student body, while more than 50 girls have a parent(s) who was born in another country and for whom English is a second language.

All students are expected to abide by the Code of Conduct: Respect yourself, respect others, respect property, and act responsibly. In addition,

all Upper School girls sign the Honor Code, which was designed by the students and states, "As a member of the Agnes Irwin community I will promote the values of honesty and personal integrity. I will not lie, steal or cheat or tolerate this behavior in others. I will take the necessary action to defend these values." The Discipline Committee, comprising both faculty members and students, handles serious violations of the Code.

ACADEMIC FACILITIES
Agnes Irwin is located on 18 acres, with two gyms; a fitness center; a library for each division; a new Arts and Sciences Center, including a 300-seat theater; a Lower School building; and a combined Middle and Upper School building. There are seven tennis courts and three playing fields.

Each classroom is equipped with seven data ports, one telephone port, and one coaxial cable TV connection. A 1-gigabyte fiber-optic backbone provides 100-megabit speed to the classroom. The network has seven servers, including five rack-mounted PIII Compaq servers.

The Upper School library contains 25,000 volumes and 183 computer ports, providing access to the Schoolwide network, Internet, and the Web-based library patron catalog. Three hundred computers are available for instruction, including Pentium and Power Mac machines.

ATHLETICS
Physical education and athletics have a strong tradition at Agnes Irwin. In the elementary years, girls have physical education three times per week, and, starting in the fifth grade, it increases to five times per week. Interscholastic competition begins in the seventh grade when the School competes in the Interacademic Athletic Association. The sports offered include basketball, crew (Upper School only), cross-country, field hockey, golf, lacrosse, soccer, softball, squash, swimming, tennis, and volleyball.

Those students who do not wish to participate in athletics have the option of working out in the Fitness Center as well as taking yoga and dance for their physical education requirement. About 25 percent of the girls choose this option.

EXTRACURRICULAR OPPORTUNITIES
Girls participate in concerts, dance recitals, plays, art exhibits, photography shows, and more, increasing their interest as both creators and patrons of art. Girls act, sing, design and decorate sets, and work lighting and soundboards. The School's proximity to Philadelphia enables its teachers to arrange visits to cultural events, such as art museums, concerts, and the opera.

There are numerous student-run clubs, including the yearbook, literary magazine, and school newspaper, and girls have the opportunity to start clubs of their own. In addition to longstanding favorites such as Model UN, SADD, and debate club, girls have recently started a drill team, a fencing club, and a robotics club. There are more than ninety leadership opportunities through clubs, athletic teams, and student government.

Service is an integral part of The Agnes Irwin School community. The emphasis of the program is on hands-on projects with a minimal amount of fundraising. Service activities include tutoring underserved children at urban schools, visiting senior citizens in nursing homes, learning American Sign Language, and participating in organized programs, such as Habitat for Humanity, Philadelphia Cares Day, Special Olympics, and Martin Luther King, Jr. Day of Service.

DAILY LIFE
The School day begins with homeroom at 8:10 and ends at 3:30, with ten 42-minute periods. Athletic teams practice and play games after school. Most games are on weekdays, although a few may be scheduled on the weekends.

SUMMER PROGRAMS
Summer Session is a seven-week summer program offering arts, athletics, and academics for boys and girls entering kindergarten–grade 12. Academic courses for credit include Biology, Chemistry, Geometry, Greek I, Latin I, Photography I, and Physics. Enrichment courses for high school students include America on Film, SAT Prep, Pottery and Sculpture, and Journalism for Print and Web.

COSTS AND FINANCIAL AID
Tuition for the 2005–06 school year for grades 9–12 was $21,050. Additional expenses included uniforms, textbooks, and lunch (optional). Tuition is paid in two installments—60 percent in August and 40 percent in January—or families can arrange for a ten-month installment plan through Higher Education Services, with the first payment due in May.

The School is committed to making its educational opportunities available to bright, motivated, and talented girls regardless of their family's ability to pay. Agnes Irwin offered $1,400,000 in financial aid for the 2005–06 school year to 16 percent of its student body. Although financial aid is available in all grades, 50 percent of the budget was awarded to Upper School students. The awards ranged from $500 to full tuition.

Applicants for grades 6–9 applying for financial aid are encouraged to take the scholarship exam, typically held on a Saturday in mid-November. Winners are awarded the full cost of textbooks as well as the full amount (up to 100 percent) of financial aid for tuition as determined by the School and Student Service for Financial Aid (SSS) each year until graduation.

ADMISSIONS INFORMATION
The three main entry years are kindergarten, sixth grade, and ninth grade, although students are admitted at all grade levels if space is available. For 2005–06, 93 new girls enrolled, including 14 each in the sixth and ninth grades. The application process includes a parent interview, standardized testing (ISEE or SSAT), school transcripts, teacher recommendations, and a full-day student visit. Each visitor is matched with a hostess and attends her classes and activities for the day so that she can better appreciate the level of course work as well as the culture of the School.

APPLICATION TIMETABLE
Applications should be submitted starting in September of the year before the student wishes to enter and should be completed by mid-January. Decision letters are mailed on February 1. Those girls offered admission must secure their place in the grade by March 1. The parent or guardian signs an enrollment contract and submits it along with a $1000 nonrefundable deposit. If space becomes available after March 1, late applications as well as those on the waiting list are considered.

ADMISSIONS CORRESPONDENCE
Joan M. Brennan
Director of Admissions and Financial Aid
The Agnes Irwin School
Ithan Avenue and Conestoga Road
Rosemont, Pennsylvania 19010
Phone: 610-525-8400
E-mail: jbrennan@agnesirwin.org
Web site: http://www.agnesirwin.org

THE ALBANY ACADEMY AND ALBANY ACADEMY FOR GIRLS

Albany, New York

Type: Day college-preparatory school; boys' boarding (grades 9–12)
Grades: PK–grade 12 and postgraduate: Lower School, Prekindergarten–4; Middle School, 5–8; Upper School, 9–12 and postgraduate (boys)
Enrollment: School total: 675; Lower School: 169; Middle School: 186; Upper School: 320
Head of School: Caroline B. Mason

THE SCHOOL

The Albany Academy and Albany Academy for Girls are independent college-preparatory day schools. They were founded in 1813 and 1814, respectively, by the granting of a charter signed by Mayor Philip Schuyler Van Rensselaer and the city council of Albany.

The Albany Academy (AA) strives to create an environment rich in possibilities that encourages and inspires each student to attain the level of mastery of which he is capable and to develop those personal qualities and talents that make him a unique individual, a leader, and a contributing member of society. Albany Academy for Girls (AAG) seeks to engage each student in academics, the arts, and athletics through a rigorous program that challenges students to become creative and independent thinkers and fosters responsible citizenship and lifelong learning. The two schools share a Coordinate Program in the Upper School, affording each other a greater number of courses and faculty members, shared facilities, and a common sense of community.

The adjacent 47-acre campuses are located in the University Heights section of Albany, approximately 2 miles from the city center. Several colleges, the state capitol, the state museum and library, and the cultural resources of the city are easily accessible from the campus.

A postgraduate program at the Albany Academy provides students (boys only) with an exceptional opportunity to enhance their intellectual growth while they strengthen their academic transcript. The boarding program at the Albany Academy affords qualified students—boys in grades 9 through postgraduate who live a great distance from the school—the opportunity to receive an Albany Academy education.

Each school is governed by a Board of Trustees composed of community leaders, alumni, and parents. The Albany Academy's annual operating budget is approximately $7 million, with annual giving and capital fund-raising by alumni, parents, and friends amounting to more than $700,000 annually. At Albany Academy for Girls, operating expenses amount to more than $5 million, with more than $355,000 raised in unrestricted gifts through the Annual Giving Program.

The Albany Academy and Albany Academy for Girls are accredited by the New York State Association of Independent Schools (NYSAIS) and approved by the New York Department of Education. The schools hold memberships in the College Board, the Cum Laude Society, NYSAIS, the National Association of Independent Schools, the Educational Records Bureau, the Capital Region Independent Schools Association, the Secondary Schools Admission Test Board, and the National Association for College Admission Counseling. The Albany Academy is a member of the Association of Boys Schools and the New England Prep School Athletic Association. Albany Academy for Girls is a member of the National Association of Principals of Schools for Girls and the National Coalition of Girls' Schools.

ACADEMIC PROGRAMS

The Academy offers an early-childhood program for 3-year-olds. Physical education, music, story time, movement, and art are integral parts of a program that stresses active, meaningful interaction with the environment, peers, and adults.

The Lower School (prekindergarten–grade 4) offers children a stimulating academic program designed to foster a love of learning. Classes are kept small so that each youngster can receive individual attention. Teachers attend to learning-readiness skills and nurture children's enthusiasm, social skills, and creative talents. Grades 1–4 feature instruction in mathematics, English, social studies, science, world language, and computers. There are frequent field trips and assemblies. In the daily athletics period, children receive systematic instruction in several sports to develop motor and coordination skills. Lower School students also attend art, music, reading, and library classes. World language instruction begins in pre-K.

The Middle School offers age-appropriate experiences to help students learn to meet challenges, take risks, and solidify organizational skills. While they share academic experiences, the Academies recognize that at perhaps no other time are single-gender classrooms more valuable than during the middle school years. Students in grades 5–8 take on the core curriculum of language arts, history, mathematics, and science. Concentrated study of a world language (Latin, French, or Spanish) begins in grade 5. Students participate in a comprehensive arts program and a physical education program that introduces interscholastic team competition in grades 7 and 8. Students in all grades participate in experiential education programs in the wilderness of northern New England and the Adirondacks as well as in Canada, Boston, and Washington, D.C.

The Upper School curriculum provides sound preparation for college. Students must earn 20 credits to graduate, including core courses in English, world language, history, mathematics, science, and the fine arts. Remaining credits may be acquired through electives, such as economics, computer programming, creative writing, astronomy, psychology, and studio art. Seventeen Advanced Placement courses are also offered. More than half of the junior and senior classes take the Advanced Placement examinations. Honors tutorials are available in several subjects, and seniors are encouraged to undertake independent-study projects or internships. The normal class size is 17 students or fewer, and the student-teacher ratio is 9:1. Through the schools' Coordinate Program, students may enroll in more than sixty additional courses and participate in numerous joint extracurricular activities.

The academic year is divided into trimesters; trimester grade reports are sent to parents. Interim reports are sent to parents at regular intervals and whenever a student's progress requires special attention.

FACULTY AND ADVISERS

There are 113 teachers and administrators at the two schools. Seventy-five hold master's degrees and 8 hold Ph.D. degrees. In addition to interacting with students in the classroom, faculty members serve as advisers to activities, clubs, and classes as well as serving as athletic coaches. Every instructor teaches five sections daily and holds a student-advisory responsibility.

Caroline B. Mason is the Head of Schools. She holds a B.A. from Denison University and an M.A. from Case Western Reserve University. She was formerly Head of Mount St. Mary High School in Nashua, New Hampshire, and a teacher at several schools, including the Laurel School for Girls in Cleveland, Ohio; Boston Conservatory of Music; and Harvard University.

COLLEGE PLACEMENT

The goal of the college counseling office is to provide Upper School students with a comprehensive and individualized program to enable them to choose the best college for themselves. College advising and placement education begin in grade 9. More than 60 representatives of various colleges visit the eleventh and twelfth grades. Private conferences with students, parents, and the Directors of College Counseling ensure that college choices are appropriate. All students are instructed in effective ways to apply to and visit colleges.

All students take the ACT and SAT exams in the eleventh and twelfth grades. Strong scores on the SAT, SAT Subject Tests, and Advanced Placement exams have led to their acceptance by highly competitive colleges and institutions. Students from the class of 2005 are attending such colleges and universities as Carnegie Mellon, Colby, Cornell, Middlebury, Northwestern, NYU, Rensselaer, and the University of Pennsylvania.

STUDENT BODY AND CONDUCT

Drawn from a six-county area and from within a radius of 65 miles, the student body is ethnically, religiously, and economically diverse. The total 2005–06 school population of 340 boys and 335 girls included 82 boys and 87 girls in the Lower School, 71 boys and 115 girls in the Middle School, and 187 boys and 133 girls in the Upper School.

Students are encouraged to actively participate in all aspects of school life; they are expected to conduct themselves responsibly and treat each other and their teachers with respect. Students are responsible for upholding school rules. The Albany Academy adheres to a schoolwide honor code.

Student Council members, especially seniors, occupy important leadership positions at Albany Academy for Girls. The Albany Academy's Leadership Development Program prepares students to hold leadership positions at school and beyond by providing formal classes on leadership, advising/student mentoring, community service, and involvement in cocurricular programs—all within the structure of a British-based house system.

ACADEMIC FACILITIES

The Albany Academy's main building (1931) was designed by Marcus Reynolds and modeled after the original building, which was designed by Philip Hooker. It houses forty classrooms that are fully equipped with full video and high-speed Internet

capacity, two libraries, a dining room, an auditorium, administrative offices, a student lounge, the school's archives, computer labs, art and music studios, the Black Box Theatre, a wellness center, a gymnasium, and a science wing. The Field House contains the main gymnasium, a wrestling room, a team room, a state-of-the-art fitness center, an Olympic-size hockey rink, an indoor pool, twelve locker rooms, a training room, and coaching staff offices.

Albany Academy for Girls underwent extensive renovations in 2001. The fully automated library houses more than 16,000 print and audiovisual materials. Other resources include six state-of-the-art classrooms in the Middle School. There are four totally renovated science labs, an auditorium, an acoustically engineered music room, an art suite, and a student lounge. The building also contains two computer labs, and all classrooms have full video capabilities, with a wireless network for high-speed Internet access throughout the school. AAG's laptop program, pioneered in 2001, begins in the sixth grade to introduce students to the integration of technology and learning in all their classes.

BOARDING AND GENERAL FACILITIES
A registered nurse is on duty at each school throughout the school day. At the Albany Academy, a twelve-bed, six-bedroom residence house, complete with a living room, kitchen, common room, laundry, and live-in resident apartment, was added in 2003.

ATHLETICS
Athletics and physical education are a vital part of the daily experience at the Albany Academy and contribute to the spirit and tone of the school. All students in prekindergarten through grade 12 participate in a physical education and athletic program supervised by 4 full-time physical education instructors, 18 faculty coaches, and a full-time athletic trainer. On all levels, the focus is on skill building and sportsmanship. Upper School team sports include baseball, basketball, cross-country, football, golf, hockey, lacrosse, soccer, swimming, tennis, track and field, and wrestling. All Upper School students are required to play two interscholastic sports.

In addition to a complete physical education program, students at Albany Academy for Girls participate in a variety of competitive athletics. Students in grades 7–12 may choose among basketball, diving, field hockey, lacrosse, soccer, softball, swimming, tennis, track, and volleyball; 85 percent of Upper School girls play a competitive sport. Club track, tennis, and skating are also available. In addition to the gymnasium, the school has three playing fields.

The Academies offer students an array of athletic facilities that is unmatched by any high school in the region. At AA, facilities include an indoor swimming pool, an indoor ice rink, nine tennis courts, a training room, a fitness center, an all-weather 400-meter track, and 15 acres of athletic fields. AAG's state-of-the-art athletic facility includes an indoor suspended track over a full-size gymnasium, two international squash courts, a weight room, and an aerobics room. The two schools have access to each other's facilities.

EXTRACURRICULAR OPPORTUNITIES
Students enthusiastically lead and participate in special-interest organizations. At Albany Academy for Girls, art club, dance workshop, dramatics association, glee club, ski club, and athletics committees plan and perform special events several times during the year. Class spirit is enhanced through a traditional sports and songfest event each September. A traditional evening of music, dance, and holiday spirit—the Wassail—occurs in late December. The school newspaper, yearbook, and literary magazine reflect the students' academic and athletic achievements and highlight the spirit and moods of the year.

Several student organizations have been in existence for many years and have strong traditions at the Albany Academy, such as the school newspaper, yearbook, and literary magazine. Students are also involved in community service, student council, peer advising, chorus, stage band, drum line, chess club, yo-yo club, Model UN, Mock Trial, and Amnesty International. Regular social activities include weekend dances at the Academies, ski trips, skating parties, holiday get-togethers, and a formal ball in April.

DAILY LIFE
The Academies hold classes five days a week. Classes meet in block periods from 8 a.m. to 3:15 p.m. Nutritious lunches for students and faculty members are served daily. Upper School athletics take place after classes until 5 p.m. Sports teams also meet on Saturday for practice or competition.

COSTS AND FINANCIAL AID
The 2004–05 tuition charges ranged from $10,000 for prekindergarten to $16,500 for grade 12. Public school districts within 15 miles of the Academy transport the students to school; private busing is also available.

The Academies' need-based financial aid program assists 30 percent of the student body. To apply for financial aid, parents must file a Parents' Financial Statement with the School and Student Service for Financial Aid in Princeton, New Jersey, and submit a copy of the previous year's federal tax return to the school. Families are required to re-apply each year. In addition to grants, the Academy offers a loan program in the Middle and Upper Schools. There is also a monthly tuition payment

option. Entering ninth graders at Albany Academy for Girls may also compete for one of two $6000 Betsy Foot Merit Scholarships each year. The Albany Academy offers two scholarships for children of Academy alumni per year.

An enrollment agreement with a nonrefundable deposit of $1000 is due at the time of enrollment. Half of the tuition is due on or before August 1; the remainder is due on December 1. Monthly tuition payments may be arranged through the Academic Management Services Program, and long-term loans are available.

ADMISSIONS INFORMATION
The Academies welcome applications from all students who are likely to benefit from and contribute to the life of the school community. The schools do not discriminate on the basis of race, creed, color, or national or ethnic origin in the administration of their admissions or educational policies, financial aid programs, or athletics or other school-administered programs.

Transcripts of all academic work and the applicant's attendance record, health record, and standardized test records must be sent from the former school. Admissions testing, teacher recommendations, and an interview are required of all candidates. Admission is based on academic performance, recommendations, and standardized test scores. Applicants are encouraged to spend a day visiting the school while classes are in session.

APPLICATION TIMETABLE
Inquiries are welcome year-round. Interested parents and prospective students may attend one of the Open Houses, or they should call to schedule a visit. Applicants for the Middle and Upper Schools are interviewed on campus and are required to make a full-day visit. Applications are due by February 15. Applications received after that date are accepted on a space-available basis.

ADMISSIONS CORRESPONDENCE
Christine Amitrano
Director of Admissions
The Albany Academy
135 Academy Road
Albany, New York 12208-3196

Phone: 518-465-1461
Fax: 518-427-7016
E-mail: admission@albany-academy.org
Web site: http://www.albany-academy.org

Katherine Howell
Director of Admissions
Albany Academy for Girls
140 Academy Road
Albany, New York 12208-3196

Phone: 518-463-2201
Fax: 518-463-5096
E-mail: admission@albanyacademyforgirls.org
Web site: http://www.albanyacademyforgirls.org

AMERICAN HERITAGE SCHOOL

Plantation and Delray Beach, Florida

Type: Coeducational, day, independent, nonsectarian
Grades: Pre-K3–12
Enrollment: 2,400, Plantation campus; 1,104, Boca/Delray campus
Head of School: William Laurie, President and Founder

THE SCHOOL

American Heritage School's mission is to graduate students who are prepared in mind, body, and spirit to meet the requirements of the colleges of their choice. To this end, the School strives to offer a challenging college preparatory curriculum, opportunities for leadership, and superior programs in the arts and athletics. American Heritage is committed to providing a safe and nurturing environment for learning so that children of average to gifted intelligence may achieve their full potential to be intelligent, creative, and contributing members of society. Students receive a well-rounded education that provides opportunities for leadership and character building and extensive opportunities for growth in the arts, athletics, and new technology.

ACADEMIC PROGRAMS

The curriculum for the preprimary child is developmental and age appropriate at each level. Daily language, speech, and auditory development activities help children to listen, understand, speak, and learn effectively. The program seeks to maximize the academic potential of each child, while fostering a positive self-image and providing the skills necessary for the next level of education.

The Lower School is committed to developing a student's basic skills, helping the student master content areas, and maintaining the student's enthusiasm for learning. Students learn the fundamentals of reading, process writing, mathematics, and English through a logical progressive sequence, and they learn social studies, handwriting, spelling, science, and health, with an emphasis on the development of good study skills. In math and reading, students are grouped according to ability. Enrichment classes in computer education, art, media center, music, Spanish, physical education, and investigative science lab are offered. Field trips, special projects and events, and assemblies supplement the work introduced in class.

Math, reading, grammar, literature, social studies, and science are the core subjects of the junior high curriculum, where critical-thinking skills become increasingly important. Writing skills are emphasized, helping students become literate and articulate thinkers and writers. Enrichment courses are an important part of the junior high curriculum, with courses rotated on a nine-week basis. Honors classes are available in all core subject areas.

At the high school level, emphasis is placed on college preparation and on higher-level thinking skills. Students are challenged by required research and speech and writing assignments in all subject areas. An extensive variety of classes in all areas of the fine arts is available. A selection of electives—from astronomy to world religions to musical theater—rounds out the students' schedules, allowing them to explore other interests and talents. In addition to traditional lecture and discussion, teachers supplement the text curriculum with activities, projects, and field trips that make subjects more relevant and meaningful to the students.

Honors and Advanced Placement (AP) courses are available to qualified students. Students may gain college credit as a benefit of the successful completion of AP courses, which include American government, American history, biology, calculus, chemistry, economics, English language, English literature, environmental studies, European history, French, music theory, physics, psychology, Spanish, and world history.

American Heritage School offers unique premedical and prelaw programs to qualified high school students. Both programs challenge those ninth- through twelfth-grade students who have an interest in medicine or legal studies and encourage students to consider these areas as potential career choices. The many course offerings are most often taught by local physicians or well-known area attorneys. In addition to course work for both programs, there are required internships that match students with professionals in their area of study.

Through the international program, in addition to an international student's regular academic classes, one to two hours of English language instruction is provided daily. Living with an American family produces more opportunity for language development and practice.

FACULTY AND ADVISERS

The students at American Heritage are served by 186 teachers, counselors, and administrators at the Plantation location and 91 teachers, counselors, and administrators at the Delray campus. Sixty-five percent hold master's or doctoral degrees. Teachers actively seek out both school-year and summer workshops to attend, and they return with creative ideas for their teaching. Faculty turnover is minimal. The faculty is also committed to the Heritage philosophy of developing good character and self-esteem as well as the reinforcement of traditional values in students. Teachers maintain close communication with parents regarding their child's progress, with frequent written progress reports, phone calls, and scheduled conference days. Classes are small, with a 17:1 student-teacher ratio.

COLLEGE PLACEMENT

At American Heritage, the goal is to send seniors to colleges that match their goals and expectations for college life. There are 6 full-time guidance counselors in the high school, including a Director of College Placement and a Scholarship Specialist.

The college placement process begins in seventh grade with academic advising about curriculum and course selection and continues through high school with college-preparation advising. The counselors keep abreast of current admissions trends through attendance at national and local conferences and frequent contact with college admissions representatives.

The preparation for college intensifies as students in grades 9 through 12 follow a three-step program designed to help them score well on the SATs. The program includes SAT prep mini-exercises in their English and math classes. In tenth grade and above, students may take an intensive daily SAT prep class taught on campus during the regular school day. In addition, high school students participate in Kaplan Test Prep's "online tutorial" which interactively takes students through SAT preparation and test-taking strategies. It provides personalized diagnostics on student progress and is monitored by each student's English and math teachers. Students may access the program via computers at school or at home.

At this level, academic counseling gives consideration to graduation requirements and course selection, study skills and time management, leadership and club involvement, and referral to mentoring or professional tutoring, if needed. College advising is offered in the classroom on topics such as standardized test taking, the college application process, resume and essay writing, and searching for colleges and majors. The School reviews all college applications sent, writes letters of recommendation, finds scholarships for students, prepares students for college interviews, invites college admission representatives to campus, hosts a college fair, and proctors Advanced Placement (AP) exams. A guidance resource room with catalogs, videos, and guidebooks is available for students and parents.

Virtually all graduates continue their educations and are admitted to the nation's finest colleges and universities. In recent years, graduates have been admitted to such schools as Columbia, Boston College, Colgate, Cornell, Duke, Georgetown, MIT, NYU, Pepperdine, Princeton, Rutgers, Tufts, Wake Forest, Yale, and the Universities of Connecticut, Maryland, Pennsylvania, and Southern California.

STUDENT BODY AND CONDUCT

In the Lower School, the PK-3 classes enroll about 16 students; PK-4, 17; kindergarten, 18; grades 1 and 2, 21; grades 3 and 4, 22; and grades 5 and 6, 23. Each PK-3, PK-4, kindergarten, grade 1, and grade 2 class has a teacher and a full-time assistant. Classes in grades 3 through 6 have a teacher and a half-time assistant. Grades 7 through 12 in the Upper School average 17 students.

The Plantation campus has 2,400 students, with 1,170 in the Lower School and 1,230 in the Upper School. The Boca/Delray student population totals 1,104, with 557 students in the Lower School and 547 in the Upper School. The School's day population is culturally diverse, with students representing forty-three countries from around the world.

ACADEMIC FACILITIES

The Plantation campus includes a fully equipped science lab, five state-of-the-art computer rooms, and a recently constructed $25-million Center for the Arts that houses a state-of-the-art 800-seat theater, a black-box theater, spacious art studios, a graphic design lab, choral and band rooms, and individual practice rooms. The entire School uses the technologically advanced media center—a 17,000-volume library—and gymnasium/auditorium. Heritage has an excellent physical education center that includes an Olympic-sized swimming and diving facility, six tennis courts, a track, four modern locker rooms, a weight-training room, and acres of well-maintained athletic fields.

The American Heritage Boca/Delray campus provides two state-of-the-art iMac computer labs, fully equipped science labs, art studios, a college guidance computer lab, a library/media center and research lab, an Olympic-sized swimming pool with eight racing lanes, a 2,600-square-foot teaching pool, a 25,000-square-foot gymnasium/auditorium, six lighted tennis courts, a football and soccer field, fully equipped weight training room, locker rooms, two well-equipped playgrounds, acres of well-maintained baseball and softball fields, practice fields for soccer and football, and beautifully landscaped grounds and courtyards.

ATHLETICS

The athletic program is an important part of the sense of community that has developed at Heritage. Parents, teachers, administrators, and students develop a special kind of camaraderie while cheering on the Patriot teams. Awards evenings are held for athletes and parents at the conclusion of each season. Heritage offers a complete competitive sports program. A "no cut" policy allows every student who wants to participate an opportunity to play on the Patriot team of his or her choice. Coaches provide high-quality instruction in all sports. Sportsmanship, team-work, recognition of effort, and thorough training and preparation are the goals toward which the School works every day. Each year, a number of student-athletes receive financial help for their college education based on their athletic ability and their performance. More importantly, however, for those who do not have the ability—or maybe the desire—to participate at the collegiate level, athletic opportunities offer a very enjoyable and memorable experience, with accomplishments and relationships that last a lifetime. American Heritage competes as a member of the Florida High School Activities Association, and the athletics programs are consistently ranked in the top ten in the state of Florida.

EXTRACURRICULAR OPPORTUNITIES

The extensive activities offered at Heritage serve several purposes. Primarily, they assist in the growth and development of students, but they also provide opportunities for leadership and excellence, which are increasingly required for college admission. Among the activities and clubs offered to high school students are the National Honor Society, Student Council, Spanish/French Honor Society, the Modern Language Club, Mu Alpha Theta (math club), SADD, the computer club, yearbook, the student newspaper, thespians, marching band, orchestra, jazz band, and chorus. Lower School students can take after-school classes in art, dance, instrumental music, karate, cooking, computers, and other areas of interest. Students may also participate in Student Council, Junior Thespians, or Math Superstars.

American Heritage School provides an outstanding fine arts program to students in PK-3 through grade 12. The Center for the Arts is a beautiful, specially designed facility that enhances the arts program. Students participating in art, music, and drama programs have won awards at local, state, and national levels of competition in recent years. This recognition includes the Florida Vocal Association (superior ratings for choir, solo, and ensemble), Florida Orchestra Association (superior ratings for solo and ensemble/guitar and strings), American Choral Directors Award, and National Scholastic Art Competition (gold and silver medals).

Many students participate in enrichment and leadership programs offered in Broward County, including the National Conference for Community and Justice, Leadership Broward, Boys and Girls Clubs, Silver Knights, and the Institute for Math and Computer Science. Nationally, students have participated in Hugh O'Brian Youth Foundation, Freedoms Foundation, Presidential Classroom, and Global Young Leaders Conference. In addition, American Heritage School is home to two nonprofit organizations: Mosaic Theatre, an organization committed to promoting the dramatic arts, where students are able to work alongside professional actors, and the Center for the Arts Scholarship Foundation, a fund-raising organization that awards scholarships to talented students in the arts.

SUMMER PROGRAMS

American Heritage has provided summer fun for young campers since 1981. Summer camp provides activities that help build confidence and self-esteem. Campers enjoy the challenges and rewards of teamwork as they work and play. Through the numerous activities that are offered, campers continue to develop the socialization skills begun in school. Campers enjoy good relationships with the high school and college counselors, who serve as role models for them. American Heritage Day Camp afternoon sessions are available for students 13 years old and under.

For students who have failed a credit course in high school or have been required by their current school to attend summer school in order to pass to the next grade level, summer school is a necessity. However, many others can benefit from American Heritage's summer academic program, including preschoolers who need readiness skills to succeed in kindergarten or first grade; elementary and junior high students who need practice and development of basic skills in math, reading, and language arts; any students who perform one or two years below grade level; students for whom English is a second language; high school students who want to advance themselves academically by earning extra credits during the summer; and high school students who will soon take the SAT or ACT tests for college admission. An FCAT prep class is also offered for elementary students. More information can be obtained by contacting the American Heritage School.

COSTS AND FINANCIAL AID

In 2005–06, tuition and fees total between $12,050 for preschoolers and $15,166 for twelfth-grade students. The price for the international program is $32,000 for an academic school year from August through May and includes tuition, housing, three meals a day, books, uniforms, 2 hours a day of English language tutoring, SAT tutoring, and activities and trips.

American Heritage offers financial aid to parents who qualify.

ADMISSIONS INFORMATION

Enrollment at American Heritage School is limited to students who are above average to gifted in intelligence and who are working at or above grade level. Math, reading, vocabulary, and IQ tests are administered and are used to determine if the student has the background and basic skills necessary to be successful. The results of these entrance exams are discussed with the parents at a conference following the testing. I-20 visas are granted to international students who are accepted. Details are available from the Director of Admissions. Students are admitted without regard to race, creed, or national origin.

For acceptance into American Heritage's international program, families must supply complete academic records from the age of 12, translated into English; two teacher letters of recommendation, translated into English; copies of the student's passport; and a completed American Heritage School application form. The American Heritage Admissions Committee reviews the student's records and determines suitable placement. Full tuition for the school year is due upon acceptance. After tuition has been received, the School issues an I-20 form, which must be taken to the U.S. Embassy in the student's country to obtain a student visa.

APPLICATION TIMETABLE

First-semester classes begin in mid-August. For information regarding specific deadlines, students should contact the Plantation campus of the American Heritage School.

ADMISSIONS CORRESPONDENCE

Attn: Admissions
American Heritage School
12200 West Broward Boulevard
Plantation, Florida 33325

Phone: 954-472-0022
E-mail: admissions@ahschool.com
Web site: http://www.ahschool.com

American Heritage School Boca/Delray
6200 Linton Boulevard
Delray Beach, Florida 33484

Phone: 561-495-7272
E-mail: admissions@mailhost.ahschoolbd.com
Web site: http://www.ahschool.com

AMERICAN INTERNATIONAL SCHOOL SALZBURG

Salzburg, Austria

Type: Independent, nonprofit, coeducational boarding and day school
Grades: 7–12, postgraduate year, academic year abroad
Enrollment: 76
Head of School: Paul McLean, Headmaster

THE SCHOOL

The American International School Salzburg (AIS-Salzburg), founded in 1977 as the Salzburg International Preparatory School, is committed to the secondary education of students from around the world, regardless of race, nationality, or religious affiliation. The American International School Salzburg is a boarding and day school committed to the college-preparatory education of conscientious young men and women. The academic and boarding programs nurture the students' intellectual growth and artistic potential, as well as their social, physical, and personal development. The school community is guided by and dependent upon self-discipline, mutual respect, integrity, care, and compassion. The school aspires to prepare students to succeed in further studies, to exercise informed judgment and to become active and responsible members of society. The School is located within 10 minutes of the city center in a rural, parklike setting that is surrounded by the city's protective greenbelt. With a population of 150,000, Salzburg is rich in cultural tradition and history and provides an exceptional setting for secondary education. The Salzburg International Airport and main train station provide immediate access to the School campus. The American International School Salzburg Association is governed by a board of directors, which includes School administrators, teachers, parents, and experts who have volunteered their time to the School. All decisions, appointments, and negotiations that are carried out by the association are not for profit under Austrian law.

AIS-Salzburg is accredited by the Middle States Association of Colleges and Schools and is a member of the European Council of International Schools, the Association of Boarding Schools, and the College Board.

ACADEMIC PROGRAMS

AIS-Salzburg offers a rich and challenging academic program that has its foundation in the American High School Curriculum. Emphasis is placed on Advanced Placement course work for all students in an effort to provide a college-preparatory schedule of courses. Small class sizes, the dedication of the teaching faculty, academic support programs, and college placement assistance create a caring yet demanding atmosphere for intellectual growth and development. Through the effort, motivation, and devotion of the students and staff members, the School is justifiably proud of its college placement record. The School assists students in gaining acceptance to some of the most highly respected institutions of higher learning worldwide. The curricular program demands much in terms of time and energy on the part of the students. The proper motivation, along with clear academic goals, is a prerequisite for admission to the School. At

AIS-Salzburg, academics come first, and the structure of the daily and weekly schedules, the emphasis on college preparation, and the fundamental schoolwide goals and principles reflect this orientation.

Graduation requirements, teaching materials, and curricular programming reflect the standards and practices of accredited independent American secondary schools in the United States and abroad, allowing AIS-Salzburg graduates to apply to universities and colleges in North America. Enrollment in universities outside North America is possible through meeting local requirements, which generally include at least four Advanced Placement examinations with acceptable scores. The AIS-Salzburg ESL program provides tuition to those whose English language skills require improvement before they can enter universities in the United States or Canada. The School's diploma requires all students to complete 25 credits from the ninth through twelfth grades: English, foreign language, and the arts, 4; mathematics, science, and social studies, 3; elective subjects and physical education, 3; and 1 credit in a higher-level mathematics or science course. Students must maintain a load of thirty-three classroom periods per week, including one English and two foreign language course, one of which must be German, one period of physical education and health, one arts course (drama, dance, and visual art, vocal or instrumental music). A cumulative grade point average of at least 1.5 (C-), at least a 90 percent attendance rate, and a positive citizenship record are required for promotion and graduation.

Full-credit course offerings include English 7–12; English as a second language (ESL) levels 2–4 (grades 9–12); German 1–6; French 1–4; Spanish 1–4; world geography; world history; European history; United States history; AP United States history; AP European history; AP human geography; prealgebra; algebra; geometry; algebra II/ trigonometry; math analysis/precalculus; advanced mathematics; AP calculus AB; junior high school science; biology; chemistry; physics; AP biology; AP chemistry; AP environmental science; chorus; studio art; physical education and health; AIS-Salzburg healthy lifestyle requirement; ESL seminar, junior high seminar; 9/10 seminar; junior seminar; and senior seminar.

Students in the ESL diploma program are required to reach as high a level as all other students in subject areas such as science and social studies before graduation. Three levels of ESL provide from one to four periods of English instruction per academic day, and successful completion of all three levels is required for the diploma. Students who complete all three levels before the twelfth grade are mainstreamed into the regular academic program, including Advanced Placement–level courses.

FACULTY AND ADVISERS

There are 20 full- and part-time administrators, teaching faculty members, and resident-care staff members, 6 of whom live on campus. The School administration is composed of a Headmaster, who coordinates both the boarding and academic programs; a Dean of Students, who directs the resident-care staff and pastoral care program; and a college counselor. The School Headmaster is active in the coordination of the various programs and provides active day-to-day leadership in the School. The teaching faculty is composed of highly qualified instructors, most with advanced degrees in their subject areas. Although predominantly American, all foreign language teachers are native speakers of their subject languages. Several of the teaching faculty members have been at the School for more than fifteen years, and the average number of years of teaching experience is more than eleven. The average number of students in a course is 7.

COLLEGE PLACEMENT

AIS-Salzburg places great emphasis on appropriate college placement and has achieved an outstanding record over the past twenty-five years. The college counselor has more than fifteen years' experience at the School and provides full information to all students and parents. Beginning in the junior year, a series of college placement counseling sessions helps students identify potential choices for higher education, and the School helps direct students, given their academic abilities, interests, and geographic requirements. All students are required to take the PSAT examination during their sophomore and junior years and the SAT exams at least twice during their junior and senior years. All students who are nonnative English speakers take the TOEFL twice at AIS-Salzburg. The School college counselor helps ensure that all college application materials are accurate, complete, and submitted on time. All students receive guidance and assistance in program selection and course scheduling while at AIS-Salzburg in an effort to maximize their abilities and showcase their talents.

Graduates of the AIS-Salzburg class of 2005 were accepted to some of the most select universities and colleges worldwide, including Lewis and Clark, Stanford, the London School of Economics, the national universities of Austria and Germany, and the Universities of Edinburgh and Bristol.

STUDENT BODY AND CONDUCT

The School's enrollment in 2005–06 was 76. There were 15 students enrolled in the junior high school and 61 enrolled in the high school (grades 9–12). There were nearly equal numbers of girls and boys enrolled. The student body represented twenty-four nationalities. The largest

percentage of students came from North America. Student conduct is governed by the rules and regulations of the School, as specified in the *AIS-Salzburg Parent and Student Handbook*. As a boarding school, the expectations of behavior reflect the schoolwide goal that student characters be directed toward self-discipline, mutual respect, care, and compassion. The School takes a firm stand on offenses related to the misuse of drugs and alcohol in order to provide a clean, healthy environment for student development and growth. Students who break the rules and regulations of the School are subject to disciplinary actions and consequences, most often in the form of restricted free time. In serious cases, the School disciplinary committee may determine that a student withdraw temporarily or permanently. AIS-Salzburg students hold permanent seats on the disciplinary committee.

ACADEMIC FACILITIES
Sixteen specific- and general-use classrooms are located on the main campus in five separate buildings. Other academic facilities include a science laboratory, a computer laboratory with Internet and student e-mail access, a darkroom, and a 14,000-volume library.

BOARDING AND GENERAL FACILITIES
All dormitories and dining and common rooms are in the main building. Single, double, and triple rooms are available, and each is equipped with a private bathroom and shower. All of the dormitory space has been recently modernized and refurbished.

ATHLETICS
Students are provided with a physical education program that offers a wide variety of athletic opportunities. The School has access to the excellent facilities at the University of Salzburg. Students can engage in numerous activities, including track and field, swimming, diving, weight lifting, aerobics, dance, softball, baseball, rock-climbing, golf, skiing, tennis, and cross-country. The School's program of sports and physical education surpasses curricular requirements in order to provide the joy of both recreation and competition for all students. Varsity basketball and volleyball teams compete with teams from the International Schools based in Austria, Germany, Switzerland, and Italy. AIS-Salzburg teams are also active in local Salzburg state sports leagues. Competitions are held regularly in softball, soccer, volleyball, basketball, track and field, bowling, skiing, snowboarding, swimming, tennis, and golf.

Noncompetitive activities include ice-skating, hiking, rock-climbing, sailing, squash, weight training, aerobics, horseback riding, and whitewater rafting. The School also charters a bus to nearby ski resorts every Saturday during the ski season.

The School uses local facilities that include playing fields, a tennis court, and a nearby riding stable (including an indoor riding hall) and is also able to offer students participation in local athletic training that is outside of the School program.

EXTRACURRICULAR OPPORTUNITIES
AIS-Salzburg offers students several extracurricular options. Noncredit elective courses include journalism, Model UN, speech and debate, and yearbook, and provide structured involvement each trimester. Participation in various clubs and organizations is also available to the students, including German, French, and Spanish club; ski and snowboarding club; chess club; student council; National Honor Society; and the student tutorial service. The School's excursion program involves students in travel throughout Europe during each trimester. Excursion destinations have included France, Switzerland, Italy, the United Kingdom, Greece, Hungary, the Czech Republic, Germany, Spain, and most of the major cities of Europe. Students are provided with all transportation, room and board, activities, and free time to explore destinations on their own. Adequate supervision and direction is provided during all excursion periods.

DAILY LIFE
Each academic day begins with breakfast in the School's dining areas at 7 a.m., and instruction begins at 8. Seven 50-minute periods follow, with a 15-minute break between periods two and three and a 35-minute lunch period. Classes end at 3 p.m. Athletic teams practice in the afternoon seasonally. Exam preparatory sessions meet in the afternoon and are scheduled before each exam date. Faculty office hours, tutorial sessions, and various organizations and clubs meet between 3 and 4; otherwise, students have free time and the opportunity to leave the campus. Dinner is served from 5:30 to 6:30, and all boarding students are required to study in their dormitory rooms from 7 to 9:30 p.m. A staggered lights-out system mandates that students be in bed by 10 p.m. Wednesday morning is set aside for a mandatory 2-hour physical education and health period, with transportation to and from the university and a regional sports center provided by the School. All of the boarding students at AIS-Salzburg have a full schedule of commitments each day of the school year.

WEEKEND LIFE
AIS-Salzburg offers a variety of weekend activities, outings, and events. Due to the School's location, the resident care staff, directed by the Dean of Students, organizes entertaining and culturally edifying activities throughout the school year. Five skiing and snowboarding trips to the nearby Alps during the winter are included in tuition. All students are engaged in at least one cultural event per month while enrolled at the School. Student interest and feedback helps determine the schedule of activities each weekend. Day trips on weekends to various places of historical interest and scenic beauty are included in the price of tuition. Destinations include the salt mines of Salzburg, the Salzkammergut lake district, Munich, Chiemsee, and Berchtesgaden.

SUMMER PROGRAMS
The Salzburg International Language Center, now in its eighteenth year of operation, offers German and ESL courses from two to six weeks in length during the summer months (early July until mid-August). Course offerings include four levels of study in each language, from beginning to advanced. During free time, the summer program includes numerous activities, sporting events, and day trips to sites of historical and cultural interest. All students are housed in the School dormitory and have access to the School's library and computer center, along with a private e-mail and Internet account. Full room and board at the School are provided in the tuition package.

COSTS AND FINANCIAL AID
For 2005–06, the boarding tuition was €20,000 for junior high, €22,000 for grades 9 and 10, and €24,000 for grades 11–13. The tuition fee included School excursions, extracurricular activities, accident insurance, and one standardized test.

Financial assistance is provided by the School, to students and families that qualify, in the form of continuing grants or single-year scholarships. Over the past five years, approximately 5 percent of the student body has received some form of financial assistance.

ADMISSIONS INFORMATION
AIS-Salzburg admits students of above-average ability, talent, academic motivation, and maturity. Through the admissions process, the School administration identifies students who are open, tolerant, intellectually qualified, and mature who can thrive within the School. Although specific requirements are not set by the admissions committee, students with a B average or higher who participate in a wide variety of extracurricular activities and who have a strong sense of concern for others are accepted. Student candidates to AIS-Salzburg must complete an application package, including an application form, an application fee of €75, four photographs, letters of recommendation from current mathematics and English teachers, and official school transcripts from the last three years.

APPLICATION TIMETABLE
Although the School accepts applications on a rolling basis, completed application packages should be received by the School no later than June 1. An interview or English proficiency test may be required in some cases. All interested students and families are invited to visit the School campus at any time throughout the year. If vacancies exist, students may be accepted at the end of the fall trimester (late November) or at midyear.

ADMISSIONS CORRESPONDENCE
Paul McLean, Headmaster
American International School Salzburg
Moosstrasse 106
A-5020 Salzburg
Austria

Phone: 43-662-824617
Fax: 43-662-824555
E-mail: pmclean@ais-salzburg.at
Web site: http://www.ais-salzburg.at

THE AMERICAN SCHOOL IN LONDON

London, England

Type: Coeducational day college-preparatory school
Grades: PK–12: Lower School, Prekindergarten–4; Middle School, 5–8; High School, 9–12
Enrollment: School total: 1,308; High School: 462
Head of School: Dr. William C. Mules

THE SCHOOL

The American School in London (ASL), the oldest American-curriculum school in the U.K., was founded by Stephen L. Eckard in 1951 to provide an American curriculum for children of American business and government personnel on assignment in London. The School aims to provide a challenging academic program that allows graduates a wide choice of colleges and universities and the continuity of an American curriculum for students coming from and returning to American and international schools. Students of all nationalities who can meet the scholastic standards, including non-English speakers below the age of 11, are welcome to apply.

The School is situated in St. John's Wood, a residential area of London just north of Regent's Park. Underground transport and public buses are available in the neighborhood, and the School offers a door-to-door transport service. Visits to the museums, theaters, and art galleries of London are a regular part of the curriculum, and historic sites in England and Wales are easily accessible from the School. London's central location and well-connected transportation system permit easy travel for student field studies, and student trips are regularly taken in London, the U.K., and Europe.

The School is owned by the American School in London Educational Trust and is registered as a charity in the United Kingdom and as a nonprofit foundation in the United States. It is governed by a Board of Trustees, with 26 full-time members from the community. The plant is owned by the School.

The School enjoys an enthusiastic response and avid support from more than 4,000 alumni and friends of ASL.

The School is accredited by the Middle States Association of Colleges and Schools and the European Council of International Schools (ECIS) and is a member of the National Association of Independent Schools, the European Council of International Schools, the Council for the Advancement and Support of Education, the Educational Records Bureau, and ECIS.

ACADEMIC PROGRAMS

The curriculum of the High School is college preparatory. To graduate, a student must complete at least 19 credits, including 4 years of English; 3 each of social sciences and one modern language; 2 each of mathematics, science, and visual arts and/or performing arts; 1 of physical education; ½ of computer science; and ½ of health. The School recommends at least 1 additional year of modern language, science, mathematics, and fine arts. Freshmen, sophomores, and juniors must take five "academics" (English, modern language, history, mathematics, science) per year, and five are recommended for seniors. Elective courses are available in all subject areas. Some examples are Shakespeare, world literature, journalism, band, play production, digital imaging, psychology, photography, Japanese, human geography, and astronomy.

ASL offers the largest selection of Advanced Placement courses (nineteen courses) outside the U.S.; they include American history, European history, calculus (2), statistics, economics, computer science, biology, chemistry, physics (2), art history, French (2), Spanish (2), German, studio art, and music theory. Other courses can be taken on an independent-study basis.

Classes in basic academic courses are not usually grouped by grade level but tend toward ability grouping in each academic discipline. In modern languages, all classes are grouped by ability. The average class size is 15, and the student-teacher ratio 11:1.

The school year is divided into two semesters. Grade reports are sent out at the end of each semester. The grading system uses letter grades of A to F. Students who receive two unsatisfactory grades (below C–) or one failing grade for any one marking period are put on academic probation.

Once a year, High School students have a three- to five-day program called "Alternatives," which is an experiential learning program. Students can choose a course from among forty options, including tours, outdoor/indoor activities, travel, and community service activities.

FACULTY AND ADVISERS

The High School faculty consists of 26 men and 29 women. Most hold graduate degrees.

William C. Mules was appointed Head of School in July 1998. An experienced administrator and educator, Dr. Mules came to ASL from Morristown-Beard School in Morristown, New Jersey, where he had been Headmaster since 1992. Previously, he was Head of School at McDonogh School for seventeen years. Dr. Mules received his B.A. in English from Princeton University. While teaching English and coaching lacrosse at his alma mater, McDonogh School, he studied for his M.Ed. at Johns Hopkins. He earned his Ed.D. in counselor education from the University of Virginia.

The School hires teachers who are willing to devote the extra time required for excellence and are interested in working with the individual student, within a program that calls for imaginative instruction.

Sabbaticals can be applied for after seven years; three are awarded each year. The School encourages teacher exchanges.

COLLEGE PLACEMENT

The High School has 3 class deans, 4 college counselors, and 1 personal counselor, who are available to students for a range of counseling services. The class deans oversee the adviser program for grades 9 through 11, and every student in grade 12 is assigned to a college counselor. A wide selection of reference materials and catalogs is constantly updated to aid students in their college choices. The college search begins with a college information session that is held midyear for the parents of juniors. A junior class meeting in February after receipt of the PSAT results establishes a schedule for seminars and individual sessions on the application process. Individual interviews are held with each student, and summer visits to selected colleges are recommended. In addition, more than 80 college admissions representatives visit the School each year. Students may take the full range of tests required for admission to colleges at the School.

The mean scores on the SAT I for the class of 2005 were 628 verbal and 630 math. Ninety-seven percent of the 87 seniors who graduated in 2005 enrolled in college. ASL graduates are attending Cambridge, Duke, Princeton, and Yale, among others. In 2005, scores of 3 or higher were obtained on 84 percent of AP exams taken. Seven percent of ASL graduates were National Merit Commended Students.

STUDENT BODY AND CONDUCT

There are currently 462 students in the High School. The distribution is as follows: grade 9, 122; grade 10, 115; grade 11, 109; and grade 12, 116. There are nearly equal numbers of boys and girls in all grades. While the majority

of the students are U.S. citizens, more than fifty nationalities are represented in the student body.

The School has a well-defined code of conduct concerning such issues as drugs, alcohol, theft, and plagiarism. Serious violations, although rare, may result in suspension or expulsion.

ACADEMIC FACILITIES

The school building is of modular design and houses all three divisions. There are eighty classrooms and nine science laboratories; seven computer centers; five music rooms; five art studios; two theaters; two gymnasiums; a writing lab; a ceramics room; a woodworking shop; and two libraries containing more than 50,000 volumes and a large media center. A computer network with 1,600 network outlets, a state-of-the-art high-speed server, and a high-speed Internet connection were installed in 1996, linking more than 500 computers in the building.

A renovation project began in 1999 and was completed in 2001. It added 24,000 square feet of classroom space and an additional gymnasium, and ventilation and lighting were upgraded for the whole school.

ATHLETICS

The physical education program is directed toward recreational and lifetime sports, with an emphasis on fitness.

The School's varsity athletics teams compete against local British and American schools, as well as American and international schools in Europe. Boys' teams and girls' teams are organized in cross-country, soccer, volleyball, basketball, swimming, tennis, crew, and track and field. In addition, boys compete in rugby, wrestling, and baseball, and there are girls' teams in field hockey, cheerleading, and softball.

The School's playing fields, located in nearby Canons Park, comprise 21 acres and include soccer and rugby pitches, tennis courts, and a baseball diamond. Neighborhood facilities include running tracks, tennis courts, and a swimming pool.

EXTRACURRICULAR OPPORTUNITIES

Elected officers and representatives serve on the Student Council, which conveys the interests and concerns of students to the administration and organizes social activities. The council sponsors dances, public service activities, movies, and other events. Concerts and plays are scheduled regularly. Special events include a winter auction, sponsored by the Parent-Teacher Organization; a yearly alumni reception; the senior prom; and the annual music tour, which takes the student orchestra, band, madrigal singers, and choir to a European city.

Regular student activities include the yearbook; newspaper; literary magazine; drama productions; prom committee; Model United Nations; instrumental and choral groups; the photography, poetry, and debate clubs; Amnesty International; and Mock U.S. Senate. Volunteer groups serve in hospitals and work with elderly people and other groups in the local community.

DAILY LIFE

The school day begins at 8:05 a.m. and ends at 3:05 p.m., except on Wednesdays, which are early release days, ending at 2:10 p.m. The schedule is an eight-day rotating block schedule, with 80-minute periods divided over every two days. Because the periods rotate, classes meet at different times over the day over the course of an eight-day cycle. Lunch can be purchased in the cafeteria, which is open from 11 to 1. Snacks, sandwiches, and drinks can also be purchased on campus throughout the

day. The School's open campus policy also allows students to buy their lunch at nearby establishments. Sports and club activities usually take place after school; some sports tournaments are held over weekends.

SUMMER PROGRAM

An active summer program enrolls students ranging from kindergarten through grade 8. A summer program director administers the session.

COSTS AND FINANCIAL AID

Tuition is £17,730 for grades 9–12. Financial aid is awarded on the basis of need.

ADMISSIONS INFORMATION

Applicants are considered on the basis of previous academic records, standardized test results, and recommendations from the previous school. There is a nonrefundable £75 application fee, and a £1000 tuition deposit is required upon admission. The School invites each candidate to spend a day at ASL with a student host to meet teachers and prospective classmates. The American School in London does not discriminate on the basis of race, nationality, creed, or sex.

APPLICATION TIMETABLE

Applications are accepted at any time throughout the year.

ADMISSIONS CORRESPONDENCE

Jodi Coats, Dean of Admissions
The American School in London
One Waverley Place
London NW8 0NP
England
Phone: 020-7449-1221
Fax: 020-7449-1350
Web site: http://www.asl.org

THE ANDREWS SCHOOL

Willoughby, Ohio

Type: Girls' boarding and day college-preparatory school
Grades: 7–12
Enrollment: School total: 143; Upper School: 102; Middle School: 41
Head of School: David Rath, Ed.D.

THE SCHOOL

Andrews offers a strong college-preparatory program that fosters individual growth, intellectual achievement, and a desire to reach one's highest potential. The School was founded in 1910 through the generous bequest of Mr. and Mrs. Wallace Corydon Andrews and maintains its original goal of providing young women with the education they need to become self-reliant, self-supporting members of the global society. Situated on 300 acres of fields, streams, woods, and trails, Andrews is located 30 minutes east of downtown Cleveland and is convenient to museums and other cultural resources as well as major shopping areas.

A 19-member Board of Trustees (3 ex-officio), which is composed of prominent members of the business, professional, and education community, oversees the operations of the School. The Head of School and his administrative staff make all decisions concerning daily student life.

The School's endowment is $4.7 million, and the annual operating budget is approximately $6.5 million. Through Annual Giving, the School's 3,750 alumnae contribute to its scholarship program.

Andrews is accredited by the Independent Schools Association of the Central States and is approved by the Ohio State Department of Education. It holds memberships in the National Association of Independent Schools, the National Association of Principals of Schools for Girls, the Secondary School Admission Test Board, the Ohio Association of Independent Academic Schools, the Ohio Association of Secondary School Principals, the National Coalition of Girls Schools, Midwest Boarding Schools, and the Association of Independent School Admission Professionals.

ACADEMIC PROGRAMS

The Andrews curriculum is geared toward the student who is high average to gifted in ability and includes honors, Advanced Placement, and independent-study courses. All seniors are involved in the Senior Project Program, which exposes the students to a variety of career and community experiences during the last few weeks of their senior year. The class of 2005, with 23 members, took a total of 32 Advanced Placement exams, and 88 percent received a score of 3 or better. The English as a second language program serves the School's international students, with classes in ESL being required of all international students until they have scored at least 550 on the TOEFL examination.

With approximately eighty-five courses from which to choose, students in grades 9 through 12 are required to take 4 units of English; 3 units each of history, mathematics, science, and foreign language in French or Spanish; 1 unit of fine arts in art, music, or drama; 1 unit of physical education/health; and ½ unit of speech. In addition, all students must demonstrate computer literacy and acquire certification in CPR. Electives are available in all academic areas, the fine arts, computers, and equine studies. The neighboring Fine Arts Association is available to students seeking private lessons in dance, art, and vocal and instrumental music.

The grading system uses designations of A to F, with pluses and minuses for finer distinctions. There are two 9-week marking periods in each semester. Small classes, averaging 13 students, and a student-teacher ratio of approximately 6:1 enable girls to excel academically and grow as self-confident individuals. Academic progress reports are sent out midway through each semester, and parents are encouraged to discuss their daughter's progress with her teachers and/or her adviser at any time during the year.

Boarding students have a 2-hour study period nightly, with teachers available for assistance and tutoring. The library is open from 8 a.m. to 5 p.m., during the evening study hall, and during daytime hours over the weekend. It contains more than 13,000 volumes, including electronic and audio books. There is an online library catalog for Andrews, area schools, colleges, and libraries, including the Library of Congress. Daily newspapers include the *New York Times* and the *Wall Street Journal,* and periodicals are available in French and Spanish. There is 24-hour home and school access to major academic and international databases of newspapers, magazines, and reference works as well as a core collection in women's studies and an extensive Asian collection.

FACULTY AND ADVISERS

Of the 25 full-time faculty members, more than half hold advanced degrees. Each is eminently prepared for teaching and represents a rich academic background. Many faculty and staff members live on campus, and all are involved in students' lives after classes and on weekends as coaches, club advisers, weekend activity leaders, and neighbors.

Faculty and staff members are committed to the development of each student's character, intellectual potential, and well-being. All students receive extensive individual guidance on their course of study from their faculty advisers, and their progress during the year is reported regularly.

The Head of School, Dr. David N. Rath, came to Andrews from the Saint James School in Maryland, where he was Dean of Students. His educational background includes study at Kenyon College, where he received his Bachelor of Arts degree; Old Dominion University, where he earned his Master of Arts degree; and George Washington University, where he received his Doctor of Education degree with a concentration on faculty retention in schools.

COLLEGE PLACEMENT

During the sophomore year, students and parents meet with the college counselor to begin goal setting and preparing for entrance exams. A junior spends time visiting colleges, while parents attend workshops on admission and financial assistance procedures. Seniors are busy in the fall, sending applications to the colleges of their choice.

The college counseling program is individualized as much as possible for each student and family. The counselor is consulted about the academic progress of every student and maintains an open-door policy for all so that informal discussions about colleges, majors, careers, and academic preparation can be held with family members and students from every grade. The formal selection process begins in the junior year. Workshops on various topics, such as admission, financial aid, and standardized testing, are conducted. Counselors guide each student through the entire application process. In 2005, 100 percent of the School's 23 graduates were accepted at institutions of higher learning. Among these colleges and universities are Boston University, Carnegie Mellon, the College of Wooster, Emory, Hiram, Hobart and William Smith, the Universities of Michigan and Wisconsin, Vassar, Washington and Jefferson, Wells, and Xavier.

ACADEMIC FACILITIES

Academic life at Andrews is centered in three buildings. The Margaret St. John Andrews Building, which was named after one of the founders of the School, houses development and student affairs offices, including the Dean of Students, Residential Life Director, and Registrar; college counseling; Middle School classrooms and classrooms for computer science, English, English as a second language, and social studies courses; and an art studio. In the Administration Building are the Head of School's office, the business office, the 700-seat auditorium, the dining room, the music department, foreign language classrooms, and the Upper School art studio. The Roberta M. Lee Building houses the library; the Student Center; labs for biology, chemistry, and physics; and classrooms for math, history, and the School's learning specialist. The field house contains the gymnasium, the wellness center, a community room, the admission offices, and the Academic Dean's office.

BOARDING AND GENERAL FACILITIES

The spacious grounds provide a serene setting for resident students, who live in four Georgian Colonial houses separated by grade level. Each unit houses up to 20 girls as well as houseparent,

who supervises the girls, manages the household, and provides a pleasant family atmosphere. Each house has a kitchen, a living room, and a dining room, in addition to the girls' bedrooms and the houseparents' apartments. Each dormitory also has computers, a fireplace, a piano, a television set, and laundry facilities. Students may bring their own cell phones and computers. Students from distant states or countries are assigned host families in the area, with whom they may reside during open weekends or School vacations.

The Van Gorder Health Center provides modern, comfortable accommodations for students who become ill. The School nurse, who is on duty during the school day, is always on call. The School physician, who is also on call 24 hours a day, visits the School weekly. Medical emergencies are referred to a local hospital.

ATHLETICS

The physical education program is designed to promote physical vitality, sound health, teamwork skills, and School spirit. Students are required to take gym classes and are encouraged to participate in team sports. Fundamental skills in team and individual sports, including archery, badminton, basketball, golf, soccer, tennis, and volleyball, are emphasized. The School fields interscholastic teams in basketball, field hockey, lacrosse, soccer, softball, tennis, and volleyball. Andrews' no-cut policy fosters participation, making it possible for all interested students to be part of a team. A state-of-the-art field house, with two full-size courts and aerobics, fitness, and weight rooms, was completed in 1999.

The equestrian center offers two full-size indoor arenas and three outdoor arenas for year-round lessons, shows, and recreational riding. There are forty-two stalls, three tack rooms, and ten grooming areas in the main building. Approximately 30 percent of the students participate in the riding program, riding one of the School's horses or bringing one of their own. Several students compete nationally, and an academic support system is in place for riders who frequently travel for competitions.

EXTRACURRICULAR OPPORTUNITIES

Extracurricular activities are a valuable part of School life at Andrews and are open to any student who is interested in participating. Students are encouraged to participate in the wide range of organizations and activities, including choir, drama, yearbook, literary maga-

zine, Environmental Club, Outdoors Club, International Club, Mock Trial, Art Club, Blue Key, Black Cultural Awareness Club, Chess Club, Community Service Club, Equestrian Club, Ski Club, Spirit Club, and Respecters of All Diversities Club.

The School frequently sponsors field trips to museums, concerts, theaters, exhibitions, and lectures to enhance the classroom learning experience. The Willoughby School of Fine Arts, which is located on the Andrews campus, offers cultural programs and lessons in art, dance, drama, and instrumental music. Class trips are organized to build class unity and to provide enrichment in academic areas, including a senior trip to the Stratford Festival in Canada. Special interest trips are generally open to the upper grades and include trips to other countries, choir tours, athletic trips, and outdoor activities.

The campus provides ample space for jogging, bicycling, cross-country skiing, tennis, and horseback riding. Traditional annual events include a camping trip, a play, class trips, Parents' Weekend, and the Holiday Concert in the fall and winter. In the spring, there are the all-School musical, International Day, and Senior Farewell.

DAILY LIFE

Boarding students begin their day with breakfast in the dining room. Classes for all students begin at 7:55 a.m. and end at 3:15 p.m. After-school activities, horseback riding, clubs, and athletics follow. Boarding students have dinner at 5:30 and study hall from 7 to 9.

WEEKEND LIFE

Activities abound throughout the weekend. Boarding and day students may participate in dances and activities with boys' schools, shop, camp, ski, see a movie, or go to an amusement park. Cleveland offers a vast selection of museums, theaters, concert halls, sports events, and shopping gallerias. In addition, sports and equestrian teams take road trips to competitions.

SUMMER PROGRAMS

Andrews offers a Summer Adventure Program during the months of June, July, and August. This camp, for girls ages 8–14, features horseback riding for beginning to advanced riders and offers arts and crafts and recreational sports. Boarding and day camps are offered.

COSTS AND FINANCIAL AID

For 2005–06, tuition was $32,300 for international students, $27,000 for seven-day boarding students, $22,000 for five-day boarding students, $16,050 for Upper School day students, and $14,500 for Middle School day students. There are additional fees for uniforms and selected activities, including music, dance, and horseback riding lessons. A student who is accepted reserves a place by paying an enrollment deposit that is deducted from the total tuition.

Scholarships are available to qualified students entering grades 7–12, ranging from academic scholarships to those based on leadership, character, service to the School, and legacies. Financial assistance is available on the basis of need, as assessed by the Parents' Financial Statement. Payment plans and loan programs are available through the Andrews business office.

ADMISSIONS INFORMATION

Andrews seeks students from diverse backgrounds, without regard to race, color, creed, or national or ethnic origin. The admission decision is based on a variety of factors, the most important being the student's academic record, test scores, character references, and potential to make positive contributions to the School.

Candidates must take the SSAT or the ISEE entrance exam. A personal interview is required, and a campus visit is strongly recommended. References from guidance counselors and teachers are necessary to complete the application. A $40 application fee is required for domestic applicants ($50 for international students). Of 122 students who applied for admission for the 2004–05 school year, 34 were enrolled.

APPLICATION TIMETABLE

An initial inquiry is welcome at any time, and campus tours are available throughout the year. Those applying for early decision are notified in mid-December. Most applications are received by April 1; those received after April 1 are considered on a rolling basis when space is available.

ADMISSIONS CORRESPONDENCE

Kristina L. Dooley, Director of Admission
The Andrews School
38588 Mentor Avenue
Willoughby, Ohio 44090

Phone: 440-942-3606
       800-753-4683 (toll free)
Fax: 440-954-5020
E-mail: admissions@andrews-school.org
Web site: http:www.andrews-school.org

ANNIE WRIGHT SCHOOL

Tacoma, Washington

Type: Girls' day (P–12) and boarding (9–12) and boys' day (P–8) college-preparatory school
Grades: P–12: Lower School, Preschool–5; Middle School, 6–8; Upper School, 9–12
Enrollment: School total: 440; Upper School: 115
Head of School: Jayasri Ghosh, Ph.D.

THE SCHOOL

Annie Wright School (AWS), the oldest boarding school in the Pacific Northwest (1884), combines more than 120 years of rich heritage and tradition with an Upper School program designed to strengthen young women with the self-confidence, talent, and skills they will need for the future. The School was founded in 1884 under the auspices of the Episcopal Church by Charles Wright, President of the Northern Pacific Railroad, and the Right Reverend John A. Paddock, the first Episcopal bishop of the Washington Territory. The original Annie Wright Seminary developed the goal its successor, AWS, still follows today: to prepare girls for higher education by stressing academic excellence and spiritual and physical growth.

Annie Wright School's curriculum provides a structured course of study to assist students in developing their own talents, in seeking and accepting challenges, and in making decisions to discover emergent values. The School encourages and expects students to develop a concern for people in all communities and an appreciation for and sensitivity to the environment.

A student's years at Annie Wright are a time for growing intellectually, physically, culturally, and spiritually. At the Upper School, AWS is more than an academic institution offering a serious college-preparatory education; it is a community in which young women learn, live, and grow together as individuals. To grow to be strong and effective human beings, AWS believes they need a time and a place like this to concentrate on their personal development. Annie Wright encourages an intellectual environment without limits, in which there is freedom to be one's own best self and one where special strengths are nourished.

The campus is on a scenic, 10-acre site in Tacoma's historic North End with a commanding view of Commencement Bay, Puget Sound, and the snowcapped Olympic Mountains to the west. The School's Tudor architecture, red brick walls, and quiet neighborhood provide an environment that is both charming and secure. The rolling lawns gently slope down to the Kemper Center for athletics and performing arts, home to both the excellent athletic program and one of the finest drama programs on the West Coast.

Tacoma, with 200,000 people, is the second largest city in Washington and is located just 20 minutes from Sea-Tac International Airport and 45 minutes from downtown Seattle. It is also just 120 miles north of Portland and 150 miles south of Vancouver, British Columbia.

The School is a nonprofit institution owned by the Foundation Board and supervised by a 28-member Board of Trustees, which meets quarterly. Among its members are alumnae and

parents as well as interested community leaders. The bishop of the Diocese of Olympia is a permanent member.

Annie Wright is accredited by the Northwest Association of Schools and Colleges. Its memberships include the Pacific Northwest Association of Independent Schools, the National Association of Independent Schools, the Pacific Northwest Association of Independent Schools, and the National Association of Principals of Schools for Girls.

ACADEMIC PROGRAMS

The academic program combines the foundation of a strong liberal arts education with a variety of course offerings that allow investigation of personal interests. The student and an academic adviser plan individual programs depending on the student's abilities, interests, preparation, and talents. Course work is divided into trimesters, in which 83 courses are offered in ten major subject areas. The average class size is 11 students; the faculty-student ratio is 1:8.

Students are required to pursue a course of study necessary to qualify for entrance to four-year colleges. The full-year credits required for graduation are a general core curriculum of English, 4 credits; foreign language, 3; social studies, 3; mathematics, 3; laboratory science, 2; and physical education/health, 2. In addition, students must participate in two seasons of after-school athletic activity, demonstrate computer proficiency, and complete course work in art, drama, music, life skills, and religion. Some of the courses that fulfill these requirements are Shakespeare, world literature, human anatomy and physiology, and comparative political systems. English as a second language is available for international students.

All students and faculty members have their own e-mail accounts and can access the campus-wide wireless network. In addition, Annie Wright is the first all-girls' school in the country to participate in the Cisco Networking Academy, a two-year, technical lab-based course that prepares and certifies students to build and maintain networks.

Annie Wright is a member of American Secondary Schools for International Students and Teachers, Inc. (ASSIST) and the English-Speaking Union and offers students the opportunity to spend a year in England after graduation.

Grades are posted and reported to parents twice each year and comments are reported four times each year. Interim progress reports are issued at midterm. Students must maintain a minimum grade point average of 2.0 (in a 4-point system) or be placed on academic probation. Students either remove themselves from probation after one semester or face possible dismissal.

FACULTY AND ADVISERS

The AWS faculty mirrors the School's student body in that it consists of a diverse group of people with a wide range of interests, talents, and special pursuits and a dedication to the independent school. Of the 73 faculty members, 70 are full-time and 29 hold advanced degrees. Eight faculty members live on campus. Upper School faculty members are involved as advisers to extracurricular activity groups, and each is also the academic adviser for 5 to 8 students. The Director of the Upper School works closely with the faculty in counseling and advising the girls to ensure a positive environment.

Dr. Jayasri Ghosh is the Head of the School. She holds a B.A. from the University of Calcutta and received her Master of Education and Ph.D. from the University of Georgia, with a concentration in educational psychology and gifted education. She is also a certified counselor.

COLLEGE PLACEMENT

The comprehensive college-counseling process begins in the freshman year, when students are taken on a day trip to several colleges in nearby Seattle. An overnight trip to colleges in Eastern Washington during the sophomore year is followed by a trip down the West Coast during Interim Week in the spring of the junior year, in which nine schools are visited. The School's college counselor schedules regular meetings with each student throughout her stay at Annie Wright. As a result of this process, each Annie Wright senior has a clear vision of the school best suited for her well before college applications are due. All juniors are required to plan and take the PSAT, SAT, and ACT. Juniors and seniors have the opportunity to meet with representatives of a wide variety of colleges and universities from throughout the U.S. and Canada who visit the campus frequently.

Students graduating from Annie Wright in recent years have typically entered competitive colleges and universities. Among the schools now attended by AWS graduates are Boston University, Columbia, Johns Hopkins, Pepperdine, Pomona, Rensselaer, Stanford, Smith, and the University of Washington.

STUDENT BODY AND CONDUCT

Annie Wright students come from a wide variety of national, economic, racial, and religious backgrounds. In 2005–06, students from Canada, India, Korea, Lithuania, the Republic of China, Rwanda, and Taiwan joined those from Alaska, Florida, New York, Ohio, Oregon, Texas, and Washington.

Student conduct is based on respect for oneself, other students, and the community. Each student subscribes to the School Honor Code. All students wear uniforms during the academic day. The *Student Handbook,* which contains School

rules and policies, is reviewed and updated each year. The Student Council is composed of elected representatives and officers of student organizations. Its purpose is to provide leadership, encourage active engagement in the community, and suggest changes in School policy regarding living conditions, curricular and extracurricular activities, social activities, and discipline. The student Honor Board reviews disciplinary matters, and the student House Council is the governing body for boarders.

ACADEMIC FACILITIES
The academic facilities include Raynor Chapel; the library (with 19,000 volumes and multiple CD-ROM databases); 45 classrooms; three well-equipped science laboratories; a center for athletics and performing arts; a darkroom; a technology lab; a music wing; a bookstore; art, dance, and ceramics studios; a nine-room Middle School; and a heated indoor pool.

BOARDING AND GENERAL FACILITIES
The Residence Department has excellent accommodations, including spacious rooms, lounge areas, a student kitchen, laundry facilities, and apartments for the Residence Department staff. The School also has a health center, two kitchens, two dining rooms, and several elegant meeting rooms.

ATHLETICS
All students are required to participate in the physical education program and are encouraged to join varsity sports, such as basketball, crew, cross-country, golf, sailing, soccer, softball, tennis, and volleyball. The School has two gymnasiums, a swimming pool, and a weight room.

EXTRACURRICULAR OPPORTUNITIES
A wide variety of extracurricular activities are offered. In addition to theater and concerts in Tacoma and Seattle, planned and impromptu special events, and regular weekend outings, many special interest clubs are available. Among these clubs are the yearbook, student newspaper, the International and Pep clubs, and vocal ensembles. Students are required to complete 30 hours of community service in order to graduate, and most go well beyond that minimum. Annie Wright students were recognized

throughout the Puget Sound area for their quick and creative responses to the Tsunami and Hurricane Katrina disasters.

DAILY LIFE
School opens at 8 a.m. Twice each week, students attend classes in the morning with a break for chapel. On the other three school days, students break for club and class meetings. The School operates on a modified block schedule in which most classes meet four days a week for a total of 220 minutes. Lunch is 40 minutes long; day students may bring a brown-bag lunch, buy their lunch, or combine the two. Tutorials run from 3:10 to 3:45, followed by sports and drama practices. Dinner is served at 6 p.m., and there is a mandatory study period from 7 to 9 p.m. The time for lights-out varies with the age of students.

WEEKEND LIFE
South Puget Sound social and cultural offerings are rich and varied. Weekend activities at Annie Wright include outings to restaurants, museums, shops, and theaters. Special weekend-long adventures can include trips to the mountains, beaches, and forests surrounding Puget Sound for picnicking, skiing, and hiking. Social functions at Annie Wright are often held in conjunction with nearby high schools. Resident and day students are included in all weekend activities. Free weekends away from school are allowed with parental and School permission.

COSTS AND FINANCIAL AID
The 2005–06 Upper School tuition for day students was $16,438. For resident students, tuition, room, and board were $32,677. Additional expenses included textbooks and uniforms, which totaled approximately $500. Each Upper School student is also required to lease a laptop computer from the School, which carries with it an attractive purchase option at its conclusion. Each resident student typically has an allowance account at the bookstore, usually ranging from $50–$100 per month.

The nonrefundable registration deposit of $1000 for day students and $2000 for boarders is applied to tuition. There are several options for payment of the remainder: semiannual payments in July and December or a monthly payment plan beginning in May, prior to the opening of

School. Tuition for international students is due in full by Registration Day in the fall.

Students should not be discouraged from applying for admission because of an inability to meet costs. Financial aid is awarded annually, based on need as determined by the School and Student Service for Financial Aid (SSS). Parents should file a Parents' Financial Statement with the SSS as soon as possible during the academic year preceding enrollment. In the 2005–06 school year, nearly 20 percent of Annie Wright students received financial aid totaling $650,000.

ADMISSIONS INFORMATION
Annie Wright School seeks students with the aptitude to attend college and the desire to make the most of their abilities. Admission requirements include scores on the Secondary School Admission Test, recommendations from the student's current English and math teachers and the head of the school or a guidance counselor, a personal reference, academic transcripts, and an interview.

Annie Wright encourages applicants of any race, color, or national or ethnic origin. The School does not discriminate on the basis of race, color, or national or ethnic origin in the administration of its educational policies, scholarship programs, admissions policies, or athletic or other programs.

APPLICATION TIMETABLE
Inquiries are welcomed at any time during the year. Applications received by mid-March receive first consideration for any vacancies in fall classes. Thereafter, applications continue to be accepted if space is available in a particular class. Qualified applicants for a full class may be placed in a wait pool. Should that happen, they are kept apprised of their status there by the Admission Office.

ADMISSIONS CORRESPONDENCE
Robert Booth, Director of Admission
Annie Wright School
827 North Tacoma Avenue
Tacoma, Washington 98403
Phone: 253-284-8601
    800-847-1582 (toll-free)
Fax: 253-572-3616
E-mail: admission@aw.org
Web site: http://www.aw.org

ARMY AND NAVY ACADEMY

Carlsbad, California

Type: Boys' boarding and day, college-preparatory and military school
Grades: Middle School, 7–8; Upper School, 9–12
Enrollment: School total: 323; Upper School: 283
Head of School: Brig. Gen. Steve Bliss, USA (Ret.), President

THE SCHOOL

Situated on 16 oceanfront acres, Army and Navy Academy (ANA) is a private, nonprofit, college-preparatory military boarding and day school that serves grades 7 through 12. The Academy strives to develop scholarship and honorable character in young men while motivating them to realize their potential. Since its founding in 1910, ANA has subscribed to the values of loyalty, duty, respect, selfless service, honor, integrity, personal courage, and gratitude. ANA accommodates 350 students, most of whom board; the remainder commute from within a 30-mile radius. The Academy is located 85 miles south of Los Angeles and 35 miles north of San Diego. It follows a traditional ten-month academic calendar, with two optional summer program offerings. As a college-preparatory school for young men, ANA is dedicated to providing a high-quality, comprehensive educational experience in a safe and structured environment. Its academic, athletic, and leadership programs, combined with a well-rounded residential life program and spiritual and character development curriculum, promote individual responsibility and a sense of self-motivation. The programs develop honor, discipline, and integrity; cultivate strength of character, personal excellence, and responsible leadership; and prepare the ANA cadet for a lifetime of achievement. ANA is accredited by the Western Association of Schools and Colleges. It holds membership in the National Association of Independent Schools, the Western Boarding Schools Association, the California Association of Independent Schools, the Association of Boarding Schools, the Association of Military Colleges and Schools of the United States, the College Board, the National Association of Secondary School Principals, the National Association for College Admission Counseling, Boys Schools: An International Coalition, and the Western Association of College Admission Counselors.

ACADEMIC PROGRAMS

The Academy's academic curriculum is designed for college preparation, offering challenging courses, customized teaching strategies, and ample scholastic resources. Cadets must complete 6 academic units per year to graduate, including a minimum of 4 units in English, 3 units in social studies, 3 units in math, 2 units in foreign language, 2 units in laboratory science, 4 units in JROTC leadership and training, and seasonal participation in the intramural and athletics programs. Sample electives include music appreciation, music technology, art, art history, drama, advanced environmental science, band, creative writing, astronomy, photography, current events, journalism, psychology, and advanced computers. Honors courses are offered in English, geometry, algebra II, Spanish, biology, and chemistry. Advanced Placement (AP) courses are offered in biology, modern European history, calculus, art, English, physics, chemistry, Spanish, and U.S. history. The Middle School (grades 7 and 8) requires that students complete 12 units in math, science, English, social studies, physical education, and an elective in order to be admitted to the Upper School.

Class schedules are assigned based on a cadet's ability, course history, standardized test scores, and the school's graduation requirements. According to the cadet's course history and standardized test scores, the school places incoming cadets into the appropriate general, honors, or AP classes. Both peer and professional tutoring are available to students, as are daily consultations with their respective teachers during scheduled appointments. In addition, faculty members are present during evening study hall for assistance in math, English, and foreign language.

Mandatory study halls are scheduled Sunday through Thursday night from 7:15 until 9:15. Faculty and staff members supervise and assist students who have specific needs. Students who fail to achieve satisfactory grades attend a Saturday study hall, which mandates additional study and homework time.

FACULTY AND ADVISERS

There are 37 full-time teaching faculty members and academic administrators (22 men and 15 women) who serve the cadet corps. The average teacher has been at ANA for five years and has approximately seven years of teaching experience. Faculty members come from all parts of the United States and are trained to work with boys in the boarding school atmosphere. In addition, 14 members compose the Commandant's staff and are responsible for training, advising, and counseling students in all aspects of campus life outside the classroom. Faculty members also sponsor interest clubs and field trips and serve as athletic coaches. The teacher-student ratio is 1:9. Class size ranges from 6 to 20 students. ANA hires accomplished individuals who are interested in developing each young man's potential and encouraging his progression into manhood. There is no tenure at the Academy; all teachers sign yearly contracts, which are based on administrative review and performance evaluations. The ANA faculty members attend in-service training sessions to keep informed of the latest teaching methodologies. In addition, ANA recently initiated a staff professional development program to attract and retain top-quality teachers and assist with advanced education.

COLLEGE PLACEMENT

ANA currently maintains a 96 percent placement rate in colleges and universities. Through a series of consultations and instructional meetings, 1 college counselor and 3 academic advisers work closely with upper-division cadets through the selection, application, and acceptance processes. All juniors are required to take the SAT; preparation courses are offered and are strongly recommended. Because of its JROTC accreditation, the Academy is entitled to nominate 3 cadets per year to the National Military Academies (including West Point, the U.S. Air Force Academy, and the U.S. Naval Academy). Cadets receiving ANA nominations must go through an internal nomination review board. Such nominations are extended only to cadets of the highest caliber who wish to pursue a distinguished military career; this recommendation can be added as a supplement to a congressional letter of endorsement. Of the 54 cadets graduating in 2005, 96 percent (52 cadets) attended four-year colleges and universities, and 4 percent (2 cadets) attended two-year colleges. Graduates from the last four graduating classes are currently attending the American (Cairo); Boston University; California State, Fullerton; California State, Los Angeles; California State Polytechnic, Pomona; The Citadel; Cornell College; European School of Economics in Italy; Monterey Tech; Norwich; Notre Dame; Oregon Tech; Pomona College; San Diego State; Santa Clara; Tulane; the U.S. Air Force Academy; the U.S. Naval Academy; Villanova; the Virginia Military Institute; and the University of California at Berkeley, Irvine, Los Angeles, Riverside, San Diego, and Santa Barbara; and the Universities of Arizona, Michigan, Missouri, Southern California, and Utah.

STUDENT BODY AND CONDUCT

The Academy strives to create a familial, supportive atmosphere by encouraging cultural learning and spiritual enrichment through a diverse student body. Cadets emigrating from such countries as Thailand, Mexico, China, Korea, Japan, Columbia, and Taiwan aid in fostering a global learning community. Of the 323 cadets currently attending ANA, 10 are in the seventh grade, 30 in eighth, 66 in ninth, 83 in tenth, 93 in eleventh, and 41 in twelfth. The Academy enrolls students from fourteen states and thirteen other countries. ANA is a cadet-governed program; under the supervision of the Commandant Advisory staff, upper-division cadets organize and oversee the daily life of the student body. Cadets are grouped into six companies in which they are delegated positions of authority on the basis of leadership skills, academic achievement, and good citizenship. Each cadet is considered at regular intervals for advancement to higher levels of responsibility; teachers and administrators review each cadet's scholastic and citizenship standing within the corps and make appropriate recommendations. Cadet rank is granted when a leadership vacancy exists and he is deemed qualified. Academy cadets commit to an Honor Code that prohibits (but is not limited to) lying, cheating, stealing, hazing, and toleration of those who do. The school reinforces a zero-tolerance policy on alcohol and drugs by mandating that all cadets submit to alcohol and/or drug test on the first day of registration or should suspicion arise, during the school year.

ACADEMIC FACILITIES

The Thomas A. Davis Hall is the central building on campus and houses five classrooms, ten academic and administrative offices, a band room, and a performing arts stage. There are three other academic buildings that contain twelve other classrooms, as well as Fitzgerald Science Hall, which houses three laboratories. The Samuel Warfield Peterson Library contains more than 3,000 volumes and maintains approximately forty subscriptions to worldwide periodicals and newspapers. Students working on extensive research projects benefit from the Carlsbad Inter-Library Loan Program that

makes nearby college resources available to ANA students. Within the Academy library is the school computer lab, containing twenty Dell models and six other PCs, all of which serve cadets' online needs. Students may obtain an e-mail address through the school and, under supervision, use on-line services for research and obtaining course-related data.

BOARDING AND GENERAL FACILITIES

Students are housed 2 per room in Crean, Atkinson, Lewis, McIntosh, McClendon, Hoover, Fegan, and Anderson Halls. Six 4-room cottages supplement boarding accommodations, A senior-ranking cadet is assigned to each dormitory for leadership, and a 24-hour staff of Commandant Advisors supervises cadets and safeguards the campus. Fegan Hall houses the Health Center, dining hall, admissions office, development office, and alumni coordinator. Atkinson Chapel is used for weekly assemblies and weekend religious services. A newly remodeled oceanfront recreational facility offers video games, billiard and Ping-Pong tables, a television lounge, and an adjoining snack bar. The bookstore, uniform store, barbershop, photo and yearbook lab, art studio, and school newspaper office are also housed in the recreation hall. The Health Center is staffed 24 hours a day, and a morning health call is held daily. A practicing physician visits the campus Monday through Friday between 7 and 9 a.m. and is also on call for additional services. Professional counseling with a registered psychologist is available to students for additional fees.

ATHLETICS

The Athletic Department is an integral part of the development of each cadet at the Academy. Each student is encouraged to participate in a varsity or junior varsity sport or in an intramural program that offers noncompetitive activities. Varsity and junior varsity sports are dictated by season. Fall choices include football, cross-country, and water polo. Winter sports include soccer, wrestling, basketball, and rifle team; spring options are baseball, swimming and diving, golf, tennis, and track and field. These teams compete in Division IV of the California Interscholastic Federation, San Diego Section. Cadets may opt for an intramural program that includes soccer, team handball, Ultimate Frisbee, flag football, 3-on-3 basketball competitions, floor hockey, and volleyball. ANA's athletic facilities include a full-size gymnasium, a swimming pool, private Pacific Coast beachfront, a track and field house, two tennis courts, a combination football/baseball/soccer field, a weight training room, wrestling room, and a rifle range.

EXTRACURRICULAR OPPORTUNITIES

Students are encouraged to participate in as many extracurricular activities as is practical. The Military Department offers Color Guard and Drill Team, as well as an Officer Candidacy School. Students involved with *The Warrior* and *Adjutant* clubs work on publishing the school newspaper and yearbook, respectively. Harvard Model Congress, drama club, Academic Decathlon, Model Club, Navy/Marine Club, Chess Club, SCUBA Dive Club, Outdoor Adventure/Racing Club, debate, and marching band are among the various organizations that meet regularly. Two formal balls are held each year in addition to informal monthly dances that involve girls from local public and private schools. Two drama productions, two orchestral performances, and fine arts classes allow students to participate in the arts.

DAILY LIFE

A typical day begins at 6:30 a.m. Students shower, dress, and report to a formation assembly at 6:45. After attendance is taken and the flag is raised, cadets have breakfast until 7:10, at which point commuting day students arrive. Following the conclusion of classes at 2:30, students are welcome to visit with their teachers for additional help during a tutorial period or have free time until 3. Varsity, junior varsity, and intramural sports begin at 3:15 and conclude, depending on game and practice schedules, around 5:30 p.m. Dinner is served between 5:30 and 6:30. Clubs often meet between 6 and 7, but this time also gives cadets an opportunity to begin their assignments, use the telephone, or check e-mail. An evening formation is held at 6:45 for attendance, announcements, and the lowering of the flag. Evening study hall begins at 7:15 and ends at 9:15; all students must be in their rooms completing the average 2 hours of homework assigned each night. Cadets who need a supervised environment join one of three faculty-proctored study halls. Cadets also benefit from having an English, math, foreign language, and science faculty member on campus during evening study hall Monday through Thursday. Cadets prepare for bed at 10, and lights-out is promptly at 10:15.

WEEKEND LIFE

ANA observes a policy of frequent weekend leave periods. On average, three weekends per month are open for cadets to leave; the closed weekend requires cadets to stay for scheduled special events. A variety of activities are available to those students staying on campus during open weekends. Cadet eligibility for leave is a privilege and is based on satisfactory academic performance and good citizenship. On- and off-campus activities include school dances, trips to movie theaters and shopping malls, athletics, and club activities. Many trips to local theme and amusement parks are planned throughout the year. Parades and other activities are scheduled during closed weekends, such as Parents' Weekend, Grandparents' Weekend, Alumni Weekend, and Military Ball Weekend.

SUMMER PROGRAMS

The Army and Navy Academy offers a summer program called Academy by the Sea. The Academy by the Sea's nonmilitary, five-week boarding session is a coeducational program that balances academics and recreation for a fulfilling experience. Designed especially for students in grades 7–10, the academic program helps students prepare for the upcoming school year and for the academic experiences that lie ahead in secondary education. Credit classes are available. Academy by the Sea also offers two-week recreational camps and one-week surf and bodyboarding camps for students ages 8–16.

COSTS AND FINANCIAL AID

In the 2005–06 academic year, the enrollment fee, annual tuition, room, and board cost $26,950. Additional first-year costs of approximately $2350 covered uniforms and books. Annual day student tuition was $16,600, with additional fees of $1500. Approximately 5 percent of returning students receive some need-based financial aid.

ADMISSIONS INFORMATION

Application for the fall semester begins during the previous fall and continues through late spring. Applicants for 2005–06 were required to supply the admissions officers with the necessary documents, including the application, the applicant's cumulative transcript, results of all recent standardized and specialized testing, math and English teachers' evaluation forms, discipline record, birth certificate, immunization records, and a $100 application fee. If applicants do not have a recent standardized test score, they must take the Independent School Entrance Exam (ISEE) at a hosting school; the cost of the exam is $63, and it is given throughout the year. Notification of acceptance is made when ANA has received all supporting materials.

ADMISSIONS CORRESPONDENCE

Admissions Department
Army and Navy Academy
P.O. Box 3000
Carlsbad, California 92018-3000
Phone: 760-729-2385 Ext. 400
        800-762-2338 (toll-free)
Fax: 760-434-5948
E-mail: admissions@armyandnavyacademy.org
Web site: http://www.armyandnavyacademy.org

ASHEVILLE SCHOOL

Asheville, North Carolina

Type: Coeducational boarding and day college-preparatory school
Grades: 9–12 (Forms III–VI), postgraduate year
Enrollment: 240
Head of School: Archibald R. Montgomery IV

THE SCHOOL

Asheville School was founded in 1900 by Newton M. Anderson and Charles A. Mitchell, who had previously founded the University School in Cleveland, Ohio. Located on 300 wooded acres at the western edge of Asheville, the School is easily accessible by interstate highways and the nearby Asheville regional airport.

As a traditional boarding and day preparatory school, Asheville brings together motivated young men and women from across the country and around the world to form a community dedicated to excellence. Asheville is committed to high academic standards and seeks to encourage intellectual curiosity, sound scholarship, integrity, and service to others. Although the School is not church-affiliated, it teaches Judeo-Christian values. Nondenominational services are held on Tuesday and Friday for all students and on Sunday for boarding students.

The Mountaineering Program, a special feature of the School, is a year-round outdoor activity conducted as an integral part of the overall educational program. The mountaineering experience is available as an afternoon activity, as a project, or through many School-sponsored weekend camping trips.

The School is incorporated not-for-profit and is governed by a self-perpetuating board of 30 trustees, most of whom are alumni, parents, or parents of alumni. The endowment is approximately $30 million. The current operating budget is $9.7 million, toward which annual gifts from alumni, faculty members, and parents contribute more than $850,000.

Asheville School is accredited by the Southern Association of Colleges and Schools. It holds memberships in, among others, A Better Chance, the College Board, Educational Records Bureau, English-Speaking Union, National Association of Independent Schools, Secondary School Admission Test Board, Southern Association of Independent Schools, Southern Association for College Admission Counseling, North Carolina Association of Independent Schools, and the Council for Advancement and Support of Education.

ACADEMIC PROGRAMS

The overall student-teacher ratio is 7:1, and the average class has 11 students. Supervised evening study hall is part of the daily schedule for boarders, and extra help is available for those who want or need it. Grades are issued every eight weeks when reports are sent to parents.

Eighteen credits are required for graduation, including 4 years of English, 3 of one foreign language, 4 of history (including 1 of U.S. history), 3 of laboratory science, 4 of math (including 2 of algebra and 1 of plane geometry), and ½ credit each in art and music. All students take five courses per year.

The curriculum includes an integrated humanities program, which incorporates literature and history with art and music for a full comprehension of the development of civilization; French, Latin, Chinese, or Spanish; algebra, geometry, precalculus, calculus, finite math, statistics, and combinatorics; biology, chemistry, and physics; and music, art, and studio art. Independent study is available. Advanced Placement courses are offered in English, history, mathematics, foreign language, science, music, and computers. All students enrolled in Advanced Placement (AP) classes take the AP exams.

FACULTY AND ADVISERS

There are 58 faculty members, 36 of whom live at the School; 14 live in the dormitories. Twenty-three faculty members hold graduate degrees. Each faculty member has approximately 5 advisees and writes comments to parents at the end of each marking period about each student's involvement in all areas of School life.

Archibald R. Montgomery IV, a graduate of Westminster School (1971), the University of Pennsylvania (B.A., 1975), Monterey Language School (Russian, 1976), and the University of Texas School of Law (J.D., 1982), was appointed Head of School in 2002. He began his career in education as a history teacher at St. George's School where he also served as Director of Summer School, coach, hall parent, and chair of the History Department. He most recently served as Headmaster of Gilman School in Baltimore for nine years.

COLLEGE PLACEMENT

Asheville's College Office employs a full-time Director of College Counseling. Students are prepared for college admission by individual conferences. College visits are encouraged during the summer of the Fifth Form year, and more than 40 college admission officers from all parts of the country visit the campus each year to talk with prospective students.

From 2001 to 2005, 50 percent of Asheville School seniors scored above 600 on the verbal section of the SAT I, and 50 percent scored above 600 on the math section.

Graduating seniors are continually accepted for entrance into a variety of outstanding colleges and universities throughout this country and overseas. Recent graduates are currently attending Auburn, Clemson, Columbia, Cornell, Dartmouth, Davidson, Duke, Furman, Harvard, Howard, Lewis and Clark, Mercer, Ohio State, Purdue, Rhodes, Savannah College of Art and Design, Stanford, University of the South, Vanderbilt, Vassar, Wake Forest, Washington and Lee, and the Universities of North Carolina at Chapel Hill, South Carolina, and Virginia.

STUDENT BODY AND CONDUCT

In the Third Form (ninth grade), there are 47 students; in the Fourth Form, 74 students; in the Fifth Form, 59 students; and in the Sixth Form, 60 students. Students come from twenty-eight states and thirteen countries.

Fundamental to the Asheville School community are the expectations of honesty, integrity, and empathy and respect for others. While it is recognized that making mistakes is a part of the learning process, certain behavior is considered serious enough, by itself or by repetition, to warrant dismissal from the School. Infractions of the rules governing conduct are dealt with at the dormitory level by hallmasters and prefects or by the Conduct Council, when appropriate.

ACADEMIC FACILITIES

The main academic building, Mitchell Hall, built in 1903, contains classrooms, offices, four science laboratories, and one computer laboratory. The Walker Arts Center has a 380-seat auditorium and theater, an art gallery, chorale rooms, and an art studio. The Skinner Library houses 18,000 volumes, in addition to a computer lab and reading rooms for student use.

All classrooms and dorm rooms are wired for connection to the School's network. Students may bring their own computers for their dorm rooms. The network provides students and faculty members with access to e-mail, the Internet, and popular software.

BOARDING AND GENERAL FACILITIES

Fifth and Sixth Formers have their own rooms, while many Third and Fourth Formers share a double room. There are four dormitories with faculty apartments on each corridor, in Anderson Hall (1900), Lawrence Hall (1907), Bement House (1937), and Kehaya House (1990).

William Spencer Boyd Memorial Chapel, Sharp Dining Hall, Tyrer Student Center, and several faculty homes are also located near the three main buildings. An infirmary staffed by 2 nurses is open 24 hours a day; a doctor is on call at all times.

ATHLETICS

Participation in competitive athletics is required for all Third and Fourth Formers, who must participate for one season each year. Varsity and junior varsity teams compete with other independent and public schools in football, cross-country, field hockey, soccer, volleyball, basketball, swimming, wrestling, golf, tennis, track, and baseball. A life fitness program and equestrian, art, music, drama, dance, and mountaineering options complement interscholastic athletics. The Mountaineering Program is conducted year-round. It provides training in hiking, rock-

climbing, kayaking, camping, and caving. A ropes course and an Alpine Tower are located on campus.

The Rodgers Memorial Athletic Center, renovated in 2003, has facilities for basketball, volleyball, wrestling, and swimming and includes team rooms, a state-of-the-art fitness center, a training room, and conference space. Stables and the Ireland Riding Rink are maintained on the campus for equestrian studies.

EXTRACURRICULAR OPPORTUNITIES

Students are encouraged to become involved in clubs, publications, student government, and social and cultural events. The student council serves as a liaison between students and faculty and as the nucleus of student activities. Students publish a newspaper, *The Ashnoca*; a yearbook, *The Blue and White*; and a literary magazine, *The Review*. The School has a chapel choir, a handbell choir, and a chorus. Plays are produced by the dramatic society. Other active organizations include the Mitchell Cabinet, the School's philanthropic organization; the Hoste Society, a student tour guide association; a Christian fellowship group; and the Students for Environmental Awareness club.

DAILY LIFE

A typical academic day runs from 8 to 3:15. Included in the day is an all-school convocation or chapel as well as a midmorning break, a community-wide seated lunch, and academic class meetings. The days end earlier on Tuesdays and Fridays to allow for adviser meetings, mountaineering trips, and travel to off-campus athletic events. Saturday classes, held approximately every other week, begin at 9 and end at 12. Athletics are from 3:30 to 5:30, Monday through Friday. Boarding students have free time before and after the evening buffet dinner at 6. Evening study hall begins at 8. Students study in their rooms, the library, or a supervised study hall in the main academic building.

WEEKEND LIFE

Asheville provides many cultural activities usually found only in larger cities. These include the Asheville Symphony, Community Concert Series, Asheville Art Museum, community theater, and performances by nationally known popular musicians. Dances are hosted on campus by student organizations. Students may be away from campus on Saturday and Sunday afternoon and Saturday evening with proper permission. A shopping center is within walking distance. Special cultural events are held on campus throughout the year. Each student may choose two weekends each semester to leave campus, in addition to regularly scheduled holidays. In addition, "honors weekends" may be earned.

COSTS AND FINANCIAL AID

For the 2005–06 year, tuition was $30,675 for boarding students and $17,500 for day students. There are alternative payment schedules, and tuition refund insurance is available.

Each year, Asheville is able to offer financial assistance to more than one third of the students because of the continuing generosity of alumni, parents, and friends of the School, including foundations. Financial aid is awarded on the basis of need. The School awarded $1.6 million in 2004–05. Parents seeking aid must complete the Parents' Financial Statement (the School and Student Service for Financial Aid form) by the February deadline. Final decisions are made by the Financial Aid Committee; confidentiality is assured.

ADMISSIONS INFORMATION

Applicants are required to submit a completed application, a transcript from their current school, recommendations from their present English and mathematics teachers, and SSAT, WISC, or ISEE scores. All candidates are required to visit the campus in order to meet with faculty, students, and admission personnel.

Since English is not taught as a second language, international applicants should have a good command of the English language. A TOEFL score is required.

The School does not discriminate on the basis of race, creed, or ethnic background in its policies or programs.

APPLICATION TIMETABLE

Prospective students are encouraged to come to the campus while the School is in session. Most visits include sitting in on a class, having lunch, and touring the facilities. Since regular classes are held on some Saturdays, appointments are welcomed then as well as during the week.

The deadline for early decision is December 10. Early decision applications are binding. Applicants who are accepted agree to enroll in Asheville School and withdraw all applications to other schools. All early decision applicants are notified of an admission decision by January 10. Applicants requiring financial aid may not apply for early decision.

The deadline for regular decision is February 1. All regular decision applicants are notified of an admission decision by March 10. A deposit and reservation agreement are due by April 10. All financial aid applicants must apply for regular decision.

Applications are considered after February 10 on a space-available basis only.

ADMISSIONS CORRESPONDENCE

Director of Admission
Asheville School
360 Asheville School Road
Asheville, North Carolina 28806

Phone: 828-254-6345
Fax: 828-252-8666
E-mail: admission@asheville-school.org
Web site: http://www.ashevilleschool.org

THE ATHENIAN SCHOOL

Danville, California

Type: Coeducational day and boarding college-preparatory school
Grades: 6–12: Middle School, 6–8; Upper School, 9–12
Enrollment: School total: 450; Upper School: 297
Head of School: Eleanor Dase, Head

THE SCHOOL

Athenian was founded in 1965 by Dyke Brown, a graduate of Yale Law School and Vice President of the Ford Foundation. Mr. Brown envisioned a school with the goal of the full development of each citizen. Athenian's objectives for each student are intellectual growth, commitment to humane values and character, aesthetic sensitivity, physical fitness, and readiness for adult citizenship and leadership.

Since its founding, Athenian has been recognized for its exceptional integration of strong, innovative, college-preparatory academics with extraordinary programs that develop students' character as citizens of the world. An Athenian education goes far beyond academic excellence to make learning meaningful, interesting, exciting, and motivating. Classes average 15 to 16 students and teachers know each student. The diverse student body comes from throughout the East Bay and around the world. The international programs broaden students' perspectives, with classmates from twelve countries and opportunities across the globe for exchanges, service projects, interim trips, and conferences. Students build important skills as participants in activities such as an airplane construction project, a championship robotics team, community service, athletics, and art, music, chorus, and theater. Few schools offer an experience as academically and personally enriching as Athenian's.

Most Athenian graduates gain admission to their first-choice college or university, with nearly 100 percent admitted to an outstanding array of four-year schools. Most importantly, Athenian inspires students to become lifelong learners and confident, successful adults. Athenian equips graduates with a deep understanding of themselves, extraordinary skills for achievement, and the compassion to make a positive difference in the world.

The Athenian School opened at the foot of Mt. Diablo State Park on a site that was previously part of the Blackhawk Ranch. The 75-acre campus of rolling hills is located 36 miles east of San Francisco, and the cultural resources of the San Francisco Bay Area are accessible via school bus and public transportation. The Pacific Coast and the Sierra are within a few hours' drive.

A nonprofit institution, Athenian is governed by a 25-member Board of Trustees. The School's operating budget is $9.9 million for 2005–06. The endowment is $2.3 million.

The Athenian School is fully accredited by the Western Association of Schools and Colleges. It is a member of the National Association of Independent Schools, the California Association of Independent Schools, the National Network of Complementary Schools, A Better Chance, Western Boarding Schools, the College Board, the National Association for College Admission Counseling, and the Round Square Conference of International Schools.

ACADEMIC PROGRAMS

The broad curriculum develops analytical thinking and communication skills in all disciplines, offering a wide variety of enriching courses in English, history, math, science, fine arts, foreign language, and physical education. The ninth-grade humanities program studies major world cultures through literature, history, and art courses. Sophomores focus on American studies using history and literature. Juniors and seniors take seminars in history and literature. Advanced Placement and/or honors courses are offered in all disciplines.

The academic year is divided into two semesters. The daily schedule includes six academic periods, ranging from 45 to 85 minutes each. Each course meets four times a week.

Courses required for graduation are as follows: English, 4 years; laboratory science, 3 years; mathematics, 3 years; history, 3 years (including freshman humanities, American studies, and three 1-semester elective history seminars in the junior or senior year); 3 years of a foreign language; and 2.5 years of fine arts. Most students exceed these requirements.

Some of the electives offered are studio arts, drama workshops, modern jazz, and computer science. Required seminars (chosen by students) for English and history may include Shakespeare, science fiction, Russian fiction, Latin American fiction, African-American studies, creative writing, or women writers, among others.

Class size varies from 5 to 18, and the average class has 15 students. The overall student-teacher ratio is 10:1. Study is supervised by faculty members assigned to dormitories during the evenings.

Athenian offers intermediate and advanced English as a second language to international students. ESL students are also integrated into the regular curriculum and go on special field trips that serve to introduce them to American life and culture.

Opportunities for independent study are provided for selected students by the academic departments. Student exchanges can be arranged either domestically or internationally. The Athenian School belongs to the National Network of Complementary Schools, which arranges short-term exchanges of students across the country between member schools that have diverse strengths and resources. International exchanges are also possible for Athenian students through the Round Square Consortium.

Class field trips in the San Francisco Bay Area are frequent. Students may also participate in off-campus internships oriented toward community service and career exploration. Qualified seniors may take advantage of an accelerated high school program arrangement at the University of California at Berkeley.

A distinctive element of the curriculum is the Athenian Wilderness Experience, required of all students in their junior year. AWE enhances self-

confidence, communication skills, and perseverance in addition to fostering an appreciation of the environment.

FACULTY AND ADVISERS

There are 55 full-time and 15 part-time faculty members, 42 of whom hold advanced degrees. Twenty-five faculty members live on-campus with their families.

Eleanor Dase, Head since 1992, graduated from the University of Michigan with a degree in mathematics. Since 1974, she has been a math teacher at Athenian; she also held responsibilities as Director of College Counseling for five years and was Assistant Head from 1987 to 1992.

The Athenian School maintains an excellent faculty by seeking the most talented people in their respective fields, by encouraging teachers to continue their education, and by providing financial support for professional growth. Enthusiasm for teaching this age group is a quality also sought in faculty members.

Faculty members perform dormitory supervision and take charge of activities several weekends a year. Each faculty member also acts as an adviser for 8 to 10 students.

COLLEGE PLACEMENT

A college counselor provides expert advice to students choosing colleges. College counseling starts in the junior year and includes sessions with each student and with parents, as well as preparation for the PSAT and SAT. Trips to campuses throughout the country are available. The Athenian School is visited by numerous college representatives each year.

The following is a representative list of the institutions to which graduates have been admitted: Amherst, Brown, Columbia, Cornell, Dartmouth, Duke, Evergreen State, Georgetown, Johns Hopkins, MIT, NYU, Occidental, Pomona, Princeton, Reed, Stanford, Yale, and the Universities of California (all campuses), Chicago, and Pennsylvania.

STUDENT BODY AND CONDUCT

In 2005–06, there were 70 freshmen (36 boys and 34 girls), 77 sophomores (39 boys and 38 girls), 76 juniors (36 boys and 40 girls), and 73 seniors (34 boys and 39 girls). Of these 296 students, 40 (20 boys and 20 girls) are boarders and 256 (125 boys and 131 girls) are day students.

Eighty-nine percent of the students are from California, and 10 percent are international students from nine different countries. Thirty-six percent are members of ethnic minority groups.

Living as a community—especially a community as democratic as the one at Athenian—requires cooperation, social responsibility, and a sense of having a real influence on the quality of life and the decision-making process. An informal atmosphere promotes a good rapport between stu-

dents and faculty members, but it also requires that students develop their own sense of appropriate behavior.

The rules encourage high ethical standards and the ability to live with others harmoniously. The use of tobacco, alcohol, and illegal drugs is prohibited. Cheating and stealing are also major rule violations. Infractions of these rules often result in expulsion or referral by the Dean of Students to the Student Discipline Committee. Town Meeting is the student government of the School and provides a forum for the discussion of community issues and standards.

ACADEMIC FACILITIES
Academic facilities include classrooms; a science building with four labs; a new library holding 15,000 print volumes, forty-three periodical subscriptions, and six electronic subscriptions; art, drama, and music studios; and a computer lab with more than thirty-five state-of-the-art computers for student use.

BOARDING AND GENERAL FACILITIES
There are two dormitories and eleven faculty homes. A number of faculty members reside in apartments or town houses on campus.

Returning students in grades 11 and 12 generally choose single rooms. The Dean of Students matches the new and younger students with roommates for the double rooms. Ninth graders are placed in dorms in which carefully selected seniors provide support and guidance through this all-important transition. Supervision of each dorm at the School is the responsibility of a faculty dorm head, assisted by older students who act as proctors.

Students most often arrange to spend vacations during the school year with nearby relatives or friends if they do not travel to their homes. The campus is closed during those periods. The School assists international students in finding suitable homes to visit at these times. Some trips are also provided during vacations.

The Fuller Commons Building serves as the student recreation and meeting center. The Dyke Brown Main Hall contains the kitchen, dining area, and administrative offices. The Boarding Center provides a gathering place for resident students.

The School nurse visits the dorms each day and advises what action should be taken for any students reported ill. She is available for emergencies as well as drop-in visits during scheduled hours.

ATHLETICS
Physical education, interscholastic sport, or dance is required of all students.

Athenian teams compete with other schools in the North Bay Conference of the California Interscholastic Federation. The School fields interscholastic teams in thirteen sports—seven for boys and six for girls. These are soccer, volleyball, basketball, tennis, swimming, cross-country, and baseball (for boys). There are also junior varsity teams in soccer, basketball, and girls' volleyball.

Noncompetitive activities include rock-climbing, hiking, downhill and cross-country skiing, bicycling, and jazz dance.

Campus facilities include a gym, two tennis courts, a 25-meter pool, a soccer field, a second playing field, and baseball and softball diamonds.

EXTRACURRICULAR OPPORTUNITIES
The School plans frequent trips to museums, plays, the opera, concerts, art exhibits, and lectures in the Bay Area. There are also skiing trips to the Sierra Nevada and excursions to spots on the coast.

On-campus activities include the School newspaper, debate, interweave, yearbook, and Multicultural Alliance.

Community service is required of all students. Service projects include cross-country skiing with the visually handicapped, running the scholarship auction, helping at soup kitchens in San Francisco, working with disadvantaged children or the elderly, and working on environmental projects.

DAILY LIFE
A typical day begins with breakfast between 7:30 and 8 a.m. Day students arrive in time for classes, which begin at 8:10. A hot lunch, prepared at the School, is served at noon. Classes end at 2:40 and are followed by sports and performing arts. Dinner is at 6. Clubs, activities, School meetings, and study occupy a portion of each day.

Faculty-supervised evening study hours are from 7:30 to 9:30, when the dormitories are kept quiet. All boarding students are in their dorms by 10:30 p.m., Sunday through Thursday, and by midnight on Friday and Saturday.

WEEKEND LIFE
Weekend activities are arranged by faculty members on duty. They may include hikes on Mt. Diablo, visits to San Francisco and Berkeley, trips to the coast or the Sierra, and an attendance of the Oregon Shakespeare Festival. Boarding students may spend weekends off campus with permission from the Dean of Students and their parents.

Day students are encouraged to participate in all activities available to boarding students and to spend the night on campus from time to time. An outdoor education program is available throughout the year.

COSTS AND FINANCIAL AID
Tuition for 2005–06 was $36,846 for boarding students (an additional $2858 was charged for international program students) and $23,202 for day students. Additional expenditures are estimated at $1000 for boarders and $500 for day students. They include such expenses as books, music lessons, field trips, and athletic uniforms. Tuition insurance and a tuition payment plan are available.

Financial aid is based on need; eligibility is determined by the School and Student Service for Financial Aid. For 2005-06, scholarship aid of nearly $1.3 million was awarded to 89 students.

ADMISSIONS INFORMATION
Admission is open to all qualified and motivated persons without regard to race, creed, or color. Athenian seeks students who will best profit from an informal, caring environment and who want a rigorous academic course of studies. Admission is selective and based upon the applicant's intellectual ability, academic achievement, character, motivation, creativity, talents, and interests. The School seeks a student body that represents a diversity of geographical, economic, cultural, and ethnic backgrounds.

Each applicant must submit an application, including transcripts and recommendations, have a personal interview, and take an entrance examination, the ISEE, or the SSAT. ESL candidates must take the TOEFL, IELTS, or SLEP.

Priority is given to ninth graders and then to tenth graders. Admission is granted to a smaller number of eleventh graders and occasionally to a twelfth grader.

APPLICATION TIMETABLE
Initial inquiries should be made in the fall of the year preceding anticipated entrance. The School catalog and application forms are available from the Admission Office upon request. Campus visits and interviews may be arranged at any time during the academic year on weekdays between 8:30 a.m. and 3 p.m. The application deadline is January 10, and notification of admission is given no later than March 16. After this date, applications may still be received and reviewed until all places are filled.

ADMISSIONS CORRESPONDENCE
Christopher Beeson, Director of Admission
The Athenian School
2100 Mt. Diablo Scenic Boulevard
Danville, California 94506

Phone: 925-362-7223
Fax: 925-362-7228
E-mail: admission@athenian.org
Web site: http://www.athenian.org

AVON OLD FARMS SCHOOL

Avon, Connecticut

Type: Boys', boarding and day, college-preparatory school
Grades: 9–12, postgraduate year
Enrollment: 382
Head of School: Kenneth H. LaRocque, Headmaster

THE SCHOOL

Avon Old Farms (AOF), founded in 1927 by Theodate Pope Riddle (1868–1946), is a school for boys located on 840 woodland acres in the Farmington River Valley, 12 miles west of Hartford and 30 minutes from Bradley Airport. Avon enjoys the best of both rural and suburban surroundings. In addition to campus trails and a fishing pond (used in fall and spring for fishing and in winter for skating), there are restaurants, movie theaters, retail stores, and two girls' schools nearby. There are 382 students who bring cultural and ethnic diversity and an interesting variety of talents and skills to the school community. Avon is attuned and responsive to the unique needs and learning styles of boys and is fully committed to the development of young men as students and citizens. Avon is a community where traditions live, scholarship flourishes, and boys become men.

The physical surroundings of the School are uniquely handsome and represent Mrs. Riddle's deep appreciation for what is good and enduring about the past. The School's architecture is influenced by the English Cotswold style of building. It is inspiring for its craftsmanship, simplicity, and careful attention to detail. While the School's founder was influenced by the time-honored system of traditional English boarding schools, the approach to the education of today's boys is supportive and lively. At Avon, education occurs not only in the classroom, but also on the playing fields, through participation in the arts, extracurricular activities, community service, and in daily campus life. Avon's core values govern day-to-day life and ensure that moral growth accompanies intellectual and personal development. Mrs. Riddle was fond of referring to her school as a "village" and, even today, the sense of community, vitality, and purpose make it a fitting term for Avon Old Farms School.

The Board of Directors numbers 24 and includes 13 alumni and 11 parents of present or former students. The School's operating budget was $14 million in 2004–05. Annual Giving and the Capital Campaign totaled $4 million in the same year. The total market value of the endowment is $31 million.

Avon Old Farms is accredited by the New England Association of Schools and Colleges and is a member of the National Association of Independent Schools, the Connecticut Association of Independent Schools, the WALKS consortium of schools, the International Boys' Schools Coalition, and the Secondary Schools Admission Test Board.

ACADEMIC PROGRAMS

The School year is divided into two semesters, and grades and comments are sent home to parents four times annually. The average class size is 12, and the student-teacher ratio is 6:1. Graduation requirements are dictated by college admissions preferences for 4 years of English, 3 of mathematics, 2 of the same foreign language, 3 of science (including biology) with intensive laboratory work, 3 of social science (including U.S. history), 1 of art, and at least 3 additional credits. Students are expected to carry a minimum of five courses per semester.

Honors and Advanced Placement sections in each discipline provide additional challenge for qualified students. AP course work prepares students to take exams in nineteen subject areas.

Academic honors are awarded on the basis of cumulative average and range from Headmaster's List to Dean's List to Honor Roll. The Cum Laude Society recognizes students who have demonstrated outstanding scholarship by their junior or senior year. Grades are A–F; A and B are honors, D is passing.

Courses are offered in English; ancient, European, and U.S. history; economics; public speaking; biology; chemistry; physics; environmental science; physical science; geology; government; the Afro-American experience; moral philosophy; computer programming in Java and C++; fundamentals of information technology; World Wars I and II; Civil War in film and fiction; criminal law and the legal process; algebra I and II; geometry; advanced math; precalculus and calculus; and probability and statistics. Courses in the fine arts are numerous and include design, ceramics, woodworking, architecture, photography, digital arts, and individualized studio courses. Music courses include chorale, jazz band, chamber music, music theory, and individual music and voice lessons. Advanced Placement courses are offered in biology, calculus AB, calculus BC, chemistry, computer programming, economics, English language, English literature, environmental science, French language, French literature, physics, Spanish language, Spanish literature, statistics, studio art-drawing portfolio, studio art-general portfolio, U.S. government and politics, and U.S. history.

FACULTY AND ADVISERS

Fifty-four talented, energetic faculty members teach, advise, and coach Avon students. They are also directly involved in the supervision of the dorms. Avon faculty members are committed to providing the support, attention, and guidance necessary to help students—both boarding and day—meet the demands of each day. Avon strongly supports the professional development of its faculty. Currently, 85 percent of the faculty members either hold or are actively pursuing an advanced degree.

Kenneth H. LaRocque (B.A., Harvard College, 1975; M.Ed. Harvard University, 1981) was appointed Headmaster in 1998. During his twenty-five years at Avon Old Farms, Mr. LaRocque has served in various capacities, including mathematics teacher, coach, Assistant Headmaster, Director of College Counseling, and Dean of Students. In his tenure, Avon completed an extensive strategic planning process and has initiated a comprehensive building program. The Ordway Science and Technology Center was completed in 2002. By winter 2005, Avon will have completed three additional facilities: a 100,000-square-foot student center/athletic complex, a woodworking/digital arts building, and a performing arts center.

COLLEGE PLACEMENT

Avon Old Farms prepares students for the college-application process through individual conferences

beginning in the spring of the junior year. In April, juniors and their parents are invited to a college-planning seminar in which they are introduced to all phases of the process. A suggested list of colleges is mailed to the student and his parents in June with the recommendation that the student familiarize himself with the schools, either through personal visits or research. Meetings with the college counselors continue into the senior year. More than 130 representatives visit the campus each fall, presenting a variety of college and university programs. Both juniors and seniors attend these meetings.

The PSAT is taken once during the sophomore year and again in the fall of the junior year. The SAT is taken during the junior year and again in the senior year (opportunities are available for additional testing). The SAT II Subject Tests are taken in the spring of the junior and/or senior year. The ACT is also offered. AP exams are taken in the spring of the junior and/or senior year. The math and English curriculums provide excellent preparation for this important standardized testing. In 2004–05, the mean score on the SAT was 541 verbal, 612 math.

All graduates are admitted to a college or university. Among many other schools, Avon graduates are currently attending Bates, Brown, Clemson, Colgate, Cornell, Dartmouth, Duke, Hamilton, Harvard, Hobart, Holy Cross, Howard, Trinity, the U.S. Coast Guard Academy, the U.S. Military Academy, the U.S. Naval Academy, William and Mary, Williams, Yale, and the Universities of Connecticut, Delaware, Iowa, New Hampshire, Pennsylvania, Vermont, and Virginia.

STUDENT BODY AND CONDUCT

Of the 382 students enrolled in 2005–06, 283 are boarding students and 99 are day students. They represent twenty-eight states and eleven other countries and present an interesting array of cultural, ethnic, and racial backgrounds. Seventy-four are freshmen (48 boarding, 26 day); 99 are sophomores (76 boarding, 23 day); 98 are juniors (74 boarding, 24 day); 92 are seniors (66 boarding, 26 day), and 19 are postgraduates (all boarding).

Avon's daily life is governed by the core values of integrity, scholarship, civility, tolerance, altruism, sportsmanship, responsibility, and self-discipline. School regulations prohibit hazing, cheating, stealing, or the use of drugs or alcohol. The violation of any of these rules requires an appearance before the Disciplinary Committee (composed of the student government president and members of the faculty and administration).

Students are expected to wear a jacket and tie to all classes, meals, and other formal occasions.

ACADEMIC FACILITIES

The Ordway Science and Technology Building opened in 2002 and offers state-of-the-art facilities for the teaching of science, math, and computer programming. The English and history departments also use classrooms within this facility. Each classroom is equipped with a SMART Board®, which offers teachers the opportunity to add ani-

mation, audio, and video clips to their classroom presentations and also allows students access to outlines, class notes, or other materials presented by the teacher in class and posted to Avon's Web site. The building contains a language lab (completed in 2005), two computer labs, six science labs, and four AP science labs. Each lab contains a SMART Board®, computers, and, where necessary, industrial-quality venting equipment. Every science lab station includes an IBM laptop for more precise lab work and lab reports. The entire campus is networked, and students have immediate access to the AOF Web through an Internet port in their room or computers located in various buildings on campus.

Classrooms are located on the first floors of the four quadrangle buildings and Jamerson House. The Estabrook Fine Arts Center is the home of studio art, photography, architecture, and ceramics facilities. Instrumental music has its own classroom and practice facility. Dramatic productions, morning meetings, and school assemblies are currently held in the 400-seat Adams Theater, which adjoins the Baxter Library (25,000 volumes, 60 periodicals). The library, including a quiet study room, is available to all boarding and day students during evening study hours. In fall 2005, an additional studio building is scheduled to open and house a new digital arts program and an expanded woodworking shop. A new performing arts center will open in fall 2006, providing expanded facilities for music and theater.

ATHLETICS
Within the last sixteen years, Avon has won more than thirty league and New England championships. Avon's athletes attend many of the nation's best Division I, II, and III collegiate programs. As a member of the Founders League, Avon's competition includes Choate, Deerfield, Hotchkiss, Kent, Loomis Chaffee, Taft, Trinity-Pawling, and Westminster. Athletic success is attributed to experienced coaches, excellent facilities, strong competition, and an emphasis on the values of teamwork, sportsmanship, and self-discipline. Two full-time trainers and fully equipped weight-training and cardiovascular fitness facilities are available to all students. In fall 2006, a new athletic complex/student center of more than 100,000 square feet is scheduled to open. It will contain three basketball courts, one of which will be a showcase court; a wrestling suite; a fitness center; a squash pavilion with seven international courts, including an exhibition court; team and training rooms; a full field house; spaces for social activities and parties; a bookstore; a game room; and a snack bar. Currently, the campus includes 65 acres of playing fields; an NHL-quality ice arena; Globe Foundation Tennis Center, with nine courts (opened in 2003); and an all-weather, eight-lane track (opened in 2004).

A wide range of sports and team levels are available to suit the talents and abilities of all students. Students are required to play in two out of three athletic seasons. Because of the time required, involvement in dramatic productions, community service, the rock band, the newspaper, or the yearbook are considered a substitute for an athletic season. Recreational skiing and recreational golf are also athletic options.

Interscholastic team sports include baseball, basketball, cross-country, football, golf, ice hockey, lacrosse, riflery, skiing, soccer, squash, swimming, tennis, track and field, and wrestling.

EXTRACURRICULAR OPPORTUNITIES
Community service is a voluntary, active component of extracurricular activity at Avon. Some of the projects include tutoring Hartford-area school children and participating in Habitat for Humanity, Toys for Tots (a Christmas toy/clothing drive), and an annual blood drive. Other clubs and organizations include the award-winning yearbook, a quarterly newspaper, *Hippocrene* (literary and art journal), Creative Writing Club, Technology Club, Stock Market Club, Nimrod Club (the school's oldest club—for boys interested in the outdoors), Fly-Tying and Fishing Club, Rock Band, Art Club, International Club, Ultimate Frisbee, Big Band, Math League, Chess Club, Crossfire (political debate), and Scuba Club. A musical and a dramatic production are performed each year in collaboration with students from Miss Porter's School, a nearby girls' school.

DAILY LIFE
Each day begins with breakfast, which is available from 6:40 to 7:30. The entire School meets each weekday morning for morning meeting at 7:55; twice a week, morning meeting takes the form of a simple, nondenominational chapel service at which a student or faculty member speaks to the assembled school community. Classes begin after morning meeting and continue until early afternoon. On Wednesday and Saturday afternoons, athletic contests are scheduled. An activities period held three afternoons a week allows for participation in drama, community service, or clubs and is followed by athletics. After dinner, an academic enrichment hour is scheduled during which teachers are available to assist students. A 2-hour, supervised study hall follows in the dormitories; students may sign out to work in the library if they prefer.

Day students are required to attend morning meeting and are welcome to remain on campus through study hall (9:45 p.m.). They are encouraged to participate in all aspects of School life, including evening meals and weekend social events, both on and off campus.

WEEKEND LIFE
Students are just minutes away from movie theaters, restaurants, supermarkets, and shops. Two girls' schools—Miss Porter's School and the Ethel Walker School—are nearby; students can also attend theater productions or athletic events in Hartford, 12 miles away. Dances and other social events are held almost every weekend, either on campus or at another school. The Social Activities Committee organizes amusement park trips, shuttles to movies and the mall, the annual Fall and Spring Flings (outdoor concert, barbecue, and games), skiing and snowboarding trips, and weekly Open Mic Nights, among other activities. Transportation to area churches is available every weekend.

Freshmen and sophomores are allowed four weekend leaves per semester; juniors are allowed five; and seniors are allowed six.

COSTS AND FINANCIAL AID
The annual tuition/room and board fee for the 2005–06 year was $34,650. The tuition fee for day students was $24,800. Additional fees total approximately $2800. For the school year 2005–06, Avon awarded $2.2 million in financial aid to 33 percent of the student population.

ADMISSIONS INFORMATION
Acceptance is based on academic achievement, motivation, and the potential for success in Avon's college-preparatory course of study. Additional consideration is given to involvement in athletics, community service, and extracurricular activities as well as personal character and standardized test results. The SSAT is required as well as a personal interview. A student application (including an essay), an official school transcript, and letters of reference (from math and English teachers and from the student's present school) are also required. In September 2005, 147 new students enrolled: 73 as freshmen, 36 as sophomores, 19 as juniors, and 19 as seniors and postgraduates.

APPLICATION TIMETABLE
A campus interview is required prior to the application deadline of February 1. The student's application, transcript, letters of recommendation, and test scores are also due by this date. All candidates are notified of their status by March 10. Accepted students must notify the school of their decision by April 10. Following that date, openings are filled on a rolling admissions basis. An online application is available at Avon's Web site. Avon Old Farms accepts the Common Application, which is also available at the School Web site.

ADMISSIONS CORRESPONDENCE
Brendon A. Welker
Director of Admissions
Avon Old Farms School
500 Old Farms Road
Avon, Connecticut 06001

Phone: 800-464-2866 (toll-free)
Fax: 860-675-6051
E-mail: admissions@avonoldfarms.com
Web site: http://www.avonoldfarms.com

THE BALDWIN SCHOOL

Bryn Mawr, Pennsylvania

Type: Girls' day college-preparatory school
Grades: PK–12: Lower School, PK–5; Middle School, 6–8; Upper School, 9–12
Enrollment: School total: 591
Head of School: Blair D. Stambaugh

THE SCHOOL

Stressing both scope and depth in learning, the Baldwin School ultimately hopes to endow each student with the ability and enthusiasm for a life of continuing growth as a scholar, a woman, and a human being. The School strives to provide a challenging academic program in a lively, creative environment. The excellence of this program was recognized in 1984, when Baldwin was named by the U.S. Department of Education as an Exemplary Private School. Baldwin is known for its rigorous academic program, diverse student body, and genuinely committed and excellent teaching faculty.

Founded in 1888 by Florence Baldwin to prepare girls for admission to Bryn Mawr College, Baldwin expanded rapidly from its opening class of 13. It now enrolls 591 girls. Baldwin celebrated its centennial in 1988. The School has had boarding students for much of its history, but in 1972 the decision was made to phase out the boarding program. Today, day students come from throughout the Philadelphia area, including Montgomery, Chester, and Delaware counties in Pennsylvania and New Jersey and Delaware as well. The School is located 11 miles west of Philadelphia in the Main Line community of Bryn Mawr (population 8,400). Bryn Mawr College and Haverford College are within walking distance. Nearby bus and rail services provide access to the historic, cultural, and recreational resources of Philadelphia.

The Baldwin School is a nonprofit institution governed by a 25-member, self-perpetuating Board of Trustees, which meets five times a year. An active Alumnae Association maintains contact with the more than 4,000 graduates and plays a direct role in fund-raising and school events. The School has an endowment of $5.9 million. Annual Giving raised $1,265,360 last year.

The Baldwin School is accredited by the Middle States Association of Colleges and Schools and the Pennsylvania Association of Private Academic Schools. It is a member of the National Association of Independent Schools, the Association of Delaware Valley Independent Schools, the Secondary School Admission Test Board, and the Pennsylvania Association of Independent Schools.

ACADEMIC PROGRAMS

Students are expected to take 5 units of credit each year in addition to physical education. Graduation requirements include 4 units of English; 3 units of one foreign language or 2 units each of two languages; 3 units of history, 1 unit each of U.S. history, ancient history, and medieval history; 3 units of mathematics; 3 units of science; 2 units of fine arts; 1 trimester course each of speech, health, and human development; and 5 units of electives.

Among the Upper School courses offered are English I–IV, Shakespearean comedy, Vietnam War and literature, creative writing, and poetry; Latin

I–III, Virgil, AP Latin, AP French I–V, and AP Spanish I–V; modern European history, economics, and comparative world issues; algebra I, algebra and consumer mathematics, geometry, algebra II and trigonometry, calculus, logic, and topics in advanced mathematics; advanced integrated science, biology I–II, chemistry I–II, and physics I–II; and art I–IV, art history, ceramics, design, architecture, photography, jewelry I–IV, theater I–III, instrumental ensemble, chorus, handbell choir, theory, and harmony. Honors courses and independent study are available in several subjects. Baldwin also has a partnership with the Notre-Dame de Mongre School in France.

Technology is strongly supported. Students have access to 250 computers on campus, laptops are available for students to sign out to take home, and mobile computer labs are available for use in individual classrooms. All faculty members have been given a laptop computer and extensive opportunities for training.

The average class size at Baldwin is 16, with an overall student-faculty ratio of about 7:1. Students who need extra work are recommended for either the math or writing labs, which provide supplemental work. In addition, the math lab provides enrichment for those with exceptional ability.

FACULTY AND ADVISERS

Faculty members include 79 full-time teachers and 15 part-time teachers, 85 women and 9 men. They hold ninety baccalaureate and seventy-nine advanced degrees from such institutions as Bryn Mawr, Columbia, Curtis Institute of Music, French University of Beirut, Johns Hopkins, Princeton, Rhode Island School of Design, Rice, Temple, and the Universities of Pennsylvania and Yale. Faculty turnover is low.

Blair D. Stambaugh (B.A., Wheaton, 1961) was appointed Head of the School in 1980. Prior to her appointment, Mrs. Stambaugh served as Head of Bryn Mawr School, as an instructor in Latin at Williams College, and as an instructor in Latin at Williams College, Pine Cobble School, and Abbot Academy. She is a former trustee of Springside School, Valley Forge Military Academy, Westhill Nursery School, and St. Catherine's School in Virginia. She was a trustee of PAIS and NAIS and is past president of the Head Mistresses of the East, National Association of the Principals of Schools for Girls, Headmasters' Association. Currently, she is on the Board of the Wyndcroft School and is president of the Country Day School Headmaster's Association and vice president of the National Coalition of Girls' Schools.

Beyond their dedication to teaching in their discipline, the Baldwin faculty members are known for their extraordinary commitment to the individual development of each girl. Many faculty members serve as advisers to individual students (with approximately 10 advisees each), grade ad-

visers, or club advisers. Every adult in the Baldwin community is seen as a role model for the students, and faculty members are supported by the school counselor and the administration in their roles outside the classroom.

COLLEGE PLACEMENT

The college placement process at Baldwin begins in the junior year with a College Night for students and their parents. Each girl and her parents meet with the College Adviser to define individual goals, realistic choices, and special interests as they pertain to the college admission process. There is a full-time Director of College Counseling.

The class of 2006 averaged Sat I scores of 673 verbal and 670 math with five National Merit Semifinalists and nine National Merit Commended Students. Among the college choices for the class of 2005 were University of Pennsylvania (4), Boston University (4), Williams College (2), Yale University (2), University of the Arts, Middlebury College, Claremont-McKenna College, New York University, and Emory University (2).

STUDENT BODY AND CONDUCT

In 2005–06, the School enrolled 591 girls in prekindergarten through grade 12 as follows: 20 in prekindergarten, 30 in kindergarten, 37 in grade 1, 44 in grade 2, 45 in grade 3, 41 in grade 4, 37 in grade 5, 44 in grade 6, 57 in grade 7, 47 in grade 8, 52 in grade 9, 51 in grade 10, 42 in grade 11, and 44 in grade 12. Students represented a variety of ethnic, religious, socioeconomic, cultural, and racial backgrounds. Of the total school population, 23 percent were students of color. Almost half of this year's new students came from public schools.

At Baldwin, all members of the school community are responsible for knowing the rules governing behavior, academics, and honesty. Minor infractions incur Friday and Saturday detentions (depending on the severity of the infraction), while more serious violations are heard by the Discipline Committee, which is made up of the Head of the School, the Director of the Upper School, 3 faculty members, and 4 grade-12 student senators.

ACADEMIC FACILITIES

The 25-acre campus includes three playing fields, indoor and outdoor swimming pools, two playgrounds, three tennis courts, two gymnasiums, and an Early Childhood Center.

The Residence (1896) houses administrative offices, a reception area, an assembly room, the dining room, the kitchen, the Music Wing, the Middle School music room, an extensive arts facility (1984–86), an Early Childhood Center (1998), and a bookstore. A former resort hotel designed by Frank Furness and featuring distinctive Victorian architecture, the Residence is listed on the National Register of Historic Places. The School-

house (1925, renovated 1998) contains Upper and Middle School classrooms, the library, and offices for the Head of the School as well as the Middle and Upper School directors. The Science Building (1961), expanded and renovated in 1995, provides a variety of science laboratories. Additional school facilities include the Mrs. Cornelius Otis Skinner Dramatic Workshop, the Cottage, and Krumrine House (the residence of the Head of the School). The School-owned plant is valued at $30 million.

The Baldwin Library is an integral part of each student's educational experience. The librarians at Baldwin are trained teachers who work to develop in each student the ability to locate and utilize all types of print and nonprint materials; to instill an appreciation of the different kinds of literature and media; and to help each student on her way to becoming a lifelong, independent library user. The Baldwin libraries have 30,000 volumes, on-line database searching through the Access Pennsylvania network, and membership in the local PREP consortium for resource sharing.

ATHLETICS

At Baldwin, team sports and physical education classes provide an important opportunity for students to compete in interschool and interclass competitive settings. Girls may choose each season between playing a team sport or joining a physical education class. In many sports, teams are fielded at varsity, junior varsity, and third-team levels so that girls of every level of athletic ability may participate. Baldwin competes in a girls' interscholastic league with Agnes Irwin, Episcopal Academy, Notre Dame, Germantown Academy, Springside, and Penn Charter. Teams are fielded in basketball, crew, cross-country, dance, diving, field hockey, golf, lacrosse, soccer, softball, squash, swimming, tennis, volleyball, and winter track. Noncompetitive athletic activities include aerobics, dancercise, lifesaving, and recreational games. Athletic facilities include indoor and outdoor swimming pools, three fields, three tennis courts, and two gymnasiums. Baldwin offers a scholar-athlete grant to students with superior academic and athletic potential and demonstrated financial need.

EXTRACURRICULAR OPPORTUNITIES

Student organizations, clubs, and activities form an important part of the Baldwin experience. Most Baldwin students participate in at least one extracurricular activity; many are involved in more. The four organizations are Student Senate, Class Officers, the Athletic Association Board, and Service League. Clubs include Lamplighters (student tour guides), Peer Counseling, SADD, the Maskers (drama), Chorus, B-Flats (a cappella group), *Roman Candle* (literary magazine), *The Hourglass* (newspaper), *The Prism* (yearbook), Contemporary Club, Debate Club, Amnesty International,

Ecology Club, Investment Club, Black Students' Union, French Club, and Society of Latin Lovers.

There is also a wide range of activities and traditions that punctuate the year. These include dances, Book Fair, Pumpkin Sale, Father-Daughter Phillies Game, Athletic Association Halloween Party, Student/Faculty Hockey/Soccer Game, IX Banner Assembly, Ring Day, Middle School Ski Trip, Café Internationale, Service Day, Alumnae Association Gift Wrap Sale, Annual Student Art Show, Marching-In Dinner, Senior Project Presentations, Alumnae Luncheon for Seniors, and Class Night.

Because of Baldwin's proximity to Philadelphia, to historic sites in Pennsylvania, and to New York City, clubs and classes frequently take part in field trips.

All of these activities constitute a vital part of the Baldwin education. Girls learn to lead as well as to be intelligent, committed members of a group. Through events sponsored by its groups, the School reaches out to the community beyond the School itself.

DAILY LIFE

The school day begins at 8:15, when students meet with advisers in homeroom to hear the daily announcements. Class periods vary in length from 42 to 75 minutes. Monday through Thursday, classes are over at 3:30; Friday classes end at 2:45. Students in grades 9 and 10 must attend study hall during a free period, while students in grades 11 and 12 have choices to make regarding free time. Girls may bring their own lunch or purchase a hot meal, salad, sandwich, or soup in the dining room. Baldwin has adopted a two-week rotating schedule that allows for club and class meetings during the school day and provides for lengthened periods for laboratory classes. There are no bells and no passing time.

Built into the weekly schedule are assemblies, a full period for meeting with advisers, and time for assignments to math or writing lab.

COSTS AND FINANCIAL AID

Tuition in grades 9–12 for the academic year 2005–06 was $21,100. Expenses such as lunch, books, lab fees, uniforms, and optional music lessons were billed separately. A tuition insurance plan is available.

For 2005–06, Baldwin awarded more than $1.14 million in financial aid to 16 percent of the students. The number of students awarded financial aid was 96, and the average grant was $11,833. All aid is allocated according to the need analysis procedures of the School and Student Service office in Princeton, New Jersey. Each year, entering students may choose to compete for a grant awarded on the basis of need and merit by taking part in the Competitive Scholarship Examination held in

early November. Renewal of all financial aid is made annually after the Financial Aid Committee has reviewed the most recent Parents' Financial Statement, tax forms, and student record for each family seeking continued assistance. Baldwin values diversity in its student body and seeks to make its education available to academically talented girls regardless of parental income level. Baldwin is committed to a policy of nondiscrimination and anti-harassment in all aspects of its members' actions and relationships on any basis, including, but not limited to, race, religion, ancestry, color, age, gender, sexual orientation, familial status, disability, veteran status, or national origin.

ADMISSIONS INFORMATION

Each year, Baldwin admits students to grades from PK–12. The School seeks girls with demonstrated academic motivation and achievement who love to learn. Individual talents and diversity of background and interests are also valued. Students are admitted on the basis of a written application, standardized test scores (WPPSI-III for prekindergarten and kindergarten, WISC-IV for grades 1–5, and SSAT or ISEE for grades 6–12), a personal interview and school visit, previous school records, two recommendations, a letter to the Head of the School, and the results of an English Placement Test (grades 6–12). Although Baldwin does not use any cutoff score on standardized tests, the Admissions Committee looks for a pattern of strong achievement in the school records. Motivation is also carefully assessed, as are the student's contributions to the previous school. There is a $50 application fee.

APPLICATION TIMETABLE

Admission inquiries should be made in the fall preceding the September of desired enrollment. Initially, parents should make an appointment to meet with the Director of Admissions and tour the School. After this visit, the application should be filed, testing should be scheduled, and the candidate should plan to come to Baldwin to visit classes. The admission deadline is February 1 for grades 2–12 and January 9 for PK, kindergarten, and grade 1. March 1 is the parents' reply date once a student has been accepted. The Baldwin admissions team strongly encourages applicants to grades 2–12 to complete their applications by early January, prior to the February 1 deadline.

ADMISSIONS CORRESPONDENCE
Sarah J. Goebel
Director of Admissions and Financial Aid
The Baldwin School
701 West Montgomery Avenue
Bryn Mawr, Pennsylvania 19010
Phone: 610-525-2700
Web site: http://www.baldwinschool.org/

BALDWIN SCHOOL OF PUERTO RICO

Guaynabo, Puerto Rico

Type: Coeducational, college-preparatory, English-language day school
Grades: Early (pre-K and kindergarten), Elementary (grades 1–6), Middle/Upper (grades 7–12)
Enrollment: 842
Head of School: Dr. Günther Brandt

THE SCHOOL

Founded in 1968, the Baldwin School of Puerto Rico is a private, English-language institution that provides a college-preparatory program for children in Pre-K through twelfth grades. The School offers an enriched curriculum and a variety of instructional methods that are geared to the learning and growth of the individual in a changing society. The School optimizes the benefits found in an intercultural community and effectively involves members of its administration and staff, parents, and the students in the total educational process.

Baldwin takes pride in its mission to be the school of choice on the island for students and families who seek a rigorous college-preparatory education. Year after year, graduating students gain entrance to highly regarded and selective universities. The School continues to build on these secure foundations and ensure a challenging and demanding education in the years ahead.

The Baldwin School of Puerto Rico is accredited by the Puerto Rico Department of Education and the Middle States Association of Colleges and Schools.

ACADEMIC PROGRAMS

The Baldwin School offers a highly demanding curriculum and its teachers use a variety of educational methods and techniques to develop students' academic skills, creative talents, critical-thinking skills, and potential strengths. The School strives to continually improve basic skills in English and language arts, mathematics, science, Spanish/Spanish as a second language (SSL), and the social sciences.

The educational program in Baldwin's Oxman Early Childhood Center (pre-K–kindergarten) is based on the premise that growth occurs as an interaction between what the child brings to learning and what is out there to be experienced. The School nurtures children's cognitive, emotional, and physical growth through developmentally appropriate activities within a supportive environment. The teaching practices are structured to promote independence, foster decision-making, and encourage involvement. These teaching areas are organized with materials related to a given theme, which help in the teaching of the academic subjects.

In the Elementary School (grades 1–6), emphasis is placed on the development of written and oral English language skills. Every student in grades 1–6 takes two periods of English language arts each day. For grades 7–12, the Middle/Upper School English department believes that language arts are basic to humanity and central to all learning, and the English curriculum incorporates all concepts integral to the language arts, emphasizes writing and reading, and exposes students to a wide variety of literary genres. From ninth to twelfth grade, students are grouped in honors or

regular classes. An Advanced Placement (AP) English literature course is offered in twelfth grade.

The Spanish curriculum, in the Elementary as well as the Middle/Upper School, includes both regular Spanish courses as well as Spanish as a second language courses. This curriculum also emphasizes the teaching of writing, reading, speaking, and listening skills. From ninth to twelfth grade, students are grouped in honors or regular classes. Advanced Placement Spanish literature and Spanish language courses are offered at the Upper School level. Under the umbrella of the Middle/Upper School Spanish department, French and Portuguese courses are offered as electives to students in grades 7–12. Students are successfully taught to speak, read, and write these foreign languages.

Baldwin School's math curriculum follows the guidelines and standards established nationally by the National Council of Teachers of Mathematics. Beginning in third grade, students are grouped homogenously based on their specific level of math instruction. One group in the grade level is placed in an enriched math program, which they continue to follow until they reach seventh grade. In seventh grade, students who are recommended are placed in the honor math tract. Calculus AB is offered at the twelfth-grade level.

The science curriculum focuses on providing the conceptual framework, factual knowledge, and analytical skills necessary to deal critically with the rapid changes in science and technology. At the Elementary level, a hands-on approach is emphasized. The main goal of the science department is to focus on understanding important relationships, processes, mechanisms, and applications of scientific concepts and of the scientific method. Advanced Placement chemistry and Advanced Placement biology courses are offered to Middle/Upper School students.

The social studies curriculum prepares students so that they may become thoughtful citizens in a multicultural world. This curriculum helps to develop an in-depth understanding of geography, history, culture, economics, and citizenship. At the Middle/Upper School level, the curriculum focuses on the humanistic formation of students through the presentation of historical models and the discussion of economic, political, and cultural change. An Advanced Placement European history course is offered to Upper School students.

In grades pre-K to 6, the curriculum is enhanced by special courses such as music and art, allowing the School to further develop an appreciation for the fine arts. Students also receive instruction in computers and physical education. Students in these grades are exposed to these four special areas on a weekly basis. At the Middle/Upper School level, students are offered a variety of elective courses that they may opt to take. Elective courses presently offered are French (levels

I–AP), computers I and II, art, music (band, vocal music, string), psychology, sociology, and writing for college.

Standardized tests are used to evaluate the effectiveness of the School's curriculum and instructional practices. The Stanford Achievement Test is used for grades 1–8, PSATs are given to students in grades 9–11, and the APRENDA test is offered to measure the skills of Spanish-speaking students in grades 2, 4, and 6. In grade 12, students are required to take the SAT, ACT, and/or any other College Board exams that are required for college acceptance. The administration and teachers analyze the results obtained by students on these standardized tests in order to set appropriate educational goals and assess the effectiveness of the School's educational program.

FACULTY AND ADVISERS

From prekindergarten through twelfth grade, students benefit from dedicated, caring professionals who teach a rigorous curriculum. Teachers use a variety of educational methods and techniques to develop students' academic skills, creative talents, critical-thinking skills, and potential strengths.

Baldwin School employs 75 full time teachers, 12 teacher aides, 1 Middle/Upper School guidance/college counselor, 2 psychologists, 2 librarians, and 3 principals.

Dr. Günther Brandt was appointed Head of School in 2004. Dr. Brandt is a native of Germany who obtained a B.A. in history from Stanford University and an M.A. and Ph.D. in history from Princeton University. He has previously served in international and private schools in Europe, Africa, Central and South America, and the United States. He joined Baldwin after serving as Head of School of Frankfurt International School from 1998–2004.

COLLEGE PLACEMENT

Every year, students are accepted into top universities, both on the island and abroad. Baldwin students' standardized test scores are well above the national averages. In 2005, Baldwin School students from the class of 2005 obtained on average the highest scores island-wide in the Advanced Placement Exams offered by the College Board. In the graduating classes of 2000 and 2001, there were 9 National Hispanic Recognition Program Finalists, and 3 National Merit Scholarship Finalists.

Baldwin School students have been accepted to colleges and universities such as Amherst, Babson, Barnard, Boston College, Boston University, Brown, Columbia, Cornell, Duke, Duquesne, George Washington, Georgetown, Georgia Tech, Harvard, Manhattanville, Marquette, MIT, NYU, Northeastern, Penn State, Pratt, Princeton, Rice, Swarthmore, Syracuse, Tufts, Universidad Interamericana, U.S. Military Academy, U.S. Naval Academy, Villanova, Yale, and the Universities of

Chicago; Florida; Miami; Pennsylvania; Puerto Rico, Rio Piedras and Mayaguez Campus; and Sagrado Corazón.

STUDENT BODY AND CONDUCT

The student population for the 2005–06 academic year was approximately 75 percent local students and 25 percent international students, with representation from nineteen different countries, including France, the United Kingdom, Switzerland, Finland, Japan, Argentina, Venezuela, Mexico, Canada, and the continental United States.

As stated in its philosophy, Baldwin School emphasizes personal as well as social growth, sound physical development, intercultural values, and mutual respect. The School strives to involve its administration, staff members, parents, and students in this educational process; this is why the School promotes student and School activities that are consistent with its philosophy, mission, and objectives.

ACADEMIC FACILITIES

Baldwin is located on 23 tree-shaded acres of land in the San Juan metropolitan area of Bayamón/Guaynabo. Facilities include a science center; a seminar room; two media centers; two computer centers; art rooms; music and band studios; tennis, volleyball, and basketball courts; soccer, softball, and baseball fields; an air-conditioned cafeteria; a 25-meter swimming pool; and a covered court. The School's libraries and media center house more than 12,000 volumes, forty-two periodical subscriptions, and twelve computers with Internet access. All of the classrooms are air-conditioned.

In 2004, the construction of a new building for high school classes was completed and offers new state-of-the-art science and computer laboratories. Several smaller projects include improvements to the School entrances and security, a new playground for the Elementary School, and new elementary classrooms to be finished in summer 2006.

ATHLETICS

The Baldwin School's athletic program is designed to provide experiences, skills, and knowledge of sports and to develop and promote physical fitness. Students are also encouraged to participate in the School's interscholastic athletic program, which offers a wide range of sports that students can join.

Baldwin School of Puerto Rico is a member of the Liga Atletica Mini de Escuelas Privadas, Inc. (LAMPEI), which serves grades 4 through 6, and the Puerto Rico High School Athletic Alliance (PRHSAA), which serves grades 7 through 12. LAMPEI sports are basketball, cross-country, soccer, swimming, tennis, and volleyball. The PRHSAA

offers baseball, basketball, golf, indoor and outdoor soccer, softball, swimming, tennis, and volleyball.

EXTRACURRICULAR OPPORTUNITIES

The School's activities program is very extensive and has high student participation. The administration and teachers are very supportive of the extracurricular activities. Several teachers at the Elementary as well as the Middle/Upper School level participate as moderators of clubs or organizations, class advisers, or as team coaches. The wide variety of activities that exists in the School's program offers students the opportunity to build a special and unique rapport with their teachers and administrators. These activities also foster responsibility, character, social skills, and citizenship.

The Elementary and Middle/Upper Schools' student councils are responsible for organizing many important activities that help to foster school spirit. One activity that has become an important tradition at the School is Spirit Week. This activity involves students, teachers, administrators, and parents and lasts a whole week during the month of October. Everyone looks forward to this week, and the competition for spirit points is great fun for all. Students in both the Elementary and Middle/Upper School join together in a final Color Pep Rally that demonstrates the very high School spirit shared by everyone. Other activities organized by the student councils include casual days, dances, pep rallies, Sports Fest, penny wars, and Rock and Bowl.

The extracurricular program offers a wide variety of activities for the tastes of all students; therefore there is a high rate of student participation. In the Elementary School, these activities include Third-Grade Opera, Talent Show, Student of the Month, Spanish Week, field trips, Fun Day, class parties, band, choir, and team sports: baseball, basketball, cross-country, soccer, swimming, tennis, and volleyball. In the Middle/Upper School, activities include band, forensics, Golden Key Club, Science Club, Photography Club, United Nations Club, Math Club, National Junior Honor Society, National Honor Society, Yearbook, School newspaper, REACH, and team sports: basketball, golf, indoor soccer, softball, swimming, tennis, and volleyball.

DAILY LIFE

All students should be in their respective classrooms by 8:25 a.m. The dismissal time is 3 p.m. for all students from grades 1 through 12. The Oxman Early Childhood Center is dismissed at 2:45. The library is open until 5:30 p.m., allowing students time to do their homework and work on projects. The After Care Program is offered to the students of the Oxman Early Childhood Center and the Elementary School (grades 1–4) from 3 to 5:30 p.m. for an additional cost.

COSTS AND FINANCIAL AID

Annual tuition is $7810 for students enrolled in the Oxman Early Childhood Center (grades pre-K to kindergarten), $8020 for grades 1–3, $8440 for grades 4–6, $8970 for grades 7–10, and $9500 for grades 11–12. Tuition does not include materials, lunch, uniforms, or transportation. Other fees include a one-time initial enrollment fee of $2000 per family, an annual building fee for the ongoing construction and improvement of the School's facilities of $1400 per family, and the technology fee of $175 for grades pre-K through 12. A tuition deposit of $1000 is due upon enrollment and re-enrollment in order to reserve space. The tuition deposit and building fee are due upon submission of the registration documents.

The School does not offer financial aid except in extraordinary hardship cases. As part of the School's Outreach Program, a scholarship program was implemented for a limited number of local students seeking entry into the seventh grade or beyond.

ADMISSIONS INFORMATION

Parents of students in all levels must submit the completed application, the nonrefundable application fee of $150, a copy of the child's birth certificate and social security card, the parents' questionnaire, the child's school health record, the immunization record PVAC-3 form (provided by any licensed physician), proof of a complete hearing and eye examination (pre-K through grade 3 only), and a letter from the previous school regarding payment history. The required age for pre-K is 4 years by September 1 and for kindergarten, 5 years by September 1.

Pre-K and kindergarten applicants must take the Brigance Assessment Test of Basic Skills and submit two recommendations, one from a teacher and one from someone who is not a relative. Applicants in grades 1 through 12 must take standardized entrance exams and submit two teacher recommendations (mathematics and English), the applicant's questionnaire (grades 5–12 only), and a letter of conduct.

APPLICATION TIMETABLE

As spaces are limited, it is extremely important that the application be submitted in a timely manner. Admission of a student is based on space availability, academic achievement, records of conduct, and recommendations made by the Admission Committee.

ADMISSIONS CORRESPONDENCE

Ely Mejías, Director of Admission
Baldwin School of Puerto Rico
P.O. Box 1827
Bayamón, Puerto Rico 00960-1827

Phone: 787-720-2421 Ext. 239
Fax: 787-790-0619
E-mail: admission@baldwin-school.org
Web site: http://www.baldwin-school.org/

BAYLOR SCHOOL

Chattanooga, Tennessee

Type: Coeducational day (6–12) and boarding (9–12) college-preparatory school
Grades: 6–12: Lower School, 6–8; Upper School, 9–12
Enrollment: School total: 1,069; Upper School: 739
Head of School: Dr. Bill Stacy, Headmaster

THE SCHOOL

Founded in 1893, Baylor School's mission is to instill in students the desire and ability to make a positive difference in the world. Since the School also believes that much growth occurs through the interaction of peers, it strives to create an interesting vital mix in the student population. Baylor School actively seeks students who bring different geographic, economic, social, ethnic, and racial backgrounds to its community. The School also believes that students in this age group benefit from a coeducational learning environment. At Baylor—as in the real world—both girls and boys occupy leadership positions within the School and participate fully in the life of the School. All of Baylor's students benefit from the global and cultural perspectives that the boarding students bring. In fact, the School's 200 boarders hail from places as close as Alabama and as far away as Korea.

In addition to an excellent academic program, great care has been applied over the years to maintain and preserve the 670 acres of land and the turn-of-the century buildings that overlook the Tennessee River gorge. Upper School classes are spread out among various academic buildings that are all within walking distance. Each element of the campus is beautiful, safe, and functional. Together, they are nothing less than spectacular.

The scenic backdrop for Baylor's campus is the dynamic city of Chattanooga, Tennessee, a model for urban revitalization. A midsized city (population of 312,000 in Hamilton County), Chattanooga residents enjoy abundant recreational and cultural opportunities, such as the Tennessee Aquarium (the largest freshwater aquarium in the United States), the Hunter Art Museum, Chattanooga Symphony Orchestra, forty-nine parks totaling 1,266 acres, white-water rafting, kayaking, sailing, boating, eight private and nineteen public golf courses, minor-league baseball, hiking, rock climbing, and hang gliding. For Baylor students and faculty members, Chattanooga is a remarkable home and an invaluable educational resource.

Baylor is accredited by the Southern Association of Colleges and Schools. It holds membership in the Educational Records Bureau, the Mid-South Association of Independent Schools, the National Association of Independent Schools, the Southern Association of Independent Schools, the Southeastern Association of Boarding Schools, the College Board, and the National Association of College Admission Counselors. The School is eligible for participation in the Morehead Scholarship program, the Jefferson Scholars program, the Boston University Trustee Scholarships program, and the Emory University Awards.

ACADEMIC PROGRAMS

Baylor's small classes of 13 are just one of the things that make its academic program strong. At Baylor, students quickly find peers who value academic achievement and are surrounded by faculty members who are committed to helping them reach their full academic potential.

Graduation requirements include at least 4 years of English, 3 years of mathematics, 3 years of science, 3 years of social studies, 2 years of one foreign language, and 1 year of fine arts. A total of 22 credits is needed to graduate. In addition to these required courses, Baylor offers approximately fifty electives. Typical elective programs include creative writing, computer programming, film history and criticism, visual literacy, drawing, painting, curricular theater, photography, graphic design, current world topics, video production, pottery, and vocal and instrumental music.

Baylor students can choose from college-level AP courses in twenty-two subjects, including English (language and literature), Latin, French, German, Spanish, American history, European history, U.S. government and politics, calculus (AB and BC levels), biology, chemistry, physics, computer science, art history, and studio art. More than 80 percent of Baylor students who take the AP exams qualify for college credit or waivers.

Beginning in grade 6 and all the way through the senior year, students have an adviser. Extra-help sessions are also built into the daily schedule, so students can receive immediate attention if they are experiencing difficulty. The Writing Center is also open daily for students who need help improving their writing. The library is open for study seven days a week and at night. New students attend proctored day study hall with access to the study skills director and peer tutors until the end of the first marking period, at which time their study needs are reevaluated. All boarding students are expected to study nightly, and quiet is maintained in the dorms by student proctors and residential faculty members.

FACULTY AND ADVISERS

More than 70 percent of Baylor faculty members hold advanced degrees from such schools as Boston University, Cornell, Duke, Emory, Harvard, Notre Dame, and Vanderbilt (including many with Ph.D. degrees). As part of Baylor's important advisory program, teachers also serve as advisers, regularly interacting closely with students in all aspects of their school life. Baylor instructors have been selected to help write the National Spanish Exam and to grade Advanced Placement English and math exams. Tennessee Governor's School for the Arts has named members of Baylor School's art and music programs as Outstanding Educators. One of the School's celebrated textbook authors received the Presidential Award for Excellence in Science and Mathematics teaching. In addition, Fulbright Scholarships have been awarded to Baylor faculty members in both social studies and Latin.

COLLEGE PLACEMENT

Baylor has a comprehensive College Counseling program beginning in the ninth grade. Individual sessions with students and their parents are also an integral part of the college counseling process. Seniors are encouraged to visit colleges and are provided the opportunity to do so while school is in session.

Baylor's 2005 graduates were offered scholarships with a value of more than $6.5 million, including 113 seniors (63 percent) who were offered scholarships totaling more than $6 million in merit awards for excellence in academics, fine arts, leadership, community service, and athletics. Colleges that have accepted Baylor graduates recently include Amherst, Brown, Columbia, Cornell, Dartmouth, Davidson, Duke, Emory, Furman, Georgetown, Harvard, Northwestern, Princeton, Rhodes, Sewanee, Stanford, Tulane, the U.S. Air Force Academy, the U.S. Military Academy, the U.S. Naval Academy, Vanderbilt, Williams, Yale, and the Universities of Alabama, Georgia, North Carolina, Tennessee, and Virginia.

STUDENT BODY AND CONDUCT

Baylor considers that the roots of leadership extend beyond a year of service as a team captain, club leader, or student officer. While these roles and opportunities are certainly significant, the Leadership Baylor Program is woven into the curriculum at each grade level so students can discover their own unique leadership potential.

Baylor was also one of the first secondary schools to establish an Honor Code, and to this day it remains central to the Baylor experience. At the beginning of each school year, students sign a pledge indicating that they will not lie, cheat, steal, or plagiarize. This community of trust is fostered by students who conduct themselves with integrity and expect the same from their peers. An elected student Honor Council investigates alleged honor offenses and suggests appropriate punishments to the School's administration.

ACADEMIC FACILITIES

The academic and residential facilities at Baylor comprise a physical plant worth $110 million. Barks Hall contains a 50,000-volume library (one of the largest among Southeastern schools), classrooms, and laboratories. In 1998, the School opened a $5-million fine arts center consisting of three separate buildings for music, studio arts, and performing arts. In 1999, the Katherine and Harrison Weeks Science Building was completed. The 41,000-square-foot, $6.5-million building provides state-of-the-art technology with 100 computers, fourteen laboratories, computer classrooms, and an interactive SMART board.

BOARDING AND GENERAL FACILITIES

Six dormitories house boarding students and resident faculty members. Most dormitory rooms

house 2 people, although there are some single rooms. Room assignments are usually made according to the students' preference. Telephones, free laundry facilities, and television lounges are available in all dorms, as are a centrally located refrigerator, microwave oven, and soft drink machine. Student proctors aid the resident adult in keeping order in the dorms.

At least 1 nurse is on duty in the infirmary 24 hours a day, seven days a week. Baylor maintains a close relationship with several local doctors, and the nurses in the infirmary arrange for any necessary medical attention that boarding students may need.

ATHLETICS

Sports Illustrated magazine recently named Baylor's athletic program the top program in Tennessee and among the top twenty-five in the country. Central to the School's athletic philosophy are the lessons learned through teamwork and good sportsmanship. In addition, Baylor strives to instill in students the lifelong enjoyment that comes from an active lifestyle. The School's athletic curriculum emphasizes both interscholastic and intramural activities, and participation is required of every student each semester.

Baylor fields seventy-four teams in seventeen sports, thirteen of which are sanctioned by the state athletic association. These teams include baseball, basketball, bowling, cross-country, football, golf, soccer, softball, tennis, track and field, volleyball, and wrestling. Other sports in which Baylor teams compete interscholastically are cheerleading, crew, dance, fencing, and swimming. In addition to these organized teams, Baylor offers intramural activities each athletic season during the school day.

Baylor's athletic facilities include two gyms and a field house complex containing three basketball courts (in addition to a varsity basketball arena), volleyball courts, badminton courts, a Nautilus and free-weights room, a new wrestling facility, locker rooms, an equipment room, cardio room, and coaches' and instructors' classrooms and offices. This complex also contains the only indoor 50-meter pool within a 130-mile radius. This new pool has been designed utilizing current state-of-the-art techniques and is considered a fast water pool.

Baylor's 670-acre campus provides the School with ample space for a football stadium with a seven-lane track, baseball fields, a softball field, four practice football fields, soccer fields, a cross-country course, fourteen outdoor and seven indoor tennis courts, and an outdoor pool. A new golf short game practice center features six stations for players to hit shots from 120 yards. It also has a 3,700-square-foot chipping green with bunkering and a 4,000-square-foot putting green. Crew team members also enjoy Baylor's proximity to the river, launching their boats directly from a campus dock.

EXTRACURRICULAR OPPORTUNITIES

Basic to Baylor's philosophy of educating the whole person is the belief that students should participate in a variety of activities. To that end, almost sixty clubs and activities are offered each year, including language clubs, film and literary societies, student advisory committees, math and chemistry clubs, concert choir, forensics, and Red Circle admissions guides. Students are active in community service projects, religious fellowship groups, and environmental awareness through school clubs. Four publications are produced every year by Baylor students, including a yearbook, a student newspaper, and two literary magazines. Students may also run for Student Council, Honor Council, and Dorm Council in order to represent their peers at the administrative level.

DAILY LIFE

Buffet-style breakfast is served on weekdays each morning. Before classes begin, boarding students prepare their rooms for daily inspection. Students are expected to enroll in five academic classes, unless they carry several AP courses or hold an elected office. One period of a student's schedule is devoted to lunch and one to free time for study or intramural recreation. Students are required to participate in either an athletic activity or other activities, such as community service, each afternoon following the academic day. Dinner is served in the evening in the dining hall, followed by evening study hall and quiet hours.

WEEKEND LIFE

Boarding students are allowed day, overnight, and weekend leaves starting on Friday night and ending on Sunday at 7 p.m. Upon returning from their leaves, students are required to check in personally with a resident faculty member. Typically, students go shopping, out to eat, to Baylor athletic events, to movies, home with day school friends, or on dates. School-sponsored activities are planned each weekend by a full-time staff member in the Student Center. Such activities include van trips to nearby shopping malls and movie theaters, restaurant trips with faculty members, bus trips to athletic events, cookouts, concerts, and trips to amusement parks and nearby attractions. The Student Center is also open during the weekend, providing games, movies, and a grill.

Baylor's unique Walkabout outdoor program schedules at least two trips each weekend, providing an opportunity for students to become proficient at rock climbing, hiking, camping, canoeing, rafting, kayaking, and many other outdoor activities.

Students are encouraged to attend Sunday school or worship services each week at one of the congregations in the Chattanooga area. The School provides transportation for this purpose.

COSTS AND FINANCIAL AID

For 2006–07, tuition and comprehensive fees total $16,945 for day students and $32,990 for boarding students. Baylor subscribes to the School and Student Service for Financial Aid, and awards are made on the basis of need. In 2004, Baylor awarded $2.5 million in need-based financial aid. A merit-based scholarship is available on a competitive basis for qualified ninth-grade boarding students.

ADMISSIONS INFORMATION

Baylor seeks boys and girls of high moral character who are willing to compete in a rigorous college-preparatory curriculum. Students are accepted in grades 6 through 11. Transcripts, recommendations, a personal interview and visit, Secondary School Admission Test scores, and an application fee complete the application. Baylor School does not discriminate on the basis of color, race, religion, or national or ethnic origin.

APPLICATION TIMETABLE

Inquiries are welcome at any time, and required campus tours and interviews are available by appointment year-round. Baylor operates under a rolling admission policy. The review of completed files begins in January and continues until all available spaces are filled. The application fee is $75; for international applicants, the fee is $100. Office hours are 8 a.m. to 4 p.m., Monday through Friday. Prospective students are encouraged to visit the School while it is in session to experience a regular day of classes and activities.

ADMISSIONS CORRESPONDENCE

Matt Radtke
Director of Boarding Admissions
Baylor School
171 Baylor School Road
Chattanooga, Tennessee 37405

Phone: 423-267-8505
    800-2-BAYLOR (toll-free)
Fax: 423-757-2525
E-mail: matt_radtke@baylorschool.org
Web site: http://www.baylorschool.org

THE BEEKMAN SCHOOL AND THE TUTORING SCHOOL

New York, New York

Type: Coeducational day college-preparatory and general academic school
Grades: 9–12, postgraduate year
Enrollment: 80
Head of School: George Higgins, Headmaster

THE SCHOOL

The Beekman School/The Tutoring School of New York was founded by George Matthew in 1925. The School was organized to offer a college-preparatory school curriculum with the advantage of highly individualized instruction. Since no 2 students have the same abilities, learning issues, or goals, teaching is geared to the needs of the individual student. Thus, classes are limited to a maximum of 10 students in The Beekman School and a maximum of 3 students in The Tutoring School.

In addition to having small classes, The Beekman School combines a traditional academic education with a flexible yet structured approach. For instance, some students are eager to complete high school in less than four years for reasons that range from having been retained in a grade earlier in their education to feeling a natural desire to move ahead to college. If there appears (to all concerned) to be a readiness to accomplish this, the School proceeds with a program that will achieve this goal. This is done by adding one or two extra classes to the student's schedule and/or through attendance in the summer session.

In order for students to move effectively at their own pace, the School provides them with the proper level of classes in as many subjects as seem appropriate. Some students require more support to facilitate their learning in the state-mandated academic curriculum. Teachers have several periods free each day to meet with students, and there are supervised study halls each period throughout the day until 5 p.m. In addition, all homework assignments are posted on the School's Web site daily. Upon request, tutors are available through The Tutoring School.

The Tutoring School is a program within The Beekman School. The Director of The Tutoring School is Lisa Chasin. This program specializes in educating students who require private or semiprivate classes. The Tutoring School teaches college-level courses as well as standard courses. Its mission is to provide a supportive environment in which students can realize their academic potential and achieve their educational goals. Generally, incoming students follow The Beekman School's college-preparatory curriculum and receive credit from The Beekman School. However, if necessary, The Tutoring School can follow any school's course syllabus, and course credit is granted by that school upon successful completion of all course work. After-school or home tutoring is available for midterm and final exam preparation, SAT preparation, or academic support in any subject. In addition, The Tutoring School can arrange at-home schooling, if necessary.

The Beekman School is registered by the Board of Regents of the State of New York and is a member of the College Entrance Examination Board and the Educational Records Bureau.

ACADEMIC PROGRAMS

The requirements of the Board of Regents of the State of New York form the core of the college-preparatory curriculum at The Beekman School and The Tutoring School. It is strongly advised, however, that students exceed these requirements, especially in the areas of mathematics, the sciences, and humanities. In addition to the requirements, The Beekman School faculty has developed many interesting and challenging elective courses from which students may choose. Some of these are psychology, bioethics, ecology, computer animation, creative writing, modern politics, filmmaking, darkroom photography, Eastern and Western philosophy, poetry, and art. Students also participate in after-school activities, such as the literary magazine, yearbook projects, and the School's volunteer program. Students can elect to study music, music theory, voice, various musical instruments, or composition at the Turtle Bay Music School, which is a 2-block walk from The Beekman School. If 6 or more students wish to form a particular course, the administration offers the course at The Beekman School. If 1 to 3 students wish to take a particular course, it can be offered through The Tutoring School. Otherwise, students are encouraged to take specialized elective courses at various institutions throughout the city.

If students take an elective course off campus, they must complete 48 course hours to earn a semester credit and 96 course hours to earn a full-year credit. For the college-bound student, the suggested academic high school program consists of the following courses: 4 years of English, 4 years of history (including a senior-year program that consists of a semester of U.S. government and a semester of economics), 3 years of mathematics (through algebra II/trigonometry), 3 years of science (including 1 year of lab science), 3 years of a foreign language, 1 year of art or music, several elective courses, and 1 semester of health education and computer science.

The grading system of the School is A to D (passing) and F (failing). Sixty percent is the minimum passing grade. Midway through each quarter, an interim progress report is mailed home to any student who is earning below 70 percent in any course. Weekly updates by phone can be arranged so that parents always know the academic status of their child.

Because of the independent nature and small size of the School community, the scheduling of classes and the number of classes in which a student enrolls are flexible. Students can begin their day with the first, second, or third period. For the same reasons of independence and adaptability, the School also tries to accommodate any reasonable requests of the students for additional courses. Similarly, tutoring for study and organizational skills and remediation courses in English and math are offered through The Tutoring School, in addition to the regular core curriculum.

FACULTY AND ADVISERS

There are 14 full-time members at The Beekman School faculty.

The current headmaster, George Higgins, has been at the School since 1980, first as a teacher, then as Assistant Headmaster, before serving the School as Headmaster.

Lisa Chasin has been with the School since 1991, first as a teacher, then as Assistant Head, before being appointed Director of The Tutoring School.

All faculty members have graduate degrees or are enrolled in a graduate degree program. In addition to teaching, faculty members also act as advisers to small groups of students. Faculty advisers review progress reports with students and hold meetings periodically to listen to student concerns and discuss upcoming events and projects. Parent conferences are held as frequently as they are needed or requested. Twice during the school year, parents are invited to the School to attend open-house evenings, at which time they can discuss their child's progress with the teachers. When necessary, the Headmaster or classroom teacher calls parents to keep them informed of their child's homework and general behavior.

The School's offices are open to the students almost all day, every day. Students feel welcome to visit the Headmaster or the Director to talk, complain, laugh, or ask questions.

COLLEGE PLACEMENT

Each year, approximately 95 percent of the graduating class attends college. The aim of the School's college guidance program is to find the right college for each graduating senior. Major considerations include how competitive an environment is desirable for a particular student, what area of study the student is leaning toward, what size of school would be conducive to success, and where the student would like to live (city, suburb; East Coast, West Coast). In the past five years, graduates of the School have been accepted at the following colleges and universities: Bard, Boston University, Columbia University, Harvard, Ithaca, NYU, Sarah Lawrence, School of Visual Arts, Smith, SUNY at Purchase, and the University of Colorado, to name a few. The Beekman School's staff and faculty members make every effort to examine not just where a student will likely be admitted but where that student will learn, grow, and feel successful for the next four years.

The senior class numbers approximately 25 students. Each student is carefully guided through the college application process, as are his or her parents. A Parents' College Evening, hosted by the School's college guidance counselor, is held each fall for the parents of seniors. It is always an informative evening for parents; the guest speaker is an administrator from the admissions office of a nearby university who is also there to answer questions. The college guidance counselor also schedules individual appointments with all seniors in order to help them navigate the college application process.

STUDENT BODY AND CONDUCT

Each year, The Beekman School begins the fall term with approximately 70 students. Its rolling admissions policy means that the School adds members to the student body until it reaches its maximum enrollment of 80 students. The enrollment is generally evenly divided between boys and girls. All students are from the immediate tristate area of Connecticut, New Jersey, and New York and its

suburbs. The success of The Beekman School's philosophy is proven by the distance students gladly travel in order to be in a school where the enrollment and class size are small, the faculty is supportive and caring, and the education is paced according to the student's abilities and needs.

There is a School code of behavior that has been shaped by the students and teachers of the School. The main tenet of the code is based on the Golden Rule—"Do unto others as you would have others do unto you." The small, intimate environment makes any type of behavior problem untenable; if the code of the School is violated, there is always an appropriate response. There have been no serious discipline or behavior issues at the School; Beekman students respect their School and its philosophy and recognize the need for tolerance and respect in an increasingly global community.

ACADEMIC FACILITIES
The School is located in an East Side Manhattan town house. There are eight classrooms; a small library; a state-of-the-art laboratory for biology, chemistry, and physics; a darkroom; a computer lab updated with the latest technology; a study hall equipped with computers; a beautifully landscaped garden; and a student lounge where students can eat lunch and socialize. Rapid Internet access is available throughout the School. Each administrator and teacher has an e-mail address so that parents and students can easily communicate with staff members.

ATHLETICS
The Beekman School meets the New York State requirements for physical education by providing a gym program at a nearby athletic facility. Students may participate in the School's program or may choose to design their own program; for example, they may wish to attend their neighborhood gym while being supervised by a private trainer, or they may decide to take dance lessons, karate lessons, or other lessons. Students must exercise for 2 hours each week. In the School's program, an instructor is provided, and students begin the year with aerobics and weight training. Activities in the gym program vary throughout the year and include swimming, volleyball, basketball, cardiovascular exercise, and track. If a student is seriously involved in an intramural activity outside the School, such as soccer or tennis, he or she may be excused from the School's sports program.

EXTRACURRICULAR OPPORTUNITIES
The School's Manhattan location gives it the opportunity to use New York City and its immediate environs as an extension of the classroom. Groups from the School attend plays, films, operas, and dance performances and visit the city's various museums, exhibitions, historical sites, and other points of interest in and around Manhattan and as far away as Philadelphia.

In addition to day trips, the School plans several overnight trips. Each spring, the history department plans a trip to Washington, D.C. During spring break, the School plans a trip to Europe (usually Paris and Rome).

Any student who wants to work on the yearbook or school literary magazine is welcome to do so, and about one third of the student body participates in one way or another. Additional after-school activities include the drama club and photography club. Upperclassmen can also take part in a community volunteer program if the desire and maturity are present.

DAILY LIFE
Students' schedules reflect their individual needs. The school day begins at 8:45 a.m. and continues until 3:50 p.m. When possible, students who have a long distance to commute are scheduled to begin classes at 9:30 or 10:15. Students with professional programs outside of school can have classes arranged for mornings or afternoons. Supervised study halls are provided throughout the day from 8:45 a.m. to 5 p.m. Lunch periods are scheduled throughout the day on a staggered basis.

SUMMER PROGRAMS
The Beekman School is in session almost year-round. When the academic year is over in June and the seniors' graduation festivities are over, the School begins a three-week minisession of intensive work for students who want or need private tutoring in a specific subject area, who need to make up work in a course for which they received an incomplete, or who exceeded the School's attendance policy (sixteen absences are allowed in a year course and eight are allowed in a semester course).

Following the minisession, The Beekman School operates a six-week summer session, which is attended by the School's students and by students from boarding and other private day schools who wish to accelerate in any major academic course, enrich their knowledge of a particular subject, or repeat a course. Each summer class is 90 minutes long; there are four classes each day, and the program lasts for thirty-two days. The Beekman School's summer session is approved by the New York State Education Department.

COSTS AND FINANCIAL AID
The annual tuition is $23,500, which is divided into four installments. In addition, an activity fee and an administrative fee ($250 each) and a refundable book fee ($400) are charged. All twelfth-grade students pay a senior fee of $300.

The tuition for the minisession depends upon the individual's length of study. The tuition for the six-week summer session is $1600 per 90-minute course.

If a student wishes to take a course in The Tutoring School (average student-teacher ratio is 2:1), tuition is $6150 for each yearlong course and $3075 for each semester course. The average load in The Tutoring School consists of four courses, for a total cost of $24,600. Activity and administration fees range from $125 to $600. Currently, there is no financial aid.

ADMISSIONS INFORMATION
It is a reflection of the School's philosophy that it does not use admissions tests as a means to determine a prospective student's eligibility to attend the School. The Headmaster or Director meets with each prospective student and his or her parents in an intensive interview so that all may better understand each other. Together, they try to assess whether the School would be a good match for the student. Previous school transcripts and records of testing are reviewed to determine the proper class placements, but they are never solely used to determine a course of study. Prospective students are also welcome to observe for a half or full day so that they can gain a clearer understanding of the style of the School. Informal evaluations in math and English may be administered to determine the best course placement for various students.

APPLICATION TIMETABLE
Since there are several different types of secondary schools offering many different programs, it is advisable that interviews take place during the early spring of the year prior to entry. Selecting a school in which to study and socialize is an important process, and students and their families should take the time to look closely at several schools before coming to a final decision. Occasionally, students choose a school that is not a good fit for them. Because Beekman has a rolling admission policy, even if the traditional day program is filled, students can begin their day in the afternoon and take their required courses through The Tutoring School. These courses use the Beekman School's syllabi and textbooks. The School believes that a successful secondary education is of vital importance to all young adults; the School is available to any student who wishes to actively participate in his or her education.

ADMISSIONS CORRESPONDENCE
George Higgins, Headmaster
The Beekman School
or
Lisa Chasin, Director
The Tutoring School
220 East 50th Street
New York, New York 10022
Phone: 212-755-6666 (Beekman School)
   212-755-6665 (Tutoring School)
Fax: 212-888-6085
E-mail: georgeh@beekmanschool.org
Web site: http://www.beekmanschool.org

BERKELEY PREPARATORY SCHOOL

Tampa, Florida

Type: Coeducational independent college-preparatory day school
Grades: PK–12: Lower Division, Prekindergarten–5; Middle Division, 6–8; Upper Division, 9–12
Enrollment: School total: 1,170; Lower Division: 400; Middle Division: 300; Upper Division: 470
Head of School: Joseph A. Merluzzi, Headmaster

THE SCHOOL

The Latin words *Disciplina, Diligentia,* and *Integritas* in Berkeley's motto describe the School's mission to nurture students' intellectual, emotional, spiritual, and physical development so they can achieve their highest human potential. Episcopal in heritage, Berkeley was founded in 1960 and opened for grades 7–12 the following year. Kindergarten through grade 6 were added in 1967, and prekindergarten began in 1988. Berkeley's purpose is to enable its students to achieve academic excellence in preparation for higher education and to instill in students a strong sense of morality, ethics, and social responsibility.

Berkeley is located on a 64-acre campus in the suburban Town 'N Country area of Tampa, a location that attracts students from Hillsborough, Pinellas, and Pasco Counties and throughout the greater Tampa Bay area. Private bus transportation is available.

Berkeley is incorporated as a nonprofit institution and is governed by a 32-member Board of Trustees that includes alumni, parents of current students, and parents of alumni. The presidents of the Alumni Association and Parents' Club are also members of the board. The value of Berkeley's campus is assessed at $24 million.

ACADEMIC PROGRAMS

The school year runs from the end of August to the first week of June and includes Thanksgiving, Christmas, and spring vacations. The curriculum naturally varies within each division.

In the Lower Division, the program seeks to provide appropriate, challenging learning experiences in a safe environment that reflects the academic, social, moral, and ethical values the School espouses in its philosophy. Curricular emphasis is on core subjects of reading and mathematics. An interdisciplinary approach is used in foreign language and social studies, and manipulatives are used extensively in the science and mathematics programs. Each student also receives instruction in library skills and computers.

Academic requirements in the Middle Division, where classes average 16–20 students, are English, English expressions, mathematics, history, foreign language, science, computers, physical education, art, drama, and music. All grade 6 students and all new grade 8 students take Latin. Continuing grade 8 students have the option of Latin, French, or Spanish. Every class meets five days a week and has one weekly scheduled makeup period. Extra help is available from teachers, and grades are sent to parents four times a year.

The Upper Division program, with average classes of 15 to 18 students meeting five days a week, requires students to take four or five credit courses a year in addition to fine arts and physical education requirements. To graduate, a student must complete 22 credits, including 4 in English and 3 each in mathematics, history, science, and foreign language. Students must also complete one year of personal fitness/health and an additional year of physical education, one year of microcomputers, two years of fine arts, and one elective. In addition, Berkeley students are required to take a course in public speaking and complete 70 hours of community service. Several Advanced Placement courses are offered.

FACULTY AND ADVISERS

There are 145 full-time faculty members and administrators, of whom 43 are men and 102 are women. Forty-four percent hold master's degrees, and 5 percent have earned doctoral degrees. Headmaster Joseph A. Merluzzi, who joined Berkeley in 1987, received his bachelor's degree from Western Connecticut State University and his master's degree in mathematics from Fairfield University. He came to Berkeley from the Cranbrook Kingswood School in Michigan.

In addition to teaching responsibilities, faculty members are involved in Berkeley's cocurricular programs as coaches and student activity advisers. In the Upper Division, 4 teach part-time and serve as academic grade advisers for each level. Berkeley faculty members receive support for professional development opportunities, and a number have been recipients of National Endowment for the Humanities grants.

COLLEGE PLACEMENT

Traditionally, Berkeley's entire graduating class goes on to attend college. Although Berkeley does not rank its students, more than 100 colleges visit the School each year to recruit the graduates. The mean SAT I scores for the class of 2004 were 643 verbal and 659 math. Berkeley's college counseling department works to assist students and their families in selecting colleges that best suit their academic, financial, and social needs.

Recent graduates are attending Auburn, Boston College, Carnegie Mellon, Cornell, Clemson, Dartmouth, Duke, Georgetown, Harvard, Johns Hopkins, MIT, Northwestern, Princeton, Stanford, Tulane, UCLA, Xavier, and the Universities of Colorado, Florida, Michigan, North Carolina, Pennsylvania, Tennessee, Texas, and Wisconsin. Seven seniors were named National Merit Scholarship Finalists, 1 was a National Hispanic Scholar, and 1 was a Presidential Scholar. Scholarship offers totaling more than $3.6 million were made to the class of 2004, and 20 percent of the graduates committed to pursuing athletic competition at the collegiate level.

STUDENT BODY AND CONDUCT

In all divisions, Berkeley students are expected to maintain high standards. Mature conduct and use of manners are expected, and an honor code outlines students' responsibilities. In exchange, students are entrusted with certain privileges, such as direct access to the administration and the opportunity to initiate School-sponsored clubs. Students wear uniforms to class. In a typical year, Berkeley has 400 students in the Lower Division, 300 in the Middle Division, and 470 in the Upper Division.

ACADEMIC FACILITIES

The 64-acre campus is located in the Town 'N Country suburb of Tampa. It consists of classrooms, a Fine Arts Wing, a Science Wing, two libraries, computer labs, general convocation rooms, physical education fields, a 19,000-square-foot student center, a prekindergarten wing, a kindergarten cottage, and administrative offices for Lower, Middle, and Upper Divisions.

The arts program was enhanced in 1997 with the addition of a 634-seat performing arts center that also includes a gallery for visual arts displays, a flex studio for both dance recitals and small drama productions, dressing rooms, and an orchestra pit.

ATHLETICS

Varsity sports for boys include baseball, basketball, crew, cross-country, diving, football, golf, soccer, swimming, tennis, track, weight lifting, and wrestling. Girls compete in basketball, crew, cross-country, diving, golf, soccer, softball, swimming, tennis, track, volleyball, and weight lifting. The campus has several playing fields. Upper Division teams are members of the Bay Conference, while Middle and Lower Division teams compete in the Florida West Coast League and the Youth Sports League.

Athletes use two gymnasiums, a wrestling/gymnastics room, a weight-lifting room, a rock-climbing wall, a stadium (for track meets and football and soccer games), baseball and softball diamonds, tennis courts, and a junior Olympic swimming pool.

Seasonal sports award banquets and a homecoming football game are scheduled annually.

EXTRACURRICULAR OPPORTUNITIES

In addition to its broad-based commitment to student organizations and clubs and its community service requirements, Berkeley offers its students a vast array of outside-the-classroom possibilities. Berkeley's Pipe and Drum Corps continues to make a significant impact in the community by performing at several special events, including an appearance in the Boston St. Patrick's Day Parade. Student artwork is accepted each year into the prestigious Scarfone Gallery Art Show. An after-school Lower Division Chess

Club attracts close to 50 students from kindergarten through fifth grade. Middle and Upper Division students, as well as many faculty members, participate in several international experiences, with trips to France, Costa Rica, China, Mexico, and Scotland.

DAILY LIFE

Students in prekindergarten through grade 5 attend classes from 8 a.m. to 3:10 p.m. Middle and Upper Division students begin at 8 and end at 3:19. Teachers are available to assist students and offer extra help during activity periods, which are scheduled into each class day. Supervised study halls are also scheduled for some students.

SUMMER PROGRAMS

A six-week summer academic program for prekindergarten through grade 12 students is offered. Tuition ranges from $900 to $1500.

COSTS AND FINANCIAL AID

The tuition schedule for 2004–05 was as follows: $11,450 for prekindergarten–grade 5, $13,260 for grades 6–8, and $14,550 for grades 9–12. Tuition is payable in eight installments and must be paid in full by January 1. Tuition payments do not cover costs of uniforms, supplies, transportation, special event admission fees, or other expenses incurred in the ordinary course of student activities at Berkeley.

Berkeley makes all admission decisions without regard to financial status. Financial aid in the form of partial tuition scholarships is available for families who demonstrate need. The School and Student Scholarship for Financial Aid (SSS) guidelines are used in determining need. Berkeley may not be able to accommodate all financial aid applicants in a given year, but once a student is awarded aid, the aid continues until graduation as long as the student remains in good standing and demonstrates need. An SSS form, available from the admissions office, must be submitted annually, and Berkeley's financial aid committee determines all awards by mid-March.

Berkeley also has twelve scholarships that are available to students.

ADMISSIONS INFORMATION

In considering applicants, Berkeley evaluates a student's talent, academic skills, personal interests, motivation to learn, and desire to attend. Special consideration is given to qualified applicants who are children of faculty members or alumni or who have siblings currently attending Berkeley.

Lower Division candidates visit age-appropriate classrooms and are evaluated for placement by Berkeley teachers. Middle and Upper Division candidates are required to take the Secondary School Admissions Test (SSAT) and should register for a December or January test date. Entering juniors and seniors may submit PSAT or SAT scores in place of sitting for the SSAT.

The admission process is selective and is based on information gathered from the application form, interviews, the candidate's record, admission tests, and teacher recommendations.

Berkeley admits students of any race, color, sex, religion, and national or ethnic origin and does not discriminate on the basis of any category protected by law in the administration of its educational policies, admission policies, and scholarship, financial aid, athletic, and other School-administered programs.

APPLICATION TIMETABLE

Applications should be submitted by the fall one year prior to the student's entrance to Berkeley. Applications are considered in the order received, and decisions are made in early March. Parents are notified of their child's status as soon as possible thereafter. All applications after the initial selection process are considered on a space-available basis.

Berkeley welcomes inquiries from families throughout the year. However, because of the competitive nature of the admission process, families are encouraged to visit the campus as early as possible to become familiar with the School, its programs, and its admission procedure.

ADMISSIONS CORRESPONDENCE

Janie McIlvaine
Director of Admissions
Berkeley Preparatory School
4811 Kelly Road
Tampa, Florida 33615

Phone: 813-885-1673
Fax: 813-886-6933
Web site: http://www.berkeleyprep.org

BERKSHIRE SCHOOL

Sheffield, Massachusetts

Type: Coeducational boarding and day college-preparatory school
Grades: 9–12 (Forms III–VI), postgraduate year
Enrollment: 372
Head of School: Michael Maher

THE SCHOOL

In 1907, Mr. and Mrs. Seaver B. Buck, graduates of Harvard and Smith respectively, rented the building of Glenny Farm at the foot of Mt. Everett and founded Berkshire School. For thirty-five years, the Bucks devoted themselves to educating young men to the values of academic excellence, physical vigor, and high personal standards. In 1969, this commitment to excellence was extended to include girls.

Berkshire School is a vigorous college-preparatory institution that has flourished for almost a century in a New England setting of extraordinary natural beauty. It is a welcoming and supportive environment where a diverse group of young men and women can develop intellectual foundations and traits of character and leadership that will permit them, in the words of the school's motto, to learn not for school, but for life. A medium-sized boarding school with a distinctly global character, Berkshire is home to 372 students from across the country and around the world and experienced teachers who are dedicated to their craft.

Situated at the base of Mt. Everett, the second highest mountain in Massachusetts, Berkshire's campus spans 500 acres of woods, meadows, and playing fields. It is a 90-minute drive to both Albany International Airport and Hartford's Bradley International Airport and just over 2 hours from Boston and New York City.

Berkshire School is incorporated as a not-for-profit institution, governed by a 28-member self-perpetuating Board of Trustees. The School has a $49-million endowment. Annual operating expenses exceed $12.5 million. Annual Giving in 2004–05 exceeded $1.2 million. The Berkshire Chapter of the Cum Laude Society was established in 1942.

Berkshire School is accredited by the New England Association of Schools and Colleges and holds memberships in the Independent School Association of Massachusetts, the National Association of Independent Schools, the College Entrance Examination Board, the National Association for College Admission Counseling, the Secondary School Admission Test Board, and the Association of Boarding Schools.

ACADEMIC PROGRAMS

The academic program at Berkshire in many respects defines the School itself: it is formal, structured, and demanding. The program of studies centers on the five principal scholastic disciplines—English, mathematics, ancient and modern languages (including Mandarin Chinese), the sciences, and history—and also includes extensive course offerings in philosophy and religion, computer science, and the visual and performing arts. The Ritt Kellogg Mountain Program uses Mt. Everett as a backdrop to encourage understanding of natural surroundings through curricular and extracurricular activities. Believing that the best preparation for college is the acquisition of knowledge from a variety of disciplines, Berkshire requires the following credits: 4 years of English; 3 years each of mathematics, a foreign language, and history; 2 years of science; and 1 year of the visual or performing arts. All departments provide for accelerated sections, and students are placed at a level commensurate with their skills and talent. Many students take one or more of the sixteen Advanced Placement courses offered.

Berkshire's entire senior and postgraduate classes participate in the intensive Leadership and Character Development Program, underscoring Berkshire's commitment to producing leaders for the twenty-first century. Seniors lead underformers in the Green Campus Initiative, the School's environmental conservation project.

Most students carry five courses. The average number of students in a class is 12, and the student-teacher ratio is 6:1. The academic year is divided into two semesters, each culminating with an assessment period. Students receive grades, teacher comments, and adviser letters twice each semester. Berkshire uses a traditional letter-grading system of A–F (D is passing).

Independent-study programs may be undertaken by Sixth Formers, with the understanding that no student may participate in more than one such project a year.

FACULTY AND ADVISERS

The Berkshire teaching faculty numbers 62, 51 of whom live on campus. Twenty-eight teachers hold a master's degree and 4 hold doctorates. Faculty members contribute to both the academic and personal development of each student. The small size of the Berkshire community permits faculty members to become involved in students' lives outside, as well as inside, the classroom. Each student is paired with a faculty adviser who provides guidance, monitors academic progress, and serves as a liaison with the student's family. Faculty members take their roles seriously, aware of the influence they have on the attitudes and values of the students they teach and with whom they live. Berkshire also retains the services of 4 pediatricians, a nurse practitioner, 4 registered nurses, and 2 certified athletic trainers.

Michael Maher was named Berkshire's fifteenth head of school in the spring of 2004. He holds a bachelor's degree in political science from the University of Vermont and a master's degree in liberal studies from Wesleyan University. Mr. Maher is in his second year at Berkshire, following an eighteen-year tenure as administrator, teacher, and hockey coach at The Taft School. He and his wife, Jean, an associate director of admission and a member of the Foreign Language Department, have three children.

COLLEGE PLACEMENT

College counseling at Berkshire is the responsibility of 2 full-time and 2 part-time professionals who assist students and their parents in the search for an appropriate college or university. The formal process begins in the Fifth Form, with the selection of a rigorous course of study, individual conferences with the college counselors, and the opportunity to meet with some of the approximately 100 college admissions representatives who visit the campus. In May, Fifth Formers and their parents attend a weekend seminar on the college admission process. Admission strategies are discussed and specific institutions are identified for each student's consideration. During the summer, students are encouraged to visit colleges and write the first draft of their college application essay. The application process is generally completed by winter vacation in the Sixth Form year.

The 115 graduates of the Class of 2005 are now attending four-year colleges or universities, including American, Art Institute of Chicago, Boston College, Boston University, Cornell, Dartmouth, Elon, Hamilton, Lehigh, Rhode Island School of Design, St. Michael's (Vermont), Trinity, Tufts, the United States Military Academy, and the Universities of Michigan, Pennsylvania, Vermont, and Wisconsin.

STUDENT BODY AND CONDUCT

In the 2005–06 academic year, there were 322 boarders and 50 day students; 4 students were participating in international study abroad. The student body is drawn from twenty-two states and twenty-two other countries.

The goal of student life at Berkshire is responsible participation. Students contribute directly to the life of the school community through involvement in the Student Government, Prefect Program, the School's Community and School Service Program, dormitory life, and various clubs and activities. Participation gives students a positive growth experience supporting the School motto, "Learning—not just for school, but for life." The rules at Berkshire are simple and straightforward and are consistent with the values and ideals of the School. They are designed to help students live orderly lives within an environment of mutual trust and respect.

ACADEMIC FACILITIES

The focal point of academic life on the campus is Berkshire Hall. It contains all of the classrooms, the science laboratories, computer centers, and a theater. The computer centers feature the latest hardware and software programs. Music facilities—four soundproofed, air-conditioned practice rooms, a piano teaching studio, and classroom-rehearsal space—are located in Memorial Hall. Near Berkshire Hall is the 400-seat Allen Theater, and there are several darkrooms located in Godman House.

The Geier Library, open 65 hours per week, is central to intellectual life on the campus. The library contains approximately 40,500 volumes in open stacks, an extensive reference collection in both print and electronic format, numerous periodicals, and a fine audiovisual collection. The library has eighteen computers with Internet access and an online card catalog for student use. ProQuest Direct, the Expanded Academic Index ASAP, the New York Times full text (1994 to present), and the current ninety days' full text of 150 Northeastern newspapers, including the Wall Street Journal online, keep the library fully up-to-date on breaking information.

At the Dixon Observatory, computer synchronized telescopes make it possible to view and photograph objects in the solar system and beyond.

Given the combination of equipment, software, and location, Berkshire's observatory is among the best in New England.

BOARDING AND GENERAL FACILITIES

Berkshire has ten residential houses, including two girls' dormitories that were completed in the fall of 2002. Three faculty families, many with small children, generally reside in each house. Each also has a prefect: Sixth Formers whose primary responsibility is to assist dorm parents with daily routines, such as study hall and room inspection. Dorm rooms are equipped with access to the Internet and private phone lines. There is a common room in each house, where students may relax or study. Benson Commons, the school center, features a dining hall capable of seating the entire School, a post office, the School bookstore, the Student Life office, and recreational spaces.

ATHLETICS

Berkshire enjoys a proud tradition of athletic excellence. The School provides competition in twenty-seven interscholastic sports, including baseball, basketball, crew, cross-country running, field hockey, football, golf, ice hockey, lacrosse, skiing, soccer, softball, squash, tennis, track and field, and volleyball. Students may also participate in the Ritt Kellogg Mountain Program, a program that utilizes Berkshire's natural environment and its proximity to the Appalachian Trail to present athletic challenges, teach leadership, and foster environmental responsibility.

A major emphasis of the athletic program is fitness and conditioning. The Athletic Center houses basketball, volleyball, and squash courts; a climbing wall; and a weight room with Nautilus and free weights. Other facilities include two new synthetic turf fields for field hockey and soccer; a hockey rink, which converts to indoor tennis courts; twelve outdoor tennis courts; an outdoor recreation park for basketball, volleyball, rollerblading, and skateboarding; an all-weather track; an extensive ropes course; and numerous playing fields.

EXTRACURRICULAR OPPORTUNITIES

Berkshire offers students a variety of opportunities to express their talents and passions. Students take responsibility for publishing a newspaper; a literary magazine that features writing, art, and photography; and a yearbook. The Ritt Kellogg Mountain Program offers hiking, rock climbing, and boat-building.

There are a number of active clubs, including the Drama Club, the International Club, the Investment Club, the Maple Syrup Program, and a Student Activities Committee.

Berkshire's student-run FM radio station, WBSL, operates with a power of 250 watts and is capable of reaching 10,000 listeners. Berkshire is one of the few secondary schools to hold membership in the Intercollegiate Broadcasting System and the only one affiliated with both the Associated Press wire service and its radio service.

Berkshire students pursue the arts in the classroom and in extracurricular activities. The theater program offers two plays in the fall and spring as well as a winter musical. There are three choral groups: Ursa Major, an all-school chorus; Ursa Minor, a girls' a cappella group; and Greensleeves, an all male chorus. There are two music groups: a jazz band and a chamber music ensemble. Students can also take private voice and instrumental lessons. Each season the Berkshire community looks forward to various performances, such as dance and music recitals, a jazz café, and poetry readings. Visual arts include painting, drawing, sculpture, digital arts, photography, and ceramics. Students display their work in galleries in the Student Center and in Berkshire Hall.

DAILY LIFE

The first of the six class periods in a school day begins at 8 a.m., and the final class concludes at 2:35 p.m., except on Wednesday and Saturday, when the last class ends by noon. Berkshire follows a rotating schedule in which classes meet at different times each day.

Athletics, outdoor experiences, and art activities occupy the afternoon. Clubs often meet after dinner, before the 2-hour supervised study period.

The Community and School Service Program is an integral part of life at Berkshire School. Students must commit a certain number of hours toward community service, with options available on and off campus.

WEEKEND LIFE

Weekend activities are planned by a student committee and include first-run movies, dances with live bands, and other dances hosted by DJs. There are trips to local amusement parks and theaters as well as shopping trips to Hartford and Albany. In addition, students and faculty members journey to New York and Boston to visit museums, attend theater and music productions, or take in professional sports events.

COSTS AND FINANCIAL AID

For the 2005–06 academic year, tuition was $35,300 for boarding students and $25,870 for day students. For most students, $100 a month is sufficient personal spending money. Ten percent of the tuition is paid upon enrollment, 50 percent is payable on July 1, and 40 percent is payable on November 30. Various tuition payment plans are available.

Financial aid is awarded on the basis of need to about 26 percent of the student body. The total financial aid spent in 2004–05 was $2 million. The School and Student Service (SSS) Parents Financial Statement and a 1040 form are required. Merit scholarships were also awarded.

ADMISSIONS INFORMATION

Berkshire adheres to the principle that in diversity there is strength and, therefore, actively seeks students from a broad range of geographic, ethnic, religious, and socioeconomic backgrounds. Admission is most frequent in the Third and Fourth Forms, and the School enrolls about 15 postgraduates each year.

In order to assess the student's academic record, potential, character, and contributions to his or her school, Berkshire requires a personal interview, a transcript, test scores, and recommendations from English and mathematics teachers. Candidates should have their Secondary School Admission Test (SSAT) scores forwarded to Berkshire School (school code 1612).

APPLICATION TIMETABLE

Interested families are encouraged to visit the campus in the fall or winter preceding the September in which admission is desired. Visits are arranged according to the academic schedule, Monday through Friday, from 8 a.m. to 1:45 p.m. and Saturday from 8 to 10 a.m. February 1 is the deadline for submitting applications; late applications are accepted as long as space is anticipated. Berkshire adheres to the standard notification date of March 10 and the parents' reply date of April 10. Applications for openings available after that time are processed on a rolling basis. Applications for admission are now available online at the School's Web site at http://www.berkshireschool.org.

ADMISSIONS CORRESPONDENCE

Andres Bogardus, Director of Admission
Berkshire School
245 North Undermountain Road
Sheffield, Massachusetts 01257

Phone: 413-229-1003
Fax: 413-229-1016

E-mail: admission@berkshireschool.org
Web site: http://www.berkshireschool.org

BISHOP'S COLLEGE SCHOOL

Lennoxville, Quebec, Canada

Type: Independent coeducational boarding school
Grades: 7–12
Enrollment: 250

THE SCHOOL

Bishop's College School (BCS) was founded in 1836. In 1972, it amalgamated with King's Hall, a well-respected girls' boarding school. Today, BCS is one of eastern Canada's foremost coeducational boarding schools. Some 250 girls and boys from all parts of the world share a beautiful 300-acre campus located in Lennoxville, Quebec, in the heart of the Eastern Townships, 120 kilometers east of Montreal and 40 kilometers north of Vermont.

The School has a 12:1 student-teacher ratio, which ensures individual attention and the recognition of different learning styles. Students benefit from the use of thirty buildings, including a modern sports facility, a theatre, a chapel, student houses, playing fields, a 40-foot indoor climbing wall, and many acres of woods and trails. The School is adjacent to Bishop's University, with all its additional academic and athletic facilities, including an Olympic-size indoor swimming pool.

BCS embraces internationalism as a long-standing member of the Round Square, an organisation of schools around the world that promotes international understanding, the principles of democracy, outdoor adventure, service to the community, and responsibility for the environment. International exchange opportunities with thirty-one other Round Square schools, in grade 9 and as a post–grade 12 option, are also offered.

The School is nonprofit and is overseen by a nonsalaried board of governors, although the day-to-day management of the School is the responsibility of the Head. The annual operating budget is $8.5 million, and the School's endowment, from which bursary and scholarship money is generated, is currently valued at $14 million.

BCS is accredited by the Canadian Educational Standards Institute and is a member of the National Association of Independent Schools (U.S.) and the Canadian Association of Independent Schools.

ACADEMIC PROGRAMME

The very essence of BCS is the strength of its academic program. BCS is not only dedicated to preparing young people for university but for a lifetime of achievement and fulfillment as well. It offers a well-rounded education that is internationally recognized and focuses on a healthy learning environment. The Ministry of Education in Quebec (MEQ) diploma of secondary studies forms the basis of the academic programme; however, BCS students are encouraged to go well beyond the mandatory requirement of the MEQ.

Courses offered at each grade level include English, French, math, moral and religious education, physical education, fine arts, sciences, and social sciences. Beyond these, BCS offers a wide range of optional courses, such as art, music, drama, Spanish, computers, introduction to technology, sociology, political science, philosophy, economics, and organizational studies.

As a dynamic Quebec school, BCS offers a unique bilingual programme in which certain courses at various levels are taught in French, enabling students to have the opportunity to improve their linguistic abilities. These courses include géographie, histoire, expression dramatique, and education économique.

Every second week, students are assessed by their teachers on the basis of academic effort. Effort ratings are posted on an Academic Notice Board every second Tuesday. Students are rewarded for achieving an Effort List status. The Advanced Placement program (AP), a challenging academic program designed to provide motivated high school students with college-level academic courses is available at BCS. The program was introduced at the School almost twenty years ago to benefit high-achieving students keen on studying university-level courses. Students are exposed to university-level content and expectations in AP courses, allowing them to feel more comfortable and have more confidence once they reach the academic setting of university. Students presenting qualifying grades on AP exams may earn anywhere from 3–6 credits in a given subject, thereby earning second-year university standing in that subject. At BCS, AP content is taught concurrently with the School's curriculum and compliments the university preparation courses already offered.

BCS has made the transition to Tablet PC-based instruction and learning, so all BCS students receive their own Tablet PC from the School upon arrival. Unlike other types of computers or laptops but more like a paper notebook, students can use the portable Tablet PC to write or draw directly on the screen, enabling them to take notes in all classes, including subjects such as math and science where there are many diagrams and symbols that are not always easily registered on a laptop. The Tablet PC has the ability to convert handwritten notes to text. International students are able to write notes to themselves in their own alphabet. With this new technology, all BCS students work with multimedia content in wireless classrooms and, as such, are connected to the technological world that is their future.

The academic year is divided into two terms, September to December and January to June. Midterm reports are sent to parents twice a year, in November and in March. Each midterm report has a mark, an effort letter, a written comment for each subject, and a sport activity comment. End-of-term reports are sent to parents at the end of each term. Each end-of-term report has a mark, a class average, an effort letter, and a written comment for each subject, activity, and sport. The Houseparent and Head of School also write comments on these report cards. All reports are sent to parents via e-mail as well as through regular mail.

FACULTY AND ADVISERS

The School employs 34 teachers; 33 are full time. There are 14 women and 20 men. Sixteen teachers live on the campus. All teachers actively participate as coaches in the athletic programme. All teachers also perform duty at school or in the residences.

The Headmaster, Lewis Evans, who was born and brought up at BCS, began his teaching career at St. John's Ravenscourt School in Winnipeg, MB. He returned to Lennoxville in 1976 to teach English and drama at his old school and has since served as Houseparent, Head of Fine Arts, and Director of Development and Alumni Relations. He has a degree from Queen's University and a teaching credential from the University of Manitoba. His association with BCS is broad and deep. His two children, both graduates, were the fifth generation of the family to attend BCS. His wife is Head of English, as was his father in the 1950s and 1960s.

COLLEGE PLACEMENT

All students receive expert preparation and personal guidance to encourage them to make realistic and appropriate choices. BCS is extremely proud of its placement of graduating students at some of the finest universities in the world. Recent Canadian university placements include Acadia, Brescia, Carleton, Dalhousie, Guelph, King's Halifax, Lakehead, Laurentian, McMaster, Memorial, Mount Allison, NSCAD, Ottawa, Queen's at Kingston, Ryerson, Simon Fraser, St. Mary's, Toronto, Toronto/Trinity, Trent, UBC, Victoria, Waterloo, Western, Wilfrid Laurier, Windsor, and York. Internationally, BCS students have gone to Boston University, Cornell, Dartmouth, Harvard, MIT, Princeton, USC, Brown, and Yale in the United States and Cambridge, Edinburgh, Oxford, and St. Andrew's in the United Kingdom.

STUDENT BODY AND CONDUCT

There are 250 students currently enrolled in grades 7–12, of whom 57 percent are boys and 43 percent are girls. The School has a strong day population, which complements the population of boarding students who come from Canada, the U.S., and from more than twenty-five other countries around the world. The large population of Canadian francophone students contributes to the bilingual Canadian flavour of the School.

ACADEMIC FACILITIES

The latest addition to the campus, the Molson Hall building, was constructed in 2004 and features a beautiful 100-seat black box theatre/classroom with computer-controlled lighting, a

workshop, and a studio that is home to the digital filmmaking program. This building also houses a modern, sound-proofed music facility, a 22,000-volume library with CD-ROM capabilities, and a student centre complete with a recreational lounge. The recently renovated Pattison science building has a computer lab and nine science labs, including newly designed electronics and optics labs. In addition, BCS has an eclectic art studio.

BOARDING AND GENERAL FACILITIES

BCS has eight residences, called houses, run by live-in houseparents. Each room is shared by 2 students. Every evening, students spend 2 hours at their desks doing homework under the supervision of the teacher on duty. Each house has a common room with a tuckshop run by the students.

There is an infirmary with a full-time nurse situated on campus. There are two hospitals within 10 minutes of the School.

ATHLETICS

The philosophy of learning through playing characterizes the physical education programme at BCS. Emphasis is placed on participation so that there is no pressure on the less competitive to excel. Those who aspire to compete at a higher level are supported by specialised instruction from the local community. Each student must select three sports from a long list of options that includes football, soccer, cross-country running, adventure training, gymnastics, basketball, ice hockey, alpine/cross-country skiing, snowboarding, swimming, squash, rugby, softball, track and field, golf, tennis, riding, climbing, cycling, and yoga.

The School's modern double gymnasium has one of the most challenging indoor-climbing walls in the nation. The weight room has a full range of Nautilus and free-weight machines. Canada's oldest covered ice rink is connected to the sports complex and is available to the students during their free time. In addition to the main sports complex, there are also seven playing fields, three tennis courts, two squash courts, and a beach volleyball court.

EXTRACURRICULAR OPPORTUNITIES

BCS has a strong, diverse, cocurricular programme. Activities include band, student council, drama club, yearbook, and the nationally acclaimed *Inscape* literary magazine. Because every activity has at least one faculty adviser, students know their teachers in many different ways, and they know that the standards of these teachers are high no matter what the activity.

BCS is one of the few schools in Canada to have maintained its cadet corps. The BCS Cadet Corps #2, formed in 1861, holds the record for the longest period of uninterrupted service. This compulsory activity is an integral part of the School's character-building programme. It teaches teamwork, leadership, and community service and reinforces the value of tradition.

DAILY LIFE

The School day begins with a 10–20 minute chapel/assembly between breakfast and the first class of the day. Chapel consists of a hymn, a reading, prayers, and silence. Chapel is followed by daily announcements. Classes begin immediately following chapel and continue until 3 p.m. The daily schedule is based on 50-minute classes, a 15-minute break, and a 1-hour lunch period. From 3:30 to 5:30 students participate in compulsory athletics (crease). Dinner is served from 5:30 to 6:30; after dinner, students take part in the numerous activities. Each day ends with 2 hours of homework (prep).

WEEKEND LIFE

BCS students have busy lives, and the School respects their need for free time. The town of Lennoxville and the city of Sherbrooke are within 10 minutes of BCS. Stores, theatres, restaurants, and concert halls are all easily accessible. The Student Activities Coordinator at BCS helps students to organize on-campus leisure activities, such as coffee houses, dances, talent shows, and theme days, and off-campus excursions, especially during long weekends or breaks.

BCS is also in the heart of ski country. Organized, staff-supervised trips occur regularly throughout the winter term, and arrangements can be made for the students to rent ski equipment.

Free time on weekends includes Friday evening, Saturday afternoon and evening, and Sunday morning and afternoon. Depending on the student's age and grade level, some restrictions apply to off-campus visits.

COSTS AND FINANCIAL AID

Total fees cover tuition, board and lodging, textbooks, and personal services. The 2005–06 tuition fees are Can$15,500 for day students and Can$32,500 for boarding students (Can$37,700 for international boarding students). Fees are subject to revision each year. Scholarships and need-based financial aid are available.

ADMISSIONS INFORMATION

BCS is proud of the fact that its students come from all over the world, from all races and national origins. Admission evaluation is based on the application, which includes a Can$100 application fee; confidential reports from the student's current school; transcripts of all school marks; an interview; and placement tests in English and math. Students and parents are encouraged to visit the campus. The Admissions Office is open Monday to Friday from 8:30 until 4:30.

APPLICATION TIMETABLE

BCS accepts applications throughout the year. Appointments for visits can be arranged through the Admissions Office. Complete application materials must be submitted before admission decisions are made. Parents are asked to reply for confirmation of enrollment within three weeks of the date that the student is accepted.

ADMISSIONS CORRESPONDENCE

Theo Brinckman, Director of Advancement
Bishop's College School
80 Moulton Hill Road, P.O. Box 5001
Lennoxville, Quebec J1M 1Z8
Canada

Phone: 819-566-0227
Fax: 819-566-8123
E-mail: admissions@bishopscollegeschool.com
Web site: http://www.bishopscollegeschool.com

THE BISHOP STRACHAN SCHOOL

Toronto, Ontario, Canada

Type: Girls' boarding (grades 7–12) and day (JK–12), college-preparatory school
Grades: JK–12: Junior School, JK–6; Senior School, 7–12
Head of School: Kim Gordon

THE SCHOOL

The Bishop Strachan School (BSS) is the leading girls' day and boarding school in Canada, with nearly 140 years' experience educating women, who routinely go on to extraordinary heights in a vast array of pursuits. A rigorous academic curriculum coupled with a creative, nurturing, and expressive approach to educating the whole girl gives BSS a uniquely successful environment specifically developed to bring out the very best in each of its girls.

BSS was founded in 1867, an auspicious year for Canada, upon the principle held by Dr. John Langtry that women should have access to the same kind of classical education provided to young men. The current site in the heart of Toronto's exquisite Forest Hill neighborhood was purchased in 1913. The buildings, campus, and athletics and arts facilities are unparalleled. A new addition housing, among other things, a wellness and health facility and expanded music studios, which opened in the fall of 2004, adding significantly to the resources and unique living environment for the boarders as well as the day students.

The School is governed by a Board of Trustees and a Board of Governors, both elected bodies representing parents, alumnae, and community leaders. They duly uphold the deeply felt values of BSS that honour its tradition of excellence, its commitment to integrity and compassion, and its ambition to remain the school of choice for the world's brightest and most gifted young women and girls. The operating budget generated by tuition fees is $11 million, and the endowment stands at $11 million. Annual giving is increasing steadily, and fund-raising campaigns are well supported. With ambitious building and capital improvements nearing completion, the School remains debt free.

BSS is an accredited member of CIS, CAIS, TABS, NAIS, SSATB, and the National Coalition of Girls' Schools. Its programs are inspected and accredited by the Ministry of Education in Ontario and the Canadian Educational Standards Institute.

ACADEMIC PROGRAMS

The Junior School program (JK–6) provides sequential learning experiences that incorporate expectations for the cognitive, social, emotional, physical, and spiritual development of students, through Reggio-inspired, inquiry-based learning. The Junior School curriculum sets the standard of excellence required to ensure that students achieve the mission set out by the School. Entry years for the Junior School are JK and grade 3.

In the Senior School, all programs are offered at the advanced and enriched levels. Community service is a part of the curriculum from grades 7 to 12. A strong emphasis is placed on the

development of competent writing skills in all subject areas. Students in grades 9–12 are involved in the laptop program that fully integrates technology into the curriculum. Entry years for the Senior School (day) are grades 7 and 9. Boarders are admitted for grades 7–12.

As required by the province of Ontario for graduation, a student must obtain a total of 30 credits from grades 9–12. Compulsory credits at BSS are 4 courses in English; 1 in physical education; 3 in math (with at least 1 credit in grades 11 or 12); 1 civics and career studies; 2 credits in science; 1 science credit at the eleventh or twelfth grade level or a technology credit (grades 9–12); 1 Canadian history credit; 1 Canadian geography credit; 1 arts credit; 1 credit that is either an additional English, a third language, social science, or Canadian and world studies; and 1 credit that is either a physical education, music, art, drama, dance, or business studies. The rest comprise a wide choice of electives, which include four other foreign languages, economics, law, science, and arts. Grading is based on the following scale: 80–100, honours (A); 70–80, very good (B); 60–70, satisfactory (C); 50–60, poor (D); and under 50, failure.

Advanced Placement exams are offered in calculus, U.S. history, microeconomics and macroeconomics, French, Spanish, German, chemistry, biology, psychology, statistics, computer science, and English language and literature.

Students at the School have been involved with the mentorship program at the University of Toronto. They can also go on various exchange programs around the world. The School has also developed programs for experiential education in grades 8 to 10.

FACULTY AND ADVISERS

There are more than 100 faculty members representing a wide spectrum of teaching experience. All of the teaching staff members hold degrees; the majority hold additional degrees or diplomas in education, while many have higher or advanced degrees. The Horizon Fund is available for professional development projects.

All staff members participate in co-curricular activities, bringing their expertise and assistance according to their interests and skills. Since the student body is divided into smaller units of Forms and Houses, staff members meet with their students at the beginning of each day. A Teacher-Advisor Program has been added to provide students with an opportunity to develop a personal profile. Teachers meet with 8 to 12 students once per week.

COLLEGE PLACEMENT

One part-time and 4 full-time counsellors are available to assist students in personal goals, academic choices, and career planning. Visits to

universities are arranged each year, and representatives from Canadian, United States, and United Kingdom universities and colleges come to the School.

All graduating students are offered places in respected Canadian universities. A large number are also offered places at prestigious universities in the United States and the United Kingdom, including Columbia, Cornell, Edinburgh, Georgetown, Harvard, the London School of Economics, MIT, Princeton, St. Andrews, and the University of Pennsylvania.

STUDENT BODY AND CONDUCT

Almost 100 boarders come from places such as Canada, the Caribbean, the Pacific Rim, Africa, the Middle East, Europe, and Mexico. Each year there are exchange students from Quebec, New Zealand, Australia, Japan, and South Africa. Although the School has Anglican affiliations, many religions are represented in the faculty and student body.

The School has an Honour Code that is clearly understood by parents and students. The underlying principle is that students are expected to conduct themselves according to legality, safety, courtesy, and consideration for others.

Prefects, elected by staff and students from the graduating class, are the School leaders. There is an elected student council. Appointment as form advisers and Ambassadors or election to club headships provides further opportunities for leadership training.

ACADEMIC FACILITIES

The traditional, grey stone buildings of the School and its playing fields occupy a 7½-acre site in the quiet residential area of Forest Hill. The Junior School is in a separate wing but shares the sports and dining facilities with the Senior School. The five science laboratories are fully modernized. There are facilities for music and drama, classrooms, three computer labs, two libraries, and a 250-seat theatre and chapel. The School is completely networked and connected to the Internet. There are two large art studios, gyms, a weight room, a pool, tennis courts, a climbing wall, and a high ropes course. The design and technology lab for grades 4–8 is used to enhance the science curriculum. In fall 2004, BSS opened a magnificent new addition to the campus, a new building housing spacious classrooms, a new gym, fitness and wellness facilities, a new arts studio, underground parking, and many other amenities. The expansion also enables the School to use the existing facilities more effectively to promote an improved learning atmosphere.

BOARDING AND GENERAL FACILITIES

The residence staff aims to make the boarding school a home away from home for the boarding

students. The residence wing is part of the main school and provides easy access to all School facilities, many of which are used in the evenings for study and recreation. As part of the recent school renovations, the washrooms on each floor were enlarged and upgraded. Supervised study occurs four times a week. Students are grouped by grade on each floor. The boarders have their own dining room, and all meals are served buffet-style with plenty of choice. Students from other countries are required to have local guardians. Each student can be contacted through her private voice mail, and all rooms are networked for e-mail and the Internet.

Security of the students is a priority, but the students' need to develop independence is recognized, so privileges are carefully related to age and responsibility. A staff of 10 provides excellent supervision, and the health centre has a nurse on duty daily. Four full-time staff members have housing in the residence.

ATHLETICS
Athletics play an integral role in fostering the development of the whole student, thereby enriching the School community. The innovative program ensures exposure to a variety of physical activities and health issues, encouraging the development of healthy lifestyles. The School has thirty-nine interscholastic teams. These allow almost 50 percent of the senior student body to participate each term. Teams include badminton, basketball, cross-country, field hockey, gymnastics, ice hockey, skiing, soccer, swimming, and volleyball.

EXTRACURRICULAR OPPORTUNITIES
There are seventeen student-run clubs in the School. These range from Third Wave to Amnesty International, from the Roots Club to robotics. Meetings are usually at lunchtime. Choral, string, and instrumental groups increase the choices. Every year there is a visiting Canadian author, as well as a Writer in Residence. Many departments invite speakers and lead field trips to local places and abroad. Debating, drama, and music provide frequent collaboration with other local private schools. The Duke of Edinburgh Award Program and the Outers Club attract many participants. A "crazy sports day" fosters community spirit early in the year. Each House is involved in a social service project under the direction of a prefect, and the

whole School is committed to raising money for community projects at home and abroad on an ongoing basis.

Students are encouraged to participate actively through the elected residence and student council, the organization of social activities, the publication of a newspaper, and a big sister/little sister program. Social, dramatic, and athletic events are often run in conjunction with Upper Canada College, a neighbouring independent boys' school.

DAILY LIFE
The school day begins at 8:30, with students assembling in Houses and Forms. From 8:50 to 9:10 there is a full assembly of the Senior School in the chapel for a short service, presentations, and announcements. The timetable operates on a five-day cycle and four-period day ending at 3:30. Lunch is from 12:00 to 1:00; half of the lunch hour is used for recreational sport and club activities. Lunch is provided for the Junior School and the boarders; day girls may purchase lunch from the cafeteria or bring a packed lunch. Extra help is available in all subjects by appointment or after school. Extramural sports are played in the afternoon and after school.

WEEKEND LIFE
The School is close to a small shopping area known as Forest Hill Village. Since Toronto is a safe and cosmopolitan city, students are encouraged to take advantage of its diversely enriching opportunities of theatre, museums, art galleries, concerts, sports, and cultural experiences. Staff members, with the assistance of students, organize activities for each weekend. Alternative in-residence activities are also available, and, with advance parental permission, students may visit friends or family. Special interest programs are occasionally arranged during the school week.

Students can make arrangements to attend the place of worship of their choice on weekends.

COSTS AND FINANCIAL AID
For 2005–06, the tuition fee is Can$19,950 for day students. Tuition and full boarding fees are Can$38,360. Additional costs include uniforms, laptop computers, books, field trips, and lunches (senior day girls only). A one-time nonrefundable fee of Can$5000 is charged to all students as a contribution to the existing infrastructure of the School. Private music lessons and tutoring are optional extras.

Upon acceptance, registration fees are Can$1000 for day students and Can$1500 for boarding students, of which half is refundable if the student withdraws before July 1. The balance of the account may be paid in two installments (August and December) or via a preauthorized monthly payment plan.

Entrance and merit scholarships are awarded to students entering grades 7 and 9 and a student who is gifted in the arts in grade 7 or 9. The Twenty-First Century scholarship is awarded to a student entering grade 9 who excels at academics, athletics, or the arts and who requires bursary assistance. These scholarships, based on tests and interviews, are applied to fees and are retained as long as the student maintains a strong academic standing each year. Bursary assistance is also available to qualified applicants.

ADMISSIONS INFORMATION
Admission is based on previous school reports, references, and a personal interview. Grade 7–12 applicants also take the SSAT. Applicants for grades 11 and 12 are required to write a more extensive English paper and take a math placement test. Students who live too far away to visit write the test at their own schools. International students applying to grades 11 and 12 and whose first language is not English must take the TOEFL. An application and brochure describing the School and the admission process are available upon request.

APPLICATION TIMETABLE
Applications may be submitted anytime, but the admissions process begins in early October for admission the following September. The entry-year application deadline is January 13. On receipt of the application, arrangements are made for a tour of the School, personal interviews with the student and parents/guardians, and assessments (grades 11 and 12). The Admissions Team makes final decisions and offers places in early March to day students. Boarders are accepted on an ongoing basis with conditional offers, pending SSAT results.

ADMISSIONS CORRESPONDENCE
The Admissions Assistant (Junior School) or
The Admissions Assistant (Senior School)
The Bishop Strachan School
298 Lonsdale Road
Toronto, Ontario M4V 1X2
Canada

Phone: 416-483-4325 Ext. 1750 (Junior) or
      1220 (Senior)
Fax: 416-481-5632
E-mail: admissions@bss.on.ca
Web site: http://www.bss.on.ca

BLAIR ACADEMY
Blairstown, New Jersey

Type: Coeducational boarding and day college-preparatory school
Grades: 9–12, postgraduate year
Enrollment: 436
Head of School: T. Chandler Hardwick III

THE SCHOOL

Blair Academy is situated on 315 hilltop acres adjacent to the village of Blairstown in Warren County, one of the most scenic counties in New Jersey. The school is 10 minutes from the Appalachian Trail and the Delaware Water Gap, yet it is only 1½ hours from New York City and 2 hours from Philadelphia.

Blair was founded in 1848 by a group of prominent local merchants and clergymen headed by John Insley Blair. The school was coeducational until 1915, when it became an all-boys school. Coeducation was reinstated in 1970 with great success, and girls now make up almost half of the school's population. Although the day-student population is small, it is important, adding a strong dimension to the student body.

Blair maintains an enrollment of 436 students, large enough to support a broad program of studies, activities, and athletics, yet small enough so that everyone can receive ample individual help and attention. The small class size (about 8–12 to a class) and the programs for guidance and counseling also make for close relationships between students and members of the faculty and staff.

A Board of Trustees directs the school, and alumni are well represented on the Board. The school's endowment is estimated at approximately $55 million. Receipt of capital gifts for 2004–05 was $2 million. Operating expenses for 2004–05 totaled approximately $18 million. The Blair Fund raised more than $1.4 million.

Blair Academy is accredited by the Middle States Association of Colleges and Schools. Its memberships include the Cum Laude Society, New Jersey Association of Independent Schools, National Association of Principals of Schools for Girls, National Association of Independent Schools, the Association of Boarding Schools, Council for Advancement and Support of Education, and Secondary School Admission Test Board.

ACADEMIC PROGRAMS

Blair Academy's academic program follows the traditional four-year college-preparatory plan. Diploma requirements at Blair are governed by college entrance requirements, and they ensure that all students graduate with an exposure to a wide variety of disciplines.

The academic year is divided into two semesters. To graduate, a four-year student must successfully complete the following units (with each semester yielding 1.5 credits): English, 12; mathematics, 9; modern or classical language, 6; laboratory science, 6; world history, 3; U.S. history, 6; arts, 4.5; religion, 1.5; and health, 1.5. Electives include area studies in Africa, Asian history, politics and government, computer science, environmental science, and the philosophy of religion. A full complement of courses is offered in the visual and performing arts. In addition, for every year a student attends Blair, he or she must complete 3 units of physical education or athletics.

Blair Academy offers a broad spectrum of courses, from the introductory level through Advanced Placement.

Individual participation is encouraged in small classroom sections. Day and evening study periods are supervised by faculty members in the dormitory. Every student is assigned a class monitor who oversees his or her academic life at school. In addition, for the fall term freshmen receive help from faculty members in managing study time and prioritizing academic tasks.

Blair uses a 6.0 grading system in which 2.0 is passing and 6.0 is an exceptional grade reserved for truly outstanding work.

Full reports are sent home at the end of each quarter, and interim reports are sent at any time for students who are experiencing difficulty. The full reports include grades and comments from each of the student's teachers. In addition, there are two formal reports (fall and spring) from the student's adviser and one from his or her class monitor.

FACULTY AND ADVISERS

For the 2005–06 academic year, Blair Academy employed 78 faculty members and administrators, of whom more than half hold graduate degrees. The vast majority of faculty members and administrators live on campus, many as houseparents in the dormitories. More than two thirds also coach sports or serve as academic monitors.

T. Chandler Hardwick III was appointed the Academy's fifteenth Headmaster in 1989. A graduate of the University of North Carolina (B.A., 1975) and Middlebury College (M.A., 1983), Mr. Hardwick previously taught English and was Senior Dean at The Taft School, as well as the Director of The Taft Summer School.

Blair makes available to members of its faculty financial assistance for continuing study and enrichment, in particular through grants from the Lafayette Butler Fund, the E.E. Ford Foundation, and the James Howard and the Lillian and Samuel Tedlow funds.

COLLEGE PLACEMENT

College counselors begin working with students and their families during the winter term of their junior year. Each student has at least four to six private meetings with a college counselor to map out the college search and application process. Counselors communicate regularly with parents to keep them informed and involved. Blair hosts on campus representatives from at least seventy colleges and universities each year.

Students from recent graduating classes are attending such colleges and universities as Brown, Colgate, Columbia, Cornell, Dartmouth, Davidson, Duke, Georgetown, Harvard, Lehigh, Middlebury, NYU, Princeton, U.S. Military Academy, U.S. Naval Academy, Wellesley, Williams, Yale, and the Universities of Pennsylvania and Virginia.

STUDENT BODY AND CONDUCT

Blair attempts to maintain a diverse student body geographically, ethnically, and socioeconomically. For 2005–06, Blair welcomed students from twenty-eight states and fourteen countries. The composition of the 2005–06 student body is as follows: senior class and postgraduate year, 74 boys, 55 girls;

junior class, 70 boys, 58 girls; sophomore class, 52 boys, 44 girls; and freshman class, 54 boys, 29 girls. Of the total enrollment of 436, there are 102 day and 334 boarding students.

School rules originate from and infractions are adjudicated by the Rules and Discipline Committee, which is composed of students and faculty members, each elected by peers. A pamphlet, *Blair Academy School Rules, Academic Expectations, and Disciplinary Procedures,* is distributed before the opening of school, and all students and their parents are expected to be familiar with its contents.

ACADEMIC FACILITIES

At the center of the campus are the four major classroom buildings: Clinton Hall, Bogle Hall, Timken Library, and the Armstrong-Hipkins Center for the Arts. Bogle Hall, dedicated in 1989, provides laboratories and classrooms for the math and science departments and includes a state-of-the-art computer laboratory and a 150-seat auditorium. Armstrong-Hipkins Center for the Arts was dedicated in 1997. The renovated Timken Library, a state-of-the-art facility that includes classrooms and a computer center, opened in 1998. A girls' dormitory opened in fall 1999. Athletic fields and a roadway system were completed in 1997, the Romano Dining hall was completed in the fall of 2000, and renovation of Insley Hall was completed in 2001. Most recently, Locke Hall, East Hall, Davies Hall, and South Cottage have been renovated.

BOARDING AND GENERAL FACILITIES

Nine dormitories house boarding students. Generally, the housing philosophy has ninth and tenth graders grouped in underclass dorms, while eleventh and twelfth graders occupy the upperclass dorms. Each dormitory has its own dorm council with faculty and elected student members.

In addition to having a housemaster (sometimes a faculty couple), each underclass dormitory unit has in residence senior prefects, and each student chooses a faculty member to be his or her adviser. Advisers are available to help students with personal and social growth.

A registered nurse is in charge of the infirmary (or on call) at all times, with a staff of RNs or LPNs on regular tours of duty. There are twenty beds, an examining room, and a dispensary. The home and office of the school physician are just 3 miles from campus.

ATHLETICS

Because Blair believes that physical education is beneficial and important, all students must take part in a program of athletics or supervised recreational sports in order to be awarded a Blair diploma.

Blair fields twenty-eight competitive varsity teams in baseball, basketball, crew, cross-country, field hockey, football, golf, ice hockey, lacrosse, skiing, soccer, softball, squash, swimming, tennis, wrestling, and winter and spring track. Participation is the key to Blair's sports program, so second- and third-level teams are fielded in most sports. An

extensive outdoor-skills program includes basic outdoor skills, canoeing, and kayaking.

Sports facilities include a football field, three soccer fields, field hockey and lacrosse fields, two baseball diamonds, and one softball diamond. There are also fourteen tennis courts, three international squash courts, a ¼-mile track, a golf course, two basketball courts, wrestling rooms, a weight-lifting and fitness room, a six-lane pool, and a nearby ice hockey rink.

EXTRACURRICULAR OPPORTUNITIES

The Nevett Bartow Series brings to the campus some twenty programs each year, which include such offerings as Rockapella, Solid Brass, Loudon Wainwright III, the David Grisman Quintet, Tom Chapin, Judy Collins, Arlo Guthrie, and visiting lecturers. Trips are arranged to the theater, concerts, the opera, and the ballet and to museums in New York City.

Among popular campus organizations are the Blair Academy Singers, the Blair Academy Players, the Wind Symphony, the Community Service and Environmental Clubs, and the Ski Club. The outdoor skills group takes full advantage of Blair's proximity to the Delaware Water Gap and the Appalachian Trail. There are also a student-written newspaper, yearbook, and literary publication; International Awareness Club; Model UN; Math Team; the Society of Skeptics, a college-level weekly lecture series sponsored by the history department; and service-oriented organizations, such as the Blue and White Key.

Groups vary from year to year depending on interests; they have included clubs devoted to photography, chess, recycling, electronics, and debating.

DAILY LIFE

Classes are 55 minutes long and meet four times during a six-day week. Four days per week, classes end at 3 p.m. Wednesday and Saturday are shortened days, with afternoons dedicated to athletics and drama. Extra help blocks are scheduled several times per week, and teachers are always available by appointment. All students participate in the weekly campus recycling program.

Afternoons are devoted to athletics practices and games, drama, recreational sports, or activities. Formal dinner for boarding students is at 6:15 two to four days per week. The hours from 8 to 10 p.m. are reserved for supervised room study or, for some students, monitored study hall.

WEEKEND LIFE

Closed weekends during examinations and the month of September require all boarding students to remain on campus. Otherwise, underclass students are allowed to take weekends away from campus according to a scale based on their grade in school.

Blair provides a stimulating, engaging weekend activities program. Each weekend, teams made up of faculty members and students coordinate a comprehensive list of activities and events. Highlights include International Weekend, the midwinter formal, a taste-off between local pizzerias, and Peddie Week. Such standards as trips to area shopping malls and movies occur every weekend. Blair also takes advantage of its location to organize trips to New York City as well as hiking, camping, and canoeing trips in the area countryside.

COSTS AND FINANCIAL AID

The annual charge for 2005–06 was $35,000 for boarders; this fee covered tuition, room and board, and ordinary infirmary care. For day students, the charge was $26,000, which covered tuition, study rooms, and meals. Additional deposits or fees are charged for the use of certain equipment, private music lessons, and extra medical services.

Financial aid is awarded on the basis of demonstrated financial need and proven personal and academic merit in accordance with procedures established by the School and Student Service for Financial Aid.

ADMISSIONS INFORMATION

Blair is interested in students who want to be a part of an independent school community and who are committed to improving their academic background.

Blair enrolls students in grades 9–11 each year and also admits a limited number of high school graduates who wish to pursue a postgraduate year of study.

In addition to a personal interview, several written components complete the formal application. To complement the school transcript and teachers' recommendations, Blair requests results from a standardized test: the SSAT for grades 9–11 and the SAT or ACT for postgraduates. Application forms must be accompanied by a nonrefundable fee of $50. The deadline is February 1.

APPLICATION TIMETABLE

The initial inquiry is welcome at any time. The Admissions Office is open for interviews and tours by appointment on weekdays and some Saturdays. Applicants who complete the admissions process prior to February 1 are notified of the decision on March 10.

ADMISSIONS CORRESPONDENCE

Barbara H. Haase, Dean of Admissions
Blair Academy
P.O. Box 600
Blairstown, New Jersey 07825-0600
Phone: 908-362-2024
          800-462-5247 (toll-free)
Fax: 908-362-7975
E-mail: admissions@blair.edu
Web site: http://www.blair.edu

BLUE RIDGE SCHOOL

St. George, Virginia

Type: Boys' boarding college-preparatory school
Grades: 9–12
Enrollment: 182
Head of School: David A. Bouton, Ph.D., Headmaster

THE SCHOOL

Blue Ridge School was founded in 1909 as an Episcopal mission school. In 1962, the School reorganized as an independent boarding school and adopted its present mission. While the required chapel program remains at the center of the spiritual life of the School, students of all religious backgrounds are welcome. A nonprofit institution, Blue Ridge is governed by a national self-perpetuating Board of Trustees. The School's recorded endowment is $5.69 million, and strong annual giving provides funds for financial aid and for support of the operating budget.

Blue Ridge is the right school for capable college-bound students of good character and integrity who possess tremendous, if yet untapped, potential and a positive attitude; who thrive in a small setting with a structured routine; who may benefit from learning to manage their time better and from developing more productive study habits; who are eager to be part of a supportive community that encourages them to take risks and to try new things; and who not only plan to go to college, but also want to be prepared to succeed in every aspect of their lives there.

Located 18 miles northwest of Charlottesville and the University of Virginia, the School is 1½ hours from Richmond and 2 hours from Washington, D.C., allowing for frequent and easy access to the tremendous cultural resources of those historic cities. The School's scenic campus, featuring lakes, ponds, streams, and a system of trails, is situated on 800 acres on the eastern face of the Blue Ridge Mountains. Its location, 5 miles from the Appalachian Trail and Shenandoah National Park, offers a wealth of opportunities for outdoor activities both on and off campus.

Blue Ridge School is accredited by the Southern Association of Colleges and Schools and by the Virginia Association of Independent Schools. It holds memberships in the National Association of Independent Schools, the Association of Boarding Schools, the Small Boarding School Association, the Secondary Admission Test Board, the Council for the Advancement and Support of Education, the National Association for College Admission Counseling, the National Association of Episcopal Schools, and the National Honor Society.

ACADEMIC PROGRAMS

Blue Ridge School is college preparatory. Students are not treated as though they are in college, nor are they expected to arrive at Blue Ridge with the skills and habits of a college student; but, when Blue Ridge students graduate, they are fully prepared to go on to college, armed with the skills, habits, and confidence necessary to succeed.

Blue Ridge School offers a college preparatory curriculum that is designed for young men who learn best in small classes with a supportive faculty. The academic program challenges students while also recognizing that study skills, support, and a solid academic routine are essential for success.

To graduate from Blue Ridge School, students must complete a minimum of 4 units of English; 4 units of mathematics, including 2 of algebra and 1

of geometry; 3 units of history, including 2 of U.S. history and 1 of non-U.S. history; 3 units of laboratory science, including 1 of biology; 3 units of the same foreign language; 2 units of physical education; 1 unit of life skills; and 2 electives. Students typically take six subjects each year. All students participate in Synergy, a three-year program in the use of technology for educational purposes designed at the University of Richmond.

The average class size at Blue Ridge is 9 students, the maximum is typically 13 students, and the student-teacher ratio is 6:1. The School calendar is based on trimesters. Classroom teachers prepare written academic comments to be mailed to parents at the middle and end of each trimester. Report cards are sent home at the end of each trimester.

Classes meet Monday through Friday, with each class meeting four times a week. All students participate in evening study hall Sunday through Thursday from 8 to 10 p.m. When it comes to the students' academic success at the School, evening study hall may be considered to be the most important 2 hours of the day. Students study in the setting that is most suitable for them: their room, the library or computer lab, a supervised study hall, or in the Learning Center. All freshmen and new sophomores start out in a traditional, supervised study hall setting. Students who have not completed all of their homework are assigned to Homework Lab after dinner to complete the missing work.

The Junius Fishburne Learning Center works with faculty and students to ensure that every student is provided the appropriate level of support necessary to realize his academic potential. The Director of Studies determines eligibility for such services, generally as part of the admission process, and space is limited.

FACULTY AND ADVISERS

Each student has a faculty adviser who serves as that student's surrogate parent and advocate. Because the adviser/advisee relationship is the cornerstone of both academic and residential life at the School, the adviser role is the single most important role that a faculty member has in the School community. Students meet with their adviser during a daily advisee period and sit with them at chapel and assemblies. Families communicate with the School through their son's adviser.

The professional staff is made up of 37 men and 10 women. Three hold a doctoral degree and 16 have master's degrees. Faculty members are selected not only for their competencies in their academic and nonacademic fields, but also for their strong commitment to the Blue Ridge mission and to its students. Nearly all have had previous boarding school teaching experience, and their continued professional development is generously supported by the School.

David A. Bouton, a graduate of the University of Notre Dame (B.B.A., M.A.) and Virginia Commonwealth University (Ph.D.), was appointed Headmaster in 2000. From 1993 to 1999, Dr. Bouton headed Benedictine High School in Richmond, Virginia. From 1990 to 1993, he was Academic Dean

at the U.S. Military War College in Carlisle, Pennsylvania, where he had served in a number of positions since 1986. Dr. Bouton's career working with young men in the U.S. Army spanned more than thirty years. He and his wife, Sheila, are the parents of 6 grown children (5 sons and 1 daughter).

COLLEGE PLACEMENT

College counseling is an important and integral part of the School's program. Typically 100 percent of the School's graduates go on to attend four-year colleges or universities. Blue Ridge School graduates attend a wide variety of schools. The goal of the College Counseling Office is to help students identify and gain admission to colleges and universities that offer a good fit: a place where they will be successful and fulfilled and continue to grow. To aid in that process, the School employs a full-time college counselor. Representatives from numerous and varied colleges and universities visit Blue Ridge School to meet with students. Members of the class of 2002 are currently attending Boston University, Brown, Hampden-Sydney, James Madison, Lynchburg College, Radford, Rhode Island School of Design, Roanoke, Rollins, Virginia Military Institute, Wesleyan, William and Mary, and the Universities of Alabama, California (Santa Cruz), Miami, Mississippi, and Virginia.

STUDENT BODY AND CONDUCT

All students and nearly all faculty members and administrators live on campus, making Blue Ridge a true residential community. In 2003–04, Blue Ridge students came from twenty states, the District of Columbia, and eleven countries. Fourteen percent are international students and another 18 percent are students of color.

Life at Blue Ridge is guided by the Code of Conduct, which comprises the core values of the School community: being honorable and accountable; being willing to invest oneself and to try new things, persevering and maintaining a positive attitude, displaying mutual respect and tolerance, being a good citizen, and developing habits of mind, body, and spirit. Senior Prefects act as the oldest brother on each of the residence halls, and as a group they serve as leaders and role models in all areas of school life. Cases involving possible honor or disciplinary infractions are heard by the Honor Council and Student-Faculty Disciplinary Committee, respectively. These boards, made up of seniors and faculty members, make recommendations to the Headmaster concerning what action should be taken. Blue Ridge maintains a traditional dress code of coat and tie attire for class.

ACADEMIC FACILITIES

A central feature of the Blue Ridge campus is the proximity of all of the buildings to one another. All classes are held in what is soon to be a completely renovated, state-of-the-art facility, including a science wing, the Junius Fishburne Learning Center, and a technology center. The 230-seat Mayo Auditorium, the dining hall, and administrative offices are located in Loving Hall, attached to the Academic Building. Music classes, lessons, and re-

hearsals are held in the Music Barn, and spacious art studios are located in the New York Auxiliary Student Center.

Built in 1993, the Hatcher C. Williams Library contains some 11,000 volumes. Students also have online access to the collections at the University of Virginia libraries and other regional libraries and to numerous research databases.

BOARDING AND GENERAL FACILITIES

All students live in one of two newly renovated dormitories; each hall in the dormitories is home to members of all four classes. All rooms are designed as doubles, except for those occupied by Prefects, and students typically have a roommate from the same class. Each hall functions as a family, and faculty members and their families, who reside on each hall, serve as hall parents. All halls operate under a similar set of guidelines, but as with all families, each hall family develops its own unique personality. Among the values shared by every hall family is the importance of creating a happy, warm, and safe living environment founded on mutual respect and tolerance. Students are also expected to take care of their homes and to keep their rooms clean and organized. Students have phone and Internet connections in their rooms.

The New York Auxiliary Student Center is home to the Center Court Snack Bar, the Game Room, the Tuck Shop, and the post office. The Game Room features a large, wide-screen home-theater system; several pool, Ping Pong, and foosball tables; an air hockey table; and video games. The Tuck Shop is the School store, where students may purchase textbooks, school supplies, Blue Ridge sportswear, personal items, and other necessities. Chapel services are held in Gibson Memorial Chapel, a state and national landmark.

A ten-bed infirmary is staffed 24 hours a day by 2 nurses. The School doctor is affiliated with Martha Jefferson Hospital in Charlottesville, one of the nation's top-ranked hospitals.

ATHLETICS

All students are required to participate in the athletics program throughout the year, including at least two team sports. Teams are available at all levels so that no student is excluded, and the program emphasizes a tradition of good sportsmanship. Cross-country, football, golf, and soccer are offered in the fall season; basketball, indoor soccer, and wrestling in the winter; and baseball, golf, lacrosse, tennis, and track and field in the spring. The Outdoor Program is offered as a team sport in each of the three seasons. As alternatives to team sports, students may participate in intramurals, drama, art, strength and conditioning, or community improvement and recycling during one of the three seasons.

The Outdoor Program is designed to give students opportunities to take full advantage of the School's unique mountain setting and location. All students, whether novices or accomplished outdoorsmen, are encouraged to participate. On campus, students have access to a 40-foot climbing tower; a ropes course; a zip line; an indoor bouldering room; a lake for fishing, canoeing, and kayaking; and a system of mountain trails for hiking and mountain biking. Through the Outdoor Pro-

gram, students enjoy off-campus trips to go overnight camping, white-water rafting, mountain biking, skiing and snowboarding, rock climbing, and caving.

A modern athletics complex includes a gymnasium, team meeting rooms, and a laundry facility. The newly renovated field house contains four indoor tennis courts, three basketball courts, a large wrestling room, fully equipped weight rooms, dressing rooms, and a training room. In addition, there are two practice fields; three game fields for football, soccer, and lacrosse; a 400-meter track; a baseball diamond with dugouts; four all-weather tennis courts; a golf driving range; and a 25-meter outdoor swimming pool. Students play golf on two local eighteen-hole courses. The School's certified athletic trainer is part of the doctoral program at the University of Virginia.

EXTRACURRICULAR OPPORTUNITIES

Blue Ridge students participate in a variety of clubs and organizations, including the Choir, the Multicultural Club, the Chess Club, the yearbook, the literary magazine, the Library Committee, the Food Committee, the Social Activities Committee, and the Boy Scouts of America Explorer Post.

Because of Blue Ridge's history as a mission school, community service has always played an important role at the School. Students have many opportunities to participate in a variety of community service projects. Students put on a musical theater production each winter as well as a major art show in the spring.

DAILY LIFE

Classes are held five days a week. Tuesdays and Fridays are half days to allow for interscholastic sports events in the afternoons. The academic day begins at 8 a.m. with assembly or chapel and ends at 3:10 p.m. All six class periods meet on Monday, Wednesday, and Thursday and last for 50 minutes. On Tuesday and Friday, only three class periods meet, lasting 75 minutes. Each day, students meet with their advisers and have the opportunity to meet with their teachers for extra help during conference period. Sports and extracurricular activities begin at 4 p.m. Dinner is served at 6 p.m. and is followed by a study hall from 7:30–9:30. Students must be in their rooms by 10:45 and have their lights out by 11 p.m.

WEEKEND LIFE

Because Blue Ridge is a seven-day all-boarding community, weekend activities play an important role in the life of the School. Weekends generally begin after lunch on Saturday and end with study hall on Sunday evening. Saturday mornings are devoted to the Saturday Program, which has four components: residential curriculum (life skills), fine arts, community service, and outdoor programs. All students are required to participate in the Saturday Program.

The Student Activities Director, along with the students on the Student Activities Committee, develops a diverse slate of offerings, both on and off campus, every weekend. The Outdoor Program sponsors several adventurous activities each weekend. There are frequent trips to Wizards, Capitals, and Orioles games, as well as to UVA soccer and

lacrosse games. Every weekend, students can attend a social event at one of the BSSAC schools, a group of girls' and boys' boarding schools located throughout Virginia, Maryland, and the D.C. area. There are also weekly excursions into nearby Charlottesville for shopping, dinner, movies, paintball, ice skating, and more.

COSTS AND FINANCIAL AID

For 2004–05, tuition is $29,358. Families should also budget about $2000 a year for the student account, which covers books, school supplies, allowance, activities, and other miscellaneous expenses incurred during the year. An enrollment deposit, which is credited toward tuition, is due with the return of the Enrollment Agreement. The balance of the tuition may be paid in full by the opening of school or in two installments, in August and in December. The second option requires participation in the Tuition Refund Plan.

The School awards need-based financial aid. In 2003–04, the School awarded $614,800 to 38 students. The School also participates in various monthly payment and loan programs.

ADMISSIONS INFORMATION

The admissions process at Blue Ridge is one of matchmaking. Blue Ridge seeks to enroll students who will be successful at the School. While the Admissions Committee considers past performance in making admissions decisions, they are primarily concerned with the candidate's potential and the likelihood that the School's program will enable the candidate to realize that potential.

Blue Ridge admits young men of good character who are committed to living according to the Blue Ridge School Code of Conduct and who, by investing themselves in the School's program and in the overall life of the School, will thrive in the Blue Ridge program. As the greatest benefit can be gained by attending Blue Ridge for at least three years, most students enter in the ninth and tenth grades. Some spaces are generally available in the eleventh grade, but it is rare for the School to admit students to the twelfth grade.

APPLICATION TIMETABLE

Initial inquiries are welcome at any time. The most important piece of the application process is the campus visit and personal interview. Arrangements for these visits should be made early in the year prior to the desired year of entry. Visits can be scheduled on weekdays while the School is in session.

A formal application with a $50 fee ($100 for international students) should be submitted by February 1. Notification on all applications received by February 1 is March 10. Families are requested to reply to an acceptance by April 10. Candidates completing applications after February 1 are reviewed on a rolling admission basis.

ADMISSIONS CORRESPONDENCE

David E. Hodgson
Director of Admissions
Blue Ridge School
St. George, Virginia 22935
Phone: 434-985-2811
Fax: 434-985-7215
E-mail: admissions@blueridgeschool.com
Web site: http://www.blueridgeschool.com

THE BOLLES SCHOOL

Jacksonville, Florida

BOLLES

Type: Coeducational boarding (7–12) and day (PK–12) college-preparatory school
Grades: PK–12: Lower Schools, PK–5; Middle School, 6–8; Upper School, 9–12
Enrollment: School total: 1,740; Lower Schools, 518; Middle School, 432; Upper School, 790
Head of School: John E. Trainer Jr., President and Head of School

---

THE SCHOOL

Bolles offers a comprehensive college-preparatory program. Bolles prepares students for the future by providing them with challenges that promote growth and development in academics, the arts, activities, and athletics. Moral development is encouraged by an emphasis on respect for self and others, volunteerism, and personal responsibility.

Bolles has served as the educational inspiration for three generations, with a strong and unshakable commitment to providing the finest preparatory education possible for each student. Located in Jacksonville, Florida, Bolles was founded in 1933 as an all-boys military school on the San Jose Campus. In 1962, the School dropped its military status, and in 1971, it began admitting girls.

In 1981, the Lower School Whitehurst Campus for grades K–5 was begun. A separate campus for middle schoolers in grades 6–8 was achieved in 1991 with the acquisition of Bartram School, an independent girls' school operating since 1934 and now known as the Bolles Middle School Bartram Campus. In 1998, the Bolles Lower School Ponte Vedra Beach Campus opened its doors to serve students in pre-kindergarten through grade 5.

Today, with more than 1,700 students at four locations, Bolles is recognized as one of the finest college-preparatory institutions in the nation. All of its students are college-bound. Bolles students consistently place in the top 10 percent of Advanced Placement scores from throughout the country. The School prepares students for the future by providing them with a variety of activities and a myriad of challenges that promote growth and development in four primary areas: academics, arts, activities, and athletics. Students learn to make decisions and budget time by balancing homework, sports, extracurricular, family, and community service responsibilities.

Students from all walks of life, cultures, religions, and races learn together at Bolles, a microcosm of the world that they will inherit. The School's excellent academic and athletic offerings attract students from sixteen countries and eight states to participate in the resident program for the 2005–06 school year. This blend of cultures and interests sets Bolles apart from other independent college-preparatory institutions in the Southeast and fosters a level of mutual respect that is crucial in learning how to meet global challenges.

The School's locations are in suburban neighborhoods. The Upper School San Jose Campus and the Lower School Whitehurst Campus occupy 52 acres on the St. Johns River. Five miles to the northeast, the Middle School Bartram Campus is set on 23 acres. The Bolles

Lower School Ponte Vedra Beach Campus is located on 12 acres in Ponte Vedra Beach, east of Jacksonville.

Jacksonville, a major metropolitan area in northeast Florida, is home to the Jaguars National Football League team and many cultural associations, such as the Jacksonville Symphony, the Florida Ballet, several professional theater companies, three major museums, the Jacksonville Zoo, and several professional sports teams. Downtown Jacksonville is located approximately 35 minutes from the Jacksonville Beach area, which includes Ponte Vedra Beach, and about an hour from St. Augustine, the oldest city in the United States.

A not-for-profit institution, Bolles is governed by a self-perpetuating board of 29 trustees. The School also works with a 30-member Board of Visitors and an Alumni Board that represents more than 7,600 living graduates.

The School's operating budget is more than $25 million. The annual giving goal for 2004–05 was $1.5 million, which included more than $1.3 million in unrestricted dollars. The School's endowment is nearly $9.5 million.

The School is accredited by the Southern Association of Colleges and Schools and the Florida Council of Independent Schools and holds membership in the National Association of Independent Schools, the Council for Spiritual and Ethical Education, the Secondary School Admission Test Board, and the Southeastern Association of Boarding Schools.

ACADEMIC PROGRAMS

The Middle School curriculum includes English, government, world cultures, world geography, U.S. history, mathematics through algebra, and science. Students may select from a varied fine- and performing-arts program and may choose among band, chorus, drama, dance, graphics, drawing and painting, ceramics and sculpture, computers, foreign language, and language arts on a rotating basis throughout the year. Each student has an adviser, and a full-time, on-campus guidance counselor assists with decision-making skills, peer relations, and alcohol and drug abuse awareness.

Upper School students must earn 22 credits for graduation, with a college-certifying grade of at least C-. Specific requirements are 4 years of English; 2 of a single foreign language; 3 of social studies, including U.S. and world history; 3 of mathematics through algebra II; 3 of science, including biology and chemistry; 2 of physical education; 1 of fine arts; one-half year of life management skills; and 3½ years of additional electives. The average class size is 18 students.

Among the full-year courses are English, French, Latin, Spanish, German, Japanese, Mandarin Chinese, world and U.S. history, algebra, geometry, precalculus, physical science, biology,

chemistry, marine science, environmental science, band, introduction to dance, intermediate dance, upper-level dance, AP drawing, portfolio AP, advanced visual studies, portfolio development honors, men's chorus, women's chorus, concert choir, and symphonic band. There are honors sections in English, geometry, algebra, biology, chemistry, physics, foreign languages, and social studies. Courses designed to prepare students for Advanced Placement examinations are available in English, U.S. and European history, American and comparative government and politics, foreign languages, calculus, biology, chemistry, physics, computer science, statistics, portfolio art, and drawing. A postgraduate program is available to students seeking an additional year of academics prior to entering college.

Students choose from such semester electives as foundations of studio art, drawing and painting, ceramics and sculpture, creative writing, acting, directing, production, public speaking, computer applications, AP statistics, algebra III, introduction to programming, Web site development, American government and politics, economics, human anatomy, marine science, neurobiology honors, drama, drawing, painting, ceramics, sculpture, and driver education.

Opportunities for off-campus projects sponsored directly by the School include the Outdoor Academy and the French, Spanish, and Japanese Exchange Programs.

Grades, with narrative reports from faculty advisers, are sent to parents twice each quarter.

FACULTY AND ADVISERS

Dr. John E. Trainer Jr. was appointed President and Head of School in 2001. He holds a Bachelor of Science degree in biology from Muhlenberg College in Allentown, Pennsylvania; a master's in biology from Wake Forest University in Winston-Salem, North Carolina; and a doctorate in zoology from the University of Oklahoma in Norman, Oklahoma. Dr. Trainer was selected for this position because of his strong people skills and innovative thinking and for his extensive experience in working effectively with academic professionals, community leaders, executives, and legislators.

Bolles has 153 full-time faculty members and 3 part-time faculty members; 89 hold master's degrees and 10 hold doctorates.

Each student in the Middle and Upper Schools is assigned to a faculty member whose primary responsibility is to serve as an adviser. A minimal class load makes the adviser readily accessible to both students and parents. The School maintains an Office of Student Counseling to assist students in addressing issues that fall outside the traditional categories of academic advising.

COLLEGE PLACEMENT

The aim of the college counseling program is to help students and their families to find college options and ultimately to find the most appropriate college choice. At the start of the second semester of the junior year, a daylong meeting is held to begin the more structured aspect of the process, and each student is assigned a college placement adviser. An evening parent meeting provides additional information. The Williams Guidance Center offers a full range of up-to-date college reference materials, which include catalogs, videotapes, and computer search programs. In addition, approximately 100 college representatives visit the campus each year to meet with students, counselors, and parents.

In each of the past five years, 98 percent of graduates have attended four-year colleges and universities. A small number of students defer admission, and a small percentage attend two-year schools.

The mean scores for the last five graduating classes on the SAT I are 591 verbal and 599 math. The ACT composite mean is 25. Teachers in English and mathematics classes work with students in preparation for college admission testing.

STUDENT BODY AND CONDUCT

The Upper School numbers 790 students, with between 190 and 202 students in each grade. There are 100 boarding students.

There are an Honor Code and a Values Statement, and the Honor Council of Upper School students administers the Code and serves as the judiciary court for infractions against the Code. The Student Council is very active and serves as a proactive body for legislation of student privileges, organizes activities, and offers advice to the Upper School administration.

ACADEMIC FACILITIES

On the Upper School San Jose Campus, Bolles Hall houses classrooms, boys' dormitory rooms, a dining room and kitchen, offices, and three meeting rooms. Other academic buildings are Clifford G. Schultz Hall, with seventeen classrooms; the Michael Marco Science Center, which houses three science labs; the Joan W. and Martin E. Stein Computer Laboratory; the Hirsig Life Science Center; Ulmer Hall, which includes fifteen classrooms, a language lab, and two science labs; and a marine science classroom along the St. Johns River.

The Swisher Library houses the Meadow Multimedia Center, with a large-screen television, two satellite dishes, and computer labs. Other facilities include the 660-seat McGehee Auditorium and the Cindy and Jay Stein Fine Arts Center, which contains the Independent Life Music Building, the Lucy B. Gooding Art Gallery, and the Lynch Theater.

Middle School academic facilities include the Curry-Hicks Computer and Science Center, the Murchison-Lane Hall for classrooms and administrative offices, Williams Building, the Art Barn, a marine science classroom along Pottsburg Creek, girls' dormitory rooms, a multipurpose auditorium for performances, and the Pratt Library.

The Lower School Whitehurst Campus houses each grade separately in homelike classrooms set around a natural playground. The Lower School located at Ponte Vedra Beach is a modern campus that includes an administration/classroom facility, as well as the McLauchlan-Evans Building, housing classrooms, and the River Branch Building, which is the location of both the Ullman Family Art Room and the Loeb-Lovett Family Music Room.

BOARDING AND GENERAL FACILITIES

All boarding students are housed in rooms that accommodate two students. Boys and girls reside on separate campuses. Students are assigned roommates based upon age and interests.

Upper School athletic facilities include Collins Stadium at the Donovan Baseball Field, Hodges Field, the Bent Tennis Complex, the Baker-Gate Petroleum Company Track Facility, and Skinner-Barco Stadium. The Davis Sports Complex includes the Houston Student Center, basketball and volleyball courts, the 25-yard Lobrano and 50-meter Uible swimming pools, the Cassidy Aquatic Fitness Center, and the Garces Diving Facility. The Agnes Cain Gymnasium features a wrestling room and athletic offices.

Among the Middle School athletic facilities are a football and soccer field, Lane Courts, the Conroy Athletic Center, a small pool, and Meninak Field, which includes Collins Baseball Stadium.

ATHLETICS

Bolles is a member of the Florida High School Athletic Association. Boys' teams compete in baseball, basketball, crew, cross-country, football, golf, lacrosse, soccer, swimming, tennis, track, volleyball, and wrestling. Girls' teams compete in basketball, cheerleading, crew, cross-country, golf, soccer, softball, swimming, tennis, track, and volleyball. Middle School boys' teams compete in baseball, basketball, crew, football, lacrosse, soccer, swimming, track, and wrestling. Middle School girls' teams compete in basketball, cheerleading, crew, soccer, softball, swimming, track, and volleyball.

EXTRACURRICULAR OPPORTUNITIES

Extracurricular activities offered include Student Government; National Honor Society; language honor societies; Amnesty International; Interact, a boys' service club; Gamma Girls Service Club; Royal Pointe, which works with a YWCA after-school day-care center; a mentor program; D-Fy-Ince, the drug-free youth initiative program; three student after-school tutoring programs; Student Advocate Council, which promotes community spirit among the students; an array of other community service opportunities; language clubs; special interest clubs; Community Service Leadership Council; Sophomore Leadership Council; class-sponsored activities; *Turris* (yearbook); *The Bugle* (newspaper); and *Perspective* (literary magazine).

DAILY LIFE

The daily schedule for the Upper School, which lasts from 8 a.m. until 3:45 p.m., includes seven 45-minute periods and "Zero Hour," a 30-minute period reserved for individual conferences and extra help. Boarders have evening study in their rooms, with faculty members available for extra help, and supervised study halls are provided for students needing more structured assistance.

WEEKEND LIFE

Resident students are strongly encouraged to take advantage of the excellent recreational facilities at Bolles. On weekends, the waterfront is open for resident students, weather permitting. In addition, regular off-campus trips are organized, as are, from time to time, special trips.

COSTS AND FINANCIAL AID

Upper School tuition costs for the 2005–06 school year were as follows: tuition, room, and meals for boarding students (grades 7–12) totaled $30,750, and tuition for day students (grades 9–12) totaled $14,500 Additional fees include $500–$750 for books, $30–$35 per gym uniform set, $350 for driver education, a $500 facilities fee, and $40–$45 for the yearbook. Essential services fees for boarding students include $175 for the School clinic, $100 for emergency escrow, and an allowance of $35 per week ($1260 per school year) for students in grades 7–8, $40 per week ($1440 per school year) for students in grades 9–11, and $45 per week ($1620 per school year) for students in grade 12. Lunches and snacks are available for purchase by day students.

The School awarded $1.85 million in financial aid for the 2005–06 academic year.

ADMISSIONS INFORMATION

The School seeks students who demonstrate the ability to meet the requirements of the college-preparatory curriculum. In addition, special talents and strengths that would allow the applicant to achieve distinction within the applicant pool are desired. The ISEE or its equivalent is required of all applicants, as are a personal interview, teacher recommendations, and transcripts. There is a $45 application fee for day students and a $75 application fee for international students.

APPLICATION TIMETABLE

The Admission Office accepts applications beginning in the fall, with a rolling admission policy. Upon acceptance, the applicant must respond with a deposit of 10 percent of the total tuition and pay the facilities fee within two weeks.

ADMISSIONS CORRESPONDENCE

The Bolles School
7400 San Jose Boulevard
Jacksonville, Florida 32217

Phone: 904-256-5032
Fax: 904-739-9929
Web site: http://www.bolles.org

BOSTON UNIVERSITY ACADEMY

Boston, Massachusetts

Type: Coeducational day college-preparatory school
Grades: 9–12
Enrollment: 156
Head of School: Dr. James Tracy

THE SCHOOL

Boston University Academy is committed to providing an excellent secondary education, optimizing the respective strengths of its small school community and its inclusion within a world-class research university.

Since 1993, Boston University Academy has welcomed students, faculty members, and parents who care deeply about intellectual life. The school atmosphere provides a safe and nurturing community where teachers and students all know and support each other in enthusiastic scholarly inquiry. At the Academy, students take courses in small class settings with master teachers, while enjoying regular lectures by university professors and access to the vast resources at Boston University.

Primary texts, experimental practice, and free discussion drive the curriculum, ensuring that students graduate with strong content knowledge, analytical skills, and writing ability in the humanities and sciences. Students join the conversations that have engaged the great minds of Western civilization for three millennia. Classes conducted in seminar format foster active dialogue among teachers, students, and texts. Students write in every course and develop their own ideas and responses to the material.

Boston University Academy offers students unparalleled preparation for the college experience. With the oversight and support of the Academy community, upper-level students take courses at Boston University, typically graduating with at least one year of university course credit. The core curriculum prepares students to excel in their university-level classes, allowing students to pursue advanced studies in a dazzling array of fields and to engage in individual research projects with university professors. The school's mission is not to accelerate learning or adolescence but to expand the secondary-level experience for highly capable students to include all the resources of a university within a supportive and caring environment. Students graduate already fully integrated into the modern life of the mind in all its diversity.

Boston University Academy is a place where intellectually passionate students can find a community that supports and celebrates their growth as thinkers and as people. The Academy values the ethical and character development of students in a noncreedal atmosphere, with community service, lectures, and class discussions all playing key roles in encouraging students to think out the ethical implications of ideas and actions. The Academy offers the satisfaction of a supportive secondary school community of sustained and engaged endeavor and talented and motivated peers and faculty members, utilizing the resources of a major research university.

Boston University Academy is accredited by the New England Association of Schools and Colleges. The Academy holds membership in the Secondary School Admission Test Board, the Na-

tional Association of Independent Schools (NAIS), and the Association of Independent Schools of New England.

ACADEMIC PROGRAMS

The curriculum of Boston University Academy is designed to prepare students to be thoughtful and active citizens in a culturally and racially diverse world. Students learn skills, facts, and theories while they explore the ethical dimensions of knowledge and history. Classes emphasize the need to recognize and choose rationally among competing values. Students learn to express and defend their judgments about materials they encounter in their courses. Teachers work together to create a coordinated curriculum, presenting in their classes related topics or complementary themes whenever possible so that students begin to discover how the elements of knowledge fit together.

In grades 9 through 11, students follow a common curriculum, differing only in the foreign language they elect. These core courses prepare students to make informed choices from the Boston University undergraduate curriculum in their junior and senior years. The high school curriculum includes 4 years of English and at least 3 years of math, laboratory science, history, and foreign language. All students study either Latin or Greek in the ninth and tenth grades. The average class size is 14, and the student-teacher ratio is 7:1.

For Academy students, the final year of high school marks not so much an end as a beginning. In grades 9 through 11, a prescribed classical curriculum provides a comprehensive foundation. Thus prepared, Academy seniors have the option to enroll full-time in university courses. Academy seniors choose from an extensive selection of undergraduate courses at Boston University. Seniors join college students and learn from more than 3,000 talented researchers and educators. During their senior year, students commence their work on the senior thesis, an 8,000-word research project, and work closely with a university professor and an Academy adviser.

FACULTY AND ADVISERS

Boston University Academy has attracted a first-rate teaching and administrative staff. The 2005–06 faculty included 11 men and 9 women: 16 full-time and 4 part-time. The Academy employs part-time specialty teachers in such areas as athletics, art, music, and drama. Fifteen members of the faculty hold master's degrees, 5 hold doctorates, and 2 are pursuing doctorates. Faculty members are chosen for their ability to excite their students about learning, their eagerness to expand their own knowledge of their subjects, and their interest in further developing an integrated curriculum.

Boston University Academy provides a structured but informal learning environment. Teachers are available for student-teacher conferences,

and students are encouraged to seek additional help whenever necessary. The Academy is especially concerned with the personal development of each student. Outside of the classroom, faculty members sponsor a multitude of student activities and frequently meet with their advisees.

Academy students enrolled in college courses are taught by the Boston University faculty, which has more than 3,000 members. Although the Academy and university faculties are entirely separate, there is an open and collegial relationship between the two.

The Academy's Headmaster, Dr. James Tracy, received his Ph.D. in history from Stanford University and his M.B.A. from Boston University. Prior to joining Boston University Academy, Dr. Tracy taught for many years at the Hotchkiss School. He has been a visiting fellow at Yale, is a published author, and has written extensively on issues affecting education.

COLLEGE PLACEMENT

College counseling begins formally in the junior year with numerous individual conferences and monthly class meetings. The college counselor works closely with students and their families to identify the colleges that best suit the student's individual interests and provide guidance through the admission process. Each year, more than fifty colleges visit the Academy and meet with interested juniors and seniors.

Although Academy students graduate from high school with a college transcript, they apply to college not as transfers but as freshmen with advanced standing. One hundred percent of Academy students enroll in four-year colleges and universities. Matriculations include Boston University, Brandeis, Brown, Bryn Mawr, Carnegie Mellon, Columbia, Cornell, Harvard, MIT, Northwestern, Oberlin, Smith, Washington (St. Louis), Wellesley, Yale, and the Universities of Chicago, Pennsylvania, and Vermont.

The mean SAT score for the class of 2005 was 1430 (composite math and verbal scores).

STUDENT BODY AND CONDUCT

Boston University Academy opened in 1993 with ninth- and tenth-grade classes. Eighty-four boys and 72 girls were enrolled for the 2005–06 school year: 37 ninth graders, 39 tenth graders, 43 eleventh graders, and 37 twelfth graders. Twenty-two percent were members of minority groups.

The Academy is a learning community built on trust, honesty, and respect. Students, faculty members, and administrators share a sense of family and commitment to the Academy community. During their years at the Academy, students are expected to demonstrate respect for the world in which they live and a willingness to make a positive, meaningful contribution to that world. They are encouraged to make the most of their potential by developing the qualities of passionate cu-

riosity, a honed and enlivened intellect, earnest inquiry, and a humane commitment to serve those in need.

Peer advisers serve as a support group for their classmates, helping them to locate valuable resources. Peer tutors help students who are having academic difficulty.

ACADEMIC FACILITIES

The Academy's program is enriched by Boston University's research libraries, science and computer laboratories, and arts and athletic facilities. Students conduct research in the Mugar Memorial Library and other specialized libraries in the university system; together, they house more than 2 million printed books and an additional 4 million volumes on optical disk, microfilm, and other media. Mugar also offers collections of recorded music, rare books, historical manuscripts, and correspondence. In addition to their own science labs, Academy students have access to the state-of-the-art laboratories at the Arthur G. B. Metcalf Center for Science and Engineering. The Academy's arts program benefits from Boston University's facilities, including studios, practice rooms, and auditoriums.

The Academy has two computer labs, one dedicated for class use and the other for general student use. All computers are part of the university-wide network and have full-time access to the Internet. In addition, students are given accounts on the Academy's First Class messaging system. This is where Academy faculty members post course material, facilitate discussions, and base their electronic classrooms. Each student is given file storage space, print services, and an account on Boston University's computing system. In addition to the computing resources at the Academy, students also have access to all of the services and resources provided by Boston University.

ATHLETICS

Students use university athletic facilities for physical education classes and after-school sports. The Case Athletic Center has an ice-skating rink, a swimming pool, a basketball court, rowing tanks, weight and fitness rooms, and aerobics facilities as well as outdoor facilities for tennis, soccer, baseball, and track. The Boston University Fitness and Recreation Center features 280,000 square feet of pools; a jogging track; racquetball and squash courts; volleyball, basketball, and badminton courts; a climbing wall, and a dance studio.

The Academy belongs to the Massachusetts Bay Independent League, the New England Preparatory School Athletic Conference, and the Girls Independent League. The Academy fields interscholastic teams in basketball, crew, fencing, golf, sailing, soccer, and tennis.

The physical education program offers a wide range of sports and activities, including basketball, beach volleyball, crew, dance, flag football, handball, kayaking, martial arts, power walking, sailing, skating, soccer, softball, swimming, Ultimate Frisbee, and volleyball. Intramural sports are offered every afternoon. During the annual trip to Camp Wing, students learn the value of teamwork through orienteering and adventure activities. Several optional one- to three-day ski trips are also organized each year.

EXTRACURRICULAR OPPORTUNITIES

Extracurricular activities are considered an essential part of each student's educational experience. Enthusiasm and commitment are the only prerequisites for participation in the Academy's student activities. The Academy draws upon university facilities for many of its student activities, including engineering team, student council, and art club. Other clubs include chorus, Science Olympiad, yearbook, Model UN, newspaper, literary magazine, math club, and debate. Students may also take part in the Young Critics Institute and Drama as Discovery programs at the Huntington Theatre or audition for the Greater Boston Youth Symphony Orchestra, both in residence at Boston University. All students are required to participate in a community-service project.

DAILY LIFE

The Academy holds classes from 8 a.m. to 2:50 p.m. Academic classes meet for four 50-minute periods. Art and physical education classes meet twice each week. Faculty members and students eat lunch together at the university's George Sherman Student Union in a room reserved for the Academy. Teachers are available for student-teacher conferences after school. Extracurricular activities are offered during the school day and after school, when athletics are also offered.

COSTS AND FINANCIAL AID

Tuition for 2005–06 was $22,210. The student activity fee and technology fee is not included. Families may pay in two installments in July and December or participate in a ten-month payment plan. The Academy is firmly committed to enrolling a diverse student body. In 2005–06, 40 percent of students at the Academy received financial assistance. Financial aid is awarded on the basis of need; merit scholarships are also available.

ADMISSIONS INFORMATION

Boston University Academy seeks intellectually curious students who are willing and able to meet the challenge of a rigorous academic curriculum. Applications are considered for entry into all but the twelfth-grade class. The admissions committee considers a student's entire application and will neither accept nor reject an applicant solely on the basis of scores or grades. Applicants must submit two teacher recommendations, a complete school transcript, results of the SSAT, an essay, and a graded paper. In 2005, the median SSAT score for entering students was in the 92nd percentile. Approximately 45 percent of the students who applied were offered admission.

APPLICATION TIMETABLE

The Academy welcomes inquiries throughout the year. Prospective students and their parents are encouraged to visit classes and to meet with the Director of Admissions in the fall. The deadline for admission and financial aid applications is January 31. Notifications are sent out on March 10, and replies must be received by April 10.

ADMISSIONS CORRESPONDENCE

Nancy Caruso
Director of Admissions
Boston University Academy
1 University Road
Boston, Massachusetts 02215

Phone: 617-353-9000
Fax: 617-353-8999
E-mail: admissions@buacademy.org
Web site: http://www.buacademy.org

BRENAU ACADEMY
Gainesville, Georgia

Type: Girls' boarding and day college-preparatory school
Grades: 9–PG
Enrollment: 80
Head of School: Frank M. Booth, Headmaster

THE SCHOOL
Founded in 1928 on the campus of Brenau College by Dr. H. J. Pearce, Brenau Academy was established to provide high-quality secondary education for young women. Brenau Academy's program is designed to foster the growth of an open and inquiring mind and to prepare graduates for admission to college.

The purpose of the Academy is implemented by means of small classes that allow for individual attention. The small student body provides greater opportunity for leadership experiences. Because of Brenau Women's College's proximity, its facilities, faculty members, and cultural programs are available to Academy students.

Brenau's 56-acre campus, with its forty-six buildings, is located very near the downtown Gainesville area; shopping is within walking distance. Gainesville is located in the foothills of the beautiful Blue Ridge Mountains on the Chattahoochee River. Lake Lanier, Georgia's largest lake, is close by. Atlanta is 50 miles to the southwest.

The governing body for both the Academy and the college is a 36-member Board of Trustees.

The endowment for the Academy is $50 million. The annual operating budget is $1.5 million.

The Academy is accredited by the Southern Association of Colleges and Schools and approved by the Georgia Department of Education. It is a member of the Georgia Independent School Association, the National Association of Independent Schools, and the National Association of Boarding Schools.

ACADEMIC PROGRAMS
The curriculum is designed to prepare students for successful college experiences. Brenau offers the standard college-preparatory program. The following courses are generally pursued for graduation: English, 4 years; mathematics, 4 years; history, 3 years; science, 3 years; foreign language, 2 years; physical education, 2 years; fine arts, 1 year; and electives, 3 units. Brenau places special academic emphasis on mastery of the English language. Every student is expected to earn more than 1 credit in English each year. Electives available include music, art, drama, dance, and student publications. All students are expected to take at least five courses each term. In addition, courses are offered to advanced students, at no extra expense, in all departments of Brenau Women's College; students can earn dual credit for these courses.

Numerical grades are used at the Academy, and grades below 70 are considered failing. Progress reports are sent to parents and students every four weeks. The student's absences and teachers' comments are recorded on the report.

Classes are grouped according to course selection only. The average class has approximately 12 students, and there is an overall student-teacher ratio of 8:1. Study time is designed to assist students in developing sound study habits. Instructors are available throughout the day for individual assistance. Evening study time, monitored by housemothers, takes place in the dorm rooms, Monday through Thursday from 7:45 to 9:30, and on Sundays from 8:30 to 9:30.

Students who need extra academic help may visit with the teacher during a tutorial period built into the school day. For advanced students who need the extra challenge, the tutorial period is also of service. Teachers may require students in academic difficulty to attend help sessions during this period. Tutoring beyond what is offered at the Academy is available at the student's expense.

The Brenau Academy Learning Center is designed for the college-preparatory student with a diagnosed learning difference. The student learns how to compensate for her learning differences in a highly supportive environment, including one-on-one tutoring by trained professionals in the field. The learning center is limited to 15 students. Early application is recommended.

FACULTY AND ADVISERS
The faculty has 6 full-time and 8 part-time members. The full-time faculty consists of 2 men and 4 women. The Assistant Dean lives on campus in addition to the house directors and security personnel. Five faculty members have master's degrees, and 4 have doctoral degrees.

The Headmaster, Frank M. Booth, graduated from Hampden-Sydney College and holds two master's degrees and a doctoral degree. He has thirty-two years of experience as a teacher, a coach, Athletic Director, Director of Studies, and Principal in single-sex, coeducational, boarding, and day schools.

Criteria for the selection of new faculty members include strong character, sound academic preparation, demonstration of subject knowledge, teaching ability, maturity, professionalism, and, above all, a desire to teach and guide young women in high school. Faculty members serve as advisers to various student groups and as chaperones and participate in intramurals and other campus activities. Personal advising is handled primarily through the counselor, but any faculty or staff member may be sought out by a student for guidance and support.

COLLEGE PLACEMENT
An adviser or guidance counselor provides assistance to all students seeking college admission. Current information is cataloged on colleges and universities, SAT and ACT procedures, and financial aid. All 13 graduates of the

class of 2004 were offered entry into colleges and universities. Recent graduates elected to attend institutions such as Atlanta College of Art, Auburn, Brenau, Furman, George Washington, Georgia Tech, Marshall, Mercer, Tufts, and the Universities of Georgia, North Carolina, Texas at Austin, and Wyoming.

STUDENT BODY AND CONDUCT
Brenau Academy enrolls 80 young women. Brenau students come from all parts of the United States and from several other countries. The majority of students are drawn from the southeastern United States.

The Academy strives to limit enrollment to students who are mature and responsible. The Student Government Association plays an integral part in directing student life and provides leadership opportunities through the Student Council and Student Judiciary Board. The Academy provides structure and positive values for student life without excessive restriction. Brenau is not designed to serve students who have major disciplinary problems, severe learning handicaps, or substance dependencies. Students who enter Brenau recognize rules and regulations as necessary factors in cooperative living and welcome opportunities for mature, independent growth.

ACADEMIC FACILITIES
The three student dormitories are connected to classrooms, recreation rooms, and administrative offices. The dining hall, Victorian performing arts theater, auditorium, gymnasium, bookstore, pool, and post office are separate facilities shared with the college. Academic facilities include spacious classrooms, a student publications office, dance studios, a $3-million library, and two computer laboratories.

BOARDING AND GENERAL FACILITIES
The Academy has three major dormitories. Girls room with other students of a similar grade level. Adult female house directors reside in each dormitory; the ratio of students to house directors is 15:1. Students are assigned to rooms by the Dean, but requests with regard to rooms and roommates may be submitted for consideration.

ATHLETICS
Both intramural and interscholastic programs are available at Brenau. The Academy fields competitive teams in volleyball and tennis. Weekly intramural activities include soccer, softball, basketball, flag football, tennis, and volleyball. Other activities include hiking, jogging, rafting, skiing, billiards, and swimming. Modern physical education facilities include a gymnasium with an indoor track, steam and sauna rooms, an exercise

and weight room, an AAU-size indoor swimming pool, and a modern tennis complex.

EXTRACURRICULAR OPPORTUNITIES
In an effort to achieve its goal of providing leadership experiences and an enriching social environment, the Academy makes many extracurricular opportunities available, particularly in the fine arts. The Atlanta Symphony and the Atlanta Ballet make regular appearances at Brenau, as well as numerous local and international performing arts groups. Convocations, both formal and informal, are also regularly scheduled on campus. Community groups in drama, art, dance, and music often include Academy students. Students participate in a variety of clubs and student interest groups. Student journalism groups publish a yearbook, a student newspaper, and a literary magazine. Driver's education is also offered when available.

Traditional activities include a Halloween party, Christmas traditions, closed weekends, Senior Vespers, and dances and activities with a local boys' academy.

Many students belong to community service and campus leadership organizations. The Key Club sponsors a Halloween party for underprivileged young girls in the community, a food drive before Thanksgiving, and a winter clothing drive. In addition, the Key Club also takes shifts ringing the Salvation Army bell during the holidays and collects for the Heart Fund. The Student Environmental Association (SEA) Club volunteers with the local Humane Society and sponsors school clean-up projects and a recycling program. An integral part in directing student life is the Student Government Association, made up of two components: the Student Council and the Judiciary Board.

Graduating seniors are honored with a year-end banquet provided by their "little sisters." An Awards Night and Fine Arts Performance precedes Graduation. Seniors wear white dresses and carry red roses at Graduation—a tradition as old as the school.

DAILY LIFE
A typical day for the Brenau student begins with breakfast, followed by the first class at 8 a.m. Generally, each class lasts 50 minutes. Classroom learning experiences may extend from 8 a.m. to 7:30 p.m., depending upon a student's schedule. Lunch is in the dining room, where students may enjoy selections from a hot food line in addition to salad, soup, baked potato, and sandwich bars. The dining room is furnished with small tables with linen tablecloths and freshly cut flowers at every meal.

Intramural and other sports and club meetings take place in the afternoon. Plenty of time is allowed for lunch and dinner, and a brief free period after dinner is followed by a 2-hour room study session. More free time is provided in the dorms before lights-out.

WEEKEND LIFE
The Academy arranges planned, supervised activities most weekends. This activity may range from a trip to the movies and a restaurant to snow-skiing trips, trips to amusement parks in Atlanta, visits to Lake Lanier Islands, or fall hikes in the north Georgia mountains. Many of these activities are offered at no cost to students. Sundays include chaperoned trips to a nearby boys' military school for its weekly parade and chapel service. Transportation is provided to take students to nearby churches, which they are encouraged to attend. Most activities are optional to the student.

All students are required to sign in and out whenever leaving the Academy. This activity is closely monitored by the house directors.

COSTS AND FINANCIAL AID
The Brenau fee for 2005–06 was $21,500 for boarding students and $9350 for day students. All meals are provided for boarders. Other expenses include books and supplies (approximately $500 per year), private music lessons, ballet lessons, and driver's education. All students pay a $2000 confirmation deposit (deducted from the tuition), and the balance is paid in August and December. Other payment plans may be arranged.

Financial aid is awarded on the basis of need, as determined by the guidelines of the School and Student Service for Financial Aid.

ADMISSIONS INFORMATION
The selection of new students at Brenau is based on a comprehensive review of the previous school's transcript of grades, three letters of recommendation, and an interview with the Dean. Brenau accepts students of all levels of academic ability. Because of the small enrollment at Brenau, admission is competitive and selective.

APPLICATION TIMETABLE
Initial inquiries are welcome at any time. Campus visits may be scheduled by appointment for any time during the week. Office hours are from 8:30 a.m. to 5 p.m., Monday through Friday. There are no application deadlines, but students are encouraged to submit an application as soon as possible to ensure an assignment to the Academy. The application fee is $25 and should be submitted with the application. Notification of acceptance can be made usually within a week of completion of the application process, and parents are expected to reply to acceptances within two weeks of notification.

ADMISSIONS CORRESPONDENCE
Director of Admissions
Brenau Academy
500 Washington Street SE
Gainesville, Georgia 30501

Phone: 770-534-6140
Fax: 770-534-6298
E-mail: enroll@brenau.edu
Web site: http://www.brenauacademy.org

BRENTWOOD COLLEGE SCHOOL

Mill Bay, British Columbia, Canada

Type: Coeducational boarding and day university-preparatory school
Grades: 8–12
Enrolment: 420
Head of School: Andrea M. Pennells

THE SCHOOL

Brentwood College School, founded in 1923, is a university-preparatory boarding school for boys and girls in grades 8 through 12, which also enrols a limited number of day students. Mill Bay, the small village in which the School is located, is 30 miles north of Victoria (population 200,000) and 10 miles south of Duncan (population 15,000). The School's oceanfront location and the surrounding countryside afford opportunities for a variety of outdoor sports and activities, while the proximity of Victoria provides access to numerous cultural facilities.

While the pursuit of academic excellence is the fundamental aim of Brentwood College School, the School also places a high value on fine arts and athletic pursuits as a means to broaden its students' outlook and appreciation and build their confidence. These philosophical goals are met through a challenging and innovative tripartite syllabus combining academic, artistic, and athletics programs while emphasizing full personal commitment, good conduct, humour, tolerance, and consideration of others.

Registered as a nonprofit association under the British Columbia Societies Act, the School is guided by a Board of Governors, 24 in number, many of whom are alumni. The full board meets three times annually, while the Executive, Finance, and Building committees meet more frequently.

Brentwood College School is a member of the Independent Schools Association of British Columbia, the Canadian Association of Independent Schools, and the Headmasters' Conference.

ACADEMIC PROGRAMS

The academic year, which usually begins in early September and ends in the third week of June, is divided into three terms with Christmas (three weeks) and spring (two weeks) vacations. Classes are held six days a week.

In the Senior School (grades 11 and 12), instructional groups have 18 to 22 students each, whereas in the Junior School (grades 8 through 10), the range is 16 to 20. Each student meets regularly with a designated faculty member who acts as an adviser for academic guidance and counselling purposes. Academic progress is discussed with students monthly, and academic reports, showing both percentage grades and comments, are sent to parents at the end of each term.

Members of the graduating class choose six courses from the following list, their choices depending upon the particular universities and faculties to which they are applying for postsecondary study: English (grammar, composition, and literature), mathematics (algebra, geometry, calculus, and computer science), history, geography, French, Spanish, economics, law, and science (chemistry, physics, and biology). The course of studies below grade 12 is designed to prepare students for their senior program; thus, all students at all grade levels are required to take English, foreign language studies, mathematics, the three science disciplines, history, and geography.

The development of skills in the fine arts and in information technology represents an important aspect of a Brentwood education. Courses offered include drawing and painting, ceramics, sculpture, choral and instrumental music, drama, photography, dance, computer graphics, Web page design, and business management. All students in each year must enrol in at least one of these courses—up to a maximum of four—and may vary their decisions from year to year to develop a general background of experience. On the other hand, for students seriously interested in the fine arts as a career, year-to-year specialization is possible, leading to the development of the portfolios necessary to support applications to fine arts schools at the postsecondary level.

FACULTY AND ADVISERS

Andrea M. Pennells, Head of School, holds a Master of Arts degree from the University of Edinburgh and a Master of Education degree from the University of British Columbia. Prior to her appointment as Head, she served at Brentwood for eighteen years in successive roles as teacher, Houseparent, Head of the English Department, Director of Fine Arts, and Assistant Head.

The full-time faculty consists of 42 teachers (31 men and 11 women), 18 of whom live on campus. They hold thirty-three baccalaureate degrees, sixteen master's degrees, and one doctorate, representing study at major universities in Canada, England, Ireland, and Scotland. Thirteen part-time instructors teach visual and performing arts, and additional part-time instructors assist in coaching major sports.

COLLEGE PLACEMENT

It is expected that all students will wish to pursue postsecondary studies. A university entrance planning department provides comprehensive advice about all major schools in North America and in Europe and supervises all aspects of the application process, including registration for SATs and application for university scholarships. Senior students who register in enriched courses in calculus, physics, biology, economics, English literature, French, and history may also choose to participate in the Advanced Placement Program administered by the College Board in Princeton, New Jersey.

Recent Brentwood graduates have studied at all major Canadian universities; at American universities, including Berkeley, Harvard, Princeton, Stanford, the University of Washington, and Yale; and at prestigious institutes of higher learning in Europe.

STUDENT BODY AND CONDUCT

Brentwood has 196 boarding boys, 144 boarding girls, and 80 day students. Students come primarily from British Columbia and Alberta; others come from the remaining Canadian provinces and from the United States and other countries. The student body typically represents more than twenty nationalities. Day students come from the Duncan and Mill Bay areas.

The School expects of its students the self-discipline, mutual respect, and consideration for others that is fundamental to an orderly, wholesome daily life in the School community.

ACADEMIC FACILITIES

The main School buildings are located on the 70-acre campus, 28 acres of which are situated on the seafront. In addition to the current classroom block and auditorium, the Academic Centre is a modern three-storey facility that houses well-furnished classrooms, an expanded library, administrative and counselling offices, an art gallery, and exhibition spaces. The classrooms are designed to form distinct teaching areas and include six fully appointed science laboratories, two computer systems instruction centres, an audiovisual language laboratory, and separate studios for dance, pottery, sculpture, photography, painting, and drawing. A raked Conference/Lecture Theatre is equipped for mixed-media presentations and also serves as a recital room and recording facility. In addition, a 20,000-square-foot performing arts facility that opened in 2003, equipped with a 431 seat theatre, a dance studio, a media arts room, a music study area, and other amenities has been a welcome addition to the campus.

BOARDING AND GENERAL FACILITIES

Campus residential facilities include four houses for boys, designed to accommodate an average of 2 or 3 students per room, and three houses for girls, designed to accommodate 2 or 3 students per room. In each case, the houses provide recreation rooms, snack kitchens, and house reference libraries. All residences have faculty advisers serving as houseparents, counsellors, and tutors. The campus also includes a dining hall that seats 450 and full laundry services.

The school doctor is regularly on call, 24-hour daily nursing service is provided, and full hospital facilities are available. By arrangement, regular and specialized dental needs can be accommodated.

ATHLETICS

Athletics opportunities offered to students on a term-by-term basis are intended to promote

---

sportsmanship, bodily health, and skill development through team and individual sports and through outdoor noncompetitive activities. All students, regardless of their ability, receive the same instructional program, and all must participate. Activities offered include badminton, basketball, cross-country running, cycling, field hockey, ice hockey, golf, rugby, rowing, sailing, soccer, squash, tennis, track and field, triathlon, and volleyball. The outdoor program emphasizes climbing, orienteering, kayaking, and canoeing, and students may take advantage of School or local community programs. Residences compete in an intramural program in most sports.

The campus has a sports complex, an indoor rowing centre, eight tennis courts, three squash courts, and sports and recreation fields.

EXTRACURRICULAR OPPORTUNITIES
Members of the grade 12 class, through prefectorial appointments, are responsible for many aspects of daily school life. Prefects are expected to provide leadership for younger members of the School and support for the staff in administering the daily routine. In addition, a Student Activities Council, representative of each grade level, consults and works with staff members to plan social events, special concerts, and student involvement in community charities.

Parents are encouraged to visit the School at any time. Traditionally, they attend such events as seasonal celebrations, performing arts shows and concerts, the Annual Brentwood Regatta, the Graduation Dinner and Dance, and the Awards Day Ceremonies.

DAILY LIFE
Academic classes are held six days a week between 8:15 a.m. and 1:15 p.m. Whereas the academic programs are featured during the morning hours, sports and fine arts opportunities are offered on alternate afternoons in hour-long periods, to which a student is expected to make a minimum 2-hour commitment.

A quiet, controlled study session is held in the residences from 6:45 to 8:45 p.m. This study time, while adequate for Junior School students, is increased by student initiative to meet Senior School academic needs.

At least once a week, there is an all-school assembly. Meals are taken in a pleasant, modern dining room.

WEEKEND LIFE
In each of the three terms, a midterm break of five days is provided to accommodate students who wish to visit their family. In addition, a number of other Sunday- and weekend-leave privileges may be obtained by request from the Houseparent.

For students remaining on campus, the School provides numerous recreational and sports activities. Dances, concerts, and similar entertainment are scheduled weekly, often with nearby independent schools. Weekend skiing trips are planned regularly during the second term. In addition, students participate in School-sponsored trips to Victoria for music, theatre, and other cultural events.

COSTS AND FINANCIAL AID
For Canadian students entering all grades, tuition and boarding fees are Can$30,300. For American students entering all grades, the fees are Can$36,300; for residents of other countries, the fees are Can$39,000, payable at the time of acceptance is confirmed. Canadian-based parents may elect to pay the annual fee in full before the beginning of the first term or in three segments in advance of each term. Day student tuition is Can$16,300. There is a 5 percent reduction on aggregate annual fees for siblings during their joint enrolment. Tuition insurance is required, the premium for which is waived should the entire annual fee be paid in advance. Parents are responsible for transportation costs between the student's home and the School. Arrangements for

such travel, including transportation to and from the airport, are provided by the School's travel office.

Scholarship awards are based on academic standing and the scholarship exam and are available only to new Canadian Grade 8 and 9 boarding students. Bursary Awards are based on financial need and are available to all new Canadian students.

ADMISSIONS INFORMATION
Students capable of succeeding in a university-preparatory program are best suited to the School's course of studies. Admission, however, is based not only on an applicant's academic potential but also on his or her character and willingness to participate actively in the fine arts and athletics sections of the School's program. In addition to taking the required entrance examination and having an interview, candidates must submit previous school records and a recommendation from the principal of their present school. Brentwood makes arrangements for the entrance test to be taken at the home location of a student should distance make a campus visit impractical.

APPLICATION TIMETABLE
Applications should be submitted as early as possible in the preceding year for September entrance. On behalf of a student granted a place, a $750 registration fee and a $2000 deposit against fees must be paid at the time acceptance is finalized. Registration charges and fee deposits paid in advance are fully refunded should acceptance not be confirmed.

ADMISSIONS CORRESPONDENCE
Mr. Andy Rodford, Director of Admissions
Brentwood College School
2735 Mount Baker Road
Mill Bay, British Columbia V0R 2P1
Canada

Phone: 250-743-5521
Fax: 250-743-2911
E-mail: admissions@brentwood.bc.ca
Web site: http://www.brentwood.bc.ca

BREWSTER ACADEMY

Wolfeboro, New Hampshire

1820

Type: Coeducational boarding and day independent college-preparatory school
Grades: 9–12, postgraduate year
Enrollment: 361
Head of School: Dr. Michael E. Cooper

THE SCHOOL

Brewster Academy was founded in 1820 and in the past decade has become known worldwide for innovation and performance in secondary education. The Brewster program, which is based on the School Design Model[SM], provides students with a highly personalized education within a vigorous college-preparatory environment. The program is designed to meet students at their current level of performance and accelerate them in their mastery of skills and knowledge, ensuring that a Brewster graduate leaves the Academy prepared for the challenges of college and life after college. The Brewster program is comprehensive and multilayered and combines the best established practices in teaching, curriculum, and resources. An academic support program offers daily individual course instruction by learning-skills teachers who work with subject teachers to support and develop strategies for motivated students with high potential who have learning-style differences.

Central to the program is a philosophy that challenges and supports each student appropriately and recognizes the need for each student to pursue a sequence of four interrelated goals: the building of self-confidence by developing an individual's most effective learning style, the cultivation of responsibility and a lifelong love of learning, the development of learning skills so that students can learn for themselves in a variety of academic mediums, and the acquisition of skills and content that predict success in college.

Brewster's location on Lake Winnipesaukee, just south of the White Mountains, offers the ideal setting for outdoor activities. The 80-acre campus encompasses a half mile of the lake's southeastern shoreline, including beaches and docks. Wolfeboro is 1¾ hours from Boston and 1 hour from Manchester and Portsmouth. Nearby airports are in Manchester and Laconia.

A nonprofit corporation, the Academy is directed by the Head of School for a 25-member Board of Trustees that meets four times annually. Among the trustees are representatives of the Parents' Association, the Alumni Association, and the John Brewster Estate. The Academy's endowment is $12 million. Plant valuation is $37 million.

Brewster Academy is accredited by the New England Association of Schools and Colleges, Inc. It is a member of the Independent Schools Association of Northern New England, the National Association of Independent Schools, the Association of Boarding Schools, and the Secondary School Admission Test Board.

ACADEMIC PROGRAMS

The Brewster program is based on the School Design Model[SM], a successful education reform model that was implemented in 1993 and has caught the attention of educators nationally and

internationally. The model combines established best teaching practices with a mastery-based curriculum developed for individual learning styles, within a technology-rich environment that offers students a highly personalized education. Since its implementation, SAT scores have increased 92 points (*International Journal of Educational Reform*, April 2000), and Brewster's success has been documented in education, technology, and mainstream publications, including the *New York Times*, *USA Today*, and *Worth* magazine.

Learning skills receive special emphasis through academic support programs. Brewster was one of the first preparatory schools in the country with such a program, and its success has made it a model for the independent school world. In this program, students who have high potential but need additional support in their studies have their classroom instruction complemented and enhanced through active, ongoing communication among instructional support and course instructors.

Brewster offers honors-level classes in all courses and eight Advanced Placement classes. Parents receive student evaluations six times yearly and weekly interim progress reports when necessary. Students are required to follow a schedule of five courses, most of which meet five times weekly. Study hours are from 8 to 10 p.m. most nights.

A variety of fine and performing arts classes are offered—some as part of the required curriculum and others as academic enrichment classes. Offerings include studio arts, painting, drawing, pottery, photography, and drama as well as art foundation, history, and theory classes. Students who are interested in music have four ensemble choices, including HOWL (the school's award-winning eclectic chorus), Clearlakes Chorale, the Chamber Orchestra, and a jazz band.

The Brewster class size averages 11. The overall student-teacher ratio is 6:1.

FACULTY AND ADVISERS

Head of School Michael E. Cooper, Ph.D., leads a faculty of 63 full-time teachers. Dr. Cooper received his doctorate in child and family studies from Syracuse University and received his M.Ed. from St. Lawrence University and his B.A. from the State University of New York.

The Academy's teachers are prepared and trained at the Brewster Summer Institute, a six-week professional development program that is designed to assist teachers in accelerating student growth. Each instructor is placed on a 9-member teaching team. Each team teaches and advises students in a single grade, allowing for constant communication and interaction. Teams meet three times weekly to discuss each student's

progress and performance. The adviser serves as the major link among students, parents, teachers, and administrators.

COLLEGE PLACEMENT

Preparing students for college may be best expressed by the extent to which they return after their first year. A recent survey showed that Brewster graduates recorded approximately 95 percent retention from their freshman to sophomore year. The national average is about 75 percent. Colleges attended by the class of 2005 include American, Boston University, Cornell, Dartmouth, George Washington, NYU, Providence, Skidmore, Stanford, the U.S. Air Force Academy, the University of Virginia, and Wake Forest.

College advising begins in the eleventh grade, with the college counseling dean and faculty advisers assisting juniors and seniors in selecting colleges.

STUDENT BODY AND CONDUCT

The 2005–06 student body included 361 students: 191 boarding boys, 89 boarding girls, 45 day boys, and 36 day girls. There were 16 postgraduates. Students came from thirty states and twelve countries.

The Student Leadership Program fosters student involvement in the operation of the Academy. Since the Academy is central to the entire student community for most of the year, it has the responsibility to offer students the opportunity to realize and develop leadership traits. The Student Council oversees student residential life and at times makes recommendations to the faculty concerning changes in rules and regulations. The Student Judicial Review Board was established to help each student develop self-discipline and personal strength. The board hears cases of student violations of school rules, clarifies the circumstances surrounding the situations, and recommends possible disciplinary actions to the Dean of Students.

ACADEMIC FACILITIES

Each grade has its own academic center complete with classrooms, a laboratory, and student and teacher work areas. In addition to the physical work space, all students and faculty members use laptop computers, and teachers use a powerful suite of software tools to design and implement curriculum and to ensure constant communication among students, parents, and administrators. Through online portfolios, students post their work to be reviewed and evaluated by faculty members and to share with parents. Students also have online access to grades to help them evaluate their own progress.

An art center is home to pottery, photography, and visual art studios. A computer graphics center features the latest computers and software,

while the journalism and desktop publishing room features the latest in publishing software, scanners, and digital equipment.

BOARDING AND GENERAL FACILITIES
Twenty family-style dormitories (most overlooking Lake Winnipesaukee) house Brewster's boarding students. The environment is family oriented. Each dorm plans community and social activities through their weekly meetings. An upperclass proctor and faculty community-life parents ensure constant communication and availability within this small setting. The Spaulding-Emerson Student Center, with a snack bar, a lounge area, and recreation facilities, is in Estabrook Hall.

ATHLETICS
All students participate in at least one season of interscholastic sports. Students choose to participate in the school's enrichment program during the other two seasons. The enrichment program provides choices in academic and athletic/fitness classes that each meet three days per week, providing students with a six-day program. Academic enrichment opportunities include drama, studio art, pottery, music, and computer graphics.

Athletic programs include baseball, basketball, crew, cross-country running, field hockey, golf, horseback riding, ice hockey (girls' and boys'), lacrosse, outdoor skills, recreational skiing and snowboarding, sailing, skiing (Alpine and Nordic), soccer, softball, strength training and conditioning, student athletic training, tennis, and yoga.

The Smith Center for Athletics and Wellness opened in September 2002. This 50,000-square-foot facility features a four-lane, 200-meter indoor track; a convertible surface turf; two basketball courts; a fitness center; and floor-to-ceiling netting for baseball and lacrosse practice. A climbing wall is in the Haines Climbing Barn.

Outdoor facilities include seven athletic fields and a boathouse (with panoramic views of the lake and cove), which provides storage and work areas for rowing shells and "420" racing sailboats. The Outdoor Skills Program takes advantage of the White Mountain National Forest for hiking, canoeing, camping, and rock climbing.

EXTRACURRICULAR OPPORTUNITIES
Through Brewster's Leadership Program, students are responsible, under faculty member guidance, for the cleanliness of dormitories and grounds, for dormitory government through floor proctors, and for school discipline set by the Student Judicial Review Board. Journalism students produce and publish the school newspaper, yearbook, and literary magazine. Other student groups include the National Honor Society, the Gold Key Society, the debate team, Interact Club, Faith Community, Brewster Big Friends, the Gay Straight Alliance, and an improv club. Each year, the drama program presents three stage productions, focusing on acting and the technical aspects of theater.

DAILY LIFE
Weekdays begin with breakfast at 7 a.m.; classes start at 8 and run 50 minutes each for eight periods. There are five periods on Wednesday and Saturday. School assemblies for information, discussions, or entertainment are held biweekly. Athletics begin after the last class. Community family-style meals are served once a week, and other meals are served cafeteria-style. Supervised evening study is from 8 to 10 p.m. Lights are out at 10:30 (11 for seniors and postgraduates).

Interscholastic athletic competitions are held Wednesday and Saturday after classes, which end at noon.

WEEKEND LIFE
Social activities include gatherings at the student center, concerts and dances, and weekend movies. Trips are planned to concerts, theaters, museums, and professional sports events around New England. Winter Carnival is at the end of January, and Family Weekends are in October and April. Coed intramural football is played in the fall, and coed intramural softball is played in the spring. Students may be granted permission for time away on some weekends.

COSTS AND FINANCIAL AID
Tuition for 2005–06 was $34,980 for boarders and $20,720 for day students. A tuition payment plan is available. Laundry service and a drawing account for allowances are optional. Reservation deposits of $2000 for boarding, $600 for day, and $3450 for international students are applied toward books, athletics supplies, and trips.

Brewster subscribes to the School and Student Service for Financial Aid. Scholarships are granted on the basis of need. In 2005–06, 28 percent of the students received financial aid totaling $1.6 million. Under the Work Grant Program, students work in offices on campus to defray tuition charges.

ADMISSIONS INFORMATION
Candidates are evaluated based on their previous school record, interests and nonacademic accomplishments, and commitment to scholastic and social growth. References and recommendations are considered carefully. Results of the SSAT form part of the admissions review. An interview is required for both the candidate and parents. Admission is granted according to the Academy's judgment of the candidate's entire record, without regard to sex, race, religion, color, or national or ethnic origin.

APPLICATION TIMETABLE
The initial inquiry should be made as soon as a student and family begin to consider private school. A campus tour is part of the interview. Thereafter, a formal application with a $35 nonrefundable fee ($75 for international students) should be submitted. After December, transcripts and recommendations from the candidate's principal or headmaster and teachers are requested. Applicants should take the SSAT in December or January. Brewster notifies students of acceptance on March 10 and offers rolling admissions thereafter, contingent upon openings.

ADMISSIONS CORRESPONDENCE
Lynne M. Palmer, Director of Admission
Brewster Academy
80 Academy Drive
Wolfeboro, New Hampshire 03894

Phone: 603-569-7200
Fax: 603-569-7272
E-mail: admissions@brewsteracademy.org
Web site: http://www.brewsteracademy.org

BRIDGTON ACADEMY

North Bridgton, Maine

Type: Boys' boarding and day college-preparatory school
Enrollment: 190
Head of School: David N. Hursty

THE SCHOOL

Bridgton Academy is the only college-preparatory school in the nation that is devoted exclusively to the education of young men in a postgraduate year of study. Its mission is to provide the opportunity to develop the academic skills, study skills, self-discipline, maturity, and confidence that is necessary to succeed in college. This one-year program is a transitional one, designed to replicate the college experience and environment as much as possible, yet with more structure and support than that offered by colleges. As a result of this focused year, graduates of Bridgton Academy are better prepared to meet the challenges of college.

Bridgton Academy was established by the Massachusetts legislature in 1808, when Maine was still part of Massachusetts. The impetus for founding the school came from a group of 37 local residents who provided financial support. Its original purpose was to provide secondary education for boys and girls. In 1964, a new academic plan was adopted whereby lower grades were dropped and girls were no longer enrolled; Bridgton Academy became a one-year college-preparatory school offering specific programs for older boys in grade 12 or a postgraduate year. Bridgton is now a school for postgraduate study, and students enter for one year only. Academics, guidance, athletics, and student life are planned to meet the needs of the student who is capable of college-level work and will benefit from an additional year of study and growth before college entrance.

The 50-acre campus is located in North Bridgton, Maine, on the shore of Long Lake in the foothills of the White Mountains, 40 miles west of Portland, Maine.

A nonprofit and nonsectarian institution, Bridgton Academy is directed by a self-perpetuating Board of Trustees. Approximately 6,000 graduates participate in an active alumni association, class reunions, Alumni Day, and regional alumni meetings.

Bridgton Academy is accredited by the New England Association of Schools and Colleges. It holds memberships in the National Association of Independent Schools, Independent Schools Association of Northern New England, Maine Association of Independent Schools, National Association of Secondary School Principals, National Association for College Admission Counseling, and Council for Advancement and Support of Education.

ACADEMIC PROGRAMS

A special feature of Bridgton Academy that no other New England independent school offers is the College Articulation Program (CAP). In cooperation with neighboring colleges, the Bridgton faculty teaches courses on the school's campus that carry college credit. The CAP offerings include calculus, college chemistry, college English, constitutional history of the United States, introductory computer, introduction to environmental issues, introduction to political science, introduction to the Internet/World Wide Web, marine biology/oceanography, precalculus, sociology, and Western civilization. The program enables students to enter college with credit toward graduation and/or to eliminate required col-

lege courses. CAP credit has been accepted by most of the colleges and universities that Bridgton graduates are currently attending. Students may also elect to take the CAP courses without registering for college credit.

All students are required to take a minimum of four major courses. Some students take five classes.

SAT/ACT preparation is provided in the classroom. An SAT/ACT prep program is also offered each fall at additional cost.

For students with learning disabilities, Bridgton offers the Program for Academic Support (PAS), a learning skills program offering individual and small group instruction.

Grades and teacher comments are issued in October, December, March, and May. Interim reports are mailed to parents when appropriate. The Academy operates on a typical two-semester college calendar, with final examinations in December and May.

Students receive a certificate validating completion of a fifth-year program of studies. Classes range in size from 6 to 15 students.

FACULTY AND ADVISERS

There are 20 faculty members who teach full-time and hold twenty baccalaureate and four master's degrees. Seventeen faculty members and administrators live on the campus, with at least one faculty member in each dormitory.

Bridgton Academy faculty members are committed seven days a week to their students and to the postgraduate year. In addition to teaching, most members serve as coaches, dorm parents, and activity leaders, and they accompany students on weekend outings and field trips. All serve as advisers to groups of 6 to 8 students each.

Headmaster David N. Hursty earned a B.S. from Salem State College and an M.A. from Georgetown University. Prior to his arrival at Bridgton Academy fifteen years ago, Mr. Hursty had served as headmaster at two other college-preparatory schools. During his fifteen-year tenure at Bridgton Academy, he has served in a variety of roles, including Director of External Affairs, Director of Technology, Academic Dean, teacher, and coach, prior to assuming his current position during the 2002 year.

COLLEGE PLACEMENT

The college counseling program begins early in the fall. Each student is assigned to 1 of 3 experienced counselors, who gives personal counseling throughout the year on the college admissions process. Using a student's career plans, desired college characteristics, and activities, each counselor helps prepares a list of appropriate colleges.

The Academy has an extensive library of college catalogs and college reference materials, including computer-based lists of college programs. Students are encouraged to participate in group meetings with the many college admissions representatives who visit the campus each year. The College Counseling Office helps make appointments for visits to colleges and strongly advises students to visit all the colleges in which they are seriously interested. The student adviser also writes a thought-

ful letter of recommendation for each advisee that accompanies the Academy transcript and provides supplemental, meaningful information. Open communication among the student, parents, the adviser, and the college counselor is stressed.

SAT and ACT examinations are administered at the Academy in November, December, and January. The median scores on the SAT for the class of 2005 were 500 verbal and 480 math.

There were 177 graduates in the class of 2005. These students are attending eighty-six colleges and universities, including Assumption, Bentley, Bryant, Clarkson, Colby, Colgate, Colorado College, Denison, Fordham, George Washington, Gettysburg, Hartwick, Loyola, Ohio Wesleyan, Providence, Saint Michael's, Skidmore, Stonehill, Union, the U.S. Naval Academy, Worcester Polytechnic, and the Universities of Maine, Massachusetts, New Hampshire, North Carolina, Rhode Island, Southern Maine, and Vermont.

STUDENT BODY AND CONDUCT

The 2004–05 student body consisted of 190 students. Students come from twenty-six states, with a majority from Massachusetts and the other New England states. The Academy also enrolls students from outside the United States.

The Academy acts on the assumption that students enter the school with a serious purpose and that their conscience and good judgment are sufficient guides to behavior. The Academy's discipline is not adapted to students who require severe restriction. Its government is one of principles, although rules and penalties for infractions exist and are enforced.

ACADEMIC FACILITIES

The Cyrus Hamlin Study Center contains eight classrooms, an anatomy and physiology science laboratory, a chemistry lab, a physics and oceanography lab, a writing center, and a computer center equipped with nineteen IBM-compatible microcomputers.

Since 1995, the Hamlin Study Center has been networked to form a campus local area network (LAN). More than thirty public-access computers in this building and 180 dormitory nodes are connected by fiber optics to a fast Ethernet network. In addition, the campus has a T1 connection to the Internet. Students and faculty members make extensive use of this network to access the resources of the Internet to communicate via e-mail and to use technology as part of the classroom experience.

The Academy has also wired its dormitories so that students may connect personal computers directly to the Academy's network, including the Internet.

The Ernest N. Stevens Library maintains a 900-volume reference collection, 8,000 circulating volumes, several online databases, and forty periodicals. Eleven computers in the library offer access to the Internet, several research databases, local and statewide catalogs, and word processing.

The Anne Weston Twitchell Memorial Chapel is used for assemblies and music and drama activi-

ties. The Spratt-Mead Museum contains many collections of historical value, including Native American artifacts.

BOARDING AND GENERAL FACILITIES
The boarding students are housed in nine dormitories ranging in capacity from 6 to 40 students each. Most rooms are doubles, but there are some singles and triples. All dormitories include faculty apartments. Homes for the Headmaster, the Dean of Students, the Director of Admission, and the Director of Athletics are also located on the school property.

The Richard L. Goldsmith Student Center provides a dining hall, a student lounge, a game room, and a school store.

ATHLETICS
Bridgton Academy's athletic teams compete in Alpine skiing baseball, basketball, football, golf, ice hockey, lacrosse, soccer, and tennis with college and university freshman and junior varsity teams and with some other prep schools. There are no structured physical education classes, but students are encouraged to participate on teams or in the skiing, intramural, or Outing Club activities each afternoon during the week.

Memorial Gymnasium houses a basketball court, two locker rooms, a weight room, a training room, a cardio room, and an Outing Club activity room. Outdoor facilities consist of a football field, soccer field, baseball field, practice field, and two all-weather tennis courts. In 1998, the Bridgton Ice Arena was constructed on the Bridgton Academy campus. Shawnee Peak ski area is within 5 miles of the Academy, and the Alpine ski teams, as well as recreational skiers, may ski every afternoon. A golf course is located within 2 miles of the Academy.

EXTRACURRICULAR OPPORTUNITIES
Guest lecturers or performances are scheduled throughout the year. An art studio is available for student use each afternoon.

Many clubs and organizations vary from year to year, depending on student interest, but certain activities remain constant. Students participate in the Student Dorm Council, the production of the yearbook, drama, and community service projects, including the Big Brother program. The Outing Club, directed by an experienced faculty member, provides daily and weekend activities. The club has its own cabin on Stearns Pond, 8 miles from the campus. The Academy also offers recreational skiing on a daily basis at Shawnee Peak. A season's pass to Shawnee Peak is distributed free of charge to all students who want one.

DAILY LIFE
The school day is divided into seven 50-minute classes meeting from 7:45 a.m. until 2:25 p.m. Monday through Friday. On Sunday through Thursday, there is a mandatory supervised study period from 7:30 to 9:30 p.m. All students must be in their dormitories no later than 10:30 p.m. Sunday through Thursday. Quiet hours in the dormitories begin at 11 p.m.

WEEKEND LIFE
Frequent weekend trips are planned for shopping, sports events, and numerous other entertainment opportunities. Transportation is provided for those wishing to attend churches in the area. All campus facilities are available to the students throughout the weekend. Day students are welcome at all events.

Those students who are in good academic standing and who have written permission from their parents may receive weekend permission from the Dean of Students to leave campus. Some weekends are not open. All students who have weekend permission are required to be back on campus for study hall at 7:30 on Sunday evening.

COSTS AND FINANCIAL AID
For 2006–07, tuition for boarding students is $33,500, which includes room and board; tuition for day students is $15,000. A $1500 enrollment deposit must accompany the enrollment agreement. This deposit is credited toward the first payment and is nonrefundable. There are three payment plans: Plan A requires payment of 100 percent of the tuition and charges on August 1; Plan B requires three payments due July 1, September 1, and November 1; Plan C, a seven-payment plan, requires a one-time fee of $40 for administration and authorization to debit checking accounts for each payment.

Partial scholarships are offered to a limited number of students each year on the basis of financial need. The Financial Aid PROFILE Form must be filed with the College Scholarship Service in Princeton, New Jersey, to qualify for financial aid. Bridgton Academy's code number is 3269. Those candidates applying for financial aid at prep schools only may obtain the Parents Financial Statement (PFS) of the School and Student Service for Financial Aid or from the Academy and may submit this form in lieu of the CSS PROFILE form, using Bridgton Academy's code number, 1840.

ADMISSIONS INFORMATION
Bridgton Academy seeks students who are seriously interested in preparing for college and who will be mature members of the student body. Candidates must submit a completed application, SAT/ACT scores, a transcript of the high school record, recommendations from teachers, and other references. On-campus interviews are required unless the applicant lives in a distant region of the United States.

The admission staff is as interested in a candidate's personal qualities and enthusiasm as in the SAT/ACT scores and high school grades. The staff depends upon recommendations from current teachers, guidance counselors, and other friends to evaluate the applicant's personality, motivation, and potential abilities. Bridgton Academy does not discriminate on the basis of race, color, or national or ethnic origin in the administration of its educational policies, admission policies, scholarships, or sports or other school-administered programs.

APPLICATION TIMETABLE
The application fee is $50. The Academy has a rolling admission policy. Applicants are notified of the admission decision as soon as all required materials have been reviewed. Interviews and campus tours may be arranged Monday through Thursday from 9:30 a.m. to 1:30 p.m., and Friday at 10:30 and 11:30 a.m.

ADMISSIONS CORRESPONDENCE
Lisa M. Antell, Director of Admission and
   Financial Aid
Bridgton Academy
P.O. Box 292
North Bridgton, Maine 04057

Phone: 207-647-3322
Fax: 207-647-8513
E-mail: admit@bridgtonacademy.org
Web site: http://www.bridgtonacademy.org

THE BROOK HILL SCHOOL

Bullard, Texas

Type: Coeducational boarding (grades 8–12 and day (grades PK–12) college-preparatory school
Grades: Lower School, pre-K–5; Middle School, 6–8; and Upper School, 9–12
Enrollment: School total: 310; Upper School: 125
Head of School: Rod Fletcher, Headmaster

THE SCHOOL

What began in the early 1990s as one man's dream is today a reality: a vibrant, independent Christian school, set on a beautiful 120-acre campus in east Texas, with a threefold mission that permeates every aspect of Brook Hill's existence. Its mission is to provide excellence in college-preparatory education, affirm the gifts and challenge the potential of each student, and encourage students to honor God through Christlike character. Although Brook Hill is a nondenominational Christian school, the Bible is studied for credit, and students attend Chapel services weekly.

The School's academic doors were opened in fall 1997 with 31 students in grades 6, 7, and 8. A grade level was then added each year, reaching a full complement of 5 through 12 in fall 2001. The Lower School, with grades pre-K–5, opened its doors in the fall of 2005. An international/domestic boarding program was established in summer 2003, and Brook Hill has now hosted more than 30 students from China, Japan, Korea, Kosovo, Mexico, South Africa, Taiwan, and Vietnam. Less than a 2-hour drive from Brook Hill is Dallas, a major multicultural city and a hub for national and international flights. Students enjoy the day-to-day benefits of Brook Hill's quiet country setting as well as its proximity to all that Dallas has to offer. The Brook Hill School is a nonprofit corporation directed by a self-perpetuating 12-member Board of Trustees made up of community leaders and parents of Brook Hill students. The School has earned accreditation through the Southern Association of Colleges and Schools and is also affiliated with the Association of Christian Schools International, the College Board, the National Association of Independent Schools, the National and Texas Association of College Admission Counselors, and the Texas Association of Private and Parochial Schools.

ACADEMIC PROGRAMS

The academic year consists of two semesters, totaling thirty-six weeks (176 days) of instruction. The current class schedule for Middle and Upper School students includes the seven-period day, with each class meeting for 50-minute periods. Most courses meet four days per week (one day per week is double blocked), while some meet one, two, or perhaps three days per week. Courses in grades 9–12 include a college-preparatory program accredited by the Southern Association of Colleges and Schools. As Brook Hill is a nondenominational Christian school, formal courses in Bible are required. Tutorial sessions are scheduled within the academic day to help the struggling student.

The Brook Hill School offers a college-preparatory program, including honors, pre-Advanced Placement (AP), and Advanced Placement courses and dual-credit classes. Brook Hill has expanded its honors/pre-AP/AP program in the last two years. Courses currently offered include honors Spanish I, II, and III; honors French I, II, and III; honors algebra I (eighth grade only); honors algebra II; honors geometry; pre-AP precalculus; AP calculus; honors chemistry; pre-AP biology; AP anatomy and physiology; honors physics; pre-AP history 9 and 10; honors history 11; AP government and economics; pre-AP English 9 and 10; honors English 11; AP language and composition 11; AP European history 11; AP U.S. history; and AP literature and composition 12.

Students enrolled in AP courses are expected to take the College Board's AP exam each May.

Brook Hill offers a classically based, liberal arts education from a Christian worldview based on universal truths, foundational principles, enduring traditions, and the great literature of history, taught in a multisensory, integrated format. Brook Hill's history/English program focuses on an intensive study of great writings, people, events, works, and ideas that have formed and reformed civilization as we know it. Normative works of Western culture are studied within their historical settings, helping the students understand how the works and the people who wrote them were influenced by their time. It also reveals the universal nature of the great works, which are classics because they somehow speak to all people at all times. The courses are organized chronologically, moving from ancient civilizations to modern times. Emphasis is placed upon reading, writing, and speaking/listening skills. A full selection of fine arts and athletic options also exists. Art, vocal music, drama, and orchestra programs are offered. A strings academy is also being designed. Athletic options include soccer, football, volleyball, basketball, golf, tennis, baseball, softball, and physical conditioning. Electives such as yearbook are also offered.

Middle School students in grades 6–8 are required to take a liberal selection of classes that expose them to academics, the arts, and athletics as well as provide a rich developmental experience that prepares them for the Upper School years. Foreign language, Latin, and Bible classes are required of all students. Frequent field trips and hands-on projects enrich the Middle School experience, and technology is incorporated into many group and individual projects.

The Lower School program provides the foundation for the Middle and Upper School college-preparatory experience. Instruction is based on time-proven methods and valuable insights into cognitive and developmental processes that are framed by the Christian worldview that permeates the academic program. The Lower School strives to develop the intellectual skills and personal traits of students that produce lifelong learners and responsible citizens. The program includes both curricular and extracurricular programs, including foreign language, fine arts, and athletics. Grades are reported to parents four times per year, and detailed comments on performance are written two times per year. Parents and students have access to grades and homework assignments via the Web 24 hours a day, seven days per week.

The average Upper School class size is 18; the student-teacher ratio is 7:1. Each spring, several educational trips are planned, including an eighth-grade trip to the Washington, D.C., area and an Upper School trip to Italy.

FACULTY AND ADVISERS

The Upper and Middle School faculty consists of 27 members, each holding baccalaureate degrees. Sixty percent of the faculty members hold graduate degrees. One holds a doctoral degree. Several support staff members assist the administration and teachers, and an RN is also on staff. Eleven Lower School faculty members who hold a minimum of a bachelor's degree were added during the summer of 2005,

and more faculty members will be added as Brook Hill School moves toward full capacity.

Faculty members not only interact with the students in the classroom, but also monitor study hours, assume responsibility for the boarders during weekend shifts, offer their time to students each morning from Monday through Friday during the "Backwork" period, share meals with the students, and act as advisers for small, grade-level groups. The Brook Hill School offers faculty members medical and retirement plans, leaves, and absences. Teachers are encouraged to continue postgraduate studies, receive AP training, and become lifelong learners.

COLLEGE PLACEMENT

College preparation at the Brook Hill School is based on a developmental guidance program targeting students in grade 8 for college preparation. Individualized conferences are held at the end of each year to evaluate and assess students' progress. Each fall, numerous college representatives visit the School for interviews. In the spring of the junior year, during interviews with the Academic Guidance Counselor, each student is assisted with making tentative college choices, arrangements for college visits and interviews, and application procedures. Each student is encouraged to visit as many colleges as possible throughout their years in high school. In the senior year, students' college choices are correlated with SAT scores, grade point averages, major areas of study, and career choices. Parents are encouraged to participate in all of these decisions. The mean SAT scores for the graduating class of 2004 were 614 verbal and 568 math, which is a total composite of 1182. The median score was 1180. Graduates of the Brook Hill School have been accepted to colleges and universities such as Agnes Scott, Auburn, Barnard, Baylor, Cornell, Embry-Riddle, Mount Holyoke, Randolph Macon, Smith, Texas A&M, Trinity, Tulane, Wellesley, and the University of Texas.

STUDENT BODY AND CONDUCT

In 2005–06, grade 6 enrolled 30 students; grade 7, 17; and grade 8, 35 (2 boarding students). Upper School students in grade 9 included 20 boys and 15 girls (4 boarding boys and 4 boarding girls); grade 10 hosted 18 boys and 12 girls (4 boarding boys and 1 boarding girl); grade 11, 24 boys and 14 girls (4 boarding boys and 3 boarding girls); and grade 12, 18 boys and 8 girls (3 boarding boys and 2 boarding girls).

Boarding students have represented seven countries: China, Japan, Kosovo, Mexico, the Republic of Korea, Taiwan, and the United States. The School is also actively recruiting additional American boarding students and is expanding recruitment efforts to South America. The student body represents diverse racial, social, economic, and religious backgrounds. The community is small enough to maintain a family feel, yet rich enough in depth to provide a multicultural experience for both day and boarding students. Both boarding and day students participate in chores, helping to maintain the beautiful campus through a sense of ownership.

Students at Brook Hill School are not just taught by Christian faculty members; they are encouraged to develop the disciplines that lead to spiritual maturity. Chapel, Bible classes, and service projects are incorporated into the curriculum to energize students to discover and mature in their spiritual life.

Students must sign an honor code and are expected to maintain the integrity of the School and its philosophy both during the school day and away from the campus. Disciplinary infractions are addressed by both teacher advisers and the Dean of Students. A student-elected Honor Council works closely with the Dean of Students regarding matters of peer discipline.

ACADEMIC FACILITIES

There are currently four academic buildings on campus, consisting of approximately 75,000 square feet. Among these are The Cabin (1995), originally used as office space but now devoted to guest use and small-group meetings; Ornelas Hall (1997), which houses the Middle School classrooms, a science lab, and a library, as well as orchestra group facilities and individual practice space; Herrington Sportscenter (1997), which consists of a gymnasium, boys' and girls' dressing facilities plus visitors' locker room, a concession stand, and weight rooms; and Lauderdale Hall (1999), the Upper School building, containing The Commons (used for fine arts performances and dining), a computer lab, administrative offices, general classroom space, and two indoor science labs as well as an outdoor laboratory space. State-of-the-art facilities for the Brook Hill Lower School and athletic programs are in the works. The Lower School will house more than 350 students in grades pre-K–5. Athletic facility additions include grandstands, a scorekeepers' box, and lights to support the state champion baseball team. A field house and lighted stadium with "field turf" are excellent additions that complement the new football program.

BOARDING AND GENERAL FACILITIES

Boarding suites in two residential homes (Wayne Dement and Ruth Dement), each of which contains 7,800 square feet of living space, can accommodate 16 boarding students each (32 students total). Faculty members live and build a familylike relationship in each home. Both homes include spacious student rooms, private bathrooms for each room, a common kitchen, a TV/game room, a laundry room, a reading room with fireplace, wireless Internet facilities, and separate houseparent living quarters. The homes are within walking distance of grocery stores, a movie rental store, a barber shop, a post office, a bank, and restaurants. A registered nurse is on staff, and several physicians are on call in the event of an emergency. An additional home is in the works for the 2007–08 school year, and additional boarding homes will be built as the program grows.

ATHLETICS

All students may select from a variety of sports to help fulfill their physical education requirement. Interscholastically, boys' teams compete in baseball, basketball, golf, soccer, and tennis; girls' teams compete in basketball, golf, softball, tennis, and volleyball. Intramural sports are also an option for all students. The Herrington Sportscenter is home to basketball and volleyball courts, a weight room, and locker room facilities for boys, girls, and visitors. The sports complex also includes a soccer field, baseball and softball fields, and a covered, lighted batting cage that can be utilized year-round.

EXTRACURRICULAR OPPORTUNITIES

At Brook Hill, students have multiple opportunities to participate outside of the academic school day. A full array of performing arts, as well as athletics, exists to inspire student involvement. A school yearbook and literary magazine are produced each year. Drama productions, such as dinner theater and a spring musical, involve many students from the vocal, orchestral, and theater programs. These same students participate annually in regional, solo, and ensemble competitions. The Brook Hill School chapter of the National Honor Society was established in 2001 and annually inducts sophomores, juniors, and seniors who exhibit exceptional characteristics of scholarship, leadership, service, and character. The students participate in numerous service activities throughout the year, both on and off campus. A student prefect system plays a major role in planning for student activities throughout the year. Weekend and after-school events such as movies, game night, Family Day, Homecoming activities, and the prom are held each year. Trips to Dallas and Houston are planned for cultural enrichment and student fellowship. Annual festivities, such as Festival of the Guard and Christmas and Spring at the Brook, highlight the talents of performing artists.

DAILY LIFE

Breakfast for boarding students is served in The Commons of Lauderdale Hall each morning, Monday through Friday from 6:45 to 8 a.m., giving each boarder the opportunity to come and go for the first meal of the day. For Upper and Middle School students, beginning at 8:20, seven 50-minute class periods rotate each day with an advisory break period on Mondays, Tuesdays, and Thursdays. On Wednesday, students enjoy a 50-minute Chapel service, in which special guests, faculty members, and students lead in worship and in Word. Lunch is served buffet style for all students. At the end of the academic day at 3:35 p.m., athletic practice and events begin. Dinner for boarders, served buffet style, begins at 6:15 and is followed by a study time from 7 to 8:30. Study times are mandatory for each boarder from Sunday through Thursday nights. Lower School students follow a similar schedule, with the exception of pre-K students who meet for only half a day.

WEEKEND LIFE

Movies, shopping trips, dances, field trips to Dallas, hayrides, community service projects, sports activities, Bible study opportunities, get-togethers, sports events, and other activities contribute to weekend life at the Brook Hill School.

SUMMER PROGRAMS

During the summer, Brook Hill offers a variety of academic, recreational, and athletic activities. Programs offered during the summer include baseball, basketball, cheerleading, and fine arts (strings, art, and drama). In addition, a summer program was implemented in 2004 to host English language students from the Joy Children's English Language School in Taiwan. Also offered in the summer is Brook Hill's Summer Immersion Program for new international boarding students. This program is designed to provide students with an orientation time to assist with their adjustment to life in the United States as well as to life at the Brook Hill School.

COSTS AND FINANCIAL AID

Tuition at Brook Hill in 2005–06 was $25,915 for seven-day boarding students enrolled in the Summer Immersion Program and $18,165 for five-day boarding students. Day students in Middle School paid $6995 and in Upper School paid $7395. Tuition may be paid in full before the school year begins or through a bank draft, as prearranged with the business office. Student Tuition Assistance (STA) is awarded to Middle and Upper School day students on the basis of financial need as determined by the School and Student Service for Financial Aid and a review by the STA Committee of Brook Hill. More than 30 percent of students receive financial aid. The financial aid fund is limited, and families are encouraged to apply early. Tuition covers most expenses incurred by the families, including textbooks. There is a lunch fee of $600 per year. Some expenses not covered include the School uniform, school supplies, student insurance, and some class fees.

ADMISSIONS INFORMATION

The Brook Hill School seeks students who desire to achieve excellence and challenge their potential academically, athletically, spiritually, and artistically. New students are accepted on the basis of their transcripts, recommendations from English and mathematics teachers and principals, and a personal interview. New day students are accepted in all grade levels, and boarding students are accepted in grades 8–11. A visit to the School is a requirement for all students living in the United States.

APPLICATION TIMETABLE

Initial inquiries are welcome throughout the year. Campus tours and interviews can be arranged by appointment. Each application must be accompanied by a nonrefundable $50 registration fee for day students and a $150 registration fee for boarding students. Acceptances are determined after application forms have been reviewed and an interview has taken place.

ADMISSIONS CORRESPONDENCE

Ginger Bell, Director of Admissions
Terry Ellis, Assistant to Admissions
The Brook Hill School
P.O. Box 668
Bullard, Texas 75757

Phone: 903-894-5000
Fax: 903-894-6332
E-mail: tellis@brookhill.org
Web site: http://www.brookhill.org

BROOKS SCHOOL

North Andover, Massachusetts

Type: Coeducational boarding and day college-preparatory school
Grades: 9–12 (Forms III–VI): Middle School, Forms III and IV; Upper School, Forms V and VI
Enrollment: 354
Head of School: Lawrence W. Becker, Headmaster

THE SCHOOL

Brooks School was founded in 1926 by the Reverend Endicott Peabody, founder and Headmaster of Groton School. Named for Phillips Brooks, Bishop of Massachusetts and a native of North Andover, the School opened for its first term in 1927 with Frank Davis Ashburn, a 24-year-old graduate of Yale, as Headmaster. Mr. Ashburn was succeeded by H. Peter Aitken in 1973 and, in 1986, by Lawrence W. Becker.

With a broad academic curriculum, including many Advanced Placement (AP) courses, the School provides a rigorous college-preparatory program with varied opportunities for challenge. A school of great spirit and pride, Brooks is committed to addressing each student's interests and challenges through flexible schedules, close student-faculty relationships, and small class size. Although nonsectarian, Brooks has traditionally maintained a strong relationship with the Episcopal Church.

Situated on the shores of Lake Cochichewick, the 251-acre campus offers a rural setting of open land, fields, and woods, while also having ready access to the cultural, intellectual, and sports activities of Greater Boston, only 40 minutes away.

A nonprofit institution, the School is governed by a self-perpetuating 30-member Board of Trustees. The endowment is estimated at $61 million, supplemented by Annual Giving of $1.7 million. The School's 2,500 alumni play a continuing role in the support of the School.

The School is accredited by the New England Association of Schools and Colleges and is a member of the Cum Laude Society, the Association of Independent Schools in New England, the National Association of Independent Schools, and the Secondary School Admission Test Board.

ACADEMIC PROGRAMS

The curriculum includes offerings in art, classical languages, computer, drama, English, history, mathematics, modern languages, music, science, and theology, together with interdisciplinary courses, such as robotics. A student's level of accomplishment, not simply the number of years of study may determine placement in a particular subject. Considerable flexibility exists in class scheduling.

Class size averages 12 students, with an overall student-teacher ratio of 5:1. Extra help is readily available during the day and evening. The library is open every day and six evenings a week.

The minimum course load per year for students in grades 11 and 12 is five major courses or their equivalent and in grades 9 and 10, four major courses and two minors. A total of 80 credits, including electives, is required for a diploma. Departmental requirements are the successful completion of English every year, algebra II, one foreign language through the third-year level, two years of history, two laboratory sciences, a year of study in the arts, a computer course, and ninth and tenth grade theology minor courses. Most students elect to take courses well beyond the minimum requirements.

Students may choose from a wide range of elective courses in completing the credit requirements for their diploma. Those capable of doing so are strongly encouraged to undertake the Advanced Placement work that is offered in all academic departments. Independent study is available. Brooks is an associate member of the School Year Abroad program and also runs an exchange program with schools in Kenya, South Africa, Hungary, Uganda, Botswana, and Scotland. Examinations are given twice yearly and reports sent home at each midterm and semester's end.

FACULTY AND ADVISERS

The Brooks faculty numbers 74 members—39 men and 35 women. Fifty-seven hold master's degrees, and 3 have earned Ph.D.'s.

The Headmaster, Lawrence W. Becker, graduated from Amherst in 1963. In 1964, he received a Master of Arts in Teaching from Harvard.

In what is primarily a residential community, the experience of the faculty both in and out of the classroom is essential. In part, Brooks has recognized this fact by steadily increasing salaries over recent years. There is much more to encouraging faculty members to choose to remain at Brooks than salary, however, and much attention has been paid to other factors as well. For example, maintaining and improving the quality of faculty housing during these years has been a major priority, and considerable effort has been directed to providing a substantial and growing benefits package for all faculty members each year.

While annual turnover is small, in selecting its new faculty members, Brooks actively seeks men and women eager to communicate their knowledge, passion, curiosity, and talent in their various capacities as teachers, coaches, dormitory masters, and advisers. In the role of adviser, each faculty member has an overall responsibility for each student's academic and general progress. Advisers are the chief contacts between school and home. While the School assigns each new student an adviser at the beginning of the year, a student may switch at a later date if a better match proves to be the case with someone else. The considerable majority of initial adviser assignments hold until a student graduates.

COLLEGE PLACEMENT

College counseling is handled by 4 experienced professionals: the director, with twenty years of college placement experience; an associate director, and 2 gifted office assistants who handle the flow of paperwork in addition to providing moral support for many seniors. The office provides support and counsel. The counselors seek to help students do useful research and make sound decisions through the college selection process, with the ultimate goal of a good match between college and graduate. The program of counseling begins in the second semester of the junior year. The active participation of both students and parents is encouraged by the School. Admission officers from a wide range of colleges come to Brooks each fall to meet with seniors.

Students take SAT Subject Tests beginning in the ninth grade, and the SAT Reasoning Test beginning in the junior year. The College Board tests are completed in either the junior or senior year. The average verbal score for the 2005 graduating class was 598; the average mathematics score was 606.

All Brooks students who wish to go directly to college gain admission. Typically, 3 or 4 postpone matriculation for a year, and the College Office continues to work with them during that year. Colleges currently attended by Brooks students include Bates, Bowdoin, Brown, Colby, Colgate, Dartmouth, Duke, Georgetown, Harvard, Trinity, Wesleyan, Williams, and Yale.

STUDENT BODY AND CONDUCT

The student body is composed of 85 students in the ninth grade, 90 in the tenth grade, 94 in the eleventh grade, and 85 in the twelfth grade. Of the 160 girls and 194 boys, 246 are boarders and 118 are day students.

Over a four-year period, boarding students at Brooks have represented thirty-two states and twenty-six countries. The majority of Brooks students have traditionally come from the eastern part of the United States, but in recent years the School has experienced significant increases in enrollment from other areas. Brooks strongly believes in developing diversity in its student body, and students represent many religious, racial, and socioeconomic backgrounds.

School rules and codes of conduct are designed to maintain an orderly life for every member of the school community. Foremost in the School's expectations are respect for others and pride in oneself. Minor disciplinary matters are dealt with by the Deans of Students in conjunction with a student's faculty adviser. Violations of a major school rule are decided upon by a Discipline Committee made up of equal numbers of faculty members and students.

ACADEMIC FACILITIES

The School's thirty-eight classrooms are contained in one large building. Also included in the building are six science laboratories, a modern computer lab, and a new multimedia language lab. Elsewhere on campus are an auditorium with a well-equipped stage, a Black Box theater, the art studios, and the music rooms. The Henry Luce III Library and Robert Lehman Art Center were built in 1995. Situated next to the classroom building, these buildings combine to form the academic heart of the campus.

BOARDING AND GENERAL FACILITIES

Brooks houses its boarding students in ten recently renovated dormitories, each of which is supervised by 2, 3, or 4 faculty members. One third of the boarding students have single rooms; two thirds live in doubles. All students have their own voice mail boxes and the option to have their own phones in their rooms, and the dormitories are wired for computer network communication.

Health services are provided in the fifteen-bed Health Center, which is staffed around the clock by registered nurses. The school doctor holds clinics two mornings a week and is on call at all other times. There are two hospitals within 15 minutes of the campus. Mental health services are provided by a counselor who visits the School on a weekly basis and is on call for consultation at all other times.

ATHLETICS

Brooks is proud of its very strong athletics tradition, which includes recent championship teams in boys' crew, cross-country, hockey, soccer, and wrestling and girls' basketball, crew, hockey, soccer, and softball. The School believes that exercise, team play, and sportsmanship are valuable parts of each student's development. Brooks endeavors to offer its sports at sufficient depth to ensure that each student is able to participate at a level that provides the greatest enjoyment. Full interscholastic schedules are played at two or three levels, including varsity, in each of the School's major sports, and there are some intramural opportunities as well.

The School completed Phase I of a new athletic complex in the fall of 2005. Phase I included the construction of a new athletic center, which houses three basketball courts, a wrestling center, a fitness room, and new locker rooms. Phase II of the complex, the renovation of the School's current gymnasium into squash and rowing centers is scheduled to be completed in late 2005. The new athletic complex will dramatically improve the already impressive outdoor facilities, which include six soccer fields, two football fields, two field-hockey fields, two lacrosse fields, two baseball fields, a softball field, two boathouses, an indoor hockey arena, and eight tennis courts. In addition, a good eighteen-hole golf course is nearby, three stables are in the immediate area, and a small ski area is within a 10-minute drive of the campus.

EXTRACURRICULAR OPPORTUNITIES

Leadership training, emphasizing student initiative and responsibility, is an important part of the School's program. One of the most exciting things about Brooks is the range of opportunities that it affords its students to explore new areas of interest outside of the classroom and to develop those areas in which they already have interest and knowledge. The list of extracurricular activities varies from year to year, depending upon the changing patterns and directions of interest in the student body. Every student is free to initiate a new organization or extracurricular activity if such a program does not already exist. Most activities have faculty advisers with both interest and experience. Popular activities include Art As-sociation, language clubs, singing groups, chess club, literary magazine, ski club, math club, peer tutoring, stage crew, entertainment committee, model U.N., political groups, music groups, yearbook, gospel choir, newspaper, radio station, and international student club.

DAILY LIFE

Classes meet four or five times a week in 45-minute periods, from 8 a.m. to 3 p.m. on Monday, Tuesday, Thursday, and Friday and from 8 a.m. to about 12 noon on Wednesday and Saturday. An all-school assembly for announcements is held in the morning on Friday. On Tuesday and Thursday, a 30-minute period is set aside for extra-help sessions, conferences, and meetings.

The afternoon program, athletics, the play production, and community service are scheduled from the end of the class day until dinner time. A family-style dinner, led by the Headmaster, is held at 6:15 on Tuesdays and Thursdays in the fall and spring. All other meals are served cafeteria style.

A free hour from 7 to 8 p.m. is frequently used for meetings of extracurricular organizations, visiting between dormitories, or simply relaxing. Study hours run from 8 to 10 p.m. Those students who need a more supervised study environment may be required to attend a formal study hall during those hours. Freshmen begin the year in supervised study hall. All students must be in their dorm at 10, and lights-out for the ninth and tenth grades is normally at 10:30 on study nights. "Late lights" for added study time are granted with permission.

WEEKEND LIFE

The Student Activities Committee meets weekly to explore, plan, and arrange weekend activities. There are regularly scheduled trips off campus that take advantage of Boston's many cultural resources. On campus, there is a weekly program of major motion pictures. A lively drama program puts on an average of three productions a year, and dances are held at the School.

While the majority of Brooks students remain on campus for weekends, with parental permission a student may elect to leave campus any weekend from the time all obligations are fulfilled on Saturday until Sunday evening. Long weekends may be taken on occasion, with the express permission of each instructor of a missed class or practice. All day students are encouraged to participate in the weekend assortment of movies, dances, plays, concerts, or trips to Boston and the surrounding area.

COSTS AND FINANCIAL AID

Tuition costs for boarders for 2005–06 were $34,440; for day students, costs were $25,400. A flat charge of $2280 for boarders and $1880 for day students covered books, athletic equipment, health care, School-sponsored trips, and most other incidentals. Tuition payment plans are available upon request.

Financial aid was awarded on the basis of need to 21 percent of the student body. The grants total more than $1.71 million annually, with awards that ranged from $1000 to full tuition. In addition, Brooks offers a loan program.

ADMISSIONS INFORMATION

Brooks admits students on the basis of proven scholastic ability, on the promise of academic success while at Brooks, and on evidence of sound character. The School especially seeks students who are likely to make real contributions to the life at Brooks and take advantage of the opportunities offered by the School.

The most important requirements for admission are a student's essay and transcript and recommendations from the applicant's present school. A personal interview and a visit to the School are also important parts of the admission procedure. Candidates are expected to take the SSAT, preferably in November or December. Older candidates may submit the results of the PSAT or SAT. Approximately 95 percent of any given year's new students enter into grades 9 and 10. Students may also apply for grade 11.

APPLICATION TIMETABLE

The fall prior to a candidate's prospective admission is usually the best time for a visit, which includes a student-guided tour of the School. Appointments should be made well in advance, by telephone or letter. The Admission Office hours run from 8:30 a.m. to 4:30 p.m. Monday through Friday and from 8:30 a.m. to 12 noon on Saturday.

An application for admission should be submitted along with a nonrefundable registration fee of $50 to the Admission Office by February 1. Day students and students who are applying for financial aid need to complete applications by January 15. Applicants are also encouraged to apply after that date, if necessary. In accordance with the SSAT Board acceptance and reply dates, Brooks notifies the majority of its candidates of its admission decision on March 10.

ADMISSIONS CORRESPONDENCE

Judith S. Beams
Director of Admission
Brooks School
1160 Great Pond Road
North Andover, Massachusetts 01845

Phone: 978-725-6272 or 6271
Fax: 978-725-6298
E-mail: admission@brooksschool.org
Web site: http://www.brooksschool.org

THE BULLIS SCHOOL

Potomac, Maryland

Type: Coeducational day college-preparatory
Grades: 3–12; Lower School, 3–5; Middle School, 6–8; Upper School, 9–12
Enrollment: School total: 624; Upper School: 356
Head of School: Thomas B. Farquhar, Headmaster

THE SCHOOL

The Bullis School is an independent, coeducational college-preparatory day school offering girls and boys in grades 3 through 12 an educational program of excellence in a community that values integrity, respect, responsibility, diversity, and service. A caring and supportive faculty fosters a positive attitude about learning and challenges students to achieve their highest potential in academics, the arts, and athletics.

Situated on a beautiful, spacious 80-acre campus in Potomac, Maryland, The Bullis School is about 12 miles from the nation's capital and is conveniently close to the District of Columbia, its Maryland suburbs, and most Northern Virginia communities. This central location provides easy access to the rich resources of the metropolitan area.

The School has a proud heritage. Founded in 1930 by Commander William F. Bullis in downtown Washington, D.C., Bullis was originally established as a preparatory school for the United States Naval Academy. Having outgrown its city facility, the School moved to Silver Spring, Maryland, in 1934 and subsequently began to offer a four-year college-preparatory program. Since then, Bullis has evolved into an independent, coeducational, ten-year college-preparatory school.

The Bullis School is governed by an independent Board of Trustees that includes several alumni as well as parents. Bullis' annual expenses are met through tuition, the annual giving program, and endowment. The Alumni Association, which represents more than 4,000 graduates, and the Parents Association contribute significantly to the ongoing programs.

Bullis is accredited by the Middle States Association of Colleges and Schools and the Maryland Department of Education. It is a member of the National Association of Independent Schools, the Association of Independent Schools of Greater Washington, the Association of Independent Maryland Schools, the Secondary School Admission Test Board, and The Black Student Fund.

The Bullis School provides bus transportation to a variety of geographic regions in the metropolitan Washington, D.C., area. Bus routes typically include stops in McLean, Virginia; northwest D.C.; and Chevy Chase, Bethesda, Potomac, Rockville, and Gaithersburg, Maryland. Approximately 15 percent of the students ride the bus. Specific pick-up points and fees can be viewed on the School's Web site. In addition to morning and afternoon buses, an after-activities bus departs from the campus at 5:45 p.m. Car pools are encouraged and families may request a zip code list to help facilitate the formation of car pools. Public transportation is also available via the T2 Metrobus, which stops directly in front of the campus gate.

ACADEMIC PROGRAMS

Bullis operates three divisions, each guided by its own Principal. The average class size of 15 encourages active student engagement in learning and allows the teachers to know their students individually.

The Lower and Middle Schools emphasize strong preparation in English, mathematics, science, history, art, music, classical and modern languages, and computer literacy. They also focus on skill development, with students learning study techniques, effective use of the library, critical thinking, and oral skills.

The Upper School provides appropriate challenges for college-bound students. The curriculum includes both traditional and innovative courses. The four years of required English emphasize writing and literary analysis. Students must take three years of math (courses range from algebra to AP calculus), three years of laboratory sciences (biology, chemistry, and physics), and three years of social studies (one of which must be U.S. history). Upper School students are required to complete at least two years of one language at the high school level and must study that language through a Level III course. Students may choose from a variety of art courses and from technology courses ranging from fundamentals to AP programming. Honors and Advanced Placement courses and tests are offered in seventeen subject areas.

The arts program encourages all students to appreciate and develop their creative talents. All Lower and Middle School students take art and music. Middle schoolers participate in the performing and production aspects of a yearly musical. A schoolwide Festival of Light is performed in December. Upper School students meet Bullis' full credit fine arts requirement through studio work and history survey courses offered in art, music, and theater. Beginning and advanced courses in painting, drawing, sculpture, ceramics, mixed media, chorus, music theory, acting, stagecraft, and set design are offered. Exhibits and musical or theater performances provide venues for students to learn and enjoy the arts. Field trips to the area's many artistic resources, such as the National Gallery of Art, the Folger Theatre, and the Kennedy Center also enhance the arts program.

FACULTY AND ADVISERS

The 96 faculty members are dedicated professionals who share a deep, personal concern for their students. They are the School's most important asset and are supported by a performance-based compensation program as well as opportunities for continuing their education. Faculty members serve as academic advisers in the Middle and Upper Schools. For all three divisions, there are designated counselors and learning specialists.

The Bullis Headmaster, Thomas B. Farquhar, has spent over twenty-five years in the field of education. He received his undergraduate degree from Earlham College and holds a master's degree in education from the University of Pennsylvania. Prior to his arrival at Bullis, Mr. Farquhar was head of Westtown School for thirteen years. His experience includes eleven years at Sidwell Friends School where he was the assistant principal for the upper school and also served as dean of students, physics teacher, and head coach of the track and field and cross-country teams.

COLLEGE PLACEMENT

The goal of the Bullis College Counseling Office is to provide students with the necessary tools to make good, informed decisions. Fit is the primary criterion for choosing a college. The process is not driven by a manufactured list based on prestige or "name", but by the hope of helping Bullis students find schools that are right for them, where they will be happy and productive throughout their entire college experience. Members of the class of 2004 attend the following schools: American, Bates, Boston University, Brigham Young, Brown, Bucknell, Carnegie Mellon, Davidson, Dickinson, Duke, Florida A&M, Franklin & Marshall, George Washington, Harvard, Indiana Bloomington, Johns Hopkins, Kenyon, Lafayette, Middlebury, Northwestern, Penn State, Swarthmore, Syracuse, Tufts, Vanderbilt, Wesleyan, and the Universities of Chicago, Texas at Austin, Virginia, and Wisconsin–Madison.

STUDENT BODY AND CONDUCT

The Lower School enrolled 85 students in grades 3, 4, and 5. The Middle School enrolled 175 students in grades 6–8. There are about 90 students in each grade in the Upper School. The majority of Bullis' students come from Maryland, the District of Columbia, and northern Virginia. In 2004–05, 143 students were members of minority groups, and 29 held international citizenship. Of the total enrollment of 624 students, the Upper School had 356 students (168 girls and 188 boys).

Students are required to wear a uniform/dress code and sign the Bullis Honor Code. They participate in Student Council and the National Honor Society and may choose from twenty cocurricular clubs. Students are required to participate in sports, publications, and/or theater after school for two trimesters each year.

ACADEMIC FACILITIES

The School's large suburban campus offers ample space for regular and summer programs and includes playing fields, woods, and a pond.

The newest building at Bullis is the Bullis Community and Arts Center, which opened in

April 2002. The new arts center and auditorium demonstrates the importance of the performing and visual arts at Bullis. The design promotes interdisciplinary teaching in the arts, providing teaching spaces for vocal and instrumental music, theater arts, dance, drawing, painting, photography, sculpture, and ceramics. In addition, the Arts Center has its own multimedia computer lab and three multipurpose classrooms. At the heart of the center is a 750-seat theater that accommodates the entire student body and faculty. The space incorporates a flexible design providing an ideal situation for both large and small productions.

The Marriott Family Library, which was dedicated in October 1998, is a 15,000-square-foot online digital library that combines the best of a traditional library with access to new technology and information media. Additional classroom space and thirty new computers are housed in the facility, along with designated areas for the Lower, Middle, and Upper Schools.

Academic buildings include Founders' Hall, with administrative offices, a dining hall, five classrooms, and the school's bookstore. North Hall contains sixteen classrooms, three science labs, a computer lab, and a student commons as well as guidance and college counseling offices. South Hall, center of most of the Lower and Middle School activities, has fourteen classrooms, three science labs, a computer lab, and an art studio. Bullis also maintains a fleet of school buses and vans to transport students to school-sponsored events and to offer transportation to and from school on a limited basis.

The physical plant and grounds are valued at about $30 million.

ATHLETICS

Athletics and physical education are an integral part of learning at Bullis. Beginning in the Lower School, students are involved in a physical education curriculum designed to improve skill development, exercise and fitness, social and emotional development, and sportsmanship. Competitive sports are introduced as students move into the Middle School. Beginning in grade 6, students have the opportunity to choose from a variety of sports and compete in leagues composed of area private schools. The Middle School fields approximately twenty teams similar to those offered in the Upper School.

Upper School students participate in interscholastic sports in the IAC (boys) and the ISL (girls). They may choose from football, cheerleading, boys' and girls' soccer, girls' tennis, field hockey, and cross-country in the fall; aerobics, basketball, wrestling, swimming, ice hockey, and fitness training in the winter; and softball,

baseball, lacrosse, boys' tennis, track and field, and golf in the spring. The Bull equestrian team competes year-round with other independent schools. Students are required to take one trimester of health and may elect to take a first aid/CPR training course.

The Bullis Athletic Center features a 1,000-seat gym, three basketball courts, a wrestling room, a recently renovated cardiovascular fitness and weight center, and locker facilities. Bullis also has a 2,000-seat stadium with a football field and an eight-lane, all-weather track. The campus includes seven outdoor and four indoor tennis courts, outdoor basketball courts, three baseball diamonds, three soccer fields, a field hockey and lacrosse field, a softball diamond, and a football practice field.

EXTRACURRICULAR OPPORTUNITIES

In keeping with the Bullis philosophy of the well-rounded individual, the School provides a variety of activities, including participation in the student-produced yearbook, newspaper, and literary magazine. Students may also be elected to class or schoolwide offices.

Among the most active clubs in the Upper School are Students Against Destructive Decisions (SADD), the Outing Club, Tour Guides, and the Multicultural Student Union. The Science Club and "It's Academic" team are also popular. Community service is a vital part of Bullis with projects sponsored by the Key Club and individual classes. Some of these programs include Peer Leadership, Adopt-A-Grandparent Program, Freshmen-Senior(Citizen) Theater Party, and Peer Tutoring Program.

Special events include Homecoming, Bullympics, Mr. Bulldog, Recognition Day, and the Junior-Senior Prom. Weekly Tuesday morning all-school assemblies and special assemblies feature speakers from a variety of fields as well as student performances and cultural activities.

DAILY LIFE

The academic day, which begins at 8 a.m., is divided into 45-minute blocks. Three mornings a week, students meet with their faculty advisers. Lunch is served family-style, with students helping in the serving and clearing of the meal. An activity period is incorporated into the schedule for breaks and assemblies as well as club and class meetings. Sports practices and play rehearsals occur when the academic day ends. Time is set aside for teachers to meet with advisees and students who may require supplemental instruction.

An Extended Day program is available for students in the Lower and Middle Schools until 6 p.m. Activities include a snack, outdoor time,

and a supervised study hall. There is an additional fee for this service. Students may enroll in the program by the week, month, trimester, or for the entire year.

SUMMER PROGRAMS

The Bullis School offers a comprehensive schedule of academic and athletics programs open to school-age children attending both Bullis and outside schools. The Bullis Summer Programs include a six-week academic summer school and summer camp programs for school-age children in soccer, tennis, basketball, baseball/softball, volleyball, and lacrosse. In addition, Bullis runs the Bulldog Day Camp for school-age children with programs in a variety of athletics, nature exploration, arts and crafts, swimming, special events, and field trips.

COSTS AND FINANCIAL AID

The range of tuition for the 2005–06 school year is $21,600–$24,170. An initial deposit is required of all students at the time an enrollment contract is submitted. Bullis is committed to need-based financial aid. All recipients of financial aid are reviewed annually. For the 2004–05 school year, the average financial aid grant was $15,000. A separate brochure, *Affording a Bullis School Education*, details various payment plans, financial options, and financial aid. Admission decisions are made without regard to financial aid consideration.

ADMISSIONS INFORMATION

Bullis seeks students who are excited about learning, able and willing to meet the challenges of college-preparatory work, and who will be contributing members of the school community. Admission is selective.

Scores on the Secondary School Admission Test, the Independent School Entrance Exam, or the Educational Records Bureau test; transcripts; a writing sample; and a minimum of three school recommendations must be submitted to the School. Interviews are required for students applying to grades 6–12.

APPLICATION TIMETABLE

The application deadline and the financial aid deadline are February 1. Parents are notified of admission decisions in mid-March and are asked to reply by early April. The Admission Office is open from 8 to 4 during the week.

ADMISSIONS CORRESPONDENCE

Director of Admission and Financial Aid
The Bullis School
10601 Falls Road
Potomac, Maryland 20854

Phone: 301-983-5724
E-mail: info@bullis.org
Web site: http://www.bullis.org

BUXTON SCHOOL

Williamstown, Massachusetts

Type: Coeducational college-preparatory boarding and day school
Grades: 9–12
Enrollment: 90
Head of School: C. William Bennett, Director

THE SCHOOL

In 1928, Ellen Geer Sangster founded Buxton School as a coeducational day school in Short Hills, New Jersey. In 1947, she moved the high school to her family estate in Williamstown, Massachusetts, and formed it anew as a boarding school.

From the beginning, Buxton has been a progressive school, one devoted to innovation and change. Today, that devotion remains steadfast. At Buxton, students' pursuits help them develop the clear vision they need to comprehend the world they live in and to define their future lives. Each student's bridge to the larger world is the informed, skilled, confident self that he or she develops while at Buxton.

Buxton places great importance on the composition and character of its student body. Foremost, a young person must want to be at Buxton. In addition, Buxton seeks students who have intelligence, motivation, creativity, and intellectual curiosity to succeed there. Prior to coming to Buxton, students have experienced positive relationships with adults as well as peers. Buxton students take a responsible and ambitious role in shaping their own lives and wish to make significant and mature social contributions. They are conscious of the importance of being useful and contributory, of serving as an asset to others, and of aiding in others' efforts to enrich the life of the group. One of the first tasks Buxton students encounter is that of developing and maintaining a sound, compassionate, stimulating environment for oneself and for the entire group.

Buxton promotes personal growth and cultivates students' abilities to understand and manage their lives. Presenting a way of life that students can come to understand and manage is of primary importance. The student body is diverse; life at the School is flexible, noninstitutional, and open to change. Opportunities often arise for collective deliberation of life's most pressing challenges. Buxton life reflects the fundamental premise that a mature individual must be morally and actively committed, each in his or her own way, to the creation and betterment of a healthy society.

The 150-acre campus of Buxton overlooks historic Williamstown, located approximately 170 miles north of New York City and 150 miles west of Boston. Nearby are Williams College, the Clark Art Institute, and the Massachusetts Museum of Contemporary Art (MASS MoCA), which are all exceptional resources for Buxton students.

Buxton is a nonprofit, nonsectarian institution governed by a 20-member self-perpetuating Board of Trustees. The board includes the Director, faculty members, alumni, parents of students and alumni, and friends of the School.

The physical plant at Buxton is valued at $6 million. The operating budget is $3.2 million annually. The current endowment is $1.2 million, and the Annual Fund for 2004–05 raised $287,255.

Buxton is accredited by the New England Association of Schools and Colleges and is approved by the Massachusetts Department of Education. It is a member of the Secondary School Admission Test Board, the Association of Boarding Schools, the Association of Independent Schools of New England, the National Association of Independent Schools, and the Small Boarding School Association as well as other professional organizations.

ACADEMIC PROGRAMS

Academic courses, activities, and community life are all essential parts of a Buxton education. Each offers the opportunity for unique and vital growth and, therefore, each is of educational significance.

Buxton's academic curriculum is broad and demanding, offering an unusual combination of traditional subjects, courses in the arts, and electives in subjects usually only encountered at the college level. Students collaborate with teachers to design their course programs. Although they are advised to design a course schedule that will prepare them for higher education, students have considerable freedom of choice about what courses they take and when they take them.

Sixteen credits are required for graduation. Students must take 4 years of English and 1 year of American history. They are also counseled to complete a minimum of 3 years of mathematics, 2 years of social science, 2 years of laboratory science, and at least 2 years of a foreign language, although 3 years are strongly recommended. Students are also encouraged to pursue courses in studio art; ceramics; black-and-white and digital photography; music theory, composition, and performance; and beginning and advanced drama. Buxton offers a range of elective courses; those offered recently include writing workshops, the Great Depression, Vietnam War history, Latin America studies, Middle East in the twentieth century, Africa, globalization, cultural history of the twentieth century, rights and the law, equality and/or freedom, existentialism in European philosophy, comparative religions, economics, contemporary social movements, social documentary, psychology, geology, marine science, astronomy, film history, and video production.

Buxton divides its academic year into two semesters. The School has a 5:1 student-teacher ratio and classes average 9 students. Faculty-supervised study periods are held daily during class hours and for 2 hours in the evening. Students may be required to attend.

Each year in March, the whole School travels to a major North American city. Atlanta, Chicago, Toronto, Mexico City, Havana, San Juan, and Washington, D.C., are among those visited in recent years. This event is of central importance in the school year, and students are involved in all aspects of planning and executing the weeklong trip. Social, economic, and political issues are the focus of project groups, and the entire Buxton community takes part in the All-School Play, which is performed several times during the trip. Upon returning to Buxton, students present their projects to the School and publish their reports as a book.

FACULTY AND ADVISERS

There are 18 faculty members—9 men and 9 women. Three hold master's degrees, and 1 has earned a doctorate. Fourteen live on campus. C. William Bennett, Director of the School since 1983, is a graduate of Williams College and has been at Buxton since 1969.

All teaching families and most teachers live at the School, interweaving their daily lives with those of the Buxton community. Along with teaching in the classroom, faculty members have advisory, leadership, administrative, and caretaking responsibilities. As advisers, faculty members are in regular contact with parents.

Compassionate adult action and reaction form the foundation of education at Buxton. Teachers seek to motivate students to engage in sincere intellectual commitment and self-evaluation. The adults are available and open to young people and are concerned with their growth in academic disciplines as well as in every other respect. Buxton faculty and staff members react to young people knowledgeably, deeply, and personally. Developing honest and caring friendships between Buxton adults and students is an educational goal in itself.

COLLEGE PLACEMENT

Buxton faculty members counsel students as they form their college plans. Students are assigned faculty advisers in the spring of their junior year. The advisers guide students in making appropriate college choices and help students with the application process.

In recent years, Buxton graduates have attended Amherst, Bennington, Colorado College, Cornell, Dartmouth, Macalaster, Mount Holyoke, Oberlin, Rhode Island School of Design, Smith, Spelman, Wellesley, and the University of Chicago.

STUDENT BODY AND CONDUCT

Enrollment at Buxton averages 90 students, with an equal number of boys and girls. In 2005–06, eighteen states, the District of Columbia, and the countries of Ecuador, Jamaica, Japan, South Korea, Spain, Taiwan, and Uzbekistan were represented among the student population.

ACADEMIC FACILITIES

The campus contains four classroom buildings (one housing science labs and a computer writing lab), a library with Internet-access computers and extra Ethernet ports for students' portable computers, an art studio, a ceramics studio, a darkroom, a music classroom and practice rooms, and a theater. Designated campus areas are equipped for wireless Internet access.

BOARDING AND GENERAL FACILITIES

In addition to the academic facilities, there are a number of other buildings on campus. The Main House contains a girls' dormitory, the School dining room, and administrative offices. The Gate House serves as an additional girls' dormitory; the boys' dormitory is a converted barn. The School has additional buildings for administrative offices and for faculty and staff housing. Williamstown Medical Associates provides medical services to students.

ATHLETICS

At Buxton, competitive and recreational sports programs do not merely fulfill physical education requirements; they also expose students to the challenges inherent in disciplined physical activity and different kinds of team play. Students acquire personal confidence and a sense of mastery as well as leadership skills through participation in these activities.

Competitive sports are not mandatory, but regular outdoor activity is expected of everyone. Interscholastic soccer, basketball, and track take place on a scheduled and supervised basis. Other activities include intramural basketball, skiing and snowboarding at a local area, cross-country skiing, sledding, skating, volleyball, karate, aerobics and yoga classes, swimming, kayaking, softball, running, biking, hiking, horseback riding, skateboarding, indoor soccer and rock-climbing, Ultimate Frisbee, and spring soccer.

The campus has its own playing fields, a basketball court, a weight room, three ponds for ice-skating, and a hill for sledding and skiing. Hiking trips are scheduled when there is student interest. Riding lessons can be arranged.

EXTRACURRICULAR OPPORTUNITIES

In keeping with the Buxton philosophy that all aspects of school life are valuable to the education of a student, activities play a prominent role at Buxton. Students of every degree of interest and ability are urged to take part and are counted on to support the efforts of each other as coparticipant, audience, or encouraging friend. All of Buxton's activities, which include art, music, drama, dance, drumming, and creative writing, are designed to foster personal expression and commitment through a combination of self-discipline, patient practice, interpersonal skill, and astute observation of life. The art studio has an extensive array of two- and three-dimensional media. Painting, drawing, figure drawing, printmaking, sculpture, work with fabric or found objects, mixed media, ceramics, and black-and-white and digital photography are available. Chorus, chamber orchestra, and ensembles are offered at Buxton as music activities. Drama includes acting, working on technical crews, and costuming. Each year, seniors raise funds for and produce the School yearbook, which they present as a gift to the Buxton community.

An essential part of a Buxton education is Work Program, which takes place on Tuesday afternoons and Saturday mornings. At these times, students engage in tasks such as forestry work and gardening, construction projects, office work, and cooking. Administered by volunteer students and faculty members, Work Program requires a great deal of planning, budgeting, and managing. What is done and who does it are always changing, but it is a consistent, direct challenge to everyone that Work Program can and must fill a major part of Buxton's nonprofessional needs.

The annual Thanksgiving Festival offers students' families the opportunity to share in Buxton life. There is no vacation at this time; instead, families are invited to visit and celebrate Thanksgiving at the School. Over the three days of this event, the School hosts a traditional dinner plus chorus and orchestra performances, chamber music ensembles, performances of student composers' work, drama productions, and readings of students' creative writing. The School also exhibits its student art work. In addition, there is ample time for parent-faculty conferences. The Spring Arts Weekend in May is similar in structure and activities. Independent and joint science projects are often presented on this weekend as well.

The proximity of Williams College is particularly significant, as it provides a source of stimulation and example as well as the opportunity to occasionally attend lectures and events and use the college library. Bordering the Buxton campus is the Clark Art Institute, one of the finest small art museums in the country.

DAILY LIFE

Each day before classes, students clean their rooms and complete minor housekeeping tasks around the School. Classes begin at 8 a.m. and are held until 3 p.m., five days a week. Sports and activities are offered from 3 to 5 p.m. Students attend study hall, study on their own, or participate in rehearsals or other activities from 7 to 9 p.m. Meals are family-style; students attend lunch at 12:30 and dinner at 6 p.m. in the School dining room.

WEEKEND LIFE

Weekends at Buxton are considered just as important as weekdays. Students plan and organize Friday night activities, which include outdoor sports and games, dances, swimming, and theme events. On Saturday mornings, everyone in the School participates in Work Program. Students are free to go into Williamstown to buy necessities or attend a movie or cultural event on Saturday afternoons and evenings. All Saturday meals are planned and prepared by students. Sundays begin with brunch and typically are devoted to academic work. Sunday evenings feature a formal dinner and presentations concerning social issues and arts events. Students remain at Buxton on weekends except for a designated Home Weekend each semester.

Students who wish to do so may attend religious services locally.

COSTS AND FINANCIAL AID

Tuition and fees for 2005–06 were $33,500 for boarding students and $20,700 for day students. This included tickets for approved cultural events, athletics (including a ski pass), and all other School-sponsored activities. The School offers a tuition-installment plan.

Buxton is committed to maintaining the diversity of its student body. Approximately 37 percent received need-based financial aid; $934,000 was awarded for 2005–06.

ADMISSIONS INFORMATION

Buxton admits students into grades 9 through 11. Interested parents and prospective students may request an information packet by calling or writing the Admissions Office. An on-campus interview is required and the student's most recent SSAT scores should accompany the application.

APPLICATION TIMETABLE

Inquiries are welcome anytime. Applications should be submitted by February 1, although they are accepted later if space is available. The application fee is $50 for U.S. students and $100 for international students.

ADMISSIONS CORRESPONDENCE

Admissions Office
Buxton School
291 South Street
Williamstown, Massachusetts 01267

Phone: 413-458-3919
Fax: 413-458-9427
E-mail: Admissions@BuxtonSchool.org
Web site: http://www.BuxtonSchool.org

THE CAMBRIDGE SCHOOL OF WESTON

Weston, Massachusetts

Type: Coeducational day and boarding college-preparatory school
Grades: 9–12, postgraduate year
Enrollment: 325
Head of School: Jane Moulding, Head of School

THE SCHOOL

Established in 1886 by the founders of Radcliffe College, the Cambridge School of Weston (CSW) is a coeducational college-preparatory school with a tradition of innovative education. The School is distinguished by a rigorous academic curriculum, active student engagement in classes, extensive offerings in the visual and performing arts, both recreational and team sports, and experience-based learning, including wilderness and off-campus courses, such as marine biology on Cape Cod.

CSW holds that sound and appropriate college preparation emphasizes the process of inquiry and encourages love of learning. The School is committed to the personal growth of students and believes that individual excellence does not have to come at someone else's expense; thus, competition between students is not emphasized.

CSW is an innovatively structured community built on genuine rapport between teacher and student and deep mutual respect and accountability. Students and faculty members discuss community issues at the School's Town Meeting, and both student and faculty representatives sit on all planning and judicial committees and on the Board of Trustees. The School prizes the diversity and individual voices of its students in a framework of social awareness and responsibility. It strives to give students a stake both in their own learning and in the well-being of the larger community.

The Cambridge School of Weston is located on a 65-acre suburban campus, 20 minutes by automobile or train from Boston and Cambridge. The School is a nonprofit corporation managed by a 25-member Board of Trustees.

The Cambridge School of Weston is accredited by the New England Association of Schools and Colleges and is a member of the Association of Independent Schools in New England, the National Association of Independent Schools, the Association of Boarding Schools, the Secondary School Admission Test Board, the Educational Records Bureau, A Better Chance, the College Board, the School and Student Service for Financial Aid, and the National Association for College Admission Counseling.

ACADEMIC PROGRAMS

Created by the faculty in 1973, the Module Plan, also known as the Mod Plan, simultaneously allows students to meet high standards and pursue individual passions. Its structure allows individuals to deeply explore a few topics at a time through access to laboratories, hands-on experiences, and off-campus research.

The Mod Plan creates a unique school day and school year. Rather than semesters, the CSW academic year consists of seven 5-week modules. During each module, students schedule three blocks of academic subjects, 90 minutes in length each day. Courses in the arts are scheduled along with traditional academics, carrying equal weight and high expectations. A fourth block allows students to pursue individual interests by selecting sports, activities, performing and visual arts, community service projects, independent study, or additional courses.

Each year, students take four blocks in each academic area, which equals a full year of study in a traditional semester system. Some subjects occur in single blocks throughout the year, while others, such as math and foreign language, are typically taught in consecutive modules. Students may spend an entire Mod studying science, history, art, and other topics off campus or while traveling in another country. Choices abound. No two schedules are identical; each is designed to meet individual interests as well as departmental requirements. Ultimately, each schedule created through the Mod Plan provides balance, rigor, and stimulation throughout the year.

CSW offers more than 300 unique and exciting classes each year, including American Sign Language, Art and Community, Zoology, Animal Behavior, Black Studies, Child Development, Gay and Lesbian Literature, Caribbean Dance, Rock/Pop Ensemble, Playwriting, and Digital Collage, just to name a few. The School also offers various integrated-studies courses, such as the Art of Prediction and the Meanings of Love. Off-campus study opportunities are available in France, Africa, and Latin America.

Class size ranges from 8 to 14 students. The grading system uses A–F designations. Teachers' grades and comments are reported to students and parents seven times per year, with seven additional mid-module reviews of each student's progress and communication about any difficulties.

FACULTY AND ADVISERS

Of the approximately 60 teachers and teacher-administrators, more than 70 percent hold advanced degrees and approximately 30 percent have taught at the school for more than ten years.

In selecting teachers, The Cambridge School of Weston looks for men and women who are excited by the Module Plan's potential for intensive learning and creative teaching, who convey their intellectual enthusiasm and curiosity, and who are comfortable with warmth and honesty between students and adults.

Each faculty member also advises 5 to 8 students a year. Advisers communicate regularly with parents and have a scheduled meeting with their advisees every day.

COLLEGE PLACEMENT

Each student chooses one of the 3 college counselors in the spring of the junior year. The college counselor helps students choose appropri-ate colleges and organize paperwork and writes a lengthy recommendation to accompany each application packet.

The middle 50 percent of SAT scores for the class of 2005 were 560 to 690 on the verbal section and 550 to 670 on the math section. Based on PSAT scores in the past four years, 32 Cambridge School of Weston students have been recognized as Commended Scholars, and 6 have qualified as National Merit Semifinalists.

Recent CSW graduates have been accepted to such institutions as Brown, Columbia, Cornell, Dartmouth, Hampshire, Harvard, Johns Hopkins, Oberlin, Rhode Island School of Design, Sarah Lawrence, Stanford, Swarthmore, University of Chicago, Wellesley, Wesleyan, and Yale.

STUDENT BODY AND CONDUCT

Of the 325 students enrolled, there are 77 ninth graders, 79 tenth graders, 96 eleventh graders, and 73 twelfth graders. There are 78 boarders and 247 day students. Home states of CSW students in the past three years include Alaska, California, Georgia, Illinois, Maryland, New Mexico, New York, North Carolina, Pennsylvania, South Carolina, Virginia, and all six New England states. In the past three years, international students have come from Canada, China, Germany, the Ivory Coast, Japan, Korea, Malaysia, Mexico, Spain, and Taiwan. Day students commute from sixty nearby towns. Sixteen percent of those enrolled are students who are members of minority groups (U.S. citizens), and an additional 10 percent are international students.

The Cambridge School of Weston Student Handbook outlines the rules governing life on campus. A student-faculty Judicial Board makes recommendations to the Head of School on most rule infractions. CSW maintains a smoke-free campus.

ACADEMIC FACILITIES

The academic facilities surround a tree-shaded quadrangle and include nine buildings housing classrooms, the library, a computer center, five science laboratories, the computerized foreign languages laboratory, and the Mugar Center for the Performing Arts. Wireless Internet connections are available in all academic buildings and dormitories.

BOARDING AND GENERAL FACILITIES

Each of the four dormitories houses 15 to 25 students and two dorm-parent families. Six other faculty members live on campus. Most students live in double rooms, but some singles are available. Rooms for new students are assigned by the boarding department in consultation with the Admissions Office.

A registered nurse staffs the five-bed Health Center during school hours and is on call at other times. The School physician is affiliated

with the Newton Wellesley Hospital, 15 minutes from the School, with emergency room physicians on duty at all times.

ATHLETICS
The athletic program is designed to help students develop habits of good health and good sportsmanship and learn to be cooperative members of a group effort. Students satisfy their physical activity requirement each year by choosing at least one season of any combination of interscholastic team or recreational sports, wilderness trips, and dance courses. CSW's baseball, basketball, cheerleading, cross-country, field hockey, soccer, tennis, and Ultimate Frisbee teams compete interscholastically. There are also opportunities for aerobics, biking, dance, downhill skiing, fencing, martial arts, triathlon training, volleyball, weight training, and yoga.

Campus athletic facilities include three playing fields, a tennis court, two outdoor swimming pools, a gymnasium, two dance studios, and a fitness center.

EXTRACURRICULAR OPPORTUNITIES
CSW values lively student participation in community affairs and governance. Thriving campus organizations include the Administrative Advisory Board; Amnesty International; Anarchist Social Club; Boarding Life; Computer, Curriculum, and Diversity Committees; four Dorm Boards; Gay-Straight Alliance; Hip-Hop Troupe; Judicial Board; Law Day Committee; Literary Magazine; Math Team; student newspaper *(The Gryphon's Eye)*; SALSA—Students Advocating Life without Substance Abuse; United Students of Color; and Yearbook. The Module Plan's yearly calendar and rich offerings allow seven major dramatic productions; two lunch hour and Sunday afternoon recital series for soloists and the classical, rock, and jazz ensembles; concerts by the School chorus; several dance performances; and seven major student art shows each year.

DAILY LIFE
Breakfast is served from 7:30, with required check-in for boarders; day students are welcome. Classes begin at 8:30 and end at 2:30, followed by athletics and activities until 4:30 or 5. All advisers and advisees meet at mid-morning every day, and there is an all-school assembly twice each week. The hour-long lunch period allows time for student-faculty activities, performances, committee meetings, individual meetings for students with teachers and advisers, and writing, math, and language workshops for extra help and practice. Required supervised study hours for boarders in the dorm, library, or any other campus facility last from 7 to 9 p.m. on school nights. Before and after study hours, boarding and day students mix in evening activities, including poetry writing workshops, music performances by students and faculty members, indoor soccer, basketball, and a nightly coffeehouse in the Student Center. On school nights, in-dorm time is 10, with a weekly dorm meeting; in-room time is 11.

WEEKEND LIFE
The Director of Student Activities and interested students plan the weekend activity offerings and three Community Days for service projects and community building. CSW's proximity to Boston and Cambridge allows trips to theater, dance, and concert productions; Patriots, Revolution, Bruins, Celtics, and Red Sox games; museums; and shopping areas. The Wilderness Program ranges farther a field in New England for biking, rock climbing, mountain trekking and survival camping, canoeing, river rafting, and sea kayaking. Students also participate in drama and dance rehearsals and enjoy access to the gym, fitness center, library, computer center, and all the visual arts, dance, and music studios. Integrating the boarding and day communities for the benefit of all is a CSW priority, and a high level of day student participation broadens and enriches all weekend and evening activities. Boarders may visit day students' families, and day students may stay overnight at school with friends, with permission of the students' parents and dorm parents.

SUMMER PROGRAMS
CSW's five-week summer art and academic day program, the Eighth Module, mirrors the intellectual and creative approaches that distinguished the School. Students pursue interests in dance, drama, music, writing, visual arts, math, science, foreign languages, American Sign Language, and history for credit or enrichment. Recreational activities such as weight training, Ultimate Frisbee, and swimming are available. The Eighth Module brings together master artist-teachers and students ages 12–18 to train, create, collaborate, and perform. Students also interact with guest performers. The Eighth Module accepts about 75 students.

COSTS AND FINANCIAL AID
Day tuition for 2005–06 was $27,000, and the boarding tuition was $36,300. Books, school supplies, and music lessons are extra.

Financial aid is based strictly on family need. For 2005–06, more than $1.3 million was awarded to 22 percent of the CSW families. Grants include a work-study component.

ADMISSIONS INFORMATION
The Cambridge School of Weston seeks students who demonstrate strong intellectual potential, who are intrigued by the Module Plan's possibilities for working in depth, who wish to explore a wide range of academic and creative interests, who are independent thinkers, who seek an active role in their own learning, and who are ready to participate as thoughtful, energetic, and caring individuals in this school community.

The application process is designed to help both the applicant and the School assess the appropriateness of CSW. Interested families and students are asked to schedule a visit on a school day for a campus tour and an interview with an admissions staff member. In addition, the student's application and essay, teacher recommendations, school record over the past three years, a parent statement, and standardized test scores are required. Applicants are strongly encouraged to share recent examples of their academic or creative work.

The Cambridge School of Weston values the diversity of its students and faculty and does not discriminate on the basis of race, color, gender, religion, sexual orientation, or ethnic or national origin in the administration of its educational, admissions, and other School-administered programs.

APPLICATION TIMETABLE
February 1 is the application deadline for March 10 decisions, with an April 10 reply date for acceptances. Thereafter, applications are considered if space permits. The Admissions Office is open between 8:30 a.m. and 3:30 p.m., Monday through Friday, throughout the year.

ADMISSIONS CORRESPONDENCE
Trish Saunders, Director of Admissions and Financial Aid
Judith Tauriac, Admissions Counselor
Julie Blazar, Admissions Counselor
David Mountcastle, Admissions Counselor
Shelby Bleiweis, Admissions and Financial Aid Coordinator
The Cambridge School of Weston
Georgian Road
Weston, Massachusetts 02493

Phone: 781-642-8650
Fax: 781-398-8344
E-mail: admissions@csw.org
Web site: http://www.csw.org

CAMDEN MILITARY ACADEMY

Camden, South Carolina

Type: Boys' boarding college-preparatory military school
Grades: 7–12, PG
Enrollment: School total: 300
Head of School: Col. Eric Boland, Headmaster

THE SCHOOL

While the Camden Military Academy tradition dates back to 1892, operations on the current campus began with the 1958–59 school year. The Academy combines the traditions of three institutions—Carlisle Military School, which operated in Bamberg, South Carolina, from 1892 to 1977; Camden Academy, which was located on the current campus from 1949 to 1957; and Camden Military Academy. Camden Military Academy, which was founded by Col. James F. Risher and his son, Col. Lanning P. Risher, has operated as a nonprofit tax-exempt institution since 1974 and is governed by a self-perpetuating board of trustees.

Today, the Academy enjoys a capacity enrollment of 300 young men from around the United States and the world. The school's modern campus is located in historic Camden, South Carolina. The Academy is a fully accredited member of the Southern Association of Colleges and Schools. It holds membership in the National Association of Independent Schools, the Southern Association of Independent Schools, the Palmetto Association of Independent Schools, and the Association of Military Colleges and Schools in the United States. The Corps has been designated by the Department of the Army as a Junior Army ROTC Honor Unit with Distinction.

ACADEMIC PROGRAMS

Camden Military Academy enrolls young men in grades 7 through the postgraduate year. The academic program at the high school level (grades 9–12) is strictly college preparatory. All high school students must earn 24 units for graduation. These include 4 units of English; algebra I, geometry, and algebra II, plus a fourth math unit (precalculus and AP calculus are also available); three sciences (two of which must be lab sciences); 4½ units of history; and 3 units of a modern foreign language (all ninth graders are required to take Latin before taking a modern foreign language; French and Spanish are offered). Students must also take a course in computer literacy and in JROTC. Additional units must be earned from approved academic electives.

The academic program is structured around a traditional class day, with all students taking six classes per day as well as JROTC. All class sections are small, with typically fewer than 15 students per class. Students are apprised of their academic progress every two weeks. Those students who earn less than a C for the two-week grading period in any class are required to attend a two-week tutorial period with their teacher. In addition, a mandatory teacher-supervised study period is conducted five nights per week. All students are monitored, and assignments are checked. Students who maintain a B or better

average may elect to study in the Cline Library. The library is available to other students during this time by faculty permission and is open daily to all students. The Academy encourages library use and has a full-time professional librarian available to assist in that usage.

FACULTY AND ADVISERS

Col. Eric Boland was appointed Headmaster in 2003. He has been employed by the Academy for more than twenty years. He has served as an instructor, a Tactical Officer, and the Academy's athletic director. Col. Boland earned his B.A. degree as well as his master's degree in secondary education from the University of South Carolina.

Lt. Col. Pat Armstrong, also a West Point graduate, is the Commandant of Cadets, while Lt. Col Don Parrotte serves as the Dean of Academic Affairs.

The faculty consists of 22 men and 4 women. Fifteen hold master's degrees and 11 hold bachelor's degrees.

COLLEGE PLACEMENT

Camden Military Academy has offered only a college-preparatory curriculum for many years. More than 95 percent of Camden graduates are accepted to four-year colleges and universities. All juniors are required to take the PSAT, which is available to sophomores as well. The Academy provides students with the opportunity to take the SAT and ACT at each administration. All students are encouraged to take an SAT preparatory seminar that is offered twice each year. Students and parents work with college advisers to select the college or university best suited to each graduate. Among the colleges and universities that recent graduates have attended are The Citadel, Clemson, Emory & Henry, George Washington, Hillsdale, North Carolina State, Norwich, Ohio State, the United States Military Academy at West Point, Virginia Military Institute, Wake Forest, and the Universities of North Carolina and South Carolina.

STUDENT BODY AND CONDUCT

Camden currently operates at a capacity of 300 boarding boys in grade 7 through the postgraduate year. Students represent seventeen states and two other countries; however, most students are from the Southeast, with the greatest concentration coming from the Carolinas.

While Camden Military Academy is a military boarding school, its strength lies in its ability to work personally with each student, meet his needs, and help him realize his potential. Because all students are seven-day boarding boys, all live by the same rules and experience daily life in the same way. Students are usually housed 2 to a room in five companies. Each company is composed of 58 to 62 young men. Each company is supervised by an adult Tactical Officer who

lives on the campus with his family. He serves as the counselor, mentor, encourager, and disciplinarian for each young man in his charge. He also serves as the communications liaison with the parents. These men bring a positive dimension to the Camden experience. Their background, professional training, and personal commitment make them uniquely qualified to help one's son develop personally as well as academically. In addition, students benefit from being part of a cadet ranking structure. The organization gives each young man the opportunity to develop personal responsibility and leadership and management skills. All students are also required to participate in JROTC and attend religious services each Sunday.

ACADEMIC FACILITIES

The campus is composed of twelve buildings. There are two academic buildings and the Cline Library dedicated to academic pursuits. Housed in these buildings are all classrooms, a computer lab, and a science lab. The Cline Library houses the school's 9,000-volume collection as well as periodicals and computer information services.

BOARDING AND GENERAL FACILITIES

The Academy's 350-seat dining hall allows for family-style meals, and the entire cadet corps eat at one time. The modern infirmary, resident nurse, and school physician meet all cadet medical needs. The gym complex houses the gym, dressing rooms, and shower facilities for all athletic teams as well as the school's band room. Each of the cadet barracks features 2- or 3-man rooms that are air-conditioned and heated and individual combination door locks.

The Carlisle House serves as the center for cadet recreational time. The Carlisle House amenities include a game room, a snack bar, a TV room, and a cadet lounge. On campus, there are three tennis courts, two athletic fields, and a state-of-the-art track complex that features one of the nation's premier running tracks.

ATHLETICS

The Academy offers eleven different sports: baseball, basketball, cross-country, drill team, football, golf, rifle team, soccer, tennis, track and field, and wrestling.

EXTRACURRICULAR OPPORTUNITIES

The Academy offers a school band, Key Club, Boy Scout troop, and Honor Society. Cadets are also welcomed to participate in community and church-sponsored activities. In addition to these activities, the Academy offers weekly outings to area restaurants and movie theaters. There are also trips to go white-water rafting and snow skiing and to other day and overnight activities.

DAILY LIFE

All students follow the same daily schedule. In addition to the academic day, there is drill three days per week, athletic practice, free time, and evening study period.

WEEKEND LIFE

All weekends offer both structured activities as well as free time. Inspections, a Sunday Dress Parade, all meals, and Sunday church services are required of all students. Cadets may spend their free time Saturday afternoon and Sunday afternoon in the gym, the fully equipped weight room, the student center, or in their rooms. All cadets are permitted to bring personal items such as clothes, a TV, video games, and a stereo. Use of these items is strictly monitored and permitted only during a cadet's free time. High school cadets are also permitted to go into the town of Camden on weekend afternoons for shopping, a meal, or a movie. The Academy provides all transportation; students are not permitted vehicles. Day or overnight trips are also planned during the weekends that cadets are on campus. Cadets are granted furloughs (the opportunity to stay overnight away from the campus) based on several factors. Certain furloughs are given and others must be earned. Furloughs may be earned either through merits or academic performance. All cadets have the opportunities to earn furloughs. Those who maximize their opportunities may go home about once a month.

SUMMER PROGRAMS

The Academy offers a summer academic program as well as a summer camp. Students should contact the Director of Admissions for summer program information.

COSTS AND FINANCIAL AID

The cost for a new student for the 2004–05 school year was $14,995. This included tuition, room and board, and uniforms. The cost of laundry and dry cleaning, books, and miscellaneous charges is extra. Limited financial aid is available.

ADMISSIONS INFORMATION

All applicants are examined on an individual basis. Only young men who have demonstrated a desire to enroll and are capable of undertaking college-preparatory work will be considered. An on-campus interview is required of all applicants. A catalog and video are available from the Admissions Office. Camden Military Academy admits students of any race, color, and national or ethnic origin. The Academy is a private, nonprofit educational institution with admission limited to young men.

APPLICATION TIMETABLE

Admission is offered on a rolling basis. Admission for the second semester is offered strictly on a space available basis. There is a $100 nonrefundable application fee.

ADMISSIONS CORRESPONDENCE

R. Casey Robinson
Director of Admissions
Camden Military Academy
520 Highway 1, North
Camden, South Carolina 29020

Phone: 803-432-6001
    800-948-6291 (toll-free)
Fax: 803-425-1020
E-mail: admissions@camdenmilitary.com
Web site: http://www.camdenmilitary.com

CAMPBELL HALL (EPISCOPAL)

North Hollywood, California

Type: Coeducational day college-preparatory school
Grades: K–12: Lower School, K–6; Middle School, 7–8; Upper School, 9–12
Enrollment: School total: 1,073; Upper School: 509
Head of School: The Reverend Julian Bull, Headmaster

THE SCHOOL

Campbell Hall is an independent, K–12, coeducational, nonprofit day school affiliated with the Episcopal Church. It offers college-preparatory academic training within the perspective of the Judeo-Christian tradition. Campbell Hall was founded in 1944 by the Reverend Alexander K. Campbell as a school dedicated not only to the finest in academic education but also to the discovery of the values of a religious heritage. Campbell Hall enrolls students in kindergarten through the twelfth grade.

The school's 15-acre campus is located in a residential suburb 10 miles north of Los Angeles. Students take advantage of the school's proximity to museums, missions, historic sites, science centers, and universities.

The basic structure and operation of the school and the formulation of educational and other school policies are guided by a 15-member Board of Directors. The board is composed of community leaders and parents of students at Campbell Hall. The Headmaster has traditionally served as a liaison between the board and the various segments of the school community.

The school's development programs include annual and capital campaigns.

Campbell Hall is accredited by the Western Association of Schools and Colleges and the California Association of Independent Schools. It holds memberships in the National Association of Independent Schools, National Association of Episcopal Schools, Episcopal Diocesan Commission on Schools, Educational Records Bureau, National Association of College Admission Counselors, Council for Advancement and Support of Education, College Board, Council for Religion in Independent Schools, and Cum Laude Society.

ACADEMIC PROGRAMS

Students must complete 7½ units in the humanities, including 4 units of the English component, 3 units of the social science component, and ½ unit of senior seminar. Other requirements for graduation include 3 units of mathematics, 3 of foreign language, 3 of laboratory sciences, 2 years of physical education, ½ year of art history, and ½ year of music history. In addition to the required courses, students must complete at least 3½ additional units chosen from electives, such as music theory, calculus honors, discrete math, ethics, physiology, poetry, political science, precalculus/trigonometry, psychology, and visual and performing arts.

A number of special academic options attract qualified students. Advanced Placement courses are offered in every department and include physics, calculus, probability and statistics, computer science, English, French, Spanish, European history, world geography, music theory, U.S. history, American government, biology, chemistry, psychology, and computer science. In addition, qualified seniors may take college-level courses through the Talented High School Student Program of the California State University at Northridge, through local community colleges, and through the UCLA High School Scholars' Program.

Classes range in size from 8 or fewer students in advanced courses to 22 in some of the required courses.

The school's grading system uses percentages: 100–90 is an A; 89–80 is a B; 79–70 is a C; 69–60 is a D, and no credit is given for a grade below 59. Report cards, which are issued twice each semester, include evaluations of work habits and cooperation. Five weeks after the beginning of each quarter, students who are in academic difficulty in one or more courses are notified, as are their parents.

Each semester, students receiving all A's in academic classes are eligible for the Headmaster's List; students receiving a 3.7 academic average, with no grade lower than a B– for all courses, qualify for the Scholastic Honor Roll. On the basis of semester grades, students may qualify for recognition by the California Scholarship Federation, and academically outstanding juniors and seniors are chosen for membership in the Cum Laude Society.

FACULTY AND ADVISERS

There are 108 full-time faculty members (72 women and 36 men); 48 hold master's degrees, and 7 have doctorates. Faculty members are encouraged to attend seminars and conferences in their fields. In addition to giving academic and social guidance to individual students, faculty advisers work closely with class officers to ensure unity and success in various class projects and social activities.

Julian Bull was appointed Headmaster in 2003. A graduate of Dartmouth (B.A., 1982) and Boston College (M.A., 1988), he expects to receive his M.Div. from Virginia Theological Seminary in June 2006. Mr. Bull was formerly Head of School at Trinity Episcopal in New Orleans, Louisiana.

COLLEGE PLACEMENT

In October, all sophomores and juniors take the PSAT. Throughout their high school years, students receive extensive college counseling through group workshops and in-depth individual conferences with the college counseling staff members. High school families are invited to the annual Senior College Night at which the college admissions process is delineated and college-financing strategies are explained. During the fall semester, juniors and seniors have the opportunity to hear presentations from a nationwide selection of college admission officers who visit Campbell Hall.

All Campbell Hall students attend college. Graduates of the class of 2005 are attending such colleges as Boston University; Brown; Claremont McKenna; Columbia; Cornell; Emory; Georgetown; Harvard; MIT; Northwestern; NYU; Occidental; Pomona; Smith; Stanford; the University of California at Berkeley, Los Angeles, and San Diego; and the Universities of Michigan and Southern California.

STUDENT BODY AND CONDUCT

Of the 509 boys and girls in the Upper School (grades 9–12), 127 are in the ninth grade, 132 in the tenth, 124 in the eleventh, and 126 in the twelfth. Most students live in the suburban areas of Los Angeles.

Because Campbell Hall is concerned with the formation of character traits and values that reflect a sense of responsibility as well as a concern for the needs of others, misconduct is subject to disciplinary action. Violation of school rules and regulations may result in suspension or expulsion.

ACADEMIC FACILITIES

Campus academic facilities include classroom complexes, a math-science building, seven science labs, four computer labs, the Fine Arts Building, and a theater. A 22,000-square-foot library and academic center serves as the hub for technological resources. Every classroom has computers available. Students and faculty members have e-mail accounts and can send e-mail worldwide. The Internet is available as are research tools on CD-ROM. Web pages can be reached at http://www.campbellhall.org.

ATHLETICS

There are two basic components to the athletics program. First, required physical education courses provide basic and advanced instruction for sports that are in season; and second, Campbell Hall is a member of the California Interscholastic Federation (Gold Coast Athletic Association) and fields teams in baseball, basketball, cheerleading, cross-country, 11-man football, equestrian, golf, soccer, softball, tennis, track and field, and volleyball.

The school has two well-equipped gymnasiums, two tennis courts, a baseball diamond, two softball fields, and five outdoor basketball/volleyball courts.

EXTRACURRICULAR OPPORTUNITIES

The students have an active student government with elected officers representing the entire student body. Among the student-planned events are the upperclassman–freshman activities, dances, Homecoming, and Halloween, Christmas, and Valentine's Day celebrations. The year's social schedule culminates in a spring prom, planned by the junior class to honor the senior class.

The environmental education program currently includes a fourth-grade trip to Sycamore Canyon, a fifth-grade trip to Leo Carrillo State Beach, and weeklong trips to the Malibu Creek State Park for the sixth grade, to Camp Hess Kramer for the seventh grade, and to Canyon Creek for the eighth grade. There are trips to Joshua Tree for the ninth grade, to the Catalina Island for the tenth grade, and Sequoia for the eleventh grade, as well as a senior retreat. These programs encourage the development of a positive interest in learning by doing, a deeper appreciation of the natural environment, and bonds of mutual respect, self-respect, and community trust.

There are also many curriculum-related field trips and about sixty special interest groups, such as the Math Team; Highlanders, the school service club; the Cultural Awareness Club; the Spirit Club; Thespians; the Creative Writing Club; Amnesty International; Junior Statesmen of America; GSA; and the Community Service Committee.

DAILY LIFE

Monday through Thursday, there are four 80-minute academic classes that meet between 8:15 and 3:30. On Friday, each class meets for 80 minutes, between 8:15 and 2:20. Every day, one-half hour is devoted either to chapel (every Tuesday and Thursday) or to advisee meetings or clubs. There is a 35-minute lunch break. Interspersed among the academic courses are electives that provide enrichment in the fine arts (painting, ceramics, sculpture, and photography); the performing arts (chorus, drama, and dance); sports (physical education and team sports); and computer programming. Also available as classes are positions on the yearbook and the newspaper staffs.

SUMMER PROGRAMS

The school offers a full complement of summer programs for students in kindergarten through grade 12, including summer school courses, a creative arts camp, and sports camps. Additional information may be obtained by writing to the Summer Programs Director at Campbell Hall.

COSTS AND FINANCIAL AID

Tuition for 2005–06 was $15,610 to 20,670. Additional expenses included a fee of $600; $1400 per year for books, supplies, and activities; and a student body fee of $65 per year for grades 9–12. Tuition payments may be made biannually or, at an additional charge to cover interest costs, in ten monthly installments. Students may either bring their own lunches to school or purchase them from a caterer at the school at lunchtime. Parents purchase school uniforms for their children and provide transportation.

Financial aid is available and is awarded on the basis of family need. Continuing students have priority for renewal. In 2005–06, 21 percent of Middle and Upper School students received financial aid.

ADMISSIONS INFORMATION

The school seeks students who are able to benefit from a rigorous college-preparatory curriculum and who will contribute to extracurricular as well as academic activities. The school does not discriminate against applicants on the basis of race, religion, or national or ethnic origin.

An entrance examination is required, as are recommendations from 2 teachers, a transcript from the school in which the applicant is currently enrolled, and an on-campus interview.

APPLICATION TIMETABLE

The Admissions Office is open from 8 to 4, Monday through Friday, to answer inquiries and to arrange interviews and campus visits. Applicants should file an application, accompanied by a $100 fee, by February 1 of the year entrance is desired. Most applications are submitted by December of the year preceding the desired entrance. Applicants take the Independent School Entrance Examination.

The school makes most decisions concerning new admissions by March. Parents are expected to reply to an offer of acceptance within three weeks and to pay a $1000 registration fee, which is credited toward the first semester's tuition.

ADMISSIONS CORRESPONDENCE

Alice Fleming, Director of Admissions
Jennifer Foley, Director of Admissions
Campbell Hall
4533 Laurel Canyon Boulevard
P.O. Box 4036
North Hollywood, California 91617-9985
Phone: 818-980-7280
Web site: http://www.campbellhall.org

CANTERBURY SCHOOL
New Milford, Connecticut

Type: Coeducational boarding and day college-preparatory school conducted by lay faculty and administrators
Grades: 9–12 (Forms III–VI), postgraduate year
Enrollment: 358
Head of School: Thomas J. Sheehy III, Headmaster

THE SCHOOL

Canterbury was founded in 1915 by Henry O. Havemeyer, Clarence H. Mackay, and Nelson Hume to give Roman Catholic boys the kind of college preparation offered by the best nonsectarian boarding schools. It was named for an English school established by Saint Dunstan, Archbishop of Canterbury, in the tenth century. After fifty-five years as a boys' school, Canterbury began admitting girls as day students in 1972 and as boarding students in 1973.

The hallmark of a Canterbury education is the School's willingness to accept students as they are, support them where necessary, stretch them where appropriate, and inspire them to become moral leaders in a secular world. Canterbury's spiritual tradition informs all aspects of the program, including academics, the arts, athletics, and community service, which aims to inspire in students a commitment to lifelong volunteer service.

New Milford, a western Connecticut town (population 25,000), is 45 miles from Hartford, 35 miles from New Haven, and 85 miles from New York City. Canterbury's proximity to the Berkshires, the Appalachian Trail, and the Housatonic River provides opportunities for outdoor activities, while the nearby urban areas offer concerts, plays, and other cultural events.

A nonprofit corporation, Canterbury operates under the patronage of the Archbishop of Hartford and is directed by a self-perpetuating Board of Trustees. Many of the 3,800 alumni contribute to the Annual Alumni Giving Program and actively participate in the admissions process.

Canterbury is accredited by the New England Association of Schools and Colleges and is a member of the National Association of Independent Schools, the Connecticut Association of Independent Schools, the Secondary School Admission Test Board, and the Council for Religion in Independent Schools.

ACADEMIC PROGRAMS

The academic requirements and curriculum of the School have been planned to provide preparation for entrance into colleges in the United States. For graduation, Canterbury requires 20 credits, including 4 credits in English; 3 each in foreign languages, mathematics, and history; 2 each in theology and science; and 1 in fine arts. Five major courses per semester are required of all students.

Elective courses are offered each semester; some semester courses offered in past years have been Asian studies, modern playwrights, women's studies, economics, Shakespeare, criminal justice, oceanography, anthropology, film, and theater workshop. Courses in religion are concerned with such topics as Christian doctrine, human relations, ethical living, the New Testament, and comparative religion.

Qualified students may take Advanced Placement courses in English language, English literature, AB and BC calculus, American history, European history, economics, biology, chemistry, studio arts, music theory, French language, French literature, Latin, Spanish language, Spanish literature, and statistics.

Each year is divided into five 5-week marking periods, for which students and parents receive grade reports. At the end of each semester, parents receive detailed grade reports accompanied by comments from faculty advisers. In Canterbury's grading system, D represents passing; C is a college-recommending grade; B is honors; B+, high honors; and A, highest honors.

Canterbury has a student-faculty ratio of 6:1, and the average recitation class contains 11 students. Generally, classes are grouped heterogeneously; in most subject areas, however, honors sections are offered.

Faculty members are readily available for individual assistance, as 80 percent of them live on campus. In Forms III and IV, students are required to attend supervised study halls during the school day unless they maintain an acceptable grade average.

During the spring semester, seniors with sound academic records who have been accepted at college may undertake independent study projects. These senior projects involve students in vocational, educational, and social service programs of their choice.

Canterbury offers a program in English as a second language (ESL) to qualified students. Students in the ESL program are tested at the beginning of the year and are placed into an appropriate level of instruction. They are tested periodically to determine whether their progress warrants placement in a more advanced section. The goal of the ESL program is to channel students into the academic mainstream.

FACULTY AND ADVISERS

The full-time faculty, including administrators who teach, numbers 76. These 42 men and 34 women hold seventy-six baccalaureate degrees and forty-eight advanced degrees.

Thomas J. Sheehy III was appointed as Canterbury's fifth headmaster in December 1989 and assumed his duties in July 1990. He previously served for seven years as Headmaster of Old Westbury School of the Holy Child in New York. He is a graduate of Bowdoin College (B.A., 1969) and Pennsylvania State University (M.A., 1976). His concentrations were American history and classics, respectively. Mr. Sheehy and his wife, Betsy, live on campus with 1 of their 4 children.

Each faculty member advises a group of 6 to 8 students. The School retains a counselor, and the services of local psychologists and physicians are available. Two registered nurses supervise the infirmary, a local doctor is on call, and the facilities

of the New Milford Hospital are available. A resident chaplain is appointed by the Archbishop of Hartford, or, with his permission, by the Provincial of a Catholic order.

COLLEGE PLACEMENT

Canterbury prepares students for college through individual conferences beginning in the Fifth Form. A full-time college counselor conducts at least two conferences during the senior year. All Fourth and Fifth Formers take the PSAT in the fall and meet with the college counselor in late spring. More than 100 college admissions officers come to the School each fall for interviews and the annual college fair. The School works with each student in assembling an intelligent choice of colleges to which to apply.

Of the 100 members of Canterbury's 2005 graduating class, 100 percent were accepted by colleges. They are attending U.S. colleges and universities, including Boston College, Colby, Cornell, Dartmouth, Georgetown, Holy Cross, the U.S. Military Academy, and the Universities of Notre Dame and Pennsylvania.

STUDENT BODY AND CONDUCT

In 2004–05, 140 day students and 218 boarding students enrolled as follows: 68 in Form III, 85 in Form IV, 100 in Form V, and 105 in Form VI.

Approximately two thirds of the students are from Connecticut and New York; the remainder come from twenty other states and many other countries, including Bermuda, Canada, France, Germany, Hong Kong, Jamaica, Japan, Korea, Spain, Taiwan, and Thailand.

Students at Canterbury are expected to follow the code of conduct specifically outlined in the *Student-Parent Handbook.* Offenses are handled by the Dean of Students in most cases, but when a breach of proper conduct may lead to a student's dismissal, an ad hoc disciplinary committee composed of students and faculty members is convened to recommend a course of action to the Headmaster.

ACADEMIC FACILITIES

Nelson Hume Hall (1967) houses ten classrooms, two biology labs, a chemistry lab, a physics lab, a new science lecture room, and the 400-seat Maguire Auditorium. The Old Schoolhouse (1938), which concluded a $2-million renovation in 1998, contains fifteen classrooms and seminar and tutorial rooms. Robert Markey Steele Hall (1983) houses the administrative offices, the dining room, a snack bar, a ninety-eight-seat auditorium, and the 20,000-volume David Casey Copley Library, which includes two computer rooms equipped with Macintosh and IBM computers, a study center, and an audiovisual room. The Duffy Art Center is located in Duffy House. A choral facility was completed in 2001.

BOARDING AND GENERAL FACILITIES

Students and faculty members reside in Carter House (1926), Duffy House (1928), Sheehan House (1937), Ingleside House (1950), Havemeyer House (1964), Carmody House (1968), and Hickory Hearth (1985). Internet access is available in dormitory common areas and classrooms. The Dean of Students assigns all students to rooms, accommodating parent requests when feasible. Supplementary facilities on the campus include the Health Center, the Study Center, the snack bar, and the School store.

ATHLETICS

The School regards athletics as an integral part of student life. All students participate in one of the many sports offered. Students may compete on any of three levels in most sports. The program is designed to accommodate players of various ages, sizes, and abilities in competition with boys and girls of other western New England schools.

The Alumni Memorial Gymnasium houses a basketball court, wrestling rooms, squash courts, two weight rooms, a training room, an equipment room, a swimming pool, and locker room facilities. A $4-million annex was completed in 1999; additions include five international squash courts, a weight room, an aerobic/fitness room, locker rooms, and a training room. The Field House contains three courts that can be used for basketball, tennis, and volleyball. The Draddy Arena provides artificial ice for the School hockey program, local hockey leagues, and figure-skating instruction. Nine playing fields and six tennis courts offer ample space for outdoor practices.

EXTRACURRICULAR OPPORTUNITIES

The Student Government, composed of elected student and faculty representatives, forms a liaison between the student body and the administration. Senior proctors in the dormitories assist the dorm faculty.

Among the nonathletic activities are the Dramatic Society, which performs two shows a year; the monthly newspaper *(The Tabard);* the yearbook *(Cantuarian);* and the literary magazine *(Carillon).* There are also several clubs and groups in which students may participate, including Environmental Club, Outdoors Club, Women of Canterbury, Canterbury Blue, Chorale, and Admissions Tour Guides. For those interested in community service, there is work in a home for senior citizens, a swimming program for the mentally handicapped, and a children's day-care center. Eighty-five percent of Canterbury's students volunteer for community service.

Movies, dances, and field trips supplement Canterbury's regular program. On-campus events include a concert series, lectures, dramatic productions, the Spring Musical, Parents' Weekends, Homecoming, and Alumni Day.

DAILY LIFE

A student's day begins with breakfast, served from 7 to 7:45 a.m. Classes consist of seven 45-minute periods during the School day. Extra-help sessions are scheduled four mornings a week and can be scheduled at other times. The kitchen staff serves a cafeteria luncheon at noon. Following afternoon classes, athletic practices run from 3 to 5:15. A family-style dinner is served on Thursday; on the other nights of the week, a less formal cafeteria-style meal is served. There is an optional Mass each day at 5:45. Each evening, except Saturday, the students study in their rooms or in the Copley Library from 7:30 to 9:30. Faculty members in the dormitory supervise evening study hours, ensuring that students work independently. Lights are turned out at 11 p.m.

WEEKEND LIFE

The weekend begins after a student's last academic or athletics commitment on Saturday and ends at 7:30 p.m. on Sunday. Fifth and Sixth Formers are allowed two free weekends per semester. Third and Fourth Formers are allowed one weekend per semester. Third, Fourth, and Fifth Formers are allowed four Saturday overnights away from campus; Sixth Formers are permitted six. College visits are also allowed for Sixth Formers, who are permitted two absences from school for this purpose in their Sixth Form year.

Visitors are welcome in the common rooms of the dormitories at the discretion of the dorm parents. Both boarders and day students are encouraged to take part in a variety of weekend activities on Saturday night and Sunday afternoon. Activities range from dances and movies to cultural trips and shopping ventures. Students are also given permission to walk into New Milford for a late afternoon dinner on Saturday or to see a movie and shop on Sunday. Day students participate in all weekend activities.

COSTS AND FINANCIAL AID

In 2004–05, tuition at Canterbury was $33,300 for boarding students and $24,400 for day students. Tuition insurance and tuition payment plans are available.

In 2004, approximately $2.4 million in financial aid was awarded on a grant-in-aid basis. Each scholarship is renewable yearly as the student proves he or she is deserving of aid. For the 2004–05 school year, 45 percent of the students received awards ranging from $1000 to $20,000. The criteria of the School and Student Service for Financial Aid are used to determine need, the sole basis for granting student aid.

ADMISSIONS INFORMATION

Canterbury seeks students who can compete academically at the college-preparatory level, will contribute their talents and abilities to the school community, and will participate in school activities. Applicants must submit SSAT scores, a transcript and reference from their former school, and letters of recommendation. In almost all cases, a personal interview is required. New students are accepted in all forms, with a limited number entering Form VI as postgraduates.

APPLICATION TIMETABLE

Canterbury welcomes early inquiry, in the fall if possible. Campus tours are conducted six days a week by student guides, usually on the day of the interview, Monday through Friday from 7:45 a.m. to 2 p.m. and Saturday from 7:45 a.m. to noon. A nonrefundable fee of $50 is required with the student's application, which is due by January 20. On March 10, the School notifies prospective students of acceptance and expects parents' replies by April 10.

ADMISSIONS CORRESPONDENCE

Keith R. Holton, Director of Admission
Canterbury School
101 Aspetuck Avenue
New Milford, Connecticut 06776

Phone: 860-210-3832
Fax: 860-350-1120
E-mail: admissions@cbury.org
Web site: http://www.cbury.org

CARSON LONG MILITARY INSTITUTE

New Bloomfield, Pennsylvania

Type: Boys' boarding preparatory school with Junior ROTC
Grades: 6–12: Middle School, 6–8; Upper School, 9–12
Enrollment: School total: 205; Upper School: 157; Middle School: 48
Head of School: Col. Carson E. R. Holman, AUS Ret, President

THE SCHOOL

Carson Long Military Institute is the direct descendant of the New Bloomfield Academy, which was founded by Robert Finly as a Latin grammar school in 1836. The new school consisted of one room over a local tavern.

The school soon outgrew its small beginnings, and, by 1840, it had moved to the present campus overlooking the small town of New Bloomfield. The school was located in a brand-new building that is now "The Maples," which houses the school museum and the reception hall.

In 1842, the academy became a boarding school for both boys and girls. During the period from 1842 to 1914, the academy continued to grow. In 1914, the academy was sold to one of its alumni, Theodore K. Long, a prosperous Chicago attorney and a native of Millerstown, Pennsylvania. Long bought the school as a memorial to his son, William Carson Long, who had died at an early age. His first step in this direction was to rename the academy in remembrance of his son. Under its new name and with Long's business knowledge, the school continued to grow and prosper.

The year 1919 was a watershed time for the school. It was at that time that Carson Long was turned into a full-fledged military school with an all-male student body. To head the new military unit, Colonel Long's nephew, Second Lieutenant Edward Lee Holman, a graduate of Bloomfield Academy, was appointed to the faculty. In 1921, Carson Long Institute was incorporated, and its motto—How to Learn, How to Labor, How to Live—was used for the first time. Under the spirited and knowledgeable leadership of now Lieutenant Colonel Edward L. Holman, the school reached its apex of strength and became one of the leading military schools in the United States. When Colonel Edward Holman stepped down as President, his son, Colonel Carson E. R. Holman, a graduate of Carson Long, became President and Head of the School.

The main campus in New Bloomfield is composed of 50 acres that include five dormitory buildings, a Cadet Chapel with a social hall, a gymnasium, an infirmary, a museum, and a library. There is also a camp of 351 acres located 8 miles from the main campus, situated on Sherman's Creek. Even though the academy is in a small-town rural setting, it is only 28 miles from Harrisburg, the state capital, which allows the students access to that city's cultural and educational benefits.

The educational philosophy of the school is "To build and graduate young men with sound bodies, high faith, stout hearts, sound character, and alert minds; with deep love for all mankind and high loyalty to the flag and the country; well grounded in all those qualities which make for good leaders in time of war and great citizens in time of peace; and high in the resolve to be ashamed to die until millions yet unborn will find a better world because Carson Long boys lived."

Carson Long Military Institute is chartered under Pennsylvania state laws as a nonprofit corporation and is governed by a 15-member Board of Trustees. There is an active and supportive alumni association.

Carson Long Military Institute has been accredited by the Middle States Association of Colleges and Schools (MSA) since 1929. It is a member of the Association of Military Schools and Colleges of the United States (AMSCUS), the National Association of Independent Schools (NAIS), the Association of Boarding Schools (TABS), and the Pennsylvania Association of Independent Schools (PAIS).

ACADEMIC PROGRAMS

The academic program is designed to prepare a student for life and, if this requires a college education, to prepare him for any college in the country, including the service academies. Physical education and JROTC training are required for all cadets. The graduates of Carson Long Military Institute are required to complete 21 credits for graduation: English (4 units), mathematics (3 units), science (3 units), social studies (3 units), arts or humanities (2 units), computer science (1 unit), health and physical education (1 unit), and four electives. Electives include such courses as the Bible, speech, computer keyboarding, and political geography.

Expository writing is stressed in all courses, and speech and comprehension are stressed in the language courses. The JROTC military training curriculum is prescribed by the Department of the Army. The following subjects are covered: military courtesy, customs, organization, history, and traditions of the army; health and first aid; map reading; and leadership and moral guidance. Military training instills self-discipline, which teaches a boy to do his job (and study assignments) right, to do it on time, and to do it without being told. In short, military training is designed as a leadership training course "to motivate young people to be better citizens."

The average class size is 13 cadets, and the ratio of teachers to students is 1:9. Students and parents receive report cards every six weeks. Cadets have supervised evening study hall in their classrooms each evening, Monday through Friday, with one teacher for every 30–40 boys.

FACULTY AND ADVISERS

The President, Colonel Carson E. R. Holman, was appointed in 1971 after serving as a member of the faculty since 1957. He is a graduate of Carson Long Military Institute. Colonel Holman received his B.S. from the United States Military Academy at West Point, his Pennsylvania teaching certificate from Dickinson College, and his Master of Arts degree in education supervision from Bucknell University. He is very active in several educational and service organizations.

The faculty consists of 3 administrators and 21 teachers, 4 of whom are women. Thirty-seven percent of the faculty members have advanced degrees. The male faculty members serve not only as classroom teachers but also as live-in dormitory supervisors and military tactical officers. For this reason, they are able to give round-the-clock counseling services. The administrative staff consists of an office supervisor, a bookkeeper, 3 secretaries, a librarian, 3 nurses, and 3 maintenance engineers.

COLLEGE PLACEMENT

The Dean of the School and the Assistant Dean coordinate all educational and college counseling. The school's testing and guidance program is carried on in conjunction with the Educational Records Bureau and includes standardized career interest, aptitude, and subject tests. Cadets are strongly encouraged to take the PSAT, ACT, SAT, and/or CAT. Using this data, the Dean and the Assistant Dean plan a program that ensures excellent academic preparation for the right college.

In the last five years, more than 85 percent of the graduating students were accepted at college. Colleges and universities that recent graduates have entered include Clemson, Hofstra, Moravian, Norwich, NYU, Pace, Penn State, Rensselaer, Rutgers, St. John's, the State University of New York, Syracuse, Temple, and The Citadel.

STUDENT BODY AND CONDUCT

The total school enrollment is 205. There are 9 students in grade 6, 12 in grade 7, 27 in grade 8, 40 in grade 9, 38 in grade 10, 49 in grade 11, and 30 in grade 12. All of these cadets are boarding students. Of the total enrollment, 60 percent of the cadets come from Pennsylvania, New York, New Jersey, and other eastern states; a total of seventeen states and ten other countries are represented.

The student council consists of two governing bodies: the House of Representatives and the Senate, whose weekly meetings are supervised by faculty members. The student council may recommend punishments; however, the Commandant and his faculty assistants (tactical officers) actually award all routine punishments. The Commandant's Board reviews and acts on all serious offenses.

It is assumed that every cadet is of good character and a gentleman whose actions are always honorable and whose sense of moral and social responsibility can be depended upon at all times to maintain a high level of behavior, morale, and loyalty to the school. This is emphasized by the taking of the Cadet Pledge that the cadet "will not lie, cheat, or steal."

The Cadet Corps is organized into a battalion of three companies and a drum and bugle corps. The cadet officers, under the strict guidance of the faculty tactical officers and the Commandant of Cadets, are directly responsible for the discipline, appearance, and performance of the battalion at all formations, parades, and ceremonies. The Corps of Cadets attend a weekly nondenominational chapel service that is conducted by the cadets and faculty officers. The cadets are required to attend local church services. Special attention is given to cadets of the Jewish, Islamic, and Buddhist faiths for services in those faiths.

ACADEMIC FACILITIES

All buildings are brick with a colonial style. Building '49 contains classrooms and a laboratory as well as dorms for the cadets and living quarters for

3 faculty members. Willard Hall, the Middle School, contains classrooms and dorms for the cadets as well as living quarters for 4 members of the faculty. Centennial Hall contains the dining room, uniform storage space, the bookstore, record storage, military storage room, three faculty member apartments, and a day room for the cadets as well as two classrooms. The rifle range and computer classroom are in Belfry Hall. Building Annex contains a biology and earth science laboratory. The library contains more than 8,000 volumes. The auditorium of the chapel is used on a weekly basis for public speaking activities.

BOARDING AND GENERAL FACILITIES
Building '49 contains dormitory space for 40 cadets plus a dayroom. Centennial Hall has a dorm for 32 cadets and a dayroom. Belfry Hall houses 35 cadets, a dayroom, and 2 faculty member apartments. The Annex Building has dorm space for 35 cadets. There are 2 boys in the high school rooms, sometimes 3. There are 3 boys in the eighth grade rooms, sometimes 4. The sixth and seventh graders sleep in an open bay barracks, but they are separated into 3 squad areas with 8 boys to a squad. Building '49 and Willard Hall each contain living quarters for 3 faculty members. The Holman Memorial Chapel, named in honor of Colonel Edward Lee Holman, President of Carson Long Military Institute for sixty-one years, contains a sanctuary for the weekly chapel services. In addition, it has a social hall for dances and a War Memorial in honor of those Carson Long cadets who gave their lives in defense of the United States, and the JROTC Department.

The Maples, which was the original school building in 1840, houses the School museum and reception hall.

The infirmary has 3 nurses who provide 24-hour coverage; several doctors are on call. The local health center is 15 minutes away, four hospitals are 45 minutes away, and an ambulance and fire company are one block away.

ATHLETICS
Carson Long Military Institute offers a wide range of varsity and intramural sports. The school philosophy states that every cadet should have the opportunity to take part in sports regardless of his athletic ability. The Kate Carson Gymnasium contains three basketball courts, the Athletic Director's office, lockers, and showers. It also has dressing rooms for visiting and home teams. On campus are five tennis courts and fields for football, soccer, baseball, and intramural athletics.

The school competes on the interscholastic level with other independent schools. The interscholastic sports are baseball, basketball, football, rifle, soccer, tennis, and wrestling. Intramural sports include basketball, Frisbee football, ice hockey, softball, table tennis, touch football, and volleyball. All cadets are encouraged to participate in some sport.

EXTRACURRICULAR OPPORTUNITIES
School organizations include drum and bugle corps, Scholastic Honor Society, dance committee, school newspaper, drama club, yearbook, glee club, weight lifting club, fencing, and ski club. Students may take piano lessons. Additional activities include debating, declamation, hiking, and JROTC activities such as military police, raiders (military skills), color guard, and drill team. Social events include formal and informal dances (including the military ball), outside entertainment programs, alumni homecoming, two parents' days, an overnight camping trip to Camp Carson, plays presented by cadets, a military "Dining In," and trips to Philadelphia, Lancaster, Hershey, Gettysburg, and Washington, D.C., and to movies in the vicinity of Harrisburg. Cadets may volunteer for community service to rake leaves or shovel snow for senior citizens.

DAILY LIFE
The daily schedule includes reveille at 6:40 a.m., outside calisthenics at 7, inspection of quarters at 8:05, and classes at 8:30. Classes run for 40 minutes, and there are seven periods a day, plus a military drill period after class. From 4 until 5:15 p.m., there are intramural games and varsity practice. At 5:30, there is Retreat Formation and dinner. All three meals are served family-style, with faculty members eating at the tables with the cadets. From 6 until 7 p.m., those cadets who are not restricted to campus may visit the town of New Bloomfield. Study hall is from 7 until 9:25 p.m. (8:45 for Middle School). Taps is at 9:45 for the Upper School (9:15 for the Middle School). On Saturday mornings, there is always a formal inspection and dress parade at 10 a.m. Church attendance in town is required on Sunday.

WEEKEND LIFE
The school has a liberal policy on town permission. Unless a student is on restriction, he is permitted to walk into town two times a week. Off-campus movie trips are scheduled at least once a month. Each dormitory dayroom has its own television set and VCR. The school selects and provides appropriate movies for weekend student viewing.

Dances are held about every three weeks. There are exchange dances with two independent girls' schools that are within approximately 50 miles of the campus.

Interscholastic and intramural athletic games are sometimes played on Saturday afternoon. Since the school is located in the beautiful foothills of the Blue Ridge Mountains, hiking is a very popular weekend activity.

COSTS AND FINANCIAL AID
Tuition and room and board were $15,400 in 2005–06, and extra charges were approximately $950. There is a $500 room deposit and a two-payment plan, with payments due on August 1 and November 1. The school operates its own monthly payment plan after the first payment on August 1. The average scholarship award is $1200. Scholarships are for returning students only.

ADMISSIONS INFORMATION
The school admits students of any race, color, creed, and national or ethnic origin. New students are accepted in grades 6–12. The Admissions Committee selects students who are of good character and who have average or above-average ability. Students who have been arrested, have been before the courts, or have been expelled from any school are not accepted at Carson Long. No entrance tests are required. Although it is preferred to have students who can handle college-preparatory work, this is not a requirement. Two character references are required: one from the assistant school principal and the other from the school counselor. In addition, a transcript and a personal interview are required.

APPLICATION TIMETABLE
Inquiries are welcome at any time. The academy has a rolling admissions policy, and applications are considered in order of receipt. Applications are available online. Campus tours can be conducted anytime during the year except Christmas Day; however, Saturday morning at 10 a.m. is a good time to visit the school and to see a dress parade. (Cadet parades are scheduled only between September 15 and May 31.)

ADMISSIONS CORRESPONDENCE
Lieutenant Colonel David M. Comolli
Director of Admissions
Carson Long Military Institute
P.O. Box 98-DD
New Bloomfield, Pennsylvania 17068
Phone: 717-582-2121
Fax: 717-582-8763
E-mail: carson6@pa.net
Web site: http://www.carsonlong.org

THE CASCADILLA SCHOOL

Ithaca, New York

Type: Coeducational boarding and day college-preparatory school
Grades: 9–12, postgraduate year
Enrollment: 60
Head of School: Patricia A. Kendall, Headmistress

THE SCHOOL

The Cascadilla School was founded in 1870 as a preparatory school for Cornell University. In 1939, it was reorganized as a nonprofit corporation under a Board of Trustees and granted an absolute charter by the Board of Regents of the State of New York.

The philosophy of education at Cascadilla is to provide a flexible, accelerated program within which each individual can achieve his or her goals in preparation for a successful college career. This learning experience emphasizes the steady development of an adult viewpoint and a mature approach to life.

The School is located in the heart of the Finger Lakes region in Ithaca, a city of 50,000 people, 20,000 of whom are college and university students. This scenic college town provides many cultural activities as well as athletics events. The School is located on the edge of the Cornell University campus, and students are encouraged to take advantage of the community's outstanding offerings, which include restaurants, shops, theater, and recreational facilities. There is direct air and bus service from New York City and other major U.S. cities.

The Cascadilla School is run by a 5-member Board of Trustees that is drawn from the business and professional community. Patricia A. Kendall is currently President of the Board and also Headmistress.

The School is privately endowed and nondenominational and has assets of approximately $1.2 million. Tuition charges provide more than 90 percent of its funding, and gifts from alumni and friends make up the remainder.

The Cascadilla School is registered with the New York State Board of Regents.

ACADEMIC PROGRAMS

The Cascadilla School offers a complete high school curriculum as well as an English as a second language program approved by the U.S. Immigration and Naturalization Service. The School's goal is to prepare students for college in an accelerated program. Full-unit high school courses are taught by the semester; the typical student completes between 7 and 8 units per year.

Twenty-three units are required for graduation, including 5 in English, 4 in social sciences, 3 in math, 3 in science, 1 in a language other than English, 1 in art and/or music, 2 in physical education, ½ in health, and 3½ in electives. All courses are taught on the New York State Regents level. In addition to taking Advanced Placement courses, seniors may enroll in actual college course work at Cornell, Ithaca College, or Tompkins Cortland Community College.

Extra help and supervised study are available in the afternoon until 5 p.m. The library and the laboratories are open until then. No evening study hall is required unless a student's academic performance falls below acceptable standards.

All class grouping is heterogeneous. Class size averages 8 students, and the student-teacher ratio is 6:1.

The Cascadilla School uses a numerical grading system that runs from 0 to 100, with 70 the minimum passing grade and 75 the start of college-recommending grades. Reports, with individual comments, are sent home monthly; more-frequent reports are developed in special situations.

Certain reading and writing skills are required for entrance into English III. A three-level skills program is used for students who do not meet these requirements.

The Cascadilla School is proud of its sixty-seven years of experience in providing a high-quality intensive English as a second language program. Cascadilla offers classes in reading, conversation, grammar, and writing at all levels of language ability. Students are enrolled in daily 1-hour-long classes and offered an optional elective course designed to prepare them for the Test of English as a Foreign Language (TOEFL).

Cascadilla offers three levels of study: beginning, intermediate, and advanced. Classroom instruction by teachers who are experienced in all areas of language education ensures that students make steady progress to the next level. The key to the success of Cascadilla School's ESL program is a curriculum that meets the individual needs of each student; classes average 5 students. In addition, students are assisted in their process of application to American universities and colleges.

FACULTY AND ADVISERS

The Cascadilla School has 9 full-time and 6 part-time teachers. All have bachelor's degrees, and 14 have master's degrees. The small size and personal nature of the School make every teacher an adviser. An attempt is made to make time in the school day for personal contact outside of regularly scheduled classes.

There is very little turnover in the full-time staff. The part-time staff is drawn from the Cornell and Ithaca college communities and changes as courses demand.

The Headmistress' academic background includes a B.S. degree from Syracuse University, an M.S. degree from Nazareth College, and an administrative degree in education from the State University of New York at Cortland. Mrs. Kendall brings thirty-five years of experience in education to Cascadilla School.

COLLEGE PLACEMENT

Planning for college begins almost as soon as a student enters Cascadilla. The School has entered a partnership with Kaplan Educational Centers, where Cascadilla students are provided prepara-

tion for the SAT exams on campus. Kaplan tailors its SAT preparation program to meet the needs of Cascadilla students. A section of the library is devoted to college catalogs and career information. College visits are encouraged, and the School provides transportation for them. Involvement with the Cornell University community provides valuable stimulation for most Cascadilla students.

Students in the class of 2005 ranged in SAT composite math and verbal scores from 1150 to 1500. The average combined score for graduating seniors was 1150 or better. Approximately one third of the graduating seniors also took the ACT. The ACT is taken only when a student wishes to travel south or west to college.

The School averages between 15 and 20 graduates per year. Ninety-nine percent go on to further education, and about 90 percent attend four-year colleges. Recent graduates are attending Binghamton, Boston University, Cornell, Georgetown, Ithaca, NYU, RIT, St. John's, Tufts, and various SUNY colleges.

STUDENT BODY AND CONDUCT

The Cascadilla School attracts students from a wide geographic area. In 2005–06, students came from six states and five other countries. The School has room for 25 boarders; day students and adult ESL students make up the rest of the School population. Seventy percent of the students are juniors, seniors, and postgraduates; unlike many private schools, Cascadilla is interested primarily in students who are planning to be at the School for one or two years. The accelerated program works best when the students have the emotional maturity to establish goals and work toward them. Most freshmen and sophomores are day students.

ACADEMIC FACILITIES

The classroom building was opened in 1880. It contains eight classrooms, a science laboratory, a language laboratory, a computer room with IBM-compatible computers, and a library of nearly 9,000 volumes.

Students who are interested in music or the visual arts may use the programs and facilities of Cornell University or Ithaca College.

BOARDING AND GENERAL FACILITIES

The two dormitories are designed to bring together the elements of a family environment, college life, and apartment living. Single and double rooms are available, each with its own refrigerator; each dormitory has a snack kitchen and a TV lounge. Supervision is provided by dorm parents, and college students also live in the dorms. The School tries to create a living environment that reinforces its academic programs.

The Cascadilla School has no formal dining facilities of its own; therefore, most students use the dorm facilities for breakfast and take the fourteen-meal option of the Cornell University Meal Plan for lunch and dinner, although a twenty-one-meal option is available. This daily exposure to the university helps them to become familiar with its programs and facilities.

ATHLETICS

Cascadilla's physical education program offers bowling, cross-country skiing, rowing, and sailboarding. Students are also encouraged to join the YMCA, which includes the weight room and aerobics, swimming, and racquetball facilities. The Cascadilla School does not have an interscholastic athletic program. Crew is offered through the Cascadilla Boat Club (a nonprofit educational organization).

EXTRACURRICULAR OPPORTUNITIES

Most extracurricular opportunities are available through the university and the community. The area is rich in cultural events that range from lectures and plays to musical performances of all types.

DAILY LIFE

Most students have 5 hours of academic course work between 8 a.m. and 4 p.m. All students and faculty members share a common lunch period. The afternoon program varies from day to day and may include physical education; special courses, such as SAT preparation through Kaplan, photography, drawing, and driver's education; and opportunities to get extra help or tutoring. After dinner, evenings typically involve study, recreation, and a movie or TV.

WEEKEND LIFE

The School sponsors movies and occasional parties. There may also be ski trips that include transportation, instruction, and rental of equipment. In addition, as is true of extracurricular activities during the week, students may take advantage of the wide range of opportunities at Cornell and other local schools and colleges.

SUMMER PROGRAMS

The Cascadilla School has offered a six-week summer session for the last seventy-five years. The program attracts both students who are interested in repeating courses and students hoping to shorten the length of time necessary to complete secondary school graduation requirements. Students are enrolled in advanced classes, repeat classes, and tutorials as well as the Driver Education course. A pamphlet is published that explains the program in detail.

COSTS AND FINANCIAL AID

Tuition, a double room, and board for the 2005–06 school year were $26,000. Additional charges are made for single rooms and for unusually heavy course loads.

The Cascadilla School is interested in attracting good students from all cultures and socioeconomic groups. Last year, 40 percent of the School's students received some type of financial aid or scholarship, averaging $1000 per student per semester. There are also several opportunities for part-time work at the School.

ADMISSIONS INFORMATION

The Cascadilla School is looking for students who are ready to put their high school program together and prepare for college. The SSAT is not required. The School, however, seeks students with academic potential, if not achievement. An admission interview is required for all U.S. applicants, and a $50 application fee is required of all U.S. applicants. An application fee is also required of international applicants.

The Cascadilla School admits students of any race, color, national or ethnic origin to all the rights, privileges, programs, and activities generally accorded or made available to students at the School. It does not discriminate on the basis of race, color, or national and ethnic origin in administration of its educational policies, admissions policies, scholarship programs, athletic and other School-administered programs.

APPLICATION TIMETABLE

Application deadlines are January 15, June 30, and September 1, depending on the term in which a student wishes to begin. A $4000 deposit is required upon acceptance. It is strongly suggested that applications be submitted by June 1 for September entrance, as the amount of dormitory space is extremely limited.

ADMISSIONS CORRESPONDENCE

Patricia A. Kendall, Headmistress
The Cascadilla School
P.O. Box 878
116 Summit Street
Ithaca, New York 14850

Phone: 607-272-3110
Fax: 607-272-0747
E-mail: admissions@cascadillaschool.org
Web site: http://www.cascadillaschool.org/

CATE SCHOOL

Carpinteria, California

Type: Coeducational boarding and day college-preparatory secondary school
Grades: 9–12
Enrollment: 265
Head of School: Benjamin D. Williams IV, Headmaster

THE SCHOOL

Cate School, established in 1910, is a four-year, coeducational, college-preparatory boarding school outside Santa Barbara, California. In addition to a highly rigorous academic curriculum that features a combined thirty-eight Advanced Placement (AP) offerings and honors courses, all students participate in an extracurricular program that includes athletics, drama, music, dance, community service, and an extensive outdoor program. The class size averages between 10 and 12 students. The student body of 265 students (83 percent are boarders) comes from twenty-three states and twelve other countries and is both academically talented and remarkably diverse (33 percent are members of minority groups). A typical applicant to Cate has strong character, a history of high academic achievement, and is mature, curious, adventurous, and willing to assume increasing responsibility and independence. An ability to communicate comfortably and well with peers and adults is important in this small, tight-knit community where students and faculty members work and live closely together.

A not-for-profit organization, Cate School is directed by a board of 28 trustees, including 2 faculty advisory trustees, 4 ex officio, 13 alumni, and 1 Alumni Council President. The endowment is currently valued at $60 million and is supplemented by an Annual Fund that totaled more than $1.5 million in 2004–05. This generous support comes from an alumni body of nearly 2,700, friends of the school, and current students. Forty-one percent of the alumni participate in the Annual Fund, and 80 percent of current families support the Annual Fund as well.

Cate is accredited by the Western Association of Schools and Colleges and is affiliated with the National Association of Independent Schools, the California Association of Independent Schools, the Western Boarding Schools Association, the Cum Laude Society, the California Interscholastic Federation, A Better Chance, and the Secondary School Admission Test Board.

ACADEMIC PROGRAMS

Through commitment, scholarship, companionship, and service, each member of the Cate community contributes to what Mr. Cate called "the spirit of this place ... all compounded of beauty and virtue, quiet study, vigorous play, and hard work."

The specific purposes of the rigorous curriculum, in order of priority, are to stimulate curiosity and interest, to develop the skills needed for the effective continuation of learning, to encourage intellectual independence, to foster the responsible use of knowledge and ability, and to engage students in a range of scholarly pursuits, including the arts, English, foreign languages, mathematics, science, computer science, human development, and social studies.

The order of these purposes is important. It reflects a set of priorities that is understood by every teacher and is inherent in the design of every course. At Cate, of more importance than what students learn is that students come to understand how to learn. Throughout the four years, a student develops both the skills and the desire to continue learning.

Graduation requirements are generally as follows: Foundation Arts, plus either a yearlong arts course or two semester-long arts courses; an English course per year; 3 years of a foreign language (French, Spanish, Chinese, or Japanese) or, for students entering with advanced standing through the sophomore year, the successful completion of a third-year foreign language course; a history course in each of the first two years and U.S. history in the Upper School (grades 11 and 12); a mathematics course per year through the junior year, with the final course determined by the level at which the student entered Cate; physics, chemistry, and biology. Cate has a four-year, sequential, nationally recognized Human Development Program consisting of Freshman, Sophomore, and Junior Seminars and the Senior Teaching Assistant Program.

In addition to this core curriculum, students may choose from electives in all disciplines. Examples include sculpture, creative writing, anthropology, computer programming, marine biology, international relations, and Asian studies. Advanced Placement preparation is offered in all disciplines.

A typical class contains 10 students, and the student-faculty ratio is 5:1. The academic year is divided into two semesters of two marking periods each, and parents are apprised of student progress in the early fall, as well as at the end of each marking period.

FACULTY AND ADVISERS

The Cate faculty includes 55 full- and part-time members. The Headmaster, Benjamin D. Williams IV, who has a B.A. from Williams College and a master's degree from Brown University, was appointed in 1997. The faculty is firmly committed to the residential program, and therefore more than 90 percent live on campus. The advising system is based on the constant contact that occurs formally and informally between classes, at meals, and on the athletics field between students and their faculty advisers. The adviser is assigned by student preference. The advisory system serves as a formal assurance that every student receives regular support and guidance. Advisers keep track of students' academic performance, athletic accomplishments, and general well-being. They open their homes and their lives to their advisees and take them on group activities regularly.

COLLEGE PLACEMENT

The college-counseling program has two major objectives: to help provide students with a range of college choices and to help them clarify these choices in view of their own academic and personal strengths. The result is students who are solidly supported and well informed. Some of the most popular college selections of Cate graduates over the past four years are Berkeley (17); USC (12); Colorado (7); NYU (7); Princeton (7); California, San Diego (6); California, Santa Cruz (6); Colorado College (6); Pennsylvania (6); Stanford (5); Columbia (4); and Tufts (4).

STUDENT BODY AND CONDUCT

In 2005–06, Cate's enrollment of 265 included 58 freshmen, 70 sophomores, 70 juniors, and 67 seniors. This total included 45 day students. Twenty-two states and twelve other countries are represented, and 40 percent of the boarding students are from outside California. The School seeks to enroll a geographically and socioeconomically diverse student body. Students of color account for 35 percent of the student body.

The goal of the School's policies and practices is to provide students with a set of community standards that define daily expectations, set limits for social behavior, and foster a sense of responsibility for the School and themselves. The breaking of a major school rule results in the convening of the Disciplinary Committee, which considers all circumstances. Students may be separated from the School for a first violation.

ACADEMIC FACILITIES

Cate offers extensive facilities in every academic area. The Seeley G. Mudd building, erected in 1984, provides an exceptionally well designed facility for instruction in the laboratory sciences. The Keck Computer Lab has Macs, Power Macs, and Pentium PCs. In addition, Cate maintains a schoolwide network with ports in the library, in all dorm rooms and faculty apartments, and in most classrooms and offices. This network provides access to e-mail, file servers, and the Internet. In all, there are more than fifty microcomputers networked on the Mesa. The Arts Center offers modern facilities for a full range of fine and dramatic arts, including a computer graphics and video workshop. The Ceramics Barn is the latest addition to the arts facilities. The McBean Library contains a selection of 115 current periodicals, open stacks for 30,000 volumes, and subscriptions to 13 online databases.

BOARDING AND GENERAL FACILITIES

Central to any boarding school experience is the quality of life in the dormitory—the basic unit of

Cate's residential program. The average dormitory houses 20 students, and each dorm is supervised by 3 faculty members. Seniors are distributed evenly throughout the campus and play an important leadership role in developing the spirit of cooperation and the sense of being part of an extended family that typifies the Cate dormitory. The Cate Health Center is staffed by a nurse, who resides on campus. Meals are served in a central dining commons. Two nights a week is reserved for formal dinners, while the rest of the meals are served cafeteria-style.

ATHLETICS

Athletics are an integral part of the overall program at Cate, and each student participates in one of the many after-school options offered in each of the three seasons. The entire program is characterized by participation and a general commitment to excellence. For the competitive athlete, Cate offers an extensive slate of team sports and competes against a range of public and private schools, including many California Interscholastic Federation schools from the Los Angeles area. Interscholastic offerings for both boys and girls include cross-country, lacrosse, soccer, tennis, track, volleyball, basketball, squash, and water polo. Eight-man football and baseball are offered for boys, and softball is offered for girls. Intramural options include aerobics, dance, surfing, Ultimate Frisbee, and weight training.

Facilities include the Fleischmann and Sprague Gymnasiums, with squash courts, basketball courts, three athletics fields, an all-weather track, baseball and softball diamonds, a swimming pool, eight tennis courts, and a weight-training room.

EXTRACURRICULAR OPPORTUNITIES

Cate believes strongly that education extends beyond the classroom. An extensive Community Service Program encourages students to tutor in local public elementary schools, work with physically and developmentally disabled children and adults in foster homes in the local community, or teach swimming to handicapped students. The School also participates in the Los Niños Program, taking frequent weekend trips to help poverty-stricken children of Tijuana, Mexico. Clubs and organizations include Amnesty International, the California Math League, the Environmental Club, Jazz Band, Mock Trial Competition, and Destination Imagination. Other activities include the school yearbook, newspaper, and literary magazine.

The Student-Faculty Senate is responsible for determining major school policy. The senate consists of 13 students and 5 faculty members and is responsible for formulating ideas, reviewing policy, and representing student and faculty opinion on all aspects of school life.

DAILY LIFE

Classes meet five days a week and on alternate Saturdays in 45-minute periods, with a shortened day on Wednesday and Saturday. Classes, which begin at 8, are preceded by daily chores that range from kitchen duty to dormitory and campus cleanup. Each morning at 9:40, the community gathers either for an assembly in the theater, Tuesday Talks in the chapel, or by advisory group in an adviser's office or home. Athletics are scheduled at the end of the academic day and before dinnertime. Study hours take place every day, except Saturday, from 8:30 to 10:30 p.m. Seniors choose how they spend their evening study hours and may remain out of the dorm until 11. One day each week the School gathers for a short evening convocation, which involves student and faculty participation as well as presentations by outside speakers.

WEEKEND LIFE

Most weekend activities are determined by a student activities committee and a faculty adviser. In addition to interscholastic sports, activities might include dances, beach trips, activities in Santa Barbara, plays or concerts in Los Angeles, local day hikes, movies on campus, or special events such as the Cate Fair, a Los Niños trip, dramatic productions, or the Talent Show. In addition, eight times a year the entire weekend is reserved for more extensive activities such as kayaking, sailing, fishing, skiing, and camping. These weekends also provide the opportunity to visit cultural centers outside of the immediate area.

COSTS AND FINANCIAL AID

The 2005–06 tuition, room, and board fees for boarding students were $34,750, and the day student tuition of $26,250 includes any meals that the student eats on campus. Personal expenses for students vary and include textbooks. Financial aid is based on need. Applications for admission and for financial aid are considered independently. Cate provides financial assistance to approximately 30 percent of the students each year from a budget of $1.9 million.

ADMISSIONS INFORMATION

Most students enter Cate in the ninth or tenth grade. Each year, a limited number of exceptionally well qualified students are admitted into the eleventh grade. It is highly unusual for the School to offer admission to a new twelfth grader. The Admission Committee considers a student's previous record, recommendations of teachers, personal references, scores on the Secondary School Admission Test or Independent School Entrance Exam, extracurricular interests and strengths, and impressions and information obtained in the personal interview. The committee strives to enroll able students who bring a wide variety of talents, skills, interests, and backgrounds to the Cate community.

APPLICATION TIMETABLE

Campus visits, which include a class visit, observing an assembly or Tuesday Talk, campus tour, and personal interviews should be scheduled and applications should be filed in the fall or early winter. The Office of Admission is open from 8:30 a.m. until 4 p.m., Monday through Friday. Campus visits are offered in the mornings only on Monday, Tuesday, Wednesday, and Friday. The application deadline is January 15. Notifications of the Admission Committee's decisions are mailed on March 10. Acceptance to Cate assumes that a student will satisfactorily complete the current school year.

ADMISSIONS CORRESPONDENCE

Peter J. Mack, Director of Admission and
   Enrollment
Cate School
P.O. Box 5005
Carpinteria, California 93014-5005

Phone: 805-684-4127 Ext. 217
Fax: 805-684-2279
E-mail: admission@cate.org
Web site: http://www.cate.org

CATLIN GABEL SCHOOL

Portland, Oregon

Type: independent, coeducational college-preparatory day school
Grades: P–12
Enrollment: School total: 705; Upper School: 270
Head of School: Lark P. Palma, Ph.D.

THE SCHOOL

Catlin Gabel School is an independent, coeducational day school accredited through the National Association of Independent Schools and the Northwest Association of Schools and Colleges. The School was founded in 1957, when the Catlin Hillside School and Gabel Country Day School merged. At Catlin Gabel School, each person's effort, imagination, and positive contributions to the community are valued. The faculty and staff members and trustees are dedicated to individuality, academic excellence, multiculturalism, and lifelong learning.

The School's program has been carefully and thoughtfully designed to educate the total person, incorporating academics along with arts, physical education, and a strong sense of community service. Through a wide range of interscholastic sports, exchange programs, and extracurricular activities, students are encouraged to take risks and to participate in a wide variety of experiences, and they are given the opportunity and responsibility to share in the creation and leadership in many of these special programs.

The Catlin Gabel School campus is a safe and inspiring place that sets the stage for learning. The 54-acre campus is in a rural setting 5 miles west of downtown Portland. The serene, pastoral atmosphere adds to the educational curriculum and the School's identity. Special places on campus, such as the peaceful Fir Grove and the inviting open space of the Paddock, create transition zones for teachers and students alike. Sculptures by Northwest artists are carefully placed throughout the campus. These areas create natural boundaries and express the School's high regard for natural beauty and art. The buildings are arranged in clusters around the community center known as the Barn, formerly an integral part of the Honey Hollow Farm. While some of the other buildings are also part of the original farm, there are also many contemporary structures that blend in with the environment.

ACADEMIC PROGRAMS

The Upper School offers a broad and demanding arts and sciences curriculum. The educational experience of each student encompasses the progressive mastery of the tools of inquiry and expression, understanding of fundamental mathematical and scientific ideas and techniques, active participation in the arts, and development of coordination as well as a sense of working with others through physical education. The School believes that these skills are fundamental to the development of each student's "fullest powers as an individual and as a group member." Community service, civic responsibility, and a commitment to using one's education wisely and well are core values of the School. Discussions about rights, responsibilities, and choices are integrated into every facet of the School program.

The Upper School's four-year plan of studies seeks to recognize and develop individual strengths as well as to build competence in areas of weakness. Pace and schedule vary with the individual. Teachers are interested in how their students learn and in helping them establish learning strategies. Through the enriched curriculum, students gain knowledge and self-esteem. Catlin Gabel encourages competence over competition. Therefore, letter grades are assigned only at the end of Upper School courses for the purpose of preparing manuscripts for college. Written evaluations and teacher-student/teacher-parent conferences take the place of periodic grading. Students at Catlin Gabel embrace learning in an informal atmosphere of respect.

Catlin Gabel's Upper School program fosters a lifelong love of learning and prepares students for productive experiences in college and beyond. All students must complete minimum core requirements before graduation. In addition, they may choose elective courses of special interest or usefulness. The program is designed to introduce each student to a wide spectrum of scholastic endeavor while encouraging in-depth study in fields of major interest. Each student, in consultation with the adviser, is encouraged to plan as broad a program as possible, taking into consideration possible requirements for further education after high school.

The minimum requirements for graduation are eighteen academic courses, including the departmental requirements and electives chosen by the student, and completion of an annual community service requirement. The minimum departmental requirements are 4 years of English; 3 years of math; 3 years of history; 3 years of science; 3 years of language (French, Spanish, or Japanese); 2 years of course work in music, theater, and the visual arts; and 3 years of physical education and health.

Computer literacy is an imperative component of the Catlin Gabel curriculum. Students are taught to access the Internet to conduct research, to use e-mail responsibly, and to utilize standard computer applications, including spreadsheet, presentation, and word-processing software. Upper School students also receive instruction in computer programming as part of a four-year progression of computer science courses and computer graphics within the visual arts program.

As an integral part of the Upper School educational experience, students may pursue independent study projects. These may be undertaken several times in a student's career and may be of short or long duration.

Catlin Gabel offers study-abroad programs and School-sponsored trips to such countries as Costa Rica, France, Italy, Japan, Mexico, the People's Republic of China, and Spain. The School also offers two- to six-week exchanges to schools throughout the U.S.

FACULTY AND ADVISERS

The faculty at Catlin Gabel School comprises well-qualified, thoughtful people who love teaching and have a genuine affection for young people. They are fully vested in every aspect of their students' experiences at the School. Each student's style and speed of learning, background influences, and individual interests and needs are taken into account as teachers plan courses, counsel advisees, and work with students. Teachers also participate wholeheartedly in student activities, environmental and community projects, class trips, excursions, and school traditions. Teachers become friends who care about what is happening to their students outside the classroom, and they encourage their students to think deeply and to test themselves in all areas. In addition to before- and after-school hours, teachers are available three of the seven class periods each day plus lunch to work individually with students.

Each student is assigned to a faculty member who serves as his or her primary counselor and academic adviser throughout the Upper School years. The faculty advisers also serve as the conduit for communication between school and home. An adviser's advisees form a group of mixed ages. The group meets each morning to take attendance and exchange daily news.

Lark P. Palma, Ph.D. has been the Head of Catlin Gabel School since 1995. She is a native South Carolinian and a graduate of an independent school in South Carolina. She earned a doctorate in twentieth-century British literature and women's studies at the University of South Carolina while teaching at Heathwood Hall Episcopal School.

COLLEGE PLACEMENT

Catlin Gabel's college counseling program, with its emphasis on personalized guidance, helps each student explore the many college opportunities available. Through individual counseling sessions throughout the junior and senior years, Catlin Gabel's 2 college counselors help students identify those colleges that best suit their interests, abilities, and goals. Counselors guide students through all aspects of the college admission process, from developing appropriate college lists to completing applications, writing essays, and applying for financial aid. Parents are kept informed and involved in the college counseling process through written communication as well as parent information sessions.

College counseling begins in the Upper School with a group meeting in the fall of the junior year. During winter term, juniors fill out an extensive questionnaire and write a self-descriptive essay. These are used as the basis for individual conferences with a college counselor and are designed to help each student define his or her direction after Catlin Gabel. Students and parents are then given checklists and deadlines to guide them through the college admission application process. Juniors and their parents are invited to a meeting in the winter to discuss all aspects of applying to college. During spring term, juniors meet weekly in small groups with a college counselor as well as in individual appointments.

Generally 65 percent of the seniors attend their first choice college. Of the students who apply to three or more colleges, most receive at least two acceptances. Recent graduates are attending such schools as Brown, Columbia, Cornell, Dartmouth, Emory, Scripps, Skidmore, Stanford, Yale, and the Universities of Chicago, Colorado, Ohio, Oregon, and Pennsylvania.

STUDENT BODY AND CONDUCT

There are 705 students enrolled at Catlin Gabel: 270 students in the Upper School (grades 9–12), 180 students in the Middle School (grades 6–8), 200 students in the Lower School (grades 1–5), and 55 students in Beginning School (preschool and kindergarten). Students represent a variety of backgrounds and cultures—coming from as many as fifty different neighborhoods throughout the greater Portland and Vancouver area. Students and teachers are actively dedicated to making Catlin Gabel a diverse and open-spirited community in which talented and motivated students of all kinds can thrive.

ACADEMIC FACILITIES

The Upper School academic campus consists of six major buildings around a central grass Commons. The science building includes five labs that support the integrated science curriculum and provide space for individual student research. The Math and Modern Languages buildings provide modern facilities for laptop teaching in small classes. The Humanities building houses English and history classes and the Learning Center, which offers both learning-style testing and study skills help and is an invaluable resource for students and their families. The James F. Miller Library, completed in 2003, has a collection of more than 10,000 volumes, as well as periodicals, online databases, reference titles, and an online catalog designed to meet the research and curricular needs of students and the faculty. The library building also includes a state-of-the-art multimedia auditorium and a computer lab for the teaching of computer science and graphic design courses. The arts facilities include studios for visual arts, instrumental music, choral music, woodworking, and ceramics. The Cabell Center for the Performing Arts, a 600-seat professional theater, supports classes in acting and technical theater and is used by all students for assemblies and theater productions.

At Catlin Gabel, technology is integrated into each division. The School is a dual-platform campus, supporting both Macintosh and Windows computers. The nearly 300 computers on the campus network comprise a Lower School lab, a Middle School lab, and two Upper School labs. In the fall of 2002, the Upper School implemented a comprehensive laptop program, making computer technology accessible to every student.

ATHLETICS

The Miller Swigert Gymnasium offers classrooms, weight training facilities, and modern locker rooms to complement the gymnasium, indoor and outdoor tennis courts, the track, and playing fields. The athletics program is open to all Middle and Upper School students and features a "no cut" policy, with the exception of varsity-level teams. The School fields intramural and interscholastic teams in baseball, basketball, cross-country, golf, racquetball, soccer, tennis, and volleyball (girls only). Student athletes, teams, and coaches have been honored nationally and statewide as state champions, All-Americans, coaches of the year, and players of the year as well as with all-state and district honors.

EXTRACURRICULAR OPPORTUNITIES

A wide range of extracurricular opportunities are available to foster students' interests, involvement, leadership skills, and intellectual and emotional development. These include community service, athletics, performing arts, concerts, lectures, gallery exhibits, publications (yearbook, literary magazine, student newspaper), Model U.N., mock trials, robotics, the social committee, and clubs. In the Upper School, each organization is run by a group of students who are elected to leadership positions. They work closely with the student activities director and a faculty adviser.

One annual event, Winterim, occurs in February when for three days the Upper School suspends regular classes and offers a variety of opportunities. Winterim allows students and faculty members to share concentrated exploration of academic and/or community service themes and activities outside the regular curriculum. Students generate ideas and collaborate with faculty members and alumni to create thirty different experiential learning opportunities. These have included working for Habitat for Humanity, the Humane Society, and the U.S. Forest Service and learning about robotics, printing techniques, and investment management. An educational or community service orientation is the expected focus for these projects. At the conclusion of Winterim, students report on their group's activities.

Sharing their time and talents in many ways helps students develop awareness of needs outside themselves. An important goal of Catlin Gabel's program is to support student awareness of the value of community involvement and service. Accordingly, students are asked to donate time to the community through Schoolwide required activities, Schoolwide optional activities, and individual community service. All Upper School students are required to complete at least 15 hours of service to both the School community and the larger, surrounding community. Service is integrated into the yearly calendar as students work collectively on School-sponsored projects. Campus Day is one example when Upper School students and faculty members work in small groups to enhance the campus with painting, planting, and building projects. Students are expected to fulfill a designated number of hours of community service each year working on a project suitable to their own schedule and interests. Students submit documentation for their community service during the year. Service opportunities include the Rummage Sale, which supports financial aid programs; tutoring; food drives; and the Bloodmobile.

DAILY LIFE

School begins at 8 a.m. with a 15-minute homeroom period where students meet with their adviser group. There are seven class periods that meet on a weekly block schedule, a 10-minute morning break, and a 40-minute lunch period. Three of the seven class periods meet four times per week for 45 minutes, plus one time per week for 75 minutes. The other four class periods meet three times per week for 45 minutes and one time per week for 75 minutes. Classes end and after-school activities begin at 3:15 p.m., three days per week, and 2:50 p.m., two days per week.

Students in the Upper School follow a modular schedule, which allows them to study independently. During open periods, students may use the time as they see fit. Students utilize these periods for such activities as studying, conducting research, meeting with faculty members, and working in small study groups.

COSTS AND FINANCIAL AID

In 2004–05, Upper School tuition was $18,150. There are three payment plans available. Parents may pay 100 percent by August 1, 60 percent in August and 40 percent in January, or monthly. The monthly option carries an interest charge. Limited need-based financial aid is available.

ADMISSIONS INFORMATION

The match between student and school is critical to success. Catlin Gabel asks each family to provide information that would be helpful in ascertaining whether the School is a right fit for their child. In addition, students are asked to visit the School and meet with faculty members, either alone or, in the case of young children, in small groups. Standardized admissions tests are administered to students applying to the Middle or Upper School. Once the School is aware of the number of openings in a particular grade, faculty and Admission Office personnel read each applicant file and decide whether the match is right. Enrollment is offered based on qualifications and available space.

APPLICATION TIMETABLE

Applicants may apply to the School one year in advance. Applications are due before January 15 of the desired year of enrollment for the Beginning and Lower Schools and by the end of the business day on February 15 for the Middle and Upper Schools.

ADMISSIONS CORRESPONDENCE

The Catlin Gabel School
8825 SW Barnes Road
Portland, Oregon 97225-6599

Phone: 503-297-1894
Fax: 503-297-0139
Web site: http://www.catlin.edu

CCI THE RENAISSANCE SCHOOL

Lanciano, Italy

Type: Coeducational boarding general academic and college-preparatory school
Grades: Secondary, 10–graduation
Enrollment: 120
Head of School: Marisa Di Carlo D'Alessandro, M.B.A.

THE SCHOOL

CCI The Renaissance School was founded in 1995 by a Canadian teacher with the purpose of giving students the opportunity to study in English within their own curriculum while living in Italy. The aim of the School is to provide excellent education and offer small class sizes, state-of-the-art facilities, a rich extracurricular program, and a strong mentorship program. The mission statement of the School is "to inspire students, through rigorous teaching and sensitive, collegial mentoring, to actualize their highest intellectual and moral potential, and become fully ready for effective university study and responsible adult life, while living communally at the historic center of our modern civilization." The School presently has 120 students but has a total capacity of 150.

The School occupies several buildings, combining the ancient and the modern. The buildings, all in the historical center of the town and all within a short walking distance of each other, include the School, the residences, the inn, the drama theater, and staff apartments. Lanciano is located 2½ hours directly east of Rome on the Adriatic coast. Due to the central geographic location, biweekly Saturday excursions take students to visit most of the country during their stay at the School. Lanciano is very famous for its classical music concerts, and students are encouraged to take music lessons from the local masters.

Teachers are all trained in Canada and the United States and are on leave from their local boards for a period of up to five years. The School is a federal nonprofit organization and is governed by a Board of Directors. The majority of board members are representatives of both European and North American universities. The annual operating expenses of €1.5 million are covered largely by school fees. The School is inspected and accredited by the Ministry of Education and Training in Ontario, Canada. The School is a member of ECIS and is presently seeking accreditation from the European Council of International Schools and the New England Association of Schools and Colleges.

ACADEMIC PROGRAMS

The academic year is divided into two semesters. The first semester starts at the end of August and finishes with examinations at the end of December. Second semester starts the end of January and finishes in mid-June.

Students take a maximum of four credit courses per semester and a total of eight courses during the full academic year. The School presently offers the Ontario Secondary School Diploma as well as Advanced Placement courses for the Advanced Placement International Diploma. The School is also a center for SAT examinations. The School offers a strong college-preparatory program. The School does not have a program for students with special needs, nor does it offer English as a second language.

FACULTY AND ADVISERS

The School has 13 full-time teachers. All have university degrees and teacher training degrees, and many have master's degrees. The teachers are all trained in North America with the exception of the Italian language teacher, who is European-trained. The head of the School is Mrs. Marisa Di Carlo D'Alessandro (Director of the College). She is a graduate of the University of Toronto and holds a teaching degree and an international M.B.A. degree from a European university.

COLLEGE PLACEMENT

Ninety-eight percent of all students continue on to universities and colleges. A guidance counsellor helps students choose appropriate courses and directs their college and university applications. The guidance library includes calendars and information packages from universities across North America and Europe. The graduates are presently attending various universities in Canada and the United States, including Boston College, Cornell, Dalhousie, Dartmouth, King's, McGill, Mount Allison, Queen's, York, and the Universities of British Columbia, Montreal, Ottawa, Toronto, and Western Ontario.

STUDENT BODY AND CONDUCT

All students board in the college residences. Presently, the majority of students are in senior grades; 60 percent are girls. Students are required to wear a school uniform during class time only. Uniforms are not worn during study hall or on evenings or weekends. The elected Student Council has a voice in making school rules, which are enforced by the staff. Smoking and drinking of alcoholic beverages are forbidden on school grounds. A school policy forbids the use of all harmful substances.

ACADEMIC FACILITIES

The main school building at Via Cavour 13 is a newly restored fourteenth-century building with an interior atrium. The building houses the school library (10,000 volumes), the computer room, offices, the tuckshop, the infirmary, and classrooms. The theater room for drama is located a short walk away from the main school building.

The School's art workshops for painting, sculpting, silk screening, jewellery, and photography are located on campus.

BOARDING AND GENERAL FACILITIES

The School presently has three residences: Cavour, Santa Maria, and Maggiore. All are located in the medieval center of the city, only a 5-minute walk from the main school. All rooms have been newly restored, are spacious, and have a great deal of natural light. Many of them have balconies. There is a common room in each residence equipped with kitchen facilities, T.V. and VCR, and laundry rooms. Students share rooms, although there are some single rooms available for senior students. Residence dons live with the students in each residence and create a caring and supportive environment for students by assisting them with time management skills, discussing their problems, and helping them with their homework. There are supervised study periods five days a week.

The School's inn, Allegria, is where students have all their meals. It is just a short walk away from the residences and the main school building. The second floor of the inn has nine bedrooms, and parents and friends are welcome to visit with the students. The inn has interior terraces, a cappuccino bar, a fireplace, and a lounge area. Two chefs and 3 assistants prepare hot meals for staff and students daily.

ATHLETICS

Students are encouraged to participate in the intramural program for basketball and volleyball, which is held after school in one of the local high school gymnasiums. Rugby, soccer, swimming, and cycling are also popular. Most of the students join the fitness club and participate in daily weightlifting and aerobics. The School does not have sports teams; however, exhibition games are encouraged with other schools. The skiing in the area is superb.

EXTRACURRICULAR OPPORTUNITIES

A wide variety of activities and clubs offer students many possibilities outside the classroom. These include photography, drama, music/voice lessons, computer, math, poetry, debating, and yearbook. All students are encouraged to participate in extracurricular activities.

DAILY LIFE

The day begins with a wake-up call at 7 a.m., followed by breakfast at 7:30 in the dining hall. There is a morning assembly at the School at 8:15. There are three 80-minute classes in the morning, with a 20-minute break between periods 2 and 3. Lunch is served in the dining hall from 1 to 1:50 p.m., and period 4 class ends at 3:10. There are extracurricular activities and personal time from 5 to 6:30. Dinner in the dining hall is served at 6:30 p.m., and there is mandatory study time in the residence from 8:30 to 10:30, Sunday through Thursday. Residence curfew is 10:30 p.m. during the week and 12 midnight on weekends.

WEEKEND LIFE

There is a day excursion every other weekend to different cities throughout Italy. Two excursions per semester are overnight trips, and students stay in first-class hotels. All trips compliment classroom study. On the weekends when there are no scheduled trips, students are free to travel in small groups on their own. There is easy access by buses or trains into Rome. Skiing is a popular weekend activity during the winter months. Rock climbing and hiking are popular in the spring and fall. The ocean is minutes away for swimming during the warmer fall and spring seasons.

COSTS AND FINANCIAL AID

Tuition for the entire year is €19,500. Tuition for one semester is €10,500. The tuition fee covers all educational and boarding costs. It does not include the cost of travel to Italy, holiday travel, uniforms, books, and the weekend trips with an overnight stay. There are four overnight trips per year at a total cost of €1200. Students who choose to join the health club are charged €30 per month. The School recommends a monthly allowance of €150. Students are invoiced three times a year. Bursaries are also available for students.

ADMISSIONS INFORMATION

There are no entrance examinations for admission. A student's previous school record and recommendations from teachers are considered in the application process. A personal interview is recommended.

APPLICATION TIMETABLE

The School accepts applications for students throughout the year. Students may enter the School in August or January. The School attracts students internationally, many with a focus on admission to a university in Canada or the United States. Interested families are encouraged to visit the School while it is in session. There is a nonrefundable application fee of €85. Families are notified of acceptance soon after application. An application fee of €1500 (part of the tuition fee) is invoiced upon acceptance.

ADMISSIONS CORRESPONDENCE

Jocelyn Manchee, Admissions Officer
CCI The Renaissance School
59 Macamo Court
Maple, Ontario L6A 1G1
Canada

Phone: 905-508-7108
      800-422-0548 (toll-free)
Fax: 905-508-5480
E-mail: cciren@rogers.com
Web site: http://www.ccilanciano.com

CFS, THE SCHOOL AT CHURCH FARM

Paoli, Pennsylvania

Type: Boys' boarding and day college-preparatory school
Grades: 7–12; Middle School, 7–8; Upper School, 9–12
Enrollment: School total: 188; Upper School: 139
Head of School: Charles W. Shreiner III, Headmaster

THE SCHOOL

For more than eighty years, CFS, The School at Church Farm, has been committed to providing the best in college preparation for qualified and deserving boys and young men. The school, located in Paoli, Pennsylvania, 25 miles west of Philadelphia, was founded in 1918 by the Reverend Charles W. Shreiner, D.D., who dreamed of a college-preparatory school for boys of ability and promise who otherwise might not have an opportunity to attend one.

The school is distinguished by one of the largest endowments per student of any educational institution in the country. As a result, CFS is able to offer an unusually broad spectrum of learning and teaching resources. These resources include members of a unique dormitory faculty who live with the students and mentor them on a daily basis; a fully equipped library; several modern science laboratories; a completely networked computer system; excellent athletic facilities for competitive and recreational sports; and a choice of courses that is extensive and challenging.

Approximately eighty buildings, spread over a 350-acre campus, are used for the School's comprehensive programs. The Administration Building houses electronically connected classrooms, offices, the library, the kitchen, and a recently renovated dining hall. The Science Building contains four well-equipped laboratories, six electronic classrooms, a projection room, and the Art Department. Ten bright, hard-wired, cottage-style dormitories house the boarding population (80 percent of the students) in small groups supervised by dorm faculty members. Athletic facilities include soccer and baseball fields, a quarter-mile track, six tennis courts, a basketball gymnasium, a modern multipurpose field house, and an adjoining outdoor swimming pool. Also on campus are the School's chapel, a twelve-bed infirmary, faculty members' homes, shop buildings, a barn, and a variety of outbuildings.

CFS is incorporated as a not-for-profit organization. It is governed by a 17-member Board of Directors, whose honorary chairman is the Bishop of the Episcopalian Diocese of Pennsylvania. The Alumni Association contributes time and resources to the School. CFS is accredited by the Middle States Association of Colleges and Schools. The School is a member of the National Association of Independent Schools, the National Association of Episcopal Schools, the Pennsylvania Association of Independent Schools, the College Board, and the Secondary School Admissions Test Board.

ACADEMIC PROGRAMS

All CFS students take a minimum of 4 years of social studies, 4 years of English, 3 years of math and science, and 2 years of a foreign language.

The core curriculum is bolstered by an outstanding program of computer training.

The academic year, from early September to early June, includes thirty-six weeks of instruction, with holidays at Thanksgiving, Christmas, and in the spring. Parents receive grade reports and teachers' comments four times a year, in addition to mid-marking-period progress reports.

Minimum graduation requirements at CFS include 23.1 credits, distributed as follows: English, 4 credits; mathematics, 3 credits; social studies, 4 credits; laboratory science, 3.2 credits; modern foreign language, 2 credits; fine art, 1 credit; technology education, 1 credit; religion, 0.5 credit; health, 0.4 credit; physical education, 1 credit; and free electives, 3 credits.

AP courses are offered by the major academic departments.

Students may choose among numerous electives, including African-American history, nineteenth and twentieth century United States history, government, evolution of warfare, world literature, journalism, public speaking, mythology, Shakespeare, anatomy and physiology, environmental studies, physical geology, precalculus, calculus, Spanish III and IV, French III and IV, 2-D and 3-D design, photography, clay, weaving, history of Western music, history of jazz, musicianship, music theory, engineering and design, power technology, fine furniture construction, values and ethics, and psychology.

The student-faculty ratio is a low 8:1. Classes are small, averaging 11 students.

FACULTY AND ADVISERS

Charles W. Shreiner III, grandson of the founder, was appointed Headmaster in 1987. Mr. Shreiner graduated from Westtown School, Nichols College (B.S.), and Villanova University (M.A.). His leadership embraces the precept that learning in the age of the Internet modifies the role of the teacher, as students work together on projects, with the faculty member doing less lecturing and serving more as coach and sounding board. Faculty members perform accordingly, giving and overseeing assignments that engage students in Web-based activities.

The teaching faculty and members of the Administration also participate in the admissions process, curriculum revision, and staff development. In total, the school is led academically by 30 men and women, 70 percent of whom have advanced degrees. The school is committed to the Faculty Evaluation and Renewal System developed by Independent School Management, a rigorous peer and departmental evaluation process.

All faculty members participate in the School's adviser/advisee program. As a mentor to a group of 7 or 8 students, the adviser is genuinely interested in the welfare of each boy and

communicates regularly with his parents. Advisers and students see each other several times during the week, and funds are provided on a monthly basis for social activities. The adviser/advisee relationship promotes an atmosphere of courtesy and respect between adults and students at CFS, and is a vitally important part of the educational program at the School.

COLLEGE PLACEMENT

Every young man who graduates from CFS, The School at Church Farm, receives a comprehensive college-preparatory education. All tenth, eleventh, and twelfth graders take the PSAT, SAT, and SAT Subject Tests as needed. Faculty members assist students in preparing for these standardized tests.

CFS emphasizes college counseling to help students understand the options available to them and guide them in making informed choices about those options. The School also provides families with information about financial aid application procedures.

College placement is between 90 and 95 percent. Recent graduating classes are represented at such colleges and universities as Colgate, Columbia, Cornell, Dartmouth, Emory, Fordham, Lafayette, Morehouse, Rutgers, St. John's, and the United States Naval Academy.

STUDENT BODY AND CONDUCT

CFS has a current enrollment of 154 boarders and 34 day students. Because of its generous financial aid policy, the School is unusually diverse, with minority students making up more than 40 percent of the population. There are 22 seventh graders, 27 eighth graders, 40 freshmen, 31 sophomores, 33 juniors, and 35 seniors at the school.

CFS expects its students to develop self-discipline and to honor the School's rules and regulations. The disciplinarians handle day-to-day infractions. Disciplinary measures include counseling, detention, probation, suspension, and dismissal. The school is committed to preventing disciplinary problems through counseling.

ACADEMIC FACILITIES

Greystock Hall, the central administration and classroom building, houses electronically connected classrooms, the library, administration offices, a student recreation room, the kitchen, and the recently renovated dining hall. Greystock is home to the English, social studies, and foreign language departments. Math and science courses are taught in the adjacent Wilkins Science Center, which contains four well-equipped laboratories, six electronic classrooms, and a study room. The fine arts department shares space in Wilkins. Music is taught in a spacious facility below the chapel.

BOARDING AND GENERAL FACILITIES

Ten bright, hard-wired cottage-style dormitories house the boarding population (80 percent of the students) in small groups supervised by dorm faculty members. Each cottage is wired into the CFS Connected Learning Community, so students are able to pursue their projects from practically anywhere on campus. All students are under the supervision of cottage faculty members, who are responsible for their well-being. Cottage life offers a unique opportunity for a young man to learn to live with and understand people from different social, cultural, and ethnic groups.

ATHLETICS

CFS, The School at Church Farm, views athletics as a major component in the education of every student. There is much to be learned from teamwork, from competing head-to-head in an individual sport, from improving little by little over time, and from refusing to quit no matter what the circumstances. Consequently, some kind of interscholastic or intramural athletic activity is required of all students.

Athletic facilities include soccer and baseball fields, a basketball gymnasium, a quarter-mile track, six tennis courts, an outdoor swimming pool, and a state-of-the-art multipurpose field house known as Founders' Pavilion. Teams at the middle school, junior varsity, and varsity levels have extensive interscholastic game schedules. The School participates in the Keystone Scholastic Athletic Conference, with excellent programs in baseball, basketball, cross-country, soccer, tennis, track, and wrestling. A program of intramural competition complements the interscholastic schedule.

EXTRACURRICULAR OPPORTUNITIES

The School offers a wide variety of extracurricular activities to give each boy the chance to test and find himself. Students can work on the school newspaper, *Greystock News,* and on the school yearbook, *The Griffin.* They can participate in the Distributive Education Club (DECA),

the astronomy club, and the Headmaster's Advisory Council; they can also assist with chapel services. In addition, they can mentor younger students as members of Griffin Odyssey and represent the school as a CFS Ambassador. Those students who qualify may become members of the CFS chapter of the National Honor Society.

The Challenge of Required Experience (CORE) is also an important supplement to the academic curriculum. Students are required to complete one community service learning experience each year and one outdoor experience. Currently, the CFS Community Service Program has close associations with more than thirty local organizations and agencies. The Outdoor Experience Program offers many exciting opportunities, both on and off campus, with activities that include backpacking, canoeing, cross-country and downhill skiing, fishing, hiking, sailing, white-water rafting, and wilderness survival.

The School also sponsors on-campus speakers as well as off-campus trips into Philadelphia to plays, concerts, museums, and other cultural activities.

DAILY LIFE

Most days begin at 6:30 a.m. with cottage chores; breakfast follows at 7. Students attend assembly and chapel twice a week. Classes last 45 minutes and continue through midafternoon. During the school day, participation in the work program or community service is required of all students. Sports programs extend from 4 to 6 p.m. After dinner all students concentrate on their academic studies during a 2-hour study hall. Bedtimes vary depending on the group and the ages of the cottage residents.

WEEKEND LIFE

Students who have a good academic record and who have conducted themselves responsibly have the opportunity to go home over the weekend. Those who remain on campus may participate in various social or intramural activities and in cultural and recreational trips. Some interscholastic sports events take place on weekends. Boys

may be visited or taken off campus on Sunday afternoon; they must return by 6 p.m. Students who spend the weekend on campus must attend chapel on Sunday.

COSTS AND FINANCIAL AID

CFS fully expects every family to be invested in its son's education, but the School is committed to the proposition that no qualified applicant should be denied the opportunity to attend the School because of financial hardship. The tuition ranges from a minimum family contribution of $4000 per year to a maximum of $12,500 per year for day students and $18,000 for boarding students. Tuition assistance over the past five years has been in excess of $5 million a year.

ADMISSIONS INFORMATION

CFS, The School at Church Farm, seeks to attract students who have a genuine interest in preparing for college study, who are enthusiastic about learning, interested in being involved, and willing to contribute to the welfare of the entire School community. Most new students are admitted to grades 7, 8, and 9. As space permits, a few new students may also be admitted to grades 10 and 11. Candidates are evaluated on the basis of previous academic records, school citizenship, standardized test results, teacher references, and a personal interview.

APPLICATION TIMETABLE

Applications and all supporting information should be submitted by May 1. All candidates are asked to schedule an appointment with the Admissions Office for an interview and a campus tour.

ADMISSIONS CORRESPONDENCE

Richard Lunardi, Admissions Director
CFS, The School at Church Farm
P.O. Box 2000
Paoli, Pennsylvania 19301

Phone: 610-363-5347
Fax: 610-280-6746

Web site: http://www.gocfs.net

CHATHAM HALL

Chatham, Virginia

Type: Girls' boarding and day college-preparatory school
Grades: 9–12
Enrollment: 132
Head of School: Gary J. Fountain, Rector

THE SCHOOL

An all-girls college-preparatory boarding school, Chatham Hall, offers students a rigorous academic environment, a rich extracurricular program, and a beautiful campus. In small classes, teachers challenge and encourage students to excel academically. Students also have opportunities to expand their talents and strengthen their self-confidence through sports, art, riding, drama, music, and dance.

Chatham Hall benefits from its proximity to educational and cultural centers in Raleigh, Durham, Chapel Hill, and Greensboro, North Carolina; and Charlottesville, Lynchburg, and Roanoke, Virginia. Located in the Piedmont section of Virginia, its 362-acre campus has rolling countryside with woods, streams, and pasturelands.

Chatham Hall is governed by a national, self-perpetuating Board of Trustees. The school's recorded endowment is valued at $16.6 million, and the average gift to the school is one of the highest among girls' schools.

Accredited by the Southern Association of Colleges and Schools and the National Association of Independent Schools, Chatham Hall holds memberships in the National Association of Principals of Schools for Girls, the National Association of College Admission Counselors, the National Coalition of Girls' Schools, the Secondary School Admission Test Board, the Council for the Advancement and Support of Education, and the Virginia Association of Independent Schools.

ACADEMIC PROGRAMS

The school's curriculum emphasizes analytical reasoning, expressive abilities, character and vision, and physical vigor. To graduate from Chatham Hall, students must complete their senior year at the school and fulfill the following minimum distribution requirements: 4 years of English, 3 years of mathematics, 3 years of history (1 of which must be U.S. history), 3 years of one foreign language, 3 years of lab science (2 of which must be biology and chemistry), 1 year of fine or performing arts, 1 trimester of religion, and 1 trimester of ethics. In addition, students must participate in the physical fitness program each trimester. A total of 20 credits are required. Advanced Placement courses are offered in each department, and students may apply to the Discovery Challenge independent-study program. Electives include such courses as DNA Science and Veterinary Science.

Classes meet five days per week for 45-minute periods. The average class size is 8 students, and the overall student-teacher ratio is approximately 6:1. Typically, students carry five to six academic courses each trimester. Grading is on a scale of A to F with pluses and minuses. Grade reports with teacher comments are sent home at the middle and end of each trimester. Parents also have regular communication with the student's adviser.

FACULTY AND ADVISERS

In 2005–06, the faculty consisted of 35 teaching members. Fifty-seven percent have advanced degrees. Nearly all faculty members live on campus, and each serves as an adviser to a small group of girls, meeting with each girl individually and helping her to define and realize her goals for the year and for the future.

Dr. Gary Fountain is Chatham Hall's ninth rector in its 110-year history. He received an A.B. degree from Brown University, a Master of Arts in Religion from Yale Divinity School, and a Ph.D. from the Department of English and American Literature at Boston University. Prior to coming to Chatham Hal, Fountain was an associate professor of English and Director of English Teacher Education at Ithaca College in New York. He also has served in faculty or administration positions at Saint Joseph's College, Miss Porter's School, and Ethel Walker School.

COLLEGE PLACEMENT

Chatham Hall is a college-preparatory school; as such, students prepare for college from the moment they enter Chatham Hall. Students begin working formally with the school's college counselor early in their Chatham Hall experience and meet frequently with her throughout the process. Recently, Chatham Hall graduates have attended such schools as Colgate, Cornell, Dartmouth, Duke, Georgetown, Johns Hopkins, Stanford, Swarthmore, Wellesley, and the Universities of North Carolina and Virginia.

STUDENT BODY AND CONDUCT

Chatham Hall is one of the few girls' schools in which more than 80 percent of the students are seven-day boarders. In 2005–06, the student body consisted of 132 girls from twenty states and eight countries. The breakdown was as follows: 32 freshmen, 31 sophomores, 29 juniors, and 40 seniors.

The entire Chatham Hall community upholds the Honor Code as the foundation upon which the school is built. In matters of daily living, Chatham Hall students also depend on a clear statement of citizenship, known as the Purple and Golden Rule. Chatham Hall does not subscribe to a demerit system. Rather, Chatham Hall students value a system of implicit understandings over explicit and restrictive rules. The school believes in each girl's innate ability to make good choices and to lead herself according to her conscience. Under the Purple and Golden Rule, each girl is responsible for her actions and accepts the consequences of them, and she embraces the concept of White Flag—respect for people and property. The Purple and Golden Rule establishes a framework by which each girl governs herself and her peers throughout the school year. As a custodian of these principles, she sets an example for others and counsels others when they are not living up to these principles.

ACADEMIC FACILITIES

The Chatham Hall Intranet connects the school community electronically. Each dorm room has two data ports and two phone ports. Each classroom and office is also networked. A full-time Director of Instructional Technology works with faculty members on integrating technology into their curricula. Pruden Hall contains offices, formal sitting rooms, two dormitory floors, a nine-bed Health Care Center, and a darkroom facility. Dabney Hall contains eleven classrooms; a computer lab; two dormitory floors; a day student room; and a student center, including a kitchen, a viewing room, mail boxes, the bookstore, and a fitness center. The Shaw Science and Technology building has four state-of-the-art laboratory classrooms, a sophisticated technology classroom, a seminar room, and a wireless computer network. The Holt Language Building has four foreign language classrooms. Boasting award-winning architecture, the Edmund and Lucy Lee Library contains 30,000 holdings, is fully computerized, and allows students online access to virtually every resource in the country through VLIN, Dialog, OCLC, and Internet connections. The Whitner Dance/Art Studio has large, flexible spaces that are well equipped for modern dance and ballet; for painting, pottery, sculpture, and

weaving; and for drama in the black box theater. Willis Hall contains two large classrooms and the Advancement Office.

BOARDING AND GENERAL FACILITIES

Students live on one of four dormitory floors located in Pruden and Dabney. They generally share a room, but some may live in a single. Houseparents live on each floor, as do members of the Student Council. Both dormitories have phone and Internet access and individual heating/air conditioning units in each room. St. Mary's Chapel is a focal point of the school, hosting three weekly services, Senior Chapel Talks, choir rehearsals, and piano and voice lessons. Chatham Hall's forty-stall riding facility features the Mars Riding Arena, a 125-foot by 250-foot indoor riding facility that is among the best on the East Coast. The physical plant is valued at $25.2 million.

ATHLETICS

Physical fitness is a vital part of the Chatham Hall experience. All students participate in athletics each trimester. The school supports varsity teams in basketball, cross-country, field hockey, riding, soccer, swimming, tennis, and volleyball. In addition to these, softball and lacrosse are played intramurally. Aerobics is also offered. Chatham Hall's Riding Program offers hunt seat riding and features a competitive, varsity show team that participates in AA shows in USEF Zone 3.

The Commons serves as both an athletic facility for basketball and volleyball and as a recreation and performance space for mixers, aerobics, and dance. The school also has three playing fields and six all-weather tennis courts. Riding facilities include forty stalls, a 125-foot by 250-foot indoor arena, a 275-foot by 175-foot show arena, a permanent hunter trial course, three large schooling and teaching fields, and extensive trails.

EXTRACURRICULAR OPPORTUNITIES

Chatham Hall students belong to more than thirty organizations representing a wide range of interests, including FOCUS; various art, language, and riding clubs; the environmental club; and numerous student publications. All students and faculty are members of one of the branches of the Service League: Community Life, School Life, or Church Life.

Students have performance and academic instruction opportunities in theater, dance, and music. The Sherwood Dramatic Club performs two major productions a year. Panache, Chatham Hall's modern dance ensemble, performs on and off campus several times a year. Singers perform in St. Mary's Choir, the Chamber Choir, Sextet, and the Gospel Choir.

DAILY LIFE

Classes begin at 8 a.m. and end at 3:30 p.m. Afternoons are devoted to athletics. Required chapel services are held three times each week. The community gathers in the Front Hall in Pruden on Monday and Thursday mornings for an all-school assembly. The school eats meals together; most meals are buffet-style. There are three seated meals each week: lunch on Wednesday and Thursday and dinner on Monday. Students sit with faculty advisers. Clubs generally meet after dinner. There are required study hours from 7:30 to 9:30 on school nights. Students may study in their rooms, the library, special group study rooms, or one of the computer labs. Room bell in the dormitories is at 10:25 p.m.

WEEKEND LIFE

Chatham Hall is a seven-day boarding school, and offers a variety of fun and enriching activities both on and off campus. Taking advantage of the school's location, Chatham Hall students spend weekends hiking or white-water rafting in the Blue Ridge Mountains, attending concerts and theater and art shows in nearby cities, or going out to dinner

and movies with friends. Chatham Hall also participates in the Boarding Schools Social Activities Committee (BSSAC), which coordinates mixers and other events with boarding schools throughout Virginia.

COSTS AND FINANCIAL AID

The comprehensive fee for 2005–06 was $33,800, which included tuition, room, and board. Books, transportation, private music lessons, English as a second language, swimming, and riding carry additional charges.

Chatham Hall is committed to bringing qualified girls to the school. To this end, the school offers financial aid grants to families who demonstrate need under the guidelines of the School and Student Service for Financial Aid. Chatham Hall also offers several payment plans.

ADMISSIONS INFORMATION

Chatham Hall admits young women whose character and integrity, academic and intellectual promise, motivation, and enthusiasm for participating in the life of the school will predictably make them successful members of the school community.

APPLICATION TIMETABLE

Chatham Hall's application deadline is February 10. After that date, students are admitted on a rolling basis. Candidates should plan to visit the school early in the process for an interview and tour and to spend the night in a dorm. In addition to completing the application forms, candidates must also submit standardized test scores, such as those from the Secondary School Admission Test (SSAT).

ADMISSIONS CORRESPONDENCE

S. Victoria Muradi
Director of Admission and Financial Aid
Chatham Hall
800 Chatham Hall Circle
Chatham, Virginia 24531
Phone: 434-432-2941
Fax: 434-432-2405
E-mail: admission@chathamhall.com
Web site: http://www.chathamhall.org

CHESHIRE ACADEMY

Cheshire, Connecticut

Type: Coeducational boarding (grades 9–12, postgraduate year) and day (grades 6–12, postgraduate year) college-preparatory school
Grades: Middle School, 6–8; Upper School, 9–12; postgraduate year
Enrollment: School total: 386; Upper School: 331
Head of School: Ralph Van Inwagen

THE SCHOOL

Cheshire Academy was founded in 1794 as the Episcopal Academy, a coeducational community school. It became a boys' boarding school in the mid-1800s and adopted a military program during the Civil War. In the early 1900s, it gave up both its military program and its religious affiliation. The Academy returned to coeducation in 1969, and in 1975 boarding girls were admitted for the first time. Academically, the school's goal is to give a full and well-rounded college-preparatory education to students of above-average intellectual ability. The 105-acre campus is located in a small-town setting, 15 miles northwest of New Haven.

Cheshire's Middle School offers grades 6 through 8 for day students. The Middle School has a separate faculty and separate athletics and extracurricular programs for its students. Where appropriate, Middle School students may take courses offered in the Upper School. Facilities shared with the Upper School include the dining room, field house, library, and Charles Harwood Student Center.

Cheshire Academy is a nonprofit corporation directed by a self-perpetuating 17-member Board of Trustees, which includes alumni and parents and meets three times a year.

Cheshire Academy is accredited by the New England Association of Schools and Colleges and approved by the Connecticut State Board of Education. Memberships are held in the National Association of Independent Schools, the Connecticut Association of Independent Schools, the Educational Records Bureau, the Secondary School Admission Test Board, the Council for Religion in Independent Schools, the Council for Women in Independent Schools, and Independent School Management.

ACADEMIC PROGRAMS

Cheshire's academic program is a traditional college-preparatory curriculum. The following disciplines and credits are required: English, 4; mathematics, 3; foreign language, 2; laboratory science, 2; history, 3 (1 in U.S. history); art or music, 1; reading, 1; and electives, 2. Most students take 4 mathematics, 3–4 foreign language, and 3 laboratory science credits.

The Roxbury Support Center is offered to select individuals who fit the appropriate profile. It is designed to aid in strengthening students' learning skills and develop better connections with class materials through modifying core curricula instruction without altering course work.

The grading system uses A to F designations with pluses and minuses. Each student also receives a grade for effort, ranging from 1 to 5 (high to low). The school year is divided into semesters, with examinations at the end of each semester. Term reports are sent home six times a year.

Class size averages 12, and students are randomly selected except for honors and Advanced Placement courses. The overall student-teacher ratio is 12:1. The average course load is five academic subjects (some elective courses are ten weeks in length, while others extend for the entire year). Advanced Placement courses are available in English, mathematics, science, history, and fine arts.

FACULTY AND ADVISERS

The faculty is composed of 64 members, including 34 women and 30 men. Thirty-nine faculty members hold master's degrees.

The Academy makes every effort to find men and women who truly want to teach and who appreciate the opportunity to serve as counselors and advisers to young people. Each member of the faculty contributes his or her own special talent toward the goals of caring for each student and encouraging that student to grow intellectually, socially, and morally.

Faculty members play a vital role in all phases of the Academy. They serve on the Admissions, Financial Aid, Curriculum, and Discipline committees. Each faculty member also serves as an adviser for a group of 6 students and as a liaison between family and school.

COLLEGE PLACEMENT

A full-time college counseling team helps students in the selection of colleges. More than 150 college representatives visit the campus each year to interview interested students. In 2005, 98 percent of the graduates entered college. They are attending such institutions as Carnegie Mellon, Cornell, Georgetown, and the University of Chicago.

STUDENT BODY AND CONDUCT

In 2005–06, the Academy enrolled 115 boarding boys, 77 boarding girls, 88 day boys, and 51 day girls as follows: 62 in grade 9, 77 in grade 10, 74 in grade 11, 107 in grade 12, and 11 in a postgraduate year. Boarding students represented eighteen states, Puerto Rico, the U.S. Virgin Islands, and twenty-five other countries. The Middle School enrolled 55 day students in grades 6–8.

Discipline at Cheshire Academy provides a suitable environment for the academic and social growth of the individual and the Cheshire Academy community in general. This basic philosophy encourages the development of a sense of self-discipline and responsibility within each student. All Cheshire Academy students are expected to commit themselves to an Honor Code that demonstrates concern for themselves and others. Offenses are handled by a faculty-student Judicial Committee.

The Student Council is composed of all the Student Proctors plus the 4 officers from each class. The Student Council elects its own officers. The Student Proctors are nominated by the previous year's Proctors and selected by faculty members.

ACADEMIC FACILITIES

The Humanities Building houses classrooms for English, foreign languages, and the Academic Support Center. Bronson Hall houses the Music Department. The John J. White '38 Science and Technology Center opened in 1998 and added eight classrooms, four laboratories, faculty offices, seminar rooms, and a 216-seat lecture hall. The Arthur N. Sheriff Field House also has classroom wings for history and the fine arts studios. The Middle School building was constructed in 1997 and houses grades 6–8.

A new addition to the campus, which opened in fall 2003, is the Library and Humanities Building, adding twelve new classrooms, a library that holds 22,000 books, and additional computer stations.

BOARDING AND GENERAL FACILITIES

The Academy has six dormitories. The newest, which opened in 2001, accommodates 44 students and five faculty families. Most of the faculty members live on campus in dormitories and single-dwelling homes. All meals are served in the Gideon Welles Dining Commons. Breakfast and dinner are served cafeteria-style, and, at noon, the whole school gathers for lunch.

The newly renovated Richmond Building houses the new Student Health Center, which is staffed by 2 nurses throughout the day. A local physician visits the school regularly and

---

is on call at other times. Cheshire is located near several outstanding medical facilities at which students may be hospitalized, if necessary.

The Charles Harwood Student Center is a three-story structure encompassing 7,600 square feet. Features include meeting rooms for clubs, practice rooms for music and drama, a game room, a snack bar, and a greenhouse. The bookstore and office of the Director of Student Activities are located there. The top floor has a large hall designed for school dances and receptions.

ATHLETICS

An important part of a student's life at Cheshire is physical education, whether recreational or competitive. Students may participate in interscholastic or intramural programs. The Arthur N. Sheriff Field House holds two basketball courts, a six-lane pool, an exercise room, a weight room, and a state-of-the-art athletic training room. Outdoor facilities include ten tennis courts; several playing fields for soccer, football, field hockey, and lacrosse; baseball and softball diamonds; a ¼-mile track; and trails for cross-country running. In addition, a ropes course was built during summer 2002.

EXTRACURRICULAR OPPORTUNITIES

Extracurricular activities at the Academy are as varied as student interests and are often organized in response to student requests and participation. There are many clubs, including the Cheshire Academy Ambassadors Club, Dramatic Society, Peer Listeners, National Honor Society, and International Club. A school newspaper, literary magazine, and yearbook provide much practical experience in writing, editing, and photography for students. The Health and Wellness Committee, the Board of Programmers, and student proctors provide opportunities for students to take on leadership roles in the community.

DAILY LIFE

Classes are held five days a week, with shorter classes on Wednesday to allow for midweek athletics contests. The day begins with breakfast between 7 and 7:30 a.m. Extra help is from 7:35 to 7:55, homeroom is held from 8 to 8:25, and classes begin at 8:30. Classes end at 2:55 p.m. and afternoon extra help is from 2:55 to 3:25. Afternoon activities are from 3:30 to 5:30. Dinner is from 5:45 to 6:30, followed by study hall from 7:15 to 9:15. Dorm meetings are held at 10, and lights out is at 10:30 and 11.

WEEKEND LIFE

Boarding students may have weekend privileges after the first week of school, with the permission of their parents, the dormitory faculty, and the Dean. Many on-campus activities are offered, and students may attend concerts, plays, and athletics contests in such cities as Boston and New York. Nearby New Haven offers many of the advantages of a university town. Day students are encouraged to participate in weekend activities.

SUMMER PROGRAMS

The Academy has offered a traditional five-week summer program for more than ninety-two years. It is intended to provide review and enrichment instruction and to give students a chance to make up needed credits. There is a daily 2½-hour clinic in language arts for students having difficulty reading and writing. Study skills classes are also offered. English as a second language is required for international students prior to acceptance in September. This intensive English program ensures proper placement in classes and helps students adjust to a new academic environment.

COSTS AND FINANCIAL AID

Tuition at Cheshire Academy in 2005–06 was $35,375 for boarding students and $24,675 for day students in the Upper School. Middle School tuition was $21,175. Tuition may be paid in full before the school year begins or in two installments, one half by August 1 and the second half by December 1.

Scholarships are awarded on the basis of financial need as determined by the School and Student Service for Financial Aid and a review by the Academy's Financial Aid Committee. Applications must be submitted each year for review. Thirty percent of the students receive financial aid. Though $1.4 million in financial aid was awarded in 2005–06, the financial aid fund is limited and applicants are urged to apply as early as possible.

ADMISSIONS INFORMATION

Cheshire Academy accepts young men and women who can contribute to, as well as benefit from, life at Cheshire. A visit to the school is required of all applicants living in the United States. Acceptance of a candidate is based on the previous school record, recommendations of teachers, and the candidate's potential as indicated by his or her performance on standardized tests, including the ISEE or the SSAT. Applicants to the senior and postgraduate years should submit scores from the PSAT or the SAT. Applicants are accepted in all grades, but the largest incoming group is in tenth grade.

APPLICATION TIMETABLE

Initial inquiries are welcome at any time. Campus tours are coordinated with the interview, from 8:30 to 2:30 on weekdays. Saturday appointments may be arranged as needed.

The Academy has rolling admissions, which begin in March. Parents are allowed one month to reply to an acceptance received by April 15. They must reply within two weeks to an acceptance received between April 15 and June 30 and within one week after June 30. If dormitory and class space are available, a well-qualified candidate may be admitted on a very selective basis after the term has begun.

ADMISSIONS CORRESPONDENCE

Michael D. McCleery
Dean of Admission
Cheshire Academy
Cheshire, Connecticut 06410

Phone: 203-272-5396

Fax: 203-250-7209

E-mail: michael.mccleery@cheshireacademy. org

Web site: http://www.cheshireacademy.org

CHOATE ROSEMARY HALL

Wallingford, Connecticut

Type: Coeducational boarding and day college-preparatory school
Grades: 9–12, postgraduate year (Forms III–VI): Third Form, 9; Fourth Form, 10; Fifth Form, 11; Sixth Form, 12, postgraduate year
Enrollment: 860 on campus; 20 abroad
Head of School: Edward J. Shanahan, Ph.D., Headmaster

THE SCHOOL

Choate Rosemary Hall's rigorous academic program, through its small classes, both challenges and supports its students. This approach is the root of the school's reputation for academic excellence. At Choate, talented students and teachers from diverse backgrounds live and learn together creatively. Community spirit builds from this richness of difference in persons, cultures, and traditions to prepare students for an increasingly interdependent world.

The school's hope for its graduates is that they go forth from a school that valued each of them for particular talents and enthusiasms, affirmed the importance of personal integrity and a sense of self-worth, inspired and nourished joy in learning and love of truth, and provided the intellectual stimulation that generates independent thought, confident expression, and worthwhile commitments. Ideally, they will have acquired an understanding of life's journey as an evolution from bold ignorance to thoughtful uncertainty.

Choate Rosemary Hall was established through the merger of Rosemary Hall, a girls' school founded by Caroline Ruutz-Rees in 1890 in Wallingford, Connecticut, and The Choate School, a boys' school founded by Judge William Choate in 1896 in the same town. In 1971, the trustees of each school announced their coordination, and, in 1974, the two boards joined to form The Choate Rosemary Hall Foundation, Inc. Since 1977, the school has functioned as a single coeducational institution. The 400-acre campus is 12 miles north of New Haven, 20 miles south of Hartford, and a 2-hour drive from Boston and New York City.

The school is governed by a Board of Trustees, most of whose 30 members are alumni. The endowment is currently valued at $213 million.

Choate Rosemary Hall is accredited by the New England Association of Schools and Colleges. It holds memberships in the National Association of Independent Schools, the Connecticut Association of Independent Schools, A Better Chance, the Secondary School Admission Test Board, and the School Scholarship Service.

ACADEMIC PROGRAMS

A student's schedule for the three-term academic year is planned individually. The student chooses from more than 240 courses with the help of the house adviser, the Dean, and college counselors. Course levels are chosen according to academic preparedness, ability, and talent in an academic area, not necessarily by age or grade level.

Students must carry five courses each term. To receive a diploma, a student must earn at least 16 course credits, including 4 credits in English, 2 in science, 2 in social science, and 1 in art plus 1 term of psychology and 1 term of either philosophy or religion. In addition, a student must complete the third level in a foreign language and in mathematics. A student must also fulfill the physical education and athletics requirements.

Each of the six academic departments offers courses that prepare students for Advanced Placement work. Special features are a strong economics program; a science research program and an arts concentration program, both for selected students; full integration of technology into the academic curriculum; a two-term creative writing seminar for

qualified seniors; and the Capstone Program, an opportunity for talented seniors to explore an area of the curriculum in depth.

A number of opportunities are available for study abroad during the academic year, including immersion programs in China, France, and Spain; term-long study in Rome; and summer programs in China, France, and Spain.

The average class size is 12. Students are graded six times a year on an A–F scale; D– is the lowest passing grade. Written comments by teachers and advisers are sent home at the end of each trimester.

FACULTY AND ADVISERS

There are 64 men and 45 women on the teaching faculty, 65 percent of whom hold advanced degrees. Each serves as academic, athletic, and personal adviser to 8 to 10 students. Most also coach and are involved in extracurricular pursuits. Choate Rosemary Hall supports the same breadth in its faculty members as in its students.

Edward J. Shanahan (St. Joseph's College, 1965; M.A., Fordham University, 1968; Ph.D., University of Wisconsin, 1982), Headmaster, came to the school after nine years as Dean of the College at Dartmouth.

COLLEGE PLACEMENT

College counseling is facilitated by a director and 6 associates and generally begins in the winter for the Fourth Form, when students receive assistance in registering for Subject Tests. The counselors work closely with students beginning in winter of the Fifth Form year, conduct interviews with them and their parents, accompany them to college fairs, and help them prepare for formal interviews with college representatives, 200 of whom visit the campus each year. In the winter, juniors attend mock interviews held by college admissions officials who visit the school, and their parents are invited to the campus for a weekend of programs with the College Counseling Office and various university admission officers about the process of applying to college.

From 2001 through 2005, the most popular college choices included Georgetown (40), the University of Pennsylvania (40), Cornell (35), Yale (35), Harvard (33), Brown (29), George Washington (27), Boston University (25), NYU (25), and Columbia (24).

STUDENT BODY AND CONDUCT

In 2005–06, the school had 615 boarders and 245 day students from forty-three states and twenty-four countries.

The Student Council, which is composed of elected members of each form, provides a forum in which students can address school-related topics and plans, and it conducts and oversees social events and community matters.

Students are expected to follow school rules. Violations of the basic honor code or major school rules, or the accumulation of a number of violations of other rules, generally lead to suspension or dismissal. Rule violations are investigated by the Judicial Committee—a committee of elected students, deans, and an appointed faculty member—which makes recommendations to the Dean of Students.

ACADEMIC FACILITIES

Most campus academic facilities are the result of generous gifts from alumni and parents. The Carl C.

Icahn Center for Science (1989), a $14-million, three-story building designed by I. M. Pei, includes twenty-two classrooms and laboratories, a 150-seat auditorium, and a conservatory. Another I. M. Pei building, the Paul Mellon Arts Center (1971), houses two theaters, a recital hall, music classrooms and practice rooms, art studios, dance and film facilities, offices, and an art gallery. Each spring, a major musical is produced.

The Andrew Mellon Library, which opened in 1926, was renovated in 2002 to integrate technological innovations with traditional library resources. The collection includes more than 60,000 volumes, more than 150 magazine subscriptions, English- and foreign-language newspapers, and thousands of reels of microfilm, videos, DVDs, and sound recordings. The collection is steadily growing. Electronic resources include a wide variety of databases and indexes that are also available via MEL—the virtual branch of the Mellon Library. Special collections include those pertaining to Adlai Stevenson '18 and John F. Kennedy '35, along with the Rare Book, Thomas Hardy, and the Haffenreffer Autograph Collections and the school's extensive archives.

The Paul Mellon Humanities Center houses a computer center and a digital video production studio. Other facilities provide a total of forty-three classrooms as well as several computer centers with 120 fully networked workstations. All student rooms have telephone and computer wiring, with direct access to the Internet.

BOARDING AND GENERAL FACILITIES

Resident faculty members, their families, and Sixth Form house prefects live and work with small groups of students in residential settings that house as few as 7 students or as many as 75. Larger dormitories are divided into smaller sections, with 1 faculty member advising approximately 8–10 students to ensure feelings of community and warmth. Some students live in double rooms; others choose singles. Trained student peer counselors are an intrinsic part of the support system for students.

The Pratt Health Center is open all day every day. Registered nurses are on duty 24 hours a day; the school physician lives on campus and is always on call.

The Student Activities Center houses the school store and post office and has a cyber cafe, games, large-screen TVs, and spaces for coffeehouses and dances.

ATHLETICS

There is an appropriate level of athletics for every student. Some athletes come from very competitive programs and want to hone their skills with dedicated coaches and a serious sports program. Other students take advantage of the breadth of offerings and begin a new sport at the introductory level. The physical education and athletic program emphasizes acquiring lifetime skills, shaping positive attitudes about oneself as an individual and as a contributing member of a group, and developing a sense of honesty and fair play. All students participate in class-day or after-school sports each term.

There are varsity, JV, and third-level interscholastic teams in most sports, as well as intramural teams. The program also includes all major sports and such activities as scuba, CPR, and weight training.

The Johnson Athletic Center includes three basketball courts, three volleyball courts, ten international squash courts, a wrestling room, team weight rooms, and a suspended 1/10-mile track. A new addition (2002) contains a fitness center, a sports medicine suite, and a dance studio as well as the school's Athletics Hall of Fame. There are twenty-three outdoor tennis courts, the Hunt Tennis Center, thirteen athletic fields, a cross-country course, tracks, a hockey arena, a boathouse, and an Olympic-size swimming pool. Students also use a nearby golf course and a riding stable.

EXTRACURRICULAR OPPORTUNITIES

The school has more than sixty extracurricular activities, clubs, and organizations through which students may pursue special interests that range from astrophysics to conservation and from various publications to debating. Because each group requires club officers, leadership positions abound. Students are required to commit 30 hours to community service. The school's proximity to major cities provides access to numerous cultural events, museums, and exhibits.

DAILY LIFE

Classes are held five days per week and on seven Saturdays. They are scheduled in seven 50-minute periods and one 55-minute period between 8 a.m. and 2:50 p.m. four days per week; on Wednesdays and Saturdays, classes are held in four 50-minute periods and the academic day ends at 12:30. The afternoon sports program follows. Late afternoon provides time for study or extracurricular activities, and dinner is served between 5 and 7.

Students return to their dorm by 7:30 for a 1½-hour study time but may sign out to use the library or other academic facilities. There is a break from 9 to 9:45, with final dorm check-in at 9:30. There is a second study period from 9:45 to 10:30.

WEEKEND LIFE

Weekend social and recreational events and activities, in addition to those already scheduled at the Arts Center or by student organizations, are planned for all students. Every weekend there are dances, movies, and excursions to New York, Boston, or other nearby towns and cities. There are such seasonal activities as Harvest Fest and Spring Fest, and shuttle vans provide transportation to local ski areas.

SUMMER PROGRAMS

The five-week summer session is designed primarily for students of day schools who are seeking enrichment of skills-oriented courses that are not offered in their home schools. Summer programs include the Writing Project, John F. Kennedy Institute of Government, English Language Institute, and Connecticut Scholars Program (a public/private collaboration). Also offered are programs for middle school students, including FOCUS, an enrichment program for boys and girls who have completed grades 6–8; CONNECT, a mathematics/science institute for girls who have completed grades 6–8; and the Young Writers Workshop. Classroom work is supplemented by such activities as lecture series, field trips, and sports. About 600 boys and girls attend. A five-week Arts Conservatory program is offered, with options in theater, playwriting, and the visual arts.

The school also sponsors study trips to China, France, Spain, and the Navajo Nation. Requests for information should be sent to Summer Programs, 333 Christian Street, Wallingford, Connecticut 06492.

COSTS AND FINANCIAL AID

For 2005–06, the total cost for boarders was $35,360 and for day students, $25,680. Books are extra. An optional laundry service is available at an additional cost. Financial aid and loans are available for students whose families qualify. Decisions are mailed March 10. In 2005–06, 27 percent of the students received financial aid totaling $6 million, with the average award amounting to 70 percent of tuition.

Choate Rosemary Hall seeks students of diverse geographic, economic, social, ethnic, and racial backgrounds. The SSAT is required of applicants for grades 9 and 10 and should be taken in December if possible. The median score for ninth and tenth graders is at the 85th percentile. Most entering students test between the 80th and 99th percentiles. The PSAT/SAT is required for candidates for grades 11 and 12 and postgraduates. The TOEFL is suggested for those whose native language is not English. Applicants should be motivated achievers in their schools, attaining at least a B average on schoolwork.

For September 2005 entry, there were 1,550 final applications. The 2005–06 total enrollment of 860 included 265 new on-campus students. Students are accepted at all levels.

APPLICATION TIMETABLE

Students may submit a pre-interview form on paper or online at the school's Web site at any time. A personal interview is required, preferably in the fall prior to the year of proposed enrollment. A final application, including recommendations, a transcript, and a $50 nonrefundable fee, must be completed by January 15.

The Admission Office schedules appointments from 9 to 2, Monday through Friday, and 8 to 1 on selected Saturdays.

The Admission Committee reviews a student's records, recommendations from teachers and the principal, test results, extracurricular interests, and interview. If all materials have been completed by January 15, applicants are notified of the decision on March 10.

ADMISSIONS CORRESPONDENCE

Raymond M. Diffley III
Director of Admission
Choate Rosemary Hall
333 Christian Street
Wallingford, Connecticut 06492-3800

Phone: 203-697-2239
Fax: 203-697-2629
E-mail: admissions@choate.edu
Web site: http://www.choate.edu

CHRISTCHURCH SCHOOL
Christchurch, Virginia

Type: Boys' boarding and coeducational day college-preparatory school
Grades: 8–12, postgraduate year
Enrollment: 220
Head of School: John E. Byers, Headmaster

THE SCHOOL

Founded in 1921 by the Episcopal Church in the Diocese of Virginia, Christchurch School was named in honor of Christ Church Parish by the Reverend F. Ernest Warren, rector of the adjacent parish and first Headmaster of the School. One of five church schools owned by the Episcopal Diocese of Virginia, Christchurch is a college-preparatory school for boarding boys and day boys and girls in grades 8 through 12. A postgraduate year is also offered. Located on a 120-acre campus in historic Tidewater Virginia, the School is 40 minutes from Colonial Williamsburg, 1 hour from downtown Richmond, and 135 miles south of Washington, D.C. Christchurch is also adjacent to the Rappahannock River, approximately 12 nautical miles from the Chesapeake Bay.

Christchurch School provides a personal and supportive environment that presents students with opportunities for self-direction and success. This atmosphere of understanding and encouragement, complemented by continuous challenges, not only sustains confidence in students who have experienced academic success, but it also nurtures a positive self-image in students whose previous frustrations may have resulted from overcrowded classrooms and an overemphasis on academic competition.

Because it is affiliated with the Episcopal Church and operates within the context of a Christian community, Christchurch School offers its students the opportunity to discover themselves through spiritual as well as intellectual growth. All religious beliefs are accepted; chapel services, although Episcopal, are nonproselytizing.

A 21-member Board of Trustees serves as the School's governing body, and 1,900 active alumni contribute financially and spiritually to the School's growth.

Christchurch is accredited by the Virginia Association of Independent Schools. Memberships include the National Association of Independent Schools, the National Association of Episcopal Schools, the Secondary School Admissions Test Board, and the Association of Boarding Schools.

ACADEMIC PROGRAMS

Christchurch School has a flexible curriculum that challenges students of varying abilities. Because of small class sizes (the average number of students in a class is 12) and a student-teacher ratio of 6.6:1, students receive a great deal of individual attention. In consultation with the Academic Dean and the Director of College Counseling, a student and his or her family can chart a unique and appropriate course of study from the initial admissions interview until graduation.

The minimum required course load is five subjects, and the maximum load is six. Academic achievement is awarded on an alphabetical (A–F) system. Grades are supplemented by periodic written progress reports as well as effort and attitude

(E/A) evaluations. Reports are sent to parents at the end of each of the four marking periods. The school year is divided into semesters; exams are held twice a year. The Christchurch curriculum follows the traditional college-preparatory program of study: 4 years of English, 3 years of history and the social sciences, 3 years of mathematics, 3 years of science, 2 years of one foreign language (French or Spanish), and 1 year each of fine arts, theology, health, and three electives. Advanced Placement courses are offered in twelve disciplines.

Electives and additional course work are offered in each academic area. Christchurch School offers a comprehensive Marine Science Program. Marine science and AP environmental studies are electives that introduce students to the Chesapeake Bay and its ecosystem. Students in the Marine Science Program are involved in bona fide research on the bay's ecology and in direct efforts to improve the quality of the bay through independent research projects. The Marine Science Program is supported with research equipment that includes a 25-foot open boat and ten canoes. Lab equipment includes an aquaculture unit and other holding tanks.

Faculty members hold extra-help sessions each day. These sessions supplement daily classroom instruction and provide students the opportunity to work closely with teachers on specific problem areas. For students who have special learning needs, the Learning Skills Program supports daily classwork and long-term skill building. The Learning Skills Program is a leading example of academic collaboration in a traditional college-preparatory curriculum and environment. In addition, an English as a second language (ESL) program is offered for international students with limited English proficiency.

FACULTY AND ADVISERS

The faculty consists of 34 teachers; 21 hold a master's degree or higher. Seventy-five percent of faculty members reside on campus.

Members of the faculty and the administration participate in all phases of School life. Resident faculty members supervise each dormitory floor, and every student has a faculty adviser. Advisers play an important role in counseling students regarding their personal, social, and academic lives at Christchurch, and they also stay in close contact with parents regarding each child's progress.

COLLEGE PLACEMENT

Christchurch, as a college-preparatory school, provides all students with the curriculum and guidance necessary for admission to a four-year institution of higher learning. Typically, 100 percent of Christchurch graduates are accepted to four-year colleges. The Director of Counseling works individually with each student and his or her par-

ents to achieve admission to a college of their choice. College admissions representatives make frequent visits to the Christchurch campus, and seniors are encouraged to visit the schools in which they are interested.

Recent Christchurch seniors have been accepted by Auburn, Charleston, Clemson, Elon, Gettysburg, Hampden-Sydney, James Madison, Lynchburg, Mary Washington, Penn State, Randolph-Macon, Rensselaer, Roanoke, Syracuse, the United States Naval Academy, University of the South, Virginia Commonwealth, Virginia Military Institute, Virginia Tech, William and Mary, and the Universities of Georgia, North Carolina, and Virginia.

STUDENT BODY AND CONDUCT

The School currently enrolls 220 students. In recent years, most boarding students have come from Virginia, Texas, Maryland, Florida, Kentucky, Georgia, Louisiana, and the Carolinas. Several students from other countries are enrolled each year. On average, 40 percent of the student body are day students.

The Honor Code is the foundation of student life. The code states that students will not lie, cheat, deceive, or steal. All Christchurch students sign their names in the Honor Book. The Honor Council, which is composed of appointed students and faculty members, adjudicates situations involving honor violations and submits decisions to the Headmaster for consideration. Together, the faculty and the students lead the School community in matters of respectful concern for others.

ACADEMIC FACILITIES

The main academic facility is the Miller Building, which houses six classrooms, the Marine Science Laboratory, and the Carl A. Olsson Science Laboratory. Historic Bishop Brown Hall, a four-story building that was completely renovated in 1998, is the home of a state-of-the-art, fully computerized library; an expanded student center; the renowned Learning Skills Program Center; six classrooms; a computer center; and a lecture hall. Newly renovated Marston Hall houses the David and Wendy Charlton Performing Arts Center, which includes a large multipurpose performance area as well as a darkroom, an art studio, music rooms, and one general-purpose classroom.

BOARDING AND GENERAL FACILITIES

Christchurch has three residence halls for boys: Faye Hall houses eighth and ninth graders; John G. Scott Hall and Murrell Hall house sophomores and upperclassmen. Two students share a room. Murrell Hall houses a six-bed infirmary that is staffed by 3 nurses. The School store, snack bar, and post office are located at the center of the campus. Cameron Dining Hall is on the lower floor of Scott Hall. Faculty apartments open onto each floor of the halls, and other faculty members

live on campus. The School boathouses and dock are on Urbanna Creek, ¼ mile up the river from the main campus.

ATHLETICS

Athletics are an integral part of the program at Christchurch and provide students with the opportunity for interscholastic and intramural competition as well as the chance to learn and master sports for lifelong enjoyment. All faculty members serve as coaches, which allows students to learn from their teachers on a different level and helps to balance the relationship between teacher and student. Among the sports offered are baseball, basketball, crew, cross-country, football, golf, lacrosse, sailing, soccer, tennis, track, and wrestling. Athletically, Christchurch School is affiliated with the Virginia Prep League, Old Dominion Football Conference, Virginia Commonwealth Conference, Virginia Interscholastic Sailing Association, and National Capital Area Scholastic Rowing Association.

Special features of the Christchurch athletics program include its waterfront opportunities, such as sailing and crew. Sailing is offered in the fall and spring for both competition and enjoyment on the beautiful Rappahannock River. The highly successful crew team races in local, regional, and national competitions.

Campus facilities for the athletics program include Yarbrough Gymnasium; the Robert S. Phipps Field House, which facilitates indoor basketball, tennis, and volleyball; an all-weather track; a weight room; Bermuda fields for baseball, field hockey, football, lacrosse, and soccer; an outdoor swimming pool; and lighted tennis courts.

EXTRACURRICULAR OPPORTUNITIES

In addition to academics and athletics, Christchurch offers students a variety of extracurricular activities, such as student government and student ambassadors. Student publications include the yearbook and literary magazine. The Drama Department produces annual plays, with an open call to all students. A combined chorus of boys and girls meets several times each week and participates regularly in chapel services and other special occasions. Many students begin or continue their study of a musical instrument while at Christchurch; the most popular choices are guitar and piano.

DAILY LIFE

The school day begins with breakfast at 7 a.m. and chapel at 8. Classes meet Monday through Friday and run from 8:30 until 2:30 p.m. Activity periods are scheduled three days per week for student organization meetings, visiting guest speakers, and all-School activities. Lunch is cafeteria-style except on Wednesdays, when all students join their advisory group for a seated lunch. A daily tutorial period is offered each day after classes, followed by athletic activities and team sport practices.

During the day, student attire is neat casual. The School uniform is worn on Wednesdays. Required evening study hall is from 8 to 10, Sunday night through Thursday night, and is followed by free time before dorm check-in at 10:15.

WEEKEND LIFE

As a boarding school, Christchurch schedules a variety of weekend activities. The faculty members sponsor and chaperone trips off campus that combine social, recreational, and cultural themes. Outings to theaters, golf courses, museums, amusement parks, shopping malls, and cinemas are frequent options and may be jointly sponsored with girls' schools. Fishing, hiking, and camping excursions are also offered. Mixers, concerts, and other large events are coordinated through the Boarding Schools Social Activity Committee (BSSAC), which is made up of twenty-one boarding and day schools from Maryland, Virginia, and North Carolina. Weekend participation in community service projects is encouraged. Organized by the Director of Community Service, projects include Habitat for Humanity, primary school mentoring, river and road cleanups, Christmas Friends, and gleaning.

Periodically, students may leave the campus. Six overnights or weekends are granted each semester in addition to the scheduled holidays and long weekends.

COSTS AND FINANCIAL AID

Charges for 2006–07 are $35,500 for boarders and $15,000 for day students. Additional expenses include Tuition Refund Insurance and the student account deposit of approximately $2400 for books, social activities, student accident insurance, and school supplies.

Newly accepted students must send a deposit of $2500 to hold their place. Two thirds of the remaining tuition is due by July 15 and one third by January 1. A monthly payment plan is also available.

For 2006–07, more than $950,000 in financial aid is expected to be awarded to Christchurch students. Financial aid grants are awarded on the basis of need and merit, as indicated by the guidelines of the School and Student Service for Financial Aid. Approximately 30 percent of the students receive aid.

Families are eligible for a tuition freeze for the subsequent academic year if a reenrollment agreement is filed prior to April 1.

ADMISSIONS INFORMATION

Admission to Christchurch School is offered to qualified candidates who have the potential for academic success. Standardized test scores, teacher and personal recommendations, and, if the need exists, additional educational testing are considered. A personal interview with a prospective student and his or her family is required. Christchurch School values diversity and therefore admits qualified students of any race, religion, or national or ethnic origin.

APPLICATION TIMETABLE

Inquiries are welcome at any time. Interviews and tours of the campus are offered during weekdays at 9 a.m. or 1 p.m., preferably when school is in session. A $50 nonrefundable application fee ($75 for international students) is required. Applications received by February 10 are notified of first-round admission decisions on March 10. After February 10, applications are welcome; consideration is on a space-available basis. A rolling admission policy is used until all available spaces for each grade are filled.

ADMISSIONS CORRESPONDENCE

Director of Admission
Christchurch School
Christchurch, Virginia 23031

Phone: 804-758-2306
Fax: 804-758-0721
E-mail: admission@christchurchschool.org
Web site: http://www.christchurchschool.org

CHRIST SCHOOL

Arden, North Carolina

Type: Boys' boarding and day college-preparatory school
Grades: 8–12
Enrollment: 190
Head of School: Paul M. Krieger, Headmaster

THE SCHOOL

Christ School was founded in 1900 by the Reverend and Mrs. Thomas Wetmore on the site of an old plantation called Struan. During its early years, the School educated the children of the region, but in the 1920s it evolved into a boys' boarding school.

Affiliated with the Episcopal Church, Christ School is dedicated to providing a superior preparation for college as well as developing within each boy a firm confidence in his own worth. The School fosters education of the whole human being in a social environment of Christian character, physical activity, and a well-structured program.

Christ School is located on 500 acres of land outside the small town of Arden, in the Blue Ridge Mountains, 11 miles south of Asheville, North Carolina. The "land of the sky" abounds with lakes, golf courses, ski resorts, hiking trails, and white-water rivers. The School is located 10 minutes from the spectacular Blue Ridge Parkway, yet has easy access to cultural activities in Asheville, Atlanta, Charlotte, and Greenville.

A not-for-profit organization, the School is governed by a Board of Trustees. The 31 members meet quarterly.

All of the School's endowment, approximately $8 million, is in productive funds and is supplemented by an Annual Fund. There are approximately 2,200 living graduates who support the School both financially and through a variety of other efforts.

Christ School is accredited by the Southern Association of Colleges and Schools. It is a member of the National Association of Independent Schools, National Association of Episcopal Schools, Southern Association of Independent Schools, North Carolina Association of Independent Schools, Secondary School Admission Test Board, College Board, and the Episcopal Diocese of Western North Carolina.

ACADEMIC PROGRAMS

Preparing boys academically for college is Christ School's primary objective. The curriculum is designed to provide students with a firm foundation in both the academic subjects and the study skills they will need in college. The School's curriculum also stresses the knowledge and skills that will enable a student to become an informed and intelligent citizen of his community. The School has always believed that these objectives can best be fulfilled through a concentration in the traditional arts and sciences.

Small classes and individual attention are the key to a boy's academic development. A structured program of independent and supervised study enables a student to better achieve his potential.

Requirements for graduation include the completion of 20 credits: English (4), mathemat-ics (4), science (3), history (3), foreign language— Latin, French, or Spanish (2), fine arts (1), religious studies (.5), computer (.5), and electives (3). Electives include Advanced Placement courses in the arts, computer programming, English, foreign languages, history, mathematics, and science. General elective courses include choir, economics, government, history of Vietnam, journalism, marine biology, music of Western civilization, music practicum, music theory and composition, studio art I and II, and theater.

Most students carry a course load of five academic subjects, independent or supervised study, and a choice of extracurricular activities.

The average class size is 10–12 students; the student-faculty ratio is 6:1. Students are placed in classes on the basis of their achievement levels, their interests, and the requirements for gradua-tion. Marks are posted and sent home to parents eight times during the year.

Christ School's Learning Resource Program offers academic support in English, math, and study skills within the context of a rigorous college-preparatory curriculum. The program serves those who can meet the challenges of a full academic schedule while benefiting from the program's supportive techniques.

FACULTY AND ADVISERS

The faculty consists of 40 full-time members, 29 with advanced degrees. Thirty reside on campus.

Paul M. Krieger was appointed the twelfth Headmaster of Christ School in 2003. He had previously served as the school's Principal since August of 2000. Before coming to the Christ School, he served as Head of the Middle School at Montgomery Academy in Chester Springs, Pennsylvania. Following an extensive career in marketing, much of which was spent in the Eastern Mediterranean and the Middle East, he chose to leave the business field in 1989 for education. At The Hill School, in Pottstown, Pennsylvania, he served as Assistant Director of Development and Alumni Affairs, as Assistant Director of Admissions, was Founder and Director of The Hill Sports Camp, and held the Knobloch Chair in Economics, teaching Ad-vanced Placement courses. Mr. Krieger has a Bachelor of Arts degree from Gettysburg College, and a Master of Education Leadership from Immaculata College.

The School seeks teachers who are dedicated to the spiritual, academic, and social well-being of students and who share the common interest in self-improvement that sets boys upon the path to maturity and manhood. A student's progress throughout his years at Christ School is moni-tored closely by the faculty. Each boy has an adviser for guidance in his academic and personal life at the School.

A strong relationship between the student and adviser is formed through meetings and frequent gatherings for meals and recreation. In addition, each new student is matched with an outstanding upperclassman as a Big Brother. This is to further help the adjustment to boarding school life.

COLLEGE PLACEMENT

In a student's junior and senior years, the Dean and College Counselor work with the student and his family to assist him in securing admission to the college most suited to his needs. In addition, college representatives visit the campus in the fall and winter to discuss college admission requirements and procedures with students.

Christ School graduated 43 seniors in 2005, all of whom attended four-year colleges and universities. The School administered sixty-three Advanced Placement exams.

Graduates have been accepted at a variety of colleges and universities. Among them are American University, Art Institute of Boston, Brown, Clemson, Duke, Furman, George Wash-ington, Georgia Tech, Howard, Indiana Univer-sity at Bloomington, Macalester College, More-house College, Northeastern, Presbyterian, Rensselaer Polytechnic Institute, Southern Meth-odist, the University of the South, Wake Forest, Washington and Lee, Wheaton, Wofford, and the University of North Carolina at Chapel Hill.

STUDENT BODY AND CONDUCT

Christ School has a maximum boarding student population of 160 boarders and 30 day students. Fifteen states and nine countries are represented among the student body, and boys come from various religious backgrounds.

The responsibility for student life and con-duct at Christ School is largely in the hands of the students themselves. A student council, composed of prefects appointed by the Headmas-ter and members elected by the various forms, makes recommendations to the Headmaster regarding discipline and other aspects of School life. Sixth Formers (twelfth graders) guide and help supervise various activities, such as house life and the self-help work program.

ACADEMIC FACILITIES

The academic facilities are housed mainly in Wetmore Hall, which contains classrooms, four science labs, a computer lab, and a music room. St. Dunstan's Library houses the main reading and research room, with a state-of-the-art computer center that links an in-house service with the Internet global community. The Pingree Fine Arts Auditorium was dedicated in 1992.

BOARDING AND GENERAL FACILITIES

Christ School students reside in five houses. Two boys are assigned to a room. Each house is supervised by prefects and proctors under the direction of a resident faculty master. All houses

are fully equipped with computer networking capabilities. Students in grades 8 and 9 live separately from students in grades 10 through 12. A student center includes a game room, lounge, fireplace, snack shop, barbershop, bookstore, and forty-seat theater/TV room. St. Joseph's chapel, built in 1907, began complete renovations June 1, 2005.

ATHLETICS
Physical development, sportsmanship, cooperation, and self-esteem are all fostered by organized athletics. The various levels in all team sports allow each boy to choose those activities that best meet his interests and competence.

On the School grounds are six hard-surfaced tennis courts, a football field, a baseball field, a soccer field, an all-weather track, and a 3-acre lake that is used for kayaking, canoeing, fishing, and swimming. Indoor athletics facilities are housed in a modern field house containing a basketball court and three full-sized practice courts. The remodeled Memorial Gymnasium contains a wrestling gym, three racquetball courts, a new weight room, a training room, an equipment room, four locker rooms, and offices for coaches.

The School fields interscholastic teams in football, cross-country, soccer, basketball, wrestling, swimming, lacrosse, baseball, tennis, golf, and track. In lieu of athletics, students have the option to participate in the theater program, debate, an intramural program, or the outdoor program.

An outdoor education program provides instruction and trips in white-water canoeing, climbing, hiking, camping, mountain-biking, and initiatives on a low ropes course. The outdoor program is available as an alternative to team sports.

EXTRACURRICULAR OPPORTUNITIES
Daily periods are set aside for extracurricular activities. On weekends, a wide range of planned activities is available for students to explore other interests.

The primary musical group on campus is the choir. The choir performs at chapel services and on tours outside the School.

For students who are learning to play musical instruments, private lessons in guitar, drums, keyboards, and other instruments can be arranged. The School yearbook and literary magazine provide opportunities for creative writing, photography, and art. The student newspaper is produced using the latest computer technology

and appears on the School Web site. A theater program produces three plays a year, enabling students to express their talents in acting, set designing, and stage managing. The art studio contains tools and equipment for extracurricular painting, woodworking, drawing, and ceramics.

Because of the School's proximity to various winter resorts, there are many opportunities for Christ School students to ski on designated ski days and weekends.

DAILY LIFE
The Angelus bell rings at 7 a.m., and breakfast is served from 7 to 7:30. From 7:40 to 7:55, room inspection is held while boys complete School jobs. At 10:30 the student body comes together for chapel and assembly.

Christ School has a rotating schedule that allows for classes to meet four or five times a week. The academic day ends at 3, and boys are dismissed for sports, the outdoor program, conditioning and exercise, or theater. Dinner is served at 6 p.m.

A self-help work program, in which students do jobs to maintain the campus, is an integral part of everyday student life.

Teacher-supervised and independent study periods are held during the academic day and at night. Faculty members and advisers monitor a student's progress and make recommendations based on a boy's individual progress.

WEEKEND LIFE
Weekends offer a less structured environment that allows participation in sports, planned activities, and free time to pursue a wide variety of interests. Christ School has a student activities director to coordinate weekend and coeducational activities. Weekends provide opportunities for interscholastic athletics; white-water rafting; taking in a concert or a movie; trips to cultural events in Asheville, Atlanta, Charlotte, and Knoxville; attending professional and collegiate sporting events; shopping; dances; and course work.

COSTS AND FINANCIAL AID
For 2005–06, tuition and room and board are $31,500 for seven-day boarders and $15,800 for day students. In addition, a $400 deposit must be placed in an account to cover each boy's weekly allowance and extracurricular activities. Expenses for clothing, travel, laundry, and other needs vary considerably according to the individual and are

the responsibility of each boy's parents. Tuition insurance and tuition payment plans are available.

The School aims, within its means, to ensure that no boy deemed suitable to Christ School be turned away because of financial need.

Financial aid and merit scholarships are available to qualified students. In 2004–05, the School awarded $815,000 in aid and scholarships.

ADMISSIONS INFORMATION
Christ School accepts students in grades 8–12. Admission policies are based on academic ability and personal qualifications. The School looks for students who can realize their full potential in a school that emphasizes the value of structure and discipline. Equally important is the ability of the potential student to fit into a small, caring community.

The School requires of candidates a campus visit, teacher recommendations, a transcript, and an application essay. The SSAT or other standardized test is required.

Campus visits are scheduled to suit each individual family and usually require a 3-hour commitment. This includes a tour of the campus, an appointment with the admission office, and visitation with the Headmaster.

A small number of students are accepted for the second semester. The School encourages families to set up a campus visit in the fall.

APPLICATION TIMETABLE
Application should be made as early as possible. Final decisions are made within two weeks by the admission committee after the applicant's file is complete. The majority of incoming students are determined before the end of the previous school year. There are a limited number of openings after June 1.

ADMISSIONS CORRESPONDENCE
Denis Stokes
Director of Admission
Christ School
500 Christ School Road
Arden, North Carolina 28704

Phone: 828-684-6232, Ext. 106
    800-422-3212 (toll-free)
Fax: 828-684-4869
E-mail: dstokes@christschool.org
Web site: http://www.christschool.org

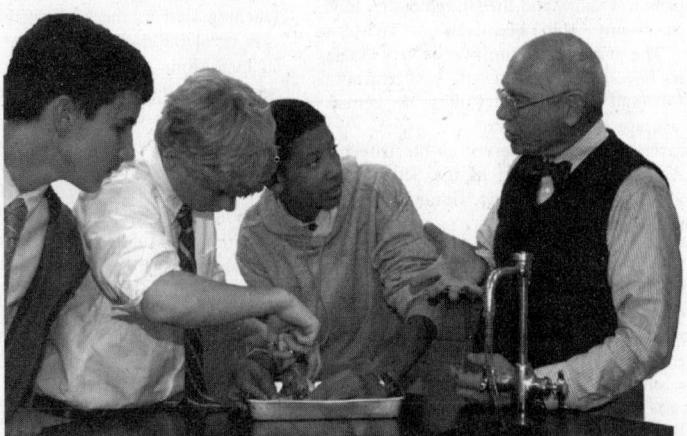

COLLEGE DU LEMAN INTERNATIONAL SCHOOL

Versoix (Geneva), Switzerland

Type: Coeducational boarding and day college-preparatory school
Grades: Kindergarten–age 5; Primary, 1–5; Junior High School, 6–8; High School, 9–13
Enrollment: School total: 1,850
Head of School: Francis A. Clivaz, Director General

THE SCHOOL

Collège du Léman International School is located on an 18-acre campus in Versoix, a city of about 10,000 on the shores of Lake Geneva, about 5 miles from the center of Geneva. It was founded in 1960 by Francis A. Clivaz to help serve the needs of the growing diplomatic and international business community located in the Geneva area.

Geneva, one of the leading international cities in Europe, is the site of the European headquarters of the United Nations and many other international organizations and businesses. Being centrally located in Europe, it is relatively close to places of historical and cultural interest. The advantages of its location are used as much as possible to implement the philosophy of the School, which is to provide a stimulating and effective college-preparatory education enriched by the wealth of cultural experiences offered by its international community. In so doing, the School hopes to develop internationally minded young people who can appreciate the accidental differences, but basic oneness, of all peoples.

The School, a registered company, is overseen by an Advisory Board. Operating and capital expenditures come almost solely from student tuition and fees.

Collège du Léman International School is accredited by the New England Association of Schools and Colleges and by the Council of International Schools.

ACADEMIC PROGRAMS

The School has two academic programs: one with instruction in French, preparing for the French Baccalauréat, the Swiss Federal Maturité, and the bilingual Swiss Federal Maturité; the other with instruction in English, preparing students for entrance into colleges and universities and A-level examinations. The information contained below pertains mainly to the Anglo-American college-preparatory curriculum.

All students in the High School are required to take a complete schedule of courses consisting of from six to ten subjects, each meeting between two and six times per week, in addition to physical education. Twelfth-grade students generally take six subjects, most meeting five times a week. Students who are taking Advanced Placement or International Baccalaureate (IB) Diploma courses are permitted to take fewer courses. A normal selection of courses would include English, mathematics, social studies, laboratory science, French and possibly another language, art, and computer studies. Twenty-two credits (18 of which must be academic) are required to earn a Graduating Diploma; 4 must be in English, 3 in laboratory science, 3 in mathematics, 3 in social studies, and 3 in modern languages. French is required of all students every year. Classes are grouped according to ability in English, mathematics, and languages. Science is taught in mixed international groups. Advanced Placement and International Baccalaureate (IB) Diploma are offered in literature, French language, French literature, American history, economics, European history, calculus, computer (AP), physics, chemistry, biology, German, Spanish, management of business psychology, management, and art. Students may sit for Advanced Placement and IB examinations in grades 11, 12, and 13.

An Intensive English Program for non-native speakers of English is scheduled into the regular timetable.

Class sizes vary from 3 to 24 students; the average class size is 13. The student-teacher ratio is about 11:1. Small classes facilitate individual participation and attention. Evening study by boarders is done in their rooms, indirectly supervised by the residence staff. Students with academic difficulties have a formally supervised study hall. The library is open from 8:30 a.m. to 5 p.m.

Academic reports are sent to parents six times a year. Written reports for each subject are included with the semester grades. Written reports are sent at other times for students who do not do as well as expected. Parents are invited to conferences during both semesters. The letter grades A through F are used. A grade of N indicates no grade was given because of insufficient knowledge of English. Examinations are given at the end of each semester.

FACULTY AND ADVISERS

Of the 197 teaching staff members, 170 are full-time. Approximately 70 percent are women. In addition, 12 resident staff members are responsible for the boarding students. Thirty-three nationalities are represented on the teaching staff. Most teachers are from Switzerland, Great Britain, France, and the United States. One hundred twenty hold licentiates or master's degrees. The annual staff turnover is very small. Teachers have an average of ten years' teaching experience and have been at Collège du Léman for an average of eleven years.

Francis A. Clivaz has served as the Director General since the founding of the School. He received his degree in business administration in Lausanne, Switzerland.

COLLEGE PLACEMENT

Students are prepared for their college selection and application by a college guidance counselor, who meets regularly with eleventh graders during their second semester and with twelfth graders during their first semester. The students have at their disposal a comprehensive library of reference materials on universities throughout the world, including college-selection computer software and videos. Approximately 50 college admissions officers visit the School each year.

The PSAT is administered to eleventh graders. The native-English-speaking 2004 graduates' mean SAT I scores were 509 verbal and 550 math (all nationalities). Mean SAT I and SAT II scores were 592 verbal and 504 math (all nationalities).

One hundred twenty-two graduates entered universities and colleges in fall 2004, including Queens in Canada; Stanford, Tufts, and Yale in the United States; the London School of Economics, Cambridge; HEC–Lausanne and Geneva in Switzerland; and institutions in other countries.

STUDENT BODY AND CONDUCT

There are 1,850 students on campus: 1,213 students are in the Anglo-American program, and 697 students are in the French program.

There are 123 nationalities represented. The nationality with the largest representation is Swiss, followed by American, English, French, Russian, and Japanese. The American students are generally from diplomatic and international business families living in countries throughout the world. The non-American students also generally come from diplomatic and business families. They come to Collège du Léman to prepare for eventual entry into American and other universities. Students coming directly from the United States generally do so in order to profit from an international experience that cannot be found in their own country.

A code of conduct exists that emphasizes the student's personal responsibility in maintaining a considerate and effective School community. Students are expected to be well dressed and to maintain a good personal appearance. Minor infractions of the rules of conduct are dealt with on an ascending chain of authority, through the teaching staff to the administration. An infraction involving the use of alcohol or drugs results in expulsion. A Student Council, which represents the High School students in both the American and the French programs, is elected annually by the students in the High School. Through its various committees, the council is responsible for the organization and efficient running of a wide variety of extracurricular activities. A Middle School Student Council is also elected each year.

A Boarding House Council plans activities for and represents the interests of resident students.

ACADEMIC FACILITIES

During the past five years, a new High School building and French Section building have been constructed to update the campus facilities and support the increased enrollment.

BOARDING AND GENERAL FACILITIES

There are six residence facilities to accommodate 200 boarding students. All but one of these are villas. For the most part, the students live 2 or 3 to a room. Lounges are in each residence; a commons area and a snack bar are open during the students' free time. There is one infirmary for boys and one for girls. Two full-time nurses are on duty, and a doctor with residence and office facilities adjacent to the campus is on call.

ATHLETICS

The School recognizes the importance of physical activity in the overall development of the individual. It recognizes also that there is a correlation between physical activity and mental growth and that the physical interests and abilities of the adult are fostered during one's youth. Considerable emphasis is therefore put on sports. All students are required to follow a physical education course, and sports activities are a regular part of the after-class hours. Competitive sports include basketball, cricket, cross-country, rugby, skiing, soccer, swimming, tennis, track and field, and volleyball. Noncompetitive sports include bowling, gymnastics, horseback riding, jogging, judo, softball, swimming, and yoga. One week of ski classes is scheduled for each grade. In addition, skiing is a regular weekend activity during the winter months.

There are three covered tennis/basketball courts, a soccer field, a softball field, a running track, a swimming pool, a judo room, and a weight-training room.

EXTRACURRICULAR OPPORTUNITIES

Extracurricular activities include the yearbook and school newspaper; music lessons and choir; drama, math, cinema, and debate; Model United Nations, National Honor Society, and many Student Council activities. Individual classes schedule field trips to museums and places of historical and cultural interest in the area. Resident students regularly attend dramatic and musical performances in Geneva. School trips are organized to places of interest in Europe or Africa during the Easter vacation. An annual International Day is sponsored by the Student Council, in which members of each nationality represented in the student body are invited to exhibit or provide something typical of their country.

DAILY LIFE

There are seven 45-minute periods scheduled each day, extending from 8:25 a.m. to3:30 p.m. One hour is allowed for lunch. A hot lunch is optional for day students; the alternatives are eating in the snack bar or bringing a picnic lunch. Sports and other activities take place after school hours.

WEEKEND LIFE

There are regularly planned weekend activities, including intramural sports and major athletics events, movies, dances, excursions to places of cultural interest, ski trips, hiking, shopping and leisure trips to Geneva, and musical and dramatic productions. Eleventh- and twelfth-grade students are allowed one weekend evening in Geneva. All planned activities are supervised. Groups of students going to Geneva all leave and return together. Younger students are accompanied by staff members. Day students are welcome to participate in planned weekend activities.

SUMMER PROGRAMS

English, French, and German studies are taught as noncredit courses during July and August to students coming from all parts of the world. A number of these students stay to continue their education during the following school year, but it is not a prerequisite or an obligation. Students may enroll for three- or six-week sessions. Language instruction is given during 3 hours in the morning. A separate, more personalized academic program in mathematics, physics, chemistry, and biology gives an opportunity for credit award. Afternoons, evenings, and weekends are taken up with organized sports activities and excursions to places of interest in Geneva and other parts of Switzerland. Summer-school faculty members are generally drawn from the regular teaching staff. Particulars can be obtained by writing to the School.

COSTS AND FINANCIAL AID

The annual charges for the 2005–06 school year were 16,500–21,800 Swiss francs for day students and Sfr. 50,000–55,000 for boarding students. Costs for textbooks, pocket money, accident insurance, and other fees add approximately Sfr. 5000. The hot lunch (about Sfr. 2750) and bus service (approximately Sfr. 3200–4000) are optional for day students. Pocket money is given to boarding students according to the wishes of their parents. School trips are not included in the annual fees, and they are optional. Charges for the initial trimester and all subsequent trimesters are billed and due in advance.

Financial aid can be given, based on need, to students with good recommendations and past performance.

ADMISSIONS INFORMATION

Students are admitted on the basis of previous academic records and recommendations indicating that they are capable of successfully following a college-preparatory curriculum and that they possess no character or psychological problems that would be incompatible with an international boarding community. Students who do not have a mastery of English must pass tests of English proficiency before being admitted to regular classes. Required for admission are the academic record, letters of recommendation, and a medical report. Generally, about 90 percent of the applicants are admitted.

APPLICATION TIMETABLE

Inquiries, campus visits, and interviews are welcome throughout the year. Students may be admitted during the school year if there are places available. The application form may be downloaded from the School's Web site. Applications for the fall semester should be submitted by April to ensure a place. For day students, an application fee of Sfr. 250 is required as well as a refundable security deposit of Sfr. 500. For residential students, the application fee is Sfr. 1000, with a refundable security deposit of Sfr. 5000. Notification of acceptance is sent shortly afterward.

ADMISSIONS CORRESPONDENCE

Collège du Léman International School
1290 Versoix (Geneva)
Switzerland

Phone: 41-22-775-55-55
Fax: 41-22-775-55-59
E-mail: info@cdl.ch
Web site: http://www.cdl.ch

COLORADO TIMBERLINE ACADEMY

Durango, Colorado

Type: Coeducational boarding and day college-preparatory school
Grades: 9–12, ages 13–19
Enrollment: 44
Head of School: Daniel J. Coey, Director

THE SCHOOL

Colorado Timberline Academy (CTA) was founded in 1975 by Claire Raines, Robert Therrell, and Joseph Maceyak, who evolved their ideas about education while teaching at another private school. These ideas included the belief that a small community, centered on learning and work and situated in a beautiful mountain setting, could provide special opportunities for students and faculty members to grow.

The CTA community is located on 50 acres 12 miles north of Durango, in the picturesque Animas Valley. Directly to the north of the campus are the peaks of the San Juan Mountains, one of the most spectacular ranges in Colorado. These mountains provide an outstanding resource that the community uses for backpacking trips, rock climbing, mountain biking, and skiing. Durango is also located close to the dramatic desert country of Utah and Arizona.

The Academy is governed by the Director and faculty with the guidance of a Board of Trustees. The board consists of parents, alumni, and faculty members and welcomes objective participation from citizens, such as businesspeople, who have no direct connection with the school. Operating expenses for 2004–05 were approximately $850,000, and Annual Giving supported about 2 percent of those expenses. The Academy has no endowment.

Colorado Timberline Academy is in good standing with the Colorado Department of Education.

ACADEMIC PROGRAMS

Rather than requiring a specific number of credits in various academic areas, CTA requires that students reach eight basic academic goals and focus on two of them. The eight goals are in the areas of mathematics, English, history, science, arts, psychology and philosophy, foreign languages, and computers. To graduate, students must prove by passing certain tests, writing certain papers, and accomplishing certain tasks that they are proficient at the levels of each of the eight goals.

The curriculum is designed to be equivalent to a four-year high school program. Because students work at differing rates, some students are able to graduate in fewer than four years. The time it takes students to meet the goals is influenced by their background and motivation. Depending on their academic background, students who transfer to CTA from another school may be able to reach some of the goals almost immediately or may need extra time in order to reach them. Although credits are not required for graduation, CTA keeps records of transferable Carnegie units so that students who wish to transfer to other schools will have the proper number of credits.

Another unusual aspect of the CTA academic program is the use of a block scheduling system that divides the academic year into seven 4- or 5-week blocks. A student registers for three academic classes during a block, and classes meet for 1½ hours each day. This scheduling leads to greater concentration on a smaller number of subjects.

Although traditional letter grades are used, they are supplemented by written evaluations that describe all aspects of a student's performance and are sent out seven times a year. These evaluations provide a complete description of progress and effort, and the school believes they are more helpful than letter grades alone.

FACULTY AND ADVISERS

The faculty consists of 10 teachers (7 men and 3 women). Some have master's degrees. Most faculty members live on campus. The faculty members share in all aspects of the school, including weekend activities, sports and recreation, and maintenance and improvements. Close faculty-student relationships are characteristic of the community.

COLLEGE PLACEMENT

Each student selects a faculty member to act as his or her adviser. This adviser is the student's chief contact for academic counseling. In addition, a faculty member serves in the official capacity of college counselor. The PSAT is given at CTA, and students are given assistance in preparing for the SAT.

The 12 members of the class of 2004 are all attending college. Graduates are attending, among other schools, Alfred, American, Colorado, Fort Lewis, and Maine Maritime Academy.

STUDENT BODY AND CONDUCT

The student body consists of 42 boarding boys and girls and 2 day students. At CTA, students are not separated by grade level. Students vary in age from 13 to 19; the majority are between 16 and 18. Students come from many parts of the United States and abroad.

The faculty determines most of the campus rules at the beginning of the year. Disciplinary decisions are made by the faculty or by the entire community, depending on the rules violated.

ACADEMIC FACILITIES

In the 1930s, a hot springs resort was developed on the land that is now the CTA campus. The lodge building is now the main classroom facility, containing several small rooms, the library, the computer system, the dining area, and the central meeting room. The old bathhouse to the south of the lodge is the foreign language, science, and arts building, containing a science lab and a darkroom.

BOARDING AND GENERAL FACILITIES

Students are housed in fifteen small log cabins, most holding 2 students. These cabins were originally tourist facilities at the resort. Two additional dormitory buildings each house 5 students in private rooms. A duplex cabin was recently built to hold 4 students.

ATHLETICS

CTA emphasizes the sports most appropriate to mountain towns. Soccer, mountain biking, kayaking, rock climbing, and softball are popular in the warm weather. Skiing, both downhill and cross-country, and snowboarding are the main activities during the winter months. Classes are scheduled Tuesday through Saturday, with Sunday and Monday set aside as the weekend, so that students can take advantage of less crowded downhill ski slopes at the Purgatory ski area. The school provides transportation to the slopes on Sunday and Monday. If there is interest, ski and snowboard teams can be formed. These teams are coached by the Purgatory staff, and they have participated in competitions in the Rockies.

EXTRACURRICULAR OPPORTUNITIES

CTA plans three major trips each year. A backpacking trip to the Weminuche Wilderness Area, adjacent to Durango, begins the year for the entire community; in the fall there is a one-week trip to a desert environment in southern Utah, and in the spring small groups of students take trips to a variety of areas. Spring trips have included river-rafting, hiking in the Grand Canyon, mountain-biking, and houseboating on Lake Powell.

The school yearbook, including all photography and layout, is produced by students and faculty members. Photography, in general, is a popular activity at CTA. The Academy encourages students to develop their own hobbies and activities.

DAILY LIFE

Breakfast begins at 7:30. The first class is held from 8:30 to 10. Teachers and students participate in a daily maintenance of the facilities between 10 and 10:30. The second class meets from 11 to 12:30. Lunch lasts from 12:30 to 1:30, and the third class meets from 1:30 to 3. A period is set aside three afternoons a week for athletics and arts and crafts. These classes meet at 3:30 and last varying amounts of time. There are scheduled study halls Monday through Friday from 7:30 to 8 p.m.

With parental permission, students may sign out and leave campus after classes. They must return by 10 on weeknights and by 11:45 on weekends.

The entire community meets Tuesday evenings for announcements and to discuss concerns

and issues. Dress at CTA is informal. Saturday night dinners are usually more formal events.

WEEKEND LIFE

On weekends, students may sign out during the day to go to town, to go skiing, to go hiking, or to take part in a similar activity. Overnight sign-out is at the discretion of parents. Weekend activities are planned by the duty faculty members and interested students. These varied activities might include skiing, bowling, soaking at local hot springs, trips to town and to the movies, and softball games. Day trips are sometimes planned to such places as Mesa Verde National Park and Navajo Lake. Faculty members accompany students on overnight trips throughout the year that might include camping, a ski trip to Telluride, a Denver Broncos or Colorado Rockies game in Denver, a cookout and slumber party at a faculty member's off-campus home, or a weekend in Santa Fe, New Mexico.

COSTS AND FINANCIAL AID

Tuition, room, and board for the 2004–05 school year were $24,800. A $3000 deposit is due upon acceptance. One refundable deposit of $500, to be used in case of damage to property and for books and supplies, is required as well. All fees are payable before the school year begins, but an installment plan, for which there is a late-payment fee, permits payment to be made in two installments. Some spring trips and personal skills require extra money, but such trips are optional. A full-season ski pass is included in the cost of tuition.

A few scholarships are available and are awarded on the basis of need.

ADMISSIONS INFORMATION

CTA seeks students who excel in an area—in academics, sports, or the arts. The Academy does not discriminate on the basis of race, religion, or national or ethnic background.

The following is a general description of the types of students who experience success at CTA: the high achiever, who wants the support, structure, and challenge of a small school to reach his or her potential; the average achiever, who wants to improve performance through closer personal attention from teachers; the underachieving yet capable student, who needs daily structure to provide an incentive for success; and all students who enjoy a wide variety of outdoor activities and experiences.

Applicants are expected to submit, in addition to the application form, transcripts of previous grades and four letters of recommendation from teachers, friends, and employers. No test scores are required. The Academy requires applicants to visit the campus for an interview.

APPLICATION TIMETABLE

Initial inquiries are welcome at any time. Application forms can be obtained and interviews can be scheduled by writing or calling the CTA office, which is open from 9 to 4, Monday through Saturday, during the academic year and from 9 to 3, Monday through Friday, during the summer. There is a $35 application fee. Applications are reviewed as they are completed. In most cases, decisions are reached within a few weeks. Final acceptance occurs when the Academy receives the $3000 deposit.

CTA occasionally has openings during the course of the year and, if space is available, accepts new students at the beginning of any block.

ADMISSIONS CORRESPONDENCE

Daniel J. Coey, Director
Alexander J. Schuhl, Director of Admission
Colorado Timberline Academy
35554 Highway 550
Durango, Colorado 81301

Phone: 970-247-5898
Fax: 970-259-8067
E-mail: adm@ctaedu.org
Web site: http://www.ctaedu.org

COLUMBIA GRAMMAR AND PREPARATORY SCHOOL

New York, New York

Type: Coeducational day college-preparatory school
Grades: PK–12: Grammar School, Prekindergarten–6; High School, 7–12
Enrollment: School total, 1,071; High School, 546
Head of School: Dr. Richard Soghoian, Headmaster

THE SCHOOL

Columbia Grammar was founded in 1764, just ten years after the founding of Kings College (later Columbia College) by King George II. Its original purpose was to prepare students for the rigors of Columbia College, and its earliest curriculum embraced, according to the first Headmaster, David Ogilby, "everything useful for the comfort and convenience and elegance of life, as well as everything that contributes to true happiness, both here and hereafter."

The School was incorporated as a nonprofit institution in 1941, and it joined with the Leonard School for Girls in 1956 to become coeducational. The School is governed by a Board of Trustees.

The School provides a rigorous, stimulating, and structured academic program in a warm and relatively informal atmosphere. It aims to instill in students the skills and habits of thought to enable them to benefit fully from college and at the same time to provide them with a rich and pleasurable intellectual and social experience during their school years. Music, theater, and the visual arts occupy an important place at all levels of the program. The values of tolerance of others and of responsibility for oneself and for one's community are likewise critical to the program. Decision making about one's education is gradually increased under careful guidance until, by the senior year, students are prepared for the choices facing them in college.

The School is accredited by the New York State Association of Independent Schools and the New York State Board of Regents. It maintains memberships in the National Association of Independent Schools, the New York State Association of Independent Schools, the Guild of Independent Schools of New York City, and the Independent Schools Admissions Association of Greater New York.

ACADEMIC PROGRAMS

Students in grades 7 and 8 study a core curriculum in academic subjects and the arts. In grades 9–12, they must complete a rigorous college-preparatory program of 4 years of English, 4 years of mathematics, 4 years of history, 3 years of science, 3 years of a foreign language, and a semester each of music literature and art history, plus a rich choice of electives. The goal of the English Department is to produce students who enjoy reading and who are accustomed to talking and writing intelligently about what they read. In grade 9, a full-year course addresses through literature the fundamental theme of coming of age and includes separate time for writing. In grade 10, students focus on writing clear and well-organized essays and read a selection of British and American literature. In grades 11 and 12, students choose from semester-long electives, with a major research paper each

fall. Typical electives include Modernist Literature, English Literature of the Early 19th Century, Shaw and Ibsen, and the Art of Poetry. The History Department has a two-year requirement in Western civilization for grades 9 and 10 as well as a required U.S. history course in grade 11. Some electives for grades 11 and 12 include a course taught with Tufts University, economics, psychology, the Holocaust, and Latin American politics.

All students are required to take four consecutive years of high school mathematics. Computer science is required, with a number of additional electives. Science offerings include biology, chemistry, physics, Advanced Placement courses, and semester electives such as electronics, ecology, organic chemistry, genetics, human evolution, and anatomy and physiology. The foreign language department offers French, Japanese, Latin, and Spanish. Students are free to start a second language at any point in their high school career.

Students in grades 9–12 may also choose from a wide range of offerings in the arts: studio courses in ceramics and sculpture, painting and drawing, jewelry making, and woodworking; courses in acting and photography; and participation in the chorus and instrumental ensembles.

Advanced Placement courses are offered in all the academic departments: American and European history, art history, biology, calculus AB and BC, chemistry, computer science, English, French, government, music theory, physics, and Spanish.

Students are grouped by ability in science and mathematics. In other academic areas, students are mixed.

The student-teacher ratio is 7:1, and the average class size is 10–15. Teachers are available to work with students during their free periods, and close student-teacher relations characterize the School. Juniors and seniors can initiate tutorials in areas not covered by courses.

In the sophomore year, students who participate in the science research course choose and explore a topic of personal interest, learn to search electronic databases, read appropriate literature, define an experimental project, and seek the guidance of a mentor from within the community of practicing scientists. Their junior year is spent refining the experimental protocol and collecting data. As seniors, they present their research in public forums of scientific symposia and competitions.

The academic year is divided into two semester units, each roughly sixteen weeks long. Students receive letter grades as well as written evaluations in paragraph form at the end of each semester. Progress reports are sent in mid-semester when students are new to the School or when they are experiencing academic difficulties. Parent-teacher-student conferences take place

twice a year, but parents are encouraged to meet with teachers whenever problems arise during the school year.

Students are required to perform 100 hours of service in order to graduate. Many students earn service credit by tutoring other students under the supervision of a faculty member or by helping with classes in the Grammar School. Students are encouraged to earn service credit in volunteer work outside the School, and half of their service must be done outside the School. Many have worked in local neighborhood centers tutoring and helping with day care. Others have worked for hospitals, the ASPCA, or the Central Park Conservancy or have earned service credit by working through the volunteer services of their own religious organizations.

FACULTY AND ADVISERS

The full-time High School faculty consists of 32 men and 33 women. In addition to baccalaureate degrees, faculty members also hold fifty-five master's degrees and one doctorate. Some faculty members hold more than one master's degree. There are also 9 part-time teachers, including 8 full-time administrators who also teach.

The Headmaster, Richard Soghoian, was appointed in 1981. He is a graduate of the University of Virginia and holds a Ph.D. in philosophy from Columbia University, where he was an International Fellow in the School of International Affairs. Prior to his appointment, Dr. Soghoian taught philosophy at the University of Denver, was Assistant Dean at Columbia College, was Director of the Graduate School at Pratt Institute, and most recently served as the Vice President for Academic Affairs at Manhattanville College in Purchase, New York.

Most full-time faculty members in the High School are assigned as advisers to a small group of students. Advisers meet daily with their students and also supervise a range of extracurricular activities.

In addition to faculty advisers, there are 6 deans in the High School, one for each grade, as well as 2 student counselors and 2 college counselors.

COLLEGE PLACEMENT

College counseling begins in the junior year, when students meet with the college counselors to discuss basic questions about the type of college in which they are interested, field of study, geographical location, and other concerns. A meeting is held for parents in February of the junior year to give them the basic outline of the college guidance program. Students are encouraged to begin visiting colleges during the spring and summer vacations before the senior year, and several Fridays are set aside during the fall of senior year for college visits. Early in the fall of the senior year, students and parents meet with

the college counselors to establish a firm list of colleges to which the student can apply.

SAT mean scores for the class of 2005 were 640 verbal and 640 math. Graduates of the class of 2005 are attending the following colleges and universities: Arizona State, Art Institute of Chicago, Bard, Bates, Boston University, Brooklyn Polytechnic, Brown, Clark, Colgate, Columbia, Connecticut College, Cornell, Emerson, Emory, Fordham, George Washington, Gettysburg, Goucher, Johns Hopkins, Lafayette, Lehigh, Muhlenberg, NYU, Northeastern, Northwestern, Oberlin, Parsons School of Design, Princeton, RIT, Rollins, Skidmore, Syracuse, Tulane, Vanderbilt, Vassar, Washington (St. Louis), Wesleyan, Wheaton, and the Universities of Arizona, Indiana, Iowa, Michigan, Pennsylvania, Rochester, Southern California, Vermont, and Wisconsin.

STUDENT BODY AND CONDUCT

There are currently 40 boys and 36 girls in grade 7, 39 boys and 36 girls in grade 8, 54 boys and 51 girls in grade 9, 53 boys and 44 girls in grade 10, 51 boys and 50 girls in grade 11, and 42 boys and 50 girls in grade 12. The majority of the students reside in Manhattan, but there is also representation from the other boroughs, Long Island, northern New Jersey, and Westchester. Approximately 15 percent of the students are members of minority groups, and the School has a strong commitment to the Prep for Prep program, which brings minority students into the School in the seventh grade.

The rules of conduct for the student body are set forth in the *Student Handbook* and stress consideration for others.

There is an active student government, with representatives from grades 7 to 12, which functions as the vehicle through which student discussion of School issues and policies can take place and student positions and policies can be articulated to the faculty and administration. Similarly, it becomes a forum in which the faculty and administration can raise problems and discuss areas of future planning with students. The student government plays a major role in organizing and supporting other extracurricular activities and groups.

ACADEMIC FACILITIES

The School has four separate buildings: the Grammar School's five connected brownstones on 94th Street; the original Columbia Grammar School building on 93rd Street, which contains the cafeteria, a swimming pool, a gymnasium, and two art studios; a High School building containing fifteen classrooms, three science labs, three music practice rooms, a library, a computer room, and a full-sized gymnasium; and a building, completed in 1996, containing classrooms for grades 5–7, three science rooms, and two computer rooms, plus five art studios, drama practice and performance space, and a cafeteria for grades 5–12. Another building that connects to the High School building was completed in 2001. It contains a third gym for the School, a state-of-the-art theater, and three floors of classrooms and science labs. Another brownstone, purchased in August 2004 at 36 West 94th Street, includes the admissions office and the development office.

ATHLETICS

The aim of the physical education program is to provide a broad range of activities that build enduring skills, provide interests for leisure time, and contribute to social adjustment and fitness. In addition to the regular physical education program, there are varsity teams in boys' baseball, basketball, golf, hockey, soccer, and tennis; girls' basketball, soccer, softball, swimming, and volleyball; and coed cross-country and track. The School makes use of the playing fields in Randall's Island as well as its own swimming pool and two gymnasiums.

EXTRACURRICULAR OPPORTUNITIES

In addition to the student government (described above), club periods are scheduled in the six-day cycle to encourage student involvement in extracurricular activities (students must choose at least one), such as a literary and art magazine, the yearbook, a School paper, women's issues, a debate club, Model UN, bridge, an environmental club, and Cartoon and Comic Creation. There is also an active theater department that presents three or more productions each year, including musicals and other theatrical works.

A Moving Up Day ceremony in June brings the Preparatory School together for class jingles and an award ceremony for the senior class.

DAILY LIFE

The school day begins at 8 and ends at 2:55. Classes meet on a six-day cycle, with time built in for chorus and orchestra rehearsals.

COSTS AND FINANCIAL AID

Tuition and fees for grades 9 through 11 in 2004–05 were $25,500; for grade 12 they were $25,700.

The School offers two payment plans: one with a 20 percent nonrefundable deposit upon signing the contract, plus 50 percent on August 1 and 30 percent on January 1; or a ten-month payment plan, with 20 percent deposit and a 10 percent interest charge on the remaining balance, which is divided into ten equal monthly payments commencing August 1.

In 2004–05, 27 percent of the preparatory school student body received some form of financial assistance. Awards were based strictly on need, and the average ranged from $5000 to $6000. Preference in awarding scholarships is given to students already attending the School as opposed to new applicants.

ADMISSIONS INFORMATION

The School enrolls students without discrimination on the basis of race, religion, color, or national or ethnic origin. Students are chosen for their emotional maturity, ability to work in a demanding program, talents, concern for others, and potential for growth.

The School requires the Educational Records Bureau test for admission. While the School does not have a strict cutoff point for these tests, low scores on the test may indicate that the student would have academic difficulties in the School.

APPLICATION TIMETABLE

Most students apply to the School in the fall preceding the year of entrance. Prior to an interview, students and parents are invited to special orientation meetings with the Director of the Preparatory School, teachers, and students. A tour of the School is included. Interviews are required, as are English and math teacher recommendations. Notification of acceptance for all candidates whose files are complete is on a common reply date in mid-February, and parents have until March 15 to reply.

ADMISSIONS CORRESPONDENCE

Terry Centeno, Admissions Coordinator
Columbia Grammar and Preparatory School
5 West 93rd Street
New York, New York 10025
Phone: 212-749-6200, Ext. 362
E-mail: info@cgps.org
Web site: http://www.cgps.org

COMMONWEALTH SCHOOL

Boston, Massachusetts

Type: Coeducational day college-preparatory school
Grades: 9–12
Enrollment: 155
Head of School: William Wharton, Headmaster

THE SCHOOL

The Commonwealth School was founded in 1957 by Charles Merrill, who was Headmaster until his retirement in 1981. His insistence on self-respect and independence of mind and his commitment to the cause of civil rights gave the School the focus on distinction in scholarship and on activism in public affairs for which it has been known. Today, the School continues to build its arts, diversions, academics, sports, and sense of community on imagination and enterprise.

Commonwealth occupies a pair of extensively rebuilt town houses on the corner of Commonwealth Avenue and Dartmouth Street in the Back Bay area of Boston. Its immediate neighborhood is an urban mixture of residences, art galleries, large and small businesses, restaurants, theaters, museums, and libraries. Students can serve as teachers' assistants in Boston schools, take part in political campaigns, and engage in a wide variety of special projects in businesses, hospitals, laboratories, and studios.

The School is a nonprofit organization whose 31-member Board of Trustees includes faculty, alumni/ae, parents, and nonvoting student and faculty representatives. The School's endowment is $10 million; the operating budget for 2005–06 was about $4.9 million. Annual Giving in 2004–05 was about $490,000.

The Commonwealth School is accredited by the New England Association of Independent Schools and holds memberships in the Council for the Advancement and Support of Education, the Association of Independent Schools of New England, and the National Association of Independent Schools.

ACADEMIC PROGRAMS

Commonwealth offers students exceptional training through close contact with outstanding teachers. Learning takes place in small classes in which every opinion counts. The curriculum is designed to teach the essential disciplines as well as topics of interest in various fields.

Full-credit courses meet four times a week; half-credit courses meet twice. A minimum of 16 academic credits is required for graduation, including 4 in English, 3 in mathematics, 3 in a foreign language, 3 in science, and 3 in history (including U.S. history). Ninth graders take a half-year course on the city of Boston. All ninth and twelfth graders take courses with the Headmaster; all ninth graders take health and community workshops and perform 70 hours of community service. In addition, students are required each year to take one course in the arts and to participate in two of three sports seasons.

Full-credit courses include English 9–12, ancient history, medieval world history, U.S. history, modern European history, French 1–4, Spanish 1–4, Latin 1–5, biology 1–2, chemistry 1–2, physics 1–2, fundamentals of physics,

computer programming, algebra 2, geometry, introduction to calculus, theoretical and applied calculus, and economics. Half-credit courses include introduction to creative writing, the novel, poetry, fiction writing, modernism, short story, film, literature of the Bible, constitutional law, African-American history, history of Japan, current history, Latin American history, probability and statistics, ancient philosophy, data structures and algorithms, computers, abstract algebra, linear algebra, biology 3, chemistry 3, environmental science, astronomy, French 5, Spanish 5, Latin 5, and Greek 1 and 2. Music theory, the symphony, composition, conducting, and jazz theory are offered. Arts courses include ceramics, chorus, chorale, orchestra, jazz band, acting, basic drawing, drawing and painting, life drawing, printmaking, art history, and photography.

Commonwealth does not rank its students or give prizes.

The average class size is 12. The student-teacher ratio is approximately 5:1.

FACULTY AND ADVISERS

Commonwealth has a teaching faculty of 34 teachers and administrators who also teach. Twenty-two (11 men and 11 women) are full-time and 12 are part-time. More than half of the full-time faculty members hold advanced degrees; 14 hold doctorates.

William D. Wharton was appointed Headmaster in July 2000. A graduate of Brown University, he received his B.A. in 1979 and M.A. in 1981, both in classics. After teaching Latin for five years at the Lincoln School in Providence, Rhode Island, he joined the Commonwealth faculty in 1985 as a teacher of history, Latin, and Greek. Since then, he has also taught ancient philosophy, ethics, and world religions and has served as Faculty Trustee, College Advisor, Acting Head, and Director of Admissions. In 1988, he was awarded a Grant for Independent Study in the Humanities from the Council for Basic Education and National Endowment for the Humanities and in 1992 was one of 38 recipients of Teacher-Scholar Grants from the NEH and DeWitt-Wallace Reader's Digest Fund, an award that funded a year's sabbatical study.

Commonwealth teachers spend most of their time out of class giving extra tutorials, conferring on essays, and meeting with advisees. Students choose their advisers. The School considers the sustained, sympathetic support of a faculty adviser to be essential for every student. The School makes available the services of a consulting psychologist. Students and teachers eat lunch together, office doors are open, and informality is the rule.

The School has regularly granted paid sabbatical leave to faculty members and provided funds for additional courses and degrees. Four

faculty members have won summer-study grants from the National Endowment for the Humanities.

COLLEGE PLACEMENT

A faculty member serves as College Advisor, working closely with students from the spring of their junior year on every aspect of the admissions process. All 32 graduates of the class of 2005 attend college. The institutions attended include Amherst, Barnard, Brown, Bryn Mawr, Carlton, Columbia, Cornell, George Washington, Hampshire, Juilliard, Macalester, McGill, NYU, Oberlin, Pitzer, Pomona, Reed, Sarah Lawrence, Smith, Swarthmore, Tufts, Wellesley, Wesleyan, Yale, and the Universities of Chicago, Illinois, and Pennsylvania.

Median SAT scores for the class of 2005 were 720 verbal and 690 math. Six of the 36 members of the class of 2006 are National Merit Semifinalists, and 14 are National Merit Commended Students.

STUDENT BODY AND CONDUCT

Forty-seven of Commonwealth's students are freshmen, 36 are sophomores, 36 are juniors, and 36 are seniors. Thirty students are members of minority groups.

The School has no formal student government; issues are discussed in weekly class meetings and a weekly all-School meeting. A boy and a girl from the senior class serve as representatives of the student body on the School's Board of Trustees, and student opinion is sought both privately and publicly by the faculty and the Head of School in shaping School policy and in making decisions. Suggestions of students with particular interests lead on occasion to the creation of new courses.

ACADEMIC FACILITIES

Commonwealth's two Back Bay town houses are connected to form a single five-story building that houses classrooms; offices; a library; laboratories for physics, biology, and chemistry; a computer room; studios for art and ceramics; a darkroom; a kitchen; a student lounge; and a lunchroom that also serves as a small gymnasium, concert hall, and theater. Facilities for some productions, concerts, and sports are located in nearby churches, theaters, clubs, and colleges. The School's 6,000-volume library is supplemented by the resources of the Boston Public Library, which is two blocks away. Commonwealth has computer linkups with many of the greater Boston public libraries as well as wireless Internet access throughout the building.

ATHLETICS

Commonwealth believes that the hard work, high spirits, and competitive grit of sports give young people an essential sense of pride and vitality. Its

program is designed to suit a range of interests and to teach both resilience of body and resilience of mind.

Major interscholastic sports are soccer, basketball, and Ultimate Frisbee. Students taking fencing, sailing, and squash also have the opportunity to compete. Noncompetitive sports include dance, sailing, and running. All sports are open to all grades and to both boys and girls.

The School has the use of a local field for soccer and of nearby courts for basketball, dance, and squash. Arrangements are made for sailing at the Community Boating Club on the Charles River.

EXTRACURRICULAR OPPORTUNITIES
Commonwealth participates in three-week exchange programs with schools in Spain and France; financial aid for these programs is provided for students demonstrating need. Twice a year, in September and May, the entire school adjourns to a camp in Maine for a four-day weekend. In January, students participate in weeklong projects that range from hospital work to teaching to working in a senator's Washington office. Seniors engage in similar projects during March. A wide variety of public figures, artists, musicians, travelers, and experts in various fields perform or speak before the School at its weekly assembly. Students also participate in a debate team.

Student publications include a literary magazine and yearbook. For many students, extra art courses are a major item of extracurricular interest. Students participate in winter and spring concerts, fall and spring plays, a dance concert, a jazz concert, and an art show. Other traditional yearly events for the Commonwealth community include a ninth-grade outing, an open house, a new parents' evening, parent-teacher evenings for

each grade, museum day, alumni/ae reunions in Boston and other cities, and an all-School beach day.

DAILY LIFE
The school day begins at 8:30. Class periods are normally 40 minutes long, with a 15-minute midmorning recess and 45 minutes for lunch. Refreshments are offered at recess, and a full meal is served at lunchtime. On Monday, Wednesday, and Friday, classes end at 2:45 and are followed by sports. Tuesday classes end at 3:10. On Thursday, class meetings and an assembly extend the day to 4:05. Thursday afternoon ends with an all-School tea.

All students take part in the jobs program, doing chores such as dusting and dishwashing that might otherwise be done by a custodial staff. The School sees this as an opportunity for down-to-earth self-reliance.

Supervised study halls are required for first-term freshmen and for students in academic difficulty; a Saturday study hall is run for those with work outstanding.

Students commute to Commonwealth from as far away as Sherbourne, Rockport, and Providence. A number of MBTA bus and subway lines run through Copley Square, which is two blocks from the School; the Back Bay Station, serving Amtrak, commuter rail, and major bus lines, is also nearby.

COSTS AND FINANCIAL AID
In 2005–06, the tuition and lunch fee was $24,855, with additional expenses of $910 for books and special weekends and a $675 activities fee. A total of more than $760,000 in scholarship aid was awarded to 45 students; awards ranged from $2000 to $26,200. A small number of

student jobs are also available. A technology grant program is offered to new students who receive financial aid.

ADMISSIONS INFORMATION
The Commonwealth School seeks boys and girls of character and intelligence, without regard to race, color, or national or ethnic origin, who are willing to work hard for a good education. Applicants are asked to submit recommendations, transcripts, and Secondary School Admission Test (SSAT) scores. In 2005, the median total SSAT score for entering students was in the 96th percentile. For the ninth grade, 160 applications were received, of which 70 were accepted.

APPLICATION TIMETABLE
Initial contact with the School, preferably in the fall, can be made by telephone, mail, or e-mail. An interview with the applicant and his or her parents and a full-day visit by the applicant (both required) will be arranged. Applications for fall admission should be completed by January 1, although the School accepts new students later in the year if places remain. All supplemental materials are due February 1. Notifications are mailed on March 10, and replies must be received by April 10. Commonwealth holds an open house for prospective students and their parents in early November and another in April for admitted students and their parents.

ADMISSIONS CORRESPONDENCE
Helene Carter
Director of Admissions
Commonwealth School
151 Commonwealth Avenue
Boston, Massachusetts 02116
Phone: 617-266-7525
Fax: 617-266-5769
E-mail: admissions@commschool.org
Web site: http://www.commschool.org/

CONSERVE SCHOOL

Land O'Lakes, Wisconsin

Type: Coeducational, nonsectarian boarding school
Grades: 9–12
Enrollment: 140
Head of School: Mr. Stefan Anderson, Headmaster

THE SCHOOL

Conserve School is an interdisciplinary, college-preparatory boarding school for academically talented students in grades 9 through 12, emphasizing the environment, ethics, and innovation. At Conserve School, students combine traditional subject areas with the unique areas of environmental science, technology, and outdoor recreation. The program prepares all graduates to be ethical and environmentally sensitive leaders and stewards within their career choice.

Conserve School is located in the Northwoods resort community of Land O' Lakes, Wisconsin. The town is in a county with 1,300 lakes and borders on the Sylvania Wilderness of Michigan's Upper Peninsula. The campus is approximately 360 miles north of Chicago and 260 miles northeast of Minneapolis. The nearest commercial airport is a 1-hour drive away in Rhinelander, Wisconsin.

Conserve School was established in 1996 as the wish of the late James R. Lowenstine, who had been Chairman of the Board and President of Central Steel & Wire Company in Chicago. Realizing the importance of conserving the area's natural resources, Mr. Lowenstine bequeathed his wealth and 1,200 acres of pristine woodlands in northern Wisconsin to found a school that would teach young people the importance of stewardship and ethical, environmental leadership.

The nonprofit Conserve School Corporation is headquartered in Chicago, Illinois, at Central Steel & Wire Company. The top executives of Central Steel & Wire form the School's 5-member Board of Directors.

Conserve School has new school status with the Independent Schools Association of the Central States (ISACS) and is on the three-year track for accreditation. Conserve is also a member of the National Association of Independent Schools (NAIS), Midwest Boarding Schools, and the National Consortium for Specialized Secondary Schools of Mathematics, Science, and Technology.

ACADEMIC PROGRAMS

Conserve School's curriculum uses an interdisciplinary approach focusing on active learning. This holistic program blends traditional and nontraditional education with interdisciplinary, hands-on engagement and problem solving.

The graduation requirements include 4 credits of English; 3 credits each of modern language, mathematics, science, and history; 2 credits of fine arts; 2.5 credits of wellness, health, and athletics; .5 credit of introduction to research methods; and 2 elective credits in accordance with each student's individual four-year plan.

The curriculum is based on student mastery of thirty program outcomes organized around six central focus points: environment, ethics and community, innovation, critical thinking, effec-

tive communication, and creative expression. There are several courses offered at the Advanced Placement level. Parents receive student evaluations six times yearly. Normally, a student takes seven classes per semester. Underclassmen have study hours four nights a week. Those students experiencing academic difficulties are assigned to supervised study hall.

Conserve School classes average 15 students per section. The overall student-teacher ratio is 8:1.

FACULTY AND ADVISERS

Stefan Anderson was named Headmaster in February 2003. Stefan received his B.A. in physics at St. Olaf College and his M.S. in physics at the Massachusetts Institute of Technology. Prior to moving to Conserve School in the summer of 2001, he was the Dean of Studies for students in grades 9–12 at Breck School in Minneapolis, Minnesota.

Most Conserve School teachers hold advanced degrees. Conserve teachers and administrators act as surrogate parents and mentors, living in residence houses as houseparents. This model ensures that students benefit from the direct involvement of mentors in every aspect of daily life.

COLLEGE PLACEMENT

Students prepare for college during their tenure at Conserve School. During their junior year, students take a class to prepare them for choosing and applying to colleges and taking standardized tests. College visits and fairs are arranged through the counseling office, which focuses on individual attention and consistent parent involvement.

STUDENT BODY AND CONDUCT

Conserve School welcomes students of any race, color, national, or ethnic origin and has students with a broad range of socioeconomic backgrounds.

Students and staff members work together to live and learn in accordance with the values expressed in the Conserve School Code. This code was developed in consultation with Dr. Rushworth Kidder, founder of the Institute for Global Ethics. The Conserve School Code is built around five values: compassion, honesty, justice, respect, and responsibility. Together, these values serve the entire School as an ethical guidepost.

ACADEMIC FACILITIES

The Lowenstine Academic Building (LAB) is centered on an expansive student gathering space. The lake view through the large wall of windows helps the interior decor and the surrounding natural landscape merge seamlessly.

The LAB contains twenty-three teaching spaces with thirteen classrooms, four science laboratories, a spacious visual arts studio and

photographic darkroom, a performing arts center (500-seat theater, large musical ensemble room, eight private practice rooms), two electronic learning labs, a 16,000-volume library, and impressive dining facilities.

Across the campus are the Technology Center and the Green Machine. The Green Machine uses natural processes to treat campus wastewater before it is returned to the ground. Bacteria and plants remove contaminants from the water, making it safe and clean without the chemicals used in conventional water treatment. Students can witness the maintenance and monitoring of the Green Machine, learning about biology and chemistry in a fully operational laboratory.

BOARDING AND GENERAL FACILITIES

Each residence house contains four student wings and four houseparent apartments. Each student wing has ten individual rooms (with a shared bath for every two rooms). Every wing has a large, comfortable commons area, with a gas fireplace, ample study and lounge space, and a small kitchenette. There are 2 houseparents assigned for every 10 students, which promotes a homelike environment.

Students and staff members eat in the dining hall, located in the Lowenstine Academic Building overlooking Little Donahue Lake. Most meals are served buffet style with plenty of choices.

ATHLETICS

Conserve School prides itself on academic and personal development. The School believes that individual and team sports are an integral part of the wellness experience and play a significant role in the complete development of its students. Conserve School offers recreational sports, wellness classes, intramurals, and an interscholastic sports program as venues for athletic participation. Participants on interscholastic athletic teams have an opportunity to compete against other schools in the sports of baseball, basketball, cross-country running, golf, Nordic skiing, soccer, softball, track, and volleyball. Conserve is a member of Wisconsin's Northern Lakes Athletic Conference. Recreational activities include a variety of individual, team, and coed sport options, focusing on the development of healthy lifetime leisure habits. Students utilize state-of-the-art facilities and Conserve School's beautiful outdoor resources to experience seasonal recreation activities, including canoeing, kayaking, hiking, biking, cross-country skiing, snowshoeing, tobogganing, and ice skating.

The Lowenwood Recreation Center (LRC) is located on the shore of Big Donahue Lake and serves as the hub for athletic and wellness activity. The LRC facility houses the gymnasium, climbing wall, and racquetball courts. The facility also supports a dance studio, a multipurpose

exercise room, and a fitness center (with the latest in cardio and strength-conditioning equipment).

EXTRACURRICULAR OPPORTUNITIES

Leadership development is an important element of the Conserve School experience. Extracurricular activities provide a forum for this development as well as personal growth, socialization, and recreation. A multitude of activities in the areas of outdoor adventure, fine arts, service learning, student publication, academic interest, skill building, and hobbies are offered. Students play an important role in choosing which activities they will pursue.

DAILY LIFE

At Conserve School, breakfast begins at 7 a.m. Classes typically meet for 4 hours each week, Monday through Friday, with some special field classes held occasionally on Saturday. Four days a week, students sit together at lunch with their wingmates and houseparents while an all-School community meeting is held. Interscholastic athletics occur in the afternoon and on some weekends. Late afternoons and early evenings are reserved for club activities and meetings.

Individual and group study takes place each evening in the library, classrooms, conference rooms, and student residences. All students have required study hours four nights a week. Upperclassmen with an outstanding level of academic achievement may, as a privilege, be released from these regulated, supervised study hours. Students in each wing meet with their

houseparents on Wednesday evenings for discussion and activities. Curfew is 10 p.m., Sunday through Thursday, and 11 p.m., Friday and Saturday.

WEEKEND LIFE

Weekends are an opportunity for students to learn to use leisure time appropriately. The students are encouraged to become involved in the planning and organizing of group activities. On-campus activities include movies, dances, intramural sports, and club-sponsored events. The School transports students to local theaters, shopping, and places of worship. Occasionally, students travel in chaperoned groups to larger cities for cultural events. Conserve School's location, on the edge of the Upper Peninsula of Michigan, provides convenient access to downhill skiing, canoeing, and kayaking venues. Some restrictions are placed on weekend privileges, depending on a student's age, grade level, and standing.

COSTS AND FINANCIAL AID

Tuition and supply fees include room, board, all textbooks, lab supplies, use of a laptop computer, School-sponsored campus sports and activities, and health and wellness services.

Academic merit scholarships are awarded based upon a specific set of criteria, including grades, teacher recommendations, and test scores.

Need-based financial aid is available. Need is evaluated in conjunction with the School and Student Services (SSS) Division of the National Association of Independent Schools.

ADMISSIONS INFORMATION

Conserve School seeks those students whose academic and social backgrounds are harmonious with Conserve School's mission. Students are expected to embrace the values of compassion, honesty, justice, respect, and responsibility. Conserve School accepts above-average students as determined by their grades and by their scores on a nationally standardized examination. Conserve students score in the top 25 percent nationally. The admissions process includes a school visit, student and parent interviews, teacher and counselor recommendations, and a review of the student's previous academic history as well as standardized testing.

APPLICATION TIMETABLE

Inquiries are welcome at any time. Students are encouraged to apply early in the fall. The application deadline is February 1, 2006, with admissions decisions being mailed out after March 10, 2006. Applications received after February 1 are reviewed after April 10 as space permits. No applications are accepted after July 21, 2006, for the 2006–07 school year.

ADMISSIONS CORRESPONDENCE

Admissions Office
Conserve School
5400 North Black Oak Lake Road
Land O'Lakes, Wisconsin 54540

Phone: 866-547-1300 Ext. 1321 (toll-free)
Fax: 715-547-1390
E-mail: admissions@conserveschool.org
Web site: http://www.ConserveSchool.org

CONVENT OF THE SACRED HEART

Greenwich, Connecticut

Type: Girls' private, independent day college-preparatory Catholic school
Grades: P–12: Lower School, Preschool–4; Middle School, 5–8; Upper School, 9–12
Enrollment: School total: 690; Upper School: 250
Head of School: Joan Magnetti, R.S.C.J., Headmistress

THE SCHOOL

Convent of the Sacred Heart is situated on a beautiful 110-acre wooded campus in Greenwich, Connecticut. Greenwich is a suburban town located about 30 miles from New York City and 40 minutes from New Haven. An independent, college-preparatory school for girls in preschool through grade 12, Sacred Heart was first established in New York City in 1848 and moved to Greenwich in 1945. Operated by the Religious of the Sacred Heart, Convent of the Sacred Heart is one of twenty-one Sacred Heart schools in the United States and part of an international network of schools that includes more than 200 members in forty-four countries around the world.

A Sacred Heart education provides a strong academic foundation appropriate to each student's individual talents and abilities within an environment that fosters the development of her spiritual life and a strong sense of personal values. True to its international heritage, the school welcomes students and faculty members of diverse backgrounds and faiths, so that each student will grow in her understanding of different cultures and peoples. Graduates are prepared to become leaders with broad intellectual and spiritual horizons.

Convent of the Sacred Heart is a nonprofit institution governed by a 21-member Board of Trustees, which is responsible to the Society of the Sacred Heart for the implementation of the society's educational philosophy. Parents, religious, alumnae, and educators serve on the board. Sacred Heart benefits from the active involvement and strong support of its parent and alumnae organizations.

The school is accredited by the New England Association of Schools and Colleges and approved by the Connecticut State Board of Education. It is a member of the National Association of Independent Schools, the Connecticut Association of Independent Schools, the National Coalition of Girls' Schools, and the Network of Sacred Heart Schools in the United States.

ACADEMIC PROGRAMS

Sacred Heart is committed to the development of each student's intellectual, physical, spiritual, and emotional well-being. The academic program in the Upper School provides a rigorous educational foundation that enables students to become independent and creative thinkers. Students are active participants in the learning process, expanding their experience through exploration, inquiry, and discovery. Students analyze, critique, evaluate, and make important connections with the concepts they learn.

Sacred Heart's academic program is comprehensive, rigorous, and flexible. Serious study is emphasized, and the development of essential academic skills necessary for success in college and life is encouraged. College-preparatory, honors, and advanced-placement courses are offered throughout the core curriculum, which includes mathematics, science, English, history and social sciences, foreign languages, theology, and the arts. A student is afforded opportunities for exploration of her own talents and interests through special projects, study abroad, summer programs, and independent study. Emphasizing the connection between the disciplines is critical to learning at Sacred Heart. Faculty collaboration helps students in discovering and understanding the relevance of all subject areas and the importance of their learning in relationship to society and their daily lives.

A student's schedule for the three-term academic year is planned individually. The student plans her course of study with the support of her academic adviser, the Academic Dean, and the Head of the Upper School. Course levels are chosen according to academic readiness, ability, and talent in an academic area. Each student takes between 6 and 8 credits per school year in a combination of required courses and electives.

Graduation requirements are based on the expectations of highly selective colleges and universities; all of Sacred Heart's graduates choose to attend college. To receive a diploma, students must complete 25 credits, including 4 credits of English, 4 credits in theology, 3 credits in history, 3 credits in mathematics, 3 credits in a foreign language, 3 credits in science, and 2 credits in art. Students must also complete two years of physical education and a two-year health education requirement.

All academic disciplines employ the computer as a tool for writing, research, analysis, and presentation, including the use of multimedia presentations, databases for organization and analysis, and desktop publishing and electronic slide shows. The program also addresses the possibilities and responsibilities associated with the use of technology in today's society. All students in grades 7–12 use laptop computers in the classroom and anywhere else that they study or work. Other students use desktop computers in Lower and Middle School computer laboratories and in classrooms.

FACULTY AND ADVISERS

High expectations and positive role models are important to the success of girls and young women. A student-faculty ratio of 7:1 and an average class size of approximately 15 students ensure the teachers know every student. Assured of the faculty's support, students are motivated to take risks through which confidence and self-discipline develop. Individual teaching styles are complemented by a common commitment to the goals and criteria of a Sacred Heart education.

Convent of the Sacred Heart has 109 faculty members, with 38 full-time and 9 part-time members teaching in the Upper School. Each serves as a personal and academic counselor to about 8 advisees, and many serve as club advisers and coaches as well. Students meet with their advisers regularly during a special advisory period. They also meet informally with faculty members at daily assemblies and weekly chapel services.

Teachers regularly participate in workshops, summer study, curriculum development, travel, and research. Approximately 80 percent of the faculty members hold advanced degrees.

COLLEGE PLACEMENT

The college counseling program at Sacred Heart begins informally when a student enters the Upper School. During the freshman and sophomore years, the faculty adviser guides course selection decisions, reviews PSAT scores, and helps the advisees to prepare for and plan appropriate schedules for the SAT I and SAT II tests.

Early in the junior year, students and parents meet with the Director of College Guidance to identify goals and discuss expectations about college plans. The college search process is further explained at an evening winter program, which features college representatives, the college counselor, and students as guest speakers. Juniors also attend guidance classes that explore a variety of issues surrounding the college selection process, including identifying prospective colleges, the campus visit and interview, and factors to consider in choosing a college. Students have access to a variety of college search resources, including guide books, the Internet, and software programs. Students are also encouraged to take advantage of opportunities to meet with college representatives at Sacred Heart through fall visits and an annual College Fair in late spring.

During the senior year, each student and her parents examine the more specific details of the application process: deadlines, the submission of standardized test scores, the college essay, resumes, and financial aid. In the school's 150-year history, Sacred Heart graduates have attended many of the nation's finest colleges and universities. Recent graduates are currently attending schools such as Amherst, Boston College, Brown, Columbia, Davidson, Georgetown, Harvard, Johns Hopkins, Northwestern, Notre Dame, NYU, Rice, Vanderbilt, and Yale.

STUDENT BODY AND CONDUCT

There are approximately 690 students enrolled in preschool through grade 12, with 250 students enrolled in the Upper School. Students join the high school from more than sixty-seven different communities, coming from public, private, and parochial schools in Connecticut and New York State. The student body includes a diversity of ethnic, socioeconomic, and religious backgrounds that allows for a dynamic community with a wide range of interests, talents, and passions.

School policies and practices foster the acceptance of responsibility, self-discipline, respect for the self and others, and caring for the school and wider community. The student government, student/faculty disciplinary board, and the administration work together to establish and enforce policies and minimal rules that govern the school community.

ACADEMIC FACILITIES

Overlooking Long Island Sound, the campus consists of modern classrooms, science laboratories, an observatory, playgrounds, playing fields, a media center, an auditorium, a swimming pool, a gymnasium, and a dance studio. The media center holds a collection of 22,000 books, CD-ROM resources,

online databases and encyclopedias, videos, and Internet access. A 29,000-square-foot science center has state-of-the-art laboratories for all three divisions, art studios, special space for drama and music, classrooms, and offices. Students in the astronomy class use a computerized, 16-inch telescope with 800x magnification in a state-of-the-art observatory, as well as ten 8-inch telescopes located on an outdoor pad. Students studying art, environmental science, and ecology make frequent use of the school's acres of woods, trails, and fields. The campus is further enlivened by traditions and events unique to Convent of the Sacred Heart.

ATHLETICS
The energy of the Sacred Heart community extends beyond the walls of the school buildings. The indoor competition swimming pool, tennis courts, and the playing fields outside are showcases for girls accepting challenges, testing limits, and cooperating with teammates. Sacred Heart provides a full schedule of varsity and junior varsity sports, including basketball, crew, cross-country, field hockey, golf, lacrosse, soccer, softball, squash, swimming and diving, and tennis. The teams are supported with the very best facilities and equipment. Convent of the Sacred Heart is a member of the twenty-seven-school Fairchester League and the Western New England Prep School Athletic Association (WNEPSAA). The school provides a full-time athletic trainer who oversees both the Middle and Upper School student athletes.

The physical education program is designed to develop skills for a healthy and active life. Opportunities are provided for competition, excellence, and fun in a variety of activities for all students.

EXTRACURRICULAR OPPORTUNITIES
A wide range of clubs, committees, and activities provide opportunities for students to contribute to the school community, pursue their interests, and develop leadership and team skills. Students produce major theatrical productions, govern the student body through extensive collaboration with student-elected representatives, and publish their own language newspapers, school newspaper, and literary magazine. Sacred Heart students participate in local, regional, and national competitions with their peers from other schools. These programs are designed to promote self-expression, intellectual challenge, and individual leadership opportunities.

Music, dance, dramatic readings, and gallery art shows are an important part of the Upper School experience. Diverse curricular offerings in visual arts, theater, music, and dance provide opportunities for interdisciplinary study, and core academic classes often collaborate on thematic projects with the arts departments.

Recognizing that one's own creative development emerges from exposure to the creativity of others, Sacred Heart emphasizes a balance between performance and appreciation. Guest artists, performers, and lecturers regularly visit the school. Proximity to New York City creates opportunities to investigate unlimited cultural resources, while student exhibitions and performances showcase the talents cultivated in the school's classes and studios.

The Community Service Program is also an integral part of the Upper School experience at Sacred Heart. Students study issues of poverty and racism, and, in age-appropriate ways, analyze the problems of injustice and learn how, within their world, they can be agents for change. The Community Service Program explores domestic and global issues and includes guest speakers, individual yearly projects, service trips, and retreats. While service is required for Upper School students, most exceed the required 100 hours with extra volunteer work.

The Sacred Heart Exchange Program allows students to experience different cultures in the United States and around the world. Upper School students may complete an academic exchange of two to ten weeks at another Sacred Heart school. Convent of the Sacred Heart also welcomes exchange students to its campus. Recently, Sacred Heart students have studied in California, Chicago, Houston, Miami, New Orleans, and Seattle and abroad in England, Spain, Australia, Chile, Mexico, and Nova Scotia. Upon graduating, students are given an international Sacred Heart Passport listing the Sacred Heart schools throughout the world where they are always welcome.

DAILY LIFE
The first academic period begins at 8:25 a.m. The school day includes an advisory period, assembly periods, and time for many activities and club meetings. The day concludes at 3:25. Sports and a variety of activities occur after school. Students may buy or bring their lunch. A hot lunch is provided for a yearly fee.

SUMMER PROGRAMS
Sacred Heart hosts an annual Summer Academy program for 220 boys and girls in grades 2 through 9 from low-income families. The academic program is augmented with extracurricular activities, including team sports, swimming lessons, and hands-on experience with farm animals. The Summer Science Academy is for girls who show interest and promise in science and math entering grades 6 through 9 from low-income families. The five-week program includes traditional classroom ex-

periences as well as guided scientific activities, independent investigations, and field trips.

The Summer Humanities Academy, which began in 2002, accepts girls entering grades 7 and 8 and offers a curriculum focused on writing, literature, and art. Students refined their writing skills, enhanced their reading and analytical skills, and had hands-on experiences that allowed them to understand the distinction between and the union of art and craft. Students used computers to create a literary magazine. Artists-in-residence offered workshops in writing, dance, and music. In addition, students received swimming instruction and participated in the farm program.

COSTS AND FINANCIAL AID
An education at Sacred Heart is an investment that provides many important and valuable opportunities. Tuition for 2005–06 is $24,900 for grades 9–12. The Financial Aid Committee is committed to helping families find ways to make an education at Convent of the Sacred Heart affordable. The Financial Aid Committee works with families to determine personalized need-based assistance and financial planning. Applying for financial aid has no bearing on admission to Convent of the Sacred Heart.

ADMISSIONS INFORMATION
Sacred Heart admits students without regard to race, religion, nationality, or ethnic origin. Applicants are considered on the basis of their school records, teacher recommendations, admission test scores, class visit, and personal interview. Entrance exams are administered at the school in November and at other local independent schools throughout the fall.

Families are encouraged to attend the Saturday Open House event (in November) or Thursday morning Tour Day programs (October, November, December, and January). Every October, Sacred Heart also hosts an evening Upper School Open House for students interested in grades 9–12. Individual tours and interviews are also available.

APPLICATION TIMETABLE
All application materials and visits must be completed by February 1. Decision letters are mailed by March 1. Applications for financial aid with supporting documentation are due by February 15.

ADMISSIONS CORRESPONDENCE
Pamela McKenna, Director of Admission
Convent of the Sacred Heart
1177 King Street
Greenwich, Connecticut 06831

Phone: 203-532-3534
Fax: 203-532-3301
E-mail: admission@cshgreenwich.org
Web site: http://www.cshgreenwich.org

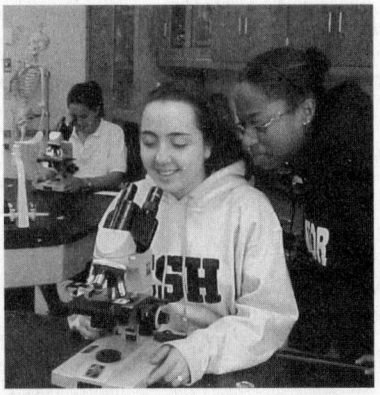

CRANBROOK SCHOOLS

Bloomfield Hills, Michigan

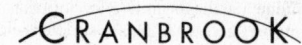

Type: Coeducational day and boarding college-preparatory school
Grades: PK–12: Brookside Lower School, Prekindergarten–5; Cranbrook Kingswood Middle School, 6–8; Cranbrook Kingswood Upper School, 9–12
Enrollment: School total: 1,620; Upper School: 766; Middle School: 340; Lower School: 514
Head of School: Arlyce M. Seibert, Director of Schools

THE SCHOOL

First established in 1922, Cranbrook Schools seek to prepare young men and women from diverse backgrounds to develop intellectually, morally, and physically; to move into higher education with competence and confidence; and to appreciate the arts. The Schools also strive to instill in their students a strong sense of social responsibility and the ability to contribute in an increasingly complex world.

Its founders, George and Ellen Scripps Booth, believed that "a life without beauty is only half lived." Critics have called the 315-acre Cranbrook campus "a masterpiece of American architecture." The buildings, gardens, and fountains were designed by Finnish architect, Eliel Saarinen, and offer students an exquisite environment in which to live and learn.

The Schools are a division of Cranbrook Educational Community, which also includes Cranbrook Institute of Science (a natural history and science museum serving Michigan and the Great Lakes region) and Cranbrook Academy of Art, known worldwide for its prestigious graduate programs in fine arts and architecture as well as its Art Museum. The entire complex has been designated a National Historic Landmark.

Cranbrook offers a comprehensive college-preparatory education that commences with Brookside (PK–5), continues in Cranbrook Kingswood Middle School (6–8, separate programs for boys and girls), and culminates in the opportunity and possibility that is provided by graduation from Cranbrook Kingswood Upper School (day and boarding, 9–12).

Bloomfield Hills is a residential suburb (population 3,985) approximately 25 minutes northwest of Detroit and 5 minutes from Birmingham and Pontiac.

A nonprofit corporation, Cranbrook is directed by a 21-member, self-perpetuating Board of Trustees, which meets four times a year. The corporation has a $150 million endowment. The plant is valued at approximately $150 million, and the operating expenses for 2004–05 were $31.7 million. The Schools received $5.6 million in gifts for fiscal year 2004, and the community gifts totaled $10.5 million.

Cranbrook Kingswood is accredited by the Independent Schools Association of the Central States. It is a member of the National Association of Independent Schools.

ACADEMIC PROGRAMS

The school year, from September to early June, is divided into semesters. Classes, which enroll an average of 16 students each, meet five days a week. Eight academic periods are scheduled daily. All boarding students participate in supervised evening study hours from Sunday through Thursday. Grades are sent to parents quarterly, written evalu-

ations are given semiannually, and progress reports for new students are issued in October.

Promotion from one class level to another is contingent upon faculty recommendations and is necessary for graduation. Each student is expected to take five academic classes each semester, along with a class chosen from the fine arts, performing arts, or computer departments. In order to graduate, students must complete the following minimum unit requirements: English, 4; mathematics, 3; foreign language, 2; social science/history, 2½; science, 2; religion and philosophy, 1; arts, 1; and computer technology, ½. (One unit is the equivalent of a full-year course.)

In addition to sixty-nine full-year courses, Cranbrook Kingswood Upper School offers seventy-eight semester courses, including surrealism, the apocalyptic other, African-American literature, anatomy, astronomy, genetics, geology, principles of psychology, human geography, eastern religious traditions, and ethics. Ninth graders have the option of fulfilling their English, history, and religion requirement in an interdisciplinary program (IDS) that asks students to discover how individual identity is projected within a social order. An extensive fine and performing arts program includes basic design, drawing, painting, sculpture, metalsmithing, ceramics, weaving, photography, dance, band, orchestra, madrigals, jazz band, mastersingers, concert choir, acting and theater, speech, and stagecraft.

Fifteen Advanced Placement (AP) courses are available in foreign languages, English, social sciences, and mathematics. Honors courses and directed-study programs are also offered for qualified students. ESL is offered for international students who demonstrate a strong academic record and a high intermediate level of English proficiency.

The Tennessee Wilderness Expedition (modeled on Outward Bound) is available to tenth graders each March. Seniors can participate in Senior May (off-campus projects) during the spring term. A fall semester exchange program with Cranbrook Kingswood's sister school, Cranbrook Kent, in Kent, England, is available to qualified juniors and seniors.

Students are graded on an A–E scale, although some elective courses are pass/fail. Students must maintain a minimum C- average to avoid academic probation. Classes are generally grouped by ability within grade level. The student-teacher ratio is 8:1.

FACULTY AND ADVISERS

Sixty-seven of the 96 full-time Cranbrook Kingswood Upper School faculty members reside on campus; 55 are men and 41 are women; 62 hold master's degrees and 12 hold doctorates.

In selecting its faculty, Cranbrook Kingswood seeks men and women with educational and intellectual curiosity. Faculty members are encour-

aged to explore special interests and talents that extend beyond their academic discipline. They are continually involved in professional advancement programs—course work, conferences, and workshops, the cost of which Cranbrook Kingswood largely underwrites. All faculty members are involved in some type of extracurricular activity, and each is an adviser to an average of 8 students, helping them in all aspects of school life from course selection to peer relationships.

Arlyce M. Seibert was appointed Vice President of Cranbrook Educational Community and the Director of Schools in 1996. Mrs. Seibert joined the Upper School in 1970 and has served in many capacities in her thirty-two years with the Schools.

COLLEGE PLACEMENT

Four full-time counselors help students select colleges, and representatives from more than 140 colleges visit Cranbrook Kingswood each year. The selection process begins in the junior year, involving both students and parents.

Among Cranbrook Kingswood's 2005 graduates, the mean SAT scores were 639 verbal and 655 quantitative. A total of 202 graduates are attending such colleges and universities as Amherst, Berkeley, Brown, Columbia, Cornell, Dartmouth, Georgetown, MIT, Mount Holyoke, Oberlin, Pratt, Princeton, Vassar, Yale, and the Universities of Chicago, Michigan, and Pennsylvania.

STUDENT BODY AND CONDUCT

The 2005–06 Upper School was composed of 154 boarding boys, 252 day boys, 104 boarding girls, and 264 day girls, distributed as follows: 174 in the ninth grade, 208 in tenth, 208 in eleventh, and 184 in twelfth. Twenty-four states and twenty countries were represented. Twenty-eight percent of students identified themselves as members of minority groups, and international students made up 11 percent of the student body.

Cranbrook Kingswood's disciplinary system is designed to be educative, not punitive. Honest conduct, regular attendance, punctual completion of assignments, and thoughtful adherence to school policies and rules are the minimum commitments expected of students. A Discipline Committee, consisting of faculty members, the deans, and elected students, assumes responsibility in matters of conduct. Major offenses may result in dismissal.

Students participate in several committees that help to shape life at Cranbrook Schools, such as the Conduct Review Board, the Dormitory Council, the Athletic Committee, the Diversity Committee, the Student Leadership Task Force, and the President's Council.

ACADEMIC FACILITIES

Students have the advantage of full access to two educational campuses. Kingswood's world-famous, Saarinen-designed building is a single con-

tinuous unit that includes a library with 23,500 volumes, a gymnasium, and six separate art studios.

Cranbrook's classrooms are located around a quadrangle in Lindquist Hall (1927) and Hoey Hall (1927). Other facilities that compose the quadrangle complex are a library with more than 21,500 volumes, a dining hall, and a student center. A recently renovated performing arts center and the Gordon Science Center are located adjacent to the quadrangle.

Students take shuttle buses from one campus to another according to their class schedules. Students also have access to the museums and other resources of Cranbrook Institute of Science and Cranbrook Academy of Art.

BOARDING AND GENERAL FACILITIES

Cranbrook Kingswood maintains single-sex boarding facilities. The campus buildings are linked by a fiber-optic network and provide telephone, computer, and video access in each dormitory room, classroom, lab, and faculty and student work area. The campus is equipped with more than ninety Smartboards.

The Kingswood dormitory for girls, adjacent to Kingswood Lake, houses 102 girls. Most live in suites that contain two single or double bedrooms with adjoining bath. The dormitory has two lounges with televisions, stereo equipment, and a piano. Two kitchenettes and laundry facilities are available, in addition to a four-lane bowling alley.

At the Cranbrook campus, there are single rooms for 163 boys, who are divided according to their grade. The student activity center has a dance floor, a snack bar, a performance space, and a small theater for videotape recording and viewing.

Many Cranbrook Kingswood faculty members live in the dormitories with their families. Others live in faculty homes clustered throughout the grounds. Resident Advisers (senior students) live on each floor and act as confidants and helpmates to their fellow boarders.

ATHLETICS

Cranbrook Kingswood Upper School provides the opportunity for participation in eighteen interscholastic sports, including baseball, basketball, cross-country, crew, fencing, field hockey, football, golf, ice hockey, lacrosse, skiing, soccer, softball, swimming, tennis, track, volleyball, and wrestling. Recent state championships include boys' and girls' tennis, girls' golf, boys' lacrosse, and boys' and girls' hockey. Among the intramural

and noncompetitive athletic activities are martial arts, modern dance, mountain biking, and volleyball.

Athletics facilities include a football stadium, a track, fifteen outdoor tennis courts, a dance studio, an indoor ice arena, three gymnasiums, and numerous playing fields. A $12-million natatorium was completed in fall 1999.

EXTRACURRICULAR OPPORTUNITIES

Cranbrook Kingswood offers thirty-nine student organizations, including Model UN, forensics, ethnic clubs, dramatics, community service, and publications, including a newspaper and an arts and literary publication. Other clubs meet to discuss topics as varied as politics and racial and sexual diversity.

The cultural and educational events on campus include the exhibitions, lectures, films, and concerts offered through the science and art museums, highlighted by regular planetarium and laser shows, a world-class collection of modern American and European paintings, and traveling exhibits. The spacious grounds, wooded areas, lakes and indoor and outdoor theaters provide a serene setting for cross-country skiing, biking, jogging, swimming, and canoeing, as well as the Cranbrook Music Festival, the American Artists Series, the Cranbrook Kingswood Film Program, the Symposium Series, and the Cranbrook Retreat for Writers and Artists.

DAILY LIFE

The school day is divided into eight 45-minute classes between 8 a.m. and 3:20 p.m., including lunch, Monday through Friday. After-school activities such as class meetings, extra-help sessions, and athletics follow. Dinner for boarders begins at 5:30 weekdays, followed by a study period from 8 to 10 p.m.

WEEKEND LIFE

Boarding students have an unusual opportunity to take part in urban and rural activities on the weekends. Although students may go home some weekends with parental permission, there are weekends during the year when all boarding students must stay on the campus for special activities. Shuttle buses drive students to nearby Birmingham for shopping and entertainment, and groups can go to Detroit, Pontiac, or Ann Arbor for professional sporting events and cultural activities. There are frequent weekend camping, hiking, rock climbing, and skiing trips during the year. On-

campus activities include dances, concerts, exhibits, lectures, sporting events, and recent movies at the student center.

SUMMER PROGRAMS

The Cranbrook Educational Community conducts several summer programs for day and boarding students and the community at large. These include day camps, a theater school, a soccer clinic, a filmmaking seminar, a compensatory educational program for youngsters from low-income families, a jazz ensemble, and ice hockey, lacrosse, and tennis camps.

COSTS AND FINANCIAL AID

The 2005–06 fees were $30,380 for boarding students and $21,730 for day students. Other expenses were for books ($400), insurance ($38), and a room deposit fee ($75). A tuition-payment plan and tuition insurance are offered.

In 2005–06, 28–30 percent of the Upper School students received some amount of tuition aid, some as much as 50 percent of day or boarding tuition. Incoming students may apply for one of several full tuition merit scholarships. Aid is based on financial need, following procedures established by the School and Student Service for Financial Aid; continuation is dependent on financial need, academic performance, and positive involvement in the school community.

ADMISSIONS INFORMATION

Cranbrook admits day students in preschool through grade 12 and boarding students in grades 9 through 12. The Schools accept students without regard to race, religion, national origin, sex, or handicap. Admission is based on recommendations, past performance, a personal interview, a writing sample, and results of the SSAT or other standardized examinations. Recommended grades for entrance are A's and B's.

APPLICATION TIMETABLE

An initial inquiry is welcome at any time. Campus tours and interviews are arranged on weekdays through the admissions office. Notification of acceptance begins in February. The application fee is $25.

ADMISSIONS CORRESPONDENCE

Drew Miller
Dean of Admission and Financial Aid
Cranbrook Schools
39221 Woodward Avenue
P.O. Box 801
Bloomfield Hills, Michigan 48303-0801

Phone: 248-645-3610
Fax: 248-645-3025
E-mail: admission@cranbrook.edu
Web site: http://www.schools.cranbrook.edu

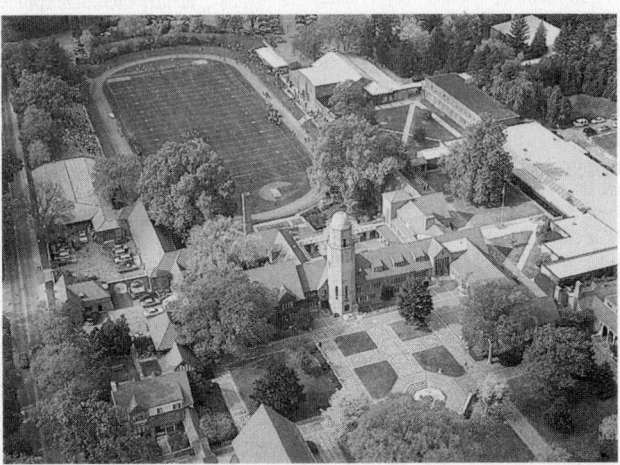

CULVER ACADEMIES

Culver, Indiana

Type: Coeducational boarding and day school
Grades: 9–12, postgraduate year
Enrollment: 767
Head of Schools: John N. Buxton

THE SCHOOLS

The Culver Academies offer a college-preparatory curriculum within a boarding school environment for boys and girls in grades 9 through 12, with select opportunities available for postgraduate study. The Academies—Culver Military Academy, founded in 1894, and Culver Girls Academy, founded in 1971—provide a coeducational academic setting, with well-developed identities, traditions, and leadership systems. In accordance with its mission statement, Culver "educates its students for leadership and responsible citizenship in society by developing and nurturing the whole individual—mind, spirit, and body—through an integrated curriculum that emphasizes the cultivation of character."

Character development is essential to the Culver mission. For more than a century, the foundation of the Culver model has been an education in the classical virtues of wisdom, courage, moderation, and justice. Given that habits of mind, spirit, and body develop over time, an education in the virtues requires understanding, self-discipline, and practice. All aspects of Culver's academic, residential, extracurricular, and athletic curricula are designed to provide students with opportunities for individual growth within a structured environment and provide opportunities for them to begin the difficult task of developing lifelong habits.

Culver Academies is located in Culver, Indiana, 2 hours east of Chicago and 2 hours north of Indianapolis. The campus is located on the north shore of Lake Maxinkuckee, and students have the opportunity to enjoy all the benefits of its location. The school community also enjoys use of the thirty-nine buildings, including the Huffington Library, one of the ten largest secondary school libraries in the country; Roberts Hall of Science; Dicke Hall of Mathematics; and Eppley Auditorium.

A 36-member Board of Trustees is the governing body of Culver. The Culver Academies endowment is valued at approximately $135 million, supplemented in 2003–04 by annual giving of more than $4.7 million.

Culver is accredited by the North Central Association of Colleges and Schools and the Independent Schools Association of the Central States and also holds a commission from the Indiana State Department of Education. Memberships include the National Association of Independent Schools, the College Board, the Secondary School Admissions Test Board, and School and Student Service for Financial Aid. Culver is a member of the National Association of College Admission Counseling.

ACADEMIC PROGRAMS

Culver is committed to intellectual growth through participation in a demanding curriculum that prepares students for success in higher education. Culver's curriculum emphasizes critical thinking, problem solving, writing, research, artistic expression, and foreign language proficiency through innovative teaching methods and technologically rich classrooms.

The curriculum incorporates a healthy combination of project-based learning and more traditional styles of education. Culver's technology initiative—issuing students laptops and establishing a wireless campus—has expanded opportunities for newer and more creative means of teaching.

The average class size is 15 students, and Culver enjoys a 9:1 student-faculty ratio. Accelerated academic sections are offered in most subjects, including Advanced Placement credit in nineteen different courses. Nineteen academic units of credit are required for a Culver diploma. The following are the minimum academic unit requirements for graduation: English, 4; mathematics, 3; history and foreign language, 5 combined (1 in U.S. history and 1 in government); science, 3; fine arts, 1; wellness, ½; leadership, ½; and electives, 2.

In addition, Culver offers comprehensive instruction in beginning, intermediate, and advanced equitation; horse training; and stable management.

The school year at Culver consists of four 8-week terms, each divided into two semesters. The grading system uses an A to F designation. Grades are sent to parents twice each term.

FACULTY AND ADVISERS

Like the student body, Culver faculty members come from a wide range of backgrounds. The faculty is composed of 87 full-time members, 6 part-time members, and 8 interns. All hold baccalaureate degrees, 79 hold master's degrees, and 8 hold Ph.D.'s. In addition to teaching, faculty members supervise dorms, coach, sponsor clubs, and act as mentors. Students benefit immensely from their close contacts with Culver's outstanding educators, coaches, and mentors.

Culver seeks to hire outstanding faculty members and allows them to continue their education in their fields and to take sabbatical leaves. In addition to the regular faculty, Culver supports one of the best-established and most extensive intern programs in private education. Each year, up to a dozen highly qualified recent college graduates join the faculty for one or two years of teaching, coaching, dorm supervision, and administrative responsibilities.

John N. Buxton has served as the head of schools since 1999. Prior to coming to Culver, Buxton was the vice-rector for administration and a member of the English faculty at St. Paul's School in Concord, New Hampshire. He is a graduate of Brown University and currently a Ph.D. candidate at Boston University.

COLLEGE PLACEMENT

Led by the Director of College Advising, Corky Miller-Strong, a full-time staff assists students in the college selection process. Nearly 100 college representatives visit Culver each year. Beginning in the junior year, weekly classes are held in college and career guidance.

Ninety-eight percent of the seniors from the class of 2005 were accepted by at least one college or university on their first- or second-choice list. The list of institutions admitting Culver students includes Boston University, Dartmouth, DePaul, Duke, Harvard, Howard, Johns Hopkins, MIT, Princeton, Purdue, SMU, Stanford, Washington (St. Louis), Yale, and the Universities of Chicago, Michigan, North Carolina at Chapel Hill, Notre Dame, and Pennsylvania.

STUDENT BODY AND CONDUCT

The 2005–06 student body represented thirty-six states and twenty countries. Enrollment was as follows: 153 freshmen, 200 sophomores, 233 juniors, 179 seniors, and 2 postgraduates. There were 433 boys and 334 girls—698 boarding and 69 day students.

Students not only learn about leadership in the classroom, they also experience it. It is this experience that helps students grow intellectually, socially, and morally. The boys' leadership program is organized around its own distinctive military system. The girls' program is designed around the traditional prefect system. Through the enactment of leadership ideals that is made possible in and through these systems, students develop confidence in their abilities to complete difficult tasks as well as habits of inquiry and self-discipline.

Each student is expected to make a positive effort to perform well academically, to develop respect for self and others, to maintain an orderly personal appearance, to meet personal responsibilities punctually and thoroughly, and to live and support the Culver Honor Code, which states, "I will not lie, cheat, or steal; and I will discourage others from such actions." Student leaders have an active role in guiding and monitoring the conduct of their fellow students.

BOARDING AND GENERAL FACILITIES

The boys' and girls' dormitories typically house 2 students per room. A number of faculty members, including the faculty interns, reside in the dormitories, and all share in supervision.

Culver students, as well as faculty and staff members and their families, eat in the Lay Dining Center. Students may visit the snack bar (the Shack) or the bookstore in the Lay Student Center. Within the Student Center, there are quiet rooms for study, lounges, and a television area for socializing and relaxation. Beason Hall (for seniors only) is the site of many social

occasions. The Health Center, which is staffed 24 hours a day, has fifty beds and is used by students and faculty members.

ATHLETICS

Culver's wellness-education programs are an integral part of the curriculum. Participation affords a significant opportunity for the development of the virtues associated with personal integrity. Culver's athletic, health, and residential curricula emphasize sound decision making through programs that include fitness, nutrition, and respect for the body. There are fifty-eight competitive sports teams supported on campus. Between 65 and 70 percent of the student body are members of one or more of these teams.

The McMillen Athletic Center contains two gymnasiums, an eight-lane pool and separate diving tank, and the athletic hall of fame. The Steinbrenner Recreation Center houses a state-of-the-art fitness center, three basketball courts, two indoor tracks, an indoor tennis court, a wrestling room, a fencing room, and squash and racquetball courts.

The Vaughn Equestrian Center is one of the largest riding halls in the nation, with stables for more than 120 horses. Culver competes in polo and hunter/jumper horse shows. The Black Horse Troop, the largest mounted cavalry unit in the United States, has appeared in fourteen presidential inaugural parades, and the girls' unit, the Equestriennes, in five.

EXTRACURRICULAR OPPORTUNITIES

Students have the opportunity to join any of the forty-five clubs, six music performance groups, and four vocal performance groups during their time at Culver. The extracurricular clubs include those that are academic, social, religious, and community-service oriented.

Each year, the Culver Concert Series brings musical, drama, and dance groups from all over the world to the campus to perform. Similarly, the Montgomery Lecture Series hosts nationally recognized speakers for both formal presentations and individual classroom discussions.

DAILY LIFE

The typical daily schedule consists of four 90-minute classes, beginning at 7:50 a.m. Athletic practices are conducted from 3:45 to 5:45 p.m., followed by dinner and an activity period for club and group meetings. Evening study is adult supervised and takes place from 7:30 to 9:30. With permission and leadership privileges, students are able to study in groups and in the library during the evening study time.

WEEKEND LIFE

Students make great use of the Culver campus and its recreational facilities. Dances, picnics, and Culver-sponsored trips are regular features of campus life. Students who have permission can spend time in town on the weekends and take periodic weekend leave to go home or to a friend's home. Weekend leave is in addition to the typical holiday and vacation schedule.

Each school year, there are two Parents Weekends, one in the fall and one in the spring. During each weekend, parents are encouraged to come to the campus to spend a day with their son or daughter, attend classes, and meet teachers. Parents are also invited to attend sporting events and lectures on the college planning process and meet with the residential supervisors throughout the weekend.

COSTS AND FINANCIAL AID

The tuition for 2005–06 was $28,900. These fees included the lease of a wireless laptop computer, academic instruction, room and board, special tutorial instruction, and most medical and other services. Textbooks cost approximately $500 per year. New student uniforms require a deposit of $850 for girls and $1500 for boys. Incidental expenses can range up to about $100 a month, depending on the student. There are additional expense requirements for horsemanship, aviation, private music lessons, and driver's training. Each payment of tuition and fees is due prior to the first day of that term. A $1000 tuition deposit is due upon acceptance.

Students are awarded grants on the basis of overall scholastic credentials and financial need, as determined by the Parent's Service for Financial Aid. In 2005–06, financial aid was awarded to 51 percent of the student body and totaled more than $6.8 million.

The Batten Scholarship, endowed by Frank Batten '45, awards 6 incoming freshmen or sophomores a renewable full tuition merit scholarship for their four-year Culver career. During the past admission cycle, more than 200 applicants competed for the six scholarships. The application process includes admission to Culver and an additional Batten application.

ADMISSIONS INFORMATION

The Admissions Committee selects students who are capable of pursuing a rigorous college-preparatory program and becoming effective and responsible citizens and leaders. Culver intends that its graduates be young men and women who are capable of clear and independent judgment and are sensitive to the rights and needs of others.

Applicants for admission must submit the results of the Secondary School Admission Test (SSAT) or other approved tests as well as four teacher evaluations and current transcripts from the previous two years. Applicants are also encouraged to visit the campus for a tour and observation of classes, to complete the personal interview, and to meet with members of the Academies' community.

APPLICATION TIMETABLE

An initial inquiry is welcome at any time. Campus tours are arranged in conjunction with interviews, from 9 a.m. to 4:30 p.m. on weekdays and on Saturday by appointment arranged at least 48 hours prior to the visit.

Applications must be accompanied by a $30 nonrefundable fee.

ADMISSIONS CORRESPONDENCE

Office of Admissions
Culver Academies
1300 Academy Road #157
Culver, Indiana 46511-1291

Phone: 800-5-CULVER (toll-free)
Fax: 574-842-8066
E-mail: admissions@culver.org
Web site: http://www.culver.org

CUSHING ACADEMY

Ashburnham, Massachusetts

Type: Coeducational boarding and day college-preparatory school
Grades: 9–12, postgraduate year
Enrollment: 410
Head of School: M. Willard Lampe II, Headmaster

THE SCHOOL

Cushing Academy, chartered in 1865, opened as a coeducational boarding school with funds provided by Thomas Parkman Cushing. Founded during a period of social change, the Academy has always sought to adapt to the needs of the students it serves. While the Academy's goals include a thorough college preparation, Cushing also seeks to create a family atmosphere and a supportive learning environment in which students can grow. As a residential school, the Academy endeavors to offer love, guidance, support, and rewards that foster sound values and positive behavior.

Cushing's 150-acre campus lies in the small, rural town of Ashburnham in north-central Massachusetts, 55 miles west of Boston and 10 miles south of the New Hampshire border. Proximity to Boston permits extensive use of the city's cultural, entertainment, and commercial resources.

The Academy is governed by a 27-member Board of Trustees, 10 of whom are alumni. The operating budget for 2003–04 was $17.5 million, and the endowment is estimated at $15.5 million. Total giving for 2003–04 realized almost $3 million in gifts of cash and kind.

Cushing is accredited by the New England Association of Schools and Colleges. The Academy is a member of the National Association of Independent Schools, the Association of Independent Schools in New England, the Secondary School Admission Test Board, and the Cum Laude Society.

ACADEMIC PROGRAMS

Each student at Cushing Academy carries four or five major courses every trimester and is required to complete a minimum of 4 course credits per year. To satisfy Cushing's diploma requirements, students must earn a total of 18 credits distributed as follows: English, 4; mathematics, 4; foreign language, 2; history and social science, 2; science, 2; fine arts, ⅓ per year at Cushing; and computer science, ⅓, or demonstrated proficiency. The remaining requirements may be filled by choosing from numerous electives, including Shakespeare, creative writing, ecology, marine biology, economics, and public speaking.

The Academy offers more than 150 full-year courses and seminars, including ten laboratory courses and fourteen Advanced Placement courses. Advanced independent study programs may be arranged through the Director of Academic Affairs.

The Cushing Network, a campuswide computer network, may be accessed from more than 500 locations throughout the school, including all classrooms and dormitory rooms. CushNet, a local area network, allows students to send e-mail, join bulletin-board discussions for many classes, communicate with teachers and friends, and submit assignments. Students have access to the Internet from 7:30 a.m. to 8 p.m. each day. A comprehensive policy guides student use.

All teachers are available daily in their classrooms during the half-hour extra help period. Informal tutoring may also take place after dinner or during free time. The Fisher-Watkins Library is open from 8 a.m. to 10 p.m. daily.

The Academy's faculty includes six learning specialists who administer developmental reading programs to roughly 18 percent of the student body. English as a Second Language is offered at various levels to 20 percent of the student body.

The academic year is divided into three terms of twelve, ten, and nine weeks in length. Most courses require final examinations. Academic evaluations are sent home seven times each term. Letters warning of academic difficulty are written at the discretion of the Academic Dean.

Cushing uses a numerical grading system (0–100); 60 is passing, 85 is honors, and 90 is high honors. Class placement is determined by the student's demonstrated ability and past performance in each subject area. The average class size is 12 students. The student-teacher ratio is approximately 7:1. On weeknights from 8 to 10, students work quietly in their rooms during a supervised study hall.

FACULTY AND ADVISERS

In 2004–05, the faculty and administration consists of 82 full-time teachers and administrators—35 women and 47 men. Forty-three faculty members have master's degrees, and 3 have earned their Ph.D.'s. In selecting new teachers, the Academy seeks men and women who believe that human growth has many facets and who possess the background, skills, human qualities, and diversity of experience needed to promote such multifaceted growth. Many faculty members reside in the dormitories. Each teacher has 5 to 7 student advisees, who generally live in the dormitory where the faculty adviser resides or has duty.

The Headmaster, M. Willard Lampe II, came to Cushing in 2000. He received an M.A. from the University of Vermont in Burlington after earning his B.A. at Muskingum College.

COLLEGE PLACEMENT

Students meet several times with the Director of College Counseling and her staff during the winter and spring of their junior year to establish a preliminary list of appropriate colleges. The following fall, a new round of interviews and meetings begin, and students are guided with great care through the college application process.

The PSAT is administered in October of the junior year. The SAT I is administered to students at Cushing in January and May of the junior year and in November of the senior year. SAT II Subject Tests are administered in June of the junior year and again in December of the senior year. The ACT is administered in April of the junior year and December (optional) of the senior year.

Nearly every member of the class of 2004 went directly to college. Among the many colleges and universities selected were American University, Bentley, Boston University, Brandeis, Brown, Carnegie Mellon, Emory, George Washington, Harvard, Northeastern, Rensselaer, Savannah College of Art, Springfield, Suffolk, Syracuse, Wheaton, and the Universities of Arizona, Colorado at Boulder, New Hampshire, Rhode Island, and Vermont.

STUDENT BODY AND CONDUCT

The 2004–05 student body was constituted as follows: freshmen: 35 boys, 27 girls; sophomores: 58 boys, 43 girls; juniors: 75 boys, 54 girls; seniors: 49 boys, 50 girls; postgraduates: 15 boys, 4 girls. Of these 410 students, 369 are boarders. Students are predominantly from Massachusetts (166), other parts of New England (50), California (21), and New York (20). Twenty-seven states and Puerto Rico, as well as twenty-two other countries, are represented. Of the total enrollment, 9 percent are African American.

Responsible behavior, respect for persons, and personal integrity are valued at Cushing. When students disregard Academy rules or the rights of others, a faculty-student Disciplinary Committee convenes to weigh evidence and submit a recommendation to the Headmaster.

The student senate is a student-based governing board. The senate's most important function is to lobby for student interests by drafting persuasive proposals for faculty consideration and approval.

ACADEMIC FACILITIES

The center of school life is the Main Building, which contains offices, a reception room, and six classrooms on the first floor; administrative offices, the Cowell Memorial Chapel, the computer center, and seven classrooms on the second floor; and three classrooms on the third floor. Located directly in front of the Main Building is the Fisher-Watkins Library, which is well equipped for research and informal reading. The Harrington Computing Center is located in the library. A new academic building, which houses mathematics, the sciences, and the performing arts, opened in January 2005. The new state-of-the-art facility has more than 56,000 square feet and features student project rooms, seminar space, wireless technology, and smart boards in every classroom. The English building houses seven newly renovated classrooms. The Emily Fisher Landau Center for the Visual Arts was completed in February 1998.

BOARDING AND GENERAL FACILITIES

The Academy has seven dormitories and six student-faculty houses (housing more than 350 students) that vary in capacity from 3 to 81 students each. Almost all rooms are doubles, and returning students select rooms through a room-draw system that favors seniority. New students are assigned rooms by the Director of Admission and the Student Life Office. The ratio of faculty to students in the dormitories is generally 1:12. All dormitories have recreational areas.

Cushing's dining facility, completed in 1987, has a student center on the lower level, which includes a recreational area, snack bar, bookstore, and post office. Formal family-style dinners are served once a month.

ATHLETICS

In the belief that physical fitness and agility enrich both the individual and the community, Cushing's athletics program is designed to involve everyone in physical endeavors. There are boys' interscho-

lastic teams in football, soccer, cross-country, basketball, skiing, ice hockey, tennis, lacrosse, baseball, track, and golf; girls compete in soccer, field hockey, ice hockey, cross-country, volleyball, basketball, skiing, softball, lacrosse, track, and tennis. Organized recreational sports include aerobics, tennis, skiing, dance, weight lifting, figure skating, riding, and volleyball.

The Heslin Gymnasium contains four locker rooms, the John Biggs Jr. Memorial Fitness Center, a training room, and a basketball court. There are also six playing fields, six tennis courts, and two local golf courses. The Theodore Iorio Ice Arena offers, in addition to year-round ice skating, boys and girls locker rooms, a dance studio, a multipurpose function room, and a pro shop.

EXTRACURRICULAR OPPORTUNITIES

Cushing offers two endowed special events series that bring a wide variety of speakers and performers to the Academy. Boston's cultural resources—ballet, opera, theater, symphony, and museums—are also tapped.

Students who enjoy active participation can choose among dozens of organized activities, including the drama society, chorus, madrigal singers, jazz ensemble, yearbook, newspaper, and a host of clubs. Major social events include Fall Parents' Day, Mountain Day, Winter Carnival, and Spring Prom.

DAILY LIFE

The Monday-through-Friday schedule, which begins with classes at 8 a.m., provides time for an extra-help period, activities, and athletics before evening study hall at 8 p.m. Lights-out is at 10:30 for underclassmen and 11 for seniors and postgraduates. Classes are 40 minutes long, and there are eight class periods each day. Courses, activities, and athletics are all centrally scheduled to avoid unnecessary conflicts. Saturday morning classes are held from 8 to noon every other week. On weekdays, the hours from 3 to 5 p.m. are reserved for athletics (interscholastic contests are played on Wednesday and Saturday).

WEEKEND LIFE

A typical weekend at the Academy is filled with opportunities for cultural enrichment, entertainment, shopping, or exercise. Chartered buses bring Boston within range most weekends, but students also frequent local shopping malls, cinemas, and, during the winter, ski areas.

Movies are shown on campus each weekend, while dances and concerts are often scheduled in the evening. Saturday night Open Houses permit boys and girls to mix in dormitory rooms with doors open and with faculty chaperones on duty. Students are permitted to spend a limited number of weekends off campus, but on any given weekend 70–75 percent of the boarding population choose to remain on campus. The first two and the last weekends of each term are restricted.

SUMMER PROGRAMS

During the six-week summer session, Cushing offers a unique boarding school experience for girls and boys ages 12–18 from throughout the United States and around the world. The program features Prep for Success for middle school students, regular and advanced college preparatory courses for high school students, and extensive English as a second language instruction; each combined with interesting artistic and athletic electives as well as exciting excursions throughout New England. For further information, students should contact Dan Frank, Director of Summer Session.

COSTS AND FINANCIAL AID

Tuition and required fees for 2005–06 are $36,135 for boarding students and $25,240 for day students. There are optional fees for skiing, music lessons, driver's education, and fine arts materials. A $3614 nonrefundable enrollment deposit is credited toward the balance due; installments are payable on or about July 15, September 15, and December 15.

In 2005–06, 78 students received $1.6 million in financial aid. Scholarships are awarded on the basis of need as demonstrated by established criteria of the School and Student Service for Financial Aid. Once need has been established, character, academic performance, and overall ability are ma-

jor considerations in making awards. Scholarships are renewed annually, subject to continued need and availability of funds.

ADMISSIONS INFORMATION

The Academy seeks boys and girls of average to superior ability who have a positive attitude and are interested in taking an active role in promoting their own social and academic growth. Admission is open to students of any race, color, and national or ethnic origin. Candidates are accepted on the basis of school performance (as indicated in the transcript and recommendations), the results of the SSAT or other tests, and a personal interview.

For 2004–05, there were 689 applications that yielded 458 acceptances, from which 180 students ultimately enrolled in the following grades: 62 in the ninth, 52 in the tenth, 45 in the eleventh, and 18 in the postgraduate year. There are 410 students in the total student body.

APPLICATION TIMETABLE

Initial inquiries are welcome at any time. Interviews and campus tours are scheduled at 9 and 10:30 a.m. and 1 p.m. Monday through Friday and at 9 and 11 a.m. on Saturday. Morning interviews are preferable.

Applicants for grades 9–11 should file for the SSAT as soon as possible, while senior and postgraduate candidates should take the November or December SAT. Completed applications should be submitted, along with the $50 nonrefundable application fee, by February 1 for early March notification. Applications may be submitted after February and will be acted on as the files are completed, subject to the availability of spaces in the class. Most places for grades 11 and 12 and the postgraduate year are filled by May 1; grades 9 and 10 are generally filled between June 15 and 30.

Students who are accepted before March 20 have a place guaranteed until April 10; students who are accepted after March 20 have two to three weeks to consider their options. A few places are usually available for the winter term.

ADMISSIONS CORRESPONDENCE

Melanie J. Connors, Director of Admission
Cushing Academy
Ashburnham, Massachusetts 01430

Phone: 978-827-7300
Fax: 978-827-6253
E-mail: admission@cushing.org
Web site: http://www.cushing.org

DANA HALL SCHOOL

Wellesley, Massachusetts

Type: Girls' boarding (9–12) and day college-preparatory school
Grades: 6–12: Middle School, 6–8; Upper School, 9–12
Enrollment: School total: 456; Upper School: 328
Head of School: Blair Jenkins

THE SCHOOL

Founded in 1881 as a preparatory school for Wellesley College, Dana Hall today sends its graduates to a variety of colleges and universities in the United States and abroad. In addition to maintaining its traditional focus on academic preparation for college, Dana Hall provides young women with opportunities to develop intellectual abilities, self-knowledge, and a sense of community in an atmosphere of women that is enriched by the diversity among its students and faculty members. Dana Hall's belief is that education should be a continuous process of personal challenges directed toward the individual's effective participation in a changing world. The School strives to provide a composite of learning through intellectually rigorous programs and independent study, through the sharing of common purposes and responsibilities for the School community, and through involvement in the world beyond the campus.

Dana Hall is located 12 miles west of Boston, offering the cultural and academic advantages of the city as well as its own attractive suburban campus. A 25-member Board of Trustees is the governing body; currently, it is composed of 16 women and 9 men. Nine members are Dana Hall graduates.

Dana Hall is accredited by the New England Association of Schools and Colleges and is a member of the Secondary School Admission Test Board, the National Association of Independent Schools, the Independent School Association of Massachusetts, A Better Chance, the National Coalition of Girls' Schools, and The Association of Boarding Schools.

ACADEMIC PROGRAMS

Students must complete 18 academic credits in grades 9–12, including the following requirements: English, 4; foreign language, 3 (through third year of the same language); mathematics, 3; laboratory science, 2; social science, 2 (including 1 credit in U.S. history and 1 credit in area studies); information science and technology, 1; performing arts, ½; and visual arts, ½. One-half credit of physical education or athletics is required each year; 20 hours of community service must be completed in grade 10.

The average class at Dana has 13 students; the student-faculty ratio is 8:1. Grades and comments are sent out to parents three times per year. Students meet with their advisers twice as a group and once a week on an individual basis, to discuss academic progress and overall well-being.

Dana Hall's academic philosophy expects students to reach beyond the School's minimum requirements and develop independence in the pursuit of learning. The School also emphasizes the links between study and experience through dynamic, interactive classroom teaching; special programs; guest lecturers; field trips; and independent projects.

Students interested in pursuing independent study in a particular area may do so under the guidance of an adviser from the corresponding academic department. Off-campus internship experiences are arranged through the Community Service Program. There is a six-week exchange program with the Ruyton Girls' School in Melbourne, Australia, and an opportunity to be part of the Rocky Mountain Semester in Leadville, Colorado. Other travel opportunities are available through spring break trips, led by faculty members, throughout the United States and to Costa Rica, France, Italy, Spain, and South Africa.

FACULTY AND ADVISERS

Dana Hall employs full-time teachers, all of whom are active in advising and counseling students. Faculty members hold graduate degrees, and many of the faculty members live on campus. In addition, there are 6 house directors and 6 house assistants who help supervise the nonacademic life of the residential students.

Mrs. Blair Jenkins, Head of School, is a graduate of Wells College and holds a master's degree from Peabody College at Vanderbilt University. Prior to becoming Head of School, she held the positions of Dean of Students, Upper School Director, and Associate Head at Dana Hall. She formerly was Head of the Middle School at Kent Denver School, Director of Counseling and Upper School Head at The Colorado Springs School, and Dean of Students at Westover School.

COLLEGE PLACEMENT

Beginning in the junior year, all students meet weekly with the college counselor as part of the Forum Program. Group discussions concerning preparation for the senior year, leadership, and social responsibility are part of the program. In addition, such topics as self-evaluation, decision-making, testing, and the college admission process are discussed. The college counselor meets with individual students and parents by appointment throughout the junior and senior years and plans a special college day for juniors and their parents each spring. Students also meet with any of the 120 college representatives who visit the Dana Hall campus annually. In addition, the college counselor plans special programs addressing issues involved in the college application and selection process for parents and students throughout the year. Seniors are encouraged to apply to colleges and universities with varying degrees of selectivity and to consider choices in terms of their own performance and goals.

The diversity of the students at Dana Hall is reflected in the variety of their college choices. In the past three years, graduates have attended more than 100 colleges and universities worldwide. The following colleges are representative of the larger number of colleges chosen by the Dana Hall graduates in the class of 2005: Brown, Cornell, Dartmouth, Georgetown, Johns Hopkins, Stanford, and the University of Pennsylvania.

STUDENT BODY AND CONDUCT

Of the 3286 students enrolled in the Upper School at Dana Hall, 139 are boarding students and 189 are day students. Each class size varies, with 80 in grade 9, 75 in grade 10, 80 in grade 11, and 93 in grade 12. While a majority of the students come from New England, fifteen states and fifteen countries are represented, including Canada, China, Ecuador, Hong Kong, Israel, Japan, Korea, Mexico, the Philippines, Sweden, Taiwan, Thailand, and the West Indies.

School life and residential affairs are regulated by the Student Senate. This group includes the Head of School, Dean of Students, all-school co-presidents, class advisers, Director of College Counseling, and several elected students. Each class has elected class officers and 2 class advisers. All students are eligible to become members of a variety of campus committees and councils.

ACADEMIC FACILITIES

Dana Hall's Shipley Science and Library Building and a renovated academic building encompass the majority of classrooms and laboratories. Also found in these buildings are the writing and math centers, the computer center, an assembly hall, a fully wired lecture hall, the art gallery, the art and ceramics studio, and a photo lab.

The Helen Temple Cooke Library offers students and faculty members a collection of more than 30,000 items, including books, books on tape, videotapes, CDs, DVDs, and CD-ROMs. Direct access to more than 5,000 full-text periodical titles is available, with almost 200 in print and others online. The library is fully automated and is a member of several shared library systems, which provide access to the resources of hundreds of libraries statewide. There are 150 computers available for student use, and connections to the campus network throughout the library enable laptop users to access a wide variety of applications. In addition to instruction in the use of traditional research tools, the library staff also offers training in audiovisual technology and educates students in media literacy.

On the edge of the 52-acre campus sits Bardwell Auditorium, where dance classes and major theatrical events take place. Across Grove Street is the Dana Hall School of Music, where students take music lessons and use practice facilities.

BOARDING AND GENERAL FACILITIES

Girls reside in six dormitories, which range in character from a modern four-building complex to small houses. The Johnston dormitories are the largest units, with up to 25 girls in each unit. In

the center of the complex is Johnston Main, a popular lounge and recreation area. Girls in the ninth and tenth grades are the primary residents of the Johnstons. In each of the houses are 14–25 girls in grades 11 and 12. Each dormitory is supervised by a set of house directors and a house assistant. A student proctor aids in house supervision.

Beveridge Hall, an attractive Greco-Roman-style building near the center of campus, is the location of the Alumnae, Development, Business, College Counseling, and Admission and Financial Aid offices. The Dining Center next door contains darkroom facilities and a photography gallery. The Health Center serves the health needs of the community. The center is open five days a week, and a nurse practitioner is on call on weekends. In-patient care is provided for Dana students at Wellesley College's Simpson Infirmary, approximately 3 minutes away.

The Wayside Student Center houses the language lab, the offices of the Learning Specialist, and the School Psychologist.

ATHLETICS
Dana Hall's athletic/fitness program is designed to meet the varying needs of students, as each student is required to participate in physical education each trimester. Students may elect to play on interscholastic teams at the varsity and junior varsity levels. Competitive teams include basketball, cross-country, fencing, field hockey, golf, ice hockey, lacrosse, riding, soccer, softball, squash, swimming, tennis, and volleyball. Fitness and physical education classes are available, which introduce all aspects of fitness including cardiovascular fitness, nutrition, weight training, and stretching exercises, or offer a chance to play in a variety of cardiovascular or sports-related activities, such as Tae-Bo, yoga, self defense, aerobics, floor hockey, and Ultimate Frisbee. The physical education requirement can also be satisfied through the dance program in the performing arts department or by programs at the Dana Hall Riding Center.

The Shipley Center for Athletics, Health & Wellness is a 93,000-square-foot facility that is scheduled to open in fall 2005 and house a swimming pool, squash courts, and a state-of-the-art fencing studio.

The Dana Hall Riding School facilities include stable capacity for forty-five horses, hunt-seat eq-

uitation, and one outdoor and two indoor arenas. The new Larson Riding Ring was completed in 2000.

EXTRACURRICULAR OPPORTUNITIES
Extracurricular activities are viewed as an important part of student life. Participation in the various activities enables students to develop interests, determine individual strengths, and encounter the outside community. Students may choose from a variety of opportunities, including athletic teams, music groups, a literary society, language clubs, student publications, student government, the activities committee, and service clubs. Also available are Blue Key, Drama, the International Student Club, Amnesty International, and Shades, Bridge, Recycling, Math, and Peer Education Clubs. These activities meet during a club period on Wednesday and are open to any student who wishes to join.

DAILY LIFE
On weekday mornings there is an adviser meeting (twice a week), an all-school assembly (three times a week), or a class meeting (once a week). Classes meet five days a week on a modular schedule from 8:30 a.m. until 3:20 or 3:45 (Monday, Tuesday, and Thursday) or 2 p.m. (Wednesday and Friday). At the end of each day there is a 45-minute conference period when students and faculty members can meet with each other, in addition to common free periods during the day. Sports practices and games, as well as club meetings, take place after regularly scheduled school hours. Assemblies, conference seminars, and special programs, such as the Wannamaker Lecture Series, may be scheduled in the evening.

WEEKEND LIFE
A student committee works closely with the Student Activities Coordinator to provide a selection of activities on and off campus. Every weekend, day and boarding students, joined by faculty members, have a choice of sports, movies, dorm events, coffeehouses, recitals, concerts, plays, and dances. Girls also participate in trips to Boston's museums, plays, concerts, and shopping areas. Coeducational weekend entertainment is frequent and well supervised.

Traditional annual events include Revels, Parents' Weekend, Alumnae Weekend, Senior-

Sophomore, Step-Sing, Cabaret, Harbor Cruise, Clambake, and Spring Carnival.

COSTS AND FINANCIAL AID
In 2005–06, Upper School tuition was $29,340 for day students and $39,000 for boarding students.

No one should hesitate to apply for admission to Dana Hall solely because of an inability to meet costs. Financial aid is awarded on the basis of need, as determined by the School, using the need assessment of the School and Student Service for Financial Aid and a family's 1040 income tax form. In 2004–05, more than $2.2 million in financial aid grants were awarded on the basis of need.

ADMISSIONS INFORMATION
Candidates for admission are often concerned about how applicants are evaluated. At Dana Hall, the first considerations are a student's academic ability and intellectual curiosity, as reflected by her school record and recommendations. Dana Hall is also interested in a student's spirit, motivation, personal growth, and ability to work with others.

All candidates must take the ISEE or the SSAT. International students must take the TOEFL. Test results are very helpful in determining patterns of strengths or weaknesses, but Dana Hall does not have a test-cutoff point below which applicants are refused consideration.

In addition to test scores and school records, students must submit two teacher recommendations. A personal interview is strongly recommended for each applicant. However, if a student cannot travel to the campus, a phone interview can be arranged.

APPLICATION TIMETABLE
Completed applications should be submitted, along with the application fee, by February 1 for March 10 notification. Applications may be submitted after February and will be acted on as the files are completed, subject to the availability of places in the class.

ADMISSIONS CORRESPONDENCE
Heather A. Cameron
Director of Admission and Financial Aid
Dana Hall School
45 Dana Road
Wellesley, Massachusetts 02482

Phone: 781-235-3010
Fax: 781-235-0577
E-mail: admission@danahall.org
Web site: http://www.danahall.org

DARLINGTON SCHOOL

Rome, Georgia

Type: Coeducational boarding and day college-preparatory school
Grades: P–PG: Lower School, Prekindergarten–5; Middle School, 6–8; Upper School, 9–12, postgraduate year
Enrollment: School total: 900; Upper School: 450
Head of School: Thomas Whitworth III, President

THE SCHOOL

Darlington School offers motivated students rigorous academics, numerous fine arts opportunities, and a competitive athletics program in a nurturing environment. Named after a teacher, Darlington was founded in 1905 as a boys' school by students of Joseph James Darlington, who believed in academic excellence, insisted upon honest and diligent effort, and stressed development of character directed to the service of God and humankind. These fundamental principles, which put the student-teacher relationship at the forefront of everything the School does, have carried Darlington through nearly a century of changes, including the addition of a boarding division in 1923, the establishment of coeducation in 1973, and a emphasis on technology throughout the curriculum in the 1990s.

Stretching for 500 acres, Darlington's beautiful campus is nestled around a small lake in the foothills of the Lookout Mountain Range in Rome, Georgia, a community of 84,000. Home to Berry, Floyd, and Shorter Colleges and the medical hub of northwest Georgia, Rome is a little more than an hour's drive from Atlanta and Chattanooga, Tennessee.

Under the governance of a 36-member Board of Trustees composed of alumni, parents, and grandparents, Darlington operates on a $15.7-million budget, with some $1.35 million coming from annual giving and another $1.1 million generated from a $20-million endowment fund. The School has completed a $43-million capital campaign, the cornerstone of which is a $16-million, 96,000-square-foot student athletic and recreation center, which opened in August 2001.

Darlington, a nonprofit organization, is accredited by the Southern Association of Colleges and Schools and holds membership in the National Association of Independent Schools as well as other professional organizations.

ACADEMIC PROGRAMS

The academic year, divided into three trimesters, begins in late August and ends in late May, with extended breaks at Thanksgiving and Christmas and in the spring. Classes, held five days a week, are scheduled in eight 45-minute rotating periods between 8:10 a.m. and 3:20 p.m. A 1-hour period for athletics, fitness, fine arts, and other activities follows the class day. The schedule allows students to maintain five or more academic subjects, electives, and extracurricular activities through the day. The average class size is 13. Extra help is available every morning in classroom sessions before school. Resident students have a supervised study hall of 2 hours each evening in their rooms. Parents receive grades every four weeks, but most refer to the School Web site for daily updates. Teacher comments and conduct reports are also available on the Web site.

To graduate from the Upper School, a student must complete 24 credits, including 4 years of English, 2 of a single foreign language, 3 of history, 4 of mathematics, 3 of science, 1 of information technology, 1 of fine arts, 3 electives, 1 of life fitness, and 2 of physical education.

Darlington offers a wide range of courses. English 1–4 covers grammar, composition, literary criticism, and American, British, and world literature. Language department offerings include French 1–5 and Spanish 1–5. The history department offers full-year courses in ancient world history, modern world history, modern European history, American history, and government/economics, and electives in military history and world cultures. Math department courses include algebra 1–3, geometry, precalculus, and calculus. Courses in the science department consist of biology, chemistry, physics, environmental science, Georgia natural history, and anatomy. The fine arts department offers art 1–3, drama 1–2, musical theater, humanities, music appreciation, cinema, chorale, concert choir, instrumental music, wind ensemble, and steel band. Information technology and communications offerings include keyboarding, word processing 1–2, computer application, video production 1–2, photojournalism, publications practicum, communications, desktop publishing, graphic design, computer art, Web authoring, and computer science. Additional courses include physical education, health, and lifetime fitness.

Honors courses are available in most subjects. Advanced Placement courses are offered in seventeen subjects: American history, art history, biology, calculus AB, calculus BC, chemistry, computer science, English, European history, French, German, government, Latin, physics, studio arts, statistics, and Spanish. In 2004, 87 Darlington students took a total of 148 AP Exams; 82 percent of the exams were scored 3 or higher. In 2004, Darlington had 9 AP Scholars, 5 AP Scholars with Honors, and 8 AP Scholars with Distinction, for a total of 22 AP Scholars.

FACULTY AND ADVISERS

Darlington takes great pride in hiring faculty members who are passionate about the subjects they teach and who have a devout interest in working with young people. Sixty-two of the 87 teachers and administrators in the Upper School live on campus. All hold baccalaureate degrees, and more than half have advanced degrees. It is a common occurrence for teachers and students to work on English papers, figure out math problems, and practice foreign languages after school hours.

In July 2005, Thomas Whitworth III will become Darlington's seventh president. With twenty-five years of administrative experience, Whitworth has served as founding headmaster of Flint Hill School in Oakton, Virginia, since 1989. He has served as assistant headmaster and academic dean at St. Stephen's School in Alexandria, Virginia; headmaster at Frederica Academy on St. Simon's Island, Georgia; and assistant headmaster and upper school director at Sea Pines Academy on Hilton Head Island, South Carolina. Whitworth holds a Bachelor of Arts degree in journalism from the University of North Carolina at Chapel Hill and a Master of Education in secondary education and supervision and English from The Citadel. He is a member of the Association of Independent Schools of Greater Washington (AISGW), where he has served two

terms on the board; the Community of Concern Steering Committee; and is a founding member of the Emerging Scholars Program (ESP), where he serves on the Board.

Every Darlington student is assigned an academic adviser and is in an advisee group of about 8 students. These groups meet at least once a month and from time to time go out to dinner or meet at the adviser's home. The adviser also meets regularly with each advisee on an individual basis to discuss academic performance and other issues. The adviser is considered the parents' primary contact at the School, whether the concern is academic or personal. The adviser-advisee program is under the direction of the School's full-time personal counselor.

COLLEGE PLACEMENT

Almost all graduates go to college and are systematically counseled by the associate headmaster and dean of college guidance and a team of 12 college advisers.

The 123 graduates in the class of 2004 were accepted at 151 colleges and are attending colleges in twenty states, the District of Columbia, Canada, and Spain, such as Boston University, Davidson, Emory, Georgia Tech, Rollins, the U.S. Air Force Academy, the U.S. Military Academy, Vanderbilt, Wake Forest, Washington and Lee, and the Universities of Georgia, North Carolina, the South, and Virginia.

Sixty-two members of the class of 2004 were offered 101 academic, athletic, and special achievement scholarships valued at more than $3.4 million. More than 75 representatives from colleges and universities throughout the nation visit the campus each year to talk with the students.

STUDENT BODY AND CONDUCT

Darlington operates on the philosophy that a diverse student body gives its students a realistic perspective of the real world. Darlington typically enrolls students from sixteen states and eighteen countries, with most students hailing from the Southeast. The 165 resident students (evenly divided between boys and girls) comprise 40 percent of the student body in the Upper School.

The close ratio of resident and day students allows the two groups many excellent opportunities to influence one another. Every resident student is assigned Rome Parents, usually parents of a current day student, who take on the responsibility of making sure their resident student feels at home at Darlington and in Rome. Rome Parents often open their homes to their "adopted" students, inviting them over for dinner or to spend a weekend. A number of resident families assert that the Rome Parent program is a significant reason for choosing Darlington.

The School has a long-standing tradition of strong student leadership. The House Senate helps to formulate and implement School policy and spirit, the Honor Council helps maintain honesty and integrity, and the "Y" Cabinet generates spiritual life at the School. Darlington expects its students to be good citizens, with major disciplinary infrac-

tions turned over to a discipline committee composed of students and faculty members.

ACADEMIC FACILITIES
The Upper School buildings, grouped around a lake, are all wired for Internet access and house nearly 150 computers. Darlington's 17,000-square-foot, fully automated McCallie Kennedy Library is the focal point of the campus. The library is complemented by Kawamura Science Center, a 10,000-square-foot facility, which ensures students frequent laboratory work. Four other classroom buildings provide space for the English, history, math, foreign language, and fine arts departments as well as computer labs and the student publications center.

BOARDING AND GENERAL FACILITIES
Six houses, three for boys and three for girls, each accommodating roughly 35 resident students and 45 day students, are supervised by 6 heads of house, full-time residents, and directors of student life in each house. Through the support of student prefects (leaders), school life is mediated through the houses. Every house has a common room where students may watch TV or movies and socialize. A snack bar is open during the day. An infirmary, which is staffed 24 hours a day, is centrally located. All resident rooms have T1 Internet access; all students are assigned e-mail addresses.

ATHLETICS
Darlington's athletics program offers something for everyone, and all students are encouraged to participate in one or more of the School's many sports offerings. Varsity boys' competition is offered in baseball, basketball, cross-country, football, golf, lacrosse, soccer, swimming and diving, tennis, track, and wrestling. Varsity sports for girls comprise basketball, cheerleading, cross-country, golf, lacrosse, soccer, softball, swimming and diving, tennis, track, and volleyball. State championships have been won the last four years in cross-country (boys and girls), tennis (boys and girls), and track (girls). There are also junior varsity and freshman teams in many sports. Lifetime Fitness offers students not participating in a competitive sport a variety of noncompetitive activities such as aerobics, baseball, basketball, kayaking, lacrosse, martial arts, running, soccer, swimming, tennis, and weight lifting.

Athletics facilities include a 96,000-square-foot athletics center that houses a performance arena, field house, wrestling room, weight room, aerobics room, indoor track, and indoor swimming pool. There is also a twelve-court tennis complex, a track and stadium, and eight playing fields.

EXTRACURRICULAR OPPORTUNITIES
The Darlington Players stages three drama productions each year, with students having numerous opportunities to direct, act, produce, and build sets. Literary and Scholar Bowl teams compete successfully in tournaments throughout the state. The chorale and concert choir present traditional seasonal concerts and frequently represent the School at civic and School-related events.

Darlington students produce four award-winning student publications (newspaper, yearbook, literary magazine, and video). Eight hands-on classes are offered as electives: graphic design, creative writing, communications, desktop publishing, photojournalism, Web authoring, publications practicum, and video production. A student internship program, in which students help write and design School publications and the Darlington Web site, is also available. Darlington's student publications lab has sixteen PC computers, plus slide/film scanners, flatbed scanners, high-resolution laser printers, and a color printer.

DAILY LIFE
Breakfast is served until 7:45 a.m., and school begins with coach classes at 7:45 for those needing additional assistance. Classes, which rotate through an eight-period-per-day schedule, begin at 8:10 and last until 3:20, with a 35-minute assembly, chapel service, or break in the morning and a 45-minute lunch break. After-school activities follow the school day (3:45–4:45 p.m.), after which students are free until dinner (6–7 p.m.). Study hall lasts from 7:45 to 10, and lights out follows at 11.

WEEKEND LIFE
Every weekend, activities are offered on campus, including movies, games, tournaments, dances, cookouts, and talent shows. Among the off-campus activities are excursions to Atlanta and Chattanooga shopping malls, amusement parks, athletic contests, and cultural events.

Phoenix Quest provides outdoor adventures in backpacking, canoeing, kayaking, mountain biking, rafting, rock-climbing, and spelunking.Other activities are scheduled over vacations, from skiing trips in Colorado or Austria to hiking ventures in the Rockies or Appalachians to travel in Belize or England.

SUMMER PROGRAMS
Darlington School offers five overnight summer camps for middle school-aged boarders. Campers choose from Eco-Adventure Darlington, Rockets and Robotics, Fast Pitch Softball, Golf, or Tennis. Several outside-sponsored camps, such as Nike Volleyball, Southern Tennis Academy, National Kicking Service, and No. 1 Soccer, are often scheduled

as well. Interested students should visit the School's Web site or call the School for more information.

COSTS AND FINANCIAL AID
Tuition for 2004–05 was $28,600 for boarding students and $12,150 for day students. There was an additional charge of $2500 for ESL. Additional expenses included textbooks, school supplies, and spending money. The School has a number of different payment plans, including a student loan program, as well as a discount for early payment.

Darlington awards more than $1.4 million annually in financial aid to 17 percent of its students on the basis of need. Thirty-three percent of boarding students receive financial aid. All families applying for financial aid must complete the forms for the School and Student Service for Financial Aid.

ADMISSIONS INFORMATION
The student body is made up of students with diverse talents and interests and from various socio-economic levels. Darlington is interested in boys and girls of average to superior ability who are committed to making the most of their academic and personal potential. Students in grades 9–12 as well as those seeking a postgraduate experience may apply, although the School prefers applicants at the freshman and sophomore levels. Day students may enter grades P–12.

Applicants must submit SSAT scores, a transcript, and teacher recommendations and have an interview on campus. Applicants may take admissions tests when they visit the campus or at home.

Darlington School does not discriminate on the basis of race, color, or national or ethnic origin in the administration of its educational or admissions policies.

APPLICATION TIMETABLE
Initial inquiries are welcome at any time. Interviews are conducted between 9 a.m. and5 p.m., Monday through Friday, and before noon on Saturday. Campus tours are organized during the school day and occasionally on Saturday. There is a testing fee of $30 ($75 for international students). Although Darlington has rolling admissions, students are advised to apply during the fall and winter for the coming year. Notification of acceptance is usually given within a month of receipt of complete application materials.

ADMISSIONS CORRESPONDENCE
Casey Zimmer, Director of Admission
Darlington School
1014 Cave Spring Road
Rome, Georgia 30161-4700
Phone: 800-36-TIGER (toll-free)
Fax: 706-232-3600
E-mail: admission@darlingtonschool.org
Web site: http://www.darlingtonschool.org

DARROW SCHOOL
New Lebanon, New York

Type: Coeducational boarding and day college-preparatory school
Grades: 9–12, postgraduate year
Enrollment: 117
Head of School: Nancy M. Wolf

THE SCHOOL

Darrow School, located along the New York–Massachusetts border, offers a hands-on college-preparatory curriculum and is supplemented by active, experiential learning within a structured, supportive environment. Small classes, stimulating and friendly faculty members, individual advisers, supervised study, and a strong tutorial program ensure that each student receives individual attention.

In its educational philosophy, Darrow has historically emphasized active learning and the belief that education is not limited to the classroom. Current pedagogical theory supports that longtime tradition, and the School continually seeks to incorporate new methods and technologies that enhance its development as a community for learning.

As an outgrowth of the Shaker motto, "Hands to Work, Hearts to God," the School sets aside Wednesday morning to foster the dignity of labor and cooperative effort. All members of the community—administrators, teachers, and students—participate in such projects and tasks as wood chopping, making apple cider and maple syrup, recycling, gardening, woodworking, and Habitat for Humanity. The purpose is to encourage self-confidence, awareness of nature, and community involvement.

Darrow School is accredited by the Middle States Association of Colleges and Schools. It is a member of the National Association of Independent Schools, the New York State Association of Independent Schools, the Association of Boarding Schools, and the Secondary School Admission Test Board.

Darrow was founded in 1932 by a group of Shaker, community, and educational leaders, including the headmasters of Deerfield, Taft, and Hotchkiss. Situated in the Berkshire Mountains on the site of a Mt. Lebanon Shaker Village, Darrow is a designated National Historic Landmark.

The School occupies 365 acres adjoining the Pittsfield State Forest on the western slope of Mount Lebanon. On the campus are three playing fields, two tennis courts, extensive hiking paths, and a cross-country ski trail as well as ponds, sheep pastures, orchards, marshlands, and an expansive forest. Darrow is located 25 miles east of Albany, New York; 9 miles west of Pittsfield, Massachusetts; 150 miles north of New York City; and 150 miles west of Boston.

ACADEMIC PROGRAMS

Darrow seeks to challenge each student through an active, hands-on curriculum that contributes to the development of essential learning skills. Classes are small, averaging 9 students, and the overall student-teacher ratio is 4:1.

Darrow follows a semester system, with a unique eight-day Spring Term after the fourth quarter. The daily schedule includes half days on Wednesday and Saturday and follows a unique, modified block program comprising class blocks of 45–65 minutes.

Darrow's evaluation system reflects a variety of assessment tools, from traditional tests to oral or PowerPoint presentations, and portfolios. Academic and effort grades are given, along with extensive teacher and adviser comments, including dorm parent observations on residential life. Grade

reports are sent home four times a year. Advisers are also in direct contact with parents regularly to report on their advisees' progress.

Central to Darrow's academic structure is the tutorial program. This program is designed to motivate and enable students to produce higher-quality work through a process of feedback and frequent assessment of their skills as learners, writers, and problem solvers. The program also allows Darrow students to learn how to deal effectively with increasing academic challenges. Tutors and students meet during the class day at least two times per week. Throughout the year, information about each student's learning style and needs is garnered from teachers' observations, testing, grades, and narrative reports, contributing to the ongoing refinement of each student's individually designed tutorial program.

Extra help is also available outside of the tutorial program. Darrow considers asking for extra help a sign of strength, not weakness, and faculty members make time each day for formal and informal sessions and study halls.

As responsible citizens of the Hudson River Watershed, Darrow promotes environmentally responsible lifestyles by explicitly linking the concept of environmental sustainability throughout the curriculum and the community.

Graduation requirements include the successful completion of 20 credits, including 4 credits of English, 3 credits of social studies, 3 credits of mathematics, 3 credits of science, 2 credits of language, 2 credits of arts, 1 credit of physical education, ½ credit of health, and 1½ additional elective credits. Students typically take five academic courses per term.

FACULTY AND ADVISERS

Darrow has 29 full-time faculty members (14 men and 15 women). All hold bachelor's degrees, and 11 have graduate degrees. Nearly all faculty members, including 12 with families, reside on campus. Most serve as dorm parents in dormitories.

Head of School Nancy M. Wolf is the tenth Head at Darrow and the first woman to hold this position, which she began in July 2001. Her career in independent education started in 1970, when she was Darrow's first full-time female faculty member, during the School's transition to coeducation. Since then, she has gained a range of expertise at a select group of independent schools, including twenty-eight years as a classroom teacher and experience in nearly every administrative capacity. Mrs. Wolf has served as Math Chair and Middle and Upper School Head at Severn School in Maryland, Dean of Students at Lawrenceville School in New Jersey and, most recently, Director of Development and Assistant Head for Advancement and Operations at Oldfields School in Maryland, where she worked for thirteen years. Mrs. Wolf earned a B.A. in mathematics (cum laude) from Ithaca College and an M.Ed. in administration and supervision from Loyola College in Baltimore. She and her husband, Robert, live on the Darrow campus.

COLLEGE PLACEMENT

The curriculum at Darrow is college-preparatory, and active steps are taken to provide guidance in the college-placement process. A full-time college counselor offers individual instruction, recommendations, and advice to students to aid them in their college search and maintains a well-equipped library of college catalogs. Starting early in the eleventh grade, juniors are provided with an overview of the college selection process and are helped to formulate opinions and direction as the year progresses. Seniors work on an individual basis with the Director of College Counseling to determine the most appropriate colleges at which to apply. Faculty members prepare detailed letters of recommendation for each senior. The SAT remains an important tool in the selection process for many colleges and universities and is administered on campus during May of the junior year and November of the senior year. Because the selection process itself constantly evolves, parents are also educated and assisted throughout the entire process.

In 2005, all of the graduating seniors went on to college. Among colleges and universities that accepted Darrow students were Boston University, Clary, Connecticut College, Goucher, Hampshire, Hobart, Rhode Island School of Design, Springfield, St. Lawrence, Union, and University of Rochester.

STUDENT BODY AND CONDUCT

In 2005–06, 117 students were enrolled in grades 9–PG, 101 boarding students and 16 day students. There were 64 boys and 53 girls. Eighteen states and seven countries were represented by the student body.

A strong student leadership program offers students the opportunity to learn the value of leadership and importance of knowing how to develop a responsible leadership style. Students have several avenues by which they can pursue these goals.

The student government is composed of 12 members, including the student body president, class presidents, and dorm and day student representatives. A member of the faculty serves as an adviser. The purpose of the student government is to provide the School with an organized student group that works to serve the needs of the Darrow community and to aid the student body president in his or her role as student leader. In addition to student government positions, students serve in leadership positions as prefects and resident assistants. Prefects work with faculty advisers, and each is primarily concerned with activities or services in one area of student life, such as the library, computers, admissions, or student activities. The resident assistants work with dorm parents and help with check-in and other supervisory responsibilities. Darrow also has a Discipline Committee, composed of both student and faculty members, which meets when a serious disciplinary infraction must be addressed.

ACADEMIC FACILITIES

There are twenty-four buildings on the Darrow campus and twenty-one are original Shaker structures. Wickersham houses the administrative offices, classrooms, and one of three computer labs.

The Joline Arts Center opened for student use in September 2002. The 12,000-square-foot building provides studio and lab spaces for a broad range of fine arts programming and areas for seminars and presentations. Included are classrooms specifically designed for painting, drawing, ceramics, photography (wet and digital), and woodworking. In addition, there is extensive studio space for private work and individual projects and a public exhibition gallery for the display of student, faculty, alumni, and guest works.

Darrow's $1.8-million Samson Environmental Center cleans the School's wastewater and provides unique, hands-on learning opportunities to Darrow students and others of all ages who are interested in the process. The centerpiece of the facility is the Living Machine, an ecological wastewater treatment system that transforms the wastewater from dormitories, academic buildings, and dining hall into clean water that is released into the Hudson River Watershed. In October 2003, Darrow secured a grant from the New York State Energy Research and Development Authority to install photovoltaic panels, which now provide partial power to the center. Adjacent to the Samson Environmental Center is the science building, which houses four laboratories and faculty offices.

The gymnasium, theater, and dining hall are in the Dairy Barn, built on the site of the original Shaker dairy barn.

The Second Meeting House, built in 1824 and remodeled in 1962, houses the library, which contains more than 15,000 volumes. A computer network links the library to other libraries in the greater Albany area and to the Web site. Darrow Net, a campuswide intranet program, connects all classroom and science lab computers.

BOARDING AND GENERAL FACILITIES

Darrow's dormitories are Shaker structures that have been adapted to provide comfortable, spacious accommodations for both students and faculty members. The capacity of each dorm ranges from 12 to 28 students, with 3 faculty dorm parents. Most dorm rooms are doubles, eight of the larger rooms serve as triples, and there are also a few single rooms available.

The on-campus health services clinic is staffed by 2 nurses, and hospital facilities are 15 minutes away. A full-time School counselor offers support for students on campus.

A School store and student center are also available.

ATHLETICS

Darrow maintains a wide-ranging sports program with emphasis on inclusion. The School wants students to be actively involved, not simply watching. A number of life sports and several competitive sports are available for boys and girls. Baseball, basketball, cross-country, dance, fencing, fitness, lacrosse, outdoor education, skiing, snowboarding, soccer, softball, tennis, and Ultimate Frisbee are offered. All students are required to participate in afternoon activities, including at least one team sport each year.

Darrow's athletic program focuses on athletic skills, sportsmanship, physical fitness, and teamwork.

EXTRACURRICULAR OPPORTUNITIES

Students at Darrow have a range of cocurricular opportunities available to them. Theater is a highly popular endeavor, with three major productions each year. A student-organized coffeehouse allows students and faculty members to share their talents in music and poetry. Additional activities include design and production of the yearbook, an independent-study music program, or other activities, such as a literary magazine, initiated and driven by student interest.

DAILY LIFE

Darrow's daily schedule reflects its structured approach to academic life. Days are planned to provide not only variety but also the predictability necessary to allow students to plan ahead and achieve.

Breakfast is served starting at 7 a.m., and the academic day begins at 7:50. There are six periods—five academic periods and a conference period. Sports begin at 3:35, and dinner is served at 5:45. A daily School meeting for all students and faculty members occurs each morning where announcements and commendations are shared. The Friday morning meeting is reserved as time for quiet, personal contemplation and sharing of thoughts.

WEEKEND LIFE

A number of student activities are planned for weekends, which include both on- and off-campus events. Sports, movies, dances, coffeehouses, and trips to theaters and special events off campus occur throughout the year. Students also go to Albany or Pittsfield for shopping and Saturday dinner. Day trips to New York City and Boston are occasionally scheduled.

Students may take weekends off campus with parental permission. Special annual events include Parents' Weekend in the fall, winter, and spring.

COSTS AND FINANCIAL AID

For the 2005–06 school year, boarding student tuition was $33,700, and day student tuition was $19,225. Other expenses included $1500 for books and personal items. A tuition protection policy is required by the School. Tutorial costs were $3800 or $6900, depending on frequency.

Darrow provides financial assistance to 32 percent of its student body. Financial aid is determined by need and the availability of funds. Candidates who require aid should discuss their needs at the time of their interview and are required to fill out the Parents' Financial Statement and mail it to the School and Student Service in Princeton, New Jersey.

ADMISSIONS INFORMATION

Darrow encourages applications from students who want a successful and rewarding educational experience, who need structure and support, and who are willing to take advantage of the School's exciting and hands-on academic and cocurricular program.

Students are admitted to grades 9 through postgraduate. Applicants must submit three recommendations from guidance counselors, heads of school, principals, or teachers; school transcripts; scores on all standardized testing; and the results of the Secondary School Achievement Test, if available. A personal interview is required.

APPLICATION TIMETABLE

Decisions are made on a rolling basis beginning in February. A few midyear or immediate enrollments may be considered. Enrollment decisions are made by the Admission Committee, composed of the Head of School, the Director of Studies, the Dean of Students, 2 faculty members, and the Director of Admission.

ADMISSIONS CORRESPONDENCE

Sean Fagan
Director of Admission
Darrow School
110 Darrow Road
New Lebanon, New York 12125

Phone: 518-794-6000
Fax: 518-794-7065
E-mail: fagans@darrowschool.org
Web site: http://www.darrowschool.org

DEERFIELD ACADEMY

Deerfield, Massachusetts

Type: Coeducational boarding and day college-preparatory school
Grades: 9–12, postgraduate year
Enrollment: 608
Head of School: Eric Widmer, Headmaster

THE SCHOOL

Since its founding in 1797, Deerfield Academy has provided a unique and challenging opportunity for young people. Deerfield Academy is a vibrant learning community nurturing high standards of scholarship, citizenship, and personal responsibility. Through a demanding liberal arts curriculum, extensive cocurricular program, and supportive residential environment, Deerfield encourages each student to develop an inquisitive and creative mind, sound body, strong moral character, and a commitment to service. The setting of the campus, rich in tradition and beauty, inspires reflection, study and play, the cultivation of friendships, and the growth of a defining community spirit.

The school's 280-acre campus is located in the center of historic Deerfield, a restored Colonial village in rural western Massachusetts, 90 miles from Boston and 55 miles from Hartford. Only 20 minutes south is the five-college area that includes Amherst, Smith, Mount Holyoke, and Hampshire colleges and the University of Massachusetts, providing rich cultural and intellectual resources.

A 28-member Board of Trustees is the Academy's governing body. The endowment is valued at approximately $308 million. In 2004–05, operating expenses totaled $34.8 million, capital gifts amounted to $11.6 million, and Annual Giving was $4.3 million, with 47.9 percent of the 8,836 alumni participating.

Deerfield is accredited by the New England Association of Schools and Colleges. It is a member of the National Association of Independent Schools, the Independent School Association of Massachusetts, and the Secondary School Admission Test Board.

ACADEMIC PROGRAMS

Deerfield's curriculum is designed to enable its students to assume active and intelligent roles in the world community. Courses and teaching methods are aimed at developing logical and imaginative thinking, systematic approaches to problem solving, clear and correct expression in writing and speech, and the confidence to pursue creatively one's interests and talents. Students take five courses per trimester. Their schedules are planned individually in consultation with advisers and the Academic Dean.

Graduation requirements include English, 4 years; mathematics, 3 years; foreign language, 3 years of a language (French, Spanish, Chinese, Greek, or Latin); history, 2 years (including 1 year of U.S. history); laboratory science, 2 years; fine arts, 2 terms; and philosophy and religion, 1 term. All sophomores take a one-term course in health issues. In addition, all new students take a required course in library skills. Advanced Placement (AP) courses are offered in English, art, history, economics, math, language, computer science, and science. Last year, 245 students sat for 458 AP

exams in eighteen of the twenty-nine subject areas. Ninety percent of the tests received qualifying scores of 3 or better. Independent study is offered in all departments.

During the spring term, seniors may engage in off-campus alternate studies projects, ranging from working in a local hospital to serving as an intern for a U.S. senator in Washington, D.C. Juniors may spend half of their year at the Maine Coast Semester, which combines regular classes with studies of environmental issues; at the Mountain School in Vermont; or at a boarding school in South Africa. Sophomores and juniors may spend a semester at the Island School on Eleuthera in the Bahamas. The Swiss Semester in Zermatt is a program that gives sophomores an opportunity to study geology, European history, and foreign language at the foot of the Matterhorn. Deerfield participates in the School Year Abroad program in China, France, Italy, and Spain, which is available for juniors and seniors. Students may also choose one of seven exchange programs, including programs in Australia, Botswana, Japan, and New Zealand.

The average class size is 12. The overall faculty-student ratio is 1:5. Placement in AP courses, honors sections, and accelerated courses is based upon preparedness, ability, and interest. All students have study hours Sunday through Thursday evenings.

The school year is divided into three 11-week terms. Grades are sent at the end of each term and at midterm. In the fall and spring, the student's academic adviser prepares a formal written report, commenting extensively on the student's academic performance, attitude, work habits, dormitory life, and participation in athletics, cocurricular activities, and as a citizen of the school.

Grading is based on a numerical scale of 0 to 100; 60 is passing. The honor roll is made up of students with minimum averages of 87, and the high honor roll recognizes students with averages of 93 and above. Students in academic difficulty are reviewed by the Academic Standing Committee at the end of each term. Teachers are available during evenings, weekends, and free periods to assist students individually. In addition, the Tutoring Center, staffed entirely by students, provides assistance in all academic areas each evening. Students can also get help from the Study Skills Coordinator.

FACULTY AND ADVISERS

The high quality of Deerfield's faculty is the school's greatest endowment. The faculty consists of 122 full- and part-time members (53 women and 69 men); 70 percent hold advanced degrees. Ninety percent reside on campus or live in the village of Deerfield. All faculty members act as advisers to students, coach sports, head tables in the dining hall, and serve on various committees. Teachers

receive summer grants and time away from the Academy for advanced study, travel, and exchange teaching.

Eric Widmer (B.A., Williams College; Ph.D. in history and Far Eastern languages, Harvard) was appointed Headmaster in July 1994. Dr. Widmer came to Deerfield from Brown University where, most recently, he served as the Dean of Admissions and Financial Aid. Previously, Dr. Widmer was Assistant Professor of Chinese and Central Asian history and served as Brown's first Dean of Student Life.

COLLEGE PLACEMENT

College counseling is coordinated by 4 college advisers. Beginning in their junior year, all students attend information sessions, small-group discussions, and workshops that help them make informed decisions about college. In the spring, every junior is assigned to an individual college adviser who further develops, with parental consultation, a list of prospective colleges. In the fall of the senior year, the college advisers assist students in narrowing their college choices and in making the most effective presentation of their strengths. During the fall, representatives of approximately 135 colleges visit the Academy for presentations and interviews on occasion.

Normally, juniors take the PSAT in October; the SAT in January; SAT Subject Tests in December, May, and June; and Advanced Placement (AP) tests in May. Seniors, whenever advisable, take the SAT in the fall and additional AP tests later in the year. The midrange of SAT scores for the class of 2005 was 660–700 verbal and 660–720 math.

Of the 183 graduates in 2005, 182 are attending college and 1 student deferred admission to college for a year. Colleges attended by 4 or more students are 10 at Harvard; 9 each at Brown and Pennsylvania; 8 at Bowdoin; 7 each at Georgetown and Middlebury; 6 at Yale; 5 each at Amherst, Cornell, and USC; and 4 each at Duke, Pomona, Princeton, Tufts, Virginia, and Wesleyan.

STUDENT BODY AND CONDUCT

In fall 2005, Deerfield enrolled 608 students: 291 girls and 317 boys. There were 81 boarders and 15 day students in the ninth grade, 132 boarders and 26 day students in the tenth grade, 150 boarders and 21 day students in the eleventh grade, and 159 boarders and 24 day students in the twelfth grade (including 16 postgraduates). Recognizing that diversity enriches the school, the Academy seeks to foster an appreciation of difference. To that end, international students made up 11 percent of the student body, and those from minority groups made up 27 percent. Deerfield students came from thirty-seven states and twenty-four countries.

In all communities, a healthy tension exists between the need for individuality and the need

for common values and standards. A community's shared values define the place, giving it a distinct sense of itself. In all facets of school life, Deerfield strives to teach that honesty, tolerance, compassion, and responsibility are essential to the well-being of the individual, the school, and society. Deerfield Academy is a residential community in which students learn to conduct themselves according to high standards of citizenship. Expectations for students are clear, and the response to misbehavior is timely and as supportive as possible of the students involved.

ACADEMIC FACILITIES
Deerfield's campus has eighty-one buildings. The Frank L. Boyden Library has a collection of more than 85,000 items and approximately 400 periodicals in five languages. Most of the library's collection is accessible via a fully integrated online catalog. The 78,000-square-foot Koch Center for Science, Mathematics, and Technology, opening in winter 2006, will house thirty state-of-the-art classroom and laboratory spaces, including dedicated spaces for independent research, a 225-seat auditorium, a planetarium, the Star Terrace, and a central atrium. The Memorial Building contains the main auditorium, Hilson Gallery, Russell Gallery, the student-run FM radio station, art studios, a black-box theater, a dance facility, and music recital and practice rooms.

BOARDING AND GENERAL FACILITIES
There are seventeen dormitories. Faculty members live in apartments attached to each dorm corridor and maintain a close, supportive relationship with students. Two senior proctors also live on the freshman and sophomore corridors. Eighty percent of the boarders have single rooms.

The fifteen-bed health center, Dewey House, is staffed full-time by a physician and registered nurses.

ATHLETICS
Participation in sports—at the student's level of ability—is the athletic program's central focus. The Academy fields interscholastic teams in baseball, basketball, crew, cross-country, field hockey, football, golf, ice hockey, lacrosse, skiing, soccer, softball, squash, swimming, tennis, track, volleyball, water polo, and wrestling. Supervised recreational activities include aerobics, dance, skiing, squash, strength training, tennis, and an outdoor skills program.

Deerfield's gymnasium complex contains three basketball courts, eight squash courts, a wrestling arena, an indoor hockey rink, a fitness center, and the largest preparatory-school natatorium in New England. This facility includes an indoor, eight-lane, 25-yard pool with a separate diving well. One hundred and ten acres of playing fields include four football fields, twelve soccer/lacrosse fields, three field hockey fields, twenty-three tennis courts, two baseball fields, a softball field, paddle tennis courts, a new boathouse and crew facility, and a six-lane, 400-meter, all-weather composition track.

EXTRACURRICULAR OPPORTUNITIES
Deerfield students and faculty members are extraordinarily productive in the performing and visual arts. Musical groups include wind ensemble, chamber music, jazz ensemble, brass choir, chamber singers, a cappella groups, and the Academy Chorus. Many opportunities exist for acting as well. In addition to the three major theater productions each year, plays and scenes are also performed by advanced acting classes. Students interested in dance may explore modern, jazz, and ballet, with the opportunity to perform all three terms.

Cocurricular organizations include WGAJ-FM, Peer Counselors, the Diversity Task Force, Amnesty International, and debate, photography, and political clubs. Outing groups offer opportunities to ski, rock climb, and bike on weekends. Publications include an award-winning campus newspaper, the yearbook, and literary publications.

Students provide service as tutors, dormitory proctors, tour guides, and waiters in the dining hall. Students serve responsibly on various standing and ad hoc administrative committees and play an especially important role on the disciplinary committee. Students are also involved in various community service projects. The Community Service program encourages Deerfield students and faculty members to broaden their perspectives by sharing with and learning from people of different ages, abilities, cultures, and economic backgrounds. Ongoing projects include mentoring at nearby schools, volunteering in shelters and daycare centers, tutoring, organic farming and on-campus recycling, visiting nursing homes, and sponsoring Red Cross blood drives. Some students also serve as Big Brothers or Big Sisters to local youth.

DAILY LIFE
Students normally take five courses each term, and each course meets four times per week. The length of a class period ranges from 50 to 70 minutes. Classes begin at 7:55 and usually end at 3, except on Wednesday, when classes end at 12:30 and are followed by cocurricular activities. Classes do not meet on Saturdays. One morning a week, students and faculty members gather together for a school meeting, and students and faculty members attend seven family-style meals per week. All sports and drama activities take place after classes. Clubs and cocurricular groups meet between dinner and study hours or on weekends.

Students study in their dormitory rooms between 8 and 10 p.m., Sunday through Thursday. They may also study in the library, perform laboratory experiments, or seek help from a faculty member or the student tutoring service. During the school week, the curfew for freshmen and sophomores is 8 p.m.; for juniors and seniors, 10 p.m.

WEEKEND LIFE
In addition to athletic events on Saturday afternoon, there are films, theatrical productions, and musical performances. Social activities, sponsored by the Student Activities Committee and chaperoned by faculty members, include coffeehouses, talent shows, concerts, and dances. Deerfield's rural setting and extensive athletic facilities are ideal for recreational hiking, rock climbing, skiing, swimming, ice-skating, and other activities.

The Academy Events Committee plans and sponsors weekend events throughout the school year. The Robert Crow Lecture Series brings to the Academy leaders in politics, government, education, science, and journalism. Students attend concerts and film series. Art exhibitions and numerous dramatic productions provide recognition for promising young artists, photographers, and actors. Students also have access to cultural programs in the five-college area.

Freshmen may take two weekends off campus in the fall term and three each in the winter and spring terms; sophomores may take two weekends in fall, three in winter, and an unlimited number in spring; juniors and seniors in good standing may take unlimited weekends. On weekends, the curfew for freshmen and sophomores is at 10:30 p.m. on Friday and at 11 on Saturday. For juniors and seniors, Friday curfew is at 11; on Saturday it is at 11:30 p.m.

COSTS AND FINANCIAL AID
For 2005–06, the cost for boarding students was $34,250; for day students, $26,320. Additional fees were $1705 for books, infirmary, and technology. Parents are asked to maintain a drawing account of $75 for their child's personal expenses. Tuition is payable in two installments—on August 1 and December 1. A $1500 deposit (credited to the August tuition bill) is due within four weeks of the student's acceptance by Deerfield.

Deerfield awards financial aid to 35 percent of its students. Grant aid totals $5 million for the current academic year; amounts, based upon demonstrated need and procedures established by the School and Student Service for Financial Aid, range from $2500 to full tuition.

ADMISSIONS INFORMATION
Deerfield maintains rigorous academic standards and seeks a diverse student body—geographically, socially, ethnically, and racially. Selection is based upon academic ability and performance, character and maturity, and promise as a positive community citizen. The Admission Committee closely examines candidates' teacher and school recommendations, SSAT scores, and personal essays.

The SSAT is required of applicants for grades 9, 10, and 11 and normally should be taken in December. The SAT is required for twelfth-grade and postgraduate candidates.

Deerfield Academy does not discriminate on the basis of race, color, creed, handicap, sexual orientation, or national or ethnic origin in its admissions policies or financial aid programs.

APPLICATION TIMETABLE
Applicants normally visit the Academy in the year prior to the proposed date of entrance. Campus tours and interviews are conducted from 8:15 to 2:15 on Monday, Tuesday, Thursday, and Friday; from 8:15 to 11:40 on Wednesday; and at 9, 10, and 11 on Saturday. Weekdays are preferable. The applicant is sent formal application papers during the fall. The completed application—including teacher recommendations, the school transcript, and essays—should be postmarked no later than January 17. Applicants are sent notification of the admission decision on March 10. The candidate reply date is April 10.

ADMISSIONS CORRESPONDENCE
Patricia L. Gimbel
Dean of Admission and Financial Aid
Deerfield Academy
Deerfield, Massachusetts 01342
Phone: 413-774-1400
E-mail: admission@deerfield.edu
Web site: http://www.deerfield.edu

DELBARTON SCHOOL

Morristown, New Jersey

Type: Boys' day college-preparatory school
Grades: 7–12: Middle School, 7–8; Upper School, 9–12
Enrollment: School total: 540; Upper School: 469
Head of School: Rev. Luke L. Travers, O.S.B., Headmaster

THE SCHOOL

Delbarton School was established in 1939 by the Benedictine monks of Saint Mary's Abbey as an independent boarding and day school. Now a day school, Delbarton is located on a 400-acre woodland campus 3 miles west of historic Morristown and 30 miles west of New York City. Adjacent to the campus is Jockey Hollow, a national historic park.

Delbarton School seeks to enroll boys of good character who have demonstrated scholastic achievement and the capacity for further growth. The faculty strives to support each boy's efforts toward intellectual development and to reinforce his commitment to help build a community of responsible individuals. The faculty encourages each boy to become an independent seeker of information, not a passive recipient, and to assume responsibility for gaining both knowledge and judgment that will strengthen his contribution to the life of the School and his later contribution to society. While the School offers much, it also seeks boys who are willing to give much and who are eager to understand as well as to be understood.

The School is governed by the 8-member Board of Trustees of the Order of Saint Benedict of New Jersey, located at Saint Mary's Abbey in Morristown. Delbarton's 2005–06 annual operating expenses totaled $13.5 million. It has an endowment of $18.3 million. This includes annual fundraising support from 45 percent of the alumni.

Delbarton School is accredited by the Middle States Association of Colleges and Schools and approved by the Department of Education of the State of New Jersey. It is a member of the National Association of Independent Schools, the New Jersey Association of Independent Schools, the Council for Advancement and Support of Education, the National Catholic Educational Association, and the New Jersey State Interscholastic Athletic Association.

ACADEMIC PROGRAMS

The academic program in the Upper School is college preparatory. The course of study offers preparation in all major academic subjects and a number of electives. The studies are intended to help a boy shape a thought and a sentence, to speak clearly about ideas and effectively about feelings, and to suspend judgment until all the facts are known. Course work, on the whole, is intensive and involves about 20 hours of outside preparation each week. The curriculum contains both a core of required subjects that are fundamental to a liberal education and various elective courses that are designed to meet the individual interests of the boys. Instruction is given in all areas that are necessary for gaining admission to the liberal arts or technical institutions of higher learning.

The school year is divided into three academic terms. In each term, every boy must take five major courses, physical education, and religious studies. The specific departmental requirements in grades 9 through 12 are English (4 years), mathematics (4 years), foreign language (3 years), science (3 years), history (3 years), religious studies (2 terms, in each of 4 years), physical education and health (4 years), fine arts (1 major course, 1 term of art, and 1 term of music), and computer technology (2 terms). For qualified boys in the junior and senior years, all departments offer Advanced Placement courses, and it is also possible in certain instances to pursue work through independent study or to study at neighboring colleges.

The grading system uses 4 to 0 (failing) designations with pluses and minuses. Advisory reports are sent to parents in the middle of each term as well as at the end of the three terms. Parents are also contacted when a student has received an academic warning or is placed on probation. The average class size is 15, and the student-teacher ratio is about 7:1, which fosters close student-faculty relations.

FACULTY AND ADVISERS

In 2005–06, the faculty consisted of 12 Benedictine monks and 66 lay teachers. All were full-time members, with 43 holding advanced degrees.

Rev. Luke L. Travers, O.S.B., became Headmaster in June 1999. Fr. Luke received his B.A. from Columbia in 1979, his M.A. in theology from the Catholic University of America in 1984, and his Ed.M. from the Harvard University Graduate School of Education in 1999. He has served the School previously in the positions of campus minister, junior- and senior-year guidance counselor, and director of admissions.

The teaching tradition of the School has called upon faculty members to serve as coaches or counselors or administrators. A genuine interest in the development of people leads the faculty to be involved in many student activities. Every boy is assigned to a guidance counselor, who advises in the selection of courses that meet School and college requirements as well as personal interests. Individual conferences are regularly arranged to discuss academic and personal development. The counselor also contacts the boy's parents when it seems advisable.

COLLEGE PLACEMENT

Preparation for college begins when a boy enters Delbarton. The PSAT is given to everyone in the tenth and eleventh grades. Guidance for admission to college is directed by the senior class counselor. This process generally begins in the fall of the junior year, when the junior class counselor meets with each boy to help clarify his goals and interests. Many college admissions officers visit the School annually for conferences. Every effort is made to direct each boy toward an institution that will challenge his abilities and satisfy his interests.

The mean SAT verbal and math score for the class of 2005 was 1350. More than 25 percent of the young men in the classes of 2002, 2003, 2004, and 2005 have been named National Merit Scholars, Semifinalists, or Commended Students. In addition, 80 percent of the members of the class of 2005 were enrolled in at least one AP course.

All of the graduates of the classes of 2002, 2003, 2004, and 2005 went on to college, with 5 or more attending such schools as Boston College, Columbia, Cornell, Dartmouth, Duke, Georgetown, Harvard, Holy Cross, Johns Hopkins, Middlebury, Notre Dame, Princeton, Villanova, Williams, Yale, and the Universities of Michigan, Pennsylvania, and Virginia.

STUDENT BODY AND CONDUCT

The 2005–06 Upper School student body consisted of 125 ninth graders, 116 tenth graders, 120 eleventh graders, and 108 twelfth graders. The Middle School had 30 seventh and 41 eighth graders. All of the students are from New Jersey, particularly the counties of Morris, Essex, Somerset, Union, Bergen, Hunterdon, Passaic, and Sussex.

Regulations, academic and social, are relatively few. The School eschews the manipulative, the coercive, the negative, or the merely punitive approach to discipline. The basic understanding underlying the School's regulations is that each boy, entering with others in a common educational enterprise, shares responsibility with his fellow students and with faculty members for developing and maintaining standards that contribute to the welfare of the entire School community. Moreover, shared responsibility is essential to the growth of the community; at the same time, much of an individual boy's growth, the increase in his capacity for self-renewal, his sense of belonging, and his sense of identity spring from his eagerness and willingness to contribute to the life of the School. Each class has a moderator who is available for advice and assistance. The moderator works closely with the boys, assisting them in their progress.

ACADEMIC FACILITIES

The physical facilities include two classroom buildings, a science pavilion, a greenhouse, the church, and the dining hall. Academic facilities include thirty-four classrooms, six science laboratories, art and music studios, a language laboratory, and a library of more than 20,000 volumes. The five computer laboratories consist of 250 workstations in a networked system. Also, the music department provides twelve personal computers for the advanced study of music and composition.

ATHLETICS

Sports at the School are an integral part of student life. The School holds the traditional belief that much can be learned about cooperation, competition, and character through participating in sports. Almost 80 percent of the boys participate on one or more interscholastic athletics teams. Varsity sports offered in the fall term are football, soccer, and cross-country; in the winter term, basketball, wrestling, track, hockey, squash, bowling, and swimming (in an off-campus pool); in the spring, baseball, track, lacrosse, tennis, and golf. In most of these sports, there are junior varsity, freshman, and Middle School teams. Some intramural sports are available, depending upon interest, every year.

The facilities consist of two gymnasiums, eight athletics fields, six tennis courts, and an outdoor pool for swimming during the warm weather. Students who join the golf team are able to play at nearby golf clubs.

EXTRACURRICULAR OPPORTUNITIES

The School provides opportunities for individual development outside the classroom as well as within. The faculty encourages the boys to express their intellectual, cultural, social, and recreational interests through a variety of activities and events. For example, fine arts at Delbarton are available both within and outside the curriculum. Studio hours accommodate boys after school, and students visit galleries and museums. In the music department, vocal and instrumental instruction is available. Performing ensembles include an orchestra, band, and chorus and smaller vocal and instrumental ensembles. Under the aegis of the Abbey Players, drama productions are staged three times a year, involving boys in a wide variety of experiences.

Other activities include Deaneries (student support groups promoting School unity and spirit), the *Courier* (the School newspaper), the *Archway* (the yearbook), *Schola Cantorum* (a vocal ensemble), the Abbey Orchestra, and the Model UN, Mock Trial, Speech and Debate, Junior Statesmen, Art, History, Chess, Cycling, Stock Exchange, and Future Business Leaders clubs. In addition, faculty moderators of the Ski Club regularly organize and chaperone trips during school vacations.

To expose students to other cultures and to enhance their understanding of the world, faculty members have organized trips to Europe, Africa, and Latin America. The Campus Ministry office is active in sponsoring several outreach programs that lead boys to an awareness of the needs of others and the means to answer calls for help. The outreach programs include community soup kitchens, Big Brothers of America, Adopt-a-Grandparent, Basketball Clinic for exceptional children, and a program in which volunteers travel to Appalachia during break to contribute various services to the poor of that area.

Students' imagination and initiative are also given opportunities for expression through Student Council committees and assemblies. The students are also offered School-sponsored trips to cultural and recreational events at area colleges and in nearby cities.

DAILY LIFE

Classes begin at 8:15 a.m. and end at 2:34 p.m. The average number of classes per day for each student is six. Two classes are an hour long, while the remainder are 40 minutes each. The School operates on a six-day cycle, and each class meets five days per cycle. Physical education classes are held during the school day. After classes, students are involved in athletics and the arts. Clubs and organizations also meet after school, while many meet at night.

COSTS AND FINANCIAL AID

Charges at Delbarton for the 2005–06 academic year were $21,390. These are comprehensive fees that include a daily hot lunch as well as library and athletics fees. The only other major expenses are the bookstore bill, generally $700 a year, and transportation, the cost of which varies. Optional expenses may arise for such items as the yearbook, music lessons, or trips.

Because of the School's endowment and generous alumni and parent support, a financial aid program enables many boys to attend the School. All awards are based on financial need, as determined by the criteria set by the School and Student Service for Financial Aid. No academic or athletics scholarships are awarded. Financial aid is granted to boys in grades 7 through 12. This year, the School was able to grant $952,580 to students.

ADMISSIONS INFORMATION

Delbarton School selects students whose academic achievement and personal promise indicate that they are likely to become positive members of the community. The object of the admissions procedure is for the School and prospective student to learn as much as possible about each other. Admission is based on the candidate's overall qualifications, without regard to race, color, religion, or national or ethnic origin.

The typical applicant takes one of the four entrance tests administered by the School in October, November, and January. Candidates are considered on the basis of their transcript, recommendations, test results, and a personal interview in addition to the formal application. In 2005–06, 352 students were tested for entrance in grades 7 and 9; of these, 133 were accepted. Ninety percent of the students who were accepted for the seventh grade were enrolled; 93 percent of those accepted for the ninth grade were enrolled. Delbarton does not admit postgraduate students or students who are entering the twelfth grade.

APPLICATION TIMETABLE

The School welcomes inquiries at any time during the year. Students who apply are invited to spend a day at Delbarton attending classes with a school host. Interested applicants should arrange this day visit through the Admissions Office. Tours of the campus are generally given in conjunction with interviews, from 9 a.m. to noon on Saturdays in the fall, or by special arrangement. The formal application for admission must be accompanied by a nonrefundable fee of $70. Application fee waivers are available upon request. It is advisable to initiate the admissions process in the early fall. Acceptance notifications for applicants to grades 7 and 9 are made by February. Applicants to all remaining grades, as well as students placed in a waitpool, are given acceptance notification as late as June. Parents are expected to reply to acceptances two to three weeks after notification. A refundable deposit is also required. Application for financial aid should be made as early as possible; the committee hopes to notify financial aid applicants by the middle of March.

ADMISSIONS CORRESPONDENCE

Dr. David Donovan
Dean of Admissions
Delbarton School
Morristown, New Jersey 07960

Phone: 973-538-3231 Ext. 3019
Fax: 973-538-8836
E-mail: admissions@delbarton.org
Web site: http://www.delbarton.org/admissions

THE DELPHIAN SCHOOL™

Sheridan, Oregon

Type: Coeducational, boarding and day, college-preparatory school
Grades: K–12
Enrollment: School total: 249; Upper School: 184
Head of School: Rosemary Didear, Headmistress

THE SCHOOL

The Delphian School is the founding school and only boarding/day school in a network of nine Delphi Schools around the country. It employs an educational philosophy that has been acknowledged by parents and educators as a breakthrough in its innovation and workability. It uses the innovative study methods developed more than forty years ago by L. Ron Hubbard, the renowned American author and educator. This study methodology gives students the tools to attain high academic and ethical standards and the ability to achieve them independently. Parents and students often acknowledge these methods as the source of the program's effectiveness and the enthusiasm for learning that develops throughout the program.

A student's progress through the curriculum is not time oriented but is based on that student's ability to demonstrate competence and application. Students operate within a disciplined, fast-paced educational structure that allows them to progress independently in a personalized program that addresses their individual strengths, weaknesses, and interests. Practical application and challenging projects are stressed. A variety of laboratories, apprenticeships, and field trips ensure that students connect their education to real life.

Delphi's logo focuses on knowledge, ethics, leadership, and integrity. The School cultivates the concept that students should take increasing responsibility for their studies, their school, their environment, and their fellow man. At some point, all students participate in activities that develop these abilities. In addition, all students have responsibilities that help maintain the operation of the School and help create the standards of the School.

A charitable nonprofit institution, the School is governed by a self-perpetuating Board of Directors. Delphi is nonsectarian and welcomes students of all religions; students can attend services at nearby churches. A school magazine, *The Delphian*, is sent to parents, alumni, and friends of the School. The Delphian School is a member of the Oregon Federation of Independent Schools, is registered with the Oregon Department of Education as a private school, and is a candidate member of the Pacific Northwest Association of Independent Schools. The Delphian School is authorized under Federal law to enroll nonimmigrant alien students.

The Delphian School is licensed to use *Applied Scholastics* educational services.

ACADEMIC PROGRAM

The curriculum is divided into eight forms that span primary, elementary, middle, and high school levels. Each form has both academic and practical requirements. Weak areas that surface on quizzes or tests are restudied to full understanding. Evaluations and examinations are carried out continually to make sure that qualifications for promotion are met. Students do not receive letter grades, but reports are sent to parents three times per year, with frequent coordination occurring among faculty members, students, and parents. To ensure true academic competence, Delphi devotes a major portion of its curriculum to strengthening basics: math, reading, and writing. All students demonstrate the mastery of these fundamentals before moving on to advanced subjects. This foundation makes possible the high level of literacy and numeracy necessitated by Delphi's graduation requirements.

Several educational formats are used to achieve the academic and personal growth expected in students. Individualized courses, seminars, apprenticeships, practicals, research, and other vehicles are used to achieve graduation requirements. Advanced work is available in most disciplines. Most college-preparatory work, however, is achieved through accomplishing the School's standard high school requirements, which are rigorous.

FACULTY AND ADVISERS

There are 95 staff members at Delphi, including 54 full- and part-time teachers and 41 additional staff members who instruct, provide dorm supervision, coach, and generally advise students outside of the classroom in the afternoons and evenings. In addition to their academic degrees, all faculty members have been trained in the study methods of L. Ron Hubbard and have a broad range of practical and professional experience. All faculty and staff members have been chosen to work closely with students, and most live on campus with their families.

COLLEGE PLACEMENT

The Delphian School helps students find and apply to colleges to enable them to accomplish their life and career goals. The college-counseling process begins in the sophomore

year in coordination with the parents. The School has a career center, which is fully stocked with catalogs, pamphlets and computers for researching careers and colleges. PSAT, SAT, and ACT preparation is available as well as assistance in obtaining financial aid. Delphi graduates have gained acceptance to a variety of distinguished colleges and universities, such as Berkeley, Georgetown, Harvey Mudd, MIT, NYU, Ohio State (Honors College), Oregon State, Pepperdine, Stanford, and the Universities of Chicago, Michigan, and Southern California. Interested students may contact the School or visit Delphian's Web site for a complete list of these colleges and universities.

STUDENT BODY AND CONDUCT

The student body is quite diverse; currently enrolled students come from twenty-two states and ten other countries.

The School assumes that students enroll at Delphi with aims of achieving scholastic competence and receiving strong college or career preparation. The School, therefore, expects a high level of integrity, purpose, responsibility, and initiative from its students. The student rules are a guide to proper conduct; serious infractions may result in suspension or dismissal.

The Student Council works with the faculty and students to establish and maintain the ethical agreements that govern the community.

ACADEMIC FACILITIES

Most facilities are located in the 110,000-square-foot main building. The structure houses dormitories, classrooms, a chemistry and biology laboratory, a theater, a 10,000-volume library, music practice rooms, a career center—which is a facility for helping students select and apply to colleges and universities—a woodshop, an audiovisual lab, a computer lab, and art, ceramics, and photography studios.

BOARDING AND GENERAL FACILITIES

The dining room overlooks the oak and fir forest to the north. A dormitory with a panoramic view of the Willamette Valley houses 30 students. There are also student lounges, a recreation room, a Laundromat, a snack bar, and a bookstore. Campus housing for faculty and staff members is close by and is also located in the main building. A Medical Liaison provides liaison for students to

health-care practitioners in the area; emergency services are available in neighboring towns.

ATHLETICS

Varsity sports for boys are baseball, basketball, soccer, and tennis; girls compete in basketball, softball, and volleyball. All of these sports are also played intramurally. Noncompetitive sports include skiing, hiking, biking, snowboarding, and tennis with lighted courts. A gymnasium houses a weight-lifting and gymnastics room as well as facilities for basketball, volleyball, and racquetball.

EXTRACURRICULAR OPPORTUNITIES

The student recreation room is an informal meeting place for students in the evenings and on weekends. There are regularly scheduled dances and parties. Other weekend activities include trips to Portland and Salem for shopping, movies, concerts, sports, and cultural events as well as trips to ocean beaches, to Ashland for the Shakespearean Festival, to the Cascade Range for hiking, and to Mount Hood for skiing and snowboarding.

Traditional annual events include the Alumni Weekend, All-School Halloween Festival, Winter Bazaar and Music Festival, Sweetheart's Ball, Spring Bazaar and Music Festival, Parents' Weekend, the prom, and Commencement.

DAILY LIFE

The regular school day for Upper School students is divided into three parts. From 8:30 a.m. to 3 p.m., there is classroom work with various practical projects and seminars that cover such areas as foreign language, advanced math, science, literature, history, and current events as well as English as a second language (ESL) for international students. From 3:25 to 6 p.m., students participate in afternoon activities, including physical education, music, ceramics, computers, photography, team practice, and art. Middle

School students have similar schedules. Classroom work is from 8:30 a.m. to 1:50 p.m. Afternoon activities are from 2:10 to 5:10. The remainder of the day is spent with student activities, free time, helping with various responsibilities on campus, study hall, and activities.

WEEKEND LIFE

The Student Council in the Upper School organizes weekend activities and other special events under faculty guidance. Students publish a yearbook, and there are clubs for students with such interests as music, skiing, singing, drama, archery, dancing, chess, and computers. All students age 9 and older spend 1 hour each day in the Student Service program, helping in such places as the library, the computer center, the Lower School, or building maintenance. Special community service projects are organized at least twice a year, wherein students in the Middle and Upper Schools contribute to their community by such things as helping in the cleanup of beaches, parks, and business areas.

SUMMER PROGRAMS

Summer at Delphi is a program of four to six weeks that offers challenging study and recreational opportunities for some 260–300 students from all over the world. Students pursue advanced work, strengthen weak areas, or take part in the extensive ESL program. There is also a computer study program for beginning, intermediate, and advanced students.

The first thing a student learns at Delphi is how to study. Thus prepared, students have access to a curriculum of more than 250 courses. Students are in class in the mornings, participate in a wide range of outdoor sports and activities in the afternoons, and attend seminars and workshops or supervised study hall in the evenings. Overnight camping and river rafting trips are some of the activities planned for the weekends.

Students age 8 and older may enroll in the boarding program. More information is available from the Admissions Office.

COSTS AND FINANCIAL AID

The Delphian School offers many different programs (day school, seven-day boarding, five-day boarding, English as a second language, and summer boarding and day programs); each has its own price structure. Interested families should call the Admissions Office to request a price sheet. Tuition payment plans and financial aid are available.

ADMISSIONS INFORMATION

Students are admitted to the School on the basis of their previous academic records, results of any available standardized testing, and personal interviews. The Delphian School does not discriminate on the basis of race, religion, or national or ethnic background. Boarders must be at least 8 years of age.

APPLICATION TIMETABLE

Although most students enroll in September, the highly individualized nature of the Delphi program allows qualified students to enroll at other times during the school year, space permitting. Priority is given to those eligible students first completing the full application procedure. Tuition, room, and board are pro-rated according to the date of enrollment.

ADMISSIONS CORRESPONDENCE

Donetta Phelps, Director of Admissions
The Delphian School, Dept. P
20950 Southwest Rock Creek Road
Sheridan, Oregon 97378
Phone: 800-626-6610 (toll-free)
       503-843-3521 (outside the U.S.)
Fax: 503-843-4158
E-mail: info@delphian.org
Web site: http://www.delphian.org
      http://www.summeratdelphi.org
      http://www.eslatdelphi.org

DETROIT COUNTRY DAY SCHOOL

Beverly Hills, Michigan

Type: Coeducational day and limited boarding college-preparatory school
Grades: PK–12: Lower School, Prekindergarten–2; Junior School, 3–5; Middle School, 6–8; Upper School, 9–12
Enrollment: School total: 1,534; Upper School: 627
Head of School: Gerald T. Hansen, Headmaster

THE SCHOOL

Detroit Country Day School, founded in downtown Detroit by F. Alden Shaw in 1914, is located 14 miles north of Detroit in suburban Beverly Hills. The School has preserved its original name because it serves more than fifty areas of greater Detroit.

Originally a school for boys, Country Day became fully coeducational in 1972 and today operates four schools on four campuses, each with its own age-appropriate programs. Located within 3 miles of each other, the Upper School (grades 9–12), Middle School (grades 6–8), Junior School (grades 3–5), and Lower School (prekindergarten–grade 2) together cover an area of approximately 100 acres.

Detroit Country Day School, an independent college-preparatory school, believes in the education of the whole person—mind, body, personality, and character—so that its students can be knowledgeable and healthy, socially aware and ethical, and creative, productive, and fulfilled members of society. This philosophy is realized through the total commitment of faculty and students to the broad School program covering academics, athletics, the arts, activities, and guidance. The School further believes that this total involvement leads to the realization of individual potential by developing the abilities of each student and cultivating an increased awareness of community responsibility.

Country Day is governed by a Board of Trustees and had an operating budget for 2004–05 of $32 million. In 2004–05, Annual Giving raised $885,472.

Country Day is accredited by the Independent Schools Association of the Central States. The School is approved by the Michigan Department of Education and is a member of the National Association of Independent Schools and the Educational Records Bureau.

ACADEMIC PROGRAMS

Introduction to the Country Day philosophy begins in the Lower and Junior Schools, which foster early academic development and values through a broad-based, integrated, stimulating curriculum that includes basic instruction in language arts, math, social studies, science, French, the arts, movement education, and computer science. In Middle School, the academic program increases thinking skills through interdisciplinary activities; honors classes; and a unique, three-year approach to scientific inquiry and methods that link studies to social issues and critical thinking. A Middler is well prepared to meet the challenge of Upper School. However, many motivated students who have enrolled later have also enjoyed success at Country Day.

A program of "anywhere, anytime" learning requires all Middle and Upper School students to have laptop computers to facilitate course work,

research, and communication. A network of some 1,200 notebook computers links students, teachers, and parents.

To graduate, students must satisfy requirements in three categories: academic, athletic, and activities. Academic credit requirements are English (4), foreign language (3), history (3), mathematics (3), science (2), the fine and performing arts (1), and completion of the following required courses: Speech and Health Education. The additional requirements include sports and fitness activities and skill-oriented and service-oriented activities.

Honors courses are available at all levels. Qualified students may enroll in Advanced Placement and college-level courses as well as the International Baccalaureate program. Graduates of this rigorous, two-year liberal arts curriculum are eligible for admission at universities throughout the world or for advanced standing in most American universities and colleges.

The grading system is numerical, extending from 50 to 100. More than 60 percent of the students achieve honor-roll status, which requires a grade average of at least 80. Semesters are divided into two 8-week goals, and grades with comments are submitted by each teacher. Two-hour exams are taken at the end of each semester. The Upper School faculty reviews the progress of each student after each goal.

An Upper School student at Country Day averages about 3 hours of daily homework. Therefore, supervised study halls, especially in the freshman and sophomore years, are part of the school day. Special tutorials are always available. The student-teacher ratio is 9:1, and the average Upper School class size is 15.

An important extension of the classroom lies in participation in local, state, and national contests. Country Day students have received numerous awards in all major fields. Students attend theatrical productions on a regular basis, conduct a biannual symposium, and benefit from meeting leaders of the community in assemblies. Most seniors spend their last four weeks at Country Day working on location with a professional in a career of their choice.

FACULTY AND ADVISERS

Of the more than 190 teachers employed at Detroit Country Day School, 72 teach in the Upper School (39 men and 33 women); of these, 61 have earned master's degrees, and 14 have doctorates. In addition to conducting classroom activities, the teachers also serve as athletics coaches and directors of activities.

There have been four Headmasters in Country Day's ninety-year history: F. Alden Shaw (1914–61), W. Rodman Snelling (1961–67), Richard A. Schlegel (1967–86), and the present Headmaster, Gerald T. Hansen. Mr. Hansen joined the DCDS faculty in 1966 and has served

as math department chairman, Director of Studies, and Assistant Headmaster. He holds a B.A. from Northern Michigan University and an M.A. from Rutgers, The State University of New Jersey.

A vital part of Country Day is the adviser-advisee system. Each teacher meets with approximately 10 advisees each week to discuss academic progress, activities, and personal concerns. In addition, the adviser serves as the primary contact with the advisee's parents.

COLLEGE PLACEMENT

There are 3 full-time college counselors and a full-time assistant who serve student and family needs regarding college guidance and placement. Throughout Upper School, evening programs and in-school workshops introduce students to college preparation, college choices, and opportunities. In the junior year, students meet individually with their college counselor, who continues to work closely with them throughout the junior and senior years. The College Counseling Office offers an extensive collection of college literature and college resource publications. A bank of personal computers is loaded with the latest college guidance and scholarship software and exclusive Internet program access. Representatives from more than 150 colleges visit the campus each year.

All of the 155 graduates of the class of 2005 were accepted by four-year colleges and universities.

STUDENT BODY AND CONDUCT

The Upper School enrollment consists of 145 students in grade 9 (71 girls and 74 boys), 185 students in grade 10 (92 girls and 93 boys), 153 students in grade 11 (67 girls and 86 boys), and 144 students in grade 12 (69 girls and 75 boys). Eight other countries are represented in the student body. Three percent of the students are international; 97 percent come from more than fifty local areas. The student body represents a broad spectrum of ethnic origins, religions, parental occupations, and economic backgrounds.

School discipline rests primarily with the faculty, although the Student Council and Class Boards are very active in the School's life and are used as sounding boards for school policies. An elected Disciplinary Review Board reviews disciplinary decisions and is free to make recommendations to the administration. Country Day maintains a dress code. Juniors and seniors have their own Commons Room; seniors enjoy certain additional privileges that are much envied by underclass students.

ACADEMIC FACILITIES

The main building houses forty-two Upper School classrooms, a science wing with eight labs

and six classrooms, a language lab, two computer rooms, two music and four art studios, and a library containing 13,000 volumes and periodicals. The Seligman Family Performing Arts Center includes a 700-seat auditorium, instrumental and choral practice areas, dressing rooms, and a set shop.

BOARDING AND GENERAL FACILITIES
Four family homes on the Main Campus have enabled Country Day to offer a limited cottage boarding program with a capacity of 19 students. Boarders live in a family-style atmosphere with a faculty family. Single and double rooms are available.

ATHLETICS
Country Day's athletics facilities include a football stadium, a baseball stadium, a Tartan track, four gyms, a strength and conditioning room, ten tennis courts, and numerous practice fields. A local hockey rink, ski slope, swimming pool, and golf course supplement the on-campus facilities.

The sports program consists of thirty interscholastic sports. All students must participate in sports for two seasons; many elect to play all three seasons. All members of a team are given the opportunity to play in games.

Country Day, an independent Class B School, often competes against local Class A schools and prep schools in Ohio, Indiana, Pennsylvania, and Ontario. Country Day teams are known to be very successful.

Programs of cheerleading and strength and conditioning supplement the physical education curriculum.

EXTRACURRICULAR OPPORTUNITIES
An activity period is part of the school day, and there are some thirty-eight clubs and projects. Among these are a prize-winning newspaper and yearbook, a literary club, performing vocal and instrumental groups, and science, history, computer, language, art, debating, photography, drama, environmental, and service clubs. Each student is awarded points for participating in these clubs and must earn a minimum number to graduate. The activities and sports a student has participated in are all mentioned in the student's letter of recommendation to colleges. In addition, a student may receive points for involvement in service activities in his or her community.

Social events and a junior-senior prom are planned by social representatives of the Student Council or individual classes. Class overnights, concerts, plays, musicals, open houses, family gatherings, and sport excursions are also an important part of the social program.

DAILY LIFE
The academic day, from 8 a.m. to 3:20 p.m., is divided into seven blocks that rotate on a seven-day schedule. It is followed by a 2½-hour period set aside for activities, athletics, and tutorials. All students attend the noon meal except seniors and juniors with sign-out privileges. The School maintains a nurturing environment through close faculty-student, coach-athlete, and adviser-advisee relationships.

WEEKEND LIFE
Weekend boarding activities are arranged by faculty parents of the cottage boarding program.

SUMMER PROGRAMS
An extensive summer program is offered for children ages 3 to 18. Upper School students are offered tutorial and enrichment classes in reading, writing, and various levels of math and science. Courses in study skills, art, and computer programming are featured, as well as an Advanced Science & Mathematics Academy. Courses vary in length from two to five weeks and are conducted in the morning. Sports camps in basketball, baseball, soccer, lacrosse, field hockey, wrestling, and tennis are scheduled throughout the summer. For additional information, parents should contact the Academic or Athletic Offices.

COSTS AND FINANCIAL AID
Upper School tuition for 2004–05 was $20,690; meals are included. Boarding cost was an additional $7500. A financial loan plan is available to parents. Full tuition is due on August 31.

Financial assistance is awarded to students whose need is determined by the Tuition Aid Data Services. Including the children of faculty members, 8.5 percent of the student body receive financial aid.

ADMISSIONS INFORMATION
Country Day seeks students who show evidence of ability, ambition, achievement, character, and discipline. The School has a policy of socioeconomic diversification and admits students of any race, color, religion, and national or ethnic origin.

Admission is highly competitive and is based on previous school records, entrance examinations, teacher recommendations, and a family interview. The entrance examinations, which are given by appointment only, consist of the Educational Records Bureau achievement tests, the Otis-Lennon test, and a writing sample.

APPLICATION TIMETABLE
The Admission Committee reviews the admission portfolio of all candidates and notifies the family of its decision. The application fee is $50.

ADMISSIONS CORRESPONDENCE
Jorge Dante Hernandez Prósperi, Director of Admission
Detroit Country Day School
22305 West Thirteen Mile Road
Beverly Hills, Michigan 48025-4435

Phone: 248-646-7717
Web site: http://www.dcds.edu

THE DOANE STUART SCHOOL

Albany, New York

Type: Coeducational, Interfaith, day college-preparatory school
Grades: N–12 (Lower School N–4, Middle School 5–8, Upper School 9–12)
Enrollment: 270 (110 Upper School, 160 Middle and Lower Schools)
Head of School: Richard D. Enemark, Ph.D., Headmaster

THE SCHOOL

The Doane Stuart School is a coeducational, nursery through grade 12 day school, welcoming students of all faiths to its historic, pastoral 80-acre campus in Albany, New York. As the nation's only successfully merged Protestant-Catholic school, Doane Stuart stands as an unique model for interfaith education in America. Founded in 1975, Doane Stuart was created from the merger of the Roman Catholic Kenwood Academy of the Sacred Heart (founded in 1852) and the Episcopal St. Agnes School (founded in 1870).

The mission of Doane Stuart is education. In a college-preparatory context, where the joy of discovery is valued, Doane Stuart emphasizes serious study, educates to social responsibility, and lays the foundation for a strong faith. With 270 students, N–12, Doane Stuart is small by intent and small by design, claiming a premier college-preparatory program and unique partnerships with many organizations in its home community and beyond—including Lagan College in Belfast (the first integrated school in Northern Ireland, welcoming both Protestant and Catholic students), the University at Albany (the region's largest university), the Albany College of Pharmacy (affording Doane Stuart students premedical and prepharmacological study and research), and the Albany Institute of History and Art.

Doane Stuart is a member in good standing of the National Association of Independent Schools (NAIS). It is governed by an independent Board of Trustees with 22 members, and has an annual operating budget of more than $3 million and an endowment of approximately $1 million. Doane Stuart is fully and successfully accredited by the New York State Association of Independent Schools and the Sacred Heart Commission on Goals. It is the only school in the nation to hold simultaneous membership in the National Network of Sacred Heart Schools and the National Association of Episcopal Schools.

ACADEMIC PROGRAMS

Doane Stuart has a student-teacher ratio of 7:1 and an average class size of 14. Doane Stuart's standard Upper School course of study includes 4 years of English, 3–4 years of math, 3–4 years of science, 4 years of history, 3–4 years of foreign language, 4 years of comparative religion, 4 years of physical education, three to four elective courses (which may include fine and performing arts classes), and 25 hours per year of community service. Doane Stuart students have regular access to and classes in newly renovated, state-of-the-art science laboratories and a learning technology center.

Any junior or senior who has completed a course for which there is an AP exam may take that examination to receive college credit for his or her high school work. Doane Stuart students may pursue independent study or take courses through the School's distinct partnership with the University at Albany for high school or college credit. Students also receive exceptional preparation for such standardized tests as the SAT and SAT Subject Tests.

Doane Stuart uses a standard 4.0 grading scale; honors are earned with an average of 3.25 or higher, and high honors are earned with an average of 3.7 or higher. Upper School students work within a quarterly structure each year, while Middle and Lower School students are graded on a trimester basis. Report cards are issued at the end of each grading period, with interim or midquarter reports (as applicable) issued between report cards.

Each Doane Stuart Upper School student is assigned an adult mentor who helps his or her assigned students to manage successfully the academic, social, and emotional rigors of the Upper School years.

FACULTY AND ADVISERS

Doane Stuart has 40 faculty members (16 men, 24 women); more than 60 percent have advanced degrees. Each Upper School faculty member serves as a mentor for 5–10 students and may also serve as an adviser or coach for clubs, activities, and athletic teams. Doane Stuart has a Campus Ministry Team comprised of faculty members from all three divisions, who coordinate interfaith chapel services and help facilitate community service opportunities. The School encourages and finances continuing professional development among its teachers, and has offered sabbaticals to senior faculty members.

Doane Stuart has been headed by Dr. Richard D. Enemark since 1998. Dr. Enemark received his A.B. from Colgate University (where he was elected to Phi Beta Kappa) in 1972, his M.A. from the University of Vermont in 1978, his M.Phil. from Columbia University in 1983, and his Ph.D. in English and comparative literature, with highest distinction, from Columbia in 1986. Beginning his teaching career in the 1970s at Burke Mountain Academy in Vermont (where he was Director of Studies and now serves on its Board of Trustees as Co-Chair of the Governance Committee), Dr. Enemark has served on the boards of other independent schools and agencies, including the Eaglebrook School in Deerfield, Massachusetts.

COLLEGE PLACEMENT

Doane Stuart's Director of Admission and College Counseling provides expert direction and oversight of the college placement process, which begins in earnest during the freshman year, although college awareness offerings are provided to students throughout their Middle School and Lower School years as well. Each Upper School student and his or her parents meet, one-on-one, with the Director for a minimum of two sessions before senior year. More than 50 college admissions officers visit the School annually, while Doane Stuart staff members take students on regular visits to colleges throughout the region and beyond.

Doane Stuart students have median SAT scores more than 20 percent higher than the national average. The School's students have been admitted to some of the most prestigious colleges and universities in the country. The 20 graduates of the class of 2005 were admitted to, among others: Columbia, Davidson, Haverford, Northwestern, NYU, Oberlin, Swarthmore, Tufts, USC, and Washington (St. Louis). All of Doane Stuart's students earn admission to college, most of them to the highly selective schools of their choice.

STUDENT BODY AND CONDUCT

Doane Stuart's Upper School has 110 students, while the Lower and Middle Schools combined have 160 students, split nearly 50:50 between boys and girls. Approximately 10 percent of the School's students are from minority communities, and another 2–5 percent each year are exchange students from international programs, including the School's unique exchange with Lagan College in Belfast, or other Sacred Heart schools in America. Doane Stuart students are primarily from the eight counties surrounding Albany, from as far south as the Berkshires to as far north as Saratoga Springs. Campus safety and

behavior policies are provided to students each year via School handbooks for each division.

ACADEMIC FACILITIES

Doane Stuart is among the largest independent school properties in northeastern New York, with 80 acres of forest, formal gardens, and playing fields. Doane Stuart's academic facilities include an historically significant nineteenth-century administrative and Upper School building, outlying structures designed by A. J. Davis, an architecturally significant Gothic-Revival chapel, a newly dedicated outdoor chapel and classroom, and a main academic building built in 1966, housing classrooms, laboratories, a Lower School library, and an Upper School learning technology center.

ATHLETICS

Doane Stuart's Upper School teams compete in the Central Hudson Valley League. Doane Stuart encourages all of its students to participate in the School's athletic programs, which include basketball, cross-country, soccer, and track and field in the Middle School and basketball, cross-country, fencing, soccer, softball, tennis, and track and field in the Upper School. Doane Stuart's campus includes an acclaimed cross-country course, outdoor tennis and basketball courts, two soccer fields, a softball field, two indoor gym facilities, a swimming pool, and two new, state-of-the-art playgrounds.

EXTRACURRICULAR OPPORTUNITIES

Every Doane Stuart Middle and Upper School student participates in one or more of the School's extracurricular offerings. Programs include varsity and junior varsity athletics, drama and theater productions, community service beyond required levels (25 hours per year), the School magazine, the School newspaper, photography club, outdoor club, student government, National Honor Society, Cum Laude Society, and independent study or internships at one of Doane Stuart's exclusive partner organizations.

DAILY LIFE

A typical day consists of seven 45-minute class periods, a 50-minute lunch and activities period, and a 15-minute morning meeting period, which is used for division gatherings, all-School meetings, or chapels. School begins at 8:20 a.m. and ends at 3:20 p.m., Monday through Thursday, and 2:35 p.m. on Friday, when extracurricular activities begin. Before- and after-school programs are available for Lower and Middle School students.

COSTS AND FINANCIAL AID

For the 2005–06 school year, tuition ranged from $10,000 in nursery to $16,800 in grade 12. Extra charges include lab fees, field trips, music lessons, lunch, books (if not available from within parents' home school districts), and special tutoring. Doane Stuart offers a generous financial aid program for qualified students whose families have demonstrated financial need; more than 35 percent of Doane Stuart students received some form of financial aid in 2005–06. Financing and payment plans are available.

ADMISSIONS INFORMATION

Admission to Doane Stuart is selective. The School seeks and welcomes talented students from all backgrounds and from all faiths, expecting that new students will contribute to the School community as much as they benefit from it.

APPLICATION TIMETABLE

Due to the competitive nature of Doane Stuart's admission process, prospective families are encouraged to begin the application process in the fall before the year that their student enrolls in the School. The admission process includes tours, classroom visits, tests, letters of recommendation, transcripts, and screening reviews by the Admission Committee. Waiting lists are implemented as soon as class sizes reach expected levels.

ADMISSIONS CORRESPONDENCE

Eric G. Stahura, Director of Admission and
    College Counseling
The Doane Stuart School
799 South Pearl Street
Albany, New York 12202
Phone: 518-465-5222 Ext. 241
Fax: 518-465-5230
E-mail: admissions@doanestuart.org
Web site: http://www.doanestuart.org

DUBLIN SCHOOL

Dublin, New Hampshire

Type: Coeducational boarding and day college-preparatory school
Grades: 9–12
Enrollment: 130
Head of School: Christopher R. Horgan, Headmaster

THE SCHOOL

Dublin School was founded in 1935 by Paul and Nancy Lehmann, who sought to create an institution that would provide a demanding college-preparatory education tempered by a high degree of personal attention and a strong sense of community. Since its founding, Dublin has sought to help each student develop intellectually, physically, socially, and morally. To accomplish this, the School provides a rigorous academic program in which students gain self-confidence from success, are prepared for the demands of college, and learn the importance of teamwork. In addition to learning the responsibilities of academic independence, students receive a diverse experience that requires participation in community service, athletics, internships, and a school work program.

The School is located in southwestern New Hampshire, 1¾ hours from Boston and 4 hours from New York City. The village of Dublin, largely residential, has about 1,400 year-round residents. The Monadnock region is rich in artistic, cultural, and intellectual activities. Situated on 345 wooded acres, Dublin School's campus is conducive to a host of outdoor activities. Dublin Lake is within walking distance of campus and is available for canoeing, swimming, and sailing. Mount Monadnock, the second most frequently climbed mountain in the world, is accessible and explored often by Dublin students throughout the year.

The School is governed by a self-perpetuating Board of Trustees. Recent support has made it possible to construct Hoyt-Horner Dorm and 14,000-square-foot Whitney Gymnasium, which houses multipurpose facilities for Dublin's athletic program. In addition to a full-size basketball court and the Athletic Director's office, the building also houses a weight-training and conditioning room. The fully equipped Von Mertens Woodworking Shop was constructed by students and faculty members five years ago.

Dublin School is accredited by the New England Association of Schools and Colleges and approved by the state of New Hampshire Department of Education. It is a member of the National Association of Independent Schools, the Independent Schools Association of Northern New England, the National Association of College Admission Counselors, the Secondary School Admission Test Board, the Small Boarding Schools Association, and the Network of Complementary Schools.

ACADEMIC PROGRAMS

The School believes that the best preparation for a demanding college environment is exposure to a variety of subjects and disciplines. Students must take a minimum of 4 credits of English; 7 credits in the disciplines of mathematics and science; 6 credits in the disciplines of history and foreign languages (including at least 2 credits in one language); 2 credits in the arts; 1 credit in elective courses in English, mathematics, history, science, foreign languages, or the arts; and .3 credits in computer literacy. (Graduation requires 20.3 credits.) An Honors Diploma requires 8 credits in mathematics and science and 7 credits in history and

foreign language or 2 credits each in two different foreign languages, with a minimum of 3 credits in one language. In addition, a student seeking Honors designation must maintain a minimum GPA of 3.0 for the junior and senior years. Honors courses are weighted. Elective courses are offered in diverse areas, including marine science, American Sign Language, photography, and psychology. A senior exhibition of mastery is also available to interested students.

The teacher-student ratio is 1:5; classes average 5 to 12 students each. Dublin's classes permit a great deal of individualized instruction, which is one of the hallmarks of the School. Courses that are designed to prepare students for Advanced Placement exams are available in English, history, foreign languages, biology, and mathematics.

The academic program is enhanced by the Humanities Program, which is designed to involve the community in the exploration of contemporary issues. Artists, speakers, craftspersons, and professionals from all over the world come to the campus to share their talents and experience in this all-School activity. Themes, chosen by presenters, students, and faculty members each year, have included gender issues, storytelling, environmental awareness, and local history.

The Learning Skills Program is designed for students who are intellectually capable but who lack academic achievement. This program includes students with learning differences and those who are experiencing general academic difficulties related to a diagnosed learning disability. Students who struggle with specific areas, including reading, written expression, mathematics, or organizational skills, are typical candidates for this program. The Learning Skills Program is not an alternate curriculum; it is a structured support system for the student mainstreamed in Dublin School's curriculum.

Grades are mailed to parents during the middle, and at the end of the trimester, grades are accompanied by teacher comments and a letter from the adviser. Each student receives not only a letter grade but also an effort grade in each class. Parents may also elect for their child to be part of the Evening Study Assistance Program. This program places a small number of students in a structured academic environment under the guidance of one of the Learning Skills Program's instructors. The program allows students to meet academic challenges and complete nightly homework assignments on their own and to receive attention when they are not able to find solutions to academic questions.

FACULTY AND ADVISERS

The heart of Dublin School is its faculty members, who are deeply involved in student life and have invested in the success of each student. In addition to strong academic backgrounds, faculty members have a deep commitment to working with students and to helping them develop academically and personally. There are 31 full-time faculty members, 15 of whom hold advanced degrees. Faculty members are required to participate in ongoing professional development and are evaluated yearly by the Headmaster and the Academic Dean.

Christopher R. Horgan, appointed Headmaster in 1994, is a graduate of Bridgewater State College (B.A.) and Plymouth State College (M.Ed.). Formerly the Dean of Students and Assistant Head, Mr. Horgan teaches psychology at Dublin and is a Klingenstein Fellow at Columbia University. He has been at Dublin since 1988.

Faculty members and administrators coach athletic teams or advise special interest groups. Each faculty member and administrator also acts as an adviser to no more than 5 students, interacting with them on a daily basis. Fourteen faculty members and their families live on campus. Students also have access to a resident full-time nurse, an athletic trainer, counseling, and a learning skills specialist.

COLLEGE PLACEMENT

Dublin School's college guidance office is staffed by a full-time director who provides the information needed to help students evaluate their options and to guide through the college admission process.

During the junior year, students are given a College Assessment Form to complete and share with their parents. Students also attend a college fair and meet with college admission representatives. By the end of their junior year, students have taken their PSAT and SAT. Some juniors take their SAT Subject Tests as well. Counselors assist students and their parents in developing a list of appropriate colleges. Juniors are encouraged to begin visiting colleges of their choice during the March vacation and the summer of the junior year. Informal meetings with parents are held during the school year to discuss topics such as admissions, financial aid, and other aspects of the college admission process.

In their senior year, students have additional opportunities to take the SAT Subject Tests as well as Advanced Placement tests. Recent college choices include Bates, Bentley, Boston University, Bowdoin, Brandeis, Clarkson, Colby, Colgate, Cornell, Dartmouth, Dickinson, Evergreen, Goucher, Hamilton, Holy Cross, Ithaca, Mt. Holyoke, NYU, Pitzer, Smith, St. Lawrence, Skidmore, Stanford, Swarthmore, Tufts, Union, Wellesley, Wentworth, Wesleyan, Williams, and the Universities of California, Colorado, Illinois at Urbana-Champaign, Maine, Massachusetts, New Hampshire, Oregon, and Vermont. Dublin School students are accepted to their first-choice college 90 percent of the time.

STUDENT BODY AND CONDUCT

The student body is a remarkably heterogeneous group, coming from nine countries and seventeen states. Students come from both rural and inner-city environments. This diversity enriches the life of the School and ensures a community in which students of widely differing backgrounds and interests can feel at home. There are 82 boarding students (49 boys and 33 girls) and 48 day students (27 boys and 21 girls).

ACADEMIC FACILITIES

Classes at Dublin are held in a number of facilities around campus, including the School House, Sci-

ence Building, Arts Building, Art Studio, the Evans Library, or outside. Specialized facilities include three science labs, a computer technology center, language lab, recording studio, recital hall, theater, darkroom, the arts studio, and an audiovisual resource center. The Evans Library houses a 13,000-volume collection, provides electronic research capabilities, and is part of the interlibrary loan system of New Hampshire.

BOARDING AND GENERAL FACILITIES
There are six dormitories on campus. Most student rooms are doubles, and the dorms house 8–24 students. One or 2 faculty members and their families live in each dormitory. Each dorm also has a resident student proctor who assists with the dormitory's operation. One of the living facilities, Lehmann House, also houses the dining hall, the day student locker area, the school store, and the newly renovated student center.

ATHLETICS
Dublin's athletic program aims to instill in students a love of exercise and a commitment to good sportsmanship. Students are required to participate in the athletic program and play interscholastic sports.

The School recognizes that there are different ways of enjoying and experiencing achievement in athletics and offers a variety of competitive and recreational sports. Dublin competes interscholastically in soccer, basketball, cross-country, equestrian, lacrosse, sailing, skiing, snowboarding, and tennis. Recreational offerings include crew, sailing, tennis, and weightlifting.

In addition to the recently completed Whitney Gymnasium, the School has two large playing fields, a squash court, six tennis courts, a trainer's room, a fitness room, several kilometers of cross-country running and ski trails, and an outdoor skating facility. The sailing and crew programs are conducted on Dublin Lake.

EXTRACURRICULAR OPPORTUNITIES
Academics are just part of the overall program at Dublin School, and students are offered a wide variety of extracurricular options. These include "Dubliners," the School's choral group; dance; music lessons; the use of compact disc recording equipment; a jazz/rock band; and the option of being a part of two major theater productions each year. Other extracurricular options include student government, Amnesty International, Oxfam America, the yearbook, and student coffeehouses.

Dublin's proximity to Boston as well as other major cities presents students with a wide variety of cultural and entertainment opportunities. Recent student excursions have included trips to a renaissance fair, the historic towns of Salem and Plymouth, museums in Boston, the annual Scottish Highland Games, and Boston Cultural Day.

Students are also involved in a mandatory community service program. They teach dance at local preschool and afterschool programs; host a Halloween party for Dublin Elementary School children; clear trails at nearby state forests or on town land; serve as big brothers and sisters at Horse Power, a therapeutic riding program for young adolescents; and help staff charity booths at local fairs. Together, Dublin students donate more than 1,000 hours of community service to local charities/organizations during the school year.

DAILY LIFE
The student work program embodies the founders' belief in the importance of shared responsibilities. Student jobs include kitchen duty, cleaning buildings, emptying dormitory trash, sweeping hallways, and cleaning bathrooms. These jobs are assigned on a rotating basis and are supervised by proctors and faculty members. The academic day consists of seven periods and a daily school meeting, followed by athletics, dinner, and evening study hours from 8 to 10 p.m. Boarding students are expected to be in their dorms and day students off campus by 10 p.m.

WEEKEND LIFE
On Saturday morning, students and faculty members participate in Work Gang. Projects have included clearing trails, stacking wood, designing and planting gardens, major cleaning projects, and painting. Students also work off campus to earn credit for community service.

On Saturday afternoon, students participate in athletic competitions against other area independent schools, both on campus and away. Students who are not competing usually support friends on teams, work on class projects, relax, and spend time with friends.

Students have the chance to participate in a range of recreational offerings. Many make the most of the School's setting by enjoying Dublin Lake, climbing Mount Monadnock, and walking other area trails. There are also movies on and off campus and trips to local restaurants and shopping locations. Special events, such as an annual "all-night" shopping trip to L. L. Bean in Maine, excursions to Boston, hiking trips, museum trips, professional games, and concerts occur as well.

Three times each year, an entire weekend is devoted to family activities. Parents' Weekend in the fall provides an opportunity for parents to visit faculty members, each other, and their children's friends and to see athletic events and the results of student projects. In February, Dublin hosts Winterfest, a day of winter-related activities for students, siblings, parents, faculty members, and the local community. The third major weekend event of the year is Mayfair, an annual celebration of the arts and preparation for graduation. The online

auction held during this event is the Parents' Committee's major fund-raiser for scholarship funds.

COSTS AND FINANCIAL AID
In 2005–06, tuition, room, and board were $35,500; day students' expenses were $22,000. There are additional fees for the Learning Skills Program, the Evening Study Assistance Program, English as a Second Language, laboratory fees, some athletic offerings, and the ski/snowboarding program.

For the 2005–06 academic year, 28 percent of the student body received financial aid, with a total disbursement of $800,000. To apply for financial aid, families need to contact the School's Financial Aid Officer, fill out a Parent's Financial Aid Statement, and provide financial information to both the Financial Aid Officer and the School and Student Service for Financial Aid in Princeton, New Jersey.

ADMISSIONS INFORMATION
Dublin School seeks students who have the ability and motivation to excel in a challenging college-preparatory curriculum, who have strong character, who are enthusiastic about becoming a student at Dublin School, and who are willing to become involved in the life of the School and to work for the common good of all students. In evaluating each candidate for admission, the Admission Committee is guided by the applicant's transcript, application essay, interview, and teachers' recommendations. Applicants are encouraged to visit the campus for a tour and interview. Class visits can also be arranged and are hosted by a student tour guide.

APPLICATION TIMETABLE
Candidates for admission are encouraged to apply by January 31. Although applications are considered after that date, students who have completed the application process by January 31 are notified regarding their acceptance by March 10. They then have until April 10 to accept or decline the School's offer. The application fee is $50, due when the application is presented to the School. Candidates who apply after January 31 are notified as soon as a decision has been reached. The Admission Office is open from 8 a.m. to 4 p.m., Monday through Friday. Interviews are scheduled during regular school hours; if necessary, special arrangements can be made to schedule a tour and interview.

ADMISSIONS CORRESPONDENCE
Shiela Bogan, Director of Admission
Dublin School
18 Lehmann Way
P.O. Box 522
Dublin, New Hampshire 03444-0522

Phone: 603-563-8584 Ext. 233
Fax: 603-563-8671
E-mail: admission@dublinschool.org
Web site: http://www.dublinschool.org

THE DWIGHT SCHOOL
New York, New York

Type: Coeducational international college-preparatory day school
Grades: Nursery–12: Woodside Preschool, ages 2–5; Timothy House, K–4; Bentley House, 5–8; Franklin House, 9–10; Anglo House, 11–12
Enrollment: 430 (Preschool: 60)
Head of School: Stephen H. Spahn, Chancellor

THE SCHOOL

The Dwight School, founded in 1872, became the first school in the U.S. to offer the three International Baccalaureate (I.B.) programs, grades nursery–12. The School's motto is "every student has a spark of genius." The School's mission is to develop each student's unique capabilities. It seeks to integrate mind, body, and spirit. The program incorporates academic excellence and a commitment to educate a diverse student population in leadership and responsibility to others. The School's structured environment places emphasis on integrating the latest educational research into a traditional curriculum.

The Dwight spirit is communicated through weekly advisory meetings, Honor Council, peer leaders, house community programs, and monthly whole-school assemblies. Dwight students aim to become confident, self-motivated, disciplined, knowledgeable, and open-minded inquirers as well as caring, principled, and responsible citizens. Dwight cofounded the Institute for Civic Leadership in order to construct a school model for civic leadership, continuing the tradition of graduates Mayor Fiorello LaGuardia, Robert Moses, Walter Lippmann, Governor Herbert Lehman, and Secretary of the Treasury Henry Morganthau. Every student is immersed in a program of civic responsibility.

Dwight is accredited by the International Baccalaureate Organization, the Council of International Schools, and the Middle States Association of Schools and Colleges. Graduating students enter leading universities in the United States and abroad.

ACADEMIC PROGRAMS

The school year of thirty-eight weeks lasts from September to June. Dwight utilizes a trimester system. Grades are sent to parents three times a year, and scheduled conferences between parents and teachers are held two times per year. All students in grades 5 through 11 meet in small weekly advisory groups. These complement house meetings.

The Dwight School's student-teacher ratio of 7:1 allows for small classes.

The School is organized into four houses, each with a Dean, and a brand new nursery school, Woodside Preschool for children ages 2–5. Woodside Preschool focuses on the development of the whole child. Through structured inquiry and play, children are challenged to think, learn, and discover in a caring and nurturing environment. Spanish, music, and art are taught by specialist teachers. Timothy House (K–4) became the first I.B. Primary Years Program in the U.S. in 1998. Students master traditional math, reading, and writing skills and are immersed in 6 units of inquiry in geography, humanities, and science. All students study beginning or advanced French, as well as Chinese. Small classes allow each child to reach his or her full intellectual, physical, and social potential. More than fifteen after-school offerings extend the normal drama, music, art, foreign language, technology, and sports programs.

Problem solving utilizes multiple approaches and solutions. The faculty members strive to awaken the sense of wonder that makes learning significant and lifelong.

The Primary Years Program transitions into the I.B. Middle Years offerings at Bentley House (grades 5–8). All students study the major academic disciplines, and they also learn technology, environmental studies, civics, community activities, and health and social education across all academic disciplines. After school, there are teams, clubs, and activities that extend a student's passion. Trips to England, France, Peru, Kenya, Mexico, India, and China are another aspect of the Dwight international experience. Students are offered a highly structured curriculum with challenging interdisciplinary units. A comprehensive study skills program is integrated into all course work. Emphasis is placed on the study of grammar and composition. Essay writing is required across the curriculum. By sixth and seventh grades, students are introduced to departmentalization.

The Upper School presents a classical core of academic subjects that incorporate community service, social education, goal setting, environmental awareness, and a knowledge of human achievement and potential. In the junior year, students enroll in the International Baccalaureate Diploma Program. The I.B. Diploma can give up to one year's credit at U.S. colleges and is an acceptable entrance standard for major international universities. Students may choose to take individual I.B. courses instead of the full program and thus earn advanced-placement credit.

Franklin House (grades 9 and 10) and Anglo House (grades 11 and 12) place special emphasis on the I.B. Diploma Program. All students in grade 10 work on a personal project, of their selection, under the steady hand of an adviser. All students study I.B. subjects with the expectation that many will complete the full Baccalaureate by grade 12. Rich course offerings from theater, art, and music extend to unique programs in design technology, environmental studies, and microeconomics and business management.

All educational programs help students to reach world-class standards. The Enrichment Work Program is offered to grades K–12 in order to go beyond the standard curriculum. Students may read additional books, study art history, and be introduced to advanced studies of science and mathematics.

Mother Tongue Instruction is available to students to maintain mastery of their native language. Students study Arabic, Chinese, Dutch, French, German, Hebrew, Hindi, Italian, Japanese, Russian, and Spanish. English as a second language (ESL) is provided for students who have not achieved the necessary level of competency in English. The ESL director offers a June and August intense immersion program that helps students integrate into Dwight life. During the academic year, the director runs an international club that provides special support for international students.

The Quest Department provides a limited number of individualized mentoring programs for stu-

dents of high academic ability. These students need to enhance their skills in one particular academic discipline in order to succeed in a rigorous academic setting. Quest students operate in the traditional class setting and execute a full academic program. Quest mentors observe students in classes and consult with their teachers on an ongoing basis. There is frequent communication with parents.

A student exchange program exists with Woodside Park International School in London. The Dwight School also enjoys a rich tradition of athletic excellence. In recent years, the School has won national championships in fencing and local or state championships in basketball, track, tennis, and cross-country.

FACULTY AND ADVISERS

Stephen H. Spahn became the Headmaster in 1967 and Chancellor in 1993. Mr. Spahn received a B.A. from Dartmouth (1963) and the equivalent of an M.A. from Oxford, and he finished course work for a Ph.D. at Columbia. He was an all-American basketball player, an International Fellow, a member of Phi Beta Kappa, a Senior Fellow, and a Woodrow Wilson Fellow. He has served as Project Officer with the Special Fund of the United Nations and helped to conduct the first health survey of Nepal. Currently, he is a trustee of the Institute for Civic Leadership, the International Baccalaureate Fund, and the Rubin Museum of Himalayan Art.

The head of the high school, Arthur Samuels, is responsible for the administrative functions of the school and for maintaining a high standard of decorum.

The Dean of Student Life, Evan Flamenbaum, is responsible for the health and well-being of every student. He chairs a team of professionals who work with families and students in order to navigate the passage to adulthood. The team is comprised of the school nurse, a certified guidance counselor, and an experienced psychologist. He runs a study-skills program for new students in June to allow for a smooth transition into Dwight.

A highly talented faculty reflects and models the qualities of leadership, scholarship, character, and service. All participate in mentoring and professional development programs.

The School is organized into six departments under the educational leadership of Anthony Foster, who has been a member of the Dwight faculty for more than twenty years. As Assistant Headmaster, Mr. Foster has created a balance of classical and innovative curricula. Master teachers are always available to discuss individual programs and concerns.

COLLEGE PLACEMENT

Dwight has a comprehensive College Guidance Program under the Directors of College Guidance, Mrs. Susheila Mani and Mrs. Ryna Bab. The program involves parents, students, college admissions officers, and financial aid consultants. Dwight's success in placing students in colleges demonstrates the effectiveness of the program.

The first phase begins with ninth-, tenth-, and eleventh-grade meetings. The guidance team intro-

duces parents and students to the college process—the options, the requirements, and the many considerations involved in selecting the best school for each child.

In the junior year, the team meets with each student to help select courses, to schedule and prepare for college testing, and to discuss individual talents and concerns. A college priority list is then personally tailored to fit each student's needs.

In the senior year, students meet with college representatives who visit Dwight to discuss the academic offerings of their schools and to answer student questions. Dialogue continues with parents, students, and admissions officers until the process is complete.

For the past two years scores on the verbal and math portions of the SAT have ranged from 500 to 800, and SAT Subject Test (formerly Achievement Test) scores have ranged from 520 to 800.

Dwight graduates attend Barnard, Bowdoin, Brown, Carnegie Mellon, Colgate, Columbia, Cornell, Dartmouth, Duke, Emory, Georgetown, Harvard, Lehigh, Middlebury, Mount Holyoke, Northwestern, NYU, Oberlin, Princeton, Skidmore, Smith, Stanford, Syracuse, Tufts, Tulane, Vassar, Wellesley, Yale, and the Universities of California, Michigan, Pennsylvania, Vermont, Virginia, and Wisconsin. Students have also recently attended Hebrew University, McGill, Oxford, Queen's University, St. Andrews, the Sorbonne, and the Universities of Brussels, Edinburgh, London, Milan, and Rome.

STUDENT BODY AND CONDUCT
The enrollment at the Dwight School is 60 in the preschool, 200 in grades K–8 and 220 in grades 9–12. Two thirds of the students are from New York City.

ACADEMIC FACILITIES
The Dwight School occupies three buildings—a five-story structure built in 1912, a brownstone converted for School use in 1968 and enlarged in 1983, and a new space added in 1993 for additional classrooms and offices. In 2001, the School completed its modernization and expansion. Together, the buildings provide thirty-four classrooms, three new science laboratories with the most modern equipment, a 17,000-volume library, two computer centers, a theater, two art rooms, and two gyms. The Lower School was also newly refurbished. Woodside Preschool is situated in brand new, state-of-the-art facilities. The campus consists of eight bright classrooms, an indoor gym, and a playroom. Each class is equipped with a computer and library area. For outdoor play, children enjoy a playground a few feet away in Riverside Park.

ATHLETICS
The importance of a sound body to complement a sound mind is integral to The Dwight School's philosophy. Athletes are introduced to the best techniques of physical and mental development produced both in the East and West.

The Dwight School has a history of outstanding scholar-athletes. The Dwight School has had national championships in fencing and tennis. State championships have been won in boys' and girls' basketball. Other teams include baseball, cross-country, softball, soccer, squash, and track. Dwight has a former world and Olympic judo champion who develops individualized training programs that allow students to reach their full potential.

EXTRACURRICULAR OPPORTUNITIES
The music program includes a chorus, jazz ensemble, classical string group, and a select choir (by audition). Students are active in the Interschool Orchestra. Twelve performances for the Middle and Upper schools are held annually. The drama program has among its four productions a musical. The dance team completed a third successful year. Students in all grades participate in annual art festivals. The most recent addition to the arts program is an IB film competition on the theme Conflict Resolution—Let's Talk. An active Parents' Association runs numerous events, including a gala benefit. The student government and honor council provide students with firsthand experience in the democratic process by giving them a formal voice in School affairs.

The Dwight School believes that student awareness of and participation in the surrounding community is essential. The Community Action Service (CAS) program is incorporated into the curriculum, with independent work required of all students. CAS has established relationships with a wide variety of community organizations. This program helps run a soup kitchen for the homeless, provides toys for hospitalized children, and organizes parties at local hospitals. The Dwight Environmental Action Committee is active in School and community issues. The yearbook provides a visual commentary. The Model United Nations Association sends students to university-run General Assembly competitions. The mock trial team is consistently among the best in the region. Recently the school won the Hagoort Award, given to a school whose community service project was deemed best in this hemisphere by the International Baccalaureate North American Office.

Dwight is a cofounder of the Institute for Civic Leadership, a nonprofit organization dedicated to training future leaders for public service. Student leaders are helping to organize conferences at the American Museum of Natural history and the United Nations. The institute seeks to be a model for other schools. A strong peer leaders program is the foundation stone of the program.

Numerous publications are produced at all grade levels. The School believes in the concept of writing for publications as a necessary part of every student's education. The Outward Bound Program organizes downhill skiing and snowboarding trips. The School sponsors trips to England, France, Peru, Mexico, India, Kenya, and China, which provides students with an opportunity to experience another culture for an extended period of time. The Contemporary Arts Society offers trips to New York City's museums, theaters, and other places of interest.

The Junior Passport program at the preschool offers a wide range of extracurricular activities for students ages 3 to 5—including music, art, drama, sports, and language immersion. In addition, the Woodside Clubhouse provides an extended day program and more informal after-school activities. The Passport Program offers students in grades K–4 a rich developmental sports program in tennis, swimming, soccer, gymnastics, basketball, and fencing. The Middle School Ambassadors Program, for grades 5–8, has an early-morning training program and intramural competition. After school, students participate in fencing, track, cross-country, volleyball, soccer, basketball, student council, art, music, choir, and drama. The Dean of the Middle School, a former Ivy League basketball and soccer player, oversees each student's pastoral care.

The School has two gymnasiums and utilizes ten local athletic facilities.

DAILY LIFE
The academic schedule, from 8 to 3, includes eight 45-minute class periods. After classes, students remain for extracurricular activities, library work, conferences with faculty members, supervised study, sports, and advanced seminars. Grades K–4 are offered an extensive after school program, including swimming, karate, music, in-line skating, art, fencing, and tennis.

The school year, from early September to June, is divided into three terms and includes an orientation period, a Thanksgiving recess, winter and spring vacations, a midwinter holiday, and several long weekends.

COSTS AND FINANCIAL AID
The 2005–06 tuition ranged from $25,000 to $26,850 plus fees for books and activities. Financial aid is granted on the basis of need and academic promise. A separate charge is made for Quest. The Dwight School Foundation provides scholarships to students with financial need.

ADMISSIONS INFORMATION
The Dwight School seeks to enroll students who are interested in and can benefit from a classical and challenging academic program. New sections have been added in kindergarten and sixth, seventh, and ninth grades. Applicants must take an Educational Records Bureau admissions test (http://www.erbtest.org), submit a transcript from the previous school, and have a personal interview. Other arrangements may be made for students residing in other parts of the country and abroad. A letter of recommendation from a person who knows the student well may be included to supplement the file. This should be sent directly to the Department of Admissions.

The Dwight School is able to issue I-20 immigration forms for international applicants. Students residing abroad who cannot visit the School for an interview must send the following materials along with the application: an official school transcript, a sample of writing in English, a teacher recommendation, and standardized test results. International applicants can arrange a videoconference interview.

APPLICATION TIMETABLE
Students are notified after all admissions information has been received by the School.

ADMISSIONS CORRESPONDENCE
Zoe Hillman
Director of Admissions, Nursery–PreK
Woodside Preschool
140 Riverside Boulevard
New York, New York 10069
Phone: 212-362-2350

Gina Lipton
Director of Admissions, Grades K–6
Marina Bernstein
Director of Admissions, Grades 7–12
The Dwight School
291 Central Park West
New York, New York 10024
Phone: 212-724-2146 Ext. 206 (K–6)
    or Ext. 204 (7–12)

For a brochure and application:
Samantha Allen, Associate Director of Admissions
The Dwight School
291 Central Park West
New York, New York 10024
Phone: 212-724-2146 Ext. 1
Fax: 212-724-2539
E-mail: admissions@dwight.edu
Web site: http://www.dwight.edu

ÉCOLE D'HUMANITÉ

Hasliberg-Goldern, Switzerland

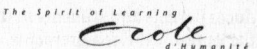

Type: Coeducational international college-preparatory boarding school
Grades: Ungraded, ages 12–20 in English-speaking program, K–Matura in Swiss/German Program
Enrollment: 148

THE SCHOOL

The founders of the École d'Humanité, Paul and Edith Geheeb, first established a school in Germany in 1910, which achieved international recognition as a successful experiment in progressive education. During the Nazi period, the Geheebs emigrated to Switzerland and rebuilt their school. In 1961, Armin and Natalie Lüthi-Peterson became directors of the School and continued many of the Geheebs' traditions. They established the American college-preparatory program, which attracts students from around the world. In 1995, the Lüthi-Petersons retired, passing their 2-person directorship on to a team of 4 teachers.

The philosophy of the École d'Humanité continues to emphasize education of the person as a whole—a balance between artistic, athletic, and rigorous academic programs. The School stresses humanistic values and responsible community living. This lifestyle in spectacular natural surroundings helps students to develop creativity and to discover their own gifts as they are not inundated by television, advertising, and constant appeals to consumerism. The School's commitment to working together rather than competing with one another extends from the classroom through the residential groups ("École family") to all aspects of School life. The search for cooperation is at the center of the École spirit.

Located in the mountain village of Hasliberg-Goldern in the heart of the Swiss Alps, the École d'Humanité lies between Lucerne and Interlaken. The campus includes twelve buildings where students and faculty members live and work together, plus nine buildings in the village with additional living space. The mountains provide an ideal setting for outdoor activities such as rock climbing, skiing/snowboarding, kayaking, and hiking.

The École d'Humanité is accredited by the Department of Youth and Education of Bern and is a member of the Swiss Group of International Schools (SGIS) and the Verein der Deutsche Landerziehungsheime. The School is also an authorized SAT testing site.

ACADEMIC PROGRAMS

The academic program manifests the School's emphasis on the development of the whole person. Students concentrate on only three academic subjects per trimester. To counterbalance this intensive academic program, they devote their afternoons to art, music, sports, and handwork, selecting from some eighty possible courses. Students learn to determine the most effective learning methods for themselves and to organize a balanced schedule. Classes are taught in both English and German.

A student takes the same three academic courses every day from Monday through Saturday. Students select their own courses with the help of faculty advisers. Those wishing to concentrate in a particular area may do so as long as university requirements and career plans are considered. Older students occasionally work independently if they have proved their ability to work on their own and have a project that meets with faculty approval. "Intensive Week" in the fall enables students to focus on one project, usually nonacademic. Those in their last two years of high school write a major research paper on a chosen subject in order to learn the techniques of note-taking, outlining, and footnoting and the self-discipline of long-term independent study as essential preparation for North American and British universities.

A graduating student must have at least 4 years of English, 3 years of mathematics, 2–3 years of foreign language, 2–3 years of laboratory science, 1 year of social science, 1 year of history, and 1 year of humanities. Arts, sports, and music courses are required throughout the student's academic career. Electives include ecology, precalculus, physics, creative writing, philosophy, psychology, French, Latin, choral and instrumental music, folk dancing, painting, weaving, woodworking, theater, computers, pottery, rock climbing, kayaking, and skiing and snowboarding.

Small classes (the student-teacher ratio is 5:1) allow individual instruction and demand students' active participation. Pupils are grouped according to ability and interest rather than by age categories. Class periods of 55 to 75 minutes encourage depth and varied approaches to the subject matter. Neither grades nor final examinations are given, though quizzes, oral presentations, and papers are common. Teachers communicate regularly with the students about their work and evaluate each one's performance every six weeks in a special "blue book." Students also evaluate themselves, which is essential if they are to see their education as primarily their responsibility. Parents receive a full report on their child's academic and social development at the end of the child's first and final terms, based on the "blue book" entries and staff conferences. An interim report can be requested as needed.

FACULTY AND ADVISERS

Thirty-four full-time teachers and teacher/administrators and 2 part-time teachers live on campus. Additional teachers are engaged part-time as needed for instruction of specialty courses such as musical instruments, ski touring, and mountain climbing. The teachers are also "family heads" who are responsible for the general well-being of the children in their family group. This regular contact engenders positive student-teacher relationships.

Kenneth C. ("KC") Hill and Kathleen Hennessy became the directors of the English program and co-directors of the School in 1995, after arriving with their 2 children in 1993. KC Hill was himself an "Écolianer" (1970–1973). He holds degrees from Vassar College (B.S.) and the University of Maryland (B.S.Ed.). Kathleen Hennessy holds degrees from Vassar College (B.A.) and the University of Maryland (M.S.W.). Ms. Hennessy stepped down from the directorship team in 2005 to become Dean of Academics and School Counselor.

Teachers are expected to enjoy a balance of academic and nonacademic pursuits, and so they offer sports, music, arts, and crafts courses as well as courses in their academic fields. The success of a student's experience at the École d'Humanité depends so much on the quality of the staff that great care is taken to hire individuals who are dedicated, well-rounded, and energetic as well as highly qualified in their academic fields. Faculty members are offered continuing education in the use of Dr. Ruth Cohn's Theme-Centered Interaction, a humanistic method for furthering effective and cooperative group work, which corresponds closely to the educational philosophy of the School.

COLLEGE PLACEMENT

The Dean of Academics meets with juniors to review college aspirations and to plan a college-visiting tour, using catalogs and online resources. Each senior meets weekly with a college adviser to complete college applications. The English program places special emphasis on preparation for the SAT. American colleges and other colleges around the world readily accept students who have had a thorough U.S. high school education combined with the experience of living abroad. Recent graduates have attended Bard, Brandeis, Clark, Guilford, McGill, San Jose State, Vassar, and the Universities of California at Santa Cruz, Richmond, Washington (Seattle), and Wisconsin.

STUDENT BODY AND CONDUCT

The student body for 2005–06 was 148: 76 boys and 72 girls. Eight were day students. More than 90 percent of the students were in the grades 6–12 age group. About 57 percent of the students came from Switzerland and the rest from twenty-one other countries. About 12 percent of the student body was non-Caucasian. Twenty-five percent received some financial assistance.

While this is a school with a demanding academic program, it is also a living community. Students take charge of such important tasks as organizing job rotations and managing committees that run the library, entertainment programs, and fire brigade. Some students are active in the student council or involved in peer counseling. Everyone participates in weekly community meetings, chaired by a student, in which individual and community concerns can be addressed.

ACADEMIC FACILITIES

Twelve buildings are used for academic purposes, including three science laboratories; a workshop each for wood, pottery, metal, silversmithing, and studio art; a flexible performance space/assembly hall; seven instrumental practice rooms; a computer room with eight IBM-compatible PCs and additional computer access at other locations on campus; a kitchen for general use; and an audiovisual room. The library houses more than 22,000 volumes in German, English, and French and subscribes to several German and English periodicals.

BOARDING AND GENERAL FACILITIES

Students live in family groups of 2 faculty members and from 4 to 12 boys and girls of varying ages. Each family lives together in one of the School houses and eats together in the common dining room. The family spends one evening a week together playing games, cooking, or working on a project. Nearly all students have double rooms, with a few having singles. Living with a mixed group including both sexes and various cultures helps everyone to see beyond stereotypes and to appreciate individual differences. Students from distant lands usually go home for the long winter and spring vacations or may be invited to stay with friends or relatives. When this is not available, the School helps to make other arrangements for them.

A trained professional assists the family heads in administering to common illnesses and ailments. A physician visits once a week. There are 2 teachers trained in psychology to consult with teachers and students as needed or to make special arrangements outside the School. There is also a psychotherapist who works closely with the School.

ATHLETICS

Physical fitness is stressed without undue emphasis on competitive sports. Living in the Swiss Alps inspires much hiking, which fosters respect for nature as well as a spirit of cooperation—the primary values that the School aims to convey through athletic activities. All students must include at least one sport course in their afternoon program. Students and faculty members often organize intramural competitions on weekends. The School has its own playing field and tennis, basketball, and volleyball courts. The School also has access to the local gymnasium, swimming pool, and riding stable in a nearby village.

EXTRACURRICULAR OPPORTUNITIES

The school year officially begins with the Blueberry Hike when the entire School goes up the mountain to gather blueberries. For four days in the fall and six days in summer, the School divides into groups for an excursion into nature, choosing among rock climbing, ski touring, kayaking, biking, horseback riding (when possible), and hiking trips that further explore Switzerland, Italy, or France.

In keeping with local culture, in late fall the School begins to bustle with preparations for the Nicholasfest, a Christmas play, and the beloved "Heinzelmaenchen Week," in which a person secretly gives gifts to another person. Advent Sundays are particularly festive. In winter a humorous "Fasnacht" festival is prepared, as is the annual Shakespeare production. A summer festival concludes the year with theater, musical, and other performances as well as exhibitions from the many handwork courses. Student theater, musical, and dance performances are presented throughout the year.

Each student has a daily cleaning task and weekly participation in community service. Students may get involved in such activities as the student council, a band or music ensemble, and the stage and lighting group, among others.

DAILY LIFE

Wake-up is at 6:30 a.m., with breakfast at 7:10. All meals are served family style by students. The first morning course begins at 8:05. The nonacademic courses take place Monday through Thursday between 2:30 and 6:15, following lunch and siesta. After dinner, there is free time until the evening Quiet Hour in the houses. Family Evening is on Wednesday. The School gathers for a community meeting on Friday afternoon and a Singing Assembly on Saturday morning.

WEEKEND LIFE

The weekend officially lasts from Saturday at midday until Sunday dinner. Students and teachers alike organize activities for the weekend, including sports events, monthly coffeehouses, films, and a biweekly disco evening that alternates with a folk-dance evening. Students and/or teachers prepare an "Andacht" for Sunday evenings as a time for reflection on ethical or social issues. Older students may visit the nearby town, and all are free to explore the surrounding natural wonders.

COSTS AND FINANCIAL AID

Tuition is dependent on the current exchange rate. The tuition for the academic year 2005–06 was SF 36,000. Tuition is payable in one payment or in three (one per term) or ten (monthly) installments. A Scholarship Committee reviews applications for financial aid.

ADMISSIONS INFORMATION

The Admissions Committee seeks students who are eager to challenge themselves academically, physically, and mentally. All applicants who live in or near Switzerland must visit the School for an interview and tour, which offers the opportunity to meet students and faculty members. Applicants who live farther away can request an interview by telephone or with someone familiar with the School in their area. The English program requires two letters of recommendation and school records.

APPLICATION TIMETABLE

Applications are accepted on a rolling basis. Applications received by May 15 have the best chance of acceptance.

ADMISSIONS CORRESPONDENCE

KC Hill, Director, English-speaking Program
Frédéric Bächtold, Director, German-speaking
    Program
École d'Humanité
CH-6085 Hasliberg-Goldern
Switzerland

Phone: +41-33-972-92-92
Fax: +41-33-972-92-11
E-mail: us.office@ecole.ch
Web site: http://www.ecole.ch

EMMA WILLARD SCHOOL

Troy, New York

Type: Girls' boarding and day college-preparatory school
Grades: 9–12, postgraduate year
Enrollment: 318
Head of School: Trudy E. Hall

THE SCHOOL

In 1814, Emma Hart Willard founded the School that now bears her name, making it the oldest institution for the higher education of young women in the United States. Her belief in women's intellectual capabilities, a radical idea for the time, is the cornerstone of a curriculum that has challenged Emma Willard students for 191 years.

The exceptionally beautiful 89-acre campus has thirty buildings. Emma Willard School is located on the edge of the city of Troy, 7 miles from Albany, at the crossroads of the Berkshires, the Adirondacks, and the Catskills.

The 30-member Board of Trustees includes 13 alumnae, 4 parents, and 1 faculty member. An operating budget of $13.5 million is supported in part through a $91-million endowment and Annual Giving that exceeds $1.5 million.

Emma Willard School is accredited by the New York State Association of Independent Schools and by the New York State Board of Regents. It is a member of the National Association of Independent Schools, the New York State Association of Independent Schools, the Cum Laude Society, and the National Coalition of Girls Schools.

ACADEMIC PROGRAMS

The Emma Willard curriculum develops those abilities and qualities of mind that are essential to the successful woman. The rigorous college-preparatory curriculum ensures a strong foundation in all major academic areas in addition to extensive exposure to the arts. Emma Willard celebrates leadership, rewards successes, offers appropriate support, and reminds girls of the limitless possibilities the world presents an educated woman.

Each student's faculty adviser helps her plan her courses in coordination with the College Counselor and the Academic Dean. Graduation requirements include a minimum of 4 years of English, completion of the third-year level in both mathematics and foreign language, 2 years of science (including biology and chemistry), 3 years of history, 3½ years of physical education, computer literacy, a health course, and 2 units of visual and performing arts.

The School offers more than 140 courses, including Advanced Placement (AP) preparation in English Literature and Composition, Spanish, French, calculus (AB and BC), statistics, computer science, chemistry, biology, physics, U.S. government, U.S. history, European history, art history, and Latin. Students may also prepare for AP tests in studio art and music theory. A student who wishes to study subjects beyond the curriculum offerings may arrange individualized tutorials with faculty supervision.

All underclass women are assigned to a daily supervised study hall during the fall term; students in good academic standing are excused from this study hall at the end of the term. There is a 2-hour evening study period Sunday through Thursday for all boarding students all year. Students may be assigned by their advisers to a supervised evening study hall. The library is open 14 hours a day, seven days a week. At least one professional librarian is on duty 67 hours a week.

Emma Willard students may take courses for credit at nearby universities. In addition, the School is a member of the National Network of Complementary Schools, which offers students an opportunity to pursue special programs on an exchange basis. Practicum, Emma Willard's independent study program, provides opportunities to earn credit and explore a career interest through hands-on experience in many industries, organizations, and professions. Recent Practicum projects have focused on broadcasting, publishing, microbiology, veterinary medicine, law, environmental engineering, photojournalism, advertising, government, and architecture. Vacation trips abroad and work with Habitat for Humanity are undertaken by students with faculty chaperones each year; groups have traveled to Belize, England, France, Germany, Greece, Ireland, Italy, Russia, and Spain.

Academic courses are graded from A to No Credit. A few courses are graded Credit/No Credit. Grades and comments are issued to parents and students at midterm and at the end of each semester.

FACULTY AND ADVISERS

The faculty numbers 69 (59 full-time and 10 part-time), 74 percent are women and 26 percent are men. There are 4 administrators who teach. The student-faculty ratio is 5:1. Fifty faculty members reside on campus. Ninety-three faculty members, administrators, and residence staff members hold sixty-four advanced degrees, including four Ph.D.'s, three J.D.'s, and fifty-seven master's, representing study at more than 104 colleges and universities. Two or more degrees were earned at American, Amherst, Boston College, Boston University, Bryn Mawr, Columbia, Dartmouth, Duke, Fairleigh Dickinson, Harvard, Macalester, Manhattanville, Massachusetts College of Liberal Arts, Middlebury, Princeton, Rensselaer, Russell Sage, Smith, St. Lawrence, Saint Rose, SUNY at Albany, Wellesley, Wesleyan, Williams, Yale, and the Universities of Chicago; Connecticut; Dublin, Trinity College; Illinois; Maryland; and New Hampshire.

Trudy E. Hall was appointed Head of School in 1999. She holds a B.S. from St. Lawrence University, an M.Ed. from Harvard University, and an M.A.L.S. from Duke University.

In selecting its teachers, Emma Willard looks for adults who are dedicated to enriching the lives of young people in and out of the classroom. The school has a full-time director of faculty development. Faculty development grants are available to those who wish to pursue advanced degrees or enrich their current areas of study and to those who wish to develop new courses. Sabbaticals and travel funds are available to all faculty members. Most dormitory staff members are full-time residence personnel and do not teach. All faculty members act as advisers to 4–6 students each. Faculty members chaperone weekend activities, sit on School committees, and advise student organizations. Annual faculty turnover is typically less than 10 percent.

COLLEGE PLACEMENT

Formal college counseling begins in the junior year. The Director of College Counseling supervises all college placement testing (the PSAT, the SAT, and Subject Tests), coordinates visits to Emma Willard by college admissions officers, assists students in planning college visits, and writes a comprehensive recommendation for each senior, based on the student's academic record and teachers' written evaluations.

SAT I scores for the class of 2005 ranged from 470 to 800 verbal and from 590 to 800 math. All of the 84 graduates in 2005 were accepted by a total of 274 colleges and universities, 26 through early decision. They are attending such schools as Bates, Boston College, Brown, Bryn Mawr, Carnegie Mellon, Columbia, Cornell, Hamilton, Harvard, Johns Hopkins, Middlebury, MIT, Northwestern, NYU, Rensselaer, Skidmore, Smith, Tufts, Vassar, Yale, and the University of Dublin, Trinity College.

STUDENT BODY AND CONDUCT

In 2005–06, Emma Willard had 199 boarding and 119 day students as follows: grade 9, 66; grade 10, 101; grade 11, 79; and grade 12, 72. Students came from twenty-five states and nineteen other countries. Eleven percent are members of minority groups.

The School seeks to enroll girls who are responsible and mature enough not to require rigid structure, but all are expected to abide by the Fundamental Rules that govern major issues of discipline.

Aside from observing standards of neatness and cleanliness, students have no dress code during the academic day or in the dormitories. Dress for plays, concerts, and academic convocations is more formal.

ACADEMIC FACILITIES

The oldest buildings, of Tudor Gothic design, include the Alumnae Chapel and Slocum Hall, which contains classrooms, offices, the main auditorium, a lab theater, and a dance studio. The Hunter Science Center, an addition to Weaver Hall, opened in 1996. Hunter includes computer equipment integrated with revolutionary fractal laboratories. Completing the main quadrangle is the art, music, and library complex designed by Edward Larabee Barnes and constructed from 1967 to 1971. Other campus buildings house an additional auditorium and dance studio, ten music practice rooms, twenty-one grand pianos, six science laboratories, an audiovisual center, two photography darkrooms, a microcomputer center, and approximately 100 computers. The William Moore Dietel Library holds more than 32,000 volumes and 108 periodical subscriptions. Microfilm and microfiche readers and reader-printers are available for student use. The collection also includes 196 CDs, a sizable art and architecture slide collection, and the School archives, which include nineteenth-century photographs and manuscripts and some medieval manuscripts.

BOARDING AND GENERAL FACILITIES

Students reside in three dormitories, with two dining halls. Sophomores, juniors, and seniors live together on various halls; ninth grade students live together on the same hall. There are single rooms, connecting singles, doubles, and suites. Ten houseparents supervise student life in the dormitories. A team of faculty affiliates, student proctors, and peer educators shares in dormitory responsibilities. Day students are assigned to residence halls to facilitate their integration into the residential program.

Other campus buildings include a variety of on-campus faculty residences.

ATHLETICS

Emma Willard encourages students to combine lifetime sports with competition; students can fulfill the physical activities requirement through team sports, individual sports, or dance. Emma Willard teams compete in a league with other local schools, both public and private, in basketball, crew, cross-

country, field hockey, lacrosse, soccer, softball, swimming, tennis, track, and volleyball. Downhill skiing is available during the winter. Recreational activities include aerobics, crew, cross-country skiing, lacrosse, skating, swimming, tennis, volleyball, and weight conditioning. In addition to the Charles Stewart Mott Gymnasium, which includes two indoor tennis courts and full facilities for basketball, volleyball, and fitness training, facilities include six outdoor tennis courts, three large playing fields, and a newly renovated all-weather 400-meter track. In 1998, the Helen S. Cheel Aquatics and Fitness Center opened with a competition-size swimming pool and state-of-the-art fitness equipment.

EXTRACURRICULAR OPPORTUNITIES
The 175th Anniversary Speakers Series brings prominent individuals to campus for 24-hour residencies. Recent 175th speakers include Poet Laureate Billy Collins; playwrights Wendy Wasserstein and Shirley Lauro; Russian poet Yevgeny Yevtushenko; National Public Radio reporter Linda Wertheimer; Herbert Hauptman, Nobel laureate in mathematics; and award-winning novelist Tobias Wolff. The EWS arts calendar features an impressive array of renowned chamber groups, dance companies, artists, and exhibitions.

The surrounding region offers performances at the historic Troy Music Hall, the Saratoga Performing Arts Center, and Tanglewood; events at the Empire State Performing Arts Center in Albany; ethnic festivals; sports events; theater; and activities at nearby colleges and universities. The School sponsors a world-class chamber music series and all students are required to attend at least two cultural events each term.

Among the twenty-three clubs and organizations are the Outing Club, Athletic Council, EMMA Green (environmental group), Peer Counseling, Foreign and American Student Organization, Black and Hispanic Awareness, and various singing groups. There are also three student publications: *Triangle,* the arts and literary magazine; *The Clock,* the School newspaper; and *Gargoyle,* the yearbook. Through Interact, girls may serve the community in volunteer projects such as Big Brothers/Big Sisters. Traditions include the opening-of-school Academic Convocation, fall and spring Senior Dinners, Holiday Eventide, Revels, the surprise holiday Principal's Playday, May Day, and the June Flame Ceremony. All students participate in a School Work Program 2 hours each week. Community service activities are required of all first-year students and encouraged for all other students. The School's recycling program is staffed by students.

DAILY LIFE
Classes are held Monday through Friday from 8 to 3:30. There is a mid-morning all-School meeting. There are eight 40-minute class periods. Team sports, choir, some dance classes, and drama rehearsals meet after 3:30. There is a double lunch period during which student clubs may meet. Dinner is served from 5:30 to 7 p.m., and quiet study hours are 7:30 to 9:30. All students must be on their floor by 10:30 and in their rooms by 11 p.m.

WEEKEND LIFE
An extensive Weekend Activities Program is developed and coordinated by a full-time staff member of Student Affairs. The Emma Willard campus is at the crossroads of New England, the Adirondacks, the Catskills, and the Berkshires. This location gives students an exciting array of cultural and recreational venues. Weekend activities include sports events, dances with boys' schools, dinner in the Capital District, movies both on and off campus, and trips to Boston, New York, and Montreal. Generally, 75 to 80 percent of the boarders remain on campus during the weekend, and day students are encouraged to participate in weekend activities. Transportation to area events and places of worship is provided upon request.

COSTS AND FINANCIAL AID
Tuition, room, and board in 2005–06 were $33,750. Day student tuition is $21,200. A smart-card fee of $600 for boarding students in grades 9–11 ($650 for seniors) and $400 for day students in grades 9–11 ($450 for seniors) covers lab fees, testing, field trips, and other class-related expenses. Families purchase text books directly from the School's online vendor. The average cost of books per year is $500. Special-fee courses include private music lessons, ballet, driver's education, skiing, and horseback riding. A $1500 deposit is required to confirm enrollment; School fees are billed in July and December, and families may elect to pay 60 percent in August, with the remainder due in January. Families who wish to make monthly tuition payments may do so through the School's ten-month installment plan.

The School is committed to maintaining the diversity of its student body and allocated more than $2.1 million in financial aid to 39 percent of the student body during 2004–05. Aid is awarded on the basis of academic promise and family financial need, as determined by the parents' financial statement of the School and Student Service for Financial Aid. Applications for financial aid must be submitted by February 15. As long as a student is in good standing and family circumstances warrant continued assistance, grants are renewed from year to year.

ADMISSIONS INFORMATION
Emma Willard seeks students of above-average to superior academic ability who are self-motivated, responsible, interested in learning, and involved in activities outside the classroom. All candidates for admission must submit an application, a personal essay, transcripts, three recommendations, and the results of the SSAT. Students for whom English is not their first language should submit the results of the TOEFL in lieu of the SSAT. An interview is strongly encouraged. Applicants for the postgraduate year should submit SAT scores.

APPLICATION TIMETABLE
Initial inquiries are welcome at any time. Campus visits include tours for parents and daughters, interviews, a class visit, and frequently a meal. On weekdays, office hours are 8:30 a.m. to 4:30 p.m. Appointments may be made at any time of year, but October through April visits are strongly recommended. Open house programs are scheduled on Columbus Day, Veteran's Day, and Martin Luther King's birthday.

The application fee of $45 ($100 for international students) is nonrefundable. The application deadline is February 15. Prospective students and their parents are notified of the Admission Committee's decision in March. Applications received after that time are accepted on a space-available basis.

ADMISSIONS CORRESPONDENCE
Director of Enrollment
Emma Willard School
285 Pawling Avenue
Troy, New York 12180

Phone: 518-833-1320
Fax: 518-833-1805
E-mail: admissions@emmawillard.org
Web site: http://www.emmawillard.org

THE EPISCOPAL ACADEMY

Merion and Devon, Pennsylvania

Type: Coeducational day college-preparatory school on two campuses
Grades: Merion Campus: Lower School, Prekindergarten–5; Middle School, 6–8; Upper School, 9–12
Enrollment: School total: 1,130; Upper School: 446
Head of School: Mr. L. Hamilton Clark, Head of School

THE SCHOOL

The Episcopal Academy believes its educational mission is to help students develop their fullest capabilities in mind, body, and spirit. Its program prepares graduates to benefit from higher education, to continue to educate themselves, and to participate in and improve the community in which they live.

The Academy was founded in 1785 by the Right Reverend William White, first Episcopal Bishop of Pennsylvania, and occupied its first building in 1787, two doors away from Independence Hall. Its original purpose was to teach Anglican doctrine and train the clergy, but Bishop White believed in free education for the poor, and in 1789 the Academy set up free schools for more than 100 children.

It occupied several sites in Philadelphia before moving in 1921 to the nearby suburb of Merion. Housed in several renovated mansions, the school prospered in its new location. A modern classroom building was opened in 1973. The adoption of co-education and the opening of a second campus in Devon (11 miles west of Merion) for the Lower School occurred simultaneously in 1974.

In 2001, the School purchased 120 acres of undeveloped farm land in Newtown Square, 10 miles west of the Merion Campus and a mile from the Devon Campus. The plan is to consolidate both current campuses onto the new one, opening in 2007–08.

Hamilton Clark joined Episcopal as Head of School for the 2002–03 school year. Previously Headmaster at Sewickley Academy in Pittsburgh for fifteen years, Clark received a B.A. degree at Trinity College and an M.Ed. at Harvard University. Prior to his tenure at Sewickley, he served as Director of College Guidance and Admission at Buckingham Browne and Nichols and as Assistant to the Director of the American School in Zurich.

Students are drawn from within a 30-mile radius, including both city and suburbs. The Merion campus has 37 acres of athletics fields and parklike areas on the edge of Philadelphia. The Lower School at Devon has 34 acres of open fields and woodlands surrounding the elementary-grade complex. The Academy is governed by a 35-member Board of Trustees. The 2002–03 budget was $21.5 million; in 2002–03, Annual Giving amounted to more than $1.6 million, of which nearly 29 percent was contributed by alumni. The endowment is $16.5 million, and the value of the school's plant is $61.5 million.

An active Parents Association sponsors events and provides services throughout the Academy. Through association activities, parents become involved in the day-to-day life of the school and contribute time and effort on behalf of their children and those of others.

The Episcopal Academy is accredited by the Middle States Association of Colleges and Schools and the Pennsylvania Association of Private Academic Schools. It holds membership in the National Association of Independent Schools, the Pennsylvania Association of Independent Schools,

the National Association of Episcopal Schools, and the National Association of Principals of Schools for Girls.

ACADEMIC PROGRAMS

The curriculum stresses clear, concise writing; reading; mathematics; the natural sciences; social studies; the arts; and foreign language proficiency. Graduation requirements are based on the expectations of highly selective colleges and universities, and nearly all graduates choose to go on to four-year colleges. A significant number of seniors are honored each year in the National Merit Scholarship competition. While academic excellence is strongly emphasized, flexible programs allow for a range of abilities and individualized instruction and enrichment where needed.

Graduation requirements include 4 credits in English, 3 in social studies, 3 in science, 3 in mathematics, 2 in foreign languages, 1 in religion, and 1 credit in the arts by participation and study in music, theater, or the visual arts. Advanced Placement courses in American history, American government and politics, biology, chemistry, computers, economics, physics, mathematics, Latin, French, and Spanish are complemented by courses in English, art history, and studio art that also prepare students for the AP examinations. In 2004, 111 students sat for 211 AP exams in seventeen subjects.

The student body is religiously diverse. Since religion plays an important role in the development of the students, chapel attendance is required three times weekly for Upper and Middle School students and once a week for Lower School students. Through chapel and required courses and electives in religion, students of all faiths learn of their similarities and differences while they explore theological, moral, and ethical issues.

The average Upper School class size is 15. Students are grouped by ability in math and foreign language, but, in general, classes are heterogeneously grouped unless they are specified as honors or advanced placement. A student-teacher ratio of 7:1 allows for frequent extra help and close faculty-student bonds. Each student has a faculty adviser who supervises his or her progress and provides counsel in times of difficulty. The adviser and parents are encouraged to remain in close touch on both academic and nonacademic matters. In addition, each grade has a dean who remains with them for all four years.

The Upper School day consists of eight periods, during which students typically attend six classes. There are electives in social studies, the classics, religion, computer science, science, English, music, theater, visual arts, woodworking, and architectural drafting. By arrangement, seniors may take courses at local colleges, including Bryn Mawr College, Saint Joseph's University, and the University of Pennsylvania. Seniors complete the year with an independent project.

The passing grade is D. Each semester is approximately ten weeks long, and reports are sent home twice each trimester. Parents may request a conference with a student's academic adviser to discuss progress at any time.

FACULTY AND ADVISERS

There are 75 faculty members in the Upper School: 58 are full-time, 13 cross over to the other units or are part-time teachers, and 8 are administrators who teach part-time. There are 3 chaplains who are ordained Episcopal priests; one chaplain is connected to the Upper School, one to the Middle School, and one is split between the two Lower Schools. Most faculty members serve as advisers to between 3 and 14 students. The Chaplain coordinates the Upper School advisory system. In addition, most faculty members coach sports or supervise students in extracurricular activities.

New faculty members are hired for their academic credentials, experience, and ability to contribute to school life beyond the classroom. Salaries are competitive, and turnover is low. Of the 178 faculty members in the entire school, 116 hold advanced degrees, including 8 who hold doctorates, and 82 have served the school for ten years or more. The school provides continuing education, enrichment, collaborative summer work, and travel grants and a sabbatical program for faculty members to continue study in their field.

COLLEGE PLACEMENT

Throughout the junior and senior years, students work closely with 2 full-time and 1 part-time College Counselors in formulating college plans. The counselors help students with all phases and aspects of the college search and application process: college entrance testing, researching and visiting colleges, interviewing, and completing applications. Representatives from more than 100 colleges typically visit Episcopal during the school year.

Episcopal students are consistently accepted by the nation's most selective colleges. The 99 graduates of the class of 2005 are attending fifty-nine institutions. Eight or more members of the classes of 2000–2004 have gone to Boston College, Boston University, Brown, Bucknell, Colgate, Cornell, Duke, Franklin and Marshall, Georgetown, George Washington, Harvard, Penn State, Princeton, Trinity College, Vanderbilt, Villanova, Williams, Yale, and the Universities of Delaware, Pennsylvania, Southern California, and Virginia.

STUDENT BODY AND CONDUCT

In 2004–05, the Upper School had 446 students. Grade 9 had 109; grade 10, 107; grade 11, 117; and grade 12, 113. Students are enrolled from Philadelphia, its northern and western suburbs as far as Lancaster, and nearby New Jersey. Students come from a broad range of social and economic backgrounds, and 16 percent are members of minority groups.

The Student Council (2 faculty members and 24 students) is the elected Upper School student government. The purpose of the organization is to give the Upper School students a voice, to develop and promote school spirit, and to plan and organize extracurricular activities.

ACADEMIC FACILITIES

At the Merion Campus, the main building contains Middle and Upper School classrooms, the Annen-

berg Library, a computer/audiovisual multimedia production studio, a photography darkroom, and three instructional computing labs. Other buildings are Christ Chapel; the Greville Haslam Science Building, with ten laboratory/classrooms; a theater; a cafeteria; and music and art buildings housing music and art computer labs. Lower School classes are housed in the main building and two former homes, Dietrich House and Wetherill House.

The Devon Campus has a facility that features classrooms, the Huston Chapel, two science laboratories, the Wike Library, an instructional computing classroom, art and woodshop studios, galleries, and a student shop. Completing the campus are music studios, a cafeteria, a gymnasium, an outdoor education ropes challenge course, and four playing fields.

With more than 500 computers on both campuses, students and faculty members have class and individual access to educational technology throughout the Academy. The Academy Intranet is fully networked between campuses with high-speed lines and full Internet access. Students, from the youngest to the oldest, have individual computer accounts and receive instruction in the use of education computing technology across the curriculum and in every grade.

The library system is composed of three libraries on the two campuses and is staffed with 7 librarians who hold at least a master's degree in library science. At Merion, the Annenberg Library–Learning Center serves students and faculty members from grades 4 to 12 and provides research resources and instructional activities that are integrated with the curriculum to develop students' beginning and advanced information literacy skills. The Dietrich House Library at Merion serves grades preK–3, and the Wike Library on the Devon campus serves grades preK–5. These elementary libraries provide programs of literature enrichment, reading development, and beginning information literacy skills. System holdings total in excess of 58,000 print and media items. Access to library resources is available through the library Web page. Resources include an online catalog, Internet-accessible subscriptions to more than two dozen research resources, and an online library of Internet sites that are professionally evaluated and coordinated with the curriculum by the library faculty.

ATHLETICS
Episcopal has a strong physical education curriculum for grades preK–5. Athletics are required for grades 6–12. Almost all sports in the extensive athletics program are coached by teachers who also see students in the classroom, and the rapport generated on the playing field transfers to other aspects of school life. The goal of competitive sports is not only to win games but also to foster participation and a lifelong respect for physical activity and to develop sportsmanship, leadership, and perseverance.

Participation in athletics is required each term for all but seniors, who may elect one season off. Boys' varsity sports are football, soccer, cross-country, winter track, basketball, ice hockey, squash, swimming, wrestling, baseball, crew, golf, lacrosse, tennis, track, and water polo. Girls' varsity sports are field hockey, tennis, basketball, squash, soccer, swimming, crew, lacrosse, winter track, track, cross-country, softball, and water polo. A weight training and fitness option is offered each season.

Athletics facilities include five full-size fields, two gymnasiums, a wrestling room, four squash courts, eight tennis courts, weight-training facilities, a dance room, and an indoor pool. The Athletic Department has full-time trainers for both boys and girls. Episcopal is a member of the boys' and girls' Inter-Academic Athletic Association.

EXTRACURRICULAR OPPORTUNITIES
Students may choose from a wide variety of organizations. There are classes for credit as well as a regularly scheduled activity period, which provides in-school time for extracurricular activities. Many groups meet after school at night and on weekends.

One of the school's most valued activities is Community Service. This program—with a full-time faculty director and assistant—is entirely voluntary yet enormously successful. Students often leave campus during the day, evenings, and weekends to work with the elderly, the disabled, and the disadvantaged. Each grade level is involved in a project either on or off campus that may include tutoring, mentoring, or hands-on assistance.

The music curriculum spans grades preK–12 and includes courses in instrumental music for grades 4–12 and sacred and secular choral ensembles for grades 2–12. There are more than 250 students who are active in the band program and nearly 500 in the choral program. The Lower School program serves as the foundation of the Kodaly methodology of music literacy for all students. At this level, all students sing in choirs, and the older students also play in the band program. In the Middle School, 40 percent of the students are enrolled in choral, band, and string ensembles as part of the curricular day. The Upper School curriculum features four choral ensembles, a concert band, a jazz combo, a chamber ensemble, and four electives, including Advanced Placement Music Theory and Music Technology.

The Upper School Domino Club and two subordinate acting ensembles provide varied theater experiences and mount two major productions yearly. The Middle School theater, the Harlequin Club, produces two main stage productions—a musical in the fall and a straight show in the spring. Another dramatic highlight in January is the Freshmen Show, a farcical spoof in which two thirds of the class act, sing, and design their way into new relationships. Theater is a required part of the curriculum for Lower School students (grades preK–5).

Other groups are the Middle School Chapel Council and the Upper School Student Vestry, which help plan and assist in chapel programs; the Student Fund, which raises money for worthwhile school projects; and a newspaper, a yearbook, a literary magazine, and a magazine of arts and opinion. An active debating society competes in intraschool and interscholastic debates. A variety of clubs develop from student and faculty interests: for example, television production, photography, Poetry Club, Amnesty International, stock market, Young Democrats, Student Council, and Young Republicans.

DAILY LIFE
The Upper School academic day, which begins with homeroom at 8:05, consists of eight periods that are 45 minutes each. There is a 35-minute lunch at midday. Students attend chapel three times weekly. Required athletics begin at 3:40 daily and end at 4:45 for those in intramural sports and approximately 5:45 for those on interscholastic teams.

SUMMER PROGRAMS
Three summer sessions are offered for students in grades K–12. Two 3-week sessions offer courses for high school credit and enrichment and skill development as well as remedial courses in core subjects. A one-week session for organizational skills and readiness is available for Middle and Upper School students. Enrollment is not limited to Episcopal students.

COSTS AND FINANCIAL AID
Upper School tuition in 2005–06 is $21,100. It is payable in two parts: 60 percent before August 1 and the balance on or before February 1. A reenrollment deposit is required on or before March 1 to reserve a space for the following year. An installment payment plan and tuition refund insurance are available through outside agencies. Tuition is all inclusive, with the exception of books and lunch. Lunch cards may be purchased for cafeteria lunches, though many students bring their own lunches. Parents are requested to contribute to a fund designated for the faculty and staff benefits fund.

The Academy offers a limited amount of financial aid based on need. Academic achievement and the student's potential contribution to the school are also taken into consideration. Need is determined by the School and Student Service for Financial Aid of Princeton, New Jersey, to which parents requesting aid must file an application. Financial aid is renewable on a yearly basis at the discretion of the Academy. In 2004–05, 291 students received financial aid. Grants ranged from $500 to full tuition. Further information on aid may be obtained in confidence from the Director of Admission.

ADMISSIONS INFORMATION
The admission process seeks to determine whether Episcopal is the right school for the candidate. Through interviews, testing, and counseling, families and the school carefully examine whether Episcopal will meet the needs of the student and if the student has the potential to benefit from the academic, physical, spiritual, and social/emotional atmosphere at Episcopal.

Applications may be received during the parental appointment, through the mail, or downloaded via the Web site. When an application is returned, the admission procedure begins. Required of all candidates are an appointment with the parents or guardians, a report or transcript from the present school, and a campus visit. In addition, independent testing is necessary for all applicants from prekindergarten through twelfth grade. Information regarding specific grade-level testing is addressed during the parental visit. Two teacher recommendations and one from a family friend are required for all applicants for grades 6–12. A comprehensive tour of the campus and facilities is included during the parental appointment.

The admission process seeks to determine whether Episcopal is the right school for the candidate. Through a review of academic records, testing, and interviews, the family and the school carefully examine whether Episcopal will meet the needs of the child. The process helps establish the candidate's potential to benefit from the academic, physical, spiritual, and social/emotional atmosphere at Episcopal.

APPLICATION TIMETABLE
Decisions on admission are made by an Admission Committee, which considers all the information, including the candidate's academic ability, achievements, and other interests. Parents of Upper School applicants are notified of the committee's decision on a rolling basis beginning in the middle of December. Due to a significantly greater number of applicants than spaces, early application is advised.

ADMISSIONS CORRESPONDENCE
Ellen M. Hay, Director of Admission
The Episcopal Academy
376 North Latches Lane
Merion, Pennsylvania 19066-1797

Phone: 610-667-9612 Ext. 3002
Fax: 610-617-2262
E-mail: adnussuib@ea1785.org
Web site: http://www.ea1785.org

EPISCOPAL HIGH SCHOOL

Alexandria, Virginia

Type: Coeducational boarding college-preparatory school
Grades: 9–12
Enrollment: 425
Head of School: F. Robertson Hershey

THE SCHOOL

Episcopal High School (EHS) opened in 1839 as the first high school in Virginia. Beginning with just 35 boys, the School has evolved into a coeducational boarding school of 425 students, with talented and motivated youth coming to Alexandria from thirty states and fourteen countries. Closed during the Civil War when the campus was used as a hospital for federal troops, the School reopened in 1866 and has been in continuous operation since.

Episcopal is dedicated to educating boys and girls who, as responsible citizens of the world, are prepared to lead lives of honor, courage, and compassion. The School emphasizes the intellectual, spiritual, physical, and moral development of every student through rigorous academics, daily athletics, regularly scheduled chapel services, and extensive activities and community service programs. The School's most enduring tradition is its Honor Code, one of the oldest among secondary schools in the nation and a tradition that remains a central part of community life.

Episcopal's 130-acre campus in Alexandria, Virginia, is just 10 minutes from the vast educational, cultural, and governmental resources of Washington, D.C., and teachers use the nation's capital as a second campus. Alexandria, situated on the Potomac River in northern Virginia, offers a spectrum of cultural, social, historical, and educational events.

Episcopal is a nonprofit corporation governed by a 30-member Board of Trustees, most of whom are alumni. The School's endowment is $120 million, and the plant is valued at $100 million. In 2004–05, contributions to the annual giving program totaled $2.4 million, and total gifts exceeded $10 million. The 4,500 living alumni, current and past parents, and the advisory council all lend their support to the School's mission.

Episcopal High School is accredited by the Southern Association of Colleges and Schools and the Virginia Association of Independent Schools. It holds membership in the National Association of Independent Schools, the National Association of Episcopal Schools, the Association of Independent Schools of Greater Washington, and the Cum Laude Society.

ACADEMIC PROGRAMS

EHS is committed to providing a liberal arts education in which students learn to think independently, analyze, and reason. The college-preparatory curriculum offers 134 courses, including forty honors and Advanced Placement (AP) courses. A minimum of 23 credits is required for graduation, including English (4), mathematics (3 or 3½), foreign language (2 or 3), social studies (2), laboratory sciences and physical education (2 each), and theology and fine arts (1 each). The passing grade is 65; a grade of 90 or better constitutes honors-level work.

In classes, students are grouped into regular, honors and AP sections of about 11 students each according to their ability and familiarity with the subject matter. Tutorial sessions are available six periods each week, and evening study hours ensure

a quiet study environment. Parents receive grades quarterly, which are accompanied by teachers' and advisers' comments.

Episcopal's Washington Program enhances classroom learning with weekly trips to museums, galleries, plays, concerts, and government agencies in Washington, D.C., and meetings with national leaders and experts of in a variety of professions. In addition, the entire school attends each presidential inauguration. Qualified seniors take part in a one-month internship in which they work in such places as Capitol Hill, banks, hospitals, social service organizations, government agencies, media companies, and law firms.

As part of the foreign language program, students may take part in summer study trips to Austria, France, Spain, and Italy. Students also have the option of studying in China, France, Italy, or Spain as part of the School Year Abroad program, and qualified seniors may take a postgraduate year in Great Britain as part of the English-Speaking Union program. In addition, Episcopal offers a semester-long cultural exchange with St. Leonard's School in St. Andrews, Scotland.

FACULTY AND ADVISERS

Nearly 90 percent of the full-time faculty of 80 men and women live on campus with their families and are available to teach and guide students while promoting community.

Rob Hershey, who was appointed Headmaster in 1998, was previously Headmaster at his alma mater, the Collegiate School in Richmond, and at Durham Academy. He received his B.A. from Williams College and his M.Ed. from the University of Virginia.

Faculty members are chosen for their interest in and dedication to young people and for their proficiency in teaching their subject area. As teachers, coaches, dorm parents, counselors, and good friends, they support and direct students' growth. Nearly all serve as advisers. Each is responsible for the academic and social progress of 6 to 8 advisees, and each maintains close contact with parents.

COLLEGE PLACEMENT

Students are encouraged to start thinking about college as early as possible. Formal college counseling begins in the spring of the sophomore year, when students meet with a college counselor to begin considering appropriate colleges and to become familiar with the application process. More than 100 colleges take part in Episcopal's annual College Fair, and representatives from about eighty-five schools conduct on-campus interviews. The 104 graduates of the class of 2005 are attending sixty colleges and universities, including Bowdoin, Duke, Harvard, Middlebury, Northwestern, Washington and Lee, Washington (St. Louis), Wesleyan, the Universities of North Carolina, Pennsylvania, and Virginia.

STUDENT BODY AND CONDUCT

Approximately 120 new students enroll each year. The student body represents more than thirty states, the District of Columbia, and fourteen other countries.

Episcopal's Honor Code is an essential part of community life and is strongly supported by the faculty and students. The Honor Code is overseen by an Honor Committee of 8 students and 4 faculty members. The code asserts that students will not lie, cheat, or steal. Out of genuine concern for and responsibility to those who do, students are asked to report violators to the Honor Committee. Students whose values and conduct prove to be irreconcilable with the Honor Code will be asked to leave.

The student body is led by student monitors who are nominated to the Headmaster by the faculty members and students. Monitors are responsible for discipline and orderliness in the day-to-day life of the School. A student-elected Dorm Council offers additional leadership opportunities.

ACADEMIC FACILITIES

Episcopal's academic facilities include seven buildings. The new Science Center will open in the fall of 2005. This is a two-story, 34,000-square foot building that features state-of-the-art laboratories for biology, chemistry, physics, and environmental science. Special features include a beautiful glass rotunda, greenhouse, science library, and auditorium with video and computer equipment to enhance any teaching situation. As a LEED Certified Green Building, the Science Center will set a new standard for energy-efficient design on campus, and this environmentally sound building will enable students to explore the world of science while simultaneously becoming stewards of their environment.

Since 2003, the Ainslie Arts Center has provided a magnificent setting for Episcopal's arts program. It features a digital photography studio, MIDI lab and 24-channel digital recording studio, professional and student galleries, along with painting, drawing, ceramics, and dance studios, plus a 540-seat auditorium and black box theater. The David H. March Library houses more than 33,000 books, videos, and CDs; 160 periodicals; twelve newspapers, microforms, and CD-ROMs; and access to seven online commercial databases and a national interlibrary loan network via OCLC.

EHS requires all students to own a laptop specified by the Technology Department. Student desks in all classrooms are wired with both power outlets and data drops, allowing any classroom to be used as a computer lab. Each classroom has a monitor for the display of both video and data. All dorm rooms are also equipped with Internet connections. EHS provides access to the Internet via a T1 line for research and recreational purposes.

BOARDING AND GENERAL FACILITIES

Residential facilities include seven dormitories. Most have double rooms, although there are a few singles and triples, and all feature common rooms and laundry facilities. A faculty member, often with a

family, lives in an apartment or town house attached to each dormitory. Together with the senior monitors who also live on each dormitory floor, they help foster a comfortable, relaxed atmosphere.

Students attend services in Patrick Henry Callaway Chapel. Health services are provided at McAllister Health Center, a fifteen-bed facility that is staffed by a registered nurse 24 hours a day and visited twice a day by a physician. Alexandria Hospital, just two blocks away, offers outstanding emergency treatment.

Other residential facilities include Laird Dining Room, where buffet- and family-style meals are served; Blackford Hall, the main coed student lounge with a snack bar, a vending area, the student post office and mailboxes, a big-screen projection unit for Friday night movies, and a jukebox; two other coed lounges, each equipped differently; and fifty-nine faculty residences.

ATHLETICS
The athletics program promotes physical fitness and good sportsmanship while instilling a healthy respect for regular exercise and competition. The School offers fifty-four athletic options per year, including forty-two teams in fifteen sports. These include junior, junior varsity, and varsity teams in many sports. Episcopal offers baseball, basketball, crew, cross-country, dance, field hockey, football, golf, lacrosse, soccer, squash, tennis, track, volleyball, and wrestling as well as aerobics, cross-training, and weight training during some seasons. Boys' teams participate in the Interstate Athletic Conference, and girls' teams take part in the Independent School League. Episcopal's teams play a full sports schedule with other independent schools in Maryland, Pennsylvania, Virginia, and Washington, D.C.

Episcopal's outstanding athletics facilities include Hummel Bowl, a 2,800-seat stadium; Flippin Field House, with three tennis courts, three basketball courts, a 200-yard track, and a batting cage; Centennial Gymnasium, which has a basketball court and fitness center; seven playing fields; and Goodman Squash Center, which houses five squash courts; Cooper Dawson Baseball International Diamond on Bryant Athletic Field; a wrestling cage; twelve all-weather tennis courts; an outdoor swimming pool; and Hoxton Track, a six-lane, 400-meter outdoor track.

EXTRACURRICULAR OPPORTUNITIES
The School makes maximum use of the opportunities of the Washington metropolitan area, and students are also encouraged to participate in and support on-campus activities with equal vigor. The

School presents at least three plays each year, one of which is a musical. Four School publications—a yearbook, a newspaper, and two literary magazines—offer opportunities for students to display their creative literary skills. Other extracurricular opportunities include three boys' and girls' a cappella groups, art, choir, community band, community service council, e-club (the varsity athletic club), environmental club, investment club, jazz ensemble, Latin club, model UN, outdoor club, performing arts group, pythonian society (student tutors), quiz bowl, spectrum (diversity group), student health awareness committee, student rock bands, student vestry, tour guides, Web publications, and youth in philanthropy, plus a varied activities program that involves students in athletic, cultural, historic, outdoor, and social activities throughout the Washington area. The School regularly provides tickets for performances at the Kennedy Center and other major theaters and concert halls in and near Washington. Qualified students may audition for the Mount Vernon Youth Symphony, which rehearses weekly at Episcopal, and the American Youth Philharmonic Orchestra.

DAILY LIFE
A buffet breakfast at 7:15 a.m. begins the day. Before the beginning of classes at 8 a.m. students put their rooms in order and participate in a work program that helps maintain the School. Four 45-minute periods precede required chapel on most days at 11:30 a.m. Chapel is followed by a seated lunch, three more class periods, and an afternoon athletics period. Students then attend dinner, which is followed by a 1-hour activities period in which students may relax or take part in extracurricular activities and clubs. The remainder of the evening is spent in study period until lights-out (10:15 p.m. for freshmen, 11 p.m. for sophomores and juniors, and 11:30 p.m. for seniors). During the evening study period, qualified students may study in their rooms, the library, or other approved study areas, while others report to supervised study hall.

All students attend chapel services three times a week and bimonthly Sunday services. Students who wish to participate more fully in the religious life of the School take part in the student vestry and a variety of community service programs. Students of other faiths are provided opportunities to attend services of their choosing in the Alexandria community.

WEEKEND LIFE
The School endeavors to make weekend life relaxing and productive. Activities include on-campus movies, dances, concerts, trips to Old Town Alex-

andria, and sports events in Washington, D.C. Faculty members regularly take students skiing, camping, hiking, and biking. The School provides tickets for performances at the Kennedy Center and other major theaters and for professional sports events.

COSTS AND FINANCIAL AID
The comprehensive fee for the 2005–06 session was $33,000. Tuition is payable in one, two, or nine installments.

Financial aid is awarded annually to those families whose need has been demonstrated through the School and Student Service for Financial Aid in Princeton, New Jersey. For the year 2005–06, scholarship funds of about $2.6 million were allocated to 30 percent of the student body. Several job opportunities enable students to supplement their personal spending money.

ADMISSIONS INFORMATION
Episcopal enrolls students with proven academic ability, strong character, and an interest in contributing significantly to the EHS community.

Typically, 110–130 new students enroll each year. In most years, roughly 40 percent of applicants are offered admission. The majority enroll in the ninth or tenth grade; a few enter in the eleventh. In special cases, a student may be admitted for his or her senior year. There are no postgraduates.

The formal application includes a personal application, recommendations from current teachers, an official school record, and a personal interview. Applicants to grades 9 and 10 are required to take the SSAT; applicants to grades 11 and 12 may submit PSAT or SAT scores.

APPLICATION TIMETABLE
Students who complete their applications ($50 fee) by January 31 are notified on March 10. Late applicants are considered on a rolling basis if space becomes available.

A personal interview and a visit to the campus are part of the admission process. Interviews and campus tours should be scheduled for class days. Classroom visits can be arranged. If a campus visit is not possible, the Admissions Office tries to coordinate other arrangements.

ADMISSIONS CORRESPONDENCE
Douglas C. Price, Director of Admissions
Episcopal High School
1200 North Quaker Lane
Alexandria, Virginia 22302

Phone: 703-933-4062
          877-933-4347 (toll-free)
Fax: 703-933-3016
E-mail: admissions@episcopalhighschool.org
Web site: http://www.episcopalhighschool.org

THE FENSTER SCHOOL

Tucson, Arizona

Type: Coeducational boarding and day college-preparatory school
Grades: 9–12
Enrollment: 161
Head of School: Don Saffer, Headmaster

THE SCHOOL

Since its founding in 1944, The Fenster School has had a single mission—to provide an environment in which students can realize their individual potential. The Fenster School provides an experience in learning for the whole person, with small classes, extracurricular activities, sports, and a supportive residential community. Seventy-five percent of Fenster's students could be defined as capable underachievers who thrive under the School's daily structure and small teacher-student ratio. Fenster not only offers students the structure that encourages academic success but also presents the rare, nurturing beauty of the desert, mountains, and forests of the Southwest. Students at Fenster live and work with people from around the world. They learn to accept challenges, solve problems, and accomplish goals. They learn about getting along with others. Perhaps more importantly, they learn about themselves.

A nonprofit independent school, Fenster occupies a 150-acre campus 3 miles outside of Tucson, Arizona, in the foothills of the Santa Catalina Mountains. The mountains have canyons, creeks, waterfalls, and, at the top of Mount Lemmon, the country's southernmost ski area. Together they form one of the world's most spectacular regions, where residents can hike, ski, camp, study nature, paint, or swim in a mountain stream—all in the same day.

Over the years, Fenster has earned a reputation for being caring and nurturing and for offering structured, supportive learning in a complete educational environment. Fenster is committed to working with students who benefit from structure.

The Fenster School is accredited by the North Central Association of Colleges and Schools and approved by the Arizona Department of Education. It is a member of the National Association of Independent Schools, the Arizona Association of Independent Schools, the Western Boarding Schools Association, the Secondary School Admission Test Board, the Southwestern Boarding Schools Association, and the Association of Boarding Schools (TABS).

ACADEMIC PROGRAMS

Classes available range from basic math and calculus to English and reading skills and American and British literature. Elective courses include art, sciences, and foreign languages. Students are enrolled in seven subject areas, including electives. Basic skills classes are offered to help students strengthen their math and English competencies. Four levels of computer skills classes, from beginning to advanced, are offered.

The academic year runs from September through May and is divided into two semesters. Grades and teacher comments are issued four times during the year. Students meet with advisers and have their academic performance monitored daily. All students are eligible each marking period for the academic and/or effort honor rolls. Juniors and seniors are eligible for election to the Saguaro Chapter of the National Honor Society.

The development of a student's program is flexible, taking into consideration previous academic experiences and the student's educational and postsecondary goals.

The average class size is 9 students, and the overall student-faculty ratio is 8:1. A faculty-supervised study hall is conducted in the evenings, Sunday through Thursday, and the library is open for individual study.

FACULTY AND ADVISERS

The 2005–06 faculty consisted of 16 full-time members and 1 part-time member, 8 of whom reside on campus. Of the total, 7 have earned master's degrees and 1 has a doctoral degree.

Mr. Don Saffer was appointed Headmaster in 1991. He holds degrees in history and business from UCLA and a master's degree in secondary education from USC.

The Fenster School seeks to employ men and women who are dedicated to the complete educational process. In addition to fulfilling teaching duties, each faculty member serves as an adviser to a small group of students and performs certain supervisory functions.

COLLEGE PLACEMENT

The college placement counselor aids students in selecting colleges that are appropriate to their interests and abilities. College representatives visit The Fenster School each year to meet with interested students. Students also have the opportunity to attend a College Night sponsored by a local high school. Full provision is made to ensure that students fulfill college entrance requirements regarding testing, including participation in the PSAT, SAT, SAT Subject Tests, ACT, and TOEFL.

Of the 38 graduates of the class of 2005, 37 went on to four-year or two-year colleges and 1 returned to his native country. Institutions that accepted Fenster graduates included Arizona State, Colorado State, LSU, Mesa Community College, Penn State, Pima Community College, Purdue, and the Universities of Arizona, San Francisco, and Washington.

STUDENT BODY AND CONDUCT

The 2004–05 student body consisted of 161 students—157 boarding and 4 day. In the total enrollment, twenty-five states and ten other countries were represented.

Like all schools, Fenster enforces reasonable rules. What separates Fenster from other, more traditional, boarding schools are the immediate consequences students face when they break the rules. With the leverage Fenster receives from parental support, a unique blend of on-campus work detail and detention study hours are used to encourage good choice making. With 150 acres available for community service, there is an endless amount of work that can be found to occupy the time of the few who choose to break the rules. Because Fenster feels that parents should not be penalized for the behavior of their children, every attempt is made to avoid expulsion of students. Parental commitment is of the utmost importance in the admission process. The School cannot deliver successful outcomes without the support of the parents.

The Student Council, an elected body, serves as a liaison between the students and the administration. It focuses on matters related to the quality of campus life and student privileges.

ACADEMIC FACILITIES

Four buildings containing nineteen classrooms are centrally located on the campus. A separate science building provides two fully equipped laboratories for biology, chemistry, and physics.

The 5,000-volume library contains several study areas for group and individual use. A computer center with twelve computers, all of which utilize CD-ROM, is also located in the library. Internet and e-mail access is available.

BOARDING AND GENERAL FACILITIES

Fenster is a close-knit community of students and faculty members working and living together. The School has eight adobe-style dormitories. Each resident lives with one roommate and shares a bathroom with two suitemates. Hopi House, the main building, contains the administrative offices, the reception lounge, the dining hall, kitchen facilities, and the Kiva Klub, the student recreation room and school store. Laundry facilities are located on campus.

ATHLETICS

All students are encouraged to participate in interscholastic athletics, including soccer, volleyball, basketball, and flag football. Fenster's sports facilities include two athletics fields, a weight room, a lighted outdoor basketball court, a swimming pool, and a spinning studio. Students also enjoy hiking, bike riding, and jogging. A ropes/challenge course is also available to students.

For many students, equestrian activities are a part of daily life; students may elect to participate in Western riding instruction. The riding area includes two large arenas, corrals, covered stalls, and tack rooms. As a member of the equestrian program, a student may compete in school- and community-sponsored events, such as Tucson's

annual Fiesta de los Vaqueros Rodeo Parade. Trail rides on campus and in Sabino Canyon are offered.

EXTRACURRICULAR OPPORTUNITIES
Participation in student government provides a useful educational experience, and all students are encouraged to become involved in the Student Council. The Student Council sponsors dances and promotes the development of student activities.

Students are responsible for the school yearbook. A variety of other clubs and activities are organized according to student interest.

DAILY LIFE
Most underachieving students simply lack the proper motivation and daily structure needed for academic success. One of the many benefits for the students is the daily monitoring of grades, attendance, homework, and behavior. Every school day, students wake up by 6:45 a.m. to perform their daily dorm duties. Breakfast follows at 7:30. Homerooms begin and end each class day. The homeroom is the cement of Fenster's academic structure. Attendance is required and strictly monitored. Staff members and students make special announcements, and behavioral transgressions from the prior evening or current day are noted. Students involved in any misconduct may be asked to join the work crew after school for a combination of landscaping, campus cleanup, and detention study hours. Students who break rules forfeit their free time for the betterment of the campus.

In the afternoon homeroom, teachers provide the Headmaster with a list of students who have performed below acceptable academic standards.

Eighth-period tutorials are utilized for students who had a grade of C-, D, or F in any subject area that day. Students starting to fall behind in their homework are also required to attend an eighth period. In the tutorials, students work one-to-one with their teachers to get back on track. Students who feel they need additional assistance may also volunteer for eighth period. If students end the class week below acceptable standards, weekend tutorials are also provided. The day-to-day consistency of the structure is what encourages success for Fenster students.

WEEKEND LIFE
A minimum of four outings are scheduled each weekend. Off-campus activities may include bowling; indoor rock-climbing; hiking in the Santa Catalinas; ski trips; field trips to Kitt Peak National Observatory, Flandrau Planetarium, and the Arizona-Sonora Desert Museum; athletics events at the University of Arizona; trail rides; trips to Mexico and the Grand Canyon; local ghost town tours; and the popular weekly trips to local shopping malls and movie theaters. Students are encouraged to take advantage of the many cultural and recreational opportunities available in Tucson.

SUMMER PROGRAMS
The Fenster School conducts a six-week summer session from July through mid-August. Credit is offered for enrichment and remedial courses.

COSTS AND FINANCIAL AID
In 2005–06, boarding tuition was $26,900; day tuition was $13,450. Additional costs include an expense deposit of $400 and a medical deposit of $200. Allowances arranged with parents range from $10 to $20 weekly.

ADMISSIONS INFORMATION
The Fenster School's program is designed for average students who want to prepare for college. Students are considered for admission if they are college-capable students who can demonstrate a willingness to learn. Applicants are admitted at all grade levels. Capable underachievers are welcome to apply.

An academic transcript is required. A personal interview is recommended.

APPLICATION TIMETABLE
An initial inquiry is welcome at any time during the year. Campus tours are scheduled, in conjunction with interviews, from 8:30 to 5 on weekdays or on weekends as needed. Candidates are encouraged to visit the School during the week so that they can observe classes in progress. Students will be accepted after the opening of school on a space-available basis.

ADMISSIONS CORRESPONDENCE
Don Saffer, Headmaster
The Fenster School
8500 East Ocotillo Drive
Tucson, Arizona 85750

Phone: 520-749-3340
      520-465-0990 (cell)
Fax: 520-749-3349
E-mail: fenadm@mindspring.com
Web site: http://www.fenster-school.com

FLORIDA AIR ACADEMY

Melbourne, Florida

Type: Boys' and girls' boarding and day college-preparatory and military school
Grades: 6–12, postgraduate year
Enrollment: 400
Head of School: Col. James Dwight, President

THE SCHOOL

Founded in 1961 by Colonel Jonathan Dwight, Florida Air Academy (FAA) turns boys and girls of promise into citizens of character. Ideally located on central Florida's high-technology Space Coast, the Academy provides an outstanding environment for learning and growth. Offering an official United States Air Force Junior Reserve Officer Training Corps (JROTC) program, FAA provides an extensive curriculum, excellent facilities, and exciting extracurricular programs. Regardless of the area of study chosen, young men and women at FAA—bolstered by superior academics and a safe, structured environment—learn the value of responsibility and self-discipline while growing into confident, well-rounded adults. From the classroom to the athletic fields to the numerous available organizations, cadets learn those traits that create a leader.

All cadets in grades 9–12 participate in JROTC for a minimum of one year, which is supervised and organized by official United States Air Force personnel. Specialized activities such as the drill team, color guard, band, and honor guard complement the Academy's program; cadets who participate in JROTC activities are rewarded through rank, ribbons, and other achievement awards while learning the value of teamwork, integrity, self-respect, dedication, and determination.

FAA is fully accredited by the Southern Association of Colleges and Schools and the Florida Council of Independent Schools and is a member of the Association of Military Colleges and Schools, the Southeastern Association of Boarding Schools, the National Honor Society, the Florida Education Association, the National Education Association, the Florida High School Activities Association, the National Bureau of Private Schools, and the Kitty Hawk Air Society.

ACADEMIC PROGRAMS

Success at all levels is achieved through the Academy's comprehensive offering of courses, structured classroom instruction, and compulsory study periods. Minimum requirements for an FAA diploma are 26 credits earned in grades 9–12, which must include the following: English, 4; mathematics, 4; science 3; social studies (which must include American Government and Economics and U.S. History), 3; foreign language, 2; computer science, 1; and physical education/ health, 1. The remaining credits may be chosen from a wide variety of electives, but must include aerospace science JROTC in the first year of attendance at the Academy. An honors program, designed to challenge academically motivated students, and seven advanced placement (AP) courses are offered.

Report cards are issued at nine-week intervals, four times during the year. Parents may also access their child's grades via the Internet. Academic progress reports are also sent four times per year. Any cadet who receives two or more failing grades for academic subjects is placed on academic probation; periodic reviews of the cadet's academic standing may remove the student from probation. Any cadet on probation for two 9-week grading periods is subject to dismissal. Each cadet is also assigned a discipline grade at the end of each grading period.

Optional special programs, offered at an additional fee, include remedial math and English, driver's education, SAT preparation, and TOEFL preparation. An intensive English as a second language (ESL) program is also available.

For cadets who dream of piloting their own aircraft, FAA's elective flight programs, offered at an additional cost, are designed to meet the skills, abilities, and ambitions of each student. A Junior Wings Flying Program is offered in grades 6–8, and a more advanced program is available to those in higher grades. Upon completion of FAA's flight training program, cadets have the opportunity to obtain a private pilot's license; once that milestone is reached, cadets can go further and become eligible for commercial, instrument, or multiengine ratings.

FACULTY AND ADVISERS

Thirty-five state-certified, degreed instructors (22 women, 13 men) challenge cadets to excel academically and to hone individual strengths. This dedicated, experienced faculty consistently emphasizes the importance of discipline and achievement and acts as role models for the student body. Twenty faculty members hold a master's degree. All flight instructors are licensed by the Federal Aviation Administration. The low teacher-student ratio of 1:15 ensures that cadets receive individualized attention in the classroom. Furthermore, each student is assisted by FAA's guidance department, with which they build an academic program that best matches their interests and abilities.

COLLEGE PLACEMENT

Seventy-one students graduated in 2004. All planned to attend colleges that include Auburn, Boston University, Florida State, Norwich, Penn State, the U.S. Coast Guard Academy, the U.S. Military Academy, and the Universities of Florida, Massachusetts, and Texas. Many FAA graduates have also gone on to highly rewarding careers in military and commercial aviation.

STUDENT BODY AND CONDUCT

The FAA student body includes 325 boarding cadets and 75 day students who range in age from 11 to 19. In the Upper School, there are 66 students in grade 9 (13 day, 53 boarding), 90 students in grade 10 (14 day, 76 boarding), 73 students in grade 11 (7 day, 66 boarding), and 70 students in grade 12 (10 day, 60 boarding). The student body represents a variety of socioeconomic and cultural backgrounds. The largest student groups come from California, Florida, Texas, Puerto Rico, and the U.S. Virgin Islands. International students come from the Bahamas, Bermuda, Costa Rica, Indonesia, Japan, Korea, and Venezuela.

The Academy expects its cadets to comply with its Honor Code as outlined in the *Cadet Handbook*. Corrective actions for those who do not follow rules and regulations include counseling, demerits, restriction to campus, and suspension. Stealing, possession of alcohol or weapons, hazing, and immoral acts (those that cause violence or physical or mental harm to another) may result in immediate dismissal from the Academy. Purchase, possession, use, intent to use, or distribution of drugs, unauthorized substances, or drug paraphernalia will result in immediate dismissal.

ACADEMIC FACILITIES

Hart, Haerle, Adeline, and Donelson Halls contain classrooms, the science laboratory, four computer labs, a language center, laundry facilities, and the tailor shop. In addition, construction of a new classroom complex was completed in 1996. This 5,000-square-foot facility, a series of three interconnected buildings, contains eight classrooms, a bell tower, and a central courtyard. A 5,500-square-foot art and music center was added in 2000.

The well-equipped library and science and computer labs enable students to add to material taught in the classroom; cadets are encouraged to use these resources to strengthen logic and research skills and to further investigate those subjects that intrigue them.

BOARDING AND GENERAL FACILITIES

The Hall of Flags contains cadet living quarters, a student lounge, a campus store, the dining room, the library, and administrative offices. Dwight, Blatt, and Phelps Halls also contain administrative offices. All living areas, classrooms, the dining room, and the library are fully air conditioned.

The campus occupies more than 30 acres, including two athletic fields, two tennis courts, an outdoor basketball court, a large swimming pool, and an air-conditioned gymnasium. A modern weight room, a sports locker room, and visiting team facilities are also available. The adjacent Melbourne Municipal Golf Course serves as the home course for the Falcon Golf Team.

A school canteen is operated on campus. An Academy nurse is on duty in the infirmary 24 hours-a-day, seven days-a-week. The campus, owned by school stockholders, is valued at more than $5 million.

Modern airplanes and state-of-the-art simulators are available less than 1 mile away at Melbourne Regional Airport.

ATHLETICS

The Academy is a member of the Florida High School Activities Association and holds an outstanding record in interscholastic competition with both private and public schools in central Florida. Many cadets compete on FAA's varsity and junior varsity teams, which include football, basketball, baseball, soccer, cross-country, track, tennis, swimming, volleyball, weightlifting, wrestling, and golf. A variety of intramural sports, such as volleyball, flag football, and softball, are also offered as well as self-challenging sports such as Tae Kwon Do and scuba. Because of its magnificent coastal location just minutes from the Atlantic Ocean and other waterways, FAA is able to offer fishing, swimming, scuba, and surfing.

EXTRACURRICULAR OPPORTUNITIES

Regular special outings include trips to the planetarium, airboat rides in the marshes, and viewing the Thunderbirds at an airshow. On-campus clubs include photography, rocketry, video production, and model-building, to name just a few. Participation in cultural events, coed functions, and civic affairs is also encouraged. A full-time Director of Activities plans social events and trips.

DAILY LIFE

After reveille, formation, squadron inspection, and day student inspection, which begin at 6:30 a.m., the academic day includes a total of seven 45-minute periods starting at 8 a.m. and ending at 2:15 p.m. All teachers are available from 3 to 3:45 for individual instruction and extra help. Evening study hall is held from 6:30 p.m. to 8:30 p.m.

WEEKEND LIFE

Weekend activities include the year-opening pool party, food and entertainment extravaganzas, trips to local attractions, and dances. Cadets enjoy trips to Kennedy Space Center, Disney World, EPCOT Center, Busch Gardens, MGM and Universal Studios, and Wet 'n Wild Water Park. Excursions to the beach, movies, mall, bowling, and roller-skating are all part of the social life at FAA.

SUMMER PROGRAMS

During the summer months (late June to early August), a full academic curriculum is offered for all grades. Courses in flight training, English as a second language, driver's education, Tae Kwon Do, and SAT preparation are also provided. Selected cadets may also enroll in an Air Force JROTC Summer Leadership School. The application deadline for summer programs is June 1.

COSTS AND FINANCIAL AID

For the 2005–06 school year, costs for tuition, textbooks, initial base exchange issue, and Academy and personal needs are $24,000 for boarding students and $7500 for day students. Tuition includes the educational program, uniforms, infirmary use, and the Academy yearbook for boarding and day students and room and board, laundry, linens, haircuts, and dry cleaning for boarding students. Fees for weekly allowance, lab and art supplies, trips, and the canteen are extra. The student's Cadet Bank ($1500 for boarding students and $500 for day students) covers the initial base exchange purchases. Tuition down payments and the Cadet Bank deposit must be received by the Academy no later than August 1 for the following school year.

Tuition payment plans are available to all students. Financial aid is based on a student's documented financial need as evaluated by an independent agency. The financial aid application process takes 4–6 weeks to complete. Financial aid awards typically range from $500 to $1500 per year. In 2004–05, 79 Upper School students applied for and received aid. A total of $394,050 in aid was awarded in 2004–05.

ADMISSIONS INFORMATION

A successful applicant must be of good moral character, supply standardized test scores and academic records that demonstrate the student's ability to perform at or above grade level, and provide good references. FAA has neither the ability to accommodate nor the inclination to accept students with a history of discipline problems. To apply for admission, students must complete the application/contract form and accompany it with two recent photographs and a nonrefundable $100 fee. An interview is also strongly recommended.

Prerequisites for applicants from outside the United States include a reasonable command of the English language or attendance at the Academy's summer session prior to fall enrollment.

APPLICATION TIMETABLE

Applications are accepted year-round, but it is best to apply by May 1. Summer school applications are due by June 1. After all information is received, FAA's Admissions Committee reviews the material to determine the candidate's qualification for acceptance; applicants are promptly notified of the committee's decision. Within two weeks of acceptance, the appropriate validation fee should be submitted ($1500 for fall term, $1500 for summer session) in order to reserve the student's space.

ADMISSIONS CORRESPONDENCE

Mr. William Orris, Director of Admissions
Florida Air Academy
1950 South Academy Drive
Melbourne, Florida 32901

Phone: 321-723-3211
Fax: 321-676-0422
E-mail: admissions@flair.com
Web site: http://www.flair.com

FORK UNION MILITARY ACADEMY

Fork Union, Virginia

Type: Boys' boarding and day college-preparatory military-style school
Grades: 6–PG: Middle School, 6–8; Upper School, 9–12, postgraduate year
Enrollment: School total: 530; Middle School: 61; Upper School: 469
Head of School: Lt. Gen. John E. Jackson Jr., President

THE SCHOOL

Fork Union Military Academy (FUMA) was founded in 1898 by Dr. William E. Hatcher, a noted Baptist minister, and was originally a coeducational "classical" school for day students who boarded in village homes. Subsequently, the school was converted into a boarding institution with a military orientation for young men. Today, Fork Union is one of the largest schools of its kind in the country.

The Academy's educational goal is to raise each cadet to his best level physically, mentally, and spiritually, thereby readying him for further educational and career opportunities and preparing him for a lifetime of success. FUMA's emphasis on Christian values and leadership skills helps promote character, integrity, teamwork, self-discipline, and pride.

The Academy is located on 1,000 acres in the gently rolling, rural Piedmont section of Virginia. Washington, D.C., is approximately 120 miles northeast; Richmond, Virginia, 50 miles east; and Charlottesville, Virginia, 30 miles northwest.

The Academy, a nonprofit institution, is governed by a 26-member Board of Trustees, 14 of whom are alumni. The trustees are responsible for the $34-million plant and $13 million in productive endowments.

During the 2004–05 academic year, Fork Union's Development Office realized $1.4 million in donations and pledges from alumni, trustees, parents, and friends.

Fork Union Military Academy is accredited by the Virginia Association of Independent Schools. It holds memberships in the National Association of Independent Schools, the Association of Military Colleges and Schools of the United States, and the Southern Association of Independent Schools.

ACADEMIC PROGRAMS

The academic program at Fork Union is designed for college preparation. Since 1950, Upper School cadets have studied under the One-Subject Plan, which allows them to concentrate on a single major subject area for approximately seven weeks per course throughout the school year.

Students must complete 21½ academic units in order to graduate; these include, at minimum, 4 units in English, 3 in social studies, 3 in mathematics, 3 in science, 2 in health, and ½ in religious studies, plus physical education. Electives include art history, astronomy, and computer science. Honors and Advanced Placement courses are offered in English, calculus, history, government, and biology.

The Middle School (grades 6–8) operates on a conventional semester plan, offering courses in math, science, English, social studies, and health and physical education. Enrichment courses are offered in art, computers, current events, drama, French, and music. Students are assigned courses on the basis of academic requirements and ability. There are 10 to 15 students in an average class. Special instruction is available for cadets who require special academic assistance.

Study periods are maintained five nights per week from 7:45 to 9:45 in the Upper School and from 7 to 8:30 in the Middle School. All cadets are required to keep these hours, during which faculty officers are on duty to maintain a quiet atmosphere for study.

FACULTY AND ADVISERS

There are 41 full-time teaching faculty members (34 men and 7 women) serving the cadet corps. Of these, 30 have advanced degrees and 40 live on campus or within the local community. In addition, 13 administrative officers assist the teachers, students, and parents in coordinating the educational program of the cadets.

Each cadet is assigned an administrator or faculty member as his adviser for the year; faculty members are assigned 7 to 11 advisees with whom they meet regularly. Faculty members also sponsor interest clubs and field trips and serve as athletics coaches.

The Academy seeks to hire for its faculty individuals who are dedicated to helping young men develop their potential for success in adult life. Fork Union faculty members must have strong academic credentials, experience in dealing with young men, and a positive attitude.

The Academy's President is Lieutenant General John E. Jackson Jr., USAF (Ret.). The general earned his baccalaureate degree from Alderson-Broaddus College and his master's degree in business and personnel management from Central Michigan University. He is a graduate of the Senior Managers in Government Course, Harvard University, and, in 1993, Alderson-Broaddus College awarded him an honorary doctorate in public administration.

COLLEGE PLACEMENT

The Director of Guidance aids Upper School cadets in the college placement process. Special courses are offered to help students prepare for the SAT, which is offered on campus four times a year. The ACT is given three times each year. A College Day is held each fall, with approximately sixty-five colleges sending representatives to the campus.

Of the 150 cadets who graduated in 2005, 99 percent are attending college. These graduates are attending such colleges and universities as The Citadel, George Mason, Virginia Military Institute, Virginia Tech, William and Mary, and the Universities of North Carolina and Virginia.

STUDENT BODY AND CONDUCT

Of the 530 cadets currently attending Fork Union, 13 are day students.

The Academy enrolls young men from thirty-one states and thirteen other countries. Approximately 70 percent of the cadets come from homes in the Eastern Seaboard region, and the remaining students come from throughout the United States and the world.

Though Fork Union is affiliated with the Virginia Baptist General Association, cadets represent twenty-seven different religious denominations. Twenty-one percent of the students come from designated minority groups.

The cadets in the Upper School operate under an Honor Code that prohibits lying, cheating, or stealing. Infractions are brought to the attention of an honor council composed of 20 cadets and a faculty adviser. The final responsibility for handling violations rests with the administration.

ACADEMIC FACILITIES

Hatcher Hall, the central building on campus, contains administrative offices and classrooms. The J. Caldwell Wicker Science Building and Planetarium and the Moretz Learning Center house modern scientific laboratory facilities, eighteen classrooms, and a planetarium. The John J. Wicker Chapel, which seats 550, is used primarily for religious services and special meetings. The Marion C. Thomas Gymnasium includes a stage for student, faculty, and guest performances. The Dorothy Thomasson Estes Dining Hall seats 750 and houses the Fork Union Cadet Store.

The Guy E. Beatty Library completed a major addition at the opening of school 2005; it contains more than 19,500 volumes and carries subscriptions to numerous periodicals and newspapers. In addition, the library houses a videotape center and the student computer facilities, which include a networked, automated library card catalog; CD-ROM reference materials; a six-station student reference/research network; and the CD-Newsbank periodical research application. Upper and Middle School cadets also enjoy access to computer laboratories that offer 300 multimedia online computer workstations.

BOARDING AND GENERAL FACILITIES

Students are housed 2 or 3 per room in Snead Hall, Memorial Hall, and the Middle School dormitory. Faculty members, a number of whom reside in the dormitory buildings, are available to supervise and counsel cadets.

A student center provides areas for informal gatherings, and the Sabre Shop contains a snack bar, post exchange, and post office. Upper School cadets' rooms are equipped with cable access for free-time viewing. There is a 4-acre lake that offers recreational activities. The Yeatman Infirmary, with a capacity of twenty-two beds, is staffed 24 hours a day by nurses and by the

school physician, who remains on call at all times. Morning sick call is held every day.

ATHLETICS
The athletics program at Fork Union takes into consideration the needs and capabilities of every cadet. Varsity (postgraduate), prep (high school), and junior prep teams compete in baseball, basketball, cross-country, football, golf, lacrosse, orienteering, riflery, soccer, swimming, tennis, track, and wrestling. The Middle School fields separate teams in baseball, basketball, football, lacrosse, soccer, swimming, and wrestling,. Fork Union competes in the Virginia Independent School League, and the postgraduate teams also compete with nationally ranked college JV and junior college teams. Cadets not involved in interscholastic competition may enroll in a variety of intramural offerings or physical conditioning.

The Academy's extensive athletics facilities include a new (2005) Olympic-size, eight-lane Aquatic Center; the 85,000-square-foot Estes Athletic Center (which houses three basketball courts, weight rooms, a 160-meter indoor track, a wrestling room, racquetball and squash courts, and a well-equipped sports medicine facility); the main 7-acre athletics field (four football fields, two baseball diamonds, and a 2,500-seat stadium); a 400-meter all-weather track; six all-weather tennis courts; an auxiliary 2-acre athletics field; a rifle range; horseshoe courts; and outdoor basketball/volleyball courts.

EXTRACURRICULAR OPPORTUNITIES
Every Fork Union cadet is encouraged to take an active role in extracurricular activities. A highly acclaimed sixty-piece marching band, men's chorales, and competitive drill teams perform regularly at Academy and local area functions. The Quadrille Club coordinates school dances, and the *Skirmisher* is the school's yearbook. In addition, other clubs meet regularly to promote a variety of interests.

Visiting speakers are frequently invited to speak to cadets during chapel services and for special programs. On-campus entertainment includes guest bands, performers, and choral groups, as well as a newly instituted Payne Greater Issues Forum.

The FUMA flight program offers cadets ground instruction and actual flying time, leading to a pilot's license.

A sense of community service is inculcated into each cadet as the corps actively participates in a local Christmas program for needy children, fund-raising for worthy projects, home visitation for community residents, and feeding the homeless.

DAILY LIFE
A typical day at Fork Union begins with reveille at 6:15 a.m., followed by breakfast at 7. The class day runs from 8 to 2, Monday through Thursday, and from 8 to 12:30 on Friday. Classes also meet on approximately six Saturdays throughout the year. In addition to the academic periods, each class day features a morning break, a chapel service (twice per week), a supervised study or study skills period, and a 45-minute lunch break. Afternoons include time for activities and clubs, military drill twice a week, and athletics. Dinner is at 5:30, with time for relaxation before the supervised study period. Taps is sounded at 10 p.m. in the Upper School and at 9:30 in the Middle School.

Inspection, held on Saturday morning, is followed by time for recreation and athletics. On Sunday morning, cadets attend religious services of their choice either on or off campus.

WEEKEND LIFE
Fork Union observes a policy of frequent weekend leaves and day passes, subject to parental permission. Student eligibility for leaves is conditional, based on satisfactory academic performance and good behavior.

On-campus activities include athletics and club activities. Frequently, faculty members sponsor trips to see a historic site, to view classic movies or enjoy a dinner theater, to explore a museum, or to have a day of fun on nearby ski slopes or at a theme park.

Book fairs, parades, and other activities are scheduled for special weekends, such as Parents' Day, the Military Ball weekend, Mother's Day, and Alumni Weekend.

SUMMER PROGRAMS
Fork Union sponsors a fully accredited nonmilitary summer school that runs for four weeks from late June to early August. Boys are admitted on a day or boarding basis.

Academic subjects are offered for grades 7–12 and are taught by Fork Union personnel, subject to full Academy standards. Courses may be taken

for enrichment, advancement, or review. The extracurricular emphasis is on intramurals. Approximately 150 students attended in 2005. For further information, students should write to the Director of the Summer School.

COSTS AND FINANCIAL AID
In 2005–06, tuition, room, and board fees were $21,190. Uniforms cost approximately $3080. The day student charge was $14,475.

Approximately 30 percent of the students in 2004–05 received some form of financial aid, which includes certain standard reductions and merit- or need-based scholarships. Scholarship money awarded amounted to more than $600,000. Affordable parent loan programs and monthly payment plans are also available.

ADMISSIONS INFORMATION
Fork Union Military Academy accepts qualified students into its college-preparatory program without regard to race, color, religion, or national origin. Applicants are admitted on the basis of previous scholastic record, academic potential, and character. If testing is required, the school helps with the arrangements.

Generally, the ninth grade class holds the largest number of new cadets. However, admission can be available at each grade level, depending on the current enrollment.

APPLICATION TIMETABLE
Applications are received on a continuing basis. A fee of $50 must accompany each application. A personal conference and interview at the school is requested; an appointment should be arranged in advance.

Notification of acceptance is made when all supporting materials have been received by the school. These materials include a transcript of previous grades, standardized test scores, teacher recommendations, and questionnaires filled out by a school official and by the parents.

ADMISSIONS CORRESPONDENCE
Lt. Col. Steve Macek
Director of Admissions
Fork Union Military Academy
P.O. Box 278
4744 James Madison Highway
Fork Union, Virginia 23055

Phone: 434-842-4205
E-mail: maceks@fuma.org
Web site: http://www.forkunion.com

FOUNTAIN VALLEY SCHOOL OF COLORADO

Colorado Springs, Colorado

Type: Coeducational boarding and day college-preparatory school
Grades: 9–12
Enrollment: 236
Head of School: Dr. John E. Creeden, Headmaster

THE SCHOOL

Fountain Valley School of Colorado (FVS) was established in 1929 and was opened the following year by a group of visionary men and women that included philanthropists, statesmen, scientists, entrepreneurs, and educators. Many had personal roots in or professional ties to the East; all shared the conviction that the Eastern independent school tradition of academic excellence, progressive ideals, individual responsibility, and creativity would thrive in the expansiveness of the Rocky Mountain West. John Dewey, the notable American educational reformer, was on the first Board of Trustees, and his grandson graduated with the class of 1940.

Fountain Valley's mission remains unchanged: to educate young people of sound character who seek high standards and a demanding course of study and to develop students emotionally, morally, and socially. Students are taught responsibility, leadership skills, and sensitivity to the needs and interests of others. The rigorous curriculum is designed to stimulate curiosity, develop intellectual stamina, and prepare students for the challenges of the finest colleges and universities.

The School is situated at the base of Pike's Peak on the former Bradley Ranch on a 1,100-acre campus in the southeastern corner of Colorado Springs. Additional property includes the 40-acre Mountain Campus deep in the San Isabel National Forest, 115 miles west of the main campus.

Fountain Valley School of Colorado is a nonprofit corporation governed by a 26-member Board of Trustees, 13 of whom are alumni. The School's endowment is valued at $27 million. In 2004–05, annual giving was $1,012,646, with capital gifts totaling $412,823. More than 2,600 alumni maintain contact with FVS, and many are actively involved. In June 2005, more than 600 alumni returned to campus to celebrate the School's seventy-fifth anniversary. In 2003, FVS completed a $24-million capital campaign, the largest in Colorado independent school history.

FVS is accredited by the Colorado State Board of Education and the Association of Colorado Independent Schools and holds memberships in the National Association of Independent Schools, the Secondary School Admission Test Board, the College Board, the Association of Boarding Schools, the Council for Advancement and Support of Education, the Colorado High School Activities Association, and the Cum Laude Society.

ACADEMIC PROGRAMS

Fountain Valley's academic program is rigorous and comprehensive, offering honors and Advanced Placement courses in all disciplines and providing a flexible approach to placing students in courses that are appropriate to their abilities. More than 100 courses were offered by six departments in the 2004–05 year.

The school year is divided into two semesters; major semester courses receive ½ credit. Twenty credits in major courses are required for graduation (most seniors graduate with more than 22 credits), with the following minimum departmental expectations: 4 credits of English; completion of the third-year level of one foreign language; 3 credits of high school mathematics, with the minimum successful completion of algebra II, 3 credits of science (including 1 credit of biology), 3½ credits of history (including 1 credit of Western civilization, 1 credit of global studies, and 1 credit of U.S. history), 1 credit of visual and performing arts, ½ credit of computer skills, ½ credit of human development, and 4 credits of physical education. Most students take one minor and five major courses per semester. In addition, English as a second language (ESL) is offered at the intermediate and advanced levels. Qualified seniors, with the approval of the Curriculum Committee, design Independent Study Projects to supplement their advanced studies. All seniors participate in the Senior Seminar, a weeklong service project culminating their FVS education.

The student-teacher ratio is 5:1. The average class size is 12 students. The small classes allow for personal attention and provide an intimate learning environment characterized by mutual respect and active participation.

Grades (letters A through E) are given at midterm and at the conclusion of each semester. Written comments are provided for each course at the fall midterm for all new students and at the end of the term for all students.

FACULTY AND ADVISERS

Forty faculty members teach full- and part-time. Thirty live on campus with their families. They hold thirty-seven graduate degrees.

Fountain Valley's sixth headmaster, John E. Creeden, assumed the leadership of the School in 1995. He graduated from Holy Cross College and earned his M.A. and Ph.D. from the University of Wisconsin (doctorate in educational administration). Prior to his appointment as Headmaster, he held several teaching and administrative positions at Phillips Andover; the University of Sussex, England; the University of Wisconsin; and Rutgers, the State University of New Jersey, where he served most recently as Associate Provost for Faculty Personnel and Planning. He serves as president of the Association of Colorado Independent Schools (ACIS) and serves on the Board of Trustees of the National Association of Independent Schools (NAIS).

Because all faculty members share responsibility for the residential and cocurricular programs at the School, Fountain Valley seeks to recruit teachers with personal idealism, a genuine respect for students, and high professional competence. An endowment and annually budgeted funds ensure continued faculty professional development.

COLLEGE PLACEMENT

Students begin to prepare for college in their first year at Fountain Valley by choosing their courses and carefully planning with the Director of Studies. Formal college counseling starts in the junior year. Sessions are planned to help students understand the complexities of the college application process and learn about the range of colleges that offer programs in which they are interested.

Each fall, Fountain Valley holds a college fair to give juniors and seniors an opportunity to talk with representatives from approximately 140 colleges and universities. Students get firsthand information from the Director of College Counseling, an extensive library of college catalogs, pamphlets, videos, various computer programs, and a workbook designed to help them with the college application process.

The Director of College Counseling begins working with individual students and small groups during the junior year. She creates an individual list of college possibilities for each junior tailored to their expressed interests and needs. She continues to work closely with each senior in refining his or her college plans.

The classes of 2002, 2003, 2004, and 2005 had an SAT range of scores (middle 50 percent) of critical reading, 540–640, math, 510–640; and writing, 530–640. Over this four-year span, FVS graduates were admitted to 238 four-year colleges and universities in forty-two states, the District of Columbia, and five other countries. They chose to enroll at 115 of these colleges, including all eight Ivy League institutions, and many other highly selective colleges and universities in the United States.

STUDENT BODY AND CONDUCT

In 2005–06, the School's enrollment was 150 boarding students and 86 day students. Students represented twenty states and nine countries.

The School works to create and maintain an environment for learning in which goodwill and mutual trust exist among all members of the campus community. At the same time, it adheres to the belief that every strong community must have a clear set of standards and defined values that all its members uphold. If a student is found to be involved in a serious disciplinary matter, the case is heard by an honor council composed of elected student representatives and faculty members. The council considers all facets of each case and recommends a course of action to the Headmaster.

A Community Council chaired by the president of the student body provides a forum in which any members of the school community can make recommendations regarding the operation of the School.

ACADEMIC FACILITIES

The majority of classes are conducted in the Froelicher Academic Building, which includes a state-of-the-art science annex and three computer labs. An arts building houses art, jewelry, and ceramics studios, an art gallery, a photo laboratory, and production rooms for the School's publications. The John B. Hawley, Jr. Library has forty-one study carrels, two seminar rooms, and a film editing and projection room. The library has an online catalog of more than 25,000 volumes and a collection of periodicals on microfilm.

BOARDING AND GENERAL FACILITIES

The School recently completed a three-year, $16-million residence hall renovation and construction master plan. There is one faculty houseparent family for every 15 boarding students.

The Hacienda, Fountain Valley's original ranch house, has dining facilities for 300, private dining rooms for meetings, and a living room for meetings and quiet conversation. The Chase Stone Infirmary is a ten-bed facility with a nurse on call at all times.

The Frautschi Campus Center, a state-of-the-art student center that was completed in 1990, has a student-operated snack bar, a campus bookstore, a post office, lounge and recreation facilities, a faculty lounge, a multimedia viewing room, and a meeting space.

ATHLETICS

Fountain Valley believes strongly in the value of sports for building physical fitness and self-confidence. Most students fulfill their requirement by participating in a variety of interscholastic sports, including basketball, cross-country, lacrosse, skiing, soccer, tennis, and track for boys and basketball, cross-country, field hockey, skiing, soccer, swimming, tennis, track, and volleyball for girls. FVS also fields the nation's only high school polocrosse team.

Students may also earn physical education credit for horseback riding and outdoor education. The School provides suitable levels of competition for students of varying abilities. FVS offers a comprehensive horsemanship program that provides diverse training in both English and Western riding. Riding facilities include the largest outdoor arena in the Colorado Springs area, a covered arena, a gymkhana field, a barn, stables, and polocrosse fields.

The Penrose Sports Center includes a gymnasium, two squash courts, a weight room, and a five-lane, 25-yard indoor swimming pool. Originally planted in Kentucky bluegrass for the polo ponies raised on the Bradley Ranch, FVS athletic fields are the finest in Colorado for soccer, field hockey, and lacrosse. Nine tennis courts; stables; and a climbing wall complete the facilities.

EXTRACURRICULAR OPPORTUNITIES

Extracurricular activities vary from season to season (fall, winter, and spring). Students perform in three major drama productions annually. Guest speakers and artists regularly visit the campus for formal presentations and lectures. There are three student publications and fourteen student activity clubs.

Special annual events include a gymkhana in which a riding team from Fountain Valley competes with teams from local riding clubs, Earth Day, and Unity Day.

During Interim, traditional classes are suspended and students participate in a variety of on- and off-campus programs. Recent Interims have included kayaking in Georgia, marine biology in Baja, and photography in Arizona's Canyon de Chelly.

DAILY LIFE

Classes meet five days per week in six 50-minute sessions between 8 a.m. and 3 p.m. Cocurricular activities are scheduled from 3:30 to 5:30 p.m. One period is used for student-adviser and all-School meetings. Students and teachers generally have at least one free period daily.

Dinner is at 5:30, and study hours run from 7 to 10 p.m. All boarding students are expected to observe study hours, although seniors in good academic standing may be excused in the spring of their senior year.

Day students are expected to be on campus before their first commitment and to remain until 5:30 p.m. on weekdays. Day students may stay overnight in a residence hall with permission from the houseparent and the student's parents.

WEEKEND LIFE

Weekends are the time for relaxation and taking advantage of campus resources and a host of opportunities in the surrounding mountain regions.

Student and faculty teams sponsor recreational activities throughout the weekend. Events include mountain climbing, skiing, and pack trips, often based at the Mountain Campus; excursions to Colorado Springs and Denver for shopping, movies, theater, concerts, and dinner; and dances, barbecues, movies, and athletics on campus.

Students with parental permission may request a weekend away from the campus. Many students visit friends or relatives or are invited to another student's home.

COSTS AND FINANCIAL AID

In 2005–06, tuition was $31,400 for boarding students and $35,500 for ESL students; the cost (including all meals and bus transportation) for day students was $17,500. A book fee of $890 covers textbooks, art supplies, lab fees, and one yearbook. Interim, a required weeklong experiential learning opportunity, varies in cost according to the student's choice of trip. There are fees for optional activities such as music lessons, horseback riding, and horse boarding. Tuition insurance and a tuition payment plan are available.

In 2005–06, 37 percent of students received approximately $1.3 million in need-based financial aid. Fountain Valley School adheres to the principles of good practice in its need-based aid distribution as part of the National Association of Independent Schools. The School also offers a number of merit-based scholarships.

ADMISSIONS INFORMATION

Students are admitted without regard to race, religion, or nationality. Fountain Valley School of Colorado seeks students who have the potential to benefit from a rigorous academic program and contribute to the school community. Students are admitted in grades 9 through 11 on the basis of previous school records, three academic recommendations, results of the Secondary School Admission Test (SSAT), an essay, and a personal interview.

APPLICATION TIMETABLE

Fountain Valley subscribes to the March 10 notification date endorsed by the SSAT Board. The application deadline is February 1. Applications are processed after that date if openings remain. The application fee is $50 for applicants residing in the United States and $100 for applicants living outside the United States.

ADMISSIONS CORRESPONDENCE

Randy Roach, Director of Admission and
    Financial Aid
Fountain Valley School of Colorado
6155 Fountain Valley School Road
Colorado Springs, Colorado 80911
Phone: 719-390-7035 Ext. 251
Fax: 719-390-7762
E-mail: admission@fvs.edu
Web site: http://www.fvs.edu

FOXCROFT SCHOOL

Middleburg, Virginia

Type: Girls' boarding and day college-preparatory school
Grades: 9–12
Enrollment: 166
Head of School: Mary Louise Leipheimer

THE SCHOOL

Foxcroft School offers a strong college-preparatory program in a challenging and supportive academic atmosphere. Charlotte Haxall Noland founded the School in 1914 and remained Director until her retirement in 1955. Miss Charlotte, as she was called by the students, valued determination, courage, and character. She sought to establish a school that would instill in its graduates high purpose, leadership, integrity, and understanding. The new generation of faculty members and students at Foxcroft continues to strive for this goal.

Located in the shadow of the Blue Ridge Mountains, Foxcroft is about an hour by car from Washington, D.C. Five hundred acres of orchards, fields, trails, and streams provide a backdrop and resource for campus life, while the proximity of Washington, D.C., enables the School community to take advantage of museums, theaters, concerts, and the halls of government.

In 1937, Foxcroft was incorporated as a non-profit institution. The 23 members of the Board of Trustees meet three times annually. The School plant is valued at $38 million, and the endowment is $24,685,000. There are approximately 2,805 graduates in the Alumnae Association and 13 alumnae on the Board of Trustees.

Foxcroft is accredited by the Virginia Association of Independent Schools and is a member of the National Association of Independent Schools, the National Association of Principals of Schools for Girls, the Council for Advancement and Support of Education, the Secondary School Admission Test Board, and the National Coalition of Girls' Schools.

ACADEMIC PROGRAMS

The minimum requirement for graduation is the successful completion of 18 academic units plus 4 years of physical education. A unit is the equivalent of a single full-year course. The Foxcroft school year is divided into two semesters; each course of one semester's length counts as ½ unit.

The minimum course requirements must be distributed as follows: English, 4 units; foreign language, 3 units; history, 3 units; mathematics, 3 units; science, 3 units; and fine arts, 1.5 units. To qualify for sequential courses beyond minimum requirements, a student must have a grade of at least 70 in the course that is the prerequisite.

The School is small, but its program is large. With ninety-four course offerings, Foxcroft's curriculum meets the needs of students' varying interests and abilities and offers a very wide variety of electives, ranging from discrete mathematics to forensics, from nineteenth-century women authors to presidential politics.

Advanced Placement courses are available in American history, mathematics (AB and BC calculus), biology, Spanish, French, English, physics, chemistry, math, economics, and U.S. government.

Classes meet according to a rotating schedule that allows for flexibility in class times and lengths depending on individual course needs. A student–teaching faculty ratio of 7:1 leads to close contact between students and teachers, and it prevents any student from going unnoticed. Similarly, regular review of students' progress during faculty meetings ensures that each student receives individualized attention. The Learning Center and Math Lab offer students the opportunity to improve their study skills, to develop strategies for learning, to find special support when they encounter academic difficulty, and to take increasing responsibility for their own learning.

Sunday through Thursday, students are in study hall from 7:30 to 9:45 p.m. They may study in their dormitory rooms or in the library; in both places, a student leader and a faculty member are present to maintain a quiet, focused atmosphere and to offer extra help.

The Foxcroft academic program is further enriched by special events such as Interim Term, which offers two weeks of seminars, events, speakers, and off-campus trips, during which the whole community pauses to explore a topic of current interest.

The Goodyear Fellowship Program brings to Foxcroft each year a person distinguished in the arts, humanities, science, or public affairs to speak and conduct seminars with students. Past speakers have included Barbara Walters, David McCullough, Andrei Codrescu, Maya Angelou, Aimee Mullins, and Doris Kearns Goodwin. In addition, the English Department sponsors an annual two-day Poetry Festival, during which published poets read from their work, lead workshops, and judge a student reading competition.

FACULTY AND ADVISERS

Foxcroft capitalizes on the fact that nearly 80 percent of the faculty and administration live on campus. The faculty members and their families are the hub of a caring community. A large part of the responsibility for counseling and advising students rests with the faculty members. Each girl has a faculty adviser in addition to her housemother.

Mary Louise Leipheimer, appointed Head in 1989, graduated from Indiana University of Pennsylvania with a B.S. in English. She has served as both a faculty member and an administrator since 1967.

Foxcroft has 52 full-time faculty members and administrators. Forty teachers and administrators live on the campus, 27 of them with their families. They hold 56 baccalaureate and 23 advanced degrees from such institutions as Colgate, Columbia, Denison, Duke, Georgetown, Harvard, Indiana University, New York Law School, Skidmore, Wellesley, William and Mary, and the Universities of California, Maryland, Massachusetts, Michigan, and Virginia.

COLLEGE PLACEMENT

During their eleventh-grade year, students meet formally with the College Counselor to begin discussing their college plans. They receive guidance on course selection, extracurricular activities, and PSAT preparation. All sophomores and juniors take the PSAT in October. Approximately fifty colleges send representatives to Foxcroft for information sessions each fall. Both juniors and seniors are encouraged to attend meetings with the colleges that are of interest to them. With the help of the College Counselor, each student begins compiling a list of colleges to research in the winter of her junior year, although the College Counselor is available to assist students and families who wish to begin the search earlier. Throughout the college admission process, the College Counseling Office provides information and workshops on topics such as evaluating colleges, writing application essays, visiting college campuses, interviewing, and preparing for standardized testing.

All Foxcroft students attend college after graduation, although a small number choose to participate in an internship or study-abroad program during an interim year with the consent of their colleges. Students in the class of 2005 matriculated at fifty-three different colleges and universities. Acceptances were received from a wide range of schools, including American, Boston College, Boston University, Bowdoin, the College of Charleston, Columbia, Connecticut College, Duke, Elon, Georgetown, Goucher, James Madison, Johns Hopkins, Princeton, Smith, Tulane, Wake Forest, Wesleyan, and the Universities of California (Irvine, Merced, Riverside, and Santa Cruz), Colorado, Pennsylvania, Richmond, the South, and Virginia.

STUDENT BODY AND CONDUCT

For the 2005–06 school year, Foxcroft enrolled 34 students in grade 9, 43 students in grade 10, 53 students in grade 11, and 36 students in grade 12. There were 111 boarders and 55 day students, representing nine countries and twenty-two states.

Student leaders and members of the faculty and administration share in the governing of the School, including the enforcement of rules and the handling of offenses. The School Council is composed of student, faculty, and administration representatives who act as a clearinghouse for new policies. Students serve on the Student and Judicial Councils.

ACADEMIC FACILITIES

The Schoolhouse has fourteen classrooms, a studio art wing, three music labs, science laboratories, lab preparation rooms, photography darkrooms, a computer room, a dance studio, and an auditorium. A science wing contains three laboratory classrooms, a science library, an animal and plant room, and facilities for permanent specimen collections.

The Currier Library contains nearly 50,000 books and bound periodicals as well as information in fourteen other formats, including DVD, videocassette, microfiche, CD, and slides. Within the three-story facility are two computer labs with e-mail and Internet access, an AV/listening room, eighty-five study carrels, a classroom, comfortable student study nooks, and the Foxcroft archives. The electronic, Web-based catalog serves as a gateway to thousands of resources, both physical and electronic, including several online research databases. The Duncan Read Observatory houses a 10-inch reflecting telescope, a tracking system, a Newtonian Cassegrain reflecting telescope, two 8-inch Celestron telescopes, and accessories for astrophotography and solar observing.

BOARDING AND GENERAL FACILITIES

Students at Foxcroft live in five dormitories. In addition to having a full-time housemother, each dormitory has 2 seniors as student leaders and counselors and 2 or 3 juniors to assist them. Usually, 2 students share a room, in which each girl has a desk, bureau, and closet. Between 2 and 4 girls share a full bath. Each dorm has a living room, sleeping areas, and kitchen and laundry facilities.

The restored Brick House, dating from the 1700s, holds the main dining hall and kitchen facilities; the newest wing (1985) enables the whole School to have a formal sit-down lunch twice a week. The Activities Building contains the gymnasium, the weight room, student lounge, snack bar, student kitchen, and dance studio. The outdoor swimming pool (1987) is open for recreational use in the early fall and spring.

ATHLETICS

Every student is required to take part in some form of athletics throughout the year. Dance, riding, and physical education classes are offered each term. The team sports program includes basketball, field hockey, lacrosse, riding, soccer, softball, tennis, and volleyball. Teams compete interscholastically in the Washington area, as well as intramurally as members of the Fox or Hound teams. The athletic facilities consist of a dance studio, a gymnasium, two playing fields (one with a softball diamond), eight tennis courts, three riding rings (one indoors), and three jump courses adjacent to the campus buildings.

McConnell Stables and Indoor Ring allow riding throughout the school year for students who range from beginners to experienced riders. Approximately 33 percent of the students participate in the riding program, riding one of the School's thirty horses or boarding their own.

With 500 acres of trails, streams, fields, and woods, as well as an active outdoors club, many opportunities exist for hiking, camping, and exploring.

EXTRACURRICULAR OPPORTUNITIES

Foxcroft has the following clubs and organizations: Activities Committee, Art Club, Astronomy, Athletic Association, CAPS tour guides, Community Service, Current Events and Debate Club, Fox-Hound, French Club, International Club, Poetry Club, Riding Officers Club, Science Club, Special Friends, and Spirituality Committee. There are three singing groups: Octet, Afternoon Delights, and Soggie Cheerios. Student publications include *Chimera* (literary magazine) and *Tally-Ho!* (yearbook).

Foxcroft also has a Leadership Program with more than fifty formal leadership positions available. This program is designed to offer every student the opportunity to become a leader. Students seeking these positions are required to obtain peer and adviser references, submit essays outlining their strengths and weaknesses, and present speeches. Once Foxcroft leaders are elected, they must attend a leadership retreat and complete specialized training to learn trust-building skills and conflict-resolution techniques.

Foxcroft has an active community service program that expects each student to give back in some way to the School and to the larger community. Students and teachers work together on a project on one of the opening weekends of the school year. Past projects have included working for an abused women's organization and for an animal shelter. Throughout the year, community service opportunities exist on campus and at the nearby elementary school, nursing home, hospital, and humane foundation.

DAILY LIFE

Classes meet five days a week according to a rotating schedule. Each academic day begins at 8 a.m. after breakfast and has six or seven periods. Morning Meeting, a student-run, all-School assembly, meets midmorning three times a week, and athletics take place daily before dinner. Study hall runs from 7:30 to 9:45 p.m., and lights-out is at 10:30 for freshmen and 11 for upperclassmen.

WEEKEND LIFE

Foxcroft's Director of Activities works closely with the students in the Activities Club to plan on- and off-campus activities. On-campus activities range from a movie and snack bar night to a Fun-Fest day. Examples of off-campus activities include trips to the theater, the mall, dances or mixers at other schools, sporting events, Kings Dominion, or the movies.

Foxcroft is located 4 miles from Middleburg, and students may shop and eat in town on the weekends or arrange a ride with a faculty member if they need to do something in town during the week. Middleburg offers a variety of restaurants, quaint shopping, a supermarket, and a pharmacy.

Day and overnight permissions allow students to take advantage of extended weekend trips to Washington, D.C.; Richmond; Williamsburg; and other cities to enjoy the many cultural and recreational opportunities available in and around Virginia.

COSTS AND FINANCIAL AID

The boarding tuition for the 2005–06 school year was $35,700; the day tuition was $25,000. Textbooks and supplies cost approximately $500. Optional riding lessons were offered for $700 per term (three terms per year).

In 2005–06, 22 percent of students received financial assistance. This assistance is awarded according to financial need as determined by the School and Student Service for Financial Aid. For 2005–06, Foxcroft awarded grants totaling approximately $890,000. Foxcroft offers two merit scholarships, a variety of payment plans, and a generous Middle Income Loan Program.

ADMISSIONS INFORMATION

Foxcroft looks for motivated young women, able to succeed in a college-preparatory program and eager to participate in all aspects of school life.

Admission decisions are based on a personal interview; recommendations from teachers, counselors, or a principal; previous academic achievement; a writing sample; and SSAT scores. Foxcroft admits students of any race, color, or national or ethnic origin to all the programs and activities generally made available to students at the School.

APPLICATION TIMETABLE

An initial inquiry is welcome anytime. Campus tours are usually given right before the interview and are best scheduled Monday, Wednesday, or Friday between 9:30 a.m. and 2:30 p.m. when school is in session. A number of Overnight Festivals are offered throughout the year to provide prospective students with an opportunity to visit classes, spend a night in the dormitory, and interview.

The application deadline is February 15, and admissions decisions are mailed March 10. Students who are accepted have until April 10 to notify the School of their decision. Should spaces remain, candidates accepted after April 10 have fifteen days to reply.

ADMISSIONS CORRESPONDENCE

Rebecca B. Gilmore, Director of Admission
Foxcroft School
P.O. Box 5555
Middleburg, Virginia 20118-5555

Phone: 540-687-5555
        800-858-2364 (toll-free, U.S.)
Fax: 540-687-3627
E-mail: admissions@foxcroft.org
Web site: http://www.foxcroft.org

GARRISON FOREST SCHOOL

Owings Mills, Maryland

Type: Girls' boarding and day college-preparatory school
Grades: P–12: Lower Division, P–5 (3-year olds–Kindergarten is coeducational); Middle School, 6–8; Upper School, 9–12
Enrollment: School total: 664; Upper School: 232
Head of School: G. Peter O'Neill Jr., Head of School

THE SCHOOL

Garrison Forest School was founded by Mary Moncrieffe Livingston in 1910. Situated 12 miles north of Baltimore at the head of the Green Spring Valley, the 115-acre campus setting is quiet and pastoral. The School's location offers convenient access to the cultural and educational opportunities of both Baltimore and Washington, D.C.

Garrison Forest School is dedicated to providing a college-preparatory education that inspires its students to approach life with intellectual awareness, enthusiasm, dedication, and spirit. Many girls find the setting that a single-sex education provides invaluable: a setting in which they can reach, stretch, lead, and learn; a setting in which all are encouraged to seek excellence and to develop their special talents, whether in science or math, the arts or athletics, languages or leadership.

Garrison Forest School is governed by a 41-member Board of Trustees. The School's operating expenses are $15 million a year. It has an endowment of $31 million. Contributions to the 2004–05 Annual Fund were more than $1 million, with 42 percent of the alumnae contributing.

Garrison Forest is accredited by the Association of Independent Maryland Schools, the Middle States Association of Colleges and Secondary Schools, the National Association of Principals of Schools for Girls, the National Coalition of Girls' Schools, the Secondary School Admission Test Board, and the Council for Advancement and Support of Education.

ACADEMIC PROGRAMS

A strong curriculum is an important aspect of the Upper School. There are 14 students in an average class. The basic diploma requirements are 4 units in English; 3 units in mathematics; 3 units in one foreign language; 3 units in science with laboratory; 2½ units in history, 1 unit of which must be U.S. history and ½ unit of which must be in a cross-cultural course; 1½ units in the arts, including ½ unit in basic design; ½ unit in decision making (grade 9 and 11); ½ unit in Transitions (grade 12); ½ unit in physical education each year; and at least 2 approved additional units.

Courses offered in the Upper School are English, French, history, Latin, Spanish, mathematics, science, economics, arts and fine arts, practical computer, child development, Decision Making, Transitions, photography, theater, music, and study skills. Advanced Placement courses are offered in English, French, Spanish, Latin, U.S. history, calculus (AB, BC), biology, chemistry, and art history. Seniors design a three-week, off-campus independent study project at the close of their senior year.

The school year is divided into two semesters. Reports and comments are sent to parents four times each year. The marking system uses A to E (failing), with B+ and above representing high honors; B, honors; and D, passing.

FACULTY AND ADVISERS

The moving spirit behind life at Garrison Forest is the affection and respect between students and the faculty. The School has attracted a strong, talented faculty, many of whom are active in the cultural life of the metropolitan area. Each girl has her own faculty adviser, and all dormitories have faculty parents. Faculty members also serve as advisers to classes, service organizations, clubs, student activities, and campus publications.

Peter O'Neill, Garrison Forest's Head of School, received his B.A. from Saint Michael's College in Vermont and holds a master's degree from Trinity College in Connecticut. In addition to holding many academic and administrative positions, Mr. O'Neill served for six years as the Headmaster of the Wooster School in Danbury, Connecticut. He has been Head of Garrison Forest since 1993.

There are 76 full-time and 15 part-time faculty members (including administrators who teach). Twenty-five members live on campus. Seventy-four percent hold advanced degrees. The Board of Trustees offers generous funds for the continuing education of the faculty through a special grant program.

COLLEGE PLACEMENT

The Director of College Counseling begins with group counseling in the eleventh grade and works on a one-to-one basis with the students and their families in the senior year. The School hosts an after-school service in SAT prep and offers sessions in both English and math, and individual teachers help the students prepare for specific Subject Tests. PSATs are given to all sophomores and juniors.

The 49 members of the class of 2005 are attending thirty-six colleges and universities this fall, including Bates; Boston University; College of Charleston; Columbia; Cornell; Duke; Elon; Johns Hopkins; Oberlin; Vanderbilt; and the Universities of Maryland, College Park; St. Andrews (Scotland); and Virginia.

STUDENT BODY AND CONDUCT

The Upper School student body consists of 42 boarding and 196 day students. Nine states and four other countries are represented in the student body. The greatest number of students come from Maryland, Pennsylvania, the District of Columbia, New Jersey, New York, and Virginia. The student body represents diversity in several areas. Forty percent come from public schools.

Students at Garrison Forest School are expected to assume a large measure of personal responsibility and self-discipline. School community life is a joint enterprise of the administration, the faculty, and the students. The major governing body of this community is the Forum. The Head of the Upper School and the Dean of Students meet regularly to help the Forum give life and meaning to the school code of conduct, which stresses individual integrity, honesty, respect, and self-discipline.

ACADEMIC FACILITIES

Most of the School and academic life centers on the Upper School Academic and Administration Building, which contains classrooms, laboratories, study areas, and offices. The 400-seat Garland Theater is home to the drama department and provides the setting for all-School assemblies as well as two plays each year. Manor House contains the Development, Alumnae, and Business offices, the bookstore, and the Student Activities Center. The McLennan Library contains audiovisual resources, computer access to the library system, and more than 16,000 volumes and periodicals as well as a four-room computer center and a 100-seat lecture hall. An art and music building, which has studios for fine arts, ceramics, jewelry, photography, and woodworking, as well as a recital hall, a choral room, and practice rooms, was completed in 1996.

The Campus Center, completed in May 2002, includes three full-length basketball courts, an indoor elevated track, locker rooms, a fitness center, a dance studio, a trainers' room, athletic offices, and a dining hall and full kitchen facility.

BOARDING AND GENERAL FACILITIES

Garrison Forest School has three dormitories: Meadowood, Senior House, and Shriver. Girls live in single and double rooms. New-girl rooming assignments are made by a Housing Committee; returning girls indicate their choices each spring. At least 4 dormitory parents or faculty families in each dorm supervise all dormitory activities, and all faculty members who live on campus dine family-style with the girls and supervise evening study halls. The Health Center offers 24-hour on-call nursing care. The Director of Residence Life and Student Activities and the Assistant to the Dean of Students both live on campus and give full-time direction to all aspects of life on campus.

ATHLETICS

Sports, with an emphasis on spirit and enthusiasm, are an integral part of Garrison Forest life. The sports program includes aerobics; badminton; basketball; cross-country; dance, including ballet, bar work, and modern dance; field hockey; horseback riding; lacrosse; polo; soccer; softball; squash; and tennis. All major sports are played

with other schools. In addition, intramural teams challenge each other in athletics and extracurricular activities. Newly remodeled and expanded riding facilities include two outdoor sand rings, two indoor arenas, a dressage arena, and two stables including ninety stalls.

EXTRACURRICULAR OPPORTUNITIES
Students are encouraged to involve themselves in many extracurricular opportunities. Through the Service League program (which is entirely voluntary), students can work both on campus and in the Baltimore community. The Connections Club heads the School's nonsectarian religious life.

Students interested in creative writing or journalism work for the School publications: *Ragged Robin* (yearbook), *Callisto* (literary magazine), and *Paw Print* (school newspaper). Those students who wish to act, produce plays, or work with lighting and scenery find an opportunity for testing theories and developing techniques in the theater program. Among other student organizations are fourteen clubs and singing groups for various classes.

Traditional events include Parents' Weekend, Grandparents' Day, Snoball, Fall Fest, and a fall and spring play.

DAILY LIFE
The school day begins with breakfast at 7:15. At 8, all students and faculty members begin class. There are eight 50-minute periods per day, Monday through Friday. The last academic class ends at 3:05, and from 3:15 to 3:45, the girls have a help-session period twice a week. Clubs and activities meet twice each week. On the other days, faculty members are available to meet with students. Dinner is at 6:15, followed by study hours (and study hall for designated students) from 7:30 to 9.

WEEKEND LIFE
Weekend activities at Garrison Forest are planned to include a combination of both on- and off-campus cultural and recreational events. The Activities Committee, along with the Director of Residential Life and Student Activities, takes full advantage of the School's proximity to the Baltimore and Washington metropolitan areas. Students have the chance to attend the symphony, theaters, and museums as well as collegiate and professional sporting events. Students also have the chance to visit Annapolis, Ocean City, Philadelphia, and New York. On-campus activities include movies, music performances, student theater productions, horse shows, dance concerts, interscholastic sports events, coffeehouses, and dances and mixers to which students from neighboring schools are invited.

In addition, Garrison Forest is one of twenty girls' and boys' boarding schools in the Middle Atlantic states that make up the Boarding School Social Activities Committee (BSSAC). BSSAC coordinates interschool activities ranging from dances and field trips to sports and cultural outings.

The Host Family program matches each boarder with a local Garrison Forest family, providing boarding students with an informal home and family setting.

COSTS AND FINANCIAL AID
Charges for 2005–06 were $33,400 for boarding students and $19,600 for day students, payable in two installments, August 1 and January 1. A monthly payment plan is also available. Instrumental music lessons, riding lessons, board for horses, and transportation are optional extras. Books and uniforms entail additional expense. There is a student activities charge that covers all activities and field trips for the year.

Garrison Forest has a generous financial aid program. Parents must complete the School and Student Service for Financial Aid form if they wish to apply for aid. Awards are based on need, with consideration given to character and scholarship. Twenty-four percent of the students receive grants and loans.

ADMISSIONS INFORMATION
Garrison Forest School's motto, "Esse Quam Videri" ("To be rather than to seem"), well summarizes the School's expectations that every girl be herself. It is a school of different individuals, one that values each girl for her diversity—for her special strengths and interests she brings to the community. The primary commitment is to a strong academic program designed to foster a spirit of inquiry, intellectual independence, and enthusiasm for learning.

Applicants must visit the campus and have an interview with a member of the admission staff. Their application folder must include a formal application, their previous school record, the recommendations of 2 teachers and the principal or Head of School, and performance on standardized tests, including the SSAT. International students are required to submit results of a WISC Test and a SLEP or TOEFL exam to determine their English proficiency level. Garrison Forest will also require international students who speak English as a second language to have a WISC evaluation completed as part of this process.

Garrison Forest does not discriminate on the basis of race, color, religion, sexual orientation, or national origin in the administration of its educational policies, admissions policies, faculty recruitment policies, scholarship or loan programs, sports, or other school-administered programs.

APPLICATION TIMETABLE
Initial inquiries by telephone, letter, or e-mail are welcome at any time. Campus interviews are conducted throughout the week, preferably between the hours of 8 a.m. and 2 p.m. when school is in session. Interviews with admission personnel are preceded by a student-conducted tour of the campus. Group overnights are offered twice in the fall. Prospective boarding students are encouraged to come to a group overnight and class visit to experience a typical 24-hour day at Garrison Forest School. Each student and parent meets with an Admission Officer for their formal interview. The application deadline is January 6. The School considers applications on a rolling admission basis after March 10, provided that space is available. In place of the School's own application, candidates may choose to submit the Boarding School Common Application Form, which can be downloaded from the Internet at http://www.schools.com. Letters of decision are mailed to candidates in early March, and candidates must reply by early April.

ADMISSIONS CORRESPONDENCE
A. Randol Benedict ('76), Director of Admission
Garrison Forest School
300 Garrison Forest Road
Owings Mills, Maryland 21117
Phone: 410-363-1500
Fax: 410-363-8441
E-mail: gfs_info@gfs.org
Web site: http://www.gfs.org

GEORGE SCHOOL

Newtown, Pennsylvania

Type: Coeducational Friends boarding and day college-preparatory school
Grades: 9–12
Enrollment: 529
Head of School: Nancy Starmer, Head of School

THE SCHOOL

Established in 1893 by the Religious Society of Friends, George School is committed to cultivating respect for differences by affirming the Light of God in everyone and to meeting the intellectual, social, and developmental needs of students.

A coeducational boarding and day school of 529 students in grades 9–12, George School was among the first secondary schools in the nation to establish foreign student exchanges, a campus co-op program, international work camps and service projects, and tuition assistance programs for families in need of financial aid. Quaker values, such as equality, social justice, and respect for others create a diverse community where academics, sports, arts, and service learning share emphasis.

Situated in historic Newtown, Pennsylvania, the 265-acre campus is conveniently located within 30 miles of the cultural centers of Princeton, New Jersey, and Philadelphia and 70 miles of New York City.

George School is under the governance of the 27-member George School Committee, the majority of whom are members of the Religious Society of Friends (Quakers); other members include 1 parent, 2 faculty members, and 2 student representatives. The School's endowment is $65.8 million, and the 2005–06 operating budget was $20.8 million. Annual Fund giving for the 2004–05 fiscal year was $878,984, of which nearly 64 percent was given by alumni.

ACADEMIC PROGRAMS

George School offers a comprehensive college-preparatory curriculum designed to prepare students for a lifetime of learning.

Every four-year George School student is expected to satisfactorily complete the following requirements: 4 years of English, 3 years of history (including U.S. history), 3 years of math, 3 years of science, third-year proficiency in a foreign language, 4 years of the arts, 4 years of physical education or sports, 4 years of co-op, 1 year of Health and the Human Spirit, and 1 term each of Bible and Quakerism or 3 terms of Theory of Knowledge. Also required are 65 hours of community service and demonstrated swimming skills.

Full-year courses are offered in English literature and composition, American literature, world literature, French I–V, Latin I–V, Spanish I–V, global interdependence, world history, U.S. history, Middle Eastern history, economics, East Asian history, European history, African-American history, twentieth-century history, physical science, chemistry, biology, physics, environmental science, computer programming and robotics, algebra I, algebra II, geometry, statistics, precalculus, and calculus. The yearlong arts courses include arts foundations, painting and drawing, photography, video production, woodworking, ceramics, orchestra, music seminar, drama, stagecraft, dance, and chorus.

George School's diverse curriculum includes Advanced Placement (AP) courses in English, history, mathematics, sciences, foreign languages, and arts as well as English as a second language (ESL) courses in English, history, and science. In addition, the School offers the International Baccalaureate (IB) Diploma Program. Recognized by universities across the country and world, the IB Program is a rigorous two-year course of study in six subjects, which leads to a second internationally recognized high school diploma. Ninety-one percent of George School IB Diploma candidates have succeeded in earning the IB Diploma over the last ten years, compared to the international average of 87 percent.

The school year is divided into three terms. Comprehensive grade reports, with teacher and adviser comments and letter grades (A–F), are sent to parents four times a year.

The student-teacher ratio is 7:1, and the average class size is 14 students. All students are required to attend meeting for worship on Tuesdays or Thursdays; boarders and day students staying on campus must also attend on Sunday mornings.

Students are required to participate in a cooperative work program each year to promote a personal and financial commitment to the School. International and domestic work camps and service projects are available to juniors and seniors during their two-week spring break and the summer. George School has recently sponsored projects to Arizona, Coastal South Carolina, Costa Rica, Cuba, France, Massachusetts, Mississippi, Nicaragua, South Africa, South Korea, Vietnam, and Virginia.

FACULTY AND ADVISERS

Appointed in 2000, Nancy Starmer is the school's seventh Head of School. Before coming to George School, she served as Principal of the Upper School at Milton Academy. During the 1999–2000 academic year, she spent her sabbatical studying issues of diversity and community as a visiting scholar at the Wellesley Centers for Women and as a visiting practitioner at Harvard Graduate School of Education. After graduating from the College of Wooster in 1970, she received a Master's in Education at Boston University.

Of the 86 faculty members, 55 have advanced degrees. Almost 40 percent of the faculty members are Quakers and 19 percent are of members of minority groups. Most faculty members reside on campus and interact with students on a full-time basis.

The adviser system is an important and effective program at George School. Advisers offer academic guidance and serve as confidants, counselors, and friends. Each adviser has approximately 8 advisees and serves as the liaison between parents and the School. Students meet with advisers daily at 8:50 a.m.

Faculty members are eligible for a sabbatical after seven years of service. A faculty enrichment fund helps cover faculty expenses for professional development whenever possible and appropriate.

COLLEGE PLACEMENT

Three college counselors work with juniors and seniors and their parents as they explore educational and career options. From the class of 2005, 143 students matriculated at 101 colleges and universities in the United States and 1 is attending university abroad. Over the past five years, 10 or more graduates have attended each of the following colleges and universities: American, Boston University, Carnegie Mellon, Guilford, Muhlenberg, NYU, Penn State, Temple, Ursinus, and the Universities of Pennsylvania and Pittsburgh.

The college counselors encourage students to meet with them often, to visit colleges, and to attend on-campus meetings with college admissions officers.

STUDENT BODY AND CONDUCT

In 2005–06, George School enrolled 286 boarders and 243 day students, including 268 girls and 261 boys. Students came from twenty-two states and twenty-seven countries. Of the total enrollment, 23 percent were members of minority groups, and Friends made up 14.4 percent of the student body.

The School's various committees include student members, providing them an opportunity to both shape and influence School policies. All decisions are reached by Quaker consensus, not majority rule. Individuals who do not abide by major School rules are considered by the Discipline Committee, which is made up of faculty members and students and makes decisions in conjunction with the deans and advisers. Minor infractions are handled by the deans. Each student is expected to accept the responsibilities inherent in George School's close-knit community.

ACADEMIC FACILITIES

There are five major academic buildings on campus. Bancroft, Retford, Hallowell Arts Center, and the Spruance-Alden Science Center house the English, mathematics, history, language, arts, and science departments; Walton Center is a 600-seat theater-auditorium with two stages, five practice rooms, a dance studio, and classroom facilities for music and drama.

The meetinghouse, originally built in Philadelphia in the 1700s, was dismantled, moved to George School, and reconstructed in 1974. It is used for Quaker meeting for worship, religion classes, and community functions. McFeely Library has an excellent collection of books (20,000 volumes), audio and video sources, electronic and hard-copy periodicals, and a broad range of scholarly online reference resources. Thirty-five computers are available for students, all with full access to the Internet. Instruction in library use and research techniques is provided. The campus is fully wired for network access, including student residential rooms. Most academic buildings, including the library, have wireless network access.

BOARDING AND GENERAL FACILITIES

Students are housed according to grade level in single-sex residence halls. There are three boys' dormitories: Campbell (ninth), Orton (tenth), and Drayton (eleventh and twelfth). The girls' dorms consist of Westwood (ninth) and three sections of Main. West Main houses sophomore girls, while juniors and seniors live in both Central and East

Main. Faculty members reside in the dorms in faculty apartments, and senior prefects live alongside students on each floor.

Marshall Center, the student activities center, houses the bookstore, the post office, a snack bar, a coffeehouse, day-student lounges and lockers, and offices for the deans and the student activities director.

The Student Health Center has a nurse practitioner and registered nurses available 24 hours a day, seven days a week. A physician and two counselors are on call at all times.

ATHLETICS

The George School physical education program offers a combination of physical education classes and interscholastic team sports, emphasizing involvement and cooperation.

Interscholastic team sports include baseball, basketball, cheerleading, cross-country, equestrian, field hockey, football, golf, lacrosse, soccer, softball, swimming, tennis, track, volleyball, and wrestling. Physical education classes include aerobics, coed intramurals, equestrian, floor hockey/soccer, instructional swimming, lifeguard training, lifetime sports, net sports, personal fitness, Ultimate Frisbee, volleyball, and yoga.

Worth Sports Center houses an eight-lane, 25-meter pool as well as facilities for indoor tennis, volleyball, and basketball. The Alumni Gym houses a basketball court, wrestling room, and weight training facilities. In addition, there are fourteen outdoor tennis courts, ten athletic fields, stables and two riding rings, a ¼-mile running track, and a cross-country course.

EXTRACURRICULAR OPPORTUNITIES

George School students are encouraged to get involved in campus organizations and to start their own interest groups that influence the quality of life of the community. Current student clubs include Amnesty International, Ceramics Club, Community Chorus, Goldfish in Java (coffeehouse music group), Model United Nations, Open Doors (gay-straight alliance), Outdoor Club, PAWS (Pets are Worth Supporting), the R&B Step Team, Students Against Drunk Driving, TERRA (Sierra Student Coalition), and Women's Issues Now.

The *Curious George,* the School's student newspaper, *Opus* (the yearbook), and *Argo* (a literary magazine) provide opportunities for creativity and self-expression. To support the needs of students from rich cultural and religious traditions, George School sponsors Havurah (Jewish culture), Latin American Student Organization, LOGOS (a Christian interest group), Pacific Rim Organization, Samosa (South Asian student society), UMOJA (culture, heritage, and ethnicity of African descendants), and Young Friends (Quaker support group).

With their adviser's permission, students interested in providing leadership to the community may apply to participate in the Discipline Committee, Diversity Steering Committee, Drug and Alcohol Coordinating Committee, George School Committee, Peer Group, Prefects, Student Council, and Students Associated for Greater Empathy (SAGE). Founded in 1971, SAGE is a student-run organization of peer counselors who are trained to address social and emotional issues common to teenagers.

DAILY LIFE

The academic day begins at 8 a.m. and ends at 3:30 p.m., except on Tuesdays and Fridays, when classes end at 2:35 p.m. Breakfast is available from 7:15 to 8 and lunch from 11 to 1. Both are served cafeteria-style. During the academic week, dinner is served between 5:30 and 6:30 p.m. A special period is set aside from 10 to 10:40 a.m. for an all-School assembly with guest speakers on Mondays and Fridays and for meeting for worship on Tuesdays and Thursdays. There are six classes each day of either 50 or 105 minutes. All students meet with their advisers in a group setting for 10 minutes every weekday morning at 8:50.

The majority of sports activities take place between 3:30 and 5:30. Clubs and committee meetings generally occur after dinner and before study hall. Study hall is scheduled between 7:30 and 9:30 p.m.; students may choose to study in their dormitory rooms or the library. They may also be assigned to a supervised study hall. All students must check into their dormitories at 10 p.m. on school nights.

WEEKEND LIFE

Under the guidance of the Director of Student Activities, weekends are organized around themes and sponsored by student organizations or faculty members. Past weekend themes included Amnesty, Outdoor Challenge, Open Doors, Pacific Rim Organization, Freedom from Chemical Dependency, Harvest, Live Music, Spring Fling, and Parents/Sibling/Alumni weekends.

Easily accessible by foot, Newtown offers a movie theater, clothing stores, shopping centers, coffee shops, and restaurants. Philadelphia and its cultural and entertainment opportunities are often a part of the weekend activities and field trips. A weekend shuttle is available to the local train station in Trenton, New Jersey.

Boarding students are free to leave campus on weekends or visit day students' homes with proper permission and parental consent. Day students are encouraged to stay overnight in the dorms for weekend activities.

COSTS AND FINANCIAL AID

The 2005–06 annual day student cost of $24,700 covered tuition, meals, activities, infirmary costs, and laboratory fees. The boarding cost of $33,500 covered room, board, tuition, activities, infirmary costs, laundry, and laboratory fees.

Students buy textbooks—new or used—at the School bookstore. Books and incidentals for the year usually cost between $500 and $750. Required athletic equipment and clothes might cost students up to $200 each year. Students can expect to spend about $750 a year on miscellaneous supplies and entertainment. An initial deposit of $2200 for boarders and $1500 for day students was required upon enrollment.

Grants and loans for scholarship assistance are awarded according to need and are based on national standards established by the School and Student Service for Financial Aid. Four $10,000 merit-based Anderson scholarships are awarded annually to students who embody the principles of social involvement, respect for others, and a commitment to academic excellence. Forty-five percent of the students received financial aid. The average award was $20,823. For 2005–06, financial aid totaled $4.8 million.

ADMISSIONS INFORMATION

George School seeks students with a high degree of academic interest and intellectual curiosity who are open to new experiences and friendships. The Admission Committee seeks a student body diverse in race, creed, and economic and social background, with some preference given to Quakers and children of alumni. The committee takes into consideration the previous school record, recommendations, writing samples, the interview, and SSAT results.

APPLICATION TIMETABLE

Inquiries are always welcome. The Admissions Office is open from 8 a.m. to 4 p.m., Monday through Friday. Student-guided tours and admissions interviews are conducted at 9 a.m., 10:45 a.m., and 1:15 p.m. daily. The application fee is $50 for domestic applicants and $75 for international applicants.

Day students should apply no later than January 15; boarding students are advised to apply before February 15. Admissions decisions are announced beginning March 10, and applicants must reply by April 10. After April, the Admissions Committee meets weekly to make decisions on a space-available basis.

ADMISSIONS CORRESPONDENCE

Director of Admissions
Box 4460
George School
Newtown, Pennsylvania 18940

Phone: 215-579-6547
Fax: 215-579-6549
E-mail: admissions@georgeschool.org
Web site: http://www.georgeschool.org

GEORGE STEVENS ACADEMY

Blue Hill, Maine

Type: Coeducational boarding and day college-preparatory school
Grades: 9–12
Enrollment: 308
Head of School: Jo Ann Douglass

THE SCHOOL

George Stevens Academy (GSA) was founded in 1803 as Blue Hill Academy. The first students, men and women from nearby towns, were taught by a preceptor and 2 teachers, and their courses of study included Greek, Latin, and navigation. The Academy flourished under the guardianship of the Congregational Church, but in 1832, George Stevens, the first non-Congregationalist to become a member of the Board of Trustees, offered money and land to the Academy on the condition that it become an equal-opportunity institution. When the Board refused, he donated 150 acres of land to build another school, the George Stevens Academy. In 1943, the two schools finally merged into Blue Hill–George Stevens Academy.

Today, the Academy consists of 20 acres, including administrative buildings and athletic fields, plus another 500 acres for future development. The mission of the Academy is to create a caring and dynamic community that educates and encourages students to reach their highest potential through a wide array of challenging academic and extracurricular programs. It is committed to academic excellence, creative thinking, and artistic expression and offers diverse opportunities for self-discovery that enable and require students to make responsible choices. The governing body includes the Head of School, the Assistant Head of School, 2 deans, and an 18-person Board of Trustees, on which many Academy alumni sit.

Academically, students from GSA rank among the best in the state. In music, the Jazz Band and the Jazz Combo have won state championships for the past two years, bringing home three first-place trophies and MVP awards. For more than seventeen years, the Jazz Band has placed in the top three spots at the State Competition. GSA's Jazz Combo, Musiquarium, won fourth place at the 2005 Berklee College of Music Jazz Festival in Boston. In athletics in 2005, students earned a state championship in sailing and the Eastern Maine Championship in baseball. In 2004, GSA won two state championships in baseball and tennis and the Eastern Maine Championship in girls' soccer.

The Academy is accredited by the New England Association of Schools and Colleges (NEAS&C) and the Maine Department of Educational and Cultural Services. GSA is also a member of the College Board and the Independent Schools Association of Northern New England.

ACADEMIC PROGRAMS

The academic year is divided into two semesters: September through December and January through June. In order to graduate, students must earn a total of 22 academic credits, including 4 English credits, 3 math credits, 3 science credits, 3 social science credits, 1 physical education credit, 1 fine art credit, ½ credit in health, and 6½ elective credits. All students are required to carry a minimum of 5 credits each semester. Juniors and seniors may also participate in a two-week Independent Study and Internship Program. Seniors must fulfill a senior debate requirement in order to graduate. Every June, seniors debate one another on a wide range of topics from current events to legal issues. Public speaking, research, cooperation with partners and team members, synthesizing an informed argument, and self-expression are important elements of the debate process. The debate is a logical culmination of the high school language arts experience and gives students an opportunity to study, in depth, a topic of their choice.

In order to accommodate different learning styles and abilities, GSA offers a varied curriculum at three different levels: skills, college-prep (CP4), and honors. Six AP courses are also available. Honors and AP courses challenge students to pursue subjects deeply, intensively, and rigorously. The foreign language program includes French, Spanish, German, and Latin. Some of the more unique courses at GSA are: earthworks, marine science, forensics, jazz, photography, modern history through sport, psychology, and lab geometry. A state-certified special education teacher is available to support students with special needs who are taking the majority of their courses in regular classes.

GSA offers a comprehensive ESL program for international students at three levels: beginner, intermediate, and advanced. Students are tested prior to placement in one of the levels. ESL courses focus on developing conversational and writing skills as well as the language necessary for regular subject classes. Special emphasis is also placed on preparing students for entry into U.S. colleges and universities.

An Alternative Course Contract (ACC) provides an opportunity for a student to take a course not offered in the regular curriculum. A student in consultation with the Office of Faculty and Student Services and a member of the GSA faculty may design the curriculum and write a course proposal that includes a description of the course, goals, and objectives and the amount of credit to be earned. An Alternative Course Contract may be taken on a pass/fail basis or for a numerical grade. Alternative Course Contracts are usually taken in addition to the required 5 academic credits. The Head of School must preapprove all Alternative Course Contracts.

FACULTY AND ADVISERS

There are 21 full-time and 9 part-time teachers at the Academy, and more than half of the instructors have advanced degrees. The faculty is composed equally of men and women. GSA faculty members are skilled, caring educators who are actively involved in students' lives. Each full-time faculty member serves as an adviser for up to 12 students to assist them in their academic, social, and emotional development. They help students set educational goals and develop the skills necessary to accomplish them. In addition, advisers assist students through the college-admission process, including the coordination of college aptitude tests and the various aspects of applying to college. Faculty members are also involved in advising student clubs and coaching athletics.

Jo Ann Douglass has a B.A. from Bates College and an M.A. from the Bread Loaf School of English at Middlebury College. Her impressive background includes experience as an Associate Admission Director at Middlebury College; Director of College Counseling at Dana Hall School; Acting Headmaster, Assistant Head of School, Dean of Faculty, and English teacher at Brooks School; and a College Counselor for School Year Abroad in Beijing, China. She was appointed Head of School in 2001 and currently serves on NEAS&C's Commission on Independent Schools. She was also recently an executive committee member and treasurer for the Maine Association of Independent Schools.

COLLEGE PLACEMENT

The Office of Faculty and Student Services meets with students on an individual and group basis to discuss and map out students' future plans, explore and refine individual goals, and organize a time-management system for the college application process. The Academy hosts a number of college admissions representatives every year as well as financial aid workshops. About 75 percent of students who graduate from the Academy attend postsecondary institutions. Within Maine, recent graduates have attended Bates, Bowdoin, Colby, and the Universities of Maine and Southern Maine. Recent graduates are attending such colleges and universities as Berklee College of Music, Harvard, NYU, Penn State, Princeton, Smith, Stanford, Yale, the University of Virginia, and the U.S. Naval Academy.

STUDENT BODY AND CONDUCT

In the 2005–06 academic year, the Academy enrolled a total of 308 students: 154 boys and 154 girls. In grade 9, there were 24 boys and 38 girls; grade 10, 59 boys and 44 girls; grade 11, 36 boys and 30 girls; and grade 12, 35 boys and 42 girls. The majority of students come from Blue Hill and the surrounding towns. The socioeconomic range is wide; students have parents in occupations ranging from lobstermen and mill workers to lawyers and doctors.

Students participate in the management of the school through the Student Council, which provides leadership, school service, a forum for student voice, and channels for student involvement. Students' rights and responsibilities are outlined in the school handbook, and both students and faculty members are expected to maintain an atmosphere of respect and encouragement for learning, take responsibility for their actions, foster a

safe and caring atmosphere, use courteous and appropriate language, abide by the highest standards of honesty, and remain chemically free. GSA's administrators and faculty members are responsible for discipline.

ACADEMIC FACILITIES

GSA's campus is located in the heart of Blue Hill and currently consists of four main buildings. The Academy's library contains a collection of more than 8,000 items for research and recreational reading. Materials are offered in a variety of formats, including books, magazines, microfiche, videotapes, and CD-ROMs. The library also includes seven computers with Internet access. In addition, there are thirty laptops in two mobile units for student use as well as sixteen computers in the campus computer lab. All of the Academy's twenty-seven classrooms are wired for the Internet, and every teacher has an in-class computer. Students also have access to the Blue Hill Library, which has more than 39,000 items, and the MERI Center for Marine Studies.

BOARDING AND GENERAL FACILITIES

GSA has a unique Host Family Program, which provides international students with the opportunity to live with a family in the community. Students become a member of that family for the school year and may spend time with their host family after school, on weekends, and during vacations. This offers students the chance to practice English intensively while experiencing life in an American household.

ATHLETICS

The Academy participates in twelve interscholastic sports throughout the year, including baseball, basketball, golf, indoor and outdoor track, sailing, soccer, tennis, and wrestling. Games and practice times take place after school during the week and sometimes in the morning on weekends. In order to play, students must be enrolled in five full-credit courses at the Academy and maintain good academic standing. Other requirements include a parents consent form, a yearly physical examination, an emergency medical card completed and on file in the Athletic Office, and attendance at a preseason meeting. In addition to a gymnasium, the Academy also has extensive athletic fields where teams play baseball, soccer, and softball.

EXTRACURRICULAR OPPORTUNITIES

There are more than twenty-five clubs and activities for students at the Academy. Some of the clubs include Amnesty International, Chamber Music Ensemble, Chess Team, Drama Club, Environmental Action Club, French Club, International Cooking Club, Jazz Band, Jazz Combo, Literary Magazine, Math Team, National Honor Society, Outing Club, Spanish Club, Student Council, and Yearbook.

The Academy sponsors an annual Arts Festival, a three-day event that celebrates arts in all its forms and allows students to show parents and friends their special accomplishments. Every year, students can take part in three days of studio-based learning at Haystack Mountain School of Crafts, which attracts some of the finest craftspeople in the nation. The Academy also offers numerous opportunities to participate in sports, performing arts, community service and other interests.

DAILY LIFE

The school day begins at 8 a.m. and ends at 2:35 p.m., with a 15-minute break at 9:20 and a 45-minute lunch beginning at 12:30 p.m. The Academy runs on an eight-period schedule. Each eight-period cycle lasts two days. Each day is divided into four periods, which are 75 minutes in length. Students may spend one of these periods in a study hall, and juniors and seniors may have the opportunity to explore an academic or vocational interest through a self-designed, two-week course of study.

WEEKEND LIFE

Students can spend their weekends in the Blue Hill Peninsula, which is known for its traditional, coastal fishing and boatbuilding history. More recently, it has become a haven for writers, painters, sculptors, and musicians. The village of Blue Hill offers shops, art galleries, pottery studios, and restaurants. Throughout the year, there are opportunities to attend or participate in classical, jazz, steel drum, and choral concerts. The Blue Hill Library hosts Friday movie nights. Students can walk along the beach, hike up Blue Hill Mountain, go canoeing and kayaking, take a bike ride through blueberry fields, kick a soccer ball in the park, and browse local shops and book stores. In the winter, there are plenty of chances for ice skating, cross-country skiing, and downhill skiing. Chaperoned weekend trips may include shopping, movies, or bowling in nearby Ellsworth or Bangor; visits to Acadia National Park and Bar Harbor; whale watching; and cultural visits to Portland and Boston. Blue Hill is an hour's drive from Acadia National Park or the Camden Snow Bowl, 3 hours from Portland or Sugarloaf Mountain, and 5 hours from Boston.

COSTS AND FINANCIAL AID

The Academy admits almost any student from Blue Hill or a neighboring town that does not have its own high school as well as international students and students from nonsupporting towns who are open to new challenges and experiences. The tuition of $25,000 per year includes tuition, the stipend for host families, book rental, and most regular school activities. Students are also expected to pay an activity fee of $500 per year or $300 per half-year; $1500 per semester for students attending an English as a second language (ESL) course; a $650 health and accident insurance fee; a technology fee of $600; and a general deposit fee of $500. Financial aid is currently not available.

ADMISSIONS INFORMATION

George Stevens Academy admits students of any race, religion, gender, national origin, or sexual orientation in the rights, privileges, programs, and activities available to students at the school. GSA does not discriminate in the administration of its educational policies, admissions policies, or any other programs administered by the school. Admission is based on the candidate's transcript, application essay, recommendations, and, when possible, PSAT, SSAT, TOEFL, or SLEP scores. GSA's Admissions Committee carefully screens all applicants to determine their level of maturity, academic competency, and ability to function successfully in the GSA community.

APPLICATION TIMETABLE

A $50 nonrefundable processing fee is required at the time of the application. A campus visit and interview are highly recommended for all applicants. Telephone interviews are arranged for candidates who are unable to visit. The Academy has a rolling admissions policy, which means that applications are accepted throughout the school year and summer. However, candidates are encouraged to complete the application process by May 15. An admissions decision is made within three weeks of receipt of the application.

ADMISSIONS CORRESPONDENCE

Sheryl Stearns
International Program Director
George Stevens Academy
23 Union Street
Blue Hill, Maine 04614
Phone: 207-374-2808 Ext. 134
Fax: 207-374-2982
E-mail: sstearns@georgestevensacademy.org
Web site: http://www.georgestevensacademy.org

GILMOUR ACADEMY

Gates Mills, Ohio

Type: Coeducational boarding (7–12) and day (P–12) college-preparatory Catholic school
Grades: P–12: Montessori Preschool; Lower School, K–6; Middle School, 7–8; Upper School, 9–12
Enrollment: School total: 760; Upper School: 442; Middle School: 83; Lower School: 235
Head of School: Br. Robert E. Lavelle, C.S.C., Headmaster

THE SCHOOL

Gilmour Academy is an independent, Catholic, co-educational college-preparatory school with a Montessori preschool program and traditional schooling from kindergarten through grade 12. It offers a day school program for all grades as well as comprehensive five-day and seven-day residential life programs for students in grades 7 through 12. Gilmour encourages and enrolls students from all faiths to be integral members of its community.

Founded in 1946 by the Brothers of Holy Cross, Gilmour Academy traces its roots through the University of Notre Dame and shares the Notre Dame spirit and commitment to scholarship, leadership, and service. Gilmour Academy builds upon the Holy Cross tradition of excellence in education. It is the Holy Cross educational mission to enable students to have "the competence to see and the courage to act in creating a more humane and just society." As a Holy Cross school, Gilmour Academy has as its core mission the education of the mind and the heart. The world students will soon lead requires individuals of great courage and moral stamina, with an enthusiastic, lifelong desire to learn. Gilmour fosters those attributes.

At Gilmour, students are active learners within a personalized and faith-based environment. For Gilmour's students, faith and life become inextricably linked. The Academy ties all of its activities, educational and otherwise, to its mission, for they are the most visible and tangible expressions of the excellence sought by the school. By instilling a strong sense of self-worth through individual achievement, Gilmour helps students reach for their personal best. The Academy regards each student as a unique learner and supports students' efforts to achieve their greatest potential, helping to make their education at Gilmour a great adventure. Students are often pleased to discover that their best is better than they ever thought possible.

The 144-acre campus is 20 miles from downtown Cleveland at the junction of four Eastern suburbs: Gates Mills, Hunting Valley, Mayfield Heights, and Pepper Pike. The outstanding artistic, musical, and theatrical activities in greater Cleveland include those at Severance Hall for classical and orchestral music, the Cleveland Museum of Art, the Cleveland Playhouse, the Great Lakes Science Center, the Cleveland Institute of Music, and the Rock and Roll Hall of Fame and Museum.

A Board of Trustees governs the school. The President of the nonprofit Gilmour corporation and the Chairman of the Board are the chief executive officers; the Headmaster is the chief administrative officer. The members of the corporation are 6 members of the Congregation of Holy Cross and 6 lay persons.

Although tuition covers only 80 percent of the cost required to educate each student, Gilmour has a solid financial base, with an endowment of $35 million, prudent fiscal management, and a generous alumni and parent donor base that is supportive of the Academy and its programs as evidenced by a successful capital campaign that has been used to augment the endowment, financial aid, and faculty compensation. Gilmour is accredited by the Independent Schools Association of the Central States and the North Central Association of Colleges and Schools and is chartered as a college-preparatory school by the state of Ohio. It is a member of the National Association of Independent Schools, the Midwest Boarding Schools Association, the Secondary School Admission Test Board, the Coalition of Essential Schools, the American Montessori Society, the Ohio High School Athletic Association, the Catholic Boarding Schools Association, the Ohio Association of Independent Schools, the College Entrance Examination Board, and the Educational Research Bureau.

ACADEMIC PROGRAMS

The curriculum at Gilmour emphasizes mastery of major curricular areas, empowering students to develop their skills as communicators, complex thinkers, and effective and collaborative problem solvers. Gilmour has incorporated into its curriculum the best of both traditional and new educational thinking to develop habits of the mind. Problem-based learning, Socratic seminars, extended classes, integration of technology, assessment by exhibition, and the creation of portfolios comprise a rigorous program that produces results. Classes are student-centered partnerships, with students as workers and teachers as coaches.

The Upper School curriculum includes both required and elective courses. The minimum number of units required for graduation from Gilmour is 4 in English, 3 in foreign language, 4 in mathematics, 3 in science, 4 in social studies, 4 in religious studies, 1 in fine and performing arts, 1 in physical education and health, and ½ in speech. Students typically take seven courses each semester. Before graduation, students must complete 60 hours of community service and present a senior exhibition to demonstrate their mastery of the curriculum. Special programs include fourteen Advanced Placement courses, independent studies, field trips, retreats, external research projects, science externships, and faculty-sponsored trips in the United States and abroad.

The student-teacher ratio is 10:1. The typical class size is 15, though certain elective or upper-level courses may enroll between 6 and 8 students. The school year, consisting of two semesters running from late August to early June, includes thirty-nine weeks of instruction, with winter and spring vacations.

Interim reports, with detailed comments by teachers and advisers, are issued at the middle of each quarter. Academic progress reports are given at the end of the quarter. Parent-student-teacher conferences are held once every semester, ensuring continuing interaction between the school and parents. Active parent organizations, a school directory, a school calendar, and various handbooks and newsletters cultivate parent and community involvement with the Academy.

FACULTY AND ADVISERS

The faculty and staff include 5 Holy Cross brothers, a Holy Cross priest, 4 nuns, and dedicated men and women chosen for their academic qualifications and ability to work effectively with students. There are 90 full-time classroom teachers and administrative personnel members. All teachers and advisers are available for extra help after each school day. Br. Robert E. Lavelle, C.S.C., the Headmaster and a Holy Cross brother, holds an M.Ed. degree from Kent State University. He has been at Gilmour for thirty years, including twenty-five as Headmaster, and has a long record of service in educational and leadership positions.

COLLEGE PLACEMENT

The Gilmour College Counseling Program begins in the ninth grade and becomes more focused each year. Each student is encouraged, through a detailed plan of action, to find the college that best matches his or her aspirations and talents, while taking into consideration family preferences and needs. In a recent five-year period, 530 Gilmour graduates chose 200 different colleges in such fields as prelaw, premedicine, film, computer engineering, and studio art. Financial aid and academic scholarship packages for Gilmour students have yielded between $3- and $4.5-million during each of the last nine years.

Members of the 2005 graduating class were admitted to such colleges and universities as Boston College, Case Western Reserve, Dartmouth, Duke, Fairfield, Georgetown, Harvard, MIT, Princeton, Vanderbilt, Yale, and the Universities of North Carolina, Notre Dame, and Virginia.

STUDENT BODY AND CONDUCT

In the Upper School, there are approximately 110 students in each grade level. The majority of the student body is drawn from the eastern suburbs of Cleveland, Ohio, but Gilmour also adds rich colors to its tapestry with boarding students from sixteen other U.S. states and from countries throughout Asia and Europe. Twelve percent of Upper School students live in the residence hall. The result is a student body with a representative population along gender, religious, cultural, ethnic, and socioeconomic lines.

All members of the Gilmour community are challenged to act in a manner that reflects the moral values of the Academy—respect for life, honesty, and a commitment to peace and justice. An Honor Code makes that expectation more explicit and calls all students to a deeper level of moral conduct. The code is intended to foster an atmosphere in which all persons aspire to hold themselves accountable to high standards of personal integrity. Students must observe the dress code, rules, and regulations outlined in the *Student Handbook*. The Dean of Students and the Honor Code Committee address breaches of conduct.

ACADEMIC FACILITIES

The 144-acre campus includes state-of-the-art academic classroom buildings including a science center and a laboratory facility, each containing a computer lab with high-speed Internet access. The Gilmour library is a universal research, writing, and communications center that includes software and professional databases. The new Fine and Perform-

ing Arts Center is a lively environment in which students draw, paint, and work on pottery, ceramics, and photography. The Fine Arts Center also includes a variety of practice and performance spaces for Gilmour's award-winning music and drama programs. Students begin their day with their adviser and the full school community in Our Lady Chapel. Physical education classes take place in the field house, gymnasiums, ice arena, and natatorium.

BOARDING AND GENERAL FACILITIES
Murphy Residence Hall—East and West House—accommodates 80 students. Boarding students live and study in single rooms or with a roommate. An expansive addition to the residence hall includes a grand family room, dining area, fitness center, and recreation areas that provide an atmosphere conducive to community building. Creating a culture of comfort and respect allows students to make Gilmour their home. The Director of Residential Life, along with a dedicated staff of professionals, guides the program with an eye to the individual needs of each student, maintaining regular communication with the important adults in each student's life, including parents, teachers, advisers, coaches, and informal mentors.

ATHLETICS
The sports program at Gilmour includes baseball, basketball, cheerleading, cross-country, fast-pitch softball, figure skating, football, golf, ice hockey, lacrosse, soccer, swimming, tennis, track and field, and volleyball. Most of these sports offer varsity, junior varsity, and freshman teams. Gilmour's philosophy maintains that participation in athletics promotes both physical and social growth. At Gilmour, there is a team for every player.

The physical education/sports center (field house) is well equipped with a batting cage and space for three full-size courts for tennis, basketball, or volleyball, and includes a 1/10-mile indoor track. Other facilities include an Athletic Center with two sheets of ice, a regulation-size gymnasium, a new fitness center staffed by a full-time strength and conditioning coach, a five-lane indoor pool, and locker and training facilities. The campus has three soccer and lacrosse fields; two baseball fields; one varsity softball field; a stadium with professional synthetic turf used for football, soccer, and lacrosse; a football practice field; six tennis courts; an all-weather eight-lane track; a cross-country course; and a driving range with practice golf green. A full-time athletic trainer is available to students.

EXTRACURRICULAR OPPORTUNITIES
Students have many opportunities to participate in more than fifty extracurricular clubs, activities, and organizations. Student organizations include the Student Council, the National Honor Society, the Blue and Gray Club (student ambassadors), and mock trial, forensics, speech, and debate programs that each year garner awards at the regional, state, and national levels. Publications include *The Lance* (newspaper), *The Prep* (yearbook), and *Impromptu* (literary magazine). Each year, students perform multiple drama productions and participate in drama competitions at the regional and state levels; twice recently, students traveled to compete in Scotland. The band and chorus present two or three concerts a year at the school as well as a number of outside performances throughout the area. School clubs exist for art, photography, student tutors, drama, cooking, chess, and other interests as they arise.

DAILY LIFE
The entire school community begins the day at 8 a.m. with convocation in the chapel, a time for announcements and reflection. The day proceeds with four extended class periods (most subjects meet every other day), allowing students and teachers to thoroughly explore their subject matter. When classes end at 3:20 p.m., students have the opportunity to meet with individual instructors who are available until 4:15 for enrichment or extra help. Sports practices, club meetings, and other interest-group meetings begin after the academic day. Students and staff members dine together in a family atmosphere in The Commons, Gilmour's dining hall. A supervised study period of 2 hours per night is required for boarding students, who gather regularly to discuss the events of the week and those ahead.

WEEKEND LIFE
Weekends in the residence hall are an opportunity for students to use their leisure time wisely. Special events include concerts, museum trips, outdoor activities such as ropes courses and canoe trips, professional sporting competitions, and amusement parks. The city of Cleveland is home to such attractions as the Cleveland Orchestra, the Rock and Roll Hall of Fame, the Great Lakes Science Center, three top-level professional sports teams, and an extensive array of shops, restaurants, world-renowned museums, and award-winning theater productions. A boarding student at Gilmour enjoys the pleasures of suburban life as well as the opportunities of an exciting, modern city.

COSTS AND FINANCIAL AID
Day student tuition and fees for 2005–06 ranged from $7365 for the Lower School to $17,460 for the Upper School. The cost of tuition, room, and board for boarding students was $30,535. There is an additional fee for students requiring ESL support. Tuition charges are due by August 1 or are paid in ten equal monthly installments through an outside agency.

A financial aid budget of $2 million is available for qualified families with demonstrated need. The school also offers both merit and named scholarships. Merit scholarships are based on a competitive examination administered in November of the preceding year for entering seventh and ninth graders. A work-study program also provides an opportunity for tuition assistance.

ADMISSIONS INFORMATION
Gilmour seeks students with strong academic ability and potential who have a demonstrated record of success in their current school community. Selection of the students is based on all-around qualifications; strong moral character is as important as a student's ability to thrive in Gilmour's challenging learning environment. Prospective students must complete an application process that includes an applicant questionnaire, three teacher recommendations, official transcripts, admissions test results (ISEE or SSAT; TOEFL if English is a second language), and a campus visit and interview with the Admissions Office. Applicants are admitted at all grade levels. Gilmour admits students of any race, color, religion, gender, or national or ethnic origin to all rights, privileges, programs, and activities generally accorded or made available to students at the school. It does not discriminate on the basis of race, color, religion, gender, or national or ethnic origin in the administration of its educational policies, scholarship and loan programs, or athletic and other school-administered programs.

APPLICATION TIMETABLE
Students are encouraged to apply as early as possible for the upcoming year. Preference is given to candidates whose applications are complete on or before November 20. Gilmour welcomes applications received after the priority deadline and considers them on a space-available basis. Typically, once an application is complete, students may expect a decision within four weeks.

A campus visit is an integral and required part of the admissions process and provides a wonderful opportunity for families to become familiar with Gilmour's motivated students, caring faculty members, and extensive opportunities.

ADMISSIONS CORRESPONDENCE
Mr. Devin K. Schlickmann
Dean of Admissions and Enrollment Management
Gilmour Academy
34001 Cedar Road
Gates Mills, Ohio 44040-9356

Phone: 440-473-8050
Fax: 440-473-8010
E-mail: admissions@gilmour.org
Web site: http://www.gilmour.org

GOULD ACADEMY

Bethel, Maine

Type: Coeducational boarding and day college-preparatory school
Grades: 9–12, postgraduate year
Enrollment: 240
Head of School: Daniel A. Kunkle, Head of School

THE SCHOOL

Gould Academy was founded in 1836 as a coeducational secondary school stressing preparation in the classics. Today, the Academy is recognized as a school small enough to know each student well and large enough to provide appropriate levels of challenge and support to the individual within a rigorous college preparatory curriculum. Gould graduates consistently go on to find success at college and in life after college.

Gould believes that the seven-day boarding school is the ideal environment for inspiring a love of ideas and learning while developing social and intellectual confidence in each individual. By exposing students to all of the benefits of a liberal arts education, Gould strives to develop leaders who are physically and morally sound, intellectually curious, and tempered by experience.

A small student-teacher ratio allows for students to know and develop adult relationships with teachers who challenge and support them to achieve their individual academic best while pursuing their passions. Gould's Learning Skills Partnership provides additional support to students who have not achieved their academic potential due to an identified learning difference or lack of good study habits.

An appreciation for the outdoors is fostered by proximity to the White Mountains, while the school's aggressive integration of technology reflects a commitment to stay abreast of societal changes. The school takes increasing advantage of the growing cultural and artistic offerings spurred by Bethel's growth as a close neighbor of Sunday River, one of the Northeast's largest ski resorts.

The Academy is 1½ hours northwest of Portland and 3½ hours north of Boston by car. Chartered buses carry students between the school and both the Portland Jetport and Boston's Logan Airport.

The Academy is governed by 30 trustees, 20 of whom are Gould graduates. The physical plant is valued at $18 million, and the school's endowment is $9.5 million. In 2004–05, the annual fund raised more than $552,000 in contributions from parents, friends, and an alumni body of more than 4,200.

Gould Academy is accredited by the New England Association of Schools and Colleges. It is a member of the Association of Boarding Schools, the National Association of Independent Schools, the Association of Independent Schools in New England, the Independent Schools Association of Northern New England, the Secondary Schools Admission Test Board, and the Educational Records Bureau.

ACADEMIC PROGRAMS

Gould's primary academic objective is to provide a varied and challenging curriculum that prepares students to succeed in college. The academic program is designed to meet students where they are and challenge them to achieve their full potential. All courses stress writing, analysis, and problem solving, and certain departments concentrate on research and oral presentation. All new students in grades 11 and 12 must enroll in an expository writing course in their first trimester.

To graduate, a Gould student must earn at least 18 credits and satisfy departmental requirements, including 4 years of English, 3 years of mathematics, 3 years of history, 3 years of a foreign language, and 2 years of laboratory science. These requirements broaden students intellectually and prepare them for the most rigorous colleges.

Departments offer elective courses designed to give breadth and allow students to pursue a subject in depth in the junior and senior years. Electives range from such art courses as design, printmaking, and silversmithing to such science courses as environmental science, astronomy, and Advanced Placement (AP) electricity and magnetism. English electives such as creative writing and Native American story provide work in literary analysis, while trimester courses in robotics, networking, and the Linux operating system expose students to leading-edge technologies.

At Gould, an average class has 12 students. The grading system is numerical; 60 is passing, 85 to 91 is Honors, and 92 and above is High Honors. Grades and teachers' comments are sent home six times a year and are also available to parents at all times via the school's information server. Gould participates in the National Honor Society.

Advanced Placement courses are offered in every core subject area, with an average of seven AP courses available at any time. A wide variety of honors courses are also available. Students who wish to do in-depth work in a discipline may pursue an independent study program in lieu of a fifth course. Upper-level foreign language students participate in international travel as a supplement to their course work. Seniors may also undertake off-campus projects of an academic or experiential nature in March.

FACULTY AND ADVISERS

Of the 40 members of the faculty, 4 have doctorates and 22 hold master's degrees. Twenty-three are men and 19 are women.

Daniel A. Kunkle was appointed Head of School in 2001 and resides on campus with his family. Mr. Kunkle received his B.A. from Brown University and holds an M.Ed. from Harvard University. Prior to coming to Gould, Mr. Kunkle spent ten years as Head of the Midland School in Los Olivos, California, where he also taught mathematics and physics. He was at Mercersburg Academy in Pennsylvania for thirteen years, where he served as a mathematics teacher, dormitory head, and Academic Dean.

Gould selects teachers who have a genuine interest in young people and have special talents that they wish to share with community members. Every faculty member also serves as a housemaster, coach, or adviser. Teachers sponsor activities and serve as surrogate parents.

COLLEGE PLACEMENT

College counseling begins in the sophomore year when students take the PSAT. Intensive counseling begins junior year with individual and group counseling sessions. Advisers help seniors complete applications, write essays, and arrange visits to colleges. Students also meet with visiting college representatives. Parents are invited to an annual spring weekend of workshops presented by expert panelists and admissions officers from various colleges on topics such as "The College Essay" and "The Interview."

Of the 51 students who graduated in 2005, 99 percent are attending college at thirty-nine different institutions. Among these are Bentley, Boston College, Lewis & Clark, RIT, and the University of Vermont. Students who graduated in the past three years are currently attending Bates, Bowdoin, MIT, Mount Holyoke, Smith, the U.S. Air Force Academy, the U.S. Naval Academy, and Yale.

STUDENT BODY AND CONDUCT

For 2004–05, 44 freshmen, 54 sophomores, 77 juniors, and 63 seniors were enrolled. This included 178 boarding students and 62 day students. While 40 percent are from Maine, students come from twenty other states and nine countries. Gould enrolls students from various socioeconomic backgrounds.

Gould has a clear disciplinary code, and students understand that major rule infractions, including drinking and use of any form of illegal drugs, are grounds for dismissal. Tobacco is not permitted, and the health staff runs educational programs on smoking and smokeless tobacco each year. Gould prefers to encourage discussions of the issues that face young people today, from AIDS and drugs to other problems of human interaction.

ACADEMIC FACILITIES

All classrooms except those for art, music, science, and drama are located in Hanscom Hall, which houses a library of 13,000 volumes, a darkroom for black-and-white photography, and twenty classrooms. New in 2002, the McLaughlin Science Center houses state-of-the-art laboratories, prep rooms, a science library, a greenhouse, and a lecture auditorium that seats sixty people. Extensive Internet, intranet, and extranet resources are available. A widely distributed switched network hosts powerful workstations and connects all school buildings, including dormitories, where each dorm resident has a network port available.

The Art Cottage houses extensive facilities for working in a wide variety of mediums, many of which are uncommon at the high school level. The pottery resources include fifteen wheels, a glaze room, a bisque kiln, and a 60-cubic-foot car kiln, and a wood-fired kiln. There are separate studios for printmaking, painting and design, photography (color and black and white), silversmithing, and blacksmithing. The James B. Owen Gallery displays five shows each year, including one by students and four by professionals; recent displays of paintings by Jamie Wyeth, Andrew Wyeth, Charles Codman, Philip Barter, and others contribute to the gallery's growing reputation.

Drama, music, and dance classes are held in the Bingham Auditorium complex, which includes a 500-seat theater with a professional stage, lighting board, practice space for instrumental and vocal music, and a musical instrument digital interface (MIDI) lab where students learn about arranging, sound synthesis, and remixing, while producing their own musical compositions and videos.

BOARDING AND GENERAL FACILITIES

Boarding students are housed in three dormitories. Gehring Hall houses 68 girls in double rooms. Holden Hall houses 55 boys in double and single rooms. Davidson Hall, which accommodates 66 boys, is arranged in suites of three rooms shared by 4 students each. Each dormitory has laundry facilities.

In accordance with Gould's policy of having the faculty interact in different ways with students, all faculty members have dormitory responsibilities.

Registered nurses supervise the eight-bed health center. Doctors are on call through the local health center.

ATHLETICS

Gould's athletics program teaches the values of sportsmanship and competition, while encouraging the development of overall physical fitness. All students must be on a team or participate in other organized activities each season; two team sports are required per year for freshmen and one is required for sophomores, juniors, and seniors.

Each team sport maintains a full competitive schedule with schools throughout the state and region. Interscholastic basketball, bicycling, cross-country running, golf, horseback riding, lacrosse, mountain biking, skateboarding, skiing, soccer, and tennis are available for both boys and girls. Field hockey and softball are additional options for girls, and baseball is available for boys. In most sports, the teams are separated by ability and skill levels. Gould offers one of the finest competitive ski and snowboarding programs available, which includes world-class training opportunities in competitive Alpine and Nordic skiing, snowboarding, freeride, freestyle, ski instructing, ski-patrol certification, and recreational skiing.

In addition to team sports, many forms of recreation are available on or near the campus, including golf, tennis, squash, skateboarding, racquetball, bicycling, hiking, and canoeing.

Farnsworth Field House contains two indoor tennis courts, two squash courts, a weight and conditioning room, basketball court, indoor climbing wall, ropes course, trampoline for training freestyle skiers and snowboarders, and full locker room facilities. There are five outdoor fields; two all-weather tennis courts; a skateboarding area, including a half-pipe; and 40 kilometers of groomed cross-country ski trails.

The Gould Academy/Sunday River Competition Center is located slope-side at Sunday River Resort and serves as the winter home for the Alpine and freestyle ski teams and the snowboarding team.

EXTRACURRICULAR OPPORTUNITIES

The theater department presents three major productions each year. The fall production is focused on coffeehouse theater, in which the students prepare short one-act plays and monologues. The winter production is a full-scale event, usually a classic comedy from the American Repertoire. The spring musical includes a full pit ensemble. The student choral group performs numbers from Bach to rock several times each year. Students may also join the band or a smaller jazz or brass ensemble. Private vocal and instrumental lessons are arranged according to students' schedules and abilities.

Throughout the year, faculty members run outdoor excursions on weekends, including hikes, canoeing, fly-fishing, rock climbing, backcountry skiing in Tuckerman's Ravine, and skeet shooting.

The extracurricular Farm and Forest program offers students hands-on agriculture and forestry experience. Members compete in woodsmen's competitions, tap trees to make maple syrup, and plant an organic vegetable garden. In addition, they help tend the sheep, goats, chickens, pigs, and draft horses that live in the Gould Academy barn.

The Herald is a student-run yearbook overseen by a faculty sponsor. Other clubs and activities include a literary magazine, a student diversity initiative, peer tutoring, and a language club. Reach Out is Gould's service organization.

For the last twenty years, the Four Points program has provided unique experiential learning opportunities for each grade in March. Ninth graders travel abroad to experience homestays in countries such as Germany and Hungary, while sophomores remain on campus and combine in-depth study opportunities and service projects. Juniors are involved in an eight-day winter mountaineering course, while seniors pursue independent learning projects off campus.

DAILY LIFE

The class day begins with a community assembly in the auditorium at 7:45. Classes are 90 minutes in length allowing in-depth inquiry in the humanities and social sciences and laboratory sessions in science courses. On Wednesdays, classes end at lunch for an extended sports and activities period in the afternoon. Classes are held on occasional Saturday mornings throughout the year. Athletics and other physical activities are scheduled every weekday afternoon. There is supervised study time every school night from 7 to 9:15; appropriate homework is assigned based on the course and grade level. Typically, students can expect 30 to 60 minutes of homework for each class. The academic schedule changes during the winter trimester to increase the time outside during the daylight hours.

WEEKEND LIFE

Weekend activities on campus include movies, concerts, dances, and coffeehouses. Many faculty members have get-togethers in their homes. There are frequent trips into the mountains for hiking, canoeing, or snowshoeing. Each weekend there is at least one off-campus trip to a nearby city for shopping and movies. Several special excursions are made to larger urban centers, such as Boston, New York City, and Quebec City. All students may spend a limited number of weekends off campus, but most remain on campus each weekend. All students are required to remain on campus during occasional "closed" weekends.

SUMMER PROGRAMS

Gould Academy hosts the Bethel Camp for the Arts, as well as two different soccer camps.

COSTS AND FINANCIAL AID

Boarding student tuition for the 2005–06 school year was $35,750. Day student tuition was $20,800. Bookstore charges amount to approximately $800 a year.

Forty percent of the students receive financial aid, which totaled more than $1.2 million for the 2004–05 school year. Financial aid is offered to qualified students based on financial need. Information regarding financial aid may be obtained from the Admissions Office.

ADMISSIONS INFORMATION

Admission to Gould is selective. The school looks for students who are likely to benefit from what the school offers and who will actively contribute to the life of the Gould community.

As guidelines for admission, the school uses those characteristics that have in the past led students to be most successful at Gould. They include a solid record of academic achievement, the potential for continued academic success, an interest in learning from the school's environment and extracurricular activities, sound moral character emphasizing honesty and caring for others, vitality, a developing self-confidence, and the potential for leadership. The school also considers a thoughtful, well-written application and the applicant's personal statement.

Gould recommends that all applicants take the SSAT. Parents are urged to bring candidates for an interview while school is in session, although visitors are welcome throughout the year. The admissions office can suggest accommodations in the Bethel vicinity and can arrange for lift tickets for skiers at Sunday River Ski Resort, 6 miles from campus.

APPLICATION TIMETABLE

As a member of the Secondary School Admission Test Board, Gould abides by the acceptance and response dates established by that organization. Students should apply by February 1 to be considered in the regular admissions process and are notified of the school's decision on March 10. Candidates have until April 10 to reply. After that date, a rolling admissions plan is in effect, and parents are notified of the decision as soon as the file is complete. There is a $30 application fee for residents of the U.S.; $60 for those living abroad.

ADMISSIONS CORRESPONDENCE

John A. Kerney, Director of Admission
Gould Academy
P.O. Box 860
Bethel, Maine 04217

Phone: 207-824-7777
Fax: 207-824-2926
E-mail: admissions@gouldacademy.org
Web site: http://www.gouldacademy.org

GOVERNOR DUMMER ACADEMY

Byfield, Massachusetts

Type: Coeducational boarding and day college-preparatory school
Grades: 9–12
Enrollment: 374
Head of School: John M. Doggett Jr., Headmaster

THE SCHOOL

Founded in 1763 by a bequest in the will of Massachusetts Bay Colony Lieutenant Governor William Dummer, Governor Dummer Academy (GDA) today successfully combines tradition with innovation. It is at once linked with great historical figures, including John Hancock, Paul Revere, and John Quincy Adams, and devoted to cutting-edge curricula and facilities.

Governor Dummer Academy expects and promotes the individual's active commitment to integrity, learning, academic excellence, and the health of the community. Enriched by tradition and beautiful surroundings, it is distinguished by its support of individual growth and achievement in academics, the arts, and athletics in a diverse community that values teamwork, service, and respect for others.

Governor Dummer Academy's location on the original 450-acre Dummer farm, 33 miles north of Boston, offers students myriad opportunities. The ocean is 5 miles due east, and the surrounding forests, marshes, and nearby Plum Island Wildlife Refuge provide both a natural laboratory and numerous recreational possibilities. The Academy's proximity to Boston also contributes significantly to a GDA education.

GDA is incorporated as a not-for-profit institution and is directed by a 24-member Board of Trustees. The current endowment is valued at more than $61 million. An active alumni constituency of 4,650 members is represented by an Alumni/ae Council.

Governor Dummer Academy is accredited by the New England Association of Schools and Colleges. It is a member of the National Association of Independent Schools, the Independent School Association of Massachusetts, and the Secondary School Admission Test Board.

ACADEMIC PROGRAMS

Governor Dummer's academic program provides both the substance and structure necessary to prepare students for college. The Academy's core curriculum equips students with a solid liberal arts education in classes of approximately 13 students each.

The Academy offers honors, accelerated, and Advanced Placement courses in English, mathematics, U.S. history, biology, physics, chemistry, studio art, French, German, Spanish, and Latin.

Each student normally carries five subjects (five major courses or four major courses and a one-semester course). Students must successfully complete 16 credits (major courses equal 1 credit, minor courses ½ credit) to graduate. By graduation, students must have fulfilled the following distribution requirements: 4 years of English, 3 years of mathematics, 3 years of a foreign language, 2 years of history, 2 years of science, 1 year of Introductory Fine Arts, and a one-semester fine arts course.

Under the humanities requirements, all students attend at least three cultural events (i.e., theater, ballet, opera) per year. The Community Service Program requires each student to spend a term engaged in endeavors ranging from tutoring homeless youths to reading to the elderly and teaching disabled children.

Each quarter, academic advisers send grades and written reports to parents. The Academy uses letter grades; D- is the minimum passing mark. Midyear and final examinations are given.

Since 1934, the Academy has been a member of the Cum Laude Society.

Independent study is available in some academic and nonacademic disciplines. Juniors and seniors may pursue self-directed projects during two of the three semesters in lieu of athletics.

FACULTY AND ADVISERS

John Martin Doggett Jr., who was appointed Headmaster in 1999, is a cum laude graduate of Williams College with a bachelor's degree in American civilization. He received his master's degree in history from New York University. Prior to his appointment, he served as Associate Headmaster and Dean of Students at the Lawrenceville School in Lawrenceville, New Jersey. He spent twenty-five years at Lawrenceville, also serving as a history and economics teacher, housemaster, and coach.

Of the 59 men and women of the GDA faculty, 40 teachers hold advanced degrees, and many are pursuing further study and enrichment with the Academy's support. In addition to being classroom instructors, faculty members are dormitory parents, coaches, and advisers. Because 80 percent of the faculty members live on campus with their families, they remain constantly available to students, helping to foster the Academy's strong sense of community.

Each student at GDA has 1 faculty member as an adviser. As adults who keep all of the different aspects of school life in focus for parents and students, advisers inform students of their grades, help them plan their course selections, address daily concerns, and are available as a resource in any capacity. In addition to faculty advising, the school counselor works with groups of students on issues of common concern and meets with students individually to discuss, in confidence, any pressures or problems. She also consults with faculty members about student needs.

COLLEGE PLACEMENT

The Academy maintains a full-time college counseling office, which is staffed by professionals. The Director and Assistant Director of College Counseling works with students, parents, and faculty advisers to evaluate academic progress and guide students toward college and career goals.

Several times during the year, the Director meets with the entire junior class to discuss college admissions, plans, and strategies. A College Day program, featuring a prominent college admissions officer as guest speaker, is also presented. Students attend a college fair in the spring of their junior year.

More than 100 representatives of colleges and universities visit the Academy annually. GDA also maintains a college resource center that includes a computerized database offering information on colleges, occupations, and financial aid; a laser network, providing videotaped views of more than 200 college campuses; and a library of college catalogs and viewbooks.

The GDA class of 2005 included 92 members, all of whom were accepted by colleges and universities.

STUDENT BODY AND CONDUCT

Governor Dummer Academy enrolled 374 students for the 2005–06 school year, including 174 girls and 200 boys. The four classes included 230 boarding students (92 girls and 138 boys) and 144 day students (82 girls and 62 boys) representing various socioeconomic groups, twenty-one states, and twelve countries. There were 84 freshmen, 105 sophomores, 99 juniors, and 86 seniors.

Of the six major school rules, paramount at GDA is the honesty rule, which demands complete integrity in all matters—personal, academic, and social. The Discipline Committee, composed of 4 students and 4 faculty members, advises the Headmaster on all discipline issues.

ACADEMIC FACILITIES

The Carl A. Pescosolido Library and the Center for the Study of Mathematics and Science opened in September 1997. Containing a combined total of 50,000 square feet of space devoted to the pursuit of academics, these state-of-the-art facilities form the nucleus of GDA's intellectual life. Parsons Schoolhouse is the focus of GDA's Foreign Language Department and contains the Wang-Goodhue Computer Center, the language library, and classrooms. The History and English Departments are centered in the Frost Building, which also contains a microcomputer-based writing laboratory.

The Kaiser Visual Arts Center houses the photography lab, art and ceramics studios, and the Carl Youngman Gallery, where student and professional work is exhibited. The new Performing Arts Center, which opened in December 2001, contains a 500-seat auditorium, eight music practice rooms, an electronic music studio, a black box theater, and a studio/classroom for jazz band and music history and theory classes.

GDA provides 150 computers for student use, and all academic and residential buildings are connected to the school network.

BOARDING AND GENERAL FACILITIES

The GDA campus includes ten dormitories that house between 12 and 39 students each. Faculty members and their families share the dormitories, living in attached apartments. Senior proctors also provide supervision. The Peter Marshall French Student Center, which was renovated and expanded in 2005, is an informal gathering place with a snack bar, lounge areas, and student mailboxes. The Duncan Health Center, which is staffed 24 hours a day by a registered nurse, provides for basic medical needs.

ATHLETICS

The Academy has long believed in the value of competitive team sports. Everyone has an opportunity to participate at GDA, where a full slate of interscholastic varsity and junior varsity sports is offered in all three seasons, including soccer, football, field hockey, and cross-country in the fall; wrestling, basketball, hockey, and volleyball in the winter; and baseball, lacrosse, softball, track, tennis, and golf in the spring. In addition, GDA offers club skiing in the winter.

Among the Academy's facilities are the 48,000-square-foot Carl A. Pescosolido, Jr. field house, featuring tennis, volleyball, and basketball courts and a track; Alumni Gymnasium, with a new state-of-the-art fitness center, training room, dance studio, wrestling room, and locker rooms; the Murphy-Frost Arena, housing an indoor ice-hockey rink and dressing rooms; and hundreds of acres of playing fields, including cross-country courses, tennis courts, a nine-hole golf course, and the lighted Barbara F. Porter Field and Huggins Track.

EXTRACURRICULAR OPPORTUNITIES

Governor Dummer Academy offers a wide range of extracurricular activities. The Academy Players stage three major theatrical productions annually. Musical performing groups include the jazz band, the Academy Chorus, The First, and the Academy Chamber Ensemble. The Music Guild, a student-organized group, produces two popular music concerts each year. The Community Service Program provides opportunities for students to work on a volunteer basis for various area service organizations. Students also publish the yearbook, the newspaper, and the literary magazine. Clubs offered are outing, poetry, photography, ski, history, debating, international, computer, art, French, German, and Spanish. Other groups are Students Against Destructive Decisions, Amnesty International, Jewish Fellowship, Harvard Model Congress, Gay-Straight Alliance, PRIDE (a multicultural group), and Irish Brotherhood.

DAILY LIFE

The daily academic schedule features 60- and 90-minute class periods, conflict-free time for fine arts, and some unscheduled time each day for students and faculty members to prepare for classes and to meet for extra help and for students to work together on group projects. The academic day begins at 7:45 and ends at 3:10 and includes scheduled time for faculty advisers and student advisees to meet and a convocation period for outside speakers or meetings of student organizations. These are in addition to three all-school meetings each week, one a nondenominational chapel service and one presided over by student-body leaders. After classes, all students are required to participate in the afternoon program, which includes competitive athletics, community service, and the drama program.

After dinner, many of the Academy's clubs and organizations hold regular meetings. The library and arts and computer facilities are all open during this time. Evening study hours follow the activity period Sunday through Thursday.

WEEKEND LIFE

During the year, there are various compulsory and optional academic, social, cultural, and sports events on campus. On Friday evening, some students attend the theater and symphony in Boston. Other students may remain on campus to enjoy a concert, play, film, lecture, or other presentation. Several times each year, the Academy's Carl Youngman Gallery hosts Friday night receptions for new art exhibits.

Classes are not held on Saturday morning in order to provide time for special interests. The photography lab and ceramic and art studios are open then, as are music rooms and computer facilities. SAT preparation, driver's education, and typing classes also are available at those times. Students may go into nearby Newburyport for shopping too.

Most students spend Saturday afternoon participating in or watching the Academy's sports teams. Saturday night activities are planned by the students' Social Committee and regularly include dances, films, plays, and talent shows.

Among Governor Dummer's unique traditions is the Saturday night open house at the Headmaster's residence, the historic Mansion House (1713).

Sunday at Governor Dummer Academy has a less formal structure than other days. Faculty members routinely take students on informal trips and to religious services of various denominations.

COSTS AND FINANCIAL AID

For boarding students, the annual charge in 2005–06 was $35,350. For day students, the annual charge was $27,900. These charges cover tuition, room and board (for boarders), lunches (for day students), outpatient and some additional health care, use of all school facilities, athletic uniforms, and other items. Additional expenses include books, laundry, school supplies, theater tickets, athletic footwear, school publications, and team pictures. A Tuition Refund Plan is required for students who are not paying full tuition in advance.

Financial aid based on need, as established through the School and Student Service for Financial Aid, is awarded annually. In 2005–06, 27 percent of Governor Dummer's students received financial aid totaling $2.2 million.

ADMISSIONS INFORMATION

The successful Governor Dummer Academy applicant is a highly motivated student who has demonstrated ability, promise, and character. The Admissions Committee takes into consideration school performance, test scores, recommendations, extracurricular involvement, and impressions from the personal interview, which is required for all applicants.

Each year, there are approximately 100 openings. While most new students enter Governor Dummer in the freshman and sophomore years, a few places open each year in the junior class. The median SSAT score for students entering for 2005–06 was in the 65th percentile.

Governor Dummer Academy actively seeks a student body that is racially, geographically, and socioeconomically diverse and welcomes applicants from all backgrounds. Differences in educational opportunities and individual circumstances are taken into consideration in the decision process. GDA does not discriminate on the basis of race, religion, gender, sexual orientation, or national or ethnic origin in admission or in the administration of other school programs.

APPLICATION TIMETABLE

Initial inquiries may be made at any time. The Academy accepts online inquiries through its Web site. The campus visit, which includes a personal interview and a tour of the Academy's facilities, should take place during the fall or early winter prior to the year of matriculation. Families are asked to telephone for an appointment. A $50 fee ($100 outside the United States) is due with the final application. All steps in the application procedure should be completed by January 15 for day students and January 31 for boarding students. All candidates are notified of the admission decision on March 10, and parents are required to reply by April 10.

ADMISSIONS CORRESPONDENCE

Peter B. Bidstrup
Director of Admission
Governor Dummer Academy
1 Elm Street
Byfield, Massachusetts 01922

Phone: 978-499-3120
Fax: 978-462-1278
E-mail: admissions@gda.org
Web site: http://www.gda.org

THE GRAND RIVER ACADEMY

Austinburg, Ohio

Type: Boys' boarding college-preparatory school
Grades: 9–12, postgraduate
Enrollment: 118
Head of School: Randy D. Blum, Headmaster

THE SCHOOL

The Grand River Academy is located on a 200-acre campus in the rural town of Austinburg, in northeastern Ohio's Western Reserve. The campus is 60 minutes east of Cleveland and 90 minutes northwest of Pittsburgh.

Founded in 1831, the Academy was known during the nineteenth and early twentieth centuries as The Grand River Institute. Carl B. Bauder reorganized the institute in 1933 as a boarding elementary school. At the beginning of a decade-long building program in the early 1960s, the Upper School was added and the elementary school phased out. Today, the Academy is again college preparatory, serving primarily boarding students in grades 9–12 and postgraduates.

As a college-preparatory boarding high school for young men, The Grand River Academy believes that responsible and educated students are developed through a structured yet flexible atmosphere for intellectual, social, and physical growth. Students, including those who are not working near their potential, are assisted in preparing for a college education after graduation from the Academy.

An integral part of the program is the dedicated staff, whose members emphasize individual attention for every student willing to make a commitment to his education, personal growth, and better understanding of the society in which he must function.

The Academy's physical plant, valued at more than $6 million, consists of nine modern brick buildings and one older but updated dormitory, which is a reminder that The Grand River Academy's roots are deep in the past.

Operated as a not-for-profit organization, the Academy is governed by a 15-member self-perpetuating Board of Trustees. Every effort is made to keep tuition as low as possible. The operating budget is supplemented by an Annual Giving campaign, which counts alumni, parents, staff, trustees, and friends as its donors.

The Grand River Academy is accredited by the Independent Schools Association of the Central States and approved by the Ohio State Department of Education. Its memberships include the National Association of Independent Schools, the Ohio Association of Independent Academic Schools, the Midwest Boarding Schools Association, the School and Student Service for Financial Aid, and the Small Boarding Schools Association.

ACADEMIC PROGRAMS

The school year is divided into two semesters. Each full-year course counts as 1 credit. Graduation requires 21 credits, including 4 credits of English, 3 of science, 3 of math, 3 of social studies (including 1 of U.S. history and 1 of government), and 1 of fine arts; two semesters of

physical education; one semester of computers; and a semester course in health. In addition, each senior must write an independent research paper, with an instructor from the English department acting as an adviser.

The curriculum includes prealgebra, algebra I and II, advanced math, precalculus, and calculus; four full-year courses in English and semester courses in creative writing, grammar and composition, essay writing, and an introduction to college writing; civics, U.S. history, ESL U.S. history, government, and world history; Spanish I–III and French I–III; anatomy, integrated science, biology I, biology II, introduction to chemistry, chemistry, and physics; English as a second language (ESL); photography; digital photography; art; ceramics; psychology; speech; computer (applications); and health.

Most students attend seven 45-minute classes a day. The student-teacher ratio is 6:1, and the average class size is 7. Study periods are held nightly for 2 hours under teacher supervision. Students who need a more structured environment attend a special study hall, and extra-help sessions are assigned to selected students on a daily basis, including Saturday. Monthly academic and social reports are sent to parents or guardians. These reports include not only a numerical evaluation of the student's progress but also comments and effort grades from each course instructor. Regular parent days are held each semester, and, whenever necessary, parent conferences are scheduled.

FACULTY AND ADVISERS

The full-time faculty consists of 15 men and 8 women. Nine instructors hold advanced degrees. All members of the full-time faculty live on campus. At least one faculty family lives in each dormitory. All instructors, however, share the responsibility of dormitory supervision. They also act as coaches, club advisers, and student counselors.

The Headmaster, Randy D. Blum, has served at the Academy since 1973 as a teacher, coach, athletics director, and Director of Admission. Mr. Blum is a graduate of Milligan College, Tennessee, and he also holds a Master of Education (M.Ed.) from Ashland University in Ohio.

COLLEGE PLACEMENT

Preparation for college placement begins in the junior year, when each student has a conference with the Academy's college guidance counselor. Individual conferences and group meetings continue throughout the senior year.

A collection of catalogs is housed in the library, and representatives of many colleges visit the campus. Seniors are encouraged to visit colleges during the summer before their senior year and during school vacations. In 2005, all of the Academy's graduates entered colleges and

universities, including Eastern Michigan, Ohio State, Ohio University, and the Universities of Dallas, Illinois at Urbana-Champaign, and Maine.

STUDENT BODY AND CONDUCT

The 2004–05 enrollment was 118 boarders. Students typically come from seventeen different states and seven countries. The school is committed to maintaining a highly diversified student body.

Rules and regulations at The Grand River Academy are limited to those necessary to promote community well-being and enhance each student's likelihood of academic success. Students are expected to respect the rights of those with whom they live, be punctual for class, and take advantage of every opportunity open to them at the Academy. A dress code promotes a comfortable image, and ties are worn during the school day.

Discipline rests primarily with the Dean of Students and is administered on a case-by-case basis. Patience is exercised in forming a sense of responsibility in each student.

ACADEMIC FACILITIES

In 1962, the Academy undertook a campaign to replace its aging wooden buildings. The facilities included Bauder Hall (1962), housing nine classrooms, a biology lab, a chemistry lab, and an ESL classroom; Green Hall (1964), housing four classrooms, two computer labs, and the school library; and a gymnasium (1966). In 1975, Armington Hall was completed, in which two classrooms, the administrative offices, the infirmary, the dining hall, and a stage are located. Skeggs Hall, a state-of-the-art science and art facility, was constructed in 2001. The classrooms provide a bright, attractive, and well-equipped workplace for the students to learn. This building features computer connectivity with SMART Board technology.

The library contains more than 8,000 volumes, a lending program, and network access. A network of Pentium computers provides T-1 Internet access as well as several software applications.

BOARDING AND GENERAL FACILITIES

A new student union is scheduled to open in fall 2006. It will house a canteen area designated for the sale of athletic apparel and gym supplies, soft drinks, and candy; plans for the new recreation area include billiards, Ping-Pong, foosball, PlayStation equipment, videos, and various electronic games. Shepard Hall (1917), the campus landmark, was totally renovated in 1983. It houses seniors, admissions, and three faculty apartments. West Hall (1969) and North Hall (1969) house freshmen and sophomores. Mastin Hall, a dormitory for juniors, was constructed in 1984. Warren Hall (1997) is home to 12 students in the

Academy's leadership training program. The Academy also owns nine houses near the campus that are used for faculty members.

Breakfast, lunch, and dinner are served daily, with choices of entrees and a salad, sandwich, and soup bar. A committee made up of class representatives and faculty members helps plan the daily menu. Student seating assignments at faculty dining tables are rotated, as are students' kitchen duties.

The school nurse is on campus every day and on call as needed. The Ashtabula Clinic is 15 minutes away. Ashtabula and Geneva hospitals, 6 miles from campus, provide round-the-clock emergency services.

ATHLETICS

The Grand River Academy fields interscholastic teams in outdoor baseball, basketball, cross-country, golf, indoor soccer, soccer, tennis, and wrestling. Games are scheduled on the junior varsity and varsity levels, and all students are encouraged to participate, regardless of age or ability. Each year, the Academy holds its own Grand River soccer and basketball tournaments. In addition to the gymnasium, sports facilities include a health and fitness center, two soccer fields, three tennis courts, one baseball fields, two outdoor basketball courts, and a beach volleyball court. Students also have the opportunity to participate in paintball on campus. A horseback riding club is available.

EXTRACURRICULAR OPPORTUNITIES

The Drama Club takes advantage of Cleveland's cultural opportunities. Students attend concerts, ballets, plays, and operas and visit museums. Student publications include the yearbook. A student council, composed of 12 boarding students, is responsible for organizing dances and sponsoring events of interest to the student body. Qualified students at the Academy are inducted into the National Honor Society.

DAILY LIFE

Classes meet five days a week, and there are seven classes per day. Extra-help sessions are scheduled daily and on Saturday morning for those students needing more individualized instruction.

At the end of the class day at 3:35, if they are not in a help session, students participate in one of the many afternoon activities: a sports team; drama; intramural sports, including soccer, bowling, basketball, tennis, weight lifting, in-line skating, skateboarding, beach volleyball, and bicycling; paintball; computers; the yearbook; horseback riding; community service; or a club.

The 2-hour teacher-supervised evening study period begins at 8 p.m. Faculty members are available at that time to check assignment books and provide extra help. The library is also open for research. Lights-out is at 11.

WEEKEND LIFE

The Academy provides a full weekend schedule. Activities include trips to the mall, movies, dances with girls' boarding schools, horseback riding, and attending Cleveland Browns, Indians, Crunch, and Cavaliers games. In the winter, daylong ski/snowboarding trips to New York's Peek 'n' Peak and Holiday Valley are arranged. If a student decides not to participate in these activities, however, he is free to hike in the Academy's wooded areas, fish in area streams and rivers, or just relax.

The Academy schedules four-day weekends twice a year in addition to the scheduled vacations at Thanksgiving, late December, and spring. Students who reside outside of the continental United States are permitted to stay on campus during the four-day weekends.

SUMMER PROGRAMS

A coeducational boarding summer program is conducted on campus from late June through early August. The six-week course of study costs $3500. Some of the students are international students who participate in an intensive English as a second language (ESL) program. All students can take advantage of a full schedule of traditional college-preparatory courses. Art, photography, and computer classes are also available. Afternoon and weekend activities involve all students in fun, education, and worthy use of leisure time.

COSTS AND FINANCIAL AID

Tuition, room, and board for 2005–06 are $26,200 for seven-day boarding students and $25,000 for five-day boarding students. Parents should expect approximately $2000 in extra expenses (laundry, books, lab fees, and entertainment), not including travel. Tuition is payable in four installments. Loan plans through Key Bank, Plato, and Prep Gate are also available. It is possible to apply for need-based financial assistance.

ADMISSIONS INFORMATION

Students are admitted to any grade on the basis of their previous school record, recommendations, and an on-campus interview. The applicant must be willing to take advantage of the Academy's program and show evidence of his ability to do college-preparatory work.

APPLICATION TIMETABLE

The Academy has a policy of accepting applications all year long. A campus tour and an interview are required and can be arranged by making an appointment with the admissions office. Students are generally accepted for enrollment on the first day of each semester. However, candidates may be considered for placement throughout the school year if openings exist. The Grand River Academy seeks students from diverse backgrounds, without regard to race, color, creed, or national or ethnic origin. There is an application fee of $35.

ADMISSIONS CORRESPONDENCE

Sam Corabi, Director of Admission
The Grand River Academy
3042 College Street
P.O. Box 222
Austinburg, Ohio 44010

Phone: 440-275-2811
Fax: 440-275-1825
E-mail: academy@grandriver.org
Web site: http://www.grandriver.org

GREENHILL SCHOOL

Addison, Texas

Type: Coeducational day college-preparatory school
Grades: Pre-K–12: Lower School, Pre-K–4; Middle School, 5–8; Upper School, 9–12
Enrollment: School total: 1,248; Upper School: 442
Head of School: Scott Griggs

THE SCHOOL

Greenhill School is a coeducational, college-preparatory day school enrolling students in pre-kindergarten through grade 12. The School is located 12 miles north of the center of Dallas and provides students with both a spacious suburban environment and convenient access to the rich cultural and educational opportunities of a lively metropolitan area.

Greenhill was founded in 1950 by Bernard L. Fulton and a group of Dallas citizens for the purpose of providing high-quality, coeducational college preparation. It attempts to prepare students not only for college but also for a lifetime of learning to follow. Greenhill combines a strong, creative academic program with a comprehensive arts and athletics program for students from diverse ethnic, religious, and racial backgrounds. Greenhill values the individuality of each child and strives to provide exceptional opportunities for academic development, intellectual growth, and artistic and athletic fulfillment.

Greenhill is governed by a Board of Trustees that is made up of parents, alumni, and community leaders. Parent and alumni associations provide monetary and volunteer support, and parents take an active role in school activities.

Greenhill School is accredited by the Independent Schools Association of the Southwest and the Texas Education Agency. Its memberships include the National Association of Independent Schools, the Texas Association of Nonpublic Schools, the Council for Advancement and Support of Education, the Council for Religion in Independent Schools, the College Board, the Secondary School Admission Test Board, and the Educational Records Bureau.

ACADEMIC PROGRAMS

Greenhill was the first independent school in Texas to be recognized as an Exemplary School by the U.S. Department of Education. Every graduate of Greenhill continues his or her studies at the college level. All students are expected to achieve a high degree of proficiency in English, history, mathematics, science, fine arts, and at least one foreign language. Because Greenhill seeks to produce self-directed learners, tutorials and independent-study projects are an important adjunct to scheduled offerings.

The year is divided into three marking periods in the Lower School, Middle School, and Upper School. Conferences are held twice annually; written comments are sent midway through the period and at the end of each marking period if necessary. Classes meet five days a week and have an average enrollment of 18 at the Upper School level.

To graduate, a student must complete 132 Upper School credits, including 12 concurrent credits for courses designated as integrated studies and cultural diversity. One credit is earned per six-week course, meaning a trimester course is a 2-credit course and a full-year course is a 6-credit course. Credits must be earned through the following courses: computer science (2), English (24), modern and classical languages (12), history and social

sciences (20), mathematics (12), laboratory science (18), physical education and wellness (16), and fine arts (10). Students typically take six courses per trimester. A coordinated curriculum from pre-K through grade 12, combined with grade-level teaching teams and integrated course materials, guides the development of each student. Teachers are available for extra help. During the last half of their final trimester, students may elect to design off-campus senior projects that combine career interests with community service.

In addition to Advanced Placement (AP) and Honors courses, the Upper School curriculum has covered such varied topics as literature of the Southwest, oceanography, East Asia in Transition, vector calculus and differential equations, philosophy, law and civil liberties, molecular biology, astronomy, chamber orchestra, ceramics, filmmaking, principles of economics, the Epic Tradition, African-American history, anatomy and physiology, religions of the world, environmental studies, and ancient and medieval history. Language offerings include French, Spanish, Chinese (Mandarin), and Latin. Emphasis throughout the grades is placed on writing well. Summer reading is required. Advanced Placement courses are available in English, Spanish, French, science, mathematics, computer science, and studio art. In 2005, 87 percent of students taking AP tests scored 3 or higher.

FACULTY AND ADVISERS

Greenhill faculty members and administrators recognize their responsibility to serve as examples for students by reinforcing the values and behaviors that support a civil community: intellectual and moral integrity, sensitivity to others, respect for difference, and a courageous and generous engagement with life. The School seeks faculty members with solid backgrounds in their subject area and genuine concern for young people and encourages them to pursue further study with financial support from the School.

Scott Griggs is Greenhill's fourth Head of School. In his more than twenty years in education, Scott has had broad and deep experience in independent schools. He has held administrative posts at the Collegiate School, the Landon School, and the Columbus Academy. He has also taught sciences and math in upper and middle schools and coached basketball and baseball. Mr. Griggs has extensive experience in college counseling and admission. Mr. Griggs received his B.S. in physics from Centre College in Kentucky and his M.A. in educational administration from Ohio State University.

Greenhill has 141 teaching faculty members; 89 are women and 52 are men. All 141 hold bachelor's degrees and 73 hold one or more advanced degrees (including nine Ph.D.'s) from such institutions as Baylor, Brown, Harvard, Middlebury, Northwestern, Purdue, Southern Methodist, Texas A&M, the University of Texas at Austin, Vanderbilt, and Xavier. The School employs 2 full-time nurses and 3 full-time learning assistants.

The advisory system is a vital component of the college-preparatory program. Each Upper School student is assigned a faculty adviser. Although the

School provides a college counselor, dean, and community service director, the adviser is the student's principal counselor and also serves as a liaison between the School and the family. He or she monitors the student's progress, schedules and conducts all parent conferences, and offers assistance as required.

COLLEGE PLACEMENT

Upper School students are assisted by the School's college counseling staff, which consists of a director, an assistant director, an assistant, and 2 faculty members. In 2005, SAT score averages were 686 verbal and 657 math. Twenty-eight of the School's 101 graduating seniors received National Merit recognition, and all matriculated to college. Institutions selected by the recent graduates include Boston University, Brown, Cornell, Dartmouth, Georgetown, Harvard, MIT, Princeton, Rice, Southern Methodist, Stanford, Texas A&M, Williams, Yale, and the Universities of Notre Dame, Pennsylvania, and Texas.

STUDENT BODY AND CONDUCT

In the 2005–06 school year, Greenhill enrolled 607 boys and 641 girls as follows: 436 in the Lower School, 370 in the Middle School, and 442 in the Upper School. Students live in Dallas and surrounding communities and come from a wide variety of ethnic, cultural, economic, and religious backgrounds. The School's minority enrollment is currently at 26.7 percent.

Greenhill accepts responsibility for the development of ethical and moral values and mature citizenship in its students. Students are encouraged to understand, respect, and communicate with peers; accept responsibility for their actions; and respect the institutions of which they are a part. Students are not required to wear uniforms at Greenhill, but neatness and cleanliness are clearly articulated expectations.

Academic integrity is of utmost importance at Greenhill. Students in the Middle and Upper Schools are required to sign an honor code stipulating that all work is original and not the product of plagiarism or copying. Students in all grades are expected to conform to this code.

ACADEMIC FACILITIES

Greenhill's campus includes the Levy Middle School, the Fulton Upper School, Crossman Hall (dining), Montgomery Library, Agnich Science Hall, the Three Chimneys (administration), and the Fine and Performing Arts Centre. A new two-story, 71,000-square-foot Lower School building opened in August 2005. The building contains state-of-the-art classroom and administrative spaces for pre-K through grade 4. In addition, a faculty child-care space is incorporated. The building was designed by Lake/Flato and F&S Partners. An addition to the Upper School also opened its doors in August 2005. The additional space provides more classrooms, lockers, administrative offices, and teacher space without increasing enrollment. In 1998, Greenhill added the Phillips Family Athletics Center, a 66,000-square-foot competition gymnasium

and athletics complex; a natatorium; and a renovated Cox Field House to its campus. The award-winning buildings were designed by such renowned architects as O'Neil Ford of Ford Carson & Associates, Ted Flato of Lake/Flato, Charles Gwathmey of Gwathmey Siegel & Associates, and Bill Hidell of Hidell & Associates. The campus spaces are characteristic of Southwestern architecture. They are contemporary and spacious, with high ceilings, exposed trusses, and large, generous windows that take advantage of indirect sunlight.

All classrooms have the latest Pentium computers. All divisions have language and computer labs that are fully equipped with PCs. Montgomery Library houses 46,000 volumes plus a virtually unlimited database of knowledge through Internet and CD-ROM resources. Library facilities also include an instructional area for Lower School students. Other facilities on campus include a before- and after-school care facility and a black-box theater.

ATHLETICS

Greenhill is a member of the Southwest Preparatory Conference (SPC), which consists of nineteen of the finest private schools in Texas and Oklahoma. Under the guidance of a top coaching staff, the School's athletic teams have enjoyed success in many of twenty-five different varsity sports. The boys' soccer team has won fourteen SPC championships since 1981, including titles in 2002, 2003, and 2004. The girls' volleyball team won the 2001, 2004, and 2005 SPC titles, while the boys' volleyball team won the title five straight years starting in 1999. Greenhill's boys' and girls' track and field teams swept the conference titles in 2001, while the girls' squad has continued as SPC champions in 2002, 2003, and 2004.

Greenhill's campus offers some of the finest facilities in the area, including two competition gymnasiums and two lighted game fields. The campus also includes ten lighted tennis courts, a six-lane indoor swimming pool, a newly resurfaced eight-lane track, baseball and softball fields, a fitness center, and an aerobics room.

Competition, though, is not the only driving force behind Greenhill's athletics program. It's also about practicing and performing as a team, with real teaching coaches. Just as the School's heart is in the arts, Greenhill's school spirit thrives in the broad reach of its athletics program.

EXTRACURRICULAR OPPORTUNITIES

Clubs are many and varied throughout the School and include community service, chess club, music club, international club, SADD, Amnesty International, ecology club, Quiz Bowl, National Honor Society, language clubs, and many others. Student government organizes school activities and provides student body representation.

Students publish literary magazines at all levels: *Peacock Pages* in the Lower School, *Horizons* in the Middle School, and *Montage* in the Upper School. Students also produce a school newspaper and yearbook. Each year since 1991, both the literary magazine and the student newspaper have received Medalist ranking from the Columbia Scholastic Press Association in New York, recognizing them as two of the finest student publications in the country. *Montage* has also received seven Gold Crowns and a Silver Crown in the past eight years as well as several top awards from the National Council of Teachers of English.

In the fine arts, students participate in dramatic and musical ensembles and stage several major productions annually in the laboratory theater. Visual artists regularly exhibit their work. In 2001, the Debate Team won the National Tournament of Champions.

DAILY LIFE

Classes meet Monday through Friday. School begins at 8 a.m. Prekindergarten and kindergarten are dismissed at 2 p.m., grades 1–4 at 3 p.m., and the Middle and Upper Schools at 3:30 p.m. Activity and study periods are included in the daily schedule. Fine arts and athletics activities often extend into the late afternoon and early evening. Competitive sports are frequently scheduled in the evening and occasionally on weekends. Greenhill's Extended Day program offers before- and after-school care for students whose parents or guardians work during the day.

SUMMER PROGRAMS

Summer on the Hill, Greenhill's summer school program, offers a wide variety of academic, enrich-ment, language, athletic, and adventure courses and camps for students who have completed grades pre-K–11. These courses are open to students from other public and private schools.

COSTS AND FINANCIAL AID

In 2005–06, tuition was $18,200 for grade 12, $18,000 for grades 7–11, $17,000 for grades 5 and 6, and $14,800 for pre-K through grade 4. Additional expenses include a $1000 facility fee for new students, an optional annual lunch program ($800 for grades 5–12; $700 for primer–grade 4), accident insurance ($58), and books (Upper School only). Tuition insurance is available. For the 2005–06 school year, 12 percent of the student body received financial aid totaling $1.9 million, awarded on the basis of need. Greenhill subscribes to the Student Scholarship Service.

ADMISSIONS INFORMATION

Greenhill School seeks students who will benefit from its structured and competitive academic program while contributing to its diverse community with individual talents and enthusiasm. The admission procedures and criteria vary according to the ages of the students and the programs to which they are applying, but they are designed to identify the following characteristics: intellectual curiosity, self-motivation and discipline, high academic expectation, capacity for diligent and sustained work, enthusiasm for contributing to the School and community, and unique talents and qualities. Valuing diversity, Greenhill School welcomes students of any race, color, or national and ethnic origin.

APPLICATION TIMETABLE

Candidates are urged to contact the Admission Office in September for admission the following August. Major testing dates are in January and February. Applicants are notified of the School's decision in March.

ADMISSIONS CORRESPONDENCE

Lynn Switzer Bozalis, '82, Director of Admission
Greenhill School
4141 Spring Valley Road
Addison, Texas 75001

Phone: 972-628-5910
Fax: 972-404-8217
Web site: http://www.greenhill.org

THE GRIER SCHOOL

Tyrone, Pennsylvania

Type: Girls' boarding college-preparatory and general course school
Grades: 7–PG: Middle School, 7–8; Upper School: 9–12, postgraduate year
Enrollment: School total: 195; Upper School: 171
Heads of School: Douglas A. Grier, Director; Andrea Hollnagel, Head of School

THE SCHOOL

The Grier School was founded in 1853 as the Mountain Female Seminary and was reincorporated in 1857 under the direction of Dr. Lemuel Grier. The School has been successfully operated under the management of four generations of the Grier family. In 1957, the School was reincorporated as a nonprofit foundation administered by an alumnae Board of Trustees. Grier is located on a 300-acre campus in the country, 3 miles from Tyrone, Pennsylvania, and halfway between State College (where Penn State University is located) and Altoona.

The School is committed to a highly supportive philosophy aimed at developing each girl's full potential as an individual. Competitive sports are offered but do not overshadow the many intramural, life-sports, and creative arts opportunities available to each girl. Grier does not seek an elitist or high-pressure label and is proud of its family-like environment. "Friendliness" is the word most often used by visitors to describe the atmosphere.

The current endowment stands at approximately $3.2 million, supplemented by $280,000 raised through the most recent Annual and Capital Giving program.

The Grier School is accredited by the Middle States Association of Colleges and Schools. It has memberships in the National Association of Independent Schools, the Pennsylvania Association of Independent Schools, and the Secondary School Admission Test Board.

ACADEMIC PROGRAMS

Grier offers a multitrack academic program. The Honors Program is well suited for high-achieving students. The A track is a rigorous college-preparatory program. The program's strength's include comprehensive study of materials designed to challenge the students. AP courses are offered in five different subject areas as class offerings and then offered as independent online courses for advanced students in subject various additional subject areas. The B track is also a college-preparatory program but is geared for students whose college choices are less competitive in nature. B track classes are tailored to meet the needs of students who require greater academic motivation and supportive classes. Every attempt is made to pace the curriculum to the needs of individual stu-

dents, and crossover is permitted between the academic tracks according to the abilities of the students.

Learning Skills, a course taught by 4 specialists, is available for students who require additional academic structure. Learning Skills provides opportunities for tutoring and the development of strong study habits. This program serves the needs of approximately 30 students at Grier. A comprehensive English as a second language program is offered to international students. Girls who test below 400 on the TOEFL are required to attend an intensive summer session.

Students are encouraged to take an elective in the arts each year. The variety of course offerings is designed to provide students with the opportunity to pursue areas of interest and to develop and enhance their individual talents. Strong programs are offered in studio art, ceramics, jewelry making, photography, weaving, costume design, dance, music, and drama. Art faculty help students assemble portfolios in preparation for higher education.

FACULTY AND ADVISERS

The full-time faculty consists of 14 men and 20 women, about half of whom have received advanced degrees.

Douglas A. Grier, Director of the School for the past twenty-three years, is a graduate of Princeton and has an M.A. and a Ph.D. from the University of Michigan. Head of School Andrea Hollnagel has an M.S. from Mankato State University of Minnesota. She is currently completing her Ph.D. in educational administration from Penn State University.

Fifty percent of the faculty members live on campus, and 18 housemothers supervise the dormitories. Faculty members are available for extra academic help on a daily basis. Faculty members also serve as advisers to students and participate in various clubs and sports activities.

COLLEGE PLACEMENT

The School has a full-time college counselor who works with students in their junior and senior years. College counseling begins in the winter term of the junior year with class discussions about colleges, admissions requirements, and application procedures. The college counselor then discusses specific colleges with each student individually and helps the student develop a preliminary list of colleges to investigate and visit over the summer, thus

refining the list. In the fall of the senior year, the counselor reviews each student's list again and encourages the student to apply to at least six colleges. Applications are usually sent by Thanksgiving, or before Christmas break at the latest.

Graduates of the Class of 2005 were accepted at various colleges and universities, including Drexel, Duquesne, Northeastern, Otis College of Art and Design, and the Universities of Michigan and Wisconsin.

STUDENT BODY AND CONDUCT

There are 12 students in grade 7, 15 in grade 8, 20 in grade 9, 43 in grade 10, 62 in grade 11, 42 in grade 12, and 1 postgraduate. Students come from twenty-two states and nineteen other countries.

Students are expected to follow the rules as defined in the student handbook. A Discipline Committee composed of students, faculty, and administrators handles all infractions. Grier believes that good citizenship should be encouraged through incentive, and girls earn merits for good conduct, honors grades, and academic effort.

The student government consists of a Student Council with representatives from each class. The council serves as a forum for student concerns and helps plan the weekend programs.

ACADEMIC FACILITIES

Trustees building is a modern facility that was completely remodeled in the summer of 2002. It houses classrooms, two science labs, a supervised study room, and studios for ceramics, batik, and photo printmaking. Adjoining buildings house computer studios, language classrooms, and a library that houses 8,000 volumes. A Fine Arts Center housing extensive facilities for music and art classes opened in January 2002. A new science center opened in August 2003. Currently under construction is a Performing Arts Center, which is expected to open in spring 2006.

BOARDING AND GENERAL FACILITIES

The living quarters consist of five dormitory areas and four senior houses. The dorms provide a modern private bath for every two rooms. Two girls share a room, and each combination of two rooms and bath is called a suite. All students must leave campus for Thanksgiving, Christmas, and spring break,

though the School does sponsor trips during Thanksgiving and spring break.

Two student lounges with games, television sets, and VCRs are available, and a School-operated snack bar is located in a remodeled eighteenth-century log cabin.

An infirmary is located on the campus and is staffed at all times for emergencies or any medical concern that may arise.

ATHLETICS

Students of all ability levels are encouraged to participate either in the interscholastic sports program, which includes soccer, basketball, tennis, and softball, or in the life-sports program of tennis, swimming, dance, weight training, and skiing. The School has an excellent horseback riding program with 2 full-time instructors. A large stable accommodates thirty-five School horses and up to ten privately owned horses. One indoor and three outdoor rings are located on the campus within an easy walking distance of the dorm.

A gymnasium incorporating a comprehensive exercise center is well suited for Rollerblading, basketball, and volleyball. Five tennis courts and ample playing fields round out the School's physical education facilities.

EXTRACURRICULAR OPPORTUNITIES

Student groups active on campus include Grier Dance, the Athletic Association, and the Post and Rail; the glee, drama, outing, Spanish, ecology, and computer clubs; and the yearbook, literary magazine, and School newspaper. In addition, students participate in "Green and Gold" intramural sports, which often include soccer, volleyball, basketball, softball, and horseback riding.

Creative arts play an important part in School life, and girls can participate in several activities for enjoyment and credit, including drama, photography, art, piano, voice, and dance.

Nearby Penn State University provides many cultural, social, and educational opportunities. A wide variety of field trips are offered each year, ranging from rock concerts to ski weekends in the Poconos to trips to Washington, D.C., and New York City. A regular schedule of visiting artists and a movie series complete the social activities.

DAILY LIFE

Classes begin at 8 and run until 2:37, Monday through Friday; sports activities are scheduled during the next 3 hours. A 20-minute period is set aside daily for student-teacher conferences, and an all-School meeting is held daily. Students have a 105-minute supervised study period in the dormitories Sunday through Thursday nights.

WEEKEND LIFE

Because all of Grier's students are boarders, a comprehensive program of weekend activities is planned. Approximately ten dances are planned annually, usually for Saturday evenings. The Outing Club uses the nearby facilities of Raystown Lake for camping, hiking, and canoeing, and white-water rafting on the Youghigheny River is also popular. Tussey Mountain Ski Resort, near Penn State University, is 40 minutes away.

COSTS AND FINANCIAL AID

Tuition, room, and board for 2006–07 are $35,900. Books cost approximately $300 a year. Off-campus entertainment is optional, with additional costs charged based on individual participation. A personal allowance of $25 a week is also recommended. A deposit of $3500 is due with the Enrollment Contract.

Parents may elect to pay the entire tuition by August 15 or pay 80 percent in August and the balance in December.

Financial aid is based primarily on need, and, to apply, parents must submit the Parents' Financial Statement to the School and Student Service for Financial Aid in Princeton, New Jersey. In 2005–06, 40 percent of the student body received a total of $1.1 million in financial aid.

ADMISSIONS INFORMATION

Grier seeks college-bound students of average to above-average ability who possess interest in sports and the arts as well as a desire to work in a challenging yet supportive academic atmosphere. Applicants are accepted in grades 7 through 12 (and occasionally for a postgraduate year) on the basis of previous record, recommendations, and, if possible, an interview. The Grier School admits students of any race, nationality, religion, or ethnic background.

Approximately 75 percent of all applicants are accepted for admission.

APPLICATION TIMETABLE

Grier has rolling admissions, and the Admissions Committee meets on a regular basis to consider students whose files are complete. Candidates are asked to file an application and transcript release form with a $25 application fee, submit two teacher's recommendations, and have a personal interview on campus. The Admissions Office is open for interviews and tours during both the academic year and the summer.

ADMISSIONS CORRESPONDENCE

Andrew Wilson, Director of Admissions
The Grier School
Tyrone, Pennsylvania 16686

Phone: 814-684-3000
Fax: 814-684-2177
E-mail: admissions@grier.org
Web site: http://www.grier.org

GROTON SCHOOL
Groton, Massachusetts

Type: Coeducational boarding and day college-preparatory school
Grades: 8–12: Lower School, Forms II and III; Upper School, Forms IV–VI
Enrollment: School total: 360; Upper School: 336
Head of School: Richard B. Commons, Headmaster

THE SCHOOL

Groton was founded in 1884 by the Reverend Endicott Peabody as a school whose aims were the intellectual, moral, and physical development of its students in preparation not only for college but also for "the active work of life." While the means of achieving these aims have changed, the aims themselves continue to govern a Groton education, and many of the original practices of the School have become valued traditions.

While Groton does not hold as its exclusive goal the preparation of students for college, it does offer a curriculum that prepares students for the most demanding of college environments. Groton is by design a small school, enabling the School community to gather together daily and to develop close personal relationships. As students adjust to life at Groton, they come to appreciate less the emblems of success and more the personal qualities of peers and faculty members. A notable characteristic of Groton is the expectation of leadership. All students are expected to grow into positions of leadership in the School, and, traditionally, every member of the Sixth Form has been a prefect of the School, with particular responsibilities in almost every aspect of School life.

The School is 40 miles northwest of Boston and a little more than a mile from the town of Groton. Its location permits the students the freedom of country life along with the accessibility of Boston and its museums, plays, concerts, and sports events. The 390-acre campus includes fields and woodlands as well as the academic buildings and dormitories that are grouped around the lawn of the Circle.

A not-for-profit corporation, Groton is governed by a 27-member Board of Trustees. The endowment is currently valued at more than $221 million and is supplemented by an Annual Fund that totaled more than $1.8 million last year. This generous support comes from parents, friends, and an alumni body of more than 3,000.

Groton is accredited by the New England Association of Schools and Colleges and is affiliated with the National Association of Independent Schools, the Independent School Association of Massachusetts, the Council for Religion in Independent Schools, and the Secondary School Admission Test Board.

ACADEMIC PROGRAMS

The Groton curriculum is predicated on the belief that certain qualities are of major importance: to be able to reason carefully and logically and to think imaginatively and sensitively; to have a command of precise and articulate communication; to be able to compute accurately and reason quantitatively; to have a grasp of scientific approaches to problem solving; to be able to identify and develop creative talents; and to acquire an understanding of the cultural, social, scientific, and political background of Western and non-Western civilizations. Students in the Second, Third, and Fourth Forms are, therefore, introduced to a wide variety of courses that draw on interests and capabilities that might otherwise be unchallenged. Older students have

choices among elective courses, independent studies, off-campus projects, and concentrations in specific areas of interest.

Minimum graduation requirements include a Lower School and an Upper School science course; English, through expository writing in the Sixth Form year; mathematics, through trigonometry; American history and European history; biblical studies and ethics; a Lower and an Upper School arts course; and three years through the end of Fifth Form in either French, Greek, Latin, Spanish, or German. Students joining Groton in eighth or ninth grade take two years of Latin in addition to their modern language.

At Groton, an average class contains between 10 and 14 students. The mathematics and language courses are sectioned on the basis of interest and ability, and Advanced Placement courses are offered in every discipline. The minimum course load for Upper Schoolers is 5 credits each term; most students take 6 or 6½. The grading system is numerical, with 60 being a passing grade and 85 or above, honors. Grades, along with teachers' comments and a letter from the faculty adviser, are sent home three times a year.

FACULTY AND ADVISERS

The Groton teaching faculty consists of 62 full- and part-time members (25 women and 37 men). The Headmaster, who was appointed in 2003, is a graduate of the University of Virginia and Stanford University (M.A.) and holds an M.A. from Middlebury College's Bread Loaf School of English.

In selecting its faculty, Groton looks for individuals who are excited by their subject, who enjoy working with adolescents, who will involve themselves in the nonacademic life of a residential school, and who have lively interests of their own. Every faculty member at Groton fills a variety of roles, taking on responsibilities in the classroom, in the dormitory, on the athletics field, in various activities, and as an adviser to students. An adviser assumes a major role in communication with the parents and is the resident expert on his or her advisees. Faculty benefits at Groton include financial support for continuing education and a ten-year sabbatical program.

COLLEGE PLACEMENT

College advising is the responsibility of 2 members of the faculty, who assist students and their families in determining what kind of environment and options the students are seeking for their college years. The median SAT scores for the class of 2005 were 677 on the verbal and 675 on the mathematics sections. The 90 members of the class of 2005 are attending forty different colleges and universities. The most popular are Harvard (7), Trinity (7), Columbia (4), Georgetown (4), Duke (3), and Princeton (3).

STUDENT BODY AND CONDUCT

In 2005–06, Groton's enrollment numbered 360 students, of whom 180 were boys and 180 were girls. Of the 360 students, 322 were boarders and 38 were day students. Students from thirty-two states

and thirteen other countries enrolled. The student body represents diversity in both geographic and socioeconomic backgrounds.

At Groton, the breaking of major School rules (lying, cheating, stealing, or using or possessing drugs or alcohol) is a serious matter and may lead to dismissal. Disciplinary action is not taken, however, without the advice of the Discipline Committee (composed of students and faculty members), which considers all circumstances. Beyond rules and regulations, the School expects all its students to offer both courtesy and respect to other students and to teachers, staff members, and their families. This expectation is one of the most important characteristics of Groton.

ACADEMIC FACILITIES

The academic heart of the School is the Schoolhouse, where most of the classrooms, the science laboratories, the woodworking shop, music rehearsal studios and performance halls, and administrative offices are found. Adjacent to the Schoolhouse is the Dillon Center for the Visual Arts, which houses ceramics, painting, sculpture, and drawing studios as well as multimedia and gallery space. The library contains approximately 60,000 volumes; 150 periodical subscriptions, including publications in French, German, and Spanish; and a rare-book collection. Local, national, and international newspapers are received daily. The library's microfilm, microfiche, and CD-ROM material and ProQuest and other Internet databases are used for periodical research.

BOARDING AND GENERAL FACILITIES

Groton houses its 322 boarding students in seventeen dormitories, all of which have been completely renovated in the last ten years. The Upper School dormitories have single, double, and some triple rooms and house from 14 to 23 students each, with a faculty member or faculty family living in the dormitory. Each dormitory's common room, which comprises a large and comfortable living room and kitchenette, adjoins the faculty residence. Student rooms are equipped with voice and intranet hookups. Use of the Internet is available in dorm rooms and common room spaces as well as in public computer space. A wireless laptop program was initiated in 2003. There is a central dining hall where faculty members and students sit down together for dinner three times a week. Other meals are more informal and are served buffet-style. Adjacent to the dining hall is the School Center, which has a snack bar, a dance floor, the student radio station, a game room, and a television-viewing room.

ATHLETICS

Sports are an essential part of the curriculum at Groton, and the School follows an "athletics for all" philosophy. It holds that, through sports, much can be learned about cooperation, competition, and character and that every student, regardless of ability, should have the opportunity to participate. Groton fields interscholastic teams in baseball, basketball, crew, cross-country running, field hockey,

football, ice hockey, lacrosse, soccer, squash, and tennis. Intramural and recreational sports include canoeing, figure skating, fives, recreational and cross-country skiing, running, soccer, softball, squash, swimming, tennis, and weight training.

Not far from the buildings on the Circle are the School's eight playing fields and Athletic Center. In 1998, the School completed the construction of a new Athletic Center, which houses twelve international squash courts, twelve outdoor and eight indoor tennis courts, three basketball courts, an indoor track, two hockey rinks, an indoor pool, a dance studio, and a fitness center as well as locker rooms and a training facility for athletic rehabilitation. The Bingham Boathouse is on the Nashua River, which flows by the campus on its western boundary.

EXTRACURRICULAR OPPORTUNITIES
A lecture series brings to Groton on numerous occasions speakers of distinction in politics, government, science, art, education, and other fields. There is also a concert series that brings to the campus various individuals and groups with special talents in the performing arts. In addition, proximity to Boston and Cambridge provides opportunities to attend concerts, lectures, plays, and sports events.

An elected Student Forum represents all Forms and dormitories, and students serve on the Discipline Committee, the Student Activities Committee, and a number of other student-faculty committees. Sixth Formers assume major responsibilities in the dormitories, the dining hall, the library, the School Center, and the work program, through which all students share responsibility for cleaning and other routine chores on campus. Students do volunteer work in the local public schools, at a local institution for retarded children, and in a nearby regional hospital, among others. Other activities include bell ringing, chess, orchestra, jazz band, choral and instrumental groups, dramatics, debating, a minority awareness society, literary magazines, a newspaper, a student vestry, and the yearbook.

DAILY LIFE
Classes at Groton meet six days a week and are 40-, 60-, or 80-minute periods, with a shortened day on Wednesday and Saturday. Four days a week, the School gathers for a short chapel service, whose centerpiece is a chapel talk given by a student and at other times by the Chaplain, the Headmaster, a member of the faculty, or a visiting speaker. While no attempt is made to indoctrinate students in any particular religious faith, the School does maintain that religious faith is as important to human life as other areas of concern.

Athletics are scheduled at the end of the class day and before dinner time. The evening hours are for study, with Second, Third, and Fourth Formers having a supervised study period. All students check in at their dormitories by 10 p.m.

WEEKEND LIFE
Weekend activities at Groton are planned by a student-faculty Social Activities Committee. In addition to interscholastic sports, these activities include coffeehouse entertainment, regular Saturday night dances, skating parties, and special events such as casino night, games, and dorm competitions. Saturday afternoon and Sunday are also times for excursions to Boston or to the mountains. Each term includes a long weekend (Friday noon to Monday evening), and, if desired, a student may take two additional weekend leaves in each of the three terms. Day students participate fully in the life at Groton, whether on weekends or in evening activities during the week.

COSTS AND FINANCIAL AID
Tuition at Groton for 2005–06 was $37,770 for boarders and $28,330 for day students. This fee covers instruction, residence, routine infirmary care, athletics, use of laboratories and studios, and admission to all athletic events, plays, lectures, and concerts held at the School. Additional costs that are not included are personal expenses, such as laundry, books, rental of sports equipment, and travel. The charges for the year are due and payable in two equal installments in August and January. Monthly payment plans, tuition-refund insurance, and accident and sickness insurance are available.

The School aims to accept students on their own qualifications, without regard to their families' financial situation. Accordingly, no student should be deterred from applying out of concern for the family's ability to pay. Financial aid grants are based on the guidelines established by the School and Student Service for Financial Aid. In 2005–06, approximately 31 percent of the students received aid that totaled more than $2.8 million.

ADMISSIONS INFORMATION
Groton accepts applications for Forms II–V (eighth through eleventh grades). Though it would be difficult to define admission policies in quantifiable terms, the School clearly favors students with plentiful spirit, significant academic ability, a willingness to participate fully in the School community, outstanding special talents, and interesting backgrounds.

Applicants must submit a school record, a writing sample, three recommendations, and the results of the SSAT. In addition, all candidates are expected to have a personal interview with a member of the admission staff or a representative of the School. Approximately 1 out of 4 applicants is offered admission.

APPLICATION TIMETABLE
The initial inquiry and a preliminary application and application fee of $40 ($75 for international students) are welcome at any time. Visits to the campus should be made during the months of September through January prior to the anticipated year of entrance. Appointments should be made by e-mail, mail or, preferably, telephone well in advance of the intended visit. The Admission Office schedules visits between the hours of 8:30 a.m. and 1:30 p.m. on weekdays and from 8 to 10:30 a.m. on Saturday. Because applications should be completed by January 15, the SSAT should be taken in November, December, or January. With the exception of late applicants (those whose applications are completed after January 15), all applicants are mailed notification letters on March 10, and parents are expected to reply by April 10.

ADMISSIONS CORRESPONDENCE
Mr. John Niles
Director of Admission
Groton School
P.O. Box 991
Groton, Massachusetts 01450

Phone: 978-448-7510
Fax: 978-448-9623
E-mail: admission_office@groton.org
Web site: http://www.groton.org

THE GUNNERY

Washington, Connecticut

THE GUNNERY
MR. GUNN'S SCHOOL ESTABLISHED 1850

Type: Coeducational boarding and day college-preparatory school
Grades: 9–12, postgraduate year
Enrollment: 290
Head of School: Susan G. Graham

THE SCHOOL

In 1850, Frederick Gunn fulfilled a lifelong dream by establishing a school for boys and girls in his home of Washington, Connecticut. In this setting, he and his wife sought to develop each student's intellect, character, and values. In 1911, The Gunnery became a school for boys, but returned to coeducation in 1977.

More than 154 years after its founding, the school's goal remains the same: the education of each student to his or her highest potential in an atmosphere of academic excellence, competitive athletics, and strong, nonsectarian moral guidance. Students are responsible for promoting their own intellectual, physical, and social development and to contribute to the well-being of others. The Gunnery's special character and strength result from the unique manner in which faculty members both challenge and support students in preparing them for the demands of college and later life.

The 220-acre campus borders the village green of Washington, a small, historic town in the foothills of the Berkshires in western Connecticut. By car, The Gunnery is about an hour from New Haven and Hartford, 2 hours from New York, and 3 hours from Boston.

A nonprofit corporation, The Gunnery is directed by a 22-member, self-perpetuating Board of Trustees. The school's physical plant is valued at $20 million. The endowment is $20.4 million and was supplemented in 2004–05 by $750,000 from the Annual Giving Program.

The Gunnery is accredited by the New England Association of Schools and Colleges and is approved by the Connecticut Association of Independent Schools and the Connecticut State Department of Education. It is a member of the National Association of Independent Schools, the Secondary School Admission Test Board, A Better Chance, and the Cum Laude Society.

ACADEMIC PROGRAMS

The curriculum reflects the school's commitment to a liberal arts education as the most appropriate vehicle for developing intellectual curiosity and the basic skills of communication and inquiry. The Gunnery aims to prepare students both for the rigors of college study and for lifetime learning. Students generally carry five courses for each of the three terms, which are approximately ten weeks in length. To graduate, students must complete 4 years of English, 3 years of mathematics, 3 years of laboratory sciences, 3 years of one foreign language, 3 years of history, and two terms of art. Additional noncredit requirements include one term of ethics in the sophomore year and one term of public speaking in the junior year.

The curriculum is unusually varied; Advanced Placement courses and many electives are offered in all disciplines. In the spring term, seniors may apply for independent study projects by submitting formal, written proposals. During independent study projects, some seniors leave campus to work full-time; others remain on campus, retaining a partial academic schedule while researching a project or working in the community. In both cases, a student designs his or her own project, works closely with a faculty adviser, and submits a written final report.

Faculty-supervised study hall is held in central locations for all students who have not yet achieved Academic Merit status. Academic Merit students may observe monitored study hall in their dormitory rooms. Study hall is held from 7:30 to 9:30 each night except Saturday; supervised study halls are also held during each class period. Classes, which average 14 students in size, provide a seminar atmosphere, allowing for maximum student-teacher interaction. In certain disciplines, students are grouped by ability.

The grading system uses the designations of distinction, high honors, honors, high pass, pass, low pass, and no credit to reflect a student's achievement in a course. Six grade reports, containing detailed written comments, are issued during the year.

Through the School Year Abroad program, students may earn a full year of credit by spending their junior or senior year studying, living with a family, and traveling in France or Spain. One or two juniors are selected each year through The Gunnery/SAGE program to spend half the academic year at a prestigious boarding school in northern India. The study culminates with six weeks of supervised travel throughout India before returning to The Gunnery in mid-January to finish the year.

FACULTY AND ADVISERS

There are 50 faculty members (28 men and 22 women). They hold twenty-six advanced degrees. Forty faculty members live on campus, 24 of them in dormitories.

In 1991, Susan G. Graham was appointed the tenth Head of School. She holds a B.S. in English and library science from Kent State University and an M.S. in counseling from Fordham University. Mrs. Graham came to The Gunnery from The Masters School in Dobbs Ferry, New York, where she served as Assistant Head for six years. Prior to that time, she worked as Dean of Students and as an English teacher there. Mrs. Graham has also taught at Lake Forest Academy and the Columbus School for Girls.

When hiring new teachers, the school carefully looks for individuals who are enthusiastic about teaching and working in a variety of roles with young people. Most faculty members live on campus, coach, and lead activities. Each student works closely with a faculty adviser, who serves as a mentor throughout the student's years at The Gunnery.

COLLEGE PLACEMENT

Careful and extensive college counseling, beginning in the winter of a student's junior year, is conducted by 1 full-time and 1 part-time college counselor. Each student's academic record, test scores, extracurricular activities, and personal promise are all evaluated at that time, and a preliminary list of colleges is drawn up by the student in conference with his or her parents and the college adviser. Juniors and seniors are encouraged to talk with college representatives who visit the campus every autumn. Students also conduct research, visit campuses, and attend college fairs. By the end of the junior year, their options are refined; in the senior year, each student files applications to approximately seven colleges, generally no later than January 1.

The 92 graduates of the class of 2005 are enrolled at Cornell, Duke, Hamilton, Tufts, the United States Naval Academy, and the University of Michigan. Mean SAT I scores for these graduates were 566 verbal and 574 math.

STUDENT BODY AND CONDUCT

In 2005–06, there were 190 boys and 100 girls (205 boarders and 85 day students) in grades 9–12, with 50 in grade 9, 74 in grade 10, 79 in grade 11, and 87 in grade 12 (including 14 postgraduates). They come from twenty-three states and thirteen other countries.

In keeping with the school's tradition of sharing responsibility, students are given opportunities to become school leaders. The student body is led by 6 elected senior prefects, who serve as liaisons with the faculty and Head of School. Selected students serve as residential assistants, working closely with dorm parents in running each dormitory and in supervising evening study halls. Students are also instrumental in implementing The Gunnery's work program and such organizations as the Red and Gray tour guides and the Student Activities Committee. Also, faculty members and students serve together on the Disciplinary Committee.

The Gunnery has clearly defined rules by which each student is expected to abide for the benefit of all. A first violation of a major school rule usually results in the student being placed on probation; a second violation may result in dismissal.

ACADEMIC FACILITIES

The Tisch Family Library has 15,000 volumes, subscriptions to seventy-five periodicals, computers for student use, and ample space for study. Recently renovated Brinsmade has four classrooms and the Schoolhouse has sixteen. The Science Building contains three laboratories, two classrooms, a lecture hall, a computer center, and a study area. The art studio and darkroom are in Memorial Hall. The Emerson Performing Arts Center has music practice and performance facilities. The Gunnery has a strong information technology program that prepares students for college and beyond. A state-of-the-art wireless network and computer facilities that include two large labs and a well-equipped library complement a schoolwide laptop program for those who wish to participate. For all students, there is ample availability of school computers, and both Internet and voice mail access are available at central locations on campus.

BOARDING AND GENERAL FACILITIES

Ten dormitories house from 12 to 48 students each. In most cases, students are grouped by class. Each dormitory, with primarily single or double student rooms, also houses faculty members and their families. The dining hall, student center, mailroom, snack

bar, and bookstore compose the newest building on campus, which was completed in 2002.

ATHLETICS
The Gunnery views required athletics as an important part of the overall development to be promoted in each student. Nearly all sports involve team participation and competition with other schools. Fall offerings include crew, cross-country, field hockey, football, and soccer. Winter offerings include basketball, ice hockey, and wrestling for boys and basketball, ice hockey, and volleyball for girls. Spring offerings include baseball, crew, golf, lacrosse, softball, and tennis.

Participation in the athletics program is mandatory. Community service, an arts option, the ski program, outdoor club, and the Independent Study Program are available alternatives for eleventh and twelfth graders for one term only.

The Ogden D. Miller Memorial Athletic Center includes two full-sized gymnasiums, the fully equipped Noto Fitness Center, a weight room, a wrestling room, and locker and shower facilities. The Linen Ice Rink was renovated and enclosed in 1996. The newly restored Haddick Field House provides additional locker, shower, and storage areas. There are four clay and four hard tennis courts, a new boathouse on Lake Waramaug, four athletic fields, and a cross-country course. In addition, students have access to the 2,000-acre Steep Rock Reservation and The Gunnery's Neergard Woods, 70 acres of woodlands, where the school cabin is located.

EXTRACURRICULAR OPPORTUNITIES
Students are strongly encouraged to participate in extracurricular activities. There are three student publications: *The Gunnery News*, *The Red and Gray* (the school yearbook), and *Stray Shot* (the literary magazine). Two major dramatic productions, one of which is a musical, are held annually, and there are opportunities in both vocal and instrumental music. Student organizations include Amnesty International and the chess, computer, international, photography, Ultimate Frisbee, and UN clubs. Members of the Community Council and student tutors help their peers with personal and academic problems. More than 45 students volunteer to serve as campus tour guides for admissions and other visitors.

DAILY LIFE
Classes are held six days a week; Wednesday and Saturday classes are held in the mornings only, followed by sports competitions in the afternoons.

Monday through Saturday, breakfast is served from 7:15 to 8:15, followed by participation in the campus job program (a commitment of approximately 20 minutes each week), dormitory jobs, and room cleanup. Seven 45-minute class periods begin at 8:30 and end at 3. Each class meets four times per week; one meeting each week is a double period. Lunch is served daily at 12:30; Tuesday and Thursday lunches are formal, family-style meals at tables headed by students' advisers.

The Gunnery community comes together for an all-school meeting every Monday, Wednesday, and Friday morning for special programs or general announcements. Sports practices take place daily between 3 and 5:30, and dinner begins at 5:30. Study hall is from 7:30 to 9:30, and students must be in their dormitories at 10.

WEEKEND LIFE
Because the school values community spirit, students are required to remain on campus during a number of weekends each term. On the remaining weekends, they are allowed to go home or visit a friend after Saturday classes and sports. Sunday on campus is a leisure day until dinner, which is followed by study hall. A late-morning brunch is served, and students are free to worship at area churches if they wish.

A four-day weekend falls near the middle of each term. The school closes during these long weekends, and all students must leave campus. The Gunnery is also closed during Thanksgiving recess, winter vacation, and spring break.

The Student Activities Committee plans many activities, including movies, dances, concerts on campus and at other schools, and open houses in faculty members' homes. Also offered are trips off campus to New York City, local shopping centers, sports events, and ski areas. The Metropolitan Opera in New York is a perennial favorite.

COSTS AND FINANCIAL AID
Tuition for 2005–06 is $35,200 for boarders and $26,000 for day students. Tuition is paid in two installments, on July 15 and December 1. A registration fee of 10 percent of the tuition is credited toward the first tuition payment. Additional costs (books, dress code items, school supplies, laundry, personal items) amount to about $1800.

The Gunnery is committed to enrolling a diverse student body. Approximately $1.9 million in financial aid has been awarded to 38 percent of the student body for 2005–06. Most awards are made on the basis of financial need, although a small number of merit scholarships are also available each year. To apply for need-based financial aid, a family should file the School and Student Service for Financial Aid (SSSFA) application, which the Admissions Office can provide after November 1. Financial aid applications are due February 10.

ADMISSIONS INFORMATION
When considering applicants for The Gunnery, the Admissions Committee considers academic aptitude and achievement, character, and extracurricular abilities and interests. The school selects applicants who can be served well by its programs and who will, in turn, enhance the community. The Gunnery seeks active and involved students with a strong desire to excel academically and to participate in sports and other activities.

Most new students enter in grade 9 or 10. A few eleventh graders are admitted and, on occasion, a highly qualified twelfth grader is accepted. Approximately 15 postgraduates also enroll each year.

An admissions decision is based on a student's academic record, a guidance counselor or adviser recommendation, two teacher references, a written application, a student writing sample, and SSAT or SAT scores. Applicants for grades 9 through 11 should take the SSAT, and twelfth grade and postgraduate candidates are asked to submit SAT I scores. A personal interview with a member of the admissions staff is required. The Gunnery also has an active network of parent and trustee volunteers who answer questions for prospective families.

APPLICATION TIMETABLE
An inquiry is welcome at any time. Campus tours and interviews can be arranged by contacting the Admissions Office in advance. Appointments are scheduled from 8:30 a.m. to 2:15 p.m., Monday, Tuesday, Thursday, and Friday and from 8:30 to 11 a.m. on Wednesday and Saturday. Applicants whose files are successfully completed by January 31 are notified of their acceptance on March 10, and students are expected to reply by April 10. After March 10, applications are considered until all places are filled.

ADMISSIONS CORRESPONDENCE
Thomas W. (Tommy) Adams
Director of Admissions
The Gunnery
99 Green Hill Road
Washington, Connecticut 06793

Phone: 860-868-7334
Fax: 860-868-1614
E-mail: admissions@gunnery.org
Web site: http://www.gunnery.org

HACKLEY SCHOOL

Tarrytown, New York

Type: Coeducational day college-preparatory school with five-day boarding available (grades 9–12)
Grades: K–12: Lower School, Kindergarten–4; Middle School, 5–8; Upper School, 9–12
Enrollment: School total: 810; Upper School: 386
Head of School: Walter C. Johnson, Headmaster

THE SCHOOL

Hackley School, founded in 1899 by Mrs. Caleb Brewster Hackley, is a nonsectarian, co-educational, college-preparatory school, enrolling day students in grades kindergarten through 12 and five-day boarding students in grades 9 through 12. For more than 100 years, the words carved in the lintel above the School's entrance, "Enter Here to Be and Find a Friend," have introduced parents and students to Hackley School's educational culture, one in which a deliberate approach to social relationships stimulates and supports the moral, intellectual, artistic, and athletic accomplishments of individuals.

At Hackley, students encounter serious classes, demanding homework assignments, and a peer environment that respects commitment and unreserved effort. Whether it is on an athletic field, in an art studio, in the theater, or in a classroom, Hackley students find arenas in which they want to do their best, where they can discover their passions, and create their character with the support of friends and teachers.

The Hackley community is one of varying backgrounds and perspectives, and that diversity of economic means, national origin, political philosophy, race, and religion enables students to appreciate the complexity and concerns of the larger community. The School believes that students grow in character and responsibility by participating in service to that larger community, and from the Lower through the Upper School, energy, time, and imagination is committed to serving the needs of people outside the spheres of home and school. Such service is another way in which teachers and parents work together to encourage students to have respect for and to act responsibly toward themselves and others. Hackley School strives to provide a social environment that supports the development of virtue, going beyond mere observance of the rules to make Hackley a civilized community where courtesy, kindness, and forbearance reign, and incivility and intolerance are shunned.

This culture, which emphasizes hard work, individual responsibility, and service to community, is expressed in the Hackley School motto: "*Iuncti Iuvamus*" or "United We Help One Another. "

Hackley is located in Tarrytown, New York (population 12,000), in the heart of the scenic Hudson River Valley, and 25 miles north of Manhattan. The School is reached easily by bus, car, or train.

A nonprofit, nonsectarian institution, Hackley is governed by a 20-member Board of Trustees. The annual operating budget is $22.8 million; the School's endowment portfolio is valued at about $23 million. The Hackley Annual Fund raises more than $2 million in operating support from parents, grandparents, alumni, and friends each year. The Hackley Parents Association enhances school life through volunteer activities and fund-raising. Hackley has completed the final year of its Centennial Campaign, which raised $50 million.

Hackley is registered by the New York State Board of Regents. It holds memberships in the National Association of Independent Schools, the College Board, the Association of College Admissions Counselors, and the New York State Association of Independent Schools.

ACADEMIC PROGRAMS

The school year, from early September to early June, is divided into semesters. There are breaks for Thanksgiving, winter, and spring vacations.

Average class size is 16 students. There are supervised study halls throughout the day for students in grades 6–12. Boarders also have supervised evening study. Teachers provide extra help as necessary; long-term tutoring is offered for an hourly fee. Grades are issued and sent to parents four times yearly, with interim reports issued as required.

The curriculum for kindergarten–grade 3 emphasizes reading and oral and written expression. Beginning in grade 3, students write a weekly theme and begin to work on research papers. The mathematics program teaches the logical structure of the number system and fosters dexterity in computation. Also included in the program are history, science, art, music, computers, and physical education. Spanish is introduced in grade 3. The Director of the Lower School is Ronald DelMoro.

The curriculum for grade 4 and the Middle School (grades 5–8) includes English, which focuses on grammar, oral expression, expository and creative writing, and literary analysis; American history (grades 4 and 6), ancient history and world history (grades 5 and 7), and Asian civilizations (grade 8); mathematics (emphasizing the four basic operations and probability, graphing, statistics and prealgebra, algebra I, and geometry); science, including the physical world (grade 6), life science (grade 7), and chemistry in biology (grade 8); art; and music. All Middle School students are required to take a computer curriculum and health education. They may also begin the study of Latin or French or continue Spanish. William Porter is Director of the Middle School.

To graduate, Upper School students must complete four years of English; three years of a foreign language (French, Spanish, or Latin); courses in practicing historical inquiry, American history to 1900, and twentieth-century world; mathematics through algebra II and trigonometry; three years of science, one of which must be a laboratory course; and one year of performing or visual arts. The Upper School puts a major emphasis on writing. The Monday composition period assigns at least twenty additional essays during the academic year.

In addition to required courses, the Upper School also offers Advanced Placement courses in twenty subjects across all departments. Other courses include contemporary issues, Shakespeare, literature of war, seminar in creative writing, electronic publishing (print and Web-based), economics, modern European history, government and politics: the U.S.A. and the world, history of rock and roll, Italian, computer science, ecology, biology, organic chemistry, plant and animal biology seminar, chemistry, ninth-grade physics, advanced physics, marine biology, environmental science, calculus, finite math, statistics, music theory, jazz improvisation, art history, studio art, advanced ceramics, photography, computer graphics, 3-D sculpture and design, and architecture and design. The Director of the Upper School is Beverley Whitaker.

English as a second language (ESL) is offered at the Middle School level with emphasis on individualized instruction. ESL students normally enter Hackley in the fall of sixth and seventh grades. Aptitude

testing in the student's first language is required for admission into this highly selective program.

FACULTY AND ADVISERS

Walter C. Johnson was appointed Headmaster in February 1995. He graduated summa cum laude from Amherst (B.A., 1974) and earned master's degrees in literature and educational administration from the University of Pennsylvania and Teachers College, Columbia University, respectively. Mr. Johnson has had educational and administrative experience at Trinity School and Collegiate School in New York City and at the American School in London.

Faculty members, including assistants and administrators who teach, number 129. Fifty percent of the full-time teachers live on campus. They hold 129 baccalaureate and 99 graduate degrees, representing study at more than 100 colleges and universities.

Each student in both the Middle School and the Upper School has an academic adviser who provides extensive course counseling for the current year as well as advice for planning a course of study for the student's entire Hackley career. Other student support services include a full-time nurse, 2 full-time psychologists, and a learning specialist.

COLLEGE PLACEMENT

A College Counseling office is staffed by 3 experienced full-time professionals. In the past four years, the following colleges and universities have enrolled the greatest number of Hackley graduates: Boston University, Columbia, Cornell, Franklin and Marshall, Georgetown, George Washington, Hamilton, Harvard, NYU, Princeton, Skidmore, University of Pennsylvania, and Yale.

STUDENT BODY AND CONDUCT

In 2005–06, the School enrolled 396 day boys, 390 day girls, 10 boarding boys, and 14 boarding girls, as follows: 240 in grades K–5, 184 in grades 6–8, and 386 in grades 9–12. Students come from ninety-four communities throughout Westchester, Orange, Putnam, Rockland, Bergen, and Fairfield counties in New York, New Jersey, and Connecticut as well as from New York City.

Hackley's philosophy challenges students to put forth their best academic effort, to maintain high standards of personal behavior, and to dress appropriately.

ACADEMIC FACILITIES

Hackley uses technology to provide resources, access information, and enhance critical-thinking skills in support of its mission. This is accomplished two ways: direct computer instruction and technological support in all academic areas. The greater focus is on the latter area since Hackley does not teach computer use as an end unto itself but rather as a supplement to its curriculum.

Three Computer Coordinators provide academic support to each of the three divisions, and the Director of Technology coordinates all of the academic initiatives of this team. Constantly reviewing the program, this team is responsible for instructing students and supporting faculty members in technology integration.

The Hackley computer network, both wired and wireless, runs throughout the entire campus and includes direct Internet access in every classroom. In the Lower School, there are workstations in every

classroom. The Middle and Upper Schools have two and three computer labs respectively, all with cutting-edge PCs and Smart Board technology. Classrooms in all divisions are outfitted with built-in LCD projectors and Smart Boards. In addition, available sets of wireless laptops allow for setting up any classroom as a mini lab, and Upper School students can also check out laptops for individual use.

A strong professional development program allows teachers to make informed decisions about technology enhancements to their courses. Faculty education work is supported by the availability of laptops through the faculty laptop loan program. This professional development work drives curricular integration. Working cooperatively with the Computer Coordinators, faculty members can use their expertise in their subject areas to determine appropriate integration of technology into the courses they teach. Research in every subject area at some point includes an Internet component. Every academic area now engages the use of technology from guided Internet research to formal application use, such as Geometer's Sketchpad in mathematics, Rosetta Stone in foreign languages, and computer-based measurements in physics labs.

The second academic component, direct computer use instruction, falls into three categories: computer applications, electronic publishing, and computer science. Hackley School believes the spark for any use of technology must come from a curricular-based decision-making process. Through improving technological infrastructure, professional development, and curricular application, academic technology gains greater use each year. The Director of Technology is Joseph E. Dioguardi III.

The Hackley library contains more than 33,000 volumes; students may also borrow items from any library in the Westchester County Library System. The library has a computerized catalog and also provides access to a number of major online databases. The librarian is Laura Pearle.

BOARDING AND GENERAL FACILITIES
The School, situated on a hilltop overlooking the Hudson, is graced by rambling, turn-of-the-century buildings in English Tudor style. The facilities include a performing arts center with a music conservatory, a new science building, an indoor swimming pool, several art studios, and a photography lab. The 285-acre campus offers six tennis courts, numerous playing fields, and several cross-country trails.

Boarders who are involved in the five-day boarding program are housed in either single or double rooms in single-sex dormitories in the main building complex. Resident faculty members live on the boarding corridors, supervising the students and providing cultural and academic enrichment programs for them. Boarding students return to their families each weekend.

ATHLETICS
Varsity sports for boys and girls include basketball, cross-country, fencing, indoor track, lacrosse, golf, soccer, squash, swimming, track and field, and ten-nis. Boys also compete in baseball, football, and wrestling, while girls play field hockey and softball. A member of the Ivy League of the metropolitan area, Hackley competes against league members and public and parochial schools. Physical education courses also include nonteam activities, such as working out in the fitness center and hiking. Swimming is required in kindergarten through grade 6.

Hackley athletic teams have accumulated recognition for their success and sportsmanship over the years. Since 1990, teams have won league championships in football, boys' and girls' soccer, field hockey, girls' basketball, boys' and girls' lacrosse, swimming, track and field, baseball, and softball. Since 1982, 20 students have received All-American accolades. Hackley has had many undefeated teams and is the home of the 2000 and 2001 New York State independent school boys' basketball and the 2003, 2004 (undefeated team) New York State independent school girls' soccer champions. In 2000, Hackley's girls' softball team was the New York State independent school champion. The girls' lacrosse team won the 2000, 2001, and 2004 Ivy League championships. In 2003 and 2004, the girls' field hockey team won the Ivy League championship. The boys' lacrosse team won the 2000, 2001, 2003, and 2004 New York Metropolitan Lacrosse Association Tournament and the Ivy League championship.

EXTRACURRICULAR OPPORTUNITIES
The Community Council, composed of student and faculty representatives from grades 6–12, organizes social and service activities. Students also participate in Model Congresses and a student-faculty judicial board. Students publish a yearbook, a newspaper, and a literary magazine. Dramatic productions include annual Lower School presentations of *St. George and the Dragon*, a Gilbert and Sullivan operetta, and a Shakespeare play. Recent Middle and Upper School drama and musical theater productions include *I Never Saw Another Butterfly, Scapin,* and the musical, *The Who's Tommy.* Students also participate in chorus, orchestra, band, and jazz bands and perform major choral works, chamber music, and vocal recitals. The Hackley Music Institute provides individual instruction for preprofessional and other music students in both vocal and instrumental music. There are also a variety of student clubs and a program for Student Teachers in Lower School classrooms.

Hackley families attend the Medieval Festival, Carnival, Spring Fair, School art shows, gym and swim nights, Book Club Evenings, and parent dinners. Hackley also holds dances and coffee house evenings for students.

Annual trips include the sixth-grade camping trip to the Delaware Water Gap, the seventh-grade visit to Boston, the eighth-grade trip to Washington, and the ninth-grade outdoor challenge experience. In addition, students take trips supplementing their courses; recent trips include visits to the Metropolitan Museum, Ellis Island, a zoology and marine biology research vessel in Long Island Sound, and numerous nearby sites in the historic Hudson River Valley.

In 2000, Hackley received a five-year grant for an annual educational trip; 29 students and faculty members have visited Cuba, China, the Galapagos Islands, Vietnam, Greece, and Italy. The School also sponsors student exchanges with nine schools in France during the spring recess.

DAILY LIFE
For students in kindergarten through grade 5, a typical day, from 8:10 a.m. to 2:20 p.m., includes seven 40-minute class periods, recess, and lunch. Students in grades 6 through 12, whose day extends until 4:30 p.m., have eight class periods, followed by sports and activities. Buses for day students depart at 2:30 and 4:45 p.m.

Hackley's five-day boarding program provides students in grades 9 through 12 with the advantages of both a traditional boarding school and weekends at home with their families. Resident faculty members, living on the boarding corridor, provide personal attention, structure, and a supportive and friendly family atmosphere.

SUMMER PROGRAMS
The Hackley Summer School offers enrichment programs in writing, history, and science as well as review work for students needing help in basic subjects and ESL. Students entering grades 5–12 are eligible to enroll. Hackley also offers football and basketball camps.

COSTS AND FINANCIAL AID
In 2005–06, tuition ranged from $22,100 for kindergarten to $25,900 for grade 12. The boarding charge was $8000. Tuition includes lunch but not the cost of Middle and Upper School books.

In the current year, a total of $2.4 million in financial aid was awarded to 117 students on the basis of demonstrated need. Low-interest loans, an installment payment plan, and tuition insurance are also available.

ADMISSIONS INFORMATION
Hackley seeks students of diverse backgrounds who demonstrate quickness of intellect and resourcefulness in problem solving, tempered by curiosity and love of truth. Students are admitted on the basis of a personal interview and written essay, a campus visit, two teacher recommendations, the transcript from the previous school, and ISEE or SSAT scores for Middle and Upper Schools. In the Lower School, candidates take Hackley's own admissions test.

APPLICATION TIMETABLE
The application deadline is December 16. There is a $55 application fee.

ADMISSIONS CORRESPONDENCE
Julie S. Core, Director of Admissions, Grades K–6
Lawrence Crimmins, Director of Admissions,
    Grades 7–12
Hackley School
293 Benedict Avenue
Tarrytown, New York 10591

Phone: 914-366-2642
Fax: 914-366-2636
E-mail: admissions@hackleyschool.org
Web site: http://www.hackleyschool.org

HAPPY VALLEY SCHOOL

Ojai, California

Type: Coeducational boarding and day college-preparatory school
Grades: 9–12
Enrollment: 90
Head of School: Mr. Paul Amadio, Director

THE SCHOOL

Founded in 1946, Happy Valley School (HVS) enjoys a rural setting on 450 acres just 90 miles north of Los Angeles. Happy Valley School was founded by a group of friends and educators that included Aldous Huxley, Dr. Guido Ferrando, Mr. J. Krishnamurti, and Mrs. Rosalind Rajagopal. The School was envisioned as an educational community that would provide an atmosphere where students could develop and discover both their intellectual and creative potential. This philosophy is still the core of the School today.

In addition to its fine academic program, Happy Valley School has an active fine arts program that is an integral part of the School curriculum. The fine arts program prepares students for a lifetime of enjoyment in the arts as well as a professional career if so desired. Music, drama, photography, studio art, digital art, and ceramics programs are all headed by experienced teachers who are professional artists in their own mediums.

Happy Valley School holds membership in the California Association of Independent Schools, the National Association of Independent Schools, and Western Boarding Schools. The School is accredited by the Western Association of Schools and Colleges.

ACADEMIC PROGRAMS

The Director of Studies is responsible for the academic life of the School. The curriculum is aimed toward college entrance. Courses of study are negotiated between the Director of Studies and individual students. The average load is five academic solids and a fine art. The teachers report to the Director of Studies, and academic issues are generally solved at the administrative level.

Students are expected to attend all classes (8 a.m.–4 p.m.), study hall, and mandatory evening activities, unless specifically excused by the staff. HVS believes that daily attendance is important to a student's success and expects students to arrive punctually to all classes every day that school is in session. The School may elect to withhold academic credit from a student if he or she falls into a pattern of excessive absenteeism. Students missing more than eight days of a class in any trimester may forfeit their credit in that class.

Class size averages 12 students. Independent study is available for especially well-motivated students, and Advanced Placement courses are offered in calculus, English, music theory, physics, and Spanish.

Happy Valley has three academic trimesters, and evaluations are sent to parents three times a year. An evening study hall is required.

In order to graduate, it is expected that students comply with the following minimum requirements from the ninth to the twelfth grades: 4 years of English, 4 years of social studies, 3 years of mathematics, 2 years of science, 2 years of a foreign language, 2 years of fine arts, and sufficient electives to complete the required number of units.

English as a second language (ESL) is also offered. This program works to improve the development of English and oral and listening comprehension skills. Concentration on vocabulary expansion, improved pronunciation, and use of idioms aid the student in understanding and participating in class. The full-year course, which requires an additional fee, is two or three periods a day and can include ESL classes in science, social studies, U.S. history, and TOEFL preparation.

FACULTY AND ADVISERS

There are 21 teachers and administrators on the Happy Valley staff. Eleven faculty members and administrators reside on campus, and all faculty and staff members are involved in the life of the community beyond the classroom. Of the 17 full-time teachers, half have advanced degrees, 2 of whom hold their doctorates.

COLLEGE PLACEMENT

All students take a college-preparatory curriculum and begin their testing program with the Preliminary SAT (PSAT) in the fall of the sophomore year. They take the PSAT again as juniors, in preparation for the SAT, which they take later that same year and then again as seniors. The SAT Subject Tests are administered to those juniors and seniors for whom it is appropriate.

The School receives annual visits from college representatives. The Director of College Guidance is on campus and begins working with students in their junior year. In 2004, all of the graduates were accepted by colleges or universities. Recent graduates are attending such colleges as Bard, Beloit, Berkeley College of Music, Cal Arts, Chicago Institute of the Arts, Mills, NYU, and various campuses of the California State University and University of California Systems.

STUDENT BODY AND CONDUCT

Of the 90 students attending Happy Valley School this year, one third are day students and two thirds are residential. Happy Valley School seeks to instill in students a lifelong love of learning. This goal is reflected in the School motto "Aun Aprendo" ("I am still learning"). The community sets reasonable limits for its members. Elected students participate in a Disciplinary Advisory Committee, along with faculty members and administrators. The School disciplinary system works on a basis of minors and majors. Students may have occasional work crew hours or more serious disciplinary action depending on the offense.

ACADEMIC FACILITIES

There are eleven buildings on campus. Networked computer stations are available in the library. The School houses a science lab, photography lab, art studio, theater, recording studio, ceramics studio, and digital media lab. The Zalk Theater houses both the drama and music departments.

BOARDING AND GENERAL FACILITIES

The Happy Valley School campus offers boarding facilities for both boys and girls. The residents are housed 2 to a room in bedrooms that contain study and storage facilities for each student. Dorm parents live in each wing of the dormitories and supervise the boarding students with the help of student prefects. Other facilities

include a modern dining hall, tennis courts, volleyball courts, basketball courts, and a soccer field.

ATHLETICS
Team experience and personal challenges through athletics are a valuable part of any education and are made available to every student. The School competes interscholastically in baseball, basketball, cross-country, soccer, softball, tennis, and volleyball.

EXTRACURRICULAR OPPORTUNITIES
The School's proximity to both the coast and the mountains provides students with a wide range of recreational activities, from surfing to rock climbing. Students can also take advantage of museums, movies, concerts, plays, skating, and bowling.

DAILY LIFE
Boarding students are responsible for cleaning their rooms and performing assigned crew jobs. Breakfast is served at 7 a.m., and the entire School meets each morning at 8 for morning assembly. Students are transported to town for shopping and leisure time during designated days of the week. Dinner is at 6 p.m., followed by supervised study hall.

WEEKEND LIFE
Weekends give students a chance to relax, catch up on their studies, or partake in planned activities by the Weekend Program Director. Weekend trips to Los Angeles, Santa Barbara, and Ventura are frequent.

Students who have parental permission may leave campus on open weekends provided they are in good standing with the School.

COSTS AND FINANCIAL AID
The cost of tuition, room, and board for the 2005–06 academic year was $33,900. Day student tuition is $17,900. A book and activity fee of $1500 is required to cover the costs of books, trips, and other expenses. The ESL fee for first-year students is $5500.

Approximately 20 percent of the School's income is given annually in scholarship and financial aid. Information on aid availability can be obtained from the Admissions Office.

ADMISSIONS INFORMATION
Students are selected on the basis of character and academic promise. Personal interviews and references are used to identify those students who are most likely to benefit from the Happy Valley School experience. Consequently, a visit to the School is strongly urged for each applicant. Acceptance is based upon records, recommendations, and a personal interview.

APPLICATION TIMETABLE
Application to Happy Valley School can be made at any time but is encouraged during school hours in the winter and spring. School hours are Monday through Friday from 8 a.m. to 4 p.m. Upon completion of the application process, acceptance of an appropriate candidate is dependent upon available space.

ADMISSIONS CORRESPONDENCE
Adrian Sweet, Director of Admission
Happy Valley School
P.O. Box 850
Ojai, California 93024
Phone: 805-646-4343
    800-900-0487 (toll-free)
Fax: 805-646-4371
E-mail: admin@hvalley.org
Web site: http://www.hvalley.org

HARGRAVE MILITARY ACADEMY

Chatham, Virginia

Type: Boys' boarding and coeducational day college-preparatory school
Grades: 7–PG: Middle School, 7–8; Upper School, 9–12, postgraduate year
Enrollment: School total: 400; Upper School: 368
Head of School: Col. Wheeler L. Baker, Ph.D., USMC (Ret.), President

THE SCHOOL

The Academy was founded in 1909 as Chatham Training School. In 1925, it was renamed to honor J. Hunt Hargrave, a founder and trustee, and to identify more clearly the school's mission and purpose. Hargrave Military Academy has long been one of the South's leading military preparatory schools, and preparing young men and women for success in college has been its primary goal.

Hargrave provides a very well structured academic environment in which college-bound students can realize their potential. The military department works hand-in-hand with the academic office and the faculty in providing an organized program. The Academy believes that student involvement in athletics, spiritual activities, and various other extracurricular activities is also an important part of intellectual and social maturity. All students are encouraged to become involved outside the classroom and to be active participants in the Hargrave community.

The Academy is attractively situated on a beautiful 214-acre campus with woods, pastures, trails, and ponds, in the hills of the Piedmont region of southern Virginia. In addition to the extensive academic and athletic facilities, the campus has a chapel as well as an airstrip. Located 15 miles north of Danville on U.S. Highway 29, the campus lies on the northwestern edge of Chatham, the county seat of Pittsylvania County. Chatham is within convenient driving distance of several larger cities, including Lynchburg and Roanoke, Virginia, and Greensboro and Chapel Hill, North Carolina.

Hargrave is governed by a Board of Trustees, many of whom are alumni and community leaders. The current endowment is nearly $4 million. In addition, Hargrave has developed its own charitable foundation to allow philanthropists another opportunity to make gifts to the school. Hargrave has not only a LAN throughout the school but also a laptop program, implemented via educational enhancement through technology. The 2004–05 school year began with all high school students receiving an IBM ThinkPad for their use—both in the classroom as well as in their rooms.

The school is accredited by the Virginia Association of Independent Schools and the Southern Association of Colleges and Schools. It is a member of the Association of Military Colleges and Schools of the United States and the National Association of Independent Schools.

ACADEMIC PROGRAMS

The Upper School has a college-type academic schedule in which students taking six subjects attend classes for three of these one day and three the next day. The academic day also allows students time to meet with their teachers should they have questions or problems in a particular area.

To earn an Advanced Studies Diploma, students must complete 24 credits: English, 4; social studies, 4; mathematics, 4; science, 4; foreign language, 3; fine arts/practical arts, 1; computer science, ½; military, 1; religion, 1; and electives, ½. Students who complete a less demanding sequence of courses may qualify for a standard diploma. The

required course in religion, which students take during the senior year, provides a general survey of the Old and New Testaments. Military drill or classes are held a total of 3½ to 4 hours per week.

Students are assigned to academic classes on the basis of their past performance and the results of placement tests administered by the guidance office. The average student-teacher ratio is 11:1. There is a 2-hour study period each night, Sunday through Thursday, which is supervised by faculty members. Students spend a considerable portion of their science class time in well-equipped labs.

Hargrave is known for its strong reading program. The program is offered to any student who wants to become more proficient and effective in reading, regardless of his or her present reading level. All students are tested upon entering Hargrave.

FACULTY AND ADVISERS

There are currently 48 full-time faculty members, 24 men and 24 women. More than 60 percent hold graduate degrees. Twenty faculty members live in campus housing.

Hargrave's President, Dr. Wheeler L. Baker, spent forty years in the U.S. Marine Corps and holds a Ph.D. in education.

Every student at Hargrave has an adviser, and every member of the faculty is required to participate in the adviser-advisee program and usually has 6 to 8 advisees. Faculty members also serve as chaperones, club sponsors, and coaches.

The school offers competitive salaries and seeks to hire faculty members with strong qualifications, experience, and the commitment that is required to teach in a boarding school.

COLLEGE PLACEMENT

Hargrave's College Placement Coordinator organizes a College Day Program for Hargrave and several other area schools.

Group sessions are held periodically for juniors and seniors to discuss the college admissions process. Individual conferences are held with each senior in the fall and with each junior in the spring to discuss individual needs and the appropriate selection of colleges.

The average SAT score for the class of 2005, with 100 percent participation, was 1051. Hargrave is a national test site; therefore, the SAT and ACT are available seven to eight times per school year. Over the past several years, more than 92.5 percent of the graduating class have been accepted to colleges and universities. The classes of 2003, 2004, and 2005 had 100 percent acceptance. Colleges and universities chosen by the graduates included The Citadel, Florida State, Purdue, the U.S. Military Academy at West Point, the U.S. Naval Academy, Vanderbilt, Virginia Tech, VMI, Wake Forest, Washington and Lee, William and Mary, and the Universities of Florida, Maryland, and Virginia.

STUDENT BODY AND CONDUCT

In 2004–05, there were approximately 400 students in the Upper and Middle Schools, including about

70 postgraduate students and 4 United States Naval Academy Foundation students.

Hargrave's student body is composed of students from thirty-four states, the District of Columbia, and four other countries. The largest number of boarding students comes from Virginia, North Carolina, Maryland, Florida, and Georgia.

A central standard of the Hargrave program is the Cadet Honor Code. Every student pledges that he or she will not lie, cheat, or steal or tolerate any violation of the code by another student. Infractions are tried by the Honor Council, a committee of 9 students elected by their classmates.

Students are able to have a voice in decisions through the Student Leadership.

ACADEMIC FACILITIES

Most classes at Hargrave are held in six main academic buildings. Laboratories for physical science, biology, chemistry, and physics are located adjacent to the lecture rooms in the new Landon-Davenport Science and Technology Building. Technology is a valued commodity at Hargrave, with wireless communications, laptop computers, a twenty-station computer learning center, an SAT prep program, a computer science teaching lab, a mathematics computer lab, two English writing labs, a social studies computer lab, computer-based library research, and state-of-the-art classroom instructional technology, including videodisc/computer interface, CD-ROM, and computer overhead. The auditorium is used for musical performances by guest artists, drama productions, and similar events.

Hargrave's library has more than 16,000 volumes, and it subscribes to nine newspapers and fifty periodicals. Back issues of 120 journals and magazines are available on microfiche. More than 200 computers are available for Internet research. All classrooms are Internet accessible.

BOARDING AND GENERAL FACILITIES

Boys are housed 2 to a room on ten dormitory floors. Special services and facilities available for boarding students include two recreation rooms (for pool, Ping-Pong, and other games), three television lounges, a student snack bar that carries various fast-food items and school supplies, a quartermaster that carries uniform parts and sports equipment, and an infirmary, open around the clock, staffed by 4 nurses. A doctor visits the campus three to four times a week. A seamstress is available to mend and alter uniforms.

ATHLETICS

Hargrave feels that all students can benefit from athletics. Students find it easier to participate at Hargrave because the school's enrollment is smaller than that of large public schools. About 70 percent of the students participate on one or more athletics teams each year. Varsity competition is available in football, soccer, cross-country, riflery, volleyball (girls only), wrestling, basketball, baseball, tennis, golf, lacrosse, and swimming. Junior varsity sports are offered in football, soccer, basketball, and base-

ball. Postgraduate competition is offered in basketball and football. Junior high sports include soccer and basketball.

Extensive facilities are available for all of these sports. In addition, a sporting clay range and a state-of-the-art weight-training facility that includes Nautilus equipment are located on campus. An addition to the gymnasium houses a sports medicine clinic, the weight-training facility, and wrestling rooms. A 50-meter indoor swimming pool is also available.

EXTRACURRICULAR OPPORTUNITIES

The Dean of Students plans on-campus entertainment at Hargrave, and he sponsors a movie Saturday night and also arranges for guest lecturers from various fields.

Nearly all Hargrave cadets are involved in one or more clubs; these include the Drama Club (HMA Players), the Beta Club, the Art Club, and the Photography Club, to name only a few. An on-campus Boy Scout Troop is very active. Boy Scout Troop Number 68 is currently the largest troop in the Blue Ridge Mountain Council. Students can also become active on the staffs of the *Cadence* (the student yearbook) and the Student Magazine Club. Students who are musically inclined may choose to be involved in the marching band, the jazz ensemble, the chorus, or the Highlanders, the school's own bagpipers.

Students also have opportunities for off-campus entertainment, such as plays, athletic events at local colleges, paintball, skiing, and white-water rafting.

DAILY LIFE

Cadets rise at 6 and have until 7:30 to complete breakfast and put their rooms in good order. An inspection is held three times a week prior to attending classes. Classes begin at 7:55 a.m. and run until 12:20 p.m. After lunch, there is additional academic time that includes academic labs and administrative time. Leadership training, a core aspect of Hargrave, is provided twice a week. Athletics or an afternoon activity is mandatory between 3:30 and 5:30 daily, and dinner is served at 6. The evening study period commences at 7:30 and ends at 9:30.

Saturday morning may be used for a special program or for a formal military inspection. Saturday afternoon and evening are free, with lights-out at 11.

WEEKEND LIFE

There are a variety of opportunities open for Hargrave cadets on weekends. Students are encouraged to take advantage of the extensive recreational facilities located on campus and the weekly movie series. Traditional festivity weekends include Parents' Weekend (October), Military Ball (March), Alumni Weekend (April), and Mothers' Day (May).

Chatham is a historic town that has received numerous beautification awards at both state and national levels. Although Chatham is small, it has several stores and restaurants that are of interest to Hargrave cadets. Students are allowed to walk downtown on Saturday and Sunday.

Students are also allowed to leave campus for day passes with authorized adults. Frequently, transportation is provided for students to attend events off campus. Weekend trips are a regular part of student activities.

SUMMER PROGRAMS

Hargrave offers a five-week nonmilitary summer program. Students can earn credit in one new subject, two enrichment courses, or two repeat subjects. As in the regular school session, all new students are required to complete a course in study skills. Selected English, math, history, science, reading, and Spanish classes are offered.

COSTS AND FINANCIAL AID

Tuition costs for day students and costs for boarding students, including tuition, room, board, laundry, uniforms, dry cleaning, bed linens, books, and fees, can be obtained from the Director of Admissions. Approximately $400 to $500 should be allowed for spending money and emergency fees. Several payment plans are available.

Scholarships are available and are awarded on the basis of need and academic achievement. Close to $250,000 in aid is given annually to 25 percent of the students. The grants range from $500 to $4000.

ADMISSIONS INFORMATION

Hargrave seeks to enroll students with average to above-average ability. The academic classes are demanding, so students who are not serious about working up to their full potential should not consider applying.

Admission decisions are based on the applicant's prior academic performance, standardized test results, teacher recommendations, and the personal interview. Poor academic performance in the past is not necessarily a deterrent to acceptance. If students show a positive attitude and have academic potential, the school encourages them to apply for admission.

APPLICATION TIMETABLE

Students are admitted, depending on the availability of classroom space, three times a year: in August with the opening of school, in January with the beginning of the second semester, and at the opening of summer school. In the fall there are three designated dates after school starts. Students should visit the Web site for details.

Because Hargrave feels that it is very important for prospective students to see the facilities, meet faculty members, and talk with students, an on-campus interview is required. Appointments can be made by contacting the Admissions Office between 8:30 and 5 weekdays and between 9 and 12 on Saturday.

Notification of the admission decision is sent within 48 hours after all necessary materials have been received and the applicant's file is complete.

ADMISSIONS CORRESPONDENCE

Comdr. Frank L. Martin III, USN Ret.
Director of Admissions
Hargrave Military Academy
Chatham, Virginia 24531

Phone: 434-432-2585
      800-432-2480 (toll-free)
Fax: 434-432-3129
E-mail: admissions@hargrave.edumartinf@hargrave.edu
Web site: http://www.hargrave.edu

THE HARKER SCHOOL

San Jose, California

HARKER
Est. 1893 · K-12 College Prep

Type: Coeducational day college-preparatory school
Grades: K–12: Lower School, Kindergarten–5; Middle School, 6–8; Upper School, 9–12
Enrollment: School total: 1,685; Lower School: 578; Middle School: 466; Upper School: 641
Head of School: Christopher Nikoloff

THE SCHOOL

The origins of The Harker School belong in the city of Palo Alto where two schools, Manzanita Hall and Miss Harker's School, were established in 1893 to provide incoming Stanford University students with the finest college-preparatory education available.

Harker's three campuses are located minutes from each other in the heart of California's famed Silicon Valley. The campuses are well maintained, beautifully landscaped, and secured with an emphasis on student safety. The Upper School campus is 16 acres, the Middle School campus is 40 acres, and the Lower School campus is 10 acres. The Harker Upper School opened in 1998 and graduated its first senior class in 2002.

Harker's suburban San Jose location attracts day students from surrounding communities, such as Los Gatos, Saratoga, Cupertino, Los Altos, and Fremont.

Harker operates as a nonprofit organization, governed by a board of directors composed of business leaders, educators, and parents. With strong support from parent volunteers, the School's Annual Fund raised more than $1 million during the 2004–05 school year. Funds are used to enhance programs such as computer science and fine arts.

Harker is accredited by the Western Association of Schools and Colleges and is a member of the California Association of Independent Schools.

ACADEMIC PROGRAMS

The Harker School is a coeducational day school for students in kindergarten through grade 12. Harker students are highly motivated, creative young people who come from families with strong commitments to educational values. The exceptional faculty, caring and qualified support staff, and modern, safe campuses give students a definite advantage in becoming top achievers. For example, students consistently score among the highest percentiles in nationally normed achievement tests. Each year, an impressive number of seventh-grade students qualify for academic recognition as Johns Hopkins University Scholars by scoring above 500 on the SAT I. Small class sizes, with an average of 16 students, enable teachers to form flexible ability groupings so that children's needs are constantly evaluated and met.

The Upper School curriculum offers a full array of academic courses, from introductory-level to Advanced Placement and honors-level courses in every discipline, from sciences and math to English, foreign language, and the fine arts. The Upper School offers a complete athletic program for boys and girls as well as a full extracurricular program, including yearbook, performing arts, newspaper, and debate.

The use of technology in teaching is an important facet of the academic program, and every student takes a year of technology as a graduation requirement. A unique aspect of the program is Harker's requirement that every student have Internet access at home. The Internet is utilized for academic research through the Harker Library's online periodical databases and access to faculty help after school hours. Grades 9–12 are also required to have a personal laptop that is linked to the School's wireless network.

Graduation requirements include 4 years of English, third-year proficiency in a foreign language (French, Spanish, Japanese, or Latin), 3 years of science (physics, chemistry, and biology), 3 years of mathematics (with a strong recommendation to take 4 years), 2 years of history, 2 years of physical education, 1 year of computer science, 1 year of fine arts, and one semester each of public speaking and ethics.

The Lower and Middle Schools' solid curriculum in both the core subjects of math and language arts and the enriching opportunities with specialists in science, expository writing, Spanish, French, Japanese, computer science, physical education, art, music, dance, and drama provides a solid foundation for the Upper School academic program.

The Lower School's full-day program allows all students ample time for learning through games, dancing, and other physical activities. Harker kindergarteners have access to teaching specialists and campus resources such as extensively equipped computer science labs and the library. In grades 1–5 the curriculum is strongly academic. In keeping with the School's commitment to treat each child as an individual, students who show special promise have ample opportunity to go beyond the standard curriculum through Harker's advanced placement grouping. Study-travel trips to Marin Headlands and California's Gold Country add field experience to the academic science offerings.

Harker's Middle School program offers students a safe and trusting atmosphere in which to grow through the challenging times of early adolescence. Special courses aid students in gaining a sense of self-worth, dealing with anxiety, understanding the risks of substance abuse, and learning about other major health issues. Student performances, field trips, art exhibitions, and assembly presentations enliven the School atmosphere. Study-travel trips to Yosemite, the Grand Canyon, and Washington, D.C., are meaningful Middle School experiences.

FACULTY AND ADVISERS

The Harker faculty is composed of 186 professionals. They hold eighteen doctoral degrees and 110 master's degrees. Christopher Nikoloff, Head of School, earned his B.A. in English literature

and his M.A.T. in education at Boston University. Faculty members serve as advisers to students on a daily basis. Many participate in after-school athletics and academic and arts enrichment activities. Continuing education is facilitated with monthly meetings and individual incentives for professional growth. Harker seeks highly qualified candidates who reflect the School's commitment to academic excellence and diversity.

COLLEGE PLACEMENT

Harker is a college-preparatory school whose rigorous curriculum prepares students for top universities. Four college counselors provide extensive guidance to students and parents in the junior and senior years regarding preparation for college admission. Over the four years of high school, there are parent workshops, family interviews, individual student interviews, classes for students, visits from college representatives, and special speakers from college admission offices.

STUDENT BODY AND CONDUCT

During the 2005–06 academic year, there were 1,685 students enrolled in kindergarten through grade 12. The student body reflects the dynamic and diverse Bay Area population, and the international programs further prepare the students as global citizens.

Harker Lower and Middle School students are required to wear uniforms. Upper School students adhere to a dress code. Students are expected to comply with rules defined in the *Student/Parent Handbook*. Good citizenship, along with academic and athletic achievement, is frequently rewarded. Discipline rests primarily with the faculty.

With leadership from its Student Council, the entire School communicates its views on codes and policies and works on community service projects. Students participate in a variety of leadership opportunities, spirit commission, and service volunteer programs.

ACADEMIC FACILITIES

Harker's a strong sense of community ties three campuses into one school, while allowing children close contact with their peers. The Lower, Middle, and Upper School campuses are within 3 miles of each other. Modern, extensively equipped facilities such as computer and science labs and art and dance studios provide enhanced learning opportunities for students at all grade levels.

The library system has 28,500 volumes among the three campuses. Each campus has its own library facility, staffed by full-time professional librarians, and equipped with electronic encyclopedias and CD-ROM information access systems. With an extensive online periodical library, students have access to a wide variety of

databases from such publishers as Gale, Oxford University Press, Grove, Encyclopedia Britannica, and others. The School's computer science laboratories are constantly updated with the latest technologies in hardware and software. In addition, computers and CD-ROM capabilities are located in each classroom.

Harker has extensive student support services. The full-time staff includes licensed school counselors, college counselors, registered school nurses, certified lifeguards, and a professional chef.

ATHLETICS
Students of all ability levels are encouraged to participate in the School's extensive athletics program. Soccer, football, volleyball, basketball, track, baseball, softball, golf, cross-country, and tennis are popular Upper School sports. Combined athletic facilities include a junior Olympic-size swimming pool and a competition-sized pool, eight tennis courts, three wood-floored gymnasiums, and expansive playing fields.

EXTRACURRICULAR OPPORTUNITIES
While the basic goal is to prepare students for future schooling by introducing them to a large body of knowledge, the focus on academics is balanced with numerous opportunities for personal development, including school spirit, sports and arts activities, and community service projects. Students take an active role in their school community, including planning school dances and rallies and participation in more than forty clubs. Harker's proximity to San Francisco makes frequent field trips to major cultural attractions and performances possible for students at all grade levels.

DAILY LIFE
Students can arrive on campus as early as 7 a.m. The school day begins and ends at staggered times between 8 a.m. and 3:30 p.m. The campus closes at 6 p.m. Supervised after-school recreation and athletics programs are available to all students at no additional cost. A professional chef supervises food service on all campuses, providing nutritious lunch selections of hot meals, fresh fruits, salad bars, and vegetarian options.

SUMMER PROGRAMS
Harker Summer Programs offers an intriguing variety of activities for boys and girls ages 4½ to 18. For students in grades K–8, day camp choices offer academic enrichment combined with sports, recreation, and computer science for a total of eight weeks. Field trips to local natural and cultural attractions such as Santa Cruz beaches, local redwood forests, and San Francisco are a popular aspect of the program. Harker's Summer Institute for students in grades 9–12 runs for 6 weeks during the summer. Students attend academic credit courses to hone existing skills or learn new topics. Offerings have included the Summer Conservatory program of music, theater, and dance; Speech and Debate Camp; rigorous math and science courses; and an enrichment courses in expository writing, Spanish, and PSAT/SAT. Annual enrollment is approximately 1,300. Enrollment in Harker's academic program is not required. Harker Summer Programs is accredited by the American Camping Association and the Western Association of Independent Camps. Further information can be obtained by contacting Summer Programs Director Kelly Espinosa at the Harker School office.

COSTS AND FINANCIAL AID
For the 2005–06 school year, tuition ranged from $19,923 to $24,968. An $800 to $900 lunch fee is added to tuition for Middle and Upper Schools. Estimated extra costs are as follows: $350 to $500 plus lunch fee for Lower School and $600 to $750 for Middle and Upper School students. A nonrefundable $700 new Lower and Middle School student fee and an enrollment deposit of $2500 for students are due within seven days of acceptance. The balance is due by July 1. Financial aid based on need is available.

ADMISSIONS INFORMATION
Harker seeks a diversified student body that reflects a range of backgrounds, aptitudes, and interests. Students performing at average to above-average levels are considered for acceptance. Student motivation and the ability to adjust comfortably to a close-knit and congenial educational community are also important factors. The specific criteria used in admissions are entrance exams, school records, and character evaluations by a teacher or principal.

APPLICATION TIMETABLE
An initial inquiry is welcome at any time, or visit the Web site for School and application information. Potential students and their families are encouraged to attend an open house or schedule a visit because there is no better way to appreciate Harker's warmth and vitality. A visit may be arranged by contacting the School offices, which are open from 8 a.m. to 5 p.m.

ADMISSIONS CORRESPONDENCE
Ms. Nan Nielsen
Director of Admission and Financial Aid
The Harker School, Saratoga Campus

Lower School (K–5)
4300 Bucknall Road
San Jose, California 95130
Telephone: 408-871-4600
Fax: 408-871-4320

Middle School (6–8)
3800 Blackford Avenue
San Jose, California 95117
Telephone: 408-248-2510
Fax: 408-248-2502

Upper School (9–12)
500 Saratoga Avenue
San Jose, California 95129
Telephone: 408-249-2510
Fax: 408-984-2325
E-mail: admissions@harker.org
Web site: http://www.harker.org

THE HARVEY SCHOOL

Katonah, New York

Type: Coeducational day and five-day residential (7–12) college-preparatory school
Grades: 6–12: Middle School, 6–8; Upper School, 9–12
Enrollment: School total: 310; Upper School: 210
Head of School: Barry W. Fenstermacher, Headmaster

THE SCHOOL

The Harvey School is a coeducational college-preparatory school that serves students in its Middle School, grades 6 through 8, and Upper School, grades 9 through 12.

The School was founded in 1916 as a school for boys "in the English manner." In 1959, the School moved to its present wooded 100-acre campus in Katonah, New York. Forty miles north of New York City in northern Westchester County, Harvey is close to major highways and the Metro North Railroad (Harlem Line). In 1976, the School became coeducational. Harvey offers an optional five-day residential program to students in grades 7 through 12.

The mission of the School is "to help students of varying abilities through a program of academic challenge, faculty support and out-of-class activities." The School believes in its students. At Harvey, students learn to succeed, often in ways and to levels that surprise them. Harvey is concerned with intellectual achievement as well as the physical, social, and emotional development of its students. Harvey offers diversity not only in its course offerings but also in the academic characteristics of its student body.

The Harvey School is chartered by the New York State Board of Regents and is accredited by the New York State Association of Independent Schools. Harvey is a member of the National Association of Independent Schools, the Independent Schools of Greater New York, the New York State Association of Independent Schools, and the Parents League of New York.

ACADEMIC PROGRAMS

The Harvey School offers a traditional curriculum in a structured but flexible environment to students of varied interests and abilities. The curriculum is enhanced by exposure to diverse points of view and activities. The sharing and exchange of ideas instills and nurtures the values of self-respect and self-reliance as well as the ability to work with others.

The Middle School creates an environment that encourages students to develop their academic skills through a structured approach. The curriculum is traditional, stressing in-depth skills development in the arts, English, mathematics, history, natural science, and foreign language. Other notable features of the Middle School program include an average class size of 12 students, a fall adventure experience, a spring trip to Boston, and programs to increase literacy and computer skills.

The Harvey School has added a meteorological center for the study of weather in partnership with WNBC-TV. This permits students to explore weather conditions worldwide by way of the Internet. The World Wide School Weather Network is comprised of more than 2,000 schools in more than 100 cities and six different countries.

Harvey's Upper School program prepares students for college and challenges students to reach beyond their perceived levels of ability. The atmosphere is structured but informal, and students are expected to take increasing responsibility for their academic progress. Thus, Harvey teaches students to learn and to work independently.

Students take a minimum of five courses each trimester, plus physical education, which is filled through participation in a team sport. Students who enroll as freshmen usually complete a typical college-preparatory curriculum, including 4 years of English; 3 years of math; 3 years of the same foreign language; 3 years of science, including biology and physics; and 3 years of history, including American history, as well as 1 year of fine arts.

Writing and test-taking skills are essential for success in college and are emphasized in all courses except art. At the end of the first and third trimester, students take exams. During the winter term, students undertake independent projects in each subject area except math. Projects offer a different type of learning experience and encourage students to delve into a subject under faculty guidance and to produce a report, display, or presentation.

Advanced Placement courses are available, including physics, chemistry, biology, calculus AB, calculus BC, computer science, American history, European history, psychology, English, French, Spanish, and Latin. All qualified students are encouraged to enroll in these courses.

Harvey's faculty members are committed to and are known for their willingness to provide extra help to students. Study halls, free periods, and meal times are often used for one-on-one or small-group help sessions for students. Review before final exams is a regular feature of most classes. This results in a group of students with a broader spectrum of abilities and interests. The School does not offer special support for students with learning disabilities; however, those who are able to function in a closely monitored mainstream environment find success at Harvey. Extra help is available from teachers throughout the school day.

Harvey's Krasne Project provides a unique approach to acquisition of computer skills and the opportunity for daily access to this technological resource. At Harvey, computer interaction is incorporated into daily instruction in English, history, Latin, geometry, Spanish, biology, physics, theater, and art. Interactive instruction and drills, combined with a video-based instructional program, amplify instruction in Spanish. Biology students perform dissections on screen, and physics students develop demonstrations and experiments using computers. History students have access to hundreds of primary and secondary documents in a variety of media, including teacher-written materials designed to support specific research. Harvey is online with the public library system of Westchester County.

All students have access to the multimedia computer centers of the Krasne Project, which are located in three different campus buildings. All of the centers are Internet-accessible. Many of the classrooms have full multimedia capability. This enhancement of most academic subjects provides students with the information and resources needed to excel in today's classrooms. Students apply this technological tool to develop, retrieve, and format information, which assists them in classes and provides a creative medium for papers, projects, and presentations.

FACULTY AND ADVISERS

The student-faculty ratio is 7:1, allowing each faculty member to work with each student as an individual both in and out of class. Faculty members serve as advisers to students. A peer counselor program provides additional support and guidance.

The Harvey School welcomes—and expects—parental involvement. The partnership between parents and teachers underscores for the students the importance placed by their family on education. A parent's best source of information and help is the teacher. When a parent presents a concern to a teacher, the teacher resolves it or, if necessary, consults an administrator or the Headmaster. The faculty responds to parents' concerns within 24 hours or as soon as possible.

COLLEGE PLACEMENT

College placement is an integral part of each student's experience during his or her junior and senior years. Four college advisers, with more than thirty years of collective experience, direct the process.

During the school year, college representatives meet with students on the campus. Recent Harvey graduates are enrolled in a number of colleges and universities, including American, Boston University, Brown, Bucknell, Cornell, Drew, Fairfield, Fordham, Hamilton, Indiana, Mount Holyoke, Roanoke, Skidmore, Smith, Springfield, Temple, Wake Forest, and the Universities of Arizona, Connecticut, Delaware, Hartford, Pennsylvania, and Richmond.

STUDENT BODY AND CONDUCT

Harvey's diverse student body reflects the social, cultural, and economic diversity of the region. Harvey accepts students who have the potential and desire to succeed, particularly those who benefit from an intimate and supportive educational setting. Approximately 20 percent of Harvey's students are in the five-day residential program, an excellent option for families with 2

working parents and for students who need a stable and structured learning-living environment.

Because Harvey is committed to traditional standards of conduct, there is a dress code. While a uniform is not required, students are expected to dress appropriately.

ACADEMIC FACILITIES

Carter Hall houses the administrative offices, admissions, a multipurpose room, a gymnasium, Upper School classrooms, and the dining room. The Upper School offices, including the Head of the Upper School, college placement, registrar's office, the business office, and the Rumbough Infirmary, are located in the "White Cottage," or Shea House. The Mennen Library also houses two computer labs that are part of the Krasne Project, named in honor of Charles A. Krasne, Treasurer of the Board of Trustees and supporter of the School. In 2001, six classrooms and a science lab were added to the Middle School as well as an additional Krasne Project computer center. The Hickrill Science Building houses science laboratories for the Upper School. In 2005, an arts center, containing space for drawing and painting, ceramics, digital photography, a dance studio, choral and music practice rooms, and a new black box theater, was completed.

BOARDING AND GENERAL FACILITIES

One of the distinctive programs offered by the Harvey School is its five-day residential program. This program provides a positive, stable environment that is focused on education. Residential students can enjoy and profit from the many aspects of School life, including proctored evening study halls and the availability of faculty members who serve as counselors, tutors, friends, and role models. However, residential students can still be with their families and friends every weekend.

ATHLETICS

Harvey's athletic program encourages participation in athletics by all students—the rule is "If you practice, you play." Teams other than the varsity teams emphasize improving skills and developing good sportsmanship. Middle School teams are organized based on skill and interest.

Fall sports include cross-country, dance, field hockey, football, and soccer. Winter sports include basketball, dance, ice hockey, skiing, and strength and conditioning. Spring sports include baseball, dance, golf, lacrosse, rugby, softball, and tennis.

EXTRACURRICULAR OPPORTUNITIES

Students in grades 6 through 11 and all residential students are required to participate in the After School Program. This program offers a wide range of activities to engage students whose interests and talents are not athletics, and it includes a well-developed visual arts program. Some examples are Harvey's nationally recognized Model United Nations team; an outstanding fine and performing arts program that produces three productions in the black box theater; studios for classes in art, digital photography, and computer graphics; *The Avatar* (literary magazine); *The Cavalier* (yearbook); *The Pulse* (School newspaper); and voice and instrumental groups. Some students are also involved in approved off-campus activities such as equestrian events and community-service projects. Individual music lessons for many instruments may also be arranged during this time.

DAILY LIFE

The School day begins at 8:15 a.m. and ends at 5 p.m. The day consists of seven academic periods, a midmorning activities/extra help period, lunch, and the After School Program.

An important part of each school day is Morning Meeting, which is an opportunity for the School community to meet and hear the results of athletic contests, learn about personal achievements, and hear general announcements made by students and faculty members. Morning Meeting is also when the School community explores the nation's heritage and the "global village" in which it lives.

Extra help is a cornerstone of the academic program and a regular part of each day. Although it is a student's responsibility to seek extra help when needed, a teacher may also require a student to meet during study halls or other free periods. Teachers may be found in their classrooms or the faculty room throughout the school day. Once a week, students also have the opportunity to work with teachers individually during an extra academic period.

Breakfast, lunch, and dinner are served in the dining room for residential and day students and faculty members. After dinner, a 2-hour supervised study hall is held for all students on campus.

WEEKEND LIFE

Weekday and weekend activities are organized by the student government, various classes, School-sponsored clubs and organizations, and the dormitories. In 2004, the student council helped organize the annual Harveypalooza, a spring carnival. Other activities included class-sponsored trips, a music festival, and several Broadway plays. The Model United Nations team participated in weekend tournaments at Harvard, Brown, and Georgetown Universities. The speech and debate team was involved in a number of weekend tournaments. The science department has also organized trips to Great Adventure as part of the theme park's Physics Day.

COSTS AND FINANCIAL AID

Tuition for 2005–06 is $23,500 for all grades. There is a student activities fee of $550. The boarding fee is $6500. Additional charges include textbooks, accident insurance, bookstore purchases, athletic supplies, and off-campus activities.

The Harvey School attempts to provide tuition grants to students who demonstrate financial need.

ADMISSIONS INFORMATION

The Harvey School admissions process is designed to allow the applicant and the School to develop clear appraisals of each other. Although students may enter at any grade level, most students enter the Middle School in grade 6 and the Upper School in grade 9. Admissions testing is not required, but the SSAT and ISEE are accepted, primarily for placement and guidance purposes. Because of its importance, a visit, which includes a student-led tour and an interview, must be scheduled. The School prefers scheduling visits in the morning so that families can attend Morning Meeting when the entire student body and faculty gather together.

The Harvey School admits students of any race, color, and national or ethnic origin to all the rights, privileges, programs, and activities generally accorded or made available to students at the School. It does not discriminate on the basis of race, color, or national or ethnic origin in the administration of its educational policies, admissions policies, scholarship and loan programs, athletics, and other School administrative programs, including its faculty and staff recruitment.

ADMISSIONS CORRESPONDENCE

Ronald Romanowicz, Director of Enrollment
The Harvey School
260 Jay Street
Katonah, New York 10536

Phone: 914-232-3161
Fax: 914-232-6034
E-mail: romanowicz@harveyschool.org
Web site: http://www.harveyschool.org

HAWAI'I PREPARATORY ACADEMY

Kamuela, Hawai'i

Type: Coeducational boarding and day college-preparatory school
Grades: K–12: Lower School, K–5; Middle School, 6–8; Upper School, 9–12
Enrollment: School total: 613; Upper School: 362
Head of School: Dr. Olaf Jorgenson, Headmaster

THE SCHOOL

Hawai'i Preparatory Academy (HPA) is one of the premier college-preparatory boarding and day schools in the Pacific Region. Its character and personality derive from six core emphases: putting students first; striving for excellence; concern for the individual; accepting, appreciating, and seeking challenges; being consistent; and exemplifying the highest moral and ethical behavior. Programs emphasize the intellectual, physical, moral, and spiritual development of students to help them achieve their highest potential as individuals and members of society.

HPA is independent and coeducational and offers a full range of opportunities for students from kindergarten through grade 12. Boarding is available for students in grades 6–12. The school is fully accredited by the Western Association of Schools and Colleges and is a member of twelve educational organizations, including the Council for the Advancement and Support of Education, College Entrance Examination Board, Cum Laude Society, and the National Association of Independent Schools.

A special aspect of HPA is its use of Hawai'i's unique geographical and social setting. Through many courses and activities, the school gives students a strong sense of Hawai'i and its culture. Offerings include programs in the visual and performing arts as well as an athletic program that stresses schoolwide participation and teaches the values of sportsmanship and fair play.

The school has two campuses in Waimea on the island of Hawai'i. The Upper School is located on 120 acres at the foot of the Kohala Mountains, in the heart of Hawai'i's ranching country. The Lower and Middle Schools are housed on a separate 8-acre campus just 2 miles away.

Small classes are taught by highly competent professional educators (more than 60 percent of them with advanced degrees, including five doctorate degrees) who utilize the latest in educational technology. Teachers take a personal interest in every student; many of them double as coaches and dorm parents, and the sense of "ohana," or family, is especially strong at the school.

ACADEMIC PROGRAMS

The college-preparatory curriculum aims at imparting basic knowledge and skills in the core subject areas. Courses include special offerings in such topics as marine biology, digital video production, economics, robotics, and sports science. Sixteen Advanced Placement courses are available.

Graduation requirements include four years of English and three years each in mathematics (through algebra II and trigonometry), laboratory science, history, modern language, humanities, and electives.

The average class size is 15 students. The school year is divided into two terms, from September to December and from January through May. Grades and written reports are sent to parents four times a year.

FACULTY AND ADVISERS

The headmaster is Dr. Olaf Jorgenson, who was appointed to the post in 2003. Prior to his appointment at HPA, Dr. Jorgenson was director of curriculum and instruction with Mesa Public Schools. Previously, he held administrative and teaching positions in public and private schools in the United States and abroad, including Honduras, Germany, and Taipei. He earned his bachelor's and master's degrees from Washington State University and his doctorate in educational leadership from Arizona State University.

The full-time faculty for grades K–12 (including teaching administrators) numbers 65 (24 men and 41 women). Almost two thirds of the faculty members hold advanced degrees, including five doctorate degrees. Twenty two Upper and Middle School faculty members live in the residence halls or in school housing. Each resident faculty member supervises between 6 and 20 students. All Upper School faculty members teach, coach, share supervisory duties, and act as advisers to boarders and day students. A librarian as well as registered nurses are also on the staff. A psychologist is available on an as-needed basis.

COLLEGE PLACEMENT

HPA's 3 professional college counselors in the College Counseling Center offer full support to students and parents, providing both individual and group counseling to help all students transition to college education. The counselors have developed working relationships with many colleges and universities around the United States and host more than 60 college representatives each year to meet with interested students. The College Counseling Center also maintains a college research library, wireless computers, and a comprehensive college-planning Web page.

All seniors are accepted by a college of their choice. About 98 percent enter college in the fall following their graduation. Many choose colleges in the western United States, favoring such schools as Lewis & Clark, Pomona, Santa Clara, Stanford, and the Universities of California, Colorado, Oregon, and Washington. Others seek experiences farther east at such institutions as Amherst, Boston University, Bowdoin, Brown, Columbia, Cornell, Dartmouth, Duke, MIT, Princeton, Yale, and the University of Pennsylvania.

STUDENT BODY AND CONDUCT

For the 2005–06 academic year, there were 613 total students in K–12, including 178 boarders and 184 day students at the Upper School and 28 boarders at the Middle School. Twenty nine international Upper and Middle School students attend the Institute of English Studies.

Students come from the Hawai'ian Islands, eighteen other states and U.S. territories, and seventeen other countries. The student body reflects the multiracial and diversified ethnic background of the Pacific Basin. About 40 percent of the students are of non-Caucasian descent.

HPA believes that a primary goal of education is the development of character. Beyond academic commitments, students are assigned a number of responsibilities that support the daily operation of a boarding school. Elected senior student representatives, teachers, and a member of the administration meet with the student and his or her adviser to determine the degree of discipline appropriate for violations of major rules.

ACADEMIC FACILITIES

Ten buildings on the Upper Campus house multiple classrooms, the Kono Institute of English Studies, Castle Lecture Hall, the Science and Technology Center, and Davenport Music Center and rehearsal rooms. Other academic facilities include the Gates Performing Arts Center, the Dyer Memorial Library, the Gerry Clark Art Center, the Davies Chapel, and a 4,100-square-foot Student Union that opened in May 2004.

Middle School students use Macintosh laboratories and two mobile wireless lab carts at the Village Campus. Upper School students use Macintosh computer laboratories at the Upper Campus. Both campuses are fully networked with fiber-optic and wireless infrastructure. Filtered Internet connection is provided in all classrooms on both campuses and in all Upper and Middle School dorm rooms.

BOARDING AND GENERAL FACILITIES

Three residence halls on the Upper Campus house students in double and triple rooms. Each room has beds and built-in closets, shelves, desks, and dressers. The rooms are equipped with telephone connections and computer access to the campuswide computer network and the Internet. Students may bring computers, stereos, and, with permission, small refrigerators. Each building has a central lounge and laundry facilities. A faculty member and 2 student prefects supervise each residence hall wing.

Twenty dorm rooms at the Village Campus house the Middle School boarders. Students share a spacious room with their own bathroom. Six to 8 students live on a hallway with boarding faculty members on each floor.

The recently renovated restaurant-style dining facilities are located in the Taylor Commons.

Also located in this building are the Academics and Student Life Center, Accounting/Business Office, Auxiliary Programs, Health Services Center, and a digital audio/video laboratory.

ATHLETICS

HPA believes that physical exercise is an integral part of daily life. Each student is required to participate in interscholastic competition, intramural sports, or noncompetitive activities each weekday. Sports include baseball, basketball, canoe paddling, cross-country, football, golf, rugby, soccer, softball, swimming, tennis, track, volleyball, water polo, and wrestling. An equestrian program, scuba diving, theater, and dance are among the other activities available.

Castle Gymnasium holds a basketball/volleyball court, a wrestling room, lockers, and equipment rooms. The Nakamaru Fitness Center is equipped with both exercise machines and free weights. Other sports facilities include the Dowsett Swimming Pool, the indoor Rutgers Tennis Center, a cross-country course, a track, a tack room, and football, baseball, soccer, and polo fields.

EXTRACURRICULAR OPPORTUNITIES

HPA encourages the pursuit of extracurricular interests—some that are traditional to boarding schools and some that are unique to HPA's program and environment. Student organizations and activities include the Student Council, the school choir, music ensembles, Amnesty International, American Red Cross Youth Group, chapel committee, environmental club, Hawai'i club, literary magazine, Red Key Guides, and the yearbook. Special interest student clubs that develop skills include robotics, sea turtle research, drama, computers, and scuba diving. Other clubs are organized according to demand. All students also participate in required service learning.

The student orientation each fall and various off-campus trips during the year focus on the special culture of Hawai'i and HPA. The School celebrates its diversity during International Students week in February, emphasizes intra-class cooperation with Olympics, a schoolwide competition among classes that precedes spring break, and teaches risk taking and self expression when the Upper School classes compete in a May Day Hawai'ian song contest that emphasizes Hawai'ian language and culture.

DAILY LIFE

Classes begin at 8 a.m. Students have an average of three classes a day that run for up to 90 minutes each. The class day ends at 2:45 p.m.; sports begin at 3:30. A formal family-style dinner is served on Monday; buffet and made-to-order cafeteria meals are served on the other nights of the week. All boarding students participate in the evening study period from 7:20 to 9:30, when they can receive help from teachers and student prefects who supervise the study hall. Boarding students are supported by residential staff members on every hall. All students participate in a campus work program to maintain school facilities.

WEEKEND LIFE

On weekends, students may take a school bus to Kona or Hilo, explore the island on chaperoned field trips, or enjoy the many recreational facilities on or near the campus. A student-government activity, such as a dance, talent show, or movie night is held on campus most Saturday nights; on Sunday, students have the option of attending a church service of their choice, catching a school shuttle to nearby Hapuna Beach, or participating in other activities after brunch.

Day students are encouraged to participate in planned weekend activities at no additional cost.

SUMMER PROGRAM

The HPA Summer Session, established in 1974, offers academic enrichment and unique study opportunities in science and humanities for boarding and day students entering grades 6 through 12. The program, which enrolls boys and girls from throughout the world, runs from June 24 to July 20, 2007.

Summer Session offers new and prospective HPA students an excellent introduction to the school's structure and environment. Many students return every summer to take advantage of Hawai'i Island's unique ecosystem and to make new friends from around the world.

Students attend classes Monday through Friday from 8 a.m. to 3 p.m., followed by sports until 5. A 1-hour study hall follows the buffet dinner and ends with a dorm activity and lights out. Weekend excursions are planned according to student interest and may include trips to state and national parks, such as Volcanoes National Park, ocean kayaking, snorkeling, camping, and hiking. Optional sports include instruction in horseback riding, scuba certification, and tennis.

COSTS AND FINANCIAL AID

Tuition for the 2005–06 school year was $30,000 for boarders and $15,000 for day students (grades 9–12). Books, supplies, testing costs, and incidental fees add about $500. A reservation deposit of $2500 for boarders and $1000 for day students is required upon acceptance. The remainder of the tuition is due on July 15. Tuition payment plans and student accident and health insurance are available.

In 2005–06, HPA granted more than $830,000 in financial aid according to need and based on the national standards of the School and Student Service for Financial Aid. About 20 percent of the student body receives financial aid.

ADMISSIONS INFORMATION

Hawai'i Preparatory Academy seeks boys and girls of good character who have demonstrated sound scholastic ability, who show promise of future accomplishment, and who will bring to the school a wide range of interests, abilities, and talents. The school does not discriminate in violation of the law on the basis of race, gender, religion, color, creed, sexual orientation, age, physical challenge, national origin, or any other characteristic in the administration of its educational and admissions policies, financial aid programs, athletics, or other school-administered programs and activities.

The application deadline is February 3, 2006. Late applications are accepted and depend upon vacancies available after the regular decision deadline. Candidates are requested to submit an application, a written essay, an official school transcript, teacher references, and the results of the SSAT, ISEE, or other standardized test. An interview, either on campus or with an alumnus in the candidate's area, is required.

APPLICATION TIMETABLE

Inquiries and interviews are welcome throughout the school year. The Office of Admission is open Monday through Friday from 8 a.m. to 4 p.m., Hawai'i Standard Time.

ADMISSIONS CORRESPONDENCE

Brian K. Chatterley, Director of Advancement
Stephanie Rutgers, Assistant Director of
    Admission
Hawai'i Preparatory Academy
65-1692 Kohala Mountain Road
Kamuela, Hawai'i 96743-8476

Phone: 808-881-4007
Fax: 808-881-4003
E-mail: admissions@hpa.edu
Web site: http://www.hpa.edu

HEBRON ACADEMY

Hebron, Maine

Type: Coeducational boarding (grades 9–12) and day college-preparatory
Grades: 6–PG: Middle School, 6–8; Upper School, 9–12; postgraduate year
Enrollment: 237; Upper School: 195
Head of School: John J. King

THE SCHOOL

Founded in 1804, Hebron Academy inspires and guides students to reach their highest potential in mind, body, and spirit. Hebron's 1,500-acre campus is an academic village, a place where students can enjoy modern facilities for research and study as well as an incomparable setting for environmental study and outdoor activities. Hebron is 6 miles from the twin towns of Norway and South Paris and 16 miles from the larger cities of Auburn and Lewiston. The Academy is an hour's drive from Portland and 2½ hours from Boston.

A self-perpetuating governing body of educational leaders, past parents, and alumni, Hebron Academy's Board of Trustees oversees a physical plant valued at $9.2 million, an annual operating budget of $5.2 million, and an endowment of $6.4 million.

Hebron Academy is accredited by the New England Association of Schools and Colleges. Hebron is a member of the National Association of Independent Schools, the College Board, the Secondary School Admission Test Board, and the Cum Laude Society.

ACADEMIC PROGRAMS

Learning and teaching at Hebron are in the active voice. Students work in a variety of contexts to develop and understand the process of inquiry and investigation. The curriculum is organized within traditional academic departments; however, learning also becomes integrated in interdisciplinary electives emphasizing ethics and humanities, mathematics, and technology.

Graduates of Hebron Academy have taken at least five classes each year and successfully completed 18 credits, including English (4 years), mathematics (3 years), language (2 years of the same language), laboratory science (2 years, including biology), history (2 years, including U.S. history), and, for four-year students, fine arts (1 year) and computer studies (1 term). Advanced Placement courses are available in seven subject areas as are honors sections in English, mathematics, and history. More than twenty electives are offered, including human anatomy and physiology, environmental ethics, world religions, international relations, and photography. Programs for students with mild learning disabilities or English as a second language serve 24 students each.

The academic day is organized by a rotating schedule of seven periods of 45 minutes each. Students are grouped by interest and ability in sections ranging from 4 to 18 students. The faculty-student ratio is 1:7. Grades are reported on a 4-point scale, with 3.0 (B) or better required for inclusion on Honor Roll and 2.3 (C+) or better to be exempt from supervised study hours. The academic year is divided into trimesters, with major exams given in the fall and spring. Advisers provide grade and progress reports for parents seven times a year, after two weeks of school and thereafter at the midpoint and close of each trimester.

Study hall is held between 8 and 10 p.m., Sunday through Thursday. The open stacks of Hupper Library and the Academy's computer center are available every weekday from 8 a.m. to 4 p.m. and again from 6:30 to 8:30 p.m.

FACULTY AND ADVISERS

Hebron's teachers represent a wonderfully diverse and talented resource combining long-tenured experience with the vigor of recent scholarship. Of 48 faculty members (27 women; 21 men), 3 hold a Ph.D. degree, and 14 hold a master's degree. Forty live on the Hebron campus, including 16 faculty members or couples that reside on-corridor in the three dormitories.

Each faculty member is the adviser for 4 to 8 students, and virtually all coach or supervise activities. Twenty faculty members have been at Hebron for ten years or more. Above all, the Hebron faculty members are a community and family of people—caring, inquiring, nurturing people invested in the lives and growth of young adults.

John J. King leads Hebron Academy as the Head of School. Mr. King's fifteen years of teaching, coaching, and administration at two independent schools as well as ten years' experience as a communications executive makes him well suited to lead Hebron into its third century.

COLLEGE PLACEMENT

Throughout a student's experience but especially during the junior and senior years, Hebron's 2 college counselors ensure that each student receives the individual attention to move confidently through the admissions process and gain admission to a college or university thoughtfully selected to be appropriate for each student's needs, goals, and talents. More than 75 college representatives visit the Hebron campus each year and students regularly attend college fairs.

In 2005, the median verbal SAT score was 540 and the median math SAT score was 540. Of 67 graduates in 2004, 66 are presently enrolled in four-year colleges and 1 deferred matriculation for a year. Among the colleges and universities currently attended by Hebron graduates are Boston College, Boston University, Bowdoin, Colby, Columbia, Cornell, Dartmouth, McGill, Purdue, Tufts, Wellesley, Wheaton, Williams, and the Universities of Maine and Miami.

STUDENT BODY AND CONDUCT

There are 195 Upper School students enrolled, 120 boarding and 75 day. There are 125 boys and 70 girls in grades 9–PG. In addition, there are 42 students in Hebron's Middle School.

With students from eighteen states and eight other countries, Hebron becomes an international community within a New England village. Most students choose Hebron because of its balance of excellent academics, competitive athletics, outdoor opportunities, and strong sense of community.

The Dean of Students, together with the student proctor group, is responsible for setting the tone of the school. Ordinary disciplinary matters are handled directly by the Dean, while major infractions are referred to a committee of student proctors and faculty members.

ACADEMIC FACILITIES

Hebron's buildings surround a spacious open area known as the Bowl. The focus of academic life is Sturtevant Hall (1894), listed on the National Register of Historic Places, which accommodates classrooms and offices. Flanking Sturtevant Hall are Treat Science Hall, which houses classrooms, laboratories, the technology center, the observatory, and the greenhouse, and Hupper Library, the center for a 16,500-volume circulating collection, reference and periodical collections, archives, and an art gallery. Overall, there are twenty-eight classrooms on campus, plus two lecture halls, five art studios, a dark room, a music recital room and private practice rooms, and an outdoor center and classroom.

BOARDING AND GENERAL FACILITIES

Students are housed in double and some single rooms in three dormitories on campus. Junior and senior boys live in the central dormitory, Sturtevant Home, which also houses the Fine Arts Center, school dining services, and the health center. Freshman and sophomore boys reside across the Bowl in Atwood Dormitory. All girls live in Halford Hall, which also houses the Leyden Student Center. All dormitories have common rooms and are supervised by resident faculty members and student proctors.

The Leyden Student Center includes a snack bar and school store as well as a game room and TV lounge.

Hebron's Health Center is staffed by 3 registered nurses; the school physicians hold office hours twice weekly and are available in case of emergency. The school also retains a psychiatrist.

ATHLETICS

Hebron fields twenty-eight varsity and junior varsity teams in fourteen interscholastic sports and seven activities. There is a place for everyone in the program; all students participate in athletics. The program serves athletes who seek a high level of competition and those who enjoy the opportunity to participate actively or try a new sport. At all levels, athletics at Hebron fosters enjoyment of physical activity and ethical competition, personal goal-setting and development, and the appreciation of working with a group to achieve common goals.

Interscholastic boys' and girls' team sports include basketball, cross-country, golf, ice hockey,

lacrosse, mountain biking, Nordic and Alpine skiing, running, snowboarding, soccer, swimming, tennis, and track and field. Additional sports for boys are baseball and football; for girls, field hockey and softball. Noncompetitive coeducational activities include drama, outdoor skills, physical conditioning, and yearbook. Hebron teams participate in the Maine Independent School League and the New England Prep School Athletic Conference. Individual athletes also compete in Junior Olympic running, skiing, and swimming.

Hebron's athletic facilities include a gymnasium with basketball court, wellness center and dance facility, an indoor ice arena, five playing fields, two diamonds, an all-weather track, six tennis courts, running and Nordic skiing trails, and a 1,500-acre Wilderness Tract with trails, sites, and low-ropes course. The swim team practices in the Carolyn E. Tarbell pool at nearby Bates College.

EXTRACURRICULAR OPPORTUNITIES
Life at Hebron is varied and active; students supplement their academic and athletics experiences with social, service, cultural, and physical activities. Campus groups abound. Student Government, the student proctors, Green Key guides, Young Women's Group, and Diversity Committee shape the life of the community.

Fine arts opportunities are equally vital. Student groups produce the *Spectator* yearbook, *Etchings* art and literary magazine, and the *Stanley Steamer* newspaper. The drama group, Heebeejeebees a cappella group, community orchestra and chorus, and the String Ensemble practice and perform throughout the year, and some performers are selected for the Maine All-State orchestra and chorus.

Hockey players teach local youngsters to skate. The Community Service Group works for service programs in surrounding communities as volunteers in food pantries, foundations, and convalescent homes. The Outing Club maintains a local hiking trail and offers hiking, canoeing, whitewater kayaking, snowshoeing, and rock-climbing trips throughout the year.

On weekends, students may participate in activities at the Leyden Center or go on trips to Auburn, Portland, or Boston for dining, seeing movies, or shopping. Winter Carnival and Casino Night are a midwinter extravaganza of games, a dance, and wacky intramural competition. Senior Prom comes in late April, and the seniors conclude the year with an overnight rafting trip in northern Maine.

DAILY LIFE
Hebron's school day begins with a morning meeting of the whole community. Seven 45-minute periods compose the day, with a midmorning break and a time for lunch. Athletics and activities occur from 3:30 to 5:30 p.m. Wednesdays throughout the year and Fridays during the winter are abbreviated to five periods ending at 12:30 p.m. to facilitate athletic competitions and trips. Saturday classes are conducted seven times each year and follow an abbreviated schedule. Regular evening study hall for all students is scheduled from 8 to 10 p.m., and check-in is at 10:30 p.m.

WEEKEND LIFE
Weekend life includes regular and special events. A faculty coordinator ensures a full calendar of activities and trips for each weekend and helps students to plan and arrange transportation for spontaneous trips beyond the regularly scheduled activities. Special activities are also scheduled, often according to the season. Trips to regional fairs, professional sports, or ski resorts are planned.

Students may sign out for weekend permissions as long as they are in good standing and have met athletic or academic obligations. Day students and boarders participate equally in planning weekends at Hebron.

COSTS AND FINANCIAL AID
Tuition and room and board for boarding students in 2005–06 were $35,500. Day student tuition was $18,500. Transportation, books, music lessons, CEEB testing, and weekend activities are additional. A nonrefundable deposit is required of all students upon enrollment to reserve a place in the class.

Tuition payment may be made in full by August 1, in two installments in August and December, or in ten monthly installments. The Dewar Tuition Refund Plan is required of all families electing to pay tuition and billed fees in two or more payments.

Forty-five percent of students received need-based financial aid that totaled more than $1 million in 2005–06.

ADMISSIONS INFORMATION
Hebron seeks students who have strong character and are motivated to acquire good preparation for college. Candidates are selected based upon academic records, interviews, recommendations, and test scores. New boarding and day students are admitted in all four classes, and postgraduates are assimilated into the senior class.

The SSAT is requested for ninth and tenth grade applicants. An interview and campus visit are encouraged for all applicants. Applicants for the postgraduate year are required to have had a college-preparatory program throughout high school.

Hebron Academy reaffirms its long-standing policy of nondiscriminatory admission of students on the basis of race, color, national or ethnic origin, religion, sex, marital or parental status, or handicap.

APPLICATION TIMETABLE
Inquiries, visits, interviews, and applications are welcome at any time throughout the year; however, most students apply for fall admission during the late fall or winter of the prior school year. Applications received after April 10 are considered as long as there is space in the class. Parental confirmation of acceptance and the enrollment deposit are requested within three weeks of acceptance.

ADMISSIONS CORRESPONDENCE
Office of Admission
Hebron Academy
P.O. Box 309
Hebron, Maine 04238
Phone: 207-966-5225
     888-432-7664 (toll-free, U.S. only)
Fax: 207-966-1111
E-mail: admissions@hebronacademy.org
Web site: http://www.hebronacademy.org

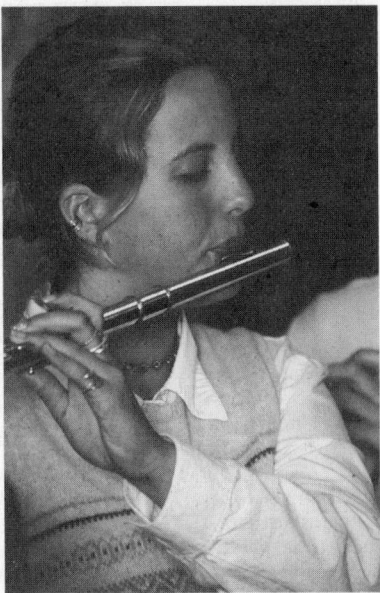

HIGH MOWING SCHOOL

Wilton, New Hampshire

Type: Coeducational boarding and day college-preparatory Waldorf school
Grades: 9–12
Enrollment: 126
Head of School: Cary A. Hughes, Dean of Students

THE SCHOOL

Beulah Hepburn Emmet (1890–1978) founded High Mowing School in 1942 as a boarding and day school that offers Waldorf education to high school students. One of more than 900 Waldorf schools worldwide, High Mowing is the only one in North America to have a boarding program.

Waldorf schools work with the educational principles of Rudolf Steiner (1861–1925), the Austrian educator, scientist, and philosopher. The Waldorf curriculum seeks to build a balance in the human capacities of intellect, imagination, and will. This balance is achieved through the combination of stimulating academic studies, challenging activities in the arts, and the development of physical and practical skills.

The School's 125-acre campus is situated on a wooded hilltop approximately 2 miles from the center of Wilton (population 3,000) in the Mount Monadnock region of southern New Hampshire. It is 12 miles from both Nashua and Peterborough, 18 miles from Manchester, and 55 miles from Boston.

Trustees named a Faculty Council to oversee day-to-day operations of the School, such as faculty development, programming, students and parents, the community, and the administration.

A nonprofit corporation, the School has a 20-member Board of Trustees, which includes 6 faculty members. The board meets four times a year. There are 1,921 graduates. The School's physical plant is valued at $8 million, and the value of the endowment is $1 million.

High Mowing School is accredited by the New England Association of Schools and Colleges and approved by the Department of Education of the State of New Hampshire. It holds memberships in the National Association of Independent Schools, the Independent Schools Association of Northern New England, the Association of Independent Schools of New England, the Secondary Schools Admission Test Board, and the Association of Waldorf Schools of North America.

ACADEMIC PROGRAMS

High Mowing awards diplomas to students who have earned 112 units. (A "unit" is roughly equivalent to one-fourth Carnegie credit.) Specific academic requirements include 16 units in English, 12 in history, 12 in mathematics, 12 in science, and 4 in a foreign language. In addition, 20 units of studio and performing arts, 4 units of physical education, and 4 units of community service are required.

Courses in literature, history, mathematics, and science are taught in "blocks" of concentrated study. There are nine blocks in the year, each block meeting for 1¾ hours each day for three or four weeks. The goal is to build a balance between the objective and the subjective aspects of experience. The content of each subject is presented at the time it will best meet the needs of the developing adolescent during the four high school years. Therefore, members of each class attend their block together.

The block courses offered for freshmen include creation myths, drama, modern history, descriptive geometry, communications and combinations, health and physiology, chemistry: plant processes, and physics: power and energy. For sophomores, block courses include Greek drama, *The Odyssey*, ancient history, dynamics, information technology, embryology, chemistry: acids and alkalis, and physics: mechanics. For juniors, block courses include Dante, Shakespeare, *Parcival*, projective geometry, geography and biology: geology, chemistry: the elements, and physics: electricity and magnetism. For seniors, block courses include Transcendentalists, Faust, drama, world religion, history through art and architecture, logic and reason, zoology and evolution, and physics: optics.

English, humanities, mathematics, foreign languages, the arts, digital arts, and science laboratories are offered in "track" classes, which are yearlong courses. These courses include English skills, French, German, Spanish, American history, global studies, economics, algebra, geometry, trigonometry, precalculus, calculus, computer science, digital arts, environmental ethics, government, seminars in philosophy and literature, The Way of the Naturalist, horticulture, digital arts, filmmaking, eurythmy, painting, drawing, weaving, batik, pottery, choral and instrumental music, and drama. Driver's education and English as a second language (ESL) are also available.

Track classes have an enrollment that ranges from 8 to 15 students. Faculty members are available for extra help, and tutoring can be arranged at an additional charge. The school year, which runs from September to June, is divided into three terms. Marks, with written comments, are sent to parents three times annually. The School uses grades of A, B, C, D, F (failing), and P (pass).

In addition, the school year includes a Projects Block for two weeks, when students and faculty members pursue their studies and interests outside the regular classroom.

FACULTY AND ADVISERS

There are 40 full- and part-time faculty and staff members at High Mowing School; more than 40 percent have advanced degrees. Fifteen faculty members, including 4 dormitory counselors, live on campus.

The School chooses faculty members who have been trained in Waldorf education as well as those who have expressed interest in doing so. They also must have the ability to relate well to adolescents and be experts in their respective fields. The faculty-student ratio is about 1:4. All faculty members are assigned to individual students as advisers.

COLLEGE PLACEMENT

College counseling is done by a faculty college counselor. Juniors take the SAT, and formal college counseling begins in spring of the junior year. The counselor advises students individually, helping them to select the colleges or other options that best meet their special needs and abilities. The counselor also assists the students in arranging to take appropriate tests and to visit college campuses.

The majority of the students go to college immediately; others take a year off for travel or other pursuits. Recent graduates are enrolled in the following schools, programs, colleges, and universities: Alfred, Audubon Expedition Institute, Antioch, Bard, Bates, Bennington, Berklee College of Music, Brown, Boston University, Caltech, Castleton State, Chester, Clark, Colby-Sawyer, College of the Atlantic, Concordia, Connecticut College, Curry, Dalhousie, Earlham, Eastman School of Music, Endicott, Evergreen State, Friends World Program, Green Mountain, Hampshire, Hendrix, International School of Geneva, Johnson and Wales, Johnson State, Keene State, King's, Macalester, McGill, Mount Holyoke, Mount Ida, National Circus School of Montreal, NYU, Oberlin Conservatory of Music, Plymouth State, Prescott, Rhode Island School of Design, Sarah Lawrence, Savannah College of Art and Design, School of the Museum of Fine Arts, Skidmore, Smith, St. Johns College, St. Olaf, Suffolk, Warren Wilson, Wheaton, and the Universities of Edinburgh, King's College (Nova Scotia), Miami (Florida), New Hampshire, and North Carolina at Asheville.

STUDENT BODY AND CONDUCT

In 2005–06, the School had an enrollment of 126 students: 70 boarding students and 56 day students. There were 28 freshmen, 32 sophomores, 37 juniors, and 29 seniors. Students came from sixteen states and eight other countries.

Both faculty members and students are strongly committed to responsible behavior. Mutual support of ideas concerning the best ways people can live and work together is an important aspect of the High Mowing community experience.

ACADEMIC FACILITIES

In fall 2003, the Dr. Bruce Bairstow Science and Technology Building, a beautiful steel-and-wood, post-and-beam classroom building, opened, offering two science labs, a small auditorium, a classroom, a recording studio, an assembly room, and state-of-the-art facilities in the digital arts classroom.

The architecture on the High Mowing campus reflects the School's New England surroundings. The Main Building, which was originally a barn built in 1787, was converted to a school building 1942. It includes two classrooms, a large assembly room, and a eurythmy studio. The Library Building (1970) includes four classrooms and a library

housing 10,000 volumes. The lower level of the boys' dormitory (1962) includes three large art studios for painting, drawing, batik, weaving, and pottery. The lower level of the girls' dormitory includes an art studio and a darkroom.

A shop was built for woodworking classes during a "barn raising" weekend in 1995. In 1990, facilities were developed for the Naturalist Program, including a traditional "longhouse" built by students. A greenhouse and hoop houses for the horticulture program were built in 1992. The gymnasium includes a basketball court and weight room.

BOARDING AND GENERAL FACILITIES
The Main Building contains the dining room, the main meeting room, offices, a student sitting room, and the student store. The girls' dormitory was completed in 1987. Both the boys' and girls' dorms include recreational and laundry facilities. Dorm counselors have apartments in the dormitories. There are double and single rooms. Students are assigned rooms by the dorm counselors. Room assignments may be changed during the year, if necessary.

Campus facilities include faculty housing units, the chapel (1973), a longhouse (1990), a greenhouse (1992), a woodworking shop (1995), a library and classroom building, and a science and technology building as well as a maintenance center, kiln shed, well house, tool shed, and recycling center.

Nearly all faculty and staff members are qualified to administer first aid. Monadnock Community Hospital in Peterborough and Milford Medical Center in Milford are nearby.

ATHLETICS
The School's athletics program helps students become aware of the importance of physical exercise, well-being, and good sportsmanship. Team sports include baseball (boys), basketball, cross-country running, cross-country skiing, lacrosse (girls), soccer, Ultimate Frisbee, and volleyball. High Mowing plays games with area private and public school athletic teams. Skiing, snowboarding, and running are some of the individual sports pursued.

EXTRACURRICULAR OPPORTUNITIES
The student government consists of the Student Council, which is composed of representatives from each class. Students and faculty members comprise the Standards Committee, which oversees the upholding of the School's standards. A Dorm Council of students and faculty members helps to plan dorm activities. In addition, each class has activities for which it is responsible. For example, the junior class works on the Halloween Party and the prom.

Students are active in social and environmental reform through the Cabin for Peace and Justice.

There are many opportunities for drama and musical performances (Jazz Band, several ensemble groups, and singing groups), and there are opportunities to attend performances in the community and in Boston. Each year, a trip is made to New York City to attend a performance at the Metropolitan Opera. There are frequent exhibitions of student and faculty artwork as well as museum trips. The art studios are open for students to work in after school. In addition, guest lecturers and performers are invited to the School.

Students in the Naturalist Program are involved in activities beyond the school day. For example, there are camping trips and treks in the White Mountains on certain weekends throughout the year.

School traditions include celebrations of several holidays. Annual events include Class Orientation Trips, Parents' Weekend, the Halloween Party, Yule Festival and many other holiday events, the prom, and Alumni Weekend. Coffee Houses, in which students and faculty members perform for each other, are held four times a year.

DAILY LIFE
The daily schedule begins at 8 a.m. with a short assembly that includes roll call and a School verse. From 12 to 1 p.m., a lunch of mostly natural and organic food, including meat, vegetarian, and non-dairy foods, is served. Block classes meet every day from 8:15 to 9:45; track classes meet every other day from 10 to 3, followed by "clean-up," in which everyone is involved, and the afternoon program from 3:30 to 4:30. In the winter months, skiing is available every weekday during the afternoon and on the weekends. From 4:30 to 6, students may return to the art studios or have free time. Following dinner, supervised study periods for boarding students are scheduled from 7 to 9, Monday through Thursday. Boarding students must be in their dormitory by 10.

WEEKEND LIFE
On-campus weekend activities include plays, dances, coffeehouses, movies, and concerts. Students may also attend off-campus plays and concerts or go shopping, camping, and skiing in the area. There is an active trekking program in the fall, winter, and spring. Students also make visits to Boston for special cultural events or for field trips to museums and sites of particular interest. With permission, individual students may leave the campus on weekends. Day students also participate in most weekend activities.

COSTS AND FINANCIAL AID
Tuition for boarding students was $34,291 in 2005–06. Day student tuition was $21,485. Additional charges for supplies and activities amounted to $1000. Tuition payments are due upon enrollment (10 percent), on August 1 (40 percent), and on December 10 (50 percent), unless special arrangements are made with the business office.

In 2005–06, High Mowing students received approximately $370,000 in financial aid. Aid is awarded on the basis of need and is given in the form of grants.

ADMISSIONS INFORMATION
High Mowing School looks for students who are bright and open, with curiosity and imagination, as well as a willingness to contribute actively in the classroom and to community life. Applicants are admitted in grades 9, 10, and 11 for the boarding and day programs. The admissions decision is based on an interview, previous school records, and recommendations.

APPLICATION TIMETABLE
Candidates for fall enrollment who complete applications by February 15 have their admissions decision sent to them on March 10. Applications for admission received after mid-February are welcome and are considered on a space-available basis. Students are occasionally enrolled at midyear if vacancies exist. There is a $50 application fee.

ADMISSIONS CORRESPONDENCE
Director of Admissions
High Mowing School
Abbot Hill Road
222 Isaac Frye Highway
Wilton, New Hampshire 03086
Phone: 603-654-2391
Fax: 603-654-6588
E-mail: admission@highmowing.org
Web site: http://www.highmowing.org

THE HILL SCHOOL

Pottstown, Pennsylvania

The Hill School

Type: Coeducational boarding and day college-preparatory school
Grades: 9–12 (Forms III–VI)
Enrollment: 485
Head of School: David R. Dougherty, Headmaster

THE SCHOOL

The Hill School was founded in 1851 by the Reverend Matthew Meigs, LL.D., a Presbyterian minister, and the Meigs family was instrumental in guiding the course of the School for three generations. In 1920, ownership was transferred to the alumni, who now operate the School as a not-for-profit institution through a 31-member Board of Trustees. In 1998, the School began admitting young women as a coeducational institution.

The Hill School's 200-acre campus extends from a residential area of the town into open country. Eight miles from the School is a 100-acre weekend camp with a small lake, campsites, and skeet and trapshooting ranges.

The Hill School continues to emphasize both structure and guidance in the quest for academic excellence. The School's commitments are to develop a student's respect for both mind and body, to instill an awareness of accountability for all decisions, and to teach those standards of personal conduct that are expected throughout life.

Pottstown is located 37 miles northwest of Philadelphia and 15 miles from Valley Forge National Park. Because of its Middle Atlantic location, students at The Hill can take advantage of a balanced climate, including warm autumn weather and a winter season that makes possible such activities as interscholastic ice hockey and skiing in the nearby Pocono Mountains.

The School's endowment is $108 million. The amount of Annual Giving for 2004–05 was more than $1.9 million, with 27 percent of the living alumni participating.

The Hill School is accredited by the Middle States Association of Colleges and Schools and is a member of the Secondary School Admission Test Board and the National Association of Independent Schools.

ACADEMIC PROGRAMS

The Hill School's principal academic goal is to instill in each student the capacity and desire to learn. The School maintains a student-faculty ratio of approximately 7:1 and an average class size of 12 students.

Sixteen academic credits in grades 9 through 12 are required to earn a diploma, and the distribution of courses includes no fewer than four in English (4 years), three in mathematics (algebra I, geometry, and algebra II), three in one foreign language (or two in each of two languages), U.S. history, two in laboratory science (biology, chemistry, or physics), and a course in the arts as well as one in theology or philosophy. Foreign language offerings include 6 years of Latin, 5 years of Spanish and French, and 4 years of Chinese Mandarin, German, and Greek. Courses offered within the Department of History include ancient and medieval, European,

and modern European history; U.S. Civil War, World War II, and Vietnam history; history of minorities; economics; and other electives. Department of Mathematics offerings include algebra I and II, geometry, analysis, analytic geometry, calculus, and advanced topics. Science courses available to all students include 2 years of biology, 2 years of chemistry, 2 years of physics, 2 years of computer science, and environmental science. Other science electives include sports medicine, kinesiology, and environmental ecology. Microsoft certified systems engineering courses are offered in addition to programming and Adobe digital arts certification.

Academic reports are sent home at the conclusion of each of the three terms. Comments from instructors, the hall parent, and the academic adviser are mailed to parents after each term. Throughout the school year, faculty members are available to provide supplemental instruction. Students have easy access to the teaching faculty through daily extra help periods, evening study periods, and weekend consultation. The main School library is open 12 hours each school day as well as weekends.

FACULTY AND ADVISERS

The faculty consists of 56 men and 30 women, and 98 percent of faculty members live on campus with their families. Faculty members hold ninety-six bachelor's degrees and sixty-one master's degrees and above from many major universities in the United States and abroad.

David R. Dougherty was appointed Headmaster in 1993. He received a B.A. in English from Washington and Lee University in 1968. He earned an M.A. in English from Georgetown University and a master's in literature from the Bread Loaf School, Middlebury College, and Lincoln College of Oxford University. Prior to becoming The Hill's tenth Headmaster, Mr. Dougherty had been Headmaster of North Cross School in Roanoke, Virginia, since 1987. From 1982 to 1987, he was Assistant Headmaster of Episcopal High School in Alexandria, Virginia. He began his teaching career at Episcopal High School in 1968.

COLLEGE PLACEMENT

For more than 150 years, The Hill School has prepared students for colleges and universities throughout the United States. The College Advising Office, staffed by 5 individuals, serves an important educational function in the selection of appropriate college and university choices and in the preparation of college admission materials.

Each year, more than 100 representatives from colleges and universities visit The Hill to present information about their institutions. Interested students are invited to attend these sessions, and Sixth Form students may schedule

formal interviews with college representatives. A variety of workshops concerning the college application process are offered to students as well. Topics covered include decision making, career interest identification, essay writing, interview techniques, and methods of quality assessment.

A complete range of standardized tests is administered on campus, including SAT and SAT Subject Tests, ACT, Advanced Placement, and TOEFL; students generally take those exams at regular intervals during the Fifth and Sixth Form years. The middle 50 percent ranges on the SAT for the class of 2005 were 560–680 critical reading and 580–690 math.

Recent graduates are attending such colleges and universities as Boston College, Boston University, Colgate, Cornell, Drexel, Duke, Franklin and Marshall, Georgetown, Harvard, Johns Hopkins, MIT, Princeton, Stanford, the United States Naval Academy, Trinity, Williams, and the Universities of Chicago, North Carolina, Pennsylvania, Richmond, St. Andrews (Scotland), and Virginia.

STUDENT BODY AND CONDUCT

In the Third Form, there are 47 boarding and 41 day students; in the Fourth Form, there are 92 boarding and 43 day students; in the Fifth Form, there are 112 boarding and 26 day students; and in the Sixth Form, there are 131 boarding and 1 day student. Students come from twenty-eight states and thirteen other countries. Sixty-nine percent of the students come from Middle Atlantic states, with the rest of the students coming in equal measure from New England, the Southeast, and Midwestern and Western states. Of the total School population, 16 percent of the students are members of minority groups.

The Hill School's orientation requires each student to maintain high standards of conduct as well as a strong sense of commitment to positive values and worthwhile goals. In 1997, the Hill School students and faculty members voted to adopt an Honor Code to promote an environment of mutual trust and respect and to uphold the principles of trust, honor, and integrity in all intellectual, athletic, and social pursuits. Disciplinary matters within the School community are handled by the Discipline Committee, a committee of students and 9 faculty members; both groups are elected by peers.

ACADEMIC FACILITIES

The Hill School's fifty-five academic buildings include the 40,000-volume John P. Ryan Library, the Alumni Chapel, Harry Elkins Widener Memorial Science Building, Theodore N. Danforth Computer Center, the 31,000-square-foot Center for the Arts, and the $12-million Academic and Student Center.

BOARDING AND GENERAL FACILITIES

The Hill School's eleven major dormitory structures are divided into residential units that most often house 12 students and one faculty family. Housing has been designed for 2 students per dormitory room. Two selected Sixth Form prefects, who share some supervisory responsibilities with the residential faculty family, live on each dormitory corridor. New students are assigned roommates by the Residential Life and Admission Offices; in subsequent years, however, roommate selections are made by each student. There is a formal dining room where students and faculty families enjoy seated family-style and buffet meals.

The Student Health Service is staffed by full-time registered nurses and 2 physicians who are on call around the clock.

ATHLETICS

Physical education is an integral part of The Hill's educational offering. A program of forty-two sports enables each student to compete and develop expertise in the sports of their choice.

The athletic facilities at The Hill include a 34,000-square-foot fieldhouse and seven squash courts, a gymnasium complex, four basketball courts, a six-lane swimming pool, and a fitness center that includes a complete Nautilus system and sixteen cardiovascular machines. Additional structures include a covered hockey rink and a building for wrestling. The Hill shares an eighteen-hole golf course and owns eleven tennis courts and 90 acres of playing fields for baseball, cross-country, field hockey, football, lacrosse, and soccer.

EXTRACURRICULAR OPPORTUNITIES

Students at The Hill are involved in many pursuits that take them well beyond the classroom and frequently beyond the campus itself. The students publish a newspaper, a literary magazine, and a yearbook. Community-action programs enable students to tutor elementary school children. Other diverse opportunities for student involvement include the Choir, the Hilltones and Hilltrebles, the jazz band, the orchestra, and thirty-five other organizations that reflect such specific interests as law, hiking, skiing, photography, archaeology, computers, classics, and sailing.

The Hill School Humanities Fund provides students with tickets and transportation to hear the Philadelphia Orchestra and makes possible other cultural excursions as well. In addition, numerous on-campus lectures, concerts, plays, and exhibits are scheduled to stimulate and enrich students' cultural life.

DAILY LIFE

Classes are held six days a week, with a mid-morning chapel service on Monday and Thursday. A full academic day is divided into eight 40-minute periods, beginning at 7:55 a.m. and ending at 3:10 p.m. Wednesday and Saturday classes meet in the morning only. Athletic practice takes place between 3:45 and 5:45 p.m. Conference periods are scheduled during free periods and in the evening; student organizations meet after dinner. Evening study hours are supervised by faculty members and prefects and vary in length by Form level.

Every Hill student must complete a specifically assigned job for the School community each day. The time required for this job averages approximately 40 minutes daily, but the collective effort is beneficial to both the School and the individual.

WEEKEND LIFE

Weekend activities are numerous and varied. Major athletic events, concerts, informal dances, and current films are regular Saturday events. Weekend excursions to Baltimore, Philadelphia, New York City, and Washington, D.C., for concerts, the theater, professional athletics, museum visits, and noteworthy events are planned by the Student Activities Committee and open to all. School organizations and special interest clubs also schedule activities and outings on the weekends. Sunday services, held in the evening, frequently feature guest clergy from a variety of faiths.

In addition, such School facilities as the Center for the Arts, athletic areas, computer laboratories, music rooms, the library, and the Student Center are open for all. Students in good academic standing may request off-campus weekends with parental permission.

COSTS AND FINANCIAL AID

The annual charge for boarding students in 2005–06 was $34,300. This fee covered instruction, board, room, concerts, lectures, movies, athletic contests, services of the School physician and nurses at daily dispensaries, and athletic equipment on an issue basis. It also includes subscriptions for the newspaper and the literary magazine. There is an optional laundry service for an additional fee.

The day student tuition in 2005–06 was $23,300, which included lunch for every day except Sunday. All day students are required to board for one year.

Financial aid is awarded to students whose parents are unable to meet the full tuition and is granted without regard to race, color, or ethnic origin. Financial aid grants are based on the guidelines established by the School and Student Service for Financial Aid. Grants are renewed annually; parents must submit the School and Student Service for Financial Aid form each year. For 2005–06, approximately $3.5 million was awarded. Applications for financial aid should be submitted by January 20.

ADMISSIONS INFORMATION

The Hill School seeks to enroll students who show academic promise, intellectual curiosity, and strong character. The School encourages students to apply who demonstrate involvement in the arts, athletics, and community service. The following credentials are required for admission: a formal application; a writing sample; a transcript of grades; results from the SSAT, PSAT, or SAT; a letter of recommendation from the school counselor and English and mathematics teachers; and an interview.

APPLICATION TIMETABLE

During the year preceding the applicant's proposed entrance, a formal application for admission should be filed, accompanied by a nonrefundable application fee of $50 ($100 for international students). February 1 is the deadline for consideration in the first round; late applications are considered on a space-available basis.

Families are requested to visit The Hill during the school term to meet members of the faculty and student body. An appointment should be made in advance.

ADMISSIONS CORRESPONDENCE

Sally B. Keidel
Director of Enrollment Management
The Hill School
717 East High Street
Pottstown, Pennsylvania 19464

Phone: 610-326-1000
Fax: 610-705-1753
E-mail: admission@thehill.org
Web site: http://www.thehill.org

THE HOCKADAY SCHOOL

Dallas, Texas

Type: Girls' day college-preparatory (Prekindergarten to grade 12) and boarding (grades 8–12) school
Grades: Prekindergarten–12: Lower School, Prekindergarten–4; Middle School, 5–8; Upper School, 9–12 (Forms I–IV)
Enrollment: School total: 1,020
Head of School: Jeanne P. Whitman, Eugene McDermott Headmistress

THE SCHOOL

The Hockaday School, which was founded in 1913, provides a nationally recognized college-preparatory education for girls of strong potential who may be expected to assume positions of responsibility and leadership in a rapidly changing world. Ela Hockaday dedicated herself to giving each girl a foundation for living based on scholarship, character, courtesy, and athletics—the traditional four cornerstones that remain the dominant influence in the School's educational philosophy.

Hockaday's campus extends over 100 acres of open fields and wooded creeks in a pleasant residential area of northwest Dallas. The School's contemporary architectural setting features an academic quadrangle built so as to provide views of exterior gardens and landscaped terraces. The science center and Clements Lecture Hall opened in 1983, the Ashley Priddy Lower School Building in 1984, the Biggs Dining Room and Whittenburg Dining Terrace in 1985, the Fine Arts Wing in 1987, the Lower School addition in 2001, and the Liza Lee Academic Research Center in 2002. The 52,000-square-foot center hosts two expansive libraries, several computer labs, and a versatile hall that doubles as a lecture facility and audiovisual theater. In the academic area are classrooms; laboratories for languages, computers, and reading; and a study center. The new Wellness Center, completed in 2003, includes the 5,000-square-foot Hill Family Fitness Center, a 1,800-square-foot aerobics room with state-of-the-art aerobic and resistance equipment, and athletic training facilities that are fully equipped for the treatment of sports-related injuries.

A Board of Trustees is the governing body. The School's endowment is $95 million, and the operating income is supplemented by Annual Fund giving of $1.2 million. The Alumnae Association, with more than 7,000 graduates and former students, contributes significantly to the ongoing programs of the School.

The Hockaday School is accredited by the Independent Schools Association of the Southwest. It holds membership in the National Association of Independent Schools, the National Association of Principals of Schools for Girls, the College Board, the National Association for College Admission Counseling, the Educational Records Bureau, the National Coalition of Girls' Schools, and the Secondary School Admission Test Board.

ACADEMIC PROGRAMS

Students are exposed to a rigorous academic curriculum that offers core educational subjects as well as unique offerings in technology, the arts, and leadership and personal development. Graduation requirements (in years) include English, 4; mathematics, 3; history, 2.5; foreign language, 2; laboratory science, 2; fine arts, 1.5; physical education and health, 4; and academic electives from any department, 2, plus basic proficiency in computer usage. Hockaday offers 121 courses, including many honors courses. Advanced Placement courses are offered in nineteen subjects, including English, modern European history, U.S. history, AB and BC

calculus, statistics, physics, chemistry, biology, studio art, Latin, French, Spanish, computer science, and economics. For some selected courses, Hockaday has a cooperative program with St. Mark's School of Texas, a boys' school in Dallas. Private lessons are available in cello, flute, guitar, piano, violin, and voice.

A one-year English as a second language (ESL) program is offered to students on intermediate and advanced levels. Intensive language training in writing, reading, listening, and speaking skills is the focus of the program. Students may continue at Hockaday after the first year, following acceptance into the regular academic program. International students with intermediate or advanced English proficiency may study at Hockaday. Along with these special classes, students may study math, science, fine arts, and other courses in the mainstream curriculum. First-year students travel to Washington, D.C., and the Texas Hill Country.

Class sizes average 15 students, with an overall student-teacher ratio of 10:1.

The grading system in grades 7–12 uses A to F designations with pluses and minuses. Reports are sent to parents at the end of each quarter period. High achievement in the Upper School is recognized by inclusion on the Headmistress's List and by initiation into a number of honor societies, including the Cum Laude Society.

Each student receives careful counseling throughout her Hockaday career. Academic counseling begins even in the admissions process and continues under the supervision of the counseling office, which coordinates the faculty adviser system and general counseling program. Each student has an interested, concerned faculty adviser to assist her with academic or personal matters on a daily basis.

FACULTY AND ADVISERS

The Hockaday faculty is represented by accomplished individuals, most of whom have advanced degrees, with 6 holding Ph.D.'s.

Ms. Jeanne P. Whitman, the Eugene McDermott Headmistress, is a magna cum laude graduate of Wake Forest University. She earned her master's degree in English from the University of Virginia and a second master's degree in business from Wake Forest University.

Hockaday's teachers are chosen for depth of knowledge in their fields of specialization, personal integrity, and the ability to facilitate the progress of individual students. Many are successful writers, lecturers, artists, musicians, photographers, or composers; many regularly assist colleagues in other schools by giving workshops and lectures. Summer study grants are awarded to faculty members to encourage both research and professional development.

COLLEGE PLACEMENT

The college counselors work directly with Upper School students in their college planning. Each student participates with her parents in conferences with the counselor concerning applications and final selection.

For the middle 50 percent of the class of 2005, SAT I scores ranged from 600 to 740 in verbal and 620 to 730 in math. Ranges of SAT II Subject Test scores were 630–750, Writing; 610–720, Math 1C; 650–760, Math 2C; 650–720, American History; and 600–720, Spanish. In the class of 2005, 18 students were named as National Merit Finalists. One hundred percent of the class went on to college. They matriculated at sixty-five different colleges and universities, including Amherst, Cornell, Dartmouth, Georgetown, Harvard, Johns Hopkins, NYU, Pomona, Princeton, Rhodes, Rice, SMU, Stanford, Tufts, Vanderbilt, Wake Forest, Wellesley, Yale, and the Universities of North Carolina, Pennsylvania, Southern California, and Texas at Austin.

STUDENT BODY AND CONDUCT

The student body is composed of 1,020 girls (close to 60 of whom board) from six states and ten countries outside of the United States. The Upper School is composed of 434 students, the Middle School 308 students, and the Lower School 278 students. Twenty-seven percent of the girls are members of minority groups.

The Upper School Student Council and the Honor Council exert strong, active, and responsible leadership in student affairs. In addition to planning activities, allocating funds, and serving as a forum for student concerns, these councils promote and exemplify the School's written Honor Code.

Students are expected to abide by the guidelines set forth in the Upper School manual. Disciplinary measures rest primarily with the Head of the Upper School and the Headmistress.

ACADEMIC FACILITIES

Hockaday's $53-million educational complex includes the new Academic Research Center, which houses the Lower, Middle, and Upper School libraries; the Technology Center; two computer labs; a science exploration lab; student publications workrooms; the School bookstore; extensive audiovisual facilities; alumnae archives; and group meeting rooms. In addition, the science center; the Clements Lecture Hall; the Fine Arts Wing, with a complete ceramics studio with outdoor kilns, a photography lab, an art studio, and music practice rooms; the 560-seat Esther Hoblitzelle Auditorium; more than 500 computer stations campuswide; and pleasant classrooms in the academic quadrangle provide a rich and inviting atmosphere for learning. The new Lower School wing includes prekindergarten and kindergarten classrooms, art and music rooms, performance and meeting areas, science labs, and a play yard. Recent renovations, which were completed in 2005, increased the size of all Middle and Upper School classrooms by 50 percent. The new classrooms are equipped with Smartboard™ technology for use in conjunction with students' laptops, which are required for every girl in grades 6–12. The campus is completely wireless.

BOARDING AND GENERAL FACILITIES

Accommodations for boarding students are attractive, comfortable dormitories connected by a glass-

enclosed recreation and study area. Each form is normally housed on a separate hall with its own lounge, kitchen, television, VCR, and laundry room. Other facilities include an aerobics center, two computer rooms (IBM and Macintosh), and an exercise-equipment room. An additional common lounge overlooks an outdoor swimming pool. Two students share a room, and each hall contains a small suite for the adult counselor in charge. The dormitories are closed for Thanksgiving, Christmas, and spring vacations.

An infirmary is located on the ground floor of the dormitory area, with a registered nurse on duty at all times and the School doctor on call. Campus security is maintained 24 hours a day.

The new Wellness Center features an aerobics center, a fitness testing area, a trainer's facility, and the Hill Fitness Center, a 4,000-square-foot, state-of-the-art facility offering aerobic, resistance, and circuit training equipment.

ATHLETICS

The Athletic and Physical Education Departments offer a full spectrum of individual, recreational, and team sports opportunities. Their goal is to help each girl develop a positive self-image, refine motor skills, experience the enjoyment of physical activity, and acquire competence in athletic pursuits of her choice. Interscholastic sports include basketball, crew, cross-country, field hockey, golf, lacrosse, soccer, softball, swimming and diving, tennis, track, and volleyball. The Penson Athletic Center contains three full-size basketball courts, two racquetball courts, a weight room, and spectator seating for more than 1,000 people. Another gymnasium houses an indoor swimming pool and a dance studio. The Ashley H. Priddy Tennis Center includes a covered gallery overlooking an exhibition court. There are nine more tennis courts, several of which are lighted for evening use.

EXTRACURRICULAR OPPORTUNITIES

Thirty-three special interest organizations and honor societies, plus eight elected boards, including Student Council, the Athletic Board, and the Fine Arts Board, augment the academic and sports programs. Upper School interest groups that meet weekly are concerned with a wide variety of areas, changing from year to year according to student and faculty choices. To encourage student creativity, the Upper School sponsors an English and a Spanish literary and journalistic magazine, a news-paper, and the Hockaday yearbook. These publications are edited by students with the guidance of faculty advisers.

Service to the School and its surrounding community is an important part of a girl's life at Hockaday. Each Upper School student is asked to contribute a minimum of 15 volunteer hours per year in service to the wider community.

DAILY LIFE

Upper School classes begin at 8 a.m. and end at 3:45 p.m. Monday through Friday. The daily schedule provides time for academic help sessions and club meetings.

Varsity sports meet after the close of the regular school day. Boarding students have a 2-hour required study time, Sunday through Thursday nights.

WEEKEND LIFE

Off-campus activities each weekend enable boarding students to take advantage of the many cultural and recreational resources in the Dallas–Fort Worth area. Faculty members are frequently involved in boarding activities, as are families of the Hockaday Parents Association, who sponsor girls who are new to Hockaday and include them in family activities. Each boarder is matched with a local Dallas family through the Host Family Program. The host families offer local support for the boarders and encourage their participation in social activities outside of school.

SUMMER PROGRAMS

A six-week coed academic summer session is offered for day and boarding students. Students may attend three- or six-week sessions beginning in June and July. Summer boarding is limited to girls ages 12–17. Programs in language immersion, math and science enrichment, computers, sports, SAT preparation, study skills, English, creative writing, and arts/theater are offered. Academic courses focus on enrichment opportunities. English as a second language, an international program lasting three weeks, begins in July. Information on the summer session is available in late spring. Applications are accepted until all spaces are filled, although students are encouraged to apply early to ensure their preferred course selection.

COSTS AND FINANCIAL AID

In 2005–06, tuition for Upper School day students averaged $18,000. For resident students, costs were approximately $34,000 for tuition, room, and board.

Additional expenses for both day and resident students include, among others, those for books and uniforms. A deposit of $1000 is due with the signed enrollment contract, and the balance of tuition and fees is due by July 1 prior to entrance in August. Partial payment for room and board for resident students is also made at this time. The room and board balance for resident students is payable by December 1 following entrance in August.

The Hockaday Financial Aid Program offers assistance based on financial need. Parents of all applicants for financial aid must provide financial information as required by the Financial Aid Committee. A total of $1,535,000 was awarded to students in 2003–04. Details of the programs are available from the Admission Office.

ADMISSIONS INFORMATION

Applicants to Hockaday's Upper School are considered on the basis of their previous academic records, results of aptitude and achievement testing, teacher and head of school evaluations, and, in most cases, a personal interview. There is no discrimination because of race, creed, or nationality. Because the School requires a student to attend the School for at least two years to be eligible for graduation, new students are not normally admitted to the senior class. In order to qualify for admission and have a successful experience at Hockaday, a girl needs to possess a strong potential and desire to learn.

APPLICATION TIMETABLE

Initial inquiries are welcome at any time, and applications are received continuously. The nonrefundable application fee is $175 for both day-student and boarding-student applications. Entrance tests are scheduled in December, January, and February and periodically throughout the spring and summer. Campus tours are available at convenient times during the year. Notification of the admission decision is made approximately six weeks after the testing. Parents are expected to reply to an offer of admission within two weeks.

ADMISSIONS CORRESPONDENCE

Jen Liggitt, Director of Admission
The Hockaday School
11600 Welch Road
Dallas, Texas 75229-2999

Phone: 214-363-6311
Fax: 214-265-1649
E-mail: admissions@mail.hockaday.org
Web site: http://www.hockaday.org

HOLDERNESS SCHOOL

Plymouth, New Hampshire

 HOLDERNESS

Type: Coeducational boarding and day college-preparatory school
Grades: 9–12
Enrollment: 276
Head of School: R. Phillip Peck

THE SCHOOL

Holderness School was founded in 1879 by a group of Episcopal clergymen who sought "to combine the highest degree of excellence in instruction and care-taking with the lowest possible rate for tuition and board." For 127 years, this charge has been carried out by extraordinarily dedicated and capable men and women, and the reputation of the School continues to prosper.

The geographical setting has been significant in shaping both the attitudes and the types of programs at Holderness. Much of the 600-acre campus is wooded, and its proximity to the White Mountain National Forest leads to a natural emphasis on the outdoors. Plymouth, a college town of 8,500, is ¾ mile away, and Logan Airport in Boston can be reached by car in 2 hours.

Holderness is governed by a self-perpetuating Board of Trustees, of which the Bishop of New Hampshire is an ex officio member. Annual expenses are met through tuition, endowment, and Annual Giving. The endowment currently totals $32.8 million. Additional funds were contributed by friends of the School.

Holderness School is accredited by the New England Association of Schools and Colleges and is a member of the Secondary School Admission Test Board, the Cum Laude Society, the National Association of Independent Schools, the Association of Independent Schools of New England, and the Independent Schools Association of Northern New England.

ACADEMIC PROGRAMS

The Holderness curriculum includes 4 years of English; AP composition and AP literature; public speaking; mathematics through AP calculus; Web programming; foreign languages through AP French, Spanish, and Latin; chemistry, honors chemistry; physics, honors physics; biology, advanced environmental science, AP biology, human anatomy and physiology, and biotechnology; ancient, modern European, contemporary world, U.S., and AP U.S. history; cold war, economics, civil rights, women's history, and global crises: instability and extremism in the post–cold war world; music, music theory and composition, AP music theory and composition, and black music in twentieth-century America; drawing, sculpture, painting, photography, ceramics, woodworking, media studies and video production, and printmaking; and ethics and religion. Advanced Placement courses are offered in eleven of the fourteen test areas.

A minimum of 48 credits is required for graduation: English, 12 credits; mathematics, 9 credits; foreign language, 6 credits; history, 6 credits; science, 6 credits; and electives, 9 credits.

Most students take more than the minimum requirements in science, foreign language, and mathematics.

Students are strongly encouraged to seek individual instruction whenever necessary. The student-faculty ratio is 7:1, and Holderness believes that the best education is available when there are extensive opportunities for contact between student and teacher.

Through a grant provided by the McCulloch family, each senior who has met all academic requirements has a chance to participate in a project that involves on- or off-campus study.

FACULTY AND ADVISERS

There are 44 full-time faculty members (30 men, 14 women). Ph.D.'s are held by 3 members and master's degrees are held by 24 members. All but 12 members reside in School housing, and 27 faculty members or couples supervise dormitory floors or houses.

Each faculty member is the adviser for the students in his or her dormitory, and most faculty members coach School sports. The Service Committee; the yearbook; the literary magazine and the newspaper; presentations in art, music, and drama; various clubs; study hall; evening library hours; and weekend activities are all under faculty supervision. With faculty help, a full-time librarian and a part-time assistant keep the library open 14 hours every day.

The Head of School, R. Phillip Peck, was inducted in 2001 after teaching, coaching, and dorm parenting at Holderness School for seventeen years. A former Olympic and World Cup ski coach, Peck was an adjunct lead instructor in Columbia's Klingenstein summer program from 1992 to 2001. He earned a B.A. at Dartmouth College and an M.A. at Columbia University, where his is currently pursuing his Ed.D.

COLLEGE PLACEMENT

College counseling begins in February of the junior year. A counselor meets with students individually and encourages them to think about the colleges they should visit. Spring and summer tours are suggested. Admissions officers from colleges and universities visit the campus during the school year and hold college meetings, which interested students are encouraged to attend. In the spring, parents and students are invited to attend a college fair of more than 200 colleges and universities. This fair is sponsored by independent schools and hosted by Colby Sawyer College.

Seventy-seven students graduated in 2005, and 100 percent were college bound. Among the colleges and universities currently attended by 2 or more Holderness graduates are Amherst, Bates, Boston College, Bowdoin, Brown, Colby, Colgate, Colorado College, Connecticut College, Dartmouth, Gettysburg, Hamilton, Hobart and

William Smith, Lewis & Clark, Middlebury, St. Lawrence, Whitman, Williams, and the Universities of Colorado, Connecticut, New Hampshire, and Vermont.

STUDENT BODY AND CONDUCT

There are 276 students enrolled: 25 boys and 21 girls in grade 9, 44 boys and 25 girls in grade 10, 51 boys and 32 girls in grade 11, and 53 boys and 25 girls in grade 12.

The Holderness community is built around a strong system of student government that has been in operation for fifty-two years. The School president, vice president, and student leaders are elected on a schoolwide ballot and, with faculty support, are responsible for day-to-day life at the School. The goal of student government at Holderness is to generate in each student a genuine feeling of responsibility for the community and to develop capable leadership within the student body.

Each member of the community has a daily job. Students work in the kitchen, on the School grounds, in the buildings, on the trails, and at other School facilities. The jobs usually take less than ½ hour each day.

Holderness is an Episcopal school that maintains respect for all faith traditions. There are two required all-school services each week. The first opens the week on Monday morning, and the second is on Thursday evening before a family-style dinner. Voluntary services are offered on the other mornings of the week as well as an optional Sunday night Eucharist. The student body is interdenominational. Opportunities for worship in other denominations and faiths are supported by the staff and school.

ACADEMIC FACILITIES

There are twenty-nine School buildings. Academic facilities include the Hagerman Center, a math and science building. Computer facilities are also housed there, along with a 325-seat auditorium. Other classes are held in the Schoolhouse and Carpenter Arts Center. A video-sound-light studio stocked with video equipment and cameras is open for serious students of photography and recording. This professional facility was made possible by the Jennie R. Donaldson Trust.

The Alfond Library has more than 16,000 volumes, more than 50 periodicals and newspapers, a large collection of reference works, videos, and microform files and readers. It also houses two computer labs.

BOARDING AND GENERAL FACILITIES

There are nine boys' dormitories that accommodate 4 to 36 students each; most rooms are doubles. On the South Campus, adjacent to the dining hall, there is a semicircle of seven houses,

each with accommodations for 8 to 16 girls. The students have a lounge of their own, a snack bar, and a game room.

There is a health center, including an infirmary, in which the School physician holds daily visiting hours, and a registered nurse is in attendance. Students who are too sick to stay at the School are taken to Speare Memorial Hospital in Plymouth, just a few minutes away.

ATHLETICS

Holderness's highly competitive and rigorous sports program promotes fair play and sportsmanship. New students are required to play a fall sport in their first year. Ninth and tenth graders are required to participate in a competitive sport all three terms each academic year; eleventh and twelfth graders, two terms. Upperclass students may elect noncompetitive activities in place of a competitive sport. Students may choose to pursue an interest in the arts on a per season basis, limited to one season per year. For example, students may choose to take one of the Art Department's offerings, or they may request to use the afternoon for such activities as preparing a portfolio or practicing a musical instrument.

Boys' and girls' team sports include basketball; cross-country running; cycling; golf; hockey; lacrosse; Nordic, Alpine, freestyle, and free-ride skiing; snowboarding; soccer; and tennis. Other boys' sports are baseball and football, while girls may choose field hockey and/or softball.

The Gallop Athletic Center houses basketball and squash courts, a training room with state-of-the-art equipment, and a ski-tuning room with storage lockers.

Other facilities include a gymnasium; ten playing fields, including a turf field for soccer and lacrosse; ten tennis courts; a 10-kilometer cross-country trail, with 5 kilometers lit by lamps; a covered artificial-ice rink; and 600 acres of backyard wilderness. An eighteen-hole golf course is 3 miles away.

EXTRACURRICULAR OPPORTUNITIES

Life at Holderness is varied and energetic. The range of extracurricular activities is wide. The drama group presents three major productions a year. The School offers a chorus, a band, and a group specializing in vocal music. Lessons are available in guitar, piano, strings, brass, percussion, and woodwinds, and students are encouraged to try out for the New Hampshire All-State Chorus and the Granite State Youth Orchestra. The School's art and photography programs are very strong and enjoy a high level of student participation. A video/sound light studio enables students to become acquainted with the professional equipment and techniques involved in video tape recording, sound recording using a synthesizer, and still photography. Students publish a newspaper, a literary magazine, and a yearbook.

Various outdoor activities sponsored by the Holderness School Outing Club include biking, camping, canoeing, hiking, fishing, rock climbing, and winter climbing.

Every March for the past twenty-eight years, the eleventh-grade class has snowshoed or skied away from school on Out Back, a ten-day wilderness program with Outward Bound features and philosophy. While the junior class is participating in Out Back, the two lower classes are immersed in Artward Bound, an intensive program in the arts that includes classes in art, drama, writing, and music, with evening programs ranging from movies and mime to readings by poets. An alternative to Artward Bound for sophomores is renovating houses for Habitat for Humanity. The twelfth grade spends the same period in Senior Colloquium, a rigorous seminar. Recent themes have included public speaking, writing for publication, production of paper, French cooking, classic American movies, and canoe building.

DAILY LIFE

Classes are held six days a week. Wednesday and Saturday are half days, to allow for interscholastic sports events in the afternoons. Classes begin at 8 a.m. and end at 3 p.m. during the fall and spring terms. There are six classes a day, each either 45 or 75 minutes long. Sports and extracurricular activities are from 3:30 to 5:30. During the winter term, classes run from 8 a.m. to 12:30 p.m.; the activity period is from 1 to 4; and class time follows and lasts until 6. Dinner is served at 6:10 p.m. and is followed by study hall from 7:30 to 9:30. Dorm check-in is at 10 p.m. for underclass students and at 10:30 for seniors.

WEEKEND LIFE

Weekend life at Holderness is planned by rotating faculty members and student leaders and varies with the seasons to some extent, but there are some constants. Movies are shown at the School every Saturday night, and students may walk to Plymouth, where there are shops and restaurants. Informal dances are held regularly at the School all year long. Sports events are held on Saturday afternoons.

Though there are many planned activities on Sunday, there is also the opportunity for students to organize their own free time. Day students are encouraged to participate in weekend events and social life.

COSTS AND FINANCIAL AID

Tuition for boarding students is $35,100, with additional expenses of books ($125–$200) and laundry ($120–$550). Day tuition is $20,800. Lessons for students participating in the band are free. There are separate charges for individual music lessons, driver's education, and participation in the U.S. Ski or Snowboarding Association program.

Tuition may be paid in full in July or in two installments in July and November. The latter method requires participation in the Tuition Refund Insurance Plan.

Financial aid equals 17 percent of all tuition income, and 22 percent of the students are currently receiving such assistance.

ADMISSIONS INFORMATION

Holderness looks for boys and girls who are able to benefit from the challenge Holderness offers and who are willing to take an active part in the life of the School. Holderness seeks students of demonstrated scholastic ability who will be likely to achieve in a number of areas.

The most important requirements for admission are a student transcript and letters of recommendation from the applicant's present school. Applicants are strongly urged to visit the School for a tour of the campus and a personal interview. Candidates are expected to take the SSAT, preferably in December, for admission the following September. Most applications each year are for grades 9 and 10, although Holderness will accept a few students in grades 11 and 12.

APPLICATION TIMETABLE

Inquiries about the School or requests for a catalog are welcome anytime. Interested students and their parents are invited to make an appointment for a student-led tour of the School and an interview with an admissions officer. It is strongly recommended that this visit be made at a time when school is in session. The Admissions Office schedules appointments from 8:15 a.m. to 2:15 p.m. on Monday, Tuesday, Thursday, and Friday and from 8:15 to 10:45 a.m. on Wednesday and Saturday. During the winter term, appointments are scheduled for mornings, Monday through Saturday. In addition to application and personal forms, recommendations from math and English teachers and an extracurricular source will be requested. Grades for the entire first half of the school year, the results of any testing by the home school, SSAT scores, and a $35 fee complete the application.

Applications completed by February 1 have priority over those arriving later. Decisions on all applications received by February 1 are mailed on the mid-March date established by the National Association of Independent Schools. Parental confirmation of acceptance, plus a reservation deposit of $3300 for a boarding student or $2000 for a day student, is expected as soon as possible but not later than April 10. Financial aid awards are mailed shortly after acceptances.

For those students unable to meet the February 1 deadline, the Admissions Committee will review credentials after mid-April. If there should be openings then, or during the summer, late applicants will be notified.

ADMISSIONS CORRESPONDENCE

Nancy Dalley, Admissions Administrator
Holderness School
Plymouth, New Hampshire 03264

Phone: 603-536-1747
Fax: 603-536-2125
E-mail: admissions@holderness.org
Web site: http://www.holderness.org

HOME STUDY INTERNATIONAL

Silver Spring, Maryland

Type: Christian distance education school
Grades: Preschool–college
Enrollment: 2,500
Head of School: Dr. Donald R. Sahly, President

THE SCHOOL

At the turn of the last century, educational opportunities were rare, and distance education was increasing in popularity in the United States. An educator, Frederick Griggs, envisioned teaching people around the world. His vision took shape in the establishment of The Fireside Correspondence School in 1909. His goal was to provide the benefits of an education to those unable to attend traditional schools. By 1916, the students of The Fireside Correspondence School (later renamed Home Study Institute and more recently Home Study International) represented nearly every state and province in North America as well as sixty other countries. Since then, more than 300,000 people have studied with Home Study International (HSI).

Today, Home Study International plays a distinct and vital role in the educational development of students of all ages in all parts of the world.

In 1990, the HSI board assigned names to its three academic divisions. Home Study Elementary School, Home Study High School, and Griggs University (HSI/GU) became part of HSI's terminology. In 1991, HSI/GU began offering college degrees.

In addition, HSI also helps fill in the educational gaps in private traditional schools with programs such as the Alternative Program for Learning Enrichment (APLE), which helps small private schools augment their course offerings.

People from all walks of life have discovered that the quiet conditions of distance education help develop self-reliance, independent thinking, and responsibility.

From its early years when it operated out of a one-room office, Home Study International has developed into a worldwide school that maintains the highest scholastic standards while utilizing the services of qualified professionals in all phases of its operation. While it employs modern technology, HSI still emphasizes the personal touch in its student-teacher relationships.

As of July 31, 2000, Home Study International has been granted full accreditation status by the Commission on Secondary and Middle Schools of the Southern Association of Colleges and Schools (SACS) and the Commission on Elementary Schools of the Middle States Association of Colleges and Schools (MSA). In addition HSI has also been accredited by the Commission on International and Transregional Accreditation (CITA). For many years HSI's elementary and secondary (high school) programs have also been approved by the Maryland Department of Education and accredited by the Accrediting Commission of the Distance Education and Training Council (DETC), an agency recognized by the U.S. Department of Education. At the college level Home Study International is also a member of the University Continuing Education Association and the International Council for Distance Education. HSI is affiliated with Andrews University, which is accredited by the North Central Association of Colleges and Schools; Columbia Union College, which is accredited by the Middle States Association of Colleges and Schools; and Oakwood College, which is accredited by the Commission on Colleges of the Southern Association of Colleges and Schools. HSI is approved by the Maryland Higher Education Commission and is a member of the American Association of Collegiate Registrars and Admissions Officers (AACRAO).

ACADEMIC PROGRAMS

Home Study International offers both a basic high school diploma and a college-preparatory diploma. The basic diploma requires 21 Carnegie units, which must include 4 units of English, 3 units of math, 3 units of social studies (one of which must be American history), 2 units of science, and 4 units of Bible study (students may be excused from the Bible requirement if their personal convictions and familial belief systems so dictate). One half-credit is given toward an HSI diploma for a student who has taken driver's education.

The college-preparatory diploma requires 24 units, including those listed for the basic diploma plus an additional unit in science and 2 units of a language.

Each Home Study International course comes equipped with a "teacher on paper"—the course study guide. The study guide includes all learning objectives, instructional sections, reading assignments, supplemental information, self-diagnostic tools, and lessons/submissions. The student also receives a full set of supplies, including a textbook and, sometimes, cassettes, CDs, lab equipment, and reading supplements. Experienced teachers are assigned to each course to provide positive, individual interaction with students. Students may be given phone numbers or e-mail addresses for the teachers of individual courses.

For most courses, two examinations are required each semester—a midterm and a semester examination. All examinations must be supervised by a school or community official (such as a teacher or registrar) or by a responsible adult who is not related to the student. If a student is enrolled in another school while taking HSI courses, the examinations should be taken under the direction of that school's registrar or testing department. Final grades are issued as A, B, C, D, or F. At the high school level, pluses and minuses (e.g., B+ and B–) are also used.

Because Home Study International's high school program offers year-round registration and self-paced instruction, students may adapt their class schedules to meet learning needs. The structure of the instructional materials engenders self-discipline and motivation as well as academic excellence.

Since July 2003, Home Study International has been offering high school courses online. Available courses are listed on HSI's Web site. It has been predicted that the entire high school curriculum will be online by 2005–06.

FACULTY AND ADVISERS

The course writers for Home Study International are exceptional professionals in their specialties, and most hold degrees at the master's or doctoral level. The courses are intellectually stimulating and designed to foster academic excellence. Home Study International has 1 full-time and 62 part-time faculty members. In addition, 18 full-time nonteaching professionals provide assistance to students and teachers. Of HSI's 63 teachers (25 women and 38 men), 45 have advanced degrees.

Dr. Alayne Thorpe, the vice president for education, has been with Home Study International since 1980. Dr. Thorpe has taught in the Maryland state public school system and at the University of Maryland. She has served as a master teacher, a curriculum supervisor, and a writing consultant. Dr. Thorpe holds a Ph.D. from the University of Maryland.

Faculty members are chosen on the basis of their expertise in their disciplines and their ability to counsel, advise, and instruct an international, multicultural student body.

COLLEGE PLACEMENT

Graduates of Home Study International attend colleges and universities throughout the world. The Coordinator for External Programs, the Registrar, and the Vice President for Education provide guidance counseling and college placement information to all interested students.

STUDENT BODY AND CONDUCT

Home Study International's elementary and high school enrollment is 1,800 students in grades kindergarten through 12. Because Home Study International is not limited to a traditional school year, enrollment figures may shift slightly from month to month as new students enroll and others finish their programs. Home Study International also provides opportunities for supplementing and augmenting programs for students attending traditional secondary schools.

Home Study International's student body consists of students from every state in the United States and from sixty countries.

DAILY LIFE

Home Study International students progress at their own speed. This allows most students to finish the study portion of their day early. The rest of the day is available to reinforce what is

being learned or to expand upon one's studies. The student is not held back by a classroom of other students who learn at various levels.

Full-time Home Study International students can enjoy intramural sports groups and have extra time to use the library, museums, and other learning centers near their homes.

On average, full-time students spend 4 to 5 hours a day on their studies.

COSTS AND FINANCIAL AID

HSI offered two options (grades K–8) for the 2004–05 school year—the Accredited Plan and the Non-Accredited Plan. The Accredited Plan is state approved and includes tuition, textbooks and study guides, daily lesson plans, exams, teacher assistance, grading services, record keeping, report cards, and transcript services. The 2005–06 prices for all subjects for one full year (including shipping) were preschool, $78; kindergarten, $374; Grade 1, $990; Grade 2, $948; Grade 3, $942; Grade 4, $911; Grade 5, $906; and Grade 6, $993.

The junior high program (grades 7 and 8) has been restructured to allow for more immediate interaction between parent and student. The prices for the four core courses, including shipping, were $765 for grade 7 and $785 for grade 8. High school prices (2004–05) were tuition, $172 per semester per course, plus the cost of supplies. A technology fee of $35 per semester applies for all online courses in addition to supply costs and tuition. College prices were $245 per semester hour per course, plus the cost of supplies.

The Non-Accredited Plan (K–8 only) is for those who do not choose to use HSI's teaching, grading, advising, or recordkeeping services. However, this plan does offer parents' or study guides/activity sheets/tests (no answer keys for tests) and placement advising for the student if necessary. Prices for the Non-Accredited Plan are substantially lower. Financial aid is not available. All prices are subject to change July 1 of each year.

Home Study International accepts applications for admission at any time. Applications/enrollments can now be completed online through the HSI Web site at the address listed in this In-Depth Description.

ADMISSIONS CORRESPONDENCE

Anita Jacobs, Director of Admissions/Registrar
Home Study International
12501 Old Columbia Pike
Silver Spring, Maryland 20904

Phone: 301-680-6570
     800-782-4769 (toll-free; enrollment inquiries only)
E-mail: enrollmentservices@hsi.edu
Web site: http://www.hsi.edu

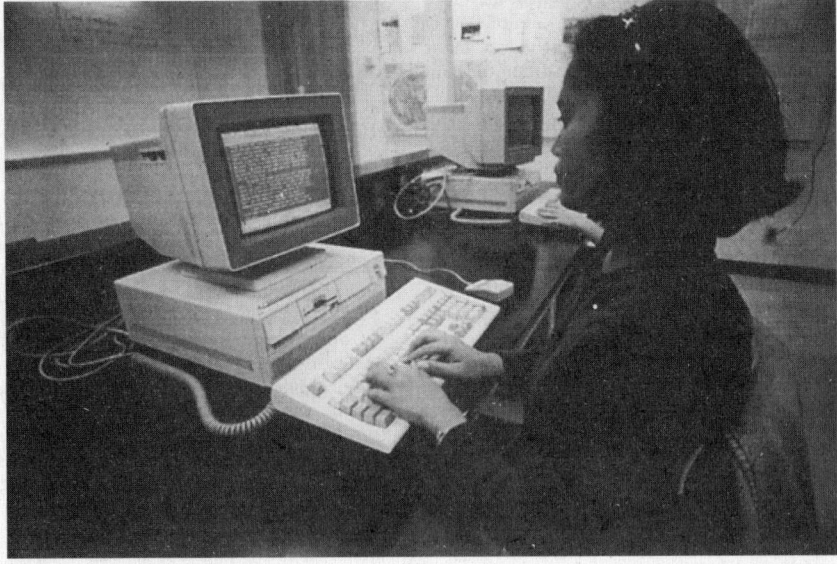

HOOSAC SCHOOL

Hoosick, New York

Type: Coeducational boarding college-preparatory school
Grades: 8–12, postgraduate year
Enrollment: 125
Head of School: Richard J. Lomuscio, Headmaster

THE SCHOOL

Hoosac is an independent coeducational boarding school. Founded in 1889, the School still follows many of the traditions for which it is well-known—for example, the nation's first student work program, in which students participate in the maintenance of their environment, and the Boar's Head and Yule Log Christmas Celebration, in which Burgess Meredith ('26) performed as a student.

Hoosac School is well suited to students who are academically motivated and are seeking a small-school environment, those who have not lived up to their potential in larger school settings, students with mild to moderate learning differences or attention deficit disorder, and students who have talent but have received poor training through the years.

Hoosick is a rural community located 30 miles northeast of Albany, New York; 7 miles west of Bennington, Vermont; and 13 miles northwest of Williamstown, Massachusetts. The name of the town, like that of the School, is one of several spellings of a Native American word meaning "Place of the Owl."

Hoosac's setting amid 350 acres of fields and woods at the head of the Taconic Valley allows for a variety of outdoor activities, and the proximity of Williams College and Rensselaer Polytechnic Institute and the larger centers of Albany and Troy provides access to a wide range of cultural and educational opportunities.

Hoosac follows the Episcopal tradition in the short chapel services offered several times a week.

The School is operated by the Headmaster for an independent, self-perpetuating Board of Trustees. The plant is valued at $11 million.

Hoosac is accredited by the Middle States Association of Colleges and Schools and chartered by the New York State Board of Regents. It is a member of the National Association of Independent Schools, the Secondary School Admission Test Board, the National Association of Episcopal Schools, and the New York State Association of Independent Schools.

ACADEMIC PROGRAMS

The student-faculty ratio of 5:1 ensures that classes are kept small and that students receive a great deal of individual attention. One-to-one tutorials, independent study, and Advanced Placement courses are all available.

The curriculum consists of English I-IV, French I-II, ancient and modern European history, global studies, U.S. history, early American history, algebra I and II, geometry, precalculus, biology, chemistry, physics, psychology, earth science, computer literacy, art, photography, drama, music, film appreciation, criminology, fashion design, dance, and health. Advanced Placement courses are offered in calculus, U.S. history, and English.

In addition, the Oasis Program provides individual instruction to students with mild learning problems or attention deficit, relying on tutorials to establish healthy patterns of self-reliance.

Graduation requirements include the following: 4 years of English, 3 of science, 3 of mathematics, 3 of history and social studies (including 1 of U.S. history), 2 of a foreign language, 1 of a lab science, 1 of health, 1 of ethics, 1 of computers, and 1 trimester each of music, drama, and art. A 3-year ESL program is available for international students.

Hoosac uses "Mastery Teaching." The concept of mastery education is older than the one-room schoolhouse where it was practiced; only the name is new. Mastery is an approach commonly used in every walk of life except formal education. For example, a person who wants to learn how to play tennis would not say, "I have 40 minutes to learn to serve. If I cannot do it in this time, I will never play tennis." Learning to serve a tennis ball well may take time. Therefore, a person would keep practicing until he or she mastered it. As in tennis, many things in life require time and repetition to learn. Given enough time and exposure, most people can master most things. Given enough exposure and support, students can learn almost anything.

Mastery uses testing as part of the instructional process. Each test reveals what a student does not know. On the basis of this, he or she is redirected and retaught in the weak areas. Each test, therefore, is a review of a student's knowledge for the purpose of reteaching. For example, a student takes a test, which is corrected and returned in class. The student is then retaught the information that they did not understand and tested again. Students also get extra help outside of class.

Mastery is an old and proven technique. It is used all over the United States, and it is a successful approach for most students. It allows the student to develop self-confidence and self-reliance.

FACULTY AND ADVISERS

Hoosac's Headmaster is Richard J. Lomuscio. Mr. Lomuscio is a graduate of NYU. He has been a newspaper editor and taught in both public and private schools. Mr. Lomuscio has served Hoosac for twenty-eight years in many capacities—teacher of math, French, science, history, and English; housemaster; coach; college counselor; Director of Athletics; Director of Studies; Dean; and Headmaster.

The faculty numbers 20, of whom 8 are women. Faculty members live on campus. They and their families participate fully in all activities.

The School's adviser system is one more example of the individual attention given to students. The system provides the structure and

support students need to be successful. A faculty member is responsible for up to 8 advisees, whom he or she sees at least twice a week—once in a private meeting and once in a group meeting. Advisers receive biweekly reports on each student from the student's teachers so that any changes or problems that arise can be handled quickly. Parents also play a significant role in this system; they can monitor their child's progress by keeping in close contact with his or her adviser.

COLLEGE PLACEMENT

College counseling, supervised by the Headmaster, begins in the junior year, and students visit colleges in the summer and during the fall. Admissions officers from many colleges and universities visit Hoosac.

In the last several years graduates have been accepted to Bennington, Berklee College of Music, Boston College, Boston University, Bowdoin, Clarkson, Connecticut College, Cornell, Drexel, Hamilton, Hartwick, Manhattan, Northeastern, NYU, Penn State, Rensselaer, St. Lawrence, Syracuse, Texas A&M, Trinity (Hartford), Vassar, Vanderbilt, Washington and Jefferson, Wheaton, and the Universities of Hartford, New Hampshire, Southern California, and Vermont.

STUDENT BODY AND CONDUCT

Hoosac enrolls approximately 110 boarding boys and girls. Most students come from the northeastern United States; others are from Georgia, Virginia, Pennsylvania, Idaho, California, and Florida and from several other countries.

Students are represented in school affairs through a traditional prefect system and play major leadership roles in important areas of school life. The kitchen and dining hall are supervised by student stewards. All class bells are rung by a student bell ringer, and the coaches are helped by student assistants. The work program is supervised by student proctors, as are the dormitory facilities. The faculty and administration offer careful guidance in order to strengthen the lessons of leadership and responsibility.

Minor infractions of Hoosac's rules and regulations result in an obligation to donate work for the benefit of the School community; more serious infractions of the regulations can result in suspension, and very serious cases can lead to dismissal. Possession or use of illegal drugs results in automatic expulsion from school, even for a first offense.

ACADEMIC FACILITIES

Tibbits Hall, built in 1828 and remodeled in 1860, is a freestone Gothic castle containing offices, classrooms, a dormitory, and faculty apartments. Wood Hall contains the School's library, a faculty apartment, and a dormitory

area. Crosby Arts Center provides facilities for theater, art, music, and dance.

Other buildings include Memorial Dining Hall (1963), which houses a spacious dining area and student lounge as well as classrooms. Blake Hall (1969) is the science building and includes classrooms, laboratories, a darkroom, a lecture hall, and an observatory equipped with two telescopes.

BOARDING AND GENERAL FACILITIES

Lewisohn and Dudley houses are small dormitories. Whitcomb Hall houses the chapel, a dormitory, and a faculty residence.

Several more recent buildings complete the campus. Pitt Mason Hall (1967) is the largest of the dormitories, housing 30 students; it includes apartments for three faculty families. Lavino House (1969) also serves as a dormitory. The Edith McCullough House (1990) holds 8 students and a faculty family, as does Cannon House, built in 1970.

About half the dormitory rooms are doubles, and the rest are singles. At least one faculty family lives in every dormitory.

ATHLETICS

Every student is required to participate in athletics or an athletics alternative during the afternoon. The School fields teams at the varsity level in soccer, ice hockey, lacrosse, basketball, tennis, baseball, and volleyball and offers skiing and flag football as intramural sports. Modern dance and fitness classes are also available. Hoosac's teams participate in league competition.

Campus sports facilities include three soccer fields, one baseball diamond, a skating pond, 6 miles of cross-country running and skiing trails, and tennis courts. Students can also fish in nearby trout streams and hike and camp in Tibbits Forest. The School's sports complex includes a gymnasium, a locker and shower area, and a swimming pool. Hoosac has a ski slope on campus as well.

EXTRACURRICULAR OPPORTUNITIES

Because the student body is small, individual interests and casual groups, rather than formal clubs, are emphasized. Extracurricular activities include student publications, academic clubs, music, and art. The students present theatrical productions and participate annually in the century-old Boar's Head and Yule Log Christmas Celebration.

The Student Activities Committee works with a faculty member to provide weekend opportunities. Informal organized activities include hiking, camping, horseback riding, fishing, skiing, and skating. Traditional events for the School community include two Parents' Weekends. There is a banquet with a speaker every Friday evening.

A driver's education course is offered, as is a Red Cross lifeguarding course.

DAILY LIFE

Breakfast is served at 7:20 a.m. Chapel is at 8:05, followed by a schoolwide meeting. Classes run from 8:35 to 2:50; there is a break at noon for a family-style sit-down lunch. Sports take place in the afternoon after classes. Dinner is at 6, followed each evening by a required study period. Lights-out is at 10:30.

Classes meet six days a week for 45 minutes each period; Wednesday and Saturday are half days to leave time for special activities and free time.

WEEKEND LIFE

Dances, concerts, lectures, and other special activities are planned with local schools, such as Emma Willard, Stoneleigh-Burnham, Miss Hall's, and Doane Stuart. On Saturday evenings, students go to movies or the mall in Pittsfield, Albany, and Saratoga or at the School or participate in other leisure-time activities. They may also attend musical, theatrical, and educational programs at local colleges, particularly Williams and Rensselaer in Troy.

Following brunch on Sunday, students explore the woodlands, climb, hike, fish, or ski on campus or at nearby resort areas. One long weekend is scheduled during each trimester, and students may take additional weekend leaves.

COSTS AND FINANCIAL AID

Boarding tuition for 2005–06 is approximately $26,200. Hoosac, which subscribes to the School and Student Service for Financial Aid, grants financial aid on the basis of demonstrated need. Approximately 30 percent of the students receive aid totaling more than $400,000 per year.

ADMISSIONS INFORMATION

New students are accepted at all grade levels on the basis of previous academic records and a personal interview. The first step for interested students and their families is to request a catalog and application and schedule a visit to the campus.

APPLICATION TIMETABLE

Candidates are encouraged to apply by March 15, although applications are considered at any time during the year as long as there are spaces available.

ADMISSIONS CORRESPONDENCE

Dean S. Foster, Assistant Headmaster
Hoosac School
Hoosick, New York 12089
Phone: 800-822-0159 (toll-free)
Fax: 518-686-3370
E-mail: info@hoosac.com
Web site: http://www.hoosac.com

Photo by Gabriel Amadeus Cooney

Photo by Gabriel Amadeus Cooney

THE HOTCHKISS SCHOOL

Lakeville, Connecticut

Type: Coeducational boarding and day college-preparatory school
Grades: 9–12 (Prep, Lower Middle, Upper Middle, Senior), postgraduate year
Enrollment: 567
Head of School: Robert H. Mattoon Jr.

THE SCHOOL

The Hotchkiss School was founded by Maria Bissell Hotchkiss in 1891 at the urging of President Timothy Dwight of Yale. The School was established to prepare young men in the basic skills of the classical curriculum then in vogue so that they might go on to attend Yale. The Hotchkiss tradition of academic excellence prevails today but with a much broader scope of course offerings and within a coeducational community.

A small-school community with a large-school diversity, Hotchkiss strives to develop in students a lifelong love of learning, responsible citizenship, and personal integrity. The Hotchkiss School's Statement of Goals and Purposes is as follows: The School is a community based on trust, mutual respect, and compassion, and it holds all members of the community accountable for upholding these values. The School is committed to mastery of learning skills, development of intellectual curiosity, excellence, and creativity in all disciplines, and enthusiastic participation in athletics and other school activities. The School encourages students to develop clarity of thought, confidence and facility in expressing ideas, and artistic and aesthetic sensitivity. In and out of the classroom, all members of the community are expected to subject their views and actions to critical examination and to accept responsibility for them. The School hopes that graduates will leave Hotchkiss with a commitment to environmental stewardship and service to others and with a greater understanding of themselves and of their roles in a global society.

The village of Lakeville is in the Township of Salisbury, a community of 3,700 people in rural northwestern Connecticut. The School is situated on 545 acres of hills and woodlands bordering on two lakes. The campus is 2¼ hours from New York City; 1½ hours from Hartford, Connecticut; and 3 hours from Boston.

The Hotchkiss School is a nonprofit corporation governed by a 25-member Board of Trustees. The School's endowment is currently valued at more than $317 million. In celebration of the School's centennial, a $100-million capital campaign was completed, allowing for enhancement of academic programs and renovation and enlargement of campus facilities. In addition to the $10-million renovation of the science building, the School has enlarged and remodeled the athletic facilities, raised increased funding for financial assistance, completed a $20-million state-of-the-art music facility, and has plans to renovate the dorms. The Annual Fund generates more than $3 million for the yearly operating budget. The Hotchkiss Alumni Association maintains contact with more than 8,550 alumni, many of whom provide substantial financial support and are active in student recruiting activities.

The School is accredited by the New England Association of Schools and Colleges and the Connecticut Association of Independent Schools. It holds membership in the National Association of Independent Schools, the National Association of Principals of Schools for Girls, and the Council for Advancement and Support of Education.

ACADEMIC PROGRAMS

The curriculum at Hotchkiss has evolved over the years from a classical, formal, and prescriptive set of courses with limited sectioning to an increasingly diverse but interwoven learning opportunity, offering a choice of more than 225 separate courses, some of them interdisciplinary and many offered as seminars. Classes begin in September and end in June, with time off for Thanksgiving Break, Winter Break, and Spring Break.

Seventeen courses, including 4 years of English; 3 years of mathematics; 3 years of one language; 1 year of American history; 1 year of art, including art, dance, drama, music, or photography; and 1 year of biology, chemistry, or physics, are required of four-year students for graduation. Advanced Placement courses are available in many subject areas. Incoming students are given placement exams to determine the level at which they should begin their studies.

Students carry an average of five courses per semester. The average class size is 12. The School uses a letter grading system, and reports are sent to parents four times a year, or more often if the situation warrants it. Faculty members provide extra help in and out of the classroom setting and student tutors are available to help their peers. In addition, a comprehensive study skills program supports students who find some difficulty with an intensive academic program.

Qualified upperclass students may participate in a School Year Abroad program in China, France, Italy, or Spain; the Maine Coast Semester program; the Rocky Mountain Semester program; or the CityTerm program at the Masters School. They may also apply through the English-Speaking Union for a postgraduate year of study at an English boarding school.

FACULTY AND ADVISERS

In 2004–05, the Hotchkiss faculty consisted of 128 faculty members and administrators. Ninety-four faculty members lived on the campus. Collectively, they held more than 100 advanced degrees, including seven doctorates.

Hotchkiss seeks a diverse and experienced faculty dedicated not only to teaching academic courses but also to aiding the full personal growth of each student. In addition to their teaching and administrative responsibilities, they are dormitory parents, academic advisers, and coaches.

COLLEGE PLACEMENT

Hotchkiss seeks to provide each student with the advice, support, and information necessary to make appropriate choices for future education. Three advisers guide students through the selection of colleges and the application process. More than 100 college representatives visit the School each year to conduct group meetings or interviews with students. The middle 50 percent of students taking the SAT in the class of 2004 had scores of 590 to 680 verbal and 600 to 700 math. All but 3 members of the class of 2004 are attending college. Four or more graduates of the class of 2004 are attending the following schools: Boston College, Bowdoin, Cornell, Davidson, Duke, Georgetown, Harvard, Middlebury, NYU, Princeton, Stanford, Union (New York), Williams, Yale, and the Universities of Southern California and Vermont.

STUDENT BODY AND CONDUCT

The enrollment for 2005–06 consisted of 507 boarding students and 60 day students (274 girls and 293 boys) as follows: ninth grade—95, tenth grade—152, eleventh grade—158, and twelfth grade—162. In addition, there were 18 postgraduates. Students came from thirty-three states and eighteen other countries. International students constituted 12 percent and students who are members of minority groups accounted for 26 percent of the student body.

The day-to-day life at Hotchkiss is governed by several important principles: concern for others, respect for all members of the community, and understanding and adherence to the rules as stated in the Hotchkiss School Handbook. The actions and attitudes of each student at Hotchkiss should be governed by concern for others, with the rules serving as guidelines for expected behavior. Composed of students and faculty members, the Hotchkiss Discipline Committee reviews reports of possible infractions of School rules and in each case makes recommendations for action to the Head of School.

ACADEMIC FACILITIES

A great advantage of the Hotchkiss campus is the centralization of the academic facilities. Handsomely renovated and significantly enlarged in 1995, the Main Building is the hub of campus life. Main Building has wings accommodating the student center, chapel, auditorium, and dining hall; two computer labs; the Cullman Art Center; the Tremaine Art Gallery, dance studio, and black-box theater; and the Edsel Ford Library, which holds a collection of more than 80,000 volumes. In fall 2005, a new wing of the Main Building was completed, which houses the School's state-of-the-art music and art facilities. All classes other than those in science are held in the Main Building. The recently renovated Griswold Science Building has a full range of laboratories and areas for independent study, extensive photographic facilities, a weather station, and a radio station with full broadcasting capabilities.

BOARDING AND GENERAL FACILITIES

Hotchkiss has ten dormitories. About two thirds of the students reside in single rooms on corridors organized by class, averaging 15 to 20 students per corridor. Faculty members and senior proctors reside on each corridor and provide extensive supervision and guidance.

The School has one dining hall, a student center with a snack bar, a bookstore that carries a full line of supplies, and a number of areas for informal gatherings. The fully equipped, recently renovated Wieler Infirmary on campus is open 24 hours a day and the Sharon Hospital is 7 miles down the road.

ATHLETICS

The athletics program is one of the School's great strengths and a major source of its spirit. All students participate in the program every season, and they pursue an activity of their choice at a level to suit their abilities.

The School prides itself on its ability to compete equally with other New England secondary schools. Hotchkiss also regularly takes part in annual coeducational New England championship meets in cross-country, field hockey, football, swimming, squash, track, volleyball, water polo, and boys' wrestling.

The School's athletic facilities are superb. A 212,000-square-foot athletic and fitness center opened in 2002. The Hotchkiss community now enjoys a second indoor ice rink, a field house with three basketball/volleyball courts and an elevated track, an expanded wrestling/multipurpose room, eight international-style squash courts, and a ten-lane swimming facility with a separate diving well. Other existing athletic facilities include a nine-hole golf course, a 400-meter all-weather track, a regulation baseball field, two football fields, four field hockey fields, five soccer/lacrosse fields, two paddle tennis courts, and twenty all-weather and three indoor tennis courts as well as a lakefront with a boathouse.

EXTRACURRICULAR OPPORTUNITIES

Because Hotchkiss is not adjacent to a metropolitan area, extensive efforts are made to bring cultural events to the campus and encourage students to participate in the wide variety of clubs. Among the most active organizations are the Hotchkiss Dramatic Association, which schedules three major productions per year and presents as many as twelve student plays; the music department, which sponsors and encourages a wide range of informal musical groups; and the various student publications.

The community service club, the St. Luke's Society, is involved in volunteer community affairs, including tutoring the handicapped, helping the aging, working in the Sharon Hospital, and working with the local volunteer ambulance service. Hotchkiss is a campus chapter member of Habitat for Humanity. Hotchkiss also has a School service program, whereby each student is expected to perform service within the School community for at least one semester each year.

DAILY LIFE

Classes are held six days a week, with Wednesdays and Saturdays as half-days to accommodate interscholastic athletic competitions. A typical day begins with breakfast served cafeteria-style between 7 and 8:30 a.m. The first period begins at 8, with 45-minute class periods thereafter. Students eat lunch during their free noontime period. Classes end at 3 p.m., and sports begin at 3:30. The dining hall is open for dinner between 5:30 and 6:45. Evening study times are set for ninth and tenth graders between 8 and 10.

WEEKEND LIFE

Students are permitted to take weekends away from the campus, but most choose to remain at the School and join the variety of activities taking place. The standard weekend events include sports competitions, movies, dances, concerts, and other scheduled activities. As students move from the lower classes to the senior year, they are permitted more weekends away from campus.

COSTS AND FINANCIAL AID

Tuition for 2005–06 was $33,310 for boarding students and $28,315 for day students. Tuition payments are due twice yearly at the start of each semester.

Hotchkiss offered more than $4.7 million in scholarships for the 2005–06 school year. In 2005–06, 35 percent of enrolled students received some level of financial assistance. Awards are made to families on the basis of family financial need, as determined by the School and Student Service for Financial Aid in Princeton, New Jersey. Those who do not qualify for direct assistance or who need additional assistance above the amount awarded may apply for loans.

ADMISSIONS INFORMATION

The School seeks to enroll students of good will and strong character who will be examples of integrity and decency. The School seeks students who provide evidence of academic ability and intellectual curiosity. Hotchkiss students should be prepared for and are expected to take advantage of the academic and cocurricular opportunities available at the School. The School aims to attract students from among the most accomplished and promising young people of diverse backgrounds, experiences, and expectations.

Applicants must complete a formal application of admission, which includes a writing sample and applicant project as well as recommendations from three teachers and an official school record. Applicants to the ninth, tenth, and eleventh grades are also required to submit results of the SSAT or ISEE. Applicants to the senior or postgraduate year are required to submit scores from the PSAT or SAT. An interview is a required part of the admission process.

APPLICATION TIMETABLE

Initial inquiries are welcome at any time. Visits to the campus include a tour (usually given by a student guide) and an interview with an admission counselor. It is strongly recommended that candidates and their parents visit when the School is in session. If this is impossible, an interview may be arranged at the School or elsewhere through the Office of Admission.

A final application and a $40 nonrefundable application fee must be submitted by January 15. Hotchkiss notifies candidates and their families of admission decisions by March 10, with a reply date of April 10.

ADMISSIONS CORRESPONDENCE

William D. Leahy, Dean of Admission
The Hotchkiss School
Box 800
Lakeville, Connecticut 06039

Phone: 860-435-3102
Fax: 860-435-0042
E-mail: admission@hotchkiss.org
Web site: http://www.hotchkiss.org

HOWE MILITARY SCHOOL

Howe, Indiana

Type: Coeducational boarding college-preparatory and military school
Grades: 5–12: Junior High, 5–8; High School, 9–12
Enrollment: School total: 189; High School: 120
Head of School: Dr. Duane VanOrden, Superintendent

THE SCHOOL

Howe Military School is a private, college-preparatory boarding school for boys and girls in grades 5 through 12. Situated in the northernmost part of the state, the village of Howe (population 500) is midway between LaGrange, Indiana, and Sturgis, Michigan. Accessible via the Indiana Toll Road (Interstate 80/90), the School is an hour from South Bend, Indiana, 3 hours from Chicago and Detroit, and 5 hours from Cincinnati.

The School was established in 1884 as the result of a bequest to the Episcopal Church by the Honorable John Badlam Howe. The military program was instituted in 1895, and since 1920, the School has had a Junior ROTC unit sponsored by the Department of the Army. Howe has been designated an Honor Military School with Distinction by the Department of Defense.

Howe Military School seeks to provide a balanced education that affords opportunities for college preparation through the academic program, physical development through the athletics program, leadership through the military program, and spiritual development through Christian worship and activities. Howe maintains its historic affiliation with the Episcopal Church and welcomes young people of all faiths.

A nonprofit institution, Howe is governed by a self-perpetuating Board of Trustees, 20 in number, which meets quarterly. Included on the board are the Bishop of the Episcopal Diocese of Northern Indiana (its head), the Superintendent, parents, and alumni. The Alumni Association, which represents the more than 3,100 living graduates, elects the 2 alumni board members.

Howe Military School is accredited by the state of Indiana and the North Central Association of Colleges and Schools. Howe is accredited by the Independent Schools Association of the Central States. Howe has memberships in the Association of Military Colleges and Schools of the United States, the Council for Advancement and Support of Education, the National Association of Independent Schools, and the Association of Boarding Schools (TABS).

ACADEMIC PROGRAMS

The school year, from late August to early June, is divided into semesters, with Thanksgiving, Christmas, and Spring Break vacations. Classes, which have a maximum enrollment of 16, meet five days a week.

The average class size is 8 to 10 students. Cadets may receive extra help from teachers during the daily extra help period. To encourage academic growth, each cadet is assigned a Potential Achievement Rating, based on objective test results, teacher ratings, and a self-evaluation. The cadet is expected to attain and maintain this goal, which is revised periodically to reflect changes in performance. Grades are sent to parents every six weeks.

Computers are integrated into all classes, with two full labs (one of which is a multimedia lab) and a computer for every teacher. All are networked into each High School barracks room, where each cadet also has his or her own computer. All High School cadets are required to lease a personal computer through the School.

To graduate, High School cadets must complete 21 academic units, including 4 of English; 3 of mathematics, including algebra I and geometry; 3 of science; 3 of social studies, including United States history and government; 2 of the same foreign language; 1 of computer science; 1½ of health/physical education; and 1–4 years of leadership excellence training. The additional units are taken in elective courses. The High School curriculum includes full-year courses in English I–IV, prealgebra, algebra I–II, geometry, college algebra/trigonometry, calculus, French I–III, German I–III, Spanish I–IV, biology, advanced biology, chemistry, physical science, physics, environmental science, U.S. history, world history, accounting I–II, band, choir, and woods I–II. Semester courses are offered in computer programming, computer graphics, keyboarding, multimedia graphics, health (substance-abuse prevention included), electricity, power mechanics, biochemistry, organic chemistry, economics, Christian ethics (required), and sociology.

Military training for the younger cadets consists of drill, "the manual of arms, the school of the soldier, and other instructions contributing to the precision and poise of the individual and the esprit de corps of the group." High School courses cover a variety of topics, such as drill, hygiene, first aid, weapons safety, land navigation, and military history.

FACULTY AND ADVISERS

The full-time faculty consists of 26 men and 9 women. Six Tactical Officers and their families live in the barracks, and many of the faculty members live on campus or in the village of Howe. The faculty holds 16 baccalaureate degrees and 11 master's degrees. Faculty benefits include insurance and retirement plans, payment for advanced study, and Social Security. Two retired army officers and 2 noncommissioned officers conduct the JROTC program. The infirmary is staffed during the day by a registered nurse. Evening and night care is provided by EMTs. Physician checks are scheduled as needed.

COLLEGE PLACEMENT

Annually, nearly 97 percent of Howe graduates go on to higher education. From the 2005 graduating class, 97 percent were accepted to the schools of their choosing and enrolled in colleges and universities across the United States. Recent graduates are attending such schools of higher learning as DePauw, Kenyon, Loyola Chicago, Miami (Ohio), Michigan State, Norwich, Ohio State, Purdue, Rose Hulman, St. Mary's, Spelman, the United States Air Force Academy, the United States Merchant Marine Academy, the United States Military Academy, the United States Naval Academy, Valparaiso, Virginia Military Institute, Wooster, and the Universities of Arizona, Chicago, Illinois, Indiana, Miami, Michigan, Tampa, and Washington.

STUDENT BODY AND CONDUCT

Most of the students come from Illinois, Indiana, Michigan, and Ohio. The School also accepts students from all fifty states and around the world.

The Corps of Cadets is governed by the rules and regulations of the School. It is also expected to live up to the Cadet's Personal Code of Honor, which states: "I will not lie, steal or cheat, nor tolerate among us anyone who does." The School motto is "Faith and Honor."

ACADEMIC FACILITIES

Classes are held in the Memorial Academic Building and annex, which together provide twenty classrooms and four science laboratories. The main biology lab was completely remodeled in 1996. Junior High classes are held in White Hall. The Grace Libey Library contains 14,000 volumes and three reference computers with CD-ROM capability; limited Internet access is available in the library. Other School buildings are Bouton Auditorium, the Industrial Arts Building, St. James Chapel, All Saints' Chapel, Memorial Gym, the Quartermaster Store, and Herrick Administration Building.

BOARDING AND GENERAL FACILITIES

Junior High cadets reside in the Frank M. Little Barracks, which provides quarters for 2 Tactical Officers and their families. High School cadets are housed in four barracks that also provide quarters for the Tactical Officers and their families. Each High School barracks room allows one computer per student. Cadets eat in the Major Merritt Dining Hall; in addition, cadets may visit the canteen and Fr. Jennings Recreational Center. The Drs. Wade Infirmary has thirty beds and is staffed day and night.

ATHLETICS

The 150-acre campus includes a 50-acre athletics complex, sports fields, and six tennis courts. Indoor athletics facilities are located in the gymnasium, which provides a wrestling room, a basketball court, and a weight room that was totally refurbished in 1999. An indoor swimming pool is adjacent to the gymnasium and was renovated in 2000. Varsity teams in baseball,

basketball, cross-country, golf, soccer, girls' softball, tennis, track, girls' volleyball, and wrestling compete with those of other independent and public high schools. There are intramural teams in volleyball, swimming, basketball, softball, and touch football. Cadets may also play tennis. Junior High cadets participate in basketball, cross-country, wrestling, soccer, golf, and track.

EXTRACURRICULAR OPPORTUNITIES

Many extracurricular activities reflect the military nature of the School. Among the cadet organizations are the Rangers, the Hussars (drill team), the rifle team, VHC (the lettermen's club), the Old Guard (cadets in attendance four or more years), and the Color Guard.

Cadets may join the staff of the School newspaper and the yearbook. Cadets may participate in the Howe Military School radio station, WHWE-FM, where they put together shows and perform other aspects of managing a radio station. They may also participate in Howe's chapter of the National Forensic League or the National Thespians. Qualified cadets are elected to the Cum Laude Society. Cadets who consistently earn a 3.5 GPA are entered in the Alpha Delta Tau Society. Musical groups include the marching band, the concert band, and the chapel choir. Cadets of all ages may receive acolyte training and participate regularly in chapel services.

DAILY LIFE

A typical day begins with First Call at 6 a.m. and First Mess from 7 to 7:45. Regular academic classes begin at 8 and continue until 3 p.m., with a break for lunch from 11:40 until 12:15. For those who need or want it, an extra-help period immediately follows classes, from 3 until 3:35. Athletics begin at 4 and continue until 5:30. At 6:05 the Cadets form up for the ceremony to lower the flag (Retreat). From 6:15 until 6:30 on Monday, Tuesday, Thursday, and Friday evenings, there is a prayer service in one of the chapels. Third Mess begins at 6:35. Evening study hall runs from 7:30 until 9:15. Junior High taps is at 9:30, at 10 for underclassmen, and at 11 for seniors.

WEEKEND LIFE

Cadets have free time on Friday evenings and Saturday and Sunday afternoons, for a half hour each evening, and for brief periods during the school day. Social activities include movies, occasional professional entertainment, three sockhops and two formal dances each year, numerous club dinners, a trip to Cedar Point, mall shopping, theater productions, and bowling parties. Among the traditional annual events are a Family Picnic, Founders' Day, Boar's Head Dinner, family weekends in September and February, Alumni Weekend, and Mother's Day Weekend. Field trips are arranged to such places as nearby zoos, the Football Hall of Fame, Greenfield Village, the Henry Ford Museum, Cedar Point Amusement Park, and Chicago museums.

COSTS AND FINANCIAL AID

It is understood that once a cadet is enrolled, he or she remains for the entire academic year or, in cases of late enrollment, for the balance of the year. The overall cost for the 2005–06 year was $23,000, plus a computer fee of $535 for High School cadets. The School does not provide health and accident insurance, so this should be taken care of by the parents.

Transportation to and from school during vacation periods and on open weekends is over and above the estimated cost. A cadet should be provided with a weekly allowance or spending money; the School recommends a moderate amount.

There are some additional charges according to the cadet's interests, such as fees for band instrument rental or private music lessons.

There are three payment plans available. The Basic Payment Plan requires full payment of $23,000 by the entrance date. The Deferred Payment Plan and the Monthly Payment Plan are available at costs of $400 and $600, respectively. The Deferred Payment Plan requires 60 percent of the total cost to be paid at registration, with the remaining 40 percent due on or before December 10. The Monthly Payment Plan requires payment in ten installments. These program payments are due commencing March 10 and ending December 10. This plan may be selected during any month, by issuing payment for months missed and continuing payment through December 10. Parents who are interested in a tuition loan or further information should call the Admissions Office.

The School has a limited amount of scholarship funds available through endowments from friends of Howe. These funds are awarded on the basis of academic ability and performance, conduct, general attitude, and family financial need. Parents wishing to apply for scholarship funds should contact the Director of Admissions for a Financial Aid Application Form.

ADMISSIONS INFORMATION

Howe seeks boys and girls of good character who have the ability to do college-preparatory work. Howe Military School is neither a correctional facility nor a therapeutic school. Howe is a traditional, private, college-preparatory boarding school. Howe's military orientation is not intended to prepare students for the military service. The military program is used to teach Howe's students self-discipline, focus, organization, and authority. Cadets are accepted in grades 5–12 on the basis of admission test results, school records, and three school references. Admission tests are administered at Howe at the time of the campus visit; if candidates cannot take the tests at the School, they may arrange to do so under supervision at a more convenient location. There is a $100 application fee.

APPLICATION TIMETABLE

Initial inquiries are welcome at any time. Campus tours are arranged, in conjunction with interviews, from 8 a.m. to 4:30 p.m. Indiana time on weekdays and by appointment on weekends.

ADMISSIONS CORRESPONDENCE

Dr. Brent Smith, Director of Admissions
Howe Military School
P.O. Box 240
Howe, Indiana 46746

Phone: 260-562-2131 Ext. 221
    888-GO-2-HOWE (toll-free)
Fax: 260-562-3678
E-mail: admissions@howemilitary.com
Web site: http://www.howemilitary.com

THE HUN SCHOOL OF PRINCETON

Princeton, New Jersey

Type: Coeducational boarding (grades 9–PG) and day (grades 6–12) college-preparatory school
Grades: 6–PG: Middle School, 6–8; Upper School, 9–12, postgraduate year
Enrollment: School total: 580; Upper School: 492
Head of School: Dr. James M. Byer '62, Headmaster

THE SCHOOL

The Hun School of Princeton was established as the Princeton Math School in 1914 by Dr. John Gale Hun, an assistant professor of mathematics at Princeton University. The School expanded its curriculum and facilities as colleges implemented higher standards of admission. In 1925, the The Hun School moved to its present location, a 45-acre campus in Princeton's residential western section. The School was incorporated under the direction of a board of trustees in 1944. Today, the board consists of 31 members.

Students enjoy the advantages of a town that is home to one of the greatest universities in the country and yet preserves the flavor of a small community. The School is within walking distance of Princeton University, and New York and Philadelphia are both about an hour away by train, bus, or automobile.

The Hun School is dedicated to providing a strong college-preparatory program that leads to informed college choices. A full range of athletics and activities supplement a strong curriculum designed to stimulate critical thinking and analysis and to inspire curiosity. Competent, caring faculty members work closely with students to promote excellence and self-esteem in an environment of high but fair expectations. The faculty and curriculum are responsive to individual learning styles and interests. The total program is committed to the development of solid scholarship and sound character in an environment dedicated to timeless values: honor, service, perseverance, responsibility, compassion, respect, and leadership.

The Hun School enjoys strong support from parents, trustees, alumni, faculty and staff members, foundations, and friends of the School. Through this support, the School recently completed major additions to the library, dining hall, and academic building and has built an ecosystem pond and a health and fitness center. The School is now embarking on a fund-raising campaign to finance the construction of a new athletic complex.

The Hun School is accredited by the Middle States Association of Colleges and Schools and approved by the Department of Education of the state of New Jersey. It is a member of the College Board, National Association of Independent Schools, the Association of Boarding Schools, National Association for College Admission Counseling, Council for Advancement and Support of Education, Cum Laude Society, and National Association for Foreign Student Affairs.

ACADEMIC PROGRAMS

The Hun School requires 19½ units for graduation, including 4 in English, 3 in mathematics, 3 in history, 3 in laboratory science, 2 in foreign language, and ½ in fine arts. Students may choose from more than ninety-five courses, including government, economics, the arts, and public speaking. Foreign language study includes French, Latin, and Spanish.

Upper School offerings also include independent study, honors, accelerated, and Advanced Placement courses. Qualified students may take courses at Princeton University. Hun has one of the oldest international student programs in the country and an Academic Learning Skills Program for students with mild learning differences.

The grading system uses numerals; 60 is the minimum passing grade. The academic year is divided into eighteen-week semesters, each containing two marking periods. Term examinations are given at the end of each semester, and academic reports are issued to parents four times a year. Written progress reports are also issued three or more times annually.

Classes average 14 students each. Five is the average number of courses taken each term. During the day, some students may have a free period available for study; in the evening, boarding students study in their rooms or in the library. For academic reasons, some students may be assigned to a supervised study hall during the school day. Students may also use their free time in the Writing and Study Strategies Centers. There is a period scheduled at the end of each day when all faculty members are available to meet students individually or in small groups to review, clarify, or expand classroom learning.

FACULTY AND ADVISERS

The faculty consists of 63 men and 52 women, all of whom serve full-time. There are 47 faculty members who hold master's or doctoral degrees. Thirty of the faculty members live on campus. They have an average of twelve years of teaching experience. Faculty turnover is low.

Headmaster James M. Byer '62, Ed.D., was appointed in 1994. A graduate of Marietta College, Rider College, and Nova University, Dr. Byer is an alumnus of The Hun School and was the Headmaster of the University School of Nova University. He has also held teaching and administrative positions at the Pine Crest School in Fort Lauderdale, Florida, and at The Hun School earlier in his career.

The School supports the professional development of the staff by providing grants for graduate study and by encouraging the faculty to participate in workshops and conferences. Faculty members coach, counsel, and supervise extracurricular activities in addition to teaching.

COLLEGE PLACEMENT

The College Counseling Office arranges group and individual meetings with students, starting in the sophomore year. By the senior year, regular individual meetings are conducted that center on the selection of institutions that meet the academic and extracurricular interests of the students. All students are encouraged to visit colleges, attend college fairs, and meet with the representatives of more than 200 institutions that visit The Hun School annually.

During the spring semester, the School, in conjunction with other local independent schools, hosts a college fair, inviting representatives from more than 300 colleges and universities to the Princeton area. The Hun School also sponsors a special evening program in the fall of the junior year and again in the fall of the senior year to explain the college selection process. In the past, the programs have featured college directors of admission, Educational Testing Service representatives, and financial aid experts. In the summer sessions, Hun also conducts briefings on preparing for the SAT.

In 2005, 140 graduates entered college. Students attend Boston College, Colgate, Dartmouth, Duke, Florida State, Harvard, Penn State, Princeton, Rutgers, Stanford, Tufts, Wellesley, Yale, the Universities of Notre Dame and Pennsylvania, and others.

STUDENT BODY AND CONDUCT

The composition of the Upper School is as follows: 106 students in grade 9, 121 in grade 10, 135 in grade 11, 117 in grade 12, and 13 postgraduates. While the largest group of students comes from New Jersey, New York, and Pennsylvania, seventeen states and fourteen countries are represented; about 7 percent of the students are from other countries.

Each member of the School community is expected to be responsible, self-disciplined, and concerned for the welfare of all. The Hun School has an Honor Code, and, through School agencies, students have a voice in the determination and enforcement of rules. The Discipline Committee, with voting student representation, makes recommendations to the Headmaster. The Honor Council, composed of students and faculty members, hears cases relating to the Honor Code and makes recommendations to the Headmaster, teachers, and students.

ACADEMIC FACILITIES

The Chesebro Academic Center and the Buck Activities Center, the two academic buildings, contain thirty-two classrooms, six science laboratories, three computer centers (thirty-six stations), photography darkrooms, an art studio, a ceramics and sculpture studio with a potter's wheel and kiln, and a music studio. Other academic facilities include a renovated 50,000-volume library with more than 45 online and CD-ROM databases, a greenhouse, a vocal music room, a wet laboratory, an aquarium, project rooms, and television and radio broadcast studios.

BOARDING AND GENERAL FACILITIES

Boys at The Hun School live in two dorms, one of which is for older students, and girls reside in a third dorm. All dorms are supervised by resident faculty members and student proctors. The dorms have lounges equipped with televisions and cooking facilities. Resident faculty families and students eat together in the centrally located dining hall. A bookstore and clinic are available on campus. The Student Activities Center houses a snack bar and a game room.

ATHLETICS

Every student can find a niche in the variety of individual and team sports offered at The Hun School at freshman, junior varsity, and varsity interscholastic levels and on intramural teams. The primary aims of the coaching staff are to teach individual skills, to

develop leadership and teamwork on the field, and to instill the concept of fair play. Track and field, cross-country, golf, swimming, and fencing teams are open to boys and girls on a competitive basis. In addition, boys compete in baseball, basketball, crew, football, ice hockey, lacrosse, soccer, tennis, and wrestling. Girls compete in basketball, crew, field hockey, lacrosse, soccer, softball, and tennis.

Coeducational intramural programs are offered in seasonal sports, weight lifting, dance, and other exercises promoting physical fitness. Through recreational sports programs and weekend events, students also enjoy skiing, horseback riding, hiking, fishing, canoeing, bowling, and in-line skating.

Athletics facilities include a gymnasium, a health and fitness center, eight tennis courts, a cross-country course, six playing fields, and a 400-meter all-weather track.

EXTRACURRICULAR OPPORTUNITIES

Through extracurricular activities, students may pursue special interests and develop social as well as personal skills. Clubs and other student activities, often organized around curricular and career interests, are under the direction of faculty advisers. Resident and day students work on the student newspaper, *The Mall*, and the yearbook, *Edgerstounian*, and take part in annual plays, dance performances, bands, photography, foreign-language dinners, regional math and national science competitions, student elections, and campus dances. Students also run various snack concessions at sporting events.

In response to student interest, the School arranges excursions to Broadway shows, the Metropolitan Opera, historic landmarks, or professional sports events in New York and Philadelphia.

Hun students are required to complete at least 10 hours of community service during the school year. They may serve as volunteers at local medical facilities, participate in programs such as Habitat for Humanity, or give of their time and effort to the Hun community.

DAILY LIFE

Classes for the Upper School commence at 8 a.m. and end at 2:33 p.m. Classes are 43 minutes long, except labs, which are 88 minutes. There are no Saturday classes. The academic day includes lunch and an extra-help or activity period, which ends at 3:15 p.m. Upper School athletics continue from 3:30 until 5:30. Day students share in all activities.

WEEKEND LIFE

Weekends at The Hun School involve a broad range of activities. On campus, students participate in athletic and theatrical events, visit with faculty members in a relaxed atmosphere, and have full use of the School's facilities. Taking advantage of the Princeton location, students spend time watching Ivy League sporting events or visiting McCarter Theatre. Excursions to Philadelphia and New York City are also popular, allowing for shopping, sightseeing, and enjoying the latest Broadway plays. The nearby Pocono Mountain range area offers outdoor activities, such as skiing, white-water rafting, and paintballing. Student input is essential to planning, and there is always something to do.

SUMMER PROGRAMS

Noncredit enrichment courses and credit courses for make up or acceleration are offered during a five-week summer session starting in early July. The courses are open to anyone, and about 100 students attend. About 10 members of the School's regular faculty teach. Study skills and the development of good work habits are integral parts of the program. Classes are offered in English, mathematics, foreign languages, history, and SAT preparation.

A Day Camp for students aged 6–12 is also held at the School. Sessions run from two to five weeks. A theater arts program, dance workshops, and the International Student Program, which provides ESL classes and cultural trips, are also offered.

COSTS AND FINANCIAL AID

Day student tuition for 2005–06 was $24,020. Boarding student tuition was $34,970. There are additional fees for the Academic Learning Skills Program ($13,320) and the English as a Second Language Program ($7580) and a health fee for all residents ($325). Between $390 and $590 should be budgeted for Upper School books, while Middle School students should expect to spend between $250 and $300. The School recommends a weekly allowance of between $30 and $40. At the time of contract signing, a $1000 tuition deposit is required. Commercial laundry service for resident students is available for an additional fee.

A student with a strong record who is seriously interested in the opportunities offered at The Hun School should not be deterred from applying because of financial considerations. Financial aid, which is expended mainly from the School's operating budget, is granted by the School's Financial Aid Committee on the basis of need as determined by the School and Student Service (SSS). Because student aid resources are limited, they are distributed in the most careful and equitable manner possible. Approximately 25 percent of the students receive $2 million in financial aid on the basis of need. Application forms for financial aid may be obtained from the Admissions Office.

ADMISSIONS INFORMATION

Individuals who are motivated and able to do college-preparatory work and who exhibit promise of being well-adjusted and responsible campus citizens are encouraged to apply to The Hun School. All candidates must complete and return an application to the Admissions Office. Also required are three Confidential Reference Forms (recommendations) and a school transcript, complete with any available test data and related commentary. An interview at the School is highly recommended.

All applicants take the Secondary School Admission Test, administered by the Secondary School Admission Test Board. The entrance difficulty level at Hun is considered moderately difficult. Admission is determined by the applicant's previous record, entrance tests, and potential for college matriculation. Of the 559 students who applied for grades 6–PG in a recent year, 281 were accepted and 164 enrolled.

The Hun School does not discriminate against applicants or students on the basis of race, religion, sex, color, or national or ethnic origin.

The School welcomes all applications. Because of campus layout and the age and design of some buildings, however, The Hun School may not be suitable for certain handicapped students. Wherever possible, the School will attempt to accommodate handicapped applicants in accordance with each applicant's needs and the School's ability to serve the student within the scope of its overall educational program and goals.

APPLICATION TIMETABLE

Inquiries are welcome at all times. The deadline for the first round of admissions decisions is January 31. Admission after that time is on a rolling basis. Students and their families are welcome to visit the School, meet the admissions staff, and tour the campus. The preferred times to visit the School are between 9 a.m. and 2 p.m. on weekdays when school is in session.

New applicants are notified of acceptance on a continuous basis from March 10 through August. The Parents' Reply Date is normally April 10, but it can be later, depending upon when the applicant is accepted.

ADMISSIONS CORRESPONDENCE

P. Terence Beach, Director of Admissions
The Hun School of Princeton
176 Edgerstoune Road
Princeton, New Jersey 08540

Phone: 609-921-7600 Ext. 4954
E-mail: admiss@hunschool.org
Web site: http://www.hunschool.org

HYDE SCHOOLS

Bath, Maine
Woodstock, Connecticut

Type: Coeducational boarding and day college-preparatory schools
Grades: Bath campus, 9–12; Woodstock campus, 9–12
Enrollment: Total, 400; Bath campus, 210; Woodstock campus, 190
Heads of Schools: Bath campus, Laurie G. Hurd; Woodstock campus, Duncan F. McCrann

THE SCHOOL

Educator Joseph Gauld founded Hyde School in 1966 in deliberate reaction to a system of education he believed had become overly preoccupied with students' abilities and insufficiently focused on their character.

For more than thirty-five years, Hyde has been developing its program in accordance with a simple premise: "Let us value attitude over aptitude, effort over ability, and character over talent." The program has evolved to focus on three emphases: character development, family renewal, and college preparation. Character development is fully integrated into School life. Family renewal results from real parent participation. Parents are not here to support the work of the faculty; they are here to develop their own character. Hyde has established a parallel curriculum for students and parents. This family-student partnership has, in fact, become the trademark of Hyde. More than 95 percent of Hyde's graduates attend four-year colleges.

The Bath campus has 145 acres of meadowland and forest that provide an inspiring background for athletics and outdoor challenges, as well as daily campus life. Bath's heritage as an important shipbuilding port provides an interesting historical environment. Bath is located on the Maine coast, just 40 minutes from Portland and 2½ hours from Boston.

A second boarding campus opened in the summer of 1996 in Woodstock, Connecticut, located in the northeastern corner of the state, 1 hour from Boston and Hartford and ½ hour from Providence, Rhode Island. Located near five cities, Providence, Rhode Island; Worcester, Massachusetts; Boston, Massachusetts; Hartford, Connecticut; and New Haven, Connecticut, the Woodstock campus offers extensive cultural and historical opportunities. Hyde owns and operates a fully staffed wilderness education program located in Eustis, Maine, on 600 acres at Flagstaff Lake. Both Hyde campuses utilize this property for outdoor challenges.

Hyde is governed by a self-perpetuating Board of Governors, which meets regularly.

The School plant at Bath is valued at $35 million, and the facilities at Woodstock are valued at $41 million. Annual operating expenses are approximately $15.5 million.

Both campuses are accredited by the New England Association of Schools and Colleges, Inc. (NEASC), and the school at Bath is a member of the National Association of Independent Schools (NAIS), the Maine Association of Independent Schools, and the Independent School Association of Northern New England. Hyde's Woodstock campus is a member of the National Association of Independent Schools (NAIS) and the Connecticut Association of Independent Schools.

ACADEMIC PROGRAMS

The academic curriculum at Hyde is designed to help a student think critically about the world and examine his or her moral and physical development. Emphasis is placed on critical writing and the discipline of mathematics as fundamental tools for each student's academic growth. Creative focus in the areas of science, history, and foreign language impresses upon the student the importance of breadth as well as depth of knowledge. Special emphasis is

placed in the classroom on the ties between the academic program and character development.

Advanced students may choose from a variety of courses, such as physics, advanced biology, film, art, philosophy, journalism, and calculus. A high level of faculty involvement creates an academic atmosphere that combines challenge, diversity, individuality, and support.

Perhaps the most important aspect of Hyde's academic curriculum is the emphasis placed upon effort and growth. A student receives separate evaluations each term for effort and achievement. The final grade reflects a factoring of the year's effort and achievement grades. Students at all class levels are closely supervised academically and receive special help and independent study as needed.

The academic program is divided into trimesters. Grade reports are released three times a year. Vacations are scheduled at Thanksgiving, at Christmas, and in the early spring.

The Hyde graduate has taken four years of English, three years of history, three years of mathematics, three years of science (two of which must be lab courses), and two years of foreign language, plus electives in the areas of art, computer science, and performing arts.

Senior responsibilities include tutoring, serving as mentors for students, attending faculty meetings, proctoring, and meeting with faculty candidates.

The student-faculty ratio is 6:1. The average class size is between 10 and 16. Grades are determined on a 100-point scale; 65 is a passing grade. In the evening, there is a 2-hour study hall; the privilege of independent study must be earned.

FACULTY AND ADVISERS

The Bath campus faculty consists of 14 women and 26 men; 13 hold advanced degrees. There are 10 Hyde alumni and alumni parents on the faculty. The Woodstock campus faculty consists of 10 women and 20 men; 11 hold advanced degrees. There are 13 alumni and alumni parents on the faculty. Nearly all of Hyde's faculty members live on campus and are responsible for counseling and supervision in the dormitories. All serve as advisers to students and their families and share coaching, performing arts, and community action responsibilities.

Laurie G. Hurd, Headmaster of the Bath campus, received a B.A. from Bowdoin College. She has more than twenty years of teaching, coaching, and administrative experience. Duncan F. McCrann, Head of School of the Woodstock campus, was an undergraduate at Harvard University, studying social relations. He is the founder of a graduate school at MIT, and did graduate work in education at George Mason University. He has more than six years of teaching experience.

COLLEGE PLACEMENT

Hyde's graduates traditionally attend four-year colleges. The College Counseling Office works closely with each junior and senior in planning postsecondary study. The office maintains an extensive library of college and university admissions materials and uses software programs to help students choose colleges that will best further their growth.

College applications are supervised and processed by the office. At least three faculty recommendations, the student's personal statement, an aca-

demic transcript, College Board scores, and an explanation of Hyde's curriculum accompany applications.

In the class of 2005, 42 students graduated from the Bath campus, with 41 attending colleges, including Bates, Bucknell, Clemson, Syracuse, and the University of Denver. On the Woodstock campus, 48 members of the class of 2005 graduated, with 40 attending colleges, including Bates, Boston University, George Washington, Gettysburg, Wheaton, and the University of Vermont.

STUDENT BODY AND CONDUCT

In 2005–06 on the Bath campus, there were 20 students in grade 9, 39 in grade 10, 100 in grade 11, and 51 in grade 12. On the Woodstock campus, there were 18 students in grade 9, 46 in grade 10, 88 in grade 11, and 38 in grade 12. Between both campuses, forty states were represented in the student body, as were Bermuda, Brazil, Canada, Japan, Korea, the Netherlands, Russia, Taiwan, and the Virgin Islands.

Students and faculty members share in maintaining discipline. A traditional student government does not exist at Hyde; instead, the entire student body establishes and maintains the ethics that govern the community. These ethics encourage individuals to live by conscience rather than rules.

ACADEMIC FACILITIES

On the Bath campus, the renovated academic wing contains most of the classrooms and laboratories. Additional classrooms exist in another building, the Carriage House, and a renovated barn serves as a spacious art studio. The Mansion houses the library (8,600 volumes and Internet access to the News Bank Curriculum Resource and facts.com), faculty offices, a computer lab, a darkroom, the College Counseling Office, the Family Education Office, and administrative offices. Students have access to Bath's Patten Free Library, and responsible students may conduct research at the Hawthorne-Longfellow Library at nearby Bowdoin College. The Student Union houses facilities for the School's performing arts program, the bookstore, and a dining hall.

On the Woodstock campus, the Cultural Center contains a 1,100-seat state-of-the-art theater, classrooms, a lecture hall and science labs, a computer lab, and administrative offices. The Student Center houses classrooms, the student coffee house, the dining hall, and the bookstore. Annhurst Hall, which was recently renovated, contains a new library, the media center, classrooms, the College Counseling Office, the admissions office, and the Family Learning Center. Westhaver Hall houses classrooms and administrative offices, as well as dormitory rooms.

BOARDING AND GENERAL FACILITIES

On the Bath campus, seven dormitories provide the living quarters for boarding students. Five dorms have been built since the School was established. Each dorm has faculty members in residence, and older students share in dormitory responsibilities. A health center is located on campus, and 1 full-time and 3 part-time nurses are employed. A student union was built to accommodate community activities and rehearsal and stage space for the performing arts program. The Family Renewal Center provides conference rooms and dormitories for family weekends and retreats. Some recent additions include a new

dining room, a weight-lifting room, a student activities barn, and a 600-seat theater.

On the Woodstock campus, two large three- and four-story dormitory buildings house boarding students; one is for boys and one is for girls. Each dorm has faculty members in residence. A health center is located in Warren Hall and is staffed by nurses. The Cultural Center is a 1,100-seat state-of-the-art facility, providing optimal space for the performing arts curriculum, as well as for the local community's cultural events. Annhurst Hall was recently renovated to house a new library, a computer lab, classrooms, and administrative offices; it provides housing for families participating in retreats and family weekends.

ATHLETICS
All Hyde students participate in interscholastic athletics regardless of their experience or skill level. Students learn the value of competitive sports and share the accomplishment of a genuine team effort.

On the Bath campus, a modern field house, playing fields, and a locker-room center at the track and field complex offer excellent facilities for a successful athletics program; a major renovation and expansion of the field house is scheduled to be completed this year. On the Woodstock campus, the Kreb's Family Gymnasium was constructed in 1998–99 with new basketball courts, fitness and training rooms, wrestling rooms, and athletic offices. New athletic fields have been built as well.

Hyde boys compete in basketball, crew (Bath), cross-country running, cross-country skiing (Bath), football, hockey (Woodstock), lacrosse, soccer, tennis, track, and wrestling. Hyde girls compete in basketball, cross-country running, cross-country skiing (Bath), lacrosse, soccer, tennis, and track. The Woodstock campus also has martial arts and ice hockey for both boys and girls.

EXTRACURRICULAR OPPORTUNITIES
Some activities that are traditionally regarded as extracurricular are conducted at Hyde on a cocurricular basis. These activities include the performing arts, community action, and outdoor education.

The community action program enables Hyde students to serve as volunteers in area nursing homes, local elementary schools, the animal shelter, and other community projects.

The performing arts program involves all Hyde students and faculty members in the research, development, and choreography of a musical presentation. In addition, everyone participates at the performing level, either singing, dancing, or acting. Hyde also has formal instruction in music, drama, and dance.

Outdoor education activities include wilderness trips to explore the rivers, mountains, and coastline of Maine, the majority of which are conducted at Hyde's property in northern Maine. The addition of high- and low-ropes courses on both the Bath and Woodstock campuses provides group and individual challenges for students, faculty members, parents, and alumni.

Hyde offers many opportunities for students to pursue interests beyond the scope of the usual academic program. The visual arts program offers an opportunity for students to be involved with sculpture, pottery, ceramics, art history, film, painting, sketching, and photography.

Students are encouraged to contribute to various publications created on both campuses.

DAILY LIFE
Breakfast is served at 7 a.m. After daily jobs for all students, classes begin at 8 and continue until 2:45 p.m. Sports practices are conducted after the academic day and are followed by dinner at 6. Evening study hall is from 7:30 to 9:30. Wednesday and Saturday afternoons are reserved for interscholastic sports competition.

WEEKEND LIFE
Weekends provide an opportunity for students to relax and interact on a social level. On Sunday mornings, brunch is served. Activities organized by students may include dances, movies, coffeehouses, camping, and trips into town and the surrounding cities. All facilities are open to students during their free time, and the School provides time and transportation for attendance at religious, civic, and social functions in the area. Day students are encouraged to participate in weekend activities.

SUMMER PROGRAMS
The Summer Challenge Program is an opportunity for students to experience a character-based educational program as well as an orientation for new students who will attend during the regular school year. The curriculum addresses excellence through individual and group challenges in academics, athletics, performing arts, and outdoor education. Most students begin their Hyde education with this program. The program starts in mid-July and runs for five weeks.

COSTS AND FINANCIAL AID
For 2005–06, the cost of tuition, room, and board was $34,500 for boarding students; day school tuition was $20,950. The Summer Challenge Program cost $6000.

Hyde offers a financial aid program and grants-in-aid based on need. In 2005–06, a total of $1,500,000 was awarded to students on both campuses. Hyde attempts to offer its varied educational programs to as many students as possible. Inquiries about financial aid should be addressed to the Business Office.

ADMISSIONS INFORMATION
Hyde School seeks to enroll students who have the character, potential, and enthusiasm to challenge and develop themselves within the School's diverse curriculum. While consideration is given to a candidate's past performance, the admissions process concentrates on the prospective student's hopes and desires for the future.

The SSAT is not required but is recommended. Evaluation of past academic performance is important, but acceptance is based on effort and potential, not on grades. A student should have the interest and capacity for a college career.

An in-depth family interview is the main criterion for admission and must be scheduled with the Admissions Office.

Hyde School does not discriminate on the basis of sex, handicap, race, creed, color, or national or ethnic origin. A family's income must be considered in determining financial aid allocations, but it does not have a bearing on admissions status.

APPLICATION TIMETABLE
The Admissions Office has a March 1 deadline and then operates on a rolling basis and interviews candidates throughout the balance of the year. Families of prospective students should contact the Admissions Office in order to discuss an appointment for an interview. Candidates can expect notification of the Admissions Committee's decision within two weeks after the interview. Interviews for the Summer Challenge Program are completed by June 30.

ADMISSIONS CORRESPONDENCE
Melissa Burroughs, Director of Admissions
Hyde School at Bath
616 High Street
Bath, Maine 04530-5002

Phone: 207-443-7101
E-mail: bath.admissions@hyde.edu
Web site: http://www.hyde.edu

or

Holly Thompson, Director of Admissions
Hyde School at Woodstock
P.O. Box 237
Woodstock, Connecticut 06281-0237

Phone: 860-963-4736
E-mail: woodstock.admissions@hyde.edu
Web site: http://www.hyde.edu

IDYLLWILD ARTS ACADEMY

Idyllwild, California

Type: Coeducational boarding and day college-preparatory school emphasizing the performing and visual arts
Grades: 9–12, postgraduate year
Enrollment: 268
Head of School: William M. Lowman, Headmaster

THE SCHOOL

The Idyllwild Arts Academy is a boarding and day academy offering preprofessional arts training and academic preparation for colleges and conservatories to boys and girls in grades 9 through 12 and to those taking a postgraduate year.

Dr. Max Krone and Beatrice Krone founded the Idyllwild Arts Foundation in 1946 and established the Academy as a summer program in 1950. The Academy opened for 100 students that year. The summer program, which reached an enrollment of more than 2,000 children and adults as it developed, was the Academy's focus for much of its history.

The Idyllwild Arts Academy seeks to prepare students for further education, for advanced arts studies, and for adult life as contributing, productive members of society. The Academy believes in an education of high quality that places demands on both faculty members and students, who in turn must be committed to the good of the school community.

The Academy is situated on 205 acres at an elevation of more than 5,000 feet in the San Jacinto Mountains. Strawberry Creek borders the campus, which is surrounded by more than 20,000 acres of protected forest and parkland. The village of Idyllwild, a community of 2,500 year-round residents, is a center for wilderness enthusiasts, who use the hundreds of miles of trails for hiking and cross-country skiing and the nearby lakes and creeks for boating and fishing. Idyllwild is about 100 miles from San Diego and 125 miles from Los Angeles. Its location near the junction of Routes 74 and 243 makes it accessible from all directions over freeway and highway routes. Motels, campgrounds, and bed-and-breakfast facilities are available for visitors.

The Idyllwild Arts Foundation, which administers the Academy, is a nonprofit corporation governed by a 50-member self-perpetuating Board of Trustees. The trustees elect 16 of their members to a Board of Governors, which meets as often as necessary to conduct the foundation's affairs.

The Idyllwild Arts Academy is accredited by the Western Association of Schools and Colleges and is a member of the Secondary School Admission Test Board, Western Boarding Schools, NAFSA: Association of International Educators, the Network of Performing and Visual Arts Schools, the National Association of Independent Schools, and the Federation of American and International Schools.

ACADEMIC PROGRAMS

In order to stimulate young people intellectually and to advance their knowledge in all areas, the Arts Academy provides an exciting and challenging academic program. In accordance with the thesis that artistically inclined young people tend to learn best by experiencing and doing rather than by simply reading or listening to information, the Academy's program of studies is designed to motivate students to think for themselves and to use disciplined inquiry to explore concepts in the various domains of knowledge.

Upon graduation, Arts Academy students have met or exceeded the admission requirements of the University of California System and are prepared to enter selective colleges, universities, and conservatories across the nation. Students must complete 17 academic units in addition to their arts curriculum. The academic units must include 4 units of English, 3 of mathematics, 2 of foreign language, 2 of laboratory sciences, 3 of social studies, 2 of physical education, and 1 of academic electives. In addition, students must meet the Academy's requirement for computer literacy. Postgraduates engage in a one-year intensive program in academics and the arts.

Students choose a major and plan individual schedules with faculty members and the Dean of Arts and Dean of Academics. Placement in arts courses is by level of ability and experience; students then advance according to their performance. Areas of study include creative writing, music, dance, acting, technical theater, musical theater, moving pictures, interdisciplinary arts, and the visual arts. Each program incorporates courses in four categories: theory, history, and fundamentals of the form; creation, production, presentation, or performance; specialized master classes and private instruction; and field trips to arts communities of southern California to observe professionals at work. Among the regular courses offered are tap, ballet, modern dance, pointe, jazz, men's class, pas de deux, and dance composition; music fundamentals, introduction to music literature, ear training/sight singing, music theory, music history, voice class, chamber music, orchestra, class piano, piano proficiency, accompaniment, and repertoire class; acting, voice and diction, musical theater, technical theater, drama history and literature, movement, playwriting, directing, and stage design; drawing and painting, art history, ceramics, sculpture, design and aesthetics, computer graphics illustration, and photography; and creative writing I and II, individual critique, and visiting artist workshops.

The academic year is divided into two semesters. Teachers are available to provide extra help in both the academic and the arts programs. Grades are issued and sent to parents four times a year.

FACULTY AND ADVISERS

William M. Lowman, a graduate of the University of Redlands (A.B.), is Headmaster of the Arts Academy. A recipient of the Nevada Governor's Arts Award, Mr. Lowman founded the Nevada School for the Arts. He currently serves as Executive Director of the Idyllwild Arts Foundation.

The full-time faculty, including administrators who teach, numbers 35 members. All have distinguished themselves as teachers and professional artists. They hold baccalaureate and graduate degrees from such institutions as California Institute of the Arts, Catawba, DePaul, Harvard, Juillard, New England Conservatory of Music, Oberlin, Royal College of Music (London), San Francisco Conservatory of Music, Stanford, Yale, and the Universities of California (Los Angeles and Santa Cruz) and New Mexico. Private instructors are appointed on a part-time or short-term basis to meet special needs. Prominent performing artists are scheduled to be in residence at various times during the academic year to conduct master classes and give performance examples.

COLLEGE PLACEMENT

College guidance for students is provided by their advisers and one full-time college counselor. Students take the SAT and ACT and receive coaching on auditions and portfolio presentation.

More than 95 percent of Arts Academy graduates have gone on to attend a wide range of colleges and conservatories, including Art Center College of Design, Boston Conservatory, California Institute of the Arts, Carnegie Mellon, Cornish College of the Arts, Curtis Institute, Harvard, Indiana University, Juilliard, New England Conservatory, NYU (Tisch School of the Arts), Oberlin, Peabody Conservatory of Music, Rice, Sarah Lawrence, Stanford, Yale, and the Universities of Hartford (Hartt School of Music), Michigan, Southern California, and California at Berkeley, Los Angeles, Santa Cruz, and San Diego.

Other graduates of the Arts Academy have gone directly to positions with institutions such as the San Francisco Ballet and Circle Repertory Company.

STUDENT BODY AND CONDUCT

In 2004–05, the Academy had 154 boarding girls, 85 boarding boys, 17 day girls, and 12 day boys. The student body represents thirty-three states and twenty-one other countries.

The Dean of Students is responsible for students' residential life. The Judicial Committee, comprising 2 faculty members, 1 dorm parent, and 3 students, works in cooperation with the Dean of Students to oversee the rules and regulations instituted by the Academy. There is no formal dress code.

ACADEMIC FACILITIES

The campus of the Idyllwild Arts Academy is designed to be in harmony with its forested

surroundings. Lecture halls, science laboratories, classrooms, art and dance studios, and three theaters are among the many campus facilities that enable Arts Academy students to live, study, practice, and perform in this special high school environment. The Bruce Ryan soundstage opened in 2002 for students in the moving pictures (film and video) major.

The Max and Bee Krone Library, a state-of-the-art multimedia center, opened in 2000. It includes a museum, a 6,000-volume music library, 6,564 books, and a computer graphics lab.

The Idyllwild Arts Foundation Theater, seating 350 people, is ideal for concerts, recitals, and mainstage plays.

Three dance facilities, complete with barres, mirrors, and resilient flooring, are in constant use throughout the year.

Music facilities include excellent recital and performance areas as well as practice rooms and several studios for ensemble rehearsals.

Studios for painting and drawing, design, sculpture, and photography are located near the center of the campus. A large ceramics studio has separate facilities for throwing on the wheel and hand building. A variety of kilns, including raku, Anagama, salt, gas, and wood, are available for student use.

The Raymond W. Todd Exhibition Center provides a spacious, well-lighted facility where students, faculty members, and guest exhibitors show their work.

BOARDING AND GENERAL FACILITIES
For most of the nine-month academic year, the dormitories are home to the Academy's boarding students. They share double rooms in four modern, comfortable dormitories supervised by faculty members and dorm parents. The close-knit family atmosphere provides a strong base of support for the artistic, academic, and social life of the students.

A registered nurse is available at all times, and a physician in Idyllwild is on call. Emergency medical care is available at nearby hospitals.

ATHLETICS
Owing to the type of curriculum offered at the Arts Academy, the physical education program tends to be more creative than typical standard-ized course offerings. Physical education courses are intended to inspire a lifelong commitment to fitness.

Although students are required to complete 2 years of physical education, including one semester of health education, it is recommended that they take a physical education course each semester they are enrolled.

Health education serves to promote a knowledge of nutrition and weight control as well as an understanding of stress in work and recreation, substance abuse, family issues, sexuality and relationships, and values in the decision-making process.

EXTRACURRICULAR OPPORTUNITIES
Extracurricular activities are planned by the student government and Student Services personnel. All students and faculty members are invited to make suggestions for these activities. Students sometimes go off campus for skiing, skating, and rock climbing and for trips to concerts, art museums, dance performances, theater productions, conferences, sports events, and beaches. Students who sign up for an off-campus trip are charged according to the cost of that particular event, including the costs of transportation, food consumed away from school, and entrance fees/tickets.

Students are also encouraged to become involved in student publications, including the yearbook, the literary magazine, and the photography magazine.

DAILY LIFE
Academic classes begin at 8 a.m. and are held Monday through Saturday mornings. Arts classes are held in the afternoons, Monday through Friday, until dinner at 6:30. Evenings from 7 to 10 are set aside for rehearsals, study halls, and studio time.

WEEKEND LIFE
On weekend field trips, students enjoy the outstanding cultural attractions of Los Angeles and San Diego—museums, theaters, art galleries, and concert halls—and the many world-famous recreational areas nearby, including Disneyland, Knott's Berry Farm, Magic Mountain, Sea World, and the San Diego Zoo. In addition, southern California offers a wide variety of world-class sports attractions. The Arts Academy seeks to offer its students both the renewing serenity of the mountains and the bright lights and cultural stimulation of the city—the best of two worlds.

SUMMER PROGRAMS
The Summer Arts Program offers a wide variety of courses ranging in length from a weekend to two weeks for students of all ages. These include a Children's Arts Center, Creative Writing (for junior high and high school students and adults), Native American arts, and comprehensive offerings in dance, music, theater and musical theater, and the visual arts. Steven Fraider is the Director.

COSTS AND FINANCIAL AID
In 2005–06, boarding tuition is $37,950, and day tuition is $20,775. The Academy subscribes to the School and Student Service for Financial Aid and awards more than $2 million in financial aid annually on the basis of talent and financial need. A tuition payment plan is available.

ADMISSIONS INFORMATION
The Idyllwild Arts Academy seeks dedicated, motivated, and talented students. Students are admitted in grades 9 through 12 and for a postgraduate year on the basis of academic transcripts, recommendations, a personal interview, and a demonstration of potential in the performing or visual arts through audition or portfolio.

APPLICATION TIMETABLE
Monthly application deadlines begin February 1, and applicants are accepted until quotas are filled in each major. Students may be admitted at midyear, if space is available. Priority deadlines for financial aid are February 1 and March 1. The application fee is $35.

ADMISSIONS CORRESPONDENCE
Karen R. Porter, Dean of Admission and
    Financial Aid
Academy Admission Office
Idyllwild Arts Academy
52500 Temecula Road
P.O. Box 38
Idyllwild, California 92549-0038

Phone: 951-659-2171 Ext. 2223, 2343, 2344
Fax: 951-659-2058
E-mail: admission@idyllwildarts.org
Web site: http://www.idyllwildarts.org

INDIAN SPRINGS SCHOOL

Indian Springs, Alabama

Type: Coeducational boarding and day college-preparatory school
Grades: 8–PG
Enrollment: 274
Head of School: Melville G. MacKay III, Director

THE SCHOOL

Indian Springs School (ISS) was founded in 1952 under the provisions of the will of a Birmingham industrialist, Harvey G. Woodward. Originally a boys' school, Indian Springs became coeducational in 1975. An eighth grade was added in 1976.

The School is located on a 350-acre wooded campus 15 miles south of Birmingham. Adjacent to the campus is Oak Mountain State Park, with lakes, hiking trails, and camping sites. A 12-acre, spring-fed lake on the campus is used for swimming, fishing, and canoeing.

One of the top academic day and boarding school in the United States, Indian Springs' mission is to provide an outstanding academic education in an environment in which each student can develop to his or her fullest potential. Emphasis is placed equally on the student as an individual and the student as a citizen, with the School providing the resources and encouragement for the student to identify and develop interests and assume greater personal responsibility for learning and growth. Students are urged to express their views and participate actively in School and community affairs in order to develop responsible citizenship and a feeling for group living.

In accordance with its philosophy of concern for the individual's rights and responsibilities, welfare, and dignity as a human being, the School offers students from across the United States and around the world a diverse setting where tolerance and understanding are prized and practiced. Indian Springs students learn their potential not only as scholars but as people, developing greater self-awareness and sensitivity to others. Indian Springs is an informal school, with enough structure to teach students to balance academic, artistic, athletic, and other interests without a constant regimen of rules and policies that might otherwise discourage self-determination and personal fulfillment.

Indian Springs School is owned by a nonprofit trust and governed by a 15-member Board of Governors. Exclusive of its campus, which is valued at $18 million, the School has other assets totaling $21 million. New additions include all-new dormitories and a state-of-the-art science center (2006) as well as the Town Hall, completed in 1998 and housing a 300-seat theater for plays and town meetings and a 500-seat concert hall for choir performances and other musical events.

Indian Springs is jointly accredited by the Southern Association of Colleges and Schools and the Southern Association of Independent Schools and is approved by the Alabama State Department of Education. It is a member of the National Association of Independent Schools, the Secondary School Admission Test Board, and the Council for Advancement and Support of Education.

ACADEMIC PROGRAMS

Since 1952, Indian Springs' reputation has rested largely on the extraordinary academic preparation of its graduates. All courses are taught at a level that requires dedication and instills a love of learning for its own sake.

Through the eleventh grade, the course of studies is largely prescribed for all students. Each year, students take five academic subjects, with English, history, science, math, and a foreign language forming the core. Students may elect to take art or technology, a second language, or an additional math, history, science, or English course. After this foundation, upperclass students select from a variety of electives offered by each department. Seniors may also design some of their own studies through an independent study program. The average core class size is 16, and the teacher-student ratio is 1:7.

Advanced Placement (AP) courses are offered in English language and composition, English literature, American government, European history, U.S. history, economics, French, Latin, Spanish, BC calculus, biology, chemistry, physics, environmental science, and music theory. In May 2005, 111 students took 208 AP exams, with 81 percent scoring 3 or above. All sophomores are enrolled in AP Modern European History; all juniors take both AP English Language and AP U.S. History.

Art, music, and study skills are part of the curriculum in the eighth, ninth, and tenth grades. The School's talented student body also takes advantage of further electives in ceramics, painting and drawing, instrumental music, and drama.

Indian Springs offers an advanced science curriculum in both yearlong and semester-long classes. In grade 8, students take environmental science, learning basic principles of scientific observation and experimentation while exploring the campus environment of lake, stream, wetland, and forest. In grade 9, students study biology; in grade 10, chemistry; and in grade 11, physics or a variety of electives. In grade 12 in science, as in all other departments, there are several advanced electives from which students may choose.

The English Department places a particular emphasis on literature and writing. Texts take students deeply into both the Western tradition and the explosion of new voices characterizing literature in the twentieth- and twenty-first-century world. Equally strong in the humanities are the history and language programs. Indian Springs students graduate with an understanding of the broad themes and details of history that prepares them for future work at top colleges. They learn languages not only as gateways to literature and culture but to the contemporary multilingual world.

The Mathematics Department encourages students to see mathematics as a key subject for future work in the sciences, economics and business, and social sciences. Students move through the curriculum at a pace comfortable for them; many graduate with a year or more in advanced work beyond AP calculus BC or AP statistics.

Unless students demonstrate the need for supervision, they may choose the ways in which to spend their free time. Teachers monitor the progress and needs of each student in periodic grade-level team meetings. Students who need help in organizing their time may be assigned to a supervised evening study hall or to a teacher for supervised study during free periods of the day. All boarding students use the time from 7:30 to 9 p.m. for evening study.

Letter grades and teachers' comments are sent home at the end of each semester. In addition, progress reports are sent at nine-week intervals. As a means of alerting parents to the possibility of impending difficulties, the School sends written notices to parents of students whose marks in any course fall below C-. For students who are struggling, an individual improvement plan is drawn up and followed.

FACULTY AND ADVISERS

Mr. Melville G. MacKay III is the School's fourth Director. He has an A.B. from Harvard University and an M.A.T. from the University of North Carolina at Chapel Hill.

Thirty-five of the 40 members of the faculty are full-time. Ten classroom teachers hold doctorates, and the majority hold master's degrees. Twenty-one teachers reside on the campus. Of the total of 40, 23 are men and 17 are women.

Students choose teachers to serve as their faculty counselors. In addition, the staff includes two trained guidance counselors and a professional staff of houseparents who live adjacent to, supervise, and counsel boarding students.

COLLEGE PLACEMENT

Starting in the students' junior year, the School's full-time college counselor guides students through the process of selecting and applying to colleges. A library of college catalogs and reference books is maintained. College representatives regularly make on-campus presentations.

The range of SAT I mathematics scores earned by the class of 2005 was 490–800; the mean was 649. The range of SAT I verbal scores was 510–800, with the mean at 670. Six of the 60 graduates in 2005 were National Merit semifinalists.

All members of the class of 2005 enrolled in colleges, including Duke, Emory, Georgia Tech, Harvard, Middlebury, Northwestern, Occidental, Princeton, Rhodes, the University of Toronto, Vanderbilt, Yale, and the University of Alabama Honors Program, among many other distinguished private colleges and public universities. The class of 2005 earned more than $2 million in scholarship offers.

STUDENT BODY AND CONDUCT

In 2005–06, 274 students enrolled. Of these, 34 boys and 31 girls board, and 102 boys and 107 girls attend as day students. There are 32 students in the eighth grade, 63 in the ninth, 61 in the tenth, 57 in the eleventh, and 63 in the twelfth. While the majority of the boarding students are from Alabama, many are from other states and a number of other countries. Both day and boarding students come from a wide range of socioeconomic levels, and 16 percent are members of minority groups.

A student government composed of an elected mayor, 10 commissioners, and 8 class representatives works with the faculty within the framework of a written constitution. Rules and regulations are discussed in Town Meetings and small groups. Stu-

dent opinions are heard and considered. In disciplinary matters, students are empowered as well; an elected Student Judiciary of 9 students hears cases involving minor infractions and recommends consequences.

ACADEMIC FACILITIES
Classrooms are on the ground floor. Covered walkways connect most to administrative offices, the technology lab, teachers' offices, the Town Hall, and the library, which houses more than 19,000 volumes and 45 periodicals, with access to 550 more on CD-ROM. A new science center with labs for the life and physical sciences and a greenhouse opens in August 2006. There is also an arts building with a pottery room, kiln, a drawing and painting studio, and darkroom. The Hut, a recreational facility, is located at the other end of the lake from the classrooms.

BOARDING AND GENERAL FACILITIES
Students in grades 9 through 12 may choose five- and seven-day boarding options. All-new dormitories open in August 2006, affording a mixture of double-occupancy rooms and suites. The suites contain three or four single bedrooms, and share a living room and bathroom. A commons room containing a kitchenette, large-screen TV, fireplace, and study area is centered in each dorm. Faculty members and their families live in proximity to the students, with a resulting home-like atmosphere in which students and adults practice the School's motto "Learning through living." In the dorms, student leadership opportunities exist for the student-elected commissioners of protection and faculty-appointed proctors.

International students who find it difficult to get home during School vacations are offered home-stay opportunities whenever possible, usually at the homes of day students.

The School infirmary, operated by a professional nursing staff, is open daily.

ATHLETICS
Physical education is required of each student every year, with a special emphasis in the early grades on issues involving wellness such as nutrition, fitness, and teen health. Students are exempt from this requirement, however, during the terms in which they compete on interscholastic teams. Girls' interscholastic teams are fielded in basketball, cross-country, soccer, softball, tennis, and golf. Boys' teams are fielded in baseball, basketball, cross-country, golf, soccer, tennis, and volleyball. Also popular on campus is Ultimate Frisbee. The School's small size means that regardless of athletic ability or prior experience, most students who so desire can participate in the athletic program.

Sports facilities include tennis courts, an 80-by-120 yard world-class soccer field, a softball field, baseball fields, a gymnasium housing two basketball courts, two weight-training rooms, and an aerobics/dance room.

EXTRACURRICULAR OPPORTUNITIES
More than half the students participate in vocal music, including the full Concert Choir, Men's Glee Club, the Women's Choir, and the select Chamber Choir. A highlight of the year is the annual Spring Tour; recent trips have brought the highly acclaimed choirs to New York, Washington, Orlando, and Miami as well as China and Eastern Europe.

As many as ten plays are performed each year, many directed by students. A major drama is presented in the fall, one-act plays are performed in the winter, and a musical is presented in the spring. Clubs and organizations include the Outdoor Club; French, Spanish, and Latin clubs; the student newspapers, literary magazine, and yearbook; Guitar Club; Drama Club; and a variety of clubs devoted to diversity and social justice issues, including the Multicultural Club, African American Student Caucus, the Asian Club, and Habitat for Humanity. Teams compete in Scholars' Bowl, debate, and chess. Two Development or "D" Days are set aside each year for work on campus improvement projects.

DAILY LIFE
The day begins with breakfast, served from 7 until 7:45. The first period is at 8; classes last 45 minutes each. Lunch is served from 11:15 until 1. Classes end at 3:20, followed by tenth period, when groups meet and teachers provide extra help. Students typically have one or two free periods during the day during which they may study, seek extra help from teachers, or socialize. Day students may leave at 4, although many participating in athletics, drama, or other extracurricular activities stay later. Dinner is served from 6 until 6:30. Evening Study Hall, a time for individual study for boarding students, lasts from 7:30 until 9, followed by student-managed time that lasts until lights-out, which varies from 10:45 for grade 9 to 11:30 for grades 10 and 11. Seniors must be in their rooms by midnight, but they do not have to turn their lights out by any specified time.

WEEKEND LIFE
The faculty is divided into four weekend teams, each of which sponsors weekend activities on Friday evenings and Saturdays and Sundays. Offerings include dances, movies, mall trips, concerts, ice skating and roller skating, laser tag, and a host of special events. The dynamic Birmingham metro area of 1 million is the cultural center of the state and includes several colleges and universities, the Civil Rights Institute, the Birmingham Museum of Art, a symphony orchestra, several theater companies, and a zoo and botanical garden. Atlanta is 2½ hours east, whitewater rafting a similar distance to the northeast, and the Gulf beaches four hours south.

COSTS AND FINANCIAL AID
In 2006–07, boarding student tuition is $25,695 ($23,815 for five-day boarding), and day student tuition is $14,250. Meals are included in the cost; books are extra. Boarding students set up allowance accounts in the office and withdraw spending money as needed.

Upon the School's acceptance of a student, a $1000 deposit is required of day students and a $1200 deposit required for boarding students. The deposit is credited to the total tuition cost. The remainder of the tuition is due by the opening of school. Installment payment plans are available. A monthly statement, covering books and other charges, is sent to parents.

Financial aid is awarded on the basis of need as determined by the School and the Student Service for Financial Aid. Aid requests are reassessed each year. For those qualifying for aid, aid awards are grants, which are not to be repaid. For the 2005–06 year, 78 students received a total of $686,726 in aid. Several students reduced their tuition costs by participating in the on-campus work-study program.

ADMISSIONS INFORMATION
Indian Springs welcomes applications from academically serious and talented students without regard to race, religion, or national origin. Applicants should be capable of self-motivation in a comparatively free and nonrestrictive environment.

While there are no cutoff points for grades or SSAT scores, students must demonstrate above-average ability in academics. The new ISS student scores on average at the 70th percentile on the SSAT and has maintained an A or B average.

In 2005–06, 35 students applied for the eighth grade and 32 enrolled, 60 applied for the ninth grade and 30 enrolled, 27 applied for the tenth grade and 11 enrolled, 38 applied for the eleventh grade and 11 enrolled, and 7 applied for the twelfth grade, and 6 enrolled.

APPLICATION TIMETABLE
Although inquiries are welcome at any time, most families visit the campus the year before anticipated enrollment. Campus tours and interviews are available on weekdays, and a visit when classes are in session gives a more complete picture of the School. Most day students enter in the eighth or ninth grade, and most boarding students enter in the ninth or tenth grade.

Applications, with a fee of $50, may be sent in anytime prior to the opening of school, but as most places are filled in April, students should begin applying by December or January. Parents are given one month to reply to the School's acceptance letter.

ADMISSIONS CORRESPONDENCE
E. T. Brown III
Director of Admission
Indian Springs School
190 Woodward Drive
Indian Springs, Alabama 35124

Phone: 205-988-3350
       888-VIEW-ISS (toll-free)
Fax: 205-988-3797
E-mail: admissions@indiansprings.org
Web site: http://www.indiansprings.org

KENT PLACE SCHOOL

Summit, New Jersey

Type: Girls' day college-preparatory school
Grades: N–12: Primary School, N–5; Middle School, 6–8; Upper School, 9–12
Enrollment: School total: 629; Upper School: 245; Middle School: 142; Primary School: 242
Head of School: Susan C. Bosland

THE SCHOOL

Since 1894, Kent Place School has provided a superior education for girls in a structured environment that combines tradition and innovative approaches to teaching. An independent, nonsectarian, college-preparatory day school, Kent Place's threefold mission is to provide a well-rounded curriculum in a caring atmosphere, to educate students who demonstrate scholastic and creative potential, and to encourage contributions to and success in an academically rigorous environment. The School's commitment to excellence encourages each student to achieve her maximum potential while developing a love of learning, respect for self and others in a multicultural community, self-discipline, confidence, and responsibility. Kent Place also strives to strengthen each girl's moral awareness, to prepare young women for leadership roles, and to work in partnership with parents to develop individual potential through a variety of intellectual, physical, and creative experiences and opportunities.

The School is located on a 26-acre campus in suburban Summit, New Jersey. Within easy access of New York City, Kent Place offers field trips to museums, concerts, the theater, and points of cultural and historic interest.

Kent Place is a nonprofit organization governed by a 27-member board of trustees.

Kent Place is accredited by the Middle States Association of Colleges and Schools, the New Jersey Association of Independent Schools (NJAIS), and the Council for the Advancement and Support of Education (CASE). Its memberships include the National Coalition of Girls' Schools, the National Association of Independent Schools, the New Jersey Association of Independent Schools, the Secondary School Admission Test Board, the College Board, and the Educational Records Bureau.

ACADEMIC PROGRAMS

A Kent Place education provides a solid foundation for lifelong learning. Because of its commitment to single-sex education, Kent Place is able to focus exclusively on how girls learn and to encourage its students to explore learning opportunities that they may be inclined to avoid in a coeducational setting.

The Kent Place Primary School focuses on creativity, fun, and imagination and encourages children to grow, take risks, and ask questions. Students are introduced to the larger world around them through an interdisciplinary curriculum that is enhanced and reinforced by the use of technology. Kent Place challenges the girls to stretch the boundaries of their own self-knowledge, as the School draws upon their natural curiosity, inquisitiveness, and sense of discovery to instill a love of learning.

Middle School girls are provided with an environment in which they can explore and grow. Classroom learning is rigorous, interactive, and collaborative, and girls are permitted to forge an individual approach to the learning process. Enthusiasm for science, mathematics, and technology is fostered through the academic program.

Kent Place's rigorous Upper School academic curriculum challenges all students and ensures that each gains the critical skills, knowledge, and experiences that she needs to be a successful college student and constructive member of society. Ninth through twelfth graders are immersed in the humanities, sciences, mathematics, and the fine and performing arts. Innovative teaching strategies bring speakers into the classroom and send students out of the School to gain real-world experiences. Girls who are so inspired may pursue a topic beyond the regular academic curriculum with the assistance of a faculty adviser. Academic credit is granted for such independent study. Kent Place graduates enter the world prepared for what lies ahead, equipped with the ability to question, analyze, and think abstractly while feeling confident in their own talents and abilities and comfortable with the larger world around them.

All Upper School students are required to take five courses a trimester; four of the five must be core courses. Courses are 1 credit per term, 3 credits for a full year. Total credits required for graduation are 60, including English, 13; mathematics, 9; foreign language, 6–9; history, 9; science, 9; fine arts, 6; and electives, 5–9. Noncredit requirements are physical education for all four years and women's studies (one trimester in grade 10). Electives include such classes as contemporary history, economics, environmental science, physics for calculus students, advanced drama, biomedical issues, etymologies, photography, Web page design, and computer programming.

FACULTY AND ADVISERS

The School maintains a distinguished faculty and staff of more than 100 members that both challenges and nurtures its students. Seventy-eight percent of the faculty members have advanced degrees. Susan C. Bosland, who was appointed Head of School in 1999, holds a Bachelor of Arts degree from Denison University and a Master of Arts in educational administration from Teachers College, Columbia University.

COLLEGE PLACEMENT

College advising begins upon a girl's enrollment in the Upper School. Course selections are reviewed yearly to ensure that every student completes the requirements needed for college admission. With the goal of helping each young woman find the most appropriate college based on her individual talents, the college advisers work individually with students and parents to develop a list of schools that best matches the interests of the student.

Kent Place is proud of the high quality and range of colleges chosen by its graduates, which in the last two years have included Barnard, Boston College, Brown, Columbia, Cornell, Dartmouth, Duke, Georgetown, Harvard, Middlebury, Northwestern, Princeton, the University of Pennsylvania, and Yale.

STUDENT BODY AND CONDUCT

The students of Kent Place represent more than seventy communities.

ACADEMIC FACILITIES

The Kent Place campus features a blend of historic and modern facilities. The School House, now the Upper School, was built in 1913, and the field house was constructed in 1985. The Primary Building was opened in 1993, and a dining hall was erected in 1995. Additional facilities include a 280-seat theater with an adjacent dance studio and art gallery, two art centers, music practice rooms, a recital room, computer centers, two libraries, two playing fields, and five tennis courts.

ATHLETICS

Kent Place School provides a competitive athletic program for students who choose to participate in interscholastic sports. Kent Place is a member of the Colonial Hills Conference and competes against a variety of private and public schools. Kent Place teams participate in Union County tournaments, New Jersey State Interscholastic Athletic Association (NJSIAA) state tournaments, and New Jersey Independent School Athletic Association (NJISAA) state tournaments. Student-athletes are encouraged to compete in team sports to develop physical capabilities, self-discipline, confidence, sportsmanship, and personal character. Participation in competitive sports is not required; most girls, however, choose to take part in some way, whether as athletes, team managers, or fans. A number of Kent Place athletes have gone on to compete in intercollegiate sports at all levels of college programs in a variety of sports.

Girls compete at the junior varsity or varsity level in cross-country, field hockey, soccer, tennis, and volleyball in the fall; basketball, indoor track, and swimming in the winter; and lacrosse, outdoor track, and softball in the spring. Students who participate in athletic programs not offered at the School may represent Kent Place at conference, county, and state championships as individuals. Independent athletic study is also

available in sports such as diving, equitation, fencing, figure skating, golf, gymnastics, and squash.

Physical education is a requirement at Kent Place School. Students participate in physical education six times in a ten-day cycle. The program provides enjoyment of activity while fulfilling the needs for fitness, social interaction, and knowledge of sports and exercise. When a student competes in a competitive interscholastic sport, Chamber Dancers, Dance Ensemble, or independent athletic study, the physical education department waives the physical education requirement for the trimester.

EXTRACURRICULAR OPPORTUNITIES
Each year, Kent Place's gallery program brings professional art shows to campus, through which exhibiting artists work with students. Students host their own annual art shows. Drama, dance, and music are featured throughout the curriculum, and students in all grades perform enthusiastically.

Middle School girls take part in community service programs and extracurricular activities that include Key Club, Outreach (a community service committee), the Social Committee, Student Council, dramatic productions, instrumental ensemble groups, the Minisingers, a forensics club, and several miniclubs. Middle School student publications include *The Log,* a literary magazine; *Reflections,* a foreign language publication; *Soundings,* the eighth grade yearbook; and a Middle School newsletter, *Catamaran.*

Extracurricular opportunities for Upper School girls abound. Student leadership groups include the Athletic Association, the Judiciary, the Senate, the Social Committee, and Student Affairs. Upper School publications feature the *Ballast,* the Upper School newspaper; *Cargoes,* the Upper School yearbook; *Dichos,* a foreign language magazine; and *Windward,* the literary magazine. Arts activities include the Chamber Dancers, Chamber Singers, chorale, Dance Ensemble, dramatic productions, instrumental ensemble, and the Kent Place Singers. Other clubs are the Ambassadors, Amnesty International, the Black Cultural Association, Environmental Club, Junior States, Green Key, and Voices.

Community service is not a required part of the Kent Place Upper School curriculum, but more than 95 percent of the students pursue such opportunities. Students serve on first aid squads, in hospitals, and at soup kitchens and battered women's shelters; bring food to the homeless; tutor disadvantaged children; coach physically challenged swimmers; and collect nonperishables for area food banks.

DAILY LIFE
The school day begins at 8:15 and ends at 3:10. Sports continue after school until 5:30–6 p.m.

COSTS AND FINANCIAL AID
Tuition for Kent Place School for the 2005–06 school year was as follows: nursery school, $8167; prekindergarten, $13,737; kindergarten, $18,034; primary grade 1, $20,150; primary grades 2–5, $20,178; middle grade 6, $23,420; middle grades 7–8, $23,477; and upper grades, $24,325. Tuition includes lunch for grades 1–12. After the initial deposit, which varies by grade, all fees are due in two installments, one on August 1 and one on February 1. The School offers a discount for tuitions paid in full by August 1. Other fees include a $200 publication fee for grades 9–12, a $185 activities fee for grades 9–12, a $110 activities fee for grades 6–8, and book fees, which range from approximately $150 for the Primary School to $525 for the Upper School.

All families are encouraged to consider Kent Place regardless of their economic circumstances. Financial aid is awarded yearly in the form of grants. The School uses the recommendations of the School and Student Service for Financial Aid as guidelines to determine financial need.

ADMISSIONS INFORMATION
Kent Place seeks motivated young women without regard to race, religion, color, or national origin and welcomes inquiries and applications from girls of strong character, academic promise, and purpose. Admission is contingent on previous school records, written recommendations, a student application, the results of an entrance exam (SSAT or ISEE), and a personal on-campus visit and interview.

APPLICATION TIMETABLE
A $50 application fee must be submitted with the application for admission. Applicants who have completed all application requirements by February 1 are given first consideration by the Admission Committee. Applications completed after February 1 are reviewed on a rolling admission basis. Kent Place notifies candidates and their families of admission decisions in March.

ADMISSIONS CORRESPONDENCE
Nancy J. Humick, Director of Admission and
  Financial Aid
Kent Place School
42 Norwood Avenue
Summit, New Jersey 07902-0308

Phone: 908-273-0900 Ext. 254
Fax: 908-273-9390
E-mail: admission@kentplace.org
Web site: http://www.kentplace.org

KENT SCHOOL

Kent, Connecticut

Type: Coeducational boarding and day college-preparatory Episcopal school
Grades: 9–12, PG (Forms III–VI)
Enrollment: 571
Head of School: Rev. Richardson W. Schell, Headmaster and Rector

THE SCHOOL

The Rev. Frederick H. Sill, whose vision of education centered on simplicity of life, self-reliance, and directness of purpose, established Kent School in 1906. From its beginning, Father Sill intended the School to be a place in which boys not only learned academics and athletics to prepare them for college and professional life but also learned the value of physical labor.

After a half century as a school for boys, Kent became coeducational and today is a community of learning that is dedicated to helping boys and girls develop their abilities and increase their knowledge. The School prepares students for college studies and beyond through a program that includes academics, athletics, chapel, daily work, and extracurricular activities.

The School has a strong, long-standing affiliation with the Episcopal Church, and it is committed to understanding and transmitting the values of the Judeo-Christian tradition. It is also committed to seeking truth in all its forms and welcomes students from all religious backgrounds.

Kent School is in the small town of Kent, Connecticut, which is about 90 miles north of New York City and 50 miles west of Hartford.

The School is governed by a 30-member Board of Trustees that, together with the Headmaster and Rector, oversees the operation of the School. Kent School's endowment is currently valued at $64 million, and the physical plant is valued at $87 million. Combined giving by alumni, parents, grandparents, and friends in 2004–05 exceeded $2.6 million.

Kent School is accredited by the New England Association of Schools and Colleges and is approved by the Connecticut State Department of Education. It holds memberships in the National Association of Independent Schools, the National Association of Episcopal Schools, the Connecticut Association of Independent Schools, and the Council for Advancement and Support of Education.

ACADEMIC PROGRAMS

Kent offers a strong college-preparatory program, with courses from basic to advanced levels in the liberal arts. A normal course load is five courses per term. To graduate, a student must complete English through the Sixth Form year; mathematics through algebra II and trigonometry or through the Fifth Form year (whichever comes first); three years of one foreign language; two yearlong laboratory sciences; two years of history, one of which must be U.S. history; and two term courses in theology. There are also required term courses in art and music.

One further course is required for Third Formers. This course, Third Form Seminar, is designed to help students make a smooth transition into the academic life at Kent School and focuses on the development of sound study habits. The course teaches the skills of time management, listening, reading, note taking, study methods, and test taking.

Course placement is based on ability and prior experience rather than on age or grade level; students are encouraged to progress to a high level as rapidly as possible. Small class size ensures that all

students become well known by their teachers and have ample opportunities to participate fully in discussions and other class activities. Students get a chance to demonstrate their mastery of the subject, confront new ideas, and hone their skills every day.

Working at the appropriate level through the flexible placement system, a student at Kent can complete a thorough course of study for college preparation. The more able students have opportunities to work at the college level in the Advanced Placement program. Kent offers AP courses in every discipline, including computer science.

The student-faculty ratio is 7:1; the average class size is 12. Grades range from a high of 6.0 to a passing low of 2.0; 1.0 is failure. Grade reports are submitted every five weeks; written comments are given in all courses at the end of each term after term exams and at the end of each five-week period in courses in which a failure occurs.

FACULTY AND ADVISERS

Of the 76 teaching faculty members, 29 are women; 34 have earned advanced degrees. Eight faculty members hold doctorates. Faculty members have an average of sixteen years of teaching experience. Thirty faculty members live in the dorms on campus, and 57 also serve as coaches.

Because education at Kent goes far beyond the classroom, faculty members are chosen not only for their academic ability but also for their willingness to provide support to and participate with the students in the full life of the School. Every student has a faculty adviser, and each adviser works with about 8 students. Advisory periods are scheduled twice a week.

The Rev. Richardson W. Schell assumed duties as Headmaster and Rector of Kent School in 1981. Father Schell is a graduate of Kent School, Harvard, and Yale Divinity School. Previously, he served as a parish priest in Chicago (1976–80) and as Chaplain of Kent School (1980–81).

COLLEGE PLACEMENT

From February of the Fifth Form year through the spring of the Sixth Form year, girls and boys work closely with Directors of College Placement. More than 100 college representatives visit Kent each year. All Fourth and Fifth Form students take the PSAT. The SAT is offered in both the Fifth and Sixth Form years, along with SAT Subject Tests in all major disciplines. The 163 graduates of the class of 2005 entered colleges and universities that included Brown, Colby, Cornell, Dartmouth, Emory, Georgetown, Harvard, Johns Hopkins, McGill, MIT, Princeton, Rice, Swarthmore, Tufts, the United States Naval and Military Academies, Yale, and the Universities of California at Berkeley, North Carolina, Pennsylvania, and Virginia.

STUDENT BODY AND CONDUCT

In 2005–06, there were 90 students in grade 9 (5 day and 40 boarding boys, 10 day and 35 boarding girls), 141 students in grade 10 (13 day and 74 boarding boys, 8 day and 46 boarding girls), 150 students in grade 11 (6 day and 73 boarding boys, 2 day and 69 boarding girls), and 190 students in

grade 12 (1 day and 108 boarding boys, 4 day and 77 boarding girls). About half of the students of the School were from the Northeast section of the United States; the rest came from all parts of the country and the world, including thirty-one states and twenty-five countries.

The Sixth Form prefects (5 boys and 5 girls) are appointed by the Headmaster to work closely with the dormitory masters in supervising the dormitories. Together with elected representatives from each form, these prefects comprise the Student Council. Boys and girls are represented equally on the Student Council, which serves as a forum for discussion of School life and makes recommendations to the Headmaster.

ACADEMIC FACILITIES

The Schoolhouse, Dickinson Science Center, and Gifford T. Foley '65 Hall are the center of academic life on the campus. The John Gray Park '28 Library has 57,000 volumes, and extensive periodical, microfilm, and computer databases are listed on the Kent School Web page. The library is open from 8 a.m. to 10 p.m. daily. The Fairleigh S. Dickinson Jr. Science Center houses chemistry, physics, biology, and genetics labs; a lecture hall; and a greenhouse. The entire campus, dormitory rooms, classrooms, and faculty member offices have direct Internet and e-mail access through Kent's own World Wide Web server. All students are expected to take full advantage of notebook computers in their classes and during study time. Students play important roles in training and support of computer users. The Graham D. Mattison '22 Auditorium is fully equipped for play productions, movies, and concerts and also houses the music studios. The Bruce Robinson Field '81 Dormitory houses the art studios.

BOARDING AND GENERAL FACILITIES

Boys live in three dormitories, which house from 40 to 120 students each. Girls live in three dormitories, which house from 40 to 98 students each. Several faculty members live in each of the dorms. Learning to live with students from a diversity of backgrounds is central to the Kent experience. Students live in double rooms and may change roommates twice a year if they wish.

ATHLETICS

Boys' sports include football, soccer, cross-country running, swimming, ice hockey, basketball, squash, riding, baseball, crew, lacrosse, tennis, modern dance, ballet, jazz dance, mountain biking, golf, yoga, and aquatic fitness. Girls' sports include crew, field hockey, soccer, cross-country running, basketball, ice hockey, swimming, squash, figure skating, modern dance, ballet, jazz dance, softball, tennis, lacrosse, mountain biking, riding, golf, yoga, and aquatic fitness.

The Magowan Field House contains a fitness center; two basketball courts; the Brainard Squash Courts (three); a six-lane, 25-yard swimming pool with spectator stands; Nautilus weight-training facilities; a free-weight room; and locker rooms. A separate building contains four indoor tennis courts.

Other facilities include the Kent School Riding Stables, an enclosed ice rink, six soccer and lacrosse fields, two field-hockey fields, three baseball diamonds, and thirteen outdoor tennis courts. The Benjamin Waring Partridge Rowing Center was opened in May 2005. Crews now have this state-of-the-art facility throughout the entire academic year, in addition to 4½ miles of rowing water on the Housatonic River. There are lights for evening football games.

EXTRACURRICULAR OPPORTUNITIES

Kent encourages students to initiate clubs whenever there is sufficient interest; recent popular organizations have included a debating club, a varsity math team, Habitat for Humanity, and a culture club. The student-run radio station, WKNT, airs popular music and commentary. The Art, Spanish, French, and German Clubs meet informally and sponsor trips and other events. Publications include the *Kent News;* the *Cauldron,* the student literary production; and the *Kent Yearbook.* Volunteer groups work at local rest homes. Students also train to assist the town's volunteer fire department. Instruction is offered in any band or orchestral instrument, and there are Dixieland and jazz bands, a concert band, an orchestra, chamber groups, the choir, the Kentones, the Kentettes, the Chamber Choir, and brass, string, and wind ensembles. Students produce at least three major plays each year.

DAILY LIFE

Each student's day begins with voluntary breakfast, which is followed by jobs. The academic day runs from 8 to 3, except on Wednesdays and Saturdays, when it ends at noon. Classes are 45 minutes long. While meals generally are served buffet-style, there are family-style dinners on Thursdays. Athletics practices follow the class day. Study conditions are maintained throughout the campus from 7:30 to 9:30 p.m. Third and Fourth Formers are checked in at 10:30; Fifth and Sixth Formers, at 11. Late lights may be requested. Students are free to study on campus where they please if they use the freedom responsibly.

Attendance at chapel is required of all students on Tuesdays and Thursdays. Voluntary Eucharists are held on Mondays.

WEEKEND LIFE

Saturdays are considered school days until noon and are protected as such by a small day-student population and by a policy that limits students to five weekends (Friday afternoon to Sunday evening) or ten overnights (Saturday afternoon to Sunday evening) away from Kent. These weekends do not include the fall and spring Parent Weekends. Permission from both parents and the School is required for all weekend absences. Most students take fewer weekends a year because they do not want to miss athletics, Saturday night dances and movies, and special concerts and lectures. Friday evening services are provided for Jewish and Muslim students and faculty members, and Sunday Mass is offered in town for Roman Catholics as well as for Mormon students; all other students attend an Episcopal Eucharist on Sunday morning at St. Joseph's Chapel. School-sponsored trips to concerts, plays, and museums in New Haven and New York City occur each term.

SUMMER PROGRAMS

Kent School offers a summer program in creative writing. In 2006, the program runs from July 9 to July 28.

COSTS AND FINANCIAL AID

The 2005–06 charges were $35,500 for boarding students and $28,000 for day students, payable half-yearly upon billing. There are annual fees of $1175 that cover infirmary care, publications, athletics, physical education, and technology. There is an additional fee of $100 for international students. A prescribed dress code applies to girls and boys for all School appointments. Approximately $2500 is necessary for such personal expenses as books, supplies, laboratory and art fees, special medicine or X-rays, and laundry. Students have debit cards for personal expenses.

For the 2005–06 school year, 169 students received financial aid, with a total financial aid budget of $4.3 million. Kent's financial aid is awarded on the basis of demonstrated need. However, as a result of its limited budget, the School each year has more families who qualify for assistance than it is able to fund.

ADMISSIONS INFORMATION

Kent students come from diverse cultural, economic, and geographical backgrounds, and the School does not discriminate on the basis of race, color, creed, or national origin. Kent is demanding of students in academic, athletic, extracurricular, and social areas and seeks students who have a high level of energy and are ready to participate fully in all aspects of the School community.

All candidates are required to take the SSAT; test results are valued primarily insofar as they are supported by grades and teachers' recommendations. Personal interviews are required, and a tour of the campus is recommended. Tours and interviews take about 2 hours.

APPLICATION TIMETABLE

Candidates and parents are encouraged to visit Kent from 8 to 2 on Mondays, Tuesdays, Thursdays, and Fridays or from 9 to noon on Wednesdays and Saturdays. While a few places are held for highly qualified candidates who apply after the March 10 notification date, candidates are strongly advised to submit applications during the fall of the year prior to intended entry and to complete their files by January 16. The application fee is $50. The fee for international students is $100. Families have one month following receipt of an offer of admission in which to accept the offer.

ADMISSIONS CORRESPONDENCE

Kathryn F. Sullivan
Director of Admissions
Kent School
Kent, Connecticut 06757
Phone: 860-927-6111
        800-538-5368 (toll-free)
Fax: 860-927-6109
E-mail: admissions@kent-school.edu
Web site: http://www.kent-school.edu

KENTS HILL SCHOOL

Kents Hill, Maine

Type: Coeducational boarding and day college-preparatory school
Grades: 9–12, postgraduate year
Enrollment: 232
Head of School: Rist Bonnefond

THE SCHOOL

Kents Hill School, one of the oldest coeducational boarding schools in the country, was founded by Luther Sampson and chartered in 1824. The 600-acre campus is on the summit of a high, rolling hill that overlooks the valleys and lakes of the Belgrade region in Maine. Located within easy reach of Colby, Bates, and Bowdoin colleges, Kents Hill is located 1 hour north of Portland, Maine, and 3 hours north of Boston, Massachusetts.

The School endeavors to prepare students for successful participation in higher education and encourages them to fulfill their personal goals and become active citizens in the community.

The School is governed by a self-perpetuating 30-member Board of Trustees, which meets four times a year. The School's physical plant is valued at $19.9 million and operates with a $4.5-million endowment. The School recently renovated Davis Hall and built the $7-million Alfond Athletics Center. Reed Hall, a new girls' dormitory, is scheduled to be completed in 2006.

The School is accredited by the New England Association of Schools and Colleges. It holds memberships in the Cum Laude Society, the National Association of Independent Schools, the College Board, the Secondary School Admission Test Board, the Independent Schools Association of Northern New England, the Council for the Advancement and Support of Education, the Council for Religion in Independent Schools, and the Association of Boarding Schools.

ACADEMIC PROGRAMS

Kents Hill School offers more than 100 college preparatory courses. Ten Advanced Placement courses are offered, and there are honors classes in every department. The School was one of twelve schools in the nation to receive the Siemens Foundation Award for Advanced Placement programs in science and math in 2003.

Eighteen credits are required to earn a diploma, including 4 credits in English, 3 in history (1 of which must be in U.S. history), 3 in mathematics, 3 in science (including two lab courses), and a minimum of one course each in environmental studies, performing arts, visual arts, and health. Students must also complete at least two years of the same foreign language (unless this requirement is waived by the Director of the Learning Center). Advanced Placement courses are offered in English, U.S. history, European history, calculus AB and BC, biology, chemistry, physics, environmental studies, and studio art. A comprehensive English as a second language (ESL) program is offered to international students. The Waters Learning Skills Center provides motivated students with mild or moderate learning differences with one- or two-on-one tutoring. The Learning Skills Program teaches students to develop strategies

that maximize their learning strengths. The Visual Arts department is particularly strong in ceramics, woodworking, graphic design, and photography. The Performing Arts Department was added in 2002 and offers classes in acting, stage management, and playwriting.

Classes range in size from 5 to 16 students. The academic year is divided into trimesters, with major exams given twice a year. The open-stack library and research room are available for use every weekday from 8 a.m. to 3 p.m. and again from 7 to 10 p.m. Five computer labs throughout the campus provide ongoing access to computers for all students. All dormitory rooms are wired for Internet access.

FACULTY AND ADVISERS

Most of the 50 faculty members live on campus and are readily available to assist students who are in need of extra help. Twenty-three of the 25 men and 25 women on the faculty hold master's degrees. Faculty members serve a variety of roles as teachers, coaches, advisers, and dormitory parents.

Rist Bonnefond, appointed Headmaster in 1990, is a graduate of Phillips Exeter Academy and Cornell University (B.A., 1971). He has also done graduate work at the University of Rhode Island. Before his appointment, Mr. Bonnefond was Director of College Guidance at the Loomis Chaffee School in Windsor, Connecticut.

COLLEGE PLACEMENT

The College Counseling Office begins working with students in their junior year, starting with the Junior Seminar in the fall of the junior year. The College Counseling Office continues to work closely with juniors and seniors to help with the college and university selection, the application and admissions processes, and the mechanics of interviewing. Representatives from approximately sixty colleges and universities visit Kents Hill each fall to present information to students regarding the variety of college choices and options.

All sophomores and juniors take the PSAT in the fall. Juniors take the SAT and SAT Subject Tests as necessary in the spring. Seniors take the SAT and SAT Subject Tests in the fall and additional Advanced Placement tests in the spring. ACT and TOEFL testing are also arranged.

Recent graduates are attending such colleges and universities as Babson, Bates, Bowdoin, Cornell, Colby, Connecticut College, Fordham, Harvard, Hobart, McGill, Michigan State, Pratt Institute, Rensselaer, Rhode Island School of Design, St. Lawrence, Smith, Tufts, Vassar, Wheaton, and Yale.

STUDENT BODY AND CONDUCT

In 2005–06, there were 29 freshmen, 59 sophomores, 64 juniors, 73 seniors, and 14 postgraduates. There were 169 boarding and 63 day students composing the student body of 232.

Students come to Kents Hill from twenty-six states and nineteen other countries. Most students choose Kents Hill because of the small classes, the close relationship between faculty members and students, and the opportunities afforded in the community.

Expectations for student behavior are very high. Any student who cannot abide by firm policies concerning attendance and social mores on campus will be subject to disciplinary action and possible dismissal.

ACADEMIC FACILITIES

Twenty classrooms are housed in three academic buildings: Bearce Hall, Ricker Hall, and Dunn Science Building, which includes an observatory. The Mathematics and Modern Language departments are also found in Dunn. Sampson Hall houses the Bass Art Center and the Cochrane Library. Ricker Hall houses the English Department and the Performing Arts Department, including the theater. Bearce Hall is the location of the School offices, the Social Studies Department, the School bank, Deering Chapel, and several classrooms. The Cochrane Library contains 14,000 volumes, two study rooms, microfilm machines, and the new Isaacson '69 Computer Center.

BOARDING AND GENERAL FACILITIES

Students are housed in four residence halls. All residence halls are supervised by resident faculty members, who are assisted by appointed student proctors.

Returning students have their choice of rooms and roommates. New students are assigned rooms by the Dean of Students.

The School maintains a school store, a snack bar, and a well-equipped student health center. A local physician makes regular calls and is available in case of emergency, although the School is in proximity to a major medical center.

Masterman Student Union, built in 1971, contains a large, modern dining room that is used for activities as well as for meals. The building also contains the kitchen, the Husky Den snack bar, the College Counseling Center, and comfortable lounges and serves as the social center of the campus.

ATHLETICS

Kents Hill strongly believes that participation in athletics plays a key role in the development of well-rounded individuals. The School offers a wide range of sports designed to challenge students individually and as part of a team. Interscholastic sports include Alpine skiing,

baseball, basketball, cross-country, field hockey, football, golf, ice hockey, lacrosse, mountain biking, snowboarding, soccer, softball, and tennis. The Outing Club, Nordic Ski Club, and an equestrian program are also offered.

The Alfond Athletics Center houses two basketball courts, an ice rink, a fitness center, and dressing and training rooms. The School also has seven competitive playing fields and on-campus Alpine skiing and snowboarding facilities at the Liz Cross Mellen Lodge.

The Alpine training center is lighted for night skiing and snowboarding. Natural snowfall is supplemented by state-of-the-art snowmaking and grooming. The School also has 14 kilometers of groomed cross-country ski trails for skiing and snowshoeing.

EXTRACURRICULAR OPPORTUNITIES
Students may become involved in the yearbook, newspaper, literary magazine, photography, Student Council, Kents Hill Singers, Drama Club, Environmental Club, Outing Club, riding, and Model UN. Students participate in a schoolwide community service program.

Student leadership activities include serving on the Student Council, as campus tour guides, as proctors, as peer counselors, and as student ambassadors for international students.

DAILY LIFE
Each class meets three times per week for 45 minutes and one time per week for 75 min-utes. The school day begins at 8 a.m. and ends at 3 p.m., with 45 minutes for lunch. On Wednesday, classes end at 12:40 p.m. Study hall is held between 8 and 10 p.m., Sunday through Thursday.

WEEKEND LIFE
With faculty members on duty each weekend, it is possible for the School to schedule a variety of weekend activities while providing the necessary supervision. Kents Hill School offers fishing, canoeing, backpacking, camping, and rock-climbing. Trips to nearby Augusta, Portland, Freeport, and Waterville supplement such on-campus activities as movies, dances, and concerts. Trips are also scheduled during the winter to the nearby ski areas of Sugarloaf and Sunday River. The student union and the athletics center are open on the weekends.

COSTS AND FINANCIAL AID
The tuition, room, and board costs for boarding students in 2005–06 were $35,850. Tuition for day students was $20,820. Expenses for transportation for vacations, books and supplies, and tutorial assistance are additional. A $3000 deposit is required following acceptance or re-enrollment to reserve a place. Tuition payment is due by August 1 unless a payment plan is arranged. The payment plans require purchase of a tuition insurance plan.

Approximately half of the students receive financial assistance. All financial aid awards and loans are based on need.

ADMISSIONS INFORMATION
Kents Hill School admits students, regardless of race, creed, or national origin, on the basis of a willingness to become an active school participant, motivation to succeed, and the ability to do the work. Students are admitted to any of the four grades or to the postgraduate year.

The SSAT is recommended for applicants to grades 9, 10, and 11, and the SAT is recommended for applicants to grade 12 and the postgraduate year. An interview on campus is required, unless waived by the Director of Admissions.

APPLICATION TIMETABLE
The School recommends that applications be submitted by February 15. However, inquiries and applications are welcome throughout the school year, and interviews can be arranged at any time. An application is considered as long as space is available. A $50 fee must accompany each application.

ADMISSIONS CORRESPONDENCE
Ms. Loren B. Mitchell, Director of Admissions
Kents Hill School
P.O. Box 257
Kents Hill, Maine 04349-0257

Phone: 207-685-4914
Fax: 207-685-9529
E-mail: info@kentshill.org
Web site: http://www.kentshill.org

KIMBALL UNION ACADEMY

Meriden, New Hampshire

Type: Coeducational, boarding and day, college-preparatory school
Grades: 9–12, postgraduate year
Enrollment: 311
Head of School: Michael J. Schafer

THE SCHOOL

Founded in 1813, Kimball Union Academy (KUA) is the fifteenth-oldest boarding school in the country. Kimball Union's unique location in the Upper Connecticut River Valley and its proximity to Dartmouth College have long made it the preferred choice for both boarding and day students seeking an educational experience that develops the whole person as scholar, athlete, artist, and global citizen. The Academy's mission is to "discover with each student the right path to academic mastery, to creativity, and to responsibility." Kimball Union offers its students an education that balances a challenging, dynamic curriculum with excellent programs in athletics and the arts.

Located in Meriden, New Hampshire, the Academy's 1,500-acre rural campus is 2½ hours via major highways from Boston, Massachusetts, and Hartford, Connecticut. Nearby bus, train, and plane terminals link the area directly with Boston, New York City, and Manchester, New Hampshire.

The Academy is governed by a 17-member Board of Trustees. The school's physical plant is valued in excess of $30 million, and the school is supported by an $11.5-million endowment. The 2004–05 annual fund campaign, which was generously supported by alumni and parents, raised more than $750,000.

ACADEMIC PROGRAMS

The Kimball Union curriculum includes 4 years of English; mathematics through BC calculus; classical civilization, world history, U.S. history; biology, chemistry, physics, environmental and marine sciences; language courses in French, Spanish, and Latin, from beginning through Advanced Placement; and a three-tier computer science progression.

Electives are offered in history, English, math, and the sciences. There is an extensive arts programs, with electives in music, theater, and the visual arts, including pottery and photography. Advanced Placement courses are offered for qualified students in English, mathematics, four sciences, history (European and U.S.), studio art, and art history as well as all three languages taught at the Academy.

Students must obtain a minimum of 19 credits for graduation (most four-year students complete 22 to 24 credits), including 4 credits of English, 3 of mathematics, 3 of history, 3 of a foreign language, 2 of science, and 1 of art. The normal academic load is five to six courses per trimester.

The average class size is 12 students. With a student-faculty ratio of 6:1, faculty members are able to give individual attention through appointments and regular office hours. During the evening study period, students study in their rooms under the supervision of faculty members

and student proctors. The Freshman Orientation and Strategies Program is a required course that explores a variety of material throughout the first trimester, including learning styles, technology and library resources, study skills and techniques, and writing skill development. Freshmen are in specially supervised study halls; as students move up through the school, they are progressively given more responsibility for the use of their own time.

There is a letter system for course grades, with effort evaluated on a numerical scale. Grades and teachers' comments are sent to parents three times a year, and new students are given interim reports every three weeks for the first trimester. A grade point average of at least 3.0, with no grade below a C, qualifies for the honor roll. A student with a GPA of 2.0 or below and/or low effort grades is considered in academic difficulty and is given special attention.

The Academy's curriculum is traditional at its core, but teaching methods include problem-solving techniques and cooperative learning. Both the English and the language departments have peer tutoring labs. Writing across the curriculum is a schoolwide initiative. There is an exciting environmental science program, which not only includes classes at several levels, including AP, but also integrates environmental science into other disciplines through a shared philosophy about the importance of the environment. A 750-acre tract of nearby mountain land provides an environmental classroom.

FACULTY AND ADVISERS

The Kimball Union faculty consists of 49 full-time teachers, most of whom hold advanced degrees. More than 85 percent of the faculty members live on the campus.

Michael J. Schafer, appointed Head of School in 2003, is a graduate of Colby College and holds an M.Ed. from Harvard University. He previously served as Assistant Head of School at Middlesex School. His teaching career began at Cushing Academy. Moving on to Belmont Hill School, he served as a Spanish teacher, college adviser, and coach.

Faculty members at Kimball Union fill many roles: teachers, advisers, coaches, and dormitory parents. All but a few faculty members live on campus. Faculty members each advise about 6 students for whom they oversee academic work and scheduling.

COLLEGE PLACEMENT

The college selection process begins in the junior year when each student is assigned to a college adviser. A college information weekend for parents of juniors is held in the spring.

In the college advising resource room, juniors and seniors can use various sources of information, including catalogs and computer software,

in making their college selections. Computer software and Internet access are available for applications, and college representatives visit the school regularly throughout the fall.

An SAT preparation course is available to all juniors and precedes the spring administration of the test. Kimball Union's SAT I scores are higher than the national averages. Students also have the opportunity to take the ACT Assessment on campus.

The 105 graduates of the class of 2005 are attending such colleges and universities as Bates, Boston College, Carnegie Mellon, Colby, Cornell, Johns Hopkins, Middlebury, Northeastern, Reed College, St. Lawrence, Trinity College, Tufts, Vanderbilt, Vassar, and the Universities of British Columbia, Denver, New Hampshire, Puget Sound, St. Andrews, and Vermont.

STUDENT BODY AND CONDUCT

For 2005–06, Kimball Union enrolled 311 students: 187 boys and 124 girls. There were 58 students in the ninth grade, 82 in the tenth grade, 77 in the eleventh grade, 81 in the twelfth grade, and 13 in the postgraduate year; 100 were day students. Although the majority of students are from New England, students come to the Academy from twenty-seven states and nine different countries.

Kimball Union Academy has an Honor Code intended to reflect its core values, support its mission, and guide the behavior of its community. In establishing its policies on conduct, Kimball Union considers it a priority to teach its students concern for others. Violations of major school rules are reviewed individually by a disciplinary committee of peers and faculty members, which makes a recommendation to the Head of School. Violations of minor rules are normally handled by a faculty member.

ACADEMIC FACILITIES

The original Academy building is Baxter Hall, which houses the humanities classrooms. Fitch Science Hall, for math and the sciences, has been entirely renovated, and the E. E. Just Center provides a magnificent home for the environmental science and human geography programs. There are three major computer labs and a language lab, and each academic department has an individual computer minilab.

The Flickinger Arts Center is a spacious home for all of the arts. It contains a 400-seat fully equipped theater; a dance studio; a darkroom; music rooms; practice rooms; separate ceramics, painting, and drawing studios; and an art gallery as well as a state-of-the-art computer lab/recording studio.

The Coffin Library contains 20,000 volumes, more than 100 periodicals, a large video/DVD/audio book library of more than 1,500 titles, a

considerable microfiche collection, and computer stations featuring online resources.

BOARDING AND GENERAL FACILITIES
Kimball Union operates nine residences ranging in size from 5 to 50 students. The variety in residence size gives students the opportunity to choose the environment that suits them best. There is a faculty member living on each floor of the larger halls and in each of the smaller houses. At least 60 percent of the students live in single rooms, with the rest in double rooms.

There is a health center staffed by registered nurses, and the Dartmouth Hitchcock Hospital is a 15-minute drive away. A spacious and comfortable Dining Commons is the center of daily life at Kimball Union, with the Miller Student Center providing a recreational space where students can socialize, play games, or exercise. Just across from Miller is the Meriden Village Store and Post Office.

ATHLETICS
The athletic program at KUA seeks to complement what the students are learning in the classroom and is vital to the life of a boarding school. KUA successfully competes in a variety of interscholastic sports. Sports and athletic offerings include baseball, basketball, biking, cross-country, cycling, equestrian, field hockey, fitness training, hockey, lacrosse, mountain football, rugby, skiing, soccer, softball, and a wilderness program.

In order to promote good health and ensure that all students have the opportunity to experience a team sport or activity, every student is required to participate in two group activities per year. Kimball Union offers teams at different levels, so there is a team appropriate for every student who wants to play.

Athletics facilities center on the Whittemore Athletic Center, which includes the state-of-the-art Akerstrom Ice Arena. There are five playing fields for soccer and/or lacrosse; a football field; baseball and softball diamonds; two basketball courts, an all-weather track; an ice hockey arena, with indoor turf in the off season; two weight rooms; and a swimming pool. A heated outdoor turf field is in the planning stages. The Miller Student center houses a state-of-the-art fitness center. Cross-country running and ski trails cut across portions of the campus and through surrounding woods, and there is Alpine skiing 15 minutes away.

EXTRACURRICULAR OPPORTUNITIES
The Arts Center runs a cultural events series of concerts and gallery openings. There are at least three lavishly produced student shows in the theater each year, and the Concordians (an a cappella group) and Rock and Jazz Band perform seasonally.

Student leadership is extremely active at Kimball Union and there are many opportunities for students to participate. There is an elected student government and the president runs all-school meetings. Community service activities are planned through a standing committee and weekly community dinners are sponsored by a group called the Penny Fellowship. The Academy has a fire squad that provides essential support to the Meriden Volunteer Fire Department. There is an active diversity program called Relay, and there are an Environmental Club and many other clubs and organizations.

Traditional events and celebrations include the Wildcat Challenge, class trips, Winter Carnival, the International Festival, Senior Girls' Tea, the Junior/Senior Spring Formal, and parents' weekends.

DAILY LIFE
Classes are scheduled Monday through Saturday (some Saturdays are set aside for alternative programming), with half days on Wednesdays and Saturdays to accommodate sports events. The daily schedule includes seven periods. All-school meetings take place twice a week. Scheduled community times and advisor/advisee lunches occur throughout the year.

Sports and activities meet every day for 2 hours in the afternoon, except on Wednesday and Saturdays, when games take place.

There is a dedicated period at the end of the day for performing arts and activities, enabling students to attend without scheduling conflicts. Dinner, which is served at 6 p.m., is family-style or formal on two days and cafeteria-style on five. The evening study hall is from 7:30 to 9:30, and students must check into their dorms by 10. Freshman through senior evening schedules are adjusted appropriately for age.

WEEKEND LIFE
Kimball Union is committed to providing students with a rich residential life program. Weekend activities are many and varied. Saturday evening events include trips to dinner or the movies, on-campus movies, and dances, while on Sundays there are regular shopping trips to town; trips to major ski areas, to Boston, and to concerts and sports events at Dartmouth; and outdoor activities such as apple-picking and hiking. Most day students spend a large part of the weekend on campus.

Apart from scheduled campus weekends, students may go home or, with their parents'

permission, visit friends after their last obligation on Saturday. They must return to the campus by 7 p.m. on Sunday.

COSTS AND FINANCIAL AID
Tuition for the 2005–06 school year at Kimball Union is $35,500 for boarders and $23,000 for day students. For boarders, the fee includes room, board, use of all facilities, and admission to plays, lectures, and concerts held on campus. Charges beyond the basic fee include those for books, athletics store purchases, the musical, and transportation. An initial deposit of 10 percent of tuition is requested upon confirmation of enrollment, with the balance due on August 1 and January 1. Loan plans and tuition-refund insurance are available.

Kimball Union accepts students without regard to their ability to pay and then attempts to present the family with a financial aid package to make attendance possible. Kimball Union awards financial aid based strictly on financial need as determined by the School and Student Service for Financial Aid of Princeton, New Jersey. This year, 39 percent of all Kimball Union students received a total of $1.5 million in financial aid.

ADMISSIONS INFORMATION
Kimball Union seeks students who want to grow and contribute as students and individuals within its family-oriented community. Typically, successful candidates have strong academic backgrounds, extracurricular interests in arts and athletics, or the willingness to stretch and try new things. The Admissions Committee views as most important the student's academic achievement as well as recommendations from current teachers and the personal interview. The majority of Kimball Union students enter in either the ninth or tenth grade.

APPLICATION TIMETABLE
Candidates for admission are required to visit the campus for a student-guided tour and an interview. The Admissions Office schedules appointments Monday through Saturday morning. Applications should be accompanied by standardized test scores (SSAT, PSAT, SAT I, TOEFL), an academic transcript, a parent statement, three recommendations, and a $40 fee ($75 for international applicants). The application must be received by February 1 in order for the applicant to be notified of a decision on March 10. Students are requested to reply to an acceptance by April 10. Admissions continue on a rolling basis after April 10.

ADMISSIONS CORRESPONDENCE
Rachel Tilney, Admissions Director
Kimball Union Academy
Meriden, New Hampshire 03770

Phone: 603-469-2100
Fax: 603-469-2041
E-mail: admissions@kua.org
Web site: http://www.kua.org

KINGSWOOD–OXFORD SCHOOL

West Hartford, Connecticut

Type: Coeducational day college-preparatory school
Grades: 6–12: Middle School, 6–8; Upper School, 9–12
Enrollment: School total: 595; Upper School: 393
Head of School: Lee M. Levison

THE SCHOOL

Kingswood-Oxford School is a coeducational day college-preparatory school formed by the merger in 1969 of two long-standing independent day schools: Oxford School for girls, founded by Mary Martin in 1909, and Kingswood School for boys, founded by George R. H. Nicholson in 1916. Both founders sought to provide their students with the advantages of an independent school education while allowing them to enjoy the benefits of living at home with their families.

The overall mission of Kingswood-Oxford today is to help build and strengthen the intellectual, ethical, aesthetic, and physical capabilities of young people from diverse backgrounds, inspiring them to lead lives of integrity and involvement.

Oxford School, which began in Mary Martin's home on Oxford Street in Hartford, moved in 1924 to 695 Prospect Avenue in West Hartford. In 2003, the Estes Family Middle School was opened, consolidating Kingswood-Oxford on the Kingswood Road campus.

Kingswood School, modeled after the boarding school of the same name in Bath, England, was established in Hartford and moved to a large tract of land in West Hartford in 1922. The Kingswood campus served as the home of the Upper School after the 1969 merger of Kingswood and Oxford and now houses both the Middle and Upper Schools.

In 1972, a development campaign raised funds to build the $3.5-million Roberts Science and Arts Center, the $2.1-million Brayton Athletic Center in 1980, and the $2-million renovation and expansion of campus landmark Seaverns Hall in 1987. The School's most recent Capital Campaign, which ended in June 2004, raised nearly $27 million. The campaign provided funding for the consolidation of the two campuses and construction of the Estes Family Middle School, purchase of faculty housing, renovation of existing structures, new squash courts, increased endowment, and annual fund support. An additional $3 to $5 million in endowment was also raised to support financial aid and faculty development, and a new fund-raising effort is being organized to provide funding for a new science and math building.

Kingswood-Oxford School is a nonprofit institution governed by a 20-member Board of Trustees. The 2005–06 operating budget of $12,924,556 is supported in part through an endowment of $19,385,000 and an annual giving program that provided more than $1,000,000 for the period ending June 30, 2005. The Alumni Association, consisting of 6,400 graduates and former students, contributes significantly to the support of the School.

Kingswood-Oxford School is accredited by the New England Association of Schools and Colleges and approved by the Connecticut Department of Education. It is a member of the Connecticut Association of Independent Schools and the National Association of Independent Schools.

ACADEMIC PROGRAMS

Organized along traditional departmental lines, Kingswood-Oxford's curriculum is designed to pro-

vide students with solid preparation in five basic liberal arts areas—English, history, mathematics, science, and foreign languages—while at the same time offering a wide variety of elective courses in the visual and performing arts and computer science.

The Middle School curriculum emphasizes the development of organized study skills within a full range of academic courses.

In order to receive a diploma, each student must complete 4 full-year credits in English, 3 full-year credits in mathematics, 3 consecutive full-year credits in one foreign language, 3 full-year credits in history (1 of which must be in American studies), 2 full-year credits in science, 1 full-year credit in the arts, one computer course, and additional credits in elective courses, for a total of 20 full credits. Students must also complete 30 hours of community service.

Elective courses in English, ranging from Shakespeare to modern world literature, are available to seniors. Electives in other disciplines include such courses as marine biology, political science, economics, stage craft, and graphic design.

Advanced Placement and honors courses are offered in all disciplines, and independent study programs are available for students who wish to pursue a particular interest.

Performing groups in each of the arts channel students' creative energies and develop skills in modern dance groups, singing groups, casts for plays and musicals, and instrumental ensembles as well as orchestras and bands.

Each student is expected to carry at least five academic courses each term. The average class size is 13 students. The School employs a traditional letter grading system. To be promoted to the next grade, a student must pass all courses and earn at least a C– in a minimum of two yearlong courses.

Kingswood-Oxford's academic calendar is composed of two academic terms, with an examination period at the end of each semester. Letter grades, supplemented by teachers' comments, are mailed home at the midpoint and the end of each semester, with interim reports issued as needed.

FACULTY AND ADVISERS

The Kingswood-Oxford School faculty consists of 85 full-time members and 8 part-time members; 59 hold advanced degrees. Each full-time teacher advises 9 students in a particular grade, meeting with his or her advisees three times a week, counseling students on an individual basis, and maintaining ongoing contact with parents regarding each student's academic and social progress. Teachers also serve as coaches of the School's athletic teams and as advisers to student clubs and organizations.

In hiring teachers, the School seeks individuals with outstanding academic credentials, wide intellectual interests, keen interest in young people, and strong character. The School encourages continuing intellectual growth among its teachers by providing tuition assistance for graduate courses, a grant program for summer research and study, and six-month sabbaticals for senior faculty members.

Dr. Lee M. Levison was named Head of School in 1992. He earned his B.A. in history at Amherst College, and he holds both a Master of Education and a Doctor of Education from Harvard University. Dr. Levison has served on the faculty of Landon School (Maryland) and in the dean's office at both Trinity College and Dartmouth. He came to Kingswood-Oxford from the Noble and Greenough School (Massachusetts), where he served as teacher, coach, Dean of Students, and, most recently, Academic Dean.

COLLEGE PLACEMENT

The goal of college advising at the School is to assist each student in selecting and gaining admission to a college well suited to academic, personal, and social needs. Coordinated by the Director of College Advising, the college advising process begins in the junior year, when students complete questionnaires on their personal background and interests. During the spring of the junior year, students meet with their college adviser individually and in groups. There are also opportunities for family meetings with their college adviser at this stage. During the senior year, students receive guidance in filling out admissions applications, writing self-descriptions, interviewing, and refining their college choices. College advisers write and update personal recommendations for each student throughout the year and advise each student as he or she makes a final college selection in the spring.

The members of the class of 2005 are currently attending Amherst, Bates, Boston College, Boston University, Colby, Colgate, Columbia, Connecticut College, Cooper Union, Dartmouth, George Washington, Hamilton, Harvard, Middlebury, Oberlin, Princeton, Rensselaer, Skidmore, Syracuse, Trinity, Wesleyan, William and Mary, and the Universities of Chicago, Michigan, Notre Dame, and Wisconsin.

STUDENT BODY AND CONDUCT

The Upper School student body is composed of 193 boys and 200 girls. The Middle School student body is composed of 109 boys and 93 girls.

Students from more than fifty towns and cities in Connecticut and Massachusetts attend the School, with approximately two thirds residing outside of West Hartford. The student body is enriched by students from varied economic, social, and ethnic backgrounds. Kingswood-Oxford accepts students without regard to race, creed, color, religion, or national origin.

Kingswood-Oxford students are governed by the School's Principles of Community as well as by the general tenets of good citizenship. Serious infractions of these principles are adjudicated by a student-faculty citizenship committee.

ACADEMIC FACILITIES

The new Estes Family Middle School includes twelve classrooms, four science labs, two art rooms, and a resource room with computers and a book collection geared for middle school students. The Upper School portion of the campus includes the Roberts Science and Arts Center, which houses twelve class-

rooms, eight science laboratories, four art studios, College Advising, and a professional theater complex that includes a 600-seat theater. Renovations in 2003 created a new dance studio and choral room in the adjacent Brayton Athletic Center. Twelve language and history classrooms are located in three cottages flanking the Roberts Center.

The Upper School library contains 30,000 volumes and a wide selection of other traditional resource materials. In addition, the library houses desktop computers and Internet connections for laptop computers as well as fiber-optic connections that allow for faster Internet access. The library subscribes to 30 online databases, most of which can be accessed from home by using the K-O Library Online Resources link. Finally, the library features a special collection of books written by former students of Kingswood-Oxford and a Rare Book Archive Room with hundreds of books from the 1800s and many special collections that were donated by former headmasters, other faculty members, and alumni.

Seaverns Hall provides seven English classrooms; a computer center that includes a modern language lab, an I-Mac lab, and other computers for general student use; a 70-seat tiered lecture hall; and a student lounge.

ATHLETICS

Meaningful participation by students in a wide variety of athletics at all skill levels is a fundamental goal of the School. To this end, each student is required to participate in some form of athletic activity each day.

The School offers interscholastic competition at the varsity and junior varsity levels in basketball, cross-country, golf, ice hockey, lacrosse, skiing, soccer, squash, swimming, tennis, and track for boys and girls; in field hockey, gymnastics, softball, and volleyball for girls only; and in baseball and football for boys only. Intramural play is offered in many sports; weight and conditioning training and dance are also available. The School sponsors tournaments in basketball, golf, soccer, swimming, and tennis.

The School's athletics facilities include four gyms, an indoor ice rink, six regulation playing fields, two outdoor tennis courts, four indoor tennis courts, four international squash courts, a thirty-two-station fitness center, and extensive locker facilities for boys and girls.

EXTRACURRICULAR OPPORTUNITIES

Recognizing that activities outside the classroom offer a valuable opportunity for personal development and the growth of self-confidence, the School provides a wealth of choices in both the Upper and Middle Schools that encourage students to expand current interests and discover new ones.

Middle School students participate in student government, write for the newspaper, produce a literary magazine, and undertake a number of community service projects. At the Upper School, members of Forensic Union (the debate team) learn poise in public speaking and debating through interscholastic forensic meets and mock trials. Team Tobati, a group of students and faculty members dedicated to improving the lives of the residents of Tobati, Paraguay, was named a Point of Light by President George H. W. Bush. Model UN, Math Club, and Shield and Dragon, the School's tour guide group, are also popular.

Three student publications offer students opportunities to utilize and build their writing skills and learn the techniques of editing and layout design: *K-O News*, the biweekly student newspaper; *epic*, the School literary magazine; and *Retrospect*, the School yearbook.

Each class elects officers who organize the activities of the class and represent the class in Student Government. Field trips, volunteer projects in service to the local community, dances, and other social events are typical undertakings of Student Government and individual grades.

The School also sponsors a number of annual, Schoolwide events that add to the enrichment opportunities available to students. The Goodman Banks Series (performing and visual arts), the Warren Baird English Symposium, the Stroud Science Symposium, and the Class of 1936 Lecture Series (history) provide students with the opportunity to work with noted experts in a variety of fields.

DAILY LIFE

Classes are held Monday through Friday on both campuses.

The Upper School day, which begins at 8 a.m., is divided into six 43-minute and two 48-minute academic periods that conclude at 2:49 p.m. Lunch is served in the dining room during four periods for Upper School students. Free periods are also built into the schedule to permit individual meetings with teachers. Club meetings are held in free periods during the day and occasionally in the early evening. The athletics period begins at 3 p.m. and ends at the conclusion of competitive team practices at 5:30 p.m.

The Middle School day, which begins at 8 a.m., is divided into seven 42-minute periods that conclude at 3:46 p.m., with lunch in the dining room and sports scheduled into the middle of the day.

Wednesday is a shortened day for both the Middle School and the Upper School.

Because Kingswood-Oxford is a day school, parents can be an integral part of their child's school experience. Formal contact between parents and teachers/advisers includes a Parents' Night and two Parent Conference Days in addition to quarterly report card comments and telephone calls as needed. Other activities include School events (athletic games, theatrical and musical performances, and visual arts exhibits), volunteer efforts (blood drive and book fair), Parent Association jobs (Library, Cultural, and Hospitality Committees), educational opportunities (School-sponsored lectures for parents), and social opportunities.

COSTS AND FINANCIAL AID

Tuition for the 2005–06 school year was $25,145. Students are also assessed a $325 student activity fee. All charges are payable either in advance or in two installments, 60 percent on July 1 and 40 percent on December 1. Monthly payment plans and loan payments are available.

For 2005–06 the School awarded $2,133,000 in financial aid to 167 students. Parents seeking financial assistance must submit a statement to the School and Student Service for Financial Aid in Princeton, New Jersey, before February 1 of the calendar year in which the candidate seeks admission.

ADMISSIONS INFORMATION

Kingswood-Oxford seeks to enroll students who have the academic potential to do college-preparatory work, the motivation to fulfill the requirements of a demanding program, and the desire to participate in rich opportunities for personal growth. Qualified applicants are accepted in all grades.

In order to be considered a candidate for admission, a student must have a personal interview with a member of the admissions staff, file an application, take the appropriate admissions test (SSAT for the Upper School and OLSAT for the Middle School), supply recommendations from current teachers, and authorize the release of a transcript from his or her current school.

APPLICATION TIMETABLE

Initial inquiries are welcome at any time, but most families choose to begin the process during the summer or fall preceding the year of intended enrollment. Interviews and campus tours begin in October and are conducted Monday through Friday during academic hours for both the Upper and Middle School prospective students. The "First Wave" application deadline is February 1. Notification of the admission decision is made on or before March 10 for "First Wave" applicants.

ADMISSIONS CORRESPONDENCE

James J. Skiff, Director of Enrollment or
Jane Daly Seaberg, Director of Admission
Kingswood-Oxford School
170 Kingswood Road
West Hartford, Connecticut 06119

Phone: 860-233-9631
Fax: 860-236-3651
Web site: http://www.kingswood-oxford.org

THE KISKI SCHOOL

Saltsburg, Pennsylvania

Type: Boys' boarding college-preparatory school
Grades: 9–12, postgraduate year
Enrollment: 210
Head of School: Christopher A. Brueningsen, Headmaster

THE SCHOOL

The Kiski School is located in western Pennsylvania, 30 miles east of Pittsburgh. It is situated on a plateau above the confluence of the Conemaugh River and Loyalhanna Creek, where they form the Kiskiminetas River.

Kiski was founded in 1888 by Andrew Wilson, nephew of President Woodrow Wilson, and R. W. Fair. By 1894, the School had graduated 42 students, 26 of whom were attending Dr. Wilson's alma mater, Princeton University. Dr. Wilson served as head of the School until 1930.

Throughout its history, Kiski has focused its attention on educating boys. Both the faculty and the School's leadership have a keen understanding of how boys learn, what their expectations are, and how best to support them and enable them to reach their full potential. In the classroom, in the laboratory, in their homes, and by e-mail, teachers provide individual attention and homework support. On the athletic field, boys learn cooperation, teamwork, humility, and self-discipline. In the dining hall and in extracurricular activities, boys come to know the value of civility, the importance of the rights of others, honesty, and how doing one's best can contribute to the well-being of the community. The Kiski experience prepares young men for happy and productive lives of leadership and service to others.

Incorporated as a nonprofit institution in 1941, the School is governed by a 23-member Board of Trustees. An active Alumni Association represents the more than 3,600 living graduates. The 350-acre campus is valued at $50 million. In addition, Annual Giving raises nearly $500,000.

The School is accredited by the Middle States Association of Colleges and Schools and is a member of the College Board, the National Association of Independent Schools, the Council for Advancement and Support of Education, the Secondary School Admission Test Board, the Pennsylvania Association of Independent Schools, and the Boys' School Coalition.

ACADEMIC PROGRAMS

Kiski operates on a three-term system. The required curriculum focuses on a traditional college-preparatory program with a minimum requirement of 4 years of English; 2 years of algebra and 1 of geometry; 3 years of French or Spanish; 3 years of history (1 American and 1 non-American); 3 years of laboratory science; and 1 year of an art/drama/music survey. In the junior and senior years, students may choose from fourth- and fifth-year languages, precalculus, calculus, advanced calculus, Pacesetter math IV, advanced computer programming, history, economics, studio art, music history, music theory, psychology, U.S. foreign policy, urban America, and political geography. Advanced Placement courses are offered in biology, chemistry, physics, math, English, and history. To graduate, a student must complete 20 academic credits. In addition, each senior is required to write a formal research paper. Three levels of English as a second language (ESL) are available at an extra cost.

The student-teacher ratio is 7:1, and there are 10 students in an average class. Homework is done under supervision; evening study hall is held in the dormitories from 7:30 to 9:30, Sunday through Thursday. Academic marks and effort grades are given monthly to each student in a personal meeting with the Headmaster, and term grades are sent to parents four times each year.

Periodic evening lectures on various topics are offered to the student body by faculty members and distinguished visitors.

FACULTY AND ADVISERS

There are 36 full-time faculty members—28 men and 8 women. Two hold Ph.D.'s, and 20 hold M.A.'s. Faculty members live with their families on campus, take their meals in the dining hall, advise clubs, coach athletics, and share their lives with their students.

Christopher A. Brueningsen became Kiski's fifth Headmaster in June 2002. A former Kiski mathematics and physics teacher, Mr. Brueningsen has also served as Math Department Chair at the Brunswick School in Connecticut, and Head of Upper School at the Nichols School in New York. He holds a B.S. from Muhlenberg College and an M.Ed. from Indiana University of Pennsylvania. Mr. Brueningsen received the 1996 Presidential Award for Excellence in Mathematics and Science Teaching. He and his wife Liz reside on campus.

COLLEGE PLACEMENT

More than 75 percent of the School's graduates gain admission to their first-choice college.

A full-time college guidance counselor works with juniors and seniors throughout the academic year. More than 100 college admissions officers from across the country come to the School each fall to meet with Kiski students.

The mean SAT scores for the class of 2004 were 550 verbal and 570 math.

All students are accepted by four-year colleges and universities. Recent graduates are now attending Boston University, Bowdoin, Bucknell, Carnegie Mellon, Colgate, Cornell, Dickinson, Emory, Franklin and Marshall, Harvard, Penn State, Trinity, the U.S. Naval Academy, Vanderbilt, Yale, and the Universities of Colorado, Pennsylvania, Pittsburgh, and Virginia, among others.

STUDENT BODY AND CONDUCT

Kiski's 2005–06 enrollment includes 210 students from sixteen states, with Pennsylvania and Ohio represented most frequently, and from fifteen other countries.

Student government is the responsibility of a self-perpetuating Prefect Organization, composed of seniors and juniors. This group counsels younger students, takes some of the responsibility for organizing dormitory life, helps monitor study periods, arranges social affairs, and assists the faculty in maintaining good order and good form. Part of this "good order and good form" derives from requirements involving dress (jacket, shirt, and tie required in classrooms, in assemblies, and at meals; casual but neat dress at other times), and neatness of dormitory rooms.

All disciplinary actions are handled by the Dean's Office in concert with the Headmaster and his assistants. Violations of School rules are reported to the Dean, and he may assign penalties in the form of demerits. The acquisition of demerits restricts a student's activity and freedom about the campus. Serious or repeated rule violations may cause the Dean to recommend to the Headmaster that a student be dismissed. Unauthorized use or possession of narcotics or alcoholic beverages, academic dishonesty, theft, or hazing results in immediate dismissal.

ACADEMIC FACILITIES

The majority of classes meet in Heath Hall (1967). Six separate well-equipped laboratories serve the biology, chemistry, and physics programs. In fall 1998, Kiski formally introduced the computer into all subject areas and use of a laptop computer is included in tuition. Classes remain interactive on the personal level, but now students have online access to a range of databases, the Internet, the library, and class assignments. Each student has his own data port in his room and full access to the campuswide network (including faculty members) and wireless Internet.

Drama, art, and music classes are held in the Stephen C. Rogers Fine Arts Center. The John A. Pidgeon Library (1993) has 24,000 volumes and a computer center, and it is electronically connected to more than 1,000 libraries in Pennsylvania. Each student has his own e-mail address and full access to the Internet anywhere on campus.

BOARDING AND GENERAL FACILITIES

Students are housed in eight dormitories. At least one faculty family lives in each dormitory unit, and the remainder of the faculty members live on campus. The dining hall complex also houses a snack bar, a laundry, a barbershop, a bookstore, and the infirmary.

A resident nurse staffs the infirmary and is available at any hour. A local doctor is always on call. Latrobe Hospital is 20 minutes away.

ATHLETICS

All students are required to participate in athletics. Varsity teams play in the Interstate Prep School League. Junior varsity and freshman teams also play full schedules.

The rewards a boy gains from participation on a team are vital to his Kiski educational experi-

ence. Each student must participate in three of the following sports a year: baseball, basketball, cross-country, football, golf, ice hockey, lacrosse, soccer, swimming, tennis, track, and wrestling.

Athletic facilities include the field house, a new fitness center, an indoor swimming pool, three football fields, four soccer fields, three baseball fields, a lacrosse field, a nine-hole golf course, a 400-meter all-weather track, five all-weather tennis courts, an outdoor basketball court, a ski slope, and approximately 200 wooded acres. An outdoor swimming pool is used during the summer, and the campus pond is available for fishing in the summer and ice-skating and ice hockey in the winter.

EXTRACURRICULAR OPPORTUNITIES
Among the extracurricular organizations are the Student Publications Boards, which produce a yearbook, a literary magazine, and *Cougar Online;* a 50-member glee club; chess, language, and science-fiction clubs; and other groups that reflect such special interests as astronomy, computer science, photography, and woodworking in the School's expansive wood shop. The drama club produces a selection of scenes or one-act plays in the fall and two full-length plays, one in the winter, the other in the spring. Stage crews design sets for the plays, concerts, and other cultural activities. The state-of-the-art playhouse lighting and sound systems are operated by the students. The Kiski Forum for Political Discussion and the Poetry Forum have selective and limited memberships. The Kiski Service Organization provides numerous volunteer opportunities for students and involves a majority of the student body each year, although Kiski has no public service requirement for graduation. A chapter of the Cum Laude Society consists of those seniors in the top fifth of their class and those juniors in the top 10 percent of their class who are elected for membership. The Kiski chapter of the National Forensic League is the largest in Pennsylvania. Members have qualified to attend the national tournament for the past several years. Kiski's radio station, 100.9 WKRC FM, enables students to experience the radio business by learning about formatting and structuring radio programming and conducting Internet broadcasts of Kiski athletic contests.

DAILY LIFE
Classes meet five days a week. A typical day includes five 45-minute classes in a six-period day extending from 8 a.m. until 2:30, athletics from 3 to 5:30, and proctored evening study for underclassmen from 7:30 to 9:30. Students are encouraged, and at times are required, to seek extra help from any teacher on campus during this time. Clubs and other groups generally meet after dinner and before study hall.

WEEKEND LIFE
Ninety percent of the students board, and many are far from home, so Kiski offers numerous weekend trips and off-campus events. Taking full advantage of Kiski's location in the beautiful western Pennsylvania Laurel highlands, some of the most popular trips include canoeing, white-water rafting, camping, fishing, snowboarding, skiing, spelunking, and hiking. Cultural and social excursions to Pittsburgh and the surrounding area include museums and art galleries, dinner theaters and playhouses, and professional and collegiate sporting events. Other popular activities and trips include movies, shopping, bowling, paintball, go-karts, and dining out. Student "mixers" with three nearby girls' schools are also regular events. All off-campus trips are properly supervised by Kiski faculty members.

SUMMER PROGRAMS
For students entering grades 5 through 8, Kiski offers a four-week program designed to show that learning can be fun. Each student is issued a laptop computer to use in cross-curricular projects. The $3000 fee includes room and board, technology, and all activities and off-campus trips and excursions.

Kiski also offers an outstanding ESL program during the month of August that is designed to prepare international students for an American boarding school. The $4500 fee includes tuition, room and board, technology, and all activities and off-campus trips and excursions.

Several athletic camps are typically held on campus, most notably Kiski's Golf Camp, which is internationally known for its excellence. Other camps include soccer, football, and wrestling.

COSTS AND FINANCIAL AID
In 2006–07, boarding tuition is $31,000, which includes use of a laptop computer. International student tuition is $33,000. Extra expenses for students are about $600. Parents deposit spending money for boys with the Kiski business office. A tuition payment plan is offered through FACTS Tuition Management Company.

Approximately $1 million in financial aid is awarded each year on the basis of need, academic promise, and evidence of leadership. For 2004–05, 40 percent of the students were awarded financial aid. The amounts of these awards are determined by standards set by the School and Student Service for Financial Aid. Kiski offers four merit scholarships each year to freshmen. These awards are renewable from year to year, as long as certain minimum standards of academics and conduct are maintained.

ADMISSIONS INFORMATION
Mindful of its demanding academic and competitive athletics program, Kiski seeks responsible students with above-average ability. New students are admitted into grades 9–12 and PG. An interview, transcripts from previous schools, and a written essay are required of all applicants. Students applying for grades 9 and 10 must submit results of the SSAT or ISEE.

APPLICATION TIMETABLE
The admissions office is open throughout the year to meet with families and conduct interviews and campus tours. Four open houses, plus several regional receptions, are also held each year. Coaches, teachers, and students are available to correspond directly with prospective students and their families by e-mail, telephone, or in person.

The application fee is $50. Transcripts and standardized tests from the student's current school and teacher recommendations should be secured after the first semester but not later than mid-January. Applicants are notified on March 10; applications are accepted after that date until fall classes are filled.

ADMISSIONS CORRESPONDENCE
Mr. Lawrence J. Jensen
Director of Admissions
The Kiski School
1888 Brett Lane
Saltsburg, Pennsylvania 15681
Phone: 877-547-5448 (toll-free)
Fax: 724-639-8596
E-mail: admissions@kiski.org
Web site: http://www.kiski.org

THE KNOX SCHOOL

St. James, New York

Type: Coeducational boarding and day college-preparatory and general academic school
Grades: 6–12: Middle School, 6–8; Upper School, 9–12
Enrollment: School total: 115; Upper School: 92
Head of School: David B. Stephens, Head of School

THE SCHOOL

The Knox School is dedicated to its mission of providing the opportunity for capable students to excel within a liberal arts program infused with artistic and athletic pursuits, in preparation for higher education at selective colleges and universities. Its purpose is to inspire in each student a love of learning and the desire to continually develop the skills necessary to lead a happy, confident, and successful life in a complex and changing world. The School enthusiastically supports a philosophy providing a diverse student body with a traditional, structured, and familial environment that fosters academic, intellectual, and character development while celebrating individual strength and talents. In addition, the School is guided by its Core Values and Principles of Action, which aim to develop responsibility and respect for self, others, and the community in which students live and learn.

Knox was founded in 1904 in Briarcliff Manor, New York, by Mary Alice Knox. Always located in New York State, the School was established in Tarrytown and relocated to Cooperstown prior to moving to its present location in St. James in 1954. The School's 68-acre wooded campus overlooks Stony Brook Harbor on Long Island's North Shore, and its proximity to New York City allows for frequent trips to athletic events, concerts, theaters, museums, and other cultural opportunities.

Incorporated as a nonprofit organization, Knox is directed by a 15-member Board of Trustees. The School's 2,500 alumni are dedicated to maintaining the School's traditions and its growth.

The Knox School is accredited by the Middle States Association of Colleges and Schools and by the New York State Board of Regents. It holds memberships in the National Association of Independent Schools, the New York State Association of Independent Schools, the Association of Boarding Schools, the Secondary School Admission Test Board, and the National Association for College Admission Counseling.

ACADEMIC PROGRAMS

The Knox curriculum includes college preparatory, honors, and Advanced Placement courses. The School follows a trimester calendar. All students take a minimum of six courses each term. The minimum requirement for graduation is the successful completion of 18½ credits distributed as follows: 4 credits in English, 3 in math, 3 in history (U.S. history is required), 2 in lab science (biology is required), 2 in a foreign language (at least a two-year sequence of a single language is required), 1 in art, and ½ in health. In addition to satisfying their distribution of credits, students must complete a three-year sequence in two disciplines other than English and history. An elective program with offerings in creative writing, journalism, contemporary literature, speech, debate, psychology, environmental science, music

history, art history, art, photography, vocal music, and computers complements the academic curriculum. Grades are issued to students on a bi-weekly basis, and grade reports with written comments are sent to parents six times per year. Letter designations from A to F are used for course grades and effort grades are given a numerical value from 1 to 5.

In addition to its traditional academic program, Knox offers English as a Second Language (ESL) for international students in grades 7 and 8 and ACCESS for a limited number of average to above-average students. The ESL program includes courses from beginning through advanced ESL, as well as ESL sections in Middle School humanities. The ACCESS program is designed to provide additional support in a small class environment for students in reading, writing, math, and study skills, and is scheduled as a class period within the student's academic day. An additional fee is charged for both the ESL and ACCESS programs.

Students benefit from a 4:1 student-faculty ratio; small classes, which range from 3 to 12 students; and an extra help period which is built into the academic day. For boarding students, a 2-hour evening study period is held Sunday through Thursday. During this time, students study in their rooms and are monitored by dorm faculty, or they may be assigned to a structured classroom study hall supervised by faculty proctors.

The Knox School participates in an exchange program with Bedstone College, a private boarding school in England. Each year, 2–4 Knox pupils apply to spend their fall trimester studying in England. In turn, Bedstone students study at Knox during their spring term.

FACULTY AND ADVISERS

There are 27 full-time and 4 part-time faculty members; 24 are women and 7 are men. Of these, 17 hold advanced degrees and 23 reside on campus. In addition to teaching, faculty members and administrators serve as dorm parents, coaches, and club sponsors. Each faculty member advises a small number of students, providing them with guidance while maintaining open lines of communication with their parents.

David B. Stephens, who was appointed Headmaster in 2005, holds a B.S. from Hobart and William Smith College and an M.S. from Syracuse University. During his career, he most recently served as the Headmaster at Rivermont Collegiate School in Bettendorf, Iowa, and he has served in various administrative and faculty positions at other independent schools.

COLLEGE PLACEMENT

The Director of College Counseling coordinates and schedules PSATs, SATs, and ACTs for all students in their sophomore through senior years, and the TOEFL for international students. Me-

dian SAT and ACT scores for the class of 2003 fell within the range of national averages.

In the spring of the junior year, each student is provided with a College Guidelines binder, which has been designed by the Knox college counseling professionals to guide the student through each step of the college admissions process. Combined with one-on-one sessions with the student's primary counselor, this system ensures that students explore various options when choosing colleges, learn to identify and emphasize their strengths and attributes in the preparation of application materials, and, with their families, make informed choices in the college selection process. In the fall, the School hosts an on-campus college fair for more than sixty colleges.

Recent graduates have been accepted at and are attending Boston College, Boston University, Clemson, Drew, Fordham, Franklin and Marshall, George Washington, Haverford, Lafayette, Lake Forest, Manhattanville, NYU, Parsons School of Design, St. John's, Susquehanna, Syracuse, SUNY at Stony Brook, Temple, Tulane, Wheaton, and the Universities of North Carolina at Chapel Hill and UC San Diego.

STUDENT BODY AND CONDUCT

The enrollment in 2005–06 was 115; 71 boys and 44 girls. Forty-five percent are day students. There are 18 seniors, 26 juniors, 18 sophomores, 29 freshmen, and 24 Middle School students. The student body represents seven countries and ten states.

The Knox School's Core Values have been designed to serve the well-being of all students. The values are based on the principles of integrity, kindness, respect, courage, responsibility, and scholarship. As an institution, Knox has no tolerance for drug, alcohol, or tobacco use.

A student council is elected each year to serve as a liaison between the students and administration, recommend proposals for changes in programs and procedures, plan and preside over weekly School meetings, and propose and sponsor student activities.

Students are required to wear the Knox School uniform during the academic day, while a more casual style is allowed at dinner and on weekends.

ACADEMIC FACILITIES

The Dann Administration and Classroom Building accommodates administrative offices, classrooms, an art studio, a computer lab, a photography studio, and the library. Lawrence Hall houses science labs, classrooms, and a second computer lab. Bancroft-Phinney Hall is a multipurpose building that includes facilities for theater, music, dance, and the gym.

BOARDING AND GENERAL FACILITIES

Houghton Hall, the main building of the campus, houses the dining room, the Health and Wellness Center, school store (The Falcon's Nest), meeting

hall, and living quarters for 35 girls and resident faculty dorm parents. In addition to the main building, there are four dormitories that accommodate 12 to 30 students each and include apartments for resident faculty families. Each dormitory has a student lounge and laundry facilities. All rooms have Internet access and students are encouraged to bring their own computers. An on-call doctor and 24-hour nursing staff provide health care.

ATHLETICS

The athletic program encourages sportsmanship, team spirit, and fair play. All students are required to participate in a competitive or noncompetitive sport each trimester. Girls may choose from crew, soccer, volleyball, basketball, tennis, softball, dance, cross-country, and riding. Boys may choose from crew, soccer, basketball, baseball, tennis, cross-country, dance, and riding. The athletic program also provides an opportunity for students to do an independent study in a sport not available at Knox. Approval by the Athletic Director is required. Students who participate in the riding program, and who qualify, may participate in both local and national horse shows. The School is divided into two teams—the Red and the White—and friendly competition between these teams is ongoing throughout the year.

In addition to the gymnasium, Knox has three athletic fields, five tennis courts, a 3.1-mile cross-country trail, stables, and outdoor and covered riding rings.

EXTRACURRICULAR OPPORTUNITIES

A wide range of extracurricular activities offers students the opportunity to explore new talents and interests. Club offerings include debate, environmental, filmmaking, Film Society, Spanish, French, jazz/rock improv, library, visual arts, performing arts, table tennis, cartooning, yoga, cooking, community service, fishing, and technology. Students publish a literary magazine, *Scribblers*, and the yearbook, *Roseleaves*. The performing arts department stages one dramatic and one musical production each year. Other on-campus activities include movies, dances, recitals, and presentations by visiting artists and speakers.

DAILY LIFE

Morning classes begin at 8 a.m., followed by lunch at 11:45 for Middle School and 12:30 for Upper School. Each day has time set aside in the schedule for class/advisory meetings. On Fridays, an all-School meeting is held prior to lunch. Athletics for Upper School are from 3 to 4:30 and Middle School sports are held from 2 to 3. Middle School students have a support/enrichment period from 3:15 to 4:15 daily. All boarding students return to their dorms and attend dinner at 5:30. Meals are served buffet-style with faculty members or a senior class member heading each table.

From 7:00 until 9:00, Sunday through Thursday, students study in their rooms or in a classroom study hall, under the supervision of dorm parents and faculty proctors. Lights-out is at 10 for the Middle School, 10:30 for ninth through eleventh grades, and 11 for twelfth grade.

WEEKEND LIFE

Weekend activities, which are open to both boarding and day students, provide a wide variety of required and optional cultural, social, and athletic events both on and off campus. With New York City only 55 miles away, Knox schedules frequent Saturday trips to concerts, Broadway shows, artistic and cultural events, museums, and professional sporting events. All activities are chaperoned by faculty members.

On many weekends, boarding students have the opportunity to go home or to visit at a classmate's home from 3:45 p.m. Friday through 6 p.m. Sunday evening. On most Sundays of the remaining weekends, students are allowed to leave campus to attend religious services or to join in off-campus family activities with their families or as invited guests of other students. Parental permission and the School's approval are required for all off-campus weekends and Sundays.

COSTS AND FINANCIAL AID

For 2005–06, the cost of tuition, room, and seven-day boarding was $31,000, and it was $29,600 for a five-day boarding experience. Day student tuition is $15,325. An initial deposit of 10 percent of the tuition is due within ten days of acceptance. The major tuition payment is due July 1, and the balance of tuition and fees is payable in two installments due September 1 and December 1. Charges for books, activities, and personal expen-

ditures average between $1800 and $4000 per year. Students may choose to participate in the riding program or take private music lessons for an additional fee. A limited number of financial aid grants are awarded each year. Scholarship applicants' parents must file a Parents' Financial Statement with the School and Student Service for Financial Aid.

ADMISSIONS INFORMATION

Knox seeks capable students who would benefit from a traditional environment, who are committed to achieving academic success, and who demonstrate a willingness to participate in and contribute to all aspects of the School community. Knox values the diversity of its student population and does not discriminate on the basis of race, color, gender, religion, or ethnic origin.

Candidates must visit the School for an interview, submit SSAT scores, and file a completed application that includes a current transcript, writing sample, and English and math teacher recommendations. Knox accepts the Boarding School Common Application Form.

APPLICATION TIMETABLE

Applicants are encouraged to apply by February 1 in order to be eligible for the March 10 notification date. From then on and throughout early summer, Knox accepts applications if space in the fall enrollment is available. The Admission Committee believes that an appropriate match for both the candidate and the School is the first step in helping a student achieve his or her goals. The School works closely with parents and students during the application process to confirm that the student's values, interests, and abilities align with the School's program.

ADMISSIONS CORRESPONDENCE

Meredith Stanley
Director of Admissions
The Knox School
541 Long Beach Road
St. James, New York 11780

Phone: 631-686-1600 Ext. 412
Fax: 631-686-1650
E-mail: mstanley@knoxschool.org
Web site: http://www.knoxschool.org

LAKE FOREST ACADEMY

Lake Forest, Illinois

Type: Coeducational boarding and day college-preparatory school
Grades: 9–12
Enrollment: 377
Head of School: John Strudwick

THE SCHOOL

Lake Forest Academy is located on a 160-acre campus on Chicago's North Shore, 35 miles from the Loop and 5 miles from Lake Michigan.

Lake Forest Academy for boys was founded in 1857 and the Ferry Hall School for girls in 1869 by a group of Chicago businessmen interested in initiating "a learning institution of higher order." The two schools, originally administered by the trustees of Lake Forest University, adopted autonomous administrations with separate boards of trustees in the 1920s but maintained cultural and social interaction. In the late 1960s, the schools' curricula were coordinated, and this led to the merger in 1974.

The school is committed to providing the kind of education that enables students to accomplish their ultimate goals. It is a community that provides the support and caring needed to develop confidence and strong values, and where learning is a constant adventure. It has created an atmosphere that builds character and fosters respect for individuality.

The 25-member Board of Trustees is the governing body. The endowment is currently valued at approximately $17 million; it is supplemented by $1 million raised through the 2005–06 Annual Fund Drive. Many of Lake Forest Academy's alumni contribute significantly to the Scholarship Fund in addition to making unrestricted gifts.

Lake Forest Academy is accredited by the Independent Schools Association of the Central States and recognized by the state of Illinois. It has memberships in the National Association of Independent Schools, the National Association of College Admission Counselors, the College Board, the Cum Laude Society, the Independent School Association of Greater Chicago, the Secondary School Admission Test Board, the National Association for Foreign Student Affairs, the Council for Advancement and Support of Education, the Midwest Association of Boarding Schools, and the Council for Advancement of Education.

ACADEMIC PROGRAMS

Students are required to carry five courses per year. Graduation requirements include English, 4 years; mathematics, 3; and fine arts, 1. In the history, science, and foreign language disciplines, students are required to complete 3 years in two departments and 2 in the other. Two additional credits are required for graduation. Requirements may be adjusted for students entering after the ninth grade.

Elective courses are offered in journalism, history (African-American History, History of Women in America, World Religions), science (current issues in science, astronomy, environmental science, and anatomy), and fine arts (theater, music theory, film). Advanced Place-ment courses are available in calculus, physics, chemistry, statistics, biology, English, foreign language, U.S. history, European history, and music.

The average class size is 12; the student-teacher ratio is 7:1. Freshmen and sophomores have a proctored study hall during some of their unassigned periods. Juniors and seniors with a sufficient GPA may be granted honor-study privileges. The school library is open during the school day and in the evening. An interlibrary loan system gives students access to more than 2 million volumes.

The grading system uses A to F, with pluses and minuses. Examinations are held twice a year, with grades and teachers' comments sent to parents after each exam. In addition, midterm grades and comments are mailed for all students in the middle of each semester.

FACULTY AND ADVISERS

The faculty is composed of 45 men and women, of whom 76 percent have advanced degrees.

Eighty percent of the faculty members live on the campus. These teachers are responsible for counseling and supervision in the dormitories. Faculty members serve as advisers to students, meeting with them and communicating with their parents on a regular basis. In addition to teaching, faculty members are responsible for extracurricular activities, usually coaching or club sponsorship.

COLLEGE PLACEMENT

Three college counselors work with students to guide them through the college selection process. Students take the PSAT in tenth grade and again in eleventh. The SAT is taken in the spring of the junior year, as well as in the fall of the senior year. Students' SAT verbal and mathematics scores range from the 500s to 800. Representatives of more than 150 colleges visit the campus in the fall of each year. Counselors work very closely with students from the spring of the junior year through the senior year to help them with the decision-making process.

Recent graduates currently attend such institutions as Columbia, Cornell, Dartmouth, Georgetown, Harvard, NYU, Northwestern, Princeton, Rhode Island School of Design, St. Andrew's University (Scotland), UCLA, Williams, and the University of Chicago as well as many other outstanding colleges and universities.

STUDENT BODY AND CONDUCT

There is approximately the same number of boarding students as day students, and the percentage of boys and girls is approximately 50 percent each. Reflecting in part the school's diversity, students come to Lake Forest Academy from seventeen states and thirteen other coun-tries. Thirty percent of the students are members of minority groups, including African American, Asian, and Hispanic.

Students are expected to behave according to prescribed standards. Violations that may lead to dismissal of a student are dealt with by the Dean of Students and the Head of School. All other violations are handled by the Dean or the Judiciary Board, a group composed of students, faculty members, and administrators.

A class president and 8 representatives from each class, forming four student committees, compose the Student Council. The council plans activities, allocates funds, makes recommendations to the Office of the Headmaster, and serves as a forum for students' concerns.

ACADEMIC FACILITIES

Corbin Center is the hub of academic life, with its classrooms, science labs, lecture hall, language lab, photography lab, art studio, computer center, and the school library, which contains 22,000 volumes. Reid Hall houses the writing center and the English department, as well as administrative offices. The auditorium/theater and Hutchinson Commons (the dining room) are housed in an adjacent building. A student center is located in another building. The Cressey Center for the Arts houses the theater and performing and fine art spaces.

BOARDING AND GENERAL FACILITIES

Four dormitories constitute the living quarters for boarding students. Two students share each room, and every dormitory has a commons room for informal gatherings. Each dorm has faculty members in residence. An infirmary is located on the campus. All students must leave the campus for the Thanksgiving, Christmas, and spring vacations.

ATHLETICS

Students at all ability levels are required to participate in athletics in order to experience team involvement and competition. Interscholastic sports for the boys include baseball, basketball, cross-country, football, golf, ice hockey, soccer, swimming and diving, tennis, track, volleyball, and wrestling. Sports for the girls include basketball, cheerleading, cross-country, field hockey, golf, ice hockey, swimming and diving, softball, soccer, tennis, track, and volleyball. In addition, the physical education program offers opportunities to participate in aerobics, weight training, and various intramural sports.

Glore Memorial Gymnasium has a pool, basketball court, wrestling room, locker rooms, and a trainer's room. The campus has football, soccer, baseball, and field hockey fields, as well as a track, an indoor ice arena, practice fields, and four tennis courts. A new fitness center opened in spring 2004 and contains weight machines, free

weights, cardio-machines, and a full-time fitness and weight-lifting expert.

EXTRACURRICULAR OPPORTUNITIES

The proximity of Lake Forest Academy to Chicago provides a wide variety of opportunities for students to participate in cultural events. Trips are made to many of the major theatrical and musical productions that come to Chicago, as well as to museums and exhibits. Other activities on campus include working on the staffs of the yearbook, newspaper, and literary magazine and being involved in various clubs (computer, poets and writers, photography, academic quiz bowl, ski, bridge, and video). Traditional annual events include Homecoming, International Fair, the Prom, Winter Fest, and three plays.

DAILY LIFE

Classes are held from 8:30 to 3. Time is set aside each week for club and class meetings and assemblies. Student-adviser meetings are held three times a week. Students have a 2-hour supervised study hall in the dormitory Sunday through Thursday nights.

WEEKEND LIFE

Both boarders and day students are encouraged to join in weekend activities. Trips are planned every weekend, often to events in Chicago. Trips include visits to various concerts, museums, restaurants, shows, and sports events. Seasonal weekend trips include skiing, camping, biking, and sailing on Lake Michigan. Transportation is provided to nearby shopping centers, where students may shop, eat, or see a movie.

COSTS AND FINANCIAL AID

Costs for 2005–06 were $22,550 for day students and $31,950 for boarding students. Books cost approximately $600 for the year, and there were additional fees for music lessons and tutoring. For boarding students, an allowance of $25 to $30 per week is recommended. An initial deposit is due with the signed Enrollment Contract. Parents then have the option of paying the entire tuition by June 15 and receiving a discount, paying the total amount on August 1, or using a ten-month payment plan available through Academic Management Services.

Financial aid is awarded to qualified students based on parents' financial need. In 2005–06, 35 percent of the students received more than $1.9 million in financial aid. Financial aid is renewed on a yearly basis; parents must submit the Parents' Financial Statement to the School and Student Service for Financial Aid in Princeton, New Jersey.

ADMISSIONS INFORMATION

All applicants to Lake Forest Academy are considered by the Admission Committee on the basis of their academic record, a personal interview, recommendations, and the result of the SSAT. Lake Forest Academy admits students of any race, nationality, religion, or ethnic background to all rights, privileges, programs, and activities generally accorded or made available to students, and the school does not discriminate on the basis of race in administration of its educational policies, admissions policies, scholarship programs, or school-administered programs.

Applicants take the SSAT. Approximately 40 percent of all applicants are accepted for admission.

APPLICATION TIMETABLE

Lake Forest Academy's application deadline is February 15. Early submission of materials is strongly encouraged. Waiting lists form as soon as a class is fully enrolled. In addition to taking the SSAT, students must file an application and transcript release form with a $50 application fee, submit personal and teachers' recommendations, and visit the campus for a tour and an interview. The Admission Office is open for interviews and tours Monday through Friday from 8 to 4 during the academic year and during the summer. Under special circumstances, interviews may be arranged for other times.

ADMISSIONS CORRESPONDENCE

Karen M. Cegelski, Dean of Admission
Lake Forest Academy
Lake Forest, Illinois 60045

Phone: 847-615-3267
Fax: 847-615-3202

LA LUMIERE SCHOOL

La Porte, Indiana

Type: Coeducational boarding and day college-preparatory school
Grades: 9–12
Enrollment: 122
Head of School: Michael H. Kennedy, Headmaster

THE SCHOOL

Founded by Catholic families in 1963 on a strikingly beautiful rural campus of rolling hills and a quiet lake, La Lumiere School provides a rigorous college-preparatory education for young men and women from a rich diversity of backgrounds. Here, faculty members and students work cooperatively in a caring and structured atmosphere to develop the skills necessary for a lifelong pursuit of character, scholarship, and faith.

Situated in northwest Indiana 60 miles southeast of Chicago and 30 miles west of the college town of South Bend, Indiana (Notre Dame, St. Mary's, Holy Cross, Indiana University (South Bend), and Bethel), La Lumiere enjoys easy access to scholastic and cultural facilities, while maintaining the serene separation of its 155-acre rural setting.

The School is governed by a Board of Trustees composed of involved parents and alumni. It is independently Catholic (not under the sponsorship of a particular religious order) and strives to be faithful to that heritage and to the vision and commitment of its lay founders.

La Lumiere is accredited by the North Central Association of Colleges and Schools and by the Independent Schools Association of the Central States. It holds active membership in the Catholic Boarding Schools Association, the National Association of Independent Schools, the Midwest Boarding Schools Association, and the Association of Boarding Schools.

ACADEMIC PROGRAMS

The academic year is divided into semesters that begin in August and end in May. Traditional college-preparatory courses are taught by involved and enthusiastic faculty members to classes of 6 to 16 students. Study skills, writing, critical thinking, and creative problem solving are emphasized.

To graduate, a student must complete 4 years of English, 4 years of math, 2½ years of social studies, 2 years of foreign language, 2 years of science with labs, 2 years of theology, one semester of fine arts, and 2 years of electives. Among the courses offered are the following: English I–IV; ESL; French I–IV; Spanish I–IV; geography; U.S. history; government; algebra I, II, and algebra II/trigonometry; geometry; precalculus; calculus; Java programming; Internet research and design; biology and advanced biology; physics;

chemistry; Old Testament; New Testament; ethics; various art courses; drama; study skills; SAT/ACT/TOEFL preparation; world history; and yearbook. English electives change each semester. Advanced Placement courses are available in English, French, and U.S. history.

Supervised evening study halls in a classroom setting are required for all first- and second-level students as well as those on academic probation. Upper-level students study in their rooms with a faculty proctor present in the dormitory. Weekend remedial sessions are required for those who have submitted homework late during the preceding week. Weekly three-page, cross-curricular writing assignments are required of all students. A study skills course and teacher/peer tutorials provide students with the resources to achieve maximum academic results.

La Lumiere provides a program in English as a second language (ESL) to qualified international students. In order to gain acceptance into the program, applicants should have studied English in their home country and scored above 400 on the paper-based or 97 on the computer-based Test of English as a Foreign Language (TOEFL) or at least 39 on the Secondary Level English Proficiency Test (SLEP). The ESL program is a one-year, fully integrated, intensive curriculum emphasizing language, social studies, and study skills. Each ESL student is mainstreamed during at least two class periods per day. Levels are determined by ability. La Lumiere's goal is to assist and support ESL students in moving as quickly as possible into the School's common program.

FACULTY AND ADVISERS

A qualified faculty consisting of 10 men and 9 women is committed to student development. All are full-time, and 13 live on campus. All of the faculty members hold baccalaureate or master's degrees in the subjects they teach. In addition to their teaching and coaching duties, they are also the sponsors of extracurricular activities.

Students consult with faculty advisers at least once per week. Advisers assist their 6 to 8 advisees in reaching their full potential, while serving as the parents' primary contact with the School. Academic reports are sent to parents quarterly (or weekly by the Academic Dean, if the student is on academic probation).

Michael H. Kennedy is La Lumiere's sixth Headmaster. Mr. Kennedy, who received his undergraduate degree from Boston College and his master's degree from the University of Notre Dame is also a graduate of La Lumiere and taught at the School in the early 1990s. Mr. Kennedy completed his first year as Headmaster in July 2005, after seven years working at The Latin School of Chicago.

COLLEGE PLACEMENT

The focus on college placement begins with the scheduling of courses when a student enters La Lumiere. Annual standardized testing assists in planning each student's academic program and assesses progress toward college/university entrance. Throughout each year, college representatives visit the School in order to inform and speak with students. All sophomores take the PSAT or TOEFL. Juniors review the School's college planning guide and prepare for taking the SAT/ACT Assessment. Seniors value the help of the college counselor to guide them through the college selection and application process. Members of the past two years' graduating classes are attending such schools as the Art Institute of Chicago, Boston College, Denison, Holy Cross, Hope, Indiana, Illinois Benedictine, IIT, Loyola (Chicago), Miami (Ohio), Marquette, Purdue, Regis, St. Joseph's, St. Mary's, Seattle, Valparaiso, Xavier, and the Universities of Denver, Michigan, and Wisconsin.

STUDENT BODY AND CONDUCT

The student body in 2005–06 was composed of 122 students. Just over 50 percent of the student body resides on campus, and the boy-to-girl ratio is evenly split.

The deep appreciation and valuing of different backgrounds and experiences is one of the School's sure strengths.

ACADEMIC FACILITIES

The majority of the instructional areas are organized in one large multilevel complex that includes ten classrooms, two science labs, an art studio, one computer lab, and a library. The library itself occupies most of the second floor. It houses more than 15,000 books and has a large reading room and an adjoining audiovisual room. Additional curriculum support is provided by a reference collection containing extensive periodical holdings, Newsbank, SIRS, and interlibrary access. CD-ROM

units are available for student research, with access to numerous multimedia programs.

The School has classrooms with state-of-the-art technology as well as a computer lab with a T-1 connection and a dual-processing server.

BOARDING AND GENERAL FACILITIES

There are five dormitories where students enjoy spacious double rooms and a homelike atmosphere that encourages the growth of lifelong friendships. Each dormitory is also home to a faculty member and his/her family.

Full health care is provided by the school nurse, the campus infirmary, standing appointments with nearby physicians, and emergency hospital facilities 15 minutes from the campus.

ATHLETICS

La Lumiere regards athletics as an integral part of its program. All students participate in one of several sports offerings each season.

Two hours of participation on sports teams follow classes each weekday. Programs are designed to teach skills and to give every student the experience of representing the School, demonstrating sportsmanship, and enjoying teamwork. Students can choose from a variety of sports programs, including baseball, basketball, football, soccer, tennis, track, and volleyball.

Marsch Gymnasium provides facilities for basketball, volleyball, track, and tennis. In addition, there is an extensive weight-training building and a practice gym with lockers. There are four tennis courts on a hill overlooking the football field. A track beside the campus lake encircles the soccer field.

EXTRACURRICULAR OPPORTUNITIES

Every Wednesday afternoon the normal academic schedule is set aside for special interest activities. Offerings arise from teacher and student interests and expertise. Some of the offerings in 2005–06 included the yearbook, drama production, photography darkroom, computer gaming, portfolio preparation, golf, Science Olympiad, fitness and weight training, chess, and multiple opportunities for community service.

A student council with a president, a vice president, and 2 representatives from each class is elected by the students. The council sponsors activities and represents student interests to the faculty and Headmaster. Admissions tour guides and National Honor Society members are chosen annually.

Scheduled throughout the year are all-school and class trips, athletic events, and speech and drama competitions and performances. The Parents Association provides special events such as cookouts and Halloween and Christmas parties.

DAILY LIFE

The school day, which runs from 7:40 a.m. to 2:35 p.m., is made up of seven 50-minute class periods. A daily school meeting at 7:40 allows for announcements and beginning each day with a prayer. From 3:15 to 5:00 p.m., athletic practices occur. Usually around 6:00, meals are served in the open-beamed Main House. After the 7:30 to 9:45 p.m. study halls, students prepare for lights out at 10:30 (11:00 for seniors). On Friday mornings an all-school assembly features faculty and guest speakers. Mass is celebrated every Sunday and Holy Day.

WEEKEND LIFE

Any student in good standing may leave campus, with parental permission, on any open weekend. For students who choose to stay on campus, the weekend faculty team designs a variety of activities. These might include off-campus trips to theaters, museums, shopping malls, sporting events, movies, and parks.

COSTS AND FINANCIAL AID

Tuition, room, and board in 2005–06 for resident students were $21,885. Day student tuition was $6905, and international students paid $23,060. A deposit of $1000 is due upon acceptance and is deductible from the total. Additional costs include book fees averaging at least $350, a yearbook fee of $90, mandatory insurance ($16 for day students, $78 for boarders), and an annual technology fee of $150. Additional charges are assessed for standardized tests, school uniforms, and any cultural excursions. A monthly deposit of $60 in the school bank is usually sufficient to cover laundry and snacks and supplies at the school store. Fees are payable in full August 1 or in two installments of 60 percent by August 1 and 40 percent by December 1 (plus a $500 carrying charge). A monthly payment alternative is available either through bank transfer or through a loan from Key Education Resources.

Financial aid in the form of need-based assistance is awarded on a first-come, first-served basis to applicants who show need, and merit in academics, athletics, or character.

ADMISSIONS INFORMATION

La Lumiere seeks students who can perform academically at the college-preparatory level and who will contribute their talents and abilities toward enriching the school community. The School values its diverse student body and admits qualified applicants without regard to race, creed, color, sex, or national origin. Applicants must submit a transcript and standardized test scores as well as three recommendations. An interview on campus is required, unless waived by the Director of Admissions. Campus tours and interviews can be arranged by contacting the Admissions Office. It is preferred that visits be scheduled on a school day so that prospective students and their families can experience the life of the School in full operation.

APPLICATION TIMETABLE

La Lumiere welcomes inquiries and visits throughout the year. Admission decisions begin in February and proceed dependent on space availability. Entrance is normally at the beginning of each school year; however, entrance at other times, especially for spring semester, is considered on an individual basis. Upon admission, the School provides international students with the documents necessary to obtain an entry visa.

ADMISSIONS CORRESPONDENCE

Office of Admissions
La Lumiere School
6801 North Wilhelm Road
La Porte, Indiana 46350
Phone: 219-326-7450
Fax: 219-325-3185
E-mail: admissions@lalumiere.org
Web site: http://www.lalumiere.org

LAWRENCE ACADEMY

Groton, Massachusetts

Type: Coeducational boarding and day nondenominational college-preparatory school
Grades: 9–12
Enrollment: 393
Head of School: D. Scott Wiggins

THE SCHOOL

Lawrence Academy was founded in 1793 as Groton Academy. The school changed its name in 1845 in honor of Amos and William Lawrence, the school's major benefactors during that era. Lawrence has earned a reputation for excellent college preparation through a curriculum designed to stimulate creative thinking and active participation and to motivate students to take responsibility for their education. Academics include the new Ansin Academic Building (2004); an expanded arts program housed in the Williams Art Center; an athletics program, based in the Stone Athletic Center; and a variety of on- and off-campus programs to allow for a personal commitment to social and cultural activities.

The campus consists of 100 acres in a classic New England town 31 miles northwest of Boston and 8 miles south of New Hampshire. Easily accessible by public transportation and major highways, it is close enough to several urban centers for students to take advantage of a variety of social, cultural, and recreational offerings, and it is far enough removed for all to enjoy the safe and quiet character of the New England countryside.

The Academy is a nonprofit corporation directed by a self-perpetuating Board of Trustees, which meets three times yearly. Endowment in productive funds totals $14.5 million, and the school plant is valued at $45 million. The 2004–05 Annual Fund raised a total of $735,000. The Alumni Council represents 4,000 graduates and assists the school in fund-raising, recruiting, and long-range planning. The Parents Association works closely with faculty members on a variety of projects.

Lawrence Academy is accredited by the New England Association of Schools and Colleges and is a member of the National Association of Independent Schools, the Association of Independent Schools of New England, the Secondary School Admission Test Board, the Principals of Girls Independent Schools, and the Council for Advancement and Support of Education.

ACADEMIC PROGRAMS

Lawrence Academy encourages the commitment and resourcefulness that will enable students to develop their intellectual skills and curiosity and apply these in the synthesis of information and experience. The goal is to increase students' ability to master higher levels of learning and help them embrace education as a lifelong process.

To graduate, students must complete 18 credits and their Winterim courses. Minimum credit requirements are English, 4; mathematics, 3; foreign language, 2; history, 2 (3 for ninth graders); science, 2 (including 1 of biology); and arts, 2.

The curriculum is a combination of yearlong and trimester courses. Yearlong courses include a ninth-grade program (an integrated study of English, history, science, and the arts); a combined studies course; sophomore and junior English and senior English seminar; French 1–5, Latin 1–6, and Spanish 1–5; sophomore history, U.S. history, and senior history honors seminar; math 1–5 (through Advanced Placement calculus); and biology, chem-

istry, physics, and AP environmental science. Honors courses are offered in English, history, math, and science, senior independent. Typical trimester electives are English composition, creative writing, women's studies, African-American writers, and Shakespeare; the Cold War, psychology, and Native Americans; electronics, tropical biology, marine biology, limnology, nuclear issues, the cosmos, ecology, and ornithology; computer science; and drawing, drama, painting, photography, understanding music, chorus, concert choir, song writing, and instrumental music. Advanced Placement preparation courses are available in environmental science, English, French, Latin, Spanish, calculus, music, and computer science. Also offered is a year-round English as a second language (ESL) program with a full-time faculty and director.

The extended independent study option permits students to pursue on- or off-campus projects for a full term. Students may also present proposals for independent study courses in lieu of regular courses in particular departments.

Winterim is a two-week period of intensive experiential learning. Typical Winterim projects are backpacking in the Superstition Mountains; mountain biking in Utah; going on cultural study trips to Russia, Italy, and Ireland; quilting; pursuing field studies in marine biology in Central America; or performing volunteer work with the homeless in Worcester.

The Independent Immersion Program is an alternative curricular structure for students who are capable of assuming the major responsibility for their own education. With the help of faculty members, each student designs a program of study to meet particular needs and interests. Students work largely on their own but are supervised and evaluated by the faculty.

The average class size is 12; the overall student-teacher ratio is 7:1. Class enrollments are determined on the basis of students' abilities, needs, and interests. Most students take five courses each term. Instruction is provided in small classes and through seminars, independent study, and individual instruction. Extra help is available in all subjects. Supervised study is provided for students in academic difficulty. The library, computer rooms, laboratories, and studios for independent study are open from 8 a.m. to 10 p.m.

Letter grades (A to F) are awarded. Standards for high honors–honors and minimum acceptable performance are set by the faculty. Progress reports from each teacher, including performance and effort marks, are given to students and advisers weekly; parents are sent midterm and term grades six times a year and adviser letters three times a year.

FACULTY AND ADVISERS

The full-time faculty consists of 41 men and 34 women. They hold seventy-five baccalaureates, forty-eight master's, and two doctoral degrees. All faculty members hold at least one baccalaureate and two thirds hold advanced degrees. Thirty-five faculty members and their families live on campus.

D. Scott Wiggins became Head of School in 2003. He is a graduate of Boston University (B.A.,

1977) and Arizona State University College of Law (J.D., 1988). Mr. Wiggins worked as an associate attorney and as an assistant district attorney in Chester County, Pennsylvania. Mr. Wiggins' experience in independent schools includes Athletic Director at The Fessenden School, Director of Admissions at Fountain Valley School, and, most recently, Upper School Head at Metairie Park Country Day School in New Orleans.

Most faculty members coach, supervise dormitory and student activities, and act as advisers. Guidance services are provided by a full-time counselor, the director of student life, and faculty members. A faculty intervention team and a sophomore sexuality program are additional guidance services. Lawrence seeks diversity within its faculty and supports professional growth opportunities during the school year as well as in the summer.

COLLEGE PLACEMENT

College counseling procedures begin in the junior year with individual conferences. Each student spends considerable time with one of the 4 college counselors, and a list of possible colleges is developed. Juniors are encouraged to read a variety of college publications and to visit schools during spring break and the summer prior to their senior year. Parents are involved in the process from the beginning.

Application procedures begin early in the senior year after each student, his or her parents, and one of the college counselors have discussed thoroughly that student's interests, abilities, academic credentials, and other related criteria. Consistent with the Academy's policy of diversity among students and faculty, Lawrence graduates have matriculated at a wide range of colleges in recent years.

The middle 50 percent of the most recent class scored between 500 and 610 on the verbal SAT and between 520 and 640 on the quantitative. Ninety-eight percent of all graduates enter college the fall following graduation, and virtually all have entered college within two years of graduation.

STUDENT BODY AND CONDUCT

Lawrence has 216 boys and 177 girls. Grade distribution is as follows: 79 in grade 9, 101 in grade 10, 112 in grade 11, and 101 in grade 12. Day students come from nearby towns in Massachusetts and New Hampshire. Boarders are from eighteen states and seventeen other countries.

Students play a responsible role in governing themselves and participate on a variety of policy-making and advisory committees related to curriculum and campus life. An active student government provides formalized procedures for student involvement in the decision-making process, and a proctor system enables students to provide support, structure, and leadership in dormitories. School rules are described and defined in the *Omnibus Lucet* mailed to students' homes before the opening of school.

ACADEMIC FACILITIES

The Ansin Academic Building opened in the fall of 2004, complete with several new classrooms, com-

puter rooms, and science laboratories. This new building supplements the existing academic building, which includes new biology and chemistry laboratories. Classrooms with computers are equipped with seven workstations with PCs and a teacher workstation, an HP printer, and access to the Ethernet network. In addition, students may independently use three more rooms that contain computers with Internet and e-mail access and online resources similar to those in the library. The Ferguson Building contains the library (with 20,000 volumes, fifty-two periodical subscriptions, and computers with educational software, online resources, CD-ROM databases, Internet access, and an automated card catalog), an art gallery, the theater, the studies office, and the college office. The Williams Art Center provides classrooms for visual and performing arts, a performance studio for the Academy's expanded dance and theater program, a recital hall, five practice rooms, an art library, a photography lab, a state-of-the-art recording studio, a radio station, and the art faculty offices.

BOARDING AND GENERAL FACILITIES

Students live in ten dormitories, seven of which are Colonial homes that date from 1793 to 1839. A new dormitory was opened in fall 2003. All dormitories are networked for Internet access from rooms. Four new faculty homes were built and opened to families in 1997. Students generally are assigned to double rooms, but a few singles are available. There are two school nurses in the expanded health center, and 2 doctors are on call. A 102-bed hospital is 4 miles from campus.

ATHLETICS

The Academy competes in the Independent School League (ISL). Lawrence supports a varied athletics program in which all students are required to participate. In the fall this includes football, boys' and girls' soccer, boys' and girls' cross-country, and field hockey. In the winter, Lawrence competes in boys' and girls' basketball and ice hockey, wrestling, and volleyball; in the spring, in baseball and golf, boys' and girls' lacrosse and tennis, and softball. Outdoor programs, offered in the fall and spring term, include rock climbing, hiking, camping, bicycling, cross-country skiing, and snowshoeing. Dance is offered every term. An intramural program develops skills in a variety of sports.

The Academy's facilities include the new Shumway athletic fields. In addition, the Stone Athletic Center has locker rooms for boys and girls, visitors, and officials as well as a weight room, Nautilus equipment, a training room, a wrestling room, offices, a meeting room, and a large gymnasium with two basketball courts, a climbing wall, and a volleyball court on a wood floor. The athletics department also utilizes 14 acres of playing fields, ten newly renovated outdoor tennis courts, and a covered artificial-ice skating rink.

EXTRACURRICULAR OPPORTUNITIES

At least three student dramatic productions and dance, music, and visual art performances are presented in the school's 420-seat theater or black box theater each year. Movies are shown frequently. Art exhibits are displayed in the gallery throughout the year. Speakers and performing artists are brought to the campus. Recent programs included Secrets, an AIDS awareness performance; Mixed Company, an a cappella group from Yale; and Marion Stoddart, Chair of Nashoba Watershed Program.

The Program Committee plans weekend entertainment and social activities, such as movies, dances, and open houses. With approval, students may attend off-campus functions or go home on weekends. Among the traditional school events are Merrimack Rep. Theater Day, Fall Parents' Day, the Spring Carnival, and Mountain Day.

Student organizations include the Amnesty International, Students Concerned about Rainforests, SADD, and Multi-Cultural Alliance clubs. Students interested in music have opportunities to join the chorus, concert choir, SLACS, stage band, and the brass, wind, string, and jazz ensembles. Additional organizations include the Athletic Council, Student Government, Health Committee, and the staffs of the yearbook, school newspaper, and literary magazine.

DAILY LIFE

The daily schedule begins with an optional breakfast, followed by adviser-advisee meetings or all-school meetings at 7:45. Classes meet from 8 a.m. until 3:30 p.m. three days a week and until 2 p.m. twice a week, with a special class period three times a week with extra time for first-year language students, full choral and instrumental group rehearsals, extra help, and class or extracurricular meetings. Four to six academic periods of varying lengths are scheduled daily; each class meets four times a week on a rotating basis. A hot meal, a deli selection, and a salad bar are offered at noon. From 3:30 to 5:30 p.m., students participate in athletics. After a buffet supper, residents have ample time for academic work and socializing. The hours 8–10 p.m. are study hours on campus, and a supervised study hall is provided for students who need it.

WEEKEND LIFE

Saturdays provide opportunities for a variety of extracurricular, social, and academic activities (including SAT preparation, computer literacy classes, reading and study skills classes, and driver education) and for athletics competition and outdoor program trips. Opportunities for off-campus activities with faculty chaperones are announced during the week, and students are urged to participate. Trips to Boston, beaches, hockey games, dances; skiing; and continual activities are planned by a full-time director of student activities. With parental permission, boarding students may leave campus most weekends if all school commitments have

been met and the adviser's and dormmaster's approval have been obtained.

COSTS AND FINANCIAL AID

In 2005–06, tuition was $36,900 for boarding students and $28,000 for day students. Additional expenses for books, class trips, art fees, and school and athletic supplies range from $150 to $300 per term. Transportation for boarders and optional expenses for tutoring or music lessons are extra. A 10 percent tuition deposit is due in May; half the remaining total is due on August 1 and the rest on December 1. A tuition payment plan is also available.

Approximately 30 percent of the student body receives $2 million in scholarships and loans each year. Lawrence subscribes to the School and Student Service for Financial Aid and grants aid on the basis of need. Candidates indicating an interest in financial aid on the application form receive a Parents' Financial Statement from the Academy.

ADMISSIONS INFORMATION

Lawrence Academy seeks talented and motivated college-bound students who will contribute to the community as well as benefit from it. New students are accepted in all grades except grade 12, unless applying to the Independent Immersion Program. An interview, SSAT, PSAT, SAT or TOEFL scores, transcripts, and academic references are required.

APPLICATION TIMETABLE

An application packet containing pertinent information and step-by-step procedures and the school catalog are provided on request. Candidates for fall entrance should apply the preceding fall. February 1 is the deadline for consideration in the first round; late applications are considered if vacancies exist. Acceptances are mailed by March 10. The Parents' reply date is April 10. There is a nonrefundable $50 application fee (international application fee is $100).

Candidates should contact the Admissions Office (8 a.m.–4:30 p.m., Monday–Friday) to arrange for a visit. If the distance is too great, an attempt will be made to arrange a telephone interview or an interview with a nearby parent or alumnus.

ADMISSIONS CORRESPONDENCE

Andrea O'Hearn, Director of Admissions
Admissions Office
Lawrence Academy
P.O. Box 992
Groton, Massachusetts 01450-0992

Phone: 978-448-6535
Fax: 978-448-9208
E-mail: admiss@lacademy.edu
Web site: http://www.lacademy.edu

THE LAWRENCEVILLE SCHOOL

Lawrenceville, New Jersey

Type: Coeducational boarding and day college-preparatory school
Grades: 9–PG (Forms II–V): Lower School, Form II; Circle/Crescent Level, Forms III–IV; Fifth Form
Enrollment: 807
Head of School: Elizabeth A. Duffy, Head Master

THE SCHOOL

The Lawrenceville School was established in 1810 as an academy by the pastor of the village church, whose elders had sons to educate. By 1885, the physical plant was greatly enlarged, the present House System adopted, and the enrollment expanded. Lawrenceville, a small historic town, is 55 miles from New York City and 40 miles from Philadelphia.

In 1987, Lawrenceville became coeducational, enrolling girls at all grade levels. Girls account for 46 percent of the student population.

Life at Lawrenceville emphasizes individual responsibility for self-development and for community living. The purpose of the School as an academic institution is to offer an education that helps students not only to gain admission to college but also to become active and thoughtful members of society.

Twenty-six of the 32 members of the Board of Trustees are alumni of Lawrenceville. The School endowment is more than $200 million, the 2004–05 gifts amounted to more than $5 million, and the 2004–05 operating expenses totaled more than $40 million. Fiscal year-end gifts for 2004–05 amounted to more than $16 million. Of this, the Annual Fund contributed some $5.2 million, with 4,085 of the more than 11,093 living alumni participating.

Lawrenceville is accredited by the Middle States Association of Colleges and Schools and is a member of the Secondary School Admission Test Board, the National Association of Independent Schools, the New Jersey Association of Independent Schools, and the Council for Religion in Independent Schools.

ACADEMIC PROGRAMS

Each student at Lawrenceville carries up to five courses per term, for a minimum total of 14 units per year. Forty-two units must be taken as follows: English, 10; language, 7; mathematics, through algebra IIB; history, 5; science, 5; arts, 3; religion, 2; geography, 1; non-Western cultures, 1; and two interdisciplinary courses. Fifty-two units are required for graduation. Students are required to give at least 40 hours of community service before they graduate.

Lawrenceville offers approximately 280 courses plus twenty-seven laboratory courses. Electives include law as literature, bioethics, Spanish, theater, and history of China. Lawrenceville offers sixteen Advanced Placement (AP) courses.

Individual participation is encouraged in small classroom sections averaging 12 students. Classes are grouped randomly except for the honors sections and are taught around a large oval table called the Harkness Table. Evening study periods, held in the houses, are supervised by the Housemaster, the Assistant Housemaster, or an Associate Housemaster.

Students with a particular interest in exploring new fields or in testing themselves against the challenge of a job may apply for Independent Study, off-campus projects, or the Term Abroad Program (France, Spain, and the Bahamas). Driver's education is available.

Lawrenceville uses a letter grading system (A–F) in which D– is passing and B+ qualifies for honors.

The school year is divided into three 10-week terms. Full reports are sent home at the end of each term, with interim reports at midterm. The full reports include comments and grades from each of a student's teachers indicating his or her accomplishments, efforts, and attitudes. Less formal progress reports are also written by teachers throughout the term as needed. Students in academic difficulty are placed on academic review, which entails close supervision and additional communication with parents.

FACULTY AND ADVISERS

Of the 142 faculty members, 135 are full-time. Eighty-four faculty members hold master's degrees, and 18 hold doctorates. Most reside on the campus, and many serve as residential housemasters, coaches, and club advisers.

Elizabeth A. Duffy was appointed the twelfth Head Master of The Lawrenceville School in 2003. Ms. Duffy graduated magna cum laude from Princeton University in 1988 with an A.B. in molecular biology. In 1993, she received an M.B.A. from the Graduate School of Business at Stanford University and an A.M. in administration and policy analysis from the School of Education there. She has spent her entire career working with educators at all levels.

Faculty members take advantage of the School's policy of providing financial help for continuing education. They have summers free, and each year 3 or 4 faculty members take a trimester off with full pay to pursue scholarly activities. All are active in advising and counseling students.

COLLEGE PLACEMENT

The goal of the College Counseling Office is to educate students and families about the nuances of college admissions, advise students about a range of interesting college options that best suit their individual needs, and support and encourage students as they complete the application process.

Lawrenceville's experienced college counselors provide timely advice to families and help students present their abilities, talents and experiences to the colleges in the most appropriate manner. Families and students receive information through newsletters, class-wide meetings and parent weekend programming. They also have access to a detailed Blackboard based college counseling program via the Web which gives them unlimited access to relevant topics on college admission and links to important sources of information and support, as well as overall advice on selecting and applying to college. These resources are designed to ensure that students and their families are well prepared to embrace the college counseling process when students are officially assigned to individual counselors in the middle of their Fourth Form year. Over the course of their junior and senior years all students engage in a series of college related standardized testing, a self-reflective process, college visits, on-campus college fairs, visits and/or interviews

with more than 150 colleges, and individual meetings with college counselors to discuss their goals and aspirations.

The class of 2005's median SAT scores were 670 verbal and 680 math. The 233 graduates are represented at 94 colleges and universities. Five or more members of the class matriculated at Princeton (14), Cornell (9), Georgetown (9), Vanderbilt (8), Duke (7), Harvard (7), NYU (7), Boston College (6), Columbia (6), GWU (6), Colgate (5), Dartmouth (5), Stanford (5), UNC Chapel Hill (5), U. Penn (5), and Yale (5).

STUDENT BODY AND CONDUCT

For 2005–06, there were 807 students, 266 of whom were day students. There were 149 students in the Second Form, 211 students in the Third Form, 212 students in the Fourth Form, and 235 students (including postgraduates) in the Fifth Form. Students came from thirty-three states and twenty-eight countries. Most boarders are from New Jersey, New York, Pennsylvania, California, Illinois, Georgia, Connecticut, Virginia, Texas, Massachusetts, Florida, and North Carolina.

Lawrenceville expects its students to achieve good records and develop self-control, systematic study habits, and a clear sense of responsibility. The School has a high regard for energy, initiative, a positive attitude, and active cooperation. Students accepting this premise have no trouble following the basic regulations.

The School separates disciplinary action into three categories. They are, in decreasing order of severity, the breaking of a rule for which dismissal from School is a possible consequence, general misbehavior deemed inappropriate by the School community, and house-related offenses that reflect a lack of cooperation in the day-to-day working of the house. A student-faculty committee makes recommendations to the Head Master in regard to disciplinary action for offenses in the first category.

The student body elects 5 governing officers from among students in the Fifth Form, and each house elects its own Student Council.

ACADEMIC FACILITIES

There are thirty-four major buildings on Lawrenceville's 700-acre campus, including the Bunn Library (with space for 100,000 volumes), which opened in 1996. The Bunn Library offers sophisticated computer research facilities, a state-of-the-art electronic classroom, and greatly expanded study areas. A 56,000-square-foot science building opened in spring 1998, a visual arts center opened in fall 1998, a history center reopened in fall 1999, and a music center opened in fall 2000.

Lawrenceville's computer network links all academic and administrative buildings. All Lawrenceville students have network ports in their dorm rooms.

BOARDING AND GENERAL FACILITIES

Lawrenceville's most distinguishing feature is its House System. In each of the nineteen houses, the housemaster maintains close contact with the residents. House athletics teams compete intramurally,

and house identity is maintained through separate dining rooms in the Dining Center for the underformers. This distinctive system provides a small social environment in which each student's contribution is important and measurable.

At Lawrenceville, the ninth graders live in four Lower School Houses; the tenth and eleventh graders live in ten Circle Houses, six for boys and four for girls; and the seniors live in five Fifth Form Houses and eat as a class in the Abbott Dining Hall. Five residential houses for girls opened in 1987.

Services in Edith Memorial Chapel are nondenominational. The McGraw Infirmary has a full-time resident physician and a round-the-clock nursing staff.

ATHLETICS

Because many physical, social, and moral values can be instilled through the disciplines and demands of team sports, competitive athletics, at both the interscholastic and house levels, are the core of the physical education program. There are interscholastic teams in baseball, basketball, crew, cross-country, diving, fencing, field hockey, football, golf, hockey, indoor and outdoor track, lacrosse, soccer, softball, squash, swimming, tennis, volleyball, water polo, and wrestling. An extensive lifetime sports program is offered, as are a variety of intramural sports among the houses, including 8-man tackle football for boys' Circle Houses.

The Edward J. Lavino Field House is an unusually fine one for a secondary school. The main arena area has been completely refinished with a synthetic surface and includes a permanent banked 200-meter track and three tennis/basketball/volleyball courts. The arena can also be used for rainy-day indoor practice. Two additional hardwood basketball courts, a six-lane swimming pool, a wrestling room, two fitness centers with a full-time strength and conditioning coach, and a training-wellness facility are housed in the wings of the building. A new squash court facility, hosting ten new internationally zoned courts, opened in 2003.

Lawrenceville has eighteen athletics fields, a golf course, sixteen outdoor tennis courts, a ¼-mile all-weather track, an indoor ice-hockey rink, a boathouse, and a state-of-the-art ropes and mountaineering course.

EXTRACURRICULAR OPPORTUNITIES

Lawrenceville offers students numerous opportunities for extracurricular activities. Students can choose from more than fifty organizations in debating, drama, music (the Lawrenceville Orchestra, the Lawrenceville Chorus, Jazz Ensemble, and Sotto

Voice), art, history, religion, science, language, video (the Yearbook), and photography. The largest single student enterprise is the Periwig Club, whose dramas, comedies, and musicals attract more than a third of the students. Publications include *The Lawrence*, the *Lit*, and a yearbook. Exhibits occur throughout the year. Two lecture programs bring to the campus authoritative speakers and artists from many fields. Student clubs have their own guest lecturers.

There is a required Community Service Program in which students may serve as tutors, elementary school study center supervisors, directors of sports, and group activity counselors. Other community services include the Chapel Ushers, Campus Guides, the School Camp, the Open Door, and the Library Associates. The School sponsors organized educational and cultural trips to New York City and Washington, D.C.

Annual events include Parents' Weekend in the fall, Parents' Winter Gathering, and Alumni Weekend in the spring.

DAILY LIFE

Each class is 45 minutes long. Classes are held six days a week, and the average number of classes per day for each student is four. Classes begin at 8 a.m. and end at 3 p.m. except on Wednesday and Saturday, when classes are over at 11:30. Students engage in sports in the afternoon; most clubs and groups meet in the evening. Students take lunch at their adviser's table on Friday.

WEEKEND LIFE

The School's location provides numerous opportunities for social, cultural, and entertainment activities. Regular weekends begin after the last class on Saturday; honors weekends, after the last class on Friday. Students may go out for dinner with responsible adults. Drama and musical performances are often held on weekends, as are major sports events, mixers, and dances. Day students are welcome at all of these.

COSTS AND FINANCIAL AID

The annual charges for 2005–06 were $34,570 (plus a $500 medical fee and $300 technology fee) for boarding students and $28,180 (plus a $300 medical fee and $200 technology fee) for day students.

Through the generosity of alumni, friends, and foundations, approximately $6 million in funds are available to provide scholarships and financial assistance to qualified students. Currently, 232 students receive assistance. Awards are made on the basis of character, ability, past performance, and future promise. Amounts are based solely on need,

range from $1000 to the full annual cost, and are determined by procedures established by the School and Student Service for Financial Aid.

ADMISSIONS INFORMATION

All students who enter must be able to meet the academic standards. But Lawrenceville also looks for students who possess the potential to become vitally interested members of the student body—students who make individual contributions.

Selection is based on all-around qualifications without regard to race, creed, or national origin. Character, seriousness of purpose, future promise as well as past performance, the recommendation of a headmaster or principal, and the results of the SSAT are all taken into consideration by the Admission Committee.

For fall 2005, there were 1,612 formal applications for grades 9 through 12, of which 399 were accepted, and 248 enrolled in the following grades: grade 9, 149; grade 10, 59; grade 11, 16; and grade 12, 24 (including postgraduates).

Required for admission is the formal application, which includes a written essay, a transcript of the applicant's school record, and a letter of recommendation from the head of the current school, plus three reference letters, SSAT or ISEE and/or TOEFL scores, and an on-campus interview.

APPLICATION TIMETABLE

Campus interviews are conducted throughout the week from 9 a.m. to 2 p.m. Monday through Friday and from 8:45 to 11:45 a.m. on Saturday. (Interviews are not conducted on Saturday during the summer months.)

The application deadline is January 31 for boarding students and January 15 for day students, at which times three teacher recommendations, student transcripts, SSAT scores, and the head of school recommendation must be submitted. All campus interviews should also be completed by this date.

The notification date is March 10, and parents reply by April 10.

ADMISSIONS CORRESPONDENCE

Dean of Admission
The Lawrenceville School
P.O. Box 6008
2500 Main Street
Lawrenceville, New Jersey 08648
Phone: 609-895-2030
       800-735-2030 (toll-free outside
          New Jersey)
Fax: 609-895-2217
E-mail: admissions@lawrenceville.org
Web site: http://www.lawrenceville.org

LEYSIN AMERICAN SCHOOL IN SWITZERLAND

Leysin, Switzerland

Type: Coeducational boarding college-preparatory school
Grades: 9–13/PG
Enrollment: 350
Head of School: Dr. K. Steven Ott, Executive Director; Mr. Vladimir Kuskovski, Headmaster

THE SCHOOL

As an international university-preparatory high school committed to excellence, the Leysin American School in Switzerland (LAS) educates students to respect people of other cultures and to be responsible, productive, and ethical citizens with the skills to think creatively, reason critically, and communicate effectively. This is achieved because students live in a family-like global community with high standards. LAS offers both an International Baccalaureate (I.B.) program and a U.S. high school curriculum. LAS teachers are highly qualified, dedicated international educators.

The School is located in Leysin, an alpine resort above Lake Geneva. About 90 minutes from the Geneva International Airport, Leysin is easily accessible by car or train. The magnificent beauty, serenity, and healthy environment of Leysin are enhanced by the cultural wealth of Europe and unlimited opportunities for outdoor enjoyment.

LAS strives to foster a harmonious community of young people who represent approximately fifty nationalities. By living and learning together, students develop into "citizens of the world," with an appreciation for other cultures and languages. The School provides a challenging college-preparatory program within a supportive framework. A large percentage of students take I.B. certificate courses, while a limited number pursue the International Baccalaureate Diploma. Virtually all students continue their studies in excellent universities in the United States, Canada, Europe, and Asia.

The Leysin American School was founded in 1961 by Mr. and Mrs. Fred C. Ott and was solely owned and operated by the Ott family until June 2005. Today, the newly formed Foundation for the Advancement of International Education owns Leysin American, but the School continues under the family's leadership. It is governed by a 5-person Foundation Board under the chairmanship of Dr. K. Steven Ott.

LAS is accredited by the European Council of International Schools, the Middle States Association of Colleges and Schools, and the Department of Swiss Private Education. LAS holds membership in the Swiss Group of International Schools, Advanced Placement, College Board, and the International Baccalaureate organization. In 1999, the Leysin American School became the first high school worldwide to be certified ISO 9001 by the Swiss Association of Quality and Management Systems (SQS).

ACADEMIC PROGRAMS

The school year is divided into two semesters. The first extends from late August to mid-December and the second from January to early June. The grading system is based upon a standard A to F, 4-point scale. LAS was the first school outside of the United States to provide Powerschool Web access to parents interested in communicating directly with teachers, administrators, and the student. Powerschool provides real-time information for students and parents and includes complete grade access, attendance records, discipline and health information, financial accounts, and the daily school bulletin.

Students follow a demanding college-preparatory curriculum, including International Baccalaureate study. AP calculus AB and BC are also offered.

The college-preparatory curriculum meets admission requirements for colleges and universities in the U.S. and Canada. The diploma is granted on the basis of the following criteria: a minimum of two semesters of LAS residency, including the two semesters of the final year, and completion of a minimum of 24 credits, which include 4 credits in English, 3 in social studies, 3 in modern languages, 3 in sciences, 3 in mathematics, 2 in creative arts, 1 in senior humanities, 1 in physical education, 1 in computer studies, and 2 electives. ESL students must earn 7 ESL course credits, which thus fulfills the English and modern languages requirements.

The International Baccalaureate, a challenging program open to qualified students, can be followed during the last two years of high school. Students take courses leading to external exams in six areas (three higher level and three standard level); enroll in the Theory of Knowledge course; write an extended essay; and participate in creativity, action, and service requirements. The I.B. Diploma is recognized by universities throughout the world and, in some cases, allows up to one year of advanced standing in U.S. universities. I.B. graduates are also awarded the U.S. high school diploma.

Students in all of the diploma programs are encouraged to take a full range of courses to enrich their education. LAS offers electives such as visual arts, band, choir, drama, photography, private piano lessons, yearbook, additional modern languages, social studies electives, and computer science studies. The average class size is 12–15 students. The academic staff–student ratio is 1:7. Students take seven courses per semester.

The annual educational travel program includes two cultural excursions designed to acquaint students with the history and culture of Switzerland and major European cities. The students travel in small groups to various regions and submit a cultural report.

FACULTY AND ADVISERS

LAS has 63 faculty members and administrators. Ninety percent are from countries whose native language is English, and more than 70 percent hold advanced degrees. The School is firmly committed to its "in loco parentis" philosophy. Faculty members reside on campus, taking on a strong parenting role for the students. They share in dormitory and study period supervision, sponsor sports and recreational activities, and supervise excursions.

Faculty members also serve as sponsors for Faculty Families, which play an important role in providing a caring, family-oriented environment for students. Two faculty members "adopt" 10 to 15 students of different nationalities and ages and serve as personal/academic advisers, guiding the students through all aspects of boarding school life. Families meet regularly during the week and join in activities and excursions on weekends.

Dr. K. Steven Ott was appointed Executive Director of the School in 1982. He served in numerous capacities at LAS from 1970 to 1977, at which point he was appointed professor and charged with curriculum development at the newly founded King Faisal University in Saudi Arabia. He earned his B.S., M.S., and Ph.D. degrees at Stanford University.

Marc Frédéric Ott was appointed Director of External Relations in 2005. He earned his master's degree in teaching business, economics, and accounting at the University of St. Gallen, Switzerland. He is currently a doctoral candidate at Teachers College at Columbia University.

COLLEGE PLACEMENT

A full-time college counselor gives advice and guidance to students as they prepare for admission to universities. Current college materials and online resources are available in the College Counseling Office. Students have many opportunities to meet college admissions officers from American and European campuses during their visits to Switzerland. There are, on average, 35 school representatives who visit LAS each year.

LAS is a regional testing center for SAT and SAT Subject Tests, ACT, IB, AP, and TOEFL examinations. Graduating students continue their education in leading U.S. and Canadian universities such as Bates, Boston University, Cornell, Dartmouth, Duke, Harvard, McGill, Stanford, U.S. Air Force Academy, and Yale.

International placements include the Federal Institute of Technology (Switzerland), Cambridge and King's College (England), Keio University (Tokyo), and the Universities of Bremen (Germany), Durham (England), and St. Andrew's (Scotland).

STUDENT BODY AND CONDUCT

In 2004–05, 320 students were enrolled from approximately fifty countries. Just over 30 percent were U.S. citizens, many of whom had families living abroad. Some of the other countries represented included Brazil, Germany, Japan, Kazakhstan, Mexico, Mongolia, Norway, Russia, Saudi Arabia, Spain, and Taiwan. Approximately one third of the student body was enrolled in LAS's English as a second language program.

The LAS publications explain community standards and behavioral expectations. LAS fosters a sense of responsibility for the School community and the individual with honesty, respect, and fairness as key concepts. Both on and off campus, LAS is a nonsmoking school at all times. LAS has a zero-tolerance policy on drug use and related activities and imposes testing.

ACADEMIC FACILITIES

The LAS campus offers excellent facilities in every academic area. There are two main academic complexes and five additional residential halls. The Savoy Complex has thirty classrooms, administrative offices, and an Information and Technology Center that includes a teaching lab and an additional lab of thirty computers, all of which are under two years old. There is a newly renovated library with 20,000 volumes, CD-ROM online data bank, and Internet access. The Savoy also houses the dining room; the health center; the new Visual Arts Center, which includes a darkroom for photography; a ceramics studio; and a beautiful painting studio with terraces overlooking the Rhone Valley. There is also a state-of-the-art black box theater, a music room with recording technology, and two new art galleries. The athletic facilities, next to the Savoy, feature a gymnasium, a squash court, a fitness center, and a dance studio.

The Beau Site houses the Science Center with four new labs and a lecture hall. The Admissions Office and the primary reception area are located in Beau Site. Students can relax in the student center,

named the Red Frog, and dance in the Valley View multipurpose hall, which is frequently the LAS Disco. The Vermont Complex, located directly between the Savoy and the Beau Site, includes a bookstore, Activities and Travel offices, and a newly renovated math chalet with six classrooms.

In 2005, the Beau Reveil facility was opened after a two-year renovation. This facility now houses the six classes of the Modern Languages department, offices, and a new computer language lab. The language lab features twenty computers with networked online Auralog TeLL me More® language software in French, German, Spanish, and ESL.

BOARDING AND GENERAL FACILITIES
The LAS campus blends into the friendly, picturesque village of Leysin. From every building there is a spectacular view of the Alps.

Residence halls are the key to the well-being and positive functioning of the School community. Teachers and their families have apartments in the residence halls and create a homelike atmosphere. Students have comfortable rooms, sharing them with 1 or 2 others of different nationalities. The girls live in the Beau Site Vermont and Eden dormitories. Boys live in the Savoy, Esplanade, and Beau Reveil dormitories. Every room has private toilets and showers. Students enjoy wireless Internet access from anywhere on campus and have their own personal LAS cell phone. Every dormitory has recreation/television rooms, community kitchens, and laundry facilities.

ATHLETICS
Sports and physical education are an integral part of the balanced program designed to develop lifelong skills and to promote health and vitality, teamwork, and school spirit. During the fall and spring terms, students devote at least two afternoons a week to instructional sports. Team sports include basketball, volleyball, soccer, tennis, swimming, and cross-country. Individual sports include ice-skating, swimming, rock-climbing, mountain biking, aerobics, hiking, weight lifting, and horseback riding.

LAS uses its own gymnasium as well as two local sports centers. Facilities include a full-size skating rink, 25-meter indoor swimming pool, gymnasium, indoor and outdoor tennis courts, soccer field, indoor squash courts, two indoor climbing walls, fitness center, exercise room, and cross-country running track.

Beginning in January, students enjoy two afternoons a week during the winter term skiing and snowboarding on the Leysin slopes. More than twenty ski lifts offer unlimited access to more than 60 kilometers of downhill trails and 20 kilometers of cross-country trails that are right at LAS's front door. Professionally trained members of the Swiss Ski School provide lessons.

EXTRACURRICULAR ACTIVITIES
LAS provides many leadership opportunities through Student Council, National Honor Society, Model United Nations, and dormitory/student life committees. There are several groups active in global awareness projects, including Peace Corps, Amnesty International, Habitat for Humanity, and OXFAM.

Students attend classical and popular concerts, visit museums, go to plays, and enjoy festivals, fairs, and special events.

Three major LAS-sponsored excursions introduce Europe's wealth of culture and history. The first, September Weekend, is a three-day outing organized by Faculty Families. Swiss Cultural Excursions acquaint students with the host country, with small groups traveling to a variety of destinations. Seniors and thirteenth graders participate in a separate trip to Rome, Florence, or Venice as part of their Senior Humanities course. The five-day European Cultural Excursions introduce the historic and cultural richness of neighboring countries. Typical destinations are Budapest, Istanbul, Munich, Paris, Prague, Salzburg, and Vienna. Students may join one of the humanitarian trips to Hungary, Poland, and Romania. Seniors have the choice of a humanitarian trip or a special senior trip, with typical destinations being London and Barcelona.

DAILY LIFE
Classes are held five days a week from 8 a.m. to 3:30 p.m., followed by sports and activities or free time. Faculty Families meet two times a week within the school day. There are two weekly assemblies for all students and faculty members. Monitored study time is held in the students' rooms from 7:30 to 10, Sunday through Thursday evenings. The library, computer labs, and music and art studios are open throughout the day.

WEEKEND LIFE
Weekends offer many options, including sports tournaments; trips to Lausanne, Geneva, and other nearby cities; Faculty Family excursions; and special outings. There are regular hiking and biking trips sponsored by the faculty. Students may go to the village after classes and on weekends. Friday and Saturday evenings, students may attend the local cinema, School-sponsored dances, sports events, or cultural activities.

SUMMER PROGRAMS
Summer in Switzerland (SIS) is the Leysin American School's well-established summer academic enrichment, recreation, and travel program. Boys and girls from more than forty-five countries participate in one of three programs: Alpine Adventure for ages 9–12, Alpine Exploration for ages 13–15, and Alpine Challenge for ages 16–19. All three programs offer challenging academic/language courses, a choice of excursions, creative arts, and exciting sports, all in the spectacular setting of the Swiss Alps.

SIS provides courses appropriate to the age group served, including French (in native French-speaking Leysin), Spanish, English literature, math, computer studies, and SAT preparation. High school credit is offered in courses such as algebra, English, French, Spanish, chorus, and writing workshop.

The creative arts program offers theater, music, and art. The theater program schedules two productions in one 3-week session. Musicians and visual artists develop individual skills in their chosen instrument or discipline.

In the mornings, students attend classes, while the afternoons are devoted to sports activities and excursions. Choices include tennis, soccer, skating,

paragliding, and alpine activities such as climbing, hiking, rafting, and glacial snowboarding. Weekend excursions permit students to explore cities such as Geneva, Lausanne, Lucerne, Zermatt, and Montreux, as well as Paris and Milan for the Alpine Challenge participants.

In addition to the regular SIS program, students with special needs, aged 9 to 19, may enroll in the Dyslexia Summer School Program. This program gives students an opportunity to be professionally evaluated by a certified psychologist. Students participate in the Dyslexia program during the morning class time, and the rest of the day is spent in the regular SIS program.

SIS also offers three specialized programs for 13- to 19-year olds. Theatre International enables students to focus on their theatrical skills and credits in an international setting. Outdoor Leadership Adventure, an intensive outdoor leadership program, allows students to explore the beauty of the Swiss Alps while learning to lead others and work as part of a close-knit group. The Alpine Chamber Music program provides an outstanding opportunity for talented young musicians to immerse themselves in the study and performance of music. There are two 3-week sessions, beginning in late June and ending in early August. Optional faculty-supervised week-long excursions to France or Italy are also offered for Alpine Exploration and Alpine Challenge students.

COSTS AND FINANCIAL AID
In 2005–06, enrollment, tuition, room, and board fees were €33,500 for the full school year. Fees covered all regular instruction and laboratory fees, book charges, dormitory facilities, full board, LAS health plan (accident and health insurances and use of health center), residence permit, three major LAS-sponsored excursions, weekend activities, social events, spring prom, and a sports/ski pass with ski/snowboard lessons.

Parents establish a personal account for disbursement of weekly pocket money and extra expenses. Financial aid is available. Families living or transferring overseas and receiving educational allowances from their employers, may apply for the LAS Corporate Plan based on company policy.

ADMISSIONS INFORMATION
Students who demonstrate good character and academic potential may apply for admission. LAS requires a school transcript, three recommendations, personal essay, and completed application form. An interview is recommended. Applicants are notified without delay regarding acceptance status. LAS encourages prospective students to visit the campus.

APPLICATION TIMETABLE
LAS encourages candidates to apply between late fall and early spring, but accepts applications on a rolling admissions basis, space permitting.

ADMISSIONS CORRESPONDENCE
Admissions Office
Leysin American School
CH-1854 Leysin
Switzerland

Phone: 41-24-493-3777 (Swiss)
      609-431-7654 (U.S.)
      888-642-4142 (U.S. toll-free)
Fax: 41-24-494-1585 (Swiss)
E-mail: admissions@las.ch
Web site: http://www.las.ch

LINDEN HALL SCHOOL FOR GIRLS

Lititz, Pennsylvania

Type: Girls' boarding and day college-preparatory school
Grades: 6–12, postgraduate year
Enrollment: 120

THE SCHOOL

Founded in 1746, Linden Hall is a boarding and day school for girls located in the small, picturesque town of Lititz, Pennsylvania (population 8,000). Linden Hall provides a challenging curriculum in a supportive academic atmosphere for college-bound young women in grades 6 through 12 and postgraduates. At Linden Hall, each student is encouraged to reach her optimal level of scholarship and self-esteem. She is expected to work hard, both academically and personally, and strive to be a well-educated, productive human being. Young women come to Linden Hall to learn about the world and themselves and to prepare for the future.

The school is located on a 47-acre campus in the heart of Pennsylvania Dutch country. The campus is 7 miles from Lancaster (population 100,000), which is served by train, bus, and commercial airlines. It is also within easy driving distance of several major cities, including Baltimore, Philadelphia, New York, and Washington, D.C. Pittsburgh is 4–5 hours due west.

Linden Hall is accredited by the Middle States Association of Colleges and Schools and approved by the Pennsylvania Department of Education. It is a member of the National Association of Independent Schools, the Secondary School Admission Test Board, the National Coalition of Girls' Schools, the Pennsylvania Association of Independent Schools, Advancement for Delaware Valley Schools, the Parents League of New York, the Association of Boarding Schools, and the Small Boarding School Association.

ACADEMIC PROGRAMS

Linden Hall is a college-preparatory school providing a place for the average to above-average student to excel. In addition to the normal college-preparatory curriculum, Linden Hall offers a wide selection of honors and advanced-placement courses. Some students also take courses at local colleges, such as Franklin and Marshall and Lebanon Valley.

The Upper School requires a minimum of 23 credits for graduation, including 4 credits in English; 3 credits each in social studies, science, and math; and 2 in the same foreign language. The additional credits are satisfied by taking electives in art, photography, acting, music, computer technology, and physical education, dance, sports, or riding. The Upper School students also participate in daily academic help sessions and are also required to do community service for graduation.

Middle School students study the major subject areas, including English/language arts, reading, math, science, social studies, and foreign language. Middle School students also take electives in art, music, physical education (including riding), computer literacy, study skills, health,

and ethics. In addition, they participate in a daily academic help period, sustained silent reading (SSR), community service, and interscholastic sports.

Tutoring for remedial or supplemental instruction is available. There is also an English as a second language (ESL) course of study for international students who wish to develop fluency and competence in the English language.

Class size averages 8 to 12 students, and the overall student-teacher ratio is 4:1. The grading system uses A to F (failing) with pluses and minuses. Reports are sent home six times a year. The school year is divided into trimesters.

The academic day has seven 47-minute periods plus time for academic help, class meeting period, physical activities/sports/riding, and an activity period. Faculty-supervised study hall takes place each evening for 2 hours for those students needing extra study time.

FACULTY AND ADVISERS

Linden Hall employs 36 full-time and 5 part-time teaching faculty members. Many of the faculty members live on campus either in the dormitories or in faculty apartments adjacent to the dorms. Faculty and staff members provide students with incentive, support, and encouragement to help each young woman become her own person. Advisers meet frequently with all of their advisees. The advisers support students, monitor their academic progress, and serve as friends and parents. A weekly meeting keeps all faculty and staff members immediately informed of any student's status, both in school and in the dorms.

COLLEGE PLACEMENT

The College Advisor at Linden Hall guides students and parents through the college selection and application process. Individual conferences and college seminars beginning in the junior year help girls to select colleges best suited to their interests, abilities, and achievements and to understand the intricacies of applications—essay writing, interviewing, campus visitations, admissions testing, and financial aid. Students also have the opportunity to meet with many college and university representatives who visit Linden Hall each year. The College Advisor keeps parents informed throughout the college selection and application process and may meet with them or consult by phone at any time. Available for students' use is a resource room with catalogs, view books, videos, and a computer search program addressing colleges, financial aid, scholarships, and careers.

Virtually all graduates pursue their education at the college level. Recent graduates are attending American University, Bryn Mawr, George Washington, Hollins, Mary Washington, MIT, Mount Holyoke, NYU, Penn State, Pratt,

Sarah Lawrence, Simmons, Tufts, and the Universities of Chicago and Michigan.

STUDENT BODY AND CONDUCT

In 2005–06, the composition of the student body was as follows: 3 in sixth grade, 8 in seventh grade, 20 in eighth grade, 16 in ninth grade, 26 in tenth grade, 22 in eleventh grade, and 25 in twelfth grade. There were 79 boarding students and 41 day students. Students came from sixteen states and ten countries, representing five continents.

Guidelines for student conduct are defined in the parent, student, and dormitory handbooks. An Honor Code Committee comprised of faculty members and students recommends the appropriate disciplinary action to the Headmaster when a major infraction occurs. There is an active Student Council.

ACADEMIC FACILITIES

Stengel Hall houses both the Middle and Upper Schools, as well as the administrative offices and two computer labs. The Frueauff Library contains 12,000 volumes. The Carr Arts Center, a multipurpose room, is located on the first floor of the Mary Dixon Chapel. Linden Hall recently opened its newly constructed sports and fitness center on the campus. This center includes a new dance studio, fitness center, and a regulation size gymnasium. The new visual and performing arts center features a theater, a gallery, and the art and photography departments.

BOARDING AND GENERAL FACILITIES

The Byron K. Horne Dormitory, divided into four separate dormitory areas, has double rooms for 84 students. There are laundry facilities in each dormitory, and every student has Internet access in her room. The Annex, an independent living dormitory, has single room space for 17 students, with Internet access in each room. Five student lounges are each equipped with a VCR, television, and microwave. An indoor pool is located in the lower level of the Annex, and testing rooms are located on the third floor. The school infirmary is also located in the Annex. A full-time school nurse holds regular infirmary hours.

ATHLETICS

Linden Hall is a member of the Pennsylvania Interscholastic Athletic Association (PIAA). At Linden Hall, participation in the athletic program is a vital part of a student's education. Students are encouraged to participate in any sport for which they have an aptitude or an interest. These sports, both intramural and interscholastic, include tennis, volleyball, riding, soccer, basketball, and lacrosse. Weight lifting, running, golf, bowling, and swimming are among the noncompetitive activities offered at Linden Hall.

One third of the students at Linden Hall participate in the riding program. There are opportunities for students to compete at every level, as well as to ride just for fun on the school's cross-country course. An indoor riding ring was added in 1996. Linden Hall hosts its own events, and students travel to other schools for competition.

EXTRACURRICULAR OPPORTUNITIES
In addition to riding and other sports and noncompetitive athletics, students are urged to become active in a wide variety of extracurricular activities, including Linden Hall Chorus, quiz bowl, handbell choir, HOBY, *The Echo* (the oldest continuously published secondary school literary magazine in the United States), the Middle School newsletter, swimming, yearbook, student council, dance, and drama. Three plays are produced each year. The choir performs regularly in the community; art and photographic works are exhibited continuously and are entered and recognized in national competitions.

DAILY LIFE
Breakfast is served from 7 to 7:45; classes begin at 8. An all-faith chapel is held once a week during the academic day. School assemblies are held three times per week to provide an opportunity to exchange information, for student public speaking, and for announcements. Lunch is scheduled for all students and faculty members after the fourth period. There are extended periods for labs weekly. The daily academic help period is a chance for students to seek help independently from a teacher or adviser. Athletics are scheduled at the end of the academic day.

Breakfast, lunch, and dinner are served cafeteria-style. Students study in their rooms under faculty supervision each evening from 7:30 to 9:30, unless assigned to proctored study hall.

WEEKEND LIFE
Faculty members work in rotating teams to plan, supervise, and provide transportation for the numerous and varied weekend activities that are offered at Linden Hall. Cultural activities may include the theater, a musical or dance concert, or a trip to a museum. Other weekend activities may include hikes, skiing, dances, rafting, videos, shopping, or day trips to Philadelphia, Baltimore's Inner Harbor, New York City, or Washington, D.C. If students choose to attend church or synagogue, transportation is provided. Day students are encouraged to participate in any or all of the weekend activities.

SUMMER PROGRAMS
Riding camps for students of all proficiencies are offered each summer. A Summer Adventure Day Camp is offered to local girls ages 7 through 12.

COSTS AND FINANCIAL AID
Yearly tuition, room, and board for the 2005–06 school year were $32,690 for five-day boarders and $34,720 for seven-day boarders. Day students' tuition costs were $15,530. Additional required fees included $700 for books and supplies, $150 for breakage and loss, and $25 for the Parents' Association. Other expenses included the purchase of uniforms and students' allowance. Optional fees included $1500 to $3000 for riding and $4110 per year for tutoring programs. A nonrefundable deposit of $2000 is due at the time of acceptance. Tuition is payable in full, or in installments. All accounts must be paid in good faith or students will not be allowed to continue to attend school. All outstanding accounts must be completely settled before the student is allowed to attend the following semester. An installment fee is charged if payment is made in installments.

Financial aid from Linden Hall is available for those families who demonstrate need. Awards are restricted to a maximum of 50 percent of tuition, room, and board. The family is responsible for all expenses, plus the remainder of the tuition, room, and board. To apply for financial aid, the family must fill out the Linden Hall financial aid application and return it to the Admissions Office. In addition, they must complete the Parents' Financial Statement and submit it to the School and Student Service for Financial Aid. Copies of the most recent W-2 and 1040 tax return are also required. The school attempts to help families in need afford a Linden Hall education for their daughters. Early applications are encouraged.

ADMISSIONS INFORMATION
Admission to Linden Hall is dependent on the quality of each applicant. The school seeks young women of average to superior ability, with good character and a strong desire to work hard to achieve their personal goals and potential. Race, color, creed, and nationality are not considered, nor is ability to pay. The school welcomes young women who demonstrate a willingness to better themselves through academic and social involvement, contribute in a positive way to the school community, and work closely with their peers and teachers to reach their personal goals. In selecting students for admission, Linden Hall places great importance on the personal interview. Every application is reviewed by an admission committee. The school also requires academic transcripts, educational testing results, and teacher evaluations.

APPLICATION TIMETABLE
The application must be accompanied by the nonrefundable fee of $75 ($100 for international students). Linden Hall accepts qualified students until all spaces are filled. For maximum financial aid benefits, application should be made as early as possible.

ADMISSIONS CORRESPONDENCE
Director of Admission
Linden Hall School for Girls
212 East Main Street
Lititz, Pennsylvania 17543

Phone: 717-626-8512
      800-258-5778 (toll-free)
Fax: 717-627-1384
E-mail: admissions@lindenhall.org
Web site: http://www.lindenhall.org

LITTLE RED SCHOOL HOUSE
and ELISABETH IRWIN HIGH SCHOOL

New York, New York

Type: Coeducational day college-preparatory school
Grades: N–12: Lower School (N–4); Middle School (5–8); High School (9–12)
Enrollment: School total (N–12): 560; High School: 162
Head of School: Philip Kassen, Director

THE SCHOOL

The Little Red School House and Elisabeth Irwin High School (LREI) was founded in 1921 by Elisabeth Irwin, a progressive educator who, along with colleagues such as John Dewey, spearheaded the development of new learning strategies and educational innovations. Elisabeth Irwin's experiment with active child-centered classrooms proved to be extraordinarily successful in producing well-educated, thinking, caring young students—so much so that in 1932, when the Board of Education, beset by the Depression, threatened to close the School, parents pledged their own resources to establish Little Red School House as an independent elementary school. Ten years later, the program required an upper division; Elisabeth Irwin High School, which was named after its founder, who died the next year, opened its doors in 1941. Since then, Little Red and Elisabeth Irwin has been the only independent fourteen-year college-preparatory school in Lower Manhattan. The Lower School (grades N–4) and the Middle School (5–8) are based at 272 6th Avenue. The High School (9–12) is located at 40 Charlton Street, three blocks south of Bleecker Street.

Many LREI students are drawn from the Greenwich Village–Soho–Chelsea areas, but students looking for progressive education come from throughout New York City. Because of the School's proximity to the PATH trains, it also attracts students from New Jersey.

The School is governed by a Board of Trustees. Parents, teachers, alumni, and 2 High School student representatives sit on the Board. The School raises $800,000 a year through its development program. The School buildings are owned outright by the School and are valued at more than $7.5 million.

LREI is accredited by the New York State Board of Regents and the New York State Association of Independent Schools. Professional affiliations include the National Association of Independent Schools, the Independent Schools Admissions Association of Greater New York, the National Association for College Admission Counseling, and the Guild of New York City Independent Schools.

ACADEMIC PROGRAMS

Elisabeth Irwin and other progressive educators introduced ideas that were revolutionary in their time, such as learning-by-doing, collaborative learning, the project method, and the integration of the arts and contemporary life into the curriculum. The LREI curriculum continues to reflect and build upon this tradition. Classes are problem-based, inquiry-driven, and student-centered. The goal is to motivate students to become active learners and decision makers.

The academic program at the High School provides students with broad and meaningful

intellectual and artistic experiences and a solid foundation in the academic skills and disciplines required for admission to and success in college. Electives allow students to concentrate in-depth in fields that interest them and to engage in the kind of advanced inquiry that is not usually available to high school students.

Required courses include English (4 years), history (4 years), the arts (4 years), science (3 years), mathematics (4 years), foreign language (3 years), urban studies, community service, and physical education. AP classes are offered in calculus, biology, English, foreign language, and history. Electives include filmmaking, urban studies, art history, technology, media studies, computer graphics, desktop publishing, journalism, photography, theater, sports, jazz band, chorus, and dance. Students may also conduct independent studies, take courses at NYU, and enter into internships. In the spring of the senior year, students must present graduation portfolios, which sum up their intellectual, artistic, and personal growth over the course of their high school careers.

LREI students may take elective courses in the College of Arts and Sciences at New York University through a special arrangement between the schools. In the past, LREI students have taken courses in anthropology, creative writing, history, and literature. It is a short walk from the Charlton Street building to Washington Square. This proximity makes possible a partnership that provides valuable educational opportunities and a taste of college life for the High School students.

The academic year is organized into trimesters rather than semesters. Designed with the needs of high school students in mind, the school day is less fragmented and more focused. Students are able to put more attention and energy into the subjects they are studying and sustain a greater sense of momentum and purpose. Longer blocks of time allow activities to reach their natural conclusions: students have time to finish the lab in science, complete the panel discussion in history, or perform a play in English. Teachers have more time to concentrate on students' needs and to communicate their assessments of students' work. Periodically, there are Exhibition Days for formal presentations, to which parents and outside experts are invited.

A student's program is planned in close consultation with a faculty adviser. Programs are designed both to encourage students' individual interests and to satisfy college entrance requirements. Grades of A through F are given, with D being the lowest passing grade. Report cards are issued three times a year.

FACULTY AND ADVISERS

There are 30 High School faculty members. The average class size is 15 students. Faculty members

are selected for their scholarly expertise, teaching skills, and ability to relate to students outside the classroom. Among the teachers are authors, professors of graduate-level classes, and professionals in the visual and performing arts.

Every High School teacher serves as an adviser to about 7 students and functions as their advocate in every aspect of school life. The Middle School/High School psychologist, along with the High School learning specialist, coordinates the guidance program and arranges for any testing or tutoring an individual student may require.

The budget for professional development is substantial. Each member of the faculty is encouraged to attend or lead at least one conference or workshop each year, offered by NYSAIS, ATIS, NAIS, NSTA, ASCD, NCTM, and others.

Philip Kassen, the School's Director, was appointed in 2004. He holds an M.A. in education administration from Teachers College, Columbia University and a B.A. in biology from Oberlin College.

COLLEGE PLACEMENT

College counseling is highly individualized, beginning in the junior year under the direction of the college counselor. In addition to helping students identify the colleges that are best suited to their interests and goals, the counselor makes arrangements for visits to colleges and appropriate testing, assists in the filing of applications, and advises students on successful interviewing.

All members of the class of 2005 were accepted into college. Recent acceptances include Amherst, Bard, Boston College, Columbia, Dartmouth, Hampshire, Oberlin, Sarah Lawrence, Tufts, Vassar, Wesleyan, Yale, and the Universities of Pennsylvania and Michigan.

STUDENT BODY AND CONDUCT

The 2005–06 High School enrollment was as follows: 42 ninth graders, 46 tenth graders, 45 eleventh graders, and 29 twelfth graders. The student body reflects the city: students of all races, ethnic backgrounds, religions, and socioeconomic status come together to form the most diverse independent school in New York.

Students play a central role in the governance of the School community as they gain practice in becoming responsible citizens. They do this in a number of ways: by performing school service, by serving on the Student Government, by participating in Town Meeting (the High School assembly), and by serving on the Community Service Roundtable.

The Student Government is made up of 2 class representatives elected from each class and 3 officers elected by the entire High School student body (president, secretary/vice president, and treasurer) and meets weekly with a faculty

adviser. The president and vice president serve as ex officio members of the School's Board of Trustees. The officers of the Student Government chair the Town Meeting and prepare its agenda.

The Honor Board, which is made up of the Principal, 2 teachers, and 2 students (the faculty and the student body each elect 1 teacher and 1 student), is convened to review charges and evidence in cases of infraction of School rules. The Honor Board makes recommendations of disciplinary action to the Director of the School.

ACADEMIC FACILITIES

The High School's facilities include spacious classrooms, a computer/media center, a gymnasium, a cafeteria, a photo lab, an art studio, a theater, a music room, a technology center, and two science labs. The library has more than 10,000 books and 52 periodicals; its computers provide access to the book collection of the Lower and Middle Schools, as well as the catalogs of the New York Public Library, through the Internet.

ATHLETICS

All students are encouraged to participate in sports. LREI is a member of the Independent Schools Athletic League. It sponsors interscholastic teams in basketball, cross-country, golf, soccer, softball, tennis, track, and volleyball.

EXTRACURRICULAR OPPORTUNITIES

High School students are offered a wide range of clubs and activities that are sponsored by various faculty members, often from student suggestions. The current roster of clubs includes the Human Rights Club, Chess Club, Environment Club, literary journal, yearbook, and newspaper. Students participate in the School's jazz band, the EI Rhythm Machine, the Step Team, and the School's chorus, the Elisabeth Irwin Singers. These are performance groups that appear throughout the year in and out of school. Students participate in the High School musical and High School play. High School students also participate in traditional all-school events: Founder's Day, Senior Appreciation Day, and a Middle School/High School Arts Festival.

DAILY LIFE

The school day begins at 8:25 a.m. and ends at 3:35 p.m. Each day contains five 60-minute academic blocks.

COSTS AND FINANCIAL AID

Tuition in 2005–06 ranged from $22,800 to $25,905; this included all fees. The School awards approximately $1.4 million in financial aid each year. All grants are made on the basis of need.

ADMISSIONS INFORMATION

The admissions procedures are designed to give full consideration to each applicant. An interview is scheduled after the student's application is received. A complete application also includes a current school transcript, two teacher recommendations, and ISEE test results from the Educational Records Bureau. Decisions are made in committee and are based on a careful review of the candidate's academic and personal qualifications. The School does not discriminate on the basis of race, creed, sex, national origin, or sexual orientation. Parents and candidates are welcome to tour the School and observe classes by appointment during the admissions process.

APPLICATION TIMETABLE

Inquiries are welcome at any time. For a February 1 decision, applications must be received by November 30. Formal applications should be sent as early as possible in the fall of the year preceding anticipated entrance. The application fee is $50. Application materials are available from the Admissions Office on request.

ADMISSIONS CORRESPONDENCE

Samantha Kirby Caruth, Director of Admissions
Little Red School House and Elisabeth Irwin
   High School
272 6th Avenue (Lower and Middle Schools)
40 Charlton Street (High School)
New York, New York 10014
Phone: 212-477-5316
Fax: 212-675-3595
Web site: http://www.LREI.org

THE LOOMIS CHAFFEE SCHOOL

Windsor, Connecticut

Type: Coeducational boarding and day college-preparatory school
Grades: 9–12, postgraduate year
Enrollment: 710
Head of School: Russell H. Weigel, Head of School

THE SCHOOL

The precursor of The Loomis Chaffee School, The Loomis Institute, was established in Windsor, Connecticut, in 1914 as a coeducational boarding and day school. The School's founders were 4 Loomis brothers and their sister, who united their considerable estates to found an institution for secondary education. The School was built on the site of the Loomis family homestead at the confluence of the Farmington and Connecticut rivers.

The charter, unusual for the time, stipulated that the institute should offer a vocational as well as college-preparatory curriculum, not discriminate against staff or students because of their religious or political beliefs, and offer "free and gratuitous education" as far as the endowment would permit.

In order to emphasize the education of young women, the girls' division moved to another part of Windsor in 1926, becoming The Chaffee School, with the boys' school becoming The Loomis School. The two schools were reunited in 1972 and became The Loomis Chaffee School.

In keeping with the vision of the founders, the School strives to develop independence of mind, a sensitivity to others, a capacity for hard work, and strong values.

The 300-acre campus is 6 miles from Hartford, 45 from New Haven, 110 from New York, and 100 from Boston.

The School is governed by a Board of Trustees, the majority of whom are alumni. The physical plant is valued at $150 million and the endowment at approximately $115 million.

The School is accredited by the New England Association of Schools and Colleges and is approved by the Connecticut Education Association and the Connecticut Department of Education. It is a member of A Better Chance, the Albert G. Oliver program, the Cum Laude Society, the National Association of Independent Schools, and the Secondary School Admission Test Board.

ACADEMIC PROGRAMS

The highly diverse and rigorous curriculum comprises more than 200 courses and is designed not only to prepare students for college admission but also more generally to provide skills, instill curiosity, and encourage a love of books and ideas. Instruction in the freshman and sophomore years concentrates on basic skills of communication and computation, preparing students for the wider program of electives available in the junior and senior years.

Subject requirements are 4 years of English, 3 years of mathematics, third-level proficiency in one foreign language, 2 years of history (1 year at the freshman-sophomore level and 1 year of U.S. history), 2 years of laboratory science (1 of which must be biology), 3 terms of the arts, and 2 terms of philosophy and religion. Students must earn 16 credits in grades 9–12; most earn 19 or 20.

Independent study for academic credit is available in each discipline. Students are also encouraged to undertake extradepartmental, off-campus projects. Advanced-level and Advanced Placement courses are available in all areas of study. All students and faculty members also participate in a work program.

Through the School Year Abroad program, students may earn a full year of credit by spending their junior or senior year abroad in France, Spain, or Beijing, studying, living with a family, and traveling. German language students are given the opportunity to spend the winter term of their senior year studying in a German boarding school. Loomis Chaffee students may also participate in the Mountain School Program of Milton Academy, living and studying for half a year on a 300-acre farm in Vershire, Vermont. Students may also participate in City Term, a semester-long, interdisciplinary urban studies program that was founded by the Masters School.

The school year is divided into three terms. The daily schedule operates within an eleven-day cycle, and Saturday classes are held every other week. The average class size is 14, and the student-faculty ratio is 5:1. The ratio of boarders to on-campus faculty members is 4:1.

The grading system uses traditional letter grades of A to F with pluses and minuses; D is passing. Grades are given at midterm and at the end of each term. An adviser works closely with each student.

Study conditions are maintained in each dormitory on class nights from 7:45 to 9:45 p.m. and resumed at 10 p.m.; a supervised study hall is also held during the day.

FACULTY AND ADVISERS

There are 150 faculty members (50 percent men and 50 percent women). One hundred twenty-three hold advanced degrees, nine of which are doctorates.

Loomis Chaffee believes that faculty members must be dedicated to the task of educating the whole student, as classroom teaching, coaching, dormitory supervising, advising, and working with various campus clubs and organizations are all part of the job. Professional growth is encouraged through sabbatical leaves, travel and summer-study grants, and endowed chairs.

In 1996, Russell H. Weigel became the sixth Head of the Loomis Chaffee School after having served on the faculty at Amherst College for more than twenty years as professor of psychology as well as Dean of New Students. He holds the following degrees: B.A. from Bowdoin, M.A. from George Washington, and a Ph.D. from the University of Colorado.

COLLEGE PLACEMENT

Four full-time college counselors provide expert advice in helping students choose colleges. College counseling starts in the junior year and continues in the senior year until a student is accepted at college. Grades, test scores, extracurricular activities, and personal interests are used as guides to help juniors make tentative decisions about colleges.

All juniors take the PSAT in the fall and the SAT in the following spring and again in the senior year. In 2005, the middle 50 percent ranges of the SAT I scores were 560–700 (verbal) and 580–700 (math).

Eighty-eight percent of the class of 2005 were admitted to colleges and universities deemed most selective or highly selective by Barron's Profiles of American Colleges. In the last five years (2001–05), the following numbers of students were accepted at these representative colleges and universities: Amherst (22), Boston College (60), Brown (22), Columbia (26), Cornell (42), Dartmouth (12), Emory (27), Harvard (8), Middlebury (22), Pennsylvania (27), Princeton (5), Smith (20), Stanford (5), Washington (St. Louis) (32), Wellesley (8), Wesleyan (20), Williams (15), Yale (14), and the University of Chicago (13).

STUDENT BODY AND CONDUCT

In 2005–06, Loomis Chaffee had students from thirty states and fifteen countries. There were 710 students, including 400 boarding and 310 day students, representing many different racial, religious, and economic backgrounds.

The immediate purpose of Loomis Chaffee's rules and regulations is to promote order, mutual respect, and academic excellence. The long-range goal is to prepare students for their roles in society. School policy fosters increased responsibility as students mature and advance from class to class.

Students take an active leadership role through the Student Council and the prefect system, serve on the Disciplinary and Curriculum committees, and have representatives on the Board of Trustees.

ACADEMIC FACILITIES

The Katharine Brush Library contains 60,000 volumes, an extensive research and reference collection, 160 periodicals, a large record collection, microfilm holdings, music-listening rooms, a microfilm-reading room, a typing room, and an entire floor devoted to audiovisual facilities.

The Richmond Visual Arts Center was completed in 1992. Housing printmaking, drawing, painting, and ceramics studios, the center also includes a fourteen-station black-and-white darkroom, a color darkroom, an extensive video production facility, two exhibition galleries, a fully equipped computer graphics center, and an art history lecture hall.

The Clark Science Center houses ten fully equipped laboratory complexes, several smaller laboratories, a science and math library, a planetarium, an observatory, a greenhouse, an animal room, a lecture hall (equipped with closed-circuit television), darkrooms, and classrooms.

Thirty-three computer stations, located in the library, computer room, science center, and School newspaper office, are available to students and faculty. Basic computer studies are required of all sophomores, and students are encouraged to take more advanced programming courses. Additional academic facilities include Founders and Chaffee halls (with thirty-four classrooms), eight music practice rooms, a dance studio, and the Norris Ely Orchard Theatre.

BOARDING AND GENERAL FACILITIES

The School has ten dormitories, which make up the Grubbs and Rockefeller Quadrangles. Each dormitory houses 30 to 40 students and 3 or 4 faculty members and their families. There are 5 additional faculty members associated with each dorm. Acting both as personal and academic counselors, faculty members maintain close contact with students through small advisory groups. The members of a dormitory function as a group, competing in informal athletics contests, sharing dining tables, and planning social activities.

In 1997, the tenth dormitory (Harman Hall) was completed and houses 40 girls and three faculty families. In 1995, Kravis Hall was completed and houses 48 boys and four faculty families. All dormitory rooms on campus are wired for computers and telephone access.

A multimillion-dollar student center was completed in 1989. The facilities include a snack bar, a game room, an enlarged School store, and an outdoor amphitheater. The bookstore and snack bar are open to students during the class day. The School also has a well-staffed infirmary.

ATHLETICS

All students are required to participate in the program. Coaching responsibilities are shared by 5 full-time physical educators, 4 part-time physical educators, and 63 faculty members. Two athletic trainers are on the staff.

Interscholastic sports include football, soccer, field hockey, cross-country, water polo, swimming, wrestling, basketball, hockey, volleyball, skiing, track, baseball, softball, lacrosse, golf, tennis, riflery, and squash. Intramural sports include soccer, hockey, basketball, volleyball, tennis, cycling, and softball. Also available are aquatics, physical fitness programs, ice-skating, modern dance, aerobics, and cross-country skiing.

Facilities include three gymnasia (basketball and volleyball courts); a 25-meter, six-lane swimming pool; an enclosed hockey rink; six international squash courts; seventeen tennis courts; a 3.1-mile cross-country course; two baseball diamonds; two softball diamonds; seventeen fields for football, soccer, lacrosse, and field hockey; and a golf practice driving range, putting green, and sand trap. With the fall 2002 completion of a construction project, the School made renovations to the hockey rink and added a double gymnasium; a 6,500 square-foot fitness center; two additional international squash courts; a 400-meter, eight-lane all-weather track; and new locker rooms.

EXTRACURRICULAR OPPORTUNITIES

There are myriad extracurricular opportunities. Many students volunteer their time in the local communities through the Community Service Program and the Service Club.

There are four student publications: two bi-weekly School newspapers, the yearbook, and a literary magazine. The School also has its own separate theater building, and as many as 50 or 60 students may take part in one of the four major annual productions of the Theatre Associates.

The chorus, orchestra, concert band, jazz band, and small-group ensembles provide opportunities for the musically inclined, as well as academic credit.

There are about thirty-six clubs to suit a wide variety of special interests, including the debate society, the computer club, an outing club, and PRISM, a club promoting multicultural awareness. The Student Activities Committee organizes social and cultural programs. Students may also elect to serve as tour guides during their junior and senior years.

DAILY LIFE

The class day runs from 8:10 to 3:10. Students generally take five subjects per term, each of which meets eight times in an eleven-day cycle. Some class periods are short (45 minutes), and some are longer (70–90 minutes) to allow more focused work in a discipline as well as laboratory work, projects, group work, research, and class trips. The School is committed to employing a wide variety of pedagogical techniques to reach students of all learning styles. Classes end at lunchtime on Wednesdays and alternate Saturdays to allow time for interscholastic games. The School meets as a whole several times per month for all-School meetings and convocations.

WEEKEND LIFE

Weekends are an important part of School life. Sports contests, dances, coffeehouses, concerts, theatrical and musical performances, and movies are held. Dormitories often plan their own cookouts and excursions. Faculty-chaperoned trips are frequently arranged. Bicycling, hiking, rock-climbing, windsurfing, and boating are popular in the fall and spring. The School owns 104 acres of woodland in East Hartland, Connecticut.

COSTS AND FINANCIAL AID

Tuition, room, and board for 2004–05 were $34,800; tuition for day students was $26,200. This was paid in two installments on August 1 and January 1. For new students, a registration fee is held as a deposit, with half returned on January 1 and the other half at the conclusion of the school year.

Financial aid is available for students who complete the School and Student Service for Financial Aid form and demonstrate need. In 2005–06, more than $4.6 million in financial aid was allocated to 30 percent of the students.

ADMISSIONS INFORMATION

The School seeks boys and girls of sound character and much promise, whose previous record, character, and potential indicate that they can contribute to, as well as benefit from, life at Loomis Chaffee. The School considers the previous school record, recommendations by teachers and friends, a candidate's potential as judged during the interview, and performance on standardized tests.

Each applicant must submit an application, have a personal interview, and take the SSAT. Candidates who have completed their junior year or beyond are expected to take either the PSAT or the SAT.

For the 2005–06 school year, 1,200 students applied for 240 places. The median SSAT score of those accepted was in the seventy-seventh percentile, and 64 percent of all students entered in the ninth or tenth grade. Ten to 20 postgraduate students are also admitted each year.

APPLICATION TIMETABLE

Contacting the Admission Office begins the admission process. Complete sets of application materials are sent to those who have made a formal inquiry. Campus tours and interviews are conducted from 8 a.m. to 2:30 p.m. on Monday, Tuesday, Thursday, and Friday and from 8 a.m. to noon on Wednesday and alternating Saturdays. Appointments should be made well in advance. The application deadline is January 15; students applying after this date are considered on a rolling admission basis, according to the availability of space.

Notices of admission are mailed on March 10. Students are not required to confirm the admission until April 10.

ADMISSIONS CORRESPONDENCE

Thomas D. Southworth, Director of Admission
The Loomis Chaffee School
Windsor, Connecticut 06095
Phone: 860-687-6400

THE LOWELL WHITEMAN SCHOOL

Steamboat Springs, Colorado

Type: Coeducational boarding and day college-preparatory school
Grades: 9–12
Enrollment: 104
Head of School: Walter H. Daub, Headmaster

THE SCHOOL

The Lowell Whiteman School was founded in 1957 by Lowell Whiteman, who wished to provide a traditional and structured college-preparatory school in an informal rustic western setting that also ensured an international exposure for all students and faculty members. Now approaching its fiftieth year, Whiteman continues to emphasize these features.

The School's location on the western slope of the Continental Divide contributes much to its atmosphere. All-School outings and camping trips into the mountain, river, and desert country of Colorado and Utah provide varied Western outdoor experiences. Informal dress and manners at Whiteman balance a conservative and structured academic curriculum. Whiteman's 180-acre campus lies 5 miles north of the ski-resort and ranching town of Steamboat Springs and 160 miles northwest of Denver. Easy access has been provided in recent years by the establishment of a 45-minute airplane flight between Steamboat Springs and Denver that departs several times a day. Direct flights to Steamboat Springs are available during the ski season from Atlanta, Chicago, Dallas, Denver, Houston, Los Angeles, Minneapolis, Salt Lake City, St. Louis, and San Francisco.

An annual international trip has been a feature of education at Whiteman since the School's initial year. Every spring, faculty members and all students (except those in the competitive ski/snowboarding program) travel in small groups to a wide variety of other countries chosen for that year.

A nonprofit corporation, The Lowell Whiteman School is governed by a Board of Trustees that meets three times annually. Operating expenses of $2.1 million are covered by tuition. Capital campaigns are supported by the 750 alumni and by friends and foundations.

The Lowell Whiteman School is accredited by the Association of Colorado Independent Schools and the Colorado State Board of Education. It is a member of the National Association of Independent Schools and the Western Boarding Schools Association.

ACADEMIC PROGRAMS

The Lowell Whiteman School requires a minimum of 18 credits for graduation. These credits can be completed in four years. Students must take five subjects each year, and they may take up to six. The minimum graduation requirements are as follows: 4 credits of English (students must take English every year), 3 credits of math, 3 credits of social studies, 2 credits of a foreign language, 2 credits of science, 1 credit of art, and 1 credit of computers. Varied advanced-placement courses are offered. Credit is given for physical education through the ski/snowboarding and activities programs, and participation is required.

Daily and evening supervised study halls are held for all students. Those who achieve honors averages may opt to study outside of the proctored study halls.

The average class size at Whiteman is 9 students. The student-teacher ratio is approximately 7:1. Those periods when a student does not have a class are spent in a study hall. Evening study hall is also required on Sunday through Thursday nights.

The school year is divided into semesters. The first semester ends at Christmas break, and the second runs from January to June (with an interruption for Intersession in the spring). Each semester is divided into two 7-week grading periods, with grades and comments sent to parents at the end of each period. The seven-week grades are used to determine the Dean's and Honor's lists. The Lowell Whiteman School uses a numerical grading scale from 0 to 100.

The spring Intersession provides an opportunity for Whiteman students to travel abroad. With the exception of competitive skiers and snowboarders, all Whiteman students participate in the annual international trip. In the months prior to the trip, a minicourse in the language, geography, and culture of the country to be visited is required of the students. Although regular classes are not continued during the international travel, students study the culture of the country and participate in community service projects. In recent years, students have visited Bhutan, Chile, China, Costa Rica, Ecuador, the Galapagos Islands, the Himalayas of Nepal, Indonesia, Mongolia, Samoa, South Africa, Vietnam, and much of Western Europe.

Intersession also provides an opportunity for competitive winter athletes to make up classwork that was missed because of heavy competition schedules and training during the winter. Students drop two classes during the winter competition season. The same course work is then covered during four weeks of intensive classes during Intersession. This schedule ensures that winter athletes do not compromise their education by pursuing their ski/snowboard ambitions.

FACULTY AND ADVISERS

There are 18 full-time and 6 part-time faculty members. Dorm parents do not teach but serve as advisers. Three interns assist the dorm parents.

Walter H. Daub was appointed Headmaster in 1998. Before coming to Whiteman, Mr. Daub served the Albuquerque Academy for seventeen years in the positions of Upper School Head, Assistant Head, and Academic Dean. He received a B.A. in philosophy from Hamilton College and an M.A. in English from the University of Delaware. In 1986, he was presented with an Exemplary Teacher Award by President Reagan.

COLLEGE PLACEMENT

Students participate in a step-by-step process of researching colleges, visiting campuses, and applying to institutions appropriate to their needs and abilities. Serious exploration begins in a student's junior year.

In the class of 2005, all 22 graduating seniors who applied to four-year colleges and universities were accepted. Recent graduates are currently enrolled at Bates, Boston University, Bowdoin, Colorado College, Cornell, Dartmouth, Fort Lewis, Harvard, McGill, Middlebury, Mount Holyoke, New England, NYU, Reed, St. Lawrence, Stanford, Texas A&M, Tulane, and the Universities of California, Colorado, Denver, Montana, Texas, Utah, Vermont, Washington, and Wyoming.

All seniors and juniors take the SAT and the ACT. Average SAT scores for the 2005 graduating class were 550 verbal and 570 mathematics. Advanced Placement examinations are administered in May of each year.

STUDENT BODY AND CONDUCT

In 2005–06, there were 35 freshmen, 24 sophomores, 23 juniors, and 23 seniors; about 45 percent of the students are girls.

The largest numbers of boarders come from Colorado; smaller numbers of students come from Alaska, Arizona, California, Idaho, Kentucky, Massachusetts, Michigan, Minnesota, Montana, Nevada, New Mexico, New York, Oregon, South Carolina, Texas, Virginia, Washington, Wisconsin, and Wyoming. Canada, England, Germany, Korea, Mexico, Spain, Sweden, Switzerland, and United Arab Emirates are also represented. Each year, the enrollment includes some international and minority students. There were 5 international students in 2005–06.

The Lowell Whiteman School's rules are written by the faculty and administered by the Dean of Students and the disciplinary committee. A point system is used as a guideline to determine the seriousness of an offense; accumulation of 125 points by a student results in dismissal.

ACADEMIC FACILITIES

The classroom buildings have nine classrooms and a variety of project labs, including a computer lab, a life science laboratory, and a physical science laboratory. They also house the 3,000-volume library, a new language lab, computers with software, periodicals, and a darkroom. Art classes are held in a studio adjacent to the classroom building. Study halls are held in the School's 125-seat lecture hall/theater. An improved library, updated for twenty-first-century technologies and standards, including state-of-the-art Internet access, was renovated four years ago.

BOARDING AND GENERAL FACILITIES

There are three dormitories. The girls' dorm houses a maximum of 25 girls; rooms vary in size and

accommodate 2–3 girls. The freshman and sophomore boys' dorm houses a maximum of 15 boys; most rooms accommodate 2–3 boys, with two single rooms. The junior and senior boys' dorm houses a maximum of 19 boys; most rooms are doubles, but some are singles. Each dorm has at least 2 live-in dorm parents who supervise the activities and hours of its occupants.

The School has a student store to provide many of the items required for everyday life.

ATHLETICS
Because of The Lowell Whiteman School's Rocky Mountain environment, athletics are centered around the activities one would expect to do in the mountains. Students may choose from the following: Alpine and Nordic skiing, freestyle skiing and snowboarding, backpacking, camping, canoeing, kayaking, hockey, horseback riding, ice-skating, mountain biking, rock climbing, soccer, tennis, cross-country, volleyball, softball, and basketball. There is an on-campus gymnasium, an athletic field, a climbing wall, and a skateboard ramp.

There are opportunities for competition in most high school sports. Those students capable of skiing or snowboarding at a high competitive level are eligible to train with and compete for the renowned Steamboat Springs Winter Sports Club at the USSA and USASA levels. Introductory competitive programs are also available. The Steamboat Springs Winter Sports Club was awarded the United States Ski Association Club of the Year Award in 2004. Sixteen alumni of the LWS Ski and Ride Program have gone on to compete in the Olympics and the XGames.

EXTRACURRICULAR OPPORTUNITIES
Opportunities include concerts in town, music, painting, pottery, photography, camping, backpacking, the School yearbook committee, dances, and community service. Whiteman's drama program presents theater performances for the student body and parents during Parents' Weekend in February.

In order to take advantage of especially fine weather, classes are canceled one day each autumn for treks to mountain lakes and other picturesque areas. Students also participate in three camping trips in the fall.

During the winter months, students have daily opportunities to take advantage of the world-class Steamboat Springs Ski Area and its surrounding facilities. When the famous deep snows arrive in Steamboat, two days are set aside to enjoy the superb powder skiing. In the winter, skiing and snowboarding constitute credits in physical education, and students may ski and ride as often as six times per week.

DAILY LIFE
Daily life at The Lowell Whiteman School is structured but allows for some flexibility. A typical weekday begins with breakfast at 7:15 a.m., followed by six 45-minute classes, lunch, and afternoon activities from 3 to 5. Dinner is at 6:15, followed by a supervised study hall from 7:15 to 9:15. Students with honors averages are not required to attend this study hall but are expected to study on their own. There is an hour of free time before students return to their dormitories at 10:15. Lights are out by 11.

Students are expected to contribute to the care of community facilities and dormitories. Therefore, participation in some work crews is required.

WEEKEND LIFE
Students have considerable time to themselves from Friday evening to Sunday afternoon, provided that they have done their work during the week. Juniors and seniors may take trips on their own with parental and faculty permission. Freshmen and sophomores have more restrictions. The School also offers a variety of faculty-sponsored outings on weekends during the fall term to such places as the Mt. Zirkel Wilderness Area, the Flat Tops Wilderness Area, Browns Park, and Colorado National Monument. Students often go to movies in town on Friday and Saturday nights.

Students have the opportunity to attend church services in Steamboat Springs on Sunday.

COSTS AND FINANCIAL AID
Tuition with room and board for 2005–06 is $29,900. Day student tuition is $15,950. The annual international trip (transportation and room and board) ranges from $3200 to $4000. For 2004–05, trips to Chile, China, Costa Rica, and East Africa were arranged. The total of the other costs, including books and a season ski pass to the local ski area, should not exceed $2000 annually; a miscellaneous student account is billed three times a year. Tuition is payable on the opening day of each school year, although $3000 of this amount is deposited upon acceptance. International trip costs are assessed and payable about February 15. The School recommends that an additional $20–$25 per week be allotted for spending money for each student.

In 2005–06, 30 percent of the students received some form of financial aid. Loans and tuition installment schedules can be arranged, and students achieving at B level or higher are eligible for scholarship consideration.

ADMISSIONS INFORMATION
Applications are considered as they are received in the Admission Office, but prospective students are encouraged to apply by March 15. A personal interview and a campus visit are normally required, although distance has exempted some applicants. A decision is normally made within two weeks of the interview if the admissions file (recommendations, transcript, personal essay, etc.) is complete.

APPLICATION TIMETABLE
Applications are welcome throughout the year, although the School reached full enrollment in late July for the 2005–06 year. The personal interview may be scheduled anytime, but an interview on campus during the school year, when classes are in session, is preferred. An off-campus interview is possible on occasion. Office hours are 9 a.m. to 5 p.m. during the school year and during the summer. A $40 application fee is required of all applicants.

ADMISSIONS CORRESPONDENCE
Travis Jones
Director of Admission
The Lowell Whiteman School
42605 RCR 36
Steamboat Springs, Colorado 80487

Phone: 970-879-1350 Ext. 15
Fax: 970-879-0506
E-mail: admissions@lws.edu
Web site: http://www.lws.edu

LUTHER COLLEGE HIGH SCHOOL

Regina, Saskatchewan, Canada

Type: Coeducational Lutheran boarding and day college-preparatory school
Grades: 9–12
Enrollment: 430
Head of School: Dr. Bruce Perlson, President

THE SCHOOL

Luther College has both a high school and a university campus. It is a great place for students who wish to study in Canada to gain entrance to North American universities.

Over the years, Luther College High School has earned a reputation for its high-quality academic program; small, friendly community; and safe, supportive atmosphere.

Luther attracts students from around the world. International students live in the College's dormitories. An ESL Program is offered for students whose first language is not English.

Luther College was founded in 1913 in Melville, Saskatchewan. In 1926, the College moved to Regina, the capital city of the province of Saskatchewan. At that time, the College provided a full high school curriculum and first-year university courses. In 1945, the first students from outside of Canada began attending Luther.

In 1971, the College expanded its university program and established a separate campus at the University of Regina. Luther College High School continues to operate at the original campus on Royal Street in the west-central area of Regina.

ACADEMIC PROGRAMS

Luther's curriculum is approved by the province of Saskatchewan, and the school is an accredited member of the Canadian Association of Independent Schools.

Luther College High School offers students a strong academic program to prepare them for college and university entrance. The required core focus includes English, math, computer science, the natural sciences, languages, and social sciences. Languages taught include Latin, German, French, and special courses in French for students from a French immersion background.

Luther has a strong fine arts program, including vocal music and the award-winning Luther College Choir, Canada's first high school program on film and motion picture production, instrumental music and band, visual arts, music appreciation, drama, and the school's annual production of a Broadway musical.

Luther College is one of a number of schools in the world that is approved to offer the International Baccalaureate program (I.B.). Luther's I.B. program offers individual courses or a full diploma program and provides

students with entrance and advanced standing at universities and colleges around the world.

Students whose first language is not English are required to enroll in the ESL Program. Students in ESL classes have opportunities to enhance their English skills with tutoring, conversation partners, and field trips. Living in residence also assists students in learning English.

FACULTY AND ADVISERS

Luther College has 34 faculty members. The student-teacher ratio is 16:1, and the average class size is 16 to 25 students. Faculty members demonstrate a commitment to the College by serving as academic advisers, athletic coaches, and cocurricular leaders.

COLLEGE PLACEMENT

For more than ninety years, Luther College has earned a reputation both in Canada and abroad for providing superior education. The quality of Luther's academic program is evident in the achievements of its graduates. Ninety-six percent of graduates continue in postsecondary education, and 80 percent of graduates go directly into university. Three former students have become presidents of Canadian universities, 5 have won the coveted Rhodes scholarship, and graduate Henry Taube received the 1983 Nobel Prize in chemistry.

STUDENT BODY AND CONDUCT

About 400 students enroll in Luther College each year. Approximately 90 to 100 of the students live in the College's residences. Most students come from Regina and Saskatchewan, and 20 percent of the students come from countries other than Canada. In recent years, students have come from such places as Austria, Brazil, Eritrea, Ethiopia, Germany, Hong Kong, India, Japan, Korea, Kuwait, Mexico, Portugal, Saudi Arabia, Singapore, Spain, Switzerland, Taiwan, Thailand, Turks and Caicos Islands, the United States, and Zimbabwe. Luther students have participated in regular exchange programs with schools in Germany and Quebec.

Luther College is a Christian-centered school with daily chapel and Christian ethics courses that encourage students to reflect on questions of morality, ethics, and faith. The College's small size helps to create a caring environment where students feel safe and

supported. Students from all faith backgrounds are welcomed at Luther.

Church music is a vital part of the College. The Luther College Choir travels each year and has toured Europe, North America, and Cuba, winning international acclaim.

ACADEMIC FACILITIES

The buildings, which are all connected, include Old Main, where the boys' dormitory and cafeteria are located; Federation Hall, the girls' dorm; the academic wing, which was built in 1989 and contains classrooms and the computer lab; and the gymnasium, where many special school events are held. The campus also includes the President's House, where the President of the College and his family live; Christ Lutheran Church; a football field; two soccer fields; a softball diamond; and many acres of open meadows.

BOARDING AND GENERAL FACILITIES

Luther College has two residences—one for boys and one for girls. Both residences offer wireless Internet connections. Students must provide their own computers. In total, 100 students can live in residence at the College. International students are encouraged to apply early because of the limited residence space.

The province of Saskatchewan has an excellent health-care system. The government provides basic health-care coverage for all international students. Coverage is in effect according to the date on the student's visa, but students must apply for a health-care card upon arrival.

There is a hospital two blocks from Luther College, where doctors are available at all times for emergencies. In addition, the College has a nurse who works every morning during the school week and pays special attention to any health problems reported by students living in residence.

ATHLETICS

Luther College is the home of L.I.T., the leading basketball tournament in western Canada. Luther fields teams in a wide variety of major sports, including football, basketball, volleyball, hockey, cross-country running, soccer, curling, badminton, softball, track and field, and cheerleading. In addition to the activities offered at Luther, the city of Regina provides many opportunities to participate in other specialized sports.

EXTRACURRICULAR OPPORTUNITIES

Luther College is large enough to offer a wide range of special activities but small enough so that all of the students can participate. The range of offerings in clubs and programs includes field trips, cultural exchanges, social and ecological advocacy, school newspaper and yearbook, debating, chess, and many other activities.

DAILY LIFE

The school year begins around Labour Day and finishes at the end of June. Students may begin their studies in September or at the start of February, when the second semester begins. The dormitories are closed in July and August, and during the Christmas holiday. The College can assist students in finding another place to stay during these periods. Some students use the breaks to travel to other cities.

Boarding students rise for breakfast at 7:30 a.m. Classes begin at 8:25 and end at 3:30. There are six periods in the class day. Students attend a daily chapel service. Residents dine at 5:30 p.m. Lights must be out in the residence halls by 11 p.m.

WEEKEND LIFE

The city of Regina, with 200,000 people, is the provincial capital of Saskatchewan. The city is large enough to offer a wide variety of cultural opportunities but small enough to avoid many of the problems that are found in larger urban centres. Regina is served by an international airport that has direct flights every day to such important connecting cities as Vancouver, Toronto, and Minneapolis. Luther College is about 5 minutes from the airport.

There is a city bus stop at a corner by the school. Students can take the bus to downtown Regina for shopping and cultural attractions, and taxis are also available.

COSTS AND FINANCIAL AID

Because Luther College receives financial donations from alumni and friends, the College attempts to keep costs as reasonable as possible. International students are eligible for the many scholarships and awards that are won by Luther students every year.

The required costs for students from outside Canada include Can$7200 to Can$7700 for tuition and Can$6500 for room and board. The Residence Activity Fee of Can$200, a room damage deposit of Can$200, and an application deposit of Can$300 are also required. The annual fee for the ESL Program is Can$1700.

Additional fees are charged if students decide to participate in special activities, such as the International Baccalaureate Program, sports, trips, choir tour, and graduation, and for any other special services not provided to all students.

ADMISSIONS INFORMATION

Students who are applying to be admitted to grades 11 and 12 must have a score of at least 450 on the TOEFL examination. Although the TOEFL test is not required for students who enter grades 9 and 10, students applying for those grades must have a good working knowledge of English.

Students who complete grades 10, 11, and 12 at Luther College are not required to write an English entrance examination in order to enter a university. Students who do not complete all three of these years at Luther must pass an English examination in order to be admitted to a university.

APPLICATION TIMETABLE

Students who wish to begin their studies in September are strongly encouraged to apply in January or February to ensure that visas and other documents are completed and received from the necessary offices. Applications are accepted until the dormitory is full.

ADMISSIONS CORRESPONDENCE

Admissions
Luther College High School
1500 Royal Street
Regina, Saskatchewan S4T 5A5
Canada

Phone: 306-791-9174
Fax: 306-359-6962
E-mail: admissions@luthercollege.edu
Web site: http://www.luthercollege.edu

LYNDON INSTITUTE

Lyndon Center, Vermont

Type: College preparatory and general academic coeducational day and boarding school
Grades: 9–12
Enrollment: 668
Head of School: Richard D. Hilton, Headmaster

THE SCHOOL

Lyndon Institute (LI) was founded in 1867 in the tradition of the New England academy. The Institute still shows the effects of the shaping hand of T. N. Vail, founder of AT&T, who served as president of LI in the early 1900s and was responsible for considerable growth in its programs and facilities.

An accomplished faculty that includes published authors, noted artists, college faculty members, and others active in their professional fields provides a challenging, comprehensive educational program in a picturesque Vermont village setting. Lyndon students enjoy personal attention from the faculty members, genuine respect for their individuality and unique talents, a truly inclusive environment, and outstanding preparation for their choices of colleges and careers.

Lyndon Institute consists of three campuses on 150 acres centered on the village green of historic Lyndon Center, Vermont, along the banks of the Passumpsic River. Academic buildings surround a tree-lined common marked by the village church's steeple and the Institute's bell tower. It is a safe, supportive community of exceptional beauty. In addition, the school owns Binney Woods, a 360-acre preserve on nearby Burke Mountain. LI is located 10 miles north of St. Johnsbury on Interstate 91. Boston and Hartford are 3–4 hours away by car. Burlington, Vermont, and Montreal are only 2 hours from the campus. Airline service to Burlington, Montreal, or Manchester, New Hampshire, provides easy access. Burke Mountain Ski Area is 7 miles away. Stowe and Jay Peak Ski Areas are within an hour's drive. The school is 1 mile from Lyndon State College (LSC). The two institutions have been historically linked from the time of their founding, and together they form a unique cultural setting in Vermont's beautiful Northeast Kingdom.

LI is governed by a 27-member board of trustees, who are elected from a group of 150 corporators. The board meets four times per year. Each trustee sits on one of five standing committees. The school's operating budget is $10.1 million; parents, friends, and an active alumni group raise about $300,000 in annual support. The endowment is $7.9 million.

Lyndon Institute is accredited by the New England Association of Schools and Colleges and approved by the Vermont Department of Education. Memberships include the Independent School Association of Northern New England, the Vermont Independent School Association, the Secondary School Admission Test Board, and The Association of Boarding Schools.

ACADEMIC PROGRAMS

Lyndon Institute is a comprehensive secondary school offering college-preparatory and fine arts programs of study as well as education in business, information, and vocational technology areas. Twenty-one credits are required for graduation, with the following distribution: English, 4 credits; social studies, 3 credits; mathematics, 3 credits; science, 3 credits; fine arts, 1 credit; health and physical education, 2 credits; and electives, 5 credits.

Other course offerings include French, 4 years; Latin, 4 years; Spanish, 4 years; band, 4 years; art, 4 years; advanced math, 1 year; algebra, 3 years; geometry, 1 year; trigonometry, 1 year; biology, 2 years; chemistry, 2 years; physics, 1 year; computer science, 7 courses; technology, 14 courses; drafting, 5 courses, including computer-aided design; word processing, 3 courses; and office technology, 3 courses. Honors courses are offered in English literature, advanced senior writing, classics, algebra 1 and 2, geometry, advanced math, origins of human culture, U.S. history, world civilizations, biology, chemistry, and advanced art. Advanced Placement tests are offered in English, chemistry, and art. Students are required to take five courses or the credit equivalent each year but are encouraged to take up to seven courses each year.

The fine arts program allows students to take a series of courses within the fine arts concentration, which includes concert band, jazz band, improvisation, music theory, chorus, select chorus, art, art 4, advanced art, book arts, painting, printmaking, design, 2-D and 3-D art, photography, dance, jazz dance, lyrical ballet, foundations of theater, directing, playwriting, and Shakespeare.

With special permission, students may take courses at LSC and receive academic credit from both LI and LSC. Advanced students may also pursue independent study with a faculty sponsor. Students have access to the library from 7:30 a.m. to 4:30 p.m. each day and from 7 to 9 p.m. in the evening. Research is also conducted from many classrooms using the computer network and library computer search features.

Classes are grouped on the basis of ability. The student-teacher ratio is 10:1, with an average class size of 16. The grading system ranges from A to F: A, 90–100; B, 80–89; C, 70–79; D, 60–69; and F, 59 and below. The academic year is divided into two semesters consisting of three 6-week marking periods each. Exchange trips are available during vacation times, and many opportunities for class travel are offered throughout the year.

FACULTY AND ADVISERS

There are 59 full-time and 7 part-time faculty members at Lyndon Institute (34 men and 32 women). Thirty-three percent have earned a master's degree or higher.

Richard D. Hilton was appointed Headmaster in 1999. He holds a B.A. in English from Notre Dame and a master's degree from Villanova. Prior to coming to Lyndon Institute, Mr. Hilton was at the Hill School in Pottstown, Pennsylvania, where he worked for twenty years, holding a variety of positions, most recently Assistant Headmaster for Academics.

New faculty members are selected on the basis of academic quality and experience within their academic discipline, any special skills that may enhance the school's environment, and individual pursuit of academic excellence. The school has a very stable faculty employment rate. All faculty members participate in extracurricular activities, serving as coaches or advisers to clubs and activities, and act as advisers to students.

COLLEGE PLACEMENT

College planning is accomplished through individual and small-group counseling beginning in the freshman year. Two full-time counselors work in concert with students and families to develop postsecondary plans. In a student's junior year, he or she is assigned to 1 of 5 faculty college advisers, who help with coordinating college applications and essay writing. Students use computer software and other informational tools to aid in their searches and career planning.

Representatives from more than thirty colleges visit Lyndon Institute annually. LI cosponsors the Northeast Kingdom College Night program each spring with representatives from more than 100 colleges and universities in attendance.

In the last two years, nearly 70 percent of LI graduates have pursued postsecondary options. Within Vermont, graduates have attended Middlebury, Norwich, Saint Michael's, Vermont, and colleges in the Vermont State College System, including Lyndon State and Vermont Tech. Outside Vermont, students have attended Berklee, Clarkson, Dartmouth, Harvard, Rensselaer, Smith, St. Lawrence, Union, Virginia Wesleyan, Washington State, and the Universities of Maine and New Hampshire.

STUDENT BODY AND CONDUCT

The total enrollment is 668 students, who come from the surrounding communities in Vermont and New Hampshire and from countries around the globe. The school implemented a boarding program in 2003–04, which has the capacity for 50 students in grades 9–12. Countries represented in the international program in the last five years include Taiwan, Japan, Korea, and Germany.

The Code of Conduct is established by the faculty members, the administration, and the Board of Trustees and is based on common courtesy, mutual respect, and socially acceptable behavior.

Student involvement is vested in each class's elected officials and the Student Council. These officials are elected at the beginning of each year. As each student is a valued member of the community, the Headmaster is available to all students at any time.

ACADEMIC FACILITIES

Lyndon Institute comprises three campuses that surround Lewis Field, which is used for football and track. The Darling Campus consists of the Main Building (1922), containing ten classrooms, four science labs, a small performing arts space, administrative offices, and a multilevel media center (renovated in 1992), which houses 13,000 volumes, 90 current periodicals, and CD-ROM information technology; Pierce Hall (1978), containing seven classrooms, a computer lab, and a 250-seat cafeteria; Alumni Wing, which houses a 550-seat gymnasium and a 650-seat auditorium; and Lewis Field, home to the Vikings' championship football and track and field programs. In addition, the Town House, which the school leases from the town of Lyndon, is an historic building used for dance and small drama practices and performances.

The Harris Campus consists of five main buildings, including Prescott House, home of the school's health center; Daniels Hall (1997), which houses the math department; Brown Business Center (renovated in 1993), which houses business and information technology classrooms; Harris Building (renovated in 1999), which has English classrooms and a weight-training facility; Sanborn Hall (1988), which provides locker rooms, athletic training facilities, and a full-size auxiliary gymnasium; and Bean Cottage, which serves as a dormitory. The Harris Campus also includes a softball field.

The Vail Campus comprises ten buildings, eight of which house technology classrooms, laboratories, and workshops, including a fully networked computer-aided design (CAD) lab and drafting studio, a newly dedicated art center (2003), and three residence dormitories. The Vail Campus also includes the Forrest Field complex, where Lyndon Institute's football, soccer, field hockey, and baseball teams practice and compete. The Institute also uses Binney Woods, a 360-acre nature preserve located on Burke Mountain, for study and recreation.

BOARDING AND GENERAL FACILITIES
The residential facilities are housed in Mathewson House, Collison Cottage, and the Tavern Dormitory on the Vail Campus and Bean Cottage on the Harris Campus. The four dormitories can accommodate 50 students in single or double rooms and 4 resident dorm parents. After-school and weekend activities center on the residence areas, the gymnasiums, and the Pierce Hall cafeteria.

ATHLETICS
All students are urged to supplement their classroom experience by participating in interscholastic competition. In the 2004–05 school year, roughly 40 percent of the student body participated in the fall sports program. Lyndon Institute participates in the Vermont Principal's Association in Division II for baseball, basketball, cross-country running, cross-country skiing, football, golf, ice hockey, soccer, and track and field; and in Division III for field hockey. Interscholastic athletics are held on the varsity, junior varsity, and freshman levels (when appropriate). Cheerleading is also offered, as are lifetime fitness activities. Facilities include Alumni Gym, Sanborn Hall, Lewis Field, Brown Field, Forrest Fields, and the Harris weight-training facility. Ice hockey athletes practice and play at the Fenton Chester Ice Arena, which is adjacent to the school. Alpine and Nordic ski teams train and race at Burke Mountain Ski Area, which is 7 miles from the campus. The golf team practices at nearby St. Johnsbury Country Club's championship golf course. The baseball team plays at the LSC field. In the last five years, LI teams have won state championships in baseball, cross-country running, football, golf, Nordic skiing, softball, and track.

EXTRACURRICULAR OPPORTUNITIES
Student clubs and organizations run the gamut of student interests. Organizations include Student Council, National Honor Society, Future Business Leaders of America, and USA Skills/Vocational Industrial Clubs of America. Students may join the jazz ensemble; choral and drama groups; French, Latin, and Spanish clubs; the forensics team, and the scholars bowl team. The award-winning *Janus* magazine, an art and literature magazine that has won All-New England honors in the annual Boston University competition in four of the five years it was submitted; the *Viking Voice*, LI's student newspaper; *Cynosure*, the yearbook; and the Writers Workshop offer students writing, editing, and desktop publishing opportunities. Other clubs include the volunteer club and SADD (Students Against Destructive Decisions).

The French and Spanish clubs organize trips abroad in alternating years. Students can take advantage of the cultural events and concerts at LSC, the Catamount Film and Arts Center in St. Johnsbury, and the Hopkins Center at Dartmouth College, which is only an hour away. The Music, Dance, and Art Departments offer students opportunities to work and perform with guest artists-in-residence. In addition to dances, plays, concerts, and athletics events, Spirit Week and Winter Carnival are two schoolwide events that engage the entire student body. Kingdom Trails offers a network of trails in the region for mountain biking in the summer and fall, and cross-country skiing and snowshoeing in the winter. Numerous field trips throughout Vermont, New England, and Canada are offered throughout the year. LI also hosts the statewide Kingdom Awards in literature, and in 2004, it hosted the first annual Vermont Dance Festival, which it has continued to host.

DAILY LIFE
Classes begin each day at 7:55 a.m. and end at 2:30 p.m. There are seven class periods of 45 minutes each. Faculty members remain in their classrooms until 3 p.m. to assist students. Activities are scheduled at 3 p.m. or later to allow students additional time to meet with faculty members as needed. The library is open from 7:30 a.m. to 4:30 p.m. during the day and from 7 to 9 p.m. during the evening.

WEEKEND LIFE
Weekends in the Northeast Kingdom are always an adventure. Many interscholastic events take place on Saturday. Trips are scheduled to nearby ski areas and to the urban centers of Burlington; Hanover, New Hampshire; and Montreal. Catamount Film and Arts Center in St. Johnsbury always has a special event or series in the area, and some of these are scheduled at LI and Lyndon State College. Students in good standing and with advance permission have the option to spend the weekend with a host family in the area or to travel home.

SUMMER PROGRAMS
Lyndon Institute sponsors a summer program in July, which offers programs in English as a second language (ESL) for students aged 14–17. There are also day camps for football, basketball, and soccer in late July and August.

Tuition for boarding students for 2006–07 is $28,150. A deposit of $1500 is due by May 31 to reserve a place. The Institute works with parents to arrange alternative payment schedules when needed.

Financial aid is based on need as determined by the School's Financial Aid Committee. Financial aid consists of both grants and loans. Special talent scholarships in music and art may be available.

ADMISSIONS INFORMATION
Acceptance to Lyndon Institute is based on academic performance and potential, school citizenship, and motivation. The SSAT is required for domestic students. The TOEFL or SLEP is required for international students whose native language is not English. A minimum score of 42 on the SLEP is necessary for acceptance.

Lyndon Institute admits students of any race, color, or national or ethnic origin to all the rights, privileges, programs, and activities generally accorded or made available to students at the school. LI does not discriminate on the basis of race, color, or national or ethnic origin in the administration of its educational policies, admission policies, scholarships, and loan programs or athletics and other school-administered programs.

APPLICATION TIMETABLE
Inquiries are welcome at any time. An interview is strongly suggested. Interviews and tours are scheduled between 10 a.m. and 2 p.m. Monday through Friday. Weekend appointments are available by special arrangement. Admissions decisions are made on a rolling basis. Since the boarding program is limited in enrollment, early application is recommended.

ADMISSIONS CORRESPONDENCE
Mary B. Thomas
Assistant Head for Admissions
Lyndon Institute
P.O. Box 127
Lyndon Center, Vermont 05850-0127

Phone: 802-626-5232
Fax: 802-626-6138
E-mail: admissions@lyndon.k12.vt.us
Web site: http://www.lyndoninstitute.org

THE MACDUFFIE SCHOOL

Springfield, Massachusetts

Type: Coeducational boarding (9–12) and day college-preparatory school
Grades: 6–12: Middle School, 6–8; Upper School, 9–12
Enrollment: School total: 226; Upper School: 166
Head of School: Kathryn P. Gibson

THE SCHOOL

The MacDuffie School was founded in 1890 by Dr. John MacDuffie, a Harvard alumnus, and his wife Abby, a member of Radcliffe's first graduating class, to provide "a fine education" for girls preparing for college. Today, MacDuffie continues its commitment to academic excellence in preparing both boys and girls for college and for life. The School emphasizes the development of the individual within a supportive community that recognizes and welcomes diversity.

The MacDuffie campus occupies 14 acres in a historic residential area. Downtown Springfield is within walking distance of the School and offers access to the city's cultural resources, including museums, a theater, a symphony orchestra, a large public library, and a civic center. Local colleges, including Amherst, Hampshire, Mount Holyoke, Smith, and the University of Massachusetts provide further intellectual and cultural opportunities.

MacDuffie is 25 miles from Hartford, Connecticut, and 20 miles from Bradley International Airport. Boston is 90 miles from Springfield, and New York City is 150 miles away; both cities are accessible by bus, rail, and air transportation.

A nonprofit institution, MacDuffie is governed by a 21-member Board of Trustees. Many of the more than 3,300 alumni assist with recruitment efforts and provide support through the Annual Fund.

The MacDuffie School is accredited by the New England Association of Schools and Colleges. It holds memberships in the National Association of Independent Schools, the Council for Advancement and Support of Education, and the Secondary School Admission Test Board.

ACADEMIC PROGRAMS

A defining principle of MacDuffie's academic program is that learning is an ongoing and intrinsic part of life. Students explore intellectual and artistic possibilities, debate differences of opinion, question assumptions, and take the kind of risks that help them to grow into informed, involved, articulate, and self-confident adults.

Middle School students benefit from an integrated curriculum that combines the study of English, history, math, science, Latin, and modern foreign languages, along with performing and visual arts and physical education. Multicultural themes provide an appreciation of varied cultural backgrounds. Students develop learning skills such as critical thinking and creative problem solving as well as computer use, effective study habits, and the art of test taking. The goal for the sixth, seventh, and eighth graders is to become confident and articulate learners ready for the challenges of the Upper School.

Upper School students choose from a solid core curriculum and have the chance to broaden their horizons through a variety of electives. To graduate, students must complete a minimum of 18 academic credits in grades 9–12 plus physical education. One credit equals one full year of work. The required credits include English, 4; mathematics, 3; U.S. history plus one other history course, 2; science, 2 (laboratory science); foreign language, 2 (with at least 3 credits of one language recommended); performing or visual arts, 1; and electives, 4. Students may study five years of French or Spanish as well as four years of Latin. English as a second language courses are available at the intermediate and advanced levels. Students must take at least four academic courses each year.

Electives may include creative writing, publications, women in literature, SAT review, African-American history, peace studies, political science, and Western philosophy. Arts electives include acting, communications, dance and choreography, vocal and instrumental music, and a variety of visual arts such as design, illustration, and photography.

Honors and Advanced Placement (AP) courses are available. In a typical year, more than half of the senior class and several underclass students take AP examinations in such subjects as English, French, Spanish, U.S. history, calculus, chemistry, and physics. Independent study is also available.

The average class size is about 11 students, and the student-teacher ratio is 6:1. There are faculty-supervised study halls during the school day and regularly scheduled extra-help sessions after school without charge. The school year is divided into semesters. Examinations take place at the end of the first semester and at the end of the year. Students receive letter grades and teacher and adviser comments four times a year. Progress reports are provided as necessary during the school year.

FACULTY AND ADVISERS

Kathryn P. Gibson was appointed Head of School in 1999. She is a graduate of Vassar College (A.B., magna cum laude) and Columbia University (M.A.). Prior to coming to MacDuffie, Mrs. Gibson served as the Associate Director of Development at Springfield College and as a regional officer at the National Endowment for the Humanities in Washington, D.C.

There are 36 full-time faculty members; 16 men and 20 women. Twenty-five faculty members have master's degrees, and 1 holds a Ph.D. Faculty members serve as academic advisers to an average of 7 students, overseeing their progress throughout the year. Faculty members also advise student organizations, organize class activities, and coach sports teams. Several staff and faculty members live on campus as do the Head of School's family and the families that host students in the Ames Hill boarding program.

COLLEGE PLACEMENT

The Director of College Counseling guides students through the college selection and application process. Individual and group meetings are held frequently with students and their parents beginning in the junior year. More than 60 college representatives visit the campus each year to meet with interested students.

The median SAT I scores of last year's graduates were 580 verbal and 610 math. An SAT preparation course is offered to juniors and seniors.

Of the 36 members of the class of 2005, 36 are attending four-year colleges and universities such as Amherst, Fairfield, Holy Cross, and Rensselaer.

STUDENT BODY AND CONDUCT

The total Upper School enrollment is 166; there are 90 girls and 76 boys. Of the total, 35 (15 girls and 20 boys) are boarding students. Enrollments in the various grades are as follows: 44 in grade 9, 39 in grade 10, 48 in grade 11, and 35 in grade 12. Day students reside in Springfield and nearby Massachusetts and northern Connecticut towns. Boarding students currently come from Ethiopia, Germany, Hong Kong, Japan, Korea, St. Lucia, Spain, Taiwan, Venezuela, Vietnam, and the United States.

ACADEMIC FACILITIES

School life revolves around Rutenber Hall, named for Ralph D. Rutenber, the Headmaster from 1941 to 1972. It houses the classrooms, science laboratories, the Holly Fisher Computer Laboratory, the Sadowsky Family Library, the Sally Fenelon-Young Auditorium, the Jostrom Multimedia Room, and the Guided Study Room. The dance, music, theater, and visual arts departments are located in the Arts Center.

BOARDING AND GENERAL FACILITIES

MacDuffie's innovative approach to cultural exchange is known as the Ames Hill Boarding Program. It combines the best of a homestay experience with a small boarding school program. Girls and boys from the United States and around the world live on campus with faculty families in five gracious homes named Castle, Caswell, Lemire, Tifft, and Young Houses. From the time students arrive, they share in the daily life of a family and of the larger School community.

Other facilities on campus include the dining room in South Hall; the student lounge, Finn's Bin; Young House, the admissions and administrative offices; and Wallace Hall, development offices and where several faculty and staff members reside. A hospital is located 1 mile from campus.

ATHLETICS

The School encourages but does not require involvement in athletics. The emphasis is on individual challenge and competing as part of a team. Interscholastic teams for girls include basketball, field hockey, lacrosse, softball, tennis, and volleyball. Boys' teams include baseball, basketball, soccer, and tennis. Coed teams include cross-country and junior varsity and varsity soccer. Activities offered as part of the physical education program include those listed above plus archery, badminton, and dance. The School participates in private-school sports clinics and playdays (all-star games and tournaments) in field hockey, lacrosse, tennis, and volleyball.

Athletic facilities include Downing Gymnasium, athletic fields, and tennis courts. Local facilities for bowling, swimming, skiing, gymnastics, hockey, ice skating, and horseback riding are available for recreational purposes.

EXTRACURRICULAR OPPORTUNITIES

A wide variety of clubs and activities offers students the opportunity to get involved and share interests. Student Admission Representatives (STARS), Dance Ensemble, Student Cultural Alliance, Ibero-Hispanic Club, Drama Club, Jazz Ensemble, Mathletes, STOP (Student/ Teacher Organization for Peace), MacDuffie Singers, Chess Club, and Key Club are just a few of the choices. Students publish a yearbook, *The Magnolia;* a newspaper, *The Magnet;* and a literary magazine, *The Unicorn.* The Student Council plans activities for the School community and offers leadership opportunities. Students also volunteer as tutors in local schools.

Traditional annual events include Mountain Day, Parents' Back to School Night, Grandparents' Day, Winter Carnival, Diversity Day, School plays and performances, International Meals, and activities sponsored by the Parents' Association.

DAILY LIFE

MacDuffie's school day begins with an all-School assembly at 8:15. Classes meet five days a week until 3:15 p.m. every day except Wednesday, when the school day ends at 1:50. There are eight class periods in the school day. Supervised study periods may be scheduled during the day. Ames Hill students have an evening study period as well. An activity period is scheduled during the school day for clubs to meet, while sports and other club activities take place after school or on weekends.

Students and faculty members eat lunch in the dining room in South Hall. Ames Hill students and their MacDuffie families prepare and eat breakfast and dinner in their homes on campus.

WEEKEND LIFE

Weekend activities for boarding students may include going to the movies or restaurants, on shopping trips, to concerts, plays, sporting events, or dances held at MacDuffie and at other nearby schools.

Supervised day or weekend trips are planned to such places as Boston, New York City, and Washington, D.C.

COSTS AND FINANCIAL AID

In 2005–06, tuition for day students was $16,795 in grades 6, 7, and 8 and $17,675 in grades 9 to 12. Tuition, room, board, and an activities fee for Ames Hill Boarding Program students were $30,025. Payment plans are available. Financial assistance is given in the form of aid and scholarships for tuition only.

ADMISSIONS INFORMATION

MacDuffie seeks a diverse, college-bound student body and has a policy of admitting students without regard to race, color, national or ethnic origin, or sexual orientation. The School considers recommendations, results of the SSAT, and previous school records in the selection of applicants. An interview is required and a visit is strongly encouraged. The Admissions Office is open Monday through Friday from 8:30 a.m. to 4:30 p.m., but appointments for interviews and visits can be arranged in the evening or on weekends as well.

APPLICATION TIMETABLE

Although there is no closing date for applications, candidates for September entrance should apply during the previous winter or early spring. If space is available, students may enroll at the beginning of the second semester in January. There is a $50 application fee; for boarding students, the application fee is $100.

ADMISSIONS CORRESPONDENCE

Linda Keating
Director of Admissions and Financial Aid
The MacDuffie School
One Ames Hill Drive
Springfield, Massachusetts 01105
Phone: 413-734-4971 Ext. 140
Fax: 413-734-6693
E-mail: lkeating@macduffie.com

MAINE CENTRAL INSTITUTE

Pittsfield, Maine

Type: Coeducational boarding and day college-preparatory and comprehensive curriculum
Grades: 9–12, postgraduate year
Enrollment: 522
Head of School: Joanne Szadkowski

THE SCHOOL

Founded in 1866 by Free Will Baptists, Maine Central Institute (MCI) retains much of its original spirit and philosophy but no longer has a formal affiliation with the church. The school is concerned with the welfare of all of its students, regarding each as an individual with individual needs and aspirations. In keeping with its belief in individuality, the school community strives to foster an atmosphere of mutual respect and cooperation among all of its members and with the surrounding community and to provide its students with varied educational opportunities. Similarly, the school encourages each student to develop a moral and social consciousness.

The rural town of Pittsfield (population 4,500) is situated in an area that provides opportunities for hiking, skiing, biking, fishing, skating, and snowmobiling. It is 35 miles from the Atlantic Ocean and 70 miles from the mountains of western Maine.

Maine Central Institute is accredited by the New England Association of Schools and Colleges and approved by the State of Maine Department of Education. MCI is also a member of the College Board and the National Association of Independent Schools.

ACADEMIC PROGRAMS

MCI offers a rigorous, comprehensive curriculum to accommodate various learning styles and academic abilities.

For grades 9–12, 20 credits are required for graduation. Students must successfully complete units in English (4), mathematics (4), social studies (3, including U.S. history), science (4), physical education (1), fine arts (1), humanities (2), computer science (½), and health (½). Students are required to take the equivalent of at least 5 units each semester.

MCI's math and science programs exceed national standards and utilize state-of-the-art technology. Students in MCI's well-known humanities program understand the culture of an era through a study of its history, literature, art, and music.

The foreign language program includes four levels of French and Spanish. In addition to the traditional offerings, students may take courses in psychology, music composition, the Internet, sociology, child development, computer-assisted drawing, human sexuality, vocational subjects, and philosophy.

MCI offers a structured ESL program for the international student who is planning for a university education. Students receive individual testing before placement at one of three levels of ESL. The extensive ESL program includes American history for international students and carefully structured math classes that focus on the development of math language skills.

MCI offers a strong program in instructional support. Students who have a diagnosed learning difference and have struggled in academic content areas may receive individual or group support with a learning specialist. These services are available for an additional cost.

FACULTY AND ADVISERS

The 2005–06 faculty consisted of 48 members. Twenty-eight percent of the faculty and staff members live on campus.

Faculty members are selected on the basis of three main criteria. They must possess a strong subject-matter background, the ability to relate to students, and an educational philosophy consistent with that of the institution. Faculty members are also expected to become actively involved in coaching, supervising dormitories, advising, counseling, and student affairs.

COLLEGE PLACEMENT

A guidance team of 2 counselors is available for students. Counselors are responsible primarily for helping students with postsecondary placement, academic program planning, and personal counseling. Approximately 75 college admissions representatives visit MCI's campus annually. Career counseling is also an integral part of the guidance department. Financial aid workshops for seniors, postgraduates, and their parents are offered. Preparation for the SAT and ACT is offered within the math and English curricula.

MCI has sent 78 percent of its graduates to postsecondary schools. Schools attended by recent graduates include Boston College, Bowdoin, Colby, Colgate, Cornell, Fairleigh Dickinson, Georgetown, Harvard, Maine Maritime Academy, Marquette, Miami, Providence, Purdue, Tufts, U.S. Naval Academy, Wellesley, and the Universities of Connecticut, Maine, New Hampshire, and Rhode Island.

STUDENT BODY AND CONDUCT

The 2005–06 enrollment of 522 included 415 day students, 99 boarding students, and 8 private day students. Students came to MCI from thirteen states and fifteen other countries.

Students at MCI are expected to be good citizens and are held responsible for their behavior. The rules that provide the structure for the school community are written in the student handbook. Disciplinary issues are the responsibility of the administration, the faculty, and the residence hall staff.

ACADEMIC FACILITIES

Currently, there are seven main academic buildings. The new Math and Science Center is a 23,000-square foot, state-of-the-art building that provides fourteen instructional spaces, two computer classrooms, and a botany area. More than 210 computers are available for student use campuswide, many of which have Internet and e-mail access. The 12,000-volume Powell Memorial Library has a computerized card catalogue and Infotrac as well as Internet access. The Pittsfield Public Library and the Pittsfield Community Theater are also available for school use.

BOARDING AND GENERAL FACILITIES

Boarding students are housed in single-sex residence halls on campus, supervised by resident faculty and staff members. Each residence hall has its own recreation room and laundry facilities.

Weymouth Hall houses the Student Services Center, consisting of the student lounge, snack machines, a bookstore, and a post office.

MCI offers a unique Host Family Program. Participating students are assigned to a family from the community that will make the student a part of the family for the school year. Students may spend time with their host family on weekends, after school, and during vacations, if so desired.

ATHLETICS

MCI believes that athletics not only provide a wholesome outlet for youthful energies but also help students apply and further develop their skills in various sports. The school strives to furnish opportunities for participation by students of all abilities.

There are seventeen sports teams for boys and girls, including football, field hockey, soccer, basketball, golf, skiing, softball, track, wrestling, cheering, rifle, baseball, and tennis.

Wright Gymnasium and Parks Gymnasium are multiple-use athletic facilities, and each contains a weight room and locker facilities. Located on the main campus are a football field, a practice field, a ¼-mile track, two tennis courts, and a rifle range. Manson Park has fields for soccer, field hockey, baseball, and softball as well as three tennis courts. The school has the use of a local golf course and ski areas for competitive teams and recreation.

EXTRACURRICULAR OPPORTUNITIES

MCI students may choose from among more than thirty campus organizations, which represent some of the following interests: drama production; foreign languages and travel to places such as Spain, England, and Russia; chess; hiking; weight lifting; science and reading clubs; Key Club, which is the school's community service organization; computer science; and public speaking. Students may participate in Student Council; MCI's strong, award-winning music program includes concert band, concert choir, chamber choir, vocal jazz ensemble, instrumental jazz ensemble, jazz combo, percussion ensemble, and pep band; and the Math Team and the Science Olympiad, which compete locally and statewide.

Bossov Ballet Theatre now offers MCI students a unique opportunity to study classical ballet as part of the academic curriculum. Ballet classes are taught by Andrei Bossov, a renowned, world-class teacher who previously taught at the Vaganova Academy in Saint Petersburg, Russia. The program consists of a preprofessional-level syllabus that prepares students for a professional ballet career.

DAILY LIFE

The school day begins at 7:45 and ends at 2:53, with a 48-minute lunch break beginning at 11:41. Classes run from Monday through Friday, with dinner served at 5 to 6:30 p.m.

Sunday through Thursday, there is a mandatory supervised study hall from 7 to 8:30 p.m. for all boarding students.

WEEKEND LIFE

Supervised weekend trips may include visits to places of interest, such as Acadia National Park, Bar Harbor, Canada, and Portland's Old Port. Whale watching, white-water rafting, hiking, and skiing at Sugarloaf are also offered. Students also may attend local college athletic, educational, and cultural activities. The town of Pittsfield has a movie theater, stores, and restaurants. On-campus activities include sporting events, concerts, plays, and dances. The gymnasiums and Student Services Center are available for student use as well.

With parental permission, students are allowed to go home on weekends or visit the home of their host family.

COSTS AND FINANCIAL AID

The 2005–06 tuition was $31,000 for boarding students and $10,000 for private day students. The cost for ESL support was $2500 for the first class and $1500 for each additional class. The nonrefundable deposit of $2000 is due within two weeks of an offer of admission. A variety of payment plans are available.

Financial aid is awarded on a need basis, determined by information shown on the Parents' Confidential Statement and any additional financial information that is requested.

ADMISSIONS INFORMATION

MCI's Admissions Committee screens all applicants to determine their compatibility with MCI's philosophy that students should assume a mature responsibility for their own education. No entrance tests are required, but an on-campus interview with each student and his or her parents is strongly recommended. School transcripts and results of standardized tests are used to determine academic ability and appropriate academic placement in classes in accordance with the student's individual needs, abilities, and interests.

Maine Central Institute does not discriminate on the basis of race, sex, age, sexual preference, disability, religion, or national or ethnic origin in the administration of its educational and admission policies, financial aid programs, and athletic or other school-administered programs and activities.

APPLICATION TIMETABLE

Inquiries and applications are welcome at any time; however, applying by June 1 is recommended. Visits may be scheduled at any time during the year but are most effective when school is in session. Tours and interviews can be arranged by calling the Admissions Office, which is open Monday through Friday from 8 a.m. to 5 p.m. A nonrefundable application fee of $50 is required.

ADMISSIONS CORRESPONDENCE

Clint M. Williams, Director of Admission
Maine Central Institute
125 South Main Street
Pittsfield, Maine 04967

Phone: 207-487-2282
Fax: 207-487-3512
E-mail: cwilliams@mci-school.org
Web site: http://www.mci-school.org

MARIANAPOLIS PREPARATORY SCHOOL

Thompson, Connecticut

Type: Coeducational boarding and day Roman Catholic college-preparatory school
Grades: 9–12, postgraduate year
Enrollment: 280
Head of School: Marilyn S. Ebbitt, Headmistress

THE SCHOOL

Located on a 300-acre arboretum, Marianapolis Preparatory School prides itself on its sense of community and academia. Founded in 1926, Marianapolis is situated in the heart of Connecticut's antique district. The School is 1 hour from Boston, 45 minutes from Hartford and Providence, and 3 hours from New York City.

The School's 280 students, representing twenty countries, contribute to an enriching academic and cultural experience. Athletics and Advanced Placement (AP) courses abound, with thirteen AP courses offered and more than thirty clubs and sports to choose from.

Marianapolis Preparatory School's aim and purpose is to encourage scholarship and mature character, develop analytical and critical-thinking skills, build communication and problem-solving skills, promote a love of learning and the highest standards of academic achievement, foster aesthetic sensitivity and creativity, encourage the classical ideal of *mens sana in corpore sano* (a sound mind and body), enable students to appreciate the value of cultural diversity, nurture active and intelligent citizenship in the world, and affirm Catholic principles through ethical and moral values.

Marianapolis is a Catholic school that is inclusive of all faiths. In every student, Marianapolis fosters a commitment to compassionate values, which can be felt in the School's genuine dedication to service—service to the world community, the local community, fellow students, and oneself. This commitment to fundamental values helps to develop the confidence, inner purpose, and well-being that are important building blocks in life.

Marianapolis Preparatory School is accredited by the New England Association of Schools and Colleges and is a member of the Connecticut Association of Independent Schools, the Secondary School Admission Test Board, and the Catholic Boarding School Association. Marianapolis is also registered and approved as an independent secondary school by the Department of Education of the state of Connecticut.

ACADEMIC PROGRAMS

To achieve a Marianapolis diploma, all students are required to fulfill 4 years of English, 3 years of math, 3 years of history, 3 years of lab science, 3 years of foreign language, six semesters of theology, 1 year of either art or music, and one semester of computer applications.

Advanced Placement courses are offered in American history, art and music theory, biology, calculus AB and BC, chemistry, English literature, European history, government, physics, psychology, and Spanish.

Reporting of grades occurs four times a year, once at the end of each academic quarter. Full academic grades, teacher comments, and adviser comments are written at the end of the first and third marking periods. At the end of the second and fourth marking periods, academic grades and adviser comments are written; course comments are required only for those students who have earned below a C- in any course. In addition, every student who is new to Marianapolis receives an interim progress report after the first four weeks of classes.

FACULTY AND ADVISERS

The faculty consists of 28 members, who serve as educators, advisers, coaches, and mentors.

Marilyn S. Ebbitt was named Headmistress in 2001. She holds an A.B. from Marquette University and an M.S. from Georgetown University and has been an educator for more than thirty years.

COLLEGE PLACEMENT

During their junior and senior years, students are given a college guide complete with the essentials of the application process. Students meet with the College Placement Director to investigate various college possibilities, and they can also practice their college interview. Dozens of college representatives visit during the school year to meet with interested students. Juniors and seniors are also encouraged to visit college campuses throughout the year.

Assistance is offered at all stages of the college placement process, including the formation of realistic expectations, filling out application forms, and understanding financial aid procedures.

All of the 2005 graduates were accepted into colleges. Recent graduates are attending such colleges and universities as Boston College, Bowdoin, Brown, Fairfield, Holy Cross, Johns Hopkins, Middlebury, Notre Dame, RIT, the Universities of Connecticut and Michigan, Williams, and Worcester Polytechnic.

BOARDING AND GENERAL FACILITIES

Marianapolis has three dormitories located on campus, all supervised by live-in faculty members. Bayer House and St. Albert's Hall are restored historic mansions that house boarding girls. Recreational lounges within the various halls offer a combination of wireless Internet access, television, board games, air hockey, and table tennis. Laundry facilities are located in each of the dormitories.

St. John's Hall houses boarding boys and has a capacity of 85 students. Boys have the use of two recreational lounges with wireless Internet access, television, a Foosball table, table tennis, and a billiards table. A student store sells snacks and other items.

The dormitories are closed during the Thanksgiving, Christmas, and spring recesses. Arrangements with local families are provided for international students who, because of distance, cannot travel home during vacations.

A laundry service with dry cleaning is available at an extra charge for students wishing to enroll in the program.

ATHLETICS

At Marianapolis, athletics are an integral part of the School's mission to nurture the mind, body, and spirit of each student. The athletic program is seen as an extension of the values and ideals developed in the academic classroom and reflects the School's underlying philosophy. Interscholastic sports at various skill levels enable students to practice and understand the values of teamwork, commitment, and sportsmanship as well as to develop a positive work ethic. Sports provide students the opportunity to learn how to work with others for a common goal and how to gain confidence in their own abilities. All freshmen and sophomores are required to participate in a minimum of two interscholastic sports. Juniors and seniors are required to participate in a minimum of one interscholastic sport at the varsity, junior varsity, or thirds level and in an alternative sport.

Athletic offerings include cross-country, volleyball, and soccer in the fall; basketball and wrestling in the winter; and baseball, softball, golf, lacrosse, and tennis in the spring.

EXTRACURRICULAR OPPORTUNITIES

Various extracurricular clubs and activities are offered throughout the school year, depending upon the needs and interests of the students. Clubs and activities include music appreciation, Amnesty International, computer, debate, math center, writing center, yearbook, science quiz bowl, peer leadership, drama, chorus, band, Ski Club, Student Government, and Student Council. Traditional events each year include the Annual Rake Day, Sports Day, Spirit Week, Breakfast with Santa, Halloween Dress-Down Day, and Mardi Gras. All events involve students in spirit-building activities.

DAILY LIFE

School begins each weekday with a small-group advisory at 8 a.m., and the academic day concludes at 2:45 p.m. There are five 1-hour periods each day. Classes meet on a rotating schedule. Club meetings and extra help sessions are scheduled during a half-hour period each day. Athletic practices are scheduled after school from 3:30 to 5:15.

Boarding students are served three meals daily in the dining room and have required night study hours from 7 to 9 p.m. Depending on their individual academic achievement, as determined by their GPA, students are placed in an appropriate study-hall environment. Students with a GPA of 95 percent or higher earn the right

to study independently. Students with a GPA of at least 85 percent are permitted to study in their dormitory rooms, and students with a GPA under 85 percent have structured study hall, which is supervised by faculty members in the academic building. After study, students have free time to enjoy their friends, call home, or surf the Web with wireless Internet access. Lights-out is at 11 p.m. in the dormitory.

WEEKEND LIFE
While most students enjoy taking part in events planned on campus, boarding students are also offered a variety of activities on the weekends. Friday night and Saturday activities can range from trips to Boston or Providence to a night at the movies. School dances are sponsored by various clubs and classes each month. On Sundays, students are required to attend mass in the chapel, followed by brunch. Off-campus activities extend into Sunday; however, study hours are enforced on Sunday evenings.

COSTS AND FINANCIAL AID
Tuition for the 2005–06 academic year was $8915 for day students and $26,770 for boarding students. Tuition covers all expenses except textbooks, supplies, and medical insurance for boarding students. There is also a nominal technology fee. Financial aid is available, and all families are encouraged to complete a financial aid form. The financial aid application deadline is March 1.

ADMISSIONS INFORMATION
Marianapolis Preparatory School seeks qualified applicants of average and above-average academic ability. The School does not discriminate on the basis of race, creed, gender, nationality, or disability. Applicants are considered on the basis of previous school transcripts, recommendations from teachers and school officials, results of the entrance examination, and a personal interview.

Marianapolis has the approval of the Department of State, Washington, D.C., for the admission of immigrant students under the Immigration Act of 1924.

APPLICATION TIMETABLE
Initial inquiries are welcome at any time, and campus visits are encouraged. The first round of boarding school applications is due March 1; after that date, applications are accepted on a rolling-admissions basis. An application fee must accompany the completed application.

ADMISSIONS CORRESPONDENCE
Daniel Harrop
Director of Admissions
Marianapolis Preparatory School
P.O. Box 304
Thompson, Connecticut 06277

Phone: 860-923-9565
Fax: 860-923-3730
E-mail: dharrop@marianapolis.org
Web site: http://www.marianapolis.org

THE MARVELWOOD SCHOOL

Kent, Connecticut

Type: Coeducational boarding and day college-preparatory school
Grades: 9–12, PG
Enrollment: 148
Head of School: Scott E. Pottbecker

THE SCHOOL

The Marvelwood School, founded in 1957 by Robert A. Bodkin, is for average to above-average students who have not yet reached their potential as well as for young people who have not been successful in traditional school settings. The School's small, supportive, familylike environment is ideal for students who are struggling to reach their potential but are seriously committed to their education and development.

Marvelwood students have a wide variety of backgrounds and learning styles requiring a flexible curriculum. Small classes, dedicated faculty members, a strong adviser program, and supervised study time ensure that each student receives the individual attention he or she needs. "Hands-on learning" in every facet of the academic program is a major emphasis at Marvelwood.

Marvelwood is located in the foothills of the Berkshire Mountains. It is 55 miles from Hartford, 80 miles from New York City, and 150 miles from Boston. The 83-acre campus sits atop Skiff Mountain and is surrounded by many acres nearby that are available for the School's use. Because of the rural nature of Kent, hiking, mountain biking, camping, skiing, and field study are normal activities at Marvelwood.

The School is governed by the Board of Trustees, composed mainly of alumni and parents of current or past students. The School's budget is $5 million. Each year, the Annual Fund raises upward of $150,000. Capital funds are sought continually to enlarge the School's endowment and expand and improve the School's facilities.

Marvelwood is accredited by the New England Association of Schools and Colleges and is a member of the National Association of Independent Schools and the Connecticut Association of Independent Schools.

ACADEMIC PROGRAMS

Currently, a minimum of 20 academic and arts credits are required for graduation, in the following distribution: 4 credits of English, 4 credits of mathematics, 3–4 credits of history, 3–4 credits of science, 2–3 credits of foreign language, and 2–3 credits in the arts. A full-year course is awarded 1 credit. Certain students may be exempted from required foreign language courses. The School has an expanded arts program, with course work in drawing and painting, creative writing, ceramics, design, photography, film, drama, and journalism. Participation in athletics is also required each term; a full year's credit in sports is a graduation requirement.

The overall student-teacher ratio is 4:1. Class sizes range from 5 to 14 students, with an average size between 8 and 10. During the freshman and sophomore years, there are two levels of academic difficulty. During the junior and senior years, the School offers three academic levels.

Classes at Marvelwood operate on a modified block schedule. Each student is involved in course work for the entire academic day. There are no free periods. Study halls are held in the afternoon as needed and in the evening. During the evening, each dormitory's study hall is supervised by 2 faculty members.

Report cards are issued every three weeks and include separate grades in academic achievement and effort. At the end of the fall, winter, and spring terms, comprehensive reports with comments from the student's teachers, coach, adviser, and the Head of School are sent to parents. Students also complete a self-evaluation and meet with their adviser at the end of each trimester to discuss this evaluation, the reports, and goals for the following term.

Students with learning difficulties may enroll in the Strategies Program, an intensive transitional support program in which they work on basic writing, reading, and organizational and study skills. The Math Tutorial Program addresses basic needs in mathematics. Marvelwood does not accept students who have either severe learning problems or serious dyslexic conditions. Students are placed in the Strategies Program on the basis of testing, prior school records, teachers' observations, and by recommendation of the Admissions Office. Most students meet individually with their Strategies teacher. Each year, approximately 50 students are enrolled in the Strategies Program, which is a full-credit course. Placement is reviewed periodically, and regroupings are made as students progress.

There are ESL classes at beginning and intermediate levels of ability as well as two ESL history classes.

FACULTY AND ADVISERS

Marvelwood currently employs 35 full-time teachers and 6 part-time faculty members. Of these, 20 are men and 21 are women. Sixteen hold master's degrees and 2 hold Ph.D.'s.

The current Head of School, Scott E. Pottbecker, was appointed Marvelwood's fifth Headmaster in 2005. Previously, he had been the Assistant Head of School and Chief Financial Officer at Forman School in Litchfield, Connecticut. Mr. Pottbecker has held administrative and teaching roles in boarding schools for more than fifteen years. He is a graduate of the University of Connecticut and holds a master's degree in public administration from the University of Hartford. Mr. Pottbecker and his wife, Amy, have 4 children. The family resides in the Headmaster's house on the Marvelwood campus.

Marvelwood's faculty members have had anywhere from one to twenty-five years of experience in private school education. All faculty members and most administrators assume duties in all School areas, including teaching, dorm supervision, coaching, and advising. Every faculty member advises 4

to 5 students, oversees their progress, and communicates with their parents.

COLLEGE PLACEMENT

Preparation for college placement begins in the junior year. This extensive and prescriptive process emphasizes individual attention for students and their families. Attention is given to helping students fine-tune their writing skills, thus enabling them to write their best college essay.

The Director of College Counseling and his assistant meet with students to help them select colleges that answer their personal needs and interests. Future career choices are also explored. Students and parents fill out questionnaires that assist counselors in identifying appropriate colleges. Students have the opportunity to hear about colleges from representatives who visit during the year. During the summer before senior year, students and parents are encouraged to visit those colleges in which they are interested.

SAT I score averages for the class of 2005 were 480 verbal and 490 math. Of the 41 students in the class of 2005, 40 matriculated in colleges and universities. Colleges and universities recently attended include Colby-Sawyer, Hamilton (New York), Johnson & Wales, Manhattanville, Michigan, NYU, Purdue, Rutgers, Syracuse, Utica, and the University of Connecticut.

STUDENT BODY AND CONDUCT

Of the 148 students at Marvelwood, 101 are boarding boys, 42 are boarding girls, 2 are day boys, and 3 are day girls. There are 25 freshmen, 31 sophomores, 47 juniors, and 45 seniors. Students come from twenty-one states and eleven countries.

Students at Marvelwood are expected to observe basic community principles. Trust, honesty, and community involvement are important values within the School. Disciplinary offenses are handled by a faculty Disciplinary Committee. A recommendation is then passed on to the Headmaster, who makes the final decision. Violation of major School rules or consistent disregard for general community principles can lead to suspension or expulsion. Any recommendation of expulsion is reviewed by the Headmaster.

A Student Council is elected by the student body and provides input regarding School life. Its members also help organize special events.

ACADEMIC FACILITIES

Classes are held in the main schoolhouse in fifteen classrooms including two up-to-date science labs. The Bodkin Library contains more than 9,000 books and 70 periodicals. It also houses a computer lab. The gymnasium building contains a large stage, student lounge, and music room as well as the main indoor athletic facilities.

BOARDING AND GENERAL FACILITIES

Marvelwood's comfortable dormitories are supervised by faculty members, who have apartments in each of the buildings. Each dormitory houses students from all grade levels. With only a few exceptions, roommates are of the same grade level or age. During School vacations, the School does not provide dormitory facilities. Students who cannot go home may arrange to spend time with another student who lives in the area.

ATHLETICS

Marvelwood believes that participation in athletics is an important part of a student's growth. Students participate in sports in lieu of gym classes. One full-year's credit in sports is required of students during each year of their enrollment at Marvelwood. Marvelwood competes with other schools at the varsity and junior varsity levels. In the fall, teams are fielded in cross-country (coed), volleyball (girls'), and soccer (boys' and girls'); in the winter, in wrestling (boys'), basketball (boys' and girls'), and downhill skiing (coed); and in the spring, in lacrosse (boys' and girls'), softball (girls'), tennis (boys' and girls'), and golf (coed).

In addition to the competitive team and individual sports, there are also recreational activities, such as a Wilderness Ways program that offers hiking and wilderness skills. In support of this program, a low-ropes course was professionally constructed on campus. Other noncompetitive offerings include mountain biking and rock climbing in the fall. Winter offerings include a skiing/snowboarding program, which uses nearby Mohawk Mountain, and yoga. In the spring, there is an Ultimate Frisbee program and white-water canoeing on the Housatonic River.

The School has five playing fields, eight tennis courts, and a gymnasium.

EXTRACURRICULAR OPPORTUNITIES

Marvelwood believes that interest and participation in extracurricular activities are important parts of every student's life. Recently, interests and activities have included the yearbook, drama, guitar lessons, photography, chess, student government, admissions tour guides, driver's education, literary magazine, creative writing, and private music lessons. Students also attend the Hartford Stage subscription series.

A special part of students' education at Marvelwood is participation in the School's Community Service Program. Most of the students are transported off campus to volunteer in day-care centers, elementary schools, nursing homes, soup kitchens, nature conservancies, an animal shelter, and Habitat for Humanity. Marvelwood's pro-

gram receives strong local recognition and was recently given an award by the governor of Connecticut.

DAILY LIFE

The academic program runs from September through June, with vacations at Thanksgiving, in the winter, and in the spring. School days begin at 7:45 a.m. with breakfast. Classes begin at 8:30, and there is an all-school meeting at 9:50. Then classes resume, there is a 40-minute lunch break, and classes are over at 2:40. Sports practice begins at 3 p.m. and is followed by dinner, evening study hall, and staggered lights-out times, depending on grade.

Community Service takes place on Wednesday mornings. On Wednesday afternoons, there are games or other sports activities. On Saturdays, three classes are held in the morning, followed by a cafeteria-style lunch and athletics in the afternoon. Sunday is a more relaxed day during which students attend a 10:30 brunch, followed by a free afternoon. Sunday evening's schedule is the same as that on the weekdays, with dinner followed by a dorm clean-up and then study hall from 7:30 until 9:15.

WEEKEND LIFE

Marvelwood's rural campus provides opportunities for numerous out-of-doors activities on weekends. These include camping trips, hikes, bicycling trips, fishing, and skiing. On Saturday evenings, students have a choice of movies, off-campus trips, plays, concerts, or other special events. Weekend activities are supervised by faculty members. Occasionally, students attend dances at other schools. Skiing at nearby Mohawk Mountain also provides an opportunity for social interaction with students from other schools. Day students are welcome to participate in weekend activities and may stay overnight at the School if they have permission. Attendance at religious services is not required, but transportation to services is available for those who wish to attend.

SUMMER PROGRAMS

For boys and girls entering grades 7–10, The Marvelwood Summer is designed to meet the individual needs of students in reading, writing, mathematics, and study skills. Extensive pretesting and posttesting, an ungraded curriculum that emphasizes skills building, and the close supervision of a friendly and supportive faculty help many young students "turn the corner" academically. Swimming, tennis, hiking, cycling, and many other activities are included in a lively extracurricular program.

COSTS AND FINANCIAL AID

In 2005–06, the cost of tuition, room, and board was $34,500. Tuition insurance was $2381. Day student tuition was $20,700, with a tuition insurance cost of $1429. The cost of the daily one-on-one Strategies Program was $6400 per year, billed separately by trimester as needed. The optional Math Tutorial Program costs $6400. A tuition deposit of $3000 is due within thirty days of acceptance. The first major payment is due on July 1, with the remainder due on December 1.

Need-based financial aid is available. Parents must file a Parents' Financial Statement with the School and Student Service for Financial Aid in Princeton, New Jersey. Forms are available through the Admissions Office. Approximately 25 percent of Marvelwood's students receive financial aid. In 2005–06, more than $500,000 was awarded.

ADMISSIONS INFORMATION

To be considered for admission, applicants must visit the campus for an interview, file an application, provide a transcript from their current school, and submit three recommendations. SSAT scores or results from other standardized tests may be submitted but are not required.

Marvelwood seeks students of average to above-average intelligence who would thrive in a small school with structure and support. Students enter Marvelwood in the ninth, tenth, or eleventh grade. Occasionally, a student may enter as a senior.

APPLICATION TIMETABLE

Inquiries are welcome Monday through Friday during the school year. Campus tours and interviews can be arranged (a call should be made while the School is in session). Interviews may be scheduled Monday through Friday, on Saturday mornings when the School is in session, or on any weekday when the School is not in session. Following receipt of all necessary information, students are notified of the Admissions Committee's decision. Following notification of acceptance, parents have thirty days to respond.

ADMISSIONS CORRESPONDENCE

Todd Holt
The Marvelwood School
P.O. Box 3001
Kent, Connecticut 06757-3001

Phone: 860-927-0047
Fax: 860-927-0021
E-mail: admissions@marvelwood.org
Web site: http://www.marvelwoods.org

MARYMOUNT SCHOOL

New York, New York

MARYMOUNT SCHOOL

Type: Girls' independent college-preparatory Catholic day school
Grades: N–12: Lower School, Nursery–3; Middle School, 4–7; Upper School, 8–12
Enrollment: School total: 530; Upper School: 220
Head of School: Concepcion R. Alvar

THE SCHOOL

Marymount School is an independent Catholic day school that educates girls in the tradition of academic excellence and moral values. The School promotes in each student a respect for her own unique abilities and provides a foundation for exploring and acting on questions of integrity and ethical decision making. Founded by Mother Joseph Butler in 1926 as part of a worldwide network of schools directed by the Religious of the Sacred Heart of Mary, Marymount remains faithful to its mission to educate young women who question, risk, and grow; young women "who care, serve, and lead; young women prepared to challenge, shape, and change the world." Committed to its Catholic heritage, the School welcomes and values the religious diversity of its student body and seeks to give all students a deeper understanding of the role of the spiritual in life. The School also has an active social service program and integrates social justice and human rights into the curriculum.

Marymount occupies three adjoining landmark Beaux Arts mansions located on Fifth Avenue's historic Museum Mile and a fourth mansion at 2 East 82nd Street. The Metropolitan Museum of Art and Central Park, both located directly across the street from the School, provide resources that are integral to the School's academic and extracurricular programs. As part of the humanities curriculum, students visit the museum regularly, as often as twice a week in the Upper School. Central Park is used for science and physical education classes as well as extracurricular activities. Other nearby sites, such as the United Nations, the Tenement Museum, Ellis Island, the New York Zoological Society, the American Museum of Natural History, and the Hayden Planetarium are used as extensions of the classroom.

Since 1969, the School has been independently incorporated under the direction of a 30-member Board of Trustees made up of parents, alumnae, educators, and members of the founding order. The School benefits from a strong Parents' Association; an active Alumnae Association; the involvement of parents, alumnae, and student volunteers; and a successful Annual Giving Program.

Marymount is chartered by the New York State Board of Regents and accredited by the New York State Association of Independent Schools. The School holds membership in the National Association of Independent Schools, the New York State Association of Independent Schools, the Independent Schools Admissions Association of Greater New York, the National Catholic Education Association, the National Coalition of Girls' Schools, and the Educational Records Bureau.

ACADEMIC PROGRAMS

Emphasizing classic disciplines and scientific inquiry, the challenging college-preparatory curriculum provides students with the skills necessary to succeed in competitive colleges and in life beyond. Through its rigorous academic program and its focus on the education of young women, Marymount seeks to instill in its students confidence, self-esteem, leadership ability, a risk-taking spirit, and a love of learning. Financial literacy is a strong commitment; the School offers investment and philanthropic opportunities through its math and economic classes as well as its extracurricular activities.

The School's commitment to technology is reflected in its curriculum, which fully integrates information and communication technologies into all subject areas. Students have access to wired and wireless desktop and laptop computers throughout the School. Upper School students have their own e-mail accounts, and students and teachers throughout the School use computers to carry out research, create presentations, publish work, communicate, and demonstrate ideas and concepts. All students learn to use HTML authoring tools to create and publish academic Web sites. Via e-mail, videoconferencing, and the Marymount Web site, students collaborate on projects with other Marymount Schools and with students and researchers from around the globe.

High school graduation requirements include satisfactory completion of 4 years of English, 3 years of history, 3 years of math, 3 years of laboratory science, 3 levels of one foreign language, 4 years of religious studies, 4 years of physical education, 1 year of studio art, 4 semesters of health education, and 1 semester of speech. These requirements are structured to provide a broad, solid base of knowledge while sharpening problem-solving and research skills and promoting critical and creative thinking.

The School offers strong honors and Advanced Placement programs. Electives include AP art history, economics, Greek, medieval history, music history, political thought, AP portfolio art, studio art, and studies in Africa. Hybrid online courses offered include astronomy, meteorology, and multimedia and programming languages. In senior English, students choose from seminars that cover topics from Shakespeare's history plays to modern Irish literature to the literature of African-American women writers. Most students elect to take a fourth year of math, which includes AP calculus and AP statistics, and a fourth year of science, which includes AP biology, AP chemistry, AP physics B or C, and advanced physics with calculus applications. The science program connects with and utilizes the research of numerous institutions, including the New York Academy of Sciences and Princeton University.

A leader in science and technological education, Marymount is also committed to the study of humanities. All Class IX students take part in the Integrated Humanities Program, an interdisciplinary curriculum that focuses on history, literature, the major world religions, art history, and studio art in the study of ancient world civilizations. Classes are held at the Metropolitan Museum of Art at least once a week, and the program culminates in a World Civilizations Festival. As part of this program, students work in groups to create a virtual museum on the Web site.

The Visual Arts Department offers studio art courses every year culminating in AP portfolio art. The performing arts program includes the school chorus, a chamber choir, music history courses, and speech and interpretive readings.

The religious studies program includes Hebrew scriptures, the New Testament, social encyclicals of the Catholic Church, comparative religions, and world issues, with a focus on moral and ethical decision making. Students analyze social systemic issues and immerse themselves in the community through numerous service projects. The Catholic-Jewish Initiative provides students with a deeper understanding of the Judeo-Christian tradition. This program includes Holocaust studies and a trip to the National Holocaust Museum in Washington, D.C.

Each spring, senior seminars provide career information from visiting alumnae. During the last four weeks of the academic year, seniors participate in an off-campus internship to gain significant exposure to a specific career of interest. Students have interned at hospitals, research laboratories, law firms, theaters, schools, nonprofit organizations, and corporations.

As members of a worldwide network of schools, students may opt to spend a semester at Marymount International Schools in London or Rome. In addition, students have participated in exchanges with the Santa Fe Indian School in New Mexico and Chiba Higashi School in Japan as well as American Field Service summer immersion programs around the globe. Annual faculty-led spring and summer trips have recently explored the theater and literature of London and the cities, countryside, language, and culture of Italy, France, and Spain. The school chorus has an annual concert tour in Europe over the spring vacation. Most recently, they performed in churches and concert halls in Rome, Florence, and Bologna.

Upper School students are formally evaluated four times a year, using an A–F grading system. The evaluation process includes written reports and parent/student/teacher conferences.

The Middle School curriculum welcomes the diverse interests of young adolescents and is structured to channel their energy and natural love of learning. The integrated core curriculum gradually increases in the degree of departmentalization at each grade level, and challenging learning activities and flexible groupings in main subject areas ensure that the students achieve their full potential. Foreign language study begins in Class IV. Students choose a four-year sequence of either French or Spanish as well as an introduction to Latin in Class V. The Middle School years culminate in a study tour to France that increases the students' knowledge of language, culture, architecture, and history. In addition, and as a complement to Class VII's study of women's issues, a trip to Seneca Falls, New York, focuses on the inspiring history of the women's rights movement.

Twice weekly speech classes prepare the girls for drama presentations such as *Revolutionary Voices, Greek Mythology, Canterbury Tales,* and a performance of a Shakespearean play. Uptown Broadway productions in the fall and spring allow the students to perform onstage in a full-scale musical.

The Lower School provides child-centered, creative learning within a challenging, structured environment. The Lower School curriculum focuses on the acquisition of foundational skills, often through an interdisciplinary approach. Innovative programs engage students in the exciting process of learning about themselves, their surroundings, and the larger world. An after-school program is also available in the Lower School.

FACULTY AND ADVISERS

There are 83 full-time and 3 part-time faculty members, allowing for a 6:1 student-teacher ratio. Seventy-one percent of the faculty members hold master's degrees, and 6 percent hold doctoral degrees. In Nursery through Class I, each class has a head teacher and

---

an assistant teacher. In the Middle School, students make the transition from homeroom teachers to advisers. In Classes IV and V, each class has two homeroom teachers. In Classes V–XII, each student has a homeroom teacher and an adviser, usually one of her teachers, who follows her academic progress and provides guidance and support. Technology integrators, museum integrators, a school nurse, learning resource specialists, a school counselor, a school psychologist, and a consulting psychologist work with students throughout the School.

Concepcion Alvar was appointed Headmistress in 2004 after serving thirteen years as the Director of Admissions, sixteen years as the Director and Supervisor of Marymount Summer, and three years as a head teacher. She holds a B.S. from Maryknoll College (Philippines) and an M.A. from Columbia University, Teachers College.

COLLEGE PLACEMENT
Under the guidance of the Director of College Counseling, the formal college counseling program begins during the junior year. In the second semester, two College Nights are held for students and parents. Individual counseling throughout the semester directs each student to those colleges that best match her abilities and aspirations. Students participate in weekly sessions to learn about general requirements for college admission, the application process, and the SAT testing process. During the fall of their senior year, students continue the weekly sessions, focusing on essay writing, admissions interviews, and financial aid applications.

Graduates from recent classes are attending the following colleges and universities: Amherst, Barnard, Boston College, Boston University, Bowdoin, Brown, Columbia, Cornell, Dartmouth, Davidson, Duke, Fordham, George Washington, Georgetown, Harvard, Holy Cross, NYU, Oberlin, Princeton, Skidmore, Smith, Trinity, Vanderbilt, Villanova, Wellesley, Wesleyan, Wheaton, Williams, Yale, and the Universities of Pennsylvania and Virginia.

STUDENT BODY AND CONDUCT
Marymount's enrollment is 530 students in Nursery through Class XII, with 220 girls in the Upper School. Most students reside in New York City; however, Upper School students also commute from Long Island, Staten Island, New Jersey, and Westchester. Students wear uniforms, except on special days; participate in athletic and extracurricular activities; and attend chapel services and annual class retreats.

Marymount fosters active participation by the students in their own education and in the life of the School community. Students seek out leadership and volunteer opportunities, serving as advocates for one another through peer assistance, peer mentoring, Houses, Retreat Team, and Big Sister/Little Sister programs within the School. Student government and campus ministry provide social and service opportunities that enable students to broaden their perspectives, sharpen public-speaking skills, and form lasting friendships.

Teachers and administrators encourage each student to respect herself and others and to be responsible members of the community. While there are relatively few rules, those that exist are consistently enforced to promote freedom and growth for the individual and the entire School community.

ACADEMIC FACILITIES
The turn-of-the-century mansions provide spacious rooms for the Nursery–Class XII educational program. Facilities include wired and wireless smart classrooms, a networked library complex, five state-of-the-art science laboratories, three computer centers, a math laboratory, an art center, a chapel, a language lab, a music lab, an auditorium, a courtyard playground, a gymnasium, and the Commons.

ATHLETICS
The athletic program promotes good health, physical fitness, coordination, skill development, confidence, and a spirit of competition and collaboration through its physical education classes, electives program for Classes X–XII, and individual and team sports.

In the Middle School, students stay two days per week for an after-school sports program. As part of this program, they are trained in techniques and strategies to prepare for competition on interscholastic teams within the Athletic Association of Independent Schools League. Marymount provides a full schedule for varsity and junior varsity sports as well as Middle School teams at the V/VI and VII/VIII class levels. The sports offered are badminton, basketball, cross-country, fencing, field hockey, lacrosse, soccer, softball, swimming, tennis, track and field, and volleyball.

In addition to its gymnasium, the School utilizes the fields in Central Park, tennis clubs, swimming pools, and athletic facilities throughout New York City.

EXTRACURRICULAR OPPORTUNITIES
A wide range of clubs and activities complement the academic program and provide students with the opportunity to contribute to the School community, pursue their individual interests, and develop communication, cooperation, and leadership skills. Activities offered include Amnesty International, campus ministry, cultural awareness, drama, environmental awareness, film, finance, forensics, Marymount Singers, mock trial, Model United Nations, National Honor Society, philosophy club, Science Bowl, Science Olympiad, set design/tech crew, student government, the New York Medical College Club, and women's issues. Student publications include a yearbook, a newspaper, and an award-winning literary/arts journal. A wide range of Friday noontime clubs includes Student Council, Italian, Latin, Handbells, Environmental Science, Art, Drama, Handwork, and the literary magazine, *Chez Nous*.

Each year, the Upper School presents two dramatic productions, including a musical; produces Harambee Night during Black History Month; and participates in numerous community service projects. Marymount participates in local and national competitions and conferences with other schools.

The Vincent A. Lisanti Speakers Series brings people of stature and achievement to the School, including poet-laureate Billy Collins, athlete Tegla Laroupe, author Jhumpa Lahiri, bioethicist Ronald Green, and feminist Gloria Steinem.

Students have the opportunity to interact with boys from neighboring schools through exchange days, drama productions, community service projects, coffee houses, and other student-run social activities.

DAILY LIFE
Upper School classes are held from 8:20 a.m. to 3:30 p.m. on Monday, Tuesday, and Thursday. To accommodate electives, extracurricular activities, and team sports, classes end at 2:45 p.m. on Wednesdays and Fridays. Classes are each 45 minutes in length and typically meet nine out of ten days in a two-week cycle, with a double period each week in each course. Students meet daily with their advisory group, gather with the entire Upper School every Friday for assembly, and have the opportunity to meet individually with their classroom teachers. After classes have ended, most students remain for sports, extracurricular activities, and/or independent study.

COSTS AND FINANCIAL AID
Tuition for the 2005–06 academic year is $25,850 for Classes K–XII. In February, parents are required to make a deposit of $4000, which is credited toward the November tuition. The Key Education Resources Payment Plan is available.

More than $1.2 million in financial aid was awarded in 2005–06 to students of outstanding academic promise after need was established by School and Student Services.

ADMISSIONS INFORMATION
As a college-preparatory school, Marymount aims to enroll young women of academic promise and sound character who are seeking a challenging educational environment and multiple opportunities for learning outside the classroom. Educational Records Bureau tests, school records, and interviews are used in selecting students.

The School admits students of any race, color, or national or ethnic origin to all the rights, privileges, programs, and activities generally accorded or made available to students at the School and does not discriminate on these bases in the administration of its educational policies, admissions policies, scholarship or loan programs, or athletic or other School-administered programs.

APPLICATION TIMETABLE
Interested students are encouraged to contact the Admissions Office as early as possible in the fall for admission the following year. The application deadline is December 15, and notifications of acceptance are sent during February and March.

ADMISSIONS CORRESPONDENCE
Lillian Issa
Director of Admissions
Marymount School
1026 Fifth Avenue
New York, New York 10028

Phone: 212-744-4486
Fax: 212-744-0163 (general)
212-744-0716 (admissions)
E-mail: Admissions@marymount.k12.ny.us
Web site: http://www.marymount.k12.ny.us

MASSANUTTEN MILITARY ACADEMY

Woodstock, Virginia

Type: Coeducational boarding college-preparatory school with an Army JROTC program
Grades: 7–12, postgraduate year
Enrollment: School total: 194; Upper School: 168; Middle School: 26
Head of School: Col. Roy F. Zinser, President

THE SCHOOL

Massanutten Military Academy's (MMA) mission is to provide every cadet with an academic, character, leadership, and physical education of excellence, which ensures their development and readiness for college, leadership, and citizenship. The mission is implemented with discipline, fostered with structure, and enhanced by a supportive environment. The mission is established on the founding motto of the Academy, "Non nobis solum" ("Not for ourselves alone"), and based on the principles of Courage, Purity, and Industry.

Massanutten's cadets are young men and women who desire advanced preparation for college within a structured, military environment. Established in 1899, the Academy adopted a military program in 1917. Today, the military structure plays a crucial role in the education of every cadet by creating a stable environment that is conducive to learning.

Situated on 40 acres in the small 250-year-old town of Woodstock, Virginia, in the heart of the Shenandoah Valley, the Academy is only 90 minutes from downtown Washington, D.C., and 2 hours from Baltimore, Maryland.

Massanutten's maximum enrollment is 242 cadets, 186 male and 56 female, enrolled in grades 7–12 and one year of postgraduate study. Massanutten provides both boarding and day cadet programs. The corps of cadets is diverse, with cadets from many countries and more than twenty states. This diversity is one of Massanutten's greatest strengths.

Massanutten Military Academy is accredited by the Southern Association of Colleges and Schools (SACS) and the Virginia Association of Independent Schools (VAIS). The Academy meets all of the academic standards of the Commonwealth of Virginia. It is a member of the National Honor Society, the Association of Military Colleges and Schools of the United States (AMC-SUS), and the Association of Boarding Schools (TABS).

ACADEMIC PROGRAMS

At Massanutten, the small class size (9:1 student-teacher ratio) encourages faculty members and cadets to develop positive relationships that foster greater success in the classroom. A daily tutorial period offers cadets the opportunity to return to their teachers for additional instruction. A mandatory, supervised evening study period is held each class night. Individual tutoring is available through a separate contract. The Academy library and computer lab are open during the afternoon and evening study periods and during the weekends for research or computer use. Each cadet is assigned a faculty mentor who keeps parents informed of progress throughout the year by telephone, e-mail, and mail.

Cadets at Massanutten have three diploma options available to them. The advanced college-

preparatory diploma may, in addition to the Academy's transcript, include a transcript of courses taken through Shenandoah University. The college-preparatory diploma is the standard Academy diploma, which requires the cadet to earn the necessary course credits in preparation for attendance at a major college or university. The basic high school diploma is offered to cadets enrolled at Massanutten who do not have enough credits for a college-preparatory diploma but have the course credits necessary to meet all of the Virginia high school standards for graduation.

The Middle School program concentrates on developing academic skills and knowledge necessary for the cadet's success in high school. In addition to the four core subjects, cadets are required to take art, health, and physical education. Advanced eighth graders may take high school–level courses, such as a foreign language or algebra I.

The Commandant's Department has the primary responsibility for the character, discipline, and leadership education of the corps of cadets. The Commandant of Cadets directs 15 dorm supervisors (called CDOs, Cadet Development Officers). The 3 retired Army leaders in the JROTC Department work closely with the Commandant's Department.

The Army Junior ROTC Program at Massanutten has consistently earned the designation of Honor Unit with Distinction, which means that it is one of the best programs in the nation. The mission of the JROTC program is to motivate each cadet to be a better citizen. JROTC's objectives include having each cadet develop an appreciation of the ethical values and principles that underlie good citizenship, including integrity, acceptance of responsibility, and a respect for constituted authority. JROTC cadets are under no obligation to enter the military. The completion of one or more years of JROTC may provide cadets with college-level ROTC credit. The fact that MMA earned the Honor Unit with Distinction designation allows the Academy to nominate selected, qualified cadets to the service academies. In addition, the JROTC Department assists cadets in competing for ROTC scholarships to major universities.

Grades are issued based on the percentage of points available versus points earned; A=90–100, B=80–89, C=70–79, D=65–69.

FACULTY AND ADVISERS

Massanutten's faculty consists of 23 full-time and 3 part-time instructors. Of this number, 18 hold bachelor's degrees and 8 hold advanced degrees. There are 3 full-time JROTC Army Instructors. Faculty members are hired based on their education, experience, and ability to truly teach their assigned subjects.

Faculty members take advantage of many continuing education programs, including those of-

fered by George Mason, James Madison, and Shenandoah Universities.

Col. Roy F. Zinser, President, received his bachelor's degree in business administration from The Citadel and holds three master's degrees: one in business administration, one in strategic policy, and one in international relations. He served for more than twenty-nine-years as an active-duty Army leader. He has been a leader in military secondary education for eight years and is committed to the education and success of young people.

COLLEGE PLACEMENT

Cadets begin receiving guidance in college selection in October of their junior year. The process continues until the cadets have chosen and been accepted at the college they plan to attend. The task of guiding students toward college placement is overseen by the Academic Dean. Cadets take the PSAT once during their junior year in preparation for the SAT. Cadets may take the SAT once in their junior year and at least once during their senior year. In the last three years, 100 percent of the graduates were accepted to colleges or universities, including The Citadel, Mary Baldwin, Penn State, the United States Military Academy, the United States Naval Academy, the University of Virginia, Virginia Military Institute, and Virginia Tech.

STUDENT BODY AND CONDUCT

Massanutten's enrollment is 194 cadets. There are 15 cadets in the seventh grade, 11 in the eighth grade, 29 in the ninth grade, 31 in the tenth grade, 52 in the eleventh grade, 47 in the twelfth grade, and 9 postgraduates.

There are 8 international cadets representing four different countries. The remaining cadets represent more than twenty states and every region of the continental United States.

The *Cadet Handbook* provides each cadet with the guidelines for life at the Academy, including each cadet's duties and responsibilities and the Academy's rules and regulations. Cadets are required to adhere to the strict guidelines of behavior established in the *Cadet Handbook*. The handbook also outlines the Cadet Honor Code, which states, "A cadet will not lie, cheat or steal nor tolerate those who do."

The corps of cadets is organized into a battalion with six companies. Cadets who lead the corps have earned rank by demonstrating leadership potential, academic success, strong character, and athletic or extracurricular performance.

ACADEMIC FACILITIES

The academic facilities include twenty-seven classrooms, three science laboratories, and an art studio. All of the classrooms were renovated during 2005, and there are five computer labs used to teach computer courses, support the teaching of

language and other courses, produce the school yearbook, and teach the SAT/PSAT/ACT preparatory courses. The computer labs are open at designated times for cadets to check e-mail or complete academic assignments under adult supervision. Every teacher has a laptop computer with wireless capabilities for classroom use.

Lantz Hall contains a 300-seat auditorium and laboratory classrooms for biology, chemistry, and physics.

BOARDING AND GENERAL FACILITIES

Male cadets are housed in Benchoff, Harrison, and Lantz Halls. Generally, two cadets of the same age and grade level are assigned to a room. All of the Academy's dorms have been renovated and provide cadets with first-class living conditions.

Female cadets are housed in Rosedrey Warehime Dormitory, which was built in 1988 and is fully air conditioned. The building can house 56 female cadets in double rooms. A woman dormitory supervisor is on duty 24 hours a day, seven days a week. A woman staff member lives in Warehime to provide additional supervision and mentorship. The building is protected by a security system. Female residents have access to the laundry room, kitchen, minigym, television lounge, and computer lab located in the dormitory.

The Infirmary is housed in the former Carriage House. A nurse is on duty between the hours of 6 a.m. and 11 p.m. every day and on call during the night. A local physician pays scheduled visits to the Academy for medical care.

ATHLETICS

Physical fitness is a vital part of the educational program at Massanutten—teaching good sportsmanship, teamwork, and an appreciation of regular exercise. All cadets are required to play on an athletic team or participate in the Academy's physical development program. Varsity and junior varsity athletics are offered to both male and female cadets in grades 7 to 12. Postgraduates may participate on sports teams but may not compete in conference events. The sports program includes basketball, cross-country, fencing, football, golf, soccer, softball, swimming, tennis, track and field, and volleyball. Many Massanutten athletes have succeeded on college and professional teams. In 2003, Massanutten launched a Postgraduate Basketball Program for men. The teams compete against junior college and college junior varsity teams.

The Academy's athletics facilities include a football field and stadium, a 440-yard track, a 30,000-square-foot gymnasium, three weight rooms, an indoor swimming pool, three tennis courts, a baseball field, a softball field, two outdoor basketball courts, an on-campus cross-country course, four practice fields, a rifle range, and a pistol range.

EXTRACURRICULAR OPPORTUNITIES

Cadets may participate in a variety of extracurricular clubs, including a BSA Venturing crew and a Boy Scout troop. These clubs take full advantage of the Shenandoah Valley and nearby state and national parks. The Academy sponsors a very active Volunteer Community Service program.

Cadets who remain on the campus for the weekend are required to attend either a local church service of their faith or an on-campus character-development class each Sunday morning.

DAILY LIFE

Reveille sounds at 6 a.m. Monday through Friday, and breakfast is served from 6:15 to 7:15. Cadets clean their rooms and participate in a morning room and uniform inspection from 7:15 until 8:30. Seven 45-minute classes begin at 8:30. Lunch is served at 12. Classes end at 3:45. All students must report to their chosen sport or intramural activity by 4. Dinner is served at 6. Students are required to be in their rooms by 8 for a 90-minute study session. Lights-out is at 10.

WEEKEND LIFE

Cadets in good standing with the Academy may enjoy the many options available to them on the weekends. Downtown Woodstock is only a 5-minute walk from the campus. Cadets can see a movie at the theater, eat at one of the restaurants, go bowling, or shop in one of the stores. Off-campus trips offered to cadets include amusement parks, local caverns, battlefield tours, music or dramatic productions, professional or college athletic events, and visits to attractions in Washington, D.C., or Baltimore. Seasonal activities include paintball exercises, horseback riding, golfing, camping, fishing, white-water rafting, indoor water parks, and snow skiing.

On-campus activities include the use of the new Cadet Activities Center, the company lounges, and planned events each weekend, such as swimming, outdoor court sports, dances, intercompany athletic competitions, and other group activities.

SUMMER PROGRAMS

Massanutten operates one of the nation's only summer cadet programs in late June and July. The emphasis is on academic success. This is supported by the traditional military structure that provides cadets with the opportunity to learn discipline (doing what is right even when no one is watching), responsibility, and respect. In addition, the Academy offers the nation's only summer JROTC program, where cadets may receive a high school credit for JROTC in just five weeks. Enrollment in the regular session is not required for participation in the summer program.

COSTS AND FINANCIAL AID

The 2005–06 tuition was $20,710. This included tuition, seven-day room and board, initial issue of uniforms, laundry, haircuts, activities, technology, and basic infirmary needs. An appropriate personal spending allowance is not more than $25 per week. Because of Massanutten's rolling admissions policy, the tuition is prorated based on the date of entry. If applying for admission after September 30, students should inquire about the current tuition rate.

Financial aid, tuition credits, and scholarships are available. All awards are assessed and granted on an annual basis.

ADMISSIONS INFORMATION

Students who are accepted to Massanutten must show a determination and willingness to comply with a structured program and must be average to above-average students. The parents or guardians of the cadets must also be willing to comply with and support the Academy's rules and policies.

APPLICATION TIMETABLE

Massanutten Military Academy operates on a rolling admissions, space-available basis. Inquiries are always welcome. All applicants must complete an application form, forward transcripts to the Admissions Office; an academic achievement test may be required. A campus tour and interview are strongly recommended and can be scheduled on weekdays or weekends to accommodate those interested in giving their son or daughter the opportunity to attend MMA.

ADMISSIONS CORRESPONDENCE

Jed Davis, Director of Admissions
Massanutten Military Academy
614 South Main Street
Woodstock, Virginia 22664

Phone: 540-459-2167 Ext. 262
       877-466-6222 (toll-free)
Fax: 540-459-5421
E-mail: admissions@militaryschool.com
Web site: http://www.militaryschool.com

THE MASTERS SCHOOL

Dobbs Ferry, New York

Type: Coeducational boarding (grades 9–12) and day (grades 5–12) college-preparatory school
Grades: 5–12: Middle School, 5–8; Upper School, 9–12
Enrollment: School total: 540; Upper School: 402
Head of School: Dr. Maureen Fonseca

THE SCHOOL

The Masters School, founded in 1877 as a school for girls by Eliza Bailey Masters and her sister, Sallie, became coeducational in 1996. The Masters School offers an all-girls Middle School as well as a parallel all-boys Middle School. The Upper School (grades 9–12) provides a coeducational framework utilizing the Harkness Table method of teaching, which features an oval table in each classroom around which students and teacher actively engage in learning. The Harkness Table approach encourages significant student participation, cooperation, and collaboration.

Dobbs Ferry, a town of some importance during the Revolutionary War, lies on the east bank of the Hudson River in culture-rich Westchester County, 20 miles north of New York City, 100 miles southwest of Hartford, and 200 miles southwest of Boston. The proximity of these and other major cities of the Northeast enables the School to use them as valuable resources in the implementation of its curriculum and activities.

The Masters School is committed to an educational experience that not only prepares students for college but also instills the joy of learning as an end in itself.

The 22 members of the Board of Trustees include graduates, parents of present and former students, and friends of the School. The School's endowment is approximately $20 million. Annual Giving totaled more than $1.3 million for 2004; 23 percent of the 4,650 living alumnae participated. Last year's operating expenses were $12.8 million.

The Masters School is accredited by the Middle States Association of Colleges and Schools and is a member of the National Association of Independent Schools, the New York State Association of Independent Schools, and the Federation of American and International Schools.

ACADEMIC PROGRAMS

A Middle School for girls (grades 5–8) and a parallel Middle School for boys (grades 5–8) both offer a curriculum that includes English, math, science, history, Latin, art, and music. All students participate in physical education, music, and art programs for the entire year. Everett "Doc" Wilson is Head of the Middle Schools.

All students at The Masters School follow an academic year that is divided into three 10-week trimesters. Students in grades 9–12 choose some courses that span the year and others that last for one or two trimesters. The Masters School's basic requirements ensure that every student will master the fundamental skills and concepts in all the major disciplines. Accordingly, courses are required in the following disciplines: English, 4 years; mathematics, 3 years; foreign language, 3 years; science, 2 years; and history, 3 years.

Additional requirements include a 1-year minor course in world religions, 3 trimesters of fine arts, 1 trimester of speech, 2 of health, and 4 years of physical education.

The Masters School offers 121 courses, including Advanced Placement in all departments. In addition to the regular course offerings, independent studies are often arranged with individual faculty members by students who wish to pursue a special topic in depth or from an interdisciplinary perspective not offered as part of the standard curriculum. Additional courses may be developed to reflect the current interests of faculty and students.

The visual and performing arts are a featured component of the total curriculum. Arts courses as well as performances and exhibitions abound.

Many subjects are offered on two or three levels, differing in pace, content, and depth of coverage. The average class size is 12 with a student-faculty ratio of 7:1.

CITYterm, a highly selective, interdisciplinary urban studies program, was initiated in 1996. CITYterm is an innovative semester-long program that draws upon the resources of New York City in its academic and experiential curriculum. CITYterm is based on The Masters School campus and accepts applications from its own students and juniors and seniors from the program's national consortium of public and private schools.

The Masters School uses a numerical grading system with 60 as passing and 83 qualifying for honors. The School operates on the trimester system. Parents receive grades and comments from teachers and dorm directors at the end of each term and an initial report within the first months of the fall term. Teachers are available for conferences at specified times during the academic day and also by appointment.

FACULTY AND ADVISERS

The Masters School faculty, approximately 57 percent of whose members reside on campus, includes 80 full-time and 10 part-time teachers; they hold four doctoral degrees and fifty-two master's degrees.

Dr. Maureen Fonseca was appointed Head of School in 2000. Dr. Fonseca holds a B.A. from Vassar and a Ph.D. in French literature from Fordham. Prior to her appointment, Dr. Fonseca was the Founding Head of St. Philips Academy in Newark, New Jersey.

Many faculty members take advantage of opportunities given to them for professional advancement through the sabbatical program and the financing of continuing educational programs. All faculty members are involved in advising students, and several also serve as dormitory directors in addition to their class-

room duties. Each student has a faculty adviser. The staff includes professional health and guidance personnel.

COLLEGE PLACEMENT

In the junior year, each student has individual and group conferences with college counseling personnel. This program is augmented by on-campus interviews with college representatives as well as college-visiting weekends during the senior year. Juniors take the PSAT in the fall. The SAT I verbal and mathematics scores ranged last year from the mid-500s to just under 800. Ninety students took 150 Advanced Placement exams and 83 percent scored 3 or better.

In 2005, 78 students graduated and are now attending such colleges and universities as Brown, Cornell, NYU, Oberlin, Wesleyan, Yale, and the Universities of Chicago and Michigan.

STUDENT BODY AND CONDUCT

In 2005–06, 40 percent of the Upper School students at The Masters School are boarders, and 60 percent are day students. There are 138 students enrolled in the Middle School in grades 5–8. While the majority of the students reside in the northeastern United States, fifteen states and fifteen countries are represented.

The Masters School is committed to a curriculum that allows students to develop their individual talents and abilities. Four principles are basic to life at the School: integrity, consideration, cooperation, and responsibility. Disciplinary problems are handled by the Dorm Council or, in serious matters, by the Disciplinary Committee, which is composed of an equal number of adults and students. The Community Government is operated by the students and functions according to the School's constitution.

ACADEMIC FACILITIES

Masters Hall, the main academic and administration building, houses all disciplines with the exception of science, physical education, and music. Departments have their own commons, which contain faculty offices as well as reference materials and study areas. The Pittsburgh Library, containing 25,000 volumes, is located on the main floor. A Computer Research Center within the library provides state-of-the-art computer research stations. This networked system incorporates access to library materials and CD-ROM resources. Access to e-mail, the Internet, and community information is also provided on each computer research station. The Claudia Boettcher Theater has a seating capacity of 450 and adjoins the spacious visual arts studio. Strayer Hall houses the physical education and music departments. A new science and technology facility opened in September 2004.

BOARDING AND GENERAL FACILITIES

There are six dorms on campus, some accommodating students in adjoining single rooms and others in double rooms. All dorms contain student lounges, kitchens, faculty apartments, and dorm directors' apartments used for informal gatherings throughout the year. Over the vacation periods, students from other countries often visit the homes of their American classmates or take School-sponsored trips in the United States and abroad.

A student recreation center and private meeting rooms are located in the Cameron Mann Dining Hall. The Health Center has a full-time nurse, a nonresident physician, and immediate access to medical facilities in Westchester and New York City.

ATHLETICS

The Masters School considers physical education to be an integral part of each student's experience at the School, not only for physical well-being but also for the development of the social and moral values of fair play and sportsmanship. For girls, there are teams in field hockey, lacrosse, softball, soccer, tennis, basketball, volleyball, and fencing. Sports for boys include soccer, cross-country, basketball, fencing, tennis, and baseball.

The School has field hockey, lacrosse, and soccer fields and has added additional fields to accommodate boys' baseball and soccer. Other athletic facilities include nine tennis courts, a large three-bay gymnasium, a fencing room, and an expansive weight-training and conditioning room.

The School has a dance studio and an excellent dance program. Students may elect dance classes for physical education credit or they may audition for various levels of technique-oriented classes. Experienced dancers may audition for Dance Company, which performs throughout the year.

EXTRACURRICULAR OPPORTUNITIES

The Masters School offers a full program of extracurricular activities, with more than thirty organizations from which a student can choose. These include clubs in the performing arts, languages, and mathematics, the literary publications, and athletics. Many of these groups take advantage of the proximity of New York City by attending concerts, dance performances, plays, and various other events.

Special programs bring outstanding lecturers, artists, and performers from many fields to the School. Community service groups include Gold Key and Masters Interested in Sharing and Helping (MISH). A well-organized Community Service Program ensures every student of the opportunity to help others through volunteer work at hospitals, children's homes, schools, and other community organizations.

Different groups within the School traditionally organize special annual events. The Senior Halloween Party, the Sophomore Fair, the International Club's Model UN, and the Glee Club's Candlelight Service are among the high points of the year.

DAILY LIFE

Most school days begin with a student-led all-school gathering at 8 a.m., followed by class periods ranging from 55 to 110 minutes in length. The cocurricular program begins at 3:30. Students can choose from a variety of activities, including athletics, theater, community service, and arts offerings. Evening study hours for boarding students run from 8 to 10 p.m.

The Student Activities Center is open throughout the day for Ping-Pong, pool, Foosball, air hockey, and big-screen TV. The dining hall has extended hours for breakfast, lunch, and dinner and offers a variety of delicious options at each meal.

WEEKEND LIFE

There are many opportunities for on- and off-campus activities during the weekends, with frequent trips to New York City; hiking, canoeing, skiing, and camping outings; and attendance at college or professional games. The Social Activities Committee plans dances, trips, and informal events with several other schools. In addition, there are numerous concerts, plays, and recitals at the School and in the surrounding community. All activities are open to nonresidents, and they can arrange to spend the night in the dorms after a late-night function. There are numerous open weekends during the year, and any student in good social and academic standing may leave campus during those times after having obtained parental permission.

COSTS AND FINANCIAL AID

Charges for 2005–06 were $33,950 for residents (grades 9–12) and $24,650 (which includes lunch) for nonresidents in the Upper School; Middle School nonresidents paid $23,950. Books and supplies are estimated at $650. Art is required of all students, with studio and lab fees ranging from $50 to $325 per year. An initial deposit of $1000 is required with the Enrollment Agreement, and tuition installments are due July 31 and November 30.

Twenty-six percent of the student body currently receives financial aid based on need. Grants range from $2200 to $31,700. The total financial aid budget is $2.5 million in 2005–06. The Masters School also offers a payment plan to help families spread tuition costs over a period of time.

ADMISSIONS INFORMATION

The Masters School seeks students who not only show academic promise but also possess those characteristics that indicate they will be vital and contributing members of the School community. Students are selected without regard to race, creed, or national origin. An application form (including a short essay), the application fee, an official school transcript covering at least the last two years, two teacher recommendations, and results from the SSAT or ISEE are required of all applicants for grades 5–12. Applicants whose first language is not English must take the TOEFL as well as the SSAT (if available in their country).

APPLICATION TIMETABLE

It is suggested that a formal application with the $50 fee ($100 for international students) be sent as early as possible. Tour and interview dates should be scheduled during school hours while the School is in session. All applicants should plan to visit the campus. Students wishing to be considered in the first round of decisions should submit all admission materials by January 5 for all day applicants and February 5 for all boarding applicants. All other applications are reviewed on a space-available basis. Applications are accepted as long as places are available. Admission Office hours are from 8 a.m. to 4 p.m. during the week.

ADMISSIONS CORRESPONDENCE

Office of Admission
The Masters School
49 Clinton Avenue
Dobbs Ferry, New York 10522

Phone: 914-479-6420
Fax: 914-693-7295
E-mail: admission@themasersschool.com
Web site: http://www.themasersschool.com

THE MCCALLIE SCHOOL

Chattanooga, Tennessee

Type: Boys' boarding (9–12) and day (6–12) college-preparatory school
Grades: 6–12: Middle School, 6–8; Upper School, 9–12
Enrollment: School total: 890; Upper School: 630; Middle School: 260
Head of School: Dr. R. Kirk Walker, Headmaster

THE SCHOOL

McCallie School, located on the western slope of Missionary Ridge in Chattanooga, Tennessee, was founded in 1905 and today is recognized as one of the South's preeminent college-preparatory schools. It accepts young men with above average to exceptional academic abilities, and those students matriculate at some of the best colleges and universities in the nation. In recent years, McCallie has been recognized for its innovative educational programs and its overall standards of excellence. Recently, the Atlanta Journal/Constitution called McCallie "one of the leading secondary educational institutions in the United States." McCallie's alumni are leaders in business, politics, art, science, and religion throughout the South and the entire country.

The mission of the School has not changed since its founding in 1905. McCallie's purpose is to prepare students for entrance into and successful academic work at college. McCallie stresses high academic standards and believes that challenging work best develops useful intellectual ability. Although not affiliated with any religious organization, McCallie supports the spiritual growth of its students and believes that response to the Christian gospel builds a strong moral foundation and a sense of civic and social duty. The School teaches and values personal integrity, intellectual honesty, and a strong work ethic. McCallie promotes the development of leadership skills and the ability to be both a self-confident individual and a dynamic member of a community. The School values and promotes an energetic response to the contemporary world and a respect for tradition.

McCallie's campus comprises 100 acres on Missionary Ridge, the site of a major battle during the Civil War. It is located 3 miles east of downtown Chattanooga. A major expansion program over the past few years has extended the campus southward and doubled the number of athletic fields available to students.

McCallie's endowment is $50 million, with an annual operating budget of about $23 million. The Annual Sustaining Fund drive raises about $2.5 million a year.

McCallie is an all-boys school and believes that the educational, physical, and social needs of secondary school students can best be met in a single-sex educational environment. To complement its single-sex commitment, McCallie has a coordinate program with Girls' Preparatory School (GPS) in Chattanooga. McCallie and GPS students participate in a wide variety of afternoon and weekend social activities.

McCallie is accredited by the Southern Association of Colleges and Schools and is a member of the National Association of Independent Schools, the Southern Association of Independent Schools, the Tennessee Association of Independent Schools, the International Coalition of Boys Schools, the Independent Schools Innovation Consortium, the Secondary School Admission Test Board, the Education Records Bureau, and the Council for the Advancement and Support of Education.

ACADEMIC PROGRAMS

McCallie's academic program centers on a strong core curriculum of math, sciences, English, foreign languages, and history. This curriculum is further strengthened by eighteen Advanced Placement courses and numerous honors courses.

Students are required to earn 19 course credits distributed as follows: English, 4 credits; mathematics, 3 credits; science, 3 credits; foreign language, 3 credits in the same language; history, 3 credits; Bible, 1 credit; fine arts, 1 credit; public speaking, ¼ credit; human development, ¼ credit; and electives, 1½ to 2 credits. Electives are offered in all core disciplines and in music, computer science, economics, writing, and world religions.

Advanced Placement courses are stressed at McCallie and nearly half the members of every graduating class receive college placement or credit for AP courses taken at McCallie.

Classes, grouped by age and ability, average 14 students. The academic year consists of two 18-week semesters. Each day consists of a seven-period rotating schedule, with each class meeting four times a week. At the teacher's discretion, students can be required to attend special "backwork" sessions during the school day.

Foreign languages offered by McCallie include Spanish, French, Latin, ancient Greek, and Japanese. German is available through independent study.

The School offers an elaborate academic support system to students. Among its many resources are the Caldwell Writing Center, several computer centers, and the Learning Center, where academic counselors and tutors are available throughout the day to assist students. The Upper and Middle School libraries, which are fully computerized, have subscriptions to 30 online databases and house more than 32,000 volumes.

In recent years, McCallie has expanded its academic offerings to include travel/study abroad programs. The School sponsors exchange programs with schools in places such as Japan, Latin America, and France.

FACULTY AND ADVISERS

McCallie has 108 full-time faculty members, 12 part-time faculty members, 4 full-time academic counselors, and numerous adjunct faculty members and tutors. More than half of the faculty members have advanced degrees in their disciplines. Nearly half of the faculty and staff members live on campus, either in dormitories or nearby houses.

When a student enrolls in McCallie, he is assigned an Academic Dean who follows his academic and extracurricular achievement throughout the year and provides feedback to the parents. The Academic Dean, the Dean of Students, the Dean of Residential Life, the guidance counselors, and other administrators also act as advisers. In the dormitories, selected seniors act as Resident Advisers to underclassmen.

McCallie has four endowed chairs on its faculty: the Sen. Howard Baker Jr. Chair of American History, the Sherrill Chair of Bible, the Caldwell Chair of Composition, and the Alumni Chair of Mathematics.

COLLEGE PLACEMENT

A principal part of McCallie's mission is to help students identify, gain admission to, and successfully graduate from the college or university that is best for them. A full-time college guidance staff, made up of 2 counselors and an administrative assistant, works with juniors and seniors in a comprehensive guidance program. They hold several individual sessions with each student, at least one session with the student and his parents, and numerous seminars and group sessions.

Students are encouraged to use the college admissions process to explore their specific goals and tastes. The School makes a distinction between gaining admission to the best colleges and gaining admission to the college that is best for the individual student. Therefore, many students matriculate at colleges outside the South that may not be as well known as larger state universities. More than 125 colleges and universities send representatives to McCallie and GPS each year to talk personally to students.

STUDENT BODY AND CONDUCT

Boarding students in the 2005–06 student body came from twenty-two different states and six international countries. The largest student groups are from Georgia, North Carolina, Tennessee, Mississippi, Kentucky, Alabama, and Texas. Minority enrollment is about 10 percent.

A central part of the School's culture is the Honor Code. All students are held to this code, which proclaims that lying, cheating, and stealing are unacceptable for a McCallie student. The code also stipulates that McCallie students are trusted by their teachers and administrators to tell the truth in all circumstances. The code is structured to encourage a life of honor and integrity and to establish a McCallie student as one whose word is his bond, whose work is always his own, and around whom the property of others is safe. Every student is required to sign his name to the Honor Pledge on all written schoolwork: "On my honor I have neither given nor received aid on this test (or work, examination, etc.)."

The Student Senate, a group elected by the students, administers the Honor Code.

ACADEMIC FACILITIES

McCallie's campus is considered one of the best preparatory campuses in the South, with a dozen major buildings and several smaller structures. The main academic building is the Robert L. Maclellan Academic Center, which rises five stories on the ridge. This building houses the library, the Burns Learning Center, the Brock Humanities Center, the McIlwaine Mathematics Center, the Chapin Science Center, and the Caldwell Writing Center. Other buildings related to the academic program include the Hunter Arts Center; the McCallie Chapel, where the music department is located; Tate Hall; and Caldwell Hall, the administration building. In 1999, McCallie opened McDonald Hall, which houses boys in grades 6–8. In the winter of the 2003–04 school year, the School opened a $7-million dining hall.

All academic buildings and all dormitories have fiber-optic connections with Internet access. Numerous computer centers are located throughout the academic facilities, with students having access to more than 125 PCs. In addition, McCallie has Ethernet ports and a wireless network in strategic locations.

BOARDING AND GENERAL FACILITIES

Boarding students live in five different dormitories that are located adjacent to the academic quadrangle. Freshmen live in Belk Hall; sophomores, juniors, and seniors live in either North or South Hutcheson Halls, Maclellan Hall, or Founders Home. McCallie is breaking ground for a new dorm in fall 2005.

Most of the dorm rooms are doubles, and soft-drink machines, washing machines, and television lounges are available in all dorms.

ATHLETICS

In addition to its academic program, McCallie is committed to the physical development of its students. The School participates in fourteen varsity sports (football, baseball, basketball, cross-country, track, tennis, swimming, lacrosse, rowing, wrestling, soccer, golf, bowling, and rock-climbing).

In recent years, the School has expanded its athletic program to make more opportunities available to students who do not wish to compete on the varsity level. An elaborate intramural program offers such opportunities as judo, karate, fencing, and juggling, as well as nonvarsity competition in traditional sports.

Over the last few years, McCallie has expanded beyond traditional "Southern" athletics. It was the first school in the state, and among the first in the South, to offer interscholastic competition in sports such as crew (rowing) and lacrosse.

In 1993, McCallie opened the 180,000-square-foot Sports and Activities Center, which has been recognized as one of the finest high school athletic facilities in the nation. The $13-million facility contains five performance courts, a 25-yard-by-25-meter indoor pool, a wrestling room, a weight room, an aerobics room, an indoor track, racquetball courts, and a climbing gym. The center is open late at night and on weekends to accommodate boarding students. It also contains a large Student Center, complete with a snack bar, pool and Ping-Pong tables, televisions, a movie room, and a video arcade.

Other athletic facilities include the 4,000-seat Spears stadium with a six-lane track, the outdoor swimming area (known as McCallie Lake), six intramural fields, a tennis center with two indoor and twelve outdoor courts, a baseball field, and a soccer field.

EXTRACURRICULAR OPPORTUNITIES

Students participate in the many musical and drama presentations held throughout the year. These include five plays a year, one musical play, and two musical performances. Many of these are performed in McCallie's new black-box theater. Formal music groups include the Men's Glee Club, Handbells, the Pep Band, the Jazz Ensemble, the McCallie and GPS Select Chorus, the Honors Orchestra, and the Wind Ensemble. McCallie's instrumental department practices in a newly renovated facility with professionally calibrated acoustics. The Hunter Gallery includes the artwork of McCallie students in its periodically updated displays.

An organized effort by the faculty introduces students to cultural activities in the surrounding community. Students also contribute to charitable organizations in the Chattanooga area, where they lend a hand and learn the importance of service. The senior class annually builds a Habitat for Humanity house in an inner-city neighborhood.

Throughout the year, students participate in a variety of special events, many of which are co-ordinated with Girls Preparatory School. These include the Wintersend and Springfest concerts. The unannounced "Duck Day" in the spring is one of the most awaited occurrences and marks the beginning of a weeklong rag-tag softball tournament in which virtually every student and faculty member participates.

During school breaks and in the summers, students are offered a variety of travel opportunities. Annual trips include skiing in the Rockies, diving in the Caribbean, backpacking in the Appalachians, and travel/study trips to such places as France, Japan, Italy, and Costa Rica.

DAILY LIFE

McCallie believes that a boy matures best when he is challenged and busy. It is an achievement-oriented, work-ethic school. Therefore, from the time they wake until lights out, students stay busy. For boarding students, the day begins at 7 a.m. with a full breakfast that is served in the cafeteria. Classes begin at 8, and each of the seven periods of the day last 50 minutes. If a student has a free period, he can study in the library, the Learning Center, or the Writing Center; or he can relax in the Student Center.

All students attend assembly once a week and chapel three days a week, at midmorning. Chapel services consist of nondenominational talks by students, faculty members, or guest speakers. Lunch is served from 11 a.m. to 1:30 p.m. and includes a variety of choices, including several entrées, a deli bar, a salad bar, a pasta bar, and a hamburger and pizza area. Academic classes end at 3, and students then attend athletics, drama, or music practice or work on student publications. These activities conclude at 5:15, at which time day students leave campus. Dinner is served from 5:30 to 6:30, and the period from 7 to 9:30 is set aside for study. McCallie also serves a "fourth meal," which runs from 9:30 to 10:30 on weeknights. Lights out is at 10:30 for freshmen and is later by 30-minute intervals for each grade.

WEEKEND LIFE

With a full-time Activities Director, McCallie offers boarders one of the most elaborate activities programs in the nation. Throughout the school year, students take advantage of more than 125 opportunities, ranging from trips to major sporting events and concerts to off-the-wall activities, such as paintball or cosmic bowling. At least one group goes to events and attractions in Atlanta, Nashville, Knoxville, Charlotte, or other major southeastern cities virtually every weekend. Likewise, the Outdoor Program takes advantage of the mountains that and rivers near Chattanooga. Groups go backpacking, skiing, fly-fishing, sailing, hunting, rock-climbing, canoeing, and kayaking.

On-campus activities include frequent concerts by some of the most up-and-coming bands in the country. In addition, weekend interdorm competitions are frequent, including football, softball, basketball, sand volleyball, and battleball tournaments.

Boarding students are required to attend Sunday worship services of their choice. Student-led services are often held on campus, and McCallie Buses transport students to off-campus churches, temples, mosques, and other places of worship.

SUMMER PROGRAMS

McCallie operates a two-week residential academic camp for boys rising into grades 8–10. Camp includes athletic and recreational activities and is designed to introduce students to McCallie's academic offerings. McCallie also offers an action-oriented sports camp for boys ages 9 through 15. This boarding program emphasizes fun and team participation regardless of athletic ability. The toll-free telephone number for summer activity information is 800-MSC-CAMP.

COSTS AND FINANCIAL AID

Boarding charges for 2005–06, including tuition, room, board, and activities, were $31,500. Day tuition was $16,410.

McCallie offers approximately $1.8 million in need-based financial aid annually. A full-time Director of Financial Aid assists families in applying for financial aid.

In 1998–99, McCallie introduced the McCallie Honors Scholarship. This $12-million-endowed program offers approximately twenty merit-based scholarships each year to boys who display leadership both inside and outside the classroom.

ADMISSIONS INFORMATION

McCallie's entrance requirements are good character, satisfactory school records, and evidence of the ability and willingness to work at competitive standards. McCallie welcomes applicants of every race, religion, and national origin. The Secondary School Admissions Test is required.

Admissions decisions are handled on a rolling basis, and there is a $50 application fee.

APPLICATION TIMETABLE

Inquiries are welcome at any time and campus tours and interviews are available by appointment year-round. The Admission Office sponsors Visitors Days in the fall and winter that enable parents and prospective students to see the School in session.

ADMISSIONS CORRESPONDENCE

Troy Kemp
Dean of Admission and Financial Aid
The McCallie School
500 Dodds Avenue
Chattanooga, Tennessee 37404

Phone: 423-624-8300
       800-234-2163 (toll-free)
Fax: 423-493-5426
E-mail: admission@mccallie.org
Web site: http://www.mccallie.org

THE MEETING SCHOOL

Rindge, New Hampshire

Type: Coeducational boarding and day college-preparatory school
Grades: 9–12, postgraduate year
Enrollment: 38
Head of School: Jacqueline Stillwell

THE SCHOOL

The Meeting School (TMS) was founded by New England Quakers in 1957. It is located in rural Rindge, New Hampshire, on 140 acres of field, pasture, and forest. The campus is 65 miles from Boston and about 45 miles from Amherst, Massachusetts, and Brattleboro, Vermont. The nearest city is Keene, New Hampshire, 20 miles from the School.

TMS offers a strong program of academic and experiential learning. Most students go on to college. A good number of students take a year or two between high school and college to work and/or travel. The School accepts 33 boarding students and 12 day students; 5 to 7 boarding students live in each of the five faculty homes. Most meals are eaten in the community dining room. All community members take part in growing food, providing care for the farm animals, meal preparation, and housekeeping.

The Meeting School day begins with a time of singing and reflection. Community life is based on traditional Quaker values of respect for the integrity of individuals, peaceful response to conflict, stewardship of the land, dignity of physical work, importance of community process, and persistent practice of intellectual and spiritual openness. What graduates of the Meeting School report as most remembered is the experience of personal transformation within a safe and loving community in which effective problem-solving skills are learned and where all are engaged in striving to live with integrity.

Faculty members and students participate in a weekly Community Meeting at which important community decisions are made. Patient discussion and careful listening are emphasized, and a sense of the meeting (similar to consensus) is required for the Community Meeting to reach a decision.

Meeting School students are not required to believe in God, although they must be respectful of those who do. No formal religious instruction is required. An all-School silent Meeting for Worship is held each week.

Students with initiative and the capacity for self-discipline are likely to be successful at TMS even if they have experienced difficulty in traditional educational settings. Students who are gifted academically will find a knowledgeable faculty to challenge them further. Students who have fewer academic skills will find the dedication of the faculty and the small class sizes helpful. The School is not remedial or tutorial.

The Meeting School is approved by the New Hampshire State Department of Education and is accredited by the New England Association of Schools and Colleges and the National Association for the Legal Support of Alternative Schools. It is a member of the Friends Council on Education, the Independent Schools Association of Northern New England, and the National Coalition of Alternative Community Schools.

ACADEMIC PROGRAMS

The educational program at the Meeting School is based on close cooperation between faculty members and students. Faculty members encourage students to take increasing initiative and responsibility for acquiring the knowledge and skills necessary to meet challenging academic standards. The faculty-student ratio at the Meeting School is 1:3. Class size ranges from 3 to 12 students.

The Meeting School academic program uses experiential methodology throughout its curriculum whenever possible. The farm and environment are highly integrated with academic studies. Chemistry classes may test soil. Math classes can be involved in counting the harvest; social science classes often examine the impact of policy on food production. Real-life situations in world, national, and local events are often used in the classroom.

The school year, which runs from early September through late May, is divided into trimesters. Intensive courses are offered within each trimester. Typically, a class meets for 1½ hours four mornings per week. Students generally take two intensive courses each term. Most courses are ½ credit. In addition, students are involved in daily writing and math classes.

To graduate, a student must receive credit for a full range of requirements in English, social studies, arts, health, science, and math. Every student is required to research, write, and revise at least one extensive term paper each year. Students must also successfully complete and receive credit for community work, home economics, exercise, and intersession each year that they attend the School. Foreign languages are offered but are not required for graduation.

Academic subject areas that are offered regularly include history, biology, literature, persuasive and creative writing, geography, peace studies, algebra, geometry, consumer math, physics, human sexuality, and health (most often presented in creative ways). Teachers and students create other classes according to their interests. Subject areas that have been added to regular class offerings in recent years include ancient civilizations, ethics, theater, mythology, photography, art, weaving, Native American spirituality, music, anthropology, psychology, and pottery. Students who have demonstrated a clear ability to take initiative and manage their academic time may take independent study courses if they have interests not represented in the course offerings.

During the winter intersession, each student undertakes a four-week independent study project designed by the student and approved by faculty members and parents. As part of the planning process, students research areas of interest, contact sponsoring organizations or individual mentors, and arrange placements that will allow them to work full-time on vocational, service, or educational projects. In recent years, student projects have included travel to Costa Rica, Cuba, and Thailand; midwifery; recording studio training; solar energy internship; forestry; home building; working with AIDS orphans; and an internship at the Smithsonian.

FACULTY AND ADVISERS

There are 15 full-time faculty members at the Meeting School. Six hold master's degrees. Faculty members have graduated from Antioch New England, Boston College, Bryn Mawr, Carleton (Ottawa), College of the Holy Cross, Columbia, Earlham School of Religion, Franklin Pierce College, Friends World College, Germain Photo School of Photography, Harvard, Houghton, Marlboro, Monadnock School of Natural Cooking, New England College, Princeton, Radford, St. Michael's (Toronto), Wilmington College, and the Universities of East Carolina and Maine.

COLLEGE PLACEMENT

Students work with their advisers to make and carry out plans for future work or study. Faculty members assist students with preparation for the SAT tests and going through the college application process. Roughly 80 percent of TMS graduates are college bound. Graduates from the last five years have attended Antioch, Ausberg, California College of Arts and Crafts, California Culinary Academy, Clark, College of the Redwoods, CUNY, Earlham, Eugene Lang, Friends World College, Goddard, Guilford, Hampshire, Johnson State, Marlboro, NYU, Quinghua (Beijing), Smith, Sterling, Syracuse, Warren Wilson, and the Universities of California, Maine, Oregon, and Vermont

STUDENT BODY AND CONDUCT

Meeting School students have a wide variety of backgrounds and personal histories. Most are from New England or the Middle Atlantic States. Over the past ten years, about 25 percent have had some Quaker background, 10 percent have been international students, and 10 percent have been of Native American, Hispanic, or African-American descent. About 25 percent have had some degree of home schooling, 30 percent have spent some years in other alternative schools, and many have a parent who has worked professionally in education.

TMS attracts young people who share the community's commitments to honesty, integrity, equality, simplicity, nonviolence, and care for the earth. Many Meeting School students have done well academically and are looking for a school in which a deeper community life can be experienced. Many students are bright and persuasive, possess leadership potential, and prize personal independence and yet have been bored or otherwise unsatisfied with their previous educational experiences. Prospective students are often passionate about music, art, environmental concerns, and animals, though they may have worked hard only on courses they considered relevant. TMS is well suited for these students because it offers personal attention in small classes that combine experiential education with traditional academics.

At the Meeting School, there are carefully upheld community agreements not to use drugs, tobacco, or alcohol and not to engage in sex while under the care of the School. Students work with each other and with faculty members to improve interpersonal communications and to resolve difficulties as they arise. A variety of issues, including personal, academic, and disciplinary problems, are addressed through Clearness Meetings. In these meetings, 2 community members are asked to lis-

ten to and offer support and advice to those involved in the particular concern. The faculty members make final decisions regarding disciplinary matters.

A Community Meeting is held each week. During this meeting, faculty members and students make decisions about many aspects of community life. Students serve on various School committees actively involved in the daily running of the School, such as Ministry and Counsel, the Curriculum Committee, and the Farm Committee. Student representatives also participate in meetings of the School's Board of Trustees.

ACADEMIC FACILITIES
Many classes meet in the informal atmosphere of household living rooms and dining rooms. Other classrooms include a greenhouse, a pottery/art studio, a weaving room, a darkroom, a wood shop, and a gathering room. Each residential house holds a part of the School book collections. Regular use is made of nearby Franklin Pierce College library. Every house has a computer with e-mail access available for student use. The farm buildings and the land are an important part of the School's educational program. Rare-breed cattle, sheep, chickens, turkeys, and pigs make up the livestock.

BOARDING AND GENERAL FACILITIES
There are five faculty-student houses and three faculty houses. The renovated eighteenth- and nineteenth-century buildings are warm, large, and homelike. Other buildings include a working barn, an art studio, a music building, a recreation building, three yurts (round wooden houses), and a cabin in the woods.

ATHLETICS
While physical activities are an important part of Meeting School life, competitive sports are not emphasized. Common physical activities include hiking, Ultimate Frisbee, downhill and cross-country skiing, skating, volleyball, soccer, basketball, biking, yoga, swimming, weight lifting, aerobics, and contra dancing.

EXTRACURRICULAR OPPORTUNITIES
Students attending the Meeting School are surrounded by the vibrant culture of New England and are encouraged to take an active part in the ongoing life of the larger community.

Each year there are several all-School field trips to Boston museums, state parks, Mount Monad-

nock, and the ocean. Smaller groups of students and faculty members organize numerous other events and trips.

Parents' Weekend, just before the Thanksgiving break, is a time when parents come to share in the life of the School. At graduation, all parents and students, the trustees, the alumni, and friends of the School join to celebrate the completion of the school year.

DAILY LIFE
The normal school day begins with breakfast at 7 a.m. Opening, held at 7:45, includes singing and music, brief worship time, and announcements. Classes are held in 1½-hour blocks. During the afternoon, math, writing, work-study assignments, special-interest activities, and physical exercise take place. In the evenings, there are trips to college libraries, meetings with interest groups (e.g., art, music, drama, and chess groups), study halls, and free time. Students can expect 1 to 2 hours of reading, writing, and research assignments daily.

Daily life at TMS presents all members of the community with the challenge of honestly living up to the values they affirm and the agreements they make. Often, new insights will change the way students look at themselves, at others, and at what they think they know. The process of transformation that this involves can be uncomfortable and difficult, yet ultimately awesome.

A supportive family atmosphere within a small community, consistent practice of life skills, rigorous academic experiences, and daily attention to the development of problem-solving and communication skills result in students gaining significant competencies, confidence, close friendships with faculty members and other students, and an increased sense of purpose and self-worth.

WEEKEND LIFE
The Meeting School has a 5½-day academic week. Weekly Forum, held on Saturday morning, is an integral part of the academic program. Often Forum includes a guest presentation from someone who has a particular area of expertise or special life experience to share. Occasionally, Forum engages the students directly in farm or community service projects. It may also involve a field trip to a museum or other place of educational interest.

With parental permission, students may leave campus between Saturday at noon and Sunday evening. Students remaining on campus may take town trips to shop, see a movie or concert, bowl, contra dance, or participate in other community

events. Weekend activities on campus include homespun coffeehouse entertainment, dancing, or special celebrations.

Sunday is the only unstructured day in the school week. Some students and faculty members choose to attend the Monadnock Friends Meeting or other nearby churches; others use the opportunity to sleep in.

COSTS AND FINANCIAL AID
The cost of tuition, room, and board at the Meeting School was $32,800 for the 2005–06 school year. Day tuition was $18,500. Middle-income families often qualify for significant tuition assistance.

A mandatory student activity fund of $400 per year covers the costs of school activities, lab fees, and incidental expenses.

Need-based financial aid, approximately 35 percent of the School's annual income from tuition, is awarded each year. The School is committed to maintaining a student body that is economically and culturally diverse.

ADMISSIONS INFORMATION
Interested students are encouraged to visit the Meeting School to get a sense of its academic and community life. Applicants respond in writing to a set of questions that help explore the students' past social and academic experiences and their possible response to life at TMS. The prospective student is interviewed by a committee that includes faculty members and seniors.

Admissions decisions are based on references and the interviewing committee's sense of the applicant. Transcripts from other schools are required but are not determinative in the admissions process. Transferring students receive credit for grades of C and better from other educational institutions.

APPLICATION TIMETABLE
Applications for the fall trimester should be made in the spring or earlier. Financial aid awards are generally completed by August 15. Students may be admitted throughout the academic year if openings exist.

ADMISSIONS CORRESPONDENCE
Admissions Coordinator
The Meeting School
120 Thomas Road
Rindge, New Hampshire 03461
Phone: 603-899-3366
Fax: 603-899-6216
E-mail: office@meetingschool.org
Web site: http://www.meetingschool.org

MERCERSBURG ACADEMY

Mercersburg, Pennsylvania

Type: Coeducational boarding and day college-preparatory school
Grades: 9–12, postgraduate year
Enrollment: 442
Head of School: Douglas Hale, Headmaster

THE SCHOOL

With roots dating to 1836, and chartered in 1865, Mercersburg Academy was transformed into a college-preparatory school on the "Exeter Model" in 1893 by William Mann Irvine, Ph.D. A graduate of Phillips Exeter Academy and Princeton University, Dr. Irvine wished to create an institution in which excellence was sought and honored. This vision remains intact at a school that prepares students for the rigors of highly competitive four-year colleges and universities. Mercersburg retains a strong sense of community, ethics, dedication to academic achievement, and commitment to a balanced education that includes extensive opportunities in arts and athletics.

The borough of Mercersburg is located in south central Pennsylvania and offers amenities from pizza and sub eateries to fine dining, and skiing and golf at nearby Whitetail Resort. The school offers an expansive 300-acre campus, which includes running trails, excellent facilities similar to many colleges, and access to the outdoors with the Tuscarora and Appalachian Trails nearby. Mercersburg is convenient to the museums, professional athletics teams, entertainment, and airports of Washington, D.C., and Baltimore, Maryland. Hagerstown, Maryland, offers extensive shopping, with major department stores and bookstores, restaurants, and a regional airport with connections to most cities in the United States and Europe.

The school is a nonprofit corporation governed by a 27-member Board of Regents. The market value of the endowment stood at $160 million in September 2005 and was supplemented by annual giving of $2 million by alumni, parents, and friends of the school. With such remarkable resources, Mercersburg has a history of recruiting outstanding faculty members and a strong commitment to financial aid.

Mercersburg is accredited by the Middle States Association of Colleges and Schools and is approved by the Pennsylvania Department of Education. The school is a member of the National Association of Independent Schools, the Association of Boarding Schools, the Association of Independent Schools of Greater Washington, the Council for Spiritual and Ethical Education, the Pennsylvania Association of Independent Schools, and the Secondary School Admission Test Board.

ACADEMIC PROGRAMS

The school year is divided into three terms of approximately twelve weeks each. To graduate, a four-year student is required to complete the following 57 credits: English, 12 credits; mathematics, through 30-level mathematics; foreign language, through the 30-level at a particular language; science, 9 credits; history, 9 credits; religion, 1 credit; fine arts, 2 credits; and physical education, 4 credits.

Students are required to take 42 credits of work in the tenth grade, 27 credits of work in the eleventh grade, and 14 credits of work in the twelfth grade. In the senior year, students may organize an independent study project. Students of superior promise may prepare for Advanced Placement examinations by taking Advanced Placement courses,

offered in all academic areas, or a suitable program of upper-level electives. Mercersburg is an associate member of School Year Abroad, a program sponsored by Exeter, Andover, and St. Paul's that allows qualified students to spend their eleventh- or twelfth-grade year in China, France, Italy, or Spain.

The student-faculty ratio is approximately 5:1, and the average class size is 12. At enrollment, students take placement tests in mathematics and a foreign language and are placed in individual classes according to the strength of their background in a particular area. The passing grade at Mercersburg is 60; 80 constitutes honors, and 90 high honors. Reports of grades and comments on students' progress are sent to parents six times a year, at six-week intervals. Supervised study hours are maintained in the dormitories Sunday through Thursday evenings. All students (except returning seniors) have required study hours.

FACULTY AND ADVISERS

In 2005–06, there were 89 full-time faculty members, 56 with master's degrees and 3 with doctorates. Seventy percent of the faculty members live in campus housing, serving in the dormitories as advisers and resident masters. Nonresident faculty members live on the periphery of the campus in town and also serve as advisers in the dormitories.

Douglas Hale was appointed Head of School in 1997. He is a graduate of the University of Tennessee (B.A., 1973) and Middlebury College (M.A., 1997). A committed independent school administrator, he served in various faculty and administrative capacities at Baylor School, including Headmaster (1994–97), since 1973.

In selecting new members of the faculty, the Head of School and others involved in the selection process look not only for academic and teaching competence but also for the personal qualities and varied interests that make a boarding school a dynamic place to learn. Faculty members serve as classroom teachers, coaches, and advisers to individual students and in extracurricular student activities. Through weekly faculty meetings and numerous standing committees, the faculty has a strong and direct role in the operation of the school.

Various faculty members attend in-service workshops and conferences each academic year, and professional activity outside the Academy is encouraged. Summer study grants allow faculty members to pursue graduate study and course-related travel.

COLLEGE PLACEMENT

Led by William R. McClintick Jr., past vice president of the National Association for College Admission Counseling (NACAC), the college counseling office has 3 professional staff members. Each student has a college counselor. The formal counseling process begins in the eleventh-grade year, when student and counselor discuss the student's needs, past record, and projected academic program. Students at Mercersburg apply to a wide variety of institutions of higher learning; the overall goal of the counseling process is to seek the best

possible match between a student's abilities and needs and a particular college or university.

The SAT I 50th percentile range was 550–670 (verbal) and 565–670 (math) for the class of 2005. Virtually all members of each class go on to college.

Mercersburg graduates are currently enrolled at Columbia, Cornell, Harvard, Johns Hopkins, Middleburg, MIT, Princeton, Tufts, the U.S. Military Academy, the U.S. Naval Academy, Washington and Lee, Wesleyan, Yale, and the Universities of Michigan, Pennsylvania, and Virginia.

STUDENT BODY AND CONDUCT

The 2005–06 student body was made up of 233 boys and 209 girls in the following classes: ninth grade, 83; tenth grade, 107; eleventh grade, 122; and twelfth grade, 130. Of the total number, only 70 were day students. In 2005–06, students attended the Academy from twenty-nine states and twenty-two countries.

Students have important responsibilities in all aspects of school life, serving in student government, as dormitory prefects, as dining hall proctors, and on student-faculty committees.

Mercersburg expects students to conduct themselves well at all times and in all places. All matters of discipline serious enough to warrant a student's dismissal are referred to the student-faculty Conduct Review Committee by the Dean of Students. The committee recommends a response to the Head of School.

ACADEMIC FACILITIES

The main academic and residential campus occupies 160 acres in a larger property of 300 acres. Lenfest Hall, the Library/Learning Center, also houses the history department and classrooms. The Burgin Center for the Arts, which opened in fall 2006, includes two theaters, music and drama practice rooms, and dance and visual arts studios. The major classroom building, Irvine Hall, houses art and music facilities, classrooms, science facilities, and a writing center. The 1938 Observatory opened in 2002.

BOARDING AND GENERAL FACILITIES

Seven buildings provide outstanding dormitory rooms, each designed to accommodate 2 students. New students are assigned to rooms, giving consideration to requests made on individual rooming questionnaires. There is at least one faculty apartment on each floor in each dormitory. Lunch and dinner are served family style at one sitting in the dining hall, where all students take turns waiting on tables. Faculty members and their families are assigned to individual tables with 6 or 7 students. The Edward E. Ford Hall, which houses the dining room, also houses the student lounge, post office, and two school stores.

ATHLETICS

The athletics program has two major objectives: to allow all students to compete in interscholastic sports and to engender a lasting interest in physical fitness and lifetime sports. The interscholastic program provides competitive opportunities for all age groups

in baseball, basketball, cross-country, field hockey, football, golf, lacrosse, skiing, soccer, softball, squash, swimming and diving, tennis, track and field, volleyball, winter track, and wrestling. Although students are not required to participate in athletics at Mercersburg, 70 percent of the student body chose to compete in interscholastic sports.

The modern gymnasium facilities include a fitness center, a nine-lane swimming pool, three basketball courts, a ten-court Davenport Squash Center, exercise rooms, a wrestling room, and locker rooms. Other facilities include the fourteen-court Smoyer Tennis Center and Franz Pavillion; a 400-meter, all-weather track; a 5-kilometer cross-country course on campus; jumping pits; ten playing fields, including two baseball diamonds and a softball diamond; and an outdoor sand volleyball court.

The Mercersburg Outdoor Education Program (MOE) uses local, national, and international environments to offer experience-based, growth-inspiring opportunities and activities. In the process, MOE reaches across all facets of the school: academic, residential, athletic, and extracurricular. The programs range from teaching introductory skills in areas such as paddling, rock climbing, and wilderness living/travel to advanced outdoor-skills classes, leadership training programs, winter travel and climbing, and extended expeditions.

EXTRACURRICULAR OPPORTUNITIES

The music department offers a varied instrumental and choral extracurricular program. Stony Batter Dramatic Club and the dance program produce several major performances each year. Students also publish a weekly newspaper, a literary review, and a yearbook. In addition, more than thirty extracurricular clubs and organizations, including a new outdoor education program, represent a wide range of student and faculty interests and talents from computer science to photography. Whitetail Ski and Golf Resort is located 6 miles from campus and is used by the Academy's recreational golf and ski clubs. Throughout the year, students are also involved in community service projects.

DAILY LIFE

Classes at Mercersburg are held five days a week. Classes meet from 8 a.m. until 3:40 p.m., except on Wednesday when classes end at 12:50. Students are expected to take five academic courses each term. Classes meet four times a week, Monday through Friday, for 50- or 70-minute periods. The class day on Monday includes an all-school community gathering in the chapel, at which a selected student addresses the entire school on a topic chosen for its relevance and meaning to the community. On Friday, an invited guest speaks on moral, ethical, or spiritual issues during the weekly chapel program. An afternoon athletics period is held from 4 until 6 (with interscholastic competitions on Wednesday and Saturday afternoons). Family-style meals are served for lunch (Monday through Friday) and dinner (Monday, Tuesday, and Thursday). Study hours in dormitories are maintained Sunday through Thursday, from 8 to 10 p.m.

WEEKEND LIFE

Numerous on- and off-campus activities are planned for the weekends by Mercersburg's full-time Student Activities Director and the Student Activities Committee. On-campus events include movies, dances, athletic competitions, student drama, dance and musical performances, and special performances sponsored by Second Story Wheat, the student-run coffee house. The Student Activities Director takes full advantage of the Academy's proximity to Baltimore and Washington, D.C., for concerts, theater performances, museum exhibitions, sporting events, and shopping. Off-campus excursions also include frequent skiing, biking, hiking, and kayaking trips.

Mercersburg also plans and sponsors guest speakers throughout the school year. A lecture series brings leaders in education, government, journalism, politics, and science to campus.

With written permission from their parents, students may spend ten weekends off campus, including a four-day weekend, each term.

COSTS AND FINANCIAL AID

The annual fee for boarding students for the 2005–06 academic year was $34,700, which covered tuition, room, and board. The fee for day students was $26,500. Extra costs included an estimated $800 per year for books and supplies.

In 2005–06, Mercersburg awarded more than $3.7 million in need-based financial aid. Further aid was offered in the form of merit-based scholarships, which are determined by outstanding records of academic achievement and standardized test scores, regardless of need. Awards are also made on a competitive basis to boys and girls of proven capacity and achievement and according to financial need as indicated by School and Student Service for Financial Aid guidelines.

Through the generosity of the Independence Foundation, alumni, parents, and friends of the Academy, funds are available for small low-interest loans to be offered as part of a larger financial aid award to families who qualify for aid.

ADMISSIONS INFORMATION

Scholastic promise, as indicated by an applicant's current academic record, standardized test scores, and recommendations, is of primary importance when an applicant is considered for admission. It is not in itself sufficient, however, to ensure success in the closely knit life of a school like Mercersburg. Character, personality, motivation, extracurricular interests, and the ability to live compatibly with others are important.

While Mercersburg accepts applications for all grade levels (9–PG), the primary entry grade is grade 9. The postgraduate program is meant to give students an extra year of academic preparation before entering college.

Applicants for the ninth and tenth grades must take the SSAT or the Educational Records Bureau's Independent Schools Entrance Examination (ISEE). Eleventh and twelfth graders and postgraduate applicants must provide either PSAT or SAT scores. Thirty-six percent of those who applied in 2005–06 were accepted.

APPLICATION TIMETABLE

Students are encouraged to apply for admission in the fall and winter of the year prior to matriculation; there is a February 1 application deadline. Inquiries are welcomed at any time, and appointments for campus tours and interviews may be made through the Admission Office from 8:30 to 4:30, Monday through Friday. An on-campus interview is required.

Students are notified about acceptance in early March, and parents are requested to reply one month after notification. After March, admission decisions are made and relayed to a family as soon as the application is complete.

ADMISSIONS CORRESPONDENCE

Director of Admission and Financial Aid
Mercersburg Academy
300 East Seminary Street
Mercersburg, Pennsylvania 17236

Phone: 717-328-6173
Fax: 717-328-6319
E-mail: admission@mercersburg.edu
Web site: http://www.mercersburg.edu

MIAMI COUNTRY DAY SCHOOL

Miami, Florida

Type: Coeducational day college-preparatory school
Grades: P–12: Lower School, Junior Kindergarten–5; Middle School, 6–8; Upper School, 9–12
Enrollment: School total: 1,000; Upper School: 400
Head of School: Dr. John Davies, Head of School

THE SCHOOL

"We are so thankful that our children had the opportunity to be educated at this fine school. You have nourished them intellectually, morally, and athletically, and they have reaped the benefits. It's been eighteen years of fond memories."—Miami Country Day School (MCDS) alumni parents

Miami Country Day's success derives from a learning environment that values and respects each individual member of the School community. This is a community characterized by faith, hope, and love. MCDS believes in the education of the whole person, recognizing that every individual is endowed with six potentials: the intellectual, spiritual, social, aesthetic, physical, and emotional. The School is committed to providing all students with the experiences that inspire them to develop fully their individual gifts.

Miami Country Day School is proud of its sixty-five-year history of providing a high-quality educational experience for children in south Florida. During this time, it has had a dramatic history of growth and change as it has developed into a coeducational college-preparatory school for grades JK–12. The School was started in 1938 as an elementary boarding school for boys and was founded by Mr. L. B. Sommers and C. W. "Doc" Abele. In the 1950s, day students were added. In 1972, Miami Country Day School became coeducational. In 1977, the School was incorporated as a nonprofit institution with a Board of Trustees as its governing body. Alumni have attained positions of prominence in society, and the most recent graduates are attending colleges and universities in Florida and throughout the country. MCDS serves students of all faiths living in the greater Miami area. Committed to the values and beliefs of a rich Judeo-Christian heritage, the School offers a strong college-preparatory curriculum enhanced by a professional faculty and modern facilities. The U.S. Department of Education has twice recognized Miami Country Day as a National Exemplary School.

A Board of Trustees governs the School. The administration of the School is carried out by the Head of School; the Directors of the Lower, Middle, and Upper Schools and the Academic Center; the Academic Dean; the deans of students; the Business Manager; the Director of Development; the Director of Admission/Financial Aid; and the Director of College Counseling.

Through its Annual Giving Program, MCDS is able to offer up-to-date computer labs, an award-winning environmental studies program, state-of-the-art language and science labs, and high-quality music, art, and athletics programs. These educational enhancements are made possible with the participation in the Annual Fund by trustees, parents, faculty and staff members, alumni, and friends of the School.

MCDS is accredited by the Southern Association of Colleges and Schools and the Florida Council of Independent Schools. It is a member of the National Association of Independent Schools, National Association for College Admission Counseling, Southern Association of Independent Schools, Florida Kindergarten Council, National Association of Secondary School Principals, Council for Advancement and Education, Educational Records Bureau, American Library Association, Council for Spiritual and Ethical Education, College Board, Southern Association of College Admissions Counselors, and the Southeast Florida Information Network (SEFLIN).

ACADEMIC PROGRAMS

Miami Country Day offers an extensive program made up of core curriculum and elective courses. Students are required to take 4 credits of English and a language arts seminar, 4 credits of mathematics, and 3 credits each of history, foreign language, and science. In addition, there is a rich and varied list of elective courses from which students may choose. Included in the core subject areas are course offerings at the AP level in calculus, physics, chemistry, biology, English literature, English language, world history, U.S. history, Spanish language, French language, Spanish literature, and French literature. In addition, AP courses are offered in studio art and music theory. A number of advanced online computer courses are offered through the Florida Virtual Schools program.

In conjunction with the core curriculum, students take courses in the fine arts, humanities, physical education, and computer science. Life skills seminars, peer counseling, and a proactive guidance/counseling department contribute to the overall development of each student in preparation for college and lifelong learning. In addition, MCDS offers a Comprehensive Outdoor Educational Program (COEP) for students in grades 6–9.

FACULTY AND ADVISERS

MCDS has 116 full-time and 14 part-time faculty members. Fifty percent hold advanced degrees. It is the School's belief that faculty members must continue to learn throughout their careers, and it provides a comprehensive professional-growth program as well as funds to support the program.

In 2000, Dr. John Davies was appointed Head of School. Dr. Davies has an A.A. from La Salette Seminary, a B.S. from Merrimack College, an M.A. in history from Texas A&M, and an Ed.D. in educational leadership from Florida International University.

Counseling programs at MCDS center on the adviser-advisee system, which provides a system of close academic support and encouragement for students in the Upper School. As in most independent schools, the teachers provide the backbone of one-to-one student advising services. Trained peer counselors also assist in the guidance program. When indicated, referrals to outside professionals are made, with liaison maintained between the professionals, the parents, and the School counselors. Career and social issues are dealt with in both individual and group settings. Assemblies and special meetings are used to present speakers and special information related to personal decision making, values clarification, and career choices.

COLLEGE PLACEMENT

The College Counseling Program focuses on finding the college that best suits each student's individual needs and goals. College selection is therefore a process that begins in the eighth grade and continues throughout high school.

Personal contact, sound advice, and professional guidance are at the heart of the MCDS college counseling program. Beginning in the eighth grade, professional guidance concerning academic scheduling and college options are discussed in small seminars. At that time, college counseling software and the college counseling resource center are introduced. As freshmen, students begin the preliminary standardized testing process with the PLAN. Once the scores are received, seminars are held to discuss how to interpret the results and how to better utilize the College Counseling Center's resources. Seminars are also conducted to assist students in course selection for the following school year. As sophomores, students continue with preliminary testing by taking the PSAT and the PLAN. Seminars are held again to interpret results, plan for college admissions, and select courses. During the year, students and their parents attend formal large-group presentations as well as annual college fairs. As juniors, students take the PSAT and, during the second semester, the SAT and ACT. While seminars, formal programs, and college fairs are held during the first semester, the contact time during the second semester among the college counselor, the student, and the student's parents intensifies. Individual meetings are held to research and evaluate the student's goals, needs, and options. Colleges and possible career opportunities are reviewed, student profiles are assembled, and meetings with college admission officers are scheduled. As seniors, students continue meeting with their college counselor as they complete the selection and application process.

All MCDS students attend college upon graduation. Among the institutions at which graduates have recently matriculated are American, Amherst, Babson, Barnard, Boston College, Boston University, Carnegie Mellon, Claremont McKenna, Columbia, Cornell, Dartmouth, Duke, Emory, Florida International, Florida State, Georgetown, George Washington, Harvard, Kenyon, Loyola, MIT, NYU, Princeton, Smith, Tufts, Tulane, Washington (St. Louis), Wellesley, Yale, and the Universities of California at Los Angeles, Central Florida, Florida, Miami (Florida), Michigan,

North Carolina at Chapel Hill, Pennsylvania, San Diego, Southern California, and Virginia.

STUDENT BODY AND CONDUCT

There are 400 students in the Upper School. Students come from the village of Miami Shores and from such local suburbs as Aventura, Miami Beach, North Miami, North Miami Beach, Miami Lakes, and Miami Springs. They are diverse in religion, race, and national background.

The School strives to be a community of individuals who develop a spirit of cooperation and mutual respect. The community is deeply committed to its Honor Code, which stresses that honesty, respect for self, and respect for others and their property are fundamental values. Discipline is built on principles rather than on a catalog of rules and penalties. Under faculty leadership, students are expected to develop a sense of responsibility for their own conduct and achievement and the well-being of the larger School community. An Honor Council, composed of 4 students and 4 faculty members, deals with major School rule infractions.

An International Student Services program has been integrated into the curriculum, JK–12, to support students academically and socially. International students are provided a unique opportunity to grow in an American school that fosters sensitivity to multiculturalism. To facilitate the transition from homeland to Miami Country Day, the Director of International Student Services acts as a liaison between families and the School community.

Applicants are tested to determine their level of English proficiency. English as a Second Language (ESL) is offered in grades 6–11. The ESL program is available at an additional charge.

Information about MCDS is provided in French, German, Hebrew, Italian, Japanese, Portuguese, Spanish, Russian, and Arabic.

ACADEMIC FACILITIES

MCDS is located on a beautiful 16-acre campus bordered by the Biscayne Canal and the Miami Shores Country Club. In 1980, the School began a major construction program, based on a master plan that was adopted for campus improvement. The School opened the doors of a two-story, u-shaped, thirty-six-classroom building in August 2000; the Lower School and part of the Middle School are accommodated in this facility. Other facilities that resulted from the master plan include the Garner Activities Center (1984), which houses music, art, and drama facilities; a cafeteria; the Admission and Financial Aid Offices; and the International Student Services Office. The Michael J. Franco Upper School Complex (1992) contains computer labs, Smurfit Hall (an auditorium), the Abess Center for Environmental Studies, and science laboratories featuring modern equipment. The Abess Center is a unique, hands-on laboratory that houses more than 150 animals; it is a favorite of students and parents alike. The College Counseling Office is located near the Upper School classrooms. The campus libraries reflect the academic mission of MCDS. The Lower School library is administered by a professional librarian and staff, and it houses approximately 18,000 books and journals. Complete library services are offered for junior kindergarten through fifth grade. Computers, Accelerated Reader, specialized databases, story hours, and other services are offered daily. The Middle/Upper School library is administered by a Director of Campus Library Services and staff; it offers a collection of approximately 28,000 volumes. Laptops, interlibrary loans, spe-

cialized databases, and access to Questia and SE-FLIN represent some of the services available for faculty and staff members. The campus is cabled with fiber optics and is networked, with readily available access to the Internet and e-mail for all faculty and staff members. For a virtual tour of MCDS, students should visit the School's Web site.

ATHLETICS

MCDS believes that a participatory philosophy of athletics—one that stresses important values rather than winning for winning's sake—best serves its students. This is not to say that experience in winning is unimportant; in fact, the School feels that mental maturity and teamwork are key ingredients in any winning activity.

In addition to intramural and physical education programs, MCDS offers competitive sports for boys in baseball, basketball, cross-country, football, golf, lacrosse, soccer, swimming, tennis, track and field, and water polo. Sports for girls include basketball, cheerleading, cross-country, soccer, softball, swimming, tennis, track and field, volleyball, and water polo.

In 2005, MCDS opened its latest addition, a state-of-the-art athletic complex. The Spartan Athletic Complex is made up of baseball, softball, soccer, lacrosse, and football facilities, complete with an artificial-turf surface. Also on campus is an outdoor recreational/practice court. The golf and tennis teams practice at a local country club.

The J. Calvin Rose Athletic Center includes offices for the athletic department, a collegiate-size basketball court, three volleyball courts, a classroom, a training room, boys' and girls' locker rooms, and a fitness center.

In July 2002, MCDS opened a state-of-the-art 25-yard by 25-meter Aquatic Center, which includes a Colorado timing scoring system and ten lanes of competition.

EXTRACURRICULAR OPPORTUNITIES

The School's extracurricular program is designed to broaden each student's appreciation of life and to help each to discover his or her own special talents and interests. Among the many activities are ceramics, drama, rock band, computer club, newspaper, literary magazine, and service clubs (including Key Club, Operation Smile, and Anchor Club).

MCDS believes that its students have a responsibility to the community. Consequently, MCDS has a community service component as a requirement for graduation. Students are required to complete 30 service hours per year. Students are encouraged to exceed that number as their interest and commitment grow.

DAILY LIFE

Some students arrive for an early class in orchestra at 7:30 a.m., although the regular school day begins at 8 with a 10-minute homeroom period. Academic classes are on a rotating block schedule, with 40-minute classes on the two-day cycle and 75-minute classes on the three-day cycle. An additional period is scheduled during the week for assemblies and meetings between students and their advisers. Students also have a 10- to 30-minute break each day. A choice of a hot lunch, a sandwich, or the salad bar is provided daily in the spacious, air-conditioned dining room. Sports practices, athletic competitions, performing arts activities, and extra help sessions are held following dismissal.

SUMMER PROGRAMS

MCDS offers a summer program that provides students with enriched academics as well as camp activities. Daily instruction is provided in arts and crafts, music, drama, computers, fishing, canoeing, swimming, and other sports. Field trips are conducted each week.

Among the academic enrichment programs are workshops in photography, art, and music. The School also offers studies in marine biology and computers. Reinforcement in reading, math, and composition skills is offered to students seeking extra help in basic academic areas. Courses for Upper School credit are taught at various levels in math, science, history, English, foreign languages, computer sciences, and English as a second language. Online elective courses are also offered. Courses are taught by Miami Country Day faculty members.

COSTS AND FINANCIAL AID

Tuition for students in the ninth grade is $17,400; it is $17,810 for students in grades 10–12. Tuition does not include lunch, textbooks, or uniform shirts. It does include lab fees and entrance to all athletic and fine arts productions for students and their immediate family.

The financial aid budget, including tuition remission, for the 2005–06 academic year was $1.2 million. This is 8.2 percent of the operating budget and provides assistance for 16.2 percent of the student population in the Lower, Middle, and Upper School divisions. Aid is awarded on the basis of need and the School's ability to project success for the student within the guidelines set forth in the School's mission statement. The financial aid program uses the services of the School and Student Services for Financial Aid in Princeton, New Jersey, to assess the financial need of families applying for aid.

ADMISSIONS INFORMATION

MCDS welcomes all qualified applicants without regard to race, religion, ethnic origin, or disability. Admission evaluations are based on test scores, letters of recommendation, past academic records, and a personal interview. Students entering grades 5–11 are required to take the ISEE for entrance into MCDS. Admission is open to all students who possess the motivation, ability, and character that will enable them to succeed in a college-preparatory program. All interested persons are encouraged to contact the Admission Office for additional information.

APPLICATION TIMETABLE

The deadline date for admission and need-based financial aid applications is February 17. Admission decisions are made in early March and financial aid grants are made in late April. Candidates applying after that date are processed on a first-come, first-served basis.

ADMISSIONS CORRESPONDENCE

J. Victor McGlone, Ph.D.
Director of Admission
Miami Country Day School
P.O. Box 380608
Miami, Florida 33238-0608
Phone: 305-779-7230
Fax: 305-758-5107
E-mail: admissions@miamicountryday.org
Web site: http://www.miamicountryday.org

MIDDLESEX SCHOOL

Concord, Massachusetts

Type: Coeducational boarding and day nondenominational college-preparatory school
Grades: 9–12
Enrollment: 340
Head of School: Kathleen C. Giles, Head

THE SCHOOL

Since opening in 1901 as a nonsectarian boarding school, Middlesex School has grown to become one of the most highly regarded small boarding schools in the country, steadily expanding academic offerings, cultivating lively and professional faculty members, taking the lead in fostering diversity, and welcoming girls in 1974. Through a century of challenge and change, Middlesex has always dedicated itself to developing the whole individual, nurturing personal and intellectual growth as well as inculcating a sense of purpose and responsibility. Accordingly, Middlesex has defined itself as a college-preparatory school in the most holistic sense—an environment in which teaching and learning only begin in the classroom.

The well-preserved history of Concord, Massachusetts, makes the town an inspiring setting for the spirited intellectual activity that characterizes the Middlesex School community. Concord's Old Manse—whose former residents include Nathaniel Hawthorne and Ralph Waldo Emerson—and the Old North Bridge, site of the "shot heard 'round the world," lie just 2½ miles from the School's 350-acre woodland campus. With the cultural enticements of Boston and Cambridge only 20 miles away, Middlesex students find ample opportunities to take advantage of the richness and variety of metropolitan life while living in a comfortable, secure rural setting.

A nonprofit institution, Middlesex School is governed by a self-perpetuating, 30-member Board of Trustees. The endowment is estimated at $78 million, supplemented by the Annual Fund, which raised $2.4 million in 2004–05.

Middlesex is accredited by the New England Association of Schools and Colleges.

ACADEMIC PROGRAMS

In its wide range of curricular offerings, from mathematics to the natural, physical, and social sciences to the humanities and the arts, Middlesex emphasizes the value of critical thinking as the cornerstone of effective learning. The School also recognizes the value of the "verbal classroom," in which students are encouraged to join in the lively classroom discussions, enabling the type of understanding that only fully participatory education allows.

Freshmen and sophomores enroll in 5½ courses per semester; juniors and seniors typically take 5. Departmental requirements include 8 semesters of English, mathematics through trigonometry and analytic geometry, a foreign language through the third-year level, 2 years of laboratory science, 1 year of American history, a semester of European history, and ½-credit courses in the arts (freshmen and sophomores only). In addition, juniors and seniors are required to distribute their courses among the four divisions of the curriculum: 8 in the humanities, 5 in the natural sciences, 3 in the

social sciences, and 1 in the arts, with 3 unrestricted. The School's curriculum guide includes 150 courses, with electives ranging from Vietnam and the 1960s to Mandarin Chinese and from Vector Calculus to DNA: Biotechnology and Analysis.

The School also offers college-level preparation, with Advanced Placement courses in twenty-four subjects presented by the College Board. In May 2005, 203 students took 427 Advanced Placement tests; 88 percent of Middlesex seniors received scores of 3 or better. Middlesex offers opportunities for students to push their own limits, with the chance to go beyond the Advanced Placement level in formal classes and faculty-student tutorials. Middlesex encourages seniors to define their own Independent Study Projects, which in recent years have included taking courses such as individualized architectural studies, microprocessor design, and modern fiction from Africa, Ireland, and China.

International programs give students the opportunity to practice their language skills and see other parts of the world. Middlesex offers overseas immersion programs in French, Spanish, and Chinese. Teachers lead summer trips to such destinations as the northern coast of Spain, France, Ecuador, Beijing, Hong Kong, and Mexico.

Student performance is evaluated with numerical grades and comments. Courses are administered on a semester or yearlong basis.

The average class size is 11; the student-teacher ratio is 6:1. Informal, drop-in style extra help is always available from individual teachers. Formal tutoring is available at additional cost.

FACULTY AND ADVISERS

Most of Middlesex's 80 faculty members—47 of whom hold graduate degrees—live on the campus, many in the student dormitories. The easy accessibility and chance for friendship that their constant presence on campus affords help faculty members gain a thorough knowledge of each student's strengths, weaknesses, interests, and goals.

In 2003, Kathleen C. Giles (B.A., Harvard College; J.D., Harvard Law School) became the fifth Head of Middlesex School.

Middlesex faculty members are integrated into their students' experiences at every level. Students at Middlesex choose their own adviser to assist with course selection and provide support and counsel on other concerns.

COLLEGE PLACEMENT

Beginning early in the fall of the junior year, two full-time Directors of College Counseling work closely with each student to help him or her make sound judgments about college interests at each step of the application process. The Directors meet frequently with parents as well as with students. More than 80 college representatives visit Middlesex to meet with students each fall.

The median scores on the SAT for Middlesex's class of 2005 were 670 verbal and 680 math.

The members of the class of 2005 are attending forty-six colleges and universities. The top five choices for the class are Boston College, Brown, Harvard, Trinity, and the University of Pennsylvania.

STUDENT BODY AND CONDUCT

Middlesex's 340 girls and boys, 75 percent of whom board on campus, are a talented and eclectic group representing nineteen states and twelve countries. Students of color constitute 18 percent of the student body. In 2005–06, boys made up 52 percent of the student population.

Middlesex's commitment to high individual and collective achievement hinges on the honesty and high moral and intellectual standards of all members of the School community. A Discipline Committee consisting of faculty members and students deals with infractions of major School rules. Students gain experience with responsibility, leadership, and consequential decision making through involvement with student government, the proctor system, the Peer Support Group, student-faculty committees on discipline and admissions, and a range of extracurricular clubs and organizations.

ACADEMIC FACILITIES

Most classes and administrative activities take place in Eliot Hall, one of the eight Georgian brick buildings that surround an oval green known as "The Circle." With its extensive studio space, large main stage, and small teaching theater, the Cornelius Ayer Wood '13 Theatre Arts Center has served as a model for a number of secondary schools. The Warburg Library supports student research with 41,000 carefully selected volumes, nearly 100 periodical subscriptions, 100 audiobooks, 20 online databases, and 1500 DVDs and videos. The Warburg Library has its own wide area network (WAN) that includes the online card catalog as well as access to the Internet, CD-ROM multimedia information, and word processing software. The new Clay Centennial Center opened in the fall of 2003; it includes lab/classrooms, math classrooms, an observatory with a research-grade 18-inch Centurion telescope and seven smaller rooftop telescopes, a project room to support independent study, and a student lounge.

Technology and computers play a significant role in the lives of students and faculty members at Middlesex. Two state-of-the-art technology centers contain multimedia computers and full Internet access. Middlesex also has several lab classrooms equipped with interactive computers for the study of mathematics, computer science, modern languages, science, and economics. In addition, all dormitory rooms have access to the School's academic and library networks, the Internet, and e-mail.

BOARDING AND GENERAL FACILITIES

Residential life at Middlesex centers around the nine dormitories on the campus. Proctors live on each floor, so they are available for all students. Two to three faculty families live in every Middlesex house and oversee the activities of the 24–30 resident students. New students are often assigned single rooms, but many students live in a double or triple at some point in their Middlesex career.

The beautiful campus was designed by the firm of famed landscape architect Frederick Law Olmsted. Beyond the dormitories, the academic facilities, and the athletic center, the simple dignified chapel provides the campus its stately center. Four of the dormitories, the athletic center, and the chapel have all been recently renovated. The dining hall includes a student center complete with snack bar, game rooms, and lounge area. The health center is affiliated with Emerson Hospital, which is located less than 5 miles from the campus.

ATHLETICS

For most students, athletics are a vital part of their Middlesex experience, offering a welcome balance to their academic work. In addition to the recognition of the importance of exercise and fitness, the School seeks to teach its students a love of fair play and respect for their opponents—lessons that enable them to better know themselves and meet the challenges of the world.

Most ninth- and tenth-grade students play three seasons of team sports. Students in the upper classes participate in one or two seasons. Interscholastic competition is available at all levels for boys and girls in cross-country running, soccer, Alpine skiing, basketball, ice hockey, squash, lacrosse, crew, golf, and tennis. Boys also participate in football, wrestling, and baseball; girls play field hockey in the fall and softball in the spring.

The Atkins Athletic Center houses the School's basketball and indoor practice facilities, with team and officials' rooms as well as two basketball courts. Athletic facilities include a fitness center, a dance studio, eight international squash courts, an indoor hockey rink that converts to indoor tennis courts, eight outdoor tennis courts, and a wrestling arena. Middlesex enjoys some of the best playing fields in the Independent School League. Across the campus, there are a boathouse and a ½-mile rowing course.

EXTRACURRICULAR OPPORTUNITIES

From a multicultural student alliance to student government to community outreach and an award-winning Model United Nations delegation, extracurricular endeavors flourish at Middlesex because of the energy and commitment students and faculty members bring to them. The School encourages an "if we don't have it, start it" approach to extracurricular activities, which allows the program to remain as lively and creative as the students involved.

More than a third of the student body participates each year in two full-length dramatic productions, a one-act play festival, and Green Rooms. The music program attracts nearly half of the student body, either in one of four different singing groups, the jazz orchestra, the chamber ensemble, a variety of bands, or in private studio voice or instrument lessons.

In 1990, the School implemented a campus-wide community service program, which now engages many students in invigorating, socially responsible projects. Middlesex seeks to expand the process of learning beyond the classroom and athletic field to include an understanding of the value and importance of service to others.

One of the School's oldest traditions requires that every senior carve a wooden plaque. The week before graduation, each plaque is mounted on the walls in the corridors of the School buildings. Dating back to the School's first graduates, the plaques bear witness to the unique impression that each student has made in the academic, athletic, or cultural life of the School.

DAILY LIFE

Classes meet four or five times a week in 40-minute periods, from 8 a.m. to 3 p.m. on Monday, Tuesday, Thursday, and Friday and from 8 to 12:10 on Wednesday and Saturday. All-School assemblies on Tuesday and Saturday set aside time for announcements, student group meetings, and presentations by distinguished visiting speakers. Wednesday morning chapel provides a more intimate and serene gathering place in which students and faculty members give talks on issues of ethical and personal significance and engage the School in group singing and quiet reflection.

Athletic practices follow the end of classes at 3:15 each day. Most interscholastic competition takes place on Wednesday and Saturday afternoons.

Breakfast (7:15 to 8:30), lunch (11:30 to 12:45), and dinner (5:30 to 6:45) are served each day in Ware Hall. Dinner is followed by either free time or club meetings. During the regular evening study period, which runs from 7:30 until 9:30, students are required to be in the dormitory or the Warburg Library. On Monday through Thursday, freshman and sophomore students must be checked into their dormitories by 7:30 p.m. (10 p.m. for sophomores during the spring semester), juniors by 10:15, and seniors by 10:30. On Friday, all students are free at 9; check-in for juniors, sophomores, and freshmen is 10:15 and seniors 10:30. All students are required to be in their dorms by 11 p.m. on Saturdays. On Sundays, check-in for juniors and seniors is 10 p.m. Freshmen and sophomores must be in their rooms by 10:30 on weeknights. Freshmen must have their lights out by 10:30 p.m. Occasional requests for one half hour of "late lights" may be made to the faculty member on duty. Day students participate in all activities and may remain on campus until 10:15 p.m.

WEEKEND LIFE

The Student Activities Committee, a joint student-faculty venture, plans exciting events for students on nonschool days. The committee organizes dances, parties, weekend movies, and live music performances. Major dramatic and musical presentations in the theater arts center draw full houses of students, parents, and visitors. The proximity of Cambridge and Boston provides an almost inexhaustible supply of interesting off-campus cultural options for students and accompanying faculty members. Due to Saturday classes and athletic obligations, most weekends at Middlesex consist of one free night. Four weekends during the school year are designated campus weekends, requiring all boarding students to stay on campus. Four weekends are long weekends and open to all boarders. Of the remaining weekends, ninth graders may choose to leave the campus four weekends a semester; sophomores, five weekends; and juniors and seniors, six weekends.

Most of the weekend activities enjoyed by boarding and day students are informal. Many students use the School's extensive woodlands for hiking, running, biking, and cross-country skiing.

The School's athletic facilities are open for spirited student and faculty competition. In the winter, students skate in the rink and on the pond. On weekends, students are active in the woodworking, metal-welding, ceramics, and photography studios and in the music rooms.

COSTS AND FINANCIAL AID

The fee for tuition and residence for 2005–06 was $36,800. Day student tuition, which includes breakfast, lunch, and dinner, was $29,450. These charges are payable in two installments, the first due August 1 and the second, January 1. When a student enrolls, a deposit is required to hold the place. Essential additional costs, such as books and laboratory and studio fees, are estimated at $1200.

As Middlesex continues to seek talented students who represent the widest possible geographic, social, ethnic, and economic range, the financial aid budget increases with the availability of School funds. In 2005–06, Middlesex administered $2.8 million to 101 students based on demonstrated need. Students can earn extra money through Middlesex Student Services, which employs students in various jobs on campus.

ADMISSIONS INFORMATION

Middlesex seeks to enroll motivated students who demonstrate academic promise, a willingness to take risks, curiosity, imagination, maturity, and concern for others. The School looks for applicants eager to contribute to the shared life of the community and to take advantage of the School's many opportunities. Intellectual curiosity, as well as the ability to meet the demands of the School's academic program, is closely evaluated. In addition, Middlesex is committed to enrolling students from a wide range of cultural, racial, and socioeconomic backgrounds from across the United States and around the world.

All students at Middlesex are admitted based on their academic merit and personal credentials, without regard to their family's ability to pay the School's tuition and fees. Prospective students submit four recommendations, a transcript, and SSAT scores with their application. A campus visit and personal interview are strongly recommended. In 2005, Middlesex had 774 applicants for 101 openings; 68 students entered grade 9, 30 joined grade 10, and 3 entered grade 11.

APPLICATION TIMETABLE

Families are encouraged to visit Middlesex between 9 and 3 on weekdays (between 9 and 12 on Wednesday and Saturday) in the fall preceding the year in which they would like to see their children matriculate. The completed application is due on January 15 for day students and January 31 for boarding students. A $50 application fee must accompany the application. For applicants residing outside the United States, the fee is $100. Appointments for campus tours and interviews should be made well in advance. Admissions decisions are mailed on March 10, and the last date for acceptance of an offer of admission is April 10.

ADMISSIONS CORRESPONDENCE

Sibyl F. Cohane, Director of Admissions
Middlesex School
1400 Lowell Road
P.O. Box 9122
Concord, Massachusetts 01742-9122

Phone: 978-371-6524
Fax: 978-402-1400
E-mail: scohane@middlesex.edu
Web site: http://www.middlesex.edu

MILLBROOK SCHOOL
Millbrook, New York

NON SIBI SED CUNCTIS
1931

Type: Coeducational boarding and day college-preparatory school
Grades: 9–12 (Forms III–VI)
Enrollment: 252
Head of School: Drew Casertano, Headmaster

THE SCHOOL

Millbrook School was established in 1931 by Edward Pulling, who served as Headmaster until his retirement in 1965. Millbrook became known for the high quality of its teaching, the close relationships formed between students and faculty members, and the important work of all students in contributing to the daily functioning of the School through community service. Millbrook has always been, and intends to remain, a small school. What was established by Mr. Pulling continues: excellence in teaching, the building of productive relationships, and a daily program of service to the School community, through which students operate their own store, bank, recycling program, and zoo, to name but a few of the many services.

As the student body is diverse, so are the reasons for each individual's choice of Millbrook. For many, the appeal is the small size combined with the strength of the academic program. The AZA-accredited Trevor Zoo, with such auxiliary features as a forest canopy walkway, a wetlands sanctuary, and a center for the captive breeding of endangered species and for the recovery of sick and injured animals, draws students with related interests. Community service is also of interest as it offers a student the opportunity to have a significant, positive impact on the daily lives of others in the School. For the athlete, there is the promise of active, frequent team participation that in much larger schools might be available only to a limited number. For the arts enthusiast, there is ample opportunity to study, exhibit, and perform.

For years all male, Millbrook admitted girls as day students in 1971 and as boarders in 1975. The current boy-girl ratio is 55:45.

The campus of 800 acres is located in the rolling hills of Dutchess County, New York: 90 miles north of New York City, 20 miles northeast of Poughkeepsie, and 8 miles from the Connecticut border. Woods, fields, streams, and ponds are the dominant features of the land, all central to the natural science and recreational interests of many Millbrook students and faculty members.

The School is incorporated not-for-profit and is governed by a self-perpetuating Board of Trustees, many of whom are alumni. Millbrook has an endowment of $14 million and is not encumbered by long-term debts. Annual contributions from the Board of Trustees, parents, and the 2,400 alumni generally total in excess of $4 million. These funds are used to make up the difference between tuition income and per-student expense, as well as to support capital projects.

Millbrook School is accredited by the New York State Association of Independent Schools and the Board of Regents of the State University of New York. Institutional memberships include the Cum Laude Society, the Secondary School Admission Test Board, the National Association of Independent Schools, the New York State Association of Independent Schools, the Council for Advancement and Support of Education, and A Better Chance.

ACADEMIC PROGRAMS

Millbrook offers a traditional college-preparatory curriculum. Rigorous, varied, and comprehensive, it is oriented to the individual, includes all aspects of learning, and requires meaningful, active involvement in the daily life of the School. Every aspect of the School's curriculum is intended to embrace five core values: respect, curiosity, integrity, service, and stewardship of the natural world. All students carry a minimum of five major academic subjects throughout each year. The minimum graduation requirements are 4 years of English, 3 of mathematics, 3 of one foreign language, 2 laboratory sciences, and 1 year of fine arts. The history/social science requirement varies with the grade level at which the student enters, but all students must take U.S. history. In addition, seniors are required to participate in a Culminating Experience project.

Extensive reading and writing are the essence of the broadly based Millbrook curriculum. In addition to required courses, there are many elective opportunities in English, mathematics, science, history/social science, and the arts. Advanced Placement courses are offered to qualified juniors and seniors in most departments. Students who qualify are also able to pursue an independent study.

FACULTY AND ADVISERS

The 2005 faculty consisted of 64 members. All hold a bachelor's degree, 27 hold a master's degree, and 2 hold a doctoral degree.

Drew Casertano was appointed Headmaster of Millbrook in 1990. He is a graduate of the Choate School and Amherst College and holds an Ed.M. from Harvard University. Prior to his appointment at Millbrook, Mr. Casertano served as a teacher, a coach, a dorm parent, and the Director of Admissions and Financial Aid over the course of his ten-year tenure at the Loomis Chaffee School in Windsor, Connecticut.

Faculty members are chosen on the basis of their expertise in their own and related disciplines, their demonstrated ability to teach and work well with young people, and the human dimension they will bring to an environment where relationships are important. Students may choose their faculty advisers, who in turn become an integral part of the students' academic and social growth. Most faculty members live on campus, many occupying dormitory housing.

COLLEGE PLACEMENT

Virtually all Millbrook graduates continue their formal education on the college level. The College Counseling Office works closely with students, parents, and faculty advisers to help ensure strong and appropriate placement. Average SAT scores for the class of 2005 were 533 verbal, 545 math, and 536 writing.

The graduates of the class of 2005 entered colleges and universities that include Bates, Boston University, Bowdoin, Colorado College, Dartmouth, Denison, Dickinson, Hamilton, MIT, Rensselaer, St. Lawrence, Wheaton, and the Universities of Denver, Michigan, and Virginia.

STUDENT BODY AND CONDUCT

Of 252 students, 189 are boarders and 63 are day; 141 are boys, 111 are girls. By class, students are distributed as follows: Form III, 44; Form IV, 71; Form V, 69; and Form VI, 68. Most students come from the Northeastern states, with strong representation from the southeastern United States, the Midwest, and the West Coast. International students with well-developed English language skills are welcomed.

Behavioral and moral guidelines are simply stated. The School expects honesty and a respect for the rights and needs of others, and it does not tolerate the use or possession of nonprescribed drugs, including alcohol. The Discipline Committee, composed of elected students and faculty members, makes recommendations to the Headmaster in responding to major disciplinary infractions. The School President and Vice President, elected each year, are responsible for providing leadership to all groups related to student government, including the Student Council, the Community Service Council, and the dormitory prefects.

ACADEMIC FACILITIES

The twenty-four classrooms are distributed in several buildings. The schoolhouse contains classrooms, science laboratories, the study hall, administrative offices, the computer center, and an 18,000-volume library equipped with CD-ROM workstations and an online public access catalog. Additional laboratory space is located in the 6-acre Trevor Zoo. In addition to the chapel interior, the Flagler Memorial Chapel houses several classrooms. Construction of the $8.5-million Holbrook Arts Center was completed in the winter of 2001. The 34,000-square-foot center houses the 300-seat Chelsea Morrison Theater, the Warner Art Gallery, several classrooms and studios (two-dimensional, dance, and ceramics), a state-of-the-art photography darkroom complex, a music suite (a recital/lecture hall and practice rooms), and department offices.

BOARDING AND GENERAL FACILITIES

Seven dormitories of varying capacities house students' single; double; and, in some cases, triple rooms. Each dorm has a staff of 4 faculty members and 2 to 4 student prefects, who assist

---

the faculty members in maintaining the high quality of dormitory life. Dormitories are closed during long weekends and major School vacations.

Most meals are served buffet-style in the dining room, with a formal family-style meal once a week.

The Barn contains a student center, which includes lounges and game areas, the School store, a snack bar, and the college counseling office. Three full-time RNs staff a fully equipped health center, and a physician makes regular visits to the campus and is on call at all times. The health center also utilizes the resources of the nearby Sharon (Connecticut) Hospital, an excellent medical facility.

ATHLETICS
Athletics, like academic and community service work, are an integral part of Millbrook's program. Students participate in interscholastic team sports at least two out of three seasons; in an off season, students have several nonteam options, such as dance, riding, rec sports, and zoo squad. Varying team levels ensure a place for all, from beginners to accomplished athletes. Teams include those for baseball (boys), basketball, cross-country, field hockey (girls), golf, ice hockey, lacrosse, soccer, softball, squash, and tennis.

In September 1996, Millbrook dedicated the Bradford and Cheryl Mills Athletic Center, an 86,000-square-foot athletic complex. This facility contains an indoor hockey rink that converts into four indoor tennis courts in the off season, a basketball court, four international squash courts with a gallery for viewing, and a training complex and fitness center. Nine playing fields, a 3.2-mile cross-country trail, and a stable for student-owned horses complete Millbrook's athletic facilities.

EXTRACURRICULAR OPPORTUNITIES
Traditional clubs are largely incorporated within the framework of community service. Student interests are served, as are the needs of the School community, through work in one of the many community services, including the zoo, library, observatory, store, bank, weather station, stables, and athletic facilities, as well as work on the activities committee, newspaper, and yearbook.

Student art exhibits are presented each month throughout the academic year. The Arts Department presents three to four plays each year, including a musical, a dramatic production, and a series of one-act plays.

DAILY LIFE
The academic day consists of five periods of 45 to 90 minutes each, from early morning through midafternoon. The entire school convenes four times a week for an all-school assembly and four times a week for community service work. On Mondays, Thursdays, and Fridays, a class period dedicated to extra help. Athletic practice takes place each afternoon. On Wednesdays and Saturdays, classes meet in the morning only; sports teams compete against other schools in the afternoon.

WEEKEND LIFE
Films, dances, concerts, trips to museums, professional sports events, Broadway shows, sleeping, studying, fishing, hiking, bicycling, playing an instrument, working on an art project, watching television, listening to music, tramping the hills with camera in hand, skiing, riding, and more combine to make each weekend as active or as quiet as each individual prefers. Students with parental permission may leave campus most weekends—after their last Saturday commitment, but an energetic and creative Activities Committee plans a full array of activities and outings on and off campus.

Day students have access to all School programs and activities, are encouraged to be full participants in the life of the School, and have bed space within the dormitories.

COSTS AND FINANCIAL AID
The 2005–06 charge for boarders was $34,690; for day students, $25,240. Extra costs, such as activity and athletics fees, books, allowances, athletic equipment, linen, and insurance, added approximately $800–$1000 to the base fee for boarders, slightly less for day students.

Financial aid is awarded on the basis of a family's demonstrated need and within the confines of the School's available financial resources. In determining its awards, Millbrook consults the information provided by families to the School and Student Services for Financial

Aid. For the 2005–06 year, 25 percent of the student body shared grants totaling $1.5 million.

ADMISSIONS INFORMATION
Millbrook enrolls young men and women whose tested abilities range from average to superior, who are able to work in a school that makes considerable academic demands without being highly pressured, who are willing to participate actively in learning, and who are willing to share their talents with others through community service. As part of the application process, taking the SSAT is required. For the last several years, SSAT scores for incoming Form III and Form IV students have ranged from the low 30s to the high 90s. Mean scores for both groups have hovered at the 60th percentile mark. For entrance in fall 2005, 400 applications for admission were completed; 170 applicants were accepted, and 84 new students were enrolled.

Many factors are considered in making admissions decisions. Academic and testing information, teachers' recommendations, and a host of intangibles are evaluated carefully as part of the admissions process. In any event, no candidate is denied or offered a place solely on the basis of a particular test score or one set of grades.

APPLICATION TIMETABLE
Inquiries are welcomed at any time; interviews are welcomed and the application deadline is January 31. Admissions decisions are made and announced March 10 and on a rolling basis thereafter. It is to the advantage of the candidate and the family to visit Millbrook during the academic year. The admissions office welcomes visitors by appointment Monday, Tuesday, Thursday, and Friday between 8 a.m. and 2 p.m. and on Wednesday and Saturday morning.

ADMISSIONS CORRESPONDENCE
Cynthia S. McWilliams
Director of Admissions
Millbrook School
School Road
Millbrook, New York 12545

Phone: 845-677-8261
Fax: 845-677-1265
E-mail: admissions@millbrook.org
Web site: http://www.millbrook.org

THE MILLER SCHOOL OF ALBEMARLE

Charlottesville, Virginia

Miller School
1878
An Enduring Promise

Type: Coeducational boarding and day college-preparatory school
Grades: 7–12, postgraduate year
Enrollment: 140
Head of School: Lindsay Barnes, Headmaster

THE SCHOOL

Samuel Miller, a native of Albemarle County, had long dreamed of establishing a school near his birthplace. Although he was born into poverty, Mr. Miller had a successful, industrious life and left a large legacy to finance the establishment of The Miller School of Albemarle after his death in 1869.

Miller School is built on the democratic premise that all children can become self-reliant and contributing members of society. The School features a college-preparatory curriculum, an extensive service program, and a range of athletic options. In a fee-based system, Miller School offers a Study Skills (SS) program and individual tutoring.

Miller School's unique approach is to develop the mind, hands, and heart of each student in a structured, disciplined, and safe environment.

On the School's 1,600 acres in the foothills of the Blue Ridge Mountains are wooded areas, farmland, orchards, and a large reservoir. The main campus has lawns, a pond, sports facilities, and a swimming pool. There is also a 12-acre lake for swimming, fishing, and canoeing. The campus is located 14 miles west of Charlottesville, Virginia, and about 120 miles southwest of Washington, D.C. The School's setting is ideally suited to the pursuit of outdoor recreational interests, yet its proximity to Charlottesville and the University of Virginia, as well as to the Shenandoah Valley, provides easy access to extracurricular academic and cultural activities.

A nonprofit organization, the School is governed by a 15-member Board of Trustees. The annual operating budget is approximately $2.7 million, with total assets well in excess of $20 million.

The Alumni Association, representing the School's 1,000 living alumni, meets monthly, and its members conduct social and fund-raising events.

Miller School is accredited by the Virginia Association of Independent Schools. It is approved by the Virginia Board of Education and holds membership in the National Association of Independent Schools.

ACADEMIC PROGRAMS

Miller School's traditional college-preparatory curriculum requires 23 credits for graduation. The high school academic program includes 4 years of English, 4 years of history, 3 years of science, 3 years of a foreign language (French or Spanish), 3 years of mathematics (through at least algebra II), and 2 years of arts, whether it be studio art, drama, music, photography, or woodworking. Qualified students may take Advanced Placement courses in a variety of disciplines.

The Middle School (grades 7–8) builds into the Upper School (grades 9–12) program and offers a strong grounding in the foundational subjects of English (including spelling, grammar, and

vocabulary building), mathematics, social studies, foreign language, and the arts.

Miller's Study Skills program is staffed to provide qualified assessments of learning needs. While it is not a special-needs program, students placed in SS meet in a small group on a daily basis, at which time qualified staff members address these study skills and organizational needs. SAT prep courses and ESL courses are also offered.

Each afternoon, students are involved in a variety of athletic programs. After dinner, required evening study halls are overseen every school night by a team of faculty members, who give needed help. There are also help sessions with available faculty members between the end of classes and the start of athletics for students in need of extra help.

FACULTY AND ADVISERS

In addition to the Headmaster, there are 45 faculty and professional staff members, 22 women and 23 men. In addition to baccalaureates, 16 hold advanced degrees, with faculty members hailing from such schools as Auburn, Bridgewater, C. W. Post, Columbia, Dartmouth, Denison, Denis Diderot (Paris), Florida State, Georgetown, Hofstra, Indiana, James Madison, Laval (Quebec), Mary Baldwin, Mary Washington, Metropolitana (Caracas), Pacific, UCLA, Virginia Commonwealth, Virginia Tech, William and Mary, and the Universities of Colorado, North Carolina at Chapel Hill, Richmond, and Virginia.

Miller School employs teachers who are dedicated to working with the whole child in a residential program. Faculty benefits include Social Security, health and dental insurance, a retirement plan, and housing and meals. The proximity to the University of Virginia and three other colleges allows faculty members to pursue advanced degrees on a part-time basis.

Each student is assigned a faculty adviser, and students sit with their adviser at lunch and meet together frequently.

Lindsay R. Barnes Jr., Esq., was appointed eleventh Headmaster of Miller School in 1999. A graduate of Hampden-Sydney College and the University of Virginia School of Law, he holds a master's degree in journalism from the University of Georgia. A past member of the Board of Trustees of Miller School, he has long been active in civic affairs, including holding elective office, as well as practicing law, in Charlottesville, Virginia.

COLLEGE PLACEMENT

The college placement process is overseen by the Director of College Placement, who works closely with each student to develop a college admissions plan. This plan includes identifying particular strengths and interests of the student, reviewing his or her academic program and performance, ensuring that appropriate standardized testing takes place, building a college search strategy and ap-

plication list, and helping the student through the college application process. The goal of this process is to help students and parents find a good fit for a successful collegiate career.

The average combined SAT I score for the class of 2005 was 1057. In 1998 through 2005, 100 percent of the seniors who sought college admission were accepted at, among other schools, American, Catholic, Christopher Newport, Colgate, Dartmouth, Dickinson, Fordham, Hampden-Sydney, James Madison, Johns Hopkins, Johnson and Wales, New Mexico Tech, Old Dominion, Purdue, Providence, Roanoke, Seton Hall, Smith, Stanford, Union, VMI, Virginia Tech, William and Mary (including a Monroe Scholar), and the Universities of North Carolina at Chapel Hill, Pennsylvania, Richmond, Virginia (including a Jefferson Scholar), and Wisconsin–Madison.

STUDENT BODY AND CONDUCT

The key word for students at Miller School is involvement. The School's educational mission is best served by keeping total enrollment and individual classes small and personal. The practical effect on the student body is that all students participate fully in the life of the School, and significant leadership roles exist for interested students in all areas of School life and work. The residential program is run by a director who is assisted by appointed student leaders. The Honor Committee and Disciplinary Review Board are made up of a mix of students and faculty members.

The general student body is composed of 140 students distributed over grades 7–12, with a 6:1 student-faculty ratio and an average class size of 10. Currently, nine states and eight other countries are represented in the student body, with approximately 25 percent of the student population belonging to minority groups.

A unique aspect of Miller School is the Service Program, which is an integral part of the overall experience. Miller School was founded on the notion of community service, and today's students are an important part of that historical legacy. On alternate Wednesday afternoons, students spend 2 hours involved in their service activity. At the beginning of the school year, students choose one of a number of options in which they can participate through the year. Examples of service activities include students traveling to Charlottesville to visit nursing homes or volunteer at the SPCA, visiting area elementary schools to serve as reading tutors, archiving documents and items from Miller School's historic past for preservation and study, maintaining outdoor trails on the 1,600-acre campus, working on the yearbook or newspaper, building or repairing needed campus items in the woodshop, and working with the local Parks and Recreation Department.

ACADEMIC FACILITIES

The collegiate Victorian-style buildings of Miller School have been designated National Historic Landmarks. Old Main (1878) houses classrooms, the library, the Chapel, the Dining Hall, the Flannagan Technology Center, and administrative offices. There is also a fully equipped technology teaching lab adjoining the Flannagan Technology Center. Located in the Arts Building (1882) are the newly renovated, state-of-the-art woodshop, art studio, darkroom and photography classroom, and music room. The Science Building (1885) provides science classrooms and laboratories. The library contains more than 8,000 volumes, receives forty-five magazines and several newspapers, and has computer access to local libraries as well as the University of Virginia library. The library has both print and online reference resources and Internet access. Audiovisual equipment and computers are available for classroom and student use. Each student receives an e-mail account during Orientation.

BOARDING AND GENERAL FACILITIES

Boys reside in large dorm rooms in Old Main, with 2 to 4 boys per room. The School's dining room and chapel are also located in Old Main. The newly renovated girls' dorm holds single rooms for both Upper and Middle School girls and offers comfortable lounges, laundry facilities, a large meeting room, and two computer labs.

In 2000–01, the top floor of Old Main was renovated to include two additional classrooms and a spacious lounge with breathtaking views of the Blue Ridge Mountains and western Albemarle County. The lounge is used for student and faculty meetings of various types as well as special activities and gatherings.

Two registered nurses, one of whom is also a degreed psychological counselor, staff the health clinic and infirmary. A local doctor makes visits to the school when the need arises for the purpose of diagnosing and treating students. A family medical practice, a dentist, and a rescue squad are within 5 miles of the School, and there are three nationally ranked hospitals within 15 miles.

ATHLETICS

Miller School offers a program of interscholastic competition designed to accommodate varied skill levels and teach the important principles of good sportsmanship and cooperation. Facilities include five athletic fields; a fully equipped gymnasium with a weight room, wrestling room, and training room; a swimming pool; basketball and tennis courts; a lake; and miles of scenic cross-country trails in the surrounding hillsides.

All Upper School students participate in sports or drama during the year's three athletic seasons. Miller provides an excellent opportunity for all students to become involved in varsity, junior varsity, and Middle School athletics. Interscholastic sports include baseball, basketball, cross-country, girls' volleyball, lacrosse, soccer, tennis, and wrestling. Strength and conditioning is an option for one season each year, and drama is available as an alternate choice in the fall and winter seasons.

EXTRACURRICULAR OPPORTUNITIES

Students' extracurricular programs are limited only by their imagination and interests. The School offers a wide variety of faculty-sponsored activities, ranging from the nationwide Youth Leadership Initiative and the Student Government Association to paintball and skiing. Students may attend an array of off-campus activities, including dances, concerts, professional sports, collegiate sports, readings, and plays. Several clubs exist through the efforts of students and faculty members alike and include the Book Club, Chess Club, Debate Club, International Club, Key Club, National Honor Society, Outdoors Club, Poetry Club, and many others.

DAILY LIFE

Classes begin at 7:45 a.m. and run for 50 minutes each, with all classes meeting daily, Monday through Friday. Students faculty and staff members meet in the chapel between second and third periods for morning announcements on Monday, Wednesday, and Friday and for a nondenominational chapel program on Tuesday and Thursday. Service days (alternate Wednesdays) are shortened class days, with the afternoons devoted to service-group programs and projects. Dinner is at 6 p.m., and evening study hall is from 7:30–9:30 on Sunday through Thursday evenings, with a ten minute break in the middle.

COSTS AND FINANCIAL AID

In 2005–06, the cost of tuition was $24,865 for seven-day boarding students, $21,135 for five-day boarding students, $28,525 for international students, and $11,995 for day students. A variety of tuition-payment plans are available; arrangements must be made through the Business Office prior to registration for plans not listed on the Enrollment Agreement.

Parents wishing to apply for financial aid should contact the School by early March for aid for the following school year. Awards are based foremost on demonstrated financial need, with merit being a secondary criteria. Recipients must reapply for aid yearly. In 2004–05, students received more than $558,000 in financial aid, with an average award of $15,744 to boarding students and $5875 to day students.

ADMISSIONS INFORMATION

Miller School's academic program is designed for students of good character with average to superior ability. Miller School does not discriminate on the basis of race, color, sex, nationality, religion, or ethnic origin in the administration of its educational policies, scholarship programs, or athletic or other school-related programs.

A complete application includes: the application and fee, the Applicant Questionnaire, the Parent/Guardian Questionnaire, letters of recommendation from math and English teachers, a copy of the student's transcript or report card, standardized test scores, and a copy of the student's birth certificate or passport. An on-campus interview is required, except for out-of-state and international applicants; however, it is highly recommended for all. The application fee is $50 ($100 for international applicants).

APPLICATION TIMETABLE

Inquiries and visits are welcome year-round. Applicants who wish to be notified of the admission decision in early March must complete the application by February 20. Applications are welcome after February 20 and are reviewed on a rolling basis. In such cases, applicants are notified of the admissions decision shortly after the application process has been completed. Campus tours and interviews are generally available Monday through Friday. Arrangements can be made through the Admissions Office on weekdays from 8:30 a.m. to 5 p.m.

ADMISSIONS CORRESPONDENCE

Jay Reeves
Director of Admissions
The Miller School of Albemarle
Charlottesville, Virginia 22903-9328

Phone: 434-823-4805
Fax: 434-823-6617
Web site: http://www.millerschool.org

MILTON ACADEMY
Milton, Massachusetts

Type: Coeducational boarding and day college-preparatory school
Grades: K–12: Lower School, Kindergarten–5; Middle School, 6–8; Upper School, 9–12
Enrollment: School total: 980; Upper School: 680
Head of School: Dr. Robin Robertson

THE SCHOOL

Milton's Bicentennial in 1998 marked the Academy's charter, given in 1798 under the Massachusetts land-grant policy. It bequeathed to the school a responsibility to "open the way for all the people to a higher order of education than the common schools can supply." Milton's motto, "Dare to be True," not only states a core value, it describes Milton's culture. Milton fosters intellectual inquiry and encourages initiative and the open exchange of ideas. Teaching and learning at Milton are active processes that recognize the intelligence, talents, and potential of each member of the Academy.

For more than 200 years, Milton has developed confident, independent thinkers in an intimate, friendly setting where students and faculty members understand that the life of the mind is the pulse of the school. A gifted and dedicated faculty motivates a diverse student body, providing students with the structure to learn and the support to take risks. The faculty's teaching expertise and passion for scholarship generates extraordinary growth in students who learn to expect the most of themselves. The Milton community connects purposefully with world issues. Students graduate with a clear sense of themselves, their world, and how to contribute.

From Milton Academy's suburban 125-acre campus, 8 miles south of Boston in the town of Milton (population 26,000), students and faculty members access the vast cultural resources of Boston and Cambridge. A few minutes from campus is the Blue Hills Reservation, 6,000 wooded acres of hiking trails and ski slopes.

Milton Academy is a nonprofit organization with a self-perpetuating Board of Trustees. Its endowment is $150 million as of March 2005.

Milton Academy is accredited by the New England Association of Schools and Colleges and holds memberships in the National Association of Independent Schools, the Cum Laude Society, and the Association of Independent Schools in New England.

ACADEMIC PROGRAMS

Milton students and faculty members are motivated participants in the world of ideas, concepts, and values. Milton's curriculum provides rigorous preparation for college and includes more than 200 courses in nine academic departments. For students entering Milton in the ninth grade, a minimum of 18 credits is required for graduation. This includes 4 years of English, 2 years of history (including U.S. history), 2 years of science (physical science and one laboratory science), 1 year of an arts course, and successful completion of algebra II, geometry, and a level III foreign language course. Noncredit requirements include ethics, current events/public speaking, health, and a ninth-grade arts course (music/drama/visual arts).

Electives are offered in all academic areas; the English Department offers nineteen electives and the History Department offers twenty. Examples of electives include computer programming, American government and politics, Spanish film and social change, advanced architecture, choreography, music theory, observational astronomy, marine biology, and many more. Students may petition to take independent study courses, and the Advanced Placement courses leading to college credit are offered in most subject areas.

In January, seniors submit a proposal for a five-week spring independent project, on or off campus. Senior projects give students the opportunity to pursue in-depth interests stemming from their work at Milton.

The typical class size is 14 students, and the overall student-teacher ratio is 5:1. Nightly 2-hour study periods in the houses are supervised for ninth and tenth graders.

Faculty members are available for individual help throughout the day and in the houses at night. Students seeking assistance with assignments or help with specific skills, organization, and/or time management visit the Academic Skills Center, which is staffed early in the morning throughout the academic day and in the evening.

The school year, which is divided into two semesters, runs from early September to early June with an examination period at the end of January. Students usually take five courses per semester. Students earn letter grades from E (failure) through A+, and comments prepared by each student's teachers and adviser are sent to parents three times a year in November, February, and June.

All academic buildings and dormitories are part of a campuswide computer network. MiltONline, the Academy's e-mail and conferencing system, allows students to join conference discussions for many classes and extracurricular activities, communicate with faculty members and friends, and submit assignments. Students have access to the Milton Intranet as well as the Internet.

Eleventh grade students may apply to spend either the fall or spring semester at the Mountain School Program of Milton Academy (an interdisciplinary academic program set on a working 300-acre farm in Vermont); at CITYterm at the Master's School in Dobbs Ferry, New York; or at the Maine Coast Semester at Chewonki. Through School Year Abroad, Milton provides opportunities in Spain, France, Italy, and China. Milton also offers six- to eight-week exchange programs with schools in London, Madrid, Paris, and Beijing.

FACULTY AND ADVISERS

The deep commitment of a learned and experienced group of teachers is Milton's greatest treasure. Teaching in grades 9–12 are 160 full-time faculty members, of whom 120 hold advanced

degrees (Ph.D. and master's degrees). Eighty percent of the faculty members live in dormitories and on campus.

Robin Robertson (B.A., University of Pennsylvania; M.A. and Ph.D., Harvard) was appointed Head of School in 1999.

In addition to teaching, faculty members also serve as dorm parents, coaches, and advisers to student clubs, organizations, publications, and activities. Each faculty member is adviser to a group of 6 to 8 students and supports the students' emotional, social, and academic well-being at Milton.

COLLEGE PLACEMENT

Four college counselors work one-on-one with students, beginning in the eleventh grade, in a highly personal and effective approach toward the college admissions process.

Of the 181 students in the class of 2005, the top college choices were Harvard (12), Brown (9), Georgetown (8), Bowdoin (7), Tufts (7), Columbia (6), Trinity (6), and Wesleyan (6).

STUDENT BODY AND CONDUCT

Of the 680 students in the Upper School, 50 percent are boys and 50 percent are girls. Coming from thirty-four states and eighteen other countries, 320 students are boarding students and 360 are day students. Twenty-six percent of Milton students receive financial aid.

Elected representatives from grades 9–12 participate in the student government, led by girl and boy head monitors. Rules at Milton Academy foster the cohesion and morale of the community and enhance education by upholding standards of conduct developed by generations of students and faculty members. Elected class representatives serve with faculty members on the Discipline Committee, which recommends to the Head of School appropriate responses when infractions of major school rules occur.

ACADEMIC FACILITIES

Among the prominent buildings on the Milton campus are three primarily academic buildings; a Science Center, including a science library, laboratories, an audiovisual lab, a digital imaging lab, and the Nesto Art Gallery; the Kellner Performing Arts Center, with a 350-seat teaching theater, a studio theater, dressing rooms, scene shop, practice rooms, orchestral rehearsal room, dance studio, and speech/debate room; the Athletic and Convocation Center, opened in 1998, including a hockey rink, a fitness center, three basketball courts, and an indoor track; the Williams Squash Courts; the Ayer Observatory; and the Apthorp Chapel.

Cox Library contains more than 45,000 volumes, more than 150 periodicals with back issues on microfilm, and a newspaper collection dating back to 1704. It also provides CD-ROM sources,

Internet access and online search capabilities. Within Cox Library is one of several computer laboratories.

BOARDING AND GENERAL FACILITIES
Milton Academy students live in one of eight houses ranging in size from 30 students to 40 students; four for boys and four for girls. Single rooms house one third of the students, while the other two thirds of the students reside in double rooms. Milton houses include all four classes as well as faculty members' families. Students spend all their Milton years in one house, experiencing a family-at-school context for developing close relationships with valued adults, learning about responsibility to the community, taking leadership roles with peers, and sharing social and cultural traditions. All rooms are networked, and each student has an e-mail account, a telephone line, and a voice mailbox. School computers are available for student use in the house common rooms.

The Health and Counseling Center and the Academic Skills Center, as well as house parents in each dormitory, class deans, and the office of the school chaplain are available to meet students' needs.

ATHLETICS
Milton believes that teamwork, sportsmanship, and the pursuit of excellence are important values for everyone and that regular vigorous exercise is a foundation of good health. Milton offers a comprehensive athletic program that includes physical education classes and a range of intramural and interscholastic sports geared to the needs and interests of every student.

The school's offerings in interscholastic sports are Alpine skiing, baseball, basketball, cross-country, cycling, field hockey, football, golf, ice hockey, lacrosse, sailing, soccer, softball, squash, swimming, tennis, track, volleyball, and wrestling.

Intramural offerings include basketball, cycling, field hockey, lacrosse, self-defense, soccer, softball, squash, swimming, tennis, Ultimate Frisbee, volleyball, weight training, and windsurfing.

Sports facilities include gymnasiums, an ice hockey rink and athletic center, two indoor climbing walls, twelve playing fields, seventeen tennis courts, seven international squash courts, an all-weather track, a cross-country course, and a ropes course.

EXTRACURRICULAR OPPORTUNITIES
The breadth of extracurricular opportunities means that every student finds a niche—a comfortable place to develop new skills, take on leadership, show commitment, make special friends, and have fun. Clubs and organizations include cultural groups such as the Asian Society, Latino Association, Onyx, and Common Ground (an umbrella organization for the various groups); the Arts Board; Dance Workshop; the Outdoor Club; the Chinese, French, and Spanish clubs; the debate, math, and speech teams; and Students for Gender Equality. There are eight student publications, among them the *Asian, La Voz, MAGUS/MABUS, Mille Tonnes,* the *Milton Measure,* the *Milton Paper,* and the yearbook. Music programs include the chamber singers, the glee club, the orchestra, improvisational jazz combos, three a capella groups, and pop music groups. The performing arts are an important part of the extracurricular offerings at Milton. Main stage theater productions, studio theater productions, play readings, and speech and debate team are a few of the available opportunities. Service opportunities include the audiovisual crew, community service, Lorax (environmental group), Orange and Blue Key (admission tour guides and leaders), and the Public Issues Board.

DAILY LIFE
The academic day runs from 8 a.m. to 3:20 p.m., except on Wednesday, when classes end at 1:45. There are no classes on Saturday or Sunday. Cafeteria-style lunch is served from 11:10 to 1:30, and students eat during a free period within that time. Athletics and extracurricular activities take place from 3:30 to 5:30 p.m. Family-style dinner is at 6, and the evening study period runs from 7:30 to 9:30. Lights-out time depends on the grade level of each student.

WEEKEND LIFE
Interscholastic games are held on Wednesday, Friday, and Saturday afternoons. Social activities on Friday and Saturday evenings are planned by the Student Activities Association. Day students join boarders every weekend for events such as dances with live or recorded music, classic and new films, concerts, plays, drama readings, dormitory open houses, and trips to professional sports events, arts events, or local museums.

Prior to leaving campus, students must check their plans with dorm parents, who must approve their whereabouts and any overnight plans.

SUMMER PROGRAMS
Milton's Academy's summer programs develop, schedule, and supervise a wide range of offerings that connect with the school's mission. These programs include professional development opportunities for teachers, academic and recreational activities for students, and corporate and community-related events. In addition to hosting many outside programs, the Academy runs Sports Plus and Milton Academy Summer Hockey camps, as well as E-Cast Computer/Science School, all for students, along with the Cultural Diversity Institute and the Boarding Staff Conference for teachers from across the country.

COSTS AND FINANCIAL AID
For the 2006–07 academic year, tuition for boarding students is $34,525, and tuition for day students is $27,100.

Milton seeks to enroll the most qualified applicants regardless of their financial circumstances. To that end, more than $4.7 million will be provided in financial aid to students in the 2006–07 school year. All financial aid at Milton is awarded on the basis of need. In addition to the program of direct grants, the school offers installment payment options and two low-interest loan programs.

ADMISSIONS INFORMATION
Milton Academy seeks students who are able, energetic, intellectually curious, and have strong values and a willingness to grow. Applicants for grade 6 must submit the Independent School Entrance Examination (ISEE) scores, and applicants for grades 9–11 must submit Secondary School Admission Test (SSAT) scores. All applicants must submit a school transcript, teacher recommendations, and an application that includes the writing of two essays. An interview on or off campus is required.

APPLICATION TIMETABLE
The deadline for applying is January 15. Notification letters are sent out on March 10; the reply date is April 11. There is a $50 preliminary application fee for U.S. applicants and a $100 fee for international applicants.

ADMISSIONS CORRESPONDENCE
Paul Rebuck, Dean of Admission
Milton Academy
170 Centre Street
Milton, Massachusetts 02186
Phone: 617-898-2227
Fax: 617-898-1701
E-mail: admissions@milton.edu
Web site: http://www.milton.edu

MISS HALL'S SCHOOL

Pittsfield, Massachusetts

Type: Girls' boarding and day college-preparatory school
Grades: 9–12
Enrollment: 175
Head of School: Jeannie K. Norris

THE SCHOOL

Founded in 1898 by Mira Hinsdale Hall, Miss Hall's School was one of the first girls' boarding schools established in New England. A graduate of Smith College, Mira Hall understood the advantages to girls of having a place of their own in which to learn and grow. During her forty-year tenure, she created a learning environment based on respect for the individual student, stimulating teaching, competitive spirit, intelligent supervision, and personal warmth. Now, more than 100 years later, the School continues to educate young women and guide them toward success and fulfillment in their academic, professional, and personal endeavors.

The School's mission is grounded in a strong belief in the benefits of an all-girl educational environment. Since its founding, Miss Hall's School has remained convinced that the best learning and surest growth—in and out of the classroom—occur in a single-sex, small-school environment. The trustees, faculty members, and alumnae of the School are determined to preserve a family-style atmosphere wherein a girl can mature surely and gracefully into a bright, confident, self-reliant young woman.

Surrounded by wooded hills and New England villages, the School takes full advantage of its location in Berkshire County in western Massachusetts. The beauty of the 80-acre campus is captured in the vibrant autumns, snowy winters, colorful springs, and lush, green summers. With its rich history and natural beauty, the area has long attracted a wide array of artists, dancers, and musicians. Thousands of visitors travel to the Berkshires every year to attend festivals and special events and to visit historical sites, museums, and performing arts centers. The Clark Art Institute, *The Mount*, Tanglewood, Jacob's Pillow, Williamstown Theatre Festival, Shakespeare & Company, Hancock Shaker Village, the Norman Rockwell Museum, and the Massachusetts Museum of Contemporary Art are among the most popular attractions. The campus is just a 5-minute drive from the center of Pittsfield, a well-populated city that offers all the amenities associated with a tourist region.

A nonprofit corporation, Miss Hall's School is governed by a 28-member Board of Trustees. An active Alumnae Association of more than 3,000 members works with the administration, faculty members, and friends of Miss Hall's to ensure that the School continues to succeed in its fund-raising and recruiting efforts. Accredited by the New England Association of Schools and Colleges, Miss Hall's School is a long-standing member of the Secondary School Admission Test Board, the National Association of Independent Schools, and the National Coalition of Girls' Schools.

ACADEMIC PROGRAMS

The Miss Hall's School college-preparatory academic program includes full offerings in math, science, history, English, foreign languages, English as a second language, the arts, and athletics, as well as an off-campus experiential learning program called *Horizons*. Each student must take at least five courses per term and graduate a minimum of 18 cred-

its. Within this framework, considerable care is taken to provide students with appropriate challenges. For many students, this means acceleration into the honors and Advanced Placement courses offered in all disciplines. An average class size of 10 and a student-teacher ratio of 7:1 ensure that each student receives the individual attention and encouragement that is vital to her success.

Graduation requirements are as follows: 4 years of English; 3 years of history, including United States history; 3 years of a foreign language; 3 years of mathematics, including algebra I and II and geometry; 3 years of science; a minimum of 2 additional elective credits; successful completion of *Horizons*; and two terms each year of athletics.

To fulfill their elective credit requirements, many students choose to enroll in courses in the Miss Hall's Expressive Arts Department. The seasoned expressive arts faculty members, drawing from their own experiences as professional artists and performers, enthusiastically promote the students' aesthetic, creative, academic, and intellectual growth. Expressive arts students also develop a thorough understanding of women's significant contributions to the art world, both historically and in the present day.

Not everything girls need to learn about the world and themselves can be learned in the classroom. Each Thursday throughout the school year, all students participate in *Horizons*. This unique experiential learning program allows students to gain new skills, explore areas of interest for college majors and careers, increase financial literacy, and learn the value of service. By graduation, each girl has volunteered in her community, written a sophisticated resume, developed interview skills, and completed an individual professional internship. *Horizons* work sites include Berkshire Medical Center, Norman Rockwell Museum, Merrill Lynch, American Red Cross, Sacred Heart School, Sunshine Photographics, Pittsfield Community Television, Congressman John Olver's office, GE Plastics, Canyon Ranch, Cranwell Resort, and many more.

FACULTY AND ADVISERS

Of the 52 Miss Hall's faculty members, 26 hold advanced degrees and 19 live on campus. Using their unique talents to serve the School in multiple capacities, faculty members act as academic instructors, class advisers, club facilitators, coaches, and dorm residents. Each Miss Hall's student also has the opportunity to select a faculty adviser, who is available to her for both academic and personal guidance.

Appointed the Head of School in 1996, Jeannie K. Norris continues to guide Miss Hall's through an exciting period of growth and campus expansion. A graduate of Pittsburg State University (B.M.Ed.) and Temple University (M.M.), she has previously served as Director of Admission and Financial Aid and Assistant Head of Enrollment at the Madeira School. With twenty-four years of teaching and administrative experience in all-girls independent schools, Norris arrived well prepared for the challenges of her position. Among her greatest achievements is the success of the Centennial

Campaign, which was launched in 1998 to raise funds for the construction of new campus facilities.

COLLEGE PLACEMENT

Preparation for college begins when a girl enrolls at Miss Hall's. Formal meetings occur in the junior year, when the student and her college counselor begin to talk about her goals and accomplishments and examine the possibilities for her college experience. The college counseling staff continues to offer guidance and support to each student throughout her junior and senior years as she refines her list, visits college campuses; takes the SAT and ACT tests, completes the college application process, and decides among her acceptances.

Recent Miss Hall's graduates have gone on to attend schools such as Barnard; Boston University; Chicago Art Institute; Colby; Cornell; Dartmouth; Georgetown; George Washington; Lehigh; Middlebury; Northeastern; NYU; Smith; Williams College; Wellesley; Yale; the Universities of Massachusetts, Southern California, Virginia, and Wisconsin; and many other fine schools.

STUDENT BODY AND CONDUCT

With an enrollment of 175 students, Miss Hall's is able to maintain a small-school environment in which every girl is recognized for unique talents and encouraged to explore all of her interests. The 130 boarding students and 45 day students represent a broad spectrum of cultural and socioeconomic backgrounds, creating a valuable diversity within the student body. Of the currently enrolled students, 16 percent are students of color, 18 percent are international, and 47 percent receive financial assistance from the School. Geographically, they represent twenty-one states and fourteen countries.

At Miss Hall's, each student is encouraged to try new activities, test out her leadership ability, and play an active role in the life of the School. As athletics team captains, Student Council representatives, class officers, club presidents, and musical ensemble leaders, girls gain valuable leadership experience that will help them grow into confident and capable young women. They are also given the serious responsibility of electing student representatives to serve on the School's two disciplinary committees, the Judicial Committee, and the Student-Faculty Advisory Committee.

ACADEMIC FACILITIES

The Main Building is a 90,000-square-foot, Georgian-style building that houses classrooms, laboratories, choral and instrumental music rehearsal space, administrative offices, Humes Euston Hall Library, the Melissa Leonhardt Academic Skills Center, and the Pamela Humphrey Firman Technology Center. Other campus resources include the Anne Meyer Cross Athletic Center, Ara West Grinnell Teaching Greenhouse, Elizabeth Gatchell Klein Arts Center, and Jessie P. Quick Ski Chalet.

The Humes Euston Hall Library, a 7,200-square-foot addition extending from the Main Building, opened in 2001. It incorporates spaces for electronic and traditional research and the Gustafson

Family Lending Library. Study carrels and a periodical room designed around the Joseph Buerger Fireplace Alcove provide additional places for study and reading, while enclosed seminar rooms offer space for group work.

The Klein Arts Center also opened in 2001. This 14,000-square-foot building contains a flexible-space theater with dressing rooms, costume and prop-storage rooms, and a design workshop. Spacious dance, art, ceramics, and photography studios are housed in this impressive building.

BOARDING AND GENERAL FACILITIES

In addition to all of the resources listed above, the Main Building also houses underclass student dormitory rooms, faculty apartments, the Dining Room, the Health Center, and several living rooms and lounges. The senior dormitory, Witherspoon Hall, is located just a few yards from the Main Building.

ATHLETICS

In the new 18,720-square-foot Cross Athletic Center students enjoy the Thatcher Family Gymnasium for basketball and volleyball competitions, the Humphrey Family Aerobics and Fitness rooms, team rooms, lockers and showers, and Wilderness Program facilities.

Miss Hall's requires each student to participate in an athletic activity of her choice each term, including at least one team sport per year. Athletics teach girls valuable skills, enhance self-discipline, encourage confidence, and provide leadership opportunities. The wide variety of athletic offerings includes varsity and junior varsity sports as well as noncompetitive and recreational activities. In the fall term, students choose among soccer, field hockey, cross-country, riding, recreational tennis, modern dance and choreography, and the Wilderness Program. Winter term offerings include basketball, volleyball, fitness, aerobics, riding, both competitive and recreational skiing, and snowboarding. During the spring term, students participate in tennis, lacrosse, softball, riding, modern dance and choreography, or the Wilderness Program.

EXTRACURRICULAR OPPORTUNITIES

With clubs and organizations to match every interest, it is easy to get involved at Miss Hall's School. The Student Council, the Social Committee, the Athletic Association, the Judicial Committee, and the Student-Faculty Advisory Committee provide excellent leadership opportunities, while the Essence Diversity Club, the Environmental Club, the Photography Club, the French Club, the Latin Club, and the International Student Alliance bring together students with common interests and goals. The *Hallways* student newspaper, *Hallmark* yearbook, and *Sol* literary magazine provide ample opportunities for aspiring artists and journalists. In addition to taking private lessons on campus, musicians and vocalists can choose from several performance groups, such as Grace Notes, the School's stellar a cappella singing group; Vocal Ensemble; Merrie Melodies, a student-faculty vocal group; and various instrumental ensembles. Two major theater productions each year showcase the talent, commitment, and enthusiasm of the School's actors and technical crew members.

DAILY LIFE

Academic classes are held five days a week for 50-minute periods, beginning at 8 a.m. On Mondays and Fridays, all members of the Miss Hall's community gather at Morning Meeting to share important announcements, updates on School-related issues, and reflections on global current events. Athletics take place between 3:45 and 5:15 p.m., after which students are free to relax, chat with friends, get started on their homework, and head to the Dining Room for dinner. Various club meetings, rehearsals, and tutorials are held in the evening, followed by a 7:30 to 9:30 p.m. quiet study-hall period.

WEEKEND LIFE

The Miss Hall's campus is a lively place on the weekends. While students do have the option of returning home for an occasional weekend, most girls remain on campus in order to participate in the wide variety of social and recreational activities arranged by the School's student-run Social Committee. Day students are also involved during the weekend, often arranging a Friday or Saturday overnight stay with a boarding friend.

Weekend activities include interscholastic dances and social events, volunteer and community service opportunities, trips to Boston and New York, pick-up sports, movie trips, shopping excursions, and theater, music, and dance performances held at nearby professional venues and colleges.

COSTS AND FINANCIAL AID

Tuition for the 2005–06 school year was $35,800 for boarding students and $21,000 for day students. Strongly committed to providing need-based financial aid for deserving candidates, Miss Hall's awarded more than $1.7 million in financial aid to 47 percent of the School's 2004–05 student population.

ADMISSIONS INFORMATION

Miss Hall's welcomes applications from girls who have the intellectual capacity and academic commitment necessary to meet the challenges of a demanding college-preparatory curriculum. The School also values extracurricular involvement, a spirit of curiosity, a willingness to explore new interests, and evidence of good citizenship.

Application materials are provided by the Admission Office upon a student's request for information about the School. In order to be considered for admission to Miss Hall's, each applicant must submit a completed student questionnaire and essay, three letters of recommendation, a completed parent form, school transcripts from the past two years, and a Secondary School Admission Test score report. Each applicant is also required to schedule an interview with a member of the admission staff. While telephone interviews can be arranged, Miss Hall's School strongly encourages prospective students to visit the campus for a tour and an interview. There is a $40 application fee ($75 for international students) for each submitted application.

APPLICATION TIMETABLE

Prospective students may choose to submit an early decision application by January 1, in which case they are notified of their admission status by January 15. Students who choose to submit their applications by the regular deadline of February 15 are notified of their admission status by March 10. Applications submitted after February 15 are considered on a rolling basis, as space permits.

ADMISSIONS CORRESPONDENCE

Kimberly B. Boland, '94
Director of Admission
Miss Hall's School
492 Holmes Road
Pittsfield, Massachusetts 01201

Phone: 800-233-5614 (toll-free)
Fax: 413-448-2994
E-mail: info@misshalls.org
Web site: http://www.misshalls.org

MISS PORTER'S SCHOOL
Farmington, Connecticut

Type: Girls' boarding and day college-preparatory school
Grades: 9–12
Enrollment: 308
Head of School: M. Burch Tracy Ford

THE SCHOOL

Miss Porter's School (MPS) is located in the town of Farmington, 9 miles from Hartford, Connecticut. The 75-acre campus is close to village stores and within a 5-minute walk of the Farmington River, woods, and fields. Students are able to take advantage of the facilities of Farmington and the cultural resources of Hartford. The School's location also allows easy access to New York and Boston for social, cultural, and academic events.

A respected leader in preparing young women for competitive colleges since 1843, Miss Porter's School offers a demanding curriculum, collaborative environment, and supportive community, which distinguishes the best boarding schools in the nation. The rigorous curriculum includes Honors, Advanced Placement, and elective courses, and provides a strong educational foundation for the talented student. On- and off-campus programs for juniors and seniors provide internships and independent studies that explore traditional and nontraditional subjects in innovative ways. All seniors attend four-year colleges. Miss Porter's mission is to challenge its students to become compassionate, resourceful, informed, responsible, and ethical young women.

The School's governing board is composed of 29 trustees, both men and women, 22 of whom are alumnae. The Annual Giving Program provides 12 percent of the operating costs each year.

Miss Porter's School is accredited by the New England Association of Schools and Colleges and is approved by the Connecticut Association of Independent Schools. It holds membership in the Connecticut Association of Independent Schools, the National Association of Independent Schools, the National Coalition of Girls' Schools, the Council for Advancement and Support of Education, and the Cum Laude Society.

ACADEMIC PROGRAMS

College preparation, with emphasis on literature, expository writing, public speaking, mathematical competence, foreign languages, science, and history, is basic to the academic program. During the fall and spring semesters, 113 courses are offered. To graduate, each girl must have a total of 36 semester units, including 8 units of English; 6 units of a foreign language; 4 units of history; algebra I, geometry, and algebra II; 6 units of science; 2 units in the arts (art, music, theater, dance, art history, or photography); 1 unit in computers; and a ½-credit in Ethics and Leadership Seminar. Advanced Placement courses are available in European and American history, art history, biology, chemistry, computer science, English, environmental science, French, Latin, mathematics, music, physics, Spanish, and studio art.

The average class size is 11. Honors courses are available for exceptional students. All ninth graders attend a required study hall each evening, while upperclass students observe "quiet hours" from 7:30 to 9:30 p.m. Grades, based on the letter system, and comments are sent home four times a year, not including adviser and house faculty comments, which are mailed at the end of each semester.

Qualified students may participate in independent projects or may apply to programs such as School Year Abroad. Juniors and seniors are encouraged to investigate career opportunities by working in the Hartford area or in carefully selected internships across the country. Juniors may choose to spend either their fall or their spring semester in the Chewonki Foundation's Maine Coast Semester Program, City Term, or the Rocky Mountain Semester in the Mosquito and Sawatch mountain ranges of Colorado. They may also elect to participate in the School Year Abroad in France, Spain, or China.

FACULTY AND ADVISERS

In 2004–05, there were 55 teaching faculty members. Of these, 35 have degrees beyond the bachelor's degree.

Burch Ford began as Head of School in 1993 and brings previous boarding school experience as Dean of Students at Milton Academy. She also taught for fifteen years and served as a school counselor at Groton School. Ms. Ford graduated magna cum laude with a B.A. in English from Boston University in 1972. In 1975 she earned an M.S.W. from Simmons College and, in 1990, an Ed.M. in administration and social planning from Harvard University.

Faculty members average fourteen years of teaching experience, eleven of those years at Miss Porter's. In hiring new faculty members, the School seeks teachers who are committed both to their own academic discipline and to the intellectual, moral, and personal development of young women. Faculty members must be willing to participate fully in boarding school life. Nonteaching faculty members, known as House Directors, assist students in planning and carrying out cultural and social activities and serve as advisers to special interest clubs. Each student has her own adviser, who helps her manage her academic program and serves as her aide and ally both in the classroom and throughout her life on campus.

Summer sabbaticals for study and travel are available to faculty members who have served at the School for seven years. Assistance is also offered in financing graduate study.

COLLEGE PLACEMENT

The Director of College Counseling helps students in planning their educational futures. Responsibility for handling college applications falls ultimately on the student, but the School offers strong support and counsels parents and students from the beginning to the end of the process. Beginning in February of the students' junior year, the college counselor meets with the students in small groups to discuss the general procedure. She also confers with girls individually, helping each to understand her unique situation. When each girl leaves for spring vacation, she takes with her a list of possible colleges and is urged to visit at least one during that break.

Before June, students have usually decided on which colleges to visit during the summer. A comprehensive letter is sent to parents outlining each girl's choices, with assessments by the adviser of the student's chances for admission. During the fall, more than 130 college representatives visit the School to meet with interested girls. During Parents' Weekend in October, the college counselor holds individual conferences with parents of seniors.

For the class of 2005, the middle 50 percent of SAT I scores in were 590–690 on the verbal portion and 570–660 on the mathematics portion. Advanced Placement tests, which are graded on a scale of 1 (low) to 5 (high), were taken by 91 students in the class of 2004. Twenty-fix percent of the students scored a 5 and 74 percent achieved a score of 3 or better.

The diversity of the student body leads naturally to diverse choices for college. The class of 2005 had 79 graduating seniors. Of those attending colleges and universities, the majority elected liberal arts programs, but a small number selected specialized curricula—fine arts, architecture, engineering, and business. The largest numbers of graduates are attending the following schools: Cornell, Duke, Hamilton, Mount Holyoke, New York University, the University of Chicago, and Yale.

STUDENT BODY AND CONDUCT

In 2005–06, the student distribution by grade was as follows: grade 9, 69; grade 10, 73; grade 11, 92; and grade 12, 74. The current total of 308 students includes 203 boarding students and 105 day students from thirty states and thirteen countries.

The goal of developing self-discipline and concern for others underlies student conduct rules. Each girl is expected to understand the School rules and to agree to abide by them. An important facet of the School's structure is the student government. The Student Council serves as the judiciary board in cases of rule infractions. When rules are broken, judicial decisions are made by the council, subject to review by the Head of School.

ACADEMIC FACILITIES

Classes are held in eight buildings. History and English classes meet in the Hamilton Building. The Ann Whitney Olin Center for the Arts and Sciences centralizes academic life on campus. It houses classrooms with state-of-the-art equipment and technology for the instruction of math, science, and computer technology. Art studios for photography, painting, sculpture, printmaking, and jewelry making and a computer lab for graphic

design are also located in Olin. Theater, dance, and drama classes convene in the modern theater/gymnasium complex. Dance classes are held in the recently renovated Dance Barn. The new library opened in spring 2001. This facility has a collection of more than 20,000 volumes, extensive holdings or journals on microfilm and microfiche, and online database searching. Interlibrary loan networking supports the research curriculum. The Leila Dilworth Jones memorial has been renovated and holds a state-of-the-art language laboratory and classrooms for foreign language instruction. In fall 2003, newly resurfaced Deco Turf tennis courts were completed.

BOARDING AND GENERAL FACILITIES
Nine dormitories, most of which were formerly private homes, are supervised by House Directors, usually young couples with children. In seven of the dormitories, students from grades 9 through 11 live together; one dormitory is reserved for ninth graders, two are reserved for seniors.

The recently renovated dining room and administrative offices are located in Main (1830), a brick building with white columns, which also has a student center and snack bar. Behind it is the bookstore. The Student Health Center is staffed by registered nurses. A physician makes regular visits and is on call 24 hours a day, seven days a week.

ATHLETICS
The School believes in maintaining a healthy balance between intellectual activity and physical exercise; each student participates daily in organized sports. Tennis, crew, basketball, field hockey, soccer, lacrosse, volleyball, softball, skiing, paddle tennis, squash, cross-country, badminton, swimming, riding, aerobics, and dance workshop are offered. An extensive number of playing fields and courts, including seven DecoTurf tennis courts and squash courts, are available. An athletics/recreation center contains two gyms, an indoor track, three squash courts, a weight room, and basketball and volleyball courts. Girls who are interested in riding use a nearby stable. There is a full schedule of interscholastic and intramural sports.

EXTRACURRICULAR OPPORTUNITIES
Endowments bring concerts, speakers, drama productions, and poets to the campus. There are many weekend activities both on and off campus. Membership in campus clubs is open to any student who wishes to participate; most students belong to at least one extracurricular group. Among the organizations are *Salmagundy* (School newspaper); *Daeges Eage* (yearbook); *Chautauqua* (expository writing); *Haggis Baggis* (creative writing); French, Spanish, Archives (School history), and Glee clubs; Debate Team; Concordia (social service); Stagecrafters and Players (drama); and *Watu Wazuri* (multicultural organization). Students also operate their own radio station, which broadcasts to the School community. Special reviews written and produced by students are staged three times a year. Annually held events include Parents' Weekend, Winter Musical, Grandparents' Day, special dance weekends, and Graduation Weekend.

DAILY LIFE
Classes, held Monday through Friday, begin at 7:45 a.m., following breakfast. Each class is 50 minutes long. Lunch is served from 11:30 to 1:30. Sports begin at 3:45. In addition to the interscholastic sports program, there are daily sports periods. Morning meetings are held two times a week, and periodically the entire school community gathers for assemblies and convocation. Club meetings take place before or after the 5:30 p.m. dinner hour. Study hours begin at 7:30 and end at 9:30 p.m. Students may study in the dormitories, in the library, or in monitored study halls.

WEEKEND LIFE
During "closed" weekends, students remain on campus, except for day trips, and a variety of activities are offered, ranging from dances, movies, and trips to plays, special dinners, and concerts. On open weekends, girls may, with permission from home, leave school for the weekend, but many girls remain at school and participate in the wide variety of scheduled and other events. Day students are encouraged to take part in all weekend events. About half of a semester's weekends are open.

Coeducational events, including some drama productions, are held frequently, with students invited from schools throughout New England; in return, MPS girls visit other schools for events.

On weekends, girls are encouraged to attend one of the churches or synagogues in the village of Farmington or local communities.

COSTS AND FINANCIAL AID
The cost of tuition, room, and board in 2005–06 is $35,050. Day student tuition is $26,625. A health center fee and an activities fee are additional charges for both day students and boarders. Books, athletic uniforms, and private music, skiing, and riding lessons are extra.

For the 2004–05 school year, financial aid totaling $2.3 million was awarded to 35 percent of the students. Financial aid is given on the basis of need, as demonstrated by the School and Student Service form, available from the MPS admission office. In addition, the admission office requires a copy of the family's most recent federal income tax form 1040 as well as W-2 wage statements. Financial aid decisions are announced at the time of the admission decisions and are renewable each year if the student demonstrates continued need and meets academic and conduct standards.

ADMISSIONS INFORMATION
Admission is based on school records, aptitude and achievement, character, citizenship, and potential. A personal interview on campus is required. The Secondary School Admission Test (SSAT) should be taken in November, December, or January preceding the September in which a student wishes to enter. International students must also take the TOEFL if English is not their first language. Students apply for entrance in grade 9, 10, or 11. The School encourages able students to apply, without regard to race, color, creed, national or ethnic origin, or socioeconomic background.

APPLICATION TIMETABLE
Applicants are urged to contact the admission office to arrange for a tour, a visit to class, and an interview. The office is open Monday through Friday from 8:30 to 4:30, with the last campus tour at 2:25. Most interviews and tours take place in the fall, but they may be scheduled up to January 31. The application, including recommendations, SSAT scores, and a $50 nonrefundable fee, must be completed by January 15. Candidates are notified by March 10 of the admission committee's decision, and parents must reply by April 10. If openings are available after April 10, interested families are encouraged to complete the application process.

ADMISSIONS CORRESPONDENCE
Deborah W. Haskins
Office of Admission
Miss Porter's School
Farmington, Connecticut 06032

Phone: 860-409-3530 (admission)
860-409-3500 (general)
Fax: 860-409-3531
E-mail: admissions@missporters.org
Web site: http://www.missporters.org

MONTCLAIR COLLEGE PREPARATORY SCHOOL

Van Nuys, California

Type: Coeducational boarding and day college-preparatory school
Grades: 6–12: Lower School, 6–8; Upper School, 9–12
Enrollment: School total: 500; Upper School: 350
Head of School: Dr. Vernon E. Simpson, Director

THE SCHOOL

Montclair College Preparatory School is the oldest independent coeducational school in the San Fernando Valley. The School is divided into an Upper School (grades 9–12) and a Lower School (grades 6, 7, and 8), which share the same campus. It is conveniently located near the Roscoe exit of the San Diego freeway.

Montclair was founded in 1956 by Dr. Vernon E. Simpson, currently the Director of the School and Headmaster. The School was established to provide solid academic training to prepare students to enter college or university. Limited boarding facilities are available.

A nonprofit organization, Montclair is governed by a Board of Directors and faculty academic advisement and standards committees that work together to maintain the high caliber of academics and to provide appropriate social, athletic, and cultural outlets for the student body.

Montclair College Preparatory School is fully accredited by the Western Association of Schools and Colleges and is a member of the California Scholarship Federation, the College Board, the National Association of Secondary School Principals, and the National Honor Society.

ACADEMIC PROGRAMS

Requirements for graduation include 4 years of English (including a full year of senior composition); 3 years of a foreign language; 2 years of laboratory sciences (beginning in the tenth grade); 3 years of math; 1 year of computer science, U.S. history, and government; and 1 year of fine arts. Elective courses complete the 21-unit total.

Montclair also offers strong Advanced Placement courses. Recent students have achieved scores of 3 or better on the Advanced Placement Program tests in English, French language, Spanish language, American history, economics (microeconomics and macroeconomics), biology, chemistry, physics, calculus, and computer science.

The Upper School offers many electives, such as computer science, economics, statistics, humanities, drama, and art. All students are required to take physical education, and many participate in the athletics program.

FACULTY AND ADVISERS

Faculty members are selected for their commitment to strong academic instruction as well as their superior academic backgrounds and personal enthusiasm for the School. In addition to teaching, they act as class advisers, coaches, and club sponsors. There are 40 full-time and 8 part-time instructors. Faculty members hold forty-two baccalaureate degrees, twenty-eight master's degrees, and two doctoral degrees. Faculty members belong to a number of professional associations.

Dr. Vernon E. Simpson, the founder and Director of the School, earned his bachelor's and doctoral degrees from USC and his master's degree from California State University, Northridge.

COLLEGE PLACEMENT

College counseling begins in the tenth-grade guidance classes and continues in the junior year with a College Counseling Night for parents and students. At this meeting, all aspects of college entrance are discussed, including application procedures, requirements, and the differences among schools. Dr. Simpson, who has had more than thirty years of experience in this area, personally advises all juniors and seniors on each step of the admission process. The counseling office maintains a file of college catalogs from every major college in the country and provides application forms and scholarship applications.

During the senior year, field trips are taken to both public and private colleges and universities. College representatives are also invited to speak on the campus to interested students.

Recent Montclair graduates have been admitted to Amherst, Brown, Colgate, Harvard, MIT, Oxford, Princeton, Stanford, Swarthmore, USC, Wellesley, and Yale as well as to all campuses of the University of California and California State University.

STUDENT BODY AND CONDUCT

Student government activities are held frequently. There are class officers as well as Associated Student Body officers. The Student Council meets weekly and sets the pace of outside student activities. A Student Court also convenes regularly.

ACADEMIC FACILITIES

The 5-acre campus includes the main classroom building, erected in 1970. There are thirty-three classrooms, including four science laboratories. In 1975, the Leslie H. Green Auditorium was constructed. It serves as both auditorium and gymnasium and is used for drama and theatrical productions. The library contains 7,500 volumes and subscribes to 20 periodicals. The Annex, across the street from the main campus, contains three classrooms, an amphitheater, a computer science laboratory, an art studio, and a multimedia center. Nine classrooms were added in 1990 and an additional two in 2002.

ATHLETICS

Montclair is a competitive school, both in academics and in athletics. The sports program emphasizes fair play and sportsmanship. The coaching staff stresses skills and teamwork rather than individual performance. All students in grades 6 through 9 are required to participate in

daily physical education classes. Students in grades 11 and 12 are encouraged to participate in extracurricular sports.

Coeducational sports are tennis, track, and volleyball. Girls' teams are available in basketball, soccer, softball, and volleyball. Boys' teams are fielded in baseball, basketball, football, and soccer. Montclair also fields teams in golf.

Athletics facilities include a fully equipped gym, constructed in 1975. The building houses offices for the athletics directors, locker rooms, and a weight-training room. The campus includes a recreational field for physical education and team practice; regular games are held at local public school facilities.

The School is a member of the California Interscholastic Federation (CIF). The football team won the league championship for seven of the last eleven years and was CIF champion in 1990. The basketball team won the league championship for six of the last twelve years and was State Division V champion in 1995. The baseball team won the league championship for nine of the past several years and won the CIF championship in 1979, 1981, 1982, 1983, 1990, 1991, and 1992.

EXTRACURRICULAR OPPORTUNITIES

Life at Montclair is varied and energetic. An active drama club stages several productions each year. There are cheerleading squads and a pep squad. A newspaper is published by the journalism class, and another group assembles the yearbook. There are campus clubs in science, languages, and photography. A Ski Club conducts trips to nearby resorts on weekends and during the semester break.

Montclair provides a well-balanced social program. Major social events include Homecoming, Spirit Week, and the Junior-Senior Prom. Other social events are held by each grade level under the guidance of the administration.

DAILY LIFE

Classes begin at 8:15 a.m. There are three periods of instruction prior to a 15-minute nutrition break at 10:35. Three more periods of instruction follow before the 1 p.m. lunch break. The cocurricular classes then begin, and all students have an elective or study hall or participate in sports from 1:35 until dismissal at 2:30.

SUMMER PROGRAMS

A six-week summer program offers remedial and review work in English, math, study skills, and languages. Interested students from any school may enroll. The summer school runs from early July to mid-August. The School also sponsors a summer course in marine biology. Summer camps are available for students who are interested in football, baseball, and basketball. Further information may be obtained from the

Director of Athletics at the School address. The cost of the 2005 summer school program is $1000. The price of the summer athletics camps varies from sport to sport.

COSTS AND FINANCIAL AID
Tuition for the 2005–06 school year was $13,500 (grade 6, $11,000). Textbooks and tuition insurance were an additional $800 per year. A deposit is required upon acceptance of admission. The balance may be paid in one or two payments (due September 1 and January 1) or on a monthly basis.

A limited amount of financial aid is available and is awarded on the basis of need.

ADMISSIONS INFORMATION
The admissions process is designed to identify students who are of above-average ability and are academically motivated. A 3-hour in-house entrance exam or the ISEE is required. In addition, applicants must provide one personal reference, two teacher references, and a transcript. All factors are considered before a student is accepted. Students are not normally accepted above the tenth grade.

APPLICATION TIMETABLE
Inquiries are welcome at any time. Application forms are sent on request, and, after the completed form and a $100 application fee are received, the applicant is advised of the date for the entrance examination. Each decision concerning admission is made after the applicant has submitted all the necessary forms and taken the entrance exam. Interested students are advised to apply before April 1 if they wish to enter the School the following September.

ADMISSIONS CORRESPONDENCE
Director of Admissions
Montclair College Preparatory School
8071 Sepulveda Boulevard
Van Nuys, California 91402

Phone: 818-787-5290
Fax: 818-786-3382
Web site: http://www.montclairprep.net

MONTE VISTA CHRISTIAN SCHOOL
Watsonville, California

Type: Coeducational boarding and day secondary- and college-preparatory school
Grades: 6–12: Middle School, 6–8; High School, 9–12
Enrollment: School total: 861; Middle School: 191; High School: 670 (Boarding: 98)

THE SCHOOL

Monte Vista Christian School (MV) has a strong history, having begun as a small boarding school in 1926. The long and rich tradition developed over the years has been instrumental in its steady growth in enrollment. Growth occurs through relationships, and Monte Vista desires that each student have a caring and trusting relationship with peers, teachers, parents, and, most importantly, a personal and growing relationship with Jesus Christ.

Situated in the heart of the beautiful Monterey Bay area of California, the spacious and picturesque campus is nestled in the foothills of the Santa Cruz Mountains. The campus occupies 100 acres of rolling lawns, ponds, playing fields, equestrian facilities, and more than twenty-seven buildings. The campus provides the student with plenty of room to breathe and offers a variety of physical activities that take education beyond the classroom, making it a stimulating, enjoyable part of everyday living. The media–science center provides the atmosphere for discovery and learning, with its large, ever-expanding library, language lab, and fully equipped chemistry and biology laboratories. The administration/classroom buildings contain classrooms, the campus store, offices, and the guidance and career center. The gymnasium complex of two gymnasiums, large weight/exercise facility, pool, and spa is utilized for interscholastic athletics and physical education. In addition, weekly chapel services, occasional concerts, parties, and banquets are held in the facility. Other facilities include an outdoor amphitheater, art laboratory, a tack room and horse barns adjacent to the Western and English horse arenas, an industrial arts shop, drama building, and the boys' and girls' dormitories. The campus has a quiet country atmosphere that encourages contemplation, study, and proper physical development away from the congestion and distractions of urban life.

Monte Vista is a nonprofit organization governed by a 10-member Board of Trustees. Alumni, parents, parents of former students, and friends generously support the various building projects and scholarship programs. The surrounding area is primarily rural. It is situated 25 miles north of Monterey, 15 miles south of Santa Cruz, 40 miles south of San Jose, and 75 miles south of San Francisco. Monte Vista is accredited by the Western Association of Schools and Colleges and the Association of Christian Schools International and offers all state-required courses and a curriculum that meets all college entrance requirements.

ACADEMIC PROGRAMS

The curriculum at Monte Vista encompasses a range of courses designed not only to prepare students for entrance to higher institutions, but also to introduce them to the cultural, scientific, and business enterprises available in the future. Students taking the college-preparatory course follow the specific requirements of the college of their choice or that of a state university in California. Students who plan to complete their secondary classroom education at the end of the twelfth year are encouraged to explore career opportunities that provide further training and placement commensurate with their interests and abilities. It is an objective of the School to provide sufficient educational opportunities to enable students to obtain the basic requirements essential to prepare them for entry employment in their selected areas of specialization. Electives are provided in several areas of specialization, and the curriculum may be arranged to meet the needs of the individual pupil. Integrated with the academic program is a course in biblical studies relating the content and principles of the Bible to each area of human understanding with application to every area of life.

Monte Vista provides a comprehensive academic program with a college-preparatory emphasis designed to challenge and equip students pursuing university entrance. Advanced Placement courses are available in American government, calculus, chemistry, computer science, English, European history, physics, Spanish, statistics, and U.S. history. Electives are provided in the areas of French, German, Japanese, psychology, Web design, computer-aided drafting and design, auto/metal fabrication, art, sculpture, yearbook, music appreciation, voice technique, choir, ensemble, guitar, band, cheerleading, drama, horsemanship, industrial arts, and culinary arts. Class size ranges from 10 to 26 students and averages 21 students in mainstream classes and 7–10 in ESL classes. The student-faculty ratio is 17:1. Approximately 33 percent of the faculty members live on or near campus.

The ESL program is designed for students who need one year of ESL. The ESL course offers listening/speaking and reading/writing course work combined with a mainstream math course, earth science, and Bible choir, band, drama, or ESL Bible. ESL students mainstream in their second year at MV and possess a sufficient level of acquisition and course work to complete the requirements for a high school diploma. Many students proceed to study at four-year universities.

Grade reports are issued every eight weeks. Academic grade reports are available upon request to parents and students. Students are given both letter grades (A-F) and conduct and citizenship grades (O, S, N, U). Coded teacher comments are also included in the report.

FACULTY AND ADVISERS

Of the 68 full-time faculty members currently employed at the combined Middle School and High School campuses, 55 teach at the High School. Fifteen of the High School faculty and administrative staff members have advanced degrees.

COLLEGE PLACEMENT

College counseling is handled through the Resident Student Academic Advisor. In addition to the guidance calendar published and mailed to all parents and sponsors throughout the year, the Resident Student Academic Advisor handles counseling for university- or college-bound students. The School hosts between 30 and 40 college and university admissions representatives every school year and holds college fairs and preparatory classes for the SAT/ACT placement tests. From the class of 2004, 85 percent of the students indicated they were going to attend college.

In the past, students have enrolled at Boston University; California State Polytechnic, Pomona; California State, San Francisco, San Jose, and San Luis Obispo; Case Western Reserve; Michigan State; Northeastern; NYU, Pepperdine; Rensselaer; Saint Mary's College; Santa Clara; Seaver; Syracuse; the United States Military Academy at West Point; West-mont College; Woodbury; and the University of California at Berkeley, Davis, Los Angeles, Riverside, San Diego, and Santa Barbara; and the Universities of Illinois, Indiana, Ohio, Pennsylvania, San Francisco, and Southern California.

STUDENT BODY AND CONDUCT

Monte Vista has been educating students from around the world for almost seventy-eight years. In 2005–06 there were nine locations represented: China, Hong Kong, Indonesia, Japan, Korea, Panama, Taiwan, the United States, and Vietnam. There were 670 students enrolled in the High School, as follows: 169 in grade 9, 167 in grade 10, 186 in grade 11, and 148 in grade 12. Monte Vista can accommodate an equal number of boys and girls, and traditionally, there has been an even split between the sexes.

Monte Vista's concern for all aspects of a student's life, for character as well as intellect, is reflected in the words of D. L. Moody when he said, "Develop the head, the heart, and the hand. If one of these must be more important, let it be the heart that distinguishes education here." Monte Vista has been established with a firm commitment to God and the unfolding of His master plan for the universe. Discovery of the presence of Divine order and design in every aspect of creation leads to the recognition that God has established a meaning and purpose for life. Monte Vista challenges each student to a personal confrontation with the commitment to Jesus Christ.

Students are expected to observe high standards of good conduct, to have respect for the property of others, and to comply with the regulations of Monte Vista Christian School. The student body prides itself on good sportsmanship, good morals, friendliness, and good manners at all times. By virtue of enrollment at Monte Vista, students agree to live within the framework of the School's standards of conduct.

ACADEMIC FACILITIES

The Middle School consists of fourteen classrooms, including a new academic building, and the main office. The library, industrial arts, and gymnasium are shared with the High School. The Middle School program is enriched with a laptop computer–based program in all course work and a fully equipped computer lab.

The High School facilities consist of forty-five fully equipped classrooms (video), a computer laboratory equipped with thirty state-of-the-art computers, a fully equipped chemistry and biology laboratory, a media center/tutoring center, an amphitheater, a gymnasium, and a workout room. Computer stations located in the library and both dormitories provide Internet access for research and e-mail.

BOARDING AND GENERAL FACILITIES

The High School offers boarding facilities for 56 boys and 50 girls. Monte Vista is set on 100 acres in a country atmosphere. In addition to the facilities mentioned above, there are trails for horseback riding, a hot tub available at the pool, large televisions in both dormitories, basketball courts, walkways for in-line skating, and acres of playing fields.

There are two dormitories, one for girls and one for boys, each of which also houses the Head Deans' apartments. The boys' dormitory consists of rooms housing 2 boys. Each boy has a bed, desk, and closet with drawers inside. Newly renovated shower and

restroom facilities are located within the dorm. Additional rooms include the laundry, two TV rooms, table tennis/pool table recreation rooms, study hall room, and an interior patio. The boys' dormitory has recently been renovated with the addition of a lobby with a fireplace, a home entertainment system, an Internet café, and a kitchen.

The girls' dormitory consists of two girls per room, sharing one vanity with sink. Four girls share the shower and restroom. The girls' dorm provides a large fellowship room with a fireplace, large-screen TV, piano, study tables, and couches. The dorm also has kitchen facilities, a reference library, computers, dorm office, laundry facility, and telephones. Both boys and girls may bring bikes to school for their personal use. Students eat their meals together in the dining hall, located nearby.

ATHLETICS
Teams compete interscholastically in baseball, basketball, cross-country, diving, equestrian, football, golf, soccer, softball, swimming, tennis, track, volleyball, and wrestling events. Noncompetitive offerings include aerobics, sandpit volleyball, skiing, surfing, and weight training.

EXTRACURRICULAR OPPORTUNITIES
Students participate in band, guitar, art, drama, culinary arts, textile arts, choir, ensemble, flag girls, and cheerleading. The various clubs represented on campus include Christian Service, French, Spanish, chess, surfing, golf, bowling, Club Med (for students interested in a medical career), horsemanship, international, and Interact (offers students opportunities to do community service projects), National Honor Society, and California Scholarship Federation. The music program offers beginning and advanced choirs, ensemble, voice technique, and master's voice.

DAILY LIFE
Wake-up is at 6:30, with breakfast at 7. Dorm rooms are to be cleaned prior to leaving for school each day. School begins at 8:20 and ends at 3:10. Sports practices are offered between 3:30 and 5. Students may make arrangements with the dean to go to town during afternoon hours. Dinner is served in the din-

ing hall at 5:30. Evening study hall is held from 6:30 to 8:30. Lights out is at 10:30 on weeknights, 11 on Saturday, and 10:30 on Sunday.

WEEKEND LIFE
Weekends give students additional opportunities to explore the broad range of activities on campus or activities planned by the boarding staff. Activities on campus may include baseball, biking, football, in-line skating, sandpit volleyball, soccer, swimming, tennis, track, and volleyball. Activities planned by the boarding staff are rock climbing, the aquarium in Monterey, Santa Cruz boardwalk, Great America, Wild Waters, hiking, miniature golf, Malibu Grand Prix (mini car racing), beach trips, ice skating, plays, football games, and shopping.

All boarding students participate in a three-day fall weekend trip to Yosemite. In the winter, they enjoy skiing and snowboarding in the Lake Tahoe area.

With permission from parents or sponsors, students may leave campus on weekends, provided it does not interfere with school-related commitments.

SUMMER PROGRAMS
Monte Vista campus is as busy in the summer months as it is during the academic year. A six-week ESL summer language program is offered in the summer. This program provides intensive training in spoken English and pronunciation, listening comprehension, reading and writing, grammar, and vocabulary for high school students at both beginning and intermediate levels of English proficiency. There are seven weeks of equestrian camps offered in July and August that include a vaulting camp, rodeo camp, and pack and trail camp. A summer school program is offered at the High School level as needed. Students should contact admissions for summer offerings.

COSTS AND FINANCIAL AID
The cost of tuition, room, and seven-day boarding for the 2006–07 academic year is $28,000 for domestic students and $31,000 for international students requiring a SEVIS I-20. This includes tuition fees, room and board, textbooks, transportation by MV

(local and airport), cultural trips, ski trips, Bay Area fun trips, PE clothing, and athletic and class fees. Fees for F1 international students also include insurance. An additional fee of $2000 is charged for students needing ESL. Limited financial aid is available to resident students.

ADMISSIONS INFORMATION
Monte Vista seeks to serve students who are committed to their personal, social, spiritual, and academic growth. Parents, sponsors, or students should contact the Resident Admissions Office to obtain an application packet. Applications may also be downloaded from the School's Web site.

The following items are taken into consideration before an admissions decision is made: a complete application; academic transcripts; SSAT or other nationally recognized test results; TOEFL or SLEP score (international students); teacher, personal, and pastoral recommendations; autobiography; and personal interview (if possible). All international resident students must have a sponsor in the U.S., preferably within the San Francisco Bay Area of California. A student is evaluated as a whole person. Grades, personal goals, past performance, maturity, and desire to attend Monte Vista are considered.

Monte Vista does not discriminate on the basis of sex, race, color, creed, or national or ethnic origin. It strives to create and maintain a geographically and ethnically diverse student body.

APPLICATION TIMETABLE
Applicants should submit applications as early as January prior to the academic year they wish to attend. There is a rolling admissions policy on a space-available basis. The School prefers not to accept students after the first midquarter in the fall.

ADMISSIONS CORRESPONDENCE
Resident Admissions
Monte Vista Christian School
Two School Way
Watsonville, California 95076

Phone: 831-722-8178 Ext. 128
Fax: 831-722-6003
E-mail: admissions@mvcs.org
Web site: http://www.mvcs.org

MORAVIAN ACADEMY

Bethlehem, Pennsylvania

Type: Day college-preparatory school
Grades: PK–12: Lower School, Prekindergarten–5; Middle School, 6–8; Upper School, 9–12
Enrollment: School total: 790; Upper School: 284
Head of School: Barnaby J. Roberts, Headmaster

THE SCHOOL

Moravian Academy traces its origin back to 1742 and the Moravians who settled Bethlehem. Guided by the wisdom of John Amos Comenius, Moravian bishop and renowned educator, the Moravian Church established schools in every community in which it settled. Moravian Academy became incorporated in 1971 when Moravian Seminary for Girls and Moravian Preparatory School were merged. The school has two campuses: the Lower–Middle School campus in the historic downtown area of Bethlehem and the Upper School campus on a 120-acre estate 6 miles to the east. The school is within minutes of three major hospitals, and medical services are easily available.

For more than 250 years, Moravian Academy has encouraged sound innovations to meet contemporary challenges while recognizing the permanence of basic human values. The school seeks to promote young people's full development in mind, body, and spirit by fostering a love for learning, respect for others, joy in participation and service, and skill in decision making. Preparation for college occurs in an atmosphere characterized by an appreciation for the individual.

Moravian Academy is governed by a Board of Trustees. Six members are representatives of the Moravian Church. The school is valued at $25.3 million, of which $10.5 million is endowment. Annual Giving in 2004–05 was $440,302, and the operating expenses for that year were $10.8 million.

Moravian Academy is accredited by the Middle States Association of Colleges and Schools and the Pennsylvania Association of Private Academic Schools and is approved to issue I-20 forms for international students. The School is a member of the National Association of Independent Schools, the Association of Delaware Valley Independent Schools, the Independent School Teachers' Association of Philadelphia and Vicinity, the College Board, the Council for Spiritual and Ethical Education, the School and Student Service for Financial Aid, and the Secondary School Admission Test Board.

Moravian Academy does not discriminate on the basis of race, nationality, sex, sexual orientation, religious affiliation, or ethnic origin in the administration of its educational and admission policies, financial aid awards, and athletic or other school-administered programs. Applicants who are disabled (or applicants' family members who are disabled) requiring any type of accommodation during the application process, or at any other time, are encouraged to identify themselves and indicate what type of accommodation is needed.

ACADEMIC PROGRAMS

Students are required to carry five major courses per year. Minimum graduation requirements include English, 4 credits; mathematics, 3 credits; lab sciences, 3 credits; foreign language, 3 credits; social studies, 3 credits; fine arts, 1 credit; and physical education and health. All students must successfully complete a semester course in world religions or ethics. Community service is an integral part of the curriculum. Electives are offered in many areas, such as drama, advanced chemistry, calculus, economics, law, art, history, and Japanese language. Advanced Placement, honors, and independent study are available. The Academy also participates in a high school scholars program that enables highly qualified students to take college courses at no cost. The overall student-faculty ratio is about 9:1. Classes range from 10 to 18 students, and grouping occurs only as a result of individual programming.

Supervised study halls are held regularly during the school day. Grades in most courses are A–F; D is a passing grade. However, a C- is required to advance to the next level. Reports are sent to parents, and parent-conference opportunities are scheduled in the fall semester. Faculty and staff members are available for additional conferences whenever necessary. Examinations are held at the end of each seventeen-week semester in all major subjects. In the senior year, final examinations are given in May to allow seniors time for a two-week Post Term Experience before graduation.

FACULTY AND ADVISERS

The Upper School has 35 full-time and 6 part-time faculty members. Eighty-three percent of the full-time Upper School faculty members have advanced degrees. Several faculty members have degrees in counseling in addition to other subjects, and the entire faculty shares in counseling through the Faculty Advisor Program.

Barnaby J. Roberts was appointed Headmaster in 1998. He previously served as the head of Casady School in Oklahoma City, Oklahoma, and of Chestnut Hill Academy in Philadelphia, Pennsylvania. Mr. Roberts received his B.A. and M.A. from Cambridge University and his Diploma in Education from Oxford University.

COLLEGE PLACEMENT

The Director of Academic Counseling begins group work in college guidance in the eleventh grade. Tenth graders take the PSAT as practice and repeat it the following year. College Night is held annually for juniors and their parents. Juniors meet weekly in small groups for college counseling during the second semester and have an individual family conference in the spring. They take the PSAT, SAT Reasoning Test, and SAT Subject Tests. Seniors meet twice weekly in small groups during the first semester for additional guidance and are guided through the college application process. They take the SAT Reasoning Test and Subject Tests again, if necessary.

Mean SAT I scores of 2005 graduates were 670 verbal and 670 math. Graduates of 2005 are attending Carnegie Mellon, Columbia, Drexel, Lehigh, NYU, Princeton, Stanford, and the University of Pennsylvania. Some students participate in travel abroad or Rotary international exchange programs before attending college.

STUDENT BODY AND CONDUCT

The Upper School in 2005–06 had 138 boys and 146 girls. Since 1742, Moravians have understood the value of diversity in the educational setting. In all divisions, students and faculty members from a variety of ethnic, cultural, religious, and socioeconomic backgrounds carry on this commitment. Through classroom activities, nondenominational chapel services discussing many faiths, and active engagement with each other, students at Moravian Academy are encouraged to appreciate one another's individuality.

Students enjoy the small classes and the opportunity for participation in sports and other activities. Students are expected to wear clothing that is neat and appropriate for school. Denim is not permitted during the school day, and a school uniform is required for members of performing groups. Students participate actively in a Student Council. Serious matters of discipline come before a faculty-student discipline committee.

ACADEMIC FACILITIES

Snyder House, Walter Hall, and Heath Science Complex hold the classrooms, studios, and laboratories (chemistry, physics, biology, and computer). All of the library's resources are integrated with the instructional program to intensify and individualize the educational experience. The Richard and Lorraine Fuisz Library contains 8,500 volumes and fifty-two periodicals and features an enhanced CD-ROM reference center network that supports a strong interlibrary loan program. Internet access is also available in the library. There are dedicated computer labs, additional computers in the library, a portable wireless lab, and a computer in every classroom. SMARTboards are used in all divisions to enhance the learning process. The Couch Fine Arts Center houses the studio arts department. A 350-seat auditorium enhances the music and theater programs. There are seven colleges in the area.

ATHLETICS

A strong athletics program meets the guidelines of the school's philosophy that a person must be nurtured in body, as well as in mind and spirit, and that respect for others and participation are important goals. A large gymnasium, four athletics fields, and six tennis courts provide the school with facilities for varsity and junior varsity teams in boys' lacrosse and girls' field hockey; boys' and girls' basketball, cross-country, soccer, and tennis; coeducational golf; and a girls' varsity team in softball. A gymnasium that includes a weight room complements the physical education facilities in Walter Hall. An outdoor recreational pool is available for special student functions as well as the Academy's summer day camp program for younger children.

All students have the chance to take part in team sports—and many of them do. In any given athletic season, more than one third of the Upper School student body participate in after-school athletics at the Academy.

There are golf courses in the Lehigh Valley as well as an indoor rock-climbing facility, a bicycle velodrome, and indoor stables. Many students belong to a ski club during the winter.

EXTRACURRICULAR OPPORTUNITIES

Moravian Academy's activity program provides opportunities for varied interests and talents. Included are service projects, outdoor education, International Club, *Legacy* (yearbook), the newspaper, Model Congress, Model UN, PJAS, Scholastic Scrimmage, and a variety of activities that change in response to student interests. A fine arts series combines music, art, drama, and dance. The annual Country Fair gives students an opportunity to work with the Parents' Association to create a family fun day for the school and Lehigh Valley community. Rooted in Moravian tradition, a strong appreciation of music has continued. There are several student musical groups including chorale, MA Chamber Singers, and instrumental ensembles. A highlight of the year is the Christmas Vespers Service.

DAILY LIFE

A typical school day begins at 8 a.m., and classes run until 3:15 p.m. on Monday, Tuesday, Wednesday, and Friday. On Thursday, classes conclude at 2:45. The average length of class periods is about 40 minutes. Students usually take six classes a day.

A weekly nondenominational chapel service is held on Thursday mornings. On Monday, Tuesday, Wednesday, and Friday there is a period for class and school meetings.

COSTS AND FINANCIAL AID

Tuition is $16,510. There is an additional dining fee for students. An initial deposit of $1000 is required upon acceptance, and the remainder of the fee is to be paid in two installments, unless other arrangements are made. An additional fee for tuition insurance is recommended for all new students.

Financial aid is available, and the school uses the recommendation of the School and Student Service for Financial Aid. Once a student has been accepted for admission, aid is determined and renewed or awarded on the basis of demonstrated financial need. Aid is received by approximately 17 percent of Upper School students.

ADMISSIONS INFORMATION

Students are admitted in grades 9–11. Each applicant is carefully considered. Students who demonstrate an ability and willingness to handle a rigorous academic program, as well as such qualities as intellectual curiosity, responsibility, creativity and cooperation, are encouraged to apply. Scores on tests administered by the school are also used in the admission process. In addition, school records, recommendations, and a personal interview are required. Admissions are usually completed by May, but there are sometimes openings available after that time.

APPLICATION TIMETABLE

Inquiries are welcome at any time. The Admission Office makes arrangements for tours and classroom visits during the school week. If necessary, other arrangements for tours can be made. The application fee is $65. Test dates are scheduled on specified Saturday mornings from January through March. Notifications are sent after February 15, and families are asked to respond within two weeks.

ADMISSIONS CORRESPONDENCE

Suzanne H. Mason
Director of Admissions, Upper School
Moravian Academy
4313 Green Pond Road
Bethlehem, Pennsylvania 18020
Phone: 610-691-1600

MORRISTOWN–BEARD SCHOOL

Morristown, New Jersey

Type: Coeducational day college-preparatory school
Grades: 6–12
Enrollment: School total: 490; Upper School: 368
Head of School: Dr. Alex D. Curtis

THE SCHOOL

The Morristown-Beard School (MBS) was established in 1971 by the merger of the Morristown School (for boys) and the Beard School (for girls), both of which were founded in 1891. Three Harvard University graduates founded the Morristown School as a preparatory school for their alma mater. While the Beard School originated as a kindergarten, it continued to add grade levels and courses for girls who wanted to attend college. In 1903, the first graduate of the Beard School matriculated to Vassar College, thus establishing a standard for future graduates.

The Morristown-Beard School is located in Morristown, a historic town in northern New Jersey. Its location 25 miles west of New York City allows frequent field trips to experience the cultural and educational benefits of Manhattan. Situated on a 22-acre campus of rolling lawns and shady trees, the pristine campus reflects the heritage and beauty befitting a school on the National Registry of Historic Places.

The purpose of the School as an academic institution is to challenge and support a range of learners, with a particular emphasis on preparation for rigorous college study. The School's goal is to guide students to appreciate the life of the mind and to become creative, thoughtful, and caring individuals who possess a sense of awareness of and a responsibility for the needs, concerns, and dignity of others.

A 22-member Board of Trustees governs the School. The School endowment is more than $6 million.

Morristown-Beard School is accredited by the Middle States Association of Colleges and Schools and approved by the New Jersey State Department of Education. It is affiliated with the National Association of Independent Schools, the New Jersey Association of Independent Schools, the Educational Records Bureau, the Advanced Placement Program of the College Board, the Council for Advancement and Support of Education, the School Consortium of New Jersey, the National Association of Principals of Schools for Girls, and the National Association of College Admission Counselors.

ACADEMIC PROGRAMS

The academic year is divided into two 16-week terms. Communication is very important, so teachers send frequent reports to parents. Full grade and comment reports are provided at the end of each 8-week period, and interim reports are provided at the middle of each quarter, with additional progress reports sent as needed. Parent/adviser conferences are held twice annually. A letter grading system is used.

The Middle School (grades 6–8) is housed in one building, where an interdisciplinary approach to academics is accompanied by individual attention and an emphasis on character

building. In addition, Middle School students enjoy numerous sports and extracurricular activities that are designed to supplement and enhance the classroom experience. The major objectives in the Middle School are teaching students how to learn, challenge themselves, and appreciate an environment that is supportive of others. The Middle School core curriculum includes language arts, social studies, math, science, and world languages. Reading for challenge and enrichment is emphasized, and technology is incorporated into teaching strategies.

The Upper School daily schedule is a modified block schedule, whereby each class meets three times per week for extended periods. Extra help is readily available and is integrated into the daily schedule. In each subject, students are placed in one of three academic levels according to their aptitude and achievement. Staff learning specialists are available to provide assistance.

To graduate from the Upper School, students must complete a minimum of 4 years of English; 3 years each of history, science, mathematics, and foreign language; and additional requirements in fine arts, the senior project, community service, and health and physical education. Nearly 130 course offerings are available in the Upper School, including English; Spanish, French, and Latin; early modern world history, United States history, the twentieth century, African studies, and constitutional law; algebra, geometry, statistics, precalculus, and calculus; earth science, biology, chemistry, physics, and ecology; and art, engineering drawing, architecture, theater, choir, Chambers Singers, jazz band, and percussion group.

One-term minicourses include creative writing, a writing workshop, and speech; computer programming; photography and printmaking; art history; and studies of Africa, Asia, Russia, and the Middle East.

The School regularly offers thirteen Advanced Placement courses: English, computer science, European history, American history, calculus AB, calculus BC, statistics, biology, chemistry, studio art, French, Spanish, and Latin. An Honors Program is offered in English, French, Spanish, history, algebra, geometry, trigonometry, precalculus, chemistry, and biology. Qualified juniors and seniors may undertake independent study.

Six full-credit courses plus physical education are required each term. A typical course load includes English, math, history, science, foreign language, and physical education. Most students elect to add one or two full-credit courses or minicourses.

Independent studies are available to juniors and seniors with the approval of the Head of the Upper School. During the last two weeks of May, seniors complete their Advanced Placement and final exams and then engage in independent-study projects.

MBS is an active member in the American Field Service student exchange program, with at least 1 international student in attendance each year. The School offers many and varied educational field trips throughout the year, including three-week intensive language programs in France and Spain.

The average class size at Morristown-Beard is 12, and the ratio of students to faculty members is 7:1.

The Morristown-Beard School academic schedule comprises thirty-two weeks of instruction, divided into semesters. The schedule provides for long winter and spring vacations. Final examinations are held in June.

FACULTY AND ADVISERS

The faculty consists of 74 full-time teachers. Forty-one hold master's degrees, and 9 hold doctoral degrees.

Dr. Alex D. Curtis was appointed Head of School in 2004. Previously, he was the Director of Admission and Financial Aid at Princeton Day School. He holds a bachelor's degree from Swarthmore College and a doctoral degree in art history from Princeton University. Dr. Curtis has taught art history and Latin and has coached rugby.

At Morristown-Beard, faculty and staff members are dedicated to supporting and challenging each student. Virtually every faculty member meets the student in some capacity in addition to that of a classroom teacher: on the playing field or stage, as an adviser for various activities, and especially in the role of counselor to between 10 and 12 students.

COLLEGE PLACEMENT

Virtually every graduate of Morristown-Beard continues his or her education at a highly selective college. Students begin the personalized college application process in ninth grade with individual counseling and group information sessions. Parents, students, advisers, and college counselors work closely together throughout the process. Admissions officers from more than 100 colleges and universities visit Morristown-Beard annually to interview juniors and seniors.

Members of the class of 2005 are attending fifty-one different colleges, including Barnard, Bucknell, Colgate, Davidson, Dickinson, Hobart, Lehigh, Princeton, Rutgers, St. Lawrence, Skidmore, Syracuse, and the University of Virginia.

STUDENT BODY AND CONDUCT

In 2005–06, the School enrolled 490 day students in grades 6–12 as follows: grade 6, 37; grade 7, 33; grade 8, 52; grade 9, 100; grade 10, 93; grade 11, 81; and grade 12, 94. Students come from seventy different communities in central and northern New Jersey.

The Morristown-Beard School expects students to respect academic achievement, to be aware of differences, and to be thoughtful toward others. As a community, MBS lives by five core values: compassion, courage, integrity, respect, and responsibility. The School admires students who exhibit creative thought and intellect and who believe in serving the community at large. The School operates on the basis of honor, both inside and outside the classroom. In addition, the School insists that students appreciate a reasonable but clearly defined dress code. There is an active Student Government Association that works closely with the faculty and administration toward common goals.

ACADEMIC FACILITIES

The Morristown-Beard School campus consists of twelve buildings. Grant Hall houses the English and World Language Departments. Newly renovated Beard Hall houses the History Department and administrative offices. South Wing is home to visual arts and the alumni office. Wilke Hall houses two vocal and instrumental music classrooms, a 100-seat black-box theater, and a music computer lab. The science building houses six classrooms and labs and the dining hall. The Middle School and Math Department have their own classroom buildings.

The Anderson Library, which was completed in 2001, is home to 14,000 volumes, more than fifty printed periodicals, and many online databases, including full-text newspapers and periodicals. The library is connected to the campuswide network and the Internet. In addition, MBS participates in the interlibrary loan program to provide students with additional research and reference materials. The library is easily supplemented by resources available from the Morris County Library, which is located adjacent to the campus.

ATHLETICS

Morristown-Beard School believes that students learn the value of commitment, teamwork, and sportsmanship through their participation in athletics. Every student has the opportunity to be actively involved on teams. The Middle School athletic program emphasizes skill acquisition and participation. In the Upper School, most sports have both varsity and junior varsity squads. The boys' teams include football, soccer, cross-country, basketball, ice hockey, skiing, golf, baseball, lacrosse, tennis, track, and swimming. Girls' teams compete with other schools in field hockey, basketball, volleyball, softball, tennis, track, soccer, lacrosse, skiing, and swimming. During the summer of 2005, a new FieldTurf athletic field was installed, along with a state-of-the-art track. There are two other athletics fields and an ice-hockey rink on the campus. The William E. Simon Athletic Center and the William W. Rooke Family Pool were dedicated in 1986.

EXTRACURRICULAR OPPORTUNITIES

Involvement in extracurricular activities is a key element in a student's total development and therefore is greatly encouraged at Morristown-Beard. Students participate in student government, the School newspaper (*Crimson Sun*), the yearbook (*Salmagundi*), an art/literary magazine (*Mariah*), the band, and chorus; astronomy, chess, computer, drama, photography, and skiing clubs; and local chapters of the Cum Laude Society, American Field Service, and National Junior Honor Society. There are also School-sponsored trips to educational and cultural events in the area and in nearby cities. Opportunities for student travel are available during spring and summer vacations.

While participation in community service is a requirement, most students exceed the minimum number of hours by assisting the community in a variety of programs, some of which include assisting children in after-school programs, visiting nursing homes and veterans' hospitals, participating in Habitat for Humanity, and sponsoring Special Olympics programs on campus.

Class dances, an Upper School prom, a foreign language fair, and a fine arts festival that is shared with consortium schools are among the social activities. Special events include several dramatic productions, including musical theater and choral and band concerts, and drug and alcohol awareness programs, varied assembly presentations, and a parent/student athletics awards dinner.

DAILY LIFE

Classes are held from 8:10 a.m. to 3:15 p.m., Monday through Friday, on a modified block schedule. Students have a half-hour lunch period. Study halls, extra help, and activities periods are incorporated into the schedule. Sports competition follows the academic day.

COSTS AND FINANCIAL AID

In 2005–06, tuition was $21,765. There were very few additional fees.

Financial aid is available to all qualified students. Awards are based on character, achievement, and aptitude. Amounts granted are based on financial need. In 2004–05, $800,000 in aid was given to 52 students (11 percent of the student body), with awards ranging from $1000 to full tuition.

ADMISSIONS INFORMATION

Admissions decisions are based on recommendations, grade reports, interviews, test results, effort, potential for future achievement, and seriousness of academic curiosity. Applicants must submit a formal application, which includes a family information sheet, parent and student questionnaires, transcripts, and four letters of recommendation. In addition, students need to submit test scores from the ISEE, SSAT, or ERB CPT III. MBS administers the ISEE monthly from October to May. All applicants are considered without regard to race, creed, color, or ethnic or national origin.

APPLICATION TIMETABLE

Morristown-Beard School begins its admissions process in mid-December and continues through the spring. It is recommended that applications be made as early as possible, since places in various grades are limited. Information sessions, interviews, and campus tours are available Monday through Friday by calling the Admissions Office. Financial aid information may also be received by calling the office. Admissions decisions are made independent of financial aid considerations. Initial inquiries are welcome at any time of the year.

ADMISSIONS CORRESPONDENCE

Mrs. Alison J. Cady
Director of Admission
Morristown-Beard School
70 Whippany Road
Morristown, New Jersey 07960

Phone: 973-539-3032
Fax: 973-539-1590
E-mail: acady@mobeard.org

MOUNT SAINT MARY ACADEMY

Watchung, New Jersey

Type: Girls' day college-preparatory Roman Catholic school
Grades: 9–12
Enrollment: 353
Head of School: Sr. Lisa D. Gambacorto, Ed.S., Directress

THE SCHOOL

Having celebrated Nine Decades of Distinction in 1998, Mount Saint Mary Academy plans to mark its centennial in just a few years. Journeying toward this milestone, the Academy continues its tradition of excellence in the education of young women. With this tradition as its valuable asset and a moving force, the institution has embarked upon a new path to ready itself for a promising future. In 2001, state-of-the-art science laboratories and science and math classrooms greeted students as they began the school year. Several months later, a student center/cafeteria and school bookstore were completed in the newly renovated lower corridor of the Saint Joseph's building. Over the next few years, the strategic plan calls for further renovations that are designed to provide a well-equipped facility with the latest advances in technology, safety, and learning.

The Mount was founded in 1908 by the Sisters of Mercy of New Jersey and opened with 77 students. A fire destroyed the main building in 1911, but the school reopened in the following year and has grown steadily to its present enrollment of 360. The school's philosophy encompasses a view of human life as "a journey of people in evolution toward a final destiny which is knowable through faith and attainable through free choice." The Academy stresses the importance of having a skilled and caring faculty work with small classes within an environment in which personal integrity and moral values are nourished. All students take courses in religion each year.

The campus is situated on a ridge of the Watchung Mountains, overlooking surrounding suburban towns and the skyline of New York City, which is 23 miles to the east. Students and teachers take advantage of the many cultural and recreational offerings in the city and area.

The school, a sponsored work of the Sisters of Mercy, is a nonprofit organization governed by a Board of Trustees. Its Alumnae Association, composed of about 4,100 graduates, provides support for a number of school functions. The school's physical plant is owned by the Sisters of Mercy of New Jersey.

In 1984–85, Mount Saint Mary Academy was one of sixty-five private schools in the United States to receive the Council for American Private Education's Exemplary Private School Recognition Project award for being a "model for the nation." In a congratulatory letter, Governor Kean of New Jersey stated, "I hope that we can guarantee all of New Jersey's young people the opportunity to receive the kind of education your school provides."

Mount Saint Mary Academy is accredited by the Middle States Association of Colleges and Schools and holds membership in the National Association of Independent Schools, the New Jersey Association of Independent Schools, the National Catholic Educational Association, the College Board, and the Educational Records Bureau.

A ten-year Middle States Association special report was recently completed utilizing the Accreditation for Growth format. Mount Saint Mary Academy received highly complimentary evaluations in all areas of its study.

ACADEMIC PROGRAMS

To graduate, a student must complete 4 years of English, 4 of religion, 3 of history (2 of U.S. history), 3 of a foreign language, 3 of mathematics, 3 of science, 1 of art/music, 4 of physical education and health, and various elective courses. The school recommends that students complete 4 years each of foreign language, mathematics, and science.

Among the class offerings are English I–IV, playwriting, journalism, public speaking, and acting for the stage; American History I and II, various history electives, world civilizations, psychology, and economics; religion I–III, World Religions, Prayer, Living and Dying: A Catholic Perspective, Women's Spirituality, and directed study; algebra I and II, geometry, trigonometry, precalculus, discrete math/statistics, and calculus; Visual Basic 6.0, Technology Today, Microsoft Publisher, Microsoft FrontPage, and PowerPoint; biology I and II, chemistry, physics, and global science; Latin I and II, Italian I–IV, French I–IV, and Spanish I–IV; physical education, health I–IV, and driver's education; basic drawing, studio art, art history, painting and mixed media, and 3-D design; and music theory I and II, advanced music theory, music appreciation, music of the U.S. and the world, chorale, instrumental program, bell choir, jazz study, classical, chamber ensemble, and private lessons (available in voice and most instruments).

Honors sections are available for all English and mathematics classes as well as for the following special topics: chemistry, biology, physics, American history I and II, Cicero, Virgil, Latin II, French II–IV, Spanish II–IV, and Italian II and III. Advanced Placement courses are also offered in the following areas: English literature, English language and composition, French, Spanish, calculus, physics, biology, history, and psychology. Students take part in such competitions as the JETS-TEAMS (Junior Engineering & Technical Society–Tests of Engineering and Math/Science), Mock Trial, Odyssey of the Mind, PRISM (Project for Research in Science and Math), and ISP (Independent Student Projects).

The academic year, divided into trimesters, begins in early September and extends to early June, with vacations at Christmas, spring break, and Easter. Classes are held five days a week. The average class has 20 students. Grades are issued to students three times a year, and progress reports are sent home at midmarking period.

FACULTY AND ADVISERS

The faculty and staff consist of 52 lay teachers and 9 Sisters of Mercy. More than 60 percent of the faculty members have advanced degrees.

Sister Lisa Gambacorto, R.S.M., a graduate of Georgian Court College (B.A.) with certification in social studies education (K–12), was appointed Directress in 2000. She holds M.A. degrees from Seton Hall University in both counseling psychology and educational administration. Sister Lisa also has certification in student personnel services and is a nationally certified psychologist and a New Jersey–licensed marriage and family therapist. She has taught on the elementary, secondary, and college levels and, in addition, holds an Ed.S. from Seton Hall University.

The administrative team also consists of three Assistant Directresses whose special areas of concern include faculty, curriculum, and student activities.

The Campus Minister and a group of peer ministers work together to create a Christian atmosphere at the school. They are responsible for retreat planning, social concerns, and peer counseling, among other things. Through the ministers' efforts, faculty members and students are made aware of their responsibility to others and are encouraged to participate in a variety of service and ministry programs. The curriculum includes a community service requirement on all grade levels.

The services of a School Psychologist are available to students experiencing any adjustment difficulty. Individual sessions, family sessions, seminars for life development, and workshops for parents are some of the many services provided through student assistance. A Peer Mediator group also functions on campus to help students in need.

COLLEGE PLACEMENT

The Director of Guidance and the Guidance Counselor at Mount Saint Mary Academy become well acquainted with their students since each maintains the same counselees over a period of four years. Individual and group conferences are held to assist students and their parents in determining the best college and career choices. Students can meet individually with college representatives who visit the school or participate in a series of mini college fairs conducted during school hours. The Academy's guidance department has recently instituted the use of the COIN program for all levels.

Students also receive valuable college and scholarship information during the course of their College Skills classes taught for one trimester during the junior and senior years.

SAT scores are consistently higher than New Jersey and national averages in both the verbal and math sections. Of the 100 graduates of the class of 2005, 5 were National Merit Commended Scholars, 8 were Edward J. Bloustein Distinguished Scholars, and 1 was a National Achievement Scholar. The class achieved 100 percent college acceptance, at institutions such as Cornell, Duke, Georgetown, Harvard, NYU, Princeton, and

the University of Pennsylvania. They were awarded more than $6.1 million in scholarships and grants.

STUDENT BODY AND CONDUCT

In 2005–06, 353 girls were enrolled. Students came from sixty-eight towns within a 35-mile radius. Van transportation is available from most areas. Students are predominately Roman Catholic, but many other faiths are also represented.

Each girl receives a copy of the *Student Planner Handbook*, which outlines what is expected of her. It is her responsibility to respect the rights of others and to maintain a high regard for truth, honesty, and integrity. The Dean of Discipline reviews any infractions of the code. There is also a dress code, which requires girls to wear attractive uniforms, one for winter and another for warm weather.

ACADEMIC FACILITIES

The Mount building, a three-story structure of rough-cut Washington Valley stone, serves as the residence of the Sisters of Mercy and also contains classrooms, the computer center, the music rooms, the English-History Resource Center, and a parlor for recitals. It is connected by an arcade to Gabriel Hall (1912), a structure of similar design containing classrooms and math and science classrooms and labs. In addition, its top floors serve as a residence hall for retired Sisters of Mercy, who are a valuable resource in the life of the school community. St. Joseph Hall (1960) has a 15,000-volume technology-equipped library, classrooms, a TV studio, and an art studio. The new cafeteria, kitchen, student center, and school store are also in this building.

The school has a student infirmary. A nurse is on duty full-time during the school day. A local hospital is less than 15 minutes away.

Immaculate Conception Chapel (1954) seats 500. Beneath the chapel is Mercy Hall, used for social functions. Other buildings on the campus are the House of Prayer and McAuley Hall, which houses the McAuley School for Exceptional Children and an infirmary and retirement home for the Sisters of Mercy.

ATHLETICS

The athletics program emphasizes the development of sound health, sportsmanship, and the enjoyment and discipline of team play. The Mount is a member of the Mountain Valley Conference and the New Jersey State Interscholastic Athletic Association (NJSIAA). Varsity teams compete in basketball, cheerleading, cross-country, field hockey, lacrosse, soccer, softball, swimming, tennis, track, and volleyball. Dance and archery are part of the physical education program; skiing and golf can be pursued as extracurricular activities, according to student interest.

Athletics facilities on campus include six tennis courts (completed in 1990), a field for hockey and softball, and the Mother Mary Patrick McCallion Gymnasium (1983).

EXTRACURRICULAR OPPORTUNITIES

Students elect class officers and members of a Student Council, which organizes activities and promotes student initiative and self-government. Among the other regular student activity groups are the yearbook, newspaper, and literary magazine; National Honor Society; Cum Laude Society; language clubs; United Cultures Club; drama club; forensics; library and guidance aides; and health careers and arts and crafts groups. Other activities include the Model UN; the Academic Team; the Science League; Music Ministry; the naturalist, chess, computer, and poetry clubs; and others, according to student interest.

The school hosts monthly dances, and students participate in social exchanges with nearby Catholic boys' schools. The many varied experiences available include trips to theaters, museums, Lincoln Center, the United Nations, Philadelphia, and Washington, D.C.

Each year during the Easter vacation, the Academy sponsors a European trip, which is open to all students.

DAILY LIFE

The school day begins with classes from 7:55 to 2:40. Both hot and cold luncheons are served during three lunch periods. Extracurricular activities follow the regular school day, and vans leave the Mount after 3:15 p.m., allowing students time for involvement on campus.

COSTS AND FINANCIAL AID

Tuition and fees for the 2005–06 year were $13,650. Transportation, which is not included in the fees, ranged in cost from $2100 to $2600, depending on distance. Most townships reimburse parents for $700 of the cost if they do not actually provide the transportation. Bus and van service is available to most areas from which students commute.

Financial aid is available to parents who qualify by filing the Parents' Financial Statement with the School and Student Service for Financial Aid in Princeton, New Jersey. Scholarship aid and tuition grants totaling approximately $175,000 were awarded for the 2005–06 school year. Partial scholarships for academic excellence are awarded to incoming freshmen based upon scores on the Scholarship/Entrance Test, which is given in November.

ADMISSIONS INFORMATION

Mount Saint Mary Academy seeks students of average to above-average ability without regard to race, color, creed, or ethnic background. Admission decisions are based on entrance examination scores, transcripts of the previous three years, two letters of recommendation, and a personal interview.

New students are accepted into grades 9, 10, and 11.

APPLICATION TIMETABLE

Inquiries are welcome at any time, and prospective students are urged to spend a day at the school. An Open House is held in October, and the entrance test is given in November; additional testing is done by individual appointment. There are fees of $45 for the application and $35 for testing. Brochures are available from the Admissions Office, and appointments for interviews and tours can be made by calling that office.

ADMISSIONS CORRESPONDENCE

Donna V. Toryak, Director of Admissions
Mount Saint Mary Academy
1645 Highway 22 at Terrill Road
Watchung, New Jersey 07069

Phone: 908-757-0108 Ext. 4506
Fax: 908-756-8085
E-mail: dtoryak@mountsaintmary.org
Web site: http://www.mountsaintmary.org

MUNICH INTERNATIONAL SCHOOL

Starnberg, Germany

Type: Coeducational day college-preparatory school
Grades: PK–12: Junior School, Early Childhood (ages 4 and 5)–grade 4; Middle School, grades 5–8; Senior School, grades 9–12
Enrollment: School total: 1,255; Junior School: 442, Middle School: 406, Senior School: 407
Head of School: Mary Seppala

THE SCHOOL

Munich International School (MIS) is a non-profit coeducational primary and secondary day school that serves students from early childhood (ages 4 and 5) through grade 12, with English as the language of instruction. A total of 1,255 students who represent more than fifty countries and nationalities attend MIS. Students are accepted without regard to race, creed, nationality, or religion. The 26-acre MIS campus lies in an environmentally protected area of woodlands and farmland near scenic Lake Starnberg, some 20 kilometres (12 miles) south of Munich. School buses serve the cities of Munich and Starnberg and the surrounding region.

Founded in 1966, the School serves the international community in and around Munich, Germany, as well as those from the local community who wish to take advantage of the unique MIS educational experience. As an exemplary English language, International Baccalaureate (IB) World School, MIS inspires students to be interculturally aware and achieve their potential within a stimulating and caring learning environment. The curriculum follows the frameworks of the IB Primary Years Programme (IBPYP) and the IB Middle Years Programme (IBMYP), which culminate in the final two years with the International Baccalaureate Diploma (IBDP) or the American High School Diploma. The IBMYP overarches the two-year International General Certificate of Secondary Education (IGCSE) Programme in grades 9 and 10.

MIS regards the acquisition of knowledge, concepts, and skills as essential. They are seen as part of a broad and significant process of personal development toward independence, understanding, and tolerance. Learning is a lifelong process, and students are encouraged to cultivate a respect for learning and the ability and wisdom to use it well. Furthermore, since the School is an international and multicultural community, it seeks to develop in young people an active and lasting commitment to international cooperation.

All parents whose children attend MIS constitute the membership of the MIS Association, a tax-exempt, nonprofit organisation that elects a Board of Directors from its membership to operate the School in accordance with its Articles of Association.

Munich International School is fully accredited by the Council of International Schools (CIS) and the New England Association of Schools and Colleges (NEASC) and is approved by the German and Bavarian Educational Authorities.

ACADEMIC PROGRAMME

The academic programme throughout the School covers English language and literature, mathematics, humanities (including history, business and management, economics, geography, and social studies), sciences (including biology, chemistry, and physics), foreign languages, computer science, the fine arts, and film studies.

In the belief that students best benefit from the experience of living in Germany if they are able to communicate effectively and take part in local culture, MIS offers German language instruction to all students in early childhood classes through grade 12. Furthermore, comprehensive instruction in English as a second language (ESL) is offered to serve students who come to MIS with little or no English language skills. In the Senior School, however, English language competence is required.

The School programme is designed so that all students have the opportunity to pursue studies in the fine arts (art, music, drama, and film studies) and computing, athletic, and recreational skills.

The Junior School (early childhood–grade 4) follows the curriculum of the IBPYP, which emphasises an inquiry-based approach to learning across all core academic subjects. The children are taught in self-contained classes in a nurturing environment. The early childhood classes prepare the students for successful entry to grade 1.

The Middle School (grades 5–8) provides a caring, stable environment with a balance of challenging academic studies and opportunities for curricular and extracurricular skill development. The curriculum conforms to the frameworks of the IBMYP in grades 6, 7, and 8. The IBMYP is now also part of the curriculum in grades 9 and 10. Studies emphasise the development of thinking skills that involve moral reasoning, aesthetic judgement, and the use of scientific method. The Middle School is committed to providing students with the knowledge, learning strategies, and study skills necessary for the demanding Senior School programme. Food technology and ethics are introduced in grade 6, and French and Spanish are offered as electives from grade 6 onwards. Additional programmes that focus on health, design and technology, social skills, and the importance of the environment are also provided.

The academic programme of the Senior School (grades 9–12) is designed to prepare students for higher education, reflecting the aspirations and priorities of MIS parents. The guidance counselor especially encourages career planning to make students aware of the education and skills necessary to pursue lifetime goals.

Course requirements for the IGCSE are completed in grades 9 and 10. The academic programme culminates in grades 11 and 12, with studies leading to a full International Baccalaureate Diploma or an American high school diploma.

FACULTY AND ADVISERS

The Head of School, Dr. Mary Seppala, has taught in and administered schools for thirty-four years in the United States and abroad. At MIS, more than 150 teachers from some sixteen nations are part of this broad international experience, coming from such countries as Australia, Canada, Croatia, France, Germany, Great Britain, Ireland, Kenya, the Netherlands, New Zealand, and the United States. The faculty members are fully qualified; many have taught overseas and hold advanced degrees.

COLLEGE PLACEMENT

Students have the opportunity to prepare and sit for the American PSAT, SAT, and ACT—tests normally needed for U.S. college entrance. About 90 percent of MIS graduates continue their education at universities and colleges in the world, including Brown, Cambridge, Harvard, the London School of Economics, MIT, Oxford, Princeton, Yale, and the Universities of Munich (Germany), Melbourne (Australia), and Waseda (Japan), to cite some recent examples.

STUDENT BODY AND CONDUCT

The strong MIS community of students, teachers, and parents works together. MIS teachers and administrators understand the uncertainties and complexities that accompany a student's transition from one country to another and from one school to another, as well as the normal challenges of growing up. A coordinated support system across the School consists of homeroom teachers, grade coordinators, year coordinators, year advisers, IBPYP/IBMYP/IB coordinators, and a guidance counselor.

ACADEMIC FACILITIES

The Junior School is housed in a strikingly new and adjoining modern facility, with spacious, light-filled classrooms that radiate from a central multipurpose activity area. There are rooms for computing, German, ESL, learning support, art, and music classes as well as a large, well-equipped library. The Health Office and the School cafeteria, which serves hot meals, are also located in this building.

The Middle School meets in a modern building on campus. The architectural concept maximises the use of windows, allowing students to feel close to the natural beauty of the campus. In addition to the spacious classrooms, there are two science laboratories, a computer laboratory, and a multipurpose auditorium as well as rooms for ESL, academic support, music, and food technology.

The Senior School combines a new building and a traditional Bavarian-style building. Multipurpose classrooms are enhanced by five science laboratories, music and computer rooms, an auditorium, and a library.

The recent completion of building construction provides additional classrooms, a student lounge, larger libraries, a performing arts center, and an additional gymnasium.

Stately Schloss Buchhof, an original manor house of the area that dates back to 1875, has been renovated to house the Middle and Senior School fine arts departments as well as the administrative offices of the School.

ATHLETICS

Sports activities, which play an important role at MIS, are conducted for all ages after school and at weekends. Soccer, skiing, volleyball, basketball, track and field, tennis, cross-country, and softball are the main sports offered. Tennis courts, several sports fields, and a well-equipped triple gymnasium are available on campus.

The School competes in several ISST tournaments and participates in local leagues and events under the auspices of a School-sponsored sports club. Middle and Senior School teams represent MIS at various international school competitions across Europe.

EXTRACURRICULAR OPPORTUNITIES

In order to take advantage of the experience of living in Germany and Europe, there is a wide range of half- or full-day field trips at all school levels. There are overnight trips for the Middle and Senior School, when teachers and students travel both within Germany and beyond for educational and cultural experiences.

Students may select from a variety of activities in the fine arts, ranging from painting, drawing, and ceramics to handicrafts, drama, and dance. There are several School choirs, bands and an orchestra. Private instrumental instruction is available. A number of student drama productions are performed throughout the year. Senior and Middle School students participate in the International School Theatre Festival, the Speech and Debate Team, and several international school tournaments. Students in grades 11 and 12 have a weekly period set aside for recreational sports and service activities. They may take part in the Business@School and Model United Nations programmes.

Each year, a group of 8 to 10 students travel to Tanzania to visit project sites funded by donations from the MIS community. The travelling students present their findings at special assemblies held in each division of the School.

An active Parent-Teacher Organisation (PTO) operates as a voluntary support group for the School and fellow parents. The PTO organises a wide range of activities throughout the year, including Ski Swap, Winterfest, and in the spring, Frühlingsfest. During the winter more than 300 students, parents, and teachers take part in Ski Saturdays.

DAILY LIFE

The school year begins at the end of August and ends in late June. It is interspersed with short vacations, usually a week at the beginning of November, two weeks at Christmas, a Ski Week, and two weeks for Spring Break.

The school day starts at 9:10 a.m.; it ends at 3:15 p.m. for Junior and Middle School students and 4 p.m. for Senior School students. Buses organised by the School and serving most areas in and around Munich provide transportation for nearly 80 percent of the students.

SUMMER PROGRAMMES

A two-week daytime sports programme at the beginning of July includes a week of camping in the Dolomite Mountains in northern Italy.

COSTS AND FINANCIAL AID

In the school year 2005–06, tuition was €11,370 for pre-reception–grade 5, €12,810 for grades 6–8, and €13,960 for grades 9–12. There is also an entrance fee of €4600 per child upon initial admission and an additional €1300 per child in each of the following two school years.

ADMISSIONS INFORMATION

Applicants are advised that the School does not have the facilities to serve the educational needs of students who have mental, emotional, or physical handicaps or severe learning disabilities. The School does not have boarding facilities.

APPLICATION TIMETABLE

Interested students are required to submit a completed MIS application packet. Following submission of all required documentation, applicants are screened. Based on the School's judgment of the suitability of the educational programme for the prospective student and on space availability, applicants are admitted throughout the year. Earliest acceptance of application material is six months prior to attendance and/or January of that particular year. A nonrefundable application fee is paid in advance of admission decisions being made.

ADMISSIONS CORRESPONDENCE

Admissions Office
Munich International School
Schloss Buchhof
D-82319 Starnberg
Germany

Phone: 49-8151-366-120
Fax: 49-8151-366-129
E-mail: admissions@mis-munich.de
Web site: http://www.mis-munich.de

NEW HAMPTON SCHOOL

New Hampton, New Hampshire

Type: Coeducational boarding and day college-preparatory
Grades: 9–12, postgraduate year
Enrollment: 330
Head of School: Andrew Menke

THE SCHOOL

Founded in 1821, New Hampton School educates young people differently. Following a nationally acclaimed model for experience-based education, New Hampton's students and adults work alongside each other to create a dynamic learning community marked by nonhierarchical relationships, mutual respect, and intentional responsibility.

At New Hampton School, faculty members and students join together to share their unique talents as they learn from each other how to be better students, teachers, and friends. Students are asked to take responsibility for their success by helping shape their community in ways that benefit everyone. New Hampton nurtures the intellectual, emotional, physical, and spiritual potential of each student. New Hampton believes in developing authentic relationships based on shared experience and common goals. At New Hampton School, positive role models and relationships are crucial to a student's growth and social development. Since learning takes place within relationships that occur naturally as people live, learn, and work together, all community members play critical roles in the teaching and learning process. At New Hampton School, each child is known, needed, and cared for. The adults at New Hampton are teachers, coaches, dorm parents, mentors, and friends who help develop a passion for learning, being active, and enjoying life. The beautiful and well-equipped campus "village" is home to comprehensive, integrated, life-changing programs in academics, arts, athletics, adventure education, and community service. At New Hampton, people care about college prep and campus life, and about a code of behavior rather than a code of dress.

Within about an hour's drive of campus are Dartmouth College, Plymouth State College, the University of New Hampshire, and the city of Boston. In addition, Lake Winnipesaukee, Newfound Lake, and the foothills of New Hampshire's White Mountains are within 10 miles of the campus.

New Hampton School is accredited by the New England Association of Schools and Colleges. The School is a member of the National Association of Independent Schools, the New England Association of College Admission Officers, the National Association of College Admission Officers, the Independent Schools Association of Northern New England, and the Cum Laude Society.

ACADEMIC PROGRAMS

New Hampton's academic requirements ensure a proper distribution of courses in the basic core subjects—English, math, science, history, foreign language, and the arts. Twenty credits are recommended for a diploma; 18 are required. Sixteen of the 18 credits must be in core subjects. At least 1 credit of fine and performing arts is required.

Program development is flexible in all courses and reflects a student's proficiency. Students are encouraged to explore New Hampton's extensive academic electives, particularly in their junior and senior years. (For a list of specific electives, interested candidates and their parents should write for a course catalog.)

The average New Hampton class size is 12 students, and the overall student-teacher ratio is 5:1. Advanced Placement courses allow students to progress to college-level studies in science, computer science, math, languages, English, history, and art. The Cum Laude Society recognizes outstanding academic achievement.

New Hampton School offers an Academic Support Program for students with diagnosed language-learning disabilities. This program includes a language arts class, which focuses on reading and writing skills; a tutorial designed to assist in the general preparation of course work; and a paced history course. Students qualifying for this program are not required to take a foreign language but enroll in the regular math, science, and fine and performing arts courses. There is an additional charge for this program of $10,800 for the academic year.

An English as a second language program is also available to international students. This program focuses on the students' reading, writing, and speaking skills while incorporating an American culture class, a conversational English class, and a tutorial. A supportive ESL program is available to students who have had at least one year of English. The three levels are ESL I, ESL II, and Advanced ESL.

FACULTY AND ADVISERS

Seventy-two faculty members dedicate themselves to specific aspects of New Hampton School life. Thirty-one have advanced degrees.

Each student is assigned an adviser who becomes his or her academic counselor and personal confidant. Other faculty duties include teaching, managing, supervising activities, and advising students on the spectrum of teenage life concerns.

COLLEGE PLACEMENT

In addition to regular advisers, students work with a college adviser in the spring of the junior year. At this time, students are strongly encouraged to research colleges and arrange visits to those of interest. Many college representatives visit New Hampton School throughout the academic year.

The SAT I and ACT are administered several times each year at New Hampton. New Hampton School students have a wide range of SAT I results; the median scores are 500 verbal and 500 math.

Graduating seniors matriculate into colleges that they deem compatible with their goals. Recent graduates are attending Babson, Bennington, Boston University, Brown, Bucknell, Cornell, Dartmouth, Duke, Endicott, Harvard, Holy Cross, Lafayette, Lehigh, Lewis & Clark, Merrimack, Middlebury, MIT, Mount Holyoke, New England, Northeastern, North Carolina, Plymouth State, Reed, St. Anselm's, St. Lawrence, Skidmore, Springfield, the United States Naval Academy, Wake Forest, and the Universities of Massachusetts, New Hampshire, and Vermont.

STUDENT BODY AND CONDUCT

In 2005–06, New Hampton has 330 students. There were 100 day students and 230 boarders. Varying religious, racial, and socioeconomic backgrounds add to the well-rounded cultural atmosphere as do the thirty states and twenty countries represented by the student body. Fourteen percent of the student body are international students.

New Hampton is a structured school with a carefully thought through system of rules and governance. Community decision making is central to the New Hampton experience. From regular all-School meetings to periodic New England–style "town meetings," students and faculty members have a unique responsibility of working alongside each other to shape and set standards. Throughout the discipline code, New Hampton holds the highest standards of moral, interpersonal, and community decorum and behavior.

ACADEMIC FACILITIES

The School buildings are a blend of Federal architecture and New England Colonial style with some modern interjections. The Academic Research Center (ARC) opened in July 1997. The ARC houses a 25,000-stack library and serves as the technology hub of campus. With more than fifty computers (including three film-editing stations), 300 data ports, and a master classroom, the center is truly a library for the future. In addition, the third floor serves as a senior leadership center and houses the college counseling resources. The T. Holmes Moore Center (1987), part of the Arts and Athletic Center, is home to a 360-seat theater and houses a student lounge and patio; classrooms; art studios and a gallery; a radio station; a music center, which includes a state-of-the-art digital recording studio; and photography labs. Three other classic brick buildings house the foreign language, science, and humanities classrooms. The Gordon Nash Town Library also offers ready access to 40,000 volumes, more than 150 periodicals, eight daily newspapers, and excellent research facilities.

BOARDING AND GENERAL FACILITIES

There are fourteen dormitories; they range in capacity from 7 to 30 students. Single-room availability depends on several circumstances, such as individual living needs. Each dormitory is supervised by specific faculty members. Their supervision helps to implement a more efficient system of student accountability.

ATHLETICS

The Art and Athletic Center opened in January 1999. This facility includes a field house for basketball, volleyball, and tennis and for indoor practices for such teams as baseball, soccer, and field hockey. Interscholastic activities and the NHS recreational activities program provide students with the opportunity to develop within the School's concept of a "well-rounded education."

There are many athletic offerings at NHS, including alpine racing, baseball, basketball, cross-country, cycling, equestrian, field hockey, golf, ice hockey, kayaking, lacrosse, mountain biking, outdoor adventure, rock climbing, snowboarding, soccer, softball, tennis, volleyball, and weight training.

The School's athletic facilities include nine tennis courts, 5 miles of cross-country trails, a covered ice rink, five athletic fields, a baseball diamond, three indoor basketball courts, one outdoor basketball court, and a climbing wall. The Frederick Smith Gymnasium building contains a comprehensive weight-training and cardiovascular facility, a training room, and locker rooms. Burleigh Mountain provides 120 acres of walking and cross-country skiing trails.

Offering excellent recreational and instructional programs for skiers, the School provides the opportunity for students to participate in competitive or recreational skiing. Exceptional skiers compete at the FIS, USSA, and Junior Olympic levels.

EXTRACURRICULAR OPPORTUNITIES

The fine and performing arts program offers a variety of opportunities for students. The fine arts program includes painting, drawing, graphic design, photography, and ceramics. Classes range from introductory level to Advanced Placement for college credit. Students may display work in the Galletly Gallery on campus and compete for the Boston Globe Arts Award.

Each year, New Hampton students participate in more than twenty-five performing arts productions and presentations. Performances include full-scale theater productions, student written and directed one-act plays, touring productions, children's shows, dance performances, and musical compilations. The new arts facility includes a digital recording studio, portable film studio, three Adobe Premiere editing stations, rehearsal halls, practice rooms, a state-of-the-art theater, and a new graphics lab.

Opportunities abound for participation in activities that encompass academic goals, cultural growth, and recreational interests. All students are encouraged to participate in at least one extracurricular activity.

Participation in the various community service projects the School sponsors is required. These projects include volunteer work at the local fire department, an elderly housing facility, the community elementary school, and a local home for underprivileged teenagers.

The Burleigh Mountain Program (BUMP) is a residential, outdoor program utilizing more than 50 acres of New Hampton School's Burleigh Mountain. This program offers selected students the opportunity to engage in a group residential initiative on the mountain.

The Student Activities Director schedules weekly visits by lecturers and artists (the Vespers Program) and arranges trips to Boston and nearby cities for sports, cultural, and "just for fun" events.

Other extracurricular activities include Tour Guide, a photography club, the yearbook, the newspaper, the literary magazine, Student Council, and Student Activity Council.

DAILY LIFE

During the fall and spring terms, students attend classes Monday through Saturday. Classes begin at 7:45 a.m. and end at 2:55 p.m., except on Wednesday and Saturday, when classes end at noon to allow for interscholastic sports competition. During the winter term, the schedule is adjusted to allow skiers to be on the slopes by 2 p.m. Students are expected to attend all classes and meet all commitments.

WEEKEND LIFE

Many events take place on the weekends for day and boarding students. A weekend roster of activities might include movies, bowling, weekend ski trips, excursions to Boston, shopping trips, plays, concerts, and intramural games. With parental permission, students may leave campus on weekends.

SUMMER PROGRAMS

Summer programs are available at New Hampton School; more information can be found online at http://www.newhampton.org/summer/ or by phone at 603-677-3476.

COSTS AND FINANCIAL AID

Tuition for 2006–07 is $36,600 for boarding students and $22,300 for day students. A nonrefundable $3000 deposit is required. Extra costs include lab fees, books, driver's education, skiing, and music lessons. An optional laundry service is also available at an additional cost. Student allowance accounts are maintained at the School bookstore.

There is a need-based financial aid program designed to ensure a heterogeneous student body. Last year, students received approximately $1.5 million in financial aid. Financial aid information and application forms may be obtained from the Admissions Office.

ADMISSIONS INFORMATION

Admission to New Hampton is based on an evaluation of the prospective student's capacity to do college-preparatory work. The committee also evaluates each candidate's overall level of citizenship, sense of purpose, and potential to be a leader in New Hampton's community. Prior school records, test scores (SSAT, PSAT, and SAT I), recommendations, and interviews are carefully considered by the Admissions Committee. A personal interview is required.

APPLICATION TIMETABLE

Campus tours and interviews are arranged Monday through Friday from 8:45 a.m. to 1:30 p.m. Parents should contact the Admissions Office to set up an interview.

Applications must be sent with a nonrefundable $50 fee ($75 for international students). The first-round application deadline is February 1. Admission decisions are mailed on March 10. Applications completed after February 1 are considered on a rolling admission basis, contingent upon available space.

ADMISSIONS CORRESPONDENCE

Dean of Admission
New Hampton School
New Hampton, New Hampshire 03256

Phone: 603-677-3401
Fax: 603-677-3481
E-mail: admissions@newhampton.org
Web site: http://www.newhampton.org

THE NEWMAN SCHOOL

Boston, Massachusetts

Type: Coeducational day college-preparatory school
Grades: 9–12, postgraduate year
Enrollment: 240
Head of School: J. Harry Lynch, Headmaster

THE SCHOOL

The Newman School is a day school offering college-preparatory courses for young men and women. Located in the Back Bay district near Copley Square and the Prudential Center, it is convenient to railroad stations, bus terminals, and MBTA stations.

The Newman School, which was named in honor of John Henry Cardinal Newman, was founded in 1945 by Dr. J. Harry Lynch. He was assisted by a group of educators who felt the need for a school that would provide an alternative approach to high school education and give postgraduate students the opportunity to correct deficiencies in their preparation for higher education. Classes are offered in fall, winter, and summer sessions, enabling students to attend the School year-round, if desired. Intensive instruction for international students is also available.

Newman is incorporated as a not-for-profit organization and directed by a self-perpetuating 10-member Board of Trustees, which meets quarterly and includes several alumni.

The Newman School is approved by the Boston School Committee and the Department of Education of the Commonwealth of Massachusetts and is accredited by the New England Association of Schools and Colleges. The School holds membership in the Association of Independent Schools of New England (AISNE), the National Association of Secondary School Principals, the Massachusetts Secondary School Principals Association, the National Association of College Admission Counselors, the Secondary School Admission Test Board, and the Council for Spiritual and Ethical Education. It is approved by the U.S. Immigration and Naturalization Service for the teaching of international students.

ACADEMIC PROGRAMS

Transfer credit is given for high school work completed in other schools, but diploma candidates must take a minimum of 6 units at Newman. To graduate, a student must complete 22 units, as follows: English, 4; social studies (including U.S. history), 3; mathematics, 4; laboratory science, 3; foreign language, 2; fine/applied arts, 1; computer science, 1; and electives, 4.

The curriculum includes humanities I and II, dramatic arts, twentieth-century art, English I–IV, and English composition; French I–IV and Spanish I–IV; U.S. history, world civilization, world cultures, world geography, world religions, ethics, twentieth-century America, economics, psychology, political science, international affairs, moral reasoning, and public issues; algebra I and II, geometry, trigonometry, calculus with analytic geometry, and SAT math review; biology, marine biology, chemistry, physics, and environmental science; and business law and computer science. AP and university course enrollment are available. Qualified students may be invited to join the National Honor Society.

Grade reports are issued every four weeks. A tutorial program is available for students who fall behind in their studies, and long-term tutoring may be arranged for an additional fee. Individualized developmental reading instruction is offered at the School, and students who require extensive help are referred to a remedial reading clinic.

The International Student Advisor and the School's Guidance Department aid students from other countries who are preparing for entrance to American colleges and universities. Intermediate and advanced English courses for international students are offered in an intensive program of six classes per day for sixteen weeks in the fall and spring semesters and ten weeks in the summer session. Special attention is given to preparing for the Test of English as a Foreign Language and for College Board tests.

FACULTY AND ADVISERS

J. Harry Lynch, the Headmaster, is a graduate of the College of the Holy Cross (B.A., 1974) and Northeastern University (M.B.A., 1976). He has been Headmaster of Newman since 1985.

The faculty includes 17 full-time teachers and 3 part-time teachers. These 9 men and 11 women hold nineteen baccalaureate degrees, seven master's degrees, and one doctorate.

Members of the faculty are available each day to give students extra help with their course work.

COLLEGE PLACEMENT

The College and Career Reference Area provides students with information regarding college admissions, vocational choices, and the employment outlook in various fields.

An average graduating class has approximately 65 students, of whom more than 95 percent continue their education. Recent graduates from Newman have been accepted to the following four-year colleges and universities, among others: American, Assumption, Babson, Bates, Boston College, Boston University, California Institute of Technology, Clark, Columbia, Emerson, Fairfield, Georgetown, Grinnell, Harvard, Holy Cross, MIT, Oberlin, Regis, St. Anselm, Smith, Stonehill, Tufts, Tulane, the U.S. Air Force Academy, Vassar, Wellesley, Wheaton, Worcester Polytechnic, and the Universities of Connecticut, Delaware, Maryland, Massachusetts, Miami, New Hampshire, and Rhode Island.

STUDENT BODY AND CONDUCT

The Newman School enrolls approximately 240 day students ranging from 14 to 19 years of age. About 50 of them are out-of-town residents who are temporarily living in Boston. Current and recent students have come from California, Connecticut, Florida, Illinois, Massachusetts, New Hampshire, New Jersey, New York, Ohio, Austria, France, Germany, Greece, India, Iran, Ireland, Italy, Japan, Korea, the People's Republic of China, Poland, Russia, Saudi Arabia, Thailand, Spain, Vietnam, the West Indies, and several Central and South American countries.

Admission to and continuance in the Newman School is to be regarded as a privilege and not a right; the Board of Trustees requires the withdrawal of any student for disciplinary or scholastic reasons that it deems sufficiently grave to warrant such action. The board is the final judge in matters of admission and retention of students. Each student has the responsibility of being thoroughly informed at all times concerning the regulations and requirements of Newman; these are outlined in the School brochure and student handbook.

ACADEMIC FACILITIES

The School plant consists of two nineteenth-century town houses located on Marlborough Street that contain libraries, laboratories, classrooms, and offices. Both buildings are wireless-network accessible. The School does not maintain boarding facilities but does assist out-of-town students in finding homestay families.

ATHLETICS

The School competes interscholastically with other independent schools in such sports as boys' and girls' basketball, boys' and girls' soccer, girls' softball, and boys' baseball.

Intramural sports, which include flag football, sailing, competitive cheerleading, crew, tennis, and volleyball, are available according to student interest but may not be available each term.

EXTRACURRICULAR OPPORTUNITIES

Extracurricular activities that are available each year include a yearbook and a newspaper (247). There are drama, dance, student government, peer leadership, photography, film, recreation and outing, and science clubs, as well as chorus, ensembles, and bands that perform throughout the year. Other activities may be organized based on student interest.

DAILY LIFE

The academic year is divided into two 18-week sessions beginning in September and January and a ten-week session beginning in June. The school day starts at 8:15 and ends by 2:45. Classes are held five days a week; to permit completion of a year's work in one fall or spring session, many courses meet for two periods each day.

The summer session incorporates the same amount of work in extended class periods. Thus, summer students may earn a full year's credit for courses not previously taken.

SUMMER PROGRAMS

Newman students may continue their studies during the summer session, receiving academic credit for regular high school courses. In addition, refresher and makeup courses are offered for students from other schools who need to correct deficiencies. International students may attend the Newman School's summer program to work on their English skills and to experience many aspects of American culture within the city of Boston.

COSTS AND FINANCIAL AID

Day tuition is estimated at $10,500 to $17,000 for the 2006–07 school year, depending on the individual schedule. Additional expenses include a graduation fee ($75) and books (approximately $225 per semester). Estimated living expenses for out-of-town students are $8000 for the 2006–07 school year. Tuition for refresher and makeup courses is $900 per course.

Entering ninth graders may be given scholarships, depending on the result of the entrance examinations. The School awarded $38,000 in scholarship aid for 2004–05. Financial aid is also available.

ADMISSIONS INFORMATION

Applicants are accepted for enrollment in September, January, and June. Transcripts of any previous high school work, a personal interview, and a character reference letter from the previous school are all part of the requirements to determine acceptance. Applicants must also take a placement test that is administered at the School.

It has always been the policy of the Newman School to admit students without distinction as to race, color, creed, sex, age, ethnic background, or national origin.

APPLICATION TIMETABLE

Candidates for admission should file an application on the required form at the earliest feasible date preceding the session in which they wish to enroll. There is a $40 application fee for American students and a $300 application and processing fee for international students.

ADMISSIONS CORRESPONDENCE

Michael Dornisch
Director of Admissions
The Newman School
247 Marlborough Street
Boston, Massachusetts 02116

Phone: 617-267-4530
Fax: 617-267-7070
E-mail: mdornisch@newmanboston.org
Web site: http://www.newmanboston.org

NEW YORK MILITARY ACADEMY

Cornwall-on-Hudson, New York

Type: Coeducational, college-preparatory, military boarding and day school
Grades: 7–12: Middle School, 7–8; Upper School, 9–12
Enrollment: 213
Head of School: Capt. Robert D. Watts, Superintendent, USN (Ret.)

THE ACADEMY

Founded in 1889 by Col. Charles J. Wright, New York Military Academy (NYMA) prepares young people for success through competitive academic, athletic, character, and leadership development programs geared to set them apart for excellence in higher education and future endeavors. NYMA is a coeducational, nondenominational, independent, college-preparatory school for students in grades 7–12 from around the world. The 165-acre campus is located in Cornwall-on-Hudson, in historic Orange County, New York, just 65 miles north of New York City. The structured and disciplined approach to learning provides for small classes, tutorial assistance, and 100 percent of the graduates entering the college or university of their choice. Participation in JROTC (Junior Reserve Officer Training Corps) and character and leadership development instills a higher level of self-discipline in the cadets while enhancing overall performance through organizational structure, accountability, responsibility, and good citizenship. Outstanding performance by the Corps of Cadets has earned the Academy the highest designation awarded by the Department of the Army, "Honor Unit with Distinction". This designation allows NYMA the opportunity to directly nominate qualified seniors for admission into the United States Service Academies.

Accredited by the Middle States Association of Schools and Colleges, NYMA is also a member of the National Association of Independent Schools, The Association of Boarding Schools, New York State Association of Independent Schools, and the Association of Military Colleges and Schools of the United States.

ACADEMIC PROGRAMS

NYMA cadets are required to achieve more than the minimal graduation requirements set forth by New York State. The Academy requires a cadet to successfully complete 4 years of history, 4 years of English, 4 years of high school math, 4 years of science, 3–4 years of a foreign language, computer studies, JROTC (4 years recommended, minimum 2 years), art or music, health, and 3 electives. These requirements both meet and exceed New York State's required curriculum. Community service is a must, and all seniors must complete no less than 50 hours of volunteer work prior to graduation. An adequate number of computers are available for cadet use. Cadets requiring computer instruction attend classes in the computer center, which opened in fall 2000 and is located in the main academic building. JROTC is taught by military instructors and is required of all cadets in grades 9–12. The curriculum promotes and assists cadets in developing the self-discipline, confidence, sound morals, and high self-esteem needed to become effective and responsible citizens. English as a

second language (ESL) is available to non-English-speaking students who have completed ESL A. International applicants are required to submit the results of the TOEFL or SLEP test. A minimum score of 450 is necessary for international students to satisfactorily complete the high school curriculum in four years. The academic curriculum and the challenge of maintaining physical fitness enable each cadet to achieve strength of mind and spirit.

FACULTY AND ADVISERS

The Academy's dedicated faculty is composed of 26 men and 18 women members, who either presently hold an advanced degree or are undertaking advanced studies. In addition, faculty members also act as coaches or other activity sponsors. Due to their many duties and responsibilities to the Corps, faculty members are provided with staff housing.

Each faculty member also serves as a cadet mentor. Assigned 8 cadets, the faculty members arrange time to meet with their cadets on an individual basis to discuss performance and other issues. The Commandant and his staff oversee cadet life and provide for the cadet military code of conduct that governs all cadets at NYMA.

Capt. Robert D. Watts was appointed the thirteenth Superintendent in May 2005. Prior to his position at NYMA he served as the Commandant of the Defense Equal Opportunity Management Institute at Patrick Air force Base in Florida. Capt. Watts is a 1973 graduate of the United States Naval Academy at Annapolis and earned his Master of Science degree in national resource strategy in 1997 from the Industrial College of Armed Forces in Washington, D.C. Throughout his distinguished naval career he has trained more than 300 aviation personnel, managed 113 helicopters and 120 fixed-wing aircraft, and directed more than 1500 military and government employees. He has been awarded the Legion of Merit (three), Defense Meritorious Service Medal, Meritorious Service Medal (two), Navy Commendation Medal (two), Navy Achievement Medal, and various theater and service medals. Capt. Watts is an accomplished leader and decision maker. He is a mentor who creates professional environments that deliver optimal results. He has demonstrated success in the training and education of tomorrow's leaders and experience in building character.

COLLEGE PLACEMENT

College selection and placement are a collective effort on the part of the Headmaster, Assistant Headmaster, and Guidance Counselor at New York Military Academy. In their junior year, cadets begin to prioritize and to sort through colleges and universities based upon area of study, number of students, and geographic location. SAT preparation, essay writing, and

interview techniques are available to all junior and senior cadets. Qualified NYMA seniors may be accepted to the U.S. Military Academy at West Point as well as other U.S. Service Academies. Other graduating seniors select colleges that are nonmilitary, while others seek colleges offering an ROTC program. College placements for the class of 2005 include Bucknell; Franklin Pierce College; Hofstra; Mount Holyoke; Niagra; Norwich; Penn State; RIT; Rutgers; SUNY at Albany, Binghamton, and Stony Brook; Syracuse; and the U.S. Military Academy at West Point, to name a few.

STUDENT BODY AND CONDUCT

The Corps of Cadets, totaling 213, consists of 182 young men and 31 young women, 29 of whom are day students. The Corps comprises students from fifteen states, one U.S. territory, and twelve countries.

Through instruction in JROTC, cadets learn the proper decorum and appropriate behaviors. All cadets in grades 9–12 have the opportunity to advance in rank based upon their personal deportment, academic achievement, and participation in athletics. Top performers within the Corps are invited to attend Leadership Development School (LDS) during the month of August to compete for key leadership positions for the upcoming school year. The selected Cadet Cadre must abide by and enforce the military code of discipline as set forth in the *Cadet Manual*, which governs all cadets. The Cadet First Captain and the cadet officers are fully accountable and responsible to the Commandant and Superintendent.

ACADEMIC FACILITIES

Scarborough Hall, built in 1963, houses math and science classrooms for grades 9–12, the auditorium, Booth Library, and the Brunetti Computer Center. The main Academic Building, as it is known, was constructed in 1912 and features newly renovated classrooms for JROTC, humanities, and computer courses for grades 9–12, plus administrative offices. Also within the main building is Davis Chapel, which is adorned with magnificent stained glass windows and is available to the cadets for church services on Sundays. The chapel also serves as the setting for many prestigious ceremonies throughout the year. Dingley Hall provides dormitory housing for boys in grades 7–8, as well as classrooms and a computer center for all middle school cadets. The Cadet Activities Center, located on Brooks Road, is home to the Cadet Canteen and Recreation Center as well as the Academy Band.

BOARDING AND GENERAL FACILITIES

Dickinson Hall, donated by Fairleigh Dickinson ('37) in 1972, is the newer of the boys' dormitories. The other boys' dorms are Dingley

Hall and Jones Barracks. Jones Barracks, the larger and older building in the Quad, is able to accommodate more than 100 boy cadets in grades 9–12. Pattillo Hall, the girls' dormitory, sits just below Jones Barracks and, like Dickinson Hall, is a newer building. Improvements in the technology area allow for all dorm rooms to be equipped with telephone (with voice-mail and long-distance service) and computer connections (with access to e-mail and the Internet). Since all computers run off the Academy's main server, individual modems are not required. Pattillo Hall also houses an indoor pool, a fitness center, and an indoor rifle range. Toward the top of the Quad, adjacent to the Academic Building, is Curie Dining Hall. The hall, large enough to seat the entire Corps at each meal hour, prepares highly nutritious, well-balanced meals served cafeteria-style three times a day. Brunch is available to the cadets on Sundays.

ATHLETICS

All cadets must participate in interscholastic or intramural sports. As a result of this requirement, a wide variety of interscholastic athletics are offered at the modified, varsity, or junior varsity levels. Boys' sports include baseball, basketball, football, ice hockey, lacrosse, soccer, and wrestling. Girls' sports include basketball, soccer, softball, and volleyball. Several of the varsity sports are coed and include cross-country, golf, rifle, swimming, tennis, and track and field. Raiders, an outdoor program, and Drill Team are conducted by JROTC. D Troop, as the equestrian program is referred to, is held at a local stable. Throughout the parade season, these cadets have the opportunity to perform in several parades as a mounted unit. Cadets have the opportunity to ski, ice skate, or snowboard at nearby West Point.

Athletic facilities include the Alumni Gymnasium, an Olympic-size pool, the Munday ('27) Wrestling Room, and the Heilbrunn ('27) Training Room. Pattillo Hall includes an indoor pool, an indoor rifle range, and the Heilbrunn Fitness Center. Outdoor basketball courts, nine tennis courts, an outdoor pool, and soccer, football, lacrosse, baseball, and softball fields complete the athletic facilities.

EXTRACURRICULAR OPPORTUNITIES

On-campus activities include the National Honor Society, yearbook, chorus, marching band, drama club, and Boy Scouts. Over the years, the marching band has been fortunate to participate in New Year's Day parades abroad. The Corps of Cadets participates in the Columbus Day Parade in New York City as well as in the Memorial Day Parade in Cornwall-on-Hudson.

DAILY LIFE

Structure sets the pace for daily life at NYMA. The cadets adhere to a strict schedule, allowing for a minimum of free time. The daily regimen requires cadets to be up at 6 a.m. and attend classes from 8 a.m. to 3 p.m.; participate in athletics for 2 hours, four afternoons per week; and attend supervised evening study hall from 7:30 to 9:30. Tutorials are held daily during the academic day and evening study period. Cadets may be required to attend Saturday study hall and tutorials, as directed.

WEEKEND LIFE

Trips are planned to local malls and movie theaters, as are dances and trips to Great Adventure, athletic events, New York City, and other points of interest.

SUMMER PROGRAMS

NYMA offers students ages 12–17 a five-week boarding summer school (grades 7–11) as well as a day/boarding SAT prep course for sophomores and juniors. Additional information may be obtained by contacting the Admissions Office. International students seeking to matriculate into NYMA for the academic year are required to attend the five-week ESL program or comparable program.

COSTS AND FINANCIAL AID

In 2005–06, new cadet tuition and fees totaled $27,395; new international cadet tuition and fees totaled $29,175. Additional fees, applied where indicated, are the art fee, the laboratory science fee, the commencement fee, haircuts (for boys), textbooks, the equestrian program, and the telephone user fee. Financial aid is available and awarded on an annual basis.

ADMISSIONS INFORMATION

NYMA admits young men and women into its college-preparatory program without regard to race, religion, color, or ethnic origin. Prospective cadets should be average to above average in academic ability and able to express their desire to undertake this commitment regardless of how demanding it may become. Recommendations from prior schools, complete academic transcripts, and a personal interview are required. Interviews may be scheduled Monday through Friday mornings. Admissions open houses are held throughout the year.

APPLICATION TIMETABLE

Cadets may enter the Academy in September or January (second semester) based on grade-level placements being available. The application for admission should be completed and returned to the admissions department, with the application fee, as soon as possible.

ADMISSIONS CORRESPONDENCE

Maureen T. Kelly
Director of Admissions
New York Military Academy
78 Academy Avenue
Cornwall-on-Hudson, New York 12520

Phone: 888-ASK-NYMA (toll-free)
Fax: 845-534-7699
E-mail: admissions@nyma.ouboces.org
Web site: http://www.nyma.org

NORTHFIELD MOUNT HERMON SCHOOL

Northfield, Massachusetts

Type: Coeducational boarding and day college-preparatory school
Grades: 9–12, postgraduate year
Enrollment: 725
Head of School: Thomas K. Sturtevant

THE SCHOOL

Northfield Mount Hermon School (NMH) offers a unique educational program, diverse and talented people, a values-oriented experience, and extensive resources. Focus, opportunity, individual attention, and values form the academic program because the School believes these are the elements that allow students to learn and grow in the most balanced and effective way possible.

Students focus their minds and energy by taking fewer major courses each term in extended periods, for a total of six college-prep courses per year. These courses are complemented by enrichment minor courses. A special ninth grade program provides foundation. NMH offers an extensive choice of courses, sports teams, performing arts groups, club activities, and study-abroad options. Cutting-edge technology enhances learning in and out of the classroom; students are required to bring a computer.

Individualized attention is ensured through the Moody system of advising, which matches teachers with advisee groups of about 7 students, small class size, college counseling, and a teacher-student ratio of 1:7. NMH also challenges its students to examine their values and to develop a sense of commitment. Every student participates in the School's work program 4 hours per week, and 200 students volunteer each term in outreach activities. Multifaith beliefs are examined in religious studies courses, at school meetings, and in spiritual life groups that are supported by the faculty.

NMH began as two schools: the Northfield Seminary for Young Ladies, which opened in 1879, and the Mount Hermon School for Boys, which began in 1881. Both schools were founded by Dwight Lyman Moody, who wanted to provide an excellent secondary education for young people regardless of race, religion, and economic circumstances. In 1971, the schools became a single coeducational institution with one faculty, one administration, and two coeducational campuses.

Today, a 24-member Board of Trustees, which includes many alumni, is the governing body of the School. The endowment in productive funds has a market value of $116 million. Contributions received from approximately 25,000 alumni are the predominant force in NMH's fund-raising efforts.

In January 2004, the NMH Board of Trustees decided to reduce the size of the student body and become a one-campus school as of September 2005. The School is located on the Gill campus, which encompasses about 2,000 acres on the wooded banks of the Connecticut River in western Massachusetts, near the borders of Vermont and New Hampshire. Brattleboro, Vermont, is 13 miles north, and Greenfield, Massachusetts, is located 14 miles to the south. New York is 3½ hours south via I-91 and I-95;

Boston is 2 hours east on Route 2 or the Massachusetts Turnpike. Bradley International Airport, which serves Hartford and Springfield, is 1¼ hours south via I-91.

Northfield Mount Hermon has been designated an exemplary school by the U.S. Department of Education, is accredited by the New England Association of Schools and Colleges, and is a member of the Independent School Association of Massachusetts, the National Association of Independent Schools, and the Educational Records Bureau.

ACADEMIC PROGRAMS

A Northfield Mount Hermon education begins and ends with the individual; every student is expected to take the most rigorous course load in which he or she can succeed. With the Moody system of advising, each faculty adviser works with about 7 students. Advisers help students select challenging courses appropriate to their individual needs. More than 200 courses are offered, including Chinese, environmental science, multivariable calculus, and Russian. Additional courses are offered in English, mathematics, classics, French, German, Spanish, environmental science, religious studies, the arts, theater, music, photography, and physical education. Advanced Placement opportunities are offered in twenty-three subject areas, and there are eleven study-abroad options. The ninth grade curriculum includes a health course that focuses on age-appropriate health, wellness, and life skills and afternoon writing and history courses to improve academic preparedness. Ninth graders are required to participate in one term of interscholastic athletics.

All NMH students participate weekly in a work program designed to teach responsibility and the dignity of labor through a variety of jobs, which may include working in the student houses, the language labs, the library, the School farm, or the dining service.

The Office of International Education offers study abroad in Australia, China, Costa Rica, the Dominican Republic, France, Germany, Ireland, Italy, Greece, and New Zealand.

Ninth and tenth graders participate in a humanities course that is collaboratively planned by teachers from different disciplines and has a thematic focus.

The typical class consists of 13 students, and the student-teacher ratio is about 7:1. Reports and comments are sent to parents twice each term.

One academic credit is earned by the successful completion of a major course. Twenty-two credits are required to graduate. Students also enroll in minor courses. Participation in minor courses and activities is measured in units. A student must take 4 credits of English, 2 credits of math, 2 credits of a foreign language

(successful completion of a second-level course in a foreign language), 2 credits of science (1 credit of a lab), and 2 credits of history and social science (1 credit of U.S. history). The arts requirement depends on the length of the student's attendance at the School. Students are required to take courses in religious studies, physical education, or athletics each year and to participate satisfactorily in the work program.

FACULTY AND ADVISERS

In 2005–06, there were 111 full-time teaching faculty members. Of the full faculty, 66 percent hold advanced degrees. Faculty members coach, advise, and live in the dorms.

Thomas K. Sturtevant is the head of Northfield Mount Hermon School. Prior to work at NMH, he taught at St. Andrew's School in Delaware and was Upper School Principal at Friends Academy in New York.

COLLEGE PLACEMENT

NMH places special emphasis on college counseling. College counselors, in conjunction with each student's adviser, guide students through the entire college search process, including the taking of standardized tests. Members of the college counseling office have worked on the admission staffs of selective colleges and universities, such as Columbia and Smith. Each year more than 160 college admission officers visit the School. Colleges and universities at which Northfield Mount Hermon students were accepted in the last five years include, among others, Amherst, Brown, Columbia, Cornell, Georgetown, Harvard, Johns Hopkins, Macalester, MIT, Middlebury, Oberlin, Stanford, the U.S. Naval Academy, Wesleyan, Williams, Yale, and the University of Pennsylvania.

STUDENT BODY AND CONDUCT

The total enrollment for 2005–06 is 725, with 535 boarding students and 190 day students. Students come from thirty-five states and twenty-six countries. International students make up about 25 percent of the total student body.

All members of the NMH community are required to abide by the School's standards, policies, and procedures. Students must agree to conduct themselves according to the highest standards of integrity in all areas of School life and treat others with honesty, civility, and respect.

ACADEMIC FACILITIES

One of NMH's greatest attributes is the large array of facilities available to students. The online library system includes an advanced media center and information commons area and houses more than 78,000 print and nonprint materials, which are indexed by an online catalog. The entire campus, including student rooms, is wired to a

high-speed network. Students bring their own computers, and they can access their personalized virtual desktop through their computer, any computer on campus, or any Internet-connected computer in the world. State-of-the-art digital language labs opened in spring 2004.

NMH's arts facilities include music practice rooms, art studios, photography studios, theater spaces, and a dance studio. Master plans include a new arts center to open in fall 2008.

BOARDING AND GENERAL FACILITIES
The School encompasses privately maintained country roads, ponds, a watershed and reservoir, and a working farm with a maple sugar house.

The Blake Student Center houses a full snack bar and grill, meeting rooms, lounges, and game rooms.

Faculty members and their families live with students in the student houses. Alumni Hall, the dining hall, is centrally located.

O'Connor Health Center is an accredited hospital with 24-hour service. The medical staff includes a resident physician, three full-time psychologists, health educators, nurses, and an X-ray technician.

ATHLETICS
Boys' sports include alpine and Nordic skiing, baseball, basketball, crew, cross-country running, football, ice hockey, lacrosse, soccer, swimming and diving, tennis, track, Ultimate Frisbee, volleyball, water polo, and wrestling. Girls' sports include alpine and Nordic skiing, basketball, crew, cross-country running, field and ice hockey, gymnastics, lacrosse, water polo, soccer, softball, swimming and diving, tennis, track, and volleyball. Golf is a coeducational sport. In addition, there are physical education opportunities in swimming and lifesaving, dance, conditioning, outdoor education, and more.

Two gymnasiums with a swimming pool and fitness center, eleven playing fields, and fifteen tennis courts are available at NMH, as are a covered hockey rink, a track, a nine-hole golf course, indoor and outdoor batting cages, a boathouse and dock, and miles of cross-country and ski trails. Athletic facilities are also scheduled to be renovated and expanded as part of the School's transition to one campus.

EXTRACURRICULAR OPPORTUNITIES
Students develop many interests through the various clubs at NMH. Groups include an international students' association, a literary magazine, affinity groups, and a debate club. Students interested in communications publish an award-winning school newspaper, an art and literary magazine, and a yearbook, and they operate a campus radio station.

Music plays an important part in School life and draws continual support from alumni and friends. There are numerous musical groups, including several choirs, orchestras, and a concert band. Musicians and singers perform in about fifty events each year, including two major traditional concerts: Christmas Vespers and the Concert of Sacred Music. Classes and individual instruction are offered in voice and musical instruments.

DAILY LIFE
Classes meet five days a week. A typical routine consists of major academic courses in the morning; lunch, major or minor classes, study time, and sports in the afternoon; dinner, rehearsal, and free time in the evening; and 2 hours of supervised study from 8 to 10 p.m. Campus work jobs are part of the daily schedule.

WEEKEND LIFE
The student activities office organizes an extensive array of weekend programming. Each weekend, films are shown in the campus theaters. In addition, students may attend dances, concerts, coffeehouse gatherings, and theater productions. Other weekend options include day trips to Boston and other locations as well as hiking, mountain biking, snowboarding, and skiing.

SUMMER PROGRAMS
The Northfield Mount Hermon School offers several summer programs for motivated students in grades 7 through 12 and postgraduates. A five-week on-campus program provides academic enrichment courses (both credit and noncredit), while overseas language programs offer a travel-study-homestay experience in China and Spain.

The faculty includes teachers from NMH and other secondary schools, as well as teaching interns. Tom Pratt is the Director of NMH Summer Session.

COSTS AND FINANCIAL AID
Boarding student tuition for the academic year 2005–06 was $35,000; day tuition was $25,600, plus $675 for weekday lunches.

The financial aid program awarded approximately $5.5 million in direct grants and loans to more than 40 percent of the student body for 2005–06. Eligibility is determined by the School and Student Service for Financial Aid.

ADMISSIONS INFORMATION
Students who demonstrate good character and academic potential may apply for admission to any class. Depending on the grade of entry, students must submit the results of one of the following standardized tests: SSAT, ISEE, CTP, PSAT, SAT, or ACT. An interview is required of any family living within 200 miles of Northfield Mount Hermon School. While the School recognizes that distance may preclude a visit to the School for those living further away, it encourages an on-campus visit as an important part of the admission process.

APPLICATION TIMETABLE
Applicants completing applications by January 15 for day students and February 1 for boarding students are notified of an admission decision by March 10, and parents or guardians are expected to reply by April 10. Applications submitted after March 10 are considered as long as spaces remain available.

ADMISSIONS CORRESPONDENCE
Director of Admission
Northfield Mount Hermon School
206 Main Street
Northfield, Massachusetts 01360-1089

Phone: 413-498-3227
Fax: 413-498-3152
E-mail: admission@nmhschool.org
Web site: http://www.nmhschool.org

OAK HILL ACADEMY

Mouth of Wilson, Virginia

Type: Coeducational boarding and day college-preparatory school
Grades: 8–12
Enrollment: 123
Head of School: Michael D. Groves, President

THE SCHOOL

Oak Hill Academy was founded in 1878 by the Baptists of the New River Baptist Association of Virginia in conjunction with surrounding associations. Beginning its 127th year, the Academy continues to be supported by and affiliated with the Baptist General Association of Virginia. The Academy has developed into a nationally recognized boarding school for girls and boys in grades 8–12 and has a geographically diverse student body from many states and other countries. It accepts a small number of academically qualified local day students.

The Academy believes that the educational process should equip students for a productive role in life. It has high standards, supporting them with an individual orientation designed to elicit the potential in every student.

The school's mission is to provide a safe, secure, nurturing environment for girls and boys needing a change in school, peer, community, or family relationships. It seeks to provide a structured educational program with a curriculum that challenges the brightest students and encourages those who are unmotivated, who are underachieving, or who are experiencing difficulty in their school setting.

The Academy is still dedicated to the tasks for which it was designed. It provides a well-planned and inclusive course of accredited high school work to meet the academic needs of its students. Recognizing the vital force of Christian character and culture in life, it emphasizes the importance of student involvement in activities for growth and for the development of a well-rounded personality, as well as the importance of ethical and moral thoughts and actions.

Oak Hill Academy is located about 7 hours from Washington, D.C., and ½ mile from the village of Mouth of Wilson, Virginia, in the scenic New River Valley of the Blue Ridge Mountains. It is 45 minutes west of Galax and 45 minutes south of Marion. The campus is easily accessible from Interstates 77 and 81. Marion is served by interstate bus lines; taxi service is also available to the campus. The airport in Charlotte, North Carolina, offers the best flight scheduling and is a 2½-hour drive from the campus.

A 24-member Board of Trustees is the governing body of the Academy. All members serve three years, and 8 rotate off each year. For the 8 vacancies, 3 new members are elected by the Baptist General Association and 5 are elected by the remaining board members.

Oak Hill Academy is accredited by the Virginia Association of Independent Schools; it is approved by the Virginia Department of Education. It is also approved by the U.S. government for the teaching of international students. The Academy is a member of the National Association for Foreign Student Affairs, the Association of Boarding Schools, the Secondary School Admission Test Board, and the Southern Association of Independent Schools.

ACADEMIC PROGRAMS

Oak Hill offers all the courses required by the Virginia Department of Education for completion of high school requirements, both college-preparatory and general. A minimum of 23 units in grades 9–12 is required for graduation. In addition to classroom instruction, extra directed study sessions are held by individual teachers for their own students throughout each week. Attendance at Sunday morning church services at Young's Chapel is expected of all students.

The grading system is numerical: A equals 94–100; B, 88–93; C, 77–87; D, 70–76; and F, below 70. Each semester is divided into two 9-week grading periods. At the completion of each grading period, reports are mailed to the parents and a copy is given to the student. At the end of the first four weeks of each period, individual progress reports are mailed for any student who has grades of D, F, or Incomplete. These students are placed in tutorials until the end of each grading period, when new grades are issued and a new assessment is made regarding the student's academic performance.

The arts are important at Oak Hill Academy, and there is a complete fine arts program. Courses available to students in the visual arts department include general crafts, painting, drawing, photography, and pottery. Drama classes offer instruction in musical drama and give performances each year. There are field trips to performances of the Barter Theatre in Abingdon, Virginia.

FACULTY AND ADVISERS

Striving to meet the particular needs of its students, Oak Hill endeavors to select a well-trained and dedicated faculty and staff with the ability and desire to counsel, instruct, and inspire the young people entrusted to their care. The faculty consists of 15 full-time teachers, 11 men and 4 women, plus 2 part-time teachers who also serve in other positions. All teachers are experienced and hold bachelor's degrees; more than one third of them hold advanced degrees. The majority of the faculty members live on the campus and therefore are an integral part of the total community.

Michael D. Groves, the President, received his undergraduate degree from Marshall University and Master of Divinity and Doctor of Philosophy degrees from Southern Baptist Theological Seminary. He has also done additional study at Regent's Park College, University of Oxford, England.

COLLEGE PLACEMENT

A college counselor provides counseling, consultation, and coordination for students, parents, and teachers. Achievement, ability, reading, and vocational aptitude group tests are given. In addition, individualized testing is available where the need is indicated. The guidance staff makes a concerted effort to help each student select and gain admission to the college that is right for his or her interests and abilities. Oak Hill graduates attend colleges and universities throughout the country.

STUDENT BODY AND CONDUCT

For the 2004–05 school year, the enrollment was 120 boarding students and 3 day students. Twenty states, the District of Columbia, and eight countries were represented.

Since all students who enter Oak Hill acquire membership in its limited student body, they must assume the obligation to adhere to both the letter and the spirit of the school's guidelines. The campus is a community, and guidelines are necessary for the welfare of all students. Upon entering a child at Oak Hill, parents are asked to familiarize themselves with the routines and rules of the Academy. The school reserves the right to require the withdrawal of students who fail to meet their obligations, whether because of low standards of scholarship, risk to their health or the welfare of others, or conflict between their standards of behavior and those the Academy seeks to maintain. Oak Hill stands firmly against and prohibits the use of any form of drugs, intoxicating beverages, or tobacco; the possession or handling of fireworks or firearms; and profanity or gambling in any form.

ACADEMIC FACILITIES

A $1-million academic classroom building, the Louise Towles English Building, was dedicated in 1989. A new science wing was dedicated in 2000. Other buildings include the Turner Building, which houses the gymnasium and athletic training rooms, and the Reverend J. F. Fletcher Chapel (1974), which provides an auditorium, music practice rooms, and a conference center. The Academy's library contains 6,500 volumes.

BOARDING AND GENERAL FACILITIES

Oak Hill has five dormitories. Fields Dormitory houses 20 boys, Fletcher Dormitory houses 15 boys, and Ussery Dormitory houses 32 boys; a dormitory for 43 boys was dedicated in 1991. Hough Dormitory has facilities for 98 girls in two-room suites with connecting baths. A large recreation room is located in the lower level of the girls' dorm. Administrative offices and the school cafeteria are located in the Vaughan Building in the center of the campus. Included on the campus are fourteen houses and apartments for faculty and staff members in addition to the apartments for staff members in each dormitory.

ATHLETICS

Each student is encouraged to participate in basketball, volleyball, tennis, or soccer or in the intramural programs of football, basketball, softball, tennis, weight lifting, or running.

The school has three boys' basketball teams: a nationally ranked Gold team, which plays approximately thirty games in several states, and a Red team and a JV team, which play interscholastically in Virginia. Graduates of the Academy have received athletic grants-in-aid from Connecticut, Kentucky, Louisville, Syracuse, and Wake Forest.

The school has a recreational horseback riding program with a riding instructor, outdoor rings, and stalls for 20 horses. The school has its own horses, or students may make arrangements to board theirs. There is a nominal fee for the riding program.

Girls compete interscholastically in basketball, soccer, volleyball, and tennis. In addition to basketball, boys also compete interscholastically in tennis, soccer, baseball, and track.

EXTRACURRICULAR OPPORTUNITIES

A full slate of extracurricular activities is available to students who want to invest some of their spare time in worthwhile projects. Included are such activities as the yearbook, newspaper, photography, and participation in service organizations and special interest clubs. As the weather permits, students take advantage of their surroundings with hiking, canoeing, tubing, cookouts, and picnics on the beautiful New River or at the campus lake and pavilion.

DAILY LIFE

Classes are held five days a week, with a few Saturday class days scheduled. Because of Saturday classes, the school is able to close the campus and give longer holiday periods during the nine-month academic term. At Thanksgiving, there are ten days of vacation. During the Christmas season and again during the early spring, the school has two and three weeks of vacation time scheduled for the students.

A typical daily schedule at Oak Hill Academy is as follows: rising bell, 6:45 a.m.; breakfast, 7:15–7:45; classes, 8:05–3:45; clubs, organizations, class meetings, intramurals, and private time, 4–7:30; dinner, 5:45–6:15; study hall, 7:30–9; and lights-out, 10:30 p.m.

WEEKEND LIFE

Weekend activities include movies, ball games, dances, outings to New River for canoeing and cookouts, and trips to Grayson Highlands and Mount Rogers for hiking. Special seasonal socials include the Fall Festival, Christmas Party, Valentine Dance, and Spring Formal.

SUMMER PROGRAMS

A five-week Summer School is held each year. During this time, a student may earn 1 new unit of credit or repeat 2 failed units of credit. Classes meet from 7:15 a.m. to 12:15 each day, six days a week. Planned, supervised recreational programs are provided in the afternoons.

COSTS AND FINANCIAL AID

Charges for 2005–06 are $21,350. This amount includes $1263 for tuition insurance, $640 for weekly allowance, and $1147 for miscellaneous student expenses. Costs are payable by the session or semester or on a monthly basis.

ADMISSIONS INFORMATION

Oak Hill Academy tries to select from its applicants the students who would most benefit from its special, but limited, program. In evaluating applications, each individual is given particular consideration, whether he or she is an overachiever, underachiever, special student, or average student. The Academy does not discriminate on the basis of religion, race, age, handicap, color, sex, or ethnic or national origin. Each year, approximately three fourths of the students are returning students.

APPLICATION TIMETABLE

Applications are accepted the year round, with admissions granted for the next semester or grading period for which the applicant would be eligible. Notification of acceptance can occur within two to four weeks of the Academy's receipt of all necessary forms. International students are only admitted at the beginning of the fall and summer school terms. Parents are expected to reply to the acceptance within seven to fourteen days whenever possible. A personal interview is always preferred.

Completed application forms must be accompanied by a $50 application fee.

ADMISSIONS CORRESPONDENCE

Admissions Office, Department P
Oak Hill Academy
2635 Oak Hill Road
Mouth of Wilson, Virginia 24363-3004
Phone: 276-579-2619
Fax: 276-579-4722
E-mail: info@oak-hill.net
Web site: http://www.oak-hill.net

OAK KNOLL SCHOOL OF THE HOLY CHILD

Summit, New Jersey

Type: Girls' day college-preparatory religious school (coeducational in Lower School)
Grades: K–12: Lower School, K–6; Upper School, 7–12
Enrollment: School total: 549; Upper School: 310
Head of School: Timothy J. Saburn

THE SCHOOL

Oak Knoll School of the Holy Child, founded in 1924, is an independent Roman Catholic day school for boys and girls in grades K–6 and for young women only in grades 7–12. Located on an 11-acre campus in Summit, New Jersey, the School enjoys the cultural and historic resources of the metropolitan New York area. An additional 14 acres in nearby Chatham Township, New Jersey, was recently developed into state-of-the-art athletic fields.

Operated by the Sisters of the Holy Child Jesus, Oak Knoll helps each student develop to her fullest potential in an environment that fosters the growth of the whole child. The curriculum is designed to engage students' interests and challenge their abilities. The School aims to infuse young people not only with knowledge but also with the spiritual, aesthetic, and moral values that will prepare them for a life of achievement, service, and fulfillment.

Oak Knoll is governed by a 20-member Board of Trustees. The 2005–06 operating budget was $12.7 million, and the 2004–05 Annual Giving campaign raised $850,000. The School's endowment is approximately $8.7 million.

Oak Knoll is accredited by the Middle States Association of Colleges and Schools. It is a member of the National Association of Independent Schools, the National Coalition of Girls Schools, the New Jersey Association of Independent Schools, the School Consortium of New Jersey, the Secondary School Admission Test Board, and the Educational Records Bureau, CSEE, NAPSG, NCEA, and the Cum Laude Society.

ACADEMIC PROGRAMS

Graduation requirements include 4 years of English and theology; 3 years of mathematics, science, and social studies (including 2 years of American history and government); and 2 years of foreign language and physical education. Four additional elective courses are required from offerings in computer science, foreign languages, mathematics, science, social studies, and studio art. Yearlong courses carry 1 academic credit; 27 credits are required for graduation.

An accelerated program in mathematics begins in the seventh grade. In addition, an honors option is available in most subjects, and there are Advanced Placement studies in American history, biology, calculus, chemistry, computer science, English, European history, French, physics, Spanish, and studio art.

The program of studies lists nearly 100 courses for grades 7–12. The widest variety of electives is open to juniors and seniors. Report cards with letter grades are issued after each trimester, and exams are scheduled at the end of the year.

The School inducts students into the Cum Laude Society yearly as well as into the French and Spanish honor societies. Oak Knoll is a wireless campus and is in the third year of an individual laptop program for grades 9 through 11. Seniors may opt in. Other grades have individual laptops available for each class.

Most classes are heterogeneous, and the average class size is 15 students. With a 1:8 faculty-student ratio, the School is noted for what its Middle States Association's evaluation cited as "the personal devotion of the administration and faculty to the students. This pleasant rapport among the members of the School community and the evident responsiveness on the part of the students are perfectly in accord with the School's concept of the importance of the individual, the formation of Christian community, and the development of a sense of service to the larger world community."

FACULTY AND ADVISERS

The Upper School faculty has 51 full-time teachers and 2 part-time teachers, 11 of them men. More than 53 percent have advanced degrees.

Faculty members serve as homeroom teachers, advisers, and moderators for a variety of extracurricular activities, clubs, and student organizations.

Timothy J. Saburn, the Head of School, was appointed by the Board of Trustees in 2005. He holds a Bachelor of Arts from St. Lawrence University, was a Klingenstein Summer Fellow within Columbia University's Teachers College, and received an Ed.M. in administration, planning, and social policy from Harvard University.

COLLEGE PLACEMENT

College guidance begins in the sophomore year under the direction of the College Counselor. In the tenth grade, students take their first PSAT/NMSQT. Students attend college fairs in the metropolitan New York area, and college admissions representatives visit the School. Each September, the entire junior class takes a three-day trip to the Boston, Philadelphia, or Washington, D.C., areas to visit numerous colleges. Information sessions and tours are a part of this trip.

Oak Knoll graduates are accepted at highly competitive colleges and universities. The 58 members of the class of 2005 are now attending numerous institutions, including Boston College, Boston University, Colgate, Cornell, Dartmouth, Duke, Fairfield, Georgetown, Haverford, Middlebury, Northwestern, Santa Clara, Trinity (Hartford), Vanderbilt, Villanova, Wake Forest, Williams, and the Universities of Chicago, Indiana, Notre Dame, and Pennsylvania.

STUDENT BODY AND CONDUCT

The Upper School enrolls 310 girls in grades 7–12, drawing its students from nearly seventy communities in the suburban Summit area.

A Code of Conduct outlines the rules and regulations of the School, which are designed to facilitate the working together of faculty members and students in a community. It is the responsibility of each student to think of others, to respect their rights, and to manifest behavior that results from inner convictions and a high regard for truth, honesty, and integrity. A Conduct Review Committee made up of administrators, teachers, and students advises the Dean of Students in cases of disciplinary infractions.

The dress code requires the wearing of a school uniform while on campus.

ACADEMIC FACILITIES

Oak Knoll is situated on a wooded hill in a residential suburban neighborhood. Grace Hall provides administrative and faculty offices, six classrooms, a chapel, and a creative arts center with media, music, and art studios and a photography darkroom.

Connelly Hall includes a library, a performing arts center, a dining hall, three science laboratories, nine classrooms, a computer center, a senior class lounge, the Writing Center, a publications room, and faculty and administrative offices.

The Tisdall Hall complex houses the gymnasium; the weight training room; the dance studio; the offices of the school nurse, athletic director, athletic trainer, and the physical education staff; and two classrooms.

The Hope Memorial Library offers computerized information services and a book collection of 11,000 volumes. Additional materials are available through an interlibrary loan system.

ATHLETICS

Oak Knoll School of the Holy Child is committed to a strong athletic program that balances physical fitness with a personal commitment to good sportsmanship, which is reflected in gym classes, on the playing fields, and in individual competition. Team spirit in competitive play teaches skills in cooperative effort, and lifelong lessons are learned in victory and defeat. Involvement in the extracurricular sports program is optional.

Oak Knoll enjoys membership in a variety of athletic organizations, including the New Jersey State Interscholastic Athletic Association (NJSIAA), the New Jersey Independent School Athletic Association (NJISAA), the Union County Athletic Conference, the Mountain Valley Conference, the Central Jersey Women's Lacrosse League, and the New Jersey Catholic Track Conference.

Young women in grades 9–12 compete on eighteen teams at the varsity and junior varsity level. Fall sports are cross-country, field hockey, soccer, tennis, and volleyball. The winter season offers basketball, fencing, indoor track, and swimming. In spring, girls compete on lacrosse, outdoor track, and softball teams. During the 2004–05 school year, Oak Knoll School earned various athletic titles, including the Mountain Valley Conference championship winner in field hockey, the Mountain Valley Conference in cross-country, the Mountain Valley Conference–Valley Division and U.C.I.A.C. Counties in soccer, the NJSIAA District Overall and Districts Sabre in fencing, and the CJWLL–Logan Division and NJSIAA sectionals in lacrosse, to name a few.

Students in grades 7 and 8 experience interscholastic competition in cross-country and field hockey in the fall, basketball in the winter, and lacrosse and softball in the spring. Oak Knoll also competes annually in the cross-country and tennis events sponsored through the New Jersey Middle School Consortium.

EXTRACURRICULAR OPPORTUNITIES

Student activities and organizations appeal to a variety of interests and talents. An active Student Council provides leadership opportunities and directs the life of the School in five areas: academic, athletic, campus ministry, creative arts, and social. Student fund-raising for a charity is also done through the Student Council each year. Students publish a yearbook, newspaper, the writers' roundtables, and an award-winning literary magazine. In the creative arts, students can join the Jesters, a drama group, or the Dancers, various choral music groups, and the photography club.

Other extracurricular activities include Mock Trial, Junior Great Books, senior Peer Leaders, tour guides, the competitions of the New Jersey Science and Math Leagues, the Society of Black Scholars, and Shades. Seventh and eighth graders actively participate in the New Jersey Middle School Consortium.

"Culture Vultures" draws students interested in experiencing opera, ballet, Broadway musicals, drama, and concerts in both New Jersey and New York. There is an annual musical theater production and dance concert. The Concert Choirs are featured in the Christmas and spring concerts.

An integral part of Holy Child education is its emphasis on service to others. Students in grades 7–12 keep service portfolios. All students participate in annual service days, during which the entire School travels to a variety of sites to volunteer. Service projects organized by the School include Bridges runs, tutoring programs for inner-city children, a clowning ministry that visits hospitals, and monthly trips to a regional food bank. Ongoing outreach programs support a variety of local and national charities.

DAILY LIFE

The school runs on a six-day-cycle schedule, with the day beginning at 8:10 a.m. and ending at 3:05 p.m.; classes are 45-minute periods.

Hot/cold lunch is served daily in the School dining hall and is included in the tuition.

COSTS AND FINANCIAL AID

Tuition for the academic year is $22,250 for grades 7–12. Included in the tuition is the cost of a hot lunch program. There are additional expenses for a laptop, uniforms, transportation for contracted van service, and a book fee. Some suburban school districts provide bus service to Oak Knoll; others provide reimbursement for part of the transportation cost. A reservation agreement with a tuition deposit is due by early March. Monthly payments can be arranged through tuition payment plans.

Financial aid is available to parents who qualify by filing the Parents' Financial Statement with the School and Student Service for Financial Aid in Princeton, New Jersey. For the 2005–06 school year, tuition grants of $913,000 were awarded; the grants ranged from $1000 to full tuition.

ADMISSIONS INFORMATION

Oak Knoll seeks young women of promise, those who are achievement oriented and who have the potential to succeed in a challenging college-preparatory curriculum. The School does not discriminate on the basis of race, creed, or national origin in the administration of its educational policies, financial aid program, or athletic or other School-administered programs.

Applicants for grade 9 are required to take the SSAT, and the test is administered at Oak Knoll on two test dates in November and December. Applicants for grade 7 and 8 take the ISEE, which is also administered on campus. Transcripts of report cards and standardized test records and two current teacher recommendations must be forwarded from the sending school. An application, $50 fee, an interview at Oak Knoll, and a day spent visiting classes are also required.

APPLICATION TIMETABLE

Inquiries are always welcome. Open Houses usually occur in October and November. Interviews and visiting days run from November through January. The deadline for the entire admissions process is January 27. Decisions are mailed in mid-February. After this date, applications and visits are handled on a rolling-admission basis. Interviews and visits are conducted by appointment only. Admissions office hours are 8 a.m. to 5 p.m. during the academic year or 9 a.m. to 4 p.m., Monday through Thursday, during the summer.

ADMISSIONS CORRESPONDENCE

Suzanne Kimm Lewis, Admissions Director
Oak Knoll School of the Holy Child
44 Blackburn Road
Summit, New Jersey 07901

Phone: 908-522-8109
Fax: 908-277-1838
E-mail: admissions@oakknoll.org
Web site: http://www.oakknoll.org

THE OAKLAND SCHOOL

Pittsburgh, Pennsylvania

Type: Coeducational day college-preparatory school
Grades: 8–PG
Enrollment: 70
Head of School: Jack King, Director of Admissions

THE SCHOOL

The Oakland School, a nonprofit, independent high school, was founded in 1982 to provide a strong basic education in an environment that prepares students for success as participants in school and community life. The Oakland School has a proven record of helping students with a diversity of needs and learning styles, ranging from the academically gifted to the bright underachiever and the motivated learning disabled. The School provides experiences that help students achieve academic success, pursue artistic talents, build self-esteem, participate in positive social interactions, and develop a feeling of belonging and personal acceptance. Students work together to reach academic goals, manage School activities, provide recreation, and offer community service.

The School is located in the Oakland neighborhood of Pittsburgh, a nationally recognized, diverse urban cultural center of libraries, museums, and universities, including the University of Pittsburgh and Carnegie Mellon University.

As a nonprofit agency, the School is supported solely by tuition and is governed by a Board of Directors that determines fiscal and academic policies. The Oakland School is registered with the Pennsylvania Department of Education and is accredited by the Accrediting Commission of the United Private Academic Schools Association of Pennsylvania (UPASA). The School is a member of the Pennsylvania Association of Independent Schools (PAIS) and the Pittsburgh Association of Independent Schools (PAISTA).

ACADEMIC PROGRAMS

The School's college-preparatory curriculum helps develop academic skills, challenges students to think and question, and introduces a wide variety of subject matter. The curriculum emphasizes the mastery of fundamental skills in reading, writing, thinking, and imaginative self-expression.

Students earn 21 credits, which are distributed as English (4), mathematics (3), science (3), social science (3), arts/humanities (3), computer technology (1), health/physical education (1), and approved electives (4). Core studies are sequential in design and include four levels of English language and literature; several levels of algebra and geometry, trigonometry, precalculus, calculus, and statistics; physical science, biology, ecology, physics,

chemistry, and environmental science; social science, which includes American civics, world cultures, U.S. history, geography, anthropology, and psychology; and electives, which include studio art, music, foreign languages, street law, cooking, senior projects, orienteering, chess, math games, history of rock and roll, writer's workshop, current history, sewing, SAT prep, play production, astronomy, and computers. Advanced Placement and honors classes are available in most core subjects. Offerings in foreign language are determined by interest. French, Spanish, Latin, German, and Japanese are currently offered.

Apprenticeships, research projects, independent studies, foreign travel, college classes, and work-study programs are important components of the curriculum.

International students are welcome and add to the diversity of the student population. English as a second language, tutoring, American culture, college counseling, and TOEFL preparation are available. Limited home stays for international students are available and are an excellent opportunity for students to learn the language and culture.

There is a 6:1 student-teacher ratio, and the average class size is 6. The school year is divided into four terms, and students earn up to one credit for each course taken. Progress evaluations are issued at midterm and at the end of each term. Evaluations reflect progress by indicating the earned credit, letter grade, and the teacher's written comments.

The Oakland School Community Service Program was established in 1982 to enable students to contribute their talents and time to the needs of others within their communities. Community service with an approved agency is a requirement for graduation. The School awards one humanities credit for the successful completion of 105 hours of community service.

FACULTY AND ADVISERS

Ten full-time, certified, and experienced teachers provide the educational leadership and instruction for the student body. Eight of these teachers have earned advanced degrees in their fields. Part-time instructors complement the staff. Each student is assigned a staff mentor who serves as an informed listener and a clear voice for the student.

The School's administration leader is Jack King, Director of Academics and Counseling. King holds a B.S. from Clarion State College,

an M.Ed. from Indiana University of Pennsylvania, and a Secondary Principal's Certificate from the Pennsylvania State University. His twenty-three years at the Oakland School (twelve as an administrator) offer strong guidance and leadership for both students and faculty members.

COLLEGE PLACEMENT

The philosophy of the Oakland School holds all students to the highest possible level of education as determined by ability, vocational goals, and educational preparation. Sophomores share achievement test information and discuss college/career goals with counselors. Meetings to discuss options and to lay the groundwork for applications are held in the junior year. Most seniors enter college immediately following graduation. Some graduates enter the military, art school, computer training, or technical schools.

Sixty-one of the 92 graduates of the classes of 2000–05 are attending, among others, the following colleges and universities: Bard, Chatham, Duquesne, Indiana of Pennsylvania, Marlboro, Oberlin, Penn State, Pittsburgh, Pratt, and West Virginia. Four graduates joined branches of the United States military. Ten graduates attended community college or enrolled in technical programs. The range and median of SAT scores for the classes of 2000–05 were Math 330–800 (500) and Verbal 340–800 (527). The classes of 2004 and 2005 both graduated a finalist in the National Merit Scholarship Competition.

A large selection of resources is available to aid students in the college search and application process. Resources include collections of print and video materials about occupations, trade and technical schools, and scholarship opportunities. The School maintains a library of more than 300 college catalogs.

STUDENT BODY AND CONDUCT

The Oakland School attracts families from southwest Pennsylvania, with many students enrolling from the Pittsburgh area. The 2000–05 distribution is 15 in grade 8, 36 in grade 9, 58 in grade 10, 75 in grade 11, and 92 in grade 12. There are 3 international students. The student body represents all socioeconomic levels and usually is equally divided among boys and girls, with 15 to 20 percent who are members of minority groups.

Students have "ownership" of the School and have always cared for the property. Students are expected to show courtesy and respect to everyone in the building and in the neighborhood. The School's rules of conduct form a short list: attendance is mandatory; forms of dress that interfere with learning are unacceptable; buying, selling, and using illegal substances is forbidden; and fighting and bullying are not tolerated.

ACADEMIC FACILITIES

The School occupies a single, 2½-level former church that provides twelve teaching areas. A large commons area and stage accommodate the all-school gatherings. A separate loft houses the studio art classes. Everyone, including those in the cooking classes, shares a kitchen area. In fair weather, students may be found outdoors on the School's benches and ample lawn areas

A library of thousands of publications is maintained in appropriate classrooms; however, most research is conducted in the libraries of nearby institutions, such as the Carnegie and Hillman libraries. Apple computers are located throughout the building, and students have Internet access through a wireless DSL network.

ATHLETICS

The Oakland School does not provide interscholastic athletic competition. The physical education program promotes individual potential through programs in basketball, football, soccer, tennis, and volleyball as well as aerobics, bowling, and walking. Students may receive credit for athletic activities outside of School.

EXTRACURRICULAR OPPORTUNITIES

The School's yearbook and its literary magazine, *Utopia*, offer opportunities for artists, writers, and organizers to utilize their talents.

Writing workshops, chess groups, music jams, stargazing, and other mostly student-inspired activities, take place before and after school hours.

DAILY LIFE

Each day begins at 8:30 a.m. with two 45-minute class periods; next, there is a 15-minute break, which is followed by two classes. Two afternoon classes follow a 45-minute lunch period, with dismissal at 2 p.m. Students may leave the School during the lunch period to eat, shop, or explore the neighborhood. The School does not serve meals; students eat out, order-in, or bring their lunches.

On most Wednesday afternoons, students pursue a number of educational options, which include library research, independent study, field trips, basic studies, community service, and work-study programs.

COSTS AND FINANCIAL AID

Tuition for the 2006–07 school year is $9000. A $200 activity fee is also charged. A $100 graduation fee is charged to seniors only. International tuition is $13,000. Additional fees are charged for selective private instruction. Students provide notebooks and other supplies. A variety of payment options are available to families for financial planning

A limited number of need-based financial aid grants are awarded each year. Families may submit an application for aid with their most recent 1040 tax return for review by the Scholarship Committee. Thirty percent of the student body received financial aid grants totaling $100,200 in 2000–05.

ADMISSIONS INFORMATION

The major criterion for admission is the student's ability to participate in and benefit from the School's academic program and social environment. Needs and abilities are assessed on three fronts: academic (Does the student possess the motivation and skills necessary to complete a demanding program of study?), goals (Are the student's future personal and career plans compatible with the educational preparation provided by the school?), and conduct (Is the student willing and able to act as a responsible member of a learning community and to contribute productively?).

The Oakland School believes in equal opportunity for everyone and does not allow any form of discrimination in admission policy or in financial aid policy. The School provides a multiethnic, multiracial, nonsexist, and coeducational environment for learning.

APPLICATION TIMETABLE

The Oakland School's open admission policy accepts applications for enrollment at any time. Prospective students and their families should contact the School to schedule an introductory visit. Students are invited to personally complete formal assessments, visit classes, and meet other students. Admission is based on the School's assessment of the student's potential for success, not on their past academic record.

A $100 application fee is applied toward tuition, if the student is accepted; if not, $75 is refunded.

Approximately 90 percent of applicants are accepted annually.

ADMISSIONS CORRESPONDENCE

Admissions Desk
The Oakland School
362 McKee Place
Pittsburgh, Pennsylvania 15213-7878

Phone: 412-621-7878
Fax: 412-621-7881
E-mail: oschool@stargate.net
Web site: http://www.theoaklandschool.org

OAKLEY SCHOOL
Oakley, Utah

Type: Coeducational college-preparatory boarding school for motivated stable students in need of continued personal support
Grades: 9–12
Enrollment: 128
Head of School: James Meyer

THE SCHOOL

The Oakley School opened in 1998 to meet the academic and emotional needs of intelligent, motivated students. Oakley gives ninth- to twelfth-grade students an exceptional college-preparatory experience coupled with a strategic counseling component and a multitude of dynamic recreation opportunities. The founders of the School, Dr. Jared Balmer and Dr. Lorin Broadbent, have created a positive, supportive environment in which students who have addressed the majority of their personal or academic issues can excel. The Oakley School offers a highly structured, individualized boarding school experience for young men and women who have made the choice to invest in learning. Students are encouraged to take charge of their lives and make positive choices in a drug-, alcohol-, and tobacco-free environment. The mission of the Oakley School is to inspire each student to respect and pursue intellectual and moral growth while developing the individual skills crucial to succeed in a complex, changing world. By engaging in diverse educational experiences both in and out of the classroom, self-esteem is strengthened and life skills are promoted. The Oakley School provides students with a learning environment that challenges the mind, body, and spirit. Furthermore, it promotes service as a means to strengthen the community and achieve self-fulfillment.

The Oakley School resides on roughly 25 acres. It is located 15 miles from Park City, Utah, and 50 minutes from Salt Lake International Airport.

The Oakley School is fully accredited by the Northwest Association of Schools and Colleges.

ACADEMIC PROGRAMS

The Oakley School maintains a traditional college-preparatory curriculum tailored to meet the students' individual needs. Small classes, ranging in size from 2 to 16 students, allow tremendous personal interaction and productive working relationships between students and teachers. A student's academic ability and needs are assessed upon enrollment. Students are then paired with a teacher who acts as an academic adviser overseeing their scholastic progress. Classes are highly competitive, requiring students to challenge themselves. Supportive teachers identify learning issues and weaknesses and coordinate with the child's academic adviser and therapist to develop strategies to help overcome these obstacles. Communication among the faculty members, academic adviser, parents, and remaining staff members is extensive. Each student receives written progress reports every sixty days detailing their progress in the following four areas of the School: education, recreation, dorm life, and therapy. The minimum length of stay at Oakley is determined by two factors: six consecutive seven-week sessions and dates when credits are issued. Credits are issued at the end of the fall, winter, and spring trimesters and at the end of the summer session. The minimum length of enrollment at the Oakley School is fulfilled the next date credits are issued after the six consecutive seven-week session requirement has been met. A minimum of 24 credits is needed to graduate. Requirements include 4 credits in English, 3 credits in social science, 3 credits in mathematics, 3 credits in science (including 1 credit of lab science and 1 credit of physical science), 2 credits in foreign language, 1 credit in computer science, 1.5 credits in fine arts, 2 credits in physical education/health, and up to 4.5 credits of electives. All students are required to participate in physical education or a competitive sports team and in recreation modules on Fridays and Saturdays, regardless of credit needs. Students in every grade level complete a formal research paper and a service project.

The Oakley curriculum offers 4 years of English, creative writing, journalism, and one other elective course; 4 years of science, including environmental science, biology, chemistry, conceptual physics, anatomy, geology, honors physics, and biotechnology; 4 years of math, including algebra 1, algebra 2, geometry, precalculus, calculus, statistics, and Advanced Placement calculus; 4 years of Spanish, including Spanish 1, 2, and 3; and 4 years of social science, including world civilizations, modern European history, U.S. history, psychology, sociology, two elective courses, and modern Asian history. Oakley also offers Japanese and art history.

FACULTY AND ADVISERS

There are 11 teachers on staff, creating a student-teacher ratio of 9:1. All members of the faculty hold baccalaureate degrees, and 6 have advanced degrees. All teachers assist in recreation and artistic modules. Oakley teachers are committed to educating the whole child. All of the teachers are certified or are in pursuit of certification with letters of authorization.

James Meyer is the Head of School. Mr. Meyer received his baccalaureate degree in history from the University of Colorado at Boulder and his master's degree in education, foundations, and curriculum from Fairfield University.

COLLEGE PLACEMENT

The Oakley School provides SAT and ACT tutoring and guidance in the college application process. Students are encouraged to begin the college application process in the junior year, and all seniors make college visits in the fall of their senior year. Educational consultants are often utilized as the "torchbearers" for the college admissions process. The Oakley School provides college counseling services for any student who is pursuing college placement. This counseling is completed in coordination with a child's educational consultant. All Oakley students who applied to colleges were accepted at a college of their choice. The students are encouraged to attend small to medium-sized colleges, as Oakley students excel in an environment that encourages student-teacher interaction. Some of these colleges include Colorado College, Eckerd, Franklin and Marshall, Lehigh, New England College, Pepperdine, Seton Hall, Suffolk, and Willamette.

STUDENT BODY AND CONDUCT

The Oakley School has the capacity to enroll 128 boarding students. Students represent a great number of countries and states. All students conform to a dress code during the school day. Boys wear collared shirts and pants (no jeans), and girls may wear pants (no jeans), a skirt or dress of appropriate length, and collared shirts. Excessive makeup, jewelry, or garments reflecting a negative subculture are not allowed.

The Oakley School has a comprehensive, individualized counseling component designed to help students work through issues in a directed prosocial manner. Students have therapy counseling with a master's-level clinician who also facilitates family therapy. Students also participate in group sessions and in a variety of recovery groups. The Oakley School has a form system that uses citizenship as a gauge for responsibility and privilege.

Five basic ground rules govern behavior at the Oakley School. All students sign and are expected to respect a working honor code. Oakley is committed to a drug-, alcohol-, and tobacco-free environment in which students support each other in positive decision making.

The student council, made up of 10 to 16 students who also act as dorm proctors, helps perpetuate a positive social environment. Student council members are elected by peers, and they serve on the disciplinary committee with staff members. Oakley students are encouraged to make healthy choices through strong interpersonal interactions with staff members, peers, and parents.

ACADEMIC FACILITIES

The Oakley School's main lodge holds twelve classrooms, including two science labs and an art studio with a kiln and a darkroom. In addition, there are a full gymnasium, rock-climbing wall, weight room, dance studio, and multipurpose room that can be used for School productions and activities. Students study in a full library that offers access to more than 2,500 volumes. All classrooms and the library are computer networked, and the School has Internet access through a DSL line.

BOARDING AND GENERAL FACILITIES

There are two dormitories at Oakley, each housing up to 48 students. The dorms are divided into houses consisting of 32 students. Dominguez and Escalante Houses comprise the boys' dorm, while Powell and Bridger Houses comprise the girls' dorm. All rooms are designed to house up to 4 students. Each dorm room has its own bathroom, and each dorm has laundry facilities and a large commons area. Student proctors in each dorm assist the house coaching staff with all aspects of dorm life, including study hall supervision and dorm-run student activities. The Oakley School gymnasium is a 14,320-square-foot addition. This facility has a 9,776-square-foot gym with a basketball and volleyball court and a two-lane running track on a state-of-the-art hardwood floor. There is also 2,320 square feet of classroom space, including an art room and a multipurpose room. A storage facility and 2,220 square feet of office space finish off the building's blueprint.

ATHLETICS

In addition to traditional, competitive sports teams, Oakley targets outdoor recreation activities. The School's location in the heart of the Wasatch Mountains provides easy access to skiing, snowboarding, mountain biking, rock climbing, kayaking, backpacking, camping, and many other outdoor activities. Self-confidence, initiative, skill competence, teamwork, and leadership skills are taught and enhanced through these activities. The concept of integrating healthy lifestyle choices into daily life skills is consciously programmed into each module. Recreation modules occur as full-day activities every Friday and Saturday, with activity offerings changing every seven weeks. Fly-fishing, drama, ceramics, Indian art, geology, dance, and other special-interest modules occur as interest dictates.

Traditional competitive sports, including basketball, cross-country, golf, lacrosse, soccer, swimming, volleyball, and wrestling, are currently offered for boys and girls, with new sports added as interest dictates. Teams compete as a part of the Utah High School Activities Association, and participation on all skill levels is encouraged. Students must maintain an acceptable academic and citizenship standard to compete. Physical conditioning is required on a daily basis during the school week, emphasizing fun and fitness in activities. Traditional calisthenics intermingled with current trendy activities (aerobics, Tae-Bo, etc.) keep the classes exciting. Recreation provides a healthy outlet and is a necessary tool for stress management. The Recreation Department strives to prepare students for independent living by incorporating healthy life skills into daily habits; promoting safe, inclusive outdoor activities; and assisting in developing individual confidence, self-esteem, and environmental respect.

Service is a mandatory requirement for all students at the Oakley School. The concept of service provides an invaluable sense of gratitude and humility. Community service, school service, and service to self and family are incorporated into the module schedule. Local and national special service projects are coordinated for students who choose to participate.

EXTRACURRICULAR OPPORTUNITIES

On-campus and off-campus activities abound at Oakley, thus enriching the spirit of community. Typical school groups, such as yearbook, drama, performing arts/annual school play, school newspaper, and the literary magazine, are available. Student organizations include student council, proctorships, peer tutors, and disciplinary committee members.

In addition to the outdoor recreation events, Oakley's proximity to Salt Lake City creates a fine balance with big-city cultural opportunities. Time is available on Sundays for student-directed activities, including many outings to Salt Lake.

DAILY LIFE

Beyond academics and recreation modules, typical student days are geared toward finding a healthy balance between work and play. On-campus activities and responsibilities during the weekdays include dormitory chores, community groups, time for socializing and relaxing, exercising and weight lifting, and various pick-up sports. Weekend activities include campus work, community service projects, trips to malls, dinners, movies, concerts, theater, and sports events. Students also take advantage of Utah's brilliant outdoors, participating in water sports, biking, golf, hiking, and winter sports such as sledding, skiing, ice skating, and snowshoeing. Staff members and students conspire weekly to discuss student outings. Once a month a formal dinner is served, offering an elegant ambiance as well as special awards and guest speakers.

The Oakley School students elect a council that works to ensure that students are provided with fun activities and are held responsible for irresponsible behavior. The student council takes an active role in community events and celebrations. They also contribute to the interview process of potential students, offering camaraderie during the extended interview.

House coaching staff members are available around the clock to provide structure, role modeling, support, and encouragement with issues concerning student life. They assist students in developing personality and promoting creativity within the different dorms. Sunday through Thursday, the house coaches supervise mandatory study halls in the afternoons and evenings.

Classes are held Monday through Thursday. Classes begin at 8 a.m. on a block schedule and last until approximately 4 p.m. Fridays and Saturdays are reserved for outdoor, experiential, and artistic modules. Sunday is a student-directed day.

SUMMER PROGRAM

The Summer Session is six weeks in length, running from mid-June until late July. Classes are 50 minutes to 90 minutes in length and meet three days a week on a rotating block schedule. Students are able to make up credit or get ahead in credit during the summer. Typical course offerings include physical science, math skill builder, SAT prep, creative writing, American history, Spanish skill builder, study skills, and independent study.

COSTS AND FINANCIAL AID

The tuition, room and board, and other costs are based on the completion of at least six 7-week sessions. This is approximately ten to fourteen months, based on the day of enrollment for each individual student. The monthly cost is $5500. This is an all-inclusive rate and covers all tuition, books, therapy, module events, transportation, and equipment rental (if necessary). Tutorial services are available at an additional cost. Payment for the prorated portion of any month, the first full month, an enrollment fee of $1750, and a $12,000 deposit ($15,000 for seniors) is expected upon enrollment. Financial aid is provided on the basis of need and considered on an individual basis. Merit-based scholarships are also available for outstanding students.

ADMISSIONS INFORMATION

The Oakley School admits students who have a strong commitment to themselves. Such a student expresses that he or she wants to actively develop and solidify a healthy lifestyle through participation in the therapy provided at the Oakley School. Applicants are evaluated through psychological testing, essay questions, school transcripts, teacher recommendations, and a required on-campus interview. Oakley School has a rolling enrollment; therefore, students can apply to enroll at any time throughout the year. The Oakley School accepts students for grades 9, 10, 11, and 12. The SSAT is recommended for applicants to grade 12 and the postgraduate year.

APPLICATION TIMETABLE

The Oakley School has a rolling enrollment; therefore, there is no cut-off date for applications. The commitment of each student and family ranges between ten and fourteen months. Applications are accepted year-round, and interviews can be arranged Monday through Thursday during business hours.

ADMISSIONS CORRESPONDENCE

Carrie Thompson, Director of Admissions
The Oakley School
251 West Weber Canyon School
P.O. Box 357/367
Oakley, Utah 84055

Phone: 435-783-5001
Fax: 435-783-5010
E-mail: admissions@oakley-school.com
Web site: http://www.oakley-school.com

OAK RIDGE MILITARY ACADEMY

Oak Ridge, North Carolina

Type: Coeducational boarding and day college-preparatory and military school
Grades: 6–12
Enrollment: 240
Head of School: Col. Roy W. Berwick, Ph.D., President

THE SCHOOL

Oak Ridge Military Academy is a coeducational college-preparatory school that enrolls students in grades 6–12. The 101-acre campus, a National and State Historic District, is located on the Piedmont plateau, about 15 miles from Greensboro, Winston-Salem, and High Point, North Carolina. The campus is 6 miles north of the Piedmont Triad International Airport and is situated at the crossroads of State Highways 68 and 150.

The school was founded in 1852 as the Oak Ridge Institute by community leaders seeking to offer a superior college-preparatory education to students in the region. In 1899, Oak Ridge became the first school in North Carolina to be accredited by the Southern Association of Colleges and Schools. A Junior Reserve Officers' Training Corps (JROTC) unit was established at the school in 1926. The Academy began enrolling women in 1971, and the present name was adopted ten years later. In 1991, the North Carolina General Assembly designated Oak Ridge Military Academy "The Official Military Academy of North Carolina."

Oak Ridge Military Academy's mission is to offer, within a military structure, a college-preparatory curriculum that develops well-rounded young men and women who are equipped to succeed in college and have the self-discipline, integrity, and leadership skills necessary to reach their potential in life.

The Academy is a nonprofit institution owned by the Oak Ridge Foundation, Inc. It is accredited by the Southern Association of Colleges and Schools and holds membership in the Association of Military Colleges and Schools and the National Association of Independent Schools as well as in other associations.

ACADEMIC PROGRAMS

The academic year, divided into semesters, begins in August and extends to the end of May, with vacations of one week in October, a Thanksgiving break in November, two weeks at Christmas, one week in February, and a week over Easter in the spring. Classes meet five days a week and are scheduled in seven academic periods. The average class has 15 students.

Special provisions within the curriculum are made for the gifted and talented. Extra academic help is offered (or may be required) during "Help Classes," scheduled after the last class period every day. Academic reports are maintained online through Edline.

The Academy offers two diplomas: the Advanced College diploma and the College Preparation diploma. To graduate with the Advanced College diploma, a cadet must complete 28 units of credit, including 4 in English, 4 in history/social studies, 4 in Leadership Education Training (LET) in the U.S. Army JROTC program, 4 in mathematics, 4 in science, 3 in a foreign language, 2 in electives, 1 in health/physical education, 1 in writing, ½ in computer studies, and ½ in SAT preparation.

To graduate with the College Preparation diploma, a cadet must complete 24 units of credit, including 4 in English, 4 in Leadership Education Training in the U.S. Army JROTC program, 3 in history/social studies, 3 in mathematics, 3 in science, 2 in a foreign language, 1 in electives, 1 in health/physical education, 1 in writing, ½ in computer studies, and ½ in SAT preparation.

The curriculum includes a full range of the traditional academic subjects, from introductory courses in math, language arts, science, and social studies through fourth-year French, German, and Spanish. Advanced Placement courses are offered in French, German, Spanish, calculus, statistics, biology, environmental science, and economics. On-campus college-level courses are offered in English and history. There are a wide variety of off-campus college courses available at the University of North Carolina at Greensboro. English as a second language is available for international students.

FACULTY AND ADVISERS

Col. Roy W. Berwick, Ph.D., is a retired soldier. While on active duty, he served in the Military Police Corps in every leadership position, from squad leader to battalion executive officer, and at every staff level, from battalion to Department of the Army. In addition, he served in the Judge Advocate General's Corps as a lawyer. Upon retirement from the U.S. Army in 1993, he entered private education as the Senior Army Instructor at Oak Ridge Military Academy and has worked in the field as Commandant of Cadets, St. John's Northwestern Military Academy; President, Millersburg Military Institute; and Vice President and Academic Dean, Massanutten Military Academy. In July 2005, he returned to Oak Ridge Military Academy as President. He resides on campus with his family and the family cats, Raggs and Harper.

The full-time faculty consists of 12 men and 14 women. Eleven faculty and staff members live on campus. Many of the faculty members hold master's degrees. There are 4 part-time instructors. Faculty members serve as study hall supervisors, coaches, and advisers for classes and organizations. They are encouraged to pursue advanced degrees at several local universities and to attend conferences and seminars related to their professional development.

An infirmary on campus is staffed by qualified medical personnel. Full medical services are available at hospitals in Greensboro and Winston-Salem.

COLLEGE PLACEMENT

All juniors and seniors take the SAT. A college counselor maintains a collection of college catalogs and scholarship information and actively monitors the placement process as well as the application process. Faculty and staff members, including the President, also assist in the process of college placement. For the past twelve years, 100 percent of the Academy's graduates have been accepted to a college or service academy.

STUDENT BODY AND CONDUCT

In 2005–06, there were 188 boys and 52 girls enrolled. Fifty were day students and 190 boarded. Most students come from North Carolina. Others are from twenty-five states and twenty-one other countries.

The Corps of Cadets is organized as a battalion and is composed of four line companies, Band Company, and Headquarters Company. A cadet's rank and position within the Corps is determined by his or her academic and military performance, participation in activities, and demonstrated leadership potential. All cadets are required to adhere to the policies outlined in the *Oak Ridge Military Academy Cadet Regulations Handbook* and the Cadet Honor Code and Creed.

ACADEMIC FACILITIES

A 31,000-square-foot classroom building was constructed in 2001. The Alumni Building houses offices and a library containing a collection of 20,000 volumes. The library is equipped with twelve IBM computer workstations with Internet access and a ten-workstation computer lab, which is provided through Computer Curriculum Corporation. The system is networked to the computer lab, which has an additional fifteen workstations. A CD-ROM stack is available for access to reference materials. Cottrell Hall houses the music facility.

BOARDING AND GENERAL FACILITIES

The Cadet Dining Hall, where all meals are provided by a professional food service, is adjacent to the Cadet Lounge. A Cadet Store offers necessities. Cadets live 2 to a room in the four dormitories, Holt Hall, Whitaker Hall, Armfield Hall, and Caesar Cone Hall. All the dormitories have at least one apartment in which a staff or faculty member resides.

The Colonel Bonner Field House is the primary athletic facility. King Gymnasium is used for indoor sports. The swimming pool was built as an addition in 1934, and the whole building was remodeled in 1992. Three athletic fields, one paintball course, a challenge course, two rifle ranges, and three tennis courts are among the athletic resources. Other facilities include Linville Chapel and the Linville Infirmary.

ATHLETICS

Men's and women's teams compete against private and public schools in baseball, basketball, cross-country, golf, lacrosse, soccer, swimming, tennis, track and field, volleyball, and wrestling. The rifle and drill teams compete on a national level. Middle School students may compete for positions on junior varsity and varsity teams. Every student has the opportunity to participate in a cocurricular activity, including paintball, rappelling, and the obstacle course. Oak Ridge is a member of the Triad Athletic Conference and the North Carolina Independent Schools Athletic Association.

EXTRACURRICULAR OPPORTUNITIES

Students may participate in community service activities, clubs, leadership opportunities, and other pursuits. Among the extracurricular options are the production of the yearbook and *The Oak Leaf,* and a scouting program. Cadets are invited to take part in the Governor's Page Program, the Military Band Festival, and state and national drill competitions.

Scheduled social events include the Junior Ring Dance (junior prom) and the Military Ball (senior prom). A full range of activities is planned for every weekend. Traditional events scheduled on the school calendar include Homecoming, Parents' Days, Alumni Day, Academic Awards Day, Annual Sports Banquet, and Mother's Day.

DAILY LIFE

The student day begins with reveille at 6:30 a.m. Seven academic periods are scheduled from 8:30 to 3:45. Teachers remain in their classrooms from 3:15 to 3:45 to offer additional help. During the afternoon activity period from 4 to 6, cadets participate in extracurricular activities, character development, chapel assembly, and drill practice. Athletic practice for interscholastic sports is held between 4 and 6. Those students not participating in interscholastic sports have study time in the library during this period. Retreat is held at 6 each evening, and dinner is at 6:30. Call to quarters (mandatory study period) is from 7:30 to 9 p.m. Taps (lights-out) is at 10.

WEEKEND LIFE

Weekend activities for boarding students are closely supervised and include recreational and athletic activities designed to provide a change from the scheduled routine of the week. Off-campus trips are generally scheduled on Saturday and include travel to cultural events, athletic activities, and outdoor recreational areas as well as regular trips to a local enclosed shopping mall. Students may attend religious services of their choice. Chapel is mandatory for those remaining on campus.

COSTS AND FINANCIAL AID

In 2005–06, the cost of tuition was $19,990 for boarding students and $7900 for day students. Additional fees include books ($475), mandatory accident insurance ($130), and the cadet bank (at least $75). Haircuts, laundry, and dry cleaning are included in the price of tuition. There is a one-time fee of $1850 for uniforms. Limited merit scholarships were available in 2005–06.

ADMISSIONS INFORMATION

Oak Ridge Military Academy seeks students of average to above-average academic ability who have the motivation to succeed in a college-preparatory environment. It maintains a nondiscriminatory admission policy. New students are accepted in grades 6–12. Admission is based upon a vote of the Admissions Committee, based on a student's grades, behavior, and participation. A personal interview is not required but is recommended.

APPLICATION TIMETABLE

Applications, with a fee of $100, should be submitted as early as possible, preferably in the spring to qualify for fall enrollment. Students may be accepted at any time during the year.

ADMISSIONS CORRESPONDENCE

Mr. Jad Davis, M.A.
Director of Admissions
Oak Ridge Military Academy
P.O. Box 498
Oak Ridge, North Carolina 27310

Phone: 336-643-4131 Ext. 131
Fax: 336-643-1797
E-mail: jdavis@ormila.com
Web site: http://www.oakridgemilitary.com

OAKWOOD FRIENDS SCHOOL

Poughkeepsie, New York

Type: Coeducational boarding (grades 9–12) and day (grades 6–12) college-preparatory school
Grades: 6–12
Enrollment: 162
Head of School: Peter F. Baily

THE SCHOOL

Oakwood Friends School is dedicated to educating each student intellectually, physically, and spiritually in a culturally diverse community. Oakwood Friends is the only school under the care of the New York Yearly Meeting of the Religious Society of Friends since 1796, when it was known as the School of Nine Partners in Millbrook, New York. Oakwood Friends settled into its present campus in 1920 and continues to elicit "that of God in every person" in its rigorous educational setting.

The School is located on 63 acres in the Hudson Valley with a view of the Shawangunk Mountains—a major rock-climbing area—80 miles north of New York City.

At least 11 members of the Board of Managers, which includes 7 trustees, are Quakers appointed by the New York Yearly Meeting of the Religious Society of Friends to oversee the School, which is a nonprofit corporation. Five other board members are nominated by the Alumni Association, and 5 members-at-large are nominated by the board itself. Operating expenses for 2004–05 were $3.5 million. The endowment was $1.8 million.

Oakwood Friends School is accredited by the New York State Association of Independent Schools and chartered by the New York State Board of Regents. It is a member of the National Association of Independent Schools, the Friends Council on Education, and A Better Chance.

ACADEMIC PROGRAMS

The school year is divided into three 11-week trimesters. In the progressively challenging college-preparatory curriculum, students are placed according to their ability in mathematics and foreign language, and they progress to college freshman–level courses in the senior program.

Minimum requirements for the diploma include 4 years of English, 3 of social studies, 3 of a foreign language, 3 of mathematics, 3 of science (2 labs), 1⅓ of the arts (drama, studio arts, or music), a term course in Quakerism, a term of computer literacy, a term of health, 4 years of physical education and sports, and a community-service requirement each year.

A unified senior program is the final requirement for graduation. It begins with a camping trip in the Adirondacks to start the yearlong process of personal and group goal setting, which continues through weekly Core Group meetings. The intellectual focus of the program is provided by challenging interdisciplinary courses on topics such as the moral dilemmas for the twenty-first century, Plato's *Republic*, comparative political systems, classics of film and literature, comparative religion, and geopolitical studies.

Advanced Placement art, English, French, Spanish, calculus, and biology are available. Elective courses include drawing, painting, printmaking, playwriting, directing, ceramics, photography, drama, drama tech, vocal ensemble, jazz ensemble, music theory, musical production, art history, music history, music/art/drama portfolio, algebra, introduction to college math (precalculus), writing seminar, chemistry, biology, and physics. The senior year also includes an off-campus community service program: students volunteer at the project of their choice one day a week during periods in the winter and spring.

Ten percent of the School's students are from abroad. Students who have mild, documented learning differences receive support for at least one period each day in the Academic Support Center, where they are given one-to-one and small-group assistance with homework assignments; basic skills in reading, writing, and math; organizing study time; and academic and personal counseling.

Students are required to study in the dorms for 2 hours, Monday through Thursday nights, supervised by faculty members.

Oakwood Friends students may take courses at nearby colleges and have access to the Vassar College library collection through interlibrary loan. Independent or accelerated study may be arranged for students in good standing.

Two grading systems are used: A, B, C, D, and F in academic subjects and honors, and pass-fail in nonacademic subjects. Grades and reports are given to parents six times a year. Students achieving independent status (IS) standing are exempt from mandatory study hall and may study independently.

FACULTY AND ADVISERS

There are 26 full-time teachers and 10 administrators. Of these, most live at the School. They hold thirty-six baccalaureate and seventeen advanced degrees, including doctorates and doctor of medicine from such colleges and universities as Adelphi; Albion; Alvan Ikoku; American; Bard; Brandeis; Brooklyn; Brown; Bryn Mawr; Carleton College; Central Michigan; Colgate; CUNY; Drew; Dutchess Community College; Earlham; East Stroudsburg; Fashion Institute of Technology; Georgetown; Guilford College; Hunter College; Imo State; Manhattan School of Music; Manhattanville; Marist; Muhlenberg; Nasson; National College of Education; New Rochelle; NYU; Ohio Wesleyan; Rutgers; St. Francis; St. Lawrence; Scarritt; SUNY at Albany, Brockport, Fredonia, Geneseo, New Paltz, and Potsdam; Syracuse; Tufts; Universidad de Chile; Universite Lumiere-Lyon; Vassar; Wentworth Institute of Technology; Wesleyan; William and Mary; and the Universities of Central Florida, Colorado, Colorado Health Sciences Center, Delaware, Denver, and Tennessee. There are 6 part-time instructors.

Peter F. Baily, appointed Head of School in July 2000, is a graduate of Earlham College, Nasson College (B.A., M.E.), and Bryn Mawr College (M.A.). Prior to his last position as Interim Head of School of the Quaker School at Horsham, Mr. Baily served seven years as Head of School at Oak Lane Day School in Blue Bell, Pennsylvania.

Oakwood Friends' primary criteria for selecting faculty members are their academic background, teaching experience, and agreement with the School's philosophy, as well as the capacity to relate to students in ways that enhance intellectual, personal, and social growth.

Professional growth opportunities are available to faculty members. Many faculty members serve as student advisers, and many supervise activities or serve as coaches.

COLLEGE PLACEMENT

College counseling begins in October of the junior year with administration of the PSAT, campus visits by college representatives, and attendance at a college night at a local campus. In January and February, every junior has a conference with the college adviser to review PSAT results and begin college selection. In the spring, juniors and their parents are informed about college admissions and financial aid procedures, and individual conferences prepare students for summer college visits and final college choices. Individual advising continues in the fall, and college applications are completed before winter vacation.

Ninety-eight to 100 percent of Oakwood's graduates continue on to colleges and universities. Graduates of the class of 2005 are attending Bennington; Brandeis; Bryn Mawr; Dutchess Community College; Emerson; Haverford; Hobart and William Smith; Pratt Institute; Rutgers; St. John's; SUNY at Albany, Alfred, Buffalo, and New Paltz; Susquehanna; Swarthmore; Illinois at Urbana-Champaign; Vassar; and Washington College.

STUDENT BODY AND CONDUCT

Oakwood Friends' enrollment includes 65 day boys, 46 day girls, 28 boarding boys, and 23 boarding girls. There are 6 in grade 6, 11 in grade 7, 20 in grade 8, 22 in grade 9, 41 in grade 10, 37 in grade 11, and 25 in grade 12. Eighty-five percent are from New York State, 4 percent are from six other states, and 10 percent are from four other countries. Twenty-five percent are members of minority groups.

The Student/Parent Handbook offers guidelines of conduct for the entire Oakwood Friends community. Disciplinary responses are student-centered in nature. While addressing the actions of students, disciplinary responses allow the opportunity for individual growth and education. Each year, the development of strong community

standards through an ongoing orientation program helps students adhere to the rules. A Judicial Committee of 3 students and 3 faculty members considers violations of rules and recommends action to the Head of School. Smoking is not permitted at Oakwood Friends.

ACADEMIC FACILITIES
The main building houses administrative offices, the meeting room, four classrooms, the art room, the ceramics studio, the media arts room, and the infirmary. Stokes and Crowley classroom buildings contain Middle School classrooms. The Turner Math and Science Building, with state-of-the-art biology, chemistry, and physics laboratories, is in use by Middle and Upper School students. Lane Auditorium houses the performing arts facilities, including two music studios. Connor Gymnasium has basketball and volleyball courts and a weight room. Boys' and girls' playing fields, including new soccer and baseball fields completed in 2000, adjoin four tennis courts. Craig dormitory includes the darkroom and a photography classroom. Collins Library, completed in 1990, contains 12,000 volumes, microform materials, four classrooms, and a computer laboratory with eighteen Intel-based systems.

BOARDING AND GENERAL FACILITIES
Boys and girls live in one supervised dormitory divided by boys on one side and girls on another. Floors are separated by grades. Student proctors, chosen by dorm parents, are responsible for working with the dorm parents to nurture and support general morale of their dormitory community. All students leave the campus during long breaks; some stay for extended weekends.

ATHLETICS
All students must participate in some sport or physical education activity each term. Students are required to join one of the School's interscholastic sports teams in the fall term: cross-country (boys and girls), soccer (boys and girls), or volleyball (girls). Team sports include soccer, softball, baseball, basketball, tennis, swimming, volleyball, and cross-country running. Oakwood Friends participates in the Western New England Preparatory School Athletic Association and the Hudson Valley Athletic League. During the winter and spring, students not wishing to play on sports teams may participate in fitness training, Ultimate Frisbee, running, yoga, table tennis, aerobics, and rock climbing. Independent sports participants must be cleared by the athletic department head.

Connor Gymnasium has a full basketball court, a volleyball court, a weight-lifting room, and locker rooms. There are four outdoor tennis courts and two soccer fields. The Hunter Mountain and Catamount ski areas are used for downhill skiing instruction, and a cross-country ski trail is on campus.

EXTRACURRICULAR OPPORTUNITIES
Participation in one activity yearly is required. Two dramatic productions and one musical are presented each year. An all-School event is scheduled each term. Other activities include special interest committees; the yearbook; photography; performance with the choral, drama, and instrumental groups; Cabaret; and the *Middle School Newsletter*.

DAILY LIFE
Breakfast is served from 7:15 to 7:45 a.m., and four class periods extend from 8:15 a.m. to 3:30 p.m., with breaks for community meeting, silent meeting, campus cleanup, and lunch. Sports and physical education are from 3:30 to 5 p.m. Dinner is served from 5:30 to 6:15, and students have free time until study hall from 7:30 to 9:30. Check-in is at 10, quiet time from 10 to 11, and lights-out is at 11 p.m.

Community meeting, held once weekly with attendance required, may include announcements, sharing of concerns, brief talks by faculty members, short musical or dramatic presentations by students, and an occasional visiting speaker. Silent meeting, also required, is unprogrammed.

WEEKEND LIFE
Every weekend, staff members on duty prepare a program of events. Many events are special to the season, such as hiking, sledding, or tubing, and trips are often arranged to a play or a museum in New York City, local fairs, and the Renaissance Fair. Weekends are also a time to catch up on sleep, go to nearby shopping centers, or get ahead on assignments. Nearby colleges and the city of Poughkeepsie provide a number of cultural opportunities.

COSTS AND FINANCIAL AID
The 2005–06 tuition, including board and room, is $31,720 for seven-day boarders, $27,560 for five-day boarders, $18,300 for day students in grades 9–12, and $15,800 for day students in grades 6–8. Each term, $655 is charged for those students enrolled in Focused Instruction. The surcharges for the Academic Support Center Program and the International Student Advisor Program are $4680 and $1640 per year, respectively. Extra tutoring and lessons are billed directly to parents.

An initial, nonrefundable tuition deposit of 5 percent of the tuition is required within two weeks of contract receipt. The balance is expected by July 15.

Financial aid is available on the basis of need. Financial applications are processed through the School and Student Service for Financial Aid. Parents must also submit their IRS 1040 form to the School. In 2004–05, $447,000 was awarded in financial aid to 43 percent of the student body.

ADMISSIONS INFORMATION
Oakwood Friends seeks students who will take responsibility for their own academic, social, and spiritual growth; make a contribution to the School community; and work effectively. Admissions decisions are based on student interviews at the School, previous school records, and three references, one from a math teacher, another from an English or history teacher, and a third from a nonschool adult.

Students enter in grades 6 through 11, and a few are considered for grade 12.

APPLICATION TIMETABLE
Initial inquiries are welcome at any time. The School prefers that the interview and tour occur during a school day before May 1. Office hours are 8:30 to 4:30, Monday through Friday. A nonrefundable $40 application fee is required. Applicants are notified of a decision within two weeks of the completion of their files.

ADMISSIONS CORRESPONDENCE
Robert J. Suphan
Director of Admissions
Oakwood Friends School
22 Spackenkill Road
Poughkeepsie, New York 12603
Phone: 845-462-4200
    800-843-3341 (toll-free)
Fax: 845-462-4251
E-mail: admissions@oakwoodfriends.org
Web site: http://www.oakwoodfriends.org

OJAI VALLEY SCHOOL

Ojai, California

Type: Coeducational boarding and day secondary- and college-preparatory school
Grades: P–12: Lower School, Prekindergarten–8; Upper School, 9–12; ELP, 9–11
Enrollment: School total: 375; Upper School: 122; Lower School: 240; ELP: 13
Heads of School: Michael Hall-Mounsey, Headmaster (Lower School); Carl S. Cooper, Headmaster (Upper School)

THE SCHOOL

Ojai Valley School originated in 1911 as The Bristol School. In 1923, Headmaster Edward Yeomans built a new campus for students in grades 3 through 8 and changed the school name to Ojai Valley School. At that time, the School occupied 14 acres near the city of Ojai. Mr. Yeomans felt that the environment of the campus would "stimulate the interests of the children in a spontaneous way." The high school was built in 1961, following the acquisition of a separate 195-acre campus in the east end of the Ojai Valley. Today, the Lower School offers programs for students in prekindergarten–grade 8, and the Upper School for students in grades 9–12.

The primary objective of Ojai Valley School is to provide a traditional education in a safe and supportive environment. The complete program stresses the importance of the well-rounded individual and encompasses athletics, horsemanship, camping, art, music, and a variety of electives, activities, and field trips. The School offers a challenging curriculum for motivated students with special attention given to study skills, positive values, and character development.

Ojai Valley School is a tax-exempt, nonprofit organization governed by a 10-member volunteer Board of Trustees. Alumni, parents of current and former students, and friends generously support the Annual Giving campaign.

The city of Ojai (population 8,000) is a rural resort community bordered by the Los Padres National Forest. It is located 70 miles north of Los Angeles, 30 miles southeast of Santa Barbara, and 15 miles inland from the coastal city of Ventura.

Ojai Valley School is accredited by the Western Association of Schools and Colleges and is a member of the National Association of Independent Schools, California Association of Independent Schools, Secondary School Admission Test Board, NAIS Boarding Schools, Council for Advancement and Support of Education, National Association of College and University Business Officers, Interscholastic Equestrian League, American Camping Association, Western Association of Independent Camps, and Western Boarding Schools Association.

ACADEMIC PROGRAMS

In the primary and elementary program (prekindergarten–grade 5), a sequential curriculum emphasizing the fundamental skills in math, reading, language arts, the sciences, and social studies is supplemented with art, music, computer training, sports, horseback riding, and other outdoor activities.

The Middle School curriculum (grades 6–8) stresses fundamental skills as well as conceptual learning. Classes reflect a strongly integrated curriculum of writing, literature, math, social studies, science, and foreign language. Middle School students also receive instruction in music, art, and computers. A daily physical education program consists of sports, horseback riding, and other outdoor activities, including fall and spring camping trips.

Graduation requirements for students in the Upper School (grades 9–12) include 4 years of En-

glish, 3 years of a foreign language, 3 years of history, 3 years of mathematics, 2 years of laboratory science, 1 year of fine arts, and 1 additional year of credit from any of the five academic solids. Advanced Placement courses are available in English, French, Spanish, biology, chemistry, computer science, government, math, and studio art. Upper School students carry an average load of five courses per term.

The School seeks to provide a wide range of electives that represent the diverse interests and needs of the student body in any given year. Among the electives that have been offered at both campuses in recent years are drama, chorus, computers, study skills, ceramics, photography, painting, yearbook, and music.

Class size ranges from 4 to 15 students and averages 12 students. The student-faculty ratio is 6:1. Most faculty members reside on campus and are easily accessible for individual tutoring sessions. A student's academic and social progress is reviewed at weekly faculty meetings. Biweekly effort and academic grade reports are available upon request to parents and students.

There are four grading periods during the year. Students are given both letter grades (A–F) and effort grades (1–4). Teachers' and resident counselors' comments are also included. Students take trips, chaperoned by faculty members, to New York; Washington, D.C.; Houston Space Center; Italy; England; and the School's sister school in Mexico City.

FACULTY AND ADVISERS

Of the 55 full-time and part-time faculty members currently employed at the combined campuses, 22 teach at the Upper School. Eight of the Upper School faculty members have advanced degrees.

Each campus has its own headmaster. The Headmaster of the Lower School is Michael Hall-Mounsey, who received degrees from St. Paul's College, Bristol University, and King Alfred's College, Winchester, England. He completed his M.Ed. degree at California Lutheran University. The Headmaster of the Upper School, Carl S. Cooper, received a bachelor's degree from California State University, Northridge, and a master's degree in education from California Lutheran University. Cooper is a graduate of Ojai Valley School.

Academic guidance is coordinated by the Director of Studies at each campus. Students are assigned faculty advisers who meet with their advisees on a weekly basis. As leaders of camping trips and weekend activity trips, faculty members interact with students outside of the school environment.

COLLEGE PLACEMENT

College counseling begins in the sophomore year and continues through the student's senior year. Care is taken to ensure appropriate placement of each graduate. Approximately 45 representatives from various colleges and universities visit the campus each year.

All graduates go on to college. Recent graduates enrolled at Barnard, Boston University, Brandeis,

Brown, California State Polytechnic, Caltech, Cornell, George Washington, Johns Hopkins, Mount Holyoke, NYU, Pepperdine, Purdue, Rhode Island School of Design, Ripon, Scripps, Stanford, Syracuse, and the Universities of California (Berkeley and Los Angeles), Denver, Oregon, the Pacific, and Southern California. Most students come from the Los Angeles area and attend colleges in the West.

STUDENT BODY AND CONDUCT

Ojai Valley School nevertheless attracts students from around the world. In 2004–05, fourteen countries and ten states were represented in the student body. There were 122 students enrolled in the Upper School, as follows: 33 in grade 9, 35 in grade 10, 32 in grade 11, and 22 in grade 12. Ojai Valley School can accommodate equal numbers of boys and girls, and traditionally there has been an even split between the sexes.

Ojai Valley School seeks to give students an environment where they can learn to accept responsibility for themselves and their own education. This goal is reflected in the School's motto, "Integrity." The School has high expectations and standards, and there are specific guidelines regarding a student's responsibility for personal, social, and academic commitments. Major offenses, which can result in dismissal without tuition refund, include the use and possession of illegal drugs and alcohol, absence from school without official permission, dishonesty and other violations of integrity, and sexual misconduct. The policy on such offenses is strictly enforced.

Student prefects help oversee school activities and take a leadership role in all aspects of campus life.

ACADEMIC FACILITIES

Lower School facilities include six self-contained elementary school classrooms, five junior high school classrooms, an ESL classroom, a library, a fully equipped science lab, a technology center consisting of a four-station state-of-the-art computer room and language lab, and a fully-equipped science lab. Each classroom is equipped with its own computer as well.

Upper School facilities support the high school program. Wallace Burr Hall houses eight air-conditioned high school classrooms, a library, computer lab, science lab, and tutoring room. A new science technology center is scheduled to open in fall 2005 on the Upper School campus. Fine arts and photography facilities are housed in a separate art studio.

BOARDING AND GENERAL FACILITIES

The Lower School campus offers boarding facilities for both girls and boys. Reed Hall, which houses boarding girls, is directly across from a ten-bed infirmary staffed by two full-time nurses. Frost Hall has accommodations for boarding boys. It also houses the kitchen, dining hall, and administrative offices.

In addition, Lower School facilities include 5 acres devoted to the equestrian program, 2 acres of playing fields, baseball and soccer fields, a 25-meter

heated pool and swim center, lighted tennis and basketball courts, an art and ceramics studio, and a separate elementary and middle school playground and fitness structure. A new performing arts center is due for completion in 2005.

Upper School boys are housed in three dormitories, each of which also includes faculty apartments. Grace Smith Hobson House provides air-conditioned living quarters for boarding girls. Each girl has a roommate. The girls' dormitory provides a large living room with a fireplace and kitchen area. All Upper School dorms have laundry facilities. Students and faculty members eat their meals together in the dining hall, which is located near the boys' dormitory.

The Headmaster of the Upper School and half of the faculty members reside on the high school campus.

A large outdoor amphitheater is used for school assemblies, drama productions, and graduation ceremonies. A high and low ropes challenge course is used to develop self-confidence and team cooperation.

A student center, which consists of a swimming pool, lockers for boys and girls, and a barbecue area, is used for a multitude of activities.

ATHLETICS

Teams compete interscholastically in soccer, volleyball, baseball, softball, basketball, golf, lacrosse, track, cross-country, tennis, and equestrian events. Noncompetitive and intramural offerings include aerobics, cycling and mountain biking, fitness programs, golf, karate, ocean kayaking, rappelling, skating, skiing, surfing, swimming, walking, weight training, and yoga.

EXTRACURRICULAR OPPORTUNITIES

There are several extracurricular activities from which students may select. Students participate in drama, chorus, yearbook, mountain-biking, mountaineering, and a variety of clubs. New clubs and activities are added each year according to student interest. Community service programs include trips to Oaxaca, Mexico; peer tutoring; visiting nursing homes; Habitat for Humanity; and the Surfriders Foundation.

DAILY LIFE

A typical day begins with breakfast at 7. Students clean their room and dorm area before going to an optional morning tutorial at 8. Classes begin at 8:30. The academic day ends at 3:15, with the exception of Wednesday, when interscholastic sports contests are played in the afternoons. Sports prac-

tices and cocurricular activities are offered between 3:30 and 5. Students are transported to town for shopping and leisure. Dinner is at 6, followed by study hall from 7:30 to 9:30. The amount of time allowed for socializing and lights-out are dependent on a student's grade and academic standing.

WEEKEND LIFE

During the week, students are expected to work hard on their studies. Weekends give students a chance to play equally hard. Students and faculty members together organize activities on and off campus. Weekend trips to visit landmarks and attend cultural events and concerts in Los Angeles, Santa Barbara, and Ventura are frequent. Camping trips are a key part of student life. Recent destinations have included Yosemite, Morro Bay, Canyonlands, Arches National Park, Zion National Park, the Sierra Nevada mountain range, Mammoth Lakes, and Death Valley, as well as local beaches and wilderness areas.

Students may, with parental permission, leave campus two weekends per month provided that their absence does not conflict with school-related commitments.

SUMMER PROGRAMS

One of the few boarding schools in the West to operate year-round, Ojai Valley School hosts a variety of safe, purposeful, and fun summer programs.

In operation since 1943, Ojai Valley Summer School and Camp offers programs to students in prekindergarten through grade 12. There are three 2-week sessions, two 4-week sessions, and one 6-week session geared to students who want to preview difficult classes, take enrichment courses, earn credit toward high school graduation requirements, and take advantage of the range of recreational and camping opportunities. Afternoon and evening enrichment activities include most of the offerings available during the academic year. Many OVS faculty members are part of the summer staff. A student-faculty ratio of less than 5:1 makes a tutorial approach to enhance student motivation possible. Study for Success, a course on study skills and the psychology of self-esteem, is one of the more popular courses. English as a second language is available.

Britannia Soccer Camp, with coaches from Great Britain, is held during the first week of August at the Lower School.

Many international students ages 8 to 18 attend the August English Language Camp. This 4-week program offers intensive English instruction with

teachers and peer tutors in the morning, recreational activities in the afternoon, and day and week-long trips to southern California theme parks during the first weeks of attendance.

COSTS AND FINANCIAL AID

The cost of tuition, room, and seven-day boarding for the 2005–06 academic year is $28,700 for grades 3–5 and $35,900 for grades 6–12. Five-day boarding is also available for students in grades 3–8. Day student tuition ranges from $12,030 to $16,330, depending on the grade.

A book and activity fee, ranging from $1265 for boarding students and $740 for day students, is required to cover the costs of books, trips, weekend activities, insurance, and lab fees.

About $250,000 in aid is given annually on the basis of need and academic standing to returning students. Information on aid availability and affordability options can be obtained from the Admission Office.

ADMISSIONS INFORMATION

The School seeks applicants who are committed to their personal, social, and academic growth. Parents and prospective students should call the Admission Office to receive a current catalog, which contains admission instructions and application forms.

The following items are taken into consideration before an admission decision is made: the student's transcript, SSAT scores or nationally normed test results, teacher recommendations, and a personal interview. For international students, TOEFL scores are also required. Each applicant's potential for success and desire for involvement in the program are given careful consideration.

Ojai Valley School does not discriminate on the basis of sex, race, color, creed, or national or ethnic origin. The School welcomes a geographically and ethnically diverse student body.

APPLICATION TIMETABLE

Applicants should submit an application before February of the academic year they wish to attend. The Lower School enrolls students at any time during the academic year on a space-available basis. The Upper School also has a rolling admission policy.

ADMISSIONS CORRESPONDENCE

John H. Williamson, Director of Admission
Ojai Valley School
723 El Paseo Road
Ojai, California 93023

Phone: 805-646-1423
Fax: 805-646-0362
E-mail: jhw@ovs.org
Web site: http://www.ovs.org

OLDFIELDS SCHOOL

Glencoe, Maryland

Type: Girls', boarding and day, college-preparatory school
Grades: 8–12
Enrollment: 174
Head of School: George S. Swope Jr.

THE SCHOOL

Oldfields was founded in 1867 by Mrs. John Sears McCulloch and has continued to reflect her desire to provide young women with the opportunity to make the most of their academic and personal potential. The goal of Oldfields is to provide a family-like environment in which students can best develop intellectually, ethically, and socially by learning the values of self-discipline and self-respect.

The 225-acre campus is located in the country, 25 miles north of Baltimore, with convenient access to the cultural and recreational activities there as well as in Washington and Philadelphia.

Oldfields is governed by a self-perpetuating Board of Trustees made up of alumnae and parents of current and past students. For the 2004–05 year, the operating budget was $7 million; Annual Giving, $515,487; and the endowment, $10 million. In 2004–05, 17 percent of the alumnae, 77 percent of the parents of current students, 100 percent of the Trustees, and 80 percent of faculty members participated in the Annual Giving campaign.

Oldfields is accredited by the Middle States Association of Colleges and Schools and holds memberships in the Educational Records Bureau, the American Council on Education, the National Association of Independent Schools, and the Council for Religion in Independent Schools.

ACADEMIC PROGRAMS

Oldfields is committed to providing each student with the college-preparatory course of study most appropriate to her needs and interests.

Oldfields supports its dedicated and passionate teaching professionals with ongoing professional development. Most recently, all faculty members completed Dr. Mel Levine's Schools Attuned® training. The Schools Attuned® program is based on more 25 years of work by Dr. Levine and his colleagues at the Clinical Center for the Study of Development and Learning at the University of North Carolina School of Medicine in Chapel Hill. Through this training, faculty members acquired the knowledge and skills needed to meet the diverse learning needs of each student. Students are grouped in homogenous classes and teachers address different styles of learning in classes. Honors level courses are available to students who show outstanding potential in particular disciplines and prepare students for Advance Placement exams. Everyone at Oldfields is committed to the idea that every student learns differently and that, by understanding and working with the students' strengths, students can be lead to academic success.

Nineteen credits are required for graduation. Students must take 4 years of English, 3 years of mathematics, 2 years of laboratory science, 3 years of a foreign language, 3 years of history (including 1 year of American and 1 year of world history), 1 year of fine arts, and physical education (each

semester). In addition, students are required to take classes in health and computer proficiency.

Oldfields faculty members prefer the curricular flexibility of an honors course while they also prepare students for advanced national exams; although the AP designation does not appear on transcripts, Advanced Placement exams were taken by students in Honors French, Honors Spanish, Honors Biology, Honors Calculus AB, Honors Calculus BC, Honors English 11, Honors English 12, and Honors U.S. History.

Qualified seniors may undertake an independent study in any academic discipline. Students are required to carry at least five courses each term.

Students in each grade level at Oldfields participate in the Seminar Series. For ninth grade, the Seminar Series focuses on study skills and time management; for tenth grade, financial literacy; for eleventh grade, the college search and admission process; and for twelfth grade and postgraduate students, leadership.

The average class size is 14 students. The student-teacher ratio is 6:1.

Underclass students have room study, supervised by dormitory parents, from 7:45 to 9:30 p.m. Monday through Thursday and quiet hours on Sunday evenings. Any student needing more closely supervised study is required to attend all daytime and evening study halls under faculty supervision in the study hall in Commons.

The school year is divided into two semesters, with midyear and final exams given. Grades and comprehensive comments from faculty members and advisers are each sent home four times a year. Numerical grades are assigned. The academic and social progress of each student is reviewed at weekly faculty meetings.

During May Program, a two-week long session, students may study abroad, participate in other off-campus experiences, or choose from a variety of on campus programs offered in a wide array of academic disciplines. In 2003–04, students traveled to Costa Rica, Germany, and Italy and completed community service projects in Appalachia and Baltimore. One-week trips included hiking in New Mexico and theater-going in New York City. On the campus, students participated in twenty-three different courses, including pottery, film, dance, auto mechanics, horseback-riding, and Spanish cuisine. Several seniors created independent projects with the permission of the Director of Studies.

FACULTY AND ADVISERS

There are 31 full-time and 2 part-time faculty members, 8 of whom are men. Sixty-seven percent of the faculty members hold advanced degrees. Seventy-five percent of the full-time faculty members live on campus and serve as dormitory parents in one of the six dormitories.

George S. Swope Jr., appointed Head of Oldfields in 2003, holds a Bachelor of Arts degree in

Slavic studies from Lawrence University. He also earned a Master of Arts degree in Slavic languages and literature and a Master of Business Administration degree from Northwestern University.

COLLEGE PLACEMENT

During her junior year, each student and her parents receive the *Oldfields College Guidebook*, which outlines the step-by-step procedures for pursuing college admission. Group counseling and aptitude testing begin in the fall of the junior year. Sophomores take the PSAT, and juniors and seniors take part in the SAT and ACT programs. The college counselor coordinates on-campus visits of more than 60 college representatives as well as College Fair evenings and direct communication with colleges to which girls are applying.

Each year, Ivy League institutions, as well as large and small colleges and universities, located around the country are represented. Oldfields' commitment to academic diversity is reflected in the diversity of the colleges the students attend. Notably, 90 percent of the class of 2004 who applied to their first choice colleges were admitted. Among the colleges and universities attended by recent graduates are the College of Charleston, Gettysburg, Howard, Miami (Ohio), Rhode Island School of Design, Washington College, and the Universities of Delaware, Georgia, South Carolina, and Virginia.

STUDENT BODY AND CONDUCT

Oldfields has 113 boarding and 61 day students. The School size is limited to 190 girls in order to maintain its family-like atmosphere. Seventy percent of the girls are boarding students. In 2005–06, the student body represented twenty-four states and seven countries, including Brazil, Bulgaria, El Salvador, Jamaica, Korea, Mexico, and Saudi Arabia.

The Student Judiciary Board and Academic Judiciary Board, made up of two elected students and two faculty members each, help to formulate and implement School policy.

ACADEMIC FACILITIES

The new state-of-the-art academic center—composed of Caesar Rodney Hall, Hook Day Hall, and the fine arts wing—houses the School's library, five science labs, classrooms, academic offices, four fine arts studios, and an art gallery. Across the quadrangle from Hook Day Hall is New House, which houses the David Niven Theatre, a music wing, and the photography resource room and photography labs as well as additional classrooms. All academic areas are fully wired for Internet access in order to support the School's 100 percent integrated laptop computer program.

BOARDING AND GENERAL FACILITIES

The six campus dormitories house girls of all grade levels as well as dormitory parents. Faculty dorm

parents, aided by seniors serving as resident advisers, supervise the dorms.

During Thanksgiving, winter, and spring breaks, the School is closed and all students go home or, in the case of students who live far from school, to the home of a schoolmate.

ATHLETICS

All students are encouraged to participate in athletics suited to their various interests and ability levels. A variety of competitive and noncompetitive sports are offered on various levels. Field hockey, basketball, lacrosse, and soccer are played on the varsity, junior varsity, and squad III levels. Varsity and junior varsity teams are offered in badminton, tennis, and volleyball, and a varsity team is offered in softball. Riding teams compete with other teams throughout the Middle Atlantic states at the varsity and junior varsity levels. Dance classes (ballet, pointe, tap, modern, and jazz) and aerobics classes are also offered each afternoon. The student body and faculty are divided into the Green and White teams, which compete throughout the year in many sports and other spirited activities.

Campus facilities for athletics include four playing fields, five all-weather tennis courts, an outdoor swimming pool, and a gymnasium with an indoor court for badminton, basketball, and volleyball. The gym also houses a dance studio and a weight training/fitness room with Nautilus and fitness equipment. The riding facilities include an indoor riding arena, two outdoor show rings, and miles of trails along the Gunpowder River. In addition, the School has a thirty-two–box stall barn, seven double-fenced paddocks, two heated wash stalls, and two well-equipped tack rooms. There are more than thirty well-schooled horses available for students to ride, and a varying number of girls bring their own horses each year. Riders can participate in local and regional shows, compete at horse trials, attend on- and off-campus clinics, and fox hunt and trail ride on weekends. In 2003–04, there were three levels of competitive riding, and 21 percent of the students rode to fulfill their physical education requirement.

EXTRACURRICULAR OPPORTUNITIES

A regular program of lectures, workshops, concerts, and movies is offered on campus, along with trips off campus to local and regional areas of interest. Plays, concerts, and dances with nearby boys' schools, as well as ski weekends and hiking trips, are scheduled regularly. Student-run clubs include the Student Council, Global Awareness,

FOCUS, Gold Key, Dubious Dozen, Images, Environmental Awareness, Outing, Art, and Black Awareness clubs.

Traditional events include Parents' Weekend in the fall, Alumnae Weekend in the spring, the Garden Party, the Annual Awards Banquet, drama and music presentations, the holiday party, Green and White Night, and graduation.

Many students do volunteer work in community organizations. Regular trips are made to Baltimore, where students work with Our Daily Bread, a soup kitchen, and Kid's Place, a shelter for women and children. Girls often participate in awareness-raising events such as Race for the Cure and the Walk for the Homeless, as well.

DAILY LIFE

Classes meet in a combination of 80-minute periods, with students typically taking a six-course load. Clubs and interest groups meet daily after academic classes, a time set aside for these activities.

WEEKEND LIFE

A regular program of lectures, workshops, concerts, and movies is offered on campus, along with trips off campus to local and regional areas of interest. Plays, concerts, and dances with nearby boys' schools, as well as ski weekends and hiking trips, are also scheduled regularly. Weekends offer Oldfields students special opportunities for further enrichment and enable them to enjoy a faculty-student relationship outside of the classroom. All cocurricular events are planned by the Director of Student Activities and chaperoned by the faculty. Because of the School's proximity to Baltimore, Philadelphia, and Washington, D.C., students can attend events and programs in these cities. Theater, concert, and museum trips are scheduled, along with shopping and sports events. Current movies are shown on campus each Friday and Saturday night, and rafting trips, impromptu cookouts, restaurant trips, and faculty dinners supplement the weekend activities.

Certain weekend, day, and overnight privileges are extended to all students with parental permission. Students may participate in as many faculty-chaperoned events as they wish. Day students are included in all aspects of boarding school life and are encouraged to participate in extracurricular programs. Frequently, day students spend overnights and weekends at school.

COSTS AND FINANCIAL AID

The comprehensive fee for 2005–06 was $35,900 for boarders and $22,600 for day students. Additional expenses include textbooks, school sup-

plies, and a laptop computer. Optional expenses include photography, music, and riding lessons. A registration fee of $3500 for boarders and $2000 for day students, applicable toward the comprehensive fee, is required with the signed entrance contract. Sixty percent of the balance of the cost is due by August 1 and the remainder by November 20.

Financial aid grants and loans are available on the basis of need and a student's commitment to the academic and ethical values of Oldfields. Twenty seven percent of the student body were awarded aid totaling $1,262,300 in 2005–06. All families applying for financial aid must complete the form from the School and Student Service for financial aid and submit their 2004 and 2005 tax returns.

ADMISSIONS INFORMATION

The student body is made up of students with diverse talents and interests from various socioeconomic backgrounds. Oldfields is interested in girls of average to superior ability who are committed to making the most of their academic and personal potential.

Applicants must submit a personal essay, standardized test scores, a transcript, two teacher recommendations and a principal's recommendation, and have an interview on campus. International students are required to submit a written essay and results from TOEFL to determine their English proficiency level. Telephone interviews are required when visits are not possible.

Oldfields School does not discriminate on the basis of race, color, or national or ethnic origin in the administration of its educational policies, admissions policies, faculty recruitment policies, scholarship or loan programs, sports, or other school-administered programs.

APPLICATION TIMETABLE

An application fee of $50 (domestic) or $125 (international) must accompany the application. The application deadline is February 1. Decisions are sent on March 10, with a reply date of April 10. The School considers applications on a rolling admissions basis after March 10 provided that space is available.

ADMISSIONS CORRESPONDENCE

Kimberly C. Loughlin, Director of Admission and
    Financial Aid
Oldfields School
1500 Glencoe Road
P.O. Box 697
Glencoe, Maryland 21152-0697

Phone: 410-472-4800
Fax: 410-472-6839
E-mail: admissions@oldfieldsschool.org
Web site: http://www.oldfieldsschool.org

OLNEY FRIENDS SCHOOL

Barnesville, Ohio

Type: Coeducational boarding and day college-preparatory school
Grades: 9–12
Enrollment: 58
Head of School: Richard F. Sidwell

THE SCHOOL

Olney Friends School offers an intellectually challenging college-preparatory program within a supportive Quaker community. Founded in 1837 by the Religious Society of Friends, Olney has a 168-year tradition of educating young people to be lifelong learners. The program of academic rigor, spiritual exploration, service to others, and useful work prepares students for the challenges they are likely to face in college and beyond.

Olney Friends School embraces two community rules: Be truthful; harm no one. These rules reflect the Quaker principle of "that of God in all of us." The School community solves conflicts creatively and nonviolently, embraces differences, and strives to be a place where no one slips through cracks; its small size and rural setting ensure that each person is known.

Olney's 350-acre campus in the Appalachian foothills of southeastern Ohio includes a working dairy farm, orchard, and organic garden. The lake provides fishing, boating, and skating. The School maintains a hardwood forest preserve and is surrounded by orchards and farmland.

The governing body of Olney Friends School is an independent board of 12 members from the parent, alumni, Quaker, and professional communities. Alumni are generous with their time and support.

Olney Friends School is accredited by and is a member of the Independent Schools Association of the Central States and is chartered by the Ohio State Department of Education. Olney Friends School holds memberships in the Ohio Association of Independent Schools, Midwest Boarding Schools, the School Scholarship Service, the Friends Council on Education, the Association of Boarding Schools, and the National Association of Independent Schools.

ACADEMIC PROGRAMS

Olney Friends School's college-preparatory curriculum emphasizes integrated content and skills development. Each student spends 80 minutes per day in humanities, an integrated course that uses the disciplines of English and history to deepen understanding of major historical themes. The School's math and science programs are linked, so mathematical skill progresses as scientific depth increases. Spanish language and literature courses focus on conversation and cultural exploration. Religion courses are offered in Quakerism, biblical studies, and spirituality. In addition, academic electives are offered throughout the year.

The humanities sequence begins in the modern world and then focuses on more specific areas of study. Ninth graders explore concepts of identity and world citizenship. Tenth graders undertake a study of the American experience. In the eleventh grade, students move into ancient civilizations, and in twelfth grade they study modern European history. Math courses are offered in algebra, geometry, algebra II, precalculus, and calculus. The science sequence begins with an introduction to the laws of the universe in ninth-grade conceptual physics. Students then take chemistry and biology. Upper-level students choose between environmental science and advanced physics. Spanish is available in levels I–V and includes literature and cultural studies in each class. Advanced Placement credit is available in English literature, math, science, and Spanish. Academic electives are offered in a wide variety of subjects, including fine and performing arts (ceramics, drawing, photography, painting, woodcarving, and instrumental and vocal ensemble), humanities (media studies and environmental history), and science (chaos theory and astronomy).

The student-teacher ratio is 4:1; class sizes range from 4 to 20. The school year is divided into four quarters. Students receive grade reports and lengthy comment reports at the end of each quarter.

FACULTY AND ADVISERS

Classes are taught by a classroom faculty of 17 members, 9 women and 8 men. Most faculty members live on campus, either in apartments in the dormitories or in school-owned houses and apartments.

All students are assigned an adviser to help with academic or social issues, as well as to maintain contact with students' parents.

COLLEGE PLACEMENT

Every student is accepted to a four-year college before graduation from Olney Friends School. The college counselor meets with students individually and in small groups throughout their academic careers. Students also receive assistance with applications, testing, and arranging college visits. The college resource room houses college selection resources, test-preparation materials, and a designated computer for research and practice tests. Students are encouraged to visit colleges throughout the year. Several times each year, representatives from colleges around the country come to Olney Friends School for "college lunches."

STUDENT BODY AND CONDUCT

Olney Friends School's 2005–06 opening enrollment was 58 students, 30 girls and 28 boys. Students came from sixteen states, ranging from Maine to Texas to Alaska, and from nine other countries: China, Ecuador, Japan, Korea, Poland, Rwanda, Serbia, Uganda, and Vietnam.

To create a structured family atmosphere, Olney Friends School has rules necessary to community well-being and academic success. Students play a contributory role in making decisions for the School. Students take on leadership roles while practicing the art of responsible decision making. A Discipline Committee composed of 3 faculty members and 3 students carries out discipline for the School. Students also participate on many School committees, such as the Co-Curricular Committee, the Outdoor Education Committee, the Weekend Activities Committee, and the Spiritual Life Committee.

ACADEMIC FACILITIES

The main building, which is referred to as "the Main," houses academic classrooms, science laboratories, a new multimedia computer classroom, a library, a gymnasium, the college room, an art room, faculty offices, kitchen and dining facilities, the School store, and the School bank. Adjacent buildings house the music department, ceramics studio, and wood shop. Other facilities include the dairy farm, orchard, and greenhouse.

BOARDING AND GENERAL FACILITIES

Student residences include boys' and girls' dormitories. Each dormitory has a meeting space, a full kitchen, coin-operated laundry facilities, and a recreation room. There are three faculty apartments in each dormitory. Also located on campus are four faculty and staff homes, a guest house, and an infirmary. The School nurse is on campus each day and is on call as needed. Barnesville Hospital provides emergency services if necessary.

Dormitory life is coordinated by a dorm staff made up of faculty members and students. Each dorm has students who plan dorm activities and supervise the general upkeep of the dorm.

ATHLETICS

At Olney Friends School, everyone is a participant rather than a spectator. Sports are played primarily for fun and health. Since the School is small, everyone has a chance to learn new skills and join one of the teams. The soccer and basketball teams compete with local schools. There are also opportunities in field hockey, volleyball, tennis, softball, cooperative gymnastics, cross-country, folk dancing, Ultimate Frisbee, walking, cycling, and other sports for interested students.

EXTRACURRICULAR OPPORTUNITIES

The Dean of Students coordinates the cocurricular program, including advising, dorm life, student activities, sports, theater, clubs, and other aspects of social and community life. Activities are focused on helping students develop their ability to live in a community respectfully and truthfully. Community expectations and rules require every person to think about their health and safety and the health and safety of others in the community.

The Olney Friends School work program provides an opportunity for all students and staff members to become invested in the physical maintenance of the community. The daily chores of cleaning are done by students and staff members. Students spend about 20 minutes each day on chores, rotating between cleaning the dormitories or the Main, washing dishes, or working in the barn, garden, or greenhouse.

For five days each year, the entire community performs service instead of participating in regularly scheduled classes and activities. Projects focus on community service; work is done in local schools, food pantries, hospitals, elderly-care facilities, museums, and other locations.

Olney's outdoor education program focuses on fun, environmental awareness, and skill building. The School's location in the Appalachian foothills offers a wide variety of hiking and biking trails, scenic rivers for canoeing, and nature preserves for lessons on minimum-impact camping techniques.

The working dairy farm, garden, and orchard offer students a variety of opportunities for agricultural and environmental awareness. Elective courses give students a chance to explore topics such as organic farming and food literacy. Every student takes a course on practical skills, often involving the farm or garden.

DAILY LIFE
Each morning, students and faculty members gather around the kitchen table for optional breakfast between 7 and 7:45 a.m. The school day begins and ends with brief times of silent reflection called Collection. Classes begin at 8:20, following Collection, and end at 4:20. There are seven 40-minute academic blocks each day and two meeting blocks. Meeting blocks are used for committee meetings, Student Self-Government, and Meeting for Worship on Wednesday. Sports teams meet between 4:40 and 6. From 7 to 8:30 each evening, all students have study hall. Students who have demonstrated their academic responsibility may study in a location of their choice while students who need more structure work in quiet rooms in the Main with faculty supervision. Tutoring, small-group work, and study workshops can also happen during this time. After evening Collection, students have free time until they check into the dorms for the night.

In addition to morning and evening Collections each day, longer times of worship are held midweek and on Sunday mornings. Students may attend other religious services by arrangement.

WEEKEND LIFE
Weekends are relaxed but provide a variety of options for activities. Most students stay on campus during weekends. Movies, concerts, biking, camping, bowling, trips to nearby cities, games, sporting events, and traditional Olney events are often on the agenda. There is also time for quiet walks around campus or trips to town with friends.

On most weekends, students are permitted to take weekends or overnights away from the School if they have met their obligations and have parental permission.

COSTS AND FINANCIAL AID
The 2006–07 annual boarding cost of $23,950 covers room, board, tuition, and fees. The day student tuition of $11,975 covers tuition, fees, and breakfast and lunch five days a week. An initial deposit of $500 is required upon enrollment and is applied to tuition.

Grants for scholarship assistance are awarded according to need and availability of funds. More than half of the students receive financial aid.

ADMISSIONS INFORMATION
Students who do well at Olney Friends School are looking for a college-preparatory education in a small, supportive, caring community in which they can learn to take responsibility for their own academic, social, and spiritual growth. The goal is a student body diverse in race, culture, and economic background. The School promotes acceptance of individual differences in a community that values integrity, tolerance, and compassion. School transcripts, school test results, an admissions interview, and recommendations are taken into consideration in the admissions process.

APPLICATION TIMETABLE
The Admissions Office encourages a weekday campus visit during the academic year prior to fall enrollment. Visits may be arranged through the Admissions Office. Phone interviews can be arranged for international students. A nonrefundable application fee of $50 should be submitted with the application forms. Applications are due February 1 for the first round of admissions and financial aid awards. Students are admitted on a rolling basis after that time, as openings permit.

ADMISSIONS CORRESPONDENCE
Meg Short
Director of Admissions
Olney Friends School
61830 Sandy Ridge Road
Barnesville, Ohio 43713

Phone: Phone: 740-425-3655
      800-303-4291 (toll-free)
Fax: 740-425-3202
E-mail: admissions@olneyfriends.org
Web site: http://www.olneyfriends.org

OREGON EPISCOPAL SCHOOL

Portland, Oregon

OREGON EPISCOPAL SCHOOL
—
1869

Type: Coeducational boarding and day college-preparatory school
Grades: PK–12: Lower School, Prekindergarten–5; Middle School, 6–8; Upper School, 9–12
Enrollment: School total: 820; Upper School: 290
Head of School: Dr. Dulany O. Bennett, Head of School

THE SCHOOL

Oregon Episcopal School (OES) was founded in 1869 as St. Helens Hall by Bishop Benjamin Wistar Morris and Miss Mary Rodney. Originally a school for girls, it has undergone changes in location, name, and administration yet has always remained true to the goal of its founder: to provide, in the Episcopal tradition, the finest liberal arts education possible for young people.

In 1965, Bishop Dagwell Hall, a companion school for boys, was added. The two schools merged into one coeducational institution in 1968 and became Oregon Episcopal School in 1972.

OES is located just beyond the west hills of Portland on a 59-acre wooded campus. Students enjoy the outdoor beauty of the region and the cultural and educational resources of Oregon's largest city. Beyond the city, the Oregon coast and the Cascade Range are just an hour and a half away.

Governed by a 19-member Board of Trustees, OES operates a physical plant valued at $22 million with an annual budget of $11 million. Endowment funds total $12.1 million. Parents, faculty, alumni, and friends supported the OES Fund with contributions of more than $415,000 in unrestricted gifts last year.

OES is accredited by the Northwest Association of Schools and Colleges and the Pacific Northwest Association of Independent Schools. The School is a member of the Oregon Federation of Independent Schools, the Pacific Northwest Association of Independent Schools, the National Association of Independent Schools, the National Association of Episcopal Schools, the Association of Boarding Schools, the Western Boarding Schools Association, the Council for Advancement and Support of Education, and the Secondary School Admission Test Board.

ACADEMIC PROGRAMS

The Upper School academic program is based on the School's conviction that learning how to learn is central to real education. Students do not just read summaries in textbooks, they analyze original source documents. They do not just memorize what should happen as the result of a science laboratory experiment; they conduct independent research and perform the experiments. Precise composition is expected in laboratory reports as well as in English and history essays. Careful, analytical reading is as much a part of mathematics as it is of foreign language study. Problem solving occurs in art as well as in math and science. The academic demands are rigorous, but the "stretching" pays dividends that last a lifetime.

Classes are small. With sections averaging 15 students and a student-faculty ratio of 7:1, personal contact between students and teachers happens naturally.

The school year has forty weeks and is divided into two semesters. Grade reports and adviser comments are issued four times a year; additional reports are written if warranted. Parents' conference days are scheduled each fall and spring, but the faculty encourages additional conferences whenever the need arises.

In order to be eligible for an OES diploma, a student must earn at least 20½ credits from departmental offerings in computer science, English, fine arts, foreign language, history, mathematics, science, religion, physical education, health, and history. Specific requirements include English, 4 credits; mathematics, 3 credits; fine arts, 2 credits; foreign language, 2 credits in one language; history, 2 credits; science, 2 credits; religion, 1 credit; computer science, ½ credit; physical education and health, 2½ credits; and electives, 1 credit. Students are expected to take at least five yearlong courses as well as four electives annually. Beyond courses required for graduation, electives are offered in each academic discipline and include functions/statistics/trigonometry; science, technology, and society; and numerous art, music, drama, and physical education courses. Students are also expected to complete College Decisions for Juniors (a program on college selection) and the Senior Discovery Program (a one-week career exploration) and to participate in the School's Service Learning Program and Winterim (elective enrichment courses and trips). Service Learning helps build a strong sense of community as students work together helping others. Each sophomore, junior, and senior is expected to contribute 40 hours a year. Students also receive credit for regular off-campus community service.

FACULTY AND ADVISERS

Of the 42 Upper School instructors, 26 have advanced degrees, including four Ph.D.'s. There are 22 men (including 1 Episcopal clergyman) and 20 women on the faculty. Twelve faculty and staff members live on campus—4 with their families. The Director of Residence and 11 dorm parents live in the dormitory complex. OES has two endowed faculty chairs: the Winningstad Chair in Physical Science and the Gerlinger Chair in Mathematics.

Dr. Dulany O. Bennett, Head of School, is well known in educational circles and has more than thirty years of experience as a teacher, school administrator, and school consultant. Dr. Bennett is a graduate of Swarthmore College (A.B. in English literature), University of Pennsylvania (M.S. in educational administration), and Pacific University (Psy.D. in clinical psychology).

The Upper School administrative team, working with the Head of Upper School, coordinates the OES advisory programs. All are available for student and parent conferences. Each student works with an academic adviser, who assists with course selection and reviews grade reports each time they are issued. All of the faculty members are involved in student extracurricular activities.

COLLEGE PLACEMENT

The college counselors begin working individually with students during their junior year and introduce them to the college selection procedure through the College Decisions program, which is part of the beginning-of-the-year junior trip. In the fall, juniors are encouraged to take advantage of the more than 80 college representatives who visit the campus each year, and in the spring individual family conferences are held. The counselors help students and their parents establish priorities and gather information, and encourage them to visit colleges that are a good match.

OES does not rank its students, and grades are not weighted. A junior year grade distribution sheet is available. As part of the application materials sent to colleges, the college counselors write comprehensive secondary school reports for each student.

Virtually all of the School's graduating seniors attend college. Recent graduates have attended Boston University, Bryn Mawr, Carnegie Mellon, Columbia, Ithaca, Macalester, Middlebury, MIT, Northwestern, NYU, Oberlin, Occidental, Pomona, Reed, RIT, Scripps, Smith, Wellesley, Whitman, and the Universities of Chicago and San Francisco.

STUDENT BODY AND CONDUCT

In 2004–05, the Upper School had 290 students, half boys and half girls. Fifty-two were boarders who represented five states and eight other countries, and 238 were day students. The day students come from the Portland-Vancouver area and participate with boarding students in all school activities.

The Student Council includes a representative from each class as well as student body officers and serves as a forum for student concerns. The responsibility for discipline is shared by the Faculty/Student Discipline Committee, advisers, and the Head of the Upper School.

ACADEMIC FACILITIES

The newly renovated main Upper School building houses administrative offices, classrooms, an IBM computer lab, and the Upper School Library. The Great Hall provides students with space for meetings and casual visiting and doubles as a theater for fall, winter, and spring drama productions. The new Math, Science, and Technology building houses several science labs and classrooms as well as two computer labs. The Episcopal Parish Church of St. John the Baptist provides additional space for weekly chapel, concerts, and lectures on campus. The visual arts building contains a ceramics studio, four large multipurpose art studios, and computer-aided design, film/video, and photography facilities. A 15-acre educational wetland serves as an on-campus natural field study laboratory.

BOARDING AND GENERAL FACILITIES

Campus residents form a close-knit community. Thirteen dorm parents, including the Director of Residence, live on campus.

Two spacious dormitories house resident students and their dorm parents. There are three lounges with fireplaces, table games, two televisions, and two pianos. All students have accounts on the Computer Network and access to the Internet. Computers are available in the library, the International Student Center, and the computer lab.

All student rooms are for double occupancy, although seniors generally have singles. Each dorm has washing machines and dryers for student use.

Meals are served in the nearby dining hall. The School health center is located in the residence complex.

The campus is closed during Thanksgiving, Christmas, Memorial Day, and spring vacations. Boarding students either return to their homes or spend the holiday with guardians, friends, relatives, or host families. Students from abroad must have guardians in the United States, preferably in the Pacific Northwest, who act as surrogate parents during the school year.

ATHLETICS

Eighty percent of the Upper School students at OES play at least one competitive sport. Sports offered to both boys and girls include soccer, basketball, fencing, skiing, cross-country, lacrosse, track, and tennis; volleyball is also offered for girls. The athletic program offers all students the opportunity to participate on a team and in meaningful physical activity. The program actively promotes the health and safety of the participants and provides an opportunity for growth through individual and team participation. OES operates on a no-cut policy; there is a team for every level of experience and skill.

The School has a regulation-size gymnasium, three soccer fields, four outdoor tennis courts, and a 400-meter all-weather track. SPARC, a 43,000-square-foot athletics facility, features indoor tennis and racquetball courts, a fencing room, a basketball/volleyball court, and practice space.

EXTRACURRICULAR OPPORTUNITIES

The yearbook, *Art-Lit* (an annual featuring students' writing and art), and the student newspaper, *Blophish*, provide opportunities for publication. The choir, the Jazz Band, and twice-yearly drama productions offer experiences in the performing arts.

Other activities include Student Council, calligraphy, photography, driver's education, stage-craft, and a cappella. OES also offers many outdoor/experiential education opportunities.

DAILY LIFE

The school day begins at 8 a.m. Four times a week, students assemble for Upper School gatherings or class meetings. There are seven 47-minute class periods on Monday, Wednesday, and Friday and three or four 65-minute classes on Tuesday and Thursday. During the day, students usually have one free period in which to study, meet individually with instructors, or socialize. All Upper School students gather weekly in the Church of St. John the Baptist for chapel. Interscholastic teams practice and compete at 2:50 p.m. when classes are over.

Breakfast is served to boarding students from 7:15 to 7:45 a.m. At lunch, all students choose among three options—salad bar, hot entrée, or specialty bar—each of which has a vegetarian option. Salad, bread, dessert, and an assortment of drinks are available for all. Weeknight dinners for boarding students, from 6 to 6:30 p.m., include two hot options, one vegetarian, as well as a salad bar, bread, and dessert. Study hours are from 7:30 to 9:30 p.m. Sunday through Thursday. On weeknights, all boarding freshmen, sophomores, and juniors must be in the dorm by 10:30 and in their rooms by 11; on weekends, freshmen and sophomores are expected to be in by 11, and juniors and seniors by midnight. On Saturday and Sunday mornings, boarders have breakfast at 8, brunch or lunch at 11:30, and dinner at 6.

WEEKEND LIFE

OES offers a wide range of weekend activities throughout the year specifically for resident students: trips around Portland, outdoor programs, a regular film series, dances, speakers and performing artists, and observances of holidays, birthdays, and other special occasions. OES is close to shopping centers, restaurants, and a bus line. With pa-

rental permission, boarders may leave the campus in pairs on most weekends.

COSTS AND FINANCIAL AID

Tuition, fees, and board costs in 2004–05 were $31,550 for resident students. Tuition for day students was $17,370, including fees and lunch costs. A yearly international fee of $1000 is required of students whose parents live outside the United States. Tuition and fees are due by August 1. The School also offers installment and insurance plans. The School provides $793,000 in need-based financial aid.

ADMISSIONS INFORMATION

Admission is based on academic performance, recommendations, and standardized test scores. The SSAT is recommended. OES administers achievement and/or aptitude tests if sufficient information is not available from previous schools. The testing is scheduled twice a month in January and February and then as needed. OES also asks prospective students to write a short personal essay.

APPLICATION TIMETABLE

Initial inquiries are welcome year-round, but the application deadline for the 2005–06 school year was January 28, 2005. There is a $50 application fee, and early application is recommended. The School conducts campus tours and interviews by appointment. Prospective applicants are asked to visit on a school day in order to see the School in full operation. Contracts are issued in March. The School continues to accept applications, issuing contracts after that date only if space permits.

ADMISSIONS CORRESPONDENCE

Pam Dreisin, Assistant Head of School for
    Admissions and Advancement
Oregon Episcopal School
6300 Southwest Nicol Road
Portland, Oregon 97223

Phone: 503-768-3115
Fax: 503-768-3140
E-mail: admit@oes.edu
Web site: http://www.oes.edu

THE ORME SCHOOL

Mayer, Arizona

Type: Coeducational boarding college-preparatory school
Grades: 8–PG boarding; 7–12 day
Enrollment: 186
Head of School: Dr. Stephen P. Robinson, Headmaster

THE SCHOOL

The year 1929 was not noted for beginning new enterprises, but in that year, in the high valley of the Agua Fria River in central Arizona, Mr. and Mrs. Charles H. Orme founded the Orme School. Faced with the problem of providing an education for their three children while operating a ranch remote from any nearby community, the Ormes solved their problem with directness: arrangements were made for the opening of a county accommodation school and a teacher was hired and installed in one room of the cowboy bunkhouse. News of the teacher at Orme traveled fast, and it was not long before other ranch families were sending their children for schooling there. The number of students grew as friends in various parts of the country became interested in having their children share in the wholesome environment, home life, and outdoor living of the ranch and, at the same time, follow a rigorous college preparatory course of study.

Since the early years, the Orme School has gradually expanded. Many facilities have been added and improved, but the atmosphere of the family group and the spirit of pioneering have been preserved so that the students of today continue to be members of the school family, living vigorous, worthwhile lives in surroundings of great natural beauty.

Orme's college preparatory academic program provides its students with the foundation for entrance to competitive universities. Yet, its definition of "education" is much broader and involves three carefully blended experiences: community, academic, and leadership. These experiences result in greater awareness, clearer perspectives, better decision-making capabilities, self-discipline, and wise use of leisure time.

The Orme School is a member of the National Association of Independent Schools (NAIS) and was incorporated as a nonprofit institution in 1962. It is governed by a 32-member Board of Trustees, including parents and alumni. In 2002, a $7.3-million endowment and $450,000 Annual Fund helped subsidize the School's $6-million yearly operating budget.

The Orme School is approved by the Arizona State Committee on Accreditation within the framework of the North Central Association of Colleges and Schools. It is a member of The Association of Boarding Schools, Western Boarding School Association, the Secondary School Admission Test Board, the Arizona Association of Independent Schools, the National Association of College Admission Counselors, the Cum Laude Society, the School and Student Service for Financial Aid, and the American Camping Association.

ACADEMIC PROGRAMS

Orme provides a traditional academic program supplemented with numerous innovative learning situations. The School believes that all learning is not in classrooms and textbooks and that a good, solid academic program is not college preparation in itself. The following provide an unusual dimension to an Orme School education: an interdisciplinary approach to learning; inquiry-centered learning, with the teacher as a moderator, not a lecturer; a week-long Fine Arts Festival; and the annual Caravan trip.

The school year runs from September to June and is divided into semesters. Students' grades are posted quarterly. In addition, grades are tabulated every two weeks to show students' progress. Additional help and incentives are then provided for students with academic deficiencies. Orme uses a numerical grading system (0–100), with 60 a passing grade, 70 the minimum for gaining college entrance, and 80 the lowest to be considered for honors.

Orme's small class size (an average of 12 students per class) provides ample opportunity for flexibility and innovation, while also offering individualism, personalization, and more direct involvement with faculty members. Independent study and Advanced Placement courses in the major disciplines are available for students.

The Orme School offers two diplomas to graduating students. The College Preparatory Diploma requires 21 credits to graduate, while the Honors Diploma requires 25 credits. Standard course work requirements include 4 credits in English, 2½ credits in history and social studies, 2 credits in a single foreign language, 2 credits in laboratory science, 2 credits in mathematics, 1 credit in humanities, 1 credit in fine arts, 3 elective credits, ½ credit in computer science, 1 credit in independent reading (¼ credit for each year at Orme), 1 credit for participation in the Fine Arts Festival (¼ credit for each year at Orme), and 1 credit for Caravan (¼ credit for each year at Orme).

Classes meet four times a week and include one 90-minute period and three 45-minute periods for each class.

Students have required evening study times in several locations determined by their class levels and academic and effort marks. Students are welcome to receive help in their courses from teachers as well as from the Learning Center and informal peer tutoring arrangements.

FACULTY AND ADVISERS

A registered nurse staffs a well-equipped and modern health center. All administrators and all full-time faculty members live on the School campus. Students are welcome visitors in faculty and staff homes, and the warm, friendly relationships that develop are important in decreasing the frustrations and alienations often found in an impersonal society. Each student has an adult advisor; advisee meetings take place on a weekly basis.

Dr. Stephen P. Robinson is the School's fifth Headmaster. He follows Laurens E. Wolcott III, Todd R. W. Horn, William S. Hart Jr., and Charles H. Orme Jr., who served as Headmaster for forty-two years. Dr. Robinson is a Bethany Nazarene College graduate and holds an M.A. from Southern Nazarene University and a Ph.D. from Oklahoma State University.

COLLEGE PLACEMENT

The preparation for college entrance is structured by the Director of College Counseling through three steps. The first begins in middle school as students take the EXPLORE exam. The second occurs during the freshman and sophomore years when they take the PLAN test. The students are given an overview of the counseling process and begin individual interviews with the college counselor. Finally, juniors and seniors take the ACT and SAT and continue individual sessions according to their needs. Graduating seniors have an excellent opportunity to talk personally with many admissions officers during the Orme School college fair, which is held each year in October. The fair attracts colleges and universities from throughout the United States, with approximately forty colleges attending.

All students from the class of 2005 were accepted by colleges or universities. Recent graduates from Orme are currently attending such notable institutions as Antioch, Arizona State, Bates, California Polytechnic, Dartmouth, Hiram, Loyola Chicago, Northern Arizona, Oberlin, Occidental, Pitzer, Westpoint, and the Universities of Arizona; California, Berkeley; Rochester; San Francisco; and Colorado at Boulder. The average SAT I combined score for the class was 1050; the average ACT composite score was 21.

STUDENT BODY AND CONDUCT

Orme students are very accepting of one another. They come from several U.S. states and from many international countries. They learn about one another's culture and are respectful of differences. In this way, Orme students mirror the diverse world around them.

At the discretion of the Dean of Students, matters of major discipline lie within the jurisdiction of the Orme School Disciplinary Board, which is composed of 1 administrator, 3 other adults, and 3 students. Discipline is intended to be constructive in nature. The advisor's role is of utmost importance in aiding students to develop self-discipline and a mature understanding of community policies and responsibilities. Truthfulness, courtesy, and promptness in the conduct of living; care in speech and manor of expression; neatness and cleanliness in personal appearance; and respect for private and school property are expected at all times.

ACADEMIC FACILITIES

Most of the School buildings are built in the traditional Western ranch style: low stone and cinderblock structures with heavy, open-beam construction, featuring extensive use of glass. The Main House, an original ranch building, contains administrative offices. The Adobe (1935) and the eight other academic buildings, constructed over a thirty-year period, provide twenty classrooms and five laboratories. The Phillips Library (1974) contains 17,500 volumes, and subscriptions are carried for more than sixty magazines and ten newspapers. Audiovisual equipment and a museum and book collection for studies of the Southwest are also housed in the library. The $700,000 Julia O'Brien Wilcox Computer Learning Center and classroom computers have brought the total number of networked student computer stations on campus to sixty-four. The computer labs are fully equipped with a T-1 line, smart boards, scanners, and printers. The Mosher Math-Science Center has three science labs and a photo lab.

The Horsecollar Theater, a converted hay barn, is used for theatrical productions and cultural events. The "frontier village," a group of buildings designed with a western motif, provides facilities for both classroom studies and extracurricular activities.

BOARDING AND GENERAL FACILITIES

The seven girls' and ten boys' dormitories are modestly furnished. Generally, 2 students share one room and two rooms share one bath. Other campus facilities include the Morton Vrang Orme Memorial Chapel; Founders' Hall, the dining facility; a ten-bed

infirmary and health center; 29 faculty members' and administrators' homes; a physical education center; and four athletic fields.

ATHLETICS

The athletic program emphasizes conditioning, teamwork, and leadership. Other equally important objectives include the development of self-confidence, an understanding of and response to the demands of team effort, and an appreciation of the insights that emerge from competition.

Interscholastic sports competition is offered for both boys and girls. Orme competes as a member of the Arizona Interscholastic Association in baseball, basketball, football, softball, tennis, track, and volleyball, Orme is one of the few boarding schools in the nation that competes against public, rather than private, schools. Cheerleading is also offered during the fall and winter activity sessions.

Orme offers a comprehensive program in Western and English horsemanship and riding, including trail riding, equestrian and showmanship programs, jumping, rodeo, and roping. Facilities include a fully lit rodeo arena that includes both roping and bucking chutes as well as two additional practice arenas. Construction has started on an additional indoor arena that is expected to house 40,000 square feet under one roof. The School owns 50 horses for students to use, or they may board their own horse in the twenty-unit "Mare Motel." In addition, there are 26,000 acres of trails, all part of the Orme Quarter Circle V Bar Ranch.

Outdoor Programs fosters an appreciation for the environment, develops self-confidence, and promotes teamwork and leadership through adventure activities such as rock climbing, mountain biking, canyoneering, snowshoeing, skiing, and snowboarding.

Athletic facilities include the Willits' Gymnasium, which houses a state-of-the-art basketball court and a weight room. The campus has four tennis courts, a swimming pool, stables, a tack barn, three riding rings, a lighted rodeo arena, and athletics fields for football, softball, baseball, and soccer.

EXTRACURRICULAR OPPORTUNITIES

Clubs and activities include the student yearbook, the School newspaper, Fellowship of Christian Athletes, Theater, International Club, Native American Club, and Key Society.

Orme students are involved in a number of programs in the creative arts—drama, dance, writing, music, and art—that are directed toward developing a "climate of creativity" and encouraging a receptiveness to aesthetic value, an increase in intellectual awareness, and preparation for wise use of leisure time. The exceptional and highly successful Fine Arts Festival brings professional artists to the school for a week to live among the students and lead studio and performing arts workshops. Other annual events include Fall Outing (a weekend camping trip), the Homecoming football game, the Northern Arizona College Fair on Orme's campus, Parents' Day, Grand-

parents' Day, Caravan, (a week-long experiential learning adventure), and Orme Western Heritage Days and Rodeo.

DAILY LIFE

Students typically take five or six classes each semester. Classes begin at 8:15 a.m. and end around 3:30 p.m. Orme does not have Saturday classes. Athletics and extracurricular activities take place in the afternoon following classes. A 2-hour evening study period takes place from 7 to 9 p.m. Curfew for underclassmen is 10 p.m.; for upperclassmen, curfew is 10:30 p.m.

WEEKEND LIFE

Orme believes it is important for its students to have both an abundance of planned activities as well as time to spend with their friends in a positive atmosphere. Planned activities vary throughout the month to include a balance of athletic, community service, leadership and team building, multicultural, Southwest exploration, and social opportunities. These activities occur both on and off the campus and provide students with a chance to develop new skills while enjoying themselves. On the campus, scheduled BBQ's and Red/White team competitions provide ample social opportunities. The Commons offers students a place to call their own where they can purchase food/school items, play pool or Ping Pong, or watch TV. In addition to weekend activities, scheduled dorm trips and dinners, advisee night, and multicultural dinners offer the students a variety of ways to be involved.

SUMMER PROGRAMS

The School hosts both a summer camp and summer school program. Camp averages 150 boys and girls between the ages of 7 and 16 and has a staff-camper ratio of 1:5. Primarily a Western horsemanship program, the camp also offers a full range of camp experiences, including field and gym sports, swimming, mountain biking, drama, crafts, archery, riflery, desert survival, and numerous other activities. Through these activities, the summer program encourages the development of strong values and character that contribute to a better society. The 2004 fee for the full camp season is $4900.

The summer school program is a five-week session that provides remedial and enrichment courses for the secondary school student. A student may receive 1 academic credit for work completed. Classes are offered in math, English, and computer science through the sophomore year. In addition to the credit courses offered, tutoring is available to those campers who desire a preview of, or foundation in, a given course. Summer school students have the opportunity to participate in several camp activities during the six-week session. Costs for the five-week summer school session total $6100.

Intensive English as a second language (ESL) classes are available to the international students who want to develop their English speaking, writing, and reading skills.

Summer camp and summer school sessions begin the last week in mid-June and end in mid-August.

COSTS AND FINANCIAL AID

The annual tuition and boarding fee is $29,190. The cost of extras, such as books, special caravan trips, laundry, and spending money, is approximately $1100. The horsemanship fee is $400 per season, whether a private or rented horse is used. When the applicant is accepted, a $2500 deposit is required.

Financial aid is awarded to deserving students on the basis of financial need, academic ability, and a positive record of citizenship. These awards are determined through guidelines set by the School and Student Service for Financial Aid.

ADMISSIONS INFORMATION

The Orme School seeks students who can benefit from and contribute to a college-preparatory boarding and day school with a rigorous academic program and strengths in sports, horsemanship, fine arts, and the outdoors. Successful students exhibit honesty, integrity, and respect for themselves and others while embracing opportunities available to them at Orme. They plan on attending a college or university, show intellectual ability and curiosity, contribute to their community, and participate in extracurricular activities. Students are admitted on the basis of their previous academic record, aptitude and intelligence test scores, and references and recommendations. An interview is requested, preferably at the School. In this way, the sincerity of a candidate's commitment to academics and social responsibility can be ascertained, and, at the same time, the candidate is able to evaluate the environment, setting, and programs of the School before deciding to attend.

APPLICATION TIMETABLE

The application process begins in the fall. The complete application and the $50 application fee must be submitted by February 15; students must also complete a campus tour and interview by this date. Decision letters are sent out to families on March 10. Families are requested to respond to the decision letter by April 10. A deposit of $2500 and the signed enrollment contract reserve a space for the upcoming school year. Midyear applications and applications submitted after February 15 are considered on a space-available basis.

ADMISSIONS CORRESPONDENCE

Alex Spence, M.A.
Director of Admission
The Orme School
HC 63 Box 3040
Mayer, Arizona 86333

Phone: 928-632-7601
Fax: 928-632-7605
E-mail: admissions@ormeschool.org
Web site: http://www.ormeschool.org

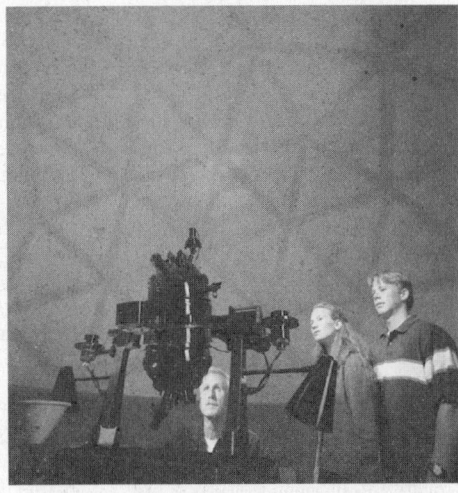

OVERSEAS FAMILY SCHOOL

Singapore

Type: Coeducational day college-preparatory school
Grades: PK–12: Prekindergarten; Kindergarten, K1–K2; Elementary School, 1–5; Middle School, 6–8; High School, 9–12
Enrollment: School total: 2,400; Middle and High Schools: 980
Head of School: Dr. Bhim P. Mozoomdar

THE SCHOOL

Overseas Family School (OFS), founded in 1991 for overseas families living in Singapore, provides classes from kindergarten to high school. The curriculum is taught in the English language. The School conducts a college-preparatory program that prepares an international body of students to return to their national educational systems or to enter colleges and universities in the country of their choice, including Australia, Canada, India, Japan, Korea, the United States, and the OFS College in Singapore, as well as institutions throughout Europe. An international faculty includes members from twenty-three different countries who have experience or training in a variety of educational systems.

The Overseas Family School offers a specialized Study Preparation Program (SPP) for students for whom English is a second or other language (ESOL). Students make international friendships in specialized programs such as SPP as well as through the academic program, extracurricular activities, and sports.

The teaching policies of the School emphasize individual needs of students. Educational growth occurs in a supportive atmosphere where students work cooperatively to achieve their school goals. A "worldwide family" approach to the School curriculum is maintained to help students overcome any biased attitudes toward other cultures. The significance of each individual's contribution to society is stressed. The School environment cultivates a flexible approach to problem solving and the development of higher thinking skills. All aspects of a student's schooling are seen as important and interdependent. Each student is encouraged to reach his or her own potential in a school where self-discipline and self-respect are the basic guidelines for behavior.

The School is located near Orchard Road and the center of Singapore. It is easily accessible from all parts of the island republic by public transportation. School buses with safety belts in each seat bring children to school from every district in Singapore.

The Overseas Family School is accredited by the Western Association of Schools and Colleges in California and is registered with the Singapore Ministry of Education.

ACADEMIC PROGRAMS

Upon entry into the Overseas Family School, students' English proficiency is assessed. Secondary students needing further preparation in English join the Study Preparation Program, which offers a full range of specially developed classes in most academic subjects, including English, science, mathematics, humanities, and computers. SPP students join the regular program for nonacademic classes and extracurricular activities. When students in the SPP have reached the appropriate level of English, they transfer to regular classes.

Students in grades 9 through 12 are required to meet School and international standards. The International Baccalaureate Middle Years Program (MYP) is offered in grades 9 and 10. The MYP curriculum includes the British-based International General Certificate of Secondary Education (IGCSE), which enables students to take IGCSE subjects as part of their MYP qualification. Students in grades 11 and 12 may prepare for the International Baccalaureate (I.B.) Program. Regular assessment and counseling provide teachers and students with an understanding of periodic progress in school subjects. Students who complete all the requirements and standards set forth by the School are awarded the OFS Diploma and participate in graduation ceremonies.

Students in Middle School (grades 6–8) follow the International Baccalaureate Middle Years Program, which prepares students for the demanding requirements of a high school curriculum. A comprehensive language program offers all students in grades 1 through 8 the opportunity to study another language among other major international languages (French, German, Japanese, Mandarin, or Spanish).

Kindergarten and Elementary School students follow the International Baccalaureate Primary Years Program, an inquiry-based approach to teaching and learning. Individual attention and regular assessment by experienced teachers prepare young students for secondary school or reentry into their national systems.

Kindergarten students (ages 3 through 5) develop social skills as well as the foundation for academic learning. Young children learn through play in a rich and stimulating School environment.

FACULTY AND ADVISERS

All 219 faculty members have required teacher training and certificates; approximately one quarter have master's degrees. Seventy-six of the faculty members are men and 143 are women. Time is allocated for support classes, and pastoral care is provided by home-base teachers and 2 academic advisers. The principals and academic advisers maintain an open-door policy for students and parents.

COLLEGE PLACEMENT

Academic advisers assist senior students in college placement but start emphasizing college counseling early in the secondary programs. Group counseling scheduled for second semester provides needed information to senior students. Tenth-grade students may choose to take the PSAT. Eleventh-grade students meet a number of college representatives to discuss college requirements, application procedures, reference building, and college selection criteria. SAT and ACT preparation workshops are presented before major testing dates. Small group presentations and individual counseling sessions assist senior-year students with final college placement arrangements.

STUDENT BODY AND CONDUCT

A significant feature of the Overseas Family School is that no one nationality dominates the School. The top ten nationality groups in the August 2005 school year were India (328), Korea (296), the United States (212), Japan (173), Britain (157), Australia (97), Denmark (90), Indonesia (69), Sweden (68), and China (52). The remainder of the student body represented a total of fifty-two other nationalities.

ACADEMIC FACILITIES

The Overseas Family School campus is situated on 11 acres, with ten buildings clustered around its sports facilities. Old trees and greenery create a pleasant and inviting learning environment.

The School has 117 classrooms, eight science labs, nine computer labs, five art studios, six music rooms, a drama theater, and an auditorium. The five School libraries have a collection of more than 35,000 volumes controlled by the Winnebago computer software system. The libraries have a collection of Proquest Periodical Database facilities. All classrooms are equipped with an Apple iMac with e-mail and Internet facilities. All rooms are air-conditioned, carpeted, linked by a

campuswide computer network, and equipped with appropriate audiovisual equipment and learning resources.

ATHLETICS

The Overseas Family School provides an extensive sports program and participates in interschool competition in badminton, cricket, rugby, soccer, softball, tennis, and volleyball. Many of these events take place at the School, or students travel by bus to other venues.

The School has two shaded basketball courts, an indoor multipurpose gymnasium, a playing field with two soccer pitches, and tennis courts. A junior pool is provided for kindergarten and elementary students, and secondary school students utilize a newly constructed swimming pool.

EXTRACURRICULAR OPPORTUNITIES

A large number of extracurricular activities are offered during the school day as well as after school and on weekends. These activities continually vary according to student request and faculty offerings. All students must choose one activity and may change their selection each quarter. Each member of the faculty is involved in at least one sport, cultural, special interest, or academic activity. Popular extracurricular activities include chess club, soccer skills, table tennis, aerobics, tae kwon do, karate, jewelry making, basketball, drama, choral music, calligraphy and crafts, Scouts, Guides, Brownies, community service, and many others.

DAILY LIFE

The school day begins at 9 a.m. and ends at 3:30 p.m., when the buses are scheduled to take students home. All students have a morning or afternoon break of approximately 15 minutes and a lunch break of 60 minutes. The school days for grades 1 through 12 are divided into five 1-hour periods. Meals and snacks may be purchased from the School canteen at break and lunchtime. Many students bring packed lunches from home. They enjoy different taste sensations by sharing their lunches with their friends from other nations.

The School maintains a closed campus; therefore, students need written permission from parents and/or their principal before they may leave the School compound during the school day.

COSTS AND FINANCIAL AID

In 2005–06, tuition fees per semester were as follows (in Singapore dollars): PK, $5500; K1–K2, $8000; grades 1–5, $9000; grades 6–8, $10,000; and grades 9–12, $11,000. There is an additional fee of $1000 for those students who enroll in the ESOL program. There are two semesters a year.

ADMISSIONS INFORMATION

Overseas Family School serves the educational needs of diplomatic, business, and professional families of the international community. The School admits students of every race, nationality, and ethnic origin and accordingly runs a strictly secular program.

APPLICATION TIMETABLE

Applications for admission are welcome throughout the year, because the School recognizes that many families have no control over the timing of their posting to Singapore.

The application is made on the School's standard application form, with two recent passport photographs and the latest copies of previous school reports. When the School registrar advises the family that a place is available, a refundable deposit equivalent to one semester's tuition fee reserves the place for that student, and the School proceeds to provide the resources necessary for the proposed start date. Tuition fees are payable on commencement and before the start of each semester.

Families are encouraged to visit the School as often as they wish to assess whether their children are happy and successful there.

ADMISSIONS CORRESPONDENCE

Mrs. Soma Mathews, Registrar
Overseas Family School
25F Paterson Road
Singapore 238515
Republic of Singapore

Phone: 65-6738-0211
Fax: 65-6733-8825
E-mail: soma_mathews@ofs.edu.sg
Web site: http://www.ofs.edu.sg

THE OXFORD ACADEMY

Westbrook, Connecticut

Type: Boys' boarding college-preparatory school for students who have not reached their academic potential
Grades: 9–12, postgraduate year
Enrollment: 48
Head of School: Philip H. Davis, Headmaster

THE SCHOOL

The Oxford Academy was founded in 1906 by Dr. Joseph M. Weidberg, who was appalled by the seeming lack of interest on the part of traditional schools in educating young men with good potential who were experiencing academic problems. He knew that some young men who do not always do well in a classroom situation can achieve acceptable, and sometimes extraordinary, academic success when given individualized attention.

After investigating different types of pedagogy, Dr. Weidberg decided to use the Socratic method of teaching. He taught his students by questioning them and stimulating them to know themselves, to think, to understand, to use initiative, and to express themselves. The school continues to do this for young men between the ages of 14 and 20 who have experienced learning difficulties in a traditional school setting. A special feature of the school is that all teaching is one-to-one—1 teacher to 1 student per class.

The school, originally located in Pleasantville, New Jersey, was destroyed by fire in 1971 and moved to a 12-acre site in Westbrook, Connecticut, along the state's shoreline. Since then, campus improvements include the Corthouts Gymnasium, Hoskins Hall, and a recreation hall as well as an academic wing built in 1999. In addition, two playing fields were developed and three tennis courts completed.

Westbrook is a 5-minute drive from Old Saybrook, which has Amtrak train service from Boston and New York, each approximately 2 hours away. Bradley International Airport, in Hartford, is an hour from school.

The school's physical plant is valued at $3.7 million.

The Oxford Academy is accredited by the New England Association of Schools and Colleges and approved by the Connecticut Department of Education. It is a member of the Connecticut Association of Independent Schools and the National Association of Independent Schools and is an associate member of the International Council of Schools.

ACADEMIC PROGRAMS

Because of its pedagogical approach, unique among boarding schools, The Oxford Academy admits students whenever there is an opening, and a boy begins his course of studies at the point dictated by his academic needs, which are determined after extensive testing. A curriculum is planned to compensate for each student's deficiencies, taking into account his individual academic needs and psychological makeup. The curriculum is geared to high school and postgraduate students and consists of courses in the five traditional academic subject areas: English, mathematics, science, social studies, and foreign languages. In addition, courses in developmental reading and mathematics, language arts, studio art, English as a second language, and other curricular areas of need can be incorporated into a boy's program.

Although the vast majority of students follow a college-preparatory curriculum, provision is made for a course of study leading to a general high school diploma. Many types of developmental learning disabilities can be addressed, but boys with severe learning disabilities are not accepted. A boy must have at least average intelligence in order to be admitted.

Every week, each student's program is evaluated, and grades for achievement and effort are handed in to the Dean of Studies. Standardized testing is used periodically to evaluate a boy's progress, and sufficient help is given to enable students to take the ACT, SAT, and the TOEFL in order to make the transition from the Academy to a traditional preparatory school or to college.

FACULTY AND ADVISERS

In 2005–06, the faculty consisted of 19 full-time and 3 part-time members; 9 hold master's degrees. Teachers at the Oxford Academy receive special instruction and supervision in one-to-one pedagogy from the Headmaster and the Dean of Studies.

The Headmaster, Philip H. Davis, has a B.A. from Middlebury College and an M.A.L.S. from Wesleyan University.

Most faculty members live on campus and thus are in constant contact with the boys to advise them not only on academic matters but also on personal and social problems.

COLLEGE PLACEMENT

The Academy offers individual help in college placement. A quarter of the school population normally stays at the Academy for up to twelve months before seeking placement in a traditional preparatory school. The remaining students, who tend to stay at the Academy for less than three years, are usually college bound. Educational consultants are kept abreast of a student's progress and thus are in a good position to evaluate college needs after a year or two at The Oxford Academy.

Graduating seniors were accepted by the following colleges and universities in 2005: Hofstra, New England College, Ohio Wesleyan, Savannah College of Art and Design, and Washington College.

STUDENT BODY AND CONDUCT

The Oxford Academy has a limited number of places. Forty-eight students is the maximum number that can be accommodated with the present facilities and staff. In September 2005, the ages of the students ranged from 14 to 19, and they came from seven states and five other countries. These boys and their parents are attracted to the Academy because of its individualized instruction and the cultural and geographical diversity of the student body, which enhances the general educational atmosphere.

Each student is required to commit himself to the program in writing before he is accepted. By this commitment, he tells the school and his parents that he is willing to work hard and to obey the rules and regulations of the Academy.

If students do not conduct themselves in a gentlemanly fashion and with good intentions after having been given a chance to succeed, they are asked to leave. It is understood that the basic regulation at The Oxford Academy is consideration for one's peers and for the adult community.

ACADEMIC FACILITIES

The main academic building, Knight Hall, named after a former Headmaster, is more than 6,500 square feet and includes offices, classrooms, a general reference library, and a state-of-the-art computer facility as well as an art studio and a darkroom. There is also a science laboratory, with a greenhouse, fully equipped for general science, biology, chemistry, and physics. The Westbrook Public Library is located directly across from the Academy.

Hoskins Hall, named in honor of an Oxford teacher who was at the school for thirty-eight years, houses three additional classrooms.

BOARDING AND GENERAL FACILITIES

The Academy has two dormitory buildings, each with facilities for 24 students. Resident faculty members live in each dormitory building with the students. Most rooms are double occupancy, and there is a common bathroom for each dormitory. One dormitory houses the dining room. Hill House, an eighteenth-century Colonial building, contains business offices, a reception center, and the admissions office. Next door is the nineteenth-century Post House, which houses faculty members. The Headmaster's residence, built in 1800, is located on the western property line next to the skating pond, which adjoins the beach area on Long Island Sound. Completing the plant is a former barn, which has been converted into a recreation center for the students.

ATHLETICS

Oxford's daily sports program aims neither to attract students nor to discourage them. Students come to Oxford for what it can do for them academically. The athletics program is designed to provide the physical activity necessary to maintain each student at his physical and psychological best. The Academy has limited interscholastic competition, usually in basketball, softball, soccer, and tennis. All other sports and

games—golf, karate, paintball, and bowling—are played on either an intramural or individual basis.

Corthouts Gymnasium was built in 1983. The foyer to the gymnasium and a weight room are located in Hoskins Hall.

EXTRACURRICULAR OPPORTUNITIES
A darkroom is available for students interested in photography. In addition to participating in the interscholastic sports program, students enjoy swimming, skiing, golf, and riding near the school. Occasional field trips are sponsored.

DAILY LIFE
Breakfast is served from 7 to 7:55 a.m., and classes begin at 8. Classes end at 3 and are followed by a scheduled athletic period. Dinner is served at 6, and the evening study period runs from 7:30 to 8:45. Lights-out is at 11 p.m.

WEEKEND LIFE
Because of the location of The Oxford Academy, students are able to take advantage of cultural events in New Haven and Hartford. Often, weekend day trips are planned to Boston and New York.

Students who have met their academic and social obligations may leave campus after testing on Saturday, with parental permission, and return by 7 p.m. on Sunday.

SUMMER PROGRAMS
In the summer, Oxford runs a program that offers the same type of work as its winter session. The program is intended primarily for students enrolled in the regular program who would like to accelerate their studies, but the Academy does accept students for the summer session only.

COSTS AND FINANCIAL AID
Tuition for the 2005–06 school year was $45,700. A security deposit of $1000 for domestic students and $2000 for international students is required. Additional expenses may include those for testing ($400), laundry, books, and field trips.

ADMISSIONS INFORMATION
Admission to The Oxford Academy is selective. The school accepts young men between the ages of 14 and 20 who have yet to realize their academic potential, who wish to make up for lost time, or are international students seeking entrance into American colleges and universities. The Oxford Academy does not discriminate on the basis of race, color, or creed. The admissions policy excludes youngsters of below-normal intelligence and students who are emotionally disturbed in the medical sense. As Oxford is not a therapeutic facility, other schools are recommended to students with severe learning disabilities or significant behavioral issues.

APPLICATION TIMETABLE
Application for admission to Oxford can be made at any time. A student begins his program the day he arrives, since he is in a class by himself. The limited number of spaces may necessitate waiting one or two months before the student begins, but the school has rolling admissions procedures. No student is accepted until all previous school records have been received and he and his parents have had an interview at the school. Exceptions have been made for international students who cannot travel to the United States but who have been interviewed by parents of former students or by alumni in their home countries.

ADMISSIONS CORRESPONDENCE
Michele M. Deane
Assistant Director of Admission
The Oxford Academy
1393 Boston Post Road
Westbrook, Connecticut 06498

Phone: 860-399-6247
Fax: 860-399-6805
E-mail: admissions@oxfordacademy.net
Web site: http://www.oxfordacademy.net

PARK TUDOR SCHOOL

Indianapolis, Indiana

PARK TUDOR
Exceptional Educators.
Extraordinary Opportunities.

Type: Coeducational day college-preparatory school
Grades: PreK–12: Hilbert Early Education Center, 3-year-old Kindergarten–Senior Kindergarten; Lower School, 1–5; Middle School, 6–8; Upper School, 9–12
Enrollment: School total: 984; Upper School: 416
Head of School: Douglas S. Jennings

THE SCHOOL

Park Tudor School was established in 1970 by a merger of Tudor Hall School for girls and Park School for boys. The Reverend James Cumming Smith and Miss Fredonia Allen founded Tudor Hall School in 1902. The Reverend Smith, formerly pastor of Tabernacle Presbyterian Church, served as the School's first Dean. Park School began in 1914 as the Brooks School for Boys. When the School moved in 1920, the name was changed to Park School because the new campus was near the Thomas Taggart Park. Both schools were founded to provide the kind of education offered by Eastern preparatory schools of the era.

Continuing the tradition established by its predecessors, Park Tudor School today offers a vigorous program in English composition and literature, laboratory science, mathematics, foreign languages, history, art, music, speech, and drama. Special interest clubs and an extensive program of athletics and physical education complement the academic program.

Park Tudor School is governed by a 22-member Board of Directors. Annual giving averages $925,000. Active alumni, mothers', fathers', athletic, and multicultural associations support the School's scholarship program.

Park Tudor School is accredited by the Independent Schools Association of the Central States and holds a continuous commission from the Indiana Department of Public Instruction. The School is a member of the National Association of Independent Schools, the College Board, the Educational Records Bureau, the Indiana Non-Public Education Association, the Council for Advancement and Support of Education, and the Secondary School Admission Test Board.

ACADEMIC PROGRAMS

The Hilbert Early Education Center provides 3-year-old, junior, and senior kindergarten students with a varied, active environment in which young learners can move and choose freely among activities, materials, and learning options. Activities include Spanish, computer instruction, art, music, books, science, math, and gym. Lower School (1–5) provides children with a program in reading, language arts, social studies, mathematics, science, music, art, and Spanish. An After-School Program is available from the time of dismissal until 6 p.m. for Park Tudor families. In the Middle School (6–8), students must take English, geography, U.S. history, mathematics, science, etymology, and physical education. Latin, French, Spanish, German, music, art, drama, and algebra are offered as electives.

Upper School students must earn 40 credits to qualify for a diploma. At least 32 credits must be earned and distributed as follows: English, 8 credits; foreign languages, 4 credits; mathematics, 6 credits; fine arts, 2 credits; science, 6 credits; social studies, 6 credits; and speech, 1 credit. Students must also complete 3 semesters of physical education and 1 semester of health.

Elective courses include government, economics, ethics, sociology, computer science, statistics, calculus, advanced chemistry, advanced physics, advanced biology, art history, film history, journalism, music theory, music history, theater history, graphic design, photography, Latin, classical Greek, French, Spanish, etymology, and creative writing. Most courses at the twelfth-grade level offer college-level instruction, and students regularly take Advanced Placement tests in English, French, Spanish, German, art history, chemistry, biology, American history, mathematics, and music theory. The School offers twenty-one Advanced Placement courses and a rigorous Global Scholars program, Park Tudor's version of the International Baccalaureate, for highly able and motivated juniors and seniors.

The student-faculty ratio in the Upper School is roughly 10:1. During the 2005–06 academic year, the average class size was 12 students.

Grades—on an A-to-F scale with pluses and minuses—are issued after each quarter, but midquarter comments are prepared for students who require encouragement or a warning. All quarter grade reports carry full written comments on student progress. Grade reports are mailed to parents, and copies are given to students in conference with their adviser. At the end of each semester, the administration reviews the progress of each student and advises the family if marked improvement is necessary. All teachers are available for additional help during a conference period at the end of the school day.

FACULTY AND ADVISERS

Of the 152 teaching faculty members, 60 percent hold master's degrees in their fields and 12 members hold Ph.D.'s. The School encourages faculty members to continue their education and assists with the costs of tuition for graduate courses and short-term seminars and workshops. Sabbaticals or fortnight study leaves are available.

Although all faculty members are involved in informal counseling, academic and personal counseling are primary responsibilities of the student's adviser and the Coordinator of Counseling Services.

Douglas S. Jennings is the School's fourth Head of School. He received his B.A. degree from Lafayette College and M.A. degrees from Montclair State College and Columbia University.

COLLEGE PLACEMENT

The Director of Guidance and Counseling assists students in selecting and applying to colleges. Almost 100 colleges and universities send representatives to the campus each year, and students are encouraged to visit colleges in which they have a particular interest. For the class of 2005, mean scores on the SAT I were 619 verbal and 624 math.

The 95 graduates of the class of 2005 were accepted by colleges and universities across the country. Their final choices included DePauw, Indiana, Miami (Ohio), Princeton, Purdue, SMU, Vanderbilt, and Washington (St. Louis).

STUDENT BODY AND CONDUCT

There are 364 students in the Hilbert Early Education Center and the Lower School and 204 in the Middle School. There are currently 60 boys and 49 girls in grade 9, 58 boys and 47 girls in grade 10, 50 boys and 45 girls in grade 11, and 52 boys and 55 girls in grade 12. Nearly all the students come from metropolitan Indianapolis, but a few students commute from neighboring towns. Each year the School hosts 1 or 2 students sponsored by American Secondary Schools for International Students and Teachers.

Rules are deliberately kept simple and few in number because the School's philosophy hinges on the concept that a strong school is one in which individuals respect the rights of others and recognize their responsibility to the School community of which they are a part. A dress code is in force schoolwide. There is an honor code in the Upper School.

Parent and student participation in School activities is a tradition at Park Tudor School. There are Student Councils in the Lower, Middle, and Upper Schools.

ACADEMIC FACILITIES

The School is located in the 55-acre Lilly Orchard, a gift to the School from the late Josiah K. Lilly and the late Eli Lilly. Six major buildings, constructed of Indiana limestone, are set among the trees and rolling hills.

The Jane Holton Upper School Building (1970; expanded and renovated in 2000) houses classrooms, four laboratories, a computer lab, central administrative offices, a lecture hall, and a 17,000-volume library. The Ruth Lilly Science Center (1989) contains four labs, a computer lab, and a science resource center. The Frederic M. Ayres Jr. Auditorium and Fine Arts Building (1976; expanded and renovated in 2000) has classrooms; music rehearsal rooms; teaching studios; a music library; studios for art, photography, ceramics, and dance; and a 425-seat auditorium. The Middle School Building (1988) has eleven classrooms, a library, and a computer lab. The Lower School Building (1967) and Hilbert Early Education Center (1997) contain twenty-five classrooms, a 17,000-volume library, and a computer lab. The Hilbert Early Education Center (1997) houses classes for 3-year-old kindergarten, junior kindergarten, and senior kindergarten. Clowes Commons (1967) provides dining, seminar, and reception facilities. The

Head of School's home is on campus, and Foster Hall (1927) provides a small conference and reception center. The gym facilities (1967, 1970, 1992) house three gyms, a fitness deck, and a suspended running track.

ATHLETICS

Practically every student in the Upper School is involved in the athletics and physical education program. Park Tudor fields varsity teams for boys in baseball, basketball, crew, cross-country, football, golf, hockey, lacrosse, soccer, swimming, tennis, track, and wrestling, and varsity teams for girls in basketball, crew, cross-country, golf, lacrosse, soccer, softball, swimming, tennis, track, and volleyball. Junior varsity teams also compete in many of these sports.

The facilities include three gymnasiums, a room for free-weight lifting, a fitness deck, locker and shower facilities, and offices. There are also six playing fields, including one with artificial turf, twelve tennis courts, a track, and an exceptionally fine cross-country course.

EXTRACURRICULAR OPPORTUNITIES

In addition to athletics and the fine arts programs, the School sponsors a wide variety of extracurricular activities. Students are encouraged to enter into the life of the School and to pursue and develop their individual interests.

New activities groups are formed whenever there is sufficient interest, while certain clubs are always included in the program. Organizations and activities include Thespians, *Chronicle* (yearbook), and *Artisan* (literary magazine); foreign language, international, science, and service clubs; and the student councils and Model UN.

DAILY LIFE

The school day extends from 8 a.m. until 3 p.m. Classes are 40 minutes long; some science classes have double periods once or twice a week. Most sports and extracurricular activities meet after the end of the school day. Except for students who are having academic difficulties, no study halls are assigned for Upper School students.

SUMMER PROGRAMS

Park Tudor School offers a nine-week summer session for youngsters ages 3 and up. Courses are offered for academic credit and for enrichment. The School also is host to soccer and basketball camps.

COSTS AND FINANCIAL AID

Tuition for the 2005–06 academic year was $14,805 for grades 6–12. This fee covered instruction, testing, and some additional activities fees. Books and lunches are extra. Tuition and fees varied for grades PreK–5.

Park Tudor School encourages qualified students, regardless of economic background, to consider the opportunity of attending. The primary basis for making grants and loans is financial need; other factors considered are academic promise and potential contributions to School life. The fact that an applicant may need financial assistance is not considered when his or her qualifications for admission are reviewed.

One student in 4 received financial aid for the 2005–06 school year; the average grant was half-tuition, and the total value of the grants was more than $2 million. The School subscribes to the School and Student Service for Financial Aid.

ADMISSIONS INFORMATION

Park Tudor School selects students for admission on the basis of intellectual aptitude, sound character, and motivation. Qualified candidates are accepted at all grade levels, depending on vacancies. Admission to grade 12 is rare and occurs only when the applicant's record is exceptionally strong. Applicants are chosen without regard to race, religion, or color.

All applicants are required to take the Independent School Entrance Exam.

The admissions record for 2005–06 was as follows: in the ninth grade, 79 applied and 47 enrolled; in the tenth grade, 12 applied and 4 enrolled; in the eleventh grade, 7 applied and 5 enrolled; and in the twelfth grade, 2 applied and 2 enrolled.

APPLICATION TIMETABLE

Initial inquiries are welcome at any time. Although applications are accepted as long as there are openings at a particular grade level, candidates have the best chance for admission if their applications are submitted by mid-December for grades 9–12 and mid-January for preschool–grade 8.

Open Houses are held in October/November, and tours of the campus may be arranged at any time. Entrance examinations are given at regular intervals, usually starting in November. The Admissions Committee informs the family of its decision in February and March. Families ordinarily have two weeks to decide whether they will accept the offer of admission.

ADMISSIONS CORRESPONDENCE

David Amstutz, Director of Admissions
Park Tudor School
7200 North College Avenue
Indianapolis, Indiana 46240-3016

Phone: 317-415-2777
Fax: 317-254-2714
E-mail: damstutz@parktudor.org
Web site: http://www.parktudor.org

PEDDIE SCHOOL

Hightstown, New Jersey

Type: Coeducational boarding and day college-preparatory school
Grades: 9–12, postgraduate year
Enrollment: 514
Head of School: John F. Green, Head

THE SCHOOL

Peddie School is recognized as one of the nation's finest boarding schools. Noted for its distinctive programs in academics, athletics, the arts, and residential life, Peddie provides a rigorous academic experience, mixing tradition with innovation, while focusing on the education of the whole child. Peddie's faculty encourages and inspires bright and enthusiastic students to reach for new levels of achievement in a uniquely friendly, supportive, and diverse community.

Peddie was established in 1864 under the auspices of the Hightstown Baptist Church. A year later it was chartered by the state legislature as the New Jersey Classical and Scientific Institute. In 1872, it was renamed to honor a benefactor, the Honorable Thomas B. Peddie. In the early 1900s it became a boys' school, but in 1970, it returned to coeducation, enrolling boarding and day girls. Although Peddie is no longer church related, its historical religious affiliation is still reflected in its twice weekly required nondenominational chapel services.

A beautiful 230-acre campus encompasses a lake and woodlands as well as extensive athletics facilities, including an eighteen-hole golf course. Peddie's location and size are both significant. As a midsized boarding school, Peddie is able to provide impressive educational resources to its students without sacrificing the personalized attention of smaller schools. In addition, Peddie is situated in the village of Hightstown, New Jersey, just east of Princeton and midway between New York City and Philadelphia, providing students with a peaceful environment only an hour away from the cultural assets of these two cities.

The School, which is nonprofit, is directed by a board of 35 trustees. The endowment totals $249 million. The value of the physical plant is $110 million. Operating expenses for 2004–05 totaled $24.5 million, and Annual Giving for the same period was $1,495,000.

Peddie School is accredited by the Middle States Association of Colleges and Schools and is a member of the Secondary School Admission Test Board, the National Association of Independent Schools, and the New Jersey Association of Independent Schools.

ACADEMIC PROGRAMS

All students receive a laptop computer as part of their tuition. The academic year is divided into three terms. In the first two terms, students study a rigorous core curriculum designed to provide a well-balanced liberal education. During the third term, most students have the opportunity to choose electives of particular interest. Qualified students are given the opportunity to enter honors programs.

In order to graduate, a student must earn a total of 47 term units. Specific area requirements are English, 11; mathematics, 8; foreign language, 6; history, 6; science, 6; and fine arts, 5.

Although teachers employ a variety of methods and techniques, the emphasis is placed on interactive learning, and students are expected to play an active role in their classes. To accommodate this approach, the average class size at Peddie is 12.

Advanced Placement courses are offered in a variety of areas: biology, chemistry, physics, European history, U.S. history, French, Spanish, Latin, calculus, computer, art history, and studio art. An Independent Study Program provides students with the opportunity to study a specialized subject in great depth; seniors may participate in off-campus projects during the spring term.

Students receive grades six times a year at the middle and end of each academic term. Grade reports are also mailed to parents on six occasions, and extensive teacher comments are produced three times a year.

FACULTY AND ADVISERS

John F. Green was appointed Head in 2001. A graduate of Wesleyan (B.A.), and Harvard (M.Ed.), Mr. Green was Dean of Faculty at St. Paul's School where he was also Director of Admission, Senior College Adviser, and head of the history department. Previously, he taught at Western Reserve Academy and The Fessenden School.

The faculty consists of 85 full-time teachers, of whom 50 are men and 35 are women, and 21 administrators. Faculty members have a median of nineteen years of teaching experience. All actively advise and counsel students. Ninety percent of the faculty members reside on campus. The faculty holds eighty-five baccalaureate and sixty-four graduate degrees (75 percent), representing study at seventy colleges and universities.

COLLEGE PLACEMENT

A college guidance staff helps to counsel students and direct them to colleges suitable for their needs and capabilities. The college counseling process begins in the junior year, and all students are expected to take the PSAT, ACT, and SAT in the junior year. Many college representatives meet with seniors and interested juniors each fall for interviews. Students are encouraged to make their college visits during the spring vacation of the junior year and the summer.

In 2005, all 135 graduates continued on to colleges and universities. Over the past five years, the most popular schools have been Boston College, Carnegie Mellon, Columbia, Cornell, George Washington, Georgetown, University of Pennsylvania, and the U.S. Naval Academy.

STUDENT BODY AND CONDUCT

Peddie enrolls 514 students—177 boarding boys, 144 boarding girls, 99 day boys, and 95 day girls—as follows: 116 in grade 9, 136 in grade 10, 130 in grade 11, and 132 in grade 12, including postgraduates. The students, who range from 13 to 19 years of age, represent twenty states and U.S. territories and twenty-two countries. Day students come from Hightstown and nearby communities—principally Cranbury, Freehold, Hamilton, Allentown, and Princeton.

The Student Council consists of elected representatives from all residence halls and day student groups. The council organizes social activities and proposes changes to the Student-Faculty Senate, which has equal representation from faculty members and students.

ACADEMIC FACILITIES

Annenberg Hall houses twenty-three classrooms, conference rooms, a computer center, and the Annenberg Library, which holds more than 30,000 volumes and has a campuswide computer network that links directly with similar networks at the Princeton University library, as well as campuswide e-mail and full access to the Internet. Students can access the library services from any residence room, from home, and anywhere they have access to the Internet. September 2005 marked the opening of the extraordinary new Walter and Leonore Annenberg Science Center, featuring eleven state-of-the-art laboratory classrooms equipped with multimedia stations, DVD players, ceiling projectors, electronic white boards, special project rooms for long-term experimentation, interactive science displays, a DNA laboratory, and a two-story greenhouse. The Swig Arts Center houses an art gallery, three painting and drawing studios, independent studio space for all advanced studio art students, three music practice rooms, a student art gallery, a state-of-the-art photography laboratory, a video imaging center, three classrooms, a large choral and instrumental performance room, an electronic music composing room, and many private studios. The present Caspersen Science Center, currently being renovated, has been renamed the Caspersen History House and is scheduled to open in fall 2006. All Peddie academic buildings have full wireless access to the Peddie network and the Internet.

BOARDING AND GENERAL FACILITIES

Boarding students reside in thirteen residence halls, the smallest of which houses 22 students and the largest, 34 students. All residence halls are supervised by resident faculty members, and almost all the rooms are doubles. The Caspersen Campus Center contains a dining hall, student lounges and recreation rooms, a snack bar, and the post office. Also on campus are the Geiger-Reeves Theater; the Hensle Health Center; Ayer Memorial Chapel; the headmaster's home; the Yu Child Care Center, which is available to the children of faculty members; and twenty-one faculty residences.

ATHLETICS

Peddie is fortunate to have one of the best-equipped facilities for athletics of any preparatory school in the country. The Athletic and Physical Education Department offers a very competitive interscholastic program of twenty-seven sports, a comprehensive physical education program emphasizing lifetime sports, and a variety of intramural activities. All students are required to participate on an interscholastic team or in one of the elective physical education activities after school.

The Athletic Center houses a swimming pool and separate diving tank, three basketball/volleyball/tennis courts surrounded by an indoor Mondo surface track, a wrestling room, an indoor soccer and lacrosse turf facility, a 2,000-square-foot fitness cen-

ter with state-of-the-art equipment, a training room, locker rooms, a kitchen, and offices. Outdoor facilities include fourteen tennis courts, eight multipurpose fields, a softball field, an Olympic-caliber ¼-mile all-weather track with Mondo track surface, a football field, three baseball diamonds, and the eighteen-hole Peddie School of Golf Club.

Peddie is a member of the New Jersey Independent Schools Athletic Association (NJISAA). Traditional rivals include Blair Academy, The Lawrenceville School, The Hill School, Mercersburg Academy, and The Hun School of Princeton.

EXTRACURRICULAR OPPORTUNITIES

Students are actively involved in a wide range of activities. A theater is used for dramatics, speaking contests, lectures, and films. Students produce a monthly news publication, a literary magazine, and a yearbook. Musical organizations include a chorus and three select singing groups, an orchestra, jazz band, and several smaller ensembles. The annual Spring Arts Festival in April focuses attention on student work in art and music and brings guest artists to the campus. There are many clubs, including those that involve students in photography, astronomy, drama, arts, chess, foreign languages, creative writing, debate, the stock market, Model UN, and social service. Students also participate in Outward Bound–type activities through the Outing Club.

DAILY LIFE

Classes meet six days a week; Wednesday and Saturday are half days. A typical daily schedule includes classes between 8 a.m. and 3 p.m. Sports are scheduled from 3:30 to 5:30. In the evening, boarders have approximately 2 hours of supervised study.

WEEKEND LIFE

A student's life at Peddie is distinguished by full, varied, and challenging involvement—academic, athletic, and social. Students actively contribute to the Peddie community in the residence halls, in the close relationships between day students and boarders, and in their extracurricular activities. The same close relationships exist between the students and their teachers and residence hall supervisors. Trips to Princeton, New York, and Philadelphia are frequent, and while weekend activities keep the students entertained and the campus active and full, boarding students have the opportunity to return home periodically between vacations. The School also allows day leaves on weekends as well as frequent Saturday overnights for boarding students. Both of these privileges are based on maintaining a good citizenship record and are allowed only with specific written parental instructions.

Typical weekend events on campus are dances, concerts, movies, residence parties, and Drama Club performances. The Outing Club schedules periodic trips to sites, such as the Poconos, the Pine Barrens, and the Delaware River. Traditional annual events include Christmas Vespers, the Geiger-Reeves Speaking Contest, Parents Day, and Alumni Day.

COSTS AND FINANCIAL AID

Charges at Peddie in 2005–06 were $33,900 for boarders and $25,250 for day students. Peddie does not charge a health center fee, tech fee, or student activity fee, and each student is provided with a laptop computer at no extra cost. Other expenses were for books ($500), insurance ($30), sports equipment ($45), allowances for boarders ($350), and travel. There were additional fees for professional tutoring, piano or organ lessons, driver education, and the photography course. A tuition payment plan is offered.

Approximately 42 percent of the students received financial aid totaling $4.5 million; the average financial aid award was $17,000. Grants are based on need, using input from the School and Student Service for Financial Aid, academic potential, and good citizenship. A limited amount of aid is awarded through competitive academic merit scholarships. Need-based low-interest student loans are also available.

ADMISSIONS INFORMATION

Peddie seeks students who demonstrate a willingness to apply themselves to their schoolwork and who appreciate the value of a broad academic and social experience. New students, including a limited number of high school graduates, are admitted to grades 9 through 12 and the postgraduate year. Most students enter in the ninth grade. For fall 2005, 1093 applications were received and 269 were accepted. New students entering in fall 2005 were as follows: 93 ninth graders, 31 tenth graders, 12 eleventh graders, and 15 postgraduates.

Applicants must submit an academic transcript, teachers' recommendations, and scores from the SSAT, ISEE, or the College Board aptitude tests. An interview on campus or with an alumni representative is also required. International applicants must demonstrate basic proficiency in English. They also should have been following a curriculum of continuous course work in mathematics and their native language (e.g., grammar, literature).

APPLICATION TIMETABLE

The application deadline is January 15 for notification on March 10. There is a $50 application fee ($100 for international students). An initial inquiry is welcome at any time. Campus interviews and tours are conducted during the school year from 9 a.m. to 3 p.m., Monday through Friday, and from 9 a.m. to noon on Saturday. During the summer, interviews are limited to weekdays only.

ADMISSIONS CORRESPONDENCE

Raymond H. Cabot, Director of Admission
Peddie School
South Main Street
P.O. Box A
Hightstown, New Jersey 08520

Phone: 609-490-7501
Fax: 609-944-7901
E-mail: admission@peddie.org
Web site: http://www.peddie.org

THE PENNINGTON SCHOOL

Pennington, New Jersey

Type: Coeducational day and boarding college-preparatory school
Grades: 6–12: Middle School, 6–8; Upper School, 9–12
Enrollment: School total: 450; Upper School: 360
Head of School: Lyle D. Rigg, Headmaster

THE SCHOOL

The Pennington School was founded in 1838 by the Southern New Jersey Conference of the United Methodist Church, making it one of the oldest Methodist secondary schools in the nation. Established as the Methodist Episcopal Male Seminary, the School became known as The Pennington School in 1926. From 1854 to 1910, Pennington was coeducational but reverted to being a boys' school in 1910, remaining so until 1972, when it again welcomed both girls and boys.

Pennington is committed to educating the whole person—mind, body, and spirit—by taking the uniqueness of the individual student into consideration.

The 54-acre campus is strategically located in a rural setting just 60 miles from New York City, 40 miles from Philadelphia, and within 8 miles of Trenton and Princeton. This makes it convenient for cultural and educational field trips.

The governing body is a 30-member Board of Trustees. The 2005–06 budget was $13.1 million, and the endowment was $20 million. Total giving by faculty, alumni, and friends in 2004–05 was $2 million.

The Pennington School is accredited by the Middle States Association of Colleges and Schools and approved by the New Jersey State Department of Education. It is a member of the National Association of Independent Schools, the National Education Association, the New Jersey Association of Independent Schools, and the Secondary School Admission Test Board. Pennington is affiliated with the University Senate and the Board of Higher Education and Ministry of the United Methodist Church.

ACADEMIC PROGRAMS

Pennington's objectives are to offer a sound academic program and to nurture the moral development of its students, helping them to acquire the kind of stable maturity that contributes to success in college and in life.

Middle School students concentrate on five major subject areas: math, English, social studies, science, and foreign language. All students rotate through a series of exploratory courses during the year, including art-o-rama, music, health, computers, writing workshop, and ethics.

Students in the Upper School usually take six classes per day. The minimum number of credits necessary for graduation is 20. Requirements include the following: English, 4; mathematics, 3; history, 3; science, 3; foreign language, 2; religion, 1; art, 1; health, 1; computers, ½; and public speaking, ¼. Honors and Advanced Placement courses are offered in all disciplines. The student-teacher ratio is 9:1, and the average class size is 13, with a maximum of 17 students in any one class. A 2-hour evening study

period for boarders is supervised. The School library is open during the day and for 2 hours each evening.

The School uses the semester system, but, with midterm evaluations, there are four marking periods. Parent-teacher-student conferences are held twice a year. Individual conferences are arranged as required.

Official grades are issued at the conclusion of each semester. Pennington uses a letter grading system in which D– (60) is the passing grade and C– (70) the minimum grade for a course to count toward graduation requirements.

The Pennington School has two unique programs: a Center for Learning, limited to 42 academically talented students with learning disabilities, and an International Student Program offering ESL.

FACULTY AND ADVISERS

The faculty consists of 47 men and 52 women, including 8 administrators. Forty-nine live on campus. The faculty holds forty-four baccalaureate, fifty master's, and five doctoral degrees. Each faculty member serves as adviser for 6 to 8 students. Other counseling is available from trained counselors. Teachers also serve as hall parents, providing the basis for yet another kind of close relationship.

Lyle D. Rigg, appointed Headmaster in 1998, earned his bachelor's degree from Miami University in Ohio, his Master of Arts degree from West Texas State University, and his Master of Education degree from Harvard University. Before coming to Pennington, he taught at West Texas State University, Lebanon High School in Ohio, and the American School of San Salvador and served as Assistant Director and history teacher at the American School of Belo Horizonte in Brazil; Assistant Headmaster and Head of the Upper School as well as Headmaster at TASIS England American School in Surrey, England; and Headmaster of the American School in Switzerland.

COLLEGE PLACEMENT

College counseling is the responsibility of trained counselors who coordinate all aspects of the college planning and placement process, including the taking of PSAT, SAT, TOEFL, and Advanced Placement tests. Representatives from almost 200 colleges visit Pennington to meet with students. Juniors and seniors meet individually with their college counselors and attend a College Ahead Program, during which a panel of returning graduates share their college experiences. Juniors attend special college programs, including two spring on-campus college fairs. In 2003, graduates earned an average verbal score of 550 and math score of 570 on the SAT.

In 2005, 95 graduates attended a college or university. Among the schools they are attending are Albright, American, Boston University, Carn-

egie Mellon, NYU, Penn State, Quinnipiac, St. Lawrence, Syracuse, University of North Carolina, U.S. Coast Guard Academy, and West Point.

STUDENT BODY AND CONDUCT

There are 87 students in grade 9, 94 in grade 10, 100 in grade 11, and 79 in grade 12. Forty-two students are in the Center for Learning program, and 12 students are in the International Student Program. The ratio of girls to boys in the Upper School is approximately 2:3, and boarding to day is 1:3. Students represent ten states and come from thirteen other countries—China, Germany, Great Britain, Guatemala, Honduras, India, Japan, Nigeria, Russia, South Africa, South Korea, Taiwan, and Thailand. Twelve percent of the students belong to minority groups.

There is a Student Council, elected by the student body, and a Boarding Council. Students are expected to follow the rules defined in the *Student Handbook*. Violations may be dealt with by the Behavior Review Board, which is made up of students and faculty members.

During class hours, Upper School boys must wear dress shirts and ties, slacks, and dress shoes; girls must wear dresses or wear slacks or skirts with blouses or sweaters. Middle School students wear Pennington polo shirts and khakis. Monday dinner and certain programs call for jackets and ties for boys and dresses or skirts and blouses for girls. The dress code permits jeans, T-shirts, and sneakers to be worn by students after class hours and on weekends but not during class time.

ACADEMIC FACILITIES

The centers of academic activities are Stainton Hall, a classroom/administration building; the new Campus Center, containing art and music studios, a theater, and the Student Center; Meckler Library, which contains the academic book collection, 10 online databases, and the Computer Center; and Old Main, which houses classrooms and five residence halls.

BOARDING AND GENERAL FACILITIES

In addition to the five residence halls mentioned above, there are two additional dormitories that contain 5 residence halls. Becher Hall can accommodate 20 students (ten double rooms) and has two faculty apartments. An 84-student dormitory has double rooms with private bathrooms. There are eight faculty apartments in this building. The School has an attractive dining facility and a health center, with 2 registered nurses in residence. Boarding facilities close for the Christmas and spring holidays and for Thanksgiving, so all students must leave the campus during those vacation periods.

ATHLETICS

The Pennington School believes that the lessons learned through athletics involvement are valuable ones. Thus, every student is expected to par-

ticipate in a team or individual sport that fits his or her own ability level. Although Pennington's athletics teams are very successful and frequently win state championships, the emphasis is on participation, collective effort, sportsmanship, and personal growth. Boarders must take three terms of activities. All students must participate in at least one sport per year. When students are not involved in a sport, they must be involved in other extracurricular activities.

The sports available for boys and girls in grades 9 to 12 are basketball, cheerleading, cross-country, golf, lacrosse, soccer, swimming, tennis, track and field, and wrestling. In addition, field hockey and softball are available for girls, while baseball, football, and ice hockey are offered for boys.

In addition to a gymnasium/swimming pool complex, Pennington has five tennis courts, 30 acres of playing fields, and an all-weather-surface 400-meter track.

EXTRACURRICULAR OPPORTUNITIES
Life at Pennington is more than classrooms, laboratories, and the library, essential as these are. Opportunities exist for participation in a wide range of extracurricular activities.

Apart from the athletics program, already described, there are many clubs and organizations that students may join. These include the choir, Mock Trial, Peer Leadership, National Honor Society, Photography Club, International Club, Outdoor Club, Drama Club, Model United Nations Club, Pennington Sports News, capoeira, and staffs of the yearbook, newspaper, and literary annual—containing creative writing of students and faculty members. All students are encouraged to do community service during the year. Students do volunteer work for hospitals and charitable organizations in Pennington, Princeton, and Trenton.

A student activities program provides for social events such as dances, professional sports, ski trips, movies, theater presentations, and visits to area places of interest.

Life at Pennington also includes a spiritual component, and all students are required to attend an interfaith weekly chapel service.

DAILY LIFE
The day's activities begin at 8 a.m. and conclude at 2:45. There is an activities period on Fridays and a bimonthly assembly on Wednesdays. There are two lunch periods. A half-hour extra help conference period follows the class day. Sports practice takes place from 3:15 to 5:15, and dinner follows at 5:30. A monitored study period for boarders from 7:30 to 9:30 completes the day. Lights are out at 10:30 p.m. on weekdays.

WEEKEND LIFE
Day students and boarders are encouraged to participate in weekend activities. These include functions on campus as well as trips off campus to attend plays, movies, or professional sports contests. The swimming pool and gymnasium are open on weekends. Transportation is provided to shopping centers, where students may shop, eat, or see a movie.

COSTS AND FINANCIAL AID
The 2005–06 charges are $22,900 for day students, $34,100 for boarding students, fees for the Center for Learning classes, and $2100 for each English as a second language course. Additional costs are a $50 application fee, a book deposit of $500 or $600, and an activity fee of $125 or $250. There are special fees for behind-the-wheel driver's education, private music lessons, and tutoring. An allowance of $15 to $25 per week is recommended for spending money for residential students.

When an enrollment contract is signed, a nonrefundable deposit of 10 percent of tuition for day students and boarders is required to hold a space for the student; it is applied toward the year's tuition. The remainder of the tuition may be paid in installments of one half on August 1 and the remaining half on November 1, or tuition may be paid through a ten-month payment plan. Tuition insurance is available.

Financial aid is based on need and student merit, except for two competitive merit scholarships. Parents applying for aid must submit the Parents' Financial Statement to the School and Student Service for Financial Aid. Financial aid is granted on an annual basis. Twenty-two percent of the students received more than $1 million in aid for the 2005–06 school year.

ADMISSIONS INFORMATION
Pennington seeks students who have strong academic ability, as demonstrated on the SSAT or other aptitude testing, good character, and a record of good citizenship. The School does not discriminate on the basis of race, color, religion, gender, or national or ethnic origin in the administration of its admission or educational policies or the financial aid, athletic, or other School-administered programs.

Approximately 35 percent of the applicants are accepted for admission. In 2005, 54 new students were enrolled in the ninth grade, 9 in the tenth grade, 8 in the eleventh grade, and 1 in the twelfth grade.

APPLICATION TIMETABLE
Students should begin the application process for Pennington early in the fall. The School uses a March 10 decision date, an April 10 reply date, and then rolling admissions as space is available. Students who wish to be considered in March should have all materials and the $50 application fee submitted and the interview completed by February 10. The Admission Office is open throughout the year for interviews and tours of the campus from 8:30 to 2, Monday through Friday, by appointment.

ADMISSIONS CORRESPONDENCE
Diane P. Monteleone
Director of Admissions
The Pennington School
Pennington, New Jersey 08534

Phone: 609-737-6128
Fax: 609-730-1405
E-mail: admiss@pennington.org
Web site: http://www.pennington.org

PERKIOMEN SCHOOL

Pennsburg, Pennsylvania

Type: Coeducational boarding and day college-preparatory school
Grades: 5–12, postgraduate year
Enrollment: 265
Head of School: George K. Allison, Headmaster

THE SCHOOL

Perkiomen School is a traditional, structured coeducational college-preparatory boarding and day school for grades 5 through 12 and the postgraduate year. Perkiomen is located in Pennsburg, a small community in eastern Pennsylvania. Founded in 1875 by a descendent of a Schwenkfelder immigrant, Perkiomen's philosophy is focused on creating an effective environment for individual growth and for the development of personal values. Perkiomen is a world community. It embraces diversity and actively pursues students and faculty members from many neighborhoods of the United States and the world.

As a school, Perkiomen strives to develop individuals who appreciate learning and who work to acquire the skills necessary to learn. The School endeavors to develop an inquisitive student who knows how to set appropriate goals and who can work independently once those goals are established. Perkiomen works to create an awareness in its students that education is a lifelong pursuit. The School helps students focus on ideals that are purposeful, reasonable, in tune with traditional values, and spiritually balanced. Perkiomen seeks to nurture common sense, a sense of justice, a sense of honor, a sense of responsibility, and a sense of humor.

A Board of Trustees directs the School. The School's endowment is estimated at $4 million, and the physical plant is valued at $40 million. The School has started construction on a $9-million academic center to house science, mathematics, and social studies. The more than 4,175 alumni contribute significantly to the School.

Perkiomen is accredited by the Middle States Association of Colleges and Schools. It is a member of the National Association of Independent Schools, the Pennsylvania Association of Independent Schools, the Secondary School Admission Test Board, and the College Board.

ACADEMIC PROGRAMS

Students in grades 5–8 participate in a challenging, traditional curriculum that prepares them for the college preparatory curriculum in the Upper School. The purpose of this curriculum is to provide the soundest possible traditional foundation in the effective use and understanding of language, mathematics, history, and science and to simultaneously quicken the students' intellectual curiosity by means of interest-oriented electives.

Upper School students may earn one of two types of diplomas. The advanced academic diploma is granted when 19 course units are earned as follows: English, 4 units; algebra, 2 units; geometry, 1 unit; foreign language, 3 units; laboratory science, 2 units; U.S. history, 1 unit; social studies, 2 units; and elective courses, 4 units (of which 1 unit must be fine arts). (However, most students elect a fourth year of mathematics and an additional unit of laboratory science.) The academic diploma is granted following the successful completion of a minimum of 19 course units earned as follows: English, 4 units; mathematics, 2 units; science, 1 unit; U.S. history, 1 unit; social studies, 2 units; and elective courses, 9 units (of which 1 unit must be fine arts).

English honors sections cover in considerable depth nonfiction, novels, drama (including Shakespeare), and poetry; writing instruction emphasizes content and style.

Advanced Placement work in English is offered to seniors who have demonstrated superior ability and the desire to do work at the college freshman level. In mathematics, those who take the course sequence through calculus may qualify for the Advanced Placement Calculus AB and BC exams.

Computer classes are offered at both the basic literacy and Advanced Placement levels.

The Developmental Language Program serves 36 highly intelligent students with mild learning disabilities.

Except for honors sections, most classes are grouped randomly, with an average of 12 in a section. Advanced language classes may have as few as 4 or 5 students, however. The overall student-teacher ratio is 7:1.

All tenth graders take a one-year introduction to the Old and New Testament class.

The fine arts program requires that all students in grades 5 through 8 take an introductory course that covers the graphic arts, music, and drama. Beyond that, major course credit is also available in various art, vocal and instrumental music, and drama electives.

Perkiomen uses a letter grading system (A, B, C, D, and F) in which D is passing. The academic year is divided into three trimesters, each composed of four marking periods. Grades and teachers' comments are sent home twelve times a year.

FACULTY AND ADVISERS

All 49 faculty members are full-time, and 41 reside on campus; many are dormitory masters. They hold forty baccalaureate and twenty-one advanced degrees from institutions such as Bryn Mawr, Haverford, Lehigh, Penn, St. Lawrence, Trinity, Villanova, and Wesleyan.

George K. Allison was appointed Headmaster in 1985. He brings to Perkiomen a wealth of experience from his teaching, coaching, and administrative responsibilities in more than thirty years of service in private secondary schools.

Instructors at Perkiomen not only must be qualified in an academic discipline but also must be able to coach a sport, assist with an extracurricular activity, and be willing to live in an apartment on one of the halls to give leadership and supervision to the students.

In addition, every teacher serves as an adviser to 4 to 8 students, and teachers who do not live on campus are identified with a house group where they have weekend responsibilities.

COLLEGE PLACEMENT

Beginning in the junior year, students meet with the Coordinator of College Counseling to discuss postsecondary possibilities. Six other faculty members work with the coordinator in developing preliminary lists of appropriate colleges for each student. Many college admissions officers visit the campus and have helpful conferences with students. Visits to college campuses are encouraged. The PSAT is given in October to all sophomores and juniors. The SAT and SAT Subject Tests are offered on campus in October, November, January, April, and May. Juniors take the January, April, and October SAT. They may take the May, June, or November SAT Subject Tests. Off-campus arrangements are made for the ACT, the TOEFL, and the November, December, March, and June SAT and SAT Subject Tests. An SAT preparation course is available to all juniors and seniors.

Graduates in the class of 2005 are enrolled at Carnegie Mellon, George Washington, Tulane, Ursinus, and the Universities of Illinois and Pennsylvania.

STUDENT BODY AND CONDUCT

The 2005–06 student body is composed as follows: fifth and sixth grade, 12 day students, of whom 5 are girls; seventh grade, 7 day and 5 boarding students, of whom 4 are girls; eighth grade, 12 day and 14 boarding students, of whom 10 are girls; ninth grade, 19 day and 19 boarding students, of whom 20 are girls; tenth grade, 19 day and 35 boarding students, of whom 22 are girls; eleventh grade, 35 day and 26 boarding students, of whom 28 are girls; twelfth grade, 23 day and 25 boarding students, of whom 15 are girls; and postgraduates, 1 day and 2 boarding students, of whom all are boys.

The students, representing a wide variety of ethnic and social backgrounds, come from eighteen states and U.S. possessions. Twenty percent are from other countries, including Bermuda, the Bahamas, Canada, China, Hong Kong, Indonesia, Japan, Korea, Russia, Spain, and Taiwan.

Rules have been established to enable the school community to function healthfully and productively. A student who flagrantly violates one of those rules may face dismissal. Less serious offenses are handled by the Dean and may result in suspension, campus restrictions, and loss of privileges.

ACADEMIC FACILITIES

Kriebel Hall houses English and foreign language, developmental language, and computer classrooms. Science and math are taught in the Hollenbach Science Center; fine arts in Kehs Hall, which houses art, ceramics, dance, fibers, and photography studios, music practice rooms, and the Kriebel Theater; and social studies in the Carnegie Library building. The library contains 17,000 volumes and is a member of Access PA, which enables students to use the collections of libraries such as Lehigh University and the University of Pennsylvania. All classrooms have computers, and the campus network has access to a T-1 line.

BOARDING AND GENERAL FACILITIES

Boarders live 2 to a room, and each floor or dormitory building is grouped according to age and grade level. There are two dormitories for girls and three for boys. Laundry facilities and lounges are located in each dormitory. All dormitory rooms are equipped with phone and data jacks.

Carl's Corner's snack bar, bookstore, and games make it the central gathering place for students.

A resident nurse lives in the infirmary building, and 2 local doctors are on call.

ATHLETICS

Broad-based participation is at the heart of the Perkiomen sports program. Perkiomen coaches are prepared to work with every willing individual. The Hollenbach Athletic Center provides two basketball courts, an indoor swimming pool, a well-equipped training room, an indoor batting cage, a wrestling room, and a weight-lifting room complete with free weights, a Universal Gym, and Nautilus equipment.

Fall sports are cross-country, dance, field hockey, football, golf, soccer, and tennis; the winter season includes basketball, cheerleading, power lifting, swimming, and wrestling; spring teams compete in baseball, lacrosse, softball, Tae Kwon Do, and tennis.

EXTRACURRICULAR OPPORTUNITIES

Drama and various choral and instrumental organizations attract many students. Three plays, one of which is always a musical, and a musical revue are presented every year. In addition to the chorus, there is a select show choir, which entertains at various conferences and meetings in eastern Pennsylvania. Both an Upper and Middle School band are offered, and a jazz combo is chosen by tryouts. Publications include *The Perkiomenite* and *Middle School Eye* (newspapers), *The Griffin* (the yearbook), and *The Palantir* (a literary magazine). There are a variety of clubs, such as the Varsity Club, that are oriented toward school and community service, including the Student Senate, a chapter of SADD, and the Environmental Club. A chapter of the International Thespian Society is also active on campus. Other groups develop in accordance with student initiative.

Lecturers, concerts, and fine arts exhibits are brought to the campus; organized trips to New York City, Baltimore, and Philadelphia provide additional cultural opportunities.

DAILY LIFE

Each school day begins at 8 a.m. with a meeting in the chapel to share information about School events. Classes are 47 minutes long, and there are seven periods and one 60-minute class each day in addition to a conference period at the end of the academic day. The athletics program runs from 3:30 to 5:30, and dinner is at 6. All boarding students are required to be in their dormitory rooms for study each weeknight from 7:30 to 9:30. Lights-out for underclass students is at 10:30.

WEEKEND LIFE

Weekend activities are planned to give students many options, both on and off campus. On campus, the student center, the gymnasiums, and the pool are open for use. Campus activities include movies, dances, athletic events, theater productions, and special entertainment.

Within walking distance of the School are restaurants, stores, and a movie theater. Students take trips off campus to go skiing, hiking, horseback riding, and skating; visit historic areas and museums; attend concerts and other cultural events; and go shopping in area malls.

On an average weekend, the majority of the boarding students stay on campus and are joined by many day students. Eight weekends are closed, and all boarding students remain on campus for special activities. Students are also expected to stay on campus on the three weekends per year prior to exams.

COSTS AND FINANCIAL AID

The 2005–06 annual charge of $32,800 for boarding students covers tuition, room, and board. Day students pay $19,200. Additional costs range up to $1500 for transportation and miscellaneous fees.

Financial aid is available to qualified students. Amounts are based on need and are determined by procedures established by the School and Student Service for Financial Aid. The deadline to apply for financial aid is March 1.

ADMISSIONS INFORMATION

Admission to Perkiomen is offered without regard to race, creed, or national origin to students who have a sincere desire to be educated in the Perkiomen fashion and to abide by Perkiomen's regulations.

Required for admission are the formal application with a $45 fee, a transcript of the previous record, results of standardized testing, letters of recommendation, and a campus visit.

APPLICATION TIMETABLE

The initial inquiry and campus visits are welcomed at any time. The transcript should be submitted on or before the day of the interview. As soon as the Admission Committee has been able to gather and examine all of the required data, applicants are notified promptly of the decision. Students may be admitted after the school year has begun.

ADMISSIONS CORRESPONDENCE

Carol S. Dougherty, Director of Admissions
Perkiomen School
P.O. Box 130
Pennsburg, Pennsylvania 18073
Phone: 215-679-9511
Fax: 215-679-1146
E-mail: admissions@perkiomen.org
Web site: http://www.perkiomen.org

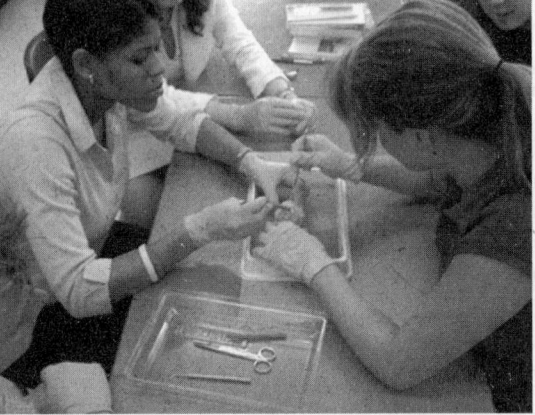

THE PHELPS SCHOOL

Malvern, Pennsylvania

Type: Boys' boarding and day school for ineffective students who may have attention issues or learning differences.
Grades: 7–12, postgraduate year
Enrollment: 140
Head of School: Norman T. Phelps Jr., Headmaster

THE SCHOOL

The Phelps philosophy of dedication to the academic, personal, and social development of each boy is accentuated by a structured family atmosphere, small classes, and daily tutorial support. Fully accredited, Phelps offers a college preparatory program for ineffective learners who may have reading, learning, or attention differences. The School is located 21 miles west of Philadelphia in the suburban community of Malvern (population 2,500). The campus is composed of 70 acres. The cultural and recreational resources of a major metropolitan center are only 30 minutes from the campus. The Phelps School is a nonprofit corporation controlled by a Board of Trustees, which is composed of 11 individuals with varying backgrounds and professions. The board has a strong alumni component. There are approximately 1,300 alumni.

The Phelps School opened its 2005–06 school year having refurbished Gains Hall, a dormitory for its secondary-school students. The School also purchased several state-of-the-art computers for its growing computer-lab facility. An enhancement was made to the Advising System which now includes a ten-minute period for students to meet with their advisers before the commencement of each academic day. This Advisor Period enables advisers to set an appropriate tone for each day's lessons thereby reinforcing the moral and cognitive development that occurs. The adviser also serves as an advocate and mentor for his or her assigned students.

The Phelps School is accredited by the Middle States Association of Colleges and Schools and is licensed by the Commonwealth of Pennsylvania. Phelps is a member of the Pennsylvania Association of Independent Schools (PAIS), Pennsylvania Association of Private Academic Schools (PAPAS), National Association of Remedial Teachers, Orton Society, the Association of Boarding Schools (TABS), Association for Delaware Valley Independent Schools (ADVIS), National Association for College Admission Counseling, CASE, APC, and the Mid-Atlantic Boarding School Association.

ACADEMIC PROGRAMS

The School requires 21 credits for graduation: English, 4; mathematics, 3; science, 3; social studies, 3; physical education, 2; and electives, 6. Students are required to carry five academic courses. Art, computers, music, woodshop, desktop publishing, culinary arts, and fitness are offered each semester. Students are placed in classes that challenge them academically. Class size averages 7 students, and the teacher-student ratio is 1:8; the Academic Support Program ratio is 1:3.

Faculty members monitor a 1½-hour evening study period in the dormitories. The computer lab is open and supervised during both the study period and the afternoon tutorial. The School's library is open and supervised in the afternoons for research, and each student is issued his own Chester County Library I.D. card, which permits him to access the computer in this major library system. Lab time for science is included in the academic day.

Grades are given on an A–F scale. Reports are sent home four times a year—two mid-semester and two semester reports.

Intensive individualized instruction is available in the Academic Support Program. Formal and informal evaluations result in the recognition of individual deficiencies and needs in the areas of reading, English, math, and organizational and study skills. One third of the student body is involved in some type of remedial or developmental work within the Academic Support Program. State-of-the-art assistive technology, such as Kurzweil 3000 and Dragon Speak, are used to help students gain independence in reading, writing, and studying. Textbooks are also available on tape and CD-ROM.

In addition to individualized remedial courses, Phelps offers English 7–12, developmental reading, American history I–III, world history, general math, geography, psychology, government, pre-algebra, algebra I–II, geometry, trigonometry, calculus, Advanced Placement calculus, consumer mathematics, life science, natural science, environmental science, biology, chemistry, physics, astronomy, earth and space science, Spanish I–III, art, desktop publishing, woodshop, computer education, music, photography, health, and physical education.

The Phelps School's English as a second language (ESL) program is designed for international students who need to improve their English proficiency. Phelps enrolls a limited number of international students each year, and the ESL program is a highly individualized one that spans all ability levels. Beginners concentrate on basic communicative competence, while more advanced students work on refining and expanding their knowledge of grammar and vocabulary. Students in this program are mainstreamed into the regular curriculum in all other subject areas so that they may qualify for an accredited high school diploma. This not only enhances their knowledge of the English language but also encourages linguistic and cultural interaction, which benefits the entire School community. In addition to the daily ESL class, special support personnel are available to assist the students who speak languages other than English.

FACULTY AND ADVISERS

The faculty is composed of 26 full-time staff members—18 men and 8 women. There are also instructors trained to work with students who require ESL courses or who have a learning or attention deficiency. The resident staff is composed of 20 members—16 men and 4 women. Of the total staff, 10 members hold master's degrees and all hold bachelor's degrees.

The Headmaster holds an M.A. from Villanova University and a B.A. from Randolph-Macon College. He also has advanced graduate credits from Harvard University and West Chester University. He has been a professional at the Phelps School for 40 years and headmaster for 30 years.

The faculty members serve as advisers to the students and are available virtually on a 24-hour basis. Many of the staff members also serve as coaches and advisers to student clubs and organizations.

COLLEGE PLACEMENT

College counseling is an important aspect of life at Phelps. Beginning in the freshman year, all students are asked to think about what they may be interested in doing once they leave school. Sophomores are urged to research different careers, visit with college representatives when their class schedules permit, and create lists of academic, athletic, and extracurricular achievements that become part of a personal profile. The work intensifies in the junior year. PSATs are administered in October, and SATs may be taken in May and/or June. For those who qualify, extended-time SATs are available through the Academic Support Program. Students also take career and interest inventories, attend college fairs, visit actual campuses, write essays, investigate academic options, and formalize a list of possibilities. In their senior year, boys complete applications, take another round of SATs, and make final decisions. Parents' participation throughout this entire process is not only encouraged but expected. The Headmaster, the Director of the Academic Support Program, and the Coordinator of College Counseling are regularly available for casual conversation or in-depth discussions. Meetings are scheduled on a more frequent basis as deadlines become imminent. Although some young men may ultimately opt for the world of work or choose to join the armed forces, it is the School's policy that upon graduation every student has the opportunity to matriculate at an institution of higher learning if he and his family so choose. Last year, 100 percent of the graduating class received formal acceptances, and 95 percent elected to attend a two- or four-year college. Phelp's boys have matriculated at Goucher, Greensboro, Lynn, West Virginia, and the University of Vermont as well as other schools.

STUDENT BODY AND CONDUCT

There are 11 boys in the Middle School, 18 in the ninth grade, 32 in the tenth grade, 39 in the eleventh grade, 35 in the twelfth grade, and 5 postgraduate students. The population of the School represents twenty-one states and nine countries. International students make up 15 percent of the enrollment and minorities represent 13 percent of students.

There is a Student Council at Phelps that works closely with the Dean of Students. Members are chosen because of their leadership abilities. Council members also serve as proctors in the dormitories, operate the School store, and act as headwaiters in the dining hall. They are expected to be available to help other students in various capacities and to assist in planning School activities.

Merit certificates are awarded to students at the recommendation of faculty members for outstanding academic, social, and personal progress. Certificates are awarded at special assemblies at the end of each term.

ACADEMIC FACILITIES

Rosengarten Hall, the main School building, contains the administrative offices. Beattie Hall has ten classrooms, the William D. L. Melcher Computer

Center, and an art room. There are two classrooms in Gains Hall and two classrooms and an auditorium in the Alumni Building. The Werner Schmitt Memorial Science Building houses two classrooms, a greenhouse, and a laboratory. The Howard H. Lyon Gymnasium also has one classroom as well as the Fitness Center.

BOARDING AND GENERAL FACILITIES

Rosengarten Hall has facilities for 13 boys and two faculty apartments. Beattie Hall houses 50 boys in three wings, each with a faculty apartment. Hilltop House provides quarters for a faculty member and 16 boys. The Farmhouse has two faculty apartments and space for 12 boys. Gains Hall, which houses 34 boys, contains two faculty apartments, the photography darkroom, and two classrooms. Founder's Hall provides housing for 20 boys, as well as a staff apartment.

A visual arts studio was completed in fall 2003. An 8,000-square-foot student center contains a student lounge, recreation areas, and the School store (Cache) where boys may purchase snacks, school supplies, toiletries, and other small items. The facility is run by students under the direction of faculty advisers.

ATHLETICS AND ACTIVITIES

Each student is required to participate in the daily afternoon activity program. The School is a member of the Tri-County Conference and offers varsity sports in soccer, basketball, lacrosse, baseball, cross-country, golf, and tennis. Golf, bowling, and fitness are also part of the sports program. A rock-climbing course began in winter 2003–04.

Five athletic fields for lacrosse, soccer, and baseball and four all-weather tennis courts are located on campus. The Lyon Gymnasium has a basketball court, and a Fitness Center. The School's indoor and outdoor riding arenas provide for year-round horseback riding.

Other activities that students can choose depend on the season. They can include ceramics, drama, rock climbing, computers, photography, publications, fitness, music, arts, crafts, or working in the library.

EXTRACURRICULAR OPPORTUNITIES

The assembly program brings guest lecturers and entertainers on campus several times a year. There are also frequent trips to plays, concerts, museums, and other special events throughout the year. Dances and other social activities occur, usually on a monthly basis. Various clubs and organizations also offer excellent activities to fill the leisure time of students, including white-water rafting, camping,

theater productions, and concerts. There are three sports/activities awards assemblies to honor students for their accomplishments in athletics and other activities. Each boy is required to complete in at least 3 hours of community service per year. Recent events included Habitat for Humanity, Walk for the Cure, beautification of the local train station, Victorian Christmas, the Devon Horse Show, and the Radnor Hunt.

Parents' Day is held in October after the first six weeks of school. Parents accompany their sons to class and have the opportunity to meet their sons' teachers, advisers, and dorm parents. The holiday program in December, to which parents are invited, is followed by a traditional candle-lighting service.

DAILY LIFE

Students wake at 7:00 and have breakfast at 7:30. There are seven 40-minute class periods in the day, the first beginning at 8:30 and the last ending at 2:45. Morning break is at 10:40, and lunch is from 12:30 to 1:15. After the last class, there is a 40-minute tutorial support period during which all staff members are available, followed by a mandatory activity period from 3:45 to 5. Dinner is at 6:30, and study hours are from 7:30 to 9. Students are to be in their dorms by 10 p.m.

WEEKEND LIFE

Since the majority of the student body is on campus during weekends, numerous activities are planned. Students with permission may walk into town on Saturday and Sunday afternoons. Movies are shown Friday and/or Saturday evenings on a large-screen T.V. in the student lounge. Each weekend, the boys have the opportunity to go to a local shopping mall. There are opportunities for boys to attend Philadelphia sports events, including 76ers basketball, Flyers hockey, Wings lacrosse, Phillies baseball, and Eagles football as well as local college games. Additional trips are planned to amusement parks, museums, plays, historical sites and events, and restaurants. During 2004–05, there were many planned outings, including golfing, canoeing, concerts, mountain biking, camping, theme parks, arcade trips, and movies.

A number of dances are held each year on and off campus. Boys attend dances at two girls' schools in the area—the Grier School and Purnell School. Girls from these schools attend dances at Phelps, including a winter holiday dance.

SUMMER PROGRAMS

Phelps conducts an intensive five-week summer program to help students with specific remedial

needs. Each student is enrolled in reading/study skills, language arts, mathematics, and computer skills classes. Enrichment workshops are held daily to build self-esteem and self-confidence. There is also a daily physical fitness/athletic period. Boys participate in weekly cultural or recreational trips. Credit for the classes is possible. Costs for the program in 2005 were $4500 for boarding students and $3500 for day students. For further information, students should contact the Director at the number listed.

COSTS AND FINANCIAL AID

The cost of tuition, room, and board for the 2006–07 academic year is $28,500, plus an activity fee of $800. A payment is due and payable in August, and the balance is due at the end of December. The cost of tuition for day students is $17,500. Students enrolled in the Academic Support Program are charged an additional $2000 per class. During the 2004–05 academic year, financial aid totaled $195,000.

ADMISSIONS INFORMATION

The Phelps School is highly qualified to help ineffective students who may have a learning or attention deficiency. Phelps accepts applicants in grade 7 through the postgraduate level. Each boy's educational program is individualized to meet his needs. The School is an equal rights educational opportunity institution; its applicants are admitted without regard to race, color, or national origin. The Test of English Proficiency is requested but not required as a prerequisite for international students. References from previous schools and/or professional advisers or counselors are sufficient, and personal interviews are waived. Attendance at the summer school ESL program is highly recommended.

APPLICATION TIMETABLE

Inquiries for application are accepted throughout the year. The interview and the accompanying campus tour may also be scheduled throughout the year. Late enrollment is possible. A fee of $50 must accompany the application. Upon acceptance, a $1000 deposit, applicable toward tuition, must be made to secure placement.

ADMISSIONS CORRESPONDENCE

F. Christopher Chirieleison
Assistant Headmaster for Enrollment
The Phelps School
583 Sugartown Road
Malvern, Pennsylvania 19355

Phone: 610-644-1754
Fax: 610-644-6679
E-mail: admis@thephelpsschool.org
Web site: http://www.thephelpsschool.org

PHILLIPS ACADEMY
Andover, Massachusetts

Type: Coeducational boarding and day college-preparatory school
Grades: 9–12, postgraduate year
Enrollment: 1,102
Head of School: Barbara L. Chase

THE SCHOOL

Phillips Academy was founded by Samuel Phillips during the Revolutionary War for the purpose of "enlarging the minds and forming the morals" of "youth from every quarter." A sister school, Abbot Female Academy, was founded in 1828, and the schools merged in 1973 to create a distinctive coeducational institution that combined the best of both traditions. Still committed to the education of mind and heart and dedicated anew to serving "youth from every quarter" in a truly multicultural community, Phillips Academy (usually called Andover) today includes 1,102 young men and women (including 18 students displaced by Hurricane Katrina) from forty-seven states and twenty-six countries. On a splendid 500-acre campus, under the tutelage of a gifted faculty, these students strive for academic excellence and moral decisiveness. The class of 2006 had 25 National Merit Semifinalists and 3 National Achievement Semifinalists.

The school is located on a hilltop in the town of Andover, Massachusetts, 21 miles north of Boston and less than an hour's drive from some of the loveliest beaches and mountains in New England. On the school's campus are a 125-acre bird sanctuary and two exceptional museums, the Addison Gallery of American Art and the Robert S. Peabody Museum of Archaeology.

The Academy's governing body is a 19-member Board of Trustees. The school has an endowment of approximately $622.8 million, as of June 2005. In the past year, Andover has received gifts totaling $22.8 million; last year's annual fund was $6.7 million.

Phillips Academy is accredited by the New England Association of Schools and Colleges. It is a member of the National Association of Independent Schools and the Secondary School Admission Test Board.

ACADEMIC PROGRAMS

Andover's curriculum encompasses 300 courses in eighteen academic departments. In all of these departments, courses are offered beyond the college entrance level and also at a variety of entry levels in order to respond sensitively to a student's incoming level of preparation.

Requirements vary according to the level at which a student enters the curriculum. In general, students receive extensive instruction in English, math, foreign language, history, and science as well as exposure to the arts, religion and philosophy, and physical education. An academic adviser guides a student throughout his or her career.

The grading is 0 (failure) through 6 (high honors). Grades are sent to parents after each of the three terms that make up the school year; comments are sent in the fall and spring. The average number of students in a classroom is 13; the overall student-teacher ratio is 5:1. Most students take five courses each term. Faculty members are available for individual help daily during the conference period and in the evenings; math study hall is open three nights a week.

Andover's Residential Education curriculum offers programs that address health and human issues. The Graham House Counseling Center offers psychological counseling, study skills courses, and student tutorial services. The school's Office of Community and Multicultural Development provides counseling and support services and sponsors workshops, lectures, and educational programs.

Several special complementary programs are also available. Qualified students may join the School Year Abroad program in China, France, Italy, and Spain. In addition, advanced language students may attend a local school in Göttingen, Germany; Burgos, Spain; Antibes, France; Kyoto, Japan; Santo Domingo, Dominican Republic; Salamanca, Spain; and Yokohama, Japan.

FACULTY AND ADVISERS

Andover has 168 full-time and 51 part-time faculty members who hold, among them, 159 Ph.D. and master's degrees and are as devoted to their students as they are passionate about their fields of expertise. Faculty members serve as students' coaches, house counselors, and advisers in addition to being classroom teachers. Roughly 98 percent of the faculty lives on campus. Turnover among faculty members at Andover is low.

The Head of School, Barbara L. Chase, came to Andover from Bryn Mawr School in 1994. She has an A.B. from Brown University and an M.L.A. from Johns Hopkins University.

COLLEGE PLACEMENT

Each Andover upper and new senior is assigned to one of the school's six college counselors who sees him or her through the college admission process. Parents are enlisted from the outset as partners in this and receive a quarterly newsletter from the College Counseling Office.

Roughly 150 college representatives visit the Andover campus each year. The mean SAT score for the 2005 graduates was 697 verbal and 691 math. The class of 2005 matriculated at ninety-eight colleges and universities, with 8 or more Andover graduates attending each of the following schools: Brown (9), Columbia (10), Cornell (14), Georgetown (13), Harvard (16), USC (9), Vanderbilt (10), Yale (9), and the University of Pennsylvania (17).

STUDENT BODY AND CONDUCT

In 2005–06, 546 boys and 556 girls from forty-seven states and twenty-six countries were enrolled at Andover. Among these students, 802 were boarders (389 boys and 413 girls) and 300 were day students (157 boys and 143 girls); 314 were seniors, 295 were upper-middlers, 279 were lower-middlers, and 214 were juniors. Forty percent of Andover's students received financial aid, 35 percent were members of minority groups, and 9 percent were international students.

Rules at Andover have a dual purpose: to preserve an atmosphere in which learning can take place and to teach students that individual freedom can be achieved only through due consideration for others. When a rule infraction involves discipline rather than counseling, the discipline is handled at the cluster level and involves the cluster dean, the house counselor, and other faculty and student representatives. Major offenses may result in dismissal.

ACADEMIC FACILITIES

Among Andover's 160 buildings are such significant academic buildings as Samuel Phillips Hall (history and language classrooms and the first all-digital language lab facility in the country), Morse Hall (mathematics), Bullfinch Hall (English and the debating room), Pearson Hall (classics), Graves Hall (music center), George Washington Hall (student center, drama laboratory, and 400-seat theater), and the Elson Art Center. The new, state-of-the-art Gelly Science Center opened in 2004. The Addison Gallery of American Art, with its collection of 12,000 works by such artists as Winslow Homer, Edward Hopper, Georgia O'Keefe, Jackson Pollack, and Andrew Wyeth, and the Robert S. Peabody Museum of Archaeology, which houses one of the country's outstanding collections of Native American artifacts, are used extensively by students for classes and exhibitions. Other academic facilities include extensive rehearsal and performance space for music, an astronomy observatory, ten science laboratories, a greenhouse, and a radio station. The Oliver Wendell Holmes Library contains Andover's main collection of 120,000 volumes, subscribes to 260 current and foreign language serials, and contains an extensive retrospective periodical collection in microform. Also in the library is the Academic Computing Center, with more than ninety computers and printers. The library is a service-oriented teaching library, open for students and faculty members more than 85 hours each week.

BOARDING AND GENERAL FACILITIES

Andover has forty-three dormitories housing from 4 to 42 students; the large dorms have several faculty families in residence. One third of boarding students live in single rooms; two thirds live in large double rooms. Currently, network access is available to all students through the dormitories and through public Technology Learning Centers (TLCs) with more than 120 computers. Every student is provided with an e-mail account, a private telephone line, and a personal voice mailbox. Seniors, uppers, and lowers live together in dormitories; juniors all live together in dorms with special study hours, visiting hours, and lights-out policies.

All Andover students and faculty members are assigned to one of the school's five clusters. At the heart of Andover's residential life and school spirit, clusters function as small schools within the school and provide the context for students' academic advising, disciplinary proceedings, personal counseling, intramural sports, weekday social functions, and Blue Key (school spirit) events.

ATHLETICS

At Andover, to play is the thing. Competitive athletics are available in all major sports at the varsity, subvarsity, and intramural levels; for students who are not interested in competitive sports, the school offers an exciting range of athletic alternatives, including dance, aerobics, yoga, kayaking, swim instruction, Search and Rescue, and many others. All lowers take one challenge-based physical education course for one term. All students participate in daily afternoon athletics and fitness activities. The athletic facilities include eighteen playing fields and eighteen tennis courts; the Sorota Track; the Borden, Memorial, and Abbot gymnasiums, with swimming and diving pools, two basketball and eight squash courts, two dance studios, a wrestling room, and a fitness center; an indoor track; two hockey rinks; a lighted varsity stadium; and a boathouse on the Merrimack River.

EXTRACURRICULAR OPPORTUNITIES

The school has four orchestras, four choral groups, several small singing groups, a Concert Band and Jazz Band, and more than forty student-run clubs, among them several literary and political magazines, a weekly newspaper, a radio station, the debate and math teams, and several drama and dance groups.

More than 700 students take part every year in the school's extensive Community Service Program. By helping others, students fulfill the mandate of Andover's motto, *non sibi*, meaning not for oneself.

DAILY LIFE

Students normally meet in four or five courses per day in 45-minute periods. Classes begin at 8 a.m. and end at 2:45 p.m., followed by athletics. There are double-block periods of 75 minutes on Wednesday and Thursday. In most courses, stu-

dents meet for one double period each week. This new schedule provides new opportunities for creative teaching and learning.

On Wednesday mornings and three Saturday mornings in both the fall and spring, classes are held, and interscholastic sports or community service are scheduled for the afternoon. All-school meetings are held once a week. Faculty-student conference periods are held three mornings a week. Extracurricular activities normally take place after dinner, and official study hours begin at 8 p.m.

WEEKEND LIFE

Dances, concerts, dramatic productions, movies, exhibits at the museums, or special cultural events are offered on campus every weekend. Students may leave campus if their parents have given them permission. Public transportation enables students to take advantage of cultural and sporting events in nearby Boston.

SUMMER PROGRAMS

The Phillips Academy Summer Session is a five-week, intensive academic program and precollege experience of both innovative and traditional courses as well as an intensive music program and focused college counseling. Also held on campus in the summer is the $(MS)^2$ Program—Math and Science for Minority Students—a three-summer program for talented public high school students. For information, those who are interested should write to the directors of these programs at Phillips Academy.

COSTS AND FINANCIAL AID

Tuition for 2005–06 was $33,000 for boarding students and $25,700 for day students. Tuition covers instruction, room, board, and admission to authorized athletic and social events but does not include textbooks, tutoring, special instruction in music or some athletics, medical expenses, some art materials, or incidentals. To reserve a place, new students pay a deposit of $1500; the tuition less that deposit is billed in two equal amounts, although additional financing options are available through the Andover Plan.

Andover is committed to admitting an economically diverse student body and awards financial aid on a basis of demonstrated need from a

financial aid budget of $10.3 million. Forty percent of Andover's students received financial aid.

ADMISSIONS INFORMATION

Andover is especially interested in accepting students with sound character and strong academic achievement who demonstrate independence, maturity, and concern for others. Valuing diversity in its student body, the school seeks to bring together a community from all parts of the country and from many nations.

Applicants for grades 9–11 must submit the results of the Secondary School Admission Test or the Independent School Entrance Exam; candidates for grade 12 and the postgraduate year must submit scores from either the PSAT or SAT I. In 2005, Andover received 2,646 preliminary applications and 2,231 final applications and offered admission to 469 students.

APPLICATION TIMETABLE

Andover welcomes initial inquiries at any time. Tours and interviews are conducted on campus from 8:45 until 2 on Monday, Tuesday, and Friday; from 10:15 until 2 on Thursday; and from 8:45 until 11:15 on Wednesday and some Saturdays. Applicants for admission to the ninth, tenth, and eleventh grades must submit the results of either the November, December, or January Secondary School Admission Test or the Independent School Entrance Exam. Senior-class and postgraduate-year applicants must submit the results of their SAT I or PSAT. Students taking later tests are considered late applicants.

For those who cannot visit the campus, interviews are also conducted elsewhere by admission representatives. The application deadline is January 15 for day students and February 1 for boarding students; the application fee is $40. Notification of acceptance is mailed on March 10, and a reply is required by April 10.

ADMISSIONS CORRESPONDENCE

Admission Office
Phillips Academy
Andover, Massachusetts 01810

Phone: 978-749-4050
Fax: 978-749-4068
E-mail: admissions@andover.edu
Web site: http://www.andover.edu

PHILLIPS EXETER ACADEMY

Exeter, New Hampshire

Type: Coeducational boarding and day college-preparatory school
Grades: 9–12, postgraduate year
Enrollment: 1,050
Head of School: Tyler C. Tingley, Principal

THE SCHOOL

Phillips Exeter Academy was founded in 1781 by John and Elizabeth Phillips. In their deed of gift, they made clear their belief in the need to link goodness with knowledge. Exeter remains a school committed to academic excellence, and the faculty members work closely with students to help them develop lifelong habits of industry and intellectual curiosity. The Academy is also committed to fostering an awareness of an individual's responsibilities toward others. *Non sibi*, "not for oneself," is the motto of the Academy.

Exeter is well known for originating Harkness teaching, whereby 12 students and a teacher join together around an oval Harkness Table. The teacher is a facilitator rather than a leader, and the learning style encourages everyone in a class to think independently, to express oneself articulately, and to understand the beliefs and viewpoints of others. As the physical table itself implies, learning at Exeter is a cooperative enterprise in which the students and instructor work together as partners. This philosophy is key to life outside the classrooms as well. The Academy strives to encourage connectedness in all areas of community life.

The Academy is located in the center of Exeter, New Hampshire, a historic town 20 minutes from the Atlantic Ocean and an hour north of Boston. Students have convenient access to charming shops, restaurants, cafés, and a movie theater, all of which are within walking distance of campus. With its proximity to the ocean, classes in science and the environment are able to make field trips to the New Hampshire seacoast to study wetlands and wildlife. Exeter is also near enough to the White Mountains for easy access to hiking and skiing.

A 20-member Board of Trustees is the Academy's governing body. The Academy's endowment, currently valued at approximately $706 million, is supplemented by an annual fund of about $5.5 million and recent noncampaign capital gifts of about $30 million. More than 20,000 graduates are members of the general alumni association and contribute significantly to the support of the Academy.

Phillips Exeter Academy is accredited by the New England Association of Schools and Colleges. It is a member of the Cum Laude Society, the Independent Schools Association of Northern New England, the National Association of Independent Schools, and the Secondary School Admission Test Board.

ACADEMIC PROGRAMS

Exeter offers a rich curriculum with more than 350 courses, including opportunities to study college-level material well beyond the Advanced Placement level. The Harkness Table is central to both the Exeter classroom and the Exeter curriculum. Though teaching and learning look different in the various disciplines and levels of study, they have in common the ideal of active, participatory, student-centered learning that values imparting to students not just a given course's content but also the skills required to become their own and each other's teachers.

The Academy's customary college-preparatory curriculum includes comprehensive instruction in English, foreign language (classical or modern), history, mathematics, and science. Other requirements include art, drama, or music; religion; health and human development; and junior studies for all entering ninth graders. Graduation requirements vary depending on a student's grade upon entry. The academic year consists of three terms.

Academic work is graded using A–E (failing) designations with pluses and minuses. Grades and teacher comments are sent to parents following each trimester.

In most cases, students are assigned to the Harkness-style classes on a random basis. Class size averages 12 students, and the student-teacher ratio is 5:1. The standard course load is five courses per term.

Exeter's international and domestic off-campus study programs offer students many distinct opportunities. Qualified eleventh and twelfth graders may undertake a year of foreign language and cultural immersion through the School Year Abroad program in China, France, Italy, or Spain. Other international study programs include a term in China, England, France, Germany, Mexico, and Russia and summer programs in France, Japan, Mexico, Spain, and Taiwan. Two domestic off-campus study programs round out the offerings: one term of study at the working farm of the Milton Mountain School in Vermont and a spring term in Exeter's Washington Intern Program.

FACULTY AND ADVISERS

Exeter faculty members are passionate about Harkness teaching and sharing their scholarly enthusiasm with students. They see themselves as counselors as well as teachers, and their interests and talents extend beyond their academic disciplines. Faculty advisers live in the dorms with their advisees and are available for academic advice and any other concerns a student may have. Faculty members also participate in the Academy's physical education program and advise student-run extracurricular activities. Annual faculty turnover is low. The faculty plays a vital role in the operation of the Academy, sharing responsibility for admissions, financial aid, discipline, and curriculum.

COLLEGE PLACEMENT

A full-time college counseling staff helps students in the selection of postsecondary institutions. More than 150 college representatives visit the Academy each year. The mid–50 percent range of SAT I scores for 2003 graduates was 620–720 verbal and 640–730 math. Ninety-nine percent of the members of the class of 2003 went on to college (a total of 106 institutions). In 2004, schools where 5 or more students matriculated were Brown (6), Columbia (12), Cornell (7), Dartmouth (8), Georgetown (10), Harvard (13), Johns Hopkins (7), McGill (5), NYU (9), Northwestern (5), Princeton (13), Smith (5), Stanford (7), Trinity (Connecticut) (5), Tufts (6), Wellesley (6), Yale (8), and the Universities of Chicago (5), North Carolina at Chapel Hill (5), Pennsylvania (15), and Virginia (5).

STUDENT BODY AND CONDUCT

When John and Elizabeth Phillips founded Phillips Exeter Academy, they stressed the importance of bringing together "youth from every quarter." In 2005–06, 538 boys and 512 girls from forty-six states, the District of Columbia, Puerto Rico, and twenty-nine other countries attended Phillips Exeter Academy. The student body consisted of the following: ninth grade, 97 boys and 93 girls; tenth grade, 118 boys and 128 girls; eleventh grade, 158 boys and 136 girls; and twelfth grade and postgraduate year, 165 boys and 155 girls. Of these totals, 840 students boarded, and 210 were day students.

Principles rather than rules are the basis for the Academy's discipline policy. The Academy acts on the assumptions that its students enter the school with a serious purpose and that their conscience and good sense are a sufficient guide to behavior. Student representatives help define and enforce essential regulations, and they hold four nonvoting seats on the Discipline Committee. Major offenses may result in the student being required to withdraw or being placed on probationary status.

ACADEMIC FACILITIES

An attractive campus of Georgian and modern buildings spreads over 471 acres. Central to campus life is the Academy's Class of 1945 Library. The award-winning structure was designed by Louis I. Kahn and is the largest secondary-school library in the world both in size and number of volumes. Exeter's performing arts facilities are state-of-the-art and include the Frederick R. Mayer Art Center, the Lamont Gallery, the Fisher Theater, and the Forrestal-Bowld Music Center. Phillips Hall houses classrooms for English and modern languages, a language media room, the Daniel Webster Debating Room, and a small theater. The Academy Building houses classrooms for mathematics, history, religion, classical languages, and anthropology; a computer lab; photography labs; the P. Phillips Foundation Anthropology Museum; and the Assembly Hall, where an all-school assembly takes place three times weekly. The Grainger Observatory has two domes with telescopes, a classroom, an observation deck, and a chart room. The multidenominational Phillips Church is the center of religious worship at Exeter, where students from eleven of the world's religions gather to express their faith.

Science classes are taught in the $38-million, award-winning Phelps Science Center, which opened in fall of 2001, bringing together two exciting pedagogies: experiential, hands-on learning and the discussion-based Harkness method. The building has many distinguishing features, including a complete humpback whale skeleton hanging in its rear atrium and a 900-gallon tropical aquarium in the lobby. The building is divided into four classroom wings serving physics, chemistry, biology, and a shared space for interdisciplinary work. There are a total of twenty classroom labs and four common labs; each classroom features its own Harkness table and state-of-the-art audiovisual system. Among the other special features found in the Phelps Science Center are a marine biology table, a teaching garden with

seven different habitats, an outdoor classroom, a rotating turntable and Dickensen runway in the physics area, and 16 feet of fume hood in the chemistry area. The building also contains the 300-seat Grainger Auditorium and the Peter Durham '85 Computer Science Lab.

BOARDING AND GENERAL FACILITIES

The Harkness spirit of collaborative learning extends to Exeter's twenty-nine centrally located residences. Twenty dormitories accommodate 30 to 60 students each and nine smaller houses board 10 to 20 students. Each residence is supervised by faculty members who serve as advisers to students and ensure that an adult is always available for assistance and counsel. Many teachers, some with their spouse and children, live in dormitory apartments and share their family lives with students. All residences have common areas for relaxation and recreation, and—depending on the residence— amenities include televisions, Ping-Pong and pool tables, kitchenettes, and laundry facilities. All rooms are equipped with individual phone, voice mail, and Internet connections.

The Lamont Health Center provides comprehensive health care 24 hours a day. The center is staffed by a Board-certified pediatrician, a nurse practitioner, registered nurses, counselors, athletic trainers, a nutritionist, and a health educator, who are available for any health concern.

Two dining halls serve the Exeter community, providing balanced, healthy meals with a wide range of choice. The Grill is a legendary spot for getting together with friends between classes, for study breaks, and for hearing bands on the weekends.

ATHLETICS

The Academy was founded on the belief that it is important to develop a sound body as well as a sound mind. More than 200 years later, the commitment remains. The Academy promotes good health and fitness by teaching skills in diverse physical activities ranging from bicycling to wrestling. There are four levels of participation available to students: competitive and intramural teams, fitness, and the ninth grade physical education program. Exeter offers thirty-three different sports from instructional to varsity level. Nine full-time physical education instructors are assisted by more than 90 faculty members, who serve as coaches at all levels and provide another opportunity for interaction among teachers and students.

The Love Gymnasium contains two indoor hockey rinks, four basketball courts, fourteen squash courts (including three international-size courts), a training room, the Ransome Conditioning Room, and an eight-lane swimming pool. The Thompson Gymnasium houses an indoor track, a wrestling room, a dance studio, two basketball courts, and a pool. Outdoor sports facilities include twenty-three tennis courts, the 4,500-seat lighted Phelps stadium, the 400-meter all-weather Lovshin track, twenty-two playing fields, and cross-country trails. Exeter's Saltonstall Boathouse houses twenty-four shells, eight ergometers, and locker rooms for the boys' and girls' teams.

EXTRACURRICULAR OPPORTUNITIES

Nearly 100 student-run clubs meet regularly and offer every student the chance to become involved.

While students take primary responsibility for organizing activities, faculty advisers meet regularly with club members and provide guidance and resources. Choices include art and performance clubs; academic, athletic, and game clubs; math, science, and computer clubs; language, cultural, and religious organizations; student publications; service organizations; and political clubs.

Exeter maintains a close connection to the local community through the student-run Exeter Social Services Organization (ESSO), which links the Academy's volunteer resources with local organizations and institutions such as schools and hospitals.

DAILY LIFE

Central to community life at Exeter is the Assembly Program. The entire Academy community gathers three times a week for programs featuring student groups, renowned speakers, alumni, and other special guests.

Classes are held five days a week and on some Saturdays; Wednesdays and Saturdays are half days. On full days, which run from 8 to 6, four class periods are held before lunch and four after lunch. Two class periods are reserved for athletics on Monday, Tuesday, Thursday, and Friday, while interscholastic contests are scheduled either on Wednesday or Saturday afternoons. Three mornings a week, there is a 30-minute all-school assembly. Student organizations meet after dinner, which is offered from 5 p.m. until 7 p.m. Evening study hours run from 8 until 10:30. Light fare is available in both dining halls from 7 a.m. until 7 p.m. Day students are fully integrated into all aspects of Academy life.

WEEKEND LIFE

Current-year events include coffeehouses, dances, films, casino and games nights, cookouts, and hiking and ski trips. Regular shuttles are available to Portsmouth and Boston. The student-run Weekend Activities Committee works closely with the Student Activities Office to schedule, plan, and implement the calendar of weekend events both on and off campus.

SUMMER PROGRAMS

The Summer School at Exeter, begun in 1919, enrolled 622 boys and girls from forty states and thirty-six countries in 2004. Able high-school students come to enrich their academic programs, to improve in particular subjects, to enjoy the challenge of rigorous college-preparatory courses, or to have an independent school experience. More than 100 faculty members from Exeter, other schools, and other countries participate in the program. Although the Academy gives no credit, students may make arrangements with their own schools for validation of their summer work. Further information may be obtained by writing to the Director of the Summer School.

COSTS AND FINANCIAL AID

In 2005–06, the tuition was $33,000 for boarding students and $25,500 for day students. These figures included most services, all meals, and admission to on-campus concerts, plays, and athletic events but excluded the cost of books and incidentals. Optional expenses were incurred for health care, private music instruction, some art materials, and off-campus programs. To reserve a place, new

students pay an initial deposit of $1700, $1500 of which is applied to the first year's tuition, and $200 of which is refunded when the student departs the Academy.

In 2005–06, Exeter offered more than $8 million in financial aid grants to 33 percent of the student body. Grants are awarded on the basis of financial need as indicated by the guidelines from the School and Student Service for Financial Aid. In addition, more than $60,000 is allocated annually to financial aid recipients for travel, books, clothing, and athletic equipment. Since its founding, the Academy has used its resources to supplement what a family contributes toward an Exeter education.

ADMISSIONS INFORMATION

Phillips Exeter Academy seeks to enroll students who combine proven academic ability and intellectual curiosity with decency and good character. Exeter wants young people who welcome the challenges and opportunities provided by a strong academic program within a diverse community. Students come from a wide range of racial, geographic, socioeconomic, ethnic, religious, and cultural backgrounds. Because what happens in the classrooms and dorms and on the stages and playing fields depends to an unusual degree upon student engagement with other students and adults, candidates are sought who demonstrate interest and involvement with others. Above all, the Academy looks for students who have the capacity to grow and who are likely to thrive at Exeter, whether they enter as four-year, three-year, two-year, or one-year students.

The SSAT is required of applicants for grades 9 or 10. The SSAT or the PSAT is required of applicants for grade 11. Senior-class and postgraduate applicants must submit results of the PSAT and the SAT, respectively. TOEFL scores are required of all applicants for whom English is not the primary language. In addition, applicants are required to have a personal interview with a member of the admissions staff or an Academy representative. Approximately 1 out of 4 students is accepted each year.

APPLICATION TIMETABLE

Interested students and their families are encouraged to visit Exeter. Campus tours and interviews are scheduled from 8 a.m. to 4 p.m. on Monday through Friday and from 8 a.m. to noon on Saturday.

All application materials must be received by January 16; completed forms must be accompanied by a nonrefundable $50 for U.S. residents or a $100 fee for non-U.S. residents. Notification of acceptance is mailed on March 10, and families are expected to reply by April 10.

ADMISSIONS CORRESPONDENCE

Michael Gary
Director of Admissions
Phillips Exeter Academy
20 Main Street
Exeter, New Hampshire 03833-2460

Phone: 603-777-3437
Fax: 603-777-4399
E-mail: admit@exeter.edu
Web site: http://www.exeter.edu

POMFRET SCHOOL

Pomfret, Connecticut

Type: Coeducational boarding and day college-preparatory school
Grades: 9–12 (Forms III–VI) and PG
Enrollment: 340
Head of School: Bradford Hastings, Headmaster

THE SCHOOL

Prospective families find 340 students and 69 faculty members learning and living together on a 500-acre campus situated in the charming northeastern corner of Connecticut. Pomfret's campus is an oasis, with boutique shopping, movie theaters, malls, and Connecticut's premier antique district all close by. Pomfret School is just 30 minutes from Providence, 40 minutes from Hartford, 1 hour from Boston, and 3 hours from New York City. Interesting and challenging academics (AP courses and independent projects offered in all disciplines) combined with competitive athletics (fourteen varsity teams, with five recent New England championships) and exciting opportunities in the creative arts (including a recent chorus tour of Spain) continue the 111-year tradition of educational excellence that defines Pomfret School. In addition to its excellent academic programs, Pomfret is particularly well known for its strong community atmosphere, which helps students develop as good citizens. Students form close relationships with their advisers and other faculty members, all of whom are devoted to guiding students in the classroom, on the playing fields, and in the art studios.

The School is governed by a Board of Trustees, most of whose 24 active members are alumni, current parents, or parents of alumni. The physical plant is valued at $47 million, and the endowment is in excess of $32 million. In 2004–05, more than $1.25 million was donated to the Annual Giving fund; 81 percent of current parents participated.

Pomfret School is accredited by the New England Association of Schools and Colleges and is approved by the Connecticut State Department of Education. Its memberships include the Connecticut Association of Independent Schools, the Headmasters' Association, the National Association of Independent Schools, the Secondary School Admission Test Board, A Better Chance (ABC), and the Cum Laude Society.

ACADEMIC PROGRAMS

Pomfret School offers a traditional college-preparatory curriculum that stresses the fundamentals. Emphasis is placed on reading, writing, math, foreign languages, science, history, and computer competence. The minimum academic requirements for graduation include 4 years of English, 4 years of mathematics, 3 years of one modern or classical foreign language, 3⅓ years of history, 3 years of a laboratory science (1 of which is biology), 1 trimester of religion, and 1 trimester of social issues. The school year is divided into trimesters, with exams in November, March, and June.

Pomfret School recognizes the value of imaginative and creative development and offers a particularly strong arts program. Students are required to enroll in an art course in two of three terms each year they attend Pomfret. Creative arts courses are offered in music, theater, painting, sculpture, film, woodworking, metalworking, dance, creative writing, photography, painting, and drawing. The religion requirement may be met through such electives as Faith and Imagination and World Religions. Pomfret encourages its students to participate in community service. Options include tutoring, day care, hospital projects, and Special Olympics.

The average class size is 12 students, and the student-faculty ratio is 6:1. The grading system uses letter grades of A to E. Grades are given twice during each trimester, and teacher comments accompany grades four times per year. A faculty adviser works closely with a group of 5 to 7 students.

FACULTY AND ADVISERS

There are 69 faculty members (41 men, 28 women); 65 are full-time, 41 have earned master's degrees, and 4 hold doctorates. All faculty members have advisees and live on campus. The average length of teaching experience is eleven years.

Pomfret employs teachers who engender enthusiasm for learning. The job of any faculty member goes beyond the classroom to include coaching, advising, and, usually, running a dormitory. Pomfret believes it is at the forefront in providing for the professional growth of its faculty members. Leaves with full pay plus travel stipends during sabbaticals enable faculty members to study in an academic area of their choice. Summer study and travel grants are also available.

Bradford Hastings became Headmaster in 1993, after serving as Assistant Headmaster at Deerfield Academy. He is a graduate of Pomfret and was on the faculty from 1972 to 1978. Mr. Hastings served on Pomfret's Board of Trustees from 1985 to 1992. His master's degree in education is from Harvard University.

COLLEGE PLACEMENT

College placement starts with college counseling, a process that begins at Pomfret midway through a student's junior year and continues as a refining and defining process until graduation. At all times it is thought of as an effort that fosters individual social maturity, academic growth, and a deeper commitment to School activities.

All juniors take the PSAT in the fall and the SAT and SAT Subject Tests in the winter and spring.

A complete portrait of each individual's life at Pomfret—social, academic, and extracurricular—and a personal understanding of each student's aspirations enable the college counseling office to provide very close personal attention.

Pomfret's graduates have chosen to attend such prestigious colleges and universities as Amherst, Columbia, Dartmouth, Duke, and Yale.

STUDENT BODY AND CONDUCT

Pomfret currently has 258 boarding and 82 day students. There are 60 in the Third Form (grade 9), 85 in the Fourth Form (grade 10), 95 in the Fifth Form (grade 11), and 100 in the Sixth Form (grade 12). The students come from twenty-nine states and fifteen countries. Twelve percent are members of minority groups.

Participation in the student government enables students to assume active leadership roles within the School. A president (a Sixth Former) chairs the government, which is made up of elected representatives from each Form and from the faculty.

Students at Pomfret are expected to follow the School rules outlined in the student handbook. Any infraction of these rules leads to an appearance before the Discipline Committee, which is composed of both students and faculty members and is chaired by the Dean of Students. The committee makes recommendations on discipline to the Headmaster.

ACADEMIC FACILITIES

The School is located on 500 acres, which consist of thirteen playing fields, rolling hills, and woodlands. The principal school buildings are grouped in the middle of the campus. The new athletic and student center, which opened in spring 2004, houses a two-floor student center, study room, snack bar, student radio station, student publications office, and bookstore. It also includes eight international-size squash courts, a wrestling room, a fitness center, locker rooms, an athletic trainer's facility, and offices for the Athletic Director and Director of Student Activities. In addition to the new athletic and student center, Pomfret recently opened a new ice-hockey rink and boathouse.

The School House contains history and foreign language classrooms, administrative offices, and the newly renovated music center. It is flanked on one side by four brick dormitories and on the other by Hard Auditorium, the center for dramatic and musical productions.

Nearby is the Monell Science Building (renovated in 1996), with laboratories for biology, chemistry, and physics as well as lecture rooms furnished with video equipment. The Centennial Building (1996) houses all mathematics and English classes as well as two- and three-dimensional art studios, metal and wood shops, and a 125-seat state-of-the-art theater.

The du Pont Library completes the current academic buildings. Along with its 22,000 volumes and the Technology Center, the library provides students with Internet access, a fully automated catalog and circulation system, and more than a dozen online subscription databases that cover a broad spectrum of disciplines with full-text and print capability. In addition, materials from outside the library are available through interlibrary loan.

Other nearby buildings include a dance studio and the Main House, which contains the dining hall, mail room, School store, and health center, which is staffed by 3 registered nurses. The School physician is at the health center in the mornings. Clark Memorial Chapel also occupies a central location on campus.

BOARDING AND GENERAL FACILITIES
Pomfret students are housed in nine dormitories on campus. Four converted homes, four large brick dormitories, and the recently renovated Pyne Hall serve as student residences. A fiber-optic backbone connects all Pomfret dormitory rooms, classrooms, faculty apartments, and offices, permitting computer and telephone networking throughout the campus as well as access to e-mail and the Internet in each dorm room. New students are assigned to double rooms, while returning students can choose to live in either single or double rooms. All dorms are supervised by live-in faculty dorm parents, each of whom supervises between 7 and 14 students on his or her floor.

The Strong Field House/Student Center has four indoor tennis courts, a student lounge, and a snack bar.

ATHLETICS
Athletics at Pomfret are an integral part of the educational experience, and all students are expected to participate each season at the level that is most challenging to them. Coaching responsibilities are shared by most faculty members. In addition, the School employs an athletics trainer.

The goal of the athletics program is to field competitive teams that exhibit discipline, the desire to excel, and pride in themselves and the School.

A varied interscholastic program is offered throughout the academic year. It includes cross-country, field hockey, football, soccer, and volleyball in the fall; basketball, ice hockey, squash, and wrestling in the winter; and baseball, crew, golf, lacrosse, softball, and tennis in the spring. In addition, aerobics, community service, dance, drama, and outdoor education are offered as athletic alternatives.

Pomfret has a fully equipped Nautilus fitness center, with nineteen individual stations, four Fitron bikes, rowing ergometers, a Stairmaster, a treadmill, and Olympic free weights. Under faculty supervision, students are able to supplement their work on the playing field with a complete resistance training or aerobic program.

Students may opt to undertake an independent project for a given season rather than engage in sports. Faculty-sponsored independent projects have included tutoring at a local school, working at a convalescent home, completing a major woodworking project, training for the Boston marathon, and working for Habitat for Humanity.

EXTRACURRICULAR OPPORTUNITIES
Pomfret also requires participation in a wide range of extracurricular activities. The *Pontefract* (newspaper), *Griffin* (yearbook), and *Manuscripts* (fiction magazine) enjoy good student leadership and participation. An active theater program presents six plays and numerous theater projects each year, including musical productions (staged each spring). Auditions are open to students, faculty members, and local artists, and performances are open to the public.

DAILY LIFE
Classes are scheduled five days a week in nine 50-minute periods from 8 a.m. to 3:15 p.m. Sports practices are scheduled in the afternoons from 3:45 to 5:45. The class day ends at 12:25 p.m. on Wednesdays and at 11:30 a.m. on class Saturdays. Evening study hours are 8 to 10 p.m., Sunday through Friday. Students study in their rooms. Lights-out is at 10:35 for Third and Fourth Formers and at 12 for Fifth and Sixth Formers.

The academic year, which is divided into trimesters, begins in early September and ends in early June, with vacations scheduled for one week at Thanksgiving, two weeks at Christmas, and three weeks in March.

WEEKEND LIFE
Most students prefer to remain at school on the weekends to enjoy time with friends and take advantage of the planned activities. On Saturday afternoons, there are interscholastic athletics contests. Students appreciate the local area, which combines rural beauty with elegant shopping and café dining. They also enjoy Sunday trips to Boston, Vermont ski slopes, and area shopping malls and movie theaters, as well as canoeing and biking excursions. Dances on campus at Pomfret School—with live music or DJs—and dances at other schools are always popular.

The student lounge, tuck shop, indoor tennis courts, squash courts, and gymnasium are open and available seven days a week. On Sundays, students are invited but not required to attend a chapel service or a local church service. Brunch is served at 10. The weekend officially ends on Sunday before dinner. There are regular study hours on Sunday evening in preparation for Monday classes.

COSTS AND FINANCIAL AID
In 2005–06, charges for boarding students were $36,200 and for day students, $23,400. Costs for textbooks, stationery, athletics equipment, laundry, and dry cleaning are charged separately through a student debit account.

Need-based financial aid is available to families who qualify. In 2005–06, close to $2 million of need-based financial aid was distributed to students.

ADMISSIONS INFORMATION
Pomfret seeks students whose past achievement indicates that they could benefit from and contribute to life at the School. Pomfret gives prime consideration to those applicants who possess academic ability, interest in the arts and athletics, and a willingness to become involved in and supportive of the Pomfret School community.

Each applicant must submit an application by January 15, come to Pomfret for an interview (preferably when school is in session), and take the SSAT. Notification to prospective students is made on March 10.

Pomfret School admits students of any race, color, creed, handicap, sexual orientation, or national origin to all the rights, privileges, programs, and activities generally accorded or made available to students at the School. The School does not discriminate on the basis of race, color, creed, handicap, sexual orientation, or national origin in the administration of its educational policies, admission policies, financial aid, or other programs administered by the School.

APPLICATION TIMETABLE
Initial inquiries are welcome at any time, and tours and interviews can be arranged by calling the Admissions Office. Office hours are 8 to 4 Monday through Friday and 8 to noon on class Saturdays. School catalogs and applications can be obtained from the Admissions Office.

Pomfret adheres to the Parents' Reply Date of April 10. Thus, a place that has been offered on March 10 is reserved until April 10. Late applications (those to which it is not possible to reply by March 10) are accepted and acted upon as soon as possible and as enrollment permits.

ADMISSIONS CORRESPONDENCE
Erik C. Bertelsen
Assistant Head for Enrollment
Pomfret School, Inc.
398 Pomfret Street
P.O. Box 128
Pomfret, Connecticut 06258-0128

Phone: 860-963-6120
Fax: 860-963-2042
E-mail: admission@pomfretschool.org
Web site: http://www.pomfretschool.org

PORTSMOUTH ABBEY SCHOOL

Portsmouth, Rhode Island

Type: Coeducational boarding and day college-preparatory school
Grades: 9–12 (Forms III–VI)
Enrollment: 349
Head of School: Dr. James M. De Vecchi, Headmaster

THE SCHOOL

Portsmouth Abbey School was founded by Benedictine monks of the English Congregation in 1926. Unique among American boarding schools, Portsmouth Abbey School has created a community rooted in the ideals of the Catholic tradition and the high scholastic standards practiced by the Benedictine community since the sixth century.

The School offers the many attractions one expects to find at a leading boarding school: a challenging college-preparatory program, talented and compassionate teachers, an international student body, fine facilities, a busy and lively student life, and a supportive residential environment.

The aim of Portsmouth Abbey School today, as it has been since Father John Hugh Diman founded it in 1926, is to help students to grow in knowledge and grace. The School seeks to embody those ideals and qualities that lie at the heart of the 1,500-year-old Benedictine tradition: reverence for God and man, respect for learning and order, and an appreciation of the shared experience of community life.

The School property covers 500 acres on Narragansett Bay. The location of the Abbey, set in a rural-suburban town, is convenient to the cultural and recreational centers of Newport (10 miles), Providence (28 miles), Boston (65 miles), and New York (190 miles). Throughout the year, students enjoy trips to athletics events, whale-watching out of Boston, and symphony and theatrical performances in Providence and Boston.

The governing body of the School is a 23-member Board of Regents. It is made up of laypersons and members of the monastic community. The total endowment is currently valued at approximately $32 million.

Portsmouth Abbey School is accredited by the New England Association of Schools and Colleges and is a member of the National Association of Independent Schools, the Association of Boarding Schools, and the Cum Laude Society.

ACADEMIC PROGRAMS

The program of studies offers young men and women of academic potential a solid foundation in the liberal arts. The School believes that these disciplines best foster the development of the skills fundamental to all learning: the ability to read with understanding, to reason clearly, and to express oneself with precision.

Students carry five full courses plus religion. To be eligible for the diploma, a student must pass a course in Christian Doctrine each year and complete a minimum of 20 college entrance units, including 4 in English, 3 in a foreign language, 3 in mathematics, 2 in a laboratory science, 1 in art/music, 1 in U.S. history, and 1 in European history or humanities. The remaining units may be obtained in any course offered for credit, including courses in art, music, photography, history, science, politics, economics, computer science, French, Spanish, Latin, and Greek.

A wide variety of noncredit courses—play production, public speaking, chorus, typing, and chamber music—are offered. Sixth Formers are encouraged to design independent study programs. Seventeen Advanced Placement courses are available.

Students are grouped by their level of achievement and ability in mathematics, language, and the sciences. The average class size is 13 students, and the student-faculty ratio is 7:1. A modern science building, a computer center, a library, and an arts center are open afternoons and evenings as well as on weekends. Faculty members are available for extra help during daily conference periods and supervised study hours.

A student's progress is carefully monitored by an advising team, the houseparent, and deans. Reports are mailed home six times a year. The median grade is 78 percent, and the passing grade is 60 percent. A learning specialist assists students in their study, reading, and writing skills and in developing a time-management program.

FACULTY AND ADVISERS

There are 45 faculty members, including 8 Benedictine monks. Forty-two advanced degrees, including eight doctorates, are held by faculty members. The majority of faculty members live on campus.

Very Reverend Dom Caedmon Holmes is Prior Administrator and Head of the School's Governing Body. Dr. James M. De Vecchi is the Headmaster. He earned an undergraduate degree from Saint Francis College, and a master's and doctorate in mathematics from the University of New Hampshire. Dr. De Vecchi joined the faculty in 1973 and has served in many capacities, including Mathematics Department Head, Registrar, Academic Dean, and Associate Headmaster.

Portsmouth Abbey's monastic community acts as a point of stability for the School. All new faculty members appointed each year are chosen because they are distinguished in their academic field, embrace the School's mission, and uphold the School's philosophy.

COLLEGE PLACEMENT

The college placement process begins in the winter of the Fifth Form year in meetings with the College Counselor and a conference to acquaint students and their parents with the process. At this time, students are encouraged to think about visiting colleges for interviews during the summer. In addition, more than 80 college representatives meet with Sixth Formers on campus during the fall. The College Counselor carefully monitors the list of colleges to which each student plans to apply.

Ninety-nine percent of the class of 2005 entered four-year colleges. The colleges and universities that have enrolled 2 or more recent graduates include Bates, Boston College, Brown, Colgate, Emory, Georgetown, George Washington, Harvard, Notre Dame, Syracuse, the United States Naval Academy, Williams, Yale, and the University of Vermont.

STUDENT BODY AND CONDUCT

Supported by the presence and example of the resident Benedictine community, the traditional ideas of Christian living and learning are intended to inform every part of school life and to guide the policies and practices of the community and its members. The School welcomes students from diverse backgrounds while encouraging an appreciation for the Catholic faith. Portsmouth thus aspires to develop informed and open-minded leaders, who are educated in the Christian tradition.

Good judgment, common sense, and consideration for others are primary guidelines for behavior in the School community. A serious breach of School rules is referred to the Discipline Committee, composed of students and faculty members. The Student Council is a forum for student concerns.

In 2004–05, Portsmouth Abbey School enrolled 349 students. They came from twenty-seven states, the District of Columbia, and twelve countries. More than 10 percent of the students are members of minority groups, and about 80 percent are Roman Catholic.

ACADEMIC FACILITIES

Surrounding the quadrangle are the Burden Classroom Building, the Science Building, and the Cortazzo Administration Building, which houses the auditorium. Other buildings include the St. Thomas More Library, the McGuire Fine Arts Center, and a Victorian manor house designed by Richard Upjohn in 1864. The library contains a 36,000-volume collection and a computerized catalog, online computers, and seminar rooms. There are more than 35,000 additional volumes housed in the monastery library.

BOARDING AND GENERAL FACILITIES

Portsmouth offers its students a structured environment built on a schedule of shared daily activities—classes, athletics, clubs, and social life—and of regular community worship. The seven Houses each contain 20 to 40 students and provide the student with a familial base, a greater amount of attention, and an identity within the School. Within each House, there are 3 houseparents and a chaplain. Such a support system proves ideal for teaching students the intrinsic values of education: compassion and morality.

Members of the Third Form (ninth grade) are housed in the same dorm; other dorms house students of mixed ages. If the houseparent is a layperson, a monk from the monastery is appointed to serve as spiritual leader of the dormi-

tory. Students in the lower forms usually share double rooms; seniors and some juniors elect singles.

Students from other countries or distant locations are welcome to spend long weekends, as well as other relatively short vacations, on campus. However, the School encourages students to take advantage of such breaks in the academic routine.

Additional School facilities include the Nesbitt Infirmary, the recently renovated Stillman Dining Hall, and the Abbey Church of St. Gregory the Great. The majority of buildings on campus are of redwood and fieldstone and were designed by Pietro Belluschi, formerly Dean of Architecture at MIT. This design has become a major architectural attraction in the state.

ATHLETICS
Portsmouth has an extensive athletics program. All students must participate in athletics as part of their education and personal development. Dispensation for projects is sometimes permitted for a season, and students with physical handicaps or injuries are asked to help in the training room or serve as team managers.

The School has varsity and junior varsity teams. Sports offered include baseball, basketball, cross-country, field hockey, football, golf, ice hockey, lacrosse, sailing, soccer, softball, squash, swimming, tennis, and track and field. A state-of-the-art fitness center includes eight squash courts. There are also six tennis courts; a six-lane, all-weather running track; an indoor ice-hockey rink; two gymnasiums; multiple outdoor playing fields; and a new equestrian center. The golf team practices at the Carnegie Abbey Golf Course, a privately owned eighteen-hole championship Scottish links golf course located on campus.

EXTRACURRICULAR OPPORTUNITIES
Outside the classroom, students are encouraged to become involved in the betterment of the Portsmouth Abbey community at large. Among the opportunities available to the students are the FM school radio station, fishing club, rocketry club, theater group, church choir, glee club, model United Nations, community service, debate club, cultural awareness group, school newspaper, yearbook, literary magazine, and equestrian program.

The School also sponsors the Dom Luke Childs lecture series, a film series, and trips to cultural, social, and sports events in the Providence and Boston areas.

DAILY LIFE
Classes begin at 8:15 and end at 2:50. On Wednesday and Saturday, the academic day is shortened to accommodate travel to athletics contests. The usual academic day includes five periods before

lunch and two academic periods after lunch. Athletics are usually scheduled from 3 to 5:45, but there are variations in the times depending on the team and season. There are buffet dinners five nights a week and formal meals twice weekly in the fall and spring terms. After dinner, there is free time for activities followed by evening study from 7:30 to 9:30. Lights-out is from 10:30 to 11:30, depending on the form. Jackets and ties for boys and blazers for girls are required for classes, assemblies, and church services.

WEEKEND LIFE
The Student Council, the Social Committee, Houses, and individual classes plan a variety of social activities both on and off campus. The Social Committee, under the supervision of the Assistant Headmaster for Student Life, coordinates dances and other social events and sponsors the Christmas semiformal and the Spring Prom. Form and House parties and trips to athletics events, movie theaters, malls, and concerts are other planned weekend activities.

Students may receive permission to leave the campus on Saturday and Sunday afternoon for Newport, Providence, and Boston. In addition to the scheduled vacations, students may take a limited number of Saturday overnights. Day students are integrated with houses and are encouraged to participate in evening and weekend activities. Their families often host students who come to Portsmouth from a distance.

SUMMER PROGRAMS
Portsmouth has operated a summer session since 1943. Courses are offered for enrichment for boys and girls entering grades 8–11. The mornings are devoted to academics and the afternoons to recreation, including sailing and daily trips to the beach. Each weekend, excursions are organized to Newport, Boston, or Cape Cod.

Courses are offered in English, history, biology, mathematics, French, Latin, Spanish, and marine biology. Available elective courses include desktop publishing, art, Web design, word processing, SAT review, public speaking, and drama. An intensive course in English as a second language is available. The student-faculty ratio in the summer session is 4:1.

In past summers, students have come from thirty states and twenty countries. The mixture of nationalities and backgrounds offers a rich cultural experience. For further information, those interested should write to the Summer School, c/o Michael Bonin.

COSTS AND FINANCIAL AID
For the 2005–06 academic year, the charge for tuition, room, and board was $33,450. Day student tuition was $23,325. Additional costs for

books, laboratory and studio fees, athletics equipment, allowances, and social events were about $1000. Fees are payable in full on August 1 or in two installments. Tuition insurance and tuition payment plans are available.

Portsmouth has an extensive financial aid program; 36 percent of the student body received a total of nearly $2 million. Awards are made on the basis of need and academic performance. The School also offers low-interest loans as part of the scholarship package. Financial aid is renewed on a yearly basis; parents must submit the School and Student Service for Financial Aid form each year. Portsmouth also offers the Reverend Hugh Diman Scholarship to a boarding student who is entering Form III; this is a full merit scholarship that covers the cost of tuition, room, and board. In addition, Portsmouth designates up to 10 highly qualified applicants each year as recipients of an Abbey Scholarship, which is a merit scholarship of up to $7000 that is renewable annually.

ADMISSIONS INFORMATION
Candidates are accepted on the basis of their personal and academic qualifications, without discrimination as to race, color, or creed. Recommendations from a student's Headmaster and teachers and the school record and test scores are all given serious consideration by the Admission Committee. A personal interview is required.

Applicants must take the SSAT. The median SSAT score for entering ninth graders is around the 80th percentile, but grades and recommendations are more significant factors in the admission decision. The following numbers of students are typically accepted annually for admission: ninth graders, 133; tenth, 29; and eleventh, 19. The School accepts midyear applications if a vacancy occurs.

APPLICATION TIMETABLE
Portsmouth Abbey School is a member of the Secondary School Admission Test Board and subscribes to the March 10 notification date and the April 10 reply date. After March 10, the Admission Committee makes every effort to notify parents of decisions as quickly as possible. Parents are encouraged to visit the campus in the fall or spring prior to the year of entry. Applications should be postmarked by January 31; early application is encouraged. There is a $50 application fee for U.S. citizens and a $75 application fee for international students.

ADMISSIONS CORRESPONDENCE
Mrs. Geri Zilian
Director of Admissions
Portsmouth Abbey School
Portsmouth, Rhode Island 02871
Phone: 401-683-2005
E-mail: admissions@portsmouthabbey.org
Web site: http://www.portsmouthabbey.org

PRINCETON DAY SCHOOL

Princeton, New Jersey

Type: Coeducational day college-preparatory school
Grades: JK–12: Lower School, Junior Kindergarten–4; Middle School, 5–8; Upper School, 9–12
Enrollment: School total: 902; Lower School: 252; Middle School: 278; Upper School: 372
Head of School: Dr. Judith Fox

THE SCHOOL

Princeton Day School (PDS) is located on a 105-acre campus just 2 miles from the center of Princeton and Princeton University. It opened its doors in 1965 after the merger of Miss Fine's School, established in 1899, and Princeton Country Day School, founded in 1924.

Princeton Day School's main goal is to offer students of above-average potential an exceptional opportunity for intellectual development, self-realization, and moral growth. The School believes its students benefit from the opportunity to complement the education they receive here with the experience gained from living at home and sharing in the life of the region's community, which has an unusually rich and diverse range of cultural and educational offerings.

As a college-preparatory school, Princeton Day School offers rigorous training in core skills of verbal and quantitative reasoning and creative self-expression. The School nurtures in its students the courage and initiative to apply these skills to problem-solving areas across the boundaries of traditional academic disciplines. Princeton Day School also strives to use the advantages of an academic continuum that spans the years from junior kindergarten through twelfth grade. It seeks to instill in its students an excitement about learning, a confidence in their own creativity, a concern for others, and a sense of commitment.

PDS is governed by a 25-member Board of Trustees that includes the President of the Alumni Board and the President of the Parents Association. Total endowment as of June 30, 2005, was $25 million. In 2004–05, the School received nearly $10 million in gifts and pledges. In addition, PDS began a $50-million "Investing in Excellence" campaign in fall 2005 with the goal of supporting compensation and professional development opportunities for teachers, financial aid, key facility enhancement and expansion, and the PDS Annual Fund.

Princeton Day School is accredited by the Middle States Association of Colleges and Schools and approved by the Department of Education of the State of New Jersey. Among the associations to which it belongs are the National Association of Independent Schools, the New Jersey Association of Independent Schools, the Educational Records Bureau, the Secondary School Admission Test Board, the Cum Laude Society, and the Council for Advancement and Support of Education.

ACADEMIC PROGRAMS

The School sets a high standard of academic excellence, and its students are expected to acquire the knowledge and skills that the School believes to be important. PDS graduates are expected to have disciplined competence in basic subjects: English language and literature, math-

ematics, at least one foreign language, history, the natural and social sciences, and the arts. They should acquire an understanding of the events and forces that shape the world: physical, intellectual, political, social, economic, religious, and aesthetic.

The school year is divided into trimesters. In each, an Upper School student must take a minimum of four major courses; most carry five major courses and at least one minor course. To earn a diploma, a student must successfully complete the equivalent of 18 full-year major courses during the Upper School years, including 4 years of English, 3 years of math, 2 years of history (including American studies in tenth grade), 2 years of one foreign language, 2 years of laboratory science, 1 year of religion, 1 year of arts, and 3 years of electives. Participation in the physical and health education program and some form of community service (50 hours by the beginning of the senior year) are also required. The requirements are designed to allow flexibility for students with special interests.

Students in sophomore through senior year are eligible to take Advanced Placement examinations in a variety of subject areas. In 2005, students took exams on eighteen topics, with the largest number taking exams in comparative government and politics, AB calculus, biology, chemistry, English literature, U.S. history, and art history.

Princeton Day School also offers its students a variety of unusual programs and projects, subject to approval, including independent study, a term away at one of six cooperating schools, driver's education, study abroad, off-campus projects, and specialized instruction. Electives include courses such as fine art, ceramics, media arts, architecture, photography, jazz ensemble, Web design, furniture design, theater, sports, music composition, and group voice lessons. Upper School students are also encouraged to serve as teaching assistants in the Lower and Middle Schools.

Small classes, with an average of 13 students, provide a close student-faculty relationship. Academic reports are sent to parents with teachers' comments and letter grades (A–F) at the end of each of the School's trimesters. Parent conferences are held each fall.

FACULTY AND ADVISERS

There are 104 full-time and 20 part-time teachers, most of whom hold advanced degrees. There are also 2 artists in residence.

Dr. Judith Fox is the Head of School. She graduated from Cornell University in 1965 with a Bachelor of Science degree in science education and biochemistry. Dr. Fox earned a master's degree in science education in 1969 and a professional diploma in administration and supervision in 1980, both from Queen's College,

CUNY. She was awarded a doctorate in education from Columbia University Teachers College in 1994.

Carlton Tucker was appointed Head of Upper School in 1993. He received his B.A. from Williams in 1977 and master's degrees from Stanford in education, history, and humanities in 1979, 1980, and 1981, respectively.

Four Deans of Students assume full responsibility for student life in the Upper School. Deans oversee a faculty-student advisory system, in which each student selects a faculty member to serve as his or her adviser.

PDS encourages professional development. In 2004–05, the School underwrote $262,100 of faculty advanced study.

COLLEGE PLACEMENT

Students are aided in their college applications by a full-time college counseling staff. In 2004–05, the graduating class averaged 2000 on their SAT verbal, math, and writing combined scores.

Twenty-eight percent of the class of 2004 was recognized by the National Merit Scholarship Program in 2003: 3 as finalists and 24 as commended scholars. The School's college placement record is strong; typically, more than 90 percent of graduates each year are accepted to colleges and universities rated "most difficult" or "very difficult" in *Peterson's Four-Year Colleges*.

STUDENT BODY AND CONDUCT

The Upper School has a target of 92 to 96 students per grade, with an overall enrollment of 372 students. These students come mainly from New Jersey, and the rest come from Pennsylvania. Students who are members of minority groups constitute 21 percent of the total enrollment.

Princeton Day School demonstrates to its students the interdependence of individuals and their community and stresses courtesy, fairness, generosity, truthfulness, and respect for others' ideas, emotions, persons, and property. The School is firmly committed to the idea of personal honor—each individual's obligation to uphold values essential to mutual well-being and trust. Upper School students bear full responsibility within the honor system, and teachers at every level work actively to help students develop moral and intellectual integrity.

The School strongly supports an Upper School community government of democratically elected student, faculty, and parent representatives and a variety of ad hoc student groups formed in response to special needs. Both faculty members and students also play an active role in evaluating the program of the School and recommending changes.

All students must adhere to the prescribed standard of dress while they are under the

jurisdiction of the School. Although dress may be casual in nature, all clothing must be neat and clean.

ACADEMIC FACILITIES
The main School building contains forty-four classrooms, twelve science laboratories, an art gallery, three art studios, a choral and orchestral rehearsal room, four music studios, a print shop, a large woodshop, an architecture drafting room, two darkrooms and a photography studio, a kiln room and ceramics studio, three computer labs, a planetarium, a greenhouse, a 400-seat theater, a 100-seat amphitheater, and three libraries housing more than 40,000 volumes.

Additional facilities include Colross, a historic Georgian house that is a short walk from the main building, and its Carriage House. In addition, students studying the natural sciences can make use of the varied habitats (gardens, streams, ponds, open meadows, and brooks) on the School grounds. An outdoor astronomical observation site, equipped with a Questar telescope, is also available to students.

ATHLETICS
Princeton Day School offers a wide variety of athletic activities, both competitive and noncompetitive, because it believes that the skills acquired through physical education and athletics are important components of individual development. There are fifty-two teams in seventeen different sports. All students are encouraged to realize their potential for physical vigor and coordination and to develop a practical understanding of the value of team effort and sportsmanship.

Competitive interscholastic sports include baseball, basketball, cross-country, fencing, field hockey, figure skating, football, golf, ice hockey, lacrosse, soccer, softball, squash, tennis, and volleyball. Crew is also offered as a spring physical education elective.

Facilities consist of three gymnasiums, ten athletic fields including a synthetic turf field, eight tennis courts, and a fully enclosed ice-skating and hockey rink. Students pursuing golf

in the spring as a team option play at Bedens Brook Country Club, while the squash team uses the facilities at the Pretty Brook Club.

EXTRACURRICULAR OPPORTUNITIES
Among the Upper School's more than thirty-five clubs and organizations are peer group, debate, community service, three foreign language groups, junior state, mock trial, model UN, science league, math league, four select singing groups, dance and drama groups, and three School publications (yearbook, newspaper, and literary magazine).

The School also brings in outside speakers, performers, and art exhibits. In addition, students are encouraged to involve themselves in the numerous cultural opportunities available locally. Taking advantage of the proximity to New York and Philadelphia, the School offers trips to theaters, musical programs, museums, historic sites, and major sports events in both cities.

DAILY LIFE
The day begins at 8 a.m. with adviser check-in and ends at 3:15 p.m. Monday through Friday. Most Upper School students take six subjects in a year. Except for team members who practice after school, students take physical education courses during the regular class day. Most clubs meet during the school day, while others are scheduled after classes.

SUMMER PROGRAMS
Princeton Day School Summer School welcomes students who seek extra study time or enrichment. Courses include photography, computer, art, and environmental studies. Interested students may write or call the Summer School Coordinator at the School.

COSTS AND FINANCIAL AID
Tuition for the 2005–06 academic year was $23,600 for the Upper School grades. This covered all educational fees other than charges for instrumental lessons, textbooks and materials, and trips. Lunches were extra.

For the 2005–06 school year, 18 percent of the student body received financial aid totaling more than $2.2 million. Eligibility, which is based on need, is determined by criteria established by the School and Student Service for Financial Aid. All families are expected to contribute toward the cost of their child's education. This amount is set at an individually affordable level. In addition, PDS received a commitment of $11 million in fall 2005 from past PDS parents to fund new financial aid grants for families who may never before have considered an independent school education.

ADMISSIONS INFORMATION
Princeton Day School seeks students who are intellectually curious and self-motivated and who can enjoy an academically challenging curriculum. Students should also be excited to be active and supportive participants in the PDS community. PDS does not discriminate on the basis of race, creed, or national origin. The School accepts students for each class, although openings in grade 12 are rare.

Applicants for the Upper School are considered on the basis of recommendations and academic records from previously attended schools, Secondary School Admission Test scores, a personal interview, and two writing samples.

APPLICATION TIMETABLE
Initial inquiries are accepted year-round. The parent questionnaire should be postmarked by January 6. The School begins to notify students March 10 or as later openings occur. Application forms and information may be obtained by visiting the School Web site or by telephoning, writing, or visiting the School.

ADMISSIONS CORRESPONDENCE
Kelly Dun
Director of Admission and Financial Aid
Princeton Day School
P.O. Box 75
Princeton, New Jersey 08542

Phone: 609-924-6700 Ext. 1200
Fax: 609-924-8944
Web site: http://www.pds.org

PROCTOR ACADEMY

Andover, New Hampshire

Type: Coeducational boarding and day college-preparatory school
Grades: 9–12
Enrollment: 344
Head of School: Michael Henriques

THE SCHOOL

Founded in 1848, Proctor Academy originally served as both the local high school and a college-preparatory boarding school. Affiliated with the Unitarian Church until 1971, Proctor retains a humanistic approach to education.

Proctor is a learning community that is committed to realizing the potential of each student. Diversity is prized in an admissions process that values a positive attitude toward work, self, and others. Academic structure demands accountability, while students are elevated in their relationships with adults. Proctor is a challenging and supportive school; its Learning Skills Program is nationally recognized, and extra help is always available. Diversity is also prized throughout the hiring process and is reflected on a Board of Trustees that includes African-American, Hispanic, and Native American members.

Andover is a small, rural town in central New Hampshire, surrounded by mountains, ski areas, lakes, and camping sites. Andover is 25 miles from Concord, 40 miles from Hanover, 45 miles from the Manchester airport, and 100 miles from Boston.

The campus includes a 250-acre central green and 3,000 acres of woodlands and mountain slopes. The property encompasses four ponds; a ski area with snow-making, three runs, a 1500 T-bar lift, and two jumps; and more than 17 miles of cross-country trails.

Proctor is a nonprofit corporation governed by a self-perpetuating 39-member Board of Trustees. The corporation has approximately $22 million in endowment, and the school plant is valued at $40 million. Total Annual Giving is more than $1.1 million.

Proctor is accredited by the New England Association of Schools and Colleges. It is a member of the National Association of Independent Schools, the Educational Records Bureau, the Association of Boarding Schools, and the Council for Advancement and Support of Education.

ACADEMIC PROGRAMS

Students earn credits by the trimester; thus, a year of English is 3 credits. To graduate, a student must earn the following credits: English, 12; math, 9; science, 9; social science, 8 (including 3 in U.S. history); modern language, 6; and fine arts, 1. Honors sections are offered and Advanced Placement courses are taught in English literature, U.S. history, U.S. government and politics, calculus, computer science, French language, Spanish language, physics, and biology. Skills courses, such as studio art, jazz band, drama, woodshop, boat building, blacksmithing, photography, and ceramics, integrate the arts into the lives of all students.

Grades are given for effort as well as academic achievement. Students must maintain an average of 60 to earn credit. Grades are issued every five weeks. The average class size is 12.

Proctor's academic program reflects the faculty's application of experiential methods to college preparation. Teaching styles favor participation over lecturing, and the diversity of student perspectives and learning styles is appreciated. Experiential offerings include the Ocean Classroom on the North Atlantic, the Mountain Classroom in the desert Southwest, and the language trimester in France or Spain. In addition, Proctor offers a term with the Country Day School of Guanacaste, Costa Rica.

Proctor faculty members oversee language study programs in Aix-en-Provence, France, and Segovia, Spain. Each student lives with a French or Spanish family. A year's language credit is earned in ten weeks. There is no additional cost for participation in this program, and 75 percent of the student body take advantage of the opportunity.

Each fall term, 20 students sail one of three 130-foot topsail schooners from Boston to San Juan, Puerto Rico, while gaining full academic credit in literature, history, navigational math, and marine biology. Ocean Classroom is an elective at no additional cost.

Each winter and spring trimester, 10 students elect to participate in the Mountain Classroom Program. Living in a separate dorm on the eastern edge of Proctor's forestlands, they prepare for a western field trip by studying Western American authors, geology, desert ecology, and Hopi and Navajo history and culture. Three weeks into the term, 2 Mountain Classroom instructors drive the group to Arizona, New Mexico, and Texas. Living with Hopi and Navajo, rock climbing in the canyonlands, and rafting on the Colorado River, students earn a full trimester of academic credit. Mountain Classroom, offered at no additional expense, is a dramatic example of Proctor's commitment to experiential education.

Learning Skills is a nonacademic elective course for students of strong aptitude who benefit from regular academic support in course work. Learning Lab provides instruction in organization, note-taking, research, and self-advocacy.

Proctor is a model school for diversity programs and is known for its inclusive community values. A full-time Diversity Coordinator spearheads student-faculty committees overseeing ethnic and racial curricular sensitivity, faculty and student workshops focusing on issues of racism and gender, and outreach programs for other New England schools. English as a second language is offered to international students.

FACULTY AND ADVISERS

Proctor has 86 full-time teachers; 39 men and 47 women. Twenty-seven teachers live on campus. Each faculty member meets daily with 5 or 6 advisees.

Mike Henriques, Head of School, holds a B.A. and M.A. from Middlebury College and has a Master of Fine Arts degree from Warren Wilson College. Mr. Henriques brings great expertise and experience in teaching and administration.

Thirty-eight faculty members have taught for ten or more years at Proctor; the school's salary structure is in the top 10 percent of northern New England schools. Full-year, full-salary sabbaticals are offered annually.

COLLEGE PLACEMENT

Proctor employs 4 College Counselors who help guide students and their families toward colleges and universities that will match students' aspirations and interests. Students begin the college process during the junior year and benefit from extensive visits to the campus by various college representatives. The class of 2004 scored an average of 551 verbal and 555 math on the SAT. Leading college placements over the past five years include Bates, Colorado College, Lewis & Clark, Skidmore, St. Lawrence, Union, and the Universities of Colorado, Denver, New Hampshire, and Vermont. Additional placements include Bowdoin, Cornell, Dartmouth, Tufts, and William and Mary.

STUDENT BODY AND CONDUCT

In 2005–06, Proctor had 344 students: 269 boarding and 75 day students. There were 66 ninth graders, 88 tenth graders, 108 eleventh graders, and 82 twelfth graders. Boarding students came primarily from Connecticut, Massachusetts, New Hampshire, New York, and California, but twenty-four other states, Cameroon, Great Britain, Jamaica, Nepal, South Africa, and other countries were also represented.

The Student Leadership Board presents issues for faculty consideration and budgets funds for student activities. Infractions of major school rules are considered by a student-faculty committee. Every student shares in the responsibility of doing necessary jobs on campus, and most students initiate services to the community, such as tutoring at the local elementary school.

ACADEMIC FACILITIES

Classrooms are clustered in four major academic buildings at the center of a village campus. The Fowler Learning Center houses the Lovejoy Library, Learning Skills and Learning Lab programs, the college counseling office, and the Faxon Computer Center, the hub of Proctor's wireless network. A laptop initiative gives all students wireless access to the Internet, e-mail, and the campus network from anywhere on

campus. Maxwell Savage is home to the English and foreign language departments. The Norris Family Theatre, dedicated in 2002, includes a 420-seat theater with black-box rehearsal space, a dance studio, dressing rooms, a costume shop, and extensive technical facilities. Shirley Hall houses sciences, social sciences, and mathematics. Ives House contains music classrooms and a 32-track recording studio. Arts and ceramics rooms are found in Slocum Hall, built in 1810 as the town's livery stable. Woodshop, boat building, machine shop, and blacksmithing are housed at the Alan Shepard Boat House.

BOARDING AND GENERAL FACILITIES

Twenty small houses, built between 1792 and 1998, provide homelike dormitories for students. Dorms, which average 12 students each, are mixed by classes. Students live in singles and doubles and enjoy much contact with dorm parents. Study halls are held in the dorms unless otherwise arranged.

The Wise Student Center, including a snack bar, is open until in-dorm time. The Health Center is staffed by a registered nurse at all times. New London and Franklin Hospitals are 15 minutes from the campus.

ATHLETICS

Skill development and sportsmanship are primary goals of the athletics program. Proctor fields varsity teams in football, soccer, cross-country, field hockey, Alpine ski racing, ski jumping, cross-country skiing, snowboarding, wrestling, ice hockey, basketball, lacrosse, baseball, tennis, and cycling. Junior varsity teams are offered in most sports. Noncompetitive afternoon activities include snowboarding, developmental skiing, horseback riding, dance, forestry, technical rock climbing, and kayaking.

The field house contains a gymnasium, ski rooms, a climbing wall, basketball courts, a Nautilus and free-weights room, and an athletics store. The Teddy Maloney Arena houses an indoor hockey rink and locker facilities. The school campus includes six playing fields, the Blackwater Ski Area, and ten tennis courts.

EXTRACURRICULAR OPPORTUNITIES

Skills courses provide hands-on activities during the school day. These include jazz band, photography, yearbook, blacksmithing, boat building, woodshop, jewelry making, ceramics, dance, drama, and many others. The drama department produces several major plays annually, including a winter student production and the spring musical. Community service, while expected of each student, is voluntary. Providing admission tours, tutoring at the elementary school, and participating in the student fire department are examples of community service involvement.

Special school events include fall and spring Family Weekends, Winter Carnival, a Head Ski Holiday, and Commencement. Early in May, Earth Day is dedicated to environmental issues. Classes, films, and panel discussions explore topics ranging from ecology, resource management, and pollution to the politics of recycling.

DAILY LIFE

Classes are held six days a week, starting at 8:15 and finishing at 3:15, in time for afternoon activities and team sports. Classes are 55 minutes in length. A schoolwide assembly at 10:10 a.m. offers an open forum for student and faculty announcements as well as skits and slide shows. Buffet meals are offered at 7:15 a.m., noon, and 5:15 p.m. Study hall runs from 8 to 10. Students study in their rooms unless alternative arrangements are made with the dorm parent to study in, for example, the Learning Center or the computer center. Wednesday and Saturday afternoons are dedicated to interscholastic team competition.

WEEKEND LIFE

After classes and games on Saturday, students are free to attend cultural events and movies both on and off campus. Several dances are held each trimester. Trips to sports or cultural events at Dartmouth College are common, and transportation is provided to cinemas in Concord each Saturday night. Camping and rock-climbing excursions and ski trips are offered frequently. Students are allowed off-campus weekends, subject to academic review and parental permission.

COSTS AND FINANCIAL AID

For 2005–06, charges were $36,000 for boarding students and $21,900 for day students, plus an additional $7800 for students in the Learning Skills Program.

Proctor subscribes to the School and Student Service for Financial Aid in awarding financial aid. Approximately $1.6 million is granted annually on the basis of need and merit. This year, 25 percent of the student body received aid.

ADMISSIONS INFORMATION

Proctor Academy offers admission to new students in grades 9–12, with the majority entering the ninth and tenth grades. A positive attitude toward work, self, and others is the highest priority in admission screening after college-bound status is confirmed. Achievement testing such as the SSAT or ISEE is used only to balance an academically diverse population. A limited number of students with above-average aptitude who have skills needs are accepted with Learning Skills tutorial support. An academic transcript, recommendations, and personal interview are required, as are results from an SSAT or ISEE. Aptitude testing such as the WISC-III is encouraged and may be requested by the Admission Committee.

APPLICATION TIMETABLE

While inquiries may be made at any time, Proctor adheres to the April 10 reply date, after which spaces are limited and admission is offered on a rolling basis. Campus tours and interviews can be scheduled for weekdays between 8:30 and 1 and Wednesday between 8:30 and 10:30. Applications for March 10 notification should be complete by February 1. The application fee is $40.

ADMISSIONS CORRESPONDENCE

Christopher Bartlett ('86), Director of
    Admission
Proctor Academy
P.O. Box 500
Andover, New Hampshire 03216

Phone: 603-735-6000
Fax: 603-735-6284
    603-735-5158
E-mail: admissions@proctornet.com
Web site: http://www.proctoracademy.org

PROFESSIONAL CHILDREN'S SCHOOL

New York, New York

Type: Coeducational day college-preparatory school
Grades: 6–12: Middle School, 6–8; High School, 9–12
Enrollment: School total: 200; Middle School: 40; High School: 160
Head of School: Dr. James Dawson

THE SCHOOL

Professional Children's School (PCS), located near Lincoln Center in New York City, is a coeducational day school for students in grades 6–12. Now in its ninety-second year, PCS offers an academic, college-preparatory education to students who are professional actors, dancers, models, or musicians; who are preparing for careers in the performing arts or sports; or who desire an environment supportive of the arts.

When Professional Children's School was founded in 1914, all the students were performing on stage as actors, dancers, jugglers, musicians, comedians, and singers. The need for young actors to have formal schooling was recognized by Mrs. Franklin W. Robinson and Deaconess Jane Harris Hall, the founders of PCS, when they discovered 5 young actors backstage playing poker instead of studying. Since the early 1900s, the composition of the student body has been broadened to reflect the development of film and television, the growth of classical and modern dance, and the importance of training for Olympic sports.

PCS is dedicated to educating its students so they are qualified to pursue any profession in which they are interested. A rigorous liberal arts program ensures that students can choose from a number of career options. While the arts are an integral part of the curriculum, students pursue professional training at such well-known schools and institutions as the Juilliard School of Music, School of American Ballet, Dance Theatre of Harlem, and Skating Club of New York. Support for artistic interest is reflected in a concentrated and flexible schedule that allows time for practice, rehearsals, and auditions.

Self-reliance is stressed. Students are given responsibility for the effective use of time to complete their work and meet their professional commitments. Scheduling and assignments often reflect a high degree of individualization.

The School is governed by a 25-member Board of Trustees. The School's endowment is valued at $1.9 million, supplemented by Annual Giving of $1.5 million during fiscal 2004–05.

Professional Children's School is accredited by the New York State Education Department and the Middle States Association of Colleges and Schools and is registered by the New York State Board of Regents. The

School is affiliated with the National Association of Independent Schools, New York State Association of Independent Schools, Guild of Independent Schools in New York, Headmistresses Association of the East, National Association of Principals of Schools for Girls, School and Student Service for Financial Aid, and Council for Advancement and Support of Education.

ACADEMIC PROGRAMS

Eighteen credits are required for graduation, not including 1 in physical education. Students usually carry 5 credits a year and may carry more, depending on their professional schedules. Requirements include 4 credits in English, 3.5 credits in history (global studies, U.S. history, and a history elective), 2 credits in a foreign language (French or Spanish), 2 credits in math, 2 credits in science, 1 credit in the arts, and ½ credit in health. In addition, students must select a three-year sequence in a foreign language, mathematics, or science.

Electives are offered in all academic areas, including the arts. Examples of electives are literature and film, constitutional law, print-making, and dramatics workshop. Seniors may also take for credit approved courses at a nearby university.

The High School also offers English as a second language, history, and mathematics courses for international students.

The school year is divided into two semesters and four marking periods. Class size ranges from 4 to 22, with an overall student-teacher ratio of about 8:1.

A special offering at PCS is the guided study program. Students who miss school for professional reasons (whether the absence is due to a morning rehearsal or a six-week theatrical tour) are provided with assignments to be completed during the time away from the classroom.

FACULTY AND ADVISERS

The 24 full-time faculty members hold five doctorates, twenty-one master's degrees, and twenty-four bachelor's degrees.

Dr. James Dawson was appointed Head of School in 1995. He is a graduate of the State University of New York at Albany (B.S., biology, 1977; Ph.D., behavior, 1982). Prior to his appointment at Professional Children's School, Dr. Dawson had been the Head of Upper School at the Spence School since 1988.

He has taught at the middle- and upper-school levels as well as at the university level since 1977.

Professional Children's School seeks faculty members who are knowledgeable in and supportive of the performing arts, who can instill academic excellence in students, and who are flexible in their teaching methodology. Faculty members are encouraged to pursue advanced degrees; compensation for relevant in-service training is offered. A grade adviser is assigned to students for academic and personal counseling. A college guidance counselor works with juniors, seniors, and alumni who are formulating college plans. In addition, all faculty members are available to counsel students. A consulting psychologist meets regularly with the faculty and is available for referrals.

COLLEGE PLACEMENT

Professional Children's School provides college counseling for juniors, seniors, and recent graduates of the School. About 75 percent of the senior class attend college directly after graduation. Of the remaining students, many enroll in college after pursuing careers or training, for several years, in the performing arts. Counseling, offered by the College Advisor, begins in the eleventh grade and extends through the time of college acceptance.

Members of the class of 2005 are attending Barnard, Duke, Fordham, Harvard, Juilliard, the Manhattan School of Music, NYU, and Sarah Lawrence.

STUDENT BODY AND CONDUCT

Of the 160 students enrolled in the High School, 45 are seniors; 55, juniors; 35, sophomores; and 25, freshmen. There are 45 boys and 115 girls enrolled in the School. The professional composition of the High School is as follows: 62 dancers, 33 musicians, 21 actors, 2 models, 21 athletes, 4 singers, 6 arts-affiliated students, and 3 film students.

There is a wide geographical distribution within the student body: eighteen states and twelve other countries are represented. International students and students of color make up 26 percent of the student enrollment. An even distribution of socioeconomic groups is represented.

Orderly, respectful conduct is expected. Rules, as described in the student handbook,

are established with the safety and well-being of the students in mind.

ACADEMIC FACILITIES

Professional Children's School is housed in an eight-story classroom building with an adjacent play yard. Eighteen classrooms, two science laboratories, a music room, an art studio, a drama room, an auditorium, a cafeteria, and a gymnasium are located in the building. (The School serves both a hot lunch and a cold buffet daily.) The library contains 15,000 volumes, a collection of phonograph albums, and basic audiovisual equipment. There are thirty computers for instructional use.

ATHLETICS

Physical education is required at PCS. Students meet the requirement either through the School's athletics program or through regularly scheduled classes at approved dance, ice-skating, or gymnastics schools. Physical education classes are focused on volleyball, basketball, movement, and calisthenics.

EXTRACURRICULAR OPPORTUNITIES

Because PCS students are so actively involved with professional organizations outside the School, extracurricular opportunities are limited to those activities initiated through joint student-faculty efforts. A yearbook and school newspaper are published annually, a drama production is staged twice a year, and students perform for each other and parents on a regular basis. An outdoor Field Day, an annual benefit, and excursions to New York City performing arts productions are also offered.

DAILY LIFE

Class hours extend from 8 to 2:45. Teachers are available from 8 until 3:15; time before and after class hours is used for extra help and makeup tests. The school day has a combination of 40-, 50-, and 100-minute class periods.

COSTS AND FINANCIAL AID

High School tuition for 2005–06 ranged from $23,500 for ninth graders to $26,000 for incoming seniors. Fees, primarily for books, are set at $512; additional costs include a graduation fee and supply costs for selected courses. Tuition payment plans offer billing one or two times during the year. A $2000 deposit, credited to the last payment, is required when the contract is signed.

Twenty-nine percent of the student body received partial tuition aid. Awards are based on financial and professional need. The 2005–06 tuition aid budget was set at $500,000.

ADMISSIONS INFORMATION

It is the admissions policy of the School not to discriminate on the basis of sex, race, color, religion, or national origin. Candidates for admission are evaluated on their academic preparation (transcript and testing required), an interview, and professional need.

The High School admits students into grades 9–12. The School prides itself on accommodating motivated young people who may be involved in some outside activity that might interfere with classroom attendance during regular school hours.

The faculty at PCS is strongly committed to a four-year education for high school students. Seniors with extra credits who have a legitimate professional need may be able to arrange a part-time program or graduate in January.

A careful screening process ensures that all students who complete the application process have a clear understanding of and desire for PCS's unique educational opportunities. From 180 applications received for 2005–06, 110 students were accepted and 76 enrolled. Twenty were enrolled in the Middle School and 56 in the High School.

APPLICATION TIMETABLE

Applications are accepted throughout the school year. Admission openings occur in September and January. Upon receipt of the application and a $50 application fee, an appointment for an interview is arranged. Families are notified of the Admissions Committee's decision by letter and, in most cases, by telephone.

ADMISSIONS CORRESPONDENCE

Sherrie Hinkle, Director of Admissions
Professional Children's School
132 West 60th Street
New York, New York 10023

Phone: 212-582-3116
Fax: 212-307-6542
E-mail: hinkle@pcs-nyc.org
Web site: http://www.pcs-nyc.org

PROVIDENCE COUNTRY DAY SCHOOL

East Providence, Rhode Island

Type: Coeducational day college-preparatory school
Grades: 5–12: Middle School, 5–8; Upper School, 9–12
Enrollment: School total: 300; Upper School: 200
Head of School: Susan M. Haberlandt

THE SCHOOL

Providence Country Day School (PCD) was founded in 1923 by a group of business leaders, educators, and parents committed to establishing a college-preparatory school in a rural setting. The Sweetland Farm in East Providence offered an ideal location. Its fresh air, open spaces, and charm quickly drew students from many communities to share in the spirit and potential of the new school.

Providence Country Day School offers a rigorous college-preparatory program through which students from diverse backgrounds grow through extensive opportunities for engaged participation and the challenges of high standards for academic achievement, ethical development, and citizenship in a democratic society. The School's hallmark, "Leadership and learning for life," underscores all of the work the School seeks to do with its students.

In 1997, the School completed an extensive campus consolidation and building project in which two historical buildings, Metcalf Hall (1927) and Chace Hall (1927), were moved to the east side of campus and renovated. That same year, the Murray House opened as the new administration building, and the Moran Annex was added to the West Field House, providing a wood-floor basketball court, a wrestling room, and a new girls' locker room. The Upper School classroom building, Lund Hall, also underwent renovations at that time.

The School's 41-acre campus is a 10-minute drive from the center of the city of Providence. A 25-member Board of Trustees, which includes the presidents of the Alumni and Parents Associations, governs PCD.

Providence Country Day School is accredited by the New England Association of Schools and Colleges (NEASC) and approved by the Department of Education of the State of Rhode Island. Among the associations to which PCD belongs are the National Association of Independent Schools (NAIS), the Association of Independent Schools of New England (AISNE), the National Center for Independent School Renewal (NCISR), the Secondary School Admission Testing Board (SSATB), the Educational Records Bureau (ERB), the Cum Laude Society, and the Greater Providence Chamber of Commerce.

ACADEMIC PROGRAMS

At Providence Country Day School, the curriculum places significant emphasis on excellent teaching and dynamic student learning. As a community of learners, the School values the symbiotic relationship that exists between teachers and students; it is, in fact, this relationship that is at the heart of the School's educational mission. The School's belief is that its small size, combined with rigorous dedication to academic excellence, creates a vibrant collective purpose

that prepares students to acquire knowledge and hone skills in pursuit of understanding themselves and the larger world.

As a college-preparatory school, the educational mission of PCD is grounded in the traditional disciplines of English, mathematics, foreign language, science, history, and visual and performing arts. In all areas of academic life, the School is committed to teaching students how to be clear thinkers and effective writers, solve problems creatively, and work together in a spirit of cooperation.

The school year is divided into semesters. In each, a student must take a minimum of five major courses. To earn a diploma, each student must successfully complete the equivalent of twenty full-year major courses during the Upper School years. This requirement includes 4 years of English, 4 years of math, 3 years of history (including U.S. history), 2 years of one foreign language, 3 years of laboratory science, 1 year of the arts, and 3 years of various electives. Participation in athletics and computer skill work are also required. The School's requirements are designed to provide a breadth of academic experience but also to allow flexibility for students with special interests; as such, students are encouraged to choose additional electives in academic areas. For example, most students opt to take 3–4 years of foreign language, while others may choose to double up in math or in English courses during the senior year.

Small classes, with an average of 12 students, provide a close student-faculty relationship. The overall student-faculty ratio of 6:1 makes certain that each student has a great deal of adult contact every day. Academic reports with teachers' comments and letter grades are sent to parents at the end of each quarter. Parent conferences are held in both the fall and spring. In addition, the School's strong adviser system ensures that each student and his or her family have a direct, close contact at the School at all times.

Students in their junior and senior years are eligible to take Advanced Placement courses and examinations in eleven different subject areas. Senior year, the culmination of a student's education at PCD, ends with the Independent Senior Project Program. In October, students begin the preliminary work that eventually leads to a three-week out-of-school project. Settings for projects include research labs, community outreach programs, law and medical offices, and elementary schools; the projects introduce students to a more experiential mode of learning. Before going on site for projects in May, students spend months reading articles, books, and other literature on their project. A substantial written and oral review of the overall experience is required before graduation.

PCD also offers its students a variety of special programs, including independent study; study abroad; Close-Up, a Washington, D.C.,

program; and off-campus community service projects. For nearly two decades, the School's Physics First curriculum has introduced students to the concepts of physics as a precursor to biology and chemistry. The relatively recent national shift to a Physics First curriculum is testimony to PCD's innovative leadership in science.

FACULTY AND ADVISERS

Of the 40 teachers at PCD, 65 percent hold advanced degrees. Teaching at PCD is not confined to the classroom. Through coaching, leadership in the arts, advising, support of student activities, and abundant participation in the life of the School, teachers at PCD know their students extremely well.

Mrs. Haberlandt began her duties as the seventh Head of School in 1998 after a distinguished career at the Kingswood-Oxford School in West Hartford, Connecticut. She holds both her B.A. and M.A. degrees from Trinity College (Hartford).

PCD strongly encourages professional development among its faculty and is committed to supporting advanced study and travel through sabbatical leaves.

COLLEGE PLACEMENT

A full-time college counselor aids students and their parents during the college application process. This formal college advising process begins in earnest during the junior year, when students and their parents meet individually with the college counselor.

Colleges and universities currently attended by PCD students include Bates, Boston College, Bowdoin, Brown, Carnegie Mellon, Colby, Culinary Institute of America, Hamilton, Hobart and William Smith, Johns Hopkins, Kenyon, Rhode Island School of Design, Rice, Savannah College of Art and Design, Tufts, Vanderbilt, and Yale.

STUDENT BODY AND CONDUCT

The Upper School has a target of 45 to 50 students per grade, with an overall enrollment of approximately 200. The majority of students come from Rhode Island and southeastern Massachusetts, and a few travel from Connecticut. Students of color constitute 15 percent of the total enrollment, and socioeconomic diversity is also valued. School rules and codes of conduct are designed to ensure the safety and comfort of every member of the School community. PCD highly values mutual respect and the basic qualities of kindness and consideration for others. The Dean of Students deals with minor disciplinary matters, and the Judicial Board, comprising students and faculty members, hears more serious cases. The Head of School makes final decisions regarding all serious disciplinary infractions. The School Council president, vice

president, and class representatives serve as the elected student governing body.

ACADEMIC FACILITIES

There are two main academic buildings on the campus. Lund Hall, the Upper School classroom building, houses a 16,000-volume library, an amphitheater, a student commons area, faculty offices, and two computer centers. The Middle School classroom building, Metcalf Hall, contains a 300-seat auditorium, a stage and greenroom, a music room, a computer center, and a photography studio with a darkroom.

ATHLETICS

Athletics at PCD are an integral part of every student's physical, social, and ethical development. Sports are not viewed solely as a vehicle for producing headlines or making champions but rather as a means for building self-confidence, learning to abide by the rules, inculcating respect for others and the values of teamwork, and reinforcing the importance of being able to both win and lose graciously. For these reasons, participation in organized sports or physical education is required. The choices each season are broad, so that each student can pursue individual interests, explore new ones, and compete at their highest level of ability.

PCD has teams in baseball, basketball, cross-country, football, golf, ice hockey, lacrosse, sailing, soccer, tennis, and wrestling. The School also offers fencing at the club level. PCD is a member of the Southeastern New England Independent School Athletics Association (SENEISAA) in most sports. The School also competes in the Rhode Island Independent School League (RIISL) in tennis, ice hockey, and baseball. All teams compete under the umbrella of the New England Prep School Athletic Conference (NEPSAC) against independent schools of comparable size throughout the region.

EXTRACURRICULAR OPPORTUNITIES

As PCD prepares young men and women to take their place in the world, the School stresses the value of pursuing individual interests and activities—in addition to discovering new ones—as a means of developing both talents and leadership skills. Theater productions are staged through the efforts of the PCD Players. The yearbook, *The Red and Black,* and *The Green Blackbird,* the School's literary magazine, are produced completely by students. An active School Council plays a vital role in the life of the School and customarily makes recommendations concerning school affairs. PCD's campus chapter of Habitat for Humanity works on restoring affordable three-story homes in South Providence, and the School's Mock Trial team competes successfully against much larger schools in the state. A few other active campus groups include Students to End Prejudice (STEP), the Investors Club, the Film Club, the Chess Club, the PCD Rock Band Club, and the Technology Club. There are approximately twenty different clubs and activities from which students may choose.

DAILY LIFE

Homeroom begins each morning at 8:05, and classes run from 8:15 until 3, with the exception of Wednesday, when the school day begins at 9 and ends at 3. Classes of either 40 or 50 minutes meet, respectively, five or four days per week. Each student has a full lunch period and generally at least one study hall during the course of each day. In the Upper School, athletic practices begin at the conclusion of the academic day and generally run until 5 to 5:30 p.m.

COSTS AND FINANCIAL AID

Upper School tuition for 2005–06 was $19,900; additional expenses included books and supplies at approximately $300 per year. A monthly payment plan is available for a small yearly charge. Tuition refund insurance is required for all new students, and need-based financial aid is available.

ADMISSIONS INFORMATION

Providence Country Day School seeks motivated students from diverse backgrounds who demonstrate high character as well as academic achievement or promise. Strong candidates are those who welcome the opportunity to be engaged, respectful members of a community and who are likely to benefit from the PCD experience and the challenging college-preparatory curriculum, while also making positive contributions to the life of the School.

To supplement supportive teacher recommendations, a writing sample, and solid achievement in current courses, applicants are also required to take either the ISEE or the SSAT. Furthermore, each prospective student must visit the School with his or her family, have an interview with a member of the admissions team, and complete a comprehensive written application. The application fee is $50.

APPLICATION TIMETABLE

Inquiries to PCD can be made either by telephone or online. School visits are arranged beginning in October. An Open House is held annually, generally in late October. The application deadline for the first round of admissions decisions is February 1. Submission of a completed application by this date is strongly encouraged, as applicant folders are subsequently read only on a rolling basis, as space allows, at each grade level. Applications submitted by February 1 ensure a response from the School by the first week of March. Accepted students then have until early April to reply.

ADMISSIONS CORRESPONDENCE

Office of Admissions
Providence Country Day School
660 Waterman Avenue
East Providence, Rhode Island 02914-1724

Phone: 401-438-5170
Fax: 401-435-4514
Web site: http://www.providencecountryday.org

RABUN GAP–NACOOCHEE SCHOOL

Rabun Gap, Georgia

Type: Coeducational boarding and day college-preparatory school
Grades: 6–12: Middle School, 6–8; Upper School, 9–12
Enrollment: School total: 314; Upper School: 210
Head of School: John D. Marshall

THE SCHOOL

Rabun Gap–Nacoochee School was formed by the 1927 merger of Rabun Gap Industrial School, founded in 1905, and Nacoochee Institute, founded in 1903, under the leadership of Harvard graduate Andrew J. Ritchie. The School enrolls students from fifteen states and fourteen countries.

Rabun Gap–Nacoochee School offers a competitive college-preparatory program enrolling boarding and day students in grades 6 through 12. The School has a covenant relationship with the Presbyterian Church (USA), hosting ecumenical chapel services twice weekly, and an active community service program assisting local charities and agencies. The School is characterized by small groups (in classes, in dorms, and with advisers) that encourage individual growth and the development of close relationships among peers, teachers, and staff members. At Rabun Gap, students are provided with opportunities to maximize their academic performance and personal development.

Rabun Gap–Nacoochee School is accredited by the Southern Association of Colleges and Schools and by the Southern Association of Independent Schools. It holds memberships in the National Association of Independent Schools, the Southern Association of Independent Schools, the Association of Boarding Schools, the Southeastern Association of Boarding Schools, the Georgia Independent School Association, the Secondary School Admission Test Board, and the Educational Records Bureau.

ACADEMIC PROGRAMS

The Rabun Gap curriculum challenges each student and prepares him or her for the college experience. Small classes, ranging in size from 4 to 17 students, promote teacher-student interaction and better peer discussions. Rabun Gap utilizes an alphabetical grading system, and progress reports are sent home to parents twice each semester. Each student has an adviser to ensure that he or she has consistent academic and personal support.

Graduation requirements include 4 units of English, 3 units of history, 4 units of mathematics, 3 units of science (including two laboratory courses), 3 units of the same foreign language, 2 units of fine arts, 1 unit of physical and health education, 1 unit of computer technology, 1 unit of Bible history, and up to 5 units of electives. Seniors are encouraged to conduct and complete a Senior Project. The regular curriculum offers 4 years of English, creative writing, journalism, and public speaking; 4 years of mathematics; physical science, environmental science, biology, chemistry, physics, and human anatomy and physiology; ancient history, modern world history, U.S. history, Biblical history, economics, and government; 4 years of French, Latin, and Spanish; 3 years of visual art, 2 years of drama, dance, chorus, Gap Singers, wind ensemble, and music preparation; 2 years of computer literacy, computer programming, and desktop publishing; 2 years of woodworking; and mechanical drawing. In addition to regular courses, Rabun Gap offers Advanced Placement courses in studio art, art history, music theory, biology, chemistry, physics, environmental science, calculus, English, European history, government, French, Spanish, and U.S. history.

Rabun Gap–Nacoochee School offers an English as a second language (ESL) program for international students who require additional help with English prior to being placed in regular classes. The multinational mix of students encourages the exchange of ideas and cultural traditions and is a vital element of the cultural education and global awareness of the Rabun Gap student.

FACULTY AND ADVISERS

There are 80 faculty and administration members; 54 live on campus. All members of the faculty and administration hold baccalaureate degrees; 43 hold advanced degrees.

John D. Marshall was appointed Head of School in 2004. Mr. Marshall holds a B.A. in history from the University of North Carolina at Chapel Hill and an M.B.A. from Duke University.

COLLEGE PLACEMENT

Rabun Gap provides an excellent counseling program that is designed to help each student select the college or university best suited to his or her needs. College testing begins in the sophomore and junior years with the administering of the PSAT, followed by the SAT in the spring of the junior year and fall of the senior year; students are also encouraged to take the ACT. Students begin their college search during the junior year and apply to colleges during the fall of the senior year.

Colleges where recent graduates have enrolled include Agnes Scott, Auburn, Berea, Brown, Brigham Young, The Citadel, Clemson, College of Charleston, Davidson, Duke, Emerson, Emory, Erskine, Florida State, Furman, Georgia Southern, Georgia Tech, Gettysburg, Guilford, Kenyon, Johns Hopkins, Lafayette, Mary Baldwin, Mercer, Morehouse, Ohio State, Presbyterian, Princeton, Rhodes, Tufts, Vanderbilt, Virginia Tech, Washington and Lee, Wofford, Yale, and the Universities of Alabama, Colorado, Florida, Georgia, Michigan, Mississippi, North Carolina, Oregon, South Carolina, Pennsylvania, and Tennessee. Typically, 100 percent of the graduating seniors attend the college or university of their choice.

STUDENT BODY AND CONDUCT

For the 2005–06 school year, Rabun Gap–Nacoochee School enrolled students from fifteen states and fourteen countries in grades 6–12. The 2005–06 enrollment was 314; 164 are girls and 150 are boys, and 53 percent are boarding students. The majority of the students come from Georgia, North Carolina, South Carolina and Florida. Other states represented are Alabama, Alaska, Arizona, California, Delaware, Illinois, Nevada, New Jersey, New York, Tennessee, Texas, and Wyoming. International students come from Germany, Jamaica, Japan, Kenya, Korea, Nigeria, Russia, Rwanda, Saudi Arabia, Spain, Taiwan, the Turks and Cacaos Islands, Uganda, and Venezuela. Rabun Gap admits students who meet academic and conduct standards without regard to race, color, gender, or national or ethnic origin.

Rules are in place to ensure the safety of all students. Students are held accountable for their own conduct and the conduct of their peers. Student prefects assist administrators and dorm parents with the legislation and administration of discipline. In addition to rules for daily living, Rabun Gap students follow an honor code in all phases of their school life.

ACADEMIC FACILITIES

Hodgson Hall contains classrooms for the Upper School, the chapel, the computer center, and school offices. The Morris Brown Science Center houses science classrooms and laboratories along with the Louise M. Gallant Herbarium. The Middle School is located in two restored homes just a short walk from the

Upper School. The Industrial Arts Building houses both wood and metal working machinery.

Two facilities were opened in January 2002. A new library offers enhanced academic resources for students, including 12,000 bound volumes, expanded computer access, and more than 300,000 volumes on CD-ROM. The new Arts and Technology Building offers state-of-the art performing and visual arts classrooms, a dance studio, a technology center, a black box theater, and a 620-seat auditorium.

Administrative offices, the Head of School's office, and the campus bookstore, along with the Gap Grill (student center), are located in the recently renovated Woodruff Memorial Administrative Building.

BOARDING AND GENERAL FACILITIES
The main campus occupies approximately 200 of the 1,400 acres owned by the School. The balance of the property consists of a working farm and forest, including a 20-acre recreational lake.

There are seven dormitories—three each for boys and girls in grades 7 through 11. Jane Hall, a "suite-style" dormitory for twelfth-grade students, was formally dedicated on June 6, 2003. Most rooms are double occupancy, and a member of the residential faculty staffs each dorm. These faculty members have no other duties at the School and serve as a resource to the students in their dorms. Student prefects assist with residential life, including evening study hall and other leadership duties.

Students and faculty members take their meals in the Addie Corn Ritchie Dining Hall, located in the middle of central campus.

ATHLETICS
The interscholastic athletics program helps foster teamwork, the improvement of physical skills, leadership, and school spirit. Coaches are also teachers; this interaction between coaches and team members helps build relationships between teachers and students in a setting outside the classroom. Competitive sports include baseball, basketball, cross-country, golf, soccer, softball, swimming, tennis, track and field, and volleyball. Rabun Gap teams maintain a distinguished record in both achievement and sportsmanship.

EXTRACURRICULAR OPPORTUNITIES
Rabun Gap takes advantage of its location by planning a full schedule of extracurricular outdoor activities. During the spring, summer, and fall, the outdoors club goes hiking, camping, white-water rafting, or mountain biking. During the winter months, students take ski trips to nearby Georgia and Carolina slopes. The School's extensive campus provides numerous opportunities for fishing, hiking, and rock climbing.

At Rabun Gap, clubs provide students with numerous educational and recreational activities. Service clubs, such as the Beta Club, offer students leadership opportunities and provide valuable services to the School and community. The Art Guild, astronomy club, environmental club, language clubs, science club, student newspaper, literary magazine, and yearbook afford learning opportunities outside of the classroom. In addition, students may choose to join recreational clubs.

DAILY LIFE
The typical student day, following academic periods, includes athletics, student work responsibilities, and other activities. Chapel services are held on Thursdays and Sundays.

Open time is available after dinner for socializing at the student center or relaxing in the dormitories. On Sunday through Thursday evenings, dorm parents and prefects supervise a mandatory 2-hour study period for boarding students.

WEEKEND LIFE
On weekends, a variety of on-campus and off-campus activities are offered, including dances, sports events, hiking, camping trips, miniature golf, bowling, and skating as well as trips to malls, concerts, amusement parks, and movies. Boarding students attend chapel every Sunday. With proper parental and administrative permission, boarding students may go home or stay with friends from school on certain "open" weekends throughout the year.

COSTS AND FINANCIAL AID
Tuition for 2005–06 was $11,250 for day students and $23,950 for boarding students. An enrollment fee of $1100 for day students, $2000 for boarding students, and $3000 for international students is also required.

The School offers payment plans by year, by semester, and by month. Financial aid is provided on the basis of need. In order to be considered for financial aid, families must complete the Parents' Financial Statement (PFS) and mail it to the School and Student Service for Financial Aid (SSS). The School uses the SSS report as a guide when making final decisions regarding the amount of aid awarded. Merit-based scholarships are also available for outstanding students.

ADMISSIONS INFORMATION
Rabun Gap seeks motivated students of good moral character who possess the skills necessary to compete in a college-preparatory environment. Candidates for admission are evaluated through school transcripts, references, on-campus interviews, and standardized testing. The School requires all applicants to take either the ISEE or the SSAT.

APPLICATION TIMETABLE
The application process begins in the fall of the year preceding entry and continues until classes are full. The Admission Office recommends initiating the process as early as possible. In addition, some applicants are admitted for the January term. Application packets and DVD presentations are available through the Admission Office.

ADMISSIONS CORRESPONDENCE
Adele Yermack
Director of Admission and Financial Aid
Rabun Gap–Nacoochee School
339 Nacoochee Drive
Rabun Gap, Georgia 30568
Phone: 706-746-7467
     800-543-7467 (toll-free)
Fax: 706-746-2594
Web site: http://www.rabungap.org

RANDOLPH–MACON ACADEMY

Front Royal, Virginia

Type: Coeducational boarding and day college-preparatory school with Air Force Junior ROTC and flight training
Grades: 6–12, PG: Middle School, 6–8; Upper School, 9–12, postgraduate year
Enrollment: School total: 396; Upper School: 323
Head of School: Maj. Gen. Henry M. Hobgood, USAF (Ret.), President

---

THE SCHOOL

Founded in 1892, Randolph-Macon Academy (R-MA) is affiliated with the United Methodist Church. R-MA is dedicated to preparing young people to succeed in top colleges and universities and in life. The Academy provides an advanced curriculum, a superior faculty and staff, and a disciplined structure in a religious and secure environment. Students learn to live together harmoniously in a supportive and diverse community while developing moral character, citizenship, and a passion for excellence and lifelong learning. The Academy accomplishes this mission by having students in grades 9–12 and postgraduates participate in Air Force Junior ROTC (AFJROTC). R-MA is the oldest coeducational boarding school in the nation that has AFJROTC. R-MA has a unique flight-training program with FAA-certified instructors and single-engine trainer aircraft.

The school is located in the beautiful Shenandoah Valley, at the north entrance to the Skyline Drive, 70 miles west of Washington, D.C. It is fully accredited by the Southern Association of Colleges and Schools and the Virginia Association of Independent Schools and is a member of the Association of Military Colleges and Schools of the United States and The Association of Boarding Schools (TABS).

ACADEMIC PROGRAMS

Randolph-Macon Academy prides itself on its high academic standards and overall educational excellence. The student-teacher ratio is 9:1; the average class size is 16. One hundred percent of R-MA seniors are accepted into college. For qualified students, nine Advanced Placement and fourteen honors courses are available. More than eighteen credits may be earned through a college dual-enrollment program.

All students have mandatory evening study hall. Students not meeting their potential may attend tutorial sessions with teachers four times a week. They may also be mandated to participate in a study improvement program. Grades are sent eight times a year.

Twenty-four credits are needed for the Advanced College Prep Diploma: English, 4; math, 4; science, 4; foreign language, 3; social studies, 3; physical education, 2; electives, 2; religion, 1; and computer applications, ½. For the standard College Preparatory Diploma, 22 credits are needed (3 credits each are needed for math and science). An International Diploma is available, which includes a full program of ESL. AFJROTC classes are required each year. The curriculum includes Power English (two periods of English in grades 8–10), opportunities to travel and study abroad, the Educational Program for Gifted Youth studies with Stanford University, speech and debate, and other electives.

In grades 6–8, cross-curricular, mentoring, and study-skills programs lay the foundation for students to build habits for high school and beyond. Fundamental core subjects are taught as well as band, drama, computer, and foreign languages (Latin, Spanish, French, and German). Middle Schoolers enjoy the security that comes from a disciplined and structured environment. Students are held accountable for their actions, with the goal of developing well-mannered, respectful, and confident young men and women.

Students participate in the annual science fair, public speaking contests, the Virginia Mathematics League, Math Counts, and the Battle of Books program. Students enjoy field trips to various museums, including the Smithsonian Institution and the national Holocaust museum. Guest speakers include Civil War re-enactors, a Holocaust survivor, and representatives from the Juvenile Diabetes Research Foundation.

FACULTY AND ADVISERS

Randolph-Macon Academy has 47 full-time teachers (30 men, 17 women). Twenty-three hold advanced degrees; 96 percent hold bachelor's degrees or higher. Faculty members are responsible for tutorial sessions in the afternoon, evening study hall, and coaching. Each faculty member mentors 3 to 9 students. Outstanding professional development is the key to retaining more than 90 percent of the faculty from year to year. R-MA provides individual and group counseling for students through the Academy's licensed clinical counselor.

Major General Henry M. Hobgood, USAF, retired, became the ninth president of Randolph-Macon Academy in 1997. He holds a B.S. from North Carolina State University, an M.S. from Troy State University, and an M.S. from Shenandoah University.

COLLEGE PLACEMENT

The R-MA staff assists graduates in finding colleges that are well matched to their abilities and interests. College representatives interview seniors on campus, while juniors attend a six-week college-counseling seminar. Students attend college fairs on and off the campus. The counselor works with students on an individual basis throughout their college search, application process, and scholarship quest.

Over the years, the Academy has experienced a near 100 percent college acceptance rate, sending more than 97 percent of its graduates to four-year institutions. Over the past four years, seniors have earned more than $14 million in college scholarships and were accepted to Bryn Mawr, Carnegie Mellon, Duke, Embry-Riddle, Purdue, Smith, Virginia Tech, William and Mary, and the University of Virginia as well as United States Service Academies such as the U.S. Air

Force Academy, West Point, and the U.S. Merchant Marine Academy.

STUDENT BODY AND CONDUCT

In 2005–06, the Upper School consisted of 323 students, and the Middle School enrolled 73 students. Randolph-Macon Academy's 396 students come from twenty-five states and eleven countries. Fifty-one percent are from Virginia and 12 percent are from Maryland. Twenty-one percent are day students, 27 percent are women, 18 percent are international students, and 22 percent are members of minority groups.

The Academy accepts students with the ability and attitude to comply with its long-standing traditions and rules. The foundation of discipline is a long-established Honor Code, supplemented by a student handbook that clearly defines the perimeters of behavior. Excellence of character is R-MA's hallmark. Emphasis is given to positive reinforcement by recognizing performance in academics, leadership, social relationships, and athletics. Students are taught effective study habits and self-discipline.

ACADEMIC FACILITIES

Crow Hall houses the math, science, language, and AFJROTC programs. Full science-laboratory facilities are available. Rives Hall houses the English, social studies, and English as a second language programs and campus photography. Three computer labs are available. The Upper School library and the Middle School library contain more than 11,500 volumes. The Fulton Fine Arts building contains a large band-rehearsal hall, practice rooms, and a music library. The Little Theatre is used for drama, poetry reading, and a student coffee house. The Middle School campus is adjacent to the Upper School and includes a classroom building with a media center and library. All buildings are air conditioned and wired for Internet access.

BOARDING AND GENERAL FACILITIES

Historic Sonner-Payne Hall, with the large gold dome and cupola, can be seen for miles. It is the main building on the campus and houses the Upper School boys' dormitory, administrative offices, the student center, a library, a pool, an infirmary, a bookstore, and a barbershop. Men and women students are housed in separate dorm facilities with well-equipped rooms and lounges. Phones and computer connections are available in each room.

On the Middle School campus, a dormitory building provides a comfortable living environment for boarding students. The activity center contains a cafeteria, a bookstore, and a gymnasium.

ATHLETICS

Each student is required to participate in athletics or in extracurricular activities. Varsity sports include baseball, basketball, cross-country, football, golf, lacrosse, riflery, soccer, softball, swimming, tennis, track, volleyball, and wrestling. The intramural program includes cheerleading, swimming, tennis, and weight lifting. Melton Memorial Gymnasium, on the Upper School campus, features basketball courts and wrestling and weight-training facilities. The campus has seven outdoor playing fields.

Middle School interscholastic sports include basketball, cheerleading, golf, soccer, and tennis. Selected students participate on Upper School teams. A variety of intramural activities and clubs are available.

EXTRACURRICULAR OPPORTUNITIES

R-MA's award-winning marching band and precision drill team perform in many national and local parades and ceremonies. The concert band and chorus perform on and off campus. The speech and debate team is nationally recognized and competes at Harvard, Yale, Princeton, Vassar, and Columbia. Students interested in theater production may take drama as an elective or audition for plays. Aspiring journalists can work on the school magazine or yearbook. Academy clubs include Student Council, Honor Council, National Honor Society, Junior Classical League, Kitty Hawk Air Society, Literary and Debating Societies, Interact Club (a community service club), Spanish, French, and Korean Clubs, Chess Club, Young Democrats and Young Republican Clubs, and the Improv Club.

Extracurricular activities for Middle School students include newspaper, yearbook, music lessons, and Student Council.

DAILY LIFE

Forty-five-minute classes are held Mondays, Tuesdays, and Fridays from 8 to 3:35. Ninety-minute block scheduling is offered on Wednesdays and Thursdays. A tutorial period is offered Monday–Thursday for twenty-five minutes. Athletics and cocurricular activities are scheduled daily between 4 and 5:45. Flight instruction is offered during the day and on selected weekends. Proctored study hours are from 7:30 to 9:30 p.m. Lights out is at 10:30 for underclassmen and at 11 for seniors and postgraduates. All Upper and Middle School students participate in chapel services.

The Middle School follows the same academic schedule as the Upper School. Afternoon activities include mentoring and tutorial sessions, sports and intramural time, and study hall. Dinner is served at 5:30 and is followed by free time and dormitory life meetings. Lights out for Middle School students is at 9:30.

WEEKEND LIFE

The Academy has a liberal weekend pass policy whereby any student who maintains high standards of conduct and academic progress may leave the campus. Closed weekends relate to semester examination times and special activities.

Students who remain on campus engage in weekend activities such as paintball, skiing, dances, trips to museums, professional sporting events, festivals, plays, movies, and amusement parks. Adults supervise all weekend activities.

SUMMER PROGRAMS

Summer courses in English, mathematics, science, social studies, Spanish, and study skills, as well as English as a second language, are offered to Upper School students. R-MA offers credit for both remedial classes and new courses. Flight training is also offered in the summer session.

Middle School students may choose from math, English, computer applications, study skills, and interactive history. A variety of sports activities are available, and there are opportunities for weekend cultural and entertainment trips.

R-MA's summer program runs for four weeks, from late June to late July. The summer program accepts students from other countries and other schools. No financial aid is available for the summer program.

COSTS AND FINANCIAL AID

Fees for room, board, and tuition for the 2005–06 year were $20,097 for Upper School boarding students, $18,751 for Middle School boarding students, $22,652 for international students, $9266 for Upper School day students, and $7370 for Middle School day students. In addition, parents should plan on approximately $3500 for books, uniforms, and other campus fees for boarding students; $1900 for day students.

Endowment funds, the United Methodist Church, and a student loan program provide the school's financial aid resources. Recipients are chosen on the basis of need as well as character, demonstrated academic achievement, and general potential. Work scholarships are also available.

ADMISSIONS INFORMATION

Applicants are accepted for all grade levels on the basis of academic potential and the ability to live by the Academy's high standards of behavior. Families are encouraged to visit the campus, view the facilities, and meet students and faculty members. Interviews are highly recommended.

APPLICATION TIMETABLE

Inquiries and applications are welcome year-round. Interviews and tours are scheduled Monday through Friday during business hours. Saturday tours may be scheduled by appointment. Open Houses are scheduled several times a year. The deadline for fall is April 1; applications received after this date are considered on a space-available basis. Financial aid is awarded in May and June. Students may be accepted for midyear enrollment if space is available.

ADMISSIONS CORRESPONDENCE

Pia G. Crandell, Ph.D.
Director of Admissions
Randolph-Macon Academy
200 Academy Drive
Front Royal, Virginia 22630

Phone: 540-636-5484
      800-272-1172 (toll-free)
Fax: 540-636-5419
E-mail: admissions@rma.edu
Web site: http://www.rma.edu

RANNEY SCHOOL

Tinton Falls, New Jersey

Type: Coeducational college-preparatory day school
Grades: BG (3 years old)–grade 12: Lower School, BG–Grade 5; Middle School, Grades 6–8; Upper School, Grades 9–12
Enrollment: School total: 750
Head of School: Lawrence S. Sykoff, Ed.D.

THE SCHOOL

Ranney School was founded in 1960 by Russell G. Ranney for the purpose of fostering high academic achievement. A former Associate Director of the New York University Reading Institute, Mr. Ranney was a firm believer in the three R's. A 12-member Board of Trustees, plus the Head of School, supervise the School's operation on its campus of more than 50 acres in a residential neighborhood located approximately 60 miles south of New York City.

The purpose of Ranney School is to prepare its students for college and to encourage them to become independent and self-reliant young adults. The School believes a well-prepared student is one who is inquisitive, knows how to acquire knowledge, and exercises sound judgment and common sense in all matters.

The Board of Trustees is the School's governing body. During 2004–05, annual giving totaled $350,000; annual operating expenses averaged $13 million.

Ranney School alumni number approximately 1200; an Alumni Council oversees alumni activities.

Ranney School is accredited by the Middle States Association of Colleges and Secondary Schools. The School maintains active membership in the National Association of Independent Schools (NAIS), the New Jersey Association of Independent Schools (NJAIS), the Counsel for the Advancement and Support of Education (CASE), the Educational Records Bureau (ERB), and the National Association for College Admission Counseling (NACAC).

ACADEMIC PROGRAMS

The Lower School (beginners [age 3] through grade 5) curriculum is designed to stimulate a child's natural love of learning. Goals are set forth in a program consistent with the early stages of child development. The primary goal is to maximize the growth of each individual. The curriculum remains rooted in the development of language arts. Course time is allotted to vocabulary building, spelling, grammar usage, reading, and the development of writing skills. Strong programs in mathematics, science, social studies, instrumental music, and computer education complement these courses. Students are also introduced to studies in the fine arts, music, and foreign languages. Aquatics and physical education complete the course of study. Teaching strategies include cooperative learning, interdisciplinary arrangements, and individual attention.

The Middle School (grades 6 through 8) curriculum is designed to provide a special community in which students can grow, learn about themselves, develop personal and group values, and prepare for the challenges of higher learning, particularly within the Ranney Upper School. The comprehensive English and math-

ematics programs initiated in the Lower School continue through the middle years along with additional concentrations in science, history, and foreign languages, including a foundation in Latin. Courses in computer fundamentals, art, music, drama, word processing, physical education, and aquatics are part of the total curriculum. To provide flexibility in instruction, some classes in math, history, and foreign languages are arranged to cover the curriculum over a two-year period.

The Upper School (grades 9 through 12) graduation requirements include a minimum of 20 academic credits, plus 4 units in health and physical education. All students are expected to take 5 full credits of course work each year. Specific requirements include English (4 credits), foreign language (3 credits), history (3 credits, 1 of which must be American history), mathematics (3 credits), science (2 credits with lab, including biology and either chemistry or physics), art (1 credit), and physical education (4 credits). In addition to required courses, a number of single-semester and full-year electives are available to sophomores, juniors, and seniors. The Upper School curriculum also offers many honors and college-level Advanced Placement courses. Eighteen AP units are available to students capable of accelerated study.

Ranney utilizes the letter grade system (A through F). The school year consists of two semesters and four marking periods, with grades and written evaluations being sent home at the end of the first and third marking periods. Report cards with grades only are sent at the end of each semester. Midterm exams are given in January and final exams in June.

FACULTY AND ADVISERS

There are 85 full-time faculty members, plus 3 part-time instructors. Thirty-two faculty members have master's degrees or higher. Each Middle and Upper School faculty member serves as an adviser to an average of 6 to 8 students. Ranney faculty members are accomplished and recognized professionals whose contributions to the growth and status of their calling often extend outside the School community.

Dr. Lawrence S. Sykoff was appointed Headmaster in June 1993. He holds degrees from the University of San Diego (Ed.D. and M.Ed.) and Baruch College of Business Administration of the City University of New York (B.B.A.).

COLLEGE PLACEMENT

The College Guidance Office assists in planning family visits to colleges. It schedules visits with college admission representatives, many of whom visit Ranney each year to interview prospective students. Juniors attend various college fairs to gather information about colleges throughout the country.

Early in the sophomore year, students take the PSATs and in the junior year, group and individual meetings with students and parents are held to assist in the college selection process. During the summer prior to their senior year, students meet with the Director of College Guidance to formulate a list of college choices and devise a plan of action for the senior year. As the application process reaches its peak in the fall of that year, students receive individual help or encouragement. All seniors receive assistance from the Director of College Guidance in writing college essays and preparing their final applications.

The mean SAT I scores for 2005 graduates are 622 verbal and 640 math.

The senior class of 2004 achieved 100 percent college acceptance at schools such as Boston College, Columbia, Cornell, Duke, Emory, George Washington, NYU, Swarthmore, Tufts, Yale, and the University of Pennsylvania.

STUDENT BODY AND CONDUCT

The 2005–06 student body consists of 750 students as follows: 201 boys and 182 girls in the Lower School; 73 boys and 76 girls in the Middle School; and 100 boys and 118 girls in the Upper School.

Ranney's families represent many different countries, including China, India, Japan, and Russia. The School sponsors an International Week of Celebration each year in all three divisions.

A Judicial Board handles routine disciplinary issues in the Upper School. The board consists of 2 faculty members and 2 students and is chaired by the Dean of Students. Recommendations are given to the Principal and the Headmaster for review and decision.

ACADEMIC FACILITIES

The Lower School is composed of three buildings and has its own computer lab, resource room, and library. Each classroom is equipped with two computers, and all computers are connected to the network and the Internet. The Middle School and Upper School are housed in Ranney's modern and high-tech academic complex. The facility offers thirty-three classrooms, state-of-the-art biology and chemistry laboratories, a foreign language laboratory, a college guidance center, a modern library, student assembly areas, 300 computers, and a unique Distance Learning Center. The entire building is wired for the Internet. In addition the Middle and Upper Schools have their own dining hall.

ATHLETICS

Ranney School encourages students to participate in sports and views athletics as an important part of the educational program. All students are eligible to participate regardless of ability. The

middle and upper divisions field teams in soccer, cross-country, tennis, basketball, swimming, baseball, softball, golf, and lacrosse. Ranney competes against other accredited public and private schools in the area and maintains active membership in the New Jersey Prep Conference. Interscholastic competition begins in the sixth grade. The School has two gymnasiums, a 25-meter indoor swimming pool, five tennis courts, two baseball fields, two soccer fields, a quarter-mile track, and a state-of-the-art fitness center with a certified athletic trainer on duty.

EXTRACURRICULAR ACTIVITIES

The Lower School offers a variety of extracurricular and after-school activities for grades 2 through 5, including computers, art instruction, creative writing, chorus, band, cooking, swimming, and other sports.

Both the Middle and Upper Schools have a broad selection of student organizations in which to participate. Both schools have a student council, foreign language clubs, and excellent forensics teams. Students in grades 6 through 9 are eligible to join the Science Olympiad Team, which travels to Rider University for participation in the New Jersey State Science Olympiad.

The Upper School has an active chapter of the National Honor Society. Students can also participate in Mock Trial, math, chess, and academic bowl teams. Chorus and drama clubs offer students an opportunity to perform for friends, parents, and peers. Publications include *Horizons* (the School's award-winning yearbook), *The Torch,* and *RSVP (Ranney School Verse & Prose),* which showcases the talents of Ranney's young artists and authors.

Throughout the year, the Ranney School Fine Arts Department and Thespian Troupe present art exhibitions, music recitals, and two major drama productions. Traditional events include Spirit Day/Homecoming, International Week, Halloween Parade, Grandparents' Thanksgiving Feast, Parents' Day Tea, and Lower, Middle, and Upper School Carnivals (fund-raisers). Field trips, both interstate and intrastate, offer cultural exposure outside the Ranney campus for students in the middle and upper divisions.

DAILY LIFE

The typical school day consists of six 45-minute academic periods and one 60-minute period, with a 10-minute break between second and third periods, plus a lunch period. Assemblies are held throughout the year. Each week, grades 6–12 meet with their advisers for approximately 20 minutes during an adviser period. School begins at 8:40 a.m. and ends at 3:20 p.m. The cafeteria serves hot and cold lunches. Bus transportation is available to most students.

SUMMER PROGRAMS

Students can enroll for six weeks to take enhancement and/or credit courses in several academic subject areas. Most courses are taught by Ranney School faculty members. In addition, an eight-, six-, or four-week summer day camp program is available for boys and girls ages 3 through 13. Ranney-in-the-Summer is fully accredited by the American Camping Association.

COSTS AND FINANCIAL AID

Tuition for 2005–06 ranges from $10,200 to $19,850. Extras include books (Lower School: $150–$450; Middle School: $300–$600; Upper School: $550–$850) and transportation ($2600–$3000). Parents of students in grades pre-K through 12 are required to purchase a $1000 bond, which is redeemed when the child either graduates or leaves Ranney School.

Ranney School is committed to awarding financial aid to those students who demonstrate a financial need. Families who feel that a need for assistance exists are encouraged to apply. The Financial Aid Committee of the Board of Trustees bases financial aid decisions on the formula provided by the School and Student Service for Financial Aid (SSS) in Princeton, New Jersey. The Financial Aid Committee diligently reviews each application in order to distribute available funds equitably. All applications are held in strict confidence. Each student applying for aid must be in good standing in all aspects of student life. Parents must complete the SSS financial aid form annually and should send it to Princeton as early as possible. Inquiries should be directed to the Associate Head for Admissions and Marketing.

Parents can arrange to pay the tuition over a ten-month period through the Knight Tuition Payment Plan. An enrollment deposit must be paid directly to the School upon registration.

Applications are also available through the Business Office for a Knight Tuition Plan Achiever Loan, which has a ten-year repayment term.

ADMISSIONS INFORMATION

Standardized placement tests are administered on an individual or small-group basis. Transferring students should forward a completed application and appropriate school records to the Admission Office prior to the scheduled date of the placement exam. All candidates must complete an interview with appropriate members of the Admission Committee. Ranney School does not discriminate on the basis of sex, race, religion, ethnic origin, or disabilities in the administration of its education, hiring, and admission policies; financial aid program; and athletic or other school-administered programs.

APPLICATION TIMETABLE

Ranney School does not stipulate a formal application deadline, but it strongly recommends that parents contact the Admission Office during the fall to enroll for the next academic year. There is a $75 application fee.

ADMISSIONS CORRESPONDENCE

Heather Rudisi, Associate Head for Admissions
    and Marketing
Ranney School
235 Hope Road
Tinton Falls, New Jersey 07724
Phone: 732-542-4777 Ext. 107
Fax: 732-460-1078
E-mail: hrudisi@ranneyschool.com
Web site: http://www.ranneyschool.org

RIVERSIDE MILITARY ACADEMY

Gainesville, Georgia

Type: Boys' boarding and day college-preparatory academy within a military structure
Grades: 7–12
Enrollment: 410
Head of School: Richard C. Moore, Interim Superintendent

THE SCHOOL

Since its establishment in 1907, Riverside Military Academy has become one of the nation's largest and most prestigious military academies, providing a distinctive and rigorous college-preparatory experience for young men in grades 7–12. Riverside's 236-acre campus is located in Gainesville, Georgia, bordering Lake Lanier in the foothills of the Blue Ridge Mountains. The moderate climate features pleasant seasonal changes in weather and allows for year-round outdoor recreation. Gainesville is a community of more than 30,000, conveniently located 1 hour north of Atlanta's Hartsfield-Jackson International Airport. Gainesville offers easy connections to I-85, I-75, and Amtrak rail service.

Riverside Military Academy provides a safe, structured educational environment to prepare young men for success in college and a lifetime of challenges. The cadet lifestyle helps develop the whole person as a self-confident leader and morally responsible citizen. Through skills development and varied experiences, cadets build manners, pride, character, honor, scholarship, and personal integrity.

Riverside is committed to building a learning alliance with parents and cadets that teaches and nurtures character-development skills that help cadets become young men of distinction in today's society. Riverside's comprehensive character-development program teaches honor instruction, respect for others, social skills, sportsmanship, and community service. The learning alliance is enriched and strengthened by Riverside's exclusive weekend leave program, which allows cadets in good standing to spend most weekends at home with their families and friends.

Riverside is jointly accredited by the Southern Association of Colleges and Schools and the Southern Association of Independent Schools. In addition, Riverside is a member of the National Association of Independent Schools, the Association of Military Colleges and Schools in the United States, the Association of Boarding Schools, and the Georgia Independent Schools Association, among others.

Cadets in grades 9–12 participate in the Academy's JROTC program, which is affiliated with the United States Army and has earned the designation of Honor Unit with Distinction for forty-eight consecutive years.

Riverside Military Academy is a nonprofit, tax-exempt corporation governed by a self-perpetuating board of trustees. Riverside's endowment enables the Academy to provide an outstanding program and facility while keeping tuition costs reasonable for parents. In some cases, Riverside's Scholarship Fund, which is supported by contributions from alumni and friends of the Academy, can provide financial assistance to students who have successfully completed at least one year at Riverside.

An interactive CD-ROM about Riverside Military Academy is available upon request.

ACADEMIC PROGRAMS

Riverside's academic program is compelling. Through a combination of small classes (the average class size is 10 students); one-on-one tutoring; a caring, highly trained senior faculty; the integration of student success study skills into the core curriculum; and the establishment of an individualized, comprehensive college-prep program, all cadets are accepted by accredited colleges or universities.

The academic year, which is divided into two semesters, begins in mid-August. The calendar includes one vacation week at Thanksgiving, two vacation weeks at Christmas, and one week in the spring.

The curriculum includes programs in algebra, American history, American literature, art, biology, calculus, chemistry, computer science, current events, economics, English, government/civics, journalism, Latin, military science, music, physics, Spanish, speech, trigonometry, world history, world literature, and writing. Twenty-four credits are required for graduation, including 18 from the following areas: English, foreign language, mathematics, science, and social studies. Honors and Advanced Placement classes are offered in English, foreign language, history, mathematics, and science. Weekly academic reports are available to parents via the Internet. The Academy also offers a five-week summer academic program for review or new credit courses.

FACULTY AND ADVISERS

There are more than 60 full-time teachers on the faculty, most of whom have advanced degrees. Faculty members are chosen on the basis of their academic credentials, personality, and ability to work successfully with boys in a wide variety of endeavors.

There is a full-time nursing staff on duty around the clock in the campus infirmary, and a physician visits the infirmary several times a week to see patients. Cadets also have access to spiritual and mental health counseling through either the Academy's chaplain or counselor.

COLLEGE PLACEMENT

Riverside graduates have a 100 percent college-acceptance rate. Graduates attend some of the country's premier colleges, including Auburn, Brown, The Citadel, Clemson, Florida State, Furman, Georgia, Georgia Tech, Johns Hopkins, North Carolina State, Penn State, Syracuse, Texas A&M, Tulane, the United States Military Academy, the United States Naval Academy, Vanderbilt, and others. Many Riverside graduates earn full scholarships to the college of their choice. In

2005, Riverside's graduates earned more than $2.2 million in merit scholarships.

STUDENT BODY AND CONDUCT

The student body is organized into a Corps of Cadets, which represents more than thirty states and ten countries. The Corps is composed of a cadet battalion staff and nine individual companies, with cadet leaders responsible for the daily nonacademic activities of each company. The Corps receives adult supervision and guidance from the office of the commandant. Every cadet has an opportunity to earn a leadership position. Each cadet is expected to be familiar with and to govern himself according to the *Code Book of Cadet Rules and Regulations,* which is available to parents, along with the *Parent Handbook.*

A system of merits and demerits offers strong incentives to boys for good and courteous conduct and academic achievement.

ACADEMIC FACILITIES

In 2004, Riverside completed a $90-million construction program to renovate the campus and build state-of-the-art academic, residential, and athletic facilities. Today, the Riverside campus rivals that of many small colleges. Riverside's primary academic facility, Elkin Hall, features bright, clean classrooms; extensive science laboratories; language labs; a computerized algebra lab; Riverside's exclusive Student Success Center; and a dedicated College Placement Center.

Riverside's Lanier Hall houses the Computer Science Department, the Military Science Department, and the Center for Character Development, which oversees the Academy's many community service projects and character education curriculum.

The newest addition to Riverside's academic facilities is the Sandy Beaver Center for Teaching and Learning, which houses a new library and reading room, art and photography classrooms, instrumental and choral rehearsal rooms, and a 790-seat auditorium. The center includes an area for on-campus faculty and professional staff development.

BOARDING AND GENERAL FACILITIES

Cadets are housed 2 to a room in new dormitories that are part of a quadrangle complex that includes an infirmary and post office. Each room is equipped with a computer with e-mail and current software applications. The dormitories have television lounges and recreation rooms. Adult advisers in each company area provide continuous supervision and monitoring to ensure an orderly and secure environment.

In the cadet grill, students may purchase refreshments, play billiards or table tennis, watch television, or participate in other activities. A

barbershop and a cadet store are also available. Riverside's stately dining hall accommodates the entire Corps for each meal.

ATHLETICS

Riverside's award-winning athletic program encourages all cadets to participate in activities that promote teamwork and physical fitness. Through physical education classes, team sports, or intramural activities, each cadet devotes an average of 2 hours daily to athletic activities. Riverside is a member of the Georgia Independent School Association's athletic league. The Academy competes interscholastically in baseball, basketball, crew, cross-country, football, golf, lacrosse, military drill, riflery, soccer, swimming, tennis, track, and wrestling.

Riverside's facilities include baseball, football, lacrosse, and soccer fields; an Olympic-size natatorium; tennis courts; indoor and outdoor basketball courts; a waterfront area on Lake Lanier; and a 45,000-square-foot field house with an indoor track. The football complex features NFL-size lockers, a film room, and a physical therapy/athletic training room. Curtis Hall, the Academy's new gymnasium complex, features a 6,000-square-foot weight-training room with customized equipment and an indoor rifle range.

EXTRACURRICULAR ACTIVITIES

Social events, off-campus trips, lecture and entertainment programs, dances, publications, movies, dramatics, and honor and leadership groups are an integral part of Riverside's program and ensure that cadets can pursue interests that are essential to well-rounded development. Excellent musical, drill, and performing organizations, including a marching band, provide opportunities for training and participation. Riverside cadets produce two publications: the campus newspaper, *The Talon*, and the yearbook, *The Bayonet*. Some of the other club activities in which cadets may participate are Boy Scouts, Fellowship of Christian Athletes, the Horton Society, Rangers/Raiders, Academic Bowl Team, chorus, and drama.

DAILY LIFE

The class day consists of eight periods that accommodate the typical assignment of five subjects, plus military science and advisement. After school, cadets participate in team sports or general athletics, followed by dinner. There is sufficient free time for relaxation, letter writing, independent study, and socializing. All cadets must participate in a 2-hour supervised study period each Sunday through Thursday evening. On Wednesday mornings, all students attend a character education assembly. Wednesday afternoons are reserved for clubs, cadet training, and other meetings. On most Tuesdays and Thursdays, cadets participate in military drill.

WEEKEND LIFE

On most weekends, boarding cadets who are in good standing may leave the campus to visit their families and friends. Weekend leaves depend on parental permission and the accumulation of merits—a means of linking privilege to academic accomplishment and good behavior. For those who remain on the campus during the weekend, Saturday and Sunday afternoons are times for relaxation, recreation, and activities on a sign-out basis. Visiting within hall units is permitted, and social events and recreation are provided on campus. In addition, the campus Activities Director schedules regular off-campus excursions and high-adventure recreation. Interdenominational chapel services are held on Sunday mornings. Alternatively, cadets may choose to attend one of many church services in the community. Periodically, the Corps conducts formal military-style parades on Sunday afternoons. Sunday evening is reserved for an in-room study period.

SUMMER PROGRAMS

Riverside offers two summer boarding programs—SOAR (Summer Opportunity and Academic Review) Program and High Adventure Camp. SOAR helps cadets earn academic credit toward high school graduation or review essential academic skills. The program is structured to give young men a holistic educational experience, including academics, character development, and athletics.

In High Adventure Camp, exciting challenges such as hiking on the world-renowned Appalachian Trail and competitive kayaking at the Olympic Rowing Venue on Lake Lanier offer a unique blend of goal-setting skills and development of character and leadership.

COSTS AND FINANCIAL AID

Riverside's comprehensive fee for the 2005–06 school year of $23,950 included tuition, room and board, books, laundry, athletic fees, haircuts, on-campus athletic events, and other incidental expenses. Uniform purchases are not included in the fee. The Academy provides parents with the opportunity to establish an allowance account for their son, which is distributed on a weekly basis. Off-campus entertainment excursions and some discretionary extracurricular activities are not covered by the basic tuition and require additional payment. A $250 medical fee is required to dispense daily medications or vitamins. Transportation fees may be incurred for travel to individual medical appointments or to the airport.

Tuition discounts are available for early tuition payment or for families with two or more brothers enrolled. A cadet is enrolled for the entire academic year. All fees and charges are due upon enrollment and are nonrefundable.

ADMISSIONS INFORMATION

Riverside Military Academy seeks boys of high moral character and academic potential who are willing to set and attain worthy goals. Applicants are admitted on the basis of school transcripts and letters of recommendation. All prospective students are required to visit the Academy for an interview with admissions counselors. Application forms can be found on the Academy's Web site.

APPLICATION TIMETABLE

Riverside accepts admission inquiries year-round for enrollment during various academic terms.

ADMISSIONS CORRESPONDENCE

Director of Admissions
Riverside Military Academy
2001 Riverside Drive
Gainesville, Georgia 30501
Phone: 770-532-6251
          800-GO-CADET (toll-free)
Web site: http://www.cadet.com

ROWLAND HALL–ST. MARK'S SCHOOL

Salt Lake City, Utah

Type: Coeducational day college-preparatory
Grades: PreK–12: Beginning School, 2-year-olds through kindergarten; Lower School, 1–5; Middle School, 6–8; High School, 9–12
Enrollment: School total: 990; Beginning School: 165; Lower School: 330; Middle School: 202; Upper School: 293
Head of School: Alan C. Sparrow

THE SCHOOL

Rowland Hall–St. Mark's School (RHSM) is Utah's oldest coeducational college-preparatory day school. In 1964, Rowland Hall (a girls' boarding and day school established in 1880) and St. Mark's (a boys' day school dating back to pre–Utah statehood) merged to become a coeducational, college-preparatory day and boarding school, housed on a block in the historic Avenues neighborhood of downtown Salt Lake City.

RHSM is committed to offering its students a broad liberal arts education with English, social studies, mathematics, science, and foreign languages at the core of its academic program. Equally important are the arts and athletics. RHSM encourages students to love learning, appreciate the arts, and strive for healthy lifestyles.

Rowland Hall–St. Mark's School is governed by a self-perpetuating Board of Trustees. The School's operating budget is $13.5 million per year. The endowment is approximately $3.75 million. An active Annual Giving program is supported by 99 percent of the faculty, more than 70 percent of the School's current parents, and many of the School's grandparents, parents of former students, and alumni.

RHSM is accredited by the Pacific Northwest Association of Independent Schools, the Northwest Association of Schools and Colleges, and the Utah Department of Education. The School is a member of the National Association of Independent Schools, the Pacific Northwest Association of Independent Schools, the National Association of Episcopal Schools, and the Utah High School Activities Association.

ACADEMIC PROGRAMS

Rowland Hall–St. Mark's builds its curriculum around a solid core of academic courses and an array of elective and specialty choices. Class size averages 14. The student-teacher ratio is 10:1.

Requirements for graduation are as follows: 4 years of English, 3 years of mathematics (2 years above algebra), 3 years of social studies, 2 years of laboratory science (1 life science and 1 physical science), 2 years of one foreign language (Spanish, Latin, or French), four trimesters of fine arts, two trimesters of health, one trimester of computer science, one trimester of world religions, one trimester of ethics, one trimester of an activity (e.g., debate, yearbook), and 2⅔ years of physical education. The minimum total of credits required for graduation is 24.

Students must be computer literate to graduate. Beginning in kindergarten, computers are regularly used in all core curriculum areas and in art, music, chess, and other specialty and elective classes. A major financial commitment by the RHSM's parent body, beginning in 1995, resulted in the availability of state-of-the-art computer hardware and software for all RHSM students, faculty members, and administration. Computers are available for student use in computer centers, classrooms, and libraries. All members of the RHSM community have access to e-mail, CD-ROM, and Internet resources.

RHSM's Beginning School is a fertile learning ground and builds a strong foundation for the elementary years. Lower School students concentrate on an integrated curriculum in reading, mathematics, science, the arts, social studies, and world cultures. RHSM takes a balanced approach to literacy in its first- and second-grade reading and writing curriculum, by which children are taught to decode words through a word study (phonics) program. The language arts curriculum used through the elementary years reinforces basic reading and writing skills, bolsters proficiency in written and oral communication, and continues to make the most of the campus's literature-rich environment. Specialty and elective classes enrich the core curriculum through music, drama, the visual arts, chess, computer science, science, environmental activities, and community service projects. During the exciting years of early adolescence, Middle School students at Rowland Hall–St. Mark's are fortunate to have programs specifically designed to meet their changing needs and developing talents. With courses in language arts, social studies, mathematics, science, computers, and foreign languages, students benefit from small, lively classes with high academic expectations. Close support is offered through the advisory program.

The Upper School mixes a challenging academic schedule with sports, the arts, community service, and social activities. RHSM students achieve a solid academic grounding through a strong liberal arts curriculum with numerous electives and are well prepared for entrance into select colleges and universities across the country. Approximately 90 percent of the Upper School student body enrolls in Advanced Placement classes, and historically, all graduating seniors enter college.

Upper school subjects offered are algebra, American history, American literature, band, biology, calculus, ceramics, chemistry, chorus, computer graphics, computer science, creative writing, dance, debate, economics, English, English literature, environmental science, ethics, European history, French, geology, geometry, health, history, journalism, Latin, math applications, music theory, photography, physical education, physics, political science, psychology, Spanish, statistics, studio art, theater/drama, trigonometry, world history, and world religion. Advanced Placement preparation in fifteen test areas, honors sections, independent study, study at local colleges for college credit, and study-abroad opportunities are available.

Parent conferences are scheduled twice a year, and parents are encouraged to confer with teachers at other times as well.

FACULTY AND ADVISERS

Of the 113 faculty members, 83 are full-time; 43 hold master's degrees and 2 hold doctorates. The Upper School total for full-time faculty members is 24. Alan C. Sparrow was appointed Headmaster of Rowland Hall–St. Mark's in 1992. He received his Bachelor of Arts degree from Brown University and Master of Arts and Master of Science degrees from the University of Rochester. In addition to teaching duties, faculty members serve as athletic

coaches, and each teacher acts as an adviser to approximately 10 students. RHSM has made a significant financial commitment to supporting faculty continuing education and professional development.

COLLEGE PLACEMENT

Eighty-three students graduated in 2005, and all planned to attend college. Institutions enrolling more than 1 member of the class of 2005 include Arizona State, Colorado College, Montana State University, New York University, Occidental, Sarah Lawrence, USC, Vassar, Westminster of Salt Lake City, Yale, and the Universities of Delaware, Pennsylvania, Puget Sound, San Francisco, and Utah. Three graduates of the Class of 2004 were National Merit Scholarship Program winners. The middle 50 percent SAT Verbal score ranges for the past three years for Rowland Hall–St. Mark's students were 580–690. The middle 50 percent SAT Math score ranges for the past three years were 520–660. The middle 50 percent ACT composite score ranges for the past three years were 24–30. The average GPA for members of the class of 2005 was 3.6.

STUDENT BODY AND CONDUCT

There are 293 students in RHSM's Upper School. Grade 9: (43 girls, 35 boys); Grade 10: (39 girls, 30 boys); Grade 11: (26 girls, 37 boys); Grade 12: (39 girls, 44 boys).

Every student who enters RHSM's Middle or Upper School is asked to declare acceptance of the responsibility to uphold ethical, honest standards of academic life by signing a copy of the Academic Honor Code. When a student is suspected of violating the Academic Honor Code, a disciplinary committee is convened to propose a course of action. All RHSM students are expected to show respect for themselves, for other people, for the School environment, and for public property.

ACADEMIC FACILITIES

For more than 121 years, RHSM's historic, 2-acre Avenues campus in downtown Salt Lake City housed the School's youngest students through grade 5. In December 2002, RHSM's preschool and Lower School moved to a new 9-acre campus on the east side of Salt Lake City. The new Beginning School facility, the two-story Lower School/administrative building, the chapel, the library, the gymnasium, and the dining hall/fine arts building—surrounded by courtyards and green fields, gardens, and playgrounds—create a residential, rather than institutional, educational environment for the youngest students. The new gymnasium comfortably accommodates home basketball games and large nonathletic events. A regulation-sized basketball court with additional room for bleachers to seat more than 400, plus boys' and girls' locker rooms, make the gym an ideal setting for Middle and Upper School practices and games. Lower School students use this facility for daily, year-round physical education classes.

The Middle School and Upper School are located on the Lincoln Street campus, approximately

¼ mile from the McCarthey Campus on Guardsman Way. Sixth through eighth graders enjoy the light and spacious environment of the Middle School, completed in 1994. It adjoins the Upper School facility, formerly a public junior high school, acquired and renovated in the 1980s. A state-of-the-art performance and assembly center, the Larimer Center for the Performing Arts, was built on the Lincoln Street campus in 1992. Science, math, and computer labs contain the latest available innovations in computer hardware and software. A library, gymnasium, playing fields, computer labs, and fine arts studios offer Middle and Upper School students many learning opportunities outside the classroom.

ATHLETICS
Physical education classes and activities throughout all grades stress the importance of lifetime fitness and taking responsibility for healthy life choices.

RHSM, a member of Region XIV of the Utah High School Activities Association, offers the following interscholastic athletic activities at the High School level: fall—coed golf, girls' soccer, girl's tennis, volleyball, cross-country running, and swimming; winter—girls' and boys' basketball, swimming, and boys' and girls' bowling; spring—track and field, boys' tennis, girls' softball, boys' soccer, golf, and boys' baseball. Coed crew if offered as a club sport. The School has 4 full-time PE instructors, 9 full-time coaches, 11 part-time coaches, and 1 part-time trainer.

Established in 1982, Rowmark Ski Academy is one of the country's top ski racing programs for young, elite Alpine ski racers. Approximately 25 high school–age student-athletes from across the U.S. and other countries participate in rigorous ski training and RHSM course work for a diploma. Students from out-of-town live with host families. Todd Brickson is the director. For more information, those interested can access the Ski Academy's Web site (http://www.rowmark.org).

EXTRACURRICULAR OPPORTUNITIES
Students are encouraged to participate in the School's rich array of extracurricular activities each year. At the Lower School, opportunities for enrichment in the visual arts, music, drama, cooking, science, community service, athletics, journalism, computer science, and chess are offered through the Extended Day Program. In the Middle School, students may choose to join the yearbook staff, the dance company, the debate team, mock trial exhibitions, chorus, band, Mathcounts, the newspaper staff, the literary magazine, and intramural and interscholastic athletic teams.

In the Upper School, student government is an important part of the extracurricular program. The Student Council serves as a channel for school communication, a voice in decision making, and a sponsor of social activities and community service. RHSM Upper School students may also become involved in the National Honor Society; the Junior Classical League; the dance company; Amnesty International; the yearbook or newspaper staff; band; debate team; the Spanish, French, and Latin clubs; Community Service Council; or the literary magazine staff.

DAILY LIFE
Students in Beginning School full-day programs and Lower School grades begin their school day at 8:30 a.m.; classes end at 3:15 p.m. Middle School students begin their day at 8:20 a.m. and are released at 3:20 p.m. Several extracurricular activities are planned beginning at 7:30 a.m. before class and after the classroom day ends.

Upper School period 1 starts at 8:15 a.m. and classes continue through 3:30 p.m. There are six 45-minute academic periods, and one 70-minute block at the end of each day is set aside for competitive athletic team practices and games, performing arts and fine arts classes, and other student activity classes. Each morning, there is a 20-minute period for assemblies and/or class meetings. Some athletic team practices and fine arts rehearsals also take place after school.

SUMMER PROGRAMS
RHSM established a summer program in 1983. Academic courses (remediation, enrichment, and advancement), sports, and computer instruction programs are offered and held on the Lincoln Street campus for RHSM Upper School students and high school students from other schools. Approximately 40 students enroll. An additional fee is charged for Summer School programs. RHSM also conducts a summer day camp, SummerWorks, for children of preschool and elementary school ages.

COSTS AND FINANCIAL AID
The cost of tuition for full-day programs for the 2005–06 school year ranges from $10,175 (4 PreK) to $13,805 (grade 12). A bundled billing fee of approximately $500 per year covers laboratory and other expenses for Middle and Upper School students. The school lunch program and transportation are available for an additional fee.

Rowland Hall–St. Mark's School offers financial aid to applicants whose families demonstrate financial need in grades 1 through 12. The financial aid application deadline is March 1. Approximately 18 percent of the student body currently receive some degree of financial aid. Financial aid decisions are made in the spring for the following year. For the 2005–06 school year, grants totaling more than $1.4 million were made to students in amounts ranging from $1000 to $13,805.

ADMISSIONS INFORMATION
Rowland Hall–St. Mark's School does not discriminate on the basis of race, religion, color, national or ethnic origin, sexual orientation, or gender in the administration of any of its programs. The admissions committee seeks motivated students who will be challenged by academic excellence and will thrive in an atmosphere of respect and concern for the individual. Applicants are required to submit an application, applicant questionnaire (grades 6 through 12), copies of school records, a current transcript or report card, and two teacher recommendations. It is also recommended that the applicant visit the School and complete a personal interview. Standardized tests are administered to applicants for grades 6 through 12. Individual assessments are required for those children applying to 2 preK to fifth grade. Previous testing information may also be required. If the child is of preschool age and has not attended school, recommendations are required from persons who know the applicant well and who have seen them in social situations.

APPLICATION TIMETABLE
Inquiries are welcome year-round. Tours and interviews are given Monday through Friday by appointment. Two admission open house events are offered in the fall and in January. Admissions applications are accepted on a rolling basis for the current year when space is available. The application deadline is March 1 for fall admission for the following year. A $50 nonrefundable fee is due with the application.

ADMISSIONS CORRESPONDENCE
Beginning School and Lower School (2 preK–
 grade 5)
Kathy Gundersen, Director of Admissions
Rowland Hall–St. Mark's School
720 Guardsman Way
Salt Lake City, Utah 84108

Phone: 801-355-7485
Fax: 801-363-5521
E-mail: kathygundersen@rowland-hall.org

Middle School and Upper School (grades 6–12)
Karen Hyde, Director of Admissions
Rowland Hall–St. Mark's School
843 South Lincoln Street
Salt Lake City, Utah 84102

Phone: 801-355-7494
Fax: 801-355-0474
E-mail: karenhyde@rowland-hall.org
Web site: http://www.rhsm.org

RYE COUNTRY DAY SCHOOL

Rye, New York

Type: Coeducational day college-preparatory school
Grades: P–12: Lower School, Prekindergarten–4; Middle School, 5–8; Upper School, 9–12
Enrollment: School total: 849; Upper School: 369
Head of School: Scott A. Nelson, Headmaster

THE SCHOOL

Founded in 1869, Rye Country Day School (RCDS) is entering its 136th year. Reflecting and reaffirming the School's purposes, the mission statement states, "Rye Country Day School is a coeducational, college preparatory school dedicated to providing students from Pre-Kindergarten through Grade Twelve with an excellent education using both traditional and innovative approaches. In a nurturing and supportive environment, we offer a challenging program that stimulates individuals to achieve their maximum potential through academic, athletic, creative, and social endeavors. We value diversity, expect moral responsibility, and promote strength of character within a respectful school community. Our goal is to foster a lifelong passion for knowledge, understanding, and service."

The 26-acre campus is located in Rye at the junction of routes I-95 and I-287, one block from the train station. The School's location, 25 miles from Manhattan, provides easy access to both New York City and to a suburban setting with ample playing fields and open spaces. Through frequent field trips, internships, and community service projects, the School takes considerable advantage of the cultural opportunities in the New York metropolitan area.

A nonprofit, nonsectarian institution, Rye Country Day is governed by a 24-member Board of Trustees that includes parents and alumni. The annual operating budget is $18.4 million, and the physical plant assets have a book value in excess of $43 million. Annual gifts from parents, alumni, and friends amount to more than $2.7 million. The endowment of the School is valued at $14 million.

Rye Country Day School is accredited by the Middle States Association of Colleges and Schools and the New York State Association of Independent Schools and is chartered and registered by the New York State Board of Regents. It is a member of the National Association of Independent Schools, the New York State Association of Independent Schools, the Educational Records Bureau, the College Board, and the National Association for College Admission Counseling.

ACADEMIC PROGRAMS

Leading to the college-preparatory program of the Upper School, the program in the Middle School (grades 5–8) emphasizes the development of skills and the acquisition of information needed for success at the secondary school level by exposing students to a wide range of opportunities. The academic program is fully departmentalized. French or Latin is taken by all fifth graders, and French, Spanish, or Latin is studied in grades 6, 7, and 8. The math, foreign language, and writing programs lead directly into

the Upper School curriculum. Programs in art, music (vocal and instrumental), computer use, and dramatics are offered in all grades. Students in these grades are scheduled for sports for 45 to 75 minutes daily, and a full interscholastic sports program is available to both boys and girls in grades 7 and 8. The instructional class size averages 15.

Sixteen courses are required for Upper School graduation, including 4 years of English, 3 years of mathematics, 3 years of one foreign language, 2 years of science, and 2 years of history. Students entering the School by grade 9 must complete ½ unit in art and music survey, and ½ unit in performance in the arts. Seniors must successfully complete an off-campus June-term community service program. In addition, seniors must satisfactorily complete 1 unit in the senior interdisciplinary humanities seminar. Students are expected to carry five academic courses per year.

Full-year courses and semester electives in English include English 9, 10, and 11; major American writers; English literature; creative writing; Shakespeare; and the short story. Required mathematics courses are algebra I, algebra II, and geometry. Regular course work extends through calculus BC, and tutorials are available for more advanced students. Yearlong courses in science are conceptual physics, environmental science, biology, chemistry, and physics. Science courses are laboratory based. The computer department offers beginning and advanced programming, software applications courses, desktop publishing, and independent study opportunities.

The modern language department offers five years of French and Spanish, and the classics department teaches five years of Latin and three years of Greek. History courses include world civilization, U.S. history, government, and modern European history. Semester electives in the humanities include philosophy, psychology, government, economics, and the twentieth century.

In the arts, full-year courses in studio art, art history, and music theory are available. Participation in the Concert Choir and Wind Ensemble earns students full academic credit. Semester courses in drawing, printmaking, sculpture, graphic design, ceramics, and photography are available. The drama department offers electives in technique, history, oral presentation, and technical theater.

Advanced Placement courses leading to the AP examinations are offered in biology, psychology, environmental science, chemistry, physics, calculus, English, government, U.S. and modern European history, French, Spanish, Latin, music, art, and computer science. Honors sections are scheduled in tenth- and eleventh-grade English, math, physics, biology, chemistry, and history and in foreign languages at all levels. Independent study is available in grades 11 and 12 in all disciplines.

The student-teacher ratio is 8:1, and the average class size in the Upper School is 12. Extra help is provided for students as needed.

The year is divided into two semesters. Examinations are given in March. Grades are scaled from A to F and are given four times a year. Written comments accompany grades at the end of each semester.

Academic classes travel to New York City and other areas to supplement classroom work. Although not a graduation requirement, all students are involved in community service programs. Semester class projects as well as individual experiences involve work with local charities and schools, YMCA, Habitat for Humanity, Midnight Run, United Cerebral Palsy, Big Brother-Big Sister, Doctors Without Borders, and AmeriCares.

FACULTY AND ADVISERS

The Upper School faculty consists of 60 full-time teachers—32 men and 28 women, the large majority of whom hold at least one advanced degree. The average length of service is eight years, and annual faculty turnover averages fewer than 6 teachers.

Scott A. Nelson became Headmaster in 1993. He holds a B.A. from Brown and an M.A. from Fordham. Prior to his appointment at Rye, he served as Upper School Director both at the Marlborough School in Los Angeles and at the Hackley School in Tarrytown, New York. Mr. Nelson and his family reside on campus.

Nearly all faculty members serve as advisers for 5 to 10 students each. In addition to helping students select courses, faculty advisers monitor the students' progress in all areas of school life and provide ongoing support. The advisers also meet with students' parents at various times throughout the year.

Rye Country Day seeks faculty members who are effective teachers in their field and who, by virtue of their sincere interest in the students' overall well-being, will further the broad goals of the School's philosophy. The School supports the continuing education of its faculty through grants and summer sabbaticals totaling more than $175,000 a year. In addition, the School provides significant support for laptop computer acquisition by faculty members.

COLLEGE PLACEMENT

The college selection process is supervised by a full-time Director of College Counseling and an Assistant College Counselor. Advising is done on an individual basis, with the staff meeting with both students and their families. More than 150 college representatives visit the campus each year.

The 82 graduates of the class of 2005 enrolled in fifty colleges and universities, including Brown, Columbia, Duke, Harvard, Northwestern,

Princeton, Stanford, Tufts, Williams, Yale, and the University of Pennsylvania.

STUDENT BODY AND CONDUCT

The Upper School enrollment for 2005–06 totaled 369—198 boys and 171 girls. There were 88 students in grade 9, 98 in grade 10, 94 in grade 11, and 89 in grade 12. Members of minority groups represent 20 percent of the student body in grades 5–12. Students come from more than thirty-five different school districts in Westchester and Fairfield Counties as well as New York City. Students holding citizenship in thirteen countries are enrolled.

While School regulations are few, the School consciously and directly emphasizes a cooperative, responsible, and healthy community life. The Student Council plays a major role in administering School organizations and activities. Minor disciplinary problems are handled by the Upper School Principal and Grade Level Dean; more serious matters are brought before the Disciplinary Committee. There is student representation on the Academic Affairs and other major committees.

ACADEMIC FACILITIES

The main academic facility is the Mary Struthers Pinkham Building. Classes are also held in the Dunn Performing Arts Center and in the Main Building. Specific facilities include five science labs, a two-room Upper School computer center, seven music rehearsal and practice rooms, a two-story art studio, a darkroom, and a student publications center.

Opened in 1984, the Klingenstein Library contains more than 30,000 volumes, with circulation and collection management fully automated. Additional resources include significant periodical and reference materials available via direct online services and the Internet, CD-ROM, a substantial videotape collection, and other audiovisual and microfiche materials.

Significant improvements have been made to the interior campus areas over the last several years. The Edward B. Dunn Performing Arts Center, a $5-million facility containing a 400-seat theater-auditorium and classroom spaces for vocal music, instrumental music, and general use, was opened in 1990. A separate dance facility is adjacent. The School continues a consistent program of technological progress. Laptop computers are required of all students in grades 7 to 12 and are used extensively throughout the curriculum. Access to the School network and the Internet is via a wireless network. In total, there are more than 550 networked computers on campus, which play a continually increasing role in curricular and general campus life.

ATHLETICS

Rye's athletics program centers on interscholastic competition, with teams in most sports on both varsity and junior varsity levels. Representative varsity sports are baseball, basketball, cross-country, fencing, field hockey, football, golf, ice hockey, lacrosse, soccer, softball, squash, tennis, and wrestling. Approximately 70 percent of the students participate in team sports. The physical education department offers classes in aerobic dancing, CPR, ice skating, kickboxing, tennis, and weight training. Athletics facilities include ample field space, two gymnasiums, and the Gerald N. LaGrange Fieldhouse (with an indoor ice rink/tennis courts, and locker facilities). In 2000, the Scott Nelson Athletic Center opened adjacent to the field house, housing two basketball courts, four squash courts, fitness facilities, and locker rooms.

EXTRACURRICULAR OPPORTUNITIES

More than thirty-five extracurricular activities are available. Students can choose vocal music (Concert Choir, Madrigal Singers, and solfeggio classes) and instrumental music (Wind Ensemble, Concert Band, and Jazz Band). Many of these offerings have curricular status. The performance groups give local concerts and occasionally travel to perform at schools and universities here and abroad. In addition, 10 professional instructors offer private instrumental and voice lessons during the school day. The drama department presents major productions three times a year.

Student publications include a yearbook, newspaper, literary magazine, and public affairs journal, each of which is composed using student publications desktop publishing facilities. The School's Web site (http://www.rcds.rye.ny.us) is an ever-changing location for student- and staff-provided information on and perspectives of the School. Students participate in Model Congress programs on campus and at other schools and colleges. The School has a dynamic community service program that embodies the RCDS motto: "Not for self, but for service." Students also participate in many other activities and School organizations, including foreign language, mock trial, debate, theater, sports, and computer clubs.

DAILY LIFE

Beginning each day at 8:05, the Upper School utilizes a six-day schedule cycle. Most courses meet five of the six days, with one or two longer, 70-minute periods per cycle. The day includes an activity/meeting period and two lunch periods as well as seven class periods. Class periods end at 2:50, and team sport practices and games begin at 3:30. Breakfast and lunch may be purchased in the school dining room; seniors may have lunch off campus. Study halls are required for grade 9.

SUMMER PROGRAMS

The Rye Country Day Summer School enrolls more than 200 students—grades 6 to postgraduate—in remedial, enrichment, and advanced-standing courses. New York State Regents exams are given in appropriate subjects. The program is six weeks long and runs on a five-period schedule from 8 a.m. to noon, Monday through Friday. Tuition averages $800 per course. A brochure is available after April 1 from the Director of the Summer School or on the School's Web site.

In addition to the Summer School, Rye conducts a summer Academic Action program for students in grades 6–8 from nearby Westchester communities. Fifty students from minority groups enroll in a four-week program that emphasizes academic enrichment in the areas of writing, math, and computer use.

COSTS AND FINANCIAL AID

Tuition for grade 9 for 2005–06 was $24,100. Additional charges were made for textbooks, lunches, sports, field trips, and private music lessons, as appropriate.

Tuition aid is available on a need basis. For 2005–06, 102 students received a total of more than $2.1 million in aid. All aid applications are processed through the School and Student Service for Financial Aid.

ADMISSIONS INFORMATION

Students are accepted in all grades. In 2005–06, 27 new students enrolled in the ninth grade, 14 in the tenth grade, and 6 in the eleventh grade. Academic readiness is a prerequisite; a diversity of skills and interests, as well as general academic aptitude, is eagerly sought. The School seeks and enrolls students of all backgrounds; a diverse student body is an important part of the School's educational environment.

Required in the admissions process are the results of the Educational Records Bureau ISEE or the Secondary School Admission Test; the student's school record; and school and faculty recommendations. A visit to the campus and an interview are also required.

APPLICATION TIMETABLE

Inquiries are welcome throughout the year. Interviews and tours of the campus begin in late September. To be considered in initial admissions decisions, applicants must fully complete the application by January 31. Candidates whose applications are complete by that date are notified by approximately February 15. Applications received after February 1 are evaluated on a rolling basis.

ADMISSIONS CORRESPONDENCE

Matthew J. M. Suzuki, Director of Admissions
Rye Country Day School
Cedar Street
Rye, New York 10580-2034

Phone: 914-925-4519
Fax: 914-921-2147
E-mail: matt_suzuki@rcds.rye.ny.us
Web site: http://www.rcds.rye.ny.us

ST. ANDREW'S SCHOOL

Barrington, Rhode Island

Type: Coeducational boarding and day college-preparatory school
Grades: 6–12: Middle School, 6–8; Upper School and Boarding, 9–12
Enrollment: School total: 206; Upper School: 167
Head of School: John D. Martin

THE SCHOOL

St. Andrew's School is a coeducational boarding and day school for students in grades 6–12. The School is located on an 83-acre campus 1 mile from the center of Barrington (population 16,000), a suburban community 10 miles southeast of Providence on Narragansett Bay. The campus contains open space and woodlands. Its proximity to Providence and Newport, Rhode Island, as well as Boston, offers a wide variety of cultural opportunities for students.

St. Andrew's School was founded in 1893 by Rev. William Merrick Chapin as a school for homeless boys. From these simple beginnings through its years as a working farm school to its present role as a coeducational boarding and day school, St. Andrew's steadfastly maintains the same sense of purpose and concern for the individual. The curriculum is designed primarily to prepare students for college, with emphasis on helping them to develop stronger academic skills, study habits, and self-esteem.

St. Andrew's was named an "Exemplary School" by learning expert Dr. Mel Levine. Dr. Levine's twenty-five years of research on learning and his groundbreaking program, Schools Attuned, are the backbone of the faculty's classroom methodology. Every St. Andrew's teacher is trained to teach using a multisensory approach for the different ways students may learn. St. Andrew's students find that when they get to college, they are well prepared to handle the course work because they have an understanding of how they learn best and the tools they need to do their best.

St. Andrew's School is a nonsectarian, nonprofit corporation. A Board of Trustees governs the School; this 21-member board meets five times a year. The School's physical plant is valued at approximately $27 million. The School's endowment is currently valued at more than $14 million.

St. Andrew's is accredited by the New England Association of Schools and Colleges. It is a member of the National Association of Independent Schools, the Association of Independent Schools in New England, and the Independent Schools Association of Rhode Island.

ACADEMIC PROGRAMS

St. Andrew's School believes that every student can find success in the classroom. With a 5:1 student-teacher ratio, the average class size at St. Andrew's is 10 to 12 students. Small classes, along with twice-daily adviser meetings, help to ensure that no student is overlooked. The homelike community, nurturing environment, and hands-on approach to learning and teaching help maintain close student-teacher relationships.

To graduate from the Upper School, a student must complete 26 credits: 24 academic credits and 2 credits in physical education. Students are expected to take course work in English, math, science, social studies, and physical education each year. Preparation in a foreign language is also highly recommended. Students may only take one study hall in their schedule. Seniors must pass the equivalent of five full-credit courses in order to graduate.

Specific minimum requirements are 4 credits in English, 3 credits in social studies (including 1 in U.S. history), 3 credits in mathematics, 3 credits in science (including 2 in a lab science), 2 credits in physical education, and 1 credit in art. Additional courses include multicultural literature, literature and writing, calculus, Advanced Placement calculus, environmental science, human physiology and anatomy, oceanography, Spanish, computer skills, study skills, art, music, and theater. An English as a second language (ESL) program is provided for international students. The School's computer network, which is available to all students, provides Internet access from all classrooms, dorm rooms, and offices.

The School's Resource Program (certified by the state of Rhode Island) for students with mild language learning disabilities is taught by certified special education teachers. All students enrolled in the Resource Program take a mainstreamed college-preparatory course of study. An Individual Education Plan (IEP) identifies which language remediation skills need to be addressed. Resource teachers work collaboratively with regular classroom teachers to develop and integrate school study skills (time management, test taking, outlining, etc.) into the existing Upper School curriculum. Middle School students receive their remediation skills during their regular language arts classes. An IEP identifies which language remediation skills need to be addressed in the Resource class. Additional programs include Focus (extra support and monitoring for attention difficulties), speech/language therapy, and the Wilson Reading System.

The school year runs on a semester basis. Students are evaluated more frequently by their teachers so that each student's progress is monitored closely throughout the year. Each advisee meets twice a day with his or her adviser to discuss issues pertaining to the student's academic progress and his or her involvement in the School community. Advisers communicate with families every three weeks by phone or e-mail.

FACULTY AND ADVISERS

The full-time faculty numbers 43: 17 men and 26 women. Eighteen reside on campus, 7 with their families. All full-time faculty members serve as advisers. John D. Martin was appointed Head of School on July 1, 1996, and has an extensive background in independent schools, including teaching and administrative positions at Sewickley Academy, Peddie School, and Tabor Academy. He holds a Master of Divinity degree from Yale University, a Master of Education degree from American International College, and a Bachelor of Arts degree from Tufts University.

COLLEGE PLACEMENT

More than 95 percent of St. Andrew's graduates enter four-year colleges, two-year colleges, or technical schools upon graduation each year. Goal setting, short- and long-term planning, and informal discussions about careers and postsecondary plans are ongoing between students and advisers from the moment a student enters the Upper School.

Formal college counseling begins in the tenth grade. The college counselor works with students and their parents to assist in determining the next steps that are best for each student. The adviser and other faculty members assist the college counselor in assessing each student's options. PSATs are given in the fall of the sophomore year and again in the junior year. SATs should be taken during the junior and senior years. College representatives visit the campus to meet with students.

St. Andrew's graduates have attended the following colleges and universities in the last three years: Curry, Drew, Emmanuel, Emory, New England College, Parsons School of Design, Pratt, Providence, Rensselaer, Rhode Island College, Savannah College of Art and Design, Simmons, Syracuse, and the Universities of Massachusetts, Rhode Island, Southern California, Vermont, and Wisconsin.

STUDENT BODY AND CONDUCT

The School enrolls both boarding and day students. More than one third of the Upper School population boards. Almost 20 percent of the School's population is enrolled in the Middle School, and 40 percent of the School's population participates in the Resource/Focus Programs.

Over the years, St. Andrew's School has attracted boarding students from all corners of the United States and several other countries, including Germany, Jamaica, Bermuda, Japan, and South Korea.

Each student receives a copy of the *Student Handbook,* which defines expectations for students within the community. Difficulties, if they arise, are handled according to degree; minor issues are handled by teachers and dorm parents, while major offenses are handled by the Director of Student Life in conjunction with a joint student-faculty disciplinary committee. Faculty advisers play a major role in working with students to help them understand the expectations of them as members of the community.

ACADEMIC FACILITIES

Stone Academic Center (1988) houses fifteen classrooms, a newly renovated resource wing with five rooms for instruction, a computer lab, academic offices, and a faculty workroom. It is also the site of a new library, which features study carrels, meeting rooms, and computer workstations. Hardy Hall (1898) was renovated in 2002 and houses the Middle School in small classrooms that are designed for interactive learning in groups of 10 to 12 students. The George M. Sage Gymnasium (2001) and the Karl P. Jones Gymnasium (1965) each house a full-size gymnasium and locker room facilities. The Annie Lee Steele Adams Memorial Student Service Center (1997) houses the Health Center, classrooms, and additional office space. The David A. Brown '52 Science Center houses four science labs and two regular classrooms. The Norman E. and Dorothy R. McCulloch Center for the Arts (2004) houses a 287-seat theater, two visual art classrooms, a music room with practice rooms, a black-

box/theater classroom, a computer graphics lab, and storage and scene construction facilities for drama productions.

BOARDING AND GENERAL FACILITIES
Upper School girls live in Cady House (1969). Upper School boys live in Bill's House (1970), Perry Hall (1927), and Coleman House (circa 1795). Girls are all assigned to single rooms, while boys are assigned to single or double rooms. Each dormitory is supervised by faculty houseparents, who are aided by the Director of Student Life. Each dorm has a common room, laundry facilities, access to a kitchen area, and ample storage space. Gardiner Hall (1926) houses the Herbert W. Spink Dining Room and the Headmaster's dining room. McVickar Hall (1913) contains the admissions office, the Headmaster's office, the development and communications department, and a reception area. Peck Hall (circa 1895) contains the business office (1993). Clark Hall (1899), which was once a library, dormitory, and classroom building, now houses the Student Center, offering students variety, entertainment, and relaxation. The second floor provides faculty housing.

Coleman House and the Rectory, the Headmaster's house, are late-eighteenth-century buildings that were acquired by the School from two local estates. Both buildings are said to have been stops for travelers on the Underground Railroad. The Rectory has a "hidden" back staircase and room.

ATHLETICS
Upper School students participate in athletics at the completion of each class day. St. Andrew's fields varsity teams in boys' basketball, cross-country, golf, lacrosse, soccer, and tennis and girls' basketball, cross-country, lacrosse, soccer, and tennis. Examples of activities offered as part of the intramural sports program are fitness training, weight training, kayaking, biking, lawn games, and Project Adventure Ropes Course.

EXTRACURRICULAR OPPORTUNITIES
Because of the School's proximity to Providence, Newport, and Boston, a wide range of cultural and recreational activities is available. Students may take advantage of museums, movies, concerts, plays, rock climbing, skating, bowling, skiing, and professional and collegiate sporting events. The School's ski club goes skiing over one long weekend in January. Among the on-campus extracurricular activities are theater, cooking club, photography, and yearbook. The St. Andrew's Parent Association (SAPA) organizes a wide variety of social activities for students throughout the year, from dances to laser tag to a canoe carnival to barbecues on the Quad.

DAILY LIFE
Boarders generally rise at about 7 each morning. Boarding students are responsible for making their beds, cleaning their rooms, and performing other assorted dorm chores. Breakfast is served at 7:30 and is a favorite gathering spot for day and boarding students. Students meet in advising groups at 8 and then proceed to Morning Meeting, a daily event that is run by students. Classes begin at 8:40. Adviser meetings are held again at the end of the day. Activities and athletics begin at 3:15 and run until approximately 4:15. Students may leave the campus between athletics and dinner if they are in good standing in the community. Dinner is at 5:30, and evening study hall is from 7:30 to 9:30. All study halls are proctored by faculty members, who are able to provide extra academic assistance if needed. During study hall, the library is open for those students who need to conduct research.

The Student Center is open on weekdays from 10 to 1. On weekends, the center is open all day Saturday and at other times depending on activities both on and off campus.

WEEKEND LIFE
Weekend activities are planned by the Director of Student Life, with student and faculty input. Students choose from an array of on- and off-campus activities, including sporting events, concerts, movies, and plays; hayrides; open gymnasium; riding; skiing; attending performances by special guests on campus; dances; skating; festivals and fairs; hiking; and shopping. Visits to nearby cities and other places of interest are also offered. Boarders may leave for the weekend, either to go home or to visit a day student's family. Each weekend, about 75 percent of the boarding community remains on campus.

COSTS AND FINANCIAL AID
Tuition for a boarder in 2005–06 was $33,600; for a day student, it was $21,075. Additional costs for the Resource and Focus Programs were $8325. The yearly book fee is about $400. Parents of a boarding student should plan to set up an account in the on-campus bank for weekly allowance needs. The amount varies from family to family and student to student.

Approximately 40 percent of the student body received financial aid for the 2005–06 academic year, with more than $1 million offered in grants and loans. Financial aid is based solely on need. St. Andrew's School is affiliated with the School and Student Service for Financial Aid in Princeton, New Jersey, and works in conjunction with this organization to provide an objective and fair basis for awarding financial aid. All required information is due to the School by February 15. Final awards are determined by the School's Financial Aid Committee.

ADMISSIONS INFORMATION
In order to assess the match between student and school and to plan an appropriate academic program, the School requires a tour, a personal interview, an application with a fee of $50 ($100 for students outside the U.S. to cover mailing/faxing costs), a current transcript covering the last three years, three teacher recommendations, and standardized test scores. For applicants to the Resource Program, an educational evaluation, a psychological evaluation, the results of a recent Test of Written Language–Version 3 (all within eighteen months), and a current Individualized Education Plan (if applicable) are required. A student applying to the Focus Program must establish a history of attention difficulties and supply the School with a medical diagnosis from a physician and appropriate testing results. There is additional information required as part of the admissions process for international students.

APPLICATION TIMETABLE
Parents and prospective students who are interested in admission to St. Andrew's School are encouraged to contact the Admissions Office (e-mail: inquiry@standrews-ri.org) for information during the fall semester. Because the School considers a visit to the campus and a personal interview with the candidate to be such a critical part of the admissions process, it asks that all families call for an appointment. It is best to visit the School during the fall or by February 1 if considering enrollment for September, although the School welcomes campus visitors throughout the year.

St. Andrew's School does not discriminate on the basis of race, creed, gender, or handicap in the administration of policies, practices, and procedures.

Applications are due by February 3. Students are notified of acceptance by March 10, and the School holds a place for accepted students until April 10. Depending on space available, rolling admission may be offered thereafter. A nonrefundable deposit of $1000 is due when students agree to matriculate and is credited toward tuition.

ADMISSIONS CORRESPONDENCE
R. Scott Telford
Director of Admissions
St. Andrew's School
63 Federal Road
Barrington, Rhode Island 02806

Phone: 401-246-1230
Fax: 401-246-0510
E-mail: inquiry@standrews-ri.org
Web site: http://www.standrews-ri.org

Type: Coeducational, boarding (grades 9–12) and day, college-preparatory school
Grades: 7–12: Middle School, 7–8; Upper School, 9–12
Enrollment: School total: 242; Middle School: 53; Upper School: 189
Head of School: Rev. William S. Wade

THE SCHOOL

With a history going back to 1868, St. Andrew's–Sewanee School (SAS) enters the twenty-first century as a dynamic learning community guided by the traditions of the Episcopal Church. Students grow personally and intellectually under the guidance of a faculty committed to caring for each student as an individual.

The School has a unique relationship with the nearby University of the South, which is consistently rated one of the top liberal arts colleges in the United States by *U.S. News and World Report.* SAS students attend university cultural events, lectures, and use university facilities; qualified students take college courses for credit in their junior and senior years.

The 550-acre campus is located on the Cumberland Plateau, a region of incredible natural beauty. SAS offers its students a wealth of outdoor recreation experiences, including caving, hiking, mountain biking, rock climbing, and kayaking. At an elevation of 2,100 feet, summers are mild and winters provide an occasional snowfall. St. Andrew's–Sewanee School is also within convenient distance of all the urban offerings in Chattanooga, Nashville, Atlanta, and Birmingham.

St. Andrew's–Sewanee is incorporated as a not-for-profit school and is led by an 18-member Board of Trustees that is appointed by the School, the University of the South, and the Episcopal Dioceses of Tennessee. Assets include a physical plant valued at $24 million and an endowment of $8.8 million. The School is fully accredited by the Southern Association of Colleges and Schools (SACS) and holds membership in the National Association of Independent Schools (NAIS), the National Association of Episcopal Schools (NAES), the Tennessee Association of Independent Schools (TAIS), and the Association of Boarding Schools (TABS). The School is also a founding member of the Southeastern Association of Boarding Schools (SABS).

ACADEMIC PROGRAMS

A member of the Coalition of Essential Schools, St. Andrew's–Sewanee School provides its students with the intellectual tools and character development necessary for lifelong success. Students are taught to take increasing responsibility for their actions as they meet academic challenges via a multidisciplinary, hands-on teaching environment. Class size ranges from 8 to 16 and the student-faculty ratio is 7:1.

SAS prepares students for the demands of college and life through a rigorous academic program that focuses on critical thinking and advanced writing. The core curriculum emphasizes English, history, mathematics, science, foreign language, and the arts. Classes focus on active learning in which teachers are facilitators and students seek answers to complex questions through experiments, demonstrations, and field trips. Writing skills are emphasized and multiple-choice testing is rarely, if ever, utilized.

Basic requirements for graduation include 4 years of English, 3 years of mathematics, 3 years of history, 2 years of a foreign language, 2 years of science, 1 year of arts, senior religion (a highly academic course focusing on student research in the great ethical traditions), and life issues (ninth grade). Traditionally, students go well beyond fulfilling minimum requirements as they partake of the many elective courses offered, which include environmental science, the study of political ideology, the history of America's civil rights movement, theater, and a multitude of independent advanced-study opportunities.

Science at SAS is lab- and field-based, which allows students to truly experience science rather than merely study its theories. In the arts, students have the opportunity to take advanced courses in all disciplines. Art, music, pottery, and theater may be taken for academic credit.

The academic year is divided into semesters, and grade reports are sent to parents six times a year. The grading scale is A–F. Students whose grades require it must attend supervised study hall during the day. Residential students have mandatory evening study hours. A tutorial period is built in every student's weekday schedule. SAS also offers a Tutoring Center for students who face extra challenges in a given subject area.

FACULTY AND ADVISERS

The Reverend William S. Wade, Head of School, was appointed in 1981. Fr. Wade received his B.A. from the University of the South and his M.Div. from Virginia Theological Seminary. He also received an honorary doctoral degree from the University of the South in 1989. He is a past President of the National Association of Episcopal Schools (1988–90).

Fr. Wade leads an experienced faculty of 49 members, 21 of whom live on campus. All SAS faculty members have bachelor's degrees; 27 hold master's degrees and 3 hold doctoral degrees. SAS teachers receive substantial support for faculty education and enrichment.

The Adviser System provides an added layer of family-style structure for students in a setting known for the strength of its faculty-student relationships. Each adviser monitors academic and social progress of between 4 to 8 students via personal talks, formal meetings, and updates by other teachers. Such one-on-one contact fosters a relationship that is based upon mutual trust and respect. Regular communication with parents is provided as an integral part of the adviser's role as St. Andrew's–Sewanee School considers the parent's involvement with and encouragement of the student to be crucial to a successful education.

COLLEGE PLACEMENT

St. Andrew's–Sewanee School places its students at colleges that are appropriate for their interests and needs. The full-time College Counselor works closely with students and parents beginning in the middle of the junior year. More than forty colleges and universities visit the campus each year, offering students the opportunity to attend information sessions and to interview by appointment. Students also attend national college fairs. Testing required by colleges begins in the sophomore year with the PSAT and is followed by the SAT and/or the ACT in the junior and senior years. Typically, 99 percent of graduating students enroll in four-year colleges and universities, and 66 percent are accepted by their first-choice colleges.

In 2005, 44 SAS graduating seniors were accepted into ninety-seven different colleges and universities and received merit-based and leadership scholarships worth $1.7 million. SAS students are attending such institutions as the Art Institute of Chicago, Brown, Bryn Mawr, Carnegie-Mellon, Cornell, Davidson, Harvard, Northwestern, Notre Dame, Rhodes, Vanderbilt, Wellesley, Yale, and the Universities of the South and Tennessee.

STUDENT BODY AND CONDUCT

The Upper School traditionally numbers 200 students, evenly divided between boarding and day. In 2005–06, students enrolled from seventeen states and had citizenship in eleven countries.

All members of the St. Andrew's–Sewanee community are expected to live by the Honor Code and other rules which provide structure and support for the whole community. Student proctors are present in each house and offer leadership and support for the entire school.

ACADEMIC FACILITIES

Bishop Bratton Hall and Simmonds Hall are the academic buildings on campus. In addition to classroom space, these buildings house the School's Computer Lab, Science Wing, Art Gallery, James Agee Memorial Library, and the Art Department.

The James Agee Memorial Library, named for alumnus James Agee, Pulitzer Prize–winning author and screenwriter, houses 35,000 volumes. In addition, the SAS library is cataloged with that of the University of the South and students may draw on the University's vast library resources. The SAS library also offers electronic research resources such as LexisNexis and ProQuest.

Natural light fills the visual arts studios, which are centrally located in Simmonds Hall. In

the spacious graphic arts studio, students work with drawing, painting, and printmaking techniques. Computer graphics is also taught. The adjoining Art Gallery provides exhibition space for the dynamic Visiting Artist Program as well as student exhibitions. New art is put on display each month during the school year.

The SAS clay facility, one of the finest in the region, includes sixteen wheels, a slab roller, and an extruder. Five kilns offer a wide range of firing techniques. Wheel-turning, slab-building, and hand-building are taught.

Located in a stand-alone building reminiscent of an off-Broadway theater, the SAS Theatre provides workspace for both acting and technical theater training for students. SAS students star in three major productions each year, one of which is always a musical. The theater program receives strong student and community support and several SAS students have gone on to successful acting careers.

St. Andrew's–Sewanee School offers a dynamic music program which includes three choruses, a stage band, and an orchestra as well as a variety of smaller ensembles. Private music lessons are available for an extra fee. More advanced music students are often invited to join the University of the South symphony orchestra.

BOARDING AND GENERAL FACILITIES
In the School's innovative Residential House system, boarding students live in residential houses where a faculty family resides as houseparents and a "family" of 12 to 15 students create a second home. Student proctors, chosen for their character and achievement, also assist in running each house. All houses have been built or renovated in the last five years and have porches with rockers. Each features a common room where microwaves, comfortable couches, televisions, and VCRs are available for use during recreational hours. All student rooms are equipped with two student phone lines and two T1 high-speed lines for Internet access. The Owen Student Union serves as the central meeting point for day and boarding student activities. Drinks and snack foods are sold in the Union and there is a small store where items such as school clothing, notebooks, and pens are available.

The Robinson Dining Hall serves three meals a day, and each meal features several hot entrée choices. Deli and grilled sandwiches, soups, and a salad bar are also offered. A vegetarian dish is served at all meals.

ATHLETICS
Participation in athletics is considered an integral component of SAS. The School offers eleven interscholastic sports, including baseball, basketball, cross-country, football, golf, soccer, swimming, tennis, track, volleyball, and wrestling. There are twenty-two teams at various levels, including separate teams for the junior varsity and Middle School.

The newly renovated Wood-Alligood Gymnasium has facilities for basketball, wrestling, weight training, volleyball, and gym classes. A six-lane all-weather track surrounds the varsity game field. In addition to a baseball diamond, St. Andrew's–Sewanee School offers six new tennis courts and many running, mountain biking, and hiking trails on the 550-acre campus.

EXTRACURRICULAR OPPORTUNITIES
The Afternoon Program provides students with options such as athletics, aerobics, community outreach, horseback riding, music, theater, weight training, yearbook, and the Outdoor Adventure Program, which makes full use of the caves, forest, bluffs, and streams of the mountain. Programs require between 6 and 12 hours each week for the duration of the twelve-week Afternoon Program term. Most students choose to participate in a program every term. Students must complete requirements in three areas—physical activity, general participation, and community service.

Many lectures and cultural events are offered at the University of the South as well as in Chattanooga and Nashville. The faculty members regularly sponsor trips to concerts, art exhibits, plays, and lectures.

DAILY LIFE
Classes are held Monday–Friday. The schedule varies daily and classes, which range in length from 45 to 90 minutes, are held three to four days a week. The Afternoon Program runs from 3:30 to 5:30. Study hours are required Sunday–Thursday from 8 to 10 p.m.

WEEKEND LIFE
SAS offers an exciting variety of activities throughout the year, including dances and movies as well as trips to museums, malls, and restaurants in Nashville and Chattanooga. Outdoor activities include caving, canoeing, and camping trips. Mountain biking is popular on campus trails.

COSTS AND FINANCIAL AID
The 2005–06 tuition for boarders was $30,825 and $12,420 for day students. There are additional fees for items such as books and allowances.

SAS offers merit scholarships, The Claiborne Scholars Program, as well as financial aid determined on the basis of demonstrated need. Since there is a limit to the amount available, early application is highly recommended. Determination of eligibility for need-based assistance is made via the School and Student Service for Financial Aid (SSS). Completion and official evaluation of the Parent Financial Statement (PFS) and other requisite forms are required. For the academic year 2005–06, students received more than $1.2 million in merit scholarships and need-based financial aid.

ADMISSIONS INFORMATION
SAS seeks a geographically, racially, socially, ethnically, and economically diverse student body. Admission is based upon a student's ability as demonstrated through past performance, academic records, testing, character, maturity, and potential as a member of the School community. A personal interview, academic records, letters of recommendation, and standardized test scores are required for review by the Admissions Committee. Acceptable test scores include the SSAT, ISEE, SAT, and ACT. International students should take the TOEFL or SLEP.

APPLICATION TIMETABLE
Inquiries, as well as appointments for interviews and tours, may be made at any time of the year. Admission Office hours are Monday–Friday from 8 to 4:30 Central time. Applications are available by contacting the Admission Office. The application fee is $50 for U.S. students and $75 for international students.

ADMISSIONS CORRESPONDENCE
Jim Tucker, Director of Admission and
    Financial Aid
St. Andrew's–Sewanee School
290 Quintard Road
Sewanee, Tennessee 37375
Phone: 931-598-5651
      866-513-8290 (toll-free)
Fax: 931-968-0208
E-mail: admissions@sasweb.org
Web site: http://www.sasweb.org

ST. ANNE'S–BELFIELD SCHOOL

Charlottesville, Virginia

Type: Coeducational five- and seven-day boarding and day college-preparatory school
Grades: P–12: Lower School, Preschool–4; Middle School, 5–8; Upper School, 9–12
Enrollment: School total: 853; Upper School: 321
Head of School: Rev. George E. Conway, Headmaster

THE SCHOOL

St. Anne's–Belfield School was formed in 1970 by the merger of St. Anne's School, a girls' boarding school founded in 1910, with the Belfield School, a coeducational elementary school established in 1955. The School is located near the University of Virginia on two campuses that total almost 50 acres. All students attend a weekly nonsectarian chapel service. The School offers a day program for boys and girls in preschool through grade 12 and five- and seven-day boarding programs for boys and girls in grades 9–12.

St. Anne's–Belfield School has a strong academic orientation. Its primary goal is to provide a solid preparation for college with concern for the individual both as a student and as a person. Small classes facilitate this dedication to individual learning.

St. Anne's–Belfield is incorporated not-for-profit under a self-perpetuating Board of Trustees. Assets include a $16.1-million plant and an endowment of more than $2.8 million. The 2004–05 operating expenses were about $12.9 million. Annual Giving for 2004–05 was more than $1.35 million.

St. Anne's–Belfield is accredited by the Virginia Association of Independent Schools. Its memberships include the Cum Laude Society, the Council for Advancement and Support of Education, the National Association of Independent Schools, and the National Association of Episcopal Schools.

ACADEMIC PROGRAMS

In agreement with the School's philosophy that both a breadth and depth of knowledge are essential for true growth, all students at St. Anne's–Belfield are encouraged to attain excellence in a variety of subjects. The requirements for graduation are 8 semesters of English, 6 of mathematics, 6 of history and government, 6 of laboratory science, 6 of one foreign language, 2 of religion, 2 of fine arts, 60 hours of community service, and the successful completion of the freshman seminar.

Freshmen, sophomores, juniors, and seniors are required to take five academic courses each semester. A significant number of students elect to carry six academic courses. The School offers honors courses in physics and chemistry and Advanced Placement (AP) courses in English, calculus, European and U.S. history, physics, chemistry, biology, Latin, French language, French literature, environmental science, Spanish language, and statistics.

The School's calendar is arranged on a semester system. Interim reports are given quarterly, and more frequent comments are provided when deemed advisable. All teachers are available for extra help five mornings a week during office hours, and every student in grades 7–12 has an adviser. The average class size is 12 students; the overall student-faculty ratio is 7:8.

St. Anne's–Belfield offers a three-day SAT preparation course to all juniors. This course reviews basic math and English skills and acquaints students with the principles of good test taking.

All students in grades 9–12 are involved in the School's Community Service Program, which is designed to develop in students an awareness of their responsibilities to the School and the community and to broaden their education by encouraging involvement with those in need.

The School offers an ESL program to students in grades 9–10. These students, many of whom participate in a seven-day boarding program, take ESL courses that are designed to prepare them to be mainstreamed into the college-preparatory program by the eleventh grade. The School employs an ESL director and a teaching staff who oversee their academic progress as well as a dorm counselor who plans and supervises their weekend activities. There is no additional fee for ESL students. At present, thirteen countries are represented in the ESL program.

FACULTY AND ADVISERS

The St. Anne's–Belfield faculty and administration consists of 44 men and 76 women. In the Upper School, 76 percent of the faculty hold graduate degrees. In selecting its faculty, the School seeks people with scholarly commitment and enthusiasm who are willing to view themselves as counselors as well as teachers. Upper School faculty members serve as advisers to groups of 10 to 12 students. The adviser is responsible for guiding a student's overall academic and social progress and serves as an important link between parents and the School.

The Rev. George E. Conway, D.Min., was appointed Headmaster of St. Anne's–Belfield in 1982. Dr. Conway earned his undergraduate degree at Wilkes College and his graduate degrees at Princeton Theological Seminary and Boston University. He was formerly Director of Admissions and Counseling at Woodberry Forest School.

COLLEGE PLACEMENT

The principal counselor in the college selection process is the Director of College Counseling, who, along with her assistants, works personally with the students, parents, and college admissions officers. The Director of College Counseling helps students in the ninth through twelfth grades in selecting a suitable yet rigorous college-preparatory curriculum and arranges for a variety of SAT preparation programs. The median combined SAT I score for the class of 2005 was 1260. Sixty percent of students taking AP exams received a score of 4 or 5.

Recent graduates of St. Anne's–Belfield are currently attending a variety of colleges and universities, including Brown, Bryn Mawr, Columbia, Dartmouth, Davidson, Duke, Harvard, Middlebury, Notre Dame, Princeton, Rhode Island School

of Design, Smith, Vanderbilt, Wake Forest, Washington and Lee, William and Mary, Williams, Yale, and the Universities of California, Colorado, Michigan, North Carolina, and Virginia.

STUDENT BODY AND CONDUCT

The 2005–06 Upper School enrollment was as follows: grade 9, 84; grade 10, 81; grade 11, 81; and grade 12, 75. There were almost equal numbers of boys and girls.

Central to the School's philosophy of promoting personal integrity is the Honor Code. The code states simply: A student is not to lie, cheat, or steal. It is the intention of the Honor Code to create and preserve an environment in which honorable behavior is the standard for all conduct. It is a system in which each case is judged individually and a student is assumed to have acted honorably unless it has been proven otherwise. The Honor Code is a student tradition. It remains the responsibility of the students to ensure that honorable behavior is encouraged and nurtured and that dishonorable behavior is not tolerated. A student Honor Council is responsible for investigating possible honor violations and recommending appropriate measures to the Headmaster.

The honor system is a method of student self-government and is separated from School discipline, which is primarily the responsibility of the faculty and administration. While the Headmaster may, at his discretion, refer a discipline case to the Disciplinary Committee for investigation and recommendation, all final decisions involving disciplinary or honor violations are made by the Headmaster. The Disciplinary Committee is appointed by the Headmaster and comprises both students and faculty members.

ACADEMIC FACILITIES

Upper School classes are held primarily in Randolph Hall, which includes twenty-three classrooms, a 325-seat chapel/auditorium, a student union, and a library with more than 10,000 volumes and various audiovisual, CD-ROM, and Internet capabilities. The Fine Arts Center houses all art, drama, and music classes. It contains a ceramics studio, a studio for two-dimensional art, a drama studio, a veranda for stone carving, and music practice rooms in addition to space for all extracurricular activities. All Upper School science facilities are housed in a 38,045-square-foot academic building. The science wing of this building includes four laboratories, three classrooms, and a computer center with two IBM computer labs with Internet access. The lower level of this building houses the new Digital Media Center, which includes photography labs and a recording studio.

BOARDING AND GENERAL FACILITIES

The Lee-DuVal Building houses administrative offices as well as the renovated dining hall and board-

ing facilities. Students in the five-day boarding program live on campus during the academic week but are able to enjoy home life on the weekends. The students leave campus Friday afternoon or Saturday morning and return to the dorms either Sunday night or Monday morning. The seven-day boarders use their time on the weekends for study, leisure, and planned activities. Residential facilities include separate halls for the girls and boys and a shared lounge and study room. Two of the 5 dormitory parents for the residential students are faculty members. Day faculty members also join residential students for dinner on a regular basis. Enrollment is intentionally limited to 45 students in an effort to maintain the program's family atmosphere.

ATHLETICS

St. Anne's–Belfield offers an interscholastic athletics program for boys and girls. Boys' teams include football and soccer in the fall, basketball and wrestling in the winter, and lacrosse, tennis, baseball, and golf in the spring. Offerings for the girls include field hockey, soccer, tennis, and volleyball in the fall; basketball in the winter; and lacrosse and softball in the spring. In addition, a coeducational cross-country team is offered in the fall, indoor track and squash in the winter, and outdoor track in the spring; conditioning is offered all three seasons.

The philosophy of the program stresses participation, regardless of a student's previous experience or level of talent. The School's goal is to have each student participate in the interscholastic program during at least one season per year. More than 85 percent of the students participate in team sports.

St. Anne's–Belfield has two gymnasiums, a field house, a weight-training facility, a wrestling room, six tennis courts, six playing fields, and a practice field.

EXTRACURRICULAR OPPORTUNITIES

The extracurricular activities and organizations at St. Anne's–Belfield School enrich and supplement the students' academic experience. Traditions foster a sense of community and provide a historic continuity for the School. Upper School traditions include the Winter Ball, Senior Easter Egg Hunt, Prom, Class Night, Thanksgiving dinner, Thanksgiving Chapel, and Madame Day.

Clubs give students with a common interest an opportunity to meet in groups in order to expand that interest. The Upper School offers the Latin Club, International Relations Club, Environmental Club, Model OAS, Gold Key Society (student guides), Spanish Club, Mathematics Club, Transcendental Society, Student-Faculty Senate, Student Government, Martial Arts Movie Club, Art Forum, Academic Team, Amnesty International, Habitat for Humanity, and Ski Club.

Publications include *Saintly Speaking*, the School newspaper; *Saints and Sinners*, the yearbook; and *Oasis*, the literary magazine.

DAILY LIFE

Classes are held five days a week, from 8 a.m. to 3:30 p.m. Monday, Wednesday, and Thursday; from 8 a.m. to 2:40 p.m. Tuesday; and from 8 a.m. to 1:45 p.m. Friday. All academic classes are held on Tuesday and Friday, but are of slightly shorter length so that athletics can be scheduled at that time. Sports practices run from 3:45 to 5:45 p.m. throughout the week.

Boarders eat breakfast at 7:15 and dinner at 6:30. In the evening, supervised study hours for boarders are from 7:15 to 9:30.

SUMMER PROGRAMS

St. Anne's–Belfield School offers a wide range of coeducational summer programs for students in preschool through grade 8. Enrollment is open to students from St. Anne's–Belfield School and other schools. Middle School offerings include classes in computer, study skills, cooking, creative writing, and an SAT preparatory course. Also offered are a Summer Camp for students in grades 1–8, lacrosse camps for boys and girls, a boys' and girls' basketball camp, a girls' field hockey camp, and soccer camps for girls and boys. The 2006 summer session begins June 12, 2006.

COSTS AND FINANCIAL AID

Tuition for 2005–06 ranged from $15,350 in the fifth grade to $17,100 in the twelfth grade. Five-day boarding students paid an additional $12,750; seven-day boarding students paid an additional $21,750. Tuition may be paid in full on or before July 31, in two equal payments that are due on July 31 and December 31 (with a $200 service charge), or in eleven equal payments from July 31 to May 31 (with a $600 service charge). A prepayment of $,000 is required to reserve a place for day students, and there is a prepayment of $1500 for five-day boarding students and $2500 for seven-day boarding students.

Financial aid for tuition charges is available. The School subscribes to the School and Student Service for Financial Aid and uses its need assessment as a major factor in determining awards. A tuition loan program augments the system of financial aid. About 33 percent of the student body receives some form of financial assistance.

ADMISSIONS INFORMATION

In an individualized admission process, St. Anne's–Belfield School seeks to enroll inquisitive, enthusiastic, and conscientious students who will bring their own special talents, energy, and skills to the School community. The goal is to enroll students who will both benefit from and contribute to the School's offerings and who will feel successful in the process. St. Anne's–Belfield does not discriminate on the basis of race, color, sex, disability, nationality, or ethnic origin in the administration of its educational policies, admission policies, scholarship and loan programs, and athletics and other School-administered programs.

All applicants and families are encouraged to visit the campus to discuss the School program and the applicant's candidacy with a member of the admissions staff. The first formal step in applying for admission is to complete an application and send it with the application fee to the Admissions Office. SSAT scores, a transcript, two teacher recommendations (from current math and English teachers), administrative recommendation, and an interview are required.

APPLICATION TIMETABLE

Preliminary application should be made in the year prior to the academic year in which the applicant wishes to be admitted. The first round of admission ends February 24, 2006. The second round of admission ends June 26, 2006. The application fee is $30. Campus interviews and tours are conducted throughout the school year. The SSAT must be taken before a candidate is considered for admission to grades 7–12. SSAT scores should be sent to St. Anne's–Belfield School. Applicants should also request the forwarding of a transcript from their current school and should ask their current teachers of mathematics and English to submit letters of recommendation to the Admissions Office. In addition, all students must supply immunization records before admittance.

ADMISSIONS CORRESPONDENCE

Jean Craig, Director of Admissions
St. Anne's–Belfield School
2132 Ivy Road
Charlottesville, Virginia 22903

Phone: 434-296-5106
Fax: 434-979-1486
E-mail: jcraig@stab.org
Web site: http://www.stab.org

ST. CATHERINE'S SCHOOL

Richmond, Virginia

Type: Girls' boarding (grades 9–12) and day college-preparatory Episcopal school
Grades: P–12: Lower School, Junior Kindergarten–5; Middle School, 6–8; Upper School, 9–12
Enrollment: School total: 820; Upper School: 292
Head of School: Auguste J. Bannard

THE SCHOOL

St. Catherine's was founded in 1890 by Virginia Randolph Ellett to prepare girls for colleges that required entrance examinations. In 1920, the Episcopal Church in the Diocese of Virginia acquired the School and changed the name to St. Catherine's School. The goal of education at St. Catherine's is to promote academic excellence through hard work, creative and critical thought, and a spirit of joy on the part of those who learn and those who teach.

The School is located on a 16-acre campus in a residential section of Richmond. Shopping, restaurants, movies, and public transportation are available within a block of the School. Students are encouraged to participate in, enjoy, and learn from the activities and facilities the city provides, such as the ballet, the youth symphony, museums, and special events. Within a 2-hour drive of the School are Washington, D.C.; the Williamsburg-Jamestown area; Virginia Beach; and ski resorts. The School owns 125 acres for regulation-size athletic fields that are located 11 miles from the campus. Four fields are in use, and a dressing room facility has been built.

A 17-member Board of Governors is the School's governing body. The endowment is valued at more than $52 million, and the yearly budget is more than $15 million. Participation by 48 percent of the alumnae and 77 percent of the parents resulted in an Annual Giving total of $1,312,550 in gifts for 2004–05.

St. Catherine's is accredited by the Virginia Association of Independent Schools. It holds memberships in the National Association of Independent Schools, the Secondary School Admission Test Board, the National Association of Principals of Schools for Girls, the National Association for College Admission Counseling, the Southern Association of Colleges and Schools, and the National Coalition of Girls' Schools.

ACADEMIC PROGRAMS

The School requires 20 credits for graduation, including English, 4; foreign language, 3 (or at least the second level of attainment in two different languages); history or social science, 3; mathematics, 3; laboratory sciences, 2; religion, 1⅓; and fine arts, 1. Computer literacy and 2 years of physical education are also required for graduation.

Coordination with St. Christopher's, a boys' school three blocks away, offers the opportunity for coeducation in all departments and an unusually wide offering of classes. Within each subject area, there are a variety of courses from which to choose to meet the requirements. Honors courses are offered in English, mathematics, science, and foreign languages. Students take Advanced Placement examinations in twelve subject areas.

Students are required to take five academic courses a year plus a physical education course or a team sport. They must also take 1⅓ credits in religion. A trimester course in biblical studies and issues is offered, followed by trimester electives in Comparative Religion, Philosophy, Church History, and Ethics. Students must also meet requirements in the fine arts by choosing among courses in music, dance, theater, or studio art. Mandarin Chinese was added to the curriculum in 1985.

The average class size is 17 students, but one course is taught by lecture followed by a seminar. In a lecture class, there may be 80 girls. The overall student-teacher ratio is 6:1. Classes are scheduled either four or six times a week for 45 minutes each. Supervised study halls are available during the day and for 2 hours in the evening. Placement in study hall is determined by a student's grade point average.

The school year is divided into three trimesters and a minimester, with an examination period after the first and third trimesters. Grades, which are based on the traditional A–F system, are sent home five times a year. Parents visit the campus in the fall for conferences. During the two-week minimester at the end of the second term, special interest courses are taught. Study-travel courses are also available. Students have spent minimesters in Texas and New York and abroad in France, England, Kenya, Mexico, Canada, China, Russia, and Guatemala.

Through the American Field Service program, students can go to other countries for the summer or the full academic year.

FACULTY AND ADVISERS

St. Catherine's has 82 full-time and 32 part-time faculty members. More than 50 percent of the faculty members hold master's degrees; 5 of the faculty members have earned a Ph.D.

Auguste J. Bannard, who was appointed Head of the School in 1989, is a graduate of St. Catherine's (1973). She received her B.A. in classics from Princeton University in 1977 and has done postgraduate work in biblical studies at St. Mary's College of the University of St. Andrews, Scotland. She taught Latin and Greek at Groton School from 1977 to 1989. From 1980 to 1989, she also served as 1 of 2 college advisers at Groton.

St. Catherine's faculty members are selected on the basis of their expertise and training in their chosen field and their ability to communicate with and enjoy young people. Faculty members average ten years each of teaching experience at St. Catherine's. Each member of the faculty serves as a sponsor for a School activity and as an adviser for 8 to 10 students. As an adviser, the faculty member is concerned not only about the student's academic progress but also about her social adjustment and involvement

in School activities. The dorm supervisors, the Dean of Students, the Chaplain, and the Director of the Upper School also serve with each adviser as a support team for the students.

COLLEGE PLACEMENT

College counselors begin contact with students and their parents during the freshman year, encouraging positive development of each student's individual interests, academic and extracurricular strengths, and self-assessment. During subsequent years, students receive guidance about selecting courses, scheduling standardized tests, investigating appropriately selected colleges, and meeting application deadlines. The School joins other private schools in the Richmond area to sponsor a local college fair that is attended by representatives from 175 colleges and universities nationwide, and admissions personnel from nearly 100 institutions visit St. Catherine's annually.

The 72 graduates of 2005 entered diverse colleges and universities, including Boston University, Cornell, Davidson, Hollins, James Madison, Sewanee, Wake Forest, Washington and Lee, William and Mary, and the Universities of Georgia, North Carolina at Chapel Hill, and Virginia.

STUDENT BODY AND CONDUCT

There are 292 students in the Upper School.

Student Government consists of the prefects, the School Council, and the Student Council. Prefects from the senior class have the responsibility of recommending and enforcing School rules. The School Council, which is composed of 6 students and 3 faculty members, deals with social and Honor Code violations. The Honor Code is a very important part of life at St. Catherine's, and any violation of the code is taken quite seriously. The Student Council, which is composed of class representatives, has the responsibility of identifying issues of concern or special interest to the students and of planning how needs can best be met.

ACADEMIC FACILITIES

Classrooms are located primarily in Turner, Ellett, Bacot, and Washington Halls and the connecting arcades. In addition, Turner Hall houses the newly renovated chapel, the Seymour and John Rennolds Gallery, the Wright Library, five new classrooms, and a Technology Center with six fully networked CD-ROM workstations with access to nearly 900 periodicals, twenty-two Internet-connected study carrels, two audiovisual screening rooms, and two computer labs. Mullen Hall contains four large laboratory classrooms. The Fine Arts Building has a photography lab and studios for painting and ceramics. An auditorium and a dance studio are located in McVey Hall. Guigon Hall contains music studios

and a small recital hall. A large addition to the Lower School was completed in 1995.

ATHLETICS
All students are expected to participate in athletics through team sports after classes or through physical education classes during the academic day. St. Catherine's offers fifteen team sports: field hockey, tennis, volleyball, cross-country, basketball, soccer, golf, squash, sailing, indoor and outdoor track, lacrosse, softball, diving, and swimming. The number of teams in each sport varies from one to four at the varsity and junior varsity levels. St. Catherine's competes against other independent and public schools in the Richmond metropolitan area and the state.

The Waterman Program, which is available in the fall and spring, offers camping, canoeing, white-water rafting, backpacking, and rappelling. Students may also meet their physical education requirements by participating in the dance class or the Joni Rodman Dance Theater.

A 70,000-square-foot Sports and Fitness Center opened in 2003. The facility includes an eight-lane, 25-yard swimming pool with two 1-meter diving boards; three gyms; a suspended fitness track; a two-story, 4,000-square-foot fitness and weight room; locker rooms; a classroom; and a training facility. In addition, 125 acres in nearby Goochland County offer playing fields for softball, field hockey, lacrosse, and soccer.

EXTRACURRICULAR OPPORTUNITIES
Extracurricular activities stimulate new interests and develop special talents in students. The dramatic arts group, which is coordinated with St. Christopher's School, produces three plays a year, ranging from musicals to new works and improvisations. The School Chorale performs regularly throughout the year, occasionally under the direction of a distinguished visiting conductor. Typically, its schedule includes a tour in the United States or abroad. In addition, the School has an a cappella group. Students may study any musical instrument for pleasure or academic credit. Especially talented students have the option of participating in the string ensemble or band (coordinated with St. Christopher's) or the Richmond Symphony Youth Orchestra. The string program is taught by a quartet-in-residence, which is composed of Richmond Symphony musicians. The School offers dance classes and a modern dance performing group. Professional dancers visiting the Richmond area teach master classes at St. Catherine's, and some students take classes at the Richmond Ballet.

Other activities include working on the yearbook, newspaper, or literary arts magazine; the Altar Guild; the Athletic Association; Unity; and the Student Activities Committee. The intramural Gold and White teams encourage sportsmanship, teamwork, and School loyalty through friendly competition and all-School cheer rallies.

Traditional events are the Sophomore Outing, Parents' Weekends, St. Catherine's Day, Candlelight Ring Service, Lower School Farewell to Seniors, Junior-Senior Banquet, and June Queen and Daisy Chain ceremonies.

DAILY LIFE
On Monday, Wednesday, and Friday, the school day begins at 7:55 a.m. with a chapel service. On numerous Tuesdays and Fridays throughout the school year, the student body assembles for special programs. On Tuesday, students assemble for class meetings. Between 8:30 a.m. and 3:30 p.m., there are seven periods. From 3:30 to 5:45, students practice competitive sports or compete in games. Other students have a short break from school routine at this time. Following the evening meal, there is a 2-hour supervised study hall.

WEEKEND LIFE
Students have many activities from which to choose on the weekends. The School organizes mixers with other schools in Virginia and Maryland; formal dances; trips to football games; ski days or weekends; shopping and cultural excursions to Washington, D.C.; and visits to the beach. In the city, the girls go out to dinner and a movie or to a shopping mall. They also attend concerts, plays, and many of the other exciting events that are available in most cities.

SUMMER PROGRAMS
St. Catherine's provides a six-week, coed summer program in the creative arts for students ages 3½ to 17 in the Richmond area. In the summer of 2003, more than 1,000 students were enrolled.

COSTS AND FINANCIAL AID
Tuition for 2005–06 was $15,820 for students in grades 9–12. Optional expenses include private music lessons.

Financial aid is available to students whose families have demonstrated financial need by making application through the School and Student Service for Financial Aid. In 2005–06, $1.1 million in financial aid was awarded to 9.6 percent of the student body. The award is made in the form of a grant and/or a low-interest loan.

ADMISSIONS INFORMATION
Because St. Catherine's seeks diversity in its student body, enrollment is open to qualified students of any race, color, religion, or national or ethnic origin. The School desires a student body of girls with varied interests and different backgrounds who are intellectually curious and have the maturity and character to benefit from their St. Catherine's experience. Admission decisions are based upon the results of the Secondary School Admission Test, the previous school record, teacher and personal recommendations, and an interview.

APPLICATION TIMETABLE
Students are encouraged to inquire and to apply for admission in the fall and winter prior to the desired September entrance. Admission decisions are made on a rolling basis beginning in early February, and applications are considered as long as space is available. Parents are asked to confirm places offered by April 10.

A campus visit is the best way to observe the program and to experience St. Catherine's learning environment. Applicants are encouraged to visit during the normal academic day, 8:30 to 3:30, Monday through Friday.

ADMISSIONS CORRESPONDENCE
Kelly J. Willbanks, Director of Admission
St. Catherine's School
6001 Grove Avenue
Richmond, Virginia 23226

Phone: 800-648-4982 (toll-free)
Fax: 804-285-8169
E-mail: admissions@st.catherines.org
Web site: http://www.st.catherines.org

ST. GEORGE'S SCHOOL
Newport, Rhode Island

Type: Coeducational boarding and day college-preparatory school
Grades: 9–12 (Forms III–VI)
Enrollment: 347
Head of School: Eric F. Peterson

THE SCHOOL

St. George's was founded in 1896 by the Reverend John B. Diman as a college-preparatory school, and, in 1901, the School moved to its present site. The 230-acre campus sits atop a promontory overlooking the Atlantic Ocean, the Sakonnet River, and the city of Newport.

St. George's is committed to the development of each student's potential. The course of study challenges students to strive for academic excellence. High standards and expectations are the norm, and the faculty is committed to assisting students in their pursuit of scholarship. The academic and extracurricular opportunities have the common goal of helping students become more effective, competent, and concerned people, dedicated to making a positive contribution in life.

Since its founding, St. George's has enjoyed a close relationship with the Episcopal Church and continues to foster the spiritual and moral development of students of every religious persuasion. In 1972, the School became coeducational.

Located 2½ miles from Newport, 35 miles from Providence, and about 70 miles south of Boston, the School encourages students and faculty members to explore the many cultural and athletic events in those cities. The School also takes advantage of its proximity to the ocean. It has developed a wide range of programs that investigate the marine environment and draw attention to ocean-related issues. Through a combination of formal academic training and exposure to superb recreational opportunities, these programs help students appreciate the interrelationship between humankind and the ocean.

St. George's is a nonprofit institution governed by a 38-member Board of Trustees. The endowment is currently $98 million and is supplemented by an annual fund that raised more than $1.92 million in 2004–05, which is ample testimony to the generosity and commitment of the 4,200 living alumni and of the friends of the School.

St. George's School is accredited by the New England Association of Schools and Colleges. The School is affiliated with the National Association of Independent Schools, the Independent School Association of Massachusetts, the Council for Religion in Independent Schools, the Secondary School Admission Test Board, and the Association of Boarding Schools.

ACADEMIC PROGRAMS

A student's course of study begins by emphasizing the mastery of fundamentals and later broadens to offer numerous elective courses. While all entering students have a strong record of academic achievement at their previous schools, relatively few have had substantial experience in planning their course of study. Consequently, careful counseling by the Dean of Academic Affairs and by faculty advisers and the College Advisors ensures that both new and returning students are able to make intelligent course selections.

Graduation requirements include English, 4 years; mathematics, 3 years (algebra I, algebra II, and geometry); laboratory sciences, 2 years; U.S. history, 1 year; Bible and theology, 1 year (for students entering after the ninth grade, ½ year); and art or music, ½ year. All students are required to complete a modern or classical language through the third level.

Advanced Placement courses are offered in twenty-two subject areas, including art, computers, economics, English, history, language, mathematics, music, and science. Students took 810 Advanced Placement exams. On 90 percent of those exams, students achieved scores of 3, 4, or 5.

Courses for grades 9 and 10 generally meet for four 50-minute class periods per week and require about the same amount of time for preparation. Courses for grades 11 and 12 usually require less classroom time and more time for assignment preparation. Because classes are small (typically 10 to 12 students), emphasis is placed on conscientious preparation and on the willingness to participate in discussion. Most students carry five full courses each semester. Grades accompanied by faculty comments and a letter from the faculty adviser are sent home three times a year.

The Off-Campus Program is predicated on the belief that students benefit from an opportunity to apply their learning to problems and questions of concern that lie outside the School community. Students initiate, plan, and evaluate these projects with the aid of the program director.

St. George's offers its students an exceptional opportunity in oceanography aboard the School-owned Research Vessel *Geronimo*, which operates year-round in coastal and offshore waters between the gulf of Maine and the northern Caribbean. There are three 6-week research cruises during the school year, and students who sail aboard *Geronimo* receive full academic credit.

FACULTY AND ADVISERS

The faculty consists of 84 full- and part-time members (39 women and 45 men). Most of the faculty members (85 percent) live on or within walking distance of the campus and, in addition to their teaching responsibilities, serve as dormitory supervisors, as advisers to individual students and extracurricular organizations, and as coaches.

Eric F. Peterson was appointed Head of School in 2004. He holds a Bachelor of Arts degree from Dartmouth College and a juris doctorate degree from Northwestern University. For the five years previous to his appointment at St. George's, he served as the Upper School head and assistant head of school, English teacher, and coach at Forsyth Country Day School.

Generous funding is available to faculty members who wish to pursue summer study or travel. A faculty fund, the gift of an anonymous donor, provides more than $30,000 each year for faculty projects.

COLLEGE PLACEMENT

St. George's students plan for college with the help of 3 college advisers, whose overriding concerns are to acquaint students with the range of options appropriate for their abilities and interests and to support them throughout their decision making.

Through individual conferences at the midpoint of the Fifth Form year, students begin the process of identifying a group of colleges and universities for investigation. Parents are involved in college planning through Fifth Form Parents' Weekend, an annual event combining formal presentations on college selection and college life by admission officers and family conferences with the college advisers.

Students are urged to visit college campuses during the summer months to interview with admission officers and see facilities. A second round of individual conferences in the fall helps Sixth Formers decide the final shape of their college lists. During an average fall, 100 colleges send representatives to St. George's, and Sixth Formers are encouraged to attend these presentations.

In conjunction with their counseling duties, the advisers work with students in selecting academic programs, registering for standardized testing, and planning summer work or study experiences. In both the Fifth and Sixth form years, the college advisers sponsor workshops to prepare students for the SAT, college interviews, and writing application essays. Every year, college admission personnel conduct mock admission committee workshops. Other representatives conduct an essay-writing workshop for students. In addition, the college advisers routinely visit college campuses and participate in regional and national admission counseling programs to enhance their professional skills.

Since its founding, the School has prepared students for the country's leading colleges and universities. The graduates of the class of 2005 are attending such colleges and universities as Boston College, Dartmouth, Georgetown, Hamilton, Harvard, Middlebury, Northwestern, Pennsylvania, Vanderbilt, and Yale.

STUDENT BODY AND CONDUCT

In 2005–06, St. George's had 347 students (173 boys and 174 girls). Of the 347 students, 85

percent were boarding students. Generally, there are 68 students in grade 9 and approximately 90 students in each of the other three grades. St. George's makes every effort to attract a student body that is diverse in geographic, economic, and racial backgrounds as well as in interests and talents. Students came from thirty-three states and sixteen countries.

St. George's believes that one of the most significant aspects of a residential school is the interaction within the school community—the students, and faculty and staff members. Rules and expectations support the principle that disciplined living leads to a sense of real freedom. Major infractions or repeated minor infractions may lead to dismissal.

ACADEMIC FACILITIES

The Schoolhouse, which contains twenty-one classrooms, is the center of campus activity during the academic day. A new $6.5-million Center for the Visual and Performing Arts was completed in September 1999. In addition to a 400-seat theater, the center contains new classrooms and studios for architecture, ceramics, dance, music, painting and drawing, photography, welding, and woodworking. Other facilities include the Dupont Science Building, which houses six well-equipped laboratories with adjoining classrooms and a new technology center, and the Smiley-Sturtevant Observatory. The Nathaniel P. Hill Memorial Library houses approximately 25,000 volumes, two audiovisual theaters, and one of four computer centers. The library subscribes to 136 periodicals, and there is access to back files, microfilms, and microfiche. Library orientation is provided for all incoming students. The library participates in the online Computer Library Center Network.

Each dormitory room is wired for access to computing, the Internet, e-mail, and voice mail. During their first year, students complete a required computer literacy course.

BOARDING AND GENERAL FACILITIES

Boarding students live in fourteen dormitories. Most entering ninth graders live in single rooms. Returning students select the type of accommodations they prefer. Some dormitories are equipped with kitchenettes. Older students are appointed as dormitory prefects and assist the faculty in supervision.

In 2002, St. George's completed a $6-million building program to provide for two new dormitories, four faculty homes, and significant improvements to other living areas. At St. George's, 70 percent of the dormitory rooms are single rooms and 30 percent are double rooms.

In 2004, St. George's completed a new campus center. The facility houses a recreation center with a game room, a grill, and spaces for dances and special events.

ATHLETICS

Because the essential mission of the School is to educate young people in mind, body, and spirit, the afternoon program is an integral part of the St. George's curriculum, and participation is required of all. As is the case with the academic program, students plan carefully with the help of advisers the activities in which they participate in each of the three seasons.

Opportunities range from interscholastic athletics to the performing arts to community service and special projects, all of which share the common goal of enabling students to expand their horizons, to test themselves, and to learn important lessons about teamwork, volunteerism, sportsmanship, competition, collaboration, and creativity.

St. George's fields forty-eight interscholastic teams: in the fall, cross-country, field hockey, football, and soccer; in the winter, basketball, ice hockey, squash, and swimming; and in the spring, baseball, lacrosse, sailing, softball, tennis, and track. In addition, there are various recreational and intramural offerings.

Facilities for athletics include a new rim-flow indoor swimming pool, new twin ice hockey rinks, and a recently completed field house, which houses four indoor tennis courts, four basketball courts, and a fully equipped weight-training facility. There are ten outdoor tennis courts, a new all-weather track, and numerous game and practice fields. The School maintains its own fleet of 420s for sailing. A squash facility housing eight international courts was completed in 1996. American squash champion Mark Talbott runs his Talbott Squash Academy summer training sessions at St. George's.

EXTRACURRICULAR OPPORTUNITIES

The creativity, imagination, and diverse talents of the student body are given full expression in the almost limitless array of extracurricular organizations, including the School newspaper, yearbook, literary magazine, St. George's Cultural Society, debate club, women's forum, entertainment committee, drama club, music guild, choir, vestry, and the St. George's dance troupe.

The student council takes a strong lead in identifying new directions for the School. The joint faculty-student Disciplinary Committee works closely with the Dean of Students and the Head of School. Student advisers welcome newcomers and serve as experienced friends.

There is a strong commitment to community service. Each term, students volunteer to work in various agencies and institutions. Each summer, 15 students act as volunteer counselors at Camp Ramleh, which provides a camp experience for children from disadvantaged backgrounds.

DAILY LIFE

The first class period is at 8 a.m. each day (8:30 on Thursdays), and the last class ends at 2:55 p.m., except on Wednesdays and Saturdays, which are half days. A typical academic day consists of four or five classes. Free periods provide time for class preparations, research projects, music lessons, and other individual pursuits. Four days a week, there is a school assembly advisory or form meetings before lunch. Sports practices are generally scheduled between 3:15 and 5:15 p.m. After dinner, an hour is set aside for extracurricular activities and visiting speakers. Evening study runs from 8 to 10 p.m. Attendance at chapel on Thursday is required. The Head of School sometimes presides over these services, but most are conducted by student and faculty volunteers. The central worship service of St. George's is on either Tuesdays or Sundays and is conducted by the chaplains. Music is provided by the choir and organist-choirmaster. Attendance at this service or at a service in Newport is required.

COSTS AND FINANCIAL AID

The tuition for 2005–06 was $34,500 for boarders and $23,200 for day students. Additional expenses include books, laundry, and travel. Students may cash checks at the Business Office on weekdays and also arrange travel plans and obtain tickets.

Financial aid awards are based on the guidelines established by the School and Student Service for Financial Aid. There is substantial aid available to qualified students. For 2005–06, St. George's awarded grants and loans in excess of $2.2 million to more than 27 percent of the student body.

ADMISSIONS INFORMATION

Applicants submit a complete school record, including two teacher evaluations, a writing sample, and the results of standardized testing. Students are required to take the Secondary School Admission Test (SSAT). When appropriate, candidates for grades 11 and 12 submit PSAT, SAT, or TOEFL scores in place of the SSAT. All candidates are expected to visit St. George's or, in exceptional situations, meet with a local representative.

The Admission Committee consists of 6 experienced staff members. In selecting students, the committee gives preference to candidates with strong records of achievement who have demonstrated a depth of interest in some area beyond the classroom.

APPLICATION TIMETABLE

A formal application and the $50 fee ($100 for international students) should be filed by February 1 in order to guarantee a decision on March 10, the notification date for applicants. In place of St. George's own application, candidates may choose to submit the Boarding School Common Application Form, which can be downloaded from the Internet at http://www.schools.com. Interviews are scheduled beginning at 8:30 a.m., Monday through Friday, and beginning at 8 a.m. on Saturdays. Appointments for an interview and a tour of the campus should be made well in advance, preferably by telephone.

ADMISSIONS CORRESPONDENCE

Jim Hamilton, Director of Admission
St. George's School
372 Purgatory Road
Middletown, Rhode Island 02842-5984

Phone: 401-842-6600
Fax: 401-842-6696
E-mail: admissions_office@stgeorges.edu
Web site: http://www.stgeorges.edu

ST. GREGORY COLLEGE PREPARATORY SCHOOL

Tucson, Arizona

Type: Coeducational day college-preparatory school
Grades: 6–12: Middle School, 6–8; High School, 9–12
Enrollment: School total: 351; High School: 205; Middle School: 146
Head of School: Bryn S. Roberts

THE SCHOOL

St. Gregory is an independent, coeducational, college-preparatory day school. It is not a parochial school. It is nonsectarian and nondenominational in its admissions, curricular, and extracurricular policies and practices. The principal purpose of the School, which has grown from a first-year enrollment of 48 students to its present size of 351, is to provide a first-rate college-preparatory education for students of all social, ethnic, and economic segments of the greater Tucson community.

The School is governed by a 20-member Board of Trustees, which, during the twenty-three years of the School's existence, has developed a campus with a capital value of $14 million and has attained the level of $350,000 in annual giving.

St. Gregory is accredited by the North Central Association of Colleges and Schools as a College Preparatory School (one of six in the state of Arizona) and by the Independent Schools Association of the Southwest. Professional memberships are held in the National Association of Independent Schools and the Educational Records Bureau.

ACADEMIC PROGRAMS

The standard academic load is six courses per semester, one of which is performance or production based. The average class size is 15. The teacher-student ratio is 1:17.

Twenty-four academic credits are required for graduation, of which the following seventeen are prescribed: English, 4 years; foreign language, 3 consecutive years of one language; mathematics, 4 years; laboratory science, 3 years; history, 2 years; and fine arts, 1 year.

Advanced Placement courses are offered in English, calculus, chemistry, biology, U.S. government, U.S. history, European history, music theory, physics (B), Spanish, and French. In AP classes and studio art, the grades are weighted.

In those rare but welcome instances in which a student's exceptional academic skills outrun the School's curriculum, independent studies are designed, or the student may take courses for credit at the University of Arizona.

Through the course of grades 6–11, students participate in a challenge course curriculum designed to enhance communication, strategic thinking, trust, leadership, and group dynamics within an enjoyable yet intensive structured program. In the spring of their junior year, students are invited to apply to be trained and serve as Peer Leaders during their senior year. This group of seniors participates in an extensive training program to learn the hard and soft skills necessary for facilitating students through St. Gregory's challenge course programs and faculty- and student-run programs for students in grades 6–11.

FACULTY AND ADVISERS

St. Gregory's faculty has 44 members. Sixty-eight percent of the 44 members of the faculty have master's degrees, and 6 hold doctorates.

Bryn S. Roberts, Head of School, is a native of Canada. Mr. Roberts graduated with honors from Mount Allison University in Sackville, Canada, and received his M.A. from the University of Western Ontario in London, Canada.

Each student is assigned to a faculty member–adviser, who is available for support in all nonacademic aspects of School life. Academic advisory functions are retained by the Head of School and his key administrative staff.

COLLEGE PLACEMENT

The School's college placement philosophy is that the best college or university for a student is one where the student can feel at home and, in addition, is challenged and stimulated intellectually, offered varied social and personal experiences, and prepared for the next step in life. The college counseling program is directed toward helping students identify the school or schools that suit them in these ways, supporting the application process, and aiding in confronting the challenges of college affordability.

The college planning program begins in the sophomore year, when students are advised on the relationship between their selection of courses and their admissibility to college.

In the fall of the junior year, the college counselor meets with students and their parents, outlining in detail the School-guided process for selecting and applying to colleges. Families receive information on the reference resources that are available in the College Counseling Center, in the form of college catalogs, directories, CD-ROMs, and Internet resources. The importance of having good grades, a challenging course selection, and sustained extracurricular activity is stressed for those students whose objective is admission to the more competitive colleges. Juniors and seniors are encouraged to visit colleges and universities to which they are considering applying.

Juniors and their parents regularly meet with the college counselor throughout the year. Juniors take the SAT or ACT tests during the last months of the academic year, as well as the appropriate SAT Subject Tests.

A weeklong class in writing the college essay is offered just before the fall semester begins. Seniors review their final lists of selected colleges with their counselor early in the fall and begin the actual application process. A highlight of the process is College Day, in mid-October, when admissions representatives of more than ninety colleges gather on the St. Gregory campus. In addition, more than 40 individual college representatives offer on-campus information sessions for St. Gregory students throughout the fall.

The colleges and universities that members of the class of 2004 are attending include Bard, Barnard, Boston University, Brandeis, Carleton, Colby, Duke, Emory, Princeton, Vassar, Yale, and the Universities of Arizona (including the Honors Program), Colorado at Boulder, Denver, Pennsylvania, Puget Sound, and Tennessee.

STUDENT BODY AND CONDUCT

Currently, there are 146 students in the Middle School, grades 6–8. There are 40 students in grade 6 in three sections and 60 to 65 students in grades 7 and 8 in four sections. There are 205 students in the High School, grades 9–12, with a goal of 60 to 65 in each class. The School operates under an Honor Code, which is overseen by an Honor Committee made up of students and faculty members.

ACADEMIC FACILITIES

The seven principal buildings on the St. Gregory campus include the Administration Building, three classroom buildings, a Middle School classroom building, a darkroom, a college counseling center, a multipurpose building named El Mirador, and a 400-seat Performing Arts Center that opened in 1997.

The theater features a gallery space for displaying student art, a thrust and side stage, and state-of-the-art lighting and sound systems. Classrooms for choral work and theater production and shop space for stage construction and storage are included in this building.

Housed in Zeskind Hall is a dining facility for 300. A full kitchen provides an extensive variety of fresh food for students and faculty and staff members throughout the day. Students may purchase a meal card for daily lunches and snacks.

The Humanities Building houses the Fine Arts and Foreign Language Departments. There are four seminar-style classrooms, an art studio, and music practice rooms.

Two new buildings house English and math classrooms and offices and the sciences, respectively. State-of-the-art laboratories and classrooms are featured in the science building, as well as storage, offices, a computer lab, and an outdoor education area. The labs include a greenhouse and space for long-term student experiments.

The refurbished Marshall building houses the newly remodeled library, a dance studio, a drama classroom, history classrooms, and offices and computer labs, one dedicated solely to student publications.

El Mirador is used for standard indoor sports (e.g., basketball and volleyball), with seating for 400.

The Louise Marshall Library houses more than 7,000 books, fifty periodicals and newspapers, and database access to 150 more journals. The facility includes two computer labs, study carrels, and an audiovisual library for student and faculty use. The computerized library is also connected to the University of Arizona library and the Tucson Pima Library System. The School's librarian, who holds a master's degree in library science, sees her task as preparing students for college-level research.

ATHLETICS

The School believes that participation in athletics is instrumental in helping students mature. In addition to promoting the objective of achieving physical fitness, the School makes an effort to develop the important skills of self-discipline, sportsmanship, and teamwork.

Interscholastic offerings are boys' and girls' soccer, boys' and girls' swimming, girls' volleyball, and boys' and girls' cross-country in the fall; boys' and girls' basketball in the winter; and baseball, softball, golf, and boys' and girls' tennis in the spring.

Athletics facilities include playing fields for soccer, baseball, and softball; an indoor gym for volleyball and basketball; and two outdoor basketball courts. The School uses the tennis courts and swimming pool at nearby Fort Lowell Park. Housed in the gym is an athletic training center that features aerobic, free-weight, and variable-resistant equipment.

EXTRACURRICULAR OPPORTUNITIES

Students are able to participate in a wide variety of extracurricular activities, and virtually 100 percent of the School is involved in the arts, publications, or other activities. A student may choose to work on the newspaper, yearbook, or literary magazine. Popular club activities include Outdoor Action, French Club, and Astronomy Club, providing students with social and leadership opportunities. The arts activities are varied, ranging from studio art and ceramics to string ensemble, musical production, and chorus.

Outdoor clubs at both the Middle School and High School levels sponsor day hiking experiences in the local area as well as extended backpacking experiences during school breaks.

Students have many opportunities to serve the Tucson community. Working as hospital volunteers or nursing home aides, serving in a crisis nursery, or participating in political internships—all of these opportunities and more are available to the St. Gregory student. The School encourages and facilitates community service as an important element of the high school years.

DAILY LIFE

A modified block schedule provides for each of eight periods to meet once a week for 40 minutes and twice a week for 75 minutes. Interscholastic sports and other activities follow in the afternoon. Only students in good academic standing may participate in interscholastic athletics.

SUMMER PROGRAMS

The School conducts summer enrichment programs that vary from two to six weeks in length. Fifth- through eleventh-grade students select from offerings in fine arts or study skills. Senior high students can choose from marine biology (a popular course that includes significant study time in the Gulf of California), creative writing, and Spanish (studied in Salamanca, Spain), among others. There is a travel and study in France program for students in grades 9–11.

COSTS AND FINANCIAL AID

Tuition for the 2005–06 school year was $14,260 for grades 9–12 and $12,980 for grades 6–8. Additional costs included books. The School provides a lunch program.

Need-based financial aid is offered. Approximately 24 percent of the students received some share of the $600,000 in financial assistance budgeted by the board.

ADMISSIONS INFORMATION

Qualification for admission is determined by the Admissions Committee on the basis of the applicant's scores on standardized testing, a transcript from the previous school, teachers' evaluations, a writing sample, and an interview.

APPLICATION TIMETABLE

Tours of the campus and visits to classes may be requested for any day the School is in regular session. Requests for visits, interview appointments, and admission materials may be made by telephone or in writing. The deadline for applications is February 10, and applicants are notified of admission by February 28. The application/testing fee is $45. The financial aid application deadline is March 10.

ADMISSIONS CORRESPONDENCE

Debby Kennedy
St. Gregory College Preparatory School
3231 North Craycroft
Tucson, Arizona 85712

Phone: 520-327-6395
Fax: 520-327-8276
E-mail: admissions@stgregoryschool.org
Web site: http://www.stgregoryschool.org

SAINT JAMES SCHOOL

St. James, Maryland

Type: Coeducational boarding and day college-preparatory school
Grades: 8–12
Enrollment: 220
Head of School: The Reverend Dr. D. Stuart Dunnan, Headmaster

THE SCHOOL

Saint James School is the oldest Episcopal boarding school founded on the English model in the United States. Founded by Bishop William Whittingham in 1842, the School originally included a preparatory school and college. In the years following the Civil War, the college was eliminated, and Saint James evolved toward its present shape. Located in a rural setting, the Georgian-style campus of Saint James sits on 600 acres of farmland containing a natural spring, fields, and streams. The campus lies 5 miles southwest of Hagerstown and is approximately 65 miles from both Baltimore and Washington, D.C. The region offers many cultural and historic points of interest, including the C&O Canal, Harpers Ferry, and Antietam and Gettysburg Battlefields. The faculty members and students enjoy the cultural resources of the Baltimore-Washington metropolitan area on regular field trips.

Throughout its history, Saint James has remained committed to the precepts of sound mind and body, emphasizing the spiritual, intellectual, physical, and moral development of each student through challenging academics, daily athletics, extensive activities, and community service. At the start of each academic day, the entire School gathers for Chapel, providing an opportunity for thought and reflection for faculty members and students of all faith traditions. Simultaneously challenged and supported, Saint James students study a traditional core curriculum, which provides a solid foundation for strong academic achievement at the collegiate level.

Saint James is governed by a self-perpetuating Board of Trustees. The School's operating budget is $7.3 million per year. The endowment is approximately $13.2 million. An active Annual Giving program is supported by better than 50 percent of the alumni.

Saint James School is accredited by the Middle States Association of Colleges and Schools and the Maryland State Department of Education. It is a member of the National Association of Independent Schools, Association of Independent Maryland Schools, Cum Laude Society, Association of Independent Schools of Greater Washington, Council for Advancement and Support of Education, and National Association of Episcopal Schools.

ACADEMIC PROGRAMS

Small classes and a student-teacher ratio of 6:1 provide an optimal learning environment at Saint James. The core curriculum encompasses courses in English, history, mathematics, science, foreign languages, art, music, and religion, with electives available to upperclassmen. Advanced Placement courses are offered in all major academic areas. Eighteen academic credits, each worth a full-year course, are required to earn a diploma, and the distribution of courses includes no fewer than En-

glish (4), history (3), mathematics (3), science (3), foreign language (3), and art/music (1). Students generally take five courses each year.

The school year is divided into three terms; examinations are given in November, March, and May. Reports and comments are sent to parents in October and at the end of each term. Students receive additional reports at the end of each six-week marking period.

FACULTY AND ADVISERS

The faculty members at Saint James are highly-talented, deeply dedicated educators with the strongest possible commitment to each student's success. The School has 33 faculty men and women; 52 percent have advanced degrees.

The Reverend Dr. D. Stuart Dunnan was appointed Headmaster in 1992. He graduated from St. Albans School and Harvard University (A.B., A.M.). He received his B.A. in theology from Christ Church of Oxford University and was awarded a certificate in Anglican studies from General Theological Seminary in New York. At Oxford, he received his M.A. and completed his D.Phil. Father Dunnan was also a member of the theology faculty of Oxford University, where he served as a research fellow and chaplain at Lincoln College.

In addition to their teaching duties, faculty members coach students in athletics and the arts, live in the dormitories, and eat with students in the dining hall. All faculty members act as advisers to 6 or 7 students, supporting and directing their academic and personal growth and achievement.

COLLEGE PLACEMENT

As a private college-preparatory institution, Saint James School believes each student and parent ultimately invests in a high-quality education, which will lead to appropriate college placement. Each year, Saint James places 100 percent of its graduating seniors in college. The Director of College Counseling has designed a college search program, which allows students the opportunity to pursue a wide range of colleges. Saint James students begin this process in the fall of the tenth grade. The School's personalized approach incorporates college admission officers, teachers, students, and parents working together to ensure every senior gets the most from his or her college search process. In addition, admission representatives from more than forty colleges and universities visit the Saint James campus annually to recruit students.

During the past four years, graduates have matriculated at the following colleges: Amherst; Boston College; Boston University; Bucknell; Davidson; Dickinson; Furman; Georgetown; George Washington; Harvard; Johns Hopkins Peabody Conservatory; McGill; Princeton; Rice; Stanford; United States Air Force, Military, and Naval Academies; Vanderbilt; Wake Forest; Wellesley; and

the Universities of California, Maryland, North Carolina, Pennsylvania, the South (Sewanee), and Virginia.

STUDENT BODY AND CONDUCT

In 2005–06, 220 students are enrolled in grades 8–12, 55 of whom are day students. The majority of students come from Maryland, Pennsylvania, Virginia, West Virginia, the District of Columbia, and a number of other states throughout the country. In addition, 10 percent of the student body comes from fifteen different countries.

A student's character is of fundamental importance at Saint James, and because of this, the School strives to foster a sense of personal and group responsibility and a high standard of honor in each student. The Honor Code (a pledge not to lie, cheat, or steal) expects each student to respect other people and their property. Furthermore, the use of alcohol and nonprescription drugs is strictly prohibited, as is the use of tobacco in any form. The Honor Council and the Disciplinary Committee, comprised largely of students, review instances of dishonor and misconduct and recommend appropriate dispositions to the Headmaster.

The Prefect Council, made up of 10 seniors elected by the students and the faculty, upholds the traditions of Saint James and assists faculty members and the Headmaster in the day-to-day operations of the School. Of this group, 1 member is elected Senior Prefect and he or she leads the Prefects in their work.

The Student Activities Committee consists of 2 prefects, both appointed by the Senior Prefect, and up to 7 underformers as selected by the Committee at the beginning of the year. The Committee serves to advise the Dean of Students and the Prefect Council on matters relating to student activities and student morale. It also organizes activities such as dances and special programs.

ACADEMIC FACILITIES

A quadrangle on the east side of campus is anchored by the John E. Owens Library, containing nearly 20,000 volumes, with the School Archives, science laboratories, and classrooms located downstairs. Powell Hall, the main academic building, contains classrooms and newly renovated science laboratories. The Bowman-Byron Fine Arts Center has a 270-seat auditorium, art studios, and stagecraft and music rooms.

BOARDING AND GENERAL FACILITIES

Claggett Hall is the main boys' dormitory, housing boys in Forms IV–VI (grades 10–12), with each form grouped together by floor. Onderdonk Dormitory is for the younger boys in Form II (grade 8) and Hershey Hall is for boys in Form III (grade 9). A common room with a TV, DVD player, and computers can be found on every hall. The Gertrude Steele Coors Hall houses girls in Forms II–IV, and Holloway House, the new girls'

dormitory, is for girls in Forms IV–VI. Faculty members who have apartments within the dormitory and student prefects supervise each dormitory. Faculty houses also surround the perimeter of the campus. A new dining hall provides seated and buffet meals for students and faculty members. Kemp Hall, housing the Detweiler Student Center, the School bookstore, and a snack bar, offers an opportunity for students to socialize together informally.

The Saint James Chapel provides for daily services. A guild of student sacristans, a student vestry, and the Chapel Choir assist and direct worship in the Chapel. The Laidlaw Infirmary houses a full-time nurse, an athletic trainer, and the office of the School Chaplain.

ATHLETICS

By requiring daily participation in the athletic program, the School seeks to enhance each student's confidence by simultaneously challenging and supporting each individual. On the field and in the field house, students develop principles of teamwork and sportsmanship and learn to stretch themselves so that they may achieve beyond their own expectations. These lessons are invaluable preparation for the challenges of life.

A program of sixteen interscholastic sports for boys and girls is offered at Saint James, and the teams play schools of similar size in the Washington-Baltimore metropolitan area. The sports available to boys include baseball, basketball, cross-country, football, golf, lacrosse, soccer, tennis, weight training, and wrestling. The sports available to girls include basketball, dance, field hockey, lacrosse, soccer, softball, tennis, volleyball, and weight training.

The Alumni Hall Athletic Center contains two wrestling rooms, locker room facilities, and a field house with three basketball courts that can be converted to tennis and volleyball courts. The Fitness Center houses a state-of-the-art weight room and dance studios that overlook the Bai Yuca. Seven athletic fields and a twelve-court tennis pavilion are also located on School grounds. In the winter, students can ski at Whitetail Ski Resort, 25 miles north of the campus.

EXTRACURRICULAR OPPORTUNITIES

Students are encouraged to participate in the School's diverse extracurricular activities each year. Saint James students may become involved in *The* *Bai Yuka* (yearbook), *Jacobite* (newspaper), Vestry, Sacristan's Guild, Choir, Lay Readers, Multi-Cultural Club, Photography Club, Ushers' Guild, Historical Society, Delta Society (math and science), Irving Society (literary), *Syrinx* (literary magazine), and the Mummers' Society (drama). In addition, there is a student tutoring group, which offers assistance to students needing additional academic support, and the Maroon Key Society, which provides tour guides for prospective students, their families, and other guests of the School. One of the strengths of the activities program is its flexibility. If a group of students has a particular interest and finds a faculty member willing to act as sponsor, the School will support new activities whenever possible.

During the school year, Saint James students hold and attend dances/mixers with other schools. A block of tickets for symphony performances in the local community is a regular offering, and additional performances at theaters in Washington and Baltimore are attended frequently.

DAILY LIFE

Breakfast for boarding students is at 7:15. Day students arrive by 8:00, at which time the School meets for chapel. The academic day begins at 8:15 with the students following a seven-period day. Two extra-help periods are offered on Tuesdays and Thursdays. Faculty members are available at this time to help students who need assistance. An athletic period follows the academic day from 3:45 until 5:45, and all students participate. Dinner is served at 6:30. The majority of meals are sit-down, family-style meals, with a faculty member heading each table.

The nightly study hall period runs from 7:30 to 9:30 for all boarding students. Lights-out is between 10:30 and 11, depending on the Form.

WEEKEND LIFE

A variety of activities on campus and in the metropolitan area can be found. Regular activities include mixers, dances, movies, and concerts, and these are augmented by field trips, informal outings, and sporting and cultural events in Washington and Baltimore. During the winter, skiing is a regular weekend event.

All activities are coordinated by the Dean of Students and the Student Activities Committee, who solicit suggestions from the student body. Saint James is affiliated with twenty boarding schools in the Baltimore–Washington, D.C., region that coordinate various social activities throughout the year. Transportation is provided by the School, and these events are supervised by faculty members.

COSTS AND FINANCIAL AID

The comprehensive fee for the 2004–05 school year was $27,000 for boarding students and $18,000 for day students. A nonrefundable 10 percent deposit is required by April 10 for new students. Tuition is payable in one, two, or ten installments.

Financial aid grants, based on need and renewed annually, are given in March for the following academic year, provided the requisite financial aid forms are returned to the Admission Office by February 10. For the 2003–04 year, $696,150 in financial aid was awarded to 25.4 percent of the students in amounts ranging from $3000 to $26,800.

ADMISSIONS INFORMATION

Saint James School accepts students without regard to race, sex, color, religion, or ethnic origin and has a diverse student body. It seeks girls and boys of good character who have the drive and curiosity to make the most of their talents and who wish to participate fully in the life of the School. Students are admitted in grades 8 through 11 on the basis of a completed application, teacher and guidance counselor recommendations, academic transcript, and the results of the SSAT, PSAT, or SAT.

APPLICATION TIMETABLE

Inquiries are welcome all year. The application deadline is January 31, and admission decisions are mailed March 10. Students have until April 10 to notify Saint James of their decision. After January 31, applications are welcomed and considered on a space-available basis.

A personal interview and visit to campus are part of the admission requirements. Appointments must be made in advance, and are scheduled between 8 a.m. and 3 p.m., Monday through Friday.

ADMISSIONS CORRESPONDENCE

Bill Ellis, Director of Admissions
Saint James School
St. James, Maryland 21781

Phone: 301-733-9330
Fax: 301-739-1310
E-mail: admissions@stjames.edu
Web site: http://www.stjames.edu

ST. JOHNSBURY ACADEMY

St. Johnsbury, Vermont

A Proud Tradition
A Bright Future

Type: Coeducational boarding and day college-preparatory, technical, and arts school
Grades: 9–12, postgraduate year
Enrollment: 958
Head of School: Thomas W. Lovett, Headmaster

THE SCHOOL

St. Johnsbury Academy is a coeducational boarding and day school enrolling students in grades 9–12 and a postgraduate year. The town of St. Johnsbury (population 8,000) is situated in a mountainous area that offers opportunities for skiing, canoeing, camping, and hiking; is a center for the state's maple sugar industry; and provides students with access to the educational and cultural resources of Dartmouth College, the University of Vermont, and Lyndon State College. The town is 180 miles north of Boston, 330 miles north of New York City, and 150 miles south of Montreal. Served by local and interstate buses, it is easily reached via Interstates 91 and 93. There is a commercial airport in Burlington, Vermont, and the school provides transportation to and from the city at vacation times.

The Academy was founded in 1842 by the three Fairbanks brothers, local residents and manufacturers, to provide "intellectual, moral, and religious training for their own children and the children of the community." Since its founding, the Academy has enrolled boarding students while also serving day students from St. Johnsbury and surrounding towns.

St. Johnsbury Academy seeks to provide an education that will serve as "a life foundation for the free citizen, enabling him to be intellectually self-reliant and to function as a constructive, moral member of society." The program, which offers college-preparatory, business, and technical courses, is designed to meet the needs of students with varied interests and abilities.

A nonprofit institution, the Academy is governed by a self-perpetuating 21-member Board of Trustees, many of whom are alumni. The operating budget for 2004–05 was $17 million. Approximately 82 percent of this amount is funded directly through tuition revenue, with the balance provided through Annual Giving, endowment, and various other programs. Of the 12,350 living graduates, 7 percent contributed to the Annual Fund last year. The school-owned facilities are valued at $58 million. In addition, endowment funds total $16.2 million.

The Academy is fully accredited by the New England Association of Schools and Colleges and approved by the Vermont State Department of Education. It is a member of the National Association of Independent Schools, the Independent Schools Association of Northern New England, and the Vermont Independent Schools Association. In addition, the Academy is a member of the College Board and has been designated by that body as an examination center.

ACADEMIC PROGRAMS

The school year, from late August to early June, is divided into two 18-week semesters and includes Thanksgiving, Christmas, winter, and spring recesses. Core classes, which have an average enrollment of 16 students each, meet five days a week. Some electives meet every other day.

Grades are sent to parents at the close of each term; interim reports are issued if a student is experiencing difficulty. Each student has a faculty adviser who provides guidance in establishing and achieving personal and educational goals. Remedial courses are offered in all academic areas at no additional cost. The Learning Center provides support to those students whose learning style requires more personal assistance and attention. Evening study support and classroom accommodations are arranged as necessary. Freshmen participate in a study skills program. Individual tutorials can be arranged.

To graduate, students must complete 26 credits. One semester of course work provides 1 credit. Specific requirements are 4 credits in English and 3 credits each in social science, mathematics, and science. All students carry four full courses each semester.

The Academy also offers an extensive English as a Second Language Program. The ESL program addresses the needs of individual students through a series of ESL, English, and social studies courses, which are directed at the specific needs of the nonnative speaker.

St. Johnsbury Academy's program is designed to provide maximum flexibility so that a student may elect a course of study that meets his or her needs. The comprehensive curriculum includes 200 courses, including seventeen advanced-placement sections. Other courses are offered at basic, standard, and accelerated levels. Eleven in-depth technical offerings and twenty-five arts courses round out the curriculum. Many technical courses have been individualized, allowing students to learn technical skills while they prepare for college admission.

FACULTY AND ADVISERS

The faculty numbers 119: 76 men and 43 women. They hold 106 bachelor's degrees and seventy-five graduate degrees, representing study at more than ninety colleges and universities. Fifteen faculty members live on the campus.

Thomas W. Lovett was appointed Headmaster in 2001. He is a graduate of Providence College (B.A.) and Brown University (M.A.). Mr. Lovett has been a member of the English faculty and has served as Acting Academic Dean, English Department Chair, and Director of the Advanced Placement Institute. He has also coached football and baseball and has been a dormitory head.

COLLEGE PLACEMENT

The Director of the Guidance Office and 5 counselors help students complete their college applications. Advising starts early in the junior year, just before the PSAT is taken. Admissions representatives from many colleges visit the Academy, and groups of students attend the college fairs held in the area. The Guidance Office maintains an extensive reference library of college catalogs and other material to help students make their selections.

In 2005, 77 percent of the Academy's 249 graduates chose to continue their education. The colleges and universities that they are attending include Bates, Carnegie Mellon, Case Western Reserve, College of the Holy Cross, Cornell, Dartmouth, George Washington, Middlebury, Stanford, Swarthmore, Vassar, Wellesley, Williams, and the Universities of Michigan, North Carolina at Chapel Hill, Pennsylvania, Vermont, and Wisconsin.

STUDENT BODY AND CONDUCT

In 2004–05, St. Johnsbury Academy had 779 day and 179 boarding students, as follows: 212 in grade 9, 226 in grade 10, 268 in grade 11, and 252 (including 5 postgraduates) in grade 12. Boarders come from seventeen states and twenty-two countries.

Discipline is handled on an individual basis; the school attempts in all cases to maintain a firm, fair, and flexible policy.

The Student Council gives students a voice in school policy. The council helps the administration by offering advice on student attitudes toward current rules and regulations and suggesting possible changes and revisions.

ACADEMIC FACILITIES

Carl Ranger Hall, the English and writing center, houses thirteen classrooms and the department's writing lab, containing twenty-five PCs. Colby Hall is the main administration building, with offices and twenty classrooms. Severance Hall contains the Boarding Students Office and eight math classrooms. Streeter Hall is the home to the science and technology departments. In addition to these state-of-the-art academic facilities, the dining hall, Common Ground Café, television studio, and a 450-seat outdoor amphitheater are located here. Fuller Hall contains an 800-seat theater and dressing rooms. Newell Hall provides the foreign language department with extensive facilities for instruction, including two Tandberg computerized language learning systems. The Charles Hosmer Morse Center for the Arts provides extraordinary facilities, consisting of six fine-arts studios and an art gallery, a print and photography studio, two music performance studios with five practice rooms, a dance studio, and a 200-seat black box theater. The Mayo Center provides space for the Grace Stuart Orcutt library (20,000 volumes), a student lounge, and the Colwell Center for Global Understanding. The nearby St. Johnsbury Athenaeum provides students with access to an additional 45,000 volumes.

BOARDING AND GENERAL FACILITIES

The Academy has nine dormitories housing 178 students. Faculty members reside in each dorm. The student-faculty ratio in the dorms is 6:1. Boarding students care for their own rooms.

A school nurse is available on campus at all times, and emergency services are available at nearby Northeastern Vermont Regional Hospital.

During vacation periods when dormitories are closed, arrangements are made for those students unable to return home to travel with an Academy group or to stay with a local family.

ATHLETICS

Varsity and junior varsity teams for boys are organized in baseball, basketball, football, lacrosse, soccer, and wrestling; there are also freshman teams in football, basketball, and soccer. Girls' varsity and junior varsity teams are formed in basketball, lacrosse, soccer, softball, and field hockey. There is also interscholastic competition in cross-country, tennis, ice hockey, golf, and track and field for boys and in golf, tennis, gymnastics, lacrosse, and track and field for girls. Nordic and Alpine skiing are offered on a coeducational basis. In addition, intramural sports are offered throughout the year. Tennis, skiing, golf, hiking, canoeing, riding, mountain climbing, and camping are among the recreational sports and activities available.

Alumni Memorial Gymnasium contains the basketball court, seating for 1,250, and locker rooms. The Academy's field house contains three multipurpose tennis, volleyball, and basketball courts; a ¹⁄₁₂-mile indoor track; and a 25-yard, 6-lane indoor swimming pool. The building also provides locker rooms; team rooms; areas for hydrotherapy and wrestling; and a weight room with a Universal Gym, nine Nautilus stations, and extensive free-weight and aerobics equipment. A 400-meter all-weather track was completed in 1996.

EXTRACURRICULAR OPPORTUNITIES

The Student Council, composed of elected representatives of each class, meets weekly to advise the administration on matters of student concern and to organize student activities.

Students publish a yearbook (*The Lamp*) and a newspaper (*The Student*). Qualified students are invited to join the National Honor Society. Other extracurricular organizations include the Academy Theatre and Lyceum and a great-books discussion group. Among the more than fifty clubs and activities are Cheerleaders and the French, Math, Band, Stage Band, Chorus, Science, Audio-Visual, Computer, Naturalist, and Chess Clubs. The International Club provides several opportunities each year for travel abroad.

DAILY LIFE

Breakfast is served at 7:15 on weekday mornings. The academic day begins with chapel, an all-school assembly, at 8. Classes begin at 8:15 and run until 2:46. Following classes, there is a conference period during which all faculty members are available to students for additional help. Extracurricular activities are scheduled between 3 and 5; dinner is at 5:30. Proctored study hall is held from 7:30 to 9; honor students are exempted from the mandatory study period. The library is open in the evening, Monday through Thursday. The quiet hours in the dormitory extend until 10:30 p.m.

WEEKEND LIFE

Brunch and dinner are served on weekends. Dances, films, concerts, plays, and sports events are typical weekend activities. Transportation is provided to area ski resorts as well as other destinations, including Boston, Montreal, and Burlington. With parental and school permission, students may leave campus on weekends.

SUMMER PROGRAMS

St. Johnsbury Academy offers an English as a Second Language Program designed to provide intensive training in spoken language, listening comprehension, reading, and writing. A unique aspect of the Academy summer program is the homestay family; each student lives with an American family during the entire six weeks of the program. During the day, the program retains the rigorous structure and numerous activities found in a high-quality boarding school. Thus, the students enjoy the advantages of a structured academic and extracurricular program combined with the benefits of living with an American family.

COSTS AND FINANCIAL AID

In 2004–05, tuition and boarding fees were $27,860; day tuition was $9760. Personal expenses for boarders totaled approximately $1500 per year.

Approximately $300,000 in financial aid is awarded annually to qualified students on the basis of need.

ADMISSIONS INFORMATION

St. Johnsbury Academy seeks to enroll students of good character who are interested in rigorous college preparation or who are serious about preparation for a vocation or trade. Candidates are accepted in all grades and occasionally for a postgraduate year, but most enter in grade 9 or 10. Admission is based on previous school records, references, a personal interview, and standardized test scores.

APPLICATION TIMETABLE

Applications are accepted throughout the year. Applying during the winter or spring prior to the anticipated fall entrance is recommended. There is a $20 application fee. Admissions are handled by the Director of Admission.

ADMISSIONS CORRESPONDENCE

John Cummings, Director of Admission and
　　Advancement
St. Johnsbury Academy
1000 Main Street
St. Johnsbury, Vermont 05819

Phone: 802-751-2130
Fax: 802-748-5463
E-mail: admissions@stjacademy.org
Web site: http://www.stjohnsburyacademy.org

ST. JOHN'S MILITARY SCHOOL

Salina, Kansas

Type: Boys' boarding college-preparatory military school
Grades: 7–12: Middle School, 7–8; Upper School, 9–12
Enrollment: School total: 215; Upper School: 170
Head of School: Col. Jack R. Fox

THE SCHOOL

St. John's Military School (SJMS) was founded in 1887 by the Right Reverend Elisha Smith Thomas, Episcopal Bishop of Kansas, and a group of Salina businessmen to provide a disciplined environment under church auspices in a military setting. The School's mission is to provide each cadet with the opportunity to grow spiritually, morally, intellectually, and physically in a structured environment.

Located in Salina, Kansas, a city with a population of 47,000, St. John's has been an integral part of the community since its inception. For 118 years, the School and the Salina community have enjoyed a close and mutually beneficial relationship. Salina is the home of three colleges. It is a progressive city and provides the cadets with many outside activities not found in smaller towns. The advantages of a larger city are combined with the small-town atmosphere to make Salina an ideal community in which to attend boarding school.

Salina has several theaters, and it offers other cultural and educational advantages through such institutions as the Salina Arts Commission, Kansas Wesleyan University, Kansas State University at Salina, and Brown-Mackie College.

St. John's is directed by a 19-member, self-perpetuating Board of Trustees. The Episcopal Bishop of the Diocese of Western Kansas is ex officio member of the board. St. John's is a nonprofit corporation.

The School has an operating budget of $3.5 million, with an Annual Giving Program providing 3 percent of this amount. The School's land and buildings are debt free and are valued at $11 million. The endowment is currently valued in excess of $10 million.

The School is accredited by the North Central Association of Colleges and Schools and the Kansas Department of Education. It is a member of the National Association of Episcopal Schools and the Association of Military Colleges and Schools of the United States.

ACADEMIC PROGRAMS

In the standard curriculum, 24 credits are required for graduation. Of these, all cadets who attend grades 9 through 12 are required to complete 4 units of language arts, 4 of mathematics, 4 of science, 4 of social science, 1 of computer science, 1 of physical education and health, 4 of JROTC, and 1 of religion. In the college-preparatory curriculum, 28 credits are required. Students must complete 2 credits of foreign language and 2 extra elective credits in addition to the standard curriculum requirements. College preparatory courses include algebra I and II, geometry, advanced mathematics (trigonometry or calculus), U.S. history, American government,

economics, world history, world government, physical science, biology I and II, chemistry, and physics.

The religion program at St. John's is predicated on the conviction that a solid religion program, rooted in the moral and ethical teachings of the Judeo-Christian heritage, is essential to any sound educational endeavor. Following the traditions of the Episcopal Church, regular worship services are conducted at St. John's on a daily basis, Sunday through Friday each week. Each cadet attends chapel four times a week (Monday, Tuesday, Thursday, and Friday). The cadets themselves conduct all aspects of the Sunday chapel service, with the exception of those functions requiring the services of a priest. Spiritual direction, advice, and guidance are available to all cadets. In addition, religion is taught as an academic subject with courses ranging from the literature, history, and geography of the ancient Middle East to courses in Judeo-Christian morals and ethics. One year of religion is required for graduation. Baptism into the Christian faith and confirmation in the Episcopal Church is voluntary and is permitted only with the consent of the cadet's parent or guardian. The chapel is open daily for personal prayer and private meditation, and visitors, including families, are always welcome to attend services with their cadet.

The School has an early graduation policy, which considers any cadet for early graduation upon successful demonstration of satisfactory completion of all SJMS graduation requirements by the combination of a previous (accredited school) and St. John's academic curriculum, a 90 percent grade on any approved course work taken outside the traditional educational school day (distance learning, college or junior college programs, and/or summer school), and a 90 percent grade on all competence (quiz out) testing while enrolled at St. John's.

The student-teacher ratio is approximately 10:1. Students have an 8-hour block schedule, which offers a total of 8 credits. Class periods are 50 minutes in length. A 45-minute tutorial period is offered daily after school. Each evening there is a 2-hour mandatory study hall period designed for academic study.

Student comprehensive academic evaluations are sent home each grading period and when either a grade or behavior is unsatisfactory.

The guidance department consists of a full-time academic counselor and a chaplain.

FACULTY AND ADVISERS

The faculty consists of 18 men and 10 women, plus 13 full-time military advisers.

The President of St. John's Military School is Col. (retired) Jack R. Fox, who was appointed in 2004. Colonel Fox has twenty-six years' military service and has spent the last eleven years in

education, with nine years in the military school arena. Colonel Fox holds a B.A. in government from New Mexico State University and a Master of Education from Georgia State University. He is also a graduate of the U.S. Army War College.

COLLEGE PLACEMENT

The academic counselor assists all cadets in managing their academic program to ensure they are on course to graduate and also assists junior and senior cadets in evaluating and selecting appropriate colleges. Parents are always highly involved in this process. All junior and senior cadets are given the opportunity to take the SAT and ACT each semester.

In typical years, 75 to 80 percent of the graduating cadets attend college or some type of post–high school educational institution. In addition to many small colleges and junior colleges, graduates attend colleges and universities such as Kansas State; the United States Military Academy at West Point; Texas A&M; Virginia Military Institute (VMI); the Universities of Colorado, Kansas, and Wyoming; and many other top-rated colleges and universities across the nation.

STUDENT BODY AND CONDUCT

The School has a total student capacity of 215 boys, 45 of whom are in the middle school. All students are boarding. The states with the largest number of boys in attendance are Colorado and Oklahoma, but boys come from more than twenty states and other countries.

An elected Cadet Court serves as an advisory body in disciplinary matters as well as for occasional special functions. Serious disciplinary infractions are handled by the Commandant of Cadets through a system of additional duties, marching tours, loss of privileges, and reduction in military rank.

ACADEMIC FACILITIES

The Upper School classes are housed in the beautiful Vanier Academic Center, which contains classrooms, labs, a theater, and the library. The center was constructed in 1980 at a cost of $1.5 million. The Lyman G. Linger Middle School is a $1-million structure that serves as the academic center for boys in grades 7 and 8. Completed in 1991, this building houses science and computer labs as well as a number of spacious classrooms.

BOARDING AND GENERAL FACILITIES

The buildings on campus include Clem-Ferris and Mize Residence Halls for the high school cadets and Sage Residence Hall for the middle school cadets. Other buildings include the Spencer Cadet Center and the Armstrong Memorial Chapel. The Stevens Center, a $3-million multipurpose facility, houses a dining facility, a

twelve-lane rifle range, a cadet recreation center, a nine-bed infirmary, the cadet staff's living quarters, and the offices of the Military Department.

Cadets are housed primarily in 2-man rooms. There is adult supervision 24 hours a day. During the three furloughs—Thanksgiving, Christmas, and spring break—the residence halls are closed.

The School has a full-time nurse in residence. A physician is available to the cadets either on campus or at his office in the city.

ATHLETICS
Athletics at St. John's are an integral part of the total program but do not interfere with organized study time or the academic schedule in any way or at any time. They are geared primarily for participation, and all cadets are encouraged to try out for an interscholastic sport sometime during the year. Middle School students in grades 7 and 8 do not participate in interscholastic sports. They do, however, participate in intramural sports programs, both on campus and in town with the YMCA programs. St. John's high school is a member of the Eisenhower League, in which the teams participate in football and basketball. The School offers an independent varsity schedule in golf, riflery, and soccer, tennis, and wrestling. The basketball team participates in substate playoffs, whereas the football team concludes its season by playing in the Saints Bowl.

Physical training is required for any cadets not in a varsity sport. The School has organized sporting events and many other activities of an athletic nature during the course of a school year.

Indoor sports are played in the Wiley T. Banes Gymnasium, and outdoor activities are scheduled on Perkins Field and on surrounding acreage, including two tennis courts.

EXTRACURRICULAR OPPORTUNITIES
Students are encouraged to participate in extracurricular activities but are advised to join no more than three student groups. Students publish a yearbook, and provide photographic support for *The Skirmisher,* a bimonthly school newspaper that is mailed to parents and St. John's alumni all over the world. There are opportunities for students to participate in art and music and perform in school plays. Students may serve as library assistants or film projectionists. The drill team and the rifle team engage in military competitions and performances throughout the Midwest. Other student organizations include the band, the Blue Berets (the top 3 academic students in the middle school and the top 3 in the high school), Cadet Patrol, Chapel Council, Chapel Choir (for which academic credit is awarded), chapters of the National Honor Society and National Junior Honor Society, Spanish Club, Spartan Program, forensics, Computer Club, French Club, Chess Club, Bicycle Club, and the Advanced Military Skills Program.

Cadets are often asked to participate in civic functions and take part in benefits for worthy causes. The School feels that the visibility and exposure of its cadets is an asset, and the cadets respond accordingly.

DAILY LIFE
A typical school day begins at 6 a.m. with "first call," followed by formation for reveille at 6:25. Cadets then march to breakfast, which starts at 6:30. All cadets attend chapel from 7:15 to 7:30 daily. Cadets get a final opportunity to square their barracks and living areas away before beginning classes at 8. Classes run until 3, with a 45-minute tutorial session from 3:15 to 4. Athletics or other activities follow until 6.

There is some free time after the evening meal before the required study time from 7 to 9. Taps sound at 9:15 for middle school students and at 10:15 for high school students.

WEEKEND LIFE
On Saturday, cadets may receive passes to go to an off-campus movie, do some shopping in town, or participate in other appropriate activities. At St. John's, Sunday is the Lord's Day. All cadets attend Sunday chapel services at Armstrong Memorial Chapel of St. John the Evangelist (Episcopal), located on campus and conducted by St. John's resident chaplain. Under special circumstances, and for valid theological reasons, cadets of other faiths may attend other services in the Salina community. The balance of Sunday is generally reserved for relaxation, study, or passes for participation in appropriate, approved, off-campus activities.

COSTS AND FINANCIAL AID
The cost of tuition, room, and board for 2005–06 was $21,663. This includes tuition, room and board, security deposit, and uniforms. There is an estimated incidentals charge during the course of the year of approximately $3000, depending on a young man's spending habits and allowance from parents. The Admissions Office is available to discuss a number of flexible payment plans and educational loans. Details can be worked out in the Business Office after a student has been accepted. Parents also have the option of using the services of a private financing institution to design other payment plans.

About $150,000 is available in scholarships each year for "old boys," or cadets returning for successive years. Scholarships are offered on a merit basis, depending on a boy's academic record and other factors, to include activities, athletics, leadership potential, and number of years attended or attending. In addition, the School has alumni members who choose to award some of the senior cadets with full scholarships every year. These are also awarded on a merit basis.

Jobs are generally not available to the cadet corps. The School prefers that cadets work strictly on School-related activities, not paid jobs. However, the dining hall can offer paying opportunities for a few boys to serve as waiters.

ADMISSIONS INFORMATION
St. John's is primarily a college-preparatory school and seeks to enroll those students who are of strong moral and ethical character and are capable of handling a tough and rigorous academic schedule. Other aspects of personality that can be important are a willingness to be at the School and to give the School's system a try. Thanks to the inherent structure of the military setting, the School works well with those who have underachieved at other schools.

No admissions pretest is given. A cadet is monitored for placement or ability grouping once he is on campus. The School requires transcripts from the student's former school. Most students who apply are accepted, but the School does careful groundwork prior to the application process to be sure that both a candidate and the School benefit from an applicant's admission.

APPLICATION TIMETABLE
St. John's has a rolling admissions policy whereby applications are welcome anytime and cadets are accepted during the school year as long as spaces are available. Personal interviews are recommended but not required.

ADMISSIONS CORRESPONDENCE
Maj. Jeffrey E. Coverdale
Director of Admissions and Development
St. John's Military School
P.O. Box 5020
Salina, Kansas 67402-5020

Phone: 785-823-7231
Fax: 785-309-5489
E-mail: jeffc@sjms.org
Web site: http://www.sjms.org

ST. JOHN'S NORTHWESTERN MILITARY ACADEMY

Delafield, Wisconsin

Type: Boys' boarding college-preparatory and military school
Grades: 7–12: Middle School, 7–8; Upper School, 9–12
Enrollment: School total: 393
Head of School: Mr. Jack H. Albert Jr., President

THE SCHOOL

The cornerstones of the St. John's Northwestern experience are academics, athletics, leadership, and character development. Together, they help students develop study skills, positive work attitudes, intellectual curiosity, cultural appreciation, good manners, self-discipline, self-motivation, teamwork, decision-making ability, personal honesty, and good character. The Academy believes that a boy must be challenged but not overwhelmed. Cadets are immersed in a structured "cadet lifestyle," in which they strengthen their academic fundamentals, are challenged to reach new heights, develop self-worth, and experience a sense of success.

The Academy uses the military program and cadet lifestyle to develop character, integrity, and leadership qualities. Each year, several students express an interest in attending the service academies or participating in college ROTC. The Academy has had a JROTC program since its inception in 1916 and has held an Honor Unit with Distinction by the United States Army since its origination.

St. John's Northwestern is located in the beautiful Kettle Moraine region of southeastern Wisconsin, just 25 miles west of Milwaukee and 95 miles northwest of Chicago. The 150-acre campus, adjacent to Lake Nagawicka and the city of Delafield, is ideally situated among rolling farmland and woods.

A nonprofit corporation, St. John's Northwestern is directed by a 22-member Board of Trustees. The school's physical plant is valued at $21 million. The Academy has the active support of the Parents' Club and more than 5,000 alumni.

St. John's Northwestern Military Academy is accredited by the Independent Schools Association of the Central States. It is a member of the National Association of Independent Schools, the Association of Military Colleges and Schools of the United States, the North Central Association, and the Midwest Boarding Schools Association.

ACADEMIC PROGRAMS

The curriculum at St. John's Northwestern is carefully designed to provide six years of academic study at the junior high and high school levels to qualified students who wish to prepare themselves for higher education. The small size of classes, averaging 12 students each, allows each student to receive individual attention and participate frequently in classroom discussions. A supervised 2-hour study period each evening, Sunday through Thursday, is an integral part of the academic program. Special morning and afternoon tutorial periods are scheduled for students who seek even more individual attention. If a student is having difficulty in a particular subject, he may be required to attend tutorial sessions for extra help. In addition, a Learning Center is available to all students to improve their reading, writing, and study skills.

English, mathematics, science, social sciences, foreign language, computers, and leadership training form the core of the academic program. These disciplines offer a variety of courses designed to meet the needs of the individual student. The required courses are supplemented by elective courses in each discipline plus art, band, choir, drama, driver's education, and aviation science. In order to ensure that each student receives the desired breadth of exposure to the many academic disciplines necessary for college preparation, the school requires students to complete a minimum of 20 units of credit plus the LET (Leadership Educational Training) sequence prior to graduation: English, 4; social studies, 3; mathematics, 3; science (lab courses), 3; foreign language, 2; computer, 1; and electives, 4. Honors courses and a special Honors Diploma are offered. Opportunities are available for students to earn college credits through an independent study program.

A 4-point grading system is employed (4.0 is equivalent to A), and a minimum average of 2.0 is required for good standing once a student is enrolled at the Academy.

FACULTY AND ADVISERS

St. John's Northwestern seeks out experienced teachers who are interested in working closely with boys, both within the classroom and in daily campus life. There are 36 full-time faculty members (30 men and 6 women). Sixteen staff members hold master's degrees, and 4 hold Ph.D.'s; 20 live on campus, most with their families.

Jack H. Albert Jr. is the president of St. John's Northwestern Military Academy. He was appointed in 2004 and has twenty years' experience in the military school arena. His experience encompasses positions of teacher, Director of Guidance, Academic Vice President, and President. Mr. Albert holds a master's degree in counseling and is a doctoral candidate in education administration.

The Academy has a college counselor to help prepare each student for college and life after high school. The academic dean, the college counselor, and the student's faculty adviser all become involved in monitoring a student's progress. All members of the staff and faculty are trained to give guidance to students, and each faculty member is assigned to advise approximately 10 students. Faculty and staff members are also involved in coaching, supervising field trips, and advising club activities.

COLLEGE PLACEMENT

St. John's Northwestern Military Academy's college counselor assists students with the college selection process. Cadets are encouraged to visit college campuses and attend college fairs. In addition, parents are actively involved as soon as a student enrolls. Each year, an average of 15 college representatives visit the school.

For more than a decade, 100 percent of Academy graduates have been accepted at colleges and universities. Schools that have accepted Academy graduates include Embry-Riddle, Emory, Florida State, Iowa State, Michigan State, Northwestern, Notre Dame, Purdue, Rose-Hulman Institute of Technology, the United States Service Academies, Vanderbilt, Williams, and the Universities of California, Illinois, Indiana, Iowa, Michigan, Ohio, and Wisconsin.

STUDENT BODY AND CONDUCT

The campus supports 393 boarding cadets. Approximately 70 are from other countries; the remainder are from twenty-two states.

The student body is organized into a Corps of Cadets composed of a Battalion Staff and six individual cadet companies, all under cadet leadership. Under the guidance of the Office of the Commandant, the Corps is self-governing, with cadet leaders responsible for the daily nonacademic activities of each company. Every cadet has an opportunity to obtain a leadership position. Each cadet is given a *Cadet Rules and Regulations Handbook* and is expected to be familiar with its contents and to govern himself accordingly.

ACADEMIC FACILITIES

Two main academic buildings, Cord Hall and the newly completed Stangeland Hall, house the classrooms, computer labs, science labs, and language labs. Stangeland Hall, a $4.5-million structure that was funded by private donations, replaced the antiquated Knight Hall and opened in 1999. Stangeland Hall provides advanced educational technology capabilities, air conditioning, and superb energy efficiency. Its twenty-first-century construction blends nicely with the English-gothic-style architecture of the existing campus, even connecting the classrooms to the barracks via an indoor walking bridge.

Following a $1.6-million renovation, newly renamed Noble Victory Memorial Chapel houses the music department and serves as the center of worship on campus for the cadets. The Old Boys' Memorial Library, built in 1894, is a national historic landmark and houses 14,000 volumes. There are a full-time librarian on staff and six networked computers with Internet access. The library is part of the fifty-two-member Waukesha County Library Association. Athletics and swimming classes are held in the newly refurbished Farrand Hall Gymnasium and Gerber Pool.

BOARDING AND GENERAL FACILITIES

The Academy's facilities include three barracks, the dining hall, a recreation center, a nine-hole golf course, two parade fields, a football stadium, a rugby/soccer field, a track, a baseball diamond, an obstacle course, a paintball course, indoor and outdoor rifle ranges, a gymnasium, an indoor swimming pool, faculty housing, and an infirmary. The school also has lake access and an island on Lake Nagawicka. The English-gothic architecture of the buildings, which are surrounded by broad lawns and towering trees, makes the campus one of the most picturesque in the United States.

There are 2 cadets to each room. Each cadet is supplied with a networked computer complete with limited access to the Internet and time- and channel-limited cable television. The cadets' rooms have new desks and bookshelves, newly installed sinks, energy-efficient windows, and individual closets. Cadets are organized into companies. Each company is staffed with a full-time, live-in TAC (Trainer, Advisor, Counselor) Officer, who resides on the same floor as the cadets.

ATHLETICS

To ensure the development of the whole person, all cadets, regardless of prior experience or ability, are required to participate in athletics. The physical education program, which emphasizes an introduction to lifetime sports, complements a comprehensive varsity and junior varsity interscholastic program of football, basketball, track, golf, baseball, soccer, wrestling, cross-country running, tennis, swimming, riflery, ice hockey, and rugby. Other team sports and activities are offered as clubs; these are downhill skiing/snowboarding, weight lifting, Raiders (military activities), chess, and Boy Scouts.

Sports facilities on campus include a nine-hole golf course, a sand volleyball court, a gymnasium, a weight room, an indoor and an outdoor rifle range, a swimming pool, tennis courts, football and soccer fields, a baseball diamond, and other outdoor athletics fields.

EXTRACURRICULAR OPPORTUNITIES

All cadets have the opportunity to participate in extracurricular activities or clubs. Among these are ACT/SAT preparation courses, the school newspaper (The Cadet Review) and yearbook (The Trumpeter), the nationally honored Silver Rifles Drill Team, the bagpipe band, and the Herald Trumpeters. Special social programs are offered throughout the year. Off-campus social, cultural, and recreational activities include movies, shopping trips, paintballing, rock climbing, water parks, professional sports, theater, music concerts, comedy clubs, annual trips to Six Flags Great America, and educational study tours, as well as other opportunities in metropolitan Milwaukee and Chicago. Some of the on-campus activities are movies, regularly scheduled dances, and high-tech interactive attractions such as laser tag, Virtual Reality, and Flight Simulators. The social highlight of the year is the Midwinter Weekend and formal Military Ball, held in the spring. Parents' Weekends are major events, as is the annual medieval Boar's Head Banquet, held before Christmas break. Opportunities for volunteerism in the Delafield community are available and encouraged.

DAILY LIFE

A typical day begins with reveille at 6 a.m., followed by room inspection and breakfast. After morning tutorial, classes start at 8:25 a.m. and end at 2:30 p.m., with a break for lunch. Following afternoon tutorial, cadets participate in sports or chapel and military training, which are followed by dinner. Supervised study begins at 7:35 p.m. and ends at 9:45 p.m. There is sufficient free time for relaxation, letter writing, independent study, and socializing.

Nondenominational chapel services are held on Sundays and Wednesdays, and all students are required to attend. In addition, cadets may sign up for Roman Catholic mass and Jewish Shabbats. High Holy Days are also observed. Transportation to other religious services and activities can be arranged.

WEEKEND LIFE

Cadets spend weekends studying, playing sports, and attending Academy-sponsored dances and social events. Sunday's activities include mandatory chapel attendance, room and personal inspection, and colorful parades. After earning leave privileges, approximately one weekend leave per month is granted.

SUMMER PROGRAMS

St. John's Northwestern Military Academy offers three types of summer programs. Camp St. John's Northwestern, a boarding military adventure camp for young men ages 10–16, is designed to promote personal growth and achievement. Young men have fun developing leadership, sportsmanship, and teamwork skills while building confidence and self-esteem. International students can attend English as a Second Language (ESL) Camp. ESL Camp helps prepare students for entrance into St. John's Northwestern Military Academy. The program improves students' fluency in English by emphasizing speaking, reading, writing, and listening skills within a classroom and during off-campus cultural activities. An Academic Camp is also offered, during which boys can earn up to ½ credit in a core academic area. Academic and ESL campers also participate in adventure camp activities daily. Students should contact Enrollment Services for dates and costs of all camps.

COSTS AND FINANCIAL AID

The comprehensive fee, which covers charges for tuition, room, board, laundry, hardcover books, the yearbook and newspaper, and haircuts for the 2005–06 school year, is $27,250. This fee does not include the cost of uniforms, deposits, personal needs, insurance, or school supplies. An initial uniform and room supply charge of $2000 covers all required uniform items as well as a blanket, backpack, and foot locker. An incidental account must be established for each cadet to cover such needs as cadet store purchases, school supplies, and social and recreational activities. This account is handled on a charge basis. In addition, parents or guardians may establish a bank account at the Academy as a means of handling the cadet's weekly allowance. An initial deposit of $200 is recommended. Monthly billings are made by the Finance Office.

A cadet is enrolled for the entire school year. All fees and charges are due and payable in full at registration; however, for those enrolling in the fall, payment plans are available through FACTS Tuition Management Company.

A limited amount of need-based financial aid is available. These limited funds are awarded to the families who are first to complete all the requirements. Sixty-six percent of the cadets were awarded scholarships or financial aid for the 2004–05 school year.

ADMISSIONS INFORMATION

St. John's Northwestern Military Academy does not discriminate on the basis of race, creed, or national or ethnic origin in the administration of their educational policies, admission policy, financial aid programs, athletics programs, or other Academy-administered programs.

When considering a young man for admission, the Academy evaluates the following factors: the student's motivation for attending the Academy, prior academic work, school officials' comments and recommendations, results of the enrollment eligibility examination administered by the Academy, results of interviews with school officials, prior citizenship and conduct, ability to successfully complete a college-preparatory curriculum, and medical fitness (an applicant should be able to participate in the major school programs: academics, physical education/athletics, and leadership development).

The Academy demands much of each cadet. A desire to succeed will help a young man achieve many goals. The Enrollment Services Department evaluates each application and all related materials in order to reach an enrollment eligibility decision. A visit to the campus is considered an integral facet of the admission process, both for the school and for the applicant and his family.

APPLICATION TIMETABLE

Applications are accepted at any time. The Enrollment Services Department is open Monday through Friday from 8 a.m. to 5 p.m. Central time. Parents and students may obtain application forms and information by contacting Enrollment Services.

ADMISSIONS CORRESPONDENCE

Maj. Charles Moore, SJNMA
Director of Enrollment Services
St. John's Northwestern Military Academy
1101 North Genesee Street
Delafield, Wisconsin 53018-1498
Phone: 262-646-7199
        800-752-2338 (toll-free)
Fax: 262-646-7128
E-mail: admissions@sjnma.org
Web site: http://www.sjnma.org

SAINT JOHN'S PREPARATORY SCHOOL

Collegeville, Minnesota

Type: Coeducational boarding and day college-preparatory school operated by the monks of the Order of St. Benedict
Grades: 9–12, postgraduate year; day program for grades 7–8
Enrollment: 316
Head of School: Father Gordon Tavis, O.S.B.

THE SCHOOL

The Benedictine monks have been educating young people and preserving the culture of Western civilization since the sixth century. Saint John's Preparatory School is a continuation of that 1,500-year-old educational system and lifestyle. During the mid-1800s, German and Irish pioneers began to settle the Minnesota territory. Saint John's was founded to minister to those early Minnesotans. Since 1857 Saint John's Prep has continuously served students from Minnesota as well as from other parts of the country and the world. The School continues to celebrate the enduring quality of education in the Benedictine tradition.

Saint John's is set on a 2,600-acre campus of woods and lakes in central Minnesota. Located on the same campus as a major university (Saint John's University), a publishing house, the largest Benedictine monastery in the world, an ecumenical and cultural research center, and the Hill Monastic Museum and Manuscript Library.

Academic excellence and spiritual growth are the pillars on which the School stands. Students learn alongside goal-directed peers from across the United States and abroad, all of whom are challenged to reach their highest potential in an environment that prepares them for college and a lifetime of learning. Students follow a college-preparatory curriculum, which often leads to a wide variety of college courses. In addition to learning in the classroom, Saint John's Prep students learn to live with others, examine individual values and aspirations, and seek God.

Saint John's is located 12 miles west of St. Cloud. Cited as one of the fastest-growing metropolitan areas in Minnesota, St. Cloud and the surrounding suburbs have a current population of 165,000. Saint John's is off Interstate 94, a 1½-hour drive from Minneapolis–St. Paul.

Saint John's Prep is accredited by the Independent Schools Association of the Central States and the North Central Association. Memberships include the Minnesota Catholic Conference, the National Association of Independent Schools, the National Catholic Educational Association, and the Midwest Boarding Schools Association.

ACADEMIC PROGRAMS

Saint John's Prep follows a traditional liberal arts curriculum. A minimum of 22½ full-year credits are required for graduation, among which the following must be included (waivers and exemptions are granted by the Academic Dean): English, 8 semesters; math, 6 semesters; fine arts, a minimum of 4 semesters; modern language, 6 semesters of one language or the equivalent; science, 6 semesters; social studies, 8 semesters; health, 1 semester; and theology, 7 semesters. Graduation requirements are met through a combination of required and elective courses. Independent study is also available. Courses for college credit in Spanish, German, English, math, science, and dozens of other subjects are available for qualified students through the School, Saint John's University, or the College of Saint Benedict.

Students take five or more classes per semester. They may also take courses at Saint John's University on the same campus and at the nearby College of Saint Benedict. Graduates of Saint John's Prep can complete a B.A. degree in three years with careful planning.

New international students are given an assessment of their English language skills as they arrive in the fall to determine their need for English as a Second Language classes and what level best fits their need.

A yearlong study-abroad program at Melk, Austria is offered to juniors, seniors, and Prep graduates. This program features a full academic curriculum enriched by travel throughout Europe. A monthlong study-abroad program to Segovia, Spain is offered in the summer.

The postgraduate program offers students the flexibility to design a course of study that best meets their needs and interests. Students may take all of their courses at the Prep School or take up to three courses each semester at Saint John's University. Credits earned at Saint John's University and the College of Saint Benedict can be transferred elsewhere when the student enrolls in college.

The grading system uses A–F designations with pluses and minuses. Student progress reports are issued several times each semester, and grade reports come out at the end of each semester. The system allows careful monitoring of students' progress throughout the semester. Parent-teacher conferences are held twice a year, and parents are invited to arrange an appointment with teachers and staff members whenever they are concerned about their son's or daughter's academic or social progress. Supervised study time during the school day is required, the amount varying according to a student's grade point average. Boarding students also have evening study hall.

FACULTY AND ADVISERS

In 2005–06, the faculty consisted of 22 men and 12 women. Twenty have earned a master's degree. Nearly all faculty members contribute to the quality of life through coaching, advising, counseling, and helping with musical, dramatic, and other special events. The faculty members are assisted by college students—paraprofessionals studying education—who work as tutors for students having academic difficulty.

Father Gordon Tavis, O.S.B., was appointed Head of School in 1998. Father Gordon is a graduate of Saint John's University (B.A., 1954) and Massachusetts Institute of Technology (M.Mgt., 1972). Prior to his appointment at Saint John's Prep, he served for seventeen years as treasurer of the Order of Saint Benedict in Collegeville, Minnesota, and for twenty years as a member of the Board of Regents; for five years as Prior of Saint John's Abbey; and for three years as a member of the Prep School staff.

COLLEGE PLACEMENT

The School employs a college placement counselor and maintains an office with a complete collection of catalogs of colleges and universities in the United

States as well as handbooks and brochures. Many college admissions representatives visit the Prep School each year, and seniors' trips to various schools are arranged through the counseling office. Ninety-eight percent of all Prep graduates pursue education at institutions of higher learning. Recent graduates are attending Babson, Boston College, Caltech, Carleton, the College of Saint Benedict, Harvard, Macalester, Saint John's, Stanford, Washington (St. Louis), Wellesley, and a variety of other schools.

STUDENT BODY AND CONDUCT

The enrollment on campus for 2005–06 included freshmen, 24 boys and 20 girls; sophomores, 39 boys and 32 girls; juniors, 35 boys and 26 girls; seniors, 31 boys and 31 girls; and postgraduates, 2 boys. Of these, 4 were studying in Austria. There were 76 students enrolled in the Middle School.

About 37 percent of the Upper School students board, 57 boys and 32 girls. Through the English Second Language Program and the Study Abroad Program, Saint John's Prep maintains an international position. This year, there are 64 international students from twelve countries living on campus. U.S. boarders come from states across the country, including Alaska, California, Iowa, Maryland, New Jersey, Texas, Wisconsin, and Wyoming as well as Minnesota. Day students come from fourteen local school districts. Approximately 45 percent of the students are not Catholic.

Students of Saint John's Preparatory School have common expectations and rights that deserve mutual support. These expectations and rights include physical safety, honesty, protection of physical and mental health, and an orderly environment in which to pursue the goals that bring Saint John's together as a school community.

In order to protect the rights of all members of the Prep community and to establish and maintain an orderly environment for the pursuit of goals that are consonant with the philosophy of the School, rules have been established and are published in the student handbook. Disciplinary action for major offenses is carried out by the Dean of Students. Consequences for major offenses might include community service, work details, fines, in-school suspension, home suspension, probation, and/or dismissal.

ACADEMIC FACILITIES

Recent additions to the Prep academic building include a fine arts center, the Weber Center, which was completed in 1997. This multipurpose facility is a theater and home for the band, choir, and string programs as well as a gathering place for all-school assemblies, dances, convocations, and prayer service or Eucharist. A science wing, consisting of four classrooms and labs, was completed in 2000. Expanded and remodeled art spaces include a new darkroom and kiln room.

Many educational facilities are shared by the Prep School and Saint John's University, including the Alcuin Library, which houses more than 250,000 volumes, microfilms, and videotapes. A technology link to the University's computer system provides

Prep students and faculty members with individual e-mail accounts, access to the Internet, and numerous online databases and software programs.

BOARDING AND GENERAL FACILITIES

At Saint John's, being in residence is viewed as much more than living in a room on campus. It brings young people together from around the world to create an exciting community accented with cultural diversity and friendships. Resident students have a peer group that values study. They also have adults who know from their own experience what study entails and what college requires of the student. Prep boarding boys are housed on the Prep School campus. Saint John's has a residential program for girls through the cooperation of the nearby College of Saint Benedict. The College of Saint Benedict, located 4 miles away in the small town of St. Joseph, Minnesota, is a premier liberal arts college for women, operating a coordinated program with Saint John's University. Each freshman student shares a room, and upper-level students are assigned single rooms on a seniority basis.

A snack bar and recreational facilities are available at the School and at Sexton Commons on the Saint John's University campus and the Haehn Center on the Saint Ben's campus. Medical attention is available at the Health Center. A doctor is available each day for appointments, and a pharmacy is located on campus. The St. Cloud Hospital is located about 20 minutes away.

Other facilities, shared by the University and the Prep School, include the Abbey Church, the Stephen B. Humphrey Auditorium, and the Warner Palaestra, which houses an indoor track, indoor tennis courts, racquetball courts, and an Olympic-size swimming pool.

ATHLETICS

At Saint John's Prep, a variety of formal and informal athletics programs provide not only an outlet for adolescent energy but also an opportunity to learn the fundamentals of teamwork and community building. On the informal level, biking, cross-country skiing, and hiking are available on campus. Ski trips are organized throughout the winter by the prefect staff. Ping-Pong, racquetball, swimming, and tennis are also popular.

Saint John's Prep is a member of the Prairie Conference, fielding varsity teams for boys in baseball, football, golf, and soccer; for girls in gymnastics, softball, and swimming; and for boys and girls in basketball, cross-country running, cross-country skiing, hockey, tennis, and track.

EXTRACURRICULAR OPPORTUNITIES

Weekly movies, college sports, cultural events, and pickup games are regular parts of student life at Saint John's Prep. The Convocation Series brings guest artists and lecturers to the School.

Several musical organizations, including the band and chorus, string ensembles, jazz band, and other clubs are open to students. Instrumental and vocal music lessons are offered at the School. The drama department produces three plays each year. Speech, *Prep World* (the student yearbook), Knowledge Bowl, student government, Mock Trial, Campus Ministry, Peer Ministry, National Honor Society, World Club, Spanish Club, and German Club are other extracurricular activities.

DAILY LIFE

Classes are held five days each week. The school day begins at 8 a.m. and ends at 3:10 p.m. Class periods are 42 minutes long. Intramural sports, driver's education, and other activities take place after school. Once each week an All-School Convocation or Mass takes place. Boarding students must study in the residence hall from 7 to 9 p.m., Sunday through Thursday.

WEEKEND LIFE

Permission to spend an evening off campus is granted at the discretion of the Dean of Students. Students may spend weekends at their own or another student's home. An average of one school-sponsored social event is held each month. There are three-, four-, or five-day Home Weekends scheduled regularly throughout the school year. The Residence Hall Life Committee plans other weekend activities, such as tournaments and special dinners, in addition to regular weekend bus trips to movie theaters and shopping areas.

SUMMER PROGRAMS

Summer Leadership Camps for boys and girls ages 10–15 are located at Prep during the summer. The camps aim to instill a sense of leadership in each camper. Small-group discussions on topics of concern to teenagers and a variety of athletics and crafts are included. German Camp, Art Camp, and Theater/Circus Camps are conducted as well. Additional information about all camps is available by calling Saint John's Prep School.

COSTS AND FINANCIAL AID

The comprehensive fee for the 2005–06 school year was $5425 for grades 7 and 8, $10,817 for Upper School day students, $22,069 for five-day boarders, $24,800 for seven-day boarders, and $28,361 for international students. This included, where applicable, room, board, tuition, fees for activities, books, and room deposit. Seniors pay a small extra fee for graduation. The comprehensive fee is due in full before the school year begins, or a deferred-payment plan, through which payments may be made in eleven installments, is available.

Financial aid is available and is granted on the basis of need, as assessed by the Financial Aid Service through its financial aid form (Parents' Financial Statement). The President's Scholarship Program offers merit scholarships for qualified students. In 2005–06, 60 percent of the U.S. students received financial aid. Each award includes a combination of a scholarship or grant and a work award.

ADMISSIONS INFORMATION

Saint John's admits students whom the Committee on Admission judges to have the intellectual capacity, character, and ability to do well in their studies, benefit their fellow students by the quality of their personal lives, and give promise of distinction in community service and leadership.

Students applying for admission must submit an application form and fee, a transcript of previous work, and two letters of recommendation using the School's form. They must take an entrance exam—the Differential Aptitude Test (DAT). Minimum expectations are a 2.0 GPA (C average) and a score in the 60th percentile on the DAT. A campus visit with an interview is normally required. Approximately 100 new students are admitted each year.

APPLICATION TIMETABLE

Inquiries are welcome at any time. Campus visits are arranged to suit the family's convenience. Normal office hours are 8 a.m. to 4:30 p.m., Monday through Friday. Visits may be arranged by calling for an appointment. Students may also visit during Discovery Days, held from October through April. The application fee is $30. The entrance exam can be taken during the campus visit. Applications are considered up to the desired date of entrance, with preference given for early registration. After parents accept an offer of admission for their children, they are requested to submit a $500 deposit to reserve a room in the residence hall; for day students, a $200 deposit is required.

ADMISSIONS CORRESPONDENCE

Bryan Backes, Director of Admission
Saint John's Preparatory School
Collegeville, Minnesota 56321
Phone: 320-363-3321
          800-525-7737 (toll-free)
Fax: 320-363-3322
E-mail: admitprep@csbsju.edu
Web site: http://www.sjprep.net

ST. MARGARET'S SCHOOL

Tappahannock, Virginia

Type: Girls' boarding and day Episcopal college-preparatory school
Grades: 8–12
Enrollment: 149
Head of School: Margaret R. Broad, Head of School

THE SCHOOL

St. Margaret's School is an Episcopal college-preparatory boarding and day school enrolling girls in grades 8 through 12. Located 45 miles northeast of Richmond in historic Tidewater Virginia, the School's picturesque 9-acre campus provides an ideal setting for academic work. Set on the banks of the Rappahannock River, St. Margaret's enjoys the recreational and educational opportunities made available by a riverfront campus while benefiting from the nearby cultural centers of Washington, D.C., and Richmond and Williamsburg, Virginia.

Founded in 1921 by the Episcopal Diocese of Virginia, St. Margaret's prepares girls for an increasingly complex and international world by supplementing a college-preparatory education with interdisciplinary seminars, town meetings, independent studies, and travel programs.

St. Margaret's is recognized as a leader among boarding schools in character and life skills education. Through a formal cocurriculum, experienced staff members and outside experts lead girls through age-appropriate explorations of identity and relationships, healthy lifestyles, and decision making.

A nonprofit institution with more than 2,000 alumnae, St. Margaret's School is governed by a Board of Governors that includes alumnae and parents. The endowment is currently valued at $6 million. The School plant is valued at more than $17.5 million.

St. Margaret's is accredited by the Southern Association of Colleges and Schools and the Virginia Association of Independent Schools. It holds membership in the National Association of Independent Schools, the National Association of Episcopal Schools, the Virginia Association of Independent Schools, the National Coalition of Girls' Schools, and a variety of other educational organizations.

St. Margaret's also is a member of the Queen Margaret of Scotland Girls' Schools Association (QMSGSA), a group of thirteen schools in nine countries, which provides opportunities for cross-cultural programs. The School offers exchanges with the St. Margaret's Schools in Berwick, Australia; and Wellington, New Zealand, for selected sophomores and juniors, respectively. In 2005, the School's vocal groups participated in a choir tour of England and Scotland with 180 girls from the other QMSGSA schools.

ACADEMIC PROGRAMS

All St. Margaret's students must earn at least 21 credits en route to their diplomas. Each student carries a minimum of five academic courses.

Eighth graders may elect a variety of courses and can earn some high school credit. Algebra I and the first year of a foreign language qualify.

St. Margaret's is committed to providing solid college preparation. The 21 required credits are distributed in the following nine academic areas: English, 4 credits; foreign language, 2–3 credits; mathematics (algebra I, algebra II, and geometry), 3 credits; laboratory science, 2 credits; history (U.S. history and government), 3 credits; religious studies, 1 credit; fine arts, ⅔ credit; health, ⅓ credit; and electives (economics, foreign policy, photography, pottery, and study skills), 2 or more credits. In addition, students must demonstrate computer proficiency and participate in physical activity twice weekly. St. Margaret's defines a credit as the completion of one year of secondary-level course work or its equivalent.

Within these areas, students can select from more than seventy courses, including English 8; introduction to literature and composition; introduction to world literature and composition; American literature; British literature; Advanced Placement English; history 8; geography; world history I and II; U.S. history and government; great books; personal finance; prealgebra; algebra I, II, and III; geometry; precalculus; calculus; Advanced Placement calculus; science 8; anatomy and physiology; biology; chemistry; ecology; Advanced Placement biology; physics (offered every other year); conceptual physics; French I–V; Advanced Placement French; Latin I–V; Spanish I–V; introduction to the Bible; comparative religion; health/physical education 8; health; driver education; art history; studio art; Treble Choir; vocal ensemble; music history; piano; beginning ESL; intermediate ESL; advanced ESL; ESL–U.S. history; ESL–science; and ESL–American culture.

To enhance academic success, St. Margaret's provides supervised, structured study time each school day and in the evening. Daytime study halls, supervised by faculty members, are for all students except those on the honor roll and seniors with in-room study privileges. The evening study period is from 7:30 to 9:30, Sunday through Thursday, and, depending on academic standing, may take place in study hall or in the student's dormitory room. Students working on special projects are encouraged to make use of the library or the computer lab or to study with another student.

Academic standing is evaluated every five weeks. Students whose performance indicates a need for additional support are assigned to math lab, writing lab, or special study halls.

The grading system uses A to F designations with pluses and minuses. Reports are sent to parents at the midpoint and end of each trimester.

To provide as many opportunities as possible for a well-rounded education, St. Margaret's offers a two-week minimester program. Every February, faculty teams teach intensive, seminar-style courses that encourage creative inquiry, experiential learning, and an exploration of cross-curricular themes.

During this time, all seniors participate in an independent off-campus project to explore a potential career or field of study. In addition, study trips are offered each year. Recent destinations include China, Greece, Peru, and the Bahamas.

FACULTY AND ADVISERS

There are 34 faculty members. The faculty members and administrators hold forty-three baccalaureate, twenty-three master's, and three doctoral degrees.

Appointed Head of School in 1989, Margaret R. Broad is a graduate of Denison University (B.A., 1970) and the University of Virginia (M.A., 1988). Prior to becoming Head, she served as Academic Dean for two years, Head of the Foreign Language Department for eight years, and a French teacher for nine years.

Each student has a faculty adviser, who provides guidance in academic as well as resident life. The School aims to know each girl well and work with her to develop her special talents to the fullest. The faculty-student ratio is 1:6, and 75 percent of the staff members are in residence.

COLLEGE PLACEMENT

St. Margaret's prepares all of its students to succeed as undergraduates in a college or university setting. All students entering eighth, ninth, and tenth grades take a trimester-long credit course in study skills. The course teaches, reinforces, and develops appropriate and consistent techniques and habits.

Throughout their last two years, students work with the college counseling staff to narrow down their choices and complete college applications. St. Margaret's publishes a college handbook that answers a number of questions about the college search, application, and selection process.

In addition, college representatives visit St. Margaret's throughout the year, and juniors attend the Richmond Independent Schools' College Fair to meet with representatives from many colleges and universities. Many juniors also elect to take the minimester course that offers SAT preparation, college application workshops, and visits to multiple college campuses. Students research colleges and manage their applications using the TCCi admission software package.

Each year, sophomores and juniors take the PSAT, and juniors and seniors take the SAT. Subject Tests are also offered, and qualified students may take Advanced Placement tests. In 2005, 2 seniors were named AP Scholars with Distinction, and a senior and a junior were named AP Scholars. Of the 29 graduates of the class of 2005, nearly all went directly to college and are attending such institutions as the College of William and Mary, Rensselaer, Smith, University of Virginia, and Virginia Tech.

STUDENT BODY AND CONDUCT

In 2005–06, the School had 149 students, 114 of whom were boarding students. Eight students were enrolled in grade 8, 37 in grade 9, 30 in grade 10,

34 in grade 11, and 40 in grade 12. The student body represents seventeen states, the District of Columbia, and eleven other countries. Although St. Margaret's is an Episcopal school, students of all faiths are enrolled, welcomed, and valued.

It is the School's belief that stressing honor, trust, and high principles builds not only a better school but also a better world. Students abide by an honor code and clearly structured system of rules, and they are accountable for their actions. Many students share in the leadership of the school community as prefects, peer leaders, school and class officers, and honor council members. Increasing maturity is accompanied by increasing privileges and responsibility.

ACADEMIC FACILITIES
St. Margaret's Hall (1820), the central building, contains administrative offices, classrooms, the chapel, an art center, and a music center. The Viola Woolfolk Learning Center (1991) contains the library, study hall, and classrooms. The library houses a collection of approximately 6,000 volumes, sixty current periodicals, a microfiche collection of fourteen periodicals, extensive reference materials, a current and substantial collection of audiovisual materials, and three daily newspapers. Additional classrooms are located in the Cottage (1923). The Community/Technology Center (1999) houses science classrooms; chemistry, physics, and biology labs; computer labs; and a spacious dining hall that overlooks the Rappahannock River.

BOARDING AND GENERAL FACILITIES
Students live in air-conditioned dormitories with resident dorm parents on each floor. In 2005, the School opened a 24-student dormitory that includes three faculty-member residences. The School fully renovated its largest dormitory in 2002. Meals are served buffet-style in the School dining room overlooking the Rappahannock River. Student rooms are wired for personal telephones and Internet and Intranet connection. Each student has her own e-mail account. A swimming pool, tennis courts, and a fitness room provide after-class recreation.

Two nurses staff the infirmary, and a doctor is on call. There is a hospital in Tappahannock.

ATHLETICS
Athletics and physical education are an integral part of St. Margaret's overall program, a challenge to each girl to grow in physical well-being and to be the best she can be. In 2004, the School purchased 42 acres of land, 5 minutes from the campus, that it plans to develop as an athletic complex.

About two thirds of the students participate on athletic teams. St. Margaret's teams do well because the students understand teamwork and team spirit. Students may try out for cross-country, field hockey, and volleyball in the fall; basketball and swimming in the winter; and crew, soccer, softball, and tennis in the spring.

In addition to team sports, plenty of other activities are designed for solo performers, such as aerobics, dance, golf, horseback riding, running, and walking.

To promote sportsmanship, school spirit, teamwork, and friendly competition, every student is a member of the either the Blue or the Grey team. Contests between these intramural teams are held throughout the year.

EXTRACURRICULAR OPPORTUNITIES
Students must pursue an after-school activity each trimester and are encouraged to try something they have not done before. The following clubs, societies, and outside organizations are active at St. Margaret's: activities committee, art club, Basic Needs (service club), *The Channel* (newspaper)*, *The Current* (yearbook)*, ensemble*, Treble Choir*, the honor council*, National Honor Society*, peer leaders*, poetry club, Quill & Scroll*, Soulful Voices (gospel music), student ambassador society*, Student Government Association*, *The Tides* (literary magazine), and Guild of Sacristans. (An asterisk denotes that students must be elected, appointed, or invited to join.)

St. Margaret's has a community service requirement of 12 hours per year that is often exceeded by the students. Last year, students participated in projects ranging from work with children in educational, athletic, and recreational programs to community beautification projects in addition to established programs such as Habitat for Humanity.

DAILY LIFE
The daily schedule begins with breakfast at 7, followed by chapel or announcements at 7:50. Classes are held from 8:20 until 3:30 and are followed by athletics and activities. Dinner is at 5:30, study hall runs from 7:30 to 9:30, and lights-out is at 10:45.

Each week consists of three 7-period days, one 3-period day, and one 4-period day. The three- and four-period days, which have 75-minute periods, allow for flexible and varied class activities. The Teachers Available period occurs after classes four days a week. At this time, all teachers are in their rooms and are available to offer extra help.

WEEKEND LIFE
On weekends, students have time for special interest programs, cultural trips, or social activities. To help students discover lifetime leisure interests, the School requires them to participate in at least one cultural or outdoor activity each trimester. For example, girls can enjoy themselves in museums in the nation's capital, take an overnight sailing trip on the Chesapeake Bay, or attend plays in Richmond. Students at St. Margaret's experience all that the area has to offer.

A varied calendar provides the opportunity for dances and social gatherings at other Virginia schools, such as Christchurch School, Episcopal High School, Woodberry Forest School, and Virginia Episcopal School. St. Margaret's is a member of the Boarding Schools Social Activities Committee, which plans social events for Virginia and Maryland boarding schools.

Students are allowed off campus five weekend nights per trimester in addition to major vacations. Juniors and seniors are granted additional time to visit colleges. Parental permission is required for all off-campus weekends.

COSTS AND FINANCIAL AID
In 2006–07, tuition for boarding students is $34,500; tuition for day students is $12,950. Boarding students must pay a $2000 deposit to cover charges for books and supplies, special testing programs, weekend trips, and other incidental expenses. Day students pay a deposit of $1000. Additional charges are made for musical instruction and ESL.

The School subscribes to the School and Student Service for Financial Aid. In 2005, financial aid was awarded to approximately 30 percent of the student body on the basis of need and academic standing.

ADMISSIONS INFORMATION
St. Margaret's School seeks students who can benefit from and contribute to the School community. The School actively admits students without regard to race, color, creed, or national or ethnic origin. Candidates are accepted in all grades on the basis of a recognized potential and achievement, completion of the SSAT, the applicant's extracurricular activities, and the recommendations of 2 teachers and 1 personal acquaintance. An interview on campus is required.

APPLICATION TIMETABLE
Although St. Margaret's conducts rolling admissions, prospective students are urged to apply in the winter. If vacancies exist, applications may be considered throughout the summer.

ADMISSIONS CORRESPONDENCE
Director of Admission
St. Margaret's School
Tappahannock, Virginia 22560

Phone: 804-443-3357
Fax: 804-443-6781
E-mail: admit@sms.org
Web site: http://www.sms.org

SAINT MARK'S SCHOOL
Southborough, Massachusetts

Type: Coeducational boarding and day college-preparatory school
Grades: 9–12 (Forms III–VI)
Enrollment: 333
Heads of School: Antony J. deV. Hill and Elsa N. Hill, Heads of School

THE SCHOOL

Saint Mark's School was founded by Joseph Burnett in 1865. His goal was to offer a high-quality education in a school affiliated with the Episcopal Church. To this day, Saint Mark's remains focused on excellent academics, providing a rigorous liberal arts program that stems from a classical tradition. Its strong tradition allows the School to provide a safe environment in which students are encouraged to explore issues of their own faith and religious beliefs.

In 1973, Saint Mark's began to coordinate operations with the Southborough School for Girls, and in 1977 it became fully coeducational through the merger of the two schools.

Saint Mark's is located in Southborough, Massachusetts, 5 minutes from both the Massachusetts Turnpike and Route 495. Its rural, 250-acre setting allows Saint Mark's to provide a wide range of athletics and activities, while its proximity to Boston, Worcester, and Providence allows students and faculty members to take full advantage of the cultural opportunities of the three cities.

Saint Mark's is governed by a 29-member Board of Trustees and eight honorary trustees. Its endowment is currently valued at more than $101 million. Last year, parents and alumni contributed more than $1.1 million to the School's Annual Fund.

The School is accredited by the New England Association of Schools and Colleges, and its memberships include the Cum Laude Society, the National Association of Independent Schools, the Secondary School Admission Test Board, and the Association of Independent Schools in New England.

ACADEMIC PROGRAMS

With a core curriculum based on a long tradition of excellence in the areas of essential learning, the School requires that each student study English, mathematics, modern or classical language, laboratory science, history, art, music, and religion. In addition, electives are offered to provide an opportunity for breadth and depth of study and to give students the chance to take an active role in their education.

The student-faculty ratio is 5:1, which allows the faculty to work closely with all students. Class sizes range from 6 to 15, with an average of 10 students. Each department offers honors and Advanced Placement sections. Students take five courses each year, working closely with their faculty advisers to determine personal goals and tailor their academic program to meet individual needs.

The School maintains the tradition of required evening study hours. With the exception of Sixth Formers, all students must study a minimum of 2 hours each night, from 8 to 10. The School's library, art and music studios, science facilities, and computer centers are open to the students during the day and in the evening.

Each student's academic progress is carefully monitored. Five times a year, comments from the student's adviser and teachers are mailed to parents. Letter grades are given six times over the course of the year, and an additional final grade is assigned at the end of each course. Parents are encouraged to contact advisers at any time to discuss a student's progress.

Students in Form VI may choose an elective Independent Study Program in the spring semester. This encourages them to follow independent academic interests. Other academic options include independent study in the arts, applied music for credit, and a carefully planned year of study abroad.

FACULTY AND ADVISERS

For the academic year 2005–06, the faculty consisted of 66 full-time members; 36 held master's degrees, 6 had earned Ph.D.'s, and 2 held law degrees.

Antony J. deV. Hill and Elsa N. Hill, Heads of School, have been at St. Mark's since 1994. Both have extensive experience in education in the United States and Australia. Mr. Hill was formerly Headmaster of Melbourne Grammar School and Christ Church Grammar School in Australia. He is a graduate of Sydney University (B.A. Honors) and Boston University. Mrs. Hill has taught English and law and practiced as an attorney and legal administrator in Washington, D.C.; Perth; and Melbourne. She is a graduate of Smith (B.A.), Harvard (M.A.T.), and the University of New South Wales (LL.B.–University Medalist).

In hiring new faculty members, the School looks for diversity of thinking, intellectual enthusiasm, and commitment to playing a full part in the life of a boarding school. Beyond teaching, faculty members act as coaches, advisers, and dorm supervisors. The faculty members bring with them an intellectual curiosity of their own, and funds are made available to them for further pursuit of education and educational travel during sabbatical leaves and summers.

COLLEGE PLACEMENT

Students begin the college selection process in the fall of Form V, working with college advisers and their personal adviser on procedures and tentative choices. In early winter, parents attend a conference and workshop at Saint Mark's so that they may understand and help with the process. This year, representatives from numerous colleges and universities are scheduled to visit Saint Mark's to inform and interview students.

The 87 graduates of the class of 2005 are attending sixty colleges and universities, including Amherst, Brown, Dartmouth, Stanford, and Yale.

STUDENT BODY AND CONDUCT

The 2005–06 student body was composed of the following: Form III, 39 boys and 37 girls; Form IV, 54 boys and 40 girls; Form V, 48 boys and 42 girls; and Form VI, 34 boys and 39 girls. Of the 333 students, 140 were boarding boys, 115 were boarding girls, 35 were day boys, and 43 were day girls. Eighteen percent included African American, Asian American, Latin American, Middle Eastern, Native American, and biracial students. Another 9 percent were international students. Twenty-one states and twelve countries were represented in the Saint Mark's community.

Student life at the School is based on trust, truth, and personal responsibility. Sixth Form Monitors lead the students, while prefects assist in the dorms, in the Admission Office, and in several other areas of the School. Student initiatives normally begin with the Student Congress, a council of 16 students advised by 2 faculty members. The central feature of the discipline system is the Student Discipline Committee, a group of 9 students and 4 faculty members who hear all major discipline cases and make recommendations to the Heads of School. While certainly a structured school, Saint Mark's offers students opportunities to define that structure and to affect the quality of their life in the School.

ACADEMIC FACILITIES

Thirty-seven classrooms, most clustered near the Forbes Student Center, are part of the School's main building. Connected by cloisters and walkways are the library, the science wing, the chapel, the art and music buildings (Taft Hall), and Benson Auditorium. Currently under construction is phase II of the Center for the Arts. Benson Auditorium, the one-time gymnasium, more recently used as a theater/wrestling room, is being completely revamped and rebuilt to create a more deserving home for the school's theater department. It is expected to include a black-box theater as well as an additional classroom for studio art. This project is slated to be complete by June 2006. The new Performing Arts Center, donated by the class of 1945, opened in February 2004. This state-of-the-art facility includes six private soundproof practice rooms and a concert hall that seats 500. The School maintains a network of fifty Macintosh computers for student access to the Internet, e-mail, and assignments and other academic work. The library contains approximately 26,000 print volumes and subscribes to 100 magazines, eight newspapers, and 6 online databases. There are twelve computers for student use that offer Internet and e-mail access as well as word processing and other programs. The library has a fully automated catalog and circulation system. Students may choose from a variety of learning environments: group study areas, quiet study areas with individual carrels, and a rare book room. The art and music building has a large and spacious art

studio, music instruction and practice rooms, a photographic darkroom, a ceramics studio, and an exhibition gallery.

BOARDING AND GENERAL FACILITIES

Approximately half of the students live in dormitories in the upper floors of the main building. The other half live in dormitories near the main building. Third Form boys and girls live in separate dormitories, but all other dorms are a mixture of Fourth, Fifth, and Sixth Formers. Supervision is provided by resident faculty members and additional faculty on dormitory duty teams. Sixth Form prefects assist the dormitory faculty with day-to-day operations in the dorms. Each student has a voice mail box and an e-mail account that is accessible from many stations around the School, including the student's dorm room.

There is a fully equipped health service building with a nurse on duty 24 hours a day. Doctors visit the School, and students can make appointments at the many medical centers and hospitals nearby. A full-time School counselor is available to meet with students daily. A selected group of Fifth and Sixth Formers supports the counseling system as peer counselors.

ATHLETICS

Saint Mark's requires all students to participate in a physical education program. The program seeks to develop specific physical skills and personal qualities, such as sportsmanship, cooperation, and confidence.

Both interscholastic and recreational sports are offered. When competing against other schools, students compete in teams commensurate with their abilities. Team sports are offered on the varsity, junior varsity, and, when needed, on the thirds level. The girls' interscholastic program includes cross-country, field hockey, and soccer in the fall; basketball, ice hockey, and squash in the winter; and crew, golf, lacrosse, softball, and tennis in the spring. Boys' teams are fielded in cross-country, football, and soccer in the fall; basketball, ice hockey, squash, and wrestling in the winter; and baseball, crew, golf, lacrosse, and tennis in the spring.

The diverse recreational program offers opportunities for individual training, creative expression, individual or intramural competition, and general fitness. Some of the offerings include dance, squash, tennis, fives, fitness training, volleyball, golf, and yoga.

The School has eight playing fields and a recently completed athletics complex that includes a hockey rink, two basketball courts, seven squash courts (one glass-backed), a weight-training room, an indoor multiuse cage that provides two indoor tennis courts, eight outdoor tennis courts, courts for fives, an outdoor swimming pool, and a nine-hole golf course.

EXTRACURRICULAR OPPORTUNITIES

Each year, the Saint Mark's Lecture Series brings to Southborough speakers who are preeminent in a variety of fields, such as government and politics, science, academia, the arts, and media.

Encouraged by the School, students take advantage of the fine cultural offerings of Boston and Providence. Each year, the School sponsors more than twenty trips to the theater, symphony, and opera. Frequently, these trips concur with material covered in English and art classrooms. In addition, the School owns a subscription to the Boston Symphony Orchestra's open rehearsals.

Saint Mark's has a wide variety of publications: the newspaper, *The Saint Marker;* the School's literary magazine, *The Vindex;* and the School yearbook, *The Lion.* Clubs and societies include, among others, opportunities for community service (St. Mark's Society) and multiculturalism (We the People), the Asian Awareness Society, the Athletic Association, an ecological group (Green Team), and a Debate Club. Recent drama productions include *The Crucible, Crimes of the Heart, To Gillian On Her 37th Birthday, Too Much Light Makes the Baby Go Blind,* and student-directed, one-act plays. The School has an outstanding choir, a boys' and girls' octet, a jazz band, and several string ensembles. Saint Mark's has also recently founded a working relationship with the New England Conservatory and a dance program.

DAILY LIFE

Classes are held six days a week. They begin at 8 a.m. and end at 2:30 p.m., except on Wednesday and Saturday, when classes end before lunch and athletic competitions are held in the afternoon. Each class lasts for 45 minutes, with double periods for laboratory and studio classes. Breakfast is served (cafeteria) from 6:45 to 8; lunch (cafeteria) from 11:30 to 1. There are formal dinners once a week and two community chapel services each week.

All students are responsible for cleaning their own rooms and contributing one job per day to the student-directed work program. Evening study is supervised by faculty members.

WEEKEND LIFE

On Saturday night, the student-based social committee plans a wide range of activities: dances, lip-sync contests, casino nights, ice-skating parties, and concerts. Also, on the weekends faculty members provide transportation to the local shopping malls and movie theaters. Other activities not restricted to Saturday night include ski trips, concerts by visiting musicians, student recitals, student drama performances, and trips to sports events and the theater.

Students wishing to take a Saturday overnight or a weekend away may do so after receiving parental permission.

COSTS AND FINANCIAL AID

The basic charge for 2005–06 boarding students, including tuition, room, and board, was $35,350 for day students, including lunch, it was $27,400. The Admission Office should be notified as early as possible if financial assistance is going to be requested.

ADMISSIONS INFORMATION

Saint Mark's seeks candidates who have demonstrated strong academic ability and good character. The Admissions Committee looks for promise of achievement and involvement in many areas of school life. The following credentials are required for admission: a formal application for admission, a student essay, a student questionnaire, a transcript of grades, records of previous achievement and aptitude tests, results of the SSAT, a school report, and three teacher recommendations. In addition, all applicants must interview with a member of the Admission Committee. If circumstances prohibit a visit to Saint Mark's, an interview with an area representative can be arranged.

APPLICATION TIMETABLE

Campus tours are arranged in conjunction with interviews. Appointments are scheduled from 8:50 a.m. to 2 p.m. on Monday, Tuesday, Thursday, and Friday; from 8 to 10 a.m. on Wednesday and Saturday.

Applicants who submit all credentials by January 31 are notified on March 10. Applicants who apply later are considered according to space availability.

ADMISSIONS CORRESPONDENCE

Anne E. Behnke, Director of Admission
Saint Mark's School
Southborough, Massachusetts 01772

Phone: 508-786-6000
Fax: 508-786-6120
E-mail: admission@stmarksschool.org

ST. MARK'S SCHOOL OF TEXAS

Dallas, Texas

Type: Boys' day college-preparatory school
Grades: 1–12: Lower School, 1–4; Middle School, 5–8; Upper School, 9–12
Enrollment: School total: 817; Upper School: 350
Head of School: Arnold E. Holtberg, Headmaster

THE SCHOOL

St. Mark's is the descendant of three former Dallas boys' schools: Terrill School (1906–1944), Texas Country Day School (1933–1950), and Cathedral School (1944–1950). St. Mark's was organized in 1950 on the Preston Road campus of Texas Country Day School (TCD) when the Cathedral School merged with TCD. The campus is located on 43 acres in the residential area of North Dallas.

St. Mark's college-preparatory program fosters intellectual, academic, and artistic excellence in young men and encourages development of the strengths in each boy's character and personality. Toward these ends, St. Mark's offers a broad range of intellectual, artistic, and athletic opportunities for its students. Challenging studies in the sciences, arts, and humanities form the basis of a St. Mark's education. Teachers work to instill an enthusiasm for learning, encourage independent and critical judgment, and demonstrate the methods for making sound inquiries and for effective communications. St. Mark's aims to prepare young men to assume leadership and responsibility in a competitive and changing world.

St. Mark's Lower School (grades 1–4) is housed in a single building and has approximately 20 faculty members. The program offers diverse learning activities, including academic instruction in Spanish language and culture, language arts, mathematics, science, and social studies; regular instruction in the arts (visual arts, music, creative dramatics); and a developmental physical education program that teaches fundamental skills at a level geared to the age and abilities of the child.

St. Mark's School of Texas is accredited by the Independent Schools Association of the Southwest. Its memberships include the National Association of Independent Schools, the Cum Laude Society, the International Boys' School Coalition, and the College Board.

ACADEMIC PROGRAMS

The academic program in the Upper School is designed to satisfy the most exacting requirements for admission to colleges and universities across the country, but it is more broadly defined by the School and the faculty as preparation for personal independence, enlightenment, and maturity.

There are required courses, Advanced Placement courses, and many electives available. Graduation requirements are 4 years of English, 3 years of a foreign language, 3 years of mathematics, 4 years of physical education or athletics, 3 years of social studies, 3 years of a laboratory science, 1 year in fine arts, a senior exhibition, and 15 hours of community service each Upper School year. Each student takes five classes per

year, and some students, with the permission of the Head of the Upper School, may take more.

The individual teaching sections average about 15 students. In most classes, the students are randomly grouped; the notable exceptions are in honors and Advanced Placement courses.

The School operates on a trimester system. Hence, grade reports are given three times a year and are mailed home to the parents with written comments. Interim reports are also written to help ensure adequate reporting to the parents. Parents are encouraged to communicate at any time with their son's adviser. Only final grades in Upper School classes are recorded for transcript purposes.

FACULTY AND ADVISERS

For the academic year 2005–06, the faculty consisted of 104 full-time members; 80 held master's degrees, and 9 had earned doctoral degrees.

The Headmaster, Arnold E. Holtberg, graduated cum laude from Princeton University in 1970 with a baccalaureate degree in sociology. He also received an M.A. degree in pastoral care and counseling in 1976 from the Lutheran Theological Seminary in Philadelphia, Pennsylvania.

The School seeks to employ faculty members who are willing to give an unusual amount of time to the School. One of the strengths and challenges of a faculty member at St. Mark's is that he or she often functions in several roles within the School.

COLLEGE PLACEMENT

The Director of College Counseling and staff members coordinate college planning and counseling. All Upper School students are encouraged to attend the College Previews, held in September, and are welcome to utilize the college office. Several required college conferences are scheduled with students and parents, beginning in the junior year. The SAT scores of the middle 50 percent for the class of 2005 were verbal, 630–750 and math, 690–780. St. Mark's graduates are attending major universities throughout the country, including Brown, Carnegie Mellon, Dartmouth, Duke, Emory, Georgetown, Harvard, Johns Hopkins, Princeton, Stanford, Yale, and the Universities of Chicago, Pennsylvania, and Texas at Austin.

STUDENT BODY AND CONDUCT

In 2005–06, there were 94 boys in grade 9, 79 in grade 10, 90 in grade 11, and 87 in grade 12. Since St. Mark's is a day school, almost all of the boys come from the Dallas area. Approximately 28 percent of the students are members of minority groups.

While the rules that govern the School are published by the School, these rules or guidelines provide only a part of the criteria that determine

student behavior. Students are also encouraged to take responsibility for their own actions, with the guidance of the faculty and class sponsors. A faculty- and student-led Discipline Council deals with some disciplinary problems.

Each boy has a faculty adviser who is available for personal counseling and advice and is responsible for reporting to the parents and the School on the student's overall performance.

ACADEMIC FACILITIES

Among the campus buildings are the Green-McDermott Science and Mathematics Quadrangle; the Cecil and Ida Green Library; Nearburg Hall; the H. Ben Decherd Center for the Arts; the St. Mark's Chapel; Thomas O. Hicks Family Athletic Center; Mullen Family Fitness Center; Wirt Davis Hall; the A. Earl Cullum, Jr., Alumni Commons; and the Athletic Center, which includes the Morris G. Spencer Gymnasium and the Ralph B. Rogers Natatorium. The Cecil and Ida Green Library seats 230 and houses 41,000 volumes, 4,000 microfilm reels, and twelve networked Pentium computers for research and Internet access, including 26 online subscription databases. Three professional librarians and a technical assistant staff the library. The School has an integrated campuswide technology network that includes video projection systems in more than 90 percent of the classrooms and numerous labs and access to extensive advanced information systems.

ATHLETICS

Every boy at St. Mark's is required to participate daily in some form of athletics. Upper School boys may select either the physical education program or one of the sports teams.

In physical education, the School is concerned with students' neuromuscular and cardiovascular development, as well as their development of an appreciation of physical fitness, through the specialty classes and intramural program.

The School provides many levels of interscholastic team sports to fit the needs of each student. There are sixteen different sports that are available to Middle and Upper School students, including baseball, basketball, crew, cross-country, cheerleading, fencing, football, golf, lacrosse, soccer, swimming, tennis, track and field, volleyball, water polo, and wrestling. In 2004–05, seven varsity teams won conference championships in their sport.

EXTRACURRICULAR OPPORTUNITIES

Students at St. Mark's are encouraged to do more than excel in their academic subjects. A boy has the opportunity to participate in speech and debate, the Student Council, the mathematics team, the robotics team, the School's yearbook and newspaper, drama activities, the environmen-

tal club, the letterman's club, the Cum Laude Society, the Lion and Sword Society, the tutorial program, the astronomy club, the School's literary magazine, and many other activities.

DAILY LIFE

The school day begins at 8 a.m. for all boys and ends at 3:45 p.m. for grades 9–12. Most of the classes, except science and fine arts, last 45 minutes. Sports and extracurricular activities for grades 9–12 are from 3:55 to 6 p.m.

COSTS AND FINANCIAL AID

In 2005–06, tuition, including textbooks and supplies, lunches, and fees, was $18,612 for grades 10 and 11, $19,216 for grade 12, and $19,812 for grade 9. Students must obtain their own uniforms at additional cost. At the time of enrollment, a deposit of $1000 is due with the

signed enrollment contract, and the balance of the tuition is due by July 1 prior to entrance in August.

The awarding of financial aid is based upon the student's financial need. Approximately 18 percent of the students receive financial aid. Parents are expected to furnish all of the financial information, as requested by the financial aid committee. Specific details are available from the Office of Admission.

ADMISSIONS INFORMATION

Applicants receive information about the School upon request or at the School's Web site at http://www.smtexas.org. Parents are asked to file an application, obtain a teacher's recommendation, and send a transcript of the applicant's prior work. Applicants take general aptitude, reading comprehension, vocabulary, and mathematics tests. A writing sample and on-campus interviews

are also required. The application fee is $100 for grade 1 and $175 for grades 2–12.

APPLICATION TIMETABLE

Inquiries are welcome at any time. Group tours and individual tours are recommended. Applications should be submitted by December for grade 1 and by November for grades 2 through 4. Applications for grades 5 through 12 are due in January. Testing and interviewing are completed in February, and decision letters are mailed in mid-March for grades 1–12.

ADMISSIONS CORRESPONDENCE

David Baker
Director of Admission
St. Mark's School of Texas
10600 Preston Road
Dallas, Texas 75230-4000

Phone: 214-346-8700
Fax: 214-346-8701
E-mail: admission@smtexas.org
Web site: http://www.smtexas.org

SAINT MARY'S HALL

San Antonio, Texas

Type: Coeducational day nondenominational college-preparatory school
Grades: P–12: Montessori Preschool/Kindergarten; Lower School, 1–5; Middle School, 6–8; Upper School, 9–12
Enrollment: School total: 919; Upper School: 314; Middle School: 182; Lower School: 269; Montessori Preschool/Kindergarten: 154
Head of School: Bob Windham, Headmaster

THE SCHOOL

Saint Mary's Hall, a coeducational college-preparatory school, was founded in 1879 by the Right Reverend Robert Woodward Barnwell Elliott, the first bishop of the Protestant Episcopal Diocese of West Texas. In 1925, the school became a nonparochial, independent school and was placed under the direction of a 25-member Board of Trustees.

Saint Mary's Hall has been at its present San Antonio location since 1968. The school is on a 60-acre wooded campus in a northeast suburb, just 3 miles east of the International Airport and within 15 minutes of downtown. The buildings of yellow Mexican brick were designed by architect O'Neil Ford in a style that features bright, airy classrooms; open courtyards; and graceful Spanish arcades. The architecture blends harmoniously with the suburban setting.

The school has an endowment of $37 million and a physical plant valued at $36.5 million. The Alumni Association maintains contact with more than 2,500 alumni throughout the world.

The Primary School is composed of a Montessori program for ages 3 to 6, a kindergarten program, and a Lower School for Forms 1 through 5. The Montessori program follows the educational philosophy developed by Dr. Maria Montessori, which calls for an environment devoted to the young child's emotional, intellectual, and physical self. Children learn to develop their sensory perceptions, acquire basic reading ability, and master simple arithmetic.

In the Lower School, the curriculum stresses language arts, mathematics, social studies, and science skills. An accelerated and enriched program provides special opportunities for advanced work. The program is designed to foster the development of critical, creative, and productive thinking. Physical education, music, art, computer science, drama, and Spanish are all part of the curriculum.

Saint Mary's Hall offers an extended care program from 7 a.m. to 6 p.m. for children in the Primary School.

The Middle School program provides a challenging curriculum with advanced courses in math and foreign language, as well as fine art classes, organized sports, clubs, a student senate, and a peer counseling program. The rigorous academics combined with a friendly environment create a well-balanced approach to education, including academic, creative, physical, and character-building activities.

Saint Mary's Hall is accredited by the Independent Schools Association of the Southwest and holds membership in the Cum Laude Society, the National Honor Society, the College Board, the National Association of College Admission Counseling, and the American Montessori Society.

ACADEMIC PROGRAMS

The Saint Mary's Hall college-preparatory curriculum places strong emphasis on writing, researching, and analytical thinking.

Students must complete 26 credits to graduate. Requirements consist of English, 4; mathematics, 3; history, 3½; foreign language, 3; science, 3; physical education, 2; fine arts, 1; and electives, 4½.

Honors courses are offered in English, drama, foreign language, math, history, and science. Advanced Placement (AP) courses are offered in art history, biology, calculus AB, calculus BC, chemistry, computer science A, computer science AB, drawing, English language, English literature, environmental science, French language, Latin Vergil, Latin literature, modern European history, music theory, physics C, Spanish literature, Spanish language, statistics, United States government and politics, and U.S. history. In May 2005, 288 AP examinations were given. Seventy-six percent of the students were awarded scores of 3 or above, which qualifies for credit hours at most colleges and universities.

The school year of thirty-six weeks is divided into two semesters, the first ending before Christmas vacation and the second at the end of May. Students are expected to carry five solid academic subjects and one elective each semester and may choose the elective from courses offered in every department. Forty-five minutes a day of outside preparation for each class is normal.

Private instrumental lessons are available for additional fees. Tutors in all disciplines are also available privately and are paid for by parents.

FACULTY AND ADVISERS

The Upper School faculty includes 49 full-time members and 4 part-time members.

The Upper School has a strong advisory program, with each faculty member having 12 advisees. The adviser provides both personal and academic support and is the student's advocate in all matters.

Bob Windham, Headmaster, attended Texas A&M University for his undergraduate degree. He received his master's degree in educational administration from the University of Houston. Bob Windham was formerly Headmaster at Trinity Valley School in Fort Worth, Texas. He has thirty years of experience in the public school setting as a teacher, coach, principal, and associate superintendent. Daily academic leadership is provided by Don Ellisor, Head of the Upper School; Mary Dickerson, Head of the Middle School; and Shirley Ellisor, Head of the Primary School.

COLLEGE PLACEMENT

Preparation for college or university entrance begins in the ninth grade, when students are assisted in designing a four-year curriculum plan that will best prepare them for college. Juniors and seniors participate in monthly college counseling sessions that are designed to identify career goals and academic interests. Every year, more than 75 college representatives visit the campus. Saint Mary's Hall hosts its own selective college fair, and students are prepared, through individual conferences, to select the college that best suits them.

The PSAT is required in the sophomore and junior years, and the SAT is taken in both the junior and senior years. Students are encouraged to include SAT preparation courses in their college-preparatory curriculum.

Mean SAT scores for the graduating class of 2005 were 614 verbal and 633 math, for a combined score of 1247. Members of the class of 2005 were accepted at Cornell, Duke, Georgetown, Harvard, Princeton, Southern Methodist, Stanford, Texas A&M, Texas Christian, Trinity, Vanderbilt, and the Universities of the Incarnate Word and Texas at Austin.

STUDENT BODY AND CONDUCT

In 2005–06, the Upper School had 72 freshmen (41 boys and 31 girls), 86 sophomores (40 boys and 46 girls), 90 juniors (48 boys and 42 girls), and 66 seniors (34 boys and 32 girls).

The Student Council works closely with the administration in planning activities for the student body and providing opportunities for the expression of student opinion. The Honor Council, comprising students and faculty members, recommends disciplinary measures for students who break school rules.

ACADEMIC FACILITIES

Educational facilities include a lecture hall with stage and projection room; three computer laboratories; ten science laboratories; two art studios; two libraries with more than 20,000 volumes; a fine arts instructional center, including studios for instrumental and choral music, photography, and theater; new Lower School and Middle School buildings and additions; a new dance building; more than seventy smart boards; an eight-lane track; and a 500-seat theater/chapel.

ATHLETICS

Competitive sports play an important part in the overall development of students, are open to all, and include baseball, basketball, cross-country, field hockey, golf, lacrosse, soccer, softball, tennis, track, and volleyball. Varsity teams compete in the Southwest Preparatory Conference, which includes private school teams from Texas and Oklahoma. They also compete against local public schools. Athletics facilities include seven lighted tennis courts; a weight room; a swimming pool; three playing fields for soccer, softball, and baseball; an NCAA regulation lighted athletic complex; and two fully equipped gymnasiums.

EXTRACURRICULAR OPPORTUNITIES

Saint Mary's Hall strongly encourages students to develop their creative talents and leadership potential through extracurricular activities. The drama department produces two major

plays a year, and the dance and choral music departments present a major cooperative production in May of each year. The choral group gives frequent performances, as do musically gifted piano students. The school sponsors the publication of a yearbook and a literary magazine. There are also language and special interest clubs.

DAILY LIFE

Classes begin at 8 and end at 3:10. There are eight class periods and an announcement time for the students and faculty members every day. In addition, there is time reserved for chapel once a week and as a meeting period for students and teachers on other days. Sports and extracurricular activities take place after school.

COSTS AND FINANCIAL AID

In 2005–06, tuition for the Upper School students was $15,495. Additional costs are for uniforms and books (estimated at $1000).

A deposit of $1000 is due with the signed enrollment agreement. The remainder of the fees must be paid by July 1 for entrance in the fall semester. Arrangements can be made to pay the tuition in two installments, the second due December 1. There is also a ten-month payment plan that can be arranged through the Business Office.

Financial aid is available for students, based on need and merit, according to an evaluation prepared by the Saint Mary's Hall

Scholarship Committee and the School and Student Service for Financial Aid. Aid is awarded in the form of grants in amounts that depend on the availability of funds.

Merit scholarship funds are also available. The Campbell Academic Scholarship Program awards full tuition scholarships to outstanding students entering the ninth grade.

ADMISSIONS INFORMATION

An application for admission includes recommendations, past school records, an admission interview, and standardized test results.

APPLICATION TIMETABLE

All highly interested applicants are encouraged to apply to Saint Mary's Hall by February 15 under the Early Action Plan. Qualified applicants in the Early Action Plan receive primary consideration for admission into the program. Applications filed after the Early Action Plan date are considered on a space-available basis.

Visits to Saint Mary's Hall are welcome at any time during the year.

ADMISSIONS CORRESPONDENCE

Elena D. Hicks
Director of Admission
Saint Mary's Hall
P.O. Box 33430
San Antonio, Texas 78265-3430

Phone: 210-483-9234
Fax: 210-655-5211
E-mail: admissions@smhall.org
Web site: http://www.smhall.org

ST. MARY'S PREPARATORY SCHOOL

Orchard Lake, Michigan

Type: Boys' boarding and day college-preparatory Catholic school
Grades: 9–12
Enrollment: 530
Head of School: James Glowacki, Headmaster

THE SCHOOL

Founded in Detroit in 1885 along with SS. Cyril and Methodius Seminary and St. Mary's College, St. Mary's Preparatory provides an education in the Catholic tradition for boys in grades 9–12. The School's founder, Fr. Joseph Dabrowski, wanted a complete educational complex for Polish immigrants interested in the priesthood. His aspiration has developed into a thriving community of three distinct schools on one campus. The present site for the schools is a beautiful 125-acre campus on the east shore of one of the state's largest lakes, Orchard Lake. The campus consists of twenty-one buildings, nine of which were present when the School moved to the site of the former Michigan Military Academy in 1909. Located in a largely affluent, suburban area 1 hour from Detroit and 10 minutes from Pontiac, St. Mary's offers a diverse, affordable, high-quality education, rich in personal contact and Catholic values, to students from Michigan, other parts of the United States, and the world.

The School is an incorporated, not-for-profit institution and is administered by a Board of Trustees. An active Moms & Dads Club and an Athletic Booster Club keep parents involved in School activities.

The emphasis at St. Mary's is on the individual student so that each student's needs are considered on a personal basis. The administration, teachers, and coaches work to develop each individual's talents and abilities at his own pace and in his own way. The average class size of 16.5 students allows teachers to understand the needs of their students and to teach to those needs in a style that stresses dialogue, not lecture. Counseling, tutoring, and supervised study are all available, but it is the personal contact and understanding directed toward each student that produces results.

ACADEMIC PROGRAMS

St. Mary's has designed an academic program that meets the basic entrance requirements for any college curriculum. Along with required courses, however, students, parents, and guidance counselors work together to determine an appropriate elective schedule. St. Mary's encourages students to create a program that addresses their individual interests and needs. Requirements for graduation are 4 years of theology and English; 3 years of mathematics, science, and social studies; 2 years of foreign language; and a semester each of computer programming, computer applications, physical education, health, fine arts, and speech. Students are required to fulfill 28 credits for graduation.

Seniors and selected juniors may take classes at St. Mary's College, which is conveniently located on the same campus. These students earn college credit directly, with no need to take an

Advanced Placement exam. St. Mary's students have graduated with more than 30 college credits.

Although students need not be Catholic to attend St. Mary's, all students are educated in the Catholic tradition. This tradition includes 4 years of theology in the classroom as well as attendance at Mass twice weekly. Students are also required to perform a certain amount of community service as determined by the theology department. In addition, students may attend class retreats, and the School Chaplain and many campus priests make their time available to students.

The scholastic year is divided into two semesters and each semester into three marking periods. Parents are advised of grades through report cards that are mailed at the end of each six-week marking period. Deficiency reports are mailed three weeks into each marking period to the parents of any student who is doing poorly in a subject. In addition, frequent, informal contact between parents and faculty members is provided to keep parents involved in their son's progress.

The grading scale at St. Mary's ranges from A+ to E. Passing grades are A+ to D–, which corresponds with a 4.0 scale of 4.3 to .7 and a percentage scale of 100 to 70 percent. Students transferring to St. Mary's from another school meet with the Counselor to determine which grades are transferable and which requirements need to be completed.

FACULTY AND ADVISERS

Mr. James Glowacki, a 1985 graduate of St. Mary's Preparatory, was named Headmaster in 1999. Mr. Glowacki earned both a B.A. and an M.A. from Wayne State University and served as the head of the English department at St. Mary's before his current appointment.

St. Mary's maintains an established and capable faculty and staff that consists of 49 teachers and several administrators. The faculty is very active in the lives of students through coaching, clubs, tutoring, and School activities.

COLLEGE PLACEMENT

A full-time guidance counselor assists students in selecting colleges and universities. Many college representatives visit St. Mary's during the year and are given the opportunity to speak to the students in groups and individually. Seniors are given frequent, personalized guidance.

Traditionally, ninety-nine percent of St. Mary's graduates are accepted to four-year colleges and universities each year. Recent graduates have attended colleges across the United States and in several other countries, including Brown, Carnegie Mellon, Columbia, Holy Cross, Kettering (formerly GMI), Loyola of Chicago, Michigan State, Notre Dame, Tufts, the United States Military Academy, Yale, and the Universities of Michigan, Pennsylvania, and Virginia.

STUDENT BODY AND CONDUCT

The 2005–06 student body consisted of 140 freshmen, 150 sophomores, 120 juniors, and 120 seniors. There were 100 boarding students representing several states and countries.

Students are guided in their attitude and conduct by St. Mary's *Parent/Student Handbook*. The Code of Conduct is based on Christian values, which must be part of the external actions of each student. The goal of the student code is to aid students in developing self-discipline. These rules apply to all students at School functions on or off campus, as participants or spectators, or when using School-sponsored transportation. The Headmaster, Dean of Students, and Dean of Resident Students determine the appropriate action to be taken for any offense against the Code of Conduct. Actions include a detention to be served after school hours, a Saturday detention to be served for 5 hours on Saturday morning, suspension, and expulsion for the most serious offenses. Most discipline is handled without formal action by the teachers. Dorm discipline also includes work crews that take care of the maintenance tasks in the dormitory.

Students follow a dress code during classes and in the chapel. On Wednesdays and Fridays, all students wear the School uniform. In addition to the regular dress code, the uniform is required for special School functions and during off-campus School-sponsored trips and consists of a blue blazer with the School crest and a School tie.

At the conclusion of the academic year, the administration reviews each student's academic and social performance. Students are invited to return to St. Mary's on a yearly basis. A positive attitude toward oneself and one's neighbor is a requirement at St. Mary's Prep.

ACADEMIC FACILITIES

The School is situated on a 125-acre campus, 70 acres of which are developed. Facilities include a three-story residence dormitory; two gymnasiums; a crew house; the campus dining commons; Shrine Chapel; the Classroom Building; the Science Center; the Alumni Library, with a new $5-million addition containing more than 75,000 volumes; the Prep Library, located in the residence dormitory; and the new $5-million St. Mary's Athletic Complex, including an ice arena, an indoor track, a weight room, a wrestling room, and concessions. The campus has a lake shoreline of 1 mile, with two docks and a swimming area.

BOARDING AND GENERAL FACILITIES

St. Mary's Prep houses students in a modern, three-story dormitory. The dormitory is under the direction of the Dean of Resident Students, and Prefects are assigned to each floor to provide direction and assistance. Students share rooms with a roommate of the same grade level. Seniors

may have single rooms if available. Each room is furnished with a bed, desk, bookshelves, dressers, and sinks. Bathroom facilities are located between every two rooms.

The dormitory contains a library and a recreation hall. The library gives boarding students access to computer facilities, while the recreation hall has a big-screen television, pool tables, and other entertainment. Other facilities include two gymnasiums, the campus dining commons, and Shrine Chapel.

ATHLETICS

Although all students participate in the physical education program at St. Mary's, interscholastic sports are not a requirement. An estimated 80 percent of students participate in varsity, junior varsity, and freshman athletics. The programs available include lacrosse, skiing, football, basketball, baseball, track, cross-country, golf, wrestling, hockey, and rowing.

The School's athletic facilities are quite extensive and include an ice arena, which includes an indoor track, a weight room, and a wrestling room. The campus also has two gymnasiums, a crew house, two football fields, two baseball diamonds, a new track, lacrosse and soccer fields, tennis courts, and many outdoor basketball courts as well as Orchard Lake, which is often used for swimming, windsurfing, fishing, ice skating, and cross-country skiing.

Athletics programs are under the direction of the Athletic Director. Interscholastic and intramural activities are coached by members of the faculty and staff as well as a staff of part-time coaches. Competitions are held against schools of similar or larger size. St. Mary's takes great pride in its tradition of competing at a level much higher than its size would indicate.

EXTRACURRICULAR OPPORTUNITIES

St. Mary's makes a serious attempt to provide for the interests of its students. Social exchanges are conducted with local schools, and field trips to places of cultural and historic interest are sponsored by various student classes or the Classmasters. Student organizations include Student Council, which sponsors a variety of activities; an Eco-club; choir; band; youth ministry; forensics; debate; Key Club (social service); SADD; *The Eaglet*, the School yearbook;

and a monthly newsletter. Additionally, clubs and other organizations are formed each year based on student interest and have included the Chess and Gaming Club, the Ski Club, the Bowling Club, and others.

A luncheon is held at the end of each marking period to celebrate the achievements of those students who have made the honor roll, while the National Honor Society has been organized to recognize the academic achievements of students who have excelled over an extended period of time. The group meets regularly and sponsors several activities throughout the year.

DAILY LIFE

Students rise at 6:45 a.m., with breakfast served until 7:30. Classes begin at 7:45 on Monday, Tuesday, and Thursday. On Wednesday and Friday, Mass is celebrated at 7:45, and classes begin promptly afterward. There are seven class periods daily, and the schedule is adjusted so that they end at 2:45 each day. After classes end, athletics activities fill the time until 5:30, when dinner is served. A supervised evening study period is held from 7 to 9. Following the study period is an activity period that usually involves intramurals, open-gym time for weight lifting or playing basketball, movies in the dorm, free time to use the recreation hall, and other activities. The Dean of Resident Students occasionally rearranges the evening schedule to accommodate such events as the Dorm Olympics, cookouts, or movie nights. Lights-out is between 10:30 and 11:30, depending upon the class.

WEEKEND LIFE

The schedule is varied on weekends, with students having free time to attend various social or cultural events or to take care of their personal needs.

With the permission of their parents and the Dean of Resident Students, students may go home after class on Friday and return by 9:15 on Sunday night. The Dean of Resident Students or his assistant coordinates recreational and social activities for students during the weekend.

COSTS AND FINANCIAL AID

The 2005–06 costs of tuition, room, board, and supervision were $8300 for day students, $16,300

for five-day boarding students, $19,500 for seven-day boarding students, and $24,500 for international students. Books and fees cost approximately $500. The initial deposit, which is nonrefundable and due at registration, is $500 and is applied to tuition. The balance may be paid before the beginning of the school year or in monthly installments.

Financial aid is available. Parents must apply through the School and Student Service for Financial Aid; awards are based on need. Forms may be obtained through the Dean of Admissions.

ADMISSIONS INFORMATION

Admission to St. Mary's Preparatory School is based on a personal interview with the Dean of Admissions; a transcript from the student's previous school; and recommendations from the principal, an English teacher, and a science or mathematics teacher. Also required are a health report, a photograph, and a $35 nonrefundable application fee. Whenever possible, SSAT or Catholic High School Placement Test results should be submitted. St. Mary's does not discriminate on the basis of race, color, creed, or national or ethnic origin in the administration of its educational policies, admissions policies, or athletics or other School-administered programs.

APPLICATION TIMETABLE

Inquiries are welcome at any time. Students are accepted for the fall semester (August) and the spring semester (January).

A personal interview with the Headmaster or Dean of Admissions is required. Parents are urged to visit St. Mary's with their son during the school term to meet members of the faculty and the students. International students should apply well in advance of the start of the new semester to comply with immigration regulations for obtaining the F-1 student visa.

ADMISSIONS CORRESPONDENCE

Kevin M. Kosco, Dean of Admissions
St. Mary's Preparatory School
3535 Indian Trail
Orchard Lake, Michigan 48324

Phone: 248-683-0532
Fax: 248-683-1740
E-mail: admissions@stmarysprep.com
Web site: http://www.stmarysprep.com

ST. PAUL'S SCHOOL

Concord, New Hampshire

Type: Coeducational boarding college-preparatory school
Grades: 9–12 (Forms III–VI)
Enrollment: 513
Head of School: William R. Matthews Jr., Interim Head of School

THE SCHOOL

St. Paul's School was founded in 1856 by Dr. George Cheyne Shattuck of Boston, who gave his country home, 3 miles west of Concord's center, as the School. St. Paul's School now encompasses 2,000 acres of woodlands, open fields, and ponds. From the beginning, the School has had an association with the Episcopal Church. Today, St. Paul's School community members come from varied faiths and many backgrounds.

St. Paul's School is committed to academic excellence and is deeply concerned with the quality of the life of its School family. The hallmarks of a successful community—trust, friendship, understanding, honest dialogue, and honorable behavior—have long been valued and continue to be priorities.

St. Paul's School actively seeks students who have the abilities, talent, and capacity to contribute to the community and who have the energy, enthusiasm, and desire to take full advantage of the School's resources.

As an all-boarding school, St. Paul's School hopes to inspire and cultivate in its students an understanding of how communities work and a willingness to make the personal sacrifices needed to sustain a community and serve those in it. The character of the School's students is as important as their intellect. Goodness outweighs knowledge in the School's scale of values, or, more precisely, the St. Paul's School community pursues knowledge for the sake of goodness.

The School's tradition and heritage are Anglican, an expression of Christianity grounded in scripture, tradition, and reason that is open to and affirming of other religions. While St. Paul's School represents the Episcopal Church, its understanding of the depth of religious experience and spirituality is not confined to any one church or faith. The School strives to be inclusive of all faith groups and recognizes that an important part of its understanding and self-identity comes from the tradition and beliefs known as religious faith. Four mornings each week, the School gathers to begin the day in the chapel, where services may include a student or faculty member speech or a student musical performance by an a cappella singing group or a string ensemble. It is a time for the entire community to join together and reflect on the events of the day in a way that enhances personal spirituality and provides a perspective for all aspects of learning.

ACADEMIC PROGRAMS

The curriculum encompasses core courses in five academic divisions: the humanities, languages, mathematics, sciences, and the arts. An innovative and student-centered residential life course is taught in each house.

The Humanities Program integrates English, history, and religious studies in a required course curriculum for students in the Third, Fourth, and Fifth Forms. Also incorporating aspects of art history, philosophy, and music, these courses involve students in an engaging interplay of imagination and intellect. This allows students to cross over the boundaries between traditional disciplines by viewing the human experience as a whole. In particular, the humanities curriculum emphasizes analytical thinking, intellectual curiosity, research, and writing by using the resources and information systems of Ohrstrom Library, technologically sophisticated classrooms, and the Internet.

The humanities curriculum offers a different focus within its three-year required program: Self, Society, and Culture (Third Form); The American Experience (Fourth Form); and European Studies from the Renaissance to the First World War (Fifth Form). Students in the Sixth Form engage in studies that build on the core curriculum. They select numerous elective courses, many of which focus on non-Western themes, religious studies, and twentieth-century issues.

Students generally take five courses each term, including an appropriate distribution among the humanities, mathematics, science, technology, languages, and arts. All students receive instruction in the use of computers, which are available in residential houses and academic buildings; a fiber-optics network connects all School buildings.

There are exceptional opportunities for language study in the Fifth and Sixth Forms through School Year Abroad, the Classical Honors Program, and the School's programs in England, France, Japan, Sweden, Denmark, and Germany.

Sixth Form students may take part in the Independent Study Program, engaging in projects that may be academic, creative, vocational, social service–oriented, or experiential in nature.

FACULTY AND ADVISERS

All 100 full-time faculty members and their families live on the School grounds with the students, teach them in the classroom, instruct them in the arts, coach them in athletics, and act as advisers. Faculty members are dedicated to the ideals of St. Paul's School, knowing that what they provide for students on the playing fields, at the boat docks, during meals, and in the houses is every bit as important as the lessons students learn in the classrooms.

COLLEGE PLACEMENT

College admissions advisers supervise college applications and related matters. About sixty-five colleges and universities send representatives to the School each year to talk with interested students. St. Paul's School students are accepted annually into all the country's major universities, including Harvard, Princeton, and Yale.

STUDENT BODY AND CONDUCT

In 2005–06, the Third Form (ninth grade) numbered 54 girls and 52 boys; Fourth Form (tenth grade), 62 girls and 78 boys; Fifth Form (eleventh grade), 82 girls and 70 boys; and Sixth Form (twelfth grade), 64 girls and 69 boys. All were boarding students and represented thirty-eight states and eighteen countries.

The Residential Life curriculum, taught during weekly meetings in the residence houses, is designed to foster the development and refinement of life skills and the spirit of working cooperatively within a community. The meetings serve to further the physical, intellectual, emotional, and spiritual development and well-being of students as they assume increasing responsibilities as young adults in the School community and the world.

ACADEMIC FACILITIES

The School's academic buildings include the Schoolhouse, with classrooms arranged in round-table format and with a comprehensive audiovisual language teaching center; Payson Laboratory; Moore Mathematics Building, which houses a computer-based teaching laboratory; separate buildings for drama, dance, and music; the Art Center in Hargate, which contains studios, photographic darkrooms, and a gallery for the visual arts; and Ohrstrom Library, with more than 65,000 volumes, 225 periodicals, and numerous online databases.

BOARDING AND GENERAL FACILITIES

The School has eighteen residence houses, with 20–36 students in each. In most houses, there are 3 resident faculty members. Faculty members not living in houses are associated with them as advisers.

Clark House, the health center, is staffed by three shifts of registered nurses and a medical director, who is the resident physician.

The Samuel Freeman Student Center features a student lounge and a snack bar. The center is open during the day and evening.

Daily chapel is viewed as a binding force in the life of the School, and the magnificent Chapel of St. Peter and St. Paul is at the center of the grounds. In addition to required morning chapel four times each week at the beginning of the day, as well as on several Sundays and evenings during the year, there are voluntary evening Compline and Sunday and weekday Eucharist services. Student involvement and participation in these services is eagerly sought and encouraged. Students also are able to explore and receive baptism, confirmation, and reception into the Episcopal Church.

ATHLETICS

Athletics is an integral part of the holistic mission of St. Paul's School. Through interscholastic and intramural sports, as well as instructional activities, the athletic program fosters the development of the mind, body, and soul. The School strives to provide a safe environment in which the values of teamwork, sportsmanship, respect, and humility are taught through healthy human interaction and competition. Moreover, the School is committed to promoting a student's appreciation for athletics and wellness beyond St. Paul's School.

All students must participate in athletic programs each term through their Fourth Form year. Students are required to fill three more terms, with two or three in their Fifth Form and/or a floating term to be taken at their discretion in their Fifth or Sixth Form year.

There are interscholastic schedules in the following twenty-seven athletics programs: basketball, crew, cross-country running, ice hockey, lacrosse, Nordic skiing, soccer, squash, tennis, and track and field for boys and girls; field hockey, softball, and

volleyball for girls; and baseball, football, and wrestling for boys. The School also offers instructional programs, such as Alpine skiing, fitness, golf, squash, and tennis. In addition to the interscholastic and instructional programs, the School has strong club programs in crew, ice hockey, and soccer.

A new state-of-the-art athletic and fitness center is equipped with two hardwood courts to accommodate fall volleyball and winter basketball; ergometer, free weight, and cardiovascular rooms with an office to ensure supervision; athletic training room to treat and nurture students in times of injury, rehabilitation, and prevention; climbing wall; two-mat wrestling rooms with adequate spectator space that can be converted to a multipurpose room for off-season activities such as yoga, tai chi, and aerobics; classroom space in which teams and groups can meet; eight-lane, 25-yard pool to support community recreation and wellness and to aid in injury prevention and rehabilitation, provide a lifelong activity option for fitness, and maximize future program flexibility; renovated cage facility with a new artificial turf floor and a three-lane indoor track; offices to support athletic department faculty and staff members for administration of programs and supervision of facilities; locker rooms to accommodate visiting interscholastic teams (while having the capacity and potential for multi-purpose use); common area/entry space to welcome all visitors to the building and to showcase the School's athletic heritage and achievements; and faculty/staff locker rooms to support all adult members of the community in a healthy lifestyle.

EXTRACURRICULAR OPPORTUNITIES

A variety of activities are available; most of them take place in the late afternoon after athletics and are run entirely by students. Some activities, such as the Debate Team, are highly structured and require intense activity. Others, such as the Bridge and Chess Clubs, meet occasionally and are informal.

The Pelican, the students' award-winning newspaper, appears approximately eight times a year and offers experience in journalism and photography. The *Horae Scholasticae*, the literary and art magazine published five times a year, encourages writers, poets, and artists, as does *The Mayflower*, published jointly by St. Paul's School and Elon College (U.K.)

Drama activities take place on the stage of Memorial Hall, in the black box experimental theater of the New Space, and often in house common rooms. Each year, the Third Form presents a Shakespeare play. In the winter, there is a lively interhouse one-act play competition open to all.

Musical groups, both instrumental and vocal, perform regularly in chapel, in the Concord area, on Parents Day, and at graduation. Groups include the Concert Band, Jazz Band, Chamber Orchestra, Chorus, Gospel Choir, Madrigal Singers, Deli Line, Mad Hatters, B-List, and T-Tones.

The St. Paul's School Ballet Company provides students with the opportunity to study classical and modern works and to perform before audiences from within and outside the School. Graduates of the program have gone on to dance professionally with major companies, including the Chicago City Ballet, the Royal Ballet of Flanders, and the New York City Ballet.

International societies and language clubs offer opportunities outside the classroom for pleasure and further development of skills.

Seasonal activities, such as fly-fishing, ice skating, in-line skating, mountain biking, boating on trout-stocked streams and ponds, and cross-country skiing on miles of forest trails provide a wonderful recreational change of pace.

DAILY LIFE

After breakfast, a regular day includes chapel at 8 a.m., followed by Reports, the announcement of daily activities made to the School by the Rector. Thereafter, classes continue until 2:30 p.m. A cafeteria lunch is served for 2 hours, allowing students and faculty members to enjoy a leisurely meal and conversation with friends. Athletics occupy a 2-hour period in midafternoon. Dinner follows, with the School in a formal assigned seating arrangement two evenings per week.

Within the six days of the academic week, a student's class meetings are distributed so that a student generally has three or four classes per day, some of which are of 90-minute duration. During evening study, from after dinner until about 10, students study alone or with one another in their rooms, in the library, or in the classroom buildings.

WEEKEND LIFE

A student committee arranges and coordinates a comprehensive schedule of social, cultural, and entertainment activities for the weekend enjoyment of the community. These may include student drama and musical performances; films, dances, and special events sponsored by a Form, a house, or a club; and presentations by an individual or group from outside the School.

Saturday night Open House at the Rectory is a regular and long-established tradition. Trips away from the School range from attending music and drama performances in Concord's Capitol Center for the Arts to hikes to the top of Mount Washington with the Outing Club.

Short or long weekends may, with parental and School permission, be taken from time to time by students whose performance is satisfactory and whose absence will not interrupt their School responsibilities. On certain weekends designated as "closed," all students are expected to be in residence.

COSTS AND FINANCIAL AID

The charge for tuition and residence for the year 2005–06 was $34,965, which is payable in one, two, or ten installments. In addition to tuition, families should anticipate variable expenses for books and academic supplies; travel to and from the School; laundry service; $800 in fees for student health, publications, and technology; spending money; and medical insurance if current coverage is not adequate.

While St. Paul's School believes that the primary responsibility for financing education rests with the parents, the School supports one of the most robust financial aid programs available at the secondary school level. For the 2005–06 school year, St. Paul's School awarded approximately $4.5 million of financial aid to 214 students, or 40 percent of the student body. Grants ranged from $1000 to approximately $34,965. Practically speaking, every St. Paul's School student receives financial aid from the School's endowment because the cost of educating each student far exceeds the full tuition. The majority of aid is awarded based on demonstrated need. Limited merit-based scholarships are offered.

Interested families should contact the Director of Financial Aid. Applicants must submit the Parents' Financial Statement to School and Student Services in Princeton, New Jersey, and supporting documentation to St. Paul's School.

ADMISSIONS INFORMATION

Candidates compete with many others for admission into St. Paul's School. Students who have demonstrated intellectual ability, motivation, and curiosity are most likely to be among those admitted. However, the School is also interested in a candidate's strength of character, leadership ability, and athletic and artistic talents.

New students are enrolled only in September and generally in the Third and Fourth Form years; a few students are admitted in the Fifth Form. All candidates are required to take the SSAT.

Personal interviews are required. Parents are urged to bring candidates to visit the School in the fall or winter of the school year prior to the September in which the student wishes to enroll. It is suggested that candidates and their families visit in the morning and plan on spending approximately 2 hours at the School. During the visit, parents and candidates talk with a member of the admissions staff and have a student-guided tour of the facilities and grounds.

APPLICATION TIMETABLE

Candidates should register and file the $50 fee by December of the year preceding enrollment. Candidates applying from abroad must pay a $100 application fee. Students who apply online pay a reduced fee of $25. The application, interview, and accompanying forms must be completed and returned to the Admissions Office by January 15. St. Paul's School notifies candidates and their families of admissions decisions on March 10. Parents are expected to notify the School of their decision by April 10.

During the academic year, visitors are encouraged to come to the School on weekdays or on Saturdays until noon. The School welcomes visitors in the summer months, when the Admissions Office is open from 9 a.m. to 4 p.m., Monday through Friday. Candidates or their parents should arrange an appointment at least three weeks before a proposed visit.

ADMISSIONS CORRESPONDENCE

Michael G. Hirschfeld
Director of Admissions
St. Paul's School
325 Pleasant Street
Concord, New Hampshire 03301-2591
Phone: 603-229-4700
Fax: 603-229-4772
E-mail: admissions@sps.edu
Web site: http://www.sps.edu

ST. STANISLAUS COLLEGE

Bay St. Louis, Mississippi

Type: Boys' day and resident college-preparatory school
Grades: 6–12: Middle School, 6–8; Upper School, 9–12
Enrollment: School total: 570
Head of School: Brother Ronald Talbot, SC, President

THE SCHOOL

St. Stanislaus College (SSC), founded in 1854, is an independent Catholic school located on the Mississippi Gulf Coast 50 miles east of New Orleans. Operated by the Brothers of the Sacred Heart, the school specializes in building character and helping young men in grades 6–12 develop to their full potential and become happy, self-confident, well-educated adults.

The mission of St. Stanislaus, a Catholic residency and day school for young men, is to teach Gospel values and to nurture the total development of each student according to the charism of the Brothers of the Sacred Heart. The school fosters character formation and integrates faith development within a curriculum that is primarily college preparatory. As an integral part of its mission, St. Stanislaus maintains a residency program that offers students opportunities for educational success and personal growth within a disciplined and structured environment.

St. Stanislaus is the largest Catholic resident high school for boys in the United States. Since boarding has been a central component and a mainstay of the school, to live at SSC is to experience the richness of a tradition of 150 years. Even fourth- and fifth-generation students have benefited from this rich tradition. Resident students come from diverse backgrounds and cultures, with eleven countries and twelve states currently represented. Over the years, students from fifty-two countries and forty-two states have profited from the rich education and character building offered by St. Stanislaus. This diversity promotes a heightened awareness of each student's value and provides opportunities for appreciation of other cultures and for lasting friendships with students from other countries.

In 1870, St. Stanislaus was recognized by the state of Mississippi as a college; however, by 1923 the curriculum became college preparatory. Since 1923, the school has been known as St. Stanislaus College and is incorporated under that name. Governed by a 10-member board of directors, the annual operating budget of the school is $6 million, with an endowment of $8 million.

St. Stanislaus is accredited by the Mississippi State Department of Education, the Southern Association of Colleges and Schools, and the Mississippi High School Activities Association. It holds membership in The Association of Boarding Schools (TABS), the Catholic Boarding Schools Association, the National Catholic Education Association, and the Association for Supervision and Curriculum Development.

ACADEMIC PROGRAMS

The school's strong core curriculum includes 4 units each of religion, English, history, science, and mathematics; 2 units of foreign language; 1 unit of art; 1 unit of computer education; and 1 unit of health and physical fitness. Electives are available in language arts, art, band, business, computer science, social studies, science, physical education, and foreign languages. Honors classes and advanced placement classes are also offered. The grading system uses A through F during four 9-week marking periods, with academic progress reports issued twice each nine weeks. After-school and evening tutoring are available.

FACULTY AND ADVISERS

The educational values of the Brothers of the Sacred Heart are exemplified by the school's 60 faculty members, the 12 residency staff members, and the 5 Brothers of the Sacred Heart active in the educational process. More than 56 percent of the faculty and resident staff members possess a master's degree or higher.

COLLEGE PLACEMENT

Ninety-eight percent of the graduating seniors attend college. The curriculum at St. Stanislaus is geared specifically toward preparation for college, and formal college guidance begins in the junior year, with each student expected to take either the ACT or the SAT. The application process for college admissions begins in August of the senior year.

Students from the most recent graduating classes have received scholarships from such institutions as Boston University, the College of Charleston, Florida State, LSU, Loyola, the Merchant Marine Academy, Mississippi State, NYU, Notre Dame, Oxford University, Spring Hill College, Tulane, the U.S. Air Force Academy, the U.S. Military Academy, the U.S. Naval Academy, and the Universities of Chicago, Florida, Miami, Pennsylvania, and Virginia. Of the 98 percent of the seniors who go on to university study, 56 percent receive academic and/or athletic scholarships.

STUDENT BODY AND CONDUCT

St. Stanislaus enrolls 550 students, of whom 180 are resident students. There are 70 resident students and 110 day students in the Middle School.

The student body is expected to adhere to a carefully delineated code of conduct that specifies the rules and regulations of the institution. The Dean of Students is responsible for maintaining student discipline. A dress code mandates that a Stanislaus shirt and designated khaki pants be worn to class. On special occasions, a white dress shirt and tie are worn. The dress code excludes jeans, shorts, and sports shoes as classroom wear.

ACADEMIC FACILITIES

The main classroom and administrative building (constructed in 1971) was enlarged significantly in 1991. The Student Chapel and the Kleinpeter-Gibbens Memorial Library (1970) are part of a building constructed in 1929. The library houses more than 13,000 volumes; a microfiche collection; numerous periodical and newspaper subscriptions; and a growing collection of local server and Internet-based reference works, including SIRS Discoverer & Researcher, Electric Library, Exegy, Infotrac, MAS Full Text Select, Welcome to the Catholic Church, and many online encyclopedias; the EBSCO abstract and full-document retrieval system for more than 400 periodicals; and supervised Internet workstations.

BOARDING AND GENERAL FACILITIES

St. Stanislaus overlooks the Gulf of Mexico, with 30 acres of campus extending from the beach into the town of Bay St. Louis. The Beach Boulevard overpass provides safe access to the 1,000-foot wooden pier from which students sail, fish, and enjoy beach sports. The Brother Aurelian Dormitory (1968) houses 230 resident students and 11 dorm staff members. This building is fully air conditioned; rooms with private baths house 2 or 3 students. The Brothers' Residence (1954, renovated in 1998) houses the 23 Brothers living on campus and the Brothers' Chapel.

The Brother Alban Dining Hall (1950), the swimming pool (1970), three lighted tennis courts, handball and basketball courts, playing fields, the Brother Peter Memorial Gymnasium (1977), and the Fitness Center (2002) complete the front campus. At the back campus, the Brother Philip Memorial Stadium includes a football field surrounded by a 400-meter all-weather track, soccer fields, a field house, and a baseball field and concession stand. Off-campus sites include two camps used for waterskiing, fishing, and relaxing.

The new Fitness Center is a two-story, 10,000-square-foot building that contains locker rooms, a state-of-the-art weight room, and an auxiliary gym as well as coaches' offices and classroom facilities. The Fitness Center provides the St. Stanislaus College athletic programs with appropriate training equipment and expands after-school recreational activities for students.

The resident staff of 12 men is directed by an experienced Director of Residency. The staff devotes full time to the care and development of the resident students. Through in-service programs and staff workshops, the prefects are trained to become effective counselors, guides, mentors, and friends. The residency curriculum is designed to nurture the development of sound study habits, self-discipline, and a Christian appreciation of others. Structured study periods with tutoring assistance constantly encourage the young men to reach their potential.

ATHLETICS

The SSC mascot, adopted in the 1920s when football and baseball became popular at SSC, is

the Rockachaw. This is the Native American name for a sticker burr indigenous to the sandy soil of south Mississippi. Playing fields were primitive and replete with the tenacious and painful Rock-A-Chaws. Unwary opponents on the playing field usually went home with hundreds of the burrs clinging to their uniforms and pricking their skin.

The school community has long encouraged student participation in both interscholastic and intramural athletics. As a member of Division 8-4A of the Mississippi High School Activities Association, SSC athletes have garnered a number of titles: the football team captured the district title in 2004; the basketball team won the district title in 2003 and 2004; the soccer team won the 4-A State Championship in 2003 and 2004; district honors went to the track, golf, and tennis teams in 2004 and 2005; the swimming team captured second place in the state in 2004; and the sailing team, after winning the Sugar Bowl Regatta, was invited to the National Regatta at Annapolis is 2004. Colonel Felix "Doc" Blanchard, '42, donated his Heisman, Maxwell, and Sullivan Trophies to SSC.

Interscholastic competition includes baseball, basketball, cross-country, football, golf, sailing, soccer, swimming, tennis, track and field, and powerlifting. Each sport fields junior high, junior varsity, and varsity teams.

Intramural sports include football, Ultimate Frisbee, beach volleyball, baseball, tennis, and swimming. The indoor sports of pool, air hockey, bumper pool, Foosball, and table tennis are also available. Athletes are encouraged to join the Fellowship of Christian Athletes.

EXTRACURRICULAR OPPORTUNITIES
SSC provides a variety of clubs and organizations appealing to students. The Student Council, the Key Club, and the Student Ministry Program provide opportunities for leadership in various phases of student life. Students publish the yearbook, the *Reflections*, and the student newspaper, *The Rock-A-Chaw*. Students who qualify are invited to join the honor organizations: the National Junior Honor Society and the National Honor Society. Other clubs and activities appealing to student interests are altar servers, Art Club,

Archaeology Club, band, Computer Club, Drama Club, fishing, literary magazine, Magic Club, Photography Club, Radio Club, Scuba Club, Sports Card Club, Varsity Quiz Bowl, and a junior high club. The Christmas and spring band concerts, the Arts Festival, spring drama productions, and beach barbecues together with frequent dances complement student activities.

The SSC band, drum line, and flag corps perform at football games and community functions and also present Christmas and spring concerts. Annually, the band and drum line participate in local parades.

Students from the neighboring girls' school participate in the swimming team, the band, dance, and the flag corps.

DAILY LIFE
Resident students are invited to attend the celebration of the Eucharist at 6:30 a.m. All rise for breakfast at 7 a.m. Class begins at 8 and ends at 3:15 p.m. Lunch is one of the eight 50-minute periods of the school day. Classes meet on a daily basis, Monday through Friday. Athletics or other extracurricular activities occupy most students' afternoons. The first study period for resident students is 5:30 to 6:30 p.m. Resident students dine at 6:30 p.m. The second study period begins at 7:30 p.m. and is preceded by prayer. Older students retire at 11 p.m., while 9:30 p.m. is lights out for the younger ones.

WEEKEND LIFE
Weekend activities for those who remain on campus are organized with the students' educational, spiritual, social, and recreational needs in mind. International students are encouraged to spend the weekend with domestic students. Students are provided travel opportunities ranging from cultural events in New Orleans to waterskiing on the Jourdan River. Attendance at Sunday Eucharist is required, and daily Eucharist with the Brothers is encouraged. A regular prayer schedule is the backdrop of each day's schedule.

COSTS AND FINANCIAL AID
The 2005–06 total for tuition and fees for resident students is $17,300 ($18,350 for international students), plus a $725 registration fee after

May 15. Day school tuition is $4600, with a $375 registration fee after May 15. There is an application fee of $100, which is applied to the registration upon acceptance. Tuition assistance for 2005–06 averages approximately $900 for day students and $2500 for resident students. The amount is based on need.

ADMISSIONS INFORMATION
The school's administrators choose carefully from the broad range of applicants who seek admission to St. Stanislaus College. The school does not discriminate on the basis of race, color, national or ethnic origin, or handicap.

The following criteria are used to admit prospective students: the student's overall school record, the recommendation of former teachers or principals, and an interview with each applicant and his parents. Consideration is given to sons of alumni and younger brothers of alumni and students presently in school. For resident students, an application form with the application fee, an unofficial copy of the transcript, recommendations from school officials, and a personal interview are required.

APPLICATION TIMETABLE
Inquiries are always welcome, and interviews and tours can be scheduled at any time during the year. March and April are the normal registration periods for resident students for the following year. Brochures and application materials may be obtained from the Admissions Office. Office hours are from 8 a.m. to 4 p.m. Requests for material and information may be made by calling the number below or sending an e-mail to the address listed in the Admissions Correspondence section.

ADMISSIONS CORRESPONDENCE
Director of Admissions
St. Stanislaus College
304 South Beach Boulevard
Bay St. Louis, Mississippi 39520
Phone: 228-467-9057 Ext. 227
       800-517-6257 (toll-free)
Fax: 228-466-2972
E-mail: admissions@ststan.com
Web site: http://www.ststan.com

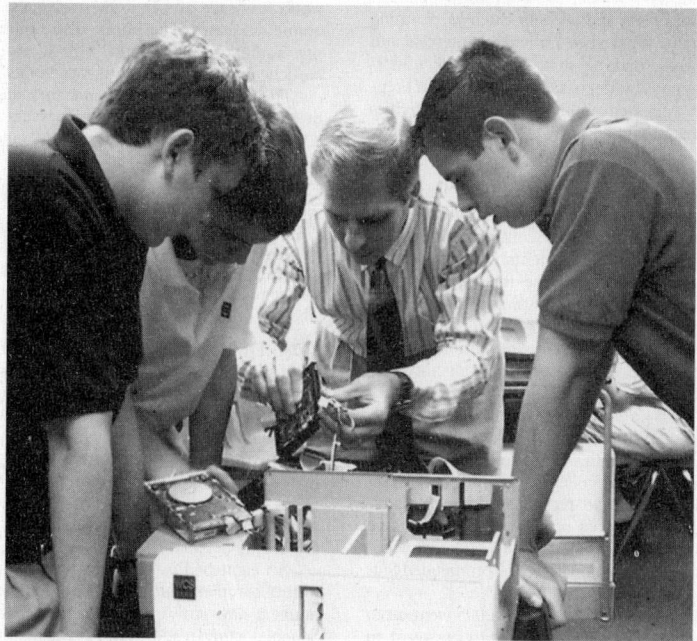

ST. STEPHEN'S EPISCOPAL SCHOOL

Austin, Texas

Type: Coeducational boarding and day college-preparatory
Grades: 6–12: Middle School, 6–8; Upper School, 9–12
Enrollment: School total: 656; Middle School: 203; Upper School: 453
Head of School: Rev. Roger Bowen

THE SCHOOL

St. Stephen's Episcopal School was opened in 1950 in response to the need for a top-quality boarding school in Texas. The Rt. Rev. John E. Hines, then Bishop Coadjutor of the Diocese of Texas and later Presiding Bishop of the Episcopal Church, chose the Austin area for the School so as to be near the University of Texas and the seat of state government. The founding vision called for the creation of a caring, diverse, Christian community with rigorous academic standards that nurtures moral growth and values the potential and dignity of every human being. The School was the first coeducational boarding school in the Episcopal Church and one of the first racially integrated boarding schools in the South. The 430-acre campus is nestled in the rolling, wooded hill country, 8 miles west of downtown Austin.

St. Stephen's Episcopal School is accredited by the Texas Education Agency and the Independent Schools Association of the Southwest. It is a member of the National Association of Independent Schools, the National Association of Episcopal Schools, the Western Boarding Schools Association, and the Cum Laude Society.

ACADEMIC PROGRAMS

St. Stephen's challenges motivated students to live intelligently, creatively, and humanely as contributing members of society. The School develops the whole person by providing rigorous academic preparation, stimulating physical activities, and rich opportunities in the fine arts.

In the St. Stephen's Upper School college-preparatory curriculum, 18 full-year credits are required for graduation. English is a required four-year sequence; a substantial number of seniors elect to take the Advanced Placement (AP) exam in literature and composition. History is a required three-year sequence, with junior and senior electives in social sciences and a senior elective in AP European history. Math is required for three years; the advanced track begins with geometry. There are AP electives in calculus and statistics, and electives are offered in multivariable analysis and computer science. Foreign language is required for three years, with advanced levels offered through Latin IV, Spanish VI, and French VII. A four-year sequence is offered in Chinese. The Classics Department offers electives in classical literature in translation and in Latin. There is a three-year requirement for science, with advanced electives in astrophysics, chemistry, and robotics. AP electives are offered in biology, physics, chemistry, and environmental science. Science students engage in independent research, field research experiences throughout Texas, science courses rarely found in high schools, and mentorship options with researchers in local laboratories. In collaboration with the Nature Conservancy of Texas, a West Texas field station has been established in the Davis Mountains.

Theology is a required one-year course stressing critical spirituality and theological reasoning. There is a one-year requirement in the fine arts, with classes in music history, photography, applied arts, music theory, and visual studies as well as AP electives in art, music, and art history.

There are three theater productions per year, including a musical and a student-directed one-act play. The Theater Focus Program inspires student artists through the study of theater and its place in society.

In addition to a core of rigorous academic classes, the curriculum includes acting, directing, musical theater, and Spartan Studios technical theater. Each student takes private or small-group lessons in acting, dance, and voice.

St. Stephen's offers a wide variety of elective courses, including many that follow Advanced Placement program syllabi. In 2005, 111 students took 179 AP examinations, making grades of 3 or higher on 86 percent of the tests.

The school year is divided into three terms. The grading system is based on marks of honors, very good, good, passing, unsatisfactory, and seriously failing. Advisers report grades to their advisees and confer with them and their parents whenever necessary.

Class size averages 16 students. The student-teacher ratio is 8:1.

St. Stephen's is an international community with students from fifteen countries. The School offers an Intensive English Program (IEP) for international students that includes an interdisciplinary course, supplemental activities, and advising. There is an extended orientation for new IEP students. St. Stephen's has an annual exchange program for tenth-grade boys with St. Andrew's Boys' High School, Osaka, Japan, and for tenth-grade girls with St. Margaret's School in Tokyo, Japan.

FACULTY AND ADVISERS

There are 75 full-time and 4 part-time faculty members. Sixty-four faculty members hold master's degrees, 12 hold doctorates, and two are doctoral candidates. Half the faculty members live on campus and supervise boarding students.

The School encourages and provides financial support for faculty professional development. Teachers serve as advisers to students and meet with them during a daily advisory period. They know their advisees well and offer special help, such as planning study programs tailored to individual interests and academic needs, making sure each advisee understands the responsibilities of school routine, and keeping parents informed about their child's activities and academic progress.

COLLEGE PLACEMENT

At St. Stephen's, the process of college planning is student centered but supported by the College Counseling Office. Individual college conferences are available to all Upper School students, with a required sequence of conferences in the junior and senior years that are crucial to the planning process. Counselors who oversee the progress of a class through the students' last two years encourage communication from families and prepare information for transmission to colleges.

The PSAT is given to all tenth and eleventh graders. The mean SAT scores for the class of 2005 were 612 verbal and 643 math. Admission representatives from the country's top colleges and universities visit the School each year to recruit students. Twenty-eight percent of the class of 2006 received national academic recognition; there were 14 National Merit Semifinalists and 16 National Merit Commended Students.

All 115 graduates of the class of 2005 went on to four-year colleges; 80 percent of the class went to colleges outside of Texas. Two or more graduates

enrolled at the following schools: Boston University, Rice, Stanford, Trinity, and the University of Texas at Austin.

STUDENT BODY AND CONDUCT

St. Stephen's enrolls a total of 453 students in the Upper School as follows: 160 boarding boys and girls and 293 day boys and girls. There are 203 students enrolled in the Middle School, including 10 boarders. Most boarding students come from Texas, but there are also students from sixteen other states. International students come from fifteen countries, including Germany, Japan, Korea, Mexico, Saudi Arabia, Syria, and Thailand. Members of minority groups (not including international students) account for 22 percent of the student population.

The rules at St. Stephen's are the guidelines to maturity, self-respect, and independence. A committee of elected students and faculty members reviews disciplinary cases and recommends action to the Head of School.

ACADEMIC FACILITIES

Academic classrooms for the Upper School are located in four single-story classroom buildings surrounding the chapel. Administrative offices and classrooms are in recently remodeled Brewster Hall. There are 120 computers available on campus for student use in the library and in the foreign language, teaching, and project labs. The campus features fast, efficient connection to the Internet through a fiber-optic network in all of the academic buildings and dorms. Wireless access is also available across campus. The Science Department is housed in Hines Hall, which has seven modern labs. The observatory features one of the largest refracting telescopes in Texas and is used for astrophysics and other classes.

Becker Library has 16,000 volumes, three banks of computers that link students to a local area network, a library of CD-ROM materials, and several online databases. The library also houses an extensive audiovisual collection, ninety periodicals, microfiche, and a collection of rare books.

The Helm Fine Arts Center includes a 400-seat theater, an eighty-seat recital hall, visual arts studios, a darkroom, an art gallery, a kiln, and teaching/practice studios.

A recent expansion to the Middle School building created four new classrooms, an art room, two science labs, three common areas, two outdoor classrooms, and restrooms. The existing Middle School facility was renovated and includes classrooms, tutoring rooms, computer labs, an additional science lab, and conference areas.

BOARDING AND GENERAL FACILITIES

St. Stephen's has six boys' and four girls' dormitory buildings, including a dorm for boys in grades 8 and 9. All boarding students have senior proctors in charge of their hallways. A majority of the rooms are doubles. New boarding boys and girls are assigned roommates; returning students may request their roommate. Faculty members and their families live in or next to the dormitories. The student-faculty ratio in the dorms is about 3:1.

An eight-bed infirmary is located near the dormitory complex, and a registered nurse is on duty 24 hours a day. An Austin practitioner serves as the School doctor. In addition, 4 psychologists and counselors serve the St. Stephen's community.

ATHLETICS

St. Stephen's requires that students in the Upper School participate in at least one interscholastic sport through their sophomore year and take part in physical education classes when not participating in a sport. St. Stephen's provides a full range of traditional varsity sports, including baseball, basketball, crew, cross-country, football, field hockey, golf, soccer, softball, tennis, track and field, and volleyball. The program also provides alternative activities for students to fulfill the athletic requirement, including caving, dance, lacrosse, mountain biking, triathlon, and rock-climbing on St. Stephen's indoor climbing wall. St. Stephen's competes in games and tournaments with schools from the Southwestern Preparatory Conference, which ranges from Houston to Oklahoma City.

St. Stephen's also offers two intensive year-round programs for soccer and tennis athletes interested in continuing their participation on the collegiate level.

The Tennis Academy offers intensive training to sectionally, nationally, and internationally ranked players who aspire to earn NCAA Division I tennis scholarships. Three private lessons per week are led by a team of coaches—former collegiate All-Americans with college coaching experience. Coaches and players travel to tournaments, and players receive coaching at every tournament. Summers include tennis camps and additional tournament travel.

The Soccer Academy has a highly qualified coaching staff directed by full-time UEFA-licensed coaches. Players participate in a highly competitive thirty-game winter high school season. In addition to individualized training sessions at the School, soccer players participate with Division I Austin clubs in the fall and spring.

Facilities include new soccer fields, modern gymnasiums with weight and conditioning rooms, a spacious dance studio, six athletic fields, an all-weather six-lane UIL track, a cross-country running trail, a sand volleyball court, and a swimming pool. A tennis facility features twelve lighted hard-surface courts and two lighted clay courts.

EXTRACURRICULAR OPPORTUNITIES

St. Stephen's, which encourages community service at home and abroad, recently launched new service programs in Haiti, El Salvador, Nicaragua, and Costa Rica.

Closer to home in Central Texas, St. Stephen's Upper School students performed more than 5,500 hours of community service at nonprofit organizations and agencies in 2004–05. Other activities include the Madrigals (an a cappella group); the St. Stephen's Choir; literary journal; the student-run, fully digital yearbook; the student newspaper; Amnesty International; the Mu Alpha Theta math honor society; the computer club; Quiz Bowl; Model U.N.,

and the Fine Arts Council. Stephen's Kids gives students a chance to participate in an educational outreach mentorship program with low-income children in Austin. The Peer Assistance Group enables St. Stephen's students to affirm and support one another, and Peer Tutoring matches student tutors with other students seeking help with academic subjects. In Mock Trial, an attorney helps students develop legal skills and understanding while they alternately play the roles of prosecutors or the defense. FACES is a support and discussion group that focuses on multicultural issues.

The Devil's Canyon Wilderness Program (DCWP) takes students climbing, caving, cycling, surfing, and backpacking throughout the United States and Mexico. The goals include fostering leadership skills and personal growth, as well as teaching students to be safe and responsible in the wilderness. Interested students should visit the DCWP Web site at http://www.dcwp.net.

DAILY LIFE

Students meet daily with their advisers before gathering in the chapel. There are eight periods in the academic day, including one or more study times.

Varsity teams and a number of extracurricular activity groups meet from 3:45 to 6 p.m., five days a week. Six nights a week, dinner is cafeteria style, and on Wednesday it is a family-style meal. There is a designated study period each evening from 8 until 10 p.m.

WEEKEND LIFE

Student life on weekends is enhanced by a full program of activities, such as town trips to movies, malls, sporting events, drama productions, and concerts. Out-of-town trips include amusement parks, theaters, sporting events, and museums. For on-campus activities, the student center is always open for movies, pool, games, television, and relaxation. The campus gyms and swimming pool are also open. Dances and other special events are planned throughout the year.

Boarding students are allowed one 3-day weekend and up to six overnights per term. To spend the weekend at a friend's house or engage in other off-campus weekend activities, the student must have parental permission. On other weekends students may sign out to go to Austin for the day or evening, but again they must have their parents' approval, and they must return to campus. Day students are invited to take part in campus activities and frequently invite boarders to their homes. In addition, a host family program provides a home away from home for out-of-state students.

SUMMER PROGRAMS

St. Stephen's offers opportunities to study and travel abroad in language-immersion, academic, cultural

exchange, and community service programs. In summer 2006, St. Stephen's students and faculty members return to Salamanca, Spain, for a language-immersion program. Plans for students during spring break 2006 include a tour of fine-arts sites in Paris, Florence, and Rome.

COSTS AND FINANCIAL AID

Charges for 2005–06 were as follows: tuition (grades 6–8), $15,900; tuition (grades 9–12), $17,300; boarding supplement, $12,200; day food service, $850; boarding food service, $1400; new student facility use fee, $1000; returning student facility use fee, $100; and international/non-U.S. resident fee, $1100. Students pay for books separately.

In support of diversity, St. Stephen's awarded more than $1.86 million in financial assistance to 18 percent of the student body in 2004–05. The average financial award was $16,014. Eligibility is based on need and determined by criteria established by the School and Student Service for Financial Aid of Princeton, New Jersey. The priority deadline to apply for financial aid is February 1.

ADMISSIONS INFORMATION

St. Stephen's seeks students of above-average ability and motivation. The School does not discriminate on the basis of race, national and ethnic origin, creed, gender, gender expression, or sexual orientation. Boarding and day students are accepted in each class annually. Applicants are considered on the basis of Independent School Entrance Exam (ISEE) scores, recommendations and academic records from previous schools, candidate and parent questionnaires, and an interview.

APPLICATION TIMETABLE

The application deadline for the first round of admission decisions is February 1. Applicants and their parents are responsible for submitting all application materials—student and parent questionnaires, teacher and personal recommendations, entrance exam results, and the student interview—by the deadline.

After the February 1 deadline, applications are considered on a rolling admission basis. When all spaces are filled, qualified candidates are placed in the wait pool.

ADMISSIONS CORRESPONDENCE

Lawrence Sampleton, Director of Admission
St. Stephen's Episcopal School
2900 Bunny Run
Austin, Texas 78746
Phone: 512-327-1213 Ext. 210
Fax: 512-327-6771
E-mail: admission@sstx.org
Web site: http://www.sstx.org

SAINT THOMAS MORE SCHOOL

Oakdale, Connecticut

Type: Boys' boarding college-preparatory school
Grades: 8–12, postgraduate year
Enrollment: 210
Head of School: James F. Hanrahan Jr., Headmaster

THE SCHOOL

Saint Thomas More School was founded in 1962 by James F. Hanrahan to assist the boy who has the ability to succeed but who has not yet shown his potential through academic achievement. The intellectual, moral, physical, and social development of each student is the focus of the School's educational design.

The goal of Saint Thomas More School is to prepare young men for college. The School believes that with the proper supervision, encouragement, and guidance from a dedicated faculty and with an environment that fosters self-discipline and responsibility, the student will develop the skills that are essential to a successful college career and a fulfilled life. Faculty members work on an individual basis with students to develop strong study habits and to foster a desire to succeed. It is the School's hope that its students will establish a record of success, build confidence through achievement, and embrace those fundamental Christian principles that enrich and dignify the human spirit.

The School is situated on 100 acres of Connecticut's most beautiful countryside bordering Gardner Lake, the largest natural lake in the eastern part of the state. While the campus and its immediate surroundings provide a rural atmosphere conducive to study and reflection, as well as to sports and outdoor recreation, the benefits of historic Connecticut and the cultural events of Hartford, New Haven, and Providence can be enjoyed only a short distance from the campus. Although Saint Thomas More School is a Catholic school, boys of all faiths are welcome. The School is a nonprofit corporation directed by a Board of Trustees composed of civic leaders, educators, alumni, and prominent business-people.

Saint Thomas More School is accredited by the New England Association of Schools and Colleges and is a member of the Connecticut Association of Independent Schools, the National Association of Independent Schools, the National Catholic Educational Association, and the NAFSA Association of International Educators.

ACADEMIC PROGRAMS

The academic requirements and curriculum have been designed to provide preparation for entrance into any U.S. college or university. All courses offered are academic in nature, and each student is required to take at least five courses per year. A total of 16 academic credits is required for graduation, including 4 in English, 3 in college-preparatory mathematics, 2 in science, 2 in foreign languages, 1 in religion, 1 in fine arts, and 1 in U.S. history. Several elective courses are available. In recent years these have included computer science, political science, presidential politics, art history, economics, and academic writing. In addition, SAT prep courses and driver's education are offered. All Catholic students are required to take a course in theology each year. The theology courses deal with the problems of personal responsibility, morality, ethics, and tradition.

Along with the normal study of content, all courses emphasize the development of study and organizational skills, such as note-taking techniques, outlining skills, and reading and vocabulary development.

The English as a second language (ESL) program offers two levels of instruction to students from other countries. In addition, TOEFL preparation is given.

The School year is divided into the traditional four marking periods. Midway through each marking period, progress reports are given to students who are not reaching their potential. These students are assigned to additional study sessions. After each marking period, parents receive report cards giving the student's numerical average, a grade for effort, and a written comment from each teacher regarding the progress of the student. Midterm examinations are administered after the return from Christmas vacation. A final examination is required before credit is awarded.

The student-faculty ratio is 8:1, and the average class size is 12 students. At the end of the class day, all teachers are available in their classrooms for a 30-minute extra-help session.

Essential to the Saint Thomas More experience is the mandatory evening study hall from 7:30 to 9:30, with a quiet time to 10:15 and lights out at 10:30. During this time, students study in their dormitory rooms under the close supervision of members of the faculty, who give individual assistance and help students to budget their study time.

FACULTY AND ADVISERS

The faculty is composed of 27 lay teachers of various denominations and 1 full-time member who is a Roman Catholic priest. All hold bachelor's degrees, and most either hold advanced degrees or are involved in graduate studies at one of the many nearby universities.

James F. Hanrahan Jr., son of the founder and Headmaster Emeritus, is a native of Oakdale, Connecticut. He holds a B.S. in mathematics from Fairfield University and an M.Ed. in educational administration from Boston College. His teaching experience began in 1976 at Saint Thomas More School, where he taught math, physics, and computers as well as coached various athletic teams. Since that time, he has held the positions of Business Manager and Assistant Headmaster. He was appointed Headmaster in 1997. Mr. Hanrahan lives on campus with his wife, Gina, and their daughters, Shannon and Casey.

All faculty members are appointed as advisers to a small group of students. In addition, faculty members direct and supervise all activities, including the evening study hall. The advisers also report each student's social progress to his parents at the end of each term.

COLLEGE PLACEMENT

The placement of students in college is a thoughtful procedure. Beginning in the junior year, conferences with students and parents help direct each student toward the colleges and universities that best suit his needs. A college placement officer helps each student develop a list of six to eight colleges that he can investigate further, often through visits during school vacations and on weekends.

For the class of 2004, the average verbal score of students taking the SAT I was 495 and the average math score was 510.

Nearly all graduates of the class of 2005 are currently enrolled in various colleges and universities throughout the country, including Assumption, Babson, Boston College, Boston University, Clark, C.W. Post, Fairfield, Northeastern, Rider, Saint Michael's, Seton Hall, Southern Connecticut State, Villanova, and the Universities of Colorado, Connecticut, Massachusetts, New Haven, Tampa, Texas, and Wisconsin.

STUDENT BODY AND CONDUCT

The School enrolls 210 boys, all of whom are boarding. There are 15 students in grade 8, 24 in grade 9, 40 in grade 10, 50 in grade 11, 55 in grade 12, and 26 postgraduates. Approximately 60 percent come from Connecticut, New Jersey, New York, Massachusetts, Rhode Island, New Hampshire, and Pennsylvania. An additional 20 percent come from Southern and Midwestern states, including Virginia, Florida, Ohio, Illinois, Texas, and Wisconsin. Approximately 20 percent of the student body is made up of students from such places as the Dominican Republic, Chile, Germany, Ghana, Japan, Korea, Mexico, Puerto Rico, Taiwan, and Turkey.

Expectations of student behavior are carefully explained in the *Student Handbook* and during the several orientation meetings that are held during Opening Weekend. All students are strictly accountable to these expectations, which are based on Christian principles of community living. Minor disciplinary measures are handled by faculty members, while serious offenses are referred to the Dean of Students. When dismissal from the School is a possible disciplinary procedure, the Dean of Students meets with the student and his adviser and submits a recommendation of procedure to the Headmaster.

ACADEMIC FACILITIES

Classes are conducted in four buildings. Saint Benedict's Hall has twelve classrooms and two

administrative offices. The Loyola Building has eight classrooms. The Aquinas Building houses a chemistry/physics lab, a biology lab, and administrative offices. The library, containing more than 8,500 volumes, online computers, and a microfiche collection, is located on the first floor of the Saint Edmund's dormitory. This building also contains four classrooms, two computer centers, and a language laboratory. An art cabin is also located on the property for art appreciation and history courses, with additional space for individual expression. The administration building includes conference rooms, the student mailroom, and all administrative offices.

BOARDING AND GENERAL FACILITIES

Students and several faculty members are housed in Saint Benedict's, Saint Edmund's, and Kennedy dorms. Most dormitory rooms are designed for double occupancy, and room assignments are made by the Dean of Students. Students may request room changes at designated times.

Other facilities include the dining hall (overlooking Gardner Lake); a health office; the Charles Hanrahan Memorial Gymnasium, which houses locker rooms; a basketball court; a weight room; student recreation areas, including a big-screen television with DVD; and a pool and Ping-Pong room. A boathouse, which houses crew boats, sailboats, canoes, and rowboats, is located on the waterfront. Our Lady's Chapel, situated on the lake shore, was dedicated in 1997. The Canisius Building, located near the entry of the campus, houses the Admissions Office.

ATHLETICS

Athletics are an integral part of the School; all students are required to participate in a sport. Interscholastic sports, offered on several levels to accommodate varying abilities and ages, are baseball, basketball, cross-country, football, golf, hockey, lacrosse, sailing, soccer, tennis, and track and field. Intramural activities include basketball, physical conditioning, sailing, softball, swimming, and weight lifting. The athletics facilities include the gymnasium, an indoor pool, an outdoor skating pond, a quarter-mile track, a football field, two soccer fields, two baseball diamonds, two all-purpose fields, and 4,000 feet of lakefront, with swimming, boating, sailing, and fishing areas.

EXTRACURRICULAR OPPORTUNITIES

The School's location allows students to pursue a wide range of cultural and recreational activities. Proximity to Hartford, New Haven, and Providence, as well as to many colleges and universities, gives students the opportunity to attend collegiate and professional sports events, concerts, shows, and plays.

On campus, students may become involved in the production of the yearbook. Other activities include the ski club, the martial arts club, the art club, the ambassador club, and driver's education. The National Honor Society participates in a variety of public service projects.

The Student Council, the formal student-government organization, composed of elected officials representing the various residence halls and classes, organizes social events and provides leadership in the dormitories. Meetings are held to plan assemblies and activities and to discuss items of importance to the student body.

DAILY LIFE

Breakfast, served from 7:20 to 8, begins the day. After dorm cleanup and room inspection, which runs from 8:05 to 8:20, the class day starts. There are seven 45-minute periods until 2 (six classes and one lunch period). Daily help is conducted from 2 to 2:30. Clubs meet from 3:30 to 4:30. Athletics begin at 3:30 and last until 5. Dinner is served from 5 to 6:15. The evening study hall is from 7:30 to 9:30. Lights-out is at 10:30.

WEEKEND LIFE

Because the academic week begins on Sunday evening at 7:30 and ends on Friday afternoon at 2:17, students are permitted to go home any weekend as long as their studies and deportment are good, but they must be back on campus by 7 on Sunday evening. Approximately one third of the students leave campus on any given weekend.

Students remaining on campus for the weekend may become involved in any number of activities. All recreational facilities are available to students and faculty members throughout the weekend. Regularly scheduled trips into town to movie theaters are available each Saturday evening. Other activities include dances with neighboring girls' schools, shows of all types in the Hartford Civic Center, collegiate and professional sports events, and concerts.

SUMMER PROGRAMS

Saint Thomas More School offers an all-boys, five-week Summer Academic Camp. Courses are offered for credit, makeup, or enrichment for students in grades 7–12. The faculty is composed of the School's regular staff. The average attendance is 60. Classes are conducted until noon, recreational activities are from 1 to 7:30, and study hall runs from 7:15 to 9:45. The all-inclusive cost for 2005 was $5495. For more information, applicants should write to the School.

COSTS AND FINANCIAL AID

The annual cost for 2005–06 was $29,250 for domestic students and $32,250 for international students. Costs include tuition, room, board, books, athletic clothing, and laundry.

Each year, approximately 20 percent of the students receive financial assistance, which is offered to qualified students based on need.

ADMISSIONS INFORMATION

Saint Thomas More School requires that applicants have a personal interview with the Director of Admissions and requires a transcript of academic work, the Otis-Lennon Test, a writing sample, two teacher's recommendations, and a guidance counselor's recommendation. The results of standardized tests are helpful, if available. The School seeks students who will be positive, contributing members of the student body and who will benefit from the special experience the School has to offer. The School admits boys throughout the school year, provided that there is space available in the grade in which entrance is sought.

APPLICATION TIMETABLE

Parents interested in Saint Thomas More School should write or call the Admissions Office to make an appointment for an interview. Interviews and tours are conducted from 8:30 to 2, Monday through Friday, by appointment. Saturday morning appointments are also available. Applications are accepted on a continuous basis, but early application is recommended to guarantee enrollment. Prospective students are notified of acceptance.

ADMISSIONS CORRESPONDENCE

Office of Admissions
Saint Thomas More School
45 Cottage Road
Oakdale, Connecticut 06370

Phone: 860-823-3861
Fax: 860-823-3863
E-mail: stmadmit@stthomasmoreschool.com

ST. TIMOTHY'S SCHOOL
Stevenson, Maryland

Type: Girls' boarding and day college-preparatory school
Grades: 9–12, postgraduate year
Enrollment: 132
Head of School: Randy S. Stevens

THE SCHOOL

St. Timothy's School was founded in Catonsville, Maryland, in 1882 by the Misses Sally and Polly Carter. In 1951, it moved to its present 145-acre site in Stevenson, just 15 minutes from the center of Baltimore, a city that serves as an extension of the campus. After merging with Hannah More Academy in 1974, St. Tim's holds the oldest Episcopal girls school charter in the United States. The School's educational philosophy is to educate and develop each student's talents, judgment, and sense of being. The college-preparatory curriculum has been designed to foster the student's higher-level analytical thinking and problem-solving skills that are often just beginning to develop during the ninth and tenth grade years. St. Timothy's School firmly believes that learning should be a joy, and the faculty works vigorously to inspire and encourage emerging enthusiasms.

A 26-member Board of Trustees is the School's governing body. There is an active Alumnae Board of Governors, and there are several alumnae branches in the United States and one in Great Britain. The value of the school property is about $7 million. The endowment is $12 million, and it is supplemented each year by the Annual Fund, which receives in excess of $700,000. The St. Timothy's–Hannah More Alumnae Association has approximately 2,700 members.

St. Timothy's School is accredited by the Middle States Association of Colleges and Schools, and it is a member of the National Association of Independent Schools, the Association of Independent Maryland Schools, the National Association of Episcopal Schools, the Federation of American and International Schools, and the National Coalition of Girls' Schools.

ACADEMIC PROGRAMS

St. Timothy's School is an all-girls boarding school in Maryland focusing exclusively on a rigorous, college-preparatory, ninth-grade through postgraduate program. The School offers a rigorous, but supported liberal arts curriculum, as well as an ESL (English as a second language) program for international students. The ESL program has an intermediate and an advanced level, and ESL students typically assimilate into the standard curriculum after one or two years. All classes are small, averaging from 10 to 12 students. The main feature of the ninth and tenth grade curriculum is the IGSCE (International General Certificate of Secondary Education), a pre-International Baccalaureate (IB) program designed by Cambridge University. St. Timothy's School is offering the International Baccalaureate to eleventh and twelfth graders in the fall of 2006, pending final approval from the International Baccalaureate Organization (IBO).

St. Tim's integrated curriculum gives students a chance to examine a subject from many different angles. Shakespeare's works, for example, may be performed onstage, studied in literature class, and given historical background in a world history class.

All students must take the PSAT/NMSQT and the SAT. Students elect to take the Subject Tests of the College Board in their junior and senior years.

The faculty-student ratio is 1:5. Most students take six courses a term, and a few take seven. There is required study hall Sunday through Thursday evenings. Exams are given at the end of each semester. Parents receive comments and grades at regular intervals throughout the year.

FACULTY AND ADVISERS

In 2005–06, there were 40 full-time and 7 part-time members of the faculty. The School's faculty members include graduates of Princeton, Harvard, Columbia, Brown, and Williams. Twenty-two faculty members hold advanced degrees. Approximately 72 percent of the faculty members live on campus with their families. Faculty members also serve as dorm parents, advisers, and coaches. Faculty members have 3 to 5 advisees and meet with them weekly during the advisory period.

COLLEGE PLACEMENT

Graduates of St. Timothy's School are accepted by highly selective colleges and universities both here and abroad. Because the School is small, the list of colleges St. Timothy's girls attend varies enormously from year to year. The School's College Counseling Office hosts selective colleges and universities to visit the campus during the course of the academic year. Each year, St. Timothy's School holds a special presentation for parents about the college admissions process. The office provides advice and assistance with all phases of the admission and selection process, and 100 percent of the girls attend college.

All students take the SAT. The SAT middle 50 percent range for the class of 2004 was verbal, 530–650, and math, 520–600.

In the class of 2004, 75 percent attended colleges ranked "very, highly, or most selective" by Barron's. The colleges attended by the class of 2004 and 2005 include Boston University, NYU's Tisch School of the Arts, Princeton University, Wake Forest, Wesleyan, and the Universities of Pennsylvania and Virginia.

STUDENT BODY AND CONDUCT

St. Timothy's School recognizes that no education is complete without regard to the development of each student's values. Honor, trust, truth, and kindness form the basis upon which this community has been built. The Honor Code

at St. Tim's is important to the students: they have been responsible for developing it and administering it, and it is held in high regard by students and faculty members alike. At St. Tim's, compassion and disciplined understanding is not only the goal but also the process of education itself.

The Student Government, with representation from all areas of the School, works as an advisory board to the Head of School. It makes recommendations to the administration and takes responsibility for the everyday life of the School. Members serve on the Honor Council and the Disciplinary Committee, along with the faculty.

ACADEMIC FACILITIES

The campus has twenty-three buildings, including a Performing Arts Center with a 350-seat theater, scene and costume shops, a dance studio, and practice rooms with pianos. The Ella R. Watkins Library has more than 22,000 volumes and computerized catalog search capabilities that link the School with the public library system. Other facilities include a Visual Arts Center for both two- and three-dimensional studies, including photography and digital imaging, and three science labs for biology, chemistry, and physics. The entire campus is networked, and St. Tim's integrates computer use in its curriculum. There are computer labs in both dorms as well as the academic building. The student-computer ratio is 2:1, and all campus computers were upgraded or replaced in 2002.

BOARDING AND GENERAL FACILITIES

Approximately 60 percent of this year's students are boarders. Students room together by class. In 2002, both dorms were fully renovated with new furniture, paint, and carpets. There are 2- and 3-girl rooms. Faculty members live in each dormitory, and each dormitory has both formal and informal living rooms. The newly renovated recreation room in Heath House is equipped with a big-screen television and a full kitchen. There is a fully equipped health center and a registered nurse on call at all times.

ATHLETICS

A state-of-the-art athletic complex opened in the spring of 2003. It includes a basketball gymnasium, fitness center, training room, home and away team locker rooms, faculty locker rooms, and a classroom.

All girls participate in the athletic program each season. The year is divided into three seasons for sports, and girls are required to join a team sport for two seasons each year. In the fall term field hockey, soccer, tennis, and volleyball are offered. In the winter, girls may choose basketball, ice hockey, indoor soccer, or squash;

in the spring, crew, lacrosse, and softball are available. Dance, fitness, and horseback riding are offered year-round.

The athletic facilities include playing fields for soccer, lacrosse, and field hockey; six all-weather tennis courts; an outdoor recreational swimming pool; and nature and cross-country jogging trails. The Hamilton-Ireland Riding Center has twenty-four stalls, two tack rooms, double-fenced turnout paddocks, and both indoor and outdoor arenas. St. Tim's owns between 15 and 20 horses at any one time.

EXTRACURRICULAR OPPORTUNITIES

St. Timothy's School is located in the Maryland countryside, just 15 minutes from downtown Baltimore and 1 hour from Washington, D.C. Students enjoy the city's cultural activities, museums, theaters, historic sites, and research facilities.

The on-campus activities allow students to pursue areas of special interest. Some of the popular choices are Drama Club, choir, the a cappella singing groups Six In The Morning and Salut!, Madrigals, *Moongate* (a literary magazine), yearbook, Environmental Action Club, Social Activities Committee, and Black Awareness Club, to name a few. The Social Services Club provides volunteer opportunities in the community. There are two major theatrical performances on campus each year as well as dance and musical performances.

DAILY LIFE

A typical day for a boarding student at St. Tim's begins at 7:15 a.m. with breakfast. Classes begin at 8 and end at 3:20, with family-style seated lunch four days each week. The afternoon includes study hall, sports, and extracurricular activities. The student self-government, the prefects, clubs, and classes all have scheduled times and days to meet. Buffet dinner begins at 5:30 p.m. One night each week, there is a formal dinner. All students have required study hall in

the evenings from 7:30 to 9:30 p.m., and the academic building and study halls remain open until 10 p.m. Girls must be in their dormitory rooms by 10:30 p.m. on weekdays.

WEEKEND LIFE

St. Tim's is committed to retaining the special qualities that distinguish a boarding school from a day school, and the extracurricular program offers a full component of weekend activities. The program is planned by the Dean of Students along with a student committee. A schedule listing all the opportunities for the weekend is posted each week. Many off-campus activities in the Baltimore and Washington area are planned. Trips to the theater, concerts, museums, and movies; hiking; dances and parties; shopping trips; and horse shows and other sports events are a few of the more popular offerings. The School is also a member of the Boarding Schools Social Activities Committee (BSSAC), which plans social events for boys' and girls' boarding schools in Maryland and Virginia. Recent BSSAC events have included a boat cruise on the Potomac River and mixers at various schools. The day girls are invited to take part in all aspects of the extracurricular program, and many choose to spend an occasional night or weekend on campus. Boarders may take weekends to go home or visit friends.

COSTS AND FINANCIAL AID

Tuition for boarding students in 2005–06 was $34,500. Day student tuition was $19,600. Several payment plans are available to fit each family's needs.

Financial aid is granted on the basis of a candidate's financial need. In 2005–06, about one third of the students received financial aid through grants and/or loans. In addition, several merit awards are available.

ADMISSIONS INFORMATION

Girls are admitted without regard to religion, race, color, or national origin. In making admissions decisions, the School considers the applicant's school transcript, recommendations from the adviser and teachers, standardized test scores (SSAT or ISEE), interview, extracurricular involvement, and application essay. Most students enter in the ninth or tenth grade.

APPLICATION TIMETABLE

An initial inquiry is welcome at any time. Campus visits include a tour and an interview and may include a classroom visit. Visitors are welcome between 8:30 a.m. and 2 p.m. when school is in session.

Applications for all students should be complete by February 10. Day student notifications are mailed March 1; boarding student notifications are mailed March 10. However, there is early notification for boarding students for whom St. Tim's is their only choice. These applications must be completed no later than January 10, with notification on February 1. St. Tim's accepts applications on a rolling basis after the March notifications, dependent upon space available.

Applicants should complete and submit the application form with a $40 application fee. Recommendations are required from the student's principal or adviser and her math and English teachers. Parents are asked to complete a parent statement. Because St. Tim's is an SSATB member, boarding students who are accepted have until April 10 to notify the School of their decision. Day students must notify the School by April 1.

ADMISSIONS CORRESPONDENCE

Patrick Finn
Director of Admissions
St. Timothy's School
8400 Greenspring Avenue
Stevenson, Maryland 21153

Phone: 410-486-7401
Fax: 410-486-1167
E-mail: admis@sttims-school.org
Web site: http://www.sttims-school.org

SALEM ACADEMY

Winston-Salem, North Carolina

Type: Girls' boarding and day college-preparatory school
Grades: 9–12
Enrollment: 183
Head of School: Dr. Wayne Burkette

THE SCHOOL

Founded in 1772 by Moravian settlers, Salem Academy has been in continuous operation for more than 230 years. Initially a day school, it added boarding facilities in 1802. During the 1860s, college-level courses were added, and Salem College was chartered in 1866. In 1930, the Academy and college were separated; both institutions remained on the original campus.

Throughout its history, Salem Academy has maintained its original commitment to the education of women. It endeavors to provide "a thorough preparation for a continuing education and a fulfilling personal life, a spiritual and ethical climate in all phases of school life, and a program promoting mental and physical well-being." While the Academy retains its affiliation with the Moravian Church, students of various religious backgrounds are enrolled.

The 64-acre campus, which is shared with Salem College, adjoins the restored eighteenth-century Moravian village of Old Salem. The Academy's grounds encompass lawns and wooded areas as well as hockey fields, a softball field, an archery range, and twelve tennis courts.

Winston-Salem (population 200,000) is located in the Piedmont region of the state, approximately 90 miles from both Charlotte and Raleigh. It is served by two airports and Interstate Highways 40, 77, and 85. A nationally recognized cultural and arts center, the city has a symphony, the Little Theater, art galleries, and four colleges—North Carolina School of the Arts, Wake Forest University, Winston-Salem State University, and Salem College—that provide cultural and educational opportunities for Academy students.

A nonprofit institution, Salem Academy is governed by a 30-member Board of Trustees, which serves as a common board for the school and Salem College. Board members are chosen by the Moravian Church, the Alumnae Association, and other organizations. Many graduates lend it financial support and refer prospective students. The endowment is approximately $6.7 million. Operating expenses were $4.6 million for 2003–04. Annual Giving contributed $480,000 for the same year. The Academy plant is valued at $15 million.

Salem Academy is accredited by the Southern Association of Colleges and Schools. It holds membership in the National Association of Independent Schools, the North Carolina Association of Independent Schools, the National Coalition of Girls Schools, the National Association of College Admission Counselors, the College Board, and the Secondary School Admission Test Board.

ACADEMIC PROGRAMS

The school year is divided into two academic terms and a 2½-week miniterm in January. There are two long weekends as well as vacations at Thanksgiving and Christmas and in the spring.

To graduate, a student must earn 20 academic credits, including English, 4 credits; mathematics, 4; science, 3; history, 3; classical language, 2; and a modern foreign language, 2. Mandatory noncredit courses are health in grade 9, religion in grade 11 or 12, and physical education in grades 9, 10, and 11. One fine arts course is required from art, drama, or music.

The curriculum includes English composition and literature I–IV; French I–III, Spanish I–III, Latin I–IV; modern European history, U.S. history, economics, political science, world history, introduction to cultural anthropology, international studies; algebra I–II, geometry, discrete mathematics, precalculus, calculus, advanced functions and modeling; biology, environmental science, chemistry, advanced chemistry, conceptual physics, advanced physics, advanced biology; biblical literature, world religions; studio art; drama; and choral and vocal instruction. Private lessons are available in piano, organ, harp, woodwind, classical guitar, harpsichord, and brass and percussion instruments. Juniors and seniors have the opportunity to take courses for credit at Salem College. Advanced Placement courses are offered in many disciplines.

The miniterm gives each student an opportunity to choose her own educational experience. Programs both on and off campus provide a variety of ways for students to pursue interests. A school-sponsored trip is offered each year to such places as England, Australia, Germany, and France. Internships and independent studies in teaching, music, medicine, banking, and other fields may be pursued under faculty supervision. In on-campus classes, teachers conduct intensive reviews and tutorials, introduce special topics not covered within the course outline, and assign and supervise independent projects.

There are 13 students in an average class. The student-faculty ratio is 9:1. Conference periods provide opportunity for individual help, and Salem College students are available to tutor. The January miniterm also offers a concentrated tutorial program. Grades are discussed with the student and sent to parents every six weeks.

FACULTY AND ADVISERS

The full-time faculty numbers 25 members. They hold twenty-five baccalaureate and eighteen master's degrees and four Ph.D.'s. Eight part-time instructors coach various athletics teams and teach. Eight House Counselors supervise the dormitories.

Dr. Wayne Burkette holds a bachelor's degree from the University of North Carolina at Chapel Hill, the M.Div. from Moravian Theological Seminary, and the Ph.D. from Union Theological Seminary. Prior to his appointment as Head of Salem Academy in 1994, he served as chaplain and Chief Planning Officer at Salem College. In 1997, he was also appointed Vice President of Salem Academy and College.

Faculty members are chosen for their solid academic training, their willingness to care for and advise students, and their talents in outside areas that can benefit the community. Each faculty member advises approximately 8 students, serves as an adviser to classes or organizations, serves on school committees, and chaperones school-sponsored activities. Faculty turnover is low.

COLLEGE PLACEMENT

The full-time College Counselor begins advising students in their freshman and sophomore years. In the second semester of the junior year, the counselor meets with each student on a one-to-one basis to discuss her college interests and to review the general admissions process. In their senior year, the students again meet individually with the College Counselor for advice on writing college applications and essays and on interviewing techniques. The counselor helps the students meet all testing deadlines and arranges their transportation. In addition, more than 50 college representatives visit Salem each year to interview interested students.

The school provides access to SAT review classes. The SAT I mean score for the class of 2005 was 1253. In the 2004–05 school year, 69 students took a total of 111 Advanced Placement exams; 90 percent received scores making them eligible for college credit.

Members of the classes of 2000 through 2005 are attending such colleges as Davidson, Duke, MIT, Northwestern, NYU, Stanford, Wake Forest, Williams, Yale, and the Universities of North Carolina and Virginia.

STUDENT BODY AND CONDUCT

In 2005–06, Salem Academy had 89 boarding girls and 94 day girls, 14 to 18 years of age, as follows: 37 in grade 9, 52 in grade 10, 49 in grade 11, and 45 in grade 12. Students came from thirteen states and six other countries. Salem welcomes students from diverse economic, racial, and geographic backgrounds.

The development of self-discipline and consideration for others is the primary concern that underlies the goals for student behavior at Salem Academy. In keeping with this philosophy, Salem operates under an honor system. The student government, which is composed of two elected bodies—the Honor Cabinet and the Student Council—is based on Salem's honor tradition. The Honor Cabinet advises and guides students by providing constructive counsel and leadership, and it may recommend disciplinary actions. The Honor Cabinet comprises elected student representatives and 2 faculty advisers.

ACADEMIC FACILITIES

Six connected buildings constitute the self-contained portion of the Academy's facilities. The main building (1930) houses administrative offices, and Weaver Building (1956) contains the library, the art studio, and the admissions office. Critz Hall (1971) houses classrooms, language and science laboratories, and faculty offices. Hodges Hall (1971) contains a music studio and library, an auditorium, and a small meditation chapel. In addition, the school shares with Salem College the Dale H. Gramley Library, the Salem Fine Arts Center, a student Commons Building, and a gymnasium and indoor swimming pool.

BOARDING AND GENERAL FACILITIES

Boarding girls live in Hodges, McMichael, Shaffner, and Bahnson residence halls. Most rooms are doubles. Seniors and some juniors live in the new wing, in which groups of 4 girls share a suite with a connecting bath.

In addition to an elected student hall representative, an adult dormitory counselor resides on each hall. New students are assigned roommates and rooms by the Dean of Students; returning students choose roommates and participate in a room lottery in the spring. Laundry and storage areas are provided, and the main building also contains reception rooms and a snack area. Weaver Building contains the dining room and school kitchen.

The Academy shares the services of physicians and a full-time infirmary staff with Salem College. The Baptist Hospital, Forsyth Memorial Hospital, and Bowman-Gray School of Medicine are nearby.

ATHLETICS

Salem believes that an active and healthy body is important to a girl's overall academic and social performance. In addition, the wholesome competition inherent in team sports is important for each girl's development.

Varsity teams in cross-country, golf, softball, swimming, and track and varsity and junior varsity teams in basketball, field hockey, soccer, tennis, and volleyball compete with other schools in the Piedmont Athletic Conference of Independent Schools. Salem also has an equestrian program. The Student Life and Fitness Center, which is shared with Salem College, houses the gymnasium and pool.

EXTRACURRICULAR OPPORTUNITIES

Students are given many opportunities to develop interests outside the classroom. They publish a newspaper, a yearbook, and a literary-art magazine. The Drama Club stages two major productions a year, and the Glee Club performs on and off campus. In 1999, the Glee Club performed in England; in January 2002, they performed in London as part of the Gala Charity Concert for the Queen's Charities. Visual arts students exhibit and compete on campus and in the community and state. Other student organizations include the Fellowship Council, which sponsors parties, campus activities, and community service projects. Traditional annual events include Opening Assembly, Ring Banquet, Senior Bazaar, Parents' Weekend, Father-Daughter Picnic, Alumnae Day, Senior Vespers, Honors Banquets, and Recognition and Graduation Exercises.

DAILY LIFE

Classes meet five days a week. A typical school day includes nondenominational devotions, six academic class periods, a recess, and an assembly period. Language and science laboratories, study halls, music, studio art, physical education, and student activities are scheduled during four afternoon class periods. Boarding students have supervised study in the evening.

WEEKEND LIFE

On the weekends, the Student Activities directors plan local trips to the theater, opera, concerts, and Wake Forest sporting events. Also scheduled are outdoor activities, such as white-water rafting, canoeing, hiking, camping, and snow skiing in the nearby mountains. Dances and other social events are planned with various boys' schools.

With written parental approval, boarding students in grade 12 may have unlimited overnight permissions on weekends; students in grades 9–11 are limited to between twelve and eighteen overnights per year. Three times a month, boarding students are expected to attend church or synagogue.

COSTS AND FINANCIAL AID

In 2005–06, room and board were $26,941; day student tuition was $14,750, including lunches. Additional expenses were books ($450), an activities fee ($125), and music lessons.

The Academy awards scholarships on the basis of financial need. Sixty-eight students received aid totaling approximately $1.1 million for the 2005–06 school year. Parents who wish their daughters to be considered for financial aid should request a School and Student Service for Financial Aid form from the Admissions Office. All applicants are automatically considered for merit-based scholarships.

ADMISSIONS INFORMATION

Salem Academy enrolls motivated students who have integrity, a positive attitude, and the desire and motivation to give their best in all phases of school life. New students are admitted in grades 9–11 and occasionally in grade 12. Candidates must submit a transcript, academic and personal recommendations, and the results of the Secondary School Admission Test (SSAT). An interview is also required.

APPLICATION TIMETABLE

Students interested in Salem Academy should contact the Admissions Office to obtain a catalog and to arrange for an interview and tour. Special visiting days are scheduled throughout the year, but students and parents may call for an interview during the work week. Students are encouraged to spend a night in the dormitory when they visit.

An application may be filed at any time during the year for the following fall. However, priority consideration is given to early applicants. As soon as the admissions folder is complete, it is sent to the admissions committee. The applicant is notified of the committee's decision promptly. Parents must notify Salem of their decision within two weeks. Later applications are acted upon as soon as they are completed, and qualified applicants are awarded enrollment on a space-available basis.

ADMISSIONS CORRESPONDENCE

Lucia Uldrick
Director of Admissions and
Financial Aid
Salem Academy
Winston-Salem, North Carolina 27101
Phone: 336-721-2644
        877-407-2536 (toll-free)
Fax: 336-917-5340
E-mail: academy@salem.edu
Web site: http://www.salemacademy.com

SALISBURY SCHOOL
Salisbury, Connecticut

Type: Boys' boarding and day college-preparatory school
Grades: 9–PG (Forms III–VI, postgraduate year)
Enrollment: 287
Head of School: Chisholm S. Chandler, Headmaster

THE SCHOOL

The Rev. Dr. George E. Quaile founded Salisbury School in 1901 after serving as Headmaster of St. Austin's School on Staten Island in New York from 1894 to 1901. After his death in 1934, Rev. Dr. Quaile was succeeded by his son, Emerson B. Quaile, whose untimely death in 1942 led to the hiring of the Rev. George D. Langdon. With the blessing of the Board of Trustees, Rev. Langdon initiated the School's first modern expansion program. After Rev. Langdon's retirement in 1965, growth continued under his successor, the Rev. Edwin M. Ward. Upon Rev. Ward's departure in 1981, the Rev. Peter W. Sipple was appointed Salisbury's fifth Headmaster. Mr. Richard T. Flood Jr. was appointed Salisbury's sixth Headmaster in 1998. Under his leadership, the School implemented a $25-million Facilities Master Plan, in conjunction with its centennial in 2001. In 2002, Chisholm S. Chandler was selected as the School's seventh Headmaster.

The Wachtmeister Mathematics and Science Building and the Harris Science Center opened in 1999, and the 65,000-square-foot Centennial Library and Humanities Classroom Building opened in 2001. In addition, the new Performing Arts Complex and the Ruger Family Visual Arts Center complete a total renovation of the School's arts facilities. The Chapel Building contains the Field Music Center, which offers space for the School's music program. It includes practice rooms for piano, band, and choral rehearsals. The completion of a new dormitory in 2004 rounds out the most recent improvements to Salisbury's physical plant.

Salisbury is an accredited college-preparatory school for approximately 285 boys from ninth through twelfth grades. Some boys are accepted for a postgraduate year. (By tradition, Salisbury refers to ninth grade as Third Form, tenth grade as Fourth Form, eleventh grade as Fifth Form, and twelfth grade as Sixth Form). The majority of students are boarders, while about 8 percent are day students from the surrounding area.

The School is set on a hilltop surrounded by 725 acres of extensive woodlands, fields, streams, and lakefront in the foothills of the Berkshire Mountains. The campus is bordered by the Appalachian Trail to the west and the Twin Lakes to the north. An active outing club and a forestry program are enhanced by the School's geographic location. Salisbury is only 1 hour from Hartford, 2 hours from New York City, and 3 hours from Boston.

The mission of Salisbury School is to instill within each student the self-confidence needed to develop intellectually, morally, and physically in an environment of personal guidance and small-group instruction. The School seeks to encourage each young man to find satisfaction and take pride in his accomplishments inside and outside the classroom and to build a sense of self-worth as he formulates goals for the future. The Salisbury School community is distinguished by a quality of life that promotes religious faith, trust, service, respect, and friendship in relationships among faculty members and students within a framework of traditional values.

Salisbury School is accredited by the New England Association of Schools and Colleges. It is a member of the National Association of Independent Schools, the Connecticut Association of Independent Schools, the Secondary School Admission Test Board, the College Board, and the Cum Laude Society.

ACADEMIC PROGRAMS

For the diploma, the following requirements must be met: English every trimester; history (ancient history in the Third Form, world history in the Fourth Form, U.S. history in the Fifth or Sixth Form); mathematics for 3 years (algebra I, geometry, and algebra II); a single foreign language for 3 years or 2 years each of two foreign languages; a laboratory science for 2 years (Fourth Formers must take at least one of their two required science courses at Salisbury); philosophy and religion for 1 full year; and art for 2 trimesters. Extensive participation in drama and gospel choir may also fulfill the art requirement, even though they are not academic courses. The student must pass all courses in the Sixth Form year.

Letter grades are issued to each student and his adviser every five weeks. Every trimester, grades are sent to parents with written comments from each of the student's teachers and his adviser. Exams are given in late November and late May.

The average class size is 12, and the student-teacher ratio is 6:1. Classes are held six days a week; each class meets for 45 minutes four times a week and for 75 minutes once a week.

There is a strong support system for students at Salisbury. Teachers are available to give extra help, and private tutoring is available to students in the Learning Center. There is a fee for this service.

Salisbury School is committed to technological development and to furthering its implementation in all academic disciplines. To that end, a campuswide computer network was completed in 1996. Significant attention has also been directed recently to expanding the arts at Salisbury and to enhancement of environmental studies (e.g., forestry, geology, freshwater ecology) and outdoor education programs.

FACULTY AND ADVISERS

The Salisbury School faculty and administration consist of 60 members. Thirty-one members hold a master's or higher degree.

Chisholm S. Chandler, the School's current Headmaster, attended Hotchkiss School, Brown University (B.A.), and Harvard University (M.Ed.). During his nearly fifteen years at Salisbury, Mr. Chandler served in a variety of capacities, including Director of Admissions, Director of College Advising, and Assistant Headmaster for External Affairs. He also served as a dorm parent, a coach, and an adviser.

The School community is close-knit and supportive. The majority of faculty members live on campus, coach, and supervise extracurricular activities.

Advising is at the core of Salisbury's dedication to its students and guarantees that each student will receive the personal attention he requires. Throughout the year, the adviser is the link between the student, his teachers, and his family.

School-funded projects include taking courses toward advanced degrees, traveling, and attending workshops and conferences relevant to one's teaching. A sabbatical program was instituted in 1984 and has thus far benefited 33 faculty members.

COLLEGE PLACEMENT

Beginning in his Fifth Form (junior) year, each student meets regularly with a college adviser. Careful attention is given to selecting colleges that best suit the student's interests and abilities. Parents may also meet with the college advising staff whenever possible. College representatives visit the campus throughout the year, and students may have interviews at the School.

The 75 members of the class of 2005 are attending a diverse group of colleges and universities, including Bowdoin, Brown, Colgate, Cornell, Georgetown, Middlebury, Princeton, Trinity, and Williams.

STUDENT BODY AND CONDUCT

The 2005–06 student body is composed of 287 boys in grades 9–12 as follows: Form III, 44; Form IV, 84; Form V, 79; and Form VI, 80. Of this number, 25 are day students. The students come from twenty-eight states and eleven other countries. The School seeks a diversity of backgrounds and interests.

The School believes that students play a vital role in leadership; thus the Student Council works closely with the Headmaster and the faculty members. Student committees deal with honor and citizenship matters and advise the Headmaster. The breaking of major School rules is punished by suspension or dismissal.

ACADEMIC FACILITIES

The Main Building contains the Admissions Office, administrative offices, and conference rooms. Academic facilities are centered in the Wachtmeister Mathematics and Science Building and the Centennial Library and Humanities Classroom Building, which contains 23,000 volumes and more than 120 periodicals. New arts facilities include the Performing Arts Complex and the Ruger Family Visual Arts Center. Other facilities include an observatory and the solar car garage. The Chapel

Building contains the Field Music Center, which offers newly renovated space for music rehearsals and piano, band, and choral practice.

BOARDING AND GENERAL FACILITIES
There are ten dormitories with faculty apartments. Single, double, and a few triple rooms are available. Returning students select their own rooms through a lottery, while new students are assigned rooms. Students live according to classes, with seniors in each dormitory serving as prefects. The remodeled Belin Lodge, a recreation center, contains a TV room and snack bar. Salisbury School provides phone service, voice mail, access to the campus computer network, and Internet services to every student's room.

A modern Health Center contains private and semiprivate rooms, a doctor's office, and faculty apartments. A full-time M.D. and a full-time athletic trainer are in residence on the campus.

ATHLETICS
Every student at Salisbury is expected to participate in the afternoon athletics program each season. The School offers a wide range of choices to students of every age and every level of athletic ability. Some students choose to take on team managerial roles.

In almost all of the following interscholastic sports, there are two or three teams: varsity, junior varsity, and third. In the fall, cross-country, football, and soccer are offered; in the winter, Alpine skiing, basketball, hockey, platform tennis, squash, and wrestling are offered; and, in the spring, baseball, crew, cycling, golf, kayaking, lacrosse, and tennis are offered. There are approximately thirty-five interscholastic teams in a given year.

The Athletic Center contains locker rooms, a training room, a basketball court, a wrestling room, various team rooms, locker rooms and showers, rooms for the ski and crew teams, new international squash courts, and a newly expanded fitness center. Two boathouses on the lakefront provide storage for racing shells and other crew equipment. Other facilities for sports include fields for football, soccer, baseball, and lacrosse; eight tennis courts, three of which are covered by a dome; two heated platform tennis courts; a lake; the Kulukundis Boathouse; and miles of cross-country trails. The Olympic-size Rudd Hockey Rink has an all-purpose playing surface for year-round use. The Class of 2003 Dome houses three indoor tennis courts and provides another indoor recreational space.

EXTRACURRICULAR OPPORTUNITIES
Salisbury's proximity to Boston, New York, and Hartford enables the School to sponsor trips off campus. In addition, the School brings speakers and entertainers to the campus. Other extracurricular activities available during free time include a variety of community service programs, Glee Club, music lessons, drama, *The Cupola* (newspaper), *The Pillar* (yearbook), *The Quill* (literary magazine), Amnesty International, Debating Club, International Club, Key Society, Outing Club, Political Club, and driver education.

DAILY LIFE
Classes are held six days a week; Wednesday and Saturday are half-days, with athletic contests taking place in the afternoons. Breakfast is served from 6:45 to 8:15. Classes run from 8 until 2:20. The class day also includes a midmorning recess and an activities period. Athletic practice takes place from 3 until 5, and dinner is from 5:30 to 6:30.

Study hall takes place from 7:30 to 9:30, and all students must be in their dormitories by 10:15. Sunday is free until dinner at 5:30. Day students eat meals at school and are invited to participate in dorm activities.

WEEKEND LIFE
After classes and sports events on Saturday, students may go into town, visit day students' homes, or remain on campus. Dances with nearby schools (Miss Porter's, Ethel Walker, Emma Willard, Master's, Westover, and Miss Hall's) are held frequently either on campus or at other schools. Transportation is provided to concerts off campus, ski areas, shopping malls, and local movie theaters. Faculty "teams" provide supervision for these trips.

Students may take weekends off campus on a limited basis. Weekends begin Saturday p.m. and end Sunday p.m.

SUMMER PROGRAMS
The Salisbury Summer School of Academic Enrichment was founded in 1946 on the belief that a student's ability to understand and use the written word determines, to a substantial degree, his academic achievement. It is the purpose of the summer school to offer intensive training in reading, writing, and study skills. This training is determined by individual needs and is conducted in a supportive and friendly environment.

Enrollment in the summer school is limited to 105 boys and girls. These students come from private and public schools across the country. Reading instruction is conducted by teachers of varied experience with sound training in this specialized field. Classes in the summer program are small; the program has a student-teacher ratio of 4:1. The school includes an extensive recreational program.

The courses offered include reading and study skills, word skills, composition, creative writing, and mathematics.

The school is under the direction of Ralph J. Menconi.

COSTS AND FINANCIAL AID
Tuition for the 2005–06 academic year was $35,750 for boarding students and $26,000 for day students. These amounts do not include incidental expenses, books, and other fees that can total an additional $700–$1000. Tutoring in the Learning Center, driver's education, and music lessons are available at extra cost. A 10 percent deposit is due at the time of enrollment, with further payments due in August and December. An initial deposit of $750 is held in escrow until the student leaves Salisbury.

During the 2005–06 academic year, 31 percent of the students received financial aid, with grants that totaled more than $1.9 million. The School uses the School and Student Service for Financial Aid in Princeton, New Jersey.

ADMISSIONS INFORMATION
The Admissions Committee seeks to accept students who have demonstrated the ability to do college-preparatory work and who can be active participants in all phases of community life.

Applicants for grades 9 through 11 should take the SSAT. The majority of students enter in grades 9 and 10, while a few twelfth graders and postgraduates are accepted. A personal interview is required.

APPLICATION TIMETABLE
An initial inquiry is welcome at any time. Campus tours are arranged when the interview appointment is made. The ideal time to visit is Monday through Friday from 9 a.m. to 2 p.m. and Saturday from 9–11 a.m., when classes are in session. The Admissions Office is open until 4:30 p.m. Applications should be received before February 1, although late applications may be considered after that time. The application should be accompanied by a nonrefundable fee of $40 ($100 for international students). Notification of acceptance is made by March 10, and parents are expected to reply by April 10.

ADMISSIONS CORRESPONDENCE
Peter B. Gilbert
Director of Admissions and Financial Aid
Salisbury School
Salisbury, Connecticut 06068

Phone: 860-435-5700
Fax: 860-435-5750
E-mail: admissions@salisburyschool.org
Web site: http://www.salisburyschool.org

SANDY SPRING FRIENDS SCHOOL

Sandy Spring, Maryland

Type: Coeducational day and five- and seven-day boarding college-preparatory school
Grades: PK–12: Lower School, PK–5; Middle School 6–8; Upper School 9–12
Enrollment: School total: 547; Lower School: 190; Middle School: 125; Upper School: 232
Head of School: Kenneth W. Smith

THE SCHOOL

Sandy Spring Friends School (SSFS) was founded by Brook Moore in 1961 under the care of the Sandy Spring Monthly Meeting of Friends. The School provides a college-preparatory liberal arts curriculum for students of varying ethnic, economic, and religious backgrounds. It is situated on a 140-acre campus that contains woodlands, a pond and stream, walking and biking paths, and playing fields. Sandy Spring is in Montgomery County and is located approximately 35 minutes from both Washington, D.C., and Baltimore.

As a Quaker school, Sandy Spring Friends School shares the Quaker concern for the unique worth of the individual. Qualities of sensitivity, inventiveness, persistence, and humor are valued, along with intellectual traits. The School's goal is to help each student develop a sense of personal integrity while growing academically and learning to be a responsible member of the community. The School offers a diverse liberal arts curriculum, with courses ranging from basic college-preparatory to Advanced Placement courses. Performing and fine arts courses and athletics are an important part of the curriculum.

The 26-member Board of Trustees includes appointments by the Baltimore Yearly Meeting, the Sandy Spring Monthly Meeting, and the Sandy Spring Friends School. The 2005–06 budget exceeded $10 million, with a growing endowment program that began in 1989.

The School is accredited by the Association of Independent Maryland Schools and approved by the State of Maryland Department of Education. It is a member of the National Association of Independent Schools, the Association of Independent Maryland Schools, the Association of Independent Schools of Greater Washington, the Association of Boarding Schools, the Friends Council on Education, the Secondary School Admission Test Board, the Education Records Bureau, A Better Chance, the National Association for College Admission Counseling, the Black Student Fund, the Potomac and Chesapeake Association of College Admissions Counselors, and the College Board.

ACADEMIC PROGRAMS

The curriculum at Sandy Spring Friends School is intended to prepare students not only for entering college but also for being valuable citizens of the world. It stresses the challenge of Quaker values, academic excellence, and personal growth in an environment that stresses personal responsibility. The school year, from early September to early June, includes Thanksgiving, winter, and spring vacations. A typical daily schedule includes six academic periods, jobs, lunch, an electives period, and sports. The school day is from 8 to 3:20, with sports and activities after school. Boarding students are required to attend dinner at 6 and study hall from 7:30 to 9:30 p.m. The average class size is 14, with a faculty-student ratio of 1:7.

Meeting for Worship is required once a week for Lower School children and twice a week for Middle and Upper School students.

The required academic load for an Upper School student is six courses. To graduate, students must earn 24 credits, including English, 4; foreign language, 3; history, 3 (including United States history); mathematics, 3; science, 3; fine arts, 3; and electives, 3. Additional requirements are participating in a physical activity two times per year, passing a semester course on Quakerism, and community service. Advanced Placement courses are available in English, Spanish, French, history, math, art, and science. The ESL program is open to students in grades 9–12; currently, 28 students are enrolled.

Intersession week in the spring gives Upper School students an opportunity to participate in off-campus activities that supplement the standard curriculum. Projects have included trips to countries such as Belize, Brazil, France, Greece, Italy, Korea, Senegal, and Turkey after intensive study; community service projects in Georgia, Maryland, New York, North Carolina, Tennessee, Virginia, and Washington, D.C.; intensive arts workshops in modern dance, improvisational theater, spinning and weaving, and other arts; and numerous opportunities for outdoor exploration by foot, bike, and boat.

The School operates on a semester schedule, and the grading systems vary by division according to the developmental needs of the students in the age group. The Lower School works within the framework of parent and teacher conferences with extensive comments; the Middle and Upper Schools use letter grades, with additional comments and parent-teacher conferences as appropriate.

FACULTY AND ADVISERS

There are 62 full-time and 6 part-time teachers and administrators who teach. Twelve live on campus, 5 with their families. Thirty-three faculty members hold advanced degrees.

Kenneth W. Smith, appointed Head of School in 1996, is a graduate of Trinity University (B.S.), Princeton Theological Seminary (M.Div., Th.M.), and Southern Methodist University (D.Min.). Prior to assuming his current position, Ken Smith worked at Friends School of Baltimore as Middle School Head and at the Pine Crest School of Ft. Lauderdale as Assistant to the Headmaster and Vice President.

Sandy Spring faculty members share a variety of nonacademic duties, including supervising student activities, proctoring the dorms, and advising students. The School encourages and supports faculty members in the pursuit of educational interests by providing funding and by supporting a professional development committee of the School.

Middle and Upper School students have a strong adviser-advisee relationship that is based on developing a mutual trust and respect. It provides parents with a personal contact when they have questions or concerns about their child's progress.

COLLEGE PLACEMENT

Active college planning begins in the junior year with individual meetings with the College Guidance Director to discuss plans and to identify colleges of interest. Parents and students attend special College Night Programs that include information regarding common admission and application for financial aid procedures. A catalogue library and a computer search program are available to students. Also, many college representatives make personal visits to students each year. The School's goal is to match the student with the right school.

All members of the class of 2005 entered college. They are attending institutions such as Bates, Bryn Mawr, Cornell, Earlham, Emory, George Washington, Guilford, Haverford, Johns Hopkins, Penn State, St. Mary's (Maryland), Spelman, Wheaton, Whittier, William and Mary, and the Universities of Maryland and Southern California.

STUDENT BODY AND CONDUCT

In 2005–06, the Upper School enrolled 232 students, 105 boys and 127 girls, as follows: 55 in grade 9, 60 in grade 10, 57 in grade 11, and 60 in grade 12. The boarding program enrolled 39 students from the mid-Atlantic region and six countries. Fifteen percent are members of the Religious Society of Friends, and 34 percent are students of color. International students represent 12 percent of the Upper School student body.

The Torch Committee, the student government organization, includes day and boarding students as well as faculty and administration representatives. The Committee, operating by consensus, considers student concerns and makes recommendations to faculty committees and to the administration. A student member of Torch is invited to attend faculty and business meetings and meetings of the Board of Trustees.

ACADEMIC FACILITIES

The School's physical plant, valued at more than $20 million, includes a state-of-the-art science center that opened in 1995, an expanded Lower School, a new Middle School building, a dormitory and dining hall, three major classroom buildings and an administration building, a new performing arts center with a fine arts wing, a new athletic complex, and Yarnall Hall, a $1.75-million resource center that houses a 20,000-volume library, a gymnasium, and an observatory. Computers are integrated into many aspects of the curriculum. Every division of the School is equipped with its own computer lab, and every classroom includes at least one computer and is wired for network and

Internet access. The School's library includes computers for online research through the public library system, subscription to online reference tools, and the Internet. A fiber-optic backbone connects the network, and a T1 line connects the Internet and e-mail accounts to students and faculty members.

BOARDING AND GENERAL FACILITIES

All of the boarding students live with their roommates in one 2-story dormitory. Boys and girls each have a separate floor. Community life for boarders includes regular dorm meetings (with decisions reached by consensus), committee-style sponsored activities, family-style dinners with resident staff members, and visits to the homes of day student friends. The dorm staff members (6 adults for 39 boarders in 2005–06) all reside in either apartments or town houses located in or near the Westview dormitory.

The School nurse assists with the appropriate care for students who may become ill. The School's infirmary is open during the school day.

ATHLETICS

Interscholastic sports and a strong physical education program are all a part of what keeps students active and healthy. The Upper School offers interscholastic sports, including baseball, basketball, cross-country, golf, lacrosse, soccer, softball, tennis, track and field, and volleyball. Other activities are weight lifting, outdoor exploration, and Ultimate Frisbee.

The athletic facilities include a new complex with a 9,000-square-foot gymnasium, a fully equipped fitness center, and state-of-the-art training and locker room facilities. The 140-acre campus includes four soccer and lacrosse fields and a 5-kilometer cross-country course.

EXTRACURRICULAR OPPORTUNITIES

Getting involved is made easy at Sandy Spring Friends by a weekly activities period that allows for students to participate in clubs such as Amnesty International (now in its tenth year at SSFS), the Multicultural Club, the International Student Club, the Open Door Club, the ski club (eight weeks of Friday-night skiing plus other trips), the chess club, and the outdoor exploration club. The yearbook and the literary magazine are also popular activities for students.

The purpose of the Community Service Program at Sandy Spring Friends School is to respond to the needs of others and to enrich the School community and the lives of its members. Every student at the School is expected to perform community service as a requirement for graduation. The programs are extremely diverse in order to allow for individual interests to be pursued.

DAILY LIFE

Breakfast for the boarding community begins at 7. Classes begin at 8 and end at 3:20; they are 45 minutes in length. A "jobs" period is scheduled daily for dorm students, advisory and tutorial periods occur once a week, and Meeting for Worship occurs two times each week. Lunch is served cafeteria-style daily.

Athletics takes place between 3:30 and 5:30, and dinner is served family-style at 6. Dorm meetings or activity groups frequently meet before the study hours, which begin nightly at 7:30, Sunday through Thursday.

WEEKEND LIFE

Weekends at the School are relaxed. Activities frequently designed by both students and faculty have included adventures such as day trips into Washington, D.C., for a museum visit, a march on the Mall, lunch at Planet Hollywood and a show at the Kennedy Center, or shopping in Georgetown. In addition, the students have visited Baltimore's Inner Harbor, Harper's Ferry, and various hot spots around the School. While boarding students are not required to stay at the School on the weekends, all students can choose the weekend activities in which they wish to participate (day students and five-day boarders would be charged an appropriate fee for the off-campus activities). One third of the weekends during the school year include on-campus activities such as School dances; student performances in theater, music, and modern dance; art shows; and special concerts and symposiums in the areas of science and the arts.

COSTS AND FINANCIAL AID

In 2005–06, tuition ranged from $14,700 to $15,800 in the Lower School, $17,200 to $18,400 in the Middle School, and $20,100 in the Upper School. Boarding tuition was $28,600 for five days and $34,700 for seven days. A hot lunch is provided beginning in the first grade. Additional costs include an incidental account for the School store, student allowances, laboratory fees, and art supplies.

Sandy Spring Friends School offers financial aid on the basis of need. The financial aid decisions for applications submitted by January 15 are made by mid-March for the following year. Twenty-one percent of the students received financial aid for the 2005–06 school year. The average award was $15,623 for boarders and $7778 for day students in the Upper School.

ADMISSIONS INFORMATION

Sandy Spring Friends School actively seeks a diverse, capable, and enthusiastic community of students. The admissions process allows prospective students and their families to become familiar with as many aspects of the School as possible. New students enter at ninth, tenth, and eleventh grades as space permits.

APPLICATION TIMETABLE

Inquiries are welcome at any time. The Admissions Office is open from 8 a.m. to 4:30 p.m., Monday through Friday. Application forms are due by January 15. The application process must be completed by February 10 to ensure first-round consideration. Applications received after January 15 are reviewed as space permits.

ADMISSIONS CORRESPONDENCE

Mecha Inman, Director of Admission
Sandy Spring Friends School
16923 Norwood Road
Sandy Spring, Maryland 20860-1199

Phone: 301-774-7455 Ext. 107
Fax: 301-924-1115
E-mail: admissions@ssfs.org
Web site: http://www.ssfs.org

SANTA CATALINA SCHOOL

Monterey, California

Type: Girls' (coeducational day, P–8) boarding and day college-preparatory school
Grades: P–12: Preschool; Lower School, 1–8; Upper School, 9–12
Enrollment: School total: 551; Upper School: 290
Head of School: Sister Claire Barone

THE SCHOOL

Santa Catalina School in Monterey, California, is dedicated to the education of young women. An independent, Catholic girls' boarding and day college preparatory school encompassing grades 9–12, Santa Catalina was founded in 1850 by Mother Mary Goemaere and established on its present site in 1950. The wooded campus on the Monterey Peninsula is convenient to the educational opportunities of Stanford University; the University of California, Santa Cruz; Santa Clara University; and the San Francisco Bay Area.

The School's philosophy integrates spiritual values with life. Christian service is emphasized through community outreach, both locally and around the world. Santa Catalina seeks to encourage students to become lifelong learners, to strive for excellence, and to develop their fullest spiritual, personal, and academic potential. In this regard, it is Santa Catalina's aim to facilitate a life where students can enjoy academic challenges while they learn to balance intellectual growth with spiritual awareness, creativity with order, and individuality with compassion.

The School seeks socioeconomic, religious, geographic, and cultural diversity. Within this Catholic and ecumenical community, each student may explore her spiritual and moral awareness and mature in her sense of responsibility to herself and to others. Students, faculty members, and the entire Santa Catalina family establish friendships and values that last throughout their lifetimes.

A nonprofit institution, Santa Catalina School is governed by a Board of Trustees. Through annual giving, the Board endeavors to implement the School's goal of maintaining academic excellence, supporting an outstanding faculty, and ensuring suitable growth.

Santa Catalina is accredited by the Western Association of Schools and Colleges and is a member of the National Association of Independent Schools, the California Association of Independent Schools, the National Coalition of Girls' Schools, the Secondary School Admission Test Board, and the Western Boarding Schools Association.

ACADEMIC PROGRAMS

The Santa Catalina curriculum provides excellent courses in the classical tradition of the liberal arts, enhanced by vigorous programs in the arts, athletics, and student leadership. Strong science, computer studies, and mathematics programs enable students to grasp the technological principles shaping modern civilization.

All students take a minimum of five academic classes as well as an elective in the arts each year. The required curriculum includes 4 years each of English, religion/philosophy, and physical education or team sports and 3 to 4 years each of history, foreign language, mathematics, and science. Honors and Advanced Placement courses are of-

fered in all disciplines, including English, history, mathematics, science, foreign language, music, and studio art. There are also numerous academic and arts electives.

Class size in both academic and elective classes ranges from 12 to 15 students. The student-faculty ratio is 7:1.

Students are assessed by letter grades ranging from A to F on a 4.0 scale. A to C are acknowledged as college-recommending grades. Students and parents receive written reports as well as grades.

FACULTY AND ADVISERS

In 2002, Sister Claire Barone assumed the position of Head of School after serving as Santa Catalina's Head of Upper School for twenty years. With a degree from the University of San Francisco, she succeeds long-standing Head Sister Carlotta O'Donnell.

Among the 41 teaching faculty members, 33 hold advanced master's degrees. Representative colleges and universities of the faculty members include Amherst, Bates, Boston College, Brown, Bucknell, California State Polytechnic, Dartmouth, Duke, Harvard, Kenyon, MIT, Middlebury, Santa Clara, Scripps, Simmons, Stanford, Tufts, Wellesley, Williams, and the Universities of California (Berkeley, San Diego, Santa Barbara), Chicago, Illinois, Montreal, North Carolina, Pennsylvania, and Wisconsin.

New faculty members are assessed on the basis of substantial academic qualifications, previous teaching experience, and willingness to participate actively in School life. Each faculty member is dedicated to helping every student develop her character and academic skills in the context of a close-knit community. A strong sense of family is provided by the resident faculty members and their families. Each freshman, sophomore, and junior has her own faculty adviser. These individuals assist and advise students in the development of their potential. Advisers write detailed letters home about a student's progress twice yearly.

COLLEGE PLACEMENT

College counseling begins in the junior year, at which time students begin regular appointments with the Director of College Counseling. Annual visits to Santa Catalina by college representatives and the extensive individual college counseling program conducted by the Head of School and the Director of College Counseling serve as significant aids in the college application process.

In addition, the English and Mathematics Departments work intensively with all juniors and seniors to strengthen verbal and mathematical skills and provide direction and growth in test-taking skills. The institutions in which graduates are currently enrolled include Bates; Boston College; Brown; Bucknell; California State, Long Beach; California State, Sonoma; Claremont McKenna; Columbia; Connecticut College; Cornell; Deni-

son; George Washington; Harvard; Harvey Mudd; Loyola Marymount; Middlebury; Mount Holyoke; Northwestern; NYU; Princeton; Santa Clara; Scripps; Stanford; Swathmore; Trinity; Tulane; UCLA; Vanderbilt; Wellesley; Williams; Yale; and the Universities of California (Berkeley, Davis, Los Angeles, and San Diego), Colorado, Michigan, North Carolina, Oregon, Pennsylvania, Virginia, and Washington.

STUDENT BODY AND CONDUCT

In 2005–06, the Upper School had 154 boarding students and 137 day students. Resident students come from California, sixteen other states, and eight other countries. Day students reside on the Monterey Peninsula and in surrounding communities.

The Student-Faculty Senate serves as a forum for student opinion, channels suggestions to the administration, and acts on suggestions in conjunction with the Head of School. Both students and faculty members serve on the Disciplinary Committee.

ACADEMIC FACILITIES

The hacienda that served as the original school building is now encircled by classrooms, dormitories, and other facilities in a blend of traditional and contemporary Spanish-style architecture. The 36-acre campus, located 1 mile from Monterey's beaches, is graced by gardens, shaded walks, and California live oaks.

There are three classroom buildings, a gymnasium, a central library, and a two-story science center. The Sister Mary Kieran Memorial Library is computerized for access to libraries and materials worldwide. It is open seven days a week and houses more than 35,000 volumes, three listening rooms for tapes and recordings, a lecture room, and art rooms. Art facilities include general art studios and a ceramics studio and a kiln as well as a photography darkroom and developing equipment. The Science Center contains chemistry, physics, and biology laboratories; a lecture amphitheater and projection room; and an observation deck equipped with a Questar telescope. In 2001, Santa Catalina was awarded a $100,000 grant from the Edward E. Ford Foundation. The grant provides several salt-water aquarium systems that are used by Santa Catalina students in marine science, AP environmental science, and biology courses. The Sister Carlotta Performing Arts Center houses a 500-seat theater with professional lighting and sound equipment. The Mary L. Johnson Music Center provides soundproof practice rooms for individual and group instruction as well as a dance studio with a spring-loaded floor. Completed in 2002, a 150-seat recital hall, a music library, and additional practice rooms enhance the School's music center. A campuswide computer network and wireless Internet access is used both in and out of the classroom. The Computer Center, Writ-

ing Center, library, science laboratories, foreign language classrooms, and dormitories are all equipped with computer technology for student use.

BOARDING AND GENERAL FACILITIES
Resident students live in three dormitory areas. Most resident students share double rooms, but there are also single rooms available. Each dormitory contains living accommodations for resident faculty families. Students change roommates three times each year.

The Bedford Athletic Complex is equipped with a gymnasium, pool, tennis courts, and field areas. A new 25-yard by 30-meter competitive pool was completed in September 2002. Health-care facilities include a Health Center and a nurse's office. An additional area for student use is the Snack Shack run by Senate members. All resident students attend mass on Sunday in the Rosary Chapel, which is also available to students for optional weekday services and individual visits.

ATHLETICS
Santa Catalina teams compete interscholastically in basketball, cross-country, field hockey, golf, lacrosse, soccer, softball, swimming and diving, track and field, tennis, volleyball, and water polo. Every girl has the opportunity to become a member of a varsity or junior varsity team. Other athletic opportunities include ballet, cardio/strength training, jazz, kickboxing, Pilates, riding, and yoga. Through its membership in the United States Lawn Tennis Association, Santa Catalina hosts an annual invitational tennis tournament in the fall that draws players from throughout the state.

EXTRACURRICULAR OPPORTUNITIES
Students publish the newspaper, the yearbook, and the school literary magazine. Activity groups at Santa Catalina include the Student Alumnae Organization, the Student-Faculty Senate, a rock-climbing club, Amnesty International, Peace and Justice, Senior Prefects, Accents (dance group), Schola, and ecco! (an a cappella group). Among numerous community outreach opportunities, girls regularly serve at local convalescent homes, a Salvation Army Day Care Center, the Boys and Girls Club, and Habitat for Humanity. Students participate in beach cleanups, raise funds for food baskets, and sponsor underprivileged children through the Santa Catalina School Children's Fund. In addition, three school days are dedicated to having the entire Santa Catalina community serve local service organizations.

Students audition for three theatrical performances, a fall and a spring musical and a midwinter drama. Recent productions have included *Good News, Anne of Green Gables,* and *The Sound of Music.* Concerts, dances, lectures, and movies

are a regular part of campus life. Periodic assemblies in the Performing Arts Center provide the opportunity to enjoy guest speakers, musicians, vocalists, choral groups, and dance and drama workshops through funding of the Edwin L. Wiegand Trust Dialogues in the Arts and Sciences.

DAILY LIFE
The Santa Catalina School day begins at 7:55 a.m. with Assembly. Academic periods, each 45 minutes long, meet from 8:15 to 2:40, five days a week. Electives in the arts and instrumental and voice lessons meet during the academic day. Team sports, physical education classes, community outreach, and drama rehearsals meet after school, and supervised study time is provided for resident students from 7:30 to 9:30 each evening. The study hall, the library, and the computer labs are available for study throughout the day and evening.

WEEKEND LIFE
Students may choose from a variety of weekend activities that are planned by the Director of Activities (a faculty member), the Activities Coordinator (an officer of the Student-Faculty Senate), and the class advisers. Traditional events scheduled throughout the year include the Halloween Party, Fall Dance, many Christmas events, Winter Formal, Spirit Day, Spring Dance, Ring Dinner, Junior/Senior Prom, Parents' Weekend, Father-Daughter Weekend, Cake Auction, Yearbook Dinner, and Class Night (held the evening before graduation).

Throughout the year there are trips to the San Francisco Bay Area for museum visits, plays, ballets, symphony concerts, sightseeing, and shopping. Other off-campus trips are taken to theme parks, ski resorts, and state and national parks for rafting, hiking, white-water rafting, and camping.

The Monterey Peninsula has many recreational and cultural opportunities that girls may enjoy as part of organized school activities or independently.

SUMMER PROGRAMS
The Santa Catalina Summer Camp, for girls entering grades 3–9, consists of a full five-week session or the choice of a two- or three-week session. A tennis clinic, musical theater workshop, riding, golf, and marine biology are offered in addition to photography, creative writing, and crafts. Recreational activities include swimming, tennis, team sports, picnics, and beach trips. Fees for summer 2005, including tuition, room and board, and activities, ranged from $1700 (boarding, two-week session) to $2600 (boarding, three-week session) to $4100 (boarding, five-week session). Inquiries should be sent to Peggy Sellars, Director of Summer Programs, at 831-655-9386.

COSTS AND FINANCIAL AID
Upper School costs for 2005–06 totaled $34,500 for resident students and $21,500 for day students. Additional fees included $600 for a bookstore deposit.

Financial aid, awarded on the basis of financial need as indicated by the School and Student Service for Financial Aid, is extended to approximately 30 percent of the student body. A merit scholarship is offered to one or two outstanding entering freshmen for up to 20 percent of tuition. In addition, the School offers low-interest loan programs to students who do not qualify for financial assistance. Families may also take advantage of several tuition payment plans.

ADMISSIONS INFORMATION
Students are selected on the basis of scholastic achievement, strong personal qualifications, three faculty recommendations, a personal interview, satisfactory scores on the SSAT, and a written essay. The Santa Catalina Upper School accepts students in the ninth, tenth, and eleventh grades. Santa Catalina School accepts students without regard to race, creed, color, or national and ethnic origins.

APPLICATION TIMETABLE
The number of new students Santa Catalina can accommodate each year is far smaller than the number of applications received. The deadline for application is February 1. Applications submitted after that date are considered if space becomes available. Applicants should complete and submit the preliminary application form with a $75 application fee and a photograph. Soon thereafter they should schedule an interview appointment during a week when school is in session. All applicants should take the SSAT at the earliest possible test date, but no later than the January test offering to be considered for admission by February 1.

A formal application, including recommendation and transcript release forms, is sent to the applicant upon receipt of the preliminary application.

Students who have completed the application process by the February 1 deadline are notified of their status by March 10. Accepted students are asked to respond to the School by April 7.

ADMISSIONS CORRESPONDENCE
Marian D. Corrigan, '72
Director, Admission
Santa Catalina School
1500 Mark Thomas Drive
Monterey, California 93940-5291

Phone: 831-655-9329
Fax: 831-655-7535
E-mail: admissions@santacatalina.org
Web site: http://www.santacatalina.org

SCATTERGOOD FRIENDS SCHOOL

West Branch, Iowa

Established 1890

Type: Coeducational boarding college-preparatory high school
Grades: 9–12
Enrollment: 60
Head of School: Jan Luchini, Director

THE SCHOOL

In addition to providing a solid foundation for higher education, Scattergood is a learning community that fosters the practical application of all kinds of knowledge through hands-on work and service. The School's mission is to provide students with a sense of global citizenship while recognizing individual self-worth. Scattergood strives to instill in students the ability to live constructively in a community as well as feel that their opinion has been heard.

Scattergood Friends School was founded in 1890 by the Religious Society of Friends (Quakers) for the purpose of educating Quaker children from the Midwest. While Scattergood students today come from many religious and backgrounds, the School is still guided by the Quaker values of equality, simplicity, integrity, and harmony with others and with nature. The School is dedicated to growth of the whole person—body, mind, and spirit—within the context of community and within a larger global context. Scattergood is 4 hours from Chicago and Omaha; 5 hours from Minneapolis, Milwaukee, Kansas City, and St. Louis; and 7–10 hours from Indianapolis, Cincinnati, and Detroit. The School's 120-acre campus in located 12 miles east of Iowa City, Iowa, and consists of a 12-acre main campus and 28-acre pond and prairie nature preserve. The 80-acre farm includes an organic fruit and vegetable garden and livestock.

Scattergood's liberal arts curriculum meets or exceeds the requirements of the Iowa Department of Public Instruction and the admissions guidelines of Iowa's state universities. Scattergood is accredited by the Iowa Department of Public Instruction, as well as the Independent Schools Association of the Central States (ISACS), and is a member of the National Association of Independent Schools (NAIS) and Midwest Boarding Schools.

ACADEMIC PROGRAMS

The academic year is divided into month-long blocks. During the weekday mornings of each block, students take two 50-minute classes and one 100-minute class. The longer classes give teachers and students the flexibility to participate in outdoor projects and field trips, as well as time to really delve into a project or discussion. Morning classes meet on alternate days much like a college schedule.

In the afternoon, students engage in projects, physical education, and sports practices. Afternoon projects are 90 minutes and include art classes such as ceramics, painting, theater, woodworking and/or welding, glass blowing, stained glass, and photography. Other projects vary from year to year but usually include off-campus community service, creative writing, dance, journalism, horticulture, and music.

Students are allowed to apply for independent study in many subjects at Scattergood but most often request studies in the areas of project and physical education classes. Some independent studies granted in the last few years include a filmmaking project, graphic design, skateboarding, iceskating, tae kwon do, and art portfolio preparation.

Every other year, the advanced Spanish students spend four weeks doing a service project in a Latin American country. This trip is alternated with a historical and service-oriented trip for the juniors and seniors to the East Coast, usually including cities such as Philadelphia, New York, and Washington, D.C. Other monthlong trips for upperclass students in recent years have included a bike trip from Mississippi back to Scattergood and a service trip to the Rosebud and Pine Ridge Native American Reservations.

Scattergood's classes are evaluated on a pass/no-pass basis; students may also do work to receive honors credit. Written evaluations are sent home every four weeks. The core curriculum includes four years of English, four years of social studies, three years of mathematics, three years of natural science, and three years of language. Advanced Placement testing is available for those seniors interested in obtaining college credit. Critical reasoning skills and the ability to communicate effectively are emphasized, including reading, writing, speaking, listening, and the capacity to consider other points of view.

FACULTY AND ADVISERS

The full-time faculty consists of 14 women and 14 men. Approximately half of the teaching staff members hold advanced degrees. However, all staff members continue their professional development while at Scattergood. Most faculty members serve as advisers to 2 or 3 students. The majority of staff members and their families live on campus. This proximity allows staff members to be available for academic help outside the classroom and to develop meaningful relationships that extend beyond the classroom. The faculty members consider themselves to be mentors as well as facilitators of the students' education.

COLLEGE PLACEMENT

All students must be accepted at an accredited four-year college or university in order to graduate from Scattergood. Beginning in their junior year, students participate in a structured search for colleges and universities that are appropriate to their needs and desires. They are encouraged to research and visit a number of schools. Over the last ten years, alumni have attended such colleges and universities as Albright, Antioch, Art Institute of Seattle, Beloit, Colorado State, Columbia, Cornell, Drake, Earlham, Evergreen State, Grinnell, Guilford, Hampshire, Haverford, Indiana, Macalester, Oberlin, Occidental, Pitzer, Reed, Smith,

Stanford, Swarthmore, Tulane, Xavier, and the Universities of Chicago, Iowa, and Wisconsin.

The Junior and Senior Seminars offer students support and assistance in taking the SAT and ACT exams as well as applying to colleges and universities. The portfolio program is further enhanced in these classes as students prepare a portfolio that will be submitted with their college applications. These seminar classes also entail the writing of an in-depth research paper over the course of one semester. During their junior year, a ten-page minimum is required. In their senior year, the minimum is twenty pages on a topic of their choice. Both of these papers have structured deadlines and individual staff readers. In their senior year, students also prepare an oral defense of their paper to be presented in front of the Director, the Academic Coordinator, and their staff reader.

STUDENT BODY AND CONDUCT

Scattergood students bring diversity from many parts of the United States and many other countries, including Bolivia, China, Japan, Korea, Mexico, Rwanda, and Turkey. Most students are from the Midwest; other states represented include Colorado, Mississippi, New Mexico, North Carolina, Pennsylvania, South Dakota, Vermont, and Wyoming.

A weekly Community Meeting allows all community members a chance to discuss issues of interest and concern and to affirm and accomplishments. The Meeting is lead by 2 students, with a staff member overseeing the process. A weekly Student Meeting is held for all students to discuss concerns and come up with possible solutions. Many times these concerns are raised again by students in the Community Meeting so that the entire community has a chance to help resolve the issue.

ACADEMIC FACILITIES

The main campus includes several buildings: an instructional building with classrooms for language and social studies; a science building with biology and chemistry labs and a photography darkroom; a large gymnasium with a weight room; two outdoor athletic fields; a main building that contains offices, the auditorium, a library, and classrooms; and two extensive art buildings with studios for drawing and painting, ceramics, stained glass, glassblowing, woodworking, and welding as well as weaving.

Each student is issued a personal laptop computer to use while attending Scattergood. A portion of the tuition is applied toward the optional purchase of the student's computer at the time the student graduates or leaves Scattergood. Each laptop is linked to the School's wireless, high-speed data network, which spans all of the academic buildings on campus as well as both dorms. The School has its own file server, allowing students and staff members the flexibility of working

on their laptops or on any of the desktops on campus while saving work to a central location. Scattergood offers free e-mail accounts to all community members for both personal and academic use.

Teachers have full access to the Grant Wood Area Education Agency. Other areas where learning takes place include the organic garden and greenhouse, the farm and orchards, and the restored prairie. Nearby cultural resources include the University of Iowa, the Herbert Hoover Presidential Library, and Hancher Auditorium in Iowa City.

BOARDING AND GENERAL FACILITIES
The primary buildings on campus form a circle, which surrounds a grassy common area that serves as a gathering place to relax and play volleyball or Frisbee or to skateboard. A large wooden deck, which is situated in front of the main building, is often a center for social interaction. Encircling the perimeter of the campus, as well as throughout, many varieties of trees provide shade and natural beauty. The main building houses the girls' dormitory on the top floor and the auditorium, a centralized social room, the library, offices, and classrooms on the main floor. The dining room and student lounge, as well as a few more offices, are located on the bottom floor. The boys' dormitory is situated directly across from the main building. Both dorms contain a comfortable lounge area. Each dormitory is staffed by 4 adult residents, called dorm sponsors, who work with the students to provide a healthy and safe dorm environment. Staff residences and offices are integrated throughout the campus in most of the buildings and at the farm. Other important buildings include Hickory Grove Meeting House and the Berquist House, which contains guest rooms, offices, and staff apartments. The newly constructed pond and sand volleyball court add to the campus as well as student and staff enjoyment.

ATHLETICS
Athletics at Scattergood are generally geared to provide recreation, physical conditioning, and enjoyment. The School has recently joined the Iowa High School Athletic Association in soccer. This allows students to play up to fourteen games in one fall season. Basketball and fencing have recently become varsity sports as well, with students participating in tournaments in both sports.

Students are required to participate in athletics each semester. Students may choose from among the following sports: basketball, dance, fencing, field hockey, roller hockey, running, soccer, tae kwon do, volleyball, and weight training. Team sports are offered in the fall, and a variety of athletics and physical activities are offered in the winter and spring seasons. Most athletics are coed.

EXTRACURRICULAR OPPORTUNITIES
There are opportunities for student involvement on campus or in the local community. Private music or dance lessons are available in West Branch and Iowa City. Students play in chess tournaments in local schools, and the fencing class goes into Iowa City twice a week to practice with the University of Iowa fencing club. Coffeehouse shows and the Arts Festival provide on-campus opportunities for community members to share their talents with others.

An all-School camping weekend in September provides relaxation and helps to strengthen the community. February Intersession replaces the usual schedule with special projects, activities, and community service projects. Students enjoy activities such as skiing and bowling, and they partake in a variety of projects and workshops. Workshop offerings have included jazz appreciation, a poetry workshop, ceramics projects, and cooking classes. Students also volunteer for service projects such as working at a nearby grade school, an animal shelter, the local public library, a restaurant for the homeless, and a women's clinic. The week is designed to provide a break from the usual routine and create an opportunity for community service. In the spring, a variety of weeklong trips are offered. Recent trips have included hiking in the Blue Ridge Mountains of Kentucky; an educational trip to Washington, D.C.; bicycling through northwest Iowa and Wisconsin; and canoe trips on nearby rivers.

DAILY LIFE
The entire School community meets together each weekday morning for Collection, a period of 15 minutes of silence. After Collection, students and staff members move out of the silence into the activity of the day. Language instruction, humanities classes, social studies, mathematics, and sciences make up the academic morning, as students and faculty members meet in small seminar-style classes. Courses are grounded in real-life activities. For example, the biology class centers its activities on living plant and animal processes, such as the birth of pigs, the spring planting, and the fall harvest. The School's farm and prairie preserve act as living laboratories, augmenting and enhancing the classroom experience.

In the afternoon, all students study art, including drawing, painting, photography, pottery, weaving, woodworking, stained glass, jewelry making, and theater, and participate in athletics such as basketball, volleyball, soccer, field hockey, and fencing. Study hall completes the day's scheduled activities.

Foregoing all institutional titles, all students and staff members are on a first-name basis. At different times during the day, staff members and students work together to prepare meals, wash dishes, maintain the buildings and grounds, and care for the livestock and garden. Through this, students come to learn that all work has value.

Special program days allow the entire community the opportunity to attend a play or dance performance in Iowa City or to go on a picnic and explore caves at the state park. Quiet walks on the prairie, swimming in the pond, bike rides into West Branch, and pool and Ping-Pong in the student recreation room also provide a break from work and study.

WEEKEND LIFE
After studying hard all week, students are usually ready for a relaxing and fairly unstructured weekend. Weekend programs feature everything from a guest speaker to a live blues band. Other offerings for weekend activities include open studio for art students, a video, or a dance. Saturday's "town-trip" provides a ride to Iowa City for shopping, a matinee, or a visit to the library.

COSTS AND FINANCIAL AID
The 2004–05 annual full board cost of $20,000 covered room, board, tuition, textbooks, and the use of a personal laptop computer. The cost for five-day boarders was $18,500, and for day students, the cost was $11,000. The work program and the generosity of Friends and alumni enable the School to maintain a low tuition cost. Each year, a considerable number of students receive tuition grants based on need. In 2004–05, more than half of the students received significant financial aid.

ADMISSIONS INFORMATION
Students are accepted without regard to race, gender, color, or creed. Some preference is given to Quakers and children of alumni in the admissions process. Admission is based on a student application and essay, a parent application, the previous school record, three recommendations, and an interview. The Admissions Committee looks for many things in its candidates, but, above all, it looks for students who are motivated and independent thinkers. Students enter Scattergood in ninth and tenth grades. Few are considered for eleventh grade.

APPLICATION TIMETABLE
Scattergood's early application deadline is December 1. Applicants are mailed their notification on December 10. The second deadline is April 1, with decisions being made on April 10. After April 10, applications are evaluated on a space-available basis. Students may contact the Admissions Office at any time to inquire about Scattergood.

ADMISSIONS CORRESPONDENCE
Rachel Thomson, Admissions Director
Scattergood Friends School
1951 Delta Avenue
West Branch, Iowa 52358-8507
Phone: 888-737-4636 (toll-free)
Fax: 319-643-7638
E-mail: admissions@scattergood.org
Web site: http://www.scattergood.org

SEISEN INTERNATIONAL SCHOOL

Tokyo, Japan

Type: Girls' day college-preparatory school with coeducational Montessori Kindergarten
Grades: K–12: Montessori Kindergarten; Elementary School, 1–6; Junior High School, 7–8; High School, 9–12
Enrollment: School total: 692; High School: 148
Head of School: Ms. Virginia Villegas, School Head

THE SCHOOL

Seisen International School began in 1949 as a kindergarten with only 4 American children. When the School moved to Gotanda in 1962, it enrolled 70 students and started a first-grade program as well. By 1970, the School included nine grades, and in 1973, when Seisen moved to its present location, its curriculum was extended to include twelve grades. The School has an enrollment of approximately 700 students representing approximately sixty nationalities.

Seisen offers a Montessori kindergarten, which is designed to take full advantage of young children's self-motivation and their sensitivity to their environment. In this program, the teacher observes each child's interests and needs and offers the stimulation and guidance that will enable him or her to experience the excitement of learning by choice. The Montessori equipment helps in the development of concentration, coordination, good working habits, and basic skills according to each child's capacities and in a noncompetitive atmosphere.

Currently, Seisen's Elementary School holds candidate status for the Primary Years Program (PYP). The Elementary School provides an environment where students are encouraged to be thinkers and inquirers and find ways to problem solve. The teachers serve as facilitators and provide the necessary coaching, information, and strategies to promote high-quality learning. Every child understands the "learning attitudes and profiles" necessary to be an integral team member and contributor to the School. This program also motivates students to become learners and participants in a collaborative international community. The effort is made to take advantage of the international nature of the student body through curriculum design and extracurricular activities. By helping students to become lifelong learners, Seisen prepares Elementary School students for success in high school and the world beyond.

Elementary-level language arts and mathematics are taught as stand-alone subjects. Music, art, and Japanese language study are integral components of the elementary curriculum. English as a second language (ESL) instruction is available for students. In addition, Seisen recognizes that the moral and spiritual development of the students is as important as academic development. The School's teachers strive to create a Christian environment that welcomes and respects children of all nationalities and creeds.

The high school program prepares young women to face the challenges of a global society with excellent academic preparation, a strong program of athletics, advanced preparation in the visual and performing arts, and an emphasis on community service. From the time that the International Baccalaureate Program was adopted at Seisen in 1988, Seisen students have consistently scored higher than the worldwide I.B. mean each year.

Seisen, a Catholic school with a Christian atmosphere in which students of all races, nationalities, and creeds can thrive, has high expectations for the students' character development, particularly respect, compassion, and international understanding.

The School is located in Tokyo's largest residential area, Setagaya-ku. It is easily accessible from downtown Tokyo and from other residential areas of the city by subway, train, public bus, or Seisen's school buses, which cover ten different routes throughout the city.

Seisen is operated by the Handmaids of the Sacred Heart of Jesus under the auspices of the Seisen Jogakuin Educational Foundation. The order was founded in 1877 by Saint Rafaela Maria Porras to dedicate its efforts to educational activities.

Seisen is accredited by the New England Association of Schools and Colleges, the Council of International Schools, and the Japanese Ministry of Education. Its memberships include the Japan Council of Overseas Schools, the Kanto Plain Association of Secondary School Principals, and the East Asia Regional Council of Overseas Schools.

ACADEMIC PROGRAMS

Seisen requires that students earn 22 credits in grades 9 through 12. Graduation requirements are as follows: English, 4 credits; social sciences, 4 credits; mathematics, 3 credits; science, 3 credits; foreign language, 3 credits; religion, 1 credit; physical education, 1 credit; and academic electives, 3 credits. Academic electives in the senior year include art, music, math, history, foreign language, and an introduction to Montessori teachings. Other electives are yearbook, journalism, library assistant, survival Japanese, computer graphics, choir, drama, 2-D art, and pottery. In grades 9 and 10, students are required to take a performing/visual arts block, drama, music, pottery, or 2-D art. Personal social health education is also a requirement at the ninth and tenth grade level. Special instruction in English as a second language is available.

Class size varies according to subject. The grading system uses letter grades (A to F) for electives and physical education and numerical grades (the highest being 100 and grades below 70 indicating failure) for other subjects. Reports are sent to parents at the end of each of the four marking periods.

Students are grouped heterogeneously, except in mathematics, in which there are regular, honors, and accelerated groups. The average course load is five classes in academic subjects and one elective. The library is open during the school day and before and after school.

To fully serve the needs of a university-bound, international student body, Seisen offers a program of studies in grades 11 and 12 that can culminate in either a full International Baccalaureate diploma or in individual subject certificates. These attainments are recognized for admission to more than 600 universities throughout the world. This includes many American colleges that accept the I.B. for advanced standing. The I.B. diploma is considered equivalent to most European university entrance requirements.

The following are administered in the School: PSAT/NMSQT, SAT and SAT Subject Tests, some IGCSE, the Iowa Test of Basic Skills, and the International School Assessment.

FACULTY AND ADVISERS

The faculty consists of 64 full-time members, of whom 50 are women and 14 are men. Thirty-one faculty members hold a master's degree or higher.

The administration and faculty members endeavor not only to educate the students in academic areas but also to foster their spiritual and emotional growth. Teachers are involved in counseling and advising students.

COLLEGE PLACEMENT

The college advisers help students in college selection and career orientation. Many college representatives visit the School each year, and some Seisen graduates return to give juniors and seniors information about various colleges.

During the junior year, all students take the PSAT and SAT. The SAT middle 50 percent range of scores for last year's graduates was 450–570 for verbal and 560–640 for mathematics.

Virtually all Seisen graduates go on to college. Some students stay in Japan, attending either Sophia University, Temple University, or International Christian University. Others attend school in their home country. A representative list of schools to which Seisen graduates have been accepted in the past several years includes Boston University, Brown, Cornell, Dartmouth, Durham, Franklin and Marshall, Harvard, Johns Hopkins, London School of Economics, McGill, Oxford, Princeton, Queens, Stanford, Tufts, Wellesley, William and Mary, Yale, and the Universities of California (Davis), Notre Dame, Pennsylvania, Prague, and Toronto.

STUDENT BODY AND CONDUCT

The 2005–06 student body included 41 in the ninth grade, 44 in the tenth, 39 in the eleventh, and 24 in the twelfth. The largest percentage of students were from the United States, Korea, the United Kingdom, and Japan, but nationalities from all over the world were represented.

Seisen expects its students to behave in such a way that maximum learning can take place. An

active Student Council involves the student body and the faculty in the educational process.

ACADEMIC FACILITIES
In addition to classrooms, the facilities include a chapel, three biology-chemistry-physics laboratories, a cafeteria, playgrounds, a music room, two art rooms, a media center, a computer center, and two tennis courts.

The School's libraries together have a collection of more than 20,000 volumes and subscribe to sixty periodicals and four newspapers. The High School library houses a multimedia center, a color printer, ten computer workstations, and ten laptops. Students have access to the library from outside the School through their home page.

ATHLETICS
In addition to the physical education program, Seisen offers basketball, cross-country, softball, tennis, track, and volleyball. Basketball, tennis, and volleyball are offered on varsity and junior varsity levels. The School has a gymnasium, tennis courts, and an outdoor playing area.

EXTRACURRICULAR OPPORTUNITIES
As a member of the Kanto Plain Association of Secondary School Principals, Seisen is active in various competitions (debate, speech, Brain Bowl, Math Field Day). There are vocal and instrumental groups and a choir and a drama group. Other organizations and activities include the National Honor Society, the Student Council, student publications, Alleluia Club (which prepares liturgy and guitar music for Mass), Bell Choir, Booster Club, Model United Nations (MUN), social service groups, and the Girls' Athletic Association (GAA).

DAILY LIFE
Students usually have eight 40-minute classes, including a study hall/activity period each day. The School cafeteria serves hot lunches, but students may choose to bring their own. Classes begin at 8:20 a.m. and end at 3:20 p.m. There are no Saturday classes. Students are encouraged to participate in competitive sports and other activities after school.

SUMMER PROGRAMS
A three-week program of remedial studies is offered in June. Enrichment programs and sports are offered on a limited basis.

COSTS AND FINANCIAL AID
The tuition, quoted in Japanese yen, fluctuates with exchange rates. In 2005–06, the High School tuition was 1.92 million yen. Transportation and lunches are available at additional cost. A registration fee of 300,000 yen and a land and building development fee of 300,000 yen are payable when a student registers.

A limited amount of financial aid is available on the basis of need and at the discretion of the School Head.

ADMISSIONS INFORMATION
Seisen International School serves the needs of diplomatic, business, and professional families of the international community. It also provides education for Japanese children who have lived abroad and wish to continue their education in English.

A completed application form, an interview with the Principal or the School Head of Seisen International School, an entrance examination, and an official transcript from the school attended previously are required of all applicants.

APPLICATION TIMETABLE
Applications are welcome at any time. Parents and prospective students are encouraged to visit the School.

ADMISSIONS CORRESPONDENCE
Ms. Virginia Villegas, School Head
Seisen International School
12-15, Yoga 1-chome
Setagaya-ku
Tokyo
Japan 158-0097

Phone: 81-3-3704-2661
Fax: 81-3-3701-1033
E-mail: sisadmissions@seisen.com
Web site: http://www.seisen.com

SHATTUCK–ST. MARY'S SCHOOL

Faribault, Minnesota

Type: Coeducational boarding and day college-preparatory school
Grades: 6–PG: Middle School, 6–8; Upper School, 9–12
Enrollment: School total: 335; Upper School: 276
Head of School: Nicholas J. B. Stoneman

THE SCHOOL

Shattuck–St. Mary's School is a coeducational boarding and day school whose rigorous academic, arts, and athletic programs foster excellence, self-confidence, and well-roundedness—all in the context of strong Midwestern values. One of the oldest boarding schools in the Midwest, Shattuck–St. Mary's has been preparing graduates for entrance into selective colleges and universities around the world for almost 150 years.

Founded as an Episcopal mission school in 1858, the School today encompasses 250 acres on a wooded hilltop overlooking the Straight River and the city of Faribault. This community of 20,000 is located 45 miles south of Minneapolis and St. Paul. These metropolitan areas provide numerous cultural opportunities for students.

The campus, with its tree-lined streets and fine neo-Gothic buildings, is a vivid reminder of old English boarding schools. Many of the buildings, constructed in the 1800s of native blue limestone, are on the National Register of Historic Places, and the entire campus has been designated a National Historic District.

In 2002–03, Shattuck–St. Mary's established a comprehensive notebook computer program. All students and faculty members use personal notebook computers on a fully wireless campus.

The primary goal of Shattuck–St. Mary's is to prepare each student not just for college but for a confident adult life. Student involvement in residential and extracurricular activities is encouraged. A new Bastian Student Leadership Development Program combines on-campus leadership positions, wilderness trips or ropes course leadership training, a speaker series, and in-class instruction to help students learn and grow as effective leaders. Weekly religious services and courses in ethics and values allow students of all faiths to explore questions of the spirit in an open, rational, and supportive atmosphere. A 20-hour-per-year community service requirement supports students' growth into responsible, contributing citizens.

Shattuck–St. Mary's School is accredited by the Independent Schools Association of the Central States and holds membership in the National Association of Episcopal Schools, the National Association of Independent Schools, the Secondary School Admission Test Board, the Council for Advancement and Support of Education, and the Midwest Boarding Schools Association.

ACADEMIC PROGRAMS

The course of study at Shattuck–St. Mary's is demanding. The curriculum includes more than 100 courses of instruction. Students carry at least five or six subjects each term.

The school year, which runs from late August to early June, is divided into trimesters and includes vacations of one week in the fall and two weeks at winter break and in the spring. Class sizes average 12 students. Faculty-supervised study halls are held during the school day and from 7:30 to 9:30 p.m. each night. Grades are available to parents online through the School's online parent com-

munity. Parents receive narrative comments at midterm and adviser letters at the end of term.

Graduation requirements for Upper School students (Grades 9–12) include 4 years of English; 3 years of mathematics; 3 years of science, including one of physical science; 3 years of history; two consecutive levels of the same language in grades 9–12; and 1 term of fine arts per year of attendance. Students must also pass a computer competency course and complete 20 hours of community service per year.

Extensive courses in choral and instrumental music, theater arts, and dance, plus numerous opportunities to perform on campus and to tour domestically and abroad, make it possible for young artists to pursue extensive arts training within a college-preparatory program. The School also offers English as a second language at five levels of proficiency and prepares students for the Test of English as a Foreign Language (TOEFL).

A competitive Honors Program challenges students to explore course work above and beyond traditional high school–level work and offers honors classes as well as AP courses in thirteen areas of study. Students who apply into this program may conduct independent study and research projects with the possibility of eventual publication.

The School's Center for Academic Achievement includes the Academic Skills Program, which is designed to recognize and enhance the potential of students with diagnosed mild learning disabilities and attention disorders. Each student enrolled receives an individualized education plan and concentrated course work specifically tailored to their educational needs. The partner Study Skills Program offers a one-half-term course for eighth and ninth grade students, providing specific instruction in study skills and strategies to successfully navigate a college-preparatory program.

The Middle School is a distinct yet integral part of the School community, with its own facility, faculty, activities, and athletic programs. The curriculum is designed to address the developmental needs of younger students and to prepare them for the academic program in the Upper School.

The School's three-week Summer Language Institute offers intensive language immersion, academics, and activities for international students interested in improving their English skills. Other summer programs include one-week camps in soccer and ice hockey.

FACULTY AND ADVISERS

At the heart of Shattuck–St. Mary's is an excellent faculty. Collectively, they offer a wealth of experiences in working with young people of diverse cultural backgrounds. By virtue of their many roles—classroom teacher, dorm parent, coach, adviser—faculty members get to know students on a personal basis. They invest themselves in their students and express personal interest in each student's growth and development. Much like parents, faculty members are there to provide encouragement, guidance, and support as needed. Each student has an adviser who serves as an academic and general counselor

and who communicates frequently with parents regarding their child's progress. Advisory meetings occur twice weekly.

Thirty-eight faculty members and administrators, along with their families, live on campus. Twenty-eight faculty members hold master's degrees, and 3 have doctoral degrees.

Nicholas J. B. Stoneman was appointed Head of School in 2003. He is a graduate of Bowdoin College and earned his master's degree at Columbia University Teacher's College. Prior to his appointment, he served as Head of the Country Day School of Arlington, Texas.

COLLEGE PLACEMENT

The School's college admissions counselors provide college information to all students, beginning in grade 11. In addition to hosting more than 50 college representatives each year, the School keeps a collection of application forms, brochures, and catalogs on hand for the students' benefit.

During the past three years, virtually all graduating seniors were accepted by at least one college institution. Ninety-five percent of seniors elected to enroll directly in a college or university. They are attending such institutions as Augsburg, Boston College, Brown, Colorado College, Carleton, Duke, Grinnell, Johns Hopkins, Macalester, MIT, Northeastern, Northwestern, Rensselaer, Sonoma State, Wellesley, Wheaten, and the Universities of California (Berkeley), Chicago, Denver, Michigan, Minnesota, North Dakota, Rochester, Vermont, and Wisconsin.

STUDENT BODY AND CONDUCT

In 2005–06, Shattuck–St. Mary's enrolled 335 students, with 234 boarders and 101 day students in grades 6–12. There were 77 students in grade 9, 93 in grade 10, 59 in grade 11, and 47 in grade 12. The Middle School had an enrollment of 59. Students came from twenty-seven states and fifteen countries.

Because Shattuck–St. Mary's is committed to traditional standards of conduct, there is a dress code. Most disciplinary matters are handled by the Middle School Director, the Upper School Director, or by a disciplinary committee. The School has a "zero tolerance" policy on the use of drugs.

ACADEMIC FACILITIES

Four academic buildings house classrooms (all with Internet access), science labs, an art studio, a dance studio, a darkroom, physical education facilities, and a library with 20,000 volumes and an extensive collection of periodicals. There is a stunning wood-paneled performing arts auditorium with a complete stage for theatrical productions.

BOARDING AND GENERAL FACILITIES

There are three girls' and two boys' dormitories for students. Most students share a room with a roommate; however, there are some single rooms available. Faculty members act as dorm parents. All dorms are equipped with private telephones and Internet and e-mail access.

Other facilities include two dining rooms, a newly renovated student center, and a school store.

The infirmary is staffed by 4 nurses who provide coverage during the academic day and are on call at night.

ATHLETICS

Three centers of excellence form the core of the Shattuck–St. Mary's athletic program. The nationally recognized hockey program has brought home four Midget Tier I National Champion banners in the past six years, and last year the girls' prep team rounded out their 51-3-8 season with a national champion title. The new soccer development program emphasizes skill development in a nine-month intensive schedule of training and tournament play. Finally, the figure skating program allows serious skaters access to daily ice times and exemplary coaching. Athletics are also offered on both interscholastic and intramural levels. The interscholastic sports include baseball, basketball, fencing, figure skating, golf, hockey, lacrosse, soccer, softball, tennis, track, and volleyball. Intramural sports focus on the individual student's recreational interests. Aerobics, biking, body conditioning, cross-country skiing, and hiking are available.

Facilities include two gymnasiums, eight tennis courts, an indoor ice arena, an all-weather outdoor track, a baseball field, three soccer fields, and an eighteen-hole golf course. A newly developed sports complex includes a second sheet of ice and a domed indoor field house for winter field sports.

EXTRACURRICULAR OPPORTUNITIES

Some fifteen clubs and organizations are supported by the School and provide opportunities for leadership, creativity, and interaction. The School hosts a full calendar of competitive sports, movies, plays, guest speakers, dances, socials, musical programs, and other cultural activities.

DAILY LIFE

Breakfast is served from 7 to 8 a.m., followed by classes from 8 until 3:30. There is a 40-minute break for a sit-down lunch, which students and teachers attend together. All teachers set aside specific times for conferences and extra help. Intramural and interscholastic athletics take place between 4 and 7:30, while drama rehearsals are held from 6 to 8. Dinner is at 5:45 and is followed by a free period until 7:30. Evening study hall, from 7:30 to 9:30, is required of all students. Lights-out and in-dorm times vary by grade.

WEEKEND LIFE

Two Student Activities Coordinators, assisted by a student committee, arrange on-campus movies, dances, and theatrical and musical performances as well as many weekend excursions. In the winter, chaperoned ski trips are frequently arranged. Special on-campus weekends are Fall Family Weekend, Winter Carnival, and Commencement. Students are allowed to go downtown during weekends. In addition, frequent chaperoned trips to Minneapolis/St. Paul expose students to theater, musicals, ballet, modern dance, sporting events, and concerts of all types.

COSTS AND FINANCIAL AID

In 2005–06, tuition for boarding students was $29,900 and covered instruction, room, board, and a notebook computer. Day-student tuition was $19,600. Tuition may be paid all at once, or a family may choose a monthly payment plan. Incidental expenses usually run from $1000 to $1500, books from $300 to $400. Each student is expected to maintain an incidental account for personal needs.

Shattuck–St. Mary's offers need-based financial aid to qualified families. All financial aid grants are based on the guidelines and principles established by the School and Student Service for Financial Aid. The School encourages all families who need tuition assistance to apply for financial aid. In 2005–06, almost 50 percent of the student body qualified for financial aid, with grants totaling just over $1 million.

The Headmaster's Scholarship Program awards scholarships to new students with outstanding academic ability and a potential for contributing to the school community in other areas, such as athletics, art, music, drama, and student government.

The Visual and Performing Arts Scholarship program awards scholarships worth up to $5000 to new students who excel in visual arts, dance, theater arts, or music. The scholarship competition is open to students entering grades 6–11. Auditions are held on campus or can be submitted on VHS or DVD.

ADMISSIONS INFORMATION

Shattuck–St. Mary's seeks students of above-average ability who are willing to take full advantage of the School's demanding academic program and broad range of extracurricular activities. The School admits qualified students without regard to race, color, or national or ethnic origin. A personal interview on campus is desirable, but a phone interview may be arranged if it is impossible for the applicant to visit the School. Previous school records, the results of the Secondary School Admission Test or other comparable tests, and recommendations are required of all candidates.

APPLICATION TIMETABLE

Admission decisions are made on a rolling basis after January 15. Interested candidates are urged to begin the application process at the earliest possible date. Inquiries may be made at any time. There is a $50 application fee ($100 for international students).

ADMISSIONS CORRESPONDENCE

Admissions Office
Shattuck–St. Mary's School
1000 Shumway Avenue
Faribault, Minnesota 55021
Phone: 507-333-1618
        800-421-2724 (toll-free)
Fax: 507-333-1661
E-mail: admissions@s-sm.org
Web site: http://www.s-sm.org

THE SHIPLEY SCHOOL

Bryn Mawr, Pennsylvania

Type: Coeducational day college-preparatory school
Grades: P–12: Lower School, Prekindergarten–5; Middle School, 6–8; Upper School, 9–12
Enrollment: School total: 856; Upper School: 334
Head of School: Dr. Steven Piltch

THE SCHOOL

The Shipley School was founded in 1894 by the Misses Hannah, Elizabeth, and Katherine Shipley to prepare girls for Bryn Mawr College. Boys were first enrolled in 1972. The School now has 856 students (441 boys and 415 girls).

The Upper and Lower Schools are located on landscaped campuses (36 acres) one block apart near the SEPTA Railroad station and directly opposite the Bryn Mawr College campus. A suburban community 12 miles west of Philadelphia, Bryn Mawr is 90 miles from New York City and 140 miles from Washington, D.C.

While Shipley places the greatest emphasis on education of the mind, it is also concerned with the moral and emotional needs of its students and is dedicated to developing in each one a love of learning and a compassionate participation in the world. Through a strong college-preparatory curriculum in the humanities and sciences, the School encourages curiosity, creativity, and respect for intellectual effort. Shipley upholds and promotes moral integrity, a sense of personal achievement and worth, and concern for others at school and in the larger community.

A nonprofit institution, Shipley is governed by a 35-member Board of Trustees, which consists of 15 men and 20 women. An active Alumni Association represents the more than 5,000 living graduates.

The School plant is valued at $60.4 million. The School endowment is estimated at $14 million.

The Shipley School is accredited by the Pennsylvania Association of Private Academic Schools and the Middle States Association of Colleges and Schools and is a member of the Secondary School Admission Test Board, the National Association of Independent Schools, and the Pennsylvania Association of Independent Schools.

ACADEMIC PROGRAMS

To graduate, a student must complete at least 16 credits in grades 9–12, including 4 years of English; 3 years of mathematics, including algebra II; 3 years of a foreign language; 2 years of history, including U.S. history; 2 years of science; and 1 year of computer science. Most graduates have many more credits than the minimum. Students in grade 9 are required to take art and music. All Upper School students must also take a seminar in health and perform 40 hours of community service.

Yearlong courses include computer science, English, French, history, Latin, mathematics, music, philosophy, science, Spanish, and studio art. Advanced Placement–level courses are available in English, studio art, history of art, U.S. history, modern European history, Latin, French language, Spanish language, biology, physics B and C, calculus AB, calculus BC, computer

(C++), music theory, and statistics. By special arrangement, seniors may take courses at Bryn Mawr College. Electives include Chinese/Japanese history, Russia and Contemporary Europe, and American Studies.

The school year is divided into semesters, and most students carry five subjects per term. Most classes are homogeneously grouped, particularly mathematics and foreign languages. There are 15 or 16 students in an average class. Students in grades 9–10 attend supervised study halls during free periods. The overall student-teacher ratio is 8:1.

Grades are discussed with the student by his or her academic adviser and then sent to parents four times a year. Reports have letter grades with comments written by individual faculty members. Extra help is often available from faculty members.

Independent service projects are required of seniors after the completion of the Advanced Placement exams in mid-May.

During spring and summer vacations, various departments offer study-travel trips, some with homestays. In the past few years, students have traveled to France, Panama, and Italy. "City Term" in New York City and the Island School are open to upperclassmen.

FACULTY AND ADVISERS

The Upper School faculty consists of 50 teachers (44 full-time and 6 part-time), including 22 men and 28 women. Six administrators who teach are part of the faculty as well. Sixty-nine percent of teachers and administrators who teach hold advanced degrees.

The Head of School, Dr. Steven Piltch, was appointed in 1992. A graduate of Williams College, Dr. Piltch has received two master's degrees in education from Harvard University, one in counseling and consulting psychology and the other in secondary and middle school administration. In 1991, he received a Doctor of Education degree from Harvard in administration, planning, and social policy.

All members of the faculty and administration are active in advising and counseling students. Many of them coach. With funds generated by a foundation and the School, faculty members are encouraged to continue their education during summer vacation.

Two nurses are on duty at the health centers, a physician is on call, and 3 consultants are at the School several days per week.

COLLEGE PLACEMENT

Three college guidance counselors and an assistant help students beginning in the eleventh grade and work with them individually throughout the process of college selection. The counselors also meet once a week with small groups of their advisees during both their junior and senior

years. College admissions officers from across the country come to the School each fall to conduct interviews, and students are assisted in making plans to visit colleges themselves. Virtually all graduates attend four-year colleges and universities. A representative list of institutions attended includes Amherst, Bates, Brown, Bucknell, Carnegie Mellon, Columbia, Cornell, Dickinson, Drexel, Duke, Franklin and Marshall, George Washington, Harvard, Middlebury, Mount Holyoke, Northwestern, Princeton, Swarthmore, Syracuse, Trinity (Connecticut), Tufts, Wesleyan, Williams, Yale, and the Universities of Michigan, Pennsylvania, Vermont, and Virginia.

STUDENT BODY AND CONDUCT

In grades 9 through 12, there are 334 students. In these grades, there are 167 boys and 167 girls.

Students come from fifty-five towns and cities in the greater Philadelphia area. Members of minority groups represent 11 percent of the total enrollment.

The Shipley School Government consists of the Executive Council, which discusses and implements decisions, and the Judicial Board, which handles all serious disciplinary matters. In addition, there is an Athletic Association, an Arts Association, and a Students' Organization for Service.

ACADEMIC FACILITIES

Two wings of the main Upper School building house classrooms, the Snyder Science Center (opened in 1995), art studios, music rooms, the library, the gymnasium, and renovated computer facilities, college counseling offices, and student and faculty lounges. Administrative offices, the dining rooms (renovated in 1998), and the kitchen are also housed in the main building. The new Lower School opened in 2001; a gym was added in 2002.

ATHLETICS

All students are members of the Athletic Association and participate in the Blue-Green intramural games. Vital to the successful development of the whole student is the belief that important physical, social, and moral values are learned through the experience of team sports and a rigorous physical education program. Cross-country, crew, field hockey, soccer, lacrosse, tennis, baseball, golf, and softball are the fall and spring varsity activities. In winter, basketball, volleyball, swimming, and squash are options. Games are scheduled with schools in suburban Philadelphia.

The Yarnall Gymnasium has two basketball courts with stands; the same area converts easily for volleyball, badminton, gymnastics, and indoor tennis. On the lower level, there are coaches' offices, locker rooms, and a fitness

center. Some games and practices also take place in the new Lower School Gym.

The Fuller fields include a separate soccer field and a hockey field, adjacent to six tennis courts. Three additional athletics fields, 2 miles away, are reached by bus. One of these fields was added in 1998.

EXTRACURRICULAR OPPORTUNITIES

Shipley offers students a variety of extracurricular activities, such as *The Beacon,* the school newspaper; *Tempora Praeterita,* the yearbook; and *The Compass,* the literary magazine; selective singing groups, the Madrigals and Madriguys, the Upper School Choir, and an All-School Choir; instrumental and jazz ensembles; the School Orchestra; Computer Club; Model UN and Youth in Government; Environmental Awareness; It's Mathematical (an interscholastic math team); jewelry and photography; Students United for Racial Equality (SURE); Amnesty International; SAT Prep; the award-winning horticultural group (the Sprouts); and the Yearbook Committee. Students also volunteer to help the Admissions Office, tutor inner-city children, rehabilitate urban housing, and work in local hospitals and nursing homes through the Students' Organization for Service (SOS). Participation in the community service program is required, including a service project at the end of the senior year.

Annual events include parents' evenings, Parents' Weekend, "Shipley Today" and "Shipley on Saturday" open houses for parents of prospective students, Alumni Day, and annual academic, character, and sports award assemblies. The Social Committee plans many on-campus activities and organizes exchange events with nearby schools. Dances and other social events are scheduled on weekends. In addition, students can be in downtown Philadelphia in 20 minutes where they can attend cultural and recreational events.

DAILY LIFE

Classes are 40 or 80 minutes long and run from 8:30 a.m. to 3:15 p.m. A hot meal and salad bar are available for lunch daily. Prepaid school lunches are required. There are nine academic periods per day. The last 20 minutes of the day are "office hours," when all students are free to meet with teachers individually.

SUMMER PROGRAMS

Summer school runs for six weeks from late June to late July. Classes offered include enrichment and remedial work for credit and recreational activities (athletics and the arts). Enrollment is about 65 students.

Shipley also offers a Summer Enrichment Camp for boys and girls ages 6–14, with a focus on sports and the arts, cooking classes, and sports clinics in soccer, lacrosse, and basketball. A transitional program for urban youth is also cosponsored every summer with the Young Scholars Fund of Philadelphia.

COSTS AND FINANCIAL AID

The 2005–06 tuition for Upper School students ranged from $14,400 to $21,675, depending on the student's grade level. Other expenses (books, lab fees, testing, athletic fees, and trips) are usually less than $500, not including lunches. Tuition insurance and a tuition payment plan are offered.

Approximately 20 percent of students receive financial aid. Grants are made possible through the generosity of certain foundations, endowment income, and the Annual Giving campaign. Grants are based on financial need and are determined by procedures established by the School and Student Service for Financial Aid. Recipients are chosen for their ability, character, past performance, and promise. Awards range from $1000 to $20,000 and total approximately $2 million per year. All families are expected to contribute to their children's educational expenses. The Centennial Scholarship Exam, given each January, provides endowed scholarships to incoming ninth graders based on need and merit.

ADMISSIONS INFORMATION

Shipley seeks responsible, self-directed students of above-average to superior ability who enjoy learning. New students are admitted at all grade levels. An interview, the School's placement testing, and reports from previous schools are required of all applicants. Students must also submit results of the SSAT, the ISEE, or the Wechsler Intelligence Scale for Children (WISC–IV). For entrance in the 2005–06 academic year, there were 114 applicants. Of these, 51 were accepted, and 30 new students enrolled in the following grades: grade 9, 22; grade 10, 4; and grade 11, 4.

APPLICATION TIMETABLE

The Admissions Office is open year-round. Campus interviews and tours are possible throughout the week during the school year from 8:30 a.m. to 4:30 p.m.

While there is no closing date for application, candidates are encouraged to submit a formal application during the fall of the year before prospective enrollment. To be considered in the first round of decisions, applications must be completed by January 15 for entrance the following September. The application fee is $50. A student should then register for the next available SSAT or ISEE or arrange to take the WISC–IV with an accredited tester. Transcripts and recommendations should be secured after the first marking period and mailed to the Director of Admissions. The first acceptances are announced in early February.

After February 1, the Shipley School works on a rolling admissions system whereby admissions decisions are announced when all necessary information has been compiled and reviewed by the Admissions Committee. Parents are expected to reply to an offer of admission within two weeks of notification. An applicant who is waiting to hear from other schools with later acceptance dates should inform the Admissions Office of the situation.

ADMISSIONS CORRESPONDENCE

Gregory W. Coleman, Director of Admissions
The Shipley School
814 Yarrow Street
Bryn Mawr, Pennsylvania 19010-3598

Phone: 610-525-4300 Ext. 4118
Fax: 610-525-5082
E-mail: admit@shipleyschool.org
Web site: http://www.shipleyschool.org

SHORECREST PREPARATORY SCHOOL

St. Petersburg, Florida

Type: Coeducational day college-preparatory school
Grades: P–12: Lower Division, Early Childhood–4; Middle Division, 5–8; Upper Division, 9–12
Enrollment: School total: 980; Upper Division: 234; Middle Division: 305; Lower Division: 441
Head of School: Michael A. Murphy

THE SCHOOL

Shorecrest Preparatory School, the oldest independent day school in Florida, was founded in 1923 as a coeducational proprietary school. Situated on 28 tree-shaded acres in northeast St. Petersburg, Shorecrest attracts academically able students from the Tampa Bay area. Originally founded to meet the educational needs of winter visitors from the North, the School was expanded in the 1940s and 1950s to offer an education of high quality to the growing number of permanent residents. In 1973, the Upper Division was added, and in 1975 Shorecrest became a not-for-profit independent institution. The Shorecrest curriculum extends from the Early Childhood Program, which enrolls 3- and 4-year-olds, to grade 12. In the upper grades, the curriculum is designed to meet the many needs of college-bound students.

Shorecrest has a child-centered approach to education, reflecting the belief that teachers and administrators should work with understanding and patience toward the fullest development of each child. The School's philosophy is that the educational development of each student is a joint venture in which the student, faculty members, and parents share responsibility. Parents are encouraged and expected to share any concerns they might have regarding their child's education with his or her teachers. The learning environment at the School is challenging yet nurturing. Students are expected to meet high standards so that they can experience the satisfaction of academic accomplishment. The School community is supportive, united by a common respect for the contributions and rights of each student and each teacher. Administrators and faculty members work together to strengthen the student's sense of self-respect and respect for others. New students are impressed by the friendliness that pervades Shorecrest and find that they become assimilated into the student body quickly and easily.

The School is governed by a board of 25 trustees who are elected by the current board to serve on a rotating basis. Alumni participate in many key operations of the School community, including service activities and development.

Shorecrest is accredited by the Southern Association of Colleges and Schools, the Florida Council of Independent Schools, the Florida Kindergarten Council, and the National Academy of Early Childhood Programs. It is a member of the College Board, the Cum Laude Society, the School and Student Service for Financial Aid, the National Association of Independent Schools, the Southern Association of Independent Schools, the Bay Area Association of Independent Schools, the Secondary School Admission Test Board, the Educational Records Bureau, and the Florida High School Activities Association.

ACADEMIC PROGRAMS

Academics are the core of the Shorecrest Preparatory School experience, and the School has a traditional college-preparatory curriculum. Students are expected to demonstrate competence in literature, writing, foreign language, history, mathematics, science, and the arts. The School has committed substantial resources to the creation of state-of-the-art technology facilities. Through its integration in the curriculum, experience in the use of technology is available to all students.

The Early Childhood Center (for 3- and 4-year-olds) uses an integrated, experiential approach to learning. Hands-on, developmentally appropriate activities promote growth in social, emotional, fine and gross motor, and cognitive development.

The kindergarten through grade 4 program emphasizes the development of a well-balanced student. The integrated reading–language arts curriculum stresses oral and written communication, reading comprehension, and vocabulary development. The mathematics curriculum focuses on developing an understanding of mathematical concepts and number sense, providing opportunities to apply higher-level critical-thinking and problem-solving skills. Science and social studies offer concrete experiences through discovery and investigation. Classroom computers, along with access to a full computer lab, enable technology to become a vehicle for enhancing all curriculum areas. Spanish, art, music, and physical education enrich the K–4 education.

The Middle Division years (grades 5 through 8) are a period of transition when academic, social, and emotional development occurs. A rigorous academic curriculum emphasizes literature, writing, higher-level mathematics, science, and social studies. Foreign language, physical education, and an arts requirement complement the curriculum. Technology is emphasized at every grade level. Personal and academic counseling are an integral part of the program.

At the secondary level, the curriculum is designed to meet—and often exceed—the course requirements for admission to the most competitive colleges and universities. For graduation, students are required to complete a minimum of 4 years each of English and mathematics; 3 years each of a foreign language, history, and science; and 1 year each of physical education and fine arts. Honors courses are offered in algebra, geometry, precalculus, calculus, biology, chemistry, English, French, Spanish, and political science. For academically able students who wish to take Advanced Placement (AP) examinations to qualify for college credit, courses are offered in English, French, Spanish, calculus, biology, chemistry, physics, computer science, U.S. history, European history, world history, economics, psychology, art history, audio art, and music

theory. In 2005, 60 students took 150 Advanced Placement exams, and 96 percent earned college-level credit based on their scores.

FACULTY AND ADVISERS

The 2005–06 Shorecrest faculty numbered 107 members. While all of the faculty members are college graduates, more than half hold master's degrees and 2 hold doctoral degrees.

COLLEGE PLACEMENT

A full-time college counselor begins guiding students in the college selection process during the junior year. Numerous individual conferences are supplemented by such events as the College Symposium, which offers panel discussions with college admission officers and workshops. Many college representatives visit the Shorecrest Preparatory campus to meet with juniors and seniors individually and in groups.

All graduates enroll in a college or university. Recent graduates have matriculated at the following institutions, among others: Amherst, Colgate, Columbia, Connecticut College, Cornell, Duke, Emory, Florida State, Georgetown, Julliard, Lehigh, Northwestern, Notre Dame, Princeton, Tufts, Tulane, the U.S. Naval Academy, Vanderbilt, Vassar, Wake Forest, Washington and Lee, William and Mary, Yale, and the Universities of Florida, Miami (Florida), and Pennsylvania.

STUDENT BODY AND CONDUCT

For the 2005–06 school year, there were 234 Upper Division students: 123 boys and 111 girls. The student body represents a diversity of ethnic and economic backgrounds.

The School fosters a sense of community among students, faculty members, and parents. School rules and regulations are set forth in the *Student/Parent Handbook* and stress the importance of the partnership between the School and the parents. Students are expected to conduct themselves in a way that promotes self-respect, tolerance of others' differences, and a sense of responsibility for the greater school community. Character education is an integral part of the Shorecrest curriculum throughout all grade levels. Believing that an education is not complete without opportunities to serve others, the School offers a broad range of community service experiences, such as opportunities to work with young children, the elderly, the homeless, and the disabled.

ACADEMIC FACILITIES

Academic facilities include sixty-five classrooms, three science labs, twelve computer labs, three language labs, and an early childhood center. The Sci-Tech Center houses biology, chemistry, and physics laboratories and two fully equipped computer classrooms. A 615-seat, state-of-the-art

theater, a gymnasium, a student center, and a newly constructed Library Media Center are shared by the Upper, Middle, and Lower Divisions.

ATHLETICS

Physical education classes emphasize the importance of physical fitness, the improvement of basic skills, and the development of self-esteem, sportsmanship, and a sense of team spirit. In addition, all students take a required health class.

The School has a varied and competitive athletics program. Boys may choose from football, cross-country, swimming, basketball, soccer, golf, tennis, track, and baseball. Girls compete in volleyball, cross-country, swimming, basketball, soccer, softball, track, golf, tennis, and cheerleading. The School is proud of its record of achievement in winning district and state championships. Since 1986, Shorecrest has been ranked in the top five among the 165 Florida schools in the I-A competitive division by the Florida Athletic Coaches Association for the overall quality of its athletics programs. In addition, Shorecrest has won the Class 2A Sportsmanship Award for the state of Florida several times.

Sports facilities include a football–soccer field with stands and lights, a practice field, indoor and outdoor basketball courts, a baseball diamond, a softball diamond, two weight rooms, and an eight-lane, all-weather track. The swim team uses the North Shore Pool, the tennis team plays at The Racquet Club, and the golf team plays at Feather Sound Country Club.

EXTRACURRICULAR OPPORTUNITIES

A wide variety of cocurricular and extracurricular activities are designed to match the varied interests of the students.

The Student Council provides a forum for the discussion of all issues concerning school government and serves as the liaison between the student body and the administration. The council, which meets weekly, also plans and sponsors numerous special social, recreational, and educational events throughout the year.

Shorecrest students are encouraged to devote time to community activities in the expectation that they will become civic-minded and public-spirited citizens. The Junior Exchange Club, Interact, SADD, and the Key Club provide opportunities for service in school, community, and international projects.

Numerous academic honor societies and clubs give students the opportunity—through field trips, special projects, and contests—to extend their interest beyond the classroom.

Shorecrest is especially proud of its student publications: *Crestviews,* the yearbook; and *The Chronicle,* the newspaper, which has won the Florida Scholastic Press Association's First Place Award for student journalism, an award for excellence from the Southern Interscholastic Press Association, and a Medalist Award from Columbia University. Shorecrest students have the professional assistance of the Poynter Institute and use the Institute's facilities in the production of the newspaper. Students who work on these publications are eligible for election into Quill and Scroll, an international honor society for high school journalists.

Shorecrest presents a fall play and a spring musical production each year. All students are invited to participate. Students with a particular interest in drama may be elected to membership in the Thespian Society.

Shorecrest also has chapters of the National Honor Society and Cum Laude Society.

DAILY LIFE

School hours are from 7:45 to 3:05. There are eight academic periods, a lunch period, and an activity period at the end of the day.

Assemblies and productions of a cultural, educational, or recreational nature are held periodically during the school year in order to broaden the students' educational experience. Students attend plays and concerts in St. Petersburg, Clearwater, and Tampa, and field trips are made to art museums and other places of interest.

COSTS AND FINANCIAL AID

The tuition for the Upper Division for the 2005–06 session was $14,190. Payment may be made monthly or in one or two payments. The cost of books and other fees increases the total by approximately $500.

A total of $350,000 is available for financial aid. Awards are made in accordance with principles established by the School and Student Service for Financial Aid. The Dewar Tuition Refund Plan is available to parents who want tuition payment insurance.

ADMISSIONS INFORMATION

Admissions decisions for grades 7 through 12 are based on previous academic records, teacher recommendations from the current school, standardized test scores, a personal interview, and results of an admissions test. Candidates should also submit a graded writing sample. In making decisions, the Admissions Committee places priority on the applicant's ability to successfully meet the academic expectations of the School's demanding college-preparatory curriculum. From among those who meet these criteria, the committee endeavors to choose those students who benefit most from attending Shorecrest and who will contribute most to making the School an interesting, enjoyable, and productive community. Shorecrest strives to be an inclusive society, and students are admitted without regard to race, creed, or national origin.

APPLICATION TIMETABLE

Applications are received and processed at any time of the year, but candidates are advised to submit their application by mid-January to ensure consideration for the limited number of places available for the following session. Prospective students may schedule visits to the campus at their convenience, and they are encouraged to spend an entire day at Shorecrest, visiting in appropriate classes and becoming acquainted with students.

ADMISSIONS CORRESPONDENCE

Diana Craig, Director of Admissions
Shorecrest Preparatory School
5101 First Street, NE
St. Petersburg, Florida 33703-3099

Phone: 727-522-2111
Fax: 727-527-4191
E-mail: admissions@shorecrest.org
Web site: http://www.shorecrest.org

SOLEBURY SCHOOL
New Hope, Pennsylvania

Type: Coeducational boarding and day college-preparatory school
Grades: 7–PG: Middle School, 7–8; Upper School, 9–12, postgraduate year
Enrollment: School total: 222; Upper School: 195
Head of School: John D. Brown, Head of School

THE SCHOOL

Solebury School was founded in 1925 by 4 teachers whose shared vision was to create an environment that would foster good learning relationships, in which there would be a close connection between teachers and pupils, in which there would be a respectful exchange of opinions and ideas, and in which the student would be well prepared for both college and their real-world responsibilities and pursuits. This dream of the Solebury's founders, Laurie Erskine, Julian Lathrop, Robert Shaw, and Arthur Washburn, has been realized; to this day Solebury continues to maintain a challenging academic curriculum that is balanced with the informal interaction of students and teachers.

The primary goal of Solebury is to provide a challenging college-preparatory curriculum that encourages students to explore and develop their academic, artistic, and athletic interests. Thoughtful attention to broadening social awareness and further development of personal responsibilities underlies the exploration in each of these areas.

The School is located in beautiful Bucks County, Pennsylvania, enjoying a rural setting on an eighteenth-century farm of more than 90 acres not far from the banks of the Delaware River. It is 65 miles from New York City and 35 miles from Philadelphia.

Solebury is a nonprofit school and is directed by a board of 26 trustees that includes 16 alumni.

Solebury School is accredited by the Middle States Association of Colleges and Schools. It is a member of the National Association of Independent Schools, Pennsylvania Association of Independent Schools, the Association of Boarding Schools, the Independent School Teachers' Association, Secondary School Admission Test Board, School and Student Services for Financial Aid, National Association of Foreign Student Advisors, and Advancement for Delaware Valley Independent Schools.

ACADEMIC PROGRAMS

Students at Solebury are required to carry a minimum academic load of 9 credits per trimester. At least 109 credits are required for graduation, including 24 credits in English, 18 in a foreign language, 18 in mathematics, 12 in science (including conceptual physics and biology), 12 in social science (including U.S. history), 6 in the arts (two full years), 1 in computer science, 1 in health, electives, 10 hours each year of community service, and three trimesters each year of a sport or activity.

About 100 lively electives are offered, as well as opportunity for independent study. These exciting courses are presented throughout all the disciplines: English, math, science, social studies, languages, arts, and English as a second language (ESL). Included in these electives are Advanced Placement and honors courses. Typical of some of these unique options are Environmental Science Fiction, Latin American Literature, the King Arthur Legends, Pilgrimage Literature: Road Trip and Nature, Line Designs, Human Anatomy and Physiology, Forensics, Gender and Society, Bioethics: Cures or Curses?, the Arab World and the West, and the Cuban Revolution: A Look at Fidel Castro's Communism.

Middle School courses preparing students for high school work in the disciplines include English, foreign language: Spanish and French 1A and 1B, pre-algebra, social studies, science, and introduction to the arts. Middle School students who qualify may take advanced courses in math, foreign language, and the arts.

In addition to local fields trips throughout the year, there are a variety of unique experiences for students to participate in during the longer school breaks, including tours of Italy, Quebec, and Costa Rica. Each year, teachers have the opportunity to design new trips, depending upon interest and availability.

Solebury's curriculum each year is highlighted by an academic theme intended to give teachers and students common experiences and to promote interdisciplinary learning. This year, the theme is environment.

Class size averages 11 students. Independent study is available for especially well motivated students, and credit can be earned for special projects. Annual senior projects focus on areas of special interest and may include apprenticeships with craftsmen, community service groups, or businesses and other organizations.

A Learning Skills Program assists 23 students who have learning differences in the basic language areas. This program is for students who possess average to above-average intelligence and need to strengthen their reading, writing, and language-related skills. Classes use multisensory Orton and Wilson models to teach phonological processing. Students also work on organization, study skills, and oral communication.

For international students, English as a second language (ESL) programs are offered during the full year, spring trimester, and summer. With small classes of 8 students, Solebury's goal is to help students develop their speaking, listening, reading, and writing skills. Classes are also offered to prepare students for the TOEFL, and the School assists them individually in college advising and placement. Solebury's main objective is to prepare students for entrance into American colleges or universities with little or no ESL support.

Solebury has three academic trimesters. Comprehensive grade reports with teacher comments are sent to parents three times per year.

FACULTY AND ADVISERS

John D. Brown was appointed Head of School in 1989. Mr. Brown is a 1967 graduate of Solebury. He was a member of the faculty from 1971 to 1980 and a member of the Board of Trustees for three years before becoming Head of School. He holds a bachelor's degree in history from Beloit College and a master's degree in educational administration from Bank Street College of Education.

There are 53 teachers and administrators on Solebury's staff, 20 of whom hold advanced degrees. Twenty-nine faculty members and administrators reside on campus, and all faculty and staff members are involved in the life of the community beyond the classroom.

The adviser system is an essential part of the life of the School, nurturing an informal relationship between teachers and students that supplements the roles filled by each in the classroom. Advisers meet weekly with their students and are the personal contacts for parents when they have questions or concerns about their child's progress. Although each new

student is assigned an adviser temporarily, all students select their own advisers.

COLLEGE PLACEMENT

The Director of College Counseling, administrators, and the faculty advisers for juniors and seniors support each student in the college-search process. Computer-assisted research, career information, and a college catalog library are maintained for student use. In addition, college representatives visit the Solebury campus yearly to speak to interested students. To assist students and parents with the completion of applications, essays, and financial aid forms, the College Counselor encourages meetings with both students and parents throughout the year. Current students are also invited to meet with recent graduates as they share their college experiences. It is recommended that sophomores and juniors take the PSATs, and juniors and seniors the SATs, and international students the TOEFL. Preparation for these tests is offered in-house through workshops and classes.

Forty-two seniors were graduated in June 2005. Graduates were admitted to a wide range of schools, including Babson, Bard, Brandeis, Bryn Mawr, Cornell, College of Wooster, Dickinson, Franklin & Marshall, George Washington, Lehigh, Northwestern, Oberlin, Skidmore, Syracuse, Ursinus, Vassar, and Washington (St. Louis).

STUDENT BODY AND CONDUCT

Of the 222 students in grades 7–PG in 2005–06, the breakdown was as follows: 35 boarding boys, 27 boarding girls, 87 day boys, and 73 day girls. There were 12 students in grade 7, 15 in grade 8, 49 in grade 9, 43 in grade 10, 49 in grade 11, 52 in grade 12, and 2 postgraduates. Students came from Pennsylvania, New Jersey, and seven other states as well as Brazil, Croatia, Germany, Hong Kong, Japan, Korea, Spain, and Taiwan.

The community sets reasonable limits for its members. The students participate with the faculty members in many areas of decision making. Students are represented on the Judiciary Committee, which makes recommendations on all serious matters of discipline. Students are also represented on the Academic Committee and the Community Council.

ACADEMIC FACILITIES

The $3-million Abbe Science Center, which opened in 2002, includes four state-of-the-art science labs, four math classrooms, and a greenhouse. The Penney International Center, opened in 2003, has five classrooms and a study lounge with eight computer stations, and a computerized active board. The Founders' Library and Art Center facilities include studios for painting, drawing, ceramics, and graphics and a darkroom for photography, which includes six enlarger stations. The library contains 13,000 items and is a member of Access Pennsylvania and P.O.W.E.R. and subscribes to ProQuest and SIRS Knowledge Source, among others. Also available is netTrekker d.i. The library, together with the adjacent multimedia room, is an integral part of reference and research orientation for students and is equipped with a large-screen video projection system, video-audio editing equipment, and computers for student use. The campus network has direct high-speed Internet access through a T-1 line, and all

classrooms and dormitory rooms are wired. There are 146 computers campuswide. The student-computer ratio is 2:1.

Classrooms for English, social studies, foreign language, and the Learning Skills Program are located in a number of other buildings on the campus.

BOARDING AND GENERAL FACILITIES

Boarding is offered to students in grades 9 through 12 and one postgraduate year. Returning students select their roommates, while new students are assigned roommates through a carefully designed questionnaire. Holmquist House, the girls' twenty-eight-bed dormitory, houses 2 girls to a room and is supervised by 2 dormitory parents. Walter Lamb Hall, the boys' thirty-six-bed dormitory, includes two-bedroom suites and baths for 4 boys and is supervised by 4 dorm parents. The School nurse is an RN and pediatric nurse practitioner. The School uses the local services of the Phillips Barber Health Center in Lambertville, New Jersey, when students need to see a physician.

Other buildings include the Farm House for administration and Boyd Dining Hall, where meals are served cafeteria-style to students, faculty members, and faculty families. The Carriage House houses offices, the music room, and the infirmary. The refurbished barn contains a 100-seat black box theater, a lounge and lockers for day students, a student café and recreation room, and offices for the deans. The Alumni Memorial Gymnasium includes a weight-training room and locker rooms. Six new faculty homes were completed in 2002. A new gym, track, and field are being planned to open spring 2007. Proposed renovations to the performing arts center are planned to open spring 2008, and proposed renovations to the student center are scheduled to open fall 2008.

ATHLETICS

At Solebury, everyone is required to participate in some form of exercise: team sports or activities. On-campus facilities include a gymnasium and a weight room, three playing fields, four tennis courts, an outdoor swimming pool, and a cross-country course. In addition, the School has the use of local stables that are 1½ miles from the campus.

Interscholastic programs are available for boys in baseball, basketball, cross-country, soccer, tennis, and track and for girls in basketball, cross-country, field hockey, lacrosse, tennis, track, soccer, and softball. In addition to competitive sports, Solebury offers aerobics, biking, dance, golf, horseback riding, rock climbing, a ski club, tae kwon do, walking club, weight training, wrestling, yoga, and a variety of recreational sports, according to the interests of the students.

EXTRACURRICULAR OPPORTUNITIES

A calendar listing the various activities is posted. Solebury's proximity to New York, Philadelphia, and Princeton allows for day trips to sports events, concerts, Broadway plays, and museums. Plays, dances, films, festivals, concerts, and the Annual Creative Thinkers Series are scheduled on campus. An eight-day Annual Arts Festival is a major highlight each spring.

Groups and activities of special interest are organized by students and teachers and have included publishing a School yearbook (*Enthymion*), School newspaper (*The Scribe*), and literary magazine (*SLAM*); singing in the chorus; and participating in the video club and the theater tech club. Other interests include conversation partners, the environmental club, AIDS Awareness Group, Diversity Club, and Amnesty International.

Solebury asks that its high school students participate in 10 hours of community service yearly as a graduation requirement. Middle School students are required to complete 5 hours per year. Many opportunities, local and international, are available.

Students have many opportunities to become involved in leadership positions in the community. Certain elected and appointed positions, including Community Council, dormitory proctors, judiciary committee reps, academic committee reps, peer leading, peer tutoring, and Sherpa (the admission tour guides), carry a formal commitment to the School's well-being.

DAILY LIFE

The academic day starts at 8 a.m. and continues until 3:30 p.m. Once a week, students have work jobs for 20 minutes. Conference time is available on Tuesdays from 12:55 to 1:25 p.m. In addition, teachers post additional office hours for conferences on other days each week. Breakfast is from 7 to 7:45, lunch is from 11:30 to 12:50, and dinner is from 5:45 to 6:15. Sports and activities are from 3:30 to 5:30, three days a week for noncompetitive sports and five days a week for competitive sports. On Sunday through Thursday, there is a required supervised evening study hall from 7:15 to 9; students who meet special criteria are entitled to study in their dormitories. Students must be in their dorms by 10:30, with lights out by 11. Seniors can have lights out at midnight.

WEEKEND LIFE

Both boarding and day students are welcome to participate in weekend activities. Activities are planned by the faculty members on duty and the students. Off-campus trips to New York City, Philadelphia, and Baltimore's Inner Harbor are offered. The New Hope area is also full of many recreational opportunities. Students often go into town or to nearby malls to shop and see movies. On-campus activities include School-sponsored dances and coffeehouses. Bonfires, roller skating, and evening games are just a few of the activities offered as well as the diversity movie series. Boarding students who have parental permission may visit day students' homes on the weekends. A shuttle is available to and from the train station in Trenton, New Jersey, on Fridays and Sundays.

SUMMER PROGRAMS

Solebury offers a summer day camp for younger children. Basketball and soccer programs and a swim club are offered for all ages. An ESL program is offered for six weeks in July and August. Brochures for programs may be obtained by writing the School.

COSTS AND FINANCIAL AID

Tuition for the 2005–06 school year was $31,200 for boarding students and $20,700 for day students. Middle School day students paid $19,300. Additional tuition for the Learning Skills Program was $8600. The additional fee for English as a second language was $8000. Additional costs are a $50 application fee ($100 for international students) and a $600 deposit for incidental expenses, which include books, school supplies, certain laboratory and art supplies, and medical expenses. Within two weeks of a student's acceptance to the full-year program, an advance deposit of 10 percent of the net annual fee must accompany the enrollment contract to reserve a place in the School. The ESL Spring Program was $14,500 and the ESL Summer Program was $6950.

Solebury has always had a generous scholarship program. Offered annually are the Trustees' Merit Scholarships: $9000 for boarding students and $6000 for day students. For 2005–06, 34 percent of the students received partial aid that totaled $1,134,000. Awards are based on financial need as determined by the School and Student Service for Financial Aid.

ADMISSIONS INFORMATION

Admission decisions are based on the candidate's potential for academic success at Solebury as well as his or her possible contributions to the School community. These characteristics are identified by a personal interview, transcripts from previous schools, and recommendations. Admission to Solebury School is open to all qualified candidates, without regard to race, sex, or national or ethnic origin.

APPLICATION TIMETABLE

Inquiries are always welcome. Candidates are strongly encouraged to visit the School for a tour and interview. The Admission Office is open Monday through Friday. Candidates who apply before January 15 are notified the week of March 10. Applications should be submitted before January 15, but those submitted after that time are considered if vacancies exist.

ADMISSIONS CORRESPONDENCE

Director of Admission
Solebury School
Phillips Mill Road
P.O. Box 429
New Hope, Pennsylvania 18938

Phone: 215-862-5261
Fax: 215-862-3366
E-mail: admissions@solebury.org
Web site: http://www.solebury.org

SOUNDVIEW PREPARATORY SCHOOL

Mount Kisco, New York

Type: Coeducational day college-preparatory school
Grades: Middle School, 6–8; Upper School, 9–12
Enrollment: Total, 80; Middle School, 20; Upper School, 60
Head of School: W. Glyn Hearn, Headmaster

THE SCHOOL

Soundview Preparatory School, a coeducational, college-preparatory school for grades 6 through 12, was founded in 1989 on the belief that the best environment for students is one where classes are small, teachers know the learning style and interests of each student, and an atmosphere of mutual trust prevails. At Soundview, students and teachers work in close collaboration in classes with an average size of 7 students.

The School's mission is to provide a college-preparatory education in a supportive and noncompetitive environment that requires rigorous application to academics, instills respect for ethical values, and fosters self-confidence by helping each student feel recognized and valued. At Soundview, students achieve not to outpace others but to reach their own goals, reflecting the School's philosophy that the best way to prepare students to succeed in a competitive world is to offer a setting where competition comes from within.

Soundview Prep opened its doors with 13 students in the spring of 1989. By 1998, the School had outgrown its original quarters in Pocantico Hills and moved to its present site in Mount Kisco. New York City, which is only an hour away, provides a wealth of cultural opportunities for Soundview students to explore on class trips.

The School is governed by an 11-member Board of Trustees. The current operating budget is $2 million, and the endowment stands at $775,000. In 2004–05, Soundview raised more than $205,000 through the Annual Fund and fund-raising events, from parents, alumni families, grandparents, friends, foundations, and corporations.

Soundview is chartered by the New York State Board of Regents and is accredited by the New York State Association of Independent Schools. The School is a member of the Education Records Bureau and the Council for Advancement and Support of Education.

ACADEMIC PROGRAMS

Soundview provides a rigorous academic program to ensure that students not only develop the skills and acquire the knowledge needed for college work but also have the opportunity to pursue their own personal goals.

The academic day is carefully structured but informal, with nurture a crucial ingredient. Soundview's student-teacher ratio of 4:1 guarantees that students are monitored closely and receive the support they need. At the same time, the School provides advanced courses for students who wish to go beyond the high school level or take a subject that is not usually offered, allowing students to soar academically and truly develop their potential.

The Middle School curriculum is designed to establish a foundation of knowledge and skills in each academic discipline, strong comprehension and communication skills, good work habits and study skills, confidence in using technology, and creativity in the arts.

The Upper School curriculum provides a traditional college-preparatory education in academics and the arts. In addition to the core subjects—English, history, math, and science—Soundview offers four languages (Latin, French, Spanish, and Italian), studio art, and electives such as history of philosophy, drama, history of art, history of architecture, psychology, government, economics, creative and expository writing, and a course that is unique to Soundview—New York! New York! (a monthly trip to New York City, where students explore history, architecture, and the arts).

AP courses are made available according to students' abilities and interests. Recently, AP courses have been offered in calculus, biology, physics, English, U.S. history, European history, government, art, French, and Spanish.

Academic requirements for graduation are 4 years each of English and history, 3 years each of math and science, 3 years of one foreign language or 2 years each of two different languages, 1 year of art, and ½ year of health.

Computer technology at Soundview is integrated into the curriculum. Teachers post assignments on the School's Web site, and students upload completed work into teachers' folders. The School is wired for wireless technology and has a well-equipped computer lab.

The language department's annual two-week trips abroad (last year's trip ventured to China, this year's to Greece) offer students experience with other cultures. Upper and Lower School trips to Washington, D.C., and Boston provide hands-on learning in history and government.

Upper School students perform community service at a day-care center, a program for senior citizens, and an after-school homework program.

The school year is divided into two semesters, with letter grades sent out at the end of each. Individual conferences with parents, students, faculty members, and the Headmaster are arranged throughout the year.

Students take the Educational Records Bureau (ERB) standardized tests every year for use by the School in monitoring each student's progress.

FACULTY AND ADVISERS

The faculty consists of 19 teachers, 15 women and 4 men; the majority hold advanced degrees. One teacher is part-time; the rest, full-time. Turnover is low, with an average of two replacements per year.

Each teacher serves as adviser to up to 5 students. Most faculty members supervise a club or publication or coach an athletic team.

W. Glyn Hearn has served as Headmaster since the School was founded in 1989. He obtained his B.A. in English at the University of Texas at Austin and his M.A. in American literature at Texas Tech University. He spent twelve years at the Awty International School of Houston, Texas, where he served as Principal of the Lower, Middle, and Upper Schools and Head of the American Section, before becoming Assistant Headmaster and then Headmaster of the American Renaissance School in Westchester County in 1987.

COLLEGE PLACEMENT

College placement at Soundview is directed by Carol Gill, president of Carol Gill Associates and one of the nation's leading college counseling experts. The process starts early on, when eighth, ninth, and tenth graders plan and refine a course sequence that is appropriate for a competitive college. In the junior year, students and their parents begin meeting with Ms. Gill to discuss the college application process, develop lists of colleges, and plan college visits. The meetings continue through the senior year to complete applications.

Because of the School's small size, the faculty and staff members know each student well and are able to assist students in selecting colleges that are the right match for them. The Headmaster writes a personal recommendation for each senior.

Colleges attended by recent Soundview graduates include Antioch, Bates, Boston Museum School, Brandeis, Carnegie Mellon, Clark, Columbia, Gettysburg, Hamilton, Hampshire, Manhattanville, Muhlenberg, NYU, Oberlin, Sarah Lawrence, Simmons, SUNY, Vassar, and the Universities of Hartford, Oregon, and Vermont.

STUDENT BODY AND CONDUCT

Soundview reflects the diversity—ethnic, religious, and economic—of American society. The 53 boys and 27 girls come from Westchester, Fairfield, Putnam, and Rockland Counties and New York City. Approximately 14 percent of the student body are members of minority groups.

Respect for ethical values such as kindness, honesty, and respect for others are paramount at Soundview, where individual responsibility and a sense of community are stressed.

The School's disciplinary structure is informal, since it is based on the assumption that students attending the School desire to be there and are therefore willing to adhere to a code of conduct that demonstrates awareness that the community is based upon a shared sense of purpose and commitment. Despite the cordiality of its atmosphere, Soundview is quite strict in its

expectations of behavior. The result of this policy is a remarkably cooperative, considerate group of students who value each other and who appreciate their teachers.

Attire appropriate for a school is expected of all students, although there is no formal dress code.

ACADEMIC FACILITIES

Soundview occupies three floors of a building in Mount Kisco, New York. The School has an assembly hall, a 200-seat theater, and twenty classrooms, including a science lab, a computer lab, and two art rooms. Students use the School's patio and garden during lunchtime.

ATHLETICS

Physical education and sports at Soundview offer students the opportunity to develop leadership and teamwork skills as well as to excel in individual sports. Students participate on coed soccer, boys' basketball, girls' basketball, and Ultimate Frisbee teams. Depending upon student interest in a given year, other sports, such as softball and baseball, are also offered. Any student who wishes to play is accepted, regardless of ability.

Golf and ski clubs offer opportunities for noncompetitive sports. In physical education class, students complete the Presidential Physical Fitness Challenge, play intramural sports, and work out on exercise equipment.

Soundview's home gym is the Brewster Sports Center, a 60,000-square-foot, state-of-the-art multisport center on a 10-acre site 20 minutes north of the School. The facility includes a 176-foot by 90-foot indoor soccer field, a regulation outdoor soccer field, three large indoor basketball courts, and exercise equipment.

EXTRACURRICULAR OPPORTUNITIES

Soundview offers a wide range of clubs and activities, with additional choices added each year by students themselves.

Drama is important at Soundview. Students perform at School functions, attend plays on Broadway, and meet backstage with theater professionals. The Language Club sponsors school-wide activities such as Cultural Heritage Week, which features speakers and banquets, and organizes trips at home and an annual trip abroad. The Student Action Club involves itself in human rights, poverty, justice, and the environment; in 2003–04, members raised money to build a school in Pakistan and sponsor a student there. Model UN focuses on political and government issues.

Other activities students are likely to sign up for include yearbook, literary magazine, student newspaper, Film Club, Chess Club, Meditation Club, yoga, ceramics, dance, photography, band, chorus, Ski Club, and Golf Club.

Major annual functions at Soundview include the Back-to-School Picnic; the Book Fair and Holiday Gift Basket Auction; the Winter Gala, a dinner and fund-raiser for the Soundview community; the Talent Show, which involves every student in the School; Texas Day, a lighthearted event featuring spoofs on American history and the Headmaster's home state; and the Graduation Dinner, an evening for Soundview parents to honor the graduating class.

DAILY LIFE

The school day begins at 8:20 a.m. with Morning Meeting, when the entire student body, faculty, and staff assemble to hear announcements about ongoing activities, listen to presentations by clubs, and discuss the day's national and international news. The Headmaster encourages students to express their views and helps them to assess events that are unfolding in the world around them.

Classes begin at 8:40 and end at 3:20 p.m. There are seven academic periods of 50 minutes each, with 50 minutes for lunch.

SUMMER PROGRAMS

Soundview offers a small summer school with classes that vary each year. A typical offering includes English, writing, math, history, a science, and a language. Some 12 to 15 students from Soundview take courses to skip ahead in a given subject or fulfill a requirement.

COSTS AND FINANCIAL AID

Tuition for 2005–06 was $27,900 for Middle School, $28,900 for ninth and tenth grade, $29,450 for eleventh grade, and $29,750 for twelfth grade. Tuition includes gym uniforms, books, literary publications, art and lab fees, and ERB exams.

In 2004–05, the School provided a total of $198,512 in financial aid to 15 percent of the student body.

ADMISSIONS INFORMATION

Soundview operates on a rolling admissions policy, with students accepted throughout the year in all grades except twelfth. Families of prospective students meet with the Admissions Director, after which the student spends a day at the School. The SSAT is not required, but portions of the ERB standardized examination are administered (unless the applicant provides the School with sufficient, current test data).

Students of all backgrounds are welcomed. The academic program is demanding, but the School's small size allows it to work with each individual student in order to develop strategies for success.

APPLICATION TIMETABLE

Soundview accepts applications on a rolling basis throughout the year. The application fee is $50.

ADMISSIONS CORRESPONDENCE

Mary E. Ivanyi
Director of Admissions and Assistant Head
Soundview Preparatory School
272 North Bedford Road
Mount Kisco, New York 10549

Phone: 914-242-9693
Fax: 914-242-9658
E-mail: info@soundviewprep.org
Web site: http://www.soundviewprep.org

SOUTH KENT SCHOOL

South Kent, Connecticut

Type: Boys' boarding college-preparatory school
Grades: 9–12 and PG (Forms III–VI)
Enrollment: 142
Head of School: Andrew J. Vadnais

THE SCHOOL

South Kent School, founded in 1923, offered young men the opportunity to develop their potential in an environment that fostered "simplicity of life, self-reliance, and directness of purpose." Committed to its original goal, the School has proven successful over the years with several types of students. First, South Kent is an excellent school for bright and imaginative students who do well academically. Second, it is a school where a student who is bright but has yet to achieve his academic potential can gain needed focus through a comprehensive study skills program beginning in grade 9. Third, for students who are motivated to learn but have had difficulties in their current school, South Kent offers, through its Student Learning Services Program, the personal attention and guidance that they need to succeed. Finally, South Kent is an excellent choice for all students who recognize the advantages provided by a small boarding school. The prefect, dorm supervisor, and Jobs Programs allow students to develop and apply their potential for leadership. Opportunities to lead are found in every aspect of school life—in the dorms, in the classrooms, in activities, and on the sports fields.

Guided by Christian principles and nurtured by an abiding respect for the worth of each person, South Kent School is a community in which young men are challenged to take responsibility for their lives. They develop, through a variety of activities, a true sense of themselves and their potential.

South Kent School is set on a hillside in the midst of 460 acres of School property. The boys have access to all of this property, which includes miles of trails for running and mountain biking, two ponds for skating and fishing, high open fields, wooded areas, and countless old stone walls. Wildlife is plentiful, and the change of seasons is arresting and inspirational. A maple syrup–making operation in the spring takes advantage of the setting; in other seasons, cider making, pumpkin carving, and the creation of toboggan and snowboard runs do the same.

South Kent's operating expenses for 2004–05 were $5 million. The endowment is currently $4.2 million. Thirty-eight percent of South Kent's alumni participated in last year's annual giving, which amounted to $850,000. A self-perpetuating Board of Trustees, which may not exceed 25 members, governs the School.

South Kent is accredited by the New England Association of Schools and Colleges and holds memberships in the Cum Laude Society, National Association of Independent Schools, National Association of Episcopal Schools, Secondary School Admission Test Board, Connecticut Association of Independent Schools, National Association for College Admission Counseling, and the International Coalition of Boys' Schools.

ACADEMIC PROGRAMS

South Kent is committed to academic excellence, and all of its students pursue postsecondary study. It provides a traditional college-preparatory program and offers Advanced Placement courses. Graduates join the larger world with the tools and

skills to accept life's challenges. In the academic curriculum, South Kent values perseverance, self-awareness, risk taking, goal setting, and self-advocacy. Essential skills instruction and practice begin in Forms III and IV (grades 9 and 10).

South Kent School's Third, Fourth, and Fifth Form Mastery Programs are integrated, interdisciplinary programs that build and reinforce strong academic and community skills, thereby nurturing self-confidence and initiative in the boys. The goal of the lower forms is to produce motivated and inquisitive students equipped to be lifelong learners. Each form program is staffed by a 5-person faculty team. In the Third Form, these faculty members come from the English, history, and science departments; the Fourth Form team combines the disciplines of English, history, and art. Using an inquiry or problem-based approach, Mastery Program teachers encourage students to become independent thinkers by teaching them to master the techniques of learning. The faculty teams meet biweekly to discuss curriculum, teaching strategies, and the progress of each boy.

In the Sixth Form, students face a more traditional classroom program, guided once again by faculty teams that oversee their academic and social progress through the upper forms. Students exercise their skills of organization, time management, and articulate communication in all of their upper-level courses. South Kent's academic program is designed to provide a broad education in English, mathematics, languages, sciences, history, and the arts and to prepare students for a successful and energetic college career. Academic requirements for graduation include 4 credits in English, 3 credits in mathematics, 2 credits in a foreign language (special considerations are provided to learning-difference students), 2 credits in laboratory science, 1 credit in U.S. history, and 2 credits in art. A student must earn a minimum of 18 credits between the beginning of the ninth grade and the end of the twelfth grade. The average student program comprises five courses per term.

FACULTY AND ADVISERS

South Kent has 31 full-time faculty members and administrators. Thirty-nine percent of the faculty members have advanced degrees. The 21 men and 10 women average seventeen years of service in education. All but 3 of the full-time teachers live on campus, many in dormitories as dorm parents.

Each student has a faculty member assigned as his adviser. A student meets with his adviser at least once a week to discuss academic progress. The size of the school, however, ensures faculty members the opportunity to have conversations with advisees almost every day.

Headmaster Andrew J. Vadnais was appointed in 2003. He received his B.A. from Williams College and his M.A. from University of Delaware. Andrew has taught at the School since 1997. His wife, Nancy Lyon, is the Fourth Form Dean and a history teacher.

COLLEGE PLACEMENT

College counseling begins formally in the Fifth Form with individual conferences and group meetings. Brian J. Mount, Director of College Counseling, works closely with each student and family to identify the colleges that best suit the student's individual interests. Every attempt is made to place students in colleges that will challenge them and where they will succeed. A computerized search is an integral part of the advising process and contributes to the diversity of schools students attend. The Internet is used to further research individual colleges, file financial aid applications, and, in some cases, apply online. About 50 college and university representatives visit South Kent each year to discuss opportunities for students.

South Kent enjoys a 99 percent college placement rate. Students generally applied to no more than five schools. Among the colleges and universities attended by recent graduates are Emory, Hobart and William Smith, Kenyon, Lafayette, Purdue, School of Visual Arts, Trinity College, and the Universities of Vermont and Wisconsin–Madison.

STUDENT BODY AND CONDUCT

During the 2004–05 school year, the Sixth Form had 40 students, the Fifth Form had 32 students, the Fourth Form had 30 students, and the Third Form had 23 students. South Kent has students from seventeen states and fourteen other countries, including the Czech Republic, England, Ireland, Japan, Korea, Nigeria, Russia, Senegal, Serbia, Switzerland, and Ukraine.

Members of the Sixth Form play an important role in the daily running of the School. Led by elected prefects, Sixth Form students work with faculty members to supervise the daily Jobs Program; they help monitor evening study periods in the dormitories, freeing resident faculty members to provide individualized attention in the form of "extra help sessions" to those students who need it. The prefects work closely with the Headmaster, meeting weekly to discuss School issues. Students' efforts are evaluated weekly; they receive Effort Ratings in the areas of academics, athletics, dormitory life, and the Jobs Program.

ACADEMIC FACILITIES

The Schoolhouse, Wittenberg Science Building, Bringhurst Complex, and the Noble and Elizabeth Richards Academic Center are at the center of academic life. Other academic buildings include the art studios and the Martin Henry Library. The Schoolhouse houses a student center, two floors of classrooms, an assembly hall, and the Winter Computer Center. Close by, the art studios have potter's wheels, kilns, and an etching press, as well as facilities for drawing, painting, sculpture, and work in batik, copper enamel, and linoleum-block prints. The newly expanded art wing enables the School to offer courses in computer art, including 3-D animation. There are two darkrooms available for photography classes as well as for general student and faculty member use. The Henry Library houses 20,000 volumes. The Wittenberg Science Building has three laboratories and two classrooms. Fifty-

five computer stations are available to students in the Winter Computer Center, the Henry Library, the Wittenberg Science Building, Bringhurst Complex, and Schoolhouse. Students are permitted their own personal computers in their rooms.

BOARDING AND GENERAL FACILITIES

Approximately 90 percent of South Kent students are boarders. Most of the Third, Fourth, and Fifth Formers live in double rooms; Sixth Formers may opt for singles, doubles, or triples. There are seven dormitories of varying sizes, housing from 8 to 20 students. St. Michael's Chapel is the spiritual center of the School. Services are held five days a week; most students take advantage of the opportunity to read at one of these services sometime in their South Kent career. Voluntary communion services are held two mornings a week before breakfast. The Old Building houses the administrative offices, the Admissions Office, the mail room, a common room, and the dining hall. The School bookstore and athletics store are located in the lower level of the Old Building. The health clinic is staffed by 2 nurses; the School doctor sees students three days a week on campus. The Tompkins Student Center offers facilities for playing pool, Ping-Pong, and air hockey and has vending machines and a large-screen television.

ATHLETICS

South Kent competes interscholastically in basketball, crew, cross-country, football, golf, hockey, lacrosse, soccer, and tennis. The golf team matches are played at The Bull's Bridge Golf Club, which was designed by Tom Fazio. Both varsity- and junior-varsity–level teams compete in games against other schools. Participation in sports is required of all students. There is an opportunity for every student, regardless of ability, to play on a competitive team with a challenging schedule. Athletics facilities include an enclosed ice rink; a gymnasium; a climbing wall; a weight room; football, soccer, and lacrosse fields; six all-weather tennis courts; a new athletic facility that boasts an open-air basketball court and a roller hockey rink; and a lake with three boathouses for the crew program.

EXTRACURRICULAR OPPORTUNITIES

Two activity periods a week are used for chorus and drama rehearsals, music lessons, or media club publications work. On weekends, there are dances and play days with neighboring schools. The School's two teams, the Cardinals and Blacks, compete in informal sports events such as volleyball, softball, and Ultimate Frisbee. Students are encouraged to generate ideas for activities on their own; in the past, they have organized weekend trips to adventure parks, rural fairs, New York City museums, Broadway plays, professional sports events, and air shows. The location of the School offers a wide variety of outdoor pursuits, including camping, canoeing, cycling, hiking, rock climbing, and skiing.

DAILY LIFE

The daily schedule is determined by the day of the week. The school day begins with a healthy breakfast at 7, Monday through Saturday, ensuring that more students eat a healthy breakfast to fuel their day. Classes are held six days a week, with half days on Wednesdays and Saturdays, when afternoon interscholastic sports contests take place. The 20–25 minutes a day devoted to jobs are scheduled either after breakfast, or immediately after lunch. During these periods, the classrooms, labs, chapel, library, offices, clinic, athletic buildings, and dining room are cleaned by students; dishwashing and some grounds work are assigned as well. Every student takes part in the Jobs Program, with the Sixth Formers working along with the underformers as well as supervising them. An all-school assembly precedes classes three mornings a week. A family-style sitdown lunch is served six days a week and is followed by afternoon classes and then sports.

Evening activities at South Kent also vary according to the day of the week. On Monday, chapel precedes formal dinner at 6:30. Formal dinner offers a time to reflect on the day with members of the faculty joining students at assigned tables. Dinners for the remainder of the week are buffet-style. Following the dinner hour, boys have time to meet with their advisers, attend club meetings and rehearsals, or relax before formal study time, which lasts from 8 until 9:45, five nights a week. During evening study hall, students may receive help from faculty proctors in tackling the day's assignments.

WEEKEND LIFE

Weekends at South Kent offer a wide variety of social events. Activities include dances with nearby girls' schools and trips to the movies, the mall, minor league ballparks, and local restaurants. Visiting musicians and lecturers come to campus several times a year for entertainment and enrichment. The area around Kent abounds with art galleries, musical performances, local theater productions, and small museums. With New York City and Boston just a few hours away, students can explore these cities and support their respective professional athletic teams. An Activities Committee made up of students and faculty members ensures that there is always a variety of outings offered.

COSTS AND FINANCIAL AID

Charges for the 2005–06 academic year were $32,000 for boarding students and $21,000 for day students. Costs of books, supplies, and personal sports equipment are charged separately. A yearly allowance of $800–$1200 for those costs is recommended. Financial aid is available and is awarded on the basis of need as recommended by the School and Student Service for Financial Aid.

ADMISSIONS INFORMATION

Although affiliated with the Episcopal Church, South Kent welcomes students of all faiths. Seventy-five percent of all students enter the Third or Fourth Forms (ninth or tenth grades); 20 percent come in the Fifth Form, and a limited few for a postgraduate year.

Participation in and contribution to all parts of school life are essential to a student's success. The program challenges the student to immerse himself in the life of the community. Admissions decisions are based both on academic ability and potential for success as well as nonacademic interests and achievements. Candidates must submit an application, a writing sample, a counselor recommendation, and a complete transcript, including teacher recommendations. In addition, applicants are required to have a personal interview at the School and take the SSAT, when possible. Candidates for the Student Learning Services Program must submit necessary documentation as requested by South Kent School.

APPLICATION TIMETABLE

South Kent adheres to the March 1 deadline for applications. Following the March deadline, the School operates on a rolling admissions basis; initial inquiries are welcome at any time. Interviews and tours can be arranged by writing to or calling the Admissions Office. Office hours are 8 a.m. to 4:30 p.m., Monday through Friday. Application forms and school brochures can be obtained from the Admissions Office. There is an application fee of $40. The first notices of acceptance for the following September are sent out in early March. After this initial date, applicants are notified of acceptance three weeks after the application process has been completed.

ADMISSIONS CORRESPONDENCE

Richard A. Brande
Director of Admissions and Financial Aid
South Kent School
40 Bull's Bridge Road
South Kent, Connecticut 06785

Phone: 860-927-3539
Fax: 860-927-0024
E-mail: admissions@southkentschool.net
Web site: http://www.southkentschool.net

SOUTHWESTERN ACADEMY

San Marino, California

Beaver Creek Ranch, Arizona

Type: Coeducational boarding and day; college-preparatory and general academic school
Grades: San Marino: 6–12, postgraduate year; Beaver Creek: 9–12, postgraduate year
Enrollment: San Marino, 140; Beaver Creek, 45
Head of School: Kenneth R. Veronda, Headmaster

THE SCHOOL

Southwestern Academy offers achievement-based, departmentalized, and supportively structured classes limited to 9 to 12 students. Small classes allow for individualized attention in a noncompetitive environment. Southwestern was founded by Maurice Veronda in 1924 as a college-preparatory program "for capable students who could do better" in small, supportive classes. While maintaining that commitment, Southwestern Academy includes U.S. and international students with strong academic abilities who are eager to learn and strengthen English-language skills as well as pursue a general scholastic program in a small, supportive school structure. Southwestern Academy is accredited by the Western Association of Schools and Colleges (WASC).

Southwestern Academy offers students the opportunity to study at either of two distinctly different and beautiful campuses. The San Marino, California, campus is situated in a historic orange grove area near Pasadena and Los Angeles. The Arizona campus, known as Beaver Creek Ranch, is located deep in a red-rock canyon in northern Arizona. Students may attend either campus and, if space permits, may divide the academic year between the two.

The San Marino campus occupies 8 acres in a residential suburb 10 miles from downtown Los Angeles and immediately south of Pasadena, home to the renowned Tournament of Roses Parade. The Beaver Creek campus is a 180-acre ranch located 100 miles north of Phoenix, 12 miles from the resort community of Sedona, and 45 miles south of Flagstaff. Although the program and philosophies are the same at both campuses, each offers a very different learning environment. Students at the California campus draw on the offerings of the urban setting. Students studying at Beaver Creek Ranch campus enjoy a living and learning environment that takes full advantage of the rich cultural, scenic, and environmentally significant region.

A mix of U.S. and international students from several countries offers a unique blend of cultural, social, and educational opportunities for all. Every effort is made to enroll a well-balanced student body that represents the rich ethnic diversity of U.S. citizens and students from around the world. The student body consists of excellent students who prefer a small, personalized education; above-average students who have the potential to become excellent academic achievers in the right learning environment; and average to underachieving students who, with a supportive structure, can achieve academic success.

Southwestern Academy is incorporated as a not-for-profit organization. Operating expenses are approximately $4.2 million per annum and are met by tuition (92 percent) and grants and annual giving (8 percent). The Academy has no indebtedness.

ACADEMIC PROGRAMS

Middle school students are placed in classes based on individual achievement levels. High school classes are divided by grade level, and students are assigned based on ability and achievement.

High school graduation requirements are based on University of California recommendations and include completion of a minimum of 200 academic credits plus 40 credit hours of physical education. The academic term is mid-September through mid-June, with a summer quarter offered at both campuses. Requirements include 4 years of English; 3 years of mathematics; 2 years of a foreign language; 2 years of laboratory sciences; 1 year each of U.S. history and world cultures, plus one semester of U.S. government and economics and 2 years of visual/performing arts. Proficiency exams in English, mathematics, and computer literacy as well as community service hours are also required for graduation.

A typical semester of course work includes six classes plus physical education. Advanced Placement classes are available in English, history, language, math, and science. Review and remedial classes are made available to students who need additional instruction. International students are offered three levels of classes in English as a second language (ESL), including an introductory class, to prepare them to enter and succeed in other academic areas.

Teachers are available daily during a midafternoon study period to work individually with students and meet with parents. There is no extra charge for this tutoring. Boarding students are required to attend a monitored evening study hall, where additional teacher assistance is available.

Student achievement is recognized with a grading system that ranges from A to F. Progress letters are sent monthly to parents and report cards are sent quarterly. The minimum college-recommending grade upon completion of academic requirements is C.

While studying at Beaver Creek Ranch campus, students attend classes on a block schedule, Monday through Thursday. Each Friday, students participate in educational, project-oriented, and assignment-based field trips. Experiential learning allows students to apply knowledge from the classroom. It also supports an integrated academic element that links core subject areas in a practical, applied manner, promoting understanding and retention of key concepts.

FACULTY AND ADVISERS

Headmaster Kenneth Veronda was born at the San Marino campus that his father founded. Mr. Veronda attended classes at Southwestern, graduated, and completed undergraduate and graduate work in American history and foreign relations at Stanford University. The majority of 31 faculty members, 22 in California and 9 in Arizona, hold advanced degrees in their subject areas. Each teacher serves as a faculty adviser to a few students and meets with them individually throughout the school year. On-campus college and career counselors are also available to meet and assist students in making post–high school graduation plans.

COLLEGE PLACEMENT

The college counselors closely monitor the advisement and placement need of each student. Beginning in the ninth grade, every effort is made to assist students in researching a variety of colleges and universities that match their interests and academic achievement levels. Students are provided a college planning handbook that offers helpful hints and suggestions regarding college application processes. A variety of college representatives are invited annually to visit each campus and meet with students.

Approximately 35 students graduate each year from Southwestern Academy. Almost all enter a U.S. college or university. Some choose to attend a local two-year community college before transferring to a four-year college or university. In recent years, Southwestern Academy graduates have been accepted to the following schools: American; Arizona State; Art Center College of Design; Azusa Pacific; Boston University; Brown; Butler; California State, Fullerton, Monterey Bay, and Northridge; California State Polytechnic, Pomona; Columbia; Hampton; Howard; Loyola; Marymount; Menlo College; Mills; Occidental; Oregon State; Parsons; Penn State; Pepperdine; Pitzer; Temple; Whittier; Woodbury; Wooster; Xavier; and the Universities of California, La Verne, Nevada, New Orleans, the Pacific, San Diego, San Francisco, Southern California, and Washington.

ACADEMIC FACILITIES

The San Marino campus includes seven buildings encircling a large open area that serves as a multisport athletic field. Lincoln Hall, the main academic building, houses morning assembly and study hall, ten classrooms, science and computer labs, and the library. Pioneer Hall includes several classrooms, a kitchen, dining rooms, and business offices. A separate building is home to large music and art studios and an additional science classroom and lab.

Newly renovated classrooms, a learning resource center, and the dormitories blend into the picturesque setting along Beaver Creek.

BOARDING AND GENERAL FACILITIES

Four dormitory halls are located on the San Marino campus. Each is designed to accommodate up to 20 boys in double and single rooms. Two off-campus dormitories (located within a mile) house a total of 30 girls. Dorm parents live in apartments adjoining each hall.

At Beaver Creek, seven stone cottages encircle the main campus area and provide faculty/staff housing. Four recently renovated residence halls accommodate up to 56 students. The Beaver Creek Ranch campus includes recreation rooms, a gymnasium, several large activity fields, and an indoor, solar-heated swimming pool.

ATHLETICS

Gyms and playing fields are available to all students at both campuses where sports opportunities exist for physical education requirements and recreation. As a member of federated leagues in California and Arizona, Southwestern Academy fields teams at both campuses in all major sports except tackle football. Athletic events are held in late afternoon, following the regular school day.

EXTRACURRICULAR OPPORTUNITIES

Southwestern offers a wide range of cocurricular and extracurricular activities and opportunities, including art, drama, music, journalism, student government, and student clubs. Current clubs include chess, Interact, International, the Southwestern Arts Society, Southwestern Environmental Associates, and tennis. Frequent class trips to Southern California and Northern Arizona places of interest, such as tide pools, museums, archaeological sites, art galleries, and live theater, are great learning experiences for students at both campuses.

DAILY LIFE

Boarding students begin each school day with a breakfast buffet at 7:30. Following breakfast, day and boarding students meet for a required assembly at 8:10, with classes following from 8:30 to 2:45. Required study halls and optional clubs and athletic events are held between 2:50 and 4:30. Dinner is served at 6 and is followed by a monitored study hall lasting until 8. Lights out is at 10:30 for middle school students and 11 for high schoolers.

WEEKEND LIFE

Students in good standing may leave the campus, with permission, during any weekend. Many students take advantage of the planned activities that are arranged for them, including theater performances, shopping at the malls and Old Town Pasadena, barbecues, beach parties, and movies. Visits are planned to Disneyland, Magic Mountain, and Big Surf, and the other attractions of the two-state areas are a part of the social program at Southwestern Academy. Day students are welcome to attend all weekend activities if space permits.

SUMMER PROGRAMS

Summer school sessions are offered at both campuses. Both offer intensive yet enjoyable individualized classes in English and other subjects, plus educational and recreational trips to interesting places in southern California and northern Arizona.

The summer program in San Marino is an excellent opportunity for domestic students to catch up, if needed, or to move ahead academically in order to take more advanced courses before graduation. For non-English-speaking international students, the summer session can provide an entire semester of the appropriate ESL level necessary to successfully complete a college-preparatory curriculum.

Summer sessions at Beaver Creek Ranch combine review and enrichment courses with experiential learning and high-adventure activities in classwork, camp-type activities, and travel in Northern Arizona. ESL is offered at the Beaver Creek campus during the summer.

COSTS AND FINANCIAL AID

Tuition for the 2006–07 U.S. boarding student is $31,500. International student tuition is $36,800. The cost for a day student (U.S. citizens and permanent residents only) is $14,800. An incidental account containing $2000 for boarding students or $1000 for day students is required of all students to cover expenses such as books, school supplies, physical education uniforms, and discretionary spending money. Payment is due in advance unless other arrangements are made with the business office.

Financial aid is awarded based on financial need. More than $630,000 was awarded in 2005–06.

ADMISSIONS INFORMATION

Southwestern Academy admits students of any race, color, national and ethnic origin, creed, or sex. A completed application packet is required, followed by a personal on-campus interview with students and parents. A day long visit to classes (and an overnight for prospective boarding students) is strongly encouraged for prospective students already living in the U.S. Interviews with prospective international students and parents are scheduled by the international admissions director and do not require a campus visit.

Each campus offers exceptional learning opportunities. Prospective students are encouraged to seriously consider both campuses and apply to the one that seems better suited to them.

Admission materials and other information can be downloaded from the Southwestern Academy Web site. It can also be obtained by contacting the Office of Admissions.

APPLICATION TIMETABLE

Admission offers are made throughout the year, as space permits. Appointments are required for interviews and campus tours at both locations. The admissions office for both campus locations is located in San Marino. Students should write or call the San Marino office for information on either campus.

ADMISSIONS CORRESPONDENCE

Office of Admissions
Southwestern Academy
2800 Monterey Road
San Marino, California 91108

Phone: 626-799-5010 Ext. 5
Fax: 626-799-0407
E-mail: admissions@southwesternacademy.edu
Web site: http://www.southwesternacademy.edu

SQUAW VALLEY ACADEMY

Olympic Valley, California

Type: Coeducational international boarding school
Grades: 6–12
Enrollment: 90
Head of School: Donald Rees, Headmaster and Founder

THE SCHOOL

Squaw Valley Academy (SVA) was founded in 1978 to offer a combination of project-based learning, outdoor education, and sports opportunities in the scenic California High Sierra. The typical Squaw Valley Academy student is highly capable but not highly motivated and needs the structure provided by small class size, evening study halls, and daily skiing and snowboarding as a reward for academic achievement. She or he may have an interest in pursuing winter sports at a recreational or competitive level. SVA offers strong preparation for college as its central focus and many outdoor sports and activities as a catalyst for personal growth and achievement.

Located 200 miles east of San Francisco and 45 miles west of Reno, SVA sits at the foot of Squaw Valley ski area, site of the 1960 Winter Olympics. At an elevation of 6,200 feet in a beautiful alpine setting, SVA offers easy access to Lake Tahoe and nearby forests, mountains, lakes, and rivers. Squaw Valley Academy is located within the small residential community of Olympic Valley, with commercial centers easily accessible 5 miles south in Tahoe City and 10 miles north in historic Truckee.

SVA's mission statement is as follows: "We challenge with rigorous academics; we support with consistent behavioral standards; we train in lifelong sports; we provide outdoor adventure; and we foster self-esteem through real accomplishment."

Squaw Valley Academy is fully accredited by the Western Association of Schools and Colleges.

ACADEMIC PROGRAMS

The Squaw Valley Academy college-preparatory curriculum focuses on hands-on, project-based learning to keep students engaged throughout the course. All core academic courses are approved by the University of California system. The curriculum includes two weeklong outdoor education trips that allow students to participate in a combined athletic and academic program in an outdoor mountain setting.

Class size and the student body remain small to allow focus on individual attention in the classroom and the dormitory. The average class size is 9 students. All boarding students are required to attend a supervised 2-hour study hall Sunday–Thursday. Honors students earn the privilege to study in their dormitory rooms.

The Squaw Valley Academy's school year is composed of two semesters. Students entering the school after September may transfer credits from their former school.

To graduate, students must complete 4 years of English, 4 years of social studies (including U.S. history and American government), 3 years of mathematics, 3 years of laboratory science, 3 years of a foreign language, 4 years of physical education, and sufficient electives each year to complete the normal five- or six-course academic load. Independent study is offered, and tutorial assistance is available to students with special needs. Transfer students at upper levels may apply for waivers in areas in which their backgrounds are deficient.

English course offerings include basic grammar and composition, American literature, British and world literature, and literary analysis. Science courses are taught as laboratory courses and include chemistry, biology, physics, and physical sciences. World history, U.S. history, world geography, U.S. government, and economics are among the social studies courses. Mathematics courses extend from algebra through calculus. Spanish is the primary foreign language taught at SVA, although French may be offered based on student interest. Electives are offered in music, studio art, photography, publications, drama, psychology, outdoor leadership, and computer literacy and programming.

Advanced Placement classes can be available in calculus, English literature and composition, chemistry, physics, Spanish, U.S. history, and other courses based on student interest and skill level. AP courses may be offered on alternate years, depending on enrollment.

Students receive letter grades, A–F. Grades are issued four times per year. Written comments supplement all grade reports. Teachers' comments identify specific strengths and weaknesses in each subject area, indicate the quality of a student's effort, and offer encouragement for improvement. Grades are based on labs, quizzes, papers, hands-on projects, tests, class participation, and a 2-hour final examination. Students earn the privilege of daily participation in athletics such as skiing and snowboarding by keeping grades up to standard.

Extra tutoring and academic guidance, as needed, are available, especially for underachieving or newly arrived students.

SVA is an international school and offers an immersion academic program for international students. Incoming students should have functional English-language skills. International students' class schedules are determined according to their English-language abilities. International students make up about 12 percent of the student population.

FACULTY AND ADVISERS

Typically, full-time teachers have a teaching credential and/or two years of previous experience in the classroom. All faculty members are assigned advisees, and many of the staff members serve as athletic coaches and dormitory parents. Most faculty members are on duty as campus supervisors one day each week.

Dormitory parents live full-time on campus in the student dormitory buildings and typically also serve as athletic coaches.

Faculty advisers mentor and guide students to become responsible, mature members of the school community and to help them develop the strong study skills that are necessary for academic success. There is an ongoing, respectful relationship between parents and advisers, and contact is frequent concerning academic, behavioral, and social matters.

SVA teachers have experience and professional competence, high personal standards and integrity, interest in athletics and outdoor adventure, and a genuine respect for their students' learning and growth.

Headmaster Donald Rees founded SVA and continues to be involved in daily activities, including student tutoring. He graduated from the University of California, Santa Barbara, with a degree in history. Mr. Rees has taught at the Polytechnic School in Pasadena, The American School in Switzerland, and Laguna Blanca School in Santa Barbara. He is the founding Executive Director of the Yosemite Institute in Yosemite Valley and the Headlands Institute near San Francisco.

COLLEGE PLACEMENT

SVA is proud of its 100 percent college acceptance rate for all graduates. Most seniors are accepted into one of their top three college or university choices.

College counseling and guidance begins early in a student's junior year. Juniors take the PSAT in the fall and the SAT and/or ACT in the spring. SVA advises juniors about the nature of different colleges and encourages students to have summer interviews at the colleges that meet their interests and needs.

Individual guidance is given to each senior, who again takes the SAT and SAT Subject Tests. College representatives visit the school throughout the school year. Seniors receive step-by-step guidance regarding the college application process. While final responsibility for college applications lies with the student and parents, the school makes every effort to help students gain acceptance at a college of their choice.

Virtually all SVA graduates go on to four-year colleges and universities. Acceptances include California State, Colby, Colorado College, Dartmouth, Middlebury, Notre Dame, Sarah Lawrence, U.S. Naval Academy, University of California campuses, and University of Colorado at Boulder.

STUDENT BODY AND CONDUCT

The school has approximately 90 coed students in grades 6–12. Students come to SVA from all over the country and the world, as SVA is authorized by the U.S. government to accept international students who wish to study at the school.

Students are expected to assume personal accountability for their behavior and self-discipline, yet the school recognizes that young men and women respond best to a positive structure. School rules and principles of conduct are clearly stated in the *Student/Parent Handbook,* and students are expected to follow the letter and spirit of these guidelines to help foster a community of mutual trust and respect. Students are assigned daily work jobs as an important part of learning responsibility, accountability, and pride in themselves and the school. Dormitory rooms are regularly inspected for tidiness and cleanliness. Violation of rules or failure to perform assigned chores may result in the loss of privileges.

Squaw Valley Academy was one of the first boarding schools on the U.S. West Coast to administer mandatory drug tests. Students are tested for five types of drugs, including marijuana. All students are tested at random throughout the year to help ensure a clean, safe campus.

ACADEMIC FACILITIES

The main building houses various classrooms, faculty and administrative offices, and kitchen-dining facilities. The campus also includes a fully equipped science laboratory, music equipment, an art studio, and a photographic darkroom.

BOARDING AND GENERAL FACILITIES

Two well-built, separate dormitories for boys and girls exist, with common areas, locker rooms, and classrooms in each building. The first three-story boys' dormitory was built in 1984, and the latest girls' dorm was built in 1997. Each room has a private bath with a tub or a shower, usually with 2 or 4 students to a room.

Dormitories have live-in house parents. The on-duty dormitory staff members set an alarm system each evening at curfew, deterring students from leaving their dormitory rooms at night. The campus also has locker rooms and other storage for ski/snowboard and bicycle equipment.

Nearby athletic facilities include a professional-size FieldTurf soccer field, indoor rock-climbing walls, mountain biking and hiking trails, world-class skiing and snowboarding resorts, and kayaking and river rafting opportunities.

A fully staffed medical clinic is located 2 miles from the school and serves the local area during the winter season. A full-service hospital is 10 miles away in Truckee.

ATHLETICS

In the fall, students choose to participate in a variety of individual or team sports. Fall sports include interscholastic soccer, rock climbing, mountain biking, yoga, skateboarding, and weight training and conditioning.

During the winter months, the academic schedule provides time each day for students to ski or snowboard—provided grades are up to standard—at Squaw Valley USA, which is located within 2 miles of the campus. Most students are recreational skiers and snowboarders. Advanced athletes may train and compete with the Squaw Valley USA Ski Team or at Alpine Meadows.

During the spring, SVA students return to sport activities similar to the fall schedule. Activities include rock climbing, soccer, golf, tennis, volleyball, basketball, fly-fishing, kayaking, and swimming. These activities depend on student and staff interest, weather, a willingness to share extra costs, and facilities and equipment.

EXTRACURRICULAR OPPORTUNITIES

The Student Council provides a forum for all members of the community to have a voice in school affairs and activities. All students are required to complete 10–15 hours of community service or service-learning. The goal and spirit of the school's community service program is to provide each student with the lifelong experience of helping those who are less fortunate than themselves and giving unselfishly to the local community or environment. Educational day trips are organized periodically for the purpose of providing a relevant and supplemental component for academic classes. Students may enroll in a service-learning elective class and plan a long-term, academic-based service project.

All students participate in the school's Outdoor Education Program. Students learn leadership, team building, and outdoor skills and experience personal growth through such diverse endeavors as backpacking, rafting, kayaking, mountaineering, backcountry skiing/snowboarding, rock climbing, fly-fishing, and other activities. Each year, all students attend two weeklong Outdoor Education trips. Supervised by SVA teachers and dormitory staff members, these trips take the curriculum into the outdoors. Past trips include marine life studies while sea kayaking at Point Reyes National Seashore, snow survival skills while snowboarding at Mammoth Mountain, and ecology and natural history while mountain biking in the Redwood National Forest.

DAILY LIFE

A typical school day in the fall or spring begins with breakfast at 8 a.m., with classes starting at the close of breakfast. Students enroll in six courses, and physical education or team sports take place for 1 to 3 hours during the day. Free time is available until dinner at 5:30 p.m., followed by evening chores and a teacher-supervised evening study hall. Day students participate in school athletics and sports activities and are welcome to remain on campus for meals and evening study hall.

During the winter season, schedules are individualized to allow for daily skiing or snowboarding.

WEEKEND LIFE

On-campus activities, recreational and adventure outings, theater, movies, music/concerts, cultural activities, shopping, and sporting events are scheduled by dormitory parents and the on-duty staff members. Dormitory parents provide transportation through the use of school vans.

A regular meal schedule is followed on Saturday; on Sunday, a brunch is served, with dinner at the regular time. Parents often visit on weekends to take advantage of the many activities in the Tahoe-Reno area. Students may visit home if homework is complete and they are in good behavioral standing.

SUMMER PROGRAMS

Summer school offers the opportunity to earn credits for one semester in three weeks or one year in six weeks. Students participate in academic classes in the morning and outdoor activities at Lake Tahoe in the afternoon.

COSTS AND FINANCIAL AID

Boarding school tuition for the 2005–06 school year was $31,916. Summer school boarding tuition for 2006 is $3990 per three-week session. Additional costs include a ski pass at Squaw Valley USA and Outdoor Education Program trips. Students should attend SVA for at least one term before applying for a reduction in tuition. Approximately 10 percent of SVA students receive financial aid.

ADMISSIONS INFORMATION

Admission centers on an applicant's ability to perform college-preparatory work, to participate fully in the school's outdoor athletic programs, and to remain drug- and alcohol-free. The school is effective with bright, active, and motivated students as well as with bright and active underachievers. The decision to accept a candidate is based on a personal interview, teacher and counselor recommendations, a school transcript, a completed application, and diagnostic testing.

APPLICATION TIMETABLE

Inquiries are welcome at any time, and a student may be accepted at any time during the academic year. Prospective students and their parents should visit on a school day to receive a firsthand view of the program and to meet faculty and staff members. An interview is conducted at that time, and diagnostic testing may be given. A nonrefundable application fee of $50 must accompany the application. Notification of admission varies with the date of application.

ADMISSIONS CORRESPONDENCE

Squaw Valley Academy
235 Squaw Valley Road
P.O. Box 2667
Olympic Valley, California 96146

Phone: 530-583-9393
Fax: 530-581-1111
E-mail: enroll@sva.org
Web site: http://www.sva.org

STANSTEAD COLLEGE

Stanstead, Quebec, Canada

Type: Coeducational boarding and day university-preparatory school
Grades: 7–12
Enrollment: 220
Head of School: Michael Wolfe, Headmaster

THE SCHOOL

Stanstead College was founded in 1872 by community leaders who wished to establish a school for superior education. Since then, Stanstead College has provided a challenging academic programme for boys and girls entering grades 7–12, without distinction as to race, language, or national or cultural origin. The mission of Stanstead College is to provide boys and girls with an education of superior quality in preparation for college and university entrance in North America. It is the College's commitment to provide a structured and supportive environment in which students can develop independence and self-reliance.

Situated just north of the American border states of Vermont and New Hampshire, in the beautiful Eastern Townships, the College offers its students a unique opportunity to experience the heritage and culture of Quebec. The school has a truly bilingual atmosphere.

The College comprises a large complex of buildings on the main campus and is surrounded by 600 acres of land. Its location 100 miles southeast of Montreal and 250 miles from Boston puts the school within easy reach of major international airports.

Stanstead College is a member of the Canadian Association of Independent Schools, the Quebec Association of Independent Schools, the New England Association of Schools and Colleges, and the Independent Schools Association of Northern New England, and is an affiliate member of the National Association of Independent Schools.

The school is governed by a Board of Trustees in close liaison with the Headmaster. There is an alumni association.

ACADEMIC PROGRAMS

Stanstead's faculty members are experienced, dedicated professionals who give generously of themselves. There is a traditional university-preparatory curriculum. Study skills are constantly reinforced through the adviser system and in the classroom. With an average class size of 12 and an overall teacher-student ratio of 1:8, communication between staff members and students is clear and personalized. Academic progress is carefully monitored and assessed continuously. Teachers and advisers are available at all times for consultation. There are three interim reports and three major end of term reports during the school year.

The academic programme at Stanstead College is divided into the junior programme (grades 7–9) and the senior programme (grades 10–12). The core subjects of English, French, and mathematics are strongly emphasized at each grade level.

Students in the junior grades must undertake a wide range of courses that include traditional academic programmes such as general science as well as practical subjects such as home economics and introduction to technology.

Senior students follow a two-year advanced programme that leads to the Quebec Secondary School Diploma. In addition to the three core subjects, all students in the senior grades must take at least one science, one humanities, and one other academic course of their choice in both grades 10 and 11. All students have their own laptop, and through the integration of information technology into all aspects of school life, Stanstead students are able to develop the skills, confidence, and creativity necessary to manage information and uncertainty in the ever-changing global environment.

The grade 12 programme at Stanstead is designed for direct entrance into universities outside the province of Quebec. The minimum requirements for the grade 12 certificate are the successful completion of six courses, which must include English.

All grade 11 and 12 students are encouraged to sit for the SAT during their final years at Stanstead. Qualified secondary 5 and grade 12 students may take Advanced Placement courses and examinations in select subject areas.

There is a study period each evening for all students. Students are placed in study hall when they receive two or more unsatisfactory effort ratings on one report. Students who maintain an A- average may be allowed the privilege of optional study.

FACULTY AND ADVISERS

Of the 32 faculty members, more than one quarter hold advanced degrees; there are 15 women members. Faculty members are involved in the athletic programme as coaches and assume dormitory and House Director responsibilities. All faculty members take on a leadership role in the various clubs and cocurricular activities. Fifteen of the faculty members live on the campus.

Michael Wolfe, M.A., M.Mgt., began as Headmaster in 2005, after three years as Director of Advancement and ten years as an active member of the Stanstead College Board of Trustees. He is a graduate of the University of Western Ontario and received his Master in Management degree from McGill University, where he was selected as a McGill-McConnell Scholar.

Every student has a faculty adviser who is there to listen, encourage, and guide his or her advisees throughout the year. Generally, a student retains the same adviser throughout his or her stay at the school.

COLLEGE PLACEMENT

A University Placement Officer is regularly available to advise and guide each graduating student on a one-to-one basis. A series of guest speakers and information sessions are also included in this programme. Graduates of the class of 2004 were accepted at colleges and universities such as Brown, Dartmouth, Emory, Guelph, McMaster, Mount Allison, Queen's at Kingston, Saint Mary's (Halifax), Smith, Stanford, and the Universities of New Brunswick, North Carolina, Ottawa, Waterloo, and Western Ontario. Every student in the graduating class of 2002 was accepted at the college or university of his or her choice.

STUDENT BODY AND CONDUCT

Stanstead enrols an average of 220 students, 165 of whom are boarders; the school has a 45 percent female enrolment. Students presently attending come from countries such as Bermuda, the Bahamas, France, Germany, Hong Kong, Hungary, Japan, Korea, Mexico, Taiwan, Thailand, the United Kingdom, and the United States. The majority of students are from Canada.

A school uniform is worn, and there is a dress code. Prefects act as leaders of the student body, and students are encouraged to become involved in the various student committees. Smoking and the use of illegal drugs or alcohol are strictly prohibited.

ACADEMIC FACILITIES

Academic facilities are located in four buildings. Colby House is the administrative and academic centre. The library (with more than 20,000 reference and general subject books), the technology centre, and six state-of-the-art science laboratories are also housed in Colby. Holmes Model School contains additional classrooms and the Art Department. LeBaron Hall is the home of the Languages Department (French and Spanish). Davis House contains several classrooms, practice rooms, and an auditorium for music studies.

BOARDING AND GENERAL FACILITIES

Boys and girls live in four different houses: Bugbee (junior boys), Colby (junior girls), Davis (senior boys), and Webster (senior girls). Each residence has a live-in House Director and Assistant Director. The well-equipped Health Centre is supervised by a live-in registered nurse. LeBaron Hall is the location of the dining hall. Rebuilt in 2001, the Student Centre houses a student lounge, tuck shop, and games room.

ATHLETICS

All students are required to participate in one of the available athletic options offered each term. Whether a team or individual sport is chosen, each student has the opportunity to participate fully and compete interscholastically or intramurally. Above all, a student is expected to exhibit the highest degree of sportsmanship. The fall season includes football, soccer, and cross-

country running; winter offers cross-country skiing, basketball, squash, hockey, and swimming; and track and field, golf, tennis, and rugby round out the school year.

The sports complex includes a full-size gymnasium with basketball, volleyball, and badminton courts. There is a fitness centre with the latest in weights and equipment. A six-lane, 25-metre swimming pool is in an adjacent building, as are two squash courts. The arena contains a full-size artificial ice surface. Stanstead also has outdoor facilities, which include tennis courts, soccer fields, a football field, softball diamonds, a basketball court, outdoor ice rink, and a ¼-mile track. Private cross-country ski trails are nearby, and some of the best Alpine ski hills in Quebec and Vermont are located within 25 miles of the school.

EXTRACURRICULAR OPPORTUNITIES

Community service, public speaking, kayaking, drama, yearbook, computer, scuba diving, outdoor education, and investment clubs are a few of the options available. The student Animation Committee plans and organizes regular social events. Activities take place on campus or at local cultural and recreational facilities and include events that range from dances and variety shows to the Winter Carnival and drama productions. Students at all levels are encouraged to join the choir or jazz band. Individual piano, guitar, and voice lessons are also available on campus.

DAILY LIFE

Weekday mornings after breakfast, faculty members and students meet for a brief assembly to preview the upcoming day. Classes begin at 8:30 a.m. Breakfast at 7:30 a.m. and dinner at 5:45 p.m. are informal, cafeteria-style meals. Weekday lunches are more formal, and students are joined by teachers and their families for a family-style meal served in LeBaron Hall. After class, from 3:30 until 5:30 p.m., sports teams practice or compete, followed by dinner at 5:30 and study at 7:30. Lights-out is at 10 p.m. for juniors and 10:45 for seniors.

WEEKEND LIFE

Students are encouraged to participate in outings such as hiking, camping, alpine skiing, and horseback riding. The city of Montreal offers opportunities for school excursions. With the exception of grade 12 students, weekend leaves are limited to three per term.

SUMMER PROGRAMS

The Stanstead College Summer Language Adventure involves students who wish to pursue French or English as a second language in an outdoor and classroom programme. The College also hosts several summer hockey schools for girls and boys.

COSTS AND FINANCIAL AID

The 2005–06 tuition fees are Can$34,660 for Canadian and American boarding students. International tuition fees for 2005–06 are Can$38,060. Parents may choose to pay fees in a single installment or by term. A number of entrance scholarships are available each year, ranging in value from Can$2000 to full fees. Scholarship examinations are written in November and February. One full-entrance scholarship is awarded annually (on the basis of a scholarship examination) to a student entering at the grade 10 level. There are student bursaries, based on need and merit, for which applications may be made. In 2004–05, 35 percent of the student body were recipients of financial aid and/or scholarship funding. The total amount awarded was Can$750,000.

ADMISSIONS INFORMATION

Stanstead College does not discriminate against any person on the basis of race, colour, sex, religion, or national or ethnic origin. Admission at all grade levels is determined by evaluation of the academic performance and potential in addition to the behaviour/character profile of the applicant. The final decision is based on scholastic records, a standardized test, confidential references, and a personal interview. Upon receipt of the completed application, the College may contact references directly. There is an application fee of Can$100. Applicants and their parents are interviewed by the Director of Admissions, and a tour of the campus is made. Applicants who cannot visit the campus are interviewed by telephone and are asked to write a letter outlining their interests and objectives.

APPLICATION TIMETABLE

Applications are received and assessed on an ongoing basis throughout the year. However, it is important to note that the number of available places is limited, and admissible applications submitted later in the year may be rejected due to space constraints.

ADMISSIONS CORRESPONDENCE

Joanne Carruthers
Director of Admissions
Stanstead College
450 Dufferin Street
Stanstead, Quebec J0B 3E0
Canada

Phone: 819-876-2223
Fax: 819-876-5891
E-mail: admissions@stansteadcollege.com
Web site: http://www.stansteadcollege.com

THE STONY BROOK SCHOOL

Stony Brook, New York

Type: Coeducational boarding and day college-preparatory school
Grades: 7–12
Enrollment: 336
Head of School: Robert E. Gustafson Jr., Headmaster

THE SCHOOL

Since its founding in 1922, the Stony Brook School has been dedicated to combining rigorous college preparation within the context of Christian faith. Although the School has no denominational affiliation, the Bible is studied for credit, and students attend daily chapel services.

The campus is situated on 52 acres of pleasant woodland in the attractive Three Village area on Long Island's North Shore. Numerous Georgian buildings, which house academic and residential facilities, grace the campus. New York City, with its many cultural opportunities, is 1½ hours away by train or car. The State University of New York at Stony Brook is within walking distance.

The Headmaster and the President of the Alumni Association are among the 18 Trustees who direct the School, a nonprofit organization. Financial support from the 3,800 living alumni and other sources totaled $1.6 million in 2004–05.

The Stony Brook School is accredited by the Middle States Association of Colleges and Schools and the New York State Board of Regents. It is a member of the National Association of Independent Schools, the New York State Association of Independent Schools, the National Association for College Admissions Counseling, the National Association of Secondary School Principals, The Association of Boarding Schools, the Council for the Advancement and Support of Education, and the College Board.

ACADEMIC PROGRAMS

The school year provides thirty weeks of instruction in two semesters. There are seven class periods each day. The curriculum, governed principally by the requirements of college preparation, includes formal study of the Bible. Courses in grades 9–12 include English (ESL courses are also available); French, Latin, and Spanish; humanities 9, humanities 10, Jewish and Islamic studies, European history, U.S. history, and political science; algebra, geometry, and advanced mathematics (through AP calculus); health, biology, physical science, chemistry, and physics; art; and music.

Electives, offered in each of the seven major departments, include topics in literature; psychology; topics in American history; marine science; computer programming, computer applications, and statistics; drawing, ceramics, painting, animation, and photography; and choir, orchestra, and jazz band. Singing lessons and instrumental music instruction are also offered.

In grades 11 and 12, individual learning programs may be arranged. Tutorials and guided study are incorporated into these programs. Honors sections in English, biology, mathematics, and physics are offered for selected students in grades 9–11. Advanced Placement courses in American history, art, comparative politics, European history, biology, chemistry, Latin, U.S. government and politics, English, French, Spanish, calculus (AB and

BC), psychology, philosophy, and physics are offered to students in grades 11 and 12. It is generally expected that juniors and seniors will take Advanced Placement courses. Seniors with high academic standing are eligible for membership in the Cum Laude Society.

The Stony Brook Middle School, for students in grades 7 and 8, provides a secure and creative environment for learning while developing the skills required for the rigorous upper school experience. The curriculum is interdisciplinary, with computers integrated into the learning process. There are also field trips and group projects.

Each year, the School sponsors the Pierson Curtis lecture series, which focuses on English literature, and the Staley Lecture Series. The Stony Brook School is the only non-college/university to be included in the Staley Lecture Series.

Marks are reported to parents four times yearly, and detailed comments on performance in each subject are written two times a year. There are 14 students in the average class; the student-teacher ratio is 7:1.

Each spring, an international educational trip is planned. Several students are chosen every year to study abroad with the English Speaking Union's academic exchange.

FACULTY AND ADVISERS

The faculty has 46 members, all of whom live on or near the campus. All teachers hold baccalaureate degrees, 25 hold master's degrees, and 2 hold doctorates. In addition, there is a full-time nursing staff that is available 24 hours a day, seven days a week.

Robert E. Gustafson Jr., Headmaster, is a graduate of the University of Virginia (B.A.), Columbia Teachers College (M.A.), and Gordon-Conwell Theological Seminary (M.A.).

Stony Brook offers faculty members medical and retirement plans, leaves of absence, and sabbaticals. A Faculty Development Grant supports faculty graduate study and conference attendance.

COLLEGE PLACEMENT

Each fall, more than 40 college representatives visit the School. Each junior meets with 5 or 6 of these representatives. This is the beginning of a two-year procedure intended to match each student with a suitable college. In the spring of the junior year, during interviews with the College Counselor, each student is assisted in making tentative college choices, with arrangements for college visits and interviews, and with application procedures. Each student is encouraged to visit as many colleges as possible during the summer preceding his or her senior year.

In the senior year, through individual conferences with the College Counselor, seniors' college choices are correlated with SAT scores, grade point

average, major area of study, and career choice. Parents are encouraged to participate in all of these procedures.

Mean SAT scores for the class of 2005 were 603 verbal and 612 math (mean 1215). Of the 68 graduates, 100 percent matriculated to competitive colleges and universities, including Davidson, Emory, Fordham, Georgetown, Gordon, Johns Hopkins, NYU, Wake Forest, Wheaton, and the Universities of Chicago and Virginia.

STUDENT BODY AND CONDUCT

In 2005–06, the total enrollment of the student body was 336. Of this total, 29 students were in seventh grade, 42 in eighth grade, 58 in ninth grade, 69 in tenth grade, 68 in eleventh grade, and 70 in twelfth grade. The Upper School maintains a student body that is equally distributed between boys and girls, with 60 percent being boarding students and 40 percent day students. These students represent twenty-two states and seventeen countries as well as a great variety of racial, social, economic, and religious backgrounds.

The community life at Stony Brook gives students freedom within structure. Students are encouraged to make their talents manifest in a large variety of ways, yet are given clear limits in which to work. Students adhere to statements of honor concerning principles of proper conduct. The Assistant Headmaster, Student Prefects, and Honor Council, in consultation with the Headmaster, consider suitable consequences for violations of acceptable conduct.

Student leadership groups include the Judicial-Honor Council and Board of Prefects, a selected group of seniors who work in a coordinate relationship with the faculty and meet to discuss peer counseling methods, listening and observation skills, and better ways of communicating. There are also maître d's, who supervise meals, and work-crew captains, who oversee work jobs.

ACADEMIC FACILITIES

There are thirty-four buildings on campus. Among these are the chapel (1927); Memorial Hall (1950), which houses classrooms, science and computer labs, the Headmaster's office, and the Admissions Center; and Carson Auditorium (1910), which houses the Visual and Performing Arts Department and is newly renovated, featuring added studio space and practice rooms. The Frank E. Gaebelein Hall (1982) contains chemistry, biology, and physics labs; general classrooms; a computer lab; and an expanded library.

BOARDING AND GENERAL FACILITIES

Double rooms are available in seven residential halls (Alexander, Barnhouse, Cleveland, Hegeman, Johnston, Monro, and Simons). Faculty members live in each residential hall and in housing adjacent to the campus. Johnston also contains a dining hall, a kitchen, two faculty apart-

ments, offices, the campus store, the post office, and other facilities. Barnhouse contains the Cellar Door, a student center with vending machines.

Registered nurses are on call 24 hours a day at the health center, and the School physician is available four days per week.

ATHLETICS

All students must elect sports and/or activities to fulfill their physical education requirement. Interscholastically, boys' teams compete in cross-country, football, golf, sailing, soccer, basketball, wrestling, lacrosse, tennis, and track, and girls' teams compete in golf, sailing, soccer, tennis, volleyball, basketball, lacrosse, softball, and track. Local public high schools and area private schools are included in the schedules. Intramural sports are also a popular pursuit.

The Swanson Gymnasium houses a basketball court, a fitness center, locker rooms, and a swimming pool. A gift to the School made possible extensive renovation and expansion that was completed for the start of the 2000–01 academic year. In 2001, other gifts added a new wood floor, an automated bleacher system, and a state-of-the-art scoreboard to the gymnasium. An additional basketball court, locker rooms, and a wrestling room are located in the Kinney Field House. In 1998, the lighted Buyers' Park stadium and Marvin Goldberg track were completed, and six tennis courts were refurbished. Fields for football, lacrosse, softball, and soccer are available for practice and competition.

EXTRACURRICULAR OPPORTUNITIES

Clubs and activities flourish at Stony Brook. Clubs include Open Studio and the Chess and International Clubs. HEART organizes community service activities, UDT promotes diversity on campus, and ICF draws Christians together for fellowship. There is also an outdoor education club and prison ministry. Publications include the yearbook, literary magazine, and *World* magazine. The Theatrical Arts Society has an ambitious program of two productions annually. The School's instrumental program offers string, brass, and pi-

ano instruction. The choir, Chamber Singers, chamber groups, and jazz band give fall and spring concerts.

Numerous weekend activities are planned and coordinated through the Student Activities Office. Students attend the theater (at a subsidized cost), concerts, and sports events; they visit galleries and museums in New York City and locally. Traditional School events include Alumni Weekend, Family Weekend, Class Challenges, Award Assemblies, Spring Fling (a schoolwide carnival benefiting a neighboring school for learning-challenged students), and the Senior Prom. SBS PARENTS, the School's parent organization, promotes parent involvement, helps integrate new parents into the School, plans two annual fund raising events, and complements the quality of the Stony Brook experience by supporting service activities and student activities.

DAILY LIFE

A buffet breakfast from 6:45 to 7:30 starts the day for boarders. There are seven 50-minute class periods that rotate each day. Friday includes adviser group sessions or an assembly for special programs. Extra academic help is available at various times of the day. A 20-minute daily chapel provides time for private devotions. Lunch is served buffet style for all students. Dinner is served family style, with students taking turns waiting on tables. After classes are over at 3:05, athletics begin. Dinner is at 6:15, and evening study is from 7:45 to 10.

WEEKEND LIFE

Faculty open houses, dances, picnics, intramurals, movies, shopping trips, field trips to New York City, retreats, community service projects, get-togethers, Bible study opportunities, and other events are planned for weekends.

SUMMER PROGRAMS

The most recent addition to the line-up of summer programs is Sound Learning, a two-week residential academic enrichment program for rising seventh-, eighth-, and ninth-grade students. Those who participate receive instruction in expository

writing and can take elective classes in marine science, theater arts, drawing and painting, and the human body. Students also take part in recreational sailing on Long Island Sound. Stony Brook also has a variety of recreational and athletic programs open to local boys and girls ages 5 to 15.

COSTS AND FINANCIAL AID

In 2005–06, the yearly charge of $31,000 for boarding students covered room, board, and tuition; the yearly charge of $18,700 for day students covered tuition. Additional expenses include textbooks, English as a Second Language, classroom supplies, special testing, and a security deposit of $200.

For 2005–06, financial aid was awarded to 30 percent of the student body on the basis of need. Applications for aid must be received by March 1 and are processed through the School and Student Service for Financial Aid.

ADMISSIONS INFORMATION

The Stony Brook School seeks students who show promise of unusual achievement. New students are accepted on the basis of scores on the SSAT, previous school record, recommendations from English and mathematics teachers, and a personal interview.

APPLICATION TIMETABLE

Initial inquiries are welcome throughout the year. Campus tours and interviews can be arranged by appointment. There is a recommended deadline of December 15 for each application, which must be accompanied by a nonrefundable $50 application fee. Acceptances begin after February 1. If vacancies become available during the school year, additional students may be admitted.

ADMISSIONS CORRESPONDENCE

Kevin M. Kunst, Director of Admissions
The Stony Brook School
1 Chapman Parkway
Stony Brook, New York 11790

Phone: 631-751-1800
Fax: 631-751-4211
E-mail: admissions@stonybrookschool.org
Web site: http://www.stonybrookschool.org

THE STORM KING SCHOOL

Cornwall-on-Hudson, New York

Type: Coeducational boarding and day college-preparatory school
Grades: 7–12, postgraduate year
Enrollment: 128
Head of School: Helen S. Chinitz

THE SCHOOL

The Storm King School was founded in 1867 as a college-preparatory school by the Reverend Louis P. Ledoux. In 1928, it was chartered by the Board of Regents of the State University of New York as a nonprofit institution governed by a self-perpetuating 18-member Board of Trustees. The School has an endowment of $1 million and an active Annual Giving campaign.

The Storm King School seeks to provide a caring, structured residential life and an academic program that prepares students for college. The School helps students stretch themselves by building upon their strengths while realistically acknowledging and addressing their weaknesses. Storm King believes that art, theater, music, and athletics are components of a good education. Therefore, they are a part of daily life at the School. Central to Storm King's philosophy is the belief that it is a learning community striving to help students live as productive members.

The School is located near the crest of Storm King Mountain on the west bank of the Hudson River. The 40-acre campus offers a serene setting and a magnificent view of a sweeping bend of the river, the Shawangunk Mountains, and the distant Catskills. The 4,000-acre Black Rock Forest, a wilderness preserved by environmentalists, adjoins the campus to the south; West Point Military reservation and Bear Mountain Preserve are nearby, as are the estates of several long-established Hudson Highlands families. New York City, about 50 miles away, is within easy reach via the Palisades Parkway.

Storm King School has a Middle School program for grades 7 and 8. The focus of this program is to help students develop and retain a sense of responsibility and individuality. The Middle School curriculum offers the basic core courses as well as technology, physical education, and performing and visual arts. Students are allowed to be creative and self-exploring while fulfilling an educationally intensive program.

The School is accredited by the Middle States Association of Colleges and Schools. It is a member of the Cum Laude Society, the National Honor Society, the New York State Association of Independent Schools, the National Association of Independent Schools, and the College Board.

ACADEMIC PROGRAMS

College preparation is a goal of Storm King School and, therefore, the School emphasizes the development of present skills and talents as the best way to prepare for the future. The School seeks to discover and extend what a student has learned and to identify and develop what he or she has not. The curriculum focuses on skill development as well as content knowledge. The English and history programs stress reading and writing skills and include both required and elective courses;

offerings range from creative writing to the British novel, and from twentieth-century Europe to psychology.

The School believes that all students can improve their mathematical skills and reasoning ability. The flexible curriculum encourages students to remedy any past deficiencies in mathematics and to move forward. Courses range from basic prealgebra through algebra and from geometry to calculus. The science program includes a basic foundations course, biology, ecology and other electives, chemistry, physics, and computer studies. The foreign language program ensures that all students become familiar with the language, history, and culture of other countries. The School offers American Sign Language, Japanese, and Spanish.

The Division of the Arts at The Storm King School is designed to unlock a student's potential through creative endeavors. The Department of Fine and Visual Arts offers courses in ceramics, drawing, painting, and sculpture, among others. Excellent faculty members encourage and inspire students to create works of art that far exceed students' personal expectations; these works are then exhibited in public art showings. The Department of Music offers chorus, digital recording and studio production, music appreciation as well as individual instruction in piano, guitar, and other instruments by special arrangement. Students learn performance techniques and are prepared for public recitals. The Dance Department offers classes in classical ballet, tap, jazz, and modern dance. Dance students also present their work in a public recital. The Department of Theatre Arts offers performance, stage craft, theater history, theater appreciation, and courses in design and production. Students apply classroom instruction in rehearsals and production work through the two or three Storm King Theatre Ensemble productions, on which the entire division collaborates. Arts education and training at the Storm King School enhance a student's education and development through academic courses in the arts and are supported by opportunities for practical application in every creative area. Each year, a student must complete a course in public speaking.

The library also houses The Learning Center (TLC), which helps selected students develop the skills and self-confidence essential for academic independence. Services include personalized/group reinforcement and assistance in the classroom setting. TLC works collaboratively with teachers in order to plan instruction that is directly related to classroom curriculum. This approach supplements the teaching skills of the classroom teachers and provides the student with a chance to link skills learned in TLC with knowledge gained from the classroom. The Learning Center focuses on building current strengths that students may not be aware of while improving academics and organization. Study skills work in-

cludes note-taking, outlining, researching, test taking, and time management.

In 2004, The Storm King School inaugurated a school within a school called The Mountain Center. This program is designed for average or above-average students who have an Individual Education Plan (IEP) developed to address the need for a different learning style. The program does not accept students who have significant emotional or behavioral problems. The Mountain Center presents core subjects (English, math, science, social studies) in a 5:1 ratio setting. The Center uses a variety of methods appropriate to the needs of each student to accomplish the desired outcome.

To graduate, a student must complete 23½ credits. The requirements include 4 years each of English and social studies, 3 years of mathematics, 3 years of science, 2 years or the equivalent of a foreign language, and a credit each in health and in visual and performing art.

The grading system uses A–F designations with pluses and minuses. An effort grade is also given. These grades are sent to parents four times a year, but, for guidance purposes, each student is evaluated in between.

FACULTY AND ADVISERS

The boarding-school teacher must not only have a genuine enthusiasm for the subject matter he or she teaches but must also relate well to the middle school and high school student. Ninety percent of the faculty members live on campus—either in the dormitories or in campus housing—and are available for extra help, especially in the evening. All faculty members are active in advising and counseling students and provide a critical link between the family and the School. Of the 18 full-time and 12 part-time faculty members, 20 hold advanced degrees. The School provides funds for continuing education.

Helen S. Chinitz was appointed the fifteenth Head of School in July 2004. She is the first woman head of The Storm King School.

COLLEGE PLACEMENT

Guidance is a continuing process that takes place throughout a student's entire stay at Storm King and quite often even after graduation. College guidance begins in the sophomore year. In group meetings, students and their advisers discuss what lies ahead; individual conferences take place frequently and often include parents. There are many "right" colleges for each student. In recent years, 2 or more graduates have attended the following colleges, among others: Bennington, Boston University, Bucknell, Emerson, George Washington, Hamilton, Iona, Northeastern, NYU, Parsons, Roger Williams, Skidmore, several campuses of the State University of New York, Syracuse, Tufts,

Virginia Tech, and the Universities of Colorado, Hartford, Massachusetts, Miami, Southern California, and Vermont.

STUDENT BODY AND CONDUCT

The Storm King School student body represents a wide spectrum of socioeconomic backgrounds and comes from eleven states and seven other countries. The student body includes 70 boarding and 58 day students. About 50 new students enroll annually.

A disciplinary committee and the Head of School determine punishments for disciplinary infractions. Major offenses may result in withdrawal. Student and faculty groups are consulted in policy formation. Students are expected to be supportive of School policies and to take an active and positive part in the School's programs and activities.

ACADEMIC FACILITIES

Stillman Hall contains mathematics and science classrooms, laboratories, a greenhouse, a darkroom, and department offices. Dyar Hall provides humanities classrooms. The Ogden Library is a split-level learning center with study carrels, an audiovisual room, and the Fox Computer Center, equipped with twenty-five microcomputers. The Walter Reade, Jr. Theatre was dedicated in 1984. The Cobb-Matthiessen Astronomy Observatory was dedicated in 1990.

The Allison Vladimer Art Center, a converted carriage house, is a beautiful facility with a spectacular view of the Black Rock wilderness area. The center was dedicated in 1994.

BOARDING AND GENERAL FACILITIES

Students, teachers, and faculty families reside in Highmount Hall, McConnell Hall, Dempsey Hall, and Cottage. Most of the rooms are doubles, but there are several singles available. The Student Commons contains lounges, a video room, modern kitchen and dining room facilities, and a recently remodeled Student Center for informal recreation. The health center is on the ground floor of Stillman Hall. An admissions/development complex opened in 1992. Also on campus are several faculty residences; the Administration Building, the second floor of which has a faculty apartment; and Spy Rock House, the Headmaster's residence. New faculty residences were completed in December 2003.

ATHLETICS

Athletics at Storm King include recreational and competitive activities as well as a physical education program that is part of the course curriculum.

Each student must participate in an approved activity in each of the three sport seasons and in a competitive sport for one of the three seasons each year.

The gymnasium provides basketball, wrestling, and weight lifting. There are also a dance studio and locker and shower facilities. There are interscholastic teams for boys in basketball, cross-country, lacrosse, tennis, and Ultimate Frisbee; and for girls in basketball, tennis, and volleyball. Coed volleyball is also offered as an interscholastic team sport. The recreational alternatives include karate, skiing, tennis, and weight lifting. The Wilderness Program takes advantage of the School's physical setting, offering outdoor-skill activities, such as mountaineering, canoeing, hiking, and rock-climbing as an alternative to sports as well as a series of weekend backpacking trips.

EXTRACURRICULAR OPPORTUNITIES

The Student Activities Committee oversees many extracurricular activities. Among the student activities are the yearbook, photography, art, the literary journal, the Environmental Club, and several dramatics productions. A work program involves students in routine chores on campus. Learning service opportunities are available on and off campus.

DAILY LIFE

Classes are 45 minutes long and meet five times a week. The day begins with breakfast from 7:15 to 7:50, followed by a morning meeting from 8:10 to 8:30 and classes from 8:35 to 3:20. This is followed by required activities from 4 to 5:30. Sit-down dinners alternate with buffet-style meals. A 2-hour supervised study period, either in the dorm or in the library, and some free time cap off the evening. The day ends at 10 p.m.

WEEKEND LIFE

The School's location provides various opportunities for social, cultural, and entertainment activities. Students may attend theater performances and concerts in New York City. The activities director and a student committee plan weekend activities, such as movies, dances, intramural athletics, hikes, skiing, horseback riding, visits to museums, and trips to special events. Students may go home any weekend after their obligations have been met.

COSTS AND FINANCIAL AID

For 2005–06, costs for boarding students totaled $29,300; for day students, costs totaled $15,800. Costs for books, insurance, and laundry are additional. Students have to pay for transportation to and from the School. The School banks an account for a student, from which spending money may be drawn.

Financial assistance totaling about $321,000 is awarded annually in the form of grants and loans, according to guidelines determined by the School and Student Service for Financial Aid, to about 27 percent of the student body.

ADMISSIONS INFORMATION

The School accepts students in grades 7 through 12 as well as some postgraduates. Selections are made without regard to race, creed, or national origin and are based upon the applicant's promise of success and past record. An interview at the School is highly desirable. The School also offers prospective students the opportunity to participate in the day program to help them feel more comfortable and to enable them to learn about the School directly from their peers. The Director of Admission recommends candidates for consideration to the Faculty Admissions Committee.

APPLICATION TIMETABLE

Initial inquiries are welcome at any time, and campus interviews can be arranged from 8:30 to 3:30 during the week. A nonrefundable $85 fee must accompany the application. Acceptance notifications are sent as soon as all information is complete and the Admissions Committee makes a decision.

ADMISSIONS CORRESPONDENCE

Stephen T. Lifrak, Ph.D.
Director of Admissions
The Storm King School
314 Mountain Road
Cornwall-on-Hudson, New York 12520-1899

Phone: 845-534-7892
          800-225-9144 (toll-free)
Fax: 845-534-4128
E-mail: admissions@sks.org
Web site: http://www.sks.org

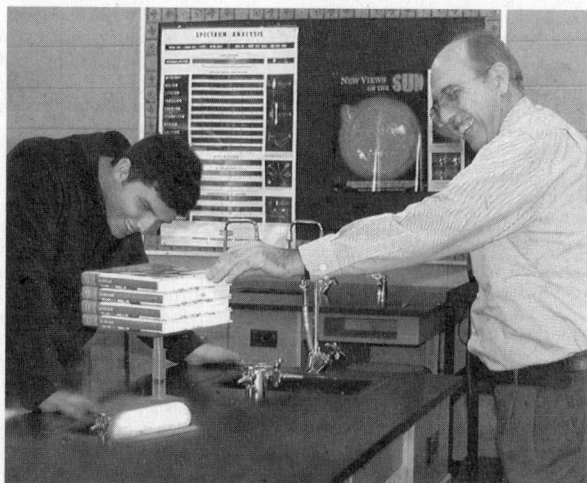

STUART COUNTRY DAY SCHOOL OF THE SACRED HEART

Princeton, New Jersey

Type: Member of the International Network of Sacred Heart Schools; College-preparatory day school (coeducational preschool)
Grades: P–12: Preschool, 3- and 4-year-olds; Lower School, K–5; Middle School, 6–8; Upper School, 9–12
Enrollment: School total: 550; Upper School: 165
Head of School: Frances de la Chapelle, R.S.C.J., Headmistress

---

THE SCHOOL

Stuart Country Day School of the Sacred Heart, situated in a 55-acre woodland section of Princeton, New Jersey, is an independent day school for girls in kindergarten through grade 12 and for both boys and girls in the preschool. The School was founded in 1963.

Operated by the Religious of the Sacred Heart, Stuart is one of the twenty-one U.S. members of the worldwide Network of Sacred Heart Schools, which was established in 1800. The Sacred Heart tradition of academic excellence and an atmosphere of affection and trust lead families of many faiths to send their children to Stuart.

A Stuart education provides a strong academic foundation that is appropriate to each student's gifts and capabilities, heightens her awareness and appreciation of the religious dimensions of life, helps her to discover her own values, and encourages a caring response to the needs and concerns of others.

Trust, openness, intellectual challenge, and personal growth—these are all characteristics of life at Stuart.

Stuart is governed by a Board of Trustees of 31 men and women from the community and the Society of the Sacred Heart, who have backgrounds in law, finance, and education.

Stuart has an endowment of more than $5.9 million.

Stuart is accredited by the Middle States Association of Colleges and Schools. It is a member of a number of organizations, including the Network of Sacred Heart Schools of the United States, the National Association of Independent Schools, the New Jersey Association of Independent Schools, the Secondary School Admission Test Board, the College Board, the Association for Supervision and Curriculum Development, and the Educational Records Bureau.

ACADEMIC PROGRAMS

The college-preparatory program requires a minimum of 70 academic credits for graduation. Students must complete 4 years of religious studies (2 trimesters each year). They must also complete 4 years of English, 3 years of one foreign language, 3 years of mathematics, 2 years of a laboratory science, 2 years of history, 1 year of fine arts, 2 trimesters of health education, and 1 trimester of computer science. The remaining credits may be electives. Every Upper School student must take physical education classes four periods per cycle and must participate in community service for all four years.

The Upper School offers a wide range of elective and honors courses in the areas of math, the sciences, social studies, religion, and art. A full range of Advanced Placement (AP) courses, including environmental science, are offered in order to provide a challenging program for seniors. The senior independent-study program provides an opportunity for students to explore some particular interest in depth while taking responsibility for their own learning. Advanced students may take courses at Princeton University.

Letter grades are used, with A+ (100) the maximum. The minimum passing grade is D (65). Stuart is on the trimester system, with about eleven weeks to the term. Written reports with grades are sent home following the end of each trimester, and interim reports are sent whenever a teacher wishes to inform parents of their daughter's progress. Upper School academic advisers meet with their students regularly to discuss courses and goals.

Students who fail a trimester course, receive an interim report indicating poor work in more than one course, or do generally poor academic work in relation to their ability are placed on academic probation until their performance improves. Probation is intended to provide help and support, not to be a punitive measure.

Students are grouped heterogeneously or homogeneously in classes, depending on the discipline. Class size varies from 6 to 18; the overall student-teacher ratio is about 7:1. The required minimum number of courses per term is five.

Students at Stuart have an opportunity to broaden their horizons socially and academically through the Exchange Program, which is made possible by the Network of Sacred Heart Schools, which exists in this country and throughout the world. In the United States, students may live for one term as resident students in the boarding schools or with host families whose children attend day schools, or they may attend a Sacred Heart school abroad for up to a full year. Stuart's International Exchange Program extends opportunities for exchanges with schools in which French or Spanish is the language of classroom instruction.

FACULTY AND ADVISERS

Stuart faculty members make learning an active and exciting process. The faculty of preschool through grade 12, a diverse group with degrees from both American and European institutions, consists of 92 teachers, including 2 from religious orders.

Eighty-two percent of the 33 Upper School faculty members have advanced degrees in their disciplines.

The Headmistress, Frances de la Chapelle, R.S.C.J., received a B.A. from Maryville College, an M.A. from Catholic University, and an M.S.A. from the University of Notre Dame. Before coming to Stuart, Sister de la Chapelle was Director of Ongoing Formation for Ministry for the United States Province of the Society of the Sacred Heart. From 1983 to 1991, she served as Headmistress of Woodlands Academy of the Sacred Heart in Lake Forest, Illinois. Prior to that, she was both a teacher and an administrator at Stuart.

Faculty members devote much time throughout the year to advising and counseling students and meeting with parents. Many are actively pursuing advanced degrees, and all are involved in in-service workshops during the school year. The annual turnover is minimal.

COLLEGE PLACEMENT

The full-time Director of College and Career Guidance works individually with students in selecting colleges. Starting with a few introductory sessions in grades 9 and 10, he advises students and their parents frequently in their junior and senior years. Representatives from many colleges and universities annually visit Stuart to talk to students, and the School maintains many college catalogs and reference sources.

Students take the PSAT or PLAN in their sophomore year as a preparation exercise, then again in their junior year. They receive guidance on how to prepare for the SAT and SAT Subject Tests. Representatives from business, the professions, and the arts assist in introducing Upper School students to various career possibilities.

In the School's forty-two-year history, Stuart graduates have entered many of the nation's finest colleges and universities. Thirty-five members of the class of 2005 entered a total of thirty-five different colleges, including Boston College, Georgetown University, George Washington University, Johns Hopkins University, Lafayette College, Massachusetts Institute of Technology, the Universities of Michigan and Pennsylvania, and Villanova.

STUDENT BODY AND CONDUCT

In 2005–06, there were 43 students in grade 9, 41 in grade 10, 40 in grade 11, and 41 in grade 12. Stuart draws its students from forty-eight communities, including central and northern New Jersey and Pennsylvania.

There is a dress code in the Upper School, and students are required to dress appropriately for school. Pants may be worn. Uniforms are worn in the Lower and Middle Schools.

The School provides an element of discipline in which a student has the freedom to explore many areas. The poise and self-discipline of the students reflect an atmosphere that depends on a shared understanding and acceptance of the policies and minimal rules drawn up by the faculty and students together.

Stuart has a Student Government, which is composed of the Executive, Outreach, School Spirit, and Social Committees. Together with members of the faculty, these bodies help to formulate and implement School rules and regulations. A Peer Leadership group serves to counsel freshmen on areas of concern to adolescents.

ACADEMIC FACILITIES

Stuart's attractive woodland setting is one of the School's finest assets. The green-glazed brick building, which was designed by Jean Labatut, Professor of Architecture Emeritus at Princeton, is well integrated with the surroundings. The simple, uncluttered design exerts a powerful influence on those who study and teach at Stuart. The entire building has been expanded and improved by means of a $10-million capital campaign.

The preschool areas are constructed as distinct units. The Lower, Middle, and Upper School classrooms, all designed to face the woods, are grouped around their Resource Centers. These centers serve the Lower and Middle School areas as gathering spaces, while the Upper School center provides students with a place in which to work or meet in-

formally in a quiet atmosphere. The building also includes a spacious reception hall, a dining room, a small chapel, a theater, a choral/instrumental music room, four state-of-the-art science laboratories, three computer rooms, numerous offices, faculty workrooms, and a seminar room. The newly renovated and expanded library houses a collection of 15,000 items and operates with the latest Internet and intranet technology. The library is a member of the regional and state library consortium. The art room includes facilities for drawing, sculpting, painting, photography, and pottery. Students studying art, environmental science, and religion make good use of the School's acres of woods, streams, recreational areas, and nature trail. A major expansion and enhancement of these facilities was completed in 2002. The 800-seat theater/chapel Cor Unum Center, which was designed by the world-renowned firm, Venturi, Scott Brown and Associates, opened in December 2004.

ATHLETICS

Stuart's size allows everyone to participate, regardless of ability, in a variety of seasonal sports. Middle and Upper School students compete interscholastically in basketball, cross-country, field hockey, ice hockey (which begins in grade 8), lacrosse, squash, tennis, and track and field.

Two large gymnasiums are equipped for indoor tennis, volleyball, gymnastics, basketball, and individual sports. Outside are two playing fields for field hockey and lacrosse and five tennis courts. The ice hockey team uses nearby rinks. Squash is offered locally. A new athletic complex includes regulation-size lacrosse and hockey fields, tennis courts for tournament play, a fitness/wellness center, locker rooms, and a field house.

EXTRACURRICULAR OPPORTUNITIES

Extracurricular organizations and activities at Stuart are varied and appeal to many interests. Some reflect academic interests (such as the Model UN and student publications). Others are geared to sports and hobbies.

School clubs at Stuart and other area schools jointly sponsor a variety of activities, including social functions. In addition, students from local schools join the Stuart Drama Club for two annual

productions. Also, a vocal ensemble, the Tartan-Tones, performs for many School activities and for civic groups.

A program of retreats augments Stuart's effort to provide an integrated approach to religion as the foundation of daily living.

Stuart's philosophy includes the belief that a responsible person must be able to care for others and minister to their needs. Therefore, participation in the community service program in the Upper School is required for graduation. Students volunteer at Stuart and in various places in the community, such as hospitals, after-school tutoring and recreation programs, nursing homes, soup kitchens, and environmental agencies. A student outreach committee in the Upper School volunteers in soup kitchens and participates during the year in hunger walks; drives for food, clothing, and toys; and beach cleanups. There are also opportunities in the summer to go to Appalachia with the Appalachia Service Project and to Trenton with Martin House and Habitat for Humanity to assist with home repairs.

DAILY LIFE

Classes are 46 minutes long. There are seven class periods five days a week. The last class ends at 3:10 p.m.

Students may bring their own lunch or subscribe to the School's dining room service.

Club and other activities are built into the school schedule. Sports practices, games, and play rehearsals are held after school.

COSTS AND FINANCIAL AID

In 2005–06, tuition ranged from $8080 to $23,150, depending upon grade level. Academic fees and testing materials are included in the tuition. There are additional expenses for such items as special instructional materials, gym uniforms, books, and some science and art materials. Payments are to be made semiannually in July and December.

Financial aid at Stuart is awarded on the basis of need as determined by the School and Student Service for Financial Aid of the Educational Testing Service. One-third-tuition academic scholarships are awarded annually to up to 3 ninth graders. Approximately 16 percent of Stuart's students receive

some financial aid, in amounts ranging from $1000 to $20,500. In order that awards may be made early in the spring, Parents' Financial Statements should be filed in the January preceding entrance or re-enrollment. All financial aid awards are reviewed annually. Awards are need-based and kept in the strictest confidence. Stuart offers a monthly payment plan administered by Academic Management Services.

ADMISSIONS INFORMATION

Admission to Stuart is determined on the basis of interviews, the student's past record, and the results of an entrance test.

Stuart does not discriminate on the basis of race in the administration of its educational policies, admissions policies, financial aid program, or athletics or other School-administered programs. Applicants for grades 1–5 must take the School's standardized test (given at the School); applicants are required to take the SSAT for grades 6–11 and are urged to take it no later than the January preceding entrance. Transcripts from a student's present school must be forwarded to Stuart along with teacher recommendations. The application deadline is January 9 for grades 1–12, January 18 for kindergarten, and January 13 for preschool.

APPLICATION TIMETABLE

Inquiries are always welcome, and the School sponsors Open Houses and conducts tours throughout the year. The submission of a completed application is the first step in the admissions process. Each prospective student is encouraged to attend an Open House with her parents and to spend a day at Stuart so that she may experience the life of the School. An interview is then set up for the student and her parents. Stuart notifies all candidates for grades 6–12 on March 10. The Admissions Committee meets regularly to act upon applications.

ADMISSIONS CORRESPONDENCE

Stephanie Lupero
Director of Admissions
Stuart Country Day School of the Sacred Heart
1200 Stuart Road
Princeton, New Jersey 08540

Phone: 609-921-2330
Fax: 609-497-0784
E-mail: admissions@stuartschool.org
Web site: http://www.stuartschool.org

STUART HALL

Staunton, Virginia

Type: Girls' boarding (8–12) and day (5–12) and boys' day (5–12) college-preparatory school
Grades: 5–12: Middle School, 5–8; Upper School, 9–12
Enrollment: 152; Upper School: 70
Head of School: Mark H. Eastham, Headmaster

THE SCHOOL

Stuart Hall, the oldest Episcopal girls' boarding school in Virginia, was founded in 1844 as Virginia Female Institute. In 1861, the school was temporarily closed and its building used by the state to house the Virginia School for the Deaf and the Blind, whose own buildings were being used as a Confederate hospital. In the 1860s, Gen. Robert E. Lee was president of the Board of Visitors, and from 1880 to 1899, Mrs. Flora Cooke Stuart, widow of Gen. J. E. B. Stuart, served as Headmistress. In 1907, Virginia Female Institute was renamed Stuart Hall in her honor.

Stuart Hall seeks to educate the whole child—mind, body, heart, and spirit—in a special context: a supportive, familylike, Christian environment that nurtures self-esteem and honor, leadership and industry, and compassion and commitment to service.

Stuart Hall provides a high-quality education through a comprehensive, integrated curriculum. Essential components of the experience at Stuart Hall include a vigorous academic program that offers a flexible sequence of individually tailored studies; the experience of life in a community; athletic and health programs; social, cultural, and service activities; and opportunities for spiritual awareness and exploration.

Stuart Hall's specific objectives and programs in all areas of school life are designed to nurture students' growth, respectfulness, discipline, leadership, independence, and creativity. Students are encouraged to contribute their time as volunteers in the community and to become active and effective participants in school life. Stuart Hall is affiliated with the Episcopal Church, and approximately 25 percent of the students are of that denomination.

The 8-acre campus is located in the small college town of Staunton, Virginia, in the Shenandoah Valley, 40 miles from Charlottesville and the University of Virginia, 20 miles from the famous Blue Ridge Parkway, and 150 miles from Washington, D.C. Mary Baldwin College and the cultural and commercial offerings of historic Staunton are only a few blocks away.

As of July 1, 2003, Stuart Hall became the sixth member of Church Schools in the Diocese of Virginia and the first new member since 1944. The other members are St. Christopher's and St. Catherine's Schools in Richmond, St. Margaret's and Christchurch Schools on the Rappahannock River, and St. Stephen's & St. Agnes School in Alexandria. Stuart Hall is a nonprofit organization governed by the Church Schools Board of Trustees and its own Board of Governors.

The Stuart Hall Foundation provides strong support for the School, as do the graduates, parents, and friends. Stuart Hall is accredited by the Virginia Association of Independent Schools and holds membership in the National Associa-

tion of Independent Schools and the National Association of Episcopal Schools, among other affiliations.

ACADEMIC PROGRAMS

Stuart Hall offers three academic tracks that lead to graduation: the traditional college preparatory track, the honors track, and the visual and performing arts track. The traditional college preparatory track is for the average to above-average student. Students have the option of taking honors and AP courses in their areas of strength. Graduation requirements for the traditional college preparatory program include art (1 credit), English (4 credits), foreign language (3 credits or through the junior year), history (4 credits), math (4 credits, at least through algebra II), philosophy/religion (1 credit), physical education/health (2 credits), and science (3 credits).

The Honors Program is for the above-average to gifted student. In order to graduate from this program and receive the Stuart Hall Honors Diploma, students must take at least three AP courses and nine Honors courses. It is a four-year program; any student entering Stuart Hall after the ninth-grade year must already have begun work in honors courses. There is an additional application required for this program.

The Visual and Performing Arts Program at Stuart Hall is specifically designed for those students with strength and ability in the arts. It prepares students who plan to attend arts or liberal arts colleges. The program focuses on three different areas: art and design, music, and theater. Art and design includes drawing, painting, ceramics, enameling, theater design, illustration, printmaking, 3-D design, and art history. Upper-level students work on independent projects. Music includes history and theory, private voice and instrumental lessons, guitar, chorus, musical theater, and performance. Theater includes literature, improvisation, voice and diction, scriptwriting, movement, stagecraft, musical theater, technical theater, chorus, performance, fitness training, and stage direction. There are also classes in theater history. Students must choose a major from one of the three areas. However, it may be possible for a student to major in one area and minor in another. Students work with their peers in morning academic sessions. Uninterrupted blocks of time in the afternoon focus on the arts. Minimum graduation requirements include English (4 credits), math (3 credits), history (5 credits), science (3 credits), foreign language (2 credits), and arts (8 credits). There is an additional application and audition process for the Visual and Performing Arts Program.

The Middle School curriculum is specifically geared toward the average to above-average student. Depending upon academic ability (deter-

mined by faculty and advisers), students in the eighth grade may opt to take algebra I and begin a foreign language.

Stuart Hall has a Learning Resource Center (LRC) that offers a time of directed study. The LRC teaches organizational and time management skills and test-taking strategies. The center serves Stuart Hall students who need help with their studies as well as those who just want a quiet place to study.

Classes average 8 to 15 students, with a student-teacher ratio of approximately 8:1. The average student's course load is five to six academic subjects. Grade reports, with extensive comments from teachers, are sent to parents at the end of each marking period.

Each year at spring break Stuart Hall Abroad offers an optional ten-day cultural immersion program to enrich the overall curriculum. Past trips have taken students to England, France, Mexico, Spain, Russia, Italy, and the Florida Keys.

FACULTY AND ADVISERS

The 2005–06 faculty consisted of 20 full-time members. Some faculty members live on campus and serve as dorm parents and hold additional responsibility with boarders. Each student is assigned a faculty adviser when they begin at Stuart Hall. This adviser serves as a contact person and mentor for the student. Students and their advisers have lunch together every Monday and Friday.

COLLEGE PLACEMENT

Beginning in their freshman year, students are aided in their applications to and selection of colleges both by their individual advisers and by a college counselor. A counseling center provides access to college selection aids, reference materials, and college catalogs. Recent graduates have attended the following colleges and universities, among others: Berklee School of Music, Bridgewater, Brown, Duke, George Mason, James Madison, Johns Hopkins, Manhattan College, Maryland Institute College of Art, Northeastern, Pratt, Randolph Macon, Rhode Island School of Design, Richmond, Stanford, Swarthmore, Sweet Briar, Virginia Commonwealth, Virginia Tech, Washington and Lee, William and Mary, University of the Arts, and the Universities of North Carolina and Virginia.

STUDENT BODY AND CONDUCT

The student body in the Upper School is composed of 40 boarding students and 30 day students. Students are from Maryland, Virginia, West Virginia, and North Carolina. Ten states and two countries are represented.

Each student is expected to uphold an honor code based on personal integrity and respect for the rights and freedoms of others. Violators of

---

the code are brought before an Honor Council made up of their fellow students. The Headmaster then acts on the recommendations of the council.

Student government organizations are active at Stuart Hall. Each class elects officers to serve as representatives in a general assembly. Students and teachers participate in workshops to form policies and make recommendations for the school.

ACADEMIC FACILITIES
The focal point of the campus is Old Main, a registered historic landmark that dates back to 1846. Old Main houses offices, a $1.1-million library, art studios, and the auditorium. The student center, a darkroom, classrooms, and a music room are contained in wings added to Old Main at various points throughout the school's history. The Tullidge Center, which houses Maxwell Science Center, Cochran Middle School classrooms, Edwards fitness center, and a gymnasium, opened in 1997.

BOARDING AND GENERAL FACILITIES
Eight residential halls in two buildings house boarding students and dorm parents. One of these is Old Main, which also contains reception areas, the dining hall, and the health center. The ratio of students to faculty members in the dormitories is approximately 6:1. Students may be assigned to double rooms, but a limited number of single rooms are available. Three balanced meals are served daily in the dining room. The television rooms, reading rooms, and lounges are available for student use. The school has access to the Episcopal church opposite the campus for its religious services and for other activities. The students may go to the church of their choice on Sunday.

The health center is staffed during school hours. A doctor and registered nurses are on call 24 hours a day, and a hospital is located nearby.

ATHLETICS
The Stuart Hall athletics department believes that the school should provide each student with the opportunity to participate in a physical activity regardless of athletic ability. Sports that most students can and will continue throughout adult life are emphasized, as is physical fitness. Varsity and junior varsity teams compete with neighbor-

ing schools in swimming, cross-country, basketball, tennis, soccer, and volleyball. Facilities include the gymnasium, the fitness center, playing fields, and tennis courts.

EXTRACURRICULAR OPPORTUNITIES
All students at Stuart Hall are invited to participate in supervised, organized, nonacademic activity. A choral group, a drama club, the ecology club, the social committee, the literary magazine, the yearbook, and volunteer services are some of the activities offered. Frequent informal activities are available, including weekend trips, movies, dances, and hiking and skiing trips. Excursions to such places as Washington, D.C., for plays and concerts are organized.

Each spring, the school observes Parents' Weekend. Art exhibits, plays, concerts, picnics, and games are shared by students and their families. There are several annual banquets, including the Junior-Senior Banquet in the spring, the seniors' Ring Banquet in the fall, and the Spring Ball.

DAILY LIFE
Monday through Friday, a typical day's schedule begins at 7:15 with a buffet breakfast until 7:45. Academic periods on Monday, Wednesday, and Friday are 47 minutes, while Tuesday's and Thursday's are 90 minutes. Students have breaks, chapel, and lunch interspersed throughout the academic day and afterward participate in athletics and may go into town if they have met their athletics requirements. Dinner is served at 6, and optional meetings may take place shortly afterward. Study hall is from 7 to 9. Freshmen and sophomores are required to be in their rooms by 10:30 with lights out by 11, and juniors and seniors are required to be in their rooms by 11 with lights out by midnight.

WEEKEND LIFE
Stuart Hall's location offers many opportunities for social, recreational, and cultural activities. School-sponsored trips to movies, dances, or picnics at nearby boys' schools, skiing in the Blue Ridge Mountains, or other activities are offered each weekend.

Most of the weekends during the year are open weekends, in which any student may take an off-campus weekend subject to approval by the student's parents and Stuart Hall adviser.

Girls remaining on campus for the weekend may receive permission to leave campus for various activities. Full-time faculty and staff members are on duty at all times to chaperone each weekend activity.

COSTS AND FINANCIAL AID
The 2005–06 general charge for tuition, room, and seven-day boarding at Stuart Hall was $32,000. Five-day boarding costs were $29,500. Costs for international students were $34,000. In addition, approximately $1000 was needed for fees, books, and supplies. Additional costs for ESL students were $4000. The Visual and Performing Arts fee was $1500. It is recommended that each student have at least $15 a week for spending money. The cost for day students was $10,500 and included five lunches per week.

In 2005–06, 32 percent of the students received a total of $400,000 in aid. Scholarships are granted on the basis of need.

ADMISSIONS INFORMATION
Stuart Hall seeks a diverse and well-rounded student body with a wide range of abilities and interests. Applicants are required to submit standardized testing results, academic records, teacher recommendations, and a personal statement. An on-campus interview is recommended. Stuart Hall does not discriminate on the basis of race, religion, or national or ethnic origin.

APPLICATION TIMETABLE
The Admissions Office welcomes inquiries at any time. Campus tours and interviews are available by appointment year round. If there is room, students who are not able to start in the fall are admitted at midyear. Students are notified of the action taken by the Admissions Office upon completion of their files, and parents are expected to respond to acceptances within one month.

ADMISSIONS CORRESPONDENCE
Admissions Office
Stuart Hall School
P.O. Box 210
Staunton, Virginia 24402-0210
Phone: 540-885-0356
        888-306-8926 (toll-free)
Fax: 540-886-2275
E-mail: admissions@stuart-hall.org
Web site: http://www.stuart-hall.org

SUFFIELD ACADEMY
Suffield, Connecticut

Type: Coeducational boarding and day college-preparatory school
Grades: 9–12, postgraduate year
Enrollment: 405
Head of School: Charles Cahn III, Headmaster

THE SCHOOL

Challenge, structure, and support characterize Suffield Academy. A rigorous college-preparatory program in academics is supported by each student's ownership of a laptop computer, beautiful new facilities for music and the visual and performing arts, and extracurricular and athletic programs that round out each student's education. The school has a tradition of academic and athletic excellence and a deep sense of community spirit.

Founded as the Connecticut Literary Institution in 1833, the school became coeducational in 1843 and provided a traditional education for 100 years as both a private academy and the town's only public high school. It took the name of Suffield Academy in 1916 and after World War II became a fully independent boarding and day school for boys. In 1974, Suffield Academy returned to coeducation.

Suffield's strength lies in the personal concern and support shown for each student. The school emphasizes small classes and a structured academic program. In this setting, faculty members encourage students to take an active role in their education and to seek creative insights and solutions.

Each student is challenged intellectually, ethically, and physically to make the best use of his or her talents while developing a sound system of personal and social values.

The Academy's beautiful 350-acre campus is located in the historic residential town of Suffield, Connecticut, a community of 13,550 people located in a region that offers excellent opportunities for bicycling and hiking. Concerts, museums, theaters, and other city offerings are easily accessible in Springfield, Massachusetts, 10 miles north of Suffield, and Hartford, Connecticut, 17 miles to the south. New York is 135 miles to the south, and Boston is 90 miles to the northeast. Bradley International Airport is 5 miles from the campus.

A nonprofit institution, Suffield is governed by a self-perpetuating 24-member Board of Trustees. It has an endowment of $21 million. Annual Giving from alumni and alumnae, parents, and friends exceeds $1 million. The annual budget is more than $10 million.

Suffield is accredited by the New England Association of Schools and Colleges. It is a member of or is affiliated with each of the following organizations: the Connecticut Association of Independent Schools, the National Association of Independent Schools, the Cum Laude Society, American Secondary Schools for International Students and Teachers (ASSIST), the Secondary School Admission Test Board, A Better Chance, the Council for Advancement and Support of Education, Hartford Area Boarding Schools, the Alumni Presidents Council, Secondary School Research Programs, and the WALKS Foundation.

ACADEMIC PROGRAMS

Suffield offers a college-preparatory curriculum that is grounded in the liberal arts. The academic program stresses acquiring the fundamental skills and knowledge needed to succeed in a variety of academic disciplines and in college. With careful guidance, students select a program of study designed to meet special interests and needs.

The school year is divided into three terms. Classes are held six days a week but end at noon on Wednesday and at 11 a.m. on Saturday, when athletics contests are scheduled in the afternoon. Classes average 11 students, and each class meets four times per week (two 45-minute periods and two extended 70-minute periods). Teachers are available for extra help on an individual basis. Students also have the support of faculty advisers and a walk-in counseling office. The student-faculty ratio is 7:1.

The Suffield Computer Initiative has enabled the school to integrate the use of technology into its traditional liberal arts curriculum. Each student possesses a laptop computer and the classrooms and dorm rooms are wired for Internet and telephone use. The campus is wireless.

The Suffield Leadership Scholar Program offers partial scholarships to students who demonstrate the potential to be leaders at Suffield, in college, and in their careers. This program is an outgrowth of the excellent leadership development opportunities already available. A 40-acre leadership training site opened in June 2000. The Suffield Leadership Initiative is a unique program that is designed to teach ways of thinking and develop skills, traits, and habits that enhance each student's leadership qualities.

Students may choose from course offerings in the visual arts (painting, sculpture, woodworking, architecture, computer graphics, and more) or the performing arts (instrument ensembles, choral groups, dance, and private instruction in voice or instrument) to satisfy the requirement of a year's study in the arts.

The Academic Support Office provides resources for students who have different learning styles or challenges, as shown by their prior academic experience. The Director of Academic Support meets regularly with each student to create strategies that will sharpen their focus and strengthen their academic performance in the classroom. The Director also works with faculty members to communicate specific student needs so that Academy teachers are better able to meet the needs of students who have a broad range of learning styles.

Freshmen and sophomores carry five or six full-credit courses; juniors and seniors carry four, five, or six. To graduate, a student must demonstrate computer literacy and complete a total of 20⅓ credits, including 4 credits in English; 4 in leadership classes; 3 in mathematics;

2 in history, including 1 in U.S. history; 2 in Latin or a modern language; 2 in science, including 1 in a laboratory science; 2 in technology portfolios; 1 in the arts; ⅓ in religion; and the balance in electives.

All major departments offer honors-level courses. Advanced Placement courses are offered in English, foreign languages, history, and science. Interest in a course may lead to individual work with a teacher. In the senior year, students may select an independent study project for credit.

Grades, based on a minimum passing grade of D-, are recorded every five weeks. Effort also plays a significant part in the grading system. Academic reports from teachers (including grade, effort rating, and detailed comments), along with an evaluation from the adviser, are sent to parents at the end of each term and at the first midterm.

Ample time is provided for uninterrupted study, both during the day and in the evening. All boarding students study in their rooms, in the library, or in the computer lab in the evening from 8 to 10. Unsatisfactory effort necessitates attendance at supervised study halls during the day and evening until the student's effort improves.

FACULTY AND ADVISERS

There are 84 dedicated men and women on the faculty at Suffield Academy, 53 of whom have or are working toward graduate degrees. With few exceptions, faculty members and their families live on campus and all serve as advisers, coaches, dormitory parents, activity supervisors, and trip leaders. They engage in training programs and workshops as well as graduate programs leading to advanced degrees and professional expertise in their academic discipline.

Charles Cahn was appointed headmaster on June 30, 2003. A native of Baltimore, Maryland, Charlie graduated from the Gilman School, received his bachelor's degree from the University of Michigan, and earned a master's degree in liberal studies at Wesleyan University. He also pursued graduate studies at Oxford University. Charlie came to Suffield in 1992 to teach in the English department. He also coached the boys' varsity lacrosse team and was a dorm parent in a girls' dorm. In 1996, Charlie took on the role of director of admissions, a position he retained until being named assistant headmaster in 1999. For the past three years, Charlie has served as associate headmaster, overseeing the day-to-day affairs of the school.

Suffield is above all a caring school, and its faculty members reflect this attitude. All faculty members serve as advisers, with an average advisee group of 5 students. Students select their advisers, meet with them on a regular basis, and confer with them when needed. Two traditional

annual events, Parents' Day in the fall and Spring Parents' Weekend, feature parental conferences with teachers and advisers that enable parents to share the results of their son's or daughter's experience at Suffield. Advisers are available to meet with parents and teachers as needed concerning a student's progress.

COLLEGE PLACEMENT

Suffield's College Counseling Office provides a comprehensive program. Preparatory testing begins in the sophomore year, and meetings between students and their college counselors begin in the spring of the junior year. Representatives of more than 100 colleges visit the school annually, and students are encouraged to visit colleges.

In 2005, graduates enrolled in eighty-one colleges and universities, including Amherst, Carnegie Mellon, Colgate, George Washington, Johns Hopkins, Middlebury, Northwestern, Santa Clara, the University of Chicago, and Williams.

STUDENT BODY AND CONDUCT

The student community of 2005–06 had an enrollment of 405 students; 144 were boarding boys, 90 were boarding girls, 71 were day boys, and 100 were day girls. Students came from twenty-two states and eighteen other countries. A wealth of understanding and enrichment is fostered through this diversity of cultural backgrounds. During school holidays and vacations, many international students stay with host families in the area.

While all students are encouraged to become constructively involved in the extracurricular life of the school, class representatives contribute to the decision-making process through participation in the Student Council and Discipline Committee. Cooperation and consideration of the rights of others are important factors in the decision-making process of each student.

The School Work Program and off-campus Community Service Program are vital parts of Suffield Academy life, promoting pride in the school and respect for other people. Everyone in the Suffield community performs a daily job that contributes to the general well-being of the school. A number of seniors and faculty members oversee this program.

ACADEMIC FACILITIES

The school occupies nineteen major buildings, including Memorial Building, the main classroom building, which houses a computer resource center with a multimedia classroom, desktop publishing center, printing stations, and a repair facility; the Alfred E. Holcomb science building, with four newly-renovated laboratories, a lecture room, and a weather satellite tracking system; and the 20,000-volume S. Kent Legare Library with a multimedia center, Tisch Auditorium, and computer resources that include fifty-five Internet drop sites located throughout the library. The Jeanice H. Seaverns Performing Arts Center is a multipurpose facility that includes a 200-seat theater, an art gallery, a music building with practice rooms, and practice space for Suffield's dance program. The Emily Hall Tremaine Visual Arts Center features a multipurpose art studio, ceramics studio, woodworking shop, graphics lab, photography lab, library office, and gallery. Nondenominational chapel services are held once a week in the town's Second Baptist Church. A wellness center and music building recently opened, and Centurion Hall, an academic building that houses class-

rooms for history, leadership, and math courses, opened in September 2002.

BOARDING AND GENERAL FACILITIES

Eleven dormitories provide double rooms for 234 students. All dorm rooms are wired for both telephone and Internet use. Five new cottage-style dorms opened in September 1998. Fuller and Spencer Halls are larger dormitories housing 46 and 50 students, respectively. There are also four homes, each shared by between 6 and 12 students. All dormitories have faculty residents, including families, and student proctors.

The downstairs part of Brewster Hall contains the school dining room, the kitchen, and the student union with lounge, TV room, game room, snack area, bookstore, and post office. Other buildings are the Fuller Hall administration building and the historic Gay Mansion, the official residence of the Headmaster.

ATHLETICS

With more than thirty-five interscholastic teams, as well as various other athletics options, all students participate in sports on a level of competition that matches individual experience and ability. Athletics at Suffield stress good sportsmanship, acquisition of skills, and leadership development. The Sherman Perry Gymnasium houses a Nautilus center, trainers' room, and facilities for basketball, wrestling, volleyball, swimming, and riflery. The campus includes a football field, five soccer fields, two baseball diamonds and a softball diamond, ten tennis courts, a hockey field, three lacrosse fields, a sand volleyball pit, and an all-weather track. Facilities for skiing and golf are available nearby. Fitness programs, outdoor programs, team management, volunteer service, or play production may be undertaken in lieu of interscholastic sports. A new squash center with four international courts opened in 1998. A state-of-the-art fitness center opened in December 2003.

EXTRACURRICULAR OPPORTUNITIES

Suffield believes that every student should become constructively involved in the life of the school outside of the classroom. In addition to weekly chapel and a varied program of assemblies, both required, the school sponsors visiting artists and professionals who share experiences with the student body that often provoke new interests.

Students may choose from more than twenty-five activities, including concert and theater series, bicycling, bands, the yearbook, drama productions, the school newspaper, photography, chess, horseback riding, community service, and computers. Suffield Outdoor Leadership Opportunities (S.O.L.O.) maintains an active program, including rock-climbing, caving, backpacking, hiking, canoeing, camping, and other seasonal activities. The school opened an outdoor leadership center in 2000. Suffield's location gives students access to plays, concerts, and museums in two major cities.

DAILY LIFE

Classes begin at 8 a.m. and conclude at 3:05 p.m. on Monday, Tuesday, Thursday, and Friday. Athletics follow the end of the academic day. Only morning classes are scheduled on Wednesday and Saturday; the afternoons are reserved for interscholastic athletics contests. Most clubs meet after dinner.

WEEKEND LIFE

The Student Union was expanded, redesigned, and renovated in 1992. The Weekend Activities and Film committees, as well as the Student Union Board of Governors, use this facility as the center of social life at the school.

On-campus weekend activities include dances, live entertainment, films, plays, and special events, such as Casino Night and Luau. Off-campus options include movies, ski and shopping trips, indoor tennis, horseback riding, and activities sponsored by the Weekend Committee.

Boarding students in good standing may, with parental permission, take an unlimited number of weekends. Rapport between day and boarding students is close, with day students sharing campus activities and many boarding students visiting day students' homes on weekends.

COSTS AND FINANCIAL AID

Charges for 2005–06 were $36,500 for boarders and $24,800 for day students. Additional expenses included books and supplies ($400–$600), spending money ($20/week), laundry, and travel. The required, subsidized computer purchase ranges in cost from $750 to $1800.

For 2005–06, 125 need-based scholarships with a total value of more than $2 million were awarded.

ADMISSIONS INFORMATION

The Admissions Committee seeks students who are committed to serious study and who have a sense of purpose, a good previous record both academically and personally, and supportive recommendations from persons who know the student well. Admissions requirements include the application form with a written essay; an academic transcript from the current school; letters of recommendation from the student's guidance counselor or placement officer, English and mathematics teachers, and a third teacher of the student's choice; and the SSAT, SAT I, PSAT, or WISC. TOEFL is required from students for whom English is not their spoken language.

APPLICATION TIMETABLE

When classes are in session, campus interviews and tours are conducted daily from 8 a.m. to 2 p.m., (8 to 10 a.m. on Wednesday and Saturday). Prospective students are encouraged to visit the campus.

Applications are due February 1 and should be accompanied by a $50 fee for domestic applicants; and a $100 fee for international applicants. The mailing of acceptances is March 10, and students are asked to reply by April 10.

ADMISSIONS CORRESPONDENCE

Terry Breault, Director of Admissions and Financial Aid
Suffield Academy
Suffield, Connecticut 06078
Phone: 860-386-4440
Fax: 860-668-2966
E-mail: saadmit@suffieldacademy.org
Web site: http://www.suffieldacademy.org

TABOR ACADEMY

Marion, Massachusetts

Type: Coeducational boarding and day college-preparatory school
Grades: 9–12
Enrollment: 485
Head of School: Jay S. Stroud, Headmaster

THE SCHOOL

Tabor Academy was founded in 1876 by Elizabeth Taber and is an independent, coeducational, residential school of approximately 485 students in grades 9 through 12. Tabor offers its students a complete educational experience founded on fundamental values of equality and opportunity for all and of kindness, directness, fairness, and honesty in one's dealings with other people.

Tabor also reflects the humility, the imagination, and the accomplishments inspired by life at sea. The Academy's unique location creates a metaphor for education. While some of the students literally study marine biology and celestial navigation, sail boats—both large and small—row crew shells, or swim off Tabor's docks, all of the students undertake voyages of the mind and spirit. At the heart of Tabor Academy stands the analogy of a good ship's crew: dedication, pursuit of knowledge, responsibility for others, lightness of spirit, and anticipation of the adventure of the future.

The Academy is distinguished by a remarkable curriculum, an exceptional faculty, and a physical facility on the shores of Sippican Harbor on Buzzards Bay. Tabor makes full use of its waterfront location in its science, literary, athletic, and naval science programs as well as in its numerous programs aboard the school's schooner, *Tabor Boy.*

Tabor's small dormitories, classrooms, and teams all bear out the school's fundamental philosophy that students must be treated as individuals. Close and personal attention to the development of each Tabor student is given by advisers who are responsible for 6 to 8 students.

Tabor is 55 miles south of Boston and 45 miles east of Providence, Rhode Island.

The current endowment is $34.6 million, and the operating budget for 2005–06 was $17 million. Annual giving in 2004–05 totaled $1,761,200, and total giving for the year was $5.1 million.

Tabor is accredited by the New England Association of Schools and Colleges and is a member of the Secondary School Admission Test Board, the National Association of Independent Schools, and the Independent School Association of New England.

ACADEMIC PROGRAMS

Tabor's curriculum is rigorous and prepares each student for the intellectual challenges of a college or university curriculum. It is comprehensive in scope and depth. Each student normally takes five major courses and may take one or two minors. Required courses include 4 years of English, at least 3 of mathematics (algebra I, algebra II, and geometry), 2 of a foreign language (chosen from a number of modern and classical languages), 2 of history, and 2 of laboratory sciences, as well as involvement in the arts each year. Twenty-four Advanced Placement courses are offered.

A variety of elective courses are offered. In the history department, for instance, courses are of-

fered in Russian, Asian, or modern American history. Nautical science electives include nautical science, marine architecture, celestial navigation, and maritime history. Science electives include astronomy (using the Academy's observatory), physiology, and various levels of oceanography.

Courses in oceanography provide an unusual opportunity for ocean research, with Buzzards Bay and the newly completed Marine and Nautical Sciences Center serving as the classrooms. Tabor has won federal and state grants to rescue endangered marine species and to conserve threatened coastal habitats. Students partner with world-class ocean scientists on cutting-edge research and work with leading organizations, such as the Woods Hole Oceanographic Institution.

The average class size is 12. Many sections are grouped by ability. Students study in their rooms under the supervision of their dormitory parents and senior proctors but may sign out to other campus facilities to do research. Those interested in pursuing an area of study outside normal curriculum offerings may request an independent-study course sponsored by a faculty member.

The Center for International Students at Tabor meets the distinctive academic and cultural needs of students from other countries.

FACULTY AND ADVISERS

The adviser system at Tabor involves every student and faculty member. The primary role of the adviser is to encourage and develop academic excellence and confidence in each advisee. Returning students have an opportunity to choose advisers, who may be coaches, teachers, or dorm parents. Few faculty members advise more than 8 students; most have fewer. The adviser writes a comprehensive report four times a year, summarizing his or her advisees' academic, social, and extracurricular progress. Throughout the year, the adviser is in close communication with the family about areas of mutual interest.

Tabor has 93 full-time faculty members; 49 hold master's degrees and 3 have doctorates. Sixty reside on campus. A discretionary fund controlled by the Headmaster enables faculty members to pursue advanced degree work, to travel, and to attend conferences in their discipline. In the words of the Headmaster, "Tabor, most importantly, is the name for a group of good teachers. They are the foundation. They recognize that interest is a crucial element in motivation and that a worthwhile education requires effort, imagination, and discipline from them and from their students."

Jay S. Stroud was appointed Headmaster in 1988, at which time he had twenty years of teaching experience in independent schools. Mr. Stroud is a graduate of Carleton, Dartmouth, and Columbia.

COLLEGE PLACEMENT

The Director of College Counseling and his staff begin working with students during the second semester of the junior year. Normally, every student and his or her family have at least three individual counseling sessions starting in the junior year, in which the student's goals, career aspirations, and performance are matched with appropriate colleges. Individual sessions with students and families continue throughout the senior year. Representatives of more than 100 colleges visit the campus annually.

Mean College Board scores for the class of 2005 were 593 verbal and 607 math.

Tabor Academy is recognized by the United States Armed Forces as an Honor Naval School, allowing Tabor to nominate annually up to 3 qualified seniors for appointments to each of the federal service academies.

Members of the class of 2005 enrolled at different colleges and universities. Some of the schools most heavily represented include Bates, Boston University, Brown, Hobart and William Smith, Middlebury, Northeastern, NYU, St. Lawrence, Trinity, Tufts, and the University of Vermont.

STUDENT BODY AND CONDUCT

Most students enter Tabor during the freshman or sophomore year. In 2005–06, the freshman class had 100 members, grade 10 had 136, grade 11 had 121, and grade 12 had 137. Students come from twenty-two states and fifteen countries.

In its relationship with students, Tabor Academy assumes that students enter with a serious purpose and believes that conscience and good sense will lead students to be responsible citizens of the school. Every member of the Academy is expected to know what is right or wrong in his or her daily living. The key precept is to conduct oneself with the rights of others in mind. Good manners, care of community property, and acceptance of responsibility are all matters that indicate one's regard for others and in no way limit individuality.

Response to infractions of the Academy's rules varies according to the offense. Serious misconduct that could lead to dismissal is reviewed by the student-faculty Discipline Committee; dorm parents and the deans adjudicate the less serious offenses.

ACADEMIC FACILITIES

The 40,000-square-foot Academic Center houses more than forty classrooms, four science laboratories, an observatory, a greenhouse, and faculty and administrative offices. The Hayden Library contains more than 23,000 volumes as well as two computer laboratories. A $4-million performing arts center was completed in 1990. The Wickenden Chapel seats 600 people and is the site of many all-school events. The newly completed

Marine and Nautical Sciences Center provides a seaside facility for in-depth ocean study.

BOARDING AND GENERAL FACILITIES

The emphasis on small boarding units is the distinguishing feature of Tabor's boarding facilities. Seventeen dormitories provide accommodations for 4 to 29 students each and are supervised by more than 50 faculty members. The house is the small unit of which all members feel a part, and the most enduring friendships are usually formed there. Freshmen live together, as do most sophomores.

The Health Center is a brand-new, well-equipped facility staffed around the clock. Students enjoy the use of The Beebe (snack bar) and Lillard Hall Commons Room in the evening after study period.

ATHLETICS

Tabor's athletics philosophy is a simple one—to offer students the chance to discover, both in themselves and in association and competition with others, the ultimate resources of their physical being. All students participate in activities of their choice at the level of their proficiency. Intramural and interscholastic teams are fielded in more than twenty sports. Alternatives to athletics may be chosen.

The school's playing fields cover 25 acres. The Fish Center for Health and Athletics opened in fall 1998 and has an indoor ice rink, a field house, a basketball court, a wrestling room, international squash courts, a weight-lifting room, an athletic training facility, and a student center. There are seven outdoor tennis courts and four indoor courts. Tabor also has an all-weather outdoor running track. Three local golf courses are available to students, one of which, the Kittansett Club, has been the scene of international competition.

The waterfront presents a superb opportunity for small-boat sailing and rowing. The Tabor small-boat fleet numbers more than forty, including Lasers and 420s for racing. All participants in the sailing program receive instruction until they are deemed capable of sailing their own craft. Faculty members supervise the waterfront with patrol launches. Tabor's fleet of deepwater cruising boats is headed by the 92-foot schooner *Tabor Boy*. Crew selection is competitive, but previous experience is not a requirement. The *Tabor Boy* takes frequent weekend cruises along the New England coast in fall and spring. The Orientation at Sea Program allows incoming students the opportunity to explore the Maine coast aboard the *Tabor Boy* each summer. Tabor's varsity rowing crew participated in the 2002 Royal Henley Regatta.

EXTRACURRICULAR OPPORTUNITIES

The Director of Student Activities and the Dean supervise more than twenty-five formal clubs and organizations. The Student Activities Committee consists of approximately 15 students who work with the Director of Activities to plan and implement weekend activities. The Tabor *Log* (newspaper), *Fore 'n' Aft* (yearbook), *Bowsprit* (literary magazine), peer tutoring, Speech and Debate, WWTA (FM radio station), Tourguide Club, Madrigal Ensemble (singing group), jazz band, string quartet, and concert band are a few of the offerings. The Drama Club attracts a large number of students; several major productions are planned for the academic year. Student-directed one-act plays conclude the year.

DAILY LIFE

The academic day runs from 8 a.m. until 3 p.m. Major courses meet four times a week at different times on different days. Students meet for assemblies on Monday and Thursday mornings in Wickenden Chapel, and a third all-school meeting takes place Friday mornings in the auditorium. Faculty members are available from 7:30 to 8 a.m. daily to provide extra help for their students. All students participate in the athletics program or in drama, art, music, or community service from 3:30 until 5:30. Dinner runs from 5:30 to 6:30 and is followed by a 2-hour study hall from 7:30 to 9:30. On Tuesday nights, a family-style dinner at 6 p.m. is required for all boarding students. Lights-out is between 10:15 and 11, depending on the student's class year, except for seniors, who have no specific hour for lights-out.

WEEKEND LIFE

Activities on the weekends include campus events as well as off-campus trips. On Saturday mornings, there are either classes or a scheduled quiet time for study in the dormitories. Interscholastic sports contests normally take place Saturday afternoons. Saturday evening dances are held, and selected films are also shown. Other weekend activities might include bands, hypnotists, and trips to Boston and Providence to visit museums, attend sporting events, and go shopping.

Tabor's proximity to Boston and Providence enables faculty members to sponsor small-group outings in their areas of interest on either weekend day. Most sports facilities as well as the library are open on Sunday, and the waterfront is available in the early fall and late spring for sailing, kayaking, and rowing.

SUMMER PROGRAMS

The Tabor Academy Summer Program enrolls boarding and day boys and girls, ages 8–15. The core program is a traditional summer camp, placing emphasis on athletics and water sports. Courses in English, EFL, reading, mathematics, and science are offered for review and for credit. The program also features courses in oceanography. The program runs for six weeks from late June until early August; half-session enrollment is possible. William Hrasky is Director of the Summer Program.

COSTS AND FINANCIAL AID

Charges for 2005–06 were $24,700 for day students and $35,000 for boarders. A $400 enrollment fee is extra.

Through the generosity of alumni and friends, Tabor is able to offer approximately $3 million in financial aid to about 34 percent of the student body annually. Awards are made on the basis of need, character, and academic performance. Applicants for financial aid must submit the Parents' Financial Statement of the School and Student Service for Financial Aid.

ADMISSIONS INFORMATION

Tabor seeks students with good character, demonstrated ability to undertake a college-preparatory course of study, and promise of attainment. Admission is based on an evaluation of these traits in each applicant, a personal interview, and results of the SSAT or the ISEE tests. Tabor accepts most of its students in grades 9 and 10. For 2005–06, there were 698 applications; 167 new students were enrolled.

APPLICATION TIMETABLE

An inquiry and a request for a catalog should be made in the fall of the year before anticipated entry. Tours and interviews are conducted Monday through Friday and on some Saturdays. The application deadline is January 31; applications received after that date are considered on a space-available basis. Tabor subscribes to the March 10 notification date and April 10 Parents' Reply Date. A $50 fee ($100 for international students) must accompany the application.

ADMISSIONS CORRESPONDENCE

Andrew L. McCain, Director of Admissions
Tabor Academy
Marion, Massachusetts 02738

Phone: 508-748-2000
Fax: 508-748-0353
E-mail: admissions@taboracademy.org
Web site: http://www.taboracademy.org

THE TAFT SCHOOL

Watertown, Connecticut

Type: Coeducational boarding and day college-preparatory
Grades: 9–PG: Lower School, 9–10; Upper School, 11–12, postgraduate year
Enrollment: 566
Head of School: William R. MacMullen, Headmaster

THE SCHOOL

The Taft School was established in 1890 as a boys' preparatory school and became coeducational in 1971. Horace Dutton Taft, brother of President and Chief Justice William Howard Taft, was the School's founder and its Headmaster for forty-six years. Because he had faith in humankind's uniqueness and educability for high purpose, his was to be a nondenominational school in which boys would receive physical, mental, moral, and spiritual training for leadership and constructive citizenship. He stressed the opportunity that is open to all individuals, and particularly to Taft students, to make a democratic society work.

The focal point of the School's educational philosophy is still on the wholeness of the student—on the essential interdependence of personal and intellectual growth. Known for its close faculty-student relationships, Taft emphasizes individual development through participation in vigorous academic, athletics, and extracurricular programs. Eighty percent of the seniors take Advanced Placement courses and are involved in at least three extracurricular organizations.

The 220-acre campus is located 30 miles from New Haven, 35 miles from Hartford, 90 miles from New York City, and 120 miles from Boston.

Since 1927, The Taft School has been governed by a Board of Trustees. The physical plant is valued at more than $158 million, and the endowment is nearly $159 million. In 2004–05, $2.9 million was raised in Annual Giving, with a 38 percent rate of participation from the alumni body of more than 7,750.

Taft is accredited by the New England Association of Schools and Colleges. Its memberships include the Connecticut Association of Independent Schools, the Cum Laude Society, the National Association of Independent Schools, the Secondary School Admission Test Board, the Educational Records Bureau, and the College Board.

ACADEMIC PROGRAMS

Taft's liberal arts education prepares its students in a community devoted to creating lifelong learners, thoughtful citizens, and caring people. The School offers more than 200 courses, each worth 1 unit, in each of two semesters. Subject requirements are 8 units of English, 6 units of one foreign language (though students may elect an additional language), 6 units of mathematics, 4 units of history or social science, 4 units of laboratory science, and 1 to 3 units of arts. Most students exceed these requirements. Thirty-six academic units are required for graduation. In grades 9 and 10, the minimum course load is five academic subjects; in grades 11 and 12, the requirement is four major subjects, though many

students carry five. Electives, honors, and Advanced Placement courses are offered in all major areas of study.

The School encourages students to express themselves clearly, purposefully, and creatively in all of their academic endeavors as well as in their arts education. The arts at Taft are incorporated into the regular academic program as well as through extracurricular and informal involvement. Visual arts, theatrical and dance classes and productions, and musical instruction and performance are offered to all students, who must fulfill the School's arts requirement for graduation.

Grades are numerical, on a scale of 1 to 6. All students must maintain an academic average of at least 2.0; a 4.5 average qualifies a student for the honor roll. Class size is generally 10 to 16, and the student-faculty ratio is 6:1. In order to appropriately challenge students, Taft closely monitors the progress of all students. Every three weeks, teachers submit academic reports. Complete grades and teachers' reports are mailed home four times per year.

The opportunity for independent study at Taft has been part of the academic offerings for more than three decades. Qualified students work individually with faculty members in such areas as fiction writing, play production, advanced computer programming, and science laboratory projects. The Senior Independent Seminar program provides opportunities for seniors to pursue intellectual endeavors that reflect their particular interest and passions, culminating with the submission of a Senior Thesis reflecting rigorous scholarship and independent thinking.

FACULTY AND ADVISERS

Of the 84 teaching faculty members, 73 have earned master's degrees and 2 hold doctorates. The full-time teaching faculty numbers 65 (44 men and 21 women), and the part-time teaching faculty numbers 19; 80 percent live on campus. The turnover of the faculty is estimated at 10 to 15 percent a year.

Members of the faculty are selected for their ability to instill enthusiasm for learning, for other inspirational qualities, and for excellence in teaching both in and out of the classroom. Taft promotes professional growth through sabbatical leaves, travel and summer study grants, teaching fellowships, and endowed chairs. Each student chooses his or her adviser at the outset of each year and then works closely with that faculty member for the duration of the year.

William R. MacMullen, Taft's fifth Headmaster, joined the faculty in 1983 upon graduating from Yale University; he earned an M.A. degree in English from Middlebury College. Mr. MacMullen was appointed Headmaster in 2001.

COLLEGE PLACEMENT

From January of the eleventh-grade year through the spring of the twelfth-grade year, students work closely with the college counselors. Parents are consulted in group and individual conferences and informed about the college admissions process and students' progress.

All eleventh graders take the PSAT in the fall and the SAT the following winter and again in the senior year. The average SAT I scores for the class of 2005 were 651 verbal and 655 math. SAT Subject Tests are offered in all major subjects.

Representatives from more than 150 colleges come to Taft each year to meet with seniors and juniors. The 165 graduates of the class of 2005 are attending eighty-three colleges, with 4 or more at Boston University, Brown, Columbia, Davidson, Denison, Georgetown, Harvard, and Middlebury.

STUDENT BODY AND CONDUCT

In 2005–06, Taft had students from thirty-four states and nineteen countries. The 566 students included 461 boarding students and 105 day students, 274 girls and 292 boys. Forty-two percent of the students are from public schools, 44 percent from private schools, and 14 percent from schools outside the United States. Taft prides itself on the geographic and economic diversity of its student body.

One out of every 7 students serves at some time in the elected student government. The president of the student body directs the honor system. A joint faculty-student Discipline Committee handles all major violations by recommending appropriate action to the Headmaster. Because Taft students are assumed to be responsible, serious, disciplined, and hardworking, the honor system guides them in all social and academic matters.

ACADEMIC FACILITIES

The center of the academic community is the Benjamin M. Belcher Learning Center, including the Library Reading Room and the Hulbert Taft Jr. Library. The library's collection includes more than 56,000 books, sound recordings, videocassettes, and DVDs, as well as an outstanding newspaper collection dating from 1704 to the present. The library's subscriptions to electronic databases provide access to full-text articles and documents from thousands of periodicals. Interlibrary loan service is offered to both students and faculty. The three-story building includes an auditorium, conference rooms, small study rooms, a computer/teaching lab, forty networked computers, and the Archives.

The Lady Ivy Kwok Wu Science and Mathematics Center, opened in 1997, contains 45,000 square feet of state-of-the-art teaching and learning space. The Charles Phelps Taft and Horace Dutton Taft buildings contain an addi-

tional thirty-five classrooms as well as Bingham Auditorium, a 595-seat theater equipped with facilities for play production, movies, and concerts.

The Arts/Humanities Center, completed in 1985, contains classrooms, faculty offices, a Macintosh computer center with nineteen stations, a student union, and facilities for teaching theater, music, dance, photography, pottery, sculpture, batik, and printmaking. The arts facilities feature an experimental theater that seats 250 people, a large dance studio, special practice rooms for the several concert bands and singing groups, an electronic music studio, and art rooms designed for work in clay, printmaking, and fabric design. Many smaller rooms are used for individual work in the arts. The student union contains a snack bar and spaces where students can socialize and relax.

The Modern Language Learning and Resource Center opened in 1992. Its Sony-equipped carrels provide facilities for playing videocassettes, audiocassettes, and laser disks. The center is linked to satellites to receive news broadcasts and programs from other countries.

BOARDING AND GENERAL FACILITIES

Taft students live in twelve dormitory units. Most students have a roommate, although single rooms are available. The four girls' dormitories have their own common rooms and laundry facilities. The boys live in self-contained groups on each of the corridors of Charles Phelps Taft and Horace Dutton Taft halls and in one smaller dormitory. Student rooms are equipped with Ethernet data parts and telephone connections. The student union is centrally located, and there are lounge areas in the dormitories.

Teachers' apartments are located among student rooms. The closeness of the central cluster of dormitory units along with the presence of faculty members establishes a strong and positive sense of community.

ATHLETICS

The Taft athletics program is sufficiently broad and varied to encourage both the physical and the psychological growth of all students. At both interscholastic and intramural levels, emphasis is placed on developing good sportsmanship, cooperation, confidence, competitiveness, and self-discipline.

Varsity and junior varsity interscholastic teams are organized in football, field hockey, wrestling, baseball, and softball; boys' and girls' soccer, cross-country, ice hockey, basketball, squash, ski racing, track, lacrosse, tennis, golf, and crew; and girls' volleyball. Lower School teams compete interscholastically in boys' basketball, ice hockey, and tennis; boys' and girls' soccer, lacrosse, and crew; and field hockey. Intramural sports are offered in soccer, golf, squash, and boys' and girls' tennis, Ultimate Frisbee, basketball, and ice hockey. Exercise programs are offered in horseback riding, aerobics, weight training, running and rock climbing, dance, and outdoor leadership.

Taft's newest athletic facility, an ice hockey arena, was completed in 2000. It contains an international-sized ice surface with seating for 600 spectators. Other facilities include a second hockey rink, an eighteen-hole golf course, twelve outdoor tennis courts, sixteen playing fields, and an all-weather, six-lane, 400-meter track. The Paul and Edith Cruikshank indoor facility houses boys' and girls' locker rooms, three international glass-backed squash courts, a wrestling room, a large up-to-date athletic trainer's area, equipment rooms, eight visiting team rooms, a state-of-the-art wood-surfaced floor for two basketball courts, three volleyball courts, and a climbing wall. A newer indoor athletics facility opened in 1993. It houses four indoor tennis courts, two basketball courts, a three-lane running track (8.5 laps to a mile), an exercise center with fifteen Cybex and Body Master machines, computerized bikes, StairMasters and free weights area, five international squash courts, a video projection room, meeting and function rooms, and the Athletic Department offices.

EXTRACURRICULAR OPPORTUNITIES

More than forty clubs and organizations are open to Taft students; opportunities range from the radio and computer clubs to filmmaking and photography. The major student publications are the *Annual*, Taft's yearbook; the *Papyrus*, the student newspaper; and a literary magazine. Active theater groups present several plays each term to the student body and the community.

The School brings writers, poets, and artists to the campus; speakers often come to address individual classes. Popular films are screened weekly as well. Many students are involved in volunteer community service.

DAILY LIFE

On Monday through Saturday, the school day begins at 7:50 a.m. There are seven class periods, one of which is used for lunch, and four or five for regular classes; the others may be used for study, music practice, art, or a conference session with a teacher. Required sports practice follows the class day. On Wednesday and Saturday, because of interscholastic games, classes are finished at lunchtime.

On two weekday mornings, the School assembles for School Meeting, at which a faculty member, student, or guest presents a brief program. On two weekday evenings per week, students share in a formal seated dinner with faculty members and their families. Various organizations and faculty-student committees often meet after dinner, but study, individually or with the help of an instructor, usually lasts 3 to 4 hours. Boarding students (except seniors) have a 2-hour required room-study period each evening.

WEEKEND LIFE

After Saturday classes, students are free to go out to dinner or, on some weekends, to spend the night away from Taft, provided that permission has been received from their parents and authorized by the Dean of Students. Most students choose to remain on campus for the weekend. The entertainment ranges from movies to dances to plays. In addition, there are often School-sponsored trips to plays and concerts in New York, New Haven, or Hartford. Day students are encouraged to join in all weekend activities. On Sundays, students may get up for a local church service or sleep until brunch is served.

SUMMER PROGRAMS

Taft offers a five-week coeducational summer program for boarding as well as day students. The courses, given for enrichment purposes and not for credit, include English, mathematics, history, languages, and science.

COSTS AND FINANCIAL AID

In 2005–06, charges for boarding students were $35,000 and for day students, $26,000. There was an additional general fee of $250 and a technology fee of $400 for boarding students, $125 for day students. An enrollment deposit of $3000 for boarding students and $2500 for day students is payable on May 15. Scholarship and loan funds were available in the amount of $4.7 million. Of the 566 students at Taft in 2005–06, 196 received some form of financial assistance, ranging from a $1000 scholarship and low-interest student loan to a full $35,000 scholarship. Financial assistance is awarded to students on the basis of financial need, as evidenced through the School and Student Service for Financial Aid form.

ADMISSIONS INFORMATION

Taft is interested in candidates as people—not just as scholars. The School seeks girls and boys who are curious, who will become involved, and who will commit themselves to a high standard of intellectual and personal growth. Because of the rigorous academic demands at the Taft School, the Admissions Committee finds that students with A and B averages who are involvement oriented and come highly recommended are usually the most successful candidates.

All candidates except prospective seniors are required to take the SSAT, preferably in December or January. The minimum percentile score accepted is generally 50. Most entering students test between the 75th and 99th percentiles. Candidates for the senior class are expected to take the PSAT and SAT. All candidates are urged to have an on-campus interview with a member of the admissions staff.

APPLICATION TIMETABLE

Admissions Office interviews may be scheduled Monday through Saturday. On Wednesdays and Saturdays, appointments are available in the morning only. Inquiries are welcome at any time. Appointments for interviews and tours should be made well in advance. The application deadline is January 31, and the application fee is $40; the fee for students living outside the U.S. is $60. Candidates are notified of the decision on March 10, and the Parents' Reply Date is April 10.

ADMISSIONS CORRESPONDENCE

Frederick H. Wandelt III
Director of Admissions
The Taft School
Watertown, Connecticut 06795
Phone: 860-945-7700
Fax: 860-945-7808
E-mail: admissions@taftschool.org
Web site: http://www.taftschool.org

TALLULAH FALLS SCHOOL

Tallulah Falls, Georgia

Type: Coeducational boarding college-preparatory
Grades: 7–12
Enrollment: 150

THE SCHOOL

Tallulah Falls School is an independent, coeducational boarding school serving a maximum of 150 students in grades 7–12. Tallulah Falls is located in northeast Georgia, approximately 90 miles from Atlanta, 100 miles west of Greenville, South Carolina, and 100 miles southwest of Asheville, North Carolina. Founded in 1909 by Mrs. Mary Ann Lipscomb, president of the Georgia Federation of Women's Clubs, the School and the Federation have deep roots in the history of secondary education in Georgia. On July 12, 1909, Tallulah Falls School opened its doors to 21 mountain children from neighboring Habersham and Rabun Counties and continued to serve as both a public and a private institution of learning for more than sixty years. To this day, Tallulah Falls School continues to provide opportunities for intellectual challenge, physical participation, and personal growth to students from the local area as well as to students from across the state of Georgia, around the nation, and throughout the world.

For all of the students, the Tallulah Falls experience is centered around community and characterized by personal attention in a nurturing environment. The setting is peaceful, yet only 90 miles from Atlanta. Classes are small, with an average of 10–12 students per class. The community consists of students and members of the faculty, staff, and administration who are committed to promoting an atmosphere of respect and encouragement that is conducive to learning and living.

Academically, students of wide-ranging ability find fulfillment and challenge at Tallulah Falls. The quality of the academic program and the success of its students as scholars and citizens form the foundation on which the School is built.

The faculty at Tallulah Falls is both highly qualified and deeply committed to helping the students discover and reach their full potential. A broad and ambitious curriculum, traditional teaching methods, and an emphasis on student involvement in the classroom all contribute to the mental development and educational achievement that students realize as they prepare for college and for life.

Situated on the slopes of Cherokee Mountain in the beautiful northeast Georgia mountains, Tallulah Falls School offers the ideal setting for learning, away from the pressure and distractions of overcrowded urban centers. Students find themselves immersed in an atmosphere that not only fosters academic excellence, but also encourages an appreciation for nature and the preservation of natural resources. Tallulah Gorge State Park, with its interpretive education center, hiking trails, and scenic vistas, is a neighbor of the School in the town of Tallulah Falls. Hiking, camping, cycling, whitewater rafting, horseback riding, and snow skiing offer students the opportunity to experience the wonders of nature. For those who prefer the sophistication and energy of the city, there are supervised weekend excursions into metro Atlanta that allow students to enjoy the best of the Southeast's premier cultural attractions, athletic events, and extensive shopping and dining.

Owned and operated by the Georgia Federation of Women's Clubs, Tallulah Falls School is a nonprofit organization and is governed by a 38-member Board of Trustees. The current operating budget is $4.6 million. The endowment exceeds $21 million. The School annually receives 10 percent of the earnings from the estate of Mrs. Lettie Pate Evans through the Lettie Pate Evans Foundation, which was approximately $2.5 million last year.

Tallulah Falls School is accredited by the Southern Association of Colleges and the Georgia Accrediting Commission. It holds membership in the Georgia Independent School Association, the Georgia High School Association, the National Association of Secondary School Principals, the Secondary School Admission Test Board, and the Small Boarding School Association.

ACADEMIC PROGRAMS

The curriculum at Tallulah Falls School has been designed to meet the needs of a broad range of students, from the average student to the academically gifted.

Twenty-one credits are required for graduation, which include 4 years of English, 4 years of math, 3 units of science, 3 years of social studies, and 1 year of physical education. In addition to the required courses needed to graduate, Tallulah Falls School requires that each senior must be in attendance the entire senior year and must complete all courses to the satisfaction of each instructor. Students seeking acceptance to selective colleges and universities are expected to complete twenty-four credits for a college preparatory diploma, including 2 years of the same foreign language and a minimum of 4 years of math.

The 12:1 student-teacher ratio ensures that students receive personal attention from each of their teachers. Tallulah Falls School operates on a six-period day, with classes running 50 minutes each. A 30-minute tutorial is held daily after sixth period to provide additional assistance. A mandatory, staff-supervised study hall is held on Sunday through Thursday evenings in the dormitories. Additional study time is assigned to all students needing academic assistance.

The school year, which begins in mid-August and ends in late May, is divided into two semesters. Grades are reported every six weeks. Tallulah Falls School uses a traditional numeric grading scale, with no credit given for a grade below D. Students whose quarterly grade point averages (GPAs) are at least 4.0, 3.5, or 3.0 (on a 4.0 scale) qualify for academic honor rolls. Students who fail to maintain an overall GPA of 2.0 and students who fail two or more subjects in a semester are placed on academic probation and are subject to dismissal unless grades improve during the following grading period.

FACULTY AND ADVISERS

Teaching at Tallulah Falls School is a highly personal commitment to helping young people succeed as scholars and citizens. Of the 25 teachers on staff, 16 hold one or more advanced degrees. Faculty members bring competence and enthusiasm to the classroom and are highly successful individuals in their own right. Faculty members serve in a multiplicity of roles, including teacher, adviser, mentor, coach, and sponsor.

The Advisory Program at Tallulah Falls School is an integral part of the educational process. Each member of the faculty serves as an adviser to a small group of students that meets once a day during the academic year. The primary purpose of these groups is to serve as an additional support service within which students can discuss personal and academic concerns. Together, these groups plan service projects and experiential learning activities and discuss developmentally appropriate issues. Advising groups afford students an extra measure of personal attention and facilitate a relationship of respect and trust between students and faculty members outside the classroom. It is this foundation that further enables students at Tallulah Falls School to meet their full potential.

COLLEGE PLACEMENT

The School counselor assumes the primary role in assisting students and their families with college selection, applications, and scholarships. Students are encouraged to begin focusing on career interests and future plans early in their high school careers.

Tallulah Falls School offers many research tools, including texts and computer-based programs, for students to use in selecting colleges, universities, technical schools, and scholarships. Juniors, seniors, and interested parents have the opportunity to attend the annual PROBE Fair, a meeting with representatives of colleges and technical schools, military personnel, and the Georgia Student Finance Authority. In addition, representatives of colleges and technical schools make campus visits throughout the year.

Students generally take the PSAT in the fall of their sophomore and junior years. For college admission purposes, students are encouraged to take either the SAT or the ACT in the fall of their senior year. Several college admission test–preparation workshops are offered to students, as is an individualized computerized tutorial program.

Of the 2005 graduates, 100 percent are attending postsecondary schools. Of those students who are attending college, many have received academic scholarships. Representative colleges and universities at which Tallulah Falls School graduates have been accepted include the Art Institute of Atlanta, Auburn, Brevard College, Dartmouth, Duke, Emory, Georgia Southern, Georgia Tech, North Georgia, Penn State, Piedmont, Presbyterian College, Reinhardt College, Southern Polytechnic State, Vanderbilt, Wesleyan College, York, and the Universities of California, Georgia, and Virginia.

STUDENT BODY AND CONDUCT

Tallulah Falls School seeks to enroll a student body that is diverse geographically, socially, academically, culturally, and economically. The School believes that diversity acts as a positive influence as it

reflects the global community, with all students learning from the others' unique backgrounds and experiences.

To help ensure the welfare of the community and its members, the School has the right and responsibility to expect certain standards of behavior. School rules are based upon common sense and good manners, with the purpose of creating an environment in which members of the community can live and work comfortably together.

The purpose of the Honor Code is to promote high ideals of personal honor and integrity. Tallulah Falls School students are expected not to lie, steal, cheat, plagiarize, or assist others in these actions. The Honor Code is modeled and enforced by the Honor Council, an autonomous organization of 5 students and an adviser appointed to review honor violations. For all other disciplinary infractions, a demerit system is utilized. The demerit system is outlined in the Student Handbook and is administered by all members of the Tallulah Falls School staff, faculty, and administration. Serious disciplinary infractions may be referred to the Disciplinary Committee for review.

ACADEMIC FACILITIES

Highlighting the historical significance of Tallulah Falls School, the original School property has been placed on the National Historic Register. The School has grown from two buildings and 5 acres of land at its inception to twenty-two buildings and approximately 500 acres of land today, 120 acres of which have been developed to form the current School campus. The physical plant is valued at approximately $17 million, excluding land values.

Most classrooms are located in the H. R. and C. R. Cannon Academic Building, which won a special award for its design from the American Institute of Architects. The academic building also includes the Briggs Computer Laboratory and the Passie Fenton Ottley Library, which houses approximately 9,000 volumes. Music and physical education classrooms, are located in the Young Matrons' Circle Building, a multipurpose fine arts facility that includes a 300-seat theater, an Olympic-size indoor swimming pool, offices, a gymnasium, practice rooms, and classrooms. The theater is a focal point for assemblies, invited lecturers, visiting artists, student performances, and School-sponsored community activities.

BOARDING AND GENERAL FACILITIES

Students are housed in two 2-story dormitories—Fitzpatrick Hall for boys and Westmoreland Hall for girls. Each dormitory is staffed by 3 full-time dormitory supervisors who are assisted by student life assistants. These students are campus leaders who serve as role models for students. They are selected based on leadership, scholarship, a written application, and interviews.

The dormitory rooms are designed for double occupancy. Roommate assignments are based on student preferences whenever possible, and students are allowed to change roommates at designated times each year if they wish. Free laundry facilities are available to students in each dormitory, or students may choose to use the School laundry service. In each dormitory, students have access to snack and drink machines, lounge areas with televisions and VCRs, and pool tables. Students also have access to the Lettie Pate Evans Student Center after school hours, on weekends, and during recreation periods.

The School infirmary is operated by a registered nurse during regular school hours. After hours, student health needs are closely monitored by dormitory supervisors.

ATHLETICS

A member of the Georgia High School Association, Tallulah Falls School competes with other independent schools and public schools in basketball, cross-country, soccer, tennis, track and field, and volleyball. All students are encouraged to participate in sports, either through membership on varsity teams, enrollment in physical education classes, or participation in the School's voluntary intramural program, which includes activities such as basketball, soccer, softball, and volleyball. Each year, all students participate in Field Day, during which students are divided into four teams and compete for a full day in a wide range of athletic events and activities. During recreation periods, students have access to the gymnasium, pool, athletic fields, and tennis courts.

EXTRACURRICULAR OPPORTUNITIES

Participation in cocurricular activities is an integral part of the overall boarding school experience. An elected Student Council is responsible for planning weekend trips and activities and also coordinates student service opportunities and community service projects.

Nonathletic competition is available to students in such areas as writing, spelling, mathematics, foreign language, word processing, geography bee, girls' trio, boys' quartet, and vocal solo. An active School chorus performs regularly. Talented art students enter several competitions each year, including the School Art Symposium, sponsored by the University of Georgia. Students with writing and design skills produce *Retrospect*, the School yearbook.

Teachers and staff members sponsor a wide range of clubs for students, including the Astronomy Club, Outdoor Club, Fishing Club, Chess Club, and Gourmet Cooking Club. The National Honor Society chapter is very active and has won five first-place awards at the NHS State Convention.

In 1989, a group of Tallulah Falls School students and faculty members entered the National Aeronautics and Space Administration's (NASA) Orbiter-Naming Program, a nationwide contest designed to name the space shuttle built to replace *Challenger*. NASA chose the Tallulah Falls entry as the national secondary school winner, and the name *Endeavour* continues to be a source of pride for the School and the nation.

DAILY LIFE

The school day begins with a buffet-style breakfast, mandatory for all students except seniors, which is served from 7 until 7:35 a.m. Classes begin at 8:15 a.m. and end at 3:30 p.m. daily, with a break of approximately 40 minutes for lunch. During the academic day, students wear School uniforms. During certain portions of the year, all students participate in the School's work program. Work program assignments vary from working in the kitchen to assisting the grounds crew. Regardless of the job, students learn the value of hard work and the importance of cooperation in maintaining the beauty and integrity of the Tallulah Falls School community. Dinner is served at 6 p.m., and is followed by recreation. Students report to the dormitories at 8 p.m. for study time. Study time is held on Sunday

through Thursday evenings from 8:10 until 9:40 p.m. Lights-out for underclassmen is at 10; senior lights-out is at 11 p.m.

WEEKEND LIFE

The Boarding Director works closely with students to plan trips and events for each weekend. Weekend activities include dances, movies, and special events on campus; trips to college and professional sports events; nature-related pursuits, including hiking, horseback riding, and kayaking; and cultural activities, including art exhibits, museums, and theater performances off campus.

All students are required to go home for long weekends or vacations approximately seven times during the school year, including Thanksgiving, Christmas, winter break, spring break, and four long weekends. Students are permitted weekend leaves on other weekends as requested by parents.

COSTS AND FINANCIAL AID

For the 2004–05 academic year, tuition was $17,850 for Georgia residents, $18,900 for out-of-state students, and $21,000 for international students. This amount includes tuition, room and board, textbook rental, group insurance, linen service, and some activities. Tuition was $7875 for day students. A student bank, funded by parents and guardians, serves as an allowance account from which students may make limited withdrawals weekly. Additional charges may include weekend activities, uniform purchases, school supplies, and long-weekend fees. Incidental charges are billed monthly throughout the year.

Financial assistance is awarded on the basis of need, as determined by a Financial Aid Committee. Last year, the School awarded more than $1 million in student assistance.

ADMISSIONS INFORMATION

The Enrollment Committee at Tallulah Falls School believes that certain criteria are essential to the ultimate success of a student seeking admission. First and foremost, the School selects students who are motivated to succeed academically, physically, socially, and spiritually, whether pursuing college preparation or the general education curriculum. A student demonstrates his or her desire to achieve through a personal essay, prior school performance, and a formal interview with a member of the Admission Office. Further, a student must be eligible to return to his or her previous educational institution and show performance at or above grade level. These criteria are evaluated based on the student's applications, official school transcripts, teacher and principal recommendations, standardized test scores, and parent questionnaires.

APPLICATION TIMETABLE

For fall enrollment, applications should be submitted by March 1. However, inquiries and applications are welcome throughout the school year and are considered on a space-available basis. A $30 fee should accompany the application. Applicant files are only considered by the Enrollment Committee when they are complete and all parts of the application have been received.

ADMISSIONS CORRESPONDENCE

Director of Admissions
Tallulah Falls School
P.O. Box 249
Tallulah Falls, Georgia 30573

Phone: 706-754-0400 Ext. 5112
Fax: 706-754-3595
E-mail: admissions@tallulahfalls.org
Web site: http://www.tallulahfalls.org

TASIS THE AMERICAN SCHOOL IN ENGLAND

Thorpe, Surrey, England

TASIS

Type: Coeducational boarding and day college-preparatory school
Grades: Nursery–13: Nursery; Lower School, Nursery–5; Middle School, 6–8; Upper School, 9–13
Enrollment: School total: 715; Upper School: 310
Head of School: Dr. James Doran, Headmaster

THE SCHOOL

TASIS England was founded in 1976 by Mrs. M. Crist Fleming as a branch of The American School in Switzerland (TASIS), which she established in 1956. The 35-acre campus is set in a country village in the Thames valley, only 18 miles from central London and 6 miles from Heathrow Airport.

The School offers a traditional, college-preparatory program. While academics are emphasized, sports, extracurricular activities, cultural excursions, and weekend trips ensure the balanced education of the whole student. The program takes full advantage of its location and the opportunities that England and Europe offer as extensions to classroom learning. The TASIS Schools and Summer Programs are owned and fully controlled by the TASIS Foundation, a Swiss, independent, not-for-profit educational foundation, registered in Delémont, Switzerland.

TASIS England is accredited by the European Council of International Schools (ECIS) and the New England Association of Schools and Colleges (NEASC) and is a member of the National Association of Independent Schools (NAIS) and The Association of Boarding Schools (TABS). It was inspected by the British Office for Standards in Education (Ofsted) in October 2004, and it received high ratings for its academic, arts, athletics, and extracurricular programs; student care, and facilities.

ACADEMIC PROGRAMS

The Upper School encompasses grades 9 to 13. The minimum requirements for graduation from the Upper School are 4 years of English, 3 years of history (including U.S. history at the eleventh- or twelfth-grade level), a third-level proficiency in a foreign language, 3 years of mathematics (through algebra II), three laboratory sciences (including biology), and 1 year of fine arts. All seniors are required to take a full-year humanities course. Students who have attended TASIS England for three years or more are expected to complete 19 credits. A normal course load consists of five courses per year. Advanced Placement courses are offered for qualified students, and the wide variety of electives include economics, environmental science, international issues, precalculus, physics, photography, music, and acting.

TASIS also offers the International Baccalaureate (IB) diploma. Students may apply to this program for their final two years at TASIS, and successful IB diploma candidates can earn both the IB diploma and the TASIS England high school diploma. Entry into the IB Program is made in consultation between the School, student, and family and is open only to highly motivated students with strong academic, time management, and study skills.

The average class size is 15, with a teacher-student ratio of 1:8. The aim is to provide an intimate learning environment that can challenge a young person to realize his or her full potential. This is heightened by the personal aspect of the Advisor Program. The advisor is charged with the social and academic well-being of each advisee.

A student's day is fully structured. Participation in supervised evening study hall for boarding students is a requirement for all but those who have earned the privilege of independent study in their rooms.

The academic year is divided into two semesters, ending in January and June, respectively. Grades and comments are mailed home to parents four times a year at midsemester and end-of-semester breaks, together with a summary report from the advisor. The grading system uses A to F, indicating achievement levels, and 1 to 5 as a measure of a student's attitude and application to his or her work.

An educational travel program during the October break is required for all boarding students and has included trips to such places as Austria, France, Germany, Greece, Hungary, Italy, Poland, Romania, Russia, Spain, and Switzerland. These school trips are also an option for day students.

FACULTY AND ADVISERS

Dr. James Doran was appointed as headmaster of TASIS in 2005. He holds a doctorate in curriculum and instruction as well as degrees in education and educational administration. A seasoned administrator who has worked in international schools for more than twenty-five years, Dr. Doran has led schools and taught in Panama, Singapore, Tokyo, Manila, Jeddah, and Tunis. He was also Executive Director at Stetson University—Celebration Campus in Florida, where, in addition to his administrative responsibilities, he taught graduate-level courses in educational leadership, research, communications, and school finance.

The faculty represents one of the School's strongest assets. Its members are a group of dedicated professionals with a true sense of vocation. Duties are not limited to teaching but encompass the responsibilities of advisors, sports coaches, dorm residents, community service aides, and trip chaperones. There are 95 full-time faculty members, 34 men and 61 women, and 13 part-time teachers; more than half of them have advanced degrees, and 16 live on campus. In addition, music specialists visit the School for private instruction by arrangement.

COLLEGE PLACEMENT

TASIS England employs 3 college counselors. They meet individually with students in their junior and senior years to discuss academic programs, careers, and college plans. Support programs include student seminars, career day, transition workshops, and a case study night. The counselors maintain a reference library of college catalogs, videos, and computer software and familiarize students with the range of opportunities available to them. The counselors coordinate visits to the School by college admissions officers from universities in the United States and Europe and administer the college admissions testing program. TASIS England is a test center for the PSAT, ACT, and SAT for juniors and seniors and all Advanced Placement examinations.

TASIS students are accepted by universities around the world and have recently attended such schools as Bates College, Boston University, Bryn Mawr, Bucknell, Cambridge (U.K.), Connecticut College, Cornell, Dartmouth, Duke, George Washington, Harvard, International Christian University (Japan), Johns Hopkins, London School of Economics (U.K.), Northwestern, Oxford (U.K.), Princeton, Rice, Rhode Island School of Design, Southern Methodist, Stanford, Tufts, University College London, University of St. Andrews (U.K.), and Yale. TASIS believes that students should be encour-

aged to think deeply about the purposes of higher education, about the intangible benefits of genuine intellectual activity, and about the range of philosophical options offered by educational institutions. The major responsibility for college choices lies with each student, but the School provides as much advice and support as possible.

STUDENT BODY AND CONDUCT

For the 2005–06 academic year, there were a total of 309 students in the Upper School (grades 9–13: 3 postgraduates, 77 seniors, 101 juniors, 66 sophomores, and 62 freshmen. Overall, the ratio of boys to girls in each grade level is close to 1:1. In some cases, the parents of boarding students are expatriates undertaking assignments overseas, in such locations as Saudi Arabia, Africa, Europe, and various parts of the British Isles. The student body is culturally diverse, with 56 percent of the students in the Upper School representing forty different countries. In the Lower School, there are 254 children, and the Middle School (grades 6–8) has a total of 153 students.

The *Student Handbook* clearly identifies the accepted codes of conduct within the School community. A dress code is required for Upper School students. Lower and Middle School students wear white and navy blue. An infraction of a major school rule is dealt with by the Upper School administration with the Disciplinary Advisory Board. TASIS England reserves the right to dismiss at any time a student who has proved to be an unsatisfactory member of the school community, even though there may have been no infraction of a specific rule.

In the Upper School, the Student Council is made up of representatives from all grade levels and is the vehicle of student government. Prefects, as student leaders, carry special responsibilities in dormitory and general school life.

ACADEMIC FACILITIES

Two large Georgian mansions and purpose-built classrooms are the focal points of the campus. There are computer and science laboratories, a library for each school division, art studios, a darkroom, music rooms, two multipurpose gymnasiums, a fitness center, two drama/dance studios, and a 400-seat theater. TASIS England has embarked on a ten-year master plan to enhance all campus facilities.

BOARDING AND GENERAL FACILITIES

Boarding students (grades 9–13) are accommodated in dormitories supervised by a faculty resident and assisted by prefects. Each unit holds 13–15 students, usually in 2- or 3-person rooms, which are located in parts of the main buildings as well as in the adjacent cottages, such as Renalds Herne, Tudor House, Orchard, and Shepherd's Cottage. The Boarding Program is coordinated by a husband and wife team, both of whom are experienced in providing boarding care and serving the needs of young people.

ATHLETICS

An awareness of physical fitness, the discipline of training the body as well as the mind, and the spirit of competition are viewed as important elements in a student's education at TASIS England. All Upper School students participate in the afternoon sports/activities program, which operates on a three-term basis, reflecting seasonal sports. The minimum requirement is participation for two afternoons a week.

Varsity sports include basketball, cross-country, soccer, tennis, and volleyball as well as boys' teams in rugby and baseball and a girls' team in softball. Other recreational sports include badminton, mountain biking, horseback riding, squash, aerobics, golf, swimming, and a conditioning program.

There are four large playing fields on campus, six all-weather tennis courts, two gymnasiums, and a fitness center that offers a complete weight-training circuit and a wide variety of cardiovascular machines. The nearby Egham Sports Center offers fine supplementary facilities.

Besides participating in local sports events, the School competes in International Schools Sports Tournaments (ISSTs) with other international schools throughout Europe and the Middle East.

EXTRACURRICULAR OPPORTUNITIES
England's capital city, London, only 18 miles away, provides an unrivaled opportunity for students to enjoy such pleasures as theater, opera, concerts, art galleries, and museums. Through course-related study or School-chaperoned trips, in the evenings and on weekends, students are regularly encouraged to participate in as many educational experiences as possible.

On-campus activities include drama productions, choir, the School newspaper, Model UN, and the Yearbook Committee as well as School dances and movies.

A committee composed of students and teachers jointly coordinates and plans on-campus and off-campus recreational activities, including day trips (sightseeing, for example) and weekends away. Traditionally, the International Festival, Christmas Dinner Dance, Spring Prom, and May Fair are the highlights of the year.

The Community Service Program aims to help each student to develop skills outside the classroom, leading to a sense of involvement and greater responsibility for others. The commitment involves approximately 1 hour a week; students serve the School community by helping in the library or tutoring younger children, and they serve the local community by visiting homes for the elderly and disabled, participating in conservation projects, and raising funds for local charities. Special summer projects are also available.

DAILY LIFE
Classes commence at 8:30 a.m. daily and end at 3:10 p.m. There are six periods with a lunch break. Each Upper School class meets four times a week (for 55-minute periods), allowing a structured tutorial period during the day. Sports/activities time is between 3:30 and 5 p.m. each day, except Fridays.

An Upper School meeting is regularly scheduled for Wednesdays. No classes are held on Saturday or Sunday.

WEEKEND LIFE
Day students as well as boarders participate freely in organized social events on the weekends. These can include trips to the theater and concerts, the ballet, and professional sports events. The Activities Coordinator and Student Council members collaborate to develop a wide variety of activities. Day trips are organized to such destinations as Stratford-upon-Avon, Salisbury, Canterbury, and Bath in the U.K., Lille in France, and a weekend trip to Christmas markets in Germany.

Excursions are chaperoned by a member of the faculty for all except seniors, who, with parental permission, enjoy the privilege of traveling in small groups.

SUMMER PROGRAMS
During the summer, six-week credit-based academic courses are offered in such subjects as Shakespeare and Theater in London, study skills, math, film production, art, photography, and performing arts. Additional offerings include preparation courses for the International Baccalaureate. Some 370 students regularly participate from schools in the United States and from international schools all over the world. Faculty members from one or more TASIS schools constitute the majority of the summer administration, while qualified teachers and counselors from the U.S. and around the world make up the remaining summer faculty. Weekend travel is included in the program.

In addition to the courses in England, TASIS offers a variety of summer programs in France, Spain, and Switzerland to students from all over the world. From intensive study of painting, photography, and architecture at Les Tapies in the Ardèche to learning Spanish in Salamanca or French at Chateaux d'Oex in Switzerland, TASIS summer courses enrich the talents, skills, and interests of its participants.

COSTS AND FINANCIAL AID
In 2005–06, tuition and fees were £5200–£15,300 per annum. Optional expenses, including costs for music lessons and horseback riding, are by private arrangement. Boarding fees, including tuition and costs for the October Travel Week were £23,600. Costs for the October Travel Week are included in the boarding fees. A recommended personal allowance is £50 per week.

There is a one-time-only Development Fund Fee of approximately £750 per student for on-campus building projects and an enrollment deposit of £1000 for day students and £1500 for boarders. The balance of fees becomes payable for each semester by July 1 and December 1.

Students are invited to apply for financial aid, which is granted on the basis of merit, need, and available funds. Early application for financial help is recommended. Each year the School awards approximately £225,000 in financial aid.

ADMISSIONS INFORMATION
Applications for admission are considered by the Admissions Committee upon receipt of a completed application form together with the application fee, three teachers' recommendations, and a transcript. Standardized test scores are requested, and a student questionnaire is required. An interview is recommended unless distance is a prohibiting factor. A decision is reached on the basis of a student's academic and social acceptability to the TASIS England School community. A student's nationality, religion, ethnic background, and gender play no part in the committee's decision, although availability of space in a certain dormitory (all are grouped by gender) is sometimes a limiting factor.

APPLICATION TIMETABLE
Applications are processed throughout the year. Visitors are welcome on campus at any time of the year. An interview by prior arrangement, even on very short notice, is recommended. It is preferable for visitors to choose days when school is in session in order to appreciate the working atmosphere of the community.

While early applications are encouraged, there is no final deadline, since a rolling admissions policy exists. Acceptances are made with the provision that students complete their current year in good standing. There is an application fee of £75.

ADMISSIONS CORRESPONDENCE
Bronwyn Thorburn
Director of Admissions
TASIS The American School in England
Coldharbour Lane
Thorpe, Nr Egham
Surrey TW20 8TE
England
Phone: 44-1932-565252
Fax: 44-1932-564644
E-mail: ukadmissions@tasis.com

The TASIS Schools
2640 Wisconsin Avenue, NW
Washington, D.C. 20007
Phone: 202-965-5800
Fax: 202-965-5816
E-mail: usadmissions@tasis.com
Web site: http://www.tasis.com

TASIS, THE AMERICAN SCHOOL IN SWITZERLAND

Montagnola-Lugano, Switzerland

TASIS

THE AMERICAN SCHOOL
IN SWITZERLAND

Type: Coeducational boarding and day college-preparatory school
Grades: 7–12, PG: Middle School, 7–8; High School, 9–12, Postgraduate year
Enrollment: School total: 338; High School: 299; Middle School: 39
Head of School: Jeffrey C. Bradley, Headmaster

THE SCHOOL

TASIS, The American School in Switzerland, was founded in 1956 by Mrs. M. Crist Fleming to offer a strong American college-preparatory education in a European setting. TASIS was the first American boarding school established in Europe. Over time, it has become a school for students from more than forty countries seeking an American independent school experience. The International Baccalaureate Program is also offered within this setting.

The objective of the School is to foster both the vital enthusiasm for learning and those habits that are essential to a full realization of each student's moral and intellectual potential. The curriculum gives special emphasis to the achievements of the Western heritage, many elements of which are easily accessible from the school's location. By providing an international dimension to education, the School stresses the need for young people to mature with confidence and competence in an increasingly interrelated world.

The beautiful campus is in the village of Montagnola, overlooking the city and the Lake of Lugano, nestled among the southernmost of the Swiss Alps in the Italian-speaking canton of Ticino. Ideally situated in the heart of Europe, the School makes the most of its location by introducing students to European cultures and languages through extensive travel programs.

The TASIS Foundation, a not-for-profit Swiss foundation, owns the School. The TASIS Foundation also has a school near London and offers summer programs in England, Spain, and Italy as well as Switzerland. Alumni provide enthusiastic support for the School's activities and participate in biennial reunions.

The European Council of International Schools (ECIS) and the New England Association of Schools and Colleges (NEASC) accredits TASIS, The American School in Switzerland. The School is a member of the National Association of Independent Schools and the Swiss Group of International Schools.

ACADEMIC PROGRAMS

The minimum requirements for graduation from the high school college-preparatory program are 4 years of English, 3 years of history (including European and U.S. history), a third-year proficiency in a modern foreign language, 3 years of mathematics (through algebra II), 3 years of laboratory science (including physical and biological sciences), and 1 year of fine arts, plus senior humanities, sports/physical education, and community service requirements. Students must satisfactorily complete a minimum of 19 credits. Students are required to enroll in a minimum of five full-credit courses per year or the equivalent. A normal course load for students consists of five or six courses. For students with recognized special needs or interests, special accommodations can sometimes be made. Such a program must follow established guidelines and requires the approval of the Academic Committee.

TASIS has an extensive ESL program, the goals of which are fluency in oral and written academic English and competence in a high school curriculum leading to the TASIS college-preparatory diploma.

TASIS offers a diverse and challenging curriculum, including the Advanced Placement Program (AP), the International Baccalaureate Diploma (I.B.), and a wide range of required and elective courses. In 2003, 111 students were involved in the Advanced Placement Program, and 202 AP exams were taken in seventeen subject areas. Students may also select from among the range of International Baccalaureate courses, either earning certificates or the full diploma. In 2003, 52 students took 196 I.B. exams; 26 of the 29 I.B. diploma candidates earned the full I.B. diploma.

The average class size is 12; the teacher-student ratio is 1:6. The student's day is fully structured, including time for academics, sports and activities, meals and socializing, and supervised evening study hours. The grading system uses A to F for performance and assigns effort grades of 1 to 5 reflecting students' attitudes and application to their work. The academic year is divided into two semesters; grades and comment reports are sent home to parents five times a year.

The postgraduate year presents an additional opportunity to high school graduates who wish to spend an interim year in Europe before going on to college. Each postgraduate student can design a tailor-made course of study with the assistance and approval of the Academic Dean that enables him or her to explore and develop new interests, strengthen academic weaknesses, or concentrate in areas of strength or particular interest. The program includes course-related, in-program travel.

FACULTY AND ADVISERS

The faculty represents one of the School's strongest assets. Its members are a group of dedicated professionals who are enthusiastic about working with young people. Forty-five percent of the faculty members have advanced degrees. There are 61 full-time teaching administrators and faculty members, of whom 27 are women and 34 are men. Twenty faculty members live on campus; the rest live nearby and participate in most campus activities. In addition to teaching, faculty members act as advisers, sports coaches, trip chaperones, and dormitory residents and help to create a warm, familylike atmosphere.

Jeffrey C. Bradley, who was appointed Headmaster in 2004, is a graduate of Georgetown University.

COLLEGE PLACEMENT

The School employs one full-time college counselor who meets with students individually and in groups during their junior and senior years. The college counseling office maintains an up-to-date reference library of college catalogs so that students can familiarize themselves with the wide variety of opportunities open to them. As a counseling resource, the School provides a small computer lab for college research. Many college admissions officers from universities in the United States and Europe visit the School and speak to students. TA-SIS is a testing center for the PSAT, SAT I, SAT II: Subject Tests, ACT, TOEFL, and all AP and I.B. examinations.

Graduates are attending such colleges and universities as Warwick University in the United Kingdom and such U.S. colleges and universities as Boston University, Brown, Colby, Duke, George Washington, Rhode Island School of Design, Tufts, and the University of Chicago.

STUDENT BODY AND CONDUCT

The total student enrollment of 338 consists of 272 boarding students (of whom 126 are boys and 146 are girls) and 66 day students. They come from fifty countries; 32 percent are American.

Each student is honor bound to abide by the rules as defined in the *Student Handbook*. The Student-Faculty Review Board deals with infractions of School rules, with more serious offenses being handled by the School administration and Governing Board.

The students at TASIS bear a serious responsibility to conduct themselves not only in a way that does credit to them, to their School, and to their country of origin, but also in a way consistent with the high standards set by the citizens of the European countries they visit. For this reason, TASIS has established reasonable but definitive standards of behavior, attitude, and appearance for all of its students. The School reserves the right to ask any student to withdraw for failure to maintain these standards.

ACADEMIC FACILITIES

The historic and architecturally interesting seventeenth-century Villa De Nobili was the original building of the School and serves as the dining hall. An extension houses the administration and the School's science laboratories. Hadsall House contains the theater, classrooms, and dormitories. Villa Monticello contains modern classrooms and the computer center and computer language lab. Additional classes are held in the dormitories of Scuderia, Belvedere, and Casa del Sole. Coach House has art and photography studios. The School's Palestra houses a sports complex containing a gymnasium, a fitness center, a dance studio, locker rooms, a recreation lounge, and music rooms. The School has completed the new 20,000-volume Mary Crist Fleming library.

BOARDING AND GENERAL FACILITIES

There are twelve dormitories on campus, housing from as few as 4 to as many as 43 students. All dormitories have faculty supervision. Rooms accommodate from 2 to 4 students each. Although School facilities are closed during winter and spring vacations, optional faculty-chaperoned trips throughout Europe are offered for students unable to return home.

Two recreation centers and a snack bar serve as focal points for student social activities. Two fully qualified nurses are in residence.

ATHLETICS

Students are required to participate in either a varsity sport three days a week or in recreational sports after classes. TASIS offers such recreational sports as soccer, basketball, fitness training, mountain biking, volleyball, rugby, tennis, track and field, squash, swimming, rock-climbing, and aerobics. Horseback riding and tennis are available at an extra cost. On weekends, students often go on hiking and mountain-climbing trips in the Swiss Alps during the fall and spring and go skiing during the winter season. During the one-week ski term in Crans-Montana or Verbier, every student takes lessons in downhill or cross-country skiing, or snowboarding. The Fleming Cup Ski Race is held during the Crans-Montana term.

Varsity sports give students the opportunity to compete against many schools in Switzerland and other countries, and to take part in tournaments sponsored by the Swiss Group of International Schools. Varsity sports include rugby, soccer, volleyball, basketball, tennis, and track and field.

Facilities include a playing field, a gym, and an outdoor basketball/volleyball area. The newly constructed sports complex includes a gymnasium with seating for up to 400 spectators, a dance studio, a fitness center, changing rooms, and a student commons lounge.

EXTRACURRICULAR OPPORTUNITIES

The School's location in central Europe offers a wide range of cultural opportunities. Trips to concerts, art galleries, and museums in Lugano, Locarno, and Milan extend education beyond the classroom. All students participate in in-program travel, which consists of a four-day, faculty-chaperoned trip in the fall and a seven-day, faculty-chaperoned trip in the spring to such cities as Athens, Barcelona, Florence, Madrid, Munich, Nice, Paris, Prague, Rome, Venice, and Vienna.

On-campus activities include drama productions, choir, Model UN and Model Congress, the Environmental Club, Student Council and peer helping, tutoring programs, the yearbook, the literary magazine, dances, weekly films, and art exhibitions. The Thanksgiving Banquet, the Christmas Dinner Dance, the Lugano Boat Dinner Dance, the Spring Prom, and the Arts Festival are major School social events.

DAILY LIFE

Classes commence at 8 a.m. and follow a rotating schedule. Classes meet from 50 to 65 minutes. There is a weekly all-school assembly, and students meet with their advisers every day. Sports and activities take place after school until 5:30 p.m. Meals are self-service except for Wednesday evening, when students share a formal dinner with their adviser. Evening study hours are from 7 until 10.

WEEKEND LIFE

Both day and boarding students are encouraged to participate in organized social events on weekends, including such options as mountain-climbing and camping trips to scenic areas in Switzerland, shopping trips to open-air markets in northern Italy, and sightseeing excursions to Zurich, Milan, Venice, or Florence. On-campus events include talent shows, coffeehouses, films, and discotheque dances.

On weekends, students have Lugano town privileges if they have no School commitments and are in good academic and social standing. All excursions beyond Lugano are chaperoned by a member of the faculty, except those for seniors and some juniors, who, with parental permission, enjoy the privilege of independent travel in groups of 2 or more.

SUMMER PROGRAMS

The TASIS Summer Language Program offers three- and four-week sessions of intensive French, Italian, German, and English as a second language at beginning, intermediate, and advanced levels of instruction for students ages 14–18. TOEFL review classes, an architecture and design course, and a photography workshop are also offered. Approximately 150 students attend each session, a small number of whom are TASIS full-year students seeking credit or enrichment. The experienced staff is drawn from TASIS and other schools, and there are visiting faculty members as well. Sports, social activities, and excursions are parts of the program.

TASIS Tuscan Academy of Art and Culture is offered to students ages 15–19 for three weeks in Tuscany, Italy. This program is ideal for students who intend to enroll in an AP art history course.

The TASIS French Language Program, located in the French-speaking canton of Vaud, offers a five-week full academic credit course as well as a four-week session for students ages 13–17 who wish to improve their language skills or develop fluency.

TASIS also offers two sessions of summer camp language programs in French and English for younger students. The Château des Enfants Program is for children ages 6–10, and the Middle School Program is for children ages 11–13.

COSTS AND FINANCIAL AID

The American all-inclusive tuition fee for U.S. citizens is $36,000; the enrollment deposit is $2000. This includes all fees necessary for attendance—room, board, tuition, eleven days of in-program travel, ski term, textbooks, laundry, and activities and lab fees. A weekly personal allowance of $50 to $80 is recommended. First-semester fees are due on July 1; second-semester fees must be paid by November 15.

Students are invited to apply for financial aid, which is granted on the basis of merit, need, and the student's ability to contribute to the School community.

ADMISSIONS INFORMATION

All applicants are considered on the basis of previous academic records, three teachers' evaluations, and a personal statement. The SSAT is recommended, and the SLEP test is required for students whose native language is not English. TASIS does not discriminate on the basis of race, color, nationality, or ethnic origin in its admissions policies and practices.

Application for entrance is recommended only for those students with sufficient academic interest and motivation to benefit from the program. The School accepts students from grades 7 to 12 and at the postgraduate level. A postgraduate applicant must have completed a high school diploma program in good standing.

APPLICATION TIMETABLE

TASIS, The American School in Switzerland, has a rolling admissions policy and considers applications throughout the year. Applicants are encouraged to make an appointment to visit the campus. Within ten days of receipt of a completed application, the $150 application fee, an official transcript from the previous school, and three teachers' evaluations, the Admissions Committee notifies the parents of its decision.

ADMISSIONS CORRESPONDENCE

Mr. William Eichner, Director of Admissions
TASIS, The American School in Switzerland
CH-6926 Montagnola-Lugano
Switzerland

Phone: 41-91-960-5151
Fax: 41-91-993-2979
E-mail: admissions@tasis.ch
Web site: http://www.tasis.com

or

The TASIS Schools
1640 Wisconsin Avenue, NW
Washington, D.C. 20007

Phone: 202-965-5800
Fax: 202-965-5816
E-mail: usadmissions@tasis.com

THE THACHER SCHOOL

Ojai, California

Type: Coeducational boarding and day college-preparatory school
Grades: 9–12
Enrollment: 240
Head of School: Michael K. Mulligan, Head

THE SCHOOL

The ranch that became the Thacher School was first named "Casa de Piedra"—house of stone. Rock-solid in its second century, Thacher has maintained founder Sherman Day Thacher's cornerstone values of hard work, both intellectual and physical, and of honesty, resourcefulness, and concern for others.

Mr. Thacher was a Yale graduate and the son of a Yale professor. His original curriculum came straight out of the New England boarding school tradition: a rigorous academic schedule, classics taught by dedicated scholar-teachers, and poetry and singing balanced by baseball and other varsity athletics. Today, the Thacher School curriculum, faculty, and college counseling are held as models for other schools, both public and private.

The Thacher School is directed by a 31-member Board of Trustees. The endowment is currently valued at $80 million. Alumni are generous in their support of Thacher; the School has won several national awards for alumni giving. Thacher is accredited by the Western Association of Schools and Colleges and holds memberships in the National Association of Independent Schools, the Council for Advancement and Support of Education, Cum Laude Society, A Better Chance, and the Western Boarding Schools Association, among many others.

Thacher's 400-acre campus is 90 miles northwest of Los Angeles and just inland from the coast at Ventura and Santa Barbara. The Los Padres National Forest is the School's backyard and offers virtually limitless outdoor adventure.

ACADEMIC PROGRAMS

Thacher takes a relatively small number of students and surrounds them with enthusiastic teachers, state-of-the-art technology, and first-rate facilities. The curriculum provides the abundant intellectual challenge that makes students seek a school like Thacher in the first place.

The academic program includes a core curriculum of requirements in English, mathematics, foreign language, the sciences, history, and fine arts as well as nearly sixty electives. Twenty-one Advanced Placement courses are offered in addition to opportunities for independent study. All seniors conduct interdisciplinary research on a topic of their choice, presenting their findings in Senior Exhibitions. Students at Thacher are offered a wide variety of opportunities for off-campus study in other countries and throughout the United States.

FACULTY AND ADVISERS

The 48 teachers at Thacher are diverse and scholarly—70 percent have earned doctoral or master's degrees in their disciplines. Because teachers fill a variety of roles on campus—serving as coaches and club advisers, heading dining room dinner tables, and sponsoring weekend activities in their own homes—relationships between the students and faculty members are strong and healthy. Ninety-five percent of the Thacher faculty members live on campus in or near a dormitory and serve as advisers to students in their dorm area, offering academic and personal guidance. The student-faculty ratio is 5:1.

Michael Mulligan was appointed Head in 1993 and holds a B.A. and M.A. from Middlebury and an Ed.M. from Harvard.

COLLEGE PLACEMENT

Thacher students explore and choose from a broad and impressive array of colleges. They have a high success rate with the applications they make: 92 percent gained admission to a college noted in *U.S. News & World Report*'s "Tier 1."

Thacher students and their parents are guided through the college process by a full-time college counselor. The College Counseling program provides individual help sessions, panel discussions with college admission directors, and workshops covering topics such as essay writing, SAT preparation, and financial aid.

SAT scores average 650 verbal and 660 math. Ninety-three percent of last year's Advanced Placement scores earned college credit. More than 100 college representatives visit Thacher each year. Thacher students have most frequently matriculated to Brown, Colorado College, Columbia, Northwestern, Stanford, and the University of California at Berkeley.

STUDENT BODY AND CONDUCT

Thacher's program encourages students to grow into leadership positions. Many seniors become dorm prefects and elected class leaders; others assume equally important leadership roles. Thacher students experience the Honor Code in concrete ways: they never receive keys to their dorm rooms, because doors at Thacher are rarely locked. Similarly, upperclass exams are unproctored, and a laptop computer left in the dining hall at lunch will still be there at dinner.

Boys and girls are equal in number at Thacher, and more than a quarter are students of color. Boarders represent 90 percent of the population, day students the remainder. Sixty percent of Thacher's boarders come from California; the others hail from more than twenty-five states and ten countries.

ACADEMIC FACILITIES

The Boswell Library stands at the heart of the campus. Home to 28,000 volumes, 120 periodicals, and 10,000 classical recordings, the library is connected by walkway to English and history seminar rooms.

Nearby is the Anson S. Thacher Humanities Building—housing classrooms, art studios and graphic design computers, darkrooms, an art gallery, and the radio station. The Seeley G. Mudd Science and Math Center is home to computer labs (one Macintosh, the other Windows based) and a digital media lab with multiple color laser printers, digital editing workstations, and access to digital and video camera equipment. In addition, there are eight laboratories, some including aquariums where students breed fish and amphibians. The newly completed Student Commons and Performing Arts Center round out the campus facilities. All dorm rooms, classrooms, and offices are connected through a schoolwide Ethernet network to the campus server and the School's multiple T1 connections to the Internet.

BOARDING AND GENERAL FACILITIES

Thacher students live by class in eight single-sex dormitories. Ninth graders nearly always live in single rooms; after the first year, some students have roommates. The dormitories are arranged in sections of 6 students to 1 senior prefect, who helps administer dormitory rules and serves as a role model and informal adviser for other students. Dormitories are run by faculty dorm heads with help from advisers and student prefects.

An Olympic-size pool, ten tennis courts, an all-weather track, a fitness complex, and a trap range are among the many athletic facilities. Arts are performed in an outdoor theater (complete with stone seats and a creek), an outdoor amphitheater, and a traditional stage auditorium. The Horse Program is complemented by 150 horses and burros, gymkhana fields, and riding rings.

ATHLETICS

Competitive athletics include tennis, soccer, track, volleyball, baseball, cross-country, lacrosse, basketball, and 8-man football, all at two or more levels. Students compete against teams fielded by other Condor League schools as well as against schools in the California Interscholastic Federation (public and private). Dance and rock-climbing programs are also offered.

All students participate each season on a formal athletic team, in the Horse Program, or in the Outdoor Program, which includes outdoor sports such as climbing, telemarking, downhill and cross-country skiing, winter camping, sea and river kayaking, and snowshoeing.

While ninth graders may participate in athletics, their primary afternoon focus is in the Horse Program—a century-long tradition. Though most new students have had little or no experience with horses, each ninth grader learns to care for and ride one of Thacher's horses. The first-year experience culminates in the Big

Gymkhana, where more than 100 riders compete in traditional events of speed, skill, and derring-do.

EXTRACURRICULAR OPPORTUNITIES
Fine arts include musical, studio art, dance, and dramatic instruction. Musical performance groups include the Concert Choir, Chamber Singers, male and female a cappella groups, and the Instrument Ensemble. The Thacher Masquers perform a play in the fall, a musical in the winter, and various one-act plays in the spring.

Students publish a newspaper, a yearbook, and a literary magazine and operate a radio station. There are active clubs for computer science, Bible study, film, trap shooting, foreign languages, environmental protection, human rights, multiculturalism, and equine interests. Student government consists of the Community Council, the Judicial Council, and elected class and dormitory leaders.

The great majority of Thacher students are involved with community service projects, such as Head Start and other elementary school tutoring programs, Habitat for Humanity, and the Humane Society. They also work in convalescent homes, homeless shelters, and an orphanage in Mexico.

DAILY LIFE
Classes are held five days a week from 8 a.m. to 3 p.m. Three days a week, the community gathers midmorning for Assembly. Athletic activities begin at 3 and are followed by rehearsals or club/committee meetings. At 6, students and faculty members and their families join together for a formal family-style meal four nights a week. Weekly evening lectures begin at 6:45. Study hours begin at 7:30 and end at 9:30, when most students congregate for a soda or snack in the new Student Commons. Faculty members are available in the evenings for extra help.

WEEKEND LIFE
A weekly film series, concerts, dances, and barbecues are just a few of the activities students enjoy on the weekends. A typical weekend might include a trip to town, athletic events, a horseback ride or hike into the mountains, social activities, and a trip off campus to a play or concert in Los Angeles or Santa Barbara. Every Saturday night, students and faculty members drop by the Head's home to play Ping-Pong, watch a movie, take a shift making cookies, or just spend time with their friends.

The tradition of camping is strong at Thacher; many weekends, a faculty member leads students by horse, mountain bike, kayak, canoe, or skis or on foot to various regions of the Southwest for an outdoor get-away.

COSTS AND FINANCIAL AID
Tuition for 2005–06 was $34,600 for boarding students and $22,950 for day students. Estimated additional expenses are $800. Tuition payments are due in the form of a $1500 deposit in April and payments on August 1 and December 1. A ten-month tuition payment plan is available.

Thacher's 2005–06 financial aid budget of $1.4 million reflected the School's commitment to a socioeconomically diverse student body. Awards are made annually to students on the basis of family need, as determined by the School and Student Service for Financial Aid in Princeton, New Jersey.

ADMISSIONS INFORMATION
Thacher has long sought motivated, highly capable students who are ready to commit their energies and talents to a dynamic, diverse community in which every individual's contribution is valued.

Most students enter in the ninth grade, though the School admits some sophomores and a few juniors. Secondary School Admission Test results are required of all applicants for the ninth and tenth grades; the PSAT or SAT is used for eleventh-grade candidates. Generally, 5 candidates submit applications for every available spot.

APPLICATION TIMETABLE
Applications received by the deadline of February 1 are acted on by March 10. Accepted students are asked to confirm their intention to enroll by April 10. Applications received after February 1 are considered as space is available.

Campus visits, which include a student-guided tour and a time to talk with a member of the Admission Office, generally take place in the fall and winter of the year preceding the September of anticipated entry. Such visits may be scheduled on Monday, Wednesday, and Friday mornings when school is in session; special interview arrangements can be made in unusual situations.

ADMISSIONS CORRESPONDENCE
Bill McMahon
Director of Admission
The Thacher School
5025 Thacher Road
Ojai, California 93023
Phone: 805-640-3210
Fax: 805-640-9377
E-mail: admission@thacher.org
Web site: http://www.thacher.org

THOMAS JEFFERSON SCHOOL

St. Louis, Missouri

Type: Coeducational boarding and day college-preparatory school
Grades: 7–12
Enrollment: 86
Head of School: William C. Rowe

THE SCHOOL

Thomas Jefferson School was founded in 1946. It has received national attention for its academic excellence and its teacher-trustee system, the two guiding ideas of the founders. It became coeducational in 1971. The campus is a 20-acre estate in Sunset Hills, a suburb 15 miles southwest of downtown St. Louis.

The School's mission is to give its students the strongest possible academic background, responsibility for their own learning, a concern for other people, and the resources to live happily as adults and become active contributors to society. Many of the School's unusual features, such as the daily schedule, are outgrowths of this mission.

The School is unique in its business organization. A majority of the members of its Board of Trustees must be teachers in the School; moreover, no one may teach full-time for more than five years without becoming a trustee. The Headmaster and the other teacher-trustees make up the administration of the School, with the exception of the Director of Development, who is not a faculty member. This structure gives teachers a greater stake in the School and a breadth of experience that produces better teaching.

Thomas Jefferson School is a member of the National Association of Independent Schools, The Association of Boarding Schools, the Independent Schools Association of the Central States, Midwest Boarding Schools, the School and Student Service for Financial Aid, and the Educational Records Bureau.

ACADEMIC PROGRAMS

Thomas Jefferson offers a challenging approach to learning, with the emphasis on the student's own efforts. Classes are short, and the teachers seldom lecture; instead, everyone is called on to answer questions and generate discussion. During afternoon and evening study time, the students have a good deal of freedom in choosing when and where to do their homework, with help readily available.

Seventh and eighth graders take English, mathematics, science, social studies, and Latin. In the ninth through twelfth grades, students take 4 years of English; 4 years of mathematics through calculus; 2 years of Greek (ninth and tenth grades); 2 years of Italian or French (tenth and eleventh); at least 2 years of science, including an AP course; and at least 2 years of history, including AP American history. Electives include more language and science courses and European history. Advanced Placement exams are a standard part of the courses in American history, European history, calculus, biology, advanced French, junior and senior English, physics, and chemistry. The faculty also helps students work toward AP exams in Latin, government, computer science, and studio art.

The English curriculum gives students intensive training in grammar, vocabulary, and writing skills. They also read and discuss a great deal of literature, including recognized classics (Shakespeare, the Bible, and epics), time-tested authors (Austen, Dickens, Dostoyevski, Fitzgerald, Manzoni, Melville, and Shaw), and more recent major authors, such as Amy Tan, Ralph Ellison, and Chaim Potok.

A special feature is the study of classical Greek, which contributes to intellectual development (including concrete benefits such as enhanced vocabulary) and cultural background. This subject, in which the School is a national leader, continues to stir curiosity and ambition. A number of graduates continue to study it in college; others do so independently or later in life.

The average class size is 10, and the overall student-teacher ratio is 7:1. During the day, teachers are accessible to everyone and are ready to help; one teacher is on duty each evening and visits the students' rooms to assist with homework. There are no study halls except for younger new students and for those in academic difficulty.

The grading system uses letter grades of A, B, C, D, and E. An average of B– is Honors. To remain in good standing, a student must have no more than one D in any marking period; students in their first year, however, are allowed extra time to adjust. One-hour examinations are given at the end of the first and third quarters (October and April), and 2- to 3-hour examinations are given at midyear and at the end of the year (January and June). Following each exam period, a student's adviser sends the parents a letter discussing the student's progress and giving the latest grades and teachers' comments. The unusually long Christmas and spring vacations (about one month each) give students an opportunity to unwind, spend time with their families, and do independent work for extra credit.

FACULTY AND ADVISERS

The faculty consists of 6 women and 6 men, including the Headmaster. Faculty members hold twelve baccalaureate degrees, nine master's degrees, and one law degree.

William C. Rowe became the third Head of School in the summer of 2000, succeeding Lawrence Morgan. Mr. Rowe attended Thomas Jefferson School and Wesleyan University (A.B., 1967) and holds a master's degree from Washington University.

All faculty members are expected to continue educating themselves by regular reading, both within and outside the subject areas they teach. They meet periodically to report on their reading and to discuss it.

Currently, 6 of the 12 faculty members live on the campus. Each teacher, whether resident or not, has several duties besides teaching, such as athletics supervision, evening study help, and advising students. Teachers meet with each of their advisees regularly to check the student's grades and to keep in touch with his or her personal development.

COLLEGE PLACEMENT

The Headmaster visits a number of colleges each year; he and other faculty members help students decide where to apply. Guidance is provided throughout the application process, and great care is taken in writing recommendations.

In fifty-nine years, the School has had 499 graduates; all have gone to college, most to well-known, selective institutions. Among the colleges and universities attended by Thomas Jefferson graduates in the past eight years are Boston University (3), Brown (3), Carnegie Mellon (1), Careleton (1), Columbia (2), Duke (2), Emory (2), Harvard (1), Haverford (2), Johns Hopkins (2), Lake Forest (4), Loyola of Chicago (3), Northwestern (4), Pennsylvania (Wharton) (2), Pomona (3), Reed (2), Stanford (2), Swarthmore (4), Vanderbilt (2), Washington (St. Louis) (8), Wesleyan (3), and the University of Missouri–Columbia (5).

For the class of 2005, the SAT I median scores were 710 verbal and 710 math.

STUDENT BODY AND CONDUCT

In 2005–06, the School had 86 students (41 boarding, 45 day), enrolled as follows: seventh grade, 9; eighth grade, 15; ninth grade, 10; tenth grade, 18; eleventh grade, 17; and twelfth grade, 17. Most students come from the region between the Appalachians and the Great Plains. Approximately 22 percent are international students from various countries (ESL instruction is available, although some knowledge of English is required for admission). Most grades have girls and boys in about equal numbers.

A Student Council, whose members are elected twice a year, brings student concerns before the faculty and helps maintain a healthy, studious atmosphere. Collectively, the council has one vote in faculty meetings on any decision concerning student life.

Demerits are given for misconduct, lateness, and other routine matters; a student who receives too many demerits in one week has to do chores around the campus on Saturday. Students may appeal any demerits, even those given by the Headmaster, before a Student Appeals Court.

ACADEMIC FACILITIES

The Main Building, a former residence, provides a comfortable, homelike setting for classes and meals; it also contains teachers' offices, the business office, the library, computer terminals, an art studio, and a darkroom. Sayers Hall, next to the Main Building, provides science laboratories, classrooms, and a library/computer annex.

BOARDING AND GENERAL FACILITIES

Boarders live in the Gables—a smaller building from the original estate—and in five modern one-story houses, built in 1960, plus one additional, similar house added in 1994. Each house has four double rooms; each room has an outside entrance, private bath, large windows, wall-to-wall carpeting, and air conditioning. The houses were designed to provide quiet, privacy, and independence. Normally, 2 boarding students share a room with 1 or 2 day students. All dorm rooms provide phone and Internet access.

ATHLETICS

Thomas Jefferson School athletics are meant to help students relax, stay healthy and in good condition, and study better. Outdoor sports include tennis (five courts), soccer, and sometimes running, walking, cycling, or ice skating at a nearby rink; indoor sports are volleyball and basketball (in the gymnasium) and sometimes aerobics. Athletics are required on Monday, Tuesday, Thursday, and Friday afternoons. There is competition with other local schools in basketball, soccer, and volleyball.

EXTRACURRICULAR OPPORTUNITIES

St. Louis has a wealth of resources in art, music, and theater, as well as an excellent zoo, a science museum, and a botanical garden. The faculty members keeps the students informed and helps provide them with transportation and tickets whenever possible. Teachers often take classes on field trips or invite students out informally. In recent years, groups have gone to the Ozarks for camping, to the Mississippi River to see bald eagles, and to many symphony concerts, ballets, and plays. Students also attend movies, sports events, and rock concerts.

Volunteer service is encouraged, and the School helps students find opportunities and use them; all students must plan and complete a required amount of voluntary community service before they graduate. Students are encouraged to pursue their own interests, such as music lessons, and the School helps make arrangements. A piano and a darkroom are available. Sometimes students organize and carry through a major project, such as producing the School yearbook (since 1981) or the student newspaper (since 1984).

DAILY LIFE

A school day begins with the 7:45 rising bell and breakfast at 8. Between 8:30 and 12:30, there are seven class periods of 35 minutes each, followed by lunch. In grades 10 and 11, students attend each of their four classes (grades 7 through 9 attend five classes) every day. Seniors, who have longer assignments, attend each class only four days a week. After lunch, a student may have a science lab, a language lab, or other supplementary academic work. Then they have an hour of athletics, perhaps a meeting with their adviser or study help from another teacher, and some independent time in which they are expected to start their homework for the next day. Supper is at 5:45, and evenings are devoted to study. On Wednesday afternoon, there are fine arts classes in such subjects as drawing, photography, ceramics, and art and music appreciation, and students may leave campus for nearby shopping centers. Day students are on campus from about 8:30 a.m. to 5 p.m.

WEEKEND LIFE

Weekends are leisure time. As long as students are in good standing academically, they have considerable freedom and may leave the campus for movies, shopping, dates, and overnights. Older students may keep cars on campus at the discretion of the faculty. The sports facilities are available for weekend use. Dances are organized periodically by the Student Council.

SUMMER PROGRAMS

Thomas Jefferson has no summer school, but there have often been summer trips to Europe, led by the Headmaster. The size of the party has varied from 2 to 10 or more students, plus adults. Thomas Jefferson groups have stayed at the same pensione in Florence for more than thirty years.

COSTS AND FINANCIAL AID

Charges for 2005–06 were $29,200 for full boarding, $27,500 for weekday boarding, and $17,800 for day students. This includes room plus all meals for boarders and all lunches for day students. The School estimates that $1300 covers books, school supplies, and other expenses related to School activities. Optional off-campus activities such as music lessons (and the necessary transportation) cost extra.

A $1000 deposit, nonrefundable but credited to tuition, is required when a student enrolls. The balance of the tuition is paid in two installments due in June and August. A monthly payment alternative is available through Academic Management Services.

Financial aid is available, based on a student's need. About one fourth of the student body currently receives some financial aid; the total amount awarded is about $500,000. An applicant's family must file a statement with the School and Student Service, and this information is used in judging need. Many middle-income families receive some assistance.

ADMISSIONS INFORMATION

The School looks for signs of native intelligence, liveliness, energy, ambition, and curiosity. Good grades and high test scores are important considerations but not always the deciding ones. The School gives its own 2-hour battery of entrance tests; as an alternative, a candidate may submit the results of the Secondary School Admission Test (SSAT) or the Independent School Entrance Examination (ISEE). International students and others living abroad follow different procedures. About two thirds of those who complete the application process are accepted.

APPLICATION TIMETABLE

Inquiries and applications are welcome at any time. When an application (mailed with the catalog) comes in, the School writes or telephones the family to arrange a visit for testing and the interview. Prospective students usually spend a day at the School visiting classes, having lunch, and taking the tests. Acceptances are sent out in early March, although parents can be notified by January 1 if they inform the Director of Admissions that their child is applying for early decision. Any remaining places are filled by a rolling admissions system. Parents should reply within two weeks of acceptance. There is a $40 fee for domestic applications and $100 fee for international applications.

ADMISSIONS CORRESPONDENCE

Marie De Jesus, Director of Admissions
Thomas Jefferson School
4100 South Lindbergh Boulevard
St. Louis, Missouri 63127

Phone: 314-843-4151
Fax: 314-843-3527
E-mail: admissions@tjs.org
Web site: http://www.tjs.org

TILTON SCHOOL

Tilton, New Hampshire

Type: Coeducational boarding and day college-preparatory
Grades: 9–12, postgraduate year
Enrollment: 210
Head of School: James R. Clements

THE SCHOOL

Tilton School challenges students to embrace and navigate a world marked by diversity and change. Through the quality of human relationships, Tilton School's faculty cultivates in its students the curiosity, the skills, the knowledge and understanding, the character, and the integrity requisite for the passionate pursuit of lifelong personal success and service.

Tilton School values people. Students, faculty, staff, parents, and alumni are the cornerstones of the School. Students are at the center of the Tilton Experience, and Tilton enrolls young men and women capable of both contributing to and benefiting from the School. Tilton is committed to recruiting and supporting faculty and staff members who are dedicated, through both education and example, to the School's mission. Tilton seeks and expects a genuine partnership with parents, working together to challenge and support the students. While encouraging the alumni to be active in their School's life, there is also a commitment to honor them and their historic relationship to the School.

Tilton School values education—the active pursuit of knowledge and the growth of intellectual curiosity. The rigorous academic program is designed to prepare graduates to be successful college students and contributing members of society. Various pathways to learning are supported; the acquisition of genuine understanding is the goal. Tilton is committed to the principle that all students can excel. Through a broad range of learning experiences, students develop problem-solving skills and self-confidence while becoming independent and critical thinkers.

Tilton School values community and believes that the well-being of the whole community is founded on the fundamental principle of respect. The current moral, ethical, spiritual, cultural, and ecological dilemmas are explored. By doing so, a just and healthy School community and wider world are promoted.

Tilton School values commitment. All members of the School have a duty to commit themselves to learning, building a respectful community, and supporting the well-being of the School to the extent each is capable.

A nonprofit corporation, Tilton is governed by the Head of School and an 18-member Board of Trustees. Annual expenses of $7.2 million are met through tuition, endowment, and annual giving. The endowment currently totals $10.4 million. The nearly 4,000 living alumni have a beneficial impact on fund raising, with gifts to the School of more than $300,000 annually.

Tilton School is accredited by the New England Association of Schools and Colleges and is a member of the National Association of Independent Schools, the Independent Schools Association of Northern New England, the Cum Laude Society, the National Honor Society, the Second-

ary School Admission Test Board, and the Council for Religion in Independent Schools.

ACADEMIC PROGRAMS

Tilton's academic program offers a traditional college-preparatory curriculum, while supporting the student's intellectual maturation and encouraging the development of academic competence. The School seeks to produce students who have a genuine interest in intellectual pursuits and to teach students self-discipline and to reinforce in students sound moral and ethical judgment.

The school year is divided into semesters. During each term, students at Tilton must take four to five full-credit courses or their equivalent in part-credit courses. Typically, freshmen and sophomores complete full-year courses, while juniors and seniors broaden their options with some one-term electives. Required credits include English, mathematics, foreign language, fine arts, laboratory science, social studies (history), and health, for a total of 18.

The program of study for ninth grade students is a team-taught integrated program (FIRST) emphasizing a strong academic foundation and supportive intellectual, personal, and social development.

The average class size is 11 students, and the student-teacher ratio is 5:1. Evening study hall is supervised. Evening study hours are designed to allow for availability of resources and a quiet, uninterrupted study atmosphere where reinforcement of learned skills can be emphasized under direct supervision by the faculty members. Academic focus is the primary purpose of evening study hours. Based on a graduated level of independence, the evening model provides for a balance of structure and self-directed study.

Tilton uses a letter grading system with numerical grades for effort (1=excellent; 5=poor). Passing is D– or above; B– qualifies for Honors and A– and above for High Honors.

The Learning Center serves approximately 34 percent of the students, complementing their regular academic instruction by identifying individual needs and helping to devise strategies that enable them to achieve academic success. The center provides specialized instructional support for students whose academic progress is limited by deficiencies in basic skills or study habits, or by distinct learning-style differences. An SAT tutorial is also offered through the center.

The English as a Second Language Program serves students who need intermediate and advanced English language support skills.

FACULTY AND ADVISERS

Tilton's faculty consists of 39 members (25 men and 14 women). The faculty members hold seventeen bachelor's degrees, sixteen master's de-

grees, and two Ph.D.s. Most members of the faculty and administration live on campus with their families.

Faculty members must have not only a high level of expertise in their academic areas but also an enthusiastic commitment to students' interests and student life. In addition to dormitory and afternoon coaching and activity duties, most faculty members have 6 to 8 student advisees. The adviser is responsible for monitoring academic progress and for counseling in other areas of school life.

James R. Clements, appointed Head of School in 1998, is a graduate of the University of New Hampshire (B.A., 1972; M.B.A., 1998). Prior to joining Tilton, Mr. Clements spent twenty-one years at the Chapel Hill–Chauncy Hall School in Waltham, Massachusetts, most recently as Head of School from 1993–98.

COLLEGE PLACEMENT

Two full-time counselors guide students in the selection of colleges and coordinate the application process, beginning in the junior year. Approximately 60 college admissions officers visit the School each year to talk with groups of students or to interview individual students.

Members of the class of 2005 were accepted at more than 150 colleges and universities, including Bowdoin, Boston University, Carnegie Mellon, Clarkson, Hobart and William Smith, Syracuse, Union, Wesleyan, and the Universities of Massachusetts, New Hampshire, and Vermont.

STUDENT BODY AND CONDUCT

In 2005–06, Tilton enrolled 210 students—80 percent are boarders and 20 percent are day students. There were 140 boys and 70 girls. Tilton students represent many racial, religious, and socioeconomic backgrounds; approximately 60 percent come from New England, 21 percent from other parts of the United States, and 19 percent from other parts of the world.

Expectations at Tilton are high and are thoroughly communicated. Although the immediate goal of School rules and regulations is to promote order, mutual respect, and academic excellence, this structure serves, in the long range, to prepare students for productive and responsible roles in a changing society. At Tilton, there is a basic faith in young people. Guided by the attitude that students can learn and want to learn, faculty members are eager to inspire commitment, pride, and responsibility in their students.

ACADEMIC FACILITIES

Plimpton Hall houses twelve classrooms, three science laboratories, and other facilities, including the Computer Center and bookstore. Eight more classrooms are contained in Pfeiffer Hall and the lower level of the chapel. Pfeiffer Hall houses the Learning Center. The Helene Grant Daly Art Cen-

ter provides excellent facilities for art classes, including ceramics, computer graphics, studio art, printmaking, sculpture, silk-screening, and photography. The Lucien Hunt Memorial Library contains approximately 17,500 volumes, including subscriptions to 40 periodicals, 4 newspapers, and an online periodical index and encyclopedias. The library features ten computers, reading and conference rooms, and extensive facilities for research. Drama and musical productions are performed in the theater in Hamilton Hall.

The Tilton campus is connected by a fiber-optic backbone that supports an Ethernet 10Base-T network. All classrooms and dormitories are wired and connected to the network, as is the library. Two CD-ROM towers service the network as well as an e-mail program. The network is serviced through a Novell parent package. All students have their own account, accessible through a password. The network supports Microsoft Works in the PC environment as well as the Macintosh environment. There are three labs—one has twelve Compaq EVO D300V machines, the second contains six Power Macintosh 6100/60 machines, and the third, in the school's library, contains ten Compaqs. The Macintosh lab is set up to support electronic music classes and computer art courses. An Internet link is available for student use in the library, PC lab, and dorm rooms with prearrangement.

BOARDING AND GENERAL FACILITIES

Five dormitories, each housing 18 to 48 students and 1 to 4 faculty members and their families, are located on campus. Students live in double or single rooms. Returning students may state their preference for room assignments. Students whose homes are a long distance from Tilton may visit with friends or family during vacations.

The school store, MARC Student Center, and the snack bar are open at various times of the day and evening. There is a six-bed health center, licensed as a hospital, with a resident nurse and a doctor on call.

ATHLETICS

The School believes that people of all ages perform best when they are active and healthy and that organized sports promote physical development, physical courage, self-discipline, and a sense of team spirit. All students must participate in an afternoon activity. Students must play at least one sport each year to fulfill their annual +5 Program requirements.

Each year, approximately twenty-five different teams are formed. Boys' sports include baseball, basketball, football, ice hockey, lacrosse, soccer, tennis, and wrestling. Girls' sports are basketball, field hockey, ice hockey, lacrosse, soccer, softball, and tennis. Coed sports include Alpine skiing, cross-country running, golf, and snowboarding.

Facilities include 25 acres of outstanding playing fields, 3 miles of cross-country trails, three tennis courts, a gymnasium, a field house with an indoor ice rink, and an outdoor swimming pool. The golf team uses a nearby eighteen-hole course.

EXTRACURRICULAR OPPORTUNITIES

Tilton's +5 Program, distinctive among independent secondary schools, requires that all students involve themselves in five areas of nonacademic campus life: art and culture, team athletics, outdoor experiences, community services, and leadership roles. These learning experiences enhance self-confidence and self-esteem.

By structuring extracurricular activities, the School broadens students' interests, enables them to develop skills that enhance their self-worth, and provides enjoyment during their free time. Faculty members' commitment to excellence and their guidance encourage and reassure students who may be doubtful of their abilities. As a result, strong relationships develop, and students and teachers work together more effectively in the classroom. Students choose afternoon activities in athletics, performing arts, and the outdoors.

Offerings in art and culture include drama; musical theater; dance, including improv jazz; tech crew; publications; ceramics; design; photography; screenprinting; woodworking; and chorus.

On virtually every weekend of the school year, there is an outdoor trip for canoeing, mountain biking, Alpine skiing, fishing, rock climbing, hiking, snowshoeing, or cross-country skiing. There are also two wilderness courses. One is a trip for all tenth graders, and a more intense weeklong program, called Winter Wilderness, is scheduled in January for students in grades 11 and 12.

Community service opportunities are available both on campus and in the Tilton community. This division of the +5 Program encourages students to commit themselves to helping others. Other projects include helping at a soup kitchen; reading to patients at the New Hampshire Veterans' Home; tutoring local children; raising funds for UNICEF, Oxfam, and Toys for Tots; and teaching in a learn-to-skate program for young children.

Leadership may be the most important of the five areas. Experience as a dorm proctor, work-program supervisor, Student Council officer, editor, or team captain offers a rigorous challenge.

Movies, plays, lectures, and concerts are regular events on campus, while trips to museums and theaters in Boston are regular off-campus activities.

DAILY LIFE

Class periods are approximately 45 minutes long. Mid-morning each day, there is a meeting either with advisee groups, special committees, or the entire School at School Meeting, which is held two times per week. Conference period and work programs are also part of daily life. The conference period is an opportunity to meet teachers for extra help or to make an appointment to meet a teacher later in the evening for more extensive work.

After classes, everyone participates in after school programs. Wednesday and Saturday schedules are a bit different in that Wednesday is a half day, which allows time for athletic competitions, and most Saturdays are scheduled with a half day of classes to make up for the short Wednesday schedule. Athletic competitions and afternoon activities are held on Saturday afternoons as well.

WEEKEND LIFE

Faculty and staff teams plan all weekend activities with student support. Saturday events include sports competitions, movies, dances, concerts, intramural or recreational athletics, and trips to shopping areas and movie theaters. The gym, field house, student center, and art center are open both Saturday and Sunday. Sunday is for scheduled activities, both on and off the campus. Day students are invited to participate and are active in weekend life.

COSTS AND FINANCIAL AID

For 2005–06, tuition, room, and board cost $34,975; tuition for day students was $20,150. Additional expenses, such as those for books and laundry, range from $600 to $1000. Private music or voice lessons, skiing, snowboarding, learning center sessions, and ESL classes are charged separately. Tuition may be paid in full in early August, or families can take advantage of one of Tilton's payment plan options.

Thirty-four percent of the students receive financial aid in the form of direct grants and/or loans. For 2005–06, more than $1.4 million in aid was granted. Applications for aid, which should be made before February 1, are reviewed separately from admission decisions.

ADMISSIONS INFORMATION

The Admissions Committee seeks to admit students who will benefit from and contribute to Tilton and those of diverse backgrounds and individual personal strengths. Students with various academic abilities who seek to challenge themselves and take advantage of Tilton's programs within and outside the classroom are excellent candidates for admission. Candidates for the ninth and tenth grades should take the SSAT and have the results sent to Tilton. Eleventh and twelfth graders and postgraduates should take the PSAT or SAT I. The most important application requirements for admission are the student's school transcript and current teacher recommendations. All prospective students are expected to visit the School and interview with the Admission Office. Students may enter at all grade levels; entry in the eleventh or twelfth grade or the postgraduate year is more competitive.

APPLICATION TIMETABLE

Initial inquiries are welcome at any time but are recommended before the late spring prior to the year in which admission is sought. Ideally, applications (accompanied by a $45 application fee) should be filed by February 1. The Admission Office is open for interviews on weekdays and on selected Saturday mornings. It is best to plan a visit while school is in session.

Admission decisions are made on a rolling basis after March 10. The School adheres to the Parents' Reply Date of April 10. A nonrefundable deposit is required to hold a place at Tilton and is applied to tuition for the year.

ADMISSIONS CORRESPONDENCE

Katherine E. Saunders
Director of Admissions
Tilton School
Tilton, New Hampshire 03276
Phone: 603-286-1733
Fax: 603-286-1705
E-mail: admissions@tiltonschool.org
Web site: http://www.tiltonschool.org

TMI–THE EPISCOPAL SCHOOL OF TEXAS

San Antonio, Texas

Type: Coeducational day (grades 6–12) and boarding (grades 9–12) college-preparatory school with optional JROTC
Grades: 6–12
Enrollment: School total: 315; Upper School: 231; Middle School: 84
Head of School: Dr. James Freeman

THE SCHOOL

The mission of TMI–The Episcopal School of Texas is to provide an excellent educational community, with values based on the teachings of Jesus Christ, challenging motivated students to develop their full potential in service and leadership. TMI is the oldest Episcopal college-preparatory school in the Southwest. Founded in 1893 by Bishop J. S. Johnston, TMI is the official school of the Episcopal Diocese of West Texas. The school became coed in 1972, and today, 45 percent of the students are girls. The JROTC-military leadership program is open to all grades and comprises approximately 30 percent of the student body.

A TMI experience is centered on the idea that a complete education requires the challenging formation of the whole person; hence, each student is expected to be a motivated scholar and to participate in daily chapel, athletics, the fine arts, and community service. All TMI graduates go on to college, and TMI's college admissions record is historically impressive. The TMI experience prepares young women and men for far more than selective college admission, however. The school watchwords are "high standards—hard work—and helping community."

TMI is accredited by the Independent Schools Association of the Southwest and is a member of the National Association of Episcopal Schools, the Southwestern Association of Episcopal Schools, and the Association of Boarding Schools.

ACADEMIC PROGRAMS

The Upper School at TMI follows a traditional four-year college-preparatory curriculum. A minimum of 23.5 credits are required for graduation: English, 4 years; mathematics, 4 years; science, 3 years; history, 3.5 years; foreign language, 3 years; fine arts, 1 year; religion, 1 year; physical education, 1 unit per year; and 3 units of electives. Fourteen Advanced Placement courses are offered in English, math, history, science, foreign language, computer programming, and studio art. Honors classes are offered in all core academic areas.

The Middle School curriculum is designed to prepare students for success in the Upper School. Middle School courses include English, literature, mathematics, history, science, foreign language, ethics, fine arts, and physical education.

The school year, thirty-six weeks, is divided into two semesters—the first ending in December and the second ending in May. Progress reports are written at three-week intervals. Formal grades are issued at the end of each nine-week period. The student-teacher ratio is 8:1, and class sizes range from fewer than 10 students to 21 students, with an average class size of 15.

FACULTY AND ADVISERS

The TMI faculty is composed of 41 full-time teachers, nearly two thirds of whom hold advanced degrees. Since the ethos of a school is determined by what actually takes place in each classroom, on each playing field, and in each performance hall, TMI faculty members are very carefully selected. Teachers are chosen not only for their learning and academic credentials, but for their commitment to the mission of the school, their classroom teaching ability, their willingness to juggle academics and extracurricular activities, and their love of young people. The school holds up the well-rounded person as an ideal; thus, the faculty members are well-rounded people. Most of the teachers also coach a sport in the Middle or Upper School or work closely with students in extracurricular programs. Eagerness to serve, a sense of vocation, an in-depth knowledge of a subject area, the personal touch, and an ability to inspire intellectual curiosity in young people—these qualities are highly valued in the TMI faculty.

It is possible for a school to set very high standards and expect each student to work hard only if there is a helping community in place. Each member of the faculty is an adviser to a small group of students. The adviser's job is to mentor students in various ways and to take a very personal interest in the progress of his or her students. The adviser/advisee relationship is a critically important element in the TMI experience.

COLLEGE PLACEMENT

The college admission process can be overwhelming, which is why TMI guides its students and places emphasis on individual college advising and placement. The Director of College Counseling begins meeting with students in their freshman year and coordinates a systematic program of information sessions, small group discussions, and workshops for students and parents. These programs help students formulate realistic college plans. A college library is open to students at all grade levels.

All TMI graduates are prepared to attend competitive colleges and universities. Students from the classes of 2004 and 2005 are now enrolled at Johns Hopkins, Princeton, Rice, Texas A&M, Tulane, University of Texas at Austin, the U.S. Naval Academy, Vanderbilt, West Point, Yale, and other fine colleges and universities.

STUDENT BODY AND CONDUCT

TMI enrolls approximately 315 coed day students in grades 6–12 and 30 coed boarding students in grades 9–12. Diverse ethnic and socioeconomic backgrounds are represented in the student body. Thirty-two percent receive financial aid or scholarships.

The students and faculty of TMI have established an Honor Code in order to foster an atmosphere of trust. The goal is to live as trustworthy people in an honorable community. Students assume the responsibility of teaching the Honor Code, living by it, and enforcing it. In addition, a strict substance abuse policy established by the Board of Governors is signed by every student and his or her family each year. Violation of this policy results in dismissal. TMI is not suitable for students who require strict disciplinary supervision or who have serious emotional problems or severe learning difficulties.

ACADEMIC FACILITIES

TMI moved to its present location in 1989. The Alkek campus is a $20-million complex located on 80 acres in the Texas hill country just inside the northwestern city limits of San Antonio. Classes are held in Coates Academic Building. The traditional college-preparatory curriculum is fortified with modern technology that includes computer labs. Ayres Hall houses a 20,000-volume library.

BOARDING AND GENERAL FACILITIES

TMI offers both a five- and seven-day program. The small, single-sex dormitories can house up to 12 students each. TMI dedicated two new state-of-the-art residence halls at the start of the 2005–06 school year. Student rooms are designed for 2 students and are furnished. Apartments for each dormitory parent (a faculty member) are adjacent to the cottage-style residences. There is a separate recreation room that also contains laundry facilities. The dorms are closed for major school vacations. An infirmary is located in the athletic building, and the school doctor is on call at all times. TMI is within 15 minutes of the Southwest Texas Medical Center and the UT Health-Science Center. The San Antonio International Airport is 25 minutes away.

ATHLETICS

Indoor athletic facilities include two gyms; an indoor six-lane, 25-meter pool; the Petty rifle range; a weight room, including Nautilus and free weights; and a training room. Outdoor facilities include football, baseball, soccer, and softball fields; a track; tennis courts; and a batting cage.

TMI recognizes that competitive sports are an integral part of the overall development of young men and women; therefore, all Upper School students are required to participate in a sport each year. Girls' sports include basketball, cross-country, diving, golf, lacrosse, soccer, softball, swimming, tennis, and volleyball. Boys compete in baseball, basketball, cross-country, diving, football, golf, lacrosse, soccer, swimming, and tennis. All teams participate in the Southwest

Preparatory Conference. In the 2006–07 school year, TMI will join the Texas Association of Private and Parochial Schools (TAPPS).

EXTRACURRICULAR OPPORTUNITIES

To help develop creative talents and leadership ability, TMI encourages all students to participate in extracurricular activities. The drama department produces two major plays (one of which is a musical) each year. The choir, which is quite active on and off the campus, uses a curriculum affiliated with the Royal School of Church Music. There are a variety of studio art offerings, including photography, ceramics, and drawing. Students publish a literary magazine and a yearbook.

Participation in a wide range of community service projects is encouraged. Projects include activities such as working with local shelters, assisting at caregiving facilities, and supporting numerous civic activities in San Antonio.

Those students electing to be cadets in the JROTC program are essentially afforded a leadership laboratory, the lessons of which have application both in and out of uniform. Topics taught include leadership, citizenship, public speaking, job interview skills, physical fitness, map reading, and first aid. Emphasis is placed on values such as integrity, dependability, self-discipline, and respect. Cadets can participate in additional opportunities including the Honor Guard, Rifle Team, Drill Team, Saber Guard, PT Platoon, Pipe and Drumline, and Cannon Crew.

DAILY LIFE

Residential life students eat together at breakfast and dinner, which is served cafeteria-style in the refectory. Lunch is served in the refectory with the day students. The weekday schedule begins with breakfast at 7 a.m. and ends with lights-out at 10:30 p.m. Study hours are from 7 to 9 p.m., Sunday through Thursday.

TMI sets out to educate the whole person, the soul no less than the mind and body. Daily chapel provides students and faculty members with the opportunity to come together as a community for a true worship experience. All students are invited to practice their religion on campus. The curriculum includes required religion courses in the belief that a complete education includes familiarity with basic theology and the Bible.

The full-time chaplain resides on the campus and is a religious leader, counselor, and teacher. TMI is an ecumenical community of faith; while the atmosphere is Christian, students of all religious backgrounds are welcome.

WEEKEND LIFE

Off-campus weekend activities are planned by the dorm council and include movies, trips, sports events, and visits to the many tourist attractions in the San Antonio area. Social highlights include the Junior/Senior Prom and the Military Ball.

COSTS AND FINANCIAL AID

Day tuition for 2005–06 was $14,150 for grades 6–8 and $15,150 for grades 9–12. The boarding tuition was $29,460 for the seven-day program and $23,000 for the five-day program. Tuition is due in August. Arrangements can be made for a monthly or semiannual payment plan.

For 2005–06, approximately 18 percent of the students received a total of $479,152 in financial aid. Eligibility is based on family need. New rising ninth-grade students may participate in the Margaret M. and Albert B. Alkek Scholarship competition. Two full-tuition four-year scholarships are awarded each year to students with outstanding academic records, leadership potential, and extracurricular involvement. In addition, two $5000 three-year Headmaster Scholarships are awarded based on the same criteria to new rising sixth-grade students. Prospective students and their families should contact the school for applications and deadline information. Merit scholarships are also available for current students.

ADMISSIONS INFORMATION

TMI seeks motivated students who are college bound. Students with behavior problems are not accepted. The comprehensive application includes school transcripts from the past two years, standardized testing, teacher recommendations, a student essay, a parent statement, and a personal interview. TMI does not discriminate on the basis of race, creed, or national origin.

APPLICATION TIMETABLE

Inquiries are welcome at any time. Because personal interviews and campus visits are required, applicants must contact the Admission Office for an appointment. Residential life space is limited, so early contact is advised. The deadline for first consideration for admission is in mid-February. There is a $50 application fee.

ADMISSIONS CORRESPONDENCE

Cynthia Schneid, Director of Admission
TMI–The Episcopal School of Texas
20955 West Tejas Trail
San Antonio, Texas 78257

Phone: 210-698-7171
Fax: 210-698-0715
Web site: http://www.tmi-sa.org

TRINITY COLLEGE SCHOOL

Port Hope, Ontario, Canada

Type: Coeducational boarding and day college-preparatory school
Grades: 5–12
Enrollment: School total: 600
Head of School: Stuart K. C. Grainger, Headmaster

THE SCHOOL

Trinity College School (TCS) was founded in 1865 when the Reverend W. A. Johnson, from Weston, Ontario, wanted to prepare his 3 sons for Trinity College, University of Toronto. After more than 130 years of independent education, university preparation is still paramount at TCS, as are the Christian values by which the Reverend Johnson lived. The mission of the School is to prepare young men and women to thrive in university and beyond and to do so in a caring, supportive community.

Academic life at TCS is rigorous. Students learn the discipline of study and the techniques of study; they learn how to learn. The student is taught how to reason and how to communicate with precision. These skills are needed not only to survive and succeed in a competitive world but also to develop mature relationships in family and everyday life. Students from across Canada and throughout the world learn, in a community of peers, how to get along and how to get ahead. In what can often be a turbulent, confusing time for young people, Trinity provides a sensitive, supportive, and safe environment for students to mature and challenge themselves. The student leaves Trinity with lifelong friendships, a genuine tolerance of others, a clear sense of self, and the sense of purpose that self-knowledge bestows. The Trinity experience fosters both leadership and a sense of service to others.

TCS is located in Port Hope, Ontario, an hour's drive from Toronto, Canada's largest city. The 100-acre campus overlooks an expansive School orchard and Lake Ontario and provides an ideal outdoor environment; yet the School is close enough to Toronto to make cultural, educational, and recreational trips to that city convenient.

The School is managed by a Board of Governors made up of leading men and women from virtually every field. The TCS Convocation comprises some 6,300 alumni, parents, and friends of the School. TCS alumni branches in cities throughout Canada and in New York, Bermuda, Nassau, and London provide alumni and other members of the TCS family with a continuing association with the School.

In 1990, the governing body approved the unanimous recommendation of its executive that Trinity College School move to become a fully coeducational boarding school, and girls were welcomed in 1991. The School has an endowment of $24 million, which makes it one of the best endowed independent coed boarding schools in Canada.

Trinity College School is inspected by the Ontario Ministry of Education and accredited by the Canadian Educational Standards Institute. It is a member of the Canadian Association of Independent Schools, the Headmasters' Conference (U.K.), the Council for Advancement and Support of Education (U.S.A.), and the Parents League of New York (U.S.A.), and it is an affiliate member of the National Association of Independent Schools (U.S.A.).

ACADEMIC PROGRAMS

The School curriculum meets all university admissions standards. Students are challenged to achieve their best through the guidance of a caring faculty. In the first two years of study, the academic program emphasizes breadth and skill development. Students are required to take a fine art and a second language for these two years (Foundation Year and Year Two). A cross-curricular approach to skill development is coordinated by faculty teams that meet regularly to discuss student and programme progress. The School's curriculum employs a number of best practices, including the integration of technology throughout. Students in FY through Y4 are required to have laptop computers. In the senior grades (Y3 and Y4), students have the option to follow the Advanced Placement programme. The ability of students to think critically and express themselves clearly is a hallmark of the English and Social Sciences departments. The high standard of learning in the maths and sciences is confirmed each year as TCS students distinguish themselves in provincial and national competitions.

Thirty credits are required for graduation, and most students choose to do this in four years. At TCS, compulsory courses include 4 English, 3 math, 2 science, 2 second language, 2 fine arts, 1 Canadian geography, 1 Canadian history, 1 senior social science, 1 health and physical education, 1 technology or business or a third science, and 1 civics/career studies. The other 10 credits are electives from a wide variety of subjects. Advanced Placement courses are offered in calculus, biology, French, English, physics, chemistry, history, studio art and art history, and Spanish.

TCS has an average class size of 16 students, with classes varying in size from 8 to 20 students. The academic year is divided into two terms. The first term runs from September to January. The second term runs from February to June, with summative assessment taking on a variety of forms. Three report cards are sent to parents each year. There is a midterm report sent in early November, a term report in February, and a final report in June. Student progress is measured numerically, and parents can compare their child's standing with subject and grade overall averages. Written comments are provided by the student's teachers, Housemaster, Faculty Adviser, Coach, and Community Service Coordinator. Year Coordinators, Deans, and the Headmaster review and comment on all student report cards as well. This support and encouragement have resulted in well above the majority of TCS students carrying an overall average of 80 percent or higher.

Each year, the School hosts a number of parent events including two Parents' Weekends. The first occurs in November, following the midterm report card, and the second occurs in February. These occasions afford the opportunity for parents to meet with teachers, Advisers, Housemasters and anyone else directly responsible for the care of their child.

FACULTY AND ADVISERS

The faculty of 47 men and 42 women plays an active role in all aspects of School life. Fifteen faculty members hold postgraduate degrees, and 2 hold a Ph.D. All are experienced teachers who meet the School's minimum requirement of holding at least a B.Ed. or the equivalent. In a fundamental sense, Trinity is its faculty. The faculty is not only qualified and proficient but also truly caring. Its hallmark is individual attention. On a personal level and in a professional way, the teacher connects with the student; they are on the same team. This special teacher-student relationship is at the heart of School life. The close involvement of faculty members with students in athletics, dramatics, debating, and clubs contributes to a healthy atmosphere in the classrooms, and TCS students usually respond to the challenge of realizing their full potential.

All students have a faculty adviser who takes an active interest in their progress and meets with them regularly. The other staff members are also available to provide counsel as required. The School retains a psychologist for counseling purposes and has a full-time chaplain.

Stuart Grainger was appointed Headmaster in 2004. He is a graduate of Ashbury College in Ottawa, Ontario and holds a B.A. and a B.Ed. from the University of Western Ontario and Queen's University, respectively. He continued on to the University of Ottawa where he secured both his M.Ed. and his M.B.A. Mr. Grainger's professional experience is highly relevant to his new role at TCS and includes pursuit of the highest academic standards and qualifications and extensive classroom and coaching experience in the independent school system. He offers administrative experience as an assistant director of studies, boarding housemaster, and director of admissions and has successfully held leadership positions as a junior school head, an assistant headmaster, and as headmaster of one of the largest coeducational preparatory schools in the country.

COLLEGE PLACEMENT

In keeping with Trinity College School's mission "to prepare promising young men and women to thrive in university and beyond," almost all

graduates choose to attend university. The Guidance Department maintains a close liaison with most Canadian universities and many in the United States. Representatives from more than thirty universities worldwide visit the School and meet with students every fall. Guidance counselors meet regularly with all Senior School students and advise them on course selection, postsecondary planning, and university admissions. Career counseling is a mandatory part of the guidance program, where all students learn to assess their own strengths, identify their special interests, and explore various career opportunities. Graduates, parents, and advisers also play important roles in the guidance of all students. All TCS students can take the SAT and SAT Subject Tests, since the School is a test centre for the College Board.

There were 133 students in the class of 2005; of these, 100 percent qualified to go on to college. TCS graduates have distinguished themselves at most Canadian universities and at many in the United States and the United Kingdom, including: Brown, Carnegie Mellon, Dartmouth, Edinburgh, Georgetown, Harvard, Middlebury, Princeton, and the University of Pennsylvania. In recent years, scholarships have been awarded to TCS graduates by most Canadian universities and by a number of major universities in the United States. Fifteen graduates have won Rhodes Scholarships.

STUDENT BODY AND CONDUCT

There are students at TCS from most provinces in Canada, from many states of the United States, and from thirty other countries. TCS is at an ideal level of enrollment, with a total of 500 students in the Senior School. The School is large enough to be able to field excellent sports teams at all levels, yet small enough for the staff to know all students well and for the students to know each other. TCS also has a Junior School, grades 5–8, with 100 day students enrolled.

Rules at TCS are kept to the minimum required to maintain order and safety. All students are expected to be considerate and to extend respect to each other and to staff members. Alcoholic beverages and illegal drugs are strictly forbidden.

ACADEMIC FACILITIES

Classrooms and laboratories are housed in two wings that adjoin the library and administrative wing. A building that houses environmental science and biology labs as well as two computer labs was added in 1991. Each computer lab is equipped with twenty-four IBM workstations, and adjacent to the labs is a twelve-station area with access to all of the functions in the main lab and library. Printers are located in each lab. The library, open seven days a week, is fully automated on a Novell network. Students can search the library database of 25,000 volumes, access fourteen CD-ROM databases, and go on line via modem to university databases; results of these searches can be downloaded to diskette and printed. Students also have the opportunity to access the Internet. There are individual study carrels and tables for 80 students. Boulden House has been renovated and is an outstanding art centre, with excellent studios for painting, printmaking, and sculpture. It is also home to the Junior School. Music classes take place in LeVan Hall, a state-of-the-art music facility with a 250-seat theater, classrooms, and ten individual practice rooms.

BOARDING AND GENERAL FACILITIES

There are three girls' boarding houses and three boys' boarding houses. Each residence is under the direction of a Housemaster and an Assistant Housemaster who live in the House with their families. All students live in double or single rooms, and each House has a common room with TV facilities. Much of the management of the School is in the hands of senior students under the guidance of the Housemasters. By learning to live with others and to accept responsibilities, young men and women at TCS develop independence and self-reliance. The House system also provides the basis for friendly competition in a variety of intramural athletics and extracurricular programs.

A well-equipped health centre is staffed by School nurses. The School's physician lives in Port Hope, and other doctors in the Port Hope area are also on call as required. The town of Cobourg, 6 miles (10 kilometres) from Port Hope, has a modern hospital in case of emergency, and Toronto, 62 miles (102 kilometres) to the west of Port Hope, is one of North America's top medical centres.

ATHLETICS

Athletics are a vital part of life at TCS, and students compete for their House and for the School. The teams are well coached and compete successfully with other schools in basketball, cricket, field hockey, football, golf, harriers, hockey, Nordic skiing, rowing, rugby, soccer, squash, swimming, tennis, track and field, and volleyball. More than 70 percent of all the students represent the School on teams, and TCS teams have earned a reputation for skill and good sportsmanship. In recent years the School and individual athletes have won senior ISAA and All Ontario championships in many sports.

The School has outstanding sports facilities. They include nine playing fields, an indoor hockey arena, two gymnasiums, a swimming pool, three new squash courts, four tennis courts, a full weight room, a harrier course, and a fitness trail. A fully equipped physical-therapy unit and 2 full-time athletic therapists provide support for student athletes.

EXTRACURRICULAR OPPORTUNITIES

A wide range of extracurricular activities is available at TCS. Debating, drama, and music are all important interests at the School. Photography, political science, philosophy clubs, hiking, mountain biking, and canoe tripping, are also popular. Many School activities are run by the students themselves, including the School magazine, the social service club, and weekend activities.

The music program includes concert bands and a jazz ensemble, as well as several other smaller musical groups and choirs, which go on tour each year. A three-act play is performed at the end of November, and a major musical or drama is produced in the winter term; these are in addition to the Writers' Craft English Plays, which takes place in the spring term, and other less formal dramatic presentations put on at various points throughout the year.

DAILY LIFE

Breakfast is served from 7:30 to 8 a.m. Clean-up is completed by 7:55, and all students attend a short chapel service at 8:15. Classes begin at 9 and are each 70 minutes in length. There are four periods per day and a double lunch period from 11:30 to 12:50. During lunch, students attend Academic Assistance, club meetings, and adviser meetings and eat at Osler Hall. Afternoon classes finish at 3:25 p.m., and sports are at 4. Supper is served from 5:30 to 6:15. Choir or band practices are usually held from 6:30 to 7:30, and supervised study runs from 7:30 to 9:30. Students with satisfactory academic records may study in their rooms; others study in supervised rooms or in the library or computer labs. Bedtime is between 9:30 and 11 p.m., depending on age.

WEEKEND LIFE

Weekends provide a healthy change of pace from a very full schedule during the week. An imaginative program of weekend activities, developed by a committee of students and staff members, includes visits to sports events, concerts, and art galleries; theatre trips; dances; and various other activities of interest. The Social Committee plans such outings as canoe trips and ski weekends. There is a Sunday morning service in the chapel.

COSTS AND FINANCIAL AID

In 2005–06, the fees for boarders were Can $37,050. Fees for day students were Can $20,860, which included a personal services fee that covers the costs of academics- and sports-related weekend travel services and selected protective equipment for players on School and league sports teams. Certain activities, such as the ice hockey and rowing programs, require a small user fee.

The School offers more than Can $1,300,000 each year in financial aid to outstanding applicants who could otherwise not attend.

ADMISSIONS INFORMATION

Admission to TCS is based on the candidates' past record, their performance on entrance examinations, and the School's assessment of their character. The School is interested in maintaining the international character of its student body, and arrangements can be made for applicants who live far from TCS to have interviews conducted by representatives of the School and to write tests.

APPLICATION TIMETABLE

Applications are received throughout the year and are frequently received for admission in future years. Applications for admission in the next school year should be received by March, but the School will consider an applicant at any time. Visits to TCS are strongly encouraged. A CD-ROM information disk is available upon request.

ADMISSIONS CORRESPONDENCE

Kathy LaBranche, Director of Admissions
Trinity College School
55 Deblaquire Street North
Port Hope, Ontario L1A 4K7
Canada

Phone: 905-885-3209
Fax: 905-885-7444
E-mail: admissions@tcs.on.ca
Web site: http://www.tcs.on.ca

TRINITY–PAWLING SCHOOL

Pawling, New York

Type: Boys' boarding (9–PG) and day (7–PG) college-preparatory school
Grades: 7–12, postgraduate year
Enrollment: 330
Head of School: Archibald A. Smith III, Headmaster

THE SCHOOL

The Pawling School was founded in 1907 by Dr. Frederick Gamage. In 1946, it was renamed Trinity-Pawling School in recognition of its ties with Trinity School of New York City. In 1978, Trinity-Pawling School became a separate educational and corporate entity. Trinity-Pawling's Episcopal background is reflected in daily chapel services and course offerings in religion, ethics, and psychology. On weekends, boarding students attend services in the School chapel, at a Roman Catholic church, or at a synagogue.

The School is located 68 miles north of New York City along the Connecticut border; regular train service is available from Grand Central Station to Pawling (population 5,000). The campus, set on 140 acres of rolling hills, is just over an hour's drive from New York's major airports. On vacations, the School transports students to and from the airports and train stations.

It is Trinity-Pawling's belief that an appreciation of one's own worth can best be discovered by experiencing the worth of others, by understanding the value of one's relationship with others, and by acquiring a sense of self-confidence that comes through living and working competently at the level of one's own potential. Trinity-Pawling respects and recognizes the differences in individuals and the different processes required to achieve their educational potential.

The School is governed by a self-perpetuating 26-member Board of Trustees. The School raises more than $1 million in Annual Giving, in part from its more than 4,000 alumni. The School's endowment exceeds $20 million, and its operating budget for 2005–06 is more than $10 million.

Trinity-Pawling is accredited by the New York State Association of Independent Schools and chartered by the New York State Board of Regents. It is a member of the National Association of Independent Schools, the Secondary School Admission Test Board, the New York State Association of Independent Schools (NYSAIS), and the National Association of Episcopal Schools.

ACADEMIC PROGRAMS

To graduate from Trinity-Pawling, a student must obtain a minimum of 112 credits. A full-year course is worth 6 credits, and a term course (trimester) is worth 2 credits. If a student enters after grade 9, his school record is evaluated and translated into Trinity-Pawling's system.

The total number of required credits is 102, distributed as follows: 24 credits in English; 18 credits in mathematics; 18 credits in a laboratory science; 18 credits in social studies; 12 credits in a foreign language; 6 credits in fine, performing, or manual arts (music, art, drafting, or drama); 4 credits in religion or philosophy; and 2 credits in health. Elective courses must be taken to make up the additional 10 credits. Advanced Placement courses are offered in English, U.S. history, Eu-

ropean history, chemistry, physics, biology, mathematics, computer science, Latin, French, and Spanish. No credit is given for physical education courses since they are required by New York State law.

Students carry a minimum of five courses per term. Evening study periods, held in student residences, are supervised by dorm masters. Students with academic difficulty have a formally supervised study hall. Teachers are available to give students extra help at any time that is agreeable to both. Reports are posted online for parents three times per term. Trinity-Pawling uses a number grading system (0–100) in which 60 is passing, 80 qualifies for honors, and 85 qualifies for high honors.

In addition to academic grades, the School utilizes a unique effort system to rank students based on overall effort in many aspects of School life, including academics, athletics, clubs, and dormitory life. A student's privileges are then tied to his overall effort ranking. This program is designed to work in conjunction with the School's philosophy of encouraging each student to work toward his own personal potential.

The Language Program, open to a maximum of 40 students, is initiated in the ninth and tenth grades. A modification of the Orton-Gillingham method, it strives to retrain students with developmental dyslexia. First-year students work in pairs with tutors. In addition, they take a skills-oriented language arts course. Phonetics, sequencing ideas, handwriting, memorization, and other language skills are emphasized. The second-year student is placed in a language skills class and a tutorial class that meets four times a week. All students in the program also take basic history, mathematics, and science courses. The program's goal is to enable students to complete Trinity-Pawling's regular college-preparatory curriculum. Students in the program are not required to take a foreign language but may elect to do so.

FACULTY AND ADVISERS

There are 49 full-time members of the faculty, all of whom reside on the campus. Members of the teaching faculty hold forty-nine baccalaureate and thirty graduate degrees. All participate in counseling and advising students. The School actively supports advanced study for its teachers during summers and other holidays.

Archibald A. Smith III was appointed Headmaster in 1990, after having served at Trinity-Pawling as a chemistry teacher, Director of College Placement, and Assistant Headmaster at various times since 1975. He is a graduate of St. John's School in Houston, Texas; Trinity College (Hartford) (B.S., 1972); and Wesleyan University (M.S., 1980). His career also includes teaching at the Northwood School in Lake Placid, New York. Mr. Smith is past president of the New York State Association of College Admissions Counselors and

he represents New York's secondary schools on the College Board's Advisory Council and its Council for Access Services. He is the past president of the New York State Association of Independent Schools, a member of the Accreditation Council of NYSAIS, and a trustee of the Dutchess Day School.

COLLEGE PLACEMENT

Trinity-Pawling's Director of College Counseling works closely with other administrators and faculty members to advise and aid students and their families with college placement. Individual meetings and group workshops are held on a regular basis, and more than 80 college representatives visit the campus each fall for presentations and interviews. More than 95 percent of the class of 2005 gained admission to their first- or second-choice college.

All of the 2005 graduates earned college or university acceptances. Among those they attend are Bates, Bentley, Boston University, Clarkson, Colby, College of Charleston, Connecticut College, Dartmouth, Drew University, Grinnell, Haverford, Kenyon, Lafayette, MIT, Saint Michael's, Skidmore, Southern Methodist University, the University of Denver, and Williams.

STUDENT BODY AND CONDUCT

Boarding students number 240, and day students number 90. Students come from twenty-nine states and thirteen countries. Students from minority groups make up 18 percent of the total enrollment. Students who choose Trinity-Pawling tend to desire a reasonably structured community that is dedicated to individual growth. A strong academic program in harmony with fine athletics and activities programs brings the School together. The School seeks students who want to actively pursue their academic and social development in a caring atmosphere.

Major violations of community rules are handled by a Faculty-Student Disciplinary Committee, which makes recommendations to the Headmaster. Less serious breaches are handled by the Dean of Students and others.

The Student-Faculty Senate is composed of School prefects and elected student and faculty representatives. The senate works to develop self-government, plans School activities, and fosters a bond between the students and the faculty. It consists of six committees, each with a responsibility for specific areas of School life.

ACADEMIC FACILITIES

The Dann Building (1964) and the Science and Technology Center (2002) house classrooms and science and computer labs. The Art Building, completed in 2004, houses the fine arts, theater, and music programs. This building contains a theater that is used for student productions, lectures, and visiting professional performances. The library fea-

tures an online catalog, 25,000 volumes, and available computers. It is located in the historic Cluett Building, which also contains administrative offices and the student center.

BOARDING AND GENERAL FACILITIES

Students reside in single or double rooms in eighteen dormitory units located in eight buildings, including Starr Hall (1984), Starr East (1987), and Cluett (renovated 1995). Each is under the supervision of 1 or more faculty members aided by senior proctors. Students are allowed to choose roommates, and, whenever possible, housing choice is granted. Students are grouped in housing units according to grade level. A student's dorm master is usually his adviser, so a strong personal relationship often develops. Trinity-Pawling stresses the value of close student-faculty relationships.

Students enjoy a School store and snack bar that are open daily. Medical services are provided by the Health Center, staffed by a resident nurse and a doctor who makes daily visits. Several hospitals serve the area. Trinity-Pawling is within walking distance of the village of Pawling.

ATHLETICS

Trinity-Pawling is a member of the New England Private School Athletic Conference and the Founders League, which affords it the opportunity to play schools in New England, such as Avon, Choate, Hotchkiss, Kent, Loomis Chaffee, Salisbury, Taft, and Westminster. Because the School believes that athletics and physical development are key ingredients in a student's growth, all students are required to participate in the program during the school year. Three or four levels of teams are formed in each interscholastic sport, including football, soccer, hockey, basketball, squash, wrestling, baseball, tennis, track and field, lacrosse, golf, and cross-country. Also offered at both the interscholastic and intramural levels are running, skiing, and weight training.

The Carleton Gymnasium contains a 50-foot by 90-foot basketball court with two cross courts for practice. The lower floor and wing contain weight-training rooms, five new international squash courts, and locker rooms. There are also six soccer fields, two football fields, two baseball fields, an all-weather track, twelve tennis courts, three lacrosse fields, ponds for skating and fishing, the McGraw wrestling pavilion, and the enclosed Tirrell Hockey Rink.

EXTRACURRICULAR OPPORTUNITIES

Each student is encouraged to participate in one or more of the twenty-four activities offered on the campus. These activities are often initiated and directed by the students with the guidance of an interested faculty adviser. Among the offerings are the student newspaper, Model United Nations, the Minority Student Union, the yearbook, the choir, the photography club, the dramatic club, the chess club, the computer club, the fishing club, foreign language clubs, jazz groups, and the outing club. Trinity-Pawling encourages student initiative in starting new activities.

The School sponsors regular trips to nearby areas of educational and cultural interest, including museums and theaters in New York City. Annual events include Parents' Weekend, Junior Parents' Weekend, and several alumni functions. The concert series, offering five concerts annually, brings a rich variety of musical talent to the campus during the school year.

Each student participates in the work program that emphasizes the School's policy of self-responsibility and economy of operation. Boys assist with parts of the routine maintenance work throughout the buildings and on the grounds.

DAILY LIFE

At 8 a.m., four mornings a week, a brief community chapel service is held for all students. Classes are scheduled from 8:20 until 2:40 four days a week and until noon on Wednesdays and Saturdays. Wednesday and Saturday afternoons are reserved for interscholastic sports events. Athletic practices take place in the afternoon, while most extracurricular activities are scheduled in the evening. Lunches are generally served cafeteria-style, dinners sit-down family-style. Students are required to study from 7:30 to 9:30 in their rooms, the library, or the study hall, depending upon their academic status.

WEEKEND LIFE

Dances, plays, concerts, trips to New York City, and informal activities are planned for weekends. The Student-Faculty Senate organizes and plans many of the weekend activities. Social activities are also arranged with girls' schools in the area. Weekend leaves from the School are based upon a group rating, which encompasses a student's record in academic effort and achievement, general citizenship, and dormitory life. In general, as

the group rating increases, so do the amount and nature of privileges. Students are evaluated twice per term.

COSTS AND FINANCIAL AID

Charges for 2005–06 are $35,000 for boarding students, $24,300 for day students in ninth through twelfth grade, and $16,800 for day students in seventh and eighth grade. Extra expenses total approximately $2000 per year. The Language Program is an additional $4700–$6800 per year, depending on the grade. A tuition payment plan and tuition insurance are available.

Thirty-five percent of the students receive a total of $1.5 million in financial aid each year. Trinity-Pawling subscribes to the School and Student Service for Financial Aid and grants aid on the basis of need.

ADMISSIONS INFORMATION

Trinity-Pawling seeks the well-rounded student who will both gain from and give to the School. New students are accepted in all grades; a limited number are accepted for the postgraduate year. Selection is based upon all-around qualifications without regard to race, color, creed, or national origin. Candidates must submit a complete transcript plus two or three teachers' recommendations, have a personal interview at the School, and take the SSAT. Candidates for the Language Retraining Program are asked to have completed a Wechsler Test (WISC-R).

In 2005, there were 385 applicants, of whom 250 were accepted and 130 enrolled.

APPLICATION TIMETABLE

Initial inquiries are welcome at any time. Campus tours and interviews (allow 1½–2 hours) can be arranged by appointment, Monday through Friday, 8:30–1:30, and on Saturday, 8:30–11. All candidates must have an interview. The completed forms must be accompanied by a nonrefundable fee of $40.

Fall is the usual time for applying, and notification of acceptance begins in early March. Parents are expected to reply to acceptances one month after notification.

ADMISSIONS CORRESPONDENCE

MacGregor Robinson
Director of Admission
Trinity-Pawling School
Pawling, New York 12564
Phone: 845-855-4825
Fax: 845-855-3816
E-mail: kdefonce@trinitypawling.org
Web site: http://www.trinitypawling.org

THE UNITED WORLD COLLEGE–U.S.A.

Montezuma, New Mexico

Type: Coeducational boarding college-preparatory school
Grades: 11–12 (International Baccalaureate Diploma Program)
Enrollment: 200
Head of School: Lisa Darling, President

THE SCHOOL

The Armand Hammer United World College–U.S.A. is one of nine secondary schools affiliated through the International Board of the United World Colleges, whose central office is in London. Other United World College (UWC) schools are located in Canada, Hong Kong, India, Italy, Norway, Singapore, Swaziland, and Wales. The term "college" is used in the British sense, meaning the last two years of schooling before entry into a university. Through national selection committee nominations, each UWC receives students ages 16 or 17 from around the world. The principal goal of the United World College schools is to promote international understanding through education.

The admissions office of the United World College–U.S.A. is responsible for the selection of U.S. students for all the United World Colleges. Fifty U.S. students are selected each year; all are awarded Davis Scholarships, which cover full tuition, room, and board at a United World College.

The UWC schools offer students of all races, creeds, and nationalities an opportunity to live, study, and work together in an intensive two-year course. The academic program prepares students for the International Baccalaureate (I.B.) exams.

Graduates traditionally enter the finest universities in the world, and students who receive I.B. diplomas may qualify for advanced standing at U.S. colleges and universities.

The United World College–U.S.A. is near the Pecos Wilderness in the Sangre de Cristo mountain range. It is a 70-mile drive from Santa Fe and 130 miles from Albuquerque. The campus is the site of the newly restored Montezuma Hotel, a century-old resort hotel developed by the Santa Fe Railroad. The building is officially known as the Davis International Center, while informally it has been known as "The Castle" for three generations. Visitors are attracted by the area's climate and nearby hot springs and historic sites.

The school is accredited by the Independent Schools Association of the Southwest (ISAS) and approved by the state of New Mexico.

ACADEMIC PROGRAMS

To earn the I.B. diploma, students must successfully complete six subjects discussed below. Of these, three are taken at the Higher Level, typically 4 hours of class work each week; the other three are taken at the Standard Level, usually 3 hours per week. Most courses last two years.

Group 1, or Language A, is the language in which the student is most fluent. Students study the literature associated with the language as well as world literature in translation. English, Spanish, and French are currently taught, and help is also provided for those who wish to prepare for

exams in other languages. Group 2, or Language B, is a second language, chosen from English, Spanish, and French. Group 3, Society and Individuals, includes economics, anthropology, history, and world religions. Group 4, Science, includes biology, environmental systems, chemistry, and physics. In Group 5, Mathematics, a variety of courses are offered to meet the needs and interests of each student. For Group 6, students may choose art, music, theater arts, or a second subject from Group 2, 3, or 4. In addition, every student takes Theory of Knowledge, an interdisciplinary course that enables students to critically examine their academic experiences at the School and to reflect on the knowledge they are acquiring.

Students are required to undertake original research and write an extended essay of 4,000 words. This project offers the opportunity to investigate a topic of special interest and acquaints students with the type of independent research and writing skills expected at a university.

FACULTY AND ADVISERS

There are 26 full-time faculty members and 4 part-time faculty members. Eighteen hold master's degrees, and 10 have doctorates from both U.S. and international universities. Twenty-six teachers and administrators live on campus. All faculty members act as academic advisers and involve themselves in activities as participants or leaders. Some faculty members are resident tutors and dormitory supervisors.

COLLEGE PLACEMENT

The University Advisor counsels students on college preparation, selection, and application. An extensive library of references and guides is available to students. Each year more than sixty American colleges and universities make on-campus presentations. Students are engaged in an active college advising program.

Graduates matriculate at some of the world's most selective universities. Approximately half of the graduates attend U.S. colleges and universities, including Carleton, Colby, Cornell, Harvard, Macalester, Middlebury, Princeton, and Wellesley. The other half of the graduates attend universities across the world, including Cambridge, the London School of Economics, and St. Andrews in the U.K.; McGill and Trent in Canada; and national and private universities of more than thirty other countries.

STUDENT BODY AND CONDUCT

About 200 students are enrolled each year at the United World College–U.S.A., with 100 in each class of the two-year program. There are about 150 international students and 50 U.S. students. More than eighty countries are represented. About 95 percent of the international students are on scholarship and represent a wide variety of

socioeconomic backgrounds. Almost 100 percent of the students receive scholarship support.

There is a written code of conduct. The Vice President and resident tutors handle disciplinary matters.

ACADEMIC FACILITIES

The Castle and the Old Stone Hotel also house classrooms, faculty and administrative offices, and the library. Various other buildings house science labs and classrooms, a technology center, a language lab and classrooms, an art studio, and music rooms. Other facilities include an auditorium with a stage and the Dwan Light Sanctuary, a nondenominational chapel.

The library has five study areas; contains 18,000 volumes, several encyclopedias, and other reference materials; and subscribes to sixty-seven magazines and thirteen newspapers. Students also have access to online reference services.

BOARDING AND GENERAL FACILITIES

There are four dormitories, each housing approximately 50 students. Students share rooms and have access to a common room with a kitchen. Men and women live in separate dorms. Resident tutors check on all students every night. Two nearby physicians are on 24-hour call. A registered nurse runs the infirmary and treats minor ailments.

ATHLETICS

The Edith Lansing Field House opened in 2002. It contains an indoor multipurpose gymnasium, weight room, dance studio, and squash and racquetball courts. There are also a small indoor pool, several playing fields, and outdoor tennis and basketball courts.

The campus is surrounded by forest and nature trails. There is a skating pond nearby and easy access to hiking, biking, running, and rock climbing. There are no interscholastic sports, but there is an active informal intramural program of basketball, volleyball, and soccer.

EXTRACURRICULAR OPPORTUNITIES

All students are expected to participate actively in the cocurricular programs.

The wilderness program, which promotes fitness and develops teamwork and leadership, consists of environmental studies, navigation, wilderness first aid, and search and rescue. Students who are part of the school's search and rescue team assist when called for emergency searches in the northern New Mexico wilderness areas.

Community service programs promote interaction with the local community. Service can involve working with the elderly, being a peer educator in the local high schools, working in the

sustainable agriculture program, or helping on construction projects like adobe church renovation.

There is an active Wellness Program in which students make presentations about health-related topics to peers and to local schools as a community service. An active Cross-cultural and Spirituality Program offers meditation, yoga, guest speakers, and student presentations on religious and cultural topics. The newly opened Bartos Institute for the Constructive Engagement of Conflict has generated an extensive Global Issues and Conflict Resolution training program.

Among the other extracurricular activities offered are programs and discussions on world affairs, an on-campus film series, weekend expeditions in conjunction with the wilderness program, cultural activities, drama, the chess club, photography, choir, and instrumental groups. Students attend cultural events in Albuquerque and Santa Fe.

Students plan and present national days—celebrations of their country's and region's heritage—with traditional foods, music and dance programs, and games.

DAILY LIFE
Six and a half hours a day, Monday through Friday, are devoted to academics. There are no scheduled classes on weekends. Most school days run from 8:50 to 5, with breaks, lunch, services, and activities scheduled into the day. Dinner is served from 6 to 7, and activities and studying take up most of the evening hours. During the 2-hour activity period in the afternoon, students are involved in sports, community service, or wilderness activities.

WEEKEND LIFE
On weekends, students participate in activities on and off campus. Off-campus activities include camping trips, ski trips, excursions, and trips to Santa Fe, Taos, or Albuquerque. Students may leave the campus on weekends with their parents' permission.

COSTS AND FINANCIAL AID
All U.S. students are awarded Davis Scholarships. The Davis Scholars competition is a national scholarship program for U.S. students. Davis Scholars receive merit scholarships covering tuition, room, and board for two years of study at a United World College school. The Davis Scholar awards are made possible through major funding to the endowment of the United World College by donors Shelby and Gale Davis. "Our contribution is intended to prepare a growing cadre of young Americans for global opportunities in the twenty-first century," says Mr. Davis, founder and CEO of Davis Selected Advisors, a major mutual fund and money management firm.

Families seeking consideration for additional need-based assistance, such as for travel and pocket money, should contact the Office of Admissions to request a Parent Financial Statement form.

ADMISSIONS INFORMATION
Students are admitted on the basis of merit. Davis Scholars are of high academic quality and also have personal attributes of responsibility, motivation, perseverance to follow through in both academic and nonacademic areas, and a tolerance and openness toward different attitudes and customs.

A candidate entering the Davis Scholar competition completes a written application and

submits academic transcripts and test scores. Standardized test scores may be from any one of the following tests: PLAN, PSAT, SSAT, SAT, or ACT. Written recommendations from a teacher and a school guidance counselor are also required.

Candidates are judged on academic record, test scores, recommendations, character, and commitment to serving others. Davis Scholars are U.S. citizens or permanent residents and must be either 16 or 17 by September 1 of the year they intend to enroll in a UWC.

Students from abroad are selected by approved national selection committees. The United World Colleges adhere to the principle that the admission of students and the employment of teachers should be conducted irrespective of race, nationality, religion, and political background.

APPLICATION TIMETABLE
Completed applications for the Davis Scholars competition must be received by January 20. After the January 20 deadline, a group of finalists are selected to advance to an interview process in March. Notifications of the results of the selection process are sent out in mid-April.

ADMISSIONS CORRESPONDENCE
Tim Smith, Director of Admission and
    University Advising
UWC-USA
P.O. Box 248
Montezuma, New Mexico 87731
Phone: 505-454-4201
        505-454-4248
Fax: 505-454-4274
E-mail: admissions@uwc.net
Web site: http://www.uwc-usa.org

VALLEY FORGE MILITARY ACADEMY AND COLLEGE

Wayne, Pennsylvania

Type: Boys' college-preparatory and co-ed junior college military boarding school
Grades: 7–PG: Middle School, 7–8; Upper School, 9–PG
Enrollment: 575
Head of School: Charles A. McGeorge, President

THE SCHOOL

The 120-acre campus of Valley Forge Military Academy includes a boys' boarding preparatory high school and a co-ed junior college, located 15 miles west of Philadelphia. The mission of Valley Forge is to educate individuals to be fully prepared to meet their responsibilities, alert in mind, sound in body, and considerate of others and to have a high sense of duty, honor, loyalty, and courage. Valley Forge fosters these goals through a comprehensive system that is built on the five cornerstones of academic excellence, character development, personal motivation, physical development, and leadership.

Eighteen of the 32 members of the Board of Trustees are Valley Forge graduates, and more than 13,000 alumni support the school. Endowment is currently $8 million, supplemented by an Annual Fund of $1 million, with 15 percent of the alumni participating.

The Academy is accredited by the Middle States Association of Colleges and Schools. It holds memberships in the Association of Military Colleges and Schools of the United States, the Council for Religion in Independent Schools, the Boarding School Headmasters' Association, and the National Association of Independent Schools. The U.S. Department of the Army designates Valley Forge as an honor unit with distinction.

ACADEMIC PROGRAMS

Valley Forge seeks to educate and develop students for college entrance, career success, and responsible citizenship. A challenging curriculum, dedicated faculty members, small classes, individual attention, and faculty-supervised evening study hall provide cadets with an environment conducive to attaining academic success. The acquisition of knowledge, the development of skills, and the shaping of attitudes are emphasized to enable cadets to excel academically and to inspire them to pursue education throughout life.

The school year extends from late August to early June and is divided into two semesters; each has two marking periods. At the end of each marking period, grades are sent to parents. Unsatisfactory grades result in special afternoon help and extra study hall, with biweekly evaluations forwarded to parents. Evening study hall is required of all students. Cadets are placed in one of three college-preparatory curricula—honors, intermediate, or standard—according to aptitude level or achievement. The grading system uses A to F with pluses and minuses. Class periods (eight per day) normally cover 45 minutes each, with double periods for laboratory courses. Twenty and a half credits are required for graduation, distributed as follows: English, 4; mathematics, 4; social studies, 3 (1 of which must be U.S. history); foreign language, 2; science, 2; laboratory science, 1; and electives, 4.5.

The average class size is 13; the student-teacher ratio is approximately 9:1. All high school cadets attend JROTC instruction. Opportunities for independent study, off-campus field trips, and enrollment in courses at Valley Forge Military College are available to cadets.

FACULTY AND ADVISERS

There are 52 full-time and 13 part-time teachers at the Academy. Thirty-one members hold master's degrees; currently, 2 have doctorates.

Charles A. McGeorge, President, is a graduate of Boston University. He earned a Master of Science degree in the dynamics of organizations from the University of Pennsylvania. He holds a certificate in advanced management from Northwestern University's Kellogg School of Business.

Experienced teachers, dedicated to educating young men, are selected primarily for their professional ability and concern for young people. Faculty members perform additional duties as athletic coaches, study hall supervisors, and advisers for extracurricular activities. Ongoing professional development is strongly encouraged.

COLLEGE PLACEMENT

The Guidance Department has 4 full-time counselors and gives continual assistance and counseling to each cadet. The department follows each cadet's academic progress and keeps in close contact with parents. College orientation and parent involvement begin during the second semester of the junior year and continue throughout the cadet's residence. College orientation sessions cover college selection, nomination to service academies, financial aid, the Army ROTC program, and contacts with college placement representatives. College test requirements are reviewed, and cadets are counseled in college application preparation and interview procedures. Ninety-seven percent of the class of 2005 went on to college, with the greatest representation at Embry-Riddle, Mercer, Penn State, Purdue, and the U.S. Air Force Academy.

STUDENT BODY AND CONDUCT

The 2004–05 Upper School student body was composed of 400 boarding cadets. The student body is diverse, and this year cadets came from twenty-five states and thirty-one countries. Eight percent were African American, 11 percent were Hispanic, 11 percent were Asian/Pacific Islanders, and 13 percent were international students.

The military structure of Valley Forge provides extraordinary opportunities for students to develop and exercise their leadership abilities in a safe environment. The Valley Forge experience is designed to foster the development of individual responsibility, self-discipline, and sound leadership skills by providing opportunities for the practical application of leadership theories in positions of increasing responsibility.

The Corps of Cadets is a self-administering body organized in eight company units along military lines, with a cadet officer and noncommissioned officer organization for cadet control and administration. Cadet leadership and positive peer pressure within this structured setting result in a brotherhood and camaraderie among cadets. Through their student representatives, cadets cooperate with the administration in enforcing regulations regarding student conduct. A Student Advisory Council represents the cadets in the school administration. The Dean's Council meets regularly to discuss aspects of academic life.

Character development and personal motivation are integral parts of the Valley Forge experience. The character development program includes weekly chapel and vesper services and monthly character development seminars that are facilitated by peer/faculty teams. Valley Forge emphasizes time-proven standards of conduct, ethical behavior, integrity, spiritual values, and service to community and country. It also motivates young men to strive for excellence, both as individuals and as members of an organization, in all areas of endeavor. Motivation is encouraged through positive competition, recognition, loyalty, teamwork, organizational pride, and the establishment of personal goals.

ACADEMIC FACILITIES

Shannon Hall is the principal academic building. In addition to classrooms, it includes biology, chemistry, and physics laboratories; a computer complex; and the military science department. The Friedman Auditorium, adjacent to Shannon Hall, serves as a large study hall, a conference and instructional center, and a center for SAT and other testing procedures. Lhotak Hall houses the Middle School and its computer center. The May H. Baker Library provides more than 60,000 books, 500 video titles, more than 60 periodical subscriptions, and more than 30 subscriptions to online research resources. To integrate library resources into the curriculum, the library faculty collaborates with the classroom faculty in implementing information literacy instruction in two fully networked computer classrooms and two seminar rooms. The educational psychologists of the Cadet Achievement Center, housed in the library, counsel and advise cadets concerning learning and personal issues.

A fiber-optic, Internet-capable network connects all classrooms, laboratories, and library and dormitory rooms on the campus.

BOARDING AND GENERAL FACILITIES

Cadets are housed by their military companies in individual dormitories, 2 cadets to a room, under the supervision of adult Tactical Officers and their cadet leaders. Cadets eat together in the Regimental Mess. The Health Center has a resident physician and a 24-hour staff; special consultants are

always available. The Alumni Chapel of St. Cornelius the Centurion seats 1,500. The service is nondenominational but Christian in nature, and services are available for all faiths. Mellon Hall provides a parents' reception room, a ballroom, piano and instrument practice rooms, a photography laboratory, a 10-point rifle and pistol range, and meeting rooms. Other facilities include the snack bar (familiarly known as the Boodle Shop), the cadet laundry, the tailor shop, and the Cadet Store. Price Athletic Center and Trainer Hall house three full-size and six intermediate-size basketball courts, a five-lane swimming pool, locker rooms, weight rooms, meeting rooms, administrative offices, and the L. Maitland Blank Hall of Fame. Also on campus are six athletic fields, nine outdoor tennis courts, an outdoor Olympic-size swimming pool, the cavalry stables, and the Mellon Polo Pavilion.

ATHLETICS

Athletics and physical well-being are important elements in a Valley Forge education. The aim of the program is to develop all-around fitness, alertness, character, esprit de corps, leadership, courage, competitive spirit, and genuine desire for physical and mental achievement. There is competition at three levels: varsity, junior varsity, and intramural. To have every cadet on a team is the constant goal. Sports opportunities include baseball, basketball, cross-country, football, golf, gymnastics, lacrosse, polo, riflery, soccer, swimming, tennis, track, and wrestling.

Valley Forge has a strong athletic tradition. Since 1986, the VFMA&C football program has sent more than 140 cadets to Division I schools on full football scholarships. Seven VF alumni currently play in the NFL. One alumnus currently plays for a major league baseball team. The Valley Forge polo team is consistently among the top-ranking polo teams in the nation. In 2003, the equestrian show jumping team participated in the Junior Olympics.

EXTRACURRICULAR OPPORTUNITIES

Clubs, honor societies, publications, intramurals, the Regimental Choir, the Anthony Wayne Legion Guard, and some thirty-five other organizations (forensic, literary, language, science, Boy Scouts, and JROTC Drill Team, to name a few) attract about 75 percent of the corps. Publications include the *Legionnaire* (a newspaper) and *Crossed Sabers* (the yearbook).

Outside lecturers visit the Academy regularly. The band and choir travel widely and have performed at the Kennedy Center, Carnegie Hall, Westminster Abbey, Lincoln Center, and the White House and have participated in inaugural events for several U.S. presidents. Various cadet units assist local communities in parades, community

events, and horse shows. Cadets participate in various public service activities in the surrounding communities; several cadet groups pay regular visits during the year to local children's homes, centers for the disabled, and nursing homes. Important traditional events are Parents' and Grandparents' Weekend, Regimental Mounted Parades, Dunaway Oratorical Contest, and frequent band and choir concerts.

DAILY LIFE

Classes (45 minutes each) are held five days a week from 7:30 a.m. to 3 p.m. The average number of classes per student is six in an eight-period day. An extra instruction period is available after the last class period. Athletics and other activities are held between 3 and 5:45 p.m. daily. Evening study hours extend from 7:30 to 9:30 p.m. Taps sounds at 10 p.m. Monday afternoon is reserved for drill, company meetings, and special activities, such as the ropes course and rappelling.

WEEKEND LIFE

Special or afternoon leaves as well as overnight and weekend privileges may be earned. Ample opportunities exist for cadets to take advantage of the cultural and entertainment opportunities in the Philadelphia area. Cadets desiring to stay at school can use all facilities and attend movies on Friday and Saturday nights in the snack bar area. The cadets frequently enjoy mixers, formal dances, plays, band concerts, special sports events, and polo games with students from neighboring schools. All events are chaperoned by faculty members.

Gold and Silver Star cadets who have earned academic achievement are granted trips into town on Wednesday afternoons and evenings. On Friday, Saturday, and Sunday, those not restricted for academic or other reasons may visit town after their last duty until early evening. Periodically during the year, weekend leaves are authorized for the entire corps; other times there are special weekend leaves for Gold and Silver Star honor students. The leaves help reinforce positive peer pressure to excel in both academics and leadership tasks. Following chapel and Regimental Parade on Sunday, cadets may leave the grounds on special dinner leave with their parents or other authorized adults.

SUMMER PROGRAMS

A four-week residential summer camp is available for young men ages 8–16. A day camp is available for young men and women ages 6–16. These programs provide them with the very best in recreational and educational opportunities.

COSTS AND FINANCIAL AID

The annual charge for 2004–05 was $28,500. This charge included tuition, room and board, uniforms, and all other fees. There is an optional charge for private music lessons, developmental reading, and driver's education. Health center stays for each period of more than 24 hours' duration are also an additional expense. A nonrefundable application fee of $100 is required with an application. At the time of acceptance, a $1000 validation fee is required.

In 2004–05, approximately 31 percent of the students received financial aid totaling more than $600,000. Merit-based scholarships are offered for academic excellence and performance in athletics, the band, and the choir. Through the generosity of many friends of Valley Forge, some special and endowed scholarships, with varying need and/or merit-based criteria, are available.

ADMISSIONS INFORMATION

Admission is based on academic aptitude as measured by the Otis-Lennon Mental Ability Test and/or the SSAT, information pertaining to grade level, personal character and scholastic references, and the recommendation of the Admissions Counselor based on a personal interview with the applicant. Applicants must present evidence of being capable of meeting the demands of a college-preparatory curriculum.

The admission policies of Valley Forge Military Academy and College are nondiscriminatory with respect to race, color, creed, and national or ethnic origin and are in compliance with federal laws.

APPLICATION TIMETABLE

Inquiries are always welcome. Those seeking further information are invited to attend periodic Sunday Campus Visitations, while applicants are hosted by appointment during the week. New cadets are enrolled in late August, and limited openings also exist for January, or midyear, entry. While there is no application deadline, it is recommended that applications be submitted three months before the desired entry date.

ADMISSIONS CORRESPONDENCE

Dean of Admissions
Valley Forge Military Academy and College
Wayne, Pennsylvania 19087-3695

Phone: 610-989-1300
    800-234-VFMA (toll-free)
Fax: 610-688-1545
E-mail: admissions@vfmac.edu
Web site: http://www.vfmac.edu

VERMONT ACADEMY

Saxtons River, Vermont

Type: Coeducational, boarding and day, college-preparatory school
Grades: 9–12, postgraduate year
Enrollment: 274
Head of School: James C. Mooney, Headmaster

THE SCHOOL

Founded in 1876, Vermont Academy is a small, independent, college-preparatory school, primarily boarding in nature, whose supportive environment offers academic and cocurricular programs that are structured for the development of confident and independent learners. Students learn the skills for oral and written expression, critical thinking and analysis, and the cultivation of good instincts—intellectual, creative, athletic, and social. Vermont Academy helps students discover their individual talents and develop the character, strength, and skills necessary to effectively handle the challenges of college and beyond.

Vermont Academy is situated on a 515-acre campus in the foothills of the Green Mountains. Its location in the southeastern part of the state provides numerous opportunities for skiing, snowboarding, hiking, and wilderness activities, as well as cultural and sports events.

A nonprofit and nondenominational institution, Vermont Academy is directed by a 25-member Board of Trustees, 12 of whom are alumni. The school endowment is $5 million, with more than $600,000 in annual gifts from alumni, parents, and friends. The Academy is nearing completion of a $22.5 million campaign that has allowed it to add many new features, including a student center, Winter Snow Park, 20-student dormitory, dance studio, and performing arts center as well as a renovated hockey rink, gym, and fitness center.

Vermont Academy is accredited by the New England Association of Schools and Colleges. Its memberships include the Cum Laude Society, the Independent Schools Association of Northern New England, the National Association of Independent Schools, the Council for Advancement and Support of Education, and the Vermont Independent Schools Association.

ACADEMIC PROGRAMS

Vermont Academy's academic program is designed for students who are planning to attend college. The average class has 11 students, and the overall student-teacher ratio is 7:1. Most students take five 1-credit courses (or their equivalent in ½-credit semester courses) each year. To achieve effective college placement, Vermont Academy students customarily acquire an average of 20 credits by graduation, including English, 4 credits; mathematics, 4 credits; foreign language, 3 credits; history, 3 credits; science, 4 credits; and visual or performing arts, 2 credits.

Vermont Academy offers advanced-level honors courses to challenge highly motivated students. Honors courses are offered in English, social studies, foreign language, math, science (including computer programming), art, and music. The science department offers organic biochemistry, advanced biology, kinesiology, and advanced physics (designed by the University of Vermont). The Conflict Resolution class participates in a national essay contest, and for the past three years, members of the class have been cited as state winners. Independent study is offered in all academic departments to help students develop portfolios as part of their college application process. In addition, Advanced Placement test preparation is offered on a tutorial basis in any subject that is part of the curriculum.

A Learning Skills program is offered to students who require help in developing basic study skills and compensatory techniques. Instructors meet students individually or in pairs one to four times per week. The course is noncredit and entails an extra fee. For students with certified learning disabilities in the language areas, a Basic Spanish course is offered, followed by Spanish 1, to meet the two-year foreign language requirement.

Vermont Academy offers an English language program for international students who have some verbal proficiency in the English language. Courses include English as a Second Language (ESL), which concentrates on language acquisition, grammar, vocabulary, and reading comprehension; English for International Students, which includes analytical and personal writing, reading, and literature discussion; and American History and Culture for International Students, an introduction to American history and society, which fulfills the U.S. history graduation requirement. A TOEFL preparation tutorial is available, and a minimum score of 500 must be attained on the TOEFL in order to qualify for a Vermont Academy diploma. With the exception of these classes, ESL students are fully integrated into the academic, athletic, and residential life of the Vermont Academy community.

Evening study periods are held in the dormitories, in the library, or at a supervised evening study program. Students may be required to attend supervised study labs in the evening between 8 and 10.

Every two weeks, Vermont Academy students are issued effort marks for discussion with students, parents, and academic advisers. In addition, letter grades (A–F, with pluses and minuses) and written comments are reported at the end of each quarter. Interim reports are sent to parents of students who are experiencing academic difficulties.

FACULTY AND ADVISERS

Vermont Academy's faculty consists of 42 members; 11 hold master's degrees, and 2 hold doctorates.

James C. Mooney was appointed Headmaster in 1993. He received his B.A. in history from Yale University in 1978 and a master's degree in education administration from Stanford University in 1984.

Most faculty members and their families live on campus with the students, creating opportunities for individual attention and greater communication.

Each student has a faculty adviser who assists with academic planning and personal development. Each adviser has approximately 6 advisees, and meets with those advisees four times a week. The adviser is the student's on-campus advocate and the liaison between the student and teachers. The Adviser monitors the progress of each advisee, helping to design a plan for academic success.

COLLEGE PLACEMENT

Counseling for college placement begins in the spring of a student's sophomore year. Meetings with the college counselors continue through the spring of the senior year. With few exceptions, Vermont Academy graduates attend four-year colleges or universities, choosing the ones that best suit their abilities and objectives. Approximately 90 percent get into their first or second choice college.

Students take the SAT, SAT Subject Tests, ACT, and various Advanced Placement tests. An intensive

SAT preparation course is available for all juniors and seniors. Advanced Placement tutorials with faculty members can be arranged for any course offered in the curriculum.

The following colleges and universities represent some of the institutions chosen by Vermont Academy graduates in the last three years: Barnard, Bates, Brown, Colby, Dartmouth, Dickinson, Georgetown, Gettysburg, Guilford, Lake Forest, Lehigh, Middlebury, Mount Holyoke, NYU, Quinnipiac, Rhode Island School of Design, St. Lawrence, St. Michael's, Savannah College of Art and Design, Simmons, Syracuse, U.S. Naval Academy, Williams, and the Universities of California, Colorado, Massachusetts, New Hampshire, and Vermont.

STUDENT BODY AND CONDUCT

The 2005–06 student body was composed of 189 boarding and 85 day students from twenty states and twelve countries. The majority of students come from California, Connecticut, Florida, Illinois, Massachusetts, New Hampshire, New York, Pennsylvania, and Vermont. Twelve percent of the students are from other countries.

Residential life is an integral part of Vermont Academy's curriculum. Community living requires certain personal obligations and restrictions that are designed to promote a healthy, safe, and comfortable atmosphere and to enhance the learning environment. Vermont Academy places a strong emphasis on mutual respect, self-discipline, and concern for others as central components of its program. High expectations exist for the entire community.

A committee of faculty and students has written an Honor Code for the Vermont Academy community. The core values of honesty, trust, respect, and responsibility by all members of the community are promoted.

The Vermont Academy Student Association (VASA) is the students' governing body. It includes representatives from all classes and meets weekly with a member of the Dean of Students' office to consider issues of concern. The meetings are open to the entire school.

All students facing major disciplinary action appear before a standards committee that consists of students and faculty members. Final action is taken by the Headmaster on the recommendation of this committee.

ACADEMIC FACILITIES

The Academy has a Tablet PC program with wireless Internet access throughout the campus, including dormitories, as well as full-time T1 access with an Internet-connected Windows XP Pro network with Windows XP Pro workstations for all computers. Tablet PCs have tremendous promise to aid in the college preparation process, and Vermont Academy is committed to being a national leader in this effort. The Tablets are an outstanding educational tool for communication, organization (with GoBinder software), notetaking, retrieving and completing assignments, etc.

Most faculty members and half of the student body use these Tablets regularly. Each department has a classroom projector for use with the Tablet. The goal is that all students will use the Tablets regularly by fall 2006. Students can purchase Tablet PCs through the Academy's Technology Department. In

addition, there are a number of computers for students' use in the library and most classrooms, as well as in a small computer lab.

Most classes are held in Fuller and Alumni Halls, with art and music classes conducted in nearby buildings. The average class size is 11, and in most classes, students and teachers sit around tables to facilitate stimulating discussion. Students are expected to be prepared and participate in the sharing of knowledge.

The Tillinghast Library contains 14,000 volumes, periodicals, study carrels, fifteen computers, the College Counseling office, and the Learning Skills Center. The library is open to students during class hours, for 3 hours in the evening, and on weekends.

As of fall 2006, the new Arts Complex will be home to the Academy's performing arts activities, including a 350-seat raked theater with state-of-the-art lighting and sound, a set shop, and dressing and practice rooms. A generous wing dedicated to studio arts will be added during the year. To date, the arts facilities include a large music room for choral and band rehearsals, five soundproof practice rooms, and a recording studio; three well-lit art studios; a pottery studio with six potters' wheels and a large gas-reduction kiln; two dark rooms for black-and-white photo developing; a new, fully-equipped filmmaking studio; and a full stage with state-of-the-art sound equipment, and a professional dance studio.

BOARDING AND GENERAL FACILITIES
Students reside in one of ten dormitories, ranging in size from 6 to 60 students. Most dorm rooms are doubles, although there are some single rooms available. A beautiful, new 20-bed girls' dormitory was recently completed. Faculty members and their families live in each dorm. All dorms have free laundry facilities and most have common rooms, as well. Roommate assignments are based on many factors, including interests, life style habits, and personality. A Roommate Questionnaire, designed with student input, is used as a guide in assigning roommates.

The Shepardson Center contains a large dining hall, a student study area, the Student Lounge, a school store, and the VA Café. Students can study, relax, and socialize, as well as snack on healthy food from 7:00 a.m. until 10:00 p.m.

ATHLETICS
Excellent coaching, enthusiastic spirit, and outstanding facilities combine to make able competitors of the Vermont Academy teams. The athletic programs support Vermont Academy's belief in developing the whole student (head, hand, and heart) by focusing on teamwork and sportsmanship, self-discipline to acquire and apply specific athletic skills and strategies, appreciation for being fit, and having fun.

Each year, students are required to earn two athletic credits during the three seasons they are in school.

The third season, they can participate in a sport or an afternoon activity (see Extracurricular Opportunities). Athletic offerings include eighteen different sports: fall—cross-country running, field hockey, football, horseback riding, mountain biking, and soccer; winter—basketball, dance, ice hockey, skiing (downhill, free-style, cross-country, and jumping), and snowboarding; and spring—baseball, golf, lacrosse, softball, tennis, and track.

Athletic facilities include the newly renovated Lucy Athletic Complex, with an outstanding basketball court and climbing wall as well as new locker rooms, fitness center, dance studio, and training room; the enclosed Michael Choukas Skating Rink with an artificial ice-making system; the Winter Snow Park, with three ski jumps, a modest alpine run, a terrain park, and 20 kilometers of cross-country trails as well as a lift, lights, and grooming equipment; the Chivers Ski and Outdoor Education Center, which includes 1,600 square feet for waxing, sharpening, and storage; seven beautifully maintained playing and practice fields, with a ¼-mile track; and six tennis courts. Ascutney, Bromley, Killington, Magic Mountain, Okemo, and Stratton ski areas are nearby.

EXTRACURRICULAR OPPORTUNITIES
Several afternoon activities are available for students during one of the three seasons they are in school. These include athletic training/weight room management, community service, outdoor challenge, photography, rock climbing, silversmithing, video drama, and yoga.

Other opportunities include yearbook, literary magazine, jazz band, guitar ensemble, vocal ensemble, private music lessons, the winter musical and other theater productions, cabarets, coffee houses, and dance performances. In addition, speakers and concert performances are brought to campus to enrich our students' experience.

Students are also involved in Vermont Academy's community service program. Possibilities include mentoring and sports clinics with local elementary schools as well as helping at the soup kitchen, nursing homes, and other locations in the community.

DAILY LIFE
In the fall and spring, the class day begins at 7:45 a.m. with adviser meetings. Classes are held until 3:15 p.m. on Monday, Tuesday, Thursday, and Friday and until noon on Wednesday and Saturday. The winter schedule is slightly modified. A modified dress code is required for classrooms, with more formal dress and assigned seating two evenings a week for Formal Dinner.

Sports and activities are scheduled from 3:45 to 5:45 p.m. Interscholastic competition with other boarding schools is scheduled on Wednesday and Saturday afternoons.

For boarding students, dinner is at 6:30 on weekday evenings and study hours are from 8 until 10 p.m. Each week, there are two or three formal dinners, with assigned seating and required formal dress.

WEEKEND LIFE
There is always something to do on the weekends. The program on weekends is varied to provide students with a change of pace, the opportunity to participate in sports and activities, and a chance to relax and enjoy the Vermont countryside. A committee of students and faculty members plan the activities, which can include movies, plays, concerts, or dances on Saturday evenings either at school or nearby and trips to Boston, Burlington, Northhampton, and New York as well as nearby ski areas (Bromley, Okemo, Stratton, etc.).

COSTS AND FINANCIAL AID
The tuition for 2005–06 is $35,300 for boarding students and $20,800 for day students. A deposit of $3,500 for boarding students and $2,000 for day students is required and is credited toward tuition.

Scholarships are available to families demonstrating financial need. More than $1.2 million is awarded each year to approximately 31 percent of the student body. A financial aid committee reviews these awards annually.

ADMISSIONS INFORMATION
Admission to Vermont Academy is made on the basis of character, potential, and previous record. Taken into consideration are a candidate's school record, recommendations from teachers of his or her current school, and standardized test results (e.g., SSAT, PLAN, ISEE) scores. An on-campus interview is required. For 2005–06, there were 368 applications, of which 231 were accepted and 108 students enrolled. Selection is based on all-around qualifications without regard to race, creed, religion, gender, sexual orientation, or national or ethnic origin.

APPLICATION TIMETABLE
Arrangements should be made early in the year for a tour of the campus and a personal interview with a member of the admissions staff. The Admissions Office is open Monday through Friday from 8:30 to 4:30 and on some Saturdays. A formal application with a $50 fee ($100 for international students) should be submitted. In November or December, students should arrange to take the SSAT, ISEE, PSAT, SAT, ACT, SLEP, or TOEFL. The application deadline is February 1, with rolling admissions thereafter if space is available.

ADMISSIONS CORRESPONDENCE
William J. Newman, Dean of Admissions
Vermont Academy
Saxtons River, Vermont 05154

Phone: 802-869-6229
        800-560-1876 (toll-free)
E-mail: admissions@vermontacademy.org
Web site: http://www.vermontacademy.org

VIEWPOINT SCHOOL
Calabasas, California

Type: Coeducational day college-preparatory school
Grades: K–12: Primary School, kindergarten–2; Lower School, 3–5; Middle School, 6–8; Upper School, 9–12
Enrollment: School total: 1,185; Upper School: 432
Head of School: Dr. Robert J. Dworkoski

THE SCHOOL

Founded in 1961, Viewpoint School offers an enriched college-preparatory program in a nurturing and wholesome environment. Located at the western end of the San Fernando Valley, Viewpoint is nestled in the foothills of the Santa Monica Mountains on a campus of 25 acres, with scenic vistas, open spaces, and heritage oak trees. Downtown Los Angeles, with its museums, libraries, and cultural attractions, is only 25 miles away.

The School's mission is to help children develop a love of learning and those qualities that provide them with strength and direction for a lifetime. Viewpoint recognizes the uniqueness of each child and is committed to the identification, preservation, and development of that individuality. While students are encouraged to pursue an accelerated academic program appropriate for each student's level, Viewpoint also stresses citizenship, moral and ethical development, and good deportment. Within this environment, students learn to value the differences among individuals and to appreciate the unique contributions each person adds to the School's diverse community. Weekly assemblies, foreign exchanges, and community service encourage such development. Student participation is high in all areas of School life, and the nurturing atmosphere encourages healthy relationships between students and faculty.

Viewpoint School is a nonprofit institution governed by a self-perpetuating Board of Trustees. The School holds accreditation from the California Association of Independent Schools and the Western Association of Schools and Colleges. The School holds memberships in the National Association of Independent Schools, the Educational Records Bureau, the Cum Laude Society, the National Association for College Admission Counseling, the National Association of Secondary School Principals, the National Association of Principals of Schools for Girls, and A Better Chance.

ACADEMIC PROGRAMS

The academic program at Viewpoint School emphasizes the traditional disciplines; provides a rich curriculum in the arts, music, computer science, and athletics; and is designed to accommodate the differing needs of each child.

The academic year, divided into semesters, begins in early September and extends to early June, with vacations of two weeks in the winter and spring. Lower, Middle and Upper School students follow a six-day rotation schedule that includes periods of varying lengths. The maximum class size in the School is 22; Upper School classes average 18 students. The School sends grades to parents four times a year and provides four additional interim reports for parents of students whose grades are C+ or below. Teachers also write annual comments for every student in each class.

To graduate, an Upper School student must complete four years of English; three and one-half years of history, including United States history and American government; three years each of mathematics, laboratory science, and a single foreign language; two sequential semesters of an art in the same discipline; the technology and human development course; eight seasons of physical education; and 45 hours of community service, along with one ninth-grade community service project. Students choose from a wide variety of electives that match their unique interests and abilities. The elective choices include women's voices in literature, neuroscience, contemporary short fiction, the novel of Africa, poetry of the Romantic period, creative writing, statistics and probability, oceanography, environmental science, modern Latin American history, contemporary politics, humanities, abnormal psychology, computer science (animation, programming, artificial intelligence, and robotics), speech, drama, history of theater, music theory, chorus, instrumental music (jazz, strings, and winds), art history, ceramics, sculpture, photography, filmmaking, and video production. Students in the Middle and Upper Schools benefit from a Laptop Program in which students receive laptop computers for use in the classrooms. The School offers twenty-two Advanced Placement courses in the following disciplines: biology, calculus, chemistry, comparative government, computer science, English, European history, French, music theory and history, physics, psychology, Spanish, studio art, and United States history. In spring 2005, 155 students sat for 337 examinations in twenty-two subject areas, with 96 percent receiving scores of 3 or above, 79 percent receiving scores of 4 or 5, and 46 percent receiving scores of 5. Viewpoint's participation in APs in May 2005 was 12.8 percent for tenth grade, 54.5 percent for eleventh grade, and 70.8 percent for twelfth grade.

The classes of 2004 and 2005 had 9 AP National Scholars, 31 AP Scholars with Distinction, 15 AP Scholars with Honors, and 22 AP Scholars.

FACULTY AND ADVISERS

The faculty consists of 131 full-time and several part-time teachers, including administrators with teaching responsibilities. The faculty members and administrators hold sixty-three baccalaureate and thirty-six advanced degrees, including six Ph.D.'s, from colleges and universities located in the United States and in several other countries. Diverse in age, background, and experience, the men and women of Viewpoint's faculty are selected for their academic expertise, for the enthusiasm and energy they bring to their teaching, and for their enjoyment of working with young people. Recently, several faculty members received awards from the National Endowment for the Humanities, the Council for Basic Education, the National Science Foundation, and the Klingenstein Summer Institute.

Dr. Robert J. Dworkoski was appointed Headmaster in 1986. He is a graduate of George Washington University (B.A., 1968), New York University (A.M., 1971), and Columbia University (M.A., 1972; Ph.D., 1979, European history). Prior to his appointment, Dr. Dworkoski taught history at Brooklyn College in New York and was Department Chairman of Social Studies at Woodmere Academy in New York. From 1980 to 1986, Dr. Dworkoski was the Head of Upper School at the Harvard School in Los Angeles. A Fulbright scholar in Europe in 1983 and a recipient of a grant from the National Endowment for the Humanities in 1993, Dr. Dworkoski has been active in the California Association of Independent Schools and the National Association of Independent Schools and sits on the Board of the Will Geer Theatricum Botanicum.

COLLEGE PLACEMENT

Working closely with parents and students, the college counseling staff clarifies the complicated process of college admission and achieves 100 percent placement of students in four-year colleges. By completing the minimum requirements for graduation, Viewpoint students exceed the basic requirements for entrance to the campuses of the University of California and to the most selective universities in the country. Graduates from the class of 2005 achieved mean SAT I scores of 637 verbal and 661 math. Recent Viewpoint graduates are currently attending such colleges and universities as Amherst, Boston, Brown, Carnegie Mellon, Cornell, Dartmouth, Duke, Emory, George Washington, Harvard, MIT, NYU, Oxford, Pepperdine, Princeton, Stanford, Tufts, Tulane, the U.S. Air Force Academy, the U.S. Naval Academy, Wellesley, Williams, Yale, and the Universities of California (Berkeley and Los Angeles), Pennsylvania, and Southern California.

STUDENT BODY AND CONDUCT

The 2005–06 enrollment totaled 1,185 students, with 205 students in kindergarten through grade 2, 224 students in grades 3 through 5, 324 students in grades 6 through 8, and 432 students in grades 9 through 12. Students come to Viewpoint from the San Fernando and Conejo Valleys, Malibu, and other neighboring communities. They represent a rich variety of ethnic, religious, socioeconomic, cultural, and linguistic backgrounds; fifteen languages are spoken in the homes of the School's families. The School hosts foreign exchanges with other countries, including China, England, France, Germany, Japan, Russia,

and Spain. All Viewpoint students benefit from a teaching and learning environment that is enriched by these diverse perspectives, talents, and interests.

Students in kindergarten through grade 8 wear uniforms. Upper School students follow a dress code.

ACADEMIC FACILITIES

Each of the four divisions has its own geographic identity, with the Primary, Lower, and Upper Schools located on the East Campus and the Middle School located on the West Campus.

The School provides each division with separate library facilities, academic classrooms, art and music studios, science laboratories, and computer laboratories with extensive access to the Internet. The newly built 41,000-square-foot Gates Academic Center houses Upper School students with state-of-the-art classrooms; art, music, and dance studios; and science and technology laboratories. The Ahmanson Foundation Black Box Theater and the 400-seat Carlson Family Theater provide a spacious environment for the School's numerous annual dance, drama, and musical productions. The combined libraries of all divisions contain approximately 20,000 volumes and offer CD-ROM access to the Los Angeles County's library collection, the Los Angeles Times Network, and ProQuest magazine collection. Additional facilities include ECOLET, an outdoor natural science laboratory and classroom for field studies on campus.

ATHLETICS

All students participate in physical education, and 80 percent of Middle and Upper School students are involved in team sports. Upper School students compete interscholastically in baseball, basketball, cheerleading, cross-country, equestrian events, football, golf, soccer, softball, swimming, tennis, and volleyball. Outdoor education and dance (modern, jazz, and ballet) are also available. The sports facilities on the 25-acre campus include several athletic fields, two regulation-size swimming pools, the Rasmussen Family Pavilion for athletics, outdoor basketball courts, batting cages, a weight-training facility, locker rooms for athletics, and playgrounds for children in the elementary grades.

EXTRACURRICULAR OPPORTUNITIES

Viewpoint students are involved in a variety of social and extracurricular activities. They include the yearbook, newspaper, literary journal, the student council, speech and debate competitions, theatrical and musical productions, foreign language presentations, and honor societies. Student clubs include mock trial, rocketry, Model UN, Junior Statesman, Amnesty International, astronomy, science fiction, film, Spanish, Chinese, community service honor society, flight simulator, poetry, Cum Laude society, multicultural, surfing, newspaper, animal rights, fashion design, and chess. Viewpoint offers formal and informal dances, domestic and international trips, and foreign exchange programs with secondary schools in seven countries. The foreign exchanges occur in Taunton, England; Paris, France; Valencia, Spain; Berlin, Germany; Osaka, Japan; Moscow, Russia; and Wenzhou, China. Student exchanges have been popular ways for students to make friends, learn about other cultures, and improve their skills in foreign language.

Outdoor Education trips provide students with additional opportunities for growth and learning. Astrocamp, in Idyllwild, is the site for the three-day fifth-grade retreat. Sixth graders camp in the mountains for three days, seventh graders travel to Catalina Island to explore marine biology, and eighth graders spend four days working through team building activities in the mountains of Arrowhead. To ease the transition from Middle to Upper School, ninth graders travel to Camp Surf, located near San Diego, to study the ecosystem of California's coastline. These trips give students the opportunity to strengthen friendships and to make new friends while enjoying outdoor activities.

Each spring, ninth and tenth graders join the Voyage of Discovery, a nine-day tour of the historic sites of the East Coast. Other trips include an East Coast tour of college campuses and trips to Europe.

The community of the School extends to include parents, alumni, and friends who are invited to the campus for a variety of special events, including Great Pumpkin Day, Open House, Homecoming, alumni reunions, sporting events, and musical and dramatic productions.

DAILY LIFE

Students travel to and from school by car pool or the bus system. The Middle and Upper Schools begin their day at 8 a.m. and conclude at 2:45 p.m. with an Academic Assistance program from 2:45 to 3:15 p.m. Students may elect to stay after school to study in the library; participate in sports, clubs, and other extracurricular activities; or work on a computer program.

SUMMER PROGRAMS

Viewpoint offers an Academic Summer Program for students entering grades 6 through 12. The School provides this session to students who are new to Viewpoint, to continuing students, and to students in the general community who can benefit from basic or advanced classes in mathematics, language, and literature. For the athletically inclined, Viewpoint also sponsors basketball, baseball, volleyball, and swimming camps each summer. Camp Roadrunner serves students in the Primary and Lower Schools.

COSTS AND FINANCIAL AID

Tuition for the 2005–06 academic year was $16,775 for kindergarten through grade 2, $16,925 for grades 3 through 5, $17,980 for grades 6 through 8, and $19,100 for grades 9 through 12. General fees were $530 for kindergarten through grade 5 and $475 for grades 6 through 12. There is a one-time new-family fee of $1,250. In addition, seventh- to twelfth-grade students purchase textbooks from the School. Tuition payment and insurance plans are available.

Financial aid is available in cases of demonstrated need. The Thelma B. Sitton Scholarship is awarded annually to an outstanding student chosen by the faculty.

ADMISSIONS INFORMATION

Viewpoint attracts highly motivated, academically talented students with diverse backgrounds, interests, and abilities. The School admits students based on a review of entrance examinations, recommendations, transcripts from previous schools, and an interview for applicants for sixth through twelfth grades. International students must demonstrate a strong command of English.

The School is committed to diversity in its student body. The School's Minority Admission Program (MAP) provides scholarships to academically able members of minority groups from families with financial need. The program works with various community organizations, local schools, and churches to identify and to recruit talented and promising students.

APPLICATION TIMETABLE

Inquiries are welcome at any time. Families should submit an application and a fee of $100 to the Admission Office no later than January 14 for kindergarten through grade 12. Later applications are considered if openings are available.

ADMISSIONS CORRESPONDENCE

Laurel Baker Tew, Director of Admission
Viewpoint School
23620 Mulholland Highway
Calabasas, California 91302
Phone: 818-340-2901
Fax: 818-591-0834
E-mail: info@viewpoint.org
Web site: http://www.viewpoint.org

WALNUT HILL SCHOOL

Natick, Massachusetts

Type: Coeducational boarding and day school for the arts and academics
Grades: 9–12
Enrollment: 289
Head of School: Stephanie B. Perrin

THE SCHOOL

Walnut Hill is internationally recognized for its program of training in the arts accompanied by a rigorous academic curriculum. Students concentrate in ballet, creative writing, music, theater, or visual art. Founded in 1893, Walnut Hill is a boarding and day school for grades 9–12, located 17 miles west of Boston in Natick, Massachusetts. The beautiful, tree-covered, 45-acre campus is within 25 minutes of Boston—a major academic and cultural center. The School has a long tradition of outstanding placement with students being offered admission to top-ranked universities, colleges, conservatories, and institutes throughout the United States and Europe.

Walnut Hill is the only high school in the nation affiliated with a major conservatory of music. The New England Conservatory of Music (NEC) at Walnut Hill is a joint program that offers students access to conservatory-level instruction while still in high school. Because of the School's proximity to Boston, students in all arts concentrations have access to a great cultural center. Students have the opportunity to attend performances by the Boston Symphony Orchestra, the Boston Lyric Opera, the Boston Ballet, the American Repertory Theater, and Huntington Theater as well as Broadway shows on tour. Art students have access to the collections of the Museum of Fine Art, the Gardner Museum, the Institute of Contemporary Art, and Harvard's Fogg Museum and other university public collections. Throughout the year, the writing program invites many guest authors to campus for workshops and readings with students.

Passion is a word often heard at Walnut Hill. The School attracts dedicated and focused students from around the world to study in an environment that is challenging and supportive. People at the School are devoted to demonstrating respect and compassion and actively pursuing learning, all in a humane and ethical community with an emphasis on the development of the whole student.

Walnut Hill is accredited by the New England Association of Schools and Colleges.

ACADEMIC PROGRAMS

The academic curriculum is designed to prepare students for admission to highly selective colleges and universities. The curriculum builds critical-thinking skills that serve students well throughout life. A well-rounded program of mathematics, science, literature, languages, and history provide a strong liberal arts foundation. Walnut Hill is a member of the Cum Laude Society.

Advanced course work is offered in biology, calculus, chemistry, English, French, Spanish, and physics. Students regularly take Advanced Placement exams. Of those students currently enrolled who took AP exams, the mean average result was

a 4. Nearly 40 percent of the members of the class of 2005 had taken either calculus or advanced calculus before graduation. English as a second language is offered from the beginning to the advanced level.

Academic requirements for graduation include 4 years of English, 3 years of mathematics, 2 years of laboratory science, 2 years of a modern world language, and 2 years of history, one of which must be United States history. Typically, a student takes two academic courses per semester. Semester-long courses, each meeting for longer instructional periods, are equal to one full year of study. Successful completion of each academic semester-long course earns an academic credit toward the graduation requirement.

Students apply for admission in one of five concentrations: ballet, creative writing, music, theater, or visual art. Ballet study at Walnut Hill develops strength and flexibility through a pure classical technique. Students have daily ballet classes, including a two-hour technique class, all taught by teachers of the highest standard. Performance opportunities are an important part of the preprofessional curriculum and training necessary for company placement. Prior to taking teaching positions at Walnut Hill, the ballet faculty members have enjoyed successful performance careers with major companies. Because of their personal experience, the instructors are prepared to assist students as they move forward in their own careers.

In creative writing, the curriculum is designed to help students acquire and refine the power of language through the practice of their craft so that they may best communicate their thoughts and feelings with both clarity and originality. Class sizes are very small and allow for effective critique and exploration of ideas. Students are exposed to the work of professional writers through frequent guests who share their work and speak about the craft of writing. Recent visiting writers have included Susan Kenny, David Budhill, David Updike, Christopher Tilghman, and Perri Klass.

In music, the curriculum is designed to provide students with an intensive level of instruction. Students study chamber music, music theory, music history, ear training, solfege, and chorus daily at Walnut Hill. Students also participate in a weekly master class with noted conductor Benjamin Zander, artistic director of the program. Through the NEC at Walnut Hill program, students participate in an orchestra at the Conservatory. Private teaching is offered by faculty members from New England Conservatory and Boston University, members of the Boston Symphony, and other noted professional musicians in greater Boston.

In theater, the curriculum is designed to develop skilled and disciplined young actors. The theater concentration includes acting and musical theater, combining rigorous training of the

mind, body, and voice, forming a solid technique and approach to the craft. Advanced acting courses combine scene study analysis and synthesis, analysis of dramatic literature, theater history, and performance. In addition to actor training, students also develop an understanding and appreciation of design and production. All theater students are expected to complement their work with courses in dance and private voice lessons.

In visual art, the curriculum is designed to expose students to a professional studio environment. Working closely with faculty members, students develop a personal artistic language while continually improving on skills such as drawing, painting, sculpture, printmaking, and photography. Students receive 10 to 15 hours of studio instruction each week. Within each studio course, they are introduced to a variety of techniques particular to that individual medium. Through this process, students continually acquire, and improve upon, fundamental skills and concepts central to all visual art: composition, form, light, color, line, shape, and texture.

FACULTY AND ADVISERS

There are 41 teaching faculty members at Walnut Hill School. The 6:1 student-faculty ratio allows for close relationships between teacher and student. Faculty members at Walnut Hill are hired for demonstrated talent in teaching their discipline and for their commitment to students. Eighty-four percent of the faculty members have earned advanced degrees. They are graduates of colleges such as Brown, Cornell, Eastman, Harvard, Michigan, Middlebury, Northwestern, Smith, Swarthmore, Tufts, Yale, and the University of Virginia.

In addition to full-time faculty members, adjunct artist teachers are drawn from local organizations such as the Boston Symphony Orchestra, the School of the Museum of Fine Arts, and the New England Conservatory.

COLLEGE PLACEMENT

The School has a full-time counseling staff who work with junior and senior students and their families throughout the college process. During the fall term, more than eighty colleges visit the Walnut Hill campus to meet with students. In the class of 2005, seniors were offered admission to a wide range of schools, including the Art Institute of Chicago, Barnard, Bennington, Carnegie-Mellon, the Cleveland Institute of Music, Cooper Union, Curtis, Juilliard, the New England Conservatory, Northwestern, NYU, Oberlin, Pratt, Princeton, Rhode Island School of Design, Smith, Tufts, Vassar, and the University of Michigan.

STUDENT BODY AND CONDUCT

The 2004–05 enrollment was 289 (219 boarding, 70 day) as follows: grade 9, 44; grade 10, 65;

grade 11, 88; and grade 12, 92. Walnut Hill is a diverse community, with 12 percent of the students identifying themselves as students of color and 26 percent as international. There are students from thirty-six states and nine different countries.

Walnut Hill provides an open and supportive environment in which students may balance their self-expression with community expectations. The School community relies upon respect, honesty, vision, flexibility, and understanding. It believes that students are responsible for their own actions and that by setting forth a common code of conduct, students can best understand the expectations and responsibilities while at the School.

Student participation in the governing of the School is an important aspect of a Walnut Hill education. Students find direct expression in the election of student officers to the Community Council.

ACADEMIC FACILITIES

The new Academic and Technology Center was opened in September 2002, with a state-of-the-art computer center and new biology and chemistry laboratories. The Creative Writing Center is housed within the Academic and Technology Center. The Eliot Library has been recently renovated and has high-speed Internet connection and a music listening room. The Music Department is housed in Highland Hall, which includes faculty offices, classrooms, Amelia Avery Hall Choral Room, and twenty-one soundproof practice rooms. The Music Department holds performances in the eighty-seat Boswell Recital Hall. In addition to on-campus facilities, music students have access to the library at New England Conservatory; the orchestra performs at NEC's Jordan Hall. The Visual Art Department is housed in the Dartley Center for the Arts, which includes faculty offices, drawing and painting studios, a print-making studio, a digital media lab, ceramics and sculpture studios, a kiln room, and private studio space for seniors. A state-of-the-art photography lab is also available. Visual art shows are displayed in Pooke Gallery in Highland Hall. The Ballet Department is housed in the Dance Center at Walnut Hill, with five large studios, offices, dressing rooms, and a costume shop. The Theater Department is housed in the Jane Oxford

Keiter Performing Arts Center, which includes the Stephanie Bonnell Perrin Theater, a black box theater, a green room, design and production facilities, a costume room and lab, and class-rooms.

BOARDING AND GENERAL FACILITIES

The School's Campus Center includes a dining hall, bookstore, offices of the Dean of Students, a conference room, lockers for day students, a mailroom, and a large social space with a fireplace and wide-screen television. Boarding students live in one of seven residence halls. All dorms have wireless Internet access and a common living room for residents. Each hall is small enough to sustain a warm and friendly atmosphere, and each hall has resident dorm parents. The health facility on campus is operated throughout the day by the nursing staff. Emergency services are available close to campus.

ATHLETICS

Walnut Hill does not participate in competitive school athletics. However, a new fitness facility, which includes two movement studios, provides students with a variety of classes and equipment such as stair climbers, stationary bikes, and weights. The campus is beautiful, and many students enjoy playing Frisbee, playing soccer, and running. Yoga classes are regularly available. There is also an outdoor pool.

WEEKEND LIFE

The School's Activities Director keeps an extensive schedule of after-school events. Regular dances, movies, parties, and social gatherings are held on campus. The town of Natick is located 5 minutes from campus. Students frequent the coffee shops, the town green, and Russ's Diner. Students also take part in the numerous cultural opportunities available in Boston. Natick is connected to Boston by commuter rail. With parental permission, students are able to enjoy the rich offerings of the city on the weekend. In addition, music students spend Saturday afternoon at New England Conservatory in orchestra or chamber music.

SUMMER PROGRAMS

Walnut Hill offers summer programs in ballet, creative writing, music, theater, and visual art. The ballet and theater programs offer intensive

training with performance opportunities, while the other three programs incorporate a European travel component. Admission to these programs is selective. In the summer, there are approximately 200 students on campus.

COSTS AND FINANCIAL AID

Tuition for the 2005–06 school year was $35,350 for boarders and $28,150 for day students. There were additional program fees varying from $1000 to $3000, depending on the program. ESL courses, if needed, are available at an additional cost. Approximately 45 percent of Walnut Hill students receive some form of financial assistance. Families are required to file a Parents' Financial Statement (PFS) to establish need, as well as submit recent tax forms. International students are not usually considered for assistance.

ADMISSIONS INFORMATION

Walnut Hill seeks applications from students who have demonstrated passion for and commitment to the arts and have a solid academic background. Each application is reviewed thoroughly, with attention paid to the individual strengths of the students. Admission is highly selective and based on a combination of audition/portfolio review, academic review, and personal qualities. It is recommended that students interview and audition on campus. Students are only admitted to a single arts concentration.

APPLICATION TIMETABLE

To be included in the primary applicant pool, students must complete their application by the deadline of February 6.

ADMISSIONS CORRESPONDENCE

Matthew A. Derr, Dean for Admission and
    College Placement
Walnut Hill School
12 Highland Street
Natick, Massachusetts 01760-2199

Phone: 508-650-5020
Fax: 508-655-3726
E-mail: admissions@walnuthillarts.org
Web site: http://www.walnuthillarts.org

WASATCH ACADEMY

Mount Pleasant, Utah

Type: Coeducational boarding and day college-preparatory school
Grades: 9–12
Enrollment: 160
Head of School: Joseph R. Loftin

THE SCHOOL

Past swerving mountain roads, farms, and undulating fields, Wasatch Academy is centered on the exact geographical center of Utah. Wasatch's location has inherently affected the institution and students alike, ultimately imbuing the community with a distinguishing spirit. The Academy provides an intimate academic experience and places attention on each individual student.

Though Wasatch Academy was founded in 1875 with a Presbyterian affiliation, the school currently holds no ties to any religious communities. A commitment to spiritual and moral growth, which includes weekly nonsectarian chapel meetings and ethics courses, has, however, endured since the school's founding.

The campus is a National Historic Site and is ensconced deep into the Sanpete Valley. The school has long been an integral part of the Mt. Pleasant City community, a city with a population of 2,700. Wasatch is 60 miles from Provo, Utah, and 95 miles away from Salt Lake City, Utah, home of the 2002 Winter Olympics. The Academy is close to many national parks and internationally renowned ski resorts.

Wasatch is a member of the Council for Spiritual and Ethical Education, the National Association of Independent Schools (NAIS), the Association of Boarding Schools (TABS), the Western Boarding Schools Association (WBSA), the Secondary School Admission Test Board (SSATB), the Council for Advancement and Support of Education (CASE), and the National Association for College Admission Counseling. Governed by a 16-member Board of Trustees composed of parents, alumni, and professional leaders from across the country and Native American nations, the Academy is a registered, nonprofit organization and is accredited by the Northwest Association of Schools and Colleges and the Pacific Northwest Association of Independent Schools.

ACADEMIC PROGRAMS

Wasatch's broad curriculum offers a wide spectrum of academic opportunities, including Advanced Placement (AP) and honors courses. Course offerings include electives in English, history, philosophy, and art history. Students are able to enroll in any of the twenty-four offered performing and visual arts courses, field-based and laboratory sciences; and Web design courses.

Wasatch is committed to teaching all students how to succeed independently with self-discipline, time-management, and learning strategies. A Learning Strategies course is taught with a student-teacher ratio of 4:1 and focuses on the above mentioned aspects of successful academic accomplishment; this course is geared toward students who need additional learning support. Exceptional students may follow an honors

curriculum and earn an honors diploma. Wasatch also offers three levels of ESL instruction: beginning, intermediate, and advanced.

The average class has 10 students, and all classes are limited to 18 students. Twenty-four credits are required for a diploma, including the following specific distributions: 4 English credits, 3 math credits, 3 history and social science credits, 3 science credits, 2 foreign language credits (3 for honors), 2 fine arts and elective credits.

Parents and students may view up-to-the-minute grade updates via the Internet through the Academy's *PowerSchool*. Parents also receive written grade reports six times a year; reports of unsatisfactory work are issued every two weeks.

Students complete homework assignments during a study hall period held in the dormitories.

FACULTY AND ADVISERS

The faculty and administration consist of 51 members. All faculty members are required to carry at least a bachelor's degree, and together, they hold eighteen master's degrees and one Ph.D. The student-teacher ratio is 6:1.

Every faculty member provides mentoring to approximately 5 students through the advising system. Advisee groups meet twice per week often over dinner or dessert. Formal dinners for advisee groups encourage the development of social poise and etiquette and create a stronger sense of community.

The majority of faculty members reside in faculty housing along the perimeter of the main Wasatch quadrangle.

Joseph R. Loftin has been a member of the faculty since 1986 and was appointed Head of School in 1988. He holds degrees from Utah State University and the University of Texas and completed the Klingenstein Fellowship at Columbia University.

COLLEGE PLACEMENT

Wasatch has a strong tradition of college placement. The college counseling office works with students to maintain a schedule of deadlines for standardized testing, scholarship competitions, and financial aid paperwork. One-on-one counseling sessions give all students an opportunity to plan college visits, refine essays, and complete applications. Wasatch also transports students to various regional college fairs and college interview sessions.

Recent graduates have matriculated to such colleges and universities as Colorado College, Emory, Gonzaga, Grinnell, Mount Holyoke, NYU, the United States Military Academy at West Point, Westminster, and the Universities of California, Pennsylvania (Wharton), Oregon, Utah, and Washington.

STUDENT BODY AND CONDUCT

Wasatch Academy is arguably situated in the most diverse location in Utah. Students come from across the U.S. and abroad, representing more than twenty-three states and twenty countries. Currently, 32 percent of the student body hails from abroad. Among the countries represented are China, El Salvador, Jamaica, Nepal, Rwanda, Tibet, and the United Kingdom.

Whether they are from urban, suburban, or rural environments, Wasatch students are fully immersed into a positive, comprehensive, and academically inclined community. Student success and benefit is attributed to the motivated environment of the school.

Student prefects assist in establishing standards of behavior on and off campus, particularly in the residence halls. Student conduct is rewarded with a citizenship-level system.

ACADEMIC FACILITIES

Wasatch's facilities are nearly as diverse as the student body. Some buildings are more than a century old, while others are recently constructed. The entire campus is networked through a high-speed wireless network.

Three buildings hold academic classrooms. The 12,000-square-foot Mathematics and Science Building houses four science labs, math classrooms, and computer centers. The Craighead School Building houses the humanities and language classrooms, the library, the auditorium, and administrative offices. The library is a member of the Utah University Interlibrary System, which makes state library and college collections available to students. The Hansen Music and Art Center provides eight music practice rooms as well as three art studios for photography, pottery, general arts, jewelry making, and oil painting. The Academy also offers a Tech Support service for student use.

BOARDING AND GENERAL FACILITIES

Students reside in six dormitories, separated by gender and age. Most students have one roommate. All rooms are equipped with Ethernet and wireless Internet connections. Dormitories are equipped with cooking and laundry facilities, television lounges, and storage rooms. Each dormitory is managed by a full-time "dorm parent" whose sole responsibility is the care of the dorm residents and the dorm.

Students and faculty members alike share meals in the newly constructed Student Center, a $3.1-million addition to campus. The Student Center provides a recreation area, a lounge, a bookstore, a cafeteria, and a snack shop.

Other facilities include two athletic centers, playing fields, tennis courts, a rock climbing room, a dance studio, a skate park, a mountain cabin and snowboarding/ski park, a health

center, a chapel, a museum, and indoor and outdoor equestrian facilities.

ATHLETICS

Varsity sport offerings include boys' and girls' basketball, cross-country, fencing, golf, skiing, snowboarding, soccer, tennis, and track. Girls may also choose from volleyball and cheerleading. Boys are offered baseball in the fall. Other athletic opportunities include mountain biking, rock climbing, skateboarding, dance, and fly fishing.

EXTRACURRICULAR OPPORTUNITIES

Extracurricular opportunities include, but are not limited to, community service, SAT prep, computer tech support, hiking, yoga, drama, painting, photography, choir, instrumental music, yearbook, Literary Magazine, snowboarding, paintball outings, dancing, orienteering, Student Ambassadors, National Honor Society, debate, Students for a Free Tibet, and Amnesty International.

Wasatch's Literary Magazine is the winner of ten consecutive first-place awards from the Association of Scholastic Periodicals. The debate team competes at the international level of competition and frequently qualifies students for the world championships. A number of Wasatch snowboarders annually qualify for the national competition.

DAILY LIFE

Breakfast begins at 7:45 a.m. Before academic classes commence, the community meets for assembly or chapel. Classes officially begin at 9:15 a.m. Each student takes three (out of a student's six total courses) academic classes per day, two before lunch, and one after. When the academic classes conclude, students are allotted two periods for athletics or extracurricular pursuits. The dinner hour begins at 5:30, thirty minutes after the conclusion of the sports and extracurricular period. Study halls are held in the dormitories between 7:30 and 9:30 p.m. "Lights-out" is either 10:30 or 11 p.m., depending on the student's year of school. The schedule, while providing free time, assumes students have to devote additional time to studying outside of the mandatory study hall hours.

WEEKEND LIFE

Wasatch offers a variety of weekend trips off campus; the costs of nearly all trips are included in tuition expenses. Regular outdoor offerings include camping, hiking, and mountain biking trips. Other trips in the past have included excursions to Salt Lake City for cultural or sporting events, snowboarding, shopping, movie-going, and musical performances. Ski and snowboarding trips are offered every weekend from Thanksgiving until early April.

SUMMER PROGRAMS

Interested students should visit the Academy's Web site and click on "Summer Programs" for more information.

COSTS AND FINANCIAL AID

Tuition for boarding and day students for the 2005–06 academic year was $31,800 and $18,350, respectively. This includes a nonrefundable deposit of $3000. A family must also make deposits for weekly student allowances and bookstore purchases. Optional expenses include private music lessons, private dance lessons, art materials, ski passes, and Learning Strategies.

For the 2005–06 academic school year, Wasatch awarded more than $590,000 in financial aid to 36 percent of its student body. Aid is granted according to need, as calculated by the School and Student Service for Financial Aid (SSS). Returning students may earn merit and effort scholarships. Wasatch also offers special payment plans and loans in order to help families manage their educational investment.

ADMISSIONS INFORMATION

Students and parents who are interested in Wasatch should contact the Office of Admissions to receive a current catalog, an application, and financial aid information.

Wasatch seeks motivated and socially responsible students. While a record of success is ideal, the Academy also gives admission consideration to an applicant who may have extenuating circumstances but shows an ambition for improvement and dedication. Ninth grade is the traditional secondary-level entrance grade.

A candidate is reviewed on the basis of school transcripts, three teacher recommendations, a personal interview, and aptitude, intelligence, and SSAT scores; TOEFL scores are required for international applicants. Wasatch Academy does not discriminate on the basis of sex, color, creed, or national or ethnic heritage.

APPLICATION TIMETABLE

Students and parents are encouraged to request admissions information throughout the year. However, most applications for fall enrollment are submitted in the spring. Families are notified of admission decisions within two weeks after completing a campus visit and interview. Wasatch traditionally reserves spaces for some students to enroll in January for the second semester.

ADMISSIONS CORRESPONDENCE

Office of Admissions
Wasatch Academy
120 South 100 West
Mount Pleasant, Utah 84647

Phone: 435-462-1400
Fax: 435-462-1450
E-mail: admissions@wacad.org
Web site: http://www.wacad.org

WASHINGTON ACADEMY

East Machias, Maine

Since 1792
Washington
Academy

Type: Coeducational boarding and day college-preparatory school; business studies and vocational training available
Grades: 9–12
Enrollment: 350
Head of School: Judson L. McBrine III, Headmaster

THE SCHOOL

As one of the oldest academies in Maine, Washington Academy (WA) has been meeting the educational needs of students in grades 9–12 since its charter was signed by John Hancock in 1792.

Originally a feeder school for Bowdoin College, the Academy has maintained an emphasis on academics and success for the individual. Taking into account each student's differences, the Academy strives to create opportunities that equip students socially and intellectually for their future endeavors. The curriculum is geared toward college preparation, but it is also flexible enough for the student who seeks a quality education that includes business, technology education, and vocational studies. Emphasis is placed on the performing and visual arts, independent study, and involvement in the community.

The Academy's 45-acre campus is located in a safe, rural community in coastal Downeast Maine. The location enhances the nurturing environment created by a low student-teacher ratio, individualized attention, and a welcoming community. Just 2 miles from the Atlantic Ocean, the area also provides excellent recreational opportunities, including kayaking, sailing, fishing, hiking, and nature walks.

The school is governed by a 15-member, self-perpetuating Board of Trustees. An active Alumni Association supports the school's Development Office in annual giving and alumni relations. The Academy's endowment is $1 million. Washington Academy is accredited by the New England Association of Schools and Colleges and the Maine Department of Education.

ACADEMIC PROGRAMS

The Academy offers a challenging and comprehensive curriculum to meet the needs of students of varying academic abilities. Courses range from training opportunities in boat building to Advanced Placement and Honors courses in many disciplines. More than 100 courses are offered, with class sizes ranging from 2 to 20. The average class size is 14 and the student-teacher ratio is 11:1.

Twenty credits are required for graduation including English (4 Carnegie units), social studies (3 units, including 1 unit of U.S. history), science (3 units), mathematics (3 units), fine arts (1 unit), physical education (1 unit), health (½ unit), computer proficiency (½ unit) and adviser/advisee (1 unit).

Students are given latitude in selecting remaining credits. Electives include many fine arts courses, including theater, digital film and video production, music appreciation and composition, band, honors art, and many more. Other electives include seven Advanced Placement courses, foreign languages (Spanish, French, and Latin), journalism, environmental science, Web design, and computer programming (C++ and Visual Basic). Students must carry at least five subjects but most opt to carry six.

The curriculum includes English as a second language (ESL). Students are provided with beginning, intermediate, and advanced ESL, as well as courses in American culture and history. International students are integrated into classes within the regular curriculum. A one-on-one personal learning lab is available to students needing help with standard curriculum courses.

The Academy operates on a two-semester system. Reports with grades and comments are sent to parents every four weeks.

FACULTY AND ADVISERS

The faculty consists of 25 full-time instructors, 13 men and 12 women, and 7 administrators. Faculty members are available after school and during prep periods for academic assistance. The faculty provides cocurricular activities during and after school.

The Academy operates an adviser/advisee program that mentors students through their four years of high school. Each faculty member oversees a group of 9 to 12 students from the time they are freshmen through graduation. Groups meet once a week to monitor student progress, discuss concerns, and facilitate character development and career planning.

Judson L. McBrine III, a graduate of the University of Maine (B.S., 1990) and University of Maine Graduate School (M.Ed., 1996), was appointed Headmaster in 1997. Mr. McBrine had formerly been the Assistant Headmaster at Washington Academy, as well as a history, health, and physical education teacher in a number of Maine schools. He is married to Paula McBrine, and they have two sons, Jacob and Landon.

COLLEGE PLACEMENT

The Guidance Office assists students in preparing for their postsecondary education and career objectives. A new guidance placement counselor who assists the guidance counselor in researching colleges, admissions and financial aid applications, and scholarship opportunities joined the staff in 2004. Visits by college representatives to the Academy are open to interested juniors and seniors. In recent years, an average of 65 percent of the graduating class applied and were accepted to colleges. Recent graduates have been accepted at American, Bates, Bowdoin, Boston University, Bryant, Ithaca, Maine Maritime Academy, Middlebury, Roger Williams, Vassar, Worcester Polytechnic Institute, and the University of Maine.

STUDENT BODY AND CONDUCT

The student enrollment at Washington Academy for 2004–05 was 350. There were 174 boys and 176 girls in grades 9–12. The ratio of boys to girls was 1:1. Of these students, 315 were day students, and 40 were international boarding students. The international students represented ten different countries, including Bermuda, Hong Kong, Hungary, Jamaica, Japan, Korea, Russia, Serbia, Taiwan, and Vietnam.

Disciplinary problems are handled by the Assistant Headmaster, in cooperation with the Headmaster, and in accordance with established policies. Policies are clearly defined in the *Student Handbook.* School policies emphasize the acceptance of responsibility, personal integrity, and zero tolerance for harassment.

ACADEMIC FACILITIES

The Academy is located on a 45-acre campus with seven buildings. Two of the buildings serve as the primary academic facilities. The original Academy Building, built in 1823 and renovated most recently in 1994, houses foreign languages, special education, and mathematics. The Alumni Building is the main facility for administrative offices and classrooms. Renovated in the early 1970s and again in 1994, the building is home to computer labs, two science labs, an art studio, cafeteria, and the Larson Library.

The library holds 10,000 volumes and is fully automated. Using the library's seven computers and services provided by the University of Maine System, students may access a suite of shared databases and journal articles.

The Gardner Gymnasium has two courts with tiered seating and a seating capacity of 1,100, a weight room, and a training room. It also contains music classrooms, practice rooms, and a computer lab for music composition. Gardner Gym houses volleyball and basketball games, assemblies, concerts and music programs, the junior prom, graduation, and other special events.

The Industrial Technology Building houses the Marine Trades Program, Industrial Arts, and Computer Networking and Repair. The facility has computerized numerical cutting equipment, a professional paint booth, fiberglass boat building resources, and a drafting lab.

The Academy's computer resources include a twenty-station computer education lab, a sixteen-station office technology lab, an eight-station marine trades drafting lab, and a twenty-station technology integration lab located within the library. Throughout the school the Academy has approximately 120 computers and a student-computer ratio of 2.5:1.

BOARDING AND GENERAL FACILITIES

Washington Academy operates two boarding facilities, the Larson Dormitory for boys and the Edwin and Linnie Cates Dormitory for girls. The Larson dorm houses up to 16 boys, with 2 students in each room. The Cates facility has the capacity to house 15 girls. Internet and cable access is available in all rooms. The Academy employs dorm parents to supervise the facilities. There

are dorm parents living in each dorm with 24-hour supervision on the weekends. Breakfast, lunch, and dinner are provided each day at the school cafeteria. Weekend and after-school activities are coordinated, including transportation, by the Director of Residential Life.

The Academy also operates an active Host Home Placement Program for both boys and girls. Families in the program have been carefully screened and matched with incoming students.

ATHLETICS

The Academy promotes sports and activities as an integral part of the educational process. Team sports include baseball, basketball, cheerleading, cross-country, golf, soccer, softball, tennis, and volleyball. The Academy competes with both private and public schools in the area. The Academy has competed in many eastern Maine and state championships. Due to the rural setting, the community is very involved in the Academy's athletic program. The amount of support and pride from fans is tremendous.

Athletic fields occupy the rear portion of the campus and consist of soccer, baseball, and softball fields. The Academy has a wooded cross-country trail that covers blueberry fields and ascends a notoriously difficult hill. Outdoor basketball courts are located behind the rear parking lot. The gym, which is considered to be one of the best in the state, has two courts and a seating capacity of 1,100.

EXTRACURRICULAR OPPORTUNITIES

Students are encouraged to get involved in clubs and activities and to start their own groups that can benefit the overall student body. The Academy offers more than thirty clubs, including, but not limited to, National Honor Society, Academic Decathlon, Student Council, Envirothon, International Club, Science Outing Club, JMG Career Association, chess, yoga, ski outings, rowing club, and social issues.

The *Silver Quill* (literary magazine), the *Student's Voice* (newspaper), and the yearbook provide opportunities for artistic and written self-expression.

The WA Players, the Academy's theater troupe, compete in fall and spring competitions, often placing within the top three to five in the state. Musicians are given opportunities to learn and demonstrate musical talents through jazz band, pep band, choruses, all-state auditions, and music festivals. The Academy's music teacher is head of the state's Tri-M Music Honor Society.

DAILY LIFE

The Academy's daily schedule consists of a seven-period day, with each period running for 45 minutes. Classes begin at 7:55 a.m. and conclude at 2:15 p.m. Each week, the Academy offers an activity period within the daily schedule in which students can sign up for an activity. No classes are held on weekends and holidays. Breakfast sandwiches are served at locker-break and a cafeteria-style lunch is served at midday. Drama, music, and sports practices are held after school.

WEEKEND LIFE

Boarding students are provided with many supervised weekend activities. Weekend trips to Bar Harbor, Acadia National Park (1 hour away), Boston (6 hours away), and Canada (½ hour away) provide access to cultural and recreational events. Skiing, whale watching, and hiking on the bold coast are all within walking and driving distances. Students are provided with passes to the local University's Life Long Learning Center (3 miles away), which includes an Olympic size pool, a weight room, racquetball courts, a gym, and cardiovascular equipment. Karate, dance, and horseback lessons are all available within a couple miles of the school.

On-campus activities often include athletic competitions, concerts, plays, and special events, such as Winter Carnival and Junior Prom.

COSTS AND FINANCIAL AID

The cost of tuition, room, and board for the 2005–06 school year ranges from $22,400 for students residing with a host family to $26,400 for students living in the dormitories. Costs for ESL support are $2500 for the first class and $1000 for each additional class. An enrollment deposit of $2500 is due within thirty days of acceptance. Most parents set up accounts for weekly spending and extra expenses through a local bank or bank card.

Scholarships are based upon academic achievement, extracurricular involvement, and financial need. The Scholarship Committee determines financial awards. All submitted information is confidential.

ADMISSIONS INFORMATION

Washington Academy seeks students who are likely to both benefit from and positively contribute to the school and its student body. Entrance tests are not required; however TOEFL or SLEP scores are required for international students to determine placement for ESL courses. Admission decisions are made by an Admissions Committee after reviewing information on the candidate's academic ability, achievements, and other interests.

Washington Academy does not discriminate on the basis of race, religion, sex, national origin, or disability. The school is committed to ensuring all enrolled students are provided with equal social and academic opportunity.

APPLICATION TIMETABLE

The Admissions Office accepts applications throughout the year. Parents are notified of the committee's decision on a rolling basis. The school encourages both campus interviews and visits at anytime (by appointment). The school is open from 7:30 a.m. until 4 p.m. Students may make an initial inquiry of the school through an online admission form. There is a $50 application fee.

ADMISSIONS CORRESPONDENCE

Samra Kuseybi
Director of Admissions
Washington Academy
High Street
P.O. Box 190
East Machias, Maine 04630

Phone: 207-255-8301
Fax: 207-255-8303
E-mail: admissions@washingtonacademy.org
Web site: http://www.washingtonacademy.org

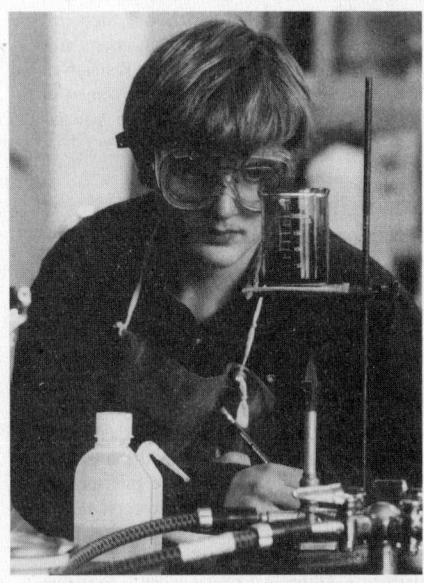

WAYLAND ACADEMY

Beaver Dam, Wisconsin

Type: Coeducational boarding and day college-preparatory school
Grades: 9–12
Enrollment: 190
Head of School: Robert L. Esten, '64, President

THE SCHOOL

Wayland Academy celebrated its sesquicentennial in 2005. Initially called Wayland University, the Academy was named in honor of Dr. Francis Wayland, a president of Brown University and education reformist.

The school seeks to foster the development of personality, responsibility, self-discipline, and friendships between young men and women as well as the acquisition of the knowledge and skills needed to appreciate the intellectual heritage of the past and to prepare for success in college and a rapidly changing world.

Wayland is located in the community of Beaver Dam (population 15,000) in southeastern Wisconsin, 160 miles northwest of Chicago, 60 miles northwest of Milwaukee, and 35 miles northeast of Madison. Beaver Dam is readily accessible via public transportation, including Amtrak service in nearby Columbus and commercial air service in Madison.

A nonprofit corporation, Wayland Academy is directed by a 23-member board of trustees through a 9-member executive committee. The school's assets include a physical plant valued at approximately $26 million and a productive endowment of more than $9 million. The Annual Gift Fund is supported by parents, alumni, trustees, faculty and staff members, and friends.

Wayland is accredited by the North Central Association of Colleges and Schools and the Independent Schools Association of the Central States. Its many memberships include the National Association of Independent Schools, The Association of Boarding Schools, the Cum Laude Society, the Council for Advancement and Support of Education, the Council for Religion in Independent Schools, the Council for Women in Independent Schools, and the Wisconsin Association of Independent Schools.

ACADEMIC PROGRAMS

Wayland's program follows the traditional four-year college-preparatory curriculum, with students taking four or five academic courses per year. To graduate, each student must complete a minimum of 19 academic units of credit. These include English, 4 units; history, 3 units; mathematics, 3 units; foreign language, 2 units; Latin, 1 unit; science, 3 units; and two elective courses. In addition to these courses, each student must complete 1 credit in the fine arts. The curriculum includes extensive offerings in English, German, Latin, Spanish, history, mathematics, and the sciences. Advanced Placement and honors sections are available in all academic departments. Additional course work is available in art, ceramics, photography, music appreciation, and English as a second language. Private music lessons are available for most instruments.

The Academy also offers a Coordinated Tutorial Program (CTP) for a limited number of high-ability students with special learning needs.

Classes are small, with 12 students in a typical section. A grading system of A–F is employed; comprehensive grade reports are issued four times a year and progress reports bimonthly. Classes are generally grouped by ability. Mandatory evening study hours are supervised by faculty members. Special help and individual conferences are scheduled throughout the school day and on weekends as needed.

FACULTY AND ADVISERS

In 2005–06, the faculty consisted of 24 members, with 23 holding advanced degrees. Approximately two thirds of the faculty members are men. Most members of the faculty live on or adjacent to the campus.

Robert L. Esten was installed as president of Wayland Academy in April 2002. Prior to his appointment, Esten was a senior partner of Phoenix Consulting, where he advised Fortune 100 clients on operations and management leadership. From 1991 to 1996, he worked in a variety of sales, managerial, and operational positions with Fox River Paper Company and International Paper Company. He is a graduate of Stanford University. Mr. Esten's family has more than a century-long association with Wayland. His grandfather began teaching at the school in 1901, he is one of eight family members to attend the Academy (graduating in 1964), and he is the parent of a Wayland alumnus. He previously served on Wayland's alumni association (1986–87) and on the board of trustees (member from 1985 to 1989 and 1991 to 2001). Esten is the school's eighteenth president, the first to have been born in Beaver Dam, and one of just four alumni to serve as the Head of Wayland Academy. Indeed, Mr. Esten has a passionate understanding for his alma mater, its heritage, and its potential.

Wayland seeks faculty members who, in addition to being scholarly, are interested in working with young people outside the typical classroom setting. Most faculty members serve as a mentor or adviser to a small group of students.

COLLEGE PLACEMENT

In a typical year, all of Wayland's graduates continue their education at colleges and universities across the nation. Wayland graduates are currently enrolled at such varied colleges and universities as Bates, Berkeley, Boston University, Brown, Carleton, Colorado College, Denison, Emory, Lawrence, Macalester, Morehouse, Northwestern, Notre Dame, Purdue, Rensselaer, Smith, U.S. Coast Guard Academy, Vanderbilt, Wake Forest, Washington (St. Louis), Yale, and the Universities of Chicago, Colorado, Illinois, Minnesota, and Wisconsin. Mean test scores for last

year's graduates on the SAT and ACT exceeded the averages for the nation, region, and state.

STUDENT BODY AND CONDUCT

The 2005–06 student body was composed of boys and girls from twelve states and ten other countries. Of the total student body, 75 percent are boarding students. Wayland strives for geographic and ethnic diversity among its students.

Wayland expects a commitment on the part of its students to academic achievement, extracurricular involvement, and positive character. The discipline system ranges from a reprimand for minor infractions to dismissal for certain major infractions. The Academy maintains a dress code, rather than having uniforms, to set an appropriate tone to the academic day and special events.

ACADEMIC FACILITIES

The academic life at Wayland revolves around three main classroom buildings. An academic building (1988) houses fifteen classrooms, twenty-one faculty offices, and workrooms. The Swan Library (1989) houses a library/media center with electronic research aids, a computer center, office suites, and the Whiting Gallery. Discovery Hall, the science building, has classrooms and laboratories for biology, chemistry, physics, science-related electives, and astronomy as well as a lecture auditorium, an observatory, preparation rooms, offices, and a plant room. Kimberly Chapel houses not only a full sanctuary but also ten practice rooms for vocal, choral, and instrumental music. The Lindsay complex (remodeled in 1994) houses a large art studio and a darkroom.

BOARDING AND GENERAL FACILITIES

Wayland has four dormitories, including Wayland Hall for underclass boys, Warren Cottage for underclass girls, and Glen Dye and Ella Dye dorms for upperclass girls and boys respectively. Faculty members and their families reside in each of the dormitories, as well as in faculty houses adjacent to the campus. New boarding students are assigned rooms by the admissions staff and the respective dormitory supervisors. All students and faculty members have their meals in Pickard Dining Hall, which seats approximately 400 people.

Other general facilities include Roundy Hall (the administration building), the Schoen House Infirmary, the day student lounge, and the campus bookstore. The Lindsay complex includes a theater-auditorium, a squash court, art facilities, a swimming pool, and the student union. The union houses a television lounge, a snack bar, and a dance floor. The Academy has a large field house and 30 acres of athletic space on its 55-acre campus.

ATHLETICS

Wayland believes that regular physical exercise is necessary for good health. Each student, therefore, is expected to participate in team sports or physical education (specific requirements exist for each grade level). The primary objective of the physical education program at Wayland is physical awareness, and major emphasis is placed upon lifetime sports. The alternatives for involvement in the athletic program are many, and nearly every student finds at least one sport that he or she enjoys.

A member of the Wisconsin Interscholastic Athletic Association, Wayland competes in state tournaments for varsity sports. In addition, there is year-round interscholastic competition for both varsity and junior varsity teams in the Midwest Classic Conference. Wayland sports for boys include baseball, basketball, football, golf, skiing, soccer, swimming, tennis, and track. Sports for girls include basketball, cheerleading, field hockey, skiing, soccer, softball, swimming, tennis, track, and volleyball.

The athletics facilities provide a quarter-mile track, two soccer fields, two football fields, baseball and softball diamonds, eleven tennis courts (two of which are lighted), and the field house. The field house features a brand new floor, Pickard Court, with space for three volleyball courts, or three basketball courts, or four tennis courts. There are also batting cages, a training room, and locker facilities. Adjacent to the Academy's swimming pool is Lindsay Gymnasium, with space for a volleyball or basketball court, locker rooms, a weight room, a squash court, and exercise rooms.

EXTRACURRICULAR OPPORTUNITIES

Wayland offers extracurricular opportunities appealing to a diversity of interests. On-campus organizations include the student newspaper and yearbook, Varsity Club (girls), W Club (boys), Thespian Troupe, Wayland Choir, jazz band, Model U.N., and Quiz Bowl teams. Additional activities include a winter carnival, spirit week, a student-faculty talent show, and the local community orchestra. Numerous outdoor activities are available, such as downhill and cross-country

skiing, ice-skating, tobogganing, fishing, paintball, rock climbing, and canoeing. Many students are also involved in community service projects in the city of Beaver Dam.

Wayland's proximity to Milwaukee and Madison allows for trips to the theater, symphony, museums, athletic events, and many other activities. A comprehensive cultural program of fine arts seminars brings lecturers, performers, and artists to the Wayland campus during the year. The Wayland Players perform several times each year, as do the choir, the jazz band, and other groups.

DAILY LIFE

The academic day begins at 8 a.m. and concludes at 3:10 p.m. with the seventh-hour class. Classes are 45 minutes long and are held five days a week. An all-school chapel is held Friday mornings and an all-school assembly on Monday mornings. The athletic period is from 3:30 to 5:30 p.m.; dinner follows and concludes at 6:30 p.m. Evening study hours, required of all students, are from 7:30 to 9:30 p.m.

WEEKEND LIFE

A broad range of cultural, aesthetic, and recreational opportunities is offered. Weekend permissions are granted if the student is in good standing socially and academically, but the school, as a policy, arranges a variety of on-campus alternatives designed to involve as many students as possible. Parents are encouraged to visit the campus at any time, but particularly for athletic events, lectures, dramatic and musical programs, and special activities, such as the Fall and Spring Parents' Weekends.

COSTS AND FINANCIAL AID

The comprehensive fee at Wayland for 2006–07 is $31,830 for boarding students and $14,110 for day students. Further expenses may be incurred for infirmary confinement and off-campus programs. A 10 percent advance tuition deposit is due upon acceptance by the school and is credited to the annual fee.

Financial aid is awarded on the basis of financial need and/or merit grant. Loans are

available for those who qualify. Each student receiving assistance is asked to work an hour each school day at a job assigned by the Dean of Students.

ADMISSIONS INFORMATION

Successful applicants for admission must express a desire to attend an independent boarding school and demonstrate that they are capable of doing the level of work expected by the faculty. Wayland seeks students who are willing to make a commitment to academic achievement and to become involved with the activities of the Wayland community.

The admissions process requires an interview, an application for admission, a transcript of prior academic work, two teachers' recommendations, and submission of standardized testing information.

APPLICATION TIMETABLE

Wayland welcomes inquiries about the Academy and its programs. A visit to the Wayland campus will be helpful to prospective students and their families. Upon completion of a student-conducted tour, the student will have an interview with a member of the admissions staff. It is suggested that prospective students consider weekday visits, as there are normally no classes during the weekend. The campus is also open for tours and interviews during the summer months. While there is no application deadline, it is strongly suggested that students submit an application as early as possible prior to the August in which they wish to enroll. Notification of the enrollment committee's decision is made as soon as a student has completed the admissions process. Parents are expected to respond promptly to the school.

ADMISSIONS CORRESPONDENCE

Office of Admissions
Wayland Academy
101 North University Avenue
Beaver Dam, Wisconsin 53916-2253

Phone: 800-860-7725
Fax: 920-887-3373
E-mail: admissions@wayland.org
Web site: http://www.wayland.org

THE WEBB SCHOOL

Bell Buckle, Tennessee

Type: Coeducational boarding and day college-preparatory school
Grades: 6–12, postgraduate year
Enrollment: 274
Head of School: Albert Cauz, Headmaster

THE SCHOOL

Webb School in Bell Buckle, Tennessee, is a coeducational college-preparatory boarding and day school for students in grades 6 through 12. The School was founded in 1870 by the noted Chapel Hill scholar, William R. "Old Sawney" Webb. It is Tennessee's oldest continuously operating college-preparatory boarding school and the South's leading producer of Rhodes scholars. Proven hallmarks of Webb's formula for success include a structured liberal arts program, individual attention, and an emphasis on honor.

The School grounds comprise 150 acres, and the overall physical plant is valued at $20 million. A nonprofit organization since 1952, Webb has an $18-million endowment, an active 43-member Board of Trustees, and more than 3,200 loyal alumni to provide a lasting framework for the School's continued growth.

Webb School is a charter member of the Southern Association of Colleges and Schools and continues to be accredited by that organization. It also holds membership in the National Association of Independent Schools, the Southern Association of Independent Schools, the Tennessee Association of Independent Schools, the Council for Religion in Independent Schools, the Secondary School Admission Test Board, and the College Board.

ACADEMIC PROGRAMS

The Webb School academic program is a traditional college-preparatory liberal arts curriculum offered in a structured environment that is conducive to the development of good academic habits. School is in session from late August to early June. Classes, which meet five days a week, range in size from 8 to 15 students.

Webb offers both a standard college-preparatory diploma track and a more rigorous Honors Diploma. The standard program requires a minimum of 4 years of English; 3 years of mathematics (algebra I and II, geometry); 2 years of the same foreign language (French, Spanish, Latin, or German), with 3 years recommended and 4–5 years offered; 2 years of history, including American history; 2 years of laboratory science, including biology; semester courses in economics, computer literacy, psychology, speech, drama, ethics, and the fine arts; and at least six full-year electives.

The Honors Diploma program increases the mathematics requirement to 4 years, foreign language to 3 years, history to 3 years, and laboratory science to 3 years. Participation in this program requires that a student undertake a minimum of two honors or Advanced Placement courses each year and receive no grade lower than 70.

The School requires that boarding students study for 2 hours in the evening five days a week. This study time is supervised by dormitory personnel. Students whose academic performance is deficient are assigned to study halls for their unscheduled periods during the day. Extra help is available from faculty members during a period that is set aside for that purpose at the end of each academic day. Students who are not working up to their potential are required to attend extra-help sessions that are scheduled at the end of the academic day.

Each student has a faculty adviser, who guides the student and acts as a liaison between the parents and the School. Parents are kept informed through regular written progress reports that are sent to them at least once every three weeks and through academic monitoring reports as required.

Whereas inadequate performance may result in increased restrictions, good academic performance yields privileges. Students on the honor roll are exempt from required study hours and may earn personal holidays away from school.

The required reading program at Webb ensures that students read widely above and beyond the assigned readings required in English classes. Books are selected from a list approved by the English faculty. This program is required of students in both the regular and the summer sessions. All Webb students are also required to declaim—recite a memorized passage before the assembled School—once a year. This program, which was instituted by Sawney Webb, is designed to teach poise in public speaking.

FACULTY AND ADVISERS

The Webb School has 42 teaching faculty members. All hold bachelor's degrees, and 63 percent hold advanced degrees. Many faculty members reside in the dormitories or in houses on campus.

Albert Cauz was appointed Headmaster in 2005. He serves as Webb's tenth Headmaster in 135 years. He received a B.A. from Boston College and an M.A. from Middlebury. Mr. Cauz brings more than twenty years of experience in independent boarding schools, including serving most recently as Abbot Residential Dean at Phillips Academy, Andover.

COLLEGE PLACEMENT

College counseling is offered to juniors and seniors, and representatives from many colleges and universities visit the campus each year. Webb's recent graduates have gone on to further study at institutions that include Auburn, Boston College, Brown, Colby, Dartmouth, Davidson, Duke, Emory, Harvard, MIT, Northwestern, Princeton, Rhodes, Transylvania, Tulane, Vanderbilt, and the Universities of Michigan, Mississippi, North Carolina, Pennsylvania, the South, Tennessee, and Virginia.

STUDENT BODY AND CONDUCT

In 2005–06, there were 46 boarding boys, 105 day boys, 28 boarding girls, and 95 day girls enrolled. The students, who come from various economic and social backgrounds, represent fifteen states and eight other countries.

An Honor Code that has been part of the School's program since its founding is administered by an Honor Council consisting of representatives from each grade.

ACADEMIC FACILITIES

Academic facilities consist of the main classroom building, which is called the Big Room; four smaller classroom buildings; a reading laboratory; a computer room with twenty personal computers; and the 22,000-volume William W. Bond Library. In addition, the School has a state-of-the-art computer and science building.

BOARDING AND GENERAL FACILITIES

Nonacademic facilities include four air-conditioned dormitories; the Webb Follin Administration Building and Chapel; the Student Health Center; and a physical education complex that houses a gymnasium, a heated pool, and a weight room. There are also three buildings on the National Register of Historic Places: the Old Library, the Son Will Admissions Building, and the Junior Room, which was erected in 1886 and is now open to the public as a museum. Also located on the campus are a bookstore, a student commons, and seventeen faculty residences.

The 25,000-square-foot Barton Athletic Complex opened in May 2002. It houses an indoor walking track, three basketball courts, a dance studio, and a weight room.

ATHLETICS
The sports program includes interscholastic competition for both boys and girls in soccer, volleyball, basketball, golf, baseball, lacrosse, softball, tennis, swimming, cross-country, and track. An extensive outdoor education program includes white-water rafting, high- and low-ropes courses, rock-climbing, spelunking, rappelling, hiking, and camping.

Athletics facilities on campus include two gymnasiums, five playing fields, five tennis courts, three outdoor education courses, an indoor swimming pool, and a trap and skeet range.

EXTRACURRICULAR OPPORTUNITIES
Student organizations include the Outer Limits Club, Trap and Skeet Club, Fly Fishing Club, Student Council, Mock Trials, the student newspaper and yearbook, Interact (a community service club), the student orientation committee, the Hamiltonians and the Platonics (student oratory societies), and the social committee. At least two major dramatic productions are performed each year by the Webb School players.

DAILY LIFE
A typical day begins at 8 a.m. and ends at 3:30 p.m. It includes seven academic periods, a chapel service, and a lunch period. Afternoon activities programs begin at 3:45 and end by 5:45 p.m.

WEEKEND LIFE
Dances and movies are scheduled at the School. Weekend activities are organized both on and off campus each weekend by the School's activities director. There are also trips to Nashville and Murfreesboro for dinner, shopping, movies, concerts, and cultural and sports events. Special events include a Christmas concert and program, Parents' Day, Grandparents' Day, College Day, Career Day, the Webb Forum, an Art and Craft Festival, and a variety of activities during Commencement Week. The Outer Limits program offers more than twenty weekend trips each year that feature white-water rafting, rock-climbing, hiking, and camping.

SUMMER PROGRAMS
A six-week Summer School offers English, mathematics, Spanish, U.S. history, field biology, reading, and basic math skills laboratories; a study-skills laboratory; nonacademic electives; and an outdoor program. Both remedial and enrichment levels are offered in these areas.

COSTS AND FINANCIAL AID
Room, board, and tuition for the 2005–06 academic year were $30,500. Day student tuition was $12,600.

Scholarships are granted to students on the basis of need. Forty percent of the student body received more than $980,000 in financial aid in 2005–06. The School also offers a Webb Legacy Scholarship and the newly announced Webb School Honors Scholarship.

ADMISSIONS INFORMATION
Webb School seeks students who desire the challenge of academic excellence in a traditional liberal arts program that emphasizes honor. The School expects students to be contributing members of the School community, have an understanding of the importance of honor and personal integrity, and possess the capability and desire to pursue a college-preparatory curriculum. With these prerequisites, Webb accepts students without regard to race, creed, or national or ethnic origin.

APPLICATION TIMETABLE
Inquiries concerning fall or summer admission are welcome at any time. Campus tours and interviews are available by appointment year-round. Students are encouraged to visit when school is in session. Office hours are from 8 a.m. to 4:30 p.m., Monday through Friday. Applications are processed continuously. There is an application fee of $35 ($50 for international students).

ADMISSIONS CORRESPONDENCE
Chad Sartini, Director of Admission and
    Financial Aid
The Webb School
Highway 82 Sawney Webb Road
Bell Buckle, Tennessee 37020
Phone: 931-389-6003
    888-SEE-WEBB (toll-free)
Fax: 931-389-6657
E-mail: admissions@webbschool.com
Web site: http://www.thewebbschool.com

WESTERN RESERVE ACADEMY

Hudson, Ohio

Type: Coeducational, boarding and day, college-preparatory
Grades: 9–12, postgraduate year
Enrollment: 401
Head of School: Dr. Henry E. Flanagan Jr., Headmaster

THE SCHOOL

Founded in 1826 as a preparatory school for Western Reserve College, Western Reserve Academy inherited its present campus in Hudson when the college moved to Cleveland in 1882 to eventually become Case Western Reserve University. In 1916, the Academy was greatly aided by a handsome endowment given by James W. Ellsworth. The school's endowment ranks among the top twenty boarding/day, independent, secondary schools in the United States.

Reserve is a traditional college-preparatory school committed to maintaining academic excellence and to offering its students a well-rounded program so that they may develop into interesting, knowledgeable, and sensitive adults. The academic part of the day is not overly structured, but an atmosphere of academic seriousness prevails. Close relationships among the adults and students are an essential and natural part of daily life.

Hudson lies between Cleveland (30 minutes away) and Akron (25 minutes away), just off the Ohio Turnpike. The main part of the Reserve campus is located one block from downtown Hudson, but most of its 190 acres extend into the surrounding countryside. Thus, outdoor activities are as much a part of life at Reserve as are those kinds of activities associated with major urban areas. Concerts (classical and otherwise), drama, art museums, outdoor activities, and cinema are a functional part of a student's life at the school.

Western Reserve Academy is governed by a board of 30 trustees who supervise the school's $81-million endowment. The annual budget of more than $15.5 million is fortified by the interest from that endowment as well as by funds from an Annual Giving Program. Parent organizations such as the Dad's Club and the Pioneer Women are actively involved in campus events as well. Approximately $3 million is allocated for financial aid, providing an opportunity for students who otherwise would be unable to attend.

Western Reserve Academy is accredited by the Independent Schools Association of the Central States. It is a member of the National Association of Independent Schools, the Secondary School Admission Test Board, the School and Student Service for Financial Aid, the Committee on Boarding Schools, the Midwest Boarding Schools, the Association of Boarding Schools, and the Ohio Association of Independent Schools.

ACADEMIC PROGRAMS

Western Reserve Academy offers a spirited four-year academic program of the highest caliber; students typically find it challenging. Structured beginning-level courses prepare younger students for what lies ahead in their final two years: opportunities to take advanced work in computer programming and Advanced Placement (AP) courses in English, Latin, French, Spanish, German, U.S. history, European history, biology, physics, chemistry, computer science, statistics, calculus, and economics, as well as the opportunity to take several courses for college credit through a special School College Articulation Program (SCAP) in conjunction with Kenyon College. Each student graduates with at least 21 credits, earned in the following configuration: 4 credits of English, 3 of mathematics, 3 of a foreign language, 3 of a lab science, 2½ of history (including U.S. history), 1 of fine arts and a Senior Seminar, and .5 each of health and ethics, athletics, with the remaining credits in electives.

For upperclass students, the AP and SCAP courses may be supplemented by independent study. Upperclass students may also participate in the School Year Abroad program. Sophomores have the opportunity to participate in a two-month exchange in the spring with Ridley College in St. Catherine's, Canada.

On the average, students take approximately 5 credits per year—in schedules arranged with their faculty advisers. The classes are small, with an average size of 12, although classes for advanced-level courses are typically smaller in size. There are no formal opportunities for remedial studies in any academic discipline.

To a great extent, students determine the use of their free periods during the academic day on an individual basis; there are no supervised study halls except during the evenings. At that time, students typically study in their dormitory rooms, although they may study in the library or in open classrooms or labs, depending on their specific needs.

Advisers work closely with students and parents to determine academic programs, daily schedules, preparation for final exams, and the need for extra help.

FACULTY AND ADVISERS

Western Reserve Academy has 68 full- and part-time faculty members, of whom all but a few live on campus in school houses or in apartments in dormitories. Many administrators teach at least one course. All faculty members have a bachelor's degree, and 52 percent have advanced degrees; 5, including the Headmaster, have doctorates.

Henry E. Flanagan Jr., the Headmaster, was appointed in 1982 and is a graduate of Rutgers (B.A.), Harvard (M.Ed.), and the University of Michigan (Ph.D.). His previous experience includes administration, teaching, and coaching at Princeton University, the University of Michigan, the Peddie School, and Avon Old Farms School, where he served as the Assistant Headmaster, the Dean, and the Director of College Guidance.

The average faculty member has been at Western Reserve Academy for more than twelve years. Typically it is the younger teachers moving on to graduate, law, or medical school who leave the staff. Almost all teachers coach a sport, serve evening duty in dormitories, supervise an activity, and advise students. Mandatory on-campus housing and meals (morning and evening meals are available for all faculty families) constitute part of each teacher's salary. A sabbatical program and summer study grants are also a part of faculty benefits.

COLLEGE PLACEMENT

College placement is handled by the College Adviser, who consults with students and their families during the junior and senior years. The school report on each student is prepared by the Faculty Guidance Committee, which is chaired by the College Adviser. Naturally, college visits are encouraged, but each year Reserve is visited by more than 85 representatives from colleges. The school library keeps on file an extensive selection of college catalogs and other admission information.

One hundred percent of the Academy's graduates attend colleges or universities each year. SAT averages have remained very high, with the current average at 1230. Recent graduates are attending such institutions as Case Western Reserve, Georgetown, Harvard, Miami (Ohio), Middlebury, Northwestern, Princeton, Stanford, the U.S. Naval Academy, Vanderbilt, Yale, and the Universities of Chicago and Pennsylvania.

STUDENT BODY AND CONDUCT

Two thirds of all students are boarders, and slightly more than half are boys. Students at Reserve come from many parts of this country and the world. The Academy is dedicated to creating and maintaining a healthy and pluralistic composition in its student body. Currently, 24 percent of the students represent minority groups (African American, Hispanic American, and Asian American).

Discipline and student conduct are handled by the Student Affairs Committee, which is made up of junior and senior class officers and selected faculty members in equal proportions and is chaired by the Dean of Students, with the final arbiter being the Headmaster. Student government officers, dorm prefects, and various other student leaders contribute their views in most matters of student conduct and general rule determination, although the school behavior and dress code is generally considered conservative.

ACADEMIC FACILITIES

Almost every building at Reserve has an academic function, but there are seven principal academic buildings: Seymour Hall, the chapel, Hayden Hall, Wilson Hall, Knight Fine Arts Center, Metcalf Center, and the John D. Ong Library. The seven buildings house classrooms, labs, music practice rooms, a lecture hall, a recital hall, dance rooms, a student lounge, woodworking and metalworking shops, a photography studio, a computer center, art studios, a publications room, administrative offices, and the school library of 45,000 volumes. The Wilson Hall Science Center was completely renovated in 2001.

Visually dominating the campus is the chapel, modeled, as were most of the buildings, on the architectural style of Yale College. Some of the buildings, such as the Loomis Observatory (circa 1838), are more than 100 years old.

BOARDING AND GENERAL FACILITIES

Western Reserve Academy has ten dormitories (four girls' and six boys') and one large dining hall for its boarding students. Monday through Thursday, evening meals are served family-style, as are lunches on Tuesday and Thursday. Lunches Monday, Wednesday, and Friday are buffet-style. Students can also purchase items at the bookstore, or they

can sign out to eat at one of Hudson's many restaurants. Most boys' dorm rooms are doubles, with some triples, and a few single rooms are available. Girls have dorms with doubles and a few singles. There are laundry facilities in five dorms.

The new school Health Center is state-of-the-art and has a dispensary, examination and waiting rooms, and six sick-bay rooms. A nurse is on duty during the day and on call at night unless needed for a student restricted to the Health Center overnight. The school doctor visits the campus every weekday to examine and talk to students.

The Student Center, located in the lower level of Ellsworth Hall, contains the Green Key snack bar, booths for eating and talking, a wide-screen television, and Ping-Pong, pool, and video games. Next door are the radio station and one of the publications rooms, where the literary magazine and the newspaper are published.

ATHLETICS
Western Reserve Academy emphasizes athletic competition and believes student participation in team sports is an essential part of the daily program. There are two or three levels of interschool competition for boys and girls in tennis, basketball, ice hockey, diving, swimming, cross-country, track, golf, lacrosse, soccer, football, wrestling, baseball, riflery, volleyball, softball, and field hockey. Reserve is a member of the Interstate Prep School League.

The Academy's athletics facilities include a new ProTurf stadium with a six-lane all-weather track, a competition swimming pool and separate diving well with 3- and 1-meter boards, a new state-of-the-art fitness center with Nautilus equipment, two football fields, four soccer/lacrosse fields, a 3.1-mile cross-country course, two field-hockey fields, a wrestling arena, and twelve all-weather tennis courts. A new indoor athletic complex features a 45,000-square-foot fieldhouse housing a 200-meter indoor track, new varsity and four practice basketball courts, and a complete training facility.

EXTRACURRICULAR OPPORTUNITIES
Aside from participating in the Student Council, student publications, and services already mentioned, students may join a diverse and changing group of clubs and organizations: photography, debate, chess, REACH (a community service club), Green Key (the student center), skiing, drama, Student Environmental Action League, Culinary Club, and WWRA (the school radio station). The school social committee, an extension of the Student Coun-

cil, organizes dances and weekend activities on campus as well as in Cleveland and Akron.

DAILY LIFE
The class day at Reserve begins at 8 a.m. There are six 55-minute periods each day. From 3:30 to 5:45 all students participate in athletics. Dinner begins at 6:30 p.m., and study halls in dorms are from 8 until 10. Classes meet on Saturday from 8 a.m. until noon.

WEEKEND LIFE
All students may sign out for weekend leave for most weekends. Leaves begin about noon on Saturday and extend until study hours begin on Sunday evening. Less than one fourth of the students leave campus on a given weekend.

A variety of activities are presented to the student body (for both day and boarding students) for Saturday and Sunday afternoons.

The Academy is located in a thriving geographic area. Nestled in the quaint village of Hudson, Reserve is within easy walking distance of attractive shops, restaurants, and community activities. Beyond Hudson, Cleveland and Akron offer major cultural events. The world-famous Cleveland Orchestra, the Rock and Roll Hall of Fame, E. J. Thomas Hall, Playhouse Square, the Ohio Ballet, the Cleveland Institute of Art, and the Museum of Natural History are easily accessible. Weekend programs also include downhill skiing at nearby slopes, concerts, off-campus movies, trips to the Gateway Sports Complex to see professional athletics teams, and outdoor activities at the nearby Cuyahoga Valley National Recreation Area. The Academy's proximity to Case Western Reserve, Hiram, Kent State, Oberlin, and the University of Akron makes the resources of these colleges and universities available as well.

SUMMER PROGRAMS
Western Reserve Academy hosts numerous summer programs. Among them is the Encore School for Strings—an intensive music program under the direction of David Cerone that is sponsored by the Cleveland Institute of Music. It brings together some of the most talented young musicians from this nation and abroad. Sports camps in lacrosse, field hockey, soccer, basketball, swimming, and diving are also offered.

COSTS AND FINANCIAL AID
Fees for 2005–06 were $32,000 for boarders and $23,000 for day students. Extra fees of about $600 covered books and other incidental expenses. Payments are made in three installments: July, September, and December. Reserve uses the Knight Tuition Payment Plan and the Dewar Tuition Refund Plan.

For 2005–06, more than $3 million in financial aid was awarded to 33 percent of Reserve's students. In addition to awards made on the basis of family need (as established by the School and Student Service for Financial Aid), merit scholarships are also available. The average award was $11,000.

ADMISSIONS INFORMATION
Western Reserve Academy admits students of any race, sex, color, disability, or national or ethnic origin to all rights, privileges, programs, and activities generally accorded or made available to students at the Academy. It does not discriminate on the basis of race, sex, color, disability, or national or ethnic origin in the administration of its educational policies, admissions policies, scholarship and loan programs, and athletics or other school-administered programs.

Reserve requires that all applicants submit SSAT, ISEE, or SAT scores and recommendations from 2 current teachers. Applicants average in the top three deciles on the SSAT and have achieved A's and B's at their previous schools. Most students enter in grade 9 or 10. Reserve admits approximately 100 freshmen per year.

APPLICATION TIMETABLE
Most inquiries are made in the fall, with applications ($50 fee for students within the United States and $150 for international students) completed by February 1 (day students, January 15). Applicants and their families should have a campus tour and an interview. After an application is submitted, it is reviewed by the Faculty Admission Committee; families are notified after March 10 (day students, February 10) and are usually allowed four weeks to notify the school of their intentions.

ADMISSIONS CORRESPONDENCE
Gayle Kish
Admission Office
Western Reserve Academy
Hudson, Ohio 44236
Phone: 330-650-9717
        800-784-3776 (toll-free)
Fax: 330-650-5858
E-mail: admission@wra.net
Web site: http://www.wra.net

WESTMINSTER SCHOOL
Simsbury, Connecticut

Type: Coeducational boarding and day college-preparatory school
Grades: 9–12 (Forms III–VI)
Enrollment: 375
Head of School: W. Graham Cole Jr., Headmaster

THE SCHOOL

Founded in 1888 by William Lee Cushing, Westminster School was first located in Dobbs Ferry, New York. At the turn of the century, the School was moved to its present location in Simsbury, Connecticut. Westminster began admitting girls in 1971 and now has an equal number of boys and girls.

Westminster is a school with a strong sense of identity and tradition. Members of the School community recognize the importance of duties and obligations, not only to other people, but to one's own aptitudes, strengths, and opportunities as well. There is a sense of the importance of trust and of living up to one's responsibilities. And there is agreement on the importance of living cheerfully within the limits a society sets and of respecting its ceremonies and symbols. These agreements support a coherent social pattern with opportunities for many different kinds of people.

Westminster is situated on 230 acres of wooded plateau overlooking the scenic Farmington River valley, 13 miles northwest of Hartford. It is 20 minutes from Bradley International Airport and a little more than a 2-hour drive from New York and Boston.

A 27-member Board of Trustees is the governing body. Westminster's current endowment is valued at $75 million. In 2004–05, the School received $2.1 million in Annual Giving and $10.2 million in capital gifts.

Westminster is accredited by the New England Association of Schools and Colleges. It has memberships in the National Association of Independent Schools, the Connecticut Association of Independent Schools, the Secondary School Admission Test Board, the Educational Records Bureau, and the Council for Religion in Independent Schools.

ACADEMIC PROGRAMS

Westminster offers a liberal arts curriculum that emphasizes balance and depth. Eighteen credits are required for graduation; however, the vast majority of students accumulate 20 or more credits. The minimum department requirements for graduation include 4 credits of English, 3 credits of mathematics, 2 credits of laboratory science, 2 credits of Latin or a modern foreign language, 2 credits of history (including 1 credit in U.S. history at the Fifth- or Sixth-Form level), and 1 credit in the creative arts.

Each of the academic departments offers Advanced Placement (AP) courses. The English program culminates with a final trimester of electives, which have included Frost and Cummings, the American Dream, Children's Literature, Modern Literature, and Modern Drama. Three trimester electives are offered for Sixth Formers in Creative Writing. Students can continue mathematics course work through AP calculus, AP computer, and AP statistics. Latin, French, and Spanish are offered through the AP level, with tutorials available for sixth-year study. The history department provides advanced courses in twentieth-century American history and ethical philosophy as well as AP courses in economics, United States history, comparative government, modern European history, and art history. In addition to the basic courses in biology, chemistry, physics, astronomy, and geology, students can choose from AP courses in chemistry, physics, biology, and environmental science. Creative arts offerings include introductory and advanced art courses, a broad range of music and theater courses, and a noteworthy program that begins with engineering drawing and leads to architecture II.

Independent study programs may be undertaken by Fifth and Sixth Formers in lieu of athletics in any trimester, with the understanding that no student may participate in more than one such project a year.

A teacher acts as an adviser for each student. Advisers monitor both the academic progress and the social adjustment of their students, meeting regularly with them and maintaining communication with their families.

The School is on the trimester system. Students normally carry five courses per year. The grading system is numerical—60 is needed to pass and 80 to achieve honors. In order to earn promotion (and in the Sixth Form, a diploma), students must successfully complete at least four major courses and achieve a minimum general average of 70. At the end of each trimester, students' parents and advisers receive grades and teacher comments; at each mid-trimester, interim grades are provided. In addition to receiving these fixed evaluations, students, parents, and advisers are alerted to any problems that might arise. The normal class size is 12 to 13 students, and the student-faculty ratio is 5:1.

FACULTY AND ADVISERS

Of the 82 faculty members at Westminster, 49 are men and 33 are women. Master's degrees are held by 43 of the 82, and 7 members have completed their Ph.D. degrees. The average tenure of faculty members at Westminster is eight years. Virtually all live on campus, either in a dormitory or in one of the nineteen houses on the campus.

Faculty turnover is minimal each year, and new members are selected for their dedication to teaching young men and women and for their versatility, richness of background, and professional preparation. Faculty members have access to an endowed fund intended for professional improvement in such areas as advanced study and traveling.

W. Graham Cole Jr. is Westminster's seventh Headmaster. He graduated Phi Beta Kappa from Williams College in 1966 and received his M.A. in history from Columbia University. Mr. Cole is in his fourteenth year at Westminster, following a twenty-year tenure at the Lawrenceville School.

COLLEGE PLACEMENT

Three college guidance counselors work closely with students and their parents throughout the college application process. Students begin the process by taking the PSAT in the fall of the junior year, followed in the winter by an on-campus College Day, which exposes them and their parents to all aspects of the college application process. In the spring and continuing through the following year, students and parents schedule frequent individual conferences with their college Guidance Counselor. Students take the SAT and the SAT Subject Tests in the spring of the junior year and again in the fall of the senior year. In 2003–04, the average scores on the SAT I were 601 verbal and 619 in mathematics.

Westminster sends all of its graduates to four-year colleges or universities. Colleges and universities attended by the class of 2005 include Boston College, Bowdoin, Colby, Columbia, Cornell, Harvard, Michigan, Notre Dame, Pennsylvania, and William and Mary.

STUDENT BODY AND CONDUCT

In 2005–06, Westminster's student body was composed as follows: Third Form, 38 boys and 37 girls; Fourth Form, 44 boys and 50 girls; Fifth Form, 61 boys and 40 girls; and Sixth Form, 61 boys and 44 girls. Of the total of 375 students, 143 were boarding boys, 62 were day boys, 113 were boarding girls, and 57 were day girls. Students came from twenty-four states and sixteen other countries. About as many students came from independent schools as from public schools.

Seniors assume responsibility in the dorms, extracurricular programs, and work squad program. They inherit responsibilities and privileges that make them the leaders of the student body. The members of the Student Council are elected from every grade but are led by a board of prefects chosen from the senior class. Students and faculty work together on ad hoc and standing committees to determine and enforce disciplinary standards.

Westminster believes that by entering into the life of a coherent and purposeful community, students are able to develop a point of view that makes sense of the opportunities and obstacles they face. To this end, Westminster inspires young men and women of promise to cultivate a passion for learning, to explore and develop their talents in a balanced program, to reach well beyond the ordinary, to live with character and intelligence, and to commit to a life of service beyond oneself.

ACADEMIC FACILITIES

Baxter Academic Center is the hub of academic life. It contains twenty-six classrooms; six state-of-the-art science laboratories; computer facilities that access the Internet through the School's own Web site and include an equipped classroom, a working laboratory, and science computers, all with CD-ROM technology; a greenhouse facility equipped with aquariums and terrariums; a spacious library containing more than 23,000 volumes; an auditorium; and a bookstore. Students taking astronomy make use of the School's astronomical observatory, which features a computer-guided 14-inch telescope. The Centennial Performing Arts Center has a theater that seats 400; a dance studio; and rooms for music courses, private music lessons, and practice sessions. There are also studios and classrooms for art and architecture.

BOARDING AND GENERAL FACILITIES

There are six dormitories, all of which underwent complete renovations in 1996, as well as one dorm which opened for use in that same year. All dorm rooms and dorm study spaces have computer access to the local campus network as well as the Internet. Computers are provided in the common study spaces of each dorm. Every student receives a phone number that rings to a phone in the student's room or to a voice mail system. Each student normally has a roommate, but there are singles available for upperclass students. Corridors have between 10 and 15 students, and a faculty member and his or her family reside on each corridor. In addition, each floor has at least two Sixth Formers who help in supervising the underclass students.

Students spend some of their free time in the School's bookstore or student center. The bookstore, the Martlet's Nest, sells school and personal supplies and has a small café. The Timken Student Center, which was originally built by students and faculty members, has recently undergone a complete renovation. The student center contains a snack bar, an extension of the School's bookstore, a game room, and a lounge that is equipped with networked computers. The School also has a well-equipped and fully staffed infirmary.

ATHLETICS

Westminster considers athletics part of the School's curriculum and requires participation by every student. The School fields fifty-four teams in seventeen different sports: cross-country, field hockey, football, soccer, and volleyball in the fall; basketball, hockey, paddle tennis, squash, and swimming and diving in the winter; and baseball, golf, lacrosse, softball, tennis, and track in the spring.

Westminster's athletic facilities include 30 acres of playing fields, a 400-meter synthetic track, two clay and twelve all-weather tennis courts, twelve squash courts, two weight-training rooms, two paddle tennis courts, two full-sized basketball courts, a hockey rink, a swimming pool, locker room facilities, and two athletic training rooms.

In 2003, Westminster completed an $11 million state-of-the-art athletic complex that included an indoor pool, a fitness center, and a

health and counseling center. The facility houses an eight-lane, 25-yard pool complete with locker rooms, an overnight health complex, and a 4,500-square-foot fitness center with the latest fitness equipment. The building is the second of four major additions to an already significant athletic complex.

EXTRACURRICULAR OPPORTUNITIES

Westminster students have an opportunity to become involved in a variety of extracurricular activities, and students are encouraged to participate in at least one.

Activities vary from year to year according to interest, time, and student initiative. Those of an ongoing nature include the school newspaper, the *Martlet* (a creative arts magazine), and the yearbook; theater, with both acting and technical work; three choral groups; a jazz ensemble, instrumental and voice lessons; chapel services, which are conducted almost entirely by students and faculty members; and social service groups, such as a group that visits a local convalescent home each week. Clubs include the Environmental Awareness Group and the Debate and Women's Issues clubs. Off-campus activities, including trips into Hartford to see performances by the Hartford Stage Company and games at the Civic Center, take place whenever appropriate.

DAILY LIFE

Classes are held six days a week, with half days on Wednesday and Saturday. An optional buffet breakfast is offered from 7:15 to 8:30 a.m. on each school day. Classes begin at 8 and run until 2:30 on Monday, Tuesday, Thursday, and Friday and until 11:40 on the other days. Students have one or two study periods during an average day.

Each class is 40 or 60 minutes long, and all major courses meet ten times in two weeks. A cafeteria-style lunch is served for 2 hours each day. Students perform assigned work squad tasks sometime during the day, either at 2:30 after classes, during a free period, or during the evening, amounting to a contribution of about 1½ hours per week. A required afternoon commitment is scheduled for approximately 1½ hours. Chapel is mandatory for all students on Tuesday and Friday at midmorning and for all boarding students on Sunday evening.

On Monday, Tuesday, and Thursday, dinner is a formal sit-down meal at which students dine with the faculty members and their families. Following these meals, Sixth Formers join faculty members for coffee and tea in the Hinman Reading Room. All other nights, dinner is served cafeteria-style. Study period is held from 7:30 to 9:15 p.m. Students study in their own rooms or the Baxter Academic Center or work in the computer labs.

WEEKEND LIFE

After classes on Saturday, most students are involved in athletics; those who are not support the various teams by attending the games. There are always a couple of events planned by the Student Activities Committee for Saturday evenings. Typical activities include on- and off-campus dances and movies, skating parties, visits to coffeehouses, and trips into Hartford to attend plays or sports events.

Students are allotted a certain number of overnights or weekends; the allotted number increases by Form. Day students are encouraged to participate in all activities, both during the school week and on the weekend. Students who want some time off campus to buy clothes or groceries or to browse can walk to the town of Simsbury.

COSTS AND FINANCIAL AID

Tuition at Westminster for 2005–06 was $35,400 for boarding students and $26,000 for day students. Students can expect approximately $1500 in additional expenses, which include such items as books, school supplies, dry cleaning, laundry, and personal needs. New students are expected to pay an initial deposit of $2000 by April 10. The balance is payable in equal installments on July 15 and December 1.

For the 2005–06 school year, approximately $2.7 million in need-based financial assistance was awarded to approximately 29 percent of the students. Financial aid is reviewed each year, and all families applying for assistance must submit the Parents' Financial Statement to the School and Student Service for Financial Aid in Princeton, New Jersey.

ADMISSIONS INFORMATION

Students are admitted to Westminster on the basis of their ability to contribute to the School community and, in a general sense, to society beyond Westminster. The admissions committee seeks students who show a willingness and enthusiasm to grow, to become involved, to work cheerfully with others, and to meet new challenges. Experience has shown that a record of accomplishment, whether in or out of the classroom, is the best evidence that a student has the potential, the will, and the imagination needed to do more things well at Westminster.

Requirements for admission include a personal interview, recommendations from English and math teachers, a school transcript, writing samples, and the results of the SSAT. The admissions committee considers each of these requirements an essential factor in establishing a complete profile of a candidate.

Most students come to Westminster as Third or Fourth Formers (grades 9 or 10), but the School accepts a few students each year for the last two grades.

APPLICATION TIMETABLE

An initial inquiry is welcome at any time. Scheduled visits are available from 8 a.m. to 1:45 p.m. on Monday, Tuesday, Thursday, and Friday and 8 to 11 on Wednesday and Saturday. The application deadline is January 25. Fees are $50 for domestic applications, $100 for international. Candidates with all credentials on file by the deadline are notified of a decision on March 10; students are expected to reply to acceptances by April 10.

ADMISSIONS CORRESPONDENCE

Jon C. Deveaux, Director of Admissions
Westminster School
Simsbury, Connecticut 06070

Phone: 860-408-3060
Fax: 860-408-3042
E-mail: admit@westminster-school.org
Web site: http://www.westminster-school.org

WEST NOTTINGHAM ACADEMY

Colora, Maryland

17 44

Type: Coeducational boarding and day college-preparatory school
Grades: 6–12, postgraduate year
Enrollment: 140
Head of School: Dr. D. John Watson

THE SCHOOL

West Nottingham Academy was founded in 1744 on the principle that an excellent and inclusive education is vital to the future. That belief and knowledge is the Academy's heritage and philosophy. Students discover a school where everyone is respected and listened to and where every student is encouraged to participate in and be a part of an energetic and caring community.

The 120-acre campus includes 20 acres of woodland. The broad lawns are dotted by an unusual variety of trees. Located about an hour from Baltimore and Philadelphia, the Academy enjoys a quiet, rural setting and supplements its overall program with the regular use of the recreational and cultural resources of the Baltimore-Philadelphia area.

West Nottingham Academy, the oldest boarding school in the United States, is accredited by the Middle States Association of Colleges and Schools and by the Maryland State Department of Education. The Academy is a member of the National Association of Independent Schools, the Association of Independent Maryland Schools, the Association of Delaware Valley Independent Schools, the Small Boarding School Association, and the Association of Boarding Schools.

ACADEMIC PROGRAMS

The academic year is divided into trimesters and includes a Thanksgiving recess as well as winter and spring vacations. Classes are held from 8 a.m. to 3 p.m. five days a week.

An average class has 10 students; the student-teacher ratio is 5:1. Teachers are available for extra help during daily "academic assistance" periods, which students may attend voluntarily or by faculty request. Boarding students have a supervised 2-hour study period Sunday through Thursday evening. Parents are sent grades and comments eight times yearly, with interim reports issued for students experiencing academic difficulty.

The Chesapeake Learning Center at West Nottingham Academy enrolls students who have experienced learning difficulties in a traditional high school curriculum. The program's environment is tailored to meet individual learning needs with the support of a caring faculty, structured study halls, small classes, and individual attention. This is a college-preparatory curriculum, and students must be able to meet the Academy's graduation requirements to receive a diploma.

Of the 84 credits required for graduation, 22 must be in literature and composition and 12 each in history, mathematics, sciences, and foreign language. In addition, 8 credits are required in fine arts and 2 each in computer science, health, and religious thought/ethics.

Courses offered are English literature 1–4 and English composition 1–4; French 1–4, Latin 1–4, and Spanish 1–4; world history, United States his-

tory, European history, ancient history, international relations, psychology, modern Africa, modern Asia, and religious thought/ethics; algebra 1–2, geometry, precalculus, and calculus; biology, chemistry, physics, computer science, and polymers; and drawing, painting, clay, photography, sculpture, performing arts, film studies, acting, ensemble, chorus, survey of Western art, and health. Advanced Placement for possible college credit is offered in most subject areas.

FACULTY AND ADVISERS

D. John Watson, Ph.D., became Head of School in 2002. Previously, Dr. Watson was Assistant Head and Director of the CASCLE program at Cheshire Academy and held positions at the Peddie School and Darrow School. He holds a degree from Northern Michigan University and earned M.A. and Ph.D. degrees in music composition and theory at the University of Minnesota.

There are 47 members of the administrative and teaching faculty, 32 men and 15 women. More than half have earned master's degrees or beyond; 3 hold doctorates. Among their representative colleges and universities are Columbia, Dartmouth, Emory, Guilford, Haverford, Johns Hopkins, Lincoln University, Loyola, Millersville, Muhlenberg, Penn State, St. Andrews (Scotland), St. John's College, Smith, SUNY, Towson State, Vanderbilt, Virginia Tech, Washington College, West Virginia, and the Universities of Alaska, Colorado, Connecticut, Kentucky, Maine, Maryland, Michigan, New Hampshire, and Pennsylvania.

A nurse is on campus during academic hours and in the early evening; the school physician resides 3 miles away. Hospital services are available in two nearby towns.

Faculty members serve as advisers to students. They also actively participate in student clubs, accompany students on field trips and weekend outings, and share dormitory life with them. Many faculty members serve as coaches, and all are available to students for informal counseling, extra academic help, and companionship. Faculty homes are frequently open to students for movies, snacks, and casual visits.

The Academy employs teachers who are not only proficient in and passionate about their subject areas but also committed to sharing their lives with the students in a caring and supportive community. Teachers listen to students, one of the characteristics that define the Academy.

COLLEGE PLACEMENT

College counseling begins upon enrollment at the Academy and is completed upon acceptance of a college's offer of admission. The Academy provides families and students with timely, accurate information and sound counsel; individualized assistance is provided to all students. No question goes unanswered and no student is overlooked.

Recent graduates are attending such colleges and universities as Davis and Elkins, Elizabethtown, Franklin and Marshall, Georgetown, Goucher, Ithaca, Penn State, Purdue, Rhode Island School of Design, Smith, Syracuse, and the Universities of Arizona, Delaware, Maryland, and Minnesota.

STUDENT BODY AND CONDUCT

The Middle School has 14 students and is a day program only. The Upper School has 126 students across four grades and a postgraduate program.

The Academy's enrollment is drawn from all socioeconomic levels and averages 65 percent boys, 35 percent girls, and 30 percent day students. Twelve percent are members of minority groups. Most of the boarding students come from Delaware, Maryland, New Jersey, Pennsylvania, Virginia, and Washington, D.C., but there are representatives from California, Colorado, Florida, Ohio, and Texas. International students come from Ethiopia, Germany, Japan, Nigeria, South Korea, and Taiwan.

The Student Government Association provides leadership in making the Academy understood by the student body and responsive to students' needs and in identifying areas of concern to students. A Residential Life Committee identifies problems in residential life and seeks solutions that encourage cooperation among students and faculty members who live in dormitories.

The Academy considers honesty as the first rule of the school. Dishonesty, the use or possession of alcohol or illegal drugs, and disrespect for persons or property is cause of great concern to the Academy and can lead to dismissal. The Dean of Students and a faculty-student committee monitor school rules and student behavior. Advisers advocate for students and stay in touch with their families to keep them informed.

ACADEMIC FACILITIES

The Patricia A. Bathon Science Center, which opened in spring 2003, is home to three state-of-the-art science labs and classroom spaces. Renovated in 2002, the academic center of the campus is Finley Hall, which was built in 1961 in memory of the Academy's founder, Rev. Samuel Finley. It houses twenty classrooms and a writing lab. The Slaybaugh Old Academy building is used for drama performances, student variety shows, and other presentations during the school year. Magraw Hall, a 1930 structure that was refurbished in 2000, houses the library, computer lab, art studio, music room, high-technology presentation room, academic program offices, and Office of Admission.

Faculty members and students regard the entire campus as an extension of the academic facilities. Classes occasionally meet in faculty homes. The trees on the Academy's grounds come from all over the world, providing an unusual opportunity for botanical study.

BOARDING AND GENERAL FACILITIES

The 120-acre campus includes 20 acres of woodland; football, field hockey, and soccer fields; and baseball and softball diamonds. Indoor athletic facilities are housed in Ware Field House. The C. Herbert Foutz Center is the focal point of the Academy's student activity. It houses the Frank D. Brown Dining Room, the Hallock Student Union, and administrative offices.

East Dorm and West Dorm (1998) house 22 girls and 22 boys, respectively. Other dormitories are Rush for boys and Rowland for girls. The oldest building on campus is Gayley House (circa 1700), which serves as the Head of School's residence. Bechtel House, Hilltop House, and Log Cabin provide additional faculty housing. The Academy-owned plant is valued at $12.6 million.

ATHLETICS

All students participate in sports. There are interscholastic teams in baseball, basketball, cross-country, field hockey, football, golf, lacrosse, power lifting, soccer, tennis, track and field, volleyball, and wrestling; noncompetitive activities include conditioning, weight lifting (off season), horseback riding, and outdoor activities.

Athletic facilities include the Ware Field House, which contains the basketball court and weight-lifting equipment. In addition, there are fields for baseball, football, hockey, lacrosse, and soccer. Two athletic fields were debuted in 2001. Academy students have access to nearby riding stables and golf courses. The emphasis in the sports program includes not only competition but also cooperation and mutual reliance, which are important in the school community. No student gets cut from a team. Students who do not know how to play a sport are taught.

EXTRACURRICULAR OPPORTUNITIES

The Student Government Association provides a forum for matters of student concern. The Student Dormitory Council identifies issues in residential life and seeks solutions.

Club activity varies according to student interest, but all students are encouraged to take part in the activity program. Activities include the yearbook, skiing, and the Computer, Library, Canteen, Riding, and Varsity Clubs. Qualified students are invited to join the National Honor Society.

Periodic dances take place on campus and at neighboring schools. Weekend activities include outings to Baltimore, Philadelphia, and the surrounding area. Traditional events and activities include Homecoming, Parents' Weekend, the Homecoming and Winter Formal dances, and the Prom.

DAILY LIFE

The day begins at 6:45 a.m. with breakfast. At 7:40 each school day, a school assembly allows the students, faculty, and administration to present information to the school community. There are four classes in the morning and four in the afternoon. At midmorning, there is a half hour of academic assistance, during which students may see their teachers for additional help.

The remainder of the afternoon is devoted to athletics and activities, in which all students must participate. From the time dinner is over until study hall, students are free to enjoy the campus, use the game room in the Student Union, watch television, or relax with friends.

Students attend a 2-hour study hall each evening Sunday through Thursday. The student who is performing well academically is allowed to study in the dorm room with supervision by a faculty member who has been assigned to the dorm. In the supervised study hall, students are in a classroom setting, with a faculty member present at all times. They may move out of the supervised study hall when their grades attain an acceptable level. Students may utilize additional study time at the end of the regular study hall.

WEEKEND LIFE

Each Saturday and Sunday features a late-morning brunch. Cultural events are frequently held on campus. All students are invited to participate in on-campus activities, including movies, small concerts, variety shows, open gym time, and games, as well as off-campus options, such as trips to the museums in Philadelphia, local shopping malls, and the Smithsonian Institution in Washington, D.C.; snow skiing, college and professional sports, equestrian events, canoeing, sailing, and white-water rafting; and dances, concerts, movies, and amusement parks.

Faculty homes are also open to students for casual conversation and company. Ware Field House is available on weekends for basketball, volleyball, and similar sports.

COSTS AND FINANCIAL AID

In 2005–06, the cost of room, board, and tuition for students enrolling in the boarding program was $31,860; tuition for day students was $16,395. There are additional charges for the Chesapeake Learning Center and the ESL program. The tuition for West Nottingham's Middle School program for grades six through eight was $9950.

In addition to these costs, a $1200 student account covers expenses for books, room/key deposits, lab fees, and emergencies. A checking account may be established with a local bank.

All financial aid is awarded on the basis of demonstrated need. The Academy is proud of its effort to assist the sons and daughters of families who otherwise could not attend. Students should contact the Admission Office for more information.

ADMISSIONS INFORMATION

The admission decision is based on various criteria, including grades, test scores, recommendations, and an interview, with a focus on the student's experiences, interests, abilities, and willingness to be a positive member of the school community. The most important criteria for the Academy are the student's willingness to embrace what West Nottingham Academy is as a school and his or her desire to attend.

APPLICATION TIMETABLE

Inquiries are welcome at any time. The Academy's admissions office is open weekdays from 8 to 4. Meetings with families are occasionally scheduled on Saturday morning. Admission staff members review each student application and make a decision without having that student compete with other applicants. An interview is required, and the admission staff looks forward to meeting interested students.

ADMISSIONS CORRESPONDENCE

J. Kirk Russell III
Director of Admission
West Nottingham Academy
1079 Firetower Road
Colora, Maryland 21917-1599
Phone: 410-658-5556
Fax: 410-658-9264
E-mail: krussell@wna.org
Web site: http://www.wna.org

WESTOVER SCHOOL

Middlebury, Connecticut

Type: Girls' boarding and day college-preparatory school
Grades: 9–12
Enrollment: 205
Head of School: Ann S. Pollina

THE SCHOOL

Westover School, founded in 1909 by Mary Robbins Hillard, offers a challenging college-preparatory program strongly supplemented by the arts and physical education. Excellent teaching, a rigorous academic and extracurricular program, and a beautiful setting provide an optimum environment for individual development.

The 100-acre campus, 40 miles southwest of Hartford, faces a scenic village green and includes ponds and woods. The School is approximately 30 minutes from Hartford and New Haven. New York and Boston are within easy reach for day trips. Thus, outdoor activities and environmental investigation can be combined with numerous opportunities for visits to theaters, concerts, museums, and centers of scientific or political thought.

The 22 members of the Board of Trustees are varied in background, profession, and interests. The School's operating expenses are $8.9 million; parents, friends, and a base of 1,403 alumnae raised $859,000 for the 2004–05 Annual Fund. The School's endowment is $38.2 million.

The School is accredited by the New England Association of Schools and Colleges and approved by the state of Connecticut. Memberships include the National Association of Independent Schools, the National Coalition of Girls' Schools, the Connecticut Association of Independent Schools, and the College Board.

ACADEMIC PROGRAMS

The purpose of the academic program is to develop the student's capacity for thought, to provide a sound background of knowledge of the physical world and of our cultural heritage, and to cultivate creativity. A minimum of 18 credits is required for graduation, including 4 in English, 3 in mathematics, 3 in languages, 2⅓ in history, 2⅓ in science, and 2 in the arts. Computer literacy and community service are required. Seventeen AP courses are offered. Some requirements may be modified for entering juniors.

There are numerous English trimester electives for eleventh- and twelfth-grade students—for example, Contemporary Poetry; Dante's Vision; Dostoyevsky; Genesis, Job, and the Gospels; Poetics and the Iliad; Shakespeare: Comedy, Tragedy, and Romance; Nineteenth-Century British Novel; Southern Women Writers; Romantic Poetry; Inner and Outer Nature; and Tolstoy. Advanced Placement courses are offered in English, calculus, French, Spanish, Latin, U.S. history, European history, biology, physics, chemistry, computer science, art, art history, and music. In May 2005, 68 students took a total of 109 Advanced Placement tests in seventeen different areas; 92 percent received grades of 3 or better, with 72 percent receiving a 4 or 5.

The arts requirement may be fulfilled not only by numerous studio art, art history, and music courses but also by advanced trimester courses in dance and theater arts.

Three special programs enhance the curriculum at Westover. For talented musicians, there is a joint program with the Manhattan School of Music. For qualified girls who hold a strong interest in science and engineering, Westover offers the Women in Science and Engineering (WISE) program, which is a joint program with Rensselaer Polytechnic Institute. For the preprofessional dancer, there is a joint program with Brass City Ballet.

Westover School provides an advanced English as a second language program for international students who are otherwise highly qualified but who require assistance in improving their English skills.

The average class size is 12 students, and the student-teacher ratio is approximately 8:1. The full class load is five courses. Conference periods, during which teachers are available in their classrooms, are part of the weekly schedule. All of these elements in the School's academic program enhance a close student-faculty rapport. Freshmen and sophomore boarders attend a required study hall, 7–9 p.m., Monday through Thursday, with quiet conditions prevailing throughout the School. The grading system is numerical: 60 is the passing grade. Students are notified of their academic progress four times a year: in October and at the end of each trimester in November, March, and June. Seniors who have completed their required courses may seek approval for a special independent project in the final weeks of school.

FACULTY AND ADVISERS

There are 27 full-time and 9 part-time teaching faculty members. All have bachelor's degrees, 18 have master's degrees, and 1 holds a Ph.D. The majority of the teaching faculty members live in School-owned housing. Dorm parents live in apartments on the nine residential student corridors.

Ann Pollina, who holds a B.A. (Fordham University) and an M.A. (New York University), came to Westover in 1972 as an instructor in mathematics. She has since served the School as Head of the Mathematics Department and Dean of Faculty and was appointed Head of School in 1997. She has been involved in numerous research projects involving how best to instruct girls in math and science and has published several articles on gender equity in the classroom and how to teach girls math. All members of the faculty are encouraged to seek in-service training, and funds are available to do so.

While returning students may choose advisers, each new student is assigned a classroom teacher as an adviser to assist with academic and personal issues and to help in the planning of an academic program. Faculty members serve as advisers to the numerous student organizations. The Dean of Students, class advisers, and a day-student adviser coordinate and supplement the resources for advising students.

COLLEGE PLACEMENT

Through group and individual conferences beginning in the eleventh grade, a college adviser guides students in selecting colleges. The School's approach to college placement is thorough and systematic. Parents as well as students are involved. The mean score for the SAT was 637 verbal and 613 math; the mean ACT score was 28. The English and math departments review material for the ACT, SAT, and SAT Subject Tests; other departments provide reviews for Subject Tests as needed.

All 42 members of the class of 2005 attend four-year colleges. Two or more members of the classes of 2004 and 2005 are attending the following colleges and universities: Beloit, Boston College, Brown, Bucknell, Carnegie Mellon, Columbia, Cornell, Davidson, Dickinson, Emory, Kenyon, Middlebury, Rensselaer, Rhode Island School of Design, Skidmore, Smith, Villanova, Wesleyan, Yale, and the Universities of Chicago, Miami, Pennsylvania, and Vermont.

STUDENT BODY AND CONDUCT

The total enrollment of 205 young women includes 50 seniors, 51 juniors, 57 sophomores, and 47 freshmen. There are 125 boarders and 80 day students. Twenty-one states and thirteen countries are represented in the student body. Slightly more than half of the students come from public and parochial schools, and the rest come from independent schools.

Student leadership is vested in class officers and officers of other organizations. Student opinion and influence are also expressed through representation on the Faculty-Student Senate as well as the Discipline Committee, in which faculty members consult with student senior officers before recommending penalties to the Head of School for serious infractions of the rules. Junior and senior proctors live on corridors with students and work with them as friends and advisers.

ACADEMIC FACILITIES

The largest of the eight buildings that house academic facilities is the Main Building, which was designed by Theodate Pope Riddle, one of America's earliest woman architects. Constructed around a quadrangle, it houses most of the classrooms, assembly rooms, a photography studio, a language lab, and a computer center. The Mary Robbins Hillard Seminar Center houses English classes and special events. The Ceramics Studio and Virginia House contain kilns and drawing, painting, ceramics, and sculpture studios.

The Whittaker Science Center houses computers, a greenhouse, and an observatory tower, in addition to labs for physics, biology, and chemistry. The Adams Library includes 17,000 volumes; the Spectrum search system, which allows students to find books by either topic or author; and a variety of areas for study.

BOARDING AND GENERAL FACILITIES

All boarding students live in the various wings of the Main Building, which also houses the dining room and the chapel. Most students are assigned to spacious double rooms. There is a dorm parent on corridor for approximately every 14 girls. The Louise Bulkley Dillingham Student Activities Center, the School's previous gymnasium, was renovated in 2004. These renovations included construction of a theater, music practice rooms, and extensive dance studios. There is a Health Center staffed by a physician's assistant and registered nurses.

ATHLETICS

Athletics are an integral part of the culture at Westover, as student participation is required each trimester. Through group sports and individual activities, the School aims to develop in girls a lifelong appreciation for physical fitness.

There is an intensive program in interscholastic competition (varsity and JV levels) with area private schools, intramural competition, and a variety of other sports and activities for all students, regardless of athletic ability. Team sports include basketball, cross-country, dance, field hockey, lacrosse, paddle tennis, soccer, softball, squash, tennis, and volleyball. Each term, a number of options are available for students who do not play on teams. Modern dance, ballet, paddle tennis, an active outdoor program, cross-country skiing, fitness classes, and rock climbing are examples of sports courses that have been offered.

The Fuller Athletic Center, an $8-million athletic complex, opened in October 2001. This facility houses one regulation-size basketball court and one practice basketball court, four full volleyball courts, a squash pavilion with four courts, a multipurpose room, and a state-of-the-art fitness and weight-training room as well as numerous team meeting rooms and locker rooms. The School also uses nearby stables for horseback riding.

EXTRACURRICULAR OPPORTUNITIES

There are numerous clubs and organizations that support interests in the environment, social services, arts, languages, and writing. Three School publications and the Glee Club involve large numbers of students. Many students and other members of the Westover community take part in all aspects of the production of a musical. The West and Over teams—the underclass spirit teams—each devise, direct, and perform musical entertainment every spring. Opportunities for community service are provided by the School and may also develop through students' initiatives.

Classes often make trips to New York, Boston, New Haven, and other cultural centers to visit museums or to see theater productions, operas, or ballets.

DAILY LIFE

Weekday breakfasts are at 7 a.m., followed by morning assembly at 7:45 and then classes of 40 minutes' duration that continue on most days until 1:20 p.m. (with lunch offered from noon to 1). Glee Club meets until 2 three days per week. Arts programs follow, as do intramural and team sports and drama rehearsals. Dinner is at 6, followed by study hall, which is required for freshmen and sophomore boarders. Lights-out for these younger students is at 10:30, with progressively later hours for older students. Seniors have no required lights-out. All students attend an interdenominational chapel program once a week.

WEEKEND LIFE

A more relaxed schedule with many options is followed on the weekends. There are later hours for breakfast and lights-out. Many students participate in an arts program on Saturday mornings, while those on sports teams may have interscholastic competitions on Saturday afternoons. A calendar issued each week lists numerous activities, which include trips to New York, New Haven, or Boston; to performances or sports events; to other schools for dances; and to stores. Occasional festive dinners are followed by cultural or entertainment programs. There are also programs and dances on campus. An all-student Social Committee works with a faculty member to ensure that the activities are varied and interesting and that Westover students have ample opportunities to meet students from other schools. To preserve the community aspects of life, alternate weekends are closed—there are no leaves for boarders except in special circumstances.

Day students are welcomed at all scheduled events, have their own adviser and day-student head, and have lounges and lockers on corridors with boarding students.

COSTS AND FINANCIAL AID

Costs for the 2005–06 academic year were $33,900 for boarding students and $23,450 for day students. A $3390 enrollment deposit is requested by April 10 for both new and returning students. Half the balance is due July 31 and the remaining half by November 30. A ten-month payment plan is also available.

Financial aid is based on need and involves both grants and loans. Families applying for aid must submit the Parents' Financial Statement to the School and Student Service for Financial Aid in Princeton, New Jersey. For 2005–06, $1.8 million in grants was distributed to approximately half of the student body. Grants range from $1500 to full tuition. Three types of special scholarships are awarded. Daughters of teachers can receive full tuition and room and board for up to four years, and talented musicians are eligible for a joint program with the Manhattan School of Music. There is also a scholarship for students from Maine.

ADMISSIONS INFORMATION

Acceptance to Westover is based on school performance, academic potential, motivation, and character. The SSAT is required; the TOEFL is required for students whose native language is not English.

Westover School admits girls of any race, color, or national or ethnic origin to all the rights, privileges, programs, and activities generally accorded or made available to students at the School. It does not discriminate on the basis of race, color, or national or ethnic origin in the administration of its educational policies, admissions policies, scholarship and loan programs, or athletic and other School-administered programs.

APPLICATION TIMETABLE

Inquiries are always welcome. An on-campus interview, required of all candidates, should be scheduled Monday through Friday between 8 a.m. and 12 noon. The application deadline is February 1 for receipt of all materials. Admissions decisions are mailed on March 10. Applications completed after that date are considered on a rolling basis for available spaces.

ADMISSIONS CORRESPONDENCE

Sara Lynn Renda
Director of Admission and Financial Aid
Westover School
Box 847
Middlebury, Connecticut 06762-0847
Phone: 203-758-2423
Fax: 203-577-4588
E-mail: admission@westoverschool.org
Web site: http://www.westoverschool.org

WESTTOWN SCHOOL

Westtown, Pennsylvania

Type: Coeducational boarding (9–12) and day (PK–10) college-preparatory school
Grades: PK–12: Lower School, PK–5; Middle School, 6–8; Upper School, 9–12
Enrollment: School total: 782; Upper School: 394; Middle School: 158, Lower School: 230
Head of School: John W. Baird, Head of School

THE SCHOOL

Philadelphia Quakers established Westtown School in 1799 as a coeducational boarding school committed to the Quaker values of integrity, equality, respect for others, and spiritual growth. Today, Westtown offers rigorous and varied academic programs coupled with a strong residential life experience that teaches students how to live in a diverse community. Athletics, the arts, and community service provide breadth and balance to the educational experience as well as additional opportunities for teamwork, leadership, and creativity.

Westtown is located only 20 miles west of Philadelphia and 11 miles north of Wilmington, Delaware, on a beautiful 600-acre campus. Students enjoy the benefits of living and studying in a peaceful and safe rural setting, while the cultural and recreational offerings of the Philadelphia metropolitan area are within close reach.

Westtown School is governed by a Board of Trustees of 22 members, 12 of whom are appointed by the Philadelphia Yearly Meeting of the Religious Society of Friends. The School has an endowment of more than $61 million and an annual budget that exceeds $18 million.

Westtown is accredited by the Middle States Association of Colleges and Schools and by the Pennsylvania Association of Private Academic Schools. It is a member of the National Association of Independent Schools, the Educational Records Bureau, the Pennsylvania Association of Independent Schools, the Council for Spiritual and Ethical Education in Independent Schools, the Secondary School Admissions Test Board, the College Board, the National Association for College Admission Counseling, and the Association of Boarding Schools.

ACADEMIC PROGRAMS

Students at Westtown are immersed in a discussion-based approach to learning, in which each student's imagination and exploration are an essential part of the classroom experience. Discovery-based science labs take advantage of the 600-acre campus for field research. The dormitories become the living laboratory for testing ideas and principles explored in the humanities curriculum. Students develop a strong sense of initiative and independence as they apply the lessons of the classroom in a classroom and residential environment that depends on dialogue, discovery, and personal growth.

Westtown's curriculum emphasizes a strong foundation in each discipline (arts, English, foreign language, health, history, mathematics and science, and religious study) in a program that is both rigorous and flexible. Ninth and tenth grade students take a minimum of six courses per year, focusing on a core curriculum. Eleventh and twelfth grade students take a minimum of five courses per year, with flexibility for choosing electives and studying in depth. Most students graduate with 4 years of English, 3 to 4 years of history, 3 to 5 years of foreign language, 4 to 5 years of mathematics, 3 to 4 years of science, 1 to 2 years of arts, 4 years of health/religious study, and 4 years of athletics/

service/theater. Eleventh and twelfth grade students are also required to board in the dormitory for the final two years.

Full-year courses are offered in acting and improvisation, advanced biology, advanced chemistry, advanced physics, advanced reading seminar, advanced U.S. history, advanced writing seminar, African and Middle eastern history, algebra 1, algebra 2, American cultures (for international students), art minor I–III, art 9, Asian history, biology, biology 2 , calculus AB, chamber singers, chemistry, chemistry 2, chorus, clay, computer science, directing, discrete math, English, English for students of other languages (intermediate through advanced), environmental science, French 1–5, geometry, German 1–5, introduction to computer applications, introduction to studio art, jazz ensemble, Latin 1–5, Latin American history, legacy of the Holocaust (advanced), math calculus BC, modern European history, music history, music theory, orchestra, peace and justice, photography, physics, physics 2, precalculus (advanced options in algebra 1, algebra 2, geometry, and precalculus), sculpture, Spanish 1–6, statistics, studio art I–III, theater design, theater history 1–2, U.S. history, U.S. history for international students, wind ensemble, woodworking, and world history (advanced). Private music lessons are available for credit. One-term electives are offered in English in the third term for juniors and seniors.

Students from a variety of religious traditions participate in the weekly meeting for worship on Thursday. The student-teacher ratio is 8:1; the average class size is 15. A supervised study program offers students the opportunity to develop increasing responsibility and self-direction as they become more independent in the progress of their experience in high school. Westtown participates in cultural exchanges from Mexico, France, and Germany, with three- to four-week-immersion experiences for Westtown students abroad and a reciprocal residency for international visitors in the boarding community. Seniors complete an Independent Senior Project in the first two weeks of March. Through this project, seniors explore service, research, or business and government internships as well as explore personal strengths, initiative, and independence.

FACULTY AND ADVISERS

John W. Baird became Head of School in 2002. He was Head of School at Carolina Friends School in Durham, North Carolina, prior to coming to Westtown. He has an undergraduate degree in biology from Princeton and a Master of Religious Studies from Providence College in Rhode Island.

Of the 113 members of the Westtown faculty, 102 are full-time and 63 have advanced degrees. In the Upper School, most faculty members live on the campus, interacting with students in classrooms, in dormitories, and on the athletic fields and sponsoring a variety of student organizations and activities.

All full-time faculty members serve as advisers to approximately 8 Upper School students. The responsibilities of the adviser include guidance and

support of academic progress as well as awareness of the student's overall well-being in the Upper School. The adviser also represents an important liaison for communication between home and school.

COLLEGE PLACEMENT

Staffed by a full-time director and additional college counselors, the Office of College Counseling supports juniors as they begin to plan for college and seniors as they are involved in the admission process. A weekly College Counseling Seminar is part of the curriculum for juniors, beginning in the spring term, and it continues through December of the senior year. Individual counseling helps students identify colleges that fit their interests and goals. Close contact between parents and the college counselors is encouraged. Resources available to students include a computerized college search program and a library of guidebooks, videos, and college viewbooks and catalogs. More than 80 college representatives visit the School each fall to speak with students, and several conduct workshops on subjects such as writing admission essays and interviewing.

The middle 50 percent of an average senior class scores between 510 and 660 on the reading section and between 540 and 690 on the math section of the SAT Reasoning Test. Preparation for the SAT Reasoning Test is offered in-house through a course and individual tutoring. Westtown serves as a test center for the administration of the PSAT, the SAT Reasoning and Subject Tests, and the ACT. Students may take the TOEFL at nearby test centers.

The 102 members of the class of 2005 applied to 232 colleges and universities and are enrolled at seventy-three institutions, including Bates, Berklee College of Music, Boston University, Brown, Bryn Mawr, Bucknell, Carleton, Columbia, Cornell, Dartmouth, Earlham, Emory, Georgetown, Gordon, Guilford, Grinnell, Haverford, Johns Hopkins, New York University, Oberlin, Parsons, Penn State, Pomona, St. Andrews (Scotland), Washington and Lee, Wesleyan, Yale, and the Universities of Chicago, Pennsylvania, and Wisconsin-Madison.

STUDENT BODY AND CONDUCT

Upper School enrollment in 2005–06 was 394; 293 students were boarders and 101 were day students. A hallmark of Westtown School is its strong, vibrant, and diverse community. Students come to Westtown from twenty-one states and twelve countries. Twenty-two percent of the students are members of the Religious Society of Friends. Students come from a broad range of social and economic backgrounds, and 22 percent are members of minority groups. International students account for 10 percent of the Upper School student body.

Westtown has been coeducational since 1799. For every leadership position at the School, there are a boy and a girl leader. Student government plays a significant role in the operation of the School. Students serve on a number of School committees, including the Discipline Council, which considers situations involving major School rule violations.

ACADEMIC FACILITIES

The Main Building, Griffith Science Center, and Industrial Hall provide classroom areas for English, mathematics, history, languages, and the sciences. The Center for the Living Arts houses the Barton-Test Theatre, which has a 564-seat auditorium, a scene-costume shop, an art gallery, three art studios, a ceramics room, a darkroom, a chorus room, an orchestra room, and six practice rooms.

Computer facilities include four labs in the main building for Upper School students. Each contains twenty Dell-Microsoft workstations. There are additional computer workstations in the library and the science building. Internet access is available to all students and faculty members through the use of two high-speed T-1 lines. The campus network consists of 450 PCs and wireless technology utilizing a high-speed, optical-fiber backbone and Dell Xeon file servers for reliable storage. Each student dorm room has network and telephone connectivity. Students have easy access to workstations in the library, labs, classrooms, and all dormitory lounges. Teachers and students have extensive use of digital presentation tools, such as PowerPoint, Photoshop, Smartboards, digital cameras, scanners, large-format color printers, and digital projectors.

The Mary Hutton Biddle Library houses a collection of 33,000 volumes and subscribes to a variety of Web-based databases that provide campus-wide access to magazine articles and reference materials. An integrated curriculum teaches students to find, evaluate, and use information effectively in the context of their classes. The library actively participates in interlibrary loan resource sharing.

BOARDING AND GENERAL FACILITIES.

Residential life is viewed as an important part of the educational program. Ninth and tenth grade students reside in two smaller houses. Upperclass girls and boys live in two dormitories in the main building. All the dormitories on the campus have been recently renovated. All eleventh and twelfth grade students are required to live on the campus, which strengthens community life. Boarding is valued as an educational opportunity, helping students prepare for college by asking them to take on greater responsibility as a stepping stone to independence. Students form relationships with adult mentors, develop time-management skills, and learn to live and share with others on dorm—all skills needed in preparing for college.

The Student Center houses a snack bar, the School Store, student mailboxes, and a lounge. The Health Center is staffed by a Health Center Director and 3 registered nurses who are on call 24 hours per day. Two doctors visit the campus twice each week.

ATHLETICS

Athletics and physical education are integral parts of Westtown School's education program. As in the classroom, students are expected to strive for and achieve high standards. Interscholastic athletics begin in seventh grade and are required through high school. Most teams are coached by full-time teachers. Interscholastic offerings for boys are baseball, basketball, cross-country, golf, indoor track, lacrosse, soccer, swimming, tennis, track and field, and wrestling. Girls' interscholastic offerings are basketball, cross-country, diving, field hockey, golf, indoor track, lacrosse, soccer, softball, swimming, tennis, track and field, and volleyball. Coeducational noncompetitive offerings include dance, indoor soccer, lifeguard training, outdoor education, physical fitness, service, weight training, and yoga. Westtown employs a full-time athletic trainer. Athletic facilities include eight full-sized fields, a baseball field, a softball field, fourteen tennis courts, a ¼-mile track, a 26-element ropes course, a 5-kilometer cross-country course, three basketball courts, a wrestling area, an indoor pool, and a weight training area.

EXTRACURRICULAR OPPORTUNITIES

Involvement is the key to a happy experience at Westtown. There are many activity groups and clubs, including chorus, orchestra, various musical ensembles, the newspaper and yearbook staffs, Amnesty International, Model UN, the Earth Service Committee, the Student Union for Multicultural Awareness, and the Drama Club. There are groups for those interested in astronomy, camping and the outdoors, ceramics, ham radio operation, woodworking, photography, and skiing. Additional groups are developed each year to meet student interests.

Each year, the Shoemaker Lecture Series brings 4 to 6 notable guests to the campus to share their expertise and experiences with the community. During the past several years, these guests have included NBC newsman Garrick Utely (Westtown '57), Coretta Scott King, author Gloria Naylor, poet Sonia Sanchez, author and radio commentator Juan Williams, and singer-songwriter Pete Seeger.

Community service is a vital part of the Westtown experience, and the Service Network enables students to volunteer their time and talents in a variety of ways both on and off campus. Starting in grade 6, all Westtown students participate in the Work Program. The Westtown Service Committee sponsors projects that include recycling, teaching English to Spanish-speaking migrant workers, using art therapy with senior citizens, and rehabilitating abandoned houses.

DAILY LIFE

Breakfast is served cafeteria-style from 7 to 7:30 and is required for ninth, tenth, and eleventh grade boarding students. "Collection" at 8:10 begins the academic day with a gathering of the community for quiet worship, School announcements, and community sharing. Classes begin at 8:25 and end at 3:15. On Thursday mornings, the Upper School gathers in the meetinghouse for meeting for worship. Lunch is served family-style in the dining room. Organizations and clubs meet on Tuesdays and Thursdays after lunch.

Athletics, both competitive and noncompetitive, take place from 3:40 to 5:30. Dinner is served family-style at 6. Students are required to study from 7:30 until 9:30 in their rooms, the library, the arts center, or the computer labs. During the week, freshmen and sophomores turn their lights out at 10:30 p.m., juniors at 11, and seniors at 11:30.

WEEKEND LIFE

Weekends at Westtown are organized by student-faculty weekend teams. In addition to such on-campus activities as dances, coffeehouses, and lectures, the School sponsors trips to cultural and sporting events in Philadelphia; Washington, D.C.; Baltimore; and other points of interest. The Westtown Outing Club organizes camping, canoeing, hiking, and ski trips.

COSTS AND FINANCIAL AID

Charges in 2005–06 were $32,575 for tuition, room, and board and $20,100 for day tuition. Additional costs may include an incidental account at the School Store, spending allowance, laboratory fees, art supplies, music lessons, and lunch fees for day students. The charge for participating in the ESOL program is $3150. An initial 10 percent deposit is required upon enrollment.

Grants and loans for scholarship assistance are awarded according to need and are based on national standards established by the School and the Student Service for Financial Aid. Thirty-six percent of students in the Upper School receive financial aid, with the average grant equaling $18,519; $3.25 million was available for financial aid in 2005–06. In addition, the Sally Barton Leadership-Scholar Grant offers $2000 to assist Quaker families with boarding expenses.

ADMISSIONS INFORMATION

Westtown seeks to attract a diverse and talented student body that is interested in pursuing a challenging and varied academic program. The School welcomes students who look forward to the life of the community and who feel a sense of commitment to the shared values of peacemaking, equality, integrity, and personal responsibility. The Admissions Committee takes into consideration the previous school record, teacher and school recommendations, an interview, and the SSAT score.

APPLICATION TIMETABLE

Inquiries are welcome at any time. The Admissions Office is open from 8 a.m. to 4 p.m., Monday through Friday. Applicants should complete the application materials and make an appointment for an interview and a visit to the School. Tours (ideally taken in the fall the year before entering the School) are conducted by current Westtown students. There is a $40 application fee.

Prospective day students should complete the application process by January 7 and boarding students by February 1. After February 1, applications are considered on a rolling admissions basis. Boarding applicants must reply by April 10.

ADMISSIONS CORRESPONDENCE

Kate Holz
Director of Admissions and Financial Aid
Westtown School
P.O. Box 1799
Westtown, Pennsylvania 19395-1799

Phone: 610-399-7900
Fax: 610-399-7909
E-mail: admissions@westtown.edu
Web site: http://www.westtown.edu

THE WHITE MOUNTAIN SCHOOL

Bethlehem, New Hampshire

Type: Coeducational boarding and day college-preparatory school
Grades: 9–12, postgraduate year
Enrollment: 110
Head of School: Alan T. Popp

THE SCHOOL

"Small school, big outdoors," is the phrase most often used to describe the White Mountain School (WMS). WMS provides an environment for challenging academics and personal growth within a small and supportive community of approximately 110 students. The academic and cocurricular programs develop the whole person and foster personal and academic excellence. The mission of the White Mountain School is to prepare young people for rigorous college studies and for life beyond formal academics, by helping them learn who they are, how they contribute to their communities, and how they can become responsible citizens of a changing planet.

Founded in Concord, New Hampshire, in 1886, the School was relocated to Bethlehem in 1935. The move north, adjacent to the spectacular 600,000-acre White Mountain National Forest, was made to offer students an opportunity to live in and among things that were much greater than themselves, to help them form perspective, and to give them a sense of appreciation for the natural environment. The School changed its name from St. Mary's-in-the-Mountains to the White Mountain School in 1972, three years after going coed, to reflect better its commitment to a balanced college-preparatory program with the outdoor learning and recreational experiences available in a mountain setting. Although the School maintains its affiliation with the Episcopal Church, it welcomes students from diverse backgrounds and all religious traditions.

The 250-acre campus, with 150 acres of adjacent property for the School's use, is easily accessible from I-93 and is a beautiful drive from the Hartford, Boston, or Manchester airports. The School is governed by a 16-member Board of Trustees.

WMS is accredited by the New England Association of Schools and Colleges and is a member of the Secondary School Admission Test Board, the National Honor Society, the Independent Schools Association of Northern New England, and the National Association of Independent Schools.

ACADEMIC PROGRAMS

WMS has a special concern for the unique gifts and individual needs of each student. Students and teachers share an abundance of intangibles—trust, encouragement, and the adventure of learning. WMS teachers work hard to create an atmosphere of interdisciplinary learning, and to enliven academic study. In discussion-based classes, students learn through books, analysis, and hands-on learning. Students are well prepared for higher education through a challenging core curriculum and an array of upper-level electives. The curriculum can be seen online at the School's Web site.

WMS students experience a total living and learning environment based on the interrelatedness of the individual spirit, the community, and the physical world. The curriculum involves a wide range of courses. Extensive international and domestic community service projects, outdoor skills training, and a human development program provide an individualized and integrated approach to education.

Students and faculty members participate four times each year in outdoor learning expeditions. These expeditions explore significant places and ideas during a three- to four-day off-campus project. Such projects have included "Women in Outdoor Literature," "Walden, Thoreau and a Philosophy of Wilderness," "Timber and Wildlife Management Practices," "Sustainability of the Ski Industry," and "Fly Fishing and Fresh Water Ecology."

To graduate, students must earn 20 academic credits, including 4 credits in English, 4 credits in history and human values, 3 credits in mathematics, 2 credits in science, 2 credits in world language, and 2 credits in the arts. Independent study courses are an option for qualified students. The student-faculty ratio is 4:1, with an average class size of 8. Grade reports and adviser comments are sent to parents approximately every four weeks.

WMS also offers a Learning Assistance Program for approximately 25 students each year. This program provides additional tutorial and/or remedial help for students who have met with academic challenges. This program is designed to give each student the tools needed to become an involved learner as well as to understand his or her own strengths, weaknesses, and distinct learning styles. Students and parents receive weekly progress reports. English as a second language (ESL) is also offered to international students.

FACULTY AND ADVISERS

The School employs 29 full-time faculty members, 18 of whom have a master's degree or higher. Many are certified as Wilderness First Responders or Wilderness EMTs.

Individual attention is a basic part of the WMS approach to education. Students and faculty are on a first name basis, living and learning in a community of friends. Every student has a faculty adviser.

COLLEGE PLACEMENT

The college counselor works extensively with each junior and senior to explore educational options. Graduates normally attend college within the first year after graduation. Graduates of the past five years have attended colleges and universities that include Boston University, Bryn Mawr, Carnegie Mellon, Colorado College, Cornell, Dartmouth, Emerson, Hampshire, Ithaca,

Lewis & Clark, Loyola University, Mount Holyoke, Northeastern, Oberlin, Pratt, Sarah Lawrence, Smith, Swarthmore, and Syracuse.

STUDENT BODY AND CONDUCT

The White Mountain School enrolls approximately 110 students from twenty states and nine other countries, including Canada, Ethiopia, Germany, India, Japan, Korea, St. Lucia, Slovakia, and Zambia. Students who attend the White Mountain School value the personal attention, academic challenges, and the support they receive from enthusiastic and talented teachers.

The White Mountain School believes that each member of the community is important and shares the responsibility for the well-being of the School. The Community Handbook outlines expectations to help provide structure for personal support, academic success, and boundaries for safety. Through the Student-Faculty Citizenship Committee, students participate in the disciplinary process of the School. Student Council and the Student Social Committee serve as forums for student ideas. They also make recommendations to the administration regarding school policies, curriculum, activities, and other aspects of community life. Opportunities are provided for responsible leadership, individual initiative, and group decision making. In addition, all students share in community responsibilities. Duties include being on kitchen crew, serving at community dinners, or helping in the library. In addition to their campus jobs, all students have rotating work assignments in their respective dormitories.

ACADEMIC FACILITIES

The Main Building houses the classroom wing, science labs, multimedia center, learning labs, and extensive studio art facilities. A new science center is planned to open in fall 2006. The Library and Information Center was completely renovated, re-equipped, and significantly expanded in 2001. It contains a comprehensive collection of books and periodicals, CD's and videos, and is fully equipped to utilize online resources for research and instruction. Each student has a computer account and access to the Internet. In 2002, WMS opened a new language and classroom lab.

BOARDING AND GENERAL FACILITIES

Student residences include clapboard and field-stone dormitories. Each dorm has a full-time dorm head responsible for residential life. There are several faculty apartments in each dormitory, along with six faculty homes on campus.

A new student center was constructed in 2000, providing a central location for students to gather. The School is staffed by a registered nurse

and an assistant. The Littleton Hospital is only a 10-minute drive for around-the-clock emergency services.

ATHLETICS
WMS offers students a special opportunity to learn and develop outdoor/wilderness skills as part of their education. In the fall and spring, students can choose from hiking, rock climbing, mountain biking, white-water and open-water paddling, and conditioning. Interscholastic team sports for the fall and spring include boys' and girls' soccer and lacrosse.

The White Mountain School's rock-climbing program is the first and only high school program, public or private, to earn accreditation from the American Mountain Guides Association. The focus of the program is skills building, not "stress challenge." Students who choose a wilderness activity as their sports option learn the technical aspects of their activity. They also explore such important topics as minimum impact travel, first aid, navigation, orienteering, trip planning, and natural history. Team building and leadership are important components of the program. It is the goal that students will develop skills in the outdoors that they can use throughout their lives.

During the winter sports term, students choose among ski/snowboard program options that include Alpine, cross-country, and back-country skiing as well as a freeride program. The recreational ski program includes Nordic skiing, backcountry skiing, Alpine skiing, and snowboarding. Students snowboard and ski at nearby Loon Mountain at least four afternoons per week.

In 2002, the School opened a new, state-of-the-art indoor climbing wall as part of an indoor sports center outfitted with Nautilus, free weights, aerobic equipment, and running track.

EXTRACURRICULAR OPPORTUNITIES
Extracurricular opportunities vary from year to year depending upon the interests of the student body and faculty. The yearbook, *The Pendulum*, is designed and produced by students. Students interested in the performing arts are given the opportunity to perform in the chorus and theater productions. A strong cultural events series brings professional performers and artists to the School, with a focus on international song and dance. Occasionally, the White Mountain School offers special trips during vacations or the summer with an outdoor or educational focus.

The White Mountain School has received local, state, and national recognition for its Community Service Program. It has two components: local service opportunities and Community Service Odysseys, which have taken place recently in Costa Rica, the Dominican Republic, Nicaragua, and Peru. Student participate in on-campus community service through the Work Jobs program and the Farm and Forest Crew.

DAILY LIFE
Breakfast begins at 7 a.m. There is an all-School morning meeting at 7:45 for announcements, a reading, and a short period of quiet reflection. Classes begin at 8:05. The academic day is based on a rotating block schedule. Each class meets three times per week, with two long blocks weekly to allow student project work, films, outdoor activities, or labs to take place without interruption. A special block is incorporated into each day's schedule, allowing students to meet with faculty members for extra assistance. After classes, all students must participate in afternoon sports or activities for approximately 2 hours. Dinner is served at 6 p.m. Supervised study time is set aside for all students from 7:30 to 9:30 p.m. Sundays through Thursdays during which time the library and computer lab are open for student use. Lights out in the dorms is 11.

WEEKEND LIFE
Activities are planned by faculty and students, and include dances, intramural games, board game nights, mock casino nights, bonfires, cider making, theater rehearsals, and art workshops. Studios in the art wing are usually open. Trips are made to Dartmouth College, Boston, Portland, Burlington, or Montreal for a variety of cultural and sporting events. Students can also go to nearby Littleton to shop, have lunch, or attend the movies. On weekends, transportation is provided to take students to religious services. There is a network of trails on campus available for hiking, running, biking, and cross-country skiing. Overnight wilderness trips are usually offered twice a month. Students are permitted to take weekends or overnights away from campus if they have parental permission and all academic and community responsibilities have been met.

COSTS AND FINANCIAL AID
Tuition and room and board for 2005–06 are $35,500. Day student tuition is $15,300. A student expense account is required in the amount of $1500. The Learning Assistance Program and the ESL Program each have separate tuition fees.

Approximately 43 percent of the students receive financial aid. Eligibility is based on need as established by the School and Student Service for Financial Aid. Academic achievement, citizenship, and future promise are also taken into consideration when awards are made.

In keeping with the tradition of the School, an Episcopal Woman's Scholarship is offered annually to a deserving young woman. Please contact the School for more information regarding WMS scholarship applications and deadlines.

ADMISSIONS INFORMATION
The White Mountain School seeks to admit students who wish to challenge themselves and to enrich and broaden their educational experience by becoming involved in the academic, cocurricular, creative, and personal opportunities at WMS. Admissions candidates should have above average to high average ability and the intellectual curiosity and motivation needed to perform college-preparatory work. Students come from varying geographical, cultural and economic backgrounds, have diverse personal strengths, and contribute a variety of interests and talents to the School community.

To complete the application process, the student needs to submit the application form and fee, references, a writing sample, and an official transcript of school records. The SSAT is requested. Admissions staff members look forward to meeting and getting to know prospective students and their families through the campus visit and interview. The campus is in an area of exceptional beauty. Admission candidates are expected to visit the campus. Telephone interviews can be arranged for overseas candidates.

APPLICATION TIMETABLE
Inquiries are always welcome. Candidates are encouraged to apply by February 1. The application fee is $50. Students who submit their applications by February 1 are notified by March 10. Students who are accepted by March are requested to respond by April 10. Applications that are made after the deadline will be considered on a rolling basis as space permits. During the spring and summer a "No Wait" admissions option is available to candidates who submit their applications and materials for review prior to the interview.

ADMISSIONS CORRESPONDENCE
Amy Broberg
Director of Admissions
The White Mountain School
371 West Farm Road
Bethlehem, New Hampshire 03574

Phone: 603-444-2928
    800-545-7813 (toll free)
Fax: 603-444-5568
E-mail: admissions@whitemountain.org
Web site: http://www.whitemountain.org

WILBRAHAM & MONSON ACADEMY

Wilbraham, Massachusetts

Type: Coeducational boarding and day college-preparatory
Grades: 6–PG: Middle School, 6–8 (day only); Upper School, 9–12; postgraduate year
Enrollment: School total: 315; Upper School: 268
Head of School: Rodney J. LaBrecque

THE SCHOOL

Wilbraham & Monson Academy (WMA) was established by the merger of two early-nineteenth-century academies: Monson Academy, founded in 1804, and Wesleyan (Wilbraham) Academy, founded in 1817 in South Newmarket, New Hampshire. Wesleyan Academy was relocated to Wilbraham in 1825. The two academies merged in 1971.

The Academy is in the center of the town of Wilbraham, located in southwestern Massachusetts, 7 miles east of Springfield. It occupies 300 acres of what was formerly rich farmland and wooded hillsides. The town itself, incorporated in 1763, is essentially suburban, though many residents commute to nearby Springfield and Hartford, Connecticut.

Among the ten area colleges are Smith, Amherst, Hampshire, Mount Holyoke, and the University of Massachusetts. Students and faculty members take advantage of the cultural events held on those campuses.

A Board of Trustees is the governing body. Its annual operating budget is $8,664,415, and its endowment is currently valued at $4.2 million. An Annual Giving Program nets the Academy approximately $1 million yearly. There are approximately 6,000 alumni.

Wilbraham & Monson Academy is accredited by the New England Association of Schools and Colleges. Its memberships include the Cum Laude Society, the Independent School Association of Massachusetts, the National Association of Independent Schools, the New England Association of Schools and Colleges, the College Board, the Secondary School Admission Test Board, and the National Association for College Admission Counseling.

ACADEMIC PROGRAMS

The Academy requires 57 credits for graduation. Departmental requirements include 12 credits in English; 9 credits in math (algebra I, geometry, and algebra II); 6 credits in history, including 1 year of U.S. history; 6 credits of laboratory science; 6 credits in languages, with two years of the same language; 3 credits in the fine and performing arts, including art and music; and 15 additional credits in any discipline.

Honors-level courses are available in all departments. Advanced Placement courses are available in art, biology, calculus, chemistry, English, economics, environmental science, European history, French, Latin, music, Spanish, statistics, and U.S. history. All students are required to take five courses per trimester. A full staff of learning consultants and instructors is available for students with diagnosed learning differences. All students with academic difficulties are assigned to the directed study program, and all students observe study hours in the

evening. Advanced ESL and a U.S. history course are available to international students needing language support.

The Center for Entrepreneurial & Global Studies (CEGS) is a program designed to give students a comprehensive introduction to the world of global economics, entrepreneurship, and finance. The CEGS faculty uses a variety of teaching methods, including case studies and round-table discussion facilitated by a Harkness table. Frequent visitors and guest lecturers from the business and financial world enhance the curriculum. Moreover, students have the opportunity to travel to financial centers in Boston and New York during the school year and to international financial capitals such as Bangkok and Brussels in the summer.

In place of a study hall system, the Academy's Directed Study encourages students to seek help from their teachers and peer tutors, both during the day and in the evening. Faculty members in each discipline are available to students at designated times during the day in addition to the help period and at a central location in the evening from 7:30 to 9:30. All students are encouraged to use the system. Students who are experiencing difficulty in a particular course may be assigned to a specific number of Directed Study sessions for clarification or reinforcement of concepts.

The average class has 12–15 students. The student-teacher ratio is 7:1. The grading system uses A to F (failing) with pluses and minuses. Reports with teachers' comments are sent to parents six times a year. Three trimesters of approximately eleven weeks each make up the school year.

FACULTY AND ADVISERS

There are 52 full- and part-time faculty members (27 men and 25 women). Sixty percent of the faculty members hold advanced degrees. Approximately 64 percent of the faculty members live on the campus.

Rodney J. LaBrecque was appointed Head of School in 2002. He holds a B.A. and M.A. from Clark University. He was a Klingenstein Fellow in 1982 and is the author of *Effective Department and Team Leaders: A Practical Guide.*

In selecting its faculty, the Academy seeks men and women who are able to demonstrate full mastery of their subject, are committed to careers in secondary education, and are truly interested in the intellectual and social development of young people. The Academy assists with continuing education for its faculty. In addition to teaching, faculty members supervise dormitories, coach, and serve as advisers.

COLLEGE PLACEMENT

A college counseling staff assists students throughout the college selection process. More than 100

college admission officers visit the campus each year. Formal parental involvement in the college selection process begins in the winter of a student's junior year.

Eighty-three of the 84 graduates in 2005 are currently attending college. Nearly sixty colleges and universities are represented, including Assumption, Babson, Bates, Boston University, Brandeis, Colgate, George Washington, Rensselaer, Rochester, Smith, and Trinity.

STUDENT BODY AND CONDUCT

The 2005–06 student body was composed of 72 day boys, 96 boarding boys, 63 day girls, and 37 boarding girls in grades 9 through 12 and the postgraduate year. There were 47 students in the Blake Middle School. Eleven states and sixteen countries were represented in the enrollment. Both of the original schools, Wilbraham Academy and Monson Academy, are ethnically and socioeconomically diverse. The first Chinese students and, later, the first Japanese and Thai students, to study in America studied at the Academy. That tradition continues in the school today.

It is the assumption of the Academy that the students it serves are willing to be accountable for their own education. Students are given responsibilities and personal freedom commensurate with their level of maturity. The social expectations are designed to foster a harmonious community.

ACADEMIC FACILITIES

There are five major academic buildings. Old Academy (1824) houses classrooms for English and world languages. Some rooms are furnished as traditional classrooms, others as seminar rooms. Fisk Hall (1851) contains the school theater and classrooms for mathematics and history. Binney Fine Arts Center (1857), which was fully renovated in 1991, houses the art department. Binney contains several studios for the visual arts, a photography studio, and an art gallery. Music classes are held in the Pratt Room in Rich Hall. Mattern Science Center (1972) contains classrooms and science laboratories. Nearby are Gill Memorial Library (20,000 volumes, research computers with a variety of databases, a video/DVD collection, and a student-run writing center) and Alumni Memorial Chapel. Gill Memorial Library has automated its catalog to enable students and faculty and staff members to better access the collection. Blake Middle School and a spacious campus center were completed in 1997.

BOARDING AND GENERAL FACILITIES

The Academy has three dormitories that are capable of housing students in single and double rooms. In addition, there are six homes along Main Street that provide faculty housing. Watts

House is a guest facility with accommodations for up to 10 guests. Faculty members and their families live in the dormitories as well. Normally, there are 10 students under the supervision of a single faculty member. The Dean assigns student rooms on the basis of student choice. All students take their meals cafeteria-style in Lak Dining Hall; a snack bar is located in the campus center. Health Services (Benton House) is staffed by 3 registered nurses. There is a medical doctor on call, and a psychologist is available for scheduled appointments.

ATHLETICS

The first principal of the Academy, Wilbur Fisk, believed that physical exercise is essential to healthy growth, and, from the outset, the Academy has required all students to participate in some form of activity. There are varsity programs in baseball, basketball, cross-country, field hockey, football, golf, lacrosse, riflery, skiing, soccer, softball, swimming, tennis, track and field, volleyball, water polo, and wrestling. Students who do not qualify for varsity teams may participate in junior varsity sports.

The Greenhalgh Athletic Center contains three basketball/volleyball courts and a fitness center. Attached to the center is Cowdrey Memorial Pool. The outdoor athletics facilities include one football field, one football practice field, six soccer fields, two baseball diamonds, one softball field, and nine tennis courts.

EXTRACURRICULAR OPPORTUNITIES

The school's proximity to ten colleges and universities makes a variety of extracurricular events easily available. In addition, the Director of Student Activities, under the guidance of the Student Activities Board, arranges numerous outings, such as theater and concerts, professional sports competitions, lectures and cultural events, hiking, camping, and numerous outdoor adventures as well as sightseeing tours of New York and Boston. On campus, students participate in a wide variety of extracurricular activities, including the newspaper and yearbook; theater, outing, and music clubs; student government; RISE; and others determined by student interest.

DAILY LIFE

Classes are held five days a week; Wednesday is a half day. Eight class periods meet for 40 to 75 minutes each. The academic day begins at 7:45 a.m. and concludes at 3 p.m. Athletics take place from 3:30 to 5:45. The period from 7:30 to 9:30 is reserved for study.

WEEKEND LIFE

The weekend begins after the last scheduled activity on Friday and concludes at 7 p.m. on Sunday. The Head Dorm Parent and the student's adviser sign weekend permissions, which are then approved by the Deans Office.

COSTS AND FINANCIAL AID

Tuition, room, and board at Wilbraham & Monson Academy for 2005–06 were $34,600 for Upper School boarding students; tuition was $22,250 for Upper School day students. Tuition for the Middle School was $19,060 (day students only; there are no Middle School boarders). Tuition bills must be paid before a student is allowed to register for the semester. All students make an enrollment deposit of $1500 or 10 percent of net tuition, which is deducted from the final payment.

For 2005–06, nearly $1.8 million in grants and loans was awarded in financial aid to 33 percent of the student body. Awards are need based, as determined by the School and Student Service for Financial Aid and WMA's policy and procedures.

The Bicentennial Scholars Program is a merit-based scholarship program designed to recognize and bring together students of outstanding potential to live and learn together at the Academy. Each year, multiple $15,000 scholarships are awarded to students entering the Upper School. Beyond receiving a monetary award, the Bicentennial Scholars enjoy an extensive extracurricular program of visiting museums and attending lectures designed to expand their horizons and enrich their lives.

ADMISSIONS INFORMATION

The Committee on Admission seeks young men and women of good character who are motivated to do well. Previous school performance and achievement are considered in the admission judgment, but character is most important.

Applicants for admission to grades 6, 7, and 8 are administered an in-house Blake Middle School admission test. Grades 9–11 must present the results of the SSAT or WISC. Candidates for grade 12 and the postgraduate program should have taken the SAT. In addition, applicants are required to have a personal interview with a member of the Admission Office.

APPLICATION TIMETABLE

An initial inquiry is always welcome. Interviews may be scheduled on weekdays from 7:45 a.m. to 2:15 p.m. The application deadline is February 1. The completed application form must be accompanied by a nonrefundable fee of $50 ($100 for international students). Beginning March 10, the school notifies applicants of admission decisions as soon as each candidate's file is completed. Applications received after the February 1 deadline are considered on a rolling admission basis.

ADMISSIONS CORRESPONDENCE

Christopher Moore, Director of Admission
Wilbraham & Monson Academy
423 Main Street
Wilbraham, Massachusetts 01095
Phone: 413-596-6811
Fax: 413-599-1749
E-mail: admission@WMAnet.org
Web site: http://WMAcademy.org

THE WILLIAMS SCHOOL
New London, Connecticut

The Williams School

Type: Coeducational day college-preparatory school
Grades: 7–12
Enrollment: School total: 330
Head of School: Charlotte Rea

THE SCHOOL

The opening of school in September 2005 marked the 114th birthday of The Williams School. It was founded by Harriet Peck Williams, who left a piece of land and her estate to endow a school "for the promotion and advancement of female education" in memory of her son Thomas H. Williams, a New London whaling merchant. In 1891, Williams Memorial Institute, as the School is legally named, opened with 150 students on Broad Street in New London.

Now located on the Connecticut College campus, The Williams School is celebrating its fiftieth anniversary on campus. The School is independent of the college but maintains close ties. Williams students have access to the college library and playing fields, and they are invited to participate in programs at the college whenever appropriate. Qualified seniors may also take courses at the college.

Williams strives to maintain close ties with the city of New London, as well as the rest of southern Connecticut, connecting students to as many cultural, historical, and educational sources as possible: Mystic Seaport, Garde Arts Center, Eugene O'Neill Memorial Theatre Center, and the U.S. Coast Guard Academy.

Williams is accredited by or is a member of the following organizations: the National Association of Independent Schools, the Connecticut Association of Independent Schools, New England League of Middle Schools, National Association of College Admission Counselors, New England Association of College Admission Counselors, Cum Laude Society, and the College Board.

ACADEMIC PROGRAMS

The school year consists of two semesters, each two quarters in length. It begins in late August and ends in early June. Teachers assess the students by letter grade and written comment every quarter and set examinations at the end of each semester. Parent conferences are also held. The calendar includes a Thanksgiving recess, a two-week vacation in winter and spring, and observances of national holidays. A strong advising program enables students to meet twice a week on an informal basis to discuss matters of social, academic, or personal concern.

The division between the Middle and the Upper School is more than a classification according to grade. The seventh- and eighth-grade curriculum is based on a middle school philosophy of the developmental needs and learning styles of younger students. The Upper School follows a traditional college-preparatory program that increases its demands throughout the four years. Students with departmental approval may gain college credit by taking Advanced Placement courses and examinations in certain subjects.

In May, each senior works on a Senior Project with the help of a faculty adviser. Oral and written presentations of project results are required for graduation.

The Williams School chapter of the Cum Laude Society, a national honor society, inducts the top 20 percent of the senior class into its membership.

To receive a diploma from the Williams School, a student must have earned a minimum of 20 credits in the college-preparatory courses: 4 credits in English, mathematics, and foreign language; 2 credits in history and laboratory science; 1 in fine arts; and 3 in electives.

A student is eligible for graduation after successfully fulfilling the Upper School minimum academic requirements, maintaining a C- or better average during the senior year, and completing an approved Senior Project. A full academic program in the senior year is also a requirement for graduation.

FACULTY AND ADVISERS

The 42 faculty members (20 women and 22 men) hold forty-two baccalaureate degrees, twenty-nine master's degrees, and three doctoral degrees. Faculty members also serve as advisers. The Williams School believes that the heart of education lies in a close relationship between students and faculty members. To this end, the School relies on an adviser system to make sure that every student has at least 1 faculty member to turn to for advice, reassurance, and friendship. Students meet weekly with their faculty adviser.

COLLEGE PLACEMENT

The Williams School has 2 full-time college counselors on its staff. The college placement program formally begins in the second semester of the junior year. An eleventh-grade College Night presents parents and juniors with an overview of the admission process, college visits, and interviews. The twelfth-grade College Night takes place in September and deals with the actual mechanics of the college admission process. The college adviser, who is also available to parents, meets frequently with juniors and seniors to discuss procedures and plans.

Virtually 100 percent of Williams' graduates go on to four-year colleges. The most recent graduates have attended such colleges and universities as Amherst, Boston College, Brown, Colby, Georgetown, Harvard, MIT, Princeton, Tufts, Wheaton, Williams, Yale, and the Universities of Connecticut and Vermont.

STUDENT BODY AND CONDUCT

The Williams School draws from forty nearby communities. There are currently 169 girls and 161 boys. The School thrives on the diversity of its students and families, who bring to the School community a breadth of experience and cultural backgrounds.

ACADEMIC FACILITIES

In September of 2002, Williams opened a new math and science wing consisting of eight new classrooms, five state-of-the-art laboratories for science, a computer lab, a digital arts lab, and a practice gymnasium. In addition, the wing houses administrative offices and additional faculty work space.

ATHLETICS

A 23-acre parcel of land 1 mile from the campus is home to The Williams School Athletic Complex. Physical education and interscholastic sports are an integral part of the Williams School educational experience. These programs assist in the development of each student through participation in organized physical activities and team sports. The interscholastic program for boys includes baseball, basketball, cross-country, indoor soccer, lacrosse, sailing, soccer, swimming, and tennis. Girls can choose from basketball, cross-country, field hockey, indoor soccer, sailing, softball, swimming, and tennis.

EXTRACURRICULAR OPPORTUNITIES

Spring and summer trips are planned on a yearly basis to such countries as Spain, France, and Greece. The School encourages students to participate in exchange programs such as AFS, NACEL, and others.

An important part of the Williams mission is to make students aware of the world beyond its walls and to help students develop a habit of service to the larger community. Through the Multicultural Club, Service Committee, and other organizations and clubs, students become more involved in meeting the local needs of their community. Students provide service to such organizations as CROP Walk, Habitat for Humanity, and local convalescent homes and soup kitchens.

Four afternoons a week, Spanish Club members go to El Centro in New London to tutor first, second, and third graders who are currently in a bilingual program, with the aim of mainstreaming them into an all-English program.

Important traditional events include fall and spring plays, Winterfest, and Compchorea. Students publish *Bending Bridges*, Williams' literary magazine, twice a year. *Legenda*, the Williams yearbook, depicts School life in photographs. Seniors produce the yearbook and finance it with advertisements.

DAILY LIFE

A day at The Williams School begins at 8 a.m. and ends at 3:25 p.m. Classes meet on a seven-day rotation schedule. Each day contains

nine periods that are approximately 45 minutes long. There is a break in classes at midmorning for assemblies and a snack. A hot lunch is served during the course of two periods from 11:30 a.m. to 1 p.m. The ninth period of the day is used for extra help from teachers or for club meetings. All athletic events and practices are scheduled after dismissal at 3:25 p.m.

COSTS AND FINANCIAL AID

The 2005–06 tuition for all grades was $19,000. Additional costs include a lunch program, transportation, books, and tuition insurance. A $1500 deposit is due upon enrollment. Payment plans are available through the School's business office. Financial assistance is based on need. All applicants are required to complete the School and Student Service for Financial Aid report, which is available through the admission office in December before the school year. In 2005–06, students received aid totaling more than $800,000.

ADMISSIONS INFORMATION

Williams seeks students who are academically able and intellectually curious, traits that enable them to take advantage of a challenging college-preparatory curriculum. In order to apply to Williams, students and their families should complete an application form and submit it with a $50 application fee. Upon receipt of the application, the School forwards a request for a transcript and two teacher recommendation forms.

A campus visit with the candidate and parent(s) is required. The visit is arranged once the School has received the application form. Applicants are invited to spend an entire day at the School, visiting classes and talking with students. Parents meet with the Director of Admission to discuss information about the Williams School program. Appointments for the visit may be arranged by calling the Admission Coordinator at the number below.

The admission process includes SSAT testing. Applicants can register for the SSAT at http://www.ssat.org. The Williams School code is 8220.

APPLICATION TIMETABLE

The application deadline is January 31. Applications are processed by the admission committee during February. All applicants are notified by mail no later than March 10. Financial aid applications are due by February 15; all awards are processed by April 15. Enrollment contracts are due by April 1.

ADMISSIONS CORRESPONDENCE

Gayle A. Holt, Director of Admission and
    Financial Aid
The Williams School
182 Mohegan Avenue
New London, Connecticut 06320-4110

Phone: 860-439-2789
E-mail: gholt@williamsschool.org

Bea Fratoni, Admission Office Coordinator
The Williams School
182 Mohegan Ave.
New London, Connecticut 06320-4110
Phone: 860-439-2756
Fax: 860-439-2796
Web site: http://www.williamsschool.org

THE WILLISTON NORTHAMPTON SCHOOL

Easthampton, Massachusetts

Type: Coeducational boarding and day college-preparatory school
Grades: 7–PG: Middle School, 7–8; Upper School, 9–12, postgraduate year
Enrollment: School total: 570; Upper School: 490
Head of School: Brian R. Wright, Headmaster

THE SCHOOL

Named in 1991 by the U.S. Department of Education as an Exemplary Secondary School as part of its Blue Ribbon Schools Program, Williston Northampton has a long history of excellence.

Williston Seminary was founded in 1841 by Samuel and Emily Williston. Initially coeducational, Williston Seminary later became a college-preparatory school for boys. The Willistons amassed a great fortune from the production of cloth-covered buttons and the manufacture of rubber webbing and thread. They also supported the local colleges both financially and personally.

Eighty-three years later, in 1924, Sarah B. Whitaker and Dorothy M. Bement founded the academic Northampton School for Girls.

In 1971, the two schools merged to form Williston Northampton, a coeducational school offering a strong secondary education to prepare interested students for the rigorous academic programs of colleges today and the demands and complexities in life afterward.

The School is located on 100 acres in the heart of the Pioneer Valley a few miles from the base of Mount Tom, 85 miles west of Boston, and 150 miles north of New York. Within a 15-mile radius are Smith, Mount Holyoke, Hampshire, and Amherst colleges and the University of Massachusetts.

A self-perpetuating 25-member Board of Trustees governs the School, which is a nonprofit institution. The current endowment is estimated at $32 million. The School's alumni body of 8,000 contributed more than $1 million in Annual Giving last year.

Williston Northampton is accredited by the New England Association of Schools and Colleges and is affiliated with the National Association of Independent Schools, the Association of Independent Schools of New England, the College Board, the School and College Conference on English, the Art Association of New England Preparatory Schools, and the Council for Advancement and Support of Education.

ACADEMIC PROGRAMS

A strong and varied academic program is the heart of the School. To strengthen, expand, and encourage students' skills and interests in the essential disciplines are the goals of the program. Care is taken to place each student in the courses and sections most appropriate to his or her abilities. A student may enroll in Honors English while working in an average section of math. Small classes of 10 to 15, which enable instructors to know each student's abilities, and the flexibility of the program make it possible for the School to structure the best program for every student.

The faculty also feels strongly that it is important for each student to experience as many academic and creative disciplines as possible so that, before having to make decisions concerning career goals, he or she will have sampled many alternatives. Therefore, Williston Northampton expects each of its students not only to satisfy the minimum basic requirements of 4 years of English, 3 years of math, 2 of science, 2 of a foreign language, and 2 in the social sciences but also to select two semester courses from the area of fine arts and one semester course from the area of religious and philosophical studies. Fifteen AP classes are available every year. Qualified students may elect to complete extra work in consultation with the teacher to prepare to take the Advanced Placement exam in two additional subject areas.

Most students choose to complete work beyond the basic requirements established by each department. In order to graduate, a student at Williston Northampton must have earned 19 academic credits (a 1-year course equals 1 credit) in grades 9–12 and must pass all courses taken during the senior year. Diploma requirements also include regular participation in the athletics program, satisfactory completion of the Senior Project for those who elect to do one, enrollment at Williston Northampton throughout the senior year, and satisfactory citizenship.

The passing and college-recommending grade at Williston Northampton is 60. Students attaining honor grades are recognized at the end of each term. The highest honor is election to the Cum Laude Society.

FACULTY AND ADVISERS

The Williston Northampton School teaching faculty numbers 82 full-time members—43 men and 39 women. Fifty-three hold master's degrees, and 4 have earned Ph.D.'s. Thirty live in dorms. The School has established programs and staff members to counsel students about academic work, personal problems, class functions, and future educational goals and opportunities. Each boarding student has a faculty adviser who is also a dorm parent and may be easily consulted on academic or personal matters. The Dean of Students, Chaplain, and Academic Dean can be consulted as the need arises. All students are encouraged to participate in a series of health workshops directed by the Health Services staff, which focuses on issues of health and personal decision making. The School also employs the services of professional counselors for those who find they require additional personal counseling.

Brian R. Wright was appointed Headmaster in 1999. Dr. Wright graduated magna cum laude and Phi Beta Kappa from Occidental College and earned his master's degree and doctorate in politics from Princeton University. He was Principal at Windward Preparatory School in Kailua, Hawaii; Head of Lower School at The Wardlaw-Hartridge School in New Jersey; Direc-tor of the Upper School at Packer Collegiate Institute in Brooklyn; Headmaster at The Birch Wathen School in New York; and Head at the Potomac School in McLean, Virginia, from 1992 until his appointment at Williston Northampton.

COLLEGE PLACEMENT

A thorough college counseling program is provided for each student making postsecondary educational plans. Two full-time counselors coordinate the program. From the beginning, the counseling process draws in both parents and students to establish a dialogue between the School and the family. During the junior year, the counselor and members of the faculty meet with students to acquaint them with standardized test taking, financial aid, roles and functions of college officials, and campus life-styles.

Of the 126 members of the class of 2005, 124 (98 percent) are attending a college or university. Eighty-four percent of the students were accepted at their first- or second-choice college. Two or more graduates are attending Brown, Carnegie Mellon, Drew, George Washington, Lehigh, Mount Holyoke, NYU, Saint Lawrence, Smith, Tufts, and the Universities of Massachusetts Amherst and Vermont.

STUDENT BODY AND CONDUCT

Most students enter Williston during the freshman or sophomore year. In 2005–06, grade 9 had 93 members (47 boys, 46 girls), of whom 52 were day students. Grade 10 had 126 members (60 boys, 66 girls), of whom 55 were day students. Grade 11 had 121 members (62 boys, 59 girls), of whom 43 were day students. Grade 12 had 130 members (58 boys, 72 girls), of whom 51 were day students. There were 20 postgraduate students. Eighteen percent of the students were students of color. Students came from twenty-seven states and twenty countries.

The regulations of the School have evolved from experience and lengthy discussion. They provide clear-cut guidelines for everyone living in the School community. It is expected that both the spirit and the letter of these regulations as described in the *Student Handbook*, which is sent to every enrolling student and is also available upon request, will be followed.

Students who are reported to have violated School rules and regulations meet with the Discipline Committee, made up of faculty and student representatives. The committee's decisions and recommendations are reviewed by the Headmaster, who makes the final decision in disciplinary matters.

ACADEMIC FACILITIES

The campus is located on approximately 100 acres. The School's thirty-eight buildings include the Reed Campus Center, the science building, the theater, the Schoolhouse, the library, the

chapel, and the Middle School building. The Williston Theatre reopened in 1995 after suffering fire damage in 1994. The internal renovation of the Schoolhouse (the major classroom building) was completed in 1984. Renovations to the old gymnasium to create a new Campus Center that includes music and fine arts classrooms were completed in 1996. The Technology and Student Publications Center, the Science Tech Lab, the library, and the math floor house four student computer labs.

BOARDING AND GENERAL FACILITIES

The buildings on campus include the Headmaster's home, the administration buildings, the chapel, the dining hall, six dormitories with facilities for 25 to 50 students, five residence houses with boarding facilities for 8 to 12 students, and faculty homes. Ford Hall, which houses 50 boys, received a million-dollar renovation in 1999, adding sun-splashed common rooms and other enhancements. All dorm rooms are wired into the campus computer network and have voice mail.

Each housing unit is supervised by resident faculty houseparents to create an environment conducive to academic achievement and a warm and pleasant home atmosphere.

ATHLETICS

Sports are an integral part of Williston Northampton life, whether interscholastic or recreational. The School requires that each student be involved in the athletics program in each of the three sports seasons. The athletics department instills the principles of fair play, good sportsmanship, teamwork, and respect for rules and authority. Most of the academic faculty members also coach team sports, and the Director of Athletics oversees the program.

In general, seventh to tenth graders participate in the basic athletics program, while older students have additional options. Interscholastic teams for girls include cross-country, field hockey, soccer, and volleyball in the fall; basketball, ice hockey, skiing, squash, swimming and diving, and wrestling in the winter; and golf, lacrosse, softball, tennis, track, and water polo in the spring. For these periods, boys may elect cross-country, football, soccer, or water polo; basketball, ice hockey, skiing, squash, swimming and diving, or wrestling; and baseball, golf, lacrosse, tennis, or track. Horseback riding at a nearby stable and modern dance are available

every season. Fitness training, aerobics, and volleyball are choices open to upperclass students.

Excellent facilities and equipment are available. An athletic center contains two basketball courts, a six-lane pool, five squash courts, a weight room and fitness center, and a wrestling room. Other facilities include a lighted, synthetic-surface football/lacrosse field, a dance studio, an indoor skating facility, ten clay and five composition tennis courts, a running track, more than 30 acres of playing fields, and a 3.4-mile cross-country course. There are several golf courses in the Easthampton area.

EXTRACURRICULAR OPPORTUNITIES

The countryside offers excellent climbing, biking, and skiing opportunities, and the proximity of five colleges provides a culturally rich environment of fine museums, libraries, and theater programs as well. The cities of Northampton and Springfield, Massachusetts, and Hartford, Connecticut, are near enough so that concerts and activities there are as readily available as those at the colleges.

DAILY LIFE

The academic day runs from 8 a.m. until 2:30 p.m. on Monday, Tuesday, Thursday, and Friday and until 12 noon on Wednesday. Classes are held every other Saturday morning as well. Students take five courses in a six-period schedule, with classes lasting 50 or 70 minutes, depending on the day. All-School assemblies for announcements and special presentations are held once each week. Sports are scheduled from the end of the class day until dinnertime. Except for theme-based formal dinners, most meals are served buffet-style. A free period from 6:40 to 8 is frequently used for meetings of extracurricular organizations, library work, theater or music rehearsals, visiting between dormitories, or simply relaxing. Supervised evening study hours run from 8 to 10 p.m. All students are checked into the dorms at 10 by the dorm faculty.

WEEKEND LIFE

While the vast majority of students remain on campus, weekends at home or at the home of a friend are permitted with parental approval after all school obligations have been met. The Student Activities Director and the students on the Activity Committee organize a variety of weekly activities, and students may take advantage of the events listed in the Five-College Calendar. Students travel off campus for such programs as

college and professional athletics contests, films, concerts, plays, dance performances, and rock concerts and to go skiing in Vermont. The many on-campus activities include dances and coffeehouse entertainment, talent shows, lectures by invited speakers, and a film series.

SUMMER PROGRAMS

During the summer, the School offers an intensive four-week Spanish program in Mexico, as well hosting many outside camps, which offer theater, music, and athletics on the campus.

COSTS AND FINANCIAL AID

Tuition for boarders for 2005–06 was $34,500; for day students, it was $24,500. Additional expenses include books, insurance, laundry, and other incidental expenses. Tuition payment and insurance plans are recommended upon request.

Financial aid is awarded on the basis of need to approximately 40 percent of the student body. The grants totaled $3 million for 2005–06. Students also have an opportunity to participate in a work-grant program.

ADMISSIONS INFORMATION

Williston Northampton seeks students who are interested in their own education and who can show solid academic performance. Students should also be positive, involved, caring contributors to life at the School. Admission is based upon an evaluation of these traits, a personal interview, and satisfactory scores on the SSAT. For 2005–06, 140 new students were enrolled in the Upper School.

APPLICATION TIMETABLE

The fall or winter prior to a candidate's prospective admission is usually the best time for a visit, which includes a student-guided tour of the School and an interview. The Admission Office is open Monday through Friday, from 8 a.m. to 4:30 p.m., and on some Saturday mornings.

An application for admission should be submitted by February 1 along with a nonrefundable fee of $40. The School abides by the March 10 notification date. After that date, a rolling admission plan is in effect.

ADMISSIONS CORRESPONDENCE

Ann C. Pickrell, Director of Admission
The Williston Northampton School
19 Payson Avenue
Easthampton, Massachusetts 01027

Phone: 413-529-3241
Fax: 413-527-9494
E-mail: admissions@williston.com
Web site: http://www.williston.com

THE WINCHENDON SCHOOL

Winchendon, Massachusetts

Type: Coeducational boarding and day college-preparatory school
Grades: 8–12, postgraduate year
Enrollment: 220
Head of School: J. William LaBelle, Headmaster

THE SCHOOL

The Winchendon School was founded in 1926 in Dexter, Maine, by Lloyd H. Hatch, whose purpose was "to create a structured and traditional atmosphere for 'good' underachievers where they may grow academically, physically, socially, and spiritually." The School was later located in Newport, Rhode Island, before moving to Winchendon in 1961. Girls were first admitted in 1973. The environment of the School remains structured, and rules are enforced sensibly. The educational philosophy of the School is conservative. Students work hard and are held accountable for their actions. The curriculum is traditional and is designed to prepare students of average to above-average ability to be successful in college, yet it is also flexible. Skills deficiencies, learning gaps, and mild learning disabilities are remediated. Strengths are challenged, and interests are developed.

Located in north-central Massachusetts in the foothills of the Monadnock Mountains, the 350-acre campus is 20 miles from Keene, New Hampshire; 35 miles from Worcester; and 65 miles from Boston. The region is noted for its skiing facilities and for its many lakes. Proximity to Boston makes that city's cultural, entertainment, and commercial resources readily available.

A nonprofit institution, the School is governed by a 17-member Board of Trustees. Most of the trustees are alumni, parents of students, and parents of alumni. The operating budget for 2005–06 exceeded $9 million. The value of the physical plant and equipment has been assessed at $25 million.

The Winchendon School is accredited by the New England Association of Schools and Colleges. It holds memberships in the Association of Independent Schools of New England, the National Association of Independent Schools, the National Honor Society, the Orton Society, and Boarding Schools.

ACADEMIC PROGRAMS

Although the School seeks to prepare its students for college-level study, the academic program is intended to provide a valuable educational experience in its own right. By using small classes, a personalized teaching approach, and a flexible structure of guidance and support, the School endeavors to create and stimulate students' interest in learning and to teach them that they are the most valuable contributors to their own education.

On the basis of its experience and capabilities in evaluating student progress and its careful analysis of all pertinent data on each student, the School makes decisions concerning each student's grade level, credit status, course requirements, and assignments.

Eighteen units, including 4 of English, 4 of mathematics, 3 of social studies (including 1 of

U.S. history), and 2 of laboratory sciences, are required for graduation. A unit is equal to one year of completed course work. French, Spanish, and Latin are offered but are not required.

Students attend classes ranging in size from 3 to 7 students each. Math and English classes are usually limited to 6 students each. Such class size allows for individualization. Learning differences can be acknowledged, needs can be addressed, and abilities can be challenged.

The grading system—the traditional A, B, C, D (supplemented by pluses and minuses), and F—is used to give constant guidance and reinforcement to the student. Each student is graded daily in each course. These daily grade slips are distributed each night to a boarding student's dorm parent, who then reviews the grades with the student during the 2-hour evening study period. Reports are mailed to parents each week so that they are equally aware of their child's progress. While academic achievement is rewarded with Honor Roll status and privileges, effort is also encouraged and rewarded in academic, athletic, and community service endeavors.

Remediation of academic deficiencies and the teaching of study skills are done within the context of each course. Instructors are trained to develop the process of learning along with the content of their courses. This "mainstream" approach is extremely effective since the study skills are immediately made relevant to the material of the course.

Tutorial assistance is available daily to assist students having difficulty with particular assignments or concepts.

FACULTY AND ADVISERS

Each member of the staff is a trained, caring, and dedicated teacher who can work well with students who need an individualized approach to education. In 2004–05, the teaching staff consisted of 20 men and 13 women. All of the dormitory parenting and athletics coaching are done by the academic staff.

J. William LaBelle was appointed Headmaster in 1988. Mr. LaBelle earned his B.S. and M.S. degrees from the University of Massachusetts at Amherst and his M.Ed. degree from Bridgewater State College. He began his career in education at Trinity-Pawling School in 1958. In 1973, he moved to Wilbraham & Monson Academy, where he served as Associate Headmaster and Dean of the Academy.

COLLEGE PLACEMENT

The college counselors, working closely with parents and staff, assist all students in selecting appropriate colleges. Representatives of various colleges visit the School, and there is a comprehensive collection of college catalogs and videos in the College Placement Office.

One hundred percent of the class of 2005 are attending colleges and universities that include Bentley, Boston University, Butler, Clark, Clarkson, Colby, Connecticut College, Curry, George Washington, Gettysburg, Hamilton, Harvard, Hobart, Hofstra, Johnson & Wales, Northeastern, Notre Dame, Parsons School of Design, Providence, RIT, Rutgers, Seton Hall, St. Lawrence, St. John's, Syracuse, Temple, Tufts, West Point, Wheaton, Worcester Polytechnic, and the Universities of Maine, Massachusetts, New Hampshire, Pennsylvania, and Vermont.

STUDENT BODY AND CONDUCT

In 2005–06, the student body consisted of 19 day boys, 150 boarding boys, 6 day girls, and 45 boarding girls. Students come from twenty-one states and nineteen countries.

Because Winchendon is a close-knit community of young people and adults, there is a need for certain rules and policies. Acts and attitudes that interfere with the educational process, that encroach on the privacy or sensitivities of others, or that violate School policies are not permitted. Rules governing conduct at Winchendon are based upon traditional values and standards of behavior. Two examples of such standards are the dress code, which requires a tie and jacket for boys and comparable dress for girls during classes and some evening meals, and the rule prohibiting tobacco use.

The Student Council, with representatives from each class, meets as the Advisory Council to the Headmaster. Students also serve on the Student-Faculty Judicial Board as Dormitory Proctors and on various committees.

ACADEMIC FACILITIES

The Winchendon School campus is highly centralized. The Science Building and two academic buildings of modern design contain a library (15,000 volumes), four laboratories, and twenty-four seminar-size classrooms. There is also an academic wing on Ford Hall.

The Computer Center contains twenty IBM microcomputer systems. The Art Center has facilities for graphic arts, photography, and ceramics. The Performing Arts Center houses facilities for dance, instrumental music, vocal music, and drama.

BOARDING AND GENERAL FACILITIES

Once a resort hotel, Ford Hall contains administrative offices, lounges, dining facilities, faculty apartments, and student living quarters. Merrell Hall, which houses boys, is a modern dormitory with a lounge and two faculty apartments. A girls' dormitory was added in 1988. A new Dining Hall and Student Center were completed in 2001.

Student rooms, furnished with draperies and wall-to-wall carpeting, are designed for comfort

and privacy. There are as many double rooms as single rooms. Nearly all rooms have direct access to baths and showers. A store and a snack bar are located in the golf course pro shop.

There is a day nurse in the School's infirmary, and a hospital is located in a neighboring town. The School also arranges for the services of a consulting clinical psychologist and a psychotherapist to be available to students.

ATHLETICS
By requiring participation in athletics, the School seeks not only to provide the proper level of physical activity for each student but also to foster physical fitness, fair play, and selfless contribution to group endeavors. Interscholastic and club sports include soccer, cross-country running, tennis, basketball, ice hockey, alpine and cross-country skiing, swimming, wrestling, lacrosse, golf, baseball, volleyball, and softball.

A new gymnasium was completed in 1990. It houses two full courts for basketball, one for volleyball, an indoor soccer area, and facilities for weight lifting, aerobic dance, and wrestling. There is also a complete athletics training room. The School also has access to the Wendell P. Clark Memorial Athletic Building in the town, which has an indoor swimming pool and an ice hockey rink.

Winchendon owns an 18-hole golf course designed by Donald Ross, several tennis courts, and an outdoor swimming pool.

EXTRACURRICULAR OPPORTUNITIES
As a small school, Winchendon provides exceptional opportunities for many students to participate in extracurricular activities, including student government, the yearbook (Vestigia), the newspaper (Progress), the literary magazine (Impressions), and the camera, computer, drama, and

outing clubs. The School has also initiated a Cultural Affairs Program, which introduces students to activities and events—chiefly in Boston—that have entertained people from all over the world.

Annual campus events include the Alumni Homecoming, Parents' Weekends in October and April, and Commencement Weekend.

DAILY LIFE
The typical daily schedule starts with breakfast at 7, room inspection at 7:30, and classes starting at 7:50. There is a midmorning all-school meeting at 10, and classes resume until lunchtime. After lunch there is a daily conference or help period, which is followed by the athletics period. Dinner is served at 5:30, and required supervised study runs from 7:15 to 9:15.

WEEKEND LIFE
A student who has met all of his or her School obligations may leave the campus on weekends with parental approval. There are many weekend activities on the campus, in nearby cities and towns, and on local college campuses. These include sports events, concerts, plays, and other cultural events as well as frequent trips to Boston and major New England ski areas and camping sites.

COSTS AND FINANCIAL AID
Tuition, room, and board for 2005–06 were $33,850; tuition for day students was $21,250. Additional fees are charged for music lessons and driver's education. Tuition payments are due twice yearly, in August and October.

Approximately 15 percent of the students receive financial aid, which is awarded on the basis of need and merit. For 2005–06, aid totaling $1 million was awarded.

ADMISSIONS INFORMATION
Winchendon accepts students of various abilities on the basis of their individual promise, avoiding stereotyped qualifications and standardized bases of judgment. A weak school record does not disqualify an applicant who shows good character and a potential for achievement in higher education.

Applicants for admission to any grade should submit recent Wechsler intelligence test (WISC or WAIS) scores and subtest scores. Postgraduate applicants should submit PSAT or SAT results as well. The SSAT is not required.

APPLICATION TIMETABLE
Initial inquiries are welcome at any time. Visits to the campus include a tour and an interview with the Headmaster. Applicants are encouraged to visit while the School is in session; if this is impossible, other arrangements can be made by the Admissions Office.

Interviews are scheduled between 8 a.m. and 4 p.m., Monday through Friday, and on Saturdays and Sundays.

Decisions on all applications are made from March 15 until all spaces are filled.

The nonrefundable application fee is $100. The initial deposit, required to reserve a place at Winchendon, is $2100.

ADMISSIONS CORRESPONDENCE
J. William LaBelle, Headmaster
The Winchendon School
172 Ash Street
Winchendon, Massachusetts 01475
Phone: 978-297-1223
      800-622-1119 (toll-free)
Fax: 978-297-0911
E-mail: admissions@winchendon.org
Web site: http://www.winchendon.org

WINDWARD SCHOOL

Los Angeles, California

Windward

Type: Coeducational day college-preparatory school
Grades: 7–12; Middle School 7–8; Upper School 9–12
Enrollment: 475
Head of School: Thomas W. Gilder

THE SCHOOL

Windward School, which was founded in 1971 through the determined efforts of Shirley Windward, a well-known educator and writer, is a self-governing independent school on the leafy west side of Los Angeles. From its founding, Windward aimed to be a bulwark of academic excellence and personal integrity, whose character could be summed up by its motto, which is found across the entrance to the School: responsible, caring, ethical, well-informed, prepared.

Through its small classes, Windward's rigorous academic program both challenges and buoys its students. This two-fold approach of rigor and support is the root of the School's well-earned reputation for academic excellence. The School's hope for its graduates is that they go forth from a school that prized each of them for their individual gifts, helped them recognize the significance of personal integrity and community service, enlivened their joy in learning, and provided the intellectual liveliness that produces independent thought, self-assured expression, and rewarding life endeavors.

A not-for-profit corporation, Windward is governed by a 20-member Board of Trustees and an administrative team centered by the Head of School. The Western Association of Schools and Colleges accredits Windward. The School holds membership in the National Association of Independent Schools, the Council for Spiritual and Ethical Education, the Independent School Alliance for Minority Affairs, A Better Chance, the Pacific Basin Consortium, Independent School Management, the Educational Records Bureau, and the California Association of Independent Schools.

ACADEMIC PROGRAMS

The energetic character of Windward's academic program is set forth on the belief that certain qualities are of primary importance. These include the ability to reason with care and logic and think outside the box, communicate well orally, compute accurately and reason quantitatively, master scientific approaches to problem solving, identify and develop aesthetic talents, and complement strong academic preparation with the development of ethics, character, and well-developed people skills.

At Windward, classes contain a maximum of 20 students. In academic areas, courses are sectioned on the basis of interest and ability, and Advanced Placement courses are offered in every discipline. The minimum course load for students in grades 7–10 is six. Students in grades 11–12 may opt for an alteration of this pattern, though approval of the grade-level deans is required, and students are actively encouraged to take six or seven classes.

In the Upper School, minimum course requirements are one English course each year through grade 12, one history course each year through grade 12 (seniors who wish to take two courses in another discipline may petition to waive the grade 12 history requirement), one mathematics course each year through grade 11, one science course each year through grade 10, one science course in either grade 11 or grade 12 (this must include one year of laboratory science), completion of Level III in one foreign language or completion of Level II in each of two foreign languages (continuation of foreign language through grade 11 is required), one arts course each year through grade 10, and one physical education course each year through grade 10 (students in grades 9 and 10 who compete in an interscholastic team sport are excused from physical education during that sport's season).

Community service has long been at the heart of the Windward tradition. Beginning in Middle School, service learning is a core component of the program, and in the Upper School, all students are required to complete two separate and extensive community service projects prior to graduation.

Windward maintains a sister school relationship with three schools, in Mexico City, Bordeaux, and Hiroshima. Students are able to attend a sister school for a three-week academic exchange once they have mastered an appropriate level of linguistic fluency. Generally, the schools exchange 15 to 20 students at a time. The culminating academic experience of a Windward education is the School's annual senior trip for one week at the School's expense. This "classroom in the field" is the capstone of six years of work and allows for an appropriate opportunity to say goodbye to one another.

FACULTY AND ADVISERS

The Windward faculty consists of 71 full- and part-time members (35 women and 36 men). Thirty-nine have advanced degrees, with 10 possessing doctorates. Thomas W. Gilder, Head of School, was appointed in 1987.

In selecting its faculty members, Windward looks for individuals who enjoy the art of teaching, who are enthusiastic about working with adolescents, who will involve themselves in the nonacademic life of the School, and who have lively personal interests of their own. Every faculty member at Windward is an integral component in the life of the School. Faculty benefits at Windward are generous on all accounts and include financial support for continuing education and the funding of faculty-generated betterment opportunities.

COLLEGE PLACEMENT

Windward places the utmost importance upon each senior having options from which to choose. Increasingly drawn toward the top colleges in the nation, students in the last several graduating classes chose between such diverse opportunities as Brown, Carleton, Colby, Columbia, Emory, Harvard, Kenyon, Princeton, the Rhode Island School of Design, Rice, Stanford, the University of California at Berkeley, the University of Pennsylvania, Vassar, Washington University (St. Louis), and Yale. College counseling begins in earnest in the fall of eleventh grade, when grade-level deans and the college counseling staff meet with students and families to map out strategies and provide advice for Subject Tests. Students are helped to prepare for interviews with college representatives, more than 100 of whom visit the School. The School offers close guidance in the application processes, essay writing, and the developmental challenge of separation from family, friends, and Windward School.

STUDENT BODY AND CONDUCT

Windward has 475 students in grades 7–12. The average class size is 17 students, allowing teachers to offer individualized attention.

The student government is directed by a group of 16 prefects, selected on the basis of community respect, personal integrity, and the ability to positively affect the life in the community. By working closely with the adults at Windward, acting as intermediaries, organizing School activities, and leading by example, the prefects help to set the tone of the School. Of primary importance is the cultivation of respect and consideration for others and their property, the enhancement of relationships between faculty members and students, and the general well-being of the student body. The prefects are expected to respect Windward's standards in their personal conduct and in the way in which they lead others.

At Windward, the breaking of major School rules (lying, cheating, stealing, or using or possessing drugs or alcohol) is a pressing matter and typically leads to dismissal. A committee headed by the appropriate division-level Dean of Students handles disciplinary matters and refers matters to the appropriate division head for final consideration. Beyond rules and regulations, however, the School's deeply ingrained code of honor expects all students to offer both civility and compassion to other students and to teachers, staff members, and their own families. In fact, this expectation is one of the defining characteristics of Windward School.

Under the oversight of the Head of School, the Middle and Upper School Directors oversee the successful operation of the School and ensure that appropriate procedures are in place for

students to enjoy their Windward experience and to be safe in the knowledge that discipline is expected of all community members.

ACADEMIC FACILITIES

The axis of School life is formed by the spacious Leichtman-Levine Bridge, built over the stream that traverses the campus, and the student pavilion, with a balcony and promenade that overlook the stream and the rest of the campus. The main academic building is the Classroom Building, with state-of-the-art technology, large light-filled classrooms, and panoramic vistas of the neighboring park at the west Los Angeles skyline. The Berrie Library provides a locus for faculty members and students to advance the use of innovative technologies and techniques to enhance teaching, learning, and research. By drawing on the strength of the members of the technology department and library and in conjunction with its faculty partners, the Berrie Library is founded upon the idea that faculty members and students work and experiment across disciplines to advance learning, explore new understandings, and develop strategies for the judicious use of technology in education. The library contains more than 7,500 volumes, subscribes to more than thirty periodicals, and provides numerous online information services, including ProQuest, EBSCO, ARTstor, and the Encyclopedia Britannica. These services provide an extensive list of magazines, journals, newspapers, and reference materials both at school and at home. In addition, the library recently expanded its services to provide a new media classroom with eighteen networked computers, an interactive whiteboard, wireless Internet access, and other digital tools.

The Irene Kleinberg Theater offers an intimate and sophisticated environment for performing arts and a spectacular venue for choral and dance performances. Separate dance and choral rehearsal halls are adjacent to each other.

The School continues its consistent program of technological progress. Laptops are used in many subject areas throughout the curriculum, and the foreign language department makes use of current audio technology in its flagship classroom. There are ample networked comput-

ers spread across the campus that play a continually increasing role in curricular and general campus life.

Three recently completed buildings contain visual and performing arts facilities and a dining pavilion.

ATHLETICS

There is a suitable level of athletics for every student. Some students seek out competitive accomplishment in one sport through years of participation, while others take advantage of Windward's breadth of offerings to begin new sports at the introductory level. The physical education and athletic programs emphasize acquiring lifetime skills, shaping confident attitudes about oneself as an individual and a contributing member of a group, and developing along the way a true sense of integrity and fairness.

There are junior varsity and varsity offerings in most sports, including football, soccer, lacrosse, baseball, cross-country, tennis, volleyball, basketball, and golf.

The Lewis Jackson Memorial Sports Center houses a weight training facility, meeting space, and trophy room display, while the gymnasium offers basketball and volleyball courts. The beauty of the playing fields, which are built to university and professional specifications, offers all participating students a chance to play at their best.

EXTRACURRICULAR OPPORTUNITIES

An array of extracurricular opportunities is available to students through period eight activity programs. Period eight is a block of scheduled time that is set aside twice a week for clubs, study hall, and other activities that provide extracurricular opportunities for Upper School students. Students choose from a wide variety of activities that include robotics, debate, yoga, ceramics, chorus, the yearbook, the newspaper, junior senate, and comedy sports. Students are encouraged to participate and to explore interests that support the development of talents and strengths that are not just limited to academic success.

DAILY LIFE

Beginning at 8 each morning and ending at 3 p.m., both Middle and Upper Schools utilize a

five-day schedule cycle. Monday mornings offer an all-School meeting for both Middle and Upper School students and faculty members, and there is a morning nutrition period five days a week. Seniors may take lunch off campus.

COSTS AND FINANCIAL AID

Tuition for 2005–06 was $23,566. The School's philosophy is to avoid extra charges for sports, field trips, or other activities offered through the School. Approximately 12 percent of the students at the School receive need-based scholarship opportunities.

ADMISSIONS INFORMATION

In every year, more students wish to become members of the Windward community than can be admitted. The admissions office works diligently to ensure that students who are accepted offer positive contributions to the community and succeed in Windward's challenging academic environment. The School seeks qualified students of diverse economic, social, ethnic, and racial backgrounds. The ISEE, recommendations from the previous school, and an interview with Windward admissions personnel are required for all applicants. Openings exist traditionally for grades 7 and 9, although students may apply for grades 8 and 10 with permission of the admissions office. Applicants to Windward should all possess admirable strengths of character, be positive contributors to school and community, and attain high grades at their present schools.

APPLICATION TIMETABLE

Inquiries are welcome throughout the year, though the deadline for application for the following year is always in the last week before winter break. Interviews and tours of the campus begin as soon as all faculty and staff members have returned in September.

ADMISSIONS CORRESPONDENCE

Sharon Pearline
Director of Admission
Windward School
11350 Palms Boulevard
Los Angeles, California 90066

Phone: 310-391-7127
Fax: 310-397-5655
Web site: http://www.windwardschool.org

WOODBERRY FOREST SCHOOL

Woodberry Forest, Virginia

Type: Boys' boarding college-preparatory school
Grades: 9–12 (Forms III–VI)
Enrollment: 391
Head of School: Dr. Dennis M. Campbell, Headmaster

THE SCHOOL

Woodberry Forest School was founded in 1889 by Robert Stringfellow Walker to educate his six sons. At the time of Captain Walker's death in 1914, the School had grown in size and influence to become one of the foremost independent schools in the South. Captain Walker was succeeded by his son J. Carter Walker, who served as Headmaster for fifty-one years. Under his leadership, the School's national reputation grew.

The School continues to emphasize strong academic preparation for college. Just as important, the School community fosters an atmosphere of civility and cooperation. The School maintains no formal church ties, but all students attend nonsectarian services each Sunday evening in St. Andrew's Chapel.

Woodberry Forest is located in a rural setting in the Piedmont section of Virginia, 3 miles north of Orange on a 1,100-acre property overlooking the Blue Ridge Mountains.

Woodberry Forest is an incorporated not-for-profit under a self-perpetuating 21-member Board of Trustees. Assets include a $58-million plant and a $180-million endowment. Annual Giving in 2004–05 totaled $2.6 million. Seventy-nine percent of the current parents and 56 percent of the alumni made gifts to the annual campaign.

Woodberry Forest is accredited by the Virginia Association of Independent Schools and by the Southern Association of Colleges and Schools. Its memberships include the Cum Laude Society and the National Association of Independent Schools.

ACADEMIC PROGRAMS

The four-year, college-preparatory curriculum requires the following courses for graduation: English, 12 trimesters; mathematics, 12 trimesters; foreign language, 9 trimesters; history, 8 trimesters; laboratory science, 9 trimesters; art and music, 2 trimesters; religion, 1 trimester; and electives, 3 trimesters. A student must earn 21 credits. The required course load is five, usually consisting of four yearlong courses and one trimester elective each term.

The curriculum contains twenty-one Advanced Placement courses and numerous electives.

Sections are grouped according to ability in most departments; honors sections begin at the ninth-grade level. The average class size is 12 students; the overall student-faculty ratio is 6:1. Woodberry uses a 4-point grading scale for passing grades (A–D); no credit is given for a failed course. Academic reports are sent home six times a year, at the midterm and end of each eleven-week trimester. All teachers are available five afternoons a week during consultation periods. Quiet is maintained in the dormitories during evening study hours by prefects and faculty duty masters.

Students in academic difficulty attend a formally supervised study hall. The library is open from 8 a.m. to 10 p.m. daily.

The School has an expansive program of outdoor education and leadership development. The first stage is the Fourth Form Leadership Program that brings all Fourth Form (tenth grade) students together and gives them tools to help their personal growth. The first part of this program is a four-day Outward Bound course in the mountains of North Carolina. Each Fourth Form class has the opportunity to take this trip.

Also included in the curriculum are a number of opportunities for overseas study. In conjunction with the Summer School, advanced language students may study under Woodberry Forest teachers in China, France, Germany, Mexico, Scotland, and Spain. Summer study is also available at Oxford University in England.

FACULTY AND ADVISERS

The full-time faculty is composed of 78 men and women; all but 3 live at the School. Seventy percent of faculty members hold advanced degrees, including six doctorates. In selecting its faculty members, the School seeks people with scholarly commitment and enthusiasm who are willing to view themselves as counselors as well as teachers and to sponsor extracurricular activities. Most faculty members coach athletics and supervise dormitories, and all serve as advisers to groups of 3 to 10 students. The adviser is responsible for guiding a student's overall academic and social progress and serves as an important link between parents and the School. The School provides financial help for continuing education and periodically grants sabbaticals to senior faculty members.

Dennis M. Campbell has a B.A. and Ph.D. from Duke University and a B.D. from Yale University. He served as dean of the Divinity School at Duke for fifteen years before being appointed headmaster of Woodberry Forest in 1997. A noted lecturer and author, Dr. Campbell has written many articles and four books on ethics and theology.

COLLEGE PLACEMENT

Beginning in tenth grade, a full-time college counselor advises students in selecting colleges and coordinates the visits of college representatives. The mean SAT scores for the class of 2005 were 630 on the verbal section and 640 on the mathematics section. One hundred percent of graduates are accepted at four-year colleges and universities. The 95 graduates of the class of 2005 are now at forty colleges and universities, including Brown, Columbia, Cornell, Davidson, Duke, Hampden-Sydney, Princeton, Vanderbilt, Wake Forest, Washington and Lee, and the Universities of North Carolina and Virginia.

STUDENT BODY AND CONDUCT

In 2004–05, the Third Form was composed of 76 students; the Fourth Form, 114; the Fifth Form, 92; and the Sixth Form, 109. Students from twenty-six states and six countries were enrolled. The School includes students from a range of economic and racial backgrounds.

Fundamental to student life at Woodberry Forest is the Honor System, which rests on the conviction that students want to be honorable and have the right to be trusted. In order to have this right, no student may lie, cheat, or steal, nor can he tolerate these offenses by others. This must be understood by anyone thinking about entering the School. The Honor System is a method of student self-government distinct from faculty-administered School discipline. The prefects are a small group of Sixth Formers appointed by the Headmaster on the basis of student and faculty nominations to maintain and nurture the Honor System. Student Council representatives are elected to canvass student opinion and make recommendations on disciplinary policy and other practical matters of student life.

ACADEMIC FACILITIES

The School's newest academic building, Armfield Hall, houses the foreign language department, a multiuse lecture hall, and a third computer center. The computer center serves as the hub for the campuswide network. Renovated Anderson Hall contains classrooms for English and history; the math-science building contains complete laboratory facilities, a computer center, two greenhouses, a lecture hall, and a rooftop deck for astronomical and meteorological observations. Hanes Hall houses the Belk Audio-Visual Center, a computer center, and the William H. White Jr. Library, which contains 60,000 volumes and maintains subscriptions to 120 periodicals. The J. Carter Walker Fine Arts Center, which recently underwent a $7-million renovation, includes a 525-seat theater, prop shops, darkrooms, a small art gallery, School publications offices, and nine studios for music, painting, drawing, sculpture, ceramics, and woodworking.

BOARDING AND GENERAL FACILITIES

The Walker Building is the main School building, housing administrative offices, the dining hall, post office, student store and recreation rooms, and dormitory rooms for about 160 boys on five halls. There are seven smaller dormitories: Turner, Taylor, Dowd, Finch, House A, House D, Terry, and Griffin House. Most students reside in double rooms, but there are a limited number of single and triple rooms. Resident nurses staff the Memorial Infirmary.

ATHLETICS

The athletics program provides outside competition for all teams at all levels—more than 300

contests per year. Almost all students, regardless of ability or experience, participate in athletics each trimester. The program seeks to promote physical fitness and develop confidence, leadership, and respect for the rules of fair play.

Foremost among the School's athletics facilities is the Harry Barbee Jr. Center. One of the finest high school athletics complexes in the nation, the building contains a 200-meter track, five basketball courts, three tennis courts, one racquetball court, three squash courts, and a 25-yard, six-lane swimming pool with a diving board.

Woodberry also has a regulation nine-hole golf course; nine fields for football, soccer, and baseball; a weight room; cardiovascular equipment; and a hardwood-floor gymnasium.

Complementing the Harry Barbee Jr. Center is the L. W. Dick Gymnasium, which contains locker and equipment rooms as well as facilities for basketball and wrestling. A state-of-the-art, two-story, $5-million fitness center is attached to the Dick Gym. Varsity football is played on Hanes Field, which has permanent bleachers for 1,500 spectators and is enclosed within a 440-yard Stratatrack track. There are seven additional football fields, four soccer fields, two baseball diamonds, four lacrosse fields, fourteen tennis courts, and varsity and junior varsity cross-country courses. The School maintains an outdoor swimming pool.

EXTRACURRICULAR OPPORTUNITIES

The more than twenty organizations at Woodberry include the Choir and Dozen, Book Club, a debate team, and Rod and Gun Club (with an automatic trap and skeet range). The Drama Department puts on three major productions a year, and smaller productions take place three times a year in the Black Box Theatre. There is also the Rapidan Program, which is highlighted by a recently completed 50-foot alpine tower for climbing and team-building activities. School publications include the *Fir Tree* (yearbook), *Oracle* (newspaper), and *Talon* (literary magazine).

The Artists and Speakers Series as well as the Fitzpatrick Lectures bring distinguished speakers and performers to the campus on a regular basis. Recent performances on campus have included the Kronos Quartet, Step Africa, and the Canadian Brass. Throughout the year, cultural and entertainment trips to Washington, Richmond, and Charlottesville are arranged in conjunction with other schools.

Each student is required to complete 60 hours of community service by graduation, and the Chapel Council and Service Committee enable students to participate in service projects in the local community.

DAILY LIFE

Classes are held six days a week—from 8 to 3:15 on Monday, Wednesday, and Thursday (seven 45-minute periods), from 8 to 12 on Tuesday and Friday (five periods), and from 8 to 11 on Saturday (four periods). A student normally has a balance between light and heavy class days, with a maximum of five classes on the latter. Athletics practices run from 3:45 to 5:30, with contests scheduled for Tuesday and Friday and an occasional Saturday. Evening study hours are from 7:45 to 10 Sunday through Friday. Club activities are scheduled for Thursday evenings and cultural programs for Friday evenings.

WEEKEND LIFE

The School sponsors frequent mixers and dances with area girls' schools. The School also sponsors frequent weekend trips to plays, concerts, and sports events in Charlottesville, Washington, and Richmond. Mixers are held with area schools for girls on most weekends.

Seniors are allowed five overnight weekends per trimester, beginning after classes Saturday to 6 p.m. Sunday. Fifth Formers are allowed four overnight weekends per trimester; Fourth Formers, three; and Third Formers, two. Students may combine two overnights and take a long weekend from Friday to Sunday. Weekend requests must be approved by the student's adviser, and parental permission is also necessary.

SUMMER PROGRAMS

The School offers basketball, lacrosse, and sports camps for boys ages 10–13. Further information can be obtained from the Director of the Summer Programs.

COSTS AND FINANCIAL AID

Charges for 2004–05 were $30,200, which covered tuition, room and board, and activities. A deposit of $3000 to reserve a place is payable by April 10. The deposit is not refundable, but is applied toward the basic fee.

A substantial financial aid budget is providing tuition assistance totaling $2.1 million for 26 percent of the student body. Scholarships ranging from partial assistance to full cost are awarded on the basis of financial need, as indicated by the guidelines of the School and Student Service for Financial Aid. A tuition loan program augments the system of financial aid, and boys who need financial assistance generally have priority in receiving paying jobs in a work program.

ADMISSIONS INFORMATION

Admission to Woodberry Forest is open to all students regardless of race, creed, or national origin. Acceptance of any candidate is based on academic capability, character, and extracurricular interests. The Admissions Committee uses teachers' recommendations, an applicant questionnaire, a transcript of grades, SSAT scores, and a personal interview at the School to assess the qualifications of every candidate. The School accepts a majority of its students into the ninth and tenth grades. Students with outstanding qualifications, however, are admitted into the eleventh grade.

In an average year, between 30 and 50 percent of the students who apply are accepted.

APPLICATION TIMETABLE

Preliminary application should be made a year prior to the year in which the applicant wishes to be admitted. In September, the final application forms are mailed to those indicating interest for the following fall. Campus interviews are conducted throughout the year from 8:30 to 1 on weekdays and from 8:30 to 10:15 on Saturday. All applicants are requested to take the SSAT on one of the November, December, or January test dates. By February 1, the candidate's folder should be complete if he is to be considered for admission. A small number of places are left open for late applicants.

ADMISSIONS CORRESPONDENCE

Office of Admissions
Woodberry Forest School
Woodberry Forest, Virginia 22989
Phone: 540-672-6023
    888-798-9371 (toll-free)

THE WOODHALL SCHOOL

Bethlehem, Connecticut

Type: Boys' boarding and day college-preparatory school for students with educational deficiencies
Grades: 9–12, postgraduate year
Enrollment: 42 boarding
Head of School: Sally Campbell Woodhall, Head of School

THE SCHOOL

The Woodhall School was founded in 1982 by Sally C. and Jonathan A. Woodhall to provide an individualized educational experience for young men of average to superior ability who have had difficulties in traditional school environments. The School's individualized approach includes an interpersonal component that recognizes the psychological dimensions of education and that permeates all aspects of the Woodhall Program: academics, communications, athletics, and student life.

The Woodhall Program is designed to meet the needs of students who manifest one or more of the following characteristics: lack of motivation, low self-confidence, difficulty with academic or study skills, problematic family- or health-related issues, a mild learning disability, attention deficit disorder, or NLD. Woodhall also admits international students who wish to prepare for entrance into American schools or colleges. An extensive admissions process enables the School to design a program for each student that takes into account his intellectual, social, neurological, and emotional needs.

The campus occupies 30 acres in the center of rural Bethlehem, Connecticut, close to nearby preparatory schools. The Woodhall School is located midway between New York and Boston and is an hour's drive from Hartford and New Haven.

The Woodhall School is a nonprofit institution governed by a 10-member Board of Trustees. The annual operating budget of $2.5 million is met primarily by tuition. The Annual Fund raised $240,000 in 2004–05.

The School is accredited by the New England Association of Schools and Colleges and approved by the Connecticut Department of Education. It is a member of the Connecticut Association of Independent Schools, the National Association of Independent Schools, and the Council for Religion in Independent Schools.

ACADEMIC PROGRAMS

The Woodhall Program offers an individualized approach to academics that allows a student to develop basic study skills and classroom skills and to learn from and with others. Each student's course of studies is designed to meet his educational needs by discovering and developing the method of learning best suited to his learning style. The program's goal is to open the door to success by meeting each student where he is and helping him move beyond that point to realize his potential. Current psychometric tests and a battery of diagnostic tests allow subsequent evaluation of his progress. Parents receive full reports at the end of each trimester and interim academic reports every three weeks.

The curriculum consists of college-preparatory classes and, in certain cases, a general secondary school program. AP courses include biology, calculus, chemistry, computer science, English language and English literature, Latin, U.S. history and European history. Graduation requires completion of 4 units of English, 3 of math, 3 of social sciences, 2 of natural sciences, 2 of a modern or classical language, and 2 of art. When necessary, remedial and language arts courses are designed to build basic skills and to fill in educational lacunae. Woodhall also offers an English as a second language program.

Each student begins his program of study in a subject at the grade level appropriate for his ability and age. The individualized and interpersonal approach within small classes allows students to work closely with other students and with a teacher. Classes of 40 minutes provide each student with a content and process approach to learning.

The Woodhall Program provides for frequent monitoring of each student's progress. Faculty members submit grades for each student every three weeks, and the Dean of School and the Dean of Faculty review each student's grades with him. This individualized approach allows for modification of the student's program as needed. Each student receives an achievement grade and an effort grade for each course, and academic honor rolls are posted every three weeks. A student must attain a grade of at least 60 to receive course credit, while 70 or above is considered appropriate for college recommendation. A grade of 80 or above is an honor grade.

The Dean of School and the Dean of Faculty monitor each student's progress and schedules conferences with teachers as necessary to explore and implement new strategies to engage the student and enable him to begin to succeed. The approach of the Woodhall Program allows discovery time to explore and develop interests as well as time to provide opportunities for success and positive reinforcement. Each student is given the opportunity to gain confidence in his ability, to learn how to learn, to proceed at his own pace, and, when necessary, to make up for time lost by completing two academic years in one year.

FACULTY AND ADVISERS

There are 16 full-time faculty members, 11 of whom live on campus. They hold fifteen baccalaureates and twelve advanced degrees. Faculty members are encouraged to participate in further professional development. They are trained in the pedagogy of the Woodhall Program upon joining the faculty.

Sally Campbell Woodhall, cofounder and Head of School, received a B. ès lettres and a C.E.L.G. from the University of Paris and holds both an M.A. in Romance languages and an M.A. in theology from Fordham University. Prior to establishing the Woodhall School, Mrs. Woodhall

taught on the college level and had administrative experience as a Director of Admissions and Associate Head.

All faculty members share responsibility for the personal and academic growth of each student and participate in all four components of the program. Woodhall seeks to recruit teachers who believe in a young person's potential and ability for growth and a learning community based on integrity and accountability.

Each student has a faculty adviser who monitors all aspects of a student's growth and needs in concert with the Head of School. If professional counseling is necessary, the Head of School arranges for it and stays in contact with the therapist.

The administration and faculty and staff members work closely together in meeting the students' needs. The intimacy of the School community means that all of the adult members act as role models for students as well as their advisers, formally and informally.

COLLEGE PLACEMENT

Many Woodhall students have been referred to the School by an educational consultant, who continues to follow his progress. It is often beneficial for the student to continue to work with the consultant for the next appropriate college or school placement. The School works closely with the student, the consultant, and the family throughout this process. A student may also choose to receive college or school guidance from the Dean of School, who assists and guides him through the process of admission to the next appropriate step after Woodhall. Students take the SSAT, the PSAT, the SAT, the ACT, and the TOEFL.

Some of the colleges and universities that recent Woodhall graduates have gone to include Beloit, Clark, Colby Sawyer, Earlham, Hartwick, New College of Florida, Ohio Wesleyan, RIT, Washington College, and Worcester Polytechnic Institute.

STUDENT BODY AND CONDUCT

For 2004–05, students came from sixteen states and two other countries. The student body is ethnically and religiously diverse. The School accepts day students.

The Communications Program offers all members of the School community the opportunity to be present and accountable to each other in a way that is built on integrity. Communications Groups on Self-Expression with Accountability meet twice weekly under the guidance of a trained faculty leader. The Committee for Accountability, composed of faculty members and students, provides a vehicle for resolving School-related issues.

The *Student Handbook* sets forth the guidelines of respectful behavior. There are appropri-

ate consequences for failure to meet responsibilities or to be respectful of people, places, and things. Major infractions, such as cheating, stealing, or substance abuse, may lead to suspension or expulsion. Students may also earn privileges on and off campus as they show themselves to be responsible members of the School community.

ACADEMIC FACILITIES

The campus was built between 1983 and 2004 and is designed to enhance the Woodhall School's individualized approach. Founders Hall houses the administration and the academic program and includes classrooms, a library, art and graphic arts rooms, a media center, and two seminar rooms. A new Athletics Center includes facilities for basketball, volleyball, wrestling, martial arts, and physical fitness.

BOARDING AND GENERAL FACILITIES

The School's academic and residential areas are architecturally conceived as a small village. The dormitories and recreational facilities are adjacent to but separate from the administrative and academic buildings. They include Velge Hall, which houses the dining hall, the science classrooms and labs, and a faculty apartment; Founders Hall, which includes the administrative offices, the library, the media center, the art and graphic arts classroom, and the art studio; the Tower Building, which houses dormitory rooms, faculty apartments, and the Student Center.

The athletics complex in the Athletics and Performing Arts Center opened in the fall of 2003 with a gymnasium, a well-equipped physical fitness room, and a room for wrestling and martial arts. The Abigail J. Woodhall Performing Arts Center is nearing completion. The campus also includes a playing field, a basketball court, and a sand volleyball court. The Head's Residence is also located on campus.

French Hall, completed in 1998, houses dorm rooms for 12 students, four faculty apartments, two seminar rooms, and the Murgio Meeting Room.

Tower Dorm houses 30 students and has four faculty apartments. The Student Center includes a large common room with a TV and a fireplace and an adjoining game room for Ping-Pong, air hockey, pool, and Foosball.

ATHLETICS

To foster physical fitness, sportsmanship, and teamwork, the School has an activities/sports program six days a week in which all students participate. The program is intended to provide students with the physical activity necessary to maintain a sound mind and a sound spirit.

Woodhall offers interscholastic competition in basketball, cross-country, lacrosse, and soccer. All students are required to participate in a group sport or activity, such as drama, outdoor education, volleyball, or physical fitness. During the winter, skiing is available.

EXTRACURRICULAR OPPORTUNITIES

The School offers various opportunities for leadership and personal growth on and off the campus. These include the Astronomy Club, the Chess Club, the Chorale, the Debate Club, the Literary Magazine, Newspaper, and the Yearbook. Students may be appointed or elected or choose to serve on committees that play an important role in the School community. These include the Student Leadership Committee, which comprises students elected by their peers to assume the responsibility and role of student leaders; the Social Activities Committee; the Student Center Committee; the Community Service Committee; and the Dorm Committee. Each student is also assigned a daily house job to develop a sense of community through shared responsibility.

Woodhall students share in social and recreational activities with nearby independent preparatory schools. Theater, concert, and educational field trips to New York, New Haven, Hartford, and Boston further enhance the educational program.

DAILY LIFE

The student begins each day with a short meeting with his faculty adviser. Following morning meeting, the academic day begins at 8:30 and ends at 3, with breaks and an hour for lunch. The class schedule is designed to integrate rhythm and structure into the class day and to allow students time with their teachers for support and guidance.

The academic day ends at noon on Wednesday and Saturday. Games and other activities take place on these afternoons. There is free time before and after the daily activities/sports period. Dinner dress is required five nights a week, and there is a supervised study period in the evening, followed by quiet time until lights-out at 11. Clubs and committees meet throughout the week during the day or evening. Day students are encouraged to participate in evening and weekend activities.

WEEKEND LIFE

Weekends begin on Saturday after School commitments have been met. The School calendar alternates between open and closed weekends. Students may sign out, with parental permission, for a Saturday overnight on an open weekend. A variety of recreational and social activities are planned for Saturdays and Sundays. These include sporting events, dances at girls' prep schools, performances of plays and music in Hartford and New Haven, movies, and shopping.

COSTS AND FINANCIAL AID

Tuition, room, and board are $47,000. Day student tuition is $36,000. The ESL program is an additional $2750. Additional billing may cover the costs of laundry, books, field trips, and certain life sports. The tuition is due in two payments. Tuition is prorated for a term of less than a year.

ADMISSIONS INFORMATION

Young men of average to superior ability, between the ages of 14 and 19, who are not experiencing success in traditional school environments may be admitted to the Woodhall School without regard to race, color, creed, or national origin. The admissions decision is based on a student's need for and ability to benefit from the School's educational program, as determined by previous school records and diagnostic and psychometric testing (when available). The School does not accept students who are chemically dependent, emotionally disturbed, or mentally handicapped.

APPLICATION TIMETABLE

Application may be made at any time. Acceptance of an appropriate candidate is dependent upon the availability of an opening. After the School has received the necessary material and a completed application form, an interview may be scheduled on campus, preferably when the School is in session. A telephone interview or an interview by Woodhall alumni or alumni parents can be arranged for international students. A student must make a commitment to the program before he can be admitted.

ADMISSIONS CORRESPONDENCE

Sally Campbell Woodhall, Head of School
The Woodhall School
P.O. Box 550
Bethlehem, Connecticut 06751

Phone: 203-266-7788
Fax: 203-266-5896
E-mail: woodhallschool@lycos.com
Web site: http://www.woodhallschool.org

WOODLANDS ACADEMY OF THE SACRED HEART

Lake Forest, Illinois

Type: Girls' boarding and day college-preparatory school
Grades: 9–12
Enrollment: 180
Head of School: Gerald J. Grossman

THE SCHOOL

Woodlands Academy of the Sacred Heart is a college-preparatory boarding and day school for girls in grades 9 through 12. It is conducted by the Religious of the Sacred Heart, an order founded in 1800 by Madeleine Sophie Barat, which now operates more than 200 educational institutions throughout the world. Woodlands Academy has been located in Lake Forest, Illinois, for almost 100 years. The Academy is currently celebrating its fortieth anniversary on the present campus. At Woodlands, students encounter what generations of young women have since 1858—an educational experience that is rigorous academically, supportive personally, and uniquely empowering of individual talents. Sacred Heart education "emphasizes serious study, educates to social responsibility, and lays the foundation of a strong faith." In relating this purpose to its own programs, Woodlands strives to educate the whole person, providing a value-based environment that supports rigorous intellectual training and opportunities for emotional, religious, and social growth. The enrollment includes girls of diverse religious backgrounds, and non-Catholic students are encouraged to pursue their own faiths. Woodlands Academy is located near Chicago and all its rich and varied cultural offerings. Many colleges and universities are located nearby, and activities for students that take advantage of these opportunities are planned frequently.

The school is a nonprofit institution under the direction of a Board of Trustees. In 2004–05, $1,337,012 was received from the Academy's Annual Giving Program. Woodlands Academy of the Sacred Heart is fully accredited by the North Central Association of Colleges and Schools and the National Association of Independent Schools.

ACADEMIC PROGRAMS

The school year is divided into quarters. Classes are held five days a week. Each girl is expected to carry five major subjects a year; well-qualified students are permitted to carry six. The minimum graduation requirements include 4 credits in English, 3 credits in history, 3 credits in religion, 3 credits in mathematics, 3 credits in foreign language, 3 credits in science, and 1½ credits in fine arts. Physical education is required for 3½ years. A sampling of the courses available includes such diverse offerings as British literature, speech, acting, ceramics, chorus, painting and drawing, photography, French, Latin, Spanish, psychology, sociology, comparative government, political theories, math functions, computer literacy, Christian ethics, peace and justice, physics, anatomy, and driver's education. Advanced Placement courses are offered in biology, calculus, English, and U.S. history.

Junior and senior girls may receive college credit for selected freshman classes at Lake Forest College. All Sacred Heart schools participate in an exchange program that enables girls to attend affiliated schools in the United States and, upon arrangement, in England, France, and other countries in which Sacred Heart schools are located.

Woodlands Academy offers an English as a second language program to meet the needs of international students who want to graduate from an American high school and then enter an American college or university or want to attend an American high school in order to learn spoken and written English. Students recently enrolled in this program have come from Brazil, Canada, Egypt, Germany, Hong Kong, Indonesia, Japan, Korea, Mexico, and Saudi Arabia. The core program includes courses in grammar, composition, American literature, reading, and vocabulary development. Students are placed according to their level of English ability, which is determined through testing. In addition, students take courses in mathematics, science, religion, history, fine arts, and physical education.

The average class is 15 students, and the ratio of students to full-time faculty members is approximately 8:1. In many courses, class sections are organized on the basis of ability and level of skill development. Assignments average 30–40 minutes per subject each day. Parents receive progress reports every five weeks. Students are given preparation for the American College Testing Program and College Board examinations; international students take the Test of English as a Foreign Language (TOEFL).

FACULTY AND ADVISERS

The faculty consists of 27 full-time teachers, the majority of whom hold advanced degrees, including doctorates.

In selecting faculty members, the administration seeks men and women who are interested in the goals and standards of the school, who can instill an intellectual curiosity and enthusiasm in students in more than a teacher-student situation, and who are willing to share their personal as well as scholarly talents.

The advisory system is an important feature of life at Woodlands Academy. Each student is a member of an advisory group that meets daily. These groups average 12 students and give each one of them an experience of personal growth within the framework of a small, stable peer group. The adviser is a counselor as well as a teacher and serves a student and her family as a resource person in all areas of school life.

COLLEGE PLACEMENT

A full-time college counselor is on campus to help students arrange to take tests, fill out applications, and apply for scholarships and to assist them in finding the information they need to select colleges. Representatives from approximately 100 colleges visited Woodlands last year, both on an individual basis and as part of the school's annual College Day, which is held in November.

In 2005, 100 percent of the Academy's graduates entered a variety of colleges and universities. Woodlands graduates are attending Boston College, Brown, Carnegie Mellon, DePaul, Emory, Fairfield, Georgetown, Harvard, Holy Cross, John Carroll, Northwestern, Notre Dame, NYU, Princeton, Providence, St. Mary's (Notre Dame), Skidmore, Syracuse, Tufts, Tulane, Washington (St. Louis), Yale, and the Universities of Chicago, Colorado, Illinois, Michigan, Southern California, and Wisconsin.

STUDENT BODY AND CONDUCT

In 2004–05, the Academy had 30 boarders and 150 day students in grades 9–12. Day students live in the nearby North Shore suburbs and surrounding areas. Resident students come from Barrington, Chicago, Oakbrook, and Palos Park as well as the surrounding states of Indiana, Michigan, and Wisconsin. Other states represented include Kentucky, Louisiana, Maryland, Oklahoma, and Texas. International students represent Brazil, Canada, Germany, Ghana, Hong Kong, Indonesia, Japan, Korea, Mexico, and Thailand.

Students are given a handbook setting out policies of the school, and their behavior is expected to comply with the rules. Violations are dealt with by the Head of School, the Dean of Students, and the Director of Resident Students. Students influence decisions concerning school life through the Woodlands Academy Council of Representatives.

ACADEMIC FACILITIES

Garden courtyards are surrounded by learning centers that house classrooms, laboratories, a small theater, three media and resource centers, art and ceramics studios (including a kiln), a darkroom, a journalism workshop, and faculty offices.

Since its opening in 1999, the Reynolds Technology Center has become vitally important to school life at all levels. The state-of-the-art facility contains a computer lab, technology classroom, publications room, and offices for technology staff featuring high-end computers, scanners, and a CD-ROM tower. The results are impressive: Woodlands has one full Internet computer for every five students. The center has also enabled faculty members to integrate more cutting-edge technology into classroom instruction and curriculum development. Using this new equipment, students are learning to complete assignments using complex software such as computer-based probes and graphing calculators.

BOARDING AND GENERAL FACILITIES

The campus is situated on rolling, heavily wooded grounds. Connected brick wings form a three-level complex that is dominated by a distinctive chapel, noted for its glass, copper, and brick design. The facilities include lounges, dining rooms, a kitchen, a canteen and student center, offices, an infirmary, and dormitories with rooms for resident students.

Dormitories consist of four halls, with private as well as double and triple rooms. New students are assigned roommates by the director, with consideration given to students' preferences as shown on a student questionnaire; returning students may choose their own roommates. Two or three houseparents are on duty; each staff member is interested in and concerned about each student. Permission for off-campus activities is prearranged by parents. School dormitories are closed during the two-week Christmas and Easter vacations as well as during Thanksgiving weekend, but arrangements for housing can be made.

ATHLETICS

Students are required to earn 3½ years of credit within the instructional physical education or sports program. Organized teams in field hockey, basketball, tennis, volleyball, soccer, and softball compete in local and regional leagues. Participation on varsity and junior varsity teams, as well as in intramural activities, is encouraged.

The campus has tennis courts, athletic fields, and a gymnasium.

EXTRACURRICULAR OPPORTUNITIES

Off-campus field trips are made to cultural events, the theater, exhibits, concerts, museums, and programs at nearby colleges or in downtown Chicago. Staff members are available to chaperone the students. Special on-campus programs with guest lecturers or performances are sponsored by the school. On-campus student programs held each year include a Fine Arts Festival in the spring, choral performances, and several dramatic productions. Traditional events, such as Ring Ceremony, May-Crowning, Father-Daughter Breakfast, and Conges (surprise holidays), are also scheduled each year.

Students may serve on the newspaper, literary magazine, or yearbook staff or participate in the chorus, the Girls Athletic Association, and the art, photography, French, Spanish, media, science, and international clubs. There are several more clubs to choose from, and new organizations are formed each year.

Girls can take part in student government either by representing their class as officers or by becoming involved in the Woodlands Academy Council of Representatives (WACOR). A council of elected officers, WACOR promotes student involvement in the school and the community (along with the dance and tradition committees) and has a say in decisions that concern school life. Its officers compose a Council Board. The Resident Community Council (RCC), an organization for boarding students only, also promotes student interest in school affairs and arranges special events in the residence halls, including a talent-variety show, a faculty dinner, birthday parties, and programs for international students. The RCC also sponsors a newspaper for resident students and does fundraising.

DAILY LIFE

The class day begins with a homeroom period at 8:15 a.m. and ends with dismissal at 3:15 p.m. Lunch is served at 11:30 and includes a variety of choices including several hot entrees, a deli bar, a salad bar, a pasta bar, and a pizza area, along with a variety of fresh fruits and desserts. The daily schedule consists of nine 40-minute periods. On Friday, there is an activity period before lunch, which provides time for Masses, special assemblies, and club meetings. Students attend Chapel every Wednesday, and school lets out at 2:30 on that day. Sports events, socials, dances, and other activities are held after school hours. Boarding students have leisure time after classes and in the evening after a required study hall from 6:30 to 8:30.

WEEKEND LIFE

Boarders visit friends on weekends, while others remain on campus where they assist in the planning of recreational activities, some of which are shared with other schools. Shows, games, special events, and trips to restaurants are among the selections available on weekends. Exercise and physical fitness activities are popular, and the nearby shores of Lake Michigan offer opportunities for running and bicycling.

COSTS AND FINANCIAL AID

The 2004–05 tuition and fees were as follows: $32,100 for boarding students and $16,100 for day students. Optional expenses are private lessons or tutoring; special programs, such as the English as a second language program or the Learning program; and bus service. The girls wear an attractive sweater and skirt uniform, which is an additional expense; however, because the clothes are worn for several years, the expense is incurred primarily in the first year.

Many members of the student body receive financial aid, which is awarded on the basis of need. Parents must submit the Parents' Financial Statement, prepared by the School and Student Service for Financial Aid in Princeton, New Jersey.

Woodlands Academy awards four-year merit scholarships on a competitive basis.

ADMISSIONS INFORMATION

Applicants to Woodlands Academy are considered on the basis of their application, previous school records, teachers' and personal recommendations, and a personal interview. Entrance or placement tests are given at the school in January. The Admissions Committee interviews prospective students and makes decisions on selection. Students of any race or ethnic origin are welcome. Woodlands seeks students striving for an excellent education, girls who recognize their self-worth and who seek to cultivate their intellectual and spiritual needs to become informed, intelligent, and enlightened young women.

APPLICATION TIMETABLE

Inquiries are welcome at any time. Tours can be arranged through the Admissions Office, from 8:30 to 4 on weekdays. Applications are accepted at any time, but admission cannot be granted after the semester has begun; a late applicant is required to wait until the next semester to enroll in classes. The completed application and necessary information should be accompanied by a $50 nonrefundable application fee. Upon notification of admission, a student's family is expected to reply, and an enrollment contract is then sent out to accepting students.

ADMISSIONS CORRESPONDENCE

Director of Admission
Woodlands Academy of the Sacred Heart
Lake Forest, Illinois 60045

Phone: 847-234-4300
Fax: 847-234-4348
E-mail: admissions@woodlandsacademy.org
Web site: http://www.woodlandsacademy.org

WOODSIDE PRIORY SCHOOL

Portola Valley, California

Type: Coeducational day and boarding college-preparatory school
Grades: 6–12
Enrollment: 350
Head of School: Timothy J. Molak, Headmaster

THE SCHOOL

Woodside Priory School is a Catholic, Benedictine coeducational college-preparatory school. Core values of spirituality, community, integrity, and individuality are practiced daily in Priory School life. The Priory combines its 60-acre campus with a rigorous and balanced college-preparatory curriculum, a 10:1 student-teacher ratio, and a full complement of athletics and extracurricular activities. Founded in 1957 by Hungarian Benedictine monks, the Priory is associated with Saint Anselm College and Abbey in New Hampshire.

The Priory is located within a 35-minute drive of San Francisco and San Jose on the San Francisco Peninsula. It is also within an hour's drive of the Pacific Ocean and the recreational areas of Santa Cruz and Monterey. The facilities of Stanford University are 4 miles east. The area is served by three international airports and is 15 minutes from the Caltrain station in Menlo Park.

The governing body of the School is the Board of Directors. Operating expenses for 2004 were $8.1 million, with $1.2 million in Annual Giving.

The Priory received a six-year accreditation by the Western Association of Schools and Colleges in June 2000. It is a member of the National Association of Independent Schools, the College Board, the National Catholic Education Association, and the Association of Boarding Schools, among other professional educational organizations.

ACADEMIC PROGRAMS

The curriculum seeks to educate well-rounded individuals who are prepared for success in college and life. The educational program and the School's sense of community take their character from the tradition of Benedictine education, which spans fifteen centuries. The school year consists of two semesters, with students carrying seven courses each semester. High school graduation requirements include 8 semesters of English literature, 1 semester of expository writing lab, 8 semesters of social studies, 6 semesters of mathematics, 6 semesters of lab sciences, 6 semesters of language (Spanish, Japanese, or French), 6 semesters of theology, 2 semesters of health and physical education, 2 semesters of humanities, 1 semester of computer science, and 2 semesters of fine arts/drama/music.

Eighteen Advanced Placement courses were offered in 2003–04 in art portfolio, biology, calculus (AB and BC), chemistry, economics, English, environmental science, French, government and politics, music, physics, Spanish language, Spanish literature, statistics, and U.S. history. Eighteen elective courses are offered in the sophomore, junior, and senior years. Honors courses are offered in the sophomore through senior years in English, mathematics, modern languages, and social studies. Students who achieve at a higher level in mathematics are placed according to their skills. Students may take course work through local colleges and universities. Close, personal faculty attention as a result of small class settings allows student's progress to be monitored and facilitates effective communication among parents, students, and teachers.

Students must maintain at least a 2.0 GPA (on a 4.0 scale) and achieve a passing grade of at least 60 percent in each course to remain in the School. Letter grades range from A through F. Parents are sent report cards quarterly and academic progress reports each midquarter.

Students participate in cultural events and field trips that enhance the academic program. They make visits to the San Francisco Symphony and art and science museums; participate in the Washington, D.C., Model United Nations Program; and take field trips to the Monterey Bay Aquarium, the Exploratorium, the Stanford Linear Accelerator Center, and the NASA-Ames Research Center. Speakers on the campus have included Senator William Bradley, anthropologist Jane Goodall, former Secretary of Defense William Perry, filmmaker Jerry Zucker, and Ambassador Shirley Temple Black.

A four-year community service program is an integral part of High School academics, requiring 80 hours of service to the outside community for students to graduate. Students work with children, young adults, the infirm, and the elderly as well as homeless and displaced persons. Middle School students work with faculty members on specific community projects and service programs. An active retreat program in each grade complements the academic program for personal and spiritual growth as well as community building.

FACULTY AND ADVISERS

Timothy J. Molak (M.A., Saint Mary's University, and M.A., Saint Thomas University) is Headmaster. He was appointed Headmaster following eight years as the Priory's Dean of Students. Before his appointment as Dean in 1990, he was the Academic Dean at Bishop Kelly High School.

With a team of 7 administrators, the Headmaster works with a faculty of 50 men and women. Most faculty members hold advanced degrees, and 3 have doctorates.

Faculty members are chosen on the basis of their qualifications, teaching experience, and willingness to participate actively in the community life of the School. Faculty members participate in counseling, coaching, and moderating activities. A monastic community of 5 along with 18 faculty families live on campus.

COLLEGE PLACEMENT

Juniors and seniors begin the college application process early in the fall of each year in group sessions, and each student receives individual counseling. Visits from college representatives provide information for students. The College Guidance Center maintains an up-to-date library of catalogs, CDs, viewbooks, and videos for student research.

Sophomores and juniors take the Preliminary Scholastic Aptitude Test (PSAT) as well as the Scholastic Assessment Test (SAT) in the spring and again in the fall of their senior year. Mean SAT scores of Priory students are significantly above national and state averages. Priory students annually earn AP scholar awards, University of California Regents scholarships, and a variety of individual college merit awards. Eighteen members of the class of 2005 received National Merit recognition by the College Board. Seven were named National Merit Semifinalists.

Priory graduates continue their undergraduate and graduate educations at colleges and universities throughout the world, including Boston College, Brown, Claremont-McKenna, California State Polytechnic, Cornell, Dartmouth, Duke, Georgetown, Harvard, Johns Hopkins, MIT, Notre Dame, NYU, Northwestern, Princeton, Reed, Santa Clara, Stanford, Syracuse, Wellesley, Williams, and Yale, as well as the Universities of Chicago, San Francisco, Southern California, and Wisconsin and the University of California campuses at Berkeley, Davis, Irvine, Los Angeles, Riverside, San Diego, Santa Barbara, and Santa Cruz.

STUDENT BODY AND CONDUCT

One third of the students are enrolled in the Middle School and two thirds are enrolled in the High School. Fifty students participate in the High School boarding program. The Priory is internationally and culturally diverse, as more than twenty-five countries are represented in the student body and faculty.

The Priory attempts to foster Christian values in each student. Honesty and a respect for others are the primary objectives of the School's mission. Serious violations may result in referral to the Student Life Advisory Committee, which consists of faculty members and students.

ACADEMIC FACILITIES

Facilities include Founders Hall, a fine arts studio, the chapel, and twenty-three classrooms. The Briggs Science Center houses full laboratories for biology, chemistry, physics, an electron microscope, and computer studies. Each lab has four Internet-connected PCs. The Assembly Hall and Theater seats 300. The 18,000-volume Panonhalma Library and Technology Center contains twenty-four computer stations that are connected to the Internet. The Priory is a totally wireless campus. There are more than 150 computer workstations throughout the campus. Computer technology is integrated into every academic department.

BOARDING AND GENERAL FACILITIES

The boarding program fosters Christian social living within a highly structured environment. Two dormitories provide living space for 45 boarders and 6 adult Housemasters. In addition, the Resident Program is supported by resident faculty members who live on campus. Students share a double room. Each dormitory has its own recreational area.

A seven-day boarding program is open to students in grades 9–12. While boarders have the option to go home for the weekends, recreation opportunities are provided for students who wish to remain on campus. The dormitories are closed during the summer vacation and the major vacation periods of the school year. International students must have a local guardian.

Generally, boarders enter in the freshman year. Transfers to the program in the sophomore and junior years are considered on a space-available basis.

ATHLETICS

Enrollment in the physical and health education curriculum is required of each student. A coed interscholastic sports program provides an opportunity for all students to compete in soccer, volleyball, cross-country, basketball, swimming, tennis, track, golf, and baseball. Facilities include a 10,000-square-foot gymnasium, a 25-meter heated pool, three soccer fields, two baseball diamonds, four tennis courts, and two outdoor basketball courts.

The Priory is a member of the Peninsula Private School Athletic League and participates with other independent schools in sixteen interscholastic teams. Athletic teams are available for Middle School and High School students.

EXTRACURRICULAR OPPORTUNITIES

Clubs and organizations play a significant role in student life. Activities include yearbook, school newspaper, drama, photography, ski, electronics, science, robotics, and computer clubs. Annual family events include the Family Picnic that opens the school year.

DAILY LIFE

Breakfast for boarding and day students is served from 7:10 to 7:45. Day students and boarders begin classes at 8:30 and end at 3:30. The academic day consists of seven classes. Class periods are on a rotating schedule and are 50 minutes long. A hot lunch and a salad bar are provided for all students.

Dinner for boarders is served at 6 p.m. Evening study periods are held Sunday through Thursday from 7 to 9:30 p.m.

WEEKEND LIFE

The Dean of Students and Dean of the Boarding Program coordinate with the student government, Dormitory Council, and various clubs in planning activities on and off campus for both day students and boarders. Dances are regularly held on campus and students are invited to dances sponsored by area schools.

The Priory is fortunate to be situated in an area of unsurpassed cultural and recreational opportunities. Communities in and around the San Francisco Bay Area and nearby Stanford University offer events throughout the year that are enjoyed by students and faculty members. The Ski Club organizes trips to Lake Tahoe. Professional football, basketball, hockey, and baseball teams are within minutes of the Priory. The School sponsors weekend trips to the Santa Cruz Beach Boardwalk, the Sierras, and nearby state and national parks.

COSTS AND FINANCIAL AID

Tuition is the cost of the academic program and general expenses, such as daily hot lunch, student government, athletics, assemblies, the yearbook, and other student publications. The tuition noted for boarders includes room and board for students enrolled in the Priory's boarding school for the academic year. Tuition for day students is $25,617 and for boarders is $34,932.

At registration, a $3000 deposit for boarders or a $1000 deposit for day students is required to ensure placement. This is a nonrefundable deposit applied to tuition. A tuition assistance program is available, and currently 22 percent of the students share more than $900,000 in financial aid. Families wishing to apply for financial aid should contact the Admissions Office. Tuition and fees are normally paid in installments in July and December. The Priory also offers a ten-month payment plan as well as a commercial loan program for tuition.

ADMISSIONS INFORMATION

Admission is based upon the applicant's school record, standardized test (ISEE, SSAT, or STS/HSPE) results, two recommendations from teachers, and the evaluation of the student by his or her principal or adviser. There is a $50 application fee.

Students are admitted into the sixth through eleventh grades each year. There are no senior transfers.

Applicants to the High School must take the SSAT or the STS/HSPE. The median SSAT score for entering students is above the 80th percentile. However, grades and recommendations are more significant factors in admission decisions. The TOEFL is required for international students, with a minimum score of 525.

The Priory seeks to admit students who are motivated learners, desiring a well-rounded college-preparatory education. The Priory is determined to provide the student with the support, opportunities, and environment necessary to meet his or her educational goals. Candidates are accepted on the basis of their personal and academic qualifications without discrimination as to race, color, or creed.

APPLICATION TIMETABLE

For admission to the 2006–07 academic year, application materials must be filed with the Priory by January 12, 2006. Candidates meeting this date are the first considered by the Admissions Committee, and notification of the committee's action is mailed on March 16, 2006. Students making application after this date are notified within two weeks after all admission forms have been received, pending available space in the class. Applicants are required to spend a class day at the Priory; an appointment may be made with the Director of Admissions. Families interested in taking a tour may do so by attending an Open House on October 22, November 19, or December 10, 2005. If attendance at an Open House is not possible, a personal tour can be arranged through the Admissions Office. A school tour and interview usually take an hour; comfortable attire and walking shoes are suggested for the visit.

ADMISSIONS CORRESPONDENCE

Al Zappelli, Dean of Admissions
Woodside Priory School
302 Portola Road
Portola Valley, California 94028-7897

Phone: 650-851-8221
Fax: 650-851-2839
E-mail: azappelli@woodsidepriory.com
Web site: http://www.woodsidepriory.com

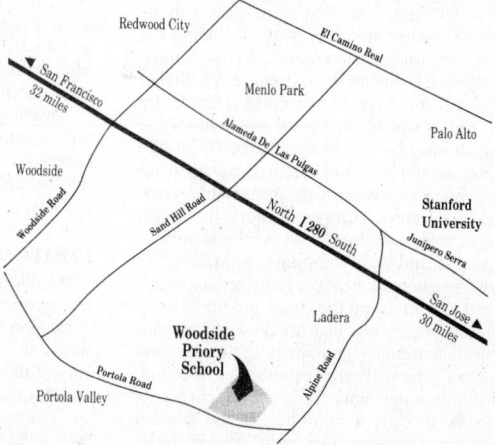

WORCESTER ACADEMY

Worcester, Massachusetts

ACHIEVE THE HONORABLE

Type: Coeducational day and boarding college-preparatory
Grades: 6–12, postgraduate year
Enrollment: 631
Head of School: Dexter Morse

THE SCHOOL

Worcester Academy was founded in 1834 by a group of Worcester citizens under the leadership of Isaac Davis. The objectives of Worcester Academy are to help students prepare for college and, most important, for life; to encourage them to take an active part in the school community and the community at large; to teach them that they have responsibilities as well as privileges; and to assure them that there is value in striving to develop their potential to the fullest.

The school, which moved to its present site in 1869, is only a 10-minute walk from the center of Worcester, home of many excellent colleges, various libraries, museums, science centers, a large number of industries, and a nationally known civic center. The main campus is a 12-acre tract on which buildings surround a central area of open lawns and shade trees. The campus includes three classroom buildings, four dormitories, a gymnasium, the Warner Memorial Theater, and the student center. A four-story academic building and library was completed in 2001 and offers additional study space, state-of-the-art classrooms, and three technology classrooms. The Alumni and Development Office is now located in a newly renovated Victorian home two blocks from the main campus.

The school is a nonprofit corporation under the direction of a self-perpetuating Board of Trustees with up to 35 members. The endowment is valued at approximately $31.5 million. Annual Fund giving for the most recent academic year amounted to more than $600,000.

Worcester Academy is accredited by the New England Association of Schools and Colleges and is affiliated with the National Association of Independent Schools, the Secondary School Admission Test Board, the Association of Independent Schools in New England, the National Association for College Admission Counseling, and the Cum Laude Society.

ACADEMIC PROGRAMS

A traditional college-preparatory curriculum is offered. To graduate, a student must earn a minimum of 18 credits in grades 9–12, including the following: English, 4; mathematics, 3 (which must include algebra I, algebra II, and geometry); foreign language, 2 (Latin, French, or Spanish); laboratory science, 2 (1 of which must be biology); history, 2 (1 of which must be U.S. history); arts, 1½ (studio art, music, or drama); and electives chosen from history (American government, American government AP, economics, European history, the Jewish Holocaust, topics in global history, the history of World War II, and understanding U.S.-Middle East relations), mathematics (advanced algebra, precalculus, and calculus), and the visual and performing arts (studio art, piano, instrumental instruction, instrumental ensemble, choral ensemble, harmony and theory, acting, theater experience, directing, and costume design and construction). Students are required to carry a minimum of five courses plus health and wellness (noncredit) in their freshman and sophomore years. Students must also fulfill an off-campus community service requirement. Special programs exist for international students.

Recent students have earned Advanced Placement credit in French, Spanish, English, chemistry, physics, Latin, music, calculus, studio art, computer science, U.S. history, European history, and world history. Honors sections, accelerated programs, and independent study are available.

Classes in mathematics, junior and senior English, junior and senior history, and science are homogeneous sections. Class size is approximately 15 students.

The new library has study carrels and books and periodicals for general reading, research, and reference. Thirty-five computers are available for student use in the library. The librarians make every effort to help students make use of the facility.

Students receive an excellent preparatory education. There are refurbished biology, geology, physics, chemistry, and biochemistry laboratories with completely modern equipment.

The school year is divided into two semesters. Each term ends with an examination period that lasts three to four days. Examinations count for approximately one third of the term grade.

Each student is provided with an adviser, with whom he or she meets once a week to review academic progress. Advisers are given a weekly update by each student's teacher, and these reports may be accessed by parents on the Academy's Web site. Grades and written comments by teachers are sent home up to four times a year. In addition, written comments from advisers are sent two times a year. Parents may request meetings with teachers or advisers at any time.

FACULTY AND ADVISERS

The full-time faculty is composed of 86 teachers, all of whom hold baccalaureate degrees. Forty-five hold advanced degrees, including three doctorates, one law degree, and one Master of Divinity degree. Thirty-five faculty members are women. There are 29 faculty members who live on campus with their families.

Dexter Morse, appointed Head of School in 1997, is a graduate of Phillips Academy in Andover, Massachusetts; Bowdoin College (A.B., 1962); and the University of Vermont (M.Ed., 1967). Mr. Morse previously served as Head of the Upper School at Phoenix Country Day School.

In selecting its faculty, the Academy looks first for classroom teaching ability. All members of the faculty are also responsible for extracurricular activities, and those living on campus are also dorm masters.

COLLEGE PLACEMENT

The College Counselor assists students in the college application process and aids them in gaining admission to, and entering, colleges suited to their needs and ambitions. It is the school's goal that each student be able to select from among several colleges extending offers of admission.

The process of college counseling at the Academy follows a general pattern. In the spring, individual conferences for each junior are scheduled to discuss college plans, and the junior class attends a college fair in Boston to obtain information about

colleges throughout the country. During the summer before their senior year, students are urged to write to colleges for literature, study college publications, and visit the colleges to which they intend to apply. In the fall of the senior year, individual conferences with the College Counselor are held to discuss final application procedures and to examine each student's goals and abilities in relation to the programs at the colleges to which he or she is applying.

The college counseling office holds individual conferences to discuss colleges, welcomes college representatives who conduct individual interviews or small informational sessions, maintains a large collection of college catalogs, provides transcripts for applications, writes statements about each student to supplement the factual information given in the transcript, gives advice on financial aid, and helps students in all areas of the college admission process.

The ranges of SAT scores in the middle 50 percent for the classes of 2000 to 2005 were 570–690 verbal and 570–700 math. Verbal scores do not include those of international students.

The SAT Reasoning Test and SAT Subject Tests are administered throughout the year by the College Counseling Office, which advises students on the appropriate testing program to highlight their strengths and satisfy the requirements of colleges. International students are registered for the TOEFL during their junior and senior years.

All of the 130 seniors who graduated in 2005 proceeded immediately to higher education. Worcester Academy graduates are enrolled at more than ninety different colleges, including Amherst, Boston College, Bowdoin, Brandeis, Brown, Carnegie Mellon, Columbia, Cornell, Emory, Harvard, Haverford, Holy Cross, MIT, Middlebury, Mount Holyoke, Oberlin, Trinity, Tufts, Washington and Lee, Wellesley, Williams, Yale, and the Universities of Chicago and Michigan.

STUDENT BODY AND CONDUCT

The 2005–06 student enrollment was distributed as follows: sixth grade, 15 boys and 15 girls; seventh grade, 37 boys and 22 girls; eighth grade, 33 boys and 29 girls; ninth grade, 45 boys and 51 girls; tenth grade, 76 boys and 45 girls; eleventh grade, 73 boys and 55 girls; twelfth grade, 53 boys and 56 girls; and postgraduate year, 23 boys and 3 girls. There were 492 day students and 139 boarding students. Students came from twelve states and eleven countries.

Students are expected to follow the rules and behave in a socially mature and responsible manner, which includes respecting the rights and property of others. The Headmaster has final authority over all disciplinary matters and has the right to dismiss any student.

ACADEMIC FACILITIES

Walker Hall houses administrative offices, classrooms, the Ackerman Media Center (containing new computer and language laboratories), the Walker Hall Gallery, the Andes Performing Arts Center, and the newly refurbished art studio. Rader

Hall, which opened in 2001, is a beautiful, state-of-the-art four-story academic building that adds eleven new classrooms and a two-story library. Kingsley Hall—renovated with a ramp and elevators to accommodate the handicapped—houses classrooms, a computer laboratory, laboratories for all sciences, and an audiovisual room. The newly renovated Warner Theater houses the music department and is used for plays, recitals, movies, and assemblies. The Megaron is a building that is also used for social events. The Kellner Student Center opened in 1991. This facility houses recreation rooms, club rooms, the mail room, the school store, and a faculty apartment. Six Worcester Academy buildings are included on the National Register of Historic Places.

BOARDING AND GENERAL FACILITIES

Dexter Hall and Davol Hall are boys' dormitories, and Heydon Hall and Stoddard Hall are girls' dormitories. In addition, Stoddard Hall also houses the infirmary. All rooms are singles or doubles. All dormitories have faculty members as dorm masters. During vacation, the dormitories are closed.

The full-time infirmary staff, including 2 nurse practitioners, is aided by a physician who visits the school twice a week. The Academy has 24-hour access to Worcester Medical Center and a family health service facility. In addition, one of the school's 2 counselors lives on campus.

ATHLETICS

Every student is required to participate in some form of physical education or sports. Athletic activities include baseball, basketball, cross-country, field hockey, football, golf, hockey, lacrosse, skiing, soccer, softball, swimming, tennis, track, volleyball, water polo, and wrestling.

Worcester Academy has a rich athletic tradition. Its alumni include many college, professional, and Olympic competitors. The boys' varsity teams compete against the Class A prep schools of New England as well as several college junior varsity teams. Girls and underclassmen compete against other independent schools.

The Daniels Gymnasium houses a swimming pool, two basketball courts, a track, a wrestling room, a weight room, a sports store, a training room, and a varsity club room. Gaskill Field, completely renovated in 1994, is an 11-acre facility with tennis courts; a track; soccer, football, and baseball fields; and a field house. The New Balance Fields, a 37-acre tract about 4 miles from campus, were completed in fall 2001 and provide additional baseball and softball diamonds, and fields for soccer, lacrosse, and field hockey.

EXTRACURRICULAR OPPORTUNITIES

Clubs are organized around common interests, such as French, Spanish, community service, mathematics, computers, history, drama, debate, public speaking, international club, science, law, investments, and chess. Students may participate in Model UN and Amnesty International. Students also publish a yearbook, the school newspaper, and a literary magazine. Students are required to participate in two clubs or sports during the year.

There are assemblies at which lecturers and performers appear. Traditional events include Homecoming, Winter Carnival, and Alumni Day. There are dances, concerts, plays, and movies throughout the year.

Located in Worcester, a city of 170,000 residents, 1 hour west of Boston, the Academy is distinctive because of its urban location. The Academy's easy access to many museums, concert halls, libraries, shopping malls, and a nationally known civic center provides its students with a number of recreational opportunities.

DAILY LIFE

Classes begin daily at 7:45 and end at 3:15 on Monday, Tuesday, Thursday, and Friday. On Wednesday, classes end at 12:30. Class periods are 49 minutes long. On Wednesday afternoons and on Saturdays, there are athletic contests. Extracurricular activities and sports practices are held from 3:15 to 6 p.m. For boarders, breakfast begins at 7, lunch is served from 11:30 to 1:30, and dinner begins at 6:15. On Sunday through Thursday evenings, there is a 2-hour required supervised study hall from 8 to 10 in the dormitories. There is free time after study hall until 10:30, when students must be back in their rooms.

WEEKEND LIFE

Friday and Saturday nights are free nights, and activities are planned and chaperoned by the faculty. A typical weekend offers two or three activities, which might be dances, movies, concerts, or field trips to points of interest. Students may also sign out to leave campus.

COSTS AND FINANCIAL AID

Tuition for the 2005–06 academic year was $18,750 for day students in grades 6–8 and $19,800 for grades 9–12 (costs include lunch); $31,725 for five-day boarders; and $35,525 for seven-day boarders. There is a minimum $800 bookstore and athletic fee for all students. Tuition refund insurance is required. Health insurance and tuition payment plans are available. Resident international students pay $3000 to cover infirmary services, activities, health insurance, TOEFL testing, and immigration support.

All financial aid is awarded on the basis of need. The Parents' Financial Statement must be filed with the School and Student Service for Financial Aid in Princeton, New Jersey. For 2004–05, scholarships amounted to approximately $2.5 million, including $20,000 allocated to a student work program.

The following job opportunities are available for students whose families qualify for financial aid: gymnasium supervision, work at athletic events, and general office help.

ADMISSIONS INFORMATION

The Academy admits each student on the basis of his or her transcript of grades, letters of recommendation, standardized test scores, and personal interview. Only college-bound students are admitted. Since each student is considered on the basis of individual college goals, no fixed grade level is required for admission. The Admission Committee evaluates candidates for admission, paying close attention to past performance as well as personal qualities. The campus visit is an important aspect of the admission process, since it gives the candidate a chance to learn a great deal about the school and to see it in operation.

Worcester Academy subscribes fully to all federal and state legislation prohibiting discrimination of any sort against applicants, students, or faculty or staff members for reasons of race, sex, religion, or national origin.

APPLICATION TIMETABLE

Worcester Academy invites inquiries at any time of the year. Campus visits may be arranged Monday through Friday from 8 a.m. to 3 p.m. The priority deadline for applying for admission is February 1; after that date applications are reviewed on a space-available basis. Notification of acceptance is mailed on March 10. The application fee is $50 for U.S. applicants and $100 for international applicants.

ADMISSIONS CORRESPONDENCE

Jonathan G. Baker, Director of Admission and
    Financial Aid
Worcester Academy
81 Providence Street
Worcester, Massachusetts 01604

Phone: 508-754-5302
Fax: 508-752-2382
E-mail: admission@worcesteracademy.org
Web site: http://www.worcesteracademy.org

WYOMING SEMINARY
COLLEGE PREPARATORY SCHOOL

Kingston, Pennsylvania

WYOMING SEMINARY
founded 1844

Type: Coeducational boarding (grades 9–12) and day college-preparatory school
Grades: PK–PG: Lower School, PK–8; Upper School, 9–12, postgraduate year
Enrollment: School total: 820; Upper School: 455
Head of School: H. Jeremy Packard, President

THE SCHOOL

Located in the Wyoming Valley of northeastern Pennsylvania, Wyoming Seminary is a coeducational college-preparatory school enrolling day students in prekindergarten (age 3) through grade 12 and boarding students in grades 9–12 and a postgraduate year. The Lower School campus is located in Forty Fort, approximately 3 miles from the Upper School campus. Kingston, a suburb of historic Wilkes-Barre, lies along the banks of the Susquehanna River. Kingston is a 2-hour drive from New York City, 2 hours from Philadelphia, and 25 minutes from the Wilkes-Barre/Scranton International Airport, which is served by major airlines.

Wyoming Seminary was founded in 1844 by leaders of the Methodist church to "prepare students for the active duties of life—for a course of professional or collegiate studies or any degree of collegiate advancement." Today, Wyoming Seminary students and teachers challenge themselves and each other to reach their academic and personal goals. Students learn to manage their time, write and speak clearly and effectively, study efficiently, and continue learning for college and life.

Five colleges, the Kirby Center for the Performing Arts, the Northeastern Pennsylvania Philharmonic, the Everhart Museum, Steamtown National Historic Park, the new Wachovia Arena, and area theater, music groups, and lecture series provide cultural opportunities. Skiing, biking, hiking, white-water rafting in nearby state parks, the Philadelphia Phillies AAA farm club games, and the Wilkes-Barre/Scranton Penguins AHL games are popular weekend activities.

Wyoming Seminary is directed by a 44-member Board of Trustees. Endowment is valued at more than $45 million, of which approximately 40 percent is used for scholarship purposes. Wyoming Seminary is accredited by the Middle States Association of Colleges and Schools, approved by the University Senate of the United Methodist Church, and a member of the National Association of Methodist Schools and Colleges, the Pennsylvania Association of Independent Schools, the Boarding Schools Association of the Philadelphia Area, the Association of Boarding Schools, the National Association of Independent Schools, the Secondary School Admission Test Board, the Council for Religion in Independent Schools, the College Board, and the National Association of College Admission Counselors.

ACADEMIC PROGRAMS

Wyoming Seminary prides itself on its high standards of academic excellence and its competitive spirit. Seminary offers more than 140 college preparatory courses, from the fundamental to the advanced, including twenty-four Advanced Placement courses in all major disciplines. Classes meet five days per week and have an average of 13 students. Advanced classes are much smaller. The student-teacher ratio is 8:1.

To be awarded a Wyoming Seminary diploma, a student must accumulate a minimum of 19.33 credits; students earn .33 credit for a term course or 1 credit for a full-year course. Specific requirements are English, 4 credits; mathematics, 3 credits; foreign language, 3 credits; history/social science, 3 credits; laboratory science, 3 credits; physical education, 4 credits; health, .33 credit; religion .33 credit; music history, .33 credit; art history, .33 credit; public speaking, .33 credit; and computer science, .33 credit. The trimester system increases the number of possible choices.

Qualified students may enroll in advanced courses at nearby Wilkes University or King's College. With faculty approval, juniors, seniors, and postgraduates may pursue independent-study programs or a school exchange abroad for one or more terms. Seniors and postgraduates have opportunities to further investigate areas of interest through internships in local businesses and professional offices.

Wyoming Seminary enrolls between 15 and 20 postgraduate students each year. All are qualified to enter college directly from their previous schools but choose to spend a year at a college-prep school to improve their college options. They take advanced courses previously unavailable to them and strengthen their skills in areas such as math or writing. Working with Seminary's postgraduate coordinator, these students enroll in two courses designed to meet their needs: The Postgraduate Experience seminar and Postgraduate English. Other than these two requirements, they have great flexibility to choose among Wyoming Seminary's multifaceted curriculum.

An ESL program is also offered for international students.

FACULTY AND ADVISERS

The teaching faculty at the Upper School includes 30 women and 39 men; 12 percent hold doctoral degrees and 57 percent hold master's degrees from a variety of colleges and universities. There are 40 women and 10 men at the Lower School; 52 percent hold master's degrees. Two thirds of the faculty members live on the campus; this gives students an opportunity to consult with their teachers beyond the usual school day.

H. Jeremy Packard, appointed tenth President of Wyoming Seminary in 1990, is a graduate of Williams College and Columbia University. He was awarded an Honorary degree of Sacred Letters from Wycliffe College, University of Toronto, in 1989.

COLLEGE PLACEMENT

Beginning in the sophomore year, students receive highly personalized counseling, which continues until they select a college or university that suits their interests, abilities, and needs. Virtually all graduates of Wyoming Seminary pursue their education in a four-year program. Most graduates are accepted by at least one highly competitive or most competitive college.

Members of the class of 2004 are currently enrolled at Boston College, Bucknell, Cornell, Denison, Lafayette, NYU, Syracuse, the United States Naval Academy, University of Pennsylvania, and Washington University.

STUDENT BODY AND CONDUCT

The current enrollment in the Upper School is 455. This includes 92 boarding boys, 62 boarding girls, 150 day boys, and 151 day girls. The students are from ten states and twenty-three countries, including Croatia, Germany, Japan, Russia, Spain, and Thailand.

The Wyoming Seminary student body is governed by a legislative assembly, made up of students and members of the faculty and administration, which is responsible for many nonacademic aspects of campus life. Within the government are four standing committees: spirit, activities, assemblies and programs, and finance.

The Dean of Upper School monitors the conduct of the student body, and, depending on the seriousness of the offense, either the Dean or a disciplinary committee determines the penalty.

ACADEMIC FACILITIES

Wyoming Seminary (Upper School) occupies an 18-acre main campus that includes traditional ivy-covered nineteenth-century buildings as well as more modern facilities. Nesbitt Hall contains science laboratories, arts studios, a Mac lab, and a dance studio. Sprague Hall includes a new addition with state-of-the-art classrooms, a conference room, computer facilities, a bookstore, and administrative offices. The 23,000-volume Kirby Library is housed in the Stettler Learning Resources Center. The Carpenter Athletic Center and Pettebone Dickson Student Center cater to athletics and student clubs. Great Hall offers performance and classroom space for the performing arts department.

BOARDING AND GENERAL FACILITIES

Boarding students live in four dormitories. Swetland, Darte, and Fleck Halls are interconnected to form one unit. Girls are housed in Swetland and Fleck and freshman and sophomore boys in Darte. Junior, senior, and postgraduate boys live in Carpenter Hall. Within each dormitory are computers for individual use and lounge areas where students can gather and relax.

Individual telephone and e-mail accounts exist for each day and boarding student, and Internet access is available in each classroom and dormitory room.

ATHLETICS
More than 75 percent of Wyoming Seminary students take part in interscholastic sports. Twenty varsity teams compete in more than 200 contests each year. Girls compete in basketball, cross-country, field hockey, golf, ice hockey, lacrosse, soccer, softball, swimming, and tennis. Boys participate in baseball, basketball, cross-country, football, golf, ice hockey, lacrosse, soccer, swimming, tennis, and wrestling. The Carpenter Athletic Center, with its swimming pool, two gymnasiums, and a new weight room, provides accommodations for both varsity and intramural sports.

EXTRACURRICULAR OPPORTUNITIES
Whether it is athletics or music, creative writing or drama, Seminary students easily find their niche. Student activities include Peer Group, *The Wyoming* (yearbook), *The Opinator* (newspaper), *Pandemonium* (literary magazine), Dance, International Club, "W" Club, Blue Key, Model United Nations, Environmental Club, Social and Gender Issues Club, Ski Club, and others. Involvement in community service is required by the EXCOLO program.

The Buckingham Performing Arts Center houses a 460-seat auditorium with high-tech stage equipment, dramatics practice area, and scenery construction shop, giving students the chance to become involved in every aspect of the theater. Three drama productions are performed each year. Orchestra and vocal performances take place in the Great Hall. Musical organizations include the 100-voice Chorale and the Madrigal Singers, a select group of 28 who tour nationally and in Europe; orchestra, jazz, and string ensembles; and a handbell choir. Music practice rooms, rehearsal studios, and a listening center give musicians a special place to perform and work. Private instruction is available in instrumental music and voice.

DAILY LIFE
A typical academic day at Seminary begins at 8 and includes four class periods in the morning followed by lunch and three classes in the afternoon in addition to weekly school meetings and chapel. Each class period is approximately 45 minutes long. A conference period is scheduled at the end of the day, giving students the opportunity to meet with teachers or advisers for extra help. During the hours between class and dinner, students participate in extracurricular activities or athletics. Family-style dinner is served in the dining hall for all boarding students and faculty families. Boarding students study in their rooms or the library from 7:30 p.m. until 9:50 p.m., Sunday through Thursday.

WEEKEND LIFE
The weekend schedules provide plenty of social activity. Along with movies, sports events, dances, and plays are white-water rafting, mountain biking, weekend ski trips, outdoor cookouts and concerts, and trips to New York and Philadelphia. Wilkes-Barre gives students additional cultural and social events to attend, and it has a great variety of restaurants and shops.

COSTS AND FINANCIAL AID
In 2005–06, Upper School tuition is $33,725 for boarding students and $17,275 for day students. Additional expenses include allowances, books, athletic clothing, a graduation fee of $60, and travel.

Financial aid is available to students who qualify on the basis of need, academic performance, and citizenship. More than $4 million in aid is awarded to about 44 percent of all students.

ADMISSIONS INFORMATION
To be accepted at Wyoming Seminary, a student must demonstrate strong character and the ability to do college-preparatory work. Applicants for grades 9, 10, and 11 must take the SSAT. A limited number of seniors and postgraduates are accepted each year, and they are asked to submit College Board scores. Each applicant is evaluated on the basis of his or her application, recommendations, and school transcripts. An interview is not required but is strongly recommended.

APPLICATION TIMETABLE
Inquiries and applications are welcome the year round. The school encourages applicants to schedule an on-campus interview. There is a charge of $75 to cover processing expenses.

ADMISSIONS CORRESPONDENCE
John R. Eidam, Dean of Admission
or
Randy Granger, Director of Admission
Wyoming Seminary
201 North Sprague Avenue
Kingston, Pennsylvania 18704-3593

Phone: 570-270-2160
    877-996-7361 (toll-free)
Fax: 570-270-2191 or 2198
E-mail: admission@wyomingseminary.org
Web site: http://www.wyomingseminary.org

YORK PREPARATORY SCHOOL

New York, New York

Type: Coeducational day college-preparatory school
Grades: 6–12: Lower School, 6–8; Upper School, 9–12
Enrollment: School total: 320
Head of School: Ronald P. Stewart, Headmaster

THE SCHOOL

York Prep is a college-preparatory school where contemporary methods enliven a strong, academically challenging, traditional curriculum. In a city known for its diversity of private schools, York Prep has developed a unique program that leads students to their highest potential. The School's approach emphasizes independent thought, builds confidence, and sends graduates on to the finest colleges and universities. York Prep believes that success breeds success. At York, every student finds opportunities to flourish. Excellence in academics, arts, or sports creates self-confidence that enhances all aspects of life, both in and out of the classroom.

York Prep was established in 1969 by its current Headmaster, Ronald P. Stewart, and his wife, Jayme Stewart, Director of College Guidance. Situated on West 68th Street between Columbus Avenue and Central Park West, the School is well served by public transportation. Consequently, it attracts students from all over the metropolitan area. The School's programs take full advantage of the prime location, with regular visits to museums, parks, and theaters, all of which are easily accessible.

York Prep is approved by the New York State Board of Regents and accredited by the Middle States Association of Colleges and Schools.

ACADEMIC PROGRAMS

The curriculum is designed to develop the superior academic skills necessary for future success. Close attention to each student's needs ensures that progress toward personal excellence is carefully guided.

Students must complete 20 credits for graduation: 4 in English, 4 in math, 4 in science, 4 in history, a minimum of 3 in foreign language, 1 in art or music, ½ in health, and ½ in community service.

Eleventh and twelfth graders choose from a number of course offerings in every subject area. In addition to selecting one course from each required category, a student must choose an elective from a variety of options that range from the creative and performing arts to the analytical sciences. Students are required to carry at least five major subjects a year plus physical education.

York Prep pioneered the requirement of community service for graduation from high school. York Prep requires 100 hours of structured and supervised community service and a final report, and the School is in close contact with the charitable agencies with which its students serve the community.

Independent study courses and Advanced Placement courses are offered. When it is appropriate, students may graduate early or enroll at local colleges for specific classes.

Classes at York are small—the average class has 15 students. There are close student-teacher relations and an advisory system. All students meet with their adviser every morning during a "house" period. Each student's academic and social progress is carefully monitored by the teachers, advisers, and deans of the Upper and Lower Schools. The deans, in turn, keep the Headmaster and the Principal informed at weekly meetings. In addition, the Headmaster and Principal maintain close relationships with the students by teaching courses and are readily available to students and parents alike. At the close of each day, there is a period when students may go to faculty members or advisers for help.

Parents are kept informed of a student's progress through individual reports posted on "Edline," a component of the York Prep Web site, every Friday. Each family signs in with a unique password and can see their child's progress in all academic subjects. The annual Curriculum Night, in which parents become students for an evening by attending their child's truncated classes, provides a good overview of the course work and the faculty members. Parent involvement is encouraged, and there is an active Parents' Association.

FACULTY AND ADVISERS

York Prep is proud of having maintained a stable faculty of outstanding and dedicated individuals. New teachers join the staff periodically, creating a nice balance between youth and experience.

There are 62 full-time faculty members, including 2 college guidance counselors, 11 reading and learning specialists, 2 computer specialists, and a librarian.

Mr. Ronald P. Stewart, the founding Headmaster, is a graduate of Oxford University (B.A., 1965; M.A., 1966; B.C.L., 1968), where he also taught.

COLLEGE PLACEMENT

York Prep has a notable college guidance program. Mrs. Jayme Stewart, the Director of College Guidance, is well known for her expertise, experience, and authorship of *How to Get into the College of Your Choice*. She meets with all tenth graders to outline the program and then meets individually with eleventh graders and their parents. The students begin working on their college essays in eleventh grade. Extensive meetings continue through the twelfth grade on an individual basis.

All of York Prep's graduating students attend college. The ultimate aim of the college guidance program is the placement of each student in the college best suited to him or her. More than 85 percent of York Prep graduates are accepted to, attend, and finish at their first-choice college. Graduates are currently attending schools that include Barnard, Berkeley, Bowdoin, Colgate, Columbia, Cornell, Franklin and Marshall, Hamilton, Hobart, MIT, Pennsylvania, Skidmore, Vassar, Wesley, and the University of Michigan. Numerous college representatives visit the School regularly to meet with interested students.

STUDENT BODY AND CONDUCT

There are 320 students enrolled at York Prep. York Prep students reside in all five boroughs of New York City as well as Long Island, northern New Jersey, and Westchester County. There are a student code of conduct and a dress code. An elected student council is an integral part of life at York Prep.

ACADEMIC FACILITIES

Located steps from Central Park at 40 West 68th Street, York Prep is a seven-story granite building housing two modern science laboratories, state-of-the-art computer equipment, performance and art studios, and a sprung hardwood gymnasium with weight and locker room facilities. The classrooms are spacious and airy, carpeted and climate controlled. All classrooms have computers and audiovisual (AV) projectors. A T1 line provides high-speed Internet access for the whole School and enables students to e-mail their teachers and review homework assignments. In addition, all classrooms are linked to the School's in-house television channel, WYRK, over which daily announcements are aired. The building is wheelchair accessible and is located near Lincoln Center on a safe and lovely tree-lined street.

ATHLETICS

All students are required to take courses in physical education and health each year. A varied and extensive program and after-school selection offer students the opportunity to participate in competitive, noncompetitive, team, and individual sports. York Prep is a playing member of several athletics leagues.

EXTRACURRICULAR OPPORTUNITIES

The Student Council organizes regular social events and trips. The School provides a wide range of extracurricular activities, including a mock trial law team, rock climbing, roller hockey, and a drama club.

DAILY LIFE

The School day begins at 8:40 with a 10-minute house period. Academic classes of 42-minute duration begin at 8:56. There is a midmorning break at 10:24. Lunch period is from 12:08 to 12:53, Mondays through Thursdays, and classes end at 3:12. Following dismissal, teachers are available for extra help. During this time, clubs and sports teams also meet. The school day ends at 1:35 on Fridays.

SUMMER PROGRAMS

The School provides workshops during the summer, both in study skills and in academic courses, most of which are set up on an individual tutorial basis. In addition, the athletic department provides summer sports camps.

COSTS AND FINANCIAL AID

Tuition for the 2005–06 academic year ranged from $25,900 to $26,400. More than 40 percent of the student body receives some financial assistance. During the previous year, $750,000 was offered in financial aid.

ADMISSIONS INFORMATION

The School seeks to enroll students of above-average intelligence with the will and ability to complete college-preparatory work. Students are accepted on the basis of their applications, ISEE test scores, writing samples, and interviews.

APPLICATION TIMETABLE

The School conforms to the notification guidelines established by the Independent Schools Admissions Association of Greater New York. Subsequent applications are processed on a rolling admissions basis. Requests for financial aid should be made at the time of application for entrance.

ADMISSIONS CORRESPONDENCE

Elizabeth Norton, Director of Enrollment
Lisa Smith, Co-Director of Admissions
Jacqueline Leber, Co-Director of Admissions
York Preparatory School
40 West 68th Street
New York, New York 10023

Phone: 212-362-0400
Fax: 212-362-7424
E-mail: admissions@yorkprep.org
Web site: http://www.yorkprep.org

Special Needs Schools

THE ACADEMY AT SISTERS

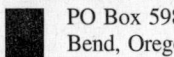

PO Box 5986
Bend, Oregon 97708-5986
Head of School: Rick O'Dell

General Information Girls' boarding general academic school; primarily serves underachievers and individuals with emotional and behavioral problems. Grades 7–12. Founded: 1994. Setting: rural. Students are housed in single-sex rooms. 20-acre campus. 6 buildings on campus. Approved or accredited by CITA (Commission on International and Trans-Regional Accreditation), Northwest Association of Schools and Colleges, and Oregon Department of Education. Total enrollment: 30. Upper school faculty-student ratio: 1:12.

Upper School Student Profile Grade 9: 3 students (3 girls); Grade 10: 10 students (10 girls); Grade 11: 10 students (10 girls); Grade 12: 5 students (5 girls). 100% of students are boarding students. 13% are state residents. 6 states are represented in upper school student body.

Faculty School total: 5. In upper school: 1 man, 4 women; 4 have advanced degrees.

Special Academic Programs Honors section; independent study; remedial reading and/or remedial writing; remedial math.

College Placement 5 students graduated in 2005.

Student Life Upper grades have uniform requirement, honor system. Discipline rests primarily with faculty.

Summer Programs Remediation programs offered; held on campus; accepts girls; not open to students from other schools. 30 students usually enrolled. 2006 schedule: June 15 to August 14.

Tuition and Aid Guaranteed tuition plan. Tuition installment plan (monthly payment plans, individually arranged payment plans). TERI Loans, Achiever Loans (Key Education Resources), prepGATE Loans available.

Admissions Traditional secondary-level entrance grade is 9. Deadline for receipt of application materials: none. Application fee required: $35. Interview required.

Athletics Intramural: aerobics, aerobics/dance, aquatics, back packing, badminton, climbing, cooperative games, dance, equestrian sports, fitness, fitness walking, hiking/backpacking, horseback riding, jogging, martial arts, modern dance, outdoor activities, outdoor adventure, outdoor education, outdoor recreation, outdoor skills, physical fitness, project adventure, rock climbing, skiing (cross-country), skiing (downhill), snowboarding, snowshoeing, soccer, volleyball, walking, wall climbing, yoga. 2 PE instructors.

Computers Computers are regularly used in all academic classes. Computer resources include on-campus library services, CD-ROMs, Internet access, DVD.

Contact Ms. Chesley Strowd, Admissions Coordinator. 541-389-2748. Fax: 541-389-2897. Web site: www.academyatsisters.org/.

ACADEMY AT SWIFT RIVER

151 South Street
Cummington, Massachusetts 01026
Head of School: Don Vardell

petersons.com

General Information Coeducational boarding college-preparatory and arts school; primarily serves students with learning disabilities, individuals with Attention Deficit Disorder, individuals with emotional and behavioral problems, and dyslexic students. Grades 9–12. Founded: 1997. Setting: rural. Nearest major city is Springfield. Students are housed in single-sex dormitories. 630-acre campus. 5 buildings on campus. Approved or accredited by Massachusetts Department of Education. Candidate for accreditation by New England Association of Schools and Colleges. Member of Secondary School Admission Test Board. Total enrollment: 100. Upper school average class size: 10. Upper school faculty-student ratio: 1:8.

Upper School Student Profile Grade 9: 25 students (20 boys, 5 girls); Grade 10: 25 students (20 boys, 5 girls); Grade 11: 25 students (20 boys, 5 girls); Grade 12: 25 students (20 boys, 5 girls). 100% of students are boarding students. 8% are state residents. 27 states are represented in upper school student body. International students from Canada and United Kingdom; 3 other countries represented in student body.

Faculty School total: 16. In upper school: 11 men, 2 women; 7 have advanced degrees.

Subjects Offered Addiction, adolescent issues, algebra, American history, American literature, art, biology, calculus, career and personal planning, career/college preparation, character education, chemistry, civics, college counseling, college placement, communication skills, community service, composition, computers, conflict resolution, current events, death and loss, decision making skills, ecology, environmental systems, English, English composition, English literature, environmental science, experiential education, fitness, geography, geometry, government/civics, health, health and wellness, history, independent study, integrated arts, interpersonal skills, lab science, life management skills, literature, martial arts, mathematics, nature study, nutrition, peer counseling, personal development, physical education, physics, pre-algebra, pre-calculus, reading/study skills, relationships, SAT/ACT preparation, science, social science, social studies, Spanish, U.S. government, weight training, wilderness experience, wilderness studies, wilderness/outdoor program, world geography, world history.

Graduation Requirements Arts and fine arts (art, music, dance, drama), English, history, mathematics, physical education (includes health), science, service learning/internship. Community service is required.

Special Academic Programs Accelerated programs; independent study; term-away projects; study at local college for college credit; study abroad; remedial reading and/or remedial writing; remedial math; programs in English, mathematics, general development for dyslexic students.

College Placement 42 students graduated in 2004; 39 went to college, including Agnes Scott College; Gannon University; Iona College; Syracuse University; University of Connecticut; University of Hartford. Other: 2 went to work. Median SAT verbal: 550, median SAT math: 510. 22% scored over 600 on SAT verbal, 15% scored over 600 on SAT math.

Student Life Upper grades have specified standards of dress, student council, honor system. Discipline rests primarily with faculty.

Tuition and Aid 7-day tuition and room/board: $69,000. Guaranteed tuition plan. Tuition installment plan (Key Tuition Payment Plan, monthly payment plans, individually arranged payment plans). Need-based scholarship grants, Sallie Mae Loan Program, Key Bank Loans, Achiever Loans (Key Education Resources) available. In 2004–05, 5% of upper-school students received aid. Total amount of financial aid awarded in 2004–05: $85,000.

Admissions Traditional secondary-level entrance grade is 11. For fall 2005, 230 students applied for upper-level admission, 118 were accepted, 100 enrolled. Battery of testing done through outside agency and Wechsler Intelligence Scale for Children required. Deadline for receipt of application materials: none. No application fee required. On-campus interview recommended.

Athletics Coed Intramural: aerobics, aerobics/dance, alpine skiing, back packing, baseball, basketball, bicycling, canoeing/kayaking, climbing, combined training, cross-country running, dance, field hockey, fishing, fitness, flag football, Frisbee, golf, hiking/backpacking, in-line skating, independent competitive sports, jogging, martial arts, mountain biking, outdoor activities, outdoor adventure, outdoor education, outdoor recreation, physical fitness, physical training, rappelling, rock climbing, roller blading, ropes courses, running, self defense, skiing (cross-country), skiing (downhill), snowboarding, soccer, softball, swimming and diving, tennis, ultimate Frisbee, walking, weight lifting, weight training, wilderness, yoga. 1 PE instructor.

Computers Computers are regularly used in English, history, science classes. Computer network features include on-campus library services, CD-ROMs, Internet access.

Contact Rhonda J. Papallo, Director of Admissions. 800-258-1770 Ext. 102. Fax: 413-634-5090. E-mail: rpapallo@swiftriver.com. Web site: www.swiftriver.com.

ANNOUNCEMENT FROM THE SCHOOL The Academy at Swift River (ASR) was the first therapeutic boarding program in the country to provide a postgraduate follow-up program for a year after graduation. The highly-skilled and dedicated staff members are committed to providing an integrated and individualized education for students. ASR offers small academic classes and strong therapeutic supports.

See full description on page 1206.

ALPINE ACADEMY

5800 South Highland Drive
Salt Lake City, Utah 84121
Head of School: Becky Schofield-Anderson

General Information Girls' boarding general academic school; primarily serves underachievers, students with learning disabilities, individuals with Attention Deficit Disorder, and individuals with emotional and behavioral problems. Grades 7–12. Founded: 2001. Setting: rural. Nearest major city is Tooele. Students are housed in single-sex dormitories. 28-acre campus. 4 buildings on campus. Approved or accredited by Northwest Association of Accredited Schools and Utah Department of Education. Upper school average class size: 8. Upper school faculty-student ratio: 1:4.

Upper School Student Profile 100% of students are boarding students. 5 states are represented in upper school student body.

Faculty In upper school: 8 reside on campus.

Subjects Offered Art, basic skills, English, health, history, life skills, mathematics, physical education, psychology, science.

Special Academic Programs Academic accommodation for the gifted; remedial reading and/or remedial writing; remedial math; special instructional classes for blind students.

Student Life Upper grades have specified standards of dress. Discipline rests primarily with faculty.

Tuition and Aid Tuition installment plan (monthly payment plans).

Admissions Psychoeducational evaluation required. No application fee required.

Athletics Interscholastic: aerobics, aerobics/dance, basketball, fitness, fitness walking, golf, outdoor activities, outdoor adventure, outdoor education, outdoor recreation, outdoor skills, outdoors, physical fitness, physical training, rock climbing, soccer, volleyball, walking, weight lifting, weight training, yoga. 2 PE instructors.

Computers Computers are regularly used in English, history, psychology, writing classes. Computer resources include CD-ROMs.

Contact Sarah Armstrong, Intake Coordinator/Education Liaison. 801-272-9980 Ext. 139. Fax: 801-272-9976. E-mail: sarmstrong@youthvillage.org. Web site: www.alpineacademy.org.

AMERICAN ACADEMY

12200 West Broward Boulevard
Plantation, Florida 33325
Head of School: William R. Laurie

General Information Coeducational day arts school; primarily serves underachievers, students with learning disabilities, individuals with Attention Deficit Disorder, dyslexic students, and slow learners, and those with poor self esteem and poor confidence. Grades 1–12. Founded: 1965. Setting: suburban. Nearest major city is Fort Lauderdale. 40-acre campus. 9 buildings on campus. Approved or accredited by Association of Independent Schools of Florida, Southern Association of Colleges and Schools, and Florida Department of Education. Total enrollment: 498. Upper school average class size: 14. Upper school faculty-student ratio: 1:12.

Upper School Student Profile Grade 9: 65 students (51 boys, 14 girls); Grade 10: 61 students (51 boys, 10 girls); Grade 11: 62 students (48 boys, 14 girls); Grade 12: 54 students (43 boys, 11 girls).

Faculty School total: 44. In upper school: 6 men, 21 women; 18 have advanced degrees.

Subjects Offered Algebra, American history, American literature, anatomy, art, band, biology, business mathematics, ceramics, chemistry, chorus, community service, computer graphics, computer science, creative writing, drafting, drama, drawing, earth science, English, English literature, environmental science, fine arts, French, geometry, health, jazz, mathematics, music appreciation, oceanography, orchestra, photography, physical education, physical science, science, sculpture, Spanish, theater, vocal music, weight training, word processing, world geography, world history, world literature, writing, yearbook, zoology.

Graduation Requirements Arts and fine arts (art, music, dance, drama), computer science, English, mathematics, physical education (includes health), science, social studies (includes history). Community service is required.

Special Academic Programs Academic accommodation for the gifted, the musically talented, and the artistically talented; remedial reading and/or remedial writing; remedial math; programs in English, mathematics, general development for dyslexic students; ESL.

College Placement 35 students graduated in 2005; all went to college, including Broward Community College; Florida Atlantic University; Lynn University; Nova Southeastern University; Palm Beach Community College.

Student Life Upper grades have uniform requirement, student council. Discipline rests primarily with faculty.

Summer Programs Remediation, enrichment, advancement, ESL, art/fine arts, computer instruction programs offered; session focuses on remediation and make-up courses; held on campus; accepts boys and girls; open to students from other schools. 400 students usually enrolled. 2006 schedule: May 30 to July 28. Application deadline: none.

Tuition and Aid Day student tuition: $16,218–$18,712. Tuition installment plan (monthly payment plans, semester payment plan, annual payment plan). Tuition reduction for siblings, need-based scholarship grants, need-based loans available. In 2005–06, 42% of upper-school students received aid. Total amount of financial aid awarded in 2005–06: $1,042,945.

Admissions Traditional secondary-level entrance grade is 9. Psychoeducational evaluation, SAT and Slosson Intelligence required. Deadline for receipt of application materials: none. Application fee required: $100. On-campus interview required.

Athletics Interscholastic: baseball (boys), basketball (b,g), cheering (g), cross-country running (b,g), dance (g), dance squad (g), diving (b,g), football (b), golf (b,g), lacrosse (b), soccer (b,g), softball (g), swimming and diving (b,g), tennis (b,g), track and field (b,g), volleyball (b,g), weight lifting (b), weight training (b,g), winter soccer (b,g), wrestling (b). 7 PE instructors, 4 coaches.

Computers Computers are regularly used in graphic arts, literary magazine, newspaper, Web site design, word processing, writing, yearbook classes. Computer network features include on-campus library services, CD-ROMs, online commercial services, Internet access, Questia.

Contact William R. Laurie, President. 954-472-0022. Fax: 954-472-3088. Web site: www.ahschool.com.

ARROWSMITH SCHOOL

245 St. Clair Avenue West
Toronto, Ontario M4V 1R3, Canada
Head of School: Ms. Barbara Arrowsmith Young

General Information Coeducational day school; primarily serves underachievers, students with learning disabilities, and dyslexic students. Ungraded, ages 6–20. Founded: 1980. Setting: urban. 1 building on campus. Approved or accredited by Ontario Ministry of Education and Ontario Department of Education. Language of instruction: English. Total enrollment: 60. Upper school average class size: 10. Upper school faculty-student ratio: 1:8.

Faculty School total: 8. In upper school: 4 women.

Special Academic Programs Remedial reading and/or remedial writing; remedial math; programs in English, mathematics for dyslexic students.

College Placement 5 students graduated in 2005; 4 went to college, including University of Toronto; York University. Other: 1 went to work.

Student Life Upper grades have specified standards of dress. Discipline rests equally with students and faculty.

Tuition and Aid Day student tuition: CAN$17,000. Tuition installment plan (monthly payment plans).

Admissions Traditional secondary-level entrance age is 14. For fall 2005, 20 students applied for upper-level admission, 20 were accepted, 20 enrolled. Achievement tests, Differential Aptitude Test, Oral and Written Language Scales, Otis-Lennon Mental Ability Test, Raven (Aptitude Test); school's own exam, Reading for Understanding, school's own test, Wide Range Achievement Test, WISC/Woodcock-Johnson and writing sample required. Deadline for receipt of application materials: none. No application fee required. On-campus interview required.

Computers Computer resources include Internet access.

Contact Ms. Andrea Peirson, Director of Admissions. 416-963-4962. Fax: 416-963-5017. E-mail: apeirson@arrowsmithprogram.ca. Web site: www.arrowsmithschool.org.

ASPEN RANCH

2000 West Dry Valley
PO Box 369
Loa, Utah 84747
Head of School: Ms. Lisa Lewis

General Information Coeducational boarding college-preparatory and general academic school; primarily serves students with learning disabilities, individuals with Attention Deficit Disorder, individuals with emotional and behavioral problems, and dyslexic students. Grades 8–12. Founded: 1995. Setting: rural. Nearest major city is Salt Lake City. Students are housed in family-style single-sex dormitories. 160-acre campus. 9 buildings on campus. Approved or accredited by Northwest Association of Schools and Colleges and Utah Department of Education. Total enrollment: 72. Upper school average class size: 10. Upper school faculty-student ratio: 1:8.

Upper School Student Profile Grade 9: 11 students (7 boys, 4 girls); Grade 10: 23 students (14 boys, 9 girls); Grade 11: 18 students (11 boys, 7 girls); Grade 12: 14 students (8 boys, 6 girls). 100% of students are boarding students. 1% are state residents. 48 states are represented in upper school student body. International students from Switzerland and United Kingdom.

Faculty School total: 10. In upper school: 7 men, 3 women; 2 have advanced degrees.

Subjects Offered Algebra, American literature, art, athletics, biology, business mathematics, calculus, career education, chemistry, creative writing, criminal justice, earth science, economics, English, English literature, environmental science, equestrian sports, equine studies, fine arts, French, geometry, guitar, health, history, information technology, life saving, mathematics, physical education, physical science, poetry, pre-algebra, pre-calculus, psychology, reading, science, social skills, social studies, Spanish, study skills, trigonometry, U.S. government, U.S. history, weight training, world civilizations.

Graduation Requirements Art, career education, English, information technology, mathematics, physical education (includes health), science, social studies (includes history), teen living.

Special Academic Programs Accelerated programs; independent study; academic accommodation for the gifted; remedial reading and/or remedial writing; remedial math.

College Placement 15 students graduated in 2005.

Student Life Upper grades have uniform requirement, student council, honor system. Discipline rests equally with students and faculty.

Tuition and Aid Tuition installment plan (monthly payment plans, individually arranged payment plans).

Admissions Traditional secondary-level entrance grade is 10. For fall 2005, 95 students applied for upper-level admission, 71 were accepted. Kaufman Test of Educational Achievement required. Deadline for receipt of application materials: none. Application fee required.

Athletics Intramural: aerobics (girls); coed intramural: archery, basketball, canoeing/kayaking, equestrian sports, fishing, fitness, flag football, hiking/backpacking, horseback riding, life saving, mountain biking, outdoor activities, outdoor adventure, outdoor skills, physical fitness, rappelling, skiing (downhill), softball, ultimate Frisbee, volleyball, water skiing, weight training, wilderness. 2 PE instructors, 1 coach.

Computers Computers are regularly used in creative writing, English, history, psychology, science classes. Computer resources include CD-ROMs, online commercial services, Internet access, desktop publishing.

Contact Aspen Ranch Admissions. 877-231-0734. Fax: 435-836-2277. Web site: www.aspenranch.com.

BEACON HIGH SCHOOL

74 Green Street
Brookline, Massachusetts 02446
Head of School: Nancy Lincoln

General Information Coeducational day college-preparatory, general academic, and arts school; primarily serves students with learning disabilities, individuals with

Attention Deficit Disorder, and individuals with emotional and behavioral problems. Ungraded, ages 15–22. Founded: 1971. Setting: urban. Nearest major city is Boston. 1-acre campus. 2 buildings on campus. Approved or accredited by Lutheran School Accreditation Commission and Massachusetts Department of Education. Total enrollment: 53. Upper school average class size: 8. Upper school faculty-student ratio: 1:2.

Faculty School total: 18. In upper school: 6 men, 9 women; 14 have advanced degrees.

Subjects Offered Algebra, American history, American literature, anatomy, art, art history, biology, ceramics, chemistry, computer math, computer programming, computer science, creative writing, earth science, economics, English, English literature, European history, geography, geometry, grammar, historical research, mathematics, music, philosophy, photography, physical education, physics, psychology, research, science, social studies, theater, trigonometry, world literature, world religions, World War II, writing.

Graduation Requirements English, historical research, mathematics, physical education (includes health), science, social studies (includes history).

Special Academic Programs Accelerated programs; independent study; programs in English, mathematics, general development for dyslexic students.

College Placement 14 students graduated in 2005; 12 went to college, including Clark University; Curry College; Franklin Pierce College; Marlboro College; Montserrat College of Art; Simmons College. Other: 2 went to work.

Student Life Upper grades have student council, honor system. Discipline rests primarily with faculty.

Summer Programs Advancement, art/fine arts programs offered; session focuses on academics; held on campus; accepts boys and girls; not open to students from other schools. 40 students usually enrolled. 2006 schedule: June 29 to July 20.

Tuition and Aid Day student tuition: $39,000. Municipal funding to special needs education (tuition paid by student's hometown) available.

Admissions Traditional secondary-level entrance age is 16. Deadline for receipt of application materials: none. No application fee required. On-campus interview required.

Athletics Coed Intramural: baseball, basketball, soccer, softball, tennis, volleyball. 2 PE instructors.

Computers Computers are regularly used in English, mathematics, music, science, Web site design classes. Computer network features include campus e-mail, CD-ROMs, online commercial services, Internet access, DVD.

Contact Nancy Lincoln, Director. 617-232-1958.

BRANDON HALL SCHOOL

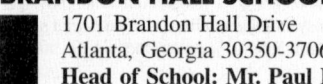

1701 Brandon Hall Drive
Atlanta, Georgia 30350-3706
Head of School: Mr. Paul R. Stockhammer

petersons.com

General Information Boys' boarding and coeducational day college-preparatory and ESL school; primarily serves underachievers, students with learning disabilities, individuals with Attention Deficit Disorder, and dyslexic students. Boarding boys grades 4–PG, day boys grades 4–PG, day girls grades 4–PG. Founded: 1959. Setting: suburban. Students are housed in single-sex dormitories. 27-acre campus. 7 buildings on campus. Approved or accredited by Georgia Accrediting Commission and Georgia Department of Education. Candidate for accreditation by Southern Association of Colleges and Schools. Member of National Association of Independent Schools. Endowment: $250,000. Total enrollment: 120. Upper school average class size: 4. Upper school faculty-student ratio: 1:3.

Upper School Student Profile Grade 9: 13 students (11 boys, 2 girls); Grade 10: 25 students (23 boys, 2 girls); Grade 11: 21 students (17 boys, 4 girls); Grade 12: 25 students (22 boys, 3 girls); Postgraduate: 1 student (1 boy). 45% of students are boarding students. 60% are state residents. 15 states are represented in upper school student body. 22% are international students. International students from Argentina, Cayman Islands, Guatemala, Netherlands Antilles, Republic of Korea, and Taiwan; 2 other countries represented in student body.

Faculty School total: 34. In upper school: 22 men, 10 women; 15 have advanced degrees; 13 reside on campus.

Subjects Offered Algebra, American literature, anatomy, art, biology, calculus, chemistry, chorus, college counseling, college planning, computer science, contemporary issues, current events, developmental math, drama, drama performance, earth science, economics, English, English composition, English literature, English-AP, ESL, expository writing, fine arts, French, geography, geometry, government/civics, grammar, health education, history, honors English, honors geometry, honors U.S. history, honors world history, human anatomy, keyboarding, mathematics, music history, music performance, physical education, physical science, physics, reading/study skills, remedial/makeup course work, research skills, SAT/ACT preparation, science, social studies, Spanish, statistics, trigonometry, U.S. history, U.S. history-AP, U.S. literature, word processing, world history, world literature, writing, writing fundamentals, yearbook.

Graduation Requirements Arts and fine arts (art, music, dance, drama), computer applications, English, mathematics, physical education (includes health), SAT preparation, science, social studies (includes history), requirements vary depending on specific disability.

Special Academic Programs Advanced Placement exam preparation in 2 subject areas; honors section; academic accommodation for the gifted; remedial reading and/or remedial writing; remedial math; programs in English, mathematics for dyslexic students; special instructional classes for blind students; ESL (12 students enrolled).

College Placement 23 students graduated in 2005; 22 went to college, including Georgia College & State University; Georgia Southern University; Truett-McConnell College. Other: 1 had other specific plans. Mean SAT verbal: 435, mean SAT math: 469. 5% scored over 600 on SAT verbal, 12% scored over 600 on SAT math.

Student Life Upper grades have uniform requirement, student council. Discipline rests primarily with faculty.

Summer Programs Remediation, enrichment, advancement, ESL programs offered; session focuses on one-to-one and group instruction (making up course credits, basic skills, enrichment, applied study skills); held on campus; accepts boys and girls; open to students from other schools. 75 students usually enrolled. 2006 schedule: June 21 to July 30. Application deadline: none.

Tuition and Aid Day student tuition: $21,500–$30,000; 5-day tuition and room/board: $35,000–$44,500; 7-day tuition and room/board: $39,500–$47,850. Tuition installment plan (individually arranged payment plans, 4-payment plan). Need-based scholarship grants available. In 2005–06, 10% of upper-school students received aid. Total amount of financial aid awarded in 2005–06: $80,000.

Admissions Traditional secondary-level entrance grade is 10. Deadline for receipt of application materials: none. Application fee required: $60. Interview required.

Athletics Interscholastic: baseball (boys), basketball (b,g), volleyball (g), wrestling (b); coed interscholastic: cross-country running, golf, soccer, tennis; coed intramural: badminton, tennis. 1 PE instructor.

Computers Computers are regularly used in English, foreign language, history, mathematics, science classes. Computer resources include on-campus library services, CD-ROMs, Internet access, wireless intranet access.

Contact Mrs. Marcia Shearer, Director of Admissions. 770-394-8177 Ext. 215. Fax: 770-804-8821. E-mail: admissions@brandonhall.org. Web site: www.brandonhall.org.

See full description on page 1208.

BREHM PREPARATORY SCHOOL

1245 East Grand Avenue
Carbondale, Illinois 62901
Head of School: Dr. Richard G. Collins

petersons.com

General Information Coeducational boarding and day college-preparatory and general academic school; primarily serves students with learning disabilities, individuals with Attention Deficit Disorder, dyslexic students, and students with language-based learning differences. Grades 6–PG. Founded: 1982. Setting: small town. Nearest major city is St. Louis, MO. Students are housed in single-sex dormitories. 80-acre campus. 11 buildings on campus. Approved or accredited by Independent Schools Association of the Central States, North Central Association of Colleges and Schools, and Illinois Department of Education. Member of National Association of Independent Schools. Total enrollment: 112. Upper school average class size: 8. Upper school faculty-student ratio: 1:4.

Upper School Student Profile Grade 9: 19 students (13 boys, 6 girls); Grade 10: 27 students (17 boys, 10 girls); Grade 11: 20 students (16 boys, 4 girls); Grade 12: 17 students (12 boys, 5 girls); Grade 13: 1 student (1 boy); Postgraduate: 20 students (10 boys, 10 girls). 97% of students are boarding students. 15% are state residents. 28 states are represented in upper school student body. International students from Saudi Arabia.

Faculty School total: 25. In upper school: 8 men, 17 women; 15 have advanced degrees.

Subjects Offered ACT preparation, algebra, American history, art, biology, calculus, chemistry, computer science, computer skills, consumer education, creative writing, current events, earth science, economics, English, environmental science, geometry, government/civics, keyboarding, learning cognition, mathematics, photography, physical education, psychology, reading/study skills, science, social studies, sociology, speech, trigonometry, weight training, world history, writing skills.

Graduation Requirements Computer science, consumer education, English, government, learning cognition, mathematics, physical education (includes health), science, social studies (includes history).

Special Academic Programs Study at local college for college credit; academic accommodation for the gifted; remedial reading and/or remedial writing; remedial math; programs in English, mathematics, general development for dyslexic students.

College Placement 21 students graduated in 2005; 11 went to college, including John A. Logan College; New England College; Southern Illinois University Edwardsville. Other: 10 entered a postgraduate year. Median composite ACT: 20. 25% scored over 26 on composite ACT.

Student Life Upper grades have specified standards of dress, student council, honor system. Discipline rests equally with students and faculty.

Tuition and Aid Day student tuition: $29,995; 7-day tuition and room/board: $48,600. PrepGATE Loans available.

Admissions Traditional secondary-level entrance grade is 9. For fall 2005, 67 students applied for upper-level admission, 50 were accepted, 42 enrolled. Wechsler

Intelligence Scale for Children III, WISC or WAIS, Woodcock-Johnson and writing sample required. Deadline for receipt of application materials: none. Application fee required: $50. On-campus interview required.

Athletics Coed Intramural: basketball, canoeing/kayaking, hiking/backpacking, horseback riding, martial arts, paint ball, physical fitness, street hockey, strength & conditioning, weight training. 1 PE instructor.

Computers Computers are regularly used in all academic, desktop publishing, graphic arts, graphic design, keyboarding, learning cognition, photography, yearbook classes. Computer network features include campus e-mail, CD-ROMs, Internet access, DVD, wireless campus network.

Contact Kim McNamee, Executive Assistant. 618-457-0371 Ext. 1304. Fax: 618-529-1248. E-mail: admissionsinfo@brehm.org. Web site: www.brehm.org.

ANNOUNCEMENT FROM THE SCHOOL Major expansion at Brehm has enhanced curriculum and campus facilities. Phase One of Brehm's 3-phase expansion plan is almost complete. The Student Activity Center, completed this summer, features a dining hall, a full gymnasium, and a stage for a variety of student activities. A new academic building, also completed this summer, houses a new science lab and computer lab. The new girls' dorm will open in August 2006.

See full description on page 1210.

BRIDGES ACADEMY

3921 Laurel Canyon Boulevard
Studio City, California 91604
Head of School: Carl Sabatino

General Information Coeducational day college-preparatory, arts, technology, and music school; primarily serves gifted students with non-verbal learning differences. Grades 6–12. Founded: 1993. Setting: suburban. Nearest major city is Los Angeles. 7-acre campus. 3 buildings on campus. Approved or accredited by California Association of Independent Schools, Western Association of Schools and Colleges, and California Department of Education. Total enrollment: 83. Upper school average class size: 9. Upper school faculty-student ratio: 1:9.

Upper School Student Profile Grade 9: 12 students (12 boys); Grade 10: 17 students (12 boys, 5 girls); Grade 11: 9 students (8 boys, 1 girl); Grade 12: 14 students (11 boys, 3 girls).

Faculty School total: 13. In upper school: 6 men, 7 women; 2 have advanced degrees.

Subjects Offered Algebra, American government, American literature, art, biology, calculus, chemistry, drama, economics, European history, European literature, film, geometry, Japanese, modern European history, music theory, non-Western literature, physics, pre-calculus, senior project, social skills, Spanish, statistics, study skills, U.S. history, world history.

Graduation Requirements Economics, English, foreign language, government, history, mathematics, science, senior seminar.

Special Academic Programs Honors section; academic accommodation for the gifted.

College Placement 14 students graduated in 2005; 11 went to college, including Berklee College of Music; California State University, Northridge; Grinnell College; Sarah Lawrence College; The Evergreen State College; University of Southern California. Other: 3 had other specific plans. 54% scored over 600 on SAT verbal, 25% scored over 600 on SAT math.

Student Life Upper grades have student council. Discipline rests primarily with faculty.

Tuition and Aid Day student tuition: $25,750. Tuition installment plan (Insured Tuition Payment Plan, monthly payment plans). Need-based scholarship grants available. In 2005–06, 8% of upper-school students received aid. Total amount of financial aid awarded in 2005–06: $110,000.

Admissions For fall 2005, 17 students applied for upper-level admission, 12 were accepted, 10 enrolled. Deadline for receipt of application materials: March 1. Application fee required: $150. On-campus interview required.

Athletics Coed Interscholastic: basketball, cross-country running. 1 PE instructor, 1 coach.

Computers Computer network features include CD-ROMs, Internet access.

Contact Doug Lenzini, Director of Admissions. 818-506-1091. Fax: 818-506-8094. E-mail: doug@bridges.edu. Web site: www.bridges.edu.

THE CEDARS ACADEMY

PO Box 103
Bridgeville, Delaware 19933
Head of School: Robin Abel

petersons.com

General Information Coeducational boarding college-preparatory and arts school; primarily serves students with learning disabilities and individuals with Attention Deficit Disorder. Grades 5–PG. Founded: 1989. Setting: rural. Nearest major city is Seaford. Students are housed in coed dormitories and single-sex dormitories. 72-acre campus. 4 buildings on campus. Approved or accredited by Delaware Department of Education. Language of instruction: English. Total enrollment: 40. Upper school average class size: 8. Upper school faculty-student ratio: 1:8.

Upper School Student Profile Grade 7: 5 students (3 boys, 2 girls); Grade 8: 6 students (3 boys, 3 girls); Grade 9: 6 students (3 boys, 3 girls); Grade 10: 6 students (3 boys, 3 girls); Grade 11: 6 students (3 boys, 3 girls); Grade 12: 6 students (3 boys, 3 girls). 100% of students are boarding students. 11 states are represented in upper school student body. 1% are international students. International students from Venezuela.

Faculty School total: 15. In upper school: 7 men, 8 women; 5 have advanced degrees.

Special Academic Programs Advanced Placement exam preparation; independent study; study at local college for college credit; academic accommodation for the musically talented and the artistically talented; remedial reading and/or remedial writing; remedial math.

College Placement 5 students graduated in 2004; 4 went to college, including Earlham College; Millersville University of Pennsylvania; The Citadel, The Military College of South Carolina; University of Delaware. Other: 1 went to work. Mean SAT verbal: 600, mean SAT math: 600.

Student Life Upper grades have specified standards of dress, honor system. Discipline rests equally with students and faculty.

Tuition and Aid 7-day tuition and room/board: $48,000. Tuition installment plan (monthly payment plans, individually arranged payment plans).

Admissions Traditional secondary-level entrance grade is 10. Deadline for receipt of application materials: none. No application fee required. On-campus interview required.

Athletics Coed Intramural: golf, horseback riding, jogging.

Computers Computer resources include on-campus library services, CD-ROMs, Internet access.

Contact Joanne Saulbury, Admissions Director. 302-337-3200 Ext. 103. Fax: 302-337-8496. E-mail: rabel@cedarsacademy.com. Web site: www.cedarsacademy.com.

See full description on page 1212.

CHATHAM ACADEMY

4 Oglethorpe Professional Boulevard
Savannah, Georgia 31406
Head of School: Mrs. Carolyn M. Hannaford

General Information Coeducational day college-preparatory, general academic, and technology school; primarily serves underachievers, students with learning disabilities, individuals with Attention Deficit Disorder, dyslexic students, and different learning styles. Grades 1–12. Founded: 1978. Setting: suburban. 5-acre campus. 1 building on campus. Approved or accredited by National Association of Private Schools for Exceptional Children, Southern Association of Colleges and Schools, and Georgia Department of Education. Endowment: $100,000. Total enrollment: 99. Upper school average class size: 10. Upper school faculty-student ratio: 1:10.

Upper School Student Profile Grade 9: 13 students (6 boys, 7 girls); Grade 10: 9 students (4 boys, 5 girls); Grade 11: 10 students (3 boys, 7 girls); Grade 12: 5 students (2 boys, 3 girls).

Faculty School total: 18. In upper school: 3 men, 5 women; 5 have advanced degrees.

Subjects Offered Algebra, American history, American literature, art, biology, earth science, economics, English, English literature, expository writing, French, geology, geometry, government/civics, grammar, history, keyboarding, mathematics, physical education, physical science, reading, SAT/ACT preparation, science, social studies, world history, world literature, writing.

Graduation Requirements Algebra, American government, American history, biology, British literature, chemistry, civics, composition, consumer economics, earth science, economics, electives, English, English composition, English literature, foreign language, French, grammar, marine biology, mathematics, physical education (includes health), physical science, reading/study skills, science, social studies (includes history), U.S. history.

Special Academic Programs Independent study; study at local college for college credit; remedial reading and/or remedial writing; remedial math; programs in English, mathematics, general development for dyslexic students.

College Placement 4 students graduated in 2005; 3 went to college, including Armstrong Atlantic State University; University of Colorado at Boulder. Other: 1 entered a postgraduate year.

Student Life Upper grades have uniform requirement, student council, honor system. Discipline rests primarily with faculty.

Summer Programs Remediation, enrichment, advancement, art/fine arts, computer instruction programs offered; session focuses on academics; held on campus; accepts boys and girls; open to students from other schools. 60 students usually enrolled. 2006 schedule: June 16 to July 25. Application deadline: June 7.

Tuition and Aid Day student tuition: $11,500. Tuition installment plan (monthly payment plans, individually arranged payment plans). Tuition reduction for siblings, need-based scholarship grants available. In 2005–06, 33% of upper-school students received aid. Total amount of financial aid awarded in 2005–06: $50,000.

Admissions Traditional secondary-level entrance grade is 10. For fall 2005, 15 students applied for upper-level admission, 8 were accepted, 6 enrolled. Achievement tests, Individual IQ, Achievement and behavior rating scale, school's own test,

Stanford Binet, Wechsler Individual Achievement Test, Wechsler Intelligence Scale for Children III, WISC or WAIS, WISC-R, Woodcock-Johnson Revised Achievement Test or writing sample required. Deadline for receipt of application materials: none. Application fee required: $50. Interview required.

Athletics Interscholastic: flag football (boys), soccer (b); coed interscholastic: basketball, fitness, flag football, soccer; coed intramural: aerobics, biathlon, cooperative games, fitness, fitness walking, flag football, jump rope, kickball, Newcombe ball, outdoor activities, outdoor recreation, paddle tennis, physical training, soccer, volleyball, walking, whiffle ball. 1 PE instructor, 1 coach.

Computers Computer network features include CD-ROMs, Internet access, file transfer, office computer access.

Contact Mrs. Carolyn M. Hannaford, Principal. 912-354-4047. Fax: 912-354-4633. E-mail: channaford@roycelearningcente.com. Web site: www.roycelearningcenter.com/ca.htm.

CHELSEA SCHOOL

711 Pershing Avenue
Silver Spring, Maryland 20910
Head of School: Anthony R. Messina Jr.

General Information Coeducational day college-preparatory, general academic, arts, bilingual studies, technology, and science school; primarily serves students with learning disabilities, individuals with Attention Deficit Disorder, and dyslexic students. Grades 5–12. Founded: 1976. Setting: suburban. 10-acre campus. 3 buildings on campus. Approved or accredited by Association of Independent Schools of Greater Washington and Maryland Department of Education. Total enrollment: 92. Upper school average class size: 8. Upper school faculty-student ratio: 1:3.

Upper School Student Profile Grade 9: 19 students (12 boys, 7 girls); Grade 10: 19 students (15 boys, 4 girls); Grade 11: 17 students (11 boys, 6 girls); Grade 12: 17 students (13 boys, 4 girls).

Faculty School total: 29. In upper school: 15 men, 13 women; 21 have advanced degrees.

Subjects Offered Advanced Placement courses, American history, American literature, anatomy and physiology, art, biology, British literature, calculus, career/college preparation, chemistry, community service, composition, computer graphics, computer technologies, computers, conceptual physics, drama, earth and space science, earth science, English, English literature, environmental science, foreign language, geometry, health, health and wellness, independent study, information technology, math review, music, personal fitness, physical education, physics, pre-algebra, pre-calculus, reading, reading/study skills, remedial study skills, science, social skills, Spanish, state government, U.S. government, U.S. history, U.S. literature, wellness.

Graduation Requirements 20th century world history, algebra, American government, American history, art, biology, career/college preparation, chemistry, earth science, electives, English, English composition, English literature, general math, geometry, health and wellness, physical education (includes health), pre-algebra, Spanish, U.S. history.

Special Academic Programs Honors section; independent study; study at local college for college credit; academic accommodation for the gifted, the musically talented, and the artistically talented; remedial reading and/or remedial writing; remedial math; programs in English, mathematics, general development for dyslexic students.

College Placement 17 students graduated in 2005; 16 went to college, including Howard University; Maryland College of Art and Design; Morgan State University; Rhode Island School of Design; University of Maryland, Baltimore County. Other: 1 entered military service.

Student Life Upper grades have student council. Discipline rests primarily with faculty.

Summer Programs Remediation, enrichment, art/fine arts, computer instruction programs offered; session focuses on remediation; held both on and off campus; held at downtown DC and local pools; accepts boys and girls; open to students from other schools. 30 students usually enrolled. 2006 schedule: July 3 to August 4. Application deadline: none.

Tuition and Aid Day student tuition: $32,020. Tuition installment plan (Key Tuition Payment Plan). Need-based scholarship grants available. In 2005–06, 12% of upper-school students received aid. Total amount of financial aid awarded in 2005–06: $90,000.

Admissions Traditional secondary-level entrance grade is 9. For fall 2005, 146 students applied for upper-level admission, 40 were accepted, 27 enrolled. Academic Profile Tests, Wechsler Individual Achievement Test, Wide Range Achievement Test, WISC III or other aptitude measures; standardized achievement test, WISC or WAIS, WISC-R or Woodcock-Johnson required. Deadline for receipt of application materials: none. Application fee required: $50. On-campus interview required.

Athletics Interscholastic: basketball (boys, girls); coed interscholastic: soccer, track and field. 1 PE instructor.

Computers Computers are regularly used in all academic classes. Computer network features include campus e-mail, on-campus library services, CD-ROMs, Internet access, file transfer, DVD, wireless campus network.

Contact Bekah D. Atkinson, Director of Cdmissions. 301-585-1430 Ext. 303. Fax: 301-585-9621. E-mail: information@chelseaschool.edu. Web site: www.chelseaschool.edu.

CHEROKEE CREEK BOYS SCHOOL

198 Cooper Road
Westminster, South Carolina 29693
Head of School: Kathy Whitmire

General Information Boys' boarding general academic and arts school; primarily serves underachievers, students with learning disabilities, individuals with Attention Deficit Disorder, individuals with emotional and behavioral problems, and dyslexic students. Grades 5–9. Founded: 2002. Setting: rural. Nearest major city is Atlanta, GA. Students are housed in single-sex dormitories. 77-acre campus. 6 buildings on campus. Approved or accredited by Southern Association of Colleges and Schools. Total enrollment: 20. Upper school average class size: 10. Upper school faculty-student ratio: 1:10.

Upper School Student Profile Grade 6: 1 student (1 boy); Grade 7: 5 students (5 boys); Grade 8: 7 students (7 boys); Grade 9: 7 students (7 boys). 100% of students are boarding students. 1% are state residents. 16 states are represented in upper school student body.

Faculty School total: 6. In upper school: 3 men, 1 woman; 1 has an advanced degree.

Special Academic Programs Remedial reading and/or remedial writing; remedial math; programs in English, mathematics, general development for dyslexic students.

Student Life Upper grades have specified standards of dress, honor system. Discipline rests primarily with faculty.

Tuition and Aid 7-day tuition and room/board: $57,600. Need-based scholarship grants available. In 2005–06, 57% of upper-school students received aid. Total amount of financial aid awarded in 2005–06: $28,800.

Admissions For fall 2005, 20 students applied for upper-level admission, 20 were accepted, 20 enrolled. Battery of testing done through outside agency or psychoeducational evaluation required. Deadline for receipt of application materials: none. Application fee required. Interview required.

Athletics 1 PE instructor.

Computers Computers are regularly used in keyboarding, mathematics, theology classes. Computer resources include CD-ROMs, online commercial services, Internet access, office computer access, DVD.

Contact Betsy Deane, Admissions Director. 864-647-1885 Ext. 105. Fax: 866-399-1869. E-mail: bdeane@cherokeecreek.net. Web site: www.cherokeecreek.net.

COMMUNITY HIGH SCHOOL

1135 Teaneck Road
Teaneck, New Jersey 07666
Head of School: Dennis Cohen

General Information Coeducational day college-preparatory school; primarily serves students with learning disabilities, individuals with Attention Deficit Disorder, and dyslexic students. Ungraded, ages 14–19. Founded: 1968. Setting: suburban. 1 building on campus. Approved or accredited by New York Department of Education and New Jersey Department of Education. Total enrollment: 170.

Subjects Offered Algebra, American history, American literature, art, biology, business, calculus, chemistry, computer science, creative writing, drama, driver education, English, English literature, European history, expository writing, fine arts, geography, geometry, government/civics, grammar, history, journalism, mathematics, music, photography, physical education, physics, psychology, science, social science, social studies, sociology, Spanish, speech, study skills, theater, trigonometry, writing.

Graduation Requirements Arts and fine arts (art, music, dance, drama), English, mathematics, physical education (includes health), science, social science, social studies (includes history).

Special Academic Programs Remedial reading and/or remedial writing; remedial math; programs in English, mathematics, general development for dyslexic students.

College Placement 39 students graduated in 2005.

Student Life Upper grades have specified standards of dress. Discipline rests primarily with faculty.

Tuition and Aid Day student tuition: $36,850.

Admissions Traditional secondary-level entrance age is 14. Deadline for receipt of application materials: none. No application fee required. On-campus interview required.

Athletics Interscholastic: baseball (boys), basketball (b), soccer (b), softball (g); intramural: baseball (b), basketball (b,g), softball (g), table tennis (b,g), track and field (b,g), volleyball (b,g). 4 PE instructors, 8 coaches.

Computers Computers are regularly used in all academic classes. Computer network features include campus e-mail, CD-ROMs, online commercial services, voice recognition systems.

Contact Toby Braunstein, Director of Education. 201-862-1796. Fax: 201-862-1791. E-mail: tbraunstein@communityhighschool.org.

THE COTTAGE SCHOOL

700 Grimes Bridge Road
Roswell, Georgia 30075
Head of School: Dr. Jacque Digieso

General Information Coeducational day college-preparatory, general academic, arts, vocational, and technology school; primarily serves students with learning disabilities, individuals with Attention Deficit Disorder, and dyslexic students. Grades 6–12. Founded: 1985. Setting: suburban. Nearest major city is Atlanta. 23-acre campus. 4 buildings on campus. Approved or accredited by Georgia Accrediting Commission, Georgia Independent School Association, Southern Association of Colleges and Schools, Southern Association of Independent Schools, and Georgia Department of Education. Total enrollment: 165. Upper school average class size: 9. Upper school faculty-student ratio: 1:10.

Upper School Student Profile Grade 9: 30 students (22 boys, 8 girls); Grade 10: 30 students (21 boys, 9 girls); Grade 11: 28 students (18 boys, 10 girls); Grade 12: 30 students (18 boys, 12 girls).

Faculty School total: 31. In upper school: 9 men, 11 women.

Subjects Offered Algebra, American history, American literature, anatomy, art, art and culture, art appreciation, art education, art history, art history-AP, athletic training, athletics, banking, baseball, basketball, biology, British literature, calculus, career and personal planning, career education, career planning, career/college preparation, careers, carpentry, ceramics, chemistry, chorus, college placement, commercial art, communication arts, computer art, computer keyboarding, computer literacy, computer processing, computer skills, consumer economics, creative writing, culinary arts, drama performance, drawing, driver education, economics, English, English composition, English literature, environmental science, equestrian sports, experiential education, experimental science, fencing, foreign language, French, general math, general science, geography, geometry, golf, grammar, graphic arts, health education, history, human anatomy, independent study, jewelry making, keyboarding/computer, language arts, library studies, literary magazine, literature, mathematics, multimedia, newspaper, personal finance, personal fitness, personal growth, physical science, political science, pre-calculus, reading/study skills, SAT preparation, science and technology, senior internship, social studies, Spanish, speech therapy, sports, stock market, tennis, trigonometry, U.S. history, video film production, vocational skills, woodworking, word processing, work experience, world geography, world history.

Graduation Requirements Algebra, American literature, art history, arts and fine arts (art, music, dance, drama), biology, British literature, careers, computer literacy, computer processing, electives, English, English composition, English literature, fitness, foreign language, mathematics, physical education (includes health), science, social studies (includes history), post-secondary plans in place prior to receiving diploma, (letter of acceptance to college, vocational school, branch of the military, or job).

Special Academic Programs Programs in English, mathematics, general development for dyslexic students.

College Placement 33 students graduated in 2005; 32 went to college, including Andrew College; Chattahoochee Technical College; Georgia Perimeter College; Kennesaw State University; Piedmont College; Reinhardt College. Other: 1 went to work. Mean SAT verbal: 392, mean SAT math: 425, mean combined SAT: 1188, mean composite ACT: 16.

Student Life Upper grades have specified standards of dress, student council. Discipline rests primarily with faculty.

Summer Programs Remediation, enrichment, advancement, computer instruction programs offered; session focuses on providing opportunities for students to strengthen or add to academic credits; held on campus; accepts boys and girls; open to students from other schools. 50 students usually enrolled. 2006 schedule: June 16 to July 25. Application deadline: June 10.

Tuition and Aid Day student tuition: $16,800. Tuition installment plan (individually arranged payment plans). Need-based scholarship grants available.

Admissions Traditional secondary-level entrance grade is 9. For fall 2005, 42 students applied for upper-level admission, 42 were accepted, 42 enrolled. ACT, battery of testing done through outside agency, Brigance Test of Basic Skills and Stanford 9 required. Deadline for receipt of application materials: none. Application fee required: $75. On-campus interview required.

Athletics Interscholastic: baseball (boys, girls), basketball (b,g), cheering (g), cross-country running (b,g), soccer (b), softball (g), tennis (b,g), track and field (b,g), volleyball (g); intramural: bicycling (b,g), cheering (b,g), cross-country running (b,g), fencing (b), Frisbee (b,g), hiking/backpacking (b,g), horseback riding (b,g), jogging (b,g), mountain biking (b,g), physical fitness (b,g), physical training (b,g), ropes courses (b,g), strength & conditioning (b,g), touch football (b,g), ultimate Frisbee (b,g), volleyball (b,g), walking (b,g); coed interscholastic: cheering, cross-country running, soccer; coed intramural: bicycling, cheering, cross-country running, fitness, fitness walking, Frisbee, hiking/backpacking, jogging, mountain biking, physical fitness, physical training, ropes courses, strength & conditioning, touch football, ultimate Frisbee, volleyball, walking.

Computers Computers are regularly used in career exploration, career technology, data processing, English, literary magazine, multimedia, music, publications, yearbook classes. Computer resources include CD-ROMs, Internet access.

Contact Dr. Jacque Digieso, Executive Director. 770-641-8688. Fax: 770-641-9026. E-mail: jacqued@cottageschool.org. Web site: cottageschool.org.

THE CRAIG SCHOOL

10 Tower Hill Road
Mountain Lakes, New Jersey 07046
Head of School: Mr. David Dennen Blanchard

General Information Coeducational day college-preparatory and general academic school; primarily serves underachievers, students with learning disabilities, individuals with Attention Deficit Disorder, and dyslexic students. Grades 3–12. Founded: 1980. Setting: suburban. Nearest major city is Lincoln Park. 1-acre campus. 2 buildings on campus. Approved or accredited by Middle States Association of Colleges and Schools and New Jersey Department of Education. Total enrollment: 162. Upper school average class size: 7. Upper school faculty-student ratio: 1:6.

Upper School Student Profile Grade 9: 13 students (13 boys); Grade 10: 12 students (7 boys, 5 girls); Grade 11: 13 students (11 boys, 2 girls); Grade 12: 22 students (13 boys, 9 girls).

Faculty School total: 45. In upper school: 8 men, 3 women; 2 have advanced degrees.

Subjects Offered Algebra, American history, art education, biology, business, chemistry, creative writing, current events, earth science, geometry, health education, literature, performing arts, physical education, physics, psychology, public speaking, SAT preparation, short story, Spanish, U.S. history, world history, writing fundamentals, writing workshop.

Graduation Requirements Arts and fine arts (art, music, dance, drama), electives, English, language, mathematics, physical education (includes health), science, social studies (includes history). Community service is required.

Special Academic Programs Remedial reading and/or remedial writing; programs in English, mathematics, general development for dyslexic students.

College Placement 8 students graduated in 2005; 3 went to college, including Lynn University. Other: 3 went to work, 2 had other specific plans. Median SAT verbal: 360, median SAT math: 410.

Student Life Upper grades have specified standards of dress, student council. Discipline rests primarily with faculty.

Summer Programs Remediation programs offered; session focuses on academics; held on campus; accepts boys and girls; open to students from other schools. 15 students usually enrolled. 2006 schedule: July 10 to August 4. Application deadline: June 5.

Tuition and Aid Day student tuition: $28,800. Tuition installment plan (monthly payment plans). Tuition reduction for siblings available.

Admissions Traditional secondary-level entrance grade is 9. For fall 2005, 28 students applied for upper-level admission, 10 were accepted, 3 enrolled. Psycho-educational evaluation or WISC/Woodcock-Johnson required. Deadline for receipt of application materials: none. Application fee required: $50. Interview required.

Athletics Coed Intramural: basketball, bowling, cross-country running, soccer. 1 PE instructor.

Computers Computers are regularly used in all classes. Computer resources include CD-ROMs, Internet access, DVD, wireless campus network.

Contact Julie Sage Day, Director of Advancement. 973-334-1295. Fax: 973-334-1299. E-mail: jday@craigschool.org. Web site: www.craigschool.org/.

ANNOUNCEMENT FROM THE SCHOOL Founded in 1980, The Craig School is an independent, nonprofit school for children of average or above-average ability who have diagnosed language-based learning differences or difficulty succeeding in the traditional classroom. The School is located on 2 campuses: grades 3–8 are in Mountain Lakes, New Jersey, and grades 9–12 are in Lincoln Park, New Jersey. Over the past 25 years, the School has promoted a solid educational program based on the most recent and effective multisensory classroom techniques, assistive technology, social skills curricula, and organizational methods. Certified specialist teachers and professionals provide individualized instruction in classes of 8 or fewer in a safe, nurturing learning environment with small, structured classrooms, positive student-teacher interaction, and strong ties to parents. Over the years, Craig School has adopted many Orton Gillingham programs to address difficulties in decoding, reading comprehension, fluency, and written expression. A hallmark of a Craig education is the integration and application of effective teaching strategies across all classrooms. For example, the speech therapist shares approaches with the reading teachers; note-taking skills are coordinated by language arts, science, and social studies teachers; and vocabulary acquisition and organizational skills are reinforced within all departments. All classrooms are equipped with desktop or wireless laptop computers that provide specialized software to assist with reading comprehension, the writing process, and computational fluency. The liberal arts curriculum at the upper school is integrated, interdisciplinary, and project-based and is designed to prepare students for college or other postsecondary experiences. The program focuses on developing solid written language skills, strategies for content acquisition and retention, and the social, behavioral, and self-advocacy skills essential for success in the extended community. Students may participate in a rich variety of social and athletic opportunities, including competitive team and intramural sports, after-school activities, and cultural arts trips.

CRAWFORD DAY SCHOOL

825 Crawford Parkway
Portsmouth, Virginia 23704
Head of School: Millie Davis

General Information Coeducational day school; primarily serves underachievers, students with learning disabilities, individuals with Attention Deficit Disorder, individuals with emotional and behavioral problems, and students with Autism Spectrum (Asperger's Syndrome), developmental delay, mental retardation (mild). Grades K–12. Founded: 1989. Setting: urban. Approved or accredited by Southern Association of Colleges and Schools. Total enrollment: 33. Upper school average class size: 8. Upper school faculty-student ratio: 1:2.

Upper School Student Profile Grade 9: 6 students (3 boys, 3 girls); Grade 10: 7 students (7 boys); Grade 11: 3 students (3 boys); Grade 12: 5 students (5 boys).

Faculty School total: 6. In upper school: 2 men, 3 women.

Student Life Upper grades have uniform requirement. Discipline rests primarily with faculty.

Summer Programs Enrichment programs offered; session focuses on maintenance of behavioral goals; held on campus; accepts boys and girls; open to students from other schools. 2006 schedule: July 3 to August 10. Application deadline: June 5.

Admissions Deadline for receipt of application materials: none. No application fee required. Interview required.

Athletics 1 PE instructor.

Computers Computer network features include Internet access, file transfer, educational programs online.

Contact Millie Davis, Director. 757-391-6675. Fax: 757-391-6651. Web site: www.absfirst.com.

CROSS CREEK PROGRAMS

150 North State Street
LaVerkin, Utah 84745
Head of School: Karr Farnsworth

petersons.com

General Information Coeducational boarding college-preparatory, arts, business, vocational, and technology school, affiliated with Christian faith; primarily serves students with learning disabilities, individuals with Attention Deficit Disorder, and individuals with emotional and behavioral problems. Grades 7–12. Founded: 1987. Setting: rural. Nearest major city is St. George. Students are housed in single-sex dormitories. 5-acre campus. 6 buildings on campus. Approved or accredited by Northwest Association of Schools and Colleges. Total enrollment: 415. Upper school average class size: 18. Upper school faculty-student ratio: 1:15.

Upper School Student Profile Grade 9: 47 students (21 boys, 26 girls); Grade 10: 114 students (49 boys, 65 girls); Grade 11: 120 students (56 boys, 64 girls); Grade 12: 109 students (52 boys, 57 girls). 100% of students are boarding students. 2% are state residents. 38 states are represented in upper school student body. 2% are international students. International students from Barbados, Bermuda, Canada, Chad, Japan, and Mexico; 2 other countries represented in student body.

Faculty School total: 23. In upper school: 8 men, 15 women; 6 have advanced degrees.

Subjects Offered 20th century American writers, 20th century world history, accounting, advanced chemistry, advanced math, algebra, American government, American government-AP, American history, American history-AP, American literature, anatomy and physiology, art, art appreciation, art history, arts and crafts, biology, biology-AP, business applications, business technology, calculus, career/college preparation, ceramics, chemistry, chemistry-AP, child development, choir, chorus, civics/free enterprise, economics-AP, English literature, gardening, general math, geography, geometry, geometry with art applications, government, health, honors algebra, honors English, honors geometry, honors U.S. history, honors world history, human anatomy, human biology, independent study, intro to computers, introduction to theater, mathematics, mathematics-AP, music, music appreciation, pre-algebra, pre-calculus, projective geometry, psychology, psychology-AP, SAT/ACT preparation, science.

Graduation Requirements 20th century world history, American government, American history, arts and fine arts (art, music, dance, drama), business skills (includes word processing), business technology, computer keyboarding, English, geography, mathematics, physical education (includes health), science, social science, social studies (includes history), senior project (including 90 hours of community or school service).

Special Academic Programs Honors section; accelerated programs; independent study; study at local college for college credit; remedial reading and/or remedial writing; remedial math; programs in English, mathematics, general development for dyslexic students.

College Placement 69 students graduated in 2005; 57 went to college, including Brigham Young University; DePaul University; Loyola Marymount University; Southern Utah University; University of California, Los Angeles; University of Colorado at Denver and Health Sciences Center—Downtown Denver Campus. Other: 2 went to work, 4 entered military service, 2 had other specific plans. Median SAT verbal: 580, median SAT math: 500; median composite ACT: 26.

Student Life Upper grades have uniform requirement, student council, honor system. Discipline rests primarily with faculty.

Summer Programs Remediation, enrichment, advancement, sports, art/fine arts, computer instruction programs offered; session focuses on advancement; held on campus; accepts boys and girls; not open to students from other schools. 390 students usually enrolled.

Tuition and Aid 7-day tuition and room/board: $53,980. Guaranteed tuition plan. Tuition installment plan (Key Tuition Payment Plan, monthly payment plans, individually arranged payment plans, discount for one year paid in-advance tuition). Tuition reduction for siblings, need-based loans, middle-income loans, prepGATE Loans available.

Admissions Traditional secondary-level entrance grade is 10. For fall 2005, 880 students applied for upper-level admission, 485 were accepted. Any standardized test, CAT 5 or Cognitive Abilities Test required. Deadline for receipt of application materials: none. Application fee required. Interview recommended.

Athletics Interscholastic: aerobics (boys, girls), aerobics/dance (b,g), aerobics/nautilus (b,g), back packing (b,g), baseball (b,g), basketball (b,g), bowling (b,g), cheering (b,g), climbing (b,g), cooperative games (b,g), cross-country running (b,g), dance (b,g), dance squad (b,g), danceline (b,g), fitness (b,g), fitness walking (b,g), flag football (b,g), hiking/backpacking (b,g), modern dance (g), outdoor activities (b,g), outdoor adventure (b,g), outdoor recreation (b,g), outdoor skills (b,g), outdoors (b,g), physical fitness (b,g), physical training (b,g), power lifting (b,g), rock climbing (b,g), softball (b,g), strength & conditioning (b,g), volleyball (b,g), walking (b,g), water skiing (b,g), weight lifting (b,g), weight training (b,g), whiffle ball (b,g), winter walking (b,g); intramural: basketball (b), cross-country running (b); coed interscholastic: aerobics/dance, baseball, dance, dance squad, danceline, softball. 3 PE instructors, 8 coaches.

Computers Computers are regularly used in all academic, keyboarding classes. Computer network features include campus e-mail, on-campus library services, CD-ROMs, Internet access, file transfer, wireless campus network.

Contact Jeni Salmi, Director of Admissions. 800-818-6228. Fax: 435-635-2331. E-mail: jeni@crosscreekprograms.com.

ANNOUNCEMENT FROM THE SCHOOL Cross Creek Programs is a residential treatment center that accommodates both girls and boys in southwestern Utah. There are separate campuses for boys and girls for college-preparatory and general academic classes. Cross Creek serves junior high– and high school–age students who have excellent potential but who are struggling at home, school, and in the community. Cross Creek Programs has developed, through years of experience, a balanced school/program that includes individual and group therapy with licensed therapists, individualized academic instruction, behavior modification, intensive seminars/workshops, physical fitness, a structured daily schedule, and emotional growth/personal development courses. Therapy is an important component of the school/program's overall design and process. Students receive one individual therapy session with a licensed therapist each week. They also participate in daily group sessions, conducted by the therapists to help incorporate emotional growth while more fully addressing the unresolved issues from the past. As the student progresses, the individual sessions will include the parents. The academic system used by Cross Creek Programs offers innovative techniques that allow the student to maximize the learning process and the earning of credits. In order for the student to earn credit for a class and move on to the next course, the class must be passed at a level of 80% or higher. Cross Creek is again expanding to meet the needs of its students. Expansion includes boys' classroom size, addition of a new dining room and kitchen, and additional Seminar Rooms. This clearly demonstrates Cross Creek's commitment to the student's academic achievement and personal success while in the program.

DALLAS ACADEMY

950 Tiffany Way
Dallas, Texas 75218
Head of School: JIm Richardson

General Information Coeducational day college-preparatory, general academic, and arts school; primarily serves students with learning disabilities, individuals with Attention Deficit Disorder, and dyslexic students. Grades K–12. Founded: 1965. Setting: suburban. 1-acre campus. 2 buildings on campus. Approved or accredited by Southern Association of Colleges and Schools, Texas Education Agency, and Texas Department of Education. Endowment: $250,000. Total enrollment: 135. Upper school average class size: 12. Upper school faculty-student ratio: 1:6.

Upper School Student Profile Grade 9: 26 students (22 boys, 4 girls); Grade 10: 20 students (15 boys, 5 girls); Grade 11: 21 students (15 boys, 6 girls); Grade 12: 26 students (20 boys, 6 girls).

Faculty School total: 24. In upper school: 4 men, 15 women; 5 have advanced degrees.

Subjects Offered American history, art, computer science, computers, drawing, economics, English, fine arts, geography, government/civics, health, history, mathematics, music, photography, physical education, physical science, science, social science, social studies, Spanish, yearbook.

Graduation Requirements Arts and fine arts (art, music, dance, drama), computer science, English, foreign language, mathematics, physical education (includes health), science, social science, social studies (includes history), 4 hours of community service per semester.

Special Academic Programs Study at local college for college credit; remedial reading and/or remedial writing; remedial math; programs in English, mathematics, general development for dyslexic students.

College Placement 23 students graduated in 2005; 19 went to college, including Benedictine College; Lon Morris College; Richland College; Sam Houston State University; Southern Methodist University. Other: 4 went to work.

Student Life Upper grades have uniform requirement, student council. Discipline rests primarily with faculty.

Tuition and Aid Day student tuition: $11,000. Tuition installment plan (monthly payment plans). Need-based scholarship grants available. In 2005–06, 23% of upper-school students received aid. Total amount of financial aid awarded in 2005–06: $95,600.

Admissions Traditional secondary-level entrance grade is 9. Admissions testing and WRAT required. Deadline for receipt of application materials: none. No application fee required. On-campus interview required.

Athletics Interscholastic: baseball (boys), basketball (b,g), cross-country running (b,g), football (b), golf (b), soccer (b,g), softball (g), track and field (b,g), volleyball (g); intramural: tennis (g); coed interscholastic: cheering, soccer. 1 PE instructor, 5 coaches, 1 trainer.

Computers Computers are regularly used in English, geography, history, library, music, SAT preparation, science, typing, writing, yearbook classes. Computer network features include on-campus library services, CD-ROMs, online commercial services, Internet access.

Contact Jim Richardson, Headmaster. 214-324-1481. Fax: 214-327-8537. E-mail: jrichardson@dallas-academy.com. Web site: www.dallas-academy.com.

DELAWARE VALLEY FRIENDS SCHOOL

19 East Central Avenue
Paoli, Pennsylvania 19301-1345
Head of School: Katherine A. Schantz

General Information Coeducational day college-preparatory, arts, and technology school, affiliated with Society of Friends; primarily serves students with learning disabilities, individuals with Attention Deficit Disorder, and dyslexic students. Grades 7–12. Founded: 1986. Setting: suburban. Nearest major city is Philadelphia. 8-acre campus. 1 building on campus. Approved or accredited by Pennsylvania Association of Private Academic Schools. Endowment: $560,696. Total enrollment: 188. Upper school average class size: 9. Upper school faculty-student ratio: 1:5.

Upper School Student Profile Grade 9: 37 students (17 boys, 20 girls); Grade 10: 33 students (23 boys, 10 girls); Grade 11: 39 students (26 boys, 13 girls); Grade 12: 29 students (20 boys, 9 girls). 7% of students are members of Society of Friends.

Faculty School total: 44. In upper school: 22 men, 22 women, 27 have advanced degrees.

Subjects Offered 20th century world history, algebra, American history, Asian studies, biology, calculus, chemistry, child development, crafts, first aid, geometry, human development, language arts, Latin, music, newspaper, photography, physical education, physics, pre-calculus, printmaking, Spanish, studio art, trigonometry, world history.

Graduation Requirements Arts and fine arts (art, music, dance, drama), English, lab science, language arts, mathematics, physical education (includes health), senior internship, social studies (includes history), at least one Adventure Based Learning (A.B.L.E.) course. Community service is required.

Special Academic Programs Remedial reading and/or remedial writing; remedial math; programs in English, mathematics, general development for dyslexic students.

College Placement 32 students graduated in 2005; 30 went to college, including Temple University; The University of Arizona. Other: 2 had other specific plans.

Student Life Upper grades have specified standards of dress, student council. Discipline rests primarily with faculty. Attendance at religious services is required.

Summer Programs Remediation, enrichment, art/fine arts programs offered; session focuses on individualized reading skills/writing tutoring using Orton-Gillingham methods; held on campus; accepts boys and girls; open to students from other schools. 50 students usually enrolled. 2006 schedule: June 26 to July 28. Application deadline: none.

Tuition and Aid Day student tuition: $27,200. Tuition installment plan (monthly payment plans, 2-payment plan (66% due May 1, 34% due January 1)). Tuition reduction for siblings, need-based scholarship grants available. In 2005–06, 28% of upper-school students received aid. Total amount of financial aid awarded in 2005–06: $330,400.

Admissions Traditional secondary-level entrance grade is 9. For fall 2005, 56 students applied for upper-level admission, 32 were accepted, 24 enrolled. Psycho-educational evaluation and WISC or WAIS required. Deadline for receipt of application materials: none. Application fee required: $100. On-campus interview required.

Athletics Interscholastic: basketball (boys, girls), Frisbee (b), lacrosse (b,g), soccer (b,g); coed interscholastic: Frisbee, golf, soccer, tennis, ultimate Frisbee, winter

walking; coed intramural: back packing, bicycling, hiking/backpacking, rock climbing, skiing (cross-country). 2 PE instructors, 5 coaches.

Computers Computers are regularly used in all classes. Computer network features include campus e-mail, CD-ROMs, online commercial services, Internet access, file transfer, office computer access, adaptive technologies.

Contact Kathryn W. Wynn, Associate Admissions Director. 610-640-4150 Ext. 2160. Fax: 610-560-4336. E-mail: wynnk@fc.dvfs.org. Web site: www.dvfs.org.

DENVER ACADEMY

4400 East Iliff Avenue
Denver, Colorado 80222
Head of School: James E. Loan

petersons.com

General Information Coeducational day college-preparatory, general academic, arts, vocational, and technology school; primarily serves underachievers, students with learning disabilities, individuals with Attention Deficit Disorder, dyslexic students, and students with unique learning styles. Grades 1–12. Founded: 1972. Setting: urban. 22-acre campus. 19 buildings on campus. Approved or accredited by Association of Colorado Independent Schools and Colorado Department of Education. Member of National Association of Independent Schools. Endowment: $1 million. Total enrollment: 429. Upper school average class size: 12. Upper school faculty-student ratio: 1:6.

Upper School Student Profile Grade 9: 81 students (62 boys, 19 girls); Grade 10: 60 students (43 boys, 17 girls); Grade 11: 76 students (61 boys, 15 girls); Grade 12: 64 students (48 boys, 16 girls).

Faculty School total: 71. In upper school: 19 men, 12 women; 10 have advanced degrees.

Subjects Offered ACT preparation, adolescent issues, algebra, American history, American literature, anatomy, art, art history, biology, botany, business, calculus, ceramics, chemistry, computer math, computer programming, computer science, creative writing, drama, earth science, English, English literature, environmental science, ethics, European history, fine arts, geography, geometry, government/civics, grammar, health, history, life skills, mathematics, music, philosophy, physical education, physics, psychology, science, social science, social studies, Spanish, speech, theater, trigonometry, values and decisions, world history, world literature, writing.

Graduation Requirements Arts and fine arts (art, music, dance, drama), English, mathematics, physical education (includes health), science, social science, social studies (includes history).

Special Academic Programs Independent study; academic accommodation for the gifted; remedial reading and/or remedial writing; remedial math; programs in English, mathematics, general development for dyslexic students.

College Placement 52 students graduated in 2005; 48 went to college, including Fort Lewis College; University of Colorado at Denver and Health Sciences Center—Downtown Denver Campus; University of Denver; University of Northern Colorado. Other: 4 went to work. Median composite ACT: 21. 10% scored over 26 on composite ACT.

Student Life Upper grades have specified standards of dress, student council, honor system. Discipline rests equally with students and faculty.

Summer Programs Remediation, enrichment, advancement, art/fine arts, rigorous outdoor training, computer instruction programs offered; session focuses on academics, remediation, and summer fun camp; held both on and off campus; held at various locations around the city and the Rocky Mountains; accepts boys and girls; open to students from other schools. 75 students usually enrolled. 2006 schedule: June to July. Application deadline: June.

Tuition and Aid Day student tuition: $18,600. Tuition installment plan (monthly payment plans). Tuition reduction for siblings, need-based scholarship grants available. In 2005–06, 21% of upper-school students received aid.

Admissions For fall 2005, 67 students applied for upper-level admission, 60 were accepted, 54 enrolled. Woodcock-Johnson and Woodcock-Johnson Educational Evaluation, WISC III required. Deadline for receipt of application materials: none. Application fee required: $75. On-campus interview required.

Athletics Interscholastic: baseball (boys), basketball (b,g), cross-country running (b,g), golf (b), soccer (b,g), volleyball (g); intramural: volleyball (g); coed interscholastic: cheering, physical fitness, physical training; coed intramural: back packing, basketball, boxing, canoeing/kayaking, climbing, cooperative games, fishing, flag football, golf, indoor hockey, indoor soccer, indoor track, jump rope, mountaineering, outdoor activities, outdoor adventure, outdoor education, outdoor recreation, outdoor skills, rafting, rock climbing, skiing (downhill), soccer, swimming and diving, track and field, wall climbing. 7 PE instructors, 7 coaches.

Computers Computers are regularly used in basic skills, career exploration, career technology, college planning, drawing and design, English, foreign language, independent study, introduction to technology, mathematics, media arts, media production, media services, multimedia, music, occupational education, SAT preparation, science, writing fundamentals, yearbook classes. Computer network features include campus e-mail, on-campus library services, CD-ROMs, online commercial services, Internet access, office computer access, DVD, wireless campus network.

Contact Janet Woolley, Admissions Counselor. 303-777-5161. Fax: 303-777-5893. E-mail: jwoolley@denveracademy.org. Web site: www.denveracademy.org.

See full description on page 1214.

DOCTOR FRANKLIN PERKINS SCHOOL

971 Main Street
Lancaster, Massachusetts 01523-2569
Head of School: Dr. Charles Conroy

General Information Coeducational boarding and day college-preparatory and general academic school, affiliated with Baptist General Conference; primarily serves underachievers, students with learning disabilities, individuals with Attention Deficit Disorder, and individuals with emotional and behavioral problems. Grades PK–12. Students are housed in single-sex dormitories. 120-acre campus. Approved or accredited by Massachusetts Department of Education. Member of National Association of Independent Schools. Upper school average class size: 10.

Special Academic Programs Remedial reading and/or remedial writing; remedial math.

Student Life Upper grades have specified standards of dress. Discipline rests primarily with faculty.

Admissions Deadline for receipt of application materials: January. No application fee required. Interview required.

Athletics Intramural: basketball (boys, girls), bicycling (b,g), physical fitness (b,g), swimming and diving (b,g); coed intramural: aerobics, aerobics/nautilus, aquatics, horseback riding.

Computers Computer network features include Internet access.

Contact Christine A. Santry, Director of Admissions. 978-368-6423. Fax: 978-368-6462. E-mail: csantry@perkinschool.org. Web site: www.perkinschool.org.

EAGLE HILL SCHOOL

45 Glenville Road
Greenwich, Connecticut 06831
Head of School: Dr. Mark J. Griffin

General Information Coeducational boarding college-preparatory, arts, and technology school; primarily serves students with learning disabilities, dyslexic students, and students with language-based learning disabilities. Grades 1–8. Founded: 1975. Setting: suburban. Nearest major city is New York, NY. Students are housed in single-sex by floor dormitories. 20-acre campus. 19 buildings on campus. Approved or accredited by Connecticut Association of Independent Schools and Connecticut Department of Education. Member of Secondary School Admission Test Board. Endowment: $17 million. Upper school average class size: 6. Upper school faculty-student ratio: 1:4.

Upper School Student Profile 30% of students are boarding students. 50% are state residents. 4 states are represented in upper school student body.

Faculty School total: 72. In upper school: 15 men, 20 women; 30 have advanced degrees; 35 reside on campus.

Subjects Offered Art, English, health, history, mathematics, music, physical education, science, technology.

Graduation Requirements Arts and fine arts (art, music, dance, drama), computer science, English, mathematics, physical education (includes health), science, social science, social studies (includes history), study skills.

Special Academic Programs Remedial reading and/or remedial writing; remedial math; programs in English, mathematics, general development for dyslexic students.

College Placement 63 students graduated in 2005; they went to Brewster Academy; Salisbury School; The Ethel Walker School; The Forman School; The Pennington School; Trinity-Pawling School.

Student Life Upper grades have specified standards of dress, student council, honor system. Discipline rests primarily with faculty.

Tuition and Aid Day student tuition: $40,750; 5-day tuition and room/board: $52,100. Tuition installment plan (Academic Management Services Plan, monthly payment plans, individually arranged payment plans). Need-based scholarship grants available. In 2005–06, 15% of upper-school students received aid. Total amount of financial aid awarded in 2005–06: $1,000,000.

Admissions For fall 2005, 78 students applied for upper-level admission, 44 were accepted, 40 enrolled. Psychoeducational evaluation and Wechsler Intelligence Scale for Children III required. Deadline for receipt of application materials: none. Application fee required: $50. On-campus interview required.

Athletics Interscholastic: baseball (boys), basketball (b,g), cheering (g), field hockey (g), lacrosse (b), softball (g); intramural: aerobics (g), aerobics/dance (g), aerobics/nautilus (b), flag football (b), football (b), lacrosse (g), strength & conditioning (b), weight lifting (b), wrestling (b); coed interscholastic: basketball, cross-country running, ice hockey, softball, tennis; coed intramural: basketball, bicycling, billiards, canoeing/kayaking, dance, fitness, fitness walking, floor hockey, Frisbee, golf, gymnastics, ice skating, jogging, judo, martial arts, outdoor activities, outdoor education, outdoor recreation, physical fitness, physical training, rhythmic gymnastics, volleyball, walking, weight training. 7 PE instructors, 21 coaches, 1 trainer.

Computers Computers are regularly used in English, history, mathematics, science classes. Computer network features include campus e-mail, on-campus library services, CD-ROMs, online commercial services, Internet access, file transfer, DVD, wireless campus network, digital lab, iMovie, intranet.

Contact Rayma-Joan Griffin, Director of Admissions and Placement. 203-622-9240. Fax: 203-622-0914. E-mail: r.griffin@eaglehill.org. Web site: www.eaglehillschool.org.

ANNOUNCEMENT FROM THE SCHOOL Eagle Hill School is a coeducational day and 5-day residential program serving children ages 6–16 with average to above-average intellectual potential with diagnosed learning disabilities. Academic programs are individually designed to meet the specific learning needs of students with learning difficulties to help the child develop the skills and strategies necessary to work to his or her potential in a more traditional learning environment. Eagle Hill School is located 35 miles northeast of New York City. The 20-acre suburban campus has 6 classroom buildings, a dormitory, and state-of-the-art technology in all buildings. A 10,000-volume library, gymnasium, and playing fields complement the classrooms. Eagle Hill is accredited by the CAIS and the state Department of Special Education in Connecticut as a school for children with language-based learning disabilities. In addition to the intense remedial program, Eagle Hill offers a full extracurricular program, including interscholastic and intramural sports, art, music, an on-campus radio station, community service, an active student council, and yearbook club.

EAGLE HILL SCHOOL

PO Box 116
242 Old Petersham Road
Hardwick, Massachusetts 01037
Head of School: Peter J. McDonald

General Information Coeducational boarding and day college-preparatory and arts school; primarily serves students with learning disabilities, individuals with Attention Deficit Disorder, dyslexic students, and students with non-verbal learning disabilities. Grades 8–12. Founded: 1967. Setting: small town. Nearest major city is Worcester. Students are housed in single-sex dormitories. 165-acre campus. 13 buildings on campus. Approved or accredited by Association of Independent Schools in New England, Massachusetts Office of Child Care Services, New England Association of Schools and Colleges, and The Association of Boarding Schools. Member of National Association of Independent Schools and Secondary School Admission Test Board. Endowment: $2 million. Total enrollment: 152. Upper school average class size: 5. Upper school faculty-student ratio: 1:5.

Upper School Student Profile Grade 9: 32 students (20 boys, 12 girls); Grade 10: 39 students (23 boys, 16 girls); Grade 11: 41 students (22 boys, 19 girls); Grade 12: 32 students (21 boys, 11 girls); Postgraduate: 1 student (1 boy). 95% of students are boarding students. 30% are state residents. 25 states are represented in upper school student body. 5% are international students. International students from Bermuda, Canada, Egypt, Hong Kong, Kuwait, and United Kingdom; 1 other country represented in student body.

Faculty School total: 40. In upper school: 17 men, 23 women; 30 have advanced degrees; 12 reside on campus.

Subjects Offered 20th century history, advanced math, algebra, American foreign policy, American government, American literature, anatomy and physiology, art, arts and crafts, biology, British literature, calculus, career/college preparation, carpentry, cell biology, ceramics, chemistry, chorus, college counseling, communication skills, composition, computer graphics, computer keyboarding, conceptual physics, contemporary issues, creative writing, culinary arts, current events, desktop publishing, drama, dramatic arts, earth science, English, English composition, English literature, environmental science, expository writing, film appreciation, film studies, filmmaking, food and nutrition, foreign policy, forensic science, French, gender issues, general science, geography, geometry, government/civics, graphic arts, graphics, guidance, health, history, history of rock and roll, Holocaust studies, Internet research, interpersonal skills, lab science, language development, Latin, leadership training, life management skills, literary magazine, mathematics, mentorship program, multicultural literature, music appreciation, music history, music theory, newspaper, outdoor education, participation in sports, peer counseling, personal finance, personal fitness, philosophy, photography, physical education, physical science, physics, poetry, pragmatics, pre-algebra, pre-calculus, printmaking, psychology, publishing, reading, relationships, Russian, SAT/ACT preparation, science, sculpture, Shakespeare, silk screening, social science, social skills, social studies, speech therapy, technology, theater arts, U.S. history, video and animation, video film production, visual and performing arts, visual arts, Web site design, women in literature, women's literature, woodworking, world history, world literature, world wide web design, writing, zoology.

Graduation Requirements Art, college counseling, computer science, electives, mathematics, physical education (includes health), pragmatics, reading, science, social studies (includes history), writing. Community service is required.

Special Academic Programs Honors section; academic accommodation for the gifted, the musically talented, and the artistically talented; remedial reading and/or remedial writing; remedial math; programs in English, mathematics, general development for dyslexic students.

College Placement 26 students graduated in 2005; 24 went to college, including Clark University; Lynn University; Mitchell College; Suffolk University; The University of Arizona; Worcester Polytechnic Institute. Other: 1 went to work, 1 entered a postgraduate year. Mean composite ACT: 30.

Student Life Upper grades have specified standards of dress, student council, honor system. Discipline rests primarily with faculty.

Summer Programs Remediation, advancement, sports, art/fine arts, computer instruction programs offered; session focuses on academics/recreation; held on campus; accepts boys and girls; open to students from other schools. 70 students usually enrolled. 2006 schedule: July 3 to August 11. Application deadline: none.

Tuition and Aid Day student tuition: $33,185; 7-day tuition and room/board: $46,885. Tuition installment plan (Key Tuition Payment Plan).

Admissions Traditional secondary-level entrance grade is 9. For fall 2005, 182 students applied for upper-level admission, 51 were accepted, 51 enrolled. Achievement tests, WISC/Woodcock-Johnson and writing sample required. Deadline for receipt of application materials: none. Application fee required: $75. On-campus interview required.

Athletics Interscholastic: basketball (boys, girls), softball (b,g); intramural: aerobics/dance (g), dance (g), yoga (g); coed interscholastic: cross-country running, golf, soccer, tennis, wrestling; coed intramural: aerobics, aerobics/nautilus, alpine skiing, basketball, bicycling, fencing, fitness, fitness walking, floor hockey, Frisbee, ice skating, jogging, mountain biking, nautilus, outdoor adventure, physical training, roller blading, roller skating, running, skiing (cross-country), skiing (downhill), snowboarding, snowshoeing, swimming and diving, touch football, weight lifting. 1 PE instructor.

Computers Computers are regularly used in college planning, English, graphic arts, keyboarding, newspaper, programming, research skills, Web site design, writing, yearbook classes. Computer network features include campus e-mail, on-campus library services, CD-ROMs, Internet access, office computer access, DVD.

Contact Dana M. Harbert, Director of Admission. 413-477-6000. Fax: 413-477-6837. E-mail: admission@ehs1.org. Web site: www.ehs1.org.

See full description on page 1216.

EAGLE HILL-SOUTHPORT

214 Main Street
Southport, Connecticut 06890
Head of School: Leonard Tavormina

General Information Coeducational day arts school; primarily serves underachievers, students with learning disabilities, individuals with Attention Deficit Disorder, and dyslexic students. Ungraded, ages 7–16. Founded: 1985. Setting: small town. Nearest major city is Bridgeport. 2-acre campus. 1 building on campus. Approved or accredited by Connecticut Association of Independent Schools and Connecticut Department of Education. Member of National Association of Independent Schools. Endowment: $3.7 million. Total enrollment: 107. Upper school average class size: 5. Upper school faculty-student ratio: 1:4.

Faculty School total: 27. In upper school: 6 men, 21 women; 16 have advanced degrees.

Subjects Offered Algebra, art, biology, creative writing, earth science, English, grammar, history, literature, mathematics, physical education, reading, social studies, writing.

Special Academic Programs Remedial reading and/or remedial writing; remedial math; programs in English, mathematics, general development for dyslexic students.

Student Life Upper grades have uniform requirement, student council. Discipline rests primarily with faculty.

Summer Programs Remediation programs offered; session focuses on academic skills reinforcement; held on campus; accepts boys and girls; open to students from other schools. 60 students usually enrolled. 2006 schedule: June 28 to August 1. Application deadline: none.

Tuition and Aid Day student tuition: $34,400. Tuition installment plan (monthly payment plans, individually arranged payment plans). Need-based scholarship grants available.

Admissions For fall 2005, 4 students applied for upper-level admission, 4 were accepted, 4 enrolled. Wechsler Intelligence Scale for Children required. Deadline for receipt of application materials: none. Application fee required: $75. On-campus interview required.

Athletics Coed Interscholastic: baseball, basketball, cross-country running, soccer, softball, tennis; coed intramural: softball.

Computers Computers are regularly used in English, writing classes. Computer resources include Internet access.

Contact Carolyn Lavender, Director of Admissions. 203-254-2044. Fax: 203-255-4052. E-mail: info@eaglehillsouthport.org. Web site: www.eaglehillsouthport.org.

EAGLE ROCK SCHOOL

PO Box 1770
Estes Park, Colorado 80517-1770
Head of School: Robert Burkhardt

General Information Coeducational boarding and day college-preparatory, general academic, arts, bilingual studies, and technology school; primarily serves underachievers, individuals with Attention Deficit Disorder, individuals with emotional and behavioral problems, dyslexic students, and students who are unsuccessful in a traditional high school. Founded: 1991. Setting: rural. Nearest major city is Boulder. Students are housed in coed dormitories. 640-acre campus. 22 buildings on campus. Approved or accredited by Accreditation Commission of the Texas Association of Baptist Schools, Association of Colorado Independent Schools, North Central Association of Colleges and Schools, and Colorado Department of Education. Upper school average class size: 8.

Faculty In upper school: 19 men, 20 women; 23 reside on campus.

Subjects Offered Algebra, American history, art, arts, biology, business skills, computer science, English, environmental science, fine arts, geography, geometry, government/civics, history, literature, mathematics, music, personal development, physical education, physical science, science, social science, social studies, speech, technology.

Graduation Requirements Arts and fine arts (art, music, dance, drama), business skills (includes word processing), computer science, English, foreign language, mathematics, personal development, physical education (includes health), science, social science, social studies (includes history).

Special Academic Programs Independent study; term-away projects; academic accommodation for the gifted; remedial reading and/or remedial writing; remedial math; programs in English, mathematics for dyslexic students.

College Placement 12 students graduated in 2005; 8 went to college. Other: 4 went to work.

Student Life Upper grades have student council, honor system. Discipline rests equally with students and faculty.

Tuition and Aid Entire tuition paid by American Honda Education Corporation available.

Admissions Deadline for receipt of application materials: none. No application fee required. Interview required.

Athletics Coed Intramural: back packing, basketball, bicycling, climbing, cross-country running, fitness, floor hockey, football, Frisbee, hiking/backpacking, jogging, juggling, life saving, martial arts, mountain biking, outdoor activities, outdoor adventure, outdoor education, outdoor recreation, outdoor skills, physical fitness, physical training, rock climbing, skiing (cross-country), soccer, softball, swimming and diving, ultimate Frisbee, volleyball, water polo, water volleyball, weight lifting. 1 PE instructor.

Computers Computers are regularly used in English, mathematics, science classes. Computer network features include campus e-mail, on-campus library services, CD-ROMs, online commercial services, Internet access.

Contact Philbert Smith, Director of Students. 970-586-7112. Fax: 970-586-4805. E-mail: philberts@aol.com. Web site: www.eaglerockschool.org.

ECKERD YOUTH ALTERNATIVES

100 North Starcrest Drive
Clearwater, Florida 33765
Head of School: Keith Philipson

General Information Coeducational boarding school, affiliated with Christian faith; primarily serves underachievers, students with learning disabilities, individuals with Attention Deficit Disorder, individuals with emotional and behavioral problems, and dyslexic students. Grades 4–12. Founded: 1968. Setting: rural. Students are housed in cabins. 250-acre campus. 48 buildings on campus. Approved or accredited by Southern Association of Colleges and Schools and Florida Department of Education. Total enrollment: 782. Upper school average class size: 12. Upper school faculty-student ratio: 1:10.

Upper School Student Profile 100% of students are boarding students. 90% are state residents. 10 states are represented in upper school student body. 1% are international students. International students from Bermuda and Switzerland.

Faculty School total: 78. In upper school: 21 men, 32 women; 10 have advanced degrees.

Subjects Offered Art history, community service, English, fine arts, humanities, mathematics, physical education, science, social science, social studies, Spanish.

Graduation Requirements Art history, arts and fine arts (art, music, dance, drama), English, foreign language, mathematics, physical education (includes health), religion (includes Bible studies and theology), science, social science, social studies (includes history). Community service is required.

Special Academic Programs Academic accommodation for the gifted; remedial reading and/or remedial writing; remedial math; programs in English, mathematics, general development for dyslexic students; ESL.

Student Life Upper grades have specified standards of dress, student council. Discipline rests equally with students and faculty.

Tuition and Aid Guaranteed tuition plan. Tuition installment plan (individually arranged payment plans). Middle-income loans available.

Admissions Traditional secondary-level entrance grade is 9. Deadline for receipt of application materials: none. No application fee required. Interview recommended.

Athletics Intramural: ice hockey (boys), skiing (downhill) (b); coed intramural: canoeing/kayaking, swimming and diving, track and field.

Computers Computers are regularly used in English, mathematics, science classes. Computer resources include CD-ROMs, Internet access.

Contact Francene Hazel, Director of Admissions. 800-914-3937 Ext. 464. Fax: 727-442-5911. E-mail: fhazel@eckerd.org. Web site: www.eckerd.org.

ELAN SCHOOL

PO Box 578
Poland, Maine 04274
Head of School: Ms. Sharon Terry

General Information Coeducational boarding college-preparatory and general academic school; primarily serves underachievers, students with learning disabilities, individuals with Attention Deficit Disorder, and individuals with emotional and behavioral problems. Grades 7–12. Founded: 1970. Setting: rural. Nearest major city is Portland. Students are housed in single-sex dormitories. 32-acre campus. Approved or accredited by Massachusetts Department of Education, New York Department of Education, and Maine Department of Education. Total enrollment: 110. Upper school average class size: 9. Upper school faculty-student ratio: 1:7.

Upper School Student Profile Grade 9: 15 students (11 boys, 4 girls); Grade 10: 25 students (20 boys, 5 girls); Grade 11: 25 students (17 boys, 8 girls); Grade 12: 43 students (30 boys, 13 girls). 100% of students are boarding students. 5% are state residents. 20 states are represented in upper school student body. 2% are international students. International students from Canada, Hong Kong, and Italy.

Faculty School total: 14. In upper school: 10 men, 4 women; 8 have advanced degrees.

Subjects Offered 20th century history, advanced math, algebra, American Civil War, American history, American literature, applied arts, art history, biology, calculus, chemistry, composition, computer tools, creative writing, critical thinking, driver education, earth science, economics, English, English literature, fine arts, French, geography, geometry, government/civics, health, history, life skills, mathematics, military history, organic chemistry, physical education, physical science, physics, pre-algebra, pre-calculus, research seminar, science, social studies, Spanish, statistics, trigonometry, world history.

Graduation Requirements American history, arts and fine arts (art, music, dance, drama), computer literacy, English, foreign language, mathematics, physical education (includes health), science, social studies (includes history).

Special Academic Programs Accelerated programs; independent study; study at local college for college credit; academic accommodation for the gifted; remedial reading and/or remedial writing; remedial math; programs in English, mathematics, general development for dyslexic students.

College Placement 35 students graduated in 2005; 24 went to college, including Dalhousie University; State University of New York at Oswego; State University of New York College at Cortland; University of Maine; University of Southern Maine. Other: 2 went to work, 2 entered military service, 1 entered a postgraduate year, 6 had other specific plans.

Student Life Upper grades have specified standards of dress. Discipline rests primarily with faculty.

Summer Programs Remediation, enrichment, advancement, sports, art/fine arts, computer instruction programs offered; session focuses on enrichment and remediation; held on campus; accepts boys and girls; not open to students from other schools. 120 students usually enrolled. 2006 schedule: June 19 to August 11. Application deadline: none.

Tuition and Aid 7-day tuition and room/board: $49,071. Tuition installment plan (monthly payment plans). Key Education Resources Achiever Loan Program, prepGATE Loan Program, Sallie Mae Loan Program available.

Admissions Traditional secondary-level entrance grade is 10. Achievement tests, any standardized test, Individual IQ, Achievement and behavior rating scale, psychoeducational evaluation, Rorschach or Thematic Apperception Test, Wechsler Individual Achievement Test, Wechsler Intelligence Scale for Children III, Wide Range Achievement Test, WISC-R, Woodcock-Johnson or WRAT required. Deadline for receipt of application materials: none. No application fee required. Interview recommended.

Athletics Interscholastic: basketball (boys, girls), cross-country running (b,g), track and field (b,g); intramural: aquatics (b,g), baseball (b,g), basketball (b,g), bicycling (b,g), track and field (b,g); coed interscholastic: golf; coed intramural: alpine skiing, bowling, canoeing/kayaking, cross-country running, figure skating, fishing, fitness, fitness walking, Frisbee, golf, hiking/backpacking, horseback riding, ice skating, jogging, kickball, nordic skiing, outdoor activities, outdoor recreation, paddle tennis, physical fitness, racquetball, rafting, roller blading, roller skating, ropes courses, running, sailing, skiing (cross-country), skiing (downhill), snowboarding, soccer, softball, strength & conditioning, swimming and diving, table tennis, telemark skiing, tennis, ultimate Frisbee, volleyball, walking, wallyball, water skiing. 1 PE instructor, 5 coaches.

Computers Computers are regularly used in English, history, life skills classes. Computer resources include CD-ROMs, Internet access.

Contact Ms. Deanna L. Valente, Admissions Director. 207-998-4666 Ext. 122. Fax: 207-998-4660. E-mail: info@elanschool.com. Web site: www.elanschool.com.

See full description on page 1218.

FAIRHILL SCHOOL

16150 Preston Road
Dallas, Texas 75248
Head of School: Ms. Jane Sego

General Information Coeducational day college-preparatory, arts, and technology school; primarily serves students with learning disabilities, individuals with Attention Deficit Disorder, and dyslexic students. Grades 1–12. Founded: 1971. Setting: urban. 16-acre campus. 2 buildings on campus. Approved or accredited by Southern Association of Colleges and Schools, Southern Association of Independent Schools, and Texas Department of Education. Endowment: $2 million. Total enrollment: 230. Upper school average class size: 12.

Upper School Student Profile Grade 9: 23 students (14 boys, 9 girls); Grade 10: 25 students (18 boys, 7 girls); Grade 11: 23 students (19 boys, 4 girls); Grade 12: 18 students (12 boys, 6 girls).

Faculty School total: 30. In upper school: 5 men, 10 women.

Subjects Offered American history, American literature, art, biology, British literature, chemistry, computer science, economics, English, government, health, journalism, mathematics, music, performing arts, physical education, physical science, physics, psychology, reading, Spanish, speech, study skills, world geography.

Graduation Requirements Arts and fine arts (art, music, dance, drama), computer science, English, mathematics, physical education (includes health), science, social studies (includes history), 60 hours of volunteer service for seniors.

Special Academic Programs Honors section; remedial reading and/or remedial writing; remedial math; programs in English, mathematics, general development for dyslexic students.

College Placement 24 students graduated in 2005; 21 went to college, including Collin County Community College District; Dallas County Community College District; Texas Tech University. Other: 1 went to work, 2 entered military service.

Student Life Upper grades have uniform requirement, student council. Discipline rests primarily with faculty.

Summer Programs Remediation, computer instruction programs offered; session focuses on academics; held on campus; accepts boys and girls; open to students from other schools. 50 students usually enrolled. 2006 schedule: June 7 to July 2. Application deadline: none.

Tuition and Aid Day student tuition: $11,000. Need-based scholarship grants available. In 2005–06, 5% of upper-school students received aid. Total amount of financial aid awarded in 2005–06: $10,000.

Admissions Traditional secondary-level entrance grade is 9. Psychoeducational evaluation required. Deadline for receipt of application materials: none. Application fee required: $100. Interview required.

Athletics Interscholastic: baseball (boys), basketball (b,g), golf (b,g), soccer (b,g), tennis (b,g), volleyball (g); intramural: cheering (b,g), jump rope (b,g); coed interscholastic: tennis. 3 coaches.

Computers Computers are regularly used in college planning, English, technology, yearbook classes. Computer network features include campus e-mail, on-campus library services, CD-ROMs, Internet access, file transfer.

Contact Mrs. Kay Wendell, Head of Upper School. 972-233-1026. Fax: 972-233-8205. E-mail: kwendell@fairhill.org. Web site: www.fairhill.org.

THE FAMILY FOUNDATION SCHOOL

431 Chapel Hill Road
Hancock, New York 13783
Head of School: Mr. Emmanuel A. Argiros

General Information Coeducational boarding college-preparatory and arts school, affiliated with Christian faith, Jewish faith; primarily serves underachievers, individuals with Attention Deficit Disorder, and individuals with emotional and behavioral problems. Grades 6–12. Founded: 1987. Setting: rural. Nearest major city is Binghamton. Students are housed in single-sex dormitories. 158-acre campus. 18 buildings on campus. Approved or accredited by Middle States Association of Colleges and Schools and New York Department of Education. Total enrollment: 225. Upper school average class size: 8. Upper school faculty-student ratio: 1:8.

Upper School Student Profile Grade 9: 18 students (13 boys, 5 girls); Grade 10: 48 students (25 boys, 23 girls); Grade 11: 84 students (56 boys, 28 girls); Grade 12: 72 students (48 boys, 24 girls). 100% of students are boarding students. 20% are state residents. 20 states are represented in upper school student body. 3% are international students. International students from Canada, Russian Federation, Thailand, and United Arab Emirates. 89% of students are Christian, Jewish.

Faculty School total: 36. In upper school: 19 men, 17 women; 14 have advanced degrees; 15 reside on campus.

Subjects Offered Advanced chemistry, algebra, American government, American history, analysis and differential calculus, ancient world history, art, Bible studies, biology, British literature, chemistry, choir, college writing, debate, drama, earth

science, economics, English, family living, geometry, global studies, health and safety, HTML design, Jewish studies, journalism, modern dance, philosophy, physics, pre-calculus, religion, religious education, sociology, Spanish, tap dance, trigonometry, world history, World-Wide-Web publishing, yoga.

Graduation Requirements New York State Board of Regents requirements, completion of emotional growth program.

Special Academic Programs Study at local college for college credit; remedial reading and/or remedial writing.

College Placement 66 students graduated in 2005; 60 went to college, including Fordham University; Loyola College in Maryland; New York University; State University of New York at Binghamton; The University of Scranton; University of Mary Washington. Other: 6 had other specific plans. Mean SAT verbal: 531, mean SAT math: 527, mean combined SAT: 1583. 27% scored over 600 on SAT verbal, 18% scored over 600 on SAT math, 16% scored over 1800 on combined SAT.

Student Life Upper grades have specified standards of dress, student council, honor system. Discipline rests primarily with faculty. Attendance at religious services is required.

Tuition and Aid 7-day tuition and room/board: $51,600. Tuition installment plan (monthly payment plans). Tuition reduction for siblings, need-based scholarship grants, paying campus jobs available. In 2005–06, 15% of upper-school students received aid. Total amount of financial aid awarded in 2005–06: $560,000.

Admissions Traditional secondary-level entrance grade is 10. Deadline for receipt of application materials: none. No application fee required. On-campus interview required.

Athletics Interscholastic: basketball (boys, girls), soccer (b,g), softball (g); intramural: aerobics (b,g), basketball (b,g); coed interscholastic: cheering, dance, golf; coed intramural: basketball, fitness walking, flag football, Frisbee, ice skating, outdoors, soccer, softball, table tennis, yoga. 4 PE instructors, 11 coaches.

Computers Computers are regularly used in English, history, journalism, science, Spanish, Web site design, yearbook classes. Computer network features include on-campus library services, CD-ROMs, online commercial services, Internet access, file transfer.

Contact Mr. Joe Lichty, Director of Admissions. 845-887-5213 Ext. 499. Fax: 845-887-4939. E-mail: jlichty@thefamilyschool.com. Web site: www.thefamilyschool.com.

See full description on page 1220.

F. L. CHAMBERLAIN SCHOOL

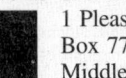

1 Pleasant Street
Box 778
Middleborough, Massachusetts 02346
Head of School: William Doherty

General Information Coeducational boarding and day college-preparatory, general academic, arts, and vocational school; primarily serves students with learning disabilities, individuals with Attention Deficit Disorder, individuals with emotional and behavioral problems, dyslexic students, students with Asperger's Syndrome, NLD Bipolar I and II, OCD, Tourettes Syndrome, depression, and anxiety, Post-Traumatic Stress Disorder, disrupted adoptions, Axis II personality disorders. Grades 6–12. Founded: 1976. Setting: rural. Nearest major city is Boston. Students are housed in coed dormitories and single-sex dormitories. 15-acre campus. 9 buildings on campus. Approved or accredited by National Association of Private Schools for Exceptional Children and Massachusetts Department of Education. Total enrollment: 102. Upper school average class size: 8. Upper school faculty-student ratio: 1:4.

Upper School Student Profile Grade 9: 14 students (10 boys, 4 girls); Grade 10: 14 students (10 boys, 4 girls); Grade 11: 31 students (19 boys, 12 girls); Grade 12: 33 students (23 boys, 10 girls). 80% of students are boarding students. 40% are state residents. 11 states are represented in upper school student body. 1% are international students. International students from Bermuda; 1 other country represented in student body.

Faculty School total: 27. In upper school: 8 men, 16 women; 2 have advanced degrees.

Subjects Offered Algebra, American history, American literature, art, biology, community service, computer math, creative writing, drama, English, English literature, environmental science, film studies, geography, geometry, government/civics, grammar, health, history, home economics, mathematics, music, peer counseling, personal growth, physical education, pre-algebra, pre-calculus, pre-vocational education, psychology, science, sex education, social education, social studies, Spanish, theater, video, world history, writing.

Graduation Requirements Computer science, English, mathematics, physical education (includes health), science, social studies (includes history). Community service is required.

Special Academic Programs Remedial reading and/or remedial writing; remedial math; programs in English, mathematics for dyslexic students; special instructional classes for students needing assistance with life skills.

College Placement 21 students graduated in 2005; 12 went to college, including Bridgewater State College; Curry College; Johnson & Wales University; New England

College; University of Massachusetts Amherst. Other: 9 went to work. Mean SAT verbal: 540, mean SAT math: 510. 30% scored over 600 on SAT verbal, 20% scored over 600 on SAT math.

Student Life Upper grades have specified standards of dress, student council. Discipline rests primarily with faculty.

Summer Programs Remediation, advancement, computer instruction programs offered; session focuses on education and recreation; held both on and off campus; held at various community facilities; accepts boys and girls; open to students from other schools. 60 students usually enrolled. 2006 schedule: July 6 to August 24. Application deadline: none.

Tuition and Aid Day student tuition: $50,350; 7-day tuition and room/board: $116,227. Tuition installment plan (monthly payment plans, individually arranged payment plans).

Admissions Traditional secondary-level entrance grade is 9. For fall 2005, 120 students applied for upper-level admission, 80 were accepted, 50 enrolled. Psycho-educational evaluation, Rorschach or Thematic Apperception Test or WAIS, WICS required. Deadline for receipt of application materials: none. No application fee required. Interview required.

Athletics Intramural: touch football (boys); coed intramural: baseball, basketball, billiards, bowling, equestrian sports, football, golf, horseback riding, skiing (downhill), soccer, softball, swimming and diving, volleyball. 1 PE instructor.

Computers Computers are regularly used in English, mathematics classes. Computer network features include campus e-mail, CD-ROMs, online commercial services, Internet access, file transfer, Online Learning.

Contact Lawrence H. Mutty, LCSW, Director of Admissions. 508-947-7825. Fax: 508-947-0944. E-mail: admissions@chamberlainschool.org. Web site: www.chamberlainschool.org.

See full description on page 1222.

FOOTHILLS ACADEMY

745 37th Street NW
Calgary, Alberta T2N 4T1, Canada
Head of School: Mr. Gordon M. Bullivant

General Information Coeducational day technology school; primarily serves underachievers, students with learning disabilities, individuals with Attention Deficit Disorder, and dyslexic students. Grades 1–12. Founded: 1979. Setting: urban. 7-acre campus. 1 building on campus. Approved or accredited by Association of Independent Schools and Colleges of Alberta and Alberta Department of Education. Language of instruction: English. Endowment: CAN$3 million. Total enrollment: 186. Upper school average class size: 12. Upper school faculty-student ratio: 1:12.

Upper School Student Profile Grade 9: 26 students (23 boys, 3 girls); Grade 10: 23 students (15 boys, 8 girls); Grade 11: 22 students (14 boys, 8 girls); Grade 12: 22 students (18 boys, 4 girls).

Faculty School total: 38. In upper school: 10 men, 15 women; 6 have advanced degrees.

Subjects Offered African American studies, algebra, animation, art education, athletics, auto mechanics, basic skills, biology, calculus, career and personal planning, chemistry, computer animation, computer education, computer keyboarding, computer literacy, computer skills, consumer mathematics, digital photography, drama, drama performance, electives, English literature, expository writing, grammar, keyboarding/computer, leadership, library research, mathematics, mechanics of writing, reading/study skills, remedial study skills, research skills, science, social skills, social studies, speech therapy, track and field.

Graduation Requirements Athletics, career and personal planning, English, English composition, English literature, expository writing, grammar, keyboarding/computer, language arts, learning strategies, mathematics, mechanics of writing, physical fitness, reading/study skills, research skills, science, social studies (includes history), study skills, Alberta Education Standards.

Special Academic Programs Remedial reading and/or remedial writing; remedial math; programs in English, mathematics for dyslexic students.

College Placement 25 students graduated in 2005; 21 went to college, including The University of Winnipeg; University of Calgary; University of Victoria. Other: 4 went to work.

Student Life Upper grades have specified standards of dress, student council, honor system. Discipline rests primarily with faculty.

Summer Programs Remediation, enrichment programs offered; session focuses on remedial reading/language/organization skills; held on campus; accepts boys and girls; open to students from other schools. 50 students usually enrolled. 2006 schedule: July 5 to August 25. Application deadline: June 30.

Tuition and Aid Day student tuition: CAN$8400. Guaranteed tuition plan. Tuition installment plan (The Tuition Plan, monthly payment plans, individually arranged payment plans). Bursaries, need-based scholarship grants available. In 2005–06, 60% of upper-school students received aid. Total amount of financial aid awarded in 2005–06: CAN$500,000.

Admissions Traditional secondary-level entrance grade is 9. For fall 2005, 35 students applied for upper-level admission, 18 were accepted, 17 enrolled. Achievement tests, CTBS, Stanford Achievement Test, any other standardized test, math, reading, and mental ability tests, Wechsler Intelligence Scale for Children, Woodcock

Language Proficiency Test, WRAT or writing sample required. Deadline for receipt of application materials: June 30. Application fee required: CAN$50. On-campus interview required.

Athletics Interscholastic: basketball (boys, girls); intramural: badminton (g), basketball (b,g), cooperative games (g), cross-country running (g); coed interscholastic: badminton, cross-country running, golf, indoor track & field, track and field, volleyball; coed intramural: badminton, ball hockey, baseball, cross-country running, curling, fitness, flag football, floor hockey, gymnastics, handball, in-line skating, indoor soccer, indoor track & field, jogging, life saving, outdoor activities, outdoor education, physical fitness, physical training, running, skiing (downhill), snowboarding, softball, strength & conditioning, tennis, touch football, track and field, volleyball, weight lifting, weight training, wilderness, wrestling. 1 PE instructor, 2 coaches, 2 trainers.

Computers Computers are regularly used in all academic, animation, career exploration, computer applications, creative writing, desktop publishing, keyboarding, library skills, research skills, Web site design, word processing, writing fundamentals, yearbook classes. Computer network features include campus e-mail, on-campus library services, CD-ROMs, online commercial services, Internet access, file transfer, office computer access, wireless campus network.

Contact Ms. K. Lenehan, Program Coordinator. 403-270-9400. Fax: 403-270-9438. E-mail: info@foothillsacademy.org. Web site: www.foothillsacademy.org.

FOREST HEIGHTS LODGE

PO Box 789
Evergreen, Colorado 80437-0789
Head of School: Linda Clefisch

General Information Boys' boarding college-preparatory and general academic school; primarily serves individuals with emotional and behavioral problems. Grades K–12. Founded: 1954. Setting: small town. Nearest major city is Denver. Students are housed in single-sex dormitories. 10-acre campus. 3 buildings on campus. Approved or accredited by Joint Commission on Accreditation of Healthcare Organizations and Colorado Department of Education. Total enrollment: 24. Upper school faculty-student ratio: 1:5.

Upper School Student Profile Grade 9: 3 students (3 boys). 100% of students are boarding students. 3 states are represented in upper school student body.

Faculty School total: 5. In upper school: 4 men, 1 woman; 3 have advanced degrees; all reside on campus.

Subjects Offered Algebra, American history, computer science, earth science, English, fine arts, grammar, mathematics, physical education, science, social studies, world history, writing.

Graduation Requirements Computer science, English, mathematics, physical education (includes health), science, social science, social studies (includes history).

Special Academic Programs Remedial reading and/or remedial writing; remedial math; programs in English, mathematics, general development for dyslexic students.

Student Life Upper grades have specified standards of dress. Discipline rests primarily with faculty.

Tuition and Aid 7-day tuition and room/board: $88,563. Tuition installment plan (monthly payment plans).

Admissions For fall 2005, 10 students applied for upper-level admission, 5 were accepted. Deadline for receipt of application materials: none. No application fee required. On-campus interview required.

Athletics Intramural: alpine skiing, aquatics, back packing, ball hockey, baseball, basketball, bicycling, blading, cooperative games, cross-country running, field hockey, fishing, football, hiking/backpacking, ice hockey, ice skating, mountain biking, nordic skiing, outdoor activities, outdoor recreation, outdoors, roller blading, skateboarding, skiing (cross-country), skiing (downhill), soccer, softball, swimming and diving, table tennis, tai chi, tennis, track and field, walking, wall climbing, weight lifting, winter walking. 1 PE instructor.

Computers Computers are regularly used in English, science classes. Computer resources include CD-ROMs, Internet access.

Contact Linda Clefisch, Executive Director. 303-674-6681. Fax: 303-674-6805.

THE FORMAN SCHOOL

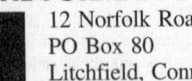

12 Norfolk Road
PO Box 80
Litchfield, Connecticut 06759
Head of School: Mark B. Perkins

General Information Coeducational boarding and day college-preparatory, arts, and technology school; primarily serves students with learning disabilities, individuals with Attention Deficit Disorder, and dyslexic students. Grades 9–12. Founded: 1930. Setting: rural. Nearest major city is Hartford. Students are housed in single-sex dormitories. 100-acre campus. 30 buildings on campus. Approved or accredited by New England Association of Schools and Colleges and The Association of Boarding Schools. Member of National Association of Independent Schools and Secondary School Admission Test Board. Endowment: $30 million. Total enrollment: 170. Upper school average class size: 11. Upper school faculty-student ratio: 1:3.

Upper School Student Profile Grade 9: 37 students (27 boys, 10 girls); Grade 10: 45 students (33 boys, 12 girls); Grade 11: 49 students (38 boys, 11 girls); Grade 12: 39 students (28 boys, 11 girls). 87% of students are boarding students. 33% are state residents. 26 states are represented in upper school student body. 13% are international students. International students from Bermuda, China, Jamaica, and Spain.

Faculty School total: 65. In upper school: 26 men, 39 women; 33 have advanced degrees; 33 reside on campus.

Subjects Offered Algebra, American history, American literature, art, art history, biology, calculus, ceramics, chemistry, computer science, creative writing, driver education, ecology, English, English literature, environmental science, European history, expository writing, fine arts, French, geography, geometry, grammar, history, history-AP, Holocaust seminar, human development, mathematics, music, photography, physical education, physics, psychology, science, social science, social studies, Spanish, trigonometry, world history, world literature, writing.

Graduation Requirements Arts and fine arts (art, music, dance, drama), English, mathematics, physical education (includes health), science, social science, social studies (includes history).

Special Academic Programs Advanced Placement exam preparation in 2 subject areas; honors section; programs in English, mathematics, general development for dyslexic students; ESL.

College Placement 47 students graduated in 2005; 42 went to college, including Lynn University; The University of Arizona; University of Vermont. Other: 2 entered a postgraduate year, 1 had other specific plans. Mean SAT verbal: 439, mean SAT math: 411, mean composite ACT: 22. 1% scored over 600 on SAT verbal, 1% scored over 600 on SAT math, .5% scored over 26 on composite ACT.

Student Life Upper grades have specified standards of dress, student council, honor system. Discipline rests primarily with faculty.

Tuition and Aid Day student tuition: $37,000; 7-day tuition and room/board: $45,000. Tuition installment plan (The Tuition Plan, Key Tuition Payment Plan, self-funded tuition, refund plan, Key Tuition Payment Plan). Need-based scholarship grants available. In 2005–06, 20% of upper-school students received aid. Total amount of financial aid awarded in 2005–06: $180,000.

Admissions Traditional secondary-level entrance grade is 9. For fall 2005, 286 students applied for upper-level admission, 110 were accepted, 71 enrolled. WISC-III and Woodcock-Johnson required. Deadline for receipt of application materials: none. Application fee required: $50. Interview required.

Athletics Interscholastic: baseball (boys), basketball (b,g), golf (b), ice hockey (b), lacrosse (b), soccer (b,g), softball (g), tennis (b,g), volleyball (g), wrestling (b); intramural: blading (g); coed interscholastic: cross-country running, football, kayaking, skiing (downhill), swimming and diving; coed intramural: bicycling, golf, kayaking, skiing (cross-country), skiing (downhill), squash, tennis, weight lifting. 1 trainer.

Computers Computers are regularly used in English, foreign language, mathematics, music, science, writing classes. Computer network features include campus e-mail, CD-ROMs, Internet access, DVD.

Contact Beth A. Rainey, Director of Admissions. 860-567-1803. Fax: 860-567-3501. E-mail: admissions@formanschool.org. Web site: www.formanschool.org.

See full description on page 1224.

FRASER ACADEMY

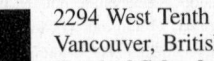

2294 West Tenth Avenue
Vancouver, British Columbia V6K 2H8, Canada
Head of School: Eleanor Nesling

General Information Coeducational day college-preparatory and general academic school; primarily serves students with learning disabilities and dyslexic students. Grades 1–12. Founded: 1982. Setting: urban. 1 building on campus. Approved or accredited by British Columbia Department of Education. Language of instruction: English. Total enrollment: 183. Upper school average class size: 8. Upper school faculty-student ratio: 1:5.

Upper School Student Profile Grade 8: 29 students (20 boys, 9 girls); Grade 9: 23 students (21 boys, 2 girls); Grade 10: 21 students (16 boys, 5 girls); Grade 11: 22 students (17 boys, 5 girls); Grade 12: 21 students (14 boys, 7 girls).

Faculty School total: 56. In upper school: 13 men, 25 women; 6 have advanced degrees.

Graduation Requirements British Columbia Ministry of Education requirements.

Special Academic Programs Remedial reading and/or remedial writing; remedial math; programs in English, mathematics, general development for dyslexic students.

College Placement 18 students graduated in 2005; 4 went to college. Other: 12 went to work, 2 had other specific plans.

Student Life Upper grades have uniform requirement, student council. Discipline rests primarily with faculty.

Tuition and Aid Day student tuition: CAN$18,550. Tuition installment plan (quarterly payment plan). Tuition reduction for siblings, bursaries available. In 2005–06, 10% of upper-school students received aid. Total amount of financial aid awarded in 2005–06: CAN$42,000.

Admissions Traditional secondary-level entrance grade is 8. For fall 2005, 27 students applied for upper-level admission, 25 were accepted, 22 enrolled. Academic

Profile Tests, admissions testing or psychoeducational evaluation required. Deadline for receipt of application materials: none. Application fee required: CAN$250. Interview required.

Athletics Interscholastic: volleyball (girls); intramural: volleyball (g); coed interscholastic: alpine skiing, ball hockey, basketball, field hockey, fitness, kickball, mountain biking, outdoor activities, outdoor education, physical fitness, rock climbing, skiing (downhill), snowboarding, soccer, softball, track and field; coed intramural: alpine skiing, basketball, fitness, mountain biking, skiing (downhill), snowboarding, soccer, softball, track and field. 1 PE instructor, 3 coaches, 1 trainer.
Computers Computer network features include campus e-mail, CD-ROMs, Internet access, various learning disabilities/dyslexic-specific software.
Contact Eleanor Nesling, Head of School. 604-736-5575. Fax: 604-736-5578. E-mail: info@fraser-academy.bc.ca. Web site: fraser-academy.bc.ca.

THE FROSTIG SCHOOL

971 North Altadena Drive
Pasadena, California 91107
Head of School: Ms. Tobey Shaw

General Information Coeducational day arts, vocational, and technology school; primarily serves underachievers, students with learning disabilities, individuals with Attention Deficit Disorder, and dyslexic students. Grades 1–12. Founded: 1951. Setting: suburban. Nearest major city is Los Angeles. 2-acre campus. 1 building on campus. Approved or accredited by National Association of Private Schools for Exceptional Children, Western Association of Schools and Colleges, and California Department of Education. Endowment: $3 million. Total enrollment: 120. Upper school average class size: 12. Upper school faculty-student ratio: 1:6.
Faculty School total: 25. In upper school: 3 men, 4 women; 4 have advanced degrees.
Special Academic Programs Remedial reading and/or remedial writing; remedial math; programs in English, mathematics, general development for dyslexic students.
College Placement 5 students graduated in 2005; 3 went to college, including Glendale Community College; Pasadena City College; Santa Monica College. Other: 2 had other specific plans.
Student Life Upper grades have specified standards of dress, student council. Discipline rests primarily with faculty.
Summer Programs Remediation programs offered; session focuses on maintaining skills obtained during the regular term; work experience for high school students; held on campus; accepts boys and girls; not open to students from other schools. 36 students usually enrolled. 2006 schedule: July 10 to August 18.
Tuition and Aid Day student tuition: $22,000. Tuition installment plan (monthly payment plans, individually arranged payment plans). Need-based scholarship grants available. Total amount of financial aid awarded in 2005–06: $50,000.
Admissions Traditional secondary-level entrance grade is 9. For fall 2005, 8 students applied for upper-level admission, 5 were accepted, 5 enrolled. Admissions testing required. Deadline for receipt of application materials: none. Application fee required: $100. On-campus interview required.
Athletics Coed Interscholastic: basketball, flag football, softball, touch football. 2 PE instructors.
Computers Computers are regularly used in all classes. Computer network features include campus e-mail, on-campus library services, CD-ROMs, Internet access, Assistive Technology Services.
Contact Ms. Barbara Mendez, Admissions Coordinator. 626-791-1255. Fax: 626-798-1801. E-mail: admissions@frostig.org. Web site: www.frostig.org.

GATEWAY SCHOOL

2570 Northwest Green Oaks Boulevard
Arlington, Texas 76012
Head of School: Mrs. Harriet R. Walber

General Information Coeducational day college-preparatory, general academic, arts, and technology school; primarily serves underachievers, students with learning disabilities, individuals with Attention Deficit Disorder, and dyslexic students. Grades 5–12. Founded: 1980. Setting: urban. Nearest major city is Fort Worth. 7-acre campus. 1 building on campus. Approved or accredited by Southern Association of Colleges and Schools, University Senate of United Methodist Church, and Texas Department of Education. Endowment: $180,000. Total enrollment: 30. Upper school average class size: 6. Upper school faculty-student ratio: 1:10.
Upper School Student Profile Grade 9: 5 students (5 boys); Grade 10: 5 students (2 boys, 3 girls); Grade 11: 6 students (6 boys); Grade 12: 2 students (2 boys).
Faculty School total: 6. In upper school: 2 men, 3 women; 4 have advanced degrees.
Subjects Offered Algebra, American literature, art, biology, British literature, career planning, chemistry, college awareness, college counseling, community service, composition, computer education, computer keyboarding, computer literacy, computer science, computer skills, developmental math, drama, earth science, economics, English, English composition, English literature, environmental science, geometry, government, government/civics, grammar, health, health education, history, intro to computers, introduction to theater, journalism, language arts, literature, mathematics, music, music performance, music theater, newspaper, physical education, pre-algebra,

reading, reading/study skills, science, social studies, Spanish, speech, state history, theater, U.S. government, U.S. history, word processing, world history, world literature, writing, writing workshop, yearbook.
Graduation Requirements Computer science, English, mathematics, physical education (includes health), science, social studies (includes history), Spanish. Community service is required.
Special Academic Programs Independent study; study at local college for college credit; domestic exchange program (with Buckingham Browne & Nichols School); remedial reading and/or remedial writing; remedial math; programs in English, mathematics, general development for dyslexic students.
College Placement 2 students graduated in 2005; all went to college, including Lon Morris College; Tarrant County College District; Texas Wesleyan University.
Student Life Upper grades have uniform requirement, student council. Discipline rests equally with students and faculty.
Tuition and Aid Day student tuition: $10,800. Guaranteed tuition plan. Merit scholarship grants, need-based scholarship grants available. In 2005–06, 15% of upper-school students received aid; total upper-school merit-scholarship money awarded: $10,000. Total amount of financial aid awarded in 2005–06: $18,000.
Admissions Traditional secondary-level entrance grade is 10. School's own test, Wechsler Intelligence Scale for Children and Woodcock-Johnson required. Deadline for receipt of application materials: none. Application fee required: $150. On-campus interview required.
Athletics Interscholastic: basketball (boys, girls), golf (g); intramural: basketball (b,g), bowling (b,g), golf (b,g), jogging (b,g); coed interscholastic: fitness walking, golf, jogging, scuba diving, tennis, triathlon; coed intramural: bowling. 1 PE instructor, 1 coach.
Computers Computers are regularly used in basic skills, English, mathematics, science classes. Computer network features include CD-ROMs, Internet access.
Contact Harriet R. Walber, Executive Director. 817-226-6222. Fax: 817-226-6225. E-mail: walberhr@aol.com. Web site: www.gatewayschool.com.

GLEN EDEN SCHOOL

8665 Barnard Street
Vancouver, British Columbia V6P 5G6, Canada
Head of School: Dr. Rick Brennan

General Information Coeducational boarding school; primarily serves underachievers, students with learning disabilities, individuals with Attention Deficit Disorder, individuals with emotional and behavioral problems, and students with Autism Spectrum Disorders. Founded: 1976. Setting: urban. 1 building on campus. Approved or accredited by British Columbia Department of Education. Language of instruction: English.
Upper School Student Profile 2% of students are boarding students. 98% are province residents. 2 provinces are represented in upper school student body.
Faculty School total: 11. In upper school: 5 men, 6 women; 2 have advanced degrees.
Special Academic Programs Remedial reading and/or remedial writing; remedial math.
Summer Programs Remediation programs offered; session focuses on outreach/group dynamics; held on campus; accepts boys and girls; not open to students from other schools. 20 students usually enrolled. 2006 schedule: July 1 to August 31. Application deadline: June 1.
Tuition and Aid Bursaries available. In 2005–06, 5% of upper-school students received aid. Total amount of financial aid awarded in 2005–06: CAN$40,000.
Admissions Deadline for receipt of application materials: none. Application fee required. Interview required.
Computers Computers are regularly used in journalism classes. Computer resources include CD-ROMs, Internet access.
Contact Dr. Rick Brennan, Director. 604-267-0394. Fax: 604-267-0544. E-mail: rbrennan@glenedeninstitute.com.

THE GLENHOLME SCHOOL

81 Sabbaday Lane
Washington, Connecticut 06793
Head of School: Gary Fitzherbert

petersons.com

General Information Coeducational boarding and day arts, vocational, technology, social skills, and study skills school; primarily serves underachievers, students with learning disabilities, individuals with Attention Deficit Disorder, individuals with emotional and behavioral problems, students with Asperger's Syndrome, and students needing social skills training and problem solving/critical thinking. Ungraded, ages 8–18. Founded: 1969. Setting: rural. Nearest major city is Hartford. Students are housed in single-sex cottages. 110-acre campus. 30 buildings on campus. Approved or accredited by Connecticut Association of Independent Schools, Connecticut Department of Children and Families, Massachusetts Department of Education, National Association of Private Schools for Exceptional Children, New Jersey Department of Education, New York Department of Education, The Association of Boarding Schools, and Connecticut Department of Education. Member of National

Association of Independent Schools. Total enrollment: 100. Upper school average class size: 12. Upper school faculty-student ratio: 1:12.

Upper School Student Profile 98% of students are boarding students. 15% are state residents. 12 states are represented in upper school student body. 2% are international students. International students from Canada, Hong Kong, Malaysia, and Mexico.

Faculty School total: 25. In upper school: 6 men, 19 women; 7 have advanced degrees.

Subjects Offered Algebra, art, biology, career education, character education, chemistry, choral music, communication skills, community service, computer education, culinary arts, decision making skills, digital photography, earth science, English, equine management, ESL, fine arts, geometry, health, life skills, mathematics, music, performing arts, photography, physical education, radio broadcasting, science, social science, Spanish, U.S. history, world history, writing.

Special Academic Programs Remedial reading and/or remedial writing; remedial math; programs in English, mathematics, general development for dyslexic students; ESL (3 students enrolled).

Student Life Upper grades have uniform requirement, student council. Discipline rests primarily with faculty.

Tuition and Aid Day student tuition: $35,475; 7-day tuition and room/board: $93,775. Tuition installment plan (Key Tuition Payment Plan). Local and state board of education funding available.

Admissions Traditional secondary-level entrance age is 13. For fall 2005, 150 students applied for upper-level admission, 38 were accepted, 32 enrolled. Admissions testing, Individual IQ, Achievement and behavior rating scale, psychoeducational evaluation or writing sample required. Deadline for receipt of application materials: none. No application fee required. Interview required.

Athletics Interscholastic: basketball (boys, girls), softball (b,g), volleyball (g); intramural: aquatics (b,g), baseball (b,g), basketball (b,g), cheering (g), floor hockey (b,g), softball (b,g), swimming and diving (b,g); coed interscholastic: baseball, soccer, tennis; coed intramural: archery, equestrian sports, horseback riding, kickball, Newcombe ball, outdoor activities, outdoor recreation, tennis, volleyball. 1 PE instructor, 2 coaches.

Computers Computers are regularly used in all academic classes. Computer network features include campus e-mail, on-campus library services, CD-ROMs, Internet access, office computer access, DVD, distance learning, Web CAM Parent Communications.

Contact Kathi Fitzherbert, Director of Admissions. 860-868-7377. Fax: 860-868-7413. E-mail: admissions@theglenholmeschool.org. Web site: www. theglenholmeschool.org/tp.

ANNOUNCEMENT FROM THE SCHOOL Glenholme is a boarding school for children with special needs that teaches varying levels of academic, social, and emotional development in a highly structured learning environment. A number of students who come to Glenholme have been unable to succeed in more traditional schools, are more emotionally fragile, and have a lack of motivation to learn. Children with ADHD, Asperger's Syndrome, and emotional, behavioral, and/or learning disabilities are successful at Glenholme because they thrive in the supportive and structured learning environment. The grades 3–12 education program at The Glenholme School provides many learning opportunities that include an individualized approach with a low student-teacher ratio, ranging from 8 to 12 students per class. In addition to Glenholme's traditional course work, there are many after-school educational opportunities in the areas of equestrian riding and care, music, drama, and art. Glenholme capitalizes on its students' creative talents and establishes more connections to learning with the use of an arts integration and values-based approach, which is incorporated into all academic classes. Students receive positive feedback and instruction in all areas of the Glenholme program through the Motivational Management Approach, which is the cornerstone of Glenholme's program both in the school and the residence. By working with this program, students learn to understand their strengths and weaknesses and begin to realize their potential. Glenholme's program assists students in setting and achieving attainable goals both academically and socially. Glenholme, as a center of The Devereux Foundation, has a rich legacy of education, care, and commitment. Helena T. Devereux, an exceptional teacher, who believed that education was not limited to the classroom but was a full-time learning experience, founded Devereux in 1912.

THE GOW SCHOOL

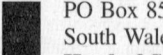

PO Box 85
South Wales, New York 14139-9778
Head of School: Mr. M. Bradley Rogers Jr.

General Information Boys' boarding college-preparatory, arts, technology, and reconstructive language school; primarily serves students with learning disabilities, individuals with Attention Deficit Disorder, dyslexic students, and students with specific language-based learning disabilities. Grades 7–PG. Founded: 1926. Setting: rural. Nearest major city is Buffalo. Students are housed in single-sex dormitories. 100-acre campus. 15 buildings on campus. Approved or accredited by New York State Association of Independent Schools, New York State Board of Regents, and The

Association of Boarding Schools. Member of National Association of Independent Schools. Endowment: $6 million. Total enrollment: 142. Upper school average class size: 5. Upper school faculty-student ratio: 1:4.

Upper School Student Profile Grade 10: 35 students (35 boys); Grade 11: 37 students (37 boys); Grade 12: 23 students (23 boys). 100% of students are boarding students. 22% are state residents. 26 states are represented in upper school student body. 7% are international students. International students from Canada, Cayman Islands, Chile, Hong Kong, Republic of Korea, and Thailand; 5 other countries represented in student body.

Faculty School total: 34. In upper school: 25 men, 5 women; 20 have advanced degrees; 26 reside on campus.

Subjects Offered Algebra, American history, American literature, art, biology, business, business applications, business skills, calculus, ceramics, chemistry, computer applications, computer keyboarding, computer literacy, computer programming, computer science, drama, earth science, economics, English, English literature, European history, expository writing, fine arts, geology, geometry, grammar, health, journalism, mathematics, metalworking, music, physics, reading, reconstructive language, robotics, science, social studies, theater, trigonometry, typing, world history.

Graduation Requirements Arts and fine arts (art, music, dance, drama), business skills (includes word processing), English, mathematics, reconstructive language, research seminar, science, senior humanities, senior seminar, social studies (includes history), outdoor experience. Community service is required.

Special Academic Programs Independent study; study at local college for college credit; academic accommodation for the musically talented; remedial reading and/or remedial writing; remedial math; programs in English, mathematics, general development for dyslexic students.

College Placement 33 students graduated in 2005; all went to college, including Embry-Riddle Aeronautical University; Lynn University; Manhattanville College; Savannah College of Art and Design; St. Lawrence University; West Virginia Wesleyan College. Median SAT verbal: 410, median SAT math: 460, median combined SAT: 1230, median composite ACT: 21. 5% scored over 600 on SAT verbal, 19% scored over 600 on SAT math.

Student Life Upper grades have specified standards of dress, student council. Discipline rests primarily with faculty. Attendance at religious services is required.

Summer Programs Remediation, enrichment, advancement, sports, art/fine arts, rigorous outdoor training, computer instruction programs offered; session focuses on remediation and course work; held both on and off campus; held at camping sites and city venues; accepts boys and girls; open to students from other schools. 100 students usually enrolled. 2006 schedule: June 25 to July 29. Application deadline: none.

Tuition and Aid 7-day tuition and room/board: $40,300. Tuition installment plan (FACTS Tuition Payment Plan, monthly payment plans, individually arranged payment plans). Need-based scholarship grants available. In 2005–06, 31% of upper-school students received aid. Total amount of financial aid awarded in 2005–06: $333,200.

Admissions Traditional secondary-level entrance grade is 10. For fall 2005, 29 students applied for upper-level admission, 26 were accepted, 22 enrolled. Wechsler Intelligence Scale for Children, Woodcock-Johnson or Woodcock-Johnson Revised Achievement Test required. Deadline for receipt of application materials: none. Application fee required: $75. On-campus interview required.

Athletics Interscholastic: basketball, crew, cross-country running, lacrosse, rowing, soccer, squash, swimming and diving, tennis, wrestling; intramural: alpine skiing, aquatics, back packing, badminton, basketball, bicycling, bowling, climbing, cross-country running, fitness, fitness walking, flag football, floor hockey, freestyle skiing, Frisbee, golf, handball, hiking/backpacking, in-line skating, indoor soccer, jogging, jump rope, lacrosse, martial arts, mountain biking, nordic skiing, outdoor education, paint ball, physical fitness, physical training, racquetball, rappelling, riflery, rock climbing, roller blading, roller hockey, ropes courses, skateboarding, skiing (cross-country), skiing (downhill), snowboarding, soccer, softball, squash, street hockey, strength & conditioning, swimming and diving, tennis, touch football, volleyball, walking, wall climbing, weight lifting, weight training.

Computers Computers are regularly used in all classes. Computer network features include campus e-mail, on-campus library services, CD-ROMs, online commercial services, Internet access, file transfer, office computer access, DVD, scanners, digital photography, voice recognition.

Contact Mr. Robert Garcia, Director of Admission. 716-652-3450. Fax: 716-687-2003. E-mail: admissions@gow.org. Web site: www.gow.org.

See full description on page 1226.

GROVE SCHOOL

175 Copse Road
PO Box 646
Madison, Connecticut 06443
Head of School: Mr. Richard L. Chorney

General Information Coeducational boarding and day college-preparatory, general academic, arts, technology, drama, and music school; primarily serves students with learning disabilities, individuals with Attention Deficit Disorder, dyslexic students, students with depression, Attention Deficit Hyperactivity Disorder, Bipolar Disorder, Tourette's Syndrome, and Asperger's Syndrome, Executive functioning disorder,

Obsessive-Compulsive Disorder, and other neuropsychiatric disorders. Grades 7–12. Founded: 1934. Setting: small town. Nearest major city is New Haven. Students are housed in single-sex dormitories. 90-acre campus. Approved or accredited by Connecticut Department of Children and Families and Connecticut Department of Education. Total enrollment: 103. Upper school average class size: 5. Upper school faculty-student ratio: 1:4.

Upper School Student Profile Grade 9: 12 students (9 boys, 3 girls); Grade 10: 25 students (18 boys, 7 girls); Grade 11: 27 students (15 boys, 12 girls); Grade 12: 31 students (18 boys, 13 girls); Postgraduate: 1 student (1 girl). 100% of students are boarding students. 18% are state residents. 20 states are represented in upper school student body. 4% are international students.

Faculty School total: 33. In upper school: 18 men, 15 women; 20 have advanced degrees; 29 reside on campus.

Subjects Offered ADL skills, algebra, American literature, art, art history, astronomy, biology, calculus, ceramics, chemistry, computer programming, computer science, creative writing, driver education, earth science, ecology, economics, English, English literature, environmental science, fine arts, geometry, health, history, industrial arts, marine biology, mathematics, music, photography, physical education, physics, psychology, science, social science, social studies, Spanish, studio art-AP, trigonometry, video film production, woodworking, world history, world literature, writing.

Graduation Requirements Algebra, arts and fine arts (art, music, dance, drama), biology, electives, English, English literature, mathematics, physical education (includes health), science, social science, social studies (includes history).

Special Academic Programs Independent study; study at local college for college credit; academic accommodation for the gifted, the musically talented, and the artistically talented; remedial reading and/or remedial writing; remedial math; programs in English, mathematics, general development for dyslexic students; special instructional classes for deaf students, blind students.

College Placement 22 students graduated in 2005; 20 went to college, including Dickinson College; Hartwick College; Muhlenberg College; Quinnipiac University; Southern Connecticut State University; Suffolk University. Other: 1 went to work, 1 entered a postgraduate year. 15% scored over 600 on SAT verbal, 15% scored over 600 on SAT math.

Student Life Upper grades have specified standards of dress, student council, honor system. Discipline rests primarily with faculty.

Summer Programs Remediation, enrichment, advancement, sports, art/fine arts, rigorous outdoor training, computer instruction programs offered; session focuses on academic courses for enhancement and obtaining necessary credits; held both on and off campus; held at US Virgin Islands; accepts boys and girls; not open to students from other schools. 103 students usually enrolled. 2006 schedule: July 11 to August 18. Application deadline: none.

Tuition and Aid Day student tuition: $59,200; 7-day tuition and room/board: $76,800. Tuition installment plan (monthly payment plans).

Admissions Battery of testing done through outside agency, WISC or WAIS or WRAT required. Deadline for receipt of application materials: none. Application fee required: $150. On-campus interview required.

Athletics Intramural: ballet (girls); coed interscholastic: baseball, basketball, ice hockey, soccer, tennis; coed intramural: aquatics, archery, back packing, badminton, baseball, basketball, bicycling, blading, bowling, canoeing/kayaking, cross-country running, dance, equestrian sports, fishing, fitness, fitness walking, floor hockey, freestyle skiing, golf, gymnastics, hiking/backpacking, horseback riding, ice hockey, ice skating, kayaking, martial arts, modern dance, mountain biking, mountaineering, nautilus, outdoor activities, outdoor adventure, outdoor education, outdoor recreation, outdoor skills, outdoors, paddle tennis, paint ball, physical fitness, physical training, racquetball, rafting, rock climbing, roller skating, ropes courses, rugby, sailing, skiing (cross-country), skiing (downhill), snowboarding, snowshoeing, soccer, strength & conditioning, swimming and diving, table tennis, tai chi, tennis, ultimate Frisbee, walking, wall climbing, water skiing, weight lifting, weight training, windsurfing. 2 PE instructors, 3 coaches.

Computers Computers are regularly used in programming classes. Computer resources include CD-ROMs, Internet access, file transfer, office computer access.

Contact Mr. Peter J. Chorney, Executive Director. 203-245-2778. Fax: 203-245-6098. E-mail: petechorney@prodigy.net. Web site: www.groveschool.org.

ANNOUNCEMENT FROM THE SCHOOL In April 2005, the Grove School was able to purchase the Madison property it has been leasing for many years. This allows the Grove School to begin an ambitious building program, as well as to undertake major renovations. An architect has been selected who will work on a master plan for the campus that will replace some existing facilities and also add facilities and/or expand program space for the arts, sciences, and technologies. As plans proceed, students and staff will be involved in the process and learn about site planning, architecture, outdoor education, and landscaping.

See full description on page 1228.

GSTAAD INTERNATIONAL SCHOOL

3780 Gstaad
Gstaad 3780, Switzerland
Head of School: Alain Souperbiet

General Information Coeducational boarding and day college-preparatory and business school; primarily serves students with learning disabilities, individuals with Attention Deficit Disorder, dyslexic students, and students with Attention Deficit and Hyperactivity Disorders. Grades 9–12. Founded: 1963. Setting: small town. Nearest major city is Bern. Students are housed in single-sex dormitories and rooms in a Swiss chalet type accommodation. 1-acre campus. 1 building on campus. Language of instruction: English. Total enrollment: 23. Upper school average class size: 6. Upper school faculty-student ratio: 1:5.

Upper School Student Profile 100% of students are boarding students. 90% are international students. International students from Bahamas, Italy, Qatar, Saudi Arabia, United Arab Emirates, and United States; 3 other countries represented in student body.

Faculty School total: 6. In upper school: 3 men, 3 women; 5 have advanced degrees; 2 reside on campus.

Subjects Offered Algebra, American history, biology, business, calculus, chemistry, computer science, economics, English, English literature, environmental science, French, geography, geometry, German, mathematics, physics, science, social science, social studies, sociology, world history.

Graduation Requirements Algebra, American history, biology, business studies, chemistry, economics, English language and composition-AP, English literature, geometry, mathematics, physics, SAT/ACT preparation, social studies (includes history), U.S. government, writing.

Special Academic Programs Advanced Placement exam preparation in 5 subject areas; accelerated programs; remedial reading and/or remedial writing; remedial math; programs in English, mathematics, general development for dyslexic students; ESL (5 students enrolled).

College Placement 7 students graduated in 2005; all went to college, including Northwestern University; Webster University. Mean SAT verbal: 550, mean SAT math: 640.

Student Life Upper grades have specified standards of dress, honor system. Discipline rests equally with students and faculty.

Summer Programs Remediation, enrichment, ESL, sports, computer instruction programs offered; session focuses on remedial classes, summer sports and culture; held on campus; accepts boys and girls; open to students from other schools. 24 students usually enrolled. 2006 schedule: July 2 to July 26. Application deadline: June 1.

Tuition and Aid Day student tuition: 38,000 Swiss francs; 7-day tuition and room/board: 45,000 Swiss francs–65,800 Swiss francs. Tuition installment plan (individually arranged payment plans, 3-payment plan). Tuition reduction for siblings available.

Admissions For fall 2005, 35 students applied for upper-level admission, 12 were accepted, 10 enrolled. Deadline for receipt of application materials: none. No application fee required. Interview recommended.

Athletics Interscholastic: basketball (boys), hiking/backpacking (b), skiing (downhill) (b), soccer (b), table tennis (b); coed interscholastic: archery, basketball, bicycling, football, gymnastics, ice hockey, ice skating, outdoors, skiing (cross-country), snowboarding; coed intramural: aerobics, archery, basketball, bicycling, football, gymnastics, horseback riding, ice hockey, ice skating, jogging, mountain biking, outdoors, physical fitness, rafting, rappelling, rock climbing, skiing (cross-country), skiing (downhill), snowboarding, soccer, squash, swimming and diving, table tennis, tennis. 1 PE instructor, 2 coaches.

Computers Computers are regularly used in English, mathematics classes. Computer resources include campus e-mail, on-campus library services, CD-ROMs, Internet access.

Contact Alain Souperbiet, Headmaster/Director/Director of Admissions. 41-33-744-2373. Fax: 41-33-744-3578. E-mail: gis@gstaad.ch. Web site: www.gstaadschool.ch.

ANNOUNCEMENT FROM THE SCHOOL A small, coed, international secondary school located in the Swiss Alps, GIS offers intensive preparation for universities in the U.S., UK, and Switzerland. At GIS, the teacher-student ratio ranges from 1:4 to 1:5. Tutorial classes are available. The curriculum includes English language, literature, U.S. and world history, international relations, U.S. government, the sciences, mathematics, business studies, law, and philosophy. Courses are developed to increase test results on the TOEFL, SAT, AP, IGSCE, and A levels. There is a special education section for students with learning differences. A comprehensive sport activities program is an integral part of school life. It includes tennis, squash, swimming, hiking, rock climbing, basketball, soccer, skiing, snowboarding, and ice skating. Admission at GIS is available to students in grades 9–12. For further information about GIS, please contact: Gstaad International School, 3780 Gstaad, Switzerland; telephone: +41 33 7442373; fax: +41 33 7443578; e-mail: gis@gstaad.ch. Web site: www.gstaadschool.ch

HAMILTON LEARNING CENTRE

1603 Main Street, West
Hamilton, Ontario L8S 1E6, Canada
Head of School: Mrs. Leia Ger-Rogers

General Information Coeducational day college-preparatory, general academic, arts, business, and vocational school; primarily serves underachievers, students with learning disabilities, individuals with Attention Deficit Disorder, and dyslexic students. Grades 3–PG. Founded: 1989. Setting: urban. Nearest major city is Toronto, Canada. 1-acre campus. 1 building on campus. Approved or accredited by Canadian Association of Independent Schools and Ontario Department of Education. Language of instruction: English. Total enrollment: 55. Upper school average class size: 8. Upper school faculty-student ratio: 1:5.

Upper School Student Profile Grade 9: 6 students (3 boys, 3 girls); Grade 10: 4 students (2 boys, 2 girls); Grade 11: 6 students (3 boys, 3 girls); Grade 12: 6 students (3 boys, 3 girls); Postgraduate: 3 students (3 boys).

Faculty School total: 20. In upper school: 2 men, 7 women; 3 have advanced degrees.

Subjects Offered 20th century world history, advanced chemistry, advanced math, advanced TOEFL/grammar, algebra, analysis and differential calculus, analytic geometry, ancient history, art, art history, basic skills, business communications, business mathematics, calculus, Canadian geography, Canadian history, Canadian literature, career and personal planning, chemistry, civics, communication skills, computer skills, consumer mathematics, English, English composition, English literature, ESL, European history, European literature, family studies, finite math, French as a second language, general business, general math, geography, geometry, grammar, honors algebra, honors English, honors geometry, honors world history, Judaic studies, keyboarding, language arts, linear algebra, literacy, literature, math applications, math methods, math review, mathematics, media studies, modern history, physical education, reading/study skills, remedial/makeup course work, science, Shakespeare, speech communications, Western philosophy, writing fundamentals.

Graduation Requirements Ontario Secondary School Diploma requirements.

Special Academic Programs Honors section; accelerated programs; independent study; academic accommodation for the gifted; remedial reading and/or remedial writing; remedial math; programs in English, mathematics, general development for dyslexic students; ESL (8 students enrolled).

College Placement 6 students graduated in 2005; 5 went to college, including MacMurray College; McMaster University; Ryerson University; The University of Western Ontario; University of Toronto; University of Waterloo. Other: 1 had other specific plans.

Student Life Upper grades have uniform requirement, honor system. Discipline rests primarily with faculty.

Summer Programs Remediation, enrichment, advancement, ESL, art/fine arts, computer instruction programs offered; session focuses on remediation; held on campus; accepts boys and girls; open to students from other schools. 15 students usually enrolled. 2006 schedule: July 5 to September 3. Application deadline: July 1.

Tuition and Aid Day student tuition: CAN$24,000. Tuition installment plan (monthly payment plans, individually arranged payment plans). Tuition reduction for siblings available. In 2005–06, 10% of upper-school students received aid. Total amount of financial aid awarded in 2005–06: CAN$15,000.

Admissions Traditional secondary-level entrance grade is 9. Academic Profile Tests, CTBS, Stanford Achievement Test, any other standardized test, grade equivalent tests, math and English placement tests, WRAT or writing sample required. Deadline for receipt of application materials: none. No application fee required. On-campus interview required.

Athletics Coed Interscholastic: baseball, basketball, floor hockey; coed intramural: aquatics, badminton, ball hockey, baseball, basketball, bicycling, climbing, cooperative games, cross-country running, dance, fitness, flag football, floor hockey, gymnastics, martial arts, outdoor activities, outdoor education, outdoor recreation, outdoor skills, roller blading, ropes courses, running, skiing (cross-country), skiing (downhill), snowshoeing, soccer, softball, swimming and diving, wall climbing. 1 PE instructor.

Computers Computers are regularly used in all classes. Computer network features include CD-ROMs, Internet access, office computer access.

Contact Ms. Lisa Palmer, Admissions Administrator. 905-521-1333. Fax: 905-521-1106. E-mail: info@hamiltonlearningcentre.com. Web site: www.hamiltonlearningcentre.com.

HIDDEN LAKE ACADEMY

830 Hidden Lake Road
Dahlonega, Georgia 30533
Head of School: Dr. Charles Cates

General Information Coeducational boarding college-preparatory, arts, and life skills school; primarily serves students with learning disabilities, individuals with Attention Deficit Disorder, individuals with emotional and behavioral problems, dyslexic students, and students with Oppositional Defiant Disorder. Grades 8–PG. Founded: 1994. Setting: rural. Nearest major city is Atlanta. Students are housed in single-sex dormitories. 210-acre campus. 17 buildings on campus. Approved or accredited by Georgia Accrediting Commission, Georgia Association of Private Schools for Exceptional Children, Georgia Independent School Association, Southern

Association of Colleges and Schools, and Georgia Department of Education. Member of National Association of Independent Schools and Secondary School Admission Test Board. Total enrollment: 141. Upper school average class size: 9. Upper school faculty-student ratio: 1:9.

Upper School Student Profile Grade 8: 3 students (2 boys, 1 girl); Grade 9: 12 students (7 boys, 5 girls); Grade 10: 38 students (24 boys, 14 girls); Grade 11: 47 students (30 boys, 17 girls); Grade 12: 40 students (26 boys, 14 girls). 100% of students are boarding students. 11% are state residents. 31 states are represented in upper school student body. 4% are international students. International students from Bermuda, Costa Rica, Italy, Mexico, United Arab Emirates, and Venezuela.

Faculty School total: 24. In upper school: 12 men, 12 women; 11 have advanced degrees; 18 reside on campus.

Subjects Offered Algebra, American history, art, biology, calculus, chemistry, earth science, economics, English, environmental science, fine arts, geography, geometry, government/civics, history, mathematics, performing arts, photojournalism, physical education, physical science, physics, science, social science, social studies, Spanish, trigonometry, world history.

Graduation Requirements Arts and fine arts (art, music, dance, drama), English, foreign language, mathematics, physical education (includes health), science, social science, family dynamics, interpersonal relationships, social dynamics.

Special Academic Programs Honors section; independent study; study at local college for college credit; academic accommodation for the gifted and the artistically talented; remedial reading and/or remedial writing; remedial math; programs in English, mathematics, general development for dyslexic students.

College Placement 30 students graduated in 2005; 19 went to college, including Brevard College; Lynn University; State University of New York College at Brockport; Warren Wilson College; Wingate University. Other: 5 entered a post-graduate year, 1 had other specific plans. Median SAT verbal: 450, median SAT math: 430, median combined SAT: 440. 8% scored over 600 on SAT verbal, 7% scored over 600 on SAT math, 7.5% scored over 1800 on combined SAT.

Student Life Upper grades have uniform requirement, student council, honor system. Discipline rests primarily with faculty. Attendance at religious services is required.

Tuition and Aid 7-day tuition and room/board: $68,400. Guaranteed tuition plan. Tuition installment plan (monthly payment plans, individually arranged payment plans, extended payment plans). Tuition reduction for siblings, need-based scholarship grants available. In 2005–06, 25% of upper-school students received aid.

Admissions Achievement tests, psychoeducational evaluation or WISC III or other aptitude measures; standardized achievement test required. Deadline for receipt of application materials: none. No application fee required.

Athletics Interscholastic: baseball (boys), basketball (b,g), cheering (g), cross-country running (b,g), golf (b), soccer (b), softball (g), tennis (b,g), track and field (b,g), volleyball (g), wrestling (b); intramural: wrestling (b); coed intramural: aerobics, aerobics/dance, aerobics/nautilus, back packing, basketball, billiards, bowling, canoeing/kayaking, climbing, cross-country running, fishing, fitness walking, flag football, Frisbee, golf, hiking/backpacking, horseshoes, jogging, kickball, outdoor activities, outdoor adventure, outdoor education, outdoor recreation, outdoor skills, physical fitness, rappelling, rock climbing, ropes courses, running, soccer, softball, strength & conditioning, table tennis, tennis, volleyball, wall climbing, weight lifting, wilderness, wilderness survival. 10 coaches.

Computers Computer network features include campus e-mail, on-campus library services, CD-ROMs, Internet access.

Contact Ms. Nicole R. Fuglsang, Director of Public Relations. 800-394-0640. Fax: 706-864-9109. E-mail: nicolef@hiddenlakeacademy.com. Web site: www.hiddenlakeacademy.com.

THE HILL CENTER, DURHAM ACADEMY

3200 Pickett Road
Durham, North Carolina 27705
Head of School: Dr. Sharon Maskel

General Information Coeducational day college-preparatory school; primarily serves underachievers, students with learning disabilities, individuals with Attention Deficit Disorder, and dyslexic students. Grades K–12. Founded: 1977. Setting: small town. 5-acre campus. 1 building on campus. Approved or accredited by North Carolina Association of Independent Schools, Southern Association of Colleges and Schools, Southern Association of Independent Schools, and North Carolina Department of Education. Member of National Association of Independent Schools. Endowment: $3.5 million. Total enrollment: 177. Upper school average class size: 4. Upper school faculty-student ratio: 1:4.

Upper School Student Profile Grade 9: 17 students (14 boys, 3 girls); Grade 10: 21 students (15 boys, 6 girls); Grade 11: 18 students (11 boys, 7 girls); Grade 12: 22 students (13 boys, 9 girls).

Faculty School total: 30. In upper school: 1 man, 10 women; 8 have advanced degrees.

Subjects Offered Algebra, American literature, calculus, English, English literature, expository writing, general math, geometry, grammar, mathematics, mechanics of writing, pre-algebra, pre-calculus, Spanish, writing.

Graduation Requirements Graduation requirements are determined by the student's home-based school.

Special Academic Programs Remedial reading and/or remedial writing; remedial math; programs in English, mathematics, general development for dyslexic students.

College Placement 20 students graduated in 2005; 17 went to college, including Clark University; Livingstone College; Meredith College; North Carolina State University; The Boston Conservatory; Western Carolina University. Other: 3 went to work. Median SAT verbal: 520, median SAT math: 490. 3% scored over 600 on SAT math.

Student Life Upper grades have student council. Discipline rests primarily with faculty.

Tuition and Aid Day student tuition: $13,850. Guaranteed tuition plan. Tuition installment plan (The Tuition Plan, Key Tuition Payment Plan, monthly payment plans, The Tuition Refund Plan). Need-based scholarship grants available. In 2005–06, 7% of upper-school students received aid. Total amount of financial aid awarded in 2005–06: $56,000.

Admissions Traditional secondary-level entrance grade is 9. For fall 2005, 32 students applied for upper-level admission, 29 were accepted, 27 enrolled. WISC-III and Woodcock-Johnson required. Deadline for receipt of application materials: March 15. Application fee required: $50. On-campus interview required.

Computers Computers are regularly used in English, foreign language, mathematics classes. Computer network features include campus e-mail, CD-ROMs, Internet access.

Contact Ms. Wendy Speir, Director of Admissions. 919-489-7464 Ext. 725. Fax: 919-489-7466. E-mail: wspeir@hillcenter.org. Web site: www.hillcenter.org.

HILLCREST SCHOOL

3510 North A Street
Building C
Midland, Texas 79705
Head of School: Mrs. Betty Noble Starnes

General Information Coeducational day college-preparatory, general academic, and technology school; primarily serves students with learning disabilities, individuals with Attention Deficit Disorder, and dyslexic students. Grades 1–12. Founded: 1993. Setting: urban. 1 building on campus. Approved or accredited by Southern Association of Colleges and Schools, Texas Education Agency, and Texas Department of Education. Total enrollment: 48. Upper school average class size: 10. Upper school faculty-student ratio: 1:10.

Upper School Student Profile Grade 9: 10 students (6 boys, 4 girls); Grade 10: 7 students (4 boys, 3 girls); Grade 11: 3 students (1 boy, 2 girls); Grade 12: 4 students (4 boys).

Faculty School total: 9. In upper school: 6 women; 1 has an advanced degree.

Graduation Requirements Computers, electives, English, history, mathematics, physical education (includes health), science.

Special Academic Programs Independent study; remedial reading and/or remedial writing; remedial math; programs in English, mathematics, general development for dyslexic students.

College Placement 4 students graduated in 2005; 3 went to college. Other: 1 went to work.

Student Life Upper grades have uniform requirement. Discipline rests primarily with faculty.

Tuition and Aid Day student tuition: $6700. Need-based scholarship grants available. In 2005–06, 25% of upper-school students received aid.

Admissions Deadline for receipt of application materials: none. Application fee required: $100. Interview required.

Athletics Coed Intramural: badminton, baseball, basketball, fitness, flag football, football, jump rope, kickball, outdoor activities, outdoor education, physical fitness, soccer, track and field, volleyball. 1 PE instructor.

Computers Computers are regularly used in all classes. Computer network features include CD-ROMs, Internet access.

Contact Mrs. Sharel Sims, Program Coordinator. 915-570-7444. Fax: 915-570-7361. Web site: www.hillcrestschool.org.

THE HILL TOP PREPARATORY SCHOOL

737 South Ithan Avenue
Rosemont, Pennsylvania 19010
Head of School: Leslie H. McLean, EdD

General Information Coeducational day college-preparatory, arts, and technology school; primarily serves students with learning disabilities, individuals with Attention Deficit Disorder, and dyslexic students. Grades 6–12. Founded: 1971. Setting: suburban. Nearest major city is Philadelphia. 25-acre campus. 4 buildings on campus. Approved or accredited by Middle States Association of Colleges and Schools and Pennsylvania Department of Education. Member of National Association of Independent Schools. Endowment: $145,000. Total enrollment: 71. Upper school average class size: 6. Upper school faculty-student ratio: 1:4.

Upper School Student Profile Grade 9: 7 students (7 boys); Grade 10: 21 students (19 boys, 2 girls); Grade 11: 11 students (9 boys, 2 girls); Grade 12: 7 students (5 boys, 2 girls).

Faculty School total: 36. In upper school: 13 men, 23 women; 22 have advanced degrees.

Subjects Offered Algebra, American history, American literature, art, biology, ceramics, chemistry, civics, college counseling, computer keyboarding, computer math, computer science, computers, creative writing, drama, earth science, economics, electives, English, English literature, environmental science, European history, geography, geometry, government/civics, grammar, health, history, journalism, mathematics, media studies, music appreciation, Native American studies, photography, physical education, physics, psychology, public speaking, science, senior project, social studies, study skills, theater, trigonometry, U.S. history, woodworking, world cultures, world history, writing.

Graduation Requirements Business skills (includes word processing), computer science, English, mathematics, physical education (includes health), science, senior project, social science, social studies (includes history), study skills.

Special Academic Programs Independent study; study at local college for college credit; academic accommodation for the gifted and the artistically talented; remedial reading and/or remedial writing; remedial math; programs in English, mathematics, general development for dyslexic students.

College Placement 20 students graduated in 2005; all went to college.

Student Life Upper grades have specified standards of dress, student council, honor system. Discipline rests primarily with faculty.

Summer Programs Remediation, enrichment programs offered; session focuses on remediation, enrichment, and recreation; held on campus; accepts boys and girls; open to students from other schools. 30 students usually enrolled. 2006 schedule: June 26 to July 21. Application deadline: none.

Tuition and Aid Day student tuition: $29,800. Need-based scholarship grants available. In 2005–06, 12% of upper-school students received aid. Total amount of financial aid awarded in 2005–06: $75,700.

Admissions Traditional secondary-level entrance grade is 9. For fall 2005, 13 students applied for upper-level admission, 10 were accepted, 9 enrolled. Achievement tests, psychoeducational evaluation, Rorschach or Thematic Apperception Test, WISC or WAIS and WISC/Woodcock-Johnson required. Deadline for receipt of application materials: none. Application fee required: $35. On-campus interview required.

Athletics Interscholastic: baseball (boys), basketball (b,g), cross-country running (b,g), soccer (b,g), softball (g), tennis (b,g), volleyball (b,g), wrestling (b,g); intramural: skiing (downhill) (b,g), soccer (b,g), softball (b,g), tennis (b,g), volleyball (b,g), weight lifting (b,g); coed interscholastic: baseball, basketball, cross-country running, golf, soccer, softball, tennis, track and field, volleyball, wrestling; coed intramural: aerobics/nautilus, badminton, ball hockey, basketball, climbing, combined training, cooperative games, Cosom hockey, fitness, flag football, floor hockey, Frisbee, indoor hockey, indoor soccer, Newcombe ball, outdoor adventure, paint ball, physical fitness, physical training, pillo polo, rock climbing, skiing (downhill), snowboarding, soccer, softball, strength & conditioning, team handball, tennis, touch football, ultimate Frisbee, volleyball, weight lifting. 2 PE instructors, 4 coaches.

Computers Computers are regularly used in English, mathematics, science, study skills classes. Computer network features include campus e-mail, on-campus library services, CD-ROMs, Internet access, file transfer, office computer access.

Contact Mrs. Cindy Falcone, Assistant Headmaster. 610-527-3230 Ext. 697. Fax: 610-527-7683. E-mail: cfalcone@hilltopprep.org. Web site: www.hilltopprep.org.

THE JOHN DEWEY ACADEMY

389 Main Street
Great Barrington, Massachusetts 01230
Head of School: Dr. Thomas E. Bratter

petersons.com

General Information Coeducational boarding college-preparatory and arts school; primarily serves underachievers, students with learning disabilities, individuals with Attention Deficit Disorder, individuals with emotional and behavioral problems, and gifted, underachieving, self-destructive adolescents. Grades 10–PG. Founded: 1985. Setting: small town. Nearest major city is Hartford, CT. Students are housed in single-sex by floor dormitories. 90-acre campus. 3 buildings on campus. Approved or accredited by New England Association of Schools and Colleges and Massachusetts Department of Education. Member of Secondary School Admission Test Board. Total enrollment: 30. Upper school average class size: 6. Upper school faculty-student ratio: 1:3.

Upper School Student Profile Grade 10: 4 students (3 boys, 1 girl); Grade 11: 20 students (10 boys, 10 girls); Grade 12: 6 students (4 boys, 2 girls). 100% of students are boarding students. 5% are state residents. 11 states are represented in upper school student body. 10% are international students. International students from Canada.

Faculty School total: 10. In upper school: 5 men, 5 women; 9 have advanced degrees; 1 resides on campus.

Subjects Offered Adolescent issues, algebra, American literature, art, art history, biology, calculus, chemistry, creative writing, drama, English, English literature, environmental science, ethics, European history, fine arts, French, geometry, government/civics, grammar, health, history, Italian, moral reasoning, philosophy, physical education, physics, psychology, sociology, Spanish, statistics, theater, trigonometry, world history, world literature, writing.

Graduation Requirements American history, arts and fine arts (art, music, dance, drama), biology, English, English literature, European history, foreign language,

leadership skills, literature, mathematics, moral reasoning, physical education (includes health), science, social studies (includes history), moral leadership qualities.

Special Academic Programs Honors section; accelerated programs; independent study; study at local college for college credit; academic accommodation for the gifted and the artistically talented; remedial reading and/or remedial writing; remedial math; programs in general development for dyslexic students.

College Placement 7 students graduated in 2005; all went to college, including Barnard College; Columbia University; Haverford College; Skidmore College; Syracuse University; University of Chicago.

Student Life Upper grades have specified standards of dress, student council, honor system. Discipline rests equally with students and faculty.

Summer Programs Session focuses on continuing college preparatory program; held on campus; accepts boys and girls; not open to students from other schools. 30 students usually enrolled.

Tuition and Aid 7-day tuition and room/board: $75,000. Tuition installment plan (monthly payment plans, individually arranged payment plans). Need-based scholarship grants available. In 2005–06, 25% of upper-school students received aid.

Admissions Traditional secondary-level entrance grade is 10. Deadline for receipt of application materials: none. No application fee required. On-campus interview required.

Computers Computer resources include Internet access.

Contact Dr. Thomas E. Bratter, President. 413-528-9800. Fax: 413-528-5662. Web site: www.jda.org.

See full description on page 1230.

THE JUDGE ROTENBERG EDUCATIONAL CENTER

240 Turnpike Street
Canton, Massachusetts 02021-2341
Head of School: Matthew L. Israel, PhD

General Information Coeducational boarding general academic school; primarily serves underachievers, students with learning disabilities, individuals with Attention Deficit Disorder, individuals with emotional and behavioral problems, dyslexic students, and autism and developmental disabilities. Founded: 1971. Setting: suburban. Nearest major city is Boston. 2 buildings on campus. Approved or accredited by Massachusetts Department of Education. Total enrollment: 130.

Student Life Upper grades have specified standards of dress. Discipline rests primarily with faculty.

Admissions Deadline for receipt of application materials: none. No application fee required. Interview recommended.

Computers Computer resources include CD-ROMs, Internet access, DVD.

Contact Julie Gomes, Director of Admissions. 781-828-2202 Ext. 4275. Fax: 781-828-2804. E-mail: j.gomes@judgerc.org. Web site: www.judgerc.org.

THE JUNE SHELTON SCHOOL AND EVALUATION CENTER

15720 Hillcrest Road
Dallas, Texas 75248
Head of School: Joyce S. Pickering

General Information Coeducational day college-preparatory and general academic school; primarily serves students with learning disabilities, individuals with Attention Deficit Disorder, and dyslexic students. Grades PS–12. Founded: 1976. Setting: suburban. 1 building on campus. Approved or accredited by Independent Schools Association of the Southwest, Southern Association of Colleges and Schools, and Southern Association of Independent Schools. Endowment: $3.7 million. Total enrollment: 833. Upper school average class size: 8. Upper school faculty-student ratio: 1:8.

Upper School Student Profile Grade 9: 69 students (47 boys, 22 girls); Grade 10: 55 students (37 boys, 18 girls); Grade 11: 61 students (32 boys, 29 girls); Grade 12: 46 students (30 boys, 16 girls).

Faculty School total: 168. In upper school: 9 men, 32 women; 20 have advanced degrees.

Graduation Requirements Arts and fine arts (art, music, dance, drama), computers, English, ethics, foreign language, mathematics, physical education (includes health), reading, science, social studies (includes history), speech.

Special Academic Programs Programs in English, mathematics, general development for dyslexic students.

College Placement 37 students graduated in 2005; 35 went to college, including Oklahoma State University; Southern Methodist University; Texas Christian University; Texas Tech University; University of Arkansas; University of North Texas. Other: 2 had other specific plans. Mean composite ACT: 22.

Student Life Upper grades have uniform requirement, student council, honor system. Discipline rests primarily with faculty.

Summer Programs Enrichment programs offered; session focuses on enrichment; held on campus; accepts boys and girls; open to students from other schools. 39 students usually enrolled. 2006 schedule: July 3 to July 27. Application deadline: May 15.

Tuition and Aid Tuition installment plan (Insured Tuition Payment Plan, Key Tuition Payment Plan). Need-based scholarship grants available. In 2005–06, 14% of upper-school students received aid. Total amount of financial aid awarded in 2005–06: $69,500.

Admissions Traditional secondary-level entrance grade is 9. WISC/Woodcock-Johnson required. Deadline for receipt of application materials: none. No application fee required. Interview required.

Athletics Interscholastic: baseball (boys), basketball (b,g), cheering (g), cross-country running (b,g), football (b), golf (b,g), softball (g), tennis (b,g), track and field (b,g), volleyball (g). 5 PE instructors, 6 coaches.

Computers Computers are regularly used in English, foreign language, information technology, lab/keyboard, library, research skills, SAT preparation, video film production classes. Computer network features include campus e-mail, on-campus library services, CD-ROMs, Internet access, file transfer, office computer access, DVD, wireless campus network.

Contact Diann Slaton, Director of Admission. 972-774-1772. Fax: 972-991-3977. E-mail: dslaton@shelton.org. Web site: www.shelton.org.

THE KARAFIN SCHOOL

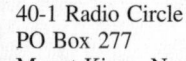

40-1 Radio Circle
PO Box 277
Mount Kisco, New York 10549
Head of School: Dr. John E. Greenfieldt

General Information Coeducational day college-preparatory and general academic school, affiliated with Mennonite Church USA; primarily serves underachievers, students with learning disabilities, individuals with Attention Deficit Disorder, individuals with emotional and behavioral problems, emotionally disabled students, and students with Tourette's Syndrome. Grades 8–12. Founded: 1958. Setting: suburban. Nearest major city is New York. 1 building on campus. Approved or accredited by New York Department of Education. Total enrollment: 82. Upper school average class size: 6. Upper school faculty-student ratio: 1:6.

Upper School Student Profile Grade 9: 19 students (19 girls); Grade 10: 18 students (18 girls); Grade 11: 18 students (18 girls); Grade 12: 15 students (15 girls).

Faculty School total: 25. In upper school: 8 men, 16 women; 23 have advanced degrees.

Subjects Offered Algebra, American history, American literature, art, art history, arts, biology, business, business skills, calculus, chemistry, computer math, computer programming, computer science, creative writing, earth science, ecology, economics, English, English literature, environmental science, European history, expository writing, fine arts, French, geography, geology, geometry, government/civics, grammar, history of ideas, history of science, Italian, Latin, mathematics, music, photography, physical education, physics, psychology, science, social science, social studies, sociology, Spanish, speech, trigonometry, typing, world history, world literature, writing, zoology.

Graduation Requirements Arts and fine arts (art, music, dance, drama), business skills (includes word processing), computer science, English, foreign language, mathematics, physical education (includes health), science, social science, social studies (includes history).

Special Academic Programs Independent study; academic accommodation for the gifted, the musically talented, and the artistically talented; remedial reading and/or remedial writing; remedial math; programs in English, mathematics, general development for dyslexic students; special instructional classes for deaf students.

College Placement 14 students graduated in 2005; 10 went to college, including City College of the City University of New York; John Jay College of Criminal Justice of the City University of New York; Pace University; University at Albany, State University of New York; Western Connecticut State University. Other: 4 went to work. Mean SAT verbal: 500, mean SAT math: 550.

Student Life Upper grades have specified standards of dress, student council. Discipline rests primarily with faculty.

Tuition and Aid Day student tuition: $22,117. Tuition installment plan (monthly payment plans).

Admissions Traditional secondary-level entrance grade is 9. For fall 2005, 500 students applied for upper-level admission, 100 were accepted, 35 enrolled. Deadline for receipt of application materials: none. No application fee required. On-campus interview required.

Athletics Coed Intramural: aerobics, aerobics/dance, archery, badminton, ball hockey, baseball, basketball, billiards, bowling, cooperative games, fitness, fitness walking, floor hockey, football, Frisbee, golf, gymnastics, jump rope, kickball, paddle tennis, physical fitness, physical training, pillo polo, power lifting, project adventure, racquetball, soccer, strength & conditioning, table tennis, team handball, tennis, touch football, volleyball, weight lifting, whiffle ball, wrestling. 1 PE instructor.

Computers Computers are regularly used in all academic classes. Computer resources include campus e-mail, CD-ROMs, Internet access, DVD.

Contact Dr. Bart A. Donow, Director. 914-666-9211. Fax: 914-666-9868. E-mail: karafin@optonline.net. Web site: bestweb.net/~karafin.

KEY SCHOOL, INC.

3947 East Loop 820 South
Fort Worth, Texas 76119
Head of School: Mary Ann Key

General Information Coeducational day college-preparatory, general academic, and technology school; primarily serves underachievers, students with learning disabilities, individuals with Attention Deficit Disorder, and dyslexic students. Grades K–12. Founded: 1966. Setting: suburban. Nearest major city is Dallas. 2-acre campus. 1 building on campus. Approved or accredited by Southern Association of Colleges and Schools and Texas Department of Education. Total enrollment: 95. Upper school average class size: 8. Upper school faculty-student ratio: 1:5.

Upper School Student Profile Grade 9: 11 students (8 boys, 3 girls); Grade 10: 10 students (10 boys); Grade 11: 11 students (8 boys, 3 girls); Grade 12: 4 students (3 boys, 1 girl).

Faculty School total: 33. In upper school: 7 men, 26 women; 12 have advanced degrees.

Subjects Offered Aviation, biology, chemistry, composition, computer applications, current events, desktop publishing, earth science, economics, electives, English, French, geometry, German, grammar, keyboarding/computer, life science, life skills, literature, mathematics, mechanics of writing, novels, physical science, physics, pre-algebra, reading, reading/study skills, SAT/ACT preparation, science, science fiction, Shakespeare, social studies, Spanish, speech communications, study skills, Texas history, U.S. history, world geography, world history, yearbook.

Graduation Requirements Graduation speech.

Special Academic Programs Study at local college for college credit; remedial reading and/or remedial writing; remedial math; programs in English, mathematics, general development for dyslexic students; ESL (1 student enrolled).

College Placement 6 students graduated in 2005; 5 went to college, including Tarrant County College District. Other: 1 went to work. Median SAT verbal: 413, median SAT math: 383.

Student Life Upper grades have specified standards of dress, honor system. Discipline rests primarily with faculty.

Summer Programs Remediation, enrichment, advancement, computer instruction programs offered; session focuses on academic enrichment; held on campus; accepts boys and girls; open to students from other schools. 150 students usually enrolled. 2006 schedule: June 1 to June 30. Application deadline: none.

Tuition and Aid Tuition installment plan (monthly payment plans, quarterly and semester payment plans).

Admissions Traditional secondary-level entrance grade is 9. For fall 2005, 17 students applied for upper-level admission, 10 were accepted, 10 enrolled. Deadline for receipt of application materials: none. No application fee required. On-campus interview required.

Computers Computers are regularly used in desktop publishing, journalism, keyboarding, newspaper, writing, yearbook classes. Computer network features include Internet access.

Contact Patricia Banks, Registrar. 817-446-3738. Fax: 817-496-3299. E-mail: administration@thekeyschool.com. Web site: www.thekeyschool.com/.

KILDONAN SCHOOL

425 Morse Hill Road
Amenia, New York 12501
Head of School: Ronald A. Wilson

General Information Coeducational boarding and day college-preparatory, general academic, arts, and technology school; primarily serves dyslexic students. Boarding grades 7–PG, day grades 2–PG. Founded: 1969. Setting: rural. Nearest major city is New York. Students are housed in single-sex dormitories. 450-acre campus. 19 buildings on campus. Approved or accredited by New York State Association of Independent Schools, The Association of Boarding Schools, and New York Department of Education. Member of National Association of Independent Schools and Secondary School Admission Test Board. Endowment: $569,200. Total enrollment: 134. Upper school average class size: 6. Upper school faculty-student ratio: 1:6.

Upper School Student Profile Grade 10: 21 students (12 boys, 9 girls); Grade 11: 20 students (14 boys, 6 girls); Grade 12: 16 students (13 boys, 3 girls); Postgraduate: 1 student (1 boy). 64% of students are boarding students. 39% are state residents. 6 states are represented in upper school student body. International students from Canada, Pakistan, Sweden, and United Kingdom; 4 other countries represented in student body.

Faculty School total: 58. In upper school: 18 men, 28 women; 12 have advanced degrees; 48 reside on campus.

Subjects Offered Algebra, American history, American literature, anthropology, art, art history, biology, botany, business skills, calculus, ceramics, chemistry, computer programming, computer science, creative writing, earth science, ecology, economics, English, English literature, environmental science, European history, expository writing, fine arts, geography, geology, geometry, government/civics, grammar, health, history, mathematics, photography, physical education, physics, science, social studies, trigonometry, typing, world history, world literature, zoology.

Graduation Requirements Arts and fine arts (art, music, dance, drama), computer science, English, mathematics, physical education (includes health), science, social studies (includes history).

Special Academic Programs Independent study; remedial reading and/or remedial writing; programs in English, mathematics, general development for dyslexic students.

College Placement 11 students graduated in 2005; 9 went to college, including Xavier University. Other: 1 went to work, 1 entered military service.

Student Life Upper grades have specified standards of dress, student council, honor system. Discipline rests primarily with faculty.

Summer Programs Remediation, art/fine arts, computer instruction programs offered; session focuses on intensive academic work for underachievers; held on campus; accepts boys and girls; open to students from other schools. 85 students usually enrolled. 2006 schedule: June 23 to August 4.

Tuition and Aid Day student tuition: $30,250; 5-day tuition and room/board: $41,250; 7-day tuition and room/board: $43,250. Tuition installment plan (Key Tuition Payment Plan). Need-based scholarship grants available. In 2005–06, 34% of upper-school students received aid. Total amount of financial aid awarded in 2005–06: $119,750.

Admissions Traditional secondary-level entrance grade is 9. SSAT required. Deadline for receipt of application materials: none. Application fee required: $50. On-campus interview required.

Athletics Coed Interscholastic: archery, basketball, bicycling, canoeing/kayaking, cross-country running, equestrian sports, golf, horseback riding, lacrosse, outdoor activities, paddle tennis, skiing (cross-country), skiing (downhill), swimming and diving, table tennis, weight lifting; coed intramural: basketball, bicycling, cross-country running, equestrian sports, golf, lacrosse, paddle tennis, skiing (cross-country), skiing (downhill).

Computers Computers are regularly used in English, mathematics classes. Computer resources include CD-ROMs.

Contact Bonnie A. Wilson, Director of Admissions. 845-373-8111. Fax: 845-373-2004.

ANNOUNCEMENT FROM THE SCHOOL Kildonan was founded in 1969 in response to an urgent need for a school for intelligent students with learning difficulties arising from dyslexia. The academic program is unique in that it revolves around intensive and daily one-on-one Orton-Gillingham tutoring for each student. Courses in mathematics, history, literature, and science are designed to meet the learning style of dyslexic students. Enhanced confidence is achieved via participation in such activities as the arts, athletics, and community life.

See full description on page 1232.

KINGSHILL SCHOOL

RR 1, Box 6125
Kingshill
St. Croix, Virgin Islands 00850
Head of School: Mrs. Janie M. Koopmans

General Information Coeducational day college-preparatory, general academic, arts, and vocational school; primarily serves underachievers, students with learning disabilities, individuals with Attention Deficit Disorder, dyslexic students, and cerebral palsy. Grades 7–12. Founded: 1997. Setting: rural. Nearest major city is Christiansted, U.S. Virgin Islands. 6-acre campus. 2 buildings on campus. Approved or accredited by Virgin Islands Department of Education. Candidate for accreditation by Middle States Association of Colleges and Schools. Total enrollment: 29. Upper school average class size: 6. Upper school faculty-student ratio: 1:4.

Upper School Student Profile Grade 9: 5 students (3 boys, 2 girls); Grade 10: 7 students (5 boys, 2 girls); Grade 11: 4 students (4 boys); Grade 12: 5 students (3 boys, 2 girls).

Faculty School total: 8. In upper school: 2 men, 6 women; 3 have advanced degrees.

Subjects Offered Algebra, American government, American history, American literature, ancient world history, applied arts, architecture, art appreciation, arts appreciation, athletics, auto mechanics, biology, bowling, career exploration, career planning, career/college preparation, Caribbean history, chemistry, civics, college admission preparation, college counseling, community service, composition, computer skills, computer technologies, consumer mathematics, current events, earth science, electives, English, English literature, entrepreneurship, environmental science, geography, geometry, health, health education, history of the Americas, keyboarding, language-AP, learning lab, learning strategies, marine biology, math applications, music appreciation, physical education, pre-algebra, remedial/makeup course work, SAT preparation, scuba diving, Spanish, world geography, world history.

Graduation Requirements Algebra, American government, American history, art history, biology, Caribbean history, chemistry, physical science, world history.

Special Academic Programs Accelerated programs; independent study; study at local college for college credit; remedial reading and/or remedial writing; remedial math; programs in English, mathematics, general development for dyslexic students.

College Placement 4 students graduated in 2005; 3 went to college. Other: 1 went to work. Median SAT verbal: 420, median SAT math: 420.

Student Life Upper grades have honor system. Discipline rests equally with students and faculty.

Tuition and Aid Day student tuition: $7700. Tuition installment plan (monthly payment plans, individually arranged payment plans). Tuition reduction for siblings, merit scholarship grants, need-based scholarship grants, paying campus jobs available. In 2005–06, 74% of upper-school students received aid; total upper-school merit-scholarship money awarded: $5200. Total amount of financial aid awarded in 2005–06: $50,000.

Admissions Traditional secondary-level entrance grade is 9. For fall 2005, 15 students applied for upper-level admission, 6 were accepted, 4 enrolled. WISC or WAIS, Woodcock-Johnson Educational Evaluation, WISC III or WRAT required. Deadline for receipt of application materials: none. No application fee required. Interview required.

Athletics Coed Intramural: basketball, bowling, canoeing/kayaking, cooperative games, fitness walking, flag football, Frisbee, hiking/backpacking, independent competitive sports, kayaking, outdoor activities, physical fitness, scuba diving, Special Olympics, surfing, swimming and diving, table tennis, volleyball, walking. 1 PE instructor.

Computers Computers are regularly used in all academic classes. Computer resources include CD-ROMs, Internet access, office computer access, DVD, wireless campus network.

Contact Mrs. Janie M. Koopmans, Director. 340-778-6564. Fax: 340-778-0520. E-mail: kingshillschool@vipowernet.net.

LA CHEIM SCHOOL

1500 D Street
Room 601
Antioch, California 94509
Head of School: Ms. Sue Herrera

General Information Coeducational day vocational school; primarily serves underachievers, students with learning disabilities, individuals with Attention Deficit Disorder, and individuals with emotional and behavioral problems. Grades 1–12. Founded: 1984. Setting: suburban. 2 buildings on campus. Approved or accredited by Western Association of Schools and Colleges and California Department of Education. Total enrollment: 42. Upper school faculty-student ratio: 1:4.

Faculty School total: 5. In upper school: 3 men, 2 women.

Subjects Offered Adolescent issues, American government, American history, art, basic skills, biology, economics, grammar, health, language arts, life science, life skills, mathematics, physical education, physical science, science, social studies, vocational skills, world history, writing skills.

Special Academic Programs Remedial reading and/or remedial writing; remedial math.

College Placement 4 students graduated in 2005; 1 went to college. Other: 3 went to work.

Student Life Upper grades have specified standards of dress. Discipline rests primarily with faculty.

Summer Programs Remediation, enrichment, advancement, sports, art/fine arts programs offered; session focuses on review of basic skills, advancement, remediation, and elective courses; held on campus; accepts boys and girls; not open to students from other schools. 50 students usually enrolled. 2006 schedule: June to August.

Tuition and Aid Tuition installment plan (Expenses covered by referring district and county agencies with no cost to parents).

Admissions Deadline for receipt of application materials: none. No application fee required. On-campus interview required.

Athletics Intramural: basketball (boys, girls), flag football (b,g), kickball (b,g), softball (b,g), volleyball (b,g), walking (b,g), weight lifting (b,g). 1 PE instructor.

Computers Computers are regularly used in all academic classes. Computer resources include CD-ROMs, Internet access, computer access in classrooms.

Contact Ms. Laurie Soucy, Registrar. 925-777-9550. Fax: 925-777-1090. E-mail: laurie@lacheim.org. Web site: www.lacheim.org/schools/index.htm.

LANDMARK EAST SCHOOL

708 Main Street
Wolfville, Nova Scotia B4P 1G4, Canada
Head of School: Timothy F. Moore

General Information Coeducational boarding and day college-preparatory school; primarily serves students with learning disabilities, individuals with Attention Deficit Disorder, and dyslexic students. Grades 6–12. Founded: 1979. Setting: small town. Nearest major city is Halifax, Canada. Students are housed in single-sex dormitories. 5-acre campus. 9 buildings on campus. Approved or accredited by Canadian Association of Independent Schools and Nova Scotia Department of Education. Language of instruction: English. Total enrollment: 60. Upper school average class size: 8. Upper school faculty-student ratio: 1:2.

Upper School Student Profile Grade 10: 13 students (9 boys, 4 girls); Grade 11: 11 students (8 boys, 3 girls); Grade 12: 11 students (9 boys, 2 girls). 80% of students are boarding students. 30% are province residents. 11 provinces are represented in upper school student body. International students from Bahamas, Bermuda, Bolivia, Canada, and Republic of Korea; 5 other countries represented in student body.

Faculty School total: 39. In upper school: 10 men, 14 women; 2 have advanced degrees; 9 reside on campus.

Subjects Offered Art, biology, career and personal planning, chemistry, computer science, drama, economics, English, entrepreneurship, geography, geology, history, integrated science, law, mathematics, physics, strategies for success.

Graduation Requirements English, mathematics, physical education (includes health), science.

Special Academic Programs Remedial reading and/or remedial writing; remedial math; programs in English, mathematics, general development for dyslexic students.

College Placement 10 students graduated in 2005; all went to college, including Bishop's University; Carleton University; University of New Brunswick Fredericton; Wilfrid Laurier University.

Student Life Upper grades have uniform requirement, student council, honor system. Discipline rests primarily with faculty.

Tuition and Aid Day student tuition: CAN$25,000; 5-day tuition and room/board: CAN$33,000; 7-day tuition and room/board: CAN$37,000. Need-based scholarship grants available. In 2005–06, 25% of upper-school students received aid. Total amount of financial aid awarded in 2005–06: CAN$200,000.

Admissions Traditional secondary-level entrance grade is 10. Achievement tests and psychoeducational evaluation required. Deadline for receipt of application materials: none. Application fee required: CAN$50. On-campus interview required.

Athletics Coed Interscholastic: aerobics, alpine skiing, aquatics, archery, badminton, basketball, bicycling, cross-country running, curling, dance, equestrian sports, fitness, gymnastics, ice skating, lacrosse, running, skiing (cross-country), skiing (downhill), snowboarding, soccer, softball, squash, swimming and diving, tennis, track and field, volleyball, weight training; coed intramural: aquatics, ball hockey, basketball, billiards, bowling, cooperative games, fitness, ice skating, indoor soccer, running, strength & conditioning, table tennis, weight training. 8 PE instructors.

Computers Computers are regularly used in art, English, mathematics, science classes. Computer resources include campus e-mail, on-campus library services, CD-ROMs, Internet access.

Contact Janet Cooper, Administrative Assistant. 902-542-2237. Fax: 902-542-4147. E-mail: jcooper@landmarkeast.org. Web site: www.landmarkeast.org.

LANDMARK SCHOOL

PO Box 227
429 Hale Street
Prides Crossing, Massachusetts 01965-0227
Head of School: Robert J. Broudo

General Information Coeducational boarding and day college-preparatory and general academic school; primarily serves students with learning disabilities and dyslexic students. Boarding grades 8–12, day grades 1–12. Founded: 1971. Setting: suburban. Nearest major city is Boston. Students are housed in single-sex dormitories. 25-acre campus. 15 buildings on campus. Approved or accredited by Association of Independent Schools in New England, Massachusetts Office of Child Care Services, National Association of Private Schools for Exceptional Children, New England Association of Schools and Colleges, The Association of Boarding Schools, and Massachusetts Department of Education. Member of National Association of Independent Schools. Endowment: $11.9 million. Total enrollment: 447. Upper school average class size: 7. Upper school faculty-student ratio: 1:3.

Upper School Student Profile Grade 8: 36 students (23 boys, 13 girls); Grade 9: 60 students (40 boys, 20 girls); Grade 10: 64 students (47 boys, 17 girls); Grade 11: 85 students (54 boys, 31 girls); Grade 12: 91 students (54 boys, 37 girls). 52% of students are boarding students. 74% are state residents. 25 states are represented in upper school student body. 3% are international students. International students from France, Greece, Mexico, Saudi Arabia, and Thailand.

Faculty School total: 150. In upper school: 69 men, 81 women; 53 have advanced degrees; 33 reside on campus.

Subjects Offered Algebra, American government, American literature, American sign language, anthropology, art, auto mechanics, basketball, biology, boat building, British literature, calculus, calculus-AP, chemistry, chorus, communications, computer science, consumer mathematics, culinary arts, cultural geography, drama, early childhood, environmental science, expressive arts, geometry, grammar, independent study, instrumental music, integrated math, language arts, literature, marine science, modern world history, multimedia design, oral expression, peer counseling, photography, physical education, physical science, physics, physiology-anatomy, portfolio art, pragmatics, pre-algebra, pre-calculus, psychology, radio broadcasting, reading, senior thesis, study skills, technical theater, television, U.S. history, weight training, woodworking, world history.

Graduation Requirements English, mathematics, physical education (includes health), science, social studies (includes history), Landmark School Competency Tests, minimum grade equivalents on standardized tests in reading and reading comprehension.

Special Academic Programs Study at local college for college credit; programs in English, mathematics, general development for dyslexic students.

College Placement 63 students graduated in 2005; 62 went to college, including Curry College; Johnson & Wales University; Lynn University; New England College; Suffolk University; University of Denver. Other: 1 went to work. Mean SAT verbal: 447, mean SAT math: 425.

Student Life Upper grades have specified standards of dress, student council. Discipline rests primarily with faculty.

Summer Programs Remediation programs offered; session focuses on academic remediation and study skills; held on campus; accepts boys and girls; open to students from other schools. 160 students usually enrolled. 2006 schedule: June 29 to August 4. Application deadline: none.

Tuition and Aid Day student tuition: $29,700–$36,700; 7-day tuition and room/board: $40,700–$47,700. Tuition installment plan (Academic Management Services Plan). Need-based scholarship grants, paying campus jobs, community and staff grants available. In 2005–06, 3% of upper-school students received aid. Total amount of financial aid awarded in 2005–06: $125,000.

Admissions For fall 2005, 213 students applied for upper-level admission, 84 were accepted, 40 enrolled. Achievement tests, psychoeducational evaluation and WISC or WAIS required. Deadline for receipt of application materials: none. Application fee required: $125. On-campus interview required.

Athletics Interscholastic: baseball (boys), basketball (b,g), dance (g), lacrosse (b,g), soccer (b,g), wrestling (b); coed interscholastic: alpine skiing, cross-country running, golf, skiing (downhill), tennis, track and field. 2 trainers.

Computers Computers are regularly used in all academic classes. Computer network features include campus e-mail, on-campus library services, CD-ROMs, Internet access, DVD.

Contact Heather Gaillard, Database Manager/Administrative Assistant. 978-236-3000 Ext. 3420. Fax: 978-927-7268. E-mail: hgaillard@landmarkschool.org. Web site: www.landmarkschool.org.

ANNOUNCEMENT FROM THE SCHOOL Professional outreach and training are an integral part of Landmark School. The Landmark School Outreach Program offers professional development (teacher training, graduate courses, and in-district programs), publications, and parent workshops. For more information, please call or visit the School's Web site (telephone: 978-236-3216; http://www.landmarkschool.org).

See full description on page 1234.

LAWRENCE SCHOOL

1551 East Wallings Road
Broadview Heights, Ohio 44147
Head of School: Mimi Mayer

General Information Coeducational day college-preparatory school; primarily serves students with learning disabilities, individuals with Attention Deficit Disorder, and dyslexic students. Grades 1–12. Founded: 1969. Setting: suburban. Nearest major city is Cleveland. 5-acre campus. 2 buildings on campus. Approved or accredited by Independent Schools Association of the Central States, North Central Association of Colleges and Schools, Ohio Association of Independent Schools, and Ohio Department of Education. Endowment: $1 million. Total enrollment: 220. Upper school average class size: 11. Upper school faculty-student ratio: 1:11.

Faculty School total: 32. In upper school: 7 men, 15 women; 7 have advanced degrees.

Subjects Offered Algebra, American history, art, biology, choir, college counseling, computer applications, consumer economics, earth science, geometry, graphic design, health, integrated math, journalism, keyboarding, language arts, life science, life skills, mathematics, music, painting, physical education, physical science, physics, pre-algebra, research skills, society, politics and law, sociology, Spanish, speech, The 20th Century, world geography, world history, yearbook.

Graduation Requirements Independent study project for seniors.

Special Academic Programs Honors section; independent study; remedial reading and/or remedial writing; remedial math; programs in English, mathematics, general development for dyslexic students.

Student Life Upper grades have specified standards of dress, student council. Discipline rests primarily with faculty.

Tuition and Aid Day student tuition: $13,750. Tuition installment plan (Key Tuition Payment Plan, monthly payment plans, individually arranged payment plans). Need-based scholarship grants available. In 2005–06, 25% of upper-school students received aid.

Admissions Traditional secondary-level entrance grade is 9. For fall 2005, 34 students applied for upper-level admission, 31 were accepted, 25 enrolled. Deadline for receipt of application materials: none. Application fee required: $50. Interview required.

Athletics Interscholastic: baseball (boys), basketball (b,g); intramural: wrestling (b); coed interscholastic: golf, soccer, track and field; coed intramural: badminton, bowling, cooperative games, flag football, floor hockey, physical fitness, running,

skiing (downhill), snowboarding, team handball, tennis, ultimate Frisbee, volleyball, walking, whiffle ball, yoga. 1 PE instructor.

Computers Computer network features include on-campus library services, CD-ROMs, Internet access, office computer access, DVD, wireless campus network.

Contact Mr. Jeffrey J. Petrulis, Dean of Admission. 440-526-0717 Ext. 2212. Fax: 440-526-0595. E-mail: jpetrulis@lawrence.pvt.k12.oh.us.

THE LEELANAU SCHOOL

One Old Homestead Road
Glen Arbor, Michigan 49636
Head of School: Mr. Richard F. Odell

General Information Coeducational boarding and day college-preparatory, general academic, and arts school; primarily serves underachievers, students with learning disabilities, individuals with Attention Deficit Disorder, dyslexic students, students with Attention Deficit Hyperactivity Disorder, language-based learning differences, and Non-verbal Learning Disabilities. Grades 9–12. Founded: 1929. Setting: rural. Nearest major city is Traverse City. Students are housed in single-sex dormitories. 50-acre campus. 12 buildings on campus. Approved or accredited by Independent Schools Association of the Central States, Michigan Association of Non-Public Schools, Midwest Association of Boarding Schools, National Independent Private Schools Association, North Central Association of Colleges and Schools, The Association of Boarding Schools, The College Board, and Michigan Department of Education. Member of National Association of Independent Schools and Secondary School Admission Test Board. Endowment: $435,200. Total enrollment: 56. Upper school average class size: 8. Upper school faculty-student ratio: 1:10.

Upper School Student Profile Grade 9: 6 students (4 boys, 2 girls); Grade 10: 8 students (8 boys); Grade 11: 27 students (14 boys, 13 girls); Grade 12: 15 students (10 boys, 5 girls). 93% of students are boarding students. 52% are state residents. 9 states are represented in upper school student body. 18% are international students. International students from Angola, Germany, Japan, and Republic of Korea.

Faculty School total: 20. In upper school: 10 men, 7 women; 7 have advanced degrees; 6 reside on campus.

Subjects Offered 20th century history, acting, Advanced Placement courses, advanced TOEFL/grammar, algebra, American Civil War, American government, American history, American literature, anatomy and physiology, ancient history, ancient world history, animation, applied arts, applied music, art, art appreciation, art education, arts, arts and crafts, arts appreciation, astronomy, athletics, audio visual/media, backpacking, basic language skills, biochemistry, biology, biotechnology, boat building, botany, British literature, business studies, calculus, calculus-AP, calligraphy, career and personal planning, career exploration, career/college preparation, cartooning, cartooning/animation, ceramics, character education, chemistry, civil war history, classical civilization, classical Greek literature, clayworking, college admission preparation, college awareness, college counseling, college placement, college planning, college writing, comedy, computer animation, computer science, conflict resolution, conservation, constitutional history of U.S., CPR, critical thinking, critical writing, decision making, decision making skills, developmental language skills, digital art, digital imaging, digital music, digital photography, drama, drama performance, dramatic arts, drawing, drawing and design, driver education, earth science, ecology, electives, English, English as a foreign language, English composition, English literature, entrepreneurship, environmental education, environmental science, environmental studies, environmental systems, epic literature, equestrian sports, equine management, equine science, equine studies, ESL, European history, experiential education, experimental science, expository writing, family living, fiction, field ecology, film and new technologies, filmmaking, fine arts, first aid, foreign language, French, French studies, general math, general science, geography, geology, geometry, golf, government/civics, grammar, great books, guitar, history, honors English, human anatomy, human biology, human relations, illustration, improvisation, independent living, independent study, instruments, integrated arts, integrated science, interpersonal skills, jazz band, jazz ensemble, jewelry making, journalism, Korean culture, language, language and composition, language arts, languages, leadership, leadership education training, leadership skills, leadership training, learning cognition, learning lab, learning strategies, life issues, life management skills, life science, life skills, literacy, literature, literature by women, marine biology, marine ecology, marine science, marine studies, mathematics, mentorship program, modern European history, modern history, modern world history, moral and social development, moral reasoning, multicultural literature, music, music appreciation, nature study, nature writers, oil painting, organizational studies, outdoor education, painting, participation in sports, photography, physics, poetry, pottery, pre-calculus, printmaking, psychology, reading/study skills, relationships, religious studies, remedial study skills, remedial/makeup course work, SAT preparation, SAT/ACT preparation, science, science and technology, science project, science research, senior thesis, Shakespeare, silk screening, social studies, Spanish, speech, sports, statistics-AP, student government, studio art, study skills, theater, TOEFL preparation, travel, trigonometry, U.S. government, U.S. government and politics, visual arts, weight training, weightlifting, wellness, wilderness camping, wilderness education, wilderness/outdoor program, world history, writing, yearbook.

Graduation Requirements Arts and fine arts (art, music, dance, drama), CPR, English, foreign language, mathematics, science, senior thesis, social studies (includes history), Senior Leadership Orientation.

Special Academic Programs Advanced Placement exam preparation in 3 subject areas; honors section; independent study; remedial reading and/or remedial writing; remedial math; programs in English, mathematics, general development for dyslexic students; ESL (8 students enrolled).

College Placement 18 students graduated in 2005; all went to college, including DePaul University; Emory University; Kalamazoo College; Michigan State University; University of Michigan; University of Oregon.

Student Life Upper grades have specified standards of dress, student council, honor system. Discipline rests primarily with faculty.

Summer Programs Remediation, enrichment, advancement, ESL programs offered; session focuses on remediation and advancement for students with learning differences; held on campus; accepts boys and girls; open to students from other schools. 20 students usually enrolled. 2006 schedule: July 8 to August 5. Application deadline: none.

Tuition and Aid Day student tuition: $15,200; 5-day tuition and room/board: $33,986; 7-day tuition and room/board: $41,500. Tuition installment plan (monthly payment plans, individually arranged payment plans). Tuition reduction for siblings, need-based scholarship grants, Beals Scholarship for legacy families available. In 2005–06, 30% of upper-school students received aid. Total amount of financial aid awarded in 2005–06: $254,922.

Admissions Traditional secondary-level entrance grade is 10. For fall 2005, 44 students applied for upper-level admission, 44 were accepted, 26 enrolled. Individual IQ, Achievement and behavior rating scale, psychoeducational evaluation, Stanford Test of Academic Skills, TOEFL or SLEP, Wechsler Intelligence Scale for Children, Wechsler Intelligence Scale for Children III, Woodcock-Johnson or writing sample required. Deadline for receipt of application materials: none. Application fee required: $50. On-campus interview required.

Athletics Interscholastic: basketball (boys), volleyball (g); coed interscholastic: dressage, equestrian sports, golf, soccer, tennis; coed intramural: alpine skiing, back packing, bicycling, canoeing/kayaking, climbing, cross-country running, fishing, fitness, flag football, fly fishing, freestyle skiing, hiking/backpacking, horseback riding, independent competitive sports, kayaking, mountain biking, outdoor activities, outdoor adventure, outdoor education, outdoor recreation, outdoor skills, outdoors, paddling, paint ball, physical fitness, rock climbing, ropes courses, running, skiing (cross-country), skiing (downhill), snowboarding, snowshoeing, table tennis, triathlon, wall climbing, yoga.

Computers Computers are regularly used in all academic classes. Computer network features include campus e-mail, on-campus library services, CD-ROMs, Internet access, DVD, wireless campus network.

Contact Mrs. Heather M. Sack, Director of Admission. 231-334-5800. Fax: 231-334-5898. E-mail: admissions@leelanau.org. Web site: www.leelanau.org.

LITTLE KESWICK SCHOOL

PO Box 24
Keswick, Virginia 22947
Head of School: Marc J. Columbus

General Information Boys' boarding arts school; primarily serves underachievers, students with learning disabilities, individuals with Attention Deficit Disorder, individuals with emotional and behavioral problems, and dyslexic students. Founded: 1963. Setting: small town. Nearest major city is Washington, DC. Students are housed in single-sex dormitories. 30-acre campus. 8 buildings on campus. Approved or accredited by Virginia Association of Independent Specialized Education Facilities and Virginia Department of Education. Total enrollment: 31. Upper school average class size: 7. Upper school faculty-student ratio: 1:4.

Upper School Student Profile 100% of students are boarding students. 30% are state residents. 17 states are represented in upper school student body.

Faculty School total: 6. In upper school: 2 men, 4 women; 2 have advanced degrees.

Subjects Offered Algebra, American history, biology, computer applications, earth science, English, geography, government/civics, health, industrial arts, mathematics, physical education, practical arts, social studies, world history.

Student Life Upper grades have specified standards of dress. Discipline rests primarily with faculty.

Summer Programs Remediation, enrichment, sports, art/fine arts, rigorous outdoor training, computer instruction programs offered; session focuses on remediation and therapy; held on campus; accepts boys; open to students from other schools. 30 students usually enrolled. 2006 schedule: July 9 to August 11. Application deadline: none.

Tuition and Aid 7-day tuition and room/board: $57,372. Need-based scholarship grants available.

Admissions WISC-III and Woodcock-Johnson required. Deadline for receipt of application materials: none. No application fee required. On-campus interview required.

Athletics Interscholastic: basketball (boys), combined training (b), soccer (b); intramural: basketball (b), cross-country running (b), equestrian sports (b), fishing (b), fitness (b), gymnastics (b), hiking/backpacking (b), horseback riding (b), lacrosse (b), outdoor activities (b), soccer (b), softball (b), swimming and diving (b), volleyball (b). 1 PE instructor, 2 coaches.

Computers Computer resources include CD-ROMs, Internet access, office computer access.

Contact Terry Columbus, Director. 434-295-0457 Ext. 14. Fax: 434-977-1892. E-mail: tcolumbuslks@littlekeswickschool.net. Web site: www.littlekeswickschool.net.

ANNOUNCEMENT FROM THE SCHOOL Little Keswick School is a therapeutic boarding school with a strong special education program serving 31 boys with significant learning, emotional, or behavioral difficulties. A warm, nurturing approach in a highly structured environment enables students to return home or to a less restrictive boarding school, generally within 2 years. The School is currently celebrating 42 years of service to children and offers a 5-week summer session that is open to non-year-round students.

MAPLEBROOK SCHOOL

5142 Route 22
Amenia, New York 12501
Head of School: Donna M. Konkolics

General Information Coeducational boarding and day general academic, vocational, and technology school; primarily serves underachievers, students with learning disabilities, individuals with Attention Deficit Disorder, and students with low average cognitive ability (70-90 I.Q.). Ungraded, ages 11–18. Founded: 1945. Setting: small town. Nearest major city is Poughkeepsie. Students are housed in single-sex dormitories. 90-acre campus. 17 buildings on campus. Approved or accredited by Middle States Association of Colleges and Schools, New York State Association of Independent Schools, and New York Department of Education. Member of National Association of Independent Schools. Endowment: $1 million. Total enrollment: 78. Upper school average class size: 6. Upper school faculty-student ratio: 1:8.

Upper School Student Profile 98% of students are boarding students. 15% are state residents. 23 states are represented in upper school student body. 5% are international students. International students from Barbados, Bermuda, India, Israel, Philippines, and Venezuela; 3 other countries represented in student body.

Faculty School total: 48. In upper school: 10 men, 20 women; 26 have advanced degrees; 27 reside on campus.

Subjects Offered Algebra, American history, art, biology, business skills, computer science, consumer economics, consumer mathematics, creative writing, drama, driver education, earth science, English, environmental science, geography, global studies, government/civics, health, home economics, industrial arts, integrated mathematics, keyboarding, mathematics, music, occupational education, performing arts, photography, physical education, physical science, science, social skills, speech, theater, typing, U.S. Presidents, world history, writing.

Graduation Requirements Career and personal planning, computer science, English, mathematics, physical education (includes health), science, social science, social skills, social studies (includes history), attendance at Maplebrook School for a minimum of 2 years.

Special Academic Programs Study at local college for college credit; remedial reading and/or remedial writing; remedial math; programs in English, mathematics, general development for dyslexic students.

College Placement 28 students graduated in 2005; 2 went to college, including Dutchess Community College; Mitchell College. Other: 6 went to work, 18 entered a postgraduate year.

Student Life Upper grades have specified standards of dress, student council, honor system. Discipline rests equally with students and faculty.

Summer Programs Remediation, enrichment, sports, art/fine arts, computer instruction programs offered; session focuses on Regents Competency Test preparation; held both on and off campus; held at various locations for New York City day and overnight trips; accepts boys and girls; open to students from other schools. 55 students usually enrolled. 2006 schedule: July 2 to August 12. Application deadline: none.

Tuition and Aid Day student tuition: $25,900; 5-day tuition and room/board: $39,400; 7-day tuition and room/board: $43,900. Tuition installment plan (Key Tuition Payment Plan, individually arranged payment plans, Tuition Management Systems Plan). Merit scholarship grants, need-based scholarship grants, need-based loans, paying campus jobs, minority and cultural diversity scholarships, day-student scholarships available. In 2005–06, 15% of upper-school students received aid. Total amount of financial aid awarded in 2005–06: $120,000.

Admissions Traditional secondary-level entrance age is 15. For fall 2005, 154 students applied for upper-level admission, 87 were accepted, 30 enrolled. Achievement tests, Bender Gestalt, Test of Achievement and Proficiency or WISC or WAIS required. Deadline for receipt of application materials: none. No application fee required. Interview required.

Athletics Interscholastic: basketball (boys, girls), cheering (g); field hockey (g); coed interscholastic: aquatics, cooperative games, cross-country running, equestrian sports, fitness, freestyle skiing, horseback riding, running, skiing (cross-country), skiing (downhill), soccer, softball, swimming and diving, tennis, track and field, weight lifting, weight training; coed intramural: alpine skiing, basketball, bicycling, bowling,

dance, figure skating, fitness, fitness walking, flag football, floor hockey, freestyle skiing, golf, hiking/backpacking, horseback riding, ice skating, indoor hockey, martial arts, outdoor education, outdoor recreation, roller blading, skiing (cross-country), skiing (downhill), soccer, softball, Special Olympics, swimming and diving, table tennis, tennis, volleyball, weight lifting, weight training, wrestling. 1 PE instructor, 18 coaches.

Computers Computers are regularly used in all academic, health classes. Computer network features include campus e-mail, on-campus library services, CD-ROMs, Internet access, office computer access, DVD, wireless campus network.

Contact Jennifer L. Scully, Dean of Admissions. 845-373-8191. Fax: 845-373-7029. E-mail: jscully@maplebrookschool.org. Web site: www.maplebrookschool.org.

ANNOUNCEMENT FROM THE SCHOOL Maplebrook's Center for the Advancement of Postsecondary Studies (CAPS) Program provides opportunities to develop independent living skills in single-gender dormitories and apartments. The vocational program offers certificate programs in a number of trades. CAPS is a laptop computer program that enables students to organize everything on their computers. The college program offers academic, social, and emotional support to students who need to develop more maturity and self-discipline prior to managing mainstream college environments.

MONTANA ACADEMY

9705 Lost Prairie Road
Marion, Montana 59925
Head of School: Dr. John Alson McKinnon

General Information Coeducational boarding school; primarily serves underachievers, students with learning disabilities, individuals with Attention Deficit Disorder, and individuals with emotional and behavioral problems. Ungraded, ages 14–18. Founded: 1997. Setting: rural. Nearest major city is Kalispell. Students are housed in single-sex dormitories. 300-acre campus. 7 buildings on campus. Approved or accredited by Northwest Association of Schools and Colleges. Total enrollment: 60. Upper school average class size: 12. Upper school faculty-student ratio: 1:2.

Upper School Student Profile 100% of students are boarding students. 1% are state residents. 15 states are represented in upper school student body. 5% are international students.

Faculty School total: 8. In upper school: 4 men, 3 women; 7 have advanced degrees; 6 reside on campus.

Subjects Offered Algebra, American government, American history, American literature, art, biology, botany, British literature, construction, creative writing, culinary arts, current events, English, field ecology, geometry, health science, literature, mathematics, music, outdoor education, physical science, political science, pre-calculus, reading, reading/study skills, remedial study skills, research skills, SAT preparation, social studies, speech communications, substance abuse, U.S. government and politics, work experience, world history, world literature, world wide web design, writing, writing fundamentals, zoology.

Graduation Requirements Completion of emotional growth program.

Special Academic Programs Advanced Placement exam preparation in 4 subject areas; honors section; independent study; academic accommodation for the gifted; remedial reading and/or remedial writing.

College Placement 21 students graduated in 2005; 14 went to college, including Lewis & Clark College; Macalester College; The Colorado College; University of Oregon; University of Portland. Other: 7 had other specific plans. Median SAT verbal: 540, median SAT math: 470.

Student Life Upper grades have specified standards of dress, student council, honor system. Discipline rests primarily with faculty.

Tuition and Aid 7-day tuition and room/board: $68,000. Guaranteed tuition plan. Tuition installment plan (monthly payment plans). Financial aid available to upper-school students. In 2005–06, 8% of upper-school students received aid. Total amount of financial aid awarded in 2005–06: $40,000.

Admissions Traditional secondary-level entrance age is 14. Psychoeducational evaluation, Rorschach or Thematic Apperception Test and WISC-R or WISC-III required. Deadline for receipt of application materials: none. No application fee required.

Athletics Interscholastic: soccer (boys); coed interscholastic: cross-country running; coed intramural: aerobics, alpine skiing, back packing, baseball, basketball, bicycling, climbing, dance, dressage, equestrian sports, fitness, fitness walking, flag football, fly fishing, hiking/backpacking, horseback riding, ice hockey, ice skating, mountain biking, nordic skiing, outdoor adventure, outdoor education, outdoor recreation, outdoor skills, physical fitness, rock climbing, ropes courses, skiing (cross-country), skiing (downhill), snowboarding, snowshoeing, softball, swimming and diving, volleyball, walking, weight training, wilderness survival, winter walking, yoga.

Computers Computers are regularly used in research skills classes. Computer resources include Internet access, office computer access.

Contact Mrs. Rosemary Eileen McKinnon, Director of Admissions. 406-755-3149. Fax: 406-755-3150. E-mail: rosemarym@montanaacademy.com. Web site: www.montanaacademy.com.

ANNOUNCEMENT FROM THE SCHOOL Montana Academy provides clinically sophisticated therapy and psychiatric care as well as competent academics for bright students who are experiencing emotional problems. Treatment takes place in the simple environment of a remote ranch, where experienced clinicians, trained teachers, and seasoned outdoorsmen integrate lessons learned in therapy into the tasks of everyday life.

MONTCALM SCHOOL

13725 Starr Commonwealth Road
Albion, Michigan 49224
Head of School: Mr. Norman Ostrum

General Information Coeducational boarding college-preparatory, general academic, and arts school, affiliated with Christian faith; primarily serves students with learning disabilities, individuals with Attention Deficit Disorder, individuals with emotional and behavioral problems, dyslexic students, and students with Asperger's Syndrome and Attachment Disorder. Grades 6–12. Founded: 2001. Setting: rural. Nearest major city is Detroit. Students are housed in single-sex dormitories. 350-acre campus. 1 building on campus. Approved or accredited by Michigan Department of Education. Total enrollment: 44. Upper school average class size: 14.

Upper School Student Profile 100% of students are boarding students. 50% are state residents. 20 states are represented in upper school student body. 80% of students are Christian faith.

Graduation Requirements Requirements determined on individual basis.

Student Life Upper grades have specified standards of dress, student council. Discipline rests primarily with faculty.

Summer Programs Remediation, enrichment, advancement, sports, art/fine arts, rigorous outdoor training programs offered; session focuses on outdoor adventure/education/trek experience; held on campus; accepts boys and girls; open to students from other schools. 16 students usually enrolled. Application deadline: May.

Tuition and Aid Guaranteed tuition plan. Tuition installment plan (monthly payment plans, individually arranged payment plans). Middle-income loans, affiliation with lending institutions, i.e., Key Lend and prepGATE available.

Admissions Comprehensive Test of Basic Skills required. Deadline for receipt of application materials: none. No application fee required. Interview recommended.

Athletics Intramural: aerobics (boys, girls), aerobics/dance (b,g), aerobics/nautilus (b,g), aquatics (b,g), back packing (b,g), ball hockey (b,g), basketball (b,g), bicycling (b,g), bowling (b,g), canoeing/kayaking (b,g), climbing (b,g), cooperative games (b,g), cross-country running (b,g), equestrian sports (b,g), field hockey (b,g), fishing (b,g), fitness (b,g), fitness walking (b,g), flag football (b), floor hockey (b), fly fishing (b), Frisbee (b), golf (b), handball (b), hiking/backpacking (b), jogging (b), life saving (b), outdoor activities (b,g), outdoor adventure (b,g), outdoor education (b,g), outdoor recreation (b,g), outdoor skills (b,g), outdoors (b,g), physical fitness (b,g), physical training (b,g), power lifting (b), racquetball (b), rappelling (b), rock climbing (b), ropes courses (b,g), running (b,g), skiing (cross-country) (b,g), soccer (b,g), softball (b,g), Special Olympics (b,g), strength & conditioning (b,g), swimming and diving (b,g), table tennis (b,g), track and field (b,g), volleyball (b,g), walking (b,g), wall climbing (b,g), wallyball (b,g), water polo (b,g), weight lifting (b,g), weight training (b,g), wilderness (b,g), wilderness survival (b,g). 4 PE instructors.

Contact Mr. Norman Ostrum, Director of Admissions. 517-629-5591 Ext. 211. Fax: 517-629-4650. E-mail: ostrumn@starr.org. Web site: www.montcalmschool.org.

MOUNT BACHELOR ACADEMY

33051 NE Ochoco Highway
Prineville, Oregon 97754
Head of School: Sharon Bitz

General Information Coeducational boarding college-preparatory and arts school; primarily serves students with learning disabilities, individuals with Attention Deficit Disorder, and individuals with emotional and behavioral problems. Grades 9–12. Founded: 1988. Setting: rural. Nearest major city is Bend. Students are housed in single-sex dormitories. 32-acre campus. Approved or accredited by Northwest Association of Schools and Colleges, Pacific Northwest Association of Independent Schools, and Oregon Department of Education. Total enrollment: 101. Upper school average class size: 8. Upper school faculty-student ratio: 1:4.

Upper School Student Profile 100% of students are boarding students. 3% are state residents. 19 states are represented in upper school student body. 2% are international students. International students from Canada and Taiwan.

Faculty School total: 16. In upper school: 9 men, 7 women; 8 have advanced degrees; 1 resides on campus.

Subjects Offered Addiction, advanced chemistry, algebra, American government, American literature, art, biology, British literature, calculus, career and personal planning, chemistry, choreography, civics, civil war history, communication skills, community service, consumer mathematics, current events, dance, developmental math, drama, earth science, English, English composition, English literature, environmental science, experiential education, foreign language, fractal geometry, geography, geometry, history, independent study, literature, mathematics, personal

growth, physical education, physical fitness, physical science, physics, poetry, political science, pre-algebra, pre-calculus, reading/study skills, remedial/makeup course work, research and reference, SAT preparation, Shakespeare, social skills, social studies, Spanish, U.S. history, values and decisions.

Graduation Requirements Completion of emotional growth program.

Special Academic Programs Accelerated programs; independent study; study at local college for college credit; study abroad; academic accommodation for the gifted; remedial reading and/or remedial writing; remedial math; programs in general development for dyslexic students.

College Placement 25 students graduated in 2005; all went to college, including Central Oregon Community College; Florida State University; Marymount College, Palos Verdes, California; University of Colorado at Boulder.

Student Life Upper grades have specified standards of dress, honor system. Discipline rests primarily with faculty.

Tuition and Aid 7-day tuition and room/board: $69,000. Tuition installment plan (Key Tuition Payment Plan, monthly payment plans). Tuition reduction for siblings, middle-income loans available.

Admissions Traditional secondary-level entrance grade is 10. For fall 2005, 1,000 students applied for upper-level admission, 122 were accepted, 122 enrolled. Psychoeducational evaluation, WISC III or other aptitude measures; standardized achievement test, WISC or WAIS, WISC-R or Woodcock-Johnson required. Deadline for receipt of application materials: none. Application fee required. On-campus interview required.

Athletics Interscholastic: basketball (boys, girls), volleyball (g), wrestling (b); intramural: aerobics (g), aerobics/dance (g), yoga (g); coed interscholastic: cross-country running, golf, soccer, winter soccer; coed intramural: alpine skiing, aquatics, back packing, basketball, bowling, canoeing/kayaking, climbing, dance, fitness, Frisbee, hiking/backpacking, outdoor activities, outdoor recreation, physical fitness, rafting, rappelling, rock climbing, ropes courses, running, sailing, skateboarding, skiing (cross-country), skiing (downhill), snowboarding, snowshoeing, soccer, swimming and diving, table tennis, ultimate Frisbee, volleyball, weight lifting, weight training, wilderness. 2 PE instructors, 3 coaches.

Computers Computer network features include Internet access, file transfer.

Contact Admissions Department. 800-462-3404. Fax: 541-462-3430. E-mail: mba@bendnet.com. Web site: www.mtba.com.

See full description on page 1236.

NAWA ACADEMY

17351 Trinity Mountain Road
French Gulch, California 96033
Head of School: David W. Hull

General Information Coeducational boarding college-preparatory, general academic, arts, vocational, and technology school; primarily serves underachievers, students with learning disabilities, individuals with Attention Deficit Disorder, dyslexic students, and students with time management, motivational and organizational problems. Grades 7–12. Founded: 1988. Setting: rural. Nearest major city is Redding. Students are housed in single-sex dormitories. 556-acre campus. 14 buildings on campus. Approved or accredited by Western Association of Schools and Colleges and California Department of Education. Languages of instruction: English and Spanish. Total enrollment: 48. Upper school average class size: 8. Upper school faculty-student ratio: 1:8.

Upper School Student Profile Grade 9: 8 students (6 boys, 2 girls); Grade 10: 12 students (6 boys, 6 girls); Grade 11: 8 students (7 boys, 1 girl); Grade 12: 13 students (11 boys, 2 girls). 100% of students are boarding students. 55% are state residents. 10 states are represented in upper school student body. 2% are international students. International students from China.

Faculty School total: 16. In upper school: 6 men, 4 women; 2 have advanced degrees.

Subjects Offered ACT preparation, algebra, alternative physical education, American literature, art, ASB Leadership, biology, calculus, chemistry, college counseling, composition, computers, earth science, economics, electives, English, ESL, experiential education, foods, forest resources, forestry, gender issues, geography, geometry, health, health education, language, language arts, leadership skills, leadership training, learning lab, life science, life skills, mathematics, metalworking, music appreciation, outdoor education, photography, physics, post-calculus, pre-algebra, pre-calculus, research, SAT preparation, SAT/ACT preparation, Spanish, training, travel, trigonometry, U.S. government, U.S. history, welding, wilderness camping, wilderness education, wilderness experience, wilderness studies, wilderness/outdoor program, world literature.

Graduation Requirements English, mathematics, physical education (includes health), science, social studies (includes history), Spanish, satisfactory completion of community service program, fulfillment of workshops in vertical rescue, swift water rescue, and leadership development.

Special Academic Programs Accelerated programs; term-away projects; study abroad; remedial reading and/or remedial writing; remedial math; programs in English, mathematics, general development for dyslexic students; ESL.

College Placement 12 students graduated in 2005; 10 went to college. Other: 2 went to work.

Student Life Upper grades have specified standards of dress, student council, honor system. Discipline rests equally with students and faculty.

Summer Programs Remediation, enrichment, advancement, art/fine arts, rigorous outdoor training programs offered; session focuses on academics through outdoor adventure, team building, abstract problem solving and thinking; held both on and off campus; held at several areas in Northern California including the Redwoods, Castle Crags and Lassen Volcanic National Park, Mt. Shasta, the Trinity Alps, and the Lost Coast; accepts boys and girls; open to students from other schools. 70 students usually enrolled. 2006 schedule: June 25 to August 19. Application deadline: none.

Tuition and Aid 7-day tuition and room/board: $32,308. Guaranteed tuition plan. Tuition installment plan (monthly payment plans, individually arranged payment plans). Tuition reduction for siblings, need-based scholarship grants, Sallie Mae Loans, Key Bank Loans available. In 2005–06, 25% of upper-school students received aid. Total amount of financial aid awarded in 2005–06: $80,000.

Admissions Traditional secondary-level entrance grade is 9. For fall 2005, 70 students applied for upper-level admission, 55 were accepted. Deadline for receipt of application materials: none. No application fee required. Interview required.

Athletics Coed Interscholastic: snowboarding; coed intramural: aerobics, alpine skiing, aquatics, archery, back packing, baseball, basketball, bicycling, billiards, canoeing/kayaking, climbing, combined training, cooperative games, cross-country running, fishing, fitness, fitness walking, flag football, fly fishing, football, freestyle skiing, Frisbee, hiking/backpacking, horseshoes, independent competitive sports, jogging, jump rope, kayaking, life saving, mountain biking, mountaineering, nordic skiing, outdoor activities, outdoor adventure, outdoor education, outdoor recreation, outdoor skills, outdoors, paddle tennis, paddling, paint ball, physical fitness, power lifting, project adventure, rafting, rappelling, rock climbing, roller blading, ropes courses, running, skateboarding, skiing (cross-country), skiing (downhill), snowboarding, snowshoeing, soccer, softball, speleology, strength & conditioning, surfing, swimming and diving, table tennis, telemark skiing, touch football, triathlon, ultimate Frisbee, volleyball, walking, wall climbing, water skiing, weight lifting, weight training, wilderness, wilderness survival, wildernessways, winter (indoor) track, winter walking. 8 PE instructors, 4 coaches, 5 trainers.

Computers Computers are regularly used in all classes. Computer network features include campus e-mail, on-campus library services, CD-ROMs, Internet access, file transfer, office computer access, DVD.

Contact Jason T. Hull, Admissions Director. 800-358-6292. Fax: 530-359-2229. E-mail: info@nawa-academy.com. Web site: www.nawa-academy.com.

NEW DOMINION SCHOOL

20700 Wagner Cutoff Road
PO Box 8
Oldtown, Maryland 21555
Head of School: Mary Porter

petersons.com

General Information Boys' boarding college-preparatory and general academic school; primarily serves underachievers, students with learning disabilities, individuals with Attention Deficit Disorder, and individuals with emotional and behavioral problems. Grades 7–12. Founded: 1981. Setting: rural. Nearest major city is Cumberland. Students are housed in single-sex villages. 340-acre campus. 5 buildings on campus. Approved or accredited by Middle States Association of Colleges and Schools and Maryland Department of Education. Total enrollment: 47. Upper school faculty-student ratio: 1:6.

Upper School Student Profile 100% of students are boarding students.

Faculty School total: 7. In upper school: 2 men, 5 women.

Subjects Offered Algebra, biology, calculus, chemistry, contemporary issues, earth science, economics, English, general math, geography, geometry, government, health, life science, life skills, physical education, physical science, physics, psychology, sociology, Spanish, trigonometry, U.S. history, world history.

Graduation Requirements English, mathematics, physical education (includes health), science, social studies (includes history).

Special Academic Programs Independent study; remedial reading and/or remedial writing; remedial math.

College Placement Median SAT verbal: 560, median SAT math: 540.

Student Life Upper grades have specified standards of dress, student council. Discipline rests equally with students and faculty.

Tuition and Aid Guaranteed tuition plan.

Admissions Deadline for receipt of application materials: none. Application fee required. Interview recommended.

Athletics Interscholastic: back packing, baseball, basketball, bicycling, bowling, canoeing/kayaking, cooperative games, field hockey, fishing, football, Frisbee, hiking/backpacking, mountain biking, outdoor activities, outdoor adventure, outdoor education, outdoor recreation, outdoor skills, outdoors, paddling, physical fitness, ropes courses, softball, ultimate Frisbee, volleyball, walking, wilderness, winter soccer, winter walking; intramural: basketball, bicycling, bowling, football.

Contact Hilary Quick, Director of Admissions. 301-478-5721 Ext. 18. Fax: 301-478-5723. E-mail: hquick@threesprings.com. Web site: www.threesprings.com.

See full description on page 1238.

NEW DOMINION SCHOOL

PO Box 540
Dillwyn, Virginia 23936
Head of School: Ben Montano

petersons.com

General Information Coeducational boarding general academic and vocational school; primarily serves underachievers, students with learning disabilities, individuals with Attention Deficit Disorder, individuals with emotional and behavioral problems, and dyslexic students. Grades 6–12. Founded: 1976. Setting: rural. Nearest major city is Richmond. Students are housed in single-sex facilities. 550-acre campus. 2 buildings on campus. Approved or accredited by Southern Association of Colleges and Schools, Virginia Association of Independent Specialized Education Facilities, and Virginia Department of Education. Total enrollment: 110. Upper school average class size: 6. Upper school faculty-student ratio: 1:6.

Upper School Student Profile 100% of students are boarding students. 70% are state residents. 10 states are represented in upper school student body.

Faculty School total: 11. In upper school: 5 men, 6 women; 1 has an advanced degree.

Subjects Offered Algebra, American government, American history, American literature, earth science, general science, geometry, home economics, industrial arts, language arts, mathematics, physical education, physical science, physics, pre-algebra, sociology, trigonometry, U.S. government, wilderness experience, work experience, world geography, world history.

Graduation Requirements Algebra, American government, American history, American literature, biology, English, geometry, mathematics, physical education (includes health), science, social studies (includes history), world history, course in either fine arts or practical arts.

Special Academic Programs Remedial reading and/or remedial writing; remedial math; programs in English, mathematics, general development for dyslexic students.

College Placement 3 students graduated in 2005; 2 went to college. Other: 1 went to work.

Student Life Upper grades have specified standards of dress. Discipline rests primarily with faculty.

Tuition and Aid 7-day tuition and room/board: $49,275. Guaranteed tuition plan.

Admissions Deadline for receipt of application materials: none. Application fee required: $300. Interview required.

Athletics Intramural: back packing (boys, girls), basketball (b,g), bicycling (b,g), bowling (b,g), canoeing/kayaking (b,g), climbing (b,g).

Computers Computer resources include Internet access.

Contact Michael Forman, Director of Admissions. 434-983-2051. Fax: 434-983-2068. E-mail: mforman@threesprings.com. Web site: threesprings.com.

See full description on page 1238.

THE NEWGRANGE SCHOOL

526 South Olden Avenue
Hamilton, New Jersey 08629
Head of School: Gordon F. Sherman, PhD

petersons.com

General Information Coeducational day college-preparatory, general academic, arts, business, and technology school; primarily serves underachievers, students with learning disabilities, individuals with Attention Deficit Disorder, dyslexic students, and students with language-based and other related learning disabilities. Ungraded, ages 7–18. Founded: 1977. Setting: urban. Nearest major city is Trenton. 2 buildings on campus. Approved or accredited by New Jersey Association of Independent Schools and New Jersey Department of Education. Total enrollment: 84. Upper school average class size: 12. Upper school faculty-student ratio: 1:3.

Faculty School total: 33. In upper school: 4 men, 29 women; 16 have advanced degrees.

Subjects Offered Algebra, American history, art, computer math, computer science, creative writing, English, fine arts, geography, geometry, health, history, keyboarding, mathematics, music, physical education, reading, science, social studies, speech, technology, writing.

Graduation Requirements Arts and fine arts (art, music, dance, drama), computer science, English, mathematics, physical education (includes health), reading, science, social studies (includes history), technology, word processing.

Special Academic Programs Academic accommodation for the gifted; remedial reading and/or remedial writing; remedial math; programs in English, mathematics, general development for dyslexic students.

College Placement 8 students graduated in 2005; 2 went to college. Other: 6 went to work.

Student Life Upper grades have specified standards of dress, student council, honor system. Discipline rests primarily with faculty.

Summer Programs Remediation, enrichment, art/fine arts programs offered; session focuses on academics; held on campus; accepts boys and girls; open to students from other schools. 50 students usually enrolled. 2006 schedule: June 26 to August 4. Application deadline: April 1.

Tuition and Aid Day student tuition: $35,500. Tuition installment plan (monthly payment plans, individually arranged payment plans). Merit scholarship grants,

need-based scholarship grants available. Total upper-school merit-scholarship money awarded for 2005–06: $10,000. Total amount of financial aid awarded in 2005–06: $10,000.

Admissions Traditional secondary-level entrance age is 11. For fall 2005, 50 students applied for upper-level admission, 15 were accepted, 15 enrolled. Psychoeducational evaluation required. Deadline for receipt of application materials: none. No application fee required. On-campus interview required.

Athletics Coed Intramural: badminton, baseball, basketball, bowling, fitness, volleyball. 2 PE instructors.

Computers Computers are regularly used in art, English, history, mathematics, reading, science classes. Computer network features include campus e-mail, CD-ROMs, Internet access, DVD.

Contact Heather Rose, School Secretary. 609-584-1800. Fax: 609-584-6166. E-mail: hrose@thenewgrange.org. Web site: www.thenewgrange.org.

ANNOUNCEMENT FROM THE SCHOOL Newgrange School, a state-approved independent school for students with learning disabilities, celebrates more than 25 years of educating students. Newgrange uses research-based multisensory structured language programs based on the Orton-Gillingham method. Students achieve academic success, improve their confidence, and are empowered to learn through an individualized, intensive, full-time day program.

NEW HORIZON YOUTH MINISTRIES

1002 South 350 East
Marion, Indiana 46953
Head of School: Mr. Timothy G. Blossom

General Information Coeducational boarding college-preparatory, general academic, religious studies, and bilingual studies school, affiliated with Christian faith, Evangelical faith; primarily serves underachievers, students with learning disabilities, individuals with Attention Deficit Disorder, individuals with emotional and behavioral problems, dyslexic students, and students with Attention Deficit Hyperactivity Disorder. Grades 7–12. Founded: 1971. Setting: rural. Nearest major city is Indianapolis. Students are housed in single-sex dormitories. 130-acre campus. 10 buildings on campus. Approved or accredited by Association of Christian Schools International, Independent Schools Joint Council, and Indiana Department of Education. Total enrollment: 24. Upper school faculty-student ratio: 1:4.

Upper School Student Profile Grade 9: 5 students (3 boys, 2 girls); Grade 10: 8 students (6 boys, 2 girls); Grade 11: 3 students (3 girls); Grade 12: 2 students (1 boy, 1 girl). 100% of students are boarding students. 15% are state residents. 11 states are represented in upper school student body. International students from Canada, Dominican Republic, and El Salvador.

Faculty School total: 9. In upper school: 2 men, 5 women; 2 reside on campus.

Subjects Offered ACT preparation, addiction, adolescent issues, algebra, American government, American literature, Bible studies, biology, Christian education, Christian ethics, Christian scripture, Christianity, decision making skills, economics, English, English composition, ethics, ethics and responsibility, general math, geography, geometry, government, grammar, health, history, math applications, pre-algebra, science, social studies, U.S. history, wilderness studies, world history.

Graduation Requirements Indiana State graduation requirements, group problem solving.

Special Academic Programs Independent study; study at local college for college credit.

College Placement 4 students graduated in 2005; 2 went to college, including Taylor University. Other: 1 went to work, 1 entered military service. Median SAT math: 510, median combined SAT: 1020, median composite ACT: 10.

Student Life Upper grades have uniform requirement, honor system. Discipline rests equally with students and faculty. Attendance at religious services is required.

Summer Programs Remediation, sports, rigorous outdoor training programs offered; session focuses on wilderness training; held off campus; held at Canada; accepts boys and girls; open to students from other schools. 40 students usually enrolled. 2006 schedule: May 15 to August 20. Application deadline: none.

Tuition and Aid 7-day tuition and room/board: $33,000–$72,000. Guaranteed tuition plan. Tuition installment plan (monthly payment plans, discount on tuition paid nine or more months in advance). Tuition reduction for siblings, need-based scholarship grants, deferred tuition until after graduation in certain cases available. In 2005–06, 36% of upper-school students received aid. Total amount of financial aid awarded in 2005–06: $252,145.

Admissions Traditional secondary-level entrance grade is 10. For fall 2005, 40 students applied for upper-level admission, 26 were accepted. Individual IQ, psychoeducational evaluation, Rorschach or Thematic Apperception Test, school's own exam and school's own exam or coop required. Deadline for receipt of application materials: none. No application fee required. Interview recommended.

Athletics Intramural: aerobics (boys, girls), aerobics/dance (g), back packing (b,g), basketball (b,g), canoeing/kayaking (b,g), climbing (b,g), combined training (b,g), cooperative games (b,g), drill team (g), fitness (b,g), fitness walking (g), Frisbee (b,g), gatorball (b,g), hiking/backpacking (b,g), indoor track & field (b,g), kickball (b,g), outdoor activities (b,g), outdoor adventure (b,g), outdoor education (b,g), outdoor recreation (b,g), outdoor skills (b,g), outdoors (b,g), physical fitness (b,g), physical

training (b,g), ropes courses (b,g), soccer (b,g), softball (b,g), strength & conditioning (b,g), team handball (b,g), track and field (b,g), ultimate Frisbee (b,g), volleyball (b,g), walking (b,g), weight lifting (b,g), weight training (b,g), whiffle ball (b,g), wilderness (b,g), wilderness survival (b,g); coed intramural: outdoor activities, outdoor adventure, outdoor education, outdoor recreation, outdoor skills, physical fitness, ropes courses, soccer, wilderness. 1 PE instructor, 1 coach.

Computers Computers are regularly used in architecture, NJROTC classes. Computer network features include on-campus library services, CD-ROMs, Internet access, file transfer, office computer access, DVD, wireless campus network.

Contact Monica Bush, Registrar. 800-333-4009 Ext. 113. Fax: 765-662-1407. E-mail: admissions@nhym.org.

NEW SUMMIT SCHOOL

PO Box 12347
Jackson, Mississippi 39216
Head of School: Dr. Nancy Boyll

General Information Coeducational day college-preparatory and general academic school; primarily serves students with learning disabilities, individuals with Attention Deficit Disorder, individuals with emotional and behavioral problems, and dyslexic students. Grades K–12. Founded: 1996. Setting: suburban. 2-acre campus. 4 buildings on campus. Approved or accredited by Southern Association of Colleges and Schools and Mississippi Department of Education. Total enrollment: 74. Upper school average class size: 8. Upper school faculty-student ratio: 1:5.

Upper School Student Profile Grade 9: 9 students (9 boys); Grade 10: 6 students (2 boys, 4 girls); Grade 11: 8 students (6 boys, 2 girls); Grade 12: 17 students (10 boys, 7 girls).

Faculty School total: 10. In upper school: 4 men, 1 woman; 4 have advanced degrees.

Subjects Offered 3-dimensional art, adolescent issues, algebra, American literature, ancient world history, applied arts, art, biology, business education, career and personal planning, career/college preparation, chemistry, computer applications, computer keyboarding, consumer mathematics, developmental language skills, developmental math, drama, earth science, economics, English, English composition, English literature, essential learning systems, family and consumer science, foreign language, general science, geography, geometry, guidance, health, history, Internet, interpersonal skills, journalism, language arts, life issues, linear algebra, literature, math methods, math review, mathematics, occupational education, personal and social education, physics, pre-algebra, psychology, public speaking, remedial study skills, remedial/makeup course work, science, sociology, Spanish, speech, state government, state history, U.S. government, U.S. history, world geography, world history, writing, yearbook.

Graduation Requirements Arts and fine arts (art, music, dance, drama), computers, electives, English, health, mathematics, science, social studies (includes history).

Special Academic Programs Accelerated programs; independent study; remedial reading and/or remedial writing; remedial math; programs in English, mathematics, general development for dyslexic students.

College Placement 18 students graduated in 2005; 16 went to college, including Hinds Community College; Holmes Community College. Other: 2 went to work. Median composite ACT: 17. 7% scored over 26 on composite ACT.

Student Life Upper grades have specified standards of dress, student council, honor system. Discipline rests primarily with faculty.

Summer Programs Session focuses on academics; held on campus; accepts boys and girls; open to students from other schools. 75 students usually enrolled. 2006 schedule: June 5 to July 16.

Tuition and Aid Day student tuition: $7200. Tuition installment plan (individually arranged payment plans). Tuition reduction for siblings available.

Admissions Traditional secondary-level entrance grade is 9. Grade equivalent tests required. Deadline for receipt of application materials: none. Application fee required. On-campus interview required.

Computers Computers are regularly used in desktop publishing, keyboarding, mathematics, media arts, reading, video film production, yearbook classes. Computer network features include campus e-mail, CD-ROMs, Internet access.

Contact Ms. Marilyn W. McGregor, Director of Counseling/Admissions. 601-982-7827. Fax: 601-982-0080. E-mail: mmcgregor@newsummitschool.com.

OAK CREEK RANCH SCHOOL

PO Box 4329
West Sedona, Arizona 86340-4329
Head of School: David Wick Sr.

petersons.com

General Information Coeducational boarding college-preparatory, general academic, technology, and ESL school; primarily serves underachievers, students with learning disabilities, and individuals with Attention Deficit Disorder. Grades 6–12. Founded: 1972. Setting: rural. Nearest major city is Phoenix. Students are housed in single-sex dormitories. 22-acre campus. 21 buildings on campus. Approved or accredited by Arizona Association of Independent Schools, National Independent Private Schools Association, North Central Association of Colleges and Schools, and

Arizona Department of Education. Total enrollment: 83. Upper school average class size: 8. Upper school faculty-student ratio: 1:8.

Upper School Student Profile Grade 9: 11 students (9 boys, 2 girls); Grade 10: 26 students (17 boys, 9 girls); Grade 11: 13 students (11 boys, 2 girls); Grade 12: 22 students (18 boys, 4 girls). 100% of students are boarding students. 10% are state residents. 15 states are represented in upper school student body. 8% are international students. International students from China, Japan, Philippines, Republic of Korea, and Thailand; 2 other countries represented in student body.

Faculty School total: 12. In upper school: 5 men, 4 women; 9 have advanced degrees.

Subjects Offered Advanced math, algebra, American literature, art, biology, business mathematics, chemistry, computer applications, computer information systems, computer multimedia, computer programming, computer science, computer skills, computer technology certification, drama, earth science, economics, English, English literature, environmental science, ESL, geography, geometry, government/civics, graphics, history, mathematics, physical education, physics, pre-algebra, reading, science, social science, social studies, Spanish, U.S. history, word processing, world history, zoology.

Graduation Requirements Computer science, electives, English, foreign language, mathematics, science, social studies (includes history), completion of a 10-page research project to be presented and defended before faculty advisors during senior year.

Special Academic Programs Honors section; accelerated programs; independent study; term-away projects; remedial reading and/or remedial writing; remedial math; programs in English, mathematics, general development for dyslexic students; ESL (6 students enrolled).

College Placement 23 students graduated in 2005; 19 went to college, including Arizona State University; Columbia College; Northern Arizona University; Purdue University; Texas Tech University. Other: 1 went to work, 1 entered military service, 2 had other specific plans. Median SAT verbal: 500, median SAT math: 490.

Student Life Upper grades have specified standards of dress, student council, honor system. Discipline rests primarily with faculty.

Summer Programs Remediation, enrichment, advancement, ESL, computer instruction programs offered; session focuses on academics; held both on and off campus; held at scenic locations in California, New Mexico, Colorado, and Arizona; accepts boys and girls; open to students from other schools. 35 students usually enrolled. 2006 schedule: June 12 to August 7. Application deadline: none.

Tuition and Aid 7-day tuition and room/board: $29,500. Tuition installment plan (individually arranged payment plans). Tuition reduction for siblings, prepGATE Loans, Key Education Resources available. Total amount of financial aid awarded in 2005–06: $28,000.

Admissions Traditional secondary-level entrance grade is 10. For fall 2005, 95 students applied for upper-level admission, 82 were accepted, 72 enrolled. Deadline for receipt of application materials: none. Application fee required: $400. Interview recommended.

Athletics Interscholastic: basketball (boys, girls), flag football (b), volleyball (g); intramural: football (b); coed interscholastic: golf, soccer, softball; coed intramural: archery, back packing, badminton, bicycling, billiards, bowling, climbing, cross-country running, dressage, equestrian sports, fishing, fly fishing, freestyle skiing, golf, hiking/backpacking, horseback riding, horseshoes, ice skating, kickball, mountain biking, nautilus, outdoor activities, outdoor adventure, outdoor education, outdoor recreation, outdoor skills, outdoors, paddle tennis, paint ball, rafting, riflery, rock climbing, roller blading, ropes courses, skateboarding, skiing (downhill), snowboarding, softball, strength & conditioning, swimming and diving, table tennis, tennis, track and field, volleyball, wall climbing, water polo, weight lifting, weight training, whiffle ball, yoga. 1 PE instructor, 1 coach.

Computers Computers are regularly used in business education, English, ESL, foreign language, information technology, literacy, mathematics, multimedia, occupational education, photography, photojournalism, psychology, publishing, science, technology, vocational-technical courses, word processing classes. Computer network features include campus e-mail, on-campus library services, CD-ROMs, Internet access, file transfer, office computer access, DVD, Electric Library (research service), Web site instruction and hosting (students only).

Contact David Wick Jr., Headmaster. 928-634-5571. Fax: 928-634-4915. E-mail: dwick@ocrs.com. Web site: ocrs.com.

ANNOUNCEMENT FROM THE SCHOOL For 32 years, Oak Creek Ranch School has been helping the academic underachiever; the child with ADD/ADHD; and teens with low self-esteem realize their true potential. Oak Creek Ranch School offers a caring and structured environment, small classes (fewer than 10 per class), individualized programs, and a focus on leadership and character development. Activities include mountain biking, hiking, competitive sports, and horseback riding. The campus is located on Oak Creek near beautiful Sedona, Arizona. Oak Creek Ranch School is a college-preparatory, NCA-accredited, coeducational boarding school for grades 7–12 (ages 12–19).

See full description on page 1240.

OAKLAND SCHOOL

Boyd Tavern
Keswick, Virginia 22947
Head of School: Mrs. Carol Smieciuch

petersons.com

General Information Coeducational boarding and day general academic school; primarily serves underachievers, students with learning disabilities, and dyslexic students. Grades 2–9. Founded: 1950. Setting: rural. Nearest major city is Richmond. Students are housed in single-sex dormitories. 450-acre campus. 25 buildings on campus. Approved or accredited by Virginia Association of Independent Specialized Education Facilities and Virginia Department of Education. Upper school average class size: 8. Upper school faculty-student ratio: 1:5.

Upper School Student Profile Grade 9: 3 students (3 boys).

Faculty School total: 16. In upper school: 3 men, 13 women; 8 have advanced degrees.

Subjects Offered Algebra, American history, earth science, English, expository writing, geometry, grammar, health, keyboarding, life science, mathematics, physical education, physical science, remedial study skills, study skills, world history.

Graduation Requirements Skills must be at or above grade/ability level.

Special Academic Programs Remedial reading and/or remedial writing; remedial math; programs in English, mathematics for dyslexic students.

Student Life Upper grades have specified standards of dress, student council. Discipline rests primarily with faculty.

Summer Programs Remediation, sports, art/fine arts, computer instruction programs offered; session focuses on academics; held on campus; accepts boys and girls; open to students from other schools. 135 students usually enrolled. 2006 schedule: June 17 to August 4.

Tuition and Aid Day student tuition: $18,900; 7-day tuition and room/board: $35,500. Tuition installment plan (monthly payment plans, individually arranged payment plans).

Admissions Wechsler Intelligence Scale for Children III required. Deadline for receipt of application materials: none. No application fee required. On-campus interview required.

Athletics Interscholastic: basketball (girls), cheering (g); intramural: yoga (g); coed interscholastic: soccer; coed intramural: archery, basketball, bicycling, billiards, cooperative games, equestrian sports, fishing, fitness, Frisbee, golf, hiking/backpacking, horseback riding, in-line skating, indoor soccer, kickball, outdoor activities, outdoor recreation, outdoors, paddle tennis, physical fitness, roller blading, roller skating, skateboarding, soccer, softball, swimming and diving, table tennis, tennis. 1 PE instructor.

Computers Computers are regularly used in English classes. Computer resources include CD-ROMs.

Contact Mrs. Carol Smieciuch, Director. 434-293-9059. Fax: 434-296-8930. E-mail: oaklandschool@earthlink.net. Web site: www.oaklandschool.net.

See full description on page 1242.

THE PATHWAY SCHOOL

162 Egypt Road
Norristown, Pennsylvania 19403
Head of School: William O'Flanagan, PhD

petersons.com

General Information Coeducational boarding and day vocational school; primarily serves underachievers, students with learning disabilities, neurologically impaired students, students with neuropsychiatric disorders, and students needing speech/language therapy and occupational therapy. Ungraded, ages 5–21. Founded: 1961. Setting: suburban. Nearest major city is Philadelphia. Students are housed in coed dormitories, single-sex dormitories, and community apartments and houses. 14-acre campus. 14 buildings on campus. Approved or accredited by National Association of Private Schools for Exceptional Children and Pennsylvania Department of Education. Total enrollment: 158. Upper school average class size: 12. Upper school faculty-student ratio: 1:6.

Upper School Student Profile 45% of students are boarding students. 13% are state residents. 11 states are represented in upper school student body.

Faculty School total: 27. In upper school: 4 men, 12 women; 7 have advanced degrees; 1 resides on campus.

Subjects Offered Language arts, mathematics, science, vocational skills.

Graduation Requirements Graduation requirements are as specified by the state of student's residence.

Special Academic Programs Study at local college for college credit; remedial reading and/or remedial writing; remedial math; programs in general development for dyslexic students.

College Placement 17 students graduated in 2005; 4 went to college. Other: 11 went to work, 2 entered a postgraduate year. Median SAT verbal: 480, median SAT math: 460.

Student Life Upper grades have specified standards of dress, student council, honor system. Discipline rests equally with students and faculty.

Summer Programs Remediation, enrichment programs offered; session focuses on students who benefit from consistency for the entire calendar year; held on campus; accepts boys and girls; not open to students from other schools. 100 students usually enrolled. 2006 schedule: July 1 to August 20. Application deadline: April 1.

Tuition and Aid Day student tuition: $34,700; 7-day tuition and room/board: $95,100. Tuition installment plan (individually arranged payment plans).

Admissions Traditional secondary-level entrance age is 13. For fall 2005, 430 students applied for upper-level admission, 20 were accepted, 15 enrolled. Deadline for receipt of application materials: none. No application fee required. On-campus interview required.

Athletics Interscholastic: basketball (boys, girls), softball (b,g); coed intramural: basketball, bowling, skiing (downhill), soccer. 2 PE instructors, 2 coaches.

Computers Computers are regularly used in basic skills, business education, business skills, career education, data processing, design, newspaper, typing classes. Computer resources include on-campus library services, CD-ROMs, Internet access.

Contact Louise Robertson, Director of External Affairs. 610-277-0660 Ext. 212. Fax: 610-539-1493. E-mail: louiser@pathwayschool.org. Web site: www.pathwayschool.org.

ANNOUNCEMENT FROM THE SCHOOL The Pathway School provides innovative programming for students who experience complex learning disabilities and neuropsychiatric disorders. A continuum of services is offered, which supports students at their current level of functioning. These services prepare students for the next step as they begin to experience themselves as competent individuals whose lives are not defined by their disabilities.

See full description on page 1244.

PINEHURST SCHOOL

10 Seymour Avenue
St. Catharines, Ontario L2P 1A4, Canada
Head of School: Mr. Dave Bird

General Information Coeducational boarding college-preparatory, arts, business, and technology school; primarily serves individuals with Attention Deficit Disorder and individuals with emotional and behavioral problems. Grades 7–12. Founded: 2000. Setting: urban. Students are housed in single-sex by floor dormitories. 5-acre campus. 2 buildings on campus. Approved or accredited by Ontario Ministry of Education and Ontario Department of Education. Language of instruction: English. Total enrollment: 25. Upper school faculty-student ratio: 1:10.

Upper School Student Profile Grade 7: 1 student (1 boy); Grade 8: 2 students (1 boy, 1 girl); Grade 9: 3 students (3 boys); Grade 10: 6 students (6 boys); Grade 11: 5 students (3 boys, 2 girls); Grade 12: 8 students (5 boys, 3 girls). 100% of students are boarding students. 80% are province residents. 4 provinces are represented in upper school student body. 20% are international students. International students from Bahamas and United States.

Faculty School total: 8. In upper school: 5 men, 2 women; 1 has an advanced degree.

Graduation Requirements 20th century world history, art, business applications, Canadian geography, English, French, geography, health education, history, math applications, mathematics, outdoor education, science.

Special Academic Programs Honors section; accelerated programs; independent study; remedial reading and/or remedial writing; remedial math.

College Placement 9 students graduated in 2005; all went to college, including Brock University; McMaster University; Queen's University at Kingston; University of Guelph; University of Toronto.

Student Life Upper grades have uniform requirement, student council, honor system. Discipline rests primarily with faculty.

Tuition and Aid 7-day tuition and room/board: CAN$29,000. Tuition installment plan (monthly payment plans).

Admissions Traditional secondary-level entrance grade is 11. For fall 2005, 6 students applied for upper-level admission, 6 were accepted, 6 enrolled. Deadline for receipt of application materials: none. No application fee required. On-campus interview required.

Athletics Coed Intramural: alpine skiing, back packing, badminton, ball hockey, baseball, basketball, bicycling, billiards, blading, bowling, canoeing/kayaking, climbing, cooperative games, field hockey, fishing, fitness, floor hockey, football, golf, hiking/backpacking, hockey, ice hockey, ice skating, indoor hockey, indoor soccer, kayaking, mountain biking, outdoor activities, outdoor adventure, outdoor education, outdoor recreation, outdoor skills, physical fitness, physical training, rock climbing, roller blading, scuba diving, skateboarding, skiing (cross-country), skiing (downhill), snowboarding, snowshoeing, soccer, softball, street hockey, strength & conditioning, swimming and diving, table tennis, touch football, volleyball, walking, wall climbing, weight lifting, weight training, wilderness, wilderness survival, wildernessways, winter soccer, winter walking, yoga. 1 PE instructor, 1 coach, 1 trainer.

Computers Computers are regularly used in all classes. Computer network features include campus e-mail, on-campus library services, CD-ROMs, Internet access, file transfer, DVD, wireless campus network.

Contact Mrs. Donna MacDonald, Admissions/Office Coordinator. 905-641-0993. Fax: 905-641-0399. E-mail: donnaatpine@aol.com. Web site: www.pinehurst.on.ca.

PINE RIDGE SCHOOL

9505 Williston Road
Williston, Vermont 05495
Head of School: Douglas Dague

General Information Coeducational boarding and day remedial school; primarily serves underachievers, students with learning disabilities, individuals with Attention Deficit Disorder, dyslexic students, and students with non-verbal learning disabilities. Ungraded, ages 13–18. Founded: 1968. Setting: rural. Nearest major city is Burlington. Students are housed in single-sex dormitories. 130-acre campus. 15 buildings on campus. Approved or accredited by Academy of Orton-Gillingham Practitioners and Educators, New England Association of Schools and Colleges, and Vermont Department of Education. Total enrollment: 98. Upper school average class size: 7. Upper school faculty-student ratio: 1:2.

Upper School Student Profile 90% of students are boarding students. 20% are state residents. 25 states are represented in upper school student body. 5% are international students. International students from Canada, Jordan, Philippines, and Thailand.

Faculty School total: 53. In upper school: 17 men, 36 women; 8 have advanced degrees; 13 reside on campus.

Subjects Offered Art history, expository writing, geography, grammar, history, social studies.

Graduation Requirements English, mathematics, physical education (includes health), science, social science, last two years of high school must be at Pine Ridge School.

Special Academic Programs Study at local college for college credit; remedial reading and/or remedial writing; remedial math; programs in English, mathematics, general development for dyslexic students.

College Placement 17 students graduated in 2005; 13 went to college, including Curry College; Lynn University; Mitchell College; New England College. Other: 1 entered a postgraduate year, 3 had other specific plans.

Student Life Upper grades have specified standards of dress, student council, honor system. Discipline rests primarily with faculty.

Summer Programs Remediation, art/fine arts, computer instruction programs offered; session focuses on language remediation; held on campus; accepts boys and girls; open to students from other schools. 45 students usually enrolled. 2006 schedule: July 2 to August 15. Application deadline: none.

Tuition and Aid Day student tuition: $36,100; 7-day tuition and room/board: $48,250. Tuition reduction for siblings available. In 2005–06, 40% of upper-school students received aid.

Admissions Traditional secondary-level entrance age is 15. For fall 2005, 51 students applied for upper-level admission, 40 were accepted, 36 enrolled. Wechsler Intelligence Scale for Children required. Deadline for receipt of application materials: none. Application fee required: $50. On-campus interview required.

Athletics Interscholastic: basketball (boys, girls); intramural: alpine skiing (b,g); coed interscholastic: indoor soccer, soccer, softball, tennis; coed intramural: climbing, cooperative games, floor hockey, golf, hiking/backpacking, indoor soccer, mountain biking, mountaineering, nordic skiing, outdoor activities, outdoor adventure, outdoor education, outdoor recreation, outdoor skills, physical fitness, rock climbing, skiing (downhill), weight lifting, wilderness survival, yoga. 2 PE instructors, 9 coaches.

Computers Computers are regularly used in English, mathematics, science, social studies classes. Computer network features include campus e-mail, on-campus library services, CD-ROMs, Internet access, Vermont Automated Libraries System.

Contact Joshua C. Doyle, Director of Admissions. 802-434-5512. Fax: 802-434-5512. E-mail: jdoyle@pineridgeschool.com. Web site: www.pineridgeschool.com.

ANNOUNCEMENT FROM THE SCHOOL Pine Ridge School was founded in 1968 to meet the needs of adolescents with dyslexia, language-based learning disabilities, and nonverbal learning disabilities. The academic program utilizes an Orton-Gillingham philosophy in the classes and an individualized, daily one-on-one tutorial. Students participate in athletics, arts, and a variety of community service activities.

See full description on page 1246.

PROVO CANYON SCHOOL

4501 North University Avenue
Provo, Utah 84603
Head of School: Kreg Gillman, PhD

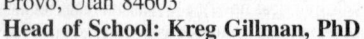

General Information Coeducational boarding college-preparatory and general academic school; primarily serves underachievers, students with learning disabilities, individuals with Attention Deficit Disorder, and individuals with emotional and behavioral problems. Grades 7–12. Founded: 1971. Setting: suburban. Nearest major city is Salt Lake City. Students are housed in single-sex dormitories. 20-acre campus. 4 buildings on campus. Approved or accredited by Joint Commission on Accreditation of Healthcare Organizations, Northwest Association of Schools and Colleges, and Utah Department of Education. Language of instruction: English. Total enrollment: 211. Upper school average class size: 12. Upper school faculty-student ratio: 1:12.

Upper School Student Profile Grade 7: 2 students (2 boys); Grade 8: 22 students (3 boys, 19 girls); Grade 9: 36 students (16 boys, 20 girls); Grade 10: 65 students (43 boys, 22 girls); Grade 11: 54 students (24 boys, 30 girls); Grade 12: 32 students (12 boys, 20 girls). 100% of students are boarding students. 2% are state residents. 21 states are represented in upper school student body. 2% are international students.

Faculty School total: 31. In upper school: 16 men, 15 women; 6 have advanced degrees.

Subjects Offered Computer science, English, mathematics, physical education, science, social science, social studies.

Graduation Requirements Computer science, English, mathematics, physical education (includes health), science, social science, social studies (includes history).

Special Academic Programs Independent study; remedial reading and/or remedial writing; remedial math.

College Placement 34 students graduated in 2004.

Student Life Upper grades have specified standards of dress. Discipline rests equally with students and faculty.

Tuition and Aid Tuition installment plan (monthly payment plans, individually arranged payment plans). Achiever Loans (Key Education Resources) available.

Admissions Deadline for receipt of application materials: none. No application fee required.

Athletics Intramural: aerobics (girls), basketball (b,g), canoeing/kayaking (b,g), fitness (b,g), hiking/backpacking (b,g), outdoor activities (b,g), outdoor adventure (b,g), physical fitness (b,g), rafting (b,g), rappelling (b,g), rock climbing (b,g), ropes courses (b,g), skiing (cross-country) (b,g), skiing (downhill) (b,g), snowboarding (b,g), soccer (b), softball (b,g), swimming and diving (b,g), tennis (b,g), volleyball (b,g), water skiing (b,g), weight training (b,g), wilderness (b,g). 3 PE instructors, 2 coaches.

Computers Computers are regularly used in all academic classes. Computer network features include on-campus library services, CD-ROMs, file transfer, office computer access.

Contact Admissions Office. 800-848-9819. Fax: 801-223-7130. E-mail: pcsinfo@provocanyon.com. Web site: www.provocanyon.com.

See full description on page 1248.

PURNELL SCHOOL

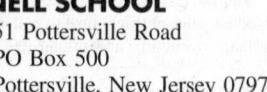

51 Pottersville Road
PO Box 500
Pottersville, New Jersey 07979
Head of School: Ms. Jenifer Fox

General Information Girls' boarding and day college-preparatory, general academic, and arts school; primarily serves students with learning disabilities and individuals with Attention Deficit Disorder. Grades 9–12. Founded: 1963. Setting: rural. Nearest major city is New York, NY. Students are housed in single-sex dormitories. 83-acre campus. 23 buildings on campus. Approved or accredited by Middle States Association of Colleges and Schools, New Jersey Association of Independent Schools, The Association of Boarding Schools, and New Jersey Department of Education. Member of National Association of Independent Schools and Secondary School Admission Test Board. Endowment: $5.5 million. Total enrollment: 116. Upper school average class size: 9. Upper school faculty-student ratio: 1:8.

Upper School Student Profile Grade 9: 27 students (27 girls); Grade 10: 24 students (24 girls); Grade 11: 30 students (30 girls); Grade 12: 35 students (35 girls). 87% of students are boarding students. 48% are state residents. 19 states are represented in upper school student body. 7% are international students. International students from Barbados, Bermuda, British Virgin Islands, China, El Salvador, and Republic of Korea; 2 other countries represented in student body.

Faculty School total: 24. In upper school: 9 men, 15 women; 14 have advanced degrees; 21 reside on campus.

Subjects Offered Algebra, American history, American literature, anatomy, art, art history, biology, botany, calculus, ceramics, chemistry, creative writing, dance, drama, earth science, ecology, English, English literature, environmental science, fine arts, French, geography, geometry, government/civics, health, history, mathematics, music, photography, physical education, science, Shakespeare, social science, social studies, Spanish, speech, statistics, theater, trigonometry, women's studies, world history, world literature, writing.

Graduation Requirements Art history, arts and fine arts (art, music, dance, drama), English, foreign language, history, mathematics, performing arts, physical education (includes health), science, study abroad, Project Exploration.

Special Academic Programs Independent study; study abroad; programs in English, mathematics, general development for dyslexic students; ESL (7 students enrolled).

College Placement 23 students graduated in 2005; 22 went to college, including American University; Drew University; Ithaca College; Ohio Wesleyan University; Saint Joseph's University; Vassar College. Other: 1 went to work.

Student Life Upper grades have specified standards of dress, student council. Discipline rests primarily with faculty.

Tuition and Aid Day student tuition: $25,250; 5-day tuition and room/board: $31,000; 7-day tuition and room/board: $34,725. Tuition installment plan (Academic Management Services Plan, Key Tuition Payment Plan, monthly payment plans,

---

individually arranged payment plans). Need-based scholarship grants, paying campus jobs, prepGATE Loans available. In 2005–06, 26% of upper-school students received aid. Total amount of financial aid awarded in 2005–06: $405,000.

Admissions Traditional secondary-level entrance grade is 9. For fall 2005, 97 students applied for upper-level admission, 94 were accepted, 58 enrolled. Deadline for receipt of application materials: none. Application fee required: $50. Interview required.

Athletics Interscholastic: basketball, dance, dance team, lacrosse, soccer, softball, tennis, volleyball; intramural: aerobics, aerobics/dance, aerobics/nautilus, ballet, equestrian sports, fitness, horseback riding, jogging, modern dance, outdoor adventure, physical training, self defense, strength & conditioning, weight training, yoga. 1 PE instructor, 4 coaches.

Computers Computers are regularly used in English, foreign language, history, mathematics, science classes. Computer network features include campus e-mail, on-campus library services, CD-ROMs, Internet access, file transfer, office computer access, DVD, wireless campus network.

Contact Ms. Valerie Gude, Associate Director of Admission. 908-439-2154. Fax: 908-439-4088. E-mail: vgude@purnell.org. Web site: www.purnell.org.

ANNOUNCEMENT FROM THE SCHOOL Purnell gives young women the gift of discovering what they are truly great at doing by recognizing different learning styles and tailoring programs to enable every student to realize her potential. Purnell offers small classes, extensive studio and performing arts, technology-rich curricula, and competitive and noncompetitive athletic offerings. At Purnell, everyone experiences success and the confidence that comes with it.

See full description on page 1250.

RANCHO VALMORA

Box 1
Valmora, New Mexico 87750
Head of School: Mr. David Braccialarghe

General Information Coeducational boarding college-preparatory, general academic, arts, bilingual studies, and technology school; primarily serves underachievers, students with learning disabilities, individuals with Attention Deficit Disorder, individuals with emotional and behavioral problems, and dyslexic students. Grades 7–12. Founded: 1994. Setting: rural. Nearest major city is Las Vegas. Students are housed in single-sex houses. 1,000-acre campus. 2 buildings on campus. Approved or accredited by North Central Association of Colleges and Schools and New Mexico Department of Education. Total enrollment: 79. Upper school average class size: 9. Upper school faculty-student ratio: 1:9.

Upper School Student Profile Grade 9: 18 students (13 boys, 5 girls); Grade 10: 23 students (12 boys, 11 girls); Grade 11: 18 students (11 boys, 7 girls); Grade 12: 14 students (6 boys, 8 girls). 100% of students are boarding students. 1% are state residents. 24 states are represented in upper school student body. 5% are international students. International students from Czech Republic, Nicaragua, Nigeria, and United Kingdom.

Faculty School total: 15. In upper school: 5 men, 8 women; 7 have advanced degrees.

Subjects Offered Algebra, American Civil War, American democracy, American government, American history, American literature, anatomy and physiology, art, art education, art history, biology, botany, calculus, career education, chemistry, civil war history, clayworking, composition, computer art, digital photography, drawing, earth science, electives, English, English composition, English literature, equine science, fine arts, foreign language, gardening, general math, general science, geography, geometry, government, health, health education, history, horticulture, human anatomy, human biology, interpersonal skills, introduction to literature, language arts, life skills, literature, mathematics, modern history, modern Western civilization, modern world history, newspaper, painting, photography, physical education, poetry, pre-algebra, pre-calculus, psychology, reading, SAT preparation, SAT/ACT preparation, science, sculpture, Spanish, standard curriculum, trigonometry, U.S. government, U.S. history, weightlifting, world history.

Graduation Requirements Must meet New Mexico State Department High School Graduation Requirements.

Special Academic Programs Accelerated programs; independent study; study at local college for college credit; academic accommodation for the gifted and the artistically talented; remedial reading and/or remedial writing; remedial math; programs in English, mathematics, general development for dyslexic students.

College Placement 9 students graduated in 2005; 4 went to college. Other: 3 entered a postgraduate year, 2 had other specific plans.

Student Life Upper grades have honor system. Discipline rests primarily with students.

Tuition and Aid Guaranteed tuition plan. Tuition installment plan (individually arranged payment plans).

Admissions Traditional secondary-level entrance grade is 10. Psychoeducational evaluation required. Deadline for receipt of application materials: none. No application fee required. Interview recommended.

Athletics Intramural: archery (boys, girls), ball hockey (b,g), baseball (b,g), basketball (b,g), bicycling (b,g), fitness (b,g), flag football (b,g), Frisbee (b,g), hiking/backpacking (b,g), horseback riding (b,g), indoor soccer (b,g), indoor track & field (b,g), kickball (b,g), outdoor activities (b,g), paddle tennis (b,g), physical fitness (b,g), rodeo (b,g), skateboarding (b,g), skiing (downhill) (b,g), snowboarding (b,g), softball (b,g), strength & conditioning (b,g), swimming and diving (b,g), table tennis (b,g), touch football (b,g), volleyball (b,g), walking (b,g), weight lifting (b,g); coed intramural: archery, ball hockey, baseball, basketball, bicycling, fitness, flag football, Frisbee, hiking/backpacking, horseback riding, indoor soccer, indoor track & field, kickball, outdoor activities, paddle tennis, physical fitness, rodeo, skateboarding, skiing (downhill), snowboarding, softball, strength & conditioning, swimming and diving, table tennis, touch football, volleyball, walking, weight lifting. 1 PE instructor.

Computers Computers are regularly used in reading, science, social studies classes. Computer resources include on-campus library services, CD-ROMs, Internet access, office computer access, DVD, wireless campus network.

Contact Ms. Angel Burch, Admissions Coordinator. 505-425-6057 Ext. 341. Fax: 505-425-0455. E-mail: angelb.ranchovalmora@starband.net. Web site: www.ranchovalmora.com.

RIVERVIEW SCHOOL

551 Route 6A
East Sandwich, Massachusetts 02537
Head of School: Mrs. Maureen B. Brenner

General Information Coeducational boarding school; primarily serves underachievers, students with learning disabilities, individuals with Attention Deficit Disorder, and adolescents and young adults with complex language, learning and cognitive disabilities. Grades 6–PG. Founded: 1957. Setting: rural. Nearest major city is Boston. Students are housed in single-sex dormitories. 16-acre campus. 20 buildings on campus. Approved or accredited by Association of Independent Schools in New England, Massachusetts Office of Child Care Services, National Association of Private Schools for Exceptional Children, New England Association of Schools and Colleges, and Massachusetts Department of Education. Member of National Association of Independent Schools. Endowment: $2.8 million. Total enrollment: 108. Upper school average class size: 8. Upper school faculty-student ratio: 1:4.

Upper School Student Profile Grade 9: 17 students (9 boys, 8 girls); Grade 10: 12 students (6 boys, 6 girls); Grade 11: 24 students (13 boys, 11 girls); Grade 12: 46 students (21 boys, 25 girls). 100% of students are boarding students. 32% are state residents. 30 states are represented in upper school student body. International students from Bahamas, Bermuda, Canada, Taiwan, Thailand, and United Kingdom; 3 other countries represented in student body.

Faculty School total: 32. In upper school: 9 men, 23 women; 19 have advanced degrees.

Subjects Offered Art, computer skills, culinary arts, history, industrial arts, language arts, mathematics, physical education, reading, science, sexuality, social skills, social studies, speech therapy, writing.

Special Academic Programs Remedial reading and/or remedial writing; remedial math; programs in English, mathematics for dyslexic students.

College Placement 38 students graduated in 2005; they went to Babson College; Cape Cod Community College; New York Institute of Technology. Other: 25 entered a postgraduate year.

Student Life Upper grades have specified standards of dress, student council. Discipline rests primarily with faculty.

Summer Programs Remediation, enrichment, sports, computer instruction programs offered; session focuses on reading, language arts, science, math, computers, fitness, sports; held on campus; accepts boys and girls; open to students from other schools. 48 students usually enrolled. 2006 schedule: July 9 to August 11. Application deadline: none.

Tuition and Aid 7-day tuition and room/board: $59,620. Tuition installment plan (initial deposit upon acceptance, 3-installment payment plan (July, August, and November)). Need-based scholarship grants available. In 2005–06, 6% of upper-school students received aid. Total amount of financial aid awarded in 2005–06: $102,500.

Admissions Traditional secondary-level entrance grade is 10. For fall 2005, 185 students applied for upper-level admission, 86 were accepted, 34 enrolled. Achievement tests, comprehensive educational evaluation, Individual IQ, Achievement and behavior rating scale, psychoeducational evaluation, WISC or WAIS, Woodcock-Johnson or writing sample required. Deadline for receipt of application materials: none. Application fee required: $75. On-campus interview required.

Athletics Interscholastic: baseball (boys), basketball (b,g), cross-country running (b,g), soccer (b,g), swimming and diving (b,g), tennis (b,g), track and field (b,g); intramural: basketball (b,g), bowling (b,g), fitness (b,g), golf (b,g), jogging (b,g), jump rope (b,g), nautilus (b,g), physical fitness (b,g), project adventure (b,g), running (b,g), softball (b,g); coed interscholastic: basketball, cross-country running, soccer, swimming and diving, tennis, track and field; coed intramural: aerobics, aerobics/dance, aerobics/nautilus, basketball, bowling, fitness, golf, jogging, jump rope, nautilus, physical fitness, project adventure, running, soccer, yoga. 2 PE instructors, 2 coaches, 2 trainers.

Computers Computers are regularly used in all academic classes. Computer network features include campus e-mail, CD-ROMs, Internet access, office computer access, digital photography, scanners, PowerPoint presentations.
Contact Ms. Monica Lindo, Admissions Assistant. 508-888-0489. Fax: 508-833-7001. E-mail: admissions@riverviewschool.org. Web site: www.riverviewschool.org.

ANNOUNCEMENT FROM THE SCHOOL Riverview School, founded in 1957, is an independent, coeducational, residential school that provides a caring community for adolescents and young adults with complex language, learning, and cognitive disabilities (70–100 IQ). The School is committed to developing student competence and confidence in academic, social, and independent living skills. Tuition: $59,620; Head of School: Maureen B. Brenner.

ROBERT LAND ACADEMY

RR #3
6726 South Chippawa Road
Wellandport, Ontario L0R 2J0, Canada
Head of School: Lt. Col. G. Scott Bowman

General Information Boys' boarding college-preparatory, arts, and business school; primarily serves underachievers, students with learning disabilities, individuals with Attention Deficit Disorder, individuals with emotional and behavioral problems, dyslexic students, and students with Oppositional Defiant Disorder. Grades 6–12. Founded: 1978. Setting: rural. Nearest major city is Niagara Falls, Canada. Students are housed in single-sex dormitories and barracks. 168-acre campus. 18 buildings on campus. Approved or accredited by Ontario Ministry of Education and Ontario Department of Education. Language of instruction: English. Total enrollment: 148. Upper school average class size: 15. Upper school faculty-student ratio: 1:15.
Upper School Student Profile Grade 11: 39 students (39 boys); Grade 12: 26 students (26 boys). 100% of students are boarding students. 65% are province residents. 19 provinces are represented in upper school student body. 25% are international students. International students from Bermuda, Cayman Islands, Hong Kong, Jamaica, United Arab Emirates, and United States; 5 other countries represented in student body.
Faculty School total: 18. In upper school: 14 men; 3 have advanced degrees.
Subjects Offered Accounting, algebra, ancient history, art, art history, biology, business, business skills, calculus, Canadian history, chemistry, computer programming, computer science, consumer education, creative writing, driver education, earth science, ecology, economics, English, English literature, environmental science, ethics, European history, expository writing, fine arts, French, geography, geology, geometry, government/civics, grammar, health, keyboarding, law, mathematics, military science, music, philosophy, photography, physical education, physics, science, social science, social studies, statistics, trigonometry, typing, world history, world literature, writing.
Graduation Requirements Arts and fine arts (art, music, dance, drama), business skills (includes word processing), English, foreign language, mathematics, physical education (includes health), science, social science, Ontario Literacy Equivalence Test.
Special Academic Programs Honors section; accelerated programs; independent study; remedial reading and/or remedial writing; remedial math; programs in general development for dyslexic students.
College Placement 24 students graduated in 2005; 23 went to college, including Brock University; McMaster University; Queen's University at Kingston; University of Ottawa; University of Toronto; University of Waterloo. Other: 1 entered military service.
Student Life Upper grades have uniform requirement, student council, honor system. Discipline rests primarily with faculty.
Tuition and Aid 7-day tuition and room/board: CAN$32,900. Tuition installment plan (individually arranged payment plans). Bursaries, merit scholarship grants, need-based scholarship grants, need-based loans, financing for American students through Key Educational Resources available. In 2005–06, 5% of upper-school students received aid.
Admissions Traditional secondary-level entrance grade is 11. Deadline for receipt of application materials: none. Application fee required: CAN$150. Interview required.
Athletics Interscholastic: badminton, basketball, cross-country running, hockey, ice hockey, rock climbing, rugby, running, soccer, track and field, volleyball, wall climbing, wrestling; intramural: aerobics/nautilus, alpine skiing, aquatics, archery, back packing, badminton, ball hockey, baseball, basketball, bicycling, boxing, canoeing/kayaking, climbing, cross-country running, drill team, fishing, fitness, fitness walking, flag football, floor hockey, football, Frisbee, hiking/backpacking, hockey, ice hockey, indoor soccer, jogging, JROTC drill, life saving, marksmanship, martial arts, mountain biking, mountaineering, nautilus, outdoor activities, outdoor adventure, outdoor education, outdoor recreation, outdoor skills, outdoors, paint ball, physical fitness, physical training, rappelling, riflery, rock climbing, rugby, running, scuba diving, self defense, skiing (downhill), skydiving, snowboarding, soccer, softball, street hockey, strength & conditioning, swimming and diving, tai chi, touch football, track and field, volleyball, wall climbing, weight training, wilderness, wilderness survival, wrestling. 3 PE instructors, 1 coach, 1 trainer.

Computers Computers are regularly used in all academic classes. Computer network features include on-campus library services, CD-ROMs, Internet access.
Contact Lt. F. Greg Hewett, Admissions Officer. 905-386-6203. Fax: 905-386-6607. E-mail: ghewett@robertlandacademy.com. Web site: www.robertlandacademy.com.

See full description on page 1252.

ROBERT LOUIS STEVENSON SCHOOL

24 West 74th Street
New York, New York 10023
Head of School: B. H. Henrichsen

General Information Coeducational day college-preparatory school; primarily serves underachievers, students with learning disabilities, individuals with Attention Deficit Disorder, individuals with emotional and behavioral problems, and dyslexic students. Grades 7–PG. Founded: 1908. Setting: urban. 1 building on campus. Approved or accredited by New York State Association of Independent Schools and New York Department of Education. Member of National Association of Independent Schools. Total enrollment: 76. Upper school average class size: 9. Upper school faculty-student ratio: 1:6.
Upper School Student Profile Grade 8: 6 students (5 boys, 1 girl); Grade 9: 17 students (13 boys, 4 girls); Grade 10: 18 students (14 boys, 4 girls); Grade 11: 19 students (14 boys, 5 girls); Grade 12: 16 students (9 boys, 7 girls).
Faculty School total: 13. In upper school: 5 men, 8 women; 8 have advanced degrees.
Subjects Offered Algebra, American history, American literature, anatomy, ancient history, art, biology, ceramics, chemistry, computer literacy, computer science, creative writing, current history, drama, earth science, English, English literature, environmental science, European civilization, European history, expository writing, film appreciation, geometry, government/civics, grammar, health, history, history of ideas, law and the legal system, mathematics, media, philosophy, physical education, physics, physiology, poetry, political science, political thought, pre-algebra, pre-calculus, psychology, science, senior project, sex education, Shakespeare, social science, social studies, theater, trigonometry, world literature, writing.
Graduation Requirements Computer literacy, English, mathematics, physical education (includes health), science, social science, social studies (includes history), portfolio of work demonstrating readiness to graduate.
Special Academic Programs Accelerated programs; independent study; academic accommodation for the gifted; remedial reading and/or remedial writing; remedial math; programs in English, mathematics; general development for dyslexic students.
College Placement 16 students graduated in 2005; 14 went to college, including City University of New York System; Pace University; State University of New York System. Other: 1 went to work, 1 entered a postgraduate year.
Student Life Upper grades have student council. Discipline rests primarily with faculty.
Summer Programs Remediation, enrichment programs offered; session focuses on tutorial work; held on campus; accepts boys and girls; open to students from other schools. 15 students usually enrolled. 2006 schedule: July 1 to August 1. Application deadline: June 20.
Tuition and Aid Day student tuition: $34,500. Tuition installment plan (Key Tuition Payment Plan, individually arranged payment plans). Need-based scholarship grants, need-based loans available. In 2005–06, 4% of upper-school students received aid. Total amount of financial aid awarded in 2005–06: $6000.
Admissions Traditional secondary-level entrance grade is 9. For fall 2005, 65 students applied for upper-level admission, 45 were accepted, 40 enrolled. Psycho-educational evaluation required. Deadline for receipt of application materials: none. No application fee required. On-campus interview required.
Athletics Coed Interscholastic: basketball, bowling, cross-country running, fitness, floor hockey, jogging, soccer, softball, yoga; coed intramural: aerobics, ball hockey, basketball, bicycling, blading, bowling, cooperative games, fitness, flag football, floor hockey, jogging, judo, juggling, martial arts, physical fitness, physical training, soccer, softball, strength & conditioning, table tennis, tennis, touch football, volleyball, weight lifting, weight training, yoga.
Computers Computers are regularly used in art, English, history, science, technology classes. Computer resources include CD-ROMs, Internet access, file transfer.
Contact B. H. Henrichsen, Headmaster. 212-787-6400. Fax: 212-873-1872. Web site: stevenson-school.org.

ANNOUNCEMENT FROM THE SCHOOL Stevenson's program for bright underachieving adolescents provides a challenging academic program combined with extensive support services. Advisers help students cope with academic, social, and emotional issues. Learning-disabled students receive help individually and in small groups. Very small classes offer individualized instruction and attention to organizational and study skills.

ROCKLYN ACADEMY

RR # 2 (Rocklyn)
Meaford, Ontario N4L 1W6, Canada
Head of School: Ms. Dale Stohn

General Information Girls' boarding college-preparatory school; primarily serves individuals with Attention Deficit Disorder and individuals with emotional and behavioral problems. Grades 9–12. Founded: 1999. Setting: rural. Nearest major city is Toronto, Canada. Students are housed in single-sex dormitories. 75-acre campus. 3 buildings on campus. Approved or accredited by Ontario Ministry of Education and Ontario Department of Education. Language of instruction: English. Total enrollment: 27. Upper school average class size: 4. Upper school faculty-student ratio: 1:3.

Upper School Student Profile Grade 9: 4 students (4 girls); Grade 10: 9 students (9 girls); Grade 11: 7 students (7 girls); Grade 12: 7 students (7 girls). 100% of students are boarding students. 66% are province residents. 14 provinces are represented in upper school student body. 34% are international students. International students from Malaysia, United Kingdom, and United States.

Faculty School total: 13. In upper school: 3 men, 8 women.

Subjects Offered Art, biology, business, calculus, career education, chemistry, civics, communication skills, computer science, contemporary history, creative writing, dramatic arts, English, equine management, ESL, family studies, fine arts, French, geography, guitar, health education, healthful living, history, humanities, law, library, life skills, literature, mathematics, music, personal growth, philosophy, physical fitness, physics, poetry, pottery, public speaking, reading/study skills, relationships, science, Shakespeare, society challenge and change, Spanish, technology.

Special Academic Programs Accelerated programs; academic accommodation for the gifted; ESL.

College Placement 8 students graduated in 2005; 7 went to college, including Trent University; University of Guelph; University of Toronto; University of Tulsa; University of Waterloo. Other: 1 went to work.

Student Life Upper grades have uniform requirement, student council, honor system. Discipline rests equally with students and faculty.

Summer Programs Sports, rigorous outdoor training programs offered; session focuses on emotional growth through outdoor activities; held on campus; accepts girls; not open to students from other schools. 9 students usually enrolled. 2006 schedule: July 6 to August 23.

Tuition and Aid 7-day tuition and room/board: CAN$42,600.

Admissions Traditional secondary-level entrance grade is 10. For fall 2005, 35 students applied for upper-level admission, 29 were accepted, 27 enrolled. Wechsler Intelligence Scale for Children required. Deadline for receipt of application materials: none. No application fee required. Interview recommended.

Athletics Intramural: aerobics, alpine skiing, badminton, baseball, cooperative games, fitness, golf, hiking/backpacking, horseback riding, ice skating, physical fitness, ropes courses, skiing (cross-country), skiing (downhill), snowboarding, soccer, softball, squash, swimming and diving, table tennis, volleyball, walking, wall climbing, weight training, yoga. 3 PE instructors.

Computers Computers are regularly used in all classes. Computer resources include CD-ROMs, Internet access.

Contact Dale Stohn, Director. 519-538-2992. Fax: 519-538-1106. E-mail: dale@rocklynacademy.com. Web site: www.rocklynacademy.com.

ANNOUNCEMENT FROM THE SCHOOL Rocklyn Academy is a private boarding high school for girls who are having difficulties in their current school setting and/or at home. Rocklyn is based on a nurturing, structured emotional growth model with therapeutic support in combination with advanced academics and a wide array of athletics. Rocklyn Academy is ministry-inspected. Rocklyn is unique in Canada.

ST. PAUL'S PREPARATORY ACADEMY

PO Box 32650
Phoenix, Arizona 85064
Head of School: Hal W. Elliott

General Information Boys' boarding and day college-preparatory school, affiliated with Episcopal Church; primarily serves underachievers, individuals with Attention Deficit Disorder, and students with motivational problems. Grades 9–12. Founded: 1961. Setting: urban. Students are housed in single-sex dormitories. 6-acre campus. 7 buildings on campus. Approved or accredited by Arizona Association of Independent Schools, National Association of Episcopal Schools, North Central Association of Colleges and Schools, Southwest Association of Episcopal Schools, and Arizona Department of Education. Member of National Association of Independent Schools and Secondary School Admission Test Board. Endowment: $350,000. Total enrollment: 75. Upper school average class size: 10. Upper school faculty-student ratio: 1:10.

Upper School Student Profile Grade 9: 15 students (15 boys); Grade 10: 15 students (15 boys); Grade 11: 20 students (20 boys); Grade 12: 25 students (25 boys). 75% of students are boarding students. 25% are state residents. 50 states are represented in upper school student body. 10% are members of Episcopal Church.

Faculty School total: 14. In upper school: 6 men, 8 women; 8 have advanced degrees.

Subjects Offered ACT preparation, addiction, adolescent issues, algebra, American government, American history, American literature, animation, art history, athletics, biology, chemistry, composition, computer graphics, computer programming, creative writing, debate, desktop publishing, drawing, economics, English, English literature, geometry, government/civics, health, keyboarding, music appreciation, painting, photojournalism, physical education, physics, pre-calculus, public speaking, Spanish, trigonometry, weight training, world history.

Graduation Requirements American government, computer science, economics, English, foreign language, mathematics, physical education (includes health), science, social studies (includes history). Community service is required.

Special Academic Programs Independent study.

College Placement 15 students graduated in 2005; all went to college, including Arizona State University; Christian Brothers University; Keene State College; Old Dominion University; Saint Mary's College of California; Whittier College. Mean SAT verbal: 566, mean SAT math: 567, mean composite ACT: 24. 35% scored over 600 on SAT verbal, 35% scored over 600 on SAT math, 25% scored over 26 on composite ACT.

Student Life Upper grades have uniform requirement, student council, honor system. Discipline rests primarily with faculty. Attendance at religious services is required.

Summer Programs Remediation, enrichment, advancement, art/fine arts, computer instruction programs offered; held on campus; accepts boys; open to students from other schools. 35 students usually enrolled. 2006 schedule: June 5 to August 11. Application deadline: none.

Tuition and Aid Day student tuition: $16,000; 7-day tuition and room/board: $39,325. Tuition installment plan (individually arranged payment plans, semester payment plan). Merit scholarship grants, need-based scholarship grants available. In 2005–06, 15% of upper-school students received aid; total upper-school merit-scholarship money awarded: $20,000. Total amount of financial aid awarded in 2005–06: $125,000.

Admissions Traditional secondary-level entrance grade is 9. For fall 2005, 95 students applied for upper-level admission, 75 were accepted, 75 enrolled. Deadline for receipt of application materials: none. No application fee required. On-campus interview required.

Athletics Interscholastic: baseball, basketball, fitness, golf, outdoor activities, physical fitness, soccer; intramural: baseball, basketball, billiards, bowling, flag football, golf, outdoor activities, rock climbing, soccer, ultimate Frisbee, volleyball, weight lifting.

Computers Computers are regularly used in art, college planning, data processing, desktop publishing, drawing and design, graphic arts, graphic design, journalism, photojournalism, research skills, SAT preparation, writing, yearbook classes. Computer resources include campus e-mail, CD-ROMs, online commercial services, Internet access.

Contact Donna Wittwer, Director of Admission. 602-956-9090 Ext. 206. Fax: 602-956-3018. E-mail: admissions@stpaulsacademy.com. Web site: www.stpaulsacademy.com.

See full description on page 1254.

SMITH SCHOOL

131 West 86 Street
New York, New York 10024
Head of School: Karen Smith

General Information Coeducational day college-preparatory school; primarily serves students with learning disabilities, individuals with Attention Deficit Disorder, students with Attention Deficit Hyperactivity Disorder, and depression and anxiety; individuals with emotional and motivational issues. Grades 7–12. Founded: 1990. Setting: urban. 1 building on campus. Approved or accredited by New York Department of Education. Total enrollment: 60. Upper school average class size: 4. Upper school faculty-student ratio: 1:4.

Upper School Student Profile Grade 9: 10 students (6 boys, 4 girls); Grade 10: 9 students (6 boys, 3 girls); Grade 11: 10 students (6 boys, 4 girls); Grade 12: 16 students (10 boys, 6 girls).

Faculty School total: 11. In upper school: 4 men, 7 women; 9 have advanced degrees.

Subjects Offered Algebra, art, biology, calculus, chemistry, computer skills, earth science, ecology, economics, English, European history, film, French, geometry, government, independent study, lab science, Latin, life science, music, philosophy, physical science, physics, pre-calculus, remedial study skills, SAT preparation, Spanish, trigonometry, U.S. history, world history, writing skills.

Graduation Requirements Algebra, American history, art, biology, chemistry, earth science, English, environmental science, European history, geometry, government, languages, physical education (includes health), physical science, pre-algebra, pre-calculus, trigonometry, world history.

Special Academic Programs Honors section; accelerated programs; independent study; academic accommodation for the gifted; remedial reading and/or remedial writing; remedial math.

College Placement 11 students graduated in 2005; 10 went to college, including Eckerd College; Fordham University; Hofstra University; Hunter College of the City University of New York; Mitchell College; Roger Williams University. Other: 1 went to work.

Student Life Upper grades have student council, honor system. Discipline rests primarily with faculty.

Summer Programs Remediation, enrichment, advancement, computer instruction programs offered; session focuses on academic courses for enrichment, remediation, or credit; held on campus; accepts boys and girls; open to students from other schools. 28 students usually enrolled. 2006 schedule: June 19 to August 22. Application deadline: June 1.

Tuition and Aid Day student tuition: $28,500. Tuition installment plan (monthly payment plans, individually arranged payment plans, quarterly payment plan). Financial aid available to upper-school students. In 2005–06, 2% of upper-school students received aid. Total amount of financial aid awarded in 2005–06: $7000.

Admissions Traditional secondary-level entrance grade is 10. For fall 2005, 35 students applied for upper-level admission, 26 were accepted, 26 enrolled. Comprehensive educational evaluation, math and English placement tests, psychoeducational evaluation, school placement exam, Wide Range Achievement Test, WRAT or writing sample required. Deadline for receipt of application materials: none. No application fee required. Interview required.

Athletics Coed Interscholastic: aerobics/dance, basketball, fitness, kickball, physical fitness, soccer; coed intramural: physical fitness. 1 PE instructor, 2 coaches.

Computers Computers are regularly used in English, research skills, study skills, writing, yearbook classes. Computer resources include CD-ROMs, Internet access, DVD.

Contact Cristina Martinez, Admissions Contact. 212-879-6317. Fax: 212-879-0962. E-mail: edu@smithschool.net.

ANNOUNCEMENT FROM THE SCHOOL The Smith School strives to bring academic success to students whose struggles with learning and/or emotional issues have prevented them from achieving their full potential. The School offers extensive support services in a nurturing, intimate setting. The staff incorporates creative and individualized teaching strategies, interactive learning, and interpersonal and social development in its practices to foster lifelong learning.

SORENSON'S RANCH SCHOOL

PO Box 440219
Koosharem, Utah 84744
Head of School: Shane Sorenson

General Information Coeducational boarding college-preparatory, general academic, arts, and vocational school; primarily serves underachievers, students with learning disabilities, individuals with Attention Deficit Disorder, and individuals with emotional and behavioral problems. Grades 7–12. Founded: 1982. Setting: rural. Nearest major city is Salt Lake City. Students are housed in single-sex dormitories. 10-acre campus. 16 buildings on campus. Approved or accredited by Joint Commission on Accreditation of Healthcare Organizations, Northwest Association of Schools and Colleges, and Utah Department of Education. Total enrollment: 95. Upper school average class size: 12. Upper school faculty-student ratio: 1:10.

Upper School Student Profile Grade 9: 21 students (11 boys, 10 girls); Grade 10: 24 students (12 boys, 12 girls); Grade 11: 25 students (14 boys, 11 girls); Grade 12: 25 students (15 boys, 10 girls). 100% of students are boarding students. 2% are state residents. 24 states are represented in upper school student body.

Faculty School total: 14. In upper school: 8 men, 4 women; 3 have advanced degrees.

Subjects Offered Animal husbandry, art, biology, chemistry, choir, computer science, drama, economics, English, home economics, leatherworking, life skills, mathematics, metalworking, music, physical education, physics, science, social studies, Spanish, theater, woodworking.

Graduation Requirements Computer science, English, mathematics, physical education (includes health), science, social studies (includes history).

Special Academic Programs Accelerated programs; independent study; remedial reading and/or remedial writing; remedial math.

College Placement 40 students graduated in 2005; 11 went to college, including Houston Community College System; Humboldt State University; Ohio University; Southern Utah University; Texas Tech University; Virginia Military Institute. Other: 15 went to work, 4 entered military service, 6 entered a postgraduate year, 4 had other specific plans. Median SAT verbal: 430, median SAT math: 420. 15% scored over 600 on SAT verbal, 15% scored over 600 on SAT math.

Student Life Upper grades have specified standards of dress. Discipline rests primarily with faculty.

Summer Programs Remediation, sports, art/fine arts, computer instruction programs offered; session focuses on recreational therapy/academics; held on campus; accepts boys and girls; not open to students from other schools. 90 students usually enrolled.

Tuition and Aid 7-day tuition and room/board: $46,800. Guaranteed tuition plan. Tuition installment plan (Key Tuition Payment Plan, monthly payment plans). Tuition reduction for siblings available.

Admissions Traditional secondary-level entrance grade is 10. Deadline for receipt of application materials: none. No application fee required.

Athletics Intramural: aerobics (girls), aerobics/dance (g), aquatics (b,g), back packing (b,g), badminton (b), baseball (b,g), basketball (b,g), bicycling (b,g), billiards (b,g), bocce (b,g), bowling (b,g), cooperative games (b,g), croquet (b), equestrian sports (b,g), fishing (b,g), fitness (b,g), flag football (b), floor hockey (b), football (b), golf (b,g), hiking/backpacking (b,g), horseback riding (b,g), ice skating (b,g), indoor hockey (b), mountain biking (b,g), outdoor activities (b,g), outdoor adventure (b,g), outdoor education (b,g), outdoor recreation (b,g), outdoor skills (b,g), outdoors (b,g), physical fitness (b,g), ropes courses (b,g), skiing (downhill) (b,g), snowboarding (b,g), softball (b,g), strength & conditioning (b,g), swimming and diving (b,g), table tennis (b,g), touch football (b), volleyball (b,g), walking (b,g), weight training (b,g), whiffle ball (b), wilderness (b,g), wildernessways (b,g), wrestling (b). 1 PE instructor.

Computers Computers are regularly used in English, keyboarding, library, SAT preparation classes. Computer resources include on-campus library services, CD-ROMs, online commercial services.

Contact Mr. Layne Bagley, Director of Admissions. 435-638-7318 Ext. 155. Fax: 435-638-7582. E-mail: layneb@sorensonsranch.com. Web site: www.sorensonsranch.com.

See full description on page 1256.

SPRING CREEK LODGE ACADEMY

1342 Blue Slide Road
Thompson Falls, Montana 59873
Head of School: Larry Ward

General Information Coeducational boarding general academic school; primarily serves underachievers and individuals with emotional and behavioral problems. Ungraded, ages 13–18. Setting: rural. Nearest major city is Spokane, WA. 25-acre campus. 13 buildings on campus. Approved or accredited by Northwest Association of Schools and Colleges and Montana Department of Education.

Subjects Offered Independent study.

Special Academic Programs Accelerated programs; independent study.

Student Life Upper grades have specified standards of dress. Discipline rests equally with students and faculty.

Admissions Deadline for receipt of application materials: none. No application fee required. Interview required.

Athletics Coed Intramural: bowling, fishing, hiking/backpacking, kayaking, rafting, skiing (cross-country).

Contact Larry Ward, Headmaster. 406-827-4344. Fax: 406-827-4346. Web site: www.saveyourteen.com/index.html.

ANNOUNCEMENT FROM THE SCHOOL Spring Creek Lodge Academy is a special-needs residential high school located in the Cabinet Mountains of northwestern Montana. The school serves 500 students who have not met with success elsewhere because of lifestyle choices. Rigorous, self-directed academics and a safe, structured, family-supportive program comprise Spring Creek's worthwhile program of study.

SPRING RIDGE ACADEMY

13690 South Burton Road
Spring Valley, Arizona 86333
Head of School: Jean B. Courtney

General Information Girls' boarding college-preparatory and arts school; primarily serves individuals with emotional and behavioral problems. Grades 9–12. Founded: 1997. Setting: rural. Nearest major city is Phoenix. Students are housed in single-sex dormitories. 27-acre campus. 6 buildings on campus. Approved or accredited by North Central Association of Colleges and Schools and Arizona Department of Education. Total enrollment: 72. Upper school average class size: 12. Upper school faculty-student ratio: 1:9.

Upper School Student Profile Grade 9: 5 students (5 girls); Grade 10: 21 students (21 girls); Grade 11: 29 students (29 girls); Grade 12: 17 students (17 girls). 100% of students are boarding students. 3% are state residents. 19 states are represented in upper school student body.

Faculty School total: 8. In upper school: 5 men, 3 women; 4 have advanced degrees.

Subjects Offered 3-dimensional art, advanced chemistry, advanced math, algebra, art, art history, biology, chemistry, choral music, clayworking, computer applications, dance, drama, ecology, economics, English, geology, geometry, health, journalism, photography, physical education, pre-calculus, Spanish, U.S. government, U.S. history, women's studies, world history.

Graduation Requirements Advanced math, algebra, American literature, arts, biology, chemistry, dance, economics, English, foreign language, geometry, life management skills, physical education (includes health), physical fitness, U.S. government, U.S. history, world history.

Special Academic Programs Accelerated programs; independent study; remedial reading and/or remedial writing; remedial math.

College Placement 11 students graduated in 2005; 8 went to college, including San Jose State University. Other: 3 went to work.

Student Life Upper grades have uniform requirement, student council, honor system. Discipline rests primarily with faculty.

Summer Programs Remediation, enrichment, advancement, art/fine arts, computer instruction programs offered; session focuses on semester courses; held on campus; accepts girls; not open to students from other schools. 65 students usually enrolled. 2006 schedule: June 5 to July 28. Application deadline: none.

Tuition and Aid 7-day tuition and room/board: $60,000. Guaranteed tuition plan. Tuition installment plan (monthly payment plans).

Admissions Psychoeducational evaluation required. Deadline for receipt of application materials: none. No application fee required.

Athletics Intramural: aerobics/dance, basketball, cooperative games, dance, fitness, fitness walking, flag football, hiking/backpacking, jogging, modern dance, physical fitness, physical training, running, soccer, softball, strength & conditioning, track and field, volleyball, walking, weight training, yoga. 1 PE instructor.

Computers Computer resources include on-campus library services, CD-ROMs, DVD.

Contact Susan Coatney, Assistant Director of Admission. 928-632-4602 Ext. 116. Fax: 928-632-7661. E-mail: scoatney@springridgeacademy.com. Web site: www.springridgeacademy.com.

STANBRIDGE ACADEMY

515 East Poplar Avenue
San Mateo, California 94401
Head of School: Mr. Martin Procaccio

General Information Coeducational day school; primarily serves underachievers, students with learning disabilities, individuals with Attention Deficit Disorder, dyslexic students, and students with non-verbal learning disorders and Asperger's Syndrome. Grades K–12. Founded: 1982. Setting: suburban. Nearest major city is San Francisco. 1-acre campus. 1 building on campus. Approved or accredited by Western Association of Schools and Colleges. Endowment: $80,000. Total enrollment: 83. Upper school average class size: 8. Upper school faculty-student ratio: 1:8.

Upper School Student Profile Grade 9: 12 students (10 boys, 2 girls); Grade 10: 8 students (6 boys, 2 girls); Grade 11: 11 students (10 boys, 1 girl); Grade 12: 10 students (7 boys, 3 girls).

Faculty School total: 18. In upper school: 7 men, 2 women; 2 have advanced degrees.

Subjects Offered Advanced Placement courses, algebra, American government, biology, calculus-AP, career/college preparation, ceramics, college admission preparation, college counseling, college planning, electronic music, English, English literature, experiential education, filmmaking, general math, geography, geometry, health education, mathematics, physical education, physics, pragmatics, pre-algebra, pre-calculus, probability and statistics, science, social science, Spanish, U.S. history, video film production, world cultures, world history, writing workshop, yearbook.

Graduation Requirements Algebra, American government, biology, English, English composition, English literature, experiential education, foreign language, geometry, health and wellness, physical education (includes health), physical science, physics, trigonometry, U.S. history, visual and performing arts, world cultures.

Special Academic Programs Remedial reading and/or remedial writing; remedial math; programs in English, mathematics for dyslexic students.

College Placement 4 students graduated in 2005; 3 went to college, including American River College; California State University, Sacramento; College of San Mateo. Other: 1 went to work.

Student Life Upper grades have specified standards of dress, honor system. Discipline rests equally with students and faculty.

Summer Programs Remediation, enrichment programs offered; held on campus; accepts boys and girls; not open to students from other schools. 20 students usually enrolled. 2006 schedule: June 20 to July 31. Application deadline: none.

Tuition and Aid Day student tuition: $20,500. Tuition installment plan (monthly payment plans). Need-based scholarship grants available. In 2005–06, 10% of upper-school students received aid. Total amount of financial aid awarded in 2005–06: $80,000.

Admissions Traditional secondary-level entrance grade is 9. For fall 2005, 20 students applied for upper-level admission, 10 were accepted, 7 enrolled. Deadline for receipt of application materials: none. Application fee required: $200. On-campus interview required.

Athletics Coed Intramural: alpine skiing, back packing, billiards, canoeing/kayaking, fitness walking, hiking/backpacking, jogging, outdoor adventure, outdoor skills, snowboarding, snowshoeing, soccer. 2 PE instructors.

Computers Computers are regularly used in all classes. Computer network features include campus e-mail, CD-ROMs, Internet access, file transfer, DVD, wireless campus network.

Contact Lisa Rying, Director of Admissions and Marketing. 650-375-5862. Fax: 650-375-5861. E-mail: lrying@stanbridgeacademy.org. Web site: www.stanbridgeacademy.org.

STONE MOUNTAIN SCHOOL

126 Camp Elliott Road
Black Mountain, North Carolina 28711
Head of School: Sam Moore

General Information Boys' boarding arts school; primarily serves underachievers, students with learning disabilities, individuals with Attention Deficit Disorder, individuals with emotional and behavioral problems, and dyslexic students. Grades 6–12. Founded: 1990. Setting: rural. Nearest major city is Asheville. Students are housed in single-sex dormitories. 100-acre campus. 19 buildings on campus. Approved or accredited by North Carolina Department of Exceptional Children and North Carolina Department of Education. Total enrollment: 58. Upper school average class size: 5. Upper school faculty-student ratio: 1:4.

Upper School Student Profile Grade 9: 17 students (17 boys); Grade 10: 14 students (14 boys); Grade 11: 6 students (6 boys); Grade 12: 2 students (2 boys). 100% of students are boarding students. 10% are state residents. 22 states are represented in upper school student body. 3% are international students. International students from Canada.

Faculty School total: 10. In upper school: 8 men, 2 women; 2 have advanced degrees.

Subjects Offered 1½ elective credits, ACT preparation, algebra, art, biology, earth science, English, family studies, geography, geometry, government/civics, history, keyboarding, mathematics, natural resources management, physical education, physical science, pre-algebra, science, social studies, Spanish, U.S. history, world history.

Graduation Requirements English, mathematics, physical education (includes health), science, social studies (includes history).

Special Academic Programs Academic accommodation for the gifted; remedial reading and/or remedial writing; remedial math; programs in English, mathematics, general development for dyslexic students.

College Placement 3 students graduated in 2005; 2 went to college. Other: 1 went to work.

Student Life Upper grades have specified standards of dress. Discipline rests primarily with faculty.

Summer Programs Remediation, rigorous outdoor training programs offered; session focuses on remediation; held on campus; accepts boys; not open to students from other schools. 12 students usually enrolled. 2006 schedule: June 6 to July 20. Application deadline: none.

Tuition and Aid 7-day tuition and room/board: $47,000. Guaranteed tuition plan. Tuition installment plan (monthly payment plans). Middle-income loans available.

Admissions Traditional secondary-level entrance grade is 9. For fall 2005, 68 students applied for upper-level admission, 53 were accepted. Achievement tests and Wechsler Intelligence Scale for Children III required. Deadline for receipt of application materials: none. No application fee required. On-campus interview recommended.

Athletics Interscholastic: back packing, canoeing/kayaking, climbing, fencing, fishing, fly fishing, Frisbee, hiking/backpacking, kayaking, mountain biking, mountaineering, outdoor activities, outdoor adventure, outdoor education, outdoor recreation, outdoor skills, outdoors, paddling, physical fitness, rafting, rappelling, rock climbing, ropes courses, skiing (downhill), snowboarding, swimming and diving, ultimate Frisbee, volleyball, wall climbing, wilderness, wilderness survival; intramural: baseball, basketball, bicycling, billiards, crew, football, paddle tennis, sailing, skiing (downhill), soccer, swimming and diving, table tennis, track and field, volleyball.

Computers Computers are regularly used in English, history, mathematics, science classes. Computer resources include campus e-mail, CD-ROMs, Internet access.

Contact Paige Thomas, Admissions Coordinator. 828-669-8639. Fax: 828-669-2521. E-mail: pthomas@stonemountainschool.com. Web site: www.stonemountainschool.com.

SUMMIT PREPARATORY SCHOOL

1605 Danielson Road
Kalispell, Montana 59901
Head of School: Rick Johnson, MSW

General Information Coeducational boarding college-preparatory and arts school; primarily serves individuals with Attention Deficit Disorder, individuals with emotional and behavioral problems, and college bound students with mild learning disabilities. Ungraded, ages 14–18. Founded: 2003. Setting: rural. Students are housed in single-sex dormitories. 530-acre campus. 3 buildings on campus. Approved or accredited by Northwest Association of Accredited Schools and Montana Department of Education. Total enrollment: 64. Upper school average class size: 12. Upper school faculty-student ratio: 1:6.

Upper School Student Profile 100% of students are boarding students. 1% are state residents. 20 states are represented in upper school student body.

Faculty School total: 9. In upper school: 5 men, 4 women; 1 has an advanced degree.

Graduation Requirements Completion of therapeutic program, which includes individual, group and family therapy, and follows the student through a series of four therapeutic stages.

Special Academic Programs Advanced Placement exam preparation in 1 subject area; accelerated programs; independent study; study at local college for college credit; academic accommodation for the musically talented and the artistically talented; remedial math.

College Placement Colleges students went to include Marymount College, Palos Verdes, California; Middle Tennessee State University; Mississippi State University; San Antonio College; The University of Tennessee; University of North Dakota.

Student Life Upper grades have specified standards of dress, student council, honor system. Discipline rests equally with students and faculty.

Tuition and Aid Need-based scholarship grants, need-based loans available. In 2005–06, 15% of upper-school students received aid.

Admissions Traditional secondary-level entrance age is 16. Psychoeducational evaluation or WISC or WAIS required. Deadline for receipt of application materials: none. Application fee required: $150. Interview required.

Athletics Interscholastic: aerobics (boys, girls), aerobics/nautilus (b,g), aquatics (b,g), back packing (b,g), ball hockey (b,g), basketball (b,g), climbing (b,g), cooperative games (b,g), fishing (b,g), fitness (b,g), floor hockey (b,g), fly fishing (b,g), hiking/backpacking (b,g), martial arts (b,g), nordic skiing (b,g), outdoor activities (b,g), outdoor adventure (b,g), outdoor education (b,g), outdoor recreation (b,g), outdoor skills (b,g), physical fitness (b,g), rafting (b,g), rock climbing (b,g), running (b,g), skiing (cross-country) (b,g), skiing (downhill) (b,g), snowboarding (b,g), snowshoeing (b,g), strength & conditioning (b,g), swimming and diving (b,g), volleyball (b,g), walking (b,g), wall climbing (b,g), water volleyball (b,g), weight training (b,g), winter walking (b,g), yoga (b,g); coed interscholastic: cooperative games, martial arts, outdoor activities, outdoor adventure, outdoor education, outdoor recreation, outdoor skills, rafting, rock climbing.

Contact Judy Heleva, B.A., Admissions Assistant. 406-758-8113. Fax: 406-758-8150. E-mail: jheleva@summitprepschool.org. Web site: www.summitprepschool.org.

TEXAS NEUROREHAB CENTER

1106 West Dittmar Road
Austin, Texas 78745
Head of School: Ms. Holly Engleman

General Information Coeducational boarding general academic school; primarily serves underachievers, students with learning disabilities, individuals with Attention Deficit Disorder, individuals with emotional and behavioral problems, dyslexic students, students with Bipolar Disorder, and medically complex patients. Grades 2–12. Setting: suburban. Students are housed in coed dormitories. 110-acre campus. Approved or accredited by Joint Commission on Accreditation of Healthcare Organizations, Southern Association of Independent Schools, Texas Education Agency, and Texas Department of Education. Upper school faculty-student ratio: 1:10.

Upper School Student Profile 100% of students are boarding students.

Faculty In upper school: 5 men, 5 women; 5 have advanced degrees.

Special Academic Programs Programs in general development for dyslexic students.

Student Life Upper grades have specified standards of dress. Discipline rests primarily with faculty.

Admissions No application fee required.

Contact Ms. Angela Haywood, Registrar. 512-464-0200 Ext. 283. Fax: 512-464-0486. E-mail: angela.haywood@psyolutions.com. Web site: www.texasneurorehab.com.

THOMAS A. EDISON HIGH SCHOOL

9020 SW Beaverton Highway
Portland, Oregon 97225
Head of School: Patrick Maguire

General Information Coeducational day college-preparatory, general academic, arts, technology, and American Sign Language school; primarily serves underachievers, students with learning disabilities, individuals with Attention Deficit Disorder, dyslexic students, and students with Nonverbal Learning Disabilities and auditory processing disorders. Grades 9–12. Founded: 1973. Setting: suburban. 1 building on campus. Approved or accredited by Northwest Association of Accredited Schools and Oregon Department of Education. Endowment: $240,000. Upper school average class size: 7. Upper school faculty-student ratio: 1:4.

Faculty School total: 15. In upper school: 6 men, 9 women; 9 have advanced degrees.

Subjects Offered Adolescent issues, algebra, American government, American literature, American sign language, art, arts, audio visual/media, biology, boat building, bowling, business skills, career and personal planning, career education, career planning, career/college preparation, choir, community service, computer applications, computer education, computer keyboarding, computer literacy, economics, English, English composition, fine arts, French, general science, geometry, government, health, keyboarding, life management skills, mathematics, physical education, physics, pre-algebra, robotics, science, social science, social studies, Spanish-AP, speech, theater, U.S. government, U.S. history, world history, yearbook.

Graduation Requirements Arts and fine arts (art, music, dance, drama), business skills (includes word processing), mathematics, science, service learning/internship, social science, social studies (includes history). Community service is required.

Special Academic Programs Remedial reading and/or remedial writing; remedial math; programs in English, mathematics, general development for dyslexic students.

College Placement 12 students graduated in 2005; they went to Portland Community College.

Student Life Upper grades have specified standards of dress, student council, honor system. Discipline rests primarily with faculty.

Tuition and Aid Day student tuition: $14,860. Tuition installment plan (quarterly payments). Need-based scholarship grants available. In 2005–06, 26% of upper-school students received aid. Total amount of financial aid awarded in 2005–06: $155,000.

Admissions Traditional secondary-level entrance grade is 9. For fall 2005, 55 students applied for upper-level admission, 26 were accepted, 26 enrolled. Deadline for receipt of application materials: March 1. Application fee required: $50. On-campus interview required.

Athletics Intramural: baseball (boys, girls), basketball (b,g), cross-country running (b,g), football (b,g), golf (b,g), skiing (downhill) (b,g), soccer (b,g), softball (g), swimming and diving (b,g), tennis (b,g), track and field (b,g), volleyball (b,g); coed interscholastic: alpine skiing.

Computers Computers are regularly used in all classes. Computer network features include campus e-mail, CD-ROMs, Internet access, file transfer, office computer access, DVD, wireless campus network.

Contact Fran Dalbey, Office Administrator. 503-297-2336. Fax: 503-297-2527. E-mail: frand@taedisonhs.org. Web site: www.taedisonhs.org.

THREE SPRINGS

1131 Eagletree Lane
Huntsville, Alabama 35801
Head of School: Sharon Laney

General Information Coeducational boarding general academic, vocational, and experiential education school; primarily serves underachievers, students with learning disabilities, individuals with Attention Deficit Disorder, and individuals with emotional and behavioral problems. Grades 6–12. Founded: 1985. Setting: rural. Students are housed in single-sex dormitories. 100-acre campus. 5 buildings on campus. Approved or accredited by Association for Experiential Education, Georgia Accrediting Commission, Joint Commission on Accreditation of Healthcare Organizations, National Association of Private Schools for Exceptional Children, Southern Association of Colleges and Schools, Virginia Association of Independent Specialized Education Facilities, and Alabama Department of Education. Upper school average class size: 12. Upper school faculty-student ratio: 1:10.

Faculty School total: 14. In upper school: 4 men, 10 women; 10 have advanced degrees.

Subjects Offered Adolescent issues, computer science, English, general science, history, home economics, mathematics, psychology, social studies.

Graduation Requirements English, general math, history.

Student Life Upper grades have specified standards of dress, student council, honor system. Discipline rests equally with students and faculty.

Summer Programs Remediation, rigorous outdoor training programs offered; session focuses on continuation of year-round program; held on campus; accepts boys; not open to students from other schools.

Tuition and Aid Guaranteed tuition plan. Tuition installment plan (Key Tuition Payment Plan, monthly payment plans).

Admissions Deadline for receipt of application materials: none. Application fee required: $350. Interview recommended.

Athletics Interscholastic: baseball (boys), basketball (b), soccer (b,g), softball (g), track and field (b); intramural: bicycling (b,g), canoeing/kayaking (b,g), equestrian sports (b,g), hiking/backpacking (b,g), outdoor activities (b,g), outdoor adventure (b,g), outdoor education (b,g), outdoor recreation (b,g), ropes courses (b,g). 4 coaches.

Computers Computers are regularly used in English classes. Computer resources include on-campus library services, CD-ROMs.

Contact Mystique Williams, Referral Counselor. 888-758-4356. Fax: 256-880-7026. E-mail: mwilliams@threesprings.com. Web site: www.threesprings.com.

THREE SPRINGS/PRINCE MOUNTAIN ACADEMY

1022 Old Fjord Road
Blue Ridge, Georgia 30513
Head of School: Mrs. Susan Reynolds

General Information Boys' boarding college-preparatory, general academic, and vocational school; primarily serves underachievers, students with learning disabilities, individuals with Attention Deficit Disorder, individuals with emotional and behavioral problems, and dyslexic students. Grades 7–12. Founded: 1993. Setting: rural. Nearest major city is Atlanta. Students are housed in single-sex dormitories. 183-acre campus. 1 building on campus. Approved or accredited by Association for Experiential Education, Georgia Association of Private Schools for Exceptional Children, Southern Association of Colleges and Schools, and Georgia Department of Education. Upper school average class size: 7. Upper school faculty-student ratio: 1:4.

Upper School Student Profile 100% of students are boarding students. 90% are state residents. 12 states are represented in upper school student body.

Faculty School total: 7. In upper school: 2 men, 5 women; 3 have advanced degrees; 4 reside on campus.

Special Academic Programs Accelerated programs; independent study; remedial reading and/or remedial writing; remedial math; programs in English, mathematics, general development for dyslexic students.

Student Life Upper grades have specified standards of dress. Discipline rests equally with students and faculty.

Summer Programs Remediation, art/fine arts programs offered; session focuses on experiential education; held on campus; accepts boys; not open to students from other schools. 50 students usually enrolled.

Tuition and Aid Tuition reduction for siblings available.

Admissions Deadline for receipt of application materials: none. Application fee required: $350. Interview recommended.

Athletics Intramural: back packing, baseball, basketball, bowling, canoeing/kayaking, climbing, cooperative games, fitness, flag football, hiking/backpacking, mountaineering, outdoor activities, outdoor adventure, outdoor education, outdoor recreation, outdoor skills, outdoors, paddling, physical fitness, rafting, soccer, softball, swimming and diving, volleyball, walking.

Computers Computer resources include CD-ROMs, DVD.

Contact Ms. Donna Boyle, Director of Admissions. 706-632-6868. Fax: 706-632-6871. E-mail: dboyle@threesprings.com. Web site: www.threesprings.com.

TIMBER RIDGE SCHOOL

1463 New Hope Road
Cross Junction, Virginia 22625
Head of School: Dr. John M. Markwood

General Information Boys' boarding vocational school; primarily serves underachievers, students with learning disabilities, individuals with Attention Deficit Disorder, and individuals with emotional and behavioral problems. Grades 6–12. Founded: 1969. Setting: rural. Nearest major city is Washington, DC. Students are housed in single-sex dormitories. 217-acre campus. 14 buildings on campus. Approved or accredited by National Commission of Accreditation of Special Education Services, Virginia Association of Independent Specialized Education Facilities, and Virginia Department of Education. Total enrollment: 75. Upper school average class size: 9. Upper school faculty-student ratio: 1:9.

Upper School Student Profile Grade 9: 17 students (17 boys); Grade 10: 20 students (20 boys); Grade 11: 9 students (9 boys); Grade 12: 11 students (11 boys). 100% of students are boarding students. 75% are state residents. 2 states are represented in upper school student body.

Faculty School total: 12. In upper school: 9 men, 1 woman.

Subjects Offered Algebra, biology, carpentry, chemistry, computer-aided design, earth science, English, fine arts, geometry, health, horticulture, journalism, keyboarding, library studies, physical education, Spanish, U.S. government, unified math, Virginia government, word processing, world geography, world history.

Graduation Requirements Arts and fine arts (art, music, dance, drama), English, mathematics, physical education (includes health), science, social science, social studies (includes history).

Special Academic Programs Independent study; study at local college for college credit; remedial reading and/or remedial writing; remedial math; programs in English, mathematics for dyslexic students.

College Placement 4 students graduated in 2005. Other: 4 went to work.

Student Life Upper grades have specified standards of dress, student council. Discipline rests primarily with faculty.

Summer Programs Remediation programs offered; session focuses on remediation; held on campus; accepts boys; not open to students from other schools. 75 students usually enrolled. 2006 schedule: June to August. Application deadline: none.

Admissions Traditional secondary-level entrance grade is 10. For fall 2005, 110 students applied for upper-level admission, 70 were accepted, 44 enrolled. Comprehensive educational evaluation or Woodcock-Johnson Revised Achievement Test required. Deadline for receipt of application materials: none. No application fee required. Interview required.

Athletics Interscholastic: basketball (boys), football (b), soccer (b), softball (b), wrestling (b); intramural: basketball (b), kickball (b), outdoor activities (b), outdoor recreation (b), Special Olympics (b), strength & conditioning (b). 1 PE instructor.

Computers Computers are regularly used in English, foreign language, library studies, mathematics classes. Computer network features include campus e-mail, on-campus library services, CD-ROMs, Internet access, office computer access.

Contact Mr. Philip E. Arlotta, Director of Admissions. 877-877-3025 Ext. 123. Fax: 540-888-4511. E-mail: arlotta@trschool.org. Web site: www.timber-ridge-school.org.

TRIDENT ACADEMY

1455 Wakendaw Road
Mt. Pleasant, South Carolina 29464
Head of School: Col. Myron C. Harrington Jr.

General Information Coeducational day college-preparatory, general academic, arts, and technology school; primarily serves underachievers, students with learning disabilities, individuals with Attention Deficit Disorder, and dyslexic students. Grades K–PG. Founded: 1972. Setting: suburban. Nearest major city is Charleston. 11-acre campus. 2 buildings on campus. Approved or accredited by Academy of Orton-Gillingham Practitioners and Educators, South Carolina Independent School Association, Southern Association of Colleges and Schools, Southern Association of Independent Schools, and South Carolina Department of Education. Member of National Association of Independent Schools. Endowment: $600,000. Total enrollment: 131. Upper school average class size: 9. Upper school faculty-student ratio: 1:4.

Upper School Student Profile Grade 9: 9 students (8 boys, 1 girl); Grade 10: 15 students (11 boys, 4 girls); Grade 11: 10 students (5 boys, 5 girls); Grade 12: 16 students (12 boys, 4 girls).

Faculty School total: 45. In upper school: 3 men, 15 women; 12 have advanced degrees.

Subjects Offered Algebra, American history, American literature, art, biology, business, calculus, chemistry, computer science, creative writing, drama, drama performance, earth science, economics, English, English literature, European history, geography, geometry, government/civics, grammar, health, history, journalism, language development, marine biology, mathematics, physical education, physics, psychology, science, social studies, Spanish, typing, writing.

Graduation Requirements Computer science, English, foreign language, mathematics, physical education (includes health), science, social studies (includes history).

Special Academic Programs Remedial reading and/or remedial writing; remedial math; programs in English, mathematics, general development for dyslexic students.

College Placement 15 students graduated in 2005; 11 went to college, including Landmark College; Limestone College; Marshall University; Savannah College of Art and Design; Trident Technical College; Wingate University. Other: 4 went to work.

Student Life Upper grades have specified standards of dress, student council, honor system. Discipline rests primarily with faculty.

Summer Programs Remediation programs offered; session focuses on remediation; held on campus; accepts boys and girls; open to students from other schools. 20 students usually enrolled. 2006 schedule: June 5 to July 14. Application deadline: May 31.

Tuition and Aid Day student tuition: $14,600–$19,900. Tuition installment plan (Key Tuition Payment Plan, monthly payment plans). Merit scholarship grants, need-based scholarship grants available. In 2005–06, 4% of upper-school students received aid; total upper-school merit-scholarship money awarded: $3000. Total amount of financial aid awarded in 2005–06: $6500.

Admissions Traditional secondary-level entrance grade is 9. For fall 2005, 13 students applied for upper-level admission, 11 were accepted, 11 enrolled. Individual IQ, Achievement and behavior rating scale, psychoeducational evaluation and WISC III or other aptitude measures; standardized achievement test required. Deadline for receipt of application materials: none. Application fee required: $150. On-campus interview required.

Athletics Interscholastic: cheering (girls), volleyball (g); coed interscholastic: basketball, cooperative games, golf, soccer, tennis, weight lifting. 1 PE instructor.

Computers Computers are regularly used in all academic classes. Computer network features include campus e-mail, on-campus library services, CD-ROMs, online commercial services, Internet access, file transfer, office computer access.

Contact Carolyn Newton, Director of Admissions. 843-884-3494. Fax: 843-884-1483. E-mail: admissions@tridentacademy.com. Web site: www.tridentacademy.com.

ANNOUNCEMENT FROM THE SCHOOL Trident Academy serves children in grades K5–12 with average to above-average intelligence who have diagnosed learning disabilities and are free from emotional disturbance. The overall teacher-student ratio is 1:4. Multisensory teaching is used in a structured, individualized environment. Trident Academy: the right school for bright students who learn differently.

VALLEY VIEW SCHOOL

91 Oakham Road
PO Box 338
North Brookfield, Massachusetts 01535
See full description on page 1258.

THE VANGUARD SCHOOL

22000 Highway 27
Lake Wales, Florida 33859-6858
Head of School: James R. Moon, PhD

General Information Coeducational boarding and day college-preparatory and general academic school; primarily serves underachievers, students with learning disabilities, individuals with Attention Deficit Disorder, and dyslexic students. Grades 5–PG. Founded: 1966. Setting: small town. Nearest major city is Orlando. Students are housed in coed dormitories, single-sex dormitories, and an honors dorm. 75-acre campus. 13 buildings on campus. Approved or accredited by Florida Council of Independent Schools, Southern Association of Colleges and Schools, and The Association of Boarding Schools. Member of National Association of Independent Schools and Secondary School Admission Test Board. Endowment: $3.8 million. Total enrollment: 93. Upper school average class size: 10. Upper school faculty-student ratio: 1:10.

Upper School Student Profile Grade 9: 18 students (11 boys, 7 girls); Grade 10: 19 students (14 boys, 5 girls); Grade 11: 24 students (19 boys, 5 girls); Grade 12: 20 students (14 boys, 6 girls). 88% of students are boarding students. 38% are state residents. 17 states are represented in upper school student body. 33% are international students. International students from Bahamas, Bermuda, Cayman Islands, Jamaica, Trinidad and Tobago, and Turks and Caicos Islands; 11 other countries represented in student body.

Faculty School total: 27. In upper school: 4 men, 18 women; 9 have advanced degrees.

Subjects Offered ACT preparation, algebra, American history, American literature, art, biology, career exploration, chemistry, computer math, computer science, construction, consumer education, creative writing, driver education, earth science, economics, English, English literature, environmental science, fine arts, geography, geometry, government, government/civics, grammar, history, humanities, industrial arts, journalism, life management skills, mathematics, physical education, physical science, reading, science, social studies, study skills, world history, world literature.

Graduation Requirements Arts and fine arts (art, music, dance, drama), biology, career exploration, computer science, economics, English, government, life management skills, literature, mathematics, physical education (includes health), reading, science, social studies (includes history), student must be on level 3 of a 5-step level system.

Special Academic Programs Remedial reading and/or remedial writing; remedial math; programs in English, mathematics, general development for dyslexic students.

College Placement 20 students graduated in 2005; 17 went to college, including Florida International University; Johnson & Wales University; Lynn University; St. Thomas University; University of Central Florida; Valencia Community College. Other: 1 went to work, 1 entered military service, 1 entered a postgraduate year.

Student Life Upper grades have specified standards of dress, student council, honor system. Discipline rests primarily with faculty.

Tuition and Aid Day student tuition: $21,450; 7-day tuition and room/board: $38,675. Tuition installment plan (monthly payment plans, individually arranged payment plans). Need-based scholarship grants available. In 2005–06, 24% of upper-school students received aid. Total amount of financial aid awarded in 2005–06: $246,100.

Admissions Traditional secondary-level entrance grade is 9. For fall 2005, 57 students applied for upper-level admission, 40 were accepted, 21 enrolled. Wechsler Intelligence Scale for Children required. Deadline for receipt of application materials: none. Application fee required: $100. On-campus interview required.

Athletics Interscholastic: basketball (boys, girls), bowling (g), cheering (g), golf (b), running (b,g), soccer (b), tennis (b), track and field (b,g), volleyball (g); intramural: basketball (b,g); coed interscholastic: cross-country running, golf, soccer, tennis; coed intramural: basketball, canoeing/kayaking, fishing, fitness, golf, physical fitness, scuba diving, skateboarding, soccer, swimming and diving, walking, weight lifting. 5 PE instructors, 5 coaches.

Computers Computers are regularly used in all classes. Computer network features include campus e-mail, on-campus library services, CD-ROMs, online commercial services, Internet access, T1 access in dormitory rooms.

Contact Melanie Anderson, Director of Admissions. 863-676-6091. Fax: 863-676-8297. E-mail: vanadmin@vanguardschool.org. Web site: www.vanguardschool.org.

See full description on page 1260.

WALDEN PREPARATORY SCHOOL

14552 Montfort Road
Dallas, Texas 75254
Head of School: Pamala Ezell

General Information Coeducational day college-preparatory, general academic, arts, and technology school; primarily serves underachievers, students with learning disabilities, individuals with Attention Deficit Disorder, individuals with emotional and behavioral problems, dyslexic students, and students with chronic illness. Grades 9–12. Founded: 1970. Setting: urban. 3-acre campus. 2 buildings on campus.

Approved or accredited by Southern Association of Colleges and Schools and Texas Education Agency. Total enrollment: 50. Upper school average class size: 8. Upper school faculty-student ratio: 1:6.

Faculty School total: 8. In upper school: 2 men, 6 women; 4 have advanced degrees.

Subjects Offered 1½ elective credits, algebra, American history, anatomy, art, biology, calculus, chemistry, computer applications, computer science, economics, English, fine arts, French, geometry, government/civics, health, history, mathematics, photography, physical education, physics, pre-calculus, science, social science, social studies, Spanish, trigonometry, world history.

Graduation Requirements Computer science, English, mathematics, physical education (includes health), science, social science, social studies (includes history).

Special Academic Programs Honors section; accelerated programs; independent study; study at local college for college credit; academic accommodation for the gifted, the musically talented, and the artistically talented; remedial reading and/or remedial writing; remedial math; programs in English, mathematics, general development for dyslexic students.

College Placement Colleges students went to include Austin College; Stephen F. Austin State University; The University of Texas at Austin; University of Colorado at Denver and Health Sciences Center—Downtown Denver Campus; University of North Texas.

Student Life Discipline rests primarily with faculty.

Summer Programs Remediation, enrichment, advancement, art/fine arts, computer instruction programs offered; session focuses on academic enrichment; held on campus; accepts boys and girls; open to students from other schools. 20 students usually enrolled. 2006 schedule: June 1 to August 6. Application deadline: none.

Tuition and Aid Day student tuition: $8500. Tuition installment plan (monthly payment plans, individually arranged payment plans).

Admissions For fall 2005, 50 students applied for upper-level admission, 50 were accepted, 50 enrolled. Deadline for receipt of application materials: none. No application fee required. On-campus interview required.

Computers Computers are regularly used in art, English, foreign language, history, mathematics, science classes. Computer resources include on-campus library services, CD-ROMs, online commercial services, Internet access, office computer access, DVD, wireless campus network.

Contact Pamala Ezell, Director. 972-233-6883. Fax: 972-458-4553. E-mail: walden@wt.net. Web site: waldenprepschool.org.

WELLSPRING FOUNDATION

21 Arch Bridge Road
PO Box 370
Bethlehem, Connecticut 06751
Head of School: Herb Hall

General Information Coeducational boarding and day college-preparatory and general academic school; primarily serves individuals with Attention Deficit Disorder, individuals with emotional and behavioral problems, and students with eating disorders and Bipolar Disorder. Grades 2–12. Founded: 1977. Setting: rural. Nearest major city is Litchfield. Students are housed in single-sex dormitories. 13-acre campus. Approved or accredited by Connecticut Department of Children and Families, Joint Commission on Accreditation of Healthcare Organizations, and Connecticut Department of Education. Total enrollment: 52.

Faculty School total: 20.

Student Life Upper grades have specified standards of dress.

Summer Programs Enrichment programs offered; held on campus; accepts boys and girls; open to students from other schools. 36 students usually enrolled.

Admissions Deadline for receipt of application materials: none. No application fee required. On-campus interview required.

Computers Computer network features include CD-ROMs, Internet access, DVD.

Contact Christa Pelletier, Admissions Coordinator. 203-266-8022. Fax: 203-266-8030. E-mail: christap@wellspring.org. Web site: www.wellspring.org.

WESTVIEW SCHOOL

2000 Stoner Avenue
Los Angeles, California 90025
Head of School: Ms. Judy Gordon

General Information Coeducational day college-preparatory, general academic, and arts school; primarily serves underachievers, students with learning disabilities, and individuals with Attention Deficit Disorder. Grades 6–12. Founded: 1990. Setting: urban. 1 building on campus. Approved or accredited by Western Association of Schools and Colleges and California Department of Education. Total enrollment: 98. Upper school average class size: 10. Upper school faculty-student ratio: 1:8.

Upper School Student Profile Grade 9: 16 students (14 boys, 2 girls); Grade 10: 24 students (18 boys, 6 girls); Grade 11: 18 students (12 boys, 6 girls); Grade 12: 14 students (10 boys, 4 girls).

Faculty School total: 16. In upper school: 10 men, 6 women; 5 have advanced degrees.

Subjects Offered Algebra, American literature, analytic geometry, art, biology, calculus, career/college preparation, chemistry, civics, community service, critical writing, current events, drama, driver education, economics, English, fine arts, geometry, literature, mathematics, physical education, pre-algebra, science, social science, social studies, Spanish, study skills, U.S. history, word processing, world geography, world history, world literature, yearbook, yoga.

Graduation Requirements Algebra, arts and fine arts (art, music, dance, drama), biology, business skills (includes word processing), career/college preparation, chemistry, economics, English, foreign language, geometry, mathematics, physical education (includes health), science, social science, social studies (includes history), Spanish, U.S. government. Community service is required.

Special Academic Programs Study at local college for college credit; remedial reading and/or remedial writing; remedial math; programs in English, mathematics, general development for dyslexic students.

College Placement 20 students graduated in 2005; 18 went to college, including California State University, Northridge; Moorpark College; Santa Barbara City College; Santa Monica College; University of Michigan; West Los Angeles College. Other: 2 went to work.

Student Life Upper grades have specified standards of dress, student council. Discipline rests primarily with faculty.

Summer Programs Remediation, enrichment, sports, art/fine arts, computer instruction programs offered; session focuses on general academics; held on campus; accepts boys and girls; open to students from other schools. 60 students usually enrolled. 2006 schedule: July 5 to August 15. Application deadline: none.

Tuition and Aid Day student tuition: $28,000. Tuition installment plan (monthly payment plans, individually arranged payment plans).

Admissions Traditional secondary-level entrance grade is 9. For fall 2005, 120 students applied for upper-level admission, 30 were accepted, 30 enrolled. Kaufman Test of Educational Achievement or Wechsler Individual Achievement Test required. Deadline for receipt of application materials: none. No application fee required. On-campus interview required.

Athletics Coed Interscholastic: baseball, basketball, golf.

Computers Computers are regularly used in all academic, data processing, video film production, Web site design classes. Computer resources include campus e-mail, CD-ROMs, Internet access, office computer access.

Contact Ms. Judy Gordon, Executive Director. 310-478-5544 Ext. 203. Fax: 310-473-5235. E-mail: jgordon@westviewschool.com. Web site: www.westviewschool.com.

ANNOUNCEMENT FROM THE SCHOOL Westview serves bright adolescents with learning differences, ADD, and/or mild emotional problems. The academically challenging curriculum is designed to meet a wide range of academic needs and learning styles. Much enrichment is offered: art, drama, computer lab, sports competition, yearbook, and more. Positive behavioral and therapeutic programs are designed to build self-esteem.

WILLOW HILL SCHOOL

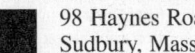

98 Haynes Road
Sudbury, Massachusetts 01776
Head of School: Dr. Rhonda Taft-Farrell

General Information Coeducational day college-preparatory, arts, and technology school; primarily serves underachievers, students with learning disabilities, individuals with Attention Deficit Disorder, dyslexic students, and students with non-verbal learning disorders and Asperger's Syndrome. Grades 6–12. Founded: 1970. Setting: suburban. Nearest major city is Boston. 26-acre campus. 3 buildings on campus. Approved or accredited by Association of Independent Schools in New England, New England Association of Schools and Colleges, and Massachusetts Department of Education. Member of National Association of Independent Schools and Secondary School Admission Test Board. Endowment: $686,672. Total enrollment: 61. Upper school average class size: 8. Upper school faculty-student ratio: 1:3.

Upper School Student Profile Grade 9: 11 students (10 boys, 1 girl); Grade 10: 8 students (6 boys, 2 girls); Grade 11: 12 students (6 boys, 6 girls); Grade 12: 9 students (6 boys, 3 girls).

Faculty School total: 17. In upper school: 6 men, 11 women; 11 have advanced degrees.

Subjects Offered 20th century world history, algebra, American government, American history, American literature, art, biology, career/college preparation, chemistry, computer science, computer technologies, conceptual physics, consumer law, creative writing, decision making skills, discrete mathematics, drama, dramatic arts, earth science, English, English composition, English literature, French, geography, geometry, grammar, integrated science, keyboarding/computer, library studies, life science, math applications, mathematics, outdoor education, physical education, physical science, pragmatics, pre-algebra, pre-calculus, science, senior composition, social studies, study skills, technology, U.S. history, U.S. literature, world history, World War II.

Graduation Requirements Art, computer keyboarding, drama, English composition, literature, mathematics, physical education (includes health), science, social studies (includes history), wilderness/outdoor program.

Special Academic Programs Independent study; study at local college for college credit; academic accommodation for the artistically talented; remedial reading and/or remedial writing; remedial math; programs in English, mathematics, general development for dyslexic students.

College Placement 6 students graduated in 2005; all went to college, including New England College; Worcester Polytechnic Institute.

Student Life Discipline rests primarily with faculty.

Tuition and Aid Day student tuition: $42,530. Tuition installment plan (Academic Management Services Plan). PrepGATE Loans available.

Admissions Traditional secondary-level entrance grade is 9. For fall 2005, 35 students applied for upper-level admission, 8 were accepted, 7 enrolled. Comprehensive educational evaluation and WISC or WAIS required. Deadline for receipt of application materials: none. No application fee required. On-campus interview required.

Athletics Coed Interscholastic: basketball, soccer, track and field; coed intramural: back packing, basketball, bicycling, canoeing/kayaking, climbing, cooperative games, croquet, cross-country running, floor hockey, Frisbee, hiking/backpacking, horseshoes, kayaking, lacrosse, martial arts, mountain biking, outdoor activities, outdoor education, rock climbing, snowshoeing, soccer, track and field, volleyball, wall climbing. 1 PE instructor.

Computers Computers are regularly used in all academic, art, library science classes. Computer network features include on-campus library services, CD-ROMs, Internet access.

Contact Nancy S. Brody, Director of Admissions. 978-443-2581. Fax: 978-443-7560. E-mail: nbrody@willowhillschool.org. Web site: www.willowhillschool.org.

WINSTON PREPARATORY SCHOOL

126 West 17th Street
New York, New York 10011
Head of School: Mr. Scott Bezsylko

petersons.com

General Information Coeducational day college-preparatory and arts school; primarily serves underachievers, students with learning disabilities, individuals with Attention Deficit Disorder, and dyslexic students. Grades 6–12. Founded: 1981. Setting: urban. 1 building on campus. Approved or accredited by New York State Association of Independent Schools. Member of National Association of Independent Schools. Language of instruction: English. Total enrollment: 220. Upper school average class size: 10. Upper school faculty-student ratio: 1:3.

Faculty School total: 66. In upper school: 24 men, 42 women; 63 have advanced degrees.

Subjects Offered Algebra, American history, American literature, art, biology, chemistry, community service, creative writing, drama, earth science, ecology, environmental systems, economics and history, English, English literature, European history, expository writing, fine arts, geography, geometry, government/civics, grammar, health, history, mathematics, music, physical education, physics, science, social skills, social studies, speech, theater, trigonometry, U.S. history, world history, world literature, writing.

Graduation Requirements Arts and fine arts (art, music, dance, drama), English, history, mathematics, physical education (includes health), science. Community service is required.

Special Academic Programs Honors section; remedial reading and/or remedial writing; remedial math; programs in English, mathematics, general development for dyslexic students.

Student Life Upper grades have specified standards of dress, student council. Discipline rests primarily with faculty.

Tuition and Aid Day student tuition: $35,500. Tuition installment plan (SMART Tuition Payment Plan, monthly payment plans, individually arranged payment plans). Need-based scholarship grants available. In 2004–05, 20% of upper-school students received aid.

Admissions Achievement tests, battery of testing done through outside agency and Wechsler Intelligence Scale for Children required. Deadline for receipt of application materials: none. Application fee required: $70. On-campus interview required.

Athletics Coed Interscholastic: basketball, cross-country running, softball; coed intramural: basketball, physical fitness, physical training, walking, yoga. 2 PE instructors.

Computers Computers are regularly used in art, English, history, mathematics, science classes. Computer network features include CD-ROMs, Internet access, file transfer.

Contact Ms. Erinn Skeffington, Director of Admissions. 646-638-2705 Ext. 634. Fax: 646-638-2706. E-mail: eskeffington@winstonprep.edu.

ANNOUNCEMENT FROM THE SCHOOL Winston Prep is a highly individualized and responsive setting for high-potential middle and high school students with learning differences, such as language-based learning difficulties, nonverbal learning difficulties, and attention deficit problems. The Winston Prep program is designed to challenge each student's strengths while developing the

essentials of reading, writing, mathematics, organization, and study skills. Independence is at the core of Winston's philosophy. To this end, individualization and the rich curricular experience happen in a climate of unwavering focus on maximizing independence and self-reliance. Each individualized educational program is based upon a continuously modified understanding of each student's dynamic learning profile that evolves as the student progresses and matures. Within the curriculum, skills are taught explicitly and directly, including 80 minutes of daily instruction in English and mathematics through grade 12. Small classes of 8–12 students help to create a comfortable learning environment and facilitate the individualization of course work. In addition to classes, students participate in a daily one-to-one instructional period called Focus, designed to serve as the diagnostic, instructional, and mentoring centerpiece of their experience. Education does not end with academics at Winston. Fostering the social and emotional growth of the students is considered an essential part of development and is addressed through specific course work and guidance in every grade. Current enrollment is 246. Art, drama, gym, and a variety of challenging enrichment choices are offered within the school day, and interscholastic athletic programs are available after school. At the high-school level, students with appropriate levels of skill mastery may participate in an academic honors program and in college courses. One hundred percent of June 2004 graduates attend college, and many students are able to mainstream before graduating.

THE WINSTON SCHOOL

5707 Royal Lane
Dallas, Texas 75229
Head of School: Dr. Pamela K. Murfin

petersons.com

General Information Coeducational day college-preparatory, arts, technology, and science school; primarily serves students with learning disabilities, individuals with Attention Deficit Disorder, and dyslexic students. Grades 1–12. Founded: 1975. Setting: suburban. 4-acre campus. 2 buildings on campus. Approved or accredited by Independent Schools Association of the Southwest and Texas Department of Education. Member of National Association of Independent Schools. Endowment: $3.4 million. Total enrollment: 239. Upper school average class size: 10. Upper school faculty-student ratio: 1:6.
Upper School Student Profile Grade 9: 34 students (25 boys, 9 girls); Grade 10: 38 students (27 boys, 11 girls); Grade 11: 40 students (29 boys, 11 girls); Grade 12: 22 students (17 boys, 5 girls).
Faculty School total: 38. In upper school: 13 men, 8 women; 12 have advanced degrees.
Subjects Offered Algebra, American history, American literature, archaeology, astronomy, biology, ceramics, chemistry, computer science, drama, economics, engineering, English, English literature, film, fine arts, geometry, government/civics, grammar, health, journalism, Latin, photography, physical education, physics, poetry, pre-calculus, Spanish, speech, technical theater, theater, trigonometry, world history, world literature, writing.
Graduation Requirements Computer science, English, foreign language, mathematics, physical education (includes health), science, social science, social studies (includes history).
Special Academic Programs Accelerated programs; independent study; study at local college for college credit; programs in English, mathematics, general development for dyslexic students.
College Placement 28 students graduated in 2005; 25 went to college, including Southern Methodist University; St. Edward's University; Texas A&M University; Texas Tech University; The University of Texas at Austin; Westminster College. Other: 2 went to work, 1 had other specific plans. Mean SAT verbal: 580, mean SAT math: 537, mean composite ACT: 24. 36% scored over 600 on SAT verbal, 25% scored over 600 on SAT math, 7% scored over 26 on composite ACT.
Student Life Upper grades have specified standards of dress, student council. Discipline rests primarily with faculty.
Summer Programs Remediation, enrichment, advancement, sports, art/fine arts, rigorous outdoor training, computer instruction programs offered; session focuses on earning academic credit; held on campus; accepts boys and girls; open to students from other schools. 80 students usually enrolled. 2006 schedule: June 5 to July 10.
Tuition and Aid Day student tuition: $17,750. Tuition installment plan (Key Tuition Payment Plan, monthly payment plans, individually arranged payment plans). Need-based scholarship grants available. In 2005–06, 18% of upper-school students received aid. Total amount of financial aid awarded in 2005–06: $269,495.
Admissions Traditional secondary-level entrance grade is 9. For fall 2005, 29 students applied for upper-level admission, 19 were accepted, 19 enrolled. Psycho-educational evaluation required. Deadline for receipt of application materials: none. Application fee required: $150. On-campus interview required.
Athletics Interscholastic: baseball (boys), basketball (b,g), fitness (b,g), flag football (b), football (b), softball (g), volleyball (g); coed interscholastic: cheering, fitness, golf, outdoor education, physical fitness, soccer, strength & conditioning, tennis, weight training. 2 PE instructors.

Computers Computers are regularly used in all academic classes. Computer resources include CD-ROMs, Internet access, DVD.
Contact Amy C. Smith, Director of Admission. 214-691-6950. Fax: 214-691-1509. E-mail: amy_smith@winston-school.org.

ANNOUNCEMENT FROM THE SCHOOL Founded in 1975, The Winston School is a coeducational, college-preparatory school enrolling *bright students who learn differently®*. Students are of average to superior intelligence in grades 1–12, with a diagnosed learning difference and/or ADHD. Based on diagnostic testing and ongoing monitoring, faculty members and staff formulate individualized academic programs that inspire students' self-confidence and self-reliance with full parental involvement. The Winston School is accredited by the Independent School Association of the Southwest and is a member of the National Association of Independent Schools. Visit www.winston-school.org.

THE WINSTON SCHOOL SAN ANTONIO

8565 Ewing Halsell Drive
San Antonio, Texas 78229
Head of School: Dr. Charles J. Karulak

General Information Coeducational day college-preparatory, general academic, arts, and technology school; primarily serves students with learning disabilities, individuals with Attention Deficit Disorder, and dyslexic students. Grades K–12. Founded: 1985. Setting: urban. 16-acre campus. 2 buildings on campus. Approved or accredited by Independent Schools Association of the Southwest, Southern Association of Colleges and Schools, Texas Education Agency, and Texas Department of Education. Total enrollment: 170. Upper school average class size: 10. Upper school faculty-student ratio: 1:10.
Upper School Student Profile Grade 9: 18 students (12 boys, 6 girls); Grade 10: 13 students (10 boys, 3 girls); Grade 11: 15 students (13 boys, 2 girls); Grade 12: 14 students (7 boys, 7 girls).
Faculty School total: 25. In upper school: 5 men, 8 women; 5 have advanced degrees.
Subjects Offered Algebra, American history, anatomy and physiology, art, biology, calculus, chemistry, computer literacy, economics, English, geometry, government, health, journalism, multimedia, music, photography, physical education, physical science, physics, pre-algebra, pre-calculus, reading, Spanish, world geography, world history, writing workshop.
Graduation Requirements Arts and fine arts (art, music, dance, drama), computer science, English, foreign language, mathematics, physical education (includes health), social science, 20 hours of community service per year.
Special Academic Programs Remedial reading and/or remedial writing; remedial math; programs in English, mathematics, general development for dyslexic students.
College Placement 20 students graduated in 2005; 15 went to college, including San Antonio College; The University of Texas at San Antonio; University of the Incarnate Word. Other: 5 went to work.
Student Life Upper grades have uniform requirement, student council. Discipline rests primarily with faculty.
Summer Programs Remediation, advancement, computer instruction programs offered; session focuses on high school classes for credit; held on campus; accepts boys and girls; open to students from other schools. 50 students usually enrolled. 2006 schedule: June 12 to July 7. Application deadline: May 30.
Tuition and Aid Day student tuition: $13,500. Tuition installment plan (individually arranged payment plans). Need-based scholarship grants available. In 2005–06, 25% of upper-school students received aid.
Admissions Traditional secondary-level entrance grade is 9. For fall 2005, 73 students applied for upper-level admission, 63 were accepted, 60 enrolled. Individual IQ, Achievement and behavior rating scale and WISC-R or WISC-III required. Deadline for receipt of application materials: none. Application fee required: $100. Interview required.
Athletics Interscholastic: aquatics (boys), basketball (b,g), football (b), volleyball (g); intramural: aquatics (b); coed interscholastic: baseball, cheering, cross-country running, golf, soccer, softball, track and field; coed intramural: ballet, cheering, dance, golf, outdoor education, physical fitness, physical training, tennis, track and field. 1 PE instructor.
Computers Computers are regularly used in all academic classes. Computer network features include campus e-mail, on-campus library services, CD-ROMs, Internet access, file transfer, office computer access, DVD, wireless campus network.
Contact Ms. Julie A. Saboe, Director of Admissions. 210-615-6544. Fax: 210-615-6627. E-mail: saboe@winston-sa.org.

WOODBRIDGE ACADEMY

251 West Second Street
Lexington, Kentucky 40507
Head of School: Mrs. Elizabeth L. Goldsworthy

General Information Coeducational day college-preparatory, arts, and technology school; primarily serves underachievers, students with learning disabilities, individu-

als with Attention Deficit Disorder, and dyslexic students. Grades 6–12. Founded: 1986. Setting: urban. 1-acre campus. 1 building on campus. Approved or accredited by Kentucky Department of Education. Total enrollment: 12. Upper school faculty-student ratio: 1:8.

Upper School Student Profile Grade 9: 1 student (1 boy); Grade 10: 3 students (1 boy, 2 girls); Grade 11: 2 students (1 boy, 1 girl); Grade 12: 1 student (1 girl).

Faculty School total: 3. In upper school: 1 man, 2 women; 2 have advanced degrees.

Subjects Offered General science, reading, reading/study skills, research skills, science and technology, science project, social sciences, social skills, social studies, society and culture, Spanish, standard curriculum.

Graduation Requirements Computers, English, foreign language, mathematics, physical education (includes health), science, social studies (includes history).

Special Academic Programs Independent study; academic accommodation for the gifted, the musically talented, and the artistically talented; remedial reading and/or remedial writing; remedial math; programs in English, mathematics, general development for dyslexic students.

College Placement 2 students graduated in 2005. Other: 2 went to work.

Student Life Upper grades have uniform requirement, student council, honor system. Discipline rests equally with students and faculty.

Summer Programs Remediation, enrichment, art/fine arts, computer instruction programs offered; session focuses on high school credit courses; held on campus; accepts boys and girls; open to students from other schools. 20 students usually enrolled. 2006 schedule: July 1 to July 31. Application deadline: June 10.

Tuition and Aid Day student tuition: $8500. Tuition installment plan (monthly payment plans). Tuition reduction for siblings available. In 2005–06, 20% of upper-school students received aid.

Admissions Traditional secondary-level entrance grade is 9. Kaufman Test of Educational Achievement required. Deadline for receipt of application materials: none. Application fee required: $100. On-campus interview required.

Computers Computers are regularly used in current events, English, French, history, humanities, independent study, information technology, introduction to technology, journalism, language development, learning cognition, life skills, literacy, mathematics, media arts, photography, reading, research skills, SAT preparation, science, social science, study skills, technology, writing, yearbook classes. Computer network features include campus e-mail, CD-ROMs, Internet access, file transfer, DVD, wireless campus network.

Contact Mrs. Carole Spicer, Administrative Assistant. 859-252-3000. Fax: 859-252-0915. E-mail: info@woodbridgeacademy.com. Web site: www.woodbridgeacademy.com.

WOODCLIFF ACADEMY

1345 Campus Parkway
Wall, New Jersey 07753
Head of School: Dr. Elizabeth J. Ferraro

General Information Coeducational day college-preparatory and general academic school; primarily serves underachievers, students with learning disabilities, individuals with Attention Deficit Disorder, individuals with emotional and behavioral problems, and dyslexic students. Grades 2–12. Founded: 1949. Setting: suburban. Nearest major city is Freehold. 1 building on campus. Approved or accredited by Middle States Association of Colleges and Schools, New York State Board of Regents, and New Jersey Department of Education. Member of Secondary School Admission Test Board. Total enrollment: 69. Upper school average class size: 8. Upper school faculty-student ratio: 1:3.

Faculty School total: 33. In upper school: 10 men, 16 women; 8 have advanced degrees.

Subjects Offered Algebra, American history, American literature, art, biology, chemistry, computer programming, computer science, creative writing, earth science, English, English literature, environmental science, expository writing, fine arts, geography, geometry, government/civics, grammar, health, history, logic, mathematics, music, physical education, physical science, science, social studies, Spanish, speech, statistics, trigonometry, typing, world history, world literature, writing.

Graduation Requirements Arts and fine arts (art, music, dance, drama), computer science, English, mathematics, physical education (includes health), science, social studies (includes history).

Special Academic Programs Academic accommodation for the gifted; remedial reading and/or remedial writing; remedial math; programs in English, mathematics, general development for dyslexic students.

College Placement 7 students graduated in 2005; 5 went to college, including Montclair State University. Other: 1 went to work, 1 entered military service.

Student Life Upper grades have specified standards of dress, student council. Discipline rests primarily with faculty.

Tuition and Aid Day student tuition: $36,000. Tuition paid by local school districts available.

Admissions Traditional secondary-level entrance grade is 9. For fall 2005, 70 students applied for upper-level admission, 10 were accepted, 10 enrolled. Deadline for receipt of application materials: none. No application fee required. On-campus interview required.

Athletics Coed Interscholastic: basketball, bowling, floor hockey, hiking/backpacking, hockey, indoor soccer, jogging, running, softball, strength & conditioning. 2 PE instructors.

Computers Computers are regularly used in all academic, writing classes. Computer network features include CD-ROMs, Internet access, office computer access.

Contact Laurie Noch, Psychologist/Clinical Director. 732-751-0240. Fax: 732-751-0243. E-mail: mail@woodcliff.com. Web site: www.woodcliff.com.

ACADEMY AT SWIFT RIVER

Cummington, Massachusetts

ACADEMY
AT
SWIFT RIVER
sssss

Type: Coeducational boarding college-preparatory therapeutic school
Grades: 9–12
Enrollment: 133
Head of School: Don Vardell, Executive Director

THE SCHOOL

The Academy at Swift River (ASR), a year-round college-preparatory boarding school for adolescents who are experiencing difficulties in more traditional environments, opened in 1997. The Academy combines the best features of established programs with the needs of today's families. Led by a visionary and highly dedicated team, ASR provides an innovative fifteen-month program that integrates college-preparatory academics with therapeutic support. ASR is a compassionate educational community with a commitment to respect the dignity and integrity of each individual.

ASR is ideally located near the cultural and educational resources of the Berkshires and the Five College area, which is home to the Tanglewood Music Center, Jacob's Pillow Dance Festival, Smith College, Mount Holyoke College, and Hampshire College. Situated on 636 rolling acres of forests, the campus was formerly operated as an inn for cross-country skiers. The facility includes 16 miles of cross-country trails, tennis and basketball courts, a fitness center, and an arts and activities center. Downhill skiing and rafting sites are located within 15 minutes of the school.

ACADEMIC PROGRAMS

The ASR program begins with Passages, a flexible four- to six-week orientation program that helps students acclimate to campus and academic life. For the majority of students coming from wilderness programs, Passages offers an experiential bridge to develop their new skills. Finally, the one-year Alumni Services portion of the ASR program assists and supports graduates as they transition back to their home, boarding school, or college environments. Regular telephone contact is provided to students and families during this year.

ASR strives to offer a memorable and challenging high school experience, drawing from the best of traditional college-preparatory curricula, combined with innovative, individualized approaches to learning. Students come to ASR with varying levels of success in their educational careers. Some have maintained consistently high grades; others have not performed to their fullest potential in a number of years. Regardless, students leave ASR with a clear sense of achievement and an understanding of who they are as learners.

The Academy's curriculum is based on the Massachusetts Frameworks, ensuring a liberal arts course of study in the major content areas of mathematics, natural sciences, humanities, and the visual arts. The core curriculum is combined with electives from these areas as well as extracurricular opportunities in athletics, community service learning, and the performing arts. Classes are taught in ten-week trimesters, which continue throughout the calendar year. The result is a well-rounded, rigorous education that prepares students for advanced college study and beyond. ASR

is proud to be able to state that 100 percent of its students who graduate high school are able to pursue higher education at the college or university of their choice.

Twenty-six credits are required for completion of a high school diploma. The following courses are available during the fifteen-month program: English language arts, social science, mathematics, science, history, government, physical education, and organizational skills, plus a variety of electives that may include photography, drawing, modern technology, dance, mythology, martial arts, and independent study.

Mandatory supervised study halls are included in the daily schedule. Students are graded daily for their participation, completion of daily assignments, and effort. The Academic Department uses a variety of methods to evaluate student success. These well-designed instruments include individual and peer-group assessments and written and oral evaluations as well as daily quizzes, which include short-answer or multiple-choice questions.

The Academy's school year consists of five trimesters of ten weeks each and a number of Alternative Curriculum Weeks (ACW). Formal progress reports are given to students, parents, and referring educational consultants twice each trimester. The grading system is as follows: A=4 points, B=3 points, and C=2 points. Each trimester, ⅓ credit is awarded for each course that is completed with a grade of C- or better.

Students are encouraged to take the PSAT in the tenth grade and the Princeton Review SAT prep class to prepare for the SAT. Scheduling arrangements for the SAT, ACT, and SSAT are made by the Academy. All ASR students take the SAT on campus.

ASR's individualized approach is relational in nature rather than confrontational, allowing the student to internalize change instead of superficially demonstrating compliance. The Academy does this through a cognitive behavioral and psychodynamic approach that is best suited to serve a student who demonstrates the ability to reflect and develop insight.

A Licensed Substance Abuse Clinician oversees individual, group, and Twelve Step programming to address addiction issues. Group therapy is led three times per week by master's-level therapists. Individual therapy is held weekly for all students by master's-level therapists.

FACULTY AND ADVISERS

The faculty members of the Academy bring dedication and many years of solid experience in the field of therapeutic education to the students. Throughout the program, academic and counseling staff members work together in an integrated approach of intellectual, emotional, and experiential learning that assists students in integrating all areas of growth and development. The Acad-

emy offers a seasoned Leadership Team that is made up of Executive, Clinical, Educational Services, and Admission Directors.

Academy Executive Director Don Vardell holds a B.A. in psychology and an M.S. from the University of Tennessee. Don has served as the Executive Director of Peninsula Village, a long-term residential treatment center for adolescents in Tennessee. For much of his career, he has been affiliated with the American Red Cross; he currently serves as an executive-level volunteer as National Chair, Health & Safety Services.

Academy Clinical Director Frank Bartolomeo is a Ph.D. candidate at Simmons College in Boston, where his research has focused on group therapy in therapeutic schools. He holds a master's degree in social work from Boston University. He brings eighteen years of experience working with adolescents in a variety of settings, including schools, residential treatment centers, outpatient clinics, psychiatric hospitals, and private practice. He has received extensive postgraduate training in the areas of group psychotherapy, adolescent psychotherapy, and the assessment and treatment of psychological trauma.

Educational Services Director Josh Becker is a candidate for an Ed.D. He has master's degrees in business administration from Boston University and in education from the University of Massachusetts, focusing on school counseling. His doctoral work in education is in progress and focuses on child and adolescent development. Josh's background includes more than sixteen years of teaching experience, predominantly of adolescents and young adults in private and public settings.

Admissions Director Rhonda Papallo holds a B.S. in therapeutic recreation from Southern Connecticut State University. She has worked as a trainer and therapist with Project Adventure and the Stonington Institute. Her work with students and families during the transition process has gained industrywide recognition.

ASR has a staff of experienced secondary-level teachers, master's-level therapists, bachelor's-level Residential Mentors, experiential education instructors, a nursing department, and a Medical Director. Three consulting adolescent psychiatrists are regularly available to students and families.

COLLEGE PLACEMENT

ASR offers the Princeton Review SAT prep class for juniors and seniors; once this class is completed, students take the SAT in preparation for college. Students who complete the ASR program at an appropriate age to enter college are assisted with the application process for the institutions of their choice. Students who complete their high school education while still involved in the therapeutic curriculum may take college courses through the local community college.

STUDENT BODY AND CONDUCT

The Academy can accommodate a maximum enrollment of 133 students. The program team structure ensures that the strong, positive peer culture that is central to the ASR curriculum is always present on campus. Positive peer influence and leadership are emphasized. Students serve as dorm leaders, interns, Ambassadors, and tutors. Students utilize school forums for both conflict resolution and peer support.

ACADEMIC FACILITIES

The academic building houses seven classrooms, two science laboratories, the computer center, and offices for teachers and the Director of Educational Services. A separate multipurpose building houses a center for arts and athletics, including an art studio, kilns, a darkroom, a gymnasium, a fitness center, and two additional classrooms.

BOARDING AND GENERAL FACILITIES

The main building consists of administrative offices, the dining hall and food-preparation areas, and separate dormitory wings for boys and girls. Two separate dormitory buildings, also gender segregated, are located adjacent to the main building. Staff housing is also available on campus. Each spacious dorm room, some of them split-level, houses 4 to 7 students. Each room has a private bath and adequate wardrobe and drawer space for each student. The rooms provide a cozy, secure atmosphere that nurtures healthy relationships that are provided by a positive peer culture. A strong work ethic is fostered by the Academy, and students are required to maintain their own rooms. Students also wash and dry the dishes and clean the kitchen after each meal and participate in general campus clean-up on Saturday mornings.

ATHLETICS

A large variety of activities, including running, soccer, basketball, biking, hiking, outdoor swimming, volleyball, Ultimate Frisbee, and tennis, are offered. Campus facilities include a fully equipped fitness center and a gymnasium. Students compete on the club level with other schools in lacrosse, basketball, and soccer. The ASR Adventure Program offers students the opportunity to explore rock climbing, kayaking, and skiing.

EXTRACURRICULAR OPPORTUNITIES

Located at the center of the Five College area, as well as in a cultural mecca for music, theater, and dance, the Academy is able to provide students with many extracurricular opportunities. Nearby lectures, workshops, and various kinds of performances offer enriching outings. In keeping with the Academy's emphasis on service to others, opportunities are also provided for students to engage in various community service projects. Recreational trips to nearby state parks, bowling alleys, miniature golf courses, and other just-for-fun spots round out the variety of extracurricular opportunities for students.

Melissa Hale, ASR's Student Life Supervisor, is committed to providing recreational activities for students on campus. Talent shows, "coffeehouse" poetry nights, dances, and more can be found by checking the activity board. The Academy is about community, and students look forward to Wednesday night family-style dinners. Students are encouraged to create proposals and develop creative interests. Students may bring musical instruments from home, and private instruction is available.

DAILY LIFE

The Academy provides a structured daily schedule to support students' academic and therapeutic goals. Days begin at 7 a.m., followed by dorm clean-up and a hot breakfast. Students follow a block schedule of three classes before lunch at noon and three after. Group therapy is scheduled three times throughout the week, alternating between day and evening blocks. Individual therapy appointments are scheduled weekly. Students have "down" time to socialize on campus and in their dorms after meals and before bed. Friday offers Academic Enhancement for all students. This creative scheduling approach allows students to participate in academic field trips and internships, schedule individualized instruction, and participate in college courses or Princeton Review SAT preparation. Lights-out is at 10 p.m. Night staff members provide security, supervision, and support during the overnight hours.

WEEKEND LIFE

After breakfast on Saturday mornings, students complete housekeeping chores from 9:30 to 12:30. After lunch, a variety of on- and off-campus activities may be offered. Some of these are privilege based and dependent upon student behavior and readiness to participate. On Sunday, a 10:30 a.m. brunch is followed by a leisurely day of recreational activities.

COSTS AND FINANCIAL AID

Tuition, room, and board cost $5950 per month. There is an enrollment fee of $2500, which includes ASR's Land's End Orientation Clothing Package. For students requiring the services of the Academy's consulting psychiatrist, a retainer fee is billed separately.

ADMISSIONS INFORMATION

The Academy at Swift River offers rolling admissions and can respond quickly to aid families in crisis. Applicants are accepted based on information provided by educational consultants, parents, and pertinent testing. Children of average or above-average ability who are experiencing social, academic, and/or familial problems are ideal candidates for admission. Such children may exhibit defiance and opposition to authority, angry outbursts, lack of confidence, low self-esteem, indications of depression, lying, stealing, and other maladaptive behaviors and traits. Histories may include adoption, divorce, death and other loss issues, or various types of abuse. ASR does not discriminate or prejudice any student's enrollment on the basis of race, religion, nationality, sex, or ethnic background. Due to the program's highly physical nature, however, children with substantial physical limitations or challenges would not be served well by the ASR program.

APPLICATION TIMETABLE

Inquiries are welcome at any time. Tours of the campus are given at the time of the interview, and parents are given the opportunity to meet with students and staff and faculty members. Students who are eligible for admission may be enrolled at any time after the interview has been completed as available spaces permit.

ADMISSIONS CORRESPONDENCE

Rhonda Papallo, Director of Admissions
Paul Ravenscraft, Associate Director of
    Admissions and Marketing
The Academy at Swift River
151 South Street
Cummington, Massachusetts 01026
Phone: 800-258-1770 (toll-free)
Fax: 413-634-5300
E-mail: admissions@swiftriver.com
Web site: http://www.swiftriver.com

BRANDON HALL SCHOOL

Atlanta, Georgia

Type: Coeducational day and boys' boarding school
Grades: 4–12, Postgraduate studies
Enrollment: 120–160
Head of School: Paul R. Stockhammer, President and Headmaster

THE SCHOOL

Originally founded as a tutorial proprietary school in 1959, Brandon Hall has historically had its focus on the individual student. The School is now a non-profit, nonsectarian, nondenominational college-preparatory school. Founded on the late Morris Brandon's summer home estate, the entire School initially was housed in what is now known as Brandon Hall. Enrollment grew, additional facilities were built, and the School's programs expanded. Brandon Hall was the first school in Georgia to be named a National School of Excellence (Blue Ribbon School).

With a focus on the individual, Brandon Hall provides both one-on-one and small group college-preparatory classes for approximately 120 to 160 students in grades 4–12 who, for a variety of reasons, have not been achieving their potential or who otherwise need a more intensive educational setting. The School is not the proper setting for students with acute behavioral or emotional problems or severe learning disabilities. Emphasizing personal attention, organization, structure, accountability, the ordering of priorities, applied study skills, and multisensory instruction, Brandon Hall seeks to motivate each student to fulfill the School's motto, "to begin anew and flourish." In addition, Brandon Hall has often been referred to as "the intensive care of education" because of its small classes and effective programs.

Brandon Hall is located on 27 acres adjacent to the Chattahoochee River in the suburban Dunwoody area of Atlanta. The facilities are attractive, air-conditioned, and appropriate to the mission of the School. The School's proximity to I-285, I-85, and GA 400 makes it easily accessible from most areas of metropolitan Atlanta. Atlanta's Hartsfield International Airport also makes the School convenient for both national and international boarding students. The Peachtree-DeKalb Airport's proximity to the School is also ideal for parents who have personal aircraft.

ACADEMIC PROGRAMS

When a student enrolls, the Office of Admissions and the academic office review the information submitted and prescribe an individual academic program that can assist the student in learning necessary skills, making up or earning essential academic credits, or taking accelerated work. Each year thereafter, the academic office meets with the student's parents and reviews the plan to establish new course projections.

The academic program at Brandon Hall School is divided into two divisions: Middle School (grades 4–8) and Upper School (grades 9–12 and postgraduate studies). Grades 4, 5, and 6 are nongraded and self-contained except for physical education, library skills, and fine arts courses. Students in grades 7 and 8 change classes. The Middle School curriculum is designed specifically for the academic and personal needs of younger students. Middle School students who need one-to-one instruction may be enrolled in tutorial classes at an additional cost.

The Upper School curriculum is college preparatory in nature, with allowances for students who are at a variety of skill levels. Graduation requirements are based on the state as well as generally understood requirements for college entrance. Brandon Hall, however, reserves the right to determine

specific graduation requirements for each student, based on the student's abilities and needs and college plans.

The school year is divided into semesters. Teachers e-mail parents weekly to apprise them of their student's progress. Nine-week grade reports are issued and contain grades along with the attendance and conduct records. At the end of a semester, grade reports are issued. The semester grades are the only grades that are placed on transcripts to reflect credit earned. The School uses letter grades as explained on the report cards. Students enrolled in honors or Advanced Placement courses earn additional credit in their courses.

The following requirements are the standard requirements that can be adjusted on an individual basis as deemed appropriate by the administration for the student's needs: English, 4 units; math, 4 units; science, 3 units (4 preferred); history, 3 units (4 preferred); foreign language, 2 units of same language (3 preferred); physical education, 1 unit; fine arts, 1 unit; electives, 5 units. Students may also enroll in computer science and SAT-prep courses based on their individual needs.

For students whose primary language is not English, Brandon Hall offers an English as a second language (ESL) program. Students who are participating in the ESL program are usually placed in small group or one-to-one classes when they first begin at Brandon Hall. Individualized instruction allows a student to progress at his or her own rate. As both written and verbal English skills develop and mature, ESL students are gradually moved into larger group classes in mathematics, English, science, and social studies.

FACULTY AND ADVISERS

Brandon Hall currently employs 35 full-time faculty members. Fifteen faculty members have advanced degrees, and 16 reside on campus.

The current headmaster, Paul R. Stockhammer, became the school's fifth president in July 2001. He received both his bachelor's and master's degrees from Mercer University in Macon, Georgia, and has more than thirty years of experience in independent education. Having begun his professional career as a classroom teacher, Mr. Stockhammer was selected in 1971 as STAR teacher of Jackson High School, where he served as Chair of the English Department. He has been a member of the administrative staffs of such well-known schools as Woodward Academy, The Lovett School, and Marist School, where he was known for his outstanding leadership, dedication, and innovation. From 1987 until 1994, Mr. Stockhammer was a senior member of the Brandon Hall administrative staff. During this period, he headed admissions, chaired the Initial Accreditation Committee, and instituted the Parents Weekend and other aspects of school life that have become traditions at the School.

COLLEGE PLACEMENT

Brandon Hall is a college-preparatory school and emphasizes preparation for college via course requirements as well as standardized test preparation. Realizing that some students may not always do well on standardized testing, the School tries to relieve test anxiety as well as to teach test-taking skills via special SAT courses during the junior and senior

years. Other standardized testing each year also helps students become acclimated to test-taking techniques. Parents and students are reminded that some students, as a result of their learning disabilities or for other reasons, do not do well on standardized tests. In such cases, it is essential that the students do their best in their academic subjects so that they may have as high a grade point average as possible. Assistance is also provided for those students taking the ACT examination for college entrance.

The School's college adviser meets with students individually to preview colleges and universities around the country that offer programs of interest to each student. Representatives from many colleges visit the School throughout the year to speak to students in group and individual settings.

Colleges and universities that have recently accepted Brandon Hall students include American, Auburn, Boston University, Duke, George Washington, Howard, Rice, RIT, Syracuse, and many others.

STUDENT BODY AND CONDUCT

Brandon Hall enrolls 120 to 160 students each year, keeping its class sizes small. In keeping with its mission and philosophy, the School has established a standard of conduct and expectations. Students are held accountable for their conduct at School and School-related activities. The School expects students and parents to treat each other and the faculty members with respect and to honor individual differences. The School reserves the right to establish rules and regulations for the general welfare of the School and its students. Brandon Hall also expects enrolled students not to bring any type of ill fame or repute to themselves or the School beyond the campus.

ACADEMIC FACILITIES

Students are able to experience the rich heritage of the buildings during different classes and extracurricular activities. Brandon Hall contains the administrative offices as well as the Great Hall for receptions. Corley Hall contains the dining room, kitchen, and several small-group classrooms. Huff Center contains the main academic and guidance offices, the gymnasium, the wellness room, Upper School classrooms, the art room, computer labs, and the Dinos Science Center. Kimbrell Hall, built in 1991, houses the library/media center, Middle School classrooms, a 300-seat auditorium, and the Rollins conference room.

BOARDING AND GENERAL FACILITIES

Brandon Hall offers metropolitan Atlanta's only traditional, college-preparatory boarding program for boys in grades 6–12 (PG). In rare exceptions, a fourth or fifth grader may board, depending on his maturity and adaptability to the program. Brandon Hall enrolls students from throughout the United States and the world. There are two types of boarders: five-day boarders who live in proximity to the school and go home on the weekends; and seven-day boarders who are full-time boarding students who go home on holidays and special weekends or occasions. The boarding program is an integral part of School life. The Director of Resident Life and his assistant work with a staff of approximately 20 faculty members and their spouses who serve on weekday and weekend teams to supervise students in the dormitory and at boarder-related weekday and weekend activi-

ties. Faculty members reside in the dormitory and are on call after hours. Other resident faculty members live in apartments on campus. Day faculty members also assist with boarding activities on the weekends. In addition, the School employs security personnel who remain awake throughout the night and monitor the halls throughout the night.

Sipple Hall is a modern air-conditioned facility containing the dormitory rooms, a commons area, a recreation room, a nurse's office and infirmary, and a study hall. The commons contains a living-room atmosphere for relaxation, reading, or television viewing. The recreation room, located on the lower level, also houses a television, drink machines, a pool table, a Ping-Pong table, an air-hockey table, and board games.

Each dormitory room features comfortable beds and study areas. Built-in closets, drawers, and shelves provide adequate space for clothes, books, and personal items. Washers and dryers are provided on each hall. Eight boys (four rooms) share bathroom facilities, which include four showers with privacy curtains, three sinks, and two commodes with doors. Boarders are responsible for keeping their rooms and assigned bathrooms clean and in good order. Students vacuum and dust their rooms, empty their trash containers, and share general responsibilities involving the common areas.

ATHLETICS
The athletic program seeks to involve students in meaningful athletic activities that teach individual and team self-discipline, responsibility, and accountability. All students may try out and participate in a sports activity, provided they are in good health, make a commitment to uphold the standards and policies, and agree to attend all practices and games. All boarders are required to participate in at least one sport activity during the school year unless otherwise approved by the administration.

Middle School athletic teams include boys' basketball, cross-country, and wrestling; girls' basketball, cross-country, and volleyball; coed soccer and track and field; and intramural coed tennis.

Upper School teams include boys' basketball (varsity and junior varsity), cross-country, tennis, and wrestling; and girls' basketball, cross-country, tennis, and volleyball; and coed baseball, golf, and varsity soccer.

EXTRACURRICULAR OPPORTUNITIES
The School provides a variety of cocurricular clubs and organizations. Each organization establishes its mission, criteria for membership, and activities for the year. All students are required to participate in at least one organization or team sport during the year. Faculty members advise the organizations and clubs and may restrict a student's membership based on lack of participation, poor attendance, or conduct.

Clubs include Art, Book Nook, Chess & Checkers (MS), Chess, Chorus, Community Service, Drama, Foreign Language, Literary Magazine, Radio Controlled, and Scrabble.

DAILY LIFE
Boarding students have a structured schedule during the weekdays to properly prepare them for classes and activities, waking each morning promptly at 6:30 before morning inspections. Classes run until mid-afternoon, followed by study time, personal time, athletics, or club activities. Dinner is held at 6 p.m., followed by additional study or recreational time. Middle School lights out is at 9:30 and Upper School lights out is at 10 p.m. Dorm students are grouped in pods of up to 8 students, headed by a student prefect and a faculty adviser.

WEEKEND LIFE
Based on the number of boarders remaining on campus, the activities available in the metropolitan Atlanta area, the students' interests, and reasonable costs of the activities (deducted from each student's supply account), the School plans both recreational and enriching weekend activities. Except where students have conduct or academic obligations, all students are required to attend at least one activity. Faculty members supervise all activities and give specific directions regarding conduct, meeting places, and expectations.

Weekend activities include professional and college sporting events, such as football, basketball, baseball, and soccer games; cultural activities, such as symphony concerts, professional theater, movies, museums, and musical performances; visits to historical sites; recreational activities, such as Six Flags Over Georgia, White Water, the Renaissance Festival, Stone Mountain, Lake Lanier, Callaway Gardens, the Georgia Aquarium, and the North Georgia Fair; and outdoor activities, including camping, canoeing, or boating. Students also have recreational activities at Brandon Hall, such as viewing movies, physical activities, and free time in the recreation room. Activities are usually planned for Friday evening, Saturday afternoon, and Sunday afternoon.

SUMMER PROGRAMS
Summer school is normally offered for those students (at Brandon Hall or other schools) who need to make up work or earn additional academic credits. Unless otherwise approved, currently enrolled students must take their summer school academic work at Brandon Hall to ensure that the curriculum standards are met. Students admitted during the middle of the school year may find that their enrollment contract or letter of invitation indicates required attendance at Brandon Hall's summer program to complete work.

COSTS AND FINANCIAL AID
For the 2005–06 academic year for grades 9–12, day students paid $23,975 for tuition, $1500 for lunch or room/boarding, and $1450 for the initial supply deposit. Five-day boarding students paid $23,975 for tuition, $15,500 for lunch or room/boarding, and $2750 for the initial supply deposit. Seven-day boarding students paid $23,975 for tuition, $17,650 for lunch or room/boarding, and $4250 for the initial supply deposit. An additional fee of $6900 was charged for each one-to-one class.

For students in grades 4–8 in 2005–06, day students paid $21,650 for tuition, $1500 for lunch or boarding, and $1450 for the initial supply deposit. Five-day boarding students paid $$21,650 for tuition, $15,500 for lunch or boarding, and $2750 for the initial supply deposit. Seven-day boarding students paid $21,650 for tuition, $17,650 for lunch or boarding, and $4250 for the initial supply deposit.

Limited financial aid is awarded on the basis of documented financial need to students of good character who have submitted an application. Prospective students and their families should contact the admissions office for the application and deadlines. Consideration for financial aid is always given first to currently enrolled students in good standing.

ADMISSIONS INFORMATION
An interview is an important component of the admission process as it provides the Admissions staff the opportunity to meet a student and his parents to determine if the School is the proper fit. Prior to the interview, the School asks parents to complete an application, have copies of transcripts and testing available for review, and look at Brandon Hall's Web site or its admissions materials so that questions can be asked and answered during the appointment. The School encourages both parents to attend the interview. Brandon Hall reserves the right to waive the interview for international students who apply through an educational consultant or who provide sufficient information to determine if the School may be a proper placement.

APPLICATION TIMETABLE
Brandon Hall adheres to a rolling admissions policy in which qualified students may be admitted throughout the year, provided space is available. For students applying for fall enrollment, the School encourages applicants to send in their information during the preceding spring.

ADMISSIONS CORRESPONDENCE
Marcia Shearer
Director of Admissions
Brandon Hall School
1701 Brandon Hall Drive
Atlanta, Georgia 30350-3706

Phone: 770-394-8177
Fax: 770-804-8821
E-mail: admissions@brandonhall.org
Web site: http://www.brandonhall.org

BREHM PREPARATORY SCHOOL

Carbondale, Illinois

Type: Coeducational boarding and day school for students with complex learning disabilities and attention deficit disorder
Grades: 6–12, postgraduate studies; ages 11–21
Enrollment: Boarding capacity limited to 96 on campus
Head of School: Dr. Richard G. Collins, Director

THE SCHOOL

Founded in 1982, Brehm Preparatory School is the only boarding school in the Midwest specifically designed to meet the academic, social, and emotional needs of students with complex learning disabilities and attention deficit disorder. Brehm's mission—to empower such students to recognize and optimize their full potential—is accomplished both through a family environment where individual needs are addressed by a focused holistic program and through the partnership developed among the staff, students, parents, board of directors, and surrounding community. Awarded the prestigious U.S. Department of Education Blue Ribbon School of Excellence honor in 1993, Brehm places a high value on student empowerment, integrity, active problem solving, ongoing communication, continuous staff and program development, and financial stability.

Brehm's 80-acre campus is located in Carbondale, a town of 27,000 in southern Illinois. Carbondale, easily reached from the major cities of St. Louis, Chicago, and Paducah, is best known as the home of Southern Illinois University. The University offers the Brehm student access to theatrical productions, sports events, concerts, and museums. Giant City State Park, the Shawnee National Forest, and many lakes provide abundant recreational areas.

A not-for-profit corporation, Brehm is governed by a board of directors that works actively with parents, faculty and staff members, and community residents to develop plans to maintain high-quality programs and increase community involvement.

Brehm is a member of the National Association of Independent Schools (NAIS) and the National Association of Private Schools for Exceptional Children (NAPSEC). Brehm is accredited by the North Central Association of Colleges and Schools and the Independent Schools Association of Central States.

ACADEMIC PROGRAMS

A full range of course work required for junior and senior high school graduation is offered in the areas of laboratory sciences, the humanities, visual arts, mathematics, microcomputers, and physical education. The maximum class size is 8 to 10 students in content-area classes, and teaching incorporates hands-on, multisensory instruction geared to meet each student's needs while allowing him or her to function as part of a group. Learning cognition classes focus on teaching students how they learn and which strategies they need to use to be successful. Maximum class size in learning cognition classes is 5 students.

Brehm recognizes that the student with learning disabilities and attention deficit disorder is affected across interrelated academic, social,

and emotional areas and is in need of simultaneous, integrated interaction within a systematically constructed environment. Brehm therefore emphasizes a holistic approach toward educating students with these complex needs, integrating all three concerns to enhance both the cognitive and the personal development of each student. Brehm's comprehensive services thus include not only instruction in core academic areas, remedial services, and guidance in compensatory strategies for skill-deficit areas but also social and life skills development, recreational therapy, cultural enrichment, career counseling, and prevocational exploration. Instruction in Orton-Gillingham, Lindamood-Bell, and the Wilson Reading Program is available, as is individual and group language therapy. Individual psychological counseling is available on an as-needed contractual basis.

The Brehm environment proactively acknowledges that new behaviors are taught when the academic, social, and emotional needs of each student are addressed in this manner. As the student demonstrates a new behavior leading to success in each area, this success provides motivation for greater changes. Acquisition of communication skills, language development, and empowered learning translate to success in all areas of development.

Assessment, parent input, teacher observation, and analysis of language deficits by a speech pathologist result in the development of an individualized program for each student. Each student receives instruction and counseling about the nature of his or her unique learning difference and learning style.

Each student's strengths and weaknesses are regularly evaluated. Using a holistic team approach, teachers meet weekly to review students, assessing standardized as well as individual testing and teacher reports. Emphasis is placed on the strengths of the individual, while introducing strategy intervention and skill building.

Brehm's postsecondary transition program OPTIONS is designed for high school graduates who need to further develop academic, organizational, or social skills. Depending on individual needs, the program provides some remediation, acquisition of learning strategies, study skills training, academic enhancement, and social skills training. College and/or career assessment are explored through John A. Logan College and Community Internship Programs.

FACULTY AND ADVISERS

One of Brehm's main objectives is to meet each student's unique needs through the provision of high-quality, individualized services delivered by highly trained, experienced, and certified staff members. Toward that end, Brehm employs certified learning disabilities instructors, certified

content instructors, and 5 full-time speech and language pathologists. The majority of staff members have master's degrees in their educational field. Brehm's academic staff averages more than ten years of professional experience. All are committed, enthusiastic professionals dedicated to the success of each student.

Teachers at Brehm are involved in decision making. They serve on curriculum committees and participate in the formulation of discipline policies and in program evaluation. Through ongoing meetings, staff members evaluate the curriculum and recommend and implement changes.

COLLEGE PLACEMENT

College entrance exam preparation and administration as well as college exploration and application counseling are provided. Also important at Brehm is the development of self-advocacy skills. These skills help students to search out their best possible postgraduation placements and to work to make these placements successful and also enable students to effectively communicate learning needs to prospective admissions directors or future employers.

Brehm graduates, bolstered by the School's commitment to and belief in their success, can currently be found at colleges, junior colleges, and vocational-technical schools around the country. Alumni have graduated from colleges and technical schools, and many are working as teachers and coaches, in the social services, and as businessmen and businesswomen. Brehm alumni can also be found in master's and Ph.D. programs throughout the country.

STUDENT BODY AND CONDUCT

Boarding enrollment at Brehm is 96 (18 boys per dorm, 18 girls per dorm, and 6 girls in Honor Dorm).

Brehm students operate under a residential tier system that rewards students who demonstrate responsibility with increased individual privileges, including free time and off-campus hours. Responsibility for personal living space and general dormitory maintenance falls to each student.

Brehm encourages student financial planning through an allowance and banking arrangement. The School acts as the student's banker through an account opened on the student's allowance, which is provided by parents.

Students are not permitted to have cars, motorcycles, or televisions on campus.

ACADEMIC FACILITIES

Brehm's campus contains three classroom buildings designed specifically to meet the needs of the program and its students. Microcomputers are used extensively in instruction. The proximity of

Southern Illinois University and John A. Logan College and access to the Internet provide opportunities for library research as well as college credit and noncredit academic experiences.

BOARDING AND GENERAL FACILITIES
A family-style living environment is designed to foster independence and responsibility. Brehm's five dormitories are designed and built much like apartment buildings, each with nine bedrooms housing 2 or 3 students per room. Each dorm has its own kitchen with ample hours for meals and snacks, a lounge area with cable television, and a laundry facility for student use.

Each dormitory is supervised by 2 dorm parents who supervise, teach, coach, counsel, console, facilitate, and regulate as needed. Emphasis is placed on group living, socialization, and development of appropriate study behaviors.

Postsecondary students in the OPTIONS program reside in supervised off-campus apartments near Southern Illinois University.

ATHLETICS
Brehm's physical education program takes place at the new Student Activity Center, which includes a full gymnasium and workout room. The campus features additional grounds for baseball, football, volleyball, soccer, and other outside games.

EXTRACURRICULAR OPPORTUNITIES
Brehm's recreation program is structured on a daily basis (1½ hours per day) and weekends. Students have the flexibility to plan individual activities and participate in scheduled group events. Clubs include but are not limited to art, dance, drama, ecology, fitness programming, gymnastics, horseback riding, karate, music lessons, and tennis. Through this program, Brehm works toward expanding student interest in hobbies and recreational involvement, enhancing social skill development, furthering group interaction and leadership skills, increasing time-management skills, facilitating community integration, and supporting students in their transi-

tion from Brehm to adult life. Recreational activities are supervised by skilled recreation staff members.

DAILY LIFE
Academic classes are held from 8:15 a.m. to 3:35 p.m. Monday through Friday. A regular school day includes seven periods of classroom instruction followed by a supervised study period on Sunday through Thursday evening.

Students are also involved in two weekly Social Skills Training sessions, which are held in individual dorms and in Campus Forum. Sessions focus on communication, listening, problem solving, and interpersonal social skills. Students explore how their learning differences may impact them in their social environment and develop strategies to overcome such issues.

WEEKEND LIFE
Students are encouraged to enjoy the southern Illinois area, "The Land between the Rivers," known for its almost unlimited access to outdoor recreational activities. A regional shopping mall as well as many small specialty shops are located in Carbondale. Numerous churches and a synagogue representing all major faiths and denominations are found in the area. Regularly scheduled transportation is provided for student activities around town and for the many weekend field trips to area activities and events. Student interests determine weekend activities.

COSTS AND FINANCIAL AID
Tuition for the 2005–06 school year was $48,600 for boarding students and $29,995 for day students. A $2000 deposit, applied toward tuition, is due at the time of acceptance. Upon enrollment, the remaining tuition balance is required.

Payment for the special services provided by Brehm Preparatory School may in many circumstances be considered by the Internal Revenue Service as a deductible expense, depending on individual circumstances. Parents are encouraged to consult with their tax consultants for further information about tuition deductibility.

ADMISSIONS INFORMATION
A current (not more than two years old) assessment of intelligence (Wechsler Scale, complete with subscores) and academic achievement data (the Woodcock-Johnson Psycho-Educational Batteries, Cognitive and Achievement, with Summary Scores pages) must be submitted with the application, along with other information pertinent to assessing the applicant's educational needs, such as previous standardized testing or school records and any medical reports containing information necessary for the student's well-being.

As a prerequisite to acceptance and enrollment, each prospective student must have a complete psychoeducational evaluation and a primary diagnosis of a specific learning difference and/or attention deficit disorder.

APPLICATION TIMETABLE
Upon receipt of the application, which must be accompanied by a $50 fee, the Admissions Committee reviews all forms and records and determines the appropriateness of the Brehm program for the student. If it is determined that Brehm and the student are a suitable match, the Director of Admissions invites the student and his or her parent(s)/guardian(s) for a campus visit. Interviews with administration and staff members are conducted at the time of this visit, as is a campus tour. An offer for admission is made by the Admissions Committee if it is determined that Brehm can meet both the educational and boarding needs of the applicant. Acceptance is confirmed by the receipt of a nonrefundable $2000 deposit, which is credited toward tuition.

ADMISSIONS CORRESPONDENCE
Donna E. Collins
Director of Admissions
Brehm Preparatory School
1245 East Grand Avenue
Carbondale, Illinois 62901

Phone: 618-457-0371
Fax: 618-549-2329
E-mail: admissionsinfo@brehm.org
Web site: http://www.brehm.org

THE CEDARS ACADEMY

Bridgeville, Delaware

Type: Coeducational residential college-preparatory boarding school for students with attention and learning difficulties and related educational and interpersonal concerns
Grades: 5–graduation, with transition year available for college credit
Enrollment: 40
Head of School: Joanne Saulsbury, Executive Director

THE SCHOOL

The Cedars Academy was founded in 1989 to provide college preparation for children of average to above average intellectual capacity who are not succeeding in the outcome-oriented educational system because of their attention, focusing, or sequencing problems. The Cedars Academy's mission is to provide a high-quality intimate setting as an alternative educational experience. These students tend to focus on step ten while working on step one.

The philosophy of the school is that it is not just an academic problem, it is a lifestyle problem. The students face a lifelong need to learn skills that will enable them to be successful not only in a classroom but also in society itself. The students who attend the Cedars Academy might be best described as "but" children. Johnny is a great kid, but he has trouble making friends. Jill has high intellectual potential but no self-confidence. Ken can do better in school, but he doesn't do his homework. All the adults like Ed, but he has no friends his own age. Sarah starts the school year with a bang, lots of high grades and lots of friends, but by the end of the first semester, she is lonely and failing. Joe behaves in school but is awful at home. Dave has lots of energy and ideas, but he never gets anything done.

The Cedars Academy's students are children who need a process-oriented, structured approach to learning so that each minute in a student's day is as important as every other minute. The Cedars Academy believes that attention in education needs to be given to the total child.

The students tend to make decisions based on what they view as "fair" or on what they "want" to do, rather than on what needs to be done. Often, these students act in a manner that is age-inappropriate. Therefore, strong emphasis is placed on social and interpersonal skill development as well as academic skill development.

There are a wide variety of activities to augment the curriculum. Classes are held five days a week. The other two days are dedicated to equestrian activities, off-campus field trips to such diverse places as the Smithsonian Museum, the Holocaust Museum, and the lovely area beaches. The Cedars Academy develops a strong sense of community awareness, with students volunteering in such places as the humane society, the community playhouse theater, and the historical society.

The Cedars Academy is located on 73 acres on the Delmarva Peninsula. Although the setting is rural, the Academy is only 2 hours from Washington, D.C.; Baltimore; and Philadelphia.

ACADEMIC PROGRAMS

The Cedars Academy is a year-round program, with regularly scheduled breaks to give the students time home with their families. The school breaks approximately every six weeks. Students receive 3 hours of homework each day during the breaks to provide real skill training in organization and independent work skills that are necessary for college. Students follow a schedule at home because it teaches internal structure that the students need, regardless of the environment.

Report cards are issued twice a year. A detailed progress report is prepared twice yearly. Parent conferences are held as needed. A weekend parent training session is held in January. Strong family involvement is important. Parents become an integral part of their child's total education and development. They are willing to learn new skills because the old approach has failed.

Classes range in size from 6 to 12. Generally students take five academic courses, with adjunct classes in the arts, music, and foreign language. Each student's educational program is designed to move the student forward and to fill in holes in their academic and developmental background. Each day at least 1½ to 2 hours of supervised homework are scheduled.

The traditional college-preparatory curriculum includes language arts (literature, English, theater), foreign language, mathematics (prealgebra through calculus), art, music, American and world history, earth science, biology, physics, chemistry, physical education, and health/nutrition. During the summer prior to senior year and continuing throughout the year, students attend selected classes at the University of Delaware. This process helps the transition to college to be a smooth one and pinpoints areas needing further skill development before graduation.

The curriculum at the Cedars Academy exceeds state of Delaware, Department of Education requirements for graduation. The facility is licensed by the state of Delaware.

FACULTY AND ADVISERS

The faculty members are chosen and trained utilizing the Cedars Academy's process-oriented approach. Because continuity is so critical, it is important that all the faculty members approach the students from the same viewpoint. All faculty members participate in academics and in the social and developmental aspects of the students' daily lives. Consistency and structure are not just catchphrases at the Cedars Academy. The students are encouraged to engage the faculty members in multidimensional ways. Faculty members are assigned to supervise the residences at night on a rotating basis.

COLLEGE PLACEMENT

Students begin college the summer before their senior year. It is possible by graduation to have 9 to 12 credits to apply to the freshman year at the college or university of choice. Students take the SAT in standard format beginning in the tenth grade. Untimed formats give a message that tells students the world will treat them differently.

At the Cedars Academy, students are taught to master their differences and be successful.

Among the colleges and universities of recent graduates are The Citadel, Elmira, Erhlam, Hendricks, Jefferson Medical, Moravian, Old Dominion, Salisbury State, Sheppard College, West Virginia Wesleyan, and the University of Delaware. The process of college selection is an individual journey based on each student's unique needs and assets.

STUDENT BODY AND CONDUCT

The Cedars Academy enrolls students from the United States and other countries. There is a code of conduct based on the reciprocity of relationships and trust among and between the students and the faculty members. One of the main facets of the approach to teaching is social learning. Teaching students to learn to live together in a homelike environment is critical in the Academy's approach. There are 16 to 18 students in each residence.

There is as much emphasis placed on the development of positive and productive relationships as on preparation for college. The students are taught the value and skill of reciprocity in gaining and maintaining friendships.

Sitting correctly at the dining room table improves the manner in which a student conducts himself or herself in the classroom. Learning only academics without social development does not make a well-rounded and successful person. There is no use of drugs or alcohol, nor is physical acting-out tolerated. A strong emphasis on the peer group is an integral aspect of life at the Cedars Academy. The Cedars Academy is a noncompetitive environment that teaches students how to work and learn together.

ACADEMIC FACILITIES

The students attend classes at the Annie Oakley Building. Organization and focusing skills are critical with ADD students, so the focus on sequential learning becomes paramount. Since the Cedars Academy's curriculum is college preparatory, the faculty-student relationship is based on learning how to learn. The students are certainly capable of learning, but they do not learn well in an outcome-oriented environment. By maintaining consistent expectations in each class and using the process approach, the native intellects of the students come to the forefront.

BOARDING AND GENERAL FACILITIES

Students reside in the Elizabeth Barrett Browning House and in the Sacajewea House. The residences are set up as "homes," and students have 2, 3, or 4 roommates who vary in age. The

Sacajewea House is a coed residence. Each residence has six bedrooms, four bathrooms, a large working kitchen, an eat-in dining room, a library with individual desks, and living room. As part of the Academy's teaching for life skills and leadership, all aspects of maintaining the home are the responsibility of the students, under the supervision of the faculty.

Hospitals and emergency-care facilities are within 7 miles of the campus.

ATHLETICS
The Cedars Academy is a noncompetitive environment. Physical activities stress the joy of participation and the cooperative aspect of play. The students are very physically active—running 30 minutes each morning, playing in the afternoon. They horseback ride each week and participate on a voluntary basis in a 5K Dover Days Race in May.

Students swim regularly in season and go camping several times during the year.

EXTRACURRICULAR OPPORTUNITIES
Since appropriate peer group relationships are important, students are taught how to work and play in groups, so many of the activities are geared toward social involvement, such as new games and other cooperative activities. There are opportunities, however, to pursue individual interests that are satisfying. Students enjoy chess, volunteering, working at the local playhouse, playing musical instruments, and other relaxing activities.

DAILY LIFE
Because the use of time is an important tool in developing life skills, the Cedars Academy maintains a daily schedule. The day is broken down sequentially to teach time management. Wake-up is at 6 a.m., followed by a morning run.

There are chores, room check, breakfast, and school preparation from 6:50 to 9:15. Morning classes begin at 9:30 and end at noon. Lunch is from noon until 1:30. Afternoon classes conclude at 3:50 p.m. Then there is a snack and an afternoon activity until 5 p.m. At that time, chores and dinner preparation, as well as homework time, are scheduled. Students have a minimum of 1½ hours per day of supervised homework. Students do not work in their rooms. Evening activity is scheduled from 8 to 8:45 p.m.

The day is specifically designed so that when students have problems or need to be taught a skill, either academic or interpersonal, they can be taught at the moment. Catching a problem at the earliest possible point makes learning a positive experience. Teaching students how to follow a schedule develops an internal structure vital for their success in life.

WEEKEND LIFE
The Academy's philosophy mandates that each day is approached in the same manner. Weekend days are scheduled as any other day. During the weekends, students participate in field trips and activities with friends on campus.

COSTS AND FINANCIAL AID
Tuition, room, and board were $49,200 for the 2005–06 academic year, September through August. A deposit of $11,020 is due upon acceptance. All tuition is paid by December 1 of the enrolled year.

There is no financial aid available from the Cedars Academy.

ADMISSIONS INFORMATION
The Cedars Academy enrolls students with problems in focusing, sequencing, and organizational and related educational concerns who have high potential that has not been realized. Parents visit the campus to discuss enrollment and to learn their role in changing the direction of their student's life. School records, a parental history, and an updated medical/dental form are necessary to complete admission and enrollment.

APPLICATION TIMETABLE
New students are interviewed and accepted throughout the year.

ADMISSIONS CORRESPONDENCE
The Cedars Academy
P.O. Box 103
Bridgeville, Delaware 19933
Phone: 302-337-3200
        866-339-0165 (toll-free)
Fax: 302-337-8496
Web site: http://www.cedarsacademy.com

DENVER ACADEMY

Denver, Colorado

Type: Coeducational day school
Grades: 1–12: Elementary, Grades 1–6; Middle School, Grades 7–8; Core High School, Grades 9–11; Progressive and Prep High School Divisions, Grades 9–12
Enrollment: School total: 480; Elementary, 88; Middle School, 120; High Schools, 272
Head of School: James Loan

THE SCHOOL

Denver Academy is an independent school that specializes in educating students with learning differences. The students are best described as having an average or better intellectual aptitude combined with a history of emotional and behavioral stability. Some of the students have identifiable sources of learning interferences, such as dyslexia or attention difficulties, while others have a history of learning difficulty or academic frustration because the strengths and weaknesses of their learning style have not been addressed in their previous setting.

Founded in 1973, Denver Academy is internationally recognized for the high quality of its program. The Academy's mission is to be a center of excellence for the education of students with learning differences in order to help them fully develop their intellectual, social, creative, physical, and moral potentials within a nurturing environment, thereby providing them with the necessary skills to be successful in life. Denver Academy is located on a 20-acre campus in the heart of Denver, minutes from downtown. Many facilities are easily accessible, including the University of Denver, the Denver Public Library, and Auraria Campus. The nearby Rocky Mountains offer many opportunities for field trips and extracurricular activities.

After enrollment, students show a significant increase in self-confidence and good study habits. Students flourish within the structured environment of Denver Academy.

A 15-member board, composed of community leaders and parents of present and former students, oversees the school. The annual operating budget is approximately $8.2 million. The school is accredited by both the Association of Colorado Independent Schools (ACIS) and the National Association of Independent Schools (NAIS).

ACADEMIC PROGRAMS

Denver Academy provides a full curriculum in which students work at their independent level of instruction so that their efforts result in a high degree of success. Students are placed in classrooms appropriate to their academic strengths and weaknesses, age, and maturity level. A variety of multisensory techniques are used in the instruction of basic academic subjects: reading, spelling, word attack, written composition, and mathematics. Students in all grades also receive instruction in science, history, social sciences, fine arts, and physical education. Class size is kept small (11–14 students), with a 7:1 student-teacher ratio. Instruction is conducted in small-group and one-on-one settings, which allows teachers to tailor lessons to specifically meet the student's needs and learning style.

The strength of Denver Academy's academic program lies in its consistency between grade levels. In addition to the content of the courses listed above, faculty members in all divisions focus on teaching respect and responsibility, homework skills, study and organizational skills, memory techniques, critical thinking, computer and library research skills, self-discipline, and self-reliance. The Academy helps the student understand his or her strengths and weaknesses.

The Elementary and Middle Schools provide a structured and nurturing environment in which students are able to maximize their learning potentials. Academic focus is weighted toward the basics, with an emphasis on language skills and mathematics as well as content courses.

Denver Academy offers three high school programs: Core, Progressive, and Prep. The Core High School focuses on language and math skills, with an increasing emphasis on content courses.

The Progressive High School combines the structure of its core curriculum with a hands-on experiential program. This program focuses on six key areas: career, creativity, community service, adventure, practical skills, and global awareness. Progressive students receive intensive one-on-one counseling to explore, prepare, and achieve their goals in the above areas. Teachers help students design projects, apply for financial assistance, and present their final products.

The Denver Academy Prep School program is college preparatory. This is a curriculum-driven program, and appropriate candidates must be at grade level or above in all subjects, be academically motivated, have developed good study skills and homework habits, and have a good foundation for independent learning.

FACULTY AND ADVISERS

Faculty members are selected for their personality and character traits as well as for their academic backgrounds and strong theoretical understanding of the teaching of exceptional learners. Qualities sought are integrity, respect for structure and discipline, organizational ability, and a genuine interest in and regard for the well-being of students. All new faculty members, regardless of prior experience, must go through an internship, learn the school's system and methods, and demonstrate their competence.

Because of their similar training experiences, Denver Academy's teachers are able to create a highly consistent school atmosphere for the students. The Academy operates under the philosophy that consistency, structure, and programming for success begin with the teachers.

There are 70 teachers at the Academy. Nineteen hold master's degrees. The Head of School, James Loan, holds an M.A. in special education from the University of Northern Colorado. He is only the second head in the school's history and has been with the Academy for thirty years, first as a teacher and then as an administrator. The Program Director, Stephan Tattum, holds an M.A. in education from George Washington University and has been with Denver Academy since 1973.

COLLEGE PLACEMENT

The Denver Academy program specializes in the placement of students into colleges that offer special programs or services to students who learn differently. Through years of experience, the Academy has also discovered schools that provide a nurturing but not separate experience for those students with learning differences.

Students attend a mandatory college-counseling course during their senior year. Included in the curriculum are time-management, study skills, and self-advocacy training. As part of the process, the Academy provides extensive career counseling services, campus tours, and summer experiences in the college environment. There are computerized databases complete with CD-ROM campus tours and college search software, all designed to help the student find a perfect match. The Academy's goal is twofold: to help students find the right school and to prepare those students for what lies ahead.

For students who qualify, extended-time administration for the college entrance exams is arranged. Recent results for the ACT show an average composite score of 20.

On average, approximately 95 percent of graduating seniors attend college in the year following graduation. Graduates attend a variety of colleges, including two-year schools, schools with learning difference support programs, and state schools, large and small. Several graduates have attended Ivy League or other highly competitive schools. The Academy prides itself on its ability to accommodate a wide range of student needs and abilities.

STUDENT BODY AND CONDUCT

In 2005–06, there are 480 students enrolled from first through twelfth grades. Students travel from all over the Denver metropolitan area and surrounding communities to attend Denver Academy.

It has been the Academy's experience that most young people respond best to a structured environment. The Academy's system of positive structure integrates consistency with a positive, supportive atmosphere.

Denver Academy has a no-tolerance policy regarding drug use, prohibits tobacco at school or school activities, and requires students to adhere to a modest dress code.

The Academy requires respectful and responsible behavior from the students. It emphasizes the reasons that underlie courteous attitudes toward others, and students respond accordingly.

ACADEMIC FACILITIES

All classes are conducted on the Academy's 20-acre campus. Each school division has its own building. Each building houses its own computer lab. All students have Internet access. In addition, there is a full-size gymnasium, a baseball field, an administrative building, and a library.

ATHLETICS

A student's self-confidence can be significantly enhanced through proper instruction in physical activities. The athletic department's emphasis is on teaching and developing skills on an individualized basis. After the individual's specific athletic skill level is improved, the student can then engage more confidently in the sport or activity.

The Academy's students discover that not only are they able to participate in a variety of physical activities but that they also perform far better than they anticipated. For those students who want more than physical education classes, the Academy offers participation in a variety of extracurricular sports teams. Students can participate in soccer, golf, basketball, baseball, wrestling, volleyball, cross-country, and club lacrosse.

EXTRACURRICULAR OPPORTUNITIES

In addition to sports, a variety of other extracurricular activities are available to students, including drama, student council, yearbook, and dances.

DAILY LIFE

Denver Academy holds classes five days a week. Students are in school at 8:15 a.m. until 3 p.m. Most students bring a lunch, although Progressive and Prep students are allowed off campus for lunch. Lunches are available if ordered and paid for in advance. Sports and extracurricular activities are scheduled after school.

SUMMER PROGRAMS

Summer School is a five-week academic program scheduled mid-June through July. Classes are offered from elementary through senior high. Half credit is awarded for each completed course. Tutoring programs are available to students with specific learning differences and for those who are not reaching their potential.

COSTS AND FINANCIAL AID

The 2005–06 tuition is $18,600. A deposit of $1000 is required. Lump-sum and monthly payment plans are available. Scholarship money is available on a need basis. Students must go through the admissions process and be officially accepted to school in addition to having a Parents' Financial Statement (forms are available at Denver Academy) submitted to the School and Student Service for Financial Aid in order to be considered for a scholarship.

ADMISSIONS INFORMATION

The applicant's needs and suitability for the program are considered on an individual basis.

Diagnostic testing, including the WISCIV and Woodcock-Johnson, is required for evaluation purposes. The application process includes an initial meeting with an admissions counselor, completing the application (requires two letters of recommendation as well as the required testing), possible classroom observation, and a family interview. An application fee of $75 is charged. (Denver Academy no longer administers the required testing.)

APPLICATION TIMETABLE

Inquiries are welcomed year-round, as are visits by prospective students and their parents. Applicants are interviewed on campus and are urged to complete diagnostic testing, if needed. Candidates are encouraged to apply by March 1; applications received after that date are considered on a rolling basis. Notification occurs in about three weeks.

ADMISSIONS CORRESPONDENCE

Dan Loan
Director of Admission
Denver Academy
4400 East Iliff
Denver, Colorado 80222

Phone: 303-777-5870
Fax: 303-777-5893
Web site: http://www.denveracademy.org

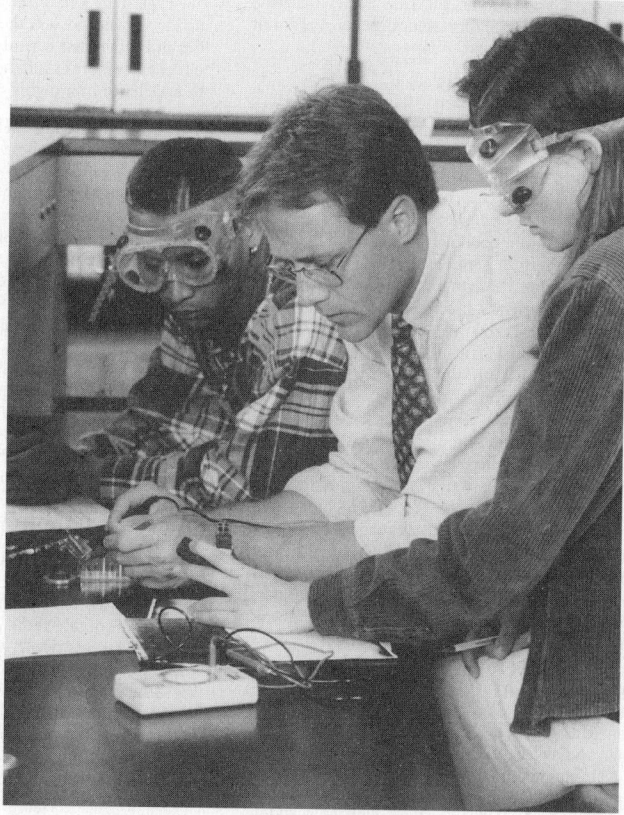

EAGLE HILL SCHOOL

Hardwick, Massachusetts

Type: Coeducational college-preparatory boarding school for adolescents with learning differences, including specific learning disabilities and/or ADD
Grades: 8–12
Enrollment: 150
Head of School: Peter J. McDonald, Headmaster

THE SCHOOL

Established in 1967, Eagle Hill School is an independent residential school located in Hardwick, Massachusetts. The School's program is designed to address the academic and social needs of students with learning differences, including specific learning disabilities (LD) and/or attention deficit disorder (ADD). Serving a coeducational population of 150 young men and women, Eagle Hill School has long been recognized for its ability to remediate academic and social deficits while continuing to develop strengths. It is the School's philosophy that every student should be given the opportunity to realize success. The faculty at Eagle Hill School truly understand the numerous challenges that face today's youth. Academic, peer, and societal demands are only a few of the hurdles that students must address on their respective paths through adolescence.

Eagle Hill School is a not-for-profit organization. It is governed by a Board of Trustees, representing alumni, parents, and prominent community members. Eagle Hill School has an exceptionally strong record of meeting the needs of LD and ADD students. Transforming years of educational frustration and deterioration into academic success and achievement has become the rule rather than the exception. The formula for attaining this goal is not left to chance.

ACADEMIC PROGRAMS

The philosophy of Eagle Hill School is to provide an individualized program of study. The Individual Education Plan (IEP) is used to define measurable objectives and provide a working plan for academic and personal growth. Each student's skill levels are determined by the review of test results, psychoeducational evaluation, previous IEPs, and a full battery of diagnostic testing performed at Eagle Hill School by the education department. The student-teacher ratio of 5:1 creates a small-class environment in which students work at their own pace with individual attention and support. These factors combine to provide an educational atmosphere that is conducive to success. The attention is focused on the individual and his or her needs.

The seven-period school day consists of two periods of English language arts and one period each of math, science, health/physical education, history, and one or more elective classes. Electives include studio art, Latin, Spanish, Chinese language and culture, Polish language and culture, Russian language and culture, woodshop, graphic arts, culinary arts, philosophy, psychology, American film, and computers. Pragmatics classes stress social skills training and work to develop both verbal and nonverbal communication skills and are also offered as electives. Students develop skills in problem solving, conflict resolution, peer mediation, and at the highest level, peer counseling strategies. Class groupings are homogeneous by age and skill level.

A fundamental component of academic growth is the need to be sufficiently challenged in the classroom. The Eagle Hill School curriculum combines process writing, metacognitive strategies, and multisensory teaching with the proven practices of a traditional curriculum. The curriculum ranges from basic math and elementary English to advanced mathematics and critical thinking. Students work together on similar goals and objectives, creating a comfortable learning environment.

The IEP establishes a baseline to measure improvement of skills. The evaluation of objectives from September through June offers a reliable and accurate depiction of a student's skills and progress. Beyond its use as an educational yardstick, the IEP is also an effective motivator. When students can visualize and understand clear objectives, they surpass everyone's expectations.

FACULTY AND ADVISERS

Eagle Hill School employs 80 full-time faculty members, including teachers, administrators, and resident counselors. The student-faculty ratio is 5:1. The cornerstone of Eagle Hill School's success is its faculty, whose members' unconditional commitment, in combination with continuous training, has made it one of the finest. Teachers and resident counselors commonly offer extra help, insightful advice, or even a shoulder to lean on during the evening hours. Dedicated, motivated, and professional are only a few of the adjectives used by students and parents to describe the faculty members. Their investment in each student's life has made Eagle Hill School an environment conducive to learning.

Eagle Hill School recruits nationally, seeking individuals who possess the qualities and characteristics of exceptional educators. These committed faculty members are experienced, certified, and dedicated to excellence in a highly challenging environment.

COLLEGE PLACEMENT

Eagle Hill School's college-preparatory program provides a full range of services designed to assist students in selecting the right environment for postsecondary education. Approximately 90 percent of graduates are accepted into colleges and universities prior to graduation. The remaining 10 percent pursue vocational and employment options. Eagle Hill School administers the ACT tests proctored and untimed to assist LD and ADD students. Preparation courses and practice tests are also offered. Vocationally, the School administers the ASVAB tests and provides the same level of service for students exploring these options. Graduates currently attend colleges and universities that include Adelphi, American, Clark, Franklin Pierce, Goucher, Hampshire, Hofstra, Ithaca, Johnson and Wales, Lesley, Mitchell, Mount Ida, Muhlenberg, WPI, and the Universities of Arizona and Hartford.

STUDENT BODY AND CONDUCT

Eagle Hill School enrolls 150 students, grades 8–12, in a coeducational environment with approximately a 3:2 boys-to-girls ratio. The current student population represents twenty-four states and seven countries. All students have been diagnosed with a learning disability and/or attention deficit disorder and range from average to above-average on diagnostic evaluations. Student behavior is governed by a code of student conduct, with emphasis placed upon personal development and individual responsibility. The expectations for student conduct are high. Positive and negative behavioral and disciplinary consequences are in place to accompany students' actions.

ACADEMIC FACILITIES

Eagle Hill School is located on the eastern edge of the Quabbin Reservoir and encompasses 165 acres. Six-teen buildings, tennis courts, soccer fields, a softball diamond, a gymnasium and fitness center, and a swimming pool occupy the grounds. Four buildings provide the thirty-eight classrooms currently used at Eagle Hill School. These include three computer labs, four science labs, a library, and culinary arts and creative arts facilities. The Norma B. Shields Library and Classroom Complex houses a spacious library and nineteen classrooms, which include a computer lab and four science laboratories.

The completion of the Richardson Classroom Complex in October 2005, connecting Greenwich Hall and the Norma B. Shields Classroom Building, brings together the majority of the school's academic resources under one roof. In addition to two new science labs, two general-use computer labs, and ten additional classrooms, the Richardson Classroom Complex is the new home for Eagle Hill's curriculum library and professional resources, a faculty library and common room, and a multiuse conference and professional development center. At the heart of the complex is a suite of college-counseling and guidance offices, a student art gallery, and the campus bookstore.

BOARDING AND GENERAL FACILITIES

Students are housed in three residential buildings. The two resident halls for underclassmen house 2 students per room and approximately 18 students per building. Upperclassmen live in the new, state-of-the-art Living and Learning Center. Opening its doors in January 2004, the facility features single rooms and multiple spacious lounges. Every student's room is equipped with Internet and telephone access. All residential buildings house full-time, live-in resident counselors who are primarily responsible for developing and maintaining a positive, community-based living environment.

ATHLETICS

Designed to complement the educational programs, athletics at Eagle Hill School are an integral part of the total development of each student. Teamwork and good sportsmanship are only two of the lifelong lessons that students learn as part of their participation in the athletic program. Beyond sports' self-esteem value, the exertion of energy serves as a positive release.

Eagle Hill School offers the interscholastic sports of basketball, cross-country running, golf, soccer, softball, tennis, and wrestling. Varsity and junior varsity teams compete against many area schools. Students who do not wish to compete on a sports team during a given semester participate in an independent aerobic activity of their choosing, including running, walking, biking, kickboxing, rollerblading, basketball, and tennis.

Facilities at Eagle Hill include a gymnasium and fitness center, an outdoor swimming pool, an adventure ropes course, and a new outdoor athletic complex, which includes two soccer fields, four tennis courts, a basketball court, a softball diamond, and a walking track.

EXTRACURRICULAR OPPORTUNITIES

Eagle Hill School offers a wide variety of clubs and activities. During the evening hours, students may participate in a formal club program or a variety of leisure activities. A sampling of clubs and activities available in the evening includes biking, tennis, out-

door/indoor basketball, guitar, weight training, student government, swimming (seasonal), literary magazine, school newspaper, environmental society, radio broadcasting, world cultures, adopt-a-grandparent, and off-campus trips. Students may choose from many different options based on individual interests. Students may also choose to relax or play a game of billiards in the Student Activity Center.

DAILY LIFE
The class day at Eagle Hill School begins at 8:30 and finishes at 3:20, followed by a 40-minute period reserved for extra help. At 4, the sports and aerobics programs round out the day, with dinner starting at 5. Students eat meals in the dining hall, conversing with faculty members. Observation of appropriate manners is emphasized. From 6 to 7:30, all students participate in mandatory study halls, which are held on each dorm floor. Resident counselors and classroom teachers provide supervision and assistance. Beginning at 7:30, students have an hour and a half of free time to spend relaxing with friends or participating in a club. A wide variety of on- and off-campus activities are offered at this time. Campus curfew is in effect at 9 for those students who have not earned no-curfew status. Bedtime is determined by age and privilege status.

WEEKEND LIFE
Eagle Hill School employs a full-time Director of Weekend Services, whose sole responsibility is to plan activities for Friday evening through Sunday evening. Weekend activities occur on and off campus, utilizing all that New England has to offer. On campus, the Student Activity Center has billiards, a widescreen TV and VCR/DVD, and a stereo system. The Athletic Center is open, complete with a full health and fitness center and a basketball court. All off-campus trips are supervised, and they are designed for the interest of the adolescent. Student participation in planning events is encouraged and solicited. During the winter months, students enjoy skiing, snowboarding, and sledding at local mountains in Massachusetts, Vermont, New Hampshire, and Maine. Those who do not choose this type of activity can participate in other options, including in-line skating, laser tag, visits to New York and Boston, and trips to movies, theaters, and sporting events. In warmer weather, students can enjoy the outdoors in many ways, including camping, hiking, deep-sea fishing, whale watching, white-water rafting, and visits to amusement and water parks.

SUMMER PROGRAMS
From early July through mid-August, Eagle Hill School offers a six-week summer program for those students who need programmatic continuity, time to make the transition into the program, and/or prevention of skill regression. The summer program limits its enrollment to 65 students, with an empha-

sis on promoting a camplike atmosphere. The program offers an eight-period class day. Four classes concentrate on reading, writing, math, and pragmatics, while the remaining four classes are designed to foster community dynamics and build self-esteem. Those classes include swimming, adventure ropes, art, woodshop, graphic arts, culinary arts, fly fishing, photography, and computers, among other subjects.

Following the class day, students enjoy a variety of afternoon activities that rotate on a daily basis. These activities may include swimming, fishing, arts and crafts, billiards, hiking, football, kickball, adventure ropes, and a wide variety of other offerings. Each evening, students participate in a club of their choice. Clubs are scheduled Monday through Thursday and do not rotate. Clubs are designed to have educational value but also incorporate fun.

Summer weekends provide the same level of structure as in the fall program but offer a wider choice of outdoor activities, given the New England summer weather. Weekend programming includes hiking, camping, amusement parks, water parks, beach trips, whale watching, deep-sea fishing, and white-water rafting.

The Eagle Hill School summer population is made up of three main groups. One group of the summer students is currently enrolled in the academic-year program as well and needs the continuity of the summer program to maintain skill levels. The second group consists of new or returning students who come just for the summer session and the academic boost it provides before returning to their home placements. The third group consists of new students who will make the transition to the academic-year program the following fall. For them, the summer program is a time of acclimation and preparation for the upcoming school year. They learn the routine, get to know the faculty members, meet some of their peers, and learn how to navigate campus life. When they return to Eagle Hill School in September to face increased academic expectations, their transition tends to be much smoother. In essence, attending the summer program reduces the anxiety and the unknown of a new situation.

The Eagle Hill Summer College program is designed for recent Eagle Hill graduates and Eagle Hill students entering their senior year. The program provides an opportunity for these students to acquire college credits, test their independence, and develop greater self-advocacy skills before they officially enter college. For six weeks, students live on the Eagle Hill campus and take two courses at nearby Anna Maria College.

COSTS AND FINANCIAL AID
Academic-year tuition, room, and board are $44,650 for the 2005–06 academic year. Student bank funds for an allowance, activities, and other expenses total $3000. A room deposit of $7500 is required upon

enrollment. Summer tuition, room, and board for 2005 are $6250, plus student bank funds totaling $500.

ADMISSIONS INFORMATION
Eagle Hill School admits students of any race, color, sexual orientation, religion, or national and ethnic origin to all of the rights, privileges, programs, and activities generally accorded or made available to students at the school. It does not discriminate on the basis of race, color, religion, sexual orientation, or national and ethnic origin in the administration of its educational policies, admission policies, athletic programs, or any other school-administered programs.

The admission procedures for both the school year and the summer programs are identical. Eagle Hill School has designed the following convenient guidelines to assist applicants in making sure their applications are processed expediently. Applications are accepted throughout the year, and qualified applicants may join the program during any semester, space permitting.

Prior to the interview process, applicants should submit a current psychoeducational evaluation to the admission department. This evaluation should include a cognitive assessment (WISC-IV) and academic achievement testing (e.g., WJ-R, WIAT), educational assessments, pertinent school records, teacher evaluations, a writing sample, IEPs, clinical evaluations, standardized testing, and official high school transcripts with school seal and signature of registrar. Following a review of the submitted records, an admission officer contacts applicants to schedule a mutually convenient time for an interview. Parents/guardians are notified of admission decisions. Should further information be needed, an admission representative contacts applicants immediately.

APPLICATION TIMETABLE
Inquiries are welcome at any time. Typically, interviews are scheduled Monday through Friday during the school year. While there is no application deadline, parents are advised to begin the admission process as soon as possible. Typically, early decisions are made in November, with two additional rounds of decisions in January and March. Once Eagle Hill School is at capacity, candidates who qualify for admission are placed in a waiting pool. Midyear enrollments are based on space availability. Admission to the summer program is rolling.

ADMISSIONS CORRESPONDENCE
Admission Office
Eagle Hill School
242 Old Petersham Road
P.O. Box 116
Hardwick, Massachusetts 01037

Phone: 413-477-6000
Fax: 413-477-6837
E-mail: admission@ehs1.org
Web site: http://www.ehs1.org

ELAN SCHOOL

Poland, Maine

Type: Coeducational boarding college-preparatory and general academic school for adolescents with emotional, behavioral, or adjustment problems
Grades: 7–12
Enrollment: 110
Head of School: Sharon Terry, Executive Director

THE SCHOOL

Founded in 1970, Elan School is a carefully conceptualized, caringly administered residential community. At its inception, it was designed as a facility that would help adolescents permanently change attitudes and life patterns, teaching them to function effectively in the mainstream of life. Students are admitted at any time year-round and stay an average of twenty-seven months. The 32-acre campus is in a rural community 20 minutes from Lewiston and 40 minutes from Portland.

The program is based on the principle that behavior cannot be changed by simply eliminating negative actions. The adolescent must not only stop antisocial acts but must also learn a new way of doing things. Elan is a closely knit, highly structured community that simulates society. The students living in each house are in charge of its operation under the supervision of direct-care staff members. There is a job hierarchy designed to instill self-respect and teach personal responsibility, honesty, consideration for others, self-control, and patience. A work ethic is stressed throughout the program, and each promotion results in new privileges and increased status. If students fail to perform with initiative, they participate in additional group and individual sessions. If this is not successful, they are demoted; this teaches them to function under adversity and to deal with failure, disappointment, and disagreement. They learn that occasionally failing is part of life, they can start again and succeed, and development of resilience is fundamental to success. Peer pressure and support teaches and enforces constructive behavior. Students learn that they must earn what they want and that they must give to receive.

The peer-oriented social structure is vital to the Elan concept. Students learn to take direction, accept criticism without taking it personally, criticize constructively, give orders reasonably, and care for and work with others; they also learn that their self-esteem is not dependent on the acceptance of others.

The most important change students can undergo at Elan is improvement of interpersonal relationship skills. Psychodynamic problems are dealt with at Elan, usually in group sessions, which are learning exercises about one's self. The exercises teach sensitivity to the needs and problems of others and foster getting in touch with feelings, understanding what touches off feelings, and controlling the acts engendered by them. Elan brings acting-out behavior into dynamic group sessions, where the goals are getting along with peers and learning how to deal with inner stresses and strains.

Elan constructs an individualized Re-Entry program for each student. During this three-month stage, students hold a paid job on campus. Emphasis is placed on a confident and productive return to the community and on coping with such realities of life as balancing time, effort, and expenditures. Students continue to participate in group sessions focusing on the anxieties involved in meeting people and building relationships with peers and authority figures outside Elan.

Elan is licensed by the Maine Department of Education as a private, residential, special-purpose school. Elan is also on the approved list of placements for several other states.

ACADEMIC PROGRAMS

Elan offers a fully approved junior high, high school, and special education program. Those students planning to continue their education in post-secondary schools are challenged through upper-level courses, while those who need intensive remediation are helped to acquire skills necessary to cope in the working world, as well as open doors to postsecondary education and training. Elan follows State of Maine credit requirements for graduation: 4 English, 3 science (including 1 lab), 3 math, 3 life skills, 3 history (including U.S. history), 1 fine arts (humanities, theater, music), 1 physical education, ½ health, and electives to total 22 credits.

Students follow a block schedule in which they take three courses per semester and earn 1 full credit in each subject. A student may earn up to 6 credits during the regular school year plus the required studies in life skills and physical education. Foreign languages are offered but are not required. Students are provided the opportunity to work in independent study programs under faculty supervision to augment their course of studies, if needed. Elan's curriculum reflects the needs of the student body and the expertise of its faculty members.

School during evening hours allows students to work through behaviors that interfere with concentration and learning during the day; students thereby arrive in class better prepared to focus.

Class size is kept small (maximum 14 students, optimum 10 students), and students are grouped by ability and course requirements. Supervised study halls and weekly grades help eliminate end-of-quarter "surprises." The passing grade is 65, and honors grades are recognized by the entire School. Each quarter, the student receives written comments from each teacher as well as numerical grades. Elan's program also includes an eight-week summer session featuring remedial work, enhancement courses, and electives. Students earn a half credit in each of the two subjects taken during summer school.

FACULTY AND ADVISERS

Faculty members at Elan are certified in their subject specialty and/or special education. Weekly faculty meetings allow continuous collaboration, brainstorming, and curriculum development. Most teachers either have earned or are working toward advanced degrees. Various professions are represented among the teaching staff, including a professional musician, a retired Army officer, a private business owner, a writer, and a psychologist.

Elan's Superintendent, Frank McDermott, was appointed to that position in July 2004. He has been Elan's Director of Education since 2000 and the Principal since 1998. He spent thirty-five years in public education, the last twenty-six as an Assistant Superintendent and Superintendent of Schools in Maine. Frank has been recognized both nationally and locally for leadership in Quality Principles application in education and the use of technology to transform schools. Mr. McDermott has a master's degree in educational administration and a Certificate of Advanced Studies in administration from the University of Maine.

Dr. Mary Waters, the Director of Special Services, joined Elan in the fall of 2005. She received her doctorate at Nova Southeastern University and has been a special education administrator in the public school system for thirty years.

Lisa Ferland, Elan's guidance counselor, joined the School in fall 2003. She received her master's degree in school psychology from the University of Southern Maine in 1997. Prior to joining Elan, Lisa was a school psychologist from 1997 until 2003, working in the public-school sector with students in all grades. She assists them in gathering teacher recommendations, filling out college applications, scheduling college visits, and determining the right college setting.

COLLEGE PLACEMENT

Elan is a closed SAT testing site. Students go on to two- and four-year colleges as well as to a variety of vocational programs and schools. More than 300 schools, colleges, and universities throughout the country have accepted Elan graduates during its thirty-five-year history. An average of 75 percent of graduates continue their education. The remainder may enter the workforce or join the armed services, but several of these students have long-range goals that include furthering their education.

STUDENT BODY AND CONDUCT

Currently, there are 3 students in grade 8, 19 students in grade 9, 23 students in grade 10, 19 students in grade 11, and 46 students in grade 12. Students who are members of minority groups make up 20 percent of the student body; 68 percent of the students are boys.

ACADEMIC FACILITIES

Elan has a central library located in the School House as well as individual house libraries, all consisting of volumes of fiction and nonfiction. Elan's iMac computer lab has been upgraded and there is a new T-1 line delivering content to the network. This lab is used by students to develop computer literacy and teachers in all subject areas use the lab as part of their course work with the students.

BOARDING AND GENERAL FACILITIES

Students live in one of two houses. Each house accommodates approximately 55 to 65 students; between 2 and 8 students share a dormitory room. The School operates year-round, and all students live on campus, even during major holidays. Academic classes are not held during standard public school vacation times.

An RN provides daily routine nursing care on-site. When she is not on campus, she is on call 24 hours a day. A physician visits one day a week, more often if necessary; he is also on call. When specialized care is indicated, students are taken to area doctors' offices or to a local hospital for emergencies.

Clothing is usually informal, but there are occasions when dress clothes are appropriate.

ATHLETICS

Elan has a certified physical education instructor. In season, an active schedule of intramural sports allows students to enjoy friendly competition. Each house has basketball, soccer, and softball teams that compete against the other house throughout the summer. An all-star game completes the season. Special trips are organized weekly during the summer for hiking on Maine's Calendar Islands, sailing, and deep-sea fishing. Additional trips are scheduled for other recreational opportunities, including bowling, canoeing, hiking, ice skating, downhill and cross-country skiing, snow tubing, whale watching, swimming, and white-water rafting

Elan currently has girls' and boys' cross-country track teams (the varsity boys won the Class D State Championship in 1997, 1999, and 2004 and were runners-up in 1998 and 2000 and the MAISAD State Championship in 2005; the junior varsity boys won the Class D State Championship in 1997, 1998, and 1999; the girls won the Class D State Championship in 2000, 2001, 2002, and 2003); boys' and girls' basketball teams (the boys' team won the Maine Principals' Association Sportsmanship of the Year Award in 1998 and the MAISAD Sportsmanship of the Year Award in 2004); a boys' golf team; and boys' and girls' track teams (the boys won the Class C State Championship in 1998), all of which compete against other area private and public schools. Elan has produced several championship teams in the MAISAD (both the boys' and girls' teams won the MAISAD Basketball Championships in 2001) and regional divisions, as well as two all-American race-walkers, who were ranked among the top 10 nationally. Peter Rowe, the cross-country and track and field coach, was named Coach of the Year in 1997, 1998, and 1999.

The School's location on Upper Range Pond affords a waterfront program of leisure swimming (supervised by a qualified lifeguard) and canoeing. In recreational activities, Elan stresses teamwork and sportsmanship. Healthy peer interaction, a cornerstone of the program, is a goal in athletics as well as in all other aspects of the program.

EXTRACURRICULAR OPPORTUNITIES

Videos are shown every week. Concerts, festivals, local fairs, exhibits, sports events, and trips out to dinner, the movies, art museums, planetariums, aquariums, and the theater are organized regularly for students who have earned the privilege. Most entertainment trips are to Portland, where professional hockey and baseball teams are among the attractions. Other trips may be to attend area football games or to go to amusement parks or places of historical or cultural interest. Field trips are scheduled to Boston annually. Trips to various state parks are organized during the summer months. In addition to the regular recreational trips, house trips include canoeing, white-water rafting, snow tubing, whale watching, roller skating, and bowling.

Elan students participate in a campuswide talent show a few times a year. Students showcase their creative side by playing musical instruments, performing comedy skits or variety acts, singing, reading poetry, or participating in any of the other performing arts. Winter and Spring Carnivals are also held; students participate in a variety of competitions, including tug-of-war, volleyball, basketball, relay races, and other athletic competitions.

DAILY LIFE

Weekday schedules begin at 8 a.m. with showers, cleaning dorm rooms, and breakfast; from 9 a.m. to 4:30 p.m. is a rotation of job functioning, physical education, group and individual sessions, administrative meetings, and other events necessary to maintain balanced structure. Lunch is at noon, dinner is at 4:30, and school is from 6 to 10:30 p.m. Students return to their dorm rooms around 11 p.m.; lights-out is half an hour after students return to their dorm rooms.

WEEKEND LIFE

Elan is a demanding place. Students are busy weekdays with group counseling, house functioning, and school. Elan recognizes the need for change of pace, so weekends and holidays are less structured. Students may sleep until 11 a.m. and have brunch at 1 p.m. The rest of the day is usually spent in recreational activities. Elan School is nonsectarian. Attendance and participation in religious services and activities is voluntary but encouraged, and transportation is provided.

SUMMER PROGRAMS

Elan's eight-week summer program is a continuation of the regular school year, except for a change in class times. (Summer program classes run from 7 to 10 p.m.) The curriculum focuses on remedial work tailored to current needs and on special electives. Full use is made of Maine's natural resources and points of interest.

COSTS AND FINANCIAL AID

The rate for the 2005–06 school year was $49,071, billed monthly at $4089. Components of the annual cost are tuition, $19,158; supportive services, $17,118; and board and care, $12,764. The daily rate is $134. Each student's personal account for sundries and entertainment (Student Bank) averages $100 per month and is billed separately each month.

No financial aid is provided by the Elan School directly; however, students not funded privately may be eligible through special education, public welfare, social services, or combinations of the above. Elan also participates in various education loan programs, including the KeyBank Achiever, Sallie Mae, and PrepGate Loan programs. At present, approximately half of Elan's students receive full or partial assistance.

If the student is privately funded, due on the date of admission are the balance of the present month (if paid after the fifteenth, the following month's fees must also be paid) plus a three-month prepayment (applied to the final three months of the program). A $200 deposit for the Student Bank is also required; this is always the parents' responsibility.

ADMISSIONS INFORMATION

Elan accepts referrals from parents/legal guardians, school districts, government agencies, therapists, educational consultants, psychologists, psychiatrists, and anyone with a personal or professional interest in the student. A current psychological evaluation and educational records are reviewed by the Admissions Committee, along with Elan's Admissions Application. Questions of appropriateness are resolved via phone; occasionally, an interview is required. If criteria are met, the referral source is notified—first by phone, and then in writing; funding is verified (if privately placed, Elan's Financial Statement is required); and details of admission are finalized. By the date of admission, school transcripts, birth certificate, immunization records, medical authorizations, health insurance information, and applicable legal documents are required. In order to maximize understanding of Elan's program, parents receive a comprehensive tour before admission (or at the time of admission in emergency placements). The tour includes a visit through one of the houses (escorted by an Elan student) and meetings with personnel from the Admissions, Education, and Medical Departments.

The successful candidate must have at least an average IQ, good reality testing, the ability to develop socialization skills, no history of violent crimes, and must not require psychotropic medications, as Elan does not administer psychotropic medications (although there may be a history of drug therapy). Mild learning disabilities and acting-out behavior are acceptable. Applicants not considered for admission are those with a major mental illness or cognitive deficits or who are actively violent, need psychotropic medications, have a physical condition requiring dietetic restriction or constant medical attention, or are non-English-speaking.

APPLICATION TIMETABLE

Inquiries and admissions occur year-round. Unless an interview is necessary, admissions decisions are usually made within three to four working days. Interviews, tours, and admissions are conducted weekdays (excluding legal holidays). Except for emergency situations, admissions are scheduled for Monday through Thursday during regular business hours. Because of Elan's rolling admissions policy, there are always students graduating from the School; therefore, if there is a waiting list, it is usually short.

ADMISSIONS CORRESPONDENCE

Deanna Valente, Admissions Director
Elan School
P.O. Box 578
Poland, Maine 04274-0578

Phone: 207-998-4666
Fax: 207-998-4660
E-mail: info@elanschool.com
Web site: http://www.elanschool.com

THE FAMILY FOUNDATION SCHOOL

Hancock, New York

Type: Coeducational college-preparatory boarding school offering a 12-step approach to responsible living for at-risk teens
Grades: 7–12
Enrollment: 250
Head of School: Emmanuel Argiros, CEO

THE SCHOOL

Founded in 1987, The Family Foundation School provides a unique opportunity for boys and girls, ages 13–18, who are experiencing difficulty in responding successfully to their home and school environments. Many of these young boys and girls have above-average intellectual aptitude. However, attention difficulties resulting from emotional and behavioral instability, often intensified by substance-abuse problems, have rendered the more traditional avenues of education ineffective. The Family School's widely recognized program, which combines the moral, academic, and psychological training necessary for a healthy maturing process, is designed to guide these young people through the difficulties of their teenage years toward responsible adulthood. The program, based on the Twelve Steps of the Anonymous Fellowships, teaches a reliance on a Higher Power and the core principles of honesty, purity, unselfishness, and love.

Upon arrival at The Family School, each student is assigned a peer sponsor as well as a staff mentor. Positive peer pressure is one of the most effective realities of Family School life, engendering a sense of trust, responsibility, and caring in the new student. In addition, all students participate in one counseling group and two Living Skills classes each week. These groups and classes augment the peer and staff review of attitudes and behavior that constitutes the "personal inventory" work done at mealtimes.

Located on 150 hilltop acres in the Catskill Mountains of upstate New York, The Family School overlooks the Upper Delaware River Valley National Scenic Park. A heightened sense of tranquility and peacefulness is a characteristic response in Family School students to the beauty of the surrounding fields, woodlands, ponds, and streams and the magnificence of the changing seasons. Hiking, canoeing, and winter and summer sports of all kinds, as well as ready access to the cultural events and activities that are a must for a well-developed educational experience, help to create an atmosphere that strongly conduces to a new and healthier approach to life.

ACADEMIC PROGRAMS

The Family School college-preparatory curriculum is accredited by the Middle States Association of Colleges and Schools. It is designed to instill in students a love for learning and to prepare them for the demands and requirements of continuing education. Upon arrival, all students are tested and evaluated for appropriate class placement. Core courses for grades 7–12 include biology, chemistry, earth science, math (through calculus), physics, four years of Spanish, and standard four-year sequences in history and English. In addition, seven college-credit courses are offered on-site, enabling students who need to stay to complete the emotional

growth part of the program to do so with no loss of educational opportunity. A wide range of electives, including art, drama, forensics, journalism, music, physical education, and Web design, supports the development of a true spirit of excellence.

Students generally take a minimum of five academic classes, an elective, and physical education each semester and take part in one or more extracurricular activities. Class size averages 12–15 students, and the student-teacher ratio is 8:1. Grades are mailed to parents each month, and students are required to maintain at least a 75 percent average in order to pass their academic courses.

To accommodate ongoing enrollment throughout the year, there are two graduations: December and June. The two 6-month semesters also allow more review time than is available in traditional school years.

FACULTY AND ADVISERS

A sense of compassion and a genuine interest in the well-being of the students are hallmarks of The Family School faculty members, who are selected for their social work skills as well as their academic backgrounds. Three members of The Family School faculty have Ph.D.'s, and many have a master's in their field. In addition, noted children's author Jan Cheripko is a member of the School's English department. Approximately half of the faculty members are in recovery themselves and are willing and able to share their experience, strength, and hope with the students. All faculty members, regardless of past experience, attend weekly staff training sessions in which the principles of integrity, responsibility, and reliance upon a Higher Power are developed. All teachers are available for extra work, and peer tutors are assigned when necessary. In addition, the teachers work closely with members of the counseling department in a coordinated effort to ensure the students' growth and development.

Members of the counseling department, under the direction of a licensed M.S.W. and supported by a psychiatrist and a psychologist who are in regular attendance, conduct weekly sessions with all students and are in regular contact with parents via the telephone or in face-to-face family groups. They also arrange visits for the students with their parents to facilitate reconciliation with the family, which is one of the primary goals of The Family School program.

COLLEGE PLACEMENT

During their junior and senior years, students are offered a two-day SAT-prep class, following which they take the SAT. Some students take SAT Subject Tests and the ACT, as well.

Members of the School's college guidance office guide the students through the process of

choosing the right college and submitting their applications. Time is then made available for students, accompanied by their parents, to visit the schools they are most interested in attending.

Over the last five years, 100 percent of Family School graduates have been accepted at postsecondary institutions, 85 percent to four-year colleges and 15 percent to two-year schools or professional training. Many of these students came to The Family School with little hope of graduating from high school. Recent graduates have applied to and were accepted by various colleges and universities, including Culinary Institute of America, Kent State, Mary Washington, Marywood, New York Institute of Technology, Purdue, Rutgers, St. John's, Steubenville, Wake Forest, the U.S. Naval Academy, and the Universities of Florida, South Carolina, and Virginia.

STUDENT BODY AND CONDUCT

The Family School population is approximately 250 students, boys and girls, enrolled in grades 7–12. Students come from all over the country and from several international countries as well, making for a richly diverse cultural experience.

The School is structured on the basis of eight individual family units, each with its own family leaders or parents, 10–12 nonrotating staff members, and 30–35 students. Each of these individual families has its own dining, living, studying, and sleeping quarters and enjoys a number of special-event field trips throughout the year. The smaller family groups allow an atmosphere of intimacy in which the student can grow and nurture friendships with his or her peers and develop relationships built on trust and sharing with the adult staff members.

The principles of honesty, purity, unselfishness, and love are fostered through student-led work crews, dorm management, conduct review, and the mutual support that derives from positive peer pressure. Older students "buddy" the newer and younger members from the day of the new student's arrival. This emphasis on sharing, as one of the primary means of dealing with one's own day-to-day problems, creates a new and enlivening sense of responsibility for others and the satisfaction and self-respect that result from taking care of others. Boys and girls are encouraged to relate to each other as sisters and brothers and as friends, without the often-disastrous rush to sexual relationship.

ACADEMIC FACILITIES

The academic building on The Family School's 150-acre mountaintop campus houses twelve classrooms, five of which provide network connections to the School's T-1 Internet link; a regulation-sized gymnasium; a full stage for dramatic and choral productions, equipped with dressing rooms, costume-making facilities, and a

computer-operated lighting system; two science labs; a fine arts studio; and the administrative, guidance, and counseling offices. A separate building, also equipped with a T-1 connection for student research, houses the School's 11,000-volume library, which is part of New York State's interlibrary loan system. Other facilities include a choral- and dance-rehearsal building, a woodcarving shop, and T-1-linked evening study quarters.

BOARDING AND GENERAL FACILITIES

Members of the individual family units, separated by sex, sleep in modern and attractive housing located on the hillside above the main building and just below the School's nondenominational chapel, which overlooks the entire campus and the Upper Delaware River National Scenic Park.

A new multifamily boys' dorm was completed in 2004, and a similar unit for girls will be constructed.

The main building contains the dining, living, and study quarters for each of the eight families. A separate facility houses the School store, fully equipped laundry, and a hair-cutting salon. In addition, a happy and colorful day-care center, serving children of Family School staff members, overlooks the School's swimming pond and enhances the atmosphere of family that pervades the campus.

ATHLETICS

Interscholastic champion soccer and basketball teams highlight a wide-ranging athletic program that promotes good sportsmanship and honest effort above simply winning. Family School teams and fans have been singled out for special mention for the level of good sportsmanship and spirit that they exhibit during league contests. A high-flying, coed cheerleading squad directs the enthusiasm and loyalty of these fans. Interscholastic sports include basketball and soccer, both boys' and girls' teams; coed golf; and girls' softball.

A large, fully equipped gymnasium; soccer and softball fields; outdoor basketball and volleyball courts; numerous paths and trails for hiking; a skating rink; and ready access to the Delaware River encourage active participation in intramural basketball, softball, volleyball, and a wealth of outdoor activities, including horseshoe tossing, hiking, ice-skating, sleigh-riding, rafting, and canoeing.

EXTRACURRICULAR OPPORTUNITIES

A "spirit of excellence" permeates and defines the extracurricular activities that are offered to Family School students on campus. Yearly participation in the North American Music Festival has resulted in superior ratings for the School's mixed, men's, and women's choruses and for the show-stopping Family School show choir. Two major theatrical performances each year, a drama in spring and a musical in the fall, showcase the dance, chorus, and drama students. In addition, a classically trained icon artist and a master woodcarver make available a professional-level fine arts program, while courses in forensics, journalism, novel writing, Web design, and yearbook provide an active forum for, the communications students.

Field trips to the Gettysburg Battlefield, Plymouth Rock, Hershey Park, and Amish country, as well as to Broadway plays, the Mystic Aquarium, and various ballets and concerts presented through the State University of New York at Binghamton's cultural center, are taken by the individual family groups each year. In addition, local visits to nearby bowling alleys, skating rinks, state parks, and ice-cream stands provide for the just-for-fun needs of 250 teenagers.

DAILY LIFE

The weekday begins at 6 a.m. with time for personal hygiene and student-led dorm jobs. This is followed by morning chapel; a rotating schedule of varying denominational services gives students an opportunity to pray and meditate with members of other faiths. Breakfast at 7:45 is followed by academic classes until noon. Lunch includes time for review of the students' conduct and personal difficulties. This "inventory" work is one of the most important activities of The Family School day and is repeated during supper. Staff members and students actively engage in this sharing of experience, strength, and hope.

Weekday afternoons are filled with more academic classes; extracurricular activities, including interscholastic athletic events; various work crews; and study hall. In the evening, mandatory study hall is followed by evening chores, and the day is concluded with a prayer and meditation time in the individual families.

WEEKEND LIFE

Saturdays are given to a mix of chores, study halls, and free time for basketball, volleyball, Frisbee, or just taking a walk. Saturday evenings are generally spent presenting skits and watching movies. Church choir and study halls make up Sunday mornings, while the afternoons are an ongoing and eclectic presentation of yoga, Tae-bo, Native American dancing, arts and crafts, talent shows, barbeques, and sports tournaments. Sunday evenings are dedicated to church services and AA meetings to round out the week on a reflective note.

COSTS AND FINANCIAL AID

Tuition, room, and board cost $4300 per month. There are no application or orientation fees. A $110 personal expense deposit, a $200 medical expense deposit, and a $4300 security deposit are due on admission. Special activities, including educational field trips and SAT-prep courses, may add $600 to $1000 per year.

ADMISSIONS INFORMATION

The Family School offers rolling admissions. The School interviews parents, not students. Interested parents should contact the Director of Admissions, Joseph Lichty. If space is available, the School is able to move quickly to assist families in crisis.

APPLICATION TIMETABLE

Inquiries are welcome at any time. A tour of the campus is given at the time of the interview, and parents have the opportunity to meet with students and staff members and sit in on the "inventory" work that is done at lunch time. Students who are eligible for admission may be enrolled at any time after the interview has been completed, as space permits.

ADMISSIONS CORRESPONDENCE

Joseph Lichty, Director of Admissions
The Family Foundation School
431 Chapel Hill Road
Hancock, New York 13783

Phone: 845-887-5213
Fax: 845-887-4939
E-mail: jlichty@thefamilyschool.com
Web site: http://www.thefamilyschool.com

F. L. CHAMBERLAIN SCHOOL

Middleborough, Massachusetts

Type: Coeducational day and boarding college-preparatory school for students with special emotional and educational needs
Grades: Postgraduate
Enrollment: 92 boarding students
Head of School: William Doherty, Executive Director

THE SCHOOL

F. L. Chamberlain School is a private, nonprofit, coeducational residential school for adolescents, ages 11–18. Many students have emotional and/or behavioral problems with overlapping learning and communication disorders. Chamberlain was founded in 1976 and has always based its treatment upon interdisciplinary service goals.

Chamberlain School's philosophy is based upon the belief that all children are capable of achieving success in vital areas of their lives no matter how adverse or traumatic their lives may have been thus far. A strong principle of the School is to protect, engage, and teach children and their families to develop the skills and confidence to manage their own lives to their highest potential.

The therapeutic treatment goal is to focus upon, contain, and modify maladaptive behavior; promote development of greater competence; and build a stronger and more valued sense of self for academically and emotionally challenged students.

The therapeutic treatment model is cognitive behavioral and reality-based. The strategies utilized include the provision of intensive clinical and psychiatric intervention and treatment, small-group remedial education, a highly structured residential setting, and a therapeutic management system with positive growth and achievement-oriented, nonpunitive consequences and rewards. A strong community network of services and family involvement throughout the course of treatment underscores the program's commitment to the best possible outcomes.

Located on a beautiful 14-acre campus between Cape Cod and Boston, F. L. Chamberlain School serves students from a wide geographic area. The School is licensed by the Massachusetts Office of Child Care Services and approved by the Massachusetts Department of Education.

The School is a member of the National Association of Private Schools for Exceptional Children and the Massachusetts Association of Approved Private Schools. Chamberlain School is under the direction of the board of the directors of the nonprofit corporation.

ACADEMIC PROGRAMS

F. L. Chamberlain School, a diploma-granting institution, offers an education program designed to meet the specific academic needs of each student. The comprehensive curriculum enables students to benefit from a wide variety of learning experiences in order to build classroom skills and promote social growth. A low student-teacher ratio enables students to receive the individualized attention they require in order to be successful.

The School provides a comprehensive and exciting curriculum tailored to each student's needs. Individual and small-group instruction focuses on traditional subjects required for a high school diploma. Extensive and varied electives include computer lab and drama. Students may prepare for college placement. Credit requirements for graduation are determined according to individual academic goals, but each student must achieve standard criteria prior to receiving a high school diploma.

FACULTY AND ADVISERS

The faculty and staff members include 140 professionals chosen for their expertise in specific treatment areas. The academic staff includes certified special education teachers and teacher assistants. The Director of Studies holds an advanced degree and coordinates the overall day program. The clinical staff includes a psychiatrist and 8 licensed therapists. The Clinical Director supervises the ongoing weekly individual and group therapy. There are 3 School nurses to attend to students' health needs.

COLLEGE PLACEMENT

Certified special education teachers assist the students in selecting colleges, filling out applications, and arranging to take the SAT. Teachers take students to area colleges to visit the campuses and interview, if desired. Average SAT scores for last year's college-bound graduating class were 540 verbal and 590 math.

STUDENT BODY AND CONDUCT

The School enrolls 92 students in the boarding component. Additional area students attend the day program. Advanced students who have completed the basic School requirements may prepare for the transition to living independently. Students represent a cross section of ethnic backgrounds and socioeconomic levels.

The therapeutic management system utilizes a structured level system, with repair contracts and proactive contracts to help students improve individual behavior and develop age-appropriate social skills. Feedback from staff members and peers allows students to chart growth, earn rewards for positive efforts, learn from mistakes, and find ways to take responsibility for their behavior in a safe, accepting, and therapeutic environment.

ACADEMIC FACILITIES

The academic classrooms, dining hall, and counseling offices are located in nine colonial-style buildings on the 14-acre main campus, which is very quiet and peaceful. There are designated areas for the computer lab and theater classes.

BOARDING AND GENERAL FACILITIES

Students at Chamberlain School live in large, New England–style houses, usually with 4 students per room. The houses have kitchen facilities and indoor recreation areas. Students are supervised 24 hours a day, and the student-staff ratio in the houses is 5:1 in most cases and 1:1 when necessary. Students participate in daily recreational and sports activities and are assigned daily living tasks. Educational and social outings are scheduled regularly.

EXTRACURRICULAR OPPORTUNITIES

Extracurricular opportunities include a life skills curriculum that encompasses a work-study program. Students are assessed for job readiness and may then participate according to their career planning goals.

Additional extracurricular activities include both planned activities and free-time activities. Extracurricular and recreational activities are scheduled and supervised by the School day staff and residential staff. Activities may be structured, such as bowling, horseback riding, swimming, and team sports, or they may be supervised free-time activities. Students are allowed to listen to music, read, talk with peers, write letters, or pursue individual interests during supervised free time.

DAILY LIFE

Students participate in a structured daily program that includes sharing in meal preparation and basic living chores. Students are responsible for keeping their rooms and general living areas orderly and clean. The school day runs from 8 a.m. to 3 p.m.

The after-school program includes recreational activities and other commitments for reaching individual goals. After dinner, the students complete homework assignments and then may participate in scheduled evening activities and meetings. Bedtime is variable according to the student's level.

WEEKEND LIFE

Activities are scheduled for all boarders on weekends. Activities include films, sports events, cultural events, and outdoor activities. Sunday evenings are scheduled as opportunities for families to meet with the Family Enrichment Coordinator, if desired, to relate any important information or attend workshops on specific topics that are relevant to the student's needs.

SUMMER PROGRAMS

Chamberlain School operates on a full schedule throughout the summer. Students may elect to enter the year-round 365-day program. Academics continue throughout the summer, with increased avocational and recreational activities. One-to-one tutoring is available.

COSTS AND FINANCIAL AID

The cost of tuition, room, board, and clinical services for 2005–06 was $318.43 per day. Parents may leave allowance money, which is kept secure and made available to the student as needed.

ADMISSIONS INFORMATION

Chamberlain School has a rolling admissions policy; a student may enter the 365-day program at various times throughout the year. Chamberlain School accepts referrals for students with various special needs, learning disorders, and/or specific diagnoses. Admission is based upon referral packet information, which includes academic assessments, psychological assessments, previous school history, and a student interview.

APPLICATION TIMETABLE

Application may be made at any time during the year. The Admissions Director will arrange for a campus tour and interview. Arrangements may be made to meet at a convenient geographic location for applicants traveling a long distance. The decision for placement is dependent upon availability, and students may be placed on a waiting list for the next opening.

ADMISSIONS CORRESPONDENCE

Lawrence H. Mutty, Admissions Director
F. L. Chamberlain School
1 Pleasant Street
P.O. Box 778
Middleborough, Massachusetts 02346
Phone: 508-947-7825
Fax: 508-947-0944
E-mail: admissions@chamberlainschool.org
Web site: http://www.chamberlainschool.org

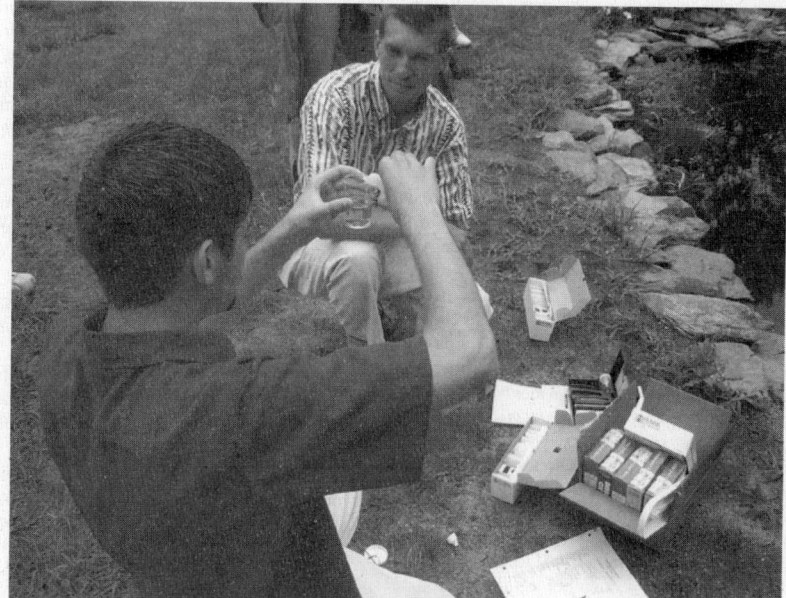

THE FORMAN SCHOOL

Litchfield, Connecticut

Type: Coeducational boarding and day college-preparatory school for students with learning differences
Grades: 9–12
Enrollment: 170
Head of School: Mark B. Perkins

THE SCHOOL

The Forman School was founded in 1930 by John and Julie Forman as a school for young boys who would benefit from close personal attention. An upper school was added in 1935. Forman became coeducational in 1942.

Forman is dedicated to helping students with learning differences achieve academic excellence. Students learn to recognize their own merit and potential and develop an appreciation for challenges as opportunities. Forman nurtures personal growth and love of learning in a caring, supportive environment. A Forman education provides opportunities for achievement and service to others.

Forman is a place where students "fit"—often for the first time in their lives. That is because Forman helps students realize that even though their brains process information differently, they are really the same as everyone else. For students, this is the difference that matters most of all.

Litchfield is a small, rural town located in the hills of northwestern Connecticut, offering an abundance of opportunities for sightseeing, recreation, shopping, dining, and cultural activities. It is famous for its historic sites and monuments and for the White Memorial Foundation, an Environmental Education Center and Nature Museum. Litchfield is 30 miles from Hartford and approximately 100 miles from Boston and New York City. The School campus occupies 100 acres. The property encompasses fields, trout streams, and ponds, with numerous hiking trails. This setting provides the Forman student with many opportunities to pursue nature-oriented interests, as well as cultural, sports, and intellectual activities in the greater Hartford area.

Forman is accredited by the New England Association of Schools and Colleges and is approved by the Connecticut State Department of Education. It is a member of the National Association of Independent Schools, the Connecticut Association of Independent Schools, the National Honor Society, the International Dyslexia Association, the Secondary School Admission Test Board, and the New England Association of College Admissions Counselors. The School is also a member of the International Association of Outdoor Recreation and Education.

The Forman School is a nonprofit corporation governed by a self-perpetuating Board of Trustees that meets four times a year. The School has an annual operating budget of $8.3 million. The School plant is valued at $17.5 million. The Annual Fund raises more than $300,000. A $7.5-million capital campaign is currently under way.

ACADEMIC PROGRAMS

Academic work at Forman is designed to prepare students for success in college. Courses are broad in focus, giving students a solid background upon which to build. Skills are taught so that students will be able to handle the rigor of the college curriculum. Learning Center teachers provide direct, explicit instruction in reading, writing, study, and self-advocacy skills. Teachers work together to provide an optimal learning experience for Forman students.

To graduate, students must earn a minimum of 20 credits, including the following: English, 4; history (including U.S. history), 3; mathematics, 3; science (including two laboratory courses, one of which must be biology I), 3; and art.

The curriculum includes English: introduction to literature, journeys of discovery, the American experience, explorations in literature, and thinking and writing for college; history: modern European, early American, modern American, Model United Nations, and screening American history; foreign languages: French, Spanish, and American sign language; science: ecology, biology, environmental (which includes rain forest research in Costa Rica), chemistry, physics, psychology, and human wellness; math: math fundamentals, consumer math, algebra I, algebra II, geometry, statistics, precalculus, and calculus; computer science; and arts: design I, II, and III, advanced portfolio, photography, ceramics, video, theater arts and production, music composition I and II, and music theory. The average class size is 12 students, and the student-teacher ratio is 3:1.

The Learning Center offers students with learning differences remedial instruction and strategies while they pursue a college-preparatory curriculum. Each student in the program spends five days a week with a trained specialist. The work focuses on skill acquisition, strategic instruction, and compensatory techniques to aid in developing learning skills. Instruction is designed to work with a student's strengths while helping to improve weak skill areas. The structured program includes critical language and study-skills instruction and self-advocacy in educational settings. The learning specialist works with the student's classroom teachers to establish a close, supportive learning environment.

Grades are given for effort as well as for achievement. Grades are available every three weeks for students. Detailed reports are mailed to parents three times a year.

The school year is made up of three 11-week terms, with examinations given at the end of the fall, winter, and spring terms.

FACULTY AND ADVISERS

There are 65 full-time faculty members and administrators who teach; one half live on campus, including 12 married faculty members. More than 50 percent of the faculty members hold advanced degrees.

Mark Perkins was appointed Head of School in 1995. He holds a Bachelor of Arts degree in mathematics from Hobart College and a master's degree in liberal studies from Dartmouth College. Mr. Perkins came to Forman from the Holderness School in New Hampshire, where he served for twenty-six years.

COLLEGE PLACEMENT

Forman has a full-time college counselor. College representatives visit the campus every fall. Students begin college planning in their junior year and receive assistance in finding colleges to match their grades, test scores, interests, and needs. Students also undertake college visits in their senior year.

In 2005, 33 of Forman's 34 graduates went on to college. They are attending such colleges and universities as Curry, Fairfield, Johnson & Wales, Lynn, Ohio Wesleyan, Savannah College of Art and Design, and the Universities of Arizona and Hartford.

STUDENT BODY AND CONDUCT

In 2005–06, the Forman School has 170 students: 152 boarding and 18 day, 125 boys and 45 girls. There are 34 ninth graders, 44 tenth graders, 51 eleventh graders, and 41 twelfth graders. Boarding students come from twenty-seven states and seven countries.

Student committees motivate community growth and provide input to the School. There is an elected student government. Students learn to serve by participating in the School's Job Program.

The School has a judicial system composed of both faculty members and students. The School strongly maintains its code of conduct. Alcohol and illegal drugs are strictly forbidden, and their possession or use is cause for immediate dismissal. All students must undergo a drug screening prior to starting the school year.

ACADEMIC FACILITIES

The expanded and renovated Thomas D. Williams Academic Center, a computer lab, and the Johnson Arts Center constitute the primary classroom facilities at Forman. Forman also has a dedicated Learning Center. The Barbara Chace Library, located in Carpenter Hall, contains 8,000 volumes, an extensive audiocassette and videocassette collection, and books on tape. The library subscribes to fifty-five periodicals and five newspapers.

BOARDING AND GENERAL FACILITIES

There are twelve dormitories on campus that are all fully wired for phones and Internet access. Three out of the twelve dormitories and a student center that includes a student lounge, snack bar, game room, and bookstore were built in the 1990s. In 2002, a new dormitory and a fully

equipped fitness center were built. The School is in the midst of a capital campaign that includes construction of a new library and technology center and the renovation of one dormitory per year.

ATHLETICS
Students are required to participate each afternoon throughout the year in Forman's after-class program. The program includes activities ranging from competitive sports to theater arts. The after-class program provides for social interaction, teamwork, caring for others, leadership opportunities, and, in many cases, physical activity. Most programs meet from 3:30 to 5:30 p.m. Monday through Saturday; however, due to special needs, some activities meet during evenings. Fall offerings include cross-country, football, soccer, and volleyball. Winter offerings include Alpine racing, basketball, ice hockey, wrestling, recreational skiing, and snowboarding. Spring offerings include baseball, golf, lacrosse, tennis, and softball. Community service, Outdoor Leadership Skills, and theater arts are offered all year.

Outdoor Leadership Skills is a program offered as an after-class program that includes canoeing, kayaking, hiking, fishing, boat-building, rock climbing, and weekend camping. A wilderness skills program is also offered throughout the year. The fitness program is offered during the winter term.

Forman has four playing fields, six outdoor tennis courts, two indoor tennis courts, a fitness center, and an 18,000-square-foot gymnasium. There is also an indoor skateboarding facility.

EXTRACURRICULAR OPPORTUNITIES
Students are encouraged to become involved with the yearbook, student government, the student leader program, and the ambassador program.

The Forman Ensemble Players of the drama department present three productions during the school year. The Gallery at the Johnson Arts Center features the work of Forman visual arts students and visiting artists. Special events include Parents' Weekend, Alumni Weekend, the Charity Benefit, the Strawberry Festival, the Junior-Senior Prom, and a winter carnival.

DAILY LIFE
Classes are held six days a week, beginning at 8:45 a.m. Monday, Tuesday, Thursday, and Friday and 9:30 a.m. on Wednesday and Saturday. The school day ends at 3 p.m. on Monday, Tuesday, Thursday, and Friday. Wednesday and Saturday classes end at 12:45. On Monday and Friday, the School comes together for morning assembly. A typical day includes breakfast, classes, lunch, sports from 3:30 to 5:30, dinner, and study hall from 7:30 to 9.

WEEKEND LIFE
The Student Activities Committee plans many activities, including movies, dances, trips to local shopping malls, plays and professional sporting events, and museum tours. Students may also go on trips for fishing, skiing, canoeing, hiking, and other chaperoned activities. A Community Life Program is integrated into the daily routine of the School, with a focus designed to draw students into discussions of topics that are currently relevant to their world, such as conflict, social interaction, and health.

COSTS AND FINANCIAL AID
For 2005–06, tuition charges were $45,000 for boarding students and $37,000 for day students. This cost included learning center instruction. The Forman School requires a Tuition Refund Plan at a cost of $1300 for boarding students and $1000 for day students. Financial aid is available to students based solely on financial need.

Parents send their financial statement form to the School and Students Service (SSS) in Princeton, New Jersey. The Forman School's Financial Aid Committee makes a final determination as to the award.

ADMISSIONS INFORMATION
Forman admits students into grades 9–12 and PG. The Admissions Committee looks for students of good character with average to above-average cognitive ability. Prior to completing the application packet, the committee requires a psychological evaluation, current within two years, which includes a cognitive and an educational evaluation, and an Individual Educational Plan, if available. After review of the evaluations, the Admissions Committee requests an application; a parent and student questionnaire; English, math, and principal/counselor recommendations; a preliminary health form; and school transcripts. The application process also includes a school tour and personal interview.

APPLICATION TIMETABLE
Students are encouraged to apply in the late fall and winter of the year prior to matriculation. There is no application deadline. Inquiries are welcome at any time, and campus tours and interviews are made through the Admissions Office from 8 a.m. to 4 p.m. Monday through Friday.

Admissions decisions are made on a rolling basis as space permits. The application fee is $50.

ADMISSIONS CORRESPONDENCE
Beth A. Rainey, Director of Admissions
The Forman School
12 Norfolk Road
P.O. Box 80
Litchfield, Connecticut 06759-0080

Phone: 860-567-1802
Fax: 860-567-3501
E-mail: admissions@formanschool.org
Web site: http://www.formanschool.org

THE GOW SCHOOL

South Wales, New York

Type: Boys' boarding college-preparatory school for young men with dyslexia/language-based learning differences
Grades: 7–PG: Middle School, 7–9; Upper School, 10–12, postgraduate year
Enrollment: School total: 143; Upper School: 94
Head of School: M. Bradley Rogers, Jr., Headmaster

THE SCHOOL

The Gow School was founded in 1926 by Peter Gow, a teacher who wanted to develop better methods for teaching young men who were experiencing scholastic failure. His work and the research of others led to the establishment of a program for students who have at least average general ability but have a developmental disability in one or more phases of language use. Reconstructive Language (RL) training, reading, writing, and other aspects of language development are stressed throughout The Gow School's college-preparatory curriculum.

There are a wide variety of extracurricular, leadership, and athletic opportunities to aid students' development outside the classroom. Attendance at weekly worship services is required; students either attend local services of their choice or participate in a nonsectarian chapel service on campus.

The School is located in South Wales, a rural community in the western portion of New York, approximately 30 miles southeast of Buffalo and 100 miles south of Toronto, Ontario. Hilly woodlands, twenty-nine buildings (including the Headmaster's residence and ten faculty houses), athletic fields, tennis courts, mountain bike trails, and a ski slope are located on the 100-acre campus, which is traversed by a stream.

The Gow School, which was incorporated not-for-profit in 1975, is governed by a self-perpetuating 23-member Board of Trustees. The board, composed of alumni, parents of alumni, parents of students, and friends of the School, meets three times annually. The School's plant is valued at approximately $14 million and the endowment is $6 million. Many alumni, parents, and friends of the School participate in the Annual Giving Program.

The School is permanently chartered by the New York State Board of Regents and accredited by the New York State Association of Independent Schools. It holds a membership in the National Association of Independent Schools and the International Dyslexia Association.

ACADEMIC PROGRAMS

The school year, which is divided into semesters, extends from early September to late May. Detailed written reports are sent to parents at the end of each marking period and semester. There is also an adviser program, with teachers serving as advisers for 3 to 6 students. Adviser reports are issued to parents four times a year.

Classes, which range in size from 3 to 6, meet six days a week. Generally, a student takes five academic courses in addition to one full-credit Reconstructive Language (RL) course. Each student's program is individualized. RL instruction, a multisensory approach emphasizing phonetics, involves training in deriving meaning from reading, in vocabulary extension, and in oral and written expression. In mathematics, a multisensory manipulative approach stressing concept understanding along with daily drill is used. Throughout the curriculum, instruction begins with the most basic operations and proceeds to more advanced concepts. Daily oral and written work is assigned as a means of promoting accurate and immediate recall.

The traditional college-preparatory curriculum includes English, U.S. history, American perspectives, global studies I and II, economics, business seminar, developmental math, pre-algebra, algebra I, algebra II, geometry, pre-calculus, calculus, earth science, biology, advanced biology, physics, chemistry, art, music, theater, computer literacy, computer programming, and robotics.

The course of study is designed to prepare students to enter college. To graduate, each student must complete 21½ academic credits in grades 9–12, including 4 in English, 3 in history, 3 in mathematics, 2 in laboratory science, and 1 in art/music. Computer literacy, which involves keyboarding, word processing (with a spell-checker), and using database programs, spreadsheets, and presentation software; Upper School health; and an outdoor camping program are all requirements for graduation.

FACULTY AND ADVISERS

The faculty consists of 35 full-time members and 2 part-time members. Ten faculty members and the Headmaster live in the dormitories or in other campus housing. Members of the faculty hold thirty-four baccalaureate degrees, eighteen master's degrees, and one doctoral degree.

M. Bradley Rogers, Jr., was elected Headmaster in 2004. He holds a B.A. degree from the University of Dayton (Ohio) and a master's degree from Johns Hopkins University. Prior to assuming his current position, Mr. Rogers was Headmaster at The Odyssey School in Maryland. He and Mrs. Rogers and their 4 sons reside on campus.

COLLEGE PLACEMENT

The Director of College Counseling begins discussions with students and parents in the junior year. Seniors can leave the campus for college visits. A large collection of college catalogs, videos, and computer search programs is available in the College Advising Center. Most seniors take the ACT and/or SAT in a nonstandard format.

Among the colleges and universities entered by recent graduates are Bates, Centre, Cornell, Davis & Elkins, Denison, Elon, Gannon, Long Beach State, Loyola New Orleans, Marshall, Mount St. Joseph, Muskingum, New England, Northeastern, Regis, RIT, St. Lawrence, Syracuse, West Virginia Wesleyan, and the Universities of Arizona, Denver, Michigan, Missouri–Kansas City, Utah, and Vermont.

STUDENT BODY AND CONDUCT

The School enrolls 143 students from twenty-nine states and twelve other countries. The 2005–06 enrollment, by grade, was 20 in grade 12, 39 in grade 11, 35 in grade 10, and 46 in the Middle School. Student leadership includes resident assistants, headwaiters, Crimson Key Club campus guides, Interact Club, and the student council.

The School does not tolerate the use of alcohol or illegal drugs. The *Student and Parents Handbook* describes the School's no-tolerance policies regarding alcohol and illegal drug use and all other rules and regulations. All disciplinary problems are handled on an individual basis.

ACADEMIC FACILITIES

The Main Building (1926) houses classrooms, the Health Care Center, the Development Office, the Business Office, and the Govian Bookstore. In February 2005, the renovations to the Thompson Building were completed. It houses the Simms Family Theatre, a ceramics studio, a painting and drawing studio, a music room, a digital lab, and the applied technology workshop for the BattleBot IQ program. The Isaac Arnold Library Building (1979) is a reference and study library with 8,000 volumes and ten online computers. In addition, the building contains seven classrooms, administrative offices, and the College Advising Center.

Orton Hall (1987) houses an all-student study hall, the Constantine Computer Center, fourteen classrooms, and the physics/chemistry laboratory.

BOARDING AND GENERAL FACILITIES

Students and dorm families reside in Green Cottage (1926); Templeton Dormitory (1961); Ellis House (1956); Cornwall House (1926); Whitcomb House (1984); and Warner House (1999), which houses 16 students and two faculty families. All of the student dormitory rooms have telephones, Internet access, and cable television. The dining hall was built in 1961.

In addition to the Health Care Center, which is staffed by 7 nurses, a local doctor serves as the School physician, and Buffalo hospitals are approximately 30 minutes away. Emergency services are provided by a local rescue facility a short distance from the School.

ATHLETICS

Athletics and participation in sports are vital parts of the School's program. Interscholastic teams are organized in soccer, crew, swimming, lacrosse, tennis, squash, wrestling, basketball, and cross-country running. The School teams compete with nearby public and other independent schools. Other programs, such as skiing, snowboarding, intramurals, and weight training are available. The outdoor education program is complete with a low- and high-ropes course and an indoor and outdoor climbing wall.

The Gow Center (2002) accommodates many of the athletic and recreational needs of the Gow students and faculty members. It houses an indoor multipurpose space for tennis (two courts), soccer, and lacrosse practices as well as intramurals; hardwood basketball courts; three international squash courts; and a 3,000-square-foot fitness center.

The building also includes an ample student union, three locker rooms, and two classrooms.

EXTRACURRICULAR OPPORTUNITIES

Extracurricular activities vary from year to year. Typical activities are the yearbook, student newspaper, theater, chess, music, in-line skating, skateboarding, and mountain biking. All students are encouraged to participate in drama activities, including the production of at least one play and one musical production each year. A Fall Weekend is scheduled in early October for parents and students. All students are required to participate in a community service program.

DAILY LIFE

The weekday schedule begins with wake-up and room inspection, breakfast, and house jobs between 6:45 and 8 a.m. Classes, supervised study, lunch, a tutorial period, and athletics are scheduled from 8 a.m. until 6 p.m. Following dinner six days each week, all students have approximately 2 hours of supervised study and a reading period before returning to their dorms. Faculty members provide assistance during these study periods, although some students work more independently in their dorm rooms if they meet certain academic standards.

WEEKEND LIFE

There are dances and social activities scheduled throughout the year. Girls from various local schools attend. Each Saturday evening, boys have dates or take a bus to a local mall to shop and see a movie. The Director of Student Activities oversees the selection of a variety of area events for Gow students to attend with faculty supervision. These have included symphony and rock concerts, theater, plays and musicals, auto shows, ethnic festivals, paintball, NHL hockey games, and NFL football games. During each semester, certain weekends are designated for students to go home or visit with a local family. Special trips and activities are planned for those who remain on campus.

COSTS AND FINANCIAL AID

Tuition, room, and board are $40,300 for the 2005–06 school year. Books, supplies, and allowances total approximately $1700.

Tuition loans and scholarships are available on a limited basis. The $4000 enrollment deposit is applied to the first year's tuition.

ADMISSIONS INFORMATION

Gow admits young men capable of traditional, intensive college-preparatory work who need specific Reconstructive Language and mathematics training. Gow is not equipped to educate those with severe physical handicaps, below-average intelligence, or serious emotional or behavioral problems. Diagnostic testing, school records, recommendations, and a personal interview are required for admission. In addition, specific skill testing to determine class placement is mandatory at the School. Testing and the interview usually require one day to complete. New students are admitted to all grades; late enrollment is possible if vacancies exist.

APPLICATION TIMETABLE

Students are interviewed throughout the year. Parents are encouraged to begin the process as early as possible by making inquiry, forwarding to the School all testing and academic records, and setting up an admissions appointment. The application fee is $75.

ADMISSIONS CORRESPONDENCE

Director of Admissions
The Gow School
P.O. Box 85
South Wales, New York 14139

Phone: 716-652-3450
Fax: 716-687-2003
E-mail: admissions@gow.org
Web site: http://www.gow.org

Photo courtesy of The Buffalo News

GROVE SCHOOL
Madison, Connecticut

Type: Coeducational boarding college-preparatory and general academic school within a therapeutic milieu
Grades: 6–PG: Middle School, 6–8; Upper School, 9–12, postgraduate year
Enrollment: School total: 105; Upper School: 60
Head of School: Richard L. Chorney, President and CEO; Peter J. Chorney, Executive Director

THE SCHOOL

Grove School was founded in 1934. The academic program is based on the "educateur" (teacher-counselor) model. Grove is a therapeutic boarding school with strong clinical support. The academic program provides an emphasis on supportive education. Teachers are also involved in residential life and activities. Classes are small and oriented to the individual. Tutoring and remediation are readily available and geared to address the best way for a student to learn.

The School is located on 90 acres of beautifully wooded land in Madison, Connecticut (population 18,719), a New England shoreline community 20 miles north of New Haven and 50 miles south of Hartford.

Grove School is a proprietary corporation with an Advisory Board composed of 12 individuals with varied backgrounds, including many noted professionals in the fields of medicine and education. The School is funded in its entirety by monies generated from tuition.

Grove School is approved by the Connecticut State Department of Education and the Connecticut State Department of Children and Families (DCF). Grove is an affiliate of the World Federation for Mental Health. The School is also a member of the National Association of Therapeutic Schools and Programs (NATSAP) and the American Academy of Child and Adolescent Psychiatry (AACAP).

ACADEMIC PROGRAMS

Grove School's program is designed to meet the academic and therapeutic needs of adolescent boys and girls between the ages of 11 and 18 who have average or above-average intelligence but who need opportunities to increase their social skills at school, at home, or with peers.

The general philosophy of Grove School is based on a supportive, psychoeducational approach delivered through academic programming in a holistic milieu. Both therapeutic and academic plans are determined to meet the needs of each child. Students who successfully complete academic requirements for the high school grades, 9 through 12, as established by the state of Connecticut and Grove School, are awarded a high school diploma.

In order to qualify for a high school diploma, all students must complete the following courses: 4 years of English; 2 years of U.S. history; 2 years of mathematics; 2 years of science, 1 of which must be biology; 1 year of computer science; and 4 years of physical education (unless excused for medical reasons). Additional elective courses in the arts, sciences, and humanities may be selected by the student with the advice of his or her administrative adviser and the Principal, to bring the total academic units required for graduation to 21.

Students are placed in classes based on their academic level, age, and social-emotional development. The student-teacher ratio is about 4:1. There is a supervised 1½-hour evening study period in the dorms. Students in need of extra help must spend additional time in a supervised after-school study hall.

Grades are given on an A to F scale (or on a pass/fail basis when indicated). Reports are sent home five times a year. Remedial assistance and additional tutoring are readily available.

The School offers a twelve-month program with four vacation periods, each of about two weeks' duration. Intensive, individualized work is carried on during the summer months as well as during the regular academic year. The therapeutic and academic work of the summer session is accompanied by extensive activities. A minimum stay of two years is generally needed in order to take full advantage of the Grove program.

FACULTY AND ADVISERS

The School's faculty (teacher-counselors) numbers 30 full-time members (men and women in equal numbers). There are also assistant teachers and part-time instructors, who expand students' experience and activities with music lessons (a variety of instruments), photography, ceramics, stained-glass craft, and sports, including snow skiing and tennis. These offerings are changed from time to time for variety.

All teachers have bachelor's degrees and are certified or in the process of obtaining certification. Forty percent of the teaching staff members have advanced degrees, and about half are actively pursuing higher education in the Grove School/Southern Connecticut State University–sponsored master's program in special education.

In addition to teachers, Grove School has 12 clinicians on its staff—4 psychiatrists, 4 psychologists, and 4 LCSWs and/or LMFTs. All students are seen twice a week in individual psychotherapy. All students and staff members meet twice daily (after breakfast and dinner) in large-group community meetings that are generally conducted by the Executive Director or Associate Director(s). Students also meet weekly in group counseling sessions of up to 8 students with a therapist and an administrator.

The President and CEO, Richard L. Chorney, has an M.S. degree in special education from Southern Connecticut State University and a B.A. in psychology from Bard College. He also has a certificate in psychiatric administration from the University of Wisconsin. He has more than forty years' experience in residential treatment and school administration. The 12 members of the administrative staff also serve as advisers to the students. Administrators carry a case load of 8 to 10 students.

The Executive Director, Peter Chorney, graduated from Bucknell University with a B.A. in psychology and school psychology and has his M.S. in special education from Southern Connecticut State University. He has been a part of Grove School since he was a teenager, as he grew up next door to the campus. As Executive Director, he manages many different aspects of the program, including the hiring and recruitment of teachers and care staff members. He also is the baseball coach and student council adviser. He has worked at Grove for more than ten years in various capacities.

COLLEGE PLACEMENT

Juniors and seniors prepare for the SAT early in the year through various practice exercises and an SAT preparation program. Senior English classes include the preparation of a college essay. The students' adviser and the School Principal help students select appropriate schools, using the numerous college catalogs available. Parents and therapists are included in the college selection process.

Special testing procedures such as untimed administration of the SAT or large-type tests are arranged when appropriate for learning-disabled students.

Recent Grove graduates are attending Berklee College of Music, Dickinson, Hartwick, Keene State, Manhattanville, Northeastern, Purdue, Roger Williams, Skidmore, and Suffolk, among others.

STUDENT BODY AND CONDUCT

There are 40 students in the Middle School, 60 in the Upper School, and 5 postgraduate students. The population of the School represents sixteen states and several other countries. International students and members of minority groups are encouraged to seek admission.

The School's code of conduct is clearly explained to all students. Much importance is attached to the relationships students establish with staff members and one another. All issues are discussed and worked through with the child's therapist and with other adults who are connected to the student. Privileges are earned, and there is a clear hierarchy of responsibilities that lead to the granting of privileges. Students help one another as peer assists, and older students often tutor younger students. The Student Council is advised and guided by the Executive Director.

ACADEMIC FACILITIES

Two main School buildings house the majority of the Upper and Middle School classes. The Redlich Building contains the Computer Program Resource Center; the Upper School houses the art complex for fine arts and ceramics, the computer program, the science laboratories, and the Middle School classrooms. The Pavilion houses the Student Union. The gymnasium contains weight-training facilities.

BOARDING AND GENERAL FACILITIES

Students live in twelve cottages and dorms that hold from 6 to 10 youngsters and 2 faculty members each. There are seven spaces for transitioning students who have earned more privileges and live more independently. Most rooms are doubles.

There is a Health Center on the campus, where registered nurses take care of students' medical needs and concerns and refer patients to local physicians and dentists as appropriate. The nurses also maintain close contact with families concerning medical and dental issues.

ATHLETICS

The School offers a complete, noncompetitive coed sports program that emphasizes participation, the benefits of physical activity in the development of a healthy body, and the social benefits derived from games and play. There are opportunities to take part in off-campus sports activities that include skiing, bowling, sailing, golf, snorkeling, diving, canoeing, rafting, waterskiing, horseback riding, biking, hiking, mountain climbing, fishing, and camping trips. There are also competitive teams in basketball, baseball, softball, and soccer as well as intramural basketball and floor hockey. Individual interests in specific activities such as tennis, racquetball, weight training, kickboxing, and golf may be pursued on an individual basis where appropriate.

In addition to its gymnasium, Grove maintains a baseball and soccer field. The Madison beaches on the Long Island Sound can be used for sailing.

EXTRACURRICULAR OPPORTUNITIES

Grove students regularly attend local plays, concerts, and movies. Frequent trips are made to New York City and Boston to pursue both cultural and sports interests. All students are expected to involve themselves in at least one of the extracurricular or athletic activities. After school and on evenings and weekends, a variety of regularly scheduled activities are offered, including ceramics, drawing and painting, stained-glass craft, photography, work-maintenance projects, culinary arts (cooking and baking), drama, creative writing (newspaper and yearbook), and journalism. Filmmaking, musical instruction, gardening and horticulture, sculpture, and model making, as well as a variety of scientific interests, are offered. Yoga, aerobics, dance, and gymnastics are also available.

A yearly parents' day is held in the spring, and a holiday program is presented in December. A graduation ceremony/banquet for all students, staff members, and parents of graduates takes place in August. A sailing or land/sea program takes 24 students and staff members to the Caribbean in the winter and/or spring aboard a large schooner (or they may be housed in a large villa). The focus is on art, adventure, science, and the sea. The history of the Caribbean is also emphasized. Generally, there are two such trips each year.

DAILY LIFE

Students awaken at 7 a.m. and have breakfast at 8. A community meeting takes place every morning after breakfast. Classes start at 8:40. There are seven 45-minute periods, ending at 3. The lunch period is from 11:54 to 12:30. Classes begin again at 12:32 p.m. A seventh period on Tuesday and Wednesday is reserved for faculty meetings. Activity periods are from 3 to 4:45 and from 6:15 to 7:30. Supper is from 5 to 5:30. Staff members meet from 5:30 to 6 daily, including weekends. Study hall runs from 7:30 to 9. All students are expected to be in their dorms by 7:30, unless permission is obtained for late privileges.

WEEKEND LIFE

Weekend programs are planned regularly with the Activities Coordinators and the staff members on duty. Most students are at Grove on any given weekend, so a wide array of events is planned. Shopping in local towns is an available activity. Students may obtain permission to visit with friends in town. Movies are shown on campus, and there are frequent seasonally oriented trips to theaters, sports events, and other activities. Trips to amusement parks, camping, waterskiing, and rafting are popular warm-weather activities. Snow skiing, cross-country skiing, skating, and sledding occur regularly during the winter.

SUMMER PROGRAMS

The Grove summer program carries on the regular activities of the year. All students attend school. There is added emphasis, however, on individual tutoring and remediation. Large-group activities, using the outdoors and the advantages of the Northeast, are promoted. Trips are taken weekly. Favored excursions include visits to amusement parks and fairs as well as deep-sea fishing and camping trips. Summer is an active, very enjoyable time at Grove.

COSTS AND FINANCIAL AID

The cost of tuition (education, room, board, and clinical services) for the 2005–06 year was $76,800. Tuition is subject to change. Two months' tuition must be paid in advance, on admission. Billing thereafter is on a monthly basis, in advance.

A deposit is also required to complete the admission process. This sum remains as a revolving fund to cover certain incidental expenses and is to be replenished monthly, depending on expenses incurred during the preceding month.

Incidental expenses include, but are not limited to, transportation, medical and dental fees, clothing purchases, school supplies, laundry, special instruction, and special recreational events (including international travel, skiing, and the Caribbean sailing program). There is an activities fee. This fee covers all activity expenses, exclusive of those mentioned above.

ADMISSIONS INFORMATION

Grove encourages inquiries and referrals from parents, therapists, educational consultants, and school representatives. Requirements include an interview and School tour with parents and the student. Appointments for interviews must be made in advance. Referral materials, including but not limited to educational transcripts and summaries, and a recent psychological, psychoeducational, and/or psychiatric assessment should be sent to the Director of Admissions after a preliminary referral call requesting information.

Grove School does not discriminate on the basis of race, sex, color, creed, or national origin in its admissions policies. Admission is determined by the Admissions Committee.

APPLICATION TIMETABLE

Initial inquiries are welcome at any time. Interviews and tours are conducted from 9 to 2, Monday through Friday. Application may be made at any time during the school year and the summer. Grove has an open, rolling admissions policy. Parents are advised of the admissions decision shortly after the interview.

ADMISSIONS CORRESPONDENCE

Director of Admissions
Grove School
175 Copse Road
P.O. Box 646
Madison, Connecticut 06443

Phone: 203-245-2778
Fax: 203-245-6098
E-mail: info@GroveSchool.org
Web site: http://www.GroveSchool.org

THE JOHN DEWEY ACADEMY

Great Barrington, Massachusetts

Type: Coeducational, year-round, college-preparatory, residential therapeutic school
Grades: 10–12, postgraduate year
Enrollment: 35
Head of School: Dr. Thomas Edward Bratter, President

THE SCHOOL

Founded in 1985 by Dr. Thomas Edward Bratter, the John Dewey Academy offers intensive, individualized instruction that stimulates academic excellence and moral integrity. The John Dewey Academy is accredited by the New England Association of Schools and Colleges. This proprietary program devotes 70 percent of its efforts to the attainment of academic excellence and 30 percent to emotional growth.

The John Dewey Academy is a residential, college-preparatory, therapeutic high school for 35 gifted and formerly alienated students who range in age from 16 to 21 and who have engaged in self-destructive behavior. These adolescents are psychologically and socially intact. Although misdiagnosed as unmotivated, they are, in fact, unconvinced. In the absence of fulfillment of affective, intellectual, and creative needs, often the gifted act out against an environment they feel is sterile and hostile. The common presenting problem for these students is a negative attitude. They are demoralized because they have compromised (and in extreme cases have seemingly destroyed) future educational, professional, and social options. Traditional educational and psychotherapeutic approaches do not work with this difficult-to-convince-and-motivate group of adolescents.

The vast majority of students arrive at JDA after multiple attempts to help them have failed. These efforts in the past of more conventional mental health practitioners generally include the prescription of a variety of psychotropic medications, none of which have been effective in slide into dysfunction. Presenting symptoms include self-medication with alcohol, prescription drugs, or illegal drugs; promiscuity; depression and suicidality; anxiety; self-mutilation; eating disorders; withdrawal into the Internet or other electronic media; anger and defiance; and deceit, including stealing, lying, or cheating. By creating constant crises with their dangerous behaviors and performing dangerous acts, students have demonstrated they need a structured, safe, and supportive residential treatment environment to help them control and curtail self-destructive behavior.

In 1902, Dewey identified three kinds of growth pragmatic that learning must address—intellectual, emotional, and moral. The John Dewey Academy achieves this ambitious mandate with a two-pronged approach. First, the school promotes intellectual growth by equipping students with the written and verbal communications skills necessary to succeed. They teach the student how to become an active learner; think conceptually, constructively, critically, and creatively and communicate their beliefs logically and persuasively; achieve written, verbal, and computational proficiency; problem solve; appreciate intellectual, cultural, and aesthetic achievement; and use, rather than continue to abuse, superior intellectual and creative potential. The school's second aim is to nurture the moral, psychological, and spiritual development of students.

These adolescents have trapped themselves in a no-win, no-exit labyrinth in which the negative self-fulfilling prophecy imprisons them. Failing begets

failure, rejecting begets rejection, betraying begets betrayal—producing the intense pain of demoralization. These adolescents are on a collision course that may result in permanent damage to their lives.

Dewey students are admitted on the basis of an interview regardless of standardized test scores, academic performance, and psychiatric reports. The school understands that such historical data are often not reflective of a student's true potential. When the students are placed in the unrelenting and uncompromising environment of John Dewey, they achieve the greatness of which they are capable.

At JDA, students often complain about feeling stressed. Expectations for academic achievement and moral integrity escalate as students improve. The school rejects mediocrity and demands excellence, both academically and morally. Only those who are ready to commit to improve by working diligently should apply. Caring confrontation by their peers forces students to accept responsibility for their behavior; thus, the stage is set for deep and lasting change.

JDA teaches the adolescent to accept responsibility for attitudes and acts; develop a positive concept of self and a proactive philosophy of life; take control by becoming independent; trust and be trusted, respect and be respected, help and be helped, and love and be loved; regain self-respect by making reasonable, responsible, and realistic decisions; and contribute to the betterment of society.

The treatment orientation is confrontation. The presenting problem, reduced to its lowest common dominator for Dewey students is that they possess toxic and often antisocial attitudes. Self-destructive behavior is symptomatic. The ultimate treatment goal is to nurture the psychological, moral, and spiritual growth of each student by creating conditions conducive to (re)gaining self-respect and personal integrity. Each adolescent is encouraged to establish a positive identity. In group work, teenagers relate to and learn from peers, learning how to establish positive and reciprocal relationships with family and adults. The group not only demands that the member accepts responsibility for stupid and self-destructive behavior but also helps the youth resolve problems. "Alone you can do it, but you can't do it alone" describes this potent psychotherapeutic principle that all self-help approaches, such as Alcoholics Anonymous, utilize.

Confrontation psychotherapy demands growth and improvement. Such growth sets up a cycle of positive reinforcement that leads to further and deeper changes/maturation in the individual. Confrontation forces the student to take control of his or her life. When the student's behavior becomes congruent with a positive value system, self-respect is a realistically attainable goal. Confrontation, though often painful, becomes a caring, creative, and constructive intervention to maximize change. Thus, the process virtually ensures future personal, educational, professional, and social success in the students who graduate from JDA.

The primary treatment goal is to help the student (re)gain self-respect. The (explicit) honor code prizes honor, respect, integrity, truth, decency, and excellence.

Group work is the primary method employed, which is supplemented by individual and family therapy. There are at least four 2-hour groups per week. There is also a weekly men's and women's group. Each night, students participate in a 1-hour self-help group. In groups, students can relate to and identify with their peers, who offer insight and suggestions that provide the catalytic conditions necessary for self-exploration and change. Each student has a primary counselor who discusses personal and family problems.

Eight times throughout the year, parents participate in therapeutic weekends at the school: first, a group in which parents can introduce themselves and discuss their concerns regarding their child; second, an intergenerational group where family members are separated so discussion can be candid and helpful; and third, a mothers' and a fathers' group where discussion focuses on role-related problems. A sibling group meets as well to help both the JDA student and his or her sibling(s) repair their relationships.

The John Dewey Academy rejects claims by psychopharmacologists and neuropsychiatrists that intrapsychic problems are caused by metabolic disorders, genetic imbalances, and cellular deficiencies. The Academy believes that the feelings of depression (which are reality based), pain, shame, inadequacy, and fear that overwhelm adolescents are caused by conscious dysfunctional, dishonest, destructive decisions not biological aberrations. The Academy believes that the assumption that people have biochemical defects ignores the impact of toxic acts and attitudes. When asked, students can provide realistic reasons why they are depressed and are consumed by self-contempt. There is no pill that teaches self-respect or cures noxious narcissism, deceit, or antisocial attitudes. The school eschews the use of all psychotropic medications at John Dewey. JDA is a drug-free environment.

ACADEMIC PROGRAMS

The quality and breadth of academics distinguishes the John Dewey Academy from other special-purpose schools.

The curriculum is designed to stimulate and inspire active learning and the development of critical-thinking skills. This learning approach helps students define the synergetic relationship between themselves and society by gaining an awareness and appreciation of science, mathematics, history, social sciences, language, and the arts. Advanced math and science courses, such as advanced calculus, linear algebra, and advanced physics, are offered. The school offers French, Italian, Spanish, Latin, and Greek. Students can study philosophy and psychology as well as multidisciplinary offerings in the social sciences. Students can take an independent study course in a subject of interest to them. Students can earn honors

credits by designing individualized projects. Class size ranges from 1 to 8 students.

To graduate, students need to complete a minimum of 24½ credits, including English (4), social studies (4), mathematics (3), science (3), foreign language (2), creative arts (2), physical education (2), health issues (½), and electives (4). Opportunities are available to take advanced courses at local colleges. There are two 18-week semesters and an 11-week summer program. Students take at least five academic courses during each semester.

The John Dewey Academy is a two- to three-year program. Depending on academic performance and attitude, the length of time for postgraduate (PG) students can be less than two years. Individualized programs for PG students can include taking college courses, serving as a congressional intern, and participating in other types of community activities.

FACULTY AND ADVISERS
There are 9 full-time faculty members, augmented by 4 part-time members. Faculty members possess B.A. degrees from Columbia, St. John's (Annapolis), the School of Visual Arts, Tulane, and the Universities of Michigan and Wisconsin. Faculty members have M.A. degrees from Columbia, New School for Social Research, Oxford, and SUNY. They have doctorates from Columbia Teachers College, NYU, Stanford, and SUNY. More than half of the faculty members have doctorates in their academic disciplines, and more than a third have college teaching experience. One third of the faculty are members of Phi Beta Kappa. One faculty member is a Rhodes Scholar.

In addition to demonstrated academic competence, the faculty members promote self-discovery, self-reliance, and respect for oneself and others.

Dr. Thomas Bratter, a graduate of Columbia College, received his master's degrees and his doctorate in counseling psychology from Columbia University, Teachers College. Dr. Bratter created and directed six community-based programs in Westchester County, New York. He maintained an independent practice of psychotherapy in Scarsdale, where he worked with adolescents and their families. He founded the John Dewey Academy, because he felt there were no rigorous academic programs that addressed the psychosocial-educational needs of gifted adolescents requiring a residential setting. Dr. Bratter has written more than 150 articles about individual, group, and family treatment for at-risk adolescents. He has coauthored four books: *The Reality Therapy Reader, How to Survive Your Adolescent's Adolescence, Alcoholism and Substance Abuse: Strategies for Intervention,* and *Smart Choices.*

COLLEGE PLACEMENT
Most students enter the John Dewey Academy with mediocre grades and inconsistent academic records. Many function more than one grade level below their chronological age, so they need intensive, individualized instruction to remedy educational deficits.

Since the first class graduated in 1987, 100 percent of graduates have attended college. Similar to elite U.S. prep schools, this academy judges itself by the reputations of the colleges that admit the graduates. Seventy percent attend some of the most selective fifty colleges in the United States. Dewey students compete successfully against 'the brightest and the best for admission to top colleges and universities.

JDA graduates excel when they reach the university setting. A third have made the dean's list at Barnard, Bates, Carleton, Columbia (College and University) Connecticut College, Cornell, George Washington, Georgetown, Hobart and William Smith, Holy Cross, Mount Holyoke, NYU, Oberlin, Ohio Wesleyan, Rensselaer, Rochester, Skidmore, Spelman, Syracuse, Trinity, Tufts, Union (New York), Vassar, Wellesley, Williams, and the Universities of Chicago, Hartford, Massachusetts, and Oregon. Seventy percent graduate from college in four years; a small percentage require longer to complete college.

After graduation from college, less than one fifth of the Academy's graduates feel the need for psychotherapy or psychopharmacology. Critics may claim that the John Dewey Academy's treatment orientation is simplistic or harsh, but the school believes that teaching students that their behavior has consequences serves the students well in later life. The records of graduates, therefore, are indistinguishable from those of the most prestigious and elite prep schools in the country. More importantly, graduates are productive and honorable members of society.

STUDENT BODY AND CONDUCT
The Honor Code is regarded as sacrosanct. Each student must agree to abide by an Honor Code that enhances the learning environment and the quality of residential life. Any violation of this contract can result in expulsion. Students assume responsibilities for the maintenance and management of the school.

Students play active roles in formulating and implementing school policies. The President retains the right to make the final determination but remains accountable to the students, staff, and parents. Students learn about leadership by often being deliberately placed in situations in which they need to render their opinions and act decisively.

Positive peer pressure encourages individual empowerment and the acceptance of responsibility for behavior; thus, staff supervision is advisory rather than authoritative. Students gain status and tangible privileges when they convince the faculty that they are responsible and productive.

ACADEMIC FACILITIES
Completed in 1887 at a cost of $2.3 million and modernized eighty years later, Searles Castle was designed by Sanford White and is listed in the National Register of Historic Places. The forty-five rooms are used for classrooms, offices, and living space. Located in an oak-paneled room, the library houses 13,000 volumes.

BOARDING AND GENERAL FACILITIES
Students live in Searles Castle. A maximum of 4 students reside in the large rooms, some of which have marble fireplaces. The recently renovated Carriage House provides additional living accommodations and classroom space for 20 students.

ATHLETICS
The John Dewey Academy has no competitive teams. Leisure-time fitness activities are emphasized, including hiking, jogging, skating, skiing, swimming, and tennis. The 40-acre campus can accommodate various team sports, such as soccer and basketball. There is a tennis court on the property as well as a small indoor gym facility with machines and free weights.

EXTRACURRICULAR OPPORTUNITIES
Students assume the responsibility to govern the John Dewey Academy. There are four teams—business, academic, kitchen, and maintenance—that provide students with pragmatic opportunities to learn how to work and develop their leadership abilities in real-world situations. Internships in a variety of community-based agencies can be arranged to augment students' learning.

DAILY LIFE
The school day begins at 8 a.m. and adheres to a college model of class scheduling. From 7 until 9 nightly, students study either individually or in small groups. There is a 3-hour Saturday study hall. Curfew is at 11:30 p.m.—except on Friday and Saturday nights, when students can stay up until 1 a.m.

WEEKEND LIFE
After a Saturday morning study hall, students have no classes until Monday, and they may go into town. As a destination resort, the Berkshires has many cultural and recreational opportunities, including classical music, theater, ballet, and lectures. During the summer, there is hiking and camping; in the winter, skiing is available 3 miles away. Those students with cars can transport peers to local movies and concerts.

COSTS AND FINANCIAL AID
The fifty-two-weeks' tuition is $75,000. The Academy is not a licensed residential treatment center; however, insurance companies generally reimburse a portion of the cost of a therapeutic program. School districts in Connecticut, Indiana, Maryland, Massachusetts, New Hampshire, New York, and Pennsylvania have reimbursed parents for tuition. Financial aid is limited.

ADMISSIONS INFORMATION
The interview is the most important determinant in the admissions process; it reveals the prospective student's current attitude and potential. Persuading the Academy that the applicant has redeeming intellectual virtues and personal qualities remains the task of the adolescent, not the family or the referral source. The candidate can plead his or her case during the mandatory on-campus interview and is expected to specifically answer the questions "Why should the John Dewey Academy admit me?" and "What am I prepared to contribute to the community?"

After admission, students undergo a probationary period. Assuming the student wants to remain and the clinical staff approves, a majority vote by the community determines full admission into the community. Acceptance is not automatic. Only those students who are able to handle rejection and are willing to work toward becoming strong, stable, and socially sophisticated should apply.

APPLICATION TIMETABLE
The Academy accepts students at any time, depending on space and scheduling considerations. For further information or to set up an interview, students should contact Dr. Lisa Sinsheimer at 917-597-7814 or via e-mail at sinsheimer@speakeasy.net.

ADMISSIONS CORRESPONDENCE
Dr. Thomas E. Bratter, President
Dr. Kenneth Steiner, Dean
The John Dewey Academy
389 Main Street
Great Barrington, Massachusetts 01230
Phone: 413-528-9800
Fax: 413-528-5662
E-mail: tbratter@jda.org
Web site: http://www.jda.org

KILDONAN SCHOOL

Amenia, New York

Type: Coeducational boarding and day college-preparatory and general academic school for students with dyslexia
Grades: 2–12, postgraduate year
Enrollment: 134
Head of School: Ronald A. Wilson, Headmaster

THE SCHOOL

The Kildonan School was founded in 1969 by Diana Hanbury King to serve the needs of dyslexic students of average to above-average intelligence. The School's threefold mission remains consistent. Kildonan strives to remediate skills in reading, writing, and spelling; provide intellectually stimulating subject matter courses in mathematics, literature, science, and social studies; and foster confidence and self-esteem.

A residential setting free from distractions is most effective in providing a unified program that is consistent with the needs of the student. Each student's day is carefully planned to include a variety of experiences designed to diminish anxiety while building confidence in mental and physical capabilities.

Central to the success of the School is a faculty committed to its philosophy and willing to work hard to implement its goals and ideals. A faculty member's respect for each student as an individual is combined with a willingness to demand the best from each student. A teacher shows regard for a student by refusing to accept any but the student's best efforts.

The School was originally established on a rented campus in Bucks County, Pennsylvania. In 1980, it acquired its own campus in Amenia, New York. The School can now accommodate more than 100 boarding students in a spacious rural setting 90 miles north of New York City; 30 miles northeast of Poughkeepsie, New York; and 55 miles west of Hartford, Connecticut. Located on a hillside, the 450-acre campus is made up of woodlands, fields, a pond, athletic fields, equine facilities, and the School facilities.

The Kildonan School is a nonprofit corporation, governed by a self-perpetuating Board of Trustees. The board is composed primarily of parents of alumni and meets three times a year.

The physical plant is valued at approximately $4.3 million. Alumni, parents, relatives, and friends of the School support the Annual Giving Fund.

The Kildonan School holds a permanent charter from the New York State Board of Regents. It is accredited by the New York State Association of Independent Schools and holds membership in the National Association of Independent Schools.

ACADEMIC PROGRAMS

The academic program is unique in that it revolves around the intensive, daily, one-to-one Orton-Gillingham tutoring for each student. The language-training instructor is responsible for devising a sequential learning program in language skills in accordance with Dr. Samuel T. Orton's principles and his belief that "such disorders should respond to specific training if we become sufficiently keen in our diagnosis and if we prove ourselves clever enough to devise the

proper training methods to meet the needs of each particular case." Orton-Gillingham tutoring is multisensory, direct, and effective. The tutorial setting makes it possible to tailor the teaching to the unique learning style of each individual. The instructor is also responsible for inculcating orderly study habits; students are held accountable for daily independent reading and writing assigned to reinforce the skills taught during the tutorial. Students learn to work through periods of frustration and even temporary failure. Ultimately, the goal is for students to become independent learners.

Subject matter courses in mathematics, history, literature, and science are designed to meet the learning style of dyslexic students. Visual, auditory, and kinesthetic presentations supplement textbooks. Class size is small; courses stimulate thinking and provide opportunities for creativity. The approach to mathematics is closely aligned with language training both in its logical, sequential approach and its daily assignments. Reading and writing demands are reduced or removed entirely from other content courses while the student is building reading and writing skills in the tutorial. Classes are structured to ensure that success is possible even for the student with minimal literacy skills.

Enhanced confidence is achieved through activities, such as the arts, athletics, and community life. Involvement in extracurricular activities that capitalize on the innate strengths of the dyslexic student often leads to lifelong interests. Leadership and service opportunities provide additional means for personal and social growth. Students become confident, experience greater success, and gain the courage to invest increasing effort in their personal and academic achievement.

Kildonan believes that learning best occurs in a structured, safe, and caring environment, which Kildonan provides in both its academic and student-life programs.

All students leave equipped with the best preparation available for the next stage of their academic development, and, of equal importance, with an appreciation for the strengths of the dyslexic mind. While most students are expected to graduate from high school and enter college or other postsecondary programs, the more severely dyslexic students achieve functional mastery of the language.

Minimum requirements for graduation are as follows: 4 units each of English, social studies, and mathematics; 3 units in science; 1 unit in art; 2 units in physical education; and elective courses that bring the total up to at least 20½ units.

FACULTY AND ADVISERS

There are 58 faculty members—22 men and 36 women. Of the total, 1 has a doctorate, 10 have master's degrees, and 47 have bachelor's degrees.

There are also 3 Fellows of the Academy of Orton-Gillingham Practitioners and Educators on staff.

Headmaster Ronald Wilson was at The Harvey School for eight years before coming to Kildonan in 1986. During his tenure at Harvey, he held the positions of Assistant Headmaster, Dean of Students, and Head of the Upper School. He also taught science and mathematics, was responsible for discipline and testing, and supervised a dormitory for four years. Before that, he taught mathematics and science at St. Agnes School in Key Biscayne, Florida. He holds a B.S. in psychology from the State University of New York College at Brockport and an M.S. in counselor education from Western Connecticut State University.

The Academic Dean is Dr. Robert A. Lane. Dr. Lane received his doctorate in Learning dis/Abilities from Teachers College at Columbia University. As an instructor in Columbia's Department of Curriculum and Teaching, he taught graduate-level courses in the Learning dis/Abilities program, coordinated the student-teaching program, and was Clinical Supervisor at the Center for Educational and Psychological Services. His career in education began at Kildonan, where he taught literature and language training and supervised a dormitory from 1992 to 1995. Before returning to Kildonan, Dr. Lane also was a Diagnostic Clinician and Educational Consultant at a private clinic in Connecticut.

COLLEGE PLACEMENT

College placement is a collaborative effort by the student, parents, the college adviser, the Academic Dean, and the Headmaster. About 95 percent of each graduating class continues in schools and colleges throughout the country. During the past five years, Kildonan students have continued their education at, among others, the following schools and colleges: Adelphi, American International, Boston University, Curry, Elon, Florida Technical, George Mason, Landmark College, Lynn University, Marshall, Muskingum, New England College, Rhode Island School of Design, RIT, SUNY at Alfred, Syracuse, Wesleyan College (Georgia), and the University of West Virginia.

STUDENT BODY AND CONDUCT

For 2005–06, Kildonan enrolled 134 students from thirteen states and three other countries.

The School does not tolerate harassment or the use of alcohol or illegal drugs. Disciplinary problems are handled on an individual basis.

ACADEMIC FACILITIES

The Schoolhouse contains ten classrooms, including a science laboratory; a computer center; development, administrative, and business of-

fices; study halls; tutoring rooms; and an auditorium/gymnasium. An elementary school classroom building opened in January 1999. It contains seven classrooms, seven tutoring rooms, and a community gathering area. The Francis St. John Library has seven tutoring rooms, two classrooms, and two large study areas. The Simon Art Studios contain two classrooms, art and ceramics studios, a printmaking studio, and a darkroom. Other academic buildings house eight tutoring rooms and an assistive technology lab. There are also two stables and a well-equipped woodworking facility on the campus.

BOARDING AND GENERAL FACILITIES

There are three student residences on campus. The main boys' residence hall houses 62 students, while 28 girls can live in the girls' residence house. There is also a small residence house that can accommodate 6 boys. The School has a fully equipped infirmary with full-time nursing coverage, and local physicians serve as the School doctors. Sharon Hospital (Connecticut) is approximately 5 miles away.

ATHLETICS

Athletics is an integral part of the Kildonan School curriculum. Each day students participate in an after-school sport that provides instruction and activities to help students develop the knowledge, motivation, and insights needed to maintain their physical fitness level throughout their lives. There is also a highly successful, long-standing ski program that culminates with a weeklong ski trip to Killington, Vermont.

The athletic program has two levels of focus: to provide a healthy, structured environment for the development of interscholastic athletic competition and to provide a program for the development of a wide range of intramural activities.

Sporting and fitness activities include intramural and interscholastic sports, such as basketball, biking, golf, hiking, horseback riding, lacrosse, skiing, soccer, softball, tennis, and weight training. Kildonan is a member of the New England Preparatory School Athletic Association.

DAILY LIFE

The weekday schedule begins with morning wake-up, room inspection, and breakfast followed by a morning assembly. Classes, sports, and supervised study are scheduled between 8:15 a.m. and 4:45 p.m. Evening study halls vary depending on grade from 1½ to 2 hours on weekdays and from 2 to 3 hours on weekends. Students participate in a community curriculum program that involves small-group, topic-based discussions.

Wednesday afternoons from 2 to 3:15 p.m. students participate in a community service project of their choosing, which may include trail clearing, building, painting, gardening, computers, cooking for the elderly, or running the bookstore.

WEEKEND LIFE

While weekend activities differ from those on academic days, the School is dedicated to the same supervision and structure. The weekend begins with small group dinners in faculty members' apartments. Often, off-campus trips are planned. These may include bowling, miniature golf, movies, biking, skiing, and white-water rafting. Occasionally students purchase tickets for professional sporting events or theater for Saturday night. Students also enjoy movies on campus or dinner out with their dorm masters. Pickup sports are also popular pastimes. Some students choose an excursion or attend church, some watch an in-house video, and some write letters or play music.

SUMMER PROGRAMS

Dunnabeck at Kildonan is a six-week summer program that was established in 1955 to meet the needs of normal, intelligent boys and girls failing or underachieving in their academic work because of specific difficulty in reading, writing, or spelling. Over the years, hundreds of students have returned from their summer of intensive work at Dunnabeck to find success in school, often for the first time.

The founder and Director Emeritus of Dunnabeck, Diana Hanbury King, was educated in England and Canada. She holds a B.A. Hons. degree from the University of London and an M.A. from George Washington University. She has taught at the Ruzawi School in Rhodesia; at Sidwell Friends School in Washington, D.C.; and at the Potomac School in Virginia. Mrs. King was the 1990 recipient of the Samuel T. Orton Award, the highest honor bestowed by the International Dyslexia Association. Publications include *Writing Skills*, *Writing Skills Teacher's Manual*, *Keyboarding Skills*, *Cursive Writing Skills*, and *English Isn't Crazy*.

Dunnabeck can accommodate 85 boys and girls, ranging in age from 8 to 16. Great care is taken to ensure that the younger campers receive sufficient attention. A number of activities are planned just for this group. They remain under the careful supervision of the counselor and the health center staff. Older students follow a schedule that allows for longer periods of study and for more intensive and challenging forms of recreation such as backpacking, canoeing, windsurfing, and waterskiing.

COSTS AND FINANCIAL AID

Tuition for the 2005–06 school year was $43,250 for boarding students, $41,250 for five-day boarding students, $30,250 for day students, and $24,500 for elementary school students. Additional expenses include athletic equipment, transportation, laundry, and special trips. Financial aid is available in the form of small grants to returning students only and is based on need.

Tuition for the 2005 Dunnabeck Program was $7300 for boarding students, $5725 for full-day students, and $3725 for half-day students. Math tutoring is available for an additional fee.

ADMISSIONS INFORMATION

Parents interested in enrolling their son or daughter should fill out the preliminary application form and send it to the School, together with all available records of educational and psychological testing as well as a transcript. As soon as the material is received, the family is invited for an interview. Acceptance at Kildonan is not competitive; students are selected on the basis of their ability to benefit from the program.

APPLICATION TIMETABLE

It is in the student's best interest to plan entrance for September, though some are admitted in January and a few at other times throughout the year as space becomes available.

ADMISSIONS CORRESPONDENCE

Bonnie A. Wilson
Director of Admissions
Kildonan School
425 Morse Hill Road
Amenia, New York 12501

Phone: 845-373-2013
Fax: 845-373-2004
E-mail: admissions@kildonan.org
Web site: http://www.kildonan.org

LANDMARK SCHOOL

Prides Crossing, Massachusetts

Type: Coeducational boarding and day school for students with language-based learning disabilities, such as dyslexia
Grades: Grades 2–12
Enrollment: 447
Head of School: Robert J. Broudo, M.Ed., Headmaster

THE SCHOOL

Landmark School's programs are designed to help emotionally sound students who are of average to above-average intelligence and who have been diagnosed as having a language-based learning disability such as dyslexia. Many of these students are failing in regular classrooms because their reading, writing, and spelling skills have not caught up with their thinking and problem-solving capacities. It is the purpose of the School to provide the special educational and social services that enable these students to return as quickly as possible to the educational mainstream as academic and social achievers.

Each student is viewed as an individual and, as such, receives an individualized course plan, starting at his or her lowest level of competency. Every activity is oriented toward a successful experience; failure to learn is considered a teaching failure rather than a learning failure. Because Landmark accepts only students who have high learning potential, each student should begin to succeed almost immediately. Once remediation is complete, however, students are well prepared to reenter public or private schools at traditional grade levels.

Landmark carries out its program on two campuses situated along the coast of Massachusetts, approximately 25 miles north of Boston. Landmark's High School campus is located in Prides Crossing. Three miles to the northeast lies the Elementary and Middle School campus in Manchester-by-the-Sea. The School's administrative offices, including admission, are located across from the High School in the Drake Administration Building. The School also owns a 500-foot ocean beachfront.

Landmark is a nonprofit, nonsectarian educational organization. It is governed by a 20-member Board of Directors. The School's operating expenses for 2004–05 were $18.8 million. Contributions and grants totaled $2.2 million.

Landmark is accredited by the New England Association of Schools and Colleges. It is a member of the Massachusetts Association of 766 Approved Private Schools, the National Association of Independent Schools, and the Association of Independent Schools of New England and is approved as a school for children with language-based learning disabilities by the Division of Special Education of the State Department of Education in the Commonwealth of Massachusetts. It is licensed as a residential facility by the Massachusetts Office of Child Care Services.

Landmark School traces its origins to the Reading Research Institute, which was founded in Berea, Kentucky, in 1956. The institute was moved to Massachusetts in 1963, where it changed its name successively to the Learning Disabilities Foundation in 1969, the Landmark Foundation in 1985, and finally, the Landmark

School, Inc. in 1998, adopting for the corporation the name of the school it had founded in 1971.

ACADEMIC PROGRAMS

Central to Landmark's Standard Academic Program is a daily one-to-one language arts tutorial focusing on oral reading, reading comprehension, spelling, composition, study skills, and handwriting. Additional core courses include language arts, mathematics (general math, prealgebra, algebra, calculus, geometry, trigonometry, and consumer math), science (biology, marine science, physical science, chemistry, environmental science, physics, and earth science), and social sciences (American history and civilization, twentieth-century America, world history, contemporary world issues, American government, civics, psychology, economics, and anthropology). Other courses include advanced communication, communication seminar, introductory communication, literature, oral expression, pragmatics, reading, and study skills. Elective classes are offered in art, auto mechanics, computers, chorus, drama, early childhood education, health, music, peer leadership, percussion, photography, physical education, radio and television broadcasting, voice, and woodworking.

Landmark also offers the Expressive Language Program for students who have a particular need to develop verbal skills. Appropriate verbalization skills are stimulated and developed in conjunction with the presentation of Landmark's Standard Academic Program.

The Landmark Preparatory Program offers a full secondary school curriculum for students who need a specialized educational environment but do not need an intensive remedial program. The program emphasizes study skills and organization development in a regular classroom setting.

The Elementary Program, for 7-, 8-, and 9-year-old day students, is a language-based program that includes language arts, oral expression, literature, science, social studies, mathematics, and computer science. The curriculum also includes physical education, art, and music. The program is located in its own building and provides a daily one-on-one tutorial; class size is limited to a maximum of 6.

Students receive a diploma from Landmark by meeting specified requirements that ensure that they are prepared to go on to meaningful education, service, or employment.

The typical course load is seven classes per day; all courses meet five times a week, and most are taken for a full year. Classes are small, ranging in size from 5 to 8 students, with an overall student-teacher ratio of 3:1. Students are grouped according to skill levels. As soon as students' progress warrants it, however, they are moved to a higher level within a course. A

schoolwide schedule review at midyear further ensures optimal placement. Prep Program students are placed in grade-appropriate levels.

Landmark uses a case management system through which each child's academic and personal development is overseen by an experienced supervisor. Additional support services are available as needed through guidance counselors, speech and language specialists, and psychological counselors.

Detailed academic reports are sent home three or four times during the school year. Parents are invited to fall and spring parents' weekends to formally consult with teachers and administrators; they may also consult as needed throughout the year.

FACULTY AND ADVISERS

Landmark employs 217 educational personnel, made up of teaching faculty members, supervisors, and department heads; more than half hold advanced degrees. The School recruits nationally, seeking intelligent, committed faculty members with appropriate experience, certification, and the ability to respond to a challenging, multifaceted educational environment.

In addition to teaching, staff members serve on rotating residential teams that monitor the nonacademic affairs of students after-school hours and on weekends. Their responsibilities include the supervision of dormitories and extracurricular activities, support of all School rules and regulations, and implementation of pertinent disciplinary policies.

Landmark faculty and staff members, through the School's Outreach Program, present workshops at schools and conferences nationwide on Landmark Methodology for students with learning disabilities. They have written and published books on teaching study skills, writing, and arithmetic. Summer training programs for parents and teachers in Landmark Methodology are offered on the Landmark campus.

COLLEGE PLACEMENT

Landmark has a full-time Guidance Director and Career/Vocational Counselor. Juniors begin the placement process in the spring. Placement guidance for seniors is accomplished through group and individual meetings; the development of skills in decision making, preparing applications, and interviewing; and preparation for and administration of untimed versions of the Scholastic Assessment Tests. College representatives come to Landmark, and students visit colleges.

Of recent graduates, 88 percent are attending colleges. Other students have gone on to postgraduate programs, vocational programs, and employment. Graduates are attending such colleges and universities as Boston College,

Colby-Sawyer, Curry, Lynn University, and the Universities of Denver, Massachusetts, and New Hampshire.

STUDENT BODY AND CONDUCT
Landmark has 447 students this year. Of these, 111 boys and 67 girls are boarders, and 179 boys and 90 girls are day students. Students come from twenty-five states and seven other countries. Approximately 19 percent of the students are members of a minority group.

Students at Landmark are immersed in learning. They have little opportunity to engage in inappropriate behavior. The Disciplinary Committee meets if a serious disciplinary infraction warrants it.

The Student Council, consisting of elected student officers and dormitory representatives, is active in planning community service activities, parties, dances, lectures, and trips.

ACADEMIC FACILITIES
Landmark's High School campus is located in an estate setting on 27 acres that overlook the Atlantic Ocean. Norrie House contains the Alexander Library, which has 8,000 volumes (twenty-seven books per student); the Tutorial Materials Resource Center, which houses approximately 8,500 volumes including reading novels, workbooks, and reference materials; the Tutorial Center; the radio station, WLMK; and the dining hall. Lopardo Hall contains boys' living space and the student center. The Health Center, the science labs, and a girls' dormitory are in Bain Hall. Other dormitories include Williston Hall, Woodside Hall (both girls' dorms), Porter Hall, Buchan House, and the Campus Cottage. In addition, there are two classroom buildings, a computer center, an art center, a woodshop, a gymnasium, and Collins Athletic Field.

The Elementary and Middle School campus is located 3 miles to the north of the High School campus. Another former estate, the main house includes classrooms, a dining hall, library, and offices. Two outbuildings house more classrooms, the art center, a woodshop, and a small engine shop. In addition, the gymnasium building includes the Elementary School classrooms and a tutorial center.

BOARDING AND GENERAL FACILITIES
Landmark has seven buildings with dormitory space on the High School campus. Students live in single, 2- or 3-person rooms. They are supervised by staff members living in the buildings and by the rotating duty teams. The newest dorm also houses a student center with recreational offerings.

ATHLETICS
As a vital part of Landmark's program, physical education is structured to develop the skills and competencies that promote physical activity and enjoyment. Opportunities for participation by all students are provided. Landmark provides an intramural program that includes basketball, floor hockey, softball, and volleyball. Interscholastically, Landmark participates in the Eastern Independent League and the Independent Girls Conference and offers baseball, basketball, cross-country, downhill skiing, golf, lacrosse, soccer, tennis, and wrestling. Both the High School and Elementary and Middle School campuses have gymnasiums.

EXTRACURRICULAR OPPORTUNITIES
The Student Council, intramurals, outdoor challenge program, drama, photography, television production, yearbook, and community service are representative of the activities and enterprises available after classes. Students may also use such facilities as the art room and the mechanics shop. Landmark has its own radio station (WLMK), which is staffed by students.

DAILY LIFE
Classes are held Monday through Friday from 8 a.m. to 2:50 p.m. There are seven 45-minute classes. All students are encouraged to participate in after-school activities of their choice. Five nights per week, high school boarding students are required to attend a supervised study hall after dinner. The boarding program encourages students to develop independence and responsibility through a system of levels with increasing privileges.

WEEKEND LIFE
Home visits are arranged individually. A full weekend schedule of supervised activities is provided for those who remain on campus. Activities include trips to the movies or nearby points of interest and overnight trips. Opportunities are plentiful for outdoor activities or trips to historic sites and cultural programs. Weekends feature skiing and hiking trips in northern New England as well as excursions to Boston. Students who wish to attend religious services are provided with transportation. Free time and social events on campus complement these activities.

SUMMER PROGRAMS
Landmark offers intensive, six-week summer programs for students who wish to explore the demonstrably beneficial effect of short-term remediation. The Elementary, the Middle, and High School Programs are offered in abbreviated formats and are supplemented with on-campus activities and recreational opportunities in the

surrounding area. One or two daily one-to-one tutorials are offered. In addition, the Seamanship Program, the Marine Science Program, the Exploration Program, and the Recreation Program are available as half-day supplements to the academic program, depending on the age of the applicant. Please contact the School for details.

COSTS AND FINANCIAL AID
The 2005–06 tuition for day students in the academic-year program was $36,700. The cost for boarding students in the academic-year program was $47,700. The Prep day program cost was $29,700, and the boarding cost was $40,700. Enrollment deposits ranging from $5700 to $7700, depending upon the program, are due upon acceptance. Half of the balance of the tuition is due July 1, and the remainder is due December 1. Parents have the option of a ten-month payment plan through AMS.

More than 50 percent of Landmark's students receive financial aid through various agencies, mainly local departments of education.

ADMISSIONS INFORMATION
To be admitted to any Landmark program, applicants must present a diagnosis of a language-based learning disability and have average to superior intellectual potential. Landmark is not equipped to work with students who have primary emotional or social difficulties. Students are admitted on the basis of medical, psychological, and educational testing. The School can assist parents in finding testing facilities. All students must visit the campus for a personal interview and admissions screening before enrollment.

APPLICATION TIMETABLE
Landmark accepts applications and admits students throughout the year if space is available. Early application for summer programs is recommended.

Students whose records suggest that they meet the admission criteria are invited to Landmark, along with at least one parent or guardian, for a full morning or afternoon session. The session includes an interview, individual testing, a tour, a discussion of test results, and a decision regarding acceptance. Since admissions are made on a rolling basis, the availability of space and an enrollment date are also addressed at this time.

A fee of $125 must accompany the application form.

ADMISSIONS CORRESPONDENCE
Carolyn Orsini Nelson, Director of Admission
Landmark School
P.O. Box 227
Prides Crossing, Massachusetts 01965-0227

Phone: 978-236-3000
Fax: 978-927-7268
E-mail: admission@landmarkschool.org
Web site: http://www.landmarkschool.org

MOUNT BACHELOR ACADEMY

Prineville, Oregon

Type: Coeducational boarding school offering college-preparatory course work for students with behavioral or motivational difficulties
Grades: Ages 14–18
Enrollment: 113
Head of School: Sharon Bitz

THE SCHOOL

Mount Bachelor Academy, founded in 1988, provides a well-rounded academic and emotional growth curriculum that is designed for children who may have academic, behavioral, emotional, or motivational problems.

The fourteen- to sixteen-month integrated curriculum at Mount Bachelor Academy encourages increased self-awareness in students, builds their self-esteem, and develops their problem-solving and decision-making skills through experiential learning.

Students are in group counseling sessions two times a week. In these sessions, students learn to deal with situational living issues as well as personal issues.

In a highly structured yet nurturing peer environment, students learn to address issues that have prevented them from achieving academic and personal success.

Mount Bachelor Academy's highly skilled teaching faculty and staff members are experienced in working with children who may have displayed behavior that is symptomatic of low self-esteem and poor self-concept.

A strong addictions recovery program serves students with substance-abuse issues through NA/AA-style meetings, addictions classes, and processing groups run by certified drug and alcohol counselors.

Mount Bachelor Academy is fully accredited by the Pacific Northwest Association of Independent Schools and the Northwest Association of Schools and Colleges. The Academy is also a member of the Aspen Education Group.

ACADEMIC PROGRAMS

Mount Bachelor Academy provides a high school academic curriculum that incorporates both classroom and individual tutoring experiences.

Each student participates in dynamic field trips that supplement their traditional course work. In addition, interpersonal skill building is emphasized, and the students' desire for learning is fostered.

College-preparatory classes, attended by 5 to 14 students, provide ample opportunities for individualized attention.

Strong emphasis is placed on each student's learning style. Students meet with one of two certified learning differences (LD) specialists on site to do a learning styles assessment and develop an individual learning plan that addresses each student's learning needs, whether LD issues or a need for challenge and academic acceleration or both.

Many classes employ experiential, hands-on techniques that keep the subject material exciting and interesting for students.

The development of caring, personal teacher-student relationships helps the faculty members to know how to better motivate their students.

Mount Bachelor Academy carefully selects experienced teachers who have enthusiasm both for their respective discipline and for working with adolescents.

Teachers are involved with student activities and counseling outside the classroom.

FACULTY AND ADVISERS

Mount Bachelor Academy has a student-faculty ratio of 4:1. Teaching faculty members and counseling staff members are involved in an on-site training program that augments their prior professional training and education.

All students are assigned to a mentor who guides them as they progress through the emotional growth component of the curriculum.

The mentor also communicates on a regular basis with the students' families.

COLLEGE PLACEMENT

Mount Bachelor Academy offers an SAT preparatory class for juniors and seniors. Once this class is completed, students take the SAT in preparation for college.

The Academy's college counselor helps students make application to the colleges of their choice.

Approximately 85 percent of graduates matriculate into and continue their education at a four-year college or university.

STUDENT BODY AND CONDUCT

The student population consists of boys and girls from twenty states and two other countries.

A strong, positive peer culture is the core of Mount Bachelor Academy's curriculum.

Students serve as dorm leaders, proctors, aides, and tutors. They utilize school forums for both conflict resolution and peer support.

ACADEMIC FACILITIES

Mount Bachelor Academy is located about an hour east of Bend, Oregon, in the Ochoco National Forest.

The school offers students the opportunity to learn and grow in a beautiful forest setting, far from the pressures and influences of the urban areas of today.

Facilities include classrooms, a library, a computer lab, a dining room, a living/social area, an art center, a multipurpose gymnasium, a weight room, an outdoor basketball court, a climbing wall, a ropes course, hiking and biking trails, an outdoor swimming pool, and twenty-two dorms.

BOARDING AND GENERAL FACILITIES

Mount Bachelor Academy students live in comfortable dorms that house 4 to 5 students each. The dorms are student-proctored, with staff oversight.

The students work together to share daily and weekly housekeeping responsibilities.

The setting of the dorms engenders a safe environment where strong and reliable friendships are built.

Staff and faculty members are part of evening student life, contributing to a warm family atmosphere.

ATHLETICS

All students participate in a variety of physical activities on campus, including basketball, climbing, cross-country skiing, dance, disc golf, downhill skiing, golf, hiking, running, soccer, swimming, volleyball, and wrestling.

Mount Bachelor Academy also competes with other area schools and teams. In addition, all students participate in wilderness challenges with their peer group in the form of backpacking, climbing, camping, and skiing.

EXTRACURRICULAR OPPORTUNITIES

Students enjoy extracurricular opportunities that include study trips to the Oregon Shakespeare Festival and political science excursions to Presidential Classroom in Washington, D.C. There are also visits to college and university activities within the state of Oregon.

In addition, there are ongoing field trips that utilize state parks and facilities.

Traditional holidays, such as Thanksgiving, Hanukkah, Christmas, Easter, Passover, and Martin Luther King Day, in addition to events unique to the school (Summer Olympics, Winter Olympics, community service days), are observed every year.

DAILY LIFE

Each student's day begins with dorm and campus housekeeping, followed by a busy academic schedule.

Tutoring and school forums take place in the late afternoons. Evenings are dedicated to study sessions and activity and social time.

WEEKEND LIFE

Saturdays and Sundays are busy on-campus project and physical activity times.

Sunday brunch is followed by a host of eventful field trips or recreational activities.

COSTS AND FINANCIAL AID

Tuition, room and board, and therapeutic costs amount to $5750 per month.

Additional one-time enrollment fees include an application, interview, and alumni services fee of $7500; a student supply pack of $482; and a wilderness clothing fee of approximately $390, depending on the season. All fees are subject to change.

ADMISSIONS INFORMATION

Applications are accepted for boys and girls, ages 14 to 18.

A full battery of psychoeducational evaluations and academic records are required as part of the enrollment process.

If a student's evaluations are incomplete, nonexistent, or more than a year old, Mount Bachelor Academy's consulting psychologist can administer the necessary tests, for an additional fee.

Children are selected to attend Mount Bachelor Academy on the basis of their ability to integrate with the school environment and their ability to receive the maximum benefit from the combined academic and emotional growth curriculum.

An interview is required.

APPLICATION TIMETABLE

Admission inquiries are welcome at any time. Parents are encouraged to schedule a tour of the campus in order to meet faculty and staff members and students.

Depending upon their individual circumstances, students may be enrolled as soon as the application process and interview are completed.

ADMISSIONS CORRESPONDENCE

Admission Department
Mount Bachelor Academy
33051 NE Ochoco Highway
Prineville, Oregon 97754

Phone: 800-462-3404 (toll-free)
Fax: 541-462-3430
Web site: http://www.mtba.com

NEW DOMINION SCHOOLS

Dillwyn, Virginia
Oldtown, Maryland

Type: Male/female residential special schools utilizing outdoor experiential education and group process to promote emotional growth
Grades: Ungraded, ages 11–17
Enrollment: Virginia boys: 72; Maryland boys: 72; Virginia girls: 48
Heads of Schools: Brooke Balch, President; Ben Montano, Administrator (Virginia); Mary Porter, Administrator (Maryland)

THE SCHOOL

New Dominion Boys School was founded in 1976 in Dillwyn, Virginia, and in 1996, the girls' campus was founded on a separate location on the 550-acre site. New Dominion School in Oldtown, Maryland, was established in 1981. The Schools, a service of Three Springs, Inc., serve students who experience emotional, behavioral, and learning problems. Operating on a year-round basis, the Schools help teenagers progress by fostering positive growth and providing education in the natural environment.

The Schools accept students who have histories of failure but are of at least average intelligence. The challenge is to reach out and encourage talent not yet tapped. The atmosphere is well disciplined, nurturing, optimistic, and conducive to bringing out the fullest potential of each student. Personal growth and education are interrelated as students build self-confidence and problem-solving skills and learn to take responsibility for themselves and their education.

The major objectives of the Schools are to help students take positive control of their lives, realize their self-worth, and develop the self-confidence and motivation to succeed both socially and academically. The Schools are committed to returning the students to their families and communities as happier, motivated, and responsible members of society.

The New Dominion School programs in Virginia are located in the rolling hills of the central part of the state, and New Dominion School in Maryland is located in the mountains of the western region of the state. The Virginia programs are licensed as alternative and special education schools and are accredited by both the Southern Association of Colleges and Schools and the Virginia Association of Specialized Education Facilities. New Dominion School in Maryland is a licensed middle and high school accredited by the Middle States Association of Colleges and Schools. Teachers certified in special education are also available to assist students with special educational needs.

Each facility is a private organization recognized by the Corporation Commission of their respective states. Three Springs, Inc., the parent organization of the programs, has a president, vice president, and secretary-treasurer. The Board of Directors meets at least quarterly to discuss items of business. Administrators from each facility also meet semiannually with a community Advisory Board made up of area professionals and community leaders. Each school currently has an operating budget of approximately $2 million.

ACADEMIC PROGRAM

The Schools' curricula are designed to meet the special needs of their students. Students enrolled at the Schools typically have a history of rejecting traditional educational approaches. Because it is often futile to continue to deal with these prob-

lems in ways that have been unsuccessful in the past, an innovative approach to education is provided. Upon enrollment in the Maryland program, students begin both their experiential and core curricula immediately. In the Virginia programs, students begin their experiential curriculum first and add the core studies approximately two months later.

Experiential life skills training in Virginia includes courses in general sociology, construction, home economics, and physical education. In Maryland, the experiential courses include sociology/citizenship, physical education, and health and life skills. These courses are incorporated in a number of group activities and outdoor programming. Academic skills are applied in meaningful ways as the group engages in making plans and carrying out projects and activities. As emotional growth progresses, a student gains the privilege of increasing academic courses.

Graduation requirements for the Virginia programs include 4 credits of English, 3 credits of social studies, 3 credits of mathematics, 3 credits of science, 2 credits of health and physical education, 1 credit of fine arts or practical arts, and 6 credits of electives. The following electives are offered: physics, chemistry, geometry, trigonometry, precalculus, world geography, general sociology, home economics, construction, carpentry, and small engine repair. The curriculum is tailored for students to earn a high school diploma, or, if appropriate, to prepare for and take the General Educational Development (GED) examination.

Graduation requirements at New Dominion School in Maryland include 4 credits of English, 3 credits of social studies, 3 credits of mathematics, 3 credits of science, 4 experiential electives, and 3 general electives. Courses offered include English I–IV; world history; U.S. history; contemporary world issues; government; geography; economics; psychology; general math; algebra I and II; geometry; trigonometry; calculus; general, earth, life, and physical science; biology; chemistry; physics; Spanish I and II; sociology/citizenship; physical education; and health and life skills. New Dominion School in Maryland's curriculum is designed to help students earn a high school diploma or, if appropriate, to prepare for and take the General Educational Development (GED) examination.

Students at the Schools may also focus on mastering basic skills if needed. Remedial education is available for learning-disabled and behavior-disordered students. In addition, students who have completed high school have the opportunity to earn college credits through distance learning programs.

FACULTY AND ADVISERS

The Schools currently employ approximately 45 full- and part-time staff members in each facility.

Thirty of the 45 are professionals who offer direct services to enrolled students.

The boys' programs in Virginia and Maryland employ 7 teachers each, while the girls' program in Virginia employs 4. All of these teachers hold certification in specialities providing K–12 curriculum and individualized instruction.

Family support staff members are assigned to each family, and a licensed psychologist is available for consultation. Each school provides drug and alcohol groups and employs the services of a professional who specializes in treating cases of sexual abuse.

COLLEGE PLACEMENT

The Schools provide guidance for postprogram schooling and vocational placement. Younger students generally continue their education at a public or private school, and older students seek either employment or college placement. Those students who do plan to attend college are helped to prepare for the SAT and to visit college campuses.

STUDENT BODY AND CONDUCT

Students enrolled in the New Dominion Schools come primarily from mid-Atlantic states, with the highest number coming from Virginia, Maryland, and Pennsylvania. The Schools also enroll students from more distant areas, including the Northeast, Southeast, and West Coast.

The boys' programs in Virginia and Maryland are licensed to accommodate an enrollment of 72 boys ranging in ages from 11 to 17. The Virginia girls' program is licensed for 48 girls ranging in age from 11–17. The girls' campus is made up of four groups, while the Virginia and Maryland boys' programs have six groups each on their campuses. Each group is composed of 10 to 12 students and 3 staff members, and at least 1 adult is in each group at all times. Factors taken into account when placing a student within a group are consideration of each student's strengths, weaknesses, and needs; the make-up of the group as a whole; and how each student's entry could affect the group's dynamic balance.

Within the framework of outdoor experiential programming, personal growth is based on a group process problem-solving model. Students' difficulties in relating to others are not dealt with in isolation from their daily actions. Instead, problems are dealt with on the spot as they occur. Group meetings are held at any time during the day when a problem arises. In addition, there are regular evening group sessions. During group meetings, students receive the help and support of their group to learn more acceptable behavior, to express emotions appropriately, and to resolve problems productively. Motivation on the part of the students is high, because they are meeting immediate primary needs and are experiencing

both the positive and negative results of their behavior immediately or soon after it occurs.

The problems that need to be solved do not affect only the students. Staff members have as much at stake as the students, as they all work together toward mutual goals. Moreover, actions taken by staff members are behaviors that students model as they progress.

As students progress in the program, they have the opportunity to begin weekend home visits. These visits are a time for healing broken trust and for practicing new positive behaviors at home and in the community.

ACADEMIC FACILITIES
Each campus has separate academic buildings. The academic buildings each house six classrooms, a library, and a video room; computers are also available for student use. The Virginia and Maryland boys' programs have separate vocational buildings with wood shop and small-engine repair classes. The Virginia girls' program has a fine arts program.

BOARDING AND GENERAL FACILITIES
Group living sites at the Schools are located within a quarter mile of the central administrative area. Each living site is autonomous. Groups build their own facilities, which are composed of three sleeping structures and eating, cooking, and personal hygiene structures. The central campus consists of administrative offices, the school building, the dining hall, and the shower house.

When necessary, enrolled students may be referred to professionals, such as dentists, doctors, and psychotherapists, who are not directly employed by the School. Staff members ensure that outside professionals comply with state statutes and are licensed practitioners in their particular professional area.

The Schools furnish groups with transportation to community, social, and cultural activities; doctor appointments; bus and train stations and airports; and special outings. Transportation is also provided for trips outside the state. All staff members are required to hold a valid driver's license and to obey all traffic laws and school regulations.

ATHLETICS
While offering traditional recreational activities including basketball, bowling, football, skating, softball, swimming, and volleyball, the Schools also offer an opportunity for students to plan extensive recreational adventure trips and outdoor activities. These trips, which include backpacking, canoeing, or bicycling, may last up to three weeks. In addition, a high- and low-ropes course is on the Maryland campus, and an Alpine tower and low-ropes course are on the Virginia campuses. Adventure activities enhance academic progress and provide significant experiences that build self-confidence, self-esteem, group cohesiveness, and trust in others.

EXTRACURRICULAR OPPORTUNITIES
The Schools provide opportunities to participate in community, social, and cultural activities on a weekly basis and to plan special outings to museums, historical sites, and other areas of interest, such as zoos, aquariums, colleges, local industries, and state parks.

DAILY LIFE
Monday through Saturday, groups at the Schools rise at 6:30. The first hour is spent taking care of the sleeping area and performing campsite responsibilities. After all individual and group responsibilities and chores are completed, the group has breakfast either at the lodge or at the campsite. Following breakfast, staff members and students have the opportunity to state their goals for the day and to recognize one another for positive actions and accomplishments. Students who have earned academic hours attend the formal classroom program. The remainder of the group then begins its chosen morning activity, which may vary from planning, building, or maintaining group site structures to participating in recreational or off-campus activities. Following lunch, the group again follows its planned activity, and some students again attend earned classroom hours. After supper, there is usually time for games or other leisure activities. At 8 p.m., a group meeting is held to evaluate the day and to deal with any unresolved personal and group issues. This meeting lasts until conflicts and issues are addressed and brought to appropriate resolution. Generally, the group is in bed by 9:30 p.m.

COSTS AND FINANCIAL AID
The per diem charge is comprehensive, and there are no additional charges for extended trips, special education, or allowance. The 2005 tuition fee for the New Dominion Schools was $135 per diem or $49,275 for a twelve-month year.

ADMISSIONS INFORMATION
Interested parents are encouraged to call for more information and are usually asked to send detailed information regarding their child's previous history. Such information should include social history; professional contacts, such as educational consultants; psychological, psychiatric, and medical history; and academic transcripts. Applications are accepted at any time, and enrollment is not limited to a specific time of year.

APPLICATION TIMETABLE
Requests to visit each campus are welcomed at any time. It is important that a call for a tour be made in advance so that staff members are available. Office hours are from 9 to 5 Monday through Friday.

ADMISSIONS CORRESPONDENCE
Mike Forman, Director of Admissions
New Dominion School
P.O. Box 540
Dillwyn, Virginia 23936

Phone: 434-983-2051
Fax: 434-983-2068
E-mail: mforman@threesprings.com

Hillary Quick, Director of Admissions
New Dominion School
P.O. Box 8
Oldtown, Maryland 21555

Phone: 301-478-5721
Fax: 301-478-5723
E-mail: ndadmissions@allconet.org
Web site: http://www.threesprings.com

OAK CREEK RANCH SCHOOL

West Sedona, Arizona

Type: Coeducational boarding school with general and college-preparatory academic programs for ADD/ADHD teens and underachievers
Grades: 7–12, postgraduate (ages 12–19)
Enrollment: School total: 85–90
Head of School: David Wick Jr., Headmaster; David Wick Sr., Director

THE SCHOOL

Oak Creek Ranch School, founded in 1972 by its director, David Wick, provides a structured environment and individualized approach that enables students to achieve their academic goals while developing self-esteem, discipline, leadership, integrity, and consideration for others. The School specializes in helping the academic underachiever, the undermotivated teen, and the student with ADD/ADHD. Oak Creek Ranch School serves as a transition school for students who have successfully completed residential treatment or other behavior modification programs.

The 20-acre campus is located on Oak Creek, near beautiful Sedona, Arizona. The rural setting, temperate climate, and adjacent Coconino National Forest provide an ideal setting for students to enjoy all facets of campus life. The School is located 100 miles north of Phoenix, Arizona.

Oak Creek Ranch School is accredited by the North Central Association of Colleges and Schools.

ACADEMIC PROGRAMS

Students must complete at least 22 credits to graduate, including classes in art, computer science, physical education, English, mathematics, science, and social studies. Foreign languages are available.

The school year is divided into semesters. However, enrollments are accepted throughout the year. After students have attended for four weeks, parents receive a progress report that describes their child's social and academic progress. Every eight weeks, a detailed report is sent to parents.

Small classes (fewer than 10 students) and experienced teachers allow the School to tailor every student's program to his or her individual needs.

FACULTY AND ADVISERS

The School's faculty includes the Headmaster, Principal, Assistant Principal, Dean of Students, and 13 certified teachers. The majority of the faculty members have advanced degrees.

COLLEGE PLACEMENT

The School provides career counseling and college placement advice and assistance to all students.

Students enrolled in the college-preparatory program are encouraged to take the SAT in January of their eleventh- and twelfth-grade years. Preparation for the SAT and/or ACT is provided through special sessions and tutoring. SAT and ACT tests are administered through Northern Arizona University in Flagstaff.

Ninety percent of OCRS graduates from last year continued their education, attending the following universities and other fine schools: Arizona State; DePaul; Marymount; Northern Arizona; Ohio State; Purdue; Texas Tech; The Illinois Institute of Art; UCLA; and the Universities of Denver; Nevada, Las Vegas; and the Pacific.

STUDENT BODY AND CONDUCT

The High School enrolls approximately 80–90 students from throughout the U.S and parts of Asia and Mexico. The largest student groups are from Arizona, California, Illinois, Nevada, and Texas.

Campus life is relaxed and informal. Most students dress in casual attire for classes. More formal dress is required for special events, such as proms and graduation.

The School has a Student Council, made up of students elected from each class. This group helps new students adjust to the School's social and academic environment, assists dormitory supervisors, and helps plan special events.

The School uses positive reinforcement to develop leadership and character. It emphasizes integrity, responsibility, loyalty, discipline, respect, and consideration for others. Opportunities exist for students to earn extra privileges. All faculty and staff members administer the program universally.

ACADEMIC FACILITIES

The main building houses administrative offices and classrooms. The School has an art building with its own kiln, a separate science lab, and a new classroom building. A state-of-the-art Macintosh computer lab, with workstations, scanners, still and video digital cameras, CD burners, and color laser printers, was added in 2004 to provide students with an opportunity to learn Web site design, video production, and graphic design. A separate PC lab is used for computer instruction, and the library's PCs are available for students to prepare homework, practice skills, and utilize Internet resources. Computer instruction focuses on the proper use of productivity office suites, graphic design, and Web site design and management. Training for certification in A+ and Microsoft applications is also offered.

BOARDING AND GENERAL FACILITIES

The campus has seventeen buildings, including the dormitories, classrooms, and recreational buildings. Other facilities include a pool, a tennis court, a basketball court, a low-ropes course, and a skateboard park. The School also has an equestrian center, where students can board their own horses for an additional fee. Instruction is provided in Western and English riding. Students are encouraged to enter local competitions and horse shows.

A supervisor in residence monitors each dormitory. All residences are centrally heated and cooled. Each dormitory contains smoke and/or fire alarm systems that have been approved by the Arizona State Fire Marshal and the state health department. A registered nurse is on duty in the School's infirmary. The School also has night security for students' safety.

ATHLETICS

Physical education is an important component of the curriculum. All students must attend a physical activity of their choice for 1 hour, four days a week. Interscholastic competitive sports include soccer, flag football, volleyball, baseball, and golf (at some of the most beautiful Sedona courses).

EXTRACURRICULAR OPPORTUNITIES

The School offers mountain biking, hiking, backpacking, horseback riding (arena and trail rides), skateboarding, rock climbing, weight lifting, tennis, swimming, and fishing. Other popular recreational activities include paintball games, overnight camping, white-water rafting, snowboarding/skiing, and trips to water parks, the Grand Canyon, concerts, and other special events in Phoenix, Flagstaff, Prescott, and Tucson.

DAILY LIFE

Students rise at 7 a.m., and breakfast is served between 8 and 9. Classes begin at 9 and continue until 3:30 p.m., with breaks for snacks and lunch. Physical education begins at 4 and last until 5 p.m. Dinner is served from 5 to 6, and evening activities, which often include a study period, last from 6 to 9 p.m. Students must be in their dorms at 9, and lights-out is at 10 on school nights.

WEEKEND LIFE

The School provides as many activities as possible to accommodate the students' diverse interests. Wilderness trips as well as excursions to rodeos, county and state fairs, concerts, college and professional football games, movies, entertainment parks, and miniature golf courses help make the weekends enjoyable. The School's horses are available for those who like cross-country trail riding in the Sedona area.

The School provides transportation to all off-campus activities, including religious services. All students are encouraged to attend the religious service of their choice. On Friday nights, a School van transports students who wish to go to movie theaters in Cottonwood or Sedona. Ice skating and skiing are also enjoyed in Flagstaff during the winter months. Parental permission is required for some off-campus activities.

With parental permission, students may sign up for weekend trips to the Grand Canyon, Oak Creek Canyon, camping in the Arizona mountains, tours of local Native American historical sites, ghost towns, and surrounding area lakes. Ski trips to local ski areas are also scheduled. Off-campus trips and other functions are supervised by residential staff and/or teaching faculty members.

SUMMER PROGRAMS

The School offers summer sessions for enrichment and for credit. Students may earn ½ credit in each of two subjects during one session. Classes are held in the morning, with study periods early in the afternoon. The remainder of the day is available for a variety of recreational activities on and off campus. Wilderness Literature and other experiential learning classes are offered during summer school. Brochures are available for those who need additional information. Transportation is furnished to and from the Sky Harbor Airport in Phoenix.

COSTS AND FINANCIAL AID

Tuition, room, board, and transportation fees for the 2005–06 school year totaled $35,500. A monthly revolving fund of $1000 is required for personal student expenditures, which may include weekly allowances, textbooks, school supplies, medical expenses, and certain activity fees. An itemized statement of the student's personal account is sent to parents monthly, and any balance is refunded within sixty days of the close of the school year. Horses can be boarded for an additional monthly fee.

ADMISSIONS INFORMATION

Information about the admissions process may be obtained through the School's admissions office. Personal visits are welcomed and encouraged. New students are accepted after a personal interview and a review of their academic records and social and behavioral issues or challenges.

There is a one-time $400 enrollment fee for both summer and regular school year enrollment. Applicants must submit a completed application form and health report. An application form may be requested through the admissions office or downloaded from the School's Web site.

APPLICATION TIMETABLE

Inquiries and enrollments are accepted throughout the year. Applications for fall enrollment should be made in the spring or summer to ensure that space is available. Visits are always welcome. Interested students should call the admissions department to schedule an appointment.

ADMISSIONS CORRESPONDENCE

Allan Popsack
Director of Admissions
Oak Creek Ranch School
P.O. Box 4329
West Sedona, Arizona 86340-4329

Phone: 928-634-5571
Fax: 928-634-4915
E-mail: admissions@ocrs.com
Web site: http://www.ocrs.com

OAKLAND SCHOOL

Keswick, Virginia

Type: Coeducational day and boarding school for children with learning disabilities or other academic problems
Grades: Ungraded, ages 8–14 at admission (curriculum through ninth grade)
Enrollment: Capacity of 60 boarding students and 26 day students
Head of School: Carol Smieciuch, Director

THE SCHOOL

Oakland School was begun as a summer reading camp in 1950 and was expanded in 1967 to include a year-round boarding and day school for average to above average children with learning problems. Located on 450 acres east of Charlottesville, Virginia, Oakland offers easy access from northern Virginia, Richmond, Tidewater, and Washington, D.C., as well as from Maryland, West Virginia, and North Carolina. Currently, Oakland serves students from eight states and three countries.

Oakland's history of successful remediation of children with learning difficulties comes from a philosophy that assumes that every child can reach his or her potential. The staff works to bring students up to their ability levels in reading, mathematics, written language, and study skills. In two to four years, students "graduate" into a public or private school to compete successfully in mainstream education. The belief that a positive self-concept is essential to future success is also an important part of Oakland's philosophy. Respect for each student as a person and encouragement and development of strengths have always been emphasized.

Oakland is licensed by the state of Virginia, approved for funded students by Virginia, Maryland, Delaware, and the District of Columbia, and accredited by the Virginia Association of Independent Specialized Education Facilities.

ACADEMIC PROGRAMS

Small classrooms and a student-teacher ratio of 5:1 provide the individual attention needed to ensure success. Each student receives at least one 30-minute period a day of one-to-one instruction. Children with severe reading disabilities often receive additional "one-to-ones" and may spend 2½ to 3 hours a day in reading instruction. Because the ability to read affects all aspects of education, teaching reading is a specialty at Oakland. Each student's reading program is designed to meet his or her individual needs. The beginning reading program is phonics based, similar to the Orton-Gillingham method. Phonics skills are reinforced during one-to-one reading periods, and reading teachers are trained in this method. Many other types of reading and comprehension instruction are utilized based on individual needs. Students typically make from 1½ to 3 years of progress in reading each year and are moved ahead as quickly as their abilities allow.

A strong basic skills emphasis is essential to future school success. Therefore, much time is spent on language, math, and study skills. English is taught as two separate courses: Grammar and Expository Writing. Students at or above a fourth-grade skill level do most of their writing on a word processor, and students are proficient by graduation. Writing is taught at different levels, beginning with the basics of writing in complete sentences and continuing through paragraphing, transitioning, and a variety of expository and creative compositions. Math classes are taught in small groups of 5 to 10 students. Courses are offered through the geometry level. All content area subjects at Oakland are taught as study skills classes and are an integral part of the process of transitioning students into general education. The curriculum includes reading for information, memory strategies, outlining, summarizing, note taking, answering essay questions, and studying for and taking tests. These skills are taught through a variety of courses in science and history.

Oakland is ungraded but provides instruction through a ninth-grade level. Grades and course credits are provided for ninth grade students. Four narrative reports a year plus several scheduled conference times and extensive telephone communication and e-mail allow parents participation in their child's school experience. The 180-day school year includes a seven-week summer camp/school program.

FACULTY AND ADVISERS

Oakland employs 12 full-time teachers and 3 teaching assistants. All teachers are certified by the state of Virginia. All reading or "main teachers" are certified in special education with endorsements in learning disabilities. There is a separate residential staff of 13 who plan after-school, evening, and weekend activities and live in the dorms. In addition, Oakland has contractual agreements with clinical psychologists and speech-language pathologists, who are an integral part of the staff. Teachers meet three times a week in the winter and daily in the summer; residential staff meet daily year-round. Each student has a "main teacher" who acts in the capacity of adviser and is aware of the student's progress in all areas of school life. Ongoing communication between staff members and a commitment to a team approach to program management ensures that each child receives the instruction and support needed.

Oakland students graduate when they are prepared for success in mainstream education. Most attend regular public or private schools; a few students continue in special education. Students graduate into the grade that will be the most appropriate for their age, maturity level, and academic skills. They may enter fifth through tenth grade after leaving Oakland, depending on their age and achievement levels. Students entering secondary school have attended Blue Ridge, Christ Church, Foreman, Grier, Phelps, and other private schools throughout the country. Many Oakland graduates return to their homes and attend public or private day schools.

STUDENT BODY AND CONDUCT

Oakland School has an enrollment of up to 60 boarding students and 26 day students. Age at admission is 8–14, and students may remain until they are 17. Although many are from mid-Atlantic states, students come from all parts of the country. A typical Oakland student has average to above-average intelligence and has not had success in prior school experiences because of a variety of reasons; these may include learning disabilities, attention deficits, or organizational problems. Oakland does not accept students with severe behavioral or emotional disorders. There are very specific behavioral expectations and school rules, combined with structure and consistency. Each dorm elects a representative to a student council, which is responsible for helping to plan activities and recommending privileges and disciplinary action. Each student works toward individual goals that are developed and frequently discussed with the residential staff.

ACADEMIC FACILITIES

Four small classroom buildings are scattered over the grounds; these contain from one to six classrooms each. There are additional classrooms in the administration building and the dining hall, which also houses a library.

BOARDING AND GENERAL FACILITIES

Oakland is located on 450 acres of rolling hills, meadows, and woods. The central building is a pre-Revolutionary farmhouse. A dining facility, gym and recreation building, five dormitories with both single and double rooms, a swimming pool, tennis courts, and a stable and riding ring, along with an extensive area of streams and fishing spots, playing fields, and riding, hiking, and bicycling trails, provide opportunities for a variety of activities.

ATHLETICS

Physical education is required Monday through Friday. In addition, there are many intramural sports, including basketball, soccer, softball, volleyball, and tennis, as well as a cheerleading squad. Basketball and soccer are played interscholastically. All students are encouraged to participate regardless of experience or athletic ability. Sportsmanship is emphasized, and, in addition to athletic awards, the trophy cases hold many Best Sportsmanship awards. Approximately 75 percent of Oakland students participate in the horseback-riding program.

EXTRACURRICULAR OPPORTUNITIES

Planning and care is taken in providing after-school and weekend activities. Evening and weekend trips to sports events; educational visits to museums and art galleries; occasional trips to Richmond or Washington, D.C.; hikes in the

Blue Ridge Mountains; or just taking in a movie and a pizza are part of the program. Other activities include arts and crafts, ceramics, cooking, and music.

DAILY LIFE

Weekday schedules begin at 7:30. Breakfast is at 8, after which students complete daily chores before school begins at 9. Lunch is from 12:30 to 1:30, and afternoon classes end at 3:35. The school day includes ten periods of 30 to 35 minutes each. Afternoon activities are from 4 to 5:15, with dinner at 5:30. Study halls and evening activities round out the day. Bedtime depends on age and may be from 9 to 10:30.

WEEKEND LIFE

In addition to trips off the farm, weekends include general cleanup, individual dorm activities, a variety of sports and games, movies, Sunday nondenominational chapel service, and special activities planned by the residential staff. Students may visit home an average of once every three or four weekends.

Oakland also has a Parent Association, which plans two weekend activities each year. This enables parents from different parts of the country to meet each other, get to know their child's school friends, and become more involved with the school.

SUMMER PROGRAMS

The seven-week summer program is part of the 180-day school year, and all winter students attend. It is also available as a summer-only option. During the summer, the residential and teaching staffs are increased to accommodate a larger enrollment, which may reach a total of 130. The summer program consists of 3½ hours of intensive academic instruction in reading, language, math, and study skills. The "Upward Lift" program for children with reading disabilities includes three 55-minute periods of reading and phonics and one period of math. The rest of the day and weekends are filled with camp activities, including swimming, riding, tennis, archery, golf, arts and crafts, nature, camping, and a variety of clubs and team sports. Summer is a fun way to be introduced to Oakland, and many year-round students choose to add seven weeks of instruction by beginning their program in June rather than September.

COSTS AND FINANCIAL AID

Total costs for the 2005–06 year (September through August) are $35,500 for boarding students and $18,900 for day students. The 2005–06 summer fees are $6900 for boarding students and $3700 for day students. Fees include all expenses except travel and minimal personal spending money. Individual and group psychological therapy and speech-language therapy are available at an additional charge and on an as-needed basis. There may also be charges for students who require additional attention from the residential staff. These fees are discussed with parents if they become necessary. Oakland does not offer financial aid at this time.

ADMISSIONS INFORMATION

Boys and girls ages 8–14 are eligible for admission. Although every child is considered individually, all students have two things in common—they are experiencing difficulty in their present school setting, and they are capable of learning successfully. Although a number of Oakland students arrive with mild emotional problems and poor social skills, the School does not accept children with extreme emotional or behavioral profiles. Many Oakland students are referred by parents of other students or by educational professionals. The application process includes a telephone interview, an application form, close inspection of records containing psychological and educational evaluations, including teacher narratives, and a personal interview. Since most applicants have been thoroughly evaluated, Oakland does not usually require additional testing. However, occasionally a session with an Oakland psychologist may be part of the interview process, and additional information may be requested.

APPLICATION TIMETABLE

Inquiries and applications are received throughout the year, and applicants are accepted on a space-available basis. Most students begin in June or September, but students can be accepted year-round as space permits.

ADMISSIONS CORRESPONDENCE

Carol Smieciuch, Director
Oakland School
Boyd Tavern
Keswick, Virginia 22947

Phone: 434-293-9059
Fax: 434-296-8930
E-mail: oaklandschool@earthlink.net
Web site: http://www.oaklandschool.net

PATHWAY SCHOOL

Norristown, Pennsylvania

Type: Coeducational therapeutic residential and day program for learning-disabled, neurologically impaired, and neuropsychiatrically disordered students
Grades: Nongraded program: Day school, ages 9 to 21; Residential program, ages 12 to 21
Enrollment: School total: 175; Day school: 120; Residential program: 55
Head of School: William O'Flanagan, Ph.D.

THE SCHOOL

Founded in 1961 by a developmental pediatrician, the Pathway School was developed to provide an environment where students could learn how to learn. As learning disabilities became more recognized and public schools became more capable of providing individualized educational programs (IEP's), the Pathway School also became more specialized. Most of the students are referred by their school districts either because it is impossible to implement an appropriate IEP or because an appropriate peer group is nonexistent within the school district. Many times the need for a more comprehensive, therapeutic program results in the referral to Pathway.

The 13-acre campus is situated within a suburban neighborhood. The School's location, 20 miles northwest of Philadelphia near historic Valley Forge, allows recreation programs to include cultural and sporting events in Philadelphia as well as trips to the nearby Lancaster County area, the Pocono Mountains, and the New Jersey shore.

The Pathway School is a member of the National Association of Private Schools for Exceptional Children and the Pennsylvania Alliance of Approved Private Schools and is licensed by the boards of education in states that the School serves.

ACADEMIC PROGRAMS

The educational program is broad in its scope. The School is a diploma-granting facility and, furthermore, is capable of preparing a student for a junior college, community college, or a small four-year college experience. A general education curriculum is also available, as is a more life skills–oriented program that results in an IEP Certificate of Completion. As many as 12 students could be in a group that is instructed by a teacher and an assistant. All students are offered a combination of academic and vocational classes to fully prepare them for greater independence.

Except for a foreign language, most levels of language arts, math, and science are available to the students. When a student demonstrates need for more advanced study, the Pathway School partners with local community colleges, area high schools, and county technical schools; at times, special tutorials are provided. Related services include reading therapy, speech/language therapy, and occupational therapy.

Vocational classes offer a variety of introductory work experiences in areas such as culinary arts, clerical and business, janitorial, horticultural, and painting and minor maintenance. Once a student has successfully completed one or several vocational classes, a work-study program in the local community is made available. More than thirty businesses in the area support the students and provide the real-life job experience that is so critical for success upon graduation.

Because the typical Pathway student has problems with self-esteem and usually does not understand his or her emotions, the structure and support of the therapeutic milieu is extremely important. When necessary, the student participates in individual, group, and family therapy. Often a behavior-modification program is designed to target specific behaviors and reinforce more age-appropriate behaviors. A multidisciplinary team approach is necessary for the student to have success across environments.

Grades are provided on a quarterly basis, with progress reports given semiannually. The IEP is reviewed at least on an annual basis, although a parent can ask for IEP meetings more frequently.

FACULTY AND ADVISERS

The professional staff is 120 in number. The students are supported by certified special educators, reading specialists, speech/language pathologists, a psychiatrist, nurses, psychologists, a librarian, and occupational therapists. In addition to this professional staff, the program is enriched by the teacher assistants, housekeepers, drivers, groundskeepers, and secretaries. These numbers ensure that the students have the attention that is necessary for them to feel secure.

COLLEGE PLACEMENT

Five to 10 percent of the student body is capable of succeeding in a college environment. Preparation for the SAT is provided, and the Pathway School is a test site for students from the School. Graduates have been enrolled in various state universities, junior colleges, community colleges, and technical schools.

STUDENT BODY AND CONDUCT

Nearly 75 percent of the student population is male. All of the day population and 25 percent of the residential students are from Pennsylvania. Currently, the remaining students reside in New Jersey, New York, New Hampshire, Vermont, Massachusetts, Connecticut, Tennessee, South Carolina, Georgia, Texas, Washington, and California.

The day student population, socioeconomically speaking, is represented mostly by middle-class families. The residential program has a higher number of upper–middle-class and upper-class income families. Because at least 95 percent of the families enjoy the benefit of full tuition funded by their sending school district, the Pathway student does not have an attitude of wealth and social advantage. Instead, the focus is placed on the development of skills, which will ensure future success.

The dress code is relaxed to help the students enjoy their youth, but clothing that could be offensive is not tolerated. Respect of themselves and of others is emphasized in the design of each cottage's level system and in the formation of a personal contract that a student may carry with them to classes and after school. Discipline is applied in the form of logical consequences for inappropriate behavior. Consequences may include removal of privileges or grounding from an off-campus trip. For serious offenses, such as hitting a peer, a suspension may occur. Expulsion results from serious behavior such as substance abuse, possession of a weapon, aggressive behavior, or elopement.

ACADEMIC FACILITIES

Seven educational buildings provide the many classrooms needed as well as a spacious gymnasium, a well-equipped recreation room, a technology center, a library, an art room, and a "practical academics center," where students may learn independent-living skills such as cooking and laundry.

BOARDING AND GENERAL FACILITIES

Pathway's attractive, open campus is always busy with student activity. By 8:50 a.m., residential students have left the four cottages on campus or the apartments located within the nearby community to join their friends who have been bussed from the local school districts. The students travel outside to change classes, eat in the cafeteria, or to have one of their therapies in the historic administrative building, known as Butera Hall.

The dormitories, known as cottages, are ranch-style brick buildings in which 10 to 12 students reside. Each room may have 2 students, and each cottage has its own kitchen, dining area, and living room for casual activities.

ATHLETICS

Development of satisfying leisure-time activities is a primary goal of both the physical education and recreational staff. Because the Pathway students have not had the past luxury of friends in their communities, they find special pleasure in playing basketball in the gym or tennis on the nearby community courts or swimming with their cottagemates at the various swim clubs. They can compete interscholastically on a soccer, basketball, or softball team. The games and practices are held within the school day so that the entire school can participate in the social event.

After-school activities may include a bowling league, ski club, DJ club, art club, chess club, weight lifting, scuba club, drama, karate, and monthly dances. Activities provide supervision with a 4:1 ratio, which encourages appropriate behavior. The adult support also gives students the support needed to manage the social environment, which is so difficult for the young people attending Pathway.

EXTRACURRICULAR OPPORTUNITIES

The community offers great variety for recreation, with nearby access to state and local parks with biking, hiking, nature trails, and other environmental areas. The students also enjoy golfing, batting facilities, in-line skating, and ice skating. Weekly trips include shopping at a large mall, browsing at a bookstore, an evening in the community library for both leisure and research purposes, and an afternoon workout at the local YMCA.

Tickets are often provided so that a group of students can attend a professional or college sporting event, a play, or musical concert. Several times each year, performances are held on campus by culturally diverse groups to broaden the experience of the students.

Community service is encouraged, and the students must participate in at least one regularly occurring activity where they are assisting someone in need. Service projects have included helping the

blind, visiting the elderly, recreation activities for underprivileged children, and activities with a veterans' home. The personal growth and development of the students' confidence is evident at each outing, and all who participate feel rewarded.

DAILY LIFE
Students are encouraged to wake up and get themselves ready for school independently. In the morning, 1 to 2 staff members are available to the students, with a housekeeper who prepares breakfast. Morning chores, such as making their bed, cleaning the kitchen, and organizing their bedroom, are completed with the staff members reinforcing mature, cooperative behavior. By 8:50 a.m. each student should be in their homeroom class with their books ready to begin an eight-period day. Depending on their ability to manage transition, the day may include 8 different teachers and movement to eight different classrooms, with the peer group changing each time. For students who have difficulty with this degree of change, Pathway offers more self-contained programs.

At midday, lunch is offered in the school cafeteria. All students enjoy a social time after lunch to talk with friends or, if weather permits, to enjoy leisure activities outside.

Most high school students have the opportunity to participate in a work-study program. This may involve a part-time job that begins in the afternoon and lasts until early evening for several days each week. Pathway drivers or public transportation are utilized to bring the students to work and back to their apartment or campus. Work-study is as broad as the interests and strengths of the current students. Past and current experience has been with employers in the hotel and restaurant industry, hospitals, auto body shops, florists, landscapers, day-care service, a library, local retail and department stores, and print shops.

After school, the residential students return to their cottage or their apartment. Three to 4 residential staff members per cottage await their return with structured activities planned to continue the development of social and independent living skills. Activities before and after dinner include a variety of interesting, socially stimulating pursuits. As during the school day, the students monitor themselves, with staff assistance, as appropriate behaviors are reinforced through personal goals that are identified on a behavioral contract. A study/rest time precedes dinner, with staff members available to assist the students if the homework assigned is presenting too much difficulty. After the evening activity, the students prepare for bed and have an assigned bedtime, depending on their level of achievement. The residential staff decreases in number as the students retire to their beds until only 1 staff member remains and is on duty through the night until the next morning.

WEEKEND LIFE
Weekends usually mean that activities that consume greater amounts of time can be scheduled. After sleeping later on Saturday morning, a bike ride through a state park with a packed picnic lunch could be the afternoon adventure. After returning to the cottage, the evening meal "made from scratch" could be the early evening entertainment. A rented movie, complete with a popcorn party, would round out the evening for the tired students and staff members. Community events, such as antique car shows and flea markets, along with the museums and multiple historic areas, lend themselves to providing interesting activities for weekend schedules.

SUMMER PROGRAMS
For students who would benefit from consistency for the entire calendar year, a seven-week summer school program is available. Academics are taught in the morning, while the afternoon is filled with activities that stimulate social growth and development. Afternoon clubs, such as tennis, swimming, chess, gardening, arts and crafts, and model building, are selected based on the interests of the students. Work-study students usually have the opportunity to work more hours in the summer and may also be able to experience new job situations. Because many of the students can enjoy a camp or are capable of staying at home, the number of summer students is less than that of the regular school term. The luxury of smaller classes and, therefore, more individual attention make this an ideal time to enroll new students.

COSTS AND FINANCIAL AID
Unfortunately, no financial aid is available at the Pathway School. Almost all students are funded entirely by their sending school district. The tuition covers costs for room and board and educational and clinical expenses. If the family lives a great distance away, the school district may also pay for the expenses of the student traveling home four times each year. Families need to supply money for the weekly allowance, personal hygiene needs, cost of special trips, and all clothing needed.

In 2005–06, the cost of a day program for ten months is $33,700 and a twelve-month program is $40,200. Residential costs for twelve months begin at $110,800 and could require more expense if a higher staffing ratio is necessary for success.

ADMISSIONS INFORMATION
The Pathway program is appropriate for students who have complex learning disabilities, may be neurologically impaired, and may experience neuropsychiatric disorders, including Asperger's disorder or P.D.D., anxiety disorders, and mood disorders. The cognitive range is typically a 70 to 100 full-scale IQ, but consideration is given to candidates who may be above average to superior intellectual capability or below a full-scale IQ of 70, as appropriate. The program is not able to serve young people who may be diagnosed with serious emotional disturbances, such as conduct disorder, personality disorder, or psychosis. Students who struggle with behaviors that include substance abuse, running away, and delinquent behaviors cannot be served at Pathway.

APPLICATION TIMETABLE
An open enrollment with a rolling admissions process is available while program space exists. It is always advisable to contact the Admissions Office to inquire about the status of available openings. If a September enrollment is anticipated, the early spring is the best time to contact the Admissions Office.

A file with all relevant and current reports is required. A screening team reviews all information that is submitted. If the team decides that it is appropriate to continue the admissions process, then an evaluation is scheduled, with participation by the student and both parents. The evaluation is multidisciplinary in nature in order to obtain the most comprehensive information. A case conference is held within three days to decide whether or not the Pathway School can offer an appropriate program.

ADMISSIONS CORRESPONDENCE
Louise Robertson, Director of External Affairs
Pathway School
162 Egypt Road
Norristown, Pennsylvania 19403-3090
Phone: 610-277-0660
Fax: 610-539-1493
E-mail: louiseR@pathwayschool.org
Web site: http://www.PathwaySchool.org

PINE RIDGE SCHOOL

Williston, Vermont

PINE RIDGE SCHOOL

Type: Coeducational boarding and day school for students with dyslexia, language-based disabilities, and nonverbal learning disabilities
Grades: Ungraded, ages 13–18
Enrollment: approximately 100
Head of School: Douglas Dague

THE SCHOOL

Pine Ridge School, founded in 1968, is a coeducational boarding school for adolescents from ages 13 to 18 who are experiencing academic difficulties as a result of dyslexia, specific language-based learning disabilities, and nonverbal learning disabilities. The School recognizes that the learning process of these students is different from that of their peers and that each student possesses individual learning needs. Thus, Pine Ridge defines its mission as "an educational community committed to empowering students with learning disabilities to define and achieve success throughout their lives."

Students are provided with a highly structured, success-oriented environment where classes are small and opportunities for teacher-student interactions are frequent. The four major components of the program—academic, remedial, residential/social, and athletic/recreational—are designed and coordinated to address every aspect of learning disabilities as they affect student growth and learning. A unique aspect of the Pine Ridge experience is the hiring of separate staff members for each of the four program areas, which allows staff members to focus all of their energy on one particular component of the program. In addition, generalized outcomes, which measure skills that are essential for success, are taught and measured across the four program areas. These outcomes include speaking, listening, organizational skills, time management, and self-advocacy.

Located at the foot of Vermont's scenic Green Mountains, the Pine Ridge Campus encompasses more than 100 acres. While the setting is rural, the School is only eight miles from Burlington, Vermont's largest city and home to the University of Vermont. Recent studies have ranked Vermont as one of the two safest states, and Burlington is regularly listed as one of America's best places to live.

The School is a nonprofit corporation directed by the Head of School for the Board of Trustees. Pine Ridge School is approved by the Vermont Department of Education as a private secondary school with diploma-granting privileges and is approved for special education funding by the Vermont State Board of Education as well as by several Association of Schools and Colleges (NEAS&C), and is a member of the Vermont Principals' Association (VPA), the International Dyslexia Association (IDA), the Independent School Association of Northern New England (ISANNE), the National Association of Independent Schools (NAIS), and the Vermont Independent School Association (VISA). In addition, the Pine Ridge School teacher/training/summer programs at the subscriber, associate, and certified levels are accredited by the Academy of Orton-Gillingham of Practitioners and Educators.

ACADEMIC PROGRAMS

Educators at Pine Ridge are specialists. They understand the needs and frustrations as well as the potential of students with learning disabilities. Students are addressed as unique individuals, with strengths and weaknesses, talents, gifts, and abilities to be recognized and developed. The School

meets the unique needs of students, building one success upon another, through small, highly structured academic classes, intensive language remediation in one-on-one tutorials, and a carefully monitored program of development in personal and social skills. Through sports, adventure activities, community service, and other explorations outside the classroom, students find their own voices and learn to speak confidently for themselves.

Pine Ridge School offers a language-based instructional program, which is presented in small classes (averaging 7 to 10 students), one-on-one tutorial sessions, and individual work in the Skills Labs. Language skills, attention, perception, cognition, and other areas that affect learning are assessed when students arrive at Pine Ridge. The faculty members then work closely with students to create a program that strengthens weaknesses and builds upon existing strengths. The small classes at Pine Ridge promote student-teacher and student-student interaction, which is essential to reinforce and sustain learning. New material is carefully presented, practiced, and reviewed using a structured, sequential, and multisensory approach.

All students spend a full period each day working one-on-one with a remedial language specialist. The Orton-Gillingham remedial approach is used in tutorials to help students understand the structure that underlies language. Tutors and students work together to improve important language-skills areas, including word identification, awareness of the phonetic aspects of language, decoding, reading comprehension, abstract reasoning, spelling, and composition of written sentences and structured paragraphs.

A period of proctored skills laboratory each day gives students an opportunity to practice and apply the skills addressed in the tutorial. In the lab, students are involved in independent learning sessions, during which they work toward goals they have set with their remedial language specialist to improve basic language skills. A trained language tutor proctors the Skills Lab, providing guidance and support as well as feedback regarding the quality of students' independent work.

To help students become better communicators, Pine Ridge students also participate in small-group social cognition sessions that aim to improve social awareness, judgment, and personal presentation. Students evaluate themselves by viewing videotapes of their social exchanges in role-playing, interviews, and other activities. Such exercises help students develop sensitivity to nonverbal communication and improve their ability to analyze social situations.

FACULTY AND ADVISERS

Pine Ridge School has 38 professionally qualified teachers and tutors. Eleven have graduate degrees. Most classroom teachers are certified in the subjects that they teach. Tutors are highly trained in the specific remedial techniques used in the one-on-one tutorial. Twelve teachers and tutors have been accredited by the Academy of Orton-Gillingham Practitioners and Educators (AOGPE). A separate, trained staff of 15 residential instructors with

college degrees, implement residential, recreational, and experiential programs during nonacademic and weekend portions of the program.

Douglas Dague, Headmaster, received his B.A. in history from the University of Wisconsin. He has been at Pine Ridge School for twenty years, spending one year as an Orton-Gillingham remedial language specialist, five years as a social studies teacher, eight years as Director of Studies, and the past seven years as Headmaster.

Jean Foss, Dean of Clinical Teaching and Research, received her M.Ed. from the University of Vermont. She has been at Pine Ridge School since 1969, and was the Founding Fellow of the Orton-Gillingham Academy and its first Vice President. She is a former President of the New England branch of the International Dyslexia Association, and she has delivered numerous lectures, papers, and workshops on the remediation of dyslexia and nonverbal learning disabilities.

COLLEGE PLACEMENT

The Pine Ridge faculty and staff members, together with Transition Services, work closely with students who are seeking postsecondary placement. The Transition Program provides students with a realistic knowledge of the world and how to adapt and grow in it. The program functions as a bridge for moving students to higher levels of community involvement, which includes helping students develop the necessary skills to succeed in the workplace, in postsecondary education, and in professional/technical training programs. Students are encouraged to visit the colleges of their choice, and Pine Ridge offers untimed versions of the SAT and the ACT on campus.

On average, 90 percent of the students who graduate from Pine Ridge School enroll in a postsecondary educational setting, including, but not limited to the Berkshire Center, Carleton University, Curry College, Essex Technical Center, Linfield College, Mitchell College, Mount Ida College, and SUNY.

STUDENT BODY AND CONDUCT

Pine Ridge students come from all across the United States and from many other countries. School guidelines and expectations are outlined in the student handbook. Serious infractions of these guidelines are referred to a disciplinary council. The School does not tolerate the use of alcohol, tobacco products, or illegal drugs. The dress code is informal, with some restrictions placed on student attire. Students are expected to care for their rooms and common living areas. Additional responsibilities are assigned on a rotating basis. Students are awarded privileges for contributing to the community through the Summit Level System.

There is a very strong sense of community at Pine Ridge between the staff and students. The School fosters a strong sense of community, emphasizing respect and relationships. Additional relationships are fostered through the leadership group and the Student Council.

ACADEMIC FACILITIES

There are ten individual buildings that form the main facilities of the campus. Two buildings are devoted to tutorial teaching areas and the skills laboratories. A large academic building with ten classrooms, a computer lab, an art room, a library, and offices was built in 1985. A separate building houses two science labs and greenhouses. The Duerr Activity Center (2001) offers numerous physical education opportunities as well as opportunities for social events and interactions. Other facilities include a health center, a social cognition classroom, and offices. It is also in the planning stages for expanding the academic building.

BOARDING AND GENERAL FACILITIES

Pine Ridge School strongly encourages students to live on campus. Currently, there are two girls' dorms and three boys' dorms. The majority of residential instructors who supervise each dorm have at least a bachelor's degree and have been trained to work with learning disabled students. The School has recently constructed two new living and learning centers housing 40 students, with plans for a third. The living and learning centers have full kitchens and a large dinning area and table to accommodate the entire dormitory for various meals throughout the week. Each dormitory has living room areas with a TV and DVD/VCR. All are equipped with a small refrigerator and microwave.

ATHLETICS

Pine Ridge School has a varied athletic program that emphasizes skill development, team spirit, cooperation, personal satisfaction, and success. All students are required to take physical education courses as part of their academic program. They may choose the sport or activity in which they wish to participate. These options include soccer, basketball, volleyball, racquetball, ropes course, aerobics, mountain biking, Alpine and Nordic skiing, snowboarding, weight training, and tennis. Many other outdoor activities, such as canoeing, rock climbing, and camping are available as adventure-based activities. The School itself has a soccer field, a softball diamond, the Duerr Activity Center, and access to a weight-training room and other fitness facilities. Many Pine Ridge students participate interscholastically in soccer, basketball, tennis, and softball.

The Pine Ridge School has developed one of the finest ropes courses in the nation. The course is certified and inspected by Northeast Adventure and provides opportunities to learn group and team-building skills, including problem solving, trust, communication, and leadership. Individuals gain self-esteem through challenging their own self-imposed limitations. The School offers experiential learning through wilderness and ropes course programs for the winter school students and the Pine Ridge Summer School. The center employs only trained and experienced adventure program leaders to work with groups. Dormitory trips include canoeing, hiking, backpacking, rock climbing, and polar camping.

EXTRACURRICULAR OPPORTUNITIES

Pine Ridge School offers extracurricular activities in the evenings and on weekends through its Residential and Transition Programs. The Residential Program focuses on activities that promote self-awareness and advocacy, interpersonal communication, self-management, personal organization, and diversity. Residential Program activities include photography, drama, school newspaper, skiing, indoor climbing, yearbook, art, music, student council, and horticulture, as well as others. The Transition Program functions as a bridge for moving students to higher levels of community involvement and work standards by developing the necessary skills to succeed in the workplace, in postsecondary education, and in professional/technical training programs. Pine Ridge is also involved in numerous civic and local volunteer projects, such as the Williston Recycling Program, Vermont Green Up Day, YMCA After School Program, Jump Rope for Heart/American Heart Association, and Burlington Kid's Day. Students also have opportunities to participate as volunteers to help the Fletcher Allen Medical Center of Vermont, United Way, Muscular Dystrophy Association, and Special Olympics.

In addition, special events are scheduled throughout the year, including a Halloween party, December holiday party, winter carnival, sports banquet, Head's Day, and the prom.

DAILY LIFE

The academic day begins at 8:40 a.m. and ends at 2:50 p.m. Transition curriculum is offered from 4:15 until 5:30, with a study hall from 3:15 to 4. Dinner is served at 6, evening activities begin at 7, and at 9:30 students return to their dormitories.

WEEKEND LIFE

Students are offered a variety of recreational and cultural programs on weekends. The School's proximity to the city of Burlington provides many recreational opportunities, including concerts, plays, movies, shopping, skating, hiking, bicycling, and mountain biking. Students can visit historic sites or sightsee both locally and in such major cities as Montreal or Boston. School trips to nearby ski areas are highlights of winter weekends.

Students may go home every other weekend if they meet academic and behavioral expectations.

Students who demonstrate maturity and commitment to their academic work can apply for the Summit Society. Members of the Summit Society may earn the privilege of a less structured weekend and plan more of their own activities.

SUMMER PROGRAMS

Pine Ridge School offers a residential program in the summer for learning disabled students ages 9 to 18. The students spend six weeks improving language-processing skills by attending 2 one-on-one Orton-Gillingham tutorials per day. In addition, they enjoy a full range of outdoor sports and regular camp activities. The Pine Ridge School teacher/training/summer programs at the subscriber, associate, and certified levels are accredited by the Academy of Orton-Gillingham of Practitioners and Educators.

COSTS AND FINANCIAL AID

The cost for the 2005–06 academic year was $48,250. This includes tuition, room, board, four content area classes, daily one-on-one tutorials, social cognition classes, one independent skills lab, art classes, athletic programs, books, selected cultural events, weekly evening activities, all meals on campus, transportation to School events and activities, and to the airport, bus, or train station. The cost for day students is $36,100. Each student has a student bank account for personal and recreational activities. Some students receive financial assistance from their local school districts and/or from their state's department of education.

ADMISSIONS INFORMATION

Pine Ridge accepts students of average to above average potential who have a diagnosed learning disability without primary emotional or behavioral problems. The School requires a completed admissions questionnaire, a student questionnaire, a transcript from the student's psychoeducational evaluation that includes a Weschler intelligence profile, and any other reports from counselors or evaluators who have worked directly with the student. Students and their families can visit informally at any time Monday through Friday, 9 a.m. to 3 p.m., by making an appointment with the Admissions Office. A formal visit is requested when the applicant is considered for placement testing and personal interviews are conducted.

APPLICATION TIMETABLE

Pine Ridge has an open admissions process. Students may be accepted into the program at any time through the end of the second term, which concludes in March, provided that a vacancy exists. Students desiring September admission should apply before June.

ADMISSIONS CORRESPONDENCE

Joshua Doyle, M.Ed.
Director of Admissions
Pine Ridge School
9505 Williston Road
Williston, Vermont 05495

Phone: 802-434-2161
Fax: 802-434-5512
E-mail: admissions@pineridgeschool.com
Web site: http://www.pineridgeschool.com

PROVO CANYON SCHOOL

Provo, Utah

Type: Adolescent residential treatment facility for boys and girls ages 12–17
Grades: 7–12
Enrollment: 242
Head of School: Kreg Gillman, Ph.D., Chief Executive Officer

THE SCHOOL

Provo Canyon School, founded in 1971, is located in Provo, Utah, approximately 40 miles south of Salt Lake City. Provo is a university town, located at the foot of majestic Mount Timpanogos, in the Wasatch Range of the Rocky Mountains.

Provo Canyon School is a 242-bed adolescent residential treatment facility with more than thirty years of experience helping teenagers with behavioral, emotional, and substance-abuse problems that preclude effective functioning in the home, school, and community. During that time, the School has established a reputation as one of the country's most respected residential treatment facilities.

Students range in age from 12 to 17. The continuum of care at Provo Canyon School includes individual, group, family, and experiential therapy. A structured, therapeutic living environment and a fully accredited middle and high school curriculum are offered. A drug and alcohol track serves the special needs of adolescents with substance-abuse and addiction problems.

Provo Canyon School has the advantage of two separate campuses. The Provo campus is located on approximately 9 acres and is the home of the boys' campus. The girls live at the Orem campus, which is about 1 mile away and is nestled in a 5-acre apple and cherry orchard.

Provo Canyon School is fully accredited by the Joint Commission on Accreditation of Healthcare Organizations (JCAHO) and the Northwest Association of Schools and Colleges and is licensed by the State of Utah Department of Human Services.

ACADEMIC PROGRAMS

A vital part of the treatment model is the role of academics. Provo Canyon students are generally of average to well-above-average intelligence. Middle and high school curricula are offered. The academic environment offers small class sizes and is designed to meet each child's individual needs, which may include learning differences. Each student arrives at Provo Canyon School with a unique level of knowledge skills and academic abilities.

Once academic ability and needs are determined through testing, an educational plan is developed to help the student progress and experience success in the classroom setting.

FACULTY AND ADVISERS

The faculty members, most of whom are certified in special education, are hired for their teaching skills and their ability to deal effectively with students with special needs. Their priorities include helping students develop self-esteem, initiative, and self-control and build a solid academic foundation.

COLLEGE PLACEMENT

Many of the high school graduates continue their education in colleges and universities. The School believes that students should leave Provo Canyon with the social and academic skills necessary for them to assume responsible roles in society.

STUDENT BODY AND CONDUCT

Provo Canyon School has high expectations for its students. The School believes that children thrive on a clear understanding of what is expected of them. Expectations are based upon the philosophy of taking responsibility for one's actions or inactions as well as consideration and respect for others. This philosophy is evident in all areas of campus life, from the cleanliness and order of personal belongings to daily interactions with staff members and peers. The School expects students to achieve their highest potential in academics and to work on the issues that resulted in placement at Provo Canyon School. Provo Canyon is committed to providing an environment conducive to success.

ACADEMIC FACILITIES

Academics are provided on both campuses. The curriculum offered on each campus is the same, and the single-sex environment allows students to focus on their academic goals. The 300-seat auditorium, located on the Provo campus, has a

full range of audiovisual equipment and provides a setting for a variety of special events.

BOARDING AND GENERAL FACILITIES

Students are housed in a dormitory-like environment. On the boys' campus, there are 4 boys to a room; they share a bathroom. On the girls' campus, there are 3 to a room; they also share a bathroom. Amenities include two gymnasiums, a swimming pool, three outdoor competitive athletic fields, tennis courts, climbing walls, and a ropes course.

ATHLETICS

Physical activity is an important component of each day at Provo Canyon School. Volleyball, soccer, basketball, tennis, swimming, weight training, and aerobics are all regular activities.

EXTRACURRICULAR OPPORTUNITIES

Utah offers unparalleled outdoor recreational opportunities. During winter, snow skiing (downhill and cross-country) and snowmobiling are both popular activities. During the summer months, hiking, caving, and trips to Lake Powell for waterskiing and camping keep the calendar full.

Provo Canyon offers opportunities for students to participate in work programs. Earnings are transferred into an account for which a paycheck stub is received detailing wages earned. This money is available to use for special outings such as skiing or other activities. Students must be at an appropriate level to participate in these different activities. Students choosing to save their money receive the entire amount in a lump sum after discharge.

DAILY LIFE

It is the School's philosophy that the students should be kept busy and supervised. From the time that the students awaken in the morning until they retire, the day is filled with specific activities. After the morning routine of personal hygiene, breakfast, and unit chores, students are off to school until late afternoon. The afternoon and evening hours are spent involved in any number of activities,

which may include therapy, homework, athletics, work, outings, letter writing, or personal reflection.

WEEKEND LIFE
The weekends are more relaxed than the weekdays. The students sleep in and, after a late breakfast, thoroughly clean their rooms and living areas. Activities may include exercise, movies, homework, free time, and coed talk time.

SUMMER PROGRAMS
During the summer months, the School offers Therapy Without Walls, an experiential component for selected adolescents who are currently enrolled at Provo Canyon School. Participation in all of these activities is dependent on behavioral stability. Different trips are offered and may include mountain backpacking, canoe-ing, mountain biking, or river rafting. The groups are limited to 8 participants per session.

COSTS AND FINANCIAL AID
The tuition varies depending on the level of care that is established by the individual therapeutic need of the adolescent. Some health insurance companies recognize Provo Canyon School as a provider and fund the placement. Some administrative financial assistance is available with completion of a financial disclosure statement.

ADMISSIONS INFORMATION
Admission to Provo Canyon School is open year-round, and an initial inquiry is welcome at any time. There are no admission processing fees. Provo Canyon School strongly encourages parents to be present at the School during the admission process. While a formal interview is not required, a complete package of information must be provided before a decision can be made.

ADMISSIONS CORRESPONDENCE
Provo Canyon School offers a proven method of turning around the lives of young people beset by emotional and behavioral problems. The caring and multi-disciplinary professional staff operates in a unique environment that can help make a positive difference in a troubled teenager's life. For more information and/or a copy of the School's video or CD, those interested should contact:

Admissions Office
Provo Canyon School
4501 North University Avenue
Provo, Utah 84603

Phone: 800-848-9819 (toll-free)
Fax: 801-223-7130
E-mail: pcsinfo@provocanyon.com
Web site: http://www.provocanyon.com

PURNELL SCHOOL

Pottersville, New Jersey

Type: Girls' boarding and day general academic and college-preparatory school
Grades: 9–12
Enrollment: 115
Head of School: Jenifer Fox

THE SCHOOL

Since 1965, Purnell has educated young women, who, for a variety of reasons, have needed a small, personal setting in which to best develop academically and socially. The 83-acre farm that is now the Purnell campus was chosen by the founders, Mr. and Mrs. Lyttleton B. P. Gould Jr., and is in the village of Pottersville, with the rolling hills of northwestern New Jersey as a backdrop and the cultural opportunities of New York City just an hour away. The core of the campus, a 20-acre area, is composed of the main administrative building; a complex housing the dining hall and three dormitories; a studio arts center with ceramics, photography, and painting labs; a performing arts center with a theater and music practice rooms; faculty housing; a health center; an athletic center with a gymnasium, dance studio, weight and workout room, and a yoga and pilates room; tennis courts, and athletic fields.

Purnell is primarily a boarding school with an emphasis on developing the whole person in a single-sex environment. A close community of learners, Purnell celebrates differences and seeks out that which is unique in each girl. The school prides itself on its feeling of family and the close personal attention promised to every girl. Meals in the dining hall are served with family-style seating, and celebrations and banquets are held throughout the year.

The educational program is designed to engage a variety of learning styles with appropriate challenge and support for a wide range of abilities. Purnell is intentionally small so that each student holds a place of individual importance in the group, no matter what her background. The curriculum prepares all girls for the university or college that is most appropriate for her. As a school that is centered on learning rather than academic competition, students are not ranked. Each student is able to find the path that best serves her needs and goals.

Purnell's Board of Trustees is composed of 18 members, many of whom are alumnae or past parents. The Head of School serves as an ex-officio member. The School depends on tuition, Annual Giving, Capital Campaigns, and Endowment income to support its budget that is annually in excess of $3.5 million. The endowment is approximately $5.5 million.

Purnell is accredited by the Middle States Association of Colleges and Schools and is a member of the National Association of Independent Schools, the New Jersey Association of Independent Schools, the National Association of Principals of Schools for Girls, the National Coalition of Girls' Schools, and the Alumni Presidents' Council.

ACADEMIC PROGRAMS

The academic program at Purnell is designed as a hands-on, integrated approach. It stresses teaching girls in the ways that allow them to flourish, as made evident by national educational research. In addition to understanding what works well for girls, faculty members are trained and certified in Mel Levine's "All Kinds of Minds" program that places the emphasis on structuring a learning environment that is dynamic, engaging, and student-centered. With a traditional university and college preparatory course sequence, students are prepared in the humanities, mathematics, science, foreign language, athletics, and performing and studio arts. Students are encouraged to participate in as challenging a course sequence as possible.

Class size ranges from 4 to 16 students. Purnell has many programs that differentiate it from other girls' schools. The Learning and Enrichment Center is integrated into the total program so that teachers are continually trained by the Learning Specialists on ways to make accommodations for different learners within the classroom. There is time built into each day for students to seek one-on-one help with their teachers. This time does not conflict with athletics or extracurricular events. All ninth graders and new students are enrolled in a guided study-time program, where, during the extra help hour, they meet with the learning specialists who help them organize their assignments, make decisions about how to prioritize work, and learn to be self-advocating, responsible students. A supervised study hall also occurs in the afternoon for students who need extra support. Tutors are available in most subject areas. An SAT preparation course is offered at an additional cost.

International students are welcomed into the curriculum and offered opportunities in the English as a Second Language course to fulfill their foreign language requirements. Purnell is flexible in their requirements for foreign language, depending on the circumstance.

The performing and studio arts programs have always attracted creative minds to Purnell. The dance troupe, acting ensemble, rock band, and singing groups have consistently been of top quality and have often led to careers in these fields. The studio arts program at Purnell is extraordinary given the size of the school. Purnell not only attracts students who already understand their artistic talent, but regularly helps a girl discover unknown talents.

An exceptional feature of Purnell's curriculum is Project Exploration, a 2½-week period set aside in February and March for experiential learning. During this time, students explore a particular topic in depth. The approach to the topic is hands-on and project-oriented. Options have included furniture alteration, a community service offering, and participation in the School musical. Eleventh graders interested in attending an art school after graduation may use this time to prepare their portfolios. Seniors and Juniors have the opportunity to live and study abroad for two weeks in a Spanish- or French-speaking country, with Purnell faculty members serving as trip leaders. Students live with host families, attend a language institute, and travel to cultural and historic sites. Students must also complete a two-week internship during the summer before their senior year, pursuing career interests of their choice. Seniors then use this internship experience in a specially designed program to prepare them for their college experiences.

Seniors are required to take a public speaking course, which culminates with a speech delivered to the entire school regarding their experiences during their four years of high school and how they have grown.

FACULTY AND ADVISERS

Purnell seeks teachers who are not only highly qualified in their fields (more than half of the faculty members hold advanced degrees) but also sensitive, compassionate, and enthusiastic people, willing to give of themselves and committed to the philosophy of the School. There are 24 full-time faculty members, most of whom reside on campus. They also serve as dorm parents, committee and publication advisers, coaches, and advisers to 2 to 5 students each. Students meet individually with their adviser, an adult friend and advocate, once a week.

Jenifer Fox began as Head of Purnell in July of 2003. A graduate of the School of Education at the University of Wisconsin–Madison, Jenifer majored in English and communications. She holds a master's degree in English from the Bread Loaf School of English at Middlebury College and a Master of Education degree, with an emphasis on curriculum and teacher supervision, from the Harvard Graduate School of Education. She is certified as a secondary teacher in English and in speech communications and drama and as a Secondary School Administrator.

Purnell has established a fund to further faculty professional growth, particularly in the study of the learning process. All faculty members attend extensive professional development workshops at the beginning and end of each school year.

Purnell's Laura McCord-Grauer Center for Excellence in Teaching Center provides training and support for new and experienced teachers across the country, and creates a space where international dialogues can take place on curriculum and teaching. Through the Center, Purnell seeks to provide the highest quality of professional development for each member of its faculty, while reaching out to educators at secondary schools, universities, and colleges around the country.

COLLEGE PLACEMENT

The Director of College Counseling works closely with students and their parents in individual and group sessions to guide choices for each student's future. Most Purnell students choose to continue their education immediately after leaving Purnell, their choices including two- and four-year liberal arts institutions and art schools. Colleges chosen in the last three years include Alfred, American, Drew, Eckerd, Elmira, Emerson, Georgetown, Gettysburg, Goucher, Guilford, Hood, Ithaca, Lynchburg, Lynn University, Marymount Manhattan College, Marshall, Michigan State, Muhlenberg, NYU, Parsons, Pratt, Rhode Island School of Design, Rollins, Rutgers, St. Joseph's University, Savannah College of Art and Design, Temple, Vassar, Washington College, Wheaton, and the Universities of Cincinnati, Denver, Hartford, New Hampshire, and Vermont.

STUDENT BODY AND CONDUCT

Approximately 115 girls make up the student body, hailing from twenty-one states and seven other countries. In 2005, the most popular feeder states included California, Connecticut, Florida, Maryland, Massachusetts, New Jersey, New York, Ohio, Pennsylvania, Texas, and Virginia. International students represent Bermuda, Barbados, Hong Kong, Korea, and Pakistan.

The guidelines of the School—use of common sense, consideration of others, and truthful relationships with all—encourage each girl to assume responsibility for the community's well-being. Breaches of this trust are dealt with on an individual basis, but

the possession or use of alcohol and/or illegal drugs in school is not tolerated and results in suspension or expulsion.

Students regularly evaluate programs, courses, and School procedures. There are many opportunities for leadership in School government, classes, sports, and activities. Senior Peer Leaders meet with peer groups throughout a student's first year at Purnell and facilitate weekly peer groups for new students.

ACADEMIC FACILITIES

The original Colonial residence of the farm-estate contains the office of the Head of School and other administrative offices. The Stringfellow Library/Media Center, a large converted barn, houses the Learning and Enrichment Center, library, computer center, and classroom wing containing teachers' offices and several smaller classrooms. The adjoining Gardner Building contains the science lab, larger classrooms, and the E. E. Ford Computer Lab. Attached to the library and classroom complex is the Johnson Art Center, an airy, fully equipped facility, where courses including oil, acrylic, and watercolor painting; pen and ink; fashion design; photography; ceramics; and drawing are held. The Bamboo Brook Art Studio provides facilities for furniture art. Independent course study opportunities and portfolio preparation studies are also offered.

Purnell's Carney Center for Performing Arts is a professionally equipped 200-seat theater. Students are encouraged to use the facility in a number of capacities, whether they are participating in one of the performing groups, working backstage and in the sound booth as a "techie," or taking private music lessons. Professional performers from the New York metropolitan area are frequently brought to Purnell.

BOARDING AND GENERAL FACILITIES

Three dormitories along one side of the residential quadrangle, opposite the Head of School's home, provide living quarters, with some single, numerous double, and a few triple rooms for students. Dorm parents, who live in apartments attached to the dormitories on every floor, are available and supportive. They work with the Director of Residential Life on the School's residential life curriculum. Student floor leaders are responsible for the smooth running of the dorms. Each dorm has a common room with a TV/VCR, laundry facilities, and a storage room. Each dorm room is wired for personal phones, the School intranet, and the World Wide Web. The Student Café and Student Store are also located in the dorm complex.

Baker Dining Hall provides gracious dining facilities as well as a place to study and socialize. The dormitory and dining hall complexes are connected, allowing students to pass safely from activity to activity in the evening.

The Deborah Gordon Nothstine Health Center is adjacent to the dormitories, housing the School nurse as well as the Director of Advising and Counseling. Facilities include an examination room and several sick rooms for students.

ATHLETICS

Purnell is committed to guiding students toward life-long personal health, and every student is required to participate in interscholastic or individual sports four days a week. Competitive offerings include basketball, lacrosse, soccer, softball, tennis, and volleyball. Noncompetitive activities include aerobics, horse-back riding, a personal fitness course, and yoga.

The 22,000-square-foot Moran Athletic Center includes a gymnasium with basketball, volleyball, and indoor tennis courts. The athletic center also has a weight room with athletic equipment, an aerobics room, and a state-of-the-art dance studio. A gallery the length of the building is used to display student and faculty artwork.

Three playing fields and five all-weather tennis courts constitute the School's outdoor athletic facilities. Horseback riding is available fall through spring at the nearby Centerline Farm.

EXTRACURRICULAR OPPORTUNITIES

Frequent field trips are taken to art and science museums, recital halls, cultural centers, and theaters in New York City, Philadelphia, and Princeton. On E. B. Osborn Artists-in-Residence Weekend, professional visual and performing artists lead workshops, and Purnell hosts a student photography exhibition involving several independent New Jersey schools.

Most students participate twice a week in the activities program, selecting from options such as Art Activity, Roots and Shoots Community Service as well as yearlong activities for the yearbook and performing groups. There are three performing groups for which students may audition: Dance Synthesis (a jazz and modern dance ensemble), Shoots & Strawberries (an a cappella singing group), and Adlibbers (an acting troupe with a rotating cast that produces a one-act play each term). Private instrumental and vocal lessons are also available, with the option of collaborating on a student ensemble.

DAILY LIFE

Classes are held Monday through Friday. A typical day starts with breakfast (optional) from 7:15 to 7:45 a.m. The academic day starts with class, dorm, or all-School meetings at 8 a.m., followed by morning classes at 8:25 a.m. and a family-style sit-down lunch at 12:55 p.m. The daily schedule is on a two-week cycle, with classes meeting for 75 minutes to facilitate cooperative learning, science labs, research, and studio work. The afternoon consists of extra help, guided study, activities, and sports, with dinner at 6 p.m. Study hours take place from 7:30 to 9, with dorm activities from 9 to 10 p.m. Students also have the opportunity to participate in a book club and a current events club once a week in the evening. Lights-out for ninth graders is 10:30 p.m. and for tenth and eleventh graders, 11 p.m.; seniors are encouraged to use good judgment.

WEEKEND LIFE

The Student Activities Committee works alongside the Director of Residential Life to plan all weekend activities. Faculty members participate fully in such activities, which include excursions to New York or Philadelphia for cultural, sports, and shopping trips; dances and sports events with boys' schools; hiking, biking, and ski trips; and crafts, movies, games, and other events on campus. About half of all weekends are "open," with students who have met their responsibilities free to leave Friday afternoon if they choose; "campus" weekends often include all-School activities as well as free time.

COSTS AND FINANCIAL AID

The combined fee for tuition, room, and board for 2005–06 was $34,725 for seven-day boarding and $31,000 for five-day boarding; day students paid $25,250. Costs for uniforms, books, and laundry averaged $1000. Such expenses as riding and music lessons, studio art lab fees, some weekend activities, and transportation are extra. Several financing options are available.

Typically, 29 percent of the students receive financial aid. In 2005–06, students received awards totaling more than $450,000.

ADMISSIONS INFORMATION

A personal interview is required along with a completed application in order for an applicant to be considered for admission. SSAT scores or other relevant educational testing results should be available, but they are not primary factors in decisions about admission to the School. Neither race nor religious faith is considered in accepting candidates.

APPLICATION TIMETABLE

Purnell has a rolling admission plan, and a candidate's file is presented to the Admission Committee after the personal interview has been completed and all paperwork has been submitted. Parents and the candidate are notified in writing of the action taken. Parents are required to reply within one month of acceptance between September and April.

ADMISSIONS CORRESPONDENCE

Darlene Snell
Director of Admission and Financial Aid
Purnell School
Pottersville, New Jersey 07979

Phone: 908-439-2154
Fax: 908-439-4088
E-mail: info@purnell.org
Web site: http://www.purnell.org

ROBERT LAND ACADEMY

Wellandport, Ontario, Canada

Type: Boys' boarding school
Grades: 6–preuniversity
Enrollment: 160
Head of School: Lt. Col. G. Scott Bowman (Ret.), Headmaster

THE SCHOOL

Robert Land Academy (RLA) is a Canadian nonprofit private boys' boarding school offering accredited courses from grade 6 through preuniversity in an environment intended to stimulate and motivate academic and personal achievement. Founded in 1978, the Academy operates with a military theme whereby a highly structured environment provides incentives and rewards for positive behaviors. Boys are accepted on the basis of their perceived potential rather than their past performance. An average class size of 16 and a student-staff ratio of 2:1 ensures attention to individual needs within a framework intended to develop self-discipline and self-directed responsibility for setting and achieving goals. Students identified as ADD, ADHD, LD, or ODD have historically responded very well to this program.

Robert Land Academy attracts students from around the world; however, the primary enrollment other than Canadian is from the United States. Located less than an hour's drive from the U.S. border at Niagara Falls and situated within a scenic rural setting, the campus provides a well-served and -equipped environment free of the distractions provided by urban living and underachieving friends. A rigorous academic program combined with a stimulating range of sports, clubs, and activities addresses the needs of the student as a whole by nourishing the body and mind in the service of building character. An average of 95 percent of the graduates over the past six years gained admission into the university or college of their first choice.

ACADEMIC PROGRAMS

The primary objective of the academic program is to provide solid foundational skills in fundamental areas of curriculum and to thereby place students in a position to maximize the range of choice for secondary education. In some instances, this requires extensive remediation or repetition of core subjects to regain choices and options. The Academy has developed a unique educational curriculum that groups students into three separate companies based on grade level. Students in grades 6, 7, and 8 are members of Alpha Company, while grades 9 and 10 are members of Bravo Company and students in grade 11 or 12 are in Charlie Company. Each company has identified the common problem areas and academic foundation targets associated with these grades and assists students to work toward the next academic level. The Academy is inspected by the Ontario Ministry of Education and offers only university-preparation courses at the advanced or academic level. With an average class size of 16 students, mandatory supervised daily study halls, and daily tutorials, the typical increase in academic standing is generally at least one full letter grade.

The grade 6, 7, and 8 program prepares boys to enter high school with the personal and academic tools necessary to make possible their future success. The program provides remediation of basic academic skills such as language, literacy, and mathematics while integrating stimulating and enjoyable outdoor activities. Boys are exposed to double the amount of instructional time normally devoted to mathematics and English literacy. Learning is taken out of the classroom, where possible, and boys are encouraged to learn by doing.

The grade 9 and 10 program focus is to continue to develop personal maturity and fundamental academic skills while preparing students for senior-level courses. The academic program is intended to create a solid foundation for success in later senior-level courses while opening up as many options and choices for future postsecondary education and career paths. Outdoor activities and adventure training are incorporated in this training program to further encourage physical fitness, initiative, and a strong self-image.

The grade 11 and 12 program focus is to provide a structured and controlled environment that provides the opportunity for students to achieve the academic foundations required to pursue postsecondary options. The objective of the company is to have boys select among future career options, work constructively toward realizing their goals, successfully complete the necessary academic prerequisites, and then gain admission to universities and colleges based upon appropriate levels of achievement.

FACULTY AND ADVISERS

The Academy's faculty consists of nearly 80 members who have been selected not only for their special abilities in their field of occupation but also for their interest in contributing to the development and education of the unique students at RLA. Of the 22 teaching staff members, all have earned baccalaureate degrees in at least one discipline of study, 4 hold master's degrees, and 2 have earned their Ph.D. In addition to classroom responsibilities and tutorials, each teacher acts as a mentor or adviser for 8 to 12 students as well as coaches a sports team and fulfills club duties.

The Academy also employs a full-time person with a Master of Social Work degree who counsels students in the areas of anger management, substance abuse, family issues, and bereavement. A clinical psychologist makes weekly visits for counseling and educational testing and assessments as required. There is a full-time nurse on staff, a doctor visits twice a week, and an athletic therapist makes weekly visits as well. All staff members are trained in preventative management of aggressive behavior and St. John's ambulance first-aid procedures, and several are first-responder certified.

The Academy's founder and Headmaster, Lt. Col. G. Scott Bowman (Ret.) holds a B.A. in philosophy and has dedicated the last twenty-five years to helping boys and young men achieve their potential and become good citizens.

COLLEGE PLACEMENT

Grade 11 and 12 students take part in a step-by-step process of researching postsecondary institutions, reviewing criteria for admittance, visiting campuses, and meeting with college representatives who are appropriate to their needs and abilities. Two experienced guidance counselors serve as advisers in this area.

The past six years have seen more than 95 percent of RLA's graduates accepted to the university or college of their choice. In 2005, 100 percent of RLA's graduates who applied were accepted to the postsecondary institution of their choice. In addition, more than $35,000 of scholarships were earned and offered to the graduates. Graduates enrolled at Brock, Carleton, Kent (England), McMaster, McGill, Ottawa, Queens, Toronto, Wilfrid Laurier, York, and the Universities of British Columbia and Western Ontario.

STUDENT BODY AND CONDUCT

In 2004–05, Robert Land Academy enrolled 160 students, all of whom were borders. The majority of students came from Ontario, Canada; 18 percent came from the United States; and another 16 percent came from countries other than Canada and the U.S., including France, Hong Kong, Mexico, Nepal, the Netherlands, Russia, Taiwan, the United Arab Emirates, Vietnam, and the West Indies.

The Academy's Code of Conduct is structured so that there is little room for misinterpretation. This allows for clear and consistent rules, consequences, privileges and rewards, and promotion in rank and responsibility. Infractions such as lack of effort, incomplete assignments, and unbecoming conduct are met with consequences in the form of healthy physical exercise ranging from push-ups to running laps. More serious breaches of the Code of Conduct result in individual review by staff members at the company level, with consequences ranging from loss of privileges or rank to community service. Students who display consistent appropriate behavior, organization, initiative, academic achievement, and physical fitness are rewarded with privileges, promotion in rank, and greater responsibility.

ACADEMIC FACILITIES

Loyalist Hall is the principal academic building with a total of ten classrooms. It includes a fully equipped computer lab with Internet access and CD-ROM library, a senior science lab, and a darkroom for photography. Loyalist Hall is complemented by a resource and leisure library, four barracks/dormitories where mandatory supervised study halls are conducted, and a 5,900-square-foot gymnasium, which includes a rock-climbing wall and a weight training room. In addition, there are rooms for art, music, and senior math, which are separate from Loyalist Hall.

BOARDING AND GENERAL FACILITIES

The Academy consists of fourteen buildings on 168 acres in a safe, rural setting. Students reside in one of four separate but closely located barracks/dormitories. Each barracks has an open-concept design where 2 students share a bunk in a cubicle or section. This arrangement facilitates easy supervision by staff members as well as fosters a community mentality with respect and tolerance for others.

Grade 11 and 12 students who demonstrate a considerable amount of maturity, initiative, responsibility, and academic achievement may earn the

privileges and responsibilities of living in Fitzgibbon Hall, which houses up to 25 students. Each student in Fitzgibbon Hall shares a room with another student and makes a transition from the constant supervision provided at the Academy to the considerably reduced supervision at university or college. Fitzgibbon Hall is the only residence where students have access to a television, DVD player, VCR, personal kitchen facilities, and a small computer lab. All residences and barracks have 24-hour staff supervision.

Landholme Hall is the Academy's dining hall, in which healthy and wholesome meals and snacks are prepared and served. Landholme Hall also provides a venue for weekly promotions, award ceremonies, formal student debates, and special events.

Ivey Hall is the Academy's gymnasium, in which 5,900 square feet provides ample space for indoor sports, special functions, and dances. Ivey Hall is fully equipped and has an indoor rock-climbing wall as well as a weight-training room. There are additional administration buildings and an admission and counseling center.

ATHLETICS
Robert Land Academy recognizes physical education and fitness as integral aspects of a student's overall education and well-being. Every school student must participate in at least one interscholastic sport over the course of the year. Grade 6, 7, and 8 students may participate in sports teams, but they are more frequently involved in intramural sports and outdoor activities. All students must maintain a certain level of cardiovascular fitness and overall health in order to be promoted and take advantage of earned privileges. The Academy engages in interscholastic competition in badminton, basketball, cross-country running, rock-climbing, rugby, soccer, track and field, volleyball, and wrestling. There is also a wide variety of intramural sports competitions, including baseball, football, ice hockey, softball, and street hockey, to name a few.

EXTRACURRICULAR OPPORTUNITIES
Robert Land Academy is large enough to offer a wide range of clubs and activities but small enough that all of the students can be involved. The list of clubs includes air-rifle target, archery, art, computers, culinary arts, fishing, life skills, martial arts, models and model rockets, mountain biking, orienteering, outdoor sports, photography, rifle drill, rock-climbing, survival skills and camping, swimming, and yearbook. Clubs meet weekly, and all students must participate in a club. Optional extracurricular activities include canoeing, driver's education, flight training, First Aid, Kendo, scuba diving, skiing, skydiving, and white-water rafting.

DAILY LIFE
Students rise at 6 a.m., Monday through Friday, and prepare their personal belongings and space for inspection. Each student has a chore to complete as a contribution to peers and the community every morning. At 7, each student and the barracks are inspected before dismissal to breakfast. Breakfast begins at 7:30 and concludes at 8:15 with the Headmaster's address, followed by 15 minutes of marching and the raising of the national flag. Classes begin at 9 a.m. and break at noon for lunch. There is a tutorial period from 1 to 2 p.m., after which regular classes resume. At 5, classes end and an activity period commences, offering additional tutorials, sports, clubs, and martial arts training. Supper begins at 6:15 and the mandatory supervised study hall runs from 7 until 8:30 p.m. At 8:30, students return to their barracks and prepare for the next day. Lights are out at 9:30 p.m.

WEEKEND LIFE
Weekends are equally structured to provide the opportunity for supervised study halls, tutorials, sports, and activities. Students rise at 8 a.m. on Saturday, and the day concludes at 10 p.m. with the completion of the Saturday night movie. Sundays allow for students to sleep in until 10 a.m. and attend brunch at 11, followed by 2 hours of study hall, 2 hours of sports, and supper at 5 p.m. Sunday evenings consist of an optional study hall and relaxed time, with lights out at 9 p.m. Students often participate in community service–oriented activities on the weekend.

SUMMER PROGRAMS
Robert Land Academy offers a summer camp program designed for boys ages 11 through 14. The program focuses on camping, canoeing, outdoor activities, adventure training, and scout-like training coupled with structure, organization skills, leadership, and team-building activities.

COSTS AND FINANCIAL AID
Tuition for 2005–06 was Can$33,750 plus a Can$500 administrative fee for international students. There was also a Can$1000 tuck account to be established for additional expenses and incidentals. Most uniforms, clothing, equipment, and academic supplies are included in the tuition fee. A breakdown of room, board, and tuition is available by request. Merit or need-based scholarships are available.

ADMISSIONS INFORMATION
Regular admissions are offered in September and January, although other admissions are considered on a case-by-case basis, with specified intake days arranged throughout the year.

Robert Land Academy accepts students without regard to race, color, religion, or national origin. Most students are accepted based on their perceived potential and suitability to the program rather than past performance. A personal interview with the applicant and at least 1 parent is usually required. Phone interviews may be arranged in some instances.

APPLICATION TIMETABLE
Applications are accepted year-round, but it is best to apply by May 15. All required materials must be received by the Admissions Department before or at the time of interview. Upon completion of the applicant's interview, consideration is made by the admissions committee. Parents are informed of the committee's decision as soon as possible. Early application is advised.

ADMISSIONS CORRESPONDENCE
Lieutenant F. Greg Hewett
Admissions Officer
Robert Land Academy
R.R. #3, 6726 South Chippawa Road
Wellandport, Ontario L0R 2J0
Canada

Phone: 905-386-6203
Fax: 905-386-6607
E-mail: 4contact@robertlandacademy.com
Web site: http://www.robertlandacademy.com

ST. PAUL'S PREPARATORY ACADEMY

Phoenix, Arizona

Type: College-preparatory boarding and day school for bright young men seeking direction and motivation to achieve academic and personal excellence
Grades: 9–12
Enrollment: 75
Head of School: Harold W. Elliott, Headmaster

THE SCHOOL

Founded in 1961, St. Paul's Preparatory Academy was developed to provide bright young men who are failing to work up to academic and personal potential with an opportunity to receive an excellent education and preparation for college while in an environment that provides structure, positive peer leadership, tools for character development, a spiritual foundation, strong faculty support, and comprehensive Life Skills Seminars.

The St. Paul's Advantage is a community of young men who are being challenged to reach their potential, with academic success, character development, and spiritual awareness and the benefit of counseling support in a structured setting. The St. Paul's Advantage is a traditional independent school with exceptional faculty and staff members, small classes, a supportive environment, healthy activities, and fulfilling volunteerism. The St. Paul's Advantage is a life in Phoenix, a vibrant metropolitan area with culture and tradition, art and theater, and major-league sports and recreation. The St. Paul's Advantage also offers a group-living situation that is much like a college setting, with supervision in homelike cottages away from the academic campus. More than anything, the St. Paul's Advantage is the people—the dedicated, talented, professional faculty and staff members who see their work as their calling—to make a difference in a young man's life. St. Paul's offers more than just a diploma—it provides improved academic performance, better family relationships, elevated self-concept, emotional centeredness, and a sense of spiritual consciousness. The St. Paul's Advantage enhances young men's outlooks, preparing them for college and for life.

The Academy is incorporated as a not-for-profit organization, governed by a 15-member volunteer Board of Trustees of prominent local community and business leaders. St. Paul's is accredited by the North Central Association of Colleges and Schools and the Southwest Association of Episcopal Schools and is a member of the National Association of Episcopal Schools, the Small Boarding Schools Association, the Western Boarding Schools Association, and the Arizona Athletic Association.

ACADEMIC PROGRAMS

St. Paul's maintains a traditional nine-month academic calendar, with a ten-week summer school program divided into two 5-week sessions. Upon admission, students are evaluated based on a review of past academic performance and testing, individual strengths and weaknesses, and social history. The staff then develops an academic blueprint that outlines the student's path of study from enrollment to graduation. The plan can be adjusted to meet the most appropriate needs of the student, including adding accelerated classes and/or independent studies. Twenty-three Carnegie units are recommended for graduation, although 22 are required. Classes are recommended, depending on the student's college requirements and career preferences.

Certified teachers dedicate themselves to the educational growth of their students. Their goal is to ensure that each student is challenged to maximize his potential utilizing his own learning style, thereby producing positive scholastic results. With only 6–12 students per class, teachers develop close, personal relationships with students and identify effective learn-

ing processes. Each student is assigned a teacher-mentor, who not only assists with academic progress but also supports the student in the social and interactive aspects of school life.

Student interest is stimulated by the rotation of teaching modalities to include visual, audio, and kinesthetic techniques. Students with attention deficits often find that the school's size and diverse teaching styles, along with block scheduling, are conducive to their learning needs. With more hands-on, experiential learning, a certified academic coach is available to work with those students with ADD/ADHD in order to recognize and appropriately compensate for their deficiencies. At St. Paul's, an attention deficit is not an excuse to fail.

St. Paul's offers a college-preparatory curriculum. Classes are rigorous and challenging, requiring students to be focused, to develop good study skills, and to be organized. Classes begin at 8 a.m. and continue until 2:30 p.m. Teachers are available each day for 1 hour after school for individual assistance, and the National Honor Society offers peer tutoring for students who need extra support, along with study skills seminars led by the academic coach. The coach also provides afternoon and evening study hall tutoring as well as study groups. Ultimately, students must take responsibility for their own effort and resulting work. Grades are monitored on a daily basis. If a student's grade drops below a C, he is notified that day and he is placed on academic probation until the grade is elevated. Academic probation consists of extra study halls and loss of extracurricular activities. Courses are offered in art, computer literacy, foreign language, humanities, language arts, mathematics, science, and social studies. Much of the success that occurs in the classroom is due to the constant communication among the faculty members, counselors, and cottage counselors. Teachers receive ongoing training in identifying and modifying behaviors that create barriers to the learning process. Counselors lend experience and support in understanding a student's emotional needs. Cottage counselors provide structure, consistency, and leadership during evenings and weekends to ensure that academic commitments are being met.

St. Paul's offers one of the nation's finest leadership and character development programs for young men. Students earn privileges and gain responsibility by demonstrating the virtues of honor, integrity, courage, patience, trust, and responsibility and then advancing through a degree system similar to the Knights Templar.

Students hold each other accountable for behaviors and actions and vote on the degree advancement of their peers. The St. Paul's student government, or Code of Conduct Council, addresses student grievances, mediates conflict, and assesses student behaviors. Members of the council pledge to the student body that they will be honest and impartial and demonstrate strong, positive values in decision making. Ten basic responsibilities form the actual Code of Conduct, which provides an outline to students for positive, respectful, and responsible living.

The core theme of the St. Paul's Advantage is that, to be a young man of character, one must make a commitment to respect oneself and others and make a consistent effort to do what is right. This theme is communicated in the classroom, in the

dorms, and out in the greater community. There is no need for locked doors or lockers because students respect each other's privacy and ownership of property. With the students directing and taking ownership of their school community, a positive peer culture motivates them to make good decisions and be accountable for their actions.

As students learn to embrace these values, they become more self-assured, take on more responsibilities, and serve as positive leaders in the St. Paul's community. Ultimately, the expectation is that young men will carry these life lessons with them beyond high school and college and into manhood.

Life Skills Seminars help students identify and deal with obstacles that interfere with positive motivation to achieve academic and social success. New students take an eight-week study skills seminar, and all students are placed in a variety of seminars based on personal needs, such as Social Strengths and Peer Relations, Stress Management and Coping Skills, 7 Habits of Highly Effective Teens, Team Building and Group Dynamics, Anger Management and Conflict Resolution, Real Relationships, Effective Communication, Successful Job Hunting, and Substance Education.

All students with any history of drug or alcohol use are required to board and participate in the substance-use Life Skills Seminar component, which includes attendance at two weekly twelve-step meetings and Substance Education Seminars. Random drug testing is done on any student who has a substance-abuse history.

FACULTY AND ADVISERS

There are 13 full-time certified faculty members, 2 full-time master's-level counselors, 1 certified academic coach, and 10 cottage counselors. It is St. Paul's philosophy to keep faculty and staff members dedicated, focused, and enthused about their specific job. Therefore, no faculty or staff members live on campus or fill more than one job description. Faculty members, using a team approach, work on the development of the curriculum and the coordination of the academic program. They pass on vital student information to the cottage counselors regarding specific evening study needs.

Cottage counselors begin their workday when school is dismissed. Their goals are to be interactive with students, to participate in evening and weekend academic and recreational activities, to be positive role models, to help young men develop problem-solving skills, and to supervise and direct students in how to make positive, productive choices. Cottage counselors are an integral part of the students' lives, providing the support, consistency, and guidance so many of them need. Overnight cottage counselors remain awake during the sleeping hours for those who wake up and need assistance or comfort during the night. Cottage counselors work closely with school counselors and faculty members to ensure that the academic structure and character development components offered on campus are fully integrated at the cottages.

Students can sense when people care about them and have concern for their futures. At St. Paul's, young men are expected to be honest with their feelings, grow in their maturity, develop sophisticated social skills, improve interpersonal relationships, and exhibit appropriate behavior, all in a safe,

supportive environment. Counselors aim to cultivate resilient, confident young men. St. Paul's enables students to take emotional risks and seek individual guidance if necessary. In addition, students are asked to participate in Life Skills Seminars that further challenge them to maturely express their thoughts and feelings. Life Skills Seminars and individual and family counseling are offered by the Academy's master's-level counselors.

COLLEGE PLACEMENT

As a college-preparatory school, it is St. Paul's goal to direct students to colleges that are appropriate for their individual needs and interests. The Academy offers a fully functional College and Career Center to assist students and their families in the selection, application, and interview process for colleges and universities. Students are able to use the center to research and apply to appropriate schools as well as meet with school representatives visiting the campus.

Each year, the Academy hosts Career Day, wherein students are able to inquire about their specific areas of interest with professionals from a variety of fields. Students also attend college fairs in the Phoenix area and are given the opportunity to speak with hundreds of representatives from nationally renowned colleges and universities.

All students at St. Paul's prepare for college entrance exams and learn testing skills and strategies by taking the PSAT. Students also take SAT- and ACT-preparation classes that are included in the junior/senior curriculum. Subsequently, juniors and seniors sit for both the SAT and ACT examinations. In addition, St. Paul's requires senior students to take a Senior Seminar course. This course teaches basic life skills such as financial management, dormitory choices, and setting boundaries that seniors need as they embark on their college experiences.

All of St. Paul's graduates in the last ten years have achieved college admission. Graduates are enrolled in such colleges and universities as American, Arizona State, Clemson, Concordia, Indiana, Ithaca, Kenyon, Roger Williams, Syracuse, Wittenburg, and the Universities of Arizona, Cincinnati, Denver, and Texas.

STUDENT BODY AND CONDUCT

St. Paul's offers a small community. Staff members have a commitment to know each student, both academically and personally, and to motivate them to become actively engaged in the small classes. For that very reason, the Academy has limited its capacity to no more than 75 students.

Students wear uniforms during school hours, have well-groomed hair, and take pride in their overall appearance. Students are not allowed to wear earrings or any self-labeling insignia. St. Paul's helps students develop an identity based on who they are on the inside rather than who they portray on the outside.

ACADEMIC FACILITIES

A new academic campus opened in 1997 and is located in a quaint, historic Phoenix neighborhood that is five blocks from the boarding campus.

BOARDING AND GENERAL FACILITIES

The 5-acre boarding campus includes four comfortable, homelike cottages, which received all-new furniture in 2005. Each cottage includes bedrooms, a kitchen, and family and laundry rooms. Also included are a workout facility, recreation center, recreation field, and full-size basketball court. The cottages and property are maintained, in part, by the students—a school expectation that teaches students to take pride in their community.

ATHLETICS

All students are required to participate in some aspect of the athletic program. Students may choose from competitive, intramural, or individual athletic activities. The Academy is a member of the Arizona Interscholastic Association and offers statewide varsity and junior varsity competitive play in baseball, basketball, golf, and soccer. Grades must be maintained at no less than a C in all classes to participate on a competitive team. Other recreational activities are offered through intramural sports and clubs such as Ultimate Frisbee, dodgeball, and bowling. Students are encouraged to exercise and participate in strength training. All students are required to participate in at least two sports or extracurricular activities each academic year.

EXTRACURRICULAR OPPORTUNITIES

Students have the opportunity to join clubs based on their interest areas and their demonstrated level of responsibility. Clubs include art, bowling, chess, spirit, drama, National Honor Society, Spanish, steel drum band, weight lifting, and yearbook.

Outings to Phoenix's cultural and professional sports events are offered regularly. Musicals, plays, the symphony, and the opera are also integrated into the classroom curriculum. Weekend activities are coordinated based on student interest and the availability of community, holiday, and seasonal events.

St. Paul's has a commitment to teaching young men about their responsibility to their community. Volunteerism is strongly emphasized at the Academy; it is an integral part of the character development component and a requirement for advancement in the degree system. Students serve those in need by volunteering with the elderly, with children, with the homeless, and with those less fortunate. Students often coordinate citywide service projects prior to graduation. Many students receive citizenship awards and have been recognized by the city, including a recent graduate who was the recipient of a $32,000 college scholarship based on community service and character.

DAILY LIFE

Students rise at 6 a.m. and begin school at 8. The school day ends at 4 p.m. Day students must remain on campus until this time and may choose to stay later for extracurricular activities. Until dinner at 5:30, students participate in clubs, sports activities, and leisure and study time. After dinner, all students participate in structured recreation, supervised study hall, and leisure time. Lights are out at 10.

WEEKEND LIFE

Weekends are structured at St. Paul's to provide students with a variety of cultural, educational, social, and recreational opportunities. At times, weekend trips are offered to hike, camp, ski, and fish. School dances, horseback riding, and barbecues are arranged with a nearby girls' school. Many off-campus

extracurricular activities, such as golf, movies, and trips to water parks and professional sports events, are arranged. Certain off-campus activities are made available to those who have earned them through their advancement in the degree system.

SUMMER PROGRAMS

Summer school is offered and includes a variety of course options. An academic curriculum is available, as are sports camps, worldwide travel experiences, and leadership opportunities. Incoming freshmen are frequently required to attend one of two summer sessions. As writing skills are vital across the St. Paul's curriculum, freshmen are assigned to a composition course that enables faculty members to assess and improve the students' composition skills.

COSTS AND FINANCIAL AID

St. Paul's tuition for the nine-month 2005–06 academic year was $42,325. This included room; board; all educational instruction; a community group; leadership meetings; an assigned master's-level counselor, who provides guidance and support; basic nursing services, including psychiatric medication assessment and monitoring; laundry expenses; and many recreational expenses. Additional Life Skills Seminars, as well as any individual or family counseling sessions, are included in the cost.

Tuition for day students was $16,000 for the nine-month school year. It included all educational instruction, a community group, leadership meetings, lunch, basic nursing services, many recreational expenses, and a certified academic coach to work on study skills.

ADMISSIONS INFORMATION

The goal of the St. Paul's admission process is to ensure that the prospective student and the school are a good match. An on-campus interview is required. By touring the campus, meeting with current students, and attending a community meeting or other on-campus functions, prospective students are given every opportunity to find out the true advantage of St. Paul's. To be accepted, not only must the school and the student agree that they are a good match, but the young man must also be able to make a personal commitment to the Academy's philosophy and academic program. Students must commit to a minimum of one year (two consecutive semesters) at the time of enrollment. However, the St. Paul's Advantage stresses the importance and benefit of at least a two-year plan to gain the maximum result toward permanent academic growth and personal development.

APPLICATION TIMETABLE

The Academy has an open admission policy based on space availability. Inquiries and applications are welcome throughout the year. New students are frequently required to attend summer sessions.

ADMISSIONS CORRESPONDENCE

Donna Wittwer, M.Ed., Director of Admission
St. Paul's Preparatory Academy
P.O. Box 32650
Phoenix, Arizona 85064-2650

Phone: 602-956-9090
Fax: 602-956-3018
E-mail: admissions@stpaulsacademy.com
Web site: http://www.stpaulsacademy.com

SORENSON'S RANCH SCHOOL

Koosharem, Utah

Type: Coeducational boarding school for troubled youths with average and above-average ability
Grades: 7–12
Enrollment: 120
Head of School: Shane Sorenson, Director

THE SCHOOL

Sorenson's Ranch School was founded by Burnell and Carrol Sorenson as a summer camp in 1959 and became a year-round school in 1982. Located on a ranch with a working farm in southern Utah at a 7,000-foot elevation, the School is situated in an open wilderness area. The surrounding valley is 3 miles wide and 14 miles long; five small canyon streams teem with beaver ponds and trout. Neighboring mountains are snow-covered year-round.

Sorenson's Ranch School serves students with histories of problems with parents, substance abuse, low or nonexistent self-esteem, learning differences, running away, dropping out of or being expelled from school, and extreme mental stress. The School's philosophy is that all children are potential successes if given the right options. The Sorenson methodology centers around consistency and firmness delivered with love and care. Working through professional counseling, group counseling, and caring staff-student relationships, the School aims to help young people function successfully both with their parents and in society. Sorenson's finds its big-wilderness setting conducive to its goal of redirecting troubled youths, with the open space serving as a deterrent to students with runaway problems and its remote locale hindering the availability of controlled substances. Parent involvement is desired but not mandatory.

Sorenson's believes that students provided with a caring atmosphere, high-quality instruction, and opportunities to experience success will enjoy and accept responsibility for their own learning. Good self-esteem and appropriate behavior are promoted by clearly defining expectations and by calling attention to acceptable behavior. The School's wilderness and work programs instill in its students the values of loyalty, respect, self-worth, personal management, respect for property, cleanliness, and trustworthiness.

Sorenson's is also a licensed residential treatment facility that includes drug and alcohol treatment. A treatment plan is developed for each child. Group counseling sessions and intensive one-on-one time with the Sorenson staff is included.

Sorenson's Ranch School is family owned and operated. It is accredited by the Northwest Association of Schools, Colleges, and Universities. It is licensed as a mental-health and substance-abuse treatment center with the Utah State Human Services Department and is accredited by the Joint Commission on Accreditation of Healthcare Organizations (JCAHO).

ACADEMIC PROGRAMS

Sorenson's program is year-round. The competency-based curriculum provides all the courses necessary for the student to earn a Utah state high school diploma. Classes are based on mastery of skills rather than on "seat time"; thus, the School features no quarter or semester system.

The educational program is designed to give students the proper guidance and counseling to learn at their own rate. Since credit is awarded when students master course objectives, Sorenson's open-entry, open-exit policy facilitates catching up in school work. Grades are based on mastery of course objectives—90 percent is an A, and 80 percent is a B. Grades lower than 80 percent are considered incomplete; students earning below this percentile are tutored until they master the material. Credit may also be earned for survival experience when students participate in licensed programs.

Small classes averaging 6–12 students are taught by caring teachers who model such values as honesty, integrity, trust, self-esteem, and concern for others.

Because this behavior modification–based educational program often requires more time than a regular school-year program for desired changes to become permanent, Sorenson's staff feels that one year in residence is an essential minimum for the student.

FACULTY AND ADVISERS

Staff members include 10 certified educators, a psychiatrist, a psychologist, 4 clinicians, 35 trained child-care specialists, and licensed social workers. The entire staff is nondrinking and nonsmoking.

Each student is assigned a personal case manager who has 3–6 students in his or her charge. The case manager comes to know each student as his or her own, acting as a personal advocate as well as a mentor. The case manager heads the student's treatment team, integrating treatment plans with other professionals and acting as a contact person with parents or placement agencies.

Shane Sorenson has directed the program for more than ten years. He graduated from Brigham Young University with a degree in psychology and received his master's degree from California Coast College. Burnell and Carrol Sorenson, the owners and founders, both hold B.S. degrees and teaching credentials and have completed advanced graduate work. They have been involved in teaching and directing education and recreation programs for more than forty years. The Education Coordinator, Chad Sorenson, has a B.S. degree and teaching credentials, has taught in public schools, and has worked in church leadership.

COLLEGE PLACEMENT

Depending on the individual, transition from the Sorenson program may be to a home, another school, or a college. Students leaving the program demonstrate renewed self-esteem and an orientation toward goal achievement, facilitating entry into the educational program of their choice.

STUDENT BODY AND CONDUCT

Sorenson's current student body of 120—50 girls and 70 boys, the largest number of whom are from California, Washington, and Oregon—is made up of youths of average and above-average ability who are 13–18 years old.

Students set weekly goals for themselves and must accept responsibility for their actions. A point system is used, and points are awarded or taken away relative to good or bad behavior. Students learn that, as a result of positive behavior, they can participate in various outings, gain more freedom within the School, and increase their allowance. Conversely, as a result of consistent negative behavior, students may find themselves digging ditches, hauling manure, and weeding. Sorenson's understands that everyone makes mistakes sometimes. At the same time, the program stresses that with choices and freedom comes personal responsibility.

The School reserves the right to expel a teen within the first thirty days if it is found that he or she is detrimental to the overall health of the School community.

ACADEMIC FACILITIES

Sorenson's Ranch School features a classroom complex, an industrial arts center with three shops, a gym, and a media center.

BOARDING AND GENERAL FACILITIES

Student housing is in rustic cabins and dorms, all with attached rest rooms. Students sleep in a ranch setting, with an average of 4 students per room.

There are also counseling offices, a kitchen, an infirmary, a game room, hiking trails, playing fields, animal/tack facilities, and the lodge, which houses a multipurpose room for dining and activities.

ATHLETICS

Sorenson's offers a noncompetitive sports program that includes horseback riding, fishing, swimming, waterskiing, skiing, outcamping, and ice skating.

EXTRACURRICULAR OPPORTUNITIES

The School's horse program is its largest special program. Students watch horses born on the farm grow and help train them for riding. Horses on the farm are suited to different types of riders and riding. An animal-care program gives students the opportunity to raise rabbits, pigeons, and domestic animals. Wilderness programs and camping are also available.

Sorenson's students may also enjoy crafts and nature-related activities as well as opportunities

to learn such vocational skills as farming, ranching, horticulture, and 4-H.

DAILY LIFE

A typical day at Sorenson's begins with a 7 a.m. wake-up call. Rooms are cleaned, chores finished, and breakfast eaten by 8:30, when classes begin. At 3 p.m., activities begin, and students with good points choose what they wish to do, such as horseback riding. Students who are behind in school have study hall, and those who have lost behavior points during the day have such consequences as work projects, mostly relating to farm and country living—hauling wood, mending fences, or digging ditches.

For the first three weeks, there is no telephone contact with outside family and friends. (Letters are permitted during this time.) Three months follow before the first on-campus visit. Follow-up home visits are usually about two or three months apart. After eight months, a student may be able to move into a home in the valley, with more freedom and responsibility.

WEEKEND LIFE

Weekends are full of activities that serve as rewards for those who have earned them and consequences for those with behavior problems. Campouts are either recreational or work oriented.

COSTS AND FINANCIAL AID

Fees for Sorenson's Ranch School are $4400 per month, plus a nonrefundable admission fee of $1700 ($6100 is due at the time of enrollment). Along with tuition, parents are billed monthly for all personal and travel expenses. Students who are 18 years old upon entry into the program require a $10,000 nonrefundable payment to ensure that they will stay in the program at least five months. If tuition becomes two months in arrears, then the student may be sent home. No scholarships are available.

It is suggested that parents not give or send any money to the student directly. Part of Sorenson's point system is to have students earn their spending money.

ADMISSIONS INFORMATION

Students may enroll at any time on an individual basis. Prospective students and their parents/guardians must complete an application for admission. Diagnostic data and background materials are helpful in determining eligibility for placement. Professional referrals are not required.

APPLICATION TIMETABLE

Since Sorenson's is a family business, the administrators are available 24 hours a day for questions. Those considering the School for their child are encouraged to arrange a visit; the most convenient hours are between 9 a.m. and 12 noon Monday through Thursday. The parent and student should not visit the campus together before the student enrolls.

ADMISSIONS CORRESPONDENCE

Layne Bagley, Admission Director
P.O. Box 440219
Koosharem, Utah 84744-0219
Phone: 435-638-7318
          800-455-4590 (toll-free)
Fax: 435-638-7582
E-mail: srs@color-country.net
Web site: http://www.sorensonsranch.com

VALLEY VIEW SCHOOL

North Brookfield, Massachusetts

Type: Boarding school for boys with moderate special needs
Grades: 5–12
Enrollment: 56
Head of School: Philip G. Spiva, Ph.D., Director

THE SCHOOL

Valley View is a private residential guidance school providing a therapeutic educational environment for 56 boys between the ages of 11 and 16 who are having difficulty getting along with their families, the world around them, and themselves. These are generally bright and healthy youngsters who differ in family and geographic backgrounds but who share the experience of functioning below their academic and social potential.

Located 1½ miles from North Brookfield, in rural central Massachusetts, Valley View is situated on a 215-acre site that was once used for farming. The School provides a relaxed yet structured environment for boys who are not able to adjust to living with their families or to life in a traditional boarding school.

The Valley View School was founded in 1970 by its present director, Dr. Philip G. Spiva, a clinical psychologist. Typical Valley View students may be boys who challenge authority to the point of psychologically intimidating their parents; others have difficulty in channeling their physical energy in meaningful ways; and a few may appear overly lethargic, bored, or depressed. The majority have had difficulty in traditional schools and, although bright, have a history of attention deficit disorder (ADD), are oppositional, and are a source of frustration to their families. Many lack an awareness of the effect that their behavior has upon others and often seem to "not get it." Although Valley View can help many boys, it is not equipped to educate overtly psychotic adolescents or alienated "streetwise" boys with histories of antisocial behavior or drug-related problems.

Dr. Spiva developed a school based on the model of a therapeutic environment for boys who show good potential but are having difficulty adjusting to the world around them. The primary objectives of the School are to provide youngsters with the skills they need to function effectively, to help them to like themselves better, and to help them achieve a higher level of success. Valley View provides a structured program that stresses a wide range of success-oriented experiences and offers the quality of interaction and instruction necessary for each boy to develop a better feeling about himself. Through this program, the School promotes self-confidence and the ability to interact with others in a more meaningful way. Boys mature socially as they gain an increased awareness of themselves and the world around them.

The School is incorporated as a nonprofit organization and is governed by a 9-member Board of Directors. It has an annual operating budget of approximately $2.7 million. Proceeds of the annual capital improvement drive assist in the development of new physical resources.

Valley View School is authorized under federal law to enroll nonimmigrant alien students.

ACADEMIC PROGRAMS

Traditional classroom methods and practices have generally frustrated rather than encouraged students who go to Valley View. These boys have been characterized as "learning disabled," "unmotivated," "hyperactive," or "disruptive" in the classroom setting. With a maximum of 56 students in the School and an average of 6 in each class, Valley View School can provide intensive remedial instruction. Classes focus on the development and strengthening of skills in basic subjects, including language arts, mathematics, social and physical sciences, physical education, history, and art. An extensive computer facility has recently been installed that integrates current technology into the entire academic curriculum.

Students who have learning difficulties in specific areas and need additional assistance may receive remedial help both from their teachers as well as from computer-aided programs. To motivate students to develop more effective study skills and habits, a study hour is required Sunday through Thursday nights.

In addition to the usual academic curriculum, music lessons are available for a variety of instruments, and boys may participate in the School's drama program.

Travel in the United States and abroad provides special intellectual challenges. Valley View students have taken a number of weeklong study tours of Washington, D.C., and Gettysburg and have visited such countries as India, Israel, the People's Republic of China, Russia, South Africa, and Vietnam.

Boys receive academic credit for all course work that is successfully completed, permitting them to progress at a normal pace. Valley View credits are transferable to more traditional public or private schools. Comprehensive quarterly reports, sent to families, address social and emotional adjustment as well as academic progress in all areas.

Valley View offers a year-round program, and boys are accepted only on that basis. The program from September to June parallels a traditional two-semester academic year, while the summer program is a combination of academic, remedial, and special-interest courses balanced with outdoor recreation.

A minimum enrollment period of two to three years is required for successful completion of the program. A student can earn a recognized high school diploma from Valley View School; however, diplomas are infrequently conferred, since most students continue their education in a standard public or private secondary school. Approximately 65 percent of departing students receive counseling to help them transfer to a more traditional boarding school.

FACULTY AND ADVISERS

Valley View's staff numbers 44. Of these, two thirds are either classroom teachers or counselors who supervise a range of activities during evenings and weekends. Responsibility for the direction of the program is shared by an administrative council of 8 senior staff members.

Philip G. Spiva, the founder and Director of Valley View School, holds a doctorate in psychology from the University of Oklahoma, is a diplomate in clinical psychology of the American Board of Professional Psychology, and is a fellow of the Academy of Clinical Psychology. He has had more than thirty years of experience in the residential treatment of emotionally maladjusted children and adolescents. He has served on the Board of Directors of the National Association of Private Schools for Exceptional Children and the American Association of Children's Residential Centers.

Eric T. Bulger, Valley View School's Associate Director, earned his Master of Social Work degree from Boston College and has worked with adolescents in residential care for sixteen years. He works closely with the director, facilitating admission interviews, and communicates extensively with parents. In addition, he closely coordinates the activities of the academic program with the Educational Coordinator, who is a certified teacher with twenty-eight years of experience, and the Program Coordinator, who has a degree in psychology and twenty-four years of experience working directly with adolescents.

There are 11 full-time academic teachers, all with appropriate degrees in their subject matter. Seventeen counselors, most of whom hold a college degree, supervise the program on evenings and weekends. This includes an extensive range of physical and recreational activities. In addition, three clinical psychologists spend a number of days at the School to see boys in individual therapy sessions. Two Board-certified psychiatrists also make regularly scheduled consultation visits to monitor psychopharmacological issues when appropriate.

COLLEGE PLACEMENT

Most alumni complete their secondary education at a more traditional school before they contemplate advanced education. If a family wishes to send their son to a private boarding school when he is ready to leave Valley View, help in selecting an appropriate school, usually one with a "counseling attitude," is provided. The majority of Valley View graduates have ultimately gone on to college after completion of their secondary education.

STUDENT BODY AND CONDUCT

Because of the need for a high level of individual attention, the student population is limited to 56 boys, who come from throughout the United States as well as a number of other countries. Although the average age at the time of enrollment is 13, boys at Valley View range in age from 11 to 16.

The School expects students to behave in an appropriate manner. Because, by nature of their difficulties, they often fall short of this expectation, the program is designed so that boys are held accountable for their actions and are expected to assume responsibility for obtaining rewards. All boys must work for their spending money through a point-earning system that is translated into cash used for activities. Parents are asked not to subsidize activities unless they have received approval from the School administration.

Although the expectations for student conduct are based on a standard of reasonableness and are not overly rigid, there is a dress code that applies during classes and at Sunday brunch. There is a high level of open and honest interaction among students, the faculty, and the administration regarding problems and issues that arise. Since it is the policy of the School to accept only those students who have a high probability of benefiting from the Valley View experience, there are very few expulsions.

ACADEMIC FACILITIES
The academic complex consists of two classroom buildings and a gymnasium. Classrooms include a computer lab that is part of an extensive campus network, a science laboratory with eight work stations designed to accommodate upper-level courses, and a creative arts studio that promotes expression in a variety of areas, including painting, sculpting, and ceramics. The gymnasium has a full-court playing surface and a locker room as well as a fully equipped weightlifting and aerobic center.

BOARDING AND GENERAL FACILITIES
The main building, a completely remodeled structure consisting of a farmhouse, a carriage house, and a barn, houses 25 students comfortably in single, double, and triple dormitory rooms. A dining room accommodates School assemblies, and a recently added stage enhances a very active dramatic arts program.

Separated from the main building are three other self-contained dormitories housing 9 to 12 students. All of the dormitories have lounge areas for reading, watching television, and other quiet activities. They are also connected to the computer network so students have access to the central file server throughout the evening and weekend.

ATHLETICS
All students are expected to take physical education classes as a component of the program. Boys are also required to participate each year in at least one varsity or junior varsity team that competes against local schools. A full-court gymnasium and adjoining athletics field provide attractive facilities for basketball, soccer, softball, lacrosse, and volleyball. In addition, there are numerous opportunities for individual sports, such as golf, skiing, snowboarding, and tennis.

EXTRACURRICULAR OPPORTUNITIES
The activity program plays a crucial role in the overall philosophy of the School, because it offers students a wide variety of success-oriented experiences. Because most of the boys who come to Valley View feel that they are—and indeed they have been—failures in some critical areas of their adjustment, their experience of success is fun and gratifying, yet challenging.

A reasonably strenuous outdoor program includes camping, rock climbing, bike trips, canoeing, and hiking. There is ample opportunity for more relaxing activities, such as photography, playing a musical instrument, painting and drawing, and fishing. Field trips are held throughout the year to various educational centers, museums, and historic sites.

DAILY LIFE
During the school year, the seven 40-minute classes begin at 8:20 and end at 2:30. Classes in traditional academic courses are held in the morning, while afternoon classes include science and math lab courses and physical education. A compulsory study hour is held Sunday evening through Thursday evening. Although certain periods of the day are free, the overall program is quite structured.

WEEKEND LIFE
During the academic year, a brunch is held each Sunday, followed by an assembly on a variety of informative subjects for student interest and enjoyment. Students also take trips away from the School, including overnight camping trips. Many activities are offered during the weekend, and all boys must elect a certain number of these options. Weekends are also most convenient for parents' visits with their sons.

SUMMER PROGRAMS
Because Valley View School has a twelve-month school year, the summer program is a component of the overall program. Classes held during July and August are somewhat less formal than those held from September through June, including summer reading and remedial programs and a number of high-interest courses such as Art, Astronomy, Birds 101, Chess, Geology, History and Science of Baseball, Life in the Middle Ages, Litera'Tours, and the Local History of Quaboag Plantation. They are balanced equally with recreational activities.

COSTS AND FINANCIAL AID
Valley View School bases its fee on the actual operating cost of $55,000 ($4583.33 per month) for a twelve-month program. Under some conditions, financial assistance may be available through programs administered by certain states. Valley View School, however, is not able to offer scholarship assistance.

ADMISSIONS INFORMATION
The majority of new students begin their experience in the summer, which provides the staff with an opportunity to thoughtfully plan their academic program. However, if space is available, a student may begin his program in September or at another time during the year. Valley View accepts qualified students without regard to race, religion, or ethnic origin.

Inquiries should be made to the Director or his associate. If, on the basis of the initial review, the applicant appears to be an appropriate candidate, a formal application for admission is requested, along with clinical summaries from professionals who are familiar with the applicant. All prospective students and their families are expected to visit the School.

APPLICATION TIMETABLE
Applications for admission are considered at any time during the year for vacancies that occur primarily in early July or September. If space is not available at the time of application, a boy may be placed on a waiting list at his family's request. If sufficient information has been submitted, parents are generally notified about acceptance when they visit the School for the personal interview.

ADMISSIONS CORRESPONDENCE
Philip G. Spiva, Ph.D., Director
Valley View School
P.O. Box 338, Oakham Road
North Brookfield, Massachusetts 01535
Phone: 508-867-6505
Fax: 508-867-3300
E-mail: valview@aol.com
Web site: http://www.valleyviewschool.org

THE VANGUARD SCHOOL

Lake Wales, Florida

Type: Coeducational boarding and day college-preparatory and general academic remedial school for students with special needs
Grades: 4–PG, ages 10–20
Enrollment: 125
Head of School: James R. Moon, Executive Director

THE SCHOOL

The Vanguard School of Lake Wales, Florida, was founded in 1966 to serve the needs of students with learning disabilities, dyslexia, attention deficit disorder, and other learning problems. At the time, the School was the residential branch of the Vanguard School of Paoli, Pennsylvania, which was founded in 1959. The Vanguard School of Lake Wales became a separate and independent corporation in 1983.

The mission of the Vanguard School is to provide an individualized program in a nurturing environment that enables students to develop to their fullest academically, socially, and personally. The School provides a safe and secure but appropriately demanding and structured environment in which students who have been unsuccessful in regular school programs are able to learn and achieve. Believing that a school's most important function is to foster and enhance the total growth of the individual, the Vanguard School focuses on both the academic and social development of its students to prepare them for a full and satisfying adult life.

Located in the heart of the Sunshine State, the School has a 75-acre campus in the city of Lake Wales. Ideally situated for access to the beaches and cultural and entertainment centers of central Florida, the School is about 70 miles east of Tampa and 45 miles south of Orlando.

A 10-member Board of Trustees, made up of prominent representatives of the local business community, oversees the School's operations and establishes its policies. The Director and administrative staff make all decisions concerning the program and daily student life. The School is a nonprofit institution, and its plant is conservatively valued at more than $7 million. The annual budget for 2002–03 was approximately $4.3 million, and the School's endowment funds exceed $3 million.

The Vanguard School of Lake Wales is accredited by the Florida Council of Independent Schools and the Southern Association of Colleges and Schools. It is a member of the International Dyslexia Association, the Learning Disabilities Association of America, the Southeastern Association of Boarding Schools, the Association of Boarding Schools, Small Boarding School Association, and SSATB.

ACADEMIC PROGRAMS

The Vanguard program is designed to prepare students for the transition from Vanguard to a regular school or the next stage in the student's progress toward self-sufficiency. It is the School's aim to prepare students to return, whenever possible, to a regular or less specialized program. The academic classes are individually oriented and based on the needs of each student. Core classes are carefully structured with no more than 8 students per class to ensure optimal attention

to individual needs. The learning activities are explicit and the steps gradual, so that each student may progress in a way that is successful and satisfying.

Additional individualized needs are met through focused educational interventions. Students with communication difficulties receive individualized instruction in language and communication. Reading specialists provide consultative services to the entire faculty.

Academic classes are held daily from 8:15 to 3:10. Students take a core curriculum of reading, language arts, and mathematics that is individually tailored to meet the specific needs of each student. Science, social studies, and elective courses are presented as group-taught subjects with minimal reading requirements. These classes emphasize audiovisual presentations, class discussions, projects, experiments, and field trips. Within this framework, the School offers the basics of a comprehensive high school curriculum; students earn credits and receive a high school diploma upon graduation.

The School offers electives in computer science, industrial arts, home economics, photography, art, yearbook design, career guidance, life management, psychology, and computer imagery. Driver's education is available. The addition of a computer network for all academic buildings enables students to access library materials and the Internet from each classroom. High school students are required to have a laptop computer.

FACULTY AND ADVISERS

James R. Moon, Ph.D., M.B.A., is the Executive Director of the Vanguard School. He holds degrees from Washington and Jefferson College (B.A., psychology, 1977), Virginia Tech (M.S., clinical psychology, 1979; Ph.D., clinical psychology, 1982), and Nova Southeastern University (M.B.A., 1997). He is a member of two professional honor societies (Psi Chi, psychology, and Sigma Beta Delta, business, management, and administration). He is a member of several professional organizations in education, psychology, and business administration and has published professional articles, book chapters, and books on a variety of topics.

The academic faculty consists of 29 teachers and specialists (20 women and 9 men). All faculty members hold bachelor's degrees, 11 hold master's degrees, and 1 holds a doctorate. The School employs 40 residential and recreational staff members who sponsor interscholastic and intramural sports, clubs, activities, weekend trips, and social events and provide structure and support in the dormitories.

The School employs a school psychologist, who conducts admissions evaluations and reevaluations and serves as counselor to the students. Individual psychological counseling may be provided through arrangements with a local,

licensed behavioral health counselor. The Vanguard School publishes the *Vanguard School LD Research Digest* on a quarterly subscription basis. A speech therapist is available to provide direct speech services to students and to provide consultative services to teachers and other staff members.

COLLEGE PLACEMENT

The majority of Vanguard students attend some form of postsecondary educational or training program, including two-year and four-year colleges and universities, vocational training programs, and transition programs. The school psychologist and faculty members counsel students and parents to help them determine the most appropriate placement for each student after Vanguard.

STUDENT BODY AND CONDUCT

The enrollment is 125, with 112 residential students and 13 day students. The residential students come from twenty states and Puerto Rico as well as twenty-one countries. They represent a cross-section of cultural, ethnic, and racial backgrounds.

The School uses a system of levels to encourage the development of independent, self-responsible behavior among its students. The goal of the level system is to provide a student the opportunity to proceed from behavior that requires external control and supervision to behavior that reflects positive, independent decision making; constructive involvement in the student's own development; and contributions to the School community. The level system incorporates a series of privileges that reflect the degree of responsibility that a student has achieved. Areas of emphasis in the system focus on the self-care, interpersonal relations, school performance, program participation, individual goals, and general behaviors that are important for the overall development of the School's students.

Within the level system there are opportunities for student involvement in the operations of the residential program as students on higher levels assume leadership responsibilities and work with the residential staff. Dormitory councils made up of representatives from each level meet regularly with residential supervisors. An active Student Council, made up of elected representatives, plans social events and addresses schoolwide student issues. Officers of the student government and dorm councils meet weekly with staff and administrators to discuss student concerns.

ACADEMIC FACILITIES

The thirteen buildings on the Vanguard campus include three classroom buildings that contain twenty-five classrooms, two science labs, and seven offices for tutorials and specialists. The

Aquatic Center consists of a 75 foot by 52 foot NCAA short pool and a bathhouse. The campus also contains three residential dormitories, the Harry E. Nelson Library/Media Center, a dining hall, a fitness center, an administration-visitors' reception center, and the Edward Bartsch Memorial Gymnasium. The grounds contain three playing fields, three lighted tennis courts, a lighted soccer field, and a fishing dock.

BOARDING AND GENERAL FACILITIES
A structured but comfortable environment surrounds Vanguard students. Housed in three spacious dormitories with students of similar ages, they are under the supervision of the residential and recreational staff. The dorms are supervised 24 hours per day. Two nurses monitor the students' health needs.

Two students share a dormitory room, which they are encouraged to personalize with their decorations. Television lounges at the center of each hall and the recreational hall, which occupies the second floor of the gym, are available for recreation and relaxation.

ATHLETICS
Vanguard provides many opportunities for students to participate in various sports, depending on the student's interests and abilities.

The Vanguard School is a member of the FHSAA, which sanctions all of the School's interscholastic athletic contests. Boys may participate in soccer, basketball, tennis, golf, weight lifting, track and field, and cross-country running. Girls are offered the opportunity to participate in volleyball, basketball, track and field, cheerleading, bowling, and cross-country running.

Vanguard also offers an opportunity for all students to participate on a less competitive basis through a program of intramurals. Games and tournaments are scheduled regularly throughout the year in softball, swimming, volleyball, tennis, indoor hockey, soccer, and basketball.

The fitness center houses a complete weight-training room with a Universal weight center, free weights, and exercise bicycles. Aerobics classes are offered as part of the physical education program, and scuba diving lessons are offered to students age 13 and older.

EXTRACURRICULAR OPPORTUNITIES
Students have excellent opportunities to participate in a variety of activities depending on their interests. Students publish a newspaper and a yearbook. Art and photography students put on an annual exhibition and enter works in local art exhibits.

In the evenings there is a regularly scheduled period for clubs and activities, during which students can participate in intramural sports,

weight lifting, aerobics, and arts and crafts projects. Key Club and the Student Government offer opportunities for leadership and community service. The Student Government sponsors dances, special activities, an annual field day, and several banquets throughout the year.

DAILY LIFE
Breakfast is served from 7:15 to 7:45, and classes begin at 8:15 and run until 3:10. Each student takes seven classes per semester. Physical education class runs from 4 until 4:50 p.m.; dinner is served at 5:30. A required study hour is held Monday to Thursday, 6:45 to 7:45, and on Sunday, 9 to 10. Clubs and activities are offered from 7:45 until 8:45, depending on the activity. Bedtimes depend on the age and level of the individual student. Students who achieve higher-level status are required to participate in community service activities.

WEEKEND LIFE
Weekends provide a change of pace and often a change of scenery for Vanguard students. Camping, canoeing, fishing, and off-campus trips are a part of the weekend activities. The School maintains a fleet of two vans and four school buses, and it is not uncommon for them to be headed to four or five different destinations on a weekend. Weekend outings offer students the opportunity to visit the beaches and many other attractions of central Florida, including Disney World, Sea World, Cypress Gardens, the Kennedy Space Center, and the metropolitan areas of Tampa and Orlando. A more relaxed atmosphere is offered on Saturday and Sunday mornings, when an extended brunch is served. Students are encouraged to attend religious services at the many places of worship in the area, and transportation is provided.

COSTS AND FINANCIAL AID
The boarding school fee for 2005–06 was $38,675, which covered tuition, room and board, and books. The fee for day students was $21,450. An academic activities/materials fee of $600 covers extra costs for field trips and materials for industrial arts, home economics, art, or humanities. An additional $650 is required for international students to cover medical and miscellaneous expenses. The $4000 enrollment deposit is applied to the current year's tuition. A monthly payment plan, which includes a deferred payment charge of $400, is available.

The Vanguard School Board of Trustees awards annual scholarship aid based on financial need. Following the interview process, families complete and submit a financial aid application and a copy of their current IRS tax return. Fourteen percent of the 2004–05 enrollment received financial assistance. As a special school,

the Internal Revenue Service allows a deduction for the cost of attendance at the Vanguard School.

ADMISSIONS INFORMATION
The Vanguard School's enrollment age is 10 through 17 and it serves students with learning disabilities, dyslexia, and attention deficit disorder who need remedial instruction. A Thirteenth-Year Program offers recent graduates an opportunity to increase basic skills and further develop social skills. The School does not accept students entering grade 12. All students must have the ability to speak and understand the English language, as the School does not offer an ESL program. Referrals to the School may originate from physicians, psychologists, educators, educational counselors, child guidance clinics, pediatricians, or other professionals who provide professional services to children, adolescents, and their families. Direct parental inquiries are also welcome.

So that the School may fully consider a student for enrollment, parents are requested to send copies of current academic records, including an official transcript for secondary-level students; a current psychoeducational evaluation (not more than two years old) that includes the Wechsler Intelligence Scales, including subtest scores; and any medical records that would assist the School's professional staff in determining a student's specific needs. The School also provides teacher and principal/counselor evaluation forms, which should be completed by the student's current school personnel. If, from this material, it appears the Vanguard program would be appropriate for the student, a visit to Lake Wales for a pre-enrollment interview and evaluation is required. Appointments for these interviews are arranged by the admissions office.

Admission to the Vanguard School is open to all applicants regardless of race, creed, color, or national or ethnic origin.

APPLICATION TIMETABLE
Inquiries are welcome at any time. Tours and evaluation interviews are scheduled throughout the year, and admission is offered based on available space. The office is open Monday through Friday from 8 to 4:30. Brochures and additional information about the School are available through the admission office.

ADMISSIONS CORRESPONDENCE
Melanie Anderson, Director of Admission
The Vanguard School
22000 Highway 27
Lake Wales, Florida 33859-6858

Phone: 863-676-6091
Fax: 863-676-8297
E-mail: vanadmin@vanguardschool.org
Web site: http://www.vanguardschool.org

Junior Boarding Schools

AMBASSADOR PREPARATORY

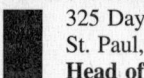

325 Dayton Avenue
St. Paul, Minnesota 55102
Head of School: Erica Roy Nyline

General Information Coeducational boarding and day college-preparatory and general academic school. Grades 6–9. Founded: 1997. Setting: urban. Nearest major city is Minneapolis/St. Paul. Students are housed in single-sex by floor dormitories. 1-acre campus. 2 buildings on campus. Approved or accredited by North Central Association of Colleges and Schools and Minnesota Department of Education. Total enrollment: 40. Upper school average class size: 5. Upper school faculty-student ratio: 1:5.

Student Profile Grade 7: 13 students (8 boys, 5 girls); Grade 8: 14 students (9 boys, 5 girls); Grade 9: 13 students (8 boys, 5 girls). 90% of students are boarding students. 10% are state residents. 1 state is represented in upper school student body. 75% are international students. International students from Brazil, China, Colombia, Japan, Republic of Korea, and Taiwan; 5 other countries represented in student body.

Faculty School total: 11. In upper school: 4 men, 5 women; 3 reside on campus.

Subjects Offered Algebra, American culture, American history, American literature, art, band, community service, ESL, geometry, history, instrumental music, language and composition, mathematics, music appreciation, physical education, physical science, reading/study skills, SAT/ACT preparation, science, social studies, strings, swimming competency, TOEFL preparation.

Special Academic Programs Honors section; ESL (20 students enrolled).

Student Life Specified standards of dress, student council, honor system. Discipline rests primarily with faculty.

Tuition and Aid 7-day tuition and room/board: $34,475. Tuition installment plan (individually arranged payment plans). Merit scholarship grants available. In 2005–06, 10% of students received aid; total merit-scholarship money awarded: $20,000. Total amount of financial aid awarded in 2005–06: $60,000.

Admissions Traditional entrance grade is 7. SLEP required. Deadline for receipt of application materials: none. Application fee required: $50. Interview recommended.

Athletics Interscholastic: basketball (boys, girls), combined training (b,g), scooter football (b,g); coed interscholastic: basketball, scooter football, volleyball; coed intramural: fitness, physical fitness, strength & conditioning, swimming and diving, tennis, weight training. 2 PE instructors, 2 coaches.

Computers Computers are regularly used in career exploration, creative writing, English, ESL, ethics, language development, research skills, SAT preparation, science, social studies, study skills, writing, writing fundamentals, yearbook classes. Computer network features include campus e-mail, Internet access, wireless campus network.

Contact Alex Thomas, Director of Admissions. 651-228-0599 Ext. 24. Fax: 651-228-0680. E-mail: athomas@academymn.com. Web site: www.academymn.com.

ANNOUNCEMENT FROM THE SCHOOL Accredited, grade 6–9, coed day/boarding program with pre–Advanced Placement curriculum. Rigorous academic and leadership development program focused on preparation for entry into selective high schools. Comprehensive ESL and cultural competency development for international students. Sports, community service, fine arts, and comprehensive high school planning in a small nurturing community.

THE BEMENT SCHOOL

Main Street
Deerfield, Massachusetts 01342
Head of School: Mrs. Shelley Borror Jackson

General Information Coeducational boarding and day college-preparatory, arts, and bilingual studies school. Boarding grades 3–9, day grades K–9. Founded: 1925. Setting: small town. Nearest major city is Springfield. Students are housed in single-sex dormitories. 12-acre campus. 11 buildings on campus. Approved or accredited by Association of Independent Schools in New England, Junior Boarding Schools Association, and The Association of Boarding Schools. Member of National Association of Independent Schools and Secondary School Admission Test Board. Language of instruction: English. Endowment: $3.1 million. Total enrollment: 245. Upper school average class size: 15. Upper school faculty-student ratio: 1:7.

Student Profile Grade 6: 25 students (11 boys, 14 girls); Grade 7: 34 students (15 boys, 19 girls); Grade 8: 33 students (14 boys, 19 girls); Grade 9: 29 students (11 boys, 18 girls). 23% of students are boarding students. 86% are state residents. 12 states are represented in upper school student body. 15% are international students. International students from Hong Kong, Jamaica, Japan, and Republic of Korea.

Faculty School total: 40. In upper school: 15 men, 10 women; 12 have advanced degrees; 11 reside on campus.

Subjects Offered Algebra, American history, art, biology, chemistry, community service, creative writing, dance, drama, earth science, English, English literature, fine arts, French, geography, geometry, grammar, health, history, Latin, literature, mathematics, music, photography, physical education, physical science, science, social studies, Spanish, theater, typing, world history, world literature, writing.

Graduation Requirements Advanced math, American history, art history, arts and fine arts (art, music, dance, drama), athletics, biology, choir, drama, English, French, geometry, guitar, health, Latin, mathematics, music history, science, social studies (includes history). Community service is required.

Special Academic Programs Honors section; special instructional classes for deaf students, blind students; ESL (5 students enrolled).

Secondary School Placement 21 students graduated in 2004; they went to Deerfield Academy; Northfield Mount Hermon School; Suffield Academy.

Student Life Specified standards of dress. Discipline rests primarily with faculty.

Tuition and Aid Day student tuition: $14,680; 5-day tuition and room/board: $26,780; 7-day tuition and room/board: $32,350. Tuition installment plan (Academic Management Services Plan, monthly payment plans, individually arranged payment plans, 60%/40% payment plan). Need-based scholarship grants available. In 2004–05, 26% of students received aid. Total amount of financial aid awarded in 2004–05: $300,000.

Admissions Traditional entrance grade is 7. For fall 2005, 95 students applied for admission, 25 were accepted, 18 enrolled. SSAT or Wechsler Intelligence Scale for Children III required. Deadline for receipt of application materials: none. Application fee required: $40. Interview required.

Athletics Interscholastic: alpine skiing (boys, girls), baseball (b), basketball (b,g), field hockey (g), lacrosse (b,g), skiing (downhill) (b,g), softball (g), swimming and diving (b,g), track and field (b,g); coed interscholastic: cross-country running, ice hockey, soccer, squash; coed intramural: dance, fitness walking, golf, ice skating, indoor soccer, jogging, modern dance, outdoor activities, outdoor recreation, outdoor skills, outdoors, physical fitness, running, skiing (cross-country), skiing (downhill), snowboarding, soccer, strength & conditioning, swimming and diving, table tennis, walking, weight training, winter soccer.

Computers Computers are regularly used in art, English, history, mathematics, science classes. Computer resources include campus e-mail, on-campus library services, CD-ROMs, Internet access, DVD.

Contact Matthew Evans, Director of Admission. 413-774-7061. Fax: 413-774-7863. E-mail: admit@bement.org. Web site: www.bement.org/.

See full description on page 1272.

CARDIGAN MOUNTAIN SCHOOL

62 Alumni Drive
Canaan, New Hampshire 03741-9307
Head of School: Mr. Thomas W. Needham

General Information Boys' boarding and day college-preparatory, arts, religious studies, and technology school, affiliated with Christian faith. Grades 6–9. Founded: 1945. Setting: rural. Nearest major city is Manchester. Students are housed in single-sex dormitories. 525-acre campus. 18 buildings on campus. Approved or accredited by New England Association of Schools and Colleges, The Association of Boarding Schools, and New Hampshire Department of Education. Member of National Association of Independent Schools and Secondary School Admission Test Board. Endowment: $11.5 million. Total enrollment: 170. Upper school average class size: 12. Upper school faculty-student ratio: 1:4.

Student Profile Grade 6: 12 students (12 boys); Grade 7: 24 students (24 boys); Grade 8: 67 students (67 boys); Grade 9: 67 students (67 boys). 93% of students are boarding students. 14% are state residents. 21 states are represented in upper school student body. 36% are international students. International students from Canada, Dominican Republic, Hong Kong, Japan, Mexico, and Republic of Korea; 4 other countries represented in student body. 90% of students are Christian.

Faculty School total: 49. In upper school: 39 men, 10 women; 22 have advanced degrees; 43 reside on campus.

Subjects Offered Algebra, American history, American literature, art, Bible studies, biology, ceramics, computer math, computer programming, computer science, creative writing, drama, earth science, ecology, English, English literature, environmental science, ethics, European history, expository writing, fine arts, French, geography, geology, geometry, grammar, health, history, industrial arts, Latin, life skills, mathematics, music, photography, physical education, physical science, reading, religion, science, social studies, Spanish, speech, study skills, theater, trigonometry, typing, world history, world literature, writing.

Graduation Requirements Arts and fine arts (art, music, dance, drama), computer science, English, foreign language, mathematics, reading, religion (includes Bible studies and theology), science, social studies (includes history), study skills.

Special Academic Programs Honors section; independent study; academic accommodation for the gifted and the artistically talented; remedial reading and/or remedial writing; remedial math; ESL (8 students enrolled).

Secondary School Placement 76 students graduated in 2005; they went to Avon Old Farms School; Berkshire School; Kent School; Pomfret School; Salisbury School; St. Paul's School.

Student Life Specified standards of dress, student council, honor system. Discipline rests primarily with faculty. Attendance at religious services is required.

Summer Programs Remediation, enrichment, ESL, sports programs offered; held on campus; accepts boys and girls; open to students from other schools. 150 students usually enrolled. 2006 schedule: June 24 to August 2. Application deadline: none.

Tuition and Aid Day student tuition: $20,000; 7-day tuition and room/board: $34,550. Tuition installment plan (The Tuition Plan, Insured Tuition Payment Plan, Academic Management Services Plan, Key Tuition Payment Plan, monthly payment plans). Need-based scholarship grants, need-based loans, prepGATE Loans available. In 2005–06, 21% of students received aid. Total amount of financial aid awarded in 2005–06: $737,250.

Admissions Traditional entrance grade is 8. For fall 2005, 174 students applied for admission, 130 were accepted, 95 enrolled. Wechsler Intelligence Scale for Children III required. Deadline for receipt of application materials: none. Application fee required: $35. On-campus interview required.

Athletics Interscholastic: alpine skiing, baseball, basketball, cross-country running, football, ice hockey, lacrosse, running, sailing, skiing (cross-country), skiing (down-hill), soccer, tennis, track and field, wrestling; intramural: archery, bicycling, bowling, boxing, climbing, equestrian sports, fitness, golf, ice hockey, martial arts, mountain biking, outdoor activities, outdoor adventure, outdoor recreation, outdoor skills, outdoors, physical training, riflery, rock climbing, ropes courses, sailing, skiing (downhill), snowboarding, swimming and diving, tennis, trap and skeet, weight lifting, whiffle ball. 1 coach, 1 trainer.

Computers Computers are regularly used in English, history, mathematics, science classes. Computer network features include campus e-mail, CD-ROMs, online commercial services, Internet access, file transfer, wireless campus network.

Contact Shirley Lester, Admissions Administrative Assistant. 603-523-3548 Ext. 3548. Fax: 603-523-3565. E-mail: rryerson@cardigan.org. Web site: www.cardigan.org.

See full description on page 1274.

EAGLEBROOK SCHOOL

petersons.com

Pine Nook Road
Deerfield, Massachusetts 01342
Head of School: Mr. Andrew C. Chase

General Information Boys' boarding and day college-preparatory, arts, and technology school. Grades 6–9. Founded: 1922. Setting: rural. Nearest major city is Springfield. Students are housed in single-sex dormitories. 750-acre campus. 26 buildings on campus. Approved or accredited by Association of Independent Schools in New England and The Association of Boarding Schools. Member of National Association of Independent Schools and Secondary School Admission Test Board. Endowment: $45 million. Total enrollment: 273. Upper school average class size: 10. Upper school faculty-student ratio: 1:4.

Student Profile Grade 6: 25 students (25 boys); Grade 7: 68 students (68 boys); Grade 8: 106 students (106 boys); Grade 9: 74 students (74 boys). 75% of students are boarding students. 35% are state residents. 28 states are represented in upper school student body. 20% are international students. International students from Bermuda, Hong Kong, Mexico, Republic of Korea, Taiwan, and Venezuela; 18 other countries represented in student body.

Faculty School total: 76. In upper school: 44 men, 24 women; 30 have advanced degrees; 50 reside on campus.

Subjects Offered Acting, African-American history, algebra, American studies, anthropology, architectural drawing, architecture, art, astronomy, band, batik, biology, ceramics, Chinese history, chorus, Civil War, civil war history, community service, computer art, computer keyboarding, computer science, computer-aided design, concert band, CPR, creative writing, current events, desktop publishing, digital music, digital photography, drafting, drama, drawing, drawing and design, earth science, ecology, English, English literature, environmental science, ESL, European history, expository writing, fine arts, first aid, French, general science, geography, geometry, grammar, health, history, industrial arts, instrumental music, journalism, Latin, mathematics, medieval history, music, newspaper, photography, physical education, pottery, pre-algebra, public speaking, publications, Russian history, science, sex education, social science, social studies, Spanish, study skills, swimming, theater, typing, U.S. history, Web site design, woodworking, world history, writing.

Graduation Requirements Arts and fine arts (art, music, dance, drama), English, foreign language, mathematics, physical education (includes health), science, social science, social studies (includes history). Community service is required.

Special Academic Programs Honors section; academic accommodation for the gifted, the musically talented, and the artistically talented; ESL (30 students enrolled).

Secondary School Placement 75 students graduated in 2005; they went to Choate Rosemary Hall; Deerfield Academy; Northfield Mount Hermon School; Phillips Exeter Academy; The Hotchkiss School; The Taft School.

Student Life Specified standards of dress, student council. Discipline rests primarily with faculty.

Summer Programs Enrichment, advancement, ESL, sports, art/fine arts, rigorous outdoor training, computer instruction programs offered; session focuses on enrichment; held on campus; accepts boys and girls; open to students from other schools. 50 students usually enrolled. 2006 schedule: July 6 to August 2. Application deadline: none.

Tuition and Aid Day student tuition: $21,900; 7-day tuition and room/board: $35,000. Tuition installment plan (individually arranged payment plans). Need-based scholarship grants available. In 2005–06, 30% of students received aid. Total amount of financial aid awarded in 2005–06: $1,200,000.

Admissions Wechsler Intelligence Scale for Children required. Deadline for receipt of application materials: none. Application fee required: $50. Interview required.

Athletics Interscholastic: alpine skiing, aquatics, baseball, basketball, cross-country running, diving, football, Frisbee, golf, hiking/backpacking, hockey, ice hockey, ice skating, in-line hockey, indoor hockey, indoor soccer, lacrosse, mountain biking, outdoor activities, outdoor recreation, ski jumping, skiing (downhill), snowboarding, soccer, squash, strength & conditioning, swimming and diving, tennis, track and field, triathlon, ultimate Frisbee, water polo, wrestling; intramural: back packing, bicycling, broomball, canoeing/kayaking, climbing, fishing, fitness, floor hockey, fly fishing, hiking/backpacking, hockey, ice hockey, ice skating, in-line skating, indoor hockey, indoor soccer, juggling, kayaking, life saving, mountain biking, nordic skiing, outdoor activities, outdoor adventure, outdoor recreation, outdoor skills, outdoors, physical training, rafting, riflery, rock climbing, roller blading, roller hockey, roller skating, ropes courses, scuba diving, ski jumping, skiing (cross-country), street hockey, table tennis, volleyball, wallyball, weight lifting, weight training, wilderness survival. 1 trainer.

Computers Computer network features include campus e-mail, on-campus library services, CD-ROMs, Internet access, DVD, wireless campus network.

Contact Mr. Theodore J. Low, Director of Admission. 413-774-9111. Fax: 413-774-9119. E-mail: tlow@eaglebrook.org. Web site: www.eaglebrook.org.

See full description on page 1276.

FAY SCHOOL

petersons.com

48 Main Street
Southborough, Massachusetts 01772-9106
Head of School: Stephen C. White

General Information Coeducational boarding and day college-preparatory, arts, and technology school. Boarding grades 6–9, day grades 1–9. Founded: 1866. Setting: small town. Nearest major city is Boston. Students are housed in single-sex dormitories. 35-acre campus. 16 buildings on campus. Approved or accredited by Association of Independent Schools in New England, The Association of Boarding Schools, and Massachusetts Department of Education. Member of National Association of Independent Schools and Secondary School Admission Test Board. Endowment: $24 million. Total enrollment: 382. Upper school average class size: 12. Upper school faculty-student ratio: 1:6.

Student Profile Grade 6: 45 students (24 boys, 21 girls); Grade 7: 61 students (33 boys, 28 girls); Grade 8: 93 students (55 boys, 38 girls); Grade 9: 59 students (35 boys, 24 girls). 42% of students are boarding students. 65% are state residents. 15 states are represented in upper school student body. 24% are international students. International students from Hong Kong, Japan, Mexico, Republic of Korea, Taiwan, and Thailand; 9 other countries represented in student body.

Faculty School total: 66. In upper school: 30 men, 35 women; 34 have advanced degrees; 32 reside on campus.

Subjects Offered Algebra, American history, American literature, art, astronomy, biology, ceramics, computer science, creative writing, drama, English, English literature, environmental science, ethics, European history, expository writing, fine arts, French, geography, geometry, government/civics, grammar, Latin, mathematics, music, photography, physical education, science, social studies, Spanish, world history, writing.

Graduation Requirements Arts and fine arts (art, music, dance, drama), computer science, English, mathematics, science, social studies (includes history).

Special Academic Programs Honors section; independent study; academic accommodation for the gifted and the musically talented; ESL (35 students enrolled).

Secondary School Placement 55 students graduated in 2005; they went to Brooks School; Choate Rosemary Hall; Phillips Exeter Academy; Saint Mark's School; St. George's School; St. Paul's School.

Student Life Specified standards of dress, student council. Discipline rests primarily with faculty. Attendance at religious services is required.

Summer Programs Enrichment, ESL, sports, computer instruction programs offered; session focuses on ESL; held on campus; accepts boys and girls; open to students from other schools. 67 students usually enrolled. 2006 schedule: June 27 to August 19. Application deadline: February 1.

Tuition and Aid Day student tuition: $15,950–$21,840; 7-day tuition and room/board: $36,500–$41,975. Tuition installment plan (Key Tuition Payment Plan, monthly payment plans, individually arranged payment plans, Key Education Resources Monthly Payment Plan). Need-based scholarship grants, Achiever Loans available. In 2005–06, 8% of students received aid. Total amount of financial aid awarded in 2005–06: $611,112.

Admissions Traditional entrance grade is 7. For fall 2005, 204 students applied for admission, 102 were accepted, 74 enrolled. WISC-R or WISC-III required. Deadline for receipt of application materials: none. Application fee required: $50. Interview required.

Athletics Interscholastic: baseball (boys), basketball (b,g), cross-country running (b,g), field hockey (g), football (b), golf (b,g), hockey (b,g), ice hockey (b,g), independent competitive sports (b,g), lacrosse (b,g), soccer (b,g), softball (g), tennis (b,g), track and field (b,g), volleyball (g), wrestling (b); intramural: basketball (b,g), climbing (b,g), dance (b,g), equestrian sports (b,g), fitness (b,g), golf (b,g), horseback riding (b,g), physical fitness (b,g), rock climbing (b,g), ropes courses (b,g), skiing

(downhill) (b,g), snowboarding (b,g), soccer (b,g), tennis (b,g), trap and skeet (b,g), weight training (b,g), yoga (b,g); coed interscholastic: basketball, cross-country running, golf, hockey, ice hockey, independent competitive sports, lacrosse, soccer, tennis, track and field, volleyball; coed intramural: aerobics/nautilus, alpine skiing, basketball, bicycling, climbing, dance, equestrian sports, fitness, golf, horseback riding, outdoor activities, outdoors, physical fitness, rock climbing, ropes courses, skiing (downhill), snowboarding, soccer, squash, tennis, trap and skeet, weight training, yoga. 2 PE instructors, 17 coaches, 1 trainer.

Computers Computers are regularly used in English, foreign language, mathematics, music, science classes. Computer network features include campus e-mail, on-campus library services, CD-ROMs, Internet access.

Contact Suzanne E. Walker Buck, Director of Admission. 508-485-0100. Fax: 508-481-7872. E-mail: fayadmit@fayschool.org. Web site: www.fayschool.org.

See full description on page 1278.

THE FESSENDEN SCHOOL

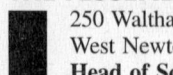

250 Waltham Street
West Newton, Massachusetts 02465-1750
Head of School: Mr. Peter P. Drake

General Information Boys' boarding and day college-preparatory, general academic, and arts school. Boarding grades 5–9, day grades K–9. Founded: 1903. Setting: suburban. Nearest major city is Boston. Students are housed in single-sex dormitories. 41-acre campus. 25 buildings on campus. Approved or accredited by Association of Independent Schools in New England, The Association of Boarding Schools, and Massachusetts Department of Education. Member of National Association of Independent Schools and Secondary School Admission Test Board. Endowment: $18 million. Total enrollment: 471. Upper school average class size: 12. Upper school faculty-student ratio: 1:7.

Student Profile Grade 7: 68 students (68 boys); Grade 8: 75 students (75 boys); Grade 9: 43 students (43 boys). 47% of students are boarding students. 70% are state residents. 8 states are represented in upper school student body. 19% are international students. International students from Bermuda, Mexico, Republic of Korea, Taiwan, and Thailand; 3 other countries represented in student body.

Faculty School total: 91. In upper school: 40 men, 51 women; 54 have advanced degrees; 43 reside on campus.

Subjects Offered Algebra, American history, American literature, anatomy, art, astronomy, biology, ceramics, chemistry, computer math, computer programming, computer science, creative writing, drama, earth science, English, English literature, European history, expository writing, fine arts, French, geography, geometry, government/civics, grammar, health, history, human sexuality, Latin, library studies, mathematics, music, photography, physical education, physics, science, social science, social studies, Spanish, theater, typing, world history, writing.

Graduation Requirements Arts and fine arts (art, music, dance, drama), computer science, English, foreign language, mathematics, science, social science, social studies (includes history).

Special Academic Programs Honors section; academic accommodation for the gifted, the musically talented, and the artistically talented; remedial reading and/or remedial writing; remedial math; ESL (14 students enrolled).

Secondary School Placement 50 students graduated in 2005; they went to Middlesex School; Milton Academy; Noble and Greenough School; Tabor Academy.

Student Life Specified standards of dress, student council, honor system. Discipline rests primarily with faculty.

Summer Programs ESL programs offered; held on campus; accepts boys and girls; open to students from other schools. 40 students usually enrolled. 2006 schedule: June 26 to July 30. Application deadline: none.

Tuition and Aid Day student tuition: $19,000–$23,750; 5-day tuition and room/board: $31,500–$32,150; 7-day tuition and room/board: $36,500–$37,150. Tuition installment plan (Academic Management Services Plan, monthly payment plans). Need-based scholarship grants available. In 2005–06, 12% of students received aid. Total amount of financial aid awarded in 2005–06: $600,000.

Admissions Traditional entrance grade is 7. For fall 2005, 112 students applied for admission, 56 were accepted, 43 enrolled. ISEE, SSAT, TOEFL, Wechsler Intelligence Scale for Children or writing sample required. Deadline for receipt of application materials: February 1. Application fee required: $50. On-campus interview required.

Athletics Interscholastic: baseball (boys), basketball (b), cross-country running (b), football (b), ice hockey (b), lacrosse (b), soccer (b), squash (b), tennis (b), track and field (b), wrestling (b); intramural: alpine skiing (b), baseball (b), basketball (b), canoeing/kayaking (b), fencing (b), football (b), golf (b), ice hockey (b), mountain biking (b), racquetball (b), sailing (b), skiing (cross-country) (b), skiing (downhill) (b), snowboarding (b), soccer (b), strength & conditioning (b), swimming and diving (b), tennis (b), weight training (b). 3 PE instructors, 1 trainer.

Computers Computers are regularly used in English, mathematics, science classes. Computer network features include campus e-mail, on-campus library services, CD-ROMs, Internet access.

Contact Mr. Caleb Thomson, Director of Admissions. 617-630-2300. Fax: 617-630-2303. E-mail: admissions@fessenden.org. Web site: www.fessenden.org.

ANNOUNCEMENT FROM THE SCHOOL The Wheeler Library, opened in fall 2004, has been relocated to an expanded space in the heart of the School for convenient access from all academic areas and direct connection to the newly updated computer classrooms. The new library features a media classroom and an upgraded 16,000-item collection, including expanded multimedia selections and enlarged professional and language collections. The library also provides a story area and reading benches and other comfortable seating for recreational reading.

See full description on page 1280.

FOX RIVER COUNTRY DAY SCHOOL

1600 Dundee Avenue
Elgin, Illinois 60120
Head of School: Mr. John Friborg

General Information Coeducational boarding and day college-preparatory and arts school, affiliated with Church of Christ, Scientist. Boarding grades 5–8, day grades PK–8. Founded: 1913. Setting: rural. Nearest major city is Chicago. Students are housed in single-sex by floor dormitories. 53-acre campus. 10 buildings on campus. Approved or accredited by Independent Schools Association of the Central States. Member of National Association of Independent Schools. Total enrollment: 180. Upper school average class size: 16. Upper school faculty-student ratio: 1:16.

Student Profile Grade 6: 5 students (4 boys, 1 girl); Grade 7: 9 students (4 boys, 5 girls); Grade 8: 19 students (11 boys, 8 girls). 51% of students are boarding students. 54% are state residents. 5 states are represented in upper school student body. 27% are international students. International students from China, Germany, Nigeria, and Republic of Korea. 5% of students are members of Church of Christ, Scientist.

Faculty School total: 32. In upper school: 5 men, 24 women; 10 have advanced degrees; 6 reside on campus.

Subjects Offered Algebra, American history, American literature, art, computer science, creative writing, earth science, English, English literature, environmental education, environmental science, fine arts, general science, geography, geology, geometry, government/civics, grammar, history, library studies, mathematics, music, physical education, social studies, Spanish, swimming, world history, world literature, writing.

Graduation Requirements Arts and fine arts (art, music, dance, drama), computer science, English, environmental education, foreign language, library studies, mathematics, physical education (includes health), science, social studies (includes history), swimming.

Special Academic Programs Academic accommodation for the gifted; remedial reading and/or remedial writing; ESL (7 students enrolled).

Secondary School Placement 6 students graduated in 2005; they went to Elgin Academy; Lake Forest Academy; Suffield Academy; Wayland Academy.

Student Life Specified standards of dress, student council, honor system. Discipline rests primarily with faculty.

Summer Programs Remediation, enrichment, ESL, sports, art/fine arts, computer instruction programs offered; session focuses on enrichment, environmental education, swimming, arts, crafts, and field trips; held on campus; accepts boys and girls; open to students from other schools. 100 students usually enrolled. 2006 schedule: June 19 to July 27. Application deadline: none.

Tuition and Aid Day student tuition: $11,450; 5-day tuition and room/board: $22,845; 7-day tuition and room/board: $26,950. Tuition installment plan (The Tuition Plan, monthly payment plans). Tuition reduction for siblings, need-based scholarship grants available. In 2005–06, 20% of students received aid.

Admissions For fall 2005, 19 students applied for admission, 15 were accepted, 12 enrolled. SLEP for foreign students and writing sample required. Deadline for receipt of application materials: none. Application fee required: $40. Interview required.

Athletics Interscholastic: basketball (boys, girls), soccer (b,g), ultimate Frisbee (b), volleyball (g); intramural: wrestling (b); coed interscholastic: basketball, cooperative games, cross-country running, swimming and diving, track and field; coed intramural: basketball, cooperative games, cross-country running, field hockey, flag football, floor hockey, gymnastics, outdoor education, physical fitness, running, soccer, softball, strength & conditioning, swimming and diving, tennis, track and field, volleyball. 2 PE instructors.

Computers Computers are regularly used in English, mathematics, science classes. Computer resources include on-campus library services, CD-ROMs, Internet access.

Contact Mr. Chuck Harvuot, Director of Admissions. 847-888-7910 Ext. 167. Fax: 847-888-7947. E-mail: charvuot@frcds.org. Web site: www.frcds.org.

ANNOUNCEMENT FROM THE SCHOOL Whether they are walking the trails of the forested campus, performing madrigals, presenting Spanish dialogues, or simply playing with friends on the playground, students at Fox River Country Day School (FRCDS) experience an atmosphere that encourages discovery and excellence. Founded in 1913, Fox River is an independent, fully accredited, coeducational day and boarding school serving students from preschool through grade 8. Located on 53 acres of rolling hills and field oaks, the country campus is a haven of learning and growing just 30 miles northwest

of Chicago. The School seeks students who are at or above grade level and who want to be a part of a learning community with a clear set of values. Fox River's mission is to educate the whole child through a values-based program, emphasizing academic excellence, enrichment, community, and ethics. The academic program at FRCDS promotes personal achievement and is as rich and varied as it is challenging—thus readying students for a college-preparatory curriculum in secondary school. The framework for this values-based program is a set of character-building qualities that are highlighted throughout the School community. Small classes enable students to receive individualized attention, and the School's philosophy fosters personal growth, respect, and a love of learning. FRCDS students reflect a broad spectrum of racial, ethnic, religious, and economic diversity. Faculty and staff strive to bring out the unlimited potential of each student and encourage them to recognize abilities in each other. Professional development encourages teachers to continue learning and to integrate new ideas into their curriculum. Faculty members, together with students and dedicated parents, create a sense of community where it is safe to grow, to be challenged, and to discover the joy of learning. A campus visit is encouraged. For more information, call 847-888-7920, e-mail admissions@frcds.org, or visit www.frcds.org.

THE GREENWOOD SCHOOL

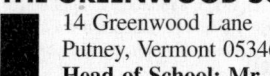

14 Greenwood Lane
Putney, Vermont 05346
Head of School: Mr. Stewart Miller

General Information Boys' boarding arts, drama, and music school; primarily serves underachievers, students with learning disabilities, individuals with Attention Deficit Disorder, and dyslexic students. Ungraded, ages 10–15. Founded: 1978. Setting: rural. Nearest major city is Boston, MA. Students are housed in single-sex dormitories. 100-acre campus. 6 buildings on campus. Approved or accredited by New England Association of Schools and Colleges, The Association of Boarding Schools, and Vermont Department of Education. Member of National Association of Independent Schools. Endowment: $1 million. Total enrollment: 40. Upper school faculty-student ratio: 1:2.

Student Profile 100% of students are boarding students. 20% are state residents. 14 states are represented in upper school student body. 9% are international students. International students from Bermuda and Japan.

Faculty School total: 20. In upper school: 11 men, 7 women; 5 have advanced degrees; 13 reside on campus.

Subjects Offered American history, American literature, art, biology, crafts, creative writing, drama, earth science, ecology, English, geography, grammar, history, mathematics, music, physical education, speech, theater, woodworking, writing.

Special Academic Programs Academic accommodation for the gifted, the musically talented, and the artistically talented; remedial reading and/or remedial writing; remedial math; programs in English, mathematics, general development for dyslexic students.

Secondary School Placement 13 students graduated in 2005; they went to The Forman School; The Gow School; Vermont Academy.

Student Life Specified standards of dress, student council, honor system. Discipline rests primarily with faculty.

Tuition and Aid 7-day tuition and room/board: $46,950. Tuition installment plan (monthly payment plans, individually arranged payment plans). Need-based scholarship grants available. In 2005–06, 10% of students received aid. Total amount of financial aid awarded in 2005–06: $47,000.

Admissions Traditional entrance age is 12. For fall 2005, 20 students applied for admission, 15 were accepted, 13 enrolled. Wechsler Intelligence Scale for Children III or Woodcock-Johnson Revised Achievement Test required. Deadline for receipt of application materials: none. Application fee required: $75. On-campus interview required.

Athletics Interscholastic: baseball (boys), basketball (b), soccer (b); intramural: alpine skiing (b), archery (b), back packing (b), badminton (b), bicycling (b), canoeing/kayaking (b), fishing (b), lacrosse (b), martial arts (b), rock climbing (b), skateboarding (b), skiing (cross-country) (b), skiing (downhill) (b), snowboarding (b). 2 PE instructors, 4 coaches.

Computers Computers are regularly used in English, mathematics classes. Computer network features include campus e-mail, on-campus library services, CD-ROMs, Internet access.

Contact Stewart Miller, Headmaster. 802-387-4545 Ext. 115. Fax: 802-387-5396. E-mail: smiller@greenwood.org. Web site: www.greenwood.org.

See full description on page 1282.

HAMPSHIRE COUNTRY SCHOOL

28 Patey Circle
Rindge, New Hampshire 03461
Head of School: William Dickerman

General Information Boys' boarding college-preparatory and general academic school; primarily serves underachievers, individuals with Attention Deficit Disorder, and students with non-verbal learning disabilities and Asperger's Syndrome. Grades 3–12. Founded: 1948. Setting: rural. Nearest major city is Boston, MA. Students are housed in single-sex dormitories. 1,700-acre campus. 7 buildings on campus. Approved or accredited by New England Association of Schools and Colleges, The Association of Boarding Schools, and New Hampshire Department of Education. Member of National Association of Independent Schools. Total enrollment: 22. Upper school average class size: 4. Upper school faculty-student ratio: 1:4.

Student Profile Grade 7: 4 students (4 boys); Grade 8: 3 students (3 boys); Grade 9: 4 students (4 boys); Grade 10: 4 students (4 boys); Grade 12: 1 student (1 boy). 100% of students are boarding students. 11 states are represented in upper school student body.

Faculty School total: 7. In upper school: 4 men, 3 women; 2 have advanced degrees; all reside on campus.

Subjects Offered Algebra, American history, American literature, ancient history, biology, chemistry, creative writing, earth science, English, English literature, environmental science, expository writing, geography, geometry, German, history, human anatomy, language arts, mathematics, physical science, science, social studies, world history, world literature, writing.

Graduation Requirements English, language arts, mathematics, science, social studies (includes history).

Student Life Specified standards of dress. Discipline rests primarily with faculty.

Tuition and Aid 7-day tuition and room/board: $39,000.

Admissions Traditional entrance grade is 7. For fall 2005, 15 students applied for admission, 5 were accepted, 3 enrolled. Individual IQ required. Deadline for receipt of application materials: none. No application fee required. On-campus interview required.

Athletics Intramural: alpine skiing, back packing, basketball, bicycling, canoeing/kayaking, cooperative games, croquet, deck hockey, fishing, fitness walking, flag football, floor hockey, hiking/backpacking, ice skating, kickball, outdoor activities, outdoor recreation, skiing (downhill), snowshoeing, soccer, softball, tennis, touch football, volleyball, walking, winter walking.

Computers Computers are regularly used in writing classes.

Contact William Dickerman, Headmaster. 603-899-3325. Fax: 603-899-6521. E-mail: hampshirecountry@monad.net. Web site: www.hampshirecountryschool.org.

ANNOUNCEMENT FROM THE SCHOOL At Hampshire Country School, a small, nurturing, well-structured boarding school, the hours outside of class are at least as important as the hours of direct classroom instruction. Afternoons and weekends are filled with well-planned activities and even the hours of relaxation and play are comfortably guided and supervised by residential faculty. Unscheduled hours are filled with outdoor play, strategy board games, informal conversation, and attention to household chores and other responsibilities. Each dorm group of about 6 students has its own living area and full-time dorm parent. The emphasis on out-of-class life is important because of the particular students who attend the school. Most have numerous scholastic strengths but these are combined with problems adapting to other people and managing the frustrations of daily life. Some students seem different from others their age because of their unusually high intellectual abilities, narrow interests, or social sensitivies. Many have received diagnoses such as Asperger's Syndrome, Nonverbal Learning Disabilities, or ADHD. Many have been unable to make friends. Some have been excluded from clubs or teams at larger schools. Many have substituted extensive reading or excessive hours on a computer for interaction with other people. Some students have received help through social skills training and other services, but such help has been only a small substitute for the learning and confidence that can come from living among peers and adults who admire their intellect, share their interests, and are not seriously bothered by their idiosyncrasies and difficulties. Hampshire Country School is designed primarily to help students who are 10 to 15 years old successfully navigate the difficult middle school years; but students as young as 8 years of age may enroll and/or remain through high school graduation.

HILLSIDE SCHOOL

Robin Hill Road
Marlborough, Massachusetts 01752
Head of School: David Z. Beecher

General Information Boys' boarding and day college-preparatory school. Grades 5–9. Founded: 1901. Setting: small town. Nearest major city is Boston. Students are housed in single-sex dormitories. 200-acre campus. 15 buildings on campus. Approved or accredited by Association of Independent Schools in New England, Junior Boarding Schools Association, New England Association of Schools and

Colleges, The Association of Boarding Schools, and Massachusetts Department of Education. Member of National Association of Independent Schools and Secondary School Admission Test Board. Endowment: $6 million. Total enrollment: 131. Upper school average class size: 10. Upper school faculty-student ratio: 1:4.

Student Profile Grade 6: 17 students (17 boys); Grade 7: 35 students (35 boys); Grade 8: 40 students (40 boys); Grade 9: 31 students (31 boys). 70% of students are boarding students. 60% are state residents. 10 states are represented in upper school student body. 10% are international students. International students from Brazil, British Virgin Islands, Mexico, Nigeria, Republic of Korea, and Saudi Arabia; 5 other countries represented in student body.

Faculty School total: 30. In upper school: 18 men, 9 women; 10 have advanced degrees; 24 reside on campus.

Subjects Offered Algebra, American government, American history, ancient history, art, computer applications, creative writing, earth science, economics, English, English literature, environmental science, ESL, French, geography, geometry, international relations, leadership skills, life science, mathematics, music, physical education, science, social skills, social studies, Spanish, woodworking, writing.

Graduation Requirements English, foreign language, mathematics, science, social studies (includes history).

Special Academic Programs Academic accommodation for the gifted; remedial reading and/or remedial writing; remedial math; programs in general development for dyslexic students; special instructional classes for students with Attention Deficit Disorder, Attention Deficit Hyperactivity Disorder, and slight dyslexia; ESL (10 students enrolled).

Secondary School Placement 25 students graduated in 2005; they went to Brewster Academy; Dublin School; The Cambridge School of Weston; Vermont Academy; Wilbraham & Monson Academy.

Student Life Specified standards of dress, student council, honor system. Discipline rests primarily with faculty. Attendance at religious services is required.

Summer Programs Remediation, enrichment, advancement, ESL, sports, art/fine arts, rigorous outdoor training, computer instruction programs offered; session focuses on academics, soccer, hockey, outdoor skills, and a farm program; held on campus; accepts boys and girls; open to students from other schools. 40 students usually enrolled. 2006 schedule: July 9 to August 4. Application deadline: none.

Tuition and Aid Day student tuition: $22,800; 5-day tuition and room/board: $36,400; 7-day tuition and room/board: $39,900. Tuition installment plan (Insured Tuition Payment Plan, SMART Tuition Payment Plan, monthly payment plans). Need-based scholarship grants available. In 2005–06, 31% of students received aid. Total amount of financial aid awarded in 2005–06: $600,000.

Admissions Traditional entrance grade is 7. For fall 2005, 95 students applied for admission, 72 were accepted, 43 enrolled. Any standardized test or WISC-III and Woodcock-Johnson required. Deadline for receipt of application materials: none. Application fee required: $50. Interview required.

Athletics Interscholastic: baseball, basketball, cross-country running, golf, hockey, ice hockey, lacrosse, running, soccer, track and field, wrestling; intramural: alpine skiing, basketball, billiards, canoeing/kayaking, climbing, deck hockey, fishing, fitness, fitness walking, flag football, floor hockey, football, Frisbee, golf, hiking/backpacking, ice skating, indoor hockey, juggling, lacrosse, mountain biking, outdoor activities, outdoor adventure, outdoor education, outdoor skills, physical training, rock climbing, ropes courses, running, sailing, skiing (downhill), snowboarding, soccer, swimming and diving, table tennis, tennis, touch football, volleyball, walking, weight training, whiffle ball, yoga.

Computers Computers are regularly used in all academic, art, music classes. Computer network features include campus e-mail, on-campus library services, CD-ROMs, Internet access.

Contact Tom O'Dell, Director of Admissions. 508-485-2824. Fax: 508-485-4420. E-mail: todell@hillsideschool.net. Web site: hillsideschool.net.

ANNOUNCEMENT FROM THE SCHOOL The Hillside School recently embarked on a multimillion-dollar campus expansion project. The first phase is complete, with the opening of the new student center/tutorial center/dining room/administration building; a new baseball field, tennis court, and swimming pool; and the Saran-Messman Library. A new dorm is now ready for occupancy. The School's proximity to Boston, superior faculty, and structured learning program remain key to its success.

See full description on page 1284.

INDIAN MOUNTAIN SCHOOL

211 Indian Mountain Road
Lakeville, Connecticut 06039
Head of School: C. Dary Dunham

General Information Coeducational boarding and day college-preparatory, general academic, arts, and ESL school. Boarding grades 6–9, day grades PK–9. Founded: 1922. Setting: rural. Nearest major city is Hartford. Students are housed in single-sex dormitories. 600-acre campus. 12 buildings on campus. Approved or accredited by Connecticut Association of Independent Schools, The Association of Boarding Schools, and Connecticut Department of Education. Member of National Association

of Independent Schools and Secondary School Admission Test Board. Endowment: $4.5 million. Total enrollment: 262. Upper school average class size: 11. Upper school faculty-student ratio: 1:4.

Student Profile Grade 7: 44 students (23 boys, 21 girls); Grade 8: 62 students (36 boys, 26 girls); Grade 9: 39 students (27 boys, 12 girls). 50% of students are boarding students. 42% are state residents. 17 states are represented in upper school student body. 15% are international students. International students from Colombia, Haiti, Hong Kong, Mexico, Republic of Korea, and Spain; 1 other country represented in student body.

Faculty School total: 64. In upper school: 27 men, 37 women; 20 have advanced degrees; 26 reside on campus.

Subjects Offered Algebra, American history, ancient history, art, biology, ceramics, computers, earth science, English, fine arts, French, general science, geometry, health, history, Latin, mathematics, music, physical science, social studies, Spanish, theater.

Graduation Requirements Arts and fine arts (art, music, dance, drama), English, foreign language, mathematics, music, science, social studies (includes history).

Special Academic Programs Honors section; ESL (8 students enrolled).

Secondary School Placement 38 students graduated in 2005; they went to Berkshire School; Choate Rosemary Hall; Millbrook School; Salisbury School; Suffield Academy; The Hotchkiss School.

Student Life Specified standards of dress, student council, honor system. Discipline rests primarily with faculty.

Tuition and Aid Day student tuition: $16,880; 7-day tuition and room/board: $31,395. Tuition installment plan (Key Tuition Payment Plan). Need-based scholarship grants available. In 2005–06, 21% of students received aid. Total amount of financial aid awarded in 2005–06: $596,189.

Admissions Traditional entrance grade is 7. For fall 2005, 118 students applied for admission, 72 were accepted, 49 enrolled. WISC-III and Woodcock-Johnson or WISC/Woodcock-Johnson required. Deadline for receipt of application materials: none. Application fee required: $45. On-campus interview required.

Athletics Interscholastic: basketball (boys, girls), football (b), ice hockey (b), lacrosse (b,g), soccer (b,g), softball (g); coed interscholastic: alpine skiing, baseball, cross-country running, ice hockey, outdoor adventure, skiing (downhill), tennis, volleyball; coed intramural: alpine skiing, back packing, skiing (downhill), tennis.

Computers Computers are regularly used in English, history, science, social studies classes. Computer network features include campus e-mail, on-campus library services, CD-ROMs, Internet access, file transfer, office computer access.

Contact Mrs. Mimi L. Babcock, Director of Admission. 860-435-0871. Fax: 860-435-1380. E-mail: admissions@indianmountain.org. Web site: www. indianmountain.org.

See full description on page 1286.

LINDEN HILL SCHOOL

154 South Mountain Road
Northfield, Massachusetts 01360-9681
Head of School: Mr. James Allen McDaniel

General Information Boys' boarding college-preparatory, general academic, technology, and ESL school; primarily serves underachievers, students with learning disabilities, individuals with Attention Deficit Disorder, dyslexic students, and students with language-based learning differences. Grades 3–9. Founded: 1961. Setting: rural. Nearest major city is Springfield. Students are housed in single-sex dormitories. 200-acre campus. 15 buildings on campus. Approved or accredited by Association of Independent Schools in New England, Junior Boarding Schools Association, Massachusetts Office of Child Care Services, New England Association of Schools and Colleges, and The Association of Boarding Schools. Member of National Association of Independent Schools. Language of instruction: English. Total enrollment: 15. Upper school average class size: 4. Upper school faculty-student ratio: 1:3.

Faculty School total: 13. In upper school: 6 men, 3 women; 5 have advanced degrees; 5 reside on campus.

Subjects Offered Arts, character education, English, ESL, experiential education, freshman seminar, general science, history, industrial arts, instrumental music, lab science, language and composition, language development, leadership and service, life skills, mathematics, outdoor education, strategies for success, woodworking, writing skills.

Special Academic Programs ESL (6 students enrolled).

Secondary School Placement 4 students graduated in 2004; they went to The Forman School; The Gow School.

Student Life Specified standards of dress. Discipline rests primarily with faculty. Attendance at religious services is required.

Tuition and Aid 7-day tuition and room/board: $38,900. Tuition installment plan (FACTS Tuition Payment Plan). Need-based scholarship grants available. In 2004–05, 25% of students received aid. Total amount of financial aid awarded in 2004–05: $75,000.

Admissions Achievement tests, Wechsler Intelligence Scale for Children III or writing sample required. Deadline for receipt of application materials: none. Application fee required: $50. On-campus interview required.

Athletics Interscholastic: basketball; intramural: alpine skiing, back packing, basketball, bicycling, blading, bowling, climbing, cooperative games, cross-country running, fishing, golf, ice skating, outdoor activities, outdoor recreation, running, skiing (downhill), snowboarding, soccer, softball, swimming and diving, wall climbing, wrestling.

Computers Computer network features include campus e-mail, CD-ROMs, Internet access, office computer access.

Contact Patricia K. Sanieski, Academic Dean. 413-498-2906. Fax: 413-498-2908. E-mail: pksanieski@lindenhs.org. Web site: www.lindenhs.org.

See full description on page 1288.

NORTH COUNTRY SCHOOL

PO Box 187
Cascade Road
Lake Placid, New York 12946
Head of School: David Hochschartner

General Information Coeducational boarding and day college-preparatory, general academic, and arts school. Grades 4–9. Founded: 1938. Setting: rural. Nearest major city is Albany. Students are housed in residential houses. 200-acre campus. 10 buildings on campus. Approved or accredited by New York State Association of Independent Schools and New York Department of Education. Member of National Association of Independent Schools and Secondary School Admission Test Board. Endowment: $6 million. Total enrollment: 75. Upper school average class size: 12. Upper school faculty-student ratio: 1:3.

Student Profile Grade 6: 8 students (1 boy, 7 girls); Grade 7: 22 students (14 boys, 8 girls); Grade 8: 26 students (18 boys, 8 girls); Grade 9: 15 students (9 boys, 6 girls). 95% of students are boarding students. 30% are state residents. 17 states are represented in upper school student body. 17% are international students.

Faculty School total: 33. In upper school: 13 men, 20 women; 9 have advanced degrees; 20 reside on campus.

Subjects Offered Algebra, American history, biology, ceramics, computer science, creative writing, earth science, English, mathematics, music, performing arts, photography, physical education, social studies, Spanish, studio art.

Special Academic Programs Remedial reading and/or remedial writing; remedial math; ESL (10 students enrolled).

Secondary School Placement 15 students graduated in 2005; they went to Gould Academy; Northwood School; The Williston Northampton School; Vermont Academy.

Student Life Specified standards of dress, student council. Discipline rests primarily with faculty.

Summer Programs Session focuses on recreation, arts, ESL, and outdoor programs; held on campus; accepts boys and girls; open to students from other schools. 150 students usually enrolled. 2006 schedule: July 1 to August 19. Application deadline: none.

Tuition and Aid Day student tuition: $14,200; 5-day tuition and room/board: $24,950; 7-day tuition and room/board: $38,300. Tuition installment plan (monthly payment plans, individually arranged payment plans, 2-payment plan). Need-based scholarship grants available. Total amount of financial aid awarded in 2005–06: $200,000.

Admissions Deadline for receipt of application materials: none. No application fee required. On-campus interview required.

Athletics Coed Interscholastic: aerobics/dance, alpine skiing, artistic gym, bicycling, climbing, curling, drill team, field hockey, fishing, Frisbee, hiking/backpacking, horseback riding, lacrosse, modern dance, mountain biking, mountaineering, nordic skiing, outdoor activities, outdoor adventure, outdoor education, outdoor recreation, outdoor skills, rappelling, rock climbing, skateboarding, ski jumping, skiing (cross-country), skiing (downhill), snowboarding, snowshoeing, swimming and diving, telemark skiing, volleyball, walking, wall climbing, wilderness survival, yoga; coed intramural: basketball, skiing (cross-country), skiing (downhill), soccer.

Computers Computer resources include campus e-mail, on-campus library services, Internet access.

Contact Christine LeFevre, Director of Admissions. 518-523-9329. Fax: 518-523-4858. E-mail: admissions@nct.org. Web site: www.nct.org/.

See full description on page 1290.

THE RECTORY SCHOOL

528 Pomfret Street
Pomfret, Connecticut 06258
Head of School: Thomas F. Army

General Information Boys' boarding and coeducational day college-preparatory, general academic, arts, and technology school, affiliated with Episcopal Church; primarily serves underachievers. Boarding boys grades 5–9, day boys grades 5–9, day girls grades 5–9. Founded: 1920. Setting: rural. Nearest major city is Hartford. Students are housed in single-sex dormitories. 135-acre campus. 20 buildings on campus. Approved or accredited by Connecticut Association of Independent Schools,

Junior Boarding Schools Association, and The Association of Boarding Schools. Member of National Association of Independent Schools and Secondary School Admission Test Board. Endowment: $9.7 million. Total enrollment: 169. Upper school average class size: 11. Upper school faculty-student ratio: 1:3.

Student Profile Grade 6: 18 students (10 boys, 8 girls); Grade 7: 38 students (30 boys, 8 girls); Grade 8: 59 students (52 boys, 7 girls); Grade 9: 35 students (34 boys, 1 girl). 63% of students are boarding students. 38% are state residents. 19 states are represented in upper school student body. 18% are international students. International students from Bermuda, Haiti, Hong Kong, Mexico, Republic of Korea, and Taiwan; 2 other countries represented in student body. 11% of students are members of Episcopal Church.

Faculty School total: 51. In upper school: 21 men, 30 women; 23 have advanced degrees; 30 reside on campus.

Subjects Offered Algebra, American history, American literature, ancient world history, art, biology, chorus, computer math, computer science, creative arts, creative writing, drama, earth science, ecology, English, English as a foreign language, English literature, environmental science, European history, expository writing, fine arts, foreign language, general science, geography, geometry, grammar, history, journalism, Latin, life science, mathematics, medieval history, medieval/Renaissance history, music, photography, physical education, physical science, reading, science, social studies, Spanish, study skills, theater, vocal music, world history, world literature, writing.

Graduation Requirements Arts and fine arts (art, music, dance, drama), English, mathematics, physical education (includes health), science, social studies (includes history).

Special Academic Programs Honors section; academic accommodation for the gifted; remedial reading and/or remedial writing; remedial math; programs in English, mathematics, general development for dyslexic students; special instructional classes for students with learning disabilities, Attention Deficit Disorder, and dyslexia; ESL (2 students enrolled).

Secondary School Placement 48 students graduated in 2005; they went to Pomfret School; Tabor College.

Student Life Specified standards of dress, student council, honor system. Discipline rests primarily with faculty. Attendance at religious services is required.

Summer Programs Remediation, enrichment, ESL, sports, art/fine arts programs offered; session focuses on study skills; held on campus; accepts boys and girls; open to students from other schools. 45 students usually enrolled. 2006 schedule: June 25 to July 29. Application deadline: none.

Tuition and Aid Day student tuition: $14,100–$16,000; 7-day tuition and room/board: $31,900. Tuition installment plan (Key Tuition Payment Plan). Need-based scholarship grants available. In 2005–06, 21% of students received aid. Total amount of financial aid awarded in 2005–06: $677,700.

Admissions Traditional entrance grade is 7. For fall 2005, 152 students applied for admission, 120 were accepted, 71 enrolled. Wechsler Intelligence Scale for Children III required. Deadline for receipt of application materials: none. Application fee required: $50. On-campus interview required.

Athletics Interscholastic: baseball (boys), basketball (b,g), cross-country running (b,g), fencing (b), football (b), ice hockey (b), lacrosse (b), soccer (b,g), softball (g), wrestling (b); intramural: basketball (b,g), football (b), lacrosse (b), rugby (b), soccer (b), softball (b), street hockey (b), strength & conditioning (b), touch football (b), weight training (b), whiffle ball (b), wrestling (b); coed interscholastic: golf, hockey, ice hockey, soccer, tennis, track and field; coed intramural: ball hockey, basketball, bowling, canoeing/kayaking, cross-country running, fishing, fitness, fly fishing, Frisbee, golf, horseback riding, ice hockey, ice skating, lacrosse, life saving, martial arts, mountain biking, nautilus, outdoor adventure, outdoor recreation, roller blading, ropes courses, running, skateboarding, skiing (cross-country), skiing (downhill), snowboarding, soccer, softball, squash, street hockey, swimming and diving, table tennis, tai chi, tennis, ultimate Frisbee, volleyball, whiffle ball. 2 trainers.

Computers Computers are regularly used in English, history, mathematics, music, science, writing classes. Computer network features include campus e-mail, on-campus library services, CD-ROMs, online commercial services, Internet access, DVD.

Contact Stephen A. DiPaolo, Director of Admission. 860-928-1328. Fax: 860-928-4961. E-mail: admissions@rectoryschool.org. Web site: www.rectoryschool.org.

See full description on page 1292.

RUMSEY HALL SCHOOL

201 Romford Road
Washington Depot, Connecticut 06794
Head of School: Thomas W. Farmen

General Information Coeducational boarding and day college-preparatory, general academic, and arts school. Boarding grades 5–9, day grades K–9. Founded: 1900. Setting: rural. Nearest major city is Hartford. Students are housed in single-sex dormitories. 147-acre campus. 29 buildings on campus. Approved or accredited by Connecticut Association of Independent Schools, National Independent Private Schools Association, The Association of Boarding Schools, and Connecticut Department of Education. Member of National Association of Independent Schools and

Secondary School Admission Test Board. Endowment: $2.5 million. Total enrollment: 307. Upper school average class size: 13. Upper school faculty-student ratio: 1:8.

Student Profile Grade 6: 31 students (25 boys, 6 girls); Grade 7: 49 students (33 boys, 16 girls); Grade 8: 68 students (46 boys, 22 girls); Grade 9: 57 students (36 boys, 21 girls). 50% of students are boarding students. 50% are state residents. 19 states are represented in upper school student body. 10% are international students. International students from Bahamas, Bermuda, Hong Kong, Japan, Mexico, and Republic of Korea; 6 other countries represented in student body.

Faculty School total: 53. In upper school: 25 men, 26 women; 25 have advanced degrees; 30 reside on campus.

Subjects Offered Algebra, American history, American literature, art, art history, biology, computer science, creative writing, drama, earth science, English, English literature, environmental science, ESL, European history, fine arts, French, geography, geometry, government/civics, grammar, health, history, Japanese history, Latin, mathematics, music, physical education, science, social studies, Spanish, theater, world history, writing.

Graduation Requirements Arts and fine arts (art, music, dance, drama), computer science, English, foreign language, mathematics, physical education (includes health), science, social studies (includes history).

Special Academic Programs Honors section; academic accommodation for the gifted; remedial reading and/or remedial writing; programs in English for dyslexic students; special instructional classes for students with learning disabilities and Attention Deficit Disorder; ESL (14 students enrolled).

Secondary School Placement 59 students graduated in 2005; they went to Choate Rosemary Hall; Kent School; St. George's School; Suffield Academy; The Gunnery; The Taft School.

Student Life Specified standards of dress, student council, honor system. Discipline rests primarily with faculty.

Summer Programs Enrichment, ESL programs offered; session focuses on academic enrichment; held on campus; accepts boys and girls; open to students from other schools. 60 students usually enrolled. 2006 schedule: June 25 to July 30. Application deadline: May 1.

Tuition and Aid Day student tuition: $15,550; 7-day tuition and room/board: $32,500. Tuition installment plan (Insured Tuition Payment Plan, Key Tuition Payment Plan, monthly payment plans, individually arranged payment plans). Need-based scholarship grants, need-based loans available. In 2005–06, 24% of students received aid. Total amount of financial aid awarded in 2005–06: $650,750.

Admissions Traditional entrance grade is 8. For fall 2005, 220 students applied for admission, 131 were accepted, 106 enrolled. ERB, Iowa Tests of Basic Skills, psychoeducational evaluation, SLEP, SSAT, TOEFL, Wechsler Intelligence Scale for Children III or writing sample required. Deadline for receipt of application materials: none. Application fee required: $40. On-campus interview required.

Athletics Interscholastic: baseball (boys), basketball (b,g), field hockey (g), football (b), lacrosse (b), softball (g), volleyball (g), wrestling (b); coed interscholastic: alpine skiing, crew, cross-country running, equestrian sports, horseback riding, ice hockey, skiing (downhill), soccer, tennis; coed intramural: alpine skiing, back packing, bicycling, canoeing/kayaking, fly fishing, Frisbee, golf, hiking/backpacking, ice skating, mountain biking, outdoor activities, outdoor adventure, outdoor education, outdoor recreation, outdoor skills, outdoors, physical fitness, physical training, project adventure, roller blading, running, skateboarding, skiing (downhill), snowboarding, street hockey, strength & conditioning, table tennis, tennis, track and field, ultimate Frisbee, weight lifting, weight training, whiffle ball, wilderness, wilderness survival, wildernessways. 1 PE instructor, 28 coaches, 1 trainer.

Computers Computers are regularly used in English, history, mathematics, science classes. Computer network features include campus e-mail, CD-ROMs, online commercial services, Internet access.

Contact Matthew S. Hoeniger, Assistant Headmaster. 860-868-0535. Fax: 860-868-7907. E-mail: admiss@rumseyhall.org. Web site: www.rumseyhall.org.

See full description on page 1294.

ST. CATHERINE'S MILITARY ACADEMY

215 North Harbor Boulevard
Anaheim, California 92805
Head of School: Sr. Mary Menegatti

petersons.com

General Information Boys' boarding and day college-preparatory and general academic school, affiliated with Roman Catholic Church. Boarding grades 3–8, day grades K–8. Founded: 1889. Setting: suburban. Students are housed in single-sex dormitories. 8-acre campus. 8 buildings on campus. Approved or accredited by National Catholic Education Association, Western Association of Schools and Colleges, and California Department of Education. Language of instruction: English. Total enrollment: 160. Upper school average class size: 19. Upper school faculty-student ratio: 1:12.

Student Profile Grade 6: 20 students (20 boys); Grade 7: 30 students (30 boys); Grade 8: 40 students (40 boys). 35% of students are boarding students. 75% are state residents. 3 states are represented in upper school student body. 15% are international students. International students from China, Hong Kong, Mexico, Philippines, Taiwan, and Thailand; 1 other country represented in student body. 70% of students are Roman Catholic.

Faculty School total: 15. In upper school: 3 men, 7 women; 3 have advanced degrees; 2 reside on campus.

Subjects Offered Art, computer science, English, fine arts, history, mathematics, music, physical education, religion, science, social studies.

Graduation Requirements Arts and fine arts (art, music, dance, drama), computer science, English, foreign language, mathematics, physical education (includes health), religion (includes Bible studies and theology), science, social studies (includes history).

Special Academic Programs Special instructional classes for students with Attention Deficit Disorder and learning disabilities; ESL (14 students enrolled).

Secondary School Placement 40 students graduated in 2004; they went to Army and Navy Academy; Mater Dei High School; New Mexico Military Institute; Servite High School.

Student Life Uniform requirement, honor system. Discipline rests primarily with faculty. Attendance at religious services is required.

Tuition and Aid Day student tuition: $8280; 5-day tuition and room/board: $21,930; 7-day tuition and room/board: $27,930. Tuition installment plan (FACTS Tuition Payment Plan). Need-based scholarship grants available. In 2004–05, 20% of students received aid. Total amount of financial aid awarded in 2004–05: $93,000.

Admissions Traditional entrance grade is 7. For fall 2005, 108 students applied for admission, 77 were accepted, 69 enrolled. Iowa Tests of Basic Skills required. Deadline for receipt of application materials: none. Application fee required: $150. Interview required.

Athletics Interscholastic: basketball, flag football, volleyball; intramural: ball hockey, basketball, bowling, cross-country running, drill team, equestrian sports, field hockey, fitness, flag football, handball, soccer, softball, swimming and diving, track and field, volleyball, water volleyball, weight lifting. 1 PE instructor, 7 coaches.

Computers Computers are regularly used in English, history, science, social studies classes. Computer network features include CD-ROMs, Internet access.

Contact Mrs. Angelique Norton, Director of Admissions. 714-772-1363 Ext. 103. Fax: 714-772-3004. E-mail: admissions@stcatherinesmilitary.com. Web site: www. stcatherinesmilitary.com.

ANNOUNCEMENT FROM THE SCHOOL St. Catherine's Military Academy, in Anaheim, California, has been addressing the needs of boys from kindergarten through grade 8 for over 116 years. Operated by the Dominican Sisters of Mission San Jose, SCMA is a Catholic school with a military tradition. The academic standards set by SCMA attract students from throughout the United States. A rigorous English as a second language (ESL) program has been successfully developed, attracting international students from all over the world. The overall student-instructor ratio is approximately 14:1. In addition to the standard academic subjects, religion, art, music, physical education, and computers are required classes for all grade levels. Technology is an important component of SCMA curriculum as is instruction in music. Piano and guitar are offered to students beginning in grade 3, and participation in the marching band is open to cadets in grades 4 through 8. Students will get a sense of St. Catherine's military program in all aspects of campus life. Self-discipline and respect for oneself and others are emphasized. Leadership training and goal setting, as well as marching, are part of a daily 40-minute military class. SCMA has dormitories in its residential program, each supervised by a Dominican Sister. Resident cadets range in age from 9 to 14; boys younger than 9 are considered on a case-by-case basis. The Academy offers a nurturing and caring environment through the Dominican Sisters' 116-year commitment to discipline-, responsibility-, and self-esteem-building through the military program; tolerance and diversity through religious formation; and the drive for academic excellence from the entire staff and faculty. St. Catherine's looks for students whose character and potential will contribute positively to the ideals of the Academy. *The prescription for success is forming young men of valor, one boy at a time.* St. Catherine's Military Academy is accredited by the Western Association of Schools and Colleges (WASC) and the Western Catholic Education Association (WCEA). SCMA has open enrollment throughout the year.

ST. THOMAS CHOIR SCHOOL

202 West 58th Street
New York, New York 10019-1406
Head of School: Rev. Charles Wallace

General Information Boys' boarding college-preparatory, general academic, arts, religious studies, technology, and music school, affiliated with Episcopal Church. Grades 4–8. Founded: 1919. Setting: urban. Students are housed in single-sex dormitories. 1 building on campus. Approved or accredited by Junior Boarding Schools Association, National Association of Episcopal Schools, New York State Association of Independent Schools, The Association of Boarding Schools, and New York Department of Education. Member of National Association of Independent Schools and Secondary School Admission Test Board. Endowment: $18 million. Total enrollment: 31. Upper school average class size: 8. Upper school faculty-student ratio: 1:3.

Student Profile Grade 7: 9 students (9 boys); Grade 8: 6 students (6 boys). 100% of students are boarding students. 47% are state residents. 9 states are represented in upper school student body. 72% of students are members of Episcopal Church.

Faculty School total: 7. In upper school: 5 men, 2 women; 6 have advanced degrees; all reside on campus.

Subjects Offered Algebra, applied music, art, choir, computers, English, French, Greek, history, Latin, mathematics, music theory, physical education, science, study skills, theology, visual arts.

Graduation Requirements Arts and fine arts (art, music, dance, drama), English, foreign language, mathematics, physical education (includes health), religion (includes Bible studies and theology), science, social studies (includes history).

Special Academic Programs Academic accommodation for the gifted and the musically talented; remedial reading and/or remedial writing; remedial math; programs in general development for dyslexic students.

Secondary School Placement 6 students graduated in 2005.

Student Life Uniform requirement. Discipline rests primarily with faculty. Attendance at religious services is required.

Tuition and Aid 7-day tuition and room/board: $9900. Tuition installment plan (individually arranged payment plans). Need-based scholarship grants available. In 2005–06, 84% of students received aid. Total amount of financial aid awarded in 2005–06: $187,950.

Admissions Admissions testing and audition required. Deadline for receipt of application materials: none. No application fee required. On-campus interview required.

Athletics Interscholastic: basketball, soccer, softball; intramural: baseball, basketball, fitness, flag football, floor hockey, independent competitive sports, indoor hockey, indoor soccer, kickball, lacrosse, Newcombe ball, outdoor recreation, physical fitness, running, soccer, softball, strength & conditioning, table tennis, track and field, ultimate Frisbee, volleyball, weight training, whiffle ball, yoga. 1 PE instructor.

Computers Computers are regularly used in art, English, foreign language, history, library, mathematics, music, science classes. Computer network features include campus e-mail, on-campus library services, CD-ROMs, online commercial services, Internet access.

Contact Ms. Fazeela Bacchus, Finance and Admissions Associate. 212-247-3311 Ext. 303. Fax: 212-247-3393. E-mail: admissions@choirschool.org. Web site: www.choirschool.org.

THE BEMENT SCHOOL

Deerfield, Massachusetts

Type: Coeducational, day (kindergarten–grade 9) and boarding (grades 3–9), general academic school
Grades: K–9: Lower School, kindergarten–5; Upper School, 6–9
Enrollment: School total: 255; Upper School: 125; Lower School: 130
Head of School: Shelley Borror Jackson

THE SCHOOL

The Bement School began in 1925 when Grace Bement agreed to a request made by Headmaster Frank Boyden of Deerfield Academy to tutor one of his students. The School grew as word spread of her effective teaching. Between 1947 and 1971, Bement was incorporated and further expanded under the direction of Katherine Bartlett and Mary Drexler. Peter Drake led the School from 1985 to 1999, during which time the School expanded its physical plant, doubled the size of its student body, and enhanced its reputation nationally and internationally.

The 12-acre campus is in historic Deerfield, an area steeped in history. Bement's proximity to five area colleges also provides a variety of learning opportunities.

The Bement School offers an education based on proven values. The pervasive atmosphere instills an understanding of the kinship of all humankind, and the School actively seeks an internationally and culturally diverse student body. The academic potential of Bement students represents a range of abilities. Adults at Bement work together to create a community that is guided by mutual respect, kindness, and honesty. The School nurtures each child's creative, academic, and emotional growth within a structured and supportive setting.

Bement is governed by a board of trustees. Alumni maintain an active role, some serving on the board in support of activities within the Alumni Association.

The Bement School is a member of the National Association of Independent Schools, the Association of Independent Schools of New England, the Junior Boarding Schools Association, the Educational Records Bureau, and the Elementary School Heads Association.

ACADEMIC PROGRAMS

The Upper School (grades 6–9) curriculum is an academic program emphasizing English, mathematics, science, history, fine arts, and foreign languages. Intermediate and advanced levels of English as a second language (ESL) are also available. Students are encouraged to apply their developing laptop computer skills in a range of courses. Classes typically have from 10 to 15 students. Tutorial help is available from a learning specialist.

Between Thanksgiving vacation and winter break, the entire School participates in a miniterm with a special schedule of courses and electives organized around a theme. The theme changes annually, yet the interdisciplinary format remains the focus of each miniterm.

Teachers evaluate student performance, participation, and effort frequently. The boarding faculty members meet weekly to review the academic and social growth of each boarder. On a triweekly basis, the School sends written comments, which include achievement and effort grades, to parents of both boarding and day students. Students review these reports in private conferences with their advisers. Comprehensive reports are mailed home at the end of each trimester.

Students in grades 7–9 may participate in Bement's cultural exchange program with L'Ermitage School in Maisons-Laffitte, a town 20 kilometers outside of Paris. In alternating years, Bement students travel to France, and their French counterparts spend three weeks at Bement, hosted by day-student families. The exchange is a living study of history, people, culture, architecture, and travel.

The Lower School (kindergarten–grade 5) strives to educate the whole child by challenging each student's intellect, creativity, and physical skills in a nurturing environment. Confidence building is a strong part of the Lower School experience. The program's goal is to instill in each student a respect for nature, mankind, and oneself while developing the skills necessary to become a productive and responsible citizen. Classes range in size from 9 to 12 students.

Teachers evaluate Lower School students' progress in a variety of ways—through conferences with parents in the fall and spring and by written reports twice each trimester. These evaluations review each child's academic progress, effort, personal development, and work habits.

FACULTY AND ADVISERS

The Bement School has 41 faculty members, 1 of whom is part-time. Thirteen live on campus, and 24 hold master's degrees. The average tenure at Bement is about nine years. The student-teacher ratio is 5:1 in the Upper School and 6:1 in the Lower School.

Shelley Borror Jackson was appointed Head of the School in 1999. She earned her Bachelor of Arts degree in English from Wheaton College and holds a Master of Arts degree in English from Ohio State University and a Certificate of Advanced Studies in education and language arts from the University of Maine.

An adviser system, in conjunction with dorm parents, guides the students in both academic and personal areas. Every Friday, Upper School students eat lunch and participate in group activities, community service projects, or a wellness program with their advisers.

Bement seeks to place each student in the appropriate secondary school. Students receive preliminary recommendations for their secondary school during the spring of their eighth-grade year. In the fall of the ninth-grade year, each student, along with parents, meets with the Head, the Assistant Head, and the Director of Secondary School Placement to consider appropriate options and to plan school visits. While the student is given the ultimate responsibility for completing admission materials, these administrators provide guidance and encouragement to ensure that all completed applications are submitted in a timely fashion. Once acceptances have been received, the student and family, with assistance from Bement, decide on the appropriate placement. Some of the schools attended in the last five years include Deerfield Academy, Northfield Mount Hermon, Phillips Exeter Academy, Suffield Academy, Westminster, and Williston-Northhampton.

STUDENT BODY AND CONDUCT

Of the total 2005–06 enrollment of 255, 224 were day students and 31 were boarders. There were 120 boys and 135 girls. Thirteen states and four other countries were represented.

Courtesy and respect for others are practiced in the classroom and throughout the School community, including the athletic fields, where sportsmanship is emphasized. Students learn that personal responsibility, good citizenship, and trust are essential components of their education.

ACADEMIC FACILITIES

The Kittredge Upper School building houses academic classrooms, science laboratories, and locker rooms. The new Clagett-McLennan Library provides the School with an all-school library facility, including two multimedia computer laboratories, an ever-expanding collection, the Grace Bement Reading Room, and a dance studio. Lower School classrooms for kindergarten–grade 2 are located in Keith Schoolhouse. The Drake School Building contains classrooms for grades 3–5 and a computer lab with fifteen Macintosh terminals. Eight mobile Macintosh computers with CD-ROM and thirty laptops are available for use in the classrooms and by faculty members. Internet access is available in each classroom and the library. The fine arts facility is the home of art classrooms, music/chorus rooms, a darkroom, band performance space, and the Barn, which houses a fully functioning stage, an assembly hall, and meeting space.

BOARDING AND GENERAL FACILITIES

Boarding students live, according to gender and age, in one of four houses. Dorm parents, who are carefully selected and often have families of their own, live with the boarders. Dorm parents commit themselves to guiding each boarder's growth as a person as well as encouraging academic achievement. While each dorm has kitchen facilities where students often gather for an after-school snack or a weekend meal, one of the cornerstones of the Bement community is the kitchen and dining hall in Bement House. Dorm parents and teachers head the tables and serve the meals.

When medical treatment is necessary, students are driven to the Deerfield Academy Health

Center, located only a few hundred yards away from Bement. In addition, the Franklin Medical Center in Greenfield is just a short drive away.

ATHLETICS

All students participate daily in some form of sport or physical education throughout the year. The Lower School program develops coordination, game skills, and a general awareness of the importance of physical fitness and sportsmanship. Grades 4 and 5 concentrate on seasonal sports, playing intramural games, and developing sport-specific skills. In the spring, students in kindergarten through grade 5 participate in an instructional swimming program.

Upper School students are involved in a variety of athletic programs suited to their age and interests. In addition to helping each student develop individual talents, coaches emphasize concepts of teamwork and good sportsmanship. During each sports season, both competitive and noncompetitive options are available. In the fall, Bement offers boys' and girls' soccer, field hockey, cross-country, golf, and dance. In the winter, the School uses nearby Deerfield Academy facilities for swimming, squash, boys' and girls' basketball, and ice hockey. The ski team travels to Berkshire East every day for training and racing events, and cross-country skiers take advantage of the New England countryside. Each Wednesday during the winter trimester, Upper School students participate in Alpine or cross-country skiing or snowboarding and have a half day of school and reduced homework that evening. In the spring, Bement offers baseball, boys' and girls' lacrosse, outdoor skills, softball, and track.

EXTRACURRICULAR OPPORTUNITIES

At Bement, students pursue their interests and develop leadership, not only in academics but also in such areas as drama, art, writing, music, and outdoor skills. Students in grades 7–9 and their advisers participate for one term in an intergenerational community service program.

Sixth graders participate in an on-campus community service program.

DAILY LIFE

In the Upper School, each day begins with a School meeting and a silent reading period. This is followed by two academic classes, a 20-minute recess, and two more classes. Lunch, which is served family-style, is followed by a class and a study hall, during which time all teachers are available for extra help. Athletic practice and games are after the academic day.

The Lower School day begins with a group meeting. Students and teachers sing, share announcements, and discuss common concerns and current events. After morning meeting, children disperse to self-contained classrooms where academic classes are taught at various times throughout the day. At noon, everyone reconvenes for Lower School lunch, served family-style with a teacher heading a table of 7 or 8 students.

WEEKEND LIFE

Weekends for boarders are carefully planned in advance by the Dean of Boarding. The social curriculum of each boarder is important, and Bement strives to provide opportunities to interact and grow while experiencing exciting and unique trips and events. Typical weekend activities include trips to points of local interest, sporting events, plays, and movies. Weekly outdoor activities include hiking, bicycle trips, and informal sports contests. Skiing and skating are emphasized when the weather permits.

COSTS AND FINANCIAL AID

For 2005–06, tuition and fees were $10,550 for day students in kindergarten–grade 2; $11,345 for day students in grades 1 and 2; $12,120 for day students in grades 3–5, and $15,415 for day students in grades 6–9. Tuition and fees were $33,970 for all boarding students. Students must have health insurance; if a student is not covered by a family health insurance policy, coverage may be purchased through the School. There is also a

one-time refundable security deposit of $500 for boarding students and $100 for day students.

Parents may indicate on the admissions application a desire to be considered for financial assistance. They will be sent a School and Student Service financial aid form to be completed and sent to the School and Student Service in Princeton, New Jersey. Decisions are based on need and available funds. Twenty-six percent of the student body received aid totaling $302,000 in 2005–06.

ADMISSIONS INFORMATION

Bement School accepts day students for kindergarten–grade 9 and boarding students for grades 3–9. The admissions committee looks for students who are likely to benefit from and contribute to the School. Decisions on admission are based on the candidate's school record, the results of the Wechsler Intelligence Scale for Children (grades 3–9), and a personal visit with the Director of Admission. Preference is given to siblings of current students. The kindergarten admissions process follows different guidelines, and those interested should contact the Admissions Director for details.

APPLICATION TIMETABLE

Inquiries and applications are welcome throughout the year. Upon their completion, boarding student folders are reviewed as part of a rolling admission process. Day students should complete application folders by February 8 in order to participate in the first round of admission decisions; notifications of decisions are mailed in early March. Kindergarten screenings take place in March and April.

ADMISSIONS CORRESPONDENCE

Matthew Evans
Director of Admission
The Bement School
Deerfield, Massachusetts 01342

Phone: 413-774-7061
Fax: 413-774-7863
E-mail: admit@bement.org
Web site: http://www.bement.org

CARDIGAN MOUNTAIN SCHOOL

Canaan, New Hampshire

Type: Boys' day and boarding junior high school
Grades: 6–9
Enrollment: 171
Head of School: Thomas Needham, Headmaster

THE SCHOOL

Cardigan Mountain School was founded in 1945 by 2 men whose vision and belief in their goal were unshakable. Harold P. Hinman, a Dartmouth College graduate, and William R. Brewster, then Headmaster of Kimball Union Academy, joined forces with legendary Dartmouth President Ernest M. Hopkins to obtain the land that is now the site of Cardigan Mountain's campus. Cardigan Mountain School opened with 24 boys, and, in 1954, upon merging with the Clark School of Hanover, New Hampshire, the School as it is known today began to emerge. Since that time, the School has grown to its current enrollment of more than 200 boys, while the philosophy and objectives set forth by the founders have remained unchanged.

Cardigan provides boys with a structured, home-like environment within which mastery of the fundamental academic skills, social and physical growth, and spiritual values can be encouraged.

The 525-acre campus, located on Canaan Street Lake, is 18 miles from Dartmouth College. Driving time from Boston is approximately 2½ hours. Some of the finest skiing in New England is only 1 hour away.

The self-perpetuating Board of Trustees and Incorporators is instrumental in guiding the School. The School's endowment is valued at more than $14.7 million. In 2004–05, Annual Giving was just under $553,161.

Cardigan Mountain is accredited by the New England Association of Schools and Colleges. Its memberships include the National Association of Independent Schools (NAIS), the Junior Boarding Schools Association, the Independent Schools Association of Northern New England (ISANNE), the Association of Independent Schools of New England (AISNE), the Secondary School Admission Test Board (SSATB), Boys' Schools, A Better Chance (ABC), the Federation of American Independent Schools, and the Educational Records Bureau (ERB).

ACADEMIC PROGRAMS

Cardigan's curriculum is designed to both support and challenge the student as he prepares for the academic programs characteristic of most independent secondary schools. In all disciplines, emphasis is placed upon the mastery of fundamental skills, content, and study skills.

The curriculum provides each student with instruction in all major courses and exposes him to a number of other subject areas that round out his education. Cardigan requires all students to take yearlong courses in English, mathematics, science, and social studies. In addition, studying a foreign language (Latin, French, or Spanish) is strongly advised.

Beyond these courses, Cardigan also requires each boy to strengthen his program of study through additional course work in reading and study skills, studio art, woodworking/sculpture and design, music history and appreciation, religion, life skills, and keyboarding.

The average class size ranges from 4 to 15 students, and, within each grade, there is ability tracking. There are normally three levels in each subject

in grades 7, 8, and 9. The extra help and conference period gives students yet another opportunity to work with faculty members on an individual basis.

In addition, a reading and study skills course is required of all students.

The Language Learning Lab is an optional tutorial program for remediation in communication skills, particularly reading and writing. Similarly, Math Lab is an optional tutorial that provides individualized enrichment or remediation in mathematics.

For students for whom English is not the primary language, English as a second language provides instruction in basic English skills.

Cardigan uses a trimester system, and grades and teacher comments are sent home at the middle and end of each of the three terms. Grading includes both achievement marks and an effort rating.

FACULTY AND ADVISERS

The faculty consists of 46 full-time and 5 part-time members, the majority of whom reside on campus. One quarter of the faculty members are women. More than one half of the faculty members have earned advanced academic degrees. All faculty members teach, coach, supervise dormitories, and serve as advisers for the students. Cardigan has a 4:1 student-faculty ratio.

Thomas Needham has been named by the Board of Trustees to serve as Cardigan's seventh Headmaster, succeeding Cameron Dewar, who retired after a fifteen-year tenure at the School. Mr. Needham served as Headmaster at Linden Hall School for Girls since 1998. Prior to that, he was Headmaster of Carroll School from 1989 to 1998 and Pine Ridge School from 1986 to 1989. He earned his B.A. at Eastern Connecticut State University and his M.Ed. from Lesley College. He is a member of a Task Force Committee for the Association of Boarding Schools (TABS) and the Independent Educational Consultants Association (IECA), working out guidelines for the relationship between educational consultants and private boarding schools.

Of the greatest importance to Cardigan are the faculty members who, by setting and attaining personal goals, serve as positive role models for the boys. Cardigan faculty members bring with them a love for learning and a variety of skills, experiences, and talents that broaden and enrich the educational experience and inject warmth and enthusiasm into campus life.

Cardigan offers extensive assistance to the students and their parents in selecting and then applying to independent secondary schools. The Secondary School Placement Office begins the counseling process in the spring of the eighth grade and continues to guide the student and his family throughout the application experience. The Placement Office offers workshops on interviewing techniques, SSAT preparation, and essay writing.

Over the past few years, a number of Cardigan graduates have matriculated to schools such as Avon Old Farms, Brooks, Deerfield, Holderness, Hotchkiss, Lawrence, Phillips Andover, Phillips Exeter, Pomfret, Salisbury, St. Mark's, St. Paul's, Tabor, Taft, and Westminster.

STUDENT BODY AND CONDUCT

For 2005–06, 171 boys enrolled at Cardigan. There were 67 boys in the ninth grade, 67 in the eighth, 24 in the seventh, and 13 in the sixth. More than 90 percent of the Cardigan students were boarders. In 2005–06, students came to Cardigan from twenty-one states and four countries.

Cardigan has a two-tiered disciplinary status system in order to inform students, their advisers, and parents when School expectations are not being met. This disciplinary system is used to correct patterns of misbehavior and to discipline those students who commit serious offenses. The Discipline Committee meets to hear cases deemed appropriate by the Headmaster and the Assistant Headmaster. Two student leaders and 3 faculty members are selected by the Assistant Headmaster to join him on the committee. The committee hears cases and makes a recommendation for consequences to the Headmaster.

Cardigan has a clearly stated Honor Code, and all students are expected to abide by the spirit of that code.

ACADEMIC FACILITIES

The numerous buildings that house academic facilities are highlighted by the Bronfman Center. Completed in 1996, Bronfman Center features, among other things, the three Freda R. Caspersen state-of-the-art science laboratories, an art studio, the Bhirombhakdi Computer Center, a School store, and class room for sixth graders. Stoddard Center is the home of both the Kirk Library and the Humann Theatre. Opened in fall 1982, the Kirk Library in Cardigan's Stoddard Center is a three-tiered, well-equipped multimedia resource center that offers students and faculty members computer software, audiotapes, and videocassettes in addition to more than 10,000 volumes and numerous journals and periodicals. Thousands of newspaper and magazine articles are available through the Infoweb NewsBank Reference Service. Computers with Internet access are available in both the Kirk Library and the adjacent writing lab. Affiliation with the New Hampshire State Library's Automated Information Access System enables users at the School to obtain materials through the interlibrary loan process. The library is staffed by 1 full-time librarian and a part-time aid. A flexible access plan allows students and faculty members to work in groups, as well as individually, throughout the day and five evenings each week. Humann, the 250-seat theater, is the site of School meetings, lectures, films, concerts, and drama performances.

Cardigan emphasizes the visual arts. The Williams Woodshop and the new Art Center are focal points for this important aspect of a boy's education. The Hinman Auditorium houses the School's music facilities, where opportunities for vocal and instrumental instruction are available.

All dormitory rooms and many classrooms are wired for access to the Internet.

BOARDING AND GENERAL FACILITIES

Eleven dormitories house from 8 to 16 students each. Each dormitory houses faculty members and

their families. Students reside in double rooms, with some singles provided. Two dormitories, referred to as "houses," were completed in fall 2000 and house 3 faculty members and their families and 12 students.

The School operates an on-campus health center, where most of the students' medical needs can be met. For extended services, Cardigan students benefit from the Dartmouth-Hitchcock Medical Center Pediatric Clinic in Canaan and the Dartmouth-Hitchcock Medical Center in Lebanon. The Morrison Health Center on the Cardigan campus has a resident nurse and a visiting physician.

ATHLETICS

The objectives of the activities program at Cardigan are to provide the boys with opportunities to experience success, to offer healthy and enjoyable activities for the boys' free-time periods and weekends, to promote the physical and athletic development of each boy, to teach cooperation with and reliance on teammates, to allow the boys to experience sports and activities that may be new or unfamiliar to them, and to encourage good sportsmanship.

Over the years, Cardigan has been fortunate to acquire extensive athletics facilities, fields, and equipment. These include five fields for soccer, football, and lacrosse; fourteen outdoor tennis courts; two baseball diamonds; a state-of-the-art hockey rink that can be converted to a multipurpose arena in the fall and spring; an on-campus, lighted ski slope; cross-country ski trails; ski team rooms; a wrestling room; an outing club room; a fully equipped weight-training room; an in-line hockey rink; and indoor and outdoor basketball courts.

As the School is situated on the shores of Canaan Street Lake, students and faculty members take full advantage of water-related activities. Sailing is pursued in the School's fleet of Flying Juniors, sailboards, ice boats, and the Hobie catamaran. Motorboats, rowboats, and canoes provide additional opportunities for students to enjoy the water. The waterfront area is well supervised, and instruction is available in all activities.

The Ragged Mountain Ski Area is close to the School and is used on weekdays by the Alpine ski team, recreational skiers, and snowboarders. On Sundays, there are daylong ski trips to major ski areas in New Hampshire and Vermont.

As in the classroom, the focus of interscholastic sports and individual activities is on learning the fundamentals. Teams are fielded on several levels in most sports, and they compete against local independent and public schools. Recreational sports are offered for the student who does not wish to compete interscholastically.

EXTRACURRICULAR OPPORTUNITIES

Many students and faculty members bring to Cardigan skills and interests that, though not included in the usual program of studies, may be pursued and developed in the informal setting of the Club Program. Clubs meet every Thursday afternoon in lieu of athletics, with the opportunity for additional meetings if the members and adviser so desire. Recent clubs have participated in community service, including visits to a local nursing home, hospital volunteer work, recycling, the Big Brother Program, and Red Cross lifeguard training; blues, jazz, and rock bands; a cappella singing groups; technical rock-climbing; horseback riding; mountain-biking; debating; painting; chess; photography; windsurfing; and conversational Chinese, French, German, Hebrew, and Japanese.

A boy may participate in the optional drama program in each of the three seasons. Each year, the drama department presents three major productions. There are extensive stage lighting and sound features, and students interested in the technical aspects of theater enjoy working in this facility.

DAILY LIFE

The typical academic day begins six days per week with a required family-style breakfast. After room inspection in the dormitories, classes begin at 8 a.m. Six class periods precede a family-style lunch. On Monday, Tuesday, Thursday, and Friday, lunch is followed by a seventh-period class and a conference/free reading/current events period. On Wednesday and Saturday, the academic day ends with lunch and is followed by a full slate of athletics and recreational activities. Dinner is a family-style meal every evening except Saturday, when a buffet is scheduled. A study period occurs each school night. Lights-out ranges from 9:15 to 10 p.m., depending on the evening and the age of the student.

WEEKEND LIFE

In addition to the regularly scheduled vacations, all boys may take weekends away from the campus and parents are invited to the campus to share in their son's experience at any time. The majority of Cardigan students are on campus on weekends, and the School provides an exciting array of options for them. A typical Saturday night's schedule might include a movie, a trip off campus, various other on-campus activities and programs, or an excursion to Dartmouth College to swim in their pool or watch a hockey game.

Cardigan is nondenominational, yet the School seeks to strengthen each boy's spiritual development within his own religious heritage. All boys are required to attend the weekly Sunday evening chapel service. Arrangements are made for students of different faiths to attend their own weekly services in the immediate area.

SUMMER PROGRAMS

The Cardigan Mountain Summer Session, a coeducational experience for 150 girls and boys, was instituted in 1951 to meet the needs of four groups of students: those who may be seeking admission to Cardigan in the fall, those who desire advanced academic work and enrichment, those who require intensive work in basic academic skills, and those who require review. The Summer Session also serves a limited number of international students for whom English is not the first language. Cardigan's outstanding range of sports and activities, along with its academic offerings, makes the Summer Session a special blend of camp and school.

Academic enrichment offerings in the sciences are a focal point for the more able students. Courses in environmental sciences were designed to better prepare youngsters for the changing world. The visual and performing arts, long a part of the Summer Session's afternoon program, achieved curricular status, allowing students to pursue drama, ceramics, and photography as part of their morning academic program of study.

The six-week program is still known for its individualized instruction, close supervision of evening study time, and general emphasis on improving study skills. Academic offerings include English, advanced English composition, computers, prealgebra, algebra I and II, geometry, reading and study skills, French, Spanish, and Latin. The Language Learning Lab is offered as a vehicle for students to improve their fundamental reading and writing skills.

The Summer Session is open to students who have completed fourth through eighth grade. The cost for the 2005 Summer Session was $7000. Need-based aid is available.

COSTS AND FINANCIAL AID

In 2005–06, charges for boarding students were $34,550 and for day students, $20,000. There are additional charges for items such as textbooks, laundry service, and athletic equipment.

Financial aid is available to families of qualified students who complete the School and Student Service for Financial Aid forms and demonstrate need. Information about loans and payment plans is available from the Cardigan Admissions Office. For 2005–06, approximately 21 percent of the student body received more than $737,250 in financial assistance.

ADMISSIONS INFORMATION

Cardigan seeks to enroll students of good character and academic promise who will contribute to and benefit from the broad range of academic and extracurricular opportunities available. The Admissions Committee reviews applications on a rolling admissions basis for students wishing to enter the sixth through the eighth grades; a few each year are admitted to the ninth grade (students in grades 4–8 are considered for the Summer Session). Decisions are based upon previous school records, teacher recommendations, aptitude testing, and a campus interview. Cardigan admits students of any race, color, nationality, or ethnic origin to all the rights, privileges, programs, and activities generally accorded or made available to students at the School.

APPLICATION TIMETABLE

Initial inquiries are welcome at any time. Office hours are 9 to 5, Monday through Friday, and 9 to noon on Saturday. School catalogs and applications can be obtained through the Admissions Office. The application fee is $35 for domestic applicants and $125 for international applicants.

ADMISSIONS CORRESPONDENCE

Richard Ryerson, Director of Admissions
Cardigan Mountain School
62 Alumni Drive
Canaan, New Hampshire 03741
Phone: 603-523-3548
Fax: 603-523-3565
E-mail: rryerson@cardigan.org
Web site: http://www.cardigan.org

EAGLEBROOK SCHOOL

Deerfield, Massachusetts

Type: Boys' day and boarding school
Grades: 6–9
Enrollment: 273
Head of School: Andrew C. Chase, Headmaster

THE SCHOOL

Eaglebrook School was opened in 1922 by its Headmaster and founder, Howard B. Gibbs, a former faculty member of Deerfield Academy. One of the earliest members of his faculty was C. Thurston Chase. When Mr. Gibbs died in 1928, Mr. Chase became Headmaster, a position he held for thirty-eight years. From 1966 to 2002, Stuart and Monie Chase assumed leadership of the School. While continuing to foster the School's traditional commitment to excellence, the Chases have encouraged and developed many components of a vital school: expansion of both academic and recreational facilities, emphasis on the arts, increased endowment and financial aid, student and faculty diversity, and a balanced, healthful diet. Stuart and Monie's son, Andrew C. Chase, now assumes leadership duties as Headmaster. Eaglebrook's goals are simple—to help each boy come into full and confident possession of his innate talents, to improve the skills needed for the challenges of secondary school, and to establish values that will allow him to be a person who acts with thoughtfulness and humanity.

The School owns more than 750 acres on Mt. Pocumtuck, overlooking the Deerfield Valley and the historic town of Deerfield. It is located 100 miles west of Boston and 175 miles north of New York City.

The Allen-Chase Foundation was chartered in 1937 as a charitable, educational trust. It is directed by a 36-member self-perpetuating Board of Trustees, representing alumni, parents, and outside professionals in many fields.

Eaglebrook is a member of the National Association of Independent Schools, the Association of Independent Schools of New England, the Valley Independent School Association, the Junior Boarding School Association, and the Secondary School Admissions Test Board.

ACADEMIC PROGRAMS

Sixth graders are taught primarily in a self-contained setting. Subjects include English, mathematics, reading, Latin, history, science, and trimester-length courses in studio art, computers, music, and woodworking. Required classes for grades 7 through 9 each year include foreign language study in Latin, French, or Spanish; a full year of mathematics; a full year of Colonial history in seventh grade, followed by a self-selected history the next two years; a full year of English; two trimesters of geography; two trimesters of science in seventh grade, followed by a full-year laboratory course; one trimester of human sexuality in eighth grade; and one trimester of ethics in the ninth grade. The School offers extensive trimester electives, including band and instrumental instruction, computer skills, word processing, current events, conditioning, chess, film classics, drama, public speaking, industrial field trips, music appreciation, first aid, publications, and a broad variety of studio arts. Drug and alcohol education is required of all students in every grade.

Class enrollment averages 8 to 12 students. Teachers report directly to a student's adviser any time the student's work is noteworthy, either for excellence or deficiency. This allows the adviser to communicate praise or concern effectively and initiate appropriate follow-up. Midway through each trimester, teachers submit brief written evaluations to the advisers of each of their students. Advisers stay in close touch with the parents of their advisees. Grades, along with full academic reports from each of the student's teachers, are given to advisers each trimester and then sent home. The reports are accompanied by a letter from the adviser discussing the student's social adjustment progress, athletic and activity accomplishments, and academic progress and study habits.

FACULTY AND ADVISERS

Andrew C. Chase, the current Headmaster, is a graduate of Deerfield Academy and Williams College. Along with his wife, Rachel Blain, a graduate of Phillips Academy at Andover and Amherst College, Andrew succeeded his father as Headmaster in 2002.

Eaglebrook's full- and part-time faculty consists of 72 men and women, 46 of whom live on campus, many with families of their own. Seventy hold undergraduate degrees, and 30 hold graduate degrees. Leaves of absence, sabbaticals, and financial assistance for graduate study are available. The ratio of students to faculty members is 4.9:1.

Teachers endeavor to make learning an adventure and watch over each boy's personal growth. They set the academic tone, coach the teams, serve as dorm parents, and are available for a boy when he needs a friend. They help each individual establish lifelong study habits and set standards for quality. Eaglebrook's teachers have the skill not only to challenge the very able but also to make learning happen for those who need close supervision. Faculty members are chosen primarily for their appreciation of boys this age, their character and integrity as role models, and competence in their subject areas. The fact that many are married and have children of their own helps to create a warm, experienced family atmosphere.

The Director of Placement assists families in selecting, visiting, and applying to secondary schools. He meets with parents and students in the spring of a boy's eighth-grade year to discuss which schools might be appropriate based on each boy's aptitude, interests, achievements, and talent. He arranges visits from secondary schools and helps with applications. Parents and the Director of Placement work together until the boy has decided upon his secondary school in April of his ninth-grade year.

Schools frequently attended by Eaglebrook graduates include Deerfield Academy, Choate Rosemary Hall School, the Hotchkiss School, Loomis Chaffee, Northfield Mount Hermon School, Phillips Andover Academy, Phillips Exeter Academy, Pomfret, St. George's, St. Paul's School, Taft School, and Westminster School.

STUDENT BODY AND CONDUCT

In the 2005–06 school year, of the 197 boarding students and 76 day students, 25 were in grade 6, 68 in grade 7, 106 in grade 8, and 74 in grade 9. Twenty-eight states and eighteen countries were represented.

There are specified standards of dress, which are neat and informal most of the time. Discipline is handled on an individual basis by those faculty members who are closely involved with the student.

ACADEMIC FACILITIES

The C. Thurston Chase Learning Center contains classrooms, an audiovisual center, and an assembly area. It also houses the Copley Library, which contains 13,000 volumes and subscriptions to eighty-five publications, books on tape, newspapers, CD-ROMs, and Internet access. The computer room is equipped with state-of-the-art computers, color printers, scanners, digital cameras, and a projection board. The Bartlett Assembly Room is an all-purpose area with seats for the entire School. The Jean Flagler Matthews Science Building houses three laboratories, classrooms, a project room, a library, an online computerized weather station, and teachers' offices. The Bryant Arts Building houses studios for drawing, painting, stained glass, architectural design, computer-aided design, stone carving, ceramics, silkscreening, printmaking, and computer art; a darkroom for photography; a woodworking shop; a band rehearsal room; a publications office; a piano studio; piano practice rooms; and a drama rehearsal room. The campus has a high-speed fiber-optic network with e-mail and access to the World Wide Web for research.

BOARDING AND GENERAL FACILITIES

Dormitories are relatively small; the five dormitories house between 18 and 36 students each, with at least one faculty family to every 8 to 10 boys.

Most students live in double rooms. A limited number of single rooms are available. After the first year, a boy may request a certain dormitory and adviser.

ATHLETICS

The athletics program is suitable for boys of all sizes and abilities. Teams are small enough to allow each boy a chance to play in the games,

master skills, and develop a good sense of sportsmanship. The School's Athletic Director arranges a competitive schedule to ensure games with teams of equal ability. Fall sports include cross-country, tennis, hiking, football, water polo, and as many as ten soccer teams. Winter sports include ice hockey, basketball, recreational and competitive skiing, swimming and diving, snowboarding, squash, and wrestling. The School maintains the Easton Ski Area, consisting of several ski trails, the Macomber chair lift, and snowmaking equipment. Spring sports are baseball, track and field, golf, Ultimate Frisbee, lacrosse, triathlon, mountain and road biking, and tennis. The School plays host to numerous students throughout the year in seasonal tournaments in ice hockey, soccer, skiing, basketball, Ultimate Frisbee, swimming, and wrestling. The Schwab Family Pool is a six-lane facility for both competitive and recreational swimming. The McFadden Rink at Alfond Arena features a state-of-the-art NHL-dimensioned 200-foot by 85-foot indoor ice surface. A multisport indoor surface is installed in the arena in the off-season to enable use of the facility for in-line skating, in-line hockey, soccer, lacrosse, and tennis. The Lewis Track and Field was dedicated in 2002.

EXTRACURRICULAR OPPORTUNITIES

Service and leadership opportunities build a sense of pride in the School and camaraderie in the student body. Elected Student Council representatives meet with the Headmaster as an advisory group and discuss School issues. Boys act as admissions guides, help with recycling, organize dances, serve as proctors in the dormitories and the dining room, act as headwaiters, and give the morning assemblies. Boys also assume responsibility, with faculty guidance, for the School newspaper, yearbook, and literary magazine.

Many of the students participate in numerous outdoor activities that are sponsored by the Mountain Club. They maintain an active weekend schedule that includes camping, hiking, backpacking, canoeing, kayaking, white-water rafting, fishing, rock climbing, and snowshoeing.

DAILY LIFE

On weekdays, students rise at 7:20 a.m.; breakfast is at 8. Academic class periods, including assembly, begin at 8:30. Lunch is at noon, and classes resume at 12:33. Study hall and special appointments begin at 2:15, athletics begin at 3:15, and tutorial periods and other activities begin at 5. Dinner is at 6, and evening activities are scheduled between 6:45 and 7:30; study hall is then held until 9:15 p.m. or later, according to the grade.

WEEKEND LIFE

A wide variety of weekend activities are available at Eaglebrook, both on campus and off, including community service, riflery, museum visits, dances, field trips, tournaments, movies, plays, concerts, town trips, Deerfield Academy games, bicycle trips, ski trips, hiking, camping, and mountain climbing. On Sunday, the Coordinator of Religion supervises a nondenominational and nonsectarian meeting for the student body. Attendance is required for boarding students. The aim is to share different beliefs and ways of worship. Transportation is provided for boys who wish to maintain their own religious commitment by attending local places of worship. Students with permission may leave the School for the weekend; 5–10 percent of the student body normally do so on a given weekend.

COSTS AND FINANCIAL AID

Eaglebrook's tuition for the 2005–06 school year was $35,000 for boarding students and $21,900

for day students. Eaglebrook seeks to enroll boys from different backgrounds from this country and abroad, regardless of their ability to pay. Approximately 30 percent of the students receive financial aid. To apply for tuition assistance, a candidate must complete the School Scholarship Service's Parents' Financial Statement, which is obtainable from the Admissions Office.

ADMISSIONS INFORMATION

Most students enter in seventh grade, although students can be admitted to any grade. Information regarding required testing and transcripts can be obtained from the Admissions Office. A School visit and interview are required.

Eaglebrook welcomes boys of any race, color, nation, or creed, and all share the same privileges and duties.

APPLICATION TIMETABLE

The School accepts applications throughout the year, but it is to the candidate's advantage to make application as early as possible. Decisions and notifications are made whenever a boy's file is complete. There is a $50 application fee ($100 for international students).

ADMISSIONS CORRESPONDENCE

Theodore J. Low
Director of Admissions
Eaglebrook School
Pine Nook Road
Deerfield, Massachusetts 01342

Phone: 413-774-9111 (admissions)
      413-774-4711 (main)
Fax: 413-774-9119 (admissions)
     413-772-2394 (main)
E-mail: admissions@eaglebrook.org
Web site: http://www.eaglebrook.org

FAY SCHOOL
Southborough, Massachusetts

Type: Coeducational high school–preparatory boarding (6–9) and day (1–9) school
Grades: 1–9: Lower School, 1–5; Upper School, 6–9
Enrollment: School total: 382; Upper School: 264; Lower School: 118
Head of School: Stephen C. White, Head of School; Michael Beck, Assistant Head of School/Director of External Affairs; Gay Larsen, Director of Development; Sarah McMillan, Head of Upper School; Anne Bishop, Head of Lower School; Christopher Schoberl, Academic Dean

THE SCHOOL

A dynamic learning environment since 1866, Fay School exemplifies a coeducational tradition of academic excellence coupled with a dedication to maximize the potential of each individual child. With a structured environment that recognizes both effort and achievement, Fay School offers both breadth and depth in academic, artistic, and athletic programs. Multilevel course offerings and the availability of tutorial support ensure each student an appropriate level of academic challenge. In small advisory groups, students receive extensive individualized attention. Relationships between students and teachers mirror those of parent and child. At Fay, faculty members and parents work as partners during the critically important adolescent years. Fay's comprehensive secondary school placement program not only provides guidance in identifying and applying to model secondary schools but also assists students and their parents in selecting the best environment for continuing their education at the next level. Exceptional facilities and a faculty committed to ongoing professional development create an environment where living and learning thrive.

Established in 1866 by two sisters, Eliza Burnett Fay and Harriet Burnett, the School is situated on 35 acres in semirural surroundings 28 miles west of Boston. Fay School's day and boarding students are drawn from twenty states and fifteen countries. The vast majority go on to graduate from independent secondary schools.

At Fay, each child's voice matters. Through its leadership opportunities, cultural program, comprehensive academic program, community service, arts, and sports offerings, the School caters to a wide range of interests and abilities. Students' endeavors are encouraged and supported by a dedicated and highly qualified faculty and monitored by an effort system that measures the level of engagement each student demonstrates in all aspects of campus life. Particular attention is given to the needs of boarding students and to making life in dormitories a "home away from home."

Fay School is a nonprofit institution and is governed by a self-perpetuating board of 27 trustees. Its endowment stands at $24 million and is supplemented by an annual fund of more than $1 million in total gifts, bridging the gap between tuition and the operating budget. Through its development efforts, the School annually receives support from more than 1,000 alumni, parents, and friends.

ACADEMIC PROGRAMS

Fay's program seeks to achieve far more than a sound foundation in course work; the emphasis is on fostering positive attitudes toward learning and living in the world beyond the campus. By limiting class size to an average of 12 Upper School students, Fay provides an environment in which children are active participants in their own education. Each student's specific needs and academic background are carefully considered when scheduling classes. A rotating block schedule and more than 200 class offerings ensure maximum flexibility in designing programs of study.

The School offers different levels in most subject areas. In the Lower School, the program emphasizes individual growth and the development of sound fundamental skills. Courses of study in the Upper School provide sequential programs grounded in strengthening basic practices in grades 6 and 7, a foundation upon which deeper conceptual understanding and application are built in the high school courses offered in grades 8 and 9. At the eighth and ninth grade levels, honors courses are available for students who qualify for this enriched experience. A full complement of courses within the five main disciplines of mathematics, English, history, science, and world languages is offered in the Upper School. Fay also provides leadership training in grades 1–9 through a full-year program that stresses the leadership skills of conflict management, social responsibility, team building, communication, and positive role modeling.

Fay School offers a comprehensive technology education program. Technology is integrated across the curriculum and throughout the grades. The School also offers technology classes to Upper and Lower School students that are designed to help students use technology to enhance their studies and to become safe, ethical, and effective computer users. Technology offerings range from Lower School introductory courses to information literacy, digital video production, and Web site design in the upper grades. All students must complete at least one term of art each year as well as a yearlong course in music.

To facilitate success in a student's academic endeavors, deliberate attention is paid to the development of study skills through a study skills curriculum administered by Learning Center staff members and reinforced in the classroom. In particular, research skills, note-taking, time management, and test-taking strategies are taught at the appropriate grade levels. In the academic and athletics programs, the School also monitors each student's progress by means of biweekly effort evaluations and by trimester reports at the middle and end of terms. Specialized help is available through the Learning Services Department for children who need support in following their regular course of study.

The International Student Program (ISP) offers English courses for students whose native language is not English. Three levels and small classes afford opportunities to tailor ISP courses to individual needs in the areas of speaking, listening, writing, reading, and skill building. As students' proficiency in English increases, they are integrated into mainstream courses. Full participation in art, music, technology classes, and sports activities helps students adapt quickly to life in their new community.

FACULTY AND ADVISERS

Children entering Fay School are welcomed into a family whose heart is the faculty. Faculty members are selected for their empathy and enthusiasm for working with students at the elementary and junior level, as well as for their expertise in a particular discipline. Students and teachers work, learn, play, and have meals together. In the boarding community they also spend weekends together, sharing many vibrant experiences both on and off campus.

Among the 88 faculty members, 3 hold doctoral degrees, 43 hold master's degrees, and 42 hold bachelor's degrees; 32 teachers reside on campus. Twelve dorm parents are directly responsible for the welfare of the boarding students.

Advisers are teachers and administrators who form the nuclei of small groups of 4 to 6 students, both day and boarding. Advisory groups meet at least three times a week. This peer support, combined with the guidance of a concerned and involved adult, makes advisory groups an important source of nurturing for youngsters at Fay. A major responsibility for advisers is communicating with parents.

Ensuring a good match between each graduating student and a secondary school is the primary objective in placement. The Director of Secondary School Placement and a second placement counselor work closely with American students, their families, their advisers, coaches, and teachers in identifying the students' needs, strengths, and talents. The Director of the International Student Program provides the same service for Fay's international students. Throughout the application process, the Placement Office provides counsel in selecting and applying to appropriate schools. Schools currently attended by Fay graduates include Berkshire School, Brooks School, Cate School, Choate Rosemary Hall, Concord Academy, Cushing Academy, Deerfield Academy, Emma Willard, Episcopal High School, Governor Dummer Academy, Groton School, Kent School, Lawrence Academy, Lawrenceville School, Loomis Chaffee School, Middlesex School, Milton Academy, Noble and Greenough School, Phillips Andover Academy, Phillips Exeter Academy, Pomfret School, Proctor Academy, Rivers School, St. George's School, St. Mark's School, St. Paul's School, Salisbury School, Suffield Academy, Tabor Academy, Thacher School, Westminster School, and Worcester Academy.

STUDENT BODY AND CONDUCT

Of the 382 students attending Fay, 110 are boarding and 272 are day students. The Upper School numbers 264; the Lower School, 118. Boys make up 55 percent and girls 45 percent of the student population. International students constitute 17 percent of the student body.

At Fay, every effort is made to establish a balance between freedom and responsibility for the young people in its care. Through small advisory groups and the Leadership Program, unstated School rules such as ethical behavior and respect for others are reinforced. Minor misconduct is dealt with by advisers or by the Dean of Students. Where infractions of major School rules are involved, the Discipline Committee, composed of the Dean of Students and 5 faculty members, may convene.

ACADEMIC FACILITIES

The Root Academic Center (1984) houses most of the Upper and Lower School classrooms. The Mars Wing (2001) includes the Learning Center, the media lab, four state-of-the-art science labs, a writing lab, and a multimedia lab. The Reinke Building (1971) contains a large auditorium and houses the Fay Extended Day Program, band room, School Counselor's office, and Summer and Special Programs office. The Picardi Art Center (1987) provides outstanding facilities for art classes, including a darkroom and ceramics studio. The Harris Events Center (1995) is home to Fay's Performing Arts Program and includes five music practice rooms, two music classrooms, a dance studio, and a 400-seat theater.

The School is completely networked and runs almost exclusively on PC technology in each classroom, in the library, the Learning Center, and in three computer labs. In addition, five multimedia

carts are outfitted with the equipment necessary to create multimedia presentations, and three mobile laptop labs provide wireless Web connection for full class lessons. The library offers 17,000 volumes and nine computers for student use. The library Web page (http://library.fayschool.org) provides access to a fully automated catalog of Fay holdings, a connection to holdings outside of Fay via the Internet or the CD-ROM Catologue of Independent Schools in Eastern Massachusetts, a subscription to 10 different databases to support teachers designing lessons and students accomplishing research, and links to many useful Web sites organized by subject and index. The library functions as a key point in the learning experience at Fay, providing students and faculty members with resources for study, research, and pleasure reading. The library program encourages a love of reading and an appreciation of quality literature, equips students with the knowledge and skills to become lifelong learners, and helps ensure that students are effective and responsible users of information and ideas.

BOARDING AND GENERAL FACILITIES

Boarding boys are housed in the Steward Dorm (1978), while girls live on the upper floors of the Dining Room Building (1924), in Webster House (1880), and in East House (circa 1895). Family-style meals are served in the dining room. An infirmary, located in the Dining Room Building, is staffed by registered nurses. Additional campus buildings include Brackett House (1860), home of the admission and development offices; Fay House (1860), the Head of School residence; and the Upjohn Building (1895), currently serving as a multiuse space.

ATHLETICS

Characterized by diversity, spirit, and sportsmanship, Fay's competitive athletics program involves all students and offers a wide range of sports and ability levels each term. Fay's interscholastic teams are noted for the high degree of pride and team spirit they bring with them. Fay's ten athletics fields and eight new tennis courts are in constant use for practices and games during the fall and spring terms, while in warmer weather the pool becomes a popular place to cool off. In snowy weather, the Harlow Gymnasium and the Mars Wrestling Room become the centers of activity, with the ice rinks at the nearby New England Sports Center providing facilities for Fay's hockey teams. Participants in the skiing program enjoy the slopes of SkiWard, a local ski area. Fay hosts annual basketball, wrestling, and tennis tournaments, and many individual athletes and teams participate in tournaments hosted by other schools. The following sports and activities are offered: fall—soccer, football, field hockey, cross-country, tennis, golf, and photography; winter—basketball, ice hockey, volleyball, wrestling, skiing, fitness, dance, drama, and woodworking; and spring—lacrosse, baseball, softball, tennis, track, golf, fitness, and squash.

The School's athletics facilities were greatly enhanced with the completion of the Harlow Gymnasium in 1993. This state-of-the-art facility incorporates four basketball courts, expanded locker room space, team rooms, a wrestling room, a weight room, and a training room.

EXTRACURRICULAR OPPORTUNITIES

Fay's academic program is augmented by a wide choice of extracurricular activities. Dramatic productions and musical groups such as band, bellringers, and chorus offer performance opportunities; aspiring journalists, photographers, and artists work on the yearbook and student newspaper; and activities such as videotaping, woodworking, community service, chess, and computers offer something for everyone. In addition, an 800-square-foot textured rock climbing wall has been added to the state-of-the-art gymnasium. The rock wall, 26 feet in height, provides an ideal setting for climbing, bouldering, and rappelling. Full advantage is taken of the School's proximity to Boston, and visits to museums, sports events, and historic sites take place throughout the year.

DAILY LIFE

Classes are held Monday through Friday in flexible blocks, starting at 8 and ending at 2:30 for all students. Grades 1 and 2 are dismissed at 3. All other students go on to sports, which continue until 3:30 for grades 3 and 4 and 4:30 for grades 5–9. Boarders have free time after sports until a family-style dinner at 6, followed by free time until 7:30 and a study period that ends at 9. Lights-out is between 9:30 and 10, depending on age.

WEEKEND LIFE

Due to the geographic diversity of Fay's boarding community, few boarding students return home on weekends. Boarders look forward to weekends, when the Weekend Coordinator schedules a wide range of activities, including daylong and weekend-long skiing, white-water rafting, and hiking trips; athletics contests; nature trips; attendance at a wide range of cultural events and performances; and visits to amusement and recreational parks, movies, Boston shops, and community service projects.

Families of day students are warmly supportive of the boarders, opening their homes to youngsters for weekends and some holidays. The number of off-campus weekends is not limited, with the exception of a few closed weekends, but permission must be granted by advisers and teachers.

SUMMER PROGRAMS

During the summer months, Fay's campus continues to be active. A six-week summer school offers academic enrichment and review courses in grades 1–9. Students ages 10–15 may live in the school dormitories. The summer school also offers a strong ESL boarding program, which combines English study with opportunities to learn about American culture. Afternoons and weekends are full of fun extracurricular activities such as travel, art, games, computers, and sports options.

In addition to the summer school, an eight-week day camp program is available for local children ages 4–12. The seven-week session combines athletics and the arts in well-supervised activities. A Counselor-in-Training program provides local teenagers with a valuable learning experience.

COSTS AND FINANCIAL AID

Tuition for 2005–06 ranged from $15,950 for day students in grades 1 and 2 to $21,840 for fifth through ninth graders. Tuition for boarding students was $36,500, and tuition for ESL boarding students in the ISP was $41,975. On enrollment, a deposit of $3500 was required for boarding students, $4000 for boarding students in the ISP, and $2000 for day students. Additional fees included $915 for laundry service (boarders only) and $410 (grades 1–5) or $565 (grades 6–9) for books. The School offers several creative payment plans.

Financial aid is awarded on the basis of need to 11 percent of the student body. Amounts based upon demonstrated need and procedures established by the School and Student Service for Financial Aid range from $1000 to nearly full tuition. The grants totaled $611,000 for 2005–06.

ADMISSIONS INFORMATION

Fay School accepts day students for grades 1–9 and boarding students for grades 6–9. The personal requirements for admission include satisfactory evidence of good character, an acceptable record of previous academic work, and the ability and motivation to successfully complete the work at Fay. All applicants must complete the application form and return it to the Director of Admission with the application fee, a transcript, and teacher recommendations. Applicants must visit the School for a personal interview and tour, on weekdays while classes are in session; interested students should call the Admission Office to arrange a time. Candidates for grades 4–9 must take the WISC-III or WISC-IV. Applicants for first grade must be 6 years of age before September 1.

APPLICATION TIMETABLE

Decisions on day student candidates whose folders are complete are announced on March 10. Fay continues to accept qualified candidates after this date until the grades are filled. Wait lists are often established. Decisions on boarding students are made once a candidate's folder is complete, beginning in January. Parents are asked to respond to the acceptance within thirty days. To hold a place for a child, a deposit and enrollment contract must be submitted. Information regarding clothing, course selection, and other pertinent items is sent upon enrollment.

ADMISSIONS CORRESPONDENCE

Suzanne Walker Buck, Director of Admission
Fay School
Box 9106, 48 Main Street
Southborough, Massachusetts 01772-9106

Phone: 508-485-0100
      800-933-2925 (toll-free)
Fax: 508-481-7872
E-mail: fayadmit@fayschool.org
Web site: http://www.fayschool.org

THE FESSENDEN SCHOOL

West Newton, Massachusetts

Type: Boys' boarding and day school
Grades: K–9: Lower School, Kindergarten–4; Middle School, 5–6; Upper School, 7–9
Enrollment: 475
Head of School: Peter P. Drake

THE SCHOOL

The Fessenden School of West Newton, Massachusetts, has enjoyed a long and rich history of providing high-quality education for boys in a supportive yet challenging environment. The School was founded in 1903 by Mr. and Mrs. Frederick J. Fessenden. The founders' original educational philosophy was "to train a boy along the right lines, to teach him how to study and form correct habits of work, and to inculcate principles, which are to regulate his daily conduct and guide his future life." The School adheres to these same principles today. The Fessenden School also recognizes the special requirements of a boy's elementary education experience and focuses on providing that experience in a nurturing environment where a boy can live up to his potential. Intellectual, physical, and emotional development share equal emphasis at Fessenden.

The Fessenden School campus is situated on 41 hilltop acres in a residential community just west of Boston. The School's proximity to the city presents a world of exciting possibilities for year-round activity, including well-known historic sites, first-class music and theater, world-renowned museums, and a multitude of professional and collegiate sports events. The Fessenden campus is convenient to all major highway routes, and Logan International Airport is only a 20-minute drive away.

The Fessenden School is a nonprofit organization. The School's endowment currently stands at $17 million and is supported by alumni and parents, both past and present, through an Annual Fund.

Fessenden's well-established Character Education Program, based on the principles of honesty, compassion, respect, and commitment to academic and athletic excellence, seeks to ensure that every member of the school community is given the support and nurturing he needs to feel secure in his academic, physical, and social ability.

Fessenden holds membership in many academic associations, including the Association of Independent Schools in New England, the National Association of Independent Schools, the Junior Boarding Schools Association, the Secondary School Admission Test Board, and the Massachusetts Association of Nonprofit Schools and Colleges.

ACADEMIC PROGRAMS

The Fessenden School's traditional curriculum is designed to be rigorous yet developmentally appropriate and supportive of each student's learning style, providing him with a foundation of skills that are imperative for the secondary school experience. Each student's needs are carefully considered by his teachers, advisers, and division heads prior to placement in an honors, regular, or moderately paced section. The average class size is 12.

Fessenden's Lower School (K–4) places a heavy emphasis on basic skills in reading, oral and written communication, and mathematics. These areas are complemented with additional work in social studies, FLES (foreign language in elementary school), science, computers, library skills, art, drama, music, sports, and games. A link to Upper School students is maintained through the Big Brother program, peer tutoring, assemblies, and other all-School activities.

In grades 5 and 6, students begin the transition from the self-contained classrooms of the Lower School to the departmentalized structure of the Upper School. Courses in English, math, social studies, geography, science, art, music, and Spanish are required for all Middle School students. Each fifth-grade student is also required to take a reading and study skills course.

The Upper School academic program ensures that each student is properly prepared for the educational programs he will encounter in secondary school. Grades 7–9 focus on the five major academic disciplines of English, history, mathematics, science, and foreign language (Spanish and Latin). Fessenden's commitment to the arts requires each student to choose a class each semester in the fine arts or performing arts. A "help and work" period each day provides additional opportunities for students to consult their teachers on an individual or small-group basis. Students must complete a half-year of computer studies and a course in personal growth and development prior to graduation. In addition, each boy is required to choose from a range of nearly twenty popular electives, including computer studies, student government, theater workshops, art courses at various levels, woodworking, photography, video production, and individual music instruction.

The Fessenden School recognizes that some students may need more specialized help with skill building and therefore offers a Skills Center staffed by professional reading and language specialists. The Skills Center provides individual skills instruction, administers tests, and makes evaluations and recommendations.

Fessenden's English as a second language program (ESL) is offered on both the intermediate and advanced levels, with the goal of mainstreaming students as their English proficiency increases. ESL students are educated using a variety of appropriate teaching resources. Class trips include visits to historic Plymouth, Mystic Seaport, whale watches, Boston's Freedom Trail, Old Sturbridge Village, and the Boston Ballet's production of *The Nutcracker*.

Fessenden's academic year is divided into two semesters. The School acknowledges that a student's effort to learn is as important as standard letter or numerical grades. Teachers give both qualitative and quantitative marks at the middle and end of each semester.

FACULTY AND ADVISERS

The 120 members of Fessenden's dedicated faculty and staff are committed to creating a family-oriented community by serving as teachers, coaches, advisers, dorm parents, and mentors. Seventy-five percent of the faculty and staff members for students in grades 5–9 live on campus, many with families of their own. Fessenden's faculty and staff members hold a combined total of eighty-nine baccalaureate and forty-three advanced degrees. The student-faculty ratio is approximately 6:1.

Each student has his own academic faculty or staff adviser. Advisers foster close relationships with each student, becoming actively involved in all facets of the student's life at school. Each adviser is responsible for communicating to parents all aspects of their sons' experiences at Fessenden.

Peter P. Drake, Interim Headmaster of the Fessenden School, was the Headmaster of the Bement School for fourteen years and then an independent educational consultant for secondary schools and colleges until the present. He was educated at Deerfield Academy, University of Virginia, and Boston University.

Fessenden seeks to provide each student with the placement guidance needed to ensure a positive secondary school experience. This is achieved by a collaboration between the student and the Director of Placement, advisers, teachers, dorm parents, and coaches. Beginning in the spring of eighth grade, families start selecting an appropriate school based on academic ability, extracurricular activities, and athletic interests. Eighth- and ninth-grade students are encouraged to take the SSAT preparatory class in English and math. The Placement Director also works with students to teach specific interviewing techniques, including mock interviews. This helps address any placement issues well in advance.

Fessenden graduates have attended a variety of secondary schools, including Avon Old Farms, Belmont Hill, Brooks, Cate School, Choate Rosemary Hall, Cushing, Deerfield, Exeter, Governor Dummer, Holderness, Loomis Chaffee, Middlesex, Noble and Greenough, Phillips Academy, Rivers, Roxbury Latin, Tabor, and Westminster. However, it is ultimately the successful match between student and school that remains essential in the placement process.

STUDENT BODY AND CONDUCT

The Fessenden School seeks boys of solid character who can grow in a supportive environment where a balanced program of academics, athletics, and social life is vigorously pursued.

Of a total enrollment of 478 students for the academic year 2005–06, 383 are day students and 95 are boarders. Fessenden students come from thirty-five cities and towns in Massachusetts, six-

teen other states, and thirteen other countries. International students represent 12 percent of the total student body.

Fessenden's Character Education Program is modeled by its faculty members, who have an extraordinary investment in the boys' care and set guidelines for the students to live by. Rewarding boys for being active and positive contributors within the community in turn places an emphasis on the reinforcement of positive role modeling. Teachers, coaches, and advisers handle disciplinary matters on an individual basis as warranted.

ACADEMIC FACILITIES

Fessenden's state-of-the-art academic building houses twenty-five new classrooms that provide multiple data points, allowing the expanding world of information into each classroom via technology. The campus features a science center, a library, a study hall, two computer centers, a photography lab, a student health center, and a performing arts center that features a theater-size wide-screen projection monitor. The Fessenden School library contains 21,000 volumes, six computers, two digital cameras, a color scanner, and a printer. The School's two computer centers include forty computers, which are networked and have color monitors and an Internet account. Students also have access to more than twenty Power PCs in their math and science classrooms to help integrate the curriculum. There are two art studios with five electric pottery wheels and two kilns, a printmaking machine, and a music center that features two band rehearsal rooms and five individual practice rooms equipped with pianos. The Skills Center contains eight classrooms for one-to-one tutoring.

BOARDING AND GENERAL FACILITIES

Fessenden's boarding students live in homelike dormitories closely supervised by residential faculty members and their families. Dormitories are made up of students in grades 3–8, with proctors who are in 9th grade. There are 11 to 19 students per hallway. Students in grade 9 live in two different dormitories. Weekday meals are served family style, with a buffet on weekends.

Students' everyday health-care needs are served at the campus Health Center. Two registered nurses are always available, and a physician makes campus visits several times a week and as needed. Newton-Wellesley Hospital is located only minutes away.

ATHLETICS

The School offers a variety of seasonal athletics for students of every age and ability level. Fessenden's long-standing tradition in sports embodies the philosophy of fair play, sportsmanship, and equal opportunity for all participants. Students may choose from competitive, intramural, or recreational activities each season. Competitive and intramural sports include baseball, basketball, cross-country, football, hockey, lacrosse, soccer, squash, tennis, track and field, and wrestling. Boys may also choose from an exciting range of recreational sports, such as Alpine skiing, cross-country skiing, fencing, golf, mountain-biking, sailing, and weight lifting and conditioning. The Fessenden School participates in several athletic tournaments each year and also hosts annual soccer, wrestling, and tennis tournaments.

Fessenden completed a state-of-the-art athletic center in spring 2002. The facility houses two basketball courts, a wrestling center with two regulation-size mats, a weight-training suite, and locker rooms for coaches and visiting teams. The facility overlooks Fessenden's six outdoor tennis courts, which are lighted. Rounding out the sports facilities are an indoor hockey rink, thirteen outdoor tennis courts, two outdoor swimming pools, and nine playing fields.

EXTRACURRICULAR OPPORTUNITIES

The Fessenden School provides a variety of opportunities for students to develop leadership skills and exhibit their talents, thus enriching and balancing their academic program. Each year, the theater arts program presents several dramatic and musical productions. Faculty members offer club programs to share specific skills and interests with students, including in-line skating, board games, cooking, floor hockey, billiards, indoor soccer, model building, volleyball, science and aeronautics, and weight lifting.

Fessenden's Student Council is formed by elected officers in grade 9. The Council meets every two weeks for regular business and calls special meetings to discuss important issues. The Student Council has a voice in implementing School rules and planning special events.

DAILY LIFE

Boarding students begin their day with a family-style breakfast. The academic day encompasses eight periods. Athletic activities take place each weekday afternoon. Day students go home after sports; for boarding students, a structured study hall follows. There are also after-dinner study halls and free activities.

WEEKEND LIFE

Fessenden's weekend program is exceptionally full, providing the balance between academic and social life by satisfying the boys' many outside interests. The residential life staff works closely with the residential faculty to offer more than twenty exciting and interesting supervised activities every weekend. A sampling of weekend trips includes college and professional sports events, museum trips, ski outings, movie nights, camping and mountain-biking trips, dances, plays, and concerts. The Fessenden School holds no religious affiliation but can provide transportation to services for all faiths.

An indispensable aspect of Fessenden's boarding life is the host family program. This program connects all new families with a family that currently has a child in the same division. A boarder's evenings, weekends, or holidays can be spent with a host family, creating friendships that can last long after their Fessenden experience is over.

SUMMER PROGRAMS

The Fessenden School's summer ESL program provides five weeks of immersion in the English language and American culture. This program is open to international boys and girls, ages 10 to 16.

The classes are offered at beginning, intermediate, and advanced levels and are designed to develop competent conversational skills and expand English vocabulary. Classes are small to enable every student to participate fully.

Fessenden's summer ESL program also offers films, videos, fun projects, and games, reinforcing classroom work and actively engaging students in the learning process. After-school and weekend trips bring students to such sites as Plymouth Plantation, Martha's Vineyard, Mystic Seaport, and Harvard University.

COSTS AND FINANCIAL AID

Day student tuition ranges from $19,000 to $23,750. Boarding tuition ranges from $31,500 to $37,150. Additional charges may be applicable to all students for supplies and laundry services.

The Fessenden School awards $600,000 in financial assistance to more than 14 percent of the student body each academic year. Scholarships are awarded on the basis of need.

ADMISSIONS INFORMATION

Catalogs, applications, and financial aid material may be obtained by contacting Fessenden's Admissions Office.

APPLICATION TIMETABLE

Admissions inquiries are welcome at any time. The application deadline for day students is February 1. Boarding student applications are processed on a rolling admissions basis.

ADMISSIONS CORRESPONDENCE

Caleb W. Thomson '79, Director of Admissions
The Fessenden School
250 Waltham Street
West Newton, Massachusetts 02465-1750

Phone: 617-630-2300
Fax: 617-630-2303
E-mail: admissions@fessenden.org
Web site: http://www.fessenden.org

THE GREENWOOD SCHOOL

Putney, Vermont

Type: Prepreparatory boarding school for boys with dyslexia or related language disabilities
Grades: Ungraded, ages 9–14 (at time of admission)
Enrollment: 40
Head of School: Stewart Miller, Headmaster

THE SCHOOL

The Greenwood School, established in 1978, is situated on a 100-acre campus outside Putney, Vermont. The current Board of Trustees includes parents of current and graduated students as well as other professionals. Located in southern Vermont, the School is 1½ hours from Bradley International Airport (Hartford, Connecticut), 2½ hours from Boston, and 4 hours from New York City. The School's mission is to remediate the language deficits of bright boys while encouraging them to develop their strengths in many areas, including art, drama, music, sports, crafts, and leadership capabilities. Students typically enter ninth or tenth grade after leaving Greenwood.

Many special educational programs do not effectively distinguish between individual aptitudes and academic deficiencies. Greenwood's curriculum recognizes that language skills are a requisite part of any education, therefore individualized remedial language training remains at its core. A true education, however, provides children with more than just skills. The ability to reason, critique, debate, and create; to enjoy a fund of general knowledge; and to set personal goals and persevere in achieving them are essential components as well.

Through a unique curriculum that is strong in creative as well as functional studies, the Greenwood School strives to reawaken the appetite for learning in its students. A full prepreparatory academic program, including science, history, literature, art, crafts, and athletics, ensures that Greenwood students are intellectually challenged, creatively stimulated, and factually informed.

The Greenwood School is accredited by the New England Association of Schools and Colleges and is approved by the state of Vermont and the New England Association of Independent Schools.

ACADEMIC PROGRAMS

The goal of Greenwood is to help students bridge the gap between their outstanding potential and present abilities. Greenwood believes that in order to raise a student's academic performance to a level appropriate for his intelligence, he must feel that he is part of the learning community. Visitors to Greenwood remark on the academic atmosphere and mutual support among the students.

A language-intensive program specially designed for Greenwood students distinguishes Greenwood from other junior boarding schools. Greenwood's remedial language program, which uses a diagnostic-prescriptive approach, including the Lindamood Bell and Orton Gillingham methods, offers individualized training in all aspects of literacy, including phonology, phonics, morphology, and orthography. Students spend 1 hour a day in a language tutorial to study and practice reading, spelling, comprehension, handwriting, and writing from dictation. All instruction is multi-

sensory, structured, sequential, and sensitive to students' individual learning styles.

Because written work is such a difficult process for most students with a language-based learning disability, Greenwood devotes an additional period to writing instruction. Classes are small and grouped according to individual ability. In writing classes, students learn grammar, punctuation, sentence and paragraph construction, and creative and expository writing. Before graduating, students receive practical instruction in writing both research and term papers. Word processors aid students in the writing process as students learn to type, edit, and structure their work.

Because many learning-disabled students also have difficulty with math, Greenwood's math classes are also small and grouped according to individual ability. Students who have particular difficulty with fundamentals receive a math tutorial. Concepts, computational skills, and beginning algebra are taught. The math program uses manipulatives, calculators, and other methods developed by the faculty to aid students in acquiring skills. The Game of Village, a creative math program, is popular with the students and unique to Greenwood.

Typically, traditional science and social studies classes require extensive reading, so that many first-year Greenwood students have fallen behind in these subjects. Through lectures, discussions, videotapes, and group projects, students learn and review important concepts. Greenwood's language-trained teachers encourage students to apply appropriate language skills to content-area work.

Although Greenwood students have specific learning disabilities that affect their performance in academic classes, they tend to excel in art, crafts, music, and drama. To develop these talents, Greenwood has a strong fine arts program. All fine arts teachers are masters in their profession and are eager to share their experiences and insights with the students.

Students are able to experience success at Greenwood because the class sizes are small—ranging from an average of 2 to 10 students—and the academic environment is highly structured. A low student-teacher ratio (2:1) ensures that Greenwood students' needs are met in all areas. Class groupings are dependent upon the student's relative language and math abilities. Consistency is built into the program because the teachers of academic classes are also the language tutors. If a student is having difficulty reading or spelling a word in the content areas, the teacher can employ strategies that the student has learned previously in his tutorial class.

A nightly study hall provides students with an opportunity to apply skills independently. Students who have demonstrated an ability to work independently earn the privilege of studying in their dorm rooms with less supervision. Since the ability to apply learned skills independently is one of the best indicators of a student's academic

progress, study hall is an important part of the overall academic program.

Although all Greenwood students receive assistance in developing an ability to use language as a communication tool, students with a greater need for remediation of this skill receive additional language therapy from a speech-language pathologist. This special training includes spoken syntax, direction following, word finding, listening comprehension, and vocabulary development.

FACULTY AND ADVISERS

There are 12 resident teachers who, in addition to teaching responsibilities, share after-school, evening, and weekend coverage. Of the 12, 4 are dorm parents. There are 13 nonresident part-time teachers who teach during the academic day. All 25 faculty members hold bachelor's degrees, 6 have master's degrees, and all have the equivalent of 9 graduate credits in the remedial application of linguistics and principles of reading comprehension. Eight teachers are women.

To ensure a unified approach throughout the curriculum, all Greenwood faculty members receive an intensive internship in linguistic principles as required for reading and spelling development taught by Louisa Moats, as well as a practicum in the Orton-Gillingham approach to remedial language teaching. A resident master and several regularly scheduled consultants provide ongoing supervision. Each student's tutor also acts as an informal adviser who helps with any difficulties that might arise. The Assistant Director and the Head of School serve as formal advisers for students preparing to leave Greenwood for a secondary school.

SECONDARY SCHOOL PLACEMENT

The Greenwood School program, through its positive emphasis on individual strengths combined with an intensive remedial program, prepares most of its students for mainstream education. As a result, a vast majority of Greenwood students advance to private and public high schools, where they succeed in meeting academic and social demands. Some graduates continue their secondary studies in specialized remedial schools. Greenwood graduates have enrolled at Cushing Academy, Eagle Hill School, the Forman School, the Gow School, Holderness School, Kents Hill School, Pine Ridge School, Putney School, and Vermont Academy.

STUDENT BODY AND CONDUCT

The Greenwood School has an enrollment of 40 boys and an average of twelve to fourteen openings per year. Students come from all across the United States. Typically, one half of the student body is from the New England region. There are normally several students from other countries.

Although the atmosphere on campus is friendly and relaxed, there are definite behavioral expec-

tations to which all students must adhere. Because trust and respect for one another are stressed at Greenwood, there is a "no-lock" policy for all but the most dangerous materials (i.e., medicines, certain tools, and flammables).

ACADEMIC FACILITIES

The Leland Best Academic Center holds nine classrooms, an auditorium, two computer labs, a science lab, an art studio, and a library. A connected wing houses the kitchen, the dining hall, and a music studio. There are also a wood shop and a ceramics studio.

BOARDING AND GENERAL FACILITIES

Students live in the newly renovated (summer 2004) Founders Hall, which has eighteen student rooms, three faculty apartments, and two common rooms. The remainder of the resident teachers live in Himmel and in the Director's and Assistant Director's houses. A gym is used for physical education and large gatherings. A wood shop and administrative building complete the list of buildings on campus.

A network of trails that wind through the 100-acre campus provides enjoyment for hikers, mountain bikers, and cross-country skiers. A 2-acre pond is available for science classes, fishing, and boating.

ATHLETICS

To balance the academic efforts of the day, 2 physical education instructors and 4 coaches head a variety of seasonal sports and outdoor activities, including interscholastic soccer, basketball, baseball, and intramural track as well as rugby, cricket, badminton, hiking, mountain biking, rock climbing, softball, volleyball, bowling, archery, outdoor leadership, martial arts, and cross-country and downhill skiing. Greenwood's sports and activity programs address the physical needs of students while fostering a sense of cooperation and respect among participants.

EXTRACURRICULAR OPPORTUNITIES

In order to provide a balanced and total experience, students take a variety of off-campus trips. Educational field trips to museums, exhibits, performances, and similar events are planned throughout the year. During the winter term, students and faculty members ski at a local ski area.

DAILY LIFE

Weekday schedules begin at 7, when students wake up and clean their rooms. Breakfast is at 7:30; morning classes run from 8:30 until lunch at 12:30, with a 20-minute break at 10:30 for a snack. Afternoon classes run from 1 until 3:35, after which students participate in a sports or outdoor program until 5. Students shower and socialize until 6, when dinner is served. Study hall begins at 7 and lasts 1 hour for boys 11 and younger and 1½ hours for boys 12 and older. The boys prepare for bed from 8:30 until 9. Lights are out at 9:05.

WEEKEND LIFE

Weekends are more relaxed. Each weekend is planned by the faculty to include a variety of directed recreational activities.

The Saturday evening meal is off campus, followed by an on-campus movie or participatory activity. Periodic dances with local public and private schools take place during the year. Sunday's schedule allows for individual worship, an all-School activity, and a Community Meeting.

Greenwood faculty members live on or near the campus and enjoy sharing their wide-ranging interests with the students. Much of this sharing occurs on weekends, when students may be invited to faculty members' homes or are taken off campus to enjoy local events.

COSTS AND FINANCIAL AID

Tuition, room, and board for the 2005–06 school year are $46,950. Limited supplemental financial aid is available. Additional charges that average $100 a month are assessed to each student's fam-

ily for personal expenses, such as laundry, entertainment, recreation, and clothing.

ADMISSIONS INFORMATION

Students between the ages of 9 and 14 are eligible for admission. The typical Greenwood student presents somewhat of an educational enigma. Intelligence tests demonstrate that Greenwood's students possess average or superior ability yet show a marked deficit in specific language or mathematical skills. Because of this inequity between ability and performance, students may be misunderstood and judged as lacking in intelligence or motivation.

Those students who have undergone emotional stress as a result of their learning problems customarily improve after experiencing academic and social success at Greenwood. The program does not accept applicants with primary or emotional behavior disorders.

Independent educational consultants or psychologists refer most candidates. These professionals administer a wide range of diagnostic tests to determine if the candidate's learning profile is compatible with Greenwood's program. In some cases, a neuropsychological report is also necessary. For students not referred by a consultant, Greenwood requires appropriate test results as part of the admission process.

APPLICATION TIMETABLE

Inquiries and applications are accepted year-round. Prospective Greenwood students and at least 1 parent or guardian are required to come to the campus for an interview. The candidate should be prepared for brief, informal testing.

ADMISSIONS CORRESPONDENCE

Stewart Miller, Headmaster
The Greenwood School
14 Greenwood Lane
Putney, Vermont 05346
Phone: 802-387-4545
Fax: 802-387-5396
E-mail: grnwood@sover.net
Web site: http://www.greenwood.org

HILLSIDE SCHOOL

Marlborough, Massachusetts

Type: Boys' boarding and day school
Grades: 5–9
Enrollment: 125
Head of School: Mr. David Z. Beecher

THE SCHOOL

Since 1901, Hillside School has continued its mission of working with boys in their formative years. Students work to develop academic and social skills while building confidence and maturity. Hillside provides small classes instructed by talented educators in a community that emphasizes personal integrity and mutual respect and is dedicated to maintaining diversity.

Hillside is situated on 200 acres of fields, forest, and ponds in Marlborough, Massachusetts. Marlborough is located just 30 miles from Boston, 70 miles from Hartford and Providence, and 3½ hours from New York City. This location is convenient for families, but it is also important to the School's educational and recreational programs. School field trips are bountiful, and weekend activity opportunities are endless. The visual arts and athletic programs at Hillside are strong and offer the boys opportunities to succeed and grow. Both boarding and day students take advantage of a high-quality residential life that is supportive, active, and exciting.

Unique to Hillside are the working farm and farmhouse dorm, tutorials available for students who need remediation and organizational skills, a daily and weekly recognition system conveying to students clear expectations regarding social and academic behavior, and excellent programs for students with minor learning disabilities or ADD/ADHD.

Hillside seeks students of average to above-average intelligence who are looking for a supportive, structured school. Family involvement is not only encouraged, it is a critical part of the School's program. Hillside's graduates matriculate at leading independent secondary boarding schools as well as local parochial and public high schools.

Hillside School is a nonprofit institution and is governed by a 24-member Board of Trustees, which includes Hillside alumni, leading citizens of Marlborough and nearby communities, and other individuals with a commitment to the School's educational mission. The School has an endowment of $4 million, with an operating budget of $5 million. Annual Giving for 2004–05 was $375,000. The physical plant is valued at more than $2.5 million.

Hillside School is a member of the National Association of Independent Schools, the Association of Independent Schools in New England, and the Junior Boarding Schools Association.

ACADEMIC PROGRAMS

Hillside School recognizes the importance of committed faculty members, small classes, and a highly structured program as factors in developing the student's self-confidence, self-esteem, individual thinking, and decision-making ability. Students in grades 5 and 6 learn in self-contained classrooms, with a core curriculum consisting of mathematics, language arts, social studies, and reading and specialized instruction in art, science, and music.

In grades 7–9, the curriculum includes English, history, science, math, studio art, music, farming, and French or Spanish.

The Skills for Life program is required of all grades, with the goal of providing a forum for students to learn and discuss issues that confront society and themselves.

Other programs were developed in recent years to help meet the needs of students who have been diagnosed with attention deficit hyperactivity disorder and/or mild learning disabilities. These students are in an environment that provides understanding and support so they may attain a level of academic and personal success.

Hillside establishes an early appreciation for the importance of organizing time and materials. This is accomplished by teaching and reinforcing such study skills as keeping a master organizational notebook in which "two-column" note-taking strategies are utilized as well as test preparation and active reading skills. The curriculum is reinforced by tutorial sessions in which study skills are developed and enhanced in small groups. Each student is provided with instruction in math, science, English, history, skills for life, and writing. French and Spanish are offered to seventh-, eighth-, and ninth-grade students. Music and studio art are also taught. Students utilize the computer lab to enhance their writing skills and creativity.

The tutorial program may be used to aid students who are having difficulty in a particular subject or to teach study skills that can be applied to all subjects.

The school year is divided into three trimesters. Students are evaluated midway through each marking period in detail by their teachers and advisers to ensure that each student's academic progress is closely monitored throughout the academic year. Parents receive student report cards three times during the academic year.

FACULTY AND ADVISERS

David Beecher, Head of the School, is a graduate of The Choate School and Lake Forest College. He served as an English and history teacher at Berkshire School as well as a coach, adviser, and dorm parent. Mr. Beecher also served Berkshire as Dean of Students and as an assistant in Admissions and Development. He also served as Director of Admission and Financial Aid at Fay School and at Wilbraham and Monson Academy.

The faculty consists of 45 full-time members; 24 reside on campus. Three counselors are available throughout the week. All 45 faculty members have bachelor's degrees and 8 have master's degrees. Faculty members and students have their meals together, live in the dormitories, and spend recreational time together on the weekends. All faculty members serve as student advisers and meet with their advisees twice per week. Fourteen faculty members coach at least one sport. Faculty members use patience, kindness, and empathy as they work alongside students.

The Director of Placement assists students and their families in selecting and applying to schools that best match a student's needs. The needs of each student are identified by the faculty members, advisers, coaches, and families at the beginning of the application process.

Schools recently attended by Hillside graduates include Brewster Academy, Chapel Hill-Chauncey Hall School, Cheshire Academy, Dublin School, Holderness School, Lawrence Academy, the Marvelwood School, New Hampton School, Pomfret School, St. Andrew's School (Rhode Island), St. Mark's School, Tilton School, and Wilbraham and Monson Academy.

STUDENT BODY AND CONDUCT

The 2004–05 student population of 125 students consisted of 83 boarding students and 42 day students. Boys enrolled at Hillside School came from ten states and five countries. There is a standard dress code for all students. Hillside School embraces the four core values of honesty, compassion, respect, and determination as the guiding principles for overseeing student behavior and achievement. Shades of Hillside Blue is a system based on these values that is designed to give students and families comprehensive and timely feedback about a boy's overall performance at school. During a biweekly period, boys are evaluated in all areas of School life using three shades of blue. Royal blue, the School color, signifies that a boy consistently meets established expectations. Sky blue signifies that a boy meets expectations with some assistance, and navy blue indicates that a boy needs frequent guidance in attempting to meet expectations. Each student has an adviser who reviews this feedback with the boy and his family. The adviser works in conjunction with the Dean of Students and other faculty members in helping boys to set and meet appropriate individual goals on an ongoing basis. Parental involvement with the Hillside system is sought and greatly encouraged so that a clear, consistent message is given to students. The Dean of Students is charged with overseeing residential life, counseling, and conduct. When infractions of major School rules occur, the Discipline Committee, composed of the Dean of Students and 4 other faculty members, may convene.

ACADEMIC FACILITIES

Simeon Stevens Hall houses fourteen classrooms, including the science laboratory. The Ernest P. Whitehead Industrial Arts Building, the Bertha

Bristol Tracy Gymnasium and Auditorium, and the Helen G. Taplin Room are all connected to Stevens Hall.

BOARDING AND GENERAL FACILITIES
The new, state-of-the-art Messman-Saran Library is located in Drinkwater Hall. The infirmary is staffed by a registered nurse. Students are housed in five dormitories: a new state-of-the-art dorm, Williams, Whittemore, Matthies, and the Farm Dorm. Living in each dormitory are at least 2 faculty members and their respective families. Additional campus buildings include Lowell House, the Headmaster's residence; Tipper House, residence of the Dean of Athletics; Emerson House, residence of the Assistant Head; and the Patten House and other buildings on the farm.

ATHLETICS
Hillside School offers an extensive athletics program and competes with other junior boarding and day schools in the area. The School population is small enough that every student is able to participate. The boys are taught basic skills and participate in a sports program that includes baseball, basketball, cross-country, eco-team, golf, ice hockey, lacrosse, soccer, tennis, track and field, and wrestling. The School also offers an outdoor program featuring hiking, canoeing, sailing, skiing, and camping. Fitness activities, weight lifting, Ultimate Frisbee, and volleyball are part of the intramural program.

EXTRACURRICULAR OPPORTUNITIES
The students and the faculty place great emphasis on service to others. Through the Skills for Life program, students learn that the true value of an individual is in the good he does for others. In this program, students visit local nursing homes and spend time with the elderly, participate in community social service projects, read to children in Head Start programs, and assist in a volunteer program for local residents.

Students participate in woodworking, painting, plays, poetry contests, and student government. They can volunteer to be on the newspaper and yearbook staffs. Students help plan and execute a Farm Day harvest festival and a Daughters of the American Revolution Day.

DAILY LIFE
During the school week, students arise at 6:30 a.m. to dress and to clean their rooms before breakfast at 7:15. Classes begin with homeroom at 8 a.m. and end at 3 p.m. Students meet with their adviser twice each week and attend community meetings five times each week. Class periods are 50 minutes long. All students participate in art, music, and the farm program as part of the academic day. Time is set aside each day from 3:30 until 5 for athletics. Dinner is at 5:45, and there is a supervised study hall from 6:30 until 8 in the main classroom building. Bedtime varies from 9 to 10, depending upon the age of the student.

WEEKEND LIFE
Weekend permission to go home is granted to seven-day boarders if they have attained minimum standards in academics and if they have no School commitments. Transportation is arranged after permission is given by parents.

A wide variety of activities are offered to boarders each weekend. The School takes full advantage of the surrounding area, including Boston, with day trips to historic sites and museums. There are evening and weekend trips to sports events, live theater, exhibits, movies, and malls. A pond, located on the farm, provides opportunities for fishing, swimming, canoeing, and winter ice-skating. Students can go roller-skating, skiing, and bowling, all within a few miles of the School.

Many families of day students welcome boarders to their homes for weekends, and a day student may spend the night, depending on the activity for that weekend.

COSTS AND FINANCIAL AID
Tuition for 2004–05 was $38,500 for a seven-day boarding student, $34,600 for a five-day boarder, and $21,700 for a day student. Hillside offers tuition payment plans. The application fee is $50. Every student has a personal account set up in the Business Office from which he receives weekly pocket money. Money can be withdrawn for special needs as long as it is approved by the Dean of Students. Funding for this account is $450 per year.

More than 30 percent of the current student population received more than $600,000 in financial aid. To apply for tuition assistance, a candidate must complete the Parents' Financial Statement (PFS) from School and Student Service for Financial Aid (SSS).

ADMISSIONS INFORMATION
The Admissions Office goes to great lengths to admit a diverse group of boys from a broad range of socioeconomic and racial backgrounds. Hillside seeks boys who are in need of a sheltered, structured, and nurturing learning environment. The School can accommodate both traditional learners and those with learning differences and/or attention problems. The boys are generally average to superior in intelligence yet have not reached their full potential. They perform best in an environment that is personalized, supportive, and challenging.

APPLICATION TIMETABLE
Parents interested in Hillside School may write, call, or e-mail the School directly for information. Enrollment is possible throughout the year, providing an opening exists. Decisions and notifications are made once an applicant's file is complete. There is a $50 application fee.

ADMISSIONS CORRESPONDENCE
Thomas O'Dell
Director of Admissions and Financial Aid
Hillside School
Robin Hill Road
Marlborough, Massachusetts 01752
Phone: 508-485-2824
Fax: 508-485-4420
E-mail: admissions@hillsideschool.net
Web site: http://www.hillsideschool.net

INDIAN MOUNTAIN SCHOOL

Lakeville, Connecticut

Indian Mountain School
life through service

Type: Coeducational boarding and day general academic school
Grades: pre-K–9
Enrollment: 262
Head of School: C. Dary Dunham, Headmaster

THE SCHOOL

In 1922, Francis Behn Riggs founded a traditional boarding school for middle school boys on his farm in Lakeville, Connecticut. Girls entered the School as day students in 1941. Indian Mountain is the focal point of the 600-acre campus, which maintains a family-centered atmosphere in a village setting. It is located 50 miles west of Hartford and 100 miles north of New York City.

On July 1, 2003, Indian Mountain merged with the Town Hill School to become one school on two separate campuses. The lower campus is home to 70 students in the Lower School, grades pre-K to the fourth grade. Students in the Middle and Upper School, totaling 190, enter the fifth grade on the Indian Mountain campus up the road.

The goal at Indian Mountain School (IMS) is to help students become confident in their own abilities and to develop the necessary academic and personal skills to be successful in secondary school. In a beautiful setting that fosters a respect for learning, the environment, and each other, students are guided through proper Middle School scholastic, athletic, and arts curricula. The IMS philosophy is to work with the whole child, providing structure, support, and challenge.

Indian Mountain School is a nonprofit institution and is governed by a self-perpetuating board of 24 trustees. IMS is accredited by the Connecticut Association of Independent Schools. Its memberships include the National Association of Independent Schools, the Secondary School Admission Test Board, the Junior Boarding School Association, the Educational Records Bureau, the Council for Religion in Independent Schools, and the National Association of Principals of Schools for Girls.

ACADEMIC PROGRAMS

At Indian Mountain, a creative and challenging academic program, combined with a system of personal support, emphasizes strong study skills and critical-thinking skills. Class size is kept small (between 10 and 12 students), and individual attention is readily available during the academic day and the evening study hall. In the Middle School, grades 5 and 6, most courses are taught in homerooms, which are set apart from the older grades, giving the younger students a sense of their own space. The Middle School curriculum includes language arts, social studies, an integrated course of math and science, computers, art, and music in the fifth grade and an introduction to French, Spanish, and Latin in the sixth grade.

A student in the Upper School, grades 7 through 9, enters a departmentalized program that is designed to accommodate his or her interests. Five core courses are required: English, science, history, math, and a choice of French, Latin, or Spanish. An alternative to a foreign language is Language Analysis and Development, which reinforces the fundamentals of English grammar, read-

ing comprehension, writing, and study skills. Elements of Orton Gillingham training are used in this course. While the philosophy throughout the School is to group students in heterogeneous classes, honors placements are possible in mathematics and foreign language in the Upper School. Computers, art, and music are a part of each student's curriculum. Help and work classes meet three afternoons per week. If more individual support is required, the Learning Skills Center offers one-on-one remedial and supportive tutoring in reading comprehension, writing skills, math, and study skills. The Orton Gillingham method is used for language-based remediation. English as a second language (ESL) is available to international students. Designed to enhance English fluency, ESL Humanities (an integration of English and American history) meets daily with an ESL specialist.

All students receive biweekly effort grades in work habits and attitude. An adviser reviews "interim" reports with advisees, giving them a timely sense of how they are meeting their responsibilities in each course and, if necessary, mapping out strategies for improvement. Middle Schoolers need this kind of supportive feedback, which offers short-term goals and encourages academic success. Letter grades and teacher comments are sent home six times during the school year, which is organized into three trimesters. On the Lower School campus, students are taught in homerooms in an intimate classroom setting. Classes are designed to build a solid academic curiosity and foundation while developing traits of good citizenship.

FACULTY AND ADVISERS

C. Dary Dunham, the School's sixth Headmaster, was appointed in 1992. Mr. Dunham graduated from Deerfield Academy and earned a B.A. from the University of Pennsylvania and an M.Ed. degree from Boston University. He started his career at the Fessenden School as a teacher, coach, and dorm parent and left, fifteen years later, as Assistant Headmaster. He went on to Kent Denver School as Upper School Head. Before coming to Indian Mountain, he was Headmaster of St. Michael's Country Day School in Newport, Rhode Island. He continues to teach ninth-grade English.

Energetic and dedicated, the IMS faculty numbers 53 (29 men, 24 women). Twenty-two members hold advanced degrees, and 75 percent live on campus. As role models and mentors, they possess the warmth, humor, and understanding to guide students academically and emotionally through adolescence. Teachers serve as advisers, athletic coaches, dorm parents, table masters, organizers of weekend activities, coordinators of the student council, overseers of the yearbook and literary magazine, and drama coaches. The relationship they build with each student carries into every aspect of School life.

The Director of Secondary School Counseling works closely with each student and his or her family to determine the best possible choices for secondary school. The counselor recommends several schools based on each student's interests and academic achievement. IMS eighth and ninth graders have the opportunity to take the SSAT twice per year on campus. Some of the schools that IMS graduates have matriculated to in the past five years include the Berkshire School, Canterbury, Choate-Rosemary Hall, Deerfield Academy, Emma Willard, Episcopal, Gunnery, Hotchkiss, Kent, Lawrenceville, Loomis Chaffee, Middlesex, Millbrook, Milton, Miss Porter's, St. George's, St. Paul's, Salisbury, Tabor, Taft, Westminster, and Williston Northampton.

STUDENT BODY AND CONDUCT

The enrollment for the 2005–06 academic year was 192 students (70 boarding, 122 day) on the Indian Mountain campus and 70 day students on the lower campus. Because the boarding program begins in the sixth grade, there is a greater concentration of day students in the Middle School. In the Upper School, there are an equal number of boarding and day students. The School had 111 boys and 81 girls. Fifteen states were represented, and 22 students from Austria, Colombia, Germany, Haiti, Hong Kong, Korea, and Mexico added to the cultural diversity. International enrollment does not exceed 12 percent of the student body.

A well-defined set of values—honesty, compassion, respect, and service—is emphasized in every area of School life. Community service is an established part of the Middle School curriculum and, in the Upper School, it is offered on a voluntary basis. Each week at the faculty meeting, students who have contributed positively to the community are awarded kudos. Each student receives a letter from the Headmaster, and a copy is sent to his or her parents. A very high honor that recognizes outstanding contributions to the community comes in the form of Mountain Cards, which are presented at Morning Meeting by the Headmaster. Conversely, if a student violates a major School rule or repeatedly disobeys smaller ones, he or she meets with the Discipline Committee, which is headed by the Dean of Students.

ACADEMIC FACILITIES

The Main Building (1928) houses the Middle School academic classes, Middle School computer room, and music room. The new wing (2000) is home to the library, which contains more than 10,000 volumes, a video collection, and audio equipment. Moreover, the library includes an automated card catalog, an electronic library, IBM-compatible computers, and access to the Internet and e-mail. In addition to three new science rooms and a new technology center, more than forty new computers have been connected to the campus-wide network. These additional computers pro-

vide access to technology not only in the library and computer labs but also in the core classrooms and the residential spaces.

Connected to the Main Building are the Upper School academic classes, Upper School computer room, study hall, assembly hall, studio art center, gymnasium, and newly expanded and renovated dining hall. A new performing arts center has been added, providing space for music and theater arts. The lower campus is located 1½ miles from the Indian Mountain campus and is situated on 10 acres. The campus comprises a building built in 1998, with a multipurpose room, an art room, and six classrooms. Outside is a large playground facility.

BOARDING AND GENERAL FACILITIES

Each of the three dormitories has its own group of dorm parents, who ensure a homelike environment. The smallest dorm, Stockton House, is dedicated to 12 sixth- and seventh-grade boys. Thirty-eight seventh-, eighth-, and ninth-grade boys reside in the newly refurbished Doolittle House, and Osgood Dorm, which is connected to the main building, houses 20 girls. Boarders are generally paired with a roommate.

The Host Family Program arranges for boarders to stay with day student families for long weekends and short vacations, if needed.

ATHLETICS

The emphasis is on building skills, good sportsmanship, and a love of the game. Everyone participates in a schedule of interscholastic competitions with many area middle and secondary schools. Fall sports include football, soccer (boys' and girls' teams), and cross-country (coed). In winter, students may choose from basketball (boys' and girls' teams), ice hockey, volleyball (coed), and competitive or recreational skiing. Spring sports include lacrosse (boys' and girls' teams), baseball (coed), and tennis. A dance program is offered in the winter.

EXTRACURRICULAR OPPORTUNITIES

Adventure Education is a dynamic part of the IMS experience that builds confidence, self-esteem, and leadership skills. Every student participates in Adventure Education at some point during the year, and each grade has a different program. A focal point is a state-of-the-art ropes course, which was built in 1988, featuring thirty-six high and low elements. Off-campus Adventure Education trips include hiking and camping in the White Mountains, canoeing, and rock climbing.

There are two major dramatic School productions per year (including a musical) plus two Middle School productions. An active Student Council organizes dances, parties, the Talent Show, spirit days, and community service projects. Volunteers work on the yearbook and literary magazine.

DAILY LIFE

On weekdays, students are awoken at 6:40 a.m. Dorm rooms are "checked out" before boarders go to breakfast at 7:30. All meals are family style. Morning Meeting for all students starts the school day, which includes six academic classes of 50 minutes in length, a recess, and lunch. Help and work classes meet three afternoons per week prior to sports, and more sports time is scheduled on Wednesdays and Fridays, which are called "game" days. Dinner is at 6, and evening study hall runs from 7 until 8:30 in one of three places: a student's dorm room, a supervised study hall, or a structured study hall. Students earn the privilege of room study if their biweekly effort marks indicate they are accomplishing their work. Supervised and structured study halls meet the needs of those students who may have difficulty organizing and completing their homework. Lights-out varies between 9:30 and 10 p.m., depending on grade.

WEEKEND LIFE

Three faculty teams alternate weekends to plan a roster of activities and trips beginning Friday evening. One study hall and two help classes, enrichment classes, or community service groups meet Saturday mornings. Students who are called to help class must attend. Choices for weekend afternoons may include trips to an Alpine slide, an amusement park, a sporting event, a mountain bike race, skiing, local movies, and malls. Campus activities include sports, hiking, fishing, camping on the mountain, biking, in-line skating, sledding, and skating. Brunch is served Sunday morning at 10:15 a.m., and an earlier continental breakfast is available in each dorm. Transportation to church services is arranged for those who wish to attend. Off-campus weekends from Saturday noon until Sunday evening are unlimited, and students are allowed to take long weekends from Friday after sports until Sunday evening six times per year.

COSTS AND FINANCIAL AID

In 2005–06, tuition for boarding students was $33,180 and for day students on the Indian Mountain campus, $17,800. Tuition in the Lower School on the lower campus ranged from $10,650 to $11,475. Tutorial and ESL fees are additional. Financial aid is awarded on a need basis to approximately 30 percent of the students. To apply for aid, families must complete the School Scholarship Services (SSS) forms, which are available upon request.

ADMISSIONS INFORMATION

Boarding students' admissions decisions in grades 5–9 are made on a rolling basis once the forms have been completed and the candidate has visited the campus for a tour and an interview. Lower School applicants in grades pre-K–4 must complete applications by February 1; decisions are sent the last week of March. IMS admits students of any race, color, nation, or creed.

APPLICATION TIMETABLE

Applications are welcome throughout the year, but candidates are encouraged to apply early and to arrange an interview during a weekday morning in the fall or winter. The application fee is $45 ($100 for international students).

ADMISSIONS CORRESPONDENCE

Mimi Babcock
Director of Admission
Indian Mountain School
211 Indian Mountain Road
Lakeville, Connecticut 06039

Phone: 860-435-0871
Fax: 860-435-1380
E-mail: admissions@indianmountain.org
Web site: http://www.indianmountain.org

LINDEN HILL SCHOOL

Northfield, Massachusetts

Type: Boarding school for young men with dyslexia and/or language-based learning differences
Grades: Ungraded, junior boarding program, along with formal freshman year, ages 9–16
Enrollment: 45
Head of School: James A. McDaniel, Headmaster and Summer Program Director

---

THE SCHOOL

Linden Hill School is an ungraded boarding school for boys between the ages of 9 and 16 with dyslexia or specific language-based differences. Located in the town of Northfield (population 3,100), in the Pioneer Valley east of the Berkshires, the School is accessible via Interstate 91; interstate buses serve the nearby town of Greenfield, and major airlines serve Bradley International Airport in Windsor Locks, Connecticut. The heavily wooded 140-acre campus overlooks the Connecticut River. The School's location offers opportunities for skiing and many other outdoor activities.

The School was founded in 1961 to provide a family atmosphere in which the Orton-Gillingham phonics approach could be implemented for the remediation of dyslexic boys. The original dairy farm estate was renovated to provide a country setting.

Today, through a multisensory approach based on a synthesis of the methods of Dr. Samuel T. Orton and Anna Gillingham, Linden Hill helps boys of inquisitive mind and good intellect strengthen areas of weakness by establishing a sound language foundation. Each student receives daily remedial language instruction tailored to meet his needs. The School endeavors to awaken creative and athletic talents through extracurricular offerings.

A nonprofit institution, Linden Hill School is governed by a self-perpetuating Board of Trustees, including parents and alumni, which meets three times annually. The School-owned plant is valued at $4 million.

Linden Hill is accredited by the New England Association of Schools and Colleges. It holds memberships in the Association of Independent Schools of New England, the National Association of Schools, the Junior Boarding School Association, the Association of Boarding Schools, and the Pioneer Valley Independent Schools Association.

ACADEMIC PROGRAMS

The Academic School Program runs from early September to late May. It includes a Thanksgiving recess, Christmas and spring vacations, and an all-school spring trip. Each year, all students study a specific topic and then, with their teachers, take a theme-based trip to further explore that topic. In recent years the entire school has traveled to Mexico, Florida, and Washington, D.C.

Classes are held five days a week and range in size from a teacher-student ratio of 2:1 in Orton-Gillingham language training sessions to 4:1, on average, in other courses.

Narrative reports, grades, and/or standardized test results are sent to parents six times per year. Individual tests are administered at the beginning and end of each year to aid in

placement and measure progress. Standardized tests, such as the Woodcock Johnson III, are administered to all students twice yearly.

FACULTY AND ADVISERS

The Head of the school, most of the full-time faculty members and their families, and additional support staff live on campus. All instructors are trained in the Orton-Gillingham method and are experienced in the teaching of students with learning differences. They hold baccalaureate and master's degrees from such institutions as American, Boston College, Canisius, Hobart and William Smith, Keene State, Kaplan, Lesley University, Medaille, Merrimack, Temple, and the Universities of Massachusetts and Tampa.

The support staff includes a psychologist and counselors, a full-time registered nurse, occupational and speech and language therapists, and Northfield Mount Hermon School Health Services, with a 24-hour clinic

SECONDARY SCHOOL PLACEMENT

At the appropriate time, Linden Hill assists each boy in the selection of a secondary school. In the past, students have gone on to attend such schools as Brewster Academy, Cardigan Mountain, Cushing Academy, Eagle Hill, Forman, Gow, The Gunnery, Kents Hill, Kildonan, Proctor Academy, St. Andrew's, South Kent, Trinity Pawling, and Vermont Academy.

Some students return to their home schools if the programs are appropriate to their needs.

STUDENT BODY AND CONDUCT

Linden Hill enrolls approximately 30 boys between the ages of 9 and 16. They represent more than ten states and four countries.

ACADEMIC FACILITIES

The main school building is the former Bennett farmhouse (circa 1835). Its ground floor houses the School's new kitchen and food storage area, offices, private meeting/dining rooms, and a music room. On the second floor are two newly renovated faculty residences.

Haskell Hall contains classrooms, an art room, a library, a greenhouse, and a large room that serves as both study hall and auditorium.

The Duplex extension (2001) has classrooms, science laboratories, a technology center, a wood shop, and housing for 16 students and three faculty apartments. A multiuse gymnasium, with a full-size hardwood floor basketball court and a climbing wall, opened in 1998.

White Cottage (1999) connects with the Headmaster's residence and houses the administrative offices, nurse's office, infirmary, and school store. In addition, there is another faculty residence, a maple-sugar shack, and several small buildings on the campus.

BOARDING AND GENERAL FACILITIES

There are three dormitories that provide students with a nurturing, "home away from home" environment.

The Bennett Farmhouse extension (2003), the school's latest million-dollar improvement, has three floors. The top floor is a dormitory with faculty residence. The main dining room, with expansive views of the surrounding valley, covers the middle floor, and a student activity center occupies the lower level.

The Hayes Hillside Dormitory (1971) provides housing for 25 students, living quarters for dormitory parents and 1 or 2 collegians, a common room, large shower/bathroom, and a locker area for each boy to store his athletic gear and other equipment.

ATHLETICS

Linden Hill teams compete with those of other schools in the Pioneer Valley in basketball, golf, soccer, softball, tennis, and wrestling. On weekends, boys choose to participate in a variety of indoor and outdoor activities, including art and woodworking projects, board games, making maple syrup, pool, reading, skating, skiing, snowboarding, table tennis, and various trips. Bicycling, cross-country skiing, flag football, hockey, horseback riding, ice skating, swimming, and track and field are offered on a recreational basis. These programs promote good motor-coordination skills and help build self-confidence.

EXTRACURRICULAR OPPORTUNITIES

Movies and concerts are provided at the School. Other extracurricular activities and events include drama, music lessons, outdoor recreation, wall climbing, and river rafting. Weekend activities include trips to nearby towns for movies, fairs and other community and sporting events, downhill and cross-country skiing, snowboarding, hiking, and Rollerblading. The students also attend area cultural events at nearby schools, colleges, town, and cities. All boys have the opportunity to attend area religious services each week.

DAILY LIFE

The daily schedule, from 6:45 a.m. to lights out at 9:30 p.m., includes seven academic periods, morning jobs, meals, athletics, free time, a 30-minute supervised free-reading session, and an 80-minute evening study hall. Each academic day, students participate in language training, literature and composition, science, math, history, and electives, including health education, art, wood shop, or computers. The structured-reading period fosters independent reading for pleasure or provides an opportunity for extra read-aloud groups. The evening study hall is a time for supervised preparation for classes.

Faculty members provide individualized assistance during both of these periods and at other times by arrangement.

SUMMER PROGRAMS
Linden Hill School offers a coed summer program from June 30 to July 30.

COSTS AND FINANCIAL AID
In 2005–06, tuition, room, and board totaled $40,750. Extras, including laundry, haircuts, allowance, other personal items, and additional clothing, amounted to approximately $1300.

Under the provisions of Public Law 94-142, boys may be eligible for state funding of the cost of a Linden Hill School education. In addition, the cost of attending the School may qualify as a medical expense.

ADMISSIONS INFORMATION
Linden Hill School enrolls bright, inquisitive, language-disabled or dyslexic boys who have become frustrated at their own shortcomings and past failures. Boys are admitted on the basis of previous academic records, teacher references, academic evaluations, and a personal interview. The school has a rolling admission policy, which permits students to enter throughout the academic year, provided there is space available.

Linden Hill has a policy of nondiscrimination on the basis of race, color, or national origin.

APPLICATION TIMETABLE
Applications are accepted throughout the year, and midyear enrollment is possible if vacancies exist. A $4750 deposit, applicable toward tuition, is due upon acceptance.

ADMISSIONS CORRESPONDENCE
Linden Hill School
154 South Mountain Road
Northfield, Massachusetts 01360
Phone: 413-498-2906
      866-498-2906 (toll-free)
Fax: 413-498-2908
E-mail: admissions@lindenhs.org
Web site: http://www.lindenhs.org

NORTH COUNTRY SCHOOL

Lake Placid, New York

Type: Coeducational, boarding, elementary school
Grades: 4–9
Enrollment: 80
Head of School: David Hochschartner

THE SCHOOL

The student body numbered 6 children when Walter and Leonora Clark started North Country School in 1938. Because construction of their new school building had been delayed, this tiny band of children and adults took temporary shelter on the property in a thin-walled summer-camp building that had neither heat nor electricity. Years later, the Clarks delighted in telling these stories about those early days: borrowing a wood stove from an obliging neighbor, hanging blankets over the windows, and breaking ice in kitchen water buckets. Thus North Country School began with children learning lessons about overcoming unexpected difficulties with energy, cooperation, and good humor.

The 165-acre campus, located in the Adirondack High Peaks, includes a working farm, organic gardens, and lakeshore and is abutted by wilderness land. Sharing in the daily chores necessary to the maintenance of the School and farm has always been at the core of a child's experience at North Country. The Clarks believed that real responsibilities fostered feelings of purpose and self-worth in children. The school they envisaged was one in which all the experiences of each day, both in the classroom and out, would have the power to teach. That same belief had informed the founding of Camp Treetops seventeen years earlier on the same site, a project in which the Clarks also participated and which to this day complements the School program, making North Country School–Camp Treetops one of the few truly year-round communities for children in the country.

Today North Country School–Camp Treetops is overseen by a Board of Trustees, who meet four times a year on the campus so that they may visit classes, talk with students and staff, and advance the institution's Long Range Plan. Gifts to the institution in 2001–02 totaled approximately $676,000, not including capital campaign contributions.

The institution is accredited by the New York State Association of Independent Schools and the American Camping Association and is a member of the Secondary School Admission Test Board, the Educational Records Bureau, and the National Association of Independent Schools.

ACADEMIC PROGRAMS

North Country School was founded on the dictum of John Dewey that "the educative process is fired and sustained by the impulse that comes from the desires, interests, and purposes of the pupil." The School structures children's study of the traditional school subjects but always encourages children to follow their own interests as they emerge. The School believes that all children are in some way gifted and creates a teaching and learning environment that is designed to find and develop those gifts. Education at North Country is a hands-on as well as a conceptual, social, and aesthetic matter. No grades are awarded; instead, teachers write comprehensive reports on each child's work twice a year.

Learning environments are highly enriched with manipulative materials and resources. There is one computer for every 4 children, and they are taught to program in HyperCard early on as well as how to use the Internet for information retrieval and global conversation. Some classes are taught by 2 or 3 teachers—1 as lead teacher and the others as coaches.

Science and math classes utilize the farm and mountain environment in their curriculum as well as the problem-solving techniques recently endorsed by the National Council of Teachers of Mathematics.

FACULTY AND ADVISERS

The Head of North Country School–Camp Treetops is David Hochschartner, a graduate of Union College and the Klingenstein Center at Columbia University Teachers College. Mr. Hochschartner has served as the Director of the Presidio Hill School in San Francisco, California, and as Assistant Director of Burgundy Farm Country Day School in Alexandria, Virginia. He has been an instructor at Colorado Outward Bound School, has served as a coach and blind racer guide for the U.S. Disabled Ski Team, and has an extensive background in outdoor sports.

The faculty members divide their time among teaching, coaching, tutoring, and the outdoors, where much of the School's program occurs year-round. Though many of the faculty members are experts and hold degrees in a particular subject area, they are primarily generalists who are prepared to work with children in all aspects of North Country School's program. A Faculty Enrichment Fund has been established to support summer study among the faculty, and time is taken before school and during the children's vacation periods for workshops and new program development.

The staff includes a nurse and a licensed social worker. The Adirondack Medical Center is 20 minutes from the School.

SECONDARY SCHOOL PLACEMENT

The ninth-grade curriculum at North Country School includes a directed program in planning for transition. Students examine themselves, their interests and skills, and their aspirations as a basis for thinking about their transition to secondary school. They receive instruction and practice in writing essays as well as in interviewing and evaluating schools.

Parents are brought into the process of school selection at the end of the seventh-grade year and stay in contact with the Secondary School Placement Director from then on.

Schools currently attended by North Country School graduates include Buxton School, Cushing Academy, Darrow School, Emma Willard, High Mowing, Masters School, Northfield Mount Herman, Proctor Academy, Putney School, Stoneleigh-Burnham, Suffield Academy, Vermont Academy, Westtown School, and Williston North Hampton.

STUDENT BODY AND CONDUCT

Of the 80 children enrolled in 2005–06, 67 were boarders and 13 were day students or faculty children. This student community included 34 girls and 46 boys from nineteen states and eight other countries. The children ranged in age from 9 to 15.

Although North Country School is in many ways a highly structured community, it is also an informal one where everyone is on a first-name basis. Respect for one another is a key prerequisite for the success of the School community and is achieved through conversation and care rather than authority.

Candy, junk food, and television are not allowed except on special occasions. Children who feel the need to test limits do so with candy rather than other substances.

The School believes in the direct arbitration of disputes between children by an adult. Houseparents are regularly in touch with the parents of their charges. When a problem exists academically, socially, or personally, conversation about it begins early and parents are asked to participate in its solution if appropriate.

ACADEMIC FACILITIES

All classes are held in one building, which was built in 1940 and has since been significantly modernized. Windows are large and rooms sunny; there are slides by three of the staircases. The art, ceramics, weaving, woodworking, and photography studio areas are contiguous and occupy the lower level of the Main Building.

The barn, greenhouse, and sugar house are also used for teaching at various times in the year. The library, a bright and many-windowed space, contains 5,000 volumes and is filled with comfortable nooks and crannies for reading as well as state-of-the-art computer retrieval and CD-ROM facilities.

BOARDING AND GENERAL FACILITIES

Students live in one of seven "houses" with resident houseparents. There are no more than 10 students to a house. Genders and ages are mixed much as they would be in a family, and most houseparents have young children of their own who complete the family circle. Two other adults are assigned to each house, as well, so that there is always plenty of coverage and the 1:3 adult-child ratio is maintained. Houseparents oversee reading period and homework for the younger students. Eighth and ninth graders attend a supervised study hall in the main building. An evening snack is often prepared by a houseparent and 1 or 2 children. Younger children are tucked into bed and often read to before going to sleep.

ATHLETICS

Part of North Country School's educational philosophy is to encourage cooperation rather than competition; this is reflected in the School's athletics and recreation program. While some soccer and basketball games are played against local schools, and North Country School's ski teams compete throughout the winter, the emphasis is on lifelong sports, free-form games, and play and mastery. Children may have riding classes once a week in the fall and spring. Children ski on the School's own ski hill and on adjacent cross-country trails. They ski each Tuesday afternoon at Whiteface Mountain and take advantage of Lake Placid's Olympic bobsled, luge, and ski-jumping venues one or two evenings

a week throughout the winter. Children sled, toboggan, build snow caves, and wee-bob most afternoons on the hill by the School's lake. Students also enjoy ice skating on the School's ponds and at the Olympic speed skating oval in town.

A major activity at North Country School is mountain climbing. Many children aim during their years at NCS-CTT to become Adirondack '46ers. There are expeditions nearly every weekend throughout the year, many on snowshoes. There is also a climbing wall in the main building that prepares children for more technical climbs in the out-of-doors.

EXTRACURRICULAR OPPORTUNITIES

The school year is built around a number of all-school special events, many of which date back fifty years. For Halloween, children make their own costumes for an evening of festivities, including a senior-run spook house and a carnival.

The fall harvests are followed by Thanksgiving, which is attended by the children's families and at which the harvest is served up. A concert and all-school performance follow.

The winter holiday celebration spans a week of special meals and treats as children go from one house to another and from one faculty residence to another.

Valentine's Day is again a time for creative manufacture and celebration as are Box Dinners later in the spring. Mountain Cakes, a monthlong escapade of spring mountaineering, is capped off by a big awards dinner, when each house is given a cake whose dimensions reflect the number of miles collectively climbed.

All children study music formally and many informally as well. Sunday dinner is a special occasion where children dress up and where the meal is followed by a student performance, often of music.

There is a requirement that all children learn to ride, ski, go on at least one overnight a term, and climb Cascade Mountain. A mounted drill team performs twice a year, and there are several horseback expeditions during the fall and spring.

Spring is maple sugar harvest time. The children split wood, gather sap, run the evaporator, and can more than 300 gallons of syrup a year.

A student newspaper and literary journal, a chorus, musical ensembles, and various student-created activities round out the extracurricular program.

DAILY LIFE

Children with barn chores are awoken at 6:30; others at 7 for other chores. All meals are served family-style. Breakfast is at 8, except on weekends when the day begins a little later. Classes follow at 8:30 Monday through Friday and run through 2:30, with a break for lunch at 12:15. There is a 15-minute "council" right after lunch at which announcements are made, afternoon activities planned, recognitions and awards given, and an occasional story is told. After lunch, children choose from a substantial list of elective courses, including photography, print shop, dance, theater, chorus, and individual music lessons. Sports follow, with various athletic opportunities, depending upon the season. Following sports, children return to their houses to relax and wind down with friends and houseparents before dinner. Occasionally there are open houses in one living unit or another or at the Head's house. Wednesdays begin with a town meeting and end with an afternoon and evening of house-related activities including a home-cooked meal.

Dinner is at 6, and following that younger children go to their houses for reading period, study time, and an evening in their houses until bedtime at 8:30. Older children remain in the building for study hall. Bedtime for them is 9:30.

WEEKEND LIFE

Weekends are nonacademic and involve field trips, hikes, sailing, and water activities in the fall and spring as well as games, horseback riding, fort building, off-campus winter competitions, sledding, skating, various homemade entertainments, dances, and free play. Ice cream is served on Saturday nights and followed by a dance or an all-school entertainment. Children never leave campus unsupervised but often go 2 or 3 at a time with a faculty member to work on a town-related project, buy fish for the aquarium, get a bicycle fixed, or go in larger groups for an occasional movie.

SUMMER PROGRAMS

North Country School and Camp Treetops are seasonal expressions of the same philosophy. Camp Treetops, founded in 1921, provides a seven-week program that, with the exception of the academic component, very much mirrors the School. Children from age 8 to 15 participate in the regular session and children from 14 to 16 in Treetops Adirondacks and Treetops Away—both mountaineering and canoeing programs.

COSTS AND FINANCIAL AID

In 2005–06, student tuition was $38,300. This fee covered such costs as textbooks, art materials, laundry service, field trips, and all ski and recreational passes. There are additional costs for the senior year, including Senior Expedition and a senior ski trip. Counseling is provided at an additional fee.

Financial aid is provided to approximately 35 percent of the students enrolled, the average grant being $15,000. Eligibility for financial aid is based upon the recommendation of the School Scholarship Service and requires submission of a copy of the applicant family's IRS filing for the previous year.

ADMISSIONS INFORMATION

North Country School looks to enroll children who are capable of using the School and the community to their advantage and who are also able to give to others from their own lives. The School is particularly successful with gifted children and children with variant learning styles. A decision to accept is based upon a child's school records, conversations with the child's parents, recommendations from those who have taught the child, the results of Wechsler Intelligence Scale for Children, and an interview with the School Director. (The interview is occasionally waived for foreign-service families.)

APPLICATION TIMETABLE

Applications to North Country School–Camp Treetops are considered on a rolling admissions basis; midyear enrollment is possible.

ADMISSIONS CORRESPONDENCE

Director of Admissions
North Country School–Camp Treetops
P.O. Box 187
Lake Placid, New York 12946

Phone: 518-523-9329
Fax: 518-523-4858
E-mail: admissions@nct.org
Web site: http://www.nct.org

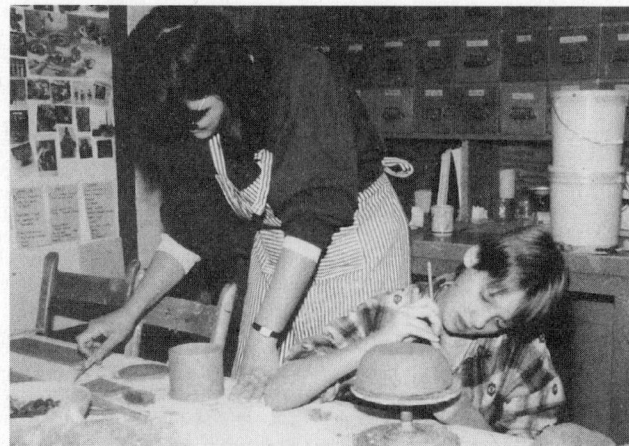

THE RECTORY SCHOOL

Pomfret, Connecticut

Type: Boys' junior boarding and coeducational day general academic school
Grades: 5–9
Enrollment: 168
Head of School: Thomas F. Army Jr., Headmaster

THE SCHOOL

The Rectory School was founded in 1920 by the Rev. Frank H. Bigelow and his wife, Mabel. In its earliest stages, the School was run out of the Bigelows' home, the Rectory of Christ Church in Pomfret. The Bigelows instituted the Individualized Instruction Program (IIP)™, which became the model for many junior boarding schools. The Rectory School welcomes students of any race, color, religion, and national or ethnic origin.

Although the School has grown considerably since its birth, its mission has remained constant. The Rectory School seeks to provide for its students an educational and social climate in which individuals, whatever their strengths and weaknesses, can develop their intellectual, ethical, physical, and social being as fully as possible. The School continues to offer an innovative combination of classic academic traditions and one-on-one tutoring in a community setting dedicated solely to middle schoolers. The U.S. Department of Education bestowed its coveted Blue Ribbon distinction for excellence in education on the Rectory School, specifically citing the School for its individualized instruction, experiential learning program, comprehensive athletic and arts programs, and computer-aided learning.

The School is situated on 138 picturesque acres in rural northeastern Connecticut. With access to three state capitals, the School enjoys a unique location; Hartford is 40 miles to the west, Providence is 30 miles to the east, and Boston is 70 miles to the northeast. The proximity of these major cities affords students the opportunity for a variety of educational trips and easy access to airports when traveling home, yet the School is in a safe, rural setting, only an hour's drive from the mountains and the coast.

Incorporated in 1935 as a nonprofit organization, the Rectory School is directed by a Board of Trustees. The endowment is $10.3 million. The approximate value of the physical plant is $21 million. Over the last several years, the School has undergone a $5 million program of capital expansion. This has resulted in two new dormitories, a library expansion and renovation, rewiring of the campus to meet technological demands, and a new performing arts center with a 214-seat auditorium. Most recently, the School dedicated its new dining hall and the art barn, with two studios and a darkroom.

The Rectory School is accredited by the Connecticut Association of Independent Schools and approved by the Connecticut State Board of Education. It is a member of the Connecticut Association of Independent Schools, the National Association of Independent Schools, the Association of Boarding Schools, the Junior Boarding School Association, the Secondary School Admission Test Board, and the Educational Records Bureau.

ACADEMIC PROGRAMS

The Rectory School's core curriculum includes major courses in English, reading, mathematics, history, and science. Minor courses in music, art, and health are required of each student. Foreign languages may be elected, with Spanish and Latin offered. Multiple sections in grades 5–9 allow opportunities for success to students with varying degrees of ability. The sections range from one with the most rigorous program of study to those with more academic support.

Students are grouped by their ability, performance, and the need for academic support. The most rigorous section is an honors track that puts students in line for advanced placement in secondary school. Using similar criteria, math sectioning is done separately from the language-based subjects. The guiding principle is that each student should feel challenged by the curriculum without being overwhelmed.

Regardless of section, every student has an equal opportunity to make the effort and the academic honor rolls. The Rectory School commends and recognizes both the gifted scholar and the dogged worker. A daily schedule rotates throughout the week. A 2-hour faculty-assisted study time is held five evenings per week. All students at the Rectory School are taught proper study skills and work habits in the small classrooms and through numerous daily contacts with faculty members.

One of the unique and critical elements of the Rectory School curriculum is the Individualized Instruction Program (IIP™). It is woven seamlessly into the normal academic day and curriculum. A tutor, provided at additional cost to any student whose parents request one, meets with the student during the academic day five times per week. The IIP™ is tailored to the specific needs of each student. The IIP™ supports the curricular, organizational, time management, and study strategies taught in the Rectory classrooms. Approximately 70 percent of the students take advantage of this program.

Classes average 10 students, with a maximum size of 12. A student-faculty ratio of 3:1 provides the perfect atmosphere for one-on-one and small group interaction.

The School's curriculum also includes a mandatory experiential learning program. The program, which operates in March, allows students to explore an area of interest in a "hands on" fashion. Topics have included visiting the site of and studying the Battle of Gettysburg; attending and reviewing Broadway musical performances; studying architecture and the history of whaling on Nantucket; studying mechanical and process engineering by touring factories; and studying ecology and natural history in Maine. Because of the wide variety of these offerings, expenses for this program cannot be included in tuition.

FACULTY AND ADVISERS

The full-time faculty consists of 32 women and 21 men. Faculty members hold sixty-two baccalaureate degrees and twenty-nine graduate degrees. Twelve faculty families and 10 single faculty members live on campus. The Rectory School seeks diversity within its faculty and supports professional growth opportunities during the school year and during the summer.

Thomas F. Army Jr. was appointed Headmaster in 1990. A graduate of Wesleyan University (B.A., 1976; M.A.L.S., 1982), he served on the Rectory School faculty from 1976 to 1978; he also served as Assistant Director of Alumni Relations at Wesleyan University and as a teacher and coach at Kent School.

The faculty members at the Rectory School are involved in all aspects of school life. Faculty members may coach, supervise a dormitory and student activities, or act as advisers. Regardless of title or job, all members of the faculty serve as role models for all students.

Every Rectory School student is assigned an adviser, usually one of his dorm parents. The adviser serves as a mentor, role model, counselor, and advocate for his or her advisee. Further guidance services are provided by School psychologist, the Director of Student Services, and other administrators.

The Rectory School provides placement counseling to all ninth-grade students and their families. The goal is to guide a student to a school where he or she may thrive academically and socially. Several schools are recommended to each student. The academic match is of primary importance, but all of a student's interests and talents are taken into consideration. In the past three years, students have matriculated to the following secondary schools: Avon, Berkshire, Blair, Blue Ridge, Brewster, Brooks, Choate, Christ, Christchurch, Darlington, Episcopal, Governor Dummer, Groton, Gunnery, Hill, Hotchkiss, Kent, Loomis–Chaffee, Milton, Peddie, Pomfret, Portsmouth Abbey, Proctor, Robert Louis Stevenson, Saint Mark's, Salisbury, St. George's, St. Paul's, Suffield, Tabor, Taft, Tilton, Trinity–Pawling, Virginia Episcopal, Westminster, Wilbraham and Monson, Williston Northampton, and Winchendon.

STUDENT BODY AND CONDUCT

The Rectory School enrolls 168 students in grades 5–9. In the ninth grade, there are 28 boarding boys and 7 day students, including 1 girl. There are 40 boarding boys and 18 day students, 7 of whom are girls, in the eighth grade. In the seventh grade, there are 24 boarding boys and 14 day students, 8 of whom are girls. There are 8 boarding boys and 10 day students, including 8 girls, in the sixth grade. In the fifth grade, there are 2 boarding boys and 17 day students, including 7 girls.

The Rectory School students come from twenty U.S. states and territories, including Alabama, California, Colorado, Connecticut, Florida, Georgia, Louisiana, Maine, Maryland, Massachusetts, Michigan, New Hampshire, New Jersey, New York, Pennsylvania, Rhode Island, Texas, Vermont, Virginia, and West Virginia. Ten other locations, including Bermuda, France, Haiti, Japan, Korea, Mexico, Nigeria, Russia, Switzerland, and Taiwan are represented in the Rectory School student body.

The School creed provides four cornerstone words that form the foundation of conduct at the Rectory School. Those principles are Responsibility, Respect, Honesty, and Compassion. All Rectory School students are required to sign a statement of understanding that describes and defines school rules and disciplinary procedures. Each week, students receive a conduct grade that evaluates their behavior over a seven-day period. Conduct grades affect privileges each week, especially weekend activities. The importance of responsibility, accountability, integrity, and concern for others is impressed upon each student throughout the day and emphasized during daily assemblies and a weekly nondenominational chapel service. Eighth-grade boarders who have distinguished themselves as leaders are selected by the faculty to serve as proctors, positions of honor and responsibility for ninth graders, in which they act as role models and provide guidance for younger students. The dress code requires jackets and ties for boys and dresses, skirts, or slacks for girls.

ACADEMIC FACILITIES

There are twenty-four buildings on campus, including the John B. Bigelow Academic Center (1983), which houses all classrooms, science labs, a greenhouse, three computer rooms that continue to be upgraded with the latest Mac hardware, and the library, which has undergone an expansion and renovation project. A new performing arts center with music rooms, M.I.D.I. labs, and a 214-seat theater has recently opened. Adjacent to the Academic Center is the Grosvenor House, which contains individualized instruction stations and administrative offices. The art barn, with two studios and a darkroom is the most recent addition to campus.

BOARDING AND GENERAL FACILITIES

Nonacademic facilities include seven dormitories, faculty residences, the Craig Calhoun Athletic Center (1987), the new Dining Hall, and the Health Center.

ATHLETICS

The Rectory School's athletic facilities include the Craig Calhoun Athletic Center (gym, weight room, wrestling room, lockers, and training room), six tennis courts, an outdoor basketball court, a street hockey court, five athletic fields, and a cross-country course as well as easy access to an ice rink.

Every student must participate in the athletic program. The School offers the opportunity to play on a competitive sports team on many levels for every season. A recreational team sport is available for those students who enjoy athletics without the competition. All students learn the valuable rewards of being part of a team, and they develop a feeling of confidence and self-esteem through their accomplishments. The Rectory School's varsity and junior varsity teams compete with middle and secondary schools in Connecticut, Rhode Island, and Massachusetts. Interscholastic teams compete in baseball, basketball, cross-country, fencing, football, golf, ice hockey, lacrosse, soccer, softball, tennis, track, and wrestling.

EXTRACURRICULAR OPPORTUNITIES

The Rectory School provides extensive opportunities for participation in arts and club programs. Club offerings include bowling, camping, weight lifting, swimming, horseback riding, squash, tennis, fishing, street hockey, hiking, skating, snowboarding, mountain biking, and in-line skating. Arts programs include an extensive music and drama program with groups for voice and band and individual lessons in all the band instruments as well as guitar, piano, and strings. Fine arts offerings include photography, painting, drawing, and ceramics.

DAILY LIFE

The rising bell rings at 6:45 a.m.; breakfast is at 7:05. The entire community assembles each morning at 8.

From 8:30 to 2:45, there are seven class periods, a cocurriculum period, chapel (Thursdays only), adviser meetings, and lunch. The cocurriculum period is a time for students to participate in activities such as band, chorus, drama, individual music lessons, fine arts, newspaper, yearbook, the literary magazine, woodshop, and model building. It is also a time when students can get extra help from subject teachers. Athletic teams practice and play games between 3 and 5. Dinner is served at 6, followed by evening study hall from 6:30 to 8:30. Bedtime is 9:30 for grades 6, 7, and 8, and it is at 10 p.m. for ninth graders.

WEEKEND LIFE

There are no Saturday classes. Five times a year an enrichment program is provided. Otherwise, the club program is run during the morning. Regular athletic practices and games are held in the afternoon. A ski program is run on both Saturdays and Sundays during the winter term. Faculty members chaperone these daylong ski trips to nearby mountains in central New England. Additional weekend activities include trips to college and professional athletic events, concerts, plays, movies, and other cultural events in nearby Hartford, Boston, Worcester, and Providence. Boarders are sometimes invited to day students' homes for the weekend.

SUMMER PROGRAMS

The five-week summer session is designed to help students develop a strong foundation in English, reading, mathematics, and study skills or to remediate specific areas of weakness. The summer program blends morning classes with camp activities each afternoon and weekend. The program can provide a student with a less stressful introduction to boarding life, allowing both the student and the School time to ascertain their mutual suitability.

The small classes, each with approximately 8 students, encourage participation and permit students to progress at their own pace. One-on-one tutoring is arranged for every student during one class period each day in order to supplement and individualize instruction and to enable the program to accommodate specific learning differences. The overall student-teacher ratio for the summer session is 3:1.

The afternoon schedule includes clinics that offer students the opportunity to try their hand at arts and crafts, tennis, Frisbee, golf, fishing, basketball, or soccer. The intramural athletics program allows all students the chance to exercise while participating in swimming, diving, baseball, basketball, touch football, soccer, softball, street hockey, and track and field events.

Weekend activities are planned to provide students the opportunity to experience some of what

New England has to offer. Recent day trips have included visits to the Museum of Science in Boston, Six Flags Theme Park, Mystic Aquarium, and the beach and attendance at Red Sox games.

COSTS AND FINANCIAL AID

The basic tuition charge for boarding students in 2005–06 was $31,900; this fee includes tuition and room and board. For those students enrolled in the IIP™, there was a tutoring fee of $6000. For boarding students, there was an additional required deposit of $2100 to open a bank account against which students may charge books, School store purchases, taxis for travel, special excursions, and similar items. The unexpended balance in the account at the year's end is refunded. Day student tuition ranged from $14,100 for grades 5 and 6 to $16,000 for the upper grades. A bank account deposit of $550 is required for day students. A limited amount of financial aid is available to qualified applicants according to need.

ADMISSIONS INFORMATION

It is the policy of the Rectory School to admit male boarding students regardless of race, color, or religion provided that they are of good character and intelligence and are capable of meeting the School's educational standards for admission. In addition, the Rectory School has day students, both boys and girls, who meet the same criteria. The Rectory School does not discriminate on the basis of race, color, or national or ethnic origin in the administration of its educational policies, admissions policies, scholarship and loan programs, and athletic and other School-administered programs.

New students are accepted in all grades, although new noninternational ninth graders are required to attend the Rectory School Summer Session. An interview, current transcripts, and testing are required.

APPLICATION TIMETABLE

Admission to the Rectory School is on a rolling basis. There is no application deadline for boarding students. Day students must have their application in by April 15. Campus interviews may be arranged by calling or writing the Admissions Office. Applications must be accompanied by a nonrefundable fee of $50 ($100 for international students). Students who are accepted are guaranteed a place when the enrollment contract is returned with an advance tuition deposit.

ADMISSIONS CORRESPONDENCE

Stephen A. DiPaolo, Director of Admission
The Rectory School
528 Pomfret Street
Pomfret, Connecticut 06258

Phone: 860-928-1328
Fax: 860-928-4961
E-mail: admissions@rectoryschool.org
Web site: http://www.rectoryschool.org

RUMSEY HALL SCHOOL

Washington Depot, Connecticut

Type: Coeducational boarding and day junior prep school
Grades: K–9: Lower School, K–5; Upper School, 6–9
Enrollment: School total: 306
Head of School: Thomas W. Farmen, Headmaster

THE SCHOOL

Rumsey Hall School was founded in 1900 by Mrs. Lillias Rumsey Sanford. Since its inception, Rumsey Hall School has retained its original philosophy: to help each child develop to his or her maximum stature as an individual, as a member of a family, and as a contributing member of society. The curriculum emphasizes basic academic skills, a complete athletic program, fine arts, computer literacy, and numerous extracurricular offerings, which are all designed to encourage individual responsibility for academic achievement, accomplishment in team sports, and service to the school community. The School believes that "effort is the key to success."

The 147-acre campus on the Bantam River provides landscaped and wooded areas in a rural environment located outside of Washington, Connecticut. Rumsey Hall School is 90 miles from New York City and within an hour of the major Connecticut cities of Hartford and New Haven. The School's location enables students to take advantage of major cultural and athletic events in New York City and Boston throughout the school year.

A nonprofit institution, Rumsey Hall School is governed by a 24-member Board of Trustees that meets quarterly. The 2003–04 operating budget totaled $5 million. Revenues include tuition and fees and contributions from alumni, parents, corporations, foundations, and friends of the School. The School's endowment is approximately $2.5 million, with the Board of Trustees' long-range planning committee examining ways to increase it. Annual giving has averaged more than $1.4 million the past three years, and a special capital campaign recently financed the purchase of 50 acres of adjacent land for athletic fields and faculty housing. Other campus improvements include two fully renovated computer labs and a new science and math building.

Rumsey Hall School is a member of the National Association of Independent Schools, the Connecticut Association of Independent Schools, the Junior Boarding Schools Association, the Educational Records Bureau, Western Connecticut Boarding Schools, and the Educational Testing Service and is a voting member of the Secondary School Admission Test Board.

ACADEMIC PROGRAMS

At Rumsey Hall, effort is as important as academic achievement. Effort as a criterion for success opens a new world to the students. Effort does not start and end with the student. It is a shared responsibility between the student and each faculty member. Just as the faculty members expect maximum effort from each student, they promise in return to give each student their very best effort.

Students in the Upper School (sixth through ninth grades) carry at least five major subjects. There are eight 40-minute periods in each day, including lunch. Extra help is available each day for students who need additional instruction or extra challenges. All classes are departmentalized.

Final examinations are given in all subjects twice a year. Report cards, with numerical grades, are

sent home every other week throughout the school year. Anecdotal comments and individualized teacher, adviser, and Headmaster comments are sent home three times each academic year.

A supplementary feature of the academic program is the Language Skills Department. This course is directed toward intellectually able students with dyslexia or learning disabilities. Students in this program carry a regular academic course load, with the exception of a foreign language. Eighteen percent of the student body is involved in this program.

The school year, divided into trimesters, begins in September and runs until the first weekend in June. Vacations are scheduled at Thanksgiving, Christmas, and in the spring.

Class size averages 13 students. Classes are heterogeneous except for some honors courses offered to exceptional ninth graders.

Students have a study hall built into their daily schedule, and there is an evening study hall for all boarding students. All study halls are supervised by faculty members, and there is ample opportunity for study assistance. The library and computer facilities adjoin the formal study hall and are available at all study times.

FACULTY AND ADVISERS

All 50 full-time faculty members (25 men and 25 women) hold baccalaureate degrees, and half have master's degrees. Most faculty members live on campus with their families. This enables Rumsey to provide the close supervision and warm family atmosphere that is an essential part of the School's culture.

Thomas W. Farmen was appointed Headmaster of Rumsey Hall School in 1985. He holds a Bachelor of Arts degree from New England College and a master's in school administration from Western Connecticut State University. He has served as President of the Association of Boarding Schools for the National Association of Independent Schools, President of the Junior Boarding Schools Association, and as a director of the Connecticut Association of Independent Schools.

The Dean of Students supervises and coordinates the advisory program. Each faculty member has 7 or 8 student advisees. Advisers meet with their advisees individually and in a weekly group setting. The adviser is the first link in the line of communication between school and home.

Faculty members at Rumsey Hall are encouraged to continue their professional development by taking postgraduate courses and attending seminars and conferences throughout the year. The School is committed to this growth and generously funds these programs.

The Director of Secondary School Placement supervises all facets of the secondary school search. Beginning in the eighth grade, a process of testing and interviewing with students and parents takes place that enables the placement director to highlight certain schools that seem appropriate. After visits and interviews with the schools, the list is pared down to those to which the student wishes to apply. The class of 2005 wrote applications to forty-

six schools, and 76 percent of the students enrolled in their first-choice schools. Members of the classes of 2003 and 2004 enrolled in the following prep schools: Blair, Brewster, Canterbury, Cheshire Academy, Deerfield, Exeter, The Gunnery, Hill, Hotchkiss, Hun, Kent, Middlesex, Miss Porters, Northfield Mount Hermon, Peddie, Phillips Exeter, Pomfret, Proctor, St. George's, Salisbury, Stevenson School, Suffield, Tabor, Taft, and Westminster.

STUDENT BODY AND CONDUCT

In 2005–06, Rumsey Hall enrolled 306 students. The Lower School (grades K–5) enrolled 84 students: 11 in kindergarten, 14 in first grade, 11 in second grade, 12 in third grade, 14 in fourth grade, and 22 in the fifth grade. The Upper School enrolled 222 students: 31 in the sixth grade, 49 in the seventh grade, 85 in the eighth grade, and 57 in the ninth grade. The Lower School consisted of 82 day students and 2 boarders, while the Upper School had 190 day students and 116 boarders. The School population was 66 percent boys and 34 percent girls.

In 2005–06, Rumsey students came from sixteen different states, eight countries, and twenty-eight local communities. Eight percent of the community was composed of international students who are enrolled in the ESL (English as a second language) program.

The Rumsey dress code requires jackets, collared shirts, and ties for boys and dresses or skirts and collared shirts or blouses for girls. There is a slight change in the winter term, when boys may wear turtlenecks and sweaters and the girls may wear slacks.

The School values of honesty, kindness, and respect comprise the yardstick by which Rumsey measures a student's thoughts and actions. Students living outside the spirit of the community are asked to meet with the Disciplinary and Senior committees. These committees represent a cross section of administrators, faculty, and students.

ACADEMIC FACILITIES

Situated alongside the Bantam River on a 147-acre campus, the School is housed in twenty-five buildings, most of which have been constructed since 1950. Nine structures house a total of thirty classrooms, including the new Dicke Family Math and Science Building. Other buildings include the library; the Sanford House, which houses the study and meeting hall; the John Seward Johnson Sr. Fine Arts Center, with spacious art and music studios; and the Satyvati Science Center. The centerpiece of the campus is the redbrick School Courtyard.

BOARDING AND GENERAL FACILITIES

The close relationship between teachers and students is a special part of Rumsey Hall School. Students live in dormitories with supportive dorm parents, and students become a part of their dorm parents' families.

Rumsey's boarding students live in one of seven dormitories. Dormitories are assigned by age, and most students have roommates, although single

rooms are available in most dorms. Each dormitory has its own common room that is the shared living space for the dorm. A School snack bar and store are open every afternoon. Laundry and dry cleaning are sent out on a weekly basis. Two registered nurses staff the School's infirmary, and the School doctor, a local pediatrician, is available on a daily basis. Emergency facilities are available at New Milford Hospital, which is 10 miles away. There are telephones in all dormitories, and every student has an e-mail account.

ATHLETICS

Athletics are a healthy and essential part of the Rumsey experience. On the playing field, lifelong attitudes, values, and habits are born. All students participate at their own level in athletics. Effort is rewarded through athletic letters and certificates at the end of the season.

Rumsey Hall fields twenty-eight interscholastic teams throughout the year. Most sports are offered on different levels so that students are able to compete with children on their own size and skill level. Interscholastic teams are fielded in baseball, basketball, crew, cross-country, field hockey, football, ice hockey, skiing, soccer, softball, tennis, volleyball, and wrestling. Other activities available include horseback riding, Outing Club, Lower School games and activities, recreational skiing and snowboarding, biking, and ice skating.

The Magnoli Gymnasium houses basketball, volleyball, and wrestling facilities. The Cornell Common Room serves as the weight training room and offers other training machines, as well as housing the athletic director and athletic training staff. The Schereschewsky Center contains three indoor tennis courts. The hockey teams skate at the indoor rinks at neighboring prep schools. In addition, there are seven outdoor playing fields and two skating ponds.

EXTRACURRICULAR OPPORTUNITIES

Throughout the year, students may participate in many activities and clubs. The choices include fishing, computer, chorus, art club, trapshooting, forestry, bicycling, fly fishing, golf, School newspaper, yearbook, art, backgammon, swimming, hiking, rocketry, lacrosse, baking, community service, intramural sports, and participation in School dramatic and musical productions.

Traditional annual events for the school community include fall and spring community work days, a Christmas concert, Parents' Days twice a year, Grandparents' Day in the spring, and a Holi-

day Carol Sing through the town. Service to the School and to the greater community is encouraged throughout the year by the community service club and the student government.

The student body is divided into red and blue color teams. These teams enjoy friendly competition throughout the school year in areas of community service, academic achievement, and athletics.

DAILY LIFE

The school day begins at 8 a.m. with an all-School meeting. The meeting is run by the Headmaster, and all administrators, faculty members, and students are in attendance. It is a time to share the news of the School and the world as well as important information and announcements with the whole community. The rest of the academic day consists of eight 40-minute periods and supervised study halls, with a 20-minute recess in the middle of the morning. Extra help is available every day after lunch. Athletic practices or contests take place at 3 p.m. Dinner is served family style at 6 and is followed by study hall from 7 to 8:30. Free time follows, with bedtimes varying depending on the grade of the child.

WEEKEND LIFE

Weekends for boarding students include a variety of activities on and off campus. There are School dances, special theme weekends, off-campus trips, and intramural activities on campus. Rumsey's proximity to four major cities—New York, Boston, Hartford, and New Haven—allows for a wide variety of cultural events, sports events (collegiate and professional), and shopping excursions. All trips are fully supervised, and an appropriate student-teacher ratio is maintained. Day students are encouraged to participate in weekend activities and are also allowed to invite boarding students home with them for the weekend.

SUMMER PROGRAMS

The five-week Rumsey Hall summer session is open to students in the third through ninth grades. The program is designed for students who desire enrichment or need additional work in a subject area in order to move on to the next grade with confidence. There is an emphasis on study skills and a heavy concentration on mathematics and language skills. The morning and evening are set aside for academic work, while the afternoon is purely recreational.

COSTS AND FINANCIAL AID

In 2005–06, tuition was $9300 to $12,300 for kindergarten, $12,650 for day students in grades 1 and 2, $15,550 for day students in grades 3–9, and $32,500 for boarding students. Additional fees included books, athletic fees, school supplies, and laundry and dry cleaning. A nonrefundable deposit of $2000 served as the student's drawing account for the year. Two thirds of the tuition was due July 15 and the balance December 15, unless the family chose to pay in ten monthly installments through KEY Educational Resources.

Rumsey Hall is a member of the School and Student Service for Financial Aid and annually awards financial aid to more than a quarter of the students.

ADMISSIONS INFORMATION

Rumsey Hall welcomes students of average to above-average intelligence and achievement. Students must show evidence of good citizenship and the willingness to live in a boarding community. Acceptance is based on past school performance, scores on standardized achievement tests, and a personal interview. Rumsey is able to accept a limited number of students with learning differences if their learning profile is compatible with the School's Orton-Gillingham–based language skills program. Rumsey Hall School admits students of any race, color, religion, or national or ethnic origin.

APPLICATION TIMETABLE

Inquiries are welcome at any time of the year, with most families beginning the admissions process in the fall or winter in anticipation of September enrollment. Admissions interviews and tours are scheduled throughout the year. Applications are accepted on a rolling basis anytime after the interview date for boarding student applicants. A February 15 due date and March 1 notification date applies to day student applicants. The Admissions Committee makes decisions on applicants within two weeks of receiving the completed application package. Families are asked to respond to an offer of acceptance in a similar time frame.

ADMISSIONS CORRESPONDENCE

Matthew S. Hoeniger, Director of Admissions
Rumsey Hall School
201 Romford Road
Washington Depot, Connecticut 06794

Phone: 860-868-0535
Fax: 860-868-7907
E-mail: admiss@rumseyhall.org
Web site: http://www.rumseyhall.org

Specialized Directories

COEDUCATIONAL DAY SCHOOLS

Academia Cotopaxi, Ecuador
Academie Sainte Cecile International School, ON, Canada
The Academy at Charlemont, MA
The Academy for Gifted Children (PACE), ON, Canada
Academy of Holy Angels, MN
The Academy of St. Joseph, NY
Academy of the Holy Names, FL
Academy of the Pacific, HI
Academy of the Sacred Heart, MI
ACS Cobham International School, United Kingdom
ACS Egham International School, United Kingdom
ACS Hillingdon International School, United Kingdom
Adelphi Academy, NY
Admiral Farragut Academy, FL
Airdrie Koinonia Christian School, AB, Canada
Akiba Hebrew Academy, PA
The Albany Academy, NY
Albert College, ON, Canada
Albuquerque Academy, NM
Alexander Dawson School, CO
Allen Academy, TX
Allendale Columbia School, NY
Alliance Academy, Ecuador
Allison Academy, FL
All Saints' Episcopal School, MS
All Saints' Episcopal School of Fort Worth, TX
The Altamont School, AL
Al-Worood School, United Arab Emirates
Ambassador Preparatory, MN
American Academy, FL
American Community Schools of Athens, Greece
American Cooperative School, Bolivia
American Heritage School, FL
The American International School, Austria
American International School in Cyprus, Cyprus
American International School of Bucharest, Romania
American International School-Riyadh, Saudi Arabia
American International School Salzburg, Austria
American Overseas School of Rome, Italy
The American School Foundation, Mexico
The American School in Japan, Japan
The American School in London, United Kingdom
American School of Doha, Qatar
The American School of Madrid, Spain
American School of Milan, Italy
American School of Paris, France
The American School of Puerto Vallarta, Mexico
The American School of The Hague, Netherlands
American School of Warsaw, Poland
Anacapa School, CA
Anglo-American School of Moscow, Russian Federation
Annie Wright School, WA
Appleby College, ON, Canada
Aquin Central Catholic High School, IL
Archbishop Mitty High School, CA
Archmere Academy, DE
Armona Union Academy, CA
Arrowhead Christian Academy, CA
Arrowsmith School, ON, Canada
Ashbury College, ON, Canada

Asheville School, NC
The Athenian School, CA
Athens Academy, GA
Atlanta International School, GA
Aurora Central High School, IL
The Awty International School, TX
Baldwin School of Puerto Rico, Inc., PR
The Baltimore Actors' Theatre Conservatory, MD
Baltimore Lutheran Middle and Upper School, MD
Bancroft School, MA
Bangor Christian School, ME
Baptist High School, NJ
Barnstable Academy, NJ
The Barstow School, MO
Battle Ground Academy, TN
Baylor School, TN
Bayside Academy, AL
Beacon High School, MA
Bearspaw Christian School, AB, Canada
Beaufort Academy, SC
Beaver Country Day School, MA
The Beekman School, NY
Beijing BISS International School, China
Bellarmine Preparatory School, WA
Bellevue Christian School, WA
The Bement School, MA
Benet Academy, IL
Ben Franklin Academy, GA
Benilde–St. Margaret's School, MN
The Benjamin School, FL
Bentley School, CA
Berkeley Carroll School, NY
Berkeley Preparatory School, FL
Berkshire School, MA
Berwick Academy, ME
The Bethany Hills School, ON, Canada
The Birch Wathen Lenox School, NY
Bishop Brady High School, NH
Bishop Brossart High School, KY
Bishop Carroll High School, PA
Bishop Eustace Preparatory School, NJ
Bishop Feehan High School, MA
Bishop Fenwick High School, OH
Bishop George Ahr High School, NJ
Bishop Guertin High School, NH
Bishop Hoban High School, PA
Bishop Ireton High School, VA
Bishop Kelly High School, ID
Bishop Kenny High School, FL
Bishop Luers High School, IN
Bishop Lynch Catholic High School, TX
Bishop McDevitt High School, PA
Bishop McGuinness Catholic High School, OK
Bishop McNamara High School, IL
Bishop Quinn High School/St. Francis Middle School, CA
Bishop's College School, QC, Canada
Bishop Verot High School, FL
Bishop Walsh Middle High School, MD
Bismark St. Mary's Central, ND
Black Forest Academy, Germany
Blair Academy, NJ

The Blake School, MN
Blueprint Education, AZ
The Bolles School, FL
Boston University Academy, MA
Boyd-Buchanan School, TN
Bradenton Christian School, FL
Brandon Hall School, GA
Breck School, MN
Brehm Preparatory School, IL
Brent School-Baguio, Philippines
Brentwood Academy, TN
Brentwood College School, BC, Canada
Brentwood School, CA
Brewster Academy, NH
Bridges Academy, CA
Bridge School, CO
British Columbia Christian Academy, BC, Canada
The British International School, Jeddah, Saudi Arabia
The British School, Muscat, Oman
Broadview Academy, IL
The Brook Hill School, TX
Brooklyn Friends School, NY
Brooks School, MA
Brookstone School, GA
Brownell-Talbot School, NE
Buckingham Browne & Nichols School, MA
The Buckley School, CA
The Bullis School, MD
Bulloch Academy, GA
Burke Mountain Academy, VT
Burr and Burton Academy, VT
The Bush School, WA
Buxton School, MA
Calgary Academy, AB, Canada
The Calhoun School, NY
Calvary Christian Academy, KY
The Calverton School, MD
Cambridge International College of Canada, ON, Canada
The Cambridge School of Weston, MA
Camelot Academy, NC
Campbell Hall (Episcopal), CA
Campion School, Athens, Greece
Canadian Academy, Japan
Cannon School, NC
Canterbury High School, IN
Canterbury School, CT
Canterbury School, FL
The Canterbury School of Florida, FL
Canyonville Christian Academy, OR
Cape Cod Academy, MA
Cape Fear Academy, NC
Cape Henry Collegiate School, VA
Cardinal Gibbons High School, FL
Cardinal Mooney Catholic College Preparatory High
    School, MI
Cardinal Newman High School, FL
Cardinal Newman School, SC
Caribbean Preparatory School, PR
Carlisle School, VA
Carlucci American International School of Lisbon, Portugal
Carolina Day School, NC

Carrabassett Valley Academy, ME
Cary Academy, NC
Casady School, OK
Cascadilla School, NY
Cascia Hall Preparatory School, OK
Cate School, CA
Cathedral High School, IN
Catholic Central High School, NY
The Catlin Gabel School, OR
CCI The Renaissance School, Italy
Centennial Academy, QC, Canada
Central Catholic High School, CA
Central Catholic Mid-High School, NE
Chadwick School, CA
Chamberlain-Hunt Academy, MS
Chaminade College Preparatory, CA
Chaminade-Madonna College Preparatory, FL
Chamisa Mesa High School, NM
Chapel Hill–Chauncy Hall School, MA
Chapel School, Brazil
Charles E. Smith Jewish Day School, MD
Charles Finney School, NY
Charles Wright Academy, WA
Charlotte Christian School, NC
Charlotte Country Day School, NC
Charlotte Latin School, NC
Chase Collegiate School, CT
Chatham Academy, GA
Chattanooga Christian School, TN
Chelsea School, MD
Cheshire Academy, CT
Cheverus High School, ME
Chinese Christian Schools, CA
Choate Rosemary Hall, CT
Christa McAuliffe Academy, WA
Christ Church Episcopal School, SC
Christchurch School, VA
Christian Brothers Academy, NY
Christian Brothers High School, CA
Christian Central Academy, NY
Christian Heritage School, CT
Christian Junior–Senior High School, CA
Christopher Dock Mennonite High School, PA
Chrysalis School, WA
Cincinnati Country Day School, OH
Coe-Brown Northwood Academy, NH
Colegio Bolivar, Colombia
Colegio Franklin D. Roosevelt, Peru
Colegio Nueva Granada, Colombia
Collège du Leman International School, Switzerland
The College Preparatory School, CA
The Collegiate School, VA
The Colorado Rocky Mountain School, CO
The Colorado Springs School, CO
Colorado Timberline Academy, CO
Columbia Academy, TN
Columbia Grammar and Preparatory School, NY
Columbia International College of Canada, ON, Canada
Columbia International School, Japan
The Columbus Academy, OH
Commonwealth School, MA

Community Christian Academy, KY
Community High School, NJ
The Community School of Naples, FL
The Concept School, PA
Concord Academy, MA
Concordia Academy, MN
Concordia Continuing Education High School, AB, Canada
Concordia High School, AB, Canada
Convent of the Visitation School, MN
Copiah Academy, MS
The Cottage School, GA
The Country Day School, ON, Canada
Covenant Canadian Reformed School, AB, Canada
The Craig School, NJ
Cranbrook Schools, MI
Crawford Adventist Academy, ON, Canada
Crawford Day School, VA
Cretin-Derham Hall, MN
Crossroads School, MO
Crossroads School for Arts & Sciences, CA
Crystal Springs Uplands School, CA
The Culver Academies, IN
Currey Ingram Academy, TN
Cushing Academy, MA
Dallas Academy, TX
Dallas Christian School, TX
The Dalton School, NY
Danube International School, Vienna, Austria
Darlington School, GA
Darrow School, NY
David Lipscomb High School, TN
Deerfield Academy, MA
De La Salle College, ON, Canada
DeLaSalle High School, MN
Delaware County Christian School, PA
Delaware Valley Friends School, PA
Delphi Academy of Los Angeles, CA
The Delphian School, OR
Denver Academy, CO
Denver Christian High School, CO
Denver Lutheran High School, CO
The Derryfield School, NH
Detroit Country Day School, MI
Devon Park Christian School, NB, Canada
Doane Stuart School, NY
Doctor Franklin Perkins School, MA
Dowling High School, IA
Dubai American Academy, United Arab Emirates
Dublin Christian Academy, NH
Dublin School, NH
Dunn School, CA
Durham Academy, NC
Dwight-Englewood School, NJ
The Dwight School, NY
Eagle Hill School, MA
Eagle Hill-Southport, CT
Eagle Rock School, CO
East Catholic High School, CT
Eastern Christian High School, NJ
Eastern Mennonite High School, VA
Eastside College Preparatory School, CA

Ecole d'Humanite, Switzerland
Edison School, AB, Canada
Elgin Academy, IL
Elyria Catholic High School, OH
Emerson Honors High Schools, CA
The Emery Weiner School, TX
The English School, Kuwait, Kuwait
The Episcopal Academy, PA
Episcopal Collegiate School, AR
Episcopal High School, TX
Episcopal High School of Jacksonville, FL
The Episcopal School of Acadiana, LA
The Episcopal School of Dallas, TX
Equilibrium International Education Institute, AB, Canada
Escola Americana de Campinas, Brazil
The Ethical Culture Fieldston School, NY
Evansville Day School, IN
Explorations Academy, WA
Ezell-Harding Christian School, TN
Fairhill School, TX
Faith Lutheran High School, NV
Falmouth Academy, MA
Father Lopez High School, FL
Father Ryan High School, TN
Fay School, MA
The Field School, DC
First Baptist Academy, TX
First Presbyterian Day School, GA
F. L. Chamberlain School, MA
Flint Hill School, VA
Florida Air Academy, FL
Foothills Academy, AB, Canada
The Forman School, CT
Forsyth Country Day School, NC
Fort Worth Christian School, TX
Fort Worth Country Day School, TX
Fountain Valley School of Colorado, CO
Fowlers Academy, PR
Fox River Country Day School, IL
Fox Valley Lutheran Academy, IL
Fox Valley Lutheran High School, WI
Francis Parker School, CA
Francis W. Parker School, IL
Franklin Road Academy, TN
Fraser Academy, BC, Canada
Frederica Academy, GA
Freeman Academy, SD
French-American School of New York, NY
Fresno Christian Schools, CA
Friends Academy, NY
Friends' Central School, PA
Friends School of Baltimore, MD
Friends Seminary, NY
The Frostig School, CA
Fryeburg Academy, ME
Fuqua School, VA
Futures High School, Oceanside, CA
Futures High School—San Diego, CA
The Galloway School, GA
Garces Memorial High School, CA
Garden School, NY

Gaston Day School, NC
Gateway Christian School, BC, Canada
Gateway School, TX
Gem State Adventist Academy, ID
The Geneva School, FL
George School, PA
George Stevens Academy, ME
Georgetown Day School, DC
George Walton Academy, GA
Germantown Academy, PA
Germantown Friends School, PA
Gill St. Bernard's School, NJ
Gilmour Academy, OH
Glades Day School, FL
Glenelg Country School, MD
The Glenholme School, CT
Gonzaga Preparatory School, WA
Gould Academy, ME
Governor Dummer Academy, MA
The Governor French Academy, IL
Grace Baptist Schools, CA
Grace Christian School, AK
The Grauer School, CA
Greater Atlanta Christian Schools, GA
Great Lakes Christian College, ON, Canada
Greenfield School, NC
Green Fields Country Day School, AZ
Greenhill School, TX
Greenhills School, MI
Greensboro Day School, NC
Greens Farms Academy, CT
Greenwood Laboratory School, MO
Grenville Christian College, ON, Canada
Groton School, MA
Grove School, CT
Gstaad International School, Switzerland
Guamani Private School, PR
Guerin College Preparatory High School, IL
Gulliver Preparatory School, FL
The Gunnery, CT
Gunston Day School, MD
Hackett Catholic Central High School, MI
Hackley School, NY
Hale O Ulu School Child and Family Service, HI
Halifax Grammar School, NS, Canada
Hamden Hall Country Day School, CT
Hamilton District Christian School, ON, Canada
Hamilton Learning Centre, ON, Canada
Hammond School, SC
Hampton Roads Academy, VA
Happy Valley School, CA
Harare International School, Zimbabwe
Harding Academy, TN
Hargrave Military Academy, VA
The Harker School, CA
The Harley School, NY
Harrells Christian Academy, NC
The Harrisburg Academy, PA
Harvard-Westlake School, CA
The Harvey School, NY
Hawaiian Mission Academy, HI

Hawaii Baptist Academy, HI
Hawai'i Preparatory Academy, HI
Hawken School, OH
Hayden High School, KS
Head-Royce School, CA
Hebrew Academy-the Five Towns, NY
Hebron Academy, ME
Heritage Christian School, ON, Canada
The Heritage School, GA
Highland Hall, A Waldorf School, CA
Highland School, VA
High Mowing School, NH
The Hill Center, Durham Academy, NC
Hillcrest Christian School, CA
Hillcrest Christian School, AB, Canada
Hillcrest School, TX
Hillfield Strathallan College, ON, Canada
The Hill School, PA
The Hill Top Preparatory School, PA
Hilton Head Preparatory School, SC
Hokkaido International School, Japan
Holderness School, NH
Holland Hall, OK
Holy Name High School, PA
Holyoke Catholic High School, MA
Holy Trinity Diocesan High School, NY
Hoosac School, NY
Hope Christian School, AB, Canada
Hopkins School, CT
The Horace Mann School, NY
Horizons School, GA
Hosanna Christian School, OR
The Hotchkiss School, CT
Houghton Academy, NY
Houston Learning Academy-Central Campus, TX
Howe Military School, IN
Hudson College, ON, Canada
The Hudson School, NJ
The Hun School of Princeton, NJ
Huntington-Surrey School, TX
Hvitfeldtska Gymnasiet, International Section, Sweden
Hyde School, CT
Hyde School, ME
Idyllwild Arts Academy, CA
Immaculata High School, NJ
Immaculate Conception School, IL
Immanuel Christian High School, AB, Canada
Indian Mountain School, CT
Indian Springs School, AL
Interlochen Arts Academy, MI
International College Spain, Spain
International Community School of Addis Ababa, Ethiopia
International High School of FAIS, CA
International Junior Golf Academy, SC
International School Bangkok, Thailand
International School Basel, Switzerland
International School Hamburg, Germany
International School of Amsterdam, Netherlands
International School of Aruba, Aruba
International School of Athens, Greece
International School of Berne, Switzerland

International School of Brussels, Belgium
The International School of Geneva, Switzerland
The International School of Kuala Lumpur, Malaysia
International School of Lausanne, Switzerland
International School of Luxembourg, Luxembourg
International School of Minnesota, MN
The International School of Monaco, Monaco
International School of Port-of-Spain, Trinidad and Tobago
International School of South Africa, South Africa
Iolani School, HI
Isidore Newman School, LA
Islamic Saudi Academy, VA
Istanbul International Community School, Turkey
Jackson Academy, MS
Jackson Preparatory School, MS
Jakarta International School, Indonesia
John Burroughs School, MO
The John Cooper School, TX
John F. Kennedy Memorial High School, WA
The June Shelton School and Evaluation Center, TX
Justin-Siena High School, CA
Kalamazoo Christian High School, MI
Kapaun Mount Carmel Catholic High School, KS
Karachi American School, Pakistan
The Karafin School, NY
Kearney Catholic High School, NE
Keith Country Day School, IL
Kent Denver School, CO
Kent School, CT
Kents Hill School, ME
Kentucky Country Day School, KY
The Key School, MD
Key School, Inc., TX
Keystone National High School, PA
Keystone School, TX
Kildonan School, NY
Kimball Union Academy, NH
Kimberton Waldorf School, PA
King & Low-Heywood Thomas School, CT
King David High School, BC, Canada
The King's Academy, TN
The King's Christian High School, NJ
Kings Christian School, CA
King's College School, ON, Canada
Kingshill School, VI
Kingsway College, ON, Canada
King's West School, WA
Kingswood-Oxford School, CT
The Kinkaid School, TX
The Knox School, NY
La Cheim School, CA
La Grange Academy, GA
Laguna Blanca School, CA
La Jolla Country Day School, CA
Lakefield College School, ON, Canada
Lake Forest Academy, IL
Lake Highland Preparatory School, FL
Lakehill Preparatory School, TX
Lakeland Christian Academy, IN
Lake Ridge Academy, OH
Lakeside School, WA

Lakewood Prep, NJ
La Lumiere School, IN
Lancaster Country Day School, PA
Landmark East School, NS, Canada
Landmark School, MA
Lansdale Catholic High School, PA
La Salle Academy, RI
La Salle High School, CA
The Latin School of Chicago, IL
Lausanne Collegiate School, TN
Lawrence Academy, MA
Lawrence School, OH
The Lawrenceville School, NJ
Lawrence Woodmere Academy, NY
Lebanon Catholic Junior / Senior High School, PA
The Leelanau School, MI
Lee-Scott Academy, AL
Lehigh Valley Christian High School, PA
Lehman High School, OH
Le Lycee Francais de Los Angeles, CA
Lexington Catholic High School, KY
Lexington Christian Academy, MA
Lick-Wilmerding High School, CA
Lifegate School, OR
Linden Christian School, MB, Canada
Linfield Christian School, CA
The Linsly School, WV
Little Red School House and Elisabeth Irwin High School, NY
Living Word Academy, PA
Long Island Lutheran Middle and High School, NY
The Loomis Chaffee School, CT
Los Angeles Baptist Junior/Senior High School, CA
Los Angeles Lutheran High School, CA
Lourdes Catholic High School, AZ
The Lovett School, GA
The Lowell Whiteman School, CO
Lower Brule High School, SD
Lower Canada College, QC, Canada
Loyola Academy, IL
Loyola School, NY
Lustre Christian High School, MT
Lutheran High North, TX
Lutheran High School, CA
Lutheran High School, IN
Lutheran High School, MN
Lutheran High School North, MO
Lutheran High School of Hawaii, HI
Lutheran High School South, MO
Luther College High School, SK, Canada
Lycee Français de New York, NY
The Lycee International, American Section, France
Lycee International de Los Angeles, CA
Lydia Patterson Institute, TX
Lyndon Institute, VT
The MacDuffie School, MA
Madison Academy, AL
Madison-Ridgeland Academy, MS
Maharishi School of the Age, IA
Maine Central Institute, ME
Malaspina International High School, BC, Canada

Manhattan Christian High School, MT
Manlius Pebble Hill School, NY
Maplebrook School, NY
Maret School, DC
Marianapolis Preparatory School, CT
Marian Central Catholic High School, IL
Marian High School, IN
Marin Academy, CA
Marion Academy, AL
Marist High School, IL
Marist High School, NJ
Marist School, GA
Marshall School, MN
Mars Hill Bible School, AL
The Marvelwood School, CT
Mary Institute and St. Louis Country Day School (MICDS), MO
Maryknoll School, HI
Marymount International School, Italy
Massanutten Military Academy, VA
The Masters School, NY
Mater Dei High School, IN
Matignon High School, MA
Maumee Valley Country Day School, OH
Maur Hill-Mount Academy, KS
Mazapan School, Honduras
McDonogh School, MD
McGill-Toolen Catholic High School, AL
McNicholas High School, OH
Meadowridge Senior School, BC, Canada
The Meadows School, NV
The Meeting School, NH
Menaul School, NM
Menlo School, CA
Mentor College, ON, Canada
Mercedes College, Australia
Mercersburg Academy, PA
Mercyhurst Preparatory School, PA
Metropolitan Preparatory Academy, ON, Canada
Miami Country Day School, FL
Middlesex School, MA
Mid-Pacific Institute, HI
Mid-Peninsula High School, CA
Milken Community High School of Stephen Wise Temple, CA
Millbrook School, NY
Miller School, VA
Milton Academy, MA
Mississauga Private School, ON, Canada
MMI Preparatory School, PA
Montclair College Preparatory School, CA
Montclair Kimberley Academy, NJ
Monte Vista Christian School, CA
Montgomery Catholic Preparatory School, AL
Mont'Kiara International School, Malaysia
Montverde Academy, FL
Moorestown Friends School, NJ
Mooseheart High School, IL
Moravian Academy, PA
Moreau Catholic High School, CA
Morgan Park Academy, IL

Morristown-Beard School, NJ
Mounds Park Academy, MN
Mountain View Christian High School, NV
Mount Saint Charles Academy, RI
Munich International School, Germany
Nacel International School, MN
National Sports Academy at Lake Placid, NY
Navajo Preparatory School, Inc., NM
Nazareth Academy, IL
Nbisiing Education Centre, ON, Canada
Nebraska Christian Schools, NE
Newark Academy, NJ
New Covenant Academy, MO
The Newgrange School, NJ
New Hampton School, NH
Newman High School, WI
The Newman School, MA
The Newport School, MD
New Summit School, MS
New York Military Academy, NY
Niagara Christian Collegiate, ON, Canada
The Nichols School, NY
Noble and Greenough School, MA
The Nora School, MD
Norfolk Academy, VA
Norfolk Collegiate School, VA
The North Broward Preparatory Upper School, FL
North Cobb Christian School, GA
North Country School, NY
Northfield Mount Hermon School, MA
The North Shore Country Day School, IL
Northside Christian School, FL
Northwest Community Christian School, AZ
The Northwest School, WA
Northwest Yeshiva High School, WA
Northwood School, NY
North Yarmouth Academy, ME
The Norwich Free Academy, CT
Notre Dame High School, LA
Notre Dame High School, NJ
Notre Dame High School, WV
Notre Dame Junior/Senior High School, PA
Notre Dame Regional Secondary, BC, Canada
Oak Hill Academy, VA
Oak Knoll School of the Holy Child, NJ
The Oakland School, PA
Oakland School, VA
Oak Mountain Academy, GA
Oak Ridge Military Academy, NC
The Oakridge School, TX
Oakwood Friends School, NY
Oakwood School, CA
The Oakwood School, NC
Ojai Valley School, CA
Okanagan Adventist Academy, BC, Canada
Oldenburg Academy, IN
Olney Friends School, OH
The O'Neal School, NC
Oneida Baptist Institute, KY
Orangewood Adventist Academy, CA
Oregon Episcopal School, OR

Orinda Academy, CA
The Orme School, AZ
Our Lady Of Fatima High School, RI
Our Lady of the Sacred Heart, PA
Our Saviour Lutheran School, NY
Out-Of-Door-Academy, FL
The Overlake School, WA
Overseas Family School, Singapore
Oxford School, CA
Pace Academy, GA
Pacific Hills School, CA
Pacific Northern Academy, AK
Padua Franciscan High School, OH
The Paideia School, GA
Palmer Trinity School, FL
Paraclete High School, CA
The Parker School, HI
Parklane Academy, MS
The Park School, MD
The Park School of Buffalo, NY
Park Tudor School, IN
The Pathway School, PA
Peddie School, NJ
The Pembroke Hill School, MO
The Pennington School, NJ
Perkiomen School, PA
Phillips Academy (Andover), MA
Phillips Exeter Academy, NH
Phoenix Christian Unified Schools, AZ
Phoenix Country Day School, AZ
Pickens Academy, AL
Pickering College, ON, Canada
Piedmont Academy, GA
Pine Crest School, FL
Pine Forge Academy, PA
Pine Ridge School, VT
The Pingree School, MA
The Pingry School, NJ
Pius X High School, NE
Polytechnic Preparatory Country Day School, NY
Polytechnic School, CA
Pomfret School, CT
Pope John Paul II High School, FL
Portland Christian Schools, OR
Portland Lutheran School, OR
Portledge School, NY
Portsmouth Abbey School, RI
Portsmouth Christian Academy, NH
The Potomac School, VA
Poughkeepsie Day School, NY
Powers Catholic High School, MI
The Prairie School, WI
Prestonwood Christian Academy, TX
Princeton Day School, NJ
Proctor Academy, NH
Professional Children's School, NY
Providence Country Day School, RI
Providence High School, CA
Providence School, FL
Pulaski Academy, AR
Punahou School, HI

Purcell Marian High School, OH
The Putney School, VT
Queen Anne School, MD
Queen Margaret's School, BC, Canada
Queensway Christian College, ON, Canada
Quigley Catholic High School, PA
Quincy Notre Dame High School, IL
Quinte Christian High School, ON, Canada
Rabbi Alexander S. Gross Hebrew Academy, FL
Rabun Gap-Nacoochee School, GA
Randolph-Macon Academy, VA
Randolph School, AL
Ranney School, NJ
Ransom Everglades School, FL
Ravenscroft School, NC
The Rectory School, CT
Regis High School, OR
Ribet Academy, CA
Ridgewood Preparatory School, LA
Ridley College, ON, Canada
Rio Lindo Adventist Academy, CA
Ripon Christian Schools, CA
Riverdale Country School, NY
Rivermont Collegiate, IA
Riverside School, Switzerland
The Rivers School, MA
Riverstone Community School, ID
Robert Louis Stevenson School, NY
The Rockland Country Day School, NY
Rock Point School, VT
Rockway Mennonite Collegiate, ON, Canada
Rocky Hill School, RI
Rocky Mount Academy, NC
The Roeper School, MI
Rolling Hills Preparatory School, CA
Roncalli High School, IN
Ron Pettigrew Christian School, BC, Canada
Rothesay Netherwood School, NB, Canada
Rotterdam International Secondary School, Wolfert van
    Borselen, Netherlands
Routt High School, IL
Rowland Hall-St. Mark's School, UT
Royal Canadian College, BC, Canada
Roycemore School, IL
Rumsey Hall School, CT
Rutgers Preparatory School, NJ
Rye Country Day School, NY
Sacramento Country Day School, CA
Sacred Heart Preparatory, CA
Sacred Heart School of Halifax, NS, Canada
Saddleback Valley Christian School, CA
Saddle River Day School, NJ
St. Agnes High School, MN
St. Andrew's College, Dublin, Ireland
St. Andrew's Episcopal School, MD
St. Andrew's Episcopal School, MS
St. Andrew's on the Marsh School, GA
Saint Andrew's School, FL
St. Andrew's School, RI
St. Andrew's–Sewanee School, TN
St. Anne's–Belfield School, VA

Saint Anthony High School, IL
St. Benedict at Auburndale, TN
St. Bernard High School, CA
Saint Cecilia High School, NE
St. Croix Country Day School, VI
St. Croix Lutheran High School, MN
St. David's School, NC
St. Dominic's International School, Portugal, Portugal
Saint Edward's School, FL
Saint Elizabeth High School, CA
Saint Francis De Sales High School, IL
St. Francis School, GA
St. George's School, RI
Saint George's School, WA
St. George's School in Switzerland, Switzerland
St. George's School of Montreal, QC, Canada
St. Gregory College Preparatory School, AZ
Saint James School, AL
Saint James School, MD
St. Johnsbury Academy, VT
St. John's College High School, DC
St. Johns Country Day School, FL
St. John's-Kilmarnock School, ON, Canada
St. John's Literary Institution at Prospect Hall, MD
Saint John's Preparatory School, MN
St. John's-Ravenscourt School, MB, Canada
Saint John's School, GU
St. John's School, PR
St. John's School, TX
St. Joseph Academy, FL
Saint Joseph Central Catholic High School, OH
St. Joseph High School, CT
Saint Joseph High School, WI
St. Joseph's Catholic School, SC
St. Leonards, United Kingdom
St. Luke's School, CT
St. Margaret's Episcopal School, CA
St. Mark's High School, DE
Saint Mark's School, MA
St. Mary's Academy, CO
St. Mary's Bundschu Memorial High School, MO
Saint Mary's College High School, CA
Saint Mary's Hall, TX
St. Mary's Hall–Doane Academy, NJ
Saint Mary's High School, AZ
Saint Mary's High School, CO
St. Mary's Ryken High School, MD
St. Mary's School, OR
St. Maur International School, Japan
St. Michael's Catholic Academy, TX
St. Michaels University School, BC, Canada
Saint Patrick—Saint Vincent High School, CA
Saint Patrick's School, KY
St. Paul Academy and Summit School, MN
Saint Paul Lutheran High School, MO
St. Paul's Episcopal School, AL
St. Pius X Catholic High School, GA
St. Pius X High School, TX
Saints Peter and Paul High School, MD
St. Stephen's & St. Agnes School, VA
Saint Stephen's Episcopal School, FL

St. Stephen's Episcopal School, TX
St. Stephen's School, Rome, Italy
St. Thomas Aquinas High School, FL
Saint Thomas Aquinas High School, KS
St. Thomas Aquinas High School, NH
Saint Viator High School, IL
St. Vincent Pallotti High School, MD
Salem Academy, OR
Salpointe Catholic High School, AZ
Saltus Grammar School, Bermuda
San Diego Jewish Academy, CA
San Domenico School, CA
Sandy Spring Friends School, MD
Sanford School, DE
San Marcos Baptist Academy, TX
Santa Catalina School, CA
Santa Fe Preparatory School, NM
Santiam Christian School, OR
Savannah Christian Preparatory School, GA
The Savannah Country Day School, GA
Sayre School, KY
Scarborough Christian School, ON, Canada
Scattergood Friends School, IA
School for Young Performers, NY
Schule Schloss Salem, Germany
Scranton Preparatory School, PA
Seabury Hall, HI
Seattle Academy of Arts and Sciences, WA
Seattle Christian Schools, WA
Second Baptist School, TX
Sedbergh School, QC, Canada
Seoul Foreign School, Republic of Korea
Seoul International School, Republic of Korea
Seton Catholic Central High School, NY
The Seven Hills School, OH
Severn School, MD
Sewickley Academy, PA
Shady Side Academy, PA
Shannon Forest Christian School, SC
Shattuck-St. Mary's School, MN
The Shipley School, PA
Shorecrest Preparatory School, FL
Shoreline Christian, WA
Sidwell Friends School, DC
Smith School, NY
Smithville District Christian High School, ON, Canada
Solebury School, PA
Soundview Preparatory School, NY
Southampton Academy, VA
Southridge School, BC, Canada
Southwest Christian School, Inc., TX
Southwestern Academy, AZ
Southwestern Academy, CA
Spar Hawk School, MA
Spartanburg Day School, SC
Squaw Valley Academy, CA
Stanbridge Academy, CA
Stanstead College, QC, Canada
Staten Island Academy, NY
Stella Maris High School and the Maura Clarke Junior High Program, NY

Stevenson School, CA
The Stony Brook School, NY
Storm King School, NY
Stratford Academy, GA
Strathcona-Tweedsmuir School, AB, Canada
Stratton Mountain School, VT
Stuart Hall, VA
The Sudbury Valley School, MA
Suffield Academy, CT
Sumiton Christian School, AL
Summerfield Waldorf School, CA
The Summit Country Day School, OH
Surabaya International School, Indonesia
Swedish Language School, AB, Canada
Tabor Academy, MA
The Taft School, CT
Taipei American School, Taiwan
Tallulah Falls School, GA
Tapply Binet College, ON, Canada
TASIS The American School in England, United Kingdom
TASIS, The American School in Switzerland, Switzerland
The Tatnall School, DE
The Tenney School, TX
Teurlings Catholic High School, LA
The Thacher School, CA
Thayer Academy, MA
Thomas A. Edison High School, OR
Thomas Jefferson School, MO
Thornton Friends School, MD
Thornton Friends School/N.V.A., VA
Tilton School, NH
Timothy Christian High School, IL
TMI—The Episcopal School of Texas, TX
Toronto District Christian High School, ON, Canada
Toronto Waldorf School, ON, Canada
Tower Hill School, DE
Town Centre Montessori School, ON, Canada
Traditional Learning Academy, BC, Canada
Trevor Day School, NY
Tri-City Christian Schools, CA
Trident Academy, SC
Trinity Academy, KS
Trinity Catholic High School, CT
Trinity Catholic High School, MA
Trinity Christian Academy, TX
Trinity Christian School, GA
Trinity College School, ON, Canada
Trinity Episcopal School, VA
Trinity High School, NH
Trinity Preparatory School, FL
Trinity School, NY
Trinity Valley School, TX
Tyler Street Christian Academy, TX
United Mennonite Educational Institute, ON, Canada
United Nations International School, NY
Universal Academy of Florida, FL
University Lake School, WI
University Liggett School, MI
University of Chicago Laboratory Schools, IL
University of Miami Online High School, FL
University of Missouri—Columbia High School, MO

University of Toronto Schools, ON, Canada
University Prep, WA
University School of Milwaukee, WI
University School of Nashville, TN
University School of Nova Southeastern University, FL
The Urban School of San Francisco, CA
Vail Mountain School, CO
Valley Christian School, CA
Valley Christian School, MT
Vandebilt Catholic High School, LA
Vanguard College Preparatory School, TX
The Vanguard School, FL
Venta Preparatory School, ON, Canada
Vermont Academy, VT
Vicksburg Catholic School, MS
Viewpoint School, CA
Village Christian Schools, CA
Villa Maria Academy, PA
Virginia Beach Friends School, VA
Virginia Episcopal School, VA
Wakefield School, VA
Walden Preparatory School, TX
The Waldorf High School of Massachusetts Bay, MA
The Waldorf School of Garden City, NY
The Walker School, GA
Walnut Hill School, MA
The Wardlaw-Hartridge School, NJ
Waring School, MA
Wasatch Academy, UT
Washington Academy, ME
Washington County Day School, MS
Washington International School, DC
Washington Waldorf School, MD
The Waterford School, UT
Watkinson School, CT
The Waverly School, CA
Wayland Academy, WI
Wayne Country Day School, NC
Waynflete School, ME
Webber Academy, AB, Canada
The Webb School, TN
Webb School of Knoxville, TN
The Wellington School, OH
Wellspring Foundation, CT
Wellsprings Friends School, OR
Wentworth Military Academy and Junior College, MO
Wesleyan School, GA
Westbury Christian School, TX
West Catholic High School, MI
Westchester Academy, NC
Western Mennonite School, OR
Western Reserve Academy, OH
The Westfield Schools, GA
Westgate Mennonite Collegiate, MB, Canada
Westhill Institute, Mexico
West Island College, AB, Canada
Westminster Christian Academy, AL
Westminster Christian Academy, LA
Westminster Christian School, FL
Westminster School, CT
The Westminster Schools, GA

Specialized Directories

Westminster Schools of Augusta, GA
West Nottingham Academy, MD
Westpark School, MB, Canada
Westtown School, PA
Westview School, CA
Wheaton Academy, IL
The Wheeler School, RI
Whitefield Academy, GA
The White Mountain School, NH
White Rock Christian Academy, BC, Canada
Whitfield School, MO
Whittier Christian High School, CA
Wichita Collegiate School, KS
Wilbraham & Monson Academy, MA
Wildwood Catholic High School, NJ
William Penn Charter School, PA
The Williams School, CT
The Williston Northampton School, MA
Willow Hill School, MA
Wilmington Christian School, DE
Wilmington Friends School, DE
Wilson Hall, SC
The Winchendon School, MA
Winchester Thurston School, PA
Windermere St. Anne's School, United Kingdom
Windhoek International School, Namibia
Windsor Christian Fellowship Academy, ON, Canada
The Windsor School, NY
Windward School, CA
Winston Preparatory School, NY
The Winston School, TX
The Winston School San Antonio, TX
Wisconsin Academy, WI
Woodbridge Academy, KY
Woodcliff Academy, NJ
The Woodlynde School, PA
Woodside International School, CA
Woodside Park International School, United Kingdom
Woodside Priory School, CA
Woodstock School, India
Wooster School, CT
Worcester Academy, MA
Worcester Preparatory School, MD
Wyoming Seminary, PA
Yeshiva Atlanta, GA
Yokohama International School, Japan
York Country Day School, PA
York Preparatory School, NY
The York School, ON, Canada
Zurich International School, Switzerland

BOYS' DAY SCHOOLS

Archbishop Curley High School, MD
Archbishop Quigley Preparatory High School, IL
Archbishop Riordan High School, CA
Army and Navy Academy, CA
Avon Old Farms School, CT
Belen Jesuit Preparatory School, FL
Bellarmine College Preparatory, CA
Belmont Hill School, MA

Benedictine High School, OH
The Boys' Latin School of Maryland, MD
Bridgton Academy, ME
Brophy College Preparatory, AZ
Brother Rice High School, MI
The Browning School, NY
Brunswick School, CT
Calvert Hall College High School, MD
Cardigan Mountain School, NH
Cathedral Preparatory School, PA
Central Catholic High School, PA
CFS, The School at Church Farm, PA
Chaminade College Preparatory School, MO
Chedar Chabad, ON, Canada
Chestnut Hill Academy, PA
Christian Brothers Academy, NJ
Christian Brothers Academy, NY
Christ School, NC
Cistercian Preparatory School, TX
Colegio San Jose, PR
Crescent School, ON, Canada
Crespi Carmelite High School, CA
De La Salle High School, CA
Delbarton School, NJ
DeMatha Catholic High School, MD
Devon Preparatory School, PA
Don Bosco High School, CA
Eaglebrook School, MA
The Fessenden School, MA
Fishburne Military School, VA
Fordham Preparatory School, NY
Fork Union Military Academy, VA
Georgetown Preparatory School, MD
Gilman School, MD
Hales Franciscan High School, IL
The Haverford School, PA
Hillside School, MA
Iona Preparatory School, NY
Jesuit College Preparatory School, TX
Jesuit High School, CA
Jesuit High School of New Orleans, LA
Jesuit High School of Tampa, FL
The Kiski School, PA
Landon School, MD
La Salle College High School, PA
Loyola-Blakefield, MD
Loyola High School, Jesuit College Preparatory, CA
Malden Catholic High School, MA
Marmion Academy, IL
Marquette University High School, WI
The McCallie School, TN
McQuaid Jesuit High School, NY
Memphis University School, TN
Montgomery Bell Academy, TN
Mount Carmel High School, IL
Mount Michael Benedictine High School, NE
O'Dea High School, WA
Palma High School, CA
The Phelps School, PA
Regis High School, NY
Riverside Military Academy, GA

The Roxbury Latin School, MA
Saint Agnes Boys High School, NY
St. Andrew's College, ON, Canada
St. Anselm's Abbey School, DC
Saint Augustine Preparatory School, NJ
St. Benedict's Preparatory School, NJ
St. Catherine's Military Academy, CA
St. Christopher's School, VA
St. Francis de Sales High School, OH
St. George's School, BC, Canada
St. John's Northwestern Military Academy, WI
St. John's Preparatory School, MA
Saint Joseph's High School, NJ
St. Joseph's Preparatory School, PA
Saint Laurence High School, IL
Saint Louis Priory School, MO
St. Mark's School of Texas, TX
St. Mary's International School, Japan
St. Mary's Preparatory School, MI
Saint Patrick High School, IL
St. Paul's High School, MB, Canada
St. Paul's Preparatory Academy, AZ
St. Peter's Preparatory School, NJ
Saint Raymond High School for Boys, NY
St. Sebastian's School, MA
St. Stanislaus College, MS
Saint Thomas Academy, MN
St. Thomas High School, TX
Saint Xavier High School, KY
Saint Xavier High School, OH
Salesian High School, NY
Salesianum School, DE
Salisbury School, CT
Selwyn House School, QC, Canada
Seton Hall Preparatory School, NJ
South Kent School, CT
Strake Jesuit College Preparatory, TX
Subiaco Academy, AR
Trinity High School, KY
Trinity-Pawling School, NY
University of Detroit Jesuit High School and Academy, MI
University School, OH
Upper Canada College, ON, Canada
Valley Forge Military Academy and College, PA
Vianney High School, MO
The Woodhall School, CT

GIRLS' DAY SCHOOLS

Academy of Mount Saint Ursula, NY
Academy of Notre Dame de Namur, PA
Academy of Our Lady of Mercy, CT
Academy of Our Lady of Peace, CA
Academy of Saint Aloysius, NJ
Academy of Saint Elizabeth, NJ
Academy of the Holy Angels, NJ
Academy of the Holy Cross, MD
Academy of the Sacred Heart, LA
The Agnes Irwin School, PA
Ahliyyah School for Girls, Jordan
The Andrews School, OH

Archbishop Blenk Girls High School, LA
The Archer School for Girls, CA
Assumption High School, KY
The Baldwin School, PA
Balmoral Hall School, MB, Canada*
Beaumont School, OH
The Bermuda High School for Girls, Bermuda
Bishop Conaty-Our Lady of Loretto High School, CA
The Bishop Strachan School, ON, Canada
The Brearley School, NY
Brenau Academy, GA
Carondelet High School, CA
Carrollton School of the Sacred Heart, FL
Castilleja School, CA
The Catholic High School of Baltimore, MD
The Chapin School, NY
Chatham Hall, VA
Colegio Puertorriqueno de Ninas, PR
Columbus School for Girls, OH
Connelly School of the Holy Child, MD
Convent of the Sacred Heart, CT
Convent of the Sacred Heart, NY
Convent of the Sacred Heart High School, CA
Cornelia Connelly School, CA
Country Day School of the Sacred Heart, PA
Crofton House School, BC, Canada
Dana Hall School, MA
Duchesne Academy of the Sacred Heart, NE
Duchesne Academy of the Sacred Heart, TX
Elizabeth Seton High School, MD
The Ellis School, PA
Emma Willard School, NY
The Ethel Walker School, CT
Fontbonne Academy, MA
Foxcroft School, VA
Garrison Forest School, MD*
Georgetown Visitation Preparatory School, DC
Girls Preparatory School, TN
Greenwich Academy, CT
The Harpeth Hall School, TN
Havergal College, ON, Canada
The Hewitt School, NY
The Hockaday School, TX
The Holton-Arms School, MD
Hutchison School, TN
Immaculata Academy, NY
Immaculate Conception High School, NJ
Incarnate Word Academy, TX
Josephinum High School, IL
Ladywood High School, MI
La Pietra–Hawaii School for Girls, HI
Linden Hall School for Girls, PA
Loretto High School, CA
Louisville High School, CA
Marlborough School, CA
Mary Help of Christians Academy, NJ
Marylawn of the Oranges, NJ
The Mary Louis Academy, NY
Marymount High School, CA
Marymount International School, United Kingdom
Maryvale Preparatory School, MD

Coeducational in lower grades

Mayfield Senior School, CA
Mercy High School, CT
Mercy High School, NE
Mercy High School College Preparatory, CA
Miss Edgar's and Miss Cramp's School, QC, Canada
Miss Hall's School, MA
Miss Porter's School, CT
Montrose School, MA
Mother McAuley High School, IL
Mount Alvernia High School, PA
Mt. Saint Dominic Academy, NJ
Mount Saint Joseph Academy, PA
Mount Saint Mary Academy, NJ
National Cathedral School, DC
Nerinx Hall, MO
Newton Country Day School of the Sacred Heart, MA
Notre Dame Academy, MA
Notre Dame High School, CA
Notre Dame High School, MO
Notre Dame High School for Girls, IL
Notre Dame Preparatory School, MD
Oldfields School, MD
Preston High School, NY
Providence High School, TX
Purnell School, NJ
Ramona Convent Secondary School, CA
Regina High School, OH
Resurrection High School, IL
Roland Park Country School, MD
Rosary High School, IL
Sacred Heart Academy, CT
Sacred Heart High School, CA
St. Agnes Academy, TX
St. Andrew's Priory School, HI
Saint Basil Academy, PA
St. Catherine's School, VA
St. Cecilia Academy, TN
St. Clement's School, ON, Canada
Saint Dominic Academy, NJ
Saint Francis School, HI
Saint Gertrude High School, VA
St. Joseph's Academy, LA
Saint Lucy's Priory High School, CA
St. Margaret's School, VA
St. Margaret's School, BC, Canada
St. Mary's Dominican High School, LA
St. Mary's Episcopal School, TN
Saint Mary's School, NC
St. Paul's School for Girls, MD
Saint Teresa's Academy, MO
St. Timothy's School, MD
Saint Vincent Ferrer High School, NY
Saint Vincent's Academy, GA
Salem Academy, NC
School of the Holy Child, NY
The Spence School, NY
Springside School, PA
Stoneleigh–Burnham School, MA
The Study School, QC, Canada
Trafalgar Castle School, ON, Canada
Trinity High School, IL

Ursuline High School, CA
Villa Maria Academy, PA
Villa Victoria Academy, NJ
Villa Walsh Academy, NJ
Westover School, CT
Westridge School, CA
The Willows Academy, IL
The Winsor School, MA
Woodlands Academy of the Sacred Heart, IL
The Woodward School, MA
Xavier College Preparatory, AZ

SCHOOLS ACCEPTING BOARDING BOYS AND GIRLS

Academie Sainte Cecile International School, ON, Canada†
The Academy at Charlemont, MA†
Academy at Swift River, MA
The Academy for Global Exploration, OR
ACS Cobham International School, United Kingdom†
Admiral Farragut Academy, FL†
Advanced Academy of Georgia, GA
Albert College, ON, Canada†
Alliance Academy, Ecuador†
All Saints' Episcopal School, MS†
Ambassador Preparatory, MN†
American International School Salzburg, Austria†
American Overseas School of Rome, Italy†
Appleby College, ON, Canada†
Argo Academy, FL
Ashbury College, ON, Canada†
Asheville School, NC†
Aspen Ranch, UT
The Athenian School, CA†
Baylor School, TN†
The Bement School, MA†
Berkshire School, MA†
Bishop's College School, QC, Canada†
Black Forest Academy, Germany†
Blair Academy, NJ†
Blue Mountain Academy, PA
The Bolles School, FL†
Brehm Preparatory School, IL†
Brent School-Baguio, Philippines†
Brentwood College School, BC, Canada†
Brewster Academy, NH†
Broadview Academy, IL†
The Brook Hill School, TX†
Brooks School, MA†
Burke Mountain Academy, VT†
Burr and Burton Academy, VT†
Buxton School, MA†
The Cambridge School of Weston, MA†
Canadian Academy, Japan†
Canterbury School, CT†
Canyonville Christian Academy, OR†
Carrabassett Valley Academy, ME†
Cascadilla School, NY†
Cate School, CA†
CCI The Renaissance School, Italy†
The Cedars Academy, DE

†Accepts day students

Chapel Hill–Chauncy Hall School, MA†
Cheshire Academy, CT†
Choate Rosemary Hall, CT†
College du Leman International School, Switzerland†
The Colorado Rocky Mountain School, CO†
Colorado Timberline Academy, CO†
Columbia International College of Canada, ON, Canada†
Columbia International School, Japan†
Concord Academy, MA†
Concordia High School, AB, Canada†
Conserve School, WI
Cranbrook Schools, MI†
Cross Creek Programs, UT
The Culver Academies, IN†
Cushing Academy, MA†
Darlington School, GA†
Darrow School, NY†
Deerfield Academy, MA†
The Delphian School, OR†
Detroit Country Day School, MI†
Doctor Franklin Perkins School, MA†
Dublin Christian Academy, NH†
Dublin School, NH†
Dunn School, CA†
Eagle Hill School, CT
Eagle Hill School, MA†
Eagle Rock School, CO
Eckerd Youth Alternatives, FL
Ecole d'Humanite, Switzerland
Elan School, ME
Emerson Honors High Schools, CA†
Episcopal High School, VA
The Family Foundation School, NY
Fay School, MA†
F. L. Chamberlain School, MA†
Florida Air Academy, FL†
The Forman School, CT†
Fountain Valley School of Colorado, CO†
Fox River Country Day School, IL†
Freeman Academy, SD†
Fryeburg Academy, ME†
Gem State Adventist Academy, ID†
George School, PA†
George Stevens Academy, ME†
Gilmour Academy, OH†
Girard College, PA
Glen Eden School, BC, Canada
The Glenholme School, CT
Gould Academy, ME†
Governor Dummer Academy, MA†
The Governor French Academy, IL†
Great Lakes Christian College, ON, Canada†
Grenville Christian College, ON, Canada†
Groton School, MA†
Grove School, CT†
Gstaad International School, Switzerland†
The Gunnery, CT†
Hackley School, NY†
Happy Valley School, CA†
The Harvey School, NY†
Hawaiian Mission Academy, HI†

Hawai'i Preparatory Academy, HI†
Hebron Academy, ME†
Hidden Lake Academy, GA
High Mowing School, NH†
The Hill School, PA†
Hokkaido International School, Japan†
Holderness School, NH†
Hoosac School, NY†
Horizons School, GA†
The Hotchkiss School, CT†
Houghton Academy, NY†
Howe Military School, IN†
The Hun School of Princeton, NJ†
Hyde School, CT†
Hyde School, ME†
Idyllwild Arts Academy, CA†
Imperial College of Toronto, ON, Canada
Indian Mountain School, CT†
Indian Springs School, AL†
Interlochen Arts Academy, MI†
International Junior Golf Academy, SC†
International School Bangkok, Thailand†
International School of South Africa, South Africa†
Island View School, UT
The John Dewey Academy, MA
John F. Kennedy Memorial High School, WA†
The Judge Rotenberg Educational Center, MA
Kent School, CT†
Kents Hill School, ME†
Kildonan School, NY†
Kimball Union Academy, NH†
The King's Academy, TN†
Kingsway College, ON, Canada†
The Knox School, NY†
Lakefield College School, ON, Canada†
Lake Forest Academy, IL†
La Lumiere School, IN†
Landmark East School, NS, Canada†
Landmark School, MA†
Lawrence Academy, MA†
The Lawrenceville School, NJ†
The Leelanau School, MI†
Leysin American School in Switzerland, Switzerland
The Linsly School, WV†
The Loomis Chaffee School, CT†
The Lowell Whiteman School, CO†
Lustre Christian High School, MT†
Luther College High School, SK, Canada†
Lyndon Institute, VT†
The MacDuffie School, MA†
Maine Central Institute, ME†
Malaspina International High School, BC, Canada†
Maplebrook School, NY
Marianapolis Preparatory School, CT†
The Marvelwood School, CT†
Massanutten Military Academy, VA†
The Masters School, NY†
Maur Hill-Mount Academy, KS†
McDonogh School, MD†
The Meeting School, NH†
Mercersburg Academy, PA†

†Accepts day students

Middlesex School, MA†

Midland School, CA

Millbrook School, NY†

Miller School, VA†

Milton Academy, MA†

Milton Hershey School, PA

Montana Academy, MT

Montcalm School, MI

Montclair College Preparatory School, CA†

Monte Vista Christian School, CA†

Montverde Academy, FL†

Mooseheart High School, IL†

Mount Bachelor Academy, OR

Nacel International School, MN†

National Sports Academy at Lake Placid, NY†

Navajo Preparatory School, Inc., NM†

Nawa Academy, CA

Nebraska Christian Schools, NE†

Neuchatel Junior College, Switzerland

New Dominion School, VA

New Hampton School, NH†

New Horizon Youth Ministries, IN

New Mexico Military Institute, NM

New York Military Academy, NY†

Niagara Christian Collegiate, ON, Canada†

Noble and Greenough School, MA†

The North Broward Preparatory Upper School, FL†

North Country School, NY†

Northfield Mount Hermon School, MA†

The Northwest School, WA†

Northwood School, NY†

Oak Creek Ranch School, AZ

Oak Hill Academy, VA†

Oakland School, VA†

Oak Ridge Military Academy, NC†

Oakwood Friends School, NY†

Ojai Valley School, CA†

Olney Friends School, OH†

Oneida Baptist Institute, KY†

Oregon Episcopal School, OR†

The Orme School, AZ†

The Pathway School, PA

Peddie School, NJ†

The Pennington School, NJ†

Perkiomen School, PA†

Phillips Academy (Andover), MA†

Phillips Exeter Academy, NH†

Pickering College, ON, Canada†

Pine Forge Academy, PA†

Pinehurst School, ON, Canada

Pine Ridge School, VT

Pomfret School, CT†

Portland Lutheran School, OR†

Portsmouth Abbey School, RI†

Proctor Academy, NH†

Professional Children's School, NY†

Provo Canyon School, UT

The Putney School, VT†

Rabun Gap-Nacoochee School, GA†

Rancho Valmora, NM

Randolph-Macon Academy, VA†

Ribet Academy, CA†

Ridley College, ON, Canada†

Rio Lindo Adventist Academy, CA†

Riverview School, MA

Rock Point School, VT†

Rockway Mennonite Collegiate, ON, Canada†

Rothesay Netherwood School, NB, Canada†

Rumsey Hall School, CT†

St. Andrew's School, DE

Saint Andrew's School, FL†

St. Andrew's School, RI†

St. Andrew's–Sewanee School, TN†

St. Anne's–Belfield School, VA†

St. Croix Lutheran High School, MN†

St. George's School, RI†

Saint James School, MD†

St. Johnsbury Academy, VT†

Saint John's Preparatory School, MN†

St. John's-Ravenscourt School, MB, Canada†

Saint John's School, GU†

Saint John's School of Alberta, AB, Canada

St. Leonards, United Kingdom†

Saint Mark's School, MA†

St. Michaels University School, BC, Canada†

Saint Paul Lutheran High School, MO†

St. Paul's School, NH

St. Stephen's Episcopal School, TX†

St. Stephen's School, Rome, Italy†

Sandy Spring Friends School, MD†

San Marcos Baptist Academy, TX†

Scattergood Friends School, IA†

Schule Schloss Salem, Germany†

Sedbergh School, QC, Canada†

Shady Side Academy, PA†

Shattuck-St. Mary's School, MN†

SICES International Academy, AB, Canada

Solebury School, PA†

Sorenson's Ranch School, UT

Southwestern Academy, AZ†

Southwestern Academy, CA†

Spring Creek Lodge Academy, MT

Squaw Valley Academy, CA†

Stanstead College, QC, Canada†

Stevenson School, CA†

The Stony Brook School, NY†

Storm King School, NY†

Stratton Mountain School, VT†

Suffield Academy, CT†

Summit Preparatory School, MT

Tabor Academy, MA†

The Taft School, CT†

Tallulah Falls School, GA†

TASIS The American School in England, United Kingdom†

TASIS, The American School in Switzerland, Switzerland†

Texas NeuroRehab Center, TX

The Thacher School, CA†

Thomas Jefferson School, MO†

Three Springs, AL

Tilton School, NH†

TMI—The Episcopal School of Texas, TX†

Trinity College School, ON, Canada†

†Accepts day students

The United World College—USA, NM
The Vanguard School, FL†
Venta Preparatory School, ON, Canada†
Vermont Academy, VT†
Virginia Episcopal School, VA†
Walnut Hill School, MA†
Wasatch Academy, UT†
Washington Academy, ME†
Wayland Academy, WI†
The Webb School, TN†
Wellspring Foundation, CT†
Wentworth Military Academy and Junior College, MO†
Western Mennonite School, OR†
Western Reserve Academy, OH†
Westminster School, CT†
West Nottingham Academy, MD†
Westtown School, PA†
The White Mountain School, NH†
Wilbraham & Monson Academy, MA†
The Williston Northampton School, MA†
The Winchendon School, MA†
Windermere St. Anne's School, United Kingdom†
Wisconsin Academy, WI†
Woodside Park International School, United Kingdom†
Woodside Priory School, CA†
Woodstock School, India†
Worcester Academy, MA†
Wyoming Seminary, PA†

SCHOOLS ACCEPTING BOARDING BOYS

The Albany Academy, NY†
Allen Academy, TX†
Army and Navy Academy, CA†
Avon Old Farms School, CT†
Belmont Hill School, MA†
The Blue Ridge School, VA
Brandon Hall School, GA†
Bridgton Academy, ME†
Camden Military Academy, SC
Cardigan Mountain School, NH†
CFS, The School at Church Farm, PA†
Chamberlain-Hunt Academy, MS†
Chaminade College Preparatory School, MO†
Chedar Chabad, ON, Canada†
Cherokee Creek Boys School, SC
Christchurch School, VA†
Christ School, NC†
Eaglebrook School, MA†
The Fessenden School, MA†
Fishburne Military School, VA†
Forest Heights Lodge, CO
Fork Union Military Academy, VA†
Georgetown Preparatory School, MD†
The Gow School, NY
The Grand River Academy, OH
The Greenwood School, VT
Hampshire Country School, NH
Hargrave Military Academy, VA†
Harrow School, United Kingdom
Hillside School, MA†

The Kiski School, PA†
Linden Hill School, MA
Little Keswick School, VA
The McCallie School, TN†
Missouri Military Academy, MO
Mount Michael Benedictine High School, NE†
New Dominion School, MD
The Oxford Academy, CT
The Phelps School, PA†
The Rectory School, CT†
Riverside Military Academy, GA†
Robert Land Academy, ON, Canada
St. Andrew's College, ON, Canada†
St. Catherine's Military Academy, CA†
St. George's School, BC, Canada†
St. John's Military School, KS
St. John's Northwestern Military Academy, WI†
St. Mary's Preparatory School, MI†
St. Michael's Preparatory School of the Norbertine Fathers, CA
St. Paul's Preparatory Academy, AZ†
St. Stanislaus College, MS†
St. Thomas Choir School, NY
Saint Thomas More School, CT
Salisbury School, CT†
South Kent School, CT†
Stone Mountain School, NC
Subiaco Academy, AR†
Three Springs/Prince Mountain Academy, GA
Timber Ridge School, VA
Trinity-Pawling School, NY†
Upper Canada College, ON, Canada†
Valley Forge Military Academy and College, PA†
Woodberry Forest School, VA
The Woodhall School, CT†

SCHOOLS ACCEPTING BOARDING GIRLS

The Academy at Sisters, OR
Academy of the Sacred Heart, LA†
Alpine Academy, UT
The Andrews School, OH†
Annie Wright School, WA†
Auldern Academy, NC
Balmoral Hall School, MB, Canada†
The Bethany Hills School, ON, Canada†
The Bishop Strachan School, ON, Canada†
Brenau Academy, GA†
Chatham Hall, VA†
Dana Hall School, MA†
Emma Willard School, NY†
The Ethel Walker School, CT†
Foxcroft School, VA†
Garrison Forest School, MD†
The Grier School, PA
Havergal College, ON, Canada†
The Hockaday School, TX†
Linden Hall School for Girls, PA†
Marymount International School, United Kingdom†
Miss Hall's School, MA†
Miss Porter's School, CT†

†Accepts day students

Oldfields School, MD†
Purnell School, NJ†
Queen Margaret's School, BC, Canada†
Rocklyn Academy, ON, Canada
St. George's School in Switzerland, Switzerland†
St. Margaret's School, VA†
St. Margaret's School, BC, Canada†
Saint Mary's School, NC†
St. Timothy's School, MD†
Salem Academy, NC†
San Domenico School, CA†
Santa Catalina School, CA†
Spring Ridge Academy, AZ
Stoneleigh–Burnham School, MA†
Stuart Hall, VA†
Trafalgar Castle School, ON, Canada†
Westover School, CT†
Woodlands Academy of the Sacred Heart, IL†

SCHOOLS WITH A RELIGIOUS AFFILIATION

Anglican Church of Canada

The Bishop Strachan School, ON, Canada
Rothesay Netherwood School, NB, Canada
St. Clement's School, ON, Canada
St. John's-Kilmarnock School, ON, Canada
Saint John's School of Alberta, AB, Canada

Apostolic Church of Pentecost

Gateway Christian School, BC, Canada

Assemblies of God

Mountain View Christian High School, NV

Baptist Church

Bangor Christian School, ME
Bradenton Christian School, FL
Calvary Christian Academy, KY
Devon Park Christian School, NB, Canada
First Baptist Academy, TX
Fork Union Military Academy, VA
Grace Baptist Schools, CA
Hawaii Baptist Academy, HI
The King's Academy, TN
Linden Christian School, MB, Canada
Los Angeles Baptist Junior/Senior High School, CA
Northside Christian School, FL
Oak Hill Academy, VA
San Marcos Baptist Academy, TX
Second Baptist School, TX
Tri-City Christian Schools, CA
Trinity Christian School, GA

Baptist General Association of Virginia

Hargrave Military Academy, VA

Baptist General Conference

Doctor Franklin Perkins School, MA

Bible Fellowship Church

Chinese Christian Schools, CA
Queensway Christian College, ON, Canada

Brethren in Christ Church

Niagara Christian Collegiate, ON, Canada

Calvinist

Ripon Christian Schools, CA

The Christian and Missionary Alliance

Westpark School, MB, Canada

Christian Reformed Church

Bradenton Christian School, FL
Denver Christian High School, CO
Eastern Christian High School, NJ
Immanuel Christian High School, AB, Canada
Kalamazoo Christian High School, MI
Manhattan Christian High School, MT
Toronto District Christian High School, ON, Canada

Christian

Adelphi Academy, NY
Ahliyyah School for Girls, Jordan
Bulloch Academy, GA
Cardigan Mountain School, NH
The Family Foundation School, NY
First Presbyterian Day School, GA
Fowlers Academy, PR
Franklin Road Academy, TN
Grace Baptist Schools, CA
Lake Highland Preparatory School, FL
Lee-Scott Academy, AL
Marion Academy, AL
New Horizon Youth Ministries, IN
North Cobb Christian School, GA
St. Croix Lutheran High School, MN
St. David's School, NC
Scarborough Christian School, ON, Canada
Shoreline Christian, WA
Smithville District Christian High School, ON, Canada
The Stony Brook School, NY
Toronto District Christian High School, ON, Canada
Trinity Academy, KS
Westminster Christian School, FL
The Westminster Schools, GA
Whittier Christian High School, CA
Woodstock School, India

Christian Nondenominational

Airdrie Koinonia Christian School, AB, Canada
Alliance Academy, Ecuador
Arrowhead Christian Academy, CA
Bearspaw Christian School, AB, Canada
Bellevue Christian School, WA
Black Forest Academy, Germany
Brentwood Academy, TN
The Brook Hill School, TX
Canterbury High School, IN
Canyonville Christian Academy, OR
Charles Finney School, NY
Charlotte Christian School, NC
Chattanooga Christian School, TN
Christian Central Academy, NY
Cross Creek Programs, UT
Darlington School, GA
Dublin Christian Academy, NH
Eckerd Youth Alternatives, FL

†Accepts day students

The Geneva School, FL
Grace Christian School, AK
Grenville Christian College, ON, Canada
Hackley School, NY
Hamilton District Christian School, ON, Canada
Hillcrest Christian School, CA
The King's Christian High School, NJ
King's West School, WA
Lakeland Christian Academy, IN
Lexington Christian Academy, MA
Lifegate School, OR
Linfield Christian School, CA
Living Word Academy, PA
Manhattan Christian High School, MT
Massanutten Military Academy, VA
The McCallie School, TN
Mid-Pacific Institute, HI
Missouri Military Academy, MO
Montcalm School, MI
Monte Vista Christian School, CA
Northwest Community Christian School, AZ
Oak Mountain Academy, GA
Phoenix Christian Unified Schools, AZ
Portland Christian Schools, OR
Portsmouth Christian Academy, NH
Ron Pettigrew Christian School, BC, Canada
Saddleback Valley Christian School, CA
St. Anne's–Belfield School, VA
Santiam Christian School, OR
Savannah Christian Preparatory School, GA
Seattle Christian Schools, WA
Seoul Foreign School, Republic of Korea
Tallulah Falls School, GA
Timothy Christian High School, IL
Trinity Academy, KS
Trinity Christian Academy, TX
Tyler Street Christian Academy, TX
Valley Christian School, CA
Valley Christian School, MT
Village Christian Schools, CA
Wesleyan School, GA
The Westfield Schools, GA
Wheaton Academy, IL
Whitefield Academy, GA
White Rock Christian Academy, BC, Canada
Windsor Christian Fellowship Academy, ON, Canada
Woodberry Forest School, VA

Church of Christ

Boyd-Buchanan School, TN
Columbia Academy, TN
Dallas Christian School, TX
David Lipscomb High School, TN
Ezell-Harding Christian School, TN
Fort Worth Christian School, TX
Greater Atlanta Christian Schools, GA
Great Lakes Christian College, ON, Canada
Harding Academy, TN
Madison Academy, AL
Mars Hill Bible School, AL
Westbury Christian School, TX

Church of Christ, Scientist

Fox River Country Day School, IL
Providence School, FL

Church of England (Anglican)

Appleby College, ON, Canada
Bishop's College School, QC, Canada
Harrow School, United Kingdom
Havergal College, ON, Canada
Lakefield College School, ON, Canada
Ridley College, ON, Canada
St. Michaels University School, BC, Canada
Saltus Grammar School, Bermuda
Trinity College School, ON, Canada

Church of God

Sumiton Christian School, AL

Episcopal Church

All Saints' Episcopal School, MS
All Saints' Episcopal School of Fort Worth, TX
Annie Wright School, WA
Berkeley Preparatory School, FL
The Blue Ridge School, VA
Breck School, MN
Brent School-Baguio, Philippines
Brooks School, MA
Campbell Hall (Episcopal), CA
The Canterbury School of Florida, FL
Casady School, OK
CFS, The School at Church Farm, PA
Chatham Hall, VA
Christ Church Episcopal School, SC
Christchurch School, VA
Christ School, NC
Doane Stuart School, NY
The Episcopal Academy, PA
Episcopal Collegiate School, AR
Episcopal High School, TX
Episcopal High School, VA
Episcopal High School of Jacksonville, FL
The Episcopal School of Acadiana, LA
The Episcopal School of Dallas, TX
Groton School, MA
Harvard-Westlake School, CA
Holderness School, NH
Holland Hall, OK
Hoosac School, NY
Howe Military School, IN
Iolani School, HI
Kent School, CT
National Cathedral School, DC
Oregon Episcopal School, OR
Palmer Trinity School, FL
Pomfret School, CT
Queen Anne School, MD
The Rectory School, CT
Rock Point School, VT
St. Andrew's Episcopal School, MD
St. Andrew's Episcopal School, MS
St. Andrew's Priory School, HI
St. Andrew's School, DE
Saint Andrew's School, FL
St. Andrew's–Sewanee School, TN
St. Catherine's School, VA
St. Christopher's School, VA
St. David's School, NC
Saint Edward's School, FL

St. George's School, RI
Saint James School, MD
St. John's Military School, KS
St. John's Northwestern Military Academy, WI
Saint John's School, GU
St. Margaret's Episcopal School, CA
St. Margaret's School, VA
Saint Mark's School, MA
St. Mary's Episcopal School, TN
St. Mary's Hall–Doane Academy, NJ
Saint Mary's School, NC
St. Paul's Episcopal School, AL
St. Paul's Preparatory Academy, AZ
St. Paul's School, MD
St. Paul's School, NH
St. Paul's School for Girls, MD
St. Stephen's & St. Agnes School, VA
Saint Stephen's Episcopal School, FL
St. Stephen's Episcopal School, TX
St. Thomas Choir School, NY
St. Timothy's School, MD
Salisbury School, CT
Seabury Hall, HI
Shattuck-St. Mary's School, MN
South Kent School, CT
Stuart Hall, VA
TMI—The Episcopal School of Texas, TX
Trinity Episcopal School, VA
Trinity-Pawling School, NY
Trinity Preparatory School, FL
Trinity School, NY
Virginia Episcopal School, VA
The White Mountain School, NH
Wooster School, CT

Evangelical Free Church of America
Hope Christian School, AB, Canada

Evangelical Friends
Quinte Christian High School, ON, Canada

Evangelical Lutheran Church in America
Faith Lutheran High School, NV

Evangelical
Hosanna Christian School, OR
New Horizon Youth Ministries, IN

Evangelical/Fundamental
Airdrie Koinonia Christian School, AB, Canada
Chinese Christian Schools, CA
Lehigh Valley Christian High School, PA

General Association of Regular Baptist Churches
Baptist High School, NJ

Jewish
Adelphi Academy, NY
Akiba Hebrew Academy, PA
Charles E. Smith Jewish Day School, MD
Chedar Chabad, ON, Canada
The Emery Weiner School, TX
The Family Foundation School, NY
Hebrew Academy-the Five Towns, NY
King David High School, BC, Canada

Milken Community High School of Stephen Wise Temple, CA
Northwest Yeshiva High School, WA
Rabbi Alexander S. Gross Hebrew Academy, FL
San Diego Jewish Academy, CA
Yeshiva Atlanta, GA

Lutheran Church
Baltimore Lutheran Middle and Upper School, MD
Concordia Continuing Education High School, AB, Canada
Concordia High School, AB, Canada
Fox Valley Lutheran Academy, IL
Long Island Lutheran Middle and High School, NY
Los Angeles Lutheran High School, CA
Lutheran High School North, MO
Lutheran High School of Hawaii, HI
Lutheran High School South, MO
Luther College High School, SK, Canada
Portland Lutheran School, OR

Lutheran Church–Missouri Synod
Concordia Academy, MN
Denver Lutheran High School, CO
Faith Lutheran High School, NV
Lutheran High North, TX
Lutheran High School, CA
Lutheran High School, IN
Lutheran High School, MN
Our Saviour Lutheran School, NY
Saint Paul Lutheran High School, MO

Mennonite Brethren Church
Christopher Dock Mennonite High School, PA
Lustre Christian High School, MT

Mennonite Church USA
Eastern Mennonite High School, VA
Freeman Academy, SD
The Karafin School, NY
Rockway Mennonite Collegiate, ON, Canada
United Mennonite Educational Institute, ON, Canada
Western Mennonite School, OR
Westgate Mennonite Collegiate, MB, Canada

Methodist Church
Kents Hill School, ME
The Pennington School, NJ
Randolph-Macon Academy, VA
Tilton School, NH
Wyoming Seminary, PA

Moravian Church
Moravian Academy, PA
Salem Academy, NC

Muslim
Ahliyyah School for Girls, Jordan
Al-Worood School, United Arab Emirates
Islamic Saudi Academy, VA
Universal Academy of Florida, FL

Pentecostal Assemblies of Canada
Queensway Christian College, ON, Canada

Pentecostal Church
Community Christian Academy, KY

Presbyterian Church

Blair Academy, NJ
Chamberlain-Hunt Academy, MS
Menaul School, NM
Rabun Gap-Nacoochee School, GA
St. Andrew's College, Dublin, Ireland
Shannon Forest Christian School, SC
Westminster Christian Academy, AL

Presbyterian Church in America

Westminster Schools of Augusta, GA

Protestant Church

Christian Junior–Senior High School, CA
Salem Academy, OR

Protestant

Fresno Christian Schools, CA
Living Word Academy, PA
Mooseheart High School, IL
Piedmont Academy, GA
Wilmington Christian School, DE

Protestant-Evangelical

Delaware County Christian School, PA
Nebraska Christian Schools, NE
Westminster Christian Academy, LA

Reformed Church

Chamberlain-Hunt Academy, MS
Covenant Canadian Reformed School, AB, Canada
Heritage Christian School, ON, Canada
Immanuel Christian High School, AB, Canada
Smithville District Christian High School, ON, Canada

Reformed Church in America

Kalamazoo Christian High School, MI

Roman Catholic Church

Academie Sainte Cecile International School, ON, Canada
Academy of Holy Angels, MN
Academy of Mount Saint Ursula, NY
Academy of Notre Dame de Namur, PA
Academy of Our Lady of Mercy, CT
Academy of Our Lady of Peace, CA
Academy of Saint Aloysius, NJ
Academy of Saint Elizabeth, NJ
The Academy of St. Joseph, NY
Academy of the Holy Cross, MD
Academy of the Holy Names, FL
Academy of the Sacred Heart, LA
Academy of the Sacred Heart, MI
Aquin Central Catholic High School, IL
Archbishop Blenk Girls High School, LA
Archbishop Curley High School, MD
Archbishop Mitty High School, CA
Archbishop Quigley Preparatory High School, IL
Archbishop Riordan High School, CA
Archmere Academy, DE
Assumption High School, KY
Aurora Central High School, IL
Beaumont School, OH
Belen Jesuit Preparatory School, FL
Bellarmine College Preparatory, CA
Bellarmine Preparatory School, WA
Benedictine High School, OH

Benet Academy, IL
Benilde–St. Margaret's School, MN
Bishop Brady High School, NH
Bishop Brossart High School, KY
Bishop Carroll High School, PA
Bishop Conaty-Our Lady of Loretto High School, CA
Bishop Eustace Preparatory School, NJ
Bishop Feehan High School, MA
Bishop Fenwick High School, OH
Bishop George Ahr High School, NJ
Bishop Guertin High School, NH
Bishop Hoban High School, PA
Bishop Ireton High School, VA
Bishop Kelly High School, ID
Bishop Kenny High School, FL
Bishop Luers High School, IN
Bishop Lynch Catholic High School, TX
Bishop McDevitt High School, PA
Bishop McGuinness Catholic High School, OK
Bishop McNamara High School, IL
Bishop Quinn High School/St. Francis Middle School, CA
Bishop Verot High School, FL
Bishop Walsh Middle High School, MD
Bismark St. Mary's Central, ND
Brother Rice High School, MI
Calvert Hall College High School, MD
Canterbury School, CT
Cardinal Gibbons High School, FL
Cardinal Mooney Catholic College Preparatory High
    School, MI
Cardinal Newman High School, FL
Cardinal Newman School, SC
Carondelet High School, CA
Carrollton School of the Sacred Heart, FL
Cascia Hall Preparatory School, OK
Cathedral High School, IN
Cathedral Preparatory School, PA
Catholic Central High School, NY
The Catholic High School of Baltimore, MD
Central Catholic High School, CA
Central Catholic High School, PA
Central Catholic Mid-High School, NE
Chaminade College Preparatory, CA
Chaminade College Preparatory School, MO
Chaminade-Madonna College Preparatory, FL
Chapel School, Brazil
Christian Brothers Academy, NJ
Christian Brothers Academy, NY
Christian Brothers Academy, NY
Christian Brothers High School, CA
Cistercian Preparatory School, TX
Colegio San Jose, PR
Connelly School of the Holy Child, MD
Convent of the Sacred Heart, CT
Convent of the Sacred Heart, NY
Convent of the Sacred Heart High School, CA
Convent of the Visitation School, MN
Cornelia Connelly School, CA
Country Day School of the Sacred Heart, PA
Crespi Carmelite High School, CA
Cretin-Derham Hall, MN
De La Salle College, ON, Canada
De La Salle High School, CA
DeLaSalle High School, MN

Delbarton School, NJ
DeMatha Catholic High School, MD
Devon Preparatory School, PA
Doane Stuart School, NY
Don Bosco High School, CA
Dowling High School, IA
Duchesne Academy of the Sacred Heart, NE
Duchesne Academy of the Sacred Heart, TX
East Catholic High School, CT
Elizabeth Seton High School, MD
Elyria Catholic High School, OH
Father Lopez High School, FL
Father Ryan High School, TN
Fontbonne Academy, MA
Fordham Preparatory School, NY
Garces Memorial High School, CA
Georgetown Preparatory School, MD
Georgetown Visitation Preparatory School, DC
Gilmour Academy, OH
Guerin College Preparatory High School, IL
Hackett Catholic Central High School, MI
Hales Franciscan High School, IL
Hayden High School, KS
Holy Name High School, PA
Holyoke Catholic High School, MA
Holy Trinity Diocesan High School, NY
Immaculata Academy, NY
Immaculata High School, NJ
Immaculate Conception High School, NJ
Immaculate Conception School, IL
Incarnate Word Academy, TX
Iona Preparatory School, NY
Jesuit High School, CA
Jesuit High School of New Orleans, LA
Jesuit High School of Tampa, FL
John F. Kennedy Memorial High School, WA
Josephinum High School, IL
Justin-Siena High School, CA
Kapaun Mount Carmel Catholic High School, KS
Kearney Catholic High School, NE
Ladywood High School, MI
Lansdale Catholic High School, PA
La Salle Academy, RI
La Salle College High School, PA
La Salle High School, CA
Lebanon Catholic Junior / Senior High School, PA
Lehman High School, OH
Lexington Catholic High School, KY
Loretto Academy, TX
Loretto High School, CA
Louisville High School, CA
Lourdes Catholic High School, AZ
Loyola-Blakefield, MD
Loyola High School, Jesuit College Preparatory, CA
Malden Catholic High School, MA
Marianapolis Preparatory School, CT
Marian Central Catholic High School, IL
Marian High School, IN
Marist High School, IL
Marist High School, NJ
Marist School, GA
Marmion Academy, IL
Marquette University High School, WI
Mary Help of Christians Academy, NJ

Maryknoll School, HI
Marylawn of the Oranges, NJ
The Mary Louis Academy, NY
Marymount High School, CA
Marymount International School, Italy
Marymount International School, United Kingdom
Marymount School, NY
Maryvale Preparatory School, MD
Mater Dei High School, IN
Matignon High School, MA
Maur Hill-Mount Academy, KS
Mayfield Senior School, CA
McGill-Toolen Catholic High School, AL
McNicholas High School, OH
Mercedes College, Australia
Mercy High School, CT
Mercy High School, NE
Mercy High School College Preparatory, CA
Mercyhurst Preparatory School, PA
Montgomery Catholic Preparatory School, AL
Montrose School, MA
Mooseheart High School, IL
Moreau Catholic High School, CA
Mother McAuley High School, IL
Mount Alvernia High School, PA
Mount Carmel High School, IL
Mount Michael Benedictine High School, NE
Mount Saint Charles Academy, RI
Mt. Saint Dominic Academy, NJ
Mount Saint Joseph Academy, PA
Mount Saint Mary Academy, NJ
Nazareth Academy, IL
Nerinx Hall, MO
Newman High School, WI
Newton Country Day School of the Sacred Heart, MA
Notre Dame Academy, MA
Notre Dame High School, CA
Notre Dame High School, LA
Notre Dame High School, MO
Notre Dame High School, NJ
Notre Dame High School, WV
Notre Dame High School for Girls, IL
Notre Dame Junior/Senior High School, PA
Notre Dame Preparatory School, MD
Notre Dame Regional Secondary, BC, Canada
Oak Knoll School of the Holy Child, NJ
O'Dea High School, WA
Oldenburg Academy, IN
Our Lady Of Fatima High School, RI
Our Lady of the Sacred Heart, PA
Padua Franciscan High School, OH
Palma High School, CA
Paraclete High School, CA
Pius X High School, NE
Pope John Paul II High School, FL
Portsmouth Abbey School, RI
Powers Catholic High School, MI
Preston High School, NY
Providence High School, CA
Providence High School, TX
Purcell Marian High School, OH
Quigley Catholic High School, PA
Quincy Notre Dame High School, IL
Ramona Convent Secondary School, CA

Regina High School, OH
Regis High School, NY
Regis High School, OR
Resurrection High School, IL
Roncalli High School, IN
Rosary High School, IL
Routt High School, IL
Sacred Heart Academy, CT
Sacred Heart High School, CA
Sacred Heart Preparatory, CA
Sacred Heart School of Halifax, NS, Canada
St. Agnes Academy, TX
Saint Agnes Boys High School, NY
St. Agnes High School, MN
St. Anselm's Abbey School, DC
Saint Anthony High School, IL
Saint Augustine Preparatory School, NJ
Saint Basil Academy, PA
St. Benedict at Auburndale, TN
St. Benedict's Preparatory School, NJ
St. Bernard High School, CA
St. Catherine's Military Academy, CA
St. Cecilia Academy, TN
Saint Cecilia High School, NE
Saint Dominic Academy, NJ
St. Dominic's International School, Portugal, Portugal
Saint Elizabeth High School, CA
Saint Francis De Sales High School, IL
St. Francis de Sales High School, OH
Saint Francis School, HI
Saint Gertrude High School, VA
St. John's College High School, DC
St. John's Literary Institution at Prospect Hall, MD
St. John's Preparatory School, MA
Saint John's Preparatory School, MN
St. Joseph Academy, FL
Saint Joseph Central Catholic High School, OH
St. Joseph High School, CT
Saint Joseph High School, WI
St. Joseph's Academy, LA
St. Joseph's Catholic School, SC
Saint Joseph's High School, NJ
St. Joseph's Preparatory School, PA
Saint Laurence High School, IL
Saint Louis Priory School, MO
Saint Lucy's Priory High School, CA
St. Mark's High School, DE
St. Mary's Academy, CO
St. Mary's Bundschu Memorial High School, MO
Saint Mary's College High School, CA
Saint Mary's High School, AZ
Saint Mary's High School, CO
St. Mary's International School, Japan
St. Mary's Preparatory School, MI
St. Mary's Ryken High School, MD
St. Mary's School, OR
St. Maur International School, Japan
St. Michael's Catholic Academy, TX
St. Michael's Preparatory School of the Norbertine Fathers, CA
Saint Patrick High School, IL
Saint Patrick—Saint Vincent High School, CA
Saint Patrick's School, KY
St. Paul's High School, MB, Canada

St. Peter's Preparatory School, NJ
St. Pius X Catholic High School, GA
St. Pius X High School, TX
Saint Raymond High School for Boys, NY
St. Sebastian's School, MA
Saints Peter and Paul High School, MD
St. Stanislaus College, MS
Saint Teresa's Academy, MO
Saint Thomas Academy, MN
St. Thomas Aquinas High School, FL
Saint Thomas Aquinas High School, KS
St. Thomas Aquinas High School, NH
St. Thomas High School, TX
Saint Thomas More School, CT
Saint Viator High School, IL
Saint Vincent Ferrer High School, NY
St. Vincent Pallotti High School, MD
Saint Vincent's Academy, GA
Saint Xavier High School, KY
Saint Xavier High School, OH
Salesian High School, NY
Salesianum School, DE
Salpointe Catholic High School, AZ
San Domenico School, CA
Santa Catalina School, CA
School of the Holy Child, NY
Seisen International School, Japan
Seton Catholic Central High School, NY
Seton Hall Preparatory School, NJ
Stella Maris High School and the Maura Clarke Junior High Program, NY
Stuart Country Day School of the Sacred Heart, NJ
Subiaco Academy, AR
The Summit Country Day School, OH
Teurlings Catholic High School, LA
Traditional Learning Academy, BC, Canada
Trinity Catholic High School, CT
Trinity Catholic High School, MA
Trinity High School, IL
Trinity High School, KY
Trinity High School, NH
Ursuline Academy, DE
Ursuline High School, CA
Vandebilt Catholic High School, LA
Vianney High School, MO
Vicksburg Catholic School, MS
Villa Maria Academy, PA
Villa Maria Academy, PA
Villa Victoria Academy, NJ
Villa Walsh Academy, NJ
Visitation Academy of St. Louis County, MO
West Catholic High School, MI
Wildwood Catholic High School, NJ
The Willows Academy, IL
Woodlands Academy of the Sacred Heart, IL
Woodside Priory School, CA
Xavier College Preparatory, AZ

Roman Catholic Church (Jesuit Order)

Academy of the Holy Angels, NJ
Brophy College Preparatory, AZ
Cheverus High School, ME
Gonzaga Preparatory School, WA
Jesuit College Preparatory School, TX

Loyola Academy, IL
Loyola School, NY
McQuaid Jesuit High School, NY
Scranton Preparatory School, PA
Strake Jesuit College Preparatory, TX
University of Detroit Jesuit High School and Academy, MI

Schwenkfelder Church

Perkiomen School, PA

Seventh-day Adventist Church

Broadview Academy, IL
Crawford Adventist Academy, ON, Canada
Gem State Adventist Academy, ID
Hawaiian Mission Academy, HI
Okanagan Adventist Academy, BC, Canada
Orangewood Adventist Academy, CA
Pine Forge Academy, PA
Rio Lindo Adventist Academy, CA
Wisconsin Academy, WI

Seventh-day Adventists

Armona Union Academy, CA
Blue Mountain Academy, PA
Kingsway College, ON, Canada

Society of Friends

Brooklyn Friends School, NY
Delaware Valley Friends School, PA
Friends Academy, NY
Friends' Central School, PA
Friends School of Baltimore, MD
Friends Seminary, NY
George School, PA
Germantown Friends School, PA
The Meeting School, NH
Moorestown Friends School, NJ
Oakwood Friends School, NY
Olney Friends School, OH
Sandy Spring Friends School, MD
Scattergood Friends School, IA
Sidwell Friends School, DC
Thornton Friends School, MD
Thornton Friends School/N.V.A., VA
Virginia Beach Friends School, VA
Wellsprings Friends School, OR
Westtown School, PA
William Penn Charter School, PA
Wilmington Friends School, DE

Southern Baptist Convention

Oneida Baptist Institute, KY
Prestonwood Christian Academy, TX

United Church of Canada

Albert College, ON, Canada
Bishop's College School, QC, Canada

United Church of Christ

United Nations International School, NY

United Lutheran Church

American Community Schools of Athens, Greece

United Methodist Church

Evansville Day School, IN
Lydia Patterson Institute, TX

Trinity Christian School, GA

Wesleyan Church

Houghton Academy, NY

Wisconsin Evangelical Lutheran Synod

Fox Valley Lutheran High School, WI
St. Croix Lutheran High School, MN

SCHOOLS BEGINNING AT JUNIOR, SENIOR, OR POSTGRADUATE YEAR

Argo Academy, FL	12
Bridgton Academy, ME	PG
Concordia Continuing Education High School, AB, Canada	11
Imperial College of Toronto, ON, Canada	11
Neuchatel Junior College, Switzerland	12
The United World College—USA, NM	11

SCHOOLS REPORTING ACADEMIC ACCOMMODATIONS FOR THE GIFTED AND TALENTED*

Academia Cotopaxi, Ecuador	G,M,A
Academie Sainte Cecile International School, ON, Canada	G,M,A
The Academy for Gifted Children (PACE), ON, Canada	G
The Academy for Global Exploration, OR	G
Academy of Holy Angels, MN	G,M,A
Academy of Mount Saint Ursula, NY	M,A
Academy of Saint Aloysius, NJ	M,A
Academy of the Holy Angels, NJ	G,M,A
Academy of the Holy Cross, MD	G,A
Academy of the Pacific, HI	A
Academy of the Sacred Heart, LA	G,M,A
Academy of the Sacred Heart, MI	A
ACS Cobham International School, United Kingdom	G
ACS Egham International School, United Kingdom	G
ACS Hillingdon International School, United Kingdom	G
Adelphi Academy, NY	G,M,A
Admiral Farragut Academy, FL	G
Advanced Academy of Georgia, GA	G,M,A
The Agnes Irwin School, PA	G
Airdrie Koinonia Christian School, AB, Canada	G
Albert College, ON, Canada	G,M,A
Alexander Dawson School, CO	G,M,A
Allison Academy, FL	G,A
All Saints' Episcopal School, MS	G,M,A
Alpine Academy, UT	G
American Academy, FL	G,M,A
American Heritage School, FL	G,M,A
American International School Salzburg, Austria	G,M
American Overseas School of Rome, Italy	G
American School of Milan, Italy	G,M,A
American School of Paris, France	G,M,A
The American School of The Hague, Netherlands	G,M,A
The Andrews School, OH	G,A
Appleby College, ON, Canada	G,M,A
Archbishop Riordan High School, CA	G
Archmere Academy, DE	G,M,A

G — gifted; M — musically talented; A — artistically talented

Asheville School, NC	G	Cardinal Gibbons High School, FL	G,M,A
Ashley Hall, SC	G,M,A	Cardinal Newman High School, FL	G
Aspen Ranch, UT	G	Carlucci American International School of Lisbon, Portugal	G
Assumption High School, KY	G		
Aurora Central High School, IL	G	Carolina Day School, NC	G
Avon Old Farms School, CT	G,M,A	Carondelet High School, CA	G
The Baldwin School, PA	G,M,A	Cary Academy, NC	G,M,A
Balmoral Hall School, MB, Canada	G	Casady School, OK	G,M,A
The Baltimore Actors' Theatre Conservatory, MD	G,M,A	Cascadilla School, NY	G,A
Baltimore Lutheran Middle and Upper School, MD	G	Cascia Hall Preparatory School, OK	G
Bancroft School, MA	G	Castilleja School, CA	G
Barnstable Academy, NJ	G,M,A	Cate School, CA	G,M,A
Baylor School, TN	G,M,A	Cathedral High School, IN	G,M,A
Beaufort Academy, SC	G	The Catlin Gabel School, OR	G,M,A
Beaumont School, OH	G	The Cedars Academy, DE	M,A
Beaver Country Day School, MA	A	Central Catholic High School, CA	G
The Beekman School, NY	G,M,A	Central Catholic High School, PA	G
Bellevue Christian School, WA	G,M	CFS, The School at Church Farm, PA	M,A
Benet Academy, IL	G	Chadwick School, CA	G,M,A
The Benjamin School, FL	G,M,A	Chamberlain-Hunt Academy, MS	G,M,A
Bentley School, CA	G,M,A	Chaminade College Preparatory School, MO	G
Berkeley Carroll School, NY	G,M,A	Chaminade-Madonna College Preparatory, FL	G,M,A
Berwick Academy, ME	G,M,A	Charles E. Smith Jewish Day School, MD	G
The Birch Wathen Lenox School, NY	G	Charles Finney School, NY	G,M,A
Bishop Eustace Preparatory School, NJ	M	Charlotte Country Day School, NC	G
Bishop Guertin High School, NH	G,M,A	Charlotte Latin School, NC	G,M,A
Bishop Ireton High School, VA	M	Chase Collegiate School, CT	G
Bishop Luers High School, IN	G,M	Chatham Hall, VA	G,M,A
Bishop Lynch Catholic High School, TX	G	Chattanooga Christian School, TN	G,M,A
Bishop McGuinness Catholic High School, OK	G,A	Chelsea School, MD	G,M,A
Bishop's College School, QC, Canada	G,M,A	Cheshire Academy, CT	M,A
Blueprint Education, AZ	G	Chestnut Hill Academy, PA	G,M,A
Boston University Academy, MA	G	Chinese Christian Schools, CA	G
The Boys' Latin School of Maryland, MD	G,M,A	Choate Rosemary Hall, CT	G,M,A
Brandon Hall School, GA	G	Christa McAuliffe Academy, WA	G
Breck School, MN	G,M,A	Christ School, NC	G
Brehm Preparatory School, IL	G	Chrysalis School, WA	G
Brenau Academy, GA	G,M,A	Colegio Bolivar, Colombia	G
Brentwood Academy, TN	G,M,A	Colegio Franklin D. Roosevelt, Peru	G,M,A
Brentwood School, CA	G,A	Colegio Nueva Granada, Colombia	G
Bridges Academy, CA	G	College du Leman International School, Switzerland	G,M,A
Bridge School, CO	G	The College Preparatory School, CA	G,M,A
The British International School, Jeddah, Saudi Arabia	G,M,A	The Colorado Rocky Mountain School, CO	G,M,A
		The Colorado Springs School, CO	G
The Brook Hill School, TX	M	Colorado Timberline Academy, CO	A
Brownell-Talbot School, NE	G	Columbia Grammar and Preparatory School, NY	G
The Browning School, NY	G	The Columbus Academy, OH	G
Brunswick School, CT	G,M,A	Commonwealth School, MA	G,M,A
The Bryn Mawr School for Girls, MD	G,M,A	The Concept School, PA	G,A
Buckingham Browne & Nichols School, MA	G,M,A	Concord Academy, MA	G,M,A
The Bullis School, MD	G	Concordia Academy, MN	G
Bulloch Academy, GA	G,M,A	Connelly School of the Holy Child, MD	G,M,A
Buxton School, MA	G,M,A	Convent of the Sacred Heart, CT	G,A
The Calhoun School, NY	G	Convent of the Sacred Heart, NY	G
Calvert Hall College High School, MD	G,M,A	Country Day School of the Sacred Heart, PA	M
Camelot Academy, NC	G	Cranbrook Schools, MI	G,M,A
Campbell Hall (Episcopal), CA	G	Cretin-Derham Hall, MN	G
Campion School, Athens, Greece	M,A	Crossroads School for Arts & Sciences, CA	G,M,A
Cape Fear Academy, NC	G	The Culver Academies, IN	G,M,A
Cape Henry Collegiate School, VA	G,M,A	Currey Ingram Academy, TN	G,M,A
Cardigan Mountain School, NH	G,A	Cushing Academy, MA	G,M,A

G — gifted; M — musically talented; A — artistically talented

Dana Hall School, MA	M,A
Darrow School, NY	M,A
Deerfield Academy, MA	G,M,A
Delaware County Christian School, PA	G,M,A
Delphi Academy of Los Angeles, CA	G
The Delphian School, OR	G,M,A
DeMatha Catholic High School, MD	G,M,A
Denver Academy, CO	G
The Derryfield School, NH	G
Detroit Country Day School, MI	G,M,A
Dowling High School, IA	G,M,A
Dublin Christian Academy, NH	M
Dublin School, NH	A
Duchesne Academy of the Sacred Heart, NE	G
Duchesne Academy of the Sacred Heart, TX	M,A
Dunn School, CA	G
Eaglebrook School, MA	G,M,A
Eagle Hill School, MA	G,M,A
Eagle Rock School, CO	G
Eastern Christian High School, NJ	G,M,A
Eastern Mennonite High School, VA	G
Eckerd Youth Alternatives, FL	G
Ecole d'Humanite, Switzerland	G,M,A
Edison School, AB, Canada	G
Elan School, ME	G
Elizabeth Seton High School, MD	G,M,A
Emerson Honors High Schools, CA	G,M,A
Emma Willard School, NY	M,A
Episcopal High School, VA	G,M,A
The Episcopal School of Acadiana, LA	G
The Ethel Walker School, CT	G,M,A
Explorations Academy, WA	G
Faith Lutheran High School, NV	M
Father Ryan High School, TN	G,M,A
Fay School, MA	G,M
The Fessenden School, MA	G,M,A
The Field School, DC	G,A
Florida Air Academy, FL	G
Forsyth Country Day School, NC	G
Fort Worth Country Day School, TX	G,M,A
Fountain Valley School of Colorado, CO	G,M,A
Foxcroft School, VA	G,M,A
Fox River Country Day School, IL	G
Fox Valley Lutheran High School, WI	G
Franklin Road Academy, TN	G,M,A
Freeman Academy, SD	M,A
Fryeburg Academy, ME	M
Fuqua School, VA	G
Futures High School, Oceanside, CA	G,M,A
Futures High School—San Diego, CA	G,M,A
The Galloway School, GA	G,M,A
Garrison Forest School, MD	G,M,A
Gaston Day School, NC	G
Gem State Adventist Academy, ID	M
George School, PA	G
George Stevens Academy, ME	G,M,A
Georgetown Preparatory School, MD	G
George Walton Academy, GA	M,A
Germantown Friends School, PA	G,M,A
Gill St. Bernard's School, NJ	G
Gilman School, MD	G
Gilmour Academy, OH	G,M,A
Glenelg Country School, MD	G
Gould Academy, ME	G,M,A
The Governor French Academy, IL	G,M,A
The Gow School, NY	M
The Grauer School, CA	G,M,A
Greater Atlanta Christian Schools, GA	G,M,A
Greenfield School, NC	G
Greenhills School, MI	G
Greensboro Day School, NC	G,A
The Greenwood School, VT	G,M,A
Grenville Christian College, ON, Canada	G
The Grier School, PA	G,M,A
Groton School, MA	G,M,A
Grove School, CT	G,M,A
Gulliver Preparatory School, FL	G,M,A
The Gunnery, CT	G,M,A
Gunston Day School, MD	G,M,A
Hackett Catholic Central High School, MI	G,M,A
Halifax Grammar School, NS, Canada	G,M,A
Hamilton Learning Centre, ON, Canada	G
Hammond School, SC	G,M,A
Happy Valley School, CA	M,A
Harare International School, Zimbabwe	G,M,A
The Harker School, CA	G
The Harpeth Hall School, TN	G,M,A
Harrow School, United Kingdom	G,M,A
Harvard-Westlake School, CA	G,M,A
The Haverford School, PA	G
Hawai'i Preparatory Academy, HI	G,M,A
Hawken School, OH	G,M
Hayden High School, KS	G,M
Head-Royce School, CA	G,M,A
Hebrew Academy-the Five Towns, NY	G,M,A
Hebron Academy, ME	G,M,A
The Hewitt School, NY	M,A
Hidden Lake Academy, GA	G,A
Highland Hall, A Waldorf School, CA	G,M,A
High Mowing School, NH	M,A
Hillfield Strathallan College, ON, Canada	G,M,A
Hillside School, MA	G
The Hill Top Preparatory School, PA	G,A
Holderness School, NH	G,M,A
The Holton-Arms School, MD	G,A
Hoosac School, NY	M,A
The Hotchkiss School, CT	G,M,A
Hudson College, ON, Canada	G
The Hudson School, NJ	G,M,A
The Hun School of Princeton, NJ	G
Huntington-Surrey School, TX	G
Hutchison School, TN	G
Idyllwild Arts Academy, CA	M,A
Immaculata Academy, NY	M,A
Indian Springs School, AL	G,M,A
Interlochen Arts Academy, MI	G,M,A
International High School of FAIS, CA	G,M,A
International School of Amsterdam, Netherlands	G,M,A
International School of Brussels, Belgium	G,M,A
The International School of Geneva, Switzerland	M,A
International School of Minnesota, MN	G
Iolani School, HI	G,M,A

G — gifted; M — musically talented; A — artistically talented

Iona Preparatory School, NY	G	The Meeting School, NH	G,A
Jackson Preparatory School, MS	G,M,A	Menaul School, NM	G,A
The John Dewey Academy, MA	G,A	Menlo School, CA	G,M,A
John F. Kennedy Memorial High School, WA	G,M,A	Mercedes College, Australia	G
Kapaun Mount Carmel Catholic High School, KS	G	Mercersburg Academy, PA	G
The Karafin School, NY	G,M,A	Mercyhurst Preparatory School, PA	G,M,A
Kearney Catholic High School, NE	G	Middlesex School, MA	G
Kent School, CT	G,M,A	Mid-Pacific Institute, HI	G,A
Kents Hill School, ME	G,A	Milken Community High School of Stephen Wise Temple,	
Kentucky Country Day School, KY	G,M,A	CA	G,M,A
The Key School, MD	G	Miller School, VA	G,M,A
Keystone National High School, PA	G	Milton Academy, MA	G,M,A
Keystone School, TX	G	Milton Hershey School, PA	M,A
Kimball Union Academy, NH	G,M,A	Miss Hall's School, MA	G,M,A
King's College School, ON, Canada	G	Missouri Military Academy, MO	M,A
King's West School, WA	M,A	MMI Preparatory School, PA	G,A
The Kinkaid School, TX	G	Montana Academy, MT	G
The Kiski School, PA	G	Montclair Kimberley Academy, NJ	G
La Grange Academy, GA	G,M,A	Morgan Park Academy, IL	G,M,A
Lakefield College School, ON, Canada	G,M,A	Mountain View Christian High School, NV	G,M
Lake Highland Preparatory School, FL	G,M,A	Mount Alvernia High School, PA	G
Lake Ridge Academy, OH	G,M	Mount Bachelor Academy, OR	G
Lakewood Prep, NJ	G,A	Mt. Saint Dominic Academy, NJ	G,M,A
Lancaster Country Day School, PA	G,M,A	Mount Saint Joseph Academy, PA	G,M,A
La Salle Academy, RI	G,M,A	Mount Saint Mary Academy, NJ	G
La Salle College High School, PA	G,M,A	Munich International School, Germany	G
The Latin School of Chicago, IL	G	Nacel International School, MN	G,M,A
Laurel School, OH	G,M,A	National Cathedral School, DC	G
Lausanne Collegiate School, TN	G,M,A	Navajo Preparatory School, Inc., NM	G
Lawrence Academy, MA	M,A	Newark Academy, NJ	G,M,A
Lehigh Valley Christian High School, PA	G	The Newgrange School, NJ	G
Leysin American School in Switzerland, Switzerland	G,M,A	New Hampton School, NH	G,M,A
Linden Hall School for Girls, PA	G,M,A	Noble and Greenough School, MA	G,M,A
The Linsly School, WV	G	The Nora School, MD	G,A
The Loomis Chaffee School, CT	G,M,A	Norfolk Academy, VA	G,M,A
Loretto High School, CA	G,M,A	Norfolk Collegiate School, VA	G
Los Angeles Lutheran High School, CA	G,M,A	The North Broward Preparatory Upper School, FL	G,M,A
The Lovett School, GA	G,M,A	North Cobb Christian School, GA	M,A
Loyola Academy, IL	G	Northfield Mount Hermon School, MA	G,M,A
Luther College High School, SK, Canada	G	The North Shore Country Day School, IL	M
Lydia Patterson Institute, TX	G	Northside Christian School, FL	G
The MacDuffie School, MA	G	The Northwest School, WA	G,M,A
Madison-Ridgeland Academy, MS	G	Northwest Yeshiva High School, WA	G
Maine Central Institute, ME	M	Notre Dame High School, LA	G
Malaspina International High School, BC, Canada	G	Notre Dame High School, MO	G,M,A
Manlius Pebble Hill School, NY	G	Notre Dame High School, WV	G,M,A
Maret School, DC	G,M,A	Notre Dame Regional Secondary, BC, Canada	G,M
Marianapolis Preparatory School, CT	M,A	The Oakland School, PA	G,A
Marin Academy, CA	G,M,A	Oak Ridge Military Academy, NC	G
Marist High School, NJ	G	The Oakridge School, TX	G,M,A
Marmion Academy, IL	G	Oakwood Friends School, NY	G
Marshall School, MN	G	Oakwood School, CA	G
Marylawn of the Oranges, NJ	G,M,A	O'Dea High School, WA	G
The Mary Louis Academy, NY	M,A	Ojai Valley School, CA	G,A
Marymount School, NY	G	Oneida Baptist Institute, KY	G,M
The Masters School, NY	G,M,A	Oregon Episcopal School, OR	G
Maumee Valley Country Day School, OH	G,M,A	Orinda Academy, CA	G
Mayfield Senior School, CA	G,M,A	The Overlake School, WA	G,M,A
The McCallie School, TN	G,M,A	The Oxford Academy, CT	G
McNicholas High School, OH	G	Pace Academy, GA	G,M,A
The Meadows School, NV	G,M,A	Pacific Northern Academy, AK	G

G — gifted; M — musically talented; A — artistically talented

Palmer Trinity School, FL	G,M,A
The Park School, MD	G,M,A
The Park School of Buffalo, NY	G
Park Tudor School, IN	G,M,A
The Pembroke Hill School, MO	G,A
The Pennington School, NJ	G
Perkiomen School, PA	G,M,A
Phillips Exeter Academy, NH	G,M,A
Polytechnic Preparatory Country Day School, NY	G,A
Pomfret School, CT	G,M,A
Portland Christian Schools, OR	G
Portledge School, NY	G,M,A
Portsmouth Abbey School, RI	G,M,A
Portsmouth Christian Academy, NH	G
Poughkeepsie Day School, NY	G,M,A
The Prairie School, WI	G,M,A
Prestonwood Christian Academy, TX	G
Princeton Day School, NJ	G,M,A
Proctor Academy, NH	G
Providence Country Day School, RI	G,A
Providence High School, CA	M,A
Providence High School, TX	G,M,A
Purcell Marian High School, OH	M,A
The Putney School, VT	G,M,A
Queen Margaret's School, BC, Canada	G,M,A
Queensway Christian College, ON, Canada	G
Rabbi Alexander S. Gross Hebrew Academy, FL	G
Ramona Convent Secondary School, CA	G,M,A
Rancho Valmora, NM	G,A
Randolph-Macon Academy, VA	G
Ravenscroft School, NC	G,M,A
The Rectory School, CT	G
Regina High School, OH	G,M,A
Ribet Academy, CA	M,A
Ridley College, ON, Canada	M,A
Ripon Christian Schools, CA	M,A
Riverdale Country School, NY	G,M,A
Rivermont Collegiate, IA	G,M
Robert Louis Stevenson School, NY	G
The Rockland Country Day School, NY	G,M,A
Rocklyn Academy, ON, Canada	G
Rockway Mennonite Collegiate, ON, Canada	G,M
Rocky Hill School, RI	G,M,A
The Roeper School, MI	G,M,A
Rolling Hills Preparatory School, CA	G
Roncalli High School, IN	G
Rothesay Netherwood School, NB, Canada	G,M,A
The Roxbury Latin School, MA	G,M,A
Rumsey Hall School, CT	G
Rutgers Preparatory School, NJ	G,M,A
Rye Country Day School, NY	G
Sacramento Country Day School, CA	G,A
Sacred Heart Academy, CT	A
Saddle River Day School, NJ	G,M,A
St. Andrew's Episcopal School, MS	G,M,A
St. Andrew's Priory School, HI	M,A
St. Andrew's School, DE	G,M,A
Saint Andrew's School, FL	G
St. Andrew's School, RI	M,A
St. Andrew's–Sewanee School, TN	G,M,A
St. Anne's–Belfield School, VA	G

St. Anselm's Abbey School, DC	G
St. Benedict at Auburndale, TN	G,M,A
St. Cecilia Academy, TN	G,M,A
St. Christopher's School, VA	G,M,A
St. Clement's School, ON, Canada	G
St. Croix Lutheran High School, MN	G,A
St. Dominic's International School, Portugal, Portugal	G,M,A
Saint Edward's School, FL	G,M,A
St. George's School, RI	G,M,A
St. George's School of Montreal, QC, Canada	G,M,A
St. Gregory College Preparatory School, AZ	G,M,A
Saint James School, AL	G,A
St. Johnsbury Academy, VT	G,A
St. John's College High School, DC	G
St. Johns Country Day School, FL	G,M,A
St. John's Preparatory School, MA	G,M,A
Saint John's Preparatory School, MN	G,M,A
St. John's School, TX	G
St. Joseph High School, CT	G
St. Joseph's Preparatory School, PA	G,M,A
St. Leonards, United Kingdom	G,M,A
Saint Louis Priory School, MO	G
St. Luke's School, CT	G
St. Margaret's Episcopal School, CA	G,M,A
St. Margaret's School, BC, Canada	G,M,A
St. Mark's High School, DE	G
Saint Mark's School, MA	G,M,A
Saint Mary's Hall, TX	G
St. Mary's Hall–Doane Academy, NJ	G,M,A
St. Mary's School, OR	G,M,A
St. Maur International School, Japan	G,M,A
Saint Patrick—Saint Vincent High School, CA	G,M,A
St. Paul's School, MD	G
St. Paul's School, NH	G,M,A
St. Paul's School for Girls, MD	G,M,A
St. Sebastian's School, MA	G,M,A
St. Stephen's & St. Agnes School, VA	G,M,A
Saint Thomas Aquinas High School, KS	G
St. Thomas Choir School, NY	G,M
Saint Xavier High School, KY	G,M,A
Salem Academy, OR	G,M,A
Salesianum School, DE	G
San Domenico School, CA	M,A
San Marcos Baptist Academy, TX	G
Santa Catalina School, CA	G,M,A
Sayre School, KY	G,A
School for Young Performers, NY	G,M,A
Schule Schloss Salem, Germany	G,M,A
Seoul Foreign School, Republic of Korea	G,M,A
Seoul International School, Republic of Korea	M,A
Seton Catholic Central High School, NY	G
The Seven Hills School, OH	G
Severn School, MD	G,M,A
Shady Side Academy, PA	G,M,A
Shattuck-St. Mary's School, MN	G,M,A
The Shipley School, PA	G
Shorecrest Preparatory School, FL	G
Smith School, NY	G
Solebury School, PA	G,M,A
Soundview Preparatory School, NY	G,M,A
Southwest Christian School, Inc., TX	G

G — gifted; M — musically talented; A — artistically talented

Spartanburg Day School, SC	G,A
Squaw Valley Academy, CA	G,A
Staten Island Academy, NY	G,M,A
Stella Maris High School and the Maura Clarke Junior High Program, NY	G
Stevenson School, CA	G,M,A
Stone Mountain School, NC	G
Stuart Country Day School of the Sacred Heart, NJ	G,M,A
Stuart Hall, VA	A
Subiaco Academy, AR	G,M,A
Suffield Academy, CT	G,M,A
Sumiton Christian School, AL	G,A
The Summit Country Day School, OH	G
Summit Preparatory School, MT	M,A
Tabor Academy, MA	G,M,A
The Taft School, CT	G,M,A
Tallulah Falls School, GA	G,M,A
TASIS The American School in England, United Kingdom	G
The Tatnall School, DE	G,M,A
The Tenney School, TX	G
The Thacher School, CA	G,M,A
Thayer Academy, MA	G,M,A
Thomas Jefferson School, MO	G
Thornton Friends School, MD	G
Thornton Friends School/N.V.A., VA	G
Trinity Academy, KS	G
Trinity Christian School, GA	G
Trinity Episcopal School, VA	G,M,A
Trinity High School, IL	G
Trinity High School, KY	G,M,A
Trinity Preparatory School, FL	G,M,A
Trinity Valley School, TX	G,M,A
United Nations International School, NY	G,M,A
University Lake School, WI	G
University Liggett School, MI	G,M,A
University of Missouri—Columbia High School, MO	G
University of Toronto Schools, ON, Canada	G
University School, OH	G,M,A
University School of Nashville, TN	G,M,A
University School of Nova Southeastern University, FL	G,M,A
Upper Canada College, ON, Canada	G,M,A
The Urban School of San Francisco, CA	G,A
Ursuline Academy, DE	G
Valley Forge Military Academy and College, PA	M,A
Vanguard College Preparatory School, TX	A
Venta Preparatory School, ON, Canada	G
Villa Victoria Academy, NJ	G,M,A
Villa Walsh Academy, NJ	G,M,A
Walden Preparatory School, TX	G,M,A
The Walker School, GA	G,A
Walnut Hill School, MA	G,M,A
The Wardlaw-Hartridge School, NJ	G,M,A
Waring School, MA	G,M,A
Wasatch Academy, UT	G,M,A
Washington Waldorf School, MD	M,A
The Waterford School, UT	G,M,A
Watkinson School, CT	G,M,A
Wayne Country Day School, NC	G
Webber Academy, AB, Canada	G,M,A
The Webb School, TN	G
The Wellington School, OH	G,M,A

Western Reserve Academy, OH	G,M,A
Westminster Christian Academy, AL	G,M,A
Westminster Christian School, FL	G,M,A
The Westminster Schools, GA	G,M,A
Westminster Schools of Augusta, GA	G
West Nottingham Academy, MD	G,M,A
Westover School, CT	G,M,A
Westtown School, PA	G,M,A
Wheaton Academy, IL	G,M,A
The White Mountain School, NH	G,A
Whitfield School, MO	G,M,A
Whittier Christian High School, CA	G,M,A
Wichita Collegiate School, KS	G
Wilbraham & Monson Academy, MA	M,A
William Penn Charter School, PA	G,M,A
The Williston Northampton School, MA	G,M,A
Willow Hill School, MA	A
Wilmington Friends School, DE	G,M,A
The Winchendon School, MA	G
Winchester Thurston School, PA	G,M,A
Windsor Christian Fellowship Academy, ON, Canada	G
The Windsor School, NY	G,M,A
Woodberry Forest School, VA	G,M,A
Woodbridge Academy, KY	G,M,A
Woodcliff Academy, NJ	G
Woodlands Academy of the Sacred Heart, IL	G
Woodside International School, CA	G,M,A
Woodside Priory School, CA	G,M,A
Woodstock School, India	G,M,A
The Woodward School, MA	A
Worcester Preparatory School, MD	G
Xavier College Preparatory, AZ	G
York Country Day School, PA	G
York Preparatory School, NY	G,M,A
The York School, ON, Canada	G,M,A
Zurich International School, Switzerland	G,M,A

SCHOOLS WITH ADVANCED PLACEMENT PREPARATION

The number of test areas, if reported, is given for each school.

The Academy for Gifted Children (PACE), ON, Canada	2
Academy of Holy Angels, MN	7
Academy of Mount Saint Ursula, NY	5
Academy of Our Lady of Peace, CA	10
Academy of Saint Elizabeth, NJ	8
The Academy of St. Joseph, NY	5
Academy of the Holy Angels, NJ	9
Academy of the Holy Cross, MD	12
Academy of the Holy Names, FL	12
Academy of the Pacific, HI	3
Academy of the Sacred Heart, LA	5
Academy of the Sacred Heart, MI	5
ACS Cobham International School, United Kingdom	10
ACS Hillingdon International School, United Kingdom	12
The Agnes Irwin School, PA	14
Akiba Hebrew Academy, PA	8
The Albany Academy, NY	17
Albert College, ON, Canada	5
Albuquerque Academy, NM	18
Alexander Dawson School, CO	15
Allen Academy, TX	14

G — gifted; M — musically talented; A — artistically talented

Allendale Columbia School, NY	15	The Benjamin School, FL	18
Alliance Academy, Ecuador	10	Bentley School, CA	15
Allison Academy, FL	4	Berkeley Carroll School, NY	9
All Saints' Episcopal School of Fort Worth, TX	9	Berkeley Preparatory School, FL	16
The Altamont School, AL	17	Berkshire School, MA	16
American Cooperative School, Bolivia	9	Berwick Academy, ME	12
American Heritage School, FL	7	The Birch Wathen Lenox School, NY	10
The American International School, Austria	9	Bishop Brady High School, NH	7
American International School Salzburg, Austria	15	Bishop Conaty-Our Lady of Loretto High School, CA	3
American Overseas School of Rome, Italy	10	Bishop Eustace Preparatory School, NJ	10
The American School Foundation, Mexico	19	Bishop Feehan High School, MA	10
The American School in Japan, Japan	19	Bishop Fenwick High School, OH	5
The American School in London, United Kingdom	19	Bishop George Ahr High School, NJ	5
American School of Doha, Qatar	13	Bishop Guertin High School, NH	12
American School of Paris, France	10	Bishop Hoban High School, PA	11
The American School of Puerto Vallarta, Mexico	3	Bishop Ireton High School, VA	11
The American School of The Hague, Netherlands	16	Bishop Kelly High School, ID	9
Anacapa School, CA	1	Bishop Kenny High School, FL	
The Andrews School, OH	7	Bishop Luers High School, IN	4
Annie Wright School, WA	8	Bishop Lynch Catholic High School, TX	13
Appleby College, ON, Canada	10	Bishop McDevitt High School, PA	6
Aquin Central Catholic High School, IL	4	Bishop McGuinness Catholic High School, OK	9
Archbishop Blenk Girls High School, LA	4	Bishop McNamara High School, IL	8
Archbishop Curley High School, MD	6	Bishop Quinn High School/St. Francis Middle School, CA	
Archbishop Mitty High School, CA	20	Bishop's College School, QC, Canada	13
Archbishop Quigley Preparatory High School, IL	12	The Bishop Strachan School, ON, Canada	16
Archbishop Riordan High School, CA	7	Bishop Verot High School, FL	9
The Archer School for Girls, CA	12	Bismark St. Mary's Central, ND	
Archmere Academy, DE	18	Black Forest Academy, Germany	10
Army and Navy Academy, CA	10	Blair Academy, NJ	17
Arrowhead Christian Academy, CA	5	The Blake School, MN	14
Asheville School, NC	15	Blue Mountain Academy, PA	2
Ashley Hall, SC	18	The Bolles School, FL	19
Assumption High School, KY	16	Boyd-Buchanan School, TN	7
The Athenian School, CA	11	The Boys' Latin School of Maryland, MD	7
Athens Academy, GA	8	Brandon Hall School, GA	2
Auldern Academy, NC		The Brearley School, NY	14
Aurora Central High School, IL	10	Breck School, MN	7
Avon Old Farms School, CT	19	Brentwood Academy, TN	8
The Baldwin School, PA	11	Brentwood College School, BC, Canada	
Baldwin School of Puerto Rico, Inc., PR	9	Brentwood School, CA	19
Balmoral Hall School, MB, Canada	12	Brewster Academy, NH	8
The Baltimore Actors' Theatre Conservatory, MD	5	Brooks School, MA	14
Baltimore Lutheran Middle and Upper School, MD	3	Brookstone School, GA	13
Bancroft School, MA	14	Brophy College Preparatory, AZ	16
Baptist High School, NJ	4	Brother Rice High School, MI	18
Barnstable Academy, NJ	5	Brownell-Talbot School, NE	13
The Barstow School, MO	16	The Browning School, NY	14
Battle Ground Academy, TN	12	Brunswick School, CT	19
Baylor School, TN	17	The Bryn Mawr School for Girls, MD	18
Bayside Academy, AL	11	Buckingham Browne & Nichols School, MA	19
Beaufort Academy, SC	5	The Buckley School, CA	17
Beaumont School, OH	6	The Bullis School, MD	17
Beaver Country Day School, MA	10	Bulloch Academy, GA	3
The Beekman School, NY	19	Burke Mountain Academy, VT	2
Belen Jesuit Preparatory School, FL	13	Burr and Burton Academy, VT	6
Bellarmine College Preparatory, CA	7	The Bush School, WA	8
Bellarmine Preparatory School, WA	8	The Calhoun School, NY	6
Bellevue Christian School, WA		Calvary Christian Academy, KY	7
Belmont Hill School, MA	10	Calvert Hall College High School, MD	19
Benedictine High School, OH	5	The Calverton School, MD	
Benet Academy, IL	12	The Cambridge School of Weston, MA	10
Ben Franklin Academy, GA		Camden Military Academy, SC	5
Benilde–St. Margaret's School, MN	11	Camelot Academy, NC	6

Campbell Hall (Episcopal), CA	19
Canadian Academy, Japan	2
Cannon School, NC	14
Canterbury High School, IN	15
Canterbury School, CT	17
Canterbury School, FL	14
The Canterbury School of Florida, FL	14
Canyonville Christian Academy, OR	4
Cape Cod Academy, MA	6
Cape Fear Academy, NC	13
Cape Henry Collegiate School, VA	12
Cardinal Gibbons High School, FL	12
Cardinal Mooney Catholic College Preparatory High School, MI	6
Cardinal Newman High School, FL	5
Cardinal Newman School, SC	3
Caribbean Preparatory School, PR	6
Carlisle School, VA	8
Carlucci American International School of Lisbon, Portugal	6
Carolina Day School, NC	18
Carondelet High School, CA	6
Carrollton School of the Sacred Heart, FL	7
Cary Academy, NC	
Casady School, OK	17
Cascadilla School, NY	10
Cascia Hall Preparatory School, OK	13
Castilleja School, CA	18
Cate School, CA	19
Cathedral High School, IN	13
Cathedral Preparatory School, PA	19
Catholic Central High School, NY	3
The Catholic High School of Baltimore, MD	5
CCI The Renaissance School, Italy	9
The Cedars Academy, DE	
Central Catholic High School, CA	8
Central Catholic High School, PA	9
CFS, The School at Church Farm, PA	3
Chadwick School, CA	16
Chamberlain-Hunt Academy, MS	2
Chaminade College Preparatory, CA	18
Chaminade College Preparatory School, MO	18
Chaminade-Madonna College Preparatory, FL	10
Chapel Hill–Chauncy Hall School, MA	2
The Chapin School, NY	17
Charles E. Smith Jewish Day School, MD	2
Charles Finney School, NY	
Charles Wright Academy, WA	12
Charlotte Christian School, NC	18
Charlotte Country Day School, NC	14
Charlotte Latin School, NC	14
Chase Collegiate School, CT	16
Chatham Hall, VA	15
Chattanooga Christian School, TN	10
Cheshire Academy, CT	12
Chestnut Hill Academy, PA	14
Cheverus High School, ME	9
Chinese Christian Schools, CA	12
Choate Rosemary Hall, CT	19
Christa McAuliffe Academy, WA	2
Christ Church Episcopal School, SC	20
Christchurch School, VA	12
Christian Brothers Academy, NJ	16
Christian Brothers Academy, NY	8

Christian Brothers Academy, NY	12
Christian Brothers High School, CA	12
Christian Central Academy, NY	3
Christian Heritage School, CT	9
Christian Junior–Senior High School, CA	7
Christopher Dock Mennonite High School, PA	2
Christ School, NC	8
Cincinnati Country Day School, OH	11
Cistercian Preparatory School, TX	19
Coe-Brown Northwood Academy, NH	4
Colegio Bolivar, Colombia	5
Colegio Nueva Granada, Colombia	15
Colegio San Jose, PR	5
College du Leman International School, Switzerland	15
The College Preparatory School, CA	11
The Collegiate School, VA	11
The Colorado Rocky Mountain School, CO	8
The Colorado Springs School, CO	8
Columbia Grammar and Preparatory School, NY	19
Columbia International College of Canada, ON, Canada	5
The Columbus Academy, OH	17
Columbus School for Girls, OH	15
Commonwealth School, MA	13
The Community School of Naples, FL	19
Concord Academy, MA	14
Concordia Academy, MN	4
Connelly School of the Holy Child, MD	9
Conserve School, WI	5
Convent of the Sacred Heart, CT	14
Convent of the Sacred Heart, NY	18
Convent of the Sacred Heart High School, CA	19
Convent of the Visitation School, MN	11
Cornelia Connelly School, CA	12
The Country Day School, ON, Canada	2
Country Day School of the Sacred Heart, PA	5
Cranbrook Schools, MI	14
Crescent School, ON, Canada	14
Crespi Carmelite High School, CA	13
Cretin-Derham Hall, MN	7
Crofton House School, BC, Canada	6
Crossroads School, MO	6
Crossroads School for Arts & Sciences, CA	13
Crystal Springs Uplands School, CA	15
The Culver Academies, IN	19
Cushing Academy, MA	14
The Dalton School, NY	11
Dana Hall School, MA	13
Darlington School, GA	16
David Lipscomb High School, TN	4
Deerfield Academy, MA	19
De La Salle College, ON, Canada	4
De La Salle High School, CA	9
DeLaSalle High School, MN	7
Delaware County Christian School, PA	8
Delbarton School, NJ	19
DeMatha Catholic High School, MD	16
Denver Lutheran High School, CO	3
The Derryfield School, NH	10
Detroit Country Day School, MI	17
Devon Preparatory School, PA	13
Doane Stuart School, NY	10
Dowling High School, IA	
Dublin School, NH	4
Duchesne Academy of the Sacred Heart, NE	5

Hebrew Academy-the Five Towns, NY	16
Hebron Academy, ME	9
The Heritage School, GA	13
The Hewitt School, NY	8
Highland School, VA	16
Hillcrest Christian School, CA	4
Hillfield Strathallan College, ON, Canada	5
The Hill School, PA	14
Hilton Head Preparatory School, SC	15
The Hockaday School, TX	19
Hokkaido International School, Japan	6
Holderness School, NH	11
Holland Hall, OK	18
The Holton-Arms School, MD	10
Holy Name High School, PA	5
Holyoke Catholic High School, MA	4
Holy Trinity Diocesan High School, NY	8
Hoosac School, NY	3
Hopkins School, CT	15
The Horace Mann School, NY	19
Horizons School, GA	2
The Hotchkiss School, CT	18
Howe Military School, IN	3
The Hun School of Princeton, NJ	14
Huntington-Surrey School, TX	6
Hutchison School, TN	16
Hyde School, CT	5
Idyllwild Arts Academy, CA	4
Immaculata Academy, NY	
Immaculata High School, NJ	5
Immaculate Conception High School, NJ	3
Immaculate Conception School, IL	4
Incarnate Word Academy, TX	10
Indian Springs School, AL	18
Interlochen Arts Academy, MI	3
International Community School of Addis Ababa, Ethiopia	
International High School of FAIS, CA	14
International Junior Golf Academy, SC	6
International School Bangkok, Thailand	14
International School Basel, Switzerland	5
International School of Aruba, Aruba	5
International School of Brussels, Belgium	7
The International School of Kuala Lumpur, Malaysia	10
International School of Minnesota, MN	20
International School of Port-of-Spain, Trinidad and Tobago	6
Iolani School, HI	19
Iona Preparatory School, NY	12
Isidore Newman School, LA	18
Islamic Saudi Academy, VA	4
Jackson Academy, MS	10
Jackson Preparatory School, MS	9
Jakarta International School, Indonesia	14
Jesuit College Preparatory School, TX	10
Jesuit High School, CA	12
Jesuit High School of New Orleans, LA	12
Jesuit High School of Tampa, FL	6
John Burroughs School, MO	7
The John Cooper School, TX	12
John F. Kennedy Memorial High School, WA	13
Justin-Siena High School, CA	5
Kalamazoo Christian High School, MI	5
Kapaun Mount Carmel Catholic High School, KS	7
Karachi American School, Pakistan	14

Keith Country Day School, IL	9
Kent Denver School, CO	16
Kent Place School, NJ	18
Kent School, CT	19
Kents Hill School, ME	11
Kentucky Country Day School, KY	12
The Key School, MD	13
Keystone School, TX	9
Kimball Union Academy, NH	15
King & Low-Heywood Thomas School, CT	17
King David High School, BC, Canada	3
The King's Academy, TN	3
The King's Christian High School, NJ	3
Kings Christian School, CA	2
King's West School, WA	4
Kingswood-Oxford School, CT	16
The Kinkaid School, TX	20
The Kiski School, PA	14
The Knox School, NY	6
La Grange Academy, GA	5
Laguna Blanca School, CA	19
La Jolla Country Day School, CA	18
Lakefield College School, ON, Canada	5
Lake Forest Academy, IL	19
Lake Highland Preparatory School, FL	20
Lakehill Preparatory School, TX	12
Lake Ridge Academy, OH	13
Lakewood Prep, NJ	5
La Lumiere School, IN	2
Lancaster Country Day School, PA	11
Landon School, MD	12
Lansdale Catholic High School, PA	6
La Pietra–Hawaii School for Girls, HI	5
La Salle Academy, RI	10
La Salle College High School, PA	17
La Salle High School, CA	6
The Latin School of Chicago, IL	17
Laurel School, OH	16
Lausanne Collegiate School, TN	14
Lawrence Academy, MA	8
The Lawrenceville School, NJ	11
Lawrence Woodmere Academy, NY	14
Lebanon Catholic Junior / Senior High School, PA	5
The Leelanau School, MI	3
Lee-Scott Academy, AL	5
Lehigh Valley Christian High School, PA	3
Lehman High School, OH	5
Le Lycee Francais de Los Angeles, CA	10
Lexington Catholic High School, KY	12
Lexington Christian Academy, MA	9
Lick-Wilmerding High School, CA	17
Lifegate School, OR	2
Linden Hall School for Girls, PA	10
Linfield Christian School, CA	5
The Linsly School, WV	7
Living Word Academy, PA	3
Long Island Lutheran Middle and High School, NY	10
The Loomis Chaffee School, CT	13
Loretto Academy, TX	6
Loretto High School, CA	6
Los Angeles Baptist Junior/Senior High School, CA	10
Los Angeles Lutheran High School, CA	
Louisville High School, CA	15
The Lovett School, GA	16

Notre Dame High School, NJ	10	The Prairie School, WI	11
Notre Dame High School, WV	7	Preston High School, NY	6
Notre Dame High School for Girls, IL	6	Prestonwood Christian Academy, TX	7
Notre Dame Junior/Senior High School, PA	4	Princeton Day School, NJ	13
Notre Dame Preparatory School, MD	16	Proctor Academy, NH	11
Oak Hill Academy, VA	2	Professional Children's School, NY	1
Oak Knoll School of the Holy Child, NJ	11	Providence Country Day School, RI	11
The Oakland School, PA	3	Providence High School, CA	11
Oak Mountain Academy, GA	5	Providence High School, TX	9
Oak Ridge Military Academy, NC	5	Providence School, FL	12
The Oakridge School, TX	17	Pulaski Academy, AR	16
Oakwood Friends School, NY	8	Punahou School, HI	14
Oakwood School, CA	17	Purcell Marian High School, OH	6
O'Dea High School, WA	2	The Putney School, VT	2
Ojai Valley School, CA	10	Queen Anne School, MD	7
Oldenburg Academy, IN	9	Queen Margaret's School, BC, Canada	7
Oldfields School, MD	8	Quigley Catholic High School, PA	3
Olney Friends School, OH	5	Quincy Notre Dame High School, IL	3
The O'Neal School, NC	10	Rabbi Alexander S. Gross Hebrew Academy, FL	8
Oneida Baptist Institute, KY	5	Rabun Gap-Nacoochee School, GA	8
Oregon Episcopal School, OR	8	Ramona Convent Secondary School, CA	13
Orinda Academy, CA	2	Randolph-Macon Academy, VA	9
The Orme School, AZ	5	Randolph School, AL	17
Our Lady of the Sacred Heart, PA	1	Ranney School, NJ	17
Our Saviour Lutheran School, NY	3	Ransom Everglades School, FL	20
Out-Of-Door-Academy, FL	13	Ravenscroft School, NC	17
The Overlake School, WA	14	Regina High School, OH	5
The Oxford Academy, CT	8	Regis High School, NY	
Oxford School, CA	1	Regis High School, OR	1
Pace Academy, GA	16	Resurrection High School, IL	9
Padua Franciscan High School, OH	6	Ribet Academy, CA	13
The Paideia School, GA	8	Ridley College, ON, Canada	10
Palma High School, CA	11	Rio Lindo Adventist Academy, CA	1
Palmer Trinity School, FL	16	Ripon Christian Schools, CA	3
Paraclete High School, CA	5	Riverdale Country School, NY	8
The Parker School, HI	5	Rivermont Collegiate, IA	8
Parklane Academy, MS	4	Riverside Military Academy, GA	6
The Park School, MD	7	Riverside School, Switzerland	16
The Park School of Buffalo, NY	11	The Rivers School, MA	15
Park Tudor School, IN	14	The Rockland Country Day School, NY	14
Peddie School, NJ	10	Rocky Hill School, RI	8
The Pembroke Hill School, MO	15	Rocky Mount Academy, NC	9
The Pennington School, NJ	14	The Roeper School, MI	14
Perkiomen School, PA	12	Roland Park Country School, MD	19
Phillips Academy (Andover), MA	14	Rolling Hills Preparatory School, CA	8
Phillips Exeter Academy, NH	19	Roncalli High School, IN	9
Phoenix Christian Unified Schools, AZ	5	Rosary High School, IL	2
Phoenix Country Day School, AZ	15	Rothesay Netherwood School, NB, Canada	11
Piedmont Academy, GA		Routt High School, IL	2
Pine Crest School, FL	19	Rowland Hall-St. Mark's School, UT	15
The Pingree School, MA	10	The Roxbury Latin School, MA	11
The Pingry School, NJ	17	Roycemore School, IL	12
Pius X High School, NE	5	Rutgers Preparatory School, NJ	19
Polytechnic Preparatory Country Day School, NY	20	Rye Country Day School, NY	15
Pomfret School, CT	19	Sacramento Country Day School, CA	12
Pope John Paul II High School, FL	6	Sacred Heart Academy, CT	5
Portland Christian Schools, OR	5	Sacred Heart Preparatory, CA	13
Portland Lutheran School, OR	1	Sacred Heart School of Halifax, NS, Canada	6
Portledge School, NY	10	Saddleback Valley Christian School, CA	
Portsmouth Abbey School, RI	14	Saddle River Day School, NJ	13
Portsmouth Christian Academy, NH	4	St. Agnes Academy, TX	12
The Potomac School, VA	15	Saint Agnes Boys High School, NY	4
Poughkeepsie Day School, NY	6	St. Agnes High School, MN	3
Powers Catholic High School, MI	8	St. Andrew's College, ON, Canada	5

School for Young Performers, NY	19
School of the Holy Child, NY	14
Seabury Hall, HI	12
Seattle Christian Schools, WA	5
Second Baptist School, TX	17
Seoul Foreign School, Republic of Korea	2
Seoul International School, Republic of Korea	13
Seton Catholic Central High School, NY	12
Seton Hall Preparatory School, NJ	16
The Seven Hills School, OH	14
Severn School, MD	11
Sewickley Academy, PA	17
Shady Side Academy, PA	6
Shannon Forest Christian School, SC	5
Shattuck-St. Mary's School, MN	14
The Shipley School, PA	17
Shorecrest Preparatory School, FL	19
Sidwell Friends School, DC	11
Solebury School, PA	9
Soundview Preparatory School, NY	5
Southampton Academy, VA	2
South Kent School, CT	5
Southridge School, BC, Canada	9
Southwest Christian School, Inc., TX	7
Southwestern Academy, AZ	2
Southwestern Academy, CA	3
Spartanburg Day School, SC	16
The Spence School, NY	2
Springside School, PA	18
Squaw Valley Academy, CA	4
Stanstead College, QC, Canada	13
Staten Island Academy, NY	12
Stella Maris High School and the Maura Clarke Junior High Program, NY	2
Stevenson School, CA	18
Stoneleigh–Burnham School, MA	9
The Stony Brook School, NY	17
Storm King School, NY	5
Strake Jesuit College Preparatory, TX	10
Stratford Academy, GA	16
Stuart Country Day School of the Sacred Heart, NJ	15
Stuart Hall, VA	
Subiaco Academy, AR	10
Suffield Academy, CT	11
Summerfield Waldorf School, CA	3
The Summit Country Day School, OH	18
Summit Preparatory School, MT	1
Surabaya International School, Indonesia	7
Tabor Academy, MA	19
The Taft School, CT	19
Taipei American School, Taiwan	17
Tallulah Falls School, GA	6
TASIS The American School in England, United Kingdom	19
TASIS, The American School in Switzerland, Switzerland	15
The Tatnall School, DE	15
The Tenney School, TX	2
Teurlings Catholic High School, LA	2
The Thacher School, CA	17
Thayer Academy, MA	13
Thomas Jefferson School, MO	12
Tilton School, NH	11
Timothy Christian High School, IL	7
TMI—The Episcopal School of Texas, TX	14
Tower Hill School, DE	17
Trafalgar Castle School, ON, Canada	2
Trevor Day School, NY	6
Tri-City Christian Schools, CA	4
Trinity Catholic High School, CT	8
Trinity Catholic High School, MA	3
Trinity Christian Academy, TX	14
Trinity Christian School, GA	2
Trinity College School, ON, Canada	9
Trinity Episcopal School, VA	14
Trinity High School, KY	
Trinity High School, NH	4
Trinity-Pawling School, NY	17
Trinity Preparatory School, FL	16
Trinity School, NY	11
Trinity Valley School, TX	15
Tyler Street Christian Academy, TX	1
University Lake School, WI	9
University Liggett School, MI	14
University of Chicago Laboratory Schools, IL	15
University of Detroit Jesuit High School and Academy, MI	7
University of Miami Online High School, FL	
University of Missouri—Columbia High School, MO	1
University of Toronto Schools, ON, Canada	1
University Prep, WA	7
University School, OH	13
University School of Milwaukee, WI	19
University School of Nashville, TN	19
University School of Nova Southeastern University, FL	20
The Urban School of San Francisco, CA	8
Ursuline Academy, DE	11
Ursuline High School, CA	4
Vail Mountain School, CO	6
Valley Christian School, CA	14
Valley Forge Military Academy and College, PA	6
Vanguard College Preparatory School, TX	6
Vermont Academy, VT	11
Vianney High School, MO	8
Vicksburg Catholic School, MS	1
Viewpoint School, CA	20
Village Christian Schools, CA	9
Villa Maria Academy, PA	5
Villa Maria Academy, PA	14
Villa Victoria Academy, NJ	6
Villa Walsh Academy, NJ	11
Virginia Beach Friends School, VA	5
Virginia Episcopal School, VA	16
Visitation Academy of St. Louis County, MO	11
Wakefield School, VA	19
The Waldorf School of Garden City, NY	4
Walnut Hill School, MA	6
The Wardlaw-Hartridge School, NJ	19
Waring School, MA	5
Wasatch Academy, UT	8
Washington Academy, ME	9
Washington Waldorf School, MD	1
The Waterford School, UT	14
The Waverly School, CA	10
Wayland Academy, WI	12
Wayne Country Day School, NC	5
Webber Academy, AB, Canada	5
The Webb School, TN	6
Webb School of Knoxville, TN	20
The Wellington School, OH	13

Wesleyan School, GA	16
Westbury Christian School, TX	13
West Catholic High School, MI	6
Westchester Academy, NC	14
Western Mennonite School, OR	1
Western Reserve Academy, OH	19
The Westfield Schools, GA	5
Westgate Mennonite Collegiate, MB, Canada	5
Westhill Institute, Mexico	6
West Island College, AB, Canada	9
Westminster Christian Academy, AL	5
Westminster Christian Academy, LA	4
Westminster Christian School, FL	13
Westminster School, CT	19
The Westminster Schools, GA	17
Westminster Schools of Augusta, GA	11
West Nottingham Academy, MD	9
Westover School, CT	17
Westridge School, CA	14
Westtown School, PA	10
Wheaton Academy, IL	5
The Wheeler School, RI	11
Whitefield Academy, GA	8
Whitfield School, MO	7
Whittier Christian High School, CA	5
Wichita Collegiate School, KS	17
Wilbraham & Monson Academy, MA	18
Wildwood Catholic High School, NJ	5
William Penn Charter School, PA	14
The Williams School, CT	7
The Williston Northampton School, MA	12
The Willows Academy, IL	7
Wilmington Christian School, DE	3
Wilmington Friends School, DE	4
Wilson Hall, SC	14
The Winchendon School, MA	5
Winchester Thurston School, PA	17
The Windsor School, NY	5
Windward School, CA	10
The Winsor School, MA	8
Woodberry Forest School, VA	19
Woodlands Academy of the Sacred Heart, IL	6
The Woodlynde School, PA	2
Woodside International School, CA	4
Woodside Priory School, CA	18
Woodstock School, India	18
The Woodward School, MA	4
Wooster School, CT	12
Worcester Academy, MA	14
Worcester Preparatory School, MD	9
Wyoming Seminary, PA	19
Xavier College Preparatory, AZ	18
Yeshiva Atlanta, GA	6
York Country Day School, PA	8
York Preparatory School, NY	3
Zurich International School, Switzerland	17

SCHOOLS REPORTING A POSTGRADUATE YEAR

Academia Cotopaxi, Ecuador
The Academy at Charlemont, MA
The Albany Academy, NY
Albert College, ON, Canada

American International School Salzburg, Austria
Avon Old Farms School, CT
The Beekman School, NY
Berkshire School, MA
Berwick Academy, ME
Blair Academy, NJ
The Bolles School, FL
Brandon Hall School, GA
Brehm Preparatory School, IL
Brenau Academy, GA
Brewster Academy, NH
Bridgton Academy, ME
Burke Mountain Academy, VT
The Cambridge School of Weston, MA
Camden Military Academy, SC
Canterbury School, CT
Carrabassett Valley Academy, ME
Cascadilla School, NY
The Cedars Academy, DE
Chapel Hill–Chauncy Hall School, MA
Cheshire Academy, CT
Choate Rosemary Hall, CT
Christchurch School, VA
Colorado Timberline Academy, CO
The Culver Academies, IN
Cushing Academy, MA
Darlington School, GA
Darrow School, NY
Deerfield Academy, MA
Emma Willard School, NY
Fork Union Military Academy, VA
Fryeburg Academy, ME
Gould Academy, ME
The Gow School, NY
The Grand River Academy, OH
The Grier School, PA
The Gunnery, CT
Hamilton Learning Centre, ON, Canada
Hargrave Military Academy, VA
Hebron Academy, ME
Hidden Lake Academy, GA
The Hill School, PA
Holderness School, NH
Hoosac School, NY
Horizons School, GA
The Hotchkiss School, CT
Houghton Academy, NY
The Hun School of Princeton, NJ
Idyllwild Arts Academy, CA
Indian Springs School, AL
Interlochen Arts Academy, MI
International Junior Golf Academy, SC
The John Dewey Academy, MA
Kent School, CT
Kents Hill School, ME
Kildonan School, NY
Kimball Union Academy, NH
The Kiski School, PA
Lakewood Prep, NJ
The Lawrenceville School, NJ
Leysin American School in Switzerland, Switzerland

Linden Hall School for Girls, PA
The Loomis Chaffee School, CT
Maine Central Institute, ME
Manlius Pebble Hill School, NY
Marianapolis Preparatory School, CT
Massanutten Military Academy, VA
Mercersburg Academy, PA
Missouri Military Academy, MO
Montverde Academy, FL
National Sports Academy at Lake Placid, NY
New Hampton School, NH
The Newman School, MA
Northfield Mount Hermon School, MA
Northwood School, NY
Oldfields School, MD
The Orme School, AZ
The Oxford Academy, CT
Peddie School, NJ
Perkiomen School, PA
The Phelps School, PA
Phillips Academy (Andover), MA
Phillips Exeter Academy, NH
Pomfret School, CT
Randolph-Macon Academy, VA
Ridley College, ON, Canada
Riverview School, MA
Robert Louis Stevenson School, NY
St. Gregory College Preparatory School, AZ
St. Johnsbury Academy, VT
Saint John's Preparatory School, MN
St. Stephen's School, Rome, Italy
Saint Thomas More School, CT
St. Timothy's School, MD
Salisbury School, CT
Scattergood Friends School, IA
Solebury School, PA
Soundview Preparatory School, NY
South Kent School, CT
Southwestern Academy, AZ
Southwestern Academy, CA
Stoneleigh–Burnham School, MA
Stratton Mountain School, VT
Suffield Academy, CT
The Taft School, CT
TASIS, The American School in Switzerland, Switzerland
Thomas Jefferson School, MO
Tilton School, NH
Trident Academy, SC
Trinity-Pawling School, NY
Valley Forge Military Academy and College, PA
The Vanguard School, FL
Vermont Academy, VT
Watkinson School, CT
Western Reserve Academy, OH
Westminster School, CT
West Nottingham Academy, MD
The White Mountain School, NH
Wilbraham & Monson Academy, MA
The Williston Northampton School, MA
The Winchendon School, MA
The Windsor School, NY

The Woodhall School, CT
Worcester Academy, MA
Wyoming Seminary, PA

SCHOOLS OFFERING THE INTERNATIONAL BACCALAUREATE PROGRAM

Academia Cotopaxi, Ecuador
Academie Sainte Cecile International School, ON, Canada
ACS Cobham International School, United Kingdom
ACS Egham International School, United Kingdom
ACS Hillingdon International School, United Kingdom
Ahliyyah School for Girls, Jordan
American Community Schools of Athens, Greece
The American International School, Austria
American International School in Cyprus, Cyprus
American International School of Bucharest, Romania
American International School-Riyadh, Saudi Arabia
American Overseas School of Rome, Italy
The American School Foundation, Mexico
The American School of Madrid, Spain
American School of Milan, Italy
American School of Paris, France
The American School of The Hague, Netherlands
American School of Warsaw, Poland
Anglo-American School of Moscow, Russian Federation
Ashbury College, ON, Canada
Atlanta International School, GA
The Awty International School, TX
Beijing BISS International School, China
The Bermuda High School for Girls, Bermuda
Brent School-Baguio, Philippines
The British International School, Jeddah, Saudi Arabia
Campion School, Athens, Greece
Canadian Academy, Japan
Cardinal Newman High School, FL
Carlisle School, VA
Carlucci American International School of Lisbon, Portugal
Chamberlain-Hunt Academy, MS
Chapel School, Brazil
Charlotte Country Day School, NC
Christ Church Episcopal School, SC
Colegio Franklin D. Roosevelt, Peru
College du Leman International School, Switzerland
Danube International School, Vienna, Austria
Detroit Country Day School, MI
Dubai American Academy, United Arab Emirates
The Dwight School, NY
Eastern Mennonite High School, VA
George School, PA
Gulliver Preparatory School, FL
Halifax Grammar School, NS, Canada
Harare International School, Zimbabwe
Hvitfeldtska Gymnasiet, International Section, Sweden
International College Spain, Spain
International Community School of Addis Ababa, Ethiopia
International High School of FAIS, CA
International School Bangkok, Thailand
International School Basel, Switzerland
International School Hamburg, Germany
International School of Amsterdam, Netherlands

International School of Athens, Greece
International School of Berne, Switzerland
International School of Brussels, Belgium
The International School of Geneva, Switzerland
The International School of Kuala Lumpur, Malaysia
International School of Lausanne, Switzerland
International School of Luxembourg, Luxembourg
The International School of Monaco, Monaco
Istanbul International Community School, Turkey
Jakarta International School, Indonesia
Leysin American School in Switzerland, Switzerland
Luther College High School, SK, Canada
Lycee Français de New York, NY
Lycee International de Los Angeles, CA
Marymount International School, Italy
Marymount International School, United Kingdom
Mercedes College, Australia
Mercyhurst Preparatory School, PA
Mid-Pacific Institute, HI
Mont'Kiara International School, Malaysia
Munich International School, Germany
Newark Academy, NJ
Overseas Family School, Singapore
Riverstone Community School, ID
Rotterdam International Secondary School, Wolfert van
  Borselen, Netherlands
St. Andrew's College, Dublin, Ireland
St. Dominic's International School, Portugal, Portugal
Saint John's School, GU
St. Leonards, United Kingdom
St. Mary's International School, Japan
St. Maur International School, Japan
Saint Paul Lutheran High School, MO
St. Paul's School, MD
St. Stephen's School, Rome, Italy
Schule Schloss Salem, Germany
Seisen International School, Japan
Seoul Foreign School, Republic of Korea
Strathcona-Tweedsmuir School, AB, Canada
Taipei American School, Taiwan
TASIS The American School in England, United Kingdom
TASIS, The American School in Switzerland, Switzerland
Trinity Episcopal School, VA
Trinity High School, IL
United Nations International School, NY
The United World College—USA, NM
Upper Canada College, ON, Canada
Washington International School, DC
Wilmington Friends School, DE
Windhoek International School, Namibia
Woodside Park International School, United Kingdom
Yokohama International School, Japan
The York School, ON, Canada
Zurich International School, Switzerland

SCHOOLS REPORTING THAT THEY AWARD MERIT SCHOLARSHIPS

Academie Sainte Cecile International School, ON, Canada
The Academy for Global Exploration, OR
Academy of Mount Saint Ursula, NY

Academy of Notre Dame de Namur, PA
Academy of Our Lady of Mercy, CT
Academy of Saint Aloysius, NJ
Academy of Saint Elizabeth, NJ
The Academy of St. Joseph, NY
Academy of the Holy Angels, NJ
Academy of the Holy Cross, MD
Academy of the Holy Names, FL
Academy of the Sacred Heart, LA
Academy of the Sacred Heart, MI
Adelphi Academy, NY
Advanced Academy of Georgia, GA
Albert College, ON, Canada
Allison Academy, FL
All Saints' Episcopal School of Fort Worth, TX
The Altamont School, AL
Ambassador Preparatory, MN
American Heritage School, FL
The American School Foundation, Mexico
The Andrews School, OH
Annie Wright School, WA
Appleby College, ON, Canada
Archbishop Blenk Girls High School, LA
Archbishop Curley High School, MD
Archbishop Quigley Preparatory High School, IL
Archbishop Riordan High School, CA
Archmere Academy, DE
Army and Navy Academy, CA
Ashbury College, ON, Canada
Ashley Hall, SC
Assumption High School, KY
Athens Academy, GA
Aurora Central High School, IL
Avon Old Farms School, CT
Balmoral Hall School, MB, Canada
Barnstable Academy, NJ
The Barstow School, MO
Battle Ground Academy, TN
Baylor School, TN
Bayside Academy, AL
Beaumont School, OH
Benedictine High School, OH
Benilde–St. Margaret's School, MN
The Benjamin School, FL
Bentley School, CA
Berkeley Preparatory School, FL
Berkshire School, MA
The Bermuda High School for Girls, Bermuda
The Birch Wathen Lenox School, NY
Bishop Brady High School, NH
Bishop Eustace Preparatory School, NJ
Bishop Feehan High School, MA
Bishop Fenwick High School, OH
Bishop George Ahr High School, NJ
Bishop Guertin High School, NH
Bishop Hoban High School, PA
Bishop Ireton High School, VA
Bishop Luers High School, IN
Bishop Lynch Catholic High School, TX
Bishop McDevitt High School, PA
Bishop McNamara High School, IL

Bishop's College School, QC, Canada
The Bishop Strachan School, ON, Canada
Bishop Verot High School, FL
Bismark St. Mary's Central, ND
Boston University Academy, MA
Brent School-Baguio, Philippines
Broadview Academy, IL
Brookstone School, GA
Brother Rice High School, MI
Calvert Hall College High School, MD
Camelot Academy, NC
Campion School, Athens, Greece
Cannon School, NC
Canterbury High School, IN
Canterbury School, FL
Canyonville Christian Academy, OR
Cape Fear Academy, NC
Caribbean Preparatory School, PR
Carlucci American International School of Lisbon, Portugal
Carrollton School of the Sacred Heart, FL
Cary Academy, NC
Casady School, OK
Cascadilla School, NY
Cathedral High School, IN
Cathedral Preparatory School, PA
The Catholic High School of Baltimore, MD
CCI The Renaissance School, Italy
Centennial Academy, QC, Canada
Central Catholic High School, CA
Chaminade College Preparatory, CA
Charlotte Latin School, NC
Chase Collegiate School, CT
Chestnut Hill Academy, PA
Cheverus High School, ME
Chinese Christian Schools, CA
Christ Church Episcopal School, SC
Christian Brothers Academy, NJ
Christian Brothers Academy, NY
Christian Brothers Academy, NY
Christ School, NC
Cincinnati Country Day School, OH
Colegio Puertorriqueno de Ninas, PR
The Colorado Rocky Mountain School, CO
The Colorado Springs School, CO
Colorado Timberline Academy, CO
Columbia International School, Japan
Concordia Academy, MN
Connelly School of the Holy Child, MD
Conserve School, WI
Convent of the Sacred Heart, CT
Cornelia Connelly School, CA
Country Day School of the Sacred Heart, PA
Cranbrook Schools, MI
Crescent School, ON, Canada
Crespi Carmelite High School, CA
Crofton House School, BC, Canada
Crossroads School for Arts & Sciences, CA
The Culver Academies, IN
Cushing Academy, MA
Danube International School, Vienna, Austria
Darlington School, GA

DeLaSalle High School, MN
The Delphian School, OR
DeMatha Catholic High School, MD
Denver Christian High School, CO
Devon Preparatory School, PA
Don Bosco High School, CA
Dowling High School, IA
Duchesne Academy of the Sacred Heart, NE
Duchesne Academy of the Sacred Heart, TX
East Catholic High School, CT
Elizabeth Seton High School, MD
Elyria Catholic High School, OH
Emma Willard School, NY
Episcopal High School, VA
Episcopal High School of Jacksonville, FL
The Episcopal School of Acadiana, LA
Falmouth Academy, MA
First Presbyterian Day School, GA
Fishburne Military School, VA
Florida Air Academy, FL
Fontbonne Academy, MA
Fordham Preparatory School, NY
Fork Union Military Academy, VA
Fort Worth Country Day School, TX
Fountain Valley School of Colorado, CO
Foxcroft School, VA
Francis Parker School, CA
Frederica Academy, GA
Freeman Academy, SD
Fuqua School, VA
Garces Memorial High School, CA
Garden School, NY
Gaston Day School, NC
Gateway School, TX
George School, PA
Georgetown Visitation Preparatory School, DC
Germantown Academy, PA
Gill St. Bernard's School, NJ
Gilmour Academy, OH
Girls Preparatory School, TN
Glenelg Country School, MD
Gonzaga Preparatory School, WA
Gould Academy, ME
The Grand River Academy, OH
The Grauer School, CA
Great Lakes Christian College, ON, Canada
Greenfield School, NC
Green Fields Country Day School, AZ
Greensboro Day School, NC
Grenville Christian College, ON, Canada
The Grier School, PA
Guerin College Preparatory High School, IL
The Gunnery, CT
Gunston Day School, MD
Hales Franciscan High School, IL
Halifax Grammar School, NS, Canada
Happy Valley School, CA
Hargrave Military Academy, VA
The Harpeth Hall School, TN
Harrow School, United Kingdom
The Harvey School, NY

Specialized Directories

Havergal College, ON, Canada
Hayden High School, KS
Hebron Academy, ME
Highland School, VA
Hillfield Strathallan College, ON, Canada
Holland Hall, OK
Hudson College, ON, Canada
The Hun School of Princeton, NJ
Immaculata Academy, NY
Immaculate Conception High School, NJ
Immaculate Conception School, IL
Incarnate Word Academy, TX
Interlochen Arts Academy, MI
International College Spain, Spain
International Community School of Addis Ababa, Ethiopia
International School of Aruba, Aruba
International School of Luxembourg, Luxembourg
International School of Port-of-Spain, Trinidad and Tobago
International School of South Africa, South Africa
Iona Preparatory School, NY
Jesuit College Preparatory School, TX
John F. Kennedy Memorial High School, WA
Josephinum High School, IL
Justin-Siena High School, CA
Keith Country Day School, IL
King & Low-Heywood Thomas School, CT
Kingshill School, VI
The Kinkaid School, TX
The Kiski School, PA
The Knox School, NY
Ladywood High School, MI
La Grange Academy, GA
Laguna Blanca School, CA
Lakefield College School, ON, Canada
Lake Forest Academy, IL
Lake Ridge Academy, OH
Lakewood Prep, NJ
La Lumiere School, IN
Lansdale Catholic High School, PA
La Salle Academy, RI
La Salle College High School, PA
La Salle High School, CA
Laurel School, OH
Lausanne Collegiate School, TN
Lawrence Woodmere Academy, NY
Lexington Christian Academy, MA
Leysin American School in Switzerland, Switzerland
Long Island Lutheran Middle and High School, NY
Loretto High School, CA
Los Angeles Baptist Junior/Senior High School, CA
Los Angeles Lutheran High School, CA
Louisville High School, CA
Lourdes Catholic High School, AZ
The Lowell Whiteman School, CO
Lower Canada College, QC, Canada
Loyola-Blakefield, MD
Loyola High School, Jesuit College Preparatory, CA
Loyola School, NY
Lutheran High School, CA
Lutheran High School, MN
Lutheran High School North, MO

Lutheran High School of Hawaii, HI
Lutheran High School South, MO
Luther College High School, SK, Canada
The MacDuffie School, MA
Maine Central Institute, ME
Malaspina International High School, BC, Canada
Malden Catholic High School, MA
Manlius Pebble Hill School, NY
Maplebrook School, NY
Marianapolis Preparatory School, CT
Marist High School, IL
Marist High School, NJ
Marlborough School, CA
Marmion Academy, IL
The Marvelwood School, CT
Mary Help of Christians Academy, NJ
Maryknoll School, HI
Marylawn of the Oranges, NJ
The Mary Louis Academy, NY
Marymount High School, CA
Marymount International School, United Kingdom
Matignon High School, MA
Maumee Valley Country Day School, OH
Maur Hill-Mount Academy, KS
Mayfield Senior School, CA
Mazapan School, Honduras
The McCallie School, TN
McNicholas High School, OH
McQuaid Jesuit High School, NY
Meadowridge Senior School, BC, Canada
The Meadows School, NV
Mentor College, ON, Canada
Mercersburg Academy, PA
Mercy High School, CT
Mercy High School, NE
Mercyhurst Preparatory School, PA
Mid-Pacific Institute, HI
Miss Edgar's and Miss Cramp's School, QC, Canada
Miss Hall's School, MA
Miss Porter's School, CT
MMI Preparatory School, PA
Montrose School, MA
Moreau Catholic High School, CA
Morgan Park Academy, IL
Morristown-Beard School, NJ
Mother McAuley High School, IL
Mount Carmel High School, IL
Mount Michael Benedictine High School, NE
Mt. Saint Dominic Academy, NJ
Mount Saint Joseph Academy, PA
Mount Saint Mary Academy, NJ
Munich International School, Germany
Nacel International School, MN
Nazareth Academy, IL
Nebraska Christian Schools, NE
Nerinx Hall, MO
Neuchatel Junior College, Switzerland
The Newgrange School, NJ
The Newman School, MA
New Mexico Military Institute, NM
Niagara Christian Collegiate, ON, Canada

Norfolk Collegiate School, VA
The North Broward Preparatory Upper School, FL
The North Shore Country Day School, IL
Notre Dame High School, MO
Notre Dame Regional Secondary, BC, Canada
Oak Knoll School of the Holy Child, NJ
The Oakland School, PA
Oak Ridge Military Academy, NC
Oldenburg Academy, IN
The O'Neal School, NC
Our Saviour Lutheran School, NY
Padua Franciscan High School, OH
Palma High School, CA
Palmer Trinity School, FL
Paraclete High School, CA
The Parker School, HI
The Park School of Buffalo, NY
Park Tudor School, IN
Peddie School, NJ
The Pembroke Hill School, MO
The Pennington School, NJ
Pickering College, ON, Canada
Pine Forge Academy, PA
The Pingree School, MA
Portland Lutheran School, OR
Portsmouth Abbey School, RI
Portsmouth Christian Academy, NH
The Prairie School, WI
Preston High School, NY
Providence High School, CA
Providence High School, TX
Punahou School, HI
Purcell Marian High School, OH
Queen Margaret's School, BC, Canada
Queensway Christian College, ON, Canada
Quigley Catholic High School, PA
Quincy Notre Dame High School, IL
Rabun Gap-Nacoochee School, GA
Ramona Convent Secondary School, CA
Randolph-Macon Academy, VA
Randolph School, AL
Ravenscroft School, NC
Regina High School, OH
Regis High School, OR
Ridley College, ON, Canada
Rio Lindo Adventist Academy, CA
Rivermont Collegiate, IA
Robert Land Academy, ON, Canada
Rocky Mount Academy, NC
Rolling Hills Preparatory School, CA
Rosary High School, IL
Rothesay Netherwood School, NB, Canada
Routt High School, IL
Rowland Hall-St. Mark's School, UT
Royal Canadian College, BC, Canada
Roycemore School, IL
Sacred Heart Academy, CT
Sacred Heart High School, CA
Sacred Heart Preparatory, CA
Sacred Heart School of Halifax, NS, Canada
Saddleback Valley Christian School, CA

Saddle River Day School, NJ
St. Agnes Academy, TX
St. Agnes High School, MN
St. Andrew's College, ON, Canada
St. Andrew's College, Dublin, Ireland
St. Andrew's Episcopal School, MS
St. Andrew's Priory School, HI
St. Andrew's–Sewanee School, TN
Saint Augustine Preparatory School, NJ
Saint Basil Academy, PA
St. Benedict at Auburndale, TN
St. Bernard High School, CA
Saint Cecilia High School, NE
St. Christopher's School, VA
St. Clement's School, ON, Canada
St. Croix Country Day School, VI
Saint Dominic Academy, NJ
St. Dominic's International School, Portugal, Portugal
Saint Elizabeth High School, CA
Saint Francis De Sales High School, IL
St. Francis de Sales High School, OH
Saint Francis School, HI
Saint George's School, WA
St. George's School, BC, Canada
St. George's School in Switzerland, Switzerland
Saint Gertrude High School, VA
Saint James School, AL
Saint James School, MD
St. John's College High School, DC
St. John's Literary Institution at Prospect Hall, MD
St. John's Military School, KS
St. John's Northwestern Military Academy, WI
St. John's Preparatory School, MA
Saint John's Preparatory School, MN
St. John's-Ravenscourt School, MB, Canada
Saint John's School, GU
Saint John's School of Alberta, AB, Canada
Saint Joseph Central Catholic High School, OH
St. Joseph High School, CT
Saint Joseph High School, WI
St. Joseph's Catholic School, SC
Saint Joseph's High School, NJ
St. Joseph's Preparatory School, PA
Saint Laurence High School, IL
St. Leonards, United Kingdom
Saint Lucy's Priory High School, CA
St. Luke's School, CT
St. Margaret's School, BC, Canada
St. Mark's High School, DE
St. Mary's Academy, CO
St. Mary's Bundschu Memorial High School, MO
St. Mary's Dominican High School, LA
Saint Mary's Hall, TX
St. Mary's Preparatory School, MI
St. Mary's Ryken High School, MD
Saint Mary's School, NC
St. Michaels University School, BC, Canada
St. Paul's High School, MB, Canada
St. Paul's Preparatory Academy, AZ
St. Paul's School, NH
St. Paul's School for Girls, MD

St. Peter's Preparatory School, NJ
St. Pius X High School, TX
Saint Raymond High School for Boys, NY
Saint Teresa's Academy, MO
Saint Thomas Academy, MN
St. Thomas High School, TX
Saint Thomas More School, CT
St. Timothy's School, MD
Saint Vincent Ferrer High School, NY
St. Vincent Pallotti High School, MD
Saint Xavier High School, KY
Saint Xavier High School, OH
Salem Academy, NC
Salesian High School, NY
Salesianum School, DE
Saltus Grammar School, Bermuda
Santa Catalina School, CA
Savannah Christian Preparatory School, GA
The Savannah Country Day School, GA
Sayre School, KY
Scattergood Friends School, IA
School of the Holy Child, NY
Schule Schloss Salem, Germany
Second Baptist School, TX
Sedbergh School, QC, Canada
Selwyn House School, QC, Canada
Seton Catholic Central High School, NY
Seton Hall Preparatory School, NJ
Shattuck-St. Mary's School, MN
Solebury School, PA
South Kent School, CT
Spartanburg Day School, SC
Springside School, PA
Stanstead College, QC, Canada
Staten Island Academy, NY
Stella Maris High School and the Maura Clarke Junior High Program, NY
Stoneleigh–Burnham School, MA
Storm King School, NY
Stratford Academy, GA
Stuart Country Day School of the Sacred Heart, NJ
Stuart Hall, VA
The Study School, QC, Canada
Subiaco Academy, AR
Suffield Academy, CT
The Summit Country Day School, OH
TASIS The American School in England, United Kingdom
Thomas Jefferson School, MO
Tilton School, NH
TMI—The Episcopal School of Texas, TX
Trafalgar Castle School, ON, Canada
Trident Academy, SC
Trinity Catholic High School, CT
Trinity Catholic High School, MA
Trinity Episcopal School, VA
Trinity High School, IL
Trinity High School, KY
Tyler Street Christian Academy, TX
The United World College—USA, NM
University Lake School, WI
University Liggett School, MI

University of Detroit Jesuit High School and Academy, MI
Ursuline Academy, DE
Ursuline High School, CA
Valley Forge Military Academy and College, PA
Venta Preparatory School, ON, Canada
Vianney High School, MO
Village Christian Schools, CA
Villa Maria Academy, PA
Villa Maria Academy, PA
Villa Victoria Academy, NJ
Villa Walsh Academy, NJ
Virginia Beach Friends School, VA
Virginia Episcopal School, VA
The Waldorf School of Garden City, NY
Walnut Hill School, MA
The Wardlaw-Hartridge School, NJ
Waring School, MA
Wasatch Academy, UT
Washington Academy, ME
Wayland Academy, WI
Webber Academy, AB, Canada
The Webb School, TN
The Wellington School, OH
Wentworth Military Academy and Junior College, MO
Westbury Christian School, TX
Westchester Academy, NC
Western Mennonite School, OR
Western Reserve Academy, OH
Westgate Mennonite Collegiate, MB, Canada
Westhill Institute, Mexico
Westminster School, CT
Wheaton Academy, IL
The White Mountain School, NH
Whittier Christian High School, CA
Wilbraham & Monson Academy, MA
Windermere St. Anne's School, United Kingdom
Woodlands Academy of the Sacred Heart, IL
The Woodward School, MA
Worcester Academy, MA
Wyoming Seminary, PA
York Preparatory School, NY
The York School, ON, Canada

SCHOOLS REPORTING A GUARANTEED TUITION PLAN

The Academy at Sisters, OR
Academy at Swift River, MA
The Academy for Global Exploration, OR
Allison Academy, FL
Armona Union Academy, CA
Auldern Academy, NC
Baldwin School of Puerto Rico, Inc., PR
Bangor Christian School, ME
Bishop Kelly High School, ID
Bishop Quinn High School/St. Francis Middle School, CA
Broadview Academy, IL
Cambridge International College of Canada, ON, Canada
Central Catholic High School, CA
CFS, The School at Church Farm, PA
Chedar Chabad, ON, Canada

Christchurch School, VA
Colorado Timberline Academy, CO
Community Christian Academy, KY
Cross Creek Programs, UT
Don Bosco High School, CA
Eckerd Youth Alternatives, FL
Ecole d'Humanite, Switzerland
Emma Willard School, NY
Equilibrium International Education Institute, AB, Canada
Explorations Academy, WA
Foothills Academy, AB, Canada
Fowlers Academy, PR
Gateway School, TX
George Stevens Academy, ME
Hackett Catholic Central High School, MI
Hargrave Military Academy, VA
Hawaii Baptist Academy, HI
Hawai'i Preparatory Academy, HI
The Hewitt School, NY
Hidden Lake Academy, GA
The Hill Center, Durham Academy, NC
Hope Christian School, AB, Canada
Imperial College of Toronto, ON, Canada
Kent School, CT
The King's Christian High School, NJ
La Pietra–Hawaii School for Girls, HI
Lehman High School, OH
The Loomis Chaffee School, CT
Lourdes Catholic High School, AZ
Marion Academy, AL
Mercy High School College Preparatory, CA
Montana Academy, MT
Montcalm School, MI
Nawa Academy, CA
New Dominion School, MD
New Dominion School, VA
New Horizon Youth Ministries, IN
Notre Dame High School, WV
Oxford School, CA
Pickens Academy, AL
Piedmont Academy, GA
Pius X High School, NE
Rancho Valmora, NM
Ribet Academy, CA
The Rockland Country Day School, NY
Saint Paul Lutheran High School, MO
Schule Schloss Salem, Germany
Selwyn House School, QC, Canada
SICES International Academy, AB, Canada
Sorenson's Ranch School, UT
Southampton Academy, VA
Spring Ridge Academy, AZ
Stone Mountain School, NC
Sumiton Christian School, AL
The Taft School, CT
Three Springs, AL
Tower Hill School, DE
Trinity High School, KY
Trinity-Pawling School, NY
The United World College—USA, NM
Universal Academy of Florida, FL

The Waterford School, UT
Wentworth Military Academy and Junior College, MO
Westminster Christian Academy, AL
Westminster Christian Academy, LA

SCHOOLS REPORTING A TUITION INSTALLMENT PLAN

Academia Cotopaxi, Ecuador
Academie Sainte Cecile International School, ON, Canada
The Academy at Charlemont, MA
The Academy at Sisters, OR
Academy at Swift River, MA
The Academy for Gifted Children (PACE), ON, Canada
The Academy for Global Exploration, OR
Academy of Holy Angels, MN
Academy of Mount Saint Ursula, NY
Academy of Notre Dame de Namur, PA
Academy of Our Lady of Mercy, CT
Academy of Our Lady of Peace, CA
Academy of Saint Aloysius, NJ
Academy of Saint Elizabeth, NJ
The Academy of St. Joseph, NY
Academy of the Holy Angels, NJ
Academy of the Holy Cross, MD
Academy of the Holy Names, FL
Academy of the Pacific, HI
Academy of the Sacred Heart, LA
Academy of the Sacred Heart, MI
ACS Cobham International School, United Kingdom
ACS Egham International School, United Kingdom
ACS Hillingdon International School, United Kingdom
Adelphi Academy, NY
Admiral Farragut Academy, FL
The Agnes Irwin School, PA
Ahliyyah School for Girls, Jordan
Airdrie Koinonia Christian School, AB, Canada
Akiba Hebrew Academy, PA
The Albany Academy, NY
Albert College, ON, Canada
Albuquerque Academy, NM
Alexander Dawson School, CO
Allen Academy, TX
Allendale Columbia School, NY
Alliance Academy, Ecuador
Allison Academy, FL
All Saints' Episcopal School, MS
All Saints' Episcopal School of Fort Worth, TX
Alpine Academy, UT
The Altamont School, AL
Al-Worood School, United Arab Emirates
Ambassador Preparatory, MN
American Academy, FL
American Community Schools of Athens, Greece
American Cooperative School, Bolivia
American Heritage School, FL
The American International School, Austria
American International School of Bucharest, Romania
American International School-Riyadh, Saudi Arabia
American Overseas School of Rome, Italy
The American School in Japan, Japan

The American School in London, United Kingdom
The American School of Madrid, Spain
American School of Milan, Italy
American School of Paris, France
The American School of Puerto Vallarta, Mexico
The American School of The Hague, Netherlands
American School of Warsaw, Poland
Anacapa School, CA
The Andrews School, OH
Annie Wright School, WA
Appleby College, ON, Canada
Aquin Central Catholic High School, IL
Archbishop Blenk Girls High School, LA
Archbishop Curley High School, MD
Archbishop Mitty High School, CA
Archbishop Quigley Preparatory High School, IL
Archbishop Riordan High School, CA
The Archer School for Girls, CA
Archmere Academy, DE
Armona Union Academy, CA
Arrowhead Christian Academy, CA
Arrowsmith School, ON, Canada
Ashbury College, ON, Canada
Asheville School, NC
Ashley Hall, SC
Aspen Ranch, UT
Assumption High School, KY
The Athenian School, CA
Athens Academy, GA
Atlanta International School, GA
Auldern Academy, NC
Aurora Central High School, IL
Avon Old Farms School, CT
The Awty International School, TX
The Baldwin School, PA
Baldwin School of Puerto Rico, Inc., PR
Balmoral Hall School, MB, Canada
The Baltimore Actors' Theatre Conservatory, MD
Baltimore Lutheran Middle and Upper School, MD
Bancroft School, MA
Bangor Christian School, ME
Baptist High School, NJ
Barnstable Academy, NJ
The Barstow School, MO
Battle Ground Academy, TN
Baylor School, TN
Bayside Academy, AL
Bearspaw Christian School, AB, Canada
Beaufort Academy, SC
Beaver Country Day School, MA
The Beekman School, NY
Bellarmine College Preparatory, CA
Bellarmine Preparatory School, WA
Bellevue Christian School, WA
Belmont Hill School, MA
The Bement School, MA
Benedictine High School, OH
Benet Academy, IL
Ben Franklin Academy, GA
Benilde–St. Margaret's School, MN
The Benjamin School, FL

Bentley School, CA
Berkeley Carroll School, NY
Berkeley Preparatory School, FL
Berkshire School, MA
The Bermuda High School for Girls, Bermuda
Berwick Academy, ME
The Birch Wathen Lenox School, NY
Bishop Brady High School, NH
Bishop Carroll High School, PA
Bishop Conaty-Our Lady of Loretto High School, CA
Bishop Eustace Preparatory School, NJ
Bishop Feehan High School, MA
Bishop Fenwick High School, OH
Bishop George Ahr High School, NJ
Bishop Guertin High School, NH
Bishop Hoban High School, PA
Bishop Ireton High School, VA
Bishop Kelly High School, ID
Bishop Kenny High School, FL
Bishop Luers High School, IN
Bishop Lynch Catholic High School, TX
Bishop McDevitt High School, PA
Bishop McGuinness Catholic High School, OK
Bishop McNamara High School, IL
Bishop Quinn High School/St. Francis Middle School, CA
Bishop's College School, QC, Canada
The Bishop Strachan School, ON, Canada
Bishop Verot High School, FL
Bishop Walsh Middle High School, MD
Bismark St. Mary's Central, ND
Black Forest Academy, Germany
Blair Academy, NJ
The Blake School, MN
The Blue Ridge School, VA
The Bolles School, FL
Boston University Academy, MA
Boyd-Buchanan School, TN
The Boys' Latin School of Maryland, MD
Bradenton Christian School, FL
Brandon Hall School, GA
The Brearley School, NY
Breck School, MN
Brenau Academy, GA
Brent School-Baguio, Philippines
Brentwood Academy, TN
Brentwood School, CA
Brewster Academy, NH
Bridges Academy, CA
Bridge School, CO
Bridgton Academy, ME
British Columbia Christian Academy, BC, Canada
Broadview Academy, IL
The Brook Hill School, TX
Brooklyn Friends School, NY
Brooks School, MA
Brookstone School, GA
Brophy College Preparatory, AZ
Brother Rice High School, MI
Brownell-Talbot School, NE
The Browning School, NY
Brunswick School, CT

The Bryn Mawr School for Girls, MD
Buckingham Browne & Nichols School, MA
The Buckley School, CA
The Bullis School, MD
Bulloch Academy, GA
Burke Mountain Academy, VT
Burr and Burton Academy, VT
The Bush School, WA
Buxton School, MA
Calgary Academy, AB, Canada
The Calhoun School, NY
Calvary Christian Academy, KY
Calvert Hall College High School, MD
The Calverton School, MD
The Cambridge School of Weston, MA
Camelot Academy, NC
Campbell Hall (Episcopal), CA
Campion School, Athens, Greece
Canadian Academy, Japan
Cannon School, NC
Canterbury High School, IN
Canterbury School, CT
Canterbury School, FL
The Canterbury School of Florida, FL
Canyonville Christian Academy, OR
Cape Cod Academy, MA
Cape Fear Academy, NC
Cape Henry Collegiate School, VA
Cardigan Mountain School, NH
Cardinal Gibbons High School, FL
Cardinal Mooney Catholic College Preparatory High
    School, MI
Cardinal Newman High School, FL
Cardinal Newman School, SC
Caribbean Preparatory School, PR
Carlisle School, VA
Carlucci American International School of Lisbon, Portugal
Carolina Day School, NC
Carondelet High School, CA
Carrabassett Valley Academy, ME
Carrollton School of the Sacred Heart, FL
Cary Academy, NC
Casady School, OK
Cascadilla School, NY
Cascia Hall Preparatory School, OK
Castilleja School, CA
Cate School, CA
Cathedral High School, IN
Cathedral Preparatory School, PA
Catholic Central High School, NY
The Catholic High School of Baltimore, MD
The Catlin Gabel School, OR
CCI The Renaissance School, Italy
The Cedars Academy, DE
Centennial Academy, QC, Canada
Central Catholic High School, CA
Central Catholic High School, PA
CFS, The School at Church Farm, PA
Chadwick School, CA
Chamberlain-Hunt Academy, MS
Chaminade College Preparatory, CA

Chaminade-Madonna College Preparatory, FL
Chamisa Mesa High School, NM
Chapel Hill–Chauncy Hall School, MA
Charles E. Smith Jewish Day School, MD
Charles Finney School, NY
Charles Wright Academy, WA
Charlotte Christian School, NC
Charlotte Country Day School, NC
Charlotte Latin School, NC
Chase Collegiate School, CT
Chatham Academy, GA
Chatham Hall, VA
Chattanooga Christian School, TN
Chedar Chabad, ON, Canada
Chelsea School, MD
Cheshire Academy, CT
Chestnut Hill Academy, PA
Cheverus High School, ME
Chinese Christian Schools, CA
Choate Rosemary Hall, CT
Christa McAuliffe Academy, WA
Christ Church Episcopal School, SC
Christchurch School, VA
Christian Brothers Academy, NJ
Christian Brothers Academy, NY
Christian Brothers Academy, NY
Christian Brothers High School, CA
Christian Central Academy, NY
Christian Heritage School, CT
Christian Junior–Senior High School, CA
Christopher Dock Mennonite High School, PA
Christ School, NC
Chrysalis School, WA
Cincinnati Country Day School, OH
Cistercian Preparatory School, TX
Colegio Bolivar, Colombia
Colegio Franklin D. Roosevelt, Peru
Colegio Nueva Granada, Colombia
Colegio Puertorriqueno de Ninas, PR
Colegio San Jose, PR
College du Leman International School, Switzerland
The College Preparatory School, CA
The Collegiate School, VA
The Colorado Rocky Mountain School, CO
The Colorado Springs School, CO
Colorado Timberline Academy, CO
Columbia Academy, TN
Columbia Grammar and Preparatory School, NY
The Columbus Academy, OH
Columbus School for Girls, OH
Commonwealth School, MA
Community Christian Academy, KY
The Community School of Naples, FL
The Concept School, PA
Concord Academy, MA
Concordia Academy, MN
Connelly School of the Holy Child, MD
Conserve School, WI
Convent of the Sacred Heart, CT
Convent of the Sacred Heart, NY
Convent of the Sacred Heart High School, CA

Convent of the Visitation School, MN
Cornelia Connelly School, CA
The Cottage School, GA
Country Day School of the Sacred Heart, PA
Covenant Canadian Reformed School, AB, Canada
The Craig School, NJ
Cranbrook Schools, MI
Crawford Adventist Academy, ON, Canada
Crescent School, ON, Canada
Crespi Carmelite High School, CA
Cretin-Derham Hall, MN
Crofton House School, BC, Canada
Cross Creek Programs, UT
Crossroads School, MO
Crossroads School for Arts & Sciences, CA
Crystal Springs Uplands School, CA
The Culver Academies, IN
Currey Ingram Academy, TN
Cushing Academy, MA
Dallas Academy, TX
Dallas Christian School, TX
The Dalton School, NY
Dana Hall School, MA
Danube International School, Vienna, Austria
Darlington School, GA
Darrow School, NY
David Lipscomb High School, TN
Deerfield Academy, MA
De La Salle College, ON, Canada
De La Salle High School, CA
DeLaSalle High School, MN
Delaware County Christian School, PA
Delaware Valley Friends School, PA
Delbarton School, NJ
Delphi Academy of Los Angeles, CA
The Delphian School, OR
DeMatha Catholic High School, MD
Denver Academy, CO
Denver Christian High School, CO
The Derryfield School, NH
Devon Preparatory School, PA
Doane Stuart School, NY
Don Bosco High School, CA
Dowling High School, IA
Dublin School, NH
Duchesne Academy of the Sacred Heart, NE
Duchesne Academy of the Sacred Heart, TX
Dunn School, CA
Durham Academy, NC
Dwight-Englewood School, NJ
The Dwight School, NY
Eaglebrook School, MA
Eagle Hill School, CT
Eagle Hill School, MA
Eagle Hill-Southport, CT
East Catholic High School, CT
Eastern Christian High School, NJ
Eastern Mennonite High School, VA
Eckerd Youth Alternatives, FL
Ecole d'Humanite, Switzerland
Edison School, AB, Canada

Elan School, ME
Elgin Academy, IL
Elizabeth Seton High School, MD
The Ellis School, PA
Elyria Catholic High School, OH
Emerson Honors High Schools, CA
The Emery Weiner School, TX
Emma Willard School, NY
The English School, Kuwait, Kuwait
The Episcopal Academy, PA
Episcopal Collegiate School, AR
Episcopal High School, TX
Episcopal High School, VA
Episcopal High School of Jacksonville, FL
The Episcopal School of Acadiana, LA
The Episcopal School of Dallas, TX
Escola Americana de Campinas, Brazil
The Ethel Walker School, CT
The Ethical Culture Fieldston School, NY
Evansville Day School, IN
Explorations Academy, WA
Ezell-Harding Christian School, TN
Faith Lutheran High School, NV
The Family Foundation School, NY
Father Lopez High School, FL
Father Ryan High School, TN
Fay School, MA
The Fessenden School, MA
The Field School, DC
First Baptist Academy, TX
First Presbyterian Day School, GA
Fishburne Military School, VA
F. L. Chamberlain School, MA
Flint Hill School, VA
Florida Air Academy, FL
Fontbonne Academy, MA
Foothills Academy, AB, Canada
Fordham Preparatory School, NY
Forest Heights Lodge, CO
Fork Union Military Academy, VA
The Forman School, CT
Forsyth Country Day School, NC
Fort Worth Christian School, TX
Fort Worth Country Day School, TX
Fountain Valley School of Colorado, CO
Fowlers Academy, PR
Foxcroft School, VA
Fox River Country Day School, IL
Fox Valley Lutheran Academy, IL
Fox Valley Lutheran High School, WI
Francis Parker School, CA
Francis W. Parker School, IL
Franklin Road Academy, TN
Fraser Academy, BC, Canada
Freeman Academy, SD
French-American School of New York, NY
Fresno Christian Schools, CA
Friends Academy, NY
Friends' Central School, PA
Friends School of Baltimore, MD
Friends Seminary, NY

The Frostig School, CA
Fryeburg Academy, ME
Fuqua School, VA
Futures High School, Oceanside, CA
Futures High School—San Diego, CA
The Galloway School, GA
Garces Memorial High School, CA
Garden School, NY
Garrison Forest School, MD
Gaston Day School, NC
Gateway Christian School, BC, Canada
Gem State Adventist Academy, ID
The Geneva School, FL
George School, PA
George Stevens Academy, ME
Georgetown Day School, DC
Georgetown Preparatory School, MD
Georgetown Visitation Preparatory School, DC
George Walton Academy, GA
Germantown Academy, PA
Germantown Friends School, PA
Gilman School, MD
Gilmour Academy, OH
Girls Preparatory School, TN
Glades Day School, FL
Glenelg Country School, MD
The Glenholme School, CT
Gonzaga Preparatory School, WA
Gould Academy, ME
Governor Dummer Academy, MA
The Governor French Academy, IL
The Gow School, NY
Grace Baptist Schools, CA
Grace Christian School, AK
The Grand River Academy, OH
The Grauer School, CA
Greater Atlanta Christian Schools, GA
Great Lakes Christian College, ON, Canada
Greenfield School, NC
Green Fields Country Day School, AZ
Greenhill School, TX
Greenhills School, MI
Greensboro Day School, NC
Greens Farms Academy, CT
Greenwich Academy, CT
Greenwood Laboratory School, MO
The Greenwood School, VT
The Grier School, PA
Groton School, MA
Grove School, CT
Gstaad International School, Switzerland
Guerin College Preparatory High School, IL
Gulliver Preparatory School, FL
The Gunnery, CT
Gunston Day School, MD
Hackett Catholic Central High School, MI
Hackley School, NY
Hales Franciscan High School, IL
Halifax Grammar School, NS, Canada
Hamden Hall Country Day School, CT
Hamilton District Christian School, ON, Canada

Hamilton Learning Centre, ON, Canada
Hammond School, SC
Hampton Roads Academy, VA
Happy Valley School, CA
Harare International School, Zimbabwe
Harding Academy, TN
Hargrave Military Academy, VA
The Harley School, NY
The Harpeth Hall School, TN
Harrells Christian Academy, NC
The Harrisburg Academy, PA
Harrow School, United Kingdom
Harvard-Westlake School, CA
The Harvey School, NY
The Haverford School, PA
Havergal College, ON, Canada
Hawaiian Mission Academy, HI
Hawaii Baptist Academy, HI
Hawai'i Preparatory Academy, HI
Hawken School, OH
Hayden High School, KS
Head-Royce School, CA
Hebrew Academy-the Five Towns, NY
Hebron Academy, ME
Heritage Christian School, ON, Canada
The Heritage School, GA
The Hewitt School, NY
Hidden Lake Academy, GA
Highland Hall, A Waldorf School, CA
Highland School, VA
High Mowing School, NH
The Hill Center, Durham Academy, NC
Hillcrest Christian School, CA
Hillcrest Christian School, AB, Canada
Hillfield Strathallan College, ON, Canada
The Hill School, PA
Hillside School, MA
Hilton Head Preparatory School, SC
The Hockaday School, TX
Holderness School, NH
Holland Hall, OK
The Holton-Arms School, MD
Holy Name High School, PA
Holyoke Catholic High School, MA
Holy Trinity Diocesan High School, NY
Hoosac School, NY
Hopkins School, CT
The Horace Mann School, NY
Horizons School, GA
Hosanna Christian School, OR
The Hotchkiss School, CT
Houghton Academy, NY
Houston Learning Academy-Central Campus, TX
Howe Military School, IN
Hudson College, ON, Canada
The Hudson School, NJ
The Hun School of Princeton, NJ
Huntington-Surrey School, TX
Hutchison School, TN
Idyllwild Arts Academy, CA
Immaculata Academy, NY

Immaculata High School, NJ
Immaculate Conception High School, NJ
Immaculate Conception School, IL
Immanuel Christian High School, AB, Canada
Incarnate Word Academy, TX
Indian Mountain School, CT
Indian Springs School, AL
Interlochen Arts Academy, MI
International College Spain, Spain
International Community School of Addis Ababa, Ethiopia
International High School of FAIS, CA
International Junior Golf Academy, SC
International School Bangkok, Thailand
International School Basel, Switzerland
International School Hamburg, Germany
International School of Amsterdam, Netherlands
International School of Aruba, Aruba
International School of Athens, Greece
International School of Berne, Switzerland
International School of Brussels, Belgium
The International School of Geneva, Switzerland
The International School of Kuala Lumpur, Malaysia
International School of Luxembourg, Luxembourg
International School of Minnesota, MN
The International School of Monaco, Monaco
International School of Port-of-Spain, Trinidad and Tobago
International School of South Africa, South Africa
Iolani School, HI
Iona Preparatory School, NY
Isidore Newman School, LA
Islamic Saudi Academy, VA
Island View School, UT
Jackson Academy, MS
Jackson Preparatory School, MS
Jakarta International School, Indonesia
Jesuit College Preparatory School, TX
Jesuit High School, CA
Jesuit High School of Tampa, FL
John Burroughs School, MO
The John Cooper School, TX
The John Dewey Academy, MA
John F. Kennedy Memorial High School, WA
Josephinum High School, IL
The June Shelton School and Evaluation Center, TX
Justin-Siena High School, CA
Kalamazoo Christian High School, MI
Karachi American School, Pakistan
The Karafin School, NY
Kearney Catholic High School, NE
Keith Country Day School, IL
Kent Denver School, CO
Kent Place School, NJ
Kent School, CT
Kents Hill School, ME
Kentucky Country Day School, KY
The Key School, MD
Key School, Inc., TX
Keystone National High School, PA
Keystone School, TX
Kildonan School, NY
Kimball Union Academy, NH

Kimberton Waldorf School, PA
King & Low-Heywood Thomas School, CT
The King's Academy, TN
The King's Christian High School, NJ
Kings Christian School, CA
King's College School, ON, Canada
Kingshill School, VI
Kingsway College, ON, Canada
King's West School, WA
Kingswood-Oxford School, CT
The Kinkaid School, TX
The Kiski School, PA
The Knox School, NY
La Cheim School, CA
Ladywood High School, MI
La Grange Academy, GA
Laguna Blanca School, CA
La Jolla Country Day School, CA
Lakefield College School, ON, Canada
Lake Forest Academy, IL
Lake Highland Preparatory School, FL
Lakehill Preparatory School, TX
Lakeland Christian Academy, IN
Lake Ridge Academy, OH
Lakeside School, WA
Lakewood Prep, NJ
La Lumiere School, IN
Lancaster Country Day School, PA
Landmark School, MA
Landon School, MD
Lansdale Catholic High School, PA
La Pietra–Hawaii School for Girls, HI
La Salle Academy, RI
La Salle College High School, PA
La Salle High School, CA
The Latin School of Chicago, IL
Laurel School, OH
Lausanne Collegiate School, TN
Lawrence Academy, MA
Lawrence School, OH
The Lawrenceville School, NJ
Lawrence Woodmere Academy, NY
Lebanon Catholic Junior / Senior High School, PA
The Leelanau School, MI
Lee-Scott Academy, AL
Lehigh Valley Christian High School, PA
Lehman High School, OH
Le Lycee Francais de Los Angeles, CA
Lexington Catholic High School, KY
Lexington Christian Academy, MA
Leysin American School in Switzerland, Switzerland
Lick-Wilmerding High School, CA
Lifegate School, OR
Linden Christian School, MB, Canada
Linden Hall School for Girls, PA
Linden Hill School, MA
Linfield Christian School, CA
The Linsly School, WV
Little Red School House and Elisabeth Irwin High School, NY
Living Word Academy, PA

Long Island Lutheran Middle and High School, NY
The Loomis Chaffee School, CT
Loretto Academy, TX
Loretto High School, CA
Los Angeles Baptist Junior/Senior High School, CA
Los Angeles Lutheran High School, CA
Louisville High School, CA
Lourdes Catholic High School, AZ
The Lovett School, GA
The Lowell Whiteman School, CO
Lower Canada College, QC, Canada
Loyola Academy, IL
Loyola-Blakefield, MD
Loyola High School, Jesuit College Preparatory, CA
Loyola School, NY
Lustre Christian High School, MT
Lutheran High North, TX
Lutheran High School, CA
Lutheran High School, MN
Lutheran High School North, MO
Lutheran High School of Hawaii, HI
Lutheran High School South, MO
Luther College High School, SK, Canada
Lycee Français de New York, NY
The Lycee International, American Section, France
Lycee International de Los Angeles, CA
Lydia Patterson Institute, TX
Lyndon Institute, VT
The MacDuffie School, MA
Madison Academy, AL
Madison-Ridgeland Academy, MS
Maharishi School of the Age, IA
Maine Central Institute, ME
Malaspina International High School, BC, Canada
Malden Catholic High School, MA
Manhattan Christian High School, MT
Manlius Pebble Hill School, NY
Maplebrook School, NY
Maret School, DC
Marianapolis Preparatory School, CT
Marian Central Catholic High School, IL
Marian High School, IN
Marin Academy, CA
Marist High School, NJ
Marist School, GA
Marlborough School, CA
Marmion Academy, IL
Marquette University High School, WI
Marshall School, MN
Mars Hill Bible School, AL
The Marvelwood School, CT
Mary Help of Christians Academy, NJ
Mary Institute and St. Louis Country Day School (MICDS), MO
Maryknoll School, HI
Marylawn of the Oranges, NJ
The Mary Louis Academy, NY
Marymount High School, CA
Marymount International School, United Kingdom
Marymount School, NY
Maryvale Preparatory School, MD

Massanutten Military Academy, VA
The Masters School, NY
Matignon High School, MA
Maumee Valley Country Day School, OH
Maur Hill-Mount Academy, KS
Mayfield Senior School, CA
Mazapan School, Honduras
The McCallie School, TN
McDonogh School, MD
McGill-Toolen Catholic High School, AL
McNicholas High School, OH
McQuaid Jesuit High School, NY
Meadowridge Senior School, BC, Canada
The Meadows School, NV
The Meeting School, NH
Memphis University School, TN
Menaul School, NM
Menlo School, CA
Mercersburg Academy, PA
Mercy High School, CT
Mercy High School, NE
Mercy High School College Preparatory, CA
Mercyhurst Preparatory School, PA
Metropolitan Preparatory Academy, ON, Canada
Miami Country Day School, FL
Middlesex School, MA
Mid-Pacific Institute, HI
Mid-Peninsula High School, CA
Milken Community High School of Stephen Wise Temple, CA
Millbrook School, NY
Miller School, VA
Milton Academy, MA
Miss Edgar's and Miss Cramp's School, QC, Canada
Miss Hall's School, MA
Mississauga Private School, ON, Canada
Missouri Military Academy, MO
Miss Porter's School, CT
MMI Preparatory School, PA
Montana Academy, MT
Montcalm School, MI
Montclair College Preparatory School, CA
Montclair Kimberley Academy, NJ
Monte Vista Christian School, CA
Montgomery Bell Academy, TN
Montrose School, MA
Montverde Academy, FL
Moorestown Friends School, NJ
Moravian Academy, PA
Moreau Catholic High School, CA
Morgan Park Academy, IL
Morristown-Beard School, NJ
Mother McAuley High School, IL
Mounds Park Academy, MN
Mountain View Christian High School, NV
Mount Alvernia High School, PA
Mount Bachelor Academy, OR
Mount Carmel High School, IL
Mount Michael Benedictine High School, NE
Mount Saint Charles Academy, RI
Mt. Saint Dominic Academy, NJ

Specialized Directories

Mount Saint Joseph Academy, PA
Mount Saint Mary Academy, NJ
Munich International School, Germany
Nacel International School, MN
National Cathedral School, DC
National Sports Academy at Lake Placid, NY
Nawa Academy, CA
Nazareth Academy, IL
Nebraska Christian Schools, NE
Nerinx Hall, MO
Newark Academy, NJ
The Newgrange School, NJ
New Hampton School, NH
New Horizon Youth Ministries, IN
The Newman School, MA
New Mexico Military Institute, NM
The Newport School, MD
New Summit School, MS
Newton Country Day School of the Sacred Heart, MA
New York Military Academy, NY
Niagara Christian Collegiate, ON, Canada
The Nichols School, NY
Noble and Greenough School, MA
The Nora School, MD
Norfolk Academy, VA
Norfolk Collegiate School, VA
The North Broward Preparatory Upper School, FL
North Cobb Christian School, GA
North Country School, NY
Northfield Mount Hermon School, MA
The North Shore Country Day School, IL
Northside Christian School, FL
The Northwest School, WA
Northwest Yeshiva High School, WA
Northwood School, NY
North Yarmouth Academy, ME
Notre Dame Academy, MA
Notre Dame High School, CA
Notre Dame High School, LA
Notre Dame High School, MO
Notre Dame High School, NJ
Notre Dame High School, WV
Notre Dame High School for Girls, IL
Notre Dame Junior/Senior High School, PA
Notre Dame Preparatory School, MD
Oak Creek Ranch School, AZ
Oak Hill Academy, VA
Oak Knoll School of the Holy Child, NJ
The Oakland School, PA
Oakland School, VA
Oak Mountain Academy, GA
Oak Ridge Military Academy, NC
The Oakridge School, TX
Oakwood Friends School, NY
Oakwood School, CA
The Oakwood School, NC
Ojai Valley School, CA
Oldenburg Academy, IN
Oldfields School, MD
Olney Friends School, OH
The O'Neal School, NC

Oneida Baptist Institute, KY
Orangewood Adventist Academy, CA
Oregon Episcopal School, OR
Orinda Academy, CA
The Orme School, AZ
Our Lady Of Fatima High School, RI
Our Lady of the Sacred Heart, PA
Our Saviour Lutheran School, NY
Out-Of-Door-Academy, FL
The Overlake School, WA
The Oxford Academy, CT
Pace Academy, GA
Pacific Hills School, CA
Pacific Northern Academy, AK
Padua Franciscan High School, OH
Palma High School, CA
Palmer Trinity School, FL
Paraclete High School, CA
The Parker School, HI
Parklane Academy, MS
The Park School, MD
The Park School of Buffalo, NY
Park Tudor School, IN
The Pathway School, PA
Peddie School, NJ
The Pembroke Hill School, MO
The Pennington School, NJ
Perkiomen School, PA
The Phelps School, PA
Phillips Academy (Andover), MA
Phillips Exeter Academy, NH
Phoenix Christian Unified Schools, AZ
Phoenix Country Day School, AZ
Pickens Academy, AL
Pickering College, ON, Canada
Piedmont Academy, GA
Pine Crest School, FL
Pine Forge Academy, PA
Pinehurst School, ON, Canada
The Pingree School, MA
The Pingry School, NJ
Pius X High School, NE
Polytechnic Preparatory Country Day School, NY
Polytechnic School, CA
Pomfret School, CT
Pope John Paul II High School, FL
Portland Christian Schools, OR
Portland Lutheran School, OR
Portledge School, NY
Portsmouth Abbey School, RI
Portsmouth Christian Academy, NH
The Potomac School, VA
Poughkeepsie Day School, NY
Powers Catholic High School, MI
The Prairie School, WI
Prestonwood Christian Academy, TX
Princeton Day School, NJ
Proctor Academy, NH
Professional Children's School, NY
Providence Country Day School, RI
Providence High School, CA

Providence School, FL
Provo Canyon School, UT
Pulaski Academy, AR
Punahou School, HI
Purcell Marian High School, OH
Purnell School, NJ
The Putney School, VT
Queen Anne School, MD
Queen Margaret's School, BC, Canada
Queensway Christian College, ON, Canada
Quigley Catholic High School, PA
Quincy Notre Dame High School, IL
Quinte Christian High School, ON, Canada
Rabbi Alexander S. Gross Hebrew Academy, FL
Rabun Gap-Nacoochee School, GA
Ramona Convent Secondary School, CA
Rancho Valmora, NM
Randolph-Macon Academy, VA
Randolph School, AL
Ranney School, NJ
Ransom Everglades School, FL
Ravenscroft School, NC
The Rectory School, CT
Regina High School, OH
Regis High School, OR
Resurrection High School, IL
Ribet Academy, CA
Ridley College, ON, Canada
Rio Lindo Adventist Academy, CA
Ripon Christian Schools, CA
Riverdale Country School, NY
Rivermont Collegiate, IA
Riverside Military Academy, GA
Riverside School, Switzerland
The Rivers School, MA
Riverstone Community School, ID
Riverview School, MA
Robert Land Academy, ON, Canada
Robert Louis Stevenson School, NY
The Rockland Country Day School, NY
Rock Point School, VT
Rockway Mennonite Collegiate, ON, Canada
Rocky Hill School, RI
Rocky Mount Academy, NC
The Roeper School, MI
Roland Park Country School, MD
Rolling Hills Preparatory School, CA
Rosary High School, IL
Rothesay Netherwood School, NB, Canada
Rotterdam International Secondary School, Wolfert van Borselen, Netherlands
Routt High School, IL
Rowland Hall-St. Mark's School, UT
The Roxbury Latin School, MA
Roycemore School, IL
Rumsey Hall School, CT
Rutgers Preparatory School, NJ
Rye Country Day School, NY
Sacramento Country Day School, CA
Sacred Heart Academy, CT
Sacred Heart High School, CA

Sacred Heart Preparatory, CA
Sacred Heart School of Halifax, NS, Canada
Saddleback Valley Christian School, CA
Saddle River Day School, NJ
St. Agnes Academy, TX
Saint Agnes Boys High School, NY
St. Agnes High School, MN
St. Andrew's College, ON, Canada
St. Andrew's College, Dublin, Ireland
St. Andrew's Episcopal School, MD
St. Andrew's Episcopal School, MS
St. Andrew's on the Marsh School, GA
St. Andrew's Priory School, HI
St. Andrew's School, DE
Saint Andrew's School, FL
St. Andrew's School, RI
St. Andrew's-Sewanee School, TN
St. Anne's-Belfield School, VA
St. Anselm's Abbey School, DC
Saint Augustine Preparatory School, NJ
Saint Basil Academy, PA
St. Benedict at Auburndale, TN
St. Bernard High School, CA
St. Catherine's Military Academy, CA
St. Catherine's School, VA
St. Cecilia Academy, TN
Saint Cecilia High School, NE
St. Christopher's School, VA
St. Clement's School, ON, Canada
St. Croix Country Day School, VI
St. David's School, NC
Saint Dominic Academy, NJ
Saint Edward's School, FL
Saint Francis De Sales High School, IL
St. Francis de Sales High School, OH
St. Francis School, GA
Saint Francis School, HI
St. George's School, RI
Saint George's School, WA
St. George's School, BC, Canada
St. George's School of Montreal, QC, Canada
Saint Gertrude High School, VA
St. Gregory College Preparatory School, AZ
Saint James School, AL
Saint James School, MD
St. Johnsbury Academy, VT
St. John's College High School, DC
St. Johns Country Day School, FL
St. John's-Kilmarnock School, ON, Canada
St. John's Literary Institution at Prospect Hall, MD
St. John's Military School, KS
St. John's Northwestern Military Academy, WI
St. John's Preparatory School, MA
Saint John's Preparatory School, MN
St. John's-Ravenscourt School, MB, Canada
Saint John's School, GU
St. John's School, PR
St. John's School, TX
St. Joseph Academy, FL
St. Joseph High School, CT
Saint Joseph High School, WI

St. Joseph's Academy, LA
St. Joseph's Catholic School, SC
Saint Joseph's High School, NJ
St. Joseph's Preparatory School, PA
Saint Laurence High School, IL
St. Leonards, United Kingdom
Saint Louis Priory School, MO
Saint Lucy's Priory High School, CA
St. Luke's School, CT
St. Margaret's Episcopal School, CA
St. Margaret's School, VA
St. Margaret's School, BC, Canada
St. Mark's High School, DE
Saint Mark's School, MA
St. Mark's School of Texas, TX
St. Mary's Academy, CO
St. Mary's Bundschu Memorial High School, MO
Saint Mary's College High School, CA
St. Mary's Episcopal School, TN
Saint Mary's Hall, TX
St. Mary's Hall–Doane Academy, NJ
Saint Mary's High School, AZ
Saint Mary's High School, CO
St. Mary's Preparatory School, MI
St. Mary's Ryken High School, MD
Saint Mary's School, NC
St. Mary's School, OR
St. Maur International School, Japan
St. Michael's Catholic Academy, TX
St. Michael's Preparatory School of the Norbertine Fathers,
    CA
St. Michaels University School, BC, Canada
Saint Patrick High School, IL
Saint Patrick—Saint Vincent High School, CA
Saint Patrick's School, KY
St. Paul Academy and Summit School, MN
Saint Paul Lutheran High School, MO
St. Paul's Episcopal School, AL
St. Paul's High School, MB, Canada
St. Paul's Preparatory Academy, AZ
St. Paul's School, MD
St. Paul's School, NH
St. Paul's School for Girls, MD
St. Peter's Preparatory School, NJ
St. Pius X Catholic High School, GA
St. Pius X High School, TX
St. Sebastian's School, MA
Saints Peter and Paul High School, MD
St. Stanislaus College, MS
St. Stephen's & St. Agnes School, VA
Saint Stephen's Episcopal School, FL
St. Stephen's Episcopal School, TX
St. Stephen's School, Rome, Italy
Saint Teresa's Academy, MO
Saint Thomas Academy, MN
Saint Thomas Aquinas High School, KS
St. Thomas Aquinas High School, NH
St. Thomas Choir School, NY
St. Thomas High School, TX
Saint Thomas More School, CT
St. Timothy's School, MD

Saint Vincent Ferrer High School, NY
St. Vincent Pallotti High School, MD
Saint Xavier High School, KY
Salem Academy, NC
Salesian High School, NY
Salesianum School, DE
Salpointe Catholic High School, AZ
Saltus Grammar School, Bermuda
San Diego Jewish Academy, CA
San Domenico School, CA
Sandy Spring Friends School, MD
Sanford School, DE
San Marcos Baptist Academy, TX
Santa Catalina School, CA
Santa Fe Preparatory School, NM
Santiam Christian School, OR
Savannah Christian Preparatory School, GA
The Savannah Country Day School, GA
Sayre School, KY
Scarborough Christian School, ON, Canada
Scattergood Friends School, IA
School of the Holy Child, NY
Schule Schloss Salem, Germany
Scranton Preparatory School, PA
Seabury Hall, HI
Seattle Academy of Arts and Sciences, WA
Seattle Christian Schools, WA
Second Baptist School, TX
Sedbergh School, QC, Canada
Selwyn House School, QC, Canada
Seoul Foreign School, Republic of Korea
Seoul International School, Republic of Korea
Seton Catholic Central High School, NY
Seton Hall Preparatory School, NJ
The Seven Hills School, OH
Severn School, MD
Sewickley Academy, PA
Shady Side Academy, PA
Shannon Forest Christian School, SC
Shattuck-St. Mary's School, MN
The Shipley School, PA
Shorecrest Preparatory School, FL
Shoreline Christian, WA
SICES International Academy, AB, Canada
Sidwell Friends School, DC
Smith School, NY
Solebury School, PA
Sorenson's Ranch School, UT
Southampton Academy, VA
South Kent School, CT
Southridge School, BC, Canada
Southwest Christian School, Inc., TX
Southwestern Academy, AZ
Southwestern Academy, CA
Spartanburg Day School, SC
The Spence School, NY
Spring Ridge Academy, AZ
Springside School, PA
Squaw Valley Academy, CA
Stanbridge Academy, CA
Stanstead College, QC, Canada

Staten Island Academy, NY
Stella Maris High School and the Maura Clarke Junior High Program, NY
Stevenson School, CA
Stoneleigh–Burnham School, MA
Stone Mountain School, NC
The Stony Brook School, NY
Storm King School, NY
Stratford Academy, GA
Strathcona-Tweedsmuir School, AB, Canada
Stratton Mountain School, VT
Stuart Country Day School of the Sacred Heart, NJ
Stuart Hall, VA
The Study School, QC, Canada
Subiaco Academy, AR
Suffield Academy, CT
Sumiton Christian School, AL
Summerfield Waldorf School, CA
The Summit Country Day School, OH
Surabaya International School, Indonesia
Tabor Academy, MA
The Taft School, CT
Tallulah Falls School, GA
TASIS The American School in England, United Kingdom
TASIS, The American School in Switzerland, Switzerland
The Tatnall School, DE
Teurlings Catholic High School, LA
The Thacher School, CA
Thomas A. Edison High School, OR
Thomas Jefferson School, MO
Thornton Friends School, MD
Thornton Friends School/N.V.A., VA
Three Springs, AL
Tilton School, NH
Timothy Christian High School, IL
TMI—The Episcopal School of Texas, TX
Toronto District Christian High School, ON, Canada
Toronto Waldorf School, ON, Canada
Tower Hill School, DE
Town Centre Montessori School, ON, Canada
Traditional Learning Academy, BC, Canada
Trafalgar Castle School, ON, Canada
Trevor Day School, NY
Tri-City Christian Schools, CA
Trident Academy, SC
Trinity Academy, KS
Trinity Catholic High School, CT
Trinity Catholic High School, MA
Trinity Christian Academy, TX
Trinity Christian School, GA
Trinity College School, ON, Canada
Trinity Episcopal School, VA
Trinity High School, IL
Trinity High School, KY
Trinity High School, NH
Trinity-Pawling School, NY
Trinity Preparatory School, FL
Trinity Valley School, TX
Tyler Street Christian Academy, TX
United Mennonite Educational Institute, ON, Canada
United Nations International School, NY

Universal Academy of Florida, FL
University Lake School, WI
University Liggett School, MI
University of Chicago Laboratory Schools, IL
University of Detroit Jesuit High School and Academy, MI
University of Miami Online High School, FL
University of Toronto Schools, ON, Canada
University Prep, WA
University School, OH
University School of Milwaukee, WI
University School of Nashville, TN
University School of Nova Southeastern University, FL
Upper Canada College, ON, Canada
The Urban School of San Francisco, CA
Ursuline Academy, DE
Ursuline High School, CA
Vail Mountain School, CO
Valley Christian School, CA
Valley Christian School, MT
Valley Forge Military Academy and College, PA
Vanguard College Preparatory School, TX
The Vanguard School, FL
Venta Preparatory School, ON, Canada
Vermont Academy, VT
Vianney High School, MO
Vicksburg Catholic School, MS
Viewpoint School, CA
Village Christian Schools, CA
Villa Maria Academy, PA
Villa Victoria Academy, NJ
Villa Walsh Academy, NJ
Virginia Beach Friends School, VA
Virginia Episcopal School, VA
Visitation Academy of St. Louis County, MO
Wakefield School, VA
Walden Preparatory School, TX
The Waldorf High School of Massachusetts Bay, MA
The Waldorf School of Garden City, NY
The Walker School, GA
Walnut Hill School, MA
The Wardlaw-Hartridge School, NJ
Waring School, MA
Wasatch Academy, UT
Washington Academy, ME
Washington County Day School, MS
Washington International School, DC
Washington Waldorf School, MD
The Waterford School, UT
Watkinson School, CT
The Waverly School, CA
Wayland Academy, WI
Wayne Country Day School, NC
Waynflete School, ME
Webber Academy, AB, Canada
The Webb School, TN
Webb School of Knoxville, TN
The Wellington School, OH
Wellsprings Friends School, OR
Wentworth Military Academy and Junior College, MO
Wesleyan School, GA
Westbury Christian School, TX

West Catholic High School, MI
Westchester Academy, NC
Western Mennonite School, OR
Western Reserve Academy, OH
The Westfield Schools, GA
Westgate Mennonite Collegiate, MB, Canada
Westhill Institute, Mexico
West Island College, AB, Canada
Westminster Christian Academy, AL
Westminster Christian Academy, LA
Westminster Christian School, FL
Westminster School, CT
Westminster Schools of Augusta, GA
West Nottingham Academy, MD
Westover School, CT
Westpark School, MB, Canada
Westridge School, CA
Westtown School, PA
Westview School, CA
Wheaton Academy, IL
The Wheeler School, RI
The White Mountain School, NH
White Rock Christian Academy, BC, Canada
Whitfield School, MO
Whittier Christian High School, CA
Wichita Collegiate School, KS
Wilbraham & Monson Academy, MA
Wildwood Catholic High School, NJ
William Penn Charter School, PA
The Williams School, CT
The Williston Northampton School, MA
Willow Hill School, MA
The Willows Academy, IL
Wilmington Christian School, DE
Wilmington Friends School, DE
Wilson Hall, SC
The Winchendon School, MA
Winchester Thurston School, PA
Windermere St. Anne's School, United Kingdom
Windhoek International School, Namibia
Windsor Christian Fellowship Academy, ON, Canada
The Windsor School, NY
Windward School, CA
The Winsor School, MA
Winston Preparatory School, NY
The Winston School, TX
The Winston School San Antonio, TX
Wisconsin Academy, WI
Woodberry Forest School, VA
Woodbridge Academy, KY
The Woodhall School, CT
Woodlands Academy of the Sacred Heart, IL
The Woodlynde School, PA
Woodside International School, CA
Woodside Priory School, CA
Woodstock School, India
The Woodward School, MA
Wooster School, CT
Worcester Academy, MA
Worcester Preparatory School, MD
Wyoming Seminary, PA

Xavier College Preparatory, AZ
Yeshiva Atlanta, GA
Yokohama International School, Japan
York Country Day School, PA
York Preparatory School, NY
The York School, ON, Canada
Zurich International School, Switzerland

SCHOOLS REPORTING THAT THEY OFFER LOANS*

The Academy at Charlemont, MA	N
Adelphi Academy, NY	M,N
Advanced Academy of Georgia, GA	M,N
The Agnes Irwin School, PA	N
The Albany Academy, NY	N
Alexander Dawson School, CO	N
American Academy, FL	N
American Heritage School, FL	N
Asheville School, NC	N
Aurora Central High School, IL	N
Avon Old Farms School, CT	N
The Barstow School, MO	N
Bearspaw Christian School, AB, Canada	N
Belmont Hill School, MA	M,N
Berwick Academy, ME	N
Bishop Kenny High School, FL	N
Bishop's College School, QC, Canada	N
Blair Academy, NJ	N
The Blake School, MN	N
The Brearley School, NY	N
Brentwood Academy, TN	N
Brookstone School, GA	M,N
The Bryn Mawr School for Girls, MD	M,N
Burke Mountain Academy, VT	N
Camelot Academy, NC	N
Canterbury School, CT	M,N
Cardigan Mountain School, NH	N
Cary Academy, NC	N
CCI The Renaissance School, Italy	N
Chestnut Hill Academy, PA	N
Choate Rosemary Hall, CT	N
The College Preparatory School, CA	N
The Colorado Rocky Mountain School, CO	M
Commonwealth School, MA	N
Concord Academy, MA	N
Connelly School of the Holy Child, MD	M
Convent of the Sacred Heart, NY	N
Cross Creek Programs, UT	M,N
Crossroads School, MO	N
Crossroads School for Arts & Sciences, CA	N
Dana Hall School, MA	N
Darlington School, GA	N
Deerfield Academy, MA	N
The Delphian School, OR	N
Detroit Country Day School, MI	N
Dwight-Englewood School, NJ	M,N
Eckerd Youth Alternatives, FL	M
Ecole d'Humanite, Switzerland	M,N
Episcopal High School, TX	M
Episcopal High School, VA	N

M — middle-income loans; N — need-based loans

The Ethical Culture Fieldston School, NY	N
Explorations Academy, WA	N
Falmouth Academy, MA	N
Fork Union Military Academy, VA	N
Foxcroft School, VA	M,N
Friends School of Baltimore, MD	M,N
Friends Seminary, NY	M,N
Garden School, NY	N
Garrison Forest School, MD	N
George School, PA	N
Georgetown Preparatory School, MD	M
Germantown Friends School, PA	N
Gilman School, MD	N
Gilmour Academy, OH	N
Girls Preparatory School, TN	N
Glades Day School, FL	N
Gould Academy, ME	N
Great Lakes Christian College, ON, Canada	M,N
Grenville Christian College, ON, Canada	N
The Grier School, PA	N
Groton School, MA	N
The Gunnery, CT	N
Hackley School, NY	N
Hamden Hall Country Day School, CT	N
The Harker School, CA	N
The Harrisburg Academy, PA	N
Hawken School, OH	N
High Mowing School, NH	M
Hoosac School, NY	N
The Hotchkiss School, CT	M
Immaculata Academy, NY	N
John Burroughs School, MO	N
The John Cooper School, TX	N
Kent Denver School, CO	N
Kent School, CT	N
Lakeside School, WA	M,N
Landon School, MD	N
The Latin School of Chicago, IL	M,N
Lawrence Academy, MA	N
Lawrence Woodmere Academy, NY	N
The Loomis Chaffee School, CT	N
Lower Canada College, QC, Canada	N
Maplebrook School, NY	N
Marin Academy, CA	N
Massanutten Military Academy, VA	N
McDonogh School, MD	M,N
The Meadows School, NV	N
The Meeting School, NH	N
Mercersburg Academy, PA	N
Middlesex School, MA	N
Midland School, CA	N
Millbrook School, NY	N
Miss Porter's School, CT	N
Montcalm School, MI	M
Moorestown Friends School, NJ	N
Moravian Academy, PA	N
Mount Bachelor Academy, OR	M
Noble and Greenough School, MA	N
Norfolk Academy, VA	N
Northfield Mount Hermon School, MA	M,N
The North Shore Country Day School, IL	M,N
Oakwood Friends School, NY	N
Ojai Valley School, CA	N
The Orme School, AZ	M,N
Pacific Hills School, CA	N
Peddie School, NJ	N
The Pembroke Hill School, MO	N
Phillips Academy (Andover), MA	M,N
Phillips Exeter Academy, NH	N
The Pingree School, MA	N
Pope John Paul II High School, FL	N
Providence High School, CA	M,N
Quincy Notre Dame High School, IL	M
Ravenscroft School, NC	N
Ridley College, ON, Canada	N
Robert Land Academy, ON, Canada	N
Robert Louis Stevenson School, NY	N
Rock Point School, VT	N
Rothesay Netherwood School, NB, Canada	N
The Roxbury Latin School, MA	N
Rumsey Hall School, CT	N
St. Andrew's School, RI	N
St. Catherine's School, VA	M,N
St. George's School, RI	M,N
St. John's School, PR	N
St. John's School, TX	N
St. Joseph's Academy, LA	N
St. Joseph's Preparatory School, PA	M,N
Saint Mark's School, MA	N
St. Paul Academy and Summit School, MN	N
St. Paul's High School, MB, Canada	N
St. Paul's School, NH	N
St. Sebastian's School, MA	N
St. Timothy's School, MD	N
Santa Catalina School, CA	N
Schule Schloss Salem, Germany	N
South Kent School, CT	M,N
Stanstead College, QC, Canada	N
Staten Island Academy, NY	N
Stone Mountain School, NC	M
Stratton Mountain School, VT	N
Suffield Academy, CT	M,N
The Summit Country Day School, OH	N
Summit Preparatory School, MT	N
The Taft School, CT	N
Tallulah Falls School, GA	N
The Tatnall School, DE	N
Tilton School, NH	N
Trinity Catholic High School, CT	M
Trinity-Pawling School, NY	N
Trinity Preparatory School, FL	M
United Mennonite Educational Institute, ON, Canada	N
Vail Mountain School, CO	N
Valley Forge Military Academy and College, PA	M
Vandebilt Catholic High School, LA	M
Visitation Academy of St. Louis County, MO	N
Wasatch Academy, UT	N
The Wellington School, OH	N
Western Reserve Academy, OH	N
Westminster School, CT	N
Westover School, CT	M,N
Westtown School, PA	N

*M — middle-income loans; N — need-based loans

Wilbraham & Monson Academy, MA   N
The Williston Northampton School, MA   N
Windward School, CA   N
Woodberry Forest School, VA   N
Woodlands Academy of the Sacred Heart, IL   N
Woodside International School, CA   M,N
Wyoming Seminary, PA   N

TOTAL AMOUNT OF UPPER SCHOOL FINANCIAL AID AWARDED FOR 2005–06

Academia Cotopaxi, Ecuador	$2500
The Academy at Charlemont, MA	$450,000
Academy of Holy Angels, MN	$600,000
Academy of Mount Saint Ursula, NY	$373,573
Academy of Our Lady of Mercy, CT	$285,000
Academy of Our Lady of Peace, CA	$566,000
The Academy of St. Joseph, NY	$66,530
Academy of the Holy Angels, NJ	$152,140
Academy of the Holy Names, FL	$400,000
Academy of the Sacred Heart, MI	$408,610
ACS Cobham International School, United Kingdom	£26,000
ACS Egham International School, United Kingdom	£18,470
ACS Hillingdon International School, United Kingdom	£65,000
Adelphi Academy, NY	$125,000
Admiral Farragut Academy, FL	$280,000
Advanced Academy of Georgia, GA	$83,700
The Agnes Irwin School, PA	$1,400,000
Ahliyyah School for Girls, Jordan	18,400 Jordanian dinars
Airdrie Koinonia Christian School, AB, Canada	CAN$15,000
Akiba Hebrew Academy, PA	$610,000
The Albany Academy, NY	$454,935
Albert College, ON, Canada	CAN$270,000
Albuquerque Academy, NM	$1,699,384
Alexander Dawson School, CO	$570,000
Allen Academy, TX	$50,000
Allendale Columbia School, NY	$528,950
Alliance Academy, Ecuador	$200,000
Allison Academy, FL	$50,000
All Saints' Episcopal School of Fort Worth, TX	$300,000
The Altamont School, AL	$521,000
Ambassador Preparatory, MN	$60,000
American Academy, FL	$1,042,945
American Heritage School, FL	$2,613,762
American International School of Bucharest, Romania	$200,000
American International School Salzburg, Austria	€26,000
The American School Foundation, Mexico	4,500,000 Mexican pesos
The American School in London, United Kingdom	£410,000
American School of Paris, France	€17,000
American School of Warsaw, Poland	$14,000
The Andrews School, OH	$401,000
Annie Wright School, WA	$300,000
Appleby College, ON, Canada	CAN$980,000
Aquin Central Catholic High School, IL	$18,000
Archbishop Blenk Girls High School, LA	$67,500
Archbishop Curley High School, MD	$180,000

Archbishop Mitty High School, CA	$265,000
Archbishop Quigley Preparatory High School, IL	$220,000
The Archer School for Girls, CA	$1,000,000
Archmere Academy, DE	$991,000
Armona Union Academy, CA	$50,000
Army and Navy Academy, CA	$150,000
Arrowhead Christian Academy, CA	$130,000
Ashbury College, ON, Canada	CAN$350,000
Asheville School, NC	$1,279,075
Ashley Hall, SC	$120,492
Assumption High School, KY	$276,475
The Athenian School, CA	$1,230,000
Atlanta International School, GA	$330,706
Aurora Central High School, IL	$80,000
Avon Old Farms School, CT	$2,400,000
The Awty International School, TX	$150,000
The Baldwin School, PA	$586,675
Baldwin School of Puerto Rico, Inc., PR	$12,000
Balmoral Hall School, MB, Canada	CAN$104,346
The Baltimore Actors' Theatre Conservatory, MD	$12,000
Baltimore Lutheran Middle and Upper School, MD	$138,150
Bancroft School, MA	$727,645
Baptist High School, NJ	$53,000
Barnstable Academy, NJ	$280,000
Battle Ground Academy, TN	$750,000
Bearspaw Christian School, AB, Canada	CAN$27,000
Beaufort Academy, SC	$62,000
Beaumont School, OH	$100,000
Beaver Country Day School, MA	$2,208,785
Belen Jesuit Preparatory School, FL	$400,000
Bellarmine College Preparatory, CA	$1,800,000
Bellarmine Preparatory School, WA	$1,636,971
Benilde–St. Margaret's School, MN	$581,585
Berkshire School, MA	$1,836,591
The Bermuda High School for Girls, Bermuda	300,000 Bermuda dollars
Berwick Academy, ME	$960,450
The Birch Wathen Lenox School, NY	$1,200,000
Bishop Carroll High School, PA	$569,502
Bishop Conaty-Our Lady of Loretto High School, CA	$300,300
Bishop Eustace Preparatory School, NJ	$520,000
Bishop Feehan High School, MA	$400,000
Bishop Fenwick High School, OH	$65,000
Bishop Guertin High School, NH	$175,000
Bishop Hoban High School, PA	$2,832,722
Bishop Ireton High School, VA	$275,000
Bishop Kelly High School, ID	$413,000
Bishop Lynch Catholic High School, TX	$190,700
Bishop McDevitt High School, PA	$100,000
Bishop McGuinness Catholic High School, OK	$65,600
Bishop McNamara High School, IL	$200,000
Bishop Quinn High School/St. Francis Middle School, CA	$232,000
Bishop's College School, QC, Canada	CAN$320,000
The Bishop Strachan School, ON, Canada	CAN$500,000
Bishop Verot High School, FL	$300,000
Bishop Walsh Middle High School, MD	$30,000
Bismark St. Mary's Central, ND	$50,000
Blair Academy, NJ	$2,264,000

M — middle-income loans; N — need-based loans

The Blake School, MN	$1,589,000	Cary Academy, NC	$568,919
Blue Mountain Academy, PA	$130,000	Casady School, OK	$428,828
Blueprint Education, AZ	$1000	Cascadilla School, NY	$60,000
The Blue Ridge School, VA	$750,000	Cascia Hall Preparatory School, OK	$350,000
The Bolles School, FL	$1,058,372	Castilleja School, CA	$600,000
Boston University Academy, MA	$545,000	Cate School, CA	$1,902,000
Boyd-Buchanan School, TN	$80,000	Cathedral Preparatory School, PA	$500,000
The Boys' Latin School of Maryland, MD	$984,900	Catholic Central High School, NY	$45,500
Bradenton Christian School, FL	$42,962	The Catholic High School of Baltimore, MD	$295,000
Brandon Hall School, GA	$80,000	The Catlin Gabel School, OR	$59,000
The Brearley School, NY	$1,340,535	CCI The Renaissance School, Italy	€30,000
Brent School-Baguio, Philippines	$78,309	Centennial Academy, QC, Canada	CAN$77,345
Brentwood Academy, TN	$362,139	Central Catholic High School, CA	$100,270
Brentwood School, CA	$2,300,000	Central Catholic High School, PA	$550,000
Brewster Academy, NH	$1,600,000	CFS, The School at Church Farm, PA	$5,464,000
Bridges Academy, CA	$110,000	Chadwick School, CA	$1,400,000
Bridge School, CO	$40,000	Chamberlain-Hunt Academy, MS	$289,700
British Columbia Christian Academy, BC, Canada	CAN$25,000	Chaminade College Preparatory, CA	$521,070
		Chaminade-Madonna College Preparatory, FL	$400,000
The British International School, Jeddah, Saudi Arabia	200,000 Saudi riyal	Chapel Hill–Chauncy Hall School, MA	$726,000
Broadview Academy, IL	$67,000	The Chapin School, NY	$1,122,020
The Brook Hill School, TX	$280,000	Charles Wright Academy, WA	$336,815
Brooklyn Friends School, NY	$764,200	Charlotte Christian School, NC	$389,150
Brooks School, MA	$1,910,000	Charlotte Country Day School, NC	$1,211,136
Brookstone School, GA	$284,310	Charlotte Latin School, NC	$809,500
Brophy College Preparatory, AZ	$1,570,000	Chase Collegiate School, CT	$838,084
Brother Rice High School, MI	$150,000	Chatham Academy, GA	$50,000
Brownell-Talbot School, NE	$280,000	Chatham Hall, VA	$980,680
The Browning School, NY	$615,750	Chattanooga Christian School, TN	$250,646
Brunswick School, CT	$828,100	Chelsea School, MD	$90,000
The Bryn Mawr School for Girls, MD	$745,000	Cherokee Creek Boys School, SC	$28,800
Buckingham Browne & Nichols School, MA	$2,334,090	Cheshire Academy, CT	$1,000,000
The Buckley School, CA	$487,400	Chestnut Hill Academy, PA	$873,500
Burke Mountain Academy, VT	$384,000	Cheverus High School, ME	$800,000
The Bush School, WA	$456,158	Chinese Christian Schools, CA	$100,000
Buxton School, MA	$934,000	Choate Rosemary Hall, CT	$5,700,000
Calgary Academy, AB, Canada	CAN$180,000	Christ Church Episcopal School, SC	$137,702
The Calhoun School, NY	$1,240,000	Christchurch School, VA	$990,300
Calvary Christian Academy, KY	$25,000	Christian Brothers Academy, NJ	$622,800
Calvert Hall College High School, MD	$1,000,000	Christian Brothers Academy, NY	$474,000
The Cambridge School of Weston, MA	$1,374,500	Christian Central Academy, NY	$20,000
Camden Military Academy, SC	$200,000	Christian Heritage School, CT	$564,000
Campbell Hall (Episcopal), CA	$1,479,425	Christian Junior–Senior High School, CA	$18,000
Canadian Academy, Japan	¥5,023,550	Christopher Dock Mennonite High School, PA	$400,000
Cannon School, NC	$192,020	Christ School, NC	$640,000
Canterbury High School, IN	$752,000	Cincinnati Country Day School, OH	$335,120
Canterbury School, CT	$1,900,000	Cistercian Preparatory School, TX	$178,650
Canterbury School, FL	$474,658	Colegio Franklin D. Roosevelt, Peru	$8840
The Canterbury School of Florida, FL	$213,000	Colegio Nueva Granada, Colombia	74,331,400 Colombian pesos
Canyonville Christian Academy, OR	$20,000		
Cape Cod Academy, MA	$275,000	Colegio Puertorriqueno de Ninas, PR	$46,550
Cape Fear Academy, NC	$146,961	Colegio San Jose, PR	$200,000
Cape Henry Collegiate School, VA	$300,000	The College Preparatory School, CA	$1,165,690
Cardigan Mountain School, NH	$737,250	The Collegiate School, VA	$571,945
Cardinal Gibbons High School, FL	$300,000	The Colorado Rocky Mountain School, CO	$75,500
Cardinal Newman School, SC	$7000	The Colorado Springs School, CO	$375,950
Caribbean Preparatory School, PR	$34,000	Colorado Timberline Academy, CO	$52,000
Carlisle School, VA	$112,000	Columbia Grammar and Preparatory School, NY	$2,007,060
Carolina Day School, NC	$161,390	The Columbus Academy, OH	$543,300
Carrollton School of the Sacred Heart, FL	$920,000	Columbus School for Girls, OH	$484,153
		Commonwealth School, MA	$782,600

The Community School of Naples, FL	$622,152	Escola Americana de Campinas, Brazil	$113,213
Concord Academy, MA	$1,800,000	The Ethel Walker School, CT	$2,000,000
Concordia Academy, MN	$75,000	The Ethical Culture Fieldston School, NY	$3,355,538
Convent of the Sacred Heart, CT	$864,150	Evansville Day School, IN	$100,000
Convent of the Sacred Heart, NY	$1,392,265	Explorations Academy, WA	$50,000
Convent of the Sacred Heart High School, CA	$700,000	Fairhill School, TX	$10,000
Convent of the Visitation School, MN	$700,000	Faith Lutheran High School, NV	$175,000
Copiah Academy, MS	$3923	Falmouth Academy, MA	$417,010
Country Day School of the Sacred Heart, PA	$300,020	The Family Foundation School, NY	$560,000
Cranbrook Schools, MI	$6,000,000	Father Lopez High School, FL	$75,000
Crawford Adventist Academy, ON, Canada	CAN$10,000	Father Ryan High School, TN	$298,000
Crescent School, ON, Canada	CAN$92,000	Fay School, MA	$611,112
Crespi Carmelite High School, CA	$276,525	The Fessenden School, MA	$600,000
Cretin-Derham Hall, MN	$1,400,000	First Baptist Academy, TX	$600,000
Crofton House School, BC, Canada	CAN$154,438	First Presbyterian Day School, GA	$140,000
Crossroads School for Arts & Sciences, CA	$1,623,980	Fishburne Military School, VA	$75,000
Crystal Springs Uplands School, CA	$1,000,000	Flint Hill School, VA	$1,012,245
The Culver Academies, IN	$1,976,620	Fontbonne Academy, MA	$720,650
Currey Ingram Academy, TN	$177,540	Foothills Academy, AB, Canada	CAN$500,000
Cushing Academy, MA	$2,100,000	Fordham Preparatory School, NY	$1,000,000
Dallas Academy, TX	$95,600	Fork Union Military Academy, VA	$600,000
Dallas Christian School, TX	$121,000	The Forman School, CT	$180,000
The Dalton School, NY	$2,014,348	Forsyth Country Day School, NC	$348,502
Dana Hall School, MA	$2,065,785	Fort Worth Christian School, TX	$138,500
Darlington School, GA	$1,172,050	Fort Worth Country Day School, TX	$662,994
David Lipscomb High School, TN	$24,877	Fountain Valley School of Colorado, CO	$1,300,000
Deerfield Academy, MA	$5,000,000	Fowlers Academy, PR	$10,500
De La Salle High School, CA	$1,029,000	Foxcroft School, VA	$890,000
DeLaSalle High School, MN	$1,102,000	Fox Valley Lutheran Academy, IL	$25,000
Delaware County Christian School, PA	$500,000	Fox Valley Lutheran High School, WI	$185,000
Delaware Valley Friends School, PA	$330,400	Francis Parker School, CA	$1,900,000
Delbarton School, NJ	$952,580	Francis W. Parker School, IL	$1,160,000
DeMatha Catholic High School, MD	$760,865	Franklin Road Academy, TN	$40,000
The Derryfield School, NH	$898,230	Fraser Academy, BC, Canada	CAN$42,000
Detroit Country Day School, MI	$2,500,000	Frederica Academy, GA	$192,430
Devon Preparatory School, PA	$629,175	Freeman Academy, SD	$5000
Doane Stuart School, NY	$625,000	French-American School of New York, NY	$270,000
Don Bosco High School, CA	$300,000	Fresno Christian Schools, CA	$300,000
Dowling High School, IA	$800,000	Friends Academy, NY	$1,000,000
Dublin School, NH	$812,000	Friends' Central School, PA	$2,485,625
Duchesne Academy of the Sacred Heart, NE	$117,000	Friends School of Baltimore, MD	$690,244
Duchesne Academy of the Sacred Heart, TX	$444,205	Friends Seminary, NY	$2,548,500
Dunn School, CA	$500,000	The Frostig School, CA	$50,000
Durham Academy, NC	$368,755	Fryeburg Academy, ME	$750,000
Dwight-Englewood School, NJ	$1,438,841	Fuqua School, VA	$44,000
The Dwight School, NY	$500,000	The Galloway School, GA	$271,860
Eaglebrook School, MA	$1,200,000	Garces Memorial High School, CA	$257,000
Eagle Hill School, CT	$1,000,000	Garrison Forest School, MD	$840,650
East Catholic High School, CT	$576,792	Gaston Day School, NC	$72,000
Eastern Mennonite High School, VA	$159,689	Gateway School, TX	$18,000
Ecole d'Humanite, Switzerland	180,000 Swiss francs	George School, PA	$4,800,000
The Ellis School, PA	$616,900	Georgetown Day School, DC	$900,000
Elyria Catholic High School, OH	$200,000	Georgetown Preparatory School, MD	$1,570,000
Emerson Honors High Schools, CA	$50,000	Georgetown Visitation Preparatory School, DC	$1,000,000
The Emery Weiner School, TX	$204,067	Germantown Academy, PA	$1,100,000
Emma Willard School, NY	$2,211,200	Germantown Friends School, PA	$624,299
Episcopal Collegiate School, AR	$525,000	Gilman School, MD	$1,100,000
Episcopal High School, TX	$1,250,000	Girls Preparatory School, TN	$847,222
Episcopal High School, VA	$2,700,000	Glen Eden School, BC, Canada	CAN$40,000
The Episcopal School of Acadiana, LA	$115,590	Glenelg Country School, MD	$375,000
The Episcopal School of Dallas, TX	$1,100,000	Gould Academy, ME	$1,242,000

Governor Dummer Academy, MA	$2,200,000
The Gow School, NY	$333,200
Grace Christian School, AK	$50,000
The Grand River Academy, OH	$100,000
The Grauer School, CA	$25,000
Great Lakes Christian College, ON, Canada	CAN$100,000
Green Fields Country Day School, AZ	$159,193
Greenhill School, TX	$922,175
Greenhills School, MI	$441,559
Greens Farms Academy, CT	$660,115
Greenwich Academy, CT	$672,100
The Greenwood School, VT	$47,000
Grenville Christian College, ON, Canada	CAN$327,384
The Grier School, PA	$1,150,000
Groton School, MA	$2,656,000
Guerin College Preparatory High School, IL	$400,000
Gulliver Preparatory School, FL	$2,000,000
The Gunnery, CT	$1,700,000
Gunston Day School, MD	$405,000
Hackett Catholic Central High School, MI	$400,000
Hackley School, NY	$2,250,000
Hales Franciscan High School, IL	$1,500,000
Halifax Grammar School, NS, Canada	CAN$184,529
Hamilton Learning Centre, ON, Canada	CAN$15,000
Hammond School, SC	$600,000
Happy Valley School, CA	$300,000
Harding Academy, TN	$227,000
Hargrave Military Academy, VA	$280,000
The Harpeth Hall School, TN	$658,450
Harrells Christian Academy, NC	$16,650
The Harrisburg Academy, PA	$450,811
Harvard-Westlake School, CA	$3,900,000
The Harvey School, NY	$900,000
The Haverford School, PA	$1,087,000
Hawaii Baptist Academy, HI	$30,315
Hawai'i Preparatory Academy, HI	$995,000
Hawken School, OH	$1,303,700
Hayden High School, KS	$55,000
Head-Royce School, CA	$889,920
Hebron Academy, ME	$1,700,000
The Heritage School, GA	$159,385
The Hewitt School, NY	$1,375,920
Highland Hall, A Waldorf School, CA	$52,200
Highland School, VA	$258,000
High Mowing School, NH	$370,000
The Hill Center, Durham Academy, NC	$56,000
The Hill School, PA	$3,500,000
Hillside School, MA	$600,000
The Hill Top Preparatory School, PA	$75,700
Hilton Head Preparatory School, SC	$200,000
The Hockaday School, TX	$786,700
Hokkaido International School, Japan	¥2,000,000
Holderness School, NH	$1,627,100
Holland Hall, OK	$720,910
The Holton-Arms School, MD	$1,674,775
Holy Name High School, PA	$233,222
Holyoke Catholic High School, MA	$287,830
Hoosac School, NY	$525,000
Hopkins School, CT	$2,245,000
The Horace Mann School, NY	$2,985,943
Horizons School, GA	$56,000
Hosanna Christian School, OR	$9000
The Hotchkiss School, CT	$4,608,000
Houghton Academy, NY	$95,000
Howe Military School, IN	$500,000
The Hudson School, NJ	$150,000
The Hun School of Princeton, NJ	$2,150,000
Hutchison School, TN	$126,822
Hyde School, CT	$750,000
Hyde School, ME	$750,000
Idyllwild Arts Academy, CA	$290,000
Immaculata Academy, NY	$34,000
Immaculate Conception High School, NJ	$12,500
Immaculate Conception School, IL	$50,000
Incarnate Word Academy, TX	$95,000
Indian Mountain School, CT	$596,189
Indian Springs School, AL	$602,377
Interlochen Arts Academy, MI	$5,000,000
International College Spain, Spain	€38,706
International High School of FAIS, CA	$748,000
International School of Aruba, Aruba	$20,000
International School of Athens, Greece	€20,000
International School of Brussels, Belgium	€671,991
International School of Lausanne, Switzerland	26,200 Swiss francs
International School of Luxembourg, Luxembourg	€1,300,000
International School of Port-of-Spain, Trinidad and Tobago	$42,000
Iolani School, HI	$950,000
Iona Preparatory School, NY	$203,000
Isidore Newman School, LA	$1,537,123
Islamic Saudi Academy, VA	$100,000
Jackson Academy, MS	$101,680
Jackson Preparatory School, MS	$158,000
Jakarta International School, Indonesia	$49,835
Jesuit College Preparatory School, TX	$1,109,175
Jesuit High School, CA	$600,000
Jesuit High School of New Orleans, LA	$350,000
John Burroughs School, MO	$1,390,000
The John Cooper School, TX	$270,408
John F. Kennedy Memorial High School, WA	$390,000
Josephinum High School, IL	$425,000
The June Shelton School and Evaluation Center, TX	$69,500
Justin-Siena High School, CA	$222,400
Kearney Catholic High School, NE	$15,000
Keith Country Day School, IL	$207,290
Kent Denver School, CO	$1,200,000
Kent Place School, NJ	$1,249,710
Kent School, CT	$4,300,000
Kents Hill School, ME	$1,600,000
Kentucky Country Day School, KY	$179,245
The Key School, MD	$320,400
Keystone School, TX	$139,390
Kildonan School, NY	$119,750
Kimberton Waldorf School, PA	$246,054
King & Low-Heywood Thomas School, CT	$496,030
The King's Academy, TN	$45,856
The King's Christian High School, NJ	$100,000
Kings Christian School, CA	$10,000
Kingshill School, VI	$50,000

Kingswood-Oxford School, CT	$1,668,175	The MacDuffie School, MA	$411,065
The Kinkaid School, TX	$486,815	Madison Academy, AL	$100,000
The Kiski School, PA	$1,250,000	Madison-Ridgeland Academy, MS	$70,000
La Grange Academy, GA	$59,820	Maharishi School of the Age, IA	$101,709
Laguna Blanca School, CA	$174,600	Maine Central Institute, ME	$1,004,395
La Jolla Country Day School, CA	$1,900,000	Malden Catholic High School, MA	$300,000
Lakefield College School, ON, Canada	CAN$1,260,000	Manlius Pebble Hill School, NY	$721,190
Lakeland Christian Academy, IN	$76,000	Maplebrook School, NY	$120,000
Lake Ridge Academy, OH	$912,743	Maret School, DC	$849,635
Lakeside School, WA	$1,904,666	Marianapolis Preparatory School, CT	$600,000
La Lumiere School, IN	$84,740	Marian Central Catholic High School, IL	$152,387
Lancaster Country Day School, PA	$360,000	Marian High School, IN	$350,000
Landmark East School, NS, Canada	CAN$200,000	Marin Academy, CA	$1,542,763
Landmark School, MA	$125,000	Marist School, GA	$762,000
Landon School, MD	$772,665	Marlborough School, CA	$551,241
La Pietra–Hawaii School for Girls, HI	$253,300	Marmion Academy, IL	$218,650
La Salle Academy, RI	$1,000,000	Marquette University High School, WI	$1,140,000
La Salle College High School, PA	$1,200,000	Marshall School, MN	$449,000
La Salle High School, CA	$550,000	Mars Hill Bible School, AL	$120,000
The Latin School of Chicago, IL	$1,571,463	The Marvelwood School, CT	$671,325
Laurel School, OH	$1,114,035	Mary Help of Christians Academy, NJ	$283,081
Lausanne Collegiate School, TN	$110,125	Mary Institute and St. Louis Country Day	
The Lawrenceville School, NJ	$600,000	School (MICDS), MO	$1,267,540
Lebanon Catholic Junior/Senior High School, PA	$126,000	Maryknoll School, HI	$360,000
The Leelanau School, MI	$254,922	Marylawn of the Oranges, NJ	$116,790
Lehigh Valley Christian High School, PA	$42,000	The Mary Louis Academy, NY	$530,225
Lehman High School, OH	$283,030	Marymount High School, CA	$824,130
Le Lycee Francais de Los Angeles, CA	$62,412	Marymount School, NY	$1,360,000
Lexington Catholic High School, KY	$325,000	Maryvale Preparatory School, MD	$247,100
Lexington Christian Academy, MA	$400,000	Massanutten Military Academy, VA	$46,000
Leysin American School in Switzerland,		The Masters School, NY	$2,336,800
Switzerland	€410,000	Matignon High School, MA	$200,000
Lick-Wilmerding High School, CA	$3,049,000	Maumee Valley Country Day School, OH	$308,150
Linden Hall School for Girls, PA	$360,000	Maur Hill-Mount Academy, KS	$100,000
The Linsly School, WV	$900,000	Mayfield Senior School, CA	$358,500
Living Word Academy, PA	$54,793	Mazapan School, Honduras	$210,204
Long Island Lutheran Middle and High School,		The McCallie School, TN	$1,800,000
NY	$170,000	McDonogh School, MD	$2,544,000
The Loomis Chaffee School, CT	$4,600,000	McGill-Toolen Catholic High School, AL	$332,450
Loretto Academy, TX	$90,000	McNicholas High School, OH	$171,500
Loretto High School, CA	$250,000	McQuaid Jesuit High School, NY	$684,000
Los Angeles Baptist Junior/Senior High School,		The Meadows School, NV	$517,260
CA	$386,950	The Meeting School, NH	$27,900
Los Angeles Lutheran High School, CA	$25,000	Memphis University School, TN	$900,000
Louisville High School, CA	$125,000	Menaul School, NM	$250,000
Lourdes Catholic High School, AZ	$2310	Menlo School, CA	$1,857,100
The Lovett School, GA	$620,700	Mentor College, ON, Canada	CAN$3002
Lower Canada College, QC, Canada	CAN$327,845	Mercersburg Academy, PA	$3,730,000
Loyola Academy, IL	$1,750,000	Mercy High School, CT	$350,275
Loyola-Blakefield, MD	$1,262,480	Mercy High School, NE	$375,000
Loyola High School, Jesuit College Preparatory,		Mercyhurst Preparatory School, PA	$159,000
CA	$900,000	Middlesex School, MA	$2,800,000
Loyola School, NY	$500,000	Midland School, CA	$603,000
Lutheran High North, TX	$200,000	Mid-Pacific Institute, HI	$644,000
Lutheran High School, CA	$10,000	Milken Community High School of Stephen	
Lutheran High School, MN	$40,000	Wise Temple, CA	$853,666
Lutheran High School North, MO	$440,135	Millbrook School, NY	$1,474,668
Lutheran High School of Hawaii, HI	$42,125	Miller School, VA	$525,000
Lutheran High School South, MO	$450,000	Miss Edgar's and Miss Cramp's School, QC,	
Lycee Français de New York, NY	$246,742	Canada	CAN$87,910
Lydia Patterson Institute, TX	$89,100	Miss Hall's School, MA	$1,620,000

Missouri Military Academy, MO	$285,720
Miss Porter's School, CT	$2,300,000
MMI Preparatory School, PA	$283,200
Montana Academy, MT	$40,000
Montclair College Preparatory School, CA	$250,000
Montclair Kimberley Academy, NJ	$2,400,000
Monte Vista Christian School, CA	$95,000
Montgomery Bell Academy, TN	$525,750
Montrose School, MA	$75,000
Montverde Academy, FL	$843,540
Moorestown Friends School, NJ	$484,320
Moravian Academy, PA	$480,950
Moreau Catholic High School, CA	$665,000
Morgan Park Academy, IL	$150,000
Morristown-Beard School, NJ	$800,000
Mother McAuley High School, IL	$333,000
Mounds Park Academy, MN	$249,040
Mountain View Christian High School, NV	$300,000
Mount Carmel High School, IL	$325,000
Mount Michael Benedictine High School, NE	$250,000
Mount Saint Charles Academy, RI	$300,000
Mount Saint Joseph Academy, PA	$309,020
Mount Saint Mary Academy, NJ	$165,000
Munich International School, Germany	€52,000
National Cathedral School, DC	$837,300
Nawa Academy, CA	$80,000
Nazareth Academy, IL	$300,000
Nebraska Christian Schools, NE	$115,000
Nerinx Hall, MO	$201,000
Neuchatel Junior College, Switzerland	10,000 Swiss francs
Newark Academy, NJ	$1,120,800
The Newgrange School, NJ	$10,000
New Hampton School, NH	$1,500,000
New Horizon Youth Ministries, IN	$252,145
The Newman School, MA	$120,000
Newton Country Day School of the Sacred Heart, MA	$1,177,245
New York Military Academy, NY	$100,000
Niagara Christian Collegiate, ON, Canada	CAN$200,000
The Nichols School, NY	$1,200,000
Noble and Greenough School, MA	$1,775,700
The Nora School, MD	$106,000
Norfolk Collegiate School, VA	$400,072
The North Broward Preparatory Upper School, FL	$805,000
North Cobb Christian School, GA	$100,025
North Country School, NY	$200,000
Northfield Mount Hermon School, MA	$5,500,000
Northside Christian School, FL	$20,000
The Northwest School, WA	$617,255
Northwest Yeshiva High School, WA	$153,680
Northwood School, NY	$960,000
North Yarmouth Academy, ME	$571,675
Notre Dame High School, CA	$600,000
Notre Dame High School, MO	$155,000
Notre Dame High School, NJ	$160,000
Notre Dame High School for Girls, IL	$990,000
Notre Dame Preparatory School, MD	$884,988
Oak Creek Ranch School, AZ	$28,000
Oak Hill Academy, VA	$335,000
Oak Knoll School of the Holy Child, NJ	$915,000
The Oakland School, PA	$51,000
Oak Mountain Academy, GA	$64,130
The Oakridge School, TX	$300,000
Oakwood Friends School, NY	$420,000
Oakwood School, CA	$789,050
The Oakwood School, NC	$91,500
O'Dea High School, WA	$260,000
Ojai Valley School, CA	$92,830
Oldfields School, MD	$1,200,000
Olney Friends School, OH	$571,450
The O'Neal School, NC	$278,920
Orangewood Adventist Academy, CA	$7000
Oregon Episcopal School, OR	$598,978
Orinda Academy, CA	$270,000
The Orme School, AZ	$695,000
Our Lady of the Sacred Heart, PA	$660,476
Our Saviour Lutheran School, NY	$30,000
Out-Of-Door-Academy, FL	$450,000
The Overlake School, WA	$389,400
Pace Academy, GA	$850,000
Pacific Hills School, CA	$1,327,190
Padua Franciscan High School, OH	$777,980
The Paideia School, GA	$642,263
The Parker School, HI	$117,000
Parklane Academy, MS	$2700
The Park School, MD	$596,615
The Park School of Buffalo, NY	$525,000
Park Tudor School, IN	$1,028,521
Peddie School, NJ	$4,500,000
The Pembroke Hill School, MO	$466,410
The Pennington School, NJ	$1,100,000
Perkiomen School, PA	$1,200,000
The Phelps School, PA	$201,500
Phillips Academy (Andover), MA	$11,321,000
Phillips Exeter Academy, NH	$8,200,000
Phoenix Christian Unified Schools, AZ	$73,000
Phoenix Country Day School, AZ	$1,272,000
Piedmont Academy, GA	$15,000
Pine Crest School, FL	$850,000
Pine Forge Academy, PA	$140,000
The Pingree School, MA	$775,000
The Pingry School, NJ	$1,159,638
Pius X High School, NE	$10,000
Polytechnic Preparatory Country Day School, NY	$3,600,000
Polytechnic School, CA	$1,039,000
Pomfret School, CT	$2,362,450
Pope John Paul II High School, FL	$370,000
Portland Christian Schools, OR	$82,000
Portland Lutheran School, OR	$19,620
Portledge School, NY	$600,000
Portsmouth Abbey School, RI	$1,900,000
Portsmouth Christian Academy, NH	$76,000
The Potomac School, VA	$630,839
Poughkeepsie Day School, NY	$302,031
The Prairie School, WI	$528,450
Prestonwood Christian Academy, TX	$217,328
Princeton Day School, NJ	$2,290,100
Proctor Academy, NH	$1,771,800
Professional Children's School, NY	$416,262
Providence Country Day School, RI	$820,000
Providence High School, CA	$192,830
Pulaski Academy, AR	$450,000

Punahou School, HI	$1,343,000
Purnell School, NJ	$405,000
The Putney School, VT	$1,205,820
Queen Anne School, MD	$200,000
Queen Margaret's School, BC, Canada	CAN$76,000
Quigley Catholic High School, PA	$279,953
Quincy Notre Dame High School, IL	$80,000
Rabbi Alexander S. Gross Hebrew Academy, FL	$300,000
Rabun Gap-Nacoochee School, GA	$2,200,000
Ramona Convent Secondary School, CA	$225,000
Randolph-Macon Academy, VA	$119,574
Randolph School, AL	$112,500
Ranney School, NJ	$17,500
Ransom Everglades School, FL	$2,050,995
Ravenscroft School, NC	$395,858
The Rectory School, CT	$677,700
Regina High School, OH	$125,000
Regis High School, OR	$53,000
Resurrection High School, IL	$90,000
Ribet Academy, CA	$100,000
Ridley College, ON, Canada	CAN$1,700,000
Rio Lindo Adventist Academy, CA	$240,000
Ripon Christian Schools, CA	$20,000
Rivermont Collegiate, IA	$309,755
Riverside School, Switzerland	300,000 Swiss francs
The Rivers School, MA	$1,346,950
Riverview School, MA	$102,500
Robert Louis Stevenson School, NY	$6000
The Rockland Country Day School, NY	$126,665
Rock Point School, VT	$150,000
Rockway Mennonite Collegiate, ON, Canada	CAN$100,000
Rocky Hill School, RI	$522,000
Rocky Mount Academy, NC	$144,960
The Roeper School, MI	$810,042
Roland Park Country School, MD	$606,475
Rolling Hills Preparatory School, CA	$650,000
Roncalli High School, IN	$450,000
Rosary High School, IL	$133,000
Rothesay Netherwood School, NB, Canada	CAN$490,000
Routt High School, IL	$26,000
Rowland Hall-St. Mark's School, UT	$549,295
The Roxbury Latin School, MA	$12,511
Roycemore School, IL	$358,000
Rumsey Hall School, CT	$650,750
Rutgers Preparatory School, NJ	$867,902
Rye Country Day School, NY	$1,218,100
Sacramento Country Day School, CA	$269,950
Sacred Heart High School, CA	$105,000
Sacred Heart School of Halifax, NS, Canada	CAN$63,150
Saddleback Valley Christian School, CA	$175,000
Saddle River Day School, NJ	$437,000
St. Agnes Academy, TX	$300,000
St. Agnes High School, MN	$514,976
St. Andrew's College, ON, Canada	CAN$858,250
St. Andrew's Episcopal School, MD	$626,510
St. Andrew's Episcopal School, MS	$176,170
St. Andrew's on the Marsh School, GA	$70,000
St. Andrew's Priory School, HI	$107,290
St. Andrew's School, DE	$3,150,000
Saint Andrew's School, FL	$1,332,000
St. Andrew's School, RI	$1,103,465

St. Andrew's–Sewanee School, TN	$1,248,000
St. Anne's–Belfield School, VA	$975,650
St. Anselm's Abbey School, DC	$500,000
Saint Augustine Preparatory School, NJ	$487,000
Saint Basil Academy, PA	$100,000
St. Benedict at Auburndale, TN	$35,000
St. Benedict's Preparatory School, NJ	$1,056,000
St. Bernard High School, CA	$200,000
St. Catherine's School, VA	$1,052,800
St. Cecilia Academy, TN	$138,150
Saint Cecilia High School, NE	$40,000
St. Christopher's School, VA	$1,423,063
St. Clement's School, ON, Canada	CAN$200,000
St. Croix Country Day School, VI	$227,700
St. David's School, NC	$430,000
Saint Dominic Academy, NJ	$100,000
St. Dominic's International School, Portugal, Portugal	€53,834
Saint Edward's School, FL	$1,486,527
Saint Elizabeth High School, CA	$380,000
Saint Francis De Sales High School, IL	$300,000
St. Francis de Sales High School, OH	$1,000,000
St. Francis School, GA	$80,000
Saint Francis School, HI	$53,000
St. George's School, RI	$2,100,000
Saint George's School, WA	$279,530
St. George's School, BC, Canada	CAN$400,000
St. George's School of Montreal, QC, Canada	CAN$175,000
St. Gregory College Preparatory School, AZ	$430,563
Saint James School, AL	$40,700
Saint James School, MD	$871,122
St. Johnsbury Academy, VT	$360,000
St. Johns Country Day School, FL	$152,635
St. John's Literary Institution at Prospect Hall, MD	$200,000
St. John's Northwestern Military Academy, WI	$404,606
St. John's Preparatory School, MA	$2,085,000
Saint John's Preparatory School, MN	$626,732
St. John's-Ravenscourt School, MB, Canada	CAN$324,500
Saint John's School, GU	$500,000
St. John's School, PR	$29,394
St. John's School, TX	$548,000
Saint John's School of Alberta, AB, Canada	CAN$130,000
St. Joseph Academy, FL	$70,000
Saint Joseph Central Catholic High School, OH	$20,000
Saint Joseph High School, WI	$48,450
St. Joseph's Academy, LA	$160,000
St. Joseph's Catholic School, SC	$100,000
Saint Joseph's High School, NJ	$85,200
St. Joseph's Preparatory School, PA	$1,300,000
Saint Laurence High School, IL	$400,000
Saint Louis Priory School, MO	$650,000
Saint Lucy's Priory High School, CA	$95,000
St. Luke's School, CT	$896,805
St. Margaret's Episcopal School, CA	$902,000
St. Margaret's School, VA	$776,700
St. Margaret's School, BC, Canada	CAN$70,000
St. Mark's High School, DE	$750,000
Saint Mark's School, MA	$2,200,000
St. Mark's School of Texas, TX	$850,245
St. Mary's Academy, CO	$346,885
St. Mary's Bundschu Memorial High School, MO	$182,000

Saint Mary's College High School, CA	$800,000	Second Baptist School, TX	$200,000
St. Mary's Episcopal School, TN	$149,153	Sedbergh School, QC, Canada	CAN$250,000
Saint Mary's Hall, TX	$577,747	Selwyn House School, QC, Canada	CAN$141,140
St. Mary's Hall–Doane Academy, NJ	$226,000	Seoul Foreign School, Republic of Korea	$60,000
Saint Mary's High School, AZ	$1,100,000	Seoul International School, Republic of Korea	$45,000
Saint Mary's High School, CO	$150,000	Seton Hall Preparatory School, NJ	$1,100,000
St. Mary's Ryken High School, MD	$450,000	The Seven Hills School, OH	$570,000
Saint Mary's School, NC	$1,000,000	Severn School, MD	$904,000
St. Mary's School, OR	$200,000	Sewickley Academy, PA	$700,000
St. Michael's Catholic Academy, TX	$60,000	Shady Side Academy, PA	$1,133,636
St. Michael's Preparatory School of the Norbertine Fathers, CA	$350,000	Shannon Forest Christian School, SC	$32,734
		Shattuck-St. Mary's School, MN	$1,300,000
St. Michaels University School, BC, Canada	CAN$620,000	The Shipley School, PA	$1,909,000
Saint Patrick High School, IL	$500,000	Shorecrest Preparatory School, FL	$256,160
St. Paul Academy and Summit School, MN	$1,624,860	Shoreline Christian, WA	$100,000
Saint Paul Lutheran High School, MO	$337,311	Sidwell Friends School, DC	$3,704,000
St. Paul's Episcopal School, AL	$326,000	Smith School, NY	$7000
St. Paul's High School, MB, Canada	CAN$140,000	Solebury School, PA	$1,134,000
St. Paul's Preparatory Academy, AZ	$125,000	Southampton Academy, VA	$85,000
St. Paul's School, MD	$638,425	South Kent School, CT	$1,370,000
St. Paul's School, NH	$5,300,000	Southwestern Academy, AZ	$316,600
St. Paul's School for Girls, MD	$575,033	Southwestern Academy, CA	$229,500
St. Peter's Preparatory School, NJ	$700,000	Spartanburg Day School, SC	$110,170
St. Pius X High School, TX	$253,024	The Spence School, NY	$987,010
St. Sebastian's School, MA	$1,401,000	Springside School, PA	$474,100
Saints Peter and Paul High School, MD	$6000	Stanbridge Academy, CA	$80,000
St. Stanislaus College, MS	$185,000	Stanstead College, QC, Canada	CAN$800,000
St. Stephen's & St. Agnes School, VA	$1,267,192	Staten Island Academy, NY	$1,000,000
Saint Stephen's Episcopal School, FL	$218,514	Stella Maris High School and the Maura Clarke Junior High Program, NY	$67,200
St. Stephen's Episcopal School, TX	$1,168,094		
St. Stephen's School, Rome, Italy	€269,000	Stevenson School, CA	$1,600,000
Saint Teresa's Academy, MO	$125,000	Stoneleigh–Burnham School, MA	$904,000
Saint Thomas Academy, MN	$1,300,000	Storm King School, NY	$400,000
St. Thomas Aquinas High School, NH	$215,000	Strake Jesuit College Preparatory, TX	$750,000
St. Thomas Choir School, NY	$187,950	Stratford Academy, GA	$205,000
St. Thomas High School, TX	$634,000	Strathcona-Tweedsmuir School, AB, Canada	CAN$50,000
Saint Thomas More School, CT	$662,000	Stratton Mountain School, VT	$425,000
St. Timothy's School, MD	$1,250,000	Stuart Country Day School of the Sacred Heart, NJ	$544,175
Saint Viator High School, IL	$650,000	Stuart Hall, VA	$800,000
Saint Xavier High School, KY	$950,000	The Study School, QC, Canada	CAN$145,000
Saint Xavier High School, OH	$1,500,000	Subiaco Academy, AR	$300,000
Salem Academy, NC	$1,098,143	Suffield Academy, CT	$1,972,930
Salesian High School, NY	$100,000	The Summit Country Day School, OH	$600,000
Salesianum School, DE	$462,000	Surabaya International School, Indonesia	$30,000
Salpointe Catholic High School, AZ	$500,000	Tabor Academy, MA	$2,894,600
Saltus Grammar School, Bermuda	350,000 Bermuda dollars	The Taft School, CT	$4,400,000
San Diego Jewish Academy, CA	$496,204	Tallulah Falls School, GA	$1,000,000
San Domenico School, CA	$1,000,000	The Tatnall School, DE	$935,000
Sandy Spring Friends School, MD	$900,000	Teurlings Catholic High School, LA	$32,513
Sanford School, DE	$586,780	The Thacher School, CA	$1,300,000
San Marcos Baptist Academy, TX	$400,000	Thomas A. Edison High School, OR	$155,000
Santa Catalina School, CA	$1,508,275	Thornton Friends School, MD	$105,035
Santa Fe Preparatory School, NM	$348,000	Thornton Friends School/N.V.A., VA	$63,490
Santiam Christian School, OR	$128,000	Tilton School, NH	$1,424,100
The Savannah Country Day School, GA	$306,807	TMI—The Episcopal School of Texas, TX	$703,457
Sayre School, KY	$250,000	Trafalgar Castle School, ON, Canada	CAN$43,000
Scattergood Friends School, IA	$360,000	Trevor Day School, NY	$2,305,279
School of the Holy Child, NY	$500,300	Tri-City Christian Schools, CA	$371,256
Scranton Preparatory School, PA	$646,300	Trident Academy, SC	$6500
Seabury Hall, HI	$499,125	Trinity Catholic High School, CT	$62,000
Seattle Christian Schools, WA	$72,601	Trinity Catholic High School, MA	$90,000

Trinity Christian Academy, TX	$250,000
Trinity Christian School, GA	$25,000
Trinity College School, ON, Canada	CAN$1,000,000
Trinity Episcopal School, VA	$660,800
Trinity High School, IL	$41,600
Trinity High School, KY	$925,000
Trinity-Pawling School, NY	$1,600,000
Trinity Preparatory School, FL	$760,180
Trinity School, NY	$1,656,360
Trinity Valley School, TX	$230,540
Tyler Street Christian Academy, TX	$120,008
United Mennonite Educational Institute, ON, Canada	CAN$4000
United Nations International School, NY	$236,872
The United World College—USA, NM	$1,600,000
University Lake School, WI	$322,395
University Liggett School, MI	$790,430
University of Chicago Laboratory Schools, IL	$465,760
University of Detroit Jesuit High School and Academy, MI	$1,100,000
University of Toronto Schools, ON, Canada	CAN$700,000
University Prep, WA	$631,254
University School, OH	$1,424,300
University School of Milwaukee, WI	$761,040
University School of Nashville, TN	$204,075
University School of Nova Southeastern University, FL	$500,000
Upper Canada College, ON, Canada	CAN$1,600,000
The Urban School of San Francisco, CA	$1,100,000
Ursuline Academy, DE	$497,000
Ursuline High School, CA	$104,000
Vail Mountain School, CO	$227,460
Valley Forge Military Academy and College, PA	$550,142
Vandebilt Catholic High School, LA	$75,000
Vanguard College Preparatory School, TX	$97,000
The Vanguard School, FL	$246,100
Vermont Academy, VT	$1,300,000
Vicksburg Catholic School, MS	$20,000
Viewpoint School, CA	$856,885
Villa Maria Academy, PA	$410,900
Villa Walsh Academy, NJ	$89,000
Virginia Episcopal School, VA	$725,000
Visitation Academy of St. Louis County, MO	$249,000
Wakefield School, VA	$83,000
The Waldorf High School of Massachusetts Bay, MA	$146,000
The Waldorf School of Garden City, NY	$140,000
The Walker School, GA	$75,000
Walnut Hill School, MA	$2,200,000
The Wardlaw-Hartridge School, NJ	$418,050
Waring School, MA	$150,000
Wasatch Academy, UT	$580,000
Washington Academy, ME	$273,762
Washington County Day School, MS	$18,000
Washington International School, DC	$556,600
Washington Waldorf School, MD	$125,000
The Waterford School, UT	$375,000
Watkinson School, CT	$766,893
The Waverly School, CA	$17,000
Wayland Academy, WI	$1,108,000
Waynflete School, ME	$639,821

Webber Academy, AB, Canada	CAN$90,000
The Webb School, TN	$900,000
Webb School of Knoxville, TN	$560,104
Wentworth Military Academy and Junior College, MO	$375,000
Wesleyan School, GA	$240,000
Westbury Christian School, TX	$48,000
West Catholic High School, MI	$330,000
Westchester Academy, NC	$59,100
Western Mennonite School, OR	$195,460
Western Reserve Academy, OH	$3,100,000
The Westfield Schools, GA	$39,500
Westgate Mennonite Collegiate, MB, Canada	CAN$36,000
Westminster Christian Academy, AL	$200,000
Westminster Christian Academy, LA	$41,395
Westminster Christian School, FL	$197,324
Westminster School, CT	$2,676,000
The Westminster Schools, GA	$1,024,591
Westminster Schools of Augusta, GA	$375,000
Westover School, CT	$1,879,500
Westpark School, MB, Canada	CAN$11,634
Westridge School, CA	$900,550
Westtown School, PA	$2,394,822
Wheaton Academy, IL	$520,000
The Wheeler School, RI	$694,435
The White Mountain School, NH	$828,600
Whitfield School, MO	$756,000
Whittier Christian High School, CA	$265,000
Wichita Collegiate School, KS	$327,347
Wilbraham & Monson Academy, MA	$1,498,433
William Penn Charter School, PA	$1,369,200
The Williams School, CT	$800,000
The Williston Northampton School, MA	$4,000,000
Wilmington Christian School, DE	$200,270
Wilmington Friends School, DE	$495,600
Wilson Hall, SC	$100,000
The Winchendon School, MA	$1,250,000
Winchester Thurston School, PA	$845,350
Windward School, CA	$720,963
The Winsor School, MA	$1,126,000
The Winston School, TX	$269,495
Wisconsin Academy, WI	$190,000
The Woodlynde School, PA	$214,660
Woodside Priory School, CA	$1,087,000
The Woodward School, MA	$61,590
Worcester Academy, MA	$2,500,000
Wyoming Seminary, PA	$4,400,000
Xavier College Preparatory, AZ	$660,000
York Country Day School, PA	$215,000
Zurich International School, Switzerland	84,800 Swiss francs

SCHOOLS REPORTING THAT THEY OFFER ENGLISH AS A SECOND LANGUAGE

Academia Cotopaxi, Ecuador
Academie Sainte Cecile International School, ON, Canada
Academy of the Sacred Heart, LA
ACS Cobham International School, United Kingdom
ACS Egham International School, United Kingdom
ACS Hillingdon International School, United Kingdom
Admiral Farragut Academy, FL

Ahliyyah School for Girls, Jordan
Albert College, ON, Canada
Allen Academy, TX
Alliance Academy, Ecuador
Allison Academy, FL
All Saints' Episcopal School, MS
Ambassador Preparatory, MN
American Academy, FL
American Community Schools of Athens, Greece
American Cooperative School, Bolivia
American Heritage School, FL
The American International School, Austria
American International School in Cyprus, Cyprus
American International School of Bucharest, Romania
American International School-Riyadh, Saudi Arabia
American International School Salzburg, Austria
American Overseas School of Rome, Italy
The American School Foundation, Mexico
The American School in London, United Kingdom
American School of Doha, Qatar
The American School of Madrid, Spain
American School of Milan, Italy
The American School of Puerto Vallarta, Mexico
The American School of The Hague, Netherlands
American School of Warsaw, Poland
The Andrews School, OH
Anglo-American School of Moscow, Russian Federation
Annie Wright School, WA
Army and Navy Academy, CA
Arrowhead Christian Academy, CA
Ashbury College, ON, Canada
The Athenian School, CA
Atlanta International School, GA
The Awty International School, TX
Baldwin School of Puerto Rico, Inc., PR
Balmoral Hall School, MB, Canada
Barnstable Academy, NJ
Baylor School, TN
The Beekman School, NY
Beijing BISS International School, China
Bellevue Christian School, WA
The Bement School, MA
Berkshire School, MA
The Bethany Hills School, ON, Canada
Bishop's College School, QC, Canada
The Bishop Strachan School, ON, Canada
Black Forest Academy, Germany
The Blue Ridge School, VA
The Bolles School, FL
Brandon Hall School, GA
Brent School-Baguio, Philippines
Brewster Academy, NH
British Columbia Christian Academy, BC, Canada
The British International School, Jeddah, Saudi Arabia
The British School, Muscat, Oman
Broadview Academy, IL
The Brook Hill School, TX
Burr and Burton Academy, VT
Buxton School, MA
Cambridge International College of Canada, ON, Canada
The Cambridge School of Weston, MA

Campion School, Athens, Greece
Canadian Academy, Japan
Canterbury School, CT
Canyonville Christian Academy, OR
Cape Henry Collegiate School, VA
Cardigan Mountain School, NH
Carlucci American International School of Lisbon, Portugal
Carrabassett Valley Academy, ME
Cascadilla School, NY
Catholic Central High School, NY
Chaminade College Preparatory School, MO
Chapel Hill–Chauncy Hall School, MA
Chapel School, Brazil
Charlotte Country Day School, NC
Chatham Hall, VA
Cheshire Academy, CT
Chinese Christian Schools, CA
Christ Church Episcopal School, SC
Christchurch School, VA
Christian Junior–Senior High School, CA
Christ School, NC
Colegio Bolivar, Colombia
Colegio Franklin D. Roosevelt, Peru
Colegio Nueva Granada, Colombia
Colegio Puertorriqueno de Ninas, PR
College du Leman International School, Switzerland
The Colorado Rocky Mountain School, CO
Columbia International College of Canada, ON, Canada
Columbia International School, Japan
Conserve School, WI
Covenant Canadian Reformed School, AB, Canada
Cranbrook Schools, MI
The Culver Academies, IN
Cushing Academy, MA
Danube International School, Vienna, Austria
Darlington School, GA
Darrow School, NY
Delaware County Christian School, PA
The Delphian School, OR
Dublin School, NH
The Dwight School, NY
Eaglebrook School, MA
Eastern Christian High School, NJ
Eckerd Youth Alternatives, FL
Ecole d'Humanite, Switzerland
Emerson Honors High Schools, CA
Emma Willard School, NY
Equilibrium International Education Institute, AB, Canada
Escola Americana de Campinas, Brazil
Fay School, MA
The Fessenden School, MA
Fishburne Military School, VA
Florida Air Academy, FL
The Forman School, CT
Forsyth Country Day School, NC
Fountain Valley School of Colorado, CO
Fowlers Academy, PR
Fox River Country Day School, IL
French-American School of New York, NY
Fryeburg Academy, ME
Garden School, NY

Garrison Forest School, MD
George School, PA
George Stevens Academy, ME
Georgetown Preparatory School, MD
Gilmour Academy, OH
The Glenholme School, CT
Gould Academy, ME
Governor Dummer Academy, MA
The Governor French Academy, IL
The Grand River Academy, OH
The Grauer School, CA
Greater Atlanta Christian Schools, GA
Great Lakes Christian College, ON, Canada
Greensboro Day School, NC
Grenville Christian College, ON, Canada
The Grier School, PA
Gstaad International School, Switzerland
Guerin College Preparatory High School, IL
The Gunnery, CT
Gunston Day School, MD
Hackley School, NY
Hamilton District Christian School, ON, Canada
Hamilton Learning Centre, ON, Canada
Happy Valley School, CA
Harare International School, Zimbabwe
Hargrave Military Academy, VA
Harrow School, United Kingdom
Hawaiian Mission Academy, HI
Hawai'i Preparatory Academy, HI
Hebron Academy, ME
High Mowing School, NH
Hillfield Strathallan College, ON, Canada
Hillside School, MA
The Hockaday School, TX
Hokkaido International School, Japan
Hoosac School, NY
Horizons School, GA
Houghton Academy, NY
Hudson College, ON, Canada
The Hudson School, NJ
The Hun School of Princeton, NJ
Hvitfeldtska Gymnasiet, International Section, Sweden
Idyllwild Arts Academy, CA
Imperial College of Toronto, ON, Canada
Indian Mountain School, CT
Interlochen Arts Academy, MI
International College Spain, Spain
International Community School of Addis Ababa, Ethiopia
International High School of FAIS, CA
International Junior Golf Academy, SC
International School Bangkok, Thailand
International School Basel, Switzerland
International School Hamburg, Germany
International School of Amsterdam, Netherlands
International School of Aruba, Aruba
International School of Athens, Greece
International School of Berne, Switzerland
International School of Brussels, Belgium
The International School of Geneva, Switzerland
The International School of Kuala Lumpur, Malaysia
International School of Lausanne, Switzerland

International School of Luxembourg, Luxembourg
International School of Minnesota, MN
The International School of Monaco, Monaco
Iolani School, HI
Islamic Saudi Academy, VA
Istanbul International Community School, Turkey
Jakarta International School, Indonesia
John F. Kennedy Memorial High School, WA
Karachi American School, Pakistan
Kent School, CT
Kents Hill School, ME
Key School, Inc., TX
The King's Academy, TN
Kingsway College, ON, Canada
The Kiski School, PA
The Knox School, NY
Lake Forest Academy, IL
La Lumiere School, IN
Lawrence Academy, MA
Lawrence Woodmere Academy, NY
The Leelanau School, MI
Le Lycee Francais de Los Angeles, CA
Leysin American School in Switzerland, Switzerland
Linden Hall School for Girls, PA
Linden Hill School, MA
Los Angeles Lutheran High School, CA
Lourdes Catholic High School, AZ
Luther College High School, SK, Canada
Lycee Français de New York, NY
Lycee International de Los Angeles, CA
Lydia Patterson Institute, TX
Lyndon Institute, VT
The MacDuffie School, MA
Maine Central Institute, ME
Malaspina International High School, BC, Canada
Manlius Pebble Hill School, NY
Marianapolis Preparatory School, CT
The Marvelwood School, CT
Mary Help of Christians Academy, NJ
Marymount International School, Italy
Marymount International School, United Kingdom
Massanutten Military Academy, VA
The Masters School, NY
Maumee Valley Country Day School, OH
Maur Hill-Mount Academy, KS
Mentor College, ON, Canada
Mercedes College, Australia
Miami Country Day School, FL
Mid-Pacific Institute, HI
Miller School, VA
Miss Hall's School, MA
Mississauga Private School, ON, Canada
Missouri Military Academy, MO
Miss Porter's School, CT
Montclair College Preparatory School, CA
Monte Vista Christian School, CA
Mont'Kiara International School, Malaysia
Montverde Academy, FL
Munich International School, Germany
Nacel International School, MN
Nawa Academy, CA

Nebraska Christian Schools, NE
New Hampton School, NH
The Newman School, MA
New York Military Academy, NY
Niagara Christian Collegiate, ON, Canada
North Country School, NY
Northfield Mount Hermon School, MA
The Northwest School, WA
Northwest Yeshiva High School, WA
Northwood School, NY
The Norwich Free Academy, CT
Oak Creek Ranch School, AZ
The Oakland School, PA
Oak Ridge Military Academy, NC
Oakwood Friends School, NY
Ojai Valley School, CA
Olney Friends School, OH
Oneida Baptist Institute, KY
Oregon Episcopal School, OR
Orinda Academy, CA
The Orme School, AZ
Overseas Family School, Singapore
The Oxford Academy, CT
Oxford School, CA
Palmer Trinity School, FL
The Park School of Buffalo, NY
The Pennington School, NJ
Perkiomen School, PA
The Phelps School, PA
Phoenix Christian Unified Schools, AZ
Pickering College, ON, Canada
Portland Christian Schools, OR
Portland Lutheran School, OR
The Prairie School, WI
Professional Children's School, NY
Purnell School, NJ
The Putney School, VT
Queen Margaret's School, BC, Canada
Queensway Christian College, ON, Canada
Rabbi Alexander S. Gross Hebrew Academy, FL
Rabun Gap-Nacoochee School, GA
Randolph-Macon Academy, VA
The Rectory School, CT
Ribet Academy, CA
Ridley College, ON, Canada
Rio Lindo Adventist Academy, CA
Riverside Military Academy, GA
Riverside School, Switzerland
Riverstone Community School, ID
Rocklyn Academy, ON, Canada
Rockway Mennonite Collegiate, ON, Canada
Rocky Hill School, RI
Rolling Hills Preparatory School, CA
Rothesay Netherwood School, NB, Canada
Rotterdam International Secondary School, Wolfert van Borselen, Netherlands
Royal Canadian College, BC, Canada
Rumsey Hall School, CT
Saddleback Valley Christian School, CA
St. Andrew's College, ON, Canada
St. Andrew's Priory School, HI

Saint Andrew's School, FL
St. Andrew's School, RI
St. Andrew's–Sewanee School, TN
St. Anne's–Belfield School, VA
St. Benedict's Preparatory School, NJ
St. Catherine's Military Academy, CA
Saint Cecilia High School, NE
St. Croix Lutheran High School, MN
St. Dominic's International School, Portugal, Portugal
Saint Francis School, HI
St. George's School in Switzerland, Switzerland
St. George's School of Montreal, QC, Canada
St. Johnsbury Academy, VT
St. John's-Kilmarnock School, ON, Canada
St. John's Northwestern Military Academy, WI
Saint John's Preparatory School, MN
St. John's-Ravenscourt School, MB, Canada
Saint John's School, GU
Saint John's School of Alberta, AB, Canada
St. Leonards, United Kingdom
St. Margaret's School, VA
St. Margaret's School, BC, Canada
Saint Mary's Hall, TX
St. Mary's International School, Japan
St. Mary's Preparatory School, MI
St. Mary's Ryken High School, MD
St. Maur International School, Japan
St. Michaels University School, BC, Canada
Saint Patrick High School, IL
St. Stanislaus College, MS
St. Stephen's Episcopal School, TX
St. Stephen's School, Rome, Italy
Saint Thomas More School, CT
St. Timothy's School, MD
Salem Academy, NC
Salem Academy, OR
San Domenico School, CA
Sandy Spring Friends School, MD
San Marcos Baptist Academy, TX
Scarborough Christian School, ON, Canada
Scattergood Friends School, IA
Schule Schloss Salem, Germany
Sedbergh School, QC, Canada
Seisen International School, Japan
Seoul Foreign School, Republic of Korea
Seoul International School, Republic of Korea
Shattuck-St. Mary's School, MN
SICES International Academy, AB, Canada
Solebury School, PA
South Kent School, CT
Southwestern Academy, AZ
Southwestern Academy, CA
Spartanburg Day School, SC
Squaw Valley Academy, CA
Stanstead College, QC, Canada
Staten Island Academy, NY
Stoneleigh–Burnham School, MA
The Stony Brook School, NY
Storm King School, NY
Stratton Mountain School, VT
Stuart Hall, VA

Subiaco Academy, AR
Suffield Academy, CT
Surabaya International School, Indonesia
Tabor Academy, MA
Taipei American School, Taiwan
Tallulah Falls School, GA
TASIS The American School in England, United Kingdom
TASIS, The American School in Switzerland, Switzerland
Thomas Jefferson School, MO
Tilton School, NH
Toronto District Christian High School, ON, Canada
Toronto Waldorf School, ON, Canada
Town Centre Montessori School, ON, Canada
Trafalgar Castle School, ON, Canada
Trinity College School, ON, Canada
Trinity-Pawling School, NY
United Nations International School, NY
The United World College—USA, NM
University School of Nashville, TN
Vail Mountain School, CO
Valley Forge Military Academy and College, PA
Vermont Academy, VT
Walnut Hill School, MA
The Wardlaw-Hartridge School, NJ
Wasatch Academy, UT
Washington Academy, ME
Washington International School, DC
Wayland Academy, WI
The Webb School, TN
Wentworth Military Academy and Junior College, MO
Westgate Mennonite Collegiate, MB, Canada
Westhill Institute, Mexico
West Nottingham Academy, MD
Westover School, CT
Westtown School, PA
The White Mountain School, NH
Whittier Christian High School, CA
Wilbraham & Monson Academy, MA
The Williston Northampton School, MA
The Winchendon School, MA
Windermere St. Anne's School, United Kingdom
Windhoek International School, Namibia
The Windsor School, NY
The Woodhall School, CT
Woodlands Academy of the Sacred Heart, IL
Woodside International School, CA
Woodside Park International School, United Kingdom
Woodstock School, India
Wooster School, CT
Worcester Academy, MA
Wyoming Seminary, PA
Zurich International School, Switzerland

SCHOOLS REPORTING A COMMUNITY SERVICE REQUIREMENT

Academia Cotopaxi, Ecuador
Academy at Swift River, MA
The Academy for Gifted Children (PACE), ON, Canada
Academy of Mount Saint Ursula, NY
Academy of Our Lady of Mercy, CT

Academy of Our Lady of Peace, CA
Academy of the Holy Angels, NJ
Academy of the Sacred Heart, LA
Academy of the Sacred Heart, MI
Admiral Farragut Academy, FL
The Agnes Irwin School, PA
Airdrie Koinonia Christian School, AB, Canada
Akiba Hebrew Academy, PA
The Albany Academy, NY
Allison Academy, FL
All Saints' Episcopal School of Fort Worth, TX
American Academy, FL
American Heritage School, FL
American International School in Cyprus, Cyprus
American International School of Bucharest, Romania
The American School Foundation, Mexico
American School of Doha, Qatar
The Andrews School, OH
Anglo-American School of Moscow, Russian Federation
Archbishop Curley High School, MD
Archbishop Riordan High School, CA
Armona Union Academy, CA
Arrowhead Christian Academy, CA
Ashbury College, ON, Canada
Assumption High School, KY
The Athenian School, CA
Atlanta International School, GA
Aurora Central High School, IL
The Awty International School, TX
Bancroft School, MA
The Barstow School, MO
Beaumont School, OH
Beaver Country Day School, MA
Belen Jesuit Preparatory School, FL
Bellevue Christian School, WA
The Bement School, MA
The Benjamin School, FL
Berkeley Carroll School, NY
Berkeley Preparatory School, FL
Berkshire School, MA
The Bethany Hills School, ON, Canada
The Birch Wathen Lenox School, NY
Bishop Brady High School, NH
Bishop Carroll High School, PA
Bishop Eustace Preparatory School, NJ
Bishop Guertin High School, NH
Bishop Ireton High School, VA
Bishop Kelly High School, ID
Bishop Lynch Catholic High School, TX
The Bishop Strachan School, ON, Canada
Bismark St. Mary's Central, ND
Black Forest Academy, Germany
Boston University Academy, MA
The Boys' Latin School of Maryland, MD
Breck School, MN
Brentwood School, CA
The Brook Hill School, TX
Brooklyn Friends School, NY
Brophy College Preparatory, AZ
The Browning School, NY
Brunswick School, CT

The Bryn Mawr School for Girls, MD
Buckingham Browne & Nichols School, MA
The Buckley School, CA
Burr and Burton Academy, VT
The Bush School, WA
The Calhoun School, NY
The Cambridge School of Weston, MA
Campbell Hall (Episcopal), CA
Cannon School, NC
Canterbury High School, IN
Canterbury School, FL
The Canterbury School of Florida, FL
Cape Cod Academy, MA
Cape Fear Academy, NC
Cape Henry Collegiate School, VA
Cardinal Newman High School, FL
Cardinal Newman School, SC
Carlucci American International School of Lisbon, Portugal
Carolina Day School, NC
Carrollton School of the Sacred Heart, FL
Cascadilla School, NY
Cascia Hall Preparatory School, OK
The Catholic High School of Baltimore, MD
The Catlin Gabel School, OR
CCI The Renaissance School, Italy
Central Catholic High School, CA
CFS, The School at Church Farm, PA
Chaminade College Preparatory, CA
Chaminade College Preparatory School, MO
Chaminade-Madonna College Preparatory, FL
Chapel Hill–Chauncy Hall School, MA
Charles Wright Academy, WA
Charlotte Country Day School, NC
Chattanooga Christian School, TN
Cheshire Academy, CT
Chestnut Hill Academy, PA
Cheverus High School, ME
Choate Rosemary Hall, CT
Christian Brothers Academy, NY
Christian Brothers High School, CA
Christian Central Academy, NY
Cincinnati Country Day School, OH
Colegio San Jose, PR
The Collegiate School, VA
The Colorado Rocky Mountain School, CO
The Colorado Springs School, CO
Columbia Grammar and Preparatory School, NY
Commonwealth School, MA
The Community School of Naples, FL
Connelly School of the Holy Child, MD
Convent of the Sacred Heart, CT
Convent of the Sacred Heart High School, CA
Cornelia Connelly School, CA
Country Day School of the Sacred Heart, PA
The Craig School, NJ
Crespi Carmelite High School, CA
Crossroads School for Arts & Sciences, CA
The Culver Academies, IN
Dallas Academy, TX
The Dalton School, NY
Dana Hall School, MA

Delaware Valley Friends School, PA
Devon Preparatory School, PA
Doane Stuart School, NY
Duchesne Academy of the Sacred Heart, NE
Duchesne Academy of the Sacred Heart, TX
Durham Academy, NC
Dwight-Englewood School, NJ
The Dwight School, NY
Eaglebrook School, MA
Eagle Hill School, MA
Eastern Christian High School, NJ
Eckerd Youth Alternatives, FL
Ecole d'Humanite, Switzerland
Elizabeth Seton High School, MD
Elyria Catholic High School, OH
Emerson Honors High Schools, CA
The Emery Weiner School, TX
Emma Willard School, NY
Episcopal High School of Jacksonville, FL
The Episcopal School of Dallas, TX
Escola Americana de Campinas, Brazil
The Ethel Walker School, CT
The Ethical Culture Fieldston School, NY
Explorations Academy, WA
Father Lopez High School, FL
First Baptist Academy, TX
F. L. Chamberlain School, MA
Flint Hill School, VA
Fontbonne Academy, MA
Forsyth Country Day School, NC
Fort Worth Country Day School, TX
Francis Parker School, CA
Francis W. Parker School, IL
Franklin Road Academy, TN
Fresno Christian Schools, CA
Friends Academy, NY
Friends School of Baltimore, MD
Friends Seminary, NY
Fryeburg Academy, ME
Fuqua School, VA
Futures High School—San Diego, CA
Garces Memorial High School, CA
Gaston Day School, NC
Gateway School, TX
George School, PA
Georgetown Day School, DC
Georgetown Preparatory School, MD
Gilmour Academy, OH
Girard College, PA
Glenelg Country School, MD
Gonzaga Preparatory School, WA
Governor Dummer Academy, MA
The Gow School, NY
The Grand River Academy, OH
The Grauer School, CA
Greenfield School, NC
Greenhill School, TX
Greenhills School, MI
Greenwich Academy, CT
Grenville Christian College, ON, Canada
Guamani Private School, PR

Gulliver Preparatory School, FL
Gunston Day School, MD
Hales Franciscan High School, IL
Hamilton District Christian School, ON, Canada
Harare International School, Zimbabwe
The Harker School, CA
The Harley School, NY
Harrells Christian Academy, NC
The Harrisburg Academy, PA
Harvard-Westlake School, CA
Havergal College, ON, Canada
Hawaiian Mission Academy, HI
Hawken School, OH
Head-Royce School, CA
The Hewitt School, NY
Highland Hall, A Waldorf School, CA
Highland School, VA
High Mowing School, NH
Hilton Head Preparatory School, SC
Holderness School, NH
Holland Hall, OK
The Holton-Arms School, MD
Holyoke Catholic High School, MA
The Horace Mann School, NY
Horizons School, GA
The Hudson School, NJ
The Hun School of Princeton, NJ
Hutchison School, TN
Immaculata Academy, NY
Immaculate Conception High School, NJ
Incarnate Word Academy, TX
International College Spain, Spain
International High School of FAIS, CA
International School Bangkok, Thailand
International School of Amsterdam, Netherlands
International School of Aruba, Aruba
International School of Athens, Greece
International School of Lausanne, Switzerland
International School of Luxembourg, Luxembourg
Iona Preparatory School, NY
Jesuit College Preparatory School, TX
Jesuit High School, CA
Jesuit High School of New Orleans, LA
Jesuit High School of Tampa, FL
Josephinum High School, IL
Justin-Siena High School, CA
Karachi American School, Pakistan
Kearney Catholic High School, NE
Keith Country Day School, IL
Kent Denver School, CO
Keystone School, TX
Kimberton Waldorf School, PA
Kings Christian School, CA
Kingswood-Oxford School, CT
Laguna Blanca School, CA
La Jolla Country Day School, CA
Lakefield College School, ON, Canada
Lake Forest Academy, IL
Lakeside School, WA
La Lumiere School, IN
La Salle Academy, RI

The Latin School of Chicago, IL
Laurel School, OH
The Lawrenceville School, NJ
Lawrence Woodmere Academy, NY
Lexington Christian Academy, MA
Linden Hall School for Girls, PA
Linfield Christian School, CA
Little Red School House and Elisabeth Irwin High School, NY
Loretto High School, CA
Louisville High School, CA
Lower Canada College, QC, Canada
Loyola High School, Jesuit College Preparatory, CA
Lutheran High School, CA
Lutheran High School North, MO
Manhattan Christian High School, MT
Maret School, DC
Marianapolis Preparatory School, CT
Marin Academy, CA
Marist School, GA
Marmion Academy, IL
Marquette University High School, WI
Marshall School, MN
Mars Hill Bible School, AL
The Marvelwood School, CT
Mary Institute and St. Louis Country Day School (MICDS), MO
Maryknoll School, HI
Marylawn of the Oranges, NJ
Marymount High School, CA
Marymount School, NY
Maryvale Preparatory School, MD
Matignon High School, MA
Maumee Valley Country Day School, OH
Mayfield Senior School, CA
McDonogh School, MD
McQuaid Jesuit High School, NY
The Meadows School, NV
Menaul School, NM
Menlo School, CA
Mercy High School, CT
Mercy High School College Preparatory, CA
Mercyhurst Preparatory School, PA
Miami Country Day School, FL
Mid-Peninsula High School, CA
Milken Community High School of Stephen Wise Temple, CA
Miller School, VA
Miss Hall's School, MA
Missouri Military Academy, MO
Miss Porter's School, CT
Moorestown Friends School, NJ
Moreau Catholic High School, CA
Morristown-Beard School, NJ
Mounds Park Academy, MN
Mount Carmel High School, IL
Mount Michael Benedictine High School, NE
Mt. Saint Dominic Academy, NJ
Mount Saint Mary Academy, NJ
Munich International School, Germany
National Cathedral School, DC

National Sports Academy at Lake Placid, NY
Nawa Academy, CA
Nazareth Academy, IL
New Hampton School, NH
Newton Country Day School of the Sacred Heart, MA
New York Military Academy, NY
Noble and Greenough School, MA
The Nora School, MD
Norfolk Academy, VA
The North Broward Preparatory Upper School, FL
The North Shore Country Day School, IL
Northside Christian School, FL
Northwest Community Christian School, AZ
Northwest Yeshiva High School, WA
Notre Dame Academy, MA
Notre Dame High School, CA
Notre Dame High School, MO
Notre Dame High School, NJ
Notre Dame Preparatory School, MD
The Oakland School, PA
Oak Mountain Academy, GA
Oak Ridge Military Academy, NC
The Oakridge School, TX
Oakwood Friends School, NY
Oakwood School, CA
O'Dea High School, WA
Oldenburg Academy, IN
Olney Friends School, OH
The O'Neal School, NC
Orinda Academy, CA
The Orme School, AZ
Out-Of-Door-Academy, FL
The Overlake School, WA
The Oxford Academy, CT
Pace Academy, GA
Pacific Hills School, CA
The Paideia School, GA
Palma High School, CA
Palmer Trinity School, FL
The Park School of Buffalo, NY
Peddie School, NJ
The Pembroke Hill School, MO
Perkiomen School, PA
Pickering College, ON, Canada
The Pingree School, MA
The Pingry School, NJ
Polytechnic Preparatory Country Day School, NY
Pope John Paul II High School, FL
Portland Christian Schools, OR
Portland Lutheran School, OR
Portledge School, NY
Poughkeepsie Day School, NY
The Prairie School, WI
Princeton Day School, NJ
Pulaski Academy, AR
Queen Margaret's School, BC, Canada
Rabbi Alexander S. Gross Hebrew Academy, FL
Ravenscroft School, NC
Ribet Academy, CA
Rio Lindo Adventist Academy, CA
Riverdale Country School, NY

The Rivers School, MA
The Rockland Country Day School, NY
Rocky Hill School, RI
Rocky Mount Academy, NC
Roland Park Country School, MD
Rosary High School, IL
Routt High School, IL
Rutgers Preparatory School, NJ
Sacramento Country Day School, CA
Sacred Heart Academy, CT
Sacred Heart High School, CA
Sacred Heart Preparatory, CA
Sacred Heart School of Halifax, NS, Canada
St. Agnes Academy, TX
St. Andrew's College, ON, Canada
St. Andrew's Episcopal School, MD
St. Andrew's Episcopal School, MS
St. Andrew's on the Marsh School, GA
St. Andrew's Priory School, HI
Saint Andrew's School, FL
St. Andrew's School, RI
St. Andrew's–Sewanee School, TN
St. Anne's–Belfield School, VA
St. Anselm's Abbey School, DC
Saint Basil Academy, PA
St. Bernard High School, CA
St. Christopher's School, VA
St. Croix Country Day School, VI
St. David's School, NC
Saint Dominic Academy, NJ
Saint Edward's School, FL
Saint Elizabeth High School, CA
St. Francis de Sales High School, OH
Saint Francis School, HI
St. George's School of Montreal, QC, Canada
Saint Gertrude High School, VA
St. Gregory College Preparatory School, AZ
Saint James School, AL
Saint James School, MD
St. John's College High School, DC
St. John's Northwestern Military Academy, WI
Saint John's School of Alberta, AB, Canada
St. Joseph High School, CT
St. Joseph's Catholic School, SC
Saint Joseph's High School, NJ
St. Luke's School, CT
St. Margaret's Episcopal School, CA
St. Margaret's School, VA
St. Mark's School of Texas, TX
St. Mary's Academy, CO
Saint Mary's High School, AZ
St. Mary's International School, Japan
St. Mary's School, OR
Saint Patrick High School, IL
Saint Patrick's School, KY
Saint Paul Lutheran High School, MO
St. Paul's Episcopal School, AL
St. Paul's Preparatory Academy, AZ
St. Paul's School, MD
St. Paul's School, NH
St. Paul's School for Girls, MD

St. Peter's Preparatory School, NJ
St. Stephen's & St. Agnes School, VA
Saint Stephen's Episcopal School, FL
St. Stephen's Episcopal School, TX
Saint Teresa's Academy, MO
St. Thomas Aquinas High School, NH
St. Timothy's School, MD
Salesian High School, NY
Salesianum School, DE
Salisbury School, CT
San Domenico School, CA
Sandy Spring Friends School, MD
Santa Fe Preparatory School, NM
Sayre School, KY
Scattergood Friends School, IA
School of the Holy Child, NY
Schule Schloss Salem, Germany
Scranton Preparatory School, PA
Seabury Hall, HI
Seattle Academy of Arts and Sciences, WA
Seton Hall Preparatory School, NJ
The Seven Hills School, OH
Severn School, MD
Sewickley Academy, PA
Shannon Forest Christian School, SC
Shattuck-St. Mary's School, MN
The Shipley School, PA
Sidwell Friends School, DC
Solebury School, PA
Southwestern Academy, AZ
Southwestern Academy, CA
Springside School, PA
Staten Island Academy, NY
Storm King School, NY
Strake Jesuit College Preparatory, TX
Stratford Academy, GA
Stratton Mountain School, VT
Stuart Country Day School of the Sacred Heart, NJ
The Study School, QC, Canada
Subiaco Academy, AR
Sumiton Christian School, AL
TASIS The American School in England, United Kingdom
The Tatnall School, DE
Thomas A. Edison High School, OR
Thomas Jefferson School, MO
Thornton Friends School, MD
Thornton Friends School/N.V.A., VA
Tilton School, NH
Tower Hill School, DE
Trevor Day School, NY
Tri-City Christian Schools, CA
Trinity Catholic High School, CT
Trinity Catholic High School, MA
Trinity Christian Academy, TX
Trinity Episcopal School, VA
Trinity High School, KY
Trinity Valley School, TX
United Nations International School, NY
The United World College—USA, NM
University Liggett School, MI
University of Chicago Laboratory Schools, IL

University of Toronto Schools, ON, Canada
University Prep, WA
University School of Milwaukee, WI
University School of Nova Southeastern University, FL
Upper Canada College, ON, Canada
The Urban School of San Francisco, CA
Vianney High School, MO
Viewpoint School, CA
Villa Maria Academy, PA
Villa Victoria Academy, NJ
Virginia Beach Friends School, VA
The Waldorf High School of Massachusetts Bay, MA
Wasatch Academy, UT
Washington International School, DC
The Waverly School, CA
Wayland Academy, WI
Wayne Country Day School, NC
Waynflete School, ME
The Wellington School, OH
Wellsprings Friends School, OR
Wentworth Military Academy and Junior College, MO
Westbury Christian School, TX
Westchester Academy, NC
Westhill Institute, Mexico
Westminster Christian School, FL
Westover School, CT
Westridge School, CA
Westview School, CA
Whitefield Academy, GA
The White Mountain School, NH
Whittier Christian High School, CA
Wilmington Christian School, DE
Wilmington Friends School, DE
Wilson Hall, SC
Winston Preparatory School, NY
The Winston School San Antonio, TX
Woodberry Forest School, VA
Woodlands Academy of the Sacred Heart, IL
Woodside International School, CA
Woodside Priory School, CA
Woodstock School, India
The Woodward School, MA
Wooster School, CT
Worcester Academy, MA
Wyoming Seminary, PA
Xavier College Preparatory, AZ
Yokohama International School, Japan
York Country Day School, PA
York Preparatory School, NY
Zurich International School, Switzerland

SCHOOLS REPORTING EXCHANGE PROGRAMS WITH OTHER U.S. SCHOOLS

Academy of the Sacred Heart, LA
Academy of the Sacred Heart, MI
Ahliyyah School for Girls, Jordan
Albuquerque Academy, NM
Appleby College, ON, Canada
The Athenian School, CA
Bishop's College School, QC, Canada

Brooklyn Friends School, NY
The Bush School, WA
The Calhoun School, NY
Caribbean Preparatory School, PR
Carrollton School of the Sacred Heart, FL
The Catlin Gabel School, OR
Convent of the Sacred Heart, CT
Convent of the Sacred Heart, NY
Convent of the Sacred Heart High School, CA
Country Day School of the Sacred Heart, PA
Doane Stuart School, NY
Dublin School, NH
Duchesne Academy of the Sacred Heart, NE
Duchesne Academy of the Sacred Heart, TX
Friends Seminary, NY
Gateway School, TX
Germantown Friends School, PA
Havergal College, ON, Canada
Marin Academy, CA
Maumee Valley Country Day School, OH
Navajo Preparatory School, Inc., NM
Newton Country Day School of the Sacred Heart, MA
Oxford School, CA
Princeton Day School, NJ
Queensway Christian College, ON, Canada
Ridley College, ON, Canada
Sacred Heart Preparatory, CA
Sacred Heart School of Halifax, NS, Canada
St. Benedict's Preparatory School, NJ
St. Paul's School for Girls, MD
St. Stephen's School, Rome, Italy
Salesianum School, DE
School of the Holy Child, NY
Schule Schloss Salem, Germany
The Shipley School, PA
Stevenson School, CA
The Study School, QC, Canada
Trafalgar Castle School, ON, Canada
The Urban School of San Francisco, CA
Windermere St. Anne's School, United Kingdom
Woodlands Academy of the Sacred Heart, IL

SCHOOLS REPORTING PROGRAMS FOR STUDY ABROAD

The Academy at Charlemont, MA
Academy at Swift River, MA
The Academy for Global Exploration, OR
Academy of Holy Angels, MN
The Academy of St. Joseph, NY
Academy of the Sacred Heart, LA
Advanced Academy of Georgia, GA
Akiba Hebrew Academy, PA
Albuquerque Academy, NM
Alexander Dawson School, CO
The Altamont School, AL
Annie Wright School, WA
Appleby College, ON, Canada
Archmere Academy, DE
Argo Academy, FL
Asheville School, NC

The Athenian School, CA
Aurora Central High School, IL
Avon Old Farms School, CT
Bancroft School, MA
Beaufort Academy, SC
Belmont Hill School, MA
Bentley School, CA
Berkeley Carroll School, NY
Berkeley Preparatory School, FL
Berkshire School, MA
Berwick Academy, ME
The Birch Wathen Lenox School, NY
Bishop Guertin High School, NH
Bishop's College School, QC, Canada
The Bishop Strachan School, ON, Canada
Blair Academy, NJ
The Blake School, MN
Boston University Academy, MA
The Brearley School, NY
Brenau Academy, GA
Brooklyn Friends School, NY
Brooks School, MA
Brophy College Preparatory, AZ
The Bryn Mawr School for Girls, MD
Buckingham Browne & Nichols School, MA
The Buckley School, CA
Burke Mountain Academy, VT
Burr and Burton Academy, VT
The Bush School, WA
The Cambridge School of Weston, MA
Campbell Hall (Episcopal), CA
Canterbury High School, IN
Canterbury School, FL
The Canterbury School of Florida, FL
Cape Cod Academy, MA
Cape Fear Academy, NC
Carrollton School of the Sacred Heart, FL
Casady School, OK
Cascia Hall Preparatory School, OK
Cate School, CA
The Catlin Gabel School, OR
CCI The Renaissance School, Italy
Chadwick School, CA
The Chapin School, NY
Charlotte Country Day School, NC
Charlotte Latin School, NC
Chatham Hall, VA
Chestnut Hill Academy, PA
Choate Rosemary Hall, CT
Christ Church Episcopal School, SC
Christian Brothers Academy, NJ
Cincinnati Country Day School, OH
The Colorado Springs School, CO
Colorado Timberline Academy, CO
Columbia International School, Japan
The Columbus Academy, OH
The Community School of Naples, FL
Concord Academy, MA
Convent of the Sacred Heart, CT
Convent of the Sacred Heart, NY
Country Day School of the Sacred Heart, PA

Cranbrook Schools, MI
Crossroads School, MO
Deerfield Academy, MA
Delaware County Christian School, PA
Doane Stuart School, NY
Duchesne Academy of the Sacred Heart, NE
Dwight-Englewood School, NJ
The Dwight School, NY
Emma Willard School, NY
The Episcopal Academy, PA
Episcopal High School, VA
Episcopal High School of Jacksonville, FL
Escola Americana de Campinas, Brazil
The Ethel Walker School, CT
Falmouth Academy, MA
Fort Worth Country Day School, TX
Foxcroft School, VA
Francis Parker School, CA
Friends School of Baltimore, MD
Friends Seminary, NY
Georgetown Preparatory School, MD
Germantown Friends School, PA
Gill St. Bernard's School, NJ
Gould Academy, ME
Governor Dummer Academy, MA
The Grauer School, CA
Greater Atlanta Christian Schools, GA
Greensboro Day School, NC
Greens Farms Academy, CT
Greenwich Academy, CT
The Grier School, PA
Groton School, MA
The Gunnery, CT
Hales Franciscan High School, IL
Hammond School, SC
Harding Academy, TN
The Harley School, NY
The Harpeth Hall School, TN
Harvard-Westlake School, CA
Havergal College, ON, Canada
Hawken School, OH
Hayden High School, KS
Head-Royce School, CA
Hebrew Academy-the Five Towns, NY
The Hewitt School, NY
Highland Hall, A Waldorf School, CA
High Mowing School, NH
The Hill School, PA
The Hockaday School, TX
Holderness School, NH
Hopkins School, CT
The Hotchkiss School, CT
The Hudson School, NJ
International High School of FAIS, CA
John F. Kennedy Memorial High School, WA
Keith Country Day School, IL
Kents Hill School, ME
Kentucky Country Day School, KY
Kimberton Waldorf School, PA
Kingswood-Oxford School, CT
The Kinkaid School, TX

The Knox School, NY
Lakefield College School, ON, Canada
Lake Forest Academy, IL
Lake Highland Preparatory School, FL
Lakeside School, WA
Landon School, MD
The Latin School of Chicago, IL
Laurel School, OH
Lawrence Academy, MA
The Lawrenceville School, NJ
Le Lycee Francais de Los Angeles, CA
Leysin American School in Switzerland, Switzerland
Linden Hall School for Girls, PA
Little Red School House and Elisabeth Irwin High School, NY
The Loomis Chaffee School, CT
The Lovett School, GA
The Lowell Whiteman School, CO
Loyola Academy, IL
Loyola School, NY
Luther College High School, SK, Canada
Lycee Français de New York, NY
Maine Central Institute, ME
Manlius Pebble Hill School, NY
Maret School, DC
Marin Academy, CA
Mary Institute and St. Louis Country Day School (MICDS), MO
The Mary Louis Academy, NY
Marymount School, NY
The Masters School, NY
Matignon High School, MA
Maumee Valley Country Day School, OH
The McCallie School, TN
Memphis University School, TN
Mercersburg Academy, PA
Mercyhurst Preparatory School, PA
Milken Community High School of Stephen Wise Temple, CA
Millbrook School, NY
Milton Academy, MA
Milton Hershey School, PA
Miss Porter's School, CT
Montgomery Bell Academy, TN
Moorestown Friends School, NJ
Morgan Park Academy, IL
Mount Bachelor Academy, OR
Nacel International School, MN
National Cathedral School, DC
Navajo Preparatory School, Inc., NM
Nawa Academy, CA
Neuchatel Junior College, Switzerland
Newark Academy, NJ
Newton Country Day School of the Sacred Heart, MA
Noble and Greenough School, MA
Norfolk Academy, VA
Northfield Mount Hermon School, MA
The North Shore Country Day School, IL
The Northwest School, WA
North Yarmouth Academy, ME
Notre Dame Academy, MA

The Oakridge School, TX
Ojai Valley School, CA
Oldfields School, MD
Oregon Episcopal School, OR
The Overlake School, WA
Oxford School, CA
Pace Academy, GA
Padua Franciscan High School, OH
Palmer Trinity School, FL
Peddie School, NJ
The Pembroke Hill School, MO
Phillips Academy (Andover), MA
Phillips Exeter Academy, NH
Princeton Day School, NJ
Proctor Academy, NH
Providence Country Day School, RI
Pulaski Academy, AR
Punahou School, HI
Purcell Marian High School, OH
Purnell School, NJ
The Putney School, VT
Ramona Convent Secondary School, CA
Randolph-Macon Academy, VA
Ravenscroft School, NC
Regina High School, OH
Regis High School, NY
Ribet Academy, CA
Ridley College, ON, Canada
Riverdale Country School, NY
Rocky Hill School, RI
Roland Park Country School, MD
Sacred Heart School of Halifax, NS, Canada
Saddleback Valley Christian School, CA
Saddle River Day School, NJ
St. Andrew's College, ON, Canada
St. Andrew's Episcopal School, MS
St. Andrew's on the Marsh School, GA
St. Anne's–Belfield School, VA
St. Catherine's School, VA
Saint Edward's School, FL
Saint Francis School, HI
St. George's School, RI
St. John's-Kilmarnock School, ON, Canada
St. John's Preparatory School, MA
Saint John's Preparatory School, MN
St. John's School, TX
St. Joseph's Preparatory School, PA
St. Luke's School, CT
St. Margaret's School, VA
St. Mark's High School, DE
Saint Mark's School, MA
Saint Mary's Hall, TX
St. Michaels University School, BC, Canada
St. Paul Academy and Summit School, MN
St. Paul's School, MD
St. Paul's School, NH
St. Paul's School for Girls, MD
St. Peter's Preparatory School, NJ
St. Stephen's & St. Agnes School, VA
St. Stephen's Episcopal School, TX
Salem Academy, NC

Salisbury School, CT
Santa Fe Preparatory School, NM
Scattergood Friends School, IA
School for Young Performers, NY
Schule Schloss Salem, Germany
Seattle Academy of Arts and Sciences, WA
Second Baptist School, TX
Sedbergh School, QC, Canada
Severn School, MD
Sewickley Academy, PA
Shady Side Academy, PA
The Shipley School, PA
SICES International Academy, AB, Canada
Sidwell Friends School, DC
Southridge School, BC, Canada
The Spence School, NY
Springside School, PA
Stanstead College, QC, Canada
Staten Island Academy, NY
Stevenson School, CA
Stuart Country Day School of the Sacred Heart, NJ
The Summit Country Day School, OH
The Taft School, CT
The Tatnall School, DE
The Thacher School, CA
Thayer Academy, MA
Toronto Waldorf School, ON, Canada
Trinity Christian Academy, TX
Trinity College School, ON, Canada
Trinity High School, KY
University Liggett School, MI
University of Toronto Schools, ON, Canada
University Prep, WA
University School, OH
University School of Nova Southeastern University, FL
Upper Canada College, ON, Canada
The Urban School of San Francisco, CA
Valley Forge Military Academy and College, PA
Vanguard College Preparatory School, TX
Vermont Academy, VT
Viewpoint School, CA
Village Christian Schools, CA
Virginia Episcopal School, VA
The Waldorf High School of Massachusetts Bay, MA
The Waldorf School of Garden City, NY
The Wardlaw-Hartridge School, NJ
Waring School, MA
Washington Academy, ME
Washington Waldorf School, MD
Wayland Academy, WI
Waynflete School, ME
The Wellington School, OH
Western Reserve Academy, OH
West Island College, AB, Canada
Westminster School, CT
The Westminster Schools, GA
Westover School, CT
The Wheeler School, RI
Wilbraham & Monson Academy, MA
The Williston Northampton School, MA
Wilmington Friends School, DE

Winchester Thurston School, PA
Windermere St. Anne's School, United Kingdom
Woodberry Forest School, VA
Woodlands Academy of the Sacred Heart, IL
Woodstock School, India
Wooster School, CT
Wyoming Seminary, PA
York Country Day School, PA
The York School, ON, Canada

SCHOOLS REPORTING SUMMER SESSIONS OPEN TO STUDENTS FROM OTHER SCHOOLS*

School	Programs
Academie Sainte Cecile International School, ON, Canada	A,F
The Academy for Global Exploration, OR	A,R,S
Academy of Holy Angels, MN	F,S
Academy of Notre Dame de Namur, PA	A,F,S
Academy of Our Lady of Peace, CA	A,C,F,S
Academy of the Holy Cross, MD	A,C,F,S
Academy of the Pacific, HI	A
Academy of the Sacred Heart, MI	A,C,F,S
ACS Cobham International School, United Kingdom	O
ACS Egham International School, United Kingdom	A,F
ACS Hillingdon International School, United Kingdom	A
Adelphi Academy, NY	A,C,F,R,S
Advanced Academy of Georgia, GA	A,F
The Agnes Irwin School, PA	A,C,F
The Albany Academy, NY	A,S
Albuquerque Academy, NM	A,C,F,S
Alexander Dawson School, CO	A,C,F,S
Allen Academy, TX	A
Allendale Columbia School, NY	A,F,S
Allison Academy, FL	A,C,F
All Saints' Episcopal School of Fort Worth, TX	A,C,F,R,S
The Altamont School, AL	A,C,F,R,S
American Academy, FL	A,C,F
American Community Schools of Athens, Greece	O
American Cooperative School, Bolivia	A,C
American Heritage School, FL	A,C,F
American International School Salzburg, Austria	A
The American School Foundation, Mexico	A,C,F
The American School in Japan, Japan	A,C,F
The American School of Madrid, Spain	A,C,S
American School of Paris, France	A,C,F,S
The American School of Puerto Vallarta, Mexico	A
The Andrews School, OH	F,S
Annie Wright School, WA	A,F,S
Appleby College, ON, Canada	A,F,S
Archbishop Curley High School, MD	A,F,S
Archbishop Mitty High School, CA	A,S
The Archer School for Girls, CA	F
Army and Navy Academy, CA	A,C,F
Ashbury College, ON, Canada	A
Asheville School, NC	A,C,F,R,S
Ashley Hall, SC	A,C,F,S
Assumption High School, KY	C,F,S
The Athenian School, CA	A,C,F,S
Athens Academy, GA	A,C
Atlanta International School, GA	A,C,F,S
Aurora Central High School, IL	A,F,S

School	Programs
Baldwin School of Puerto Rico, Inc., PR	A,C
The Baltimore Actors' Theatre Conservatory, MD	A,F
Baltimore Lutheran Middle and Upper School, MD	A,S
Bancroft School, MA	A,C,F,S
Bangor Christian School, ME	S
Barnstable Academy, NJ	A
Battle Ground Academy, TN	A,C,F,S
The Beekman School, NY	A
Beijing BISS International School, China	A,C,F,R,S
Bellarmine College Preparatory, CA	A,C,F,S
Bellarmine Preparatory School, WA	A
Benilde–St. Margaret's School, MN	S
The Benjamin School, FL	A
Berkeley Carroll School, NY	A,F,S
Berkeley Preparatory School, FL	A,C,F,S
The Bermuda High School for Girls, Bermuda	F
Berwick Academy, ME	O
Bishop Eustace Preparatory School, NJ	A,S
Bishop Ireton High School, VA	A,C
Bishop Luers High School, IN	A,F,S
Bishop McDevitt High School, PA	A,S
Bishop McNamara High School, IL	A,S
Bishop Quinn High School/St. Francis Middle School, CA	A,S
Bishop's College School, QC, Canada	A,C,F,R,S
The Bishop Strachan School, ON, Canada	A,C,F,R
Bismark St. Mary's Central, ND	A
The Blake School, MN	A,F,S
Blueprint Education, AZ	A
The Bolles School, FL	A,C,F
Boyd-Buchanan School, TN	S
The Boys' Latin School of Maryland, MD	A
Brandon Hall School, GA	A
Brentwood Academy, TN	A,C,F,S
Brentwood School, CA	A,C,F,S
Brewster Academy, NH	A,C,F,S
British Columbia Christian Academy, BC, Canada	A,C,S
The Brook Hill School, TX	A,F,S
Brooks School, MA	A,C,S
Brophy College Preparatory, AZ	A,C,F,S
Brother Rice High School, MI	A,F
Brownell-Talbot School, NE	A,S
The Bryn Mawr School for Girls, MD	A,F,S
The Buckley School, CA	A,C,F
Bulloch Academy, GA	A,C,F,S
The Bush School, WA	A
Calvert Hall College High School, MD	A,C
Cambridge International College of Canada, ON, Canada	A,F
The Cambridge School of Weston, MA	A,F
Camden Military Academy, SC	A
Camelot Academy, NC	A
Campbell Hall (Episcopal), CA	A,C,F,S
Canadian Academy, Japan	A,S
Canterbury School, CT	S
Canterbury School, FL	A,F,S
The Canterbury School of Florida, FL	A,C,F,S
Cape Fear Academy, NC	A,F,S
Cape Henry Collegiate School, VA	A,C,F,S
Cardigan Mountain School, NH	A,S
Caribbean Preparatory School, PR	A,C,S

*A — academic; C — computer instruction; F — art/fine arts; R — rigorous outdoor training; S — sports; O — other

Carlisle School, VA	A,C,F,S	Delbarton School, NJ	A,C,S
Carolina Day School, NC	A,S	Delphi Academy of Los Angeles, CA	A,C,F,S
Carrabassett Valley Academy, ME	S	DeMatha Catholic High School, MD	A,C,F,S
Cary Academy, NC	A,C,F,S	Denver Academy, CO	A,C,F,R
Casady School, OK	A,C,F	Detroit Country Day School, MI	A,C,F
Cascadilla School, NY	A,F	Don Bosco High School, CA	A,C,F,S
Cascia Hall Preparatory School, OK	S	Duchesne Academy of the Sacred Heart, TX	C,F
Cathedral Preparatory School, PA	A,S	Durham Academy, NC	A
CCI The Renaissance School, Italy	F	Dwight-Englewood School, NJ	A,C,F,S
Central Catholic High School, CA	A	The Dwight School, NY	A,C
Chadwick School, CA	A,C,F,R,S	Eaglebrook School, MA	A,C,F,R,S
Chamberlain-Hunt Academy, MS	A,R,S	Eagle Hill School, MA	A,C,F,S
Chaminade College Preparatory, CA	A,C,S	Eagle Hill-Southport, CT	A
Charlotte Christian School, NC	A,C,F,R,S	Elizabeth Seton High School, MD	A,F,S
Charlotte Country Day School, NC	A,C,F,S	Emerson Honors High Schools, CA	A,C,F,S
Charlotte Latin School, NC	A,C,F,S	Emma Willard School, NY	A,C
Chase Collegiate School, CT	A,C,F	Episcopal Collegiate School, AR	A,C,F,S
Chatham Academy, GA	A,C,F	Episcopal High School, TX	A,F
Chatham Hall, VA	S	The Episcopal School of Dallas, TX	A,C,F,R,S
Chedar Chabad, ON, Canada	A	Evansville Day School, IN	A,C,F
Chelsea School, MD	A,C,F	Explorations Academy, WA	A,F
Cheshire Academy, CT	A,C,F,S	Fairhill School, TX	A,C
Chinese Christian Schools, CA	A,S	Father Ryan High School, TN	A,C,F,S
Choate Rosemary Hall, CT	A,F	Fay School, MA	A,C,S
Christa McAuliffe Academy, WA	A,C	The Fessenden School, MA	A
Christ Church Episcopal School, SC	A,C,F,S	First Presbyterian Day School, GA	A,F,S
Christchurch School, VA	A,S	Fishburne Military School, VA	A,C
Christian Brothers Academy, NY	A,S	F. L. Chamberlain School, MA	A,C
Christian Brothers High School, CA	A,C,F,S	Flint Hill School, VA	A,C,F,R,S
Christian Junior–Senior High School, CA	A	Florida Air Academy, FL	A,C,S
Chrysalis School, WA	A,C,F	Foothills Academy, AB, Canada	A
Cincinnati Country Day School, OH	A,C,F,S	Fork Union Military Academy, VA	A,C
Cistercian Preparatory School, TX	A,C,F,S	Forsyth Country Day School, NC	A
Coe-Brown Northwood Academy, NH	A	Fort Worth Country Day School, TX	A,F,S
Colegio San Jose, PR	A,C	Fountain Valley School of Colorado, CO	R
College du Leman International School, Switzerland	A,C,F,S	Fowlers Academy, PR	A
The Collegiate School, VA	A,C,F,S	Fox River Country Day School, IL	A,C,F,S
The Colorado Springs School, CO	A,F,S	Francis Parker School, CA	A,C,F,S
Columbia International College of Canada, ON, Canada	A,S	Franklin Road Academy, TN	A,C,F,S
Columbia International School, Japan	A,C,F	Frederica Academy, GA	A,C,F,S
The Columbus Academy, OH	A,C,F	Friends Academy, NY	F
Columbus School for Girls, OH	A,C,F,R,S	Friends' Central School, PA	A
Convent of the Sacred Heart, NY	C,F,S	Friends School of Baltimore, MD	C,F
Cornelia Connelly School, CA	A	Friends Seminary, NY	O
The Cottage School, GA	A,C	Fuqua School, VA	A,S
The Country Day School, ON, Canada	A,F	Futures High School, Oceanside, CA	A,C,F
The Craig School, NJ	A	Futures High School—San Diego, CA	A,C,F
Cranbrook Schools, MI	A	The Galloway School, GA	A,S
Crawford Day School, VA	A	Garces Memorial High School, CA	A,C,F,S
Crescent School, ON, Canada	A	Garrison Forest School, MD	F,S
Crespi Carmelite High School, CA	A,F,S	Gaston Day School, NC	A,S
Cretin-Derham Hall, MN	A,C,F,S	George Stevens Academy, ME	A,C,F,S
Crossroads School for Arts & Sciences, CA	A,C,F,S	Georgetown Preparatory School, MD	A
The Culver Academies, IN	A,C,F,S	Germantown Academy, PA	A,C,F
Currey Ingram Academy, TN	A,C,F,S	Gilman School, MD	A
Cushing Academy, MA	A,C,F	Girls Preparatory School, TN	A,C,F,S
Darlington School, GA	A,S	Glenelg Country School, MD	A,S
David Lipscomb High School, TN	A,F	Gonzaga Preparatory School, WA	A,C,F
De La Salle College, ON, Canada	A	The Governor French Academy, IL	A,C,F
Delaware County Christian School, PA	F,S	The Gow School, NY	A,C,F,R,S
Delaware Valley Friends School, PA	A,F	The Grand River Academy, OH	A,C,F,S

*A — academic; C — computer instruction; F — art/fine arts; R — rigorous outdoor training; S — sports; O — other

Specialized Directories

The Grauer School, CA	A,C,F,S	Jesuit College Preparatory School, TX	A,C,F,S
Greenfield School, NC	A,C,F,S	Jesuit High School, CA	A,C
Green Fields Country Day School, AZ	S	The John Cooper School, TX	A,C,F,R,S
Greenhill School, TX	A,C,F,S	John F. Kennedy Memorial High School, WA	A
Greenhills School, MI	A	The June Shelton School and Evaluation Center, TX	A
Greens Farms Academy, CT	A,S	Justin-Siena High School, CA	A
The Grier School, PA	A,F,S	Keith Country Day School, IL	A,F,S
Gstaad International School, Switzerland	A,C,S	Kent Denver School, CO	A,C,F,S
Guamani Private School, PR	A	Kent Place School, NJ	A
Guerin College Preparatory High School, IL	A,F,S	Kent School, CT	A,F
Gulliver Preparatory School, FL	A,C,F,R	Kentucky Country Day School, KY	A,C,F,R,S
Hales Franciscan High School, IL	A,C,S	Key School, Inc., TX	A,C
Halifax Grammar School, NS, Canada	A	Keystone National High School, PA	A,C,F
Hamden Hall Country Day School, CT	A,C,F,S	Keystone School, TX	S
Hamilton Learning Centre, ON, Canada	A,C,F	Kildonan School, NY	A,C,F
Hampton Roads Academy, VA	A,F,S	Kimball Union Academy, NH	A
Harding Academy, TN	A,F,S	King & Low-Heywood Thomas School, CT	A
Hargrave Military Academy, VA	A,C,R,S	The King's Academy, TN	A
The Harker School, CA	A	The Kinkaid School, TX	A,C,F,S
The Harley School, NY	A,C,F,S	The Kiski School, PA	A,S
The Harpeth Hall School, TN	A,C,F,S	La Grange Academy, GA	A,C,F
Harrow School, United Kingdom	A,R,S	La Jolla Country Day School, CA	A,C,F,S
Harvard-Westlake School, CA	A,C,F,R,S	Lake Highland Preparatory School, FL	A,C,F,S
Hawaii Baptist Academy, HI	A,C,F	Lakehill Preparatory School, TX	A,F,S
Hawai'i Preparatory Academy, HI	A,C,F,S	Lake Ridge Academy, OH	A,C,F,S
Hawken School, OH	A,C	Lakeside School, WA	A,C
Head-Royce School, CA	A	Landmark School, MA	A
Highland School, VA	A,C,F,R,S	Landon School, MD	A,C,F,R,S
Hillcrest Christian School, CA	A,C,F,S	La Salle College High School, PA	A,C,F,S
Hillside School, MA	A,C,F,R,S	La Salle High School, CA	A,C,F,S
The Hill Top Preparatory School, PA	A	The Latin School of Chicago, IL	A,C,F,R,S
The Hockaday School, TX	A,C,F,S	Lausanne Collegiate School, TN	A,C,F,S
Holland Hall, OK	A,F,S	The Leelanau School, MI	A
Hopkins School, CT	A,C,F,R,S	Le Lycee Francais de Los Angeles, CA	A,C,F,S
The Horace Mann School, NY	A,C,F	Leysin American School in Switzerland, Switzerland	A,C,F,R,S
The Hotchkiss School, CT	F	The Linsly School, WV	A,C
Houston Learning Academy-Central Campus, TX	A,C,F	Little Keswick School, VA	A,C,F,R,S
Howe Military School, IN	A,R,S	Living Word Academy, PA	S
Hudson College, ON, Canada	A,C,F,S	Long Island Lutheran Middle and High School, NY	C,F,S
The Hudson School, NJ	F	Los Angeles Baptist Junior/Senior High School, CA	A,C,S
The Hun School of Princeton, NJ	A,C,F	Louisville High School, CA	S
Hutchison School, TN	A,C,F,S	The Lovett School, GA	A
Hyde School, CT	A,F,R,S	Loyola Academy, IL	A,C,F,S
Hyde School, ME	A,F,R,S	Loyola-Blakefield, MD	A,S
Idyllwild Arts Academy, CA	A,F	Loyola High School, Jesuit College Preparatory, CA	A,C,F,S
Immaculata Academy, NY	A,S	Lutheran High North, TX	C,F,S
Imperial College of Toronto, ON, Canada	A	Lycee International de Los Angeles, CA	A,C,F,S
Incarnate Word Academy, TX	S	Lyndon Institute, VT	A
Interlochen Arts Academy, MI	F	The MacDuffie School, MA	A,C
International College Spain, Spain	A,F	Madison-Ridgeland Academy, MS	A,S
International High School of FAIS, CA	A,F	Maine Central Institute, ME	A
International Junior Golf Academy, SC	A,S	Malaspina International High School, BC, Canada	A,C,F
International School Bangkok, Thailand	A,F	Malden Catholic High School, MA	O
International School of Aruba, Aruba	A	Manlius Pebble Hill School, NY	A,C,F,S
International School of Athens, Greece	A,C,F	Maplebrook School, NY	A,C,F,S
International School of Brussels, Belgium	A,C,F,S	Maret School, DC	A,C,F,S
The International School of Kuala Lumpur, Malaysia	A,C,F,R	Marianapolis Preparatory School, CT	A,C,F
Iolani School, HI	A,C,F	Marian Central Catholic High School, IL	S
Isidore Newman School, LA	A,C,F	Marist High School, IL	O
Jackson Academy, MS	A,C,F,S	Marlborough School, CA	A,C,F,S
Jackson Preparatory School, MS	A,C,F		

A — academic; C — computer instruction; F — art/fine arts; R — rigorous outdoor training; S — sports; O — other

Marshall School, MN	A,C,F	New York Military Academy, NY	A,C
Mars Hill Bible School, AL	A,F,S	Niagara Christian Collegiate, ON, Canada	A
The Marvelwood School, CT	A,F	The Nichols School, NY	A,C,F
Mary Institute and St. Louis Country Day School (MICDS), MO	R,S	Noble and Greenough School, MA	A
		The Nora School, MD	A,F
Maryknoll School, HI	A,C,F,S	Norfolk Academy, VA	A,F,S
The Mary Louis Academy, NY	A	Norfolk Collegiate School, VA	A,C,F,S
Marymount High School, CA	A,C,F,S	The North Broward Preparatory Upper School, FL	A,C,F
Marymount School, NY	A,F	North Cobb Christian School, GA	A,C,F,S
Massanutten Military Academy, VA	A,C,S	North Country School, NY	O
Matignon High School, MA	A	Northfield Mount Hermon School, MA	A,C,F
Maumee Valley Country Day School, OH	A,C,F,S	Northside Christian School, FL	A,C,F,S
Maur Hill-Mount Academy, KS	O	The Northwest School, WA	A,C,F,S
Mayfield Senior School, CA	A,C,F,S	Northwest Yeshiva High School, WA	S
The McCallie School, TN	A,R,S	North Yarmouth Academy, ME	A,F,S
McDonogh School, MD	C,F,S	The Norwich Free Academy, CT	A,S
The Meadows School, NV	A,F	Notre Dame High School, CA	A,C,F,S
Memphis University School, TN	A,S	Notre Dame High School, NJ	A,F,S
Mentor College, ON, Canada	A	Notre Dame High School, WV	A
Mercersburg Academy, PA	A,F,R,S	Notre Dame Regional Secondary, BC, Canada	A
Mercy High School College Preparatory, CA	A	Oak Creek Ranch School, AZ	A,C
Mercyhurst Preparatory School, PA	A,C,F,R	Oak Hill Academy, VA	A
Middlesex School, MA	F	Oakland School, VA	A,C,F,S
Mid-Pacific Institute, HI	A,C,F	The Oakridge School, TX	A,C,F,S
Mid-Peninsula High School, CA	A,F	Oakwood School, CA	A,F,S
Milken Community High School of Stephen Wise Temple, CA	A,C,F	Ojai Valley School, CA	A,C,F
		Oneida Baptist Institute, KY	A
Miller School, VA	S	Orangewood Adventist Academy, CA	A
Mississauga Private School, ON, Canada	A,C,F,S	Oregon Episcopal School, OR	A,F,S
Missouri Military Academy, MO	R,S	Orinda Academy, CA	A,S
Miss Porter's School, CT	A,C,F,S	The Orme School, AZ	A
MMI Preparatory School, PA	A	Our Saviour Lutheran School, NY	A
Montcalm School, MI	A,F,R,S	Out-Of-Door-Academy, FL	A,F,S
Montclair College Preparatory School, CA	A,C,S	The Oxford Academy, CT	A
Montclair Kimberley Academy, NJ	A,C,F,S	Pace Academy, GA	A,C,F,S
Monte Vista Christian School, CA	A,S	Pacific Hills School, CA	A
Montgomery Bell Academy, TN	A,C,F,S	Padua Franciscan High School, OH	A,C,F,S
Montverde Academy, FL	A	Palma High School, CA	A
Moravian Academy, PA	A,F	The Parker School, HI	A
Moreau Catholic High School, CA	A,S	The Park School, MD	F,R,S
Morgan Park Academy, IL	A,C,F	Park Tudor School, IN	A,C,F,R,S
Morristown-Beard School, NJ	A,C,F,S	Peddie School, NJ	A
Mother McAuley High School, IL	A,C,F,S	The Pembroke Hill School, MO	A,C,F,S
Mountain View Christian High School, NV	A,C	The Phelps School, PA	A,C,F
Mount Carmel High School, IL	A	Phillips Academy (Andover), MA	A,C,F
Mount Saint Charles Academy, RI	F,S	Phillips Exeter Academy, NH	A,C,F,S
Munich International School, Germany	R,S	Phoenix Christian Unified Schools, AZ	A
Nacel International School, MN	A,S	Phoenix Country Day School, AZ	A,C,F,S
National Cathedral School, DC	A,F,S	Pickering College, ON, Canada	A
National Sports Academy at Lake Placid, NY	S	Pine Crest School, FL	A,S
Nawa Academy, CA	A,F,R	Pine Ridge School, VT	A,C,F
Nbisiing Education Centre, ON, Canada	A	The Pingry School, NJ	A
Nebraska Christian Schools, NE	A	Polytechnic Preparatory Country Day School, NY	A,C,F,S
Newark Academy, NJ	A,C,F,S	Polytechnic School, CA	A,C,F,S
The Newgrange School, NJ	A,F	Pomfret School, CT	F
New Hampton School, NH	A,F,S	Portland Christian Schools, OR	A,C,F
New Horizon Youth Ministries, IN	A,R,S	Portledge School, NY	A,C,F,S
The Newman School, MA	A,C	Portsmouth Abbey School, RI	A,C,F,S
New Mexico Military Institute, NM	A,C,F,R	Portsmouth Christian Academy, NH	A,S
New Summit School, MS	O	The Potomac School, VA	A,F,S
Newton Country Day School of the Sacred Heart, MA	S	Poughkeepsie Day School, NY	F

A — academic; C — computer instruction; F — art/fine arts; R — rigorous outdoor training; S — sports; O — other

The Prairie School, WI	A,C,F	St. Croix Lutheran High School, MN	A
Prestonwood Christian Academy, TX	A,C,F,S	St. David's School, NC	A,C,F,S
Princeton Day School, NJ	A,C,F,S	Saint Dominic Academy, NJ	A,C
Providence High School, CA	A,C,F,S	Saint Francis De Sales High School, IL	A,S
Providence High School, TX	A,F,S	Saint Francis School, HI	A
Pulaski Academy, AR	A,C,F	St. George's School, RI	A,C,F,S
Punahou School, HI	A,C,F,S	St. George's School, BC, Canada	A,C,F,S
Purcell Marian High School, OH	A,S	St. George's School in Switzerland, Switzerland	A,C,F,R,S
The Putney School, VT	A,F	St. Gregory College Preparatory School, AZ	A,C,F,S
Queen Anne School, MD	A,C,S	Saint James School, AL	A,C,F,S
Queen Margaret's School, BC, Canada	A	St. Johnsbury Academy, VT	A
Rabun Gap-Nacoochee School, GA	A,F	St. Johns Country Day School, FL	A
Ramona Convent Secondary School, CA	A,C,F	St. John's Literary Institution at Prospect Hall, MD	C,F,S
Randolph-Macon Academy, VA	A	St. John's Northwestern Military Academy, WI	A,R
Randolph School, AL	A,C,F,S	Saint John's Preparatory School, MN	A,F
Ranney School, NJ	A,C	Saint John's School, GU	A,C,F,S
Ransom Everglades School, FL	A,C	St. John's School, PR	A
Ravenscroft School, NC	A,C,F,S	Saint John's School of Alberta, AB, Canada	A
The Rectory School, CT	A,F,S	Saint Joseph's High School, NJ	A,C,S
Regina High School, OH	A,F,S	St. Joseph's Preparatory School, PA	A,F
Regis High School, OR	S	Saint Laurence High School, IL	A,S
Resurrection High School, IL	A,C,S	Saint Louis Priory School, MO	A,C,F
Ribet Academy, CA	A,C,F,S	St. Luke's School, CT	A,C,F,S
Ridley College, ON, Canada	A	St. Margaret's Episcopal School, CA	A,S
Rivermont Collegiate, IA	A,S	St. Margaret's School, BC, Canada	A
Riverside Military Academy, GA	A,C,F,R,S	St. Mark's High School, DE	A
Riverstone Community School, ID	A,F	St. Mary's Bundschu Memorial High School, MO	A
Riverview School, MA	A,C,S	St. Mary's Episcopal School, TN	A,S
Robert Louis Stevenson School, NY	A	Saint Mary's Hall, TX	A,C,F,S
Rocky Hill School, RI	A,S	St. Mary's International School, Japan	A,C,F
Rocky Mount Academy, NC	A,C,F,S	St. Mary's Preparatory School, MI	S
The Roeper School, MI	F	Saint Mary's School, NC	A,C,F,S
Roland Park Country School, MD	A,F,S	St. Mary's School, OR	A,F,S
Rolling Hills Preparatory School, CA	A,F	St. Maur International School, Japan	A,C,F,S
Rowland Hall-St. Mark's School, UT	A	St. Michael's Catholic Academy, TX	A,C
Royal Canadian College, BC, Canada	A	St. Michaels University School, BC, Canada	A,C,F,S
Roycemore School, IL	A,F	Saint Patrick High School, IL	A,C,F,S
Rumsey Hall School, CT	A	St. Paul Academy and Summit School, MN	A,F,S
Rutgers Preparatory School, NJ	A,C	St. Paul's Episcopal School, AL	A,C,F,S
Rye Country Day School, NY	A,C,F	St. Paul's Preparatory Academy, AZ	A,C,F
Sacred Heart Preparatory, CA	C,F,S	St. Paul's School, NH	A
Saddleback Valley Christian School, CA	A	St. Peter's Preparatory School, NJ	A,F
Saddle River Day School, NJ	A,F,S	St. Stanislaus College, MS	A
Saint Agnes Boys High School, NY	A	St. Stephen's & St. Agnes School, VA	A,C,F
St. Andrew's College, ON, Canada	A,F,S	Saint Stephen's Episcopal School, FL	A,S
St. Andrew's Episcopal School, MD	A,F,S	St. Stephen's Episcopal School, TX	A,F,R,S
St. Andrew's on the Marsh School, GA	A,F,S	Saint Teresa's Academy, MO	C,F,S
St. Andrew's Priory School, HI	A,C,F,R,S	Saint Thomas Aquinas High School, KS	A,S
Saint Andrew's School, FL	A,C,F	St. Thomas High School, TX	A
St. Andrew's School, RI	F,S	Saint Thomas More School, CT	A,C,F
St. Andrew's–Sewanee School, TN	A,R	Saint Vincent Ferrer High School, NY	A
St. Anne's–Belfield School, VA	A,C,F,S	St. Vincent Pallotti High School, MD	A,S
St. Anselm's Abbey School, DC	A,F,S	Salesian High School, NY	A
Saint Augustine Preparatory School, NJ	A,C,F,S	Salisbury School, CT	A,S
St. Benedict at Auburndale, TN	A	San Domenico School, CA	A,C,F,S
St. Bernard High School, CA	A,C,F,S	Sanford School, DE	A,C,F
St. Catherine's School, VA	F,S	The Savannah Country Day School, GA	A,C,F,S
St. Cecilia Academy, TN	C,F,S	Scarborough Christian School, ON, Canada	A
Saint Cecilia High School, NE	S	School for Young Performers, NY	A,F
St. Christopher's School, VA	A	Schule Schloss Salem, Germany	A,F,S
St. Clement's School, ON, Canada	A	Scranton Preparatory School, PA	A

A — academic; C — computer instruction; F — art/fine arts; R — rigorous outdoor training; S — sports; O — other

Seabury Hall, HI	F,S
Selwyn House School, QC, Canada	S
Seton Catholic Central High School, NY	A,S
The Seven Hills School, OH	O
Severn School, MD	A,S
Sewickley Academy, PA	A,C,F,S
Shady Side Academy, PA	A,C,F
Shattuck-St. Mary's School, MN	A,C,F,S
The Shipley School, PA	A,C,F,S
Sidwell Friends School, DC	A,C,F,S
Smith School, NY	A,C
Solebury School, PA	A
Southridge School, BC, Canada	A,C,F,S
Southwest Christian School, Inc., TX	A,S
Southwestern Academy, AZ	A,F,R
Southwestern Academy, CA	A,C,F
Spartanburg Day School, SC	A,F,S
Squaw Valley Academy, CA	A,S
Stanstead College, QC, Canada	A,S
Stella Maris High School and the Maura Clarke Junior High Program, NY	A
Stevenson School, CA	A
Stoneleigh–Burnham School, MA	A,F,S
The Stony Brook School, NY	A
Storm King School, NY	A
Stratton Mountain School, VT	R
Stuart Country Day School of the Sacred Heart, NJ	A,F
Suffield Academy, CT	A,C,F
Sumiton Christian School, AL	A,S
The Summit Country Day School, OH	A,C,F,S
The Taft School, CT	A,C,F,S
Taipei American School, Taiwan	A
Tallulah Falls School, GA	A,S
TASIS The American School in England, United Kingdom	A,C,F,S
TASIS, The American School in Switzerland, Switzerland	A,F,S
The Tatnall School, DE	A,F
The Tenney School, TX	A,C
Thayer Academy, MA	A,C,F,R,S
TMI—The Episcopal School of Texas, TX	A,S
Tri-City Christian Schools, CA	A,S
Trident Academy, SC	A
Trinity Catholic High School, CT	A
Trinity Christian Academy, TX	A,C,F,S
Trinity College School, ON, Canada	A,C,F
Trinity Preparatory School, FL	A,C,F,S
Trinity Valley School, TX	A,F,R,S
United Nations International School, NY	A,S
University Lake School, WI	A,C,F,S
University Liggett School, MI	A
University of Chicago Laboratory Schools, IL	A
University of Detroit Jesuit High School and Academy, MI	A
University of Miami Online High School, FL	A,C,F,S
University School, OH	A,C
University School of Milwaukee, WI	A,C,F,S
University School of Nova Southeastern University, FL	A,F
Upper Canada College, ON, Canada	A,C,F
The Urban School of San Francisco, CA	A,C,F,S
Valley Christian School, CA	A,F,S
Valley Forge Military Academy and College, PA	A,F,R,S

Viewpoint School, CA	A,C,F,S
Village Christian Schools, CA	A,C,F
Visitation Academy of St. Louis County, MO	S
Wakefield School, VA	A,F,S
Walden Preparatory School, TX	A,C,F
The Waldorf School of Garden City, NY	A
The Walker School, GA	A,C,S
Walnut Hill School, MA	F
The Wardlaw-Hartridge School, NJ	A
Waring School, MA	F
Wasatch Academy, UT	A
Washington Academy, ME	A
Washington International School, DC	A
Washington Waldorf School, MD	S
Watkinson School, CT	A,C
Waynflete School, ME	A,F,S
The Webb School, TN	A,C,F
Webb School of Knoxville, TN	A,F,S
The Wellington School, OH	A,S
Wellspring Foundation, CT	A
Wentworth Military Academy and Junior College, MO	A,R,S
Wesleyan School, GA	A,C,F,S
Westbury Christian School, TX	S
Westchester Academy, NC	F,S
Western Mennonite School, OR	S
West Island College, AB, Canada	A,C,S
Westminster Christian School, FL	A,C
Westminster School, CT	S
The Westminster Schools, GA	A,C,F,R,S
Westminster Schools of Augusta, GA	S
Westridge School, CA	F,S
Westtown School, PA	A,F
Westview School, CA	A,C,F,S
Wheaton Academy, IL	A,C,F,S
Whitefield Academy, GA	A,S
Whitfield School, MO	C,F,S
Whittier Christian High School, CA	A,C,F
Wichita Collegiate School, KS	A,C,F,S
The Williams School, CT	S
The Williston Northampton School, MA	F,S
Wilmington Friends School, DE	A,C
The Winchendon School, MA	A,C,F,R,S
Winchester Thurston School, PA	A,S
The Windsor School, NY	A,C,F
Windward School, CA	S
The Winston School, TX	A,C,F,R,S
The Winston School San Antonio, TX	A,C
Woodbridge Academy, KY	A,C,F
The Woodlynde School, PA	A
Woodside International School, CA	A
Wyoming Seminary, PA	A,C,F,S
Yokohama International School, Japan	A,S

SCHOOLS REPORTING THAT THEY ACCOMMODATE UNDERACHIEVERS

The Academy at Sisters, OR
Ahliyyah School for Girls, Jordan
Allison Academy, FL
Alpine Academy, UT
American Academy, FL

A — academic; C — computer instruction; F — art/fine arts; R — rigorous outdoor training; S — sports; O — other

Arrowsmith School, ON, Canada
Brandon Hall School, GA
Calgary Academy, AB, Canada
Chatham Academy, GA
Cherokee Creek Boys School, SC
Colorado Timberline Academy, CO
The Craig School, NJ
Crawford Day School, VA
Denver Academy, CO
Doctor Franklin Perkins School, MA
Eagle Hill-Southport, CT
Eagle Rock School, CO
Eckerd Youth Alternatives, FL
Elan School, ME
The Family Foundation School, NY
Fishburne Military School, VA
Foothills Academy, AB, Canada
Fowlers Academy, PR
The Frostig School, CA
Futures High School—San Diego, CA
Gateway Christian School, BC, Canada
Gateway School, TX
Glen Eden School, BC, Canada
The Glenholme School, CT
The Grand River Academy, OH
The Greenwood School, VT
Hale O Ulu School Child and Family Service, HI
Hamilton Learning Centre, ON, Canada
Hampshire Country School, NH
The Hill Center, Durham Academy, NC
Hillcrest Christian School, AB, Canada
Houston Learning Academy-Central Campus, TX
The John Dewey Academy, MA
The Judge Rotenberg Educational Center, MA
The Karafin School, NY
Key School, Inc., TX
Kingshill School, VI
La Cheim School, CA
The Leelanau School, MI
Linden Hill School, MA
Little Keswick School, VA
Lower Brule High School, SD
Maplebrook School, NY
The Marvelwood School, CT
Mid-Peninsula High School, CA
Montana Academy, MT
Mooseheart High School, IL
Nawa Academy, CA
Nbisiing Education Centre, ON, Canada
New Dominion School, MD
New Dominion School, VA
The Newgrange School, NJ
New Horizon Youth Ministries, IN
Oak Creek Ranch School, AZ
The Oakland School, PA
Oakland School, VA
The Oxford Academy, CT
The Pathway School, PA
The Phelps School, PA
Pine Ridge School, VT
Provo Canyon School, UT

Rancho Valmora, NM
The Rectory School, CT
Riverview School, MA
Robert Land Academy, ON, Canada
Robert Louis Stevenson School, NY
St. John's Northwestern Military Academy, WI
St. Paul's Preparatory Academy, AZ
Saint Thomas More School, CT
Sorenson's Ranch School, UT
Spring Creek Lodge Academy, MT
Stanbridge Academy, CA
Stone Mountain School, NC
Texas NeuroRehab Center, TX
Thomas A. Edison High School, OR
Thornton Friends School, MD
Thornton Friends School/N.V.A., VA
Three Springs, AL
Three Springs/Prince Mountain Academy, GA
Timber Ridge School, VA
Toronto Waldorf School, ON, Canada
Trident Academy, SC
The Vanguard School, FL
Walden Preparatory School, TX
Wellsprings Friends School, OR
Westview School, CA
Willow Hill School, MA
The Winchendon School, MA
Winston Preparatory School, NY
Woodbridge Academy, KY
Woodcliff Academy, NJ

SCHOOLS REPORTING PROGRAMS FOR STUDENTS WITH SPECIAL NEEDS

Remedial Reading and/or Writing

Academia Cotopaxi, Ecuador
Academie Sainte Cecile International School, ON, Canada
The Academy at Sisters, OR
Academy at Swift River, MA
The Academy for Global Exploration, OR
Academy of Mount Saint Ursula, NY
The Academy of St. Joseph, NY
Academy of the Pacific, HI
Adelphi Academy, NY
Admiral Farragut Academy, FL
The Albany Academy, NY
Alliance Academy, Ecuador
Allison Academy, FL
Alpine Academy, UT
American Academy, FL
American Overseas School of Rome, Italy
The American School Foundation, Mexico
American School of Milan, Italy
American School of Paris, France
Archbishop Curley High School, MD
Army and Navy Academy, CA
Arrowsmith School, ON, Canada
Aspen Ranch, UT
Aurora Central High School, IL
Baptist High School, NJ
Barnstable Academy, NJ

The Beekman School, NY
Bellarmine Preparatory School, WA
Benedictine High School, OH
The Bermuda High School for Girls, Bermuda
Bishop Carroll High School, PA
Bishop Conaty-Our Lady of Loretto High School, CA
Bishop Hoban High School, PA
Bishop Kelly High School, ID
Bishop Luers High School, IN
Bishop Lynch Catholic High School, TX
Bishop McDevitt High School, PA
Bismark St. Mary's Central, ND
Blue Mountain Academy, PA
Blueprint Education, AZ
The Blue Ridge School, VA
Brandon Hall School, GA
Brehm Preparatory School, IL
The British International School, Jeddah, Saudi Arabia
Brother Rice High School, MI
Burr and Burton Academy, VT
Calgary Academy, AB, Canada
Calvert Hall College High School, MD
Camden Military Academy, SC
Camelot Academy, NC
Cape Henry Collegiate School, VA
Cardigan Mountain School, NH
Cardinal Newman High School, FL
Carlucci American International School of Lisbon, Portugal
Cascadilla School, NY
Cathedral High School, IN
Catholic Central High School, NY
The Catholic High School of Baltimore, MD
The Cedars Academy, DE
Central Catholic High School, CA
Chamberlain-Hunt Academy, MS
Chaminade-Madonna College Preparatory, FL
Charles E. Smith Jewish Day School, MD
Chatham Academy, GA
Chattanooga Christian School, TN
Chelsea School, MD
Cherokee Creek Boys School, SC
Cheshire Academy, CT
Christopher Dock Mennonite High School, PA
Chrysalis School, WA
Coe-Brown Northwood Academy, NH
Colegio Bolivar, Colombia
Colegio Franklin D. Roosevelt, Peru
College du Leman International School, Switzerland
Colorado Timberline Academy, CO
Columbia Grammar and Preparatory School, NY
Community High School, NJ
The Concept School, PA
Concord Academy, MA
Concordia Academy, MN
Covenant Canadian Reformed School, AB, Canada
The Craig School, NJ
Cretin-Derham Hall, MN
Cross Creek Programs, UT
Currey Ingram Academy, TN
Cushing Academy, MA
Dallas Academy, TX
Delaware Valley Friends School, PA
Delphi Academy of Los Angeles, CA
DeMatha Catholic High School, MD

Denver Academy, CO
Denver Lutheran High School, CO
Doctor Franklin Perkins School, MA
Dowling High School, IA
Dublin Christian Academy, NH
The Dwight School, NY
Eagle Hill School, CT
Eagle Hill School, MA
Eagle Hill-Southport, CT
Eagle Rock School, CO
Eastern Christian High School, NJ
Eastern Mennonite High School, VA
Eckerd Youth Alternatives, FL
Ecole d'Humanite, Switzerland
Elan School, ME
Elyria Catholic High School, OH
Fairhill School, TX
The Family Foundation School, NY
The Fessenden School, MA
Fishburne Military School, VA
F. L. Chamberlain School, MA
Florida Air Academy, FL
Foothills Academy, AB, Canada
Forest Heights Lodge, CO
Fork Union Military Academy, VA
Fox River Country Day School, IL
Fox Valley Lutheran High School, WI
Fraser Academy, BC, Canada
Fresno Christian Schools, CA
The Frostig School, CA
Fryeburg Academy, ME
Futures High School, Oceanside, CA
Futures High School—San Diego, CA
Gateway School, TX
George Stevens Academy, ME
Girard College, PA
Glades Day School, FL
Glen Eden School, BC, Canada
The Glenholme School, CT
The Gow School, NY
The Grand River Academy, OH
Greenfield School, NC
The Greenwood School, VT
The Grier School, PA
Grove School, CT
Gstaad International School, Switzerland
Hackett Catholic Central High School, MI
Hamilton District Christian School, ON, Canada
Hamilton Learning Centre, ON, Canada
Harare International School, Zimbabwe
Hargrave Military Academy, VA
The Haverford School, PA
Hawai'i Preparatory Academy, HI
Hayden High School, KS
Hebrew Academy-the Five Towns, NY
Heritage Christian School, ON, Canada
Hidden Lake Academy, GA
The Hill Center, Durham Academy, NC
Hillcrest School, TX
Hillside School, MA
The Hill Top Preparatory School, PA
Hoosac School, NY
Hosanna Christian School, OR
Houston Learning Academy-Central Campus, TX

The Hudson School, NJ
Hyde School, CT
Hyde School, ME
International Community School of Addis Ababa, Ethiopia
International School Basel, Switzerland
International School of Amsterdam, Netherlands
International School of Aruba, Aruba
International School of Athens, Greece
International School of Brussels, Belgium
The International School of Geneva, Switzerland
Islamic Saudi Academy, VA
Jakarta International School, Indonesia
John Burroughs School, MO
The John Dewey Academy, MA
John F. Kennedy Memorial High School, WA
Kapaun Mount Carmel Catholic High School, KS
The Karafin School, NY
Keith Country Day School, IL
Key School, Inc., TX
Kildonan School, NY
Kings Christian School, CA
Kingshill School, VI
The Knox School, NY
La Cheim School, CA
Lakeland Christian Academy, IN
Lakewood Prep, NJ
Landmark East School, NS, Canada
Lansdale Catholic High School, PA
La Pietra–Hawaii School for Girls, HI
The Latin School of Chicago, IL
Lawrence School, OH
Lebanon Catholic Junior / Senior High School, PA
The Leelanau School, MI
Lehman High School, OH
Le Lycee Francais de Los Angeles, CA
Lourdes Catholic High School, AZ
Lower Brule High School, SD
Lower Canada College, QC, Canada
Loyola Academy, IL
Lutheran High School, IN
Lutheran High School South, MO
Lyndon Institute, VT
Maine Central Institute, ME
Malaspina International High School, BC, Canada
Manhattan Christian High School, MT
Maplebrook School, NY
Marian Central Catholic High School, IL
Marist High School, NJ
The Marvelwood School, CT
Mary Help of Christians Academy, NJ
Marylawn of the Oranges, NJ
Massanutten Military Academy, VA
McGill-Toolen Catholic High School, AL
McNicholas High School, OH
The Meeting School, NH
Mercedes College, Australia
Mercyhurst Preparatory School, PA
Mid-Peninsula High School, CA
Milton Hershey School, PA
Montana Academy, MT
Monte Vista Christian School, CA
Moravian Academy, PA
Mount Bachelor Academy, OR
Mount Carmel High School, IL

Nawa Academy, CA
Nbisiing Education Centre, ON, Canada
New Dominion School, MD
New Dominion School, VA
The Newgrange School, NJ
New Hampton School, NH
New Summit School, MS
The Nora School, MD
Norfolk Collegiate School, VA
The North Broward Preparatory Upper School, FL
North Country School, NY
Northwest Yeshiva High School, WA
Northwood School, NY
The Norwich Free Academy, CT
Notre Dame High School, MO
Notre Dame High School, NJ
Notre Dame High School, WV
Notre Dame High School for Girls, IL
Notre Dame Regional Secondary, BC, Canada
Oak Creek Ranch School, AZ
Oak Hill Academy, VA
The Oakland School, PA
Oakland School, VA
O'Dea High School, WA
Ojai Valley School, CA
The O'Neal School, NC
Oneida Baptist Institute, KY
The Orme School, AZ
Our Lady of the Sacred Heart, PA
The Oxford Academy, CT
Oxford School, CA
Pace Academy, GA
The Pathway School, PA
The Phelps School, PA
Pinehurst School, ON, Canada
Pine Ridge School, VT
Pope John Paul II High School, FL
Portland Christian Schools, OR
Powers Catholic High School, MI
The Prairie School, WI
Providence High School, TX
Provo Canyon School, UT
Purcell Marian High School, OH
Queen Margaret's School, BC, Canada
Queensway Christian College, ON, Canada
Quincy Notre Dame High School, IL
Rancho Valmora, NM
The Rectory School, CT
Regina High School, OH
Resurrection High School, IL
Rio Lindo Adventist Academy, CA
Riverview School, MA
Robert Land Academy, ON, Canada
Robert Louis Stevenson School, NY
Routt High School, IL
Rumsey Hall School, CT
Saddleback Valley Christian School, CA
St. Andrew's College, Dublin, Ireland
St. Andrew's School, RI
St. Benedict at Auburndale, TN
St. Benedict's Preparatory School, NJ
Saint Cecilia High School, NE
St. Croix Lutheran High School, MN
Saint Dominic Academy, NJ

St. Dominic's International School, Portugal, Portugal
Saint Elizabeth High School, CA
Saint Francis De Sales High School, IL
St. Francis School, GA
St. George's School, BC, Canada
St. George's School in Switzerland, Switzerland
St. George's School of Montreal, QC, Canada
Saint James School, AL
St. Johnsbury Academy, VT
Saint Joseph Central Catholic High School, OH
Saint Laurence High School, IL
St. Leonards, United Kingdom
St. Mark's High School, DE
Saint Mary's High School, AZ
Saint Patrick High School, IL
Saint Patrick—Saint Vincent High School, CA
St. Pius X High School, TX
Saint Raymond High School for Boys, NY
St. Stanislaus College, MS
St. Thomas Aquinas High School, FL
Saint Thomas Aquinas High School, KS
St. Thomas Choir School, NY
Saint Thomas More School, CT
Saint Xavier High School, KY
Salesianum School, DE
Salpointe Catholic High School, AZ
San Marcos Baptist Academy, TX
School for Young Performers, NY
Seattle Christian Schools, WA
Sedbergh School, QC, Canada
Seoul International School, Republic of Korea
Seton Catholic Central High School, NY
Shattuck-St. Mary's School, MN
Shoreline Christian, WA
Smith School, NY
Smithville District Christian High School, ON, Canada
Solebury School, PA
Sorenson's Ranch School, UT
Spring Ridge Academy, AZ
Stanbridge Academy, CA
Stone Mountain School, NC
Storm King School, NY
Taipei American School, Taiwan
TASIS The American School in England, United Kingdom
The Tenney School, TX
Thomas A. Edison High School, OR
Three Springs/Prince Mountain Academy, GA
Tilton School, NH
Timber Ridge School, VA
Timothy Christian High School, IL
Toronto District Christian High School, ON, Canada
Trident Academy, SC
Trinity High School, KY
Trinity-Pawling School, NY
University Lake School, WI
University of Missouri—Columbia High School, MO
University School of Nova Southeastern University, FL
Valley Forge Military Academy and College, PA
The Vanguard School, FL
Venta Preparatory School, ON, Canada
Vianney High School, MO
Walden Preparatory School, TX
Washington Academy, ME
Wellsprings Friends School, OR

Wesleyan School, GA
West Catholic High School, MI
Westhill Institute, Mexico
West Nottingham Academy, MD
Westpark School, MB, Canada
Westview School, CA
Wheaton Academy, IL
The White Mountain School, NH
Whittier Christian High School, CA
Willow Hill School, MA
Wilmington Christian School, DE
The Winchendon School, MA
Windhoek International School, Namibia
Windsor Christian Fellowship Academy, ON, Canada
The Windsor School, NY
Winston Preparatory School, NY
The Winston School San Antonio, TX
Woodbridge Academy, KY
Woodcliff Academy, NJ
York Preparatory School, NY

Remedial Math
Academia Cotopaxi, Ecuador
Academie Sainte Cecile International School, ON, Canada
The Academy at Sisters, OR
Academy at Swift River, MA
The Academy for Global Exploration, OR
Academy of Mount Saint Ursula, NY
The Academy of St. Joseph, NY
Academy of the Pacific, HI
Adelphi Academy, NY
Admiral Farragut Academy, FL
Airdrie Koinonia Christian School, AB, Canada
Allison Academy, FL
Alpine Academy, UT
American Academy, FL
American Overseas School of Rome, Italy
The American School Foundation, Mexico
American School of Milan, Italy
American School of Paris, France
The American School of Puerto Vallarta, Mexico
Archbishop Curley High School, MD
Arrowhead Christian Academy, CA
Arrowsmith School, ON, Canada
Aspen Ranch, UT
Aurora Central High School, IL
Baptist High School, NJ
Barnstable Academy, NJ
The Beekman School, NY
Benedictine High School, OH
Bishop Conaty-Our Lady of Loretto High School, CA
Bishop Hoban High School, PA
Bishop Luers High School, IN
Bishop Lynch Catholic High School, TX
Bishop McDevitt High School, PA
Bishop's College School, QC, Canada
Bishop Verot High School, FL
Bismark St. Mary's Central, ND
Black Forest Academy, Germany
Blue Mountain Academy, PA
Blueprint Education, AZ
Brandon Hall School, GA
Brehm Preparatory School, IL
The British International School, Jeddah, Saudi Arabia

Brother Rice High School, MI
Burr and Burton Academy, VT
Calgary Academy, AB, Canada
Calvert Hall College High School, MD
Camelot Academy, NC
Canyonville Christian Academy, OR
Cape Fear Academy, NC
Cape Henry Collegiate School, VA
Cardigan Mountain School, NH
Cardinal Newman High School, FL
Carlucci American International School of Lisbon, Portugal
Cascadilla School, NY
Cathedral High School, IN
Catholic Central High School, NY
The Catholic High School of Baltimore, MD
The Cedars Academy, DE
Central Catholic High School, CA
Chamberlain-Hunt Academy, MS
Chaminade-Madonna College Preparatory, FL
Charles E. Smith Jewish Day School, MD
Chatham Academy, GA
Chattanooga Christian School, TN
Chelsea School, MD
Cherokee Creek Boys School, SC
Cheshire Academy, CT
Christopher Dock Mennonite High School, PA
Chrysalis School, WA
Coe-Brown Northwood Academy, NH
Colorado Timberline Academy, CO
Columbia Grammar and Preparatory School, NY
Community High School, NJ
The Concept School, PA
Concordia Academy, MN
Covenant Canadian Reformed School, AB, Canada
Cretin-Derham Hall, MN
Cross Creek Programs, UT
Currey Ingram Academy, TN
Cushing Academy, MA
Dallas Academy, TX
De La Salle High School, CA
Delaware Valley Friends School, PA
Delphi Academy of Los Angeles, CA
Denver Academy, CO
Denver Lutheran High School, CO
Doctor Franklin Perkins School, MA
Dowling High School, IA
Dublin Christian Academy, NH
The Dwight School, NY
Eagle Hill School, CT
Eagle Hill School, MA
Eagle Hill-Southport, CT
Eagle Rock School, CO
Eastern Christian High School, NJ
Eastern Mennonite High School, VA
Eckerd Youth Alternatives, FL
Ecole d'Humanite, Switzerland
Elan School, ME
Elyria Catholic High School, OH
Fairhill School, TX
Faith Lutheran High School, NV
The Fessenden School, MA
The Field School, DC
Fishburne Military School, VA
F. L. Chamberlain School, MA

Florida Air Academy, FL
Foothills Academy, AB, Canada
Forest Heights Lodge, CO
Fox Valley Lutheran High School, WI
Fraser Academy, BC, Canada
Fresno Christian Schools, CA
The Frostig School, CA
Fryeburg Academy, ME
Futures High School, Oceanside, CA
Futures High School—San Diego, CA
Gateway School, TX
George Stevens Academy, ME
Girard College, PA
Glades Day School, FL
Glen Eden School, BC, Canada
The Glenholme School, CT
The Gow School, NY
The Grauer School, CA
Greenfield School, NC
The Greenwood School, VT
The Grier School, PA
Grove School, CT
Gstaad International School, Switzerland
Hackett Catholic Central High School, MI
Hamilton District Christian School, ON, Canada
Hamilton Learning Centre, ON, Canada
Harare International School, Zimbabwe
Hargrave Military Academy, VA
The Haverford School, PA
Hawai'i Preparatory Academy, HI
Hayden High School, KS
Hebrew Academy-the Five Towns, NY
Heritage Christian School, ON, Canada
Hidden Lake Academy, GA
The Hill Center, Durham Academy, NC
Hillcrest School, TX
Hillside School, MA
The Hill Top Preparatory School, PA
Hoosac School, NY
Hosanna Christian School, OR
Houston Learning Academy-Central Campus, TX
The Hudson School, NJ
Hyde School, CT
Hyde School, ME
International Community School of Addis Ababa, Ethiopia
International School Basel, Switzerland
International School of Amsterdam, Netherlands
International School of Athens, Greece
International School of Brussels, Belgium
The International School of Geneva, Switzerland
International School of Minnesota, MN
Islamic Saudi Academy, VA
Jakarta International School, Indonesia
John Burroughs School, MO
The John Dewey Academy, MA
John F. Kennedy Memorial High School, WA
Josephinum High School, IL
Kapaun Mount Carmel Catholic High School, KS
The Karafin School, NY
Key School, Inc., TX
Keystone National High School, PA
Kings Christian School, CA
Kingshill School, VI
La Cheim School, CA

Lakeland Christian Academy, IN
Lakewood Prep, NJ
Landmark East School, NS, Canada
Lansdale Catholic High School, PA
La Pietra–Hawaii School for Girls, HI
The Latin School of Chicago, IL
Lawrence School, OH
Lebanon Catholic Junior / Senior High School, PA
The Leelanau School, MI
Le Lycee Francais de Los Angeles, CA
Lourdes Catholic High School, AZ
Lower Canada College, QC, Canada
Loyola Academy, IL
Lutheran High School, IN
Lutheran High School South, MO
Lycee International de Los Angeles, CA
Lyndon Institute, VT
Maine Central Institute, ME
Manhattan Christian High School, MT
Maplebrook School, NY
Marian Central Catholic High School, IL
Marian High School, IN
Marist High School, NJ
The Marvelwood School, CT
Mary Help of Christians Academy, NJ
Marylawn of the Oranges, NJ
Massanutten Military Academy, VA
McNicholas High School, OH
The Meeting School, NH
Mercy High School, NE
Mercyhurst Preparatory School, PA
Mid-Peninsula High School, CA
Milton Hershey School, PA
Missouri Military Academy, MO
Monte Vista Christian School, CA
Mount Alvernia High School, PA
Mount Bachelor Academy, OR
Mount Carmel High School, IL
Nawa Academy, CA
Nbisiing Education Centre, ON, Canada
New Dominion School, MD
New Dominion School, VA
The Newgrange School, NJ
New Hampton School, NH
New Summit School, MS
The Nora School, MD
Norfolk Collegiate School, VA
The North Broward Preparatory Upper School, FL
North Country School, NY
Northwest Yeshiva High School, WA
The Norwich Free Academy, CT
Notre Dame High School, MO
Notre Dame High School, NJ
Notre Dame High School for Girls, IL
Notre Dame Regional Secondary, BC, Canada
Oak Creek Ranch School, AZ
The Oakland School, PA
Oakland School, VA
Ojai Valley School, CA
The O'Neal School, NC
Oneida Baptist Institute, KY
The Orme School, AZ
The Oxford Academy, CT
Oxford School, CA

The Pathway School, PA
The Phelps School, PA
Pine Forge Academy, PA
Pinehurst School, ON, Canada
Pine Ridge School, VT
Pope John Paul II High School, FL
Portland Christian Schools, OR
Powers Catholic High School, MI
Providence High School, TX
Provo Canyon School, UT
Purcell Marian High School, OH
Queen Margaret's School, BC, Canada
Quincy Notre Dame High School, IL
Rancho Valmora, NM
The Rectory School, CT
Regina High School, OH
Resurrection High School, IL
Riverview School, MA
Robert Land Academy, ON, Canada
Robert Louis Stevenson School, NY
Roncalli High School, IN
Routt High School, IL
Saddleback Valley Christian School, CA
St. Andrew's College, Dublin, Ireland
St. Benedict at Auburndale, TN
St. Benedict's Preparatory School, NJ
St. Croix Lutheran High School, MN
Saint Dominic Academy, NJ
St. Dominic's International School, Portugal, Portugal
Saint Elizabeth High School, CA
Saint Francis De Sales High School, IL
St. Francis School, GA
St. George's School in Switzerland, Switzerland
St. George's School of Montreal, QC, Canada
St. Johnsbury Academy, VT
Saint John's School of Alberta, AB, Canada
Saint Joseph Central Catholic High School, OH
Saint Laurence High School, IL
St. Mary's Bundschu Memorial High School, MO
Saint Mary's High School, AZ
Saint Patrick—Saint Vincent High School, CA
St. Paul's High School, MB, Canada
St. Stanislaus College, MS
St. Thomas Aquinas High School, FL
Saint Thomas Aquinas High School, KS
St. Thomas Choir School, NY
Saint Thomas More School, CT
Saint Xavier High School, KY
Salesianum School, DE
Salpointe Catholic High School, AZ
San Marcos Baptist Academy, TX
School for Young Performers, NY
Sedbergh School, QC, Canada
Seton Catholic Central High School, NY
Shattuck-St. Mary's School, MN
Smith School, NY
Smithville District Christian High School, ON, Canada
Sorenson's Ranch School, UT
Spring Ridge Academy, AZ
Stanbridge Academy, CA
Stone Mountain School, NC
Storm King School, NY
Summit Preparatory School, MT
Taipei American School, Taiwan

Specialized Directories

The Tenney School, TX
Thomas A. Edison High School, OR
Three Springs/Prince Mountain Academy, GA
Tilton School, NH
Timber Ridge School, VA
Timothy Christian High School, IL
Toronto District Christian High School, ON, Canada
Trident Academy, SC
Trinity High School, KY
Valley Forge Military Academy and College, PA
The Vanguard School, FL
Venta Preparatory School, ON, Canada
Vianney High School, MO
Walden Preparatory School, TX
Washington Academy, ME
Wellsprings Friends School, OR
Wesleyan School, GA
Westhill Institute, Mexico
West Nottingham Academy, MD
Westpark School, MB, Canada
Westtown School, PA
Westview School, CA
Wheaton Academy, IL
The White Mountain School, NH
Willow Hill School, MA
Wilmington Christian School, DE
The Winchendon School, MA
Windhoek International School, Namibia
Windsor Christian Fellowship Academy, ON, Canada
The Windsor School, NY
Winston Preparatory School, NY
The Winston School San Antonio, TX
Woodbridge Academy, KY
Woodcliff Academy, NJ
York Preparatory School, NY

Deaf Students

Ahliyyah School for Girls, Jordan
Alexander Dawson School, CO
Archbishop Blenk Girls High School, LA
Baylor School, TN
The Bement School, MA
Bishop Carroll High School, PA
Bishop Hoban High School, PA
Bishop Verot High School, FL
Burr and Burton Academy, VT
Cate School, CA
Cathedral High School, IN

Coe-Brown Northwood Academy, NH
Denver Christian High School, CO
Duchesne Academy of the Sacred Heart, NE
Equilibrium International Education Institute, AB, Canada
Futures High School, Oceanside, CA
Grove School, CT
Josephinum High School, IL
Kapaun Mount Carmel Catholic High School, KS
The Karafin School, NY
King David High School, BC, Canada
Lake Ridge Academy, OH
Lawrence Academy, MA
Luther College High School, SK, Canada
North Cobb Christian School, GA
Northwest Yeshiva High School, WA
Notre Dame High School, CA
Notre Dame High School, WV
Notre Dame Regional Secondary, BC, Canada
Providence Country Day School, RI
Rye Country Day School, NY
St. George's School of Montreal, QC, Canada
School for Young Performers, NY
The Webb School, TN
Westhill Institute, Mexico
The Williston Northampton School, MA

Blind Students

Alpine Academy, UT
Appleby College, ON, Canada
Archbishop Blenk Girls High School, LA
Archbishop Riordan High School, CA
The Bement School, MA
Bishop Carroll High School, PA
Bishop Hoban High School, PA
Brandon Hall School, GA
Burr and Burton Academy, VT
Cathedral High School, IN
Coe-Brown Northwood Academy, NH
Duchesne Academy of the Sacred Heart, NE
Equilibrium International Education Institute, AB, Canada
Grove School, CT
Laguna Blanca School, CA
Lawrence Academy, MA
Notre Dame High School, CA
Notre Dame High School, WV
Notre Dame Regional Secondary, BC, Canada
Roncalli High School, IN
School for Young Performers, NY
Westhill Institute, Mexico

Index

Alphabetical Listing of Schools

In the index that follows, page numbers for school profiles are shown in regular type, page numbers for profiles accompanied by announcements are shown in *italic* type, and page numbers for full descriptions are shown in **boldface** type.

NOTES

NOTES

NOTES

6. Rate each of the following aspects of this book on a scale of 4 to 1 (4 = Excellent and 1 = Poor).

	4	3	2	1
Comprehensiveness of the information	❑	❑	❑	❑
Accuracy of the information	❑	❑	❑	❑
Usability	❑	❑	❑	❑
Cover design	❑	❑	❑	❑
Book layout	❑	❑	❑	❑
Special features (e.g., CD, flashcards, charts, etc.)	❑	❑	❑	❑
Value for the money	❑	❑	❑	❑

7. This book was recommended by:
- ❑ Guidance counselor
- ❑ Parent/guardian
- ❑ Family member/relative
- ❑ Friend
- ❑ Teacher
- ❑ Not recommended by anyone—I found the book on my own
- ❑ Other (please specify) _____

8. Would you recommend this book to others?

Yes	Not Sure	No
❑	❑	❑

9. Please provide any additional comments.

_____

_____

_____

_____

Remember, you can tear out this page and mail it to us at:

Editorial Department
Thomson Peterson's
2000 Lenox Drive
Lawrenceville, NJ 08648

or you can complete the survey online at **www.petersons.com/booksurvey.**

Your feedback is important to us at Thomson Peterson's, and we thank you for your time!

If you would like us to keep in touch with you about new products and services, please include your e-mail here: _____

Thomson Peterson's
Book Satisfaction Survey

Give Us Your Feedback

Thank you for choosing Thomson Peterson's as your source for personalized solutions for your education and career achievement. Please take a few minutes to answer the following questions. Your answers will go a long way in helping us to produce the most user-friendly and comprehensive resources to meet your individual needs.

When completed, please tear out this page and mail it to us at:

Editorial Department
Thomson Peterson's
2000 Lenox Drive
Lawrenceville, NJ 08648

You can also complete this survey online at **www.petersons.com/booksurvey.**

1. **What is the ISBN of the book you have purchased? (The ISBN can be found on the book's back cover in the lower right-hand corner.)** _____

2. **Where did you purchase this book?**
   ❑ Retailer, such as Barnes & Noble
   ❑ Online reseller, such as Amazon.com
   ❑ Petersons.com or Thomson Learning Bookstore
   ❑ Other (please specify) _____

3. **If you purchased this book on Petersons.com or through the Thomson Learning Bookstore, please rate the following aspects of your online purchasing experience on a scale of 4 to 1 (4 = Excellent and 1 = Poor).**

	4	3	2	1
Comprehensiveness of Peterson's Online Bookstore page	❑	❑	❑	❑
Overall online customer experience	❑	❑	❑	❑

4. **Which category best describes you?**
   ❑ High school student
   ❑ Parent of high school student
   ❑ College student
   ❑ Graduate/professional student
   ❑ Returning adult student

   ❑ Teacher
   ❑ Counselor
   ❑ Working professional/military
   ❑ Other (please specify) _____

5. **Rate your overall satisfaction with this book.**

Extremely Satisfied	Satisfied	Not Satisfied
❑	❑	❑

NOTES

NOTES